TELEVISION & CABLE FACTBOOK
VOLUME 80

Albert Warren
Editor & Publisher 1961-2006

Publications & Services of Warren Communications News

TELEVISION & CABLE FACTBOOK: ONLINE

CABLE & STATION COVERAGE ATLAS ON CD-ROM
Published Annually

COMMUNICATIONS DAILY

CONSUMER ELECTRONICS DAILY

GREEN ELECTRONICS DAILY

PUBLIC BROADCASTING REPORT
Published Biweekly

SATELLITE WEEK

TELECOM A.M.
Daily News Service

WARREN'S WASHINGTON INTERNET DAILY

WASHINGTON TELECOM NEWSWIRE

ISBN: 1-57696-064-1
ISSN: 0732-8648

Index to Sections
Television & Cable Factbook No. 80

TV STATIONS VOLUME

Section A

Section B

Section C – Charts

CABLE SYSTEMS VOLUME

Section D

Section E

Section F – Charts

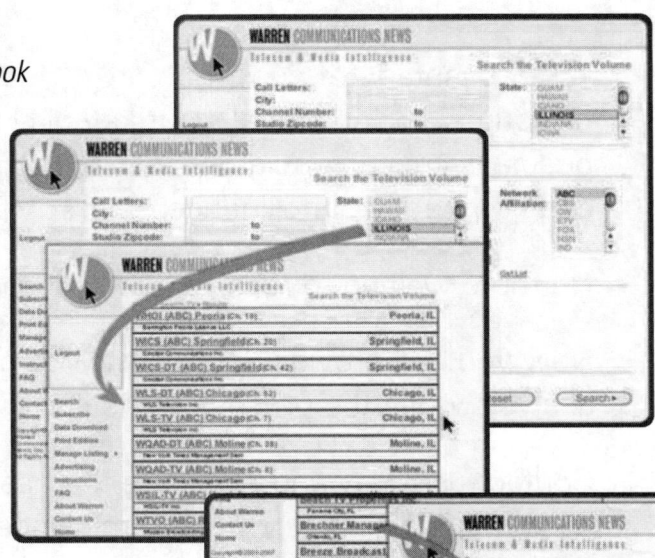

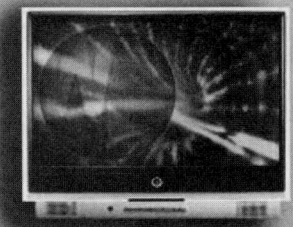

Index to Contents
Television & Cable Factbook No. 80

A

B

C

ADVANCED
TVFactbook

D

E

Access the most current data instantly.
FREE
TRIAL
@
ADVANCED
TVFactbook
www.warren-news.com/factbook.htm

F

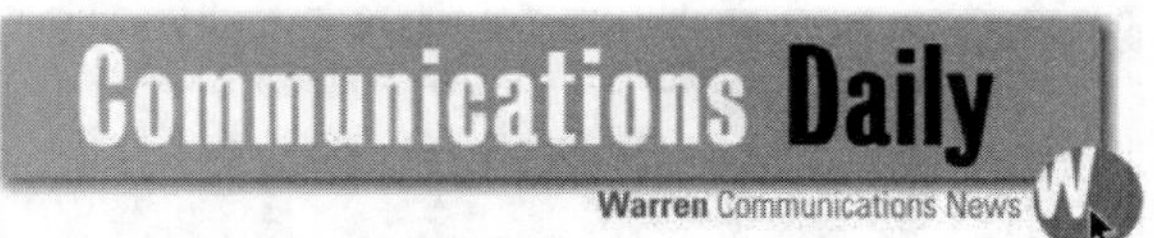
Communications Daily
Warren Communications News

G

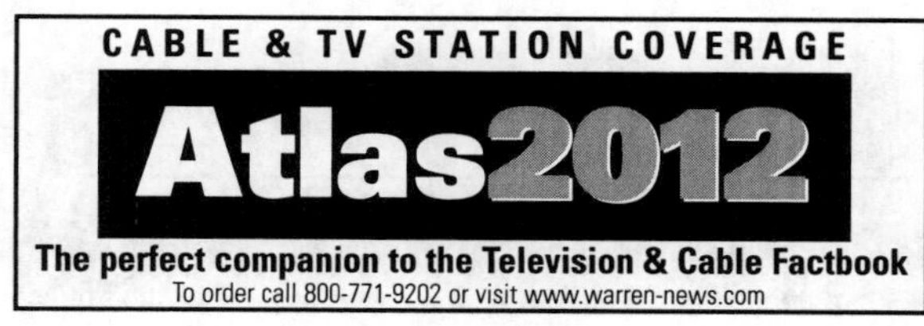

H

MediaPrints™
Map a Winning Business Strategy
Digital cable and TV coverage maps.
Visit www.warren-news.com/mediaprints.htm

I

J

K

L

FREE
TRIAL
@
Access the most current data instantly.
ADVANCED
TVFactbook
www.warren-news.com/factbook.htm

M

ADVANCED
TVFactbook

N

O

P

Q

R

S

T

ADVANCED
TVFactbook

U

V

W

X

Y

Z

Cable Systems State Index

NEW YORK

Total Systems: **86**
Total Communities Served: **1,567**
Franchises Not Yet Operating: **0**
Applications Pending: **0**
Communities with Applications: **0**
Number of Basic Subscribers: **6,514,574**
Number of Expanded Basic Subscribers: **2,688,409**
Number of Pay Units: **570,840**

Top 100 Markets Represented: Hartford-New Haven-New Britain-Waterbury-New London, CT (19); New York, NY-Linden-Paterson-Newark, NJ (1); Buffalo (24); Albany-Schenectady-Troy (34); Syracuse (35); Rochester (56).

**For a list of cable communities in this section, see the Cable Community Index located in the back of Cable Volume 2.
For explanation of terms used in cable system listings, see p. D-11.**

ADAMS (town)—Time Warner Cable. No longer in operation. ICA: NY0119.

ALBANY—Time Warner Cable, 1021 Highbridge Rd, Schenectady, NY 12303. Phones: 866-321-2225; 518-869-5500. Fax: 518-242-8948. Web Site: http://www.timewarnercable.com/albany. Also serves Alplaus, Altamont, Ames (village), Amsterdam, Argyle, Averill Park, Ballston, Ballston Lake, Ballston Spa, Berne (town), Bethlehem, Bolton, Broadalbin, Brunswick, Burnt Hills, Cambridge (village), Canajoharie (village), Castleton-on-Hudson, Charlton, Cherry Valley (village), Clifton Park, Cobleskill, Cobleskill (village), Cohoes, Colonie (village), Corinth (village), Day, Defreestville, Delanson, Delmar, Duanesburg, East Greenbush, Easton (town), Edinburg (town), Esperance (village), Fonda, Fort Ann (village), Fort Edward (village), Fort Johnson, Fort Plain (village), Fultonville, Galway, Glen (town), Glens Falls, Glenville, Gloversville, Granville, Green Island, Greenfield, Greenwich (village), Guilderland, Hadley (town), Hagaman, Halfmoon, Hartford (town), Hoosick, Hoosick Falls, Horicon, Hudson Falls (village), Jackson (town), Johnstown (city), Johnstown (town), Junction, Kingsbury (town), Knox (town), Lake George (village), Malta, Mayfield, Mayfield (town), Mayfield (village), Mechanicville, Menands, Middle Granville, Middleburgh (village), Milton, Minden (town), Mohawk (town), Nassau (village), Nelliston (village), New Scotland, Niskayuna, North Greenbush, North Hoosick, Northumberland (town), Northville, Palatine (town), Palatine Bridge (town), Perth, Pittstown (town), Poestenkill, Rensselaer, Richmondville (village), Root (town), Rotterdam, Round Lake, Salem (village), Sand Lake, Saratoga (town), Saratoga Springs, Schagticoke (village), Schenectady, Schodack, Schoharie (village), Schuylerville, Scotia, Seward, Sharon, Sharon Springs, South Glens Falls (village), St. Johnsville (village), Stillwater (village), Stuyvesant, Troy, Valatie, Valley Falls (village), Victory Mills, Voorheesville, Warrensburg (town), Watervliet, Whitehall (town) & Wilton. ICA: NY0014.

TV Market Ranking: 34 (ALBANY, Alplaus, Altamont, Ames (village), Amsterdam, Averill Park, Ballston, Ballston Lake, Ballston Spa, Berne (town), Bethlehem, Broadalbin, Brunswick, Burnt Hills, Cambridge (village), Canajoharie (village), Castleton-on-Hudson, Charlton, Clifton Park, Cobleskill, Cobleskill (village), Cohoes, Cohoes, Colonie (village), Defreestville, Delanson, Delmar, Delmar, Duanesburg, East Greenbush, Easton (town), Esperance (village), Fonda, Fort Johnson, Fultonville, Galway, Glen (town), Glenville, Gloversville, Green Island, Greenfield, Greenwich (village), Guilderland, Hagaman, Halfmoon, Hoosick, Hoosick Falls, Jackson (town), Johnstown (city), Johnstown (town), Knox (town), Malta, Mayfield, Mayfield (town), Mayfield (village), Mechanicville, Menands, Middleburgh (village), Milton, Mohawk (town), Nassau (village), New Scotland, New Scotland, Niskayuna, North Greenbush, North Hoosick, Northville, Palatine Bridge (town), Pattersonville, Perth, Pittstown (town), Poestenkill, Rensselaer, Richmondville (village), Root (town), Rotterdam, Rotterdam Junction, Round Lake, Sand Lake, Saratoga (town), Saratoga Springs, Schagticoke (village), Schenectady, Schodack, Schoharie (village), Scotia, Seward, Sharon, Sharon Springs, Stillwater (village), Stuyvesant, Troy, Valatie, Valley Falls (village), Voorheesville, Voorheesville, Watervliet, Wilton); Below 100 (Cherry Valley (village), Fort Plain (village), Hadley (town), Minden (town), Nelliston (village), Palatine (town), St. Johnsville (village)); Outside TV Markets (Argyle, Bolton, Fort Ann (village), Fort Edward (village), Glens Falls, Granville, Hartford (town), Horicon, Hudson Falls (village), Kingsbury (town), Lake George (village), Middle Granville, Salem (village), South Glens Falls (village), Warrensburg (town), Whitehall (town), Whitehall (village)). Franchise award date: N.A. Franchise expiration date: N.A. Began: July 1, 1974.

Channel capacity: N.A. Channels available but not in use: N.A.

Basic Service

Subscribers: 405,790 Includes Port Henry, Athol MA, & Pittsfield MA.

Programming (received off-air): WCWN (CW) Schenectady; WMHT (PBS) Schenectady; WNYA (MNT) Pittsfield; WNYT (NBC) Albany; WRGB (CBS) Schenectady; WTEN (ABC) Albany; WXXA-TV (FOX) Albany; WYPX-TV (ION) Amsterdam.

Programming (via satellite): Capital News 9; C-SPAN; QVC; TBS Superstation; TV Guide Network.

Fee: $38.95 installation; $10.77 monthly.

Expanded Basic Service 1

Subscribers: N.A.

Programming (via satellite): A&E Networks; ABC Family Channel; AMC; Animal Planet; BET Networks; Bravo!; Cartoon Network; CNBC; CNN; Comedy Central; Country Music TV; C-SPAN 2; Discovery Channel; Discovery Health Channel; Disney Channel; E! Entertainment Television; ESPN; ESPN 2; ESPN Classic Sports; Eternal Word TV Network; Food Network; Fox News Channel; FX; Golf Channel; Headline News; HGTV; History Channel; Lifetime; Lifetime Movie Network; MSG; MSG Plus; MSNBC; MTV; National Geographic Channel; Nickelodeon; Oxygen; ShopNBC; SoapNet; Spike TV; SportsNet New York; Style Network; Syfy; The Learning Channel; The Weather Channel; Travel Channel; truTV; Turner Classic Movies; Turner Network TV; TV Land; Univision Studios; USA Network; Versus; VH1; WE tv; Yankees Entertainment & Sports.

Fee: $10.00 installation; $31.18 monthly.

Digital Basic Service

Subscribers: 94,284 Includes Port Henry, Athol MA, & Pittsfield MA.

Programming (via satellite): America's Store; BBC America; Bloomberg Television; Cooking Channel; C-SPAN 3; Direct to You; Discovery Digital Networks; DIY Network; DMX Music; ESPNews; Fox Sports World; FSN Digital Atlantic; FSN Digital Central; FSN Digital Pacific; G4; Great American Country; GSN; Hallmark Channel; History Channel; Lifetime Real Women; MTV Networks Digital Suite; National Geographic Channel; New York 1 News; Nick Jr.; Outdoor Channel; Ovation; Speed; Toon Disney; Trinity Broadcasting Network; TV Asia; Versus; Zee TV USA.

Fee: $4.95 monthly.

Digital Pay Service 1

Pay Units: N.A.

Programming (via satellite): Cinemax; Encore (multiplexed); Flix; Fox Movie Channel; HBO (multiplexed); Showtime (multiplexed); Starz (multiplexed); The Movie Channel (multiplexed).

Fee: $14.95 monthly (HBO or Showtime & TMC).

Video-On-Demand: Yes

Pay-Per-View

Addressable homes: 21,323.

iN DEMAND; Playboy TV; NBA/WNBA League Pass (delivered digitally); NHL Center Ice/MLB Extra Innings (delivered digitally); ESPN Full Court (delivered digitally); ESPN Gameplan (delivered digitally); Fresh; iN DEMAND (delivered digitally); Playboy TV (delivered digitally); Fresh (delivered digitally); Shorteez (delivered digitally); Hot Choice (delivered digitally); Pleasure (delivered digitally); Adult PPV (delivered digitally).

Internet Service

Operational: Yes. Began: July 22, 1997.

Subscribers: 16,500.

Broadband Service: AOL for Broadband; EarthLink; Local.net; Road Runner.

Fee: $24.95 installation; $44.95 monthly.

Telephone Service

Digital: Operational

Fee: $44.95 monthly

Miles of Plant: 7,633.0 (coaxial); 357.0 (fiber optic). Miles of plant include Port Henry, Athol MA, & Pittsfield MA

Vice President, Operations: Mark Loreno. Vice President, Engineering: James Marchester. Vice President, Marketing: Tricia Buhr. Vice President, Public Affairs: Peter Taubkin. Vice President, Customer Care: Paul Ventosa. General Manager, Ad Sales: Kevin Bartlett.

Ownership: Time Warner Cable (MSO).; Advance/Newhouse Partnership (MSO).

ALBION—Time Warner Cable. Now served by BATAVIA (formerly Stafford), NY [NY0249]. ICA: NY0196.

ALDEN—Time Warner Cable. Now served by BATAVIA (formerly Stafford), NY [NY0249]. ICA: NY0197.

ALEXANDRIA BAY—Cass Cable TV Inc., 26 S Main St, PO Box 339, Hammond, NY 13646-0339. Phone: 315-482-9975. Fax: 315-324-6289. Also serves Alexandria (town), Plessis, Redwood & Theresa (town). ICA: NY0137.

TV Market Ranking: Below 100 (Alexandria (town), ALEXANDRIA BAY, Plessis, Redwood, Theresa (town)). Franchise award date: August 21, 1984. Franchise expiration date: N.A. Began: May 31, 1985.

Channel capacity: N.A. Channels available but not in use: N.A.

Basic Service

Subscribers: 1,579.

Programming (received off-air): WNYF-CA Watertown; WWNY-TV (CBS) Carthage; WWTI (ABC, CW) Watertown.

Programming (via satellite): A&E Networks; ABC Family Channel; CNN; CNN International; Country Music TV; C-SPAN; C-SPAN 2; Discovery Channel; Discovery Fit & Health; Disney Channel; DIY Network; ESPN; ESPN 2; Eternal Word TV Network; Food Network; Fox News Channel; FX; Golf Channel; Hallmark Channel; Headline News; HGTV; History Channel; Lifetime; MTV; National Geographic Channel; Nickelodeon; Outdoor Channel; QVC; SoapNet; Spike TV; Syfy; TBS Superstation; The Learning Channel; The Weather Channel; Toon Disney; truTV; Turner Classic Movies; Turner Network TV; TV Guide Network; TV Land; USA Network; VH1; WDIV-TV (NBC) Detroit; WGN America; WSBK-TV (CBS, MNT) Boston; Yankees Entertainment & Sports.

Fee: $45.00 installation; $30.50 monthly; $22.00 additional installation.

Pay Service 1

Pay Units: 246.

Programming (via satellite): Cinemax.

Fee: $7.50 monthly.

Pay Service 2

Pay Units: 316.

Programming (via satellite): HBO.

Fee: $9.00 monthly.

Video-On-Demand: No

Internet Service

Operational: Yes.

Subscribers: 100.

Broadband Service: In-house.

Fee: $45.00 installation; $34.95 monthly.

Telephone Service
None
Miles of Plant: 34.0 (coaxial); None (fiber optic).
Manager: Beverly Morley.
Ownership: Citizens Cablevision Inc.

ALFRED—Formerly served by Alfred Cable System Inc. No longer in operation. ICA: NY0154.

AMSTERDAM—Time Warner Cable. Now served by ALBANY, NY [NY0014]. ICA: NY0047.

ANDES—MTC Cable. Now served by MARGARETVILLE, NY [NY0155]. ICA: NY0192.

ANGELICA—Time Warner Cable. Now served by HORNELL, NY [NY0076]. ICA: NY0198.

ARGYLE—Now served by QUEENSBURY, NY [NY0042]. ICA: NY0271.

ASTORIA—RCN Corp. Formerly served by Queens, NY [NY0283]. This cable system has converted to IPTV, 196 Van Buren St, Herndon, VA 20170. Phone: 703-434-8200. Web Site: http://www.rcn.com. ICA: NY5300.
TV Market Ranking: 1 (QUEENS).
Channel capacity: N.A. Channels available but not in use: N.A.
Pay Service 1
Pay Units: N.A.
Fee: $11.95 monthly (Cinemaz or Starz!); $16.95 monthly (Showtime/The Movie Channel); $17.95 monthly (HBO).
Internet Service
Operational: Yes.
Fee: $38.00 monthly.
Telephone Service
Digital: Operational
Fee: $45.00 monthly
Chairman: Steven J. Simmons. Chief Executive Officer: Jim Holanda.

AUBURN—Time Warner Cable, 6005 Fair Lakes Rd, East Syracuse, NY 13057. Phone: 315-634-6100. Fax: 315-634-6219. Web Site: http://www.timewarnercable.com. Also serves Fleming, Mandana, Owasco, Sennett, Skaneateles (village), Spafford & Throop. ICA: NY0049.
TV Market Ranking: 35 (AUBURN, Fleming, Mandana, Owasco, Sennett, Skaneateles (village), Spafford, Throop). Franchise award date: N.A. Franchise expiration date: N.A. Began: June 22, 1967.
Channel capacity: N.A. Channels available but not in use: N.A.
Basic Service
Subscribers: N.A. Included in Syracuse
Programming (received off-air): WCNY-TV (PBS) Syracuse; WNYS-TV (MNT) Syracuse; WSPX-TV (ION) Syracuse; WSTM-TV (NBC) Syracuse; WSTQ-LP (CW) Syracuse; WSYR-TV (ABC) Syracuse; WSYT (FOX) Syracuse; WTVH (CBS) Syracuse; allband FM.
Programming (via satellite): C-SPAN; QVC.
Fee: $69.68 installation; $6.29 monthly; $2.10 converter.
Expanded Basic Service 1
Subscribers: N.A. Included in Syracuse
Programming (via satellite): A&E Networks; ABC Family Channel; AMC; Animal Planet; BET Networks; Bravo; Cartoon Network; CNBC; CNN; Comedy Central; Country Music TV; C-SPAN 2; Discovery Channel; Disney Channel; E! Entertainment Television; ESPN; ESPN 2; ESPN Classic Sports; Eternal Word TV Network; Food Network; Fox News Channel; FX; Golf Channel; Great American Country; Headline News; HGTV; History Channel; Lifetime; LOGO; MSG; MSG Plus; MSNBC; MTV; Nickelodeon; Spike TV; Style Network; Syfy; TBS Superstation; The Learning Channel; The Weather Channel; Travel Channel; truTV; Turner Classic Movies; Turner Network TV; TV Guide Network; TV Land; USA Network; Versus; VH1; WE tv; Yankees Entertainment & Sports.
Fee: $19.25 installation; $14.86 monthly.
Digital Basic Service
Subscribers: N.A. Included in Syracuse
Programming (via satellite): AmericanLife TV Network; BBC America; Black Family Channel; Bloomberg Television; DIY Network; ESPN HD; ESPNews; Fox Movie Channel; Fox Soccer; Fuse; G4; GAS; GSN; Hallmark Channel; Halogen Network; HD Theater; Lifetime Movie Network; MTV Networks Digital Suite; Music Choice; National Geographic Channel; Nick Jr.; Nick Too; NickToons TV; Outdoor Channel; SoapNet; Speed; The Word Network; Toon Disney; Trinity Broadcasting Network.
Digital Expanded Basic Service
Subscribers: N.A.
Programming (via satellite): Bio; Canales N; Flix; FSN Digital Atlantic; FSN Digital Central; FSN Digital Pacific; History Channel International; Independent Film Channel; Sundance Channel; Versus.
Digital Pay Service 1
Pay Units: N.A.
Programming (via satellite): Cinemax (multiplexed); Encore (multiplexed); Flix; HBO (multiplexed); Showtime (multiplexed); Showtime HD; Starz (multiplexed); Starz HDTV; The Movie Channel (multiplexed).
Video-On-Demand: No
Pay-Per-View
Playboy TV (delivered digitally); Fresh (delivered digitally); Hot Choice (delivered digitally); Movies (delivered digitally).
Internet Service
Operational: Yes.
Broadband Service: EarthLink, LocalNet, Road Runner.
Fee: $39.95 installation; $44.95 monthly.
Telephone Service
Digital: Operational
Fee: $39.95 monthly
Miles of plant included in Syracuse.
President: Mary Cotter. Vice President, Engineering: Henry Hryckiewicz. Vice President, Marketing: John Melvany. Technical Operations Director: Bruce Tompkins. Vice President, Public Affairs: Jeff Unaitis.
Ownership: Time Warner Cable (MSO).

AUGUSTA (town)—Chain Lakes Cablevision. Now served by ROME, NY [NY0037]. ICA: NY0199.

AVOCA—Time Warner Cable. Now served by HORNELL, NY [NY0076]. ICA: NY0200.

BAINBRIDGE—Time Warner Cable. Now served by ONEONTA, NY [NY0065]. ICA: NY0120.

BALDWINSVILLE—Time Warner Cable. Now served by SYRACUSE, NY [NY0013]. ICA: NY0074.

BATAVIA—Time Warner Cable, 71 Mount Hope Ave, Rochester, NY 14620. Phone: 585-756-1000. Fax: 585-756-1675. Web Site: http://www.timewarnercable.com/rochester. Also serves Akron (village), Alabama (town), Albion, Albion (village), Alden, Alexander (village), Attica (village), Avon (village), Bennington, Bergen (village), Bethany (town), Caledonia (village), Carlton (town), Castile (town), Churchville (village), Conesus (town), Corfu (village), Covington (town), Darien, Elba (village), Fillmore, Gaines (town), Gainesville (town), Genesee Falls (town), Geneseo (village), Hartland (town), Honeoye Falls (village), Hume, Java (town), Kendall, Le Roy (village), Leicester (village), Lima (village), Livonia (village), Lyndonville, Marilla (town), Medina (village), Mendon (town), Middlebury, Middleport (village), Mount Morris (village), Newstead (town), Nunda (village), Oakfield (village), Orangeville (town), Pembroke (town), Perry (village), Portage, Ridgeway (town), Riga (town), Royalton (town), Rush (town), Scottsville (village), Shelby (town), Sheldon (town), Silver Springs, Stafford, Warsaw (village), West Bloomfield (town), Wheatland (town), Wyoming, Yates (town) & York (town). ICA: NY0249.
TV Market Ranking: 24 (Akron (village), Alabama (town), Alden, Alexander (village), Attica (village), Bennington, Corfu (village), Darien, Hartland (town), Honeoye Falls (village), Java (town), Marilla (town), Medina (village), Middleport (village), Newstead (town), Orangeville (town), Pembroke (town), Ridgeway (town), Royalton (town), Rush (town), Scottsville (village), Shelby (town), Sheldon (town), West Bloomfield (town), Wheatland (town), York (town)); 24,56 (BATAVIA, Oakfield (village)); 56 (Albion, Albion (village), Avon (village), Bergen (village), Bethany (town), Caledonia (village), Carlton (town), Churchville (village), Conesus (town), Covington (town), Elba (village), Gaines (town), Geneseo (village), Kendall, Le Roy (village), Leicester (village), Lima (village), Livonia (village), Mendon (town), Middlebury, Mount Morris (village), Riga (town), Stafford, Wyoming, Wyoming (town)); Below 100 (Castile (town), Fillmore, Gainesville (town), Genesee Falls (town), Hume, Lyndonville, Nunda (village), Perry (village), Portage, Silver Springs, Warsaw (village), Yates (town)). Franchise award date: N.A. Franchise expiration date: N.A. Began: January 1, 1980.
Channel capacity: N.A. Channels available but not in use: N.A.
Basic Service
Subscribers: N.A. Included in Rochester
Programming (received off-air): WBGT-CA (MNT) Rochester; WGRZ (NBC) Buffalo; WHAM-TV (ABC, CW) Rochester; WHEC-TV (NBC) Rochester; WIVB-TV (CBS) Buffalo; WKBW-TV (ABC) Buffalo; WNED-TV (PBS) Buffalo; WNYB (IND) Jamestown; WNYO-TV (MNT) Buffalo; WPXJ-TV (ION) Batavia; WROC-TV (CBS) Rochester; WUHF (FOX) Rochester; WUTV (FOX) Buffalo; WXXI-TV (PBS) Rochester.
Programming (via satellite): QVC; TV Guide Network.
Fee: $50.00 installation; $13.17 monthly.
Expanded Basic Service 1
Subscribers: N.A.
Programming (via satellite): A&E Networks; ABC Family Channel; AMC; Animal Planet; BET Networks; Bravo; Cartoon Network; CNBC; CNN; Comedy Central; Country Music TV; C-SPAN; Discovery Channel; Disney Channel; E! Entertainment Television; ESPN; ESPN 2; ESPN Classic Sports; Eternal Word TV Network; Food Network; Fox News Channel; FX; Golf Channel; Headline News; HGTV; History Channel; Lifetime; Lifetime Movie Network; MoviePlex; MSG; MSNBC; MTV; National Geographic Channel; Nickelodeon; Oxygen; ShopNBC; SoapNet; Spike TV; Syfy; TBS Superstation; The Learning Channel; The Weather Channel; Travel Channel; truTV; Turner Classic Movies; Turner Network TV; TV Land; Univision Studios; USA Network; VH1; WE tv; Yankees Entertainment & Sports.
Fee: $33.58 monthly.
Digital Basic Service
Subscribers: N.A. Included in Rochester
Programming (via satellite): BBC America; Bloomberg Television; Cooking Channel; C-SPAN 3; Discovery Digital Networks; DIY Network; ESPNews; Fox Deportes; Fox Movie Channel; FSN Digital Atlantic; FSN Digital Central; FSN Digital Pacific; Great American Country; GSN; Lifetime Real Women; MTV2; Music Choice; Nick Jr.; Outdoor Channel; Ovation; Speed; Style Network; Tennis Channel; Toon Disney; VH1 Classic.
Fee: $11.95 monthly.
Digital Pay Service 1
Pay Units: N.A.
Programming (via satellite): Cinemax (multiplexed); Encore (multiplexed); Flix; HBO (multiplexed); Independent Film Channel; Showtime (multiplexed); Starz (multiplexed); Sundance Channel; The Movie Channel (multiplexed).
Fee: $10.95 monthly (Cinemax, HBO, Showtime, Flix/TMC, or IFC/Starz/Encore).
Video-On-Demand: Yes
Pay-Per-View
iN DEMAND (delivered digitally); Playboy TV (delivered digitally); ETC (delivered digitally); Sports PPV (delivered digitally).
Internet Service
Operational: Yes.
Broadband Service: Road Runner.
Fee: $39.95 installation; $44.95 monthly.
Telephone Service
Digital: Operational
Fee: $39.95 monthly
Miles of Plant: 985.0 (coaxial); None (fiber optic).
Division President: Terrence Rafferty. Vice President, Operations: Bruce Hennekey. Vice President, Engineering: Armando Ruiz. Vice President, Marketing: Mike Neal. Vice President, Government & Public Affairs: Chris Mueller.
Ownership: Time Warner Cable (MSO).; Advance/Newhouse Partnership (MSO).Day-to-day Operations are managed by Time Warner Cable.

BATH—Time Warner Cable. Now served by HORNELL, NY [NY0076]. ICA: NY0093.

BERKSHIRE—Haefele TV Inc. Now served by SPENCER, NY [NY0145]. ICA: NY0139.

BERLIN (town)—Charter Communications, 95 Higgins St, Worcester, MA 1606. Phone: 508-853-1515. Fax: 508-563-2696. Web Site: http://www.charter.com. Also serves Petersburg & Petersburgh (town). ICA: NY0187.
TV Market Ranking: 34 (BERLIN (TOWN), Petersburg, Petersburgh (town)). Franchise award date: N.A. Franchise expiration date: N.A. Began: January 1, 1993.
Channel capacity: 60 (not 2-way capable). Channels available but not in use: N.A.
Basic Service
Subscribers: N.A. Included in Chatham
Programming (received off-air): WCWN (CW) Schenectady; WMHT (PBS) Schenectady; WNYA (MNT) Pittsfield; WNYT (NBC) Albany; WRGB (CBS) Schenectady; WRNN-TV (IND) Kingston; WTEN (ABC)

Albany; WXXA-TV (FOX) Albany; WYPX-TV (ION) Amsterdam.
Programming (via satellite): QVC; Trinity Broadcasting Network; TV Guide Network; WPIX (CW, IND) New York.
Fee: $29.99 installation.

Expanded Basic Service 1
Subscribers: N.A.
Programming (via satellite): A&E Networks; ABC Family Channel; AMC; Animal Planet; Bravo; Cartoon Network; CNBC; CNN; Comedy Central; Country Music TV; C-SPAN; C-SPAN 2; Discovery Channel; Disney Channel; E! Entertainment Television; ESPN; ESPN 2; ESPN Classic Sports; Food Network; Fox News Channel; FX; Headline News; HGTV; History Channel; Lifetime; MTV; Nickelodeon; Speed; Spike TV; Syfy; TBS Superstation; The Learning Channel; The Weather Channel; Toon Disney; Travel Channel; truTV; Turner Classic Movies; Turner Network TV; TV Land; USA Network; Versus; VH1.
Fee: $55.00 monthly.

Digital Basic Service
Subscribers: N.A.
Programming (via satellite): BBC America; Bio; Discovery Digital Networks; DMX Music; ESPNews; Fox Soccer; Fuse; GAS; Golf Channel; History Channel International; Independent Film Channel; Lifetime Movie Network; MTV2; Nick Jr.; Style Network; Turner Classic Movies; TV Guide Interactive Inc.; WE tv.

Digital Pay Service 1
Pay Units: N.A.
Programming (via satellite): Cinemax (multiplexed); Encore (multiplexed); Flix; HBO (multiplexed); Showtime (multiplexed); Starz (multiplexed); The Movie Channel (multiplexed).

Video-On-Demand: No

Pay-Per-View
iN DEMAND (delivered digitally); Playboy TV (delivered digitally).

Telephone Service
None

Miles of Plant: 20.0 (coaxial); None (fiber optic).
Vice President & General Manager: Greg Garabedian. Technical Operations Director: George Duffy. Marketing Director: Dennis Jerome. Marketing Manager: Paula Cecchetelli.
Ownership: Charter Communications Inc. (MSO).

BINGHAMTON—Time Warner Cable, 120 Plaza Dr, Vestal, NY 13850-3658. Phone: 607-644-0646. Fax: 607-644-1501. Web Site: http://www.timewarnercable.com. Also serves Greene, Killawog, Lisle (village), Marathon (town), Marathon (village), Newark Valley (village), Owego (village), Triangle (town) & Whitney Point (village). ICA: NY0016.
TV Market Ranking: Below 100 (BINGHAMTON, Greene, Killawog, Lisle (village), Marathon (village), Owego (village), Triangle (town), Whitney Point (village)); Outside TV Markets (Newark Valley (village)). Franchise award date: N.A. Franchise expiration date: N.A. Began: September 1, 1964.
Channel capacity: 75 (operating 2-way). Channels available but not in use: N.A.

Basic Service
Subscribers: 200,000 Includes Elmira/Corning, Hornell, Jamestown, Oneonta, Montrose PA, Sayre PA, & Ulysses PA.
Programming (received off-air): WBGH-CA (NBC) Binghamton; WBNG-TV (CBS, CW) Binghamton; WBPN-LP Binghamton; WBXI-CA (CBS) Indianapolis; WICZ-TV (FOX) Binghamton; WIVT (ABC) Binghamton; WSKG-TV (PBS) Binghamton.
Fee: $47.21 installation; $4.75 monthly; $3.48 converter.

Expanded Basic Service 1
Subscribers: 62,644.
Programming (via satellite): Boomerang; Fox Soccer; ION Television; NickToons TV; ShopNBC; TBS Superstation; TV Land.

Expanded Basic Service 2
Subscribers: 59,501.
Programming (via satellite): A&E Networks; ABC Family Channel; AMC; Animal Planet; BET Networks; Bravo; Cartoon Network; CNBC; CNN; Comedy Central; C-SPAN; Discovery Channel; Discovery Fit & Health; Disney Channel; E! Entertainment Television; ESPN; ESPN 2; ESPN Classic Sports; Eternal Word TV Network; Food Network; Fox News Channel; Fuse; FX; Golf Channel; GSN; Hallmark Channel; Headline News; HGTV; History Channel; Lifetime; Lifetime Movie Network; MoviePlex; MSG; MSG Plus; MSNBC; MTV; MTV2; National Geographic Channel; Nickelodeon; Oxygen; QVC; SoapNet; Speed; Spike TV; Style Network; Syfy; The Learning Channel; The Weather Channel; Travel Channel; truTV; Turner Classic Movies; Turner Network TV; TV Guide Network; USA Network; Versus; VH1; WE tv; Yankees Entertainment & Sports.

Digital Basic Service
Subscribers: 30,000 Includes Elmira/Corning, Hornell, Jamestown, Oneonta, Montrose PA, & Sayre PA.
Programming (via satellite): American-Life TV Network; America's Store; BBC America; Bio; Bloomberg Television; CBS Sports Network; Cooking Channel; C-SPAN 3; Discovery Digital Networks; DIY Network; Encore Action; ESPNews; Fox College Sports Atlantic; Fox College Sports Central; Fox College Sports Pacific; Fox Movie Channel; G4; GAS; Great American Country; History Channel International; Independent Film Channel; Lifetime Real Women; MTV Hits; Music Choice; Nick Jr.; Outdoor Channel; Ovation; Sundance Channel; Toon Disney; Trinity Broadcasting Network; VH1 Classic; WAM! America's Kidz Network.
Fee: $8.45 monthly.

Digital Expanded Basic Service
Subscribers: N.A.
Programming (via satellite): Fox Deportes; FSN Digital Pacific; Fuel TV; HD Theater; HDNet; HDNet Movies; Howard TV; NBA TV; Tennis Channel; Turner Network TV HD.
Fee: $4.95 monthly.

Digital Pay Service 1
Pay Units: 44,194.
Programming (via satellite): Canales N; Cinemax (multiplexed); Flix; HBO (multiplexed); Showtime (multiplexed); Starz (multiplexed); The Movie Channel (multiplexed); TV Asia; Zee TV USA.
Fee: $4.95 monthly (Canales N), $11.25 monthly (Cinemax, HBO, Starz, or Flix/Showtime/TMC), $19.95 monthly (TV Asia & Zee TV).

Video-On-Demand: Yes

Pay-Per-View
Addressable homes: 21,045.
iN DEMAND (delivered digitally); Hot Choice (delivered digitally); Fresh (delivered digitally); Playboy TV (delivered digitally); Shorteez (delivered digitally); Pleasure (delivered digitally); ESPN Full Court (delivered digitally); ESPN Gameplan (delivered digitally); Sports PPV (delivered digitally).

Internet Service
Operational: Yes.
Subscribers: 80,000.
Broadband Service: Road Runner.
Fee: $39.95 installation; $44.95 monthly.

Telephone Service
Digital: Operational
Fee: $39.95 monthly

Miles of Plant: 4,741.0 (coaxial); 40.0 (fiber optic). Miles of plant include Elmira/Corning, Hornell, Jamestown, Oneonta, Montrose PA, Sayre PA, & Ulysses PA
President: Mary Cotter. Vice President & General Manager: Chris Strahm. Vice President, Public Affairs: Dave Whalen. Technical Operations Director: Bruce Tomkins. Marketing Director: John Melvany.
Ownership: Time Warner Cable (MSO).; Advance/Newhouse Partnership (MSO).

BLOOMVILLE—DTC Cable Inc., 107 Main St, PO Box 271, Delhi, NY 13753-0271. Phones: 888-898-8006; 607-746-2111. Fax: 607-746-7991. E-mail: steve@delhitel.com. Web Site: http://www.delhitel.com. ICA: NY0201.
TV Market Ranking: Outside TV Markets (BLOOMVILLE). Franchise award date: N.A. Franchise expiration date: N.A. Began: January 1, 1957.
Channel capacity: 30 (not 2-way capable). Channels available but not in use: N.A.

Basic Service
Subscribers: 111.
Programming (received off-air): WBNG-TV (CBS, CW) Binghamton; WICZ-TV (FOX) Binghamton; WIVT (ABC) Binghamton; WNBC (NBC) New York; WRGB (CBS) Schenectady; WSKG-TV (PBS) Binghamton; WSYR-TV (ABC) Syracuse.
Programming (via satellite): A&E Networks; ABC Family Channel; AMC; Animal Planet; CNN; Country Music TV; C-SPAN; CW11 New York; Discovery Channel; Disney Channel; ESPN; FX; History Channel; QVC; Spike TV; TBS Superstation; The Weather Channel; Trinity Broadcasting Network; Turner Network TV; USA Network; WGN America; Yankees Entertainment & Sports.
Fee: $39.00 installation; $19.00 monthly.

Pay Service 1
Pay Units: 30.
Programming (via satellite): HBO.
Fee: $9.00 monthly.

Video-On-Demand: No

Internet Service
Operational: No.

Telephone Service
None

Miles of Plant: 15.0 (coaxial); None (fiber optic).
General Manager: Douglas N. Edwards. Chief Technical Officer: William Trelease. Business Manager: Steve Oles.
Ownership: DTC Cable Inc. (MSO).

BOLIVAR—Time Warner Cable. Now served by HORNELL, NY [NY0076].. ICA: NY0202.

BOVINA (TOWN)—DTC Cable Inc., 107 Main St, PO Box 271, Delhi, NY 13753-0271. Phones: 607-746-1500; 607-746-2111. Fax: 607-746-7991. E-mail: steve@delhitel.com. Web Site: http://www.delhitel.com. ICA: NY0284.
TV Market Ranking: Outside TV Markets (BOVINA (TOWN)).
Channel capacity: 72 (not 2-way capable). Channels available but not in use: N.A.

Basic Service
Subscribers: 88.
Programming (received off-air): WABC-TV (ABC) New York; WBNG-TV (CBS, CW) Binghamton; WICZ-TV (FOX) Binghamton; WIVT (ABC) Binghamton; WNBC (NBC) New York; WNET (PBS) Newark; WNYT (NBC) Albany; WNYW (FOX) New York; WPIX (CW, IND) New York; WRGB (CBS) Schenectady; WSKG-TV (PBS) Binghamton; WWOR-TV (MNT) Secaucus.
Programming (via satellite): AMC; CW11 New York; ION Television; QVC; The Weather Channel.
Fee: $29.97 installation; $15.00 monthly.

Expanded Basic Service 1
Subscribers: N.A.
Programming (via satellite): A&E Networks; ABC Family Channel; Animal Planet; Bloomberg Television; Cartoon Network; CNBC; CNN; Comedy Central; Country Music TV; C-SPAN; Discovery Channel; Discovery Health Channel; Disney Channel; ESPN; ESPN 2; Eternal Word TV Network; Food Network; Fox Movie Channel; Fox News Channel; Fox Sports World; FX; G4; Golf Channel; Hallmark Channel; Headline News; HGTV; History Channel; Lifetime; MSG; MSG Plus; MSNBC; MTV; National Geographic Channel; Nickelodeon; Outdoor Channel; SoapNet; Speed; Spike TV; Syfy; TBS Superstation; Telemundo; The Learning Channel; Toon Disney; Travel Channel; Trinity Broadcasting Network; truTV; Turner Classic Movies; Turner Network TV; TV Land; USA Network; Versus; VH1; WE tv; WGN America; Yankees Entertainment & Sports.
Fee: $21.95 monthly.

Digital Basic Service
Subscribers: N.A.
Programming (via satellite): AmericanLife TV Network; BBC America; Bio; Bravo; CBS Sports Network; Discovery Digital Networks; DIY Network; DMX Music; ESPN; ESPN Classic Sports; ESPNews; Fox Movie Channel; FSN Digital Atlantic; FSN Digital Central; FSN Digital Pacific; Fuse; GAS; Great American Country; GSN; Halogen Network; History Channel International; Independent Film Channel; Lifetime Movie Network; Lifetime Real Women; Lime; LOGO; MTV Networks Digital Suite; Nick Jr.; Nick Too; NickToons TV; PBS Kids Channel; Style Network; Trio.
Fee: $11.00 monthly.

Pay Service 1
Pay Units: N.A.
Programming (via satellite): HBO.
Fee: $11.00 monthly.

Digital Pay Service 1
Pay Units: 13.
Programming (via satellite): HBO.
Fee: $11.00 monthly.

Digital Pay Service 2
Pay Units: N.A.
Programming (via satellite): Cinemax (multiplexed); Flix; Showtime (multiplexed); The Movie Channel (multiplexed).

Digital Pay Service 3
Pay Units: 6.
Programming (via satellite): Encore (multiplexed); Starz (multiplexed).
Fee: $11.00 monthly.

Video-On-Demand: No

Internet Service
Operational: No.

Telephone Service
None

General Manager: Douglas Edwards. Business Manager: Steve Oles.
Ownership: DTC Cable Inc. (MSO).

BRONX—Cablevision Systems Corp., 500 Brush Ave, Bronx, NY 10465. Phones: 516-803-2300 (Corporate office); 718-991-6000. Fax: 516-803-1183. Web Site: http://www.cablevision.com. ICA: NY0011.
TV Market Ranking: 1 (BRONX). Franchise award date: June 1, 1968. Franchise expiration date: N.A. Began: October 1, 1988.
Channel capacity: 91 (operating 2-way). Channels available but not in use: N.A.

Basic Service
Subscribers: 276,209.
Programming (received off-air): WABC-TV (ABC) New York; WCBS-TV (CBS) New York; WFUT-DT (TEL) Newark; WLIW (PBS) Garden City; WLNY-TV (IND) Riverhead; WMBC-TV (IND) Newton; WNBC (NBC) New York; WNET (PBS) Newark; WNJU (TMO) Linden; WNYE-TV (PBS) New York; WNYW (FOX) New York; WPIX (CW, IND) New York; WPXN-TV (ION) New York; WWOR-TV (MNT) Secaucus; WXTV-DT (UNV) Paterson.
Programming (via satellite): ESPN; News 12 The Bronx; QVC.
Fee: $15.52 monthly.

Expanded Basic Service 1
Subscribers: N.A.
Programming (via microwave): New York 1 News.
Programming (via satellite): ABC Family Channel; AMC; Animal Planet; BET Networks; Bravo; Cartoon Network; CNBC; CNN; Comedy Central; C-SPAN; C-SPAN 2; Discovery Channel; Discovery Fit & Health; E! Entertainment Television; ESPN 2; Fox News Channel; GalaVision; History Channel; Lifetime; MSG; MSG Plus; MSNBC; MTV; MTV2; News 12 Traffic & Weather; Nickelodeon; Spike TV; Syfy; TBS Superstation; The Learning Channel; The Weather Channel; truTV; Turner Network TV; TV Land; USA Network; VH1; WE tv.
Fee: $34.43 monthly.

Digital Basic Service
Subscribers: N.A.
Programming (via satellite): Bio; Bloomberg Television; Country Music TV; C-SPAN 3; Discovery Digital Networks; Disney Channel; ESPN Classic Sports; ESPNews; EuroNews; Fox Deportes; Fox Movie Channel; Fox Sports World; G4; GAS; Hallmark Channel; History Channel International; Independent Film Channel; MTV Networks Digital Suite; National Geographic Channel; Nick Jr.; NickToons TV; Oxygen; Toon Disney.
Fee: $10.95 monthly; $2.95 converter.

Digital Pay Service 1
Pay Units: N.A.
Programming (via satellite): Cinemax (multiplexed); Encore (multiplexed); HBO (multiplexed); Showtime (multiplexed); Starz (multiplexed); The Movie Channel (multiplexed).

Video-On-Demand: Yes

Pay-Per-View
Special events; Playboy TV.

Internet Service
Operational: Yes.
Broadband Service: Optimum Online.
Fee: $46.95 installation; $34.95 monthly.

Telephone Service
Digital: Operational
Fee: $34.95 monthly

Miles of Plant: 1,286.0 (coaxial); 100.0 (fiber optic). Additional miles planned: 10.0 (coaxial). Miles of plant include Brooklyn
Vice President, Field Operations: Thomas Monaghan.
Ownership: Cablevision Systems Corp. (MSO).

BROOKHAVEN—Cablevision Systems Corp. Now served by SUFFOLK COUNTY, NY [NY0006]. ICA: NY0015.

BROOKLYN—Cablevision Systems Corp., 1095 E 45th St, Brooklyn, NY 11234. Phone: 718-617-3500. Fax: 516-803-1183. Web Site: http://www.cablevision.com. ICA: NY0009.
TV Market Ranking: 1 (BROOKLYN). Franchise award date: June 1, 1983. Franchise expiration date: N.A. Began: August 23, 1988.
Channel capacity: N.A. Channels available but not in use: N.A.

Basic Service
Subscribers: 299,226.
Programming (received off-air): WABC-TV (ABC) New York; WCBS-TV (CBS) New York; WFTY-DT (TEL) Smithtown; WLIW (PBS) Garden City; WLNY-TV (IND) Riverhead; WMBC-TV (IND) Newton; WNBC (NBC) New York; WNET (PBS) Newark; WNJU (TMO) Linden; WNYW (FOX) New York; WPIX (CW, IND) New York; WPXN-TV (ION) New York; WRNN-TV (IND) Kingston; WWOR-TV (MNT) Secaucus; 30 FMs.
Programming (via satellite): ESPN; ESPN 2; New York 1 News; News 12 Brooklyn; QVC.
Fee: $49.95 installation; $15.52 monthly.

Expanded Basic Service 1
Subscribers: N.A.
Programming (via satellite): A&E Networks; ABC Family Channel; AMC; Animal Planet; BET Networks; Bravo; Cartoon Network; CNBC; CNN; Comedy Central; C-SPAN; C-SPAN 2; Discovery Channel; Disney Channel; E! Entertainment Television; ESPN 2; Food Network; Fox News Channel; Fuse; FX; GalaVision; GSN; Headline News; HGTV; History Channel; Independent Film Channel; Lifetime; MSG; MSG Plus; MSNBC; MTV; MTV2; News 12 Traffic & Weather; Nickelodeon; Prayer Channel; SoapNet; Speed; Spike TV; SportsNet New York; Syfy; TBS Superstation; The Learning Channel; The Weather Channel; Travel Channel; truTV; Turner Classic Movies; Turner Network TV; TV Land; USA Network; VH1; WE tv; Yankees Entertainment & Sports.
Fee: $34.43 monthly.

Digital Basic Service
Subscribers: N.A.
Programming (via satellite): Azteca America; BBC World News; Bio; Bloomberg Television; Canal Sur; Caracol TV; Cartoon Network Tambien en Espanol; Cine Latino; CNN en Espanol; CNN HD; Country Music TV; C-SPAN 3; Discovery en Espanol; Discovery Home Channel; Discovery Kids Channel; Docu TVE; Ecuavisia Internacional; ESPN 2 HD; ESPN Classic Sports; ESPN Deportes; ESPN HD; ESPNews; EuroNews; EWTN en Espanol; Food Network HD; Fox College Sports Atlantic; Fox College Sports Central; Fox College Sports Pacific; Fox Deportes; Fox Movie Channel; Fox Soccer; FSN HD; Fuel TV; G4; GameHD; Golf Channel; GolTV; Great American Country; Hallmark Channel; HD Theater; here! On Demand; HGTV HD; History Channel en Espanol; History Channel International; Howard TV; HTV Musica; ID Investigation Discovery; Infinito; Jewelry Television; La Familia Network; Latele Novela Network; LOGO; Mariavision; Military Channel; Momentum TV; MTV Hits; mun2 television; Music Choice; National Geographic Channel; National Geographic Channel HD Network; NBA TV; NHL Network; Nick Jr.; NickToons TV; Outdoor Channel; Oxygen; Science; ShopNBC; Sorpresa; Sundance Channel; Supercanal Caribe; TBS in HD; TeenNick; Telefe Internacional; Toon Disney; Toon Disney en Espanol; Tr3s; Turner Network TV HD; TV Chile; TV Colombia; TVE Internacional; TVG Network; Universal HD; Utilisima; VeneMovies; Versus; Versus HD; VH1 Classic; VH1 Soul; V-me TV; WAPA America; World Cinema HD; YES HD.
Fee: $10.95 monthly; $2.95 converter.

Pay Service 1
Pay Units: N.A.
Programming (via satellite): Cinemax; Flix; HBO (multiplexed); Showtime (multiplexed); The Movie Channel.
Fee: $9.95 monthly (Cinemax, Showtime or TMC), $11.95 monthly (HBO).

Digital Pay Service 1
Pay Units: N.A.
Programming (via satellite): CCTV-4; Channel One; Cinemax (multiplexed); Cinemax HD; Cinemax On Demand; Encore (multiplexed); HBO (multiplexed); HBO HD; HBO On Demand; Korean Channel; MBC America; Playboy TV; RAI International; Russian Television Network; Showtime (multiplexed); Showtime HD; Showtime On Demand; Society of Portuguese Television; Starz (multiplexed); Starz HDTV; The Movie Channel (multiplexed); The Movie Channel HD; TV Asia; TV Japan; TV Polonia; TV5, La Television International.
Fee: $9.95 monthly (Showtime, Cinemax, TMC, Starz/Encore, RAI, SPT, TV5 or TV Polinia), $11.95 monthly (HBO), $24.95 monthly (TV Japan).

Video-On-Demand: Yes

Pay-Per-View
iN DEMAND; Playboy TV; Club Jenna.

Internet Service
Operational: Yes.
Broadband Service: Optimum Online.
Fee: $46.95 installation; $34.95 monthly.

Telephone Service
Digital: Operational
Fee: $34.95 monthly

Miles of plant included in Bronx
Vice President, Field Operations: Samuel Magliaro.
Ownership: Cablevision Systems Corp. (MSO).

BROOKLYN—Formerly served by Cellularvision of New York. No longer in operation. ICA: NY0276.

BUFFALO—Now served by LACKAWANNA, NY [NY0216]. ICA: NY0008.

BURDETT—Haefele TV Inc. Now served by ENFIELD, NY [NY0152]. ICA: NY0158.

BURLINGTON (town)—Chain Lakes Cable. Now served by ROME, NY [NY0037]. ICA: NY0173.

CANAJOHARIE (village)—Time Warner Cable. Now served by ALBANY, NY [NY0014]. ICA: NY0103.

CARMEL—Comcast Cable, 21 Old Route 6, Carmel, NY 10512-2107. Phones: 860-505-6248 (Berlin office); 845-531-3900. Fax: 845-531-3926. Web Site: http://www.comcast.com. Also serves Beekman (town), Brewster, Heritage Hills, Mahopac, Patterson, Pawling (village), Putnam Valley (town), Somers (town) & Southeast (town). ICA: NY0051.
TV Market Ranking: 19 (Beekman (town), Brewster, CARMEL, Heritage Hills, Patterson, Pawling (village), Putnam Valley (town), Somers (town), Southeast (town)); Below 100 (Mahopac). Franchise award date: N.A. Franchise expiration date: N.A. Began: N.A.
Channel capacity: 80 (operating 2-way). Channels available but not in use: N.A.

Basic Service
Subscribers: 28,746.
Programming (received off-air): WABC-TV (ABC) New York; WCBS-TV (CBS) New York; WEDW (PBS) Bridgeport; WFSB (CBS) Hartford; WFUT-DT (TEL) Newark; WNBC (NBC) New York; WNET (PBS) Newark; WNJU (TMO) Linden; WNYE-TV (PBS) New York; WNYW (FOX) New York; WPIX (CW, IND) New York; WRNN-TV (IND) Kingston; WTBY-TV (TBN) Poughkeepsie; WWOR-TV (MNT) Secaucus; WXTV-DT (UNV) Paterson.
Programming (via satellite): C-SPAN; C-SPAN 2; ION Television; QVC.
Fee: $35.00 installation; $15.95 monthly.

Expanded Basic Service 1
Subscribers: 25,173.
Programming (via satellite): A&E Networks; ABC Family Channel; CNBC; Comedy Central; Discovery Channel; ESPN; Food Network; Fox News Channel; Lifetime; MSG; MTV; Nickelodeon; Syfy; TBS Superstation; The Weather Channel; Turner Network TV; TV Guide Network; USA Network; VH1; WE tv.
Fee: $38.95 monthly.

Digital Basic Service
Subscribers: 15,013.
Programming (via satellite): BBC America; Bio; Boomerang; Discovery Digital Networks; DIY Network; Fox Deportes; Fox Sports World; FSN Digital Atlantic; FSN Digital Central; FSN Digital Pacific; GAS; History Channel; Independent Film Channel; Lifetime; MTV Networks Digital Suite; National Geographic Channel; Nick Jr.; NickToons TV; Outdoor Channel; RAI International; Science Television; Sundance Channel.
Fee: $9.16 monthly.

Pay Service 1
Pay Units: N.A.
Programming (via satellite): Cinemax (multiplexed); HBO (multiplexed); Showtime; The Movie Channel.

Digital Pay Service 1
Pay Units: N.A.
Programming (via satellite): Cinemax (multiplexed); Encore (multiplexed); HBO (multiplexed); Showtime (multiplexed); Starz (multiplexed); The Movie Channel (multiplexed).

Fee: $15.00 monthly (each).
Video-On-Demand: No
Pay-Per-View
TEN (delivered digitally).
Internet Service
Operational: Yes.
Subscribers: 18,399.
Broadband Service: Comcast High Speed Internet.
Fee: $42.95 monthly.
Telephone Service
Digital: Operational
Miles of Plant: 880.0 (coaxial); 100.0 (fiber optic).
Vice President: Michael Parker. General Manager: Andrew McCarthy. Technical Operations Manager: Kevin Aguiere. Marketing Director: Carolyne Hannan. Marketing Manager: Judi Cyr. Marketing Coordinator: Marcia McElroy.
Ownership: Comcast Cable Communications Inc. (MSO).

CATO (town)—Time Warner Cable. Now served by SYRACUSE, NY [NY0013]. ICA: NY0207.

CATSKILL—Mid-Hudson Cablevision Inc., 200 Jefferson Hts, PO Box 399, Catskill, NY 12414-0399. Phones: 800-342-5400; 518-943-6600. Fax: 518-943-6603. E-mail: cable@mid-hudson.com. Web Site: http://www2.mhcable.com. Also serves Ashland (town) (Greene County), Athens (town), Athens (village), Bethlehem (town), Cairo (town), Catskill (town), Catskill (village), Claverack, Coeymans, Columbiaville, Coxsackie (town), Coxsackie (village), Gallatin, Greenport (Columbia County), Greenville, Hudson, Livingston (town), New Baltimore, Philmont, Prattsville (town), Ravena (village), Stockport, Stockport (town), Stottville, Westerlo & Windham (town). ICA: NY0039.
TV Market Ranking: 34 (Ashland (town) (Greene County), Athens (town), Athens (village), Bethlehem (town), Cairo (town), CATSKILL, Catskill (town), Catskill (village), Claverack, Coeymans, Columbiaville, Coxsackie (town), Coxsackie (village), Greenport (Columbia County), Greenville, Hudson, New Baltimore, Philmont, Ravena (village), Stockport, Stockport (town), Stottville, Westerlo, Windham (town)); Below 100 (Gallatin, Livingston (town), Prattsville (town)). Franchise award date: January 1, 1970. Franchise expiration date: N.A. Began: September 1, 1971.
Channel capacity: N.A. Channels available but not in use: N.A.
Basic Service
Subscribers: 20,252.
Programming (received off-air): WCWN (CW) Schenectady; WMHT (PBS) Schenectady; WNYT (NBC) Albany; WRGB (CBS) Schenectady; WRNN-TV (IND) Kingston; WSSN-LP (ION) Hudson et al.; WTEN (ABC) Albany; WXXA-TV (FOX) Albany; 21 FMs.
Programming (via satellite): C-SPAN; C-SPAN 2; Eternal Word TV Network; Fox News Channel; FX; MSNBC; MyNetworkTV Inc.; QVC; TV Guide Network.
Fee: $20.95 monthly.
Digital Basic Service
Subscribers: 873.
Programming (via satellite): BBC America; Bloomberg Television; Chiller; cloo; CMT Pure Country; Cooking Channel; Current; Discovery Fit & Health; Discovery Health Channel; Discovery Kids Channel; DMX Music; ESPNews; Fox Business Channel; Fox College Sports Atlantic; Fox College Sports Central; Fox College Sports Pacific; Fox Soccer; Great American Country; GSN; Halogen Network; History Channel International; ID Investigation Discovery; Independent Film Channel; Lifetime Movie Network; Military Channel; MTV Hits; MTV2; Nick Jr.; NickToons TV; Outdoor Channel; Ovation; PBS Kids Sprout; Planet Green; RFD-TV; RTN; Science; ShopNBC; Sundance Channel; TeenNick; The Word Network; Toon Disney; Trinity Broadcasting Network; TVG Network; VH1 Classic; VH1 Soul.
Fee: $6.95 monthly; $5.95 converter.
Digital Expanded Basic Service
Subscribers: N.A.
Programming (received off-air): WCWN (CW) Schenectady; WMHT (PBS) Schenectady; WNYT (NBC) Albany; WRGB (CBS) Schenectady; WTEN (ABC) Albany; WXXA-TV (FOX) Albany.
Programming (via satellite): A&E HD; Animal Planet HD; Bravo HD; Discovery Channel HD; ESPN HD; Food Network HD; FX HD; HD Theater; HDNet; HDNet Movies; HGTV HD; History Channel HD; National Geographic Channel HD Network; Outdoor Channel 2 HD; QVC HD; Science HD; Speed HD; Syfy HD; TBS in HD; TLC HD; Turner Network TV HD; Universal HD; USA Network HD; YES HD.
Fee: $7.50 monthly; $7.95 converter.
Pay Service 1
Pay Units: 2,250.
Programming (via satellite): Cinemax; HBO (multiplexed); Showtime.
Fee: $9.95 monthly (Cinemax), $11.95 monthly (HBO or Showtime & TMC).
Digital Pay Service 1
Pay Units: N.A.
Programming (via satellite): Cinemax (multiplexed); Cinemax HD; Encore (multiplexed); HBO (multiplexed); HBO HD; HBO On Demand; Showtime (multiplexed); Starz (multiplexed); Starz HDTV; The Movie Channel (multiplexed).
Fee: $13.40 monthly (Cinemax), $13.95 monthly (HBO, Showtime/TMC or Starz/Encore).
Video-On-Demand: Yes
Pay-Per-View
Addressable homes: 20,252.
iN DEMAND (delivered digitally); Playboy TV (delivered digitally); Fresh (delivered digitally); Spice: Xcess (delivered digitally); Club Jenna (delivered digitally).
Internet Service
Operational: Yes.
Subscribers: 6,666.
Broadband Service: In-house.
Fee: $49.95 monthly; $10.00 modem lease.
Telephone Service
Digital: Operational
Subscribers: 1,326.
Fee: $29.95 monthly
Miles of Plant: 800.0 (coaxial); 60.0 (fiber optic).
President: James M. Reynolds. Chief Technician: Edward Harter. Chief Engineer: David Fingar.
Ownership: Mid-Hudson Cablevision Inc.

CENTRAL SQUARE—Time Warner Cable. Now served by OSWEGO, NY [NY0061]. ICA: NY0091.

CHAMPLAIN—Time Warner Cable, 6005 Fair Lakes Rd, East Syracuse, NY 13057. Phone: 315-634-6100. Fax: 315-634-6219. Web Site: http://www.timewarnercable.com/CentralNY. Also serves Altona, Champlain (village), Chazy (town), Ellenburg, Ingraham, Mooers, Rouses Point, Sciota & West Chazy. ICA: NY0101.

TV Market Ranking: Below 100 (Altona, CHAMPLAIN, Champlain (village), Chazy (town), Ellenburg, Ingraham, Mooers, Rouses Point, Sciota, West Chazy). Franchise award date: February 8, 1982. Franchise expiration date: N.A. Began: November 1, 1982.
Channel capacity: N.A. Channels available but not in use: N.A.
Basic Service
Subscribers: N.A. Included in Syracuse
Programming (received off-air): WCAX-TV (CBS) Burlington; WCFE-TV (PBS) Plattsburgh; WETK (PBS) Burlington; WFFF-TV (CW, FOX) Burlington; WPTZ (NBC) Plattsburgh; WVNY (ABC) Burlington.
Programming (via satellite): ABC Family Channel; CNN; ESPN; Headline News; MSG Plus; MTV; QVC; TBS Superstation; TV Guide Network; USA Network; various Canadian stations; WGN America; YNN-Central New York.
Fee: $38.42 installation; $9.28 monthly; $.88 converter.
Expanded Basic Service 1
Subscribers: N.A. Included in Syracuse
Programming (via satellite): A&E Networks; Animal Planet; BET Networks; Cartoon Network; CNBC; Comedy Central; C-SPAN; C-SPAN 2; Discovery Channel; Discovery Fit & Health; E! Entertainment Television; ESPN 2; Eternal Word TV Network; Food Network; Fox News Channel; FX; Hallmark Channel; HGTV; ION Television; Lifetime; Lifetime Movie Network; MSNBC; Nickelodeon; Oxygen; ShopNBC; SoapNet; Spike TV; Syfy; The Learning Channel; The Weather Channel; Travel Channel; Turner Network TV; TV Land; Univision Studios; Versus; VH1; WE tv; Yankees Entertainment & Sports.
Fee: $44.34 installation; $45.50 monthly.
Digital Basic Service
Subscribers: N.A. Included in Syracuse
Programming (via satellite): AMC; AmericanLife TV Network; America's Store; ART America; BBC America; Bio; Bloomberg Television; Boomerang; Bravo; Canales N; CCTV-4; Cooking Channel; Country Music TV; C-SPAN 3; Daystar TV Network; Discovery Digital Networks; Disney Channel; DIY Network; ESPN Classic Sports; ESPNews; Fox Movie Channel; Fox Sports World; FSN Digital Atlantic; FSN Digital Central; FSN Digital Pacific; Fuel TV; Fuse; G4; GAS; Golf Channel; Great American Country; GSN; History Channel; History Channel International; Independent Film Channel; International Television (ITV); Lifetime Real Women; MSG; MTV2; Music Choice; National Geographic Channel; NBA TV; Nick Jr.; Outdoor Channel; Ovation; Russian Television Network; Saigon Broadcasting Television Network; Speed; Style Network; Sundance Channel; Tennis Channel; Toon Disney; Trinity Broadcasting Network; truTV; Turner Classic Movies; TV Asia; TV5 USA; VH1 Classic; WAM! America's Kidz Network; Zee TV USA.
Fee: $14.95 installation; $10.95 monthly.
Digital Pay Service 1
Pay Units: N.A.
Programming (via satellite): Cinemax (multiplexed); Encore (multiplexed); HBO (multiplexed); RAI International; Showtime (multiplexed); Starz (multiplexed); The Movie Channel (multiplexed).
Video-On-Demand: Yes
Pay-Per-View
Addressable homes: 1,125.
Hot Choice.
Internet Service
Operational: Yes.
Broadband Service: EarthLink, LocalNet, Road Runner.
Fee: $39.95 installation; $44.95 monthly.
Telephone Service
Digital: Operational
Fee: $39.95 monthly
Miles of plant included in Syracuse.
President: Mary Cotter. Vice President, Engineering: Henry Hryckiewicz. Vice President, Marketing: John Melvany. Vice President, Public Affairs: Jeff Unaitis. Technical Operations Director: Bruce Tompkins.
Ownership: Time Warner Cable (MSO).; Advance/Newhouse Partnership (MSO).

CHATHAM—Charter Communications, 95 Higgins St, Worcester, MA 1606. Phone: 508-853-1515. Fax: 508-854-5042. Web Site: http://www.charter.com. Also serves Ancram (town), Austerlitz (town), Canaan (town), Copake (town), Ghent (town), Hillsdale (town) & New Lebanon (town). ICA: NY0088.
TV Market Ranking: 34 (Austerlitz (town), Canaan (town), CHATHAM, Ghent (town), Hillsdale (town), New Lebanon (town)); Below 100 (Ancram (town), Copake (town)). Franchise award date: July 1, 1983. Franchise expiration date: N.A. Began: June 1, 1993.
Channel capacity: 60 (not 2-way capable). Channels available but not in use: N.A.
Basic Service
Subscribers: 5,000 Includes Berlin.
Programming (received off-air): WCWN (CW) Schenectady; WMHT (PBS) Schenectady; WNYA (MNT) Pittsfield; WNYT (NBC) Albany; WRGB (CBS) Schenectady; WRNN-TV (IND) Kingston; WTEN (ABC) Albany; WXXA-TV (FOX) Albany; WYPX-TV (ION) Amsterdam.
Programming (via satellite): C-SPAN; QVC; TBS Superstation; Trinity Broadcasting Network; TV Guide Network; WPIX (CW, IND) New York.
Fee: $29.99 installation; $4.00 converter.
Expanded Basic Service 1
Subscribers: N.A.
Programming (via satellite): A&E Networks; ABC Family Channel; AMC; Animal Planet; Bravo; Cartoon Network; CNBC; CNN; Comedy Central; Country Music TV; C-SPAN 2; Discovery Channel; Disney Channel; E! Entertainment Television; ESPN; ESPN 2; ESPN Classic Sports; Food Network; Fox News Channel; FX; GSN; Headline News; HGTV; History Channel; Lifetime; Meadows Racing Network; MSG; MSG Plus; MTV; Nickelodeon; Speed;

Spike TV; Syfy; TBS Superstation; The Learning Channel; The Weather Channel; Toon Disney; Travel Channel; Turner Network TV; TV Land; USA Network; Versus; VH1; Yesterday USA.
Fee: $55.00 monthly.

Digital Basic Service
Subscribers: N.A.
Programming (via satellite): BBC America; Bio; Discovery Digital Networks; DMX Music; ESPNews; Fox Soccer; Fuse; GAS; Golf Channel; Independent Film Channel; Lifetime Movie Network; MTV2; Nick Jr.; Style Network; Turner Classic Movies; TV Guide Interactive Inc.; WE tv.

Digital Pay Service 1
Pay Units: N.A.
Programming (via satellite): Cinemax (multiplexed); Encore (multiplexed); Flix; HBO (multiplexed); Showtime (multiplexed); Starz (multiplexed); The Movie Channel (multiplexed).

Video-On-Demand: Yes

Pay-Per-View
iN DEMAND (delivered digitally); Playboy TV (delivered digitally).

Internet Service
Operational: Yes.
Broadband Service: Charter Pipeline.

Telephone Service
Digital: Operational

Miles of Plant: 300.0 (coaxial); None (fiber optic). Additional miles planned: 30.0 (coaxial).

Vice President & General Manager: Greg Garabedian. Technical Operations Director: George Duffy. Marketing Director: Dennis Jerome. Marketing Manager: Paula Cucchetelli.

Ownership: Charter Communications Inc. (MSO).

CINCINNATUS—Chain Lakes Cablevision. Now served by CORTLAND, NY [NY0062]. ICA: NY0279.

CLYMER—Time Warner Cable. Now served by JAMESTOWN, NY [NY0030]. ICA: NY0185.

COBLESKILL (town)—Time Warner Cable. Now served by ALBANY, NY [NY0014]. ICA: NY0082.

COHOCTON—Time Warner Cable. Now served by HORNELL, NY [NY0076]. ICA: NY0177.

CONSTANTIA (town)—Time Warner Cable. Now served by ROME, NY [NY0037]. ICA: NY0117.

COOPERSTOWN—Time Warner Cable. Now served by ONEONTA, NY [NY0065]. ICA: NY0105.

CORONA—RCN Corp. Formerly served by Queens, NY [NY0283]. This cable system has converted to IPTV, 196 Van Buren St, Herndon, VA 20170. Phone: 703-434-8200. Web Site: http://www.rcn.com. ICA: NY5302.

TV Market Ranking: 1 (QUEENS).

Channel capacity: N.A. Channels available but not in use: N.A.

Pay Service 1
Pay Units: N.A.
Fee: $11.95 monthly (Cinemaz or Starz!); $16.95 monthly (Showtime/The Movie Channel); $17.95 monthly (HBO).

Internet Service
Operational: Yes.
Fee: $38.00 monthly.

Telephone Service
Digital: Operational
Fee: $45.00 monthly

Chairman: Steven J. Simmons. Chief Executive Officer: Jim Holanda.

CORTLAND—Time Warner Cable, 6005 Fair Lakes Rd, East Syracuse, NY 13057. Phone: 315-634-6100. Fax: 315-634-6219. Web Site: http://www.timewarnercable.com/CentralNY. Also serves Apulia Station, Cincinnatus, Cortlandville, Cuyler, Fabius (village), Georgetown (town), Homer (village), McGraw, North Pitcher, Otselic (town), Pitcher (town), Preble (town), Scott (town), Taylor (town), Truxton (town), Tully (town), Virgil (town) & Willet. ICA: NY0062.

TV Market Ranking: 35 (Apulia Station, CORTLAND, Cortlandville, Cuyler, Fabius (village), Georgetown (town), Homer (village), McGraw, North Pitcher, Otselic (town), Pitcher (town), Preble (town), Scott (town), Taylor (town), Truxton (town), Tully (town)); Below 100 (Cincinnatus, Virgil (town), Willet). Franchise award date: July 15, 1965. Franchise expiration date: N.A. Began: July 15, 1965.

Channel capacity: N.A. Channels available but not in use: N.A.

Basic Service
Subscribers: N.A. Included in Syracuse
Programming (received off-air): WBNG-TV (CBS, CW) Binghamton; WCNY-TV (PBS) Syracuse; WICZ-TV (FOX) Binghamton; WIVT (ABC) Binghamton; WNYS-TV (MNT) Syracuse; WSKG-TV (PBS) Binghamton; WSPX-TV (ION) Syracuse; WSTM-TV (NBC) Syracuse; WSTQ-LP (CW) Syracuse; WSYR-TV (ABC) Syracuse; WSYT (FOX) Syracuse; WTVH (CBS) Syracuse; 23 FMs.
Programming (via satellite): TV Guide Network; YNN-Central New York.
Fee: $41.10 installation; $9.28 monthly.

Expanded Basic Service 1
Subscribers: N.A. Included in Syracuse
Programming (via satellite): A&E Networks; ABC Family Channel; Animal Planet; BET Networks; Cartoon Network; CNBC; CNN; Comedy Central; C-SPAN; C-SPAN 2; Discovery Channel; Discovery Fit & Health; E! Entertainment Television; ESPN; ESPN 2; Eternal Word TV Network; Food Network; Fox News Channel; FX; Hallmark Channel; Headline News; HGTV; Lifetime; Lifetime Movie Network; MSG Plus; MSNBC; MTV; National Geographic Channel; Nickelodeon; Oxygen; QVC; ShopNBC; SoapNet; Spike TV; Syfy; TBS Superstation; The Learning Channel; The Weather Channel; Travel Channel; Turner Network TV; TV Land; Univision Studios; USA Network; Versus; VH1; WE tv; Yankees Entertainment & Sports.
Fee: $45.50 monthly.

Digital Basic Service
Subscribers: N.A. Included in Syracuse
Programming (via satellite): AMC; AmericanLife TV Network; America's Store; BBC America; Bio; Bloomberg Television; Boomerang; Bravo; Cooking Channel; Country Music TV; C-SPAN 3; Daystar TV Network; Disney Channel; DIY Network; ESPN Classic Sports; ESPNews; Fox Movie Channel; Fox Sports World; Fuse; G4; GAS; Golf Channel; Great American Country; GSN; History Channel; History Channel International; Independent Film Channel; Lifetime Real Women; Local Cable Weather; MSG; MTV2; Music Choice; National Geographic Channel; Nick Jr.; Outdoor Channel; Ovation; Speed; Style Network; Sundance Channel; Toon Disney; Trinity Broadcasting Network; truTV; Turner Classic Movies; VH1 Classic.
Fee: $10.95 monthly.

Digital Expanded Basic Service
Subscribers: N.A.
Programming (via satellite): ART America; Canales N; CCTV-4; FSN Digital Atlantic; FSN Digital Central; FSN Digital Pacific; Fuel TV; NBA TV; RAI International; Russian Television Network; Saigon Broadcasting Television Network; Tennis Channel; TV Asia; TV5 USA; Zee TV USA.
Fee: $4.95 monthly.

Digital Pay Service 1
Pay Units: 3,166.
Programming (via satellite): Cinemax (multiplexed); Encore Action (multiplexed); HBO (multiplexed); Showtime (multiplexed); Starz (multiplexed); The Movie Channel (multiplexed).
Fee: $8.00 monthly (Cinemax), $9.50 monthly (Showtime, Starz or TMC), $10.95 monthly (HBO).

Video-On-Demand: Yes

Pay-Per-View
iN DEMAND (delivered digitally); Playboy TV (delivered digitally); Fresh (delivered digitally).

Internet Service
Operational: Yes.
Broadband Service: EarthLink, LocalNet, Road Runner.
Fee: $39.95 installation; $44.95 monthly.

Telephone Service
Digital: Operational
Fee: $39.95 monthly

Miles of plant included in Syracuse.

President: Mary Cotter. Vice President, Engineering: Henry Hryckiewicz. Technical Operations Director: Bruce Tompkins. Vice President, Marketing: John Melvany. Vice President, Public Affairs: Jeff Unaitis.

Ownership: Time Warner Cable (MSO).; Advance/Newhouse Partnership (MSO).

CUYLER—Chain Lakes Cable. Now served by CORTLAND, NY [NY0062]. ICA: NY0157.

DANSVILLE—Time Warner Cable. Now served by HORNELL, NY [NY0076]. ICA: NY0208.

DE RUYTER—Chain Lakes Cablevision. No longer in operation. ICA: NY0165.

DELHI—DTC Cable Inc., 107 Main St, PO Box 271, Delhi, NY 13753-0271. Phones: 607-746-1500; 888-898-8006. Fax: 607-746-7991. E-mail: custserv@delhitel.com. Web Site: http://www.delhitel.com. ICA: NY0285.

TV Market Ranking: Outside TV Markets (DELHI). Franchise award date: N.A. Franchise expiration date: N.A. Began: N.A.

Channel capacity: N.A. Channels available but not in use: N.A.

Digital Basic Service
Subscribers: 259.
Programming (via satellite): Bloomberg Television.
Fee: $29.95 installation; $14.95 monthly.

Digital Expanded Basic Service
Subscribers: N.A.
Programming (received off-air): WNET (PBS) Newark; WNYW (FOX) New York.
Programming (via satellite): A&E Networks; ABC Family Channel; AMC; AmericanLife TV Network; Animal Planet; BBC America; Bio; Bravo; Cartoon Network; CNBC; CNN; Comedy Central; Country Music TV; C-SPAN; Discovery Channel; Discovery Digital Networks; Disney Channel; DMX Music; E! Entertainment Television; ESPN; ESPN 2; ESPN Classic Sports; ESPNews; Food Network; Fox Sports World; Fuse; FX; G4; Golf Channel; Great American Country; GSN; Halogen Network; Headline News; HGTV; History Channel; History Channel International; Independent Film Channel; Lifetime; Lifetime Movie Network; MSG; MSG Plus; MSNBC; MTV Networks Digital Suite; National Geographic Channel; Nickelodeon; QVC; Spike TV; Syfy; TBS Superstation; The Learning Channel; The Weather Channel; Toon Disney; Travel Channel; Trinity Broadcasting Network; Turner Classic Movies; Turner Network TV; TV Land; USA Network; Versus; WE tv; WGN America; Yankees Entertainment & Sports.
Fee: $17.00 monthly.

Digital Expanded Basic Service 2
Subscribers: N.A.
Programming (via satellite): Encore (multiplexed); ESPN 2; ESPN Classic Sports; ESPNews; Fox Movie Channel; Fox Sports World; FSN Digital Atlantic; FSN Digital Central; FSN Digital Pacific; Hallmark Channel; Outdoor Channel; Speed; Style Network; Trio.
Fee: $6.00 monthly.

Digital Pay Service 1
Pay Units: 47.
Programming (via satellite): HBO (multiplexed).
Fee: $9.95 monthly.

Digital Pay Service 2
Pay Units: 23.
Programming (via satellite): Flix; Showtime (multiplexed); The Movie Channel (multiplexed).
Fee: $9.95 monthly.

Digital Pay Service 3
Pay Units: 13.
Programming (via satellite): Cinemax (multiplexed).
Fee: $9.95 monthly.

Digital Pay Service 4
Pay Units: 12.
Programming (via satellite): Starz (multiplexed).
Fee: $9.95 monthly.

Video-On-Demand: No

Pay-Per-View
Playboy TV (delivered digitally).

Internet Service
Operational: Yes, DSL.

Telephone Service
None

General Manager: Douglas Edwards. Business Manager: Steve Oles.

Ownership: DTC Cable Inc. (MSO).

DELHI—Time Warner Cable. Now served by ONEONTA, NY [NY0065]. ICA: NY0140.

DEPOSIT—Formerly served by Adams Cable TV. Now served by CARBONDALE, PA [PA0067]. ICA: NY0148.

DOVER PLAINS—Cablevision Systems Corp., 1 Van Cortland Ave, Ossining, NY 10562-3309. Phone: 516-803-2300 (Corporate office). Fax: 516-803-1183. Web Site: http://www.cablevision.com. Also serves Amenia (town), Clinton (town), Dover (town), Millbrook, Millerton, North East (town), Pine Plains (town), Stanford (town), Union Vale (town), Verbank, Washington (town) & Wingdale. ICA: NY0209.

TV Market Ranking: 19 (Amenia (town), Dover (town), DOVER PLAINS, Union Vale (town), Wingdale); Below 100 (Clinton (town), Millbrook, Millerton, North East (town), Pine

Plains (town), Stanford (town), Verbank, Washington (town)). Franchise award date: N.A. Franchise expiration date: N.A. Began: January 1, 1964.
Channel capacity: N.A. Channels available but not in use: N.A.

Basic Service
Subscribers: 4,635.
Programming (received off-air): W42AE Poughkeepsie; WABC-TV (ABC) New York; WCBS-TV (CBS) New York; WFUT-DT (TEL) Newark; WMBC-TV (IND) Newton; WNBC (NBC) New York; WNET (PBS) Newark; WNJN (PBS) Montclair; WNJU (TMO) Linden; WNYW (FOX) New York; WPIX (CW, IND) New York; WPXN-TV (ION) New York; WRNN-TV (IND) Kingston; WTBY-TV (TBN) Poughkeepsie; WWOR-TV (MNT) Secaucus; WXTV-DT (UNV) Paterson.
Programming (via satellite): Disney Channel.
Fee: $49.95 installation; $15.11 monthly.

Expanded Basic Service 1
Subscribers: N.A.
Programming (via satellite): A&E Networks; ABC Family Channel; AMC; Animal Planet; BET Networks; Bravo; Cartoon Network; CNBC; CNN; Comedy Central; Country Music TV; C-SPAN; C-SPAN 2; Discovery Channel; E! Entertainment Television; ESPN; ESPN 2; Food Network; Fox News Channel; Fuse; FX; GSN; Headline News; HGTV; History Channel; Independent Film Channel; Lifetime; MSG; MSG Plus; MSNBC; MTV; MTV2; News 12 Traffic & Weather; Nickelodeon; QVC; SoapNet; Speed; Spike TV; SportsNet New York; Syfy; TBS Superstation; The Learning Channel; The Weather Channel; Travel Channel; truTV; Turner Classic Movies; Turner Network TV; TV Land; USA Network; VH1; WE tv; Yankees Entertainment & Sports.
Fee: $34.84 monthly.

Digital Basic Service
Subscribers: N.A.
Programming (via satellite): Azteca America; BBC World News; Bio; Bloomberg Television; Canal Sur; Caracol TV; Cartoon Network Tambien en Espanol; Cine Latino; CNN en Espanol; CNN HD; Country Music TV; C-SPAN 3; Discovery en Espanol; Discovery Home Channel; Discovery Kids Channel; Discovery Times Channel; Docu TVE; Ecuavisia Internacional; ESPN 2 HD; ESPN Classic Sports; ESPN Deportes; ESPN HD; ESPNews; EuroNews; EWTN en Espanol; Food Network HD; Fox College Sports Central; Fox College Sports Pacific; Fox Deportes; Fox Movie Channel; Fox Soccer; Fuel TV; G4; Golf Channel; GolTV; Great American Country; Hallmark Channel; HD Theater; here! On Demand; HGTV HD; History Channel en Espanol; History Channel International; Howard TV; HTV Musica; Infinito; Jewelry Television; La Familia Network; Latele Novela Network; LOGO; Mariavision; Military Channel; Momentum TV; MTV Hits; mun2 television; Music Choice; National Geographic Channel; National Geographic Channel HD Network; NBA TV; NDTV The Dominican Channel; NHL Network; Nick Jr.; NickToons TV; Outdoor Channel; Oxygen; Science; ShopNBC; Sorpresa; Sundance Channel; Supercanal Caribe; TBS in HD; TeenNick; Telefe International; Toon Disney; Toon Disney en Espanol; Tr3s; Turner Network TV HD; TV Chile; TV Colombia; TVE Internacional; TVG Network; Universal HD; Utilisima; VeneMovies; Versus; Versus HD; VH1 Classic; VH1 Soul; V-me TV; WAPA America; World Cinema HD; WWE 24/7; YES HD.
Fee: $10.95 monthly.

Pay Service 1
Pay Units: 180.
Programming (via satellite): Cinemax; Flix; HBO (multiplexed); Showtime (multiplexed); Starz; The Movie Channel.
Fee: $10.45 monthly.

Digital Pay Service 1
Pay Units: N.A.
Programming (via satellite): CCTV-4; Channel One; Chinese Television Network; Cinemax (multiplexed); Cinemax HD; Cinemax On Demand; Encore (multiplexed); HBO (multiplexed); HBO HD; HBO On Demand; Korean Channel; MBC America; Portuguese Channel; RAI International; Russian Television Network; Showtime (multiplexed); Showtime HD; Showtime On Demand; Starz (multiplexed); Starz HDTV; The Movie Channel (multiplexed); The Movie Channel HD; TV Asia; TV Japan; TV Polonia; TV5, La Television International; Zee TV USA.
Fee: $9.95 monthly (Showtime, Cinemax, TMC, Starz/Encore, Playboy, RAI, SPT, TV5, or TV Polonia), $11.95 monthly (HBO), $14.95 monthly (Korean Package or Chinese Package), $19.95 monthly (South Asian Package), $24.95 monthly (TV Japan), $29.95 monthly (Russian Pack.

Video-On-Demand: Yes

Pay-Per-View
Playboy TV; Sports PPV (delivered digitally); NBA TV (delivered digitally); iN DEMAND (delivered digitally); Playboy TV (delivered digitally).

Internet Service
Operational: Yes.
Broadband Service: Optimum Online.
Fee: $46.95 installation; $34.95 monthly.

Telephone Service
Digital: Operational
Fee: $34.95 monthly
Miles of Plant: 377.0 (coaxial); 42.0 (fiber optic).
Vice President, Field Operations: Mark Fitchett. Area Operations Manager: Gary Kirkland. Chief Technician: Steve Wrisley. Media Relations Director: Patrick Macelro.
Ownership: Cablevision Systems Corp. (MSO).

DOWNSVILLE—Formerly served by Downsville Community Antenna. No longer in operation. ICA: NY0210.

DRESDEN—Time Warner Cable. Now served by GENEVA, NY [NY0218]. ICA: NY0211.

DUNDEE—Time Warner Cable. Now served by ELMIRA/CORNING, NY [NY0057]. ICA: NY0212.

DUNKIRK—Time Warner Cable, 355 Chicago St, Buffalo, NY 14204-2069. Phone: 716-558-8881. Fax: 716-558-8855. Web Site: http://www.timewarnercable.com/wny. Also serves Arkwright, Chautauqua, Dunkirk (town), Forestville, Hanover, Mayville, North Harmony (town), Pomfret, Portland, Ripley, Sheridan (town), Sherman & Silver Creek. ICA: NY0064.
TV Market Ranking: 24 (DUNKIRK, Dunkirk (town), Forestville, Hanover, Sheridan (town), Silver Creek, Silver Creek); Below 100 (Arkwright, Chautauqua, Mayville, North Harmony (town), Pomfret, Portland, Ripley, Sherman). Franchise award date: N.A. Franchise expiration date: N.A. Began: October 1, 1973.
Channel capacity: N.A. Channels available but not in use: N.A.

Basic Service
Subscribers: N.A. Included in Lackawanna
Programming (received off-air): various Canadian stations; WBBZ-TV (IND) Springville; WGRZ (NBC) Buffalo; WIVB-TV (CBS) Buffalo; WKBW-TV (ABC) Buffalo; WNED-TV (PBS) Buffalo; WNLO (CW) Buffalo; WNYB (IND) Jamestown; WNYO-TV (MNT) Buffalo; WPXJ-TV (ION) Batavia; WUTV (FOX) Buffalo.
Programming (via satellite): C-SPAN; C-SPAN 2; Eternal Word TV Network; QVC; TV Guide Network.

Expanded Basic Service 1
Subscribers: 11,123.
Programming (received off-air): WUTV (FOX) Buffalo.
Programming (via satellite): A&E Networks; ABC Family Channel; AMC; Animal Planet; BET Networks; Bravo; Cartoon Network; CNBC; CNN; Comedy Central; Country Music TV; Discovery Channel; Disney Channel; E! Entertainment Television; ESPN; ESPN 2; Food Network; Fox News Channel; FX; Hallmark Channel; Headline News; HGTV; History Channel; Lifetime; MSG; MSNBC; MTV; Nickelodeon; Oxygen; ShopNBC; Spike TV; SportsNet New York; Style Network; Syfy; TBS Superstation; The Learning Channel; The Weather Channel; Travel Channel; truTV; Turner Classic Movies; Turner Network TV; TV Land; USA Network; Versus; VH1; Yankees Entertainment & Sports.

Digital Basic Service
Subscribers: N.A.
Programming (via satellite): A&E HD; AmericanLife TV Network; BBC America; BBC America On Demand; Bio; Bloomberg Television; Boomerang; Canal 52MX; CBS Sports Network; Cine Latino; CMT Pure Country; CNN en Espanol; Cooking Channel; Current; Daystar TV Network; Discovery en Espanol; Discovery Fit & Health; Discovery Health Channel; Discovery Home Channel; Discovery Kids Channel; Discovery Times Channel; DIY Network; ESPN 2 HD; ESPN Classic Sports; ESPN Deportes; ESPN HD; ESPN U; ESPNews; Exercise TV; FamilyNet; Fox Business Channel; Fox College Sports Atlantic; Fox College Sports Central; Fox College Sports Pacific; Fox Deportes; Fox Movie Channel; Fox Reality Channel; Fox Soccer; Fuel TV; Fuse; G4; GAS; GMC; Golf Channel; Great American Country; GSN; Halogen Network; HD Theater; HDNet; HDNet Movies; History Channel en Espanol; History Channel International; Howard TV; Independent Film Channel; Lifetime Movie Network; LOGO; Military Channel; MTV Hits; MTV Jams; MTV2; Music Choice; National Geographic Channel; National Geographic Channel On Demand; NBA TV; NHL Network; Nick Jr.; Nick Too; NickToons TV; Outdoor Channel; Oxygen On Demand; Palladia; ReelzChannel; Science; SoapNet; Speed; Speed On Demand; Sundance Channel; Tennis Channel; The Word Network; Toon Disney; Toon Disney en Espanol; Tr3s; Trinity Broadcasting Network; Turner Network TV HD; TV Guide SPOT; TV One; Universal HD; Versus HD; VH1 Classic; VH1 Soul; WE tv.
Fee: $57.95 monthly.

Digital Pay Service 1
Pay Units: N.A.
Programming (via satellite): Cinemax (multiplexed); Cinemax HD; Cinemax On Demand; Encore (multiplexed); Flix; HBO (multiplexed); HBO HD; HBO On Demand; Showtime (multiplexed); Showtime HD; Showtime On Demand; Starz (multiplexed); Starz HDTV; Starz On Demand; The Movie Channel (multiplexed); The Movie Channel On Demand.
Fee: $11.95 monthly (each).

Video-On-Demand: Yes

Pay-Per-View
Playboy TV (delivered digitally); Fresh (delivered digitally); NBA League Pass (delivered digitally); Sports PPV (delivered digitally); Ten Clips (delivered digitally); Ten Blox (delivered digitally); Ten Blue (delivered digitally).

Internet Service
Operational: Yes.
Broadband Service: Road Runner.
Fee: $44.95 monthly.

Telephone Service
Digital: Operational
Fee: $39.95 monthly
Miles of Plant: 177.0 (coaxial); None (fiber optic).
President: Gordon Harp. Vice President, Marketing: Steve Jaworowski. Vice President, Public Affairs: Robin Wolfgang. Technical Operations Manager: Steve Parlik. Marketing Manager: Jean Calabrese.
Ownership: Time Warner Cable (MSO).

DURHAM—Mid-Hudson Cablevision Inc., 200 Jefferson Hts, PO Box 399, Catskill, NY 12414-0399. Phones: 518-943-6653; 518-943-6600. Fax: 518-943-6603. E-mail: cable@mid-hudson.com. Web Site: http://www2.mhcable.com. Also serves Cornwallville, East Durham, Medusa, Oak Hill, Preston Hollow & Rensselaerville. ICA: NY0149.
TV Market Ranking: 34 (Cornwallville, DURHAM, East Durham, Medusa, Oak Hill, Preston Hollow, Rensselaerville). Franchise award date: N.A. Franchise expiration date: N.A. Began: June 1, 1990.
Channel capacity: 60 (operating 2-way). Channels available but not in use: N.A.

Basic Service
Subscribers: 650.
Programming (received off-air): WCWN (CW) Schenectady; WMHT (PBS) Schenectady; WNYT (NBC) Albany; WRGB (CBS) Schenectady; WTEN (ABC) Albany; WXXA-TV (FOX) Albany.
Programming (via satellite): Fox News Channel; FX; MyNetworkTV Inc.; QVC; TV Guide Network.
Fee: $50.00 installation; $20.95 monthly; $2.00 converter; $20.00 additional installation.

Expanded Basic Service 1
Subscribers: N.A.
Programming (received off-air): WRNN-LD Nyack; WSSN-LP (ION) Hudson et al.
Programming (via satellite): A&E Networks; ABC Family Channel; AMC; Animal Planet; Bio; Bravo; Cartoon Network; Cinemax; CNBC; CNN; Comedy Central; Country Music TV; C-SPAN; C-SPAN 2; Discovery Channel; Disney Channel; E! Entertainment Television; ESPN; ESPN 2; ESPN Classic Sports; Eternal Word TV Network; Food Network; Fox Movie Channel; Fox Sports Net New York; Fuse; G4; Golf Channel; GSN; Hallmark Channel; Headline News; HGTV; History Channel; Lifetime; MSG; MSNBC; MTV; National Geographic Channel; Nickelodeon; SoapNet; Speed; Spike TV; SportsNet New York; Style Network; Syfy; TBS Superstation; The Learning Channel; The Weather Channel; Travel Channel; truTV; Turner Classic Movies; Turner Network TV; TV Land; USA Network; Versus; VH1; WE tv; Yankees Entertainment & Sports.
Fee: $32.50 monthly.
Digital Basic Service
Subscribers: N.A.
Programming (via satellite): BBC America; Bloomberg Television; Chiller; cloo; CMT Pure Country; Cooking Channel; Current; Discovery Fit & Health; Discovery Health Channel; Discovery Kids Channel; DMX Music; ESPNews; Fox Business Channel; Fox College Sports Atlantic; Fox College Sports Central; Fox College Sports Pacific; Fox Soccer; Great American Country; GSN; Halogen Network; History Channel International; ID Investigation Discovery; Independent Film Channel; Lifetime Movie Network; Military Channel; MTV Hits; MTV2; Nick Jr.; NickToons TV; Outdoor Channel; Ovation; PBS Kids Sprout; Planet Green; RFD-TV; RTN; Science; ShopNBC; Sundance Channel; TeenNick; The Word Network; Toon Disney; Trinity Broadcasting Network; TVG Network; VH1 Classic; VH1 Soul.
Fee: $6.95 monthly; $6.95 converter.
Digital Expanded Basic Service
Subscribers: N.A.
Programming (received off-air): WCWN (CW) Schenectady; WMHT (PBS) Schenectady; WNYT (NBC) Albany; WRGB (CBS) Schenectady; WTEN (ABC) Albany; WXXA-TV (FOX) Albany.
Programming (via satellite): A&E HD; Animal Planet HD; Bravo HD; ESPN HD; Food Network HD; FX HD; HD Theater; HDNet; HDNet Movies; HGTV HD; History Channel HD; National Geographic Channel HD Network; Outdoor Channel 2 HD; QVC HD; Science HD; Speed HD; Syfy HD; TBS in HD; TLC HD; Turner Network TV HD; Universal HD; USA Network HD; YES HD.
Fee: $7.50 monthly; $7.95 converter.
Digital Pay Service 1
Pay Units: N.A.
Programming (via satellite): Cinemax HD (multiplexed); Cinemax HD; Cinemax On Demand; Encore (multiplexed); HBO (multiplexed); HBO HD; HBO On Demand; Showtime; Starz (multiplexed); Starz HDTV; The Movie Channel (multiplexed).
Fee: $11.95 monthly (Showtime/TMC), $13.40 monthly (Cinemax), $13.95 monthly (HBO or Starz/Encore).
Pay-Per-View
iN DEMAND (delivered digitally); Playboy TV (delivered digitally); Club Jenna (delivered digitally).
Internet Service
Operational: Yes.
Fee: $49.95 monthly.
Telephone Service
Analog: Not Operational
Digital: Operational
Fee: $29.95 monthly
Miles of Plant: 53.0 (coaxial); None (fiber optic).
President: James M. Reynolds.
Ownership: Mid-Hudson Cablevision Inc. (MSO).

EAST HAMPTON—Cablevision Systems Corp. Now served by RIVERHEAD, NY [NY0024]. ICA: NY0060.

EDINBURG (town)—Formerly served by Adelphia Communications. Now served by ALBANY, NY [NY0014]. ICA: NY0143.

ELLENVILLE—Time Warner Cable. Now served by HUDSON VALLEY (formerly Middletown), NY [NY0231]. ICA: NY0087.

ELMHURST—RCN Corp. Formerly served by Queens, NY [NY0283]. This cable system has converted to IPTV, 196 Van Buren St, Herndon, VA 20170. Phone: 703-434-8200. Web Site: http://www.rcn.com. ICA: NY5304.
TV Market Ranking: 1 (ELMHURST).
Channel capacity: N.A. Channels available but not in use: N.A.
Pay Service 1
Pay Units: N.A.
Fee: $11.95 monthly (Cinemaz or Starz!); $16.95 monthly (Showtime/The Movie Channel); $17.95 monthly (HBO).
Internet Service
Operational: Yes.
Fee: $38.00 monthly.
Telephone Service
Digital: Operational
Fee: $45.00 monthly
Chairman: Steven J. Simmons. Chief Executive Officer: Jim Holanda.

ELMIRA—Time Warner Cable. Now served by ELMIRA/CORNING (formerly Corning), NY [NY0057]. ICA: NY0215.

ELMIRA/CORNING—Time Warner Cable, 120 Plaza Dr, Vestal, NY 13850-3658. Phones: 607-644-0646; 607-739-3510 (Horseheads). Fax: 607-664-1501. Web Site: http://www.timewarnercable.com. Also serves Corning, Dundee, Lindley (town), Presho, Starkey (town) & Watkins Glen (village), NY; Deerfield Twp., East Lawrence Twp., Elkland, Lawrence Twp., Nelson Twp., Osceola & Tioga, PA. ICA: NY0057.
TV Market Ranking: Below 100 (CORNING, Deerfield Twp., Dundee, East Lawrence Twp., Elkland, ELMIRA, Lawrence Twp., Lindley (town), Nelson Twp., Osceola, Presho, Starkey (town), Tioga, Watkins Glen (village)). Franchise award date: N.A. Franchise expiration date: N.A. Began: September 1, 1954.
Channel capacity: N.A. Channels available but not in use: N.A.
Basic Service
Subscribers: N.A. Included in Binghamton
Programming (received off-air): WBNG-TV (CBS, CW) Binghamton; WENY-TV (ABC, CW) Elmira; WETM-TV (NBC) Elmira; WSKG-TV (PBS) Binghamton; WYDC (FOX, MNT) Corning; 20 FMs.
Programming (via microwave): WKBW-TV (ABC) Buffalo.
Programming (via satellite): C-SPAN; ION Television; TV Guide Network; WGN America; WPIX (CW, IND) New York.
Fee: $47.21 installation; $8.95 monthly; $3.48 converter.
Expanded Basic Service 1
Subscribers: 12,725.
Programming (via satellite): A&E Networks; ABC Family Channel; AMC; Animal Planet; BET Networks; Bravo; Cartoon Network; CNBC; CNN; Comedy Central; Country Music TV; Discovery Channel; Discovery Fit & Health; Disney Channel; E! Entertainment Television; ESPN; ESPN 2; ESPN Classic Sports; Eternal Word TV Network; Food Network; Fox News Channel; Fuse; FX; Golf Channel; Hallmark Channel; Headline News; HGTV; History Channel; Lifetime; Lifetime Movie Network; MoviePlex; MSG; MSG Plus; MSNBC; MTV; MTV2; National Geographic Channel; Nickelodeon; Oxygen; Product Information Network; QVC; ShopNBC; SoapNet; Speed; Spike TV; Style Network; Syfy; TBS Superstation; The Learning Channel; The Weather Channel; Travel Channel; truTV; Turner Classic Movies; Turner Network TV; TV Land; USA Network; Versus; VH1; WE tv; Yankees Entertainment & Sports.
Fee: $32.26 installation; $34.62 monthly.
Digital Basic Service
Subscribers: N.A. Included in Binghamton
Programming (via satellite): American-Life TV Network; America's Store; BBC America; Bio; Bloomberg Television; Cooking Channel; C-SPAN 3; Discovery Digital Networks; DIY Network; Encore Action; ESPNews; Fox Movie Channel; Fox Sports World; Fuse; G4; GAS; Great American Country; History Channel International; Independent Film Channel; Lifetime Real Women; Music Choice; Nick Jr.; Outdoor Channel; Ovation; Sundance Channel; Toon Disney; Trinity Broadcasting Network; VH1 Classic.
Fee: $8.45 monthly.
Digital Expanded Basic Service
Subscribers: N.A.
Programming (via satellite): Fox Deportes; FSN Digital Atlantic; FSN Digital Central; FSN Digital Pacific; Fuel TV; NBA TV; Tennis Channel.
Fee: $4.95 monthly.
Digital Pay Service 1
Pay Units: 2,165.
Programming (via satellite): Cinemax (multiplexed).
Fee: $11.25 monthly.
Digital Pay Service 2
Pay Units: 945.
Programming (via satellite): Starz (multiplexed).
Fee: $11.25 monthly.
Digital Pay Service 3
Pay Units: 3,340.
Programming (via satellite): HBO (multiplexed).
Fee: $11.25 monthly.
Digital Pay Service 4
Pay Units: 718.
Programming (via satellite): Flix; Showtime (multiplexed); The Movie Channel.
Fee: $11.25 monthly.
Digital Pay Service 5
Pay Units: 2,387.
Programming (via satellite): Canales N; TV Asia; Zee TV USA.
Fee: $4.95 monthly (Canales N), $19.95 monthly (TV Asia & Zee TV).
Video-On-Demand: Yes
Pay-Per-View
Addressable homes: 4,550.
Hot Choice (delivered digitally); iN DEMAND (delivered digitally); Playboy TV (delivered digitally); Fresh (delivered digitally); Shorteez (delivered digitally); Pleasure (delivered digitally); ESPN Gameplan (delivered digitally); ESPN Full Court (delivered digitally); Sports PPV (delivered digitally).
Internet Service
Operational: Yes. Began: November 1, 1996.
Broadband Service: Road Runner.
Fee: $39.95 installation; $44.95 monthly.
Telephone Service
Digital: Operational
Fee: $39.95 monthly
Miles of plant included in Binghamton
President: Mary Cotter. Vice President & General Manager: Chris Strahm. Vice President, Marketing: John Melvany. Vice President, Public Affairs: Dave Whalen. Technical Operations Director: Bruce Tomkins. Technical Operations Manager: Nancy Derr.
Ownership: Time Warner Cable (MSO).; Advance/Newhouse Partnership (MSO).

ENFIELD—Haefele TV Inc., 24 E Tioga St, PO Box 312, Spencer, NY 14883. Phone: 607-589-6235. Fax: 607-589-7211. E-mail: cs@htva.net. Web Site: http://www.htva.net. Also serves Bradford (town), Burdett, Burdett (village), Enfield (town), Hector (town), Orange (town) & Reading. ICA: NY0152.
TV Market Ranking: Below 100 (Bradford (town), BURDETT, Burdett (village), ENFIELD, Enfield (town), Hector (town), Orange (town), Reading). Franchise award date: December 27, 1984. Franchise expiration date: N.A. Began: April 1, 1985.
Channel capacity: 65 (operating 2-way). Channels available but not in use: N.A.
Basic Service
Subscribers: 2,017.
Programming (received off-air): WBNG-TV (CBS, CW) Binghamton; WCNY-TV (PBS) Syracuse; WICZ-TV (FOX) Binghamton; WNYS-TV (MNT) Syracuse; WSKG-TV (PBS) Binghamton; WSYR-TV (ABC) Syracuse; WSYT (FOX) Syracuse; WTVH (CBS) Syracuse.
Programming (via satellite): A&E Networks; ABC Family Channel; AMC; Animal Planet; Cartoon Network; CNBC; CNN; Comedy Central; Country Music TV; C-SPAN; Discovery Channel; Disney Channel; DIY Network; E! Entertainment Television; ESPN; ESPN 2; ESPN Classic Sports; Eternal Word TV Network; Food Network; Fox News Channel; FX; G4; Great American Country; Hallmark Channel; Headline News; HGTV; History Channel; ION Television; Lifetime; MSG; MSG Plus; MSNBC; MTV; Nickelodeon; QVC; Speed; Spike TV; Syfy; TBS Superstation; The Learning Channel; The Weather Channel; Travel Channel; truTV; Turner Network TV; TV Guide Network; TV Land; USA Network; VH1; WE tv; WPIX (CW, IND) New York; Yankees Entertainment & Sports.
Fee: $30.00 installation; $48.45 monthly; $1.00 converter; $10.00 additional installation.
Digital Basic Service
Subscribers: 138.
Programming (via satellite): BBC America; Bio; Bloomberg Television; Bravo; Discovery Fit & Health; DMX Music; ESPN Classic Sports; ESPNews; Fox Movie Channel; Fox Soccer; GAS; Golf Channel; GSN; History Channel International; Independent Film Channel; INSP; Lifetime Movie Network; MTV2; Nick Jr.; NickToons TV; Outdoor Channel; Style Network; Toon Disney; Turner Classic Movies.
Fee: $12.95 monthly.

Pay Service 1
Pay Units: 18.
Programming (via satellite): Cinemax.
Fee: $9.00 monthly.
Pay Service 2
Pay Units: 221.
Programming (via satellite): HBO (multiplexed).
Fee: $10.00 monthly.
Digital Pay Service 1
Pay Units: N.A.
Programming (via satellite): Cinemax (multiplexed); Encore; HBO (multiplexed); Showtime (multiplexed); Starz (multiplexed).
Fee: $9.95 monthly (Starz/Encore), $12.95 monthly (Showtime/TMC), $17.00 monthly (HBO and Cinemax).
Video-On-Demand: No
Internet Service
Operational: Yes. Began: October 1, 1999.
Subscribers: 354.
Broadband Service: In-house.
Fee: $34.50-$51.95 monthly; $9.95 modem lease; $89.00 modem purchase.
Telephone Service
Digital: Operational
Miles of Plant: 87.0 (coaxial); None (fiber optic).
President & Manager: Lee Haefele. Vice President: Denise Laue. Chief Technician: Michael McNamara.
Ownership: Haefele TV Inc. (MSO).

FORESTPORT—Now served by UTICA, NY [NY0022]. ICA: NY0217.

FREDONIA (village)—Time Warner Cable. Now served by JAMESTOWN, NY [NY0030]. ICA: NY0090.

FRESH MEADOWS—RCN Corp. Formerly served by Queens, NY [NY0283]. This cable system has converted to IPTV, 196 Van Buren St, Herndon, VA 20170. Phone: 703-434-8200. Web Site: http://www.rcn.com. ICA: NY5308.
TV Market Ranking: 1 (FRESH MEADOWS).
Channel capacity: N.A. Channels available but not in use: N.A.
Pay Service 1
Pay Units: N.A.
Fee: $11.95 monthly (Cinemaz or Starz!); $16.95 monthly (Showtime/The Movie Channel); $17.95 monthly (HBO).
Internet Service
Operational: Yes.
Fee: $38.00 monthly.
Telephone Service
Digital: Operational
Fee: $45.00 monthly
Chairman: Steven J. Simmons. Chief Executive Officer: Jim Holanda.

FRIENDSHIP—Time Warner Cable. Now served by HORNELL, NY [NY0076]. ICA: NY0166.

FULTON—Time Warner Cable. Now served by OSWEGO, NY [NY0061]. ICA: NY0063.

GENEVA—Time Warner Cable, 71 Mount Hope Ave, Rochester, NY 14620. Phone: 585-756-1000. Fax: 585-756-1675. Web Site: http://www.timewarnercable.com/rochester. Also serves Arcadia (town), Aurelius (town), Aurora (Cayuga County), Benton, Branchport, Canandaigua, Cayuga (village), Clifton Springs (village), Clyde (village), Covert (town), Dix, Dresden, East Bloomfield (town), Farmington (town), Fayette (town), Galen (village), Geneva (town), Gorham, Hammondsport, Holcomb (village), Hopewell (town), Huron (town), Interlaken (village), Ledyard, Lodi (village), Lyons (village), Macedon (village), Manchester (village), Marion (town), Middlesex, Milo, Montour, Montour Falls (village), Naples, Newark (village), Odessa (village), Ontario (town), Ovid (town), Ovid (village), Palmyra (town), Palmyra (village), Penn Yan, Phelps (town), Phelps (village), Prattsburgh (town), Pulteney, Reading (town), Red Creek (village), Romulus (town), Rose (town), Rushville, Savannah (town), Seneca (town), Seneca County (southern portion), Seneca Falls (village), Shortsville (village), Sodus (town), Sodus (village), Sodus Point (village), South Bristol (town), Springport, Tyrone, Union Springs, Varick (town), Victor (village), Walworth (town), Waterloo (village), Watkins Glen, Wayne, Williamson (town) & Wolcott (village). ICA: NY0218.
TV Market Ranking: 35 (Aurelius (town), Aurora (Cayuga County), Cayuga (village), Ledyard, Savannah (town), Seneca (town), Seneca County (southern portion), Seneca Falls (village), Springport, Union Springs); 56 (Arcadia (town), Canandaigua, Clifton Springs (village), East Bloomfield (town), Farmington (town), Holcomb (village), Hopewell (town), Lyons (village), Macedon (village), Manchester (village), Marion (town), Newark (village), Ontario (town), Palmyra (town), Palmyra (village), Phelps (town), Phelps (village), Red Creek (village), Rushville, Shortsville (village), Sodus (village), Sodus Point (village), South Bristol (town), Victor (village), Walworth (town), Williamson (town)); Below 100 (Benton, Covert (town), Dix, Dresden, Fayette (town), Gorham, Hammondsport, Interlaken (village), Lodi (village), Milo, Montour, Montour Falls (village), Odessa (village), Ovid (town), Penn Yan, Prattsburgh (town), Pulteney, Reading (town), Romulus (town), Tyrone, Watkins Glen); Outside TV Markets (Clyde (village), Galen (village), GENEVA, Geneva (town), Huron (town), Middlesex, Naples, Ovid (village), Rose (town), Varick (town), Waterloo (village), Wayne, Wolcott (village), Red Creek (village)). Franchise award date: January 20, 1966. Franchise expiration date: N.A. Began: March 1, 1972.
Channel capacity: 66 (operating 2-way). Channels available but not in use: N.A.
Basic Service
Subscribers: N.A. Included in Rochester
Programming (received off-air): WBGT-CA (MNT) Rochester; WCNY-TV (PBS) Syracuse; WHAM-TV (ABC, CW) Rochester; WHEC-TV (NBC) Rochester; WNYS-TV (MNT) Syracuse; WROC-TV (CBS) Rochester; WSTM-TV (NBC) Syracuse; WSYR-TV (ABC) Syracuse; WSYT (FOX) Syracuse; WTVH (CBS) Syracuse; WUHF (FOX) Rochester; WXXI-TV (PBS) Rochester.
Programming (via satellite): CW+; ION Television; QVC; ShopNBC.
Fee: $59.95 installation; $13.17 monthly.
Expanded Basic Service 1
Subscribers: N.A.
Programming (via satellite): A&E Networks; ABC Family Channel; AMC; Animal Planet; BET Networks; Bravo; Cartoon Network; CNBC; CNN; Comedy Central; Country Music TV; C-SPAN; C-SPAN 2; Discovery Channel; Disney Channel; E! Entertainment Television; ESPN; ESPN 2; Eternal Word TV Network; Food Network; Fox News Channel; FX; Golf Channel; Hallmark Channel; Headline News; HGTV; History Channel; Lifetime; Lifetime Movie Network; MoviePlex; MSG; MSG Plus; MSNBC; MTV; National Geographic Channel; Nickelodeon; Oxygen; SoapNet; Spike TV; Syfy; TBS Superstation; The Learning Channel; The Weather Channel; Travel Channel; Trinity Broadcasting Network; truTV; Turner Classic Movies; Turner Network TV; TV Land; Univision Studios; USA Network; VH1; WE tv; Yankees Entertainment & Sports.
Fee: $33.58 monthly.
Digital Basic Service
Subscribers: N.A. Included in Rochester
Programming (via satellite): BBC America; Bloomberg Television; Cooking Channel; C-SPAN 3; Discovery Digital Networks; DIY Network; ESPN Classic Sports; ESPNews; Fox Deportes; Fox Movie Channel; Fox Sports World; FSN Digital Atlantic; FSN Digital Central; FSN Digital Pacific; Great American Country; GSN; Lifetime Real Women; MTV2; Music Choice; Nick Jr.; Outdoor Channel; Ovation; Speed; Style Network; Tennis Channel; Toon Disney; VH1 Classic.
Digital Pay Service 1
Pay Units: N.A.
Programming (via satellite): Cinemax (multiplexed); Encore (multiplexed); Flix; HBO (multiplexed); Independent Film Channel; Showtime (multiplexed); Starz (multiplexed); The Movie Channel (multiplexed).
Fee: $9.95 monthly (Cinemax, HBO, Showtime or Flix & TMC or IFC, Starz & Encore).
Video-On-Demand: Yes
Pay-Per-View
Addressable homes: 25,135.
Playboy TV; iN DEMAND; Fresh; iN DEMAND (delivered digitally); Playboy TV (delivered digitally); ETC (delivered digitally); Sports PPV (delivered digitally).
Internet Service
Operational: Yes.
Broadband Service: Road Runner.
Fee: $39.95 installation; $44.95 monthly.
Telephone Service
Digital: Operational
Fee: $39.95 monthly
Miles of Plant: 1,290.0 (coaxial); None (fiber optic).
Division President: Terrence Rafferty. Vice President, Operations: Bruce Hennekey. Vice President, Engineering: Armando Ruiz. Vice President, Marketing: Mike Neal. Vice President, Government & Public Affairs: Chris Mueller.
Ownership: Time Warner Cable (MSO).; Advance/Newhouse Partnership (MSO).

GERMANTOWN—GTel Teleconnections, 210 Main St, PO Box 188, Germantown, NY 12526-0188. Phone: 518-537-4835. Fax: 518-537-6700. E-mail: questions@gtel.net. Web Site: http://home.gtel.net. Also serves Clermont. ICA: NY0141.
TV Market Ranking: 34 (GERMANTOWN); Below 100 (Clermont). Franchise award date: September 1, 1984. Franchise expiration date: N.A. Began: September 1, 1984.
Channel capacity: 46 (not 2-way capable). Channels available but not in use: N.A.
Basic Service
Subscribers: 923.
Programming (received off-air): WCWN (CW) Schenectady; WMHT (PBS) Schenectady; WNYT (NBC) Albany; WRGB (CBS) Schenectady; WTEN (ABC) Albany; WXXA-TV (FOX) Albany.
Programming (via satellite): A&E Networks; ABC Family Channel; Animal Planet; CNBC; CNN; Comedy Central; Country Music TV; C-SPAN; Discovery Channel; ESPN; ESPN 2; Eternal Word TV Network; Food Network; Fox News Channel; Fox Sports Net New York; History Channel; Lifetime; MSG; MTV; Nickelodeon; Outdoor Channel; QVC; Spike TV; SportsNet New York; Syfy; TBS Superstation; The Learning Channel; The Weather Channel; Turner Classic Movies; Turner Network TV; TV Guide Network; USA Network; VH1; Yankees Entertainment & Sports.
Fee: $40.00 installation; $31.85 monthly; $15.00 additional installation.
Digital Basic Service
Subscribers: 115.
Programming (via satellite): BBC America; Discovery Health Channel; Discovery Kids Channel; Encore; ID Investigation Discovery; Military Channel; Music Choice; Planet Green; Science.
Fee: $10.95 monthly.
Pay Service 1
Pay Units: 84.
Programming (via satellite): Cinemax.
Fee: $25.00 installation; $8.95 monthly.
Pay Service 2
Pay Units: 56.
Programming (via satellite): Showtime.
Fee: $25.00 installation; $9.95 monthly.
Pay Service 3
Pay Units: 138.
Programming (via satellite): HBO.
Fee: $25.00 installation; $10.95 monthly.
Digital Pay Service 1
Pay Units: 38.
Programming (via satellite): Encore Family; Starz (multiplexed).
Fee: $5.45 monthly.
Video-On-Demand: No
Pay-Per-View
Addressable homes: 122.
Playboy TV (delivered digitally); Fresh (delivered digitally); Movies (delivered digitally); special events (delivered digitally).
Internet Service
Operational: No, Both DSL & dial-up.
Telephone Service
None
Miles of Plant: 50.0 (coaxial); 8.0 (fiber optic).
President & General Manager: Bruce Bohnsack. Office Manager: Tammy Holmes. Human Resources Manager: Sherry Barringer.
Ownership: Hilltop Communications Inc. (MSO).

GLENS FALLS—Time Warner Cable. Now served by ALBANY, NY [NY0014]. ICA: NY0044.

GREENE—Time Warner Cable. Now served by BINGHAMTON, NY [NY0016]. ICA: NY0150.

GREIG—Time Warner Cable. Now served by CARTHAGE, NY [NY0206]. ICA: NY0222.

HAMDEN—DTC Cable Inc., 107 Main St, PO Box 271, Delhi, NY 13753-0271. Phones: 888-898-8006; 607-746-2111. Fax: 607-746-7991. Web Site: http://www.delhi.net/cable.htm. Also serves De Lancey & Fraser. ICA: NY0223.

TV Market Ranking: Outside TV Markets (De Lancey, HAMDEN). Franchise award date: N.A. Franchise expiration date: N.A. Began: April 1, 1958.

Channel capacity: 30 (not 2-way capable). Channels available but not in use: N.A.

Basic Service

Subscribers: 292.

Programming (received off-air): WBNG-TV (CBS, CW) Binghamton; WICZ-TV (FOX) Binghamton; WIVT (ABC) Binghamton; WNBC (NBC) New York; WRGB (CBS) Schenectady; WSKG-TV (PBS) Binghamton; WSYR-TV (ABC) Syracuse; allband FM.

Programming (via satellite): ABC Family Channel; CW11 New York; The Weather Channel; TV Guide Network; USA Network; WGN America.

Fee: $29.95 installation; $8.50 monthly.

Expanded Basic Service 1

Subscribers: N.A.

Programming (via satellite): A&E Networks; AMC; Animal Planet; CNN; Country Music TV; C-SPAN; CW11 New York; Discovery Channel; Disney Channel; ESPN; FX; History Channel; QVC; Spike TV; TBS Superstation; Trinity Broadcasting Network; Turner Network TV; Yankees Entertainment & Sports.

Fee: $12.50 monthly.

Pay Service 1

Pay Units: 93.

Programming (via satellite): HBO.

Fee: $15.00 installation; $9.00 monthly.

Video-On-Demand: No

Internet Service

Operational: No.

Telephone Service

None

Miles of Plant: 14.0 (coaxial); None (fiber optic). Additional miles planned: 3.0 (coaxial).

General Manager: Douglas Edwards. Business Manager: Steve Oles.

Ownership: DTC Cable Inc. (MSO).

HANCOCK—Hancock Video, 34 Read St, PO Box 608, Hancock, NY 13783-0608. Phones: 800-360-4664; 607-637-2568. Fax: 607-637-9999. Web Site: http://www.hancockvideo.com. Also serves Cadosia, East Branch, Fishs Eddy, Hancock Twp. & Tompkins (town). ICA: NY0147.

TV Market Ranking: Below 100 (Cadosia, HANCOCK, Hancock Twp., Tompkins (town)); Outside TV Markets (East Branch, Fishs Eddy). Franchise award date: N.A. Franchise expiration date: N.A. Began: January 2, 1959.

Channel capacity: 31 (not 2-way capable). Channels available but not in use: N.A.

Basic Service

Subscribers: 1,100.

Programming (received off-air): WBNG-TV (CBS, CW) Binghamton; WICZ-TV (FOX) Binghamton; WIVT (ABC) Binghamton; WNEP-TV (ABC) Scranton; WSKG-TV (PBS) Binghamton; WVIA-TV (PBS) Scranton; allband FM.

Programming (via satellite): A&E Networks; ABC Family Channel; AMC; CNBC; CNN; Discovery Channel; Disney Channel; ESPN; ESPN 2; History Channel; Nickelodeon; QVC; Spike TV; Syfy; TBS Superstation; The Weather Channel; Toon Disney; Turner Network TV; USA Network; WGN America; WPIX (CW, IND) New York.

Fee: $50.00 installation; $38.95 monthly; $20.00 additional installation.

Pay Service 1

Pay Units: 320.

Programming (via satellite): HBO.

Fee: $10.00 installation; $10.50 monthly.

Pay Service 2

Pay Units: N.A.

Programming (via satellite): Cinemax.

Fee: $7.00 monthly.

Video-On-Demand: No

Internet Service

Operational: No, DSL & dial-up.

Telephone Service

None

Miles of Plant: 30.0 (coaxial); None (fiber optic).

President: Robert C. Wrighter, Sr. Vice President & Treasurer: Donald C. Wrighter, Sr. Manager: Beth Miller. Chief Technician: Gary Schoonmaker. Customer Service Manager: Mary Lynn Smith.

Ownership: Hancel Inc. (MSO).

HARTFORD (town)—Now served QUEENSBURY, NY [NY0042]. ICA: NY0183.

HENDERSON (town)—Time Warner Cable. Now served by CARTHAGE, NY [NY0206]. ICA: NY0129.

HIGHLAND FALLS (village)—Time Warner Cable. Now served by HUDSON VALLEY (formerly Middletown), NY [NY0231]. ICA: NY0261.

HORNELL—Time Warner Cable, 120 Plaza Dr, Vestal, NY 13850-3658. Phones: 607-324-2487 (Hornell office); 607-644-0646. Fax: 607-644-1501. Web Site: http://www.timewarnercable.com. Also serves Alfred, Angelica, Avoca, Bath, Belfast, Bolivar, Canaseraga, Cohocton, Dansville, Friendship, Groveland (town), Jasper, North Dansville (town), Perkinsville, Sparta (town), Springwater, Troupsburg, Wayland, West Sparta (town) & Woodhull. ICA: NY0076.

TV Market Ranking: Below 100 (Avoca, Bath, Belfast, Cohocton, Friendship, HORNELL, Jasper, Troupsburg, Woodhull); Outside TV Markets (Alfred, Angelica, Bolivar, Canaseraga, Dansville, Groveland (town), North Dansville (town), Perkinsville, Sparta (town), Springwater, Wayland, West Sparta (town)). Franchise award date: January 1, 1951. Franchise expiration date: N.A. Began: July 1, 1951.

Channel capacity: N.A. Channels available but not in use: N.A.

Basic Service

Subscribers: N.A. Included in Binghamton

Programming (received off-air): WENY-TV (ABC, CW) Elmira; WETM-TV (NBC) Elmira; WHEC-TV (NBC) Rochester; WIVB-TV (CBS) Buffalo; WKBW-TV (ABC) Buffalo; WROC-TV (CBS) Rochester; WXXI-TV (PBS) Rochester; WYDC (FOX, MNT) Corning; allband FM.

Programming (via satellite): WGN America; WPIX (CW, IND) New York.

Fee: $47.21 installation; $8.95 monthly; $3.12 converter.

Expanded Basic Service 1

Subscribers: N.A.

Programming (via satellite): A&E Networks; ABC Family Channel; AMC; Animal Planet; BET Networks; Bravo; Cartoon Network; CNBC; CNN; Comedy Central; Country Music TV; C-SPAN; Discovery Channel; Discovery Fit & Health; Disney Channel; E! Entertainment Television; ESPN; ESPN 2; ESPN Classic Sports; Eternal Word TV Network; Food Network; Fox News Channel; Fuse; FX; Golf Channel; Hallmark Channel; Headline News; HGTV; History Channel; ION Television; Lifetime; Lifetime Movie Network; MoviePlex; MSG; MSG Plus; MSNBC; MTV; MTV2; National Geographic Channel; Nickelodeon; Oxygen; Product Information Network; QVC; ShopNBC; SoapNet; Speed; Spike TV; Style Network; Syfy; TBS Superstation; The Learning Channel; The Weather Channel; Travel Channel; truTV; Turner Classic Movies; Turner Network TV; TV Guide Network; TV Land; USA Network; Versus; VH1; WE tv; Yankees Entertainment & Sports.

Fee: $34.62 monthly.

Digital Basic Service

Subscribers: N.A. Included in Binghamton

Programming (via satellite): AmericanLife TV Network; America's Store; BBC America; Bio; Bloomberg Television; Cooking Channel; C-SPAN 3; Discovery Digital Networks; DIY Network; Encore Action; ESPNews; Fox Movie Channel; Fox Sports World; G4; GAS; Great American Country; History Channel International; Independent Film Channel; Lifetime Real Women; Music Choice; Nick Jr.; Outdoor Channel; Ovation; Sundance Channel; Toon Disney; Trinity Broadcasting Network; VH1 Classic.

Fee: $8.45 monthly.

Digital Expanded Basic Service

Subscribers: N.A.

Programming (via satellite): FSN Digital Atlantic; FSN Digital Central; FSN Digital Pacific; Fuel TV; NBA TV; Tennis Channel.

Fee: $4.95 monthly.

Digital Pay Service 1

Pay Units: 6,945.

Programming (via satellite): Canales N; Cinemax (multiplexed); Flix; HBO (multiplexed); Showtime (multiplexed); Starz (multiplexed); The Movie Channel (multiplexed); TV Asia; Zee TV USA.

Fee: $11.25 monthly (Cinemax, HBO, Starz, or Showtime/TMC), $19.95 monthly (TV Asia & Zee TV).

Video-On-Demand: Yes

Pay-Per-View

iN DEMAND (delivered digitally); Hot Choice (delivered digitally); Playboy TV (delivered digitally); Fresh (delivered digitally); Shorteez (delivered digitally); Pleasure (delivered digitally); ESPN Full Court (delivered digitally); ESPN Gameplan (delivered digitally); Sports PPV (delivered digitally).

Internet Service

Operational: Yes.

Broadband Service: Road Runner.

Fee: $39.95 installation; $44.95 monthly.

Telephone Service

Digital: Operational

Fee: $39.95 monthly

Miles of plant included in Binghamton

President: Mary Cotter. Vice President & General Manager: Chris Strahm. Vice President, Marketing: John Melvany. Vice President, Public Affairs: Dave Whalen. Technical Operations Director: Bruce Tomkins.

Ownership: Time Warner Cable (MSO).; Advance/Newhouse Partnership (MSO).

HUDSON VALLEY—Time Warner Cable, 2 Industrial Dr, PO Box 887, Middletown, NY 10941-0887. Phones: 845-692-5339; 212-598-7200 (New York office). Fax: 845-692-0901. Web Site: http://www.timewarnercable.com. Also serves Barryville, Bethel (town), Big Indian, Blooming Grove (town), Bloomingburg (village), Bloomington, Boiceville, Cairo, Callicoon (town), Catskill (town), Chichester, Cochecton, Colchester Twp., Cornwall (town), Cottekill, Crawford (town), Delaware (town), Denning (unincorporated areas), Denver, Dutchess County, Eldred, Ellenville, Esopus, Fallsburg (town), Fleischmanns, Forestburgh (town), Fremont, Gardiner (town), Glen Spey, Goshen (village), Grahamsville (town), Grand Gorge, Greene County (portions), Haines Falls, Hamptonburgh (town), High Falls, Highland (town), Highland Falls (village), Hortonville, Hunter (village), Hurley, Jeffersonville (village), Jewett, Kingston, La Grange (town), Lexington, Liberty (village), Livingston Manor (town), Lumberland, Mamakating (town), Marbletown, Marlboro, Maybrook (village), Middletown, Minisink Ford, Montgomery (village), Monticello (village), Mount Hope (town), Mount Tremper, Napanoch, Narrowsburg, Neversink (town), New Paltz (village), New Windsor, Newburgh, North Branch, Olive, Olivebridge, Oliverea, Otisville (village), Palenville, Phoenicia, Pine Hill, Pleasant Valley (portions), Pond Eddy, Port Jervis, Poughkeepsie, Red Hook (village), Rhinebeck (village), Rhinecliff, Rockland (town), Rosendale, Round Top, Roxbury, Saugerties (village), Shandaken, Shawangunk (town), Shokan, Stone Ridge, Sullivan County (portions), Tannersville, Thompson (town), Tillson, Tivoli (village), Tusten, Ulster (town), Walden (village), Wallkill (town), Washingtonville (village), Wawarsing, Wawayanda (town), West Hurley, West Point, West Point Military Academy, West Shokan, Woodridge, Woodstock (town), Wurtsboro (village) & Yulan. ICA: NY0231.

TV Market Ranking: 1 (Blooming Grove (town), Goshen (town), Goshen (village), Highland (town), Highland Falls (village), Highland Falls (village), West Point, West Point Military Academy); 19 (Dutchess County (portions)); 34 (Cairo, Catskill (town), Greene County (portions) (portions), Round Top); Below 100 (Barryville, Big Indian, Bloomingburg (village), Bloomington, Boiceville, Chichester, Cornwall (town), Cornwall (village), Cottekill, Crawford (town), Creek Locks, Denning (unincorporated areas), Eldred, Ellenville, Esopus, Fallsburg (town), Fallsburg (town), Fleischmanns, Gardiner (town), Glen Spey, Grahamsville (town), Haines Falls, Hamptonburgh (town), High Falls, Highland, HUDSON VALLEY, Hunter (town), Hunter (village), Hurley, Jewett, Kingston, Kingston (town), La Grange (town), Lexington, Mamakating, Mamakating (town), Marbletown, Marbletown, Marlboro, Maybrook (village), Middletown, Minisink Ford, Montgomery (town), Montgomery (village), Mount Hope (town), Mount Pleasant, Mount Tremper, Napanoch, Neversink (town), New Paltz, New Paltz (village), New Windsor, Newburgh, Newburgh (town), Olive, Olivebridge, Oliverea, Otisville (village), Palenville, Phoenicia, Pine Hill, Pleasant Valley (portions), Pond Eddy, Port Jervis, Poughkeepsie, Poughkeepsie (town), Red Hook (town), Red Hook (village), Rhinebeck (town), Rhinebeck (village), Rhinecliff, Rochester (village), Rosendale, Saugerties (town), Saugerties (village), Shandaken, Shandaken, Shawangunk (town), Shokan, Stewart AFB, Stone Ridge, Sullivan County (portions) (portions), Tannersville, Tillson, Tivoli, Tivoli (village), Tusten, Ulster (town), Walden,

Walden (village), Wallkill, Wallkill (town), Washingtonville, Washingtonville (village), Wawarsing, Wawayanda (town), West Hurley, West Shokan, Wittenburg, Woodland, Woodridge, Woodstock (town), Wurtsboro, Wurtsboro (village), Yulan, Dutchess County (portions), Greene County (portions) (portions)); Outside TV Markets (Bethel (town), Callicoon (town), Cochecton, Colchester Twp., Cooks Falls, Deerpark (town), Delaware (town), Denver, Fallsburg (town), Forestburgh (town), Fremont, Grand Gorge, Hortonville, Jeffersonville (village), Lava, Liberty (town), Liberty (village), Livingston Manor (town), Lumberland, Monticello (village), Narrowsburg, North Branch, Rockland (town), Roxbury, Sullivan County (portions) (portions), Thompson (town)). Franchise award date: June 1, 1966. Franchise expiration date: N.A. Began: February 2, 1956.

Channel capacity: N.A. Channels available but not in use: N.A.

Basic Service

Subscribers: N.A. Included in New York

Programming (received off-air): WABC-TV (ABC) New York; WCBS-TV (CBS) New York; WMBC-TV (IND) Newton; WNBC (NBC) New York; WNET (PBS) Newark; WNYW (FOX) New York; WPIX (CW, IND) New York; WPXN-TV (ION) New York; WRNN-TV (IND) Kingston; WTBY-TV (TBN) Poughkeepsie; WTEN (ABC) Albany; WWOR-TV (MNT) Secaucus; WXTV-DT (UNV) Paterson; 20 FMs.

Programming (via satellite): CNN; CW11 New York; Discovery Channel; ESPN; FX; QVC; Turner Network TV.

Fee: $26.10 installation; $26.30 monthly.

Expanded Basic Service 1

Subscribers: N.A. Included in New York

Programming (via satellite): A&E Networks; ABC Family Channel; AMC; Animal Planet; BET Networks; Bravo; Cartoon Network; CNBC; Comedy Central; Country Music TV; C-SPAN; Discovery Fit & Health; Disney Channel; E! Entertainment Television; ESPN 2; Eternal Word TV Network; Food Network; Fox News Channel; Fuse; GalaVision; Golf Channel; Hallmark Channel; Headline News; HGTV; History Channel; Lifetime; Lifetime Movie Network; MSG; MSG Plus; MSNBC; MTV; National Geographic Channel; Nickelodeon; Oxygen; ShopNBC; Spike TV; SportsNet New York; Style Network; Syfy; TBS Superstation; Telemundo; The Learning Channel; The Weather Channel; Travel Channel; truTV; Turner Classic Movies; TV Guide Network; TV Land; TV One; USA Network; Versus; VH1; Yankees Entertainment & Sports.

Digital Basic Service

Subscribers: N.A. Included in New York

Programming (via satellite): AmericanLife TV Network; BBC America; BBC America On Demand; Bio; Bloomberg Television; Boomerang; CBS Sports Network; CCTV News; CNN International; Cooking Channel; C-SPAN; C-SPAN 2; C-SPAN 3; Current; Discovery Health Channel; Discovery Home Channel; Discovery Kids Channel; DIY Network; Encore Family; ESPN 2 HD; ESPN Classic Sports; ESPN HD; ESPNews; Exercise TV; Fox Business Channel; Fox College Sports Atlantic; Fox College Sports Central; Fox College Sports Pacific; Fox Deportes; Fox Movie Channel; Fox Soccer; Fuel TV; G4; GMC; Great American Country; Great American Country On Demand; GSN; HD Theater; HDNet; HDNet Movies; History Channel International; ID Investigation Discovery; Independent Film Channel; Lifetime Real Women; LOGO; Military Channel; MTV2; Music Choice; National Geographic Channel HD Network; National Geographic Channel On Demand; NBA TV; Nick Jr.; Nick Too; Nuvo TV; Outdoor Channel; Ovation; Science; SoapNet; Speed; Speed On Demand; Sundance Channel; TBN HD; Teen-Nick; Tennis Channel; The Word Network; Toon Disney; Turner Network TV HD; Universal HD; VH1 Classic; YES HD.

Pay Service 1

Pay Units: 40,300.

Programming (via satellite): HBO.

Digital Pay Service 1

Pay Units: N.A.

Programming (via satellite): ART America; CCTV-4; Cinemax (multiplexed); Cinemax HD; Cinemax On Demand; CT-N; Encore (multiplexed); HBO (multiplexed); HBO HD; HBO On Demand; International Television (ITV); MBC America; RAI USA; RTV21; Russian Television Network; Showtime (multiplexed); Showtime HD; Showtime On Demand; Starz (multiplexed); Starz HDTV; The Movie Channel (multiplexed); The Movie Channel On Demand; TV Japan; TV Polonia; TV5 USA; Zee TV USA.

Fee: $12.95 monthly (HBO, Cinemax, Starz/Encore or Showtime/TMC).

Video-On-Demand: Yes

Pay-Per-View

Playboy TV; Spice; movies.

Internet Service

Operational: Yes.

Broadband Service: EarthLink, LocalNet, Road Runner.

Fee: $44.95 monthly.

Telephone Service

Digital: Operational

Fee: $39.95 monthly

Miles of plant included in New York

President: Howard Szarfarc. Vice President, Technical Operations: John Brown. Vice President, Marketing: David Goldberg. General Manager: Roger Wells. Public Affairs Director: Brenda Parks.

Ownership: Time Warner Cable (MSO).

HUNTER—Time Warner Cable. Now served by HUDSON VALLEY (formerly Middletown), NY [NY0231]. ICA: NY0130.

ILION—Time Warner Cable, 6005 Fair Lakes Rd, East Syracuse, NY 13057. Phone: 315-634-6100. Fax: 315-634-6219. Web Site: http://www.timewarnercable.com/CentralNY. Also serves Bridgewater, Brookfield, Columbia (town), Danube (town), Dolgeville, Earlville (village), Eaton, Frankfort (village), German Flatts, Herkimer (village), Lebanon, Leonardsville, Litchfield (town), Little Falls, Madison, Manheim (town), Mohawk, Morrisville, Plainfield, Salisbury (town), Sherburne (village), Smyrna, West Winfield & Winfield. ICA: NY0036.

TV Market Ranking: 35 (Eaton, Lebanon, Madison, Morrisville); Below 100 (Bridgewater, Brookfield, Columbia (town), Danube (town), Dolgeville, Earlville (village), Frankfort (village), German Flatts, Herkimer (village), ILION, Leonardsville, Litchfield (town), Little Falls, Manheim (town), Mohawk, Plainfield, Salisbury (town), Sherburne (village), Smyrna, West Winfield, Winfield). Franchise award date: N.A. Franchise expiration date: N.A. Began: June 15, 1964.

Channel capacity: N.A. Channels available but not in use: N.A.

Basic Service

Subscribers: N.A. Included in Syracuse

Programming (received off-air): WCNY-TV (PBS) Syracuse; WFXV (FOX) Utica; WKTV (CW, NBC) Utica; WPNY-LP Utica, etc.; WTVH (CBS) Syracuse; WUTR (ABC) Utica; allband FM.

Programming (via satellite): QVC; TBS Superstation; various Canadian stations.

Fee: $35.91 installation; $8.40 monthly.

Expanded Basic Service 1

Subscribers: N.A. Included in Syracuse

Programming (via satellite): A&E Networks; ABC Family Channel; Animal Planet; BET Networks; Cartoon Network; CNBC; CNN; Comedy Central; C-SPAN; C-SPAN 2; Discovery Channel; Discovery Fit & Health; E! Entertainment Television; ESPN; ESPN 2; Eternal Word TV Network; Food Network; Fox News Channel; FX; Hallmark Channel; Headline News; HGTV; ION Television; Jewelry Television; Lifetime; Lifetime Movie Network; MSG Plus; MSNBC; MTV; Nickelodeon; Oxygen; ShopNBC; SoapNet; Spike TV; Syfy; The Learning Channel; The Weather Channel; Travel Channel; Turner Network TV; TV Land; Univision Studios; USA Network; Versus; VH1; WE tv; Yankees Entertainment & Sports.

Fee: $35.10 monthly.

Digital Basic Service

Subscribers: N.A. Included in Syracuse

Programming (via satellite): AMC; America's Store; BBC America; Bio; Bloomberg Television; Boomerang; Bravo; Cooking Channel; Country Music TV; C-SPAN 3; Discovery Digital Networks; Disney Channel; DIY Network; Encore Action; ESPN Classic Sports; ESPNews; Fox Movie Channel; Fox Sports World; Fuse; G4; GAS; Golf Channel; Great American Country; GSN; History Channel; History Channel International; Independent Film Channel; Lifetime Real Women; Local Cable Weather; MSG; MTV2; National Geographic Channel; Nick Jr.; Nick Too; Ovation; Speed; Style Network; Sundance Channel; Toon Disney; Trinity Broadcasting Network; truTV; Turner Classic Movies; Versus; VH1 Classic.

Fee: $10.95 monthly.

Digital Expanded Basic Service

Subscribers: N.A.

Programming (via satellite): FSN Digital Atlantic; FSN Digital Central; FSN Digital Pacific; Fuel TV; NBA TV; Tennis Channel.

Fee: $4.95 monthly.

Digital Pay Service 1

Pay Units: 5,217.

Programming (via satellite): ART America; Canales N; CCTV-4; Cinemax (multiplexed); HBO (multiplexed); RAI International; Russian Television Network; Saigon Broadcasting Television Network; Showtime (multiplexed); Starz (multiplexed); The Movie Channel (multiplexed); TV Asia; TV5, La Television International; Zee TV USA.

Fee: $8.95 monthly (Cinemax, Showtime, Starz or TMC), $9.95 monthly (ART, Canales N, CCTV-4, RAI, RTN, SBN or TV 5), $10.95 monthly (HBO), $14.95 monthly (TV Asia or Zee TV).

Video-On-Demand: Yes

Pay-Per-View

iN DEMAND (delivered digitally); Playboy TV (delivered digitally); Fresh (delivered digitally).

Internet Service

Operational: Yes.

Broadband Service: EarthLink, LocalNet, Road Runner.

Fee: $39.95 installation; $44.95 monthly.

Telephone Service

Digital: Operational

Fee: $39.95 monthly

Miles of plant included in Syracuse.

President: Mary Cotter. Vice President, Engineering: Henry Hryckiewicz. Vice President, Marketing: John Melvany. Vice President, Public Affairs: Jeff Unaitis. Technical Operations Director: Bruce Tompkins.

Ownership: Time Warner Cable (MSO).; Advance/Newhouse Partnership (MSO).Day-to-Day operations managed by Time Warner Cable.

INDIAN LAKE (town)—Hamilton County Cable TV Inc., 1330 State Rt 30, Wells, NY 12190. Phones: 800-562-1560; 518-924-2013. Fax: 518-924-3410. Web Site: http://www.hcctelevision.com/. Also serves Blue Mountain Lake & Indian Lake. ICA: NY0168.

TV Market Ranking: Outside TV Markets (Blue Mountain Lake, Indian Lake, INDIAN LAKE (TOWN)). Franchise award date: January 1, 1987. Franchise expiration date: N.A. Began: December 1, 1987.

Channel capacity: 36 (operating 2-way). Channels available but not in use: N.A.

Basic Service

Subscribers: 200.

Programming (received off-air): WNYT (NBC) Albany; WPBS-DT (PBS) Watertown; WRGB (CBS) Schenectady; WTEN (ABC) Albany; WXXA-TV (FOX) Albany.

Programming (via satellite): A&E Networks; ABC Family Channel; AMC; Animal Planet; CNN; C-SPAN 2; Discovery Channel; ESPN; QVC; Spike TV; TBS Superstation; Turner Network TV; USA Network.

Fee: $49.95 installation; $33.68 monthly.

Pay Service 1

Pay Units: 80.

Programming (via satellite): HBO.

Fee: $10.00 monthly.

Pay Service 2

Pay Units: 45.

Programming (via satellite): Cinemax.

Fee: $9.00 monthly.

Video-On-Demand: No

Internet Service

Operational: No.

Telephone Service

None

Miles of Plant: 17.0 (coaxial); None (fiber optic).

Manager & Chief Technician: Brian Towers. Office Manager: Maggie Welch.

Ownership: Hamilton County/Gore Mountain Cable TV Inc. (MSO).

ISLIP—Cablevision Systems Corp. Now served by WOODBURY/ISLIP, NY [NY0001]. ICA: NY0225.

ITHACA—Time Warner Cable, 6005 Fair Lakes Rd, East Syracuse, NY 13057. Phone: 315-634-6100. Fax: 315-634-6219. Web Site: http://www.timewarnercable.com/centralNY. Also serves Candor (village), Caroline, Cayuga Heights, Covert (town), Danby, Dryden (village), Freeville, Groton (village), Lansing (village), Newfield, Tompkins County, Trumansburg (village) & Ulysses (town). ICA: NY0028.

TV Market Ranking: 35 (Groton (village)); Below 100 (Candor (village), Caroline, Cayuga Heights, Covert (town), Danby, Dryden (village), Freeville, ITHACA, Lansing (village), Newfield, Tompkins County, Trumansburg (village), Ulysses (town)). Franchise award date: N.A. Franchise expiration date: N.A. Began: May 1, 1952.

Channel capacity: N.A. Channels available but not in use: N.A.

Basic Service

Subscribers: N.A. Included in Syracuse

Programming (received off-air): WBNG-TV (CBS, CW) Binghamton; WCNY-TV (PBS) Syracuse; WENY-TV (ABC, CW) Elmira; WNYS-TV (MNT) Syracuse; WSKG-TV (PBS) Binghamton; WSPX-TV (ION) Syracuse; WSTM-TV (NBC) Syracuse; WSYR-TV (ABC) Syracuse; WSYT (FOX) Syracuse; WTVH (CBS) Syracuse; 17 FMs.

Programming (via satellite): C-SPAN; C-SPAN 2; E! Entertainment Television; LWS Local Weather Station; QVC; ShopNBC; TBS Superstation; WPIX (CW, IND) New York.

Fee: $35.00 installation; $15.81 monthly.

Expanded Basic Service 1

Subscribers: N.A. Included in Syracuse

Programming (via satellite): A&E Networks; ABC Family Channel; Animal Planet; BET Networks; Cartoon Network; CNBC; CNN; Comedy Central; Discovery Channel; Discovery Fit & Health; ESPN; ESPN 2; Eternal Word TV Network; Food Network; Fox News Channel; FX; Headline News; HGTV; Lifetime; Lifetime Movie Network; MSG Plus; MSNBC; MTV; Nickelodeon; Oxygen; Scola; Shop at Home; SoapNet; Spike TV; Syfy; The Learning Channel; The Weather Channel; Travel Channel; Turner Network TV; TV Land; Univision Studios; USA Network; Versus; VH1; WE tv; Yankees Entertainment & Sports.

Fee: $20.00 installation; $31.58 monthly.

Digital Basic Service

Subscribers: N.A. Included in Syracuse

Programming (via satellite): AMC; America's Store; BBC America; Bio; Bloomberg Television; Boomerang; Bravo; Cooking Channel; Country Music TV; C-SPAN 3; Discovery Digital Networks; Disney Channel; DIY Network; Encore Action; ESPN Classic Sports; ESPNews; Fox Movie Channel; Fox Sports World; Fuse; G4; GAS; Golf Channel; Great American Country; GSN; History Channel; History Channel International; Independent Film Channel; Lifetime Real Women; MSG; MTV2; National Geographic Channel; Nick Jr.; Nick Too; Outdoor Channel; Ovation; Speed; Style Network; Sundance Channel; Toon Disney; Trinity Broadcasting Network; truTV; Turner Classic Movies; VH1 Classic.

Fee: $10.95 monthly.

Digital Expanded Basic Service

Subscribers: N.A.

Programming (via satellite): FSN Digital Atlantic; FSN Digital Central; FSN Digital Pacific; Fuel TV; NBA TV; Tennis Channel.

Fee: $4.95 monthly.

Digital Pay Service 1

Pay Units: N.A.

Programming (via satellite): ART America; Canales N; CCTV-4; Cinemax (multiplexed); HBO (multiplexed); RAI International; Russian Television Network; Saigon Broadcasting Television Network; Showtime (multiplexed); Starz (multiplexed); The Movie Channel; TV Asia; TV5, La Television International; Zee TV USA.

Fee: $20.00 installation; $9.95 monthly (ART, Canales n, CCTV-4, RAI, RTN, SBN or TV 5), $10.95 monthly (Cinemax, HBO, Showtime, Starz or TMC), $14.95 monthly (TV Asia or Zee TV).

Video-On-Demand: Yes

Pay-Per-View

Addressable homes: 8,725.

iN DEMAND (delivered digitally); Playboy TV (delivered digitally); Fresh (delivered digitally).

Internet Service

Operational: Yes.

Broadband Service: EarthLink, LocalNet, Road Runner.

Fee: $39.95 installation; $44.95 monthly.

Telephone Service

Digital: Operational

Fee: $39.95 monthly

Miles of plant included in Syracuse.

President: Mary Cotter. Vice President, Engineering: Henry Hryckiewicz. Vice President, Marketing: John Melvany. Vice President, Public Affairs: Jeff Unaitis. Technical Operations Director: Bruce Tompkins.

Ownership: Time Warner Cable (MSO).; Advance/Newhouse Partnership (MSO).Day-to-Day operations managed by Time Warner Cable.

JACKSON HEIGHTS—RCN Corp. Formerly served by Queens, NY [NY0283]. This cable system has converted to IPTV, 196 Van Buren St, Herndon, VA 20170. Phone: 703-434-8200. Web Site: http://www.rcn.com. ICA: NY5309.

TV Market Ranking: 1 (JACKSON HEIGHTS).

Channel capacity: N.A. Channels available but not in use: N.A.

Pay Service 1

Pay Units: N.A.

Fee: $11.95 monthly (Cinemaz or Starz!); $16.95 monthly (Showtime/The Movie Channel); $17.95 monthly (HBO).

Internet Service

Operational: Yes.

Fee: $38.00 monthly.

Telephone Service

Digital: Operational

Fee: $45.00 monthly

Chairman: Steven J. Simmons. Chief Executive Officer: Jim Holanda.

JAMESTOWN—Time Warner Cable, 120 Plaza Dr, Vestal, NY 13850-3658. Phones: 607-644-1646; 716-664-7315 (Jamestown office). Fax: 607-644-1501. Web Site: http://www.timewarnercable.com. Also serves Bemus Point (village), Brocton (village), Busti (town), Carroll (town), Cassadaga (village), Celoron (village), Cherry Creek, Clymer (town), Dayton (town), Ellery (town), Ellicott (town), Ellington (town), Falconer (village), Fredonia (village), French Creek, Gerry (town), Harmony (town), Kiantone (town), Lakewood (village), Maple Springs, Mina, North Clymer, North Harmony (town), Panama (village), Pomfret (town), Portland (portions), Sinclairville (village), South Dayton (village), Stockton (town) & Villenova (town). ICA: NY0030.

TV Market Ranking: 24 (Dayton (town)); Below 100 (Bemus Point (village), Brocton (village), Busti (town), Carroll (town), Cassadaga (village), Celoron (village), Cherry Creek, Clymer (town), Ellery (town), Ellicott (town), Ellington (town), Falconer (village), Fredonia (village), French Creek, Gerry (town), Harmony (town), JAMESTOWN, Kiantone (town), Lakewood (village), Maple Springs, Mina, North Clymer, North Harmony (town), Panama (village), Pomfret (town), Portland (portions), Sinclairville (village), South Dayton (village), Stockton (town), Villenova (town)). Franchise award date: January 1, 1965. Franchise expiration date: N.A. Began: January 1, 1965.

Channel capacity: N.A. Channels available but not in use: N.A.

Basic Service

Subscribers: N.A. Included in Binghamton

Programming (received off-air): WGRZ (NBC) Buffalo; WICU-TV (NBC) Erie; WIVB-TV (CBS) Buffalo; WJET-TV (ABC) Erie; WKBW-TV (ABC) Buffalo; WNED-TV (PBS) Buffalo; WNYB (IND) Jamestown; WNYO-TV (MNT) Buffalo; WPIX (CW, IND) New York; WSEE-TV (CBS, CW) Erie; WUTV (FOX) Buffalo; allband FM.

Programming (via satellite): BET Networks; ION Television; NewsChannel 8; TBS Superstation; Telemundo; The Learning Channel; TV Guide Network; WGN America.

Fee: $47.21 installation; $13.60 monthly; $2.87 converter.

Expanded Basic Service 1

Subscribers: N.A.

Programming (via satellite): A&E Networks; ABC Family Channel; AMC; American-Life TV Network; Animal Planet; Bravo; Cartoon Network; CNN; Comedy Central; Country Music TV; C-SPAN; C-SPAN 2; Discovery Channel; Discovery Fit & Health; Disney Channel; E! Entertainment Television; ESPN; ESPN 2; ESPN Classic Sports; Eternal Word TV Network; Food Network; Fox News Channel; Fuse; FX; Golf Channel; Headline News; HGTV; History Channel; Lifetime; Lifetime Movie Network; MSNBC; MTV; Nickelodeon; QVC; ShopNBC; SoapNet; Speed; Spike TV; Style Network; Syfy; The Weather Channel; Travel Channel; truTV; Turner Classic Movies; Turner Network TV; TV Land; USA Network; VH1; WE tv; Yankees Entertainment & Sports.

Fee: $29.97 monthly.

Digital Basic Service

Subscribers: N.A. Included in Binghamton

Programming (via satellite): America's Store; BBC America; Bio; Bloomberg Television; Cooking Channel; C-SPAN 3; Discovery Digital Networks; DIY Network; Encore Action; ESPNews; Fox Movie Channel; Fox Sports World; G4; GAS; Great American Country; History Channel International; Independent Film Channel; Lifetime Real Women; Music Choice; Nick Jr.; Outdoor Channel; Ovation; Sundance Channel; Toon Disney; Trinity Broadcasting Network; VH1 Classic.

Fee: $8.45 monthly.

Digital Expanded Basic Service

Subscribers: N.A.

Programming (via satellite): Fox Deportes; FSN Digital Atlantic; FSN Digital Central; FSN Digital Pacific; Fuel TV; NBA TV; Tennis Channel.

Fee: $4.95 monthly.

Digital Pay Service 1

Pay Units: 18,949.

Programming (via satellite): Canales N; Cinemax (multiplexed); Flix; HBO (multiplexed); Showtime (multiplexed); Starz; The Movie Channel (multiplexed); TV Asia; Zee TV USA.

Fee: $4.95 monthly (Canales N), $11.25 monthly (Cinemax, HBO, Starz or Flix, Showtime &TMC), $19.95 monthly (TV Asia & Zee TV).

Video-On-Demand: Yes

Pay-Per-View

Addressable homes: 7,623.

iN DEMAND (delivered digitally); Hot Choice (delivered digitally); Playboy TV (delivered digitally); Fresh (delivered digitally); Shorteez (delivered digitally); Pleasure (delivered digitally); ESPN Full Court (delivered digitally); ESPN Gameplan (delivered digitally); Sports PPV (delivered digitally).

Internet Service

Operational: Yes.

Broadband Service: Road Runner.

Fee: $39.95 installation; $44.95 monthly.

Telephone Service

Digital: Operational

Fee: $39.95 monthly

Miles of plant included in Binghamton

President: Mary Cotter. Vice President & General Manager: Chris Stramm. Vice President, Marketing: John Melvany. Vice President, Public Affairs: Dave Whalen. Technical Operations Director: Bruce Tomkins.

Ownership: Time Warner Cable (MSO).; Advance/Newhouse Partnership (MSO).Day-to-Day operations managed by Time Warner Cable.

JASPER—Time Warner Cable. Now served by HORNELL, NY [NY0076]. ICA: NY0226.

JOHNSBURG (town)—Hamilton County Cable TV Inc., 1330 State Rt 30, Wells, NY 12190. Phones: 800-562-1560; 518-924-2013. Fax: 518-924-3410. Web Site: http://www.hcctelevision.com. Also serves Chestertown & North Creek. ICA: NY0156.

TV Market Ranking: Outside TV Markets (Chestertown, JOHNSBURG (TOWN), North Creek). Franchise award date: January 1, 1988. Franchise expiration date: N.A. Began: June 1, 1988.

Channel capacity: 36 (operating 2-way). Channels available but not in use: N.A.

Basic Service

Subscribers: 401.

Programming (received off-air): WCAX-TV (CBS) Burlington; WNYT (NBC) Albany; WTEN (ABC) Albany; WVER (PBS) Rutland.

Programming (via satellite): A&E Networks; ABC Family Channel; AMC; CNN; C-SPAN; Discovery Channel; ESPN; ESPN 2; QVC; Spike TV; TBS Superstation; Turner Network TV; USA Network; WABC-TV (ABC) New York; WFLD (FOX) Chicago; WGN America.

Fee: $49.95 installation; $33.68 monthly.

Digital Basic Service

Subscribers: 80.

Fee: $46.36 monthly.

Pay Service 1

Pay Units: 79.

Programming (via satellite): HBO.

Fee: $10.00 monthly.

Pay Service 2

Pay Units: 40.

Programming (via satellite): Cinemax.

Fee: $9.00 monthly.

Video-On-Demand: No

Internet Service

Operational: No.

Telephone Service

None

Miles of Plant: 31.0 (coaxial); None (fiber optic).

Manager & Chief Technician: Brian Towers. Office Manager: Maggie Welch.

Ownership: Hamilton County/Gore Mountain Cable TV Inc. (MSO).

JOHNSTOWN (city)—Time Warner Cable. Now served by AMSTERDAM, NY [NY0047]. ICA: NY0054.

KEENE VALLEY—Keene Valley Video Inc., 1948 State Route 73, PO Box 47, Keene Valley, NY 12943. Phone: 518-576-4510. E-mail: info@kvvi.net. Web Site: http://www.kvvi.net. Also serves Keene (town). ICA: NY0171.

TV Market Ranking: Below 100 (Keene (town), KEENE VALLEY). Franchise award date: N.A. Franchise expiration date: N.A. Began: June 15, 1982.

Channel capacity: N.A. Channels available but not in use: N.A.

Basic Service

Subscribers: 285.

Programming (received off-air): WCAX-TV (CBS) Burlington; WETK (PBS) Burlington; WFFF-TV (CW, FOX) Burlington; WPTZ (NBC) Plattsburgh; WVNY (ABC) Burlington.

Programming (via satellite): A&E Networks; ABC Family Channel; AMC; CNN; Country Music TV; C-SPAN; C-SPAN 2; Discovery Channel; Disney Channel; ESPN; ESPN 2; Headline News; History Channel; Lifetime; MTV; Nickelodeon; Outdoor Channel; QVC; Speed; Spike TV; TBS Superstation; The Learning Channel; The Weather Channel; Turner Network TV; USA Network; VH1.

Fee: $50.00 installation; $28.50 monthly.

Pay Service 1

Pay Units: 25.

Programming (via satellite): Showtime.

Fee: $5.00 monthly.

Video-On-Demand: No

Internet Service

Operational: Yes.

Subscribers: 200.

Broadband Service: In-house.

Fee: $60.00-$100.00 monthly.

Telephone Service

None

Miles of Plant: 24.0 (coaxial); None (fiber optic).

Manager & Chief Engineer: Timothy Whitney. Office Manager: Anita Hall.

Ownership: Timothy A. Whitney.

KINGSTON—Time Warner Cable. Now served by HUDSON VALLEY (formerly Middletown), NY [NY0231]. ICA: NY0038.

LACKAWANNA—Time Warner Cable, 355 Chicago St, Buffalo, NY 14204-2069. Phone: 716-558-8881. Fax: 716-558-8855. Web Site: http://www.timewarnercable.com/wny. Also serves Amherst, Angola, Barker, Blasdell, Boston, Brant (town), Buffalo, Cambria, Cheektowaga, Colden, Depew, East Aurora, Eden, Elma, Evans (town), Farnham (village), Grand Island, Hamburg (town), Holland, Kenmore (village), Lancaster (village), Lewiston (village), Lockport, Newfane (town), Niagara (town), Niagara Falls, North Tonawanda, Orchard Park (village), Pendleton, Porter, Ransomville, Sanborn, Sloan, Somerset, Tonawanda, Wales, West Seneca, Wheatfield, Williamsville, Wilson (village) & Youngstown (village). ICA: NY0216.

TV Market Ranking: 24 (Amherst, Angola, Barker, Blasdell, Boston, Brant (town), Buffalo, Buffalo, Cambria, Cheektowaga, Colden, Depew, East Aurora, Eden, Elma, Evans (town), Farnham (village), Grand Island, Hamburg (town), Holland, Kenmore (village), LACKAWANNA, Lancaster (village), Lewiston (village), Lockport, Newfane (town), Niagara (town), Niagara Falls, North Tonawanda, Orchard Park (village), Pendleton, Porter, Ransomville, Sanborn, Sloan, Somerset, Tonawanda, Wales, West Seneca, Wheatfield, Williamsville, Wilson (village), Youngstown (village)). Franchise award date: N.A. Franchise expiration date: N.A. Began: May 1, 1965.

Channel capacity: N.A. Channels available but not in use: N.A.

Basic Service

Subscribers: 320,000 Includes Dunkirk, Olean, & Westfield.

Programming (received off-air): WBBZ-TV (IND) Springville; WGRZ (NBC) Buffalo; WIVB-TV (CBS) Buffalo; WKBW-TV (ABC) Buffalo; WNED-TV (PBS) Buffalo; WNLO (CW) Buffalo; WNYB (IND) Jamestown; WNYO-TV (MNT) Buffalo; WPXJ-TV (ION) Batavia; WUTV (FOX) Buffalo.

Programming (via satellite): C-SPAN; C-SPAN 2; Eternal Word TV Network; QVC; TV Guide Network; various Canadian stations.

Expanded Basic Service 1

Subscribers: 213,270.

Programming (via satellite): A&E Networks; ABC Family Channel; AMC; Animal Planet; BET Networks; Bravo; Cartoon Network; CNBC; CNN; Comedy Central; Country Music TV; Discovery Channel; Disney Channel; E! Entertainment Television; ESPN; ESPN 2; Food Network; Fox News Channel; FX; Hallmark Channel; Headline News; HGTV; History Channel; Lifetime; MSG; MSNBC; MTV; Nickelodeon; Oxygen; Spike TV; SportsNet New York; Style Network; Syfy; TBS Superstation; The Learning Channel; The Weather Channel; Travel Channel; truTV; Turner Classic Movies; Turner Network TV; TV Land; USA Network; Versus; VH1; Yankees Entertainment & Sports.

Digital Basic Service

Subscribers: 14,762.

Programming (via satellite): A&E HD; AmericanLife TV Network; BBC America; BBC America On Demand; Bio; Bloomberg Television; Boomerang; Bridges TV; Canal 52MX; CBS Sports Network; Cine Latino; CMT Pure Country; CNN en Espanol; Cooking Channel; Current; Daystar TV Network; Discovery en Espanol; Discovery Fit & Health; Discovery Health Channel; Discovery Home Channel; Discovery Kids Channel; Discovery Times Channel; DIY Network; ESPN 2 HD; ESPN Classic Sports; ESPN Deportes; ESPN HD; ESPN U; ESPNews; Exercise TV; Familyland Television Network; Fox Business Channel; Fox College Sports Atlantic; Fox College Sports Central; Fox College Sports Pacific; Fox Deportes; Fox Movie Channel; Fox Reality Channel; Fox Soccer; Fuel TV; Fuse; G4; GAS; GMC; Golf Channel; Great American Country; GSN; Halogen Network; HD Theater; HDNet; HDNet Movies; History Channel en Espanol; History Channel International; Howard TV; Independent Film Channel; Lifetime Movie Network; LOGO; Military Channel; MTV Hits; MTV Jams; MTV2; Music Choice; National Geographic Channel; National Geographic Channel On Demand; NBA TV; NHL Network; Nick Jr.; Nick Too; NickToons TV; Outdoor Channel; Oxygen On Demand; Palladia; ReelzChannel; Science; SoapNet; Speed; Speed On Demand; Sundance Channel; Tennis Channel; The Word Network; Toon Disney; Toon Disney en Espanol; Tr3s; Trinity Broadcasting Network; Turner Network TV HD; TV Guide SPOT; TV One; Universal HD; Versus HD; VH1 Classic; VH1 Soul; WE tv; YES HD.

Fee: $57.95 monthly.

Digital Pay Service 1

Pay Units: 70,850.

Programming (via satellite): Cinemax (multiplexed); Cinemax HD; Cinemax On Demand; Encore (multiplexed); HBO (multiplexed); HBO HD; HBO On Demand; Showtime (multiplexed); Showtime HD; Showtime On Demand; Starz (multiplexed); Starz HDTV; Starz On Demand; The Movie Channel (multiplexed); The Movie Channel On Demand.

Fee: $11.95 monthly (each).

Video-On-Demand: Yes

Pay-Per-View

Playboy TV (delivered digitally); Fresh (delivered digitally); Ten Clips (delivered digitally); Ten Blox (delivered digitally); Ten Blue (delivered digitally); Sports PPV (delivered digitally); NBA League Pass (delivered digitally).

Internet Service

Operational: Yes.

Broadband Service: Road Runner.

Fee: $44.95 monthly; $3.00 modem lease.

Telephone Service

Digital: Operational

Fee: $39.95 monthly

Miles of Plant: 3,012.0 (coaxial); None (fiber optic).

President: Gordon Harp. Vice President, Marketing: Steve Jaworowski. Vice President, Public & Government Affairs: Robin Wolfgang. Vice President, Customer Operations: David Fraass. Technical Operations Manager: Steve Pawlik. Marketing Manager: Jean Calabrese.

Ownership: Time Warner Cable (MSO).

LANCASTER (town)—Now served by LACKAWANNA, NY [NY0216]. ICA: NY0043.

LIMESTONE—Atlantic Broadband, 24 Main St, Bradford, PA 16701. Phones: 888-536-9600; 814-539-8971; 814-362-2190. Fax: 814-362-2190. Web Site: http://www.atlanticbb.com. Also serves Carrollton (town), Rushford & West Valley. ICA: NY0228.

TV Market Ranking: Below 100 (Carrollton (town), LIMESTONE, Rushford, West Valley). Franchise award date: January 1, 1991. Franchise expiration date: N.A. Began: January 1, 1991.

Channel capacity: 60 (operating 2-way). Channels available but not in use: N.A.

Basic Service

Subscribers: 160.

Programming (received off-air): WGRZ (NBC) Buffalo; WICU-TV (NBC) Erie; WKBW-TV (ABC) Buffalo; WNYB (IND) Jamestown; WSEE-TV (CBS, CW) Erie; WUTV (FOX) Buffalo.

Programming (via microwave): WPSU-TV (PBS) Clearfield.

Programming (via satellite): C-SPAN; Eternal Word TV Network; INSP; Jewelry Television; PBS World; Pennsylvania Cable Network; Product Information Network; QVC; TV Guide Network; WGN America.

Fee: $25.00 installation; $18.98 monthly; $20.00 additional installation.

Expanded Basic Service 1

Subscribers: N.A.

Programming (via satellite): A&E Networks; ABC Family Channel; AMC; Animal Planet; Bravo; Cartoon Network; CNBC; CNN; Comedy Central; Country Music TV; Discovery Channel; Discovery Health Channel; Disney Channel; E! Entertainment Television; ESPN; ESPN 2; ESPN Classic Sports; Food Network; Fox News Channel; FX; G4; Golf Channel; Hallmark Channel; Headline News; HGTV; History Channel; Lifetime; Lifetime Movie Network; MSG; MSNBC; MTV; National Geographic Channel; Nickelodeon; Outdoor Channel; Oxygen; Root Sports Pittsburgh; Speed; Spike TV; Syfy; TBS Superstation; The Learning Channel; The Weather Channel; Travel Channel; truTV; Turner Classic Movies; Turner Network TV; TV Land; USA Network; VH1.

Fee: $37.47 monthly.

Digital Basic Service

Subscribers: N.A.

Programming (via satellite): A&E HD; Animal Planet HD; BBC America; Bio; Bloomberg Television; Boomerang; Chiller; CMT Pure Country; Discovery Channel HD; Discovery Kids Channel; Disney Channel HD; DIY Network; Encore; ESPN 2 HD; ESPN HD; ESPN U; ESPNews; Fuel TV; HD Theater; History Channel International; ID Investigation Discovery; Independent Film Channel; Lifetime Real Women; Military Channel; MTV Hits; MTV Jams; MTV2; Music Choice; NFL Network; NFL Network HD; Nick Jr.; Nick Too; NickToons TV; Planet Green; Root Sports Pittsburgh; Science; SoapNet; Starz; Syfy HD; TBS in HD; TeenNick; TLC HD; Toon Disney; Tr3s; Turner Network TV HD; USA Network HD; VH1 Classic; VH1 Soul; WE tv; Weatherscan.

Fee: $18.95 monthly.

Digital Pay Service 1

Pay Units: N.A.

Programming (via satellite): Cinemax (multiplexed); Flix; HBO (multiplexed); Showtime (multiplexed); The Movie Channel (multiplexed).

Fee: $15.95 monthly (HBO, Cinemax or Showtime/Flix/TMC).

Pay-Per-View

iN DEMAND (delivered digitally); Hot Choice (delivered digitally); Club Jenna (delivered digitally); Spice: Xcess (delivered digitally); Fresh (delivered digitally); Shorteez (delivered digitally); Playboy TV (delivered digitally).

Internet Service

Operational: Yes.

Broadband Service: Atlantic Broadband High-Speed Internet.

Fee: $24.95-$57.95 monthly.

Telephone Service

Digital: Operational

Fee: $44.95 monthly

Miles of Plant: 10.0 (coaxial); None (fiber optic).

Vice President: David Dane. General Manager: Mike Papasergi. Technical Operations Director: Charles Sorchillo. Chief Technician: Richard Himes. Marketing & Customer Service Director: Dara Leslie. Marketing Manager: Natalie Kurchak.
Ownership: Atlantic Broadband (MSO).

LONG ISLAND CITY—RCN Corp. Formerly served by Queens, NY [NY0283]. This cable system has converted to IPTV, 196 Van Buren St, Herndon, VA 20170. Phone: 703-434-8200. Web Site: http://www.rcn.com. ICA: NY5311.
TV Market Ranking: 1 (LONG ISLAND CITY).
Channel capacity: N.A. Channels available but not in use: N.A.

Pay Service 1
Pay Units: N.A.
Fee: $11.95 monthly (Cinemaz or Starz!); $16.95 monthly (Showtime/The Movie Channel); $17.95 monthly (HBO).

Internet Service
Operational: Yes.
Fee: $38.00 monthly.

Telephone Service
Digital: Operational
Fee: $45.00 monthly
Chairman: Steven J. Simmons. Chief Executive Officer: Jim Holanda.

LONG LAKE—Chain Lakes Cablevision, 9507 Cherokee Trail, Crossville, TN 38572. Phone: 866-788-5261. Fax: 931-788-0489. ICA: NY0172.
TV Market Ranking: Outside TV Markets (LONG LAKE). Franchise award date: N.A. Franchise expiration date: N.A. Began: January 1, 1954.
Channel capacity: 32 (not 2-way capable). Channels available but not in use: N.A.

Basic Service
Subscribers: 298.
Programming (received off-air): WNPI-DT (PBS) Norwood; WRGB (CBS) Schenectady; WTEN (ABC) Albany; WWNY-TV (CBS) Carthage; allband FM.
Programming (via satellite): Bravo; ESPN; Eternal Word TV Network; HGTV; Nickelodeon; QVC; Spike TV; Turner Network TV; WNBC (NBC) New York.
Fee: $45.00 installation; $16.67 monthly.

Expanded Basic Service 1
Subscribers: 295.
Programming (via satellite): CNN; Discovery Channel; USA Network.
Fee: $3.33 monthly.

Expanded Basic Service 2
Subscribers: 287.
Programming (via satellite): TBS Superstation; WGN America.
Fee: $2.95 monthly.

Pay Service 1
Pay Units: 57.
Programming (via satellite): The Movie Channel.
Fee: $25.00 installation; $10.95 monthly.

Video-On-Demand: No

Internet Service
Operational: No.

Telephone Service
None
Miles of Plant: 25.0 (coaxial); None (fiber optic).
Manager: Charles Himelrick. Assistant Manager: Diane Bowles.
Ownership: Phoenix Cable Inc. (MSO).

LYNBROOK—Cablevision Systems Corp. Now served by WOODBURY/ISLIP, NY [NY0001]. ICA: NY0069.

MALONE—Time Warner Cable. Now served by MASSENA, NY [NY0072]. ICA: NY0079.

MAMARONECK—Cablevision Systems Corp., 1 Van Cortland Ave, Ossining, NY 10562-3309. Phone: 516-803-2300 (Corporate office). Fax: 516-803-1183. Web Site: http://www.cablevision.com. Also serves Ardsley, Bronxville, Dobbs Ferry, Eastchester, Elmsford, Greenburgh, Hastings-on-Hudson, Irvington (village), Larchmont (village), New Rochelle, North Castle, Pelham, Pelham Manor, Rye (city), Rye Brook (village), Scarsdale, Tuckahoe & White Plains. ICA: NY0012.
TV Market Ranking: 1 (Ardsley, Bronxville, Dobbs Ferry, Eastchester, Elmsford, Greenburgh, Hastings-on-Hudson, Irvington (village), Larchmont (village), MAMARONECK, New Rochelle, North Castle, Pelham, Pelham Manor, Rye (city), Rye Brook (village), Scarsdale, Tuckahoe, White Plains). Franchise award date: N.A. Franchise expiration date: N.A. Began: November 1, 1977.
Channel capacity: N.A. Channels available but not in use: N.A.

Basic Service
Subscribers: 103,340.
Programming (received off-air): WABC-TV (ABC) New York; WCBS-TV (CBS) New York; WFTY-DT (TEL) Smithtown; WLIW (PBS) Garden City; WLNY-TV (IND) Riverhead; WNBC (NBC) New York; WNET (PBS) Newark; WNJU (TMO) Linden; WNYW (FOX) New York; WPIX (CW, IND) New York; WPXN-TV (ION) New York; WWOR-TV (MNT) Secaucus; WXTV-DT (UNV) Paterson; 28 FMs.
Programming (via satellite): News 12 Long Island; QVC; ShopNBC.
Fee: $49.95 installation; $10.58 monthly; $3.00 converter.

Expanded Basic Service 1
Subscribers: N.A.
Programming (via satellite): A&E Networks; ABC Family Channel; AMC; Animal Planet; BET Networks; Bravo; Cartoon Network; CNBC; CNN; Comedy Central; C-SPAN; C-SPAN 2; Discovery Channel; Disney Channel; E! Entertainment Television; ESPN; ESPN 2; Food Network; Fox News Channel; Fuse; FX; GalaVision; Golf Channel; Headline News; HGTV; History Channel; Lifetime; MSG; MSG Plus; MSNBC; MTV; MTV2; News 12 Traffic & Weather; Nickelodeon; SoapNet; Speed; Spike TV; SportsNet New York; Syfy; TBS Superstation; Telecare; The Learning Channel; The Weather Channel; Travel Channel; truTV; Turner Classic Movies; Turner Network TV; TV Land; USA Network; VH1; WE tv; Yankees Entertainment & Sports.
Fee: $39.37 monthly.

Digital Basic Service
Subscribers: N.A.
Programming (via satellite): Azteca America; BBC World News; Bio; Bloomberg Television; Canal Sur; Caracol TV; Cartoon Network Tambien en Espanol; Cine Latino; CNN en Espanol; CNN HD; Country Music TV; C-SPAN 3; Discovery en Espanol; Discovery Home Channel; Discovery Kids Channel; Docu TVE; Ecuavisia Internacional; ESPN 2 HD; ESPN Classic Sports; ESPN Deportes; ESPN HD; ESPNews; EuroNews; EWTN en Espanol; Food Network HD; Fox College Sports Atlantic; Fox College Sports Central; Fox College Sports Pacific; Fox Deportes; Fox Movie Channel; Fox Soccer; FSN HD; Fuel TV; G4; GameHD; Golf Channel; GolTV; Great American Country; Hallmark Channel; HD Theater; HGTV HD; History Channel en Espanol; History Channel International; Howard TV; HTV Musica; ID Investigation Discovery; Infinito; Jewelry Television; La Familia Network; Latele Novela Network; LOGO; Mariavision; Military Channel; Momentum TV; MTV Hits; mun2 television; Music Choice; National Geographic Channel; National Geographic Channel HD Network; NBA TV; NHL Network; Nick Jr.; NickToons TV; Outdoor Channel; Science; Sorpresa; Sundance Channel; Supercanal Caribe; TBS in HD; TeenNick; Telefe International; Toon Disney; Toon Disney en Espanol; Tr3s; Turner Network TV HD; TV Chile; TV Colombia; TVE Internacional; TVG Network; Universal HD; Utilisima; VeneMovies; Versus; Versus HD; VH1 Classic; VH1 Soul; V-me TV; WAPA America; World Cinema HD; YES HD.
Fee: $10.95 monthly.

Pay Service 1
Pay Units: N.A.
Programming (via satellite): Cinemax; HBO (multiplexed); Showtime (multiplexed); The Movie Channel.

Digital Pay Service 1
Pay Units: N.A.
Programming (via satellite): CCTV-4; Cinemax (multiplexed); Cinemax HD; Encore (multiplexed); HBO (multiplexed); HBO HD; Korean Channel; RAI International; Russian Television Network; Showtime (multiplexed); Showtime HD; Starz (multiplexed); Starz HDTV; The Movie Channel (multiplexed); The Movie Channel HD; TV Asia; TV Japan; TV Polonia; TV5, La Television International; Zee TV USA.
Fee: $9.95 monthly (Showtime, Cinemax, TMC, Starz/Encore, Playboy, RAI, SPT, TV5 Monde, or TV Polonia), $11.95 monthly (HBO), $24.95 monthly (TV Japan).

Video-On-Demand: Yes

Pay-Per-View
iN DEMAND; Club Jenna; Playboy TV; special events.

Internet Service
Operational: Yes.
Broadband Service: Optimum Online.
Fee: $46.95 installation; $34.95 monthly.

Telephone Service
Digital: Operational
Fee: $34.95 monthly
Miles of Plant: 1,029.0 (coaxial); 257.0 (fiber optic).
Vice President, Field Operations: Mark Fitchett.
Ownership: Cablevision Systems Corp. (MSO).

MANHATTAN—RCN Corp. Formerly served by Manhattan, NY [NY0282]. This cable system has converted to IPTV, 196 Van Buren St, Herndon, VA 20170. Phone: 703-434-8200. Web Site: http://www.rcn.com. ICA: NY5312.
Channel capacity: N.A. Channels available but not in use: N.A.

Pay Service 1
Pay Units: N.A.
Fee: $11.95 monthly (Cinemaz or Starz!); $16.95 monthly (Showtime/The Movie Channel); $17.95 monthly (HBO).

Internet Service
Operational: Yes.
Fee: $38.00 monthly.

Telephone Service
Digital: Planned
Fee: $45.00 monthly
Chairman: Steven J. Simmons. Chief Executive Officer: Jim Holanda.

MANHATTAN—RCN Corp. This cable system has converted to IPTV. See Manhattan, NY [NY5312]. ICA: NY0282.

MARGARETVILLE—MTC Cable, PO Box 260, Margaretville, NY 12455. Phone: 845-586-3311. E-mail: mtc@catskill.net. Web Site: http://www.mtctelcom.com. Also serves Andes, Arkville & Downsville. ICA: NY0155.
TV Market Ranking: Outside TV Markets (Andes, Arkville, MARGARETVILLE, Downsville). Franchise award date: N.A. Franchise expiration date: N.A. Began: January 1, 1953.
Channel capacity: 118 (operating 2-way). Channels available but not in use: N.A.

Basic Service
Subscribers: 2,200.
Programming (received off-air): WABC-TV (ABC) New York; WBNG-TV (CBS, CW) Binghamton; WBXI-CA (CBS) Indianapolis; WICZ-TV (FOX) Binghamton; WIVT (ABC) Binghamton; WNBC (NBC) New York; WNET (PBS) Newark; WNYT (NBC) Albany; WNYW (FOX) New York; WPIX (CW, IND) New York; WRGB (CBS) Schenectady; WSKG-TV (PBS) Binghamton; WWOR-TV (MNT) Secaucus; allband FM.
Programming (via satellite): QVC; The Weather Channel.
Fee: $39.00 installation; $16.95 monthly.

Digital Basic Service
Subscribers: N.A.
Programming (via satellite): AmericanLife TV Network; BBC America; Bio; Bravo; CBS Sports Network; Discovery Digital Networks; DIY Network; ESPN; ESPN Classic Sports; ESPNews; Fox College Sports Atlantic; Fox College Sports Central; Fox College Sports Pacific; Fox Movie Channel; Fuse; GAS; Great American Country; GSN; Halogen Network; HDNet; HDNet Movies; History Channel; INHD (multiplexed); Lifetime; Lifetime Real Women; Lime; MTV Networks Digital Suite; Music Choice; National Geographic Channel; Nick Jr.; Nick Too; NickToons TV; Style Network.
Fee: $27.95 monthly.

Pay Service 1
Pay Units: N.A.
Programming (via satellite): HBO.
Fee: $10.00 monthly.

Digital Pay Service 1
Pay Units: N.A.
Programming (via satellite): Encore (multiplexed); HBO (multiplexed); Showtime (multiplexed); Starz (multiplexed); The Movie Channel (multiplexed).
Fee: $9.00 monthly (each).

Video-On-Demand: No

Pay-Per-View
iN DEMAND (delivered digitally); Pleasure (delivered digitally); Hot Choice (delivered digitally).
Internet Service
Operational: Yes.
Subscribers: 1,000.
Broadband Service: In-house.
Fee: $41.95-$61.85 monthly.
Telephone Service
Digital: Operational
Fee: $39.95-$59.85 monthly
Miles of Plant: 23.0 (coaxial); None (fiber optic).
Ownership: Margaretville Telephone Co. (MSO).

MASSENA—Time Warner Cable, 6005 Fair Lakes Rd, East Syracuse, NY 13057. Phone: 315-634-6100. Fax: 315-634-6219. Web Site: http://www.timewarnercable.com/CentralNY. Also serves Bangor, Bombay (town), Brasher, Brushton, Burke (village), Canton (village), Chateaugay (village), Colton, Constable (town), De Kalb (town), Fort Covington, Fowler (town), Gouverneur (village), Harrisville, Hermon (village), Heuvelton, Hopkinton (town), Lisbon, Louisville, Madrid (town), Malone, Moira, Morristown (village), Norfolk, Norwood, Ogdensburg, Oswegatchie, Parishville, Pierrepont, Potsdam (village), Rensselaer Falls, Richville (village), Russell (town), Stockholm, Waddington (village) & Westville. ICA: NY0072.
TV Market Ranking: Below 100 (Chateaugay (village), Fowler (town), Gouverneur (village), Oswegatchie, Richville (village)); Outside TV Markets (Bangor, Bombay (town), Brasher, Brushton, Burke (village), Canton (village), Colton, Constable (town), De Kalb (town), Fort Covington, Harrisville, Hermon (village), Heuvelton, Hopkinton (town), Lisbon, Louisville, Madrid (town), Malone, MASSENA, Moira, Morristown (village), Norfolk, Norwood, Ogdensburg, Parishville, Pierrepont, Potsdam (village), Rensselaer Falls, Russell (town), Stockholm, Waddington (village), Westville). Franchise award date: June 9, 1958. Franchise expiration date: N.A. Began: November 1, 1959.
Channel capacity: N.A. Channels available but not in use: N.A.
Basic Service
Subscribers: N.A. Included in Syracuse
Programming (received off-air): WCFE-TV (PBS) Plattsburgh; WNYF-CA Watertown; WPBS-DT (PBS) Watertown; WPTZ (NBC) Plattsburgh; WWNY-TV (CBS) Carthage; WWTI (ABC, CW) Watertown.
Programming (via microwave): WSYR-TV (ABC) Syracuse.
Programming (via satellite): ABC Family Channel; CNN; ESPN; Headline News; MSG Plus; MTV; QVC; Shop at Home; TBS Superstation; USA Network; various Canadian stations.
Fee: $11.00 monthly.
Expanded Basic Service 1
Subscribers: N.A. Included in Syracuse
Programming (via satellite): A&E Networks; AMC; Animal Planet; BET Networks; Cartoon Network; CNBC; Comedy Central; C-SPAN; C-SPAN 2; Discovery Channel; Discovery Fit & Health; E! Entertainment Television; ESPN 2; Eternal Word TV Network; Food Network; Fox News Channel; FX; Hallmark Channel; HGTV; ION Television; Jewelry Television; Lifetime; Lifetime Movie Network; MSNBC; Nickelodeon; Oxygen; ShopNBC; Spike TV; Syfy; The Learning Channel; The Weather Channel; Travel Channel; Turner Network TV; TV Land; Univision Studios; Versus; VH1; WE tv; Yankees Entertainment & Sports.
Fee: $36.22 installation; $34.95 monthly.
Digital Basic Service
Subscribers: N.A. Included in Syracuse
Programming (via satellite): America's Store; BBC America; Bio; Bloomberg Television; Boomerang; Bravo; Cooking Channel; Country Music TV; C-SPAN 3; Discovery Digital Networks; Disney Channel; DIY Network; Encore Action; ESPN Classic Sports; ESPNews; Fox Movie Channel; Fox Sports World; Fuse; G4; GAS; Golf Channel; Great American Country; GSN; History Channel; History Channel International; Independent Film Channel; Lifetime Real Women; Local Cable Weather; MSG; MTV2; National Geographic Channel; Nick Jr.; Nick Too; Outdoor Channel; Ovation; Speed; Style Network; Sundance Channel; Toon Disney; Trinity Broadcasting Network; truTV; Turner Classic Movies; VH1 Classic.
Fee: $10.95 monthly.
Digital Expanded Basic Service
Subscribers: N.A.
Programming (via satellite): FSN Digital Atlantic; FSN Digital Central; FSN Digital Pacific; Fuel TV; NBA TV; Tennis Channel.
Fee: $4.95 monthly.
Digital Pay Service 1
Pay Units: N.A.
Programming (via satellite): Canales N; CCTV-4; Cinemax (multiplexed); HBO (multiplexed); RAI International; Russian Television Network; Saigon Broadcasting Television Network; Showtime (multiplexed); Starz (multiplexed); The Movie Channel (multiplexed); TV Asia; TV5, La Television International; Zee TV USA.
Fee: $9.95 monthly (ART, Canales N, CCTV-4, Cinemax, RAI, RTN, SBN, Starz, TMC or TV 5), $10.95 monthly (HBO), $12.95 (Showtime), $14.95 monthly (TV Asia or Zee TV).
Video-On-Demand: Yes
Pay-Per-View
Addressable homes: 2,502.
iN DEMAND (delivered digitally); Playboy TV (delivered digitally); Fresh (delivered digitally).
Internet Service
Operational: Yes. Began: June 1, 1998.
Broadband Service: EarthLink, LocalNet, Road Runner.
Fee: $39.95 installation; $44.95 monthly.
Telephone Service
Digital: Operational
Fee: $39.95 monthly
Miles of plant included in Syracuse.
President: Mary Cotter. Vice President, Engineering: Henry Hryckiewicz. Vice President, Marketing: John Melvany. Vice President, Public Affairs: Jeff Unaitis. Technical Operations Director: Bruce Tompkins.
Ownership: Time Warner Cable (MSO).; Advance/Newhouse Partnership (MSO).Day-to-Day operations managed by Time Warner Cable.

McDONOUGH—Formerly served by Haefele TV Inc. No longer in operation. ICA: NY0230.

MINERVA (town)—Chain Lakes Cablevision, 9507 Cherokee Trail, Crossville, TN 38572. Phone: 866-788-5261. Fax: 931-788-0489. ICA: NY0178.
TV Market Ranking: Outside TV Markets (MINERVA (TOWN)).
Channel capacity: 44 (not 2-way capable). Channels available but not in use: N.A.

Basic Service
Subscribers: 87.
Programming (received off-air): WCAX-TV (CBS) Burlington; WCDC-TV (ABC) Adams; WETK (PBS) Burlington; WFFF-TV (CW, FOX) Burlington; WPIX (CW, IND) New York; WPTZ (NBC) Plattsburgh; WVNY (ABC) Burlington.
Programming (via satellite): A&E Networks; ABC Family Channel; American Movie Classics; Cartoon Network; CNN; Country Music TV; C-SPAN; Discovery Channel; Discovery Health Channel; E! Entertainment Television; ESPN; ESPN 2; Food Network; Hallmark Channel; Headline News; HGTV; History Channel; Lifetime; Men's Channel; MSNBC; Outdoor Channel; QVC; Spike TV; Syfy; TBS Superstation; The Learning Channel; The Weather Channel; TNT; Trinity Broadcasting Network; TV Land; USA Network; WGN America.
Fee: $34.95 monthly; $25.00 converter; $8.75 additional installation.
Digital Basic Service
Subscribers: 8.
Programming (via satellite): BBC America; Bio; Bloomberg Television; Bravo; cloo; Discovery Home Channel; Discovery Kids Channel; DMX Music; ESPN Classic Sports; ESPNews; Fox Soccer; Fuse; G4; Golf Channel; GSN; History Channel International; ID Investigation Discovery; Independent Film Channel; Military Channel; Science; Speed; Style Network; Turner Classic Movies; Versus; WE tv.
Fee: $12.95 monthly.
Digital Pay Service 1
Pay Units: N.A.
Programming (via satellite): Cinemax (multiplexed); Encore (multiplexed); HBO (multiplexed); Showtime (multiplexed); Starz (multiplexed).
Fee: $10.95 monthly (Cinemax), $12.95 monthly (HBO, Showtime or Starz/Encore).
Internet Service
Operational: No.
Telephone Service
None
Miles of Plant: 16.0 (coaxial); None (fiber optic).
Manager & Chief Technician: Charles Himelrick. Assistant Manager: Diane Bowles.
Ownership: Phoenix Cable Inc. (MSO).

MINISINK—Cablevision Systems Corp. Now served by WARWICK, NY [NY0045]. ICA: NY0232.

MORAVIA—Southern Cayuga County Cablevision, PO Box 157, Locke, NY 13092-0157. Phone: 315-497-0444. Fax: 315-497-7653. Also serves Genoa Twp., King Ferry, Locke Twp. & Moravia (village). ICA: NY0233.
TV Market Ranking: 35 (Locke Twp., MORAVIA, Moravia (village)); Below 100 (Genoa Twp., King Ferry). Franchise award date: N.A. Franchise expiration date: N.A. Began: November 1, 1952.
Channel capacity: N.A. Channels available but not in use: N.A.
Basic Service
Subscribers: 950.
Programming (received off-air): WBNG-TV (CBS, CW) Binghamton; WCNY-TV (PBS) Syracuse; WENY-TV (ABC, CW) Elmira; WHAM-TV (ABC, CW) Rochester; WHEC-TV (NBC) Rochester; WNYS-TV (MNT) Syracuse; WPIX (CW, IND) New York; WSTM-TV (NBC) Syracuse; WSYR-TV (ABC) Syracuse; WSYT (FOX) Syracuse; WTVH (CBS) Syracuse; WUHF (FOX) Rochester; allband FM.
Programming (via satellite): A&E Networks; ABC Family Channel; AmericanLife TV Network; Animal Planet; CNN; Country Music TV; C-SPAN; Discovery Channel; ESPN; ESPN 2; Headline News; History Channel; KTLA (CW) Los Angeles; MSG; MTV; Nickelodeon; QVC; Spike TV; Syfy; TBS Superstation; The Learning Channel; The Weather Channel; Turner Network TV; TV Land; USA Network; VH1; WGN America; WSBK-TV (CBS, MNT) Boston.
Fee: $30.00 installation; $37.00 monthly.
Pay Service 1
Pay Units: N.A.
Programming (via satellite): Cinemax; HBO; Showtime; The Movie Channel.
Fee: $9.50 monthly (each).
Video-On-Demand: Planned
Internet Service
Operational: Yes.
Subscribers: 300.
Broadband Service: Netlink.
Fee: $54.00 installation; $34.95 monthly.
Telephone Service
None
Miles of Plant: 16.0 (coaxial); None (fiber optic).
Manager: Ray S. Dyer Jr.
Ownership: Ray S. Dyer Jr.

MORRIS—Time Warner Cable. Now served by ONEONTA, NY [NY0065]. ICA: NY0179.

MOUNT KISCO—Cablevision Systems Corp. Now served by OSSINING, NY [NY0018]. ICA: NY0067.

MOUNT TREMPER—Time Warner Cable. Now served by HUDSON VALLEY (formerly Middletown), NY [NY0231]. ICA: NY0193.

MOUNT VERNON—Time Warner Cable, 120 E 23rd St, New York, NY 10010. Phone: 212-598-7200. Fax: 212-420-4803. Web Site: http://www.timewarnercable.com. ICA: NY0032.
TV Market Ranking: 1 (MOUNT VERNON). Franchise award date: August 1, 1971. Franchise expiration date: N.A. Began: August 1, 1971.
Channel capacity: N.A. Channels available but not in use: N.A.
Basic Service
Subscribers: N.A. Included in New York
Programming (received off-air): WABC-TV (ABC) New York; WCBS-TV (CBS) New York; WEDW (PBS) Bridgeport; WFUT-DT (TEL) Newark; WLIW (PBS) Garden City; WMBC-TV (IND) Newton; WNBC (NBC) New York; WNET (PBS) Newark; WNJU

(TMO) Linden; WNYE-TV (PBS) New York; WNYW (FOX) New York; WPIX (CW, IND) New York; WPXN-TV (ION) New York; WRNN-LD Nyack; WWOR-TV (MNT) Secaucus; WXTV-DT (UNV) Paterson; allband FM.

Programming (via satellite): Bravo; C-SPAN; Disney Channel; Food Network; New York 1 News; News 12 Westchester.

Fee: $43.00 installation; $11.78 monthly.

Expanded Basic Service 1

Subscribers: N.A. Included in New York

Programming (received off-air): WLNY-TV (IND) Riverhead.

Programming (via satellite): A&E Networks; ABC Family Channel; AMC; BET Networks; Bloomberg Television; Cartoon Network; CNBC; CNN; Comedy Central; Discovery Channel; E! Entertainment Television; ESPN; ESPN 2; ESPN Classic Sports; Eternal Word TV Network; GalaVision; Headline News; HGTV; History Channel; Lifetime; Lifetime Movie Network; MSG; MSG Plus; MSNBC; MTV; National Geographic Channel; Nickelodeon; Oxygen; QVC; Spike TV; Syfy; TBS Superstation; The Learning Channel; The Weather Channel; Travel Channel; truTV; Turner Network TV; TV Guide Network; USA Network; VH1; WE tv; Yesterday USA.

Fee: $28.26 monthly.

Digital Basic Service

Subscribers: N.A. Included in New York

Programming (via satellite): AmericanLife TV Network; America's Store; BBC America; Black Family Channel; Bloomberg Television; Boomerang; CBS Sports Network; CNN International; Cooking Channel; Country Music TV; C-SPAN 3; Discovery Fit & Health; DIY Network; ESPN; ESPNews; Fox College Sports Atlantic; Fox College Sports Central; Fox College Sports Pacific; Fox Soccer; Fuel TV; Fuse; GAS; Great American Country; GSN; Hallmark Channel; HD Theater; HDNet; HDNet Movies; INHD; Lifetime Real Women; LOGO; MTV2; mun2 television; Music Choice; Nick Jr.; Nick Too; Nuvo TV; SoapNet; Tennis Channel; The Word Network; Toon Disney; Turner Network TV HD; VH1 Classic.

Fee: $9.95 monthly.

Digital Pay Service 1

Pay Units: N.A.

Programming (via satellite): CCTV-4; Cinemax (multiplexed); Deutsche Welle TV; Encore (multiplexed); HBO (multiplexed); HBO HD; National Greek Television; RAI Internacional; Russian Television Network; Showtime (multiplexed); Showtime HD; Starz (multiplexed); The Movie Channel (multiplexed); TV Asia; TV Japan; TV Polonia; TV5, La Television International; Zee TV USA.

Fee: $9.95 monthly (CCTV, RTN, RAI, Deutsche Welle or TV5), $10.95 monthly (HBO, Showtime, Cinemax, TMC, Starz or Encore), $14.95 monthly (TV Asia, Antenna or Zee TV), $17.95 monthly (TV Polonia), $24.95 monthly (TV Japan).

Video-On-Demand: Yes

Pay-Per-View

iN DEMAND (delivered digitally); Playboy TV (delivered digitally); Special events (delivered digitally); Sports PPV (delivered digitally); NBA TV (delivered digitally).

Internet Service

Operational: Yes.

Broadband Service: EarthLink, LocalNet, Road Runner.

Fee: $30.50 installation; $44.95 monthly.

Telephone Service

Digital: Operational

Fee: $39.95 monthly

Additional miles planned: 1.0 (coaxial). Miles of plant included in New York

President: Howard Szarfarc. Senior Vice President & General Manager: Barbara Kelly. Vice President, Engineering: Larry Pestana. Vice President, Technical Operations: Norberto Rivera. Vice President, Marketing: David Goldberg. Vice President, Sales: Ken Fluger. Vice President, Public Affairs: Harriet Novet. General Manager: Brien Kelley.

Ownership: Time Warner Cable (MSO).

NAPLES—Time Warner Cable. Now served by GENEVA, NY [NY0218]. ICA: NY0161.

NEW BERLIN—Time Warner Cable. Now served by ONEONTA, NY [NY0065]. ICA: NY0133.

NEW PALTZ—Time Warner Cable. Now served by HUDSON VALLEY (formerly Middletown), NY [NY0231]. ICA: NY0234.

NEW YORK—Time Warner Cable, 120 E 23rd St, New York, NY 10010. Phone: 212-598-7200. Fax: 212-420-4803. Web Site: http://www.timewarnercable.com. Also serves Astoria, Bay Ridge, Bayside, Beechhurst, Bellerose (Queens County), Brooklyn (western portion), Brooklyn Heights, Brooklyn Navy Yard, Cambria Heights, Clearview, College Point, Corona, Douglaston, East Elmhurst, Floral Park, Flushing, Forest Hills, Fort Hamilton Army Base, Fresh Meadows, Glen Oaks, Glendale, Greenpoint, Hillside, Hollis, Howard Beach, Jackson Heights, Jamaica, Kew Garden Hills, Laurelton, Linden Hill, Little Neck, Long Island City, Malba, Manhattan, Maspeth, Middle Village, Murray Hill, Oakland Gardens, Ozone Park, Park Slope, Pomonok, Queens, Queens Village, Rego Park, Richmond Hill, Ridgewood, Rockaway Beach, Rockaway Park, Rockaway Point, Roosevelt Island, Rosedale, Springfield Gardens, Sunset Park, Utopia, Whitestone, Williamsburg & Woodside. ICA: NY0235.

TV Market Ranking: 1 (Astoria, Bay Ridge, Bayside, Beechhurst, Bellerose (Queens County), Brooklyn (western portion), Brooklyn Heights, Brooklyn Navy Yard, Cambria Heights, Clearview, College Point, Corona, Douglaston, East Elmhurst, Floral Park, Flushing, Forest Hills, Fort Hamilton Army Base, Fresh Meadows, Glen Oaks, Glendale, Greenpoint, Hillside, Hollis, Howard Beach, Jackson Heights, Jamaica, Kew Garden Hills, Laurelton, Linden Hill, Little Neck, Long Island City, Malba, Manhattan, Maspeth, Middle Village, Murray Hill, NEW YORK, Oakland Gardens, Ozone Park, Park Slope, Pomonok, Queens, Queens Village, Rego Park, Richmond Hill, Ridgewood, Rockaway Beach, Rockaway Park, Rockaway Point, Roosevelt Island, Rosedale, Springfield Gardens, Sunset Park, Utopia, Whitestone, Williamsburg, Woodside). Franchise award date: August 1, 1970. Franchise expiration date: September 16, 2008. Began: January 1, 1967.

Channel capacity: N.A. Channels available but not in use: N.A.

Basic Service

Subscribers: 1,432,372 Includes Hudson Valley, Mount Vernon, Palisades Park NJ, & Staten Island.

Programming (received off-air): WABC-TV (ABC) New York; WCBS-TV (CBS) New York; WFUT-DT (TEL) Newark; WLIW (PBS) Garden City; WMBC-TV (IND) Newton; WNBC (NBC) New York; WNET (PBS) Newark; WNJU (TMO) Linden; WNYE-TV (PBS) New York; WNYW (FOX) New York; WPIX (CW, IND) New York; WPXN-TV (ION) New York; WWOR-TV (MNT) Secaucus; WXTV-DT (UNV) Paterson; 24 FMs.

Programming (via microwave): New York 1 News.

Programming (via satellite): C-SPAN; C-SPAN 2; Food Network; QVC; ShopNBC; TBS Superstation; TV Guide Network.

Fee: $43.00 installation; $14.04 monthly; $19.00 additional installation.

Expanded Basic Service 1

Subscribers: 1,285,298 Includes Hudson Valley, Mount Vernon, Palisades Park NJ, & Staten Island.

Programming (via satellite): A&E Networks; ABC Family Channel; AMC; BET Networks; Bravo; Cartoon Network; CNBC; CNN; Comedy Central; Discovery Channel; Disney Channel; E! Entertainment Television; ESPN; ESPN 2; Fox News Channel; FX; GalaVision; Hallmark Channel; Headline News; History Channel; Lifetime; Lifetime Movie Network; MSG; MSG Plus; MSNBC; MTV; Nickelodeon; Oxygen; Spike TV; Syfy; The Learning Channel; The Weather Channel; truTV; Turner Network TV; USA Network; VH1; WE tv; Yankees Entertainment & Sports.

Fee: $29.03 monthly.

Digital Basic Service

Subscribers: 1,000,000 Includes Hudson Valley, Mount Vernon, Palisades Park NJ, & Staten Island.

Programming (via satellite): America's Store; Animal Planet; BBC America; Bloomberg Television; Boomerang; CNBC; Country Music TV; C-SPAN 3; Discovery Fit & Health; DMX Music; ESPN Classic Sports; ESPNews; Fox Deportes; Fox Sports World; Fuse; G4; GAS; Golf Channel; GSN; Hallmark Channel; HGTV; Independent Film Channel; Lifetime Real Women; MTV2; mun2 television; Nick Jr.; Nick Too; Ovation; SoapNet; Speed; Style Network; Sundance Channel; Toon Disney; Travel Channel; Turner Classic Movies; TV Land; Versus; VH1 Classic; WAM! America's Kidz Network.

Fee: $9.95 monthly.

Digital Pay Service 1

Pay Units: N.A.

Programming (via satellite): CCTV-4; Cinemax (multiplexed); Deutsche Welle TV; Encore (multiplexed); HBO (multiplexed); National Greek Television; RAI USA; Russian Television Network; Showtime (multiplexed); Starz (multiplexed); The Movie Channel (multiplexed); TV Asia; TV Japan; TV Polonia; TV5, La Television International; Zee TV USA.

Fee: $9.95 monthly (CCTV, RTN, RAI, Deutsche Welle or TV5), $12.95 monthly (HBO, Showtime, Cinemax, TMC, Starz or Encore), $14.95 monthly (TV Asia, Antenna or Zee TV), $17.95 monthly (TV Polonia), $24.95 monthly (TV Japan).

Video-On-Demand: Yes

Pay-Per-View

WNBA Season Pass (delivered digitally); ESPN Gameplan (delivered digitally); ESPN Full Court (delivered digitally); MLB Extra Innings (delivered digitally); NHL Center Ice (delivered digitally); NBA League Pass (delivered digitally); special events (delivered digitally); Movies (delivered digitally); Playboy TV (delivered digitally).

Internet Service

Operational: Yes.

Subscribers: 930,246.

Broadband Service: EarthLink, LocalNet, Road Runner.

Fee: $30.50 installation; $44.95 monthly.

Telephone Service

Digital: Operational

Subscribers: 299,552.

Fee: $39.95 monthly

Miles of Plant: 9,031.0 (coaxial); None (fiber optic). Miles of plant include Hudson Valley, Mount Vernon, Palisades Park NJ, & Staten Island

President: Howard Szarfarc. Vice President & General Manager: Barbara Kelly. Vice President, Engineering: Larry Pestana. Vice President, Technical Operations: Norberto Rivera. Vice President, Marketing: David Goldberg. Vice President, Sales: Ken Fluger. Vice President, Public Affairs: Harriet Novet. Public Relations Director: Suzanne Giuliani.

Ownership: Time Warner Cable (MSO).

NEWARK VALLEY (town)—Time Warner Binghamton. Now served by BINGHAMTON, NY [NY0016]. ICA: NY0275.

NEWBURGH—Time Warner Cable. Now served by HUDSON VALLEY (formerly Middletown), NY [NY0231]. ICA: NY0029.

NEWCOMB—Chain Lakes Cablevision, 9507 Cherokee Trail, Crossville, TN 38572. Phone: 931-788-5261. Fax: 931-788-0489. ICA: NY0236.

TV Market Ranking: Below 100 (NEWCOMB). Channel capacity: 44 (not 2-way capable). Channels available but not in use: N.A.

Basic Service

Subscribers: 47.

Programming (received off-air): WCAX-TV (CBS) Burlington; WCDC-TV (ABC) Adams; WETK (PBS) Burlington; WFFF-TV (CW, FOX) Burlington; WPIX (CW, IND) New York; WPTZ (NBC) Plattsburgh; WVNY (ABC) Burlington.

Programming (via satellite): A&E Networks; ABC Family Channel; American Movie Classics; Cartoon Network; CNN; Country Music TV; C-SPAN; Discovery Channel; Discovery Health Channel; E! Entertainment Television; ESPN; ESPN 2; Food Network; Hallmark Channel; Headline News; HGTV; History Channel; Lifetime; Men's Channel; MSNBC; Outdoor Channel; QVC; Spike TV; Syfy; TBS Superstation; The Learning Channel; The Weather Channel; TNT; Trinity Broadcasting Network; TV Land; USA Network; WGN America.

Fee: $34.95 monthly; $5.00 converter; $8.75 additional installation.

Digital Basic Service

Subscribers: 5.

Programming (via satellite): BBC America; Bio; Bloomberg Television; cloo; Discovery Home Channel; Discovery Kids Channel; DMX Music; ESPN Classic Sports; ESPNews; Fox Soccer; Fuse; G4; Golf Channel; GSN; History Channel International; ID Investigation Discovery; Independent Film Channel; Military Channel; Science; Speed; Style Network; Turner Classic Movies; Versus; WE tv.

Fee: $12.95 monthly.

Digital Pay Service 1

Pay Units: N.A.

Programming (via satellite): Cinemax (multiplexed); Encore (multiplexed); HBO

(multiplexed); Showtime (multiplexed); Starz (multiplexed).
Fee: $10.95 monthly (Cinemax), $12.95 monthly (HBO, Showtime or Starz/Encore).

Internet Service
Operational: No.

Telephone Service
None

Miles of Plant: 9.0 (coaxial); None (fiber optic).
Manager & Chief Technician: Charles Himelrick. Assistant Manager: Diane Bowles.
Ownership: Phoenix Cable Inc. (MSO).

NIAGARA FALLS—Now served by LACKAWANNA, NY [NY0216]. ICA: NY0026.

NORTH SALEM—Cablevision Systems Corp. Now served by YORKTOWN, NY [NY0050]. ICA: NY0077.

NORTHVILLE—Formerly served by Adelphia Communications. Now served by ALBANY, NY [NY0014]. ICA: NY0270.

NORWICH—Time Warner Cable. Now served by ONEONTA, NY [NY0065]. ICA: NY0095.

OGDENSBURG—Time Warner Cable. Now served by MASSENA, NY [NY0072]. ICA: NY0081.

OLD FORGE—Formerly served by Adelphia Communications. Now served by UTICA, NY [NY0022]. ICA: NY0136.

OLEAN—Time Warner Cable, 355 Chicago St, Buffalo, NY 14204-2069. Phone: 716-558-8881. Fax: 716-558-8855. Web Site: http://www.timewarnercable.com/wny. Also serves Allegany (town), Allegany (village), Amity (town), Andover (town), Andover (village), Arcade (town), Arcade (village), Belmont (village), Cattaraugus, Chaffee (town), Coldspring (town), Collins (town), Collins Center (town), Concord (town), Conewango, Cuba (town), Cuba (village), Delevan (village), East Concord Twp., East Randolph (village), Ellicottville (town), Ellicottville (village), Franklinville (town), Franklinville (village), Freedom (town), Gowanda (village), Great Valley (town), Helmuth (town), Hinsdale (town), Ischua (town), Lawtons (town), Machias (town), Mansfield (town), New Albion (town), North Collins (town), North Collins (village), Olean (town), Perrysburg (town), Perrysburg (village), Persia (town), Portville (town), Portville (village), Randolph (town), Randolph (village), Sandusky (town), Sardinia (town), Scio, Springville (village), Wellsville, Wellsville (town), Wellsville (village), Willing & Yorkshire (town), NY; Ceres Twp., Eldred Borough & Eldred Twp., PA. ICA: NY0056.

TV Market Ranking: 24 (Arcade (town), Arcade (village), Chaffee (town), Collins (town), Collins Center (town), Concord (town), Delevan (village), East Concord Twp., Gowanda (village), Helmuth (town), Lawtons (town), North Collins (town), North Collins (village), Perrysburg (town), Perrysburg (village), Persia (town), Sardinia (town), Springville (village), Yorkshire (town)); Below 100 (Allegany (town), Allegany (village), Cattaraugus, Coldspring (town), Conewango, Cuba (town), Cuba (village), East Randolph (village), Ellicottville (town), Ellicottville (village), Franklinville (town), Franklinville (village), Freedom (town), Great Valley (town), Hinsdale (town), Ischua (town), Machias (town), Mansfield (town), New Albion (town), OLEAN, Olean (town), Randolph (town), Randolph (village), Sandusky (town)); Outside TV Markets (Amity (town), Andover (town), Andover (village), Belmont (village), Ceres Twp., Eldred Borough, Eldred Twp., Portville (town), Portville (village), Scio, Wellsville, Wellsville (town), Wellsville (village), Willing). Franchise award date: March 7, 1956. Franchise expiration date: N.A. Began: March 7, 1956.

Channel capacity: N.A. Channels available but not in use: N.A.

Basic Service
Subscribers: N.A. Included in Lackawanna
Programming (received off-air): WBBZ-TV (IND) Springville; WGRZ (NBC) Buffalo; WIVB-TV (CBS) Buffalo; WKBW-TV (ABC) Buffalo; WNED-TV (PBS) Buffalo; WNLO (CW) Buffalo; WNYB (IND) Jamestown; WNYO-TV (MNT) Buffalo; WONS-LP Olean; WPSU-TV (PBS) Clearfield; WPXJ-TV (ION) Batavia; 16 FMs.
Programming (via satellite): C-SPAN; C-SPAN 2; QVC; The Weather Channel; TV Guide Network; WGN America.
Fee: $23.00 additional installation.

Expanded Basic Service 1
Subscribers: 20,338.
Programming (received off-air): WUTV (FOX) Buffalo.
Programming (via satellite): A&E Networks; ABC Family Channel; AMC; Animal Planet; BET Networks; Bravo; Cartoon Network; CNBC; CNN; Comedy Central; Country Music TV; Discovery Channel; Discovery Fit & Health; Disney Channel; E! Entertainment Television; ESPN; ESPN 2; Eternal Word TV Network; Flix; Food Network; Fox News Channel; FX; Hallmark Channel; Headline News; HGTV; History Channel; Lifetime; MSG; MSNBC; MTV; Nickelodeon; Oxygen; Product Information Network; ShopNBC; Spike TV; SportsNet New York; Style Network; Syfy; TBS Superstation; The Learning Channel; Travel Channel; truTV; Turner Classic Movies; Turner Network TV; TV Land; USA Network; Versus; VH1; Yankees Entertainment & Sports.

Digital Basic Service
Subscribers: N.A.
Programming (via satellite): A&E HD; AmericanLife TV Network; BBC America; BBC America On Demand; Bio; Black Family Channel; Bloomberg Television; Boomerang; Canales N; CBS Sports Network; Cooking Channel; Country Music TV; Current; Daystar TV Network; DIY Network; ESPN 2 HD; ESPN Classic Sports; ESPN Deportes; ESPN HD; ESPNews; Exercise TV; Familyland Television Network; Fox College Sports Atlantic; Fox College Sports Central; Fox College Sports Pacific; Fox Movie Channel; Fox Reality Channel; Fox Soccer; Fuel TV; Fuse; G4; GAS; Golf Channel; Great American Country; Great American Country On Demand; GSN; Halogen Network; HD Theater; HDNet; HDNet Movies; History Channel International; Howard TV; Independent Film Channel; INHD; Lifetime Movie Network; LOGO; MTV Networks Digital Suite; Music Choice; National Geographic Channel; National Geographic Channel On Demand; NBA TV; Nick Jr.; Nick Too; NickToons TV; Outdoor Channel; ReelzChannel; SoapNet; Speed; Sundance Channel; Tennis Channel; The Word Network; Toon Disney; Trinity Broadcasting Network; Turner Network TV HD; TV One; Universal HD; WE tv.
Fee: $57.95 monthly.

Digital Pay Service 1
Pay Units: 2,522.
Programming (via satellite): Cinemax (multiplexed); Cinemax HD; Cinemax On Demand; Encore (multiplexed); Flix; HBO (multiplexed); HBO HD; HBO On Demand; Showtime (multiplexed); Showtime HD; Showtime On Demand; Starz (multiplexed); Starz HDTV; Starz On Demand; The Movie Channel (multiplexed).
Fee: $11.95 monthly (each).

Video-On-Demand: Yes

Pay-Per-View
iN DEMAND (delivered digitally); Playboy TV (delivered digitally); NBA League Pass (delivered digitally); NHL Center Ice (delivered digitally); MLB Extra Innings (delivered digitally).

Internet Service
Operational: Yes.
Broadband Service: Road Runner.
Fee: $44.95 monthly.

Telephone Service
Digital: Operational
Fee: $39.95 monthly

Miles of Plant: 491.0 (coaxial); 20.0 (fiber optic).
President: Gordon Harp. Vice President, Public Affairs: Robin Wolfgang. Vice President, Marketing: Steve Jaworski. Technical Operations Manager: Steve Pawlik. Marketing Director: Jean Calabrese.
Ownership: Time Warner Cable (MSO).

OLIVE—Time Warner Cable. Now served by HUDSON VALLEY (formerly Middletown), NY [NY0231]. ICA: NY0138.

ONEIDA—Time Warner Cable. Now served by ROME, NY [NY0037]. ICA: NY0237.

ONEONTA—Time Warner Cable, 120 Plaza Dr, Vestal, NY 13850-3658. Phone: 607-644-0646. Fax: 607-644-1501. Web Site: http://www.timewarnercable.com. Also serves Afton, Bainbridge, Butternuts, Columbus (town), Cooperstown, Coventry (town), Davenport, Delhi (village), East Guilford, Edmeston, Exeter, Franklin (village), Gilbertsville, Guilford (town), Guilford Center, Harpersfield, Hartwick, Hobart, Kortright, Laurens (village), Maryland, Masonville, Meredith, Middlefield, Milford (village), Morris (village), Mount Upton, New Berlin (village), North Norwich, Norwich, Otego (village), Otsego, Oxford (village), Pittsfield, Plymouth (town), Richfield, Richfield Springs, Rockdale, Schenevus, Sidney, Springfield, Stamford, Unadilla (village), Walton (village) & Worcester. ICA: NY0065.

TV Market Ranking: Below 100 (Afton, Bainbridge, Columbus (town), Cooperstown, Coventry (town), East Guilford, Edmeston, Exeter, Guilford (town), Guilford Center, Hartwick, Masonville, Middlefield, Mount Upton, New Berlin (village), Otsego, Oxford (village), Pittsfield, Richfield, Richfield Springs, Rockdale, Sidney, Springfield, Unadilla (village)); Outside TV Markets (Butternuts, Davenport, Delhi (village), Franklin (village), Gilbertsville, Harpersfield, Hobart, Kortright, Laurens (village), Maryland, Meredith, Milford (village), Morris (village), North Norwich, Norwich, ONEONTA, Otego (village), Plymouth (town), Schenevus, Stamford, Walton (village), Worcester). Franchise award date: N.A. Franchise expiration date: N.A. Began: August 1, 1954.

Channel capacity: N.A. Channels available but not in use: N.A.

Basic Service
Subscribers: N.A. Included in Binghamton
Programming (received off-air): WBNG-TV (CBS, CW) Binghamton; WCNY-TV (PBS) Syracuse; WFXV (FOX) Utica; WICZ-TV (FOX) Binghamton; WISF-LP Oneonta; WKTV (CW, NBC) Utica; WPNY-LP Utica, etc.; WRGB (CBS) Schenectady; WSKG-TV (PBS) Binghamton; WSYR-TV (ABC) Syracuse; WUTR (ABC) Utica; allband FM.
Programming (via satellite): ION Television; TV Guide Network; WGN America.
Fee: $47.21 installation; $10.00 monthly.

Expanded Basic Service 1
Subscribers: 18,619.
Programming (via satellite): A&E Networks; ABC Family Channel; AMC; Animal Planet; BET Networks; Bravo; Cartoon Network; CNBC; CNN; Comedy Central; Country Music TV; C-SPAN; C-SPAN 2; Discovery Channel; Discovery Fit & Health; Disney Channel; E! Entertainment Television; ESPN; ESPN 2; ESPN Classic Sports; Eternal Word TV Network; Food Network; Fox News Channel; FX; Golf Channel; Hallmark Channel; Headline News; HGTV; History Channel; Lifetime; Lifetime Movie Network; MoviePlex; MSG; MSG Plus; MSNBC; MTV; MTV2; National Geographic Channel; Nickelodeon; Oxygen; Product Information Network; QVC; ShopNBC; SoapNet; Speed; Spike TV; Style Network; Syfy; TBS Superstation; The Learning Channel; The Weather Channel; Travel Channel; truTV; Turner Classic Movies; Turner Network TV; TV Land; USA Network; Versus; VH1; WE tv; Yankees Entertainment & Sports.
Fee: $31.87 monthly.

Digital Basic Service
Subscribers: N.A. Included in Binghamton
Programming (via satellite): AmericanLife TV Network; America's Store; BBC America; Bio; Bloomberg Television; Cooking Channel; C-SPAN 3; Discovery Digital Networks; DIY Network; Encore Action; ESPNews; Fox Movie Channel; Fox Sports World; Fuse; G4; GAS; Great American Country; History Channel International; Independent Film Channel; Lifetime Real Women; Music Choice; Nick Jr.; Outdoor Channel; Ovation; Sundance Channel; Toon Disney; Trinity Broadcasting Network; VH1 Classic.
Fee: $8.45 monthly.

Digital Expanded Basic Service
Subscribers: N.A.
Programming (via satellite): Fox Deportes; FSN Digital Atlantic; FSN Digital Central; FSN Digital Pacific; Fuel TV; NBA TV; Tennis Channel.
Fee: $4.95 monthly.

Digital Pay Service 1
Pay Units: 13,060.
Programming (via satellite): Canales N; Cinemax (multiplexed); Flix; HBO (multiplexed); Showtime (multiplexed); Starz (multiplexed); The Movie Channel (multiplexed); TV Asia; Zee TV USA.
Fee: $11.25 monthly (Cinemax, HBO, Starz, or Showtime/TMC), $19.95 monthly (TV Asia & Zee TV).
Video-On-Demand: Yes
Pay-Per-View
iN DEMAND (delivered digitally); Hot Choice (delivered digitally); Playboy TV (delivered digitally); Fresh (delivered digitally); Shorteez (delivered digitally); Pleasure (delivered digitally); ESPN Full Court (delivered digitally); ESPN Gameplan (delivered digitally); Sports PPV (delivered digitally).
Internet Service
Operational: Yes.
Broadband Service: Road Runner.
Fee: $39.95 installation; $44.95 monthly.
Telephone Service
Digital: Operational
Fee: $39.95 monthly
Miles of plant included in Binghamton
President: Mary Cotter. Vice President & General Manager: Chris Strahm. Vice President, Marketing: John Melvany. Vice President, Public Affairs: Dave Whalen. Technical Operations Director: Bruce Tomkins.
Ownership: Time Warner Cable (MSO).; Advance/Newhouse Partnership (MSO).Day-to-Day operations managed by Time Warner Cable.

OSSINING—Cablevision Systems Corp., 1 Van Cortland Ave, Ossining, NY 10562-3309. Phones: 914-762-8684; 516-803-2300 (Corporate office). Fax: 516-803-1183. Web Site: http://www.cablevision.com. Also serves Armonk, Beacon, Bedford, Bedford Hills, Briarcliff Manor, Buchanan, Cortlandt, Croton-on-Hudson, East Fishkill, Fishkill (village), Garrison, Harriman, Haverstraw, Hyde Park, Katonah, La Grange, LaGrangeville, Lloyd, Marlboro, Monroe (village), Mount Kisco, Mount Pleasant (Westchester County), Nelsonville, New Castle, North Castle, North Tarrytown, Peekskill, Philipstown, Plattekill, Pleasantville, Pomona, Poughkeepsie, Stony Point, Tarrytown, Wappinger (town), Wappingers Falls, West Haverstraw & Woodbury. ICA: NY0018.
TV Market Ranking: 1 (Armonk, Bedford, Bedford Hills, Briarcliff Manor, Buchanan, Cortlandt, Croton-on-Hudson, Garrison, Harriman, Haverstraw, Katonah, Lloyd, Marlboro, Monroe (village), Mount Kisco, Mount Pleasant (Westchester County), New Castle, North Castle, North Tarrytown, OSSINING, Peekskill, Plattekill, Pleasantville, Pomona, Poughkeepsie, Ramapo, Stony Point, Tarrytown, West Haverstraw, Woodbury); Below 100 (Beacon, East Fishkill, Fishkill (village), Hyde Park, La Grange, LaGrangeville, Nelsonville, Philipstown, Wappinger (town), Wappingers Falls). Franchise award date: N.A. Franchise expiration date: N.A. Began: N.A.
Channel capacity: N.A. Channels available but not in use: N.A.
Basic Service
Subscribers: 64,217.
Programming (received off-air): WABC-TV (ABC) New York; WCBS-TV (CBS) New York; WFUT-DT (TEL) Newark; WLIW (PBS) Garden City; WMBC-TV (IND) Newton; WNBC (NBC) New York; WNET (PBS) Newark; WNJN (PBS) Montclair; WNJU (TMO) Linden; WNYW (FOX) New York; WPIX (CW, IND) New York; WPXN-TV (ION) New York; WRNN-TV (IND) Kingston; WTBY-TV (TBN) Poughkeepsie; WWOR-TV (MNT) Secaucus; WXTV-DT (UNV) Paterson.
Fee: $49.95 installation; $18.00 monthly.
Expanded Basic Service 1
Subscribers: N.A.
Programming (via satellite): A&E Networks; ABC Family Channel; AMC; Animal Planet; BET Networks; Bravo; Cartoon Network; CNBC; CNN; Comedy Central; C-SPAN; C-SPAN 2; Discovery Channel; Disney Channel; E! Entertainment Television; ESPN; ESPN 2; Food Network; Fox News Channel; Fuse; FX; GSN; Headline News; HGTV; History Channel; Lifetime; MSNBC; MTV; News 12 Traffic & Weather; Nickelodeon; QVC; SoapNet; Speed; Spike TV; SportsNet New York; Syfy; TBS Superstation; The Learning Channel; The Weather Channel; Travel Channel; truTV; Turner Classic Movies; Turner Network TV; TV Land; USA Network; VH1; WE tv.
Fee: $31.95 monthly.
Digital Basic Service
Subscribers: N.A.
Programming (via satellite): Animal Planet HD; Azteca America; Bio; Bloomberg Television; Bollywood Hits On Demand; Bravo HD; Canal Sur; Caracol TV; Cartoon Network Tambien en Espanol; CBS Sports Network; CCTV-4; Channel One; Chiller; Cine Latino; cloo; CMT HD; CNBC HD+; CNN en Espanol; CNN HD; Country Music TV; C-SPAN 3; Discovery Channel HD; Discovery en Espanol; Discovery Kids Channel; Docu TVE; Ecuavisia Internacional; ESPN 2 HD; ESPN Classic Sports; ESPN Deportes; ESPN HD; ESPNews; EuroNews; EWTN en Espanol; Filipino Channel; Food Network HD; Fox College Sports Atlantic; Fox College Sports Central; Fox College Sports Pacific; Fox Deportes; Fox Movie Channel; Fox News HD; Fox Soccer; Fuel TV; FX HD; G4; GMA Pinoy TV; Golf Channel; GolTV; Great American Country; Hallmark Channel; Hallmark Movie Channel; Hallmark Movie Channel HD; HD Theater; here! On Demand; HGTV HD; History Channel en Espanol; History Channel International; Howard TV; HTV Musica; ID Investigation Discovery; Infinito; Jewelry Television; Korean Channel; La Familia Network; Latele Novela Network; LATV Networks; LOGO; Mariavision; Military Channel; MKTV; Momentum TV; MTV Hits; MTV Networks HD; mun2 television; Music Choice; National Geographic Channel; National Geographic Channel HD Network; NBA TV; NHL Network; NHL Network HD; Nick HD; Nick Jr.; NickToons TV; Outdoor Channel; Oxygen; Planet Green; RAI USA; Russian Television Network; Science; Science HD; ShopNBC; Sino TV; Society of Portuguese Television; Sorpresa; Speed HD; Spike TV HD; Sundance Channel; Supercanal Caribe; Syfy HD; TBS in HD; TeenNick; Telefe International; Telemicro Internacional; The Jewish Channel; The Weather Channel HD; TLC HD; Toon Disney; Toon Disney en Espanol; Tr3s; Travel Channel HD; Turner Network TV HD; TV Asia; TV Chile; TV Colombia; TV Japan; TV Polonia; TV5 USA; TVE Internacional; TVG Network; Universal HD; Universal Sports; USA Network HD; Utilisima; VeneMovies; Versus; Versus HD; VH1 Classic; VH1 HD; V-me TV; WAPA America; YES HD; Zee TV USA.
Fee: $10.95 monthly.
Pay Service 1
Pay Units: N.A.
Programming (via satellite): Cinemax; Flix; HBO (multiplexed); Independent Film Channel; MSG; MSG Plus; Showtime (multiplexed); The Movie Channel; Yankees Entertainment & Sports.
Digital Pay Service 1
Pay Units: N.A.
Programming (via satellite): Cinemax (multiplexed); Cinemax HD; Cinemax On Demand; Encore (multiplexed); HBO (multiplexed); HBO HD; HBO On Demand; Showtime (multiplexed); Showtime HD; Showtime On Demand; Starz (multiplexed); Starz HDTV; Starz On Demand; The Movie Channel (multiplexed); The Movie Channel HD.
Video-On-Demand: Yes
Pay-Per-View
Addressable homes: 90,000.
iN DEMAND; Playboy TV; Club Jenna; Sports PPV (delivered digitally); NBA TV (delivered digitally); iN DEMAND (delivered digitally); Playboy TV (delivered digitally).
Internet Service
Operational: Yes. Began: December 31, 2002.
Broadband Service: Optimum Online.
Fee: $46.95 installation; $34.95 monthly.
Telephone Service
Digital: Operational
Fee: $34.95 monthly
Miles of Plant: 3,888.0 (coaxial); 70.0 (fiber optic).
Vice President, Field Operations: Mark Fitchett.
Ownership: Cablevision Systems Corp. (MSO).

OSWEGO—Time Warner Cable, 6005 Fair Lakes Rd, East Syracuse, NY 13057. Phone: 315-634-6100. Fax: 315-634-6219. Web Site: http://www.timewarnercable.com/CentralNY. Also serves Central Square, Fair Haven, Fulton, Granby, Hannibal, Hastings, Lacona, Mexico (village), Minetto, New Haven, Palermo, Parish (village), Pulaski, Richland (town), Sandy Creek, Sandy Creek (village), Scriba, Sterling & Volney. ICA: NY0061.
TV Market Ranking: 35 (Central Square, Fair Haven, Fulton, Granby, Hannibal, Hastings, Mexico (village), Minetto, New Haven, OSWEGO, Palermo, Parish (village), Scriba, Sterling, Volney); Below 100 (Lacona, Pulaski, Richland (town), Sandy Creek, Sandy Creek (village)). Franchise award date: N.A. Franchise expiration date: March 27, 2011. Began: December 15, 1965.
Channel capacity: N.A. Channels available but not in use: N.A.
Basic Service
Subscribers: N.A. Included in Syracuse
Programming (received off-air): WCNY-TV (PBS) Syracuse; WNYS-TV (MNT) Syracuse; WSPX-TV (ION) Syracuse; WSTM-TV (NBC) Syracuse; WSTQ-LP (CW) Syracuse; WSYR-TV (ABC) Syracuse; WSYT (FOX) Syracuse; WTVH (CBS) Syracuse.
Programming (via satellite): Jewelry Television.
Fee: $35.91 installation; $9.28 monthly.
Expanded Basic Service 1
Subscribers: N.A. Included in Syracuse
Programming (via satellite): A&E Networks; ABC Family Channel; Animal Planet; BET Networks; Cartoon Network; CNBC; CNN; Comedy Central; C-SPAN; C-SPAN 2; Discovery Channel; Discovery Fit & Health; E! Entertainment Television; ESPN; ESPN 2; Eternal Word TV Network; Food Network; Fox News Channel; FX; Hallmark Channel; Headline News; HGTV; Lifetime; Lifetime Movie Network; MSG Plus; MSNBC; MTV; Nickelodeon; Oxygen; QVC; ShopNBC; SoapNet; Spike TV; Syfy; TBS Superstation; The Learning Channel; The Weather Channel; Travel Channel; Turner Network TV; TV Land; Univision Studios; USA Network; Versus; VH1; WE tv; Yankees Entertainment & Sports.
Fee: $35.91 installation; $34.27 monthly.
Digital Basic Service
Subscribers: N.A. Included in Syracuse
Programming (via satellite): AMC; America's Store; BBC America; Bio; Bloomberg Television; Boomerang; Bravo; Cooking Channel; Country Music TV; C-SPAN 3; Discovery Digital Networks; Disney Channel; DIY Network; Encore Action; ESPN Classic Sports; ESPNews; Fox Movie Channel; Fox Sports World; Fuse; G4; GAS; Golf Channel; Great American Country; GSN; History Channel; History Channel International; Independent Film Channel; Lifetime Real Women; Local Cable Weather; MSG; MTV2; National Geographic Channel; Nick Jr.; Nick Too; Outdoor Channel; Ovation; Speed; Style Network; Sundance Channel; Toon Disney; Trinity Broadcasting Network; truTV; Turner Classic Movies; VH1 Classic.
Fee: $10.95 monthly.
Digital Expanded Basic Service
Subscribers: N.A.
Programming (via satellite): FSN Digital Atlantic; FSN Digital Central; FSN Digital Pacific; Fuel TV; NBA TV; Tennis Channel.
Fee: $4.95 monthly.
Digital Pay Service 1
Pay Units: N.A.
Programming (via satellite): Cinemax (multiplexed); HBO (multiplexed); Showtime (multiplexed); Starz (multiplexed); The Movie Channel (multiplexed).
Fee: $8.50 monthly (Cinemax), $9.50 monthly (Showtime, Starz or TMC), $10.95 monthly (HBO).
Video-On-Demand: Yes
Pay-Per-View
Hot Choice; Hot Choice (delivered digitally); iN DEMAND; iN DEMAND (delivered digitally); Playboy TV (delivered digitally); Pleasure (delivered digitally); Spice; Fresh (delivered digitally); Shorteez (delivered digitally).
Internet Service
Operational: Yes.
Broadband Service: EarthLink, LocalNet, Road Runner.
Fee: $39.95 installation; $44.95 monthly.
Telephone Service
Digital: Operational
Fee: $39.95 monthly
Miles of plant included in Syracuse.
President: Mary Cotter. Vice President, Engineering: Henry Hryckiewicz. Vice President, Marketing: John Melvany. Vice President, Public Affairs: Jeff Unaitis. Technical Operations Director: Bruce Tomkins.
Ownership: Time Warner Cable (MSO).; Advance/Newhouse Partnership (MSO).Day-to-Day operations managed by Time Warner Cable.

OTSELIC—Chain Lakes Cable. Now served by CORTLAND, NY [NY0062]. ICA: NY0160.

OWEGO (village)—Time Warner Cable. Now served by BINGHAMTON, NY [NY0016]. ICA: NY0104.

OXFORD (town)—Time Warner Cable. Now served by ONEONTA, NY [NY0065]. ICA: NY0142.

PENN YAN—Time Warner Cable. Now served by GENEVA, NY [NY0218]. ICA: NY0108.

PETERBORO—Chain Lakes Cablevision. Now served by ROME, NY [NY0037]. ICA: NY0238.

PHOENICIA—Time Warner Cable. Now served by HUDSON VALLEY (formerly Middletown), NY [NY0231]. ICA: NY0239.

PINE HILL—Time Warner Cable. Now served by HUDSON VALLEY (formerly Middletown), NY [NY0231]. ICA: NY0106.

PLATTSBURGH—Charter Communications, 95 Higgins St, Worcester, MA 1606. Phone: 508-853-1515. Fax: 508-854-5042. Web Site: http://www.charter.com. Also serves Au Sable (town), Beekmantown, Black Brook (town), Chesterfield (town), Dannemora (village), Elizabethtown, Jay, Keeseville (village), Lewis, Peru (town), Saranac (town), Schuyler Falls (town), Wadhams & Westport (town). ICA: NY0263.

TV Market Ranking: Below 100 (Au Sable (town), Beekmantown, Black Brook (town), Chesterfield (town), Dannemora (village), Elizabethtown, Jay, Keeseville (village), Lewis, Peru (town), PLATTSBURGH, Saranac (town), Schuyler Falls (town), Wadhams, Westport (town)). Franchise award date: January 1, 1967. Franchise expiration date: N.A. Began: December 1, 1967.

Channel capacity: N.A. Channels available but not in use: N.A.

Basic Service

Subscribers: 14,800.

Programming (received off-air): WCAX-TV (CBS) Burlington; WCFE-TV (PBS) Plattsburgh; WETK (PBS) Burlington; WFFF-TV (CW, FOX) Burlington; WGMU-CA (MNT) Burlington; WPTZ (NBC) Plattsburgh; WVNY (ABC) Burlington; WWBI-LP Plattsburgh.

Programming (via satellite): C-SPAN; C-SPAN 2; Eternal Word TV Network; INSP; QVC; TV Guide Network; WPIX (CW, IND) New York.

Fee: $29.99 installation.

Expanded Basic Service 1

Subscribers: 14,208.

Programming (via satellite): A&E Networks; ABC Family Channel; AMC; Animal Planet; BET Networks; Cartoon Network; CNBC; CNN; Comedy Central; Country Music TV; Discovery Channel; Disney Channel; E! Entertainment Television; ESPN; ESPN 2; Food Network; Fox News Channel; FX; G4; Golf Channel; Hallmark Channel; Headline News; HGTV; History Channel; Lifetime; MSG; MSG Plus; MSNBC; MTV; National Geographic Channel; Nickelodeon; Oxygen; Product Information Network; Speed; Spike TV; Syfy; TBS Superstation; The Learning Channel; The Weather Channel; Travel Channel; truTV; Turner Classic Movies; Turner Network TV; TV Land; USA Network; Versus; VH1; Yankees Entertainment & Sports.

Fee: $55.00 monthly.

Digital Basic Service

Subscribers: N.A.

Programming (via satellite): BBC America; Bio; Bloomberg Television; Discovery Digital Networks; DIY Network; ESPN Classic Sports; GAS; History Channel International; Independent Film Channel; Lifetime Movie Network; MTV Networks Digital Suite; MuchMusic Network; Music Choice; Nick Jr.; SoapNet; Style Network; Sundance Channel; Toon Disney; WE tv.

Fee: $7.41 monthly.

Digital Pay Service 1

Pay Units: 1,476.

Programming (via satellite): Cinemax (multiplexed).

Fee: $13.95 monthly.

Digital Pay Service 2

Pay Units: 2,022.

Programming (via satellite): HBO (multiplexed).

Fee: $13.95 monthly.

Digital Pay Service 3

Pay Units: 1,280.

Programming (via satellite): Showtime (multiplexed).

Fee: $13.95 monthly.

Digital Pay Service 4

Pay Units: 757.

Programming (via satellite): The Movie Channel (multiplexed).

Fee: $13.95 monthly.

Digital Pay Service 5

Pay Units: 1,246.

Programming (via satellite): Encore (multiplexed); Starz (multiplexed).

Fee: $13.95 monthly.

Video-On-Demand: Yes

Pay-Per-View

iN DEMAND (delivered digitally); Playboy TV (delivered digitally); Fresh (delivered digitally); Shorteez (delivered digitally).

Internet Service

Operational: Yes.

Broadband Service: Charter Pipeline.

Fee: $29.99 monthly.

Telephone Service

Digital: Operational

Miles of Plant: 615.0 (coaxial); None (fiber optic).

Vice President & General Manager: Greg Garabedian. Technical Operations Director: George Duffy. Chief Technician: Dan Rushford. Marketing Director: Dennis Jerome.

Ownership: Charter Communications Inc. (MSO).

PORT CHESTER—Cablevision Systems Corp., 1 Van Cortland Ave, Ossining, NY 10562-3309. Phone: 516-803-2300 (Corporate office). Fax: 516-803-1183. Web Site: http://www.cablevision.com. Also serves Harrison, Purchase & West Harrison. ICA: NY0048.

TV Market Ranking: 1 (Harrison, PORT CHESTER, Purchase, West Harrison). Franchise award date: January 25, 1979. Franchise expiration date: N.A. Began: March 1, 1980.

Channel capacity: 95 (operating 2-way). Channels available but not in use: N.A.

Basic Service

Subscribers: 13,400.

Programming (received off-air): WABC-TV (ABC) New York; WCBS-TV (CBS) New York; WFUT-DT (TEL) Newark; WLIW (PBS) Garden City; WLNY-TV (IND) Riverhead; WMBC-TV (IND) Newton; WNBC (NBC) New York; WNET (PBS) Newark; WNJU (TMO) Linden; WNYE-TV (PBS) New York; WNYW (FOX) New York; WPIX (CW, IND) New York; WPXN-TV (ION) New York; WRNN-TV (IND) Kingston; WSAH (IND) Bridgeport; WWOR-TV (MNT) Secaucus; WXTV-DT (UNV) Paterson; 30 FMs.

Fee: $49.95 installation; $10.58 monthly.

Expanded Basic Service 1

Subscribers: N.A.

Programming (via microwave): News 12 Traffic & Weather.

Programming (via satellite): A&E Networks; ABC Family Channel; AMC; Animal Planet; BET Networks; Bravo; Cartoon Network; CNBC; CNN; Comedy Central; C-SPAN; C-SPAN 2; Discovery Channel; Disney Channel; E! Entertainment Television; ESPN; ESPN 2; Eternal Word TV Network; Food Network; Fox News Channel; Fuse; FX; GalaVision; GSN; Headline News; HGTV; History Channel; Independent Film Channel; Lifetime; MSG; MSG Plus; MSNBC; MTV; MTV2; mun2 television; News 12 Westchester; Nickelodeon; QVC; ShopNBC; SoapNet; Speed; Spike TV; SportsNet New York; Syfy; TBS Superstation; The Learning Channel; The Weather Channel; Travel Channel; truTV; Turner Classic Movies; Turner Network TV; TV Land; USA Network; VH1; WE tv; Yankees Entertainment & Sports.

Fee: $39.37 monthly.

Digital Basic Service

Subscribers: N.A.

Programming (via satellite): Azteca America; Bio; Bloomberg Television; Caracol TV; Cartoon Network Tambien en Espanol; Cine Latino; CNN en Espanol; CNN HD; Country Music TV; C-SPAN 3; Discovery en Espanol; Discovery Home Channel; Discovery Kids Channel; Discovery Times Channel; Docu TVE; Ecuavisia Internacional; ESPN Classic Sports; ESPN Deportes; ESPN HD; ESPNews; EuroNews; EWTN en Espanol; Fox College Sports Atlantic; Fox College Sports Central; Fox College Sports Pacific; Fox Deportes; Fox Movie Channel; Fox Soccer; Fuel TV; G4; Golf Channel; Hallmark Channel; HD Theater; History Channel en Espanol; History Channel International; Howard TV; HTV Musica; Infinito; Jewelry Television; La Familia Network; Latele Novela Network; LOGO; Mariavision; Military Channel; MTV Hits; mun2 television; Music Choice; National Geographic Channel; National Geographic Channel HD Network; NBA TV; NDTV The Dominican Channel; NHL Network; Nick Jr.; NickToons TV; Outdoor Channel; Oxygen; Science; Sorpresa; Sundance Channel; Sur Network; TBS in HD; TeenNick; Telefe International; Toon Disney; Toon Disney en Espanol; Tr3s; Turner Network TV HD; TV Chile; TV Colombia; TVE Internacional; TVG Network; Universal HD; VeneMovies; Versus; Versus HD; VH1 Classic; VH1 Soul; V-me TV; WAPA America.

Fee: $10.95 monthly.

Pay Service 1

Pay Units: N.A.

Programming (via satellite): Cinemax; Flix; HBO (multiplexed); Showtime (multiplexed); The Movie Channel.

Digital Pay Service 1

Pay Units: N.A.

Programming (via satellite): CCTV-4; Cinemax (multiplexed); Cinemax HD; Cinemax On Demand; Encore (multiplexed); HBO (multiplexed); HBO HD; HBO On Demand; MBC America; RAI International; Russian Television Network; Showtime (multiplexed); Showtime HD; Showtime On Demand; Starz HDTV; The Movie Channel (multiplexed); The Movie Channel HD; TV Asia; TV Japan; TV Polonia; TV5, La Television International; Zee TV USA; Zhong Tian Channel.

Fee: $9.95 monthly (Showtime, Cinemax, TMC, Starz/Encore, Playboy, RAI, TV Japan, TV5, TV Polonia, TV Asia, MCB, Zee TV or CCTV), $11.95 monthly (HBO), $14.95 monthly (RTN).

Video-On-Demand: Yes

Pay-Per-View

iN DEMAND (delivered digitally); Playboy TV (delivered digitally); iN DEMAND (delivered digitally); NBA League Pass (delivered digitally).

Internet Service

Operational: Yes.

Broadband Service: Optimum Online.

Fee: $46.95 installation; $34.95 monthly.

Telephone Service

Digital: Operational

Fee: $34.95 monthly

Miles of Plant: 150.0 (coaxial); None (fiber optic).

Vice President, Field Operations: Mark Fitchett.

Ownership: Cablevision Systems Corp. (MSO).

PORT HENRY (village)—Time Warner Cable, 1021 Highbridge Rd, Schenectady, NY 12303. Phone: 518-242-8890. Fax: 518-242-8948. Web Site: http://www.timewarnercable.com/albany. Also serves Crown Point (town), Hague (town), Moriah (town), Putnam, Schroon, Schroon Lake & Ticonderoga (town). ICA: NY0123.

TV Market Ranking: Below 100 (Crown Point (town), Moriah (town), PORT HENRY (VILLAGE)); Outside TV Markets (Hague (town), Putnam (town), Schroon, Schroon Lake, Ticonderoga (town)). Franchise award date: N.A. Franchise expiration date: May 15, 2007. Began: September 1, 1983.

Channel capacity: N.A. Channels available but not in use: N.A.

Basic Service

Subscribers: N.A. Included in Albany

Programming (received off-air): WCAX-TV (CBS) Burlington; WCDC-TV (ABC) Adams; WCFE-TV (PBS) Plattsburgh; WCWN (CW) Schenectady; WETK (PBS) Burlington; WFFF-TV (CW, FOX) Burlington; WNYA (MNT) Pittsfield; WPTZ (NBC) Plattsburgh; WVNY (ABC) Burlington.

Programming (via satellite): Capital News 9; C-SPAN; QVC; TBS Superstation; TV Guide Network.

Fee: $38.25 installation; $7.75 monthly.

Expanded Basic Service 1

Subscribers: N.A.

Programming (via satellite): A&E Networks; ABC Family Channel; AMC; Animal Planet; BET Networks; Bravo; Cartoon Network; CNBC; CNN; Comedy Central; Country Music TV; C-SPAN 2; Discovery Channel; Discovery Health Channel; Disney Channel; E! Entertainment Television; ESPN; ESPN 2; ESPN Classic Sports; Eternal Word TV Network; Food Network; Fox News Channel; FX; Golf Channel; Headline News; HGTV; History Channel; Lifetime; Lifetime Movie Network; MSG; MSG Plus;

MSNBC; MTV; National Geographic Channel; Nickelodeon; Oxygen; ShopNBC; SoapNet; Spike TV; SportsNet New York; Style Network; Syfy; The Learning Channel; The Weather Channel; Travel Channel; truTV; Turner Classic Movies; Turner Network TV; TV Land; Univision Studios; USA Network; Versus; VH1; WE tv; Yankees Entertainment & Sports.
Fee: $26.35 monthly.

Digital Basic Service
Subscribers: N.A. Included in Albany
Programming (via satellite): A&E Networks; ABC Family Channel; AMC; Animal Planet; BBC America; BET Networks; Bloomberg Television; Boomerang; Bravo; Cartoon Network; CNBC; CNN; Comedy Central; Cooking Channel; C-SPAN; C-SPAN 2; C-SPAN 3; Discovery Channel; Discovery Fit & Health; Disney Channel; DIY Network; DMX Music; E! Entertainment Television; ESPN; ESPN 2; ESPN Classic Sports; ESPNews; Eternal Word TV Network; Food Network; Fox Movie Channel; Fox News Channel; Fox Sports World; FSN Digital Atlantic; FSN Digital Central; FSN Digital Pacific; Fuel TV; Fuse; FX; G4; Golf Channel; GSN; Hallmark Channel; Headline News; HGTV; History Channel; History Channel International; Independent Film Channel; Lifetime; Lifetime Movie Network; Lifetime Real Women; LWS Local Weather Station; MSG; MSG Plus; MSNBC; National Geographic Channel; NBA TV; New York 1 News; Nick Jr.; Nickelodeon; Outdoor Channel; Ovation; Oxygen; SoapNet; Speed; Spike TV; Style Network; Sundance Channel; Syfy; TBS Superstation; Tennis Channel; The Learning Channel; The Weather Channel; Toon Disney; Travel Channel; Trinity Broadcasting Network; truTV; Turner Classic Movies; Turner Network TV; TV Land; USA Network; Versus; WE tv; Yankees Entertainment & Sports.
Fee: $4.95 monthly.

Digital Pay Service 1
Pay Units: N.A.
Programming (via satellite): Cinemax (multiplexed); Encore (multiplexed); Flix; HBO (multiplexed); RAI International; Showtime (multiplexed); Starz (multiplexed); The Movie Channel (multiplexed); TV Asia; Zee TV USA.
Fee: $9.95 monthly (RAI, ZeeTV or TV Asia), $14.95 monthly (HBO, Cinemax, Showtime/TMC or Starz).
Video-On-Demand: Yes

Pay-Per-View
sports (delivered digitally); Shorteez (delivered digitally); Fresh (delivered digitally); Playboy TV (delivered digitally); iN DEMAND (delivered digitally); iN DEMAND.

Internet Service
Operational: Yes.
Broadband Service: EarthLink, LocalNet, Road Runner.
Fee: $29.95 installation; $44.95 monthly.

Telephone Service
Digital: Operational
Fee: $44.95 monthly
Miles of plant (coax & fiber) included in Albany
Vice President, Operations: Mark Loreno. Vice President, Engineering: James Marchester. Vice President, Marketing: Tricia Buhr. Vice President, Public Affairs: Peter Taubkin. Vice President, Customer Care: Paul Ventosa.
Ownership: Advance/Newhouse Partnership.; Time Warner Cable (MSO).

PORT JERVIS—Time Warner Cable. Now served by HUDSON VALLEY (formerly Middletown), NY [NY0231]. ICA: NY0240.

POTSDAM—Time Warner Cable. Now served by MASSENA, NY [NY0072]. ICA: NY0053.

POUGHKEEPSIE—Time Warner Cable. Now served by HUDSON VALLEY (formerly Middletown), NY [NY0231]. ICA: NY0035.

PRINCETOWN (town)—Princetown Cable Co., 878 Ennis Rd, Schenectady, NY 12306-5702. Phone: 518-887-5500. Fax: 518-887-2815. Web Site: http://www.princetowncable.com. Also serves Duanesburg, Mariaville, Princetown & Rotterdam (portions). ICA: NY0151.
TV Market Ranking: 34 (Duanesburg, Mariaville, Princetown, PRINCETOWN (TOWN), Rotterdam (portions)). Franchise award date: September 17, 1987. Franchise expiration date: N.A. Began: December 15, 1989.
Channel capacity: N.A. Channels available but not in use: N.A.

Basic Service
Subscribers: 750.
Programming (received off-air): WCWN (CW) Schenectady; WMHT (PBS) Schenectady; WNYT (NBC) Albany; WRGB (CBS) Schenectady; WTEN (ABC) Albany; WXXA-TV (FOX) Albany.
Programming (via satellite): A&E Networks; ABC Family Channel; AMC; America One Television; AmericanLife TV Network; Animal Planet; Bio; Bloomberg Television; Boomerang; Bravo; Cartoon Network; CNBC; CNN; Comedy Central; Country Music TV; Crime & Investigation Network; C-SPAN; C-SPAN 2; Discovery Channel; Discovery Fit & Health; Disney Channel; DIY Network; E! Entertainment Television; ESPN; ESPN 2; ESPNews; Eternal Word TV Network; FamilyNet; Food Network; Fox Movie Channel; Fox News Channel; Fox Soccer; Fox Sports Net New York; FX; G4; Golf Channel; Hallmark Channel; Headline News; HGTV; History Channel; History Channel International; ION Television; Lifetime; Military History Channel; MSG; MSNBC; MTV; National Geographic Channel; Nickelodeon; Outdoor Channel; QVC; SoapNet; Speed; Spike TV; SportsNet New York; Style Network; Syfy; TBS Superstation; The Learning Channel; The Weather Channel; Travel Channel; Trinity Broadcasting Network; truTV; Turner Classic Movies; Turner Network TV; TV Land; USA Network; VH1; Yankees Entertainment & Sports.
Fee: $25.00 installation; $41.95 monthly.

Pay Service 1
Pay Units: 174.
Programming (via satellite): Cinemax (multiplexed); HBO (multiplexed); Showtime.
Fee: $10.95 monthly (each).
Video-On-Demand: Planned

Internet Service
Operational: Yes.
Subscribers: 500.
Broadband Service: In-house.
Fee: $29.95-$49.95 monthly.

Telephone Service
None
Miles of Plant: 40.0 (coaxial); None (fiber optic).
General Manager: James F. D'Allaird. Chief Technician: Robert Motyl. Office Manager: Denise Chamberlin.
Ownership: Princetown Cable Co. Inc.

QUEENS—RCN Corp. Formerly [NY0283]. This cable system has converted to IPTV, 196 Van Buren St, Herndon, VA 20170. Phone: 703-434-8200. Web Site: http://www.rcn.com. ICA: NY5321.
TV Market Ranking: 1 (QUEENS). Franchise award date: N.A. Franchise expiration date: N.A. Began: N.A.
Channel capacity: N.A. Channels available but not in use: N.A.

Pay Service 1
Pay Units: N.A.
Fee: $11.95 monthly (Cinemaz or Starz!); $16.95 monthly (Showtime/The Movie Channel); $17.95 monthly (HBO).
Video-On-Demand: Yes

Internet Service
Operational: Yes.
Broadband Service: RCN.
Fee: $38.00 monthly.

Telephone Service
Digital: Operational
Fee: $45.00 monthly
Chairman: Steven J. Simmons. Chief Executive Officer: Jim Holanda.

QUEENS—RCN Corp. This cable system has converted to IPTV. See Queens, NY [NY5321]. ICA: NY0283.

QUEENSBURY—Formerly served by Adelphia Communications. No longer in operation. ICA: NY0042.

RAMAPO (town)—Cablevision Systems Corp., 40 Potash Rd, Oakland, NJ 07436-3100. Phones: 516-803-2300 (Corporate office); 201-651-4000. Fax: 516-803-1183. Web Site: http://www.cablevision.com. Also serves Mahwah Twp., NJ; Chestnut Ridge, Hillburn, Sloatsburg, Southfields, Suffern, Tuxedo & Tuxedo Park, NY. ICA: NY0059.
TV Market Ranking: 1 (Chestnut Ridge, Hillburn, Mahwah Twp., RAMAPO (TOWN), Sloatsburg, Southfields, Suffern, Tuxedo, Tuxedo Park). Franchise award date: January 1, 1979. Franchise expiration date: N.A. Began: June 1, 1981.
Channel capacity: N.A. Channels available but not in use: N.A.

Basic Service
Subscribers: 15,672.
Programming (received off-air): WABC-TV (ABC) New York; WCBS-TV (CBS) New York; WFME-TV (ETV) West Milford; WFUT-DT (TEL) Newark; WLIW (PBS) Garden City; WLNY-TV (IND) Riverhead; WMBC-TV (IND) Newton; WNBC (NBC) New York; WNET (PBS) Newark; WNJN (PBS) Montclair; WNJU (TMO) Linden; WNYW (FOX) New York; WPIX (CW, IND) New York; WPXN-TV (ION) New York; WRNN-TV (IND) Kingston; WWOR-TV (MNT) Secaucus; WXTV-DT (UNV) Paterson.
Programming (via satellite): News 12 New Jersey; QVC; ShopNBC.
Fee: $49.95 installation; $15.11 monthly; $2.95 converter.

Expanded Basic Service 1
Subscribers: N.A.
Programming (via satellite): A&E Networks; ABC Family Channel; AMC; Animal Planet; BET Networks; Bravo; Cartoon Network; CNBC; CNN; Comedy Central; C-SPAN; C-SPAN 2; Discovery Channel; Disney Channel; E! Entertainment Television; ESPN; ESPN 2; Food Network; Fox News Channel; Fuse; FX; GSN; Headline News; HGTV; History Channel; Lifetime; MSG; MSG Plus; MSNBC; MTV; MTV2; News 12 Traffic & Weather; Nickelodeon; SoapNet; Speed; Spike TV; SportsNet New York; Syfy; TBS Superstation; The Learning Channel; The Weather Channel; Travel Channel; truTV; Turner Classic Movies; Turner Network TV; TV Land; USA Network; VH1; WE tv; Yankees Entertainment & Sports.
Fee: $34.84 monthly.

Digital Basic Service
Subscribers: N.A.
Programming (via satellite): Azteca America; BBC World News; Bio; Bloomberg Television; Canal Sur; Cartoon Network Tambien en Espanol; Cine Latino; CNN en Espanol; CNN HD; Country Music TV; C-SPAN 3; Discovery en Espanol; Discovery Home Channel; Discovery Kids Channel; Docu TVE; ESPN 2 HD; ESPN Classic Sports; ESPN Deportes; ESPN HD; ESPNews; EuroNews; EWTN en Espanol; Food Network HD; Fox College Sports Atlantic; Fox College Sports Central; Fox College Sports Pacific; Fox Deportes; Fox Movie Channel; Fox Soccer; Fuel TV; G4; GameHD; Golf Channel; GolTV; Great American Country; Hallmark Channel; HD Theater; here! On Demand; HGTV HD; History Channel en Espanol; History Channel International; Howard TV; HTV Musica; ID Investigation Discovery; Infinito; Jewelry Television; La Familia Network; Latele Novela Network; LOGO; Mariavision; Military Channel; Momentum TV; MTV Hits; mun2 television; Music Choice; National Geographic Channel; National Geographic Channel HD Network; NBA TV; NHL Network; Nick Jr.; NickToons TV; Outdoor Channel; Oxygen; Science; ShopNBC; Sorpresa; Sundance Channel; Supercanal Caribe; TBS in HD; TeenNick; Telefe International; Toon Disney; Toon Disney en Espanol; Tr3s; Turner Network TV HD; TV Chile; TV Colombia; TVE Internacional; TVG Network; Universal HD; Utilisima; VeneMovies; Versus; Versus HD; VH1 Classic; VH1 Soul; V-me TV; WABC-TV (ABC) New York; World Cinema HD; YES HD.
Fee: $10.95 monthly; $2.95 converter.

Pay Service 1
Pay Units: N.A.
Programming (via satellite): Cinemax; Flix; HBO (multiplexed); Independent Film Channel; Playboy TV; Showtime; The Movie Channel.
Fee: $9.95 monthly (Cinemax, Playboy, Showtime, TMC or Starz & Encore), $11.95 monthly (HBO).

Digital Pay Service 1
Pay Units: N.A.
Programming (via satellite): CCTV-4; Channel One; Cinemax (multiplexed); Cinemax HD; Cinemax On Demand; Encore (multiplexed); HBO (multiplexed); HBO HD; HBO On Demand; International Television (ITV); Korean Channel; MBC America; Playboy TV; RAI International; RAI USA; Russian Television Network; Showtime (multiplexed); Showtime HD; Showtime On Demand; Society of Portuguese Television; Starz (multiplexed); Starz HDTV; The Movie Channel (multiplexed); The Movie Channel HD; TV Asia; TV Japan; TV Polonia; TV5, La Television International; Zee TV USA.
Fee: $9.95 monthly (Showtime, Cinemax, TMC, Starz/Encore, Playboy, RAI, SPT, TV5 or TV Polonia), $11.95 monthly (HBO), $24.95 monthly (TV Japan).
Video-On-Demand: Yes

Pay-Per-View
Addressable homes: 5,000.
Fresh.

Internet Service
Operational: Yes.
Broadband Service: Optimum Online.
Fee: $46.95 installation; $34.95 monthly; $299.00 modem purchase.
Telephone Service
Digital: Operational
Fee: $34.95 monthly
Miles of Plant: 222.0 (coaxial); None (fiber optic). Additional miles planned: 10.0 (coaxial).
Vice President, Field Operations: Christopher Fulton.
Ownership: Cablevision Systems Corp. (MSO).

REGO PARK—RCN Corp. Formerly served by Queens, NY [NY0283]. This cable system has converted to IPTV, 196 Van Buren St, Herndon, VA 20170. Phone: 703-434-8200. Web Site: http://www.rcn.com. ICA: NY5317.
TV Market Ranking: 1 (REGO PARK).
Channel capacity: N.A. Channels available but not in use: N.A.
Pay Service 1
Pay Units: N.A.
Fee: $11.95 monthly (Cinemaz or Starz!); $16.95 monthly (Showtime/The Movie Channel); $17.95 monthly (HBO).
Internet Service
Operational: Yes.
Fee: $38.00 monthly.
Telephone Service
Digital: Operational
Fee: $45.00 monthly
Chairman: Steven J. Simmons. Chief Executive Officer: Jim Holanda.

RENSSELAER—Time Warner Cable. Now served by ALBANY, NY [NY0014]. ICA: NY0034.

RHINEBECK (town)—Time Warner Cable. Now served by HUDSON VALLEY (formerly Middletown), NY [NY0231]. ICA: NY0094.

RIVERHEAD—Cablevision Systems Corp., 1111 Stewart Ave, Bethpage, NY 11714. Phone: 516-803-2300. Fax: 516-803-1183. Web Site: http://www.cablevision.com. Also serves Amagansett, Aquebogue, Baiting Hollow, Bay Point, Bridgehampton, Canoe Place, Cutchogue, Dering Harbor, East Hampton, East Marion, East Quogue, Flanders, Greenport, Hampton Bays, Jamesport, Laurel, Mattituck, Montauk, North Haven, North Sea, Northampton, Noyac, Orient, Orient Point, Peconic, Pine Neck, Quogue, Remsenburg, Sag Harbor, Sagaponack, Shelter Island, South Jamesport, Southampton, Southampton (village), Southold, Springs, Tiana, Wading River, Wainscott, Water Mill, West Tiana, Westhampton & Westhampton Beach. ICA: NY0024.
TV Market Ranking: 19 (Aquebogue, Baiting Hollow, Bay Point, Bridgehampton, Cutchogue, Dering Harbor, East Hampton, East Marion, Flanders, Greenport, Jamesport, Laurel, Mattituck, North Haven, North Sea, Northampton, Noyac, Orient, Orient Point, Peconic, RIVERHEAD, Sag Harbor, Sagaponack, Shelter Island, South Jamesport, Southampton (village), Southold, Wading River, Water Mill); Below 100 (Amagansett, Canoe Place, East Quogue, Hampton Bays, Pine Neck, Quogue, Remsenburg, Southampton, Springs, Tiana, Wainscott, West Tiana, Westhampton, Westhampton Beach, East Marion); Outside TV Markets (Montauk). Franchise award date: N.A. Franchise expiration date: N.A. Began: May 9, 1984.
Channel capacity: N.A. Channels available but not in use: N.A.
Basic Service
Subscribers: 57,410.
Programming (received off-air): WFTY-DT (TEL) Smithtown; WLIW (PBS) Garden City; WLNY-TV (IND) Riverhead; WNJU (TMO) Linden; WWOR-TV (MNT) Secaucus; WXTV-DT (UNV) Paterson; allband FM.
Programming (via microwave): WABC-TV (ABC) New York; WCBS-TV (CBS) New York; WNBC (NBC) New York; WNET (PBS) Newark; WNYW (FOX) New York; WPIX (CW, IND) New York; WPXN-TV (ION) New York.
Programming (via satellite): News 12 Long Island; Plum TV; QVC; ShopNBC.
Fee: $49.95 installation; $17.64 monthly; $2.95 converter.
Expanded Basic Service 1
Subscribers: 16,728.
Programming (received off-air): WVVH-CA Southampton.
Programming (via satellite): A&E Networks; ABC Family Channel; AMC; Animal Planet; BET Networks; Bravo; Cartoon Network; CNBC; CNN; Comedy Central; C-SPAN; C-SPAN 2; Discovery Channel; Disney Channel; E! Entertainment Television; ESPN; ESPN 2; Food Network; Fox News Channel; Fuse; FX; GalaVision; GSN; Headline News; HGTV; History Channel; Lifetime; MSG; MSG Plus; MSNBC; MTV; MTV2; News 12 Traffic & Weather; Nickelodeon; SoapNet; Speed; Spike TV; SportsNet New York; Syfy; TBS Superstation; Telecare; The Learning Channel; The Weather Channel; Travel Channel; truTV; Turner Classic Movies; Turner Network TV; TV Land; USA Network; VH1; WE tv; Yankees Entertainment & Sports.
Fee: $32.31 monthly.
Digital Basic Service
Subscribers: N.A.
Programming (via satellite): Azteca America; BBC World News; Bio; Bloomberg Television; Canal Sur; Caracol TV; Cartoon Network Tambien en Espanol; Cine Latino; CNN en Espanol; CNN HD; Country Music TV; C-SPAN 3; Discovery en Espanol; Discovery Home Channel; Discovery Kids Channel; Docu TVE; Ecuavisia Internacional; ESPN 2 HD; ESPN Classic Sports; ESPN Deportes; ESPN HD; ESPNews; EuroNews; EWTN en Espanol; Food Network HD; Fox College Sports Atlantic; Fox College Sports Central; Fox College Sports Pacific; Fox Deportes; Fox Movie Channel; Fox Soccer; FSN HD; Fuel TV; G4; GameHD; Golf Channel; GolTV; Great American Country; Hallmark Channel; HD Theater; here! On Demand; HGTV HD; History Channel en Espanol; History Channel International; Howard TV; HTV Musica; ID Investigation Discovery; Infinito; Jewelry Television; La Familia Network; Latele Novela Network; LOGO; Mariavision; Military Channel; Momentum TV; MTV Hits; mun2 television; Music Choice; National Geographic Channel; National Geographic Channel HD Network; NBA TV; Nick Jr.; NickToons TV; Outdoor Channel; Oxygen; Science; Sorpresa; Sundance Channel; Supercanal Caribe; TBS in HD; TeenNick; Telefe International; Toon Disney; Toon Disney en Espanol; Tr3s; Turner Network TV HD; TV Chile; TV Colombia; TVE Internacional; TVG Network; Universal HD; Utilisima; VeneMovies; Versus; Versus HD; VH1 Classic; VH1 Soul; V-me TV; WAPA America; World Cinema HD; YES HD.
Fee: $10.95 monthly; $2.95 converter.
Pay Service 1
Pay Units: N.A.
Programming (via satellite): Cinemax; Flix; HBO (multiplexed); Independent Film Channel; Showtime; The Movie Channel.
Digital Pay Service 1
Pay Units: 2,736.
Programming (via satellite): Cinemax (multiplexed); Cinemax HD; Cinemax On Demand.
Fee: $9.95 monthly.
Digital Pay Service 2
Pay Units: 7,474.
Programming (via satellite): HBO (multiplexed); HBO HD; HBO On Demand.
Fee: $11.95 monthly.
Digital Pay Service 3
Pay Units: N.A.
Programming (via satellite): CCTV-4; Channel One; Encore (multiplexed); RAI Internatiоnal; Russian Television Network; Starz (multiplexed); Starz HDTV; The Movie Channel (multiplexed); The Movie Channel HD; TV Asia; TV Japan; TV Polonia; TV5, La Television International; Zee TV USA.
Digital Pay Service 4
Pay Units: 5,572.
Programming (via satellite): Showtime (multiplexed); Showtime HD; Showtime On Demand.
Fee: $9.95 monthly.
Video-On-Demand: Yes
Pay-Per-View
iN DEMAND; Playboy TV; Club Jenna.
Internet Service
Operational: Yes.
Broadband Service: Optimum Online.
Fee: $46.95 installation; $34.95 monthly; $299.00 modem purchase.
Telephone Service
Digital: Operational
Fee: $34.95 monthly
Miles of Plant: 1,518.0 (coaxial); 143.0 (fiber optic).
Senior Vice President, Field Operations: Christopher Coffee. Corporate Communications Manager: Kristen Blank.
Ownership: Cablevision Systems Corp. (MSO).

ROCHESTER—Time Warner Cable, 71 Mount Hope Ave, Rochester, NY 14620. Phones: 585-756-1000 (Administrative office); 585-756-5000. Fax: 585-756-1675. Web Site: http://www.timewarnercable.com/rochester. Also serves Brighton, Bristol, Brockport, Byron (town), Canadice, Chili, Clarendon, Clarkson (town), East Rochester, Fairport, Gates, Greece, Hamlin (town), Henrietta, Hilton, Holley, Honeoye, Irondequoit, Murray (town), Ogden (town), Parma, Penfield, Perinton, Pittsford (village), Richmond, Riga (town), Spencerport, Sweden (town) & Webster (village). ICA: NY0003.
TV Market Ranking: 56 (Brighton, Bristol, Brockport, Byron (town), Canadice, Chili, Clarendon, Clarkson (town), East Rochester, Fairport, Gates, Greece, Hamlin (town), Henrietta, Hilton, Holley, Honeoye, Irondequoit, Murray (town), Ogden (town), Parma, Penfield, Perinton, Pittsford (village), Richmond, ROCHESTER, Spencerport, Sweden (town), Webster (village)); 56,56 (Riga (town)). Franchise award date: April 1, 1979. Franchise expiration date: N.A. Began: November 1, 1980.
Channel capacity: N.A. Channels available but not in use: N.A.
Basic Service
Subscribers: 334,713 Includes Batavia & Geneva.
Programming (received off-air): WBGT-CA (MNT) Rochester; WHAM-TV (ABC, CW) Rochester; WHEC-TV (NBC) Rochester; WROC-TV (CBS) Rochester; WUHF (FOX) Rochester; WXXI-TV (PBS) Rochester.
Programming (via satellite): Animal Planet; CW+; QVC; ShopNBC; TBS Superstation; WGN America.
Fee: $37.64 installation; $13.17 monthly; $3.13 converter.
Expanded Basic Service 1
Subscribers: 198,850.
Programming (via satellite): A&E Networks; ABC Family Channel; AMC; BET Networks; Bravo; Cartoon Network; CNBC; CNN; Comedy Central; Country Music TV; C-SPAN; C-SPAN 2; Discovery Channel; Disney Channel; E! Entertainment Television; ESPN; ESPN 2; Eternal Word TV Network; Food Network; Fox News Channel; FX; Golf Channel; Hallmark Channel; Headline News; HGTV; History Channel; ION Television; Lifetime; MoviePlex; MSG; MSG Plus; MSNBC; MTV; Nickelodeon; Spike TV; Syfy; The Learning Channel; The Weather Channel; Travel Channel; Trinity Broadcasting Network; truTV; Turner Classic Movies; Turner Network TV; TV Land; Univision Studios; USA Network; VH1; Yankees Entertainment & Sports.
Fee: $33.58 monthly.
Digital Basic Service
Subscribers: 162,000 Includes Batavia & Geneva.
Programming (via satellite): America's Store; BBC America; Bloomberg Television; Cooking Channel; C-SPAN 3; Discovery Digital Networks; DIY Network; ESPN Classic Sports; ESPNews; Fox Deportes; Fox Movie Channel; Fox Sports World; FSN Digital Atlantic; FSN Digital Central; FSN Digital Pacific; Great American Country; GSN; Independent Film Channel; Lifetime Movie Network; Lifetime Real Women; MTV2; Music Choice; National Geographic Channel; Nick Jr.; Outdoor Channel; Ovation; Oxygen; SoapNet; Speed; Style Network; Tennis Channel; Toon Disney; VH1 Classic.
Fee: $11.95 monthly.
Digital Pay Service 1
Pay Units: 22,180.
Programming (via satellite): Cinemax (multiplexed); Flix; Starz (multiplexed).
Fee: $1.95 installation; $12.95 monthly.
Digital Pay Service 2
Pay Units: 60,907.
Programming (via satellite): HBO (multiplexed).
Fee: $1.95 installation; $12.95 monthly.

Digital Pay Service 3
Pay Units: 7,854.
Programming (via satellite): Showtime (multiplexed).
Fee: $1.95 installation; $12.95 monthly.

Digital Pay Service 4
Pay Units: 2,703.
Programming (via satellite): The Movie Channel (multiplexed).
Fee: $1.95 installation; $12.95 monthly.

Digital Pay Service 5
Pay Units: 2,063.
Programming (via satellite): Encore (multiplexed).
Fee: $12.95 monthly.

Video-On-Demand: Yes

Pay-Per-View
iN DEMAND (delivered digitally); Playboy TV (delivered digitally); ETC (delivered digitally); Sports PPV (delivered digitally).

Internet Service
Operational: Yes. Began: September 21, 1998.
Subscribers: 110,000.
Broadband Service: Road Runner.
Fee: $39.95 installation; $44.95 monthly.

Telephone Service
Digital: Operational

Miles of Plant: 3,765.0 (coaxial); 1,322.0 (fiber optic).

Division President: Terrence Rafferty. Vice President, Operations: Bruce Hennekey. Vice President, Engineering: Armando Ruiz. Vice President, Marketing: Mike Neal. Vice President, Government & Public Affairs: Chris Mueller.

Ownership: Time Warner Cable (MSO).; Advance/Newhouse Partnership (MSO).Day-to-day Operations are managed by Time Warner Cable.

ROCKLAND—Cablevision Systems Corp., 40 Potash Rd, Oakland, NJ 07436-3100. Phones: 516-803-2300 (Corporate office); 201-651-4000. Fax: 516-803-1183. Web Site: http://www.cablevision.com. Also serves Montvale, NJ; Airmont (village), Chestnut Ridge, Clarkstown, Grand View-on-Hudson, Montebello, Nanuet, New Hempstead, Nyack, Orangetown (town), Piermont, Ramapo (town), Ramapo Corridor, Rockland County (unincorporated areas), South Nyack, Spring Valley, Upper Nyack, Wesley Hills & West Nyack, NY. ICA: NY0017.

TV Market Ranking: 1 (Airmont (village), Chestnut Ridge, Clarkstown, Grand View-on-Hudson, Montebello, Montvale, Nanuet, New Hempstead, Nyack, Orangetown (town), Piermont, Ramapo (town), Ramapo Corridor, ROCKLAND, Rockland County (unincorporated areas), South Nyack, Spring Valley, Upper Nyack, Wesley Hills, West Nyack). Franchise award date: N.A. Franchise expiration date: N.A. Began: November 8, 1980.

Channel capacity: N.A. Channels available but not in use: N.A.

Basic Service
Subscribers: 53,872.
Programming (received off-air): WABC-TV (ABC) New York; WCBS-TV (CBS) New York; WFME-TV (ETV) West Milford; WFUT-DT (TEL) Newark; WLIW (PBS) Garden City; WLNY-TV (IND) Riverhead; WMBC-TV (IND) Newton; WNBC (NBC) New York; WNET (PBS) Newark; WNJN (PBS) Montclair; WNJU (TMO) Linden; WNYW (FOX) New York; WPIX (CW, IND) New York; WPXN-TV (ION) New York; WRNN-TV (IND) Kingston; WWOR-TV (MNT) Secaucus; WXTV-DT (UNV) Paterson; 23 FMs.
Programming (via satellite): News 12 New Jersey.
Fee: $49.95 installation; $18.00 monthly; $2.95 converter.

Expanded Basic Service 1
Subscribers: 51,000.
Programming (via microwave): News 12 Traffic & Weather.
Programming (via satellite): A&E Networks; ABC Family Channel; AMC; Animal Planet; BET Networks; Bravo; Cartoon Network; CNBC; CNN; Comedy Central; C-SPAN; C-SPAN 2; Discovery Channel; Disney Channel; E! Entertainment Television; ESPN; ESPN 2; Food Network; Fox News Channel; Fuse; FX; GSN; Headline News; HGTV; History Channel; Independent Film Channel; Lifetime; MSG; MSG Plus; MSNBC; MTV; MTV2; Nickelodeon; QVC; SoapNet; Speed; Spike TV; SportsNet New York; Syfy; TBS Superstation; The Learning Channel; The Weather Channel; Travel Channel; truTV; Turner Classic Movies; Turner Network TV; TV Land; USA Network; VH1; WE tv; Yankees Entertainment & Sports.
Fee: $31.95 monthly.

Digital Basic Service
Subscribers: N.A.
Programming (via satellite): Animal Planet HD; Azteca America; BBC World News; Bio; Bloomberg Television; Canal Sur; Caracol TV; Cartoon Network Tambien en Espanol; CNN en Espanol; CNN HD; Country Music TV; C-SPAN 3; Discovery en Espanol; Discovery Home Channel; Discovery Kids Channel; Docu TVE; Ecuavisia Internacional; ESPN 2 HD; ESPN Classic Sports; ESPN Deportes; ESPN HD; ESPNews; EuroNews; EWTN en Espanol; Food Network HD; Fox College Sports Atlantic; Fox College Sports Central; Fox College Sports Pacific; Fox Deportes; Fox Movie Channel; Fox Soccer; FSN HD; Fuel TV; G4; GameHD; Golf Channel; GolTV; Great American Country; Hallmark Channel; HD Theater; here! On Demand; HGTV HD; History Channel en Espanol; History Channel International; Howard TV; HTV Musica; ID Investigation Discovery; Infinito; Jewelry Television; La Familia Network; Latele Novela Network; LOGO; Mariavision; Military Channel; Momentum TV; MTV Hits; mun2 television; Music Choice; National Geographic Channel; National Geographic Channel HD Network; NBA TV; NHL Network; Nick Jr.; NickToons TV; Outdoor Channel; Oxygen; Science; ShopNBC; Sorpresa; Sundance Channel; Supercanal Caribe; TBS in HD; TeenNick; Telefe International; Toon Disney; Toon Disney en Espanol; Tr3s; Turner Network TV HD; TV Chile; TV Colombia; TVE Internacional; TVG Network; Universal HD; Utilisima; VeneMovies; Versus; Versus HD; VH1 Classic; VH1 Soul; V-me TV; WAPA America; World Cinema HD; YES HD.
Fee: $10.95 monthly; $2.95 converter.

Pay Service 1
Pay Units: 8,325.
Programming (via satellite): Cinemax; Flix; HBO (multiplexed); Showtime (multiplexed); The Movie Channel.

Digital Pay Service 1
Pay Units: N.A.
Programming (via satellite): CCTV-4; Cinemax (multiplexed); Cinemax HD; Cinemax On Demand; Encore (multiplexed); HBO (multiplexed); HBO HD; HBO On Demand; Korean Channel; RAI International; Russian Television Network; Showtime (multiplexed); Showtime HD; Showtime On Demand; Starz (multiplexed); Starz HDTV; The Movie Channel (multiplexed); The Movie Channel HD; TV Asia; TV Japan; TV Polonia; TV5, La Television International; Zee TV USA.
Fee: $9.95 monthly (Showtime, Cinemax, TMC, Starz/Encore, RAI, SPT, TV5 or TV Polinia), $11.95 monthly (HBO), $24.95 monthly (TV Japan).

Video-On-Demand: Yes

Pay-Per-View
iN DEMAND (delivered digitally); Playboy TV (delivered digitally); Club Jenna (delivered digitally).

Internet Service
Operational: Yes.
Broadband Service: Optimum Online.
Fee: $46.95 installation; $34.95 monthly; $299.00 modem purchase.

Telephone Service
Digital: Operational
Fee: $34.95 monthly

Miles of Plant: 51.0 (coaxial); 1,189.0 (fiber optic).

Vice President, Field Operations: Christopher Fulton.

Ownership: Cablevision Systems Corp. (MSO).

ROME—Time Warner Cable, 6005 Fair Lakes Rd, East Syracuse, NY 13057. Phone: 315-634-6100. Fax: 315-634-6219. Web Site: http://www.timewarnercable.com/CentralNY. Also serves Annsville, Augusta (town), Ava (town), Boonville, Burlington (town), Camden, Canastota (village), Chittenango, Cleveland (village), Constableville, Constantia (town), Deansboro, Exeter (town), Fenner (town), Floyd, Garrattsville, Hamilton, Holland Patent, Kirkland (town), Lee, Lenox (town), Leyden, Lincoln (town), Lyons Falls, Lyonsdale, Lyonsdale (town), Madison (village), Marcy, Marshall, Munnsville (village), New Lisbon, Oneida, Oneida Castle (village), Oriskany Falls, Peterboro, Port Leyden, Sangerfield, Sherrill (village), Smithfield (town), Stockbridge (town), Sullivan (town), Sylvan Beach, Trenton (town) (portions), Turin, Turin (town), Vernon (village), Verona (town), Vienna, Wampsville, Waterville, West Leyden, West Monroe (town), West Turin, Western, Westmoreland & Whitestown. ICA: NY0037.

TV Market Ranking: 35 (Annsville, Augusta (town), Camden, Canastota (village), Chittenango, Cleveland (village), Constantia (town), Fenner (town), Hamilton, Lee, Lenox (town), Lincoln (town), Madison (village), Munnsville (village), Oneida, Oneida Castle (village), Peterboro, Sherrill (village), Smithfield (town), Stockbridge (town), Sullivan (town), Sylvan Beach, Vernon (village), Verona (town), Vienna, Wampsville, West Monroe (town), Western); Below 100 (Ava (town), Boonville, Burlington (town), Constableville, Deansboro, Exeter (town), Floyd, Garrattsville, Holland Patent, Kirkland (town), Leyden, Lyons Falls, Lyonsdale, Lyonsdale (town), Marcy, Marshall, Oriskany Falls, Port Leyden, ROME, Sangerfield, Turin, Turin (town), Waterville, West Leyden, West Turin, Westmoreland, Whitestown); Outside TV Markets (New Lisbon). Franchise award date: N.A. Franchise expiration date: N.A. Began: May 15, 1965.

Channel capacity: N.A. Channels available but not in use: N.A.

Basic Service
Subscribers: N.A. Included in Syracuse
Programming (received off-air): WCNY-TV (PBS) Syracuse; WFXV (FOX) Utica; WKTV (CW, NBC) Utica; WNYS-TV (MNT) Syracuse; WSPX-TV (ION) Syracuse; WSTM-TV (NBC) Syracuse; WSTQ-LP (CW) Syracuse; WSYR-TV (ABC) Syracuse; WSYT (FOX) Syracuse; WTVH (CBS) Syracuse; WUTR (ABC) Utica.
Programming (via satellite): C-SPAN; QVC; TBS Superstation; various Canadian stations; WGN America.
Fee: $99.00 installation; $9.28 monthly.

Expanded Basic Service 1
Subscribers: N.A. Included in Syracuse
Programming (via satellite): A&E Networks; ABC Family Channel; Animal Planet; BET Networks; Cartoon Network; CNBC; CNN; Comedy Central; C-SPAN 2; Discovery Channel; E! Entertainment Television; ESPN; ESPN 2; Eternal Word TV Network; Food Network; Fox News Channel; FX; Hallmark Channel; Headline News; HGTV; Jewelry Television; Lifetime; Lifetime Movie Network; MSG Plus; MSNBC; MTV; Nickelodeon; Oxygen; ShopNBC; SoapNet; Spike TV; Syfy; The Learning Channel; The Weather Channel; Travel Channel; Turner Network TV; TV Land; Univision Studios; USA Network; Versus; VH1; WE tv; Yankees Entertainment & Sports.
Fee: $32.00 installation; $36.22 monthly.

Digital Basic Service
Subscribers: N.A. Included in Syracuse
Programming (via satellite): AMC; America's Store; BBC America; Bio; Bloomberg Television; Boomerang; Bravo; Cooking Channel; Country Music TV; C-SPAN 3; Discovery Digital Networks; Disney Channel; DIY Network; Encore Action; ESPN Classic Sports; ESPNews; Fox Movie Channel; Fox Sports World; Fuse; G4; GAS; Golf Channel; Great American Country; GSN; History Channel; History Channel International; Independent Film Channel; Lifetime Real Women; Local Cable Weather; MSG; MTV2; National Geographic Channel; Nick Jr.; Nick Too; Outdoor Channel; Ovation; Speed; Style Network; Sundance Channel; Toon Disney; Trinity Broadcasting Network; truTV; Turner Classic Movies; VH1 Classic.
Fee: $10.95 monthly.

Digital Expanded Basic Service
Subscribers: N.A.
Programming (via satellite): FSN Digital Atlantic; FSN Digital Central; FSN Digital Pacific; Fuel TV; NBA TV; Tennis Channel.
Fee: $4.95 monthly.

Digital Pay Service 1
Pay Units: 11,180.
Programming (via satellite): Cinemax (multiplexed); HBO (multiplexed); Showtime (multiplexed); Starz (multiplexed); The Movie Channel (multiplexed).
Fee: $8.95 monthly (Cinemax, Showtime, Starz or TMC), $10.95 monthly (HBO).

Video-On-Demand: Yes

Pay-Per-View
iN DEMAND (delivered digitally); Playboy TV (delivered digitally); Fresh (delivered digitally).

Internet Service
Operational: Yes.
Broadband Service: EarthLink, LocalNet, Road Runner.
Fee: $39.95 installation; $44.95 monthly.

Telephone Service
Digital: Operational
Fee: $39.95 monthly

Miles of plant included in Syracuse.

President: Mary Cotter. Vice President, Engineering: Henry Hryckiewicz. Vice President, Marketing: John Melvany. Vice President, Public Affairs: Jeff Unaitis. Technical Operations Director: Bruce Tompkins.

Ownership: Time Warner Cable (MSO).; Advance/Newhouse Partnership (MSO).Day-to-day Operations are managed by Time Warner Cable.

ROSENDALE—Time Warner Cable. Now served by HUDSON VALLEY (formerly Middletown), NY [NY0231]. ICA: NY0112.

SALAMANCA—Atlantic Broadband, 24 Main St, Bradford, PA 16701. Phones: 888-536-9600; 814-539-8971. Fax: 814-362-2190. E-mail: info@atlanticbb.com. Web Site: http://www.atlanticbb.com. Also serves Great Valley, Little Valley (town), Little Valley (village) & Salamanca (town). ICA: NY0099.

TV Market Ranking: Below 100 (Great Valley, Little Valley (town), Little Valley (village), SALAMANCA, Salamanca (town)). Franchise award date: December 13, 1965. Franchise expiration date: N.A. Began: January 1, 1965.

Channel capacity: N.A. Channels available but not in use: N.A.

Basic Service
Subscribers: 2,150.
Programming (received off-air): WGRZ (NBC) Buffalo; WIVB-TV (CBS) Buffalo; WKBW-TV (ABC) Buffalo; WNED-TV (PBS) Buffalo; WNYB (IND) Jamestown; WSEE-TV (CBS, CW) Erie; WUTV (FOX) Buffalo.
Programming (via satellite): C-SPAN; INSP; QVC; TV Guide Network; various Canadian stations; WGN America.
Fee: $25.00 installation; $19.13 monthly.

Expanded Basic Service 1
Subscribers: 1,495.
Programming (via satellite): A&E Networks; ABC Family Channel; AMC; Animal Planet; Bravo; Cartoon Network; CNBC; CNN; Comedy Central; Country Music TV; Discovery Channel; Discovery Health Channel; Disney Channel; E! Entertainment Television; ESPN; ESPN 2; ESPN Classic Sports; Food Network; Fox News Channel; FX; G4; Golf Channel; Hallmark Channel; HGTV; History Channel; Lifetime; Lifetime Movie Network; MSG; MSNBC; MTV; National Geographic Channel; Nickelodeon; Outdoor Channel; Oxygen; Speed; Spike TV; Style Network; Syfy; TBS Superstation; The Learning Channel; The Weather Channel; Travel Channel; truTV; Turner Classic Movies; Turner Network TV; TV Land; USA Network; VH1.
Fee: $8.51 installation; $37.32 monthly.

Digital Basic Service
Subscribers: N.A.
Programming (via satellite): A&E HD; Animal Planet HD; BBC America; Bio; Bloomberg Television; Boomerang; Chiller; CMT Pure Country; Discovery Channel HD; Discovery Kids Channel; Disney Channel HD; DIY Network; DMX Music; Encore (multiplexed); ESPN 2 HD; ESPN HD; ESPN U; ESPNews; Fuel TV; GSN; HD Theater; History Channel International; ID Investigation Discovery; Independent Film Channel; Lifetime Real Women; Military Channel; MTV Hits; MTV Jams; MTV2; NFL Network; NFL Network HD; Nick Jr.; Nick Too; NickToons TV; Planet Green; Science; SoapNet; Starz (multiplexed); Syfy HD; TBS in HD; TeenNick; TLC HD; Toon Disney; Tr3s; Turner Network TV HD; USA Network HD; VH1 Classic; VH1 Soul; WE tv; Weatherscan.
Fee: $18.95 monthly.

Digital Pay Service 1
Pay Units: 210.
Programming (via satellite): HBO (multiplexed).
Fee: $15.95 monthly.

Digital Pay Service 2
Pay Units: 120.
Programming (via satellite): Cinemax (multiplexed).
Fee: $15.95 monthly.

Digital Pay Service 3
Pay Units: N.A.
Programming (via satellite): Flix; Showtime (multiplexed); The Movie Channel (multiplexed).
Fee: $15.95 monthly.

Video-On-Demand: No

Pay-Per-View
iN DEMAND (delivered digitally); Hot Choice (delivered digitally); Spice: Xcess (delivered digitally); Club Jenna (delivered digitally); Fresh (delivered digitally); Shorteez (delivered digitally); Playboy TV (delivered digitally).

Internet Service
Operational: Yes.
Broadband Service: Atlantic Broadband High-Speed Internet.
Fee: 24.95-$57.95 monthly.

Telephone Service
Digital: Operational
Fee: $44.95 monthly

Miles of Plant: 74.0 (coaxial); 16.0 (fiber optic).

Vice President: David Dane. General Manager: Mike Papasergi. Technical Operations Director: Charles Sorchillo. Marketing & Customer Service Director: Dara Leslie. Marketing Manager: Natalie Kurchak.

Ownership: Atlantic Broadband (MSO).

SARANAC LAKE—Time Warner Cable, 6005 Fair Lakes Rd, East Syracuse, NY 13057. Phone: 315-634-6100. Fax: 305-634-6219. Web Site: http://www.timewarnercable.com/CentralNY. Also serves Bloomingdale, Harrietstown, Lake Placid, North Elba, St. Armand, Tupper Lake & Vermontville. ICA: NY0243.

TV Market Ranking: Below 100 (Bloomingdale, Harrietstown, Lake Placid, North Elba, SARANAC LAKE, St. Armand, Tupper Lake, Vermontville). Franchise award date: N.A. Franchise expiration date: N.A. Began: January 1, 1956.

Channel capacity: N.A. Channels available but not in use: N.A.

Basic Service
Subscribers: N.A. Included in Syracuse
Programming (received off-air): WCAX-TV (CBS) Burlington; WCFE-TV (PBS) Plattsburgh; WFFF-TV (CW, FOX) Burlington; WGMU-CA (MNT) Burlington; WNPI-DT (PBS) Norwood; WPTZ (NBC) Plattsburgh; WVNY (ABC) Burlington; allband FM.
Programming (via microwave): WPIX (CW, IND) New York.
Programming (via satellite): QVC; TV Guide Network; various Canadian stations.
Fee: $40.00 installation; $5.90 monthly; $3.25 converter.

Expanded Basic Service 1
Subscribers: N.A. Included in Syracuse
Programming (via satellite): A&E Networks; ABC Family Channel; AMC; Animal Planet; Bravo; Cartoon Network; CNBC; CNN; Comedy Central; Country Music TV; C-SPAN; C-SPAN 2; Discovery Channel; Disney Channel; E! Entertainment Television; ESPN; ESPN 2; Eternal Word TV Network; Food Network; Fox News Channel; FX; Golf Channel; Hallmark Channel; Headline News; HGTV; History Channel; ION Television; Lifetime; MSG; MSG Plus; MSNBC; MTV; Nickelodeon; Oxygen; Product Information Network; ShopNBC; Speed; Spike TV; Syfy; TBS Superstation; The Learning Channel; The Weather Channel; Travel Channel; truTV; Turner Classic Movies; Turner Network TV; TV Land; USA Network; VH1; Yankees Entertainment & Sports.

Digital Basic Service
Subscribers: N.A. Included in Syracuse
Programming (via satellite): AmericanLife TV Network; BBC America; Black Family Channel; Bloomberg Television; Country Music TV; Discovery Digital Networks; DIY Network; ESPN 2 HD; ESPN Classic Sports; ESPN HD; ESPNews; Fox Movie Channel; Fox Soccer; Fuse; G4; GAS; Great American Country; GSN; Halogen Network; HDNet; HDNet Movies; Lifetime Movie Network; LOGO; MTV Networks Digital Suite; Music Choice; National Geographic Channel; NFL Network; Nick Jr.; Nick Too; NickToons TV; Outdoor Channel; SoapNet; Speed; Style Network; The Word Network; Toon Disney; Trinity Broadcasting Network; Turner Classic Movies; Versus; WE tv.

Digital Expanded Basic Service
Subscribers: N.A.
Programming (via satellite): Arabic Channel; Bio; CBS Sports Network; CCTV-4; Filipino Channel; FSN Digital Atlantic; FSN Digital Central; FSN Digital Pacific; Fuel TV; Golf Channel; History Channel International; Independent Film Channel; RAI International; Russian Television Network; Sundance Channel; TV Asia; TV Japan; TV5, La Television International; Zee TV USA; Zhong Tian Channel.

Digital Pay Service 1
Pay Units: N.A.
Programming (via satellite): Canales N; Cinemax (multiplexed); Cinemax HD; Encore; Flix (multiplexed); HBO (multiplexed); HBO HD; Showtime (multiplexed); Showtime HD; Starz (multiplexed); Starz HDTV.

Video-On-Demand: Yes

Pay-Per-View
Playboy TV (delivered digitally); Fresh (delivered digitally); Shorteez (delivered digitally); Hot Choice (delivered digitally); ESPN (delivered digitally); NHL Center Ice (delivered digitally); MLB Extra Innings (delivered digitally).

Internet Service
Operational: Yes.
Broadband Service: EarthLink, LocalNet, Road Runner.
Fee: $39.95 installation; $44.95 monthly.

Telephone Service
Digital: Operational
Fee: $39.95 monthly

Miles of plant included in Syracuse.

President: Mary Cotter. Vice President, Engineering: Henry Hryckiewicz. Technical Operations Director: Bruce Tompkins. Vice President, Marketing: John Melvany. Vice President, Public Affairs: Jeff Unaitis.

Ownership: Time Warner Cable (MSO).

SARATOGA SPRINGS—Time Warner Cable. Now served by ALBANY, NY [NY0014]. ICA: NY0027.

SAUGERTIES (town)—Time Warner Cable. Now served by HUDSON VALLEY (formerly Middletown), NY [NY0231]. ICA: NY0244.

SCHENECTADY—Time Warner Cable. Now served by ALBANY, NY [NY0014]. ICA: NY0025.

SCHROEPPEL—Time Warner Cable. Now served by SYRACUSE, NY [NY0013]. ICA: NY0128.

SCHROON (town)—Time Warner Cable. Now served by PORT HENRY (village), NY [NY0123]. ICA: NY0159.

SIDNEY—Time Warner Cable. Now served by ONEONTA, NY [NY0065]. ICA: NY0109.

SILVER CREEK—Time Warner Cable. Now served by DUNKIRK, NY [NY0064]. ICA: NY0111.

SMITHVILLE—Haefele TV Inc., 24 E Tioga St, PO Box 312, Spencer, NY 14883. Phone: 607-589-6235. Fax: 607-589-7211. E-mail: cs@htva.net. Web Site: http://www.htva.net. Also serves Greene (town) & Smithville Flats. ICA: NY0174.

TV Market Ranking: Below 100 (Greene (town), SMITHVILLE, Smithville Flats). Franchise award date: October 18, 1990. Franchise expiration date: N.A. Began: January 1, 1991.

Channel capacity: 42 (not 2-way capable). Channels available but not in use: N.A.

Basic Service
Subscribers: 179.
Programming (received off-air): WBNG-TV (CBS, CW) Binghamton; WBPN-LP Binghamton; WCNY-TV (PBS) Syracuse; WETM-TV (NBC) Elmira; WICZ-TV (FOX) Binghamton; WIVT (ABC) Binghamton; WSKG-TV (PBS) Binghamton; WSTM-TV (NBC) Syracuse.
Programming (via satellite): A&E Networks; ABC Family Channel; AMC; Animal Planet; Cartoon Network; CNBC; CNN; Country Music TV; Discovery Channel; Disney Channel; ESPN; ESPN 2; Food Network; Great American Country; Headline

News; HGTV; History Channel; Lifetime; MSNBC; Nick At Nite; Nickelodeon; QVC; Speed; Spike TV; Syfy; TBS Superstation; The Learning Channel; The Weather Channel; Travel Channel; Turner Classic Movies; Turner Network TV; USA Network; VH1.
Fee: $30.00 installation; $48.45 monthly; $1.00 converter; $10.00 additional installation.
Pay Service 1
Pay Units: 10.
Programming (via satellite): Cinemax.
Fee: $9.00 monthly.
Pay Service 2
Pay Units: 29.
Programming (via satellite): HBO.
Fee: $9.50 monthly.
Video-On-Demand: No
Internet Service
Operational: Yes.
Fee: $34.50-$51.95 monthly.
Telephone Service
Digital: Operational
Miles of Plant: 12.0 (coaxial); None (fiber optic).
President & General Manager: Lee Haefele. Vice President: Denise Lave. Chief Technician: Michael McNamara.
Ownership: Haefele TV Inc. (MSO).

SPENCER—Haefele TV Inc., 24 E Tioga St, PO Box 312, Spencer, NY 14883. Phone: 607-589-6235. Fax: 607-589-7211. E-mail: cs@htva.net. Web Site: http://www.htva.net. Also serves Alpine, Barton (town), Berkshire, Berkshire (town), Candor (portions), Caroline (town), Catharine (town), Cayuta (town), Harford (town), Newark Valley (town), Richford (town), Smithboro, Spencer (town), Tioga, Van Etten (village) & Virgil (town). ICA: NY0145.
TV Market Ranking: Below 100 (Alpine, Barton (town), BERKSHIRE, Berkshire (town), Candor, Caroline (town), Catharine (town), Cayuta (town), Harford (town), Newark Valley (town), Richford (town), Smithboro, SPENCER, Spencer (town), Tioga, Van Etten (village), Virgil (town)). Franchise award date: July 11, 1983. Franchise expiration date: N.A. Began: September 1, 1983.
Channel capacity: 65 (operating 2-way). Channels available but not in use: N.A.
Basic Service
Subscribers: 2,742.
Programming (received off-air): WBNG-TV (CBS, CW) Binghamton; WETM-TV (NBC) Elmira; WICZ-TV (FOX) Binghamton; WIVT (ABC) Binghamton; WSKG-TV (PBS) Binghamton; WSYT (FOX) Syracuse; WVIA-TV (PBS) Scranton.
Programming (via satellite): A&E Networks; ABC Family Channel; AMC; Animal Planet; Cartoon Network; CNBC; CNN; Comedy Central; Country Music TV; C-SPAN; Discovery Channel; Disney Channel; DIY Network; E! Entertainment Television; ESPN; ESPN 2; ESPN Classic Sports; Food Network; Fox News Channel; FX; G4; Great American Country; Hallmark Channel; HGTV; History Channel; ION Television; Lifetime; MSG; MSG Plus; MSNBC; MTV; Nickelodeon; QVC; Speed; Spike TV; Syfy; TBS Superstation; The Learning Channel; The Weather Channel; Travel Channel; Trinity Broadcasting Network; truTV; Turner Network TV; TV Guide Network; TV Land; USA Network; VH1; WE tv; WGN America; WPIX (CW, IND) New York; Yankees Entertainment & Sports.
Fee: $30.00 installation; $48.45 monthly; $1.00 converter; $10.00 additional installation.
Digital Basic Service
Subscribers: 279.
Programming (via satellite): BBC America; Bio; Bloomberg Television; Bravo; Discovery Fit & Health; DMX Music; ESPN Classic Sports; ESPNews; Fox Movie Channel; Fox Soccer; GAS; Golf Channel; GSN; History Channel International; Independent Film Channel; INSP; Lifetime Movie Network; MTV2; Nick Jr.; NickToons TV; Outdoor Channel; Style Network; Toon Disney; Turner Classic Movies.
Fee: $12.95 monthly.
Pay Service 1
Pay Units: 44.
Programming (via satellite): Cinemax.
Fee: $9.00 monthly.
Pay Service 2
Pay Units: 311.
Programming (via satellite): HBO (multiplexed).
Fee: $10.00 monthly.
Digital Pay Service 1
Pay Units: N.A.
Programming (via satellite): Cinemax; Encore (multiplexed); HBO; Showtime (multiplexed); Starz (multiplexed); The Movie Channel (multiplexed).
Fee: $22.90 monthly ($12.00 Starz & Encore), $25.90 monthly (Showtime & TMC), $19.00 Encore $29.95 monthly (Cinemax & HBO).
Video-On-Demand: No
Pay-Per-View
Fresh (delivered digitally); TVN Entertainment (delivered digitally).
Internet Service
Operational: Yes. Began: October 1, 1999.
Subscribers: 669.
Broadband Service: In-house.
Fee: $34.50-$51.95 monthly; $9.95 modem lease; $89.00 modem purchase.
Telephone Service
Digital: Operational
Miles of Plant: 137.0 (coaxial); None (fiber optic).
President & Manager: Lee Haefele. Vice President: Denise Laue. Chief Technician: Michael McNamara.
Ownership: Haefele TV Inc. (MSO).

SPRINGVILLE (village)—Now served by OLEAN, NY [NY0056]. ICA: NY0052.

STAMFORD—Time Warner Cable. Now served by ONEONTA, NY [NY0065]. ICA: NY0146.

STATEN ISLAND—Time Warner Cable, 120 E 23rd St, New York, NY 10010. Phone: 212-598-7200. Fax: 718-816-8433. Web Site: http://www.timewarnercable.com. ICA: NY0010.
TV Market Ranking: 1 (STATEN ISLAND). Franchise award date: July 19, 1983. Franchise expiration date: September 16, 2008. Began: August 1, 1986.
Channel capacity: N.A. Channels available but not in use: N.A.
Basic Service
Subscribers: N.A. Included in New York
Programming (received off-air): WABC-TV (ABC) New York; WCBS-TV (CBS) New York; WFUT-DT (TEL) Newark; WLIW (PBS) Garden City; WLNY-TV (IND) Riverhead; WMBC-TV (IND) Newton; WNBC (NBC) New York; WNET (PBS) Newark; WNJU (TMO) Linden; WNYE-TV (PBS) New York; WNYW (FOX) New York; WPIX (CW, IND) New York; WPXN-TV (ION) New York; WWOR-TV (MNT) Secaucus; WXTV-DT (UNV) Paterson; 4 FMs.
Programming (via satellite): A&E Networks; ABC Family Channel; AMC; BET Networks; Bravo; Cartoon Network; CNBC; CNN; Comedy Central; C-SPAN; C-SPAN 2; CTV News 1; Discovery Channel; Disney Channel; E! Entertainment Television; ESPN; ESPN 2; Food Network; Fox News Channel; FX; GalaVision; Headline News; HGTV; History Channel; Lifetime; Lifetime Movie Network; MSG; MSG Plus; MSNBC; MTV; National Geographic Channel; New York 1 News; Nickelodeon; Nuvo TV; Oxygen; QVC; ShopNBC; Spike TV; Syfy; TBS Superstation; The Learning Channel; The Weather Channel; truTV; Turner Network TV; TV Guide Network; USA Network; VH1; WE tv; Yesterday USA.
Fee: $59.00 installation; $10.59 monthly; $2.86 converter.
Expanded Basic Service 1
Subscribers: N.A. Included in New York
Programming (received off-air): WRNN-LD Nyack.
Programming (via satellite): Animal Planet; Encore Family; ESPN Classic Sports; Eternal Word TV Network; Flix; Independent Film Channel; Travel Channel; Turner Classic Movies; TV Land.
Fee: $17.84 monthly.
Digital Basic Service
Subscribers: N.A. Included in New York
Programming (via satellite): AmericanLife TV Network; America's Store; BBC America; Black Family Channel; Bloomberg Television; Boomerang; CCTV-4; CNN International; Cooking Channel; Country Music TV; C-SPAN 3; Current; Discovery Fit & Health; DIY Network; ESPN HD; ESPNews; Fox Movie Channel; Fox Soccer; Fuse; G4; GAS; Golf Channel; Great American Country; GSN; Hallmark Channel; HD Theater; HDNet; HDNet Movies; INHD; Lifetime Real Women; LOGO; MTV2; mun2 television; Music Choice; Nick Jr.; Nick Too; Nuvo TV; Shop at Home; SoapNet; Speed; Style Network; Sundance Channel; The Word Network; Toon Disney; Turner Network TV HD; Versus; VH1 Classic.
Fee: $9.95 monthly.
Digital Pay Service 1
Pay Units: N.A.
Programming (via satellite): CCTV-4; Cinemax (multiplexed); Deutsche Welle TV; Encore (multiplexed); HBO (multiplexed); HBO HD; National Greek Television; RAI International; Russian Television Network; Showtime (multiplexed); Showtime HD; Starz (multiplexed); The Movie Channel (multiplexed); TV Asia; TV Japan; TV Polonia; TV5, La Television International; Zee TV USA.
Fee: $9.95 monthly (CCTV, RTN, RAI, Deutsche Welle or TV5), $10.95 monthly (HBO, Showtime, Cinemax, TMC, Starz or Encore), $14.95 monthly (TV Asia, Antenna or Zee TV), $17.95 monthly (TV Polonia), $24.95 monthly (TV Japan).
Video-On-Demand: Yes
Pay-Per-View
Movies & Events (delivered digitally); Playboy TV (delivered digitally); Sports PPV (delivered digitally).
Internet Service
Operational: Yes.
Broadband Service: Road Runner.
Fee: $44.95 monthly.
Telephone Service
Digital: Operational
Fee: $39.95 monthly
Miles of plant included in New York
President: Howard Szarfarc. Senior Vice President & General Manager: Barbara Kelly. Vice President, Engineering: Larry Pestana. Vice President, Technical Operations: Norberto Rivera. Vice President, Marketing: David Goldberg. Vice President, Sales: Ken Fluger. Vice President, Public Affairs: Harriet Novet. General Manager: Brien Kelley. Marketing & Public Affairs Director: Gina Gutman.
Ownership: Time Warner Cable (MSO).

SUFFOLK COUNTY—Cablevision Systems Corp., 1111 Stewart Ave, Bethpage, NY 11714. Phone: 516-803-2300. Fax: 516-803-1183. Web Site: http://www.cablevision.com. Also serves Belle Terre, Bellport, Blue Point, Brightwaters, Brookhaven, Brookhaven (town), Calverton, Center Moriches, Centereach, Commack, Coram, East Moriches, Eastport, Farmingville, Fort Salonga, Head of the Harbor, Holtsville, Islandia, Islip, Kings Park, Lake Grove (village), Lake Ronkonkama, Manorville, Mastic, Mastic Beach, Medford, Moriches, Nesconset, Nissequogue, Old Field, Patchogue (village), Poquott (village), Port Jefferson, Port Jefferson Station, San Remo, Selden, Setauket, Shirley, Smithtown, St. James, Stony Brook, Village of the Branch & Yaphank. ICA: NY0006.
TV Market Ranking: 1 (Head of the Harbor); 1,19 (SUFFOLK COUNTY (portions)); 19 (Belle Terre, Calveston, Centereach, Coram, Farmingville, Fort Salonga, Holtsville, Kings Park, Lake Grove (village), Lake Ronkonkama, Manorville, Medford, Nesconset, Nissequogue, Old Field, Poquott (village), Port Jefferson, Port Jefferson Station, San Remo, Selden, Setauket, Smithtown, St. James, Stony Brook, Village of the Branch, Yaphank); Below 100 (Bellport (village), Blue Point, Brightwaters, Center Moriches, Commack, Eastport, Islandia, Islip, Mastic, Mastic Beach, Moriches, Port Jefferson, Shirley, SUFFOLK COUNTY (portions)); Outside TV Markets (SUFFOLK COUNTY (portions)). Franchise award date: N.A. Franchise expiration date: N.A. Began: January 1, 1966.
Channel capacity: N.A. Channels available but not in use: N.A.
Basic Service
Subscribers: 235,885.
Programming (received off-air): WABC-TV (ABC) New York; WCBS-TV (CBS) New York; WFTY-DT (TEL) Smithtown; WLIW (PBS) Garden City; WLNY-TV (IND) Riverhead; WNBC (NBC) New York; WNET (PBS) Newark; WNJU (TMO) Linden; WNYW (FOX) New York; WPIX (CW, IND) New York; WPXN-TV (ION) New York; WWOR-TV (MNT) Secaucus; WXTV-DT (UNV) Paterson.
Programming (via satellite): News 12 Long Island; QVC; ShopNBC.
Fee: $49.95 installation; $16.22 monthly; $2.95 converter.
Expanded Basic Service 1
Subscribers: 159,800.
Programming (via satellite): A&E Networks; ABC Family Channel; AMC; Animal Planet; BET Networks; Bravo; Cartoon Network; CNBC; CNN; Comedy Central; C-SPAN; C-SPAN 2; Discovery Channel; Disney Channel; E! Entertainment Television; ESPN; ESPN 2; Food Network; Fox News Channel; Fuse; FX; GSN; Headline News; HGTV; History Channel; Independent Film Channel; Lifetime; MSG; MSG Plus; MSNBC; MTV; News 12 Traffic & Weather; Nickelodeon; RAI USA; SoapNet; Speed; Spike TV; Syfy; TBS Superstation; Telecare; The Learning Chan-

nel; The Weather Channel; Travel Channel; truTV; Turner Classic Movies; Turner Network TV; TV Land; USA Network; VH1; WE tv; Yankees Entertainment & Sports.
Fee: $33.73 monthly; $2.95 converter.

Digital Basic Service
Subscribers: N.A.
Programming (via satellite): Animal Planet HD; Azteca America; BBC World News; Bio; Bloomberg Television; Canal Sur; Caracol TV; Cartoon Network Tambien en Espanol; CBS Sports Network; CCTV-4; Channel One; Cine Latino; CMT HD; CNN en Espanol; CNN HD; Country Music TV; C-SPAN 3; Discovery Channel HD; Discovery en Espanol; Discovery Kids Channel; Docu TVE; Ecuavisia Internacional; ESPN 2 HD; ESPN Classic Sports; ESPN Deportes; ESPN HD; ESPNews; EuroNews; EWTN en Espanol; Filipino Channel; Food Network HD; Fox College Sports Atlantic; Fox College Sports Central; Fox College Sports Pacific; Fox Deportes; Fox Movie Channel; Fox News HD; Fox Soccer; Fuel TV; FX HD; G4; GMA Pinoy TV; Golf Channel; GolTV; Great American Country; Hallmark Channel; Hallmark Movie Channel; Hallmark Movie Channel HD; HD Theater; here! On Demand; HGTV HD; History Channel en Espanol; History Channel International; Howard TV; HTV Musica; ID Investigation Discovery; Infinito; Jewelry Television; Korean Channel; La Familia Network; Latele Novela Network; LATV Networks; LOGO; Mariavision; MBC America; Military Channel; MKTV; Momentum TV; MTV Hits; MTV Networks HD; mun2 television; Music Choice; National Geographic Channel; National Geographic Channel HD Network; NBA TV; NHL Network; NHL Network HD; Nick HD; Nick Jr.; NickToons TV; NTV America; Outdoor Channel; Oxygen; Planet Green; RAI USA; Russian Television Network; Science; Science HD; Society of Portuguese Television; Sorpresa; Speed HD; Spike TV HD; Sundance Channel; Supercanal Caribe; TBS in HD; TeenNick; Telefe International; Telemicro Internacional; The Jewish Channel; The Weather Channel HD; TLC HD; Toon Disney; Toon Disney en Espanol; Tr3s; Travel Channel HD; Turner Network TV HD; TV Asia; TV Chile; TV Colombia; TV Japan; TV Polonia; TV5 USA; TVE Internacional; TVG Network; Universal HD; Utilisima; VeneMovies; Versus; Versus HD; VH1 Classic; VH1 HD; VH1 Soul; V-me TV; WAPA America; YES HD; Zee TV USA.
Fee: $10.95 monthly; $2.95 converter.

Pay Service 1
Pay Units: N.A.
Programming (via satellite): Flix; HBO (multiplexed); Showtime (multiplexed); The Movie Channel.

Digital Pay Service 1
Pay Units: 4,426.
Programming (via satellite): Cinemax (multiplexed); Cinemax HD; Cinemax On Demand; HBO HD; Showtime HD; Starz HDTV; The Movie Channel HD.
Fee: $9.95 monthly.

Digital Pay Service 2
Pay Units: 2,611.
Programming (via satellite): Playboy TV.
Fee: $9.95 monthly.

Digital Pay Service 3
Pay Units: 41,194.
Programming (via satellite): Encore (multiplexed); Starz On Demand.
Fee: $9.95 monthly.

Digital Pay Service 4
Pay Units: 38,798.
Programming (via satellite): HBO (multiplexed); HBO On Demand.
Fee: $11.95 monthly.

Digital Pay Service 5
Pay Units: 22,764.
Programming (via satellite): The Movie Channel (multiplexed).
Fee: $9.95 monthly.

Digital Pay Service 6
Pay Units: 24,534.
Programming (via satellite): Showtime (multiplexed); Showtime On Demand.
Fee: $9.95 monthly.

Video-On-Demand: Yes

Pay-Per-View
Playboy TV; Club Jenna.

Internet Service
Operational: Yes.
Broadband Service: Optimum Online.
Fee: $46.95 installation; $34.95 monthly; $299.00 modem purchase.

Telephone Service
Digital: Operational
Fee: $34.95 monthly

Miles of Plant: 3,807.0 (coaxial); 356.0 (fiber optic).
Senior Vice President, Field Operations: Christopher Coffey. Corporate Communications Manager: Kristin Blank.
Ownership: Cablevision Systems Corp. (MSO).

SULLIVAN (town)—Time Warner Cable. Now served by ROME, NY [NY0037]. ICA: NY0096.

SULLIVAN COUNTY—Time Warner Cable. Now served by HUDSON VALLEY (formerly Middletown), NY [NY0231]. ICA: NY0251.

SUMMIT (town)—Chain Lakes Cablevision, 9507 Cherokee Trail, Crossville, TN 38572. Phone: 866-788-5261. Fax: 931-788-0489. Also serves Charlotteville & Jefferson (town). ICA: NY0180.
TV Market Ranking: Outside TV Markets (Charlotteville, Jefferson (town), SUMMIT). Franchise award date: January 15, 1990. Franchise expiration date: N.A. Began: May 15, 1990.
Channel capacity: 36 (not 2-way capable). Channels available but not in use: N.A.

Basic Service
Subscribers: 36.
Programming (received off-air): WMHT (PBS) Schenectady; WNYT (NBC) Albany; WRGB (CBS) Schenectady; WRNN-TV (IND) Kingston; WTEN (ABC) Albany; WXXA-TV (FOX) Albany; WYPX-TV (ION) Amsterdam.
Programming (via satellite): A&E Networks; ABC Family Channel; AMC; Animal Planet; CNN; Country Music TV; Discovery Channel; Disney Channel; ESPN; ESPN 2; Headline News; Nickelodeon; QVC; Spike TV; TBS Superstation; The Learning Channel; The Weather Channel; Trinity Broadcasting Network; Turner Network TV; USA Network.
Fee: $50.00 installation; $32.95 monthly; $2.00 converter; $10.00 additional installation.

Pay Service 1
Pay Units: N.A.
Programming (via satellite): HBO.
Fee: $10.00 installation; $12.95 monthly.

Internet Service
Operational: No.

Telephone Service
None

Miles of Plant: 17.0 (coaxial); None (fiber optic).

Manager & Chief Technician: Charles Himelrick. Assistant Manager: Diane Bowles.
Ownership: Phoenix Cable Inc. (MSO).

SYRACUSE—Time Warner Cable, 6005 Fair Lakes Rd, East Syracuse, NY 13057. Phones: 315-634-6100; 315-634-6200. Fax: 315-634-6219. Web Site: http://www.timewarnercable.com/CentralNY. ICA: NY0021.
TV Market Ranking: 35 (SYRACUSE). Franchise award date: April 27, 1978. Franchise expiration date: June 20, 2007. Began: March 13, 1979.
Channel capacity: N.A. Channels available but not in use: N.A.

Basic Service
Subscribers: 420,000 Includes Auburn, Champlain, Cortland, Ilion, Ithaca, Massena, Oswego, Rome, Saranac Lake, Syracuse (suburbs), Utica, & Watertown.
Programming (received off-air): WCNY-TV (PBS) Syracuse; WNYS-TV (MNT) Syracuse; WSPX-TV (ION) Syracuse; WSTM-TV (NBC) Syracuse; WSYR-TV (ABC) Syracuse; WSYT (FOX) Syracuse; WTVH (CBS) Syracuse; 23 FMs.
Programming (via satellite): TV Guide Network; WGN America; YNN-Central New York.
Fee: $50.00 installation; $9.28 monthly.

Expanded Basic Service 1
Subscribers: 400,000 Includes Auburn, Champlain, Cortland, Ilion, Ithaca, Massena, Oswego, Rome, Saranac Lake, Syracuse (suburbs), Utica, & Watertown.
Programming (via satellite): A&E Networks; ABC Family Channel; Animal Planet; BET Networks; Cartoon Network; CNBC; CNN; Comedy Central; C-SPAN; C-SPAN 2; Discovery Channel; Discovery Fit & Health; E! Entertainment Television; ESPN; ESPN 2; Eternal Word TV Network; Food Network; Fox News Channel; FX; Hallmark Channel; Headline News; HGTV; Lifetime; Lifetime Movie Network; MSG Plus; MSNBC; MTV; Nickelodeon; Oxygen; QVC; Shop at Home; ShopNBC; SoapNet; Spike TV; Syfy; TBS Superstation; The Learning Channel; The Weather Channel; Travel Channel; Turner Network TV; TV Land; Univision Studios; USA Network; Versus; VH1; WE tv; Yankees Entertainment & Sports.
Fee: $33.00 installation; $45.50 monthly.

Digital Basic Service
Subscribers: 280,000 Includes Auburn, Champlain, Cortland, Ilion, Ithaca, Massena, Oswego, Rome, Saranac Lake, Syracuse (suburbs), Utica, & Watertown.
Programming (via satellite): AMC; AmericanLife TV Network; America's Store; BBC America; Bio; Bloomberg Television; Boomerang; Bravo; Cooking Channel; Country Music TV; C-SPAN 3; Discovery Digital Networks; Disney Channel; DIY Network; ESPN Classic Sports; ESPNews; Fox Movie Channel; Fox Sports World; Fuse; G4; GAS; Golf Channel; Great American Country; GSN; History Channel; History Channel International; Independent Film Channel; Lifetime Real Women; Local Cable Weather; MSG; MTV2; Music Choice; National Geographic Channel; Nick Jr.; Nick Too; Outdoor Channel; Ovation; Speed; Style Network; Sundance Channel; Toon Disney; Trinity Broadcasting Network; truTV; Turner Classic Movies; VH1 Classic.
Fee: $10.95 monthly.

Digital Expanded Basic Service
Subscribers: N.A.
Programming (via satellite): FSN Digital Atlantic; FSN Digital Central; FSN Digital Pacific; Fuel TV; NBA TV; Tennis Channel; WAM! America's Kidz Network.
Fee: $4.95 monthly.

Digital Pay Service 1
Pay Units: N.A.
Programming (via satellite): ART America; Canales N; CCTV-4; Cinemax (multiplexed); Encore (multiplexed); HBO (multiplexed); RAI International; Russian Television Network; Saigon Broadcasting Television Network; Showtime (multiplexed); Starz (multiplexed); The Movie Channel (multiplexed); TV Asia; TV5, La Television International; Zee TV USA.
Fee: $9.95 monthly (ART, Canales n, CCTV-4, RAI, RTN, SBN or TV 5), $10.95 monthly (Cinemax, HBO, Showtime, Starz or TMC), $14.95 monthly (TV Asia or Zee TV).

Video-On-Demand: Yes

Pay-Per-View
Addressable homes: 13,779.
iN DEMAND (delivered digitally); Playboy TV (delivered digitally); Fresh (delivered digitally).

Internet Service
Operational: Yes.
Subscribers: 280,000.
Broadband Service: AOL for Broadband; EarthLink; Local Net; Road Runner.
Fee: $24.95 installation; $39.95 monthly.

Telephone Service
Digital: Operational
Subscribers: 120,000.
Fee: $44.95 monthly

President: Mary Cotter. Vice President, Engineering: Henry Hryckiewicz. Vice President, Marketing: John Melvany. Vice President, Public Affairs: Jeff Unaitis. Technical Operations Director: Bruce Tompkins.
Ownership: Time Warner Cable (MSO).; Advance/Newhouse Partnership (MSO).

SYRACUSE (suburbs)—Time Warner Cable, 6005 Fair Lakes Rd, East Syracuse, NY 13057. Phones: 315-634-6000; 315-634-6100. Fax: 315-634-6219. Web Site: http://www.timewarnercable.com/centralNY. Also serves Baldwinsville, Brutus, Camillus, Cato, Cazenovia, Cicero, Clay, De Witt, East Syracuse, Elbridge, Fayetteville, Fenner (town), Geddes, Ira (town), Jordan, La Fayette, Liverpool, Lysander (town), Manlius, Marcellus, Mentz (town), Meridian, Minoa, Nelson (town), North Syracuse, Onondaga, Orwell (town), Otisco (town), Pennellville, Phoenix, Pompey, Port Byron, Salina, Schroeppel, Solvay, Tully, Van Buren (town) & Weedsport. ICA: NY0013.
TV Market Ranking: 35 (Baldwinsville, Brutus, Camillus, Cato, Cazenovia, Cicero, Clay, De Witt, East Syracuse, Elbridge,

Fayetteville, Fenner (town), Geddes, Ira (town), Jordan, La Fayette, Liverpool, Lysander (town), Manlius, Marcellus, Mentz (town), Meridian, Minoa, Nelson (town), North Syracuse, Onondaga, Otisco (town), Pennellville, Phoenix, Pompey, Port Byron, Salina, Schroeppel, Solvay, SYRACUSE (SUBURBS), Tully, Van Buren (town), Weedsport); Below 100 (Orwell (town)). Franchise award date: April 1, 1974. Franchise expiration date: June 20, 2007. Began: April 1, 1974.

Channel capacity: N.A. Channels available but not in use: N.A.

Basic Service

Subscribers: N.A. Included in Syracuse

Programming (received off-air): WCNY-TV (PBS) Syracuse; WNYS-TV (MNT) Syracuse; WSPX-TV (ION) Syracuse; WSTM-TV (NBC) Syracuse; WSTQ-LP (CW) Syracuse; WSYR-TV (ABC) Syracuse; WSYT (FOX) Syracuse; WTVH (CBS) Syracuse.

Programming (via satellite): Jewelry Television; TBS Superstation; WGN America.

Fee: $9.43 monthly; $2.00 converter.

Expanded Basic Service 1

Subscribers: N.A. Included in Syracuse

Programming (via satellite): A&E Networks; ABC Family Channel; BET Networks; Cartoon Network; CNBC; CNN; Comedy Central; C-SPAN; C-SPAN 2; Discovery Channel; Discovery Fit & Health; E! Entertainment Television; ESPN; ESPN 2; Eternal Word TV Network; Food Network; Fox News Channel; FX; Hallmark Channel; Headline News; HGTV; Lifetime; Lifetime Movie Network; MSG Plus; MSNBC; MTV; Nickelodeon; Oxygen; QVC; ShopNBC; SoapNet; Spike TV; Syfy; The Learning Channel; The Weather Channel; Travel Channel; Turner Network TV; TV Land; Univision Studios; USA Network; Versus; VH1; WE tv; Yankees Entertainment & Sports.

Fee: $37.00 installation; $36.07 monthly.

Digital Basic Service

Subscribers: N.A. Included in Syracuse

Programming (via satellite): AMC; America's Store; BBC America; Bio; Bloomberg Television; Boomerang; Bravo; Cooking Channel; Country Music TV; C-SPAN 3; Discovery Digital Networks; Disney Channel; DIY Network; Encore Action; ESPN Classic Sports; ESPNews; Fox Movie Channel; Fox Sports World; Fuse; G4; GAS; Golf Channel; Great American Country; GSN; History Channel; History Channel International; Independent Film Channel; Lifetime Real Women; MSG; MTV2; National Geographic Channel; Nick Jr.; Nick Too; Outdoor Channel; Ovation; Speed; Style Network; Sundance Channel; Toon Disney; Trinity Broadcasting Network; truTV; Turner Classic Movies; VH1 Classic; Weatherscan.

Fee: $10.95 monthly.

Digital Expanded Basic Service

Subscribers: N.A.

Programming (via satellite): FSN Digital Atlantic; FSN Digital Central; FSN Digital Pacific; Fuel TV; NBA TV; Tennis Channel.

Fee: $4.95 monthly.

Digital Pay Service 1

Pay Units: 12,600.

Programming (via satellite): Cinemax (multiplexed).

Fee: $8.00 monthly.

Digital Pay Service 2

Pay Units: 5,800.

Programming (via satellite): Starz (multiplexed).

Fee: $9.50 monthly.

Digital Pay Service 3

Pay Units: 32,600.

Programming (via satellite): HBO (multiplexed).

Fee: $10.95 monthly.

Digital Pay Service 4

Pay Units: 4,100.

Programming (via satellite): Showtime (multiplexed).

Fee: $9.50 monthly.

Digital Pay Service 5

Pay Units: 3,006.

Programming (via satellite): The Movie Channel (multiplexed).

Fee: $9.50 monthly.

Video-On-Demand: Yes

Pay-Per-View

iN DEMAND (delivered digitally); Playboy TV (delivered digitally); Fresh (delivered digitally).

Internet Service

Operational: Yes.

Broadband Service: EarthLink, LocalNet, Road Runner.

Fee: $39.95 installation; $44.95 monthly.

Telephone Service

Digital: Operational

Fee: $39.95 monthly

Miles of plant included in Syracuse.

President: Mary Cotter. Vice President, Engineering: Henry Hryckiewicz. Vice President, Marketing: John Melvany. Vice President, Public Affairs: Jeff Unaitis. Technical Operations Director: Bruce Tompkns.

Ownership: Time Warner Cable (MSO).; Advance/Newhouse Partnership (MSO).

TOMPKINS COUNTY—Time Warner Cable. Now served by ITHACA, NY [NY0028]. ICA: NY0280.

TROUPSBURG—Time Warner Cable. Now served by HORNELL, NY [NY0076]. ICA: NY0253.

TROY—Time Warner Cable. Now served by ALBANY, NY [NY0014]. ICA: NY0020.

TURIN (town)—Turin Cable TV. Now served by ROME, NY [NY0037]. ICA: NY0254.

TUSTEN—Tiime Warner Cable. Now served by HUDSON VALLEY (formerly Middletown), NY [NY0231]. ICA: NY0255.

UTICA—Time Warner Cable, 6005 Fair Lakes Rd, East Syracuse, NY 13057. Phone: 315-634-6100. Fax: 305-634-6219. Web Site: http://www.timewarnercable.com. Also serves Barneveld (village), Clayville (village), Clinton (village), Cold Brook, Deerfield, Eagle Bay, Forestport, Frankfort (town), Inlet, Kirkland (town), Marcy (town), Middleville (village), New Hartford (village), New York Mills (village), Newport (village), Old Forge, Oriskany, Paris (town), Poland, Prospect (village), Remsen (village), Russia (town), Schuyler, Thendara, Trenton (town), Westmoreland, Whitesboro (village), Whitestown & Yorkville (village). ICA: NY0022.

TV Market Ranking: Below 100 (Barneveld (village), Clayville (village), Clinton (village), Cold Brook, Deerfield, Forestport, Frankfort (town), Kirkland (town), Marcy (town), Middleville (village), New Hartford (village), New York Mills (village), Newport (village), Oriskany, Paris (town), Poland, Prospect (village), Remsen (village), Russia (town), Schuyler, Thendara, Trenton (town), UTICA, Westmoreland, Whitesboro (village), Whitestown, Yorkville (village)); Outside TV Markets (Eagle Bay, Inlet, Old Forge). Franchise award date: October 11, 1963. Franchise expiration date: N.A. Began: October 1, 1964.

Channel capacity: N.A. Channels available but not in use: N.A.

Basic Service

Subscribers: N.A. Included in Syracuse

Programming (received off-air): WCNY-TV (PBS) Syracuse; WFXV (FOX) Utica; WKTV (CW, NBC) Utica; WPNY-LP Utica, etc.; WTVH (CBS) Syracuse; WUTR (ABC) Utica.

Programming (via satellite): C-SPAN; C-SPAN 2; QVC.

Fee: $23.00 installation; $8.91 monthly.

Expanded Basic Service 1

Subscribers: N.A. Included in Syracuse

Programming (via satellite): A&E Networks; ABC Family Channel; AMC; Animal Planet; BET Networks; Bravo; Cartoon Network; CNBC; CNN; Comedy Central; Country Music TV; Discovery Channel; Disney Channel; E! Entertainment Television; ESPN; ESPN 2; Eternal Word TV Network; Food Network; Fox News Channel; FX; Headline News; HGTV; History Channel; ION Television; Lifetime; MSG; MSG Plus; MSNBC; MTV; Nickelodeon; Spike TV; Syfy; TBS Superstation; The Learning Channel; The Weather Channel; Travel Channel; truTV; Turner Classic Movies; Turner Network TV; TV Guide Network; TV Land; USA Network; VH1; Yankees Entertainment & Sports.

Fee: $19.95 monthly.

Digital Basic Service

Subscribers: N.A. Included in Syracuse

Programming (via satellite): AmericanLife TV Network; BBC America; Bio; Bloomberg Television; Discovery Fit & Health; DIY Network; ESPN Classic Sports; ESPNews; Fox Sports World; Fuse; G4; GSN; Hallmark Channel; Halogen Network; History Channel International; Music Choice; Outdoor Channel; SoapNet; Toon Disney; Trinity Broadcasting Network; Versus; WE tv.

Digital Expanded Basic Service

Subscribers: N.A.

Programming (via satellite): Fox Movie Channel; GAS; Golf Channel; Independent Film Channel; National Geographic Channel; Nick Jr.; Nick Too; Speed; Style Network; Sundance Channel; Turner Classic Movies; VH1 Classic; VH1 Country.

Digital Pay Service 1

Pay Units: N.A.

Programming (via satellite): Cinemax (multiplexed); Encore (multiplexed); Flix; HBO (multiplexed); Showtime (multiplexed); Starz (multiplexed); The Movie Channel (multiplexed).

Video-On-Demand: Yes

Pay-Per-View

Fresh (delivered digitally); Playboy TV (delivered digitally).

Internet Service

Operational: Yes.

Broadband Service: Road Runner.

Fee: $39.95 installation; $44.95 monthly.

Telephone Service

Analog: Not Operational

Digital: Operational

Fee: $39.95 monthly

Miles of plant included in Syracuse.

President: Mary Cotter. Vice President, Engineering: Henry Hryckiewicz. Vice President, Marketing: John Melvany. Vice President, Public Affairs: Jeff Unaitis. Technical Operations Director: Bruce Tompkins.

Ownership: Time Warner Cable (MSO).

WALDEN—Time Warner Cable. Now served by HUDSON VALLEY (formerly Middletown), NY [NY0231]. ICA: NY0256.

WALTON (village)—Time Warner Cable. Now served by ONEONTA, NY [NY0065]. ICA: NY0121.

WARSAW (village)—Time Warner. Now served by BATAVIA (formerly Stafford), NY [NY0249]. ICA: NY0126.

WARWICK—Cablevision Systems Corp., 683 Route 10 E, Randolph, NJ 7869. Phones: 516-803-2300 (Corporate office); 973-659-2000. Fax: 845-986-0031. Web Site: http://www.cablevision.com. Also serves Layton, Montague Twp., Sandyston Twp. & West Milford, NJ; Chester (town) (Orange County), Chester (village), Florida (village), Greenwood Lake, Greenwood Lake (village), Minisink, Sugar Loaf, Unionville, Warwick (village), Warwick Twp. & Westtown, NY. ICA: NY0045.

TV Market Ranking: 1 (Chester (town) (Orange County), Chester (village), Florida (village), Greenwood Lake, Sugar Loaf, Unionville, WARWICK, Warwick (village), Warwick Twp., West Milford); 8 (Greenwood Lake); Below 100 (Minisink, Montague Twp., Sandyston Twp., Westtown); Outside TV Markets (Layton). Franchise award date: March 1, 1977. Franchise expiration date: N.A. Began: December 2, 1978.

Channel capacity: 121 (operating 2-way). Channels available but not in use: N.A.

Basic Service

Subscribers: 25,056.

Programming (received off-air): WABC-TV (ABC) New York; WCBS-TV (CBS) New York; WFME-TV (ETV) West Milford; WFUT-DT (TEL) Newark; WMBC-TV (IND) Newton; WNBC (NBC) New York; WNET (PBS) Newark; WNJN (PBS) Montclair; WNJU (TMO) Linden; WNYW (FOX) New York; WPIX (CW, IND) New York; WPXN-TV (ION) New York; WRNN-TV (IND) Kingston; WTBY-TV (TBN) Poughkeepsie; WWOR-TV (MNT) Secaucus; WXTV-DT (UNV) Paterson.

Programming (via satellite): News 12 New Jersey; QVC; ShopNBC.

Fee: $49.95 installation; $13.96 monthly; $3.00 converter.

Expanded Basic Service 1

Subscribers: 19,903.

Programming (via microwave): News 12 Traffic & Weather.

Programming (via satellite): A&E Networks; ABC Family Channel; AMC; Animal Planet; BET Networks; Bravo; Cartoon Network; CNBC; CNN; Comedy Central; C-SPAN; C-SPAN 2; Discovery Channel; Disney Channel; E! Entertainment Television; ESPN; ESPN 2; Food Network; Fox News Channel; Fuse; FX; GSN; Headline News; HGTV; History Channel; Independent Film Channel; Lifetime; MSG; MSG Plus; MSNBC; MTV; MTV2; Nickelodeon; SoapNet; Speed; Spike TV; SportsNet New York; Syfy; TBS Superstation; The Learning Channel; The Weather Channel; Travel Channel; truTV; Turner Classic Movies; Turner Network TV; TV Land; USA Network; VH1; WE tv; Yankees Entertainment & Sports.

Fee: $35.99 monthly.

Digital Basic Service

Subscribers: N.A.

Programming (via satellite): BBC World News; Bio; Bloomberg Television; Canal

Sur; Cartoon Network Tambien en Espanol; Cine Latino; CNN en Espanol; CNN HD; Country Music TV; C-SPAN 3; Discovery en Espanol; Discovery Kids Channel; Docu TVE; ESPN 2 HD; ESPN Classic Sports; ESPN Deportes; ESPN HD; ESPNews; EuroNews; EWTN en Espanol; Food Network HD; Fox College Sports Atlantic; Fox College Sports Central; Fox College Sports Pacific; Fox Deportes; Fox Movie Channel; Fox Soccer; FSN HD; Fuel TV; G4; GameHD; Golf Channel; GolTV; Great American Country; Hallmark Channel; HD Theater; HGTV HD; History Channel en Espanol; History Channel International; Howard TV; ID Investigation Discovery; Infinito; Jewelry Television; La Familia Network; Latele Novela Network; LOGO; Mariavision; Military Channel; Momentum TV; MTV Hits; mun2 television; Music Choice; National Geographic Channel; National Geographic Channel HD Network; NBA TV; NHL Network; Nick Jr.; NickToons TV; Outdoor Channel; Oxygen; Planet Green; Science; ShopNBC; Sorpresa; Sundance Channel; Supercanal Caribe; TBS in HD; TeenNick; Telefe International; Toon Disney; Toon Disney en Espanol; Tr3s; Turner Network TV HD; TV Chile; TV Colombia; TVE Internacional; TVG Network; Universal HD; Utilisima; Versus; Versus HD; VH1 Classic; VH1 Soul; V-me TV; World Cinema HD; YES HD.
Fee: $9.95 monthly; $2.95 converter.

Pay Service 1
Pay Units: N.A.
Programming (via satellite): Cinemax; Flix; HBO (multiplexed); Showtime (multiplexed); The Movie Channel.

Digital Pay Service 1
Pay Units: 1,100.
Programming (via satellite): Cinemax (multiplexed); Cinemax HD.
Fee: $10.00 installation; $9.95 monthly.

Digital Pay Service 2
Pay Units: N.A.
Programming (via satellite): The Movie Channel (multiplexed); The Movie Channel HD.
Fee: $9.95 monthly.

Digital Pay Service 3
Pay Units: 5.
Programming (via satellite): Encore (multiplexed); Starz (multiplexed); Starz HDTV.
Fee: $7.95 monthly.

Digital Pay Service 4
Pay Units: 8,466.
Programming (via satellite): HBO (multiplexed); HBO HD.
Fee: $11.95 monthly.

Digital Pay Service 5
Pay Units: 2,640.
Programming (via satellite): Showtime (multiplexed); Showtime HD.
Fee: $9.95 monthly.

Digital Pay Service 6
Pay Units: N.A.
Programming (via satellite): Azteca America; Caracol TV; CCTV-4; Ecuavisia Internacional; Korean Channel; MBC America; Portuguese Channel; RAI International; Russian Television Network; TV Asia; TV Japan; TV Polonia; TV5, La Television International; VeneMovies; WAPA America; Zee TV USA.
Fee: $9.95 monthly (RAI, SPT, TV5 or TV Polonia), $24.95 monthly (TV Japan).

Video-On-Demand: Yes

Pay-Per-View
iN DEMAND (delivered digitally); Playboy TV (delivered digitally); Club Jenna (delivered digitally).

Internet Service
Operational: Yes.
Broadband Service: Optimum Online.
Fee: $46.95 installation; $34.95 monthly; $299.00 modem purchase.

Telephone Service
Digital: Operational
Fee: $34.95 monthly

Miles of Plant: 544.0 (coaxial); 217.0 (fiber optic). Additional miles planned: 7.0 (coaxial).
Vice President, Field Operations: Frank Dagliere. Operations Manager: Laura Cavazzi.
Ownership: Cablevision Systems Corp. (MSO).

WASHINGTONVILLE—Time Warner Cable. Now served by HUDSON VALLEY (formerly Middletown), NY [NY0231]. ICA: NY0258.

WATERTOWN—Time Warner Cable, 6005 Fair Lakes Rd, East Syracuse, NY 13057. Phone: 315-634-6100. Fax: 315-634-6219. Web Site: http://www.timewarnercable.com/CentralNY. Also serves Adams (village), Adams Center, Alexandria (town), Antwerp (village), Belleville, Black River (village), Brownville (village), Cape Vincent (village), Carthage, Castorland, Champion, Chaumont, Clayton, Copenhagen, Croghan (village), Deferiet, Denmark (town), Dexter (village), Diana (town), East Carthage, Ellisburg, Evans Mills (village), Fort Drum, Glen Park (village), Glenfield, Greig, Henderson (town), Herrings, Hounsfield (town), Indian River, Le Ray (town), Lowville, Lyme (town), Mannsville, Martinsburg, New Bremen, Orleans, Pamelia (town), Philadelphia (village), Pierrepont Manor, Pitcairn (town), Rodman (town), Rutland (town), Sackets Harbor (village), Theresa (village), Watson, Wellesley Island, West Carthage & Wilna. ICA: NY0206.
TV Market Ranking: Below 100 (Adams (village), Adams Center, Alexandria (town), Antwerp (village), Belleville, Black River (village), Brownville (village), Cape Vincent (village), Carthage, Castorland, Champion, Chaumont, Clayton, Copenhagen, Croghan (village), Deferiet, Denmark (town), Dexter (village), Diana (town), East Carthage, Ellisburg, Evans Mills (village), Fort Drum, Glen Park (village), Glenfield, Greig, Henderson (town), Herrings, Hounsfield (town), Hounsfield (town), Indian River, Le Ray (town), Lowville, Lyme (town), Mannsville, Martinsburg, New Bremen, Orleans, Pamelia (town), Philadelphia (village), Pierrepont Manor, Pitcairn (town), Rodman (town), Rutland (town), Sackets Harbor (village), Theresa (village), WATERTOWN, Watson, Wellesley Island, West Carthage, Wilna). Franchise award date: January 1, 1961. Franchise expiration date: N.A. Began: January 1, 1962.
Channel capacity: N.A. Channels available but not in use: N.A.

Basic Service
Subscribers: N.A. Included in Syracuse
Programming (received off-air): WNYF-CA Watertown; WPBS-DT (PBS) Watertown; WWNY-TV (CBS) Carthage; WWTI (ABC, CW) Watertown; allband FM.
Programming (via microwave): WSTM-TV (NBC) Syracuse.
Programming (via satellite): CW+; TBS Superstation; various Canadian stations; WGN America.
Fee: $99.00 installation; $8.29 monthly; $2.00 converter.

Expanded Basic Service 1
Subscribers: N.A. Included in Syracuse
Programming (via satellite): A&E Networks; ABC Family Channel; Animal Planet; BET Networks; Cartoon Network; CNBC; CNN; Comedy Central; C-SPAN; C-SPAN 2; Discovery Channel; Discovery Fit & Health; E! Entertainment Television; ESPN; ESPN 2; Eternal Word TV Network; Food Network; Fox News Channel; FX; Hallmark Channel; Headline News; HGTV; ION Television; Jewelry Television; Lifetime Movie Network; MSG Plus; MSNBC; Nickelodeon; Oxygen; QVC; ShopNBC; SoapNet; Spike TV; Syfy; The Learning Channel; The Weather Channel; Travel Channel; TV Land; Univision Studios; USA Network; Versus; VH1; WE tv; Yankees Entertainment & Sports.
Fee: $34.67 monthly.

Digital Basic Service
Subscribers: N.A. Included in Syracuse
Programming (via satellite): America's Store; BBC America; Bio; Bloomberg Television; Boomerang; Bravo; Cooking Channel; Country Music TV; C-SPAN 3; Discovery Digital Networks; Disney Channel; DIY Network; Encore Action; ESPN Classic Sports; ESPNews; Fox Movie Channel; Fox Sports World; Fuse; G4; GAS; Golf Channel; Great American Country; GSN; History Channel; History Channel International; Independent Film Channel; Lifetime; Lifetime Real Women; Local Cable Weather; MSG; MTV; MTV2; National Geographic Channel; Nick Jr.; Nick Too; Outdoor Channel; Ovation; Speed; Style Network; Toon Disney; Trinity Broadcasting Network; truTV; Turner Classic Movies; Turner Network TV; VH1 Classic; WAM! America's Kidz Network.
Fee: $10.95 monthly.

Digital Expanded Basic Service
Subscribers: N.A.
Programming (via satellite): FSN Digital Atlantic; FSN Digital Central; FSN Digital Pacific; Fuel TV; NBA TV; Tennis Channel.
Fee: $4.95 monthly.

Digital Pay Service 1
Pay Units: 8,048.
Programming (via satellite): ART America; Canales N; CCTV-4; Cinemax (multiplexed); HBO (multiplexed); RAI International; Russian Television Network; Saigon Broadcasting Television Network; Showtime (multiplexed); Starz (multiplexed); The Movie Channel (multiplexed); TV Asia; TV5, La Television International.
Fee: $9.95 monthly (ART, Canales N, CCTV-4, RAI, RTN, SBN or TV 5), $10.95 monthly (Cinemax, HBO, Showtime, Starz or TMC), $14.95 monthly (TV Asia or Zee TV).

Video-On-Demand: Yes

Pay-Per-View
Addressable homes: 9,390.
iN DEMAND (delivered digitally); Fresh (delivered digitally); Playboy TV (delivered digitally).

Internet Service
Operational: Yes. Began: June 1, 1998.
Broadband Service: EarthLink, LocalNet, Road Runner.
Fee: $39.95 installation; $44.95 monthly.

Telephone Service
Digital: Operational
Fee: $39.95 monthly

Miles of plant (coax & fiber) included in Syracuse
President: Mary Cotter. Vice President, Engineering: Henry Hryckiewicz. Vice President, Marketing: John Melvany. Vice President, Public Affairs: Jeff Unaitis. Technical Operations Director: Bruce Tompkins.
Ownership: Time Warner Cable (MSO).; Advance/Newhouse Partnership (MSO).

WATERTOWN—Time Warner Cable. Now served by CARTHAGE, NY [NY0206]. ICA: NY0040.

WELLESLEY ISLAND—Time Warner Cable. Now served by CARTHAGE, NY [NY0206]. ICA: NY0281.

WELLS—Hamilton County Cable TV Inc., 1330 State Rt 30, Wells, NY 12190. Phones: 800-562-1560; 518-924-2013. Fax: 518-924-3410. Web Site: http://www.hcctelevision.com. Also serves Lake Pleasant & Speculator. ICA: NY0260.
TV Market Ranking: Below 100 (WELLS); Outside TV Markets (Lake Pleasant, Speculator). Franchise award date: November 1, 1984. Franchise expiration date: N.A. Began: July 1, 1985.
Channel capacity: N.A. Channels available but not in use: N.A.

Basic Service
Subscribers: 510.
Programming (received off-air): WMHT (PBS) Schenectady; WNYT (NBC) Albany; WRGB (CBS) Schenectady; WTEN (ABC) Albany; WXXA-TV (FOX) Albany.
Programming (via satellite): A&E Networks; ABC Family Channel; AMC; Animal Planet; CNN; C-SPAN; Discovery Channel; ESPN; History Channel; Lifetime; QVC; Spike TV; TBS Superstation; Turner Network TV; USA Network; WGN America.
Fee: $49.95 installation; $33.68 monthly.

Digital Basic Service
Subscribers: 70.
Fee: $46.36 monthly.

Pay Service 1
Pay Units: 80.
Programming (via satellite): HBO.
Fee: $10.00 monthly.

Pay Service 2
Pay Units: 45.
Programming (via satellite): Cinemax.
Fee: $9.00 monthly.

Video-On-Demand: No

Internet Service
Operational: No.

Telephone Service
None

Miles of Plant: 27.0 (coaxial); None (fiber optic).

Manager & Chief Technician: Brian Towers. Office Manager: Maggie Welch.
Ownership: Hamilton County/Gore Mountain Cable TV Inc. (MSO).

WELLSVILLE—Now served by OLEAN, NY [NY0056]. ICA: NY0086.

WESTFIELD—Time Warner Cable, 355 Chicago St, Buffalo, NY 14204-2069. Phone: 716-558-8881. Fax: 716-558-8855. Web Site: http://www.timewarnercable.com/wny. ICA: NY0286.
TV Market Ranking: 24 (WESTFIELD).
Channel capacity: N.A. Channels available but not in use: N.A.
Basic Service
Subscribers: N.A. Included in Lackawanna
Programming (received off-air): WFXP (FOX) Erie; WGRZ (NBC) Buffalo; WICU-TV (NBC) Erie; WIVB-TV (CBS) Buffalo; WKBW-TV (ABC) Buffalo; WNED-TV (PBS) Buffalo; WNYB (IND) Jamestown; WPXJ-TV (ION) Batavia; WQLN (PBS) Erie; WSEE-TV (CBS, CW) Erie; WUTV (FOX) Buffalo.
Programming (via satellite): C-SPAN; C-SPAN 2; CW+; QVC; The Weather Channel; TV Guide Network.
Expanded Basic Service 1
Subscribers: N.A.
Programming (via satellite): A&E Networks; ABC Family Channel; AMC; Animal Planet; BET Networks; Bravo; Cartoon Network; CNBC; CNN; Comedy Central; Country Music TV; Discovery Channel; Disney Channel; E! Entertainment Television; ESPN; ESPN 2; Eternal Word TV Network; Food Network; Fox News Channel; Fox Sports Net Ohio; FX; Hallmark Channel; Headline News; HGTV; History Television; Lifetime; MSG; MSNBC; MTV; Nickelodeon; Oxygen; ShopNBC; Spike TV; Style Network; Syfy; TBS Superstation; The Learning Channel; The Weather Channel; Travel Channel; truTV; Turner Network TV; TV Land; USA Network; VH1.
Digital Basic Service
Subscribers: N.A.
Programming (via satellite): American-Life TV Network; BBC America; Bio; Black Family Channel; Bloomberg Television; Boomerang; Canales N; CBS Sports Network; CMT Pure Country; Cooking Channel; Current; Daystar TV Network; Discovery Digital Networks; DIY Network; ESPN Classic Sports; ESPN Deportes; ESPNews; Familyland Television Network; Fox College Sports Atlantic; Fox College Sports Central; Fox College Sports Pacific; Fox Movie Channel; Fox Reality Channel; Fox Soccer; Fuel TV; Fuse; G4; GAS; Golf Channel; Great American Country; GSN; Halogen Network; History Channel International; Independent Film Channel; Lifetime Movie Network; LOGO; MTV Networks Digital Suite; Music Choice (multiplexed); National Geographic Channel; NBA TV; Nick Jr.; Nick Too; NickToons TV; Outdoor Channel; ReelzChannel; SoapNet; Speed; Sundance Channel; Tennis Channel; The Word Network; Toon Disney; Trinity Broadcasting Network; TV One.
Fee: $57.95 monthly.
Digital Pay Service 1
Pay Units: N.A.
Programming (via satellite): Cinemax; Encore (multiplexed); Flix; HBO (multiplexed); Showtime (multiplexed); Starz (multiplexed); The Movie Channel (multiplexed).
Fee: $11.95 monthly (each).
Video-On-Demand: Yes
Internet Service
Operational: Yes.
Broadband Service: Road Runner.
Fee: $44.95 monthly.
Telephone Service
Digital: Operational
Fee: $39.95 monthly
President: Gordon Harp. Vice President, Marketing: Steve Jaworowski. Vice President, Public Affairs: Robin Wolfgang. Technical Operations Manager: Steve Pawlik. Marketing Manager: Jean Calabrese.
Ownership: Time Warner Cable (MSO).

WHITEHALL (town)—Time Warner Cable. Now served by ALBANY, NY [NY0014]. ICA: NY0134.

WHITESVILLE—Fitzpatrick Cable TV, PO Box 35, Whitesville, NY 14897-0035. Phone: 607-356-3117. Also serves Independence. ICA: NY0191.
TV Market Ranking: Outside TV Markets (Independence, WHITESVILLE). Franchise award date: N.A. Franchise expiration date: N.A. Began: January 1, 1956.
Channel capacity: 12 (not 2-way capable). Channels available but not in use: N.A.
Basic Service
Subscribers: 150.
Programming (received off-air): WENY-TV (ABC, CW) Elmira; WGRZ (NBC) Buffalo; WIVB-TV (CBS) Buffalo; WKBW-TV (ABC) Buffalo; WSTM-TV (NBC) Syracuse; 15 FMs.
Programming (via satellite): ESPN; TBS Superstation; Turner Network TV; WGN America.
Fee: $40.00 installation; $10.00 monthly.
Video-On-Demand: No
Internet Service
Operational: No.
Telephone Service
None
Miles of Plant: 3.0 (coaxial); None (fiber optic).
Manager: James W. Fitzpatrick.
Ownership: James W. Fitzpatrick.

WHITNEY POINT (village)—Time Warner Cable. Now served by BINGHAMTON, NY [NY0016]. ICA: NY0135.

WILLSBORO (town)—Cable Communications of Willsboro, 3669 Essex Rd, PO Box 625, Willsboro, NY 12996. Phone: 518-963-4116. Fax: 518-963-7405. E-mail: herb@willex.com. Also serves Essex, Essex (town), Willsboro, Willsboro Bay & Willsboro Point. ICA: NY0162.
TV Market Ranking: Below 100 (Essex, Essex (town), Willsboro, WILLSBORO (TOWN), Willsboro Bay, Willsboro Point). Franchise award date: July 27, 1987. Franchise expiration date: N.A. Began: July 5, 1988.
Channel capacity: 60 (operating 2-way). Channels available but not in use: N.A.
Basic Service
Subscribers: 453.
Programming (received off-air): various Canadian stations; WCAX-TV (CBS) Burlington; WCFE-TV (PBS) Plattsburgh; WETK (PBS) Burlington; WFFF-TV (CW, FOX) Burlington; WPTZ (NBC) Plattsburgh; WVNY (ABC) Burlington; WWOR-TV (MNT) Secaucus.
Programming (via satellite): Cartoon Network; Comedy Central; Country Music TV; ESPN 2; FX; WGN America.
Fee: $33.90 monthly.
Expanded Basic Service 1
Subscribers: N.A.
Programming (received off-air): various Canadian stations.
Programming (via satellite): A&E Networks; AMC; Animal Planet; Bravo; CNBC; CNN; Discovery Channel; Disney Channel; ESPN; Food Network; Fox News Channel; Hallmark Channel; HGTV; History Channel; Lifetime; MTV; National Geographic Channel; Nickelodeon; QVC; Spike TV; Syfy; TBS Superstation; The Learning Channel; The Weather Channel; Turner Classic Movies; Turner Network TV; TV Land; USA Network; WPIX (CW, IND) New York.
Digital Basic Service
Subscribers: N.A.
Programming (via satellite): BBC America; Bio; Bloomberg Television; Country Music TV; Discovery Digital Networks; DMX Music; E! Entertainment Television; ESPN Classic Sports; ESPNews; Fox Movie Channel; Fox Sports World; G4; GAS; Golf Channel; GSN; History Channel International; Independent Film Channel; Lifetime Movie Network; Lime; MTV Networks Digital Suite; Nick Jr.; NickToons TV; Outdoor Channel; Ovation; Speed; Toon Disney; Versus; WE tv.
Pay Service 1
Pay Units: 59.
Programming (via satellite): HBO.
Fee: $9.95 monthly.
Pay Service 2
Pay Units: 103.
Programming (via satellite): Cinemax.
Fee: $8.95 monthly.
Digital Pay Service 1
Pay Units: N.A.
Programming (via satellite): Cinemax (multiplexed); Encore (multiplexed); Flix; HBO (multiplexed); Showtime (multiplexed); Starz (multiplexed); Sundance Channel; The Movie Channel (multiplexed).
Internet Service
Operational: Yes.
Subscribers: 110.
Broadband Service: In-house.
Fee: $49.95 installation; $39.95 monthly; $5.00 modem lease.
Miles of Plant: 32.0 (coaxial); None (fiber optic).
Manager & Chief Technician: Herb Longware.
Ownership: Cable Communications of Willsboro Inc.

WINDSOR (town)—Formerly served by Adams Cable. Now served by CARBONDALE, PA [PA0067]. ICA: NY0100.
Video-On-Demand: No

WOODBURY—Cablevision Systems Corp., 1111 Stewart Ave, Bethpage, NY 11714. Phone: 516-803-2300. Fax: 516-803-1183. Web Site: http://www.cablevision.com. Also serves Albertson, Amityville, Asharoken, Atlantic Beach, Babylon, Babylon (village), Baldwin, Baxter Estates, Bay Shore, Bayville, Bellerose (Nassau County), Bellmore, Bethpage, Brookville (village), Cedarhurst, Centerport, Centre Island, Cold Spring Harbor, Copiague, Cove Neck, Deer Park, Dix Hills, East Hills, East Northport, East Rockaway, East Williston, Elmont, Elwood, Farmingdale, Floral Park, Flower Hill, Franklin Square, Freeport, Garden City, Glen Cove, Great Neck, Great Neck Estates, Great Neck Plaza (village), Greenlawn, Halesite, Hempstead (village), Herricks, Hewlett Bay Park, Hewlett Harbor, Hewlett Neck, Hicksville, Huntington, Huntington Bay, Huntington Station, Inwood, Island Park, Islip, Islip Twp., Jericho, Kensington (village), Kings Point, Lake Success (village), Lattingtown, Laurel Hollow, Lawrence, Levittown, Lindenhurst, Lloyd Harbor, Locust Valley, Long Beach, Lynbrook, Malverne, Manhasset, Manorhaven, Massapequa, Massapequa Park, Matinecock, Melville, Merrick, Mill Neck, Mineola, Munsey Park (village), Muttontown, New Hyde Park, North Hempstead, North Hills (village), North Woodmere, Northport, Oceanside, Old Bethpage, Old Brookville, Old Westbury, Oyster Bay, Oyster Bay Cove, Plainedge, Plainview, Plandome (village), Plandome Heights (village), Plandome Manor, Port Washington, Rockville Centre, Roosevelt, Roslyn, Roslyn Estates, Roslyn Harbor (village), Russell Gardens (village), Saddle Rock (village), Sands Point, Sea Cliff, Seaford, South Floral Park, Stewart Manor, Syosset, Thomaston (village), Uniondale, Upper Brookville, Valley Stream, Wantagh, Westbury, Wheatley Heights, Williston Park, Woodmere, Woodsburgh & Wyandanch. ICA: NY0001.
TV Market Ranking: 1 (Albertson, Amityville, Asharoken, Atlantic Beach, Babylon, Babylon (village), Baldwin, Baxter Estates, Bayville, Bellerose (Nassau County), Bellmore, Bethpage, Brookville (village), Cedarhurst, Centerport, Cold Spring Harbor, Copiague, Cove Neck, Deer Park, Dix Hills, East Hills, East Rockaway, East Williston, Elmont, Elwood, Farmingdale, Floral Park, Flower Hill, Franklin Square, Freeport, Garden City, Glen Cove, Great Neck, Great Neck Estates, Great Neck Plaza (village), Greenlawn, Halesite, Hempstead (village), Herricks, Hewlett Bay Park, Hewlett Harbor, Hewlett Neck, Hicksville, Huntington, Huntington, Huntington Station, Inwood, Island Park, Jericho, Kensington (village), Kings Point, Lake Success (village), Lattingtown, Laurel Hollow, Lawrence, Levittown, Lindenhurst, Lloyd Harbor, Locust Valley, Long Beach, Lynbrook, Malverne, Manhasset, Manorhaven, Massapequa, Massapequa Park, Matinecock, Melville, Merrick, Mill Neck, Mineola, Munsey Park (village), Muttontown, New Hyde Park, North Hempstead, North Hills (village), North Woodmere, Oceanside, Old Bethpage, Old Brookville, Old Westbury, Oyster Bay, Oyster Bay Cove, Plainedge, Plandome (village), Plandome Heights (village), Plandome Manor, Port Washington, Rockville Centre, Roosevelt, Roslyn, ROSLYN, Roslyn Estates, Russell Gardens (village), Saddle Rock (village), Sands Point, Sea Cliff, Seaford, South Floral Park, Stewart Manor, Syosset, Thomaston (village), Uniondale, Upper Brookville, Valley Stream, Wantagh, Westbury, Wheatley Heights, Williston Park, WOODBURY (portions), Woodmere, Woodsburgh, Wyandanch); Below 100 (Bay Shore, East Northport, Islip Twp., Northport, Plainview); Outside TV Markets (Centre Island). Franchise award date: N.A. Franchise expiration date: N.A. Began: November 1, 1973.
Channel capacity: N.A. Channels available but not in use: N.A.
Basic Service
Subscribers: 480,698.
Programming (received off-air): WABC-TV (ABC) New York; WCBS-TV (CBS) New York; WFTY-DT (TEL) Smithtown; WLIW (PBS) Garden City; WLNY-TV (IND) Riverhead; WNBC (NBC) New York; WNET (PBS) Newark; WNJU (TMO) Linden; WNYW (FOX) New York; WPIX (CW, IND) New York; WPXN-TV (ION) New York; WWOR-TV (MNT) Secaucus; WXTV-DT (UNV) Paterson.

Programming (via satellite): News 12 Long Island; QVC; ShopNBC.
Fee: $49.95 installation; $15.42 monthly.

Expanded Basic Service 1
Subscribers: 117,152.
Programming (via satellite): A&E Networks; ABC Family Channel; AMC; Animal Planet; BET Networks; Bravo; Cartoon Network; CNBC; CNN; Comedy Central; C-SPAN; C-SPAN 2; Discovery Channel; Disney Channel; E! Entertainment Television; ESPN; ESPN 2; Food Network; Fox News Channel; Fuse; FX; GalaVision; GSN; Headline News; HGTV; History Channel; Independent Film Channel; Jewelry Television; Lifetime; MSG; MSG Plus; MSNBC; MTV; MTV2; News 12 Traffic & Weather; Nickelodeon; RAI USA; SoapNet; Speed; Spike TV; SportsNet New York; Syfy; TBS Superstation; Telecare; The Learning Channel; The Weather Channel; Travel Channel; truTV; Turner Classic Movies; Turner Network TV; TV Land; USA Network; VH1; WE tv; Yankees Entertainment & Sports.
Fee: $34.53 monthly.

Digital Basic Service
Subscribers: N.A.
Programming (via satellite): Animal Planet HD; Azteca America; BBC World News; Bio; Bloomberg Television; Canal Sur; Caracol TV; Cartoon Network Tambien en Espanol; CBS Sports Network; CCTV-4; Channel One; Cine Latino; CMT HD; CNN en Espanol; CNN HD; Country Music TV; C-SPAN 3; Discovery Channel HD; Discovery en Espanol; Discovery Kids Channel; Docu TVE; Ecuavisia Internacional; ESPN 2 HD; ESPN Classic Sports; ESPN Deportes; ESPN HD; ESPNews; EuroNews; EWTN en Espanol; Filipino Channel; Food Network HD; Fox College Sports Atlantic; Fox College Sports Central; Fox College Sports Pacific; Fox Deportes; Fox Movie Channel; Fox News HD; Fox Soccer; Fuel TV; FX HD; G4; GMA Pinoy TV; Golf Channel; GolTV; Great American Country; Hallmark Channel; Hallmark Movie Channel; Hallmark Movie Channel HD; HD Theater; here! On Demand; HGTV HD; History Channel en Espanol; History Channel International; Howard TV; HTV Musica; ID Investigation Discovery; Infinito; Jewelry Television; Korean Channel; La Familia Network; Latele Novela Network; LATV Networks; LOGO; Mariavision; MBC America; Military Channel; MKTV; Mojo Mix; Momentum TV; MTV Hits; MTV Networks HD; mun2 television; Music Choice; National Geographic Channel; National Geographic Channel HD Network; NBA TV; NHL Network; Nick HD; Nick Jr.; NickToons TV; NTV America; Outdoor Channel; Oxygen; Planet Green; RAI USA; Russian Television Network; Science; Science HD; Society of Portuguese Television; Sorpresa; Speed HD; Spike TV HD; Sundance Channel; Supercanal Caribe; TBS in HD; TeenNick; Telefe International; Telemicro Internacional; The Jewish Channel; The Weather Channel HD; TLC HD; Toon Disney; Toon Disney en Espanol; Tr3s; Travel Channel HD; Turner Network TV HD; TV Asia; TV Chile; TV Colombia; TV Japan; TV Polonia; TV5 USA; TVE Internacional; TVG Network; Universal HD; Utilisima; VeneMovies; Versus; Versus HD; VH1 Classic; VH1 HD; VH1 Soul; V-me TV; WAPA America; YES HD; Zee TV USA.
Fee: $10.95 monthly.

Pay Service 1
Pay Units: N.A.
Programming (via satellite): Cinemax; Flix; HBO (multiplexed); Showtime (multiplexed); The Movie Channel.

Digital Pay Service 1
Pay Units: N.A.
Programming (via satellite): Cinemax (multiplexed); Cinemax HD; Cinemax On Demand; Encore; HBO (multiplexed); HBO HD; HBO On Demand; Playboy TV; Showtime (multiplexed); Showtime HD; Showtime On Demand; Starz HDTV; Starz On Demand; The Movie Channel (multiplexed); The Movie Channel HD.
Fee: $9.95 monthly (Starz/Encore, Showtime/TMC, Cinemax or Playboy), $11.95 monthly (HBO).

Video-On-Demand: Yes

Internet Service
Operational: Yes.
Broadband Service: Optimum Online.
Fee: $46.95 installation; $34.95 monthly; $299.00 modem purchase.

Telephone Service
Digital: Operational
Fee: $34.95 monthly

Miles of Plant: 5,636.0 (coaxial); 150.0 (fiber optic).
Senior Vice President, Field Operations: Christopher Coffey. Senior Vice President, Media Relations: Charles Schueler. Corporate Communications Manager: Kristen Blank.
Ownership: Cablevision Systems Corp. (MSO).

WOODHULL—Time Warner Cable. Now served by HORNELL, NY [NY0076]. ICA: NY0262.

WOODRIDGE (village)—Time Warner Cable. Now served by HUDSON VALLEY (formerly Middletown), NY [NY0231]. ICA: NY0153.

WOODSIDE—RCN Corp. Formerly served by Queens, NY [NY0283]. This cable system has converted to IPTV, 196 Van Buren St, Herndon, VA 20170. Phone: 703-434-8200. Web Site: http://www.rcn.com. ICA: NY5320.
TV Market Ranking: 1 (WOODSIDE).
Channel capacity: N.A. Channels available but not in use: N.A.

Pay Service 1
Pay Units: N.A.
Fee: $11.95 monthly (Cinemaz or Starz!); $16.95 monthly (Showtime/The Movie Channel); $17.95 monthly (HBO).

Internet Service
Operational: Yes.
Fee: $38.00 monthly.

Telephone Service
Digital: Operational
Fee: $45.00 monthly

Chairman: Steven J. Simmons. Chief Executive Officer: Jim Holanda.

WOODSTOCK (town)—Time Warner Cable. Now served by HUDSON VALLEY (formerly Middletown), NY [NY0231]. ICA: NY0098.

YONKERS—Cablevision Systems Corp., 1 Van Cortland Ave, Ossining, NY 10562-3309. Phone: 516-803-2300 (Corporate office). Fax: 516-803-1183. Web Site: http://www.cablevision.com. ICA: NY0019.
TV Market Ranking: 1 (YONKERS). Franchise award date: December 16, 1976. Franchise expiration date: N.A. Began: October 1, 1977.
Channel capacity: 90 (operating 2-way). Channels available but not in use: N.A.

Basic Service
Subscribers: 53,601.
Programming (received off-air): WABC-TV (ABC) New York; WCBS-TV (CBS) New York; WFUT-DT (TEL) Newark; WLIW (PBS) Garden City; WLNY-TV (IND) Riverhead; WMBC-TV (IND) Newton; WNBC (NBC) New York; WNET (PBS) Newark; WNJU (TMO) Linden; WNYW (FOX) New York; WPIX (CW, IND) New York; WPXN-TV (ION) New York; WRNN-TV (IND) Kingston; WWOR-TV (MNT) Secaucus; WXTV-DT (UNV) Paterson.
Programming (via satellite): News 12 Westchester; TV Guide Network.
Fee: $49.95 installation; $17.80 monthly.

Expanded Basic Service 1
Subscribers: N.A.
Programming (via satellite): A&E Networks; ABC Family Channel; AMC; Animal Planet; BET Networks; Bravo; Cartoon Network; CNBC; CNN; Comedy Central; Country Music TV; C-SPAN; C-SPAN 2; Discovery Channel; Discovery Fit & Health; Disney Channel; E! Entertainment Television; ESPN; ESPN 2; Food Network; Fox News Channel; Fuse; FX; GalaVision; GSN; Headline News; HGTV; History Channel; Lifetime; MSNBC; MTV; MTV2; mun2 television; News 12 Traffic & Weather; Nickelodeon; QVC; SoapNet; Speed; Spike TV; Syfy; TBS Superstation; The Learning Channel; The Weather Channel; Travel Channel; truTV; Turner Network TV; TV Land; USA Network; VH1; WE tv.
Fee: $32.15 monthly.

Digital Basic Service
Subscribers: N.A.
Programming (via satellite): Bio; Bloomberg Television; Country Music TV; C-SPAN 3; Discovery Digital Networks; ESPN Classic Sports; ESPNews; EuroNews; Fox Deportes; Fox Movie Channel; Fox Soccer; G4; Hallmark Channel; History Channel International; Mag Rack; MSG; MSG Plus; mun2 television; Music Choice; National Geographic Channel; NBA TV; Nick Jr.; Oxygen; Science Television; TeenNick; Toon Disney; VH1 Classic.
Fee: $10.95 monthly.

Pay Service 1
Pay Units: N.A.
Programming (via satellite): Cinemax; Encore; Flix; HBO (multiplexed); Independent Film Channel; MSG; MSG Plus; Showtime; Starz; The Movie Channel; Turner Classic Movies; Yankees Entertainment & Sports.

Digital Pay Service 1
Pay Units: N.A.
Programming (via satellite): Cinemax (multiplexed); Encore (multiplexed); HBO (multiplexed); Showtime (multiplexed); Starz (multiplexed); The Movie Channel (multiplexed).
Fee: $9.95 monthly (Cinemax, Showtime, TMC or Starz & Encore), $11.95 monthly (HBO).

Video-On-Demand: Yes

Pay-Per-View
Playboy TV (delivered digitally); iN DEMAND (delivered digitally); NBA TV (delivered digitally); Sports PPV (delivered digitally); Playboy TV; iN DEMAND.

Internet Service
Operational: Yes.
Broadband Service: Optimum Online.
Fee: $46.95 installation; $34.95 monthly; $299.00 modem purchase.

Telephone Service
Digital: Operational
Fee: $34.95 monthly

Miles of Plant: 300.0 (coaxial); 23.0 (fiber optic). Additional miles planned: 40.0 (fiber optic).
Vice President, Field Operations: Mark Fitchett.
Ownership: Cablevision Systems Corp. (MSO).

YORKTOWN—Cablevision Systems Corp., 1 Van Cortland Ave, Ossining, NY 10562-3309. Phones: 516-803-2300 (Corporate office); 914-768-8684. Fax: 516-803-1183. Web Site: http://www.cablevision.com. Also serves Cross River, Lewisboro, North Salem, Pound Ridge, Putnam Valley & Somers. ICA: NY0050.
TV Market Ranking: 1 (Putnam Valley, YORKTOWN); 19 (Lewisboro, North Salem, Pound Ridge, Somers); Below 100 (Cross River). Franchise award date: September 17, 1980. Franchise expiration date: N.A. Began: January 1, 1981.
Channel capacity: N.A. Channels available but not in use: N.A.

Basic Service
Subscribers: 33,436.
Programming (received off-air): WABC-TV (ABC) New York; WCBS-TV (CBS) New York; WFUT-DT (TEL) Newark; WLIW (PBS) Garden City; WNBC (NBC) New York; WNET (PBS) Newark; WNJU (TMO) Linden; WNYW (FOX) New York; WPIX (CW, IND) New York; WPXN-TV (ION) New York; WRNN-TV (IND) Kingston; WSAH (IND) Bridgeport; WTBY-TV (TBN) Poughkeepsie; WWOR-TV (MNT) Secaucus; WXTV-DT (UNV) Paterson.
Programming (via satellite): News 12 Westchester.
Fee: $49.95 installation; $18.00 monthly; $2.08 converter.

Expanded Basic Service 1
Subscribers: N.A.
Programming (via satellite): A&E Networks; ABC Family Channel; AMC; Animal Planet; BET Networks; Bravo; Cartoon Network; CNBC; CNN; Comedy Central; C-SPAN; C-SPAN 2; Discovery Channel; Disney Channel; E! Entertainment Television; ESPN; ESPN 2; Food Network; Fox News Channel; Fuse; FX; GSN; Headline News; HGTV; History Channel; Independent Film Channel; Lifetime; MSG; MSG Plus; MSNBC; MTV; MTV2; News 12 Traffic & Weather; Nickelodeon; QVC; ShopNBC; SoapNet; Speed; Spike TV; SportsNet New York; Syfy; TBS Superstation; The Learning Channel; The Weather Channel; Travel Channel; truTV; Turner Classic Movies; Turner Network TV; TV Land; USA Network; VH1; WE tv; Yankees Entertainment & Sports.
Fee: $21.95 monthly.

Digital Basic Service
Subscribers: N.A.
Programming (via satellite): Animal Planet HD; Azteca America; BBC World News; Bio; Bloomberg Television; Bravo HD; Canal Sur; Caracol TV; Cartoon Network Tambien en Espanol; CBS Sports Network; Chiller; Cine Latino; cloo; CMT HD; CNBC HD+; CNN en Espanol; CNN HD; Country Music TV; C-SPAN 3; Discovery Channel HD; Discovery en Espanol; Discovery Kids Channel; Docu TVE; Ecuavisia Internacional; ESPN 2 HD; ESPN Classic Sports; ESPN Deportes; ESPN HD; ESPNews; EuroNews; EWTN en Espanol; Food Network HD; Fox College Sports Atlantic; Fox College Sports Central; Fox College Sports Pacific; Fox Deportes; Fox Movie Channel; Fox News HD; Fox Soccer; Fuel TV; FX HD; G4; GameHD; Golf Channel; GolTV; Great American Country; Hallmark Channel; Hallmark Movie Channel; Hallmark Movie Channel HD; HD Theater; here! On Demand; HGTV HD; History Channel en Espanol; History Channel International; Howard TV; HTV Musica; ID Investigation Discovery; Infinito; Jewelry Television; La Familia Network; Latele Novela Network; LATV Networks; LOGO; Mariavision; Military Channel; Momentum TV; MTV Hits; MTV Networks HD; mun2 television; Music Choice; National Geographic Channel; National Geographic Channel HD Network; NBA TV; NHL Network; NHL Network HD; Nick HD; Nick Jr.; NickToons TV; Outdoor Channel; Oxygen; Planet Green; Science; Science HD; Sorpresa; Speed HD; Spike TV HD; Sundance Channel; Supercanal Caribe; Syfy HD; TBS in HD; TeenNick; Telefe International; The Movie Channel (multiplexed); The Weather Channel HD; TLC HD; Toon Disney; Toon Disney en Espanol; Tr3s; Travel Channel HD; Turner Network TV HD; TV Chile; TV Colombia; TVE Internacional; TVG Network; Universal HD; Universal Sports; USA Network HD; Utilisima; VeneMovies; Versus; Versus HD; VH1 Classic; VH1 HD; VH1 Soul; V-me TV; WAPA America; YES HD.
Fee: $10.95 monthly.

Pay Service 1
Pay Units: N.A.
Programming (via satellite): Cinemax; Flix; HBO (multiplexed); Showtime (multiplexed); The Movie Channel.

Digital Pay Service 1
Pay Units: N.A.
Programming (via satellite): Bollywood Hits On Demand; CCTV-4; Channel One; Chinese Television Network; Cinemax (multiplexed); Cinemax HD; Cinemax On Demand; Encore (multiplexed); Filipino Channel; GMA Pinoy TV; HBO (multiplexed); HBO HD; HBO On Demand; Korean Channel; MBC America; MKTV; Playboy TV; RAI International; Russian Television Network; Showtime (multiplexed); Showtime HD; Showtime On Demand; Society of Portuguese Television; Starz (multiplexed); Starz HDTV; Starz On Demand; Telemicro Internacional; The Movie Channel HD; TV Asia; TV Japan; TV Polonia; TV5 USA; Zee TV USA.
Fee: $9.95 monthly (Showtime, Cinemax, TMC, Starz/Encore, Playboy, RAI, SPT, TV5 or TV Polonia), $11.95 monthly (HBO), $24.95 monthly (TV Japan).

Video-On-Demand: Yes

Pay-Per-View
Playboy TV; Club Jenna.

Internet Service
Operational: Yes.
Broadband Service: Optimum Online.
Fee: $46.95 installation; $34.95 monthly.

Telephone Service
Digital: Operational
Fee: $34.95 monthly

Miles of Plant: 955.0 (coaxial); None (fiber optic).

Vice President, Field Operations: Mark Fitchett.

Ownership: Cablevision Systems Corp. (MSO).

NORTH CAROLINA

Total Systems: **104**
Total Communities Served: **879**
Franchises Not Yet Operating: **0**
Applications Pending: **0**
Communities with Applications: **0**
Number of Basic Subscribers: **2,308,235**
Number of Expanded Basic Subscribers: **818,134**
Number of Pay Units: **234,215**

Top 100 Markets Represented: Charlotte (42); Norfolk-Newport News-Portsmouth-Hampton, VA (44); Greenville-Spartanburg-Anderson, SC-Asheville, NC (46); Greensboro-High Point-Winston-Salem (47); Raleigh-Durham-Goldsboro-Fayetteville (73); Greenville-Washington-New Bern (84).

For a list of cable communities in this section, see the Cable Community Index located in the back of Cable Volume 2.
For explanation of terms used in cable system listings, see p. D-11.

AHOSKIE—Formerly served by Adelphia Communications. Now served by MURFREESBORO, NC [NC0144]. ICA: NC0081.

ALBEMARLE—Time Warner Cable, 3140 W Arrowood Rd, Charlotte, NC 28273. Phone: 704-378-2500. Fax: 704-504-1997. Web Site: http://www.timewarnercable.com/carolinas. Also serves Badin, Cabarrus County (portions), Locust, Montgomery County (portions), Mount Gilead, New London, Norwood, Oakboro, Richfield, Stanfield & Stanly County. ICA: NC0030.

TV Market Ranking: 42 (Locust, Oakboro, Stanfield, Stanly County (portions)); Below 100 (ALBEMARLE, Badin, New London, Richfield); Outside TV Markets (Cabarrus County (portions), Montgomery County (portions), Mount Gilead, Norwood, Stanly County (portions)). Franchise award date: April 8, 1980. Franchise expiration date: September 1, 2009. Began: April 1, 1981.

Channel capacity: 80 (operating 2-way). Channels available but not in use: N.A.

Basic Service

Subscribers: N.A. Included in Charlotte

Programming (received off-air): WAXN-TV (IND) Kannapolis; WBTV (CBS) Charlotte; WCCB (FOX) Charlotte; WCNC-TV (NBC) Charlotte; WFMY-TV (CBS) Greensboro; WHKY-TV (IND) Hickory; WJZY (CW) Belmont; WMYT-TV (MNT) Rock Hill; WSOC-TV (ABC) Charlotte; WTVI (PBS) Charlotte; WUNG-TV (PBS) Concord.

Programming (via satellite): QVC; TV Guide Network; WGN America.

Fee: $36.00 installation; $9.00 monthly.

Expanded Basic Service 1

Subscribers: N.A.

Programming (via satellite): A&E Networks; ABC Family Channel; AMC; Animal Planet; BET Networks; Bravo; Cartoon Network; CNBC; CNN; Comedy Central; Country Music TV; C-SPAN; C-SPAN 2; Discovery Channel; Discovery Health Channel; Disney Channel; E! Entertainment Television; ESPN; ESPN 2; ESPN Classic Sports; Food Network; Fox News Channel; Fox Sports South; FX; Golf Channel; Hallmark Channel; Headline News; HGTV; History Channel; INSP; Lifetime; Lifetime Movie Network; MSNBC; MTV; National Geographic Channel; Nickelodeon; Oxygen; Speed; Spike TV; SportSouth; Style Network; Syfy; TBS Superstation; The Learning Channel; The Weather Channel; Travel Channel; truTV; Turner Classic Movies; Turner Network TV; TV Land; USA Network; Versus; VH1; WE tv.

Fee: $40.95 monthly.

Digital Basic Service

Subscribers: 4,209.

Programming (via satellite): AmericanLife TV Network; America's Store; BBC America; Bio; Black Family Channel; Bloomberg Television; Boomerang; cloo; Cooking Channel; C-SPAN 3; Current; DIY Network; ESPN; ESPNews; FamilyNet; Fox College Sports Atlantic; Fox College Sports Central; Fox College Sports Pacific; Fox Soccer; Fuel TV; Fuse; G4; GAS; Great American Country; GSN; Halogen Network; HD Theater; HDNet; HDNet Movies; History Channel International; Independent Film Channel; INHD (multiplexed); Lifetime Movie Network; MTV2; Music Choice; NBA TV; Nick Jr.; NickToons TV; Outdoor Channel; Ovation; SoapNet; Style Network; Tennis Channel; Toon Disney; Turner Network TV HD; TV One; VH1 Classic.

Fee: $15.00 monthly.

Digital Pay Service 1

Pay Units: N.A.

Programming (via satellite): Canales N; Cinemax (multiplexed); Deutsche Welle TV; Encore (multiplexed); Flix (multiplexed); Fox Movie Channel; HBO (multiplexed); HBO HD; RAI International; Saigon Broadcasting Television Network; Showtime (multiplexed); Showtime On Demand; Starz (multiplexed); Sundance Channel (multiplexed); The Movie Channel (multiplexed); TV5, La Television International; Zee TV USA.

Fee: $9.95 monthly (Deutsche Welle, TV5 or RAI), $10.95 monthly (HBO, Cinemax, Showtime, TMC or Starz/Encore), $14.95 monthly (SBTN or Zee).

Video-On-Demand: Yes

Pay-Per-View

iN DEMAND (delivered digitally); Adult PPV (delivered digitally); ESPN Now (delivered digitally); ESPN Full Court (delivered digitally); ESPN Gameplan (delivered digitally); Sports PPV (delivered digitally); NBA League Pass (delivered digitally); MLB Extra Innings (delivered digitally); NHL Center Ice (delivered digitally).

Internet Service

Operational: Yes.

Subscribers: 4,340.

Broadband Service: Road Runner, AOL, EarthLink.

Fee: $39.95 installation; $46.95 monthly.

Telephone Service

Digital: Operational

Fee: $39.95 monthly

Miles of plant (coax & fiber) included in Charlotte

President: Mike Munley. Vice President, Technical Operations: Mike Cullim. Vice President, Engineering: Richard Newcomb. Vice President, Marketing & Sales: Eric Franey. Government Affairs Director: Michael Tanck. Public Affairs Director: Jessica Graham.

Ownership: Time Warner Cable (MSO).; Advance/Newhouse Partnership (MSO).

ANDERSON CREEK TWP.—Charter Communications. Now served by BUIES CREEK, NC [NC0194]. ICA: NC0188.

ANDREWS—Cable TV of Andrews. Now served by MURPHY, NC [NC0079]. ICA: NC0189.

ARROWHEAD BEACH—Mediacom. Now served by EDENTON, NC [NC0076]. ICA: NC0161.

ASHEBORO—Time Warner Cable. Now served by GREENSBORO, NC [NC0006]. ICA: NC0052.

ASHEVILLE—Charter Communications, 1670 Hendersonville Rd, Asheville, NC 28803. Phone: 828-209-2200. Fax: 828-277-6150. Web Site: http://www.charter.com. Also serves Barnardsville, Biltmore Forest, Black Mountain, Buncombe County (northern portion), Candler, Emma, Enka, Fairview (portions), Fletcher, Jupiter, Leicester, Mars Hill, Marshall, Montreat, Swannanoa, Weaverville & Woodfin. ICA: NC0012.

TV Market Ranking: 46 (ASHEVILLE, Barnardsville, Biltmore Forest, Black Mountain, Buncombe County, Candler, Emma, Enka, Fairview (portions), Fletcher, Jupiter, Leicester, Mars Hill, Marshall, Montreat, Swannanoa, Weaverville, Woodfin). Franchise award date: January 1, 1969. Franchise expiration date: N.A. Began: October 3, 1968.

Channel capacity: N.A. Channels available but not in use: N.A.

Basic Service

Subscribers: 31,700.

Programming (received off-air): WGGS-TV (IND) Greenville; WHNS (FOX) Greenville; WLOS (ABC) Asheville; WMYA-TV (MNT) Anderson; WSPA-TV (CBS) Spartanburg; WUNF-TV (PBS) Asheville; WYCW (CW) Asheville; WYFF (NBC) Greenville.

Programming (via satellite): C-SPAN; C-SPAN 2; INSP; ION Television; TV Guide Network; WGN America.

Fee: $29.99 installation; $1.86 converter.

Expanded Basic Service 1

Subscribers: N.A.

Programming (via satellite): A&E Networks; ABC Family Channel; AMC; Animal Planet; BET Networks; Bravo; Cartoon Network; CNBC; CNN; Comcast/Charter Sports Southeast (CSS); Comedy Central; Country Music TV; Discovery Channel; Disney Channel; E! Entertainment Television; ESPN; ESPN 2; Food Network; Fox News Channel; Fox Sports South; FX; G4; Golf Channel; GSN; Hallmark Channel; Headline News; HGTV; History Channel; Lifetime; MSNBC; MTV; National Geographic Channel; Nickelodeon; Oxygen; QVC; SoapNet; Speed; Spike TV; SportSouth; Syfy; TBS Superstation; Telemundo; The Learning Channel; The Weather Channel; Toon Disney; Travel Channel; truTV; Turner Classic Movies; Turner Network TV; TV Land; Univision Studios; USA Network; Versus; VH1.

Fee: $47.99 monthly.

Digital Basic Service

Subscribers: N.A.

Programming (via satellite): BBC America; Bio; Bloomberg Television; Boomerang; CNN en Espanol; CNN International; Cooking Channel; Discovery Fit & Health; DIY Network; ESPN; ESPN Classic Sports; Fox College Sports Atlantic; Fox College Sports Central; Fox College Sports Pacific; Fox Movie Channel; Fox Soccer; Fuel TV; GAS; HD Theater; HDNet; HDNet Movies; History Channel International; Independent Film Channel; Lifetime Movie Network; MTV Networks Digital Suite; Music Choice; NFL Network; Nick Jr.; Nick Too; NickToons TV; Outdoor Channel; Science Television; Sundance Channel; Trinity Broadcasting Network; WE tv.

Digital Pay Service 1

Pay Units: N.A.

Programming (via satellite): Cinemax (multiplexed); HBO (multiplexed); HBO HD; Showtime HD; Starz (multiplexed).

Video-On-Demand: Yes

Pay-Per-View

Playboy TV (delivered digitally); Fresh (delivered digitally); Spice Live (delivered digitally).

Internet Service

Operational: Yes.

Broadband Service: Charter Pipeline.

Fee: $29.99 monthly; $9.95 modem lease; $199.95 modem purchase.

Telephone Service

Analog: Not Operational

Digital: Operational

Fee: $29.95 monthly

Miles of Plant: 780.0 (coaxial); 20.0 (fiber optic).

Vice President & General Manager: Anthony Pope. Marketing Director: Brooke Sinclair. Sales & Marketing Manager: Karen Sims. Operations Manager: Janet Cloyde. Engineering Manager: Dean McCracken.

Ownership: Charter Communications Inc. (MSO).

AULANDER—Formerly served by Adelphia Communications. Now served by MURFREESBORO, NC [NC0144]. ICA: NC0190.

BAILEY—Time Warner Cable, 101 Innovation Ave, Ste 100, Morrisville, NC 27560. Phone: 919-573-7000. Fax: 919-573-7042. Web Site: http://www.timewarnercable.com. Also serves Middlesex, Nash County (southwestern portion), Sims & Wilson County (northwestern portion). ICA: NC0117.

TV Market Ranking: 73 (BAILEY, Middlesex, Nash County (southwestern portion) (portions), Sims); 73,84 (Wilson County (northwestern portion) (portions)). Franchise award date: October 1, 1985. Franchise expiration date: N.A. Began: January 1, 1985.

Channel capacity: 42 (not 2-way capable). Channels available but not in use: N.A.

Basic Service

Subscribers: 916.

Programming (received off-air): WITN-TV (MNT, NBC) Washington; WLFL (CW) Raleigh; WNCN (NBC) Goldsboro; WNCT-TV (CBS, CW) Greenville; WRAL-TV (CBS) Raleigh; WRAY-TV (IND) Wilson; WRAZ (FOX) Raleigh; WRDC (MNT) Durham; WRPX-TV (ION) Rocky Mount; WTVD (ABC) Durham; WUNK-TV (PBS) Greenville; WUVC-DT (UNV) Fayetteville.

Programming (via satellite): QVC.

Fee: $39.95 installation; $15.14 monthly; $1.86 converter; $19.95 additional installation.

Expanded Basic Service 1

Subscribers: 871.

Programming (via satellite): ABC Family Channel; Animal Planet; BET Networks; CNN; Country Music TV; C-SPAN; Discovery Channel; Disney Channel; ESPN; Fox News Channel; Headline News; Lifetime; MSNBC; MTV; Nickelodeon; Spike TV; Syfy; TBS Superstation; The Weather Channel; Trinity Broadcasting Network; Turner Network TV; USA Network; VH1; WGN America.

Fee: $19.69 monthly.

Digital Basic Service

Subscribers: N.A.

Programming (via satellite): BBC America; Bravo; Discovery Digital Networks; DMX Music; ESPN Classic Sports; ESPNews; Fox Soccer; Golf Channel; GSN; HGTV; History Channel; Independent Film Channel; Versus; WE tv.

Fee: $11.00 monthly.

Pay Service 1

Pay Units: N.A.

Programming (via satellite): HBO.

Fee: $14.99 monthly.

Digital Pay Service 1

Pay Units: N.A.

Programming (via satellite): Cinemax (multiplexed); Encore (multiplexed); HBO (multiplexed); Showtime (multiplexed); Starz (multiplexed); The Movie Channel (multiplexed).

Fee: $15.95 monthly (HBO, Cinemax, Showtime/TMC or Starz/Encore).

Video-On-Demand: No

Pay-Per-View

HITS 1 (delivered digitally); HITS 2 (delivered digitally); HITS 3 (delivered digitally); HITS 4 (delivered digitally); Playboy TV (delivered digitally).

Internet Service

Operational: Yes.

Broadband Service: RoadRunner.

Fee: $24.95 monthly.

Telephone Service

Digital: Operational

Fee: $24.99 monthly

Miles of Plant: 79.0 (coaxial); None (fiber optic).

President: Tom Adams. Vice President, Technical Operations: Gary Frederick. Vice President, Sales & Marketing: Tom Smith. Vice President, Government & Public Affairs: Brad Phillips.

Ownership: Time Warner Cable (MSO).

BALD HEAD ISLAND—Tele-Media, 804 Jacksonville Rd, PO Box 39, Bellefonte, PA 16823-0039. Phones: 800-533-7048; 910-842-8383. Fax: 910-842-2821. E-mail: tmilligan@tele-media.com. Web Site: http://www.tele-media.com. ICA: NC0238.

TV Market Ranking: Below 100 (BALD HEAD ISLAND). Franchise award date: July 1, 1991. Franchise expiration date: July 1, 2006. Began: September 1, 1991.

Channel capacity: 61 (not 2-way capable). Channels available but not in use: N.A.

Basic Service

Subscribers: 753.

Programming (received off-air): WBTW (CBS, MNT) Florence; WECT (NBC) Wilmington; WSFX-TV (FOX) Wilmington; WUNJ-TV (PBS) Wilmington; WWAY (ABC) Wilmington.

Programming (via satellite): A&E Networks; ABC Family Channel; AMC; Animal Planet; Cartoon Network; CNBC; CNN; Comedy Central; C-SPAN; C-SPAN 2; CW+; Discovery Channel; Disney Channel; E! Entertainment Television; ESPN; ESPN 2; Food Network; Fox News Channel; Fox Sports South; FX; Golf Channel; GSN; Hallmark Channel; Headline News; HGTV; History Channel; Lifetime; MTV; Nickelodeon; QVC; SoapNet; Spike TV; Syfy; TBS Superstation; The Learning Channel; The Weather Channel; Travel Channel; Trinity Broadcasting Network; Turner Network TV; TV Land; USA Network; VH1; WGN America.

Fee: $35.00 installation; $45.50 monthly.

Digital Basic Service

Subscribers: 59.

Programming (via satellite): BBC America; Bio; Bloomberg Television; Bravo; CMT Pure Country; Discovery Fit & Health; Discovery Health Channel; Discovery Kids Channel; DMX Music; ESPN Classic Sports; ESPNews; Fuse; G4; Great American Country; History Channel International; ID Investigation Discovery; Independent Film Channel; Lifetime Movie Network; Lime; MBC America; Military Channel; MTV2; National Geographic Channel; Nick Jr.; NickToons TV; Planet Green; Science; Style Network; TeenNick; The Word Network; Turner Classic Movies; VH1 Classic; WE tv.

Fee: $10.95 monthly.

Digital Expanded Basic Service

Subscribers: N.A.

Programming (via satellite): Fox College Sports Atlantic; Fox College Sports Central; Fox College Sports Pacific; Fox Movie Channel; Fox Soccer; Outdoor Channel; Speed; Versus.

Fee: $2.95 monthly.

Digital Pay Service 1

Pay Units: N.A.

Programming (via satellite): Cinemax (multiplexed); Encore (multiplexed); Flix; HBO (multiplexed); Showtime (multiplexed); Starz (multiplexed); The Movie Channel (multiplexed).

Fee: $7.00 monthly (Cinemax), $9.00 monthly (Starz/Encore), $11.00 monthly (Showtime/TMC/Flix), $12.00 monthly (HBO).

Video-On-Demand: No

Internet Service

Operational: Yes.

Subscribers: 118.

Telephone Service

Digital: Operational

Miles of Plant: 28.0 (coaxial); None (fiber optic).

Senior Vice President, Finance: Bob Stemler. Station Manager & Chief Technician: John Hockenberry.

Ownership: Tele-Media Corp. (MSO).

BATH—Red's TV Cable Inc., PO Box 202, Farmville, NC 27828-0202. Phone: 252-753-3074. Also serves Beaufort County (unincorporated areas). ICA: NC0173.

TV Market Ranking: 84 (BATH, Beaufort County (unincorporated areas)). Franchise award date: N.A. Franchise expiration date: N.A. Began: N.A.

Channel capacity: 90 (operating 2-way). Channels available but not in use: N.A.

Basic Service

Subscribers: 290.

Programming (received off-air): WFXI (FOX, MNT) Morehead City; WNCT-TV (CBS, CW) Greenville; WRAL-TV (CBS) Raleigh; WUNK-TV (PBS) Greenville.

Programming (via satellite): ABC Family Channel; CNN; Comcast SportsNet Mid-Atlantic; ESPN; Lifetime; QVC; TBS Superstation; The Weather Channel; Turner Classic Movies; Turner Network TV; USA Network; WGN America.

Fee: $50.00 installation; $18.00 monthly.

Expanded Basic Service 1

Subscribers: 180.

Programming (via satellite): CNBC; C-SPAN; Spike TV.

Fee: $45.00 installation; $13.00 monthly.

Digital Basic Service

Subscribers: 45.

Fee: $50.00 installation; $4.95 monthly.

Pay Service 1

Pay Units: 29.

Programming (via satellite): HBO.

Fee: $9.50 monthly.

Pay Service 2

Pay Units: 10.

Programming (via satellite): Cinemax.

Fee: $8.00 monthly.

Pay Service 3

Pay Units: 17.

Programming (via satellite): Showtime; The Movie Channel.

Fee: $10.95 monthly.

Pay Service 4

Pay Units: 12.

Programming (via satellite): Encore.

Fee: $11.00 monthly.

Internet Service

Operational: Yes.

Subscribers: 83.

Broadband Service: In-house.

Fee: $20.95 monthly.

Telephone Service

None

Miles of Plant: 16.0 (coaxial); None (fiber optic).

Manager: Frank Styers.

Ownership: Red's TV Cable Inc.

BELHAVEN—Belhaven Cable TV, 235 Pamlico St, PO Box 8, Belhaven, NC 27810. Phone: 252-943-3736. Fax: 252-943-3738. E-mail: bctv@beaufortco.com. Web Site: http://www.belhavencabletv.com. Also serves Engelhard, Fairfield, Nebraska, Ocracoke Island & Swan Quarter. ICA: NC0130.

TV Market Ranking: 84 (BELHAVEN); Below 100 (Engelhard, Nebraska); Outside TV Markets (Fairfield, Ocracoke Island, Swan Quarter). Franchise award date: N.A. Franchise expiration date: N.A. Began: February 1, 1983.

Channel capacity: 41 (operating 2-way). Channels available but not in use: N.A.

Basic Service

Subscribers: 600.

Programming (received off-air): WCTI-TV (ABC) New Bern; WFXI (FOX, MNT) Morehead City; WITN-TV (MNT, NBC) Washington; WNCT-TV (CBS, CW) Greenville; WUND-TV (PBS) Edenton.

Programming (via satellite): A&E Networks; ABC Family Channel; BET Networks; Cartoon Network; CNBC; CNN; Comedy Central; C-SPAN; Discovery Channel; Disney Channel; ESPN; Fox News Channel; Fox Sports South; Golf Channel; Headline News; HGTV; History Channel; Lifetime; MTV; Nickelodeon; Outdoor Channel; QVC; TBS Superstation; The Learning Channel; The Weather Channel; Trinity Broadcasting Network; WGN America.

Fee: $25.00 installation; $21.00 monthly; $25.00 additional installation.

Expanded Basic Service 1

Subscribers: 50.

Programming (via satellite): AMC; Country Music TV; ESPN 2; FX; Spike TV; Syfy; Turner Classic Movies; USA Network.

Fee: $6.00 monthly.

Digital Basic Service

Subscribers: 60.

Programming (via satellite): BBC America; Discovery Digital Networks; DMX Music; GAS; MTV Networks Digital Suite; Nick Jr.; Nick Too.

Fee: $9.95 monthly.

Pay Service 1

Pay Units: N.A.

Programming (via satellite): Cinemax; HBO; Showtime.

Fee: $10.00 monthly (Cinemax or Showtime), $12.00 monthly (HBO).

Digital Pay Service 1

Pay Units: N.A.

Programming (via satellite): Cinemax (multiplexed); Encore (multiplexed); Flix; HBO (multiplexed); Showtime (multiplexed); Starz (multiplexed); Sundance Channel; The Movie Channel (multiplexed).

Video-On-Demand: Yes

Internet Service

Operational: Yes, Both DSL & dial-up.

Fee: $50.00 installation; $39.95 monthly; $5.00 modem lease; $99.99 modem purchase.

Telephone Service

Analog: Operational

Fee: $51.94 monthly

Digital: Not Operational

Miles of Plant: 20.0 (coaxial); None (fiber optic).

General Manager: Ben Johnson. Chief Technologist: Jerry Stender. Office Manager: Darrell Patterson.

Ownership: Belhaven Cable TV Inc.

BELHAVEN—TriCounty Telecom, 2193 NC 99 Hwy S, PO Box 520, Belhaven, NC 27810-0520. Phone: 252-964-8000. Fax: 252-964-2211. E-mail: questions@gotricounty.com. Web Site: http://www.gotricounty.biz. Also serves Camp Leach, Douglas Crossroads, Hyde County (portions), Pamlico Beach, Pantego, Pike Road, Pinetown, Smithton, Terra Ceia & White Post. ICA: NC0182.

TV Market Ranking: 84 (BELHAVEN, Camp Leach, Douglas Crossroads, Pamlico Beach, Pantego, Pike Road, Pinetown, Smithton, Terra Ceia, White Post); Outside TV Markets (Hyde County (portions)). Franchise award date: September 9, 2007. Franchise expiration date: N.A. Began: April 19, 1993.

Channel capacity: 62 (not 2-way capable). Channels available but not in use: N.A.

Digital Basic Service

Subscribers: 803.

Programming (via satellite): C-SPAN; C-SPAN 2; CW+; DMX Music; INSP; Trinity Broadcasting Network; WGN America.

Fee: $50.00 installation; $11.95 monthly; $5.95 converter; $25.00 additional installation.

Digital Expanded Basic Service

Subscribers: N.A.

Programming (via satellite): A&E Networks; ABC Family Channel; AMC; Animal Planet; BET Networks; Boomerang; Bravo; Cartoon Network; CNBC; CNN; Comedy Central; Country Music TV; Discovery Channel; Disney Channel; E! Entertainment Television; ESPN; ESPN 2; ESPN Classic Sports; Food Network; Fox News Channel; Fox Sports Net Carolinas; FX; Headline News; HGTV; History Channel; Lifetime; Lifetime Movie Network; Mid-Atlantic Sports Network; MTV; National Geographic Channel; Nickelodeon; Oxygen; PBS Kids Sprout; Planet Green; QVC; Science; ShopNBC; Spike TV; Syfy; TBS Superstation; The Learning Channel; The Weather Channel; Travel Channel; Turner Network TV; TV Land; USA Network; VH1.

Fee: $30.00 monthly.

Digital Expanded Basic Service 2

Subscribers: N.A.

Programming (received off-air): WCTI-TV (ABC) New Bern; WITN-TV (MNT, NBC) Washington; WNCT-TV (CBS, CW) Greenville; WUND-TV (PBS) Edenton; WYDO (FOX) Greenville.

Programming (via satellite): A&E HD; ABC Family HD; AmericanLife TV Network; Animal Planet HD; BBC America; Bio; Bloomberg Television; CBS Sports Network; Chiller; cloo; CMT Pure Country; Cooking Channel; Discovery Channel HD; Discovery Fit & Health; Discovery Health Channel; Discovery Kids Channel; Disney Channel HD; DIY Network; ESPN 2 HD; ESPN HD; ESPN U; ESPNews; FamilyNet; Food Network HD; Fox Business Channel; Fox College Sports Atlantic; Fox College Sports Central; Fox College Sports Pacific; Fox Movie Channel; Fox News HD; Fox Reality Channel; Fox Soccer; Fuse; FX HD; G4; GMC; Golf Channel; Great American Country; GSN; Hallmark Channel; Hallmark Movie Channel; Hallmark Movie Channel HD; Halogen Network; HD Theater; HGTV HD; History Channel HD; History Channel International; ID Investigation Discovery; Independent Film Channel; Lifetime Movie Network; Lifetime Real Women; Military Channel; MSNBC; MTV Hits; MTV2; National Geographic Channel HD Network; Nick Jr.; NickToons TV; Outdoor Channel; Outdoor Channel 2 HD; Planet Green; RFD-TV; Science HD; SoapNet; Speed; Speed HD; Style Network; Syfy HD; TeenNick; TLC HD; Toon Disney; Travel Channel HD; truTV; Turner Classic Movies; Universal HD; USA Network HD; Versus; VH1 Classic; VH1 Soul; WE tv.

Fee: $20.00 monthly.

Digital Pay Service 1

Pay Units: 161.

Programming (via satellite): HBO (multiplexed); HBO HD.

Fee: $13.35 monthly; $5.95 converter.

Digital Pay Service 2

Pay Units: 126.

Programming (via satellite): Cinemax (multiplexed); Cinemax HD.

Fee: $11.15 monthly; $5.95 converter.

Digital Pay Service 3

Pay Units: 107.

Programming (via satellite): Showtime (multiplexed); Showtime HD; The Movie Channel (multiplexed).

Fee: $13.35 monthly; $5.95 converter.

Digital Pay Service 4

Pay Units: 134.

Programming (via satellite): Encore (multiplexed); Starz (multiplexed); Starz HDTV.

Fee: $14.50 monthly; $5.95 converter.

Digital Pay Service 5

Pay Units: 56.

Programming (via satellite): Encore (multiplexed).

Fee: $7.75 monthly; $5.95 converter.

Video-On-Demand: No

Pay-Per-View

Addressable homes: 803.

Fresh (delivered digitally); iN DEMAND (delivered digitally); Playboy TV (delivered digitally).

Internet Service

Operational: No, DSL & dial-up.

Telephone Service

None

Miles of Plant: 277.0 (coaxial); 65.0 (fiber optic).

Chief Operating Officer: Lyman Horne. Operations Manager: Greg Coltrain. Engineering Manager: Danny Britt. Marketing & Media Relations Manager: Terry Raupe.

Ownership: Tri-County Communications Inc.

BENSON—Charter Communications. Now served by BUIES CREEK, NC [NC0194]. ICA: NC0141.

BLACK MOUNTAIN—Tri-Star Communications. No longer in operation. ICA: NC0067.

BOONE—Charter Communications, 1121 Lenoir Rhyne Blvd SE, Hickory, NC 28602-5128. Phone: 828-322-2288. Fax: 828-322-5492. Web Site: http://www.charter.com. Also serves Ashe County, Avery County, Banner Elk, Beech Mountain, Blowing Rock, Caldwell County, Crossnore, Deep Gap, Elk Park, Foscoe, Grandfather Mountain, Linville Ridge, Meat Camp, Newland, Seven Devils, Sugar Grove, Sugar Mountain, Valle Crucis, Vilas, Watauga County & Zionville, NC; Carter County, Roan Mountain & Trade, TN. ICA: NC0023.

TV Market Ranking: Below 100 (Ashe County (portions), Avery County, Banner Elk, Beech Mountain, Blowing Rock, Caldwell County, Carter County, Crossnore, Elk Park, Grandfather Mountain, Newland, Roan Mountain, Seven Devils, Sugar Grove, Sugar Mountain, Valle Crucis, Vilas, Watauga County (portions), Zionville); Outside TV Markets (Ashe County (portions), BOONE, Deep Gap, Foscoe, Linville Ridge, Meat Camp, Trade, Watauga County (portions)). Franchise award date: N.A. Franchise expiration date: N.A. Began: January 1, 1968.

Channel capacity: N.A. Channels available but not in use: N.A.

Basic Service

Subscribers: 17,710.

Programming (received off-air): WAXN-TV (IND) Kannapolis; WBTV (CBS) Charlotte; WCCB (FOX) Charlotte; WCNC-TV (NBC) Charlotte; WCYB-TV (CW, NBC) Bristol; WJHL-TV (CBS) Johnson City; WJZY (CW) Belmont; WKPT-TV (ABC) Kingsport; WLFG (IND) Grundy; WLNN-LP Boone; WMYT-TV (MNT) Rock Hill; WSOC-TV (ABC) Charlotte; WUNE-TV (PBS) Linville; allband FM.

Programming (via satellite): QVC; TV Guide Network.

Fee: $29.99 installation.

Expanded Basic Service 1

Subscribers: N.A.

Programming (via satellite): A&E Networks; ABC Family Channel; AMC; Animal Planet; Bravo; Cartoon Network; CNBC; CNN; Comedy Central; Country Music TV; C-SPAN; C-SPAN 2; Discovery Channel; Disney Channel; E! Entertainment Television; ESPN; ESPN 2; Food Network; Fox News Channel; Fox Sports South; FX; G4; Golf Channel; Hallmark Channel; Headline News; HGTV; History Channel; INSP; ION Television; Lifetime; MSNBC; MTV; National Geographic Channel; Nickelodeon; Oxygen; Speed; Spike TV; SportSouth; Syfy; TBS Superstation; The Learning Channel; The Weather Channel; Travel Channel; truTV; Turner Network TV; TV Land; USA Network; Versus; VH1; WE tv.

Fee: $47.99 monthly.

Digital Basic Service

Subscribers: N.A.

Programming (via satellite): BBC America; Bio; Boomerang; CNN en Espanol; CNN International; Discovery Digital Networks; DIY Network; ESPN; ESPNews; Fox College Sports Atlantic; Fox College Sports Central; Fox College Sports Pacific; Fox Deportes; Fox Movie Channel; Fox Soccer; Fuel TV; GAS; HDNet; HDNet Movies; Independent Film Channel; Lifetime Movie Network; MTV Networks Digital Suite; Music Choice; NFL Network; Nick Jr.; Nick Too; NickToons TV; Sundance Channel.

Digital Pay Service 1

Pay Units: 512.

Programming (via satellite): Cinemax (multiplexed).

Fee: $10.00 monthly.

Digital Pay Service 2

Pay Units: 1,581.

Programming (via satellite): HBO (multiplexed); HBO HD.

Fee: $10.00 monthly.

Digital Pay Service 3

Pay Units: 322.

Programming (via satellite): Showtime (multiplexed); Showtime HD.

Fee: $10.00 monthly.

Digital Pay Service 4

Pay Units: N.A.

Programming (via satellite): Encore (multiplexed); Starz (multiplexed).

Fee: $4.95 monthly (Starz & Encore).

Video-On-Demand: Yes

Pay-Per-View

iN DEMAND (delivered digitally); Playboy TV (delivered digitally); Fresh (delivered digitally); Shorteez (delivered digitally).

Internet Service

Operational: Yes, DSL.

Subscribers: 225.

Broadband Service: Charter Pipeline.

Fee: $29.99 monthly.

Telephone Service

Digital: Operational

Fee: $29.99 monthly

Miles of Plant: 886.0 (coaxial); 176.0 (fiber optic).

Vice President & General Manager: Anthony Pope. Operations Manager: Sam Scialabba. Marketing Director: Brooke Sinclair. Sales & Marketing Manager: Karon Sims.

Ownership: Charter Communications Inc. (MSO).

BREVARD—Comporium Communications, 190 E Main St, Brevard, NC 28712. Phone: 828-884-2671. Fax: 828-885-2300. Web Site: http://www.comporium.com. Also serves Lake Toxaway, Pisgah Forest, Rosman & Transylvania County. ICA: NC0053.

TV Market Ranking: 46 (BREVARD, Lake Toxaway, Rosman, Transylvania County (portions)); Outside TV Markets (Transylvania County (portions)). Franchise award date: January 1, 1979. Franchise expiration date: August 15, 2016. Began: February 19, 1980.

Channel capacity: 56 (not 2-way capable). Channels available but not in use: N.A.

Basic Service

Subscribers: 7,539.

Programming (received off-air): WHNS (FOX) Greenville; WLOS (ABC) Asheville; WMYA-TV (MNT) Anderson; WSPA-TV (CBS) Spartanburg; WUNF-TV (PBS) Asheville; WYCW (CW) Asheville; WYFF (NBC) Greenville; allband FM.

Programming (via satellite): ABC Family Channel; C-SPAN; Lifetime; The Weather Channel.

Fee: $25.00 installation; $15.25 monthly.

Expanded Basic Service 1

Subscribers: 5,972.

Programming (via satellite): A&E Networks; AMC; Animal Planet; BET Networks; Cartoon Network; CNBC; CNN; Country Music TV; C-SPAN 2; Discovery Channel; Disney Channel; E! Entertainment Television; ESPN; ESPN 2; Fox News Channel; Fox Sports South; Golf Channel; Headline News; HGTV; History Channel; MTV; Nickelodeon; Speed; Spike TV; Syfy; TBS Superstation; The Learning Channel; Travel Channel; Trinity Broadcasting Network; Turner Network TV; USA Network; VH1; WGN America.

Fee: $30.70 monthly.

Pay Service 1

Pay Units: 493.

Programming (via satellite): HBO (multiplexed).

Fee: $11.95 monthly.

Pay Service 2

Pay Units: 161.

Programming (via satellite): Cinemax (multiplexed).

Fee: $10.95 monthly.

Pay Service 3

Pay Units: 54.

Programming (via satellite): The Movie Channel (multiplexed).

Fee: $10.95 monthly.

Pay Service 4

Pay Units: 68.

Programming (via satellite): Showtime (multiplexed).

Fee: $10.95 monthly.

Video-On-Demand: No

Internet Service
Operational: No.
Telephone Service
None
Miles of Plant: 475.0 (coaxial); None (fiber optic).
Chief Technician: Gary Butler. Customer Service Manager: Lorretta Sanders.
Ownership: Comporium Communications (MSO).

BRYSON CITY—Zito Media, 611 Vader Hill Rd, Coudersport, PA 16915. Phone: 814-260-9575. Web Site: http://www.zitomedia.com. Also serves Whittier. ICA: NC0193.
TV Market Ranking: Outside TV Markets (BRYSON CITY, Whittier). Franchise award date: February 10, 1981. Franchise expiration date: N.A. Began: October 1, 1981.
Channel capacity: N.A. Channels available but not in use: N.A.
Basic Service
Subscribers: 1,065.
Programming (received off-air): WHNS (FOX) Greenville; WLOS (ABC) Asheville; WSPA-TV (CBS) Spartanburg; WUNE-TV (PBS) Linville; WYFF (NBC) Greenville.
Programming (via satellite): Comedy Central; C-SPAN; QVC; TBS Superstation; The Learning Channel; WGN America.
Fee: $29.98 installation; $19.95 monthly; $1.78 converter.
Expanded Basic Service 1
Subscribers: N.A.
Programming (via satellite): A&E Networks; ABC Family Channel; AMC; Animal Planet; Cartoon Network; CNN; Country Music TV; Discovery Channel; Disney Channel; ESPN; ESPN 2; Fox Sports South; FX; Headline News; HGTV; History Channel; Lifetime; MTV; Nickelodeon; Spike TV; The Weather Channel; Turner Classic Movies; Turner Network TV; TV Land; USA Network; VH1.
Fee: $18.00 monthly.
Digital Basic Service
Subscribers: 47.
Programming (via satellite): AmericanLife TV Network; BBC America; Bloomberg Television; Discovery Digital Networks; DMX Music; ESPN Classic Sports; Fox Sports World; G4; Golf Channel; GSN; Halogen Network; ION Television; Outdoor Channel; Syfy; Trinity Broadcasting Network.
Fee: $13.95 monthly.
Pay Service 1
Pay Units: 106.
Programming (via satellite): HBO (multiplexed).
Fee: $11.95 monthly.
Pay Service 2
Pay Units: 152.
Programming (via satellite): Showtime (multiplexed); The Movie Channel (multiplexed).
Fee: $12.96 monthly.
Digital Pay Service 1
Pay Units: N.A.
Programming (via satellite): Cinemax (multiplexed); Encore (multiplexed); HBO (multiplexed); Showtime (multiplexed); Starz (multiplexed); The Movie Channel (multiplexed).
Fee: $7.95 monthly (Starz & Encore), $18.95 monthly (Cinemax or Showtime & TMC), $20.95 monthly (HBO).
Video-On-Demand: No
Pay-Per-View
Movies (delivered digitally); special events (delivered digitally); Sports PPV (delivered digitally).
Internet Service
Operational: Yes. Began: November 1, 2004.
Broadband Service: Rapid High Speed Internet.
Fee: $50.00 installation; $39.95 monthly.
Telephone Service
None
Miles of Plant: 87.0 (coaxial); 12.0 (fiber optic).
Chief Technician: Mark Laver.
Ownership: Zito Media (MSO).

BUIES CREEK—Charter Communications, 2516 Fayetteville St., Sanford, NC 27332. Phone: 919-708-5902. Fax: 919-774-6126. Web Site: http://www.charter.com. Also serves Anderson Creek Twp., Angier, Benson, Broadway, Bunnlevel, Chatham County (unincorporated areas), Coats, Erwin, Johnsonville Twp., Kipling, Lee County (portions), Lillington, Mamers, Moore County, Newton Grove, Plainview, Sanford, Siler City, Spivey's Corner, Vass & Whispering Pines. ICA: NC0194.
TV Market Ranking: 47 (Chatham County (unincorporated areas) (portions), Siler City); 73 (Anderson Creek Twp., Angier, Benson, Broadway, BUIES CREEK, Bunnlevel, Coats, Erwin, Johnsonville Twp., Kipling, Lee County (portions), Lillington, Mamers, Moore County (portions) (portions), Newton Grove, Plainview, Sanford, Spivey's Corner, Vass, Whispering Pines); Below 100 (Chatham County (unincorporated areas) (portions), Lee County (portions)); Outside TV Markets (Chatham County (unincorporated areas) (portions), Lee County (portions), Moore County (portions) (portions)). Franchise award date: N.A. Franchise expiration date: N.A. Began: May 1, 1984.
Channel capacity: N.A. Channels available but not in use: N.A.
Basic Service
Subscribers: 4,403.
Programming (received off-air): WFPX-TV (ION) Fayetteville; WLFL (CW) Raleigh; WNCN (NBC) Goldsboro; WRAL-TV (CBS) Raleigh; WRAY-TV (IND) Wilson; WRAZ (FOX) Raleigh; WRDC (MNT) Durham; WTVD (ABC) Durham; WUNC-TV (PBS) Chapel Hill; WUVC-DT (UNV) Fayetteville.
Programming (via satellite): C-SPAN; C-SPAN 2; QVC; Trinity Broadcasting Network; TV Guide Network; WGN America.
Fee: $35.00 installation; $7.41 monthly; $1.43 converter.
Expanded Basic Service 1
Subscribers: 4,246.
Programming (via satellite): A&E Networks; ABC Family Channel; AMC; Animal Planet; BET Networks; Bravo; Cartoon Network; CNBC; CNN; Comedy Central; Country Music TV; Discovery Channel; Disney Channel; E! Entertainment Television; ESPN; ESPN 2; Food Network; Fox News Channel; Fox Sports South; FX; G4; GalaVision; Golf Channel; Hallmark Channel; Headline News; HGTV; History Channel; Lifetime; MSNBC; MTV; National Geographic Channel; Nickelodeon; Oxygen; Speed; Spike TV; Syfy; TBS Superstation; Telemundo; The Learning Channel; The Weather Channel; Travel Channel; truTV; Turner Network TV; TV Land; USA Network; Versus; VH1; WE tv.
Fee: $35.00 installation; $12.97 monthly.
Digital Basic Service
Subscribers: N.A.
Programming (via satellite): BBC America; Bio; Boomerang; Canales N; CNN International; Discovery Digital Networks; DIY Network; Fox College Sports Atlantic; Fox College Sports Central; Fox College Sports Pacific; Fox Movie Channel; Fox Soccer; Fuel TV; GAS; History Channel International; Independent Film Channel; Lifetime Movie Network; MTV Networks Digital Suite; Music Choice; Nick Jr.; Nick Too; NickToons TV; SoapNet; Sundance Channel; Toon Disney; TV Guide Interactive Inc.
Digital Pay Service 1
Pay Units: 461.
Programming (via satellite): Cinemax (multiplexed); HBO (multiplexed); Showtime (multiplexed); The Movie Channel (multiplexed).
Fee: $9.95 monthly (each).
Digital Pay Service 2
Pay Units: N.A.
Programming (via satellite): Encore (multiplexed); Flix; Starz (multiplexed).
Video-On-Demand: Yes
Pay-Per-View
iN DEMAND (delivered digitally); Playboy TV (delivered digitally); Fresh (delivered digitally); Shorteez (delivered digitally).
Internet Service
Operational: Yes.
Broadband Service: Charter Pipeline.
Fee: $29.99 monthly.
Telephone Service
None
Miles of Plant: 1,480.0 (coaxial); 60.0 (fiber optic). Miles of plant (coax & fiber) includes Kenly & Troy
Vice President & General Manager: Anthony Pope. Operations Manager: Doug Underwood. Marketing Director: Brooke Sinclair. Marketing Manager: LaRisa Scales. Office Manager: Brenda Brinson.
Ownership: Charter Communications Inc. (MSO).

BUNCOMBE COUNTY (northern portion)—Charter Communications. Now served by ASHEVILLE, NC [NC0012]. ICA: NC0179.

BUNN—Formerly served by Adelphia Communications. Now served by HENDERSON, NC [NC0062]. ICA: NC0114.

BUNNLEVEL—Carolina Cable Partnership. Now served by BUIES CREEK, NC [NC0194]. ICA: NC0160.

BURKE COUNTY—Charter Communications. Now served by HICKORY, NC [NC0009]. ICA: NC0028.

BURLINGTON—Time Warner Cable. Now served by GREENSBORO, NC [NC0006]. ICA: NC0015.

BURNSVILLE—Charter Communications, 1670 Hendersonville Rd, Asheville, NC 28803. Phone: 828-209-2200. Fax: 828-277-6150. Web Site: http://www.charter.com. Also serves Bakersville, Micaville, Mitchell County, Pensacola, Spruce Pine & Yancey County (portions). ICA: NC0128.
TV Market Ranking: 46 (BURNSVILLE, Micaville, Mitchell County (portions), Pensacola, Spruce Pine, Yancey County (portions)); Below 100 (Bakersville, Mitchell County (portions)). Franchise award date: N.A. Franchise expiration date: N.A. Began: January 1, 1956.
Channel capacity: N.A. Channels available but not in use: N.A.
Basic Service
Subscribers: 3,900.
Programming (received off-air): WBTV (CBS) Charlotte; WCCB (FOX) Charlotte; WCNC-TV (NBC) Charlotte; WCYB-TV (CW, NBC) Bristol; WJHL-TV (CBS) Johnson City; WJZY (CW) Belmont; WLOS (ABC) Asheville; WMYA-TV (MNT) Anderson; WUNE-TV (PBS) Linville.
Programming (via satellite): ION Television; QVC; TV Guide Network; WGN America.
Fee: $29.99 installation.
Expanded Basic Service 1
Subscribers: 900.
Programming (via satellite): A&E Networks; ABC Family Channel; AMC; Animal Planet; Bravo; Cartoon Network; CNBC; CNN; Comcast/Charter Sports Southeast (CSS); Comedy Central; Country Music TV; C-SPAN; Discovery Channel; Disney Channel; E! Entertainment Television; ESPN; ESPN 2; Food Network; Fox News Channel; Fox Sports South; FX; G4; GSN; Hallmark Channel; Headline News; HGTV; History Channel; INSP; Lifetime; MSNBC; MTV; National Geographic Channel; Nickelodeon; Oxygen; Speed; Spike TV; Syfy; TBS Superstation; The Learning Channel; The Weather Channel; Travel Channel; truTV; Turner Classic Movies; Turner Network TV; TV Land; USA Network; Versus; VH1.
Fee: $47.99 monthly.
Digital Basic Service
Subscribers: N.A.
Programming (via satellite): BBC America; Bio; Bloomberg Television; Boomerang; CNN en Espanol; CNN International; Discovery Digital Networks; DIY Network; Fox College Sports Atlantic; Fox College Sports Central; Fox College Sports Pacific; Fox Movie Channel; Fox Soccer; GAS; History Channel International; Independent Film Channel; MTV Networks Digital Suite; Music Choice; Nick Jr.; Nick Too; NickToons TV; Sundance Channel; TV Guide Interactive Inc.; WE tv.
Digital Pay Service 1
Pay Units: 210.
Programming (via satellite): HBO (multiplexed).
Fee: $11.95 monthly.
Digital Pay Service 2
Pay Units: 95.
Programming (via satellite): The Movie Channel (multiplexed).
Fee: $11.95 monthly.
Digital Pay Service 3
Pay Units: 80.
Programming (via satellite): Showtime (multiplexed).
Fee: $11.95 monthly.
Digital Pay Service 4
Pay Units: N.A.
Programming (via satellite): Cinemax (multiplexed); Encore (multiplexed); Flix; Playboy TV; Starz (multiplexed).
Fee: $11.95 monthly (Cinemax).
Video-On-Demand: No
Pay-Per-View
iN DEMAND (delivered digitally); Playboy TV (delivered digitally).
Internet Service
Operational: Yes.
Fee: $19.99 monthly.
Telephone Service
None
Miles of Plant: 132.0 (coaxial); None (fiber optic).
Vice President & General Manager: Anthony Pope. Marketing Director: Brooke Sinclair. Sales & Marketing Manager: Karen Sims.

Operations Manager: Janet Cloyde. Chief Technician: Dean McCracken.
Ownership: Charter Communications Inc. (MSO).

BURNSVILLE—Country Cablevision Inc., 9449 State Hwy 197 S, Burnsville, NC 28714-9633. Phones: 800-722-4074; 828-682-4074. Fax: 828-682-6895. Web Site: http://www.ccvn.com. Also serves Little Switzerland, Madison County, Mitchell County, Spruce Pine & Yancey County. ICA: NC0099.
TV Market Ranking: 46 (BURNSVILLE, Little Switzerland, Madison County, Mitchell County (portions), Yancey County (portions)); Below 100 (Spruce Pine, Mitchell County (portions)). Franchise award date: N.A. Franchise expiration date: N.A. Began: September 1, 1990.
Channel capacity: 61 (operating 2-way). Channels available but not in use: N.A.

Basic Service
Subscribers: 4,732.
Programming (received off-air): WBTV (CBS) Charlotte; WCYB-TV (CW, NBC) Bristol; WHNS (FOX) Greenville; WJHL-TV (CBS) Johnson City; WKPT-TV (ABC) Kingsport; WLOS (ABC) Asheville; WMYA-TV (MNT) Anderson; WSPA-TV (CBS) Spartanburg; WUNC-TV (PBS) Chapel Hill; WYCW (CW) Asheville; WYFF (NBC) Greenville.
Programming (via satellite): A&E Networks; ABC Family Channel; AMC; American-Life TV Network; Animal Planet; Cartoon Network; CNBC; CNN; Comedy Central; Country Music TV; C-SPAN; C-SPAN 2; Discovery Channel; Disney Channel; E! Entertainment Television; ESPN; ESPN 2; ESPN Classic Sports; Food Network; Fox News Channel; FX; Great American Country; Hallmark Channel; Headline News; HGTV; History Channel; ION Television; Lifetime; MTV; National Geographic Channel; Nickelodeon; Outdoor Channel; QVC; Shop at Home; ShopNBC; Spike TV; SportSouth; Syfy; TBS Superstation; The Learning Channel; The Weather Channel; Travel Channel; Trinity Broadcasting Network; Turner Classic Movies; Turner Network TV; TV Guide Network; TV Land; USA Network; VH1; WGN America.
Fee: $39.00 installation; $46.39 monthly.

Digital Basic Service
Subscribers: 600.
Programming (via satellite): American-Life TV Network; BBC America; Bio; Black Family Channel; Bloomberg Television; Bravo; Discovery Fit & Health; DMX Music; ESPN 2; ESPN Classic Sports; ESPNews; Fox Movie Channel; Fox Sports World; FSN Digital Atlantic; FSN Digital Central; FSN Digital Pacific; Fuse; G4; GAS; Golf Channel; Great American Country; GSN; Halogen Network; HGTV; History Channel; History Channel International; Independent Film Channel; International Television (ITV); Lime; MTV Networks Digital Suite; National Geographic Channel; Nick Jr.; NickToons TV; Outdoor Channel; Ovation; Speed; Style Network; Syfy; Toon Disney; Trinity Broadcasting Network; Turner Classic Movies; Versus; WE tv.
Fee: $13.00 monthly.

Digital Pay Service 1
Pay Units: 201.
Programming (via satellite): HBO (multiplexed).
Fee: $13.00 monthly.

Digital Pay Service 2
Pay Units: 101.
Programming (via satellite): Cinemax (multiplexed).
Fee: $13.00 monthly.

Digital Pay Service 3
Pay Units: 183.
Programming (via satellite): Encore (multiplexed); Starz (multiplexed).
Fee: $13.00 monthly.

Digital Pay Service 4
Pay Units: 114.
Programming (via satellite): Showtime; The Movie Channel (multiplexed).
Fee: $13.00 monthly.

Video-On-Demand: No

Pay-Per-View
iN DEMAND (delivered digitally); Urban American Television Network (delivered digitally); Hot Choice (delivered digitally); Playboy TV (delivered digitally); Fresh (delivered digitally); Shorteez (delivered digitally).

Internet Service
Operational: Yes.
Subscribers: 1,339.
Broadband Service: In-house.
Fee: $29.99-$49.99 monthly; $9.95 modem lease.

Telephone Service
Analog: Not Operational
Digital: Operational
Fee: $29.99-$39.99 monthly
Miles of Plant: 600.0 (coaxial); 40.0 (fiber optic).
President: Randall Miller. Manager: Bryan Hyder. Chief Technician: James McPeters.
Ownership: Ray V. Miller Group.

BUXTON—Charter Communications. Now served by MANTEO, NC [NC0118]. ICA: NC0110.

CAMDEN COUNTY—Mediacom. Now served by CAMDEN/CURRITUCK (formerly Currituck County, southern portion), NC [NC0083]. ICA: NC0133.

CAMDEN/CURRITUCK—Mediacom, 910 NC Hwy 32 S, PO Box 580, Plymouth, NC 27962. Phone: 252-793-1570. Fax: 252-793-6135. Web Site: http://www.mediacomcable.com. Also serves Aydlett, Camden County, Coinjock, Currituck County (southern portion), Grandy, Harbinger, Jarvisburg, Point Harbor, Poplar Branch & Powells Point, NC; Northwest Naval Base, VA. ICA: NC0083.
TV Market Ranking: 44 (Camden County (portions), CURRITUCK, Northwest Naval Base); Below 100 (Aydlett, CAMDEN, Coinjock, Currituck County (southern portion), Grandy, Harbinger, Jarvisburg, Point Harbor, Poplar Branch, Powells Point, Camden County (portions)). Franchise award date: November 5, 1984. Franchise expiration date: N.A. Began: July 1, 1985.
Channel capacity: N.A. Channels available but not in use: N.A.

Basic Service
Subscribers: 4,134.
Programming (received off-air): WAVY-TV (NBC) Portsmouth; WGNT (CW) Portsmouth; WHRO-TV (PBS) Hampton-Norfolk; WITN-TV (MNT, NBC) Washington; WNCT-TV (CBS, CW) Greenville; WTKR (CBS) Norfolk; WTVZ-TV (MNT) Norfolk; WUND-TV (PBS) Edenton; WVBT (FOX) Virginia Beach; WVEC (ABC) Hampton.
Programming (via satellite): History Channel; ION Television; TV Guide Network; WGN America.
Fee: $29.50 installation; $13.25 monthly.

Expanded Basic Service 1
Subscribers: N.A.
Programming (via satellite): A&E Networks; ABC Family Channel; AMC; Animal Planet; BET Networks; Bravo; Cartoon Network; CNBC; CNN; Comedy Central; Country Music TV; C-SPAN; Discovery Channel; Discovery Fit & Health; Disney Channel; ESPN; ESPN 2; Food Network; Fox News Channel; Fox Sports Net; FX; Hallmark Channel; Headline News; HGTV; INSP; Lifetime; MSNBC; MTV; Nickelodeon; Outdoor Channel; QVC; Speed; Spike TV; Syfy; TBS Superstation; The Learning Channel; The Weather Channel; Toon Disney; Travel Channel; Turner Network TV; TV Land; USA Network; VH1; WE tv.
Fee: $34.70 monthly.

Digital Basic Service
Subscribers: N.A.
Programming (via satellite): BBC America; Bio; Discovery Digital Networks; Fox Soccer; Fuse; Golf Channel; GSN; History Channel International; Independent Film Channel; Lifetime Movie Network; Science Television; Style Network; Turner Classic Movies; Versus.

Digital Pay Service 1
Pay Units: N.A.
Programming (via satellite): Cinemax (multiplexed); Encore; Flix; HBO (multiplexed); Showtime (multiplexed); Starz (multiplexed); Sundance Channel; The Movie Channel (multiplexed).

Video-On-Demand: No

Internet Service
Operational: Yes. Began: January 1, 2002.
Broadband Service: Mediacom High Speed Internet.
Fee: $40.95 monthly.

Telephone Service
None
Miles of plant included in Plymouth
General Manager: Wayne Holiday. Office Manager: Wendy White. Marketing Analyst: Renette Ruffin.
Ownership: Mediacom LLC (MSO).

CAMP LEJEUNE—Charter Communications. Now served by HOLLY RIDGE, NC [NC0069]. ICA: NC0044.

CAMP WESLEY—Now served by GOLD HILL, NC [NC0140]. ICA: NC0159.

CAROLINA BEACH—Charter Communications. Now served by HOLLY RIDGE, NC [NC0069]. ICA: NC0041.

CARRBORO—Time Warner Cable, 101 Innovation Ave, Ste 100, Morrisville, NC 27560. Phone: 919-573-7000. Fax: 919-573-7042. Web Site: http://www.timewarnercable.com/carolinas. Also serves Hillsborough. ICA: NC0250.
TV Market Ranking: 73 (CARRBORO, Hillsborough).
Channel capacity: N.A. Channels available but not in use: N.A.

Basic Service
Subscribers: N.A.
Programming (received off-air): WFMY-TV (CBS) Greensboro; WGHP (FOX, IND) High Point; WLFL (CW) Raleigh; WNCN (NBC) Goldsboro; WRAL-TV (CBS) Raleigh; WRAY-TV (IND) Wilson; WRAZ (FOX) Raleigh; WRDC (MNT) Durham; WRPX-TV (ION) Rocky Mount; WTVD (ABC) Durham; WTVI (PBS) Charlotte; WUVC-DT (UNV) Fayetteville.
Programming (via satellite): BET Networks; QVC; Telefutura; WGN America.
Fee: $42.95 installation; $12.75 monthly; $19.95 additional installation.

Expanded Basic Service 1
Subscribers: N.A.
Programming (via satellite): A&E Networks; ABC Family Channel; AMC; Animal Planet; Bravo; Cartoon Network; CNBC; CNN; Comedy Central; Country Music TV; C-SPAN; C-SPAN 2; Discovery Channel; Discovery Fit & Health; Discovery Health Channel; Disney Channel; E! Entertainment Television; ESPN; ESPN 2; ESPN Classic Sports; Food Network; Fox News Channel; Fox Sports South; FX; Golf Channel; Hallmark Channel; Headline News; HGTV; History Channel; Lifetime; Lifetime Movie Network; MSNBC; MTV; National Geographic Channel; Nickelodeon; Oxygen; ShopNBC; SoapNet; Spike TV; Syfy; TBS Superstation; The Learning Channel; The Weather Channel; Travel Channel; truTV; Turner Classic Movies; Turner Network TV; TV Land; USA Network; Versus; VH1; WE tv.
Fee: $38.05 monthly.

Digital Basic Service
Subscribers: N.A.
Programming (via satellite): AmericanLife TV Network; America's Store; BBC America; Bio; Black Family Channel; Bloomberg Television; Boomerang; Canales N; CBS Sports Network; Cooking Channel; C-SPAN 3; Current; Daystar TV Network; DIY Network; Encore; ESPN; ESPNews; Flix; Fox College Sports Atlantic; Fox College Sports Central; Fox College Sports Pacific; Fox Movie Channel; Fox Soccer; Fuel TV; Fuse; G4; GAS; Great American Country; GSN; HD Theater; HDNet; HDNet Movies; History Channel International; Independent Film Channel; INHD (multiplexed); Lifetime Real Women; MTV Networks Digital Suite; Music Choice; NBA TV; Nick Jr.; Outdoor Channel; Ovation; Speed; Style Network; Sundance Channel; Tennis Channel; The Word Network; Toon Disney; Trinity Broadcasting Network; Turner Network TV HD; TV One.
Fee: $16.25 monthly, $2.95 monthly (Cinema Choice, Encore Movie Pak, Sports or Canales).

Digital Pay Service 1
Pay Units: N.A.
Programming (via satellite): Cinemax (multiplexed); HBO (multiplexed); Showtime (multiplexed); Starz (multiplexed); The Movie Channel (multiplexed).

Fee: $11.95 monthly (HBO, Cinemax, Showtime/TMC, or Starz).

Video-On-Demand: Yes

Pay-Per-View

iN DEMAND (delivered digitally); ESPN Full Court (delivered digitally); Ten Blox (delivered digitally); NBA League Pass (delivered digitally); NHL Center Ice (delivered digitally); NASCAR In Car (delivered digitally); Playboy TV (delivered digitally); Pleasure (delivered digitally); Ten Clips (delivered digitally); Ten Blue (delivered digitally).

Internet Service

Operational: Yes.

Broadband Service: Road Runner, EarthLink, AOL.

Fee: $99.95 installation; $46.95 monthly.

Telephone Service

Digital: Operational

Fee: $49.95 monthly

President: Tom Adams. Vice President, Technical Operations: Gary Frederick. Vice President, Sales & Marketing: Tom Smith. Vice President, Government & Public Affairs: Brad Phillips.

Ownership: Time Warner Cable (MSO).; Advance/Newhouse Partnership (MSO).

CARY—Time Warner Cable, 101 Innovation Ave, Ste 100, Morrisville, NC 27560. Phone: 919-573-7000. Fax: 919-573-7042. Web Site: http://www.timewarnercable.com/carolinas. Also serves Apex, Fuquay-Varina, Holly Springs, Johnston County (portions), Morrisville & Wake County (portions). ICA: NC0196.

TV Market Ranking: 73 (Apex, CARY, Fuquay-Varina, Holly Springs, Johnston County (portions), Morrisville, Wake County (portions)). Franchise award date: October 1, 1976. Franchise expiration date: N.A. Began: October 1, 1976.

Channel capacity: N.A. Channels available but not in use: N.A.

Basic Service

Subscribers: 35,831.

Programming (received off-air): WACN-LP Raleigh; WLFL (CW) Raleigh; WNCN (NBC) Goldsboro; WRAL-TV (CBS) Raleigh; WRAY-TV (IND) Wilson; WRAZ (FOX) Raleigh; WRDC (MNT) Durham; WRPX-TV (ION) Rocky Mount; WTVD (ABC) Durham; WUNC-TV (PBS) Chapel Hill; WUVC-DT (UNV) Fayetteville.

Programming (via satellite): Sneak Prevue; TBS Superstation; TV Guide Network; WGN America.

Fee: $42.95 installation; $12.75 monthly; $2.30 converter; $19.96 additional installation.

Expanded Basic Service 1

Subscribers: 24,875.

Programming (via satellite): A&E Networks; ABC Family Channel; AMC; Animal Planet; BET Networks; Cartoon Network; CNBC; CNN; Comedy Central; Country Music TV; C-SPAN; C-SPAN 2; Discovery Channel; Disney Channel; E! Entertainment Television; ESPN; ESPN 2; ESPN Classic Sports; Eternal Word TV Network; Food Network; Fox News Channel; Fox Sports Net; FX; Golf Channel; Hallmark Channel; Headline News; HGTV; History Channel; INSP; Lifetime; Lifetime Movie Network; MSNBC; MTV; National Geographic Channel; Nickelodeon; Oxygen; QVC; SoapNet; Spike TV; Syfy; The Learning Channel; The Weather Channel; Travel Channel; truTV; Turner Classic Movies; Turner Network TV; TV Land; USA Network; VH1; WE tv.

Fee: $38.05 monthly.

Digital Basic Service

Subscribers: N.A.

Programming (via satellite): America's Store; BBC America; Bloomberg Television; Canales N; Cooking Channel; Discovery Digital Networks; DIY Network; DMX Music; Encore; ESPNews; Flix; Fox Movie Channel; Fox Sports World; G4; GAS; Great American Country; GSN; Independent Film Channel; Lifetime Movie Network; MTV2; MuchMusic Network; Nick Jr.; Outdoor Channel; Ovation; Speed; Style Network; Sundance Channel; Toon Disney; Versus; VH1 Classic; WAM! America's Kidz Network.

Fee: $16.25 monthly.

Digital Pay Service 1

Pay Units: N.A.

Programming (via satellite): Cinemax (multiplexed); HBO (multiplexed); Showtime (multiplexed); Starz (multiplexed); The Movie Channel (multiplexed).

Fee: $11.95 monthly (each).

Video-On-Demand: Yes

Pay-Per-View

Addressable homes: 3,900.

Hot Choice; iN DEMAND; Shorteez (delivered digitally); Pleasure (delivered digitally); Movies (delivered digitally); Playboy TV (delivered digitally); ESPN Now (delivered digitally); Fresh (delivered digitally); Movies.

Internet Service

Operational: Yes.

Broadband Service: Road Runner, EarthLink, AOL.

Fee: $99.95 installation; $44.95 monthly; $3.00 modem lease.

Telephone Service

Digital: Operational

Miles of Plant: 838.0 (coaxial); 12.0 (fiber optic).

President: Tom Adams. Vice President, Technical Operations: Gary Frederick. Vice President, Sales & Marketing: Tom Smith. Vice President, Government & Public Affairs: Brad Phillips.

Ownership: Time Warner Cable (MSO).; Advance/Newhouse Partnership (MSO).

CEDAR ISLAND—Time Warner Cable, 101 Innovation Ave, Ste 100, Morrisville, NC 27560. Phones: 919-573-7000; 910-763-0004 (Wilmington office). Fax: 919-573-7042. Web Site: http://www.timewarnercable.com/carolinas. ICA: NC0249.

TV Market Ranking: Below 100 (CEDAR ISLAND).

Channel capacity: N.A. Channels available but not in use: N.A.

Basic Service

Subscribers: N.A. Included in Wilmington

Programming (received off-air): WCTI-TV (ABC) New Bern; WFXI (FOX, MNT) Morehead City; WITN-TV (MNT, NBC) Washington; WNCT-TV (CBS, CW) Greenville.

Programming (via satellite): ION Television; PBS Kids Channel; Univision Studios; WGN America.

Fee: $35.00 installation; $7.08 monthly; $18.00 additional installation.

Expanded Basic Service 1

Subscribers: N.A.

Programming (via satellite): A&E Networks; ABC Family Channel; AMC; Animal Planet; BET Networks; Bravo!; Cartoon Network; CNBC; CNN; Comedy Central; Country Music TV; C-SPAN; C-SPAN 2; Discovery Channel; Discovery Fit & Health; Discovery Health Channel; Disney Channel; E! Entertainment Television; ESPN; ESPN 2; ESPN Classic Sports; Food Network; Fox News Channel; Fox Sports South; FX; Golf Channel; Hallmark Channel; Headline News; HGTV; History Channel; Jewelry Television; Lifetime; Lifetime Movie Network; MSNBC; MTV; National Geographic Channel; Nickelodeon; Oxygen; QVC; SoapNet; Speed; Spike TV; Syfy; TBS Superstation; The Learning Channel; The Weather Channel; Travel Channel; Trinity Broadcasting Network; truTV; Turner Classic Movies; Turner Network TV; TV Guide Network; USA Network; Versus; VH1; WE tv.

Fee: $38.29 monthly.

Pay Service 1

Pay Units: N.A.

Programming (via satellite): Cinemax; HBO; Showtime; Starz (multiplexed); The Movie Channel.

Fee: $10.95 monthly (Cinemax, Starz or Showtime/TMC), $11.95 monthly (HBO).

Internet Service

Operational: Yes.

Broadband Service: RoadRunner.

Fee: $37.95 monthly.

Telephone Service

Digital: Operational

Fee: $24.99 monthly

President: Tom Adams. Vice President, Technical Services: Gary Frederick. Vice President, Sales & Marketing: Tom Smith. General Manager: Kim Cannon. Government & Public Affairs Director: Marty Feurer.

Ownership: Time Warner Cable (MSO).; Advance/Newhouse Partnership (MSO).

CHAPEL HILL—Time Warner Cable, 101 Innovation Ave, Ste 100, Morrisville, NC 27560. Phone: 919-573-7000. Fax: 919-573-7042. Web Site: http://www.timewarnercable.com/carolinas. Also serves Bynum, Chatham County, Durham County, Orange County & Pittsboro. ICA: NC0017.

TV Market Ranking: 47,73 (Chatham County (portions), Orange County (portions)); 73 (Bynum, CHAPEL HILL, Durham County, Pittsboro); Below 100 (Chatham County (portions)); Outside TV Markets (Chatham County (portions)). Franchise award date: N.A. Franchise expiration date: July 16, 2016. Began: June 7, 1980.

Channel capacity: N.A. Channels available but not in use: N.A.

Basic Service

Subscribers: 28,011.

Programming (received off-air): WLFL (CW) Raleigh; WNCN (NBC) Goldsboro; WRAL-TV (CBS) Raleigh; WRAY-TV (IND) Wilson; WRAZ (FOX) Raleigh; WRDC (MNT) Durham; WRPX-TV (ION) Rocky Mount; WTVD (ABC) Durham; WUNC-TV (PBS) Chapel Hill; WUVC-DT (UNV) Fayetteville.

Programming (via satellite): BET Networks; Country Music TV; C-SPAN 2; Discovery Fit & Health; Discovery Health Channel; Disney Channel; E! Entertainment Television; ESPN Classic Sports; Fox Sports Net; FX; Lifetime Movie Network; National Geographic Channel; Oxygen; QVC; ShopNBC; SoapNet; TBS Superstation; Turner Classic Movies; TV Guide Network; TV Land; Versus; WE tv; WGN America.

Fee: $42.95 installation; $9.20 monthly; $19.95 additional installation.

Expanded Basic Service 1

Subscribers: N.A.

Programming (via satellite): A&E Networks; ABC Family Channel; AMC; Animal Planet; Cartoon Network; CNBC; CNN; Comedy Central; Discovery Channel; ESPN; ESPN 2; Food Network; Fox News Channel; Golf Channel; Hallmark Channel; Headline News; HGTV; INSP; Lifetime; MSNBC; MTV; Nickelodeon; Spike TV; Syfy; The Learning Channel; The Weather Channel; Travel Channel; truTV; Turner Network TV; USA Network; VH1.

Fee: $38.75 monthly.

Digital Basic Service

Subscribers: N.A.

Programming (via satellite): AmericanLife TV Network; America's Store; BBC America; Bio; Bloomberg Television; Boomerang; Cooking Channel; C-SPAN 3; Discovery Digital Networks; DIY Network; ESPNews; Fox Sports World; G4; GAS; Great American Country; GSN; History Channel International; Independent Film Channel; Lifetime Real Women; MTV Networks Digital Suite; Music Choice; Nick Jr.; Outdoor Channel; Ovation; Speed; Style Network; Toon Disney; Trinity Broadcasting Network.

Fee: $16.25 monthly.

Digital Pay Service 1

Pay Units: N.A.

Programming (via satellite): Cinemax (multiplexed); Encore; Flix; Fox Movie Channel; HBO (multiplexed); Showtime (multiplexed); Sundance Channel; The Movie Channel (multiplexed).

Fee: $11.95 monthly (each).

Video-On-Demand: Yes

Pay-Per-View

iN DEMAND (delivered digitally); ESPN Gameplan (delivered digitally); ESPN Full Court (delivered digitally); NBA League Pass (delivered digitally); MLS Direct Kick (delivered digitally); MLB Extra Innings (delivered digitally); NHL Center Ice (delivered digitally); NASCAR In Car (delivered digitally); Pleasure (delivered digitally); Playboy TV (delivered digitally).

Internet Service

Operational: Yes. Began: January 1, 2000.

Subscribers: 125,000.

Broadband Service: Road Runner, EarthLink, AOL, max.inter.net.

Fee: $99.95 installation; $44.95 monthly.

Telephone Service

Digital: Operational

Miles of Plant: 808.0 (coaxial); 32.0 (fiber optic).

Vice President & General Manager: Chris Whitaker. Regional Vice President, Operations: Darrell Hegar. Vice President, Government & Public Affairs: Jack Stanley. Technical Opeartions Director: Doug Davis.

Ownership: Time Warner Cable (MSO).; Advance/Newhouse Partnership (MSO).

CHARLOTTE—Time Warner Cable, 3140 W Arrowood Rd, Charlotte, NC 28273. Phones: 704-938-5144; 704-378-2500. Fax: 704-504-1997. Web Site: http://www.timewarnercable.com/carolinas. Also serves Cabarrus, Huntersville, Lancaster, Matthews, Mecklenburg County (unincorporated areas), Mint Hill, Pineville (portions) & Weddington. ICA: NC0001.

TV Market Ranking: 42 (Cabarrus, CHARLOTTE, Huntersville, Lancaster, Matthews, Mecklenburg County (unincorporated areas), Mint Hill, Pineville (portions), Weddington). Franchise award date: February 1, 1967. Franchise expiration date: N.A. Began: February 1, 1967.

Channel capacity: N.A. Channels available but not in use: N.A.

Basic Service

Subscribers: 441,087 Includes Albemarle, Gastonia, Kannapolis, Monroe, Rockingham, Salisbury, Shelby, & Wadesboro.

Programming (received off-air): WAXN-TV (IND) Kannapolis; WBTV (CBS) Charlotte; WCCB (FOX) Charlotte; WCNC-TV (NBC) Charlotte; WHKY-TV (IND) Hickory; WJZY (CW) Belmont; WMYT-TV (MNT) Rock Hill; WNSC-TV (PBS) Rock Hill; WSOC-TV (ABC) Charlotte; WTVI (PBS) Charlotte; WUNG-TV (PBS) Concord.

Programming (via satellite): WGN America.

Fee: $28.00 installation; $10.00 monthly; $3.35 converter; $18.00 additional installation.

Expanded Basic Service 1

Subscribers: N.A.

Programming (via satellite): A&E Networks; ABC Family Channel; AMC; Animal Planet; BET Networks; Bravo; Cartoon Network; CNBC; CNN; Comedy Central; Country Music TV; C-SPAN; C-SPAN 2; Discovery Channel; Discovery Health Channel; Disney Channel; E! Entertainment Television; ESPN; ESPN 2; ESPN Classic Sports; Eternal Word TV Network; Food Network; Fox News Channel; Fox Sports South; FX; Golf Channel; Hallmark Channel; Headline News; HGTV; History Channel; INSP; Lifetime; Lifetime Movie Network; MSNBC; MTV; National Geographic Channel; Nickelodeon; Oxygen; QVC; ShopNBC; Speed; Spike TV; SportSouth; Syfy; TBS Superstation; The Learning Channel; The Weather Channel; Travel Channel; truTV; Turner Classic Movies; Turner Network TV; TV Guide Network; TV Land; Univision Studios; USA Network; Versus; WE tv.

Fee: $39.95 monthly.

Digital Basic Service

Subscribers: 65,038.

Programming (via satellite): AmericanLife TV Network; America's Store; BBC America; Bio; Bloomberg Television; Boomerang; Cooking Channel; C-SPAN 3; Discovery Fit & Health; Disney Channel; DIY Network; FamilyNet; Fuse; G4; GAS; Great American Country; GSN; History Channel International; Independent Film Channel; INSP; MTV2; Music Choice; Nick Jr.; NickToons TV; Ovation; SoapNet; Style Network; Toon Disney; VH1 Classic.

Fee: $15.00 monthly; $6.42 converter.

Digital Expanded Basic Service

Subscribers: N.A.

Programming (via satellite): ESPNews; Fox Sports World; FSN Digital Atlantic; FSN Digital Central; FSN Digital Pacific; Fuel TV; NBA TV; Outdoor Channel; Tennis Channel.

Digital Pay Service 1

Pay Units: 39,536.

Programming (via satellite): Canales N; Cinemax (multiplexed); Deutsche Welle TV; Encore (multiplexed); Flix; Fox Movie Channel; HBO (multiplexed); RAI International; Saigon Broadcasting Television Network; Showtime (multiplexed); Starz (multiplexed); Sundance Channel; The Movie Channel (multiplexed); TV5, La Television International; WAM! America's Kidz Network; Zee TV USA.

Fee: $11.95 monthly (Cinemax, HBO, Showtime/TMC or Starz), $9.95 or $14.95 monthly (international channels).

Video-On-Demand: Yes

Pay-Per-View

iN DEMAND (delivered digitally); ESPN Now (delivered digitally); ESPN Full Court (delivered digitally); ESPN Gameplan (delivered digitally); Adult (delivered digitally); Sports PPV (delivered digitally).

Internet Service

Operational: Yes.

Subscribers: 67,070.

Broadband Service: Road Runner, AOL, EarthLink.

Fee: $39.95 installation; $46.95 monthly.

Telephone Service

Digital: Operational

Fee: $39.95 monthly

Miles of Plant: 15,116.0 (coaxial); 2,174.0 (fiber optic). Miles of plant include Albemarle, Gastonia, Kannapolis, Monroe, Rockingham, Salisbury, Shelby, & Wadesboro

President, Time Warner Cable Charlotte: Mike Munley. Vice President, Engineering: Richard Newcomb. Vice President, Technical Operations: Mike Cullim. Vice President, Marketing & Sales: Eric Franey. Technical Operations Director: Donnie Stone. Government Affairs Director: Michael Tanck. Public Affairs Director: Jessica Graham.

Ownership: Time Warner Cable (MSO).; Advance/Newhouse Partnership (MSO).

CHEROKEE INDIAN RESERVATION—

Cherokee Cablevision, 55 John Crowe Rd, PO Box 487, Cherokee, NC 28719-0487. Phone: 828-497-4861. Fax: 828-497-4983. Also serves Qualla. ICA: NC0106.

TV Market Ranking: Outside TV Markets (CHEROKEE INDIAN RESERVATION, Qualla). Franchise award date: N.A. Franchise expiration date: N.A. Began: March 1, 1980.

Channel capacity: 24 (not 2-way capable). Channels available but not in use: N.A.

Basic Service

Subscribers: 2,353.

Programming (received off-air): WDEF-TV (CBS) Chattanooga; WETP-TV (PBS) Sneedville; WLOS (ABC) Asheville; WUNE-TV (PBS) Linville; WYFF (NBC) Greenville.

Programming (via satellite): CNN; Country Music TV; C-SPAN; Discovery Channel; Disney Channel; ESPN; MTV; Nickelodeon; Spike TV; TBS Superstation; The Learning Channel; The Weather Channel; Turner Network TV; USA Network; WGN America.

Fee: $25.00 installation; $19.50 monthly.

Pay Service 1

Pay Units: 375.

Programming (via satellite): Cinemax.

Fee: $10.00 monthly.

Pay Service 2

Pay Units: 361.

Programming (via satellite): Showtime.

Fee: $10.00 monthly.

Video-On-Demand: No

Internet Service

Operational: Yes.

Broadband Service: IBBS.

Telephone Service

None

Miles of Plant: 200.0 (coaxial); None (fiber optic).

Manager: Delores Murphy.

Ownership: Cherokee Cablevision Inc.

CHERRY POINT—Time Warner Cable. Now served by NEWPORT, NC [NC0013]. ICA: NC0077.

CHINQUAPIN—Charter Communications. Now served by HOLLY RIDGE, NC [NC0069]. ICA: NC0223.

CLINTON—StarVision, 3850 N Hwy US 421, PO Box 319, Clinton, NC 28329-0319. Phones: 910-564-4194; 910-564-7888. Fax: 910-564-5410. Web Site: http://www.starvisions.tv. Also serves Garland, Roseboro, Salemburg & Sampson County. ICA: NC0070.

TV Market Ranking: 73 (CLINTON, Garland, Roseboro, Salemburg, Sampson County (portions)); Outside TV Markets (Sampson County (portions)). Franchise award date: May 1, 1980. Franchise expiration date: N.A. Began: May 8, 1981.

Channel capacity: N.A. Channels available but not in use: N.A.

Basic Service

Subscribers: 6,000.

Programming (received off-air): Local News on Cable; WECT (NBC) Wilmington; WFPX-TV (ION) Fayetteville; WLFL (CW) Raleigh; WNCN (NBC) Goldsboro; WRAL-TV (CBS) Raleigh; WRAZ (FOX) Raleigh; WRDC (MNT) Durham; WTVD (ABC) Durham; WUNU (PBS) Lumberton; WUVC-DT (UNV) Fayetteville.

Programming (via satellite): C-SPAN; INSP; QVC; Trinity Broadcasting Network; TV Guide Network; WGN America.

Fee: $34.74 installation; $10.49 monthly.

Expanded Basic Service 1

Subscribers: 2,999.

Programming (via satellite): A&E Networks; ABC Family Channel; ABC News Now; AMC; Animal Planet; BET Networks; Bravo; Cartoon Network; CNBC; CNN; Comedy Central; Country Music TV; Discovery Channel; Discovery Health Channel; Disney Channel; DIY Network; E! Entertainment Television; ESPN; ESPN 2; ESPN Classic Sports; ESPN U; Food Network; Fox News Channel; Fox Sports South; FX; Gospel Music TV; Hallmark Channel; Headline News; HGTV; History Channel; Lifetime; MSNBC; MTV; National Geographic Channel; Nickelodeon; RFD-TV; SoapNet; Spike TV; Syfy; TBS Superstation; The Learning Channel; The Weather Channel; Travel Channel; Turner Network TV; TV Land; USA Network; VH1.

Fee: $36.80 monthly.

Digital Basic Service

Subscribers: N.A.

Programming (via satellite): BBC America; Bio; Bloomberg Television; CMT Pure Country; Discovery Channel HD; Discovery Fit & Health; Discovery Home Channel; Discovery Kids Channel; Discovery Times Channel; ESPN Deportes; ESPN HD; ESPNews; Fox Movie Channel; Fox Soccer; G4; GMC; Golf Channel; Great American Country; GSN; HDNet; HDNet Movies; History Channel International; Lifetime Movie Network; Lifetime Real Women; Military Channel; MTV Hits; MTV2; Music Choice; Nick Jr.; NickToons TV; Outdoor Channel; Oxygen; Science; Speed; Sundance Channel; TeenNick; Toon Disney; truTV; TV Colombia; Universal HD; Versus; VH1 Classic; VH1 Soul; WE tv.

Fee: $14.99 monthly.

Digital Expanded Basic Service

Subscribers: N.A.

Programming (via satellite): Cine Mexicano; La Familia Network; Latele Novela Network; Puma TV; TBN Enlace USA; Tr3s; TV Chile.

Fee: $7.20 monthly.

Digital Pay Service 1

Pay Units: N.A.

Programming (via satellite): Cinemax (multiplexed); Encore; Flix; HBO (multiplexed); Playboy TV; Showtime; Starz (multiplexed); The Movie Channel (multiplexed).

Fee: $8.77 monthly (Cinemax), $9.95 monthly (Starz & Encore), $10.95 monthly (Showtime/TMC/Flix or Playboy), $11.03 monthly (HBO).

Video-On-Demand: No

Pay-Per-View

Hot Choice (delivered digitally); iN DEMAND (delivered digitally); Fresh (delivered digitally); Spice: Xcess (delivered digitally).

Internet Service

Operational: Yes.

Subscribers: 903.

Broadband Service: Intistar.

Fee: $79.95 installation; $49.95 monthly.

Telephone Service

None

Miles of Plant: None (coaxial); 94.0 (fiber optic).

President: Robert G. Hester. General Manager: Randy Jacobs. Chief Technician: Johnny Eason. Marketing Manager: Vivian Lewis.

Ownership: StarVision Inc.

COLUMBIA—Mediacom. Now served by PLYMOUTH, NC [NC0085]. ICA: NC0154.

COLUMBUS COUNTY (central portion)—Formerly served by Carolina Cable Partnership. No longer in operation. ICA: NC0197.

COLUMBUS COUNTY (unincorporated areas)

—Time Warner Cable, 101 Innovation Ave, Ste 100, Morrisville, NC 27560. Phones: 910-763-0004; 919-573-7000 (Morrisville office). Fax: 919-573-7042. Web Site: http://www.timewarnercable.com. Also serves Tabor City. ICA: NC0155.

TV Market Ranking: Below 100 (COLUMBUS COUNTY (UNINCORPORATED AREAS), Tabor City). Franchise award date: N.A. Franchise expiration date: N.A. Began: September 1, 1983.

Channel capacity: N.A. Channels available but not in use: N.A.

Basic Service

Subscribers: 1,127.

Programming (received off-air): WBTW (CBS, MNT) Florence; WECT (NBC) Wilmington; WJPM-TV (PBS) Florence; WPDE-TV (ABC) Florence; WSFX-TV (FOX) Wilmington; WUNJ-TV (PBS) Wilmington; WWAY (ABC) Wilmington.

Programming (via satellite): A&E Networks; ABC Family Channel; BET Networks; CNN; Country Music TV; Discovery Channel; Disney Channel; ESPN; Hallmark Channel; Headline News; Lifetime; MTV; Nickelodeon; Spike TV; Syfy; TBS Superstation; The Learning Channel; Turner Network TV; USA Network; WGN America.

Fee: $35.00 installation; $20.50 monthly.

Pay Service 1

Pay Units: 86.

Programming (via satellite): Cinemax.

Fee: $9.95 monthly.

Pay Service 2

Pay Units: 119.

Programming (via satellite): HBO.

Fee: $10.95 monthly.

Pay Service 3

Pay Units: 57.

Programming (via satellite): Showtime.

Fee: $9.95 monthly.

Video-On-Demand: No

Internet Service

Operational: No.

Telephone Service

None

Miles of Plant: 158.0 (coaxial); None (fiber optic).

President: Tom Adams. Vice President, Technical Services: Gary Frederick. Vice President, Marketing & Sales: Tom Smith. Manager: Kim Cannon. Government & Public Affairs Director: Marty Feurer.

Ownership: Time Warner Cable (MSO).

CONWAY—Mediacom. Now served by RICH SQUARE, NC [NC0115]. ICA: NC0198.

COROLLA—Charter Communications. Now served by MANTEO, NC [NC0118]. ICA: NC0139.

CRAVEN—Now served by GOLD HILL, NC [NC0140]. ICA: NC0165.

CRESTON (southern portion)—Zito Media, 611 Vader Hill Rd, Coudersport, PA 16915. Phone: 814-260-9575. Web Site: http://www.zitomedia.com. ICA: NC0199.
TV Market Ranking: Below 100 (CRESTON). Franchise award date: N.A. Franchise expiration date: N.A. Began: N.A.
Channel capacity: N.A. Channels available but not in use: N.A.
Basic Service
Subscribers: 415.
Programming (received off-air): WBTV (CBS) Charlotte; WCYB-TV (CW, NBC) Bristol; WGHP (FOX, IND) High Point; WJHL-TV (CBS) Johnson City; WKPT-TV (ABC) Kingsport; WUNL-TV (PBS) Winston-Salem; WXII-TV (NBC) Winston-Salem.
Programming (via satellite): ABC Family Channel; CNN; Discovery Channel; ESPN; Spike TV; TBS Superstation; The Weather Channel; USA Network.
Fee: $29.95 installation; $38.00 monthly.
Digital Basic Service
Subscribers: N.A.
Programming (via satellite): AmericanLife TV Network; BBC America; Bio; Bloomberg Television; Bravo; CMT Pure Country; Discovery Fit & Health; DMX Music; Fox Movie Channel; Fox Soccer; Fuse; G4; Golf Channel; GSN; HGTV; History Channel; History Channel International; Independent Film Channel; INSP; Lifetime Movie Network; Military History Channel; MTV Networks Digital Suite; Nick Jr.; Outdoor Channel; Speed; Style Network; Syfy; TeenNick; Toon Disney; Trinity Broadcasting Network; Turner Classic Movies; Versus; WE tv.
Pay Service 1
Pay Units: N.A.
Programming (via satellite): HBO.
Fee: $12.00 monthly.
Digital Pay Service 1
Pay Units: N.A.
Programming (via satellite): Cinemax (multiplexed); Encore (multiplexed); HBO (multiplexed); Showtime (multiplexed); Starz (multiplexed); The Movie Channel (multiplexed).
Video-On-Demand: No
Pay-Per-View
iN DEMAND (delivered digitally); Hot Choice (delivered digitally); Playboy TV (delivered digitally).
Internet Service
Operational: No.
Telephone Service
None
Public Relations Manager: Mark Laver.
Ownership: Zito Media (MSO).

CRUSO—Carolina Mountain Cable. Now served by WAYNESVILLE, NC [NC0127]. ICA: NC0158.

DAVIDSON COUNTY—Time Warner Cable. Now served by GREENSBORO, NC [NC0006]. ICA: NC0040.

DAVIDSON COUNTY—Windstream Communications, 200 N State St, PO Box 808, Lexington, NC 27292. Phone: 336-249-9901. Fax: 336-238-2160. Web Site: http://www.windstream.com. Also serves Guilford County (portions) & High Point. ICA: NC0247. **Note:** This system is an overbuild.
TV Market Ranking: 47 (DAVIDSON COUNTY, Guilford County (portions), High Point). Franchise award date: January 1, 1997. Franchise expiration date: N.A. Began: October 1, 1997.
Channel capacity: 116 (operating 2-way). Channels available but not in use: N.A.
Basic Service
Subscribers: 11,500.
Programming (received off-air): WBTV (CBS) Charlotte; WCWG (CW) Lexington; WFMY-TV (CBS) Greensboro; WGHP (FOX, IND) High Point; WGPX-TV (ION) Burlington; WLXI (IND) Greensboro; WMYV (MNT) Greensboro; WUNL-TV (PBS) Winston-Salem; WXII-TV (NBC) Winston-Salem; WXLV-TV (ABC) Winston-Salem.
Programming (via satellite): CityTV; C-SPAN; C-SPAN 2; INSP; News 14 Carolina; QVC; TV Guide Network; WGN America.
Fee: $50.00 installation; $11.59 monthly.
Expanded Basic Service 1
Subscribers: 10,430.
Programming (via satellite): A&E Networks; ABC Family Channel; AMC; Animal Planet; BET Networks; Bravo; Cartoon Network; CNBC; CNN; Comedy Central; Country Music TV; Discovery Channel; Discovery Fit & Health; Discovery Health Channel; Disney Channel; E! Entertainment Television; ESPN; ESPN 2; ESPN Classic Sports; Food Network; Fox News Channel; Fox Sports South; FX; Golf Channel; Great American Country; GSN; Hallmark Channel; Headline News; HGTV; History Channel; Lifetime; Lifetime Movie Network; MoviePlex; MSNBC; MTV; National Geographic Channel; Nickelodeon; Outdoor Channel; Speed; Spike TV; SportSouth; Syfy; TBS Superstation; The Learning Channel; The Weather Channel; Toon Disney; Travel Channel; truTV; Turner Classic Movies; Turner Network TV; TV Land; Univision Studios; USA Network; VH1; WE tv.
Fee: $45.89 monthly.
Digital Basic Service
Subscribers: 3,516.
Programming (via satellite): A&E HD; ABC Family HD; AmericanLife TV Network; Animal Planet HD; BBC America; Bio; Boomerang; CMT Pure Country; CNBC World; CNN HD; Cooking Channel; Discovery Channel HD; Discovery Health Channel; Discovery Home Channel; Discovery Kids Channel; Disney Channel HD; DIY Network; DMX Music; E! Entertainment Television; ESPN 2 HD; ESPN HD; ESPN U; ESPNews; Food Network HD; Fox Business Channel; Fox Movie Channel; Fox Reality Channel; Fuel TV; FX HD; G4; GMC; Golf Channel HD; Hallmark Movie Channel; HD Theater; HDNet; HDNet Movies; Healthy Living Channel; HGTV HD; History Channel International; ID Investigation Discovery; Lifetime Movie Network HD; Lifetime Real Women; Lifetime Television HD; Military Channel; MTV Hits; MTV Jams; MTV2; National Geographic Channel HD Network; Nick Jr.; Nick Too; NickToons TV; Oxygen; RFD-TV; Science; Science HD; SoapNet; Speed HD; Style Network; TBS in HD; TeenNick; TLC HD; Travel Channel HD; Turner Network TV HD; Universal HD; Versus; Versus HD; VH1 Classic; VH1 Soul.
Fee: $58.99 monthly.
Digital Expanded Basic Service
Subscribers: N.A.
Programming (via satellite): Fox College Sports Atlantic; Fox College Sports Central; Fox College Sports Pacific; Fox Soccer; Tennis Channel.
Fee: $1.99 monthly.
Digital Expanded Basic Service 2
Subscribers: N.A.
Programming (via satellite): Cine Latino; Cine Mexicano; CNN en Espanol; Discovery en Espanol; ESPN Deportes; Fox Deportes; History Channel en Espanol; mun2 television; Sorpresa; Tr3s; VeneMovies.
Fee: $4.19 monthly.
Digital Pay Service 1
Pay Units: N.A.
Programming (via satellite): Cinemax (multiplexed); Encore (multiplexed); Flix; HBO (multiplexed); HBO HD; Showtime (multiplexed); Showtime HD; Starz; Sundance Channel; The Movie Channel (multiplexed).
Fee: $6.39 monthly (Encore), $10.29 monthly (Starz), $10.99 monthly (Cinemax or HBO), $13.99 monthly (TMC/Showtime).
Video-On-Demand: Yes
Pay-Per-View
iN DEMAND (delivered digitally); Hot Choice (delivered digitally); Pleasure (delivered digitally).
Internet Service
Operational: Yes, Both DSL & dial-up.
Subscribers: 7,808.
Broadband Service: TURBOconnect.
Fee: $21.99-$59.99 monthly.
Telephone Service
Analog: Not Operational
Digital: Operational
Subscribers: 1,150.
Fee: $39.95-$49.95 monthly
Miles of Plant: 855.0 (coaxial); None (fiber optic).
President: Richard Reese. Operations Manager: John Beck.
Ownership: Windstream Communications Inc.

DOBSON—Time Warner Cable. Now served by GREENSBORO, NC [NC0006]. ICA: NC0091.

DOVER—Formerly served by Johnston County Cable LP. No longer in operation. ICA: NC0185.

DUNCAN—Carolina Cable Partnership. No longer in operation. ICA: NC0149.

DURHAM—Time Warner Cable, 101 Innovation Ave, Ste 100, Morrisville, NC 27560. Phone: 919-572-7000. Fax: 919-573-7042. Web Site: http://www.timewarnercable.com/carolinas. Also serves Butner, Creedmoor, Durham County (portions), Gorman, Granville County (portions), Orange County (portions), Stern & Wake County (portions). ICA: NC0005.
TV Market Ranking: 73 (Butner, Creedmoor, DURHAM, Durham County (portions), Gorman, Granville County (portions), Orange County (portions), Stern, Wake County (portions)). Franchise award date: June 1, 1973. Franchise expiration date: N.A. Began: September 1, 1977.
Channel capacity: N.A. Channels available but not in use: N.A.
Basic Service
Subscribers: 58,969.
Programming (received off-air): WLFL (CW) Raleigh; WNCN (NBC) Goldsboro; WRAL-TV (CBS) Raleigh; WRAY-TV (IND) Wilson; WRAZ (FOX) Raleigh; WRDC (MNT) Durham; WRPX-TV (ION) Rocky Mount; WTVD (ABC) Durham; WUNC-TV (PBS) Chapel Hill; WUVC-DT (UNV) Fayetteville.
Programming (via satellite): BET Networks; C-SPAN; QVC; TBS Superstation; TV Guide Network; WGN America.
Fee: $42.95 installation; $9.20 monthly; $1.27 converter.
Expanded Basic Service 1
Subscribers: N.A.
Programming (via satellite): A&E Networks; ABC Family Channel; AMC; Animal Planet; Cartoon Network; CNBC; CNN; Comedy Central; Country Music TV; C-SPAN 2; Discovery Channel; Disney Channel; E! Entertainment Television; ESPN; ESPN 2; ESPN Classic Sports; Food Network; Fox News Channel; Fox Sports Net; FX; Golf Channel; Hallmark Channel; Headline News; HGTV; History Channel; INSP; Lifetime; Lifetime Movie Network; MSNBC; MTV; National Geographic Channel; Nickelodeon; Oxygen; QVC; SoapNet; Spike TV; Syfy; The Learning Channel; The Weather Channel; Travel Channel; truTV; Turner Classic Movies; Turner Network TV; TV Land; USA Network; VH1; WE tv.
Fee: $38.75 monthly.
Digital Basic Service
Subscribers: N.A.
Programming (via satellite): America's Store; BBC America; Black Family Channel; Bloomberg Television; C-SPAN 3; Discovery Digital Networks; Disney Channel; ESPNews; Fox Sports World; FSN Digital Atlantic; FSN Digital Central; FSN Digital Pacific; G4; Great American Country; GSN; Lifetime Movie Network; MTV2; MuchMusic Network; Music Choice; Nick Jr.; Outdoor Channel; Ovation; Speed; Style Network; Toon Disney; VH1 Classic.
Fee: $16.25 monthly.
Digital Pay Service 1
Pay Units: N.A.
Programming (via satellite): Cinemax (multiplexed); HBO (multiplexed); Showtime (multiplexed); The Movie Channel.
Fee: $11.95 monthly (each).
Video-On-Demand: Yes
Pay-Per-View
Hot Choice (delivered digitally); movies; special events; Sports PPV; ESPN Now; Playboy TV (delivered digitally); Playboy en Espanol; Pleasure; Spice; Shorteez.
Internet Service
Operational: Yes.
Broadband Service: Road Runner, EarthLink, AOL.
Fee: $99.95 installation; $45.95 monthly; $3.00 modem lease.
Telephone Service
Digital: Operational
Fee: $44.95 monthly
Miles of Plant: 1,158.0 (coaxial); 42.0 (fiber optic).
President: Tom Adams. Vice President, Technical Operations: Gary Frederick. Vice President, Sales & Marketing: Tom Smith. Vice President, Government & Public Affairs: Brad Phillips.
Ownership: Time Warner Cable (MSO).; Advance/Newhouse Partnership (MSO).

EDENTON—Mediacom, 910 NC Hwy 32 S, PO Box 580, Plymouth, NC 27962. Phone: 252-793-1570. Fax: 252-793-6135. Web Site: http://www.mediacomcable.com. Also serves Arrowhead Beach, Chowan Beach, Chowan County, Hertford, Perquimans County & Winfall. ICA: NC0076.

TV Market Ranking: Outside TV Markets (Arrowhead Beach, Chowan Beach, Chowan County, EDENTON, Hertford, Perquimans County, Winfall). Franchise award date: December 8, 1980. Franchise expiration date: N.A. Began: August 1, 1981.
Channel capacity: N.A. Channels available but not in use: N.A.

Basic Service
Subscribers: 4,524.
Programming (received off-air): WAVY-TV (NBC) Portsmouth; WCTI-TV (ABC) New Bern; WGNT (CW) Portsmouth; WHRO-TV (PBS) Hampton-Norfolk; WITN-TV (MNT, NBC) Washington; WPXV-TV (ION) Norfolk; WSKY-TV (IND) Manteo; WTKR (CBS) Norfolk; WTVZ-TV (MNT) Norfolk; WUND-TV (PBS) Edenton; WVBT (FOX) Virginia Beach; WVEC (ABC) Hampton; allband FM.
Programming (via satellite): History Channel; TV Guide Network; WGN America.
Fee: $45.00 installation; $14.46 monthly.

Expanded Basic Service 1
Subscribers: N.A.
Programming (via satellite): A&E Networks; ABC Family Channel; AMC; Animal Planet; BET Networks; Bravo; Cartoon Network; CNBC; CNN; Comedy Central; Country Music TV; C-SPAN; Discovery Channel; Discovery Fit & Health; Disney Channel; ESPN; ESPN 2; Food Network; Fox News Channel; Fox Sports South; FX; Hallmark Channel; Headline News; HGTV; INSP; Lifetime; MSNBC; MTV; Nickelodeon; Outdoor Channel; QVC; Speed; Spike TV; Syfy; TBS Superstation; The Learning Channel; The Weather Channel; Toon Disney; Travel Channel; Turner Network TV; TV Land; USA Network; VH1; WE tv.
Fee: $33.49 monthly.

Digital Basic Service
Subscribers: N.A.
Programming (via satellite): AmericanLife TV Network; BBC America; Bio; Bloomberg Television; DMX Music; ESPN; ESPNews; Fox Movie Channel; Fox Soccer; Fuse; G4; GAS; Golf Channel; GSN; HD Theater; HDNet; HDNet Movies; History Channel International; Independent Film Channel; Lifetime Movie Network; Lime; MTV2; National Geographic Channel; Nick Jr.; Style Network; The Word Network; truTV; Turner Classic Movies; Versus; Weatherscan.
Fee: $8.00 monthly.

Digital Pay Service 1
Pay Units: N.A.
Programming (via satellite): Cinemax (multiplexed); Encore (multiplexed); Flix (multiplexed); HBO (multiplexed); HBO HD; Showtime (multiplexed); Showtime HD; Starz (multiplexed); Starz HDTV; Sundance Channel (multiplexed); The Movie Channel (multiplexed); The Movie Channel HD.
Fee: $8.00 monthly Starz, $9.95 monthly (Showtime or Cinemax), $13.95 monthly (HBO).

Video-On-Demand: Planned

Pay-Per-View
iN DEMAND (delivered digitally); ESPN Sports PPV (delivered digitally).

Internet Service
Operational: Yes. Began: January 1, 2002.
Broadband Service: Mediacom High Speed Internet.
Fee: $59.95 installation; $40.95 monthly; $3.00 modem lease.

Telephone Service
Digital: Operational
Fee: $39.95 monthly
Miles of plant (coax & fiber) included in Plymouth
General Manager: Wayne Holiday. Marketing Analyst: Renette Ruffin. Office Manager: Wendy White.
Ownership: Mediacom LLC (MSO).

ELIZABETH CITY—Time Warner Cable, 101 Innovation Ave, Ste 100, Morrisville, NC 27560. Phone: 919-573-7000. Fax: 919-573-7042. Web Site: http://www.timewarnercable.com/carolinas. Also serves Pasquotank County. ICA: NC0043.
TV Market Ranking: 44 (Pasquotank County (portions)); Outside TV Markets (ELIZABETH CITY, Pasquotank County (portions)). Franchise award date: November 1, 1973. Franchise expiration date: N.A. Began: March 1, 1976.
Channel capacity: 62 (operating 2-way). Channels available but not in use: N.A.

Basic Service
Subscribers: 9,593.
Programming (received off-air): W18BB Elizabeth City; WAVY-TV (NBC) Portsmouth; WGNT (CW) Portsmouth; WHRO-TV (PBS) Hampton-Norfolk; WNCT-TV (CBS, CW) Greenville; WPXV-TV (ION) Norfolk; WSKY-TV (IND) Manteo; WTKR (CBS) Norfolk; WTVZ-TV (MNT) Norfolk; WUND-TV (PBS) Edenton; WVBT (FOX) Virginia Beach; WVEC (ABC) Hampton; allband FM.
Programming (via satellite): QVC; TBS Superstation; TV Guide Network.
Fee: $39.95 installation; $8.25 monthly.

Expanded Basic Service 1
Subscribers: 9,027.
Programming (via satellite): A&E Networks; ABC Family Channel; AMC; Animal Planet; BET Networks; Cartoon Network; CNBC; CNN; Comedy Central; Country Music TV; C-SPAN; C-SPAN 2; Discovery Channel; Disney Channel; E! Entertainment Television; ESPN; ESPN 2; Eternal Word TV Network; Food Network; Fox News Channel; Fox Sports South; FX; Headline News; HGTV; History Channel; INSP; Lifetime; LWS Local Weather Station; MSNBC; MTV; Nickelodeon; Spike TV; Syfy; The Learning Channel; The Weather Channel; Travel Channel; truTV; Turner Network TV; TV Land; USA Network; VH1.
Fee: $34.18 monthly.

Digital Basic Service
Subscribers: N.A.
Programming (via satellite): AmericanLife TV Network; BBC America; Bio; Bloomberg Television; Canales N; C-SPAN 3; Discovery Digital Networks; ESPN Classic Sports; ESPNews; Fox Movie Channel; Fox Sports World; G4; GAS; Golf Channel; GSN; Halogen Network; History Channel International; Independent Film Channel; MTV Networks Digital Suite; Music Choice; National Geographic Channel; Nick Jr.; Outdoor Channel; SoapNet; Speed; Style Network; Toon Disney; Trinity Broadcasting Network; Turner Classic Movies; Versus; WE tv.
Fee: $10.00 monthly.

Digital Pay Service 1
Pay Units: N.A.
Programming (via satellite): Cinemax (multiplexed); Encore (multiplexed); Flix; HBO (multiplexed); Showtime (multiplexed); Starz (multiplexed); The Movie Channel (multiplexed).
Fee: $15.95 monthly (HBO, Cinemax, Showtime, TMC or Starz), $19.95 monthly (Playboy).

Video-On-Demand: No

Pay-Per-View
Urban Extra (delivered digitally); Fresh (delivered digitally); Playboy TV (delivered digitally); Hot Choice (delivered digitally).

Internet Service
Operational: Yes. Began: September 1, 2000.
Subscribers: 10,300.
Broadband Service: Road Runner.
Fee: $44.95 monthly.

Telephone Service
Digital: Planned
Miles of Plant: 277.0 (coaxial); 80.0 (fiber optic).
Vice President & General Manager: Chris Whitaker. Vice President, Technical Operations: Gary Frederick. Vice President, Sales & Marketing: Tom Smith. Vice President, Government & Public Affairs: Brad Phillips.
Ownership: Time Warner Cable (MSO).

ELIZABETHTOWN—Time Warner Cable, 101 Innovation Ave, Ste 100, Morrisville, NC 27560. Phones: 910-763-0004 (Wilmington office); 919-573-7000. Fax: 919-573-7042. Web Site: http://www.timewarnercable.com/carolinas. Also serves Bladen County (portions), Bladenboro, Brunswick, Cerro Gordo, Chadbourn, Clarkton, Dublin, White Lake & Whiteville. ICA: NC0071.
TV Market Ranking: 73 (Bladen County (portions), Dublin, ELIZABETHTOWN); Outside TV Markets (Bladenboro, Brunswick, Cerro Gordo, Chadbourn, Clarkton, White Lake, Whiteville, Bladen County (portions)). Franchise award date: May 4, 1981. Franchise expiration date: October 12, 2007. Began: December 30, 1981.
Channel capacity: N.A. Channels available but not in use: N.A.

Basic Service
Subscribers: N.A. Included in Wilmington
Programming (received off-air): WBTW (CBS, MNT) Florence; WECT (NBC) Wilmington; WFPX-TV (ION) Fayetteville; WSFX-TV (FOX) Wilmington; WTVD (ABC) Durham; WUNJ-TV (PBS) Wilmington; WUVC-DT (UNV) Fayetteville; WWAY (ABC) Wilmington.
Programming (via satellite): ABC Family Channel; CNBC; C-SPAN; WGN America.
Fee: $35.00 installation; $8.29 monthly; $2.88 converter.

Expanded Basic Service 1
Subscribers: N.A.
Programming (via satellite): A&E Networks; AMC; Animal Planet; BET Networks; Bravo; Cartoon Network; CNN; Comedy Central; Country Music TV; C-SPAN 2; Discovery Channel; Discovery Health Channel; Disney Channel; E! Entertainment Television; ESPN; ESPN 2; ESPN Classic Sports; Eternal Word TV Network; Food Network; Fox News Channel; Fox Sports South; Fuse; FX; Golf Channel; Hallmark Channel; Halogen Network; Headline News; HGTV; History Channel; Lifetime; Lifetime Movie Network; MSNBC; MTV; National Geographic Channel; Nickelodeon; Oxygen; QVC; ShopNBC; SoapNet; Speed; Spike TV; Syfy; TBS Superstation; The Learning Channel; The Weather Channel; Travel Channel; Trinity Broadcasting Network; Turner Classic Movies; Turner Network TV; TV Guide Network; TV Land; USA Network; Versus; VH1; WE tv.
Fee: $33.87 monthly.

Digital Basic Service
Subscribers: N.A. Included in Wilmington
Programming (via satellite): AmericanLife TV Network; America's Store; BBC America; Bio; Black Family Channel; Bloomberg Television; CNBC; Cooking Channel; C-SPAN 3; Discovery Digital Networks; Disney Channel; DIY Network; ESPNews; Flix; Fox Movie Channel; Fox Sports Net (multiplexed); Fox Sports World; Fuel TV; G4; Great American Country; GSN; Halogen Network; History Channel International; Independent Film Channel; Lifetime Real Women; MTV2; Nick Jr.; Outdoor Channel; Ovation; Style Network; Sundance Channel; Tennis Channel; The Word Network; Toon Disney; TV Land; VH1 Classic.
Fee: $6.95 monthly.

Digital Pay Service 1
Pay Units: N.A.
Programming (via satellite): Cinemax (multiplexed); Encore; HBO (multiplexed); Showtime (multiplexed); The Movie Channel (multiplexed).
Fee: $11.95 monthly (Cinemax, Starz, or Showtime & TMC), $13.95 monthly (HBO).

Video-On-Demand: Yes

Pay-Per-View
Pleasure (delivered digitally); Fresh (delivered digitally); Shorteez (delivered digitally); Hot Choice (delivered digitally); iN DEMAND (delivered digitally); Playboy TV (delivered digitally).

Internet Service
Operational: Yes.
Broadband Service: Road Runner.
Fee: $69.95 installation; $44.95 monthly.

Telephone Service
Digital: Operational
Fee: $44.95 monthly
Miles of Plant: 170.0 (coaxial); 12.0 (fiber optic).
President: Tom Adams. Vice President, Technical Services: Gary Frederick. Vice President, Sales & Marketing: Tom Smith. General Manager: Kim Cannon. Public Affairs Director: Marty Feurer.
Ownership: Time Warner Cable (MSO).; Advance/Newhouse Partnership (MSO).

ELKIN—Time Warner Cable. Now served by MOUNT AIRY, NC [NC0075]. ICA: NC0095.

ENFIELD—Suddenlink Communications, 12444 Powerscourt Dr, Saint Louis, MO 63131-3660. Phone: 314-965-2020. Web Site: http://www.suddenlink.com. ICA: NC0126.
TV Market Ranking: Below 100 (ENFIELD). Franchise award date: July 1, 1978. Franchise expiration date: April 6, 2007. Began: June 1, 1980.
Channel capacity: N.A. Channels available but not in use: N.A.

Basic Service
Subscribers: N.A. Included in Scotland Neck
Programming (received off-air): WNCT-TV (CBS, CW) Greenville; WRAL-TV (CBS) Raleigh; WTVD (ABC) Durham; WUNK-TV (PBS) Greenville.
Programming (via satellite): A&E Networks; ABC Family Channel; BET Networks; Cartoon Network; CNBC; Country Music TV; E! Entertainment Television; ESPN; Food Network; Nickelodeon; QVC; Syfy; The Learning Channel; The Weather Channel; Trinity Broadcasting Network; USA Network; WGN America.
Fee: $21.99 installation; $19.95 monthly.

Expanded Basic Service 1
Subscribers: N.A. Included in Scotland Neck
Programming (via satellite): CNN; Discovery Channel; Disney Channel; Spike TV; Turner Classic Movies; Turner Network TV.
Fee: $3.45 monthly.

Pay Service 1
Pay Units: 480.
Programming (via satellite): Cinemax.
Fee: $9.75 monthly.
Pay Service 2
Pay Units: 572.
Programming (via satellite): HBO.
Fee: $8.75 monthly.
Internet Service
Operational: Yes.
Broadband Service: Suddenlink High Speed Internet.
Fee: $100.00 installation; $39.95 monthly.
Telephone Service
None
Miles of Plant: 24.0 (coaxial); None (fiber optic).
Ownership: Cequel Communications LLC (MSO).

FAIR BLUFF—Formerly served by MIM Cable. No longer in operation. ICA: NC0178.

FAISON—Charter Communications. Now served by HOLLY RIDGE, NC [NC0069]. ICA: NC0236.

FARMVILLE—Time Warner Cable, 101 Innovation Ave, Ste 100, Morrisville, NC 27560. Phone: 919-573-7000. Fax: 919-573-7042. Web Site: http://www.timewarnercable.com/carolinas. Also serves Pitt County. ICA: NC0096.
TV Market Ranking: 84 (FARMVILLE); 84,73 (Pitt County (portions)). Franchise award date: N.A. Franchise expiration date: November 26, 2006. Began: December 22, 1981.
Channel capacity: N.A. Channels available but not in use: N.A.
Basic Service
Subscribers: 1,781.
Programming (received off-air): WCTI-TV (ABC) New Bern; WLFL (CW) Raleigh; WNCT-TV (CBS, CW) Greenville; WRAL-TV (CBS) Raleigh; WTVD (ABC) Durham; WUNK-TV (PBS) Greenville; WYDO (FOX) Greenville.
Programming (via satellite): TBS Superstation; TV Guide Network; WGN America.
Fee: $42.95 installation; $14.95 monthly; $3.00 converter; $19.96 additional installation.
Expanded Basic Service 1
Subscribers: N.A.
Programming (via satellite): A&E Networks; ABC Family Channel; AMC; Animal Planet; BET Networks; Bravo; Cartoon Network; CNBC; CNN; Comedy Central; Country Music TV; C-SPAN; C-SPAN 2; Disney Channel; E! Entertainment Television; ESPN; ESPN 2; ESPN Classic Sports; Eternal Word TV Network; Food Network; Fox News Channel; Fox Sports Net; FX; Golf Channel; Hallmark Channel; Headline News; HGTV; History Channel; INSP; Lifetime; Lifetime Movie Network; MSNBC; MTV; Nickelodeon; Oxygen; QVC; SoapNet; Spike TV; Syfy; The Learning Channel; The Weather Channel; Travel Channel; Trinity Broadcasting Network; truTV; Turner Classic Movies; Turner Network TV; TV Land; USA Network; VH1; WE tv.
Fee: $33.00 monthly.
Digital Basic Service
Subscribers: N.A.
Programming (via satellite): America's Store; BBC America; Black Family Channel; Bloomberg Television; Canales N; Cooking Channel; C-SPAN 3; Discovery Digital Networks; DIY Network; Encore Action; ESPNews; Fox Sports World; FSN Digital Atlantic; FSN Digital Central; FSN Digital Pacific; Fuse; G4; GAS; Great American Country; GSN; MTV2; Music Choice; Nick Jr.; Outdoor Channel; Ovation; Speed; Style Network; Toon Disney; Versus; VH1 Classic.
Fee: $16.25 monthly.
Digital Pay Service 1
Pay Units: 57.
Programming (via satellite): Cinemax (multiplexed); Flix; Fox Movie Channel; HBO (multiplexed); Independent Film Channel; Showtime (multiplexed); Starz (multiplexed); Sundance Channel; The Movie Channel (multiplexed).
Fee: $11.95 monthly (each).
Video-On-Demand: Yes
Pay-Per-View
iN DEMAND (delivered digitally); Hot Choice (delivered digitally); Playboy TV (delivered digitally); Fresh (delivered digitally); Shorteez (delivered digitally); Pleasure (delivered digitally); ESPN Now (delivered digitally).
Internet Service
Operational: Yes. Began: December 31, 2002.
Broadband Service: Road Runner.
Fee: $99.95 installation; $44.95 monthly; $3.00 modem lease.
Telephone Service
Digital: Operational
Fee: $44.95 monthly
Miles of Plant: 92.0 (coaxial); None (fiber optic).
President: Tom Adams. Vice President, Technical Operations: Gary Frederick. Vice President, Sales & Marketing: Tom Smith. Vice President, Government & Public Affairs: Brad Phillips.
Ownership: Time Warner Cable (MSO).; Advance/Newhouse Partnership (MSO).

FAYETTEVILLE—Time Warner Cable, 6202 Raeford Rd, Fayetteville, NC 28304. Phones: 919-573-7000 (Morrisville office); 910-401-5001. Fax: 910-864-8878. Web Site: http://www.timewarnercable.com/carolinas. Also serves Autryville, Bonnie Doone, Cumberland County, Dunn, Erwin, Falcon, Fort Bragg, Godwin, Hope Mills, Parkton, Pope AFB, Spring Lake, Stedman & Wade. ICA: NC0004.
TV Market Ranking: 73 (Autryville, Bonnie Doone, Cumberland County, Dunn, Erwin, Falcon, FAYETTEVILLE, Fort Bragg, Godwin, Hope Mills, Parkton, Pope AFB, Spring Lake, Stedman, Wade). Franchise award date: January 1, 1963. Franchise expiration date: N.A. Began: September 9, 1963.
Channel capacity: N.A. Channels available but not in use: N.A.
Basic Service
Subscribers: 90,000.
Programming (received off-air): WECT (NBC) Wilmington; WFPX-TV (ION) Fayetteville; WLFL (CW) Raleigh; WNCN (NBC) Goldsboro; WRAL-TV (CBS) Raleigh; WRAZ (FOX) Raleigh; WRDC (MNT) Durham; WTVD (ABC) Durham; WUNU (PBS) Lumberton; WUVC-DT (UNV) Fayetteville.
Programming (via satellite): C-SPAN; TBS Superstation; TV Guide Network.
Fee: $42.95 installation; $9.65 monthly; $18.65 additional installation.
Expanded Basic Service 1
Subscribers: 46,000.
Programming (via satellite): A&E Networks; ABC Family Channel; AMC; Animal Planet; BET Networks; Cartoon Network; CNBC; CNN; Comedy Central; Country Music TV; Discovery Channel; Disney Channel; E! Entertainment Television; ESPN; ESPN 2; Food Network; Fox News Channel; Fox Sports South; FX; Golf Channel; Headline News; HGTV; History Channel; Lifetime; Lifetime Movie Network; MSNBC; MTV; National Geographic Channel; Nickelodeon; Oxygen; QVC; Sneak Prevue; SoapNet; Spike TV; Syfy; The Learning Channel; The Weather Channel; Travel Channel; Trinity Broadcasting Network; truTV; Turner Classic Movies; Turner Network TV; TV Land; USA Network; VH1; WE tv.
Fee: $40.20 monthly.
Digital Basic Service
Subscribers: 40,000.
Programming (via satellite): America's Store; BBC America; Black Family Channel; Bloomberg Television; Cooking Channel; C-SPAN 3; Disney Channel; DIY Network; Fox Deportes; Fox Sports Net; Fox Sports World; Fuse; G4; Great American Country; GSN; Lifetime Movie Network; mun2 television; Music Choice; Nick Jr.; Outdoor Channel; Ovation; Speed; Style Network; Toon Disney; Versus; VH1; Video Rola.
Fee: $16.25 monthly.
Digital Pay Service 1
Pay Units: 11,000.
Programming (via satellite): Cinemax (multiplexed); Encore (multiplexed); Flix; Fox Movie Channel; HBO (multiplexed); Showtime (multiplexed); Starz (multiplexed); Sundance Channel; The Movie Channel.
Fee: $11.95 monthly (each).
Video-On-Demand: Yes
Pay-Per-View
Hot Choice (delivered digitally); Playboy TV (delivered digitally); Playboy TV En Espanol delivered digitally (delivered digitally); Spice delivered digitally (delivered digitally); Shorteez (delivered digitally); Pleasure (delivered digitally); ESPN Now (delivered digitally).
Internet Service
Operational: Yes. Began: September 1, 2000.
Subscribers: 6,000.
Broadband Service: Road Runner.
Fee: $99.95 installation; $44.95 monthly.
Telephone Service
Digital: Operational
Fee: $44.95 monthly
Miles of Plant: 1,500.0 (coaxial); None (fiber optic).
Vice President & General Manager: Kim Cannon. Chief Technician: Fred Kirk. Public & Government Affairs Director: Eric Collins.
Ownership: Time Warner Cable (MSO).; Advance/Newhouse Partnership (MSO).

FOREST CITY—Northland Cable Television, 1108 W Main St, Forest City, NC 28043-2522. Phone: 828-245-1633. Fax: 828-245-8850. E-mail: forestcity@northlandcabletv.com. Web Site: http://www.northlandcabletv.com/forestcity. Also serves Alexander Mills, Bat Cave, Bostic, Chimney Rock, Cliffside, Ellenboro, Fairfield Mountain, Gerton, Henderson County (northeastern portion), Lake Lure, Polk County (northern portion), Ruth, Rutherford County (portions), Rutherfordton, Sandy Mush, Six Points & Spindale. ICA: NC0054.
TV Market Ranking: 46 (Alexander Mills, Bat Cave, Bostic, Chimney Rock, Cliffside, Ellenboro, Fairfield Mountain, FOREST CITY, Gerton, Henderson County (northeastern portion), Lake Lure, Polk County (northern portion), Ruth, Rutherford County (portions), Rutherfordton, Sandy Mush, Six Points, Spindale); Below 100 (Rutherford County (portions)). Franchise award date: February 7, 1977. Franchise expiration date: N.A. Began: August 1, 1979.
Channel capacity: 72 (not 2-way capable). Channels available but not in use: N.A.
Basic Service
Subscribers: 9,588.
Programming (received off-air): WBTV (CBS) Charlotte; WGGS-TV (IND) Greenville; WHNS (FOX) Greenville; WLOS (ABC) Asheville; WMYA-TV (MNT) Anderson; WRET-TV (PBS) Spartanburg; WSPA-TV (CBS) Spartanburg; WUNF-TV (PBS) Asheville; WYCW (CW) Asheville; WYFF (NBC) Greenville.
Programming (via satellite): A&E Networks; BET Networks; Cartoon Network; CNBC; CNN; Discovery Channel; ESPN; Food Network; Fox News Channel; Fox Sports South; Great American Country; Hallmark Channel; HGTV; QVC; SportSouth; TBS Superstation; The Learning Channel; The Weather Channel; Turner Network TV; TV Guide Network; USA Network; WGN America.
Fee: $29.99 installation; $32.49 monthly; $3.00 converter; $20.00 additional installation.
Expanded Basic Service 1
Subscribers: 6,390.
Programming (via satellite): Animal Planet; Comedy Central; C-SPAN; ESPN 2; Fox Movie Channel; FX; Headline News; History Channel; Lifetime; MTV; Nickelodeon; Outdoor Channel; Spike TV; Syfy; Turner Classic Movies.
Fee: $20.00 monthly.
Digital Basic Service
Subscribers: 1,333.
Programming (via satellite): BBC America; Bloomberg Television; Bravo; Discovery Digital Networks; DMX Music; G4; Golf Channel; GSN; Halogen Network; Independent Film Channel; National Geographic Channel; Speed; Trinity Broadcasting Network; Versus; WE tv.
Fee: $9.50 monthly.
Pay Service 1
Pay Units: 1,537.
Programming (via satellite): HBO.
Fee: $15.00 installation; $10.00 monthly.
Digital Pay Service 1
Pay Units: 2,135.
Programming (via satellite): Cinemax (multiplexed); Encore (multiplexed); Flix; HBO (multiplexed); Showtime (multiplexed); Starz (multiplexed); The Movie Channel (multiplexed).
Fee: $14.75 monthly (Cinemax, HBO, Showtime/TMC/Flix or Starz/Encore).
Video-On-Demand: No
Pay-Per-View
Special events, Addressable: No; Playboy TV (delivered digitally); Fresh (delivered digitally).
Internet Service
Operational: Yes.
Fee: $42.99 monthly.
Telephone Service
Analog: Not Operational
Digital: Operational
Fee: $29.99 monthly
Miles of Plant: 497.0 (coaxial); None (fiber optic).
Manager: Ronnie Parker. Marketing Director: Donna McCann. Office Manager: Patty Crowder.
Ownership: Northland Communications Corp. (MSO).

FOUNTAIN—Windjammer Cable, 8500 W 110th St, Ste 600, Overland Park, KS 66210. Phone: 888-495-2881. Fax: 913-563-5454. Web Site: http://www.windjammercable.com. ICA: NC0184.

TV Market Ranking: 84,73 (FOUNTAIN). Franchise award date: March 9, 1982. Franchise expiration date: N.A. Began: August 1, 1982.
Channel capacity: 42 (not 2-way capable). Channels available but not in use: N.A.

Basic Service
Subscribers: 125.
Programming (received off-air): WCTI-TV (ABC) New Bern; WEPX-TV (ION) Greenville; WITN-TV (MNT, NBC) Washington; WLFL (CW) Raleigh; WNCN (NBC) Goldsboro; WNCT-TV (CBS, CW) Greenville; WRAL-TV (CBS) Raleigh; WUNP-TV (PBS) Roanoke Rapids; WYDO (FOX) Greenville.
Programming (via satellite): QVC; Trinity Broadcasting Network.
Fee: $39.95 installation; $14.91 monthly; $2.00 converter.

Expanded Basic Service 1
Subscribers: 119.
Programming (via satellite): A&E Networks; ABC Family Channel; BET Networks; CNN; Country Music TV; C-SPAN; Discovery Channel; ESPN; HGTV; Lifetime; Nickelodeon; Spike TV; Syfy; TBS Superstation; The Weather Channel; Turner Network TV; USA Network; WGN America.
Fee: $19.71 monthly.

Digital Basic Service
Subscribers: N.A.
Programming (via satellite): Bravo; ESPN Classic Sports; History Channel; Versus; WE tv.
Fee: $10.23 monthly.

Pay Service 1
Pay Units: 37.
Programming (via satellite): HBO.
Fee: $10.00 installation; $15.95 monthly.

Digital Pay Service 1
Pay Units: N.A.
Programming (via satellite): Cinemax (multiplexed); Encore; HBO (multiplexed); Showtime (multiplexed); Starz (multiplexed); The Movie Channel.
Fee: $15.95 monthly (each).

Video-On-Demand: No

Pay-Per-View
Hits Movies & Events (delivered digitally).

Internet Service
Operational: No.

Telephone Service
None

Miles of Plant: 4.0 (coaxial); None (fiber optic).
General Manager: Timothy Evard. Operations Director: Belinda Graham. Engineering Director: Mike Earehart. Finance & Accounting Director: Cindy Johnson.
Ownership: Windjammer Communications LLC (MSO).

FRANKLIN/SYLVA—Morris Broadband, 719 S Grove St, Hendersonville, NC 28792. Phones: 800-622-6358; 828-697-3600; 888-855-9036. Web Site: http://morrisbroadband.com. Also serves Cullowhee, Dillsboro, Forest Hills, Jackson County (unincorporated areas), Macon County & Webster. ICA: NC0087.
TV Market Ranking: 46 (Jackson County (unincorporated areas) (portions)); Below 100 (Macon County (portions)); Outside TV Markets (Cullowhee, Dillsboro, Forest Hills, FRANKLIN, Macon County (portions), SYLVA, Webster, Jackson County (unincorporated areas) (portions)). Franchise award date: October 22, 1980. Franchise expiration date: N.A. Began: April 7, 1981.
Channel capacity: N.A. Channels available but not in use: N.A.

Basic Service
Subscribers: 8,546.
Programming (via satellite): INSP; TV Guide Network; WGN America.
Programming (via translator): WHNS (FOX) Greenville; WLOS (ABC) Asheville; WSPA-TV (CBS) Spartanburg; WUNE-TV (PBS) Linville; WYFF (NBC) Greenville.
Fee: $45.00 installation; $1.00 converter.

Expanded Basic Service 1
Subscribers: N.A.
Programming (via satellite): A&E Networks; ABC Family Channel; AMC; Animal Planet; BET Networks; Bravo; Cartoon Network; CNBC; CNN; Comedy Central; Country Music TV; C-SPAN; Discovery Channel; Disney Channel; E! Entertainment Television; ESPN; ESPN 2; Food Network; Fox News Channel; Fox Sports South; FX; Headline News; HGTV; History Channel; Lifetime; MSNBC; Nickelodeon; QVC; SoapNet; Speed; Spike TV; SportSouth; Syfy; TBS Superstation; The Learning Channel; The Weather Channel; Travel Channel; truTV; Turner Network TV; TV Land; USA Network; Versus; VH1; WE tv.
Fee: $51.95 monthly.

Digital Basic Service
Subscribers: N.A.
Programming (via satellite): AmericanLife TV Network; BBC America; Bio; Bloomberg Television; Discovery Digital Networks; Fox Movie Channel; Fox Soccer; Fuse; G4; GAS; Golf Channel; GSN; Halogen Network; History Channel International; Independent Film Channel; Lifetime Movie Network; Lime; MTV Networks Digital Suite; Music Choice; National Geographic Channel; Nick Jr.; NickToons TV; Outdoor Channel; Science Television; Style Network; Turner Classic Movies; Weatherscan.
Fee: $8.00 monthly.

Digital Pay Service 1
Pay Units: N.A.
Programming (via satellite): Cinemax (multiplexed); Encore (multiplexed); Flix (multiplexed); HBO (multiplexed); Showtime (multiplexed); Starz (multiplexed); Sundance Channel (multiplexed); The Movie Channel (multiplexed).
Fee: $8.00 monthly (Starz/Encore), $9.95 monthly (Cinemax or Showtime/TMC/Flix/Sundance), $13.95 monthly (HBO).

Video-On-Demand: No

Pay-Per-View
Movies (delivered digitally); ESPN (delivered digitally).

Internet Service
Operational: Yes.
Broadband Service: In-house.
Fee: $59.95 installation; $29.95-$59.95 monthly; $3.00 modem lease.

Telephone Service
Digital: Operational
Fee: $49.95 monthly

Miles of Plant: 254.0 (coaxial); None (fiber optic).
Chairman & Chief Executive Officer: William S. Morris III. Senior Vice President, Finance: Craig Mitchell. Senior Vice President & Chief Financial Officer: Steve K. Stone. Vice President: Susie Morris Baker.
Ownership: Morris Communications Co LLC (MSO).

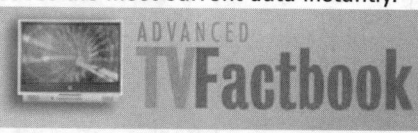

GASTONIA—Time Warner Cable, 3140 W Arrowood Rd, Charlotte, NC 28273. Phone: 704-378-2500. Fax: 704-504-1997. Web Site: http://www.timewarnercable.com/carolinas. Also serves Belmont, Bessemer City, Cherryville, Cramerton, Gaston County, Lowell, McAdenville, Mount Holly, Ranlo, South Gastonia, Spencer Mountain & Stanley, NC; Bowling Green, Clover & Lake Wylie, SC. ICA: NC0020.
TV Market Ranking: 42 (Belmont, Bessemer City, Bowling Green, Cherryville, Clover, Cramerton, Gaston County, GASTONIA, Lake Wylie, Lowell, McAdenville, Mount Holly, Ranlo, South Gastonia, Spencer Mountain, Stanley). Franchise award date: N.A. Franchise expiration date: April 24, 2012. Began: October 1, 1965.
Channel capacity: N.A. Channels available but not in use: N.A.

Basic Service
Subscribers: N.A. Included in Charlotte
Programming (received off-air): WAXN-TV (IND) Kannapolis; WBTV (CBS) Charlotte; WCCB (FOX) Charlotte; WCNC-TV (NBC) Charlotte; WHKY-TV (IND) Hickory; WJZY (CW) Belmont; WMYT-TV (MNT) Rock Hill; WSOC-TV (ABC) Charlotte; WTVI (PBS) Charlotte; WUNG-TV (PBS) Concord.
Programming (via satellite): Trinity Broadcasting Network; TV Guide Network; WGN America.
Fee: $36.00 installation; $10.00 monthly; $1.38 converter.

Expanded Basic Service 1
Subscribers: 44,519.
Programming (via satellite): A&E Networks; ABC Family Channel; AMC; Animal Planet; BET Networks; Bravo; Cartoon Network; CNBC; CNN; Comedy Central; Country Music TV; C-SPAN; C-SPAN 2; Discovery Channel; Discovery Health Channel; Disney Channel; E! Entertainment Television; ESPN; ESPN 2; ESPN Classic Sports; Food Network; Fox News Channel; Fox Sports Net; FX; Golf Channel; Hallmark Channel; Headline News; HGTV; History Channel; INSP; Lifetime; Lifetime Movie Network; MSNBC; MTV; National Geographic Channel; Nickelodeon; Oxygen; QVC; ShopNBC; Speed; Spike TV; SportSouth; Syfy; TBS Superstation; The Learning Channel; The Weather Channel; Travel Channel; truTV; Turner Classic Movies; Turner Network TV; TV Land; USA Network; Versus; VH1; WE tv.
Fee: $39.95 monthly.

Digital Basic Service
Subscribers: 14,419.
Programming (via satellite): AmericanLife TV Network; America's Store; BBC America; Bio; Black Family Channel; Bloomberg Television; Boomerang; Canales N; Cooking Channel; C-SPAN 3; Discovery Digital Networks; DIY Network; DMX Music; ESPNews; FamilyNet; Fox Movie Channel; FSN Digital Atlantic; FSN Digital Central; FSN Digital Pacific; Fuel TV; Fuse; G4; Great American Country; GSN; History Channel International; Independent Film Channel; Lifetime Real Women; MTV Networks Digital Suite; NBA TV; Nick Jr.; Outdoor Channel; Ovation; SoapNet; Style Network; Tennis Channel; Toon Disney.
Fee: $15.00 monthly.

Digital Pay Service 1
Pay Units: 5,932.
Programming (via satellite): Cinemax (multiplexed); Deutsche Welle TV; Encore (multiplexed); Flix; HBO (multiplexed); RAI International; Saigon Broadcasting Television Network; Showtime (multiplexed); Starz (multiplexed); Sundance Channel; The Movie Channel (multiplexed); TV5, La Television International; Zee TV USA.
Fee: $9.95 monthly (Deutsche Welle, TV5 or RAI), $11.95 monthly (Cinemax, HBO, Showtime, Flix/Sundance/TMC or Starz/Encore), $14.95 monthly (SBTN or ZEE).

Video-On-Demand: Yes

Pay-Per-View
Addressable homes: 14,419.
Sports PPV (delivered digitally); ESPN Now (delivered digitally); Adult PPV (delivered digitally); iN DEMAND (delivered digitally); ESPN Gameplan (delivered digitally); ESPN Full Court (delivered digitally).

Internet Service
Operational: Yes.
Subscribers: 14,869.
Broadband Service: Road Runner, AOL, EarthLink.
Fee: $39.95 installation; $46.95 monthly.

Telephone Service
Digital: Operational
Fee: $39.95 monthly

Miles of plant (coax & fiber) included in Charlotte
President: Mike Munley. Vice President, Technical Operations: Mike Cullim. Vice President, Engineering: Richard Newcomb. Vice President, Marketing & Sales: Eric Franey. Technical Operations Director: Donnie Stone. Government Affairs Director: Michael Tanck. Public Affairs Director: Jessica Graham.
Ownership: Time Warner Cable (MSO).; Advance/Newhouse Partnership (MSO).

GATES COUNTY—Charter Communications, 216 Moore Ave, Suffolk, VA 23434. Phone: 757-539-0713. Fax: 919-774-1057. Web Site: http://www.charter.com. Also serves Gatesville. ICA: NC0226.
TV Market Ranking: 44 (GATES COUNTY (portions)); Outside TV Markets (Gatesville, GATES COUNTY (portions)). Franchise award date: N.A. Franchise expiration date: N.A. Began: N.A.
Channel capacity: 54 (not 2-way capable). Channels available but not in use: N.A.

Basic Service
Subscribers: 296.
Programming (received off-air): WAVY-TV (NBC) Portsmouth; WGNT (CW) Portsmouth; WHRO-TV (PBS) Hampton-Norfolk; WPXV-TV (ION) Norfolk; WSKY-TV (IND) Manteo; WTKR (CBS) Norfolk; WTVZ-TV (MNT) Norfolk; WUND-TV (PBS) Edenton; WVBT (FOX) Virginia Beach; WVEC (ABC) Hampton.
Programming (via satellite): C-SPAN; C-SPAN 2; INSP; LWS Local Weather Station; QVC; Trinity Broadcasting Network; WGN America.
Fee: $29.99 installation.

Expanded Basic Service 1
Subscribers: 223.
Programming (via satellite): A&E Networks; ABC Family Channel; AMC; Animal Planet; BET Networks; Bravo; Cartoon

Network; CNBC; CNN; Comedy Central; Country Music TV; Discovery Channel; Disney Channel; E! Entertainment Television; ESPN; ESPN 2; Fox News Channel; Fox Sports South; FX; G4; Golf Channel; Headline News; HGTV; History Channel; Lifetime; MSNBC; MTV; Nickelodeon; Oxygen; Speed; Spike TV; Syfy; TBS Superstation; The Learning Channel; The Weather Channel; Turner Classic Movies; Turner Network TV; TV Land; USA Network; VH1; WE tv.
Fee: $47.99 monthly.

Digital Basic Service
Subscribers: N.A.
Programming (via satellite): BBC America; Bio; Bloomberg Television; Discovery Fit & Health; DIY Network; ESPN Classic Sports; ESPNews; Fox College Sports Atlantic; Fox College Sports Central; Fox College Sports Pacific; Fox Movie Channel; Fox Soccer; Fuse; GAS; GSN; History Channel International; Independent Film Channel; Lifetime Movie Network; MTV Networks Digital Suite; Music Choice; National Geographic Channel; Nick Jr.; Nick Too; NickToons TV; SoapNet; Sundance Channel; Toon Disney; TV Guide Interactive Inc.

Digital Pay Service 1
Pay Units: 37.
Programming (via satellite): Cinemax (multiplexed).
Fee: $10.95 monthly.

Digital Pay Service 2
Pay Units: 71.
Programming (via satellite): HBO (multiplexed).
Fee: $11.95 monthly.

Digital Pay Service 3
Pay Units: N.A.
Programming (via satellite): Encore (multiplexed); Flix; Showtime (multiplexed); Starz (multiplexed); The Movie Channel (multiplexed).

Video-On-Demand: No

Pay-Per-View
iN DEMAND (delivered digitally); Playboy TV (delivered digitally); Fresh (delivered digitally); Shorteez (delivered digitally).

Internet Service
Operational: No.

Telephone Service
None

Miles of Plant: 51.0 (coaxial); None (fiber optic).
Vice President & General Manager: Anthony Pope. Marketing Director: Brooke Sinclair. Marketing Manager: LaRisa Scales. Operations Manager: Tom Ross.
Ownership: Charter Communications Inc. (MSO).

GOLD HILL—Time Warner Cable. Now served by SALISBURY, NC [NC0022]. ICA: NC0140.

GOLDSBORO—Time Warner Cable, 101 Innovation Ave, Ste 100, Morrisville, NC 27560. Phone: 919-573-7000. Fax: 919-573-7042. Web Site: http://www.timewarnercable.com/carolinas. Also serves Fremont, Mount Olive, Pikeville, Seymour Johnson AFB & Wayne County (portions). ICA: NC0021.
TV Market Ranking: 73 (GOLDSBORO, Mount Olive, Pikeville, Seymour Johnson AFB); 73,84 (Fremont, Wayne County (portions) (portions)). Franchise award date: August 1, 1973. Franchise expiration date: April 28, 2018. Began: March 1, 1976.
Channel capacity: N.A. Channels available but not in use: N.A.

Basic Service
Subscribers: 23,555.
Programming (received off-air): WLFL (CW) Raleigh; WNCN (NBC) Goldsboro; WNCT-TV (CBS, CW) Greenville; WRAL-TV (CBS) Raleigh; WRAY-TV (IND) Wilson; WRAZ (FOX) Raleigh; WRDC (MNT) Durham; WRPX-TV (ION) Rocky Mount; WTVD (ABC) Durham; WUNK-TV (PBS) Greenville; WUVC-DT (UNV) Fayetteville; 14 FMs.
Programming (via satellite): C-SPAN; TBS Superstation; TV Guide Network; WGN America.
Fee: $42.95 installation; $14.50 monthly; $19.95 additional installation.

Expanded Basic Service 1
Subscribers: N.A.
Programming (via satellite): A&E Networks; ABC Family Channel; AMC; Animal Planet; BET Networks; Cartoon Network; CNBC; CNN; Comedy Central; Country Music TV; C-SPAN 2; Discovery Channel; Disney Channel; E! Entertainment Television; ESPN; ESPN 2; ESPN Classic Sports; Eternal Word TV Network; Food Network; Fox News Channel; Fox Sports Net; FX; Golf Channel; Hallmark Channel; Headline News; HGTV; History Channel; INSP; Lifetime; Lifetime Movie Network; MSNBC; MTV; National Geographic Channel; Nickelodeon; Oxygen; QVC; SoapNet; Spike TV; Syfy; The Learning Channel; The Weather Channel; Travel Channel; truTV; Turner Classic Movies; Turner Network TV; TV Land; USA Network; VH1; WE tv.
Fee: $35.35 monthly.

Digital Basic Service
Subscribers: N.A.
Programming (via satellite): America's Store; BBC America; Black Family Channel; Bloomberg Television; Canales N; Cooking Channel; C-SPAN 3; Discovery Digital Networks; DIY Network; Encore Action; ESPNews; Fox Sports World; FSN Digital Atlantic; FSN Digital Central; FSN Digital Pacific; Fuse; G4; GAS; Great American Country; GSN; MTV2; Music Choice; Nick Jr.; Outdoor Channel; Ovation; Speed; Style Network; Toon Disney; Versus; VH1 Classic.
Fee: $16.25 monthly.

Digital Pay Service 1
Pay Units: 1,051.
Programming (via satellite): Cinemax (multiplexed); Flix; Fox Movie Channel; HBO (multiplexed); Independent Film Channel; Showtime (multiplexed); Starz (multiplexed); Sundance Channel; The Movie Channel (multiplexed).
Fee: $11.95 monthly (each).

Video-On-Demand: Yes

Pay-Per-View
Hot Choice (delivered digitally); iN DEMAND (delivered digitally); Playboy TV (delivered digitally); Fresh (delivered digitally); Shorteez (delivered digitally); Pleasure (delivered digitally); ESPN Now (delivered digitally); Sports PPV (delivered digitally).

Internet Service
Operational: Yes.
Broadband Service: AOL for Broadband; EarthLink; max.inter.net; Road Runner.
Fee: $99.95 installation; $44.95 monthly; $3.00 modem lease.

Telephone Service
Digital: Operational
Fee: $44.95 monthly

Miles of Plant: 600.0 (coaxial); None (fiber optic). Additional miles planned: 32.0 (coaxial).
President: Tom Adams. Vice President, Technical Operations: Gary Frederick. Vice President, Sales & Marketing: Tom Smith. Vice President, Government & Public Affairs: Brad Phillips.
Ownership: Time Warner Cable (MSO).; Advance/Newhouse Partnership (MSO).Day-to-day operations are managed by Time Warner Cable.

GOLDSTON—Formerly served by Main Street Broadband. No longer in operation. ICA: NC0229.

GREENSBORO—Time Warner Cable, PO Box 35568, Greensboro, NC 27425. Phone: 336-665-0160. Fax: 336-665-9979. Web Site: http://www.timewarnercable.com/carolinas. Also serves Advance, Alamance (village), Alamance County, Arcadia, Archdale, Arlington, Asheboro, Bermuda Run, Bethania (portions), Biscoe, Boonville, Burlington, Candor, Clemmons, Coleridge, Colfax, Cooleemee, Courtney, Danbury, Davidson County, Davie County (portions), Denton, Dobson, East Bend, Eden, Elkin, Elon College, Forsyth County, Franklinville, Germanton, Gibsonville, Glen Raven, Graham, Haw River, High Point, Jamestown, Jonesville, Jullan, Kernersville, King, Lewisville, Lexington, Liberty, Lone Hickory, Madison, Mebane, Mocksville, Mount Airy, Oak Ridge, Pfafftown, Pilot Mountain, Pine Hall, Pinnacle, Pleasant Garden, Ramseur, Randleman, Randolph County (portions), Reidsville, Rockingham County (portions), Rural Hall, Sandy Ridge, Saxapahaw, Seagrove, Southmont, Star, Stokes County (portions), Stokesdale, Stoneville, Summerfield, Surry County, Swancreek, Swepsonville, Thomasville, Toast, Tobaccoville, Trinity, Walkertown, Wallburg, Walnut Cove, Welcome, Westfield, White Plains, Whitsett, Wilkes County, Winston-Salem & Yadkin County. ICA: NC0006.
TV Market Ranking: 47 (Advance, Alamance (village), Alamance County, Arcadia, Archdale, Arlington, Asheboro, Bermuda Run, Bethania (portions), Boonville, Burlington, Clemmons, Coleridge, Colfax, Cooleemee, Courtney, Danbury, Davidson County, Davie County (portions), Denton, Dobson, East Bend, Eden, Elkin, Elon College, Forsyth County, Franklinville, Germanton, Gibsonville, Gibsonville, Glen Raven, Graham, GREENSBORO, Haw River, High Point, Jamestown, Jonesville, Jullan, Kernersville, King, Lewisville, Lexington, Liberty, Lone Hickory, Madison, Mebane, Mocksville, Mount Airy, Oak Ridge, Pfafftown, Pilot Mountain, Pine Hall, Pinnacle, Pleasant Garden, Ramseur, Randleman, Randolph County (portions), Reidsville, Rockingham County (portions), Rural Hall, Sandy Ridge, Saxapahaw, Seagrove, Southmont, Stokes County (portions), Stokesdale, Stoneville, Summerfield, Surry County (portions), Swancreek, Swepsonville, Thomasville, Toast, Tobaccoville, Trinity, Walkertown, Wallburg, Walnut Cove, Welcome, Westfield, White Plains, Whitsett, Wilkes County (portions), Winston-Salem, Yadkin County); Outside TV Markets (Biscoe, Candor, Star, Surry County (portions), Wilkes County (portions)). Franchise award date: January 1, 1968. Franchise expiration date: May 1, 2013. Began: January 1, 1968.
Channel capacity: 77 (operating 2-way). Channels available but not in use: N.A.

Basic Service
Subscribers: 360,000.
Programming (received off-air): WCWG (CW) Lexington; WFMY-TV (CBS) Greensboro; WGHP (FOX, IND) High Point; WGPX-TV (ION) Burlington; WLXI (IND) Greensboro; WMYV (MNT) Greensboro; WUNL-TV (PBS) Winston-Salem; WXII-TV (NBC) Winston-Salem; WXLV-TV (ABC) Winston-Salem.
Programming (via satellite): WGN America.
Fee: $50.51 installation; $9.20 monthly; $18.81 additional installation.

Expanded Basic Service 1
Subscribers: 328,168.
Programming (via satellite): A&E Networks; ABC Family Channel; AMC; Animal Planet; BET Networks; Bravo; Cartoon Network; CNBC; CNN; Comedy Central; Country Music TV; C-SPAN; C-SPAN 2; Discovery Channel; Discovery Fit & Health; Disney Channel; E! Entertainment Television; ESPN; ESPN 2; Eternal Word TV Network; Food Network; Fox News Channel; Fox Sports Net; FX; Golf Channel; Hallmark Channel; Headline News; HGTV; History Channel; INSP; Lifetime; Lifetime Movie Network; MoviePlex; MSNBC; MTV; National Geographic Channel; Nickelodeon; Oxygen; QVC; ShopNBC; Spike TV; SportSouth; Syfy; TBS Superstation; The Learning Channel; The Weather Channel; Travel Channel; truTV; Turner Classic Movies; Turner Network TV; TV Guide Network; TV Land; Univision Studios; USA Network; Versus; VH1; WE tv.
Fee: $42.75 monthly.

Digital Basic Service
Subscribers: 123,103.
Programming (via satellite): America's Store; BBC America; Bio; Black Family Channel; Bloomberg Television; Boomerang; Canales N; C-SPAN 3; Discovery Digital Networks; DIY Network; Encore (multiplexed); ESPN Classic Sports; ESPNews; Flix; Fox Movie Channel; Fox Sports World; FSN Digital Atlantic; FSN Digital Central; FSN Digital Pacific; Fuse; G4; GSN; History Channel International; Independent Film Channel; Lifetime Real Women; MTV Networks Digital Suite; Music Choice; Nick Jr.; Outdoor Channel; Ovation; SoapNet; Speed; Style Network; Sundance Channel; Tennis Channel; Toon Disney.
Fee: $16.00 monthly.

Pay Service 1
Pay Units: 6,037.
Programming (via satellite): Cinemax.
Fee: $8.00 monthly.

Pay Service 2
Pay Units: 2,428.
Programming (via satellite): The Movie Channel.
Fee: $8.00 monthly.

Pay Service 3
Pay Units: 38,473.
Programming (via satellite): HBO.
Fee: $8.00 monthly.

Pay Service 4
Pay Units: 8,417.
Programming (via satellite): Showtime.
Fee: $8.00 monthly.

Digital Pay Service 1
Pay Units: N.A.
Programming (via satellite): Cinemax (multiplexed); HBO (multiplexed); Showtime (multiplexed); Starz (multiplexed); The Movie Channel (multiplexed).
Fee: $8.00 monthly (each).

Video-On-Demand: Yes

Pay-Per-View
Addressable homes: 26,122.
iN DEMAND (delivered digitally); Sports PPV (delivered digitally).

Internet Service
Operational: Yes.
Subscribers: 134,179.

Broadband Service: AOL for Broadband, EarthLink, Road Runner.
Fee: $49.95 installation; $46.95 monthly.
Telephone Service
Digital: Operational
Fee: $44.95 monthly
Miles of Plant: None (coaxial); 14,034.0 (fiber optic).
Area Vice President, Operations: Dianne Blackwood. Vice President, Marketing & Sales: David Marshall. Regional Vice President, Government Relations: Jack Stanley. Technical Operations Director: Anthony Siero. Marketing Director: Beth Alphin.
Ownership: Time Warner Cable (MSO).; Advance/Newhouse Partnership (MSO).Day-to-day operations are managed by Time Warner Cable.

GREENVILLE—Suddenlink Communications, 2120 W Arlington Blvd, Greenville, NC 27834-6487. Phones: 252-757-2200 (Administrative office); 866-999-3278; 252-756-5677. Fax: 252-756-4954. Web Site: http://www.suddenlink.com. Also serves Ayden, Battleboro, Bridgeton, Conetoe, Craven County, Edgecombe County (eastern portion), James City, Kinston, La Grange, Mildred, Nash County, Nashville, New Bern, Pitt County, Princeville, River Bend, Rocky Mount, Sharpsburg, Tarboro, Trent Woods, Vanceboro, Wayne County (portions) & Winterville. ICA: NC0014.
TV Market Ranking: 73 (Nash County (portions), Wayne County (portions)); 84 (Ayden, Bridgeton, Conetoe, Craven County, Edgecombe County (eastern portion) (portions), James City, Kinston, La Grange, Mildred, New Bern, Pitt County, Princeville, River Bend, Rocky Mount, Sharpsburg, Tarboro, Trent Woods, Vanceboro, Winterville); 84,73 (GREENVILLE); Below 100 (Battleboro, Nashville, Nash County (portions), Edgecombe County (eastern portion) (portions)). Franchise award date: August 5, 1976. Franchise expiration date: September 23, 2006. Began: June 1, 1978.
Channel capacity: 66 (operating 2-way). Channels available but not in use: N.A.
Basic Service
Subscribers: 98,639.
Programming (received off-air): WCTI-TV (ABC) New Bern; WEPX-TV (ION) Greenville; WNCT-TV (CBS, CW) Greenville; WRAL-TV (CBS) Raleigh; WUNK-TV (PBS) Greenville; WYDO (FOX) Greenville.
Programming (via satellite): QVC; WGN America.
Fee: $20.00 installation; $40.95 monthly.
Expanded Basic Service 2
Subscribers: N.A.
Programming (via satellite): CNN; Comedy Central; Disney Channel; Golf Channel; Headline News; Spike TV; Turner Classic Movies; TV Land.
Fee: $6.46 monthly.
Digital Basic Service
Subscribers: N.A.
Programming (via satellite): AmericanLife TV Network; BBC America; Black Family Channel; Bloomberg Television; Daystar TV Network; Discovery Digital Networks; Encore Action; ESPN Classic Sports; ESPNews; Eternal Word TV Network; FamilyNet; Fox Sports World; Fuse; G4; GAS; GSN; Hallmark Channel; Halogen Network; Lifetime Movie Network; MTV Networks Digital Suite; Music Choice; NBA TV; Nick Jr.; NickToons TV; Outdoor Channel; SoapNet; Speed; Sundance Channel; Telelatino Network; The Word Network; Toon Disney; truTV; Versus.
Fee: $7.95 monthly.
Pay Service 1
Pay Units: 4,951.
Programming (via satellite): Cinemax.
Fee: $13.33 installation; $10.75 monthly.
Pay Service 2
Pay Units: 6,481.
Programming (via satellite): HBO (multiplexed).
Fee: $13.33 installation; $11.50 monthly.
Pay Service 3
Pay Units: 726.
Programming (via satellite): The Movie Channel.
Fee: $13.33 installation; $10.75 monthly.
Pay Service 4
Pay Units: 2,321.
Programming (via satellite): Showtime.
Fee: $13.33 installation; $10.25 monthly.
Digital Pay Service 1
Pay Units: N.A.
Programming (via satellite): Cinemax (multiplexed); Encore (multiplexed); HBO (multiplexed); Showtime (multiplexed); The Movie Channel (multiplexed).
Fee: $10.95 monthly (Cinemax, Starz/ Encore or Showtime/TMC), $11.50 monthly (HBO).
Video-On-Demand: No
Pay-Per-View
Addressable homes: 11,893.
iN DEMAND; Playboy TV (delivered digitally); Fresh (delivered digitally); Shorteez (delivered digitally); iN DEMAND (delivered digitally); Hot Choice (delivered digitally); ESPN (delivered digitally).
Internet Service
Operational: Yes.
Broadband Service: Suddenlink High Speed Internet.
Fee: $99.95 installation; $39.95 monthly; $15.00 modem lease; $199.95 modem purchase.
Telephone Service
Digital: Operational
Fee: $39.95 monthly
Miles of Plant: 522.0 (coaxial); None (fiber optic).
Vice President & General Manager: Phil Ahlschlager. Field Operations Director: Bill Paramore. Field Operations Manager: Ken Willard.
Ownership: Cequel Communications LLC (MSO).

HALIFAX—Crystal Broadband Networks, PO Box 180336, Chicago, IL 60618. Phones: 630-206-0447; 877-319-0328. E-mail: sales@crystalbn.com. Web Site: http://www.crystalbn.com. ICA: NC0183.
TV Market Ranking: Below 100 (HALIFAX). Franchise award date: June 30, 1986. Franchise expiration date: N.A. Began: January 5, 1988.
Channel capacity: 42 (not 2-way capable). Channels available but not in use: N.A.
Basic Service
Subscribers: 172.
Programming (received off-air): WLFL (CW) Raleigh; WNCN (NBC) Goldsboro; WNCT-TV (CBS, CW) Greenville; WNVN-LP Roanoke Rapids; WRAL-TV (CBS) Raleigh; WRAY-TV (IND) Wilson; WRAZ (FOX) Raleigh; WRPX-TV (ION) Rocky Mount; WTVD (ABC) Durham; WUNP-TV (PBS) Roanoke Rapids.
Fee: $39.95 installation; $17.01 monthly; $2.00 converter.
Expanded Basic Service 1
Subscribers: 141.
Programming (via satellite): A&E Networks; ABC Family Channel; BET Networks; CNN; Country Music TV; Discovery Channel; ESPN; Headline News; Lifetime; MTV; Nickelodeon; Spike TV; Syfy; TBS Superstation; The Learning Channel; The Weather Channel; Trinity Broadcasting Network; Turner Network TV; USA Network; VH1.
Fee: $16.69 monthly.
Digital Basic Service
Subscribers: N.A.
Programming (via satellite): Bravo; ESPN Classic Sports; HGTV; History Channel; Versus; WE tv.
Fee: $10.27 monthly.
Pay Service 1
Pay Units: 28.
Programming (via satellite): HBO.
Fee: $15.95 monthly.
Digital Pay Service 1
Pay Units: N.A.
Programming (via satellite): Cinemax (multiplexed); Encore (multiplexed); HBO (multiplexed); Showtime (multiplexed); Starz (multiplexed); The Movie Channel (multiplexed).
Fee: $15.95 monthly (each).
Video-On-Demand: No
Internet Service
Operational: No.
Telephone Service
None
Miles of Plant: 7.0 (coaxial); None (fiber optic).
Ownership: Crystal Broadband Networks (MSO).

HARRIS—Northland Cable Television, 1108 W Main St, Forest City, NC 28043-2522. Phone: 828-245-1633. Fax: 828-245-8850. E-mail: forestcity@northlandcabletv.com. Web Site: http://www.northlandcabletv.com. ICA: NC0246.
TV Market Ranking: 46 (HARRIS).
Channel capacity: N.A. Channels available but not in use: N.A.
Basic Service
Subscribers: 310.
Programming (received off-air): WBTV (CBS) Charlotte; WGGS-TV (IND) Greenville; WHNS (FOX) Greenville; WLOS (ABC) Asheville; WMYA-TV (MNT) Anderson; WRET-TV (PBS) Spartanburg; WSPA-TV (CBS) Spartanburg; WUNF-TV (PBS) Asheville; WYCW (CW) Asheville; WYFF (NBC) Greenville.
Programming (via satellite): A&E Networks; Animal Planet; BET Networks; Cartoon Network; CNBC; CNN; Comedy Central; Country Music TV; C-SPAN; Discovery Channel; ESPN; ESPN 2; Food Network; Fox Movie Channel; Fox News Channel; Fox Sports South; FX; Great American Country; Hallmark Channel; Headline News; HGTV; History Channel; Lifetime; MTV; Nickelodeon; Outdoor Channel; QVC; Spike TV; Syfy; TBS Superstation; The Learning Channel; The Weather Channel; Turner Classic Movies; Turner Network TV; Turner South; USA Network; WGN America.
Fee: $32.49 monthly.
Digital Basic Service
Subscribers: N.A.
Programming (via satellite): BBC America; Bravo; Discovery Fit & Health; Discovery Home Channel; Discovery Kids Channel; Discovery Times Channel; DMX Music; ESPNews; Fox Soccer; G4; Golf Channel; Independent Film Channel; Military Channel; National Geographic Channel; NFL Network; Science; Speed; Trinity Broadcasting Network; WE tv.
Pay Service 1
Pay Units: N.A.
Programming (via satellite): HBO.
Digital Pay Service 1
Pay Units: N.A.
Programming (via satellite): Cinemax (multiplexed); Encore (multiplexed); Flix; HBO (multiplexed); Showtime (multiplexed); Starz (multiplexed); The Movie Channel (multiplexed).
Pay-Per-View
iN DEMAND (delivered digitally); Playboy TV (delivered digitally); Fresh (delivered digitally); Hot Choice (delivered digitally).
Internet Service
Operational: Yes.
Fee: $42.99 monthly.
Telephone Service
Digital: Operational
Fee: $29.99 monthly
Manager: Nick Stover. Chief Engineer: Ronnie Parker. Marketing Director: Donna McCann. Office Manager: Patty Crowder.
Ownership: Northland Communications Corp. (MSO).

HENDERSON—Time Warner Cable, 101 Innovation Ave, Ste 100, Morrisville, NC 27560. Phone: 919-573-7000. Web Site: http://www.timewarnercable.com/carolinas. Also serves Bunn, Franklin County (portions), Granville County (portions), Kittrell, Louisburg, Manson, Middleburg, Norlina, Oxford, Stovall, Townsville, Vance County (portions), Warren County (portions), Warrenton & Wise. ICA: NC0062.
TV Market Ranking: 73 (Bunn, Franklin County (portions), Granville County (portions), Kittrell, Louisburg, Oxford, Vance County (portions), Warren County (portions)); Outside TV Markets (HENDERSON (PORTIONS), Manson, Middleburg, Norlina, Stovall, Townsville, Warrenton, Wise, Vance County (portions)). Franchise award date: N.A. Franchise expiration date: N.A. Began: August 1, 1969.
Channel capacity: N.A. Channels available but not in use: N.A.
Basic Service
Subscribers: 12,440.
Programming (received off-air): WLFL (CW) Raleigh; WNCN (NBC) Goldsboro; WRAL-TV (CBS) Raleigh; WRAY-TV (IND) Wilson; WRAZ (FOX) Raleigh; WRDC (MNT) Durham; WRPX-TV (ION) Rocky Mount; WTVD (ABC) Durham; WUNP-TV (PBS) Roanoke Rapids; WUVC-DT (UNV) Fayetteville.
Programming (via satellite): C-SPAN; C-SPAN 2; Fox Sports Net; National Geographic Channel; News 14 Carolina; QVC;

Telefutura; TV Guide Network; WGN America.
Fee: $42.95 installation; $14.95 monthly; $19.96 additional installation.

Expanded Basic Service 1
Subscribers: N.A.
Programming (via satellite): A&E Networks; ABC Family Channel; AMC; Animal Planet; BET Networks; Cartoon Network; CNBC; CNN; Comedy Central; Country Music TV; Discovery Channel; Discovery Fit & Health; Discovery Health Channel; Disney Channel; E! Entertainment Television; ESPN; ESPN 2; Eternal Word TV Network; Food Network; Fox News Channel; Fox Sports South; FX; Golf Channel; Hallmark Channel; Headline News; HGTV; History Channel; INSP; Lifetime; Lifetime Movie Network; MSNBC; MTV; National Geographic Channel; Nick Jr.; Nickelodeon; Oxygen; ShopNBC; SoapNet; Spike TV; Syfy; TBS Superstation; The Learning Channel; The Weather Channel; Trinity Broadcasting Network; truTV; Turner Classic Movies; Turner Network TV; TV Land; USA Network; Versus; VH1; VH1 Classic; WE tv.
Fee: $34.90 monthly.

Digital Basic Service
Subscribers: N.A.
Programming (via satellite): America's Store; BBC America; Black Family Channel; Bloomberg Television; Canales N; Cooking Channel; C-SPAN 3; Discovery Home Channel; Discovery Kids Channel; Discovery Times Channel; Disney Channel; DIY Network; DMX Music; ESPNews; Fox Sports World; FSN Digital Atlantic; FSN Digital Central; FSN Digital Pacific; Fuse; G4; GAS; Great American Country; GSN; History Channel International; Lifetime Movie Network; Military Channel; MTV2; Nick Jr.; Outdoor Channel; Ovation; Science; Speed; Style Network; Toon Disney; Versus; VH1 Classic.
Fee: $16.25 monthly.

Digital Pay Service 1
Pay Units: N.A.
Programming (via satellite): Cinemax (multiplexed); Encore (multiplexed); Flix; Fox Movie Channel; HBO (multiplexed); Independent Film Channel; Showtime (multiplexed); Starz (multiplexed); Sundance Channel.
Fee: $11.95 monthly (Cinemax, HBO, or Showtime/TMC).

Video-On-Demand: Yes

Pay-Per-View
Pleasure (delivered digitally); Shorteez (delivered digitally); Fresh (delivered digitally); Playboy TV (delivered digitally); Hot Choice (delivered digitally).

Internet Service
Operational: Yes. Began: December 31, 2002.
Broadband Service: Road Runner.
Fee: $99.95 installation; $44.95 monthly.

Telephone Service
Digital: Operational
Fee: $44.95 monthly

Miles of Plant: 151.0 (coaxial); None (fiber optic).

Vice President & General Manager: Chris Whitaker. Vice President, Sales & Marketing: Tom Smith. Vice President, Government & Public Affairs: Brad Phillips. Technical Operations Director: Doug Davis. Customer Care Director: Kelly Robel.

Ownership: Time Warner Cable (MSO).; Advance/Newhouse Partnership (MSO).Day-to-day operations are managed by Time Warner Cable.

HENDERSONVILLE—Morris Broadband, 719 S Grove St, Hendersonville, NC 28792. Phones: 888-855-9036; 828-697-3600; 828-697-1371. Web Site: http://morrisbroadband.com. Also serves Dana, East Flat Rock, Flat Rock, Fletcher, Henderson County, Laurel Park & Mills River. ICA: NC0033.

TV Market Ranking: 46 (Dana, East Flat Rock, Flat Rock, Fletcher, Henderson County, HENDERSONVILLE, Laurel Park, Mills River). Franchise award date: June 10, 1976. Franchise expiration date: N.A. Began: February 1, 1970.

Channel capacity: N.A. Channels available but not in use: N.A.

Basic Service
Subscribers: 19,763.
Programming (received off-air): WAEN-LP Asheville; WGGS-TV (IND) Greenville; WHNS (FOX) Greenville; WLOS (ABC) Asheville; WMYA-TV (MNT) Anderson; WSPA-TV (CBS) Spartanburg; WUNF-TV (PBS) Asheville; WYCW (CW) Asheville; WYFF (NBC) Greenville; allband FM.
Programming (via satellite): QVC; WGN America.
Fee: $45.00 installation; $29.95 monthly; $1.00 converter.

Expanded Basic Service 1
Subscribers: N.A.
Programming (via satellite): A&E Networks; ABC Family Channel; AMC; AmericanLife TV Network; Animal Planet; BET Networks; Bravo; Cartoon Network; CNBC; CNN; Comedy Central; Country Music TV; C-SPAN; C-SPAN 2; Discovery Channel; Disney Channel; ESPN; ESPN 2; Eternal Word TV Network; Food Network; Fox News Channel; Fox Sports South; FX; Golf Channel; Headline News; HGTV; History Channel; INSP; Lifetime; MSNBC; MTV; Nickelodeon; ShopNBC; Speed; Spike TV; SportSouth; Syfy; TBS Superstation; The Learning Channel; The Weather Channel; Travel Channel; truTV; Turner Network TV; TV Guide Network; TV Land; Univision Studios; USA Network; VH1; WE tv.
Fee: $25.00 installation; $18.62 monthly.

Digital Basic Service
Subscribers: N.A.
Programming (via satellite): BBC America; Bio; Bloomberg Television; Bravo; DMX Music; ESPN; ESPNews; Fox Movie Channel; Fox Soccer; Fuse; G4; GAS; GSN; Halogen Network; HD Theater; HDNet; HDNet Movies; History Channel International; Independent Film Channel; Lifetime Movie Network; Lime; MTV2; National Geographic Channel; Nick Jr.; NickToons TV; Outdoor Channel; Style Network; Turner Classic Movies; Versus; VH1 Classic; Weatherscan.

Digital Pay Service 1
Pay Units: N.A.
Programming (via satellite): Cinemax (multiplexed); Encore (multiplexed); Flix (multiplexed); HBO (multiplexed); Showtime (multiplexed); Showtime HD; Starz (multiplexed); Starz HDTV; Sundance Channel (multiplexed); The Movie Channel (multiplexed).
Fee: $13.95 monthly (HBO), $9.95 monthly (Showtime or Cinemax), $8.00 monthly (Starz/Encore).

Video-On-Demand: No

Pay-Per-View
ESPN (delivered digitally); iN DEMAND (delivered digitally).

Internet Service
Operational: Yes.
Subscribers: 5,731.
Broadband Service: In-house.
Fee: $59.95 installation; $29.95-$59.95 monthly; $3.00 modem lease.

Telephone Service
Digital: Operational
Fee: $49.95 monthly

Miles of Plant: 668.0 (coaxial); 162.0 (fiber optic).

Chairman & Chief Executive Officer: William S. Morris III. Senior Vice President, Finance: Craig Mitchell. Senior Vice President & Chief Financial Officer: Steve K. Stone. Vice President: Susie Morris Baker.

Ownership: Morris Communications Co LLC (MSO).

HICKORY—Charter Communications, 1121 Lenoir Rhyne Blvd SE, Hickory, NC 28602-5128. Phone: 828-322-2288. Fax: 828-322-5492. Web Site: http://www.charter.com. Also serves Alexander County, Bethlehem, Brookford, Burke County, Cajah's Mountain, Caldwell County, Catawba (northern portion), Catawba County, Claremont, Connelly Springs, Conover, Crouse, Dallas, Denver, Drexel, Gamewell, Gaston County, Glen Alpine, Granite Falls, Hiddenite, High Shoals, Hildebran, Hudson, Icard, Kings Creek, Lenoir, Lincoln County, Lincolnton, Longview, Maiden, Mountain View, Newton, North Hickory, Northlakes, Patterson, Rhodhiss, Rutherford College, Sawmills, Stony Point, Taylorsville, Valdese, Vale & Whitnel. ICA: NC0009.

TV Market Ranking: 42 (Catawba County (portions), Crouse, Dallas, Denver, Gaston County, High Shoals, Lincoln County (portions), Lincolnton, Maiden); Below 100 (Alexander County, Bethlehem, Brookford, Burke County, Cajah's Mountain, Caldwell County, Catawba (northern portion), Claremont, Connelly Springs, Conover, Drexel, Gamewell, Glen Alpine, Granite Falls, HICKORY, Hiddenite, Hildebran, Hudson, Icard, Kings Creek, Lenoir, Longview, Mountain View, Newton, North Hickory, Northlakes, Patterson, Rhodhiss, Rutherford College, Sawmills, Stony Point, Taylorsville, Valdese, Vale, Whitnel, Catawba County (portions), Lincoln County (portions)). Franchise award date: N.A. Franchise expiration date: February 25, 2007. Began: November 15, 1976.

Channel capacity: N.A. Channels available but not in use: N.A.

Basic Service
Subscribers: 81,399.
Programming (received off-air): WAXN-TV (IND) Kannapolis; WBTV (CBS) Charlotte; WCCB (FOX) Charlotte; WCNC-TV (NBC) Charlotte; WHKY-TV (IND) Hickory; WJZY (CW) Belmont; WMYT-TV (MNT) Rock Hill; WSOC-TV (ABC) Charlotte; WSPA-TV (CBS) Spartanburg; WTVI (PBS) Charlotte; WUNE-TV (PBS) Linville.
Programming (via satellite): INSP; ION Television; QVC; Trinity Broadcasting Network; TV Guide Network; Univision Studios.
Fee: $29.99 installation.

Expanded Basic Service 1
Subscribers: 44,000.
Programming (via satellite): A&E Networks; ABC Family Channel; AMC; Animal Planet; BET Networks; Bravo; Cartoon Network; CNBC; CNN; Comedy Central; Country Music TV; C-SPAN; Discovery Channel; Disney Channel; E! Entertainment Television; ESPN; ESPN 2; Food Network; Fox News Channel; Fox Sports South; FX; G4; Golf Channel; GSN; Hallmark Channel; Headline News; HGTV; History Channel; Lifetime; MSNBC; MTV; National Geographic Channel; Nickelodeon; Oxygen; Shop at Home; SoapNet; Speed; Spike TV; SportSouth; Style Network; Syfy; TBS Superstation; Telemundo; The Learning Channel; The Weather Channel; Toon Disney; Travel Channel; truTV; Turner Classic Movies; Turner Network TV; TV Land; USA Network; Versus; VH1; WE tv.
Fee: $47.99 monthly.

Digital Basic Service
Subscribers: N.A.
Programming (via satellite): BBC America; Bio; Bloomberg Television; Boomerang; Canales N; CNN International; Discovery Digital Networks; DIY Network; ESPN; ESPN Classic Sports; ESPNews; Fox College Sports Atlantic; Fox College Sports Central; Fox College Sports Pacific; Fox Deportes; Fox Movie Channel; Fox Soccer; Fuel TV; GAS; Great American Country; HDNet; HDNet Movies; History Channel International; Independent Film Channel; Lifetime Movie Network; MTV Networks Digital Suite; Music Choice; NFL Network; Nick Jr.; Nick Too; NickToons TV; Sundance Channel; TV Guide Interactive Inc.

Digital Pay Service 1
Pay Units: N.A.
Programming (via satellite): Cinemax (multiplexed); Encore (multiplexed); Flix; HBO (multiplexed); HBO HD; Showtime (multiplexed); Showtime HD; Starz (multiplexed); The Movie Channel (multiplexed).

Video-On-Demand: Yes

Pay-Per-View
iN DEMAND (delivered digitally); NASCAR In Car (delivered digitally); NHL Center Ice (delivered digitally); MLB Extra Innings (delivered digitally); Pleasure (delivered digitally); Playboy TV (delivered digitally); Fresh (delivered digitally); Shorteez (delivered digitally).

Internet Service
Operational: Yes. Began: September 1, 2000.
Broadband Service: Charter Pipeline.
Fee: $29.99 monthly; $10.00 modem lease; $220.00 modem purchase.

Telephone Service
Digital: Operational
Fee: $29.99 monthly

Miles of Plant: 2,361.0 (coaxial); 180.0 (fiber optic).

Vice President & General Manager: Anthony Pope. Operations Manager: Sam Scialabba. Marketing Director: Brooke Sinclair. Sales & Marketing Manager: Karen Sims.

Ownership: Charter Communications Inc. (MSO).

HIGH POINT—Time Warner Cable. Now served by GREENSBORO, NC [NC0006]. ICA: NC0024.

HIGHLANDS—Northland Cable Television, 479 South St, PO Box 1087, Highlands, NC 28741. Phones: 866-978-0816; 828-526-5675. Fax: 828-526-9266. E-mail: highlands@northlandcabletv.com. Web Site: http://www.northlandcabletv.com. Also serves Cashiers, Cedar Creek Resorts, Jackson County (portions), Macon County (eastern portion), Sapphire & Sapphire Valley. ICA: NC0094.

TV Market Ranking: 46 (Jackson County (portions), Sapphire, Sapphire Valley); Below 100 (HIGHLANDS, Macon County (eastern portion) (portions), Jackson County (portions)); Outside TV Markets (Cashiers, Cedar Creek Resorts, Macon County (eastern portion) (portions), Jackson County (portions)). Franchise award date: Octo-

ber 3, 1979. Franchise expiration date: N.A. Began: July 2, 1982.
Channel capacity: 65 (operating 2-way). Channels available but not in use: N.A.

Basic Service
Subscribers: 2,900.
Programming (received off-air): WAGA-TV (FOX) Atlanta; WGTV (PBS) Athens; WHNS (FOX) Greenville; WLOS (ABC) Asheville; WMYA-TV (MNT) Anderson; WSB-TV (ABC) Atlanta; WSPA-TV (CBS) Spartanburg; WUNC-TV (PBS) Chapel Hill; WYCW (CW) Asheville; WYFF (NBC) Greenville; allband FM.
Programming (via satellite): A&E Networks; Animal Planet; Cartoon Network; CNBC; CNN; Comedy Central; C-SPAN; Discovery Channel; E! Entertainment Television; ESPN; ESPN 2; Food Network; Fox Movie Channel; Fox News Channel; Fox Sports South; FX; Golf Channel; Great American Country; Hallmark Channel; Headline News; HGTV; History Channel; Lifetime; MSNBC; National Geographic Channel; Nickelodeon; Outdoor Channel; QVC; Spike TV; Syfy; TBS Superstation; The Learning Channel; The Weather Channel; Trinity Broadcasting Network; Turner Network TV; Turner South; TV Land; USA Network.
Fee: $85.00 installation; $37.99 monthly.

Digital Basic Service
Subscribers: N.A.
Programming (via satellite): BBC America; Discovery Health Channel; Discovery Kids Channel; DMX Music; ESPNews; Fox Soccer; Independent Film Channel; Lifetime Movie Network; Science; Speed; Style Network; Versus; WE tv.

Digital Expanded Basic Service
Subscribers: N.A.
Programming (received off-air): WHNS (FOX) Greenville; WSPA-TV (CBS) Spartanburg; WYFF (NBC) Greenville.
Programming (via satellite): ESPN 2 HD; ESPN HD; HD Theater; Turner Network TV HD.
Fee: $5.99 monthly.

Pay Service 1
Pay Units: N.A.
Programming (via satellite): HBO.
Fee: $13.50 monthly.

Digital Pay Service 1
Pay Units: N.A.
Programming (via satellite): Cinemax (multiplexed); Encore (multiplexed); Flix; HBO (multiplexed); Showtime (multiplexed); Starz (multiplexed); The Movie Channel (multiplexed).
Fee: $14.75 monthly (HBO, Cinemax, Starz/Encore or Showtime/TMC/Flix).

Pay-Per-View
iN DEMAND (delivered digitally); Playboy TV (delivered digitally).

Internet Service
Operational: Yes. Began: May 1, 2004.
Broadband Service: Northland Express.
Fee: $44.99 monthly.

Telephone Service
Digital: Operational
Fee: $29.99 monthly
Miles of Plant: 113.0 (coaxial); None (fiber optic). Additional miles planned: 25.0 (coaxial).
Plant Manager: Alan Boggs. Marketing Manager: Melinda Harbin. Regional Manager: Bill Staley. Technical Manager: Marty Mashburn.
Ownership: Northland Communications Corp. (MSO).

HOLLISTER—Crystal Broadband Networks, PO Box 180336, Chicago, IL 60618. Phones: 630-206-0447; 877-319-0328. E-mail: sales@crystalbn.com. Web Site: http://www.crystalbn.com. ICA: NC0200.
TV Market Ranking: Below 100 (HOLLISTER). Franchise award date: N.A. Franchise expiration date: N.A. Began: N.A.
Channel capacity: 42 (not 2-way capable). Channels available but not in use: N.A.

Basic Service
Subscribers: 673.
Programming (received off-air): WITN-TV (MNT, NBC) Washington; WLFL (CW) Raleigh; WNCN (NBC) Goldsboro; WNCT-TV (CBS, CW) Greenville; WRAL-TV (CBS) Raleigh; WRAY-TV (IND) Wilson; WRAZ (FOX) Raleigh; WRDC (MNT) Durham; WTVD (ABC) Durham; WUNP-TV (PBS) Roanoke Rapids.
Programming (via satellite): QVC; Trinity Broadcasting Network.
Fee: $39.95 installation; $17.48 monthly; $2.00 converter.

Expanded Basic Service 1
Subscribers: 636.
Programming (via satellite): ABC Family Channel; AMC; BET Networks; CNN; Country Music TV; C-SPAN; Discovery Channel; Disney Channel; ESPN; ESPN 2; Fox News Channel; Headline News; Lifetime; MSNBC; MTV; Nickelodeon; Spike TV; Syfy; TBS Superstation; The Learning Channel; The Weather Channel; Toon Disney; Turner Network TV; USA Network; VH1.
Fee: $19.69 monthly.

Digital Basic Service
Subscribers: N.A.
Programming (via satellite): BBC America; Bravo; Discovery Digital Networks; ESPN Classic Sports; ESPNews; Fox Sports World; Golf Channel; GSN; History Channel; Independent Film Channel; Music Choice; Nick Jr.; Versus; WE tv.
Fee: $10.11 monthly.

Pay Service 1
Pay Units: 163.
Programming (via satellite): HBO.
Fee: $15.95 monthly.

Digital Pay Service 1
Pay Units: N.A.
Programming (via satellite): Cinemax (multiplexed); Encore (multiplexed); HBO (multiplexed); Showtime (multiplexed); Starz (multiplexed); The Movie Channel (multiplexed).
Fee: $15.95 monthly (each).

Video-On-Demand: No

Pay-Per-View
HITS Movies & Events (delivered digitally).

Internet Service
Operational: No.

Telephone Service
None
Miles of Plant: 68.0 (coaxial); None (fiber optic).
Ownership: Crystal Broadband Networks (MSO).

HOLLY RIDGE—Charter Communications, 2516 Fayetteville St, Sanford, NC 27332. Phone: 919-708-5902. Fax: 919-774-6126. Web Site: http://www.charter.com. Also serves Beulaville, Calypso, Camp Lejeune, Carolina Beach, Chinquapin, Duplin County, Faison, Fort Fisher AFB, Hampstead, Kenansville, Kure Beach, Magnolia, New Hanover County (unincorporated areas), North Topsail Beach, Olde Point, Onslow County, Pender County (portions), Richlands, Rose Hill, Sneads Ferry, Surf City, Tarawa Terrace, Teachey, Topsail Beach, Wallace & Warsaw. ICA: NC0069.
TV Market Ranking: 73 (Beulaville, Duplin County (portions), Kenansville, Warsaw); 74 (Calypso); 84 (Camp Lejeune, Onslow County (portions), Richlands, Tarawa Terrace); Below 100 (Carolina Beach, Chinquapin, Faison, Fort Fisher AFB, Hampstead, HOLLY RIDGE, Kure Beach, New Hanover County (unincorporated areas), North Topsail Beach, Olde Point, Pender County (portions), Sneads Ferry, Surf City, Teachey, Topsail Beach, Wallace, Duplin County (portions), Onslow County (portions)); Outside TV Markets (Magnolia, Rose Hill, Duplin County (portions)). Franchise award date: March 15, 1982. Franchise expiration date: N.A. Began: August 1, 1982.
Channel capacity: N.A. Channels available but not in use: N.A.

Basic Service
Subscribers: 13,480.
Programming (received off-air): WCTI-TV (ABC) New Bern; WECT (NBC) Wilmington; WITN-TV (MNT, NBC) Washington; WNCT-TV (CBS, CW) Greenville; WSFX-TV (FOX) Wilmington; WUNJ-TV (PBS) Wilmington; WWAY (ABC) Wilmington; allband FM.
Programming (via satellite): C-SPAN; C-SPAN 2; CW+; INSP; QVC; The Weather Channel; Trinity Broadcasting Network; TV Guide Network; WGN America.
Fee: $35.00 installation; $20.47 monthly.

Expanded Basic Service 1
Subscribers: 3,923.
Programming (via satellite): A&E Networks; ABC Family Channel; AMC; Animal Planet; BET Networks; Bravo; Cartoon Network; CNBC; CNN; Comedy Central; Country Music TV; Discovery Channel; Discovery Fit & Health; E! Entertainment Television; ESPN; Food Network; Fox News Channel; Fox Sports South; FX; G4; Golf Channel; GSN; Hallmark Channel; Headline News; HGTV; History Channel; Lifetime; MSNBC; MTV; MTV2; National Geographic Channel; Nickelodeon; Oxygen; Speed; Syfy; Telefutura; Telemundo; The Learning Channel; Toon Disney; Travel Channel; truTV; Turner Classic Movies; Turner Network TV; TV Land; Univision Studios; USA Network; Versus; VH1; WE tv.
Fee: $47.99 monthly.

Digital Basic Service
Subscribers: N.A.
Programming (via satellite): BBC America; Bio; Bloomberg Television; Canales N; Discovery Digital Networks; DIY Network; ESPN Classic Sports; ESPNews; Fox College Sports Atlantic; Fox College Sports Central; Fox College Sports Pacific; Fox Deportes; Fox Movie Channel; Fox Soccer; Fuel TV; GAS; Great American Country; History Channel International; Independent Film Channel; Lifetime Movie Network; MTV Networks Digital Suite; Music Choice; Nick Jr.; Nick Too; NickToons TV; Sundance Channel; TV Guide Interactive Inc.

Digital Pay Service 1
Pay Units: 209.
Programming (via satellite): Cinemax (multiplexed).
Fee: $25.00 installation; $10.95 monthly.

Digital Pay Service 2
Pay Units: 404.
Programming (via satellite): HBO (multiplexed).
Fee: $25.00 installation; $11.95 monthly.

Digital Pay Service 3
Pay Units: 185.
Programming (via satellite): The Movie Channel (multiplexed).
Fee: $25.00 installation; $10.95 monthly.

Digital Pay Service 4
Pay Units: 242.
Programming (via satellite): Showtime (multiplexed).
Fee: $25.00 installation; $10.95 monthly.

Digital Pay Service 5
Pay Units: N.A.
Programming (via satellite): Encore (multiplexed); Flix; Starz (multiplexed).

Video-On-Demand: Yes

Pay-Per-View
iN DEMAND (delivered digitally); Playboy TV (delivered digitally); Fresh (delivered digitally); Shorteez (delivered digitally); NASCAR In Car (delivered digitally).

Internet Service
Operational: Yes.
Broadband Service: Charter Pipeline.
Fee: $29.99 monthly.

Telephone Service
Digital: Planned
Miles of Plant: 712.0 (coaxial); None (fiber optic).
Vice President & General Manager: Anthony Pope. Technical Operations Director: Clarence Rainey. Operations Manager: Doug Underwood. Marketing Director: Brooke Sinclair. Marketing Manager: LaRisa Scales.
Ownership: Charter Communications Inc. (MSO).

IRONDUFF—Carolina Mountain Cable. Now served by WAYNESVILLE, NC [NC0127]. ICA: NC0124.

JACKSONVILLE—Time Warner Cable, 101 Innovation Ave, Ste 100, Morrisville, NC 27560. Phones: 910-763-0004 (Wilmington office); 919-573-7000. Web Site: http://www.timewarnercable.com/carolinas. Also serves Jones County (portions), Maysville, Midway Park, Pollocksville & Richlands. ICA: NC0025.
TV Market Ranking: 84 (JACKSONVILLE, Jones County (portions), Midway Park, Pollocksville). Franchise award date: December 1, 1973. Franchise expiration date: March 4, 2012. Began: July 20, 1965.
Channel capacity: N.A. Channels available but not in use: N.A.

Basic Service
Subscribers: N.A. Included in Wilmington
Programming (received off-air): WCTI-TV (ABC) New Bern; WECT (NBC) Wilmington; WFXI (FOX, MNT) Morehead City; WNCT-TV (CBS, CW) Greenville; WUNM-TV (PBS) Jacksonville; WWAY (ABC) Wilmington.
Programming (via satellite): Animal Planet; Bravo; Cartoon Network; C-SPAN 2; Disney Channel; E! Entertainment Television; ESPN 2; ESPN Classic Sports; Food Net-

work; Fox News Channel; Fox Sports South; Fuse; Golf Channel; HGTV; ION Television; Jewelry Television; Lifetime Movie Network; National Geographic Channel; Oxygen; ShopNBC; SoapNet; Speed; Travel Channel; Turner Classic Movies; TV Guide Network; Versus; WE tv.
Fee: $35.00 installation; $8.29 monthly.

Expanded Basic Service 1
Subscribers: 20,300.
Programming (via satellite): A&E Networks; ABC Family Channel; AMC; BET Networks; CNBC; CNN; Comedy Central; Country Music TV; Discovery Channel; ESPN; FX; Hallmark Channel; Headline News; History Channel; Lifetime; MSNBC; MTV; Nickelodeon; QVC; Spike TV; Syfy; TBS Superstation; The Learning Channel; The Weather Channel; Trinity Broadcasting Network; truTV; Turner Network TV; USA Network; VH1; WGN America.
Fee: $44.16 monthly.

Digital Basic Service
Subscribers: N.A. Included in Wilmington
Programming (via satellite): American-Life TV Network; America's Store; BBC America; Bio; Bloomberg Television; Cooking Channel; C-SPAN 3; Discovery Digital Networks; Disney Channel; DIY Network; ESPNews; Flix; Fox Sports Net (multiplexed); Fox Sports World; Fuel TV; G4; GSN; History Channel International; Independent Film Channel; INSP; Lifetime Real Women; MTV Networks Digital Suite; Music Choice; NBA TV; Nick Jr.; Outdoor Channel; Ovation; Style Network; Tennis Channel; The Word Network; Toon Disney; TV Land.
Fee: $6.95 monthly.

Digital Pay Service 1
Pay Units: N.A.
Programming (via satellite): Cinemax (multiplexed); Encore (multiplexed); Fox Movie Channel; HBO (multiplexed); Showtime (multiplexed); Sundance Channel; The Movie Channel (multiplexed).
Fee: $11.95 monthly (Starz, Cinemax, or Showtime/TMC), $13.95 monthly (HBO).

Video-On-Demand: Yes

Pay-Per-View
Hot Choice (delivered digitally); Pleasure (delivered digitally); iN DEMAND (delivered digitally); Fresh (delivered digitally); Shorteez (delivered digitally); Playboy TV (delivered digitally); ESPN Now (delivered digitally).

Internet Service
Operational: Yes.
Broadband Service: Road Runner.
Fee: $69.95 installation; $44.95 monthly.

Telephone Service
Digital: Operational
Fee: $44.95 monthly

Miles of Plant: 485.0 (coaxial); 66.0 (fiber optic). Additional miles planned: 25.0 (coaxial).

Vice President & General Manager: Kim Cannon. Vice President, Sales & Marketing: Tom Smith. Technical Operations Director: Joe Pell. Public Affairs Director: Marty Feurer. Customer Care Manager: Linda Bell.

Ownership: Time Warner Cable (MSO).; Advance/Newhouse Partnership (MSO).Day-to-day operations are managed by Time Warner Cable.

KANNAPOLIS—Time Warner Cable, 3140 W Arrowood Rd, Charlotte, NC 28273. Phone: 704-378-2500. Fax: 704-504-1997. Web Site: http://www.timewarnercable.com/carolinas. Also serves Cabarrus County, China Grove, Concord, Enochville, Harrisburg, Landis, Midland, Mount Pleasant, Poplar Tent & Rowan County. ICA: NC0010.

TV Market Ranking: 42 (Cabarrus County, China Grove, Concord, Enochville, Harrisburg, KANNAPOLIS, Landis, Midland, Mount Pleasant, Poplar Tent); 42,47 (Rowan County (portions)). Franchise award date: November 1, 1978. Franchise expiration date: N.A. Began: March 1, 1980.

Channel capacity: N.A. Channels available but not in use: N.A.

Basic Service
Subscribers: N.A. Included in Charlotte
Programming (received off-air): WAXN-TV (IND) Kannapolis; WBTV (CBS) Charlotte; WCCB (FOX) Charlotte; WCNC-TV (NBC) Charlotte; WHKY-TV (IND) Hickory; WJZY (CW) Belmont; WMYT-TV (MNT) Rock Hill; WSOC-TV (ABC) Charlotte; WTVI (PBS) Charlotte; WUNG-TV (PBS) Concord.
Programming (via satellite): TV Guide Network; WGN America.
Fee: $36.00 installation; $8.00 monthly.

Expanded Basic Service 1
Subscribers: N.A.
Programming (via satellite): A&E Networks; ABC Family Channel; AMC; Animal Planet; BET Networks; Bravo; Cartoon Network; CNBC; CNN; Comedy Central; Country Music TV; C-SPAN; C-SPAN 2; Discovery Channel; Discovery Health Channel; Disney Channel; E! Entertainment Television; ESPN; ESPN 2; ESPN Classic Sports; Food Network; Fox News Channel; Fox Sports South; FX; Golf Channel; Hallmark Channel; Headline News; HGTV; History Channel; INSP; Lifetime; Lifetime Movie Network; MSNBC; MTV; National Geographic Channel; Nickelodeon; Oxygen; QVC; Speed; Spike TV; SportSouth; Syfy; TBS Superstation; The Learning Channel; The Weather Channel; Travel Channel; truTV; Turner Classic Movies; Turner Network TV; TV Land; USA Network; Versus; VH1; WE tv.
Fee: $41.95 monthly.

Digital Basic Service
Subscribers: 13,768.
Programming (via satellite): AmericanLife TV Network; America's Store; BBC America; Bio; Black Family Channel; Bloomberg Television; Boomerang; Canales N; Cooking Channel; C-SPAN 3; Discovery Digital Networks; DIY Network; DMX Music; ESPNews; FamilyNet; Fox Sports World; FSN Digital Atlantic; FSN Digital Central; FSN Digital Pacific; Fuel TV; Fuse; G4; Great American Country; GSN; History Channel International; Independent Film Channel; Lifetime Real Women; MTV Networks Digital Suite; NBA TV; Nick Jr.; Outdoor Channel; Ovation; SoapNet; Style Network; Tennis Channel; Toon Disney.
Fee: $15.00 monthly.

Digital Pay Service 1
Pay Units: N.A.
Programming (via satellite): Cinemax (multiplexed); Deutsche Welle TV; Encore (multiplexed); Flix; Fox Movie Channel; HBO (multiplexed); RAI International; Saigon Broadcasting Television Network; Showtime (multiplexed); Starz (multiplexed); Sundance Channel; The Movie Channel (multiplexed); TV5, La Television International; Zee TV USA.
Fee: $9.95 monthly (Deutsche Welle, TV5 or RAI), 10.95 monthly (Cinemax, HBO, Showtime, TMC or Starz/Encore), $14.95 monthly (SBTN or Zee), $24.95 monthly (Nuestra Tele).

Video-On-Demand: Yes

Pay-Per-View
Addressable homes: 13,768.
iN DEMAND (delivered digitally); ESPN Now (delivered digitally); ESPN Full Court (delivered digitally); ESPN Gameplan (delivered digitally); Adult PPV (delivered digitally); Sports PPV (delivered digitally).

Internet Service
Operational: Yes.
Subscribers: 14,199.
Broadband Service: Road Runner, AOL, EarthLink.
Fee: $39.95 installation; $46.95 monthly.

Telephone Service
Digital: Operational
Fee: $39.95 monthly

Miles of plant (coax & fiber) included in Charlotte

President: Mike Munley. Vice President, Technical Operations: Mike Cullim. Vice President, Engineering: Richard Newcomb. Vice President, Marketing & Sales: Eric Franey. Government Affairs Director: Michael Tanck. Public Affairs Director: Jessica Graham.

Ownership: Time Warner Cable (MSO).; Advance/Newhouse Partnership (MSO).Day-to-day operations are managed by Time Warner Cable.

KENLY—Charter Communications, 2516 Fayetteville St, Sanford, NC 27332. Phone: 919-708-5902. Fax: 919-774-6126. Web Site: http://www.charter.com. Also serves Johnston County, Lucama, Micro & Princeton. ICA: NC0148.

TV Market Ranking: 73 (Johnston County, KENLY, Lucama, Micro, Princeton). Franchise award date: N.A. Franchise expiration date: N.A. Began: January 1, 1983.

Channel capacity: N.A. Channels available but not in use: N.A.

Basic Service
Subscribers: N.A.
Programming (received off-air): WARZ-LP Smithfield/Selma; WITN-TV (MNT, NBC) Washington; WLFL (CW) Raleigh; WNCN (NBC) Goldsboro; WNCT-TV (CBS, CW) Greenville; WRAL-TV (CBS) Raleigh; WRAY-TV (IND) Wilson; WRAZ (FOX) Raleigh; WRDC (MNT) Durham; WRPX-TV (ION) Rocky Mount; WTVD (ABC) Durham; WUNC-TV (PBS) Chapel Hill.
Programming (via satellite): C-SPAN; QVC; WGN America.
Fee: $35.00 installation; $2.00 converter.

Expanded Basic Service 1
Subscribers: N.A.
Programming (via satellite): A&E Networks; ABC Family Channel; AMC; BET Networks; Bravo; Cartoon Network; CNBC; CNN; Comedy Central; Country Music TV; Discovery Channel; Disney Channel; E! Entertainment Television; ESPN; ESPN 2; Food Network; Fox News Channel; Fox Sports South; FX; G4; Golf Channel; Headline News; HGTV; History Channel; Lifetime; MSNBC; MTV; Nickelodeon; Oxygen; Speed; Spike TV; Syfy; TBS Superstation; Telemundo; The Learning Channel; The Weather Channel; Trinity Broadcasting Network; Turner Classic Movies; Turner Network TV; TV Land; USA Network; VH1.
Fee: $47.99 monthly.

Digital Basic Service
Subscribers: N.A.
Programming (via satellite): BBC America; Bio; Bloomberg Television; Discovery Fit & Health; DIY Network; ESPN Classic Sports; ESPNews; Fox College Sports Atlantic; Fox College Sports Central; Fox College Sports Pacific; Fox Movie Channel; Fox Soccer; Fuse; GAS; GSN; History Channel International; Independent Film Channel; Lifetime Movie Network; MTV Networks Digital Suite; Music Choice; National Geographic Channel; Nick Jr.; Nick Too; SoapNet; Style Network; Sundance Channel; Toon Disney; TV Guide Interactive Inc.; WE tv.

Digital Pay Service 1
Pay Units: N.A.
Programming (via satellite): Cinemax (multiplexed); Encore; Flix; HBO (multiplexed); Showtime (multiplexed); Starz (multiplexed); The Movie Channel (multiplexed).

Video-On-Demand: No

Pay-Per-View
iN DEMAND (delivered digitally); Playboy TV (delivered digitally); Fresh (delivered digitally).

Internet Service
Operational: Yes.
Broadband Service: Charter Pipeline.
Fee: $29.99 monthly.

Telephone Service
None

Miles of plant (coax & fiber) included in Buies Creek

Vice President & General Manager: Anthony Pope. Marketing Director: Brooke Sinclair. Marketing Manager: LaRisa Scales. Office Manager: Brenda Brinson. Operations Manager: Doug Underwood.

Ownership: Charter Communications Inc. (MSO).

KING—Time Warner Cable. Now served by GREENSBORO, NC [NC0006]. ICA: NC0064.

KINSTON—Cox Communications. Now served by GREENVILLE, NC [NC0014]. ICA: NC0034.

LAKE GASTON—Time Warner Cable, 101 Innovation Ave, Ste 100, Morrisville, NC 27560. Phone: 919-573-7000. Web Site: http://www.timewarnercable.com/carolinas. Also serves Henrico, Northampton County (portions) & Warren County (portions). ICA: NC0121.

TV Market Ranking: Below 100 (Northampton County (portions), Warren County (portions)); Outside TV Markets (Henrico, LAKE GASTON, Northampton County (portions), Warren County (portions)). Franchise award date: January 4, 1988. Franchise expiration date: January 4, 2008. Began: January 4, 1988.

Channel capacity: 42 (not 2-way capable). Channels available but not in use: N.A.

Basic Service
Subscribers: 803.
Programming (received off-air): WLFL (CW) Raleigh; WNCN (NBC) Goldsboro; WRAL-TV (CBS) Raleigh; WRAY-TV (IND) Wilson; WRAZ (FOX) Raleigh; WRDC (MNT) Durham; WRPX-TV (ION) Rocky Mount; WTVD (ABC) Durham; WUNP-TV (PBS) Roanoke Rapids.
Programming (via satellite): QVC; Trinity Broadcasting Network.
Fee: $39.95 installation; $17.48 monthly; $2.00 converter.

Expanded Basic Service 1
Subscribers: 662.
Programming (via satellite): A&E Networks; ABC Family Channel; AMC; BET Networks; CNN; Country Music TV; C-SPAN; Discovery Channel; Disney Channel; ESPN; ESPN 2; Fox News Channel; Headline News; HGTV; Lifetime; MSNBC; MTV; Nickelodeon; Spike TV; Syfy; TBS Superstation; The Learning Channel; The Weather Channel; Turner Network TV; USA Network; VH1.
Fee: $19.69 monthly.

Digital Basic Service
Subscribers: N.A.
Programming (via satellite): BBC America; Bravo; Discovery Digital Networks; DMX Music; ESPNews; Fox Sports World; Golf Channel; GSN; History Channel International; Independent Film Channel; Nick Jr.; Versus; WE tv.
Fee: $10.11 monthly.
Pay Service 1
Pay Units: 92.
Programming (via satellite): HBO.
Fee: $15.95 monthly.
Digital Pay Service 1
Pay Units: N.A.
Programming (via satellite): Cinemax (multiplexed); Encore; HBO (multiplexed); Showtime (multiplexed); The Movie Channel (multiplexed).
Fee: $15.95 monthly (each).
Pay-Per-View
Hits Movies & Events (delivered digitally); Playboy TV (delivered digitally).
Internet Service
Operational: No.
Telephone Service
Digital: Operational
Fee: $24.95 monthly
Miles of Plant: 66.0 (coaxial); None (fiber optic).
Regional Vice President & General Manager: Dianne Blackwood. Vice President, Technical Operations: Gary Frederick. Vice President, Sales & Marketing: Tom Smith. Vice President, Government & Public Affairs: Brad Phillips. Customer Care Director: Sharon Duggins.
Ownership: Time Warner Cable (MSO).

LAKE NORMAN—Now served by MOORESVILLE, NC [NC0207]. ICA: NC0103.

LAKE TOXAWAY—Comporium Communications. Now served by BREVARD, NC [NC0053]. ICA: NC0156.

LAKE WACCAMAW—Time Warner Cable, 115 E Walter St, Whiteville, NC 28472-4135. Phones: 910-640-2288; 888-683-1000. Fax: 910-640-2303. Web Site: http://www.timewarnercable.com. Also serves Columbus County (portions) & Hallsboro. ICA: NC0201.
TV Market Ranking: Below 100 (Columbus County (portions)); Outside TV Markets (Hallsboro, LAKE WACCAMAW). Franchise award date: April 27, 1987. Franchise expiration date: N.A. Began: December 15, 1987.
Channel capacity: N.A. Channels available but not in use: N.A.
Basic Service
Subscribers: 543.
Programming (received off-air): WBTW (CBS, MNT) Florence; WECT (NBC) Wilmington; WFPX-TV (ION) Fayetteville; WILM-LD Wilmington; WSFX-TV (FOX) Wilmington; WUNJ-TV (PBS) Wilmington; WWAY (ABC) Wilmington.
Programming (via satellite): A&E Networks; ABC Family Channel; AMC; Animal Planet; BET Networks; Bravo; Cartoon Network; CNBC; CNN; Comedy Central; Country Music TV; C-SPAN; CW+; Discovery Channel; Discovery Fit & Health; Disney Channel; ESPN; ESPN 2; Eternal Word TV Network; Food Network; Fox News Channel; Fox Sports Net Carolinas; FX; Golf Channel; Hallmark Channel; Headline News; HGTV; History Channel; Home Shopping Network; Jewelry Television; Lifetime; Lifetime Movie Network; MSNBC; MTV; News 14 Carolina; Nick Jr.; Nickelodeon; OWN: Oprah Winfrey Network; Oxygen; QVC; Russia Today; SoapNet; Speed; Spike TV; Syfy; TBS Superstation; The Learning Channel; The Weather Channel; Trinity Broadcasting Network; truTV; Turner Classic Movies; Turner Network TV; TV Guide Network; TV Land; Univision; USA Network; Versus; VH1; WE tv; WGN America.
Fee: $35.00 installation; $20.50 monthly.
Digital Basic Service
Subscribers: N.A.
Programming (via satellite): A&E HD; ABC Family HD; AMC HD; AmericanLife TV Network; Animal Planet HD; Azteca America; Bandamax; BBC America; BBC HD; Bio; Bio HD; Bloomberg Television; Boomerang; Boomerang en Espanol; Bravo HD; BTN; Canal Sur; Cartoon Network HD; Cartoon Network Tambien en Espanol; CBS Sports Network; Centric; Chiller; Cine Latino; cloo; CMT HD; CNBC HD+; CNBC World; CNN en Espanol; CNN HD; Comedy Central HD; Cooking Channel; C-SPAN 3; Current; Daystar TV Network; De Pelicula; De Pelicula Clasico; Discovery Channel HD; Discovery en Espanol; Discovery Familia; Disney Channel HD; Disney XD; Disney XD en Espanol; Disney XD HD; DIY Network; ESPN 2 HD; ESPN Classic Sports; ESPN Deportes; ESPN Full Court; ESPN Gameplan; ESPN HD; ESPN U; ESPNews; ESPNews HD; ESPNU HD; EWTN en Espanol; Flix; Food Network HD; Fox Business Channel; Fox Business Channel HD; Fox College Sports Atlantic; Fox College Sports Central; Fox College Sports Pacific; Fox Deportes; Fox News HD; Fox Soccer; FSN HD; Fuel TV; Fuse; Fuse HD; FX HD; G4; GalaVision; GMC; Golf Channel HD; GolTV; Great American Country; GSN; Hallmark Channel HD; Hallmark Movie Channel; Halogen Network; HD Theater; Headline News HD; HGTV HD; History Channel en Espanol; History Channel HD; History Channel International; ID Investigation Discovery; ID Investigation Discovery HD; La Familia Network; Lifetime Movie Network HD; Lifetime Real Women; LOGO; Military Channel; MLB Extra Innings; MLB Network; MLB Network HD; MTV Networks HD; MTV2; mun2 television; Music Choice; Nat Geo WILD; National Geographic Channel HD Network; NBA League Pass; NBA TV; NBA TV HD; New England Sports Network; NHL Center Ice; NHL Network; NHL Network HD; Nick HD; NickToons TV; Nuvo TV; Outdoor Channel; Outdoor Channel HD; Ovation; Palladia; PBS Kids Sprout; Planet Green; Planet Green HD; ReelzChannel; Science; Science HD; Sorpresa; Speed HD; Spike TV HD; Style Network; Sundance Channel; Syfy HD; TBS in HD; TeenNick; Telefutura; Telemundo; Tennis Channel; The Hub; The Sportsman Channel; TLC HD; Tr3s; Travel Channel; Travel Channel HD; truTV HD; Turner Classic Movies HD; Turner Network TV HD; TV One; Univision; USA Network HD; Versus HD; VH1 HD; WE tv HD; Yankees Entertainment & Sports.
Digital Pay Service 1
Pay Units: N.A.
Programming (via satellite): Cinemax (multiplexed); Cinemax HD; HBO (multiplexed); HBO HD; Showtime (multiplexed); Showtime HD; Starz (multiplexed); Starz HDTV; Starz RetroPlex; The Movie Channel (multiplexed); The Movie Channel HD.
Video-On-Demand: No
Internet Service
Operational: No.

Telephone Service
None
Miles of Plant: 62.0 (coaxial); None (fiber optic).
Regional Manager: Kevin Barrett. Chief Technician: Donny Washington. Manager: Debra Burr.
Ownership: Time Warner Cable (MSO).

LANSING—Mediacom. Now served by WEST JEFFERSON, NC [NC0098]. ICA: NC0169.

LAURINBURG—Time Warner Cable. Now served by MYRTLE BEACH, SC [SC0007]. ICA: NC0061.

LITTLETON—Time Warner Cable, 101 Innovation Ave, Ste 100, Morrisville, NC 27560. Phone: 919-573-7000. Web Site: http://www.timewarnercable.com/carolinas. Also serves Warren County (eastern portion). ICA: NC0123.
TV Market Ranking: Below 100 (LITTLETON, Warren County (eastern portion) (portions)); Outside TV Markets (Warren County (eastern portion) (portions)). Franchise award date: September 15, 1986. Franchise expiration date: N.A. Began: September 1, 1987.
Channel capacity: 42 (not 2-way capable). Channels available but not in use: N.A.
Basic Service
Subscribers: 1,376.
Programming (received off-air): WLFL (CW) Raleigh; WNCN (NBC) Goldsboro; WNVN-LP Roanoke Rapids; WRAL-TV (CBS) Raleigh; WRAY-TV (IND) Wilson; WRAZ (FOX) Raleigh; WRDC (MNT) Durham; WRPX-TV (ION) Rocky Mount; WTVD (ABC) Durham; WUNP-TV (PBS) Roanoke Rapids.
Programming (via satellite): QVC.
Fee: $29.95 installation; $17.48 monthly; $2.00 converter.
Expanded Basic Service 1
Subscribers: 1,190.
Programming (via satellite): A&E Networks; ABC Family Channel; AMC; BET Networks; CNN; Country Music TV; C-SPAN; Discovery Channel; Disney Channel; ESPN; ESPN 2; Fox News Channel; Headline News; HGTV; INSP; Lifetime; MSNBC; MTV; Nickelodeon; Spike TV; Syfy; TBS Superstation; The Learning Channel; The Weather Channel; Trinity Broadcasting Network; Turner Network TV; USA Network; VH1.
Fee: $19.69 monthly.
Digital Basic Service
Subscribers: N.A.
Programming (via satellite): BBC America; Bravo; Discovery Digital Networks; ESPN Classic Sports; ESPNews; Fox Soccer; Golf Channel; GSN; HGTV; History Channel; Independent Film Channel; Music Choice; Nick Jr.; TV Land; Versus; WE tv.
Fee: $10.11 monthly.
Pay Service 1
Pay Units: N.A.
Programming (via satellite): HBO.
Fee: $15.95 monthly.
Digital Pay Service 1
Pay Units: N.A.
Programming (via satellite): Cinemax (multiplexed); Encore (multiplexed); HBO (multiplexed); Showtime (multiplexed); Starz (multiplexed); The Movie Channel (multiplexed).
Fee: $15.95 monthly (each).
Video-On-Demand: No
Pay-Per-View
Movies (delivered digitally); Playboy TV (delivered digitally).
Internet Service
Operational: Yes.
Fee: $24.95 monthly.
Telephone Service
Digital: Operational
Fee: $24.99 monthly
Miles of Plant: 89.0 (coaxial); None (fiber optic).
Vice President & General Manager: Chris Whitaker. Vice President, Sales & Marketing: Tom Smith. Vice President, Government & Public Affairs: Brad Phillips. Technical Operations Director: Doug Davis.
Ownership: Time Warner Cable (MSO).

LUMBERTON—Time Warner Cable, 6202 Raeford Rd, Fayetteville, NC 28304. Phones: 919-573-7000 (Morrisville office); 910-401-5001. Fax: 910-864-8878. Web Site: http://www.timewarnercable.com/carolinas. Also serves Fairmont, Lumber Bridge (portions), Pembroke, Red Springs, Rennert, Robeson County, Shannon & St. Pauls. ICA: NC0055.
TV Market Ranking: 73 (Lumber Bridge (portions) (portions), LUMBERTON, Pembroke, Red Springs, Rennert, Robeson County (portions), Shannon, St. Pauls); Below 100 (Robeson County (portions)); Outside TV Markets (Fairmont, Robeson County (portions)). Franchise award date: N.A. Franchise expiration date: June 29, 2011. Began: March 28, 1967.
Channel capacity: N.A. Channels available but not in use: N.A.
Basic Service
Subscribers: 15,378.
Programming (received off-air): WBTW (CBS, MNT) Florence; WECT (NBC) Wilmington; WFPX-TV (ION) Fayetteville; WFXB (FOX) Myrtle Beach; WRAL-TV (CBS) Raleigh; WTVD (ABC) Durham; WUNU (PBS) Lumberton; WUVC-DT (UNV) Fayetteville.
Programming (via satellite): TBS Superstation; TV Guide Network.
Fee: $42.95 installation; $10.35 monthly.
Expanded Basic Service 1
Subscribers: N.A.
Programming (via satellite): A&E Networks; ABC Family Channel; AMC; Animal Planet; BET Networks; Cartoon Network; CNBC; CNN; Comedy Central; Country Music TV; C-SPAN; Discovery Channel; Disney Channel; E! Entertainment Television; ESPN; ESPN 2; ESPN Classic Sports; Food Network; Fox News Channel; Fox Sports South; FX; Golf Channel; Headline News; HGTV; History Channel; INSP; Lifetime; Lifetime Movie Network; MSNBC; MTV; National Geographic Channel; Nick-

elodeon; Oxygen; QVC; Sneak Prevue; SoapNet; Spike TV; Syfy; The Learning Channel; The Weather Channel; Travel Channel; Trinity Broadcasting Network; truTV; Turner Classic Movies; Turner Network TV; TV Land; USA Network; VH1; WE tv.
Fee: $39.50 monthly.

Digital Basic Service
Subscribers: 4,500.
Programming (via satellite): America's Store; BBC America; Black Family Channel; Bloomberg Television; Canales N; Cooking Channel; C-SPAN 3; Discovery Digital Networks; Disney Channel; DIY Network; ESPNews; Flix; Fox Movie Channel; Fox Sports Net; Fox Sports World; G4; Great American Country; GSN; Lifetime Movie Network; MTV2; MuchMusic Network; Music Choice; Nick Jr.; Outdoor Channel; Ovation; Speed; Style Network; Sundance Channel; Toon Disney; Versus; VH1 Classic.
Fee: $16.25 monthly.

Digital Pay Service 1
Pay Units: N.A.
Programming (via satellite): Cinemax (multiplexed); Encore (multiplexed); HBO (multiplexed); Showtime (multiplexed); Starz (multiplexed); The Movie Channel (multiplexed).
Fee: $11.95 monthly (each).

Video-On-Demand: Yes

Pay-Per-View
ESPN Now (delivered digitally); Hot Choice (delivered digitally); iN DEMAND; Playboy TV (delivered digitally); Pleasure (delivered digitally); Fresh (delivered digitally); Shorteez (delivered digitally).

Internet Service
Operational: Yes. Began: October 1, 2000.
Subscribers: 1,000.
Broadband Service: AOL; EarthLink; Road Runner.
Fee: $99.95 installation; $44.95 monthly.

Telephone Service
Digital: Operational
Fee: $44.95 monthly

Miles of Plant: 491.0 (coaxial); None (fiber optic).

President: Tom Adams. Vice President, Technical Operations: Gary Frederick. Vice President, Sales & Marketing: Tom Smith. Vice President, Government & Public Affairs: Brad Phillips. General Manager: Kim Cannon. Chief Technician: Fred Kirk.

Ownership: Time Warner Cable (MSO).; Advance/Newhouse Partnership (MSO).Day-to-day operations are managed by Time Warner Cable.

MANTEO—Charter Communications, 2400 S Virginia Dare Trail, Nags Head, NC 27959. Phones: 757-539-0713 (Suffolk office); 252-441-1582. Fax: 252-441-1581. Web Site: http://www.charter.com. Also serves Avon, Buxton, Colington, Corolla, Dare County (portions), Duck, Frisco, Hatteras, Kill Devil Hills, Kitty Hawk, Manns Harbor, Nags Head, Rodanthe, Salvo, Southern Shores, Stumpy Point, Wanchese & Waves. ICA: NC0118.

TV Market Ranking: Below 100 (Avon, Colington, Corolla, Dare County (portions), Duck, Kill Devil Hills, Kitty Hawk, Manns Harbor, MANTEO, Nags Head, Rodanthe, Salvo, Southern Shores, Stumpy Point, Wanchese, Waves); Outside TV Markets (Buxton, Frisco, Hatteras). Franchise award date: N.A. Franchise expiration date: N.A. Began: May 1, 1974.

Channel capacity: N.A. Channels available but not in use: N.A.

Basic Service
Subscribers: 17,250.
Programming (received off-air): WAVY-TV (NBC) Portsmouth; WGNT (CW) Portsmouth; WITN-TV (MNT, NBC) Washington; WNCT-TV (CBS, CW) Greenville; WPXV-TV (ION) Norfolk; WSKY-TV (IND) Manteo; WTKR (CBS) Norfolk; WTVZ-TV (MNT) Norfolk; WUND-TV (PBS) Edenton; WVBT (FOX) Virginia Beach; WVEC (ABC) Hampton; allband FM.
Programming (via satellite): A&E Networks; AMC; CNBC; CNN; Comedy Central; C-SPAN; Discovery Channel; FX; Headline News; LWS Local Weather Station; MTV; MTV2; Nickelodeon; QVC; Spike TV; The Weather Channel; Trinity Broadcasting Network; Turner Classic Movies; TV Guide Network; USA Network; VH1.
Fee: $29.99 installation; $22.03 monthly.

Expanded Basic Service 1
Subscribers: 15,611.
Programming (via satellite): ABC Family Channel; Animal Planet; BET Networks; Bravo; Cartoon Network; Country Music TV; Disney Channel; E! Entertainment Television; ESPN; ESPN 2; Food Network; Fox News Channel; Fox Sports South; G4; Golf Channel; Hallmark Channel; HGTV; History Channel; Lifetime; MSNBC; National Geographic Channel; Oxygen; SoapNet; Speed; Syfy; TBS Superstation; The Learning Channel; Toon Disney; Travel Channel; truTV; Turner Network TV; TV Land; WE tv.
Fee: $47.99 monthly.

Digital Basic Service
Subscribers: N.A.
Programming (via satellite): BBC America; Bio; Bloomberg Television; Canales N; Discovery Digital Networks; DIY Network; ESPN Classic Sports; ESPNews; Fox College Sports Atlantic; Fox College Sports Central; Fox College Sports Pacific; Fox Deportes; Fox Movie Channel; Fox Soccer; Fuel TV; GAS; Great American Country; History Channel International; Independent Film Channel; Lifetime Movie Network; Mid-Atlantic Sports Network; MTV Networks Digital Suite; Music Choice; Nick Jr.; Nick Too; NickToons TV; Sundance Channel; TV Guide Interactive Inc.

Digital Pay Service 1
Pay Units: 1,136.
Programming (via satellite): Cinemax (multiplexed).
Fee: $5.00 installation; $11.95 monthly.

Digital Pay Service 2
Pay Units: 1,923.
Programming (via satellite): HBO (multiplexed).
Fee: $11.95 monthly.

Digital Pay Service 3
Pay Units: 966.
Programming (via satellite): Showtime (multiplexed).
Fee: $11.95 monthly.

Digital Pay Service 4
Pay Units: 516.
Programming (via satellite): The Movie Channel (multiplexed).
Fee: $11.95 monthly.

Digital Pay Service 5
Pay Units: N.A.
Programming (via satellite): Encore (multiplexed); Flix; Starz (multiplexed).

Video-On-Demand: No

Pay-Per-View
iN DEMAND (delivered digitally); Playboy TV (delivered digitally); Fresh (delivered digitally); Shorteez (delivered digitally); NASCAR In Car (delivered digitally).

Internet Service
Operational: Yes.
Broadband Service: Charter Pipeline.
Fee: $29.99 monthly.

Telephone Service
None

Miles of Plant: 531.0 (coaxial); None (fiber optic).

Vice President & General Manager: Anthony Pope. Operations Manager: Tom Ross. Technical Operations Director: Joel Sprout. Marketing Director: Brooke Sinclair. Marketing Manager: LaRisa Scales.

Ownership: Charter Communications Inc. (MSO).

MARION—Charter Communications, 1670 Hendersonville Rd, Asheville, NC 28803. Phone: 828-209-2200. Fax: 828-277-6150. Web Site: http://www.charter.com. Also serves McDowell County (central portion) & Old Fort. ICA: NC0068.

TV Market Ranking: 46 (MARION, McDowell County (central portion) (portions), Old Fort); Below 100 (McDowell County (central portion) (portions)). Franchise award date: N.A. Franchise expiration date: N.A. Began: November 1, 1968.

Channel capacity: N.A. Channels available but not in use: N.A.

Basic Service
Subscribers: 5,281.
Programming (received off-air): WHNS (FOX) Greenville; WLOS (ABC) Asheville; WMYA-TV (MNT) Anderson; WSPA-TV (CBS) Spartanburg; WUNF-TV (PBS) Asheville; WYFF (NBC) Greenville.
Programming (via satellite): INSP; QVC; ShopNBC; TV Guide Network; WGN America.
Fee: $29.99 installation; $3.00 converter.

Expanded Basic Service 1
Subscribers: 145.
Programming (via satellite): A&E Networks; ABC Family Channel; AMC; Animal Planet; BET Networks; Cartoon Network; CNBC; CNN; Comedy Central; Country Music TV; C-SPAN; Discovery Channel; Disney Channel; E! Entertainment Television; ESPN; ESPN 2; Food Network; Fox News Channel; Fox Sports South; FX; G4; Golf Channel; Hallmark Channel; Headline News; HGTV; History Channel; ION Television; Lifetime; MSNBC; MTV; National Geographic Channel; Nickelodeon; Oxygen; SoapNet; Speed; Spike TV; SportSouth; Syfy; TBS Superstation; The Learning Channel; The Weather Channel; Travel Channel; truTV; Turner Network TV; TV Land; USA Network; Versus; VH1.
Fee: $47.99 monthly.

Digital Basic Service
Subscribers: N.A.
Programming (via satellite): BBC America; Bio; Bloomberg Television; Boomerang; CNN en Espanol; CNN International; Discovery Digital Networks; DIY Network; ESPN Classic Sports; Fox College Sports Atlantic; Fox College Sports Central; Fox College Sports Pacific; Fox Soccer; Fuel TV; GAS; History Channel International; Independent Film Channel; Lifetime Movie Network; Lifetime Real Women; MTV Networks Digital Suite; Music Choice; NFL Network; Nick Jr.; Nick Too; NickToons TV; Sundance Channel; TV Guide Interactive Inc.; WE tv.

Digital Pay Service 1
Pay Units: 286.
Programming (via satellite): Cinemax (multiplexed); Encore (multiplexed); HBO (multiplexed); Showtime (multiplexed).
Fee: $15.00 installation.

Digital Pay Service 2
Pay Units: N.A.
Programming (via satellite): Flix; Playboy TV; Starz (multiplexed); The Movie Channel (multiplexed).

Video-On-Demand: No

Pay-Per-View
iN DEMAND (delivered digitally); Playboy TV (delivered digitally); Fresh (delivered digitally); Shorteez (delivered digitally); NASCAR In Car (delivered digitally).

Internet Service
Operational: Yes.
Broadband Service: Charter Pipeline.
Fee: $29.99 monthly.

Telephone Service
Digital: Planned

Miles of Plant: 164.0 (coaxial); None (fiber optic).

Vice President & General Manager: Anthony Pope. Operations Manager: Janet Cloyde. Chief Technician: Dean McCracken. Marketing Director: Brooke Sinclair. Sales & Marketing Manager: Karen Sims.

Ownership: Charter Communications Inc. (MSO).

MEBANE—Time Warner Cable. Now served by GREENSBORO, NC [NC0006]. ICA: NC0074.

MID LAKES TRAILER PARK—Windjammer Cable, 8500 W 110th St, Ste 600, Overland Park, KS 66210. Phone: 888-495-2881. Fax: 913-563-5454. Web Site: http://www.windjammercable.com. Also serves Edgecombe County (portions). ICA: NC0206.

TV Market Ranking: 84 (Edgecombe County (portions), MID LAKES TRAILER PARK). Franchise award date: N.A. Franchise expiration date: N.A. Began: N.A.

Channel capacity: 42 (not 2-way capable). Channels available but not in use: N.A.

Basic Service
Subscribers: 527.
Programming (received off-air): WLFL (CW) Raleigh; WNCN (NBC) Goldsboro; WNCT-TV (CBS, CW) Greenville; WRAL-TV (CBS) Raleigh; WRAY-TV (IND) Wilson; WRDC (MNT) Durham; WTVD (ABC) Durham; WUNP-TV (PBS) Roanoke Rapids; WYDO (FOX) Greenville.
Programming (via satellite): ABC Family Channel; Trinity Broadcasting Network.
Fee: $39.95 installation; $15.14 monthly; $2.00 converter.

Expanded Basic Service 1
Subscribers: 490.
Programming (via satellite): AMC; Animal Planet; BET Networks; CNN; Country Music TV; C-SPAN; Discovery Channel; Disney Channel; ESPN; ESPN 2; Fox News Channel; Headline News; HGTV; Lifetime; MSNBC; MTV; Nickelodeon; QVC; Spike TV; Syfy; TBS Superstation; The Learning Channel; The Weather Channel; Turner Network TV; USA Network; VH1.
Fee: $19.69 monthly.

Digital Basic Service
Subscribers: N.A.
Programming (via satellite): Bravo; ESPN Classic Sports; History Channel; Versus; WE tv.
Fee: $11.00 monthly.

Pay Service 1
Pay Units: 87.
Programming (via satellite): HBO.
Fee: $11.95 monthly.

Digital Pay Service 1
Pay Units: N.A.
Programming (via satellite): Cinemax (multiplexed); Encore; HBO (multiplexed);

Showtime (multiplexed); The Movie Channel (multiplexed).
Fee: $15.95 monthly (each).

Video-On-Demand: No

Pay-Per-View
Hits Movies & Events (delivered digitally).

Internet Service
Operational: No.

Telephone Service
None

Miles of Plant: 46.0 (coaxial); None (fiber optic).

General Manager: Timothy Evard. Operations Director: Belinda Graham. Engineering Director: Mike Earehart. Finance & Accounting Director: Cindy Johnson.

Ownership: Windjammer Communications LLC (MSO).

MOCKSVILLE—Time Warner Cable. Now served by GREENSBORO, NC [NC0006]. ICA: NC0080.

MONROE—Time Warner Cable, 3140 W Arrowood Rd, Charlotte, NC 28273. Phone: 704-378-2500. Fax: 704-504-1997. Web Site: http://www.timewarnercable.com/carolinas. Also serves Fairview (town), Hemby Bridge, Indian Trail, Lake Park, Marshville, Marvin, Mineral Springs (town), Stallings, Union County, Unionville (town), Waxhaw, Wesley Chapel & Wingate. ICA: NC0031.

TV Market Ranking: 42 (Fairview (town), Indian Trail, Lake Park, Marshville, Marvin, Mineral Springs (town), MONROE, Stallings, Union County, Unionville (town), Waxhaw, Wesley Chapel, Wingate); Below 100 (Hemby Bridge). Franchise award date: N.A. Franchise expiration date: June 1, 2013. Began: January 1, 1981.

Channel capacity: N.A. Channels available but not in use: N.A.

Basic Service
Subscribers: N.A. Included in Charlotte
Programming (received off-air): WAXN-TV (IND) Kannapolis; WBTV (CBS) Charlotte; WCCB (FOX) Charlotte; WCNC-TV (NBC) Charlotte; WHKY-TV (IND) Hickory; WJZY (CW) Belmont; WMYT-TV (MNT) Rock Hill; WSOC-TV (ABC) Charlotte; WTVI (PBS) Charlotte; WUNG-TV (PBS) Concord.
Programming (via satellite): TV Guide Network; WGN America.
Fee: $36.00 installation; $9.50 monthly; $1.50 converter.

Expanded Basic Service 1
Subscribers: 25,353.
Programming (via satellite): A&E Networks; ABC Family Channel; AMC; Animal Planet; BET Networks; Bravo; Cartoon Network; CNBC; CNN; Comedy Central; Country Music TV; C-SPAN; C-SPAN 2; Discovery Channel; Discovery Health Channel; Disney Channel; E! Entertainment Television; ESPN; ESPN 2; ESPN Classic Sports; Eternal Word TV Network; Food Network; Fox News Channel; Fox Sports Net; FX; Golf Channel; Hallmark Channel; Headline News; HGTV; History Channel; Lifetime; Lifetime Movie Network; MSNBC; MTV; National Geographic Channel; Nickelodeon; Oxygen; QVC; ShopNBC; Speed; Spike TV; SportSouth; Syfy; TBS Superstation; The Learning Channel; The Weather Channel; Travel Channel; Trinity Broadcasting Network; truTV; Turner Classic Movies; Turner Network TV; TV Land; Univision Studios; USA Network; Versus; VH1; WE tv.
Fee: $40.45 monthly.

Digital Basic Service
Subscribers: 8,638.
Programming (via satellite): AmericanLife TV Network; America's Store; BBC America; Bio; Black Family Channel; Bloomberg Television; Boomerang; Cooking Channel; C-SPAN 3; Deutsche Welle TV; Discovery Fit & Health; DIY Network; FamilyNet; Fuse; G4; Great American Country; GSN; History Channel International; Independent Film Channel; Lifetime Real Women; MTV2; Nick Jr.; Ovation; RAI International; Saigon Broadcasting Television Network; SoapNet; Style Network; Toon Disney; TV5, La Television International; VH1 Classic; Zee TV USA.
Fee: $15.00 monthly.

Pay Service 1
Pay Units: 9,300.
Programming (via satellite): HBO.
Fee: $11.54 monthly (each).

Digital Pay Service 1
Pay Units: N.A.
Programming (via satellite): Canales N; Cinemax (multiplexed); Encore (multiplexed); Flix; Fox Movie Channel; HBO (multiplexed); Showtime (multiplexed); Starz (multiplexed); Sundance Channel; The Movie Channel (multiplexed).
Fee: $11.54 monthly (HBO, Cinemax, Showtime/TMC or Starz/Encore).

Video-On-Demand: Yes

Pay-Per-View
Addressable homes: 8,638.
iN DEMAND (delivered digitally); Adult PPV (delivered digitally); ESPN Now (delivered digitally); ESPN Gameplan (delivered digitally); ESPN Full Court (delivered digitally); Sports PPV (delivered digitally).

Internet Service
Operational: Yes.
Subscribers: 8,908.
Broadband Service: Road Runner, AOL, EarthLink.
Fee: $39.95 installation; $46.95 monthly.

Telephone Service
Digital: Operational
Fee: $39.95 monthly

Miles of plant (coax & fiber) included in Charlotte

President: Mike Munley. Vice President, Technical Operations: Mike Cullim. Vice President, Engineering: Richard Newcomb. Vice President, Marketing & Sales: Eric Franey. Government Affairs Director: Michael Tanck. Public Affairs Director: Jessica Graham.

Ownership: Time Warner Cable (MSO).; Advance/Newhouse Partnership (MSO).Day-to-day operations are managed by Time Warner Cable.

MOORESVILLE—MI-Connection, 435 S Broad St, PO Box 90, Mooresville, NC 28115. Phones: 704-660-3840; 704-662-3255. E-mail: ahall@mi-connection.com. Web Site: http://www.mi-connection.com. Also serves Cornelius, Davidson & Mecklenburg County (unincorporated areas). ICA: NC0207.

TV Market Ranking: 42 (Cornelius, Davidson, Mecklenburg County, MOORESVILLE). Franchise award date: N.A. Franchise expiration date: N.A. Began: January 1, 1982.

Channel capacity: N.A. Channels available but not in use: N.A.

Basic Service
Subscribers: 15,800.
Programming (received off-air): WAXN-TV (IND) Kannapolis; WBTV (CBS) Charlotte; WCCB (FOX) Charlotte; WCNC-TV (NBC) Charlotte; WHKY-TV (IND) Hickory; WJZY (CW) Belmont; WMYT-TV (MNT) Rock Hill; WSOC-TV (ABC) Charlotte; WTVI (PBS) Charlotte; WUNG-TV (PBS) Concord.
Programming (via satellite): C-SPAN; INSP; QVC; ShopNBC; TV Guide Network; WGN America.
Fee: $35.00 installation; $16.00 monthly.

Expanded Basic Service 1
Subscribers: N.A.
Programming (via satellite): A&E Networks; ABC Family Channel; AMC; Animal Planet; BET Networks; Cartoon Network; CNBC; CNN; Comedy Central; Country Music TV; C-SPAN 2; Discovery Channel; Disney Channel; E! Entertainment Television; ESPN; ESPN 2; Food Network; Fox News Channel; Fox Sports South; FX; Hallmark Channel; Headline News; HGTV; History Channel; ION Television; Lifetime; MSNBC; MTV; Nickelodeon; Speed; Spike TV; SportSouth; Syfy; TBS Superstation; The Learning Channel; The Weather Channel; Travel Channel; truTV; Turner Network TV; TV Land; Univision Studios; USA Network; VH1.
Fee: $32.99 monthly.

Digital Basic Service
Subscribers: 9,096.
Programming (via satellite): AmericanLife TV Network; BBC America; Bloomberg Television; Bravo; Canal 52MX; Cine Latino; Cine Mexicano; CMT Pure Country; CNN en Espanol; Discovery en Espanol; Discovery Fit & Health; Discovery Health Channel; Discovery Home Channel; Discovery Kids Channel; Discovery Times Channel; ESPN 2 HD; ESPN Classic Sports; ESPN HD; ESPNews; Fox Deportes; Fox Movie Channel; Fox Soccer; G4; Golf Channel; GSN; Halogen Network; HD Theater; HDNet; HDNet Movies; History Channel en Espanol; La Familia Network; Latele Novela Network; Military Channel; Music Choice; Nick Jr.; NickToons TV; Outdoor Channel; Puma TV; Science; Tr3s; Trinity Broadcasting Network; TV Chile; Versus; VH1 Classic; WE tv.
Fee: $20.95 monthly.

Digital Pay Service 1
Pay Units: N.A.
Programming (via satellite): Cinemax (multiplexed); Encore (multiplexed); HBO (multiplexed); HBO HD; Playboy TV; Showtime (multiplexed); Showtime HD; Starz (multiplexed); Starz HDTV; The Movie Channel (multiplexed).
Fee: $12.95 monthly (HBO, Cinemax, Showtime/TMC or Starz/Encore), $19.95 monthly (Playboy).

Video-On-Demand: Planned

Pay-Per-View
iN DEMAND (delivered digitally); Playboy TV (delivered digitally); Club Jenna (delivered digitally); Fresh (delivered digitally); Hot Choice (delivered digitally).

Internet Service
Operational: Yes.
Broadband Service: In-house.
Fee: $44.95 monthly.

Telephone Service
Digital: Planned

General Manager: Alan Hall. Operations Manager: James R. Miller, Jr. Technical Operations Manager: Robert Lackey. Marketing Coordinator: Sandra Munsey.

Ownership: MI-Connection (MSO).

MORGANTON—CoMPAS-City of Morganton Public Antenna System, 305 E Union St, Ste A-100, Morganton, NC 28645. Phone: 828-438-5353. Fax: 828-432-2672. E-mail: compas@ci.morganton.nc.us. Web Site: http://www.compascable.net. ICA: NC0065.

TV Market Ranking: Below 100 (MORGANTON). Franchise award date: N.A. Franchise expiration date: N.A. Began: January 15, 1993.

Channel capacity: N.A. Channels available but not in use: N.A.

Basic Service
Subscribers: 5,241.
Programming (received off-air): WAXN-TV (IND) Kannapolis; WBTV (CBS) Charlotte; WCCB (FOX) Charlotte; WCNC-TV (NBC) Charlotte; WHKY-TV (IND) Hickory; WJZY (CW) Belmont; WLOS (ABC) Asheville; WMYT-TV (MNT) Rock Hill; WSOC-TV (ABC) Charlotte; WSPA-TV (CBS) Spartanburg; WUNE-TV (PBS) Linville; WYFF (NBC) Greenville.
Programming (via satellite): ABC Family Channel; QVC; TBS Superstation; The Learning Channel; The Weather Channel; Turner Network TV; TV Guide Network.
Fee: $35.00 installation; $21.95 monthly; $25.00 additional installation.

Expanded Basic Service 1
Subscribers: 4,548.
Programming (via satellite): A&E Networks; AMC; Animal Planet; BET Networks; Bravo; Cartoon Network; CNBC; CNN; Comedy Central; Country Music TV; C-SPAN; Discovery Channel; Discovery Health Channel; Disney Channel; E! Entertainment Television; ESPN; ESPN 2; ESPN Classic Sports; Food Network; Fox News Channel; Fox Sports South; FX; Golf Channel; GSN; Hallmark Channel; Headline News; HGTV; History Channel; Lifetime Movie Network; MSNBC; MTV; National Geographic Channel; Nickelodeon; Outdoor Channel; Oxygen; SoapNet; Speed; Spike TV; SportSouth; Syfy; Toon Disney; Travel Channel; Trinity Broadcasting Network; truTV; Turner Classic Movies; TV Land; Univision Studios; USA Network; Versus; VH1; WE tv; WGN America.
Fee: $40.95 monthly.

Digital Basic Service
Subscribers: 892.
Programming (via satellite): AmericanLife TV Network; BBC America; Bio; Bloomberg Television; Boomerang; cloo; Cooking Channel; C-SPAN 3; DIY Network; Fox Movie Channel; Fuse; G4; GAS; GSN; HD Theater; HDNet; HDNet Movies; History Channel International; Independent Film Channel; Lifetime Real Women; Lime; Mag Rack; MTV Networks Digital Suite; National Geographic Channel HD Network; Nick Jr.; Nick Too; NickToons TV; Outdoor Channel 2 HD; Sportskool; Style Network.
Fee: $5.00 converter.

Digital Pay Service 1
Pay Units: N.A.
Programming (via satellite): Cinemax (multiplexed); Encore; HBO (multiplexed); Showtime (multiplexed); Starz (multiplexed); The Movie Channel.
Fee: $7.00 monthly (Starz/Encore, Showtime/TMC, & Cinemax), $12.95 monthly (HBO).
Digital Pay Service 2
Pay Units: 7.
Programming (via satellite): Canales N.
Fee: $7.00 monthly.
Video-On-Demand: Yes
Pay-Per-View
Addressable homes: 1,532.
iN DEMAND (delivered digitally).
Internet Service
Operational: Yes.
Subscribers: 1,749.
Fee: $23.95-$69.95 monthly.
Telephone Service
Digital: Operational
Miles of Plant: 160.0 (coaxial); 120.0 (fiber optic).
Manager: Randy Loop.
Ownership: City of Morganton.

MORVEN—WFL Cable Television Associates Inc., 114 N Rutherford St, Wadesboro, NC 28170-2131. Phone: 704-694-9409. Fax: 704-694-9409. E-mail: wflcable@yahoo.com. Also serves Anson County (unincorporated areas), Peachland & Polkton. ICA: NC0166.
TV Market Ranking: 42 (Anson County (unincorporated areas) (portions)); Outside TV Markets (MORVEN, Peachland, Polkton, Anson County (unincorporated areas) (portions)). Franchise award date: N.A. Franchise expiration date: N.A. Began: November 1, 1987.
Channel capacity: 42 (not 2-way capable). Channels available but not in use: N.A.
Basic Service
Subscribers: 42.
Programming (received off-air): WAXN-TV (IND) Kannapolis; WBTV (CBS) Charlotte; WBTW (CBS, MNT) Florence; WCCB (FOX) Charlotte; WCNC-TV (NBC) Charlotte; WJZY (CW) Belmont; WMYT-TV (MNT) Rock Hill; WSOC-TV (ABC) Charlotte; WTVI (PBS) Charlotte; WUNG-TV (PBS) Concord.
Programming (via satellite): A&E Networks; ABC Family Channel; BET Networks; CNBC; CNN; Country Music TV; Discovery Channel; Disney Channel; ESPN; ESPN 2; FX; Hallmark Channel; Lifetime; MTV; Nickelodeon; QVC; Spike TV; Syfy; TBS Superstation; The Learning Channel; The Weather Channel; truTV; Turner Network TV; TV Land; USA Network; VH1.
Fee: $50.00 installation; $32.09 monthly; $2.00 converter.
Internet Service
Operational: No.
Telephone Service
None
Miles of Plant: 9.0 (coaxial); None (fiber optic).
Manager & Chief Technician: William F. Lee. Office Manager: Deana Wasmer.
Ownership: WFL Cable Television Associates Inc.

MOUNT AIRY—Time Warner Cable. Now served by GREENSBORO, NC [NC0006]. ICA: NC0075.

MURFREESBORO—Time Warner Cable, 101 Innovation Ave, Ste 100, Morrisville, NC 27560. Phone: 919-573-7000. Fax: 919-573-7042. Web Site: http://www.timewarnercable.com. Also serves Ahoskie, Aulander, Bertie County (portions), Cofield, Hertford County (portions) & Winton. ICA: NC0144.
TV Market Ranking: Outside TV Markets (Ahoskie, Aulander, Bertie County (portions), Cofield, Hertford County (portions), MURFREESBORO, Winton). Franchise award date: May 16, 1966. Franchise expiration date: N.A. Began: December 1, 1967.
Channel capacity: 70 (operating 2-way). Channels available but not in use: N.A.
Basic Service
Subscribers: 5,014.
Programming (received off-air): WAVY-TV (NBC) Portsmouth; WGNT (CW) Portsmouth; WHRO-TV (PBS) Hampton-Norfolk; WNCT-TV (CBS, CW) Greenville; WPXV-TV (ION) Norfolk; WRAL-TV (CBS) Raleigh; WSKY-TV (IND) Manteo; WTKR (CBS) Norfolk; WTVZ-TV (MNT) Norfolk; WUND-TV (PBS) Edenton; WVBT (FOX) Virginia Beach; WVEC (ABC) Hampton; allband FM.
Programming (via satellite): QVC; ShopNBC; WGN America.
Fee: $39.95 installation; $13.75 monthly; $3.25 converter.
Expanded Basic Service 1
Subscribers: 4,860.
Programming (via satellite): A&E Networks; ABC Family Channel; AMC; Animal Planet; BET Networks; Bravo; Cartoon Network; CNBC; CNN; Comedy Central; Country Music TV; C-SPAN; C-SPAN 2; Discovery Channel; Disney Channel; E! Entertainment Television; ESPN; ESPN 2; Food Network; Fox News Channel; Fox Sports South; FX; Hallmark Channel; Headline News; HGTV; History Channel; Lifetime; MSNBC; MTV; Nickelodeon; Oxygen; Spike TV; Syfy; TBS Superstation; The Learning Channel; The Weather Channel; Travel Channel; truTV; Turner Network TV; TV Guide Network; TV Land; USA Network; VH1.
Fee: $36.10 monthly.
Digital Basic Service
Subscribers: N.A.
Programming (via satellite): American-Life TV Network; BBC America; Bio; Black Family Channel; Bloomberg Television; Discovery Digital Networks; DIY Network; DMX Music; ESPN Classic Sports; ESPNews; Fox Movie Channel; Fox Sports World; Fuse; G4; GAS; Golf Channel; Great American Country; GSN; Halogen Network; History Channel International; Independent Film Channel; Lifetime Movie Network; MTV Networks Digital Suite; Music Choice; National Geographic Channel; Nick Jr.; Nick Too; Outdoor Channel; SoapNet; Speed; Style Network; Sundance Channel; Toon Disney; Trinity Broadcasting Network; Turner Classic Movies; Versus; WE tv.
Fee: $11.00 monthly; $4.69 converter.
Digital Pay Service 1
Pay Units: N.A.
Programming (via satellite): ART America; Canales N; CCTV-4; Cinemax (multiplexed); Encore (multiplexed); Filipino Channel; Flix; HBO (multiplexed); RAI International; Russian Television Network; Showtime (multiplexed); Starz (multiplexed); The Movie Channel (multiplexed); TV Japan; TV5, La Television International.
Fee: $10.00 monthly (ART, CCTV, Filipino, RAI, TV5 or TV Japan), $15.00 monthly (TV Russia), $15.95 monthly (HBO, Cinemax, Showtime/TMC/Flix or Starz/Encore).
Video-On-Demand: No
Pay-Per-View
Sports PPV (delivered digitally); iN DEMAND (delivered digitally); Playboy TV (delivered digitally); Fresh (delivered digitally); Shorteez (delivered digitally); Hot Choice (delivered digitally); Urban Xtra (delivered digitally).
Internet Service
Operational: Yes.
Broadband Service: Road Runner.
Fee: $44.95 monthly.
Telephone Service
Digital: Planned
Miles of Plant: 138.0 (coaxial); None (fiber optic).
Vice President & General Manager: Chris Whitaker. Vice President, Technical Operations: Gary Frederick. Vice President, Sales & Marketing: Tom Smith. Vice President, Government & Public Affairs: Brad Phillips.
Ownership: Time Warner Cable (MSO).

MURPHY—Cable TV of Cherokee County, 1421 Creekside Dr, PO Box 1000, Murphy, NC 28906-1000. Phone: 828-837-7118. Fax: 828-837-3820. E-mail: murphycabletv@cabletvonline.net. Web Site: http://www.cabletvonline.net. Also serves Andrews, Cherokee County (portions), Marble, Ranger & Topton. ICA: NC0079.
TV Market Ranking: Outside TV Markets (Andrews, Cherokee County (portions), Marble, MURPHY, Ranger, Topton). Franchise award date: N.A. Franchise expiration date: N.A. Began: March 15, 1972.
Channel capacity: N.A. Channels available but not in use: N.A.
Basic Service
Subscribers: 2,144.
Programming (received off-air): WAGA-TV (FOX) Atlanta; WDEF-TV (CBS) Chattanooga; WDSI-TV (FOX, MNT) Chattanooga; WLOS (ABC) Asheville; WRCB (NBC) Chattanooga; WSB-TV (ABC) Atlanta; WTCI (PBS) Chattanooga; WTVC (ABC) Chattanooga; WUNE-TV (PBS) Linville; WYFF (NBC) Greenville; allband FM.
Expanded Basic Service 1
Subscribers: N.A.
Programming (via satellite): 3 Angels Broadcasting Network; A&E Networks; ABC Family Channel; Animal Planet; Cartoon Network; CNBC; CNN; Country Music TV; Discovery Channel; Disney Channel; ESPN; ESPN 2; Eternal Word TV Network; Food Network; Fox News Channel; Golf Channel; Gospel Music TV; Hallmark Channel; Headline News; HGTV; History Channel; ION Television; Lifetime; MarketConnect Network; MSNBC; Nickelodeon; Outdoor Channel; QVC; SoapNet; Speed; Spike TV; SportSouth; Syfy; TBS Superstation; The Learning Channel; The Weather Channel; Toon Disney; Travel Channel; Trinity Broadcasting Network; truTV; Turner Classic Movies; Turner Network TV; Turner South; TV Land; USA Network; VH1; WGN America; WPIX (CW, IND) New York.
Fee: $69.00 installation; $42.08 monthly.
Pay Service 1
Pay Units: 140.
Programming (via satellite): HBO; Showtime.
Fee: $9.95 monthly (each).
Video-On-Demand: No
Internet Service
Operational: Yes.
Fee: $69.95 installation.
Telephone Service
None
Miles of Plant: 342.0 (coaxial); None (fiber optic). Additional miles planned: 13.0 (coaxial).
Manager: William Cook. Chief Technician: Dean Hensley.
Ownership: CND Acquisition Co. LLC (MSO).

NASH COUNTY—Crystal Broadband Networks, PO Box 180336, Chicago, IL 60618. Phones: 877-319-0328; 630-206-0447. E-mail: sales@crystalbn.com. Web Site: http://www.crystalbn.com. Also serves Castalia, Dortches, Edgecombe County (portions) & Red Oak. ICA: NC0105.
TV Market Ranking: 84 (Edgecombe County (portions) (portions)); Below 100 (Castalia, Dortches, NASH COUNTY, Red Oak, Edgecombe County (portions) (portions)). Franchise award date: October 1, 1986. Franchise expiration date: N.A. Began: January 1, 1986.
Channel capacity: 64 (not 2-way capable). Channels available but not in use: N.A.
Basic Service
Subscribers: 2,293.
Programming (received off-air): WLFL (CW) Raleigh; WNCN (NBC) Goldsboro; WNCT-TV (CBS, CW) Greenville; WRAL-TV (CBS) Raleigh; WRAZ (FOX) Raleigh; WRDC (MNT) Durham; WRPX-TV (ION) Rocky Mount; WTVD (ABC) Durham; WUNK-TV (PBS) Greenville.
Programming (via satellite): QVC; WGN America.
Fee: $39.95 installation; $15.65 monthly; $1.86 converter.
Expanded Basic Service 1
Subscribers: 2,169.
Programming (via satellite): A&E Networks; ABC Family Channel; AMC; Animal Planet; BET Networks; Bravo; Cartoon Network; CNBC; CNN; Comedy Central; Country Music TV; C-SPAN; C-SPAN 2; Discovery Channel; Disney Channel; E! Entertainment Television; ESPN; ESPN 2; Food Network; Fox News Channel; Fox Sports South; FX; Hallmark Channel; Headline News; HGTV; History Channel; Lifetime; MSNBC; MTV; Nickelodeon; Oxygen; Spike TV; Syfy; TBS Superstation; The Learning Channel; The Weather Channel; Travel Channel; truTV; Turner Network TV; TV Guide Network; TV Land; USA Network; VH1.
Fee: $22.45 monthly.
Digital Basic Service
Subscribers: N.A.
Programming (via satellite): AmericanLife TV Network; BBC America; Bio; Black Family Channel; Bloomberg Television; Canales N; Discovery Digital Networks; DIY Network; Encore (multiplexed); ESPN Classic Sports; ESPNews; Fox Movie Channel; Fox Sports World; Fuse; G4; GAS; Golf Channel; Great American Country; GSN; Halogen Network; History Channel International; Independent Film Channel; Lifetime Movie Network; MTV Networks Digital Suite; Music Choice; National Geographic Channel; Nick Jr.; Nick Too; Outdoor Channel; SoapNet; Speed; Style Network; Sundance Channel; Toon Disney; Trinity Broadcasting Network; Turner Classic Movies; Versus; WE tv.
Fee: $11.00 monthly.
Digital Pay Service 1
Pay Units: 143.
Programming (via satellite): Cinemax (multiplexed); HBO (multiplexed); Showtime (multiplexed); Starz (multiplexed); The Movie Channel (multiplexed).

Fee: $15.95 monthly (each).
Video-On-Demand: No

Pay-Per-View
Hot Choice (delivered digitally); Playboy TV (delivered digitally); Fresh (delivered digitally); Shorteez (delivered digitally); sports (delivered digitally).

Internet Service
Operational: No.

Telephone Service
None
Miles of Plant: 162.0 (coaxial); None (fiber optic).
Ownership: Crystal Broadband Networks (MSO).

NEBO—Morris Broadband, 719 S Grove St, Hendersonville, SC 28792. Phones: 888-855-9036; 828-697-3600; 828-697-1371. Web Site: http://morrisbroadband.com. ICA: NC0113.
TV Market Ranking: 46 (NEBO). Franchise award date: May 14, 1986. Franchise expiration date: N.A. Began: December 31, 1986.
Channel capacity: N.A. Channels available but not in use: N.A.

Basic Service
Subscribers: 2,130.
Programming (received off-air): WBTV (CBS) Charlotte; WHNS (FOX) Greenville; WLOS (ABC) Asheville; WSPA-TV (CBS) Spartanburg; WUNE-TV (PBS) Linville; WYFF (NBC) Greenville; allband FM.
Programming (via satellite): INSP; QVC; TV Guide Network; WGN America.
Fee: $45.00 installation; $12.93 monthly; $19.95 additional installation.

Expanded Basic Service 1
Subscribers: N.A.
Programming (via satellite): A&E Networks; ABC Family Channel; AMC; Animal Planet; Bravo; Cartoon Network; CNBC; CNN; Comedy Central; Country Music TV; C-SPAN; Discovery Channel; Disney Channel; ESPN; ESPN 2; Food Network; Fox News Channel; Fox Sports South; FX; Headline News; HGTV; History Channel; Lifetime; MTV; Nickelodeon; Outdoor Channel; ShopNBC; Speed; Spike TV; Syfy; TBS Superstation; The Learning Channel; The Weather Channel; Travel Channel; truTV; Turner Network TV; TV Land; USA Network; VH1; WE tv.
Fee: $35.02 monthly.

Digital Basic Service
Subscribers: N.A.
Programming (via satellite): BBC America; Bio; Bloomberg Television; Discovery Digital Networks; DMX Music; ESPNews; Fox Movie Channel; Fox Sports World; Fuse; G4; GAS; GSN; Halogen Network; History Channel International; Independent Film Channel; International Television (ITV); Lifetime Movie Network; Lime; MTV Networks Digital Suite; National Geographic Channel; Nick Jr.; NickToons TV; Style Network; Turner Classic Movies; Versus.

Digital Pay Service 1
Pay Units: N.A.
Programming (via satellite): Cinemax (multiplexed); Encore (multiplexed); Flix; HBO (multiplexed); Showtime (multiplexed); Starz (multiplexed); Sundance Channel; The Movie Channel.
Fee: $8.00 monthly (Starz/Encore), $9.95 monthly (Cinemax or Showtime/TMC/Flix), $13.95 monthly (HBO).
Video-On-Demand: No

Internet Service
Operational: Yes.
Broadband Service: In-house.
Fee: $59.95 installation; $29.95-$59.95 monthly.

Telephone Service
Digital: Operational
Fee: $49.95 monthly
Miles of Plant: 73.0 (coaxial); None (fiber optic). Additional miles planned: 10.0 (coaxial).
Chairman & Chief Executive Officer: William S. Morris III. Senior Vice President, Finance: Craig Mitchell. Senior Vice President & Chief Financial Officer: Steve K. Stone. Vice President: Susie Morris Baker.
Ownership: Morris Communications Co LLC (MSO).

NEW BERN—Cox Communications. Now served by GREENVILLE, NC [NC0014]. ICA: NC0029.

NEWPORT—Time Warner Cable, 101 Innovation Ave, Ste 100, Morrisville, NC 27560. Phones: 910-763-0004 (Wilmington office); 919-573-7000. Web Site: http://www.timewarnercable.com/carolinas. Also serves Atlantic, Atlantic Beach, Beaufort, Cape Carteret, Carteret County, Cedar Point, Cherry Point, Craven County, Emerald Isle, Gloucester, Harkers Island, Havelock, Hubert, Indian Beach, Marshallberg, Morehead City, Peletier, Pine Knoll Shores, Salter Path, Sealevel, Smyrna, Stacy, Stella, Swansboro & Williston. ICA: NC0013.
TV Market Ranking: 84 (Atlantic Beach, Cape Carteret, Carteret County (portions), Cedar Point, Cherry Point, Craven County, Emerald Isle, Havelock, Hubert, Indian Beach, Morehead City, NEWPORT, Peletier, Pine Knoll Shores, Salter Path, Stella, Swansboro); Below 100 (Atlantic, Beaufort, Gloucester, Harkers Island, Marshallberg, Sealevel, Smyrna, Stacy, Williston, Carteret County (portions)). Franchise award date: June 13, 1978. Franchise expiration date: N.A. Began: May 25, 1979.
Channel capacity: N.A. Channels available but not in use: N.A.

Basic Service
Subscribers: N.A. Included in Wilmington
Programming (received off-air): WCTI-TV (ABC) New Bern; WFXI (FOX, MNT) Morehead City; WITN-TV (MNT, NBC) Washington; WNCT-TV (CBS, CW) Greenville; WUNM-TV (PBS) Jacksonville.
Programming (via satellite): Discovery Channel; ION Television; ShopNBC; TBS Superstation; Turner Network TV; TV Guide Network; WGN America.
Fee: $35.00 installation; $7.08 monthly; $2.40 converter.

Expanded Basic Service 1
Subscribers: 41,718.
Programming (via satellite): A&E Networks; ABC Family Channel; AMC; Animal Planet; BET Networks; Bravo; Cartoon Network; CNBC; CNN; Comedy Central; Country Music TV; C-SPAN; C-SPAN 2; Discovery Health Channel; Disney Channel; E! Entertainment Television; ESPN; ESPN 2; ESPN Classic Sports; Food Network; Fox News Channel; Fox Sports South; FX; Golf Channel; Hallmark Channel; Headline News; HGTV; History Channel; Jewelry Television; Lifetime; Lifetime Movie Network; MTV; National Geographic Channel; Nickelodeon; Oxygen; QVC; SoapNet; Speed; Spike TV; Syfy; The Learning Channel; The Weather Channel; Travel Channel; Trinity Broadcasting Network; truTV; Turner Classic Movies; TV Guide Network; USA Network; Versus; VH1; WE tv.
Fee: $42.42 monthly.

Digital Basic Service
Subscribers: N.A. Included in Wilmington
Programming (via satellite): BBC America; Bio; Bloomberg Television; Cooking Channel; C-SPAN 3; Discovery Digital Networks; DIY Network; ESPNews; Flix (multiplexed); Fox Sports World; FSN Digital Atlantic; FSN Digital Central; FSN Digital Pacific; Fuel TV; G4; Great American Country; GSN; Halogen Network; History Channel International; Independent Film Channel; Lifetime Real Women; MTV2; Music Choice; NBA TV; Nick Jr.; Outdoor Channel; Ovation; Style Network; Sundance Channel; Tennis Channel; The Word Network; Toon Disney; TV Land; VH1 Classic.
Fee: $38.29 monthly.

Digital Pay Service 1
Pay Units: N.A.
Programming (via satellite): Cinemax (multiplexed); Encore (multiplexed); Fox Movie Channel; HBO (multiplexed); MoviePlex; Showtime (multiplexed); Starz (multiplexed); The Movie Channel (multiplexed); WAM! America's Kidz Network.
Fee: $6.95 monthly (Fox Movie Channel & Encore), $11.95 monthly (Cinemax, Starz or Showtime/TMC), $13.95 monthly (HBO).
Video-On-Demand: Yes

Pay-Per-View
iN DEMAND (delivered digitally); Hot Choice (delivered digitally); Pleasure (delivered digitally); Fresh (delivered digitally); Shorteez (delivered digitally); Playboy TV (delivered digitally); Sports PPV (delivered digitally).

Internet Service
Operational: Yes.
Broadband Service: EarthLink, Road Runner.
Fee: $69.95 installation; $44.95 monthly.

Telephone Service
Digital: Operational
Fee: $44.95 monthly
Miles of Plant: 1,011.0 (coaxial); 28.0 (fiber optic).
Vice President & General Manager: Kim Cannon. Vice President, Marketing & Sales: Tom Smith. Technical Operations Director: Joe Pell. Public Affairs Director: Marty Feurer.
Ownership: Time Warner Cable (MSO).; Advance/Newhouse Partnership (MSO).Day-to-day operations are managed by Time Warner Cable.

NEWTON GROVE—Charter Communications. Now served by BUIES CREEK, NC [NC0194]. ICA: NC0218.

NORTH WILKESBORO—Charter Communications, 1121 Lenoir Rhyne Blvd SE, Hickory, NC 28602-5128. Phone: 828-322-2288. Fax: 828-322-5492. Web Site: http://www.charter.com. Also serves Alleghany County (unincorporated areas), Cricket, Fairplains, Hays, Millers Creek, Moravian Falls, Mulberry, Roaring Gap, Roaring River, Ronda, Thurmond, Traphill, Wilkes County & Wilkesboro. ICA: NC0046.
TV Market Ranking: Below 100 (Cricket, Fairplains, Millers Creek, Moravian Falls, Mulberry, NORTH WILKESBORO, Wilkes County (portions), Wilkesboro); Outside TV Markets (Alleghany County (unincorporated areas) (portions), Hays, Roaring Gap, Roaring River, Ronda, Thurmond, Traphill, Wilkes County (portions)). Franchise award date: July 1, 1972. Franchise expiration date: N.A. Began: September 1, 1976.
Channel capacity: N.A. Channels available but not in use: N.A.

Basic Service
Subscribers: 9,103.
Programming (received off-air): WBTV (CBS) Charlotte; WCCB (FOX) Charlotte; WFMY-TV (CBS) Greensboro; WGHP (FOX, IND) High Point; WGPX-TV (ION) Burlington; WJZY (CW) Belmont; WSOC-TV (ABC) Charlotte; WUNE-TV (PBS) Linville; WXII-TV (NBC) Winston-Salem; WXLV-TV (ABC) Winston-Salem; 10 FMs.
Programming (via satellite): C-SPAN; C-SPAN 2; INSP; QVC; Shop at Home; Trinity Broadcasting Network.
Fee: $29.99 installation; $4.00 converter.

Expanded Basic Service 1
Subscribers: N.A.
Programming (via satellite): A&E Networks; ABC Family Channel; AMC; Animal Planet; Bravo; Cartoon Network; CNBC; Comedy Central; Country Music TV; Discovery Channel; E! Entertainment Television; ESPN; ESPN 2; Food Network; Fox College Sports Atlantic; Fox College Sports Central; Fox College Sports Pacific; Fox News Channel; Fox Sports South; FX; G4; Golf Channel; GSN; Hallmark Channel; HGTV; History Channel; Lifetime; MSNBC; MTV; National Geographic Channel; Nickelodeon; Oxygen; SoapNet; Speed; SportSouth; Syfy; TBS Superstation; Telemundo; The Learning Channel; The Weather Channel; Toon Disney; Travel Channel; truTV; Turner Classic Movies; Turner Network TV; TV Guide Network; TV Land; Univision Studios; USA Network; Versus; VH1; WE tv.
Fee: $47.99 monthly.

Expanded Basic Service 2
Subscribers: 8,477.
Programming (via satellite): CNN; Disney Channel; Headline News; Spike TV.
Fee: $6.45 monthly.

Digital Basic Service
Subscribers: N.A.
Programming (via satellite): BBC America; Bio; Bloomberg Television; Boomerang; Canales N; CNN International; Discovery Digital Networks; DIY Network; ESPN Classic Sports; ESPNews; Fox Deportes; Fox Movie Channel; Fox Soccer; Fuel TV; GAS; Great American Country; History Channel International; Independent Film Channel; Lifetime Movie Network; MTV Networks Digital Suite; Music Choice; NFL Network; Nick Jr.; Nick Too; NickToons TV; Sundance Channel.

Digital Pay Service 1
Pay Units: 2,025.
Programming (via satellite): HBO (multiplexed).
Fee: $30.00 installation; $11.95 monthly.
Digital Pay Service 2
Pay Units: 1,221.
Programming (via satellite): Showtime (multiplexed).
Fee: $10.95 monthly.
Digital Pay Service 3
Pay Units: N.A.
Programming (via satellite): Cinemax (multiplexed); Encore (multiplexed); Flix; Starz (multiplexed); The Movie Channel (multiplexed).
Video-On-Demand: Yes
Pay-Per-View
iN DEMAND (delivered digitally); Pleasure (delivered digitally); Playboy TV (delivered digitally); Fresh (delivered digitally); Shorteez (delivered digitally); NHL Center Ice (delivered digitally); MLB Extra Innings (delivered digitally); NASCAR In Car (delivered digitally).
Internet Service
Operational: Yes.
Broadband Service: Charter Pipeline.
Fee: $29.99 monthly.
Telephone Service
Digital: Planned
Miles of Plant: 923.0 (coaxial); 219.0 (fiber optic).
Vice President & General Manager: Anthony Pope. Marketing Director: Brooke Sinclair. Sales & Marketing Manager: Karen Sims. Operations Manager: Sam Scialabba.
Ownership: Charter Communications Inc. (MSO).

OAK CITY—Crystal Broadband Networks, PO Box 180336, Chicago, IL 60618. Phones: 877-319-0328; 630-206-0447. E-mail: sales@crystalbn.com. Web Site: http://www.crystalbn.com. Also serves Edgecombe County (portions), Halifax County (portions), Hamilton, Hassel, Hobgood & Martin County (unincorporated areas). ICA: NC0147.
TV Market Ranking: 84 (Edgecombe County (portions), Halifax County (portions), Hamilton, Hassel, Hobgood, Martin County (unincorporated areas), OAK CITY). Franchise award date: July 1, 1985. Franchise expiration date: N.A. Began: April 1, 1986.
Channel capacity: 42 (not 2-way capable). Channels available but not in use: N.A.
Basic Service
Subscribers: 527.
Programming (received off-air): WCTI-TV (ABC) New Bern; WEPX-TV (ION) Greenville; WNCN (NBC) Goldsboro; WNCT-TV (CBS, CW) Greenville; WRAL-TV (CBS) Raleigh; WTVD (ABC) Durham; WUNK-TV (PBS) Greenville; WYDO (FOX) Greenville.
Programming (via satellite): ABC Family Channel; QVC; Trinity Broadcasting Network.
Fee: $39.95 installation; $17.38 monthly; $2.00 converter; $25.00 additional installation.
Expanded Basic Service 1
Subscribers: 499.
Programming (via satellite): AMC; BET Networks; CNN; Country Music TV; C-SPAN; Discovery Channel; Disney Channel; ESPN; ESPN 2; Fox News Channel; Headline News; HGTV; Lifetime; MSNBC; MTV; Nickelodeon; Spike TV; Syfy; TBS Superstation; The Learning Channel; The Weather Channel; Turner Network TV; USA Network; VH1.
Fee: $19.69 monthly.
Digital Basic Service
Subscribers: N.A.
Programming (via satellite): BBC America; Bravo; Discovery Digital Networks; ESPNews; Fox Sports World; Golf Channel; GSN; History Channel International; Independent Film Channel; Versus; WE tv.
Fee: $10.21 monthly; $5.00 converter.
Pay Service 1
Pay Units: 91.
Programming (via satellite): HBO.
Fee: $15.95 monthly.
Digital Pay Service 1
Pay Units: N.A.
Programming (via satellite): Cinemax (multiplexed); Encore (multiplexed); HBO (multiplexed); Starz (multiplexed); The Movie Channel (multiplexed).
Fee: $15.95 monthly (each).
Video-On-Demand: No
Pay-Per-View
Playboy TV (delivered digitally).
Internet Service
Operational: No.
Telephone Service
None
Miles of Plant: 29.0 (coaxial); None (fiber optic).
Ownership: Crystal Broadband Networks (MSO).

OCEAN ISLE BEACH/BRICK LANDING—Tele-Media. Now served by SHALLOTTE, NC [NC0050]. ICA: NC0244.

OLDE POINTE—Charter Communications. Now served by HOLLY RIDGE, NC [NC0069]. ICA: NC0224.

ORRUM—Formerly served by Carolina Cable Partnership. No longer in operation. ICA: NC0208.

PAMLICO COUNTY—Time Warner Cable, PO Box 757, Bayboro, NC 28515-0757. Phones: 910-763-0004 (Wilmington office); 252-745-5842; 252-745-4938. Fax: 252-745-3437. Web Site: http://www.timewarnercable.com/carolinas. Also serves Alliance, Arapahoe, Aurora, Bayboro, Beaufort County (unincorporated areas), Edward, Grantsboro, Hobucken, Lowland, Merritt, Mesic, Minnesott Beach, Oriental, Stonewall & Vandemere. ICA: NC0192.
TV Market Ranking: 84 (Alliance, Arapahoe, Aurora, Bayboro, Beaufort County (unincorporated areas), Grantsboro, Merritt, Mesic, Minnesott Beach, Oriental, PAMLICO COUNTY, Stonewall, Vandemere). Franchise award date: January 2, 1984. Franchise expiration date: N.A. Began: December 1, 1983.
Channel capacity: 40 (not 2-way capable). Channels available but not in use: N.A.
Basic Service
Subscribers: N.A.
Programming (received off-air): WCTI-TV (ABC) New Bern; WFXI (FOX, MNT) Morehead City; WNCT-TV (CBS, CW) Greenville; WUNM-TV (PBS) Jacksonville.
Programming (via satellite): C-SPAN; QVC; TBS Superstation; Trinity Broadcasting Network; WGN America.
Fee: $30.00 installation; $17.14 monthly; $1.87 converter; $18.00 additional installation.
Expanded Basic Service 1
Subscribers: 2,357.
Programming (via satellite): A&E Networks; ABC Family Channel; BET Networks; CNN; Country Music TV; Discovery Channel; Disney Channel; ESPN; Headline News; Lifetime; MTV; Nickelodeon; Spike TV; The Weather Channel; Turner Network TV; USA Network.
Fee: $12.72 monthly.
Pay Service 1
Pay Units: 120.
Programming (via satellite): Cinemax.
Fee: $11.50 monthly.
Pay Service 2
Pay Units: 27.
Programming (via satellite): Showtime.
Fee: $11.50 monthly.
Pay Service 3
Pay Units: 201.
Programming (via satellite): HBO.
Fee: $11.50 monthly.
Pay Service 4
Pay Units: 45.
Programming (via satellite): The Movie Channel.
Fee: $11.50 monthly.
Video-On-Demand: No
Internet Service
Operational: Yes.
Broadband Service: RoadRunner.
Telephone Service
None
Miles of Plant: 143.0 (coaxial); None (fiber optic).
President: William Greene. Vice President, Engineering: Mike Connelly. Vice President, Marketing: Tom Smith. Manager: Ed Palumbo. Marketing Director: Amy Tripp. Chief Technician: Wesley Croom. Public Affairs Director: Marty Feurer.
Ownership: Time Warner Cable (MSO).; Advance/Newhouse Partnership.

PARMELE—Suddenlink Communications, 2120 W Arlington Blvd, Greenville, NC 27834-6487. Phones: 877-804-6501 (Customer service); 252-756-5677. Fax: 252-697-0157. Web Site: http://www.suddenlink.com. Also serves Beargrass, Bethel, Everetts, Martin County (central portion), Robersonville & Williamston. ICA: NC0101.
TV Market Ranking: 84 (Beargrass, Bethel, Everetts, Martin County (central portion), PARMELE, Robersonville, Williamston). Franchise award date: January 4, 1983. Franchise expiration date: N.A. Began: December 1, 1983.
Channel capacity: 35 (operating 2-way). Channels available but not in use: N.A.
Basic Service
Subscribers: 3,450.
Programming (received off-air): WCTI-TV (ABC) New Bern; WEPX-TV (ION) Greenville; WFXI (FOX, MNT) Morehead City; WITN-TV (MNT, NBC) Washington; WNCT-TV (CBS, CW) Greenville; WRAL-TV (CBS) Raleigh; WUNC-TV (PBS) Chapel Hill; WUNK-TV (PBS) Greenville; 1 FM.
Programming (via satellite): C-SPAN 2; QVC; WGN America.
Fee: $16.47 installation; $20.57 monthly.
Expanded Basic Service 1
Subscribers: 3,050.
Programming (via satellite): A&E Networks; ABC Family Channel; AMC; Animal Planet; BET Networks; Bravo; Cartoon Network; CNBC; CNN; Comedy Central; Country Music TV; C-SPAN; C-SPAN 2; Discovery Channel; Disney Channel; E! Entertainment Television; ESPN; ESPN 2; Food Network; Fox News Channel; Fox Sports South; FX; Golf Channel; Headline News; HGTV; History Channel; INSP; Lifetime; MSNBC; MTV; Nickelodeon; ShopNBC; Spike TV; Syfy; TBS Superstation; Telemundo; The Learning Channel; The Weather Channel; Travel Channel; Trinity Broadcasting Network; Turner Classic Movies; Turner Network TV; TV Guide Network; TV Land; USA Network; VH1.
Fee: $2.85 monthly.
Digital Basic Service
Subscribers: N.A.
Programming (via satellite): AmericanLife TV Network; BBC America; Black Family Channel; Bloomberg Television; Canales N; CBS Sports Network; Cooking Channel; Daystar TV Network; DIY Network; Encore (multiplexed); ESPN Classic Sports; ESPN HD; ESPNews; Eternal Word TV Network; FamilyNet; Food Network HD; Fox Soccer; Fuel TV; Fuse; G4; GAS; Great American Country; GSN; Hallmark Channel; Halogen Network; HD Theater; HDNet; HDNet Movies; HGTV HD; Lifetime Movie Network; MTV Networks Digital Suite; Music Choice; National Geographic Channel; Nick Jr.; NickToons TV; Outdoor Channel; Oxygen; SoapNet; Speed; Sundance Channel; Tennis Channel; The Word Network; Toon Disney; truTV; Turner Network TV HD; TV One; Versus.
Digital Pay Service 1
Pay Units: N.A.
Programming (via satellite): Cinemax (multiplexed); HBO (multiplexed); HBO HD; Showtime (multiplexed); Showtime HD; Starz (multiplexed); Starz HDTV; The Movie Channel (multiplexed).
Video-On-Demand: No
Pay-Per-View
iN DEMAND (delivered digitally); Playboy TV (delivered digitally); Fresh (delivered digitally); Shorteez (delivered digitally); Hot Choice (delivered digitally); ESPN (delivered digitally).
Internet Service
Operational: Yes.
Broadband Service: Suddenlink High Speed Internet.
Fee: $100.00 installation; $39.95 monthly.
Telephone Service
Digital: Operational
Fee: $49.95 monthly
Miles of Plant: 40.0 (coaxial); None (fiber optic).
Manager: Bill Paramore. Chief Technician: Ed Diehl.
Ownership: Cequel Communications LLC (MSO).

PEMBROKE—Formerly served by Carolina Cable Partnership. No longer in operation. ICA: NC0251.

PINETOPS—Crystal Broadband Networks, PO Box 180336, Chicago, IL 60618. Phones: 877-319-0328; 630-206-0447. E-mail: sales@crystalbn.com. Web Site: http://www.crystalbn.com. Also serves Crisp, Macclesfield & Maccripines. ICA: NC0204.
TV Market Ranking: 73,84 (Maccripines); 84 (Crisp, Macclesfield, PINETOPS). Franchise award date: N.A. Franchise expiration date: N.A. Began: N.A.
Channel capacity: 42 (not 2-way capable). Channels available but not in use: N.A.
Basic Service
Subscribers: 1,107.
Programming (received off-air): WCTI-TV (ABC) New Bern; WLFL (CW) Raleigh; WNCN (NBC) Goldsboro; WNCT-TV (CBS, CW) Greenville; WRAL-TV (CBS) Raleigh; WRAY-TV (IND) Wilson; WRAZ (FOX) Raleigh; WRDC (MNT) Durham; WRPX-TV (ION) Rocky Mount; WTVD (ABC) Durham; WUNK-TV (PBS) Greenville.

Programming (via satellite): QVC.
Fee: $39.95 installation; $15.14 monthly; $25.00 additional installation.

Expanded Basic Service 1
Subscribers: 1,075.
Programming (via satellite): ABC Family Channel; AMC; Animal Planet; BET Networks; CNN; Country Music TV; Discovery Channel; Disney Channel; ESPN; ESPN 2; Fox News Channel; FX; Headline News; Lifetime; MSNBC; Nickelodeon; Spike TV; Syfy; TBS Superstation; The Learning Channel; The Weather Channel; Trinity Broadcasting Network; Turner Network TV; USA Network; WPIX (CW, IND) New York.
Fee: $19.69 monthly.

Digital Basic Service
Subscribers: N.A.
Programming (via satellite): BBC America; Bravo; Discovery Digital Networks; DMX Music; Encore (multiplexed); ESPN Classic Sports; ESPNews; Fox Sports World; Golf Channel; GSN; HGTV; History Channel; Independent Film Channel; Nick Jr.; Versus; WE tv.
Fee: $11.00 monthly.

Pay Service 1
Pay Units: 97.
Programming (via satellite): HBO.
Fee: $14.99 monthly.

Digital Pay Service 1
Pay Units: N.A.
Programming (via satellite): Cinemax (multiplexed); HBO (multiplexed); Showtime (multiplexed); Starz.
Fee: $15.95 monthly (each).

Video-On-Demand: No

Pay-Per-View
Playboy TV (delivered digitally); Hits Movies & Events (delivered digitally).

Internet Service
Operational: No.

Telephone Service
None

Miles of Plant: 41.0 (coaxial); None (fiber optic).
Ownership: Crystal Broadband Networks (MSO).

PINK HILL—Time Warner Cable, 4461 Sunset Ave, Rocky Mount, NC 27804. Phones: 252-338-2029; 888-683-1000. Fax: 252-937-4572. Web Site: http://www.timewarnercable.com/carolinas. ICA: NC0210.
TV Market Ranking: 73,84 (PINK HILL). Franchise award date: N.A. Franchise expiration date: N.A. Began: N.A.
Channel capacity: 42 (not 2-way capable). Channels available but not in use: N.A.

Basic Service
Subscribers: 237.
Programming (received off-air): WNCT-TV (CBS, CW) Greenville; WRAL-TV (CBS) Raleigh; WUNM-TV (PBS) Jacksonville; WYDO (FOX) Greenville.
Programming (via satellite): ABC Family Channel; QVC; Trinity Broadcasting Network; Turner Network TV; USA Network.
Fee: $47.50 installation; $9.37 monthly; $2.00 converter; $25.00 additional installation.

Expanded Basic Service 1
Subscribers: 226.
Programming (via satellite): A&E Networks; BET Networks; CNN; Country Music TV; Discovery Channel; Disney Channel; ESPN; Headline News; Spike TV; Syfy; TBS Superstation; WGN America.
Fee: $10.89 monthly.

Pay Service 1
Pay Units: 37.
Programming (via satellite): Cinemax.
Fee: $10.95 monthly.

Pay Service 2
Pay Units: 54.
Programming (via satellite): HBO.
Fee: $11.95 monthly.

Pay Service 3
Pay Units: N.A.
Programming (via satellite): Showtime.

Video-On-Demand: No

Internet Service
Operational: Yes.

Telephone Service
None

Miles of Plant: 26.0 (coaxial); None (fiber optic).
Vice President & General Manager: Kim Cannon. Technical Operations Director: Joe Pell. Customer Care Manager: Linda Bell.
Ownership: Time Warner Cable (MSO).

PLYMOUTH (town)—Mediacom, 910 NC Highway 32 S, PO Box 580, Plymouth, NC 27962. Phone: 252-793-1570. Fax: 252-793-6135. Web Site: http://www.mediacomcable.com. Also serves Bertie County (eastern portion), Colerain, Columbia, Creswell, Jamesville, Martin County (portions), Powellsville, Roper, Tyrrell County (portions), Washington County & Windsor. ICA: NC0085.
TV Market Ranking: 84 (Bertie County (eastern portion) (portions), Jamesville, Martin County (portions), PLYMOUTH (TOWN), Roper, Washington County (portions), Windsor); Below 100 (Columbia, Tyrrell County (portions), Bertie County (eastern portion) (portions)); Outside TV Markets (Colerain, Creswell, Powellsville, Bertie County (eastern portion) (portions), Washington County (portions)). Franchise award date: December 12, 1972. Franchise expiration date: N.A. Began: June 12, 1973.
Channel capacity: N.A. Channels available but not in use: N.A.

Basic Service
Subscribers: 5,315.
Programming (received off-air): WAVY-TV (NBC) Portsmouth; WCTI-TV (ABC) New Bern; WEPX-TV (ION) Greenville; WGNT (CW) Portsmouth; WHRO-TV (PBS) Hampton-Norfolk; WITN-TV (MNT, NBC) Washington; WNCT-TV (CBS, CW) Greenville; WSKY-TV (IND) Manteo; WTKR (CBS) Norfolk; WUND-TV (PBS) Edenton; WVEC (ABC) Hampton; WYDO (FOX) Greenville.
Programming (via satellite): History Channel; TV Guide Network; WGN America.
Fee: $45.00 installation; $14.46 monthly; $3.00 converter.

Expanded Basic Service 1
Subscribers: N.A.
Programming (via satellite): A&E Networks; ABC Family Channel; AMC; Animal Planet; BET Networks; Bravo; Cartoon Network; CNBC; CNN; Comedy Central; Country Music TV; C-SPAN; Discovery Channel; Discovery Fit & Health; Disney Channel; ESPN; ESPN 2; Food Network; Fox News Channel; Fox Sports South; FX; Hallmark Channel; Headline News; HGTV; INSP; Lifetime; MSNBC; MTV; Nickelodeon; Outdoor Channel; QVC; Speed; Spike TV; Syfy; TBS Superstation; The Learning Channel; The Weather Channel; Toon Disney; Travel Channel; Turner Network TV; TV Land; USA Network; VH1; WE tv.
Fee: $33.49 monthly.

Digital Basic Service
Subscribers: N.A.
Programming (via satellite): AmericanLife TV Network; BBC America; Bio; Bloomberg Television; DMX Music; ESPN; ESPNews; Fox Movie Channel; Fox Soccer; Fuse; G4; GAS; Golf Channel; GSN; HD Theater; HDNet; HDNet Movies; History Channel International; Independent Film Channel; Lifetime Movie Network; Lime; MTV2; National Geographic Channel; Nick Jr.; Style Network; The Word Network; truTV; Turner Classic Movies; Versus; Weatherscan.
Fee: $8.00 monthly.

Digital Pay Service 1
Pay Units: N.A.
Programming (via satellite): Cinemax (multiplexed); Encore (multiplexed); Flix (multiplexed); HBO (multiplexed); HBO HD; Showtime (multiplexed); Showtime HD; Starz (multiplexed); Starz HDTV; Sundance Channel (multiplexed); The Movie Channel (multiplexed); The Movie Channel HD.
Fee: $8.00 monthly (Starz), $9.95 monthly (Showtime or Cinemax), $13.95 monthly (HBO).

Video-On-Demand: No

Pay-Per-View
iN DEMAND (delivered digitally); ESPN Sports PPV (delivered digitally).

Internet Service
Operational: Yes. Began: January 1, 2002.
Broadband Service: Mediacom High Speed Internet.
Fee: $59.95 installation; $40.95 monthly; $3.00 modem lease.

Telephone Service
Analog: Not Operational
Digital: Operational
Fee: $39.95 monthly

Miles of Plant: 1,100.0 (coaxial); None (fiber optic). Miles of plant (coax and fiber) includes Camden/Currituck, Edonton & Rich Square
General Manager: Wayne Holiday. Marketing Analyst: Renette Ruffin. Office Manager: Wendy White.
Ownership: Mediacom LLC (MSO).

POWELLSVILLE—Mediacom. Now served by WINDSOR, NC [NC0111]. ICA: NC0180.

PRINCETON—Southern Cablevision. Now served by KENLY, NC [NC0148]. ICA: NC0177.

RAEFORD—Time Warner Cable, 6202 Raeford Rd, Fayetteville, NC 28304. Phones: 919-573-7000 (Morrisville office); 910-401-5001. Fax: 910-864-8878. Web Site: http://www.timewarnercable.com. ICA: NC0108.
TV Market Ranking: 73 (RAEFORD). Franchise award date: N.A. Franchise expiration date: N.A. Began: August 1, 1989.
Channel capacity: N.A. Channels available but not in use: N.A.

Basic Service
Subscribers: 1,225.
Programming (received off-air): WECT (NBC) Wilmington; WRAL-TV (CBS) Raleigh; WRAZ (FOX) Raleigh; WRDC (MNT) Durham; WTVD (ABC) Durham; WUNJ-TV (PBS) Wilmington.
Programming (via satellite): ESPN; QVC; TBS Superstation; USA Network.
Fee: $39.95 installation; $10.10 monthly.

Expanded Basic Service 1
Subscribers: N.A.
Programming (received off-air): WBTW (CBS, MNT) Florence; WNCN (NBC) Goldsboro; WRPX-TV (ION) Rocky Mount; WUVC-DT (UNV) Fayetteville.
Programming (via satellite): ABC Family Channel; BET Networks; CNN; Country Music TV; Discovery Channel; Discovery Fit & Health; Disney Channel; ESPN 2; Fox News Channel; Headline News; Lifetime; MSNBC; MTV; Nickelodeon; Spike TV; Syfy; The Weather Channel; Trinity Broadcasting Network; Turner Classic Movies; Turner Network TV; WGN America.
Fee: $25.61 monthly.

Pay Service 1
Pay Units: N.A.
Programming (via satellite): Cinemax; HBO; Showtime; The Movie Channel.
Fee: $12.95 monthly (each).

Video-On-Demand: No

Internet Service
Operational: Yes.
Broadband Service: RoadRunner.
Fee: $24.95 monthly.

Telephone Service
Digital: Operational
Fee: $24.99 monthly

Miles of Plant: 176.0 (coaxial); None (fiber optic). Additional miles planned: 20.0 (coaxial).
President: Tom Adams. Vice President, Technical Operations: Gary Frederick. Vice President, Sales & Marketing: Tom Smith. Vice President, Government & Public Affairs: Brad Phillips. General Manager: Kim Cannon.
Ownership: Time Warner Cable (MSO).

RALEIGH—Time Warner Cable, 101 Innovation Ave, Ste 100, Morrisville, NC 27560. Phone: 919-573-7000. Fax: 919-573-7042. Web Site: http://www.timewarnercable.com/carolinas. Also serves Franklin County (portions), Franklinton, Granville County (portions), Johnston County (portions), Knightdale, Rolesville, Wake County (portions), Wake Forrest, Wendell, Youngsville & Zebulon. ICA: NC0003.
TV Market Ranking: 73 (Franklin County (portions), Franklinton, Granville County (portions), Johnston County (portions), Knightdale, RALEIGH, Rolesville, Wake County (portions), Wake Forrest, Wendell, Youngsville); Outside TV Markets (Zebulon). Franchise award date: June 1, 1983. Franchise expiration date: November 16, 2009. Began: September 14, 1968.
Channel capacity: N.A. Channels available but not in use: N.A.

Basic Service
Subscribers: 103,690.
Programming (received off-air): WLFL (CW) Raleigh; WNCN (NBC) Goldsboro; WRAL-TV (CBS) Raleigh; WRAY-TV (IND) Wilson; WRAZ (FOX) Raleigh; WRDC

(MNT) Durham; WRPX-TV (ION) Rocky Mount; WTVD (ABC) Durham; WUNC-TV (PBS) Chapel Hill; WUVC-DT (UNV) Fayetteville; 2 FMs.
Programming (via satellite): TBS Superstation; TV Guide Network; WGN America.
Fee: $42.95 installation; $18.65 monthly; $2.88 converter.

Expanded Basic Service 1
Subscribers: 55,057.
Programming (via satellite): A&E Networks; ABC Family Channel; AMC; Animal Planet; BET Networks; Cartoon Network; CNBC; CNN; Comedy Central; Country Music TV; C-SPAN; C-SPAN 2; Discovery Channel; Discovery Fit & Health; Disney Channel; E! Entertainment Television; ESPN; ESPN 2; ESPN Classic Sports; Eternal Word TV Network; Food Network; Fox News Channel; Fox Sports Net; FX; Golf Channel; Hallmark Channel; Headline News; HGTV; History Channel; INSP; Lifetime; MSNBC; MTV; National Geographic Channel; Nickelodeon; Oxygen; QVC; ShopNBC; SoapNet; Spike TV; Syfy; The Learning Channel; The Weather Channel; Travel Channel; truTV; Turner Classic Movies; Turner Network TV; TV Land; USA Network; Versus; VH1; WE tv.
Fee: $36.05 monthly.

Digital Basic Service
Subscribers: N.A.
Programming (via satellite): AmericanLife TV Network; America's Store; BBC America; Bio; Bloomberg Television; Boomerang; Canales N; Cooking Channel; C-SPAN 3; C-SPAN Extra; Discovery Digital Networks; Disney Channel; DIY Network; ESPNews; Fox Sports World; FSN Digital Atlantic; FSN Digital Central; FSN Digital Pacific; Fuse; G4; GAS; Great American Country; GSN; History Channel International; Independent Film Channel; Lifetime Real Women; MBC America; MTV Hits; MTV2; Music Choice; NBA TV; Nick Jr.; Outdoor Channel; Ovation; Speed; Style Network; Tennis Channel; Toon Disney; Trinity Broadcasting Network; VH1 Classic; WAM! America's Kidz Network.
Fee: $16.25 monthly.

Digital Pay Service 1
Pay Units: N.A.
Programming (via satellite): Cinemax (multiplexed); Encore (multiplexed); Flix (multiplexed); Fox Movie Channel; HBO (multiplexed); Showtime (multiplexed); Sundance Channel; The Movie Channel (multiplexed).
Fee: $11.95 monthly (each).

Video-On-Demand: Yes

Pay-Per-View
Pleasure (delivered digitally); ESPN Now (delivered digitally); Playboy TV (delivered digitally); Fresh (delivered digitally); Shorteez (delivered digitally); Hot Choice (delivered digitally); Sports PPV (delivered digitally).

Internet Service
Operational: Yes. Began: October 1, 2003.
Broadband Service: EarthLink, Road Runner, AOL.
Fee: $99.95 installation; $44.95 monthly; $3.00 modem lease.

Telephone Service
Digital: Operational
Fee: $44.95 monthly

Miles of Plant: 2,518.0 (coaxial); None (fiber optic).
Vice President & General Manager: Chris Whitaker. Vice President, Technical Services: Gary Frederick. Vice President, Marketing & Sales: Tom Smith. Vice President, Finance: Rick Bennett. Vice President, Government & Public Affairs: Jack Stanley. Vice President, Customer Care: Michele Varsano. Vice President, Voice: Margie Fry. Vice President, Human Resources: Ann Burford.
Ownership: Time Warner Cable (MSO).; Advance/Newhouse Partnership (MSO).Day-to-day operations are managed by Time Warner Cable.

RANGER—Haywood Cablevision. Now served by MURPHY, NC [NC0079]. ICA: NC0116.

REEDS CROSS ROADS—Piedmont Communications Services, Inc., 191 Reeds Baptist Church Rd, PO Box 2066, Lexington, NC 27295. Phone: 336-787-5433. Fax: 336-787-5246. E-mail: ptmc@ptmc.net. Web Site: http://www.ptmc.net. Also serves Churchland, Davidson County (western portion) & Tyro. ICA: NC0212.
TV Market Ranking: 47 (Churchland, Davidson County (western portion), REEDS CROSS ROADS, Tyro). Franchise award date: N.A. Franchise expiration date: N.A. Began: January 1, 1989.
Channel capacity: 65 (operating 2-way). Channels available but not in use: N.A.

Basic Service
Subscribers: 3,188.
Programming (received off-air): WBTV (CBS) Charlotte; WCWG (CW) Lexington; WFMY-TV (CBS) Greensboro; WGHP (FOX, IND) High Point; WGPX-TV (ION) Burlington; WLXI (IND) Greensboro; WMYV (MNT) Greensboro; WUNL-TV (PBS) Winston-Salem; WXII-TV (NBC) Winston-Salem; WXLV-TV (ABC) Winston-Salem.
Programming (via satellite): WGN America.
Fee: $45.00 installation; $9.95 monthly.

Expanded Basic Service 1
Subscribers: N.A.
Programming (via satellite): A&E Networks; ABC Family Channel; AMC; Animal Planet; BET Networks; Cartoon Network; CNBC; CNN; Comedy Central; Country Music TV; C-SPAN; Discovery Channel; Disney Channel; ESPN; ESPN 2; ESPN Classic Sports; Food Network; Fox News Channel; Fox Sports South; FX; Golf Channel; Great American Country; Hallmark Channel; Headline News; HGTV; History Channel; INSP; Lifetime; Lifetime Movie Network; MSNBC; MTV; National Geographic Channel; Nickelodeon; Outdoor Channel; QVC; Speed; Spike TV; SportSouth; Syfy; TBS Superstation; The Learning Channel; The Weather Channel; Toon Disney; Travel Channel; truTV; Turner Network TV; TV Guide Network; TV Land; USA Network; Versus; VH1.
Fee: $28.20 monthly.

Digital Basic Service
Subscribers: N.A.
Programming (via satellite): BBC America; Bio; Bloomberg Television; Bravo; Canales N; cloo; CMT Pure Country; C-SPAN 2; Discovery Fit & Health; DMX Music; ESPNews; Flix; Fox Movie Channel; FSN Digital Atlantic; FSN Digital Central; FSN Digital Pacific; Fuse; G4; GSN; History Channel International; Independent Film Channel; MTV2; Nick Jr.; NickToons TV; SoapNet; Style Network; TeenNick; Turner Classic Movies; VH1 Classic; WE tv.
Fee: $9.95 monthly, $8.95 monthly (Spanish Tier).

Pay Service 1
Pay Units: N.A.
Programming (via satellite): Cinemax; HBO.
Fee: $8.95 monthly (Cinemax), $9.95 monthly (HBO).

Digital Pay Service 1
Pay Units: N.A.
Programming (via satellite): Cinemax (multiplexed); Encore (multiplexed); HBO (multiplexed); Showtime (multiplexed); Starz (multiplexed); The Movie Channel (multiplexed).
Fee: $8.95 monthly (Cinemax, Showtime or TMC), $9.95 monthly (HBO), $12.95 monthly (Starz /Encore).

Video-On-Demand: No

Pay-Per-View
Playboy TV (delivered digitally); Fresh (delivered digitally); Movies (delivered digitally); iN DEMAND.

Internet Service
Operational: Yes, DSL & dial-up. Began: January 31, 2003.
Broadband Service: InfoAve.net.
Fee: $39.95 monthly.

Telephone Service
None

Miles of Plant: 250.0 (coaxial); None (fiber optic).
President: Bruce Younger. Manager: Mike Stanley. Chief Technician: Bill Purcell.
Ownership: Piedmont Telephone Membership Corp.

REIDSVILLE—Time Warner Cable. Now served by GREENSBORO, NC [NC0006]. ICA: NC0045.

RICH SQUARE—Mediacom, 910 NC Highway 32 S, PO Box 580, Plymouth, NC 27962. Phone: 252-793-1570. Fax: 252-793-6135. Web Site: http://www.mediacomcable.com. Also serves Bertie County (westhern portion), Conway, Jackson, Kelford, Lasker, Lewiston, Northampton County, Roxobel, Seaboard, Severn & Woodland. ICA: NC0115.
TV Market Ranking: 84 (Bertie County (western portion) (portions)); Below 100 (Lewiston, Northampton County, Bertie County (western portion) (portions)); Outside TV Markets (Conway, Jackson, Kelford, Lasker, Northampton County, RICH SQUARE, Roxobel, Seaboard, Severn, Woodland, Bertie County (western portion) (portions)). Franchise award date: March 1, 1984. Franchise expiration date: N.A. Began: January 23, 1985.
Channel capacity: N.A. Channels available but not in use: N.A.

Basic Service
Subscribers: 1,486.
Programming (received off-air): WAVY-TV (NBC) Portsmouth; WCTI-TV (ABC) New Bern; WGNT (CW) Portsmouth; WHRO-TV (PBS) Hampton-Norfolk; WITN-TV (MNT, NBC) Washington; WPXV-TV (ION) Norfolk; WSKY-TV (IND) Manteo; WTKR (CBS) Norfolk; WTVZ-TV (MNT) Norfolk; WUND-TV (PBS) Edenton; WVBT (FOX) Virginia Beach; WVEC (ABC) Hampton.
Programming (via satellite): History Channel; TV Guide Network.
Fee: $45.00 installation; $14.46 monthly.

Expanded Basic Service 1
Subscribers: N.A.
Programming (via satellite): A&E Networks; ABC Family Channel; AMC; Animal Planet; BET Networks; Bravo; Cartoon Network; CNBC; CNN; Comedy Central; Country Music TV; C-SPAN; Discovery Channel; Disney Channel; ESPN; ESPN 2; Food Network; Fox News Channel; Fox Sports South; FX; Hallmark Channel; HD Theater; HDNet; HDNet Movies; Headline News; Healthy Living Channel; HGTV; INSP; Lifetime; MSNBC; MTV; Nickelodeon; Outdoor Channel; QVC; Speed; Spike TV; Syfy; TBS Superstation; The Learning Channel; The Weather Channel; Toon Disney; Travel Channel; Turner Network TV; TV Land; Universal HD; USA Network; VH1; WE tv; WGN America.
Fee: $33.49 monthly.

Digital Basic Service
Subscribers: N.A.
Programming (via satellite): AmericanLife TV Network; BBC America; Bio; Bloomberg Television; Discovery Digital Networks; Fox Movie Channel; Fox Sports World; Fuse; G4; GAS; Golf Channel; GSN; History Channel International; Independent Film Channel; Lifetime Movie Network; Lime; MTV2; Music Choice; National Geographic Channel; Nick Jr.; Science Television; Style Network; The Word Network; truTV; Turner Classic Movies; Versus; Weatherscan.
Fee: $8.00 monthly.

Digital Pay Service 1
Pay Units: N.A.
Programming (via satellite): Cinemax (multiplexed); Encore (multiplexed); Flix (multiplexed); HBO (multiplexed); HBO HD; Showtime (multiplexed); Showtime HD; Starz (multiplexed); Starz HDTV; Sundance Channel (multiplexed); The Movie Channel (multiplexed); The Movie Channel HD.
Fee: $8.00 monthly (Starz/Encore), $9.95 monthly (Showtime/TMC/Flix/Sundance or Cinemax), $13.95 monthly (HBO).

Video-On-Demand: No

Pay-Per-View
Movies (delivered digitally); ESPN (delivered digitally).

Internet Service
Operational: Yes. Began: January 1, 2002.
Broadband Service: Mediacom High Speed Internet.
Fee: $40.95 monthly; $3.00 modem lease.

Telephone Service
Digital: Operational
Fee: $39.95 monthly

Miles of plant included in Plymouth
General Manager: Wayne Holiday. Office Manager: Wendy White. Marketing Analyst: Renette Ruffin.
Ownership: Mediacom LLC (MSO).

RIEGELWOOD—Time Warner Cable, 1345 Madison St. S, Whiteville, NC 28472. Phones: 866-489-2669; 910-642-7171. Web Site: http://www.timewarnercable.com. Also serves Acme, Armour, Bladen County (portions), Bolton, Brunswick County (portions), Buckhead, Columbus County (portions), Delco, East Arcadia, Northwest & Sandy Creek. ICA: NC0217.
TV Market Ranking: Below 100 (Acme, Armour, Bladen County (portions), Bolton, Brunswick County (portions), Buckhead, Columbus County (portions), Delco, East Arcadia, Northwest, RIEGELWOOD, Sandy Creek). Franchise award date: November 3, 1988. Franchise expiration date: N.A. Began: December 31, 1988.
Channel capacity: 40 (not 2-way capable). Channels available but not in use: N.A.

Basic Service
Subscribers: 581.
Programming (received off-air): WBTW (CBS, MNT) Florence; WECT (NBC) Wilmington; WSFX-TV (FOX) Wilmington; WUNJ-TV (PBS) Wilmington; WWAY (ABC) Wilmington.
Programming (via satellite): A&E Networks; ABC Family Channel; BET Networks; CNN; Country Music TV; Discovery Channel; Disney Channel; ESPN; Hallmark Channel; Headline News; Lifetime; MTV; Nickelodeon; Spike TV; Syfy; TBS Superstation; The Learning Channel; The Weather Chan-

nel; Turner Network TV; USA Network; WGN America.
Fee: $35.00 installation; $20.50 monthly.

Pay Service 1
Pay Units: 172.
Programming (via satellite): Cinemax.
Fee: $9.95 monthly.

Pay Service 2
Pay Units: 295.
Programming (via satellite): HBO.
Fee: $10.95 monthly.

Pay Service 3
Pay Units: 144.
Programming (via satellite): Showtime.
Fee: $9.95 monthly.

Video-On-Demand: No

Internet Service
Operational: Yes.
Broadband Service: RoadRunner.
Fee: $24.95 monthly.

Telephone Service
Digital: Operational
Fee: $24.99 monthly

Miles of Plant: 157.0 (coaxial); None (fiber optic).

Vice President & General Manager: Kim Cannon. Technical Operations Director: Joe Pell. Customer Care Manager: Kelly Person.

Ownership: Time Warner Cable (MSO).

ROANOKE RAPIDS—Charter Communications, 2400 S Virginia Dare Trail, Nags Head, NC 27959. Phones: 757-539-0713 (Suffolk office); 252-441-1582. Fax: 252-441-1581. Web Site: http://www.charter.com. Also serves Garysburg, Gaston, Halifax County, Northampton County & Weldon. ICA: NC0214.

TV Market Ranking: Below 100 (Halifax County (portions), Northampton County (portions), Weldon); Outside TV Markets (Garysburg, Gaston, Halifax County (portions), Northampton County (portions), ROANOKE RAPIDS). Franchise award date: N.A. Franchise expiration date: N.A. Began: March 1, 1965.

Channel capacity: N.A. Channels available but not in use: N.A.

Basic Service
Subscribers: 10,230.
Programming (received off-air): WGNT (CW) Portsmouth; WITN-TV (MNT, NBC) Washington; WLFL (CW) Raleigh; WNCT-TV (CBS, CW) Greenville; WNVN-LP Roanoke Rapids; WRAL-TV (CBS) Raleigh; WRAY-TV (IND) Wilson; WRAZ (FOX) Raleigh; WRPX-TV (ION) Rocky Mount; WTVD (ABC) Durham; WUNP-TV (PBS) Roanoke Rapids.
Programming (via satellite): C-SPAN; INSP; QVC; Trinity Broadcasting Network; TV Guide Network.
Fee: $25.00 installation; $1.79 converter.

Expanded Basic Service 1
Subscribers: N.A.
Programming (via satellite): A&E Networks; ABC Family Channel; AMC; Animal Planet; BET Networks; Bravo; Cartoon Network; CNBC; CNN; Comedy Central; Country Music TV; Discovery Channel; Disney Channel; E! Entertainment Television; ESPN; ESPN 2; Food Network; Fox News Channel; Fox Sports South; FX; G4; Golf Channel; GSN; Hallmark Channel; Headline News; HGTV; History Channel; Lifetime; MSNBC; MTV; MTV2; National Geographic Channel; Nickelodeon; Oxygen; SoapNet; Speed; Spike TV; TBS Superstation; The Learning Channel; The Weather Channel; Toon Disney; Travel Channel; truTV; Turner Network TV; TV Land; USA Network; Versus; VH1; WE tv.
Fee: $47.99 monthly.

Digital Basic Service
Subscribers: N.A.
Programming (via satellite): BBC America; Bio; Bloomberg Television; Boomerang; CNN en Espanol; CNN International; Discovery Digital Networks; DIY Network; ESPN Classic Sports; ESPNews; Fox College Sports Atlantic; Fox College Sports Central; Fox College Sports Pacific; Fox Deportes; Fox Movie Channel; Fox Soccer; Fuel TV; Fuse; GAS; Great American Country; History Channel International; Independent Film Channel; Lifetime Movie Network; Mid-Atlantic Sports Network; MTV Networks Digital Suite; Music Choice; Nick Jr.; Nick Too; NickToons TV; Sundance Channel; Turner Classic Movies; TV Guide Interactive Inc.

Digital Pay Service 1
Pay Units: N.A.
Programming (via satellite): Cinemax (multiplexed); Encore (multiplexed); HBO (multiplexed); Showtime (multiplexed); Starz (multiplexed).

Video-On-Demand: No

Pay-Per-View
Addressable homes: 5,648.
iN DEMAND (delivered digitally); Playboy TV (delivered digitally); Fresh (delivered digitally); Shorteez (delivered digitally).

Internet Service
Operational: Yes.
Broadband Service: Charter Pipeline.
Fee: $29.99 monthly.

Telephone Service
None

Miles of Plant: 201.0 (coaxial); None (fiber optic). Additional miles planned: 5.0 (coaxial).

Vice President & General Manager: Anthony Pope. Marketing Director: Brooke Sinclair. Marketing Manager: LaRisa Scales. Operations Manager: Doug Underwood. Technical Operations Manager: Joel Sprout.

Ownership: Charter Communications Inc. (MSO).

ROARING FORK—Formerly served by Almega Cable. No longer in operation. ICA: NC0213.

ROBBINS—Windjammer Cable, 8500 W 110th St, Ste 600, Overland Park, KS 66210. Phone: 888-495-2881. Fax: 913-563-5454. Web Site: http://www.windjammercable.com. Also serves Moore County (portions). ICA: NC0153.

TV Market Ranking: Outside TV Markets (Moore County (portions), ROBBINS). Franchise award date: April 1, 1983. Franchise expiration date: March 20, 2011. Began: April 1, 1984.

Channel capacity: N.A. Channels available but not in use: N.A.

Basic Service
Subscribers: 335.
Programming (received off-air): WLFL (CW) Raleigh; WNCN (NBC) Goldsboro; WRAL-TV (CBS) Raleigh; WRDC (MNT) Durham; WTVD (ABC) Durham; WUNC-TV (PBS) Chapel Hill; WUVC-DT (UNV) Fayetteville.
Programming (via satellite): ABC Family Channel; QVC; TBS Superstation; WGN America.
Fee: $42.95 installation; $12.50 monthly; $1.10 converter.

Expanded Basic Service 1
Subscribers: 320.
Programming (via satellite): CNN; Country Music TV; Discovery Channel; Disney Channel; ESPN; Headline News; MTV; Nickelodeon; Spike TV; Turner Network TV; USA Network; VH1.
Fee: $35.45 monthly.

Pay Service 1
Pay Units: 66.
Programming (via satellite): HBO.
Fee: $11.50 monthly.

Pay Service 2
Pay Units: N.A.
Programming (via satellite): The Movie Channel.
Fee: $11.50 monthly.

Pay Service 3
Pay Units: 15.
Programming (via satellite): Showtime.
Fee: $11.50 monthly.

Video-On-Demand: Yes

Internet Service
Operational: Yes.
Broadband Service: Road Runner.
Fee: $99.95 installation; $44.95 monthly.

Telephone Service
Digital: Operational
Fee: $49.95 monthly

Miles of Plant: 18.0 (coaxial); None (fiber optic). Additional miles planned: 21.0 (coaxial).

General Manager: Timothy Evard. Operations Director: Belinda Graham. Engineering Director: Mike Earehart. Finance & Accounting Director: Cindy Johnson.

Ownership: Windjammer Communications LLC (MSO).

ROBBINSVILLE—Zito Media, 611 Vader Hill Rd, Coudersport, PA 16915. Phone: 814-260-9575. Web Site: http://www.zitomedia.com. Also serves Graham County (central portion) & Santeetlah. ICA: NC0231.

TV Market Ranking: Outside TV Markets (Graham County (central portion), ROBBINSVILLE, Santeetlah). Franchise award date: September 25, 1980. Franchise expiration date: June 1, 2009. Began: October 1, 1981.

Channel capacity: 35 (not 2-way capable). Channels available but not in use: N.A.

Basic Service
Subscribers: 414.
Programming (received off-air): WLOS (ABC) Asheville; WUNE-TV (PBS) Linville; WYFF (NBC) Greenville.
Programming (via satellite): C-SPAN; QVC; The Learning Channel; The Weather Channel; WGN America; WSEE-TV (CBS, CW) Erie.
Fee: $29.95 installation; $19.95 monthly; $1.78 converter.

Expanded Basic Service 1
Subscribers: N.A.
Programming (via satellite): A&E Networks; ABC Family Channel; AMC; Cartoon Network; CNN; Comedy Central; Country Music TV; Discovery Channel; Disney Channel; ESPN; ESPN 2; Fox Sports South; FX; Headline News; Lifetime; MTV; Nickelodeon; Spike TV; SportSouth; TBS Superstation; Turner Classic Movies; Turner Network TV; USA Network.
Fee: $20.00 monthly.

Digital Basic Service
Subscribers: N.A.
Programming (via satellite): BBC America; Bio; cloo; Discovery Digital Networks; DMX Music; ESPN Classic Sports; ESPNews; Fox Soccer; Fuse; GAS; Golf Channel; GSN; History Channel International; Independent Film Channel; Lifetime Movie Network; MTV2; National Geographic Channel; Nick Jr.; Speed; Style Network; Syfy; Toon Disney; Versus; WE tv.

Digital Pay Service 1
Pay Units: N.A.
Programming (via satellite): Cinemax (multiplexed); Encore (multiplexed); HBO (multiplexed); Showtime (multiplexed); Starz (multiplexed); The Movie Channel (multiplexed).

Video-On-Demand: No

Pay-Per-View
iN DEMAND (delivered digitally); Playboy TV (delivered digitally).

Internet Service
Operational: No.

Telephone Service
None

Miles of Plant: 69.0 (coaxial); None (fiber optic).

Public Relations Manager: Mark Laver.

Ownership: Zito Media (MSO).

ROBESON COUNTY (western portion)—Formerly served by Carolina Cable Partnerships. No longer in operation. ICA: NC0215.

ROCKINGHAM—Time Warner Cable, 3140 W Arrowood Rd, Charlotte, NC 28273. Phone: 910-378-2500. Fax: 704-504-1997. Web Site: http://www.timewarnercable.com/carolinas. Also serves Dobbins Heights, East Rockingham, Ellerbe, Hamlet, Hoffman, Marston & Richmond County. ICA: NC0038.

TV Market Ranking: 73 (Richmond County (portions)); Outside TV Markets (Dobbins Heights, East Rockingham, Ellerbe, Hamlet, Hoffman, Marston, ROCKINGHAM, Richmond County (portions)). Franchise award date: April 15, 1968. Franchise expiration date: N.A. Began: January 1, 1990.

Channel capacity: N.A. Channels available but not in use: N.A.

Basic Service
Subscribers: N.A. Included in Charlotte
Programming (received off-air): WAXN-TV (IND) Kannapolis; WBTV (CBS) Charlotte; WBTW (CBS, MNT) Florence; WCCB (FOX) Charlotte; WCNC-TV (NBC) Charlotte; WHKY-TV (IND) Hickory; WJZY (CW) Belmont; WMYT-TV (MNT) Rock Hill; WRAL-TV (CBS) Raleigh; WSOC-TV (ABC) Charlotte; WUNG-TV (PBS) Concord.
Programming (via satellite): TV Guide Network; WGN America.
Fee: $36.00 installation; $8.50 monthly; $18.00 additional installation.

Expanded Basic Service 1
Subscribers: N.A.
Programming (via satellite): A&E Networks; ABC Family Channel; AMC; Animal Planet; BET Networks; Bravo; Cartoon Network; CNBC; CNN; Comedy Central; Country Music TV; C-SPAN; C-SPAN 2; Discovery Channel; Discovery Health Channel; Disney Channel; E! Entertainment Television; ESPN; ESPN 2; ESPN Classic Sports; Food Network; Fox News Channel; Fox Sports Net; FX; Golf Channel; Hallmark Channel; Headline News; HGTV; History Channel; INSP; Lifetime; Lifetime Movie Network; MSNBC; MTV; National Geographic Channel; Nickelodeon; Oxygen; QVC; ShopNBC; Speed; Spike TV; SportSouth; Syfy; TBS Superstation; The Learning Channel; The Weather Channel; Travel Channel; Trinity Broadcasting Network; truTV; Turner Classic Movies; Turner Network TV; TV Land; USA Network; Versus; VH1; WE tv.
Fee: $41.45 monthly.

Digital Basic Service
Subscribers: 4,822.
Programming (via satellite): AmericanLife TV Network; America's Store; BBC America; Bio; Black Family Channel; Bloomberg Television; Boomerang; Cooking Channel; C-SPAN 3; Discovery Digital Networks; DIY Network; DMX Music; ESPNews; FamilyNet; Fox Sports World; FSN Digital Atlantic; FSN Digital Central; FSN Digital Pacific; Fuel TV; Fuse; G4; Great American Country; GSN; History Channel International; Independent Film Channel; Lifetime Real Women; MTV2; NBA TV; Nick Jr.; Outdoor Channel; Ovation; SoapNet; Style Network; Tennis Channel; Toon Disney; VH1 Classic.
Fee: $15.00 monthly.

Digital Pay Service 1
Pay Units: 2,055.
Programming (via satellite): Canales N; Cinemax (multiplexed); Deutsche Welle TV; Encore (multiplexed); Flix; Fox Movie Channel; HBO (multiplexed); RAI International; Saigon Broadcasting Television Network; Showtime (multiplexed); Starz (multiplexed); Sundance Channel; The Movie Channel (multiplexed); TV5, La Television International; Zee TV USA.
Fee: $9.95 monthly (Deutsche Welle, TV5 or RAI), $11.95 monthly (HBO, Cinemax, Showtime, TMC or Starz/Encore), $14.95 monthly (SBTN or Zee).

Video-On-Demand: Yes

Pay-Per-View
Addressable homes: 4,822.
iN DEMAND (delivered digitally); ESPN Now (delivered digitally); ESPN Gameplan (delivered digitally); ESPN Full Court (delivered digitally); Sports PPV (delivered digitally).

Internet Service
Operational: Yes.
Subscribers: 4,972.
Broadband Service: Road Runner, AOL, EarthLink.
Fee: $39.95 installation; $46.95 monthly.

Telephone Service
Digital: Operational
Fee: $39.95 monthly

Miles of plant (coax & fiber) included in Charlotte

President: Mike Munley. Vice President, Technical Operations: Mike Cullim. Vice President, Engineering: Richard Newcomb. Vice President, Marketing & Sales: Eric Franey. Public Affairs Director: Jessica Graham. Government Affairs Director: Michael Tanck.

Ownership: Time Warner Cable (MSO).; Advance/Newhouse Partnership (MSO).Day-to-day operations are managed by Time Warner Cable.

ROCKY MOUNT—Cox Communications. Now served by GREENVILLE, NC [NC0014]. ICA: NC0016.

ROSEBORO—StarVision. Now served by CLINTON, NC [NC0070]. ICA: NC0216.

ROWLAND—Time Warner Cable. Now served by MYRTLE BEACH, SC [SC0007]. ICA: NC0174.

ROXBORO—Charter Communications, 107-B Weeks Dr, Roxboro, NC 27573. Phone: 336-599-2042. Fax: 336-599-1792. Web Site: http://www.charter.com. Also serves Caswell County (portions), Hurdle Mills, Leasburg, Milton, Person County, Semora & Timberlake. ICA: NC0059.

TV Market Ranking: 73 (Caswell County (portions), Person County (portions), ROXBORO); 75 (Hurdle Mills, Leasburg, Timberlake); Below 100 (Milton, Semora); Outside TV Markets (Caswell County (portions), Person County (portions)). Franchise award date: December 1, 1979. Franchise expiration date: N.A. Began: May 26, 1980.

Channel capacity: N.A. Channels available but not in use: N.A.

Basic Service
Subscribers: 5,872.
Programming (received off-air): WLFL (CW) Raleigh; WNCN (NBC) Goldsboro; WRAL-TV (CBS) Raleigh; WRAZ (FOX) Raleigh; WRDC (MNT) Durham; WRPX-TV (ION) Rocky Mount; WSET-TV (ABC) Lynchburg; WTVD (ABC) Durham; WUNC-TV (PBS) Chapel Hill; WUVC-DT (UNV) Fayetteville.
Programming (via satellite): INSP; QVC; ShopNBC; Trinity Broadcasting Network; TV Guide Network.
Fee: $29.99 installation; $2.50 converter.

Expanded Basic Service 1
Subscribers: N.A.
Programming (via satellite): A&E Networks; ABC Family Channel; AMC; Animal Planet; BET Networks; Cartoon Network; CNBC; CNN; Comedy Central; Country Music TV; C-SPAN; Discovery Channel; Disney Channel; E! Entertainment Television; ESPN; ESPN 2; Fox News Channel; Fox Sports South; FX; Golf Channel; Headline News; HGTV; History Channel; Lifetime; MSNBC; MTV; National Geographic Channel; Nickelodeon; SoapNet; Speed; Spike TV; Syfy; TBS Superstation; The Learning Channel; The Weather Channel; Travel Channel; truTV; Turner Network TV; TV Land; USA Network; Versus; VH1.
Fee: $47.99 monthly.

Digital Basic Service
Subscribers: 2,500.
Programming (via satellite): Bio; Discovery Digital Networks; DIY Network; G4; GAS; History Channel International; Lifetime Movie Network; MTV2; Music Choice; Nick Jr.; Sundance Channel; TV Guide Interactive Inc.

Digital Pay Service 1
Pay Units: 965.
Programming (via satellite): Cinemax (multiplexed).
Fee: $11.00 monthly.

Digital Pay Service 2
Pay Units: 440.
Programming (via satellite): Encore (multiplexed); Flix; Showtime (multiplexed); Starz (multiplexed).

Digital Pay Service 3
Pay Units: 1,758.
Programming (via satellite): HBO (multiplexed).
Fee: $11.00 monthly.

Digital Pay Service 4
Pay Units: N.A.
Programming (via satellite): The Movie Channel (multiplexed).

Video-On-Demand: No

Pay-Per-View
iN DEMAND (delivered digitally), Addressable: No; Playboy TV (delivered digitally); Fresh (delivered digitally); Shorteez (delivered digitally).

Internet Service
Operational: Yes, DSL.
Subscribers: 216.
Broadband Service: Charter Pipeline.
Fee: $29.99 monthly.

Telephone Service
None

Miles of Plant: 328.0 (coaxial); 21.0 (fiber optic). Additional miles planned: 30.0 (coaxial).

Vice President & General Manager: Anthony Pope. Marketing Director: Brooke Sinclair. Marketing Manager: LaRisa Scales. Office Manager: Brenda Brinson. Plant Manager: Barry Creasy. Chief Technician: Steve Folly. Operations Manager: Doug Underwood.

Ownership: Charter Communications Inc. (MSO).

SALISBURY—Time Warner Cable, 3140 W Arrowood Rd, Charlotte, NC 28273. Phone: 704-378-2500. Fax: 704-504-1997. Web Site: http://www.timewarnercable.com/carolinas. Also serves Camp Wesley, Cleveland, Craven, East Spencer, Faith, Gold Hill, Granite Quarry, Rockwell, Rowan County & Spencer. ICA: NC0022.

TV Market Ranking: 42 (Cleveland, Faith, Rockwell); 42,47 (East Spencer, Rowan County (portions), SALISBURY); 47 (Camp Wesley, Craven, Gold Hill, Spencer); Below 100 (Granite Quarry). Franchise award date: May 21, 1968. Franchise expiration date: N.A. Began: January 1, 1969.

Channel capacity: N.A. Channels available but not in use: N.A.

Basic Service
Subscribers: N.A. Included in Charlotte
Programming (received off-air): WAXN-TV (IND) Kannapolis; WBTV (CBS) Charlotte; WCCB (FOX) Charlotte; WCNC-TV (NBC) Charlotte; WGHP (FOX, IND) High Point; WHKY-TV (IND) Hickory; WJZY (CW) Belmont; WMYT-TV (MNT) Rock Hill; WSOC-TV (ABC) Charlotte; WTVI (PBS) Charlotte; WUNG-TV (PBS) Concord.
Programming (via satellite): Cooking Channel; TV Guide Network; WGN America.
Fee: $36.00 installation; $9.50 monthly; $2.11 converter; $18.00 additional installation.

Expanded Basic Service 1
Subscribers: N.A.
Programming (via satellite): A&E Networks; ABC Family Channel; AMC; Animal Planet; BET Networks; Bravo; Cartoon Network; CNBC; CNN; Comedy Central; Country Music TV; C-SPAN; C-SPAN 2; Discovery Channel; Discovery Health Channel; Disney Channel; E! Entertainment Television; ESPN; ESPN 2; ESPN Classic Sports; Food Network; Fox News Channel; Fox Sports South; FX; Golf Channel; Hallmark Channel; Headline News; HGTV; History Channel; INSP; Lifetime; Lifetime Movie Network; MSNBC; MTV; National Geographic Channel; Nickelodeon; Oxygen; QVC; Speed; Spike TV; SportSouth; Syfy; TBS Superstation; The Learning Channel; The Weather Channel; Travel Channel; truTV; Turner Classic Movies; Turner Network TV; TV Land; USA Network; Versus; VH1; WE tv.
Fee: $40.45 monthly.

Digital Basic Service
Subscribers: 6,738.
Programming (via satellite): AmericanLife TV Network; America's Store; BBC America; Bio; Black Family Channel; Bloomberg Television; Boomerang; Canales N; C-SPAN 3; Discovery Digital Networks; DIY Network; DMX Music; ESPNews; FamilyNet; Fox Sports World; FSN Digital Atlantic; FSN Digital Central; FSN Digital Pacific; Fuel TV; Fuse; G4; Great American Country; GSN; History Channel International; Independent Film Channel; Lifetime Real Women; MTV Networks Digital Suite; NBA TV; Nick Jr.; Outdoor Channel; Ovation; SoapNet; Style Network; Tennis Channel; Toon Disney.
Fee: $15.00 monthly.

Digital Pay Service 1
Pay Units: N.A.
Programming (via satellite): Cinemax (multiplexed); Deutsche Welle TV; Encore (multiplexed); Flix; HBO (multiplexed); RAI International; Saigon Broadcasting Television Network; Showtime (multiplexed); Starz (multiplexed); Sundance Channel; The Movie Channel (multiplexed); TV5, La Television International; Zee TV USA.
Fee: $9.95 monthly (Deutsche Welle, TV5 or RAI), $10.95 monthly (Cinemax, HBO, Showtime, Flix/Sundance/TMC or Starz/Encore), $14.95 monthly (SBTN or ZEE).

Video-On-Demand: Yes

Pay-Per-View
Addressable homes: 6,738.
iN DEMAND (delivered digitally); ESPN Now (delivered digitally); ESPN Full Court (delivered digitally); ESPN Gameplan (delivered digitally); Adult PPV (delivered digitally); Sports PPV (delivered digitally).

Internet Service
Operational: Yes.
Subscribers: 6,948.
Broadband Service: Road Runner, AOL, EarthLink.
Fee: $39.95 installation; $46.95 monthly.

Telephone Service
Digital: Operational
Fee: $39.95 monthly

Miles of plant (coax & fiber) included in Charlotte

President: Mike Munley. Vice President, Technical Operations: Mike Cullim. Vice President, Engineering: Richard Newcomb. Vice President, Marketing & Sales: Eric Franey. Public Affairs Director: Jessica Graham. Government Affairs Director: Michael Tanck.

Ownership: Time Warner Cable (MSO).; Advance/Newhouse Partnership (MSO).Day-to-day operations are managed by Time Warner Cable.

SANFORD—Charter Communications. Now served by BUIES CREEK, NC [NC0194]. ICA: NC0219.

SANTREE MOBILE HOME PARK—Formerly served by Adelphia Communications. No longer in operation. ICA: NC0220.

SCOTLAND NECK—Suddenlink Communications, 1509 Westmount Dr, Rocky Mount, NC 27803. Phones: 877-804-6501 (Customer service); 314-965-2020. Web Site: http://www.suddenlink.com. ICA: NC0146.

TV Market Ranking: Below 100 (SCOTLAND NECK). Franchise award date: April 10, 1980. Franchise expiration date: N.A. Began: April 1, 1982.

Channel capacity: N.A. Channels available but not in use: N.A.

Basic Service

Subscribers: 1,125 Includes Enfield.

Programming (received off-air): WCTI-TV (ABC) New Bern; WNCT-TV (CBS, CW) Greenville; WRAL-TV (CBS) Raleigh; WUNK-TV (PBS) Greenville; WYDO (FOX) Greenville; allband FM.

Programming (via satellite): A&E Networks; ABC Family Channel; AMC; BET Networks; Cartoon Network; CNBC; Comcast SportsNet Mid-Atlantic; C-SPAN; ESPN; ESPN 2; Food Network; History Channel; Nickelodeon; Syfy; TBS Superstation; The Learning Channel; The Weather Channel; Trinity Broadcasting Network; USA Network; WGN America.

Fee: $21.99 installation; $19.95 monthly.

Expanded Basic Service 1

Subscribers: 950 Includes Enfield.

Programming (via satellite): CNN; Discovery Channel; Disney Channel; Spike TV; Turner Classic Movies; Turner Network TV.

Fee: $3.45 monthly.

Pay Service 1

Pay Units: 265.

Programming (via satellite): Cinemax.

Fee: $9.75 monthly.

Pay Service 2

Pay Units: 337.

Programming (via satellite): HBO.

Fee: $8.75 monthly.

Video-On-Demand: No

Internet Service

Operational: Yes.

Broadband Service: Suddenlink High Speed Internet.

Fee: $100.00 installation; $39.95 monthly.

Telephone Service

None

Miles of Plant: 18.0 (coaxial); None (fiber optic).

Ownership: Cequel Communications LLC (MSO).

SELMA/GARNER—Time Warner Cable, 101 Innovation Ave, Ste 100, Morrisville, NC 27560. Phone: 919-573-7000. Fax: 919-573-7042. Web Site: http://www.timewarnercable.com/carolinas. Also serves Clayton, Four Oaks, Johnston County (portions), Pine Level, Smithfield & Wake County (portions). ICA: NC0032.

TV Market Ranking: 73 (Clayton, Four Oaks, GARNER, Johnston County (portions), Pine Level, SELMA, Smithfield, Wake County (portions)). Franchise award date: June 1, 1972. Franchise expiration date: March 27, 2011. Began: February 1, 1975.

Channel capacity: N.A. Channels available but not in use: N.A.

Basic Service

Subscribers: 14,497.

Programming (received off-air): WARZ-LP Smithfield/Selma; WLFL (CW) Raleigh; WNCN (NBC) Goldsboro; WRAL-TV (CBS) Raleigh; WRAY-TV (IND) Wilson; WRAZ (FOX) Raleigh; WRDC (MNT) Durham; WRPX-TV (ION) Rocky Mount; WTVD (ABC) Durham; WUNC-TV (PBS) Chapel Hill; WUVC-DT (UNV) Fayetteville.

Programming (via satellite): ABC Family Channel; TBS Superstation; WGN America.

Fee: $42.95 installation; $12.55 monthly.

Expanded Basic Service 1

Subscribers: N.A.

Programming (via satellite): A&E Networks; AMC; Animal Planet; BET Networks; Cartoon Network; CNBC; CNN; Comedy Central; Country Music TV; C-SPAN; C-SPAN 2; Discovery Channel; Disney Channel; DIY Network; E! Entertainment Television; ESPN; ESPN 2; ESPN Classic Sports; Eternal Word TV Network; Food Network; Fox News Channel; Fox Sports Net; FX; Golf Channel; Hallmark Channel; Headline News; HGTV; History Channel; Lifetime; Lifetime Movie Network; MSNBC; MTV; National Geographic Channel; Nickelodeon; Oxygen; QVC; SoapNet; Spike TV; Syfy; The Learning Channel; The Weather Channel; Travel Channel; truTV; Turner Classic Movies; Turner Network TV; TV Guide Network; TV Land; Univision Studios; USA Network; VH1; WE tv.

Fee: $38.25 monthly.

Digital Basic Service

Subscribers: N.A.

Programming (via satellite): America's Store; BBC America; Black Family Channel; Bloomberg Television; Canales N; CNBC; Cooking Channel; C-SPAN 3; Discovery Digital Networks; Disney Channel; ESPNews; Fox Sports World; FSN Digital Atlantic; FSN Digital Central; FSN Digital Pacific; Fuse; G4; GAS; Great American Country; GSN; Lifetime Movie Network; MTV2; Music Choice; Nick Jr.; Outdoor Channel; Ovation; Speed; Style Network; Toon Disney; Versus; VH1 Classic.

Fee: $16.25 monthly; $8.95 additional installation.

Digital Pay Service 1

Pay Units: N.A.

Programming (via satellite): Cinemax (multiplexed); Encore (multiplexed); Flix; Fox Movie Channel; HBO (multiplexed); Independent Film Channel; Showtime (multiplexed); Starz (multiplexed); Sundance Channel; The Movie Channel (multiplexed).

Fee: $11.95 monthly (each).

Video-On-Demand: Yes

Pay-Per-View

ESPN Now (delivered digitally); Pleasure (delivered digitally); Shorteez (delivered digitally); Fresh (delivered digitally); Playboy TV (delivered digitally); Hot Choice (delivered digitally); Playboy TV.

Internet Service

Operational: Yes.

Broadband Service: Road Runner.

Fee: $99.95 installation; $44.95 monthly.

Telephone Service

Digital: Operational

Fee: $44.95 monthly

Miles of Plant: 540.0 (coaxial); 67.0 (fiber optic).

Vice President & General Manager: Chris Whitaker. President, Network Operations & Engineering: Mike Munley. Vice President, Sales & Marketing: Tom Smith. Vice President, Government & Public Affairs: Brad Phillips.

Ownership: Time Warner Cable (MSO).; Advance/Newhouse Partnership (MSO).Day-to-day operations are managed by Time Warner Cable.

SHALLOTTE—Atlantic Telephone Membership Corp., 640 Whitehall Rd NW, PO Box 3198, Shallotte, NC 28459-3198. Phones: 888-367-2862; 910-754-4311. Fax: 910-754-5499. E-mail: contact@atlantictelephone.org. Web Site: http://www.atmc.net. Also serves Ash, Bolivia, Brick Landing, Brunswick County (unincorporated areas), Calabash, Longwood, Ocean Isle Beach, Sunset Beach, Sunset Harbor & Supply. ICA: NC0050.

TV Market Ranking: Below 100 (Ash, Bolivia, Brick Landing, Brunswick County (unincorporated areas), Calabash, Longwood, Ocean Isle Beach, SHALLOTTE, Sunset Beach, Sunset Harbor, Supply). Franchise award date: May 26, 1980. Franchise expiration date: January 1, 2010. Began: October 1, 1982.

Channel capacity: N.A. Channels available but not in use: N.A.

Digital Basic Service

Subscribers: 25,000.

Programming (via satellite): A&E HD; A&E Networks; ABC Family Channel; ABC Family HD; AMC; AMC HD; AmericanLife TV Network; Animal Planet HD; BBC America; BET Networks; Bio; Bio HD; Boomerang; Bravo HD; BTN; Cartoon Network; Chiller; CNBC; CNBC HD+; CNN HD; Comedy Central; Cooking Channel; Country Music TV; Crime & Investigation Network; C-SPAN; C-SPAN 2; Daystar TV Network; Discovery Channel; Discovery Channel HD; Discovery Fit & Health; Discovery Health Channel; Discovery Kids Channel; Disney Channel; Disney Channel HD; Disney XD; DIY Network; E! Entertainment Television; E! Entertainment Television HD; ESPN; ESPN 2; ESPN 2 HD; ESPN Classic Sports; ESPN HD; ESPN U; ESPNews; ESPNews HD; ESPNU HD; Eternal Word TV Network; FamilyNet; Food Network HD; Fox Business Channel; Fox Business Channel HD; Fox College Sports Atlantic; Fox College Sports Central; Fox College Sports Pacific; Fox Movie Channel; Fox News HD; FX; FX HD; G4; GMC; Golf Channel; Great American Country; GSN; Hallmark Channel; Hallmark Movie Channel; Hallmark Movie Channel HD; HDNet; Headline News; HGTV HD; History Channel; History Channel HD; History Channel International; ID Investigation Discovery; INSP; Lifetime Movie Network; Lifetime Movie Network HD; Lifetime Television HD; Military Channel; Military History Channel; MLB Network HD; MSNBC; MTV; MTV Hits; MTV2; Music Choice; MyNetworkTV Inc.; National Geographic Channel; National Geographic Channel HD Network; Nick Jr.; Nickelodeon; NickToons TV; Outdoor Channel; Ovation; Oxygen; PBS HD; PBS Kids Sprout; Planet Green; QVC; RFD-TV; RTN; Science; Science HD; SoapNet; Speed; Speed HD; Spike TV; Spike TV HD; Superstation WGN; Syfy HD; TBS in HD; TeenNick; Tennis Channel; The Learning Channel; The Weather Channel HD; The Word Network; Travel Channel HD; truTV; Turner Classic Movies; Turner Classic Movies HD; Turner Network TV; Turner Network TV HD; TV Land; USA Network HD; Versus; Versus HD; VH1; VH1 Classic; WE tv.

Fee: $54.95 monthly.

Digital Expanded Basic Service

Subscribers: N.A.

Programming (via satellite): HD Theater; HDNet Movies; Smithsonian Channel HD; Universal HD.

Fee: $4.95 monthly.

Digital Pay Service 1

Pay Units: N.A.

Programming (via satellite): Cinemax (multiplexed); Cinemax HD; Encore (multiplexed); Flix; HBO (multiplexed); HBO HD; Showtime (multiplexed); Showtime HD; Starz (multiplexed); Starz HDTV; The Movie Channel (multiplexed).

Fee: $5.50 monthly (Encore), $11.95 monthly (Cinemax or Showtime/TMC/Flix), $12.95 monthly (Starz/Encore), $14.95 monthly (HBO).

Video-On-Demand: No

Pay-Per-View

Addressable homes: 14,730.

iN DEMAND; Club Jenna (delivered digitally); ESPN (delivered digitally); MLB Extra Innings (delivered digitally).

Internet Service

Operational: Yes.

Fee: $29.95-$39.95 monthly.

Telephone Service

None

Miles of Plant: 1,200.0 (coaxial); 5,784.0 (fiber optic).

Chief Executive Officer & General Manager: Allen Russ. Marketing Director: Jody Heustess. Cable Operations Manager: Brent Dirnson.

Ownership: Atlantic Telephone Membership Corp.

SHELBY—Time Warner Cable, 3140 W Arrowood Rd, Charlotte, NC 28273. Phone: 704-378-2500. Fax: 704-504-1997. Web Site: http://www.timewarnercable.com/carolinas. Also serves Belwood, Boiling Springs, Casar, Cleveland County, Earl, Fallston, Grover, Kings Mountain, Kingstown, Lattimore, Lawndale, Light Oak, Mooresboro, Patterson Springs, Polkville & Waco. ICA: NC0027.

TV Market Ranking: 42 (Kings Mountain, Kingstown, SHELBY); 42,46 (Cleveland County (portions), Grover, Patterson Springs); 46 (Boiling Springs, Earl, Lattimore, Light Oak, Mooresboro); Below 100 (Belwood, Casar, Fallston, Lawndale, Polkville, Waco, Cleveland County (portions)). Franchise award date: August 21, 1967. Franchise expiration date: N.A. Began: October 1, 1967.

Channel capacity: N.A. Channels available but not in use: N.A.

Basic Service

Subscribers: N.A. Included in Charlotte

Programming (received off-air): WAXN-TV (IND) Kannapolis; WBTV (CBS) Charlotte; WCCB (FOX) Charlotte; WCNC-TV (NBC) Charlotte; WGGS-TV (IND) Greenville; WHKY-TV (IND) Hickory; WJZY (CW) Belmont; WMYT-TV (MNT) Rock Hill; WNSC-TV (PBS) Rock Hill; WSOC-TV (ABC) Charlotte; WSPA-TV (CBS) Spartanburg; WTVI (PBS) Charlotte; WUNG-TV (PBS) Concord.

Programming (via satellite): TV Guide Network; WGN America.
Fee: $36.00 installation; $10.00 monthly; $2.88 converter; $18.00 additional installation.
Expanded Basic Service 1
Subscribers: N.A.
Programming (via satellite): A&E Networks; ABC Family Channel; AMC; Animal Planet; BET Networks; Bravo; Cartoon Network; CNBC; CNN; Comedy Central; Country Music TV; C-SPAN; C-SPAN 2; Discovery Channel; Discovery Health Channel; Disney Channel; E! Entertainment Television; ESPN; ESPN 2; ESPN Classic Sports; Food Network; Fox News Channel; Fox Sports South; FX; Golf Channel; Hallmark Channel; Headline News; HGTV; History Channel; Lifetime; Lifetime Movie Network; MSNBC; MTV; National Geographic Channel; Nickelodeon; Oxygen; QVC; Speed; Spike TV; SportSouth; Syfy; TBS Superstation; The Learning Channel; The Weather Channel; Travel Channel; truTV; Turner Classic Movies; Turner Network TV; TV Land; USA Network; Versus; VH1; WE tv.
Fee: $39.95 monthly.
Digital Basic Service
Subscribers: 6,967.
Programming (via satellite): AmericanLife TV Network; America's Store; BBC America; Bio; Black Family Channel; Bloomberg Television; Boomerang; Canales N; Cooking Channel; C-SPAN 3; Discovery Digital Networks; DIY Network; FamilyNet; Fox Sports World; FSN Digital Atlantic; FSN Digital Central; FSN Digital Pacific; Fuel TV; Fuse; G4; Great American Country; GSN; History Channel International; Independent Film Channel; Lifetime Real Women; MTV2; Music Choice; NBA TV; Nick Jr.; Outdoor Channel; Ovation; SoapNet; Style Network; Tennis Channel; Toon Disney; VH1 Classic.
Fee: $15.00 monthly.
Digital Pay Service 1
Pay Units: N.A.
Programming (via satellite): Cinemax (multiplexed); Deutsche Welle TV; Encore (multiplexed); Flix; Fox Movie Channel; HBO (multiplexed); RAI International; Saigon Broadcasting Television Network; Showtime (multiplexed); Starz (multiplexed); Sundance Channel; The Movie Channel (multiplexed); TV5, La Television International; Zee TV USA.
Fee: $9.95 monthly (Deutsche Welle, TV5 or RAI), $11.95 monthly (HBO, Cinemax, Showtime, TMC or Starz/Encore), $14.95 monthly (SBTN or Zee).
Video-On-Demand: Yes
Pay-Per-View
Addressable homes: 6,967.
iN DEMAND (delivered digitally); ESPN Now (delivered digitally); Adult PPV (delivered digitally); Sports PPV (delivered digitally); ESPN Full Court (delivered digitally); ESPN Gameplan (delivered digitally).
Internet Service
Operational: Yes.
Subscribers: 7,184.
Broadband Service: Road Runner, AOL, EarthLink.
Fee: $39.95 installation; $46.95 monthly.
Telephone Service
Digital: Operational
Fee: $39.95 monthly
Miles of plant (coax & fiber) included in Charlotte
President: Mike Munley. Vice President, Technical Operations: Mike Cullim. Vice President, Engineering: Richard Newcomb. Vice President, Marketing & Sales: Eric Franey. Public Affairs Director: Jessica Graham. Government Affairs Director: Michael Tanck.
Ownership: Time Warner Cable (MSO).; Advance/Newhouse Partnership (MSO).Day-to-day operations are managed by Time Warner Cable.

SIMPSON—Suddenlink Communications, 2120 W Arlington Blvd, Greenville, NC 27834-6487. Phone: 877-694-9474. Web Site: http://www.suddenlink.com. Also serves Grimesland & Pitt County (portions). ICA: NC0221.
TV Market Ranking: 84 (Grimesland, Pitt County (portions), SIMPSON). Franchise award date: N.A. Franchise expiration date: N.A. Began: N.A.
Channel capacity: 39 (operating 2-way). Channels available but not in use: N.A.
Basic Service
Subscribers: 828.
Programming (received off-air): WCTI-TV (ABC) New Bern; WEPX-TV (ION) Greenville; WNCT-TV (CBS, CW) Greenville; WRAL-TV (CBS) Raleigh; WTVD (ABC) Durham; WUNK-TV (PBS) Greenville; WYDO (FOX) Greenville.
Programming (via satellite): ABC Family Channel; INSP; The Weather Channel; Trinity Broadcasting Network.
Fee: $39.95 installation; $10.10 monthly; $1.86 converter.
Expanded Basic Service 1
Subscribers: 772.
Programming (via satellite): A&E Networks; AMC; Animal Planet; BET Networks; CNN; Country Music TV; C-SPAN; Discovery Channel; Disney Channel; ESPN; ESPN 2; Fox News Channel; Headline News; HGTV; MTV; Nickelodeon; QVC; Spike TV; Syfy; TBS Superstation; The Learning Channel; Turner Network TV; USA Network; VH1; WGN America.
Fee: $25.61 monthly.
Digital Basic Service
Subscribers: N.A.
Programming (via satellite): BBC America; Bravo; Discovery Digital Networks; ESPN Classic Sports; ESPNews; Fox Sports World; Golf Channel; GSN; History Channel International; Independent Film Channel; Music Choice; Nick Jr.; Versus; WE tv.
Fee: $11.00 monthly.
Pay Service 1
Pay Units: 108.
Programming (via satellite): HBO.
Fee: $14.99 monthly.
Digital Pay Service 1
Pay Units: N.A.
Programming (via satellite): Cinemax (multiplexed); Encore (multiplexed); HBO (multiplexed); Showtime (multiplexed); Starz (multiplexed).
Fee: $15.95 monthly (each).
Video-On-Demand: No
Pay-Per-View
Playboy TV (delivered digitally).
Internet Service
Operational: Yes.
Telephone Service
None
Miles of Plant: 48.0 (coaxial); None (fiber optic).
Ownership: Cequel Communications LLC (MSO).

SMITHFIELD—Johnston County Cable LP. Now served by SELMA/GARNER (formerly Garner), NC [NC0032]. ICA: NC0072.

SNOW HILL—MediaCast, 1121 SE 2nd St, PO Box 368, Snow Hill, NC 28580-0368. Phone: 252-747-5682. Fax: 252-747-3061. E-mail: dhancock@windstream.net. Also serves Greene County (portions), Hookerton, Lenoir County (portions), Maury, Pitt County (portions) & Walstonburg. ICA: NC0073.
TV Market Ranking: 84,73 (Greene County (portions), Hookerton, Lenoir County (portions), Maury, Pitt County (portions), SNOW HILL, Walstonburg). Franchise award date: N.A. Franchise expiration date: N.A. Began: October 1, 1983.
Channel capacity: 35 (not 2-way capable). Channels available but not in use: N.A.
Basic Service
Subscribers: 892.
Programming (received off-air): WCTI-TV (ABC) New Bern; WEPX-TV (ION) Greenville; WITN-TV (MNT, NBC) Washington; WLFL (CW) Raleigh; WNCT-TV (CBS, CW) Greenville; WRAL-TV (CBS) Raleigh; WTVD (ABC) Durham; WUNK-TV (PBS) Greenville; WYDO (FOX) Greenville.
Programming (via satellite): C-SPAN; WGN America.
Fee: $29.95 installation.
Expanded Basic Service 1
Subscribers: 824.
Programming (via satellite): ABC Family Channel; AMC; BET Networks; CNN; Discovery Channel; Disney Channel; ESPN; ESPN 2; Fox Sports South; FX; Headline News; INSP; Lifetime; MTV; Nickelodeon; SoapNet; Spike TV; TBS Superstation; The Weather Channel; Turner Network TV; USA Network.
Fee: $38.95 monthly.
Digital Basic Service
Subscribers: 389.
Programming (via satellite): BBC America; Bloomberg Television; Discovery Digital Networks; DMX Music; ESPN Classic Sports; ESPNews; Fox Movie Channel; G4; GAS; Golf Channel; GSN; Halogen Network; Lifetime Movie Network; MTV Networks Digital Suite; Nick Jr.; NickToons TV; Outdoor Channel; Speed; Style Network; Toon Disney; Trinity Broadcasting Network; Turner Classic Movies; Versus.
Digital Pay Service 1
Pay Units: 457.
Programming (via satellite): Cinemax (multiplexed); Encore; Flix; HBO (multiplexed); Showtime (multiplexed); Starz; The Movie Channel (multiplexed).
Video-On-Demand: No
Pay-Per-View
Shorteez (delivered digitally); Playboy TV (delivered digitally); Fresh (delivered digitally); iN DEMAND (delivered digitally).
Internet Service
Operational: No.
Telephone Service
None
Miles of Plant: 232.0 (coaxial); None (fiber optic).
General Manager: Mark Bookout. Chief Technician: Bobby Thurman. Office Manager: Michelle Price.
Ownership: Dale-Media Inc.

SOUTHERN PINES—Time Warner Cable, 6202 Raeford Rd, Fayetteville, NC 28304. Phones: 919-573-7000 (Morrisville office); 910-401-5001. Fax: 910-864-8878. Web Site: http://www.timewarnercable.com/carolinas. Also serves Aberdeen, Beacon Ridge, Carthage, Foxfire Village, Moore County (portions), Pinebluff, Pinehurst, Pinewild, Seven Lakes, Taylortown & West End. ICA: NC0048.
TV Market Ranking: 73 (Aberdeen, Beacon Ridge, Moore County (portions), Pinebluff, Pinehurst, Pinewild, SOUTHERN PINES, Taylortown); Below 100 (Moore County (portions)); Outside TV Markets (Carthage, Foxfire Village, Seven Lakes, West End, Moore County (portions)). Franchise award date: N.A. Franchise expiration date: December 14, 2014. Began: August 1, 1972.
Channel capacity: N.A. Channels available but not in use: N.A.
Basic Service
Subscribers: 13,050.
Programming (received off-air): WECT (NBC) Wilmington; WFPX-TV (ION) Fayetteville; WLFL (CW) Raleigh; WNCN (NBC) Goldsboro; WRAL-TV (CBS) Raleigh; WRAZ (FOX) Raleigh; WRDC (MNT) Durham; WTVD (ABC) Durham; WUNU (PBS) Lumberton; WUVC-DT (UNV) Fayetteville; WYBE-CA (IND) Pinehurst.
Programming (via satellite): TBS Superstation; TV Guide Network.
Fee: $42.95 installation; $10.35 monthly.
Expanded Basic Service 1
Subscribers: N.A.
Programming (via satellite): A&E Networks; ABC Family Channel; AMC; Animal Planet; BET Networks; Cartoon Network; CNBC; CNN; Comedy Central; Country Music TV; C-SPAN; Discovery Channel; Disney Channel; E! Entertainment Television; ESPN; ESPN 2; ESPN Classic Sports; Food Network; Fox News Channel; Fox Sports South; FX; Golf Channel; Headline News; HGTV; History Channel; Lifetime; MSNBC; MTV; National Geographic Channel; Nickelodeon; Oxygen; QVC; SoapNet; Spike TV; Syfy; The Learning Channel; The Weather Channel; Travel Channel; Trinity Broadcasting Network; truTV; Turner Classic Movies; Turner Network TV; TV Land; USA Network; VH1; WE tv.
Fee: $39.50 monthly.
Digital Basic Service
Subscribers: 2,500.
Programming (via satellite): America's Store; BBC America; Black Family Channel; Bloomberg Television; C-SPAN 3; Discovery Digital Networks; Disney Channel; ESPNews; Fox Sports Net; Fox Sports World; G4; Great American Country; GSN; Independent Film Channel; Lifetime Movie Network; MTV2; MuchMusic Network; Music Choice; Nick Jr.; Outdoor Channel; Ovation; Speed; Style Network; Toon Disney; VH1 Classic.
Fee: $16.25 monthly.
Digital Pay Service 1
Pay Units: N.A.
Programming (via satellite): Cinemax; Encore; Flix; Fox Movie Channel; HBO; Showtime; Starz; Sundance Channel; The Movie Channel.
Fee: $11.95 monthly (each).
Video-On-Demand: Yes
Pay-Per-View
ESPN Now (delivered digitally); Pleasure (delivered digitally); Hot Choice (delivered digitally), Addressable: No; Playboy TV delivered digitally (delivered digitally); Spice delivered digitally (delivered digitally); Spice2 delivered digitally (delivered digitally).
Internet Service
Operational: Yes.
Broadband Service: Road Runner.
Fee: $99.95 installation; $44.95 monthly.
Telephone Service
Digital: Operational
Fee: $44.95 monthly
Miles of Plant: 468.0 (coaxial); None (fiber optic). Additional miles planned: 10.0 (coaxial).

Vice President & General Manager: Chris Whitaker. President, Residential Services: Brian Kelly. Vice President, Technical Operations: Gary Frederick. Vice President, Government & Public Affairs: Brad Phillips. Vice President, Sales & Marketing: Tom Smith. Chief Technician: Fred Kirk. Public Affairs Director: Eric Collins.

Ownership: Time Warner Cable (MSO).; Advance/Newhouse Partnership (MSO).Day-to-day operations are managed by Time Warner Cable.

SPARTA—Alleghany Cablevision Inc., 17 N Main St, PO Box 429, Sparta, NC 28675. Phone: 336-372-5801. Fax: 336-372-5801. E-mail: alleghanycablevision@yahoo.com. ICA: NC0152.

TV Market Ranking: Outside TV Markets (SPARTA). Franchise award date: March 1, 1990. Franchise expiration date: N.A. Began: August 1, 1990.

Channel capacity: 54 (not 2-way capable). Channels available but not in use: N.A.

Basic Service

Subscribers: 672.

Programming (received off-air): WBTV (CBS) Charlotte; WCCB (FOX) Charlotte; WJZY (CW) Belmont; WSOC-TV (ABC) Charlotte; WUNL-TV (PBS) Winston-Salem; WXII-TV (NBC) Winston-Salem.

Programming (via satellite): A&E Networks; ABC Family Channel; CNN; Comedy Central; Country Music TV; C-SPAN; Discovery Channel; Disney Channel; ESPN; Headline News; INSP; Lifetime; MTV; Nickelodeon; QVC; TBS Superstation; The Learning Channel; Turner Network TV; USA Network; VH1; WGN America.

Fee: $25.00 installation; $39.95 monthly.

Pay Service 1

Pay Units: 19.

Programming (via satellite): Cinemax.

Fee: $8.95 monthly.

Pay Service 2

Pay Units: 14.

Programming (via satellite): HBO.

Fee: $10.95 monthly.

Pay Service 3

Pay Units: 15.

Programming (via satellite): Showtime.

Fee: $5.95 monthly.

Video-On-Demand: No

Internet Service

Operational: No.

Telephone Service

None

Miles of Plant: 70.0 (coaxial); None (fiber optic).

Manager: George Sheets. Chief Technician: Steve Rose. Office Manager: Jennie Andrews.

Ownership: Alleghany Cablevision Inc.

SPRING HOPE—Time Warner Cable, 101 Innovation Ave, Ste 100, Morrisville, NC 27560. Phone: 919-573-7000. Web Site: http://www.timewarnercable.com/carolinas. Also serves Momeyer. ICA: NC0122.

TV Market Ranking: 73 (Momeyer, SPRING HOPE). Franchise award date: October 15, 1985. Franchise expiration date: N.A. Began: January 1, 1985.

Channel capacity: 42 (not 2-way capable). Channels available but not in use: N.A.

Basic Service

Subscribers: 717.

Programming (received off-air): WLFL (CW) Raleigh; WNCN (NBC) Goldsboro; WNCT-TV (CBS, CW) Greenville; WRAL-TV (CBS) Raleigh; WRAY-TV (IND) Wilson; WRAZ (FOX) Raleigh; WRDC (MNT) Durham; WRPX-TV (ION) Rocky Mount; WTVD (ABC) Durham; WUNK-TV (PBS) Greenville.

Programming (via satellite): QVC.

Fee: $39.95 installation; $15.14 monthly; $2.00 converter.

Expanded Basic Service 1

Subscribers: 683.

Programming (via satellite): ABC Family Channel; AMC; Animal Planet; BET Networks; CNN; Comedy Central; Country Music TV; C-SPAN; Discovery Channel; Disney Channel; ESPN; ESPN 2; Fox News Channel; Headline News; Lifetime; MSNBC; MTV; Nickelodeon; Spike TV; Syfy; TBS Superstation; The Learning Channel; The Weather Channel; Trinity Broadcasting Network; Turner Network TV; USA Network; VH1; WGN America.

Fee: $19.69 monthly.

Digital Basic Service

Subscribers: N.A.

Programming (via satellite): BBC America; Bravo; Discovery Digital Networks; ESPN Classic Sports; ESPNews; Fox Soccer; Golf Channel; GSN; HGTV; History Channel; Independent Film Channel; Music Choice; Nick Jr.; Versus; WE tv.

Fee: $11.00 monthly.

Pay Service 1

Pay Units: N.A.

Programming (via satellite): HBO.

Fee: $14.99 monthly.

Digital Pay Service 1

Pay Units: N.A.

Programming (via satellite): Cinemax (multiplexed); Encore (multiplexed); HBO (multiplexed); Showtime (multiplexed); Starz (multiplexed); The Movie Channel (multiplexed).

Fee: $15.95 monthly (each).

Video-On-Demand: No

Pay-Per-View

Playboy TV (delivered digitally); Movies (delivered digitally).

Internet Service

Operational: Yes.

Fee: $24.95 monthly.

Telephone Service

Digital: Operational

Fee: $24.99 monthly

Miles of Plant: 81.0 (coaxial); None (fiber optic).

Vice President & General Manager: Chris Whitaker. Vice President, Sales & Marketing: Tom Smith. Vice President, Government & Public Affairs: Brad Phillips. Technical Operations Director: Doug Davis. Customer Care Director: Kelly Robel.

Ownership: Time Warner Cable (MSO).

STATESVILLE—Formerly served by Adelphia Communications. No longer in operation. ICA: NC0035.

STATESVILLE—Time Warner Cable, 3140 W Arrowood Rd, Charlotte, NC 28273. Phone: 704-378-2500. Fax: 704-504-1997. Web Site: http://www.timewarnercable.com/carolinas. Also serves Iredell County (portions) & Troutman. ICA: NC0252.

TV Market Ranking: Below 100 (Iredell County (portions) (portions), STATESVILLE, Troutman); Outside TV Markets (Iredell County (portions) (portions)).

Channel capacity: N.A. Channels available but not in use: N.A.

Basic Service

Subscribers: N.A.

Programming (received off-air): WAXN-TV (IND) Kannapolis; WBTV (CBS) Charlotte; WCCB (FOX) Charlotte; WCNC-TV (NBC) Charlotte; WHKY-TV (IND) Hickory; WJZY (CW) Belmont; WMYT-TV (MNT) Rock Hill; WSOC-TV (ABC) Charlotte; WTVI (PBS) Charlotte; WUNG-TV (PBS) Concord.

Programming (via satellite): C-SPAN; INSP; News 14 Carolina; QVC; ShopNBC; TV Guide Network; WGN America.

Fee: $36.00 installation; $10.00 monthly.

Expanded Basic Service 1

Subscribers: N.A.

Programming (via satellite): A&E Networks; ABC Family Channel; AMC; Animal Planet; BET Networks; Cartoon Network; CNBC; CNN; Comedy Central; Country Music TV; C-SPAN 2; Discovery Channel; Disney Channel; E! Entertainment Television; ESPN; ESPN 2; Food Network; Fox News Channel; Fox Sports South; FX; Hallmark Channel; Headline News; HGTV; History Channel; ION Television; Lifetime; MSNBC; MTV; Nickelodeon; Speed; Spike TV; Syfy; TBS Superstation; The Learning Channel; The Weather Channel; Travel Channel; truTV; Turner Network TV; TV Land; USA Network; VH1.

Digital Basic Service

Subscribers: N.A.

Programming (via satellite): American-Life TV Network; BBC America; Bloomberg Television; Bravo; Cine Latino; Cine Mexicano; CMT Pure Country; CNN en Espanol; Discovery Channel HD; Discovery en Espanol; Discovery Fit & Health; Discovery Health Channel; Discovery Home Channel; Discovery Kids Channel; Discovery Times Channel; ESPN 2 HD; ESPN Classic Sports; ESPN HD; ESPNews; Fox Deportes; Fox Movie Channel; Fox Soccer; G4; Golf Channel; GSN; Halogen Network; HDNet; HDNet Movies; History Channel en Espanol; INHD; La Familia Network; Latin Television (LTV); Military Channel; Music Choice; National Geographic Channel; Nick Jr.; NickToons TV; Outdoor Channel; Puma TV; Science; Telemundo; Toon Disney en Espanol; Tr3s; Trinity Broadcasting Network; TV Chile; Versus; VH1 Classic; WE tv.

Digital Pay Service 1

Pay Units: N.A.

Programming (via satellite): Cinemax (multiplexed); Encore (multiplexed); HBO (multiplexed); HBO HD; Showtime (multiplexed); Showtime HD; Starz (multiplexed); Starz HDTV; The Movie Channel (multiplexed).

Video-On-Demand: Yes

Pay-Per-View

iN DEMAND (delivered digitally); Playboy TV (delivered digitally); Fresh (delivered digitally); Hot Choice (delivered digitally).

Internet Service

Operational: Yes.

Broadband Service: Road Runner.

Fee: $39.95 installation; $46.95 monthly.

Telephone Service

Digital: Operational

Fee: $39.95 monthly

President: Mike Munley. Vice President, Technical Operations: Mike Cullim. Vice President, Engineering: Richard Newcomb. Vice President, Sales & Marketing: Eric Franey. Public Affairs Director: Jessica Graham. Government Affairs Director: Michael Tanck.

Ownership: Time Warner Cable (MSO).

SUNSET HARBOR—Tele-Media. Now served by SHALLOTTE, NC [NC0050]. ICA: NC0245.

SUPPLY—Tele-Media. Now served by SHALLOTTE, NC [NC0050]. ICA: NC0243.

SYLVA—Mediacom. Now served by FRANKLIN/SYLVA (formerly Franklin), NC [NC0087]. ICA: NC0078.

TROY—Charter Communications, 2516 Fayetteville St, Sanford, NC 27332. Phone: 919-708-5902. Fax: 919-708-6126. Web Site: http://www.charter.com. ICA: NC0248.

TV Market Ranking: Outside TV Markets (TROY).

Channel capacity: N.A. Channels available but not in use: N.A.

Basic Service

Subscribers: N.A.

Programming (received off-air): WCCB (FOX) Charlotte; WCNC-TV (NBC) Charlotte; WFMY-TV (CBS) Greensboro; WGHP (FOX, IND) High Point; WGPX-TV (ION) Burlington; WMYV (MNT) Greensboro; WSOC-TV (ABC) Charlotte; WTVI (PBS) Charlotte; WUNC-TV (PBS) Chapel Hill; WXII-TV (NBC) Winston-Salem; WXLV-TV (ABC) Winston-Salem.

Programming (via satellite): C-SPAN; QVC; WGN America.

Expanded Basic Service 1

Subscribers: N.A.

Programming (via satellite): A&E Networks; ABC Family Channel; AMC; BET Networks; Bravo; Cartoon Network; CNBC; CNN; Comedy Central; Country Music TV; Discovery Channel; Disney Channel; E! Entertainment Television; ESPN; ESPN 2; Food Network; Fox News Channel; Fox Sports South; FX; G4; Golf Channel; Headline News; HGTV; History Channel; INSP; Lifetime; MSNBC; MTV; Nickelodeon; Oxygen; Speed; Spike TV; Syfy; TBS Superstation; Telemundo; The Learning Channel; The Weather Channel; Turner Classic Movies; Turner Network TV; TV Land; USA Network; VH1.

Digital Basic Service

Subscribers: N.A.

Programming (via satellite): BBC America; Bio; Bloomberg Television; Discovery Fit & Health; DIY Network; ESPN Classic Sports; ESPNews; Fox College Sports Atlantic; Fox College Sports Central; Fox College Sports Pacific; Fox Movie Channel; Fox Soccer; Fuse; GAS; GSN; History Channel International; Independent Film Channel; Lifetime Movie Network; MTV Networks Digital Suite; Music Choice; National Geographic Channel; Nick Jr.; Nick Too; NickToons TV; SoapNet; Style Network; Sundance Channel; Toon Disney; TV Guide Interactive Inc.; WE tv.

Digital Pay Service 1
Pay Units: N.A.
Programming (via satellite): Cinemax (multiplexed); Encore; Flix; HBO (multiplexed); Showtime (multiplexed); Starz (multiplexed); The Movie Channel (multiplexed).
Video-On-Demand: No
Pay-Per-View
iN DEMAND (delivered digitally); Playboy TV (delivered digitally); Fresh (delivered digitally).
Internet Service
Operational: No.
Telephone Service
None
Miles of plant included in Buies Creek
Vice President & General Manager: Anthony Pope. Marketing Director: Brooke Sinclair. Marketing Manager: Larissa Scales. Office Manager: Brenda Brinson. Operations Manager: Doug Underwood.
Ownership: Charter Communications Inc. (MSO).

TRYON—Charter Communications. Now served by GREENVILLE/SPARTANBURG, SC [SC0003]. ICA: NC0211.

VASS—Charter Communications. Now served by BUIES CREEK, NC [NC0194]. ICA: NC0222.

WADESBORO—Time Warner Cable, 3140 W Arrowood Rd, Charlotte, NC 28273. Phone: 704-378-2500. Fax: 704-504-1997. Web Site: http://www.timewarnercable.com/carolinas. Also serves Anson County, Ansonville, Ellerbe, Lilesville & Richmond County (unincorporated areas). ICA: NC0082.
TV Market Ranking: 42 (Anson County (portions)); Outside TV Markets (Ansonville, Ellerbe, Lilesville, Richmond County (unincorporated areas), WADESBORO, Anson County (portions)). Franchise award date: July 11, 1977. Franchise expiration date: N.A. Began: January 1, 1979.
Channel capacity: N.A. Channels available but not in use: N.A.
Basic Service
Subscribers: N.A. Included in Charlotte
Programming (received off-air): WAXN-TV (IND) Kannapolis; WBTV (CBS) Charlotte; WCCB (FOX) Charlotte; WCNC-TV (NBC) Charlotte; WIS (NBC) Columbia; WJZY (CW) Belmont; WMYT-TV (MNT) Rock Hill; WSOC-TV (ABC) Charlotte; WTVI (PBS) Charlotte; WUNG-TV (PBS) Concord.
Programming (via satellite): BET Networks; C-SPAN; Lifetime; ShopNBC; TBS Superstation; TV Guide Network; WGN America.
Fee: $36.00 installation; $8.50 monthly.
Expanded Basic Service 1
Subscribers: 2,223.
Programming (via satellite): A&E Networks; ABC Family Channel; AMC; Animal Planet; Bravo; Cartoon Network; CNBC; CNN; Comedy Central; Country Music TV; C-SPAN 2; Discovery Channel; Disney Channel; E! Entertainment Television; ESPN; ESPN 2; ESPN Classic Sports; Fox News Channel; Fox Sports Net; FX; Golf Channel; Headline News; HGTV; History Channel; INSP; MSNBC; MTV; Nickelodeon; Oxygen; QVC; Speed; Spike TV; SportSouth; Syfy; The Learning Channel; The Weather Channel; Travel Channel; Trinity Broadcasting Network; truTV; Turner Classic Movies; Turner Network TV; TV Land; USA Network; VH1; WE tv.
Fee: $41.45 monthly.
Digital Basic Service
Subscribers: 842.
Programming (via satellite): AmericanLife TV Network; America's Store; BBC America; Black Family Channel; Bloomberg Television; Boomerang; Cooking Channel; C-SPAN 3; Discovery Fit & Health; DIY Network; DMX Music; Food Network; Fuse; G4; Great American Country; GSN; Independent Film Channel; Lifetime Movie Network; MTV2; National Geographic Channel; Nick Jr.; Ovation; SoapNet; Style Network; Toon Disney; VH1 Classic.
Fee: $15.00 monthly.
Digital Expanded Basic Service
Subscribers: N.A.
Programming (via satellite): ESPNews; Fox Sports World; FSN Digital Atlantic; FSN Digital Central; FSN Digital Pacific; Fuel TV; Outdoor Channel; Versus.
Fee: $2.00 monthly.
Digital Pay Service 1
Pay Units: 261.
Programming (via satellite): Cinemax (multiplexed); Encore (multiplexed); Flix; HBO (multiplexed); Showtime (multiplexed); Starz (multiplexed); Sundance Channel; The Movie Channel (multiplexed).
Fee: $11.50 monthly (Cinemax, HBO, Starz/Encore or Showtime/TMC/Flix).
Video-On-Demand: Yes
Pay-Per-View
Addressable homes: 842.
iN DEMAND (delivered digitally); Adult PPV (delivered digitally).
Internet Service
Operational: Yes.
Subscribers: 869.
Broadband Service: Road Runner, AOL, EarthLink.
Fee: $39.95 installation; $46.95 monthly.
Telephone Service
Digital: Operational
Fee: $39.95 monthly
Miles of plant (coax & fiber) included in Charlotte
President: Mike Munley. Vice President, Technical Operations: Mike Cullim. Vice President, Engineering: Richard Newcomb. Vice President, Marketing & Sales: Eric Franey. Public Affairs Director: Jessica Graham. Government Affairs Director: Michael Tanck.
Ownership: Time Warner Cable (MSO).; Advance/Newhouse Partnership (MSO).

WAGRAM—Formerly served by Wagram Cable TV. No longer in operation. ICA: NC0186.

WARSAW—Charter Communications. Now served by HOLLY RIDGE, NC [NC0069]. ICA: NC0151.

WASHINGTON—Suddenlink Communications, 910 Hackney Ave, Washington, NC 27889. Phones: 877-804-6501 (Customer service); 252-946-3308. Fax: 252-443-5932. Web Site: http://www.suddenlink.com. Also serves Beaufort County, Chocowinity, River Road & Washington Park. ICA: NC0057.
TV Market Ranking: 84 (Beaufort County, Chocowinity, River Road, WASHINGTON, Washington Park). Franchise award date: March 13, 1978. Franchise expiration date: July 12, 2008. Began: May 1, 1979.
Channel capacity: 61 (operating 2-way). Channels available but not in use: N.A.
Basic Service
Subscribers: 7,458.
Programming (received off-air): WCTI-TV (ABC) New Bern; WEPX-TV (ION) Greenville; WNCT-TV (CBS, CW) Greenville; WUNK-TV (PBS) Greenville; WYDO (FOX) Greenville; 1 FM.
Programming (via satellite): QVC; WGN America.
Fee: $18.21 installation; $20.75 monthly.
Expanded Basic Service 1
Subscribers: 6,533.
Programming (via satellite): A&E Networks; ABC Family Channel; AMC; Animal Planet; BET Networks; Cartoon Network; CNBC; CNN; Comedy Central; Country Music TV; C-SPAN; C-SPAN 2; Discovery Channel; Disney Channel; E! Entertainment Television; ESPN; ESPN 2; Food Network; Fox News Channel; Fox Sports South; FX; Golf Channel; Headline News; History Channel; Lifetime; MSNBC; MTV; Nickelodeon; Spike TV; Syfy; TBS Superstation; Telemundo; The Learning Channel; The Weather Channel; Travel Channel; Trinity Broadcasting Network; Turner Classic Movies; Turner Network TV; TV Guide Network; TV Land; USA Network; VH1; Weatherscan.
Fee: $3.15 monthly.
Digital Basic Service
Subscribers: N.A.
Programming (via satellite): AmericanLife TV Network; BBC America; Black Family Channel; Bloomberg Television; Daystar TV Network; Discovery Digital Networks; Encore Action; ESPN Classic Sports; ESPNews; Eternal Word TV Network; FamilyNet; Fox Sports World; Fuse; G4; GAS; GSN; Hallmark Channel; Halogen Network; Lifetime Movie Network; MTV Networks Digital Suite; Music Choice; NBA TV; Nick Jr.; NickToons TV; Outdoor Channel; SoapNet; Speed; Sundance Channel; Telelatino Network; The Word Network; Toon Disney; truTV; Versus.
Pay Service 1
Pay Units: 1,264.
Programming (via satellite): Cinemax.
Fee: $10.75 monthly.
Pay Service 2
Pay Units: 1,669.
Programming (via satellite): HBO (multiplexed).
Fee: $10.75 monthly.
Pay Service 3
Pay Units: 1,028.
Programming (via satellite): Showtime.
Fee: $9.75 monthly.
Digital Pay Service 1
Pay Units: N.A.
Programming (via satellite): Cinemax (multiplexed); HBO (multiplexed); Showtime (multiplexed); Starz (multiplexed); The Movie Channel (multiplexed).
Video-On-Demand: No
Pay-Per-View
iN DEMAND (delivered digitally); Playboy TV (delivered digitally); Fresh (delivered digitally); Shorteez (delivered digitally); Hot Choice (delivered digitally); ESPN (delivered digitally).
Internet Service
Operational: Yes. Began: January 1, 2001.
Broadband Service: Suddenlink High Speed Internet.
Fee: $100.00 installation; $39.95 monthly.
Telephone Service
Digital: Operational
Fee: $49.95 monthly
Miles of Plant: 286.0 (coaxial); 42.0 (fiber optic).
Manager & Chief Technician: Hugh Worsley.
Ownership: Cequel Communications LLC (MSO).

WAYNE COUNTY (northern portion)—Time Warner Cable, 101 Innovation Ave, Ste 100, Morrisville, NC 27560. Phone: 919-573-7000. Web Site: http://www.timewarnercable.com/carolinas. Also serves Eureka, Johnston County (portions) & Wilson County (portions). ICA: NC0227.
TV Market Ranking: 73 (Johnston County (portions), Wilson County (portions)); 73,84 (Eureka, WAYNE COUNTY (NORTHERN PORTION)). Franchise award date: N.A. Franchise expiration date: N.A. Began: December 30, 1993.
Channel capacity: 60 (not 2-way capable). Channels available but not in use: N.A.
Basic Service
Subscribers: 1,700.
Programming (received off-air): WLFL (CW) Raleigh; WNCN (NBC) Goldsboro; WNCT-TV (CBS, CW) Greenville; WRAL-TV (CBS) Raleigh; WRDC (MNT) Durham; WTVD (ABC) Durham; WUNK-TV (PBS) Greenville; WUVC-DT (UNV) Fayetteville.
Programming (via satellite): A&E Networks; ABC Family Channel; AMC; BET Networks; CNBC; CNN; Country Music TV; C-SPAN; Discovery Channel; Disney Channel; ESPN; ESPN 2; Headline News; Lifetime; MTV; Nickelodeon; QVC; Spike TV; Syfy; TBS Superstation; The Learning Channel; The Weather Channel; Trinity Broadcasting Network; Turner Network TV; USA Network; VH1; WGN America.
Fee: $39.95 installation; $37.17 monthly.
Pay Service 1
Pay Units: N.A.
Programming (via satellite): Cinemax; HBO; Showtime.
Fee: $9.95 monthly (Cinemax or Showtime), $10.95 monthly (HBO).
Video-On-Demand: No
Internet Service
Operational: No.
Telephone Service
None
Miles of Plant: 34.0 (coaxial); None (fiber optic).
Vice President & General Manager: Chris Whitaker. President, Residential Services: Brian Kelly. Vice President, Sales & Marketing: Tom Smith. Vice President, Government & Public Affairs: Brad Phillips. Technical Operations Director: Doug Davis. Customer Care Director: Kelly Robel.
Ownership: Time Warner Cable (MSO).

WAYNESVILLE—Carolina Mountain Cablevision Inc., 4930 Jonathan Creek Rd, Waynesville, NC 28785-8302. Phone: 828-926-2288 (Main Office). Fax: 828-377-0006. E-mail: cmc@cbvnol.com. Web Site: http://www.cbvnol.com. Also serves Canton (Cruso/Bethel), Clyde, Cruso, Haywood County (unincorporated areas), Ironduff, Jonathan Creek & Maggie Valley. ICA: NC0127.
TV Market Ranking: 46 (Cruso, Haywood County (unincorporated areas), Ironduff, Jonathan Creek, WAYNESVILLE). Franchise award date: N.A. Franchise expiration date: N.A. Began: May 15, 1990.
Channel capacity: 116 (not 2-way capable). Channels available but not in use: N.A.
Basic Service
Subscribers: 2,079.
Programming (received off-air): WHNS (FOX) Greenville; WLOS (ABC) Asheville; WSPA-TV (CBS) Spartanburg; WUNC-TV (PBS) Chapel Hill; WUNF-TV (PBS) Asheville; WYFF (NBC) Greenville.
Programming (via satellite): A&E Networks; ABC Family Channel; American Movie Classics; AmericanLife TV Net-

work; Animal Planet; Cartoon Network; CNBC; CNN; Comedy Central; Cooking Channel; Country Music TV; C-SPAN; C-SPAN 2; CW+; Discovery Channel; Disney Channel; DIY Network; E! Entertainment Television; ESPN; ESPN 2; ESPN Classic Sports; ESPN U; Eternal Word TV Network; Food Network; Fox News Channel; FX; Great American Country; Hallmark Channel; Headline News; HGTV; History Channel; INSP; ION Television; Lifetime; MSNBC; MTV; MyNetworkTV Inc.; National Geographic Channel; Nickelodeon; Outdoor Channel; QVC; RFD-TV; ShopNBC; SoapNet; Spike TV; SportSouth; Syfy; TBS Superstation; The Learning Channel; The Weather Channel; Travel Channel; Trinity Broadcasting Network; truTV; Turner Classic Movies; Turner Network TV; TV Guide Network; TV Land; USA Network; VH1; WGN America.

Fee: $39.00 installation; $46.39 monthly; $5.00 converter; $15.00 additional installation.

Digital Basic Service

Subscribers: 185.

Programming (via satellite): A&E HD; ABC Family HD; BBC America; Bio; Bloomberg Television; Bravo; cloo; CMT Pure Country; Current; Discovery Fit & Health; Discovery Health Channel; Discovery Kids Channel; Disney Channel HD; DMX Music; ESPN 2 HD; ESPN HD; ESPNews; ESPNews HD; ESPNU HD; Food Network HD; Fox Business Channel; Fox Movie Channel; Fox News HD; Fox Soccer; Fuse; G4; GMC; Golf Channel; GSN; Hallmark Movie Channel; Halogen Network; HGTV HD; History Channel HD; History Channel International; ID Investigation Discovery; Independent Film Channel; Lifetime Movie Network HD; Military Channel; MTV Hits; MTV Jams; MTV2; National Geographic Channel HD Network; Nick Jr.; NickToons TV; Outdoor Channel 2 HD; Planet Green; Science; Speed; TeenNick; Toon Disney; Travel Channel HD; Universal HD; Versus; VH1 Classic; VH1 Soul; WE tv; Weatherscan.

Fee: $39.00 installation; $13.00 monthly; $5.00 converter.

Digital Pay Service 1

Pay Units: N.A.

Programming (via satellite): Cinemax (multiplexed); Encore (multiplexed); Flix; HBO (multiplexed); Showtime (multiplexed); Starz (multiplexed); Starz HDTV; The Movie Channel (multiplexed).

Video-On-Demand: No

Pay-Per-View

Addressable homes: 345.

iN DEMAND (delivered digitally); Hot Choice (delivered digitally); Club Jenna (delivered digitally); Playboy TV (delivered digitally); Fresh (delivered digitally); Spice: Xcess (delivered digitally).

Internet Service

Operational: Yes.

Subscribers: 624.

Fee: $39.00 installation; $29.99-$79.99 monthly; $69.00 modem purchase.

Telephone Service

None

Miles of Plant: 379.0 (coaxial); 67.0 (fiber optic).

General Manager: John T. Dickson. Operations Manager: Bryan Hyder. Chief Technician: Terry Sersland.

Ownership: Carolina Mountain Cablevision Inc. (MSO).

WAYNESVILLE—Charter Communications, 1670 Hendersonville Rd, Asheville, NC 28803. Phone: 828-209-2200. Fax: 828-277-6150. Web Site: http://www.charter.com. Also serves Canton, Clyde, Haywood County, Hazelwood, Lake Junaluska, Maggie Valley & West Canton. ICA: NC0042.

TV Market Ranking: 46 (Canton, Clyde, Haywood County, Hazelwood, Lake Junaluska, Maggie Valley, WAYNESVILLE, West Canton). Franchise award date: January 1, 1962. Franchise expiration date: N.A. Began: August 1, 1963.

Channel capacity: N.A. Channels available but not in use: N.A.

Basic Service

Subscribers: 14,700.

Programming (received off-air): WGGS-TV (IND) Greenville; WHNS (FOX) Greenville; WLOS (ABC) Asheville; WMYA-TV (MNT) Anderson; WSPA-TV (CBS) Spartanburg; WUNF-TV (PBS) Asheville; WYCW (CW) Asheville; WYFF (NBC) Greenville.

Programming (via satellite): C-SPAN; C-SPAN 2; INSP; ION Television; Jewelry Television; QVC; TV Guide Network; WGN America.

Fee: $29.99 installation.

Expanded Basic Service 1

Subscribers: 12,380.

Programming (via satellite): A&E Networks; ABC Family Channel; AMC; Animal Planet; BET Networks; Bravo; Cartoon Network; CNBC; CNN; Comcast/Charter Sports Southeast (CSS); Comedy Central; Country Music TV; Discovery Channel; Disney Channel; E! Entertainment Television; ESPN; ESPN 2; Food Network; Fox News Channel; Fox Sports South; FX; G4; Golf Channel; GSN; Hallmark Channel; Headline News; HGTV; History Channel; Lifetime; MSNBC; MTV; National Geographic Channel; Nickelodeon; Oxygen; SoapNet; Speed; Spike TV; SportSouth; Style Network; Syfy; TBS Superstation; Telemundo; The Learning Channel; The Weather Channel; Toon Disney; Travel Channel; truTV; Turner Classic Movies; Turner Network TV; TV Land; Univision Studios; USA Network; Versus; VH1.

Fee: $47.99 monthly.

Digital Basic Service

Subscribers: N.A.

Programming (via satellite): BBC America; Bio; Bloomberg Television; Boomerang; CNN en Espanol; CNN International; Cooking Channel; Discovery Fit & Health; DIY Network; ESPN; ESPN Classic Sports; ESPNews; Eternal Word TV Network; Fox College Sports Atlantic; Fox College Sports Central; Fox College Sports Pacific; Fox Movie Channel; Fox Soccer; Fuel TV; GAS; HD Theater; HDNet; HDNet Movies; History Channel International; Independent Film Channel; Jewelry Television; Lifetime Movie Network; Lifetime Real Women; MTV Networks Digital Suite; Music Choice; NFL Network; Nick Jr.; Nick Too; NickToons TV; Outdoor Channel; ShopNBC; Sundance Channel; Tennis Channel; Trinity Broadcasting Network; Turner Network TV HD; TV Guide Interactive Inc.; Universal HD; WE tv.

Digital Pay Service 1

Pay Units: N.A.

Programming (via satellite): Cinemax (multiplexed); Cinemax HD; Encore (multiplexed); Flix; HBO (multiplexed); HBO HD; LOGO; Showtime (multiplexed); Showtime HD; Starz (multiplexed); The Movie Channel (multiplexed).

Video-On-Demand: Yes

Pay-Per-View

iN DEMAND (delivered digitally); ESPN (delivered digitally); Playboy TV (delivered digitally); Spice Live (delivered digitally); Spice Hot (delivered digitally).

Internet Service

Operational: Yes.

Broadband Service: Charter Pipeline.

Fee: $29.99 monthly.

Telephone Service

Digital: Operational

Fee: $29.99 monthly

Miles of Plant: 434.0 (coaxial); 105.0 (fiber optic).

Vice President & General Manager: Anthony Pope. Marketing Director: Brooke Sinclair. Sales & Marketing Manager: Karen Sims. Chief Technician: Dean McCracken. Operations Manager: Janet Cloyde.

Ownership: Charter Communications Inc. (MSO).

WEST JEFFERSON—Morris Broadband, 719 S Grove St, Hendersonville, SC 28792. Phones: 888-855-9036; 828-697-3600; 828-697-1371. Web Site: http://morrisbroadband.com. Also serves Ashe County, Beaver Creek, Jefferson, Lansing & Warrensville. ICA: NC0098.

TV Market Ranking: Below 100 (Ashe County (portions)); Outside TV Markets (Ashe County (portions), Beaver Creek, Jefferson, Lansing, Warrensville, WEST JEFFERSON). Franchise award date: N.A. Franchise expiration date: June 6, 2013. Began: March 1, 1966.

Channel capacity: N.A. Channels available but not in use: N.A.

Basic Service

Subscribers: 2,744.

Programming (received off-air): WBTV (CBS) Charlotte; WCCB (FOX) Charlotte; WCYB-TV (CW, NBC) Bristol; WGHP (FOX, IND) High Point; WJZY (CW) Belmont; WSOC-TV (ABC) Charlotte; WUNL-TV (PBS) Winston-Salem; WXII-TV (NBC) Winston-Salem; allband FM.

Programming (via satellite): TV Guide Network; WGN America.

Fee: $45.00 installation; $12.93 monthly; $1.00 converter; $20.00 additional installation.

Expanded Basic Service 1

Subscribers: N.A.

Programming (via satellite): A&E Networks; ABC Family Channel; AMC; Animal Planet; Bravo; Cartoon Network; CNBC; CNN; Comedy Central; Country Music TV; C-SPAN; C-SPAN 2; Discovery Channel; Disney Channel; E! Entertainment Television; ESPN; ESPN 2; Food Network; Fox News Channel; Fox Sports South; FX; Headline News; History Channel; INSP; Lifetime; MTV; Nickelodeon; Outdoor Channel; QVC; ShopNBC; Spike TV; Syfy; TBS Superstation; The Learning Channel; The Weather Channel; Travel Channel; Trinity Broadcasting Network; truTV; Turner Network TV; TV Land; USA Network; VH1; WE tv.

Fee: $35.02 monthly.

Digital Basic Service

Subscribers: N.A.

Programming (via satellite): AmericanLife TV Network; BBC America; Bio; Bloomberg Television; Discovery Digital Networks; Fox Movie Channel; Fox Soccer; Fuse; G4; GAS; Golf Channel; GSN; Halogen Network; History Channel International; Independent Film Channel; Lifetime Movie Network; Lime; MTV Networks Digital Suite; Music Choice; National Geographic Channel; Nick Jr.; NickToons TV; Science Television; Speed; Style Network; Turner Classic Movies; Versus; Weatherscan.

Digital Pay Service 1

Pay Units: N.A.

Programming (via satellite): Cinemax (multiplexed); Encore (multiplexed); Flix; HBO (multiplexed); Showtime (multiplexed); Starz (multiplexed); Sundance Channel; The Movie Channel (multiplexed).

Fee: $8.00 monthly (Starz/Encore), $9.95 monthly (Cinemax or Showtime/TMC/Flix/Sundance), $13.95 monthly (HBO).

Video-On-Demand: No

Internet Service

Operational: Yes.

Broadband Service: In-house.

Fee: $29.95-$59.95 monthly.

Telephone Service

Digital: Operational

Fee: $49.95 monthly

Miles of Plant: 115.0 (coaxial); None (fiber optic).

Chairman & Chief Executive Officer: William K. Morris III. Senior Vice President, Finance: Craig Mitchell. Senior Vice President & Chief Financial Officer: Steve K. Stone. Vice President: Susie Morris Baker.

Ownership: Morris Communications Co LLC (MSO).

WHITAKERS—Crystal Broadband Networks, PO Box 180336, Chicago, IL 60618. Phones: 630-206-0447; 877-319-0328. E-mail: sales@crystalbn.com. Web Site: http://www.crystalbn.com. Also serves Edgecombe County (portions) & Nash County (portions). ICA: NC0164.

TV Market Ranking: 84 (Edgecombe County (portions), Nash County (portions)); Below 100 (WHITAKERS, Edgecombe County (portions), Nash County (portions)). Franchise award date: June 1, 1985. Franchise expiration date: N.A. Began: November 1, 1985.

Channel capacity: 42 (not 2-way capable). Channels available but not in use: N.A.

Basic Service

Subscribers: 372.

Programming (received off-air): WLFL (CW) Raleigh; WNCN (NBC) Goldsboro; WNCT-TV (CBS, CW) Greenville; WRAL-TV (CBS) Raleigh; WRAY-TV (IND) Wilson; WRAZ (FOX) Raleigh; WRDC (MNT) Durham; WRPX-TV (ION) Rocky Mount; WTVD (ABC) Durham; WUNP-TV (PBS) Roanoke Rapids.

Fee: $39.95 installation; $15.65 monthly; $2.00 converter; $25.00 additional installation.

Expanded Basic Service 1
Subscribers: 348.
Programming (via satellite): A&E Networks; ABC Family Channel; AMC; BET Networks; CNN; Country Music TV; C-SPAN; Discovery Channel; Disney Channel; ESPN; ESPN 2; Headline News; HGTV; Lifetime; MSNBC; MTV; Nickelodeon; Spike TV; Syfy; TBS Superstation; Trinity Broadcasting Network; Turner Network TV; USA Network; VH1.
Fee: $22.45 monthly.
Digital Basic Service
Subscribers: N.A.
Programming (via satellite): Bravo; ESPN Classic Sports; History Channel International; Versus; WE tv.
Fee: $11.00 monthly.
Digital Pay Service 1
Pay Units: N.A.
Programming (via satellite): Cinemax (multiplexed); Encore (multiplexed); HBO (multiplexed); Showtime (multiplexed); Starz (multiplexed); The Movie Channel (multiplexed).
Fee: $15.95 monthly (each).
Video-On-Demand: No
Internet Service
Operational: No.
Telephone Service
None
Miles of Plant: 27.0 (coaxial); None (fiber optic).
Ownership: Crystal Broadband Networks (MSO).

WHITEVILLE—Time Warner Cable. Now served by ELIZABETHTOWN/WHITEVILLE, NC (formerly Bladenboro) [NC0071]. ICA: NC0088.

WILMINGTON—Formerly served by Microwave Communication Services. No longer in operation. ICA: NC0228.

WILMINGTON—Time Warner Cable, 101 Innovation Ave, Ste 100, Morrisville, NC 27560. Phones: 910-763-0004 (Wilmington office); 919-573-7000 (Morrisville office). Fax: 919-573-7042. Web Site: http://www.timewarnercable.com/carolinas. Also serves Bolling Spring Lakes, Burgaw, Castle Hayne, Caswell Beach, Holden Beach, Leland, Long Beach, Navassa, New Hanover County, Ocean Isle Beach, Pender County, Southport, St. Helena, Watha, Wrightsville Beach & Yaupon Beach. ICA: NC0007.
TV Market Ranking: Below 100 (Bolling Spring Lakes, Burgaw, Castle Hayne, Caswell Beach, Holden Beach, Leland, Long Beach, Navassa, New Hanover County, Ocean Isle Beach, Pender County, Southport, St. Helena, Watha, WILMINGTON, Wrightsville Beach, Yaupon Beach). Franchise award date: N.A. Franchise expiration date: September 7, 2008. Began: April 1, 1962.
Channel capacity: N.A. Channels available but not in use: N.A.
Basic Service
Subscribers: 169,500 Includes Bayboro, Cedar Island, Elizabethtown, Jacksonville, & Newport.
Programming (received off-air): WECT (NBC) Wilmington; WSFX-TV (FOX) Wilmington; WUNJ-TV (PBS) Wilmington; WWAY (ABC) Wilmington; allband FM.
Programming (via satellite): AMC; Animal Planet; Bravo; Cartoon Network; Comedy Central; Country Music TV; C-SPAN 2; CW+; Disney Channel; E! Entertainment Television; ESPN 2; ESPN Classic Sports; Eternal Word TV Network; Food Network; Fox News Channel; Fox Sports South; FX; Golf Channel; HGTV; History Channel; INSP; ION Television; Lifetime Movie Network; MSNBC; National Geographic Channel; Oxygen; ShopNBC; SoapNet; Speed; Syfy; TBS Superstation; Travel Channel; truTV; Turner Classic Movies; TV Guide Network; TV Land; Versus; WE tv; WGN America.
Fee: $35.00 installation; $8.10 monthly.
Expanded Basic Service 1
Subscribers: 56,645.
Programming (via satellite): A&E Networks; ABC Family Channel; BET Networks; CNBC; CNN; C-SPAN; Discovery Channel; ESPN; Hallmark Channel; Headline News; Lifetime; MTV; Nickelodeon; QVC; Spike TV; The Learning Channel; The Weather Channel; Trinity Broadcasting Network; Turner Network TV; USA Network; VH1.
Fee: $36.25 monthly.
Digital Basic Service
Subscribers: 97,500 Includes Elizabethtown, Jacksonville, & Newport.
Programming (via satellite): AmericanLife TV Network; America's Store; BBC America; Bio; Bloomberg Television; Cooking Channel; C-SPAN 3; Discovery Digital Networks; DIY Network; ESPNews; Fox Sports Net (multiplexed); Fuel TV; Fuse; G4; Great American Country; GSN; History Channel International; Independent Film Channel; INSP; Jewelry Television; Lifetime Real Women; MTV2; Music Choice; NBA TV; Nick Jr.; Outdoor Channel; Ovation; Style Network; Tennis Channel; The Word Network; Toon Disney; VH1 Classic; WAM! America's Kidz Network.
Fee: $6.95 monthly.
Digital Pay Service 1
Pay Units: 57,300.
Programming (via satellite): Cinemax (multiplexed); Encore; Flix (multiplexed); Fox Movie Channel; HBO (multiplexed); MoviePlex; Showtime (multiplexed); Sundance Channel; The Movie Channel.
Fee: $11.95 monthly (Starz, Cinemax or Showtime/TMC), $13.95 monthly (HBO).
Video-On-Demand: Yes
Pay-Per-View
Hot Choice (delivered digitally); Pleasure (delivered digitally); Fresh (delivered digitally); Shorteez (delivered digitally); Playboy TV (delivered digitally); iN DEMAND (delivered digitally).
Internet Service
Operational: Yes. Began: May 1, 2000.
Subscribers: 67,000.
Broadband Service: Road Runner.
Fee: $69.95 installation; $46.95 monthly.
Telephone Service
Digital: Operational
Fee: $44.95 monthly
Miles of Plant: 1,306.0 (coaxial); 226.0 (fiber optic). Additional miles planned: 57.0 (coaxial).
President: Tom Adams. Vice President, Technical Services: Gary Frederick. Vice President, Sales & Marketing: Tom Smith. General Manager: Kim Cannon. Government & Public Affairs Director: Marty Feurer.
Ownership: Time Warner Cable (MSO).; Advance/Newhouse Partnership (MSO).

WILSON—Time Warner Cable, 101 Innovation Ave, Ste 100, Morrisville, NC 27560. Phone: 919-573-7000. Web Site: http://www.timewarnercable.com/nc. Also serves Black Creek, Elm City, Saratoga & Stantonsburg. ICA: NC0026.
TV Market Ranking: 73,84 (Black Creek, Elm City, Saratoga, Stantonsburg, WILSON). Franchise award date: February 28, 1974. Franchise expiration date: N.A. Began: June 1, 1976.
Channel capacity: N.A. Channels available but not in use: N.A.
Basic Service
Subscribers: 15,931.
Programming (received off-air): WITN-TV (MNT, NBC) Washington; WLFL (CW) Raleigh; WNCN (NBC) Goldsboro; WNCT-TV (CBS, CW) Greenville; WRAL-TV (CBS) Raleigh; WRAY-TV (IND) Wilson; WRAZ (FOX) Raleigh; WRDC (MNT) Durham; WRPX-TV (ION) Rocky Mount; WTVD (ABC) Durham; WUNK-TV (PBS) Greenville; WUVC-DT (UNV) Fayetteville.
Programming (via satellite): ShopNBC; TBS Superstation; TV Guide Network; WGN America.
Fee: $42.95 installation; $12.50 monthly; $2.30 converter.
Expanded Basic Service 1
Subscribers: 15,000.
Programming (via satellite): A&E Networks; ABC Family Channel; AMC; Animal Planet; BET Networks; Bravo; Cartoon Network; CNBC; CNN; Comedy Central; Country Music TV; C-SPAN; C-SPAN 2; Discovery Channel; Discovery Fit & Health; Discovery Health Channel; Disney Channel; E! Entertainment Television; ESPN; ESPN 2; ESPN Classic Sports; Eternal Word TV Network; Food Network; Fox News Channel; Fox Sports Net; FX; Golf Channel; Hallmark Channel; Headline News; HGTV; History Channel; Lifetime; Lifetime Movie Network; MSNBC; MTV; National Geographic Channel; Nickelodeon; Oxygen; QVC; SoapNet; Spike TV; Syfy; The Learning Channel; The Weather Channel; Travel Channel; Trinity Broadcasting Network; truTV; Turner Classic Movies; Turner Network TV; TV Land; USA Network; Versus; VH1; WE tv.
Fee: $37.35 monthly.
Digital Basic Service
Subscribers: 3,000.
Programming (via satellite): AmericanLife TV Network; America's Store; BBC America; Bio; Bloomberg Television; Boomerang; Canales N; Cooking Channel; C-SPAN 3; Discovery Digital Networks; Disney Channel; DIY Network; ESPNews; Fox Sports World; FSN Digital Atlantic; FSN Digital Central; FSN Digital Pacific; Fuel TV; Fuse; G4; GAS; Great American Country; GSN; History Channel International; Independent Film Channel; Lifetime Real Women; MBC America; MTV Hits; MTV2; Music Choice; NBA TV; Nick Jr.; Outdoor Channel; Ovation; Speed; Style Network; Tennis Channel; Toon Disney; Trinity Broadcasting Network; VH1 Classic.
Fee: $16.25 monthly.
Digital Pay Service 1
Pay Units: 7,000.
Programming (via satellite): Cinemax (multiplexed); Encore (multiplexed); Flix; Fox Movie Channel; HBO (multiplexed); Independent Film Channel; Showtime (multiplexed); Starz (multiplexed); Sundance Channel; The Movie Channel (multiplexed).
Fee: $11.95 monthly (Cinemax, HBO, Showtime, Starz, or TMC).
Video-On-Demand: Yes
Pay-Per-View
iN DEMAND (delivered digitally); Playboy TV (delivered digitally); Pleasure (delivered digitally); Sports PPV (delivered digitally).
Internet Service
Operational: Yes.
Broadband Service: Road Runner.
Fee: $99.95 installation; $44.95 monthly.
Telephone Service
Digital: Operational
Fee: $44.95 monthly
Miles of Plant: 480.0 (coaxial); 22.0 (fiber optic).
Vice President & General Manager: Chris Whitaker. Vice President, Sales & Marketing: Tom Smith. Vice President, Government & Public Affairs: Brad Phillips. Technical Operations Director: Doug Davis. Customer Care Director: Kelly Robel.
Ownership: Time Warner Cable (MSO).; Advance/Newhouse Partnership (MSO).

WINDSOR—Mediacom. Now served by PLYMOUTH, NC [NC0085]. ICA: NC0111.

WINSTON-SALEM—Time Warner Cable. Now served by GREENSBORO, NC [NC0006]. ICA: NC0002.

NORTH DAKOTA

Total Systems: **72**
Total Communities Served: **220**
Franchises Not Yet Operating: **0**
Applications Pending: **0**
Communities with Applications: **0**
Number of Basic Subscribers: **188,103**
Number of Expanded Basic Subscribers: **23,948**
Number of Pay Units: **15,609**

Top 100 Markets Represented: Fargo-Valley City (98).

For a list of cable communities in this section, see the Cable Community Index located in the back of Cable Volume 2.
For explanation of terms used in cable system listings, see p. D-11.

ARVILLA—Midcontinent Communications, PO Box 5010, Sioux Falls, SD 57117. Phones: 800-456-0564; 605-229-1775. Fax: 605-229-0478. Web Site: http://www.midcocomm.com. ICA: ND0171.
TV Market Ranking: Below 100 (ARVILLA). Franchise award date: N.A. Franchise expiration date: N.A. Began: October 1, 1985.
Channel capacity: 10 (not 2-way capable). Channels available but not in use: N.A.
Basic Service
Subscribers: 7.
Programming (received off-air): KBRR (FOX) Thief River Falls; KGFE (PBS) Grand Forks; KVLY-TV (NBC) Fargo; KXJB-TV (CBS) Valley City; WDAZ-TV (ABC, CW) Devils Lake.
Programming (via satellite): ABC Family Channel; CNN; ESPN; TBS Superstation.
Fee: $31.91 installation; $18.29 monthly; $15.96 additional installation.
Pay Service 1
Pay Units: N.A.
Programming (via satellite): HBO.
Fee: $10.20 monthly.
Video-On-Demand: No
Internet Service
Operational: No.
Telephone Service
None
Miles of Plant: 1.0 (coaxial); None (fiber optic).
Manager: Butch Motenberg. Chief Technician: Jeff Wilde.
Ownership: Midcontinent Media Inc. (MSO).; Comcast Cable Communications Inc. (MSO).

BEACH—Midcontinent Communications, PO Box 5010, Sioux Falls, SD 57117. Phones: 800-456-0564; 605-229-1775. Fax: 605-229-0478. Web Site: http://www.midcocomm.com. ICA: ND0041.
TV Market Ranking: Outside TV Markets (BEACH). Franchise award date: April 7, 1986. Franchise expiration date: April 7, 2011. Began: December 20, 1979.
Channel capacity: 61 (not 2-way capable). Channels available but not in use: N.A.
Basic Service
Subscribers: 183.
Programming (received off-air): KDSE (PBS) Dickinson; KMGH-TV (ABC) Denver; KQCD-TV (NBC) Dickinson; KXGN-TV (CBS, NBC) Glendive; KXMA-TV (CBS) Dickinson; 1 FM.
Programming (via satellite): A&E Networks; ABC Family Channel; AMC; Animal Planet; Bravo; Cartoon Network; CNBC; CNN; Comedy Central; Country Music TV; C-SPAN; C-SPAN 2; Discovery Channel; Disney Channel; E! Entertainment Television; ESPN; ESPN 2; ESPN Classic Sports; Eternal Word TV Network; Food Network; Fox News Channel; FX; GSN; Hallmark Channel; Headline News; HGTV; History Channel; INSP; ION Television; Lifetime; MSNBC; MTV; Nickelodeon; Outdoor Channel; QVC; Speed; Spike TV; Syfy; TBS Superstation; The Learning Channel; The Weather Channel; Travel Channel; Trinity Broadcasting Network; Turner Classic Movies; Turner Network TV; TV Guide Network; TV Land; USA Network; VH1; WE tv; WGN America.
Fee: $50.00 installation; $23.55 monthly.
Pay Service 1
Pay Units: 46.
Programming (via satellite): HBO.
Fee: $20.00 installation; $12.00 monthly.
Video-On-Demand: No
Internet Service
Operational: No.
Telephone Service
None
Miles of Plant: 8.0 (coaxial); None (fiber optic).
Manager: Darrell Wrege. Marketing Director: Fred Jamieson. Customer Service Manager: Kathy Furhmann.
Ownership: Midcontinent Media Inc. (MSO).; Comcast Cable Communications Inc. (MSO).

BERTHOLD—SRT Communications. Now served by VELVA, ND [ND0059]. ICA: ND0100.

BEULAH—Midcontinent Communications, PO Box 5010, Sioux Falls, SD 57117. Phones: 800-456-0564; 605-229-1775. Fax: 605-229-0478. E-mail: darrell_wrege@mmi.net. Web Site: http://www.midcocomm.com. Also serves Center, Dodge, Gladstone, Glen Ullin, Golden Valley, Halliday, Hazen, Hebron, Killdeer, New Salem, Pick City, Richardton, Riverdale, Stanton, Turtle Lake, Underwood, Washburn, Wilton & Zap. ICA: ND0017.
TV Market Ranking: Below 100 (Center, Gladstone, Hebron, Killdeer, New Salem, Richardton, Wilton); Outside TV Markets (BEULAH, Dodge, Glen Ullin, Golden Valley, Halliday, Hazen, Pick City, Riverdale, Stanton, Turtle Lake, Underwood, Washburn, Zap). Franchise award date: December 23, 1986. Franchise expiration date: N.A. Began: June 1, 1978.
Channel capacity: 63 (2-way capable). Channels available but not in use: N.A.
Basic Service
Subscribers: 4,827.
Programming (received off-air): KBMY (ABC) Bismarck; KFYR-TV (NBC) Bismarck; KNDX (FOX) Bismarck; KSRE (PBS) Minot; KXMB-TV (CBS) Bismarck.
Programming (via satellite): A&E Networks; ABC Family Channel; CNN; C-SPAN; Discovery Channel; ESPN; Lifetime; MTV; Nickelodeon; QVC; Spike TV; TBS Superstation; The Weather Channel; Turner Network TV; TV Guide Network; USA Network; VH1; WGN America.
Fee: $25.00 installation; $38.95 monthly.
Expanded Basic Service 1
Subscribers: N.A.
Programming (via satellite): AMC; Animal Planet; Cartoon Network; CNBC; Comedy Central; Country Music TV; C-SPAN 2; Discovery Health Channel; Disney Channel; E! Entertainment Television; ESPN 2; ESPN Classic Sports; Eternal Word TV Network; Food Network; Fox News Channel; Fox Sports Net North; FX; Hallmark Channel; Headline News; HGTV; History Channel; INSP; MSNBC; NFL Network; Outdoor Channel; Speed; Syfy; The Learning Channel; Travel Channel; Turner Classic Movies; TV Land; Versus; WE tv.
Digital Basic Service
Subscribers: N.A.
Programming (via satellite): AmericanLife TV Network; BBC America; Bio; Boomerang; CBS Sports Network; Cooking Channel; C-SPAN 3; Current; Discovery Fit & Health; Discovery Health Channel; Discovery Home Channel; Discovery Kids Channel; Discovery Times Channel; DIY Network; DMX Music; ESPN Classic Sports; ESPNews; Fox College Sports Atlantic; Fox College Sports Central; Fox College Sports Pacific; Fox Soccer; G4; GAS; Golf Channel; GolTV; Great American Country; GSN; Halogen Network; History Channel International; Independent Film Channel; Lifetime Movie Network; MTV Networks Digital Suite; National Geographic Channel; NFL Network; Nick Jr.; Nick Too; NickToons TV; Outdoor Channel; Pentagon Channel; Science Television; Sundance Channel; Tennis Channel; Toon Disney; Trinity Broadcasting Network; Turner Classic Movies; TV One; TVG Network; Versus; WE tv.
Fee: $47.95 monthly.
Digital Pay Service 1
Pay Units: N.A.
Programming (via satellite): Canales N; Cinemax (multiplexed); Encore; HBO (multiplexed); Showtime (multiplexed); Starz (multiplexed); The Movie Channel (multiplexed).
Video-On-Demand: No
Internet Service
Operational: Yes.
Subscribers: 1,022.
Broadband Service: Midcontinent.
Fee: $35.00 installation; $19.95 monthly; $8.00 modem lease; $39.00 modem purchase.
Telephone Service
Digital: Operational
Fee: $18.00 monthly
Miles of Plant: 140.0 (coaxial); 16.0 (fiber optic).
Manager: Darrell Wrege. Marketing Director: Fred Jamieson. Customer Service Manager: Kathy Fuhrmann.
Ownership: Midcontinent Media Inc. (MSO).; Comcast Cable Communications Inc. (MSO).

BOWDON—Dakota Central Telecommunications. Formerly [ND0139]. This cable system has converted to IPTV, 630 Fifth St N, PO Box 299, Carrington, ND 58421. Phones: 800-771-0974; 701-652-3184. Fax: 701-674-8121. E-mail: customerservice@daktel.com. Web Site: http://www.daktel.com. ICA: ND5000.
TV Market Ranking: Outside TV Markets (Bowdon).
Channel capacity: N.A. Channels available but not in use: N.A.
Internet Service
Operational: Yes.
Telephone Service
Digital: Operational
Chief Executive Officer & General Manager: Keith Larson.

BOWDON—Dakota Central Telecommunications. This cable system has converted to IPTV. See Bowdon, ND [ND5000]. ICA: ND0139.

BOWMAN—Midcontinent Communications, PO Box 5010, Sioux Falls, SD 57117. Phones: 800-456-0564; 605-229-1775. Fax: 605-229-0478. Web Site: http://www.midcocomm.com. Also serves Hettinger, Reeder, Rhame & Scranton. ICA: ND0030.
TV Market Ranking: Outside TV Markets (BOWMAN, Hettinger, Reeder, Rhame, Scranton). Franchise award date: May 6, 1986. Franchise expiration date: May 6, 2011. Began: May 1, 1980.
Channel capacity: N.A. Channels available but not in use: N.A.
Basic Service
Subscribers: 1,482.
Programming (received off-air): KDSE (PBS) Dickinson; KHSD-TV (ABC) Lead; KIVV-TV (FOX) Lead; KQCD-TV (NBC) Dickinson; KXMA-TV (CBS) Dickinson.
Programming (via satellite): A&E Networks; ABC Family Channel; AMC; Animal Planet; Cartoon Network; CNBC; CNN; Country Music TV; C-SPAN; CW+; Discovery Channel; Disney Channel; ESPN; ESPN 2; Food Network; Fox News Channel; Fox Sports Net North; FX; Headline News; HGTV; History Channel; INSP; Lifetime; MTV; Nickelodeon; QVC; Spike TV; Syfy; TBS Superstation; The Learning Channel; The Weather Channel; Turner Network TV; TV Guide Network; TV Land; USA Network; VH1; WE tv; WGN America.
Fee: $50.00 installation; $26.50 monthly.

Digital Basic Service
Subscribers: N.A.
Programming (via satellite): 3 Angels Broadcasting Network; A&E HD; ABC Family HD; AMC HD; AmericanLife TV Network; Animal Planet HD; BBC America; Bio; Bloomberg Television; Boomerang; BTN; BTN HD; Canal Sur; CBS Sports Network; Centric; Cine Latino; Cine Mexicano; cloo; CMT Pure Country; CNN en Espanol; CNN HD; Cooking Channel; C-SPAN 2; C-SPAN 3; Current; Discovery Channel HD; Discovery en Espanol; Discovery Fit & Health; Discovery Health Channel; Disney Channel HD; Disney XD; DIY Network; ESPN 2 HD; ESPN Classic Sports; ESPN Deportes; ESPN HD; ESPN U; ESPNews; EWTN en Espanol; Food Network HD; Fox Business Channel; Fox College Sports Atlantic; Fox College Sports Central; Fox College Sports Pacific; Fox Deportes; Fox Movie Channel; Fox News HD; Fox Soccer; Fuse; FX HD; G4; Golf Channel; Golf Channel HD; GolTV; Great American Country; GSN; Hallmark Channel; Halogen Network; HD Theater; HGTV HD; History Channel en Espanol; History Channel HD; History Channel International; ID Investigation Discovery; Independent Film Channel; ION Life; JCTV; Lifetime; Military Channel; MLB Network; MLB Network HD; MTV Hits; MTV Jams; MTV2; mun2 television; Music Choice; National Geographic Channel; National Geographic Channel HD Network; NFL Network; NFL Network HD; NHL Network; Nick Jr.; Nick Too; NickToons TV; Outdoor Channel; Palladia; PBS Kids Sprout; Pentagon Channel; Planet Green; Qubo; ReelzChannel; RFD-TV; Science; Science HD; SoapNet; Speed HD; Spike TV HD; Style Network; Sundance Channel; Syfy HD; TBS in HD; TeenNick; Telemundo; Tennis Channel; The Hub; The Weather Channel HD; TLC HD; Toon Disney en Espanol; Tr3s; Trinity Broadcasting Network; Turner Classic Movies; Turner Network TV HD; TV One; TVE Internacional; TVG Network; Universal HD; USA Network HD; VeneMovies; Versus; Versus HD; VH1 Classic; WE tv.

Digital Pay Service 1
Pay Units: N.A.
Programming (via satellite): Cinemax (multiplexed); Cinemax HD; Encore (multiplexed); Flix; HBO (multiplexed); HBO HD; HBO Latino; Showtime (multiplexed); Showtime HD; Starz (multiplexed); Starz HDTV; The Movie Channel (multiplexed); The Movie Channel HD.

Video-On-Demand: No

Pay-Per-View
iN DEMAND (delivered digitally); MLS Direct Kick (delivered digitally); NBA League Pass (delivered digitally); NHL Center Ice (delivered digitally); MLB Extra Innings (delivered digitally).

Internet Service
Operational: Yes.
Fee: $35.00 installation; $19.95 monthly.

Telephone Service
Digital: Operational
Fee: $18.00 monthly

Miles of Plant: 36.0 (coaxial); None (fiber optic).
Manager: Darrell Wrege. Marketing Director: Trish McCann. Customer Service Manager: Kris Virggves.
Ownership: Midcontinent Media Inc. (MSO).; Comcast Cable Communications Inc. (MSO).

CARPIO—SRT Communications. Now served by VELVA, ND [ND0059]. ICA: ND0154.

CARRINGTON—Midcontinent Communications, PO Box 5010, Sioux Falls, SD 57117. Phones: 800-456-0564; 605-229-1775. Fax: 605-229-0478. E-mail: darrell_wrege@mmi.net. Web Site: http://www.midcocomm.com. Also serves Barlow & New Rockford. ICA: ND0015.
TV Market Ranking: Below 100 (New Rockford); Outside TV Markets (Barlow, CARRINGTON). Franchise award date: May 14, 1990. Franchise expiration date: N.A. Began: March 1, 1971.
Channel capacity: N.A. Channels available but not in use: N.A.

Basic Service
Subscribers: 1,283.
Programming (received off-air): KFYR-TV (NBC) Bismarck; KGFE (PBS) Grand Forks; KJRR (FOX) Jamestown; KVLY-TV (NBC) Fargo; KXJB-TV (CBS) Valley City; WDAZ-TV (ABC, CW) Devils Lake; allband FM.
Programming (via satellite): A&E Networks; ABC Family Channel; CNN; Country Music TV; C-SPAN; Discovery Channel; Disney Channel; ESPN; ESPN 2; FX; Lifetime; Nickelodeon; QVC; Spike TV; TBS Superstation; The Learning Channel; The Weather Channel; Turner Network TV; TV Guide Network; TV Land; USA Network; VH1; WGN America.
Fee: $25.00 installation; $38.95 monthly.

Digital Basic Service
Subscribers: N.A.
Programming (via satellite): AmericanLife TV Network; BBC America; Bio; Boomerang; CBS Sports Network; Cooking Channel; C-SPAN 3; Current; Discovery Fit & Health; Discovery Health Channel; Discovery Home Channel; Discovery Kids Channel; Discovery Times Channel; DIY Network; DMX Music; ESPN Classic Sports; ESPNews; Fox College Sports Atlantic; Fox College Sports Central; Fox College Sports Pacific; Fox Soccer; Fuse; G4; GAS; Golf Channel; GolTV; Great American Country; GSN; Halogen Network; History Channel International; Independent Film Channel; Lifetime Movie Network; MTV Networks Digital Suite; National Geographic Channel; NFL Network; Nick Jr.; Nick Too; NickToons TV; Outdoor Channel; Science Television; Style Network; Sundance Channel; Tennis Channel; Toon Disney; Trinity Broadcasting Network; Turner Classic Movies; TV One; TVG Network; Versus; WE tv.
Fee: $47.95 monthly.

Pay Service 1
Pay Units: 172.
Programming (via satellite): Showtime.
Fee: $20.00 installation; $10.95 monthly.

Pay Service 2
Pay Units: 96.
Programming (via satellite): HBO.
Fee: $20.00 installation; $10.95 monthly.

Pay Service 3
Pay Units: 149.
Programming (via satellite): The Movie Channel.
Fee: $20.00 installation; $10.95 monthly.

Digital Pay Service 1
Pay Units: N.A.
Programming (via satellite): Canales N; Cinemax; Encore; Flix; HBO (multiplexed); Showtime; Starz.

Video-On-Demand: No

Internet Service
Operational: Yes.
Broadband Service: MidcoNet.
Fee: $35.00 installation; $19.95 monthly; $8.00 modem lease; $39.00 modem purchase.

Telephone Service
Digital: Operational
Fee: $18.00 monthly

Miles of Plant: 27.0 (coaxial); None (fiber optic).
General Manager: Darrell Wrege. Marketing Director: Trish McCann. Customer Service Manager: Carol Haselhorst.
Ownership: Midcontinent Media Inc. (MSO).; Comcast Cable Communications Inc. (MSO).

CARSON—Formerly served by Northland Communications. No longer in operation. ICA: ND0104.

CASSELTON—Midcontinent Communications, PO Box 5010, Sioux Falls, SD 57117. Phones: 800-456-0564; 605-229-1775. Fax: 605-229-0478. E-mail: darrell_wrege@mmi.net. Web Site: http://www.midcocomm.com. Also serves Arthur, Buffalo, Harwood, Horace, Hunter, Leonard & Mapleton. ICA: ND0039.
TV Market Ranking: 98 (Arthur, Buffalo, CASSELTON, Harwood, Horace, Hunter, Leonard, Mapleton). Franchise award date: January 5, 1988. Franchise expiration date: January 5, 2011. Began: July 1, 1981.
Channel capacity: 39 (operating 2-way). Channels available but not in use: N.A.

Basic Service
Subscribers: 1,247.
Programming (received off-air): KCPM (MNT) Grand Forks; KFME (PBS) Fargo; KVLY-TV (NBC) Fargo; KVRR (FOX) Fargo; KXJB-TV (CBS) Valley City; WDAY-TV (ABC, CW) Fargo.
Programming (via satellite): CNBC; CNN; Country Music TV; C-SPAN 2; Eternal Word TV Network; Fox News Channel; FX; INSP; Lifetime; QVC; TBS Superstation; The Learning Channel; TV Guide Network; TV Land; VH1; WGN America.
Fee: $25.00 installation; $38.95 monthly.

Expanded Basic Service 1
Subscribers: N.A.
Programming (via satellite): A&E Networks; ABC Family Channel; AMC; Animal Planet; Bravo!; Cartoon Network; Comedy Central; C-SPAN; C-SPAN 2; Discovery Channel; Disney Channel; E! Entertainment Television; ESPN; ESPN 2; Food Network; Fox Sports Net North; Hallmark Channel; Headline News; HGTV; History Channel; Home Shopping Network; MSNBC; MTV; Nickelodeon; Oxygen; Speed; Spike TV; Syfy; The Weather Channel; This TV; Travel Channel; truTV; Turner Classic Movies; Turner Network TV; USA Network.

Digital Basic Service
Subscribers: N.A.
Programming (via satellite): 3 Angels Broadcasting Network; A&E HD; ABC Family HD; AMC HD; AmericanLife TV Network; Animal Planet HD; BBC America; Bio; Bloomberg Television; Boomerang; BTN; BTN HD; Canal Sur; CBS Sports Network; Centric; Cine Latino; Cine Mexicano; cloo; CMT Pure Country; CNN en Espanol; CNN HD; Cooking Channel; C-SPAN 3; Current; Discovery Channel HD; Discovery en Espanol; Discovery Fit & Health; Discovery Health Channel; Disney Channel HD; Disney XD; Disney XD en Espanol; DIY Network; ESPN 2 HD; ESPN Classic Sports; ESPN Deportes; ESPN HD; ESPN U; ESPNews; EWTN en Espanol; Food Network HD; Fox Business Channel; Fox College Sports Atlantic; Fox College Sports Central; Fox College Sports Pacific; Fox Deportes; Fox Movie Channel; Fox News HD; Fox Soccer; FSN HD; Fuse; FX HD; G4; Golf Channel; Golf Channel HD; GolTV; Great American Country; GSN; Halogen Network; HD Theater; HGTV HD; History Channel en Espanol; History Channel HD; History Channel International; ID Investigation Discovery; Independent Film Channel; ION Life; JCTV; Lifetime Movie Network; Military Channel; MLB Network; MLB Network HD; MTV Hits; MTV Jams; MTV2; mun2 television; Music Choice; National Geographic Channel; National Geographic Channel HD Network; NFL Network; NFL Network HD; NFL RedZone; NHL Network; Nick Jr.; Nick Too; NickToons TV; Outdoor Channel; Palladia; PBS Kids Sprout; Pentagon Channel; Planet Green; Qubo; ReelzChannel; RFD-TV; Science HD; Science Television; SoapNet; Speed HD; Spike TV HD; Style Network; Sundance Channel; Syfy HD; TBS in HD; TeenNick; Telemundo; Tennis Channel; The Hub; The Sportsman Channel; The Weather Channel HD; TLC HD; Tr3s; Trinity Broadcasting Network; Turner Classic Movies; Turner Network TV HD; TV One; TVE Internacional; TVG Network; Universal HD; USA Network HD; VeneMovies; Versus; Versus HD; VH1 Classic; WE tv.
Fee: $47.95 monthly.

Digital Pay Service 1
Pay Units: N.A.
Programming (via satellite): Cinemax (multiplexed); Cinemax HD; Encore (multiplexed); Flix; HBO (multiplexed); HBO HD; Showtime (multiplexed); Showtime HD; Starz (multiplexed); Starz HDTV; The Movie Channel (multiplexed); The Movie Channel HD.

Video-On-Demand: No

Internet Service
Operational: Yes.
Fee: $35.00 installation; $19.95 monthly.

Telephone Service
Digital: Operational
Fee: $18.00 monthly

Miles of Plant: 57.0 (coaxial); None (fiber optic).
Manager: Darrell Wrege. Marketing Director: Fred Jamieson. Customer Service Manager: Kathy Fuhrmann.
Ownership: Midcontinent Media Inc. (MSO).; Comcast Cable Communications Inc. (MSO).

CLEVELAND—Dakota Central Telecommunications. Formerly [ND0162]. This cable system has converted to IPTV, 630 Fifth St N, PO Box 299, Carrington, ND 58421. Phones: 800-771-0974; 701-652-3184. Fax: 701-674-8121. E-mail: customerservice@daktel.com. Web Site: http://www.daktel.com. ICA: ND5002.
TV Market Ranking: Below 100 (CLEVELAND).
Channel capacity: N.A. Channels available but not in use: N.A.

Internet Service
Operational: Yes.

Telephone Service
Digital: Operational

Chief Executive Officer & General Manager: Keith Larson.

CLEVELAND—Dakota Central Telecommunications. This cable system has converted to IPTV. See Cleveland, ND [ND5002]. ICA: ND0162.

COOPERSTOWN—Midcontinent Communications, PO Box 5010, Sioux Falls, SD 57117. Phones: 800-456-0564; 605-229-

1775. Fax: 605-229-0478. Web Site: http://www.midcocomm.com. Also serves Aneta, Binford, Hannaford, Hope, Kensal, Page & Wimbledon. ICA: ND0054.

TV Market Ranking: 98 (Hannaford, Hope, Page, Wimbledon); Below 100 (Kensal); Outside TV Markets (Aneta, Binford, COOPERSTOWN). Franchise award date: January 13, 1988. Franchise expiration date: January 13, 2011. Began: February 1, 1981.

Channel capacity: 44 (not 2-way capable). Channels available but not in use: N.A.

Basic Service

Subscribers: 800.

Programming (received off-air): KGFE (PBS) Grand Forks; KJRR (FOX) Jamestown; KVLY-TV (NBC) Fargo; KXJB-TV (CBS) Valley City; WDAZ-TV (ABC, CW) Devils Lake; 1 FM.

Programming (via satellite): A&E Networks; ABC Family Channel; AMC; Cartoon Network; CNBC; CNN; Country Music TV; C-SPAN; Discovery Channel; Disney Channel; ESPN; ESPN 2; ESPNews; Eternal Word TV Network; Fox Sports Net North; FX; Hallmark Channel; Headline News; HGTV; History Channel; INSP; Lifetime; NFL Network; Nickelodeon; QVC; Spike TV; TBS Superstation; The Learning Channel; The Weather Channel; Turner Network TV; TV Guide Network; TV Land; USA Network; VH1; WGN America.

Fee: $50.00 installation; $26.50 monthly.

Pay Service 1

Pay Units: 87.

Programming (via satellite): HBO.

Fee: $20.00 installation; $12.00 monthly.

Pay Service 2

Pay Units: 62.

Programming (via satellite): Showtime.

Fee: $11.00 monthly.

Pay Service 3

Pay Units: 40.

Programming (via satellite): The Movie Channel.

Fee: $11.00 monthly.

Video-On-Demand: No

Internet Service

Operational: No.

Telephone Service

None

Miles of Plant: 31.0 (coaxial); None (fiber optic).

Manager: Darrell Wrege. Marketing Director: Fred Jamieson. Customer Service Manager: Kathy Fuhrmann.

Ownership: Midcontinent Media Inc. (MSO).; Comcast Cable Communications Inc. (MSO).

DEVILS LAKE—Midcontinent Communications, PO Box 5010, Sioux Falls, SD 57117. Phones: 800-888-1300 (Customer service); 800-456-0564; 605-229-1775. Fax: 605-229-0478. Web Site: http://www.midcocomm.com. Also serves Cando, Edmore & Starkweather. ICA: ND0009.

TV Market Ranking: Below 100 (Cando, DEVILS LAKE, Edmore, Starkweather). Franchise award date: December 1, 1986. Franchise expiration date: N.A. Began: April 1, 1964.

Channel capacity: 61 (operating 2-way). Channels available but not in use: N.A.

Basic Service

Subscribers: 3,338.

Programming (received off-air): KGFE (PBS) Grand Forks; KNRR (FOX) Pembina; KVLY-TV (NBC) Fargo; KXJB-TV (CBS) Valley City; WDAZ-TV (ABC, CW) Devils Lake; 5 FMs.

Programming (via satellite): A&E Networks; ABC Family Channel; AMC; Animal Planet; Cartoon Network; CNBC; CNN; Comedy Central; Country Music TV; C-SPAN; C-SPAN 2; Discovery Channel; Discovery Fit & Health; Discovery Health Channel; Disney Channel; E! Entertainment Television; ESPN; ESPN 2; ESPN Classic Sports; ESPNews; Eternal Word TV Network; Food Network; Fox News Channel; Fox Sports Net North; FX; Headline News; HGTV; History Channel; INSP; ION Television; Lifetime; MSNBC; MTV; Nickelodeon; Outdoor Channel; QVC; Speed; Spike TV; Syfy; TBS Superstation; The Learning Channel; The Weather Channel; Travel Channel; truTV; Turner Classic Movies; Turner Network TV; TV Guide Network; TV Land; USA Network; Versus; VH1; WE tv; WGN America.

Fee: $50.00 installation; $38.95 monthly.

Digital Basic Service

Subscribers: 632.

Programming (via satellite): BBC America; Bio; Bravo; Discovery Digital Networks; DMX Music; Fox Movie Channel; Fox Sports World; Fuse; G4; GAS; Golf Channel; GSN; History Channel International; Independent Film Channel; Lifetime Movie Network; Lime; MTV Networks Digital Suite; Nick Jr.; NickToons TV; Style Network; Toon Disney; Trinity Broadcasting Network.

Digital Pay Service 1

Pay Units: N.A.

Programming (via satellite): Cinemax (multiplexed); Encore; Flix; HBO (multiplexed); Showtime (multiplexed); The Movie Channel (multiplexed).

Video-On-Demand: No

Pay-Per-View

iN DEMAND (delivered digitally).

Internet Service

Operational: Yes.

Subscribers: 697.

Broadband Service: MidcoNet.

Fee: $35.00 installation; $19.95 monthly.

Telephone Service

Digital: Operational

Fee: $18.00 monthly

Miles of Plant: 76.0 (coaxial); None (fiber optic).

Manager: Darrell Wrege. Marketing Director: Fred Jamieson. Customer Service Manager: Kathy Fuhrmann.

Ownership: Midcontinent Media Inc. (MSO).; Comcast Cable Communications Inc. (MSO).

DICKINSON—Consolidated Telecommunications Co., 507 S Main Ave, PO Box 1408, Dickinson, ND 58601. Phones: 800-795-0555; 888-225-5282; 701-483-4000. Fax: 701-483-0001. Web Site: http://www.ctctel.com. Also serves Regent & Taylor. ICA: ND0005.

TV Market Ranking: Below 100 (DICKINSON, Regent, Taylor). Franchise award date: N.A. Franchise expiration date: N.A. Began: January 1, 1965.

Channel capacity: N.A. Channels available but not in use: N.A.

Basic Service

Subscribers: 5,353.

Programming (received off-air): KDSE (PBS) Dickinson; KQCD-TV (NBC) Dickinson; KXMA-TV (CBS) Dickinson.

Programming (via satellite): ABC Family Channel; C-SPAN; ESPN; Eternal Word TV Network; KMGH-TV (ABC) Denver; QVC; TBS Superstation; The Weather Channel; TV Guide Network; VH1; WGN America.

Fee: $24.00 installation; $14.49 monthly; $2.69 converter.

Expanded Basic Service 1

Subscribers: 4,436.

Programming (via satellite): A&E Networks; AMC; Animal Planet; Cartoon Network; CNBC; CNN; Discovery Channel; Disney Channel; ESPN 2; Great American Country; Headline News; HGTV; History Channel; Lifetime; MTV; Nickelodeon; Oxygen; Speed; Spike TV; Syfy; The Learning Channel; Turner Network TV; TV Land; USA Network; Versus; WE tv.

Fee: $29.95 installation; $28.00 monthly.

Digital Basic Service

Subscribers: 1,200.

Programming (via satellite): BBC America; Bio; Bloomberg Television; Discovery Digital Networks; DIY Network; DMX Music; ESPN Classic Sports; G4; History Channel International; Independent Film Channel; Style Network; Toon Disney.

Fee: $24.00 installation; $14.00 monthly; $8.43 converter.

Digital Pay Service 1

Pay Units: 1,067.

Programming (via satellite): Cinemax (multiplexed); Encore; Flix; HBO (multiplexed); Showtime (multiplexed); Starz; The Movie Channel (multiplexed).

Fee: $10.50 monthly (each).

Video-On-Demand: Planned

Pay-Per-View

Addressable homes: 1,400.

iN DEMAND.

Internet Service

Operational: Yes.

Subscribers: 3,408.

Broadband Service: In-house.

Fee: $48.00 installation; $29.95-$79.90 monthly; $10.00 modem lease; $300.00 modem purchase.

Telephone Service

Analog: Operational

Subscribers: 4,498.

Fee: $26.50 monthly

Miles of Plant: 77.0 (coaxial); None (fiber optic).

General Manager: Paul Schuetzler. Plant Manager: Forrest Mikkelsen. Chief Technician: Doug Rummel. Public Relations Manager: Rhonda Dukart.

Ownership: Consolidated Telecom.

DUNN CENTER—Formerly served by Eagle Cablevision Inc. No longer in operation. ICA: ND0174.

EDGELEY—Dickey Rural Networks. Formerly [ND0182]. This cable system has converted to IPTV, 9628 Hwy 281, PO Box 69, Ellendale, ND 58436-0069. Phones: 877-559-4692; 701-344-5000. Fax: 701-344-4300. Web Site: http://www.drtel.net. ICA: ND5020.

Channel capacity: N.A. Channels available but not in use: N.A.

Pay Service 1

Pay Units: N.A.

Fee: $11.00 monthly (HBO), $14.95 monthly (Showtime/TMC).

Internet Service

Operational: Yes.

Fee: $59.95 monthly.

Telephone Service

Digital: Operational

Fee: monthly (installation; $15.75 monthly

General Manager: Jeff Wilson. Engineering Manager: James Byerley. Marketing Manager: Janell Hauck. Plant Manager: Kent Schimke.

EDGELEY—Dickey Rural Networks. This cable system has converted to IPTV. See Edgeley, ND [ND5020]. ICA: ND0182.

ELGIN—Formerly served by Northland Communications. No longer in operation. ICA: ND0183.

ELLENDALE—Dickey Rural Networks. Formerly served by Oakes, ND [ND0026]. This cable system has converted to IPTV, 9628 Hwy 281, PO Box 69, Ellendale, ND 58436-0069. Phones: 877-559-4692; 701-344-5000. Fax: 701-344-4300. Web Site: http://www.drtel.net. ICA: ND5021.

Channel capacity: N.A. Channels available but not in use: N.A.

Basic Service

Subscribers: N.A.

Fee: $27.95 monthly.

Expanded Basic Service 1

Subscribers: N.A.

Fee: $49.95 monthly.

Pay Service 1

Pay Units: N.A.

Fee: $11.00 monthly (HBO), $14.95 monthly (Showtime/TMC).

Internet Service

Operational: Yes.

Fee: $59.95 monthly.

Telephone Service

Digital: Operational

Fee: monthly (installation; $15.75 monthly

General Manager: Jeff Wilson. Manager, Engineering: James Byerley. Manager, Marketing: Janell Hauck. Plant Manager: Kent Schimke.

ENDERLIN—MLGC, 301 Dewey St, Enderlin, ND 58027. Phone: 701-437-3300. Fax: 701-437-3022. E-mail: mandl@mlgc.com. Web Site: http://www.mlgc.com. ICA: ND0222.

TV Market Ranking: 98 (ENDERLIN). Franchise award date: N.A. Franchise expiration date: N.A. Began: N.A.

Channel capacity: N.A. Channels available but not in use: N.A.

Basic Service

Subscribers: 301.

Programming (received off-air): KFME (PBS) Fargo; KVLY-TV (NBC) Fargo; KVRR (FOX) Fargo; KXJB-TV (CBS) Valley City; WDAY-TV (ABC, CW) Fargo.

Programming (via satellite): A&E Networks; ABC Family Channel; CNN; Country Music TV; Discovery Channel; Disney Channel; ESPN; ESPN 2; Fox Sports Net; History Channel; Nickelodeon; QVC; Spike TV; Syfy; TBS Superstation; The Weather Channel; Turner Network TV; USA Network; WGN America.

Fee: $40.00 installation; $12.00 monthly.

Pay Service 1
Pay Units: N.A.
Programming (via satellite): HBO.
Fee: $11.00 monthly.
Video-On-Demand: No
Internet Service
Operational: Yes.
Telephone Service
None
Manager: Tyler Kilde.
Ownership: MLGC (MSO).

ESMOND—Midcontinent Communications, PO Box 5010, Sioux Falls, SD 57117. Phones: 800-456-0564; 605-229-1775. Fax: 605-229-0478. Web Site: http://www.midcocomm.com. ICA: ND0132.
TV Market Ranking: Outside TV Markets (ESMOND). Franchise award date: April 15, 1988. Franchise expiration date: April 15, 2011. Began: October 1, 1982.
Channel capacity: 41 (not 2-way capable). Channels available but not in use: N.A.
Basic Service
Subscribers: 64.
Programming (received off-air): KMOT (NBC) Minot; KSRE (PBS) Minot; KXMC-TV (CBS) Minot; WDAZ-TV (ABC, CW) Devils Lake.
Programming (via satellite): A&E Networks; ABC Family Channel; AMC; Animal Planet; Cartoon Network; CNBC; CNN; Country Music TV; C-SPAN; Discovery Channel; Disney Channel; ESPN; ESPN 2; Fox Sports Net North; Headline News; HGTV; History Channel; INSP; Lifetime; Nickelodeon; QVC; Spike TV; Syfy; TBS Superstation; The Learning Channel; The Weather Channel; Turner Network TV; TV Land; USA Network; VH1; WE tv; WGN America.
Programming (via translator): KVLY-TV (NBC) Fargo.
Fee: $50.00 installation; $32.95 monthly.
Pay Service 1
Pay Units: 8.
Programming (via satellite): HBO.
Fee: $20.00 installation; $12.00 monthly.
Pay Service 2
Pay Units: N.A.
Programming (via satellite): Showtime; The Movie Channel.
Fee: $20.00 installation; $11.00 monthly (each).
Video-On-Demand: No
Internet Service
Operational: No.
Telephone Service
None
Miles of Plant: 2.0 (coaxial); None (fiber optic).
Manager: Darrell Wrege. Marketing Director: Trish McCann. Customer Service Manager: Carol Haselhorst.
Ownership: Midcontinent Media Inc. (MSO).; Comcast Cable Communications Inc. (MSO).

FARGO—Cable One, 1024 Page Dr, PO Box 10757, Fargo, ND 58103-2336. Phone: 701-280-0033. Fax: 701-461-7005. E-mail: sgeston@cableone.net. Web Site: http://www.cableone.net. Also serves Dilworth, Moorhead & Oakport, MN; Briarwood, Cass County (portions), Frontier, Prairie Rose, Reed, Reile's Acres, Riverside & West Fargo, ND. ICA: ND0001.
TV Market Ranking: 98 (Briarwood, Cass County (portions), Dilworth, FARGO, Frontier, Glyndon, Moorhead, Oakport, Prairie Rose, Reed, Reile's Acres, Riverside, West Fargo). Franchise award date: July 2, 1979. Franchise expiration date: November 15, 2020. Began: November 29, 1979.
Channel capacity: 80 (operating 2-way). Channels available but not in use: N.A.
Basic Service
Subscribers: 45,578.
Programming (received off-air): KCPM (MNT) Grand Forks; KFME (PBS) Fargo; KVLY-TV (NBC) Fargo; KVRR (FOX) Fargo; KXJB-TV (CBS) Valley City; WDAY-TV (ABC, CW) Fargo.
Programming (via satellite): C-SPAN; C-SPAN 2; QVC; TV Guide Network; WGN America.
Fee: $30.00 installation; $46.00 monthly; $1.75 converter; $30.00 additional installation.
Expanded Basic Service 1
Subscribers: N.A.
Programming (via satellite): A&E Networks; ABC Family Channel; AMC; Animal Planet; Bravo; Cartoon Network; CNBC; CNN; Comedy Central; Country Music TV; Discovery Channel; Disney Channel; E! Entertainment Television; ESPN; ESPN 2; Eternal Word TV Network; Food Network; Fox News Channel; Fox Sports Net Minnesota; FX; Hallmark Channel; Headline News; HGTV; History Channel; Home Shopping Network; INSP; Lifetime; MSNBC; MTV; Nickelodeon; Oxygen; Speed; Spike TV; Syfy; TBS Superstation; The Learning Channel; The Weather Channel; This TV; Travel Channel; truTV; Turner Classic Movies; Turner Network TV; TV Land; USA Network; VH1.
Digital Basic Service
Subscribers: 13,135.
Programming (via satellite): 3 Angels Broadcasting Network; A&E HD; ABC Family HD; AMC HD; AmericanLife TV Network; Animal Planet HD; BBC America; Bio; Bloomberg Television; Boomerang; BTN; BTN HD; Canal Sur; CBS Sports Network; Centric; Cine Latino; Cine Mexicano; cloo; CMT Pure Country; CNN en Espanol; CNN HD; Cooking Channel; C-SPAN 2; C-SPAN 3; Current; Discovery Channel HD; Discovery en Espanol; Discovery Fit & Health; Discovery Health Channel; Disney Channel HD; Disney XD; Disney XD en Espanol; DIY Network; ESPN 2 HD; ESPN Classic Sports; ESPN Deportes; ESPN HD; ESPN U; ESPNews; EWTN en Espanol; Food Network HD; Fox Business Channel; Fox College Sports Atlantic (multiplexed); Fox College Sports Central (multiplexed); Fox College Sports Pacific (multiplexed); Fox Deportes; Fox Movie Channel; Fox News HD; Fox Soccer; FSN HD; Fuse; FX HD; G4; Golf Channel; Golf Channel HD; GolTV; Great American Country; Halogen Network; HD Theater; HGTV HD; History Channel en Espanol; History Channel HD; History Channel International; ID Investigation Discovery (multiplexed); Independent Film Channel; ION Life; JCTV; Lifetime Movie Network; Military Channel; MLB Network; MLB Network HD; MTV Hits; MTV Jams; MTV2; mun2 television; Music Choice; National Geographic Channel; National Geographic Channel HD Network; NFL Network; NFL Network HD; NFL RedZone; NHL Network; NHL Network HD; Nick Jr.; Nick Too; NickToons TV; Outdoor Channel; Palladia; PBS Kids Sprout; Pentagon Channel; Planet Green; Qubo; ReelzChannel; RFD-TV; Science; Science HD; SoapNet; Speed HD; Spike TV HD; Style Network; Sundance Channel; Syfy HD; TBS in HD; TeenNick; Telemundo; Tennis Channel; The Hub; The Sportsman Channel; The Weather Channel HD; TLC HD; Tr3s; Trinity Broadcasting Network; Turner Classic Movies; Turner Network TV HD; TVE Internacional; TVG Network; Universal HD; USA Network HD; VeneMovies; Versus; Versus HD; VH1 Classic; WE tv.
Fee: $75.00 installation; $9.95 monthly; $10.00 converter; $30.00 additional installation.
Digital Pay Service 1
Pay Units: 3,162.
Programming (via satellite): Cinemax (multiplexed); Cinemax HD; Encore (multiplexed); Flix; HBO (multiplexed); HBO HD; Showtime (multiplexed); Showtime HD; Starz (multiplexed); Starz HDTV; The Movie Channel (multiplexed); The Movie Channel HD.
Video-On-Demand: No
Pay-Per-View
Addressable homes: 13,135.
Movies/Specials (delivered digitally); Adult (delivered digitally); Adult (delivered digitally); Adult (delivered digitally).
Internet Service
Operational: Yes. Began: April 30, 2000.
Subscribers: 23,396.
Broadband Service: CableONE.net.
Fee: $75.00 installation; $43.00 monthly; $6.00 modem lease.
Telephone Service
Analog: Not Operational
Digital: Operational
Fee: $39.95 monthly
Miles of Plant: 756.0 (coaxial); 140.0 (fiber optic). Additional miles planned: 20.0 (coaxial); 10.0 (fiber optic).
General Manager: Scott Geston. Technical Operations Manager: Bryon Brenneman. Marketing Manager: Maxine Schmidt. Production Manager: Tamara Rostad. Office Manager: Laureen Nyborg. Advertising Manager: Cheryl Carlson. Internet Manager: Dave Barge.
Ownership: Cable ONE Inc. (MSO).

FINLEY—MLGC, 301 Dewey St, Enderlin, ND 58027. Phones: 701-797-3300; 701-437-3300. Fax: 701-437-3022. E-mail: mandl@mlgc.com. Web Site: http://www.mlgc.com. ICA: ND0184.
TV Market Ranking: Outside TV Markets (FINLEY). Franchise award date: N.A. Franchise expiration date: N.A. Began: August 1, 1981.
Channel capacity: N.A. Channels available but not in use: N.A.
Basic Service
Subscribers: 140.
Programming (received off-air): KFME (PBS) Fargo; KVLY-TV (NBC) Fargo; KVRR (FOX) Fargo; KXJB-TV (CBS) Valley City; WDAZ-TV (ABC, CW) Devils Lake.
Programming (via satellite): A&E Networks; ABC Family Channel; AMC; Animal Planet; Bio; Bravo; CNBC; CNN; Country Music TV; Discovery Channel; Disney Channel; E! Entertainment Television; ESPN; ESPN 2; Food Network; Fox News Channel; Fox Sports Net; FX; Headline News; HGTV; History Channel; Lifetime; MSNBC; MTV; Nickelodeon; Outdoor Channel; QVC; Spike TV; Syfy; TBS Superstation; The Learning Channel; The Weather Channel; Travel Channel; Turner Classic Movies; Turner Network TV; TV Land; USA Network; VH1; WGN America.
Fee: $26.50 monthly.
Pay Service 1
Pay Units: 70.
Programming (via satellite): HBO.
Fee: $11.00 monthly.
Video-On-Demand: No
Internet Service
Operational: No, DSL.
Telephone Service
None
Assistant Manager: Tyler Kilde.
Ownership: MLGC (MSO).

FLASHER—Formerly served by Flasher Cablevision Inc. No longer in operation. ICA: ND0114.

FOREST RIVER—Midcontinent Communications, PO Box 5010, Sioux Falls, SD 57117. Phones: 800-456-0564; 605-229-1775. Fax: 605-229-0478. Web Site: http://www.midcocomm.com. ICA: ND0160.
TV Market Ranking: Below 100 (FOREST RIVER). Franchise award date: N.A. Franchise expiration date: N.A. Began: January 1, 1984.
Channel capacity: 12 (not 2-way capable). Channels available but not in use: N.A.
Basic Service
Subscribers: 16.
Programming (received off-air): KGFE (PBS) Grand Forks; KNRR (FOX) Pembina; KVLY-TV (NBC) Fargo; KXJB-TV (CBS) Valley City; WDAZ-TV (ABC, CW) Devils Lake.
Programming (via satellite): ABC Family Channel; CNN; ESPN; TBS Superstation.
Fee: $35.27 installation; $18.41 monthly; $17.64 additional installation.
Pay Service 1
Pay Units: N.A.
Programming (via satellite): HBO.
Fee: $10.20 monthly.
Video-On-Demand: No
Internet Service
Operational: No.
Telephone Service
None
Miles of Plant: 3.0 (coaxial); None (fiber optic).
Manager: Butch Motenberg. Chief Technician: Jeff Wilde.
Ownership: Midcontinent Media Inc. (MSO).; Comcast Cable Communications Inc. (MSO).

FORMAN—Dickey Rural Networks. Formerly served by Milnor, ND [ND0067]. This cable system has converted to IPTV, 9628 Hwy 281, PO Box 69, Ellendale, ND 58436-0069. Phones: 877-559-4692; 701-344-5000. Fax: 701-344-4300. Web Site: http://www.drtel.net. ICA: ND5022.
Channel capacity: N.A. Channels available but not in use: N.A.
Pay Service 1
Pay Units: N.A.
Fee: $11.00 monthly (HBO), $14.95 monthly (Showtime/TMC).
Internet Service
Operational: Yes.
Fee: $59.95 monthly.
Telephone Service
Digital: Operational
Fee: monthly (installation; $15.75 monthly
General Manager: Jeff Wilson. Engineering Manager: James Byerley. Marketing Manager: Janell Hauck. Plant Manager: Kent Schimke.

GACKLE—Midcontinent Communications, PO Box 5010, Sioux Falls, SD 57117. Phones: 800-456-0564; 605-229-1775. Fax: 605-229-0478. Web Site: http://www.midcocomm.com. Also serves Streeter. ICA: ND0093.
TV Market Ranking: Below 100 (GACKLE); Outside TV Markets (Streeter). Franchise award date: April 6, 1987. Franchise expi-

ration date: April 6, 2011. Began: April 1, 1984.
Channel capacity: 41 (not 2-way capable). Channels available but not in use: N.A.

Basic Service
Subscribers: 190.
Programming (received off-air): KBMY (ABC) Bismarck; KFYR-TV (NBC) Bismarck; KJRE (PBS) Ellendale; KJRR (FOX) Jamestown; KXMB-TV (CBS) Bismarck.
Programming (via satellite): A&E Networks; ABC Family Channel; AMC; Animal Planet; Cartoon Network; CNBC; CNN; Country Music TV; C-SPAN; Discovery Channel; Disney Channel; ESPN; ESPN 2; Fox Sports Net North; Headline News; HGTV; History Channel; INSP; Lifetime; Nickelodeon; Outdoor Channel; QVC; Spike TV; Syfy; TBS Superstation; The Learning Channel; The Weather Channel; Turner Network TV; TV Land; USA Network; VH1; WE tv; WGN America.
Fee: $50.00 installation; $26.50 monthly.

Pay Service 1
Pay Units: 18.
Programming (via satellite): Showtime.
Fee: $20.00 installation; $11.00 monthly.

Pay Service 2
Pay Units: 8.
Programming (via satellite): HBO.
Fee: $20.00 installation; $12.00 monthly.

Pay Service 3
Pay Units: 13.
Programming (via satellite): The Movie Channel.
Fee: $20.00 installation; $11.00 monthly.

Video-On-Demand: No

Internet Service
Operational: No.

Telephone Service
None
Miles of Plant: 7.0 (coaxial); None (fiber optic).
Manager: Darrell Wrege. Marketing Director: Fred Jamieson. Customer Service Manager: Kathy Fuhrmann.
Ownership: Midcontinent Media Inc. (MSO).; Comcast Cable Communications Inc. (MSO).

GARRISON—Reservation Telephone Cooperative, 24 Main St N, PO Box 68, Parshall, ND 58770-0068. Phones: 888-862-3115; 701-862-3115. Fax: 701-862-3008. E-mail: kristin@rtc.coop. Web Site: http://www.reservationtelephone.com. ICA: ND0033.
TV Market Ranking: Outside TV Markets (GARRISON). Franchise award date: December 30, 1986. Franchise expiration date: December 30, 2011. Began: March 1, 1979.
Channel capacity: 41 (not 2-way capable). Channels available but not in use: N.A.

Basic Service
Subscribers: 446.
Programming (received off-air): KFYR-TV (NBC) Bismarck; KMCY (ABC) Minot; KSRE (PBS) Minot; KXMC-TV (CBS) Minot; KXND (FOX) Minot.
Programming (via satellite): A&E Networks; ABC Family Channel; AMC; Animal Planet; Cartoon Network; CNBC; CNN; Country Music TV; C-SPAN; Discovery Channel; Disney Channel; ESPN; ESPN 2; Fox Sports Net; Headline News; HGTV; History Channel; INSP; Lifetime; Nickelodeon; Outdoor Channel; QVC; Spike TV; Syfy; TBS Superstation; The Learning Channel; The Weather Channel; Turner Network TV; TV Land; USA Network; VH1; WGN America.
Fee: $20.00 installation; $32.95 monthly.

Pay Service 1
Pay Units: 40.
Programming (via satellite): Showtime; The Movie Channel.
Fee: $20.00 installation; $10.00 monthly (Showtime & TMC).

Pay Service 2
Pay Units: 16.
Programming (via satellite): HBO.
Fee: $20.00 installation; $10.00 monthly.

Video-On-Demand: Planned

Internet Service
Operational: No.

Telephone Service
None
Miles of Plant: 16.0 (coaxial); None (fiber optic).
General Manager: Royce S. Aslakson. Marketing Manager: Kristin Jaeger. Office Manager: Jan Boschee.
Ownership: Reservation Telephone Cooperative.

GILBY—Formerly served by Midcontinent Communications. No longer in operation. ICA: ND0142.

GLENFIELD—Formerly served by Dakota Central Telecommunications. No longer in operation. ICA: ND0173.

GRAFTON—Midcontinent Communications, PO Box 5010, Sioux Falls, SD 57117. Phones: 800-456-0564; 605-229-1775. Fax: 605-229-0478. Web Site: http://www.midcocomm.com. Also serves Drayton. ICA: ND0014.
TV Market Ranking: Below 100 (Drayton); Outside TV Markets (GRAFTON). Franchise award date: November 9, 1981. Franchise expiration date: August 12, 2011. Began: January 1, 1966.
Channel capacity: 68 (operating 2-way). Channels available but not in use: N.A.

Basic Service
Subscribers: 1,875.
Programming (received off-air): KGFE (PBS) Grand Forks; KNRR (FOX) Pembina; KVLY-TV (NBC) Fargo; KXJB-TV (CBS) Valley City; WDAZ-TV (ABC, CW) Devils Lake; 2 FMs.
Programming (via satellite): A&E Networks; ABC Family Channel; AMC; Animal Planet; BET Networks; Bravo; Cartoon Network; CNBC; CNN; Comedy Central; Country Music TV; C-SPAN; C-SPAN 2; Discovery Channel; Discovery Fit & Health; Discovery Health Channel; Disney Channel; E! Entertainment Television; Encore Action; ESPN; ESPN 2; ESPN Classic Sports; ESPNews; Eternal Word TV Network; Food Network; Fox News Channel; Fox Sports Net North; FX; G4; Headline News; HGTV; History Channel; INSP; ION Television; Lifetime; MSNBC; MTV; Nickelodeon; Outdoor Channel; Oxygen; QVC; Speed; Spike TV; Syfy; TBS Superstation; The Learning Channel; The Weather Channel; Trinity Broadcasting Network; truTV; Turner Classic Movies; Turner Network TV; TV Guide Network; TV Land; USA Network; Versus; VH1; WE tv; WGN America.
Fee: $50.00 installation; $23.87 monthly.

Digital Basic Service
Subscribers: N.A.
Programming (via satellite): BBC America; Bio; Bloomberg Television; Discovery Digital Networks; DMX Music; ESPN Now; Fox Sports World; Fuse; GAS; Golf Channel; GSN; History Channel International; Independent Film Channel; Lifetime Movie Network; MTV Networks Digital Suite; Nick Jr.; Science Television; Style Network; Sundance Channel; Toon Disney.

Digital Pay Service 1
Pay Units: N.A.
Programming (via satellite): Cinemax (multiplexed); Encore (multiplexed); HBO (multiplexed); Showtime (multiplexed); The Movie Channel (multiplexed).

Video-On-Demand: No

Pay-Per-View
NHL/MLB (delivered digitally); NBA TV (delivered digitally); Sports PPV (delivered digitally); Hot Choice (delivered digitally); iN DEMAND (delivered digitally).

Internet Service
Operational: Yes.
Subscribers: 212.
Broadband Service: MidcoNet.
Fee: $35.00 installation; $19.95 monthly.

Telephone Service
Analog: Not Operational
Digital: Operational
Fee: $18.00 monthly
Miles of Plant: 26.0 (coaxial); None (fiber optic).
Manager: Darrell Wrege. Marketing Director: Fred Jamieson. Customer Service Manager: Kathy Fuhrmann.
Ownership: Midcontinent Media Inc. (MSO).; Comcast Cable Communications Inc. (MSO).

GRAND FORKS—Formerly served by Microwave Communication Services. No longer in operation. ICA: ND0215.

GRAND FORKS—Midcontinent Communications, 5030 Gateway Dr, Ste B, Grand Forks, ND 58203-1116. Phones: 701-772-6411 (Local office); 800-456-0564; 605-229-1775. Fax: 605-229-0478. Web Site: http://www.midcocomm.com. Also serves Crookston & East Grand Forks, MN; Buxton, Emerado, Galesburg, Grand Forks AFB, Grandin, Hatton, Hillsboro, Mayville, Portland, Reynolds & Thompson, ND. ICA: ND0003.
TV Market Ranking: 98 (Galesburg, Grandin); Below 100 (Buxton, Crookston, East Grand Forks, Emerado, GRAND FORKS, Grand Forks AFB, Hatton, Mayville, Portland, Reynolds, Thompson); Outside TV Markets (Hillsboro). Franchise award date: N.A. Franchise expiration date: N.A. Began: November 1, 1970.
Channel capacity: 70 (operating 2-way). Channels available but not in use: N.A.

Basic Service
Subscribers: 19,948.
Programming (received off-air): KBRR (FOX) Thief River Falls; KGFE (PBS) Grand Forks; KVLY-TV (NBC) Fargo; KXJB-TV (CBS) Valley City; WDAZ-TV (ABC, CW) Devils Lake.
Programming (via satellite): ABC Family Channel; CNN; CW+; QVC; The Weather Channel; TV Guide Network; various Canadian stations; WGN America.
Fee: $25.00 installation; $38.95 monthly; $1.50 converter; $20.96 additional installation.

Expanded Basic Service 1
Subscribers: 18,212.
Programming (via satellite): A&E Networks; AMC; Animal Planet; BET Networks; Bravo; Cartoon Network; Celebrity Shopping Network; CNBC; Comedy Central; Country Music TV; C-SPAN; C-SPAN 2; Discovery Channel; Disney Channel; E! Entertainment Television; ESPN; ESPN 2; Eternal Word TV Network; Food Network; Fox News Channel; Fox Sports Net North; FX; G4; Hallmark Channel; Headline News; HGTV; History Channel; INSP; Lifetime; MSNBC; MTV; Nickelodeon; Outdoor Channel; Oxygen; Speed; Spike TV; Syfy; TBS Superstation; The Learning Channel; Travel Channel; Trinity Broadcasting Network; truTV; Turner Classic Movies; Turner Network TV; TV Land; USA Network; Versus; VH1; WE tv.
Fee: $25.00 installation; $19.97 monthly.

Digital Basic Service
Subscribers: 2,946.
Programming (via satellite): 3 Angels Broadcasting Network; A&E HD; ABC Family HD; AmericanLife TV Network; Animal Planet HD; BBC America; Bio; Bloomberg Television; Boomerang; BTN; Canal Sur; CBS Sports Network; Cine Latino; Cine Mexicano; CMT Pure Country; CNN en Espanol; CNN HD; Cooking Channel; C-SPAN 3; Current; Discovery Channel HD; Discovery en Espanol; Discovery Fit & Health; Discovery Health Channel; Discovery Kids Channel; Disney Channel HD; DIY Network; ESPN 2 HD; ESPN Classic Sports; ESPN Deportes; ESPN HD; ESPNews; EWTN en Espanol; Food Network HD; Fox Business Channel; Fox College Sports Atlantic; Fox College Sports Central; Fox College Sports Pacific; Fox Deportes; Fox Soccer; FSN HD; Fuse; G4; Golf Channel; GolTV; Great American Country; GSN; Halogen Network; HD Theater; HDNet; HDNet Movies; HGTV HD; History Channel en Espanol; History Channel HD; History Channel International; ID Investigation Discovery; Independent Film Channel; ION Life; ION Television; JCTV; Lifetime Movie Network; Military Channel; MTV Hits; MTV Jams; MTV2; mun2 television; Music Choice; National Geographic Channel; National Geographic Channel HD Network; NFL Network; NHL Network; Nick Jr.; Nick Too; NickToons TV; Outdoor Channel; Palladia; PBS Kids Sprout; Pentagon Channel; Planet Green; Qubo; ReelzChannel; RFD-TV; Science; SoapNet; Style Network; Sundance Channel; Syfy HD; TBS in HD; TeenNick; Telemundo; Tennis Channel; TLC HD; Toon Disney; Toon Disney en Espanol; Tr3s; Trinity Broadcasting Network; Turner Classic Movies; Turner Network TV HD; TV One; TVE Internacional; TVG Network; Universal HD; USA Network HD; Versus; Versus HD; VH1 Classic; VH1 Soul; WE tv.

Digital Pay Service 1
Pay Units: 2,107.
Programming (via satellite): Cinemax (multiplexed); Cinemax HD; Encore (multiplexed); HBO (multiplexed); HBO HD; Showtime (multiplexed); Showtime HD; Starz (multiplexed); Starz HDTV; The Movie

Channel (multiplexed); The Movie Channel HD.
Fee: $12.90 monthly (each).
Video-On-Demand: No
Pay-Per-View
Addressable homes: 2,946.
ESPN Now (delivered digitally); Hot Choice (delivered digitally); iN DEMAND (delivered digitally); Playboy TV (delivered digitally); Fresh (delivered digitally); sports (delivered digitally).
Internet Service
Operational: Yes.
Subscribers: 6,647.
Broadband Service: MidcoNet.
Fee: $35.00 installation; $19.95 monthly.
Telephone Service
Digital: Operational
Fee: $18.00 monthly
Miles of Plant: 327.0 (coaxial); None (fiber optic).
Manager: Butch Motenburg. Chief Technician: Mark Jensen.
Ownership: Midcontinent Media Inc. (MSO).; Comcast Cable Communications Inc. (MSO).

GRANVILLE—SRT Communications. Now served by VELVA, ND [ND0059]. ICA: ND0111.

GWINNER—Dickey Rural Networks. Formerly served by Milnor, ND [ND0067]. This cable system has converted to IPTV, 9628 Hwy 281, PO Box 69, Ellendale, ND 58436-0069. Phones: 877-559-4692; 701-344-5000. Fax: 701-344-4300. Web Site: http://www.drtel.net. ICA: ND5024.
Channel capacity: N.A. Channels available but not in use: N.A.
Pay Service 1
Pay Units: N.A.
Fee: $11.00 monthly (HBO), $14.95 monthly (Showtime/TMC).
Internet Service
Operational: Yes.
Fee: $59.95 monthly.
Telephone Service
Digital: Operational
Fee: monthly (installation; $18.00 monthly
General Manager: Jeff Wilson. Engineering Manager: James Byerley. Marketing Manager: Janell Hauck. Plant Manager: Kent Schimke.

HANKINSON—Midcontinent Communications, PO Box 5010, Sioux Falls, SD 57117. Phones: 800-456-0564; 605-229-1775. Fax: 605-229-0478. E-mail: darrell_wrege@mmi.net. Web Site: http://www.midcocomm.com. Also serves Fairmount & Lidgerwood. ICA: ND0025.
TV Market Ranking: Outside TV Markets (Fairmount, HANKINSON, Lidgerwood). Franchise award date: July 16, 1990. Franchise expiration date: December 31, 2011. Began: August 1, 1981.
Channel capacity: 41 (operating 2-way). Channels available but not in use: N.A.
Basic Service
Subscribers: 706.
Programming (received off-air): KBHE-TV (PBS) Rapid City; KCLO-TV (CBS) Rapid City; KCPM (MNT) Grand Forks; KEVN-TV (FOX) Rapid City; KFME (PBS) Fargo; KOTA-TV (ABC) Rapid City; KVLY-TV (NBC) Fargo; KVRR (FOX) Fargo; KXJB-TV (CBS) Valley City; WDAY-TV (ABC, CW) Fargo.
Programming (via satellite): A&E Networks; ABC Family Channel; AMC; Animal Planet; Bravo; Cartoon Network; CNBC; CNN; Comedy Central; Country Music TV; C-SPAN; C-SPAN 2; Discovery Channel; Disney Channel; E! Entertainment Television; ESPN; ESPN 2; Eternal Word TV Network; Food Network; Fox News Channel; Fox Sports Net North; FX; Hallmark Channel; Headline News; HGTV; History Channel; INSP; Lifetime; MSNBC; MTV; Nickelodeon; Oxygen; QVC; Speed; Spike TV; Syfy; TBS Superstation; The Learning Channel; The Weather Channel; Travel Channel; truTV; Turner Classic Movies; Turner Network TV; TV Guide Network; TV Land; USA Network; VH1; WGN America.
Fee: $50.00 installation; $38.95 monthly.
Digital Basic Service
Subscribers: N.A.
Programming (via satellite): 3 Angels Broadcasting Network; A&E HD; ABC Family HD; AmericanLife TV Network; Animal Planet HD; BBC America; Bio; Bloomberg Television; Boomerang; BTN; Canal Sur; CBS Sports Network; Cine Latino; Cine Mexicano; CMT Pure Country; CNN en Espanol; CNN HD; Cooking Channel; C-SPAN 3; Current; Discovery Channel HD; Discovery en Espanol; Discovery Health Channel; Discovery Kids Channel; Disney Channel HD; DIY Network; ESPN 2 HD; ESPN Classic Sports; ESPN Deportes; ESPN HD; ESPNews; EWTN en Espanol; Food Network HD; Fox Business Channel; Fox College Sports Atlantic; Fox College Sports Central; Fox College Sports Pacific; Fox Deportes; Fox Soccer; FSN HD; Fuse; Golf Channel; GolTV; Great American Country; GSN; Halogen Network; HD Theater; HDNet; HDNet Movies; HGTV HD; History Channel en Espanol; History Channel HD; History Channel International; ID Investigation Discovery; Independent Film Channel; ION Life; JCTV; Lifetime Movie Network; Military Channel; MTV Hits; MTV Jams; MTV2; mun2 television; Music Choice; National Geographic Channel; National Geographic Channel HD Network; NFL Network; Nick Jr.; Nick Too; NickToons TV; Palladia; PBS Kids Sprout; Pentagon Channel; Planet Green; Qubo; ReelzChannel; Science; SoapNet; Style Network; Sundance Channel; Syfy HD; TBS in HD; TeenNick; Telemundo; Tennis Channel; TLC HD; Toon Disney; Toon Disney en Espanol; Tr3s; Trinity Broadcasting Network; Turner Network TV HD; TV One; TVE Internacional; TVG Network; USA Network HD; VeneMovies; Versus HD; VH1 Classic; VH1 Soul.
Fee: $47.95 monthly.
Digital Pay Service 1
Pay Units: N.A.
Programming (via satellite): Cinemax (multiplexed); Cinemax HD; Encore (multiplexed); Flix; HBO (multiplexed); HBO HD; HBO Latino; Showtime (multiplexed); Showtime HD; Starz (multiplexed); Starz HDTV; The Movie Channel (multiplexed); The Movie Channel HD.
Video-On-Demand: No
Pay-Per-View
iN DEMAND (delivered digitally); MLS Direct Kick (delivered digitally); NBA League Pass (delivered digitally); NHL Center Ice (delivered digitally); MLB Extra Innings (delivered digitally).
Internet Service
Operational: Yes.
Broadband Service: MidcoNet.
Fee: $35.00 installation; $19.95 monthly; $8.00 modem lease; $39.00 modem purchase.
Telephone Service
Digital: Operational
Fee: $18.00 monthly
Miles of Plant: 16.0 (coaxial); None (fiber optic).
General Manager: Darrell Wrege. Marketing Director: Fred Jamieson. Customer Service Manager: Kathy Fuhrmann.
Ownership: Midcontinent Media Inc. (MSO).; Comcast Cable Communications Inc. (MSO).

HARVEY—Midcontinent Communications, PO Box 5010, Sioux Falls, SD 57117. Phones: 800-456-0564; 605-229-1775. Fax: 605-229-0478. Web Site: http://www.midcocomm.com. Also serves Anamoose, Drake, Fessenden & McHenry County (portions). ICA: ND0019.
TV Market Ranking: Below 100 (McHenry County (portions) (portions)); Outside TV Markets (Anamoose, Drake, Fessenden, HARVEY, McHenry County (portions) (portions)). Franchise award date: April 4, 1988. Franchise expiration date: April 4, 2011. Began: May 1, 1973.
Channel capacity: N.A. Channels available but not in use: N.A.
Basic Service
Subscribers: 1,120.
Programming (received off-air): KMCY (ABC) Minot; KMOT (NBC) Minot; KSRE (PBS) Minot; KXMC-TV (CBS) Minot; KXND (FOX) Minot; allband FM.
Programming (via satellite): A&E Networks; ABC Family Channel; AMC; BET Networks; Bravo; Cartoon Network; CNBC; CNN; Country Music TV; C-SPAN; CW+; Discovery Channel; Disney Channel; ESPN; ESPN 2; FX; G4; Great American Country; Hallmark Channel; Headline News; INSP; Lifetime; MTV; Nickelodeon; Oxygen; QVC; Spike TV; TBS Superstation; The Learning Channel; The Weather Channel; Trinity Broadcasting Network; truTV; Turner Network TV; TV Guide Network; TV Land; Univision Studios; USA Network; VH1; WE tv; WGN America.
Fee: $50.00 installation; $26.50 monthly.
Digital Basic Service
Subscribers: N.A.
Programming (via satellite): 3 Angels Broadcasting Network; A&E HD; ABC Family HD; AmericanLife TV Network; Animal Planet HD; BBC America; Bio; Bloomberg Television; Boomerang; BTN; Canal Sur; CBS Sports Network; Cine Latino; Cine Mexicano; CMT Pure Country; CNN en Espanol; CNN HD; Cooking Channel; C-SPAN 3; Current; Discovery Channel HD; Discovery en Espanol; Discovery Fit & Health; Discovery Health Channel; Discovery Kids Channel; Disney Channel HD; DIY Network; ESPN 2 HD; ESPN Classic Sports; ESPN Deportes; ESPN HD; ESPNews; EWTN en Espanol; Food Network HD; Fox Business Channel; Fox College Sports Atlantic; Fox College Sports Central; Fox College Sports Pacific; Fox Deportes; Fox Movie Channel; Fox Soccer; FSN HD; Fuse; G4; Golf Channel; GolTV; Great American Country; GSN; Halogen Network; HD Theater; HDNet; HDNet Movies; HGTV HD; History Channel en Espanol; History Channel HD; History Channel International; ID Investigation Discovery; Independent Film Channel; ION Life; ION Television; JCTV; Lifetime Movie Network; Military Channel; MTV Hits; MTV Jams; MTV2; mun2 television; Music Choice; National Geographic Channel; National Geographic Channel HD Network; NFL Network; Nick Jr.; Nick Too; NickToons TV; Outdoor Channel; Palladia; PBS Kids Sprout; Pentagon Channel; Planet Green; Qubo; ReelzChannel; RFD-TV; Science; SoapNet; Style Network; Sundance Channel; Syfy HD; TBS in HD; TeenNick; Telemundo; Tennis Channel; TLC HD; Toon Disney; Toon Disney en Espanol; Tr3s; Trinity Broadcasting Network; Turner Classic Movies; Turner Network TV HD; TV One; TVE Internacional; TVG Network; Universal HD; USA Network HD; Versus; Versus HD; VH1 Classic; VH1 Soul; WE tv.
Digital Pay Service 1
Pay Units: N.A.
Programming (via satellite): Cinemax (multiplexed); Encore (multiplexed); Flix; HBO (multiplexed); HBO HD; HBO Latino; Showtime (multiplexed); Showtime HD; Starz (multiplexed); Starz HDTV; The Movie Channel (multiplexed); The Movie Channel HD.
Video-On-Demand: No
Internet Service
Operational: Yes.
Fee: $35.00 installation; $19.95 monthly.
Telephone Service
Digital: Operational
Fee: $18.00 monthly
Miles of Plant: 23.0 (coaxial); None (fiber optic).
Manager: Darrell Wrege. Marketing Director: Fred Jamieson. Customer Service Manager: Kathy Fuhrmann.
Ownership: Midcontinent Media Inc. (MSO).; Comcast Cable Communications Inc. (MSO).

JAMESTOWN—Cable Services Inc., PO Box 1995, Jamestown, ND 58402-1995. Phones: 701-845-4383; 701-252-5281. Fax: 701-252-1105. Web Site: http://www.csicable.com. ICA: ND0191.
TV Market Ranking: 98 (JAMESTOWN). Franchise award date: N.A. Franchise expiration date: N.A. Began: December 24, 1964.
Channel capacity: N.A. Channels available but not in use: N.A.
Basic Service
Subscribers: 5,319.
Programming (received off-air): KFME (PBS) Fargo; KJRR (FOX) Jamestown; KVLY-TV (NBC) Fargo; KXJB-TV (CBS) Valley City; various Canadian stations; WDAY-TV (ABC, CW) Fargo; 7 FMs.
Programming (via satellite): A&E Networks; ABC Family Channel; Animal Planet; Cartoon Network; CNBC; CNN; Comedy Central; C-SPAN; C-SPAN 2; C-SPAN 3; Discovery Channel; Disney Channel; E! Entertainment Television; ESPN; ESPN 2; Food Network; Fox News Channel; Fox Sports Net; FX; Great American Country; Hallmark Channel; Headline News; HGTV; History Channel; INSP; Lifetime; MSNBC; MTV; NASA TV; Nickelodeon; QVC; Spike TV; Syfy; TBS Superstation; The Learning Channel; The Weather Channel; Trinity Broadcasting Network; Turner Classic Movies; Turner Network TV; TV Guide Network; USA Network; VH1; WGN America.
Fee: $10.00 installation; $29.95 monthly.
Pay Service 1
Pay Units: 800.
Programming (via satellite): Showtime; The Movie Channel.
Fee: $10.00 installation; $7.95 monthly.
Video-On-Demand: No
Internet Service
Operational: Yes. Began: September 1, 1999.
Broadband Service: In-house.
Fee: $30.00 installation; $29.99 monthly; $4.00 modem lease; $56.56 modem purchase.

Telephone Service
Analog: Not Operational
Digital: Planned
Miles of Plant: 125.0 (coaxial); 100.0 (fiber optic). Additional miles planned: 5.0 (coaxial).
Manager: Roy Sheppard. Chief Technician: Roger J. Nelson. Marketing Manager: Chris Sheppard.
Ownership: Cable Services Inc. (MSO).

KENMARE—Reservation Telephone Cooperative, 24 Main St N, PO Box 68, Parshall, ND 58770-0068. Phones: 888-862-3115; 701-862-3115. Fax: 701-862-3008. E-mail: kristin@rtc.coop. Web Site: http://www.reservationtelephone.com. ICA: ND0043.
TV Market Ranking: Outside TV Markets (KENMARE). Franchise award date: April 1, 1987. Franchise expiration date: September 9, 2011. Began: May 1, 1976.
Channel capacity: 42 (2-way capable). Channels available but not in use: N.A.
Basic Service
Subscribers: 342.
Programming (received off-air): KMCY (ABC) Minot; KMOT (NBC) Minot; KSRE (PBS) Minot; KXMC-TV (CBS) Minot; KXND (FOX) Minot.
Programming (via satellite): A&E Networks; ABC Family Channel; AMC; Cartoon Network; CNBC; CNN; Country Music TV; C-SPAN; Discovery Channel; ESPN; ESPN 2; ESPNews; Fox News Channel; Fox Sports Net; FX; Headline News; History Channel; INSP; Lifetime; Nickelodeon; QVC; Spike TV; TBS Superstation; The Learning Channel; The Weather Channel; Turner Network TV; TV Guide Network; TV Land; USA Network; VH1; WE tv; WGN America.
Fee: $20.00 installation; $32.95 monthly.
Pay Service 1
Pay Units: 40.
Programming (via satellite): Showtime; The Movie Channel.
Fee: $20.00 installation; $10.00 monthly (Showtime & TMC).
Pay Service 2
Pay Units: 11.
Programming (via satellite): HBO.
Fee: $20.00 installation; $10.00 monthly.
Pay Service 3
Pay Units: 21.
Fee: $20.00 installation; $11.00 monthly.
Video-On-Demand: Planned
Internet Service
Operational: No.
Telephone Service
None
Miles of Plant: 10.0 (coaxial); None (fiber optic).
General Manager: Royce S. Aslakson. Marketing Manager: Kristin Jaeger. Office Manager: Jan Boschee.
Ownership: Reservation Telephone Cooperative (MSO).

KINDRED—MLGC, 301 Dewey St, Enderlin, ND 58027. Phone: 701-437-3300. Fax: 701-437-3022. E-mail: mandl@mlgc.com. Web Site: http://www.mlgc.com. ICA: ND0223.
TV Market Ranking: 98 (KINDRED). Franchise award date: N.A. Franchise expiration date: N.A. Began: N.A.
Channel capacity: N.A. Channels available but not in use: N.A.
Basic Service
Subscribers: 155.
Programming (received off-air): KFME (PBS) Fargo; KVLY-TV (NBC) Fargo; KVRR (FOX) Fargo; KXJB-TV (CBS) Valley City; WDAY-TV (ABC, CW) Fargo.
Programming (via satellite): A&E Networks; ABC Family Channel; CNN; Country Music TV; Discovery Channel; Disney Channel; ESPN; ESPN 2; Fox Sports Net; History Channel; Nickelodeon; QVC; Spike TV; Syfy; TBS Superstation; The Weather Channel; Turner Network TV; USA Network; WGN America.
Fee: $40.00 installation; $26.50 monthly.
Pay Service 1
Pay Units: N.A.
Programming (via satellite): HBO.
Fee: $11.00 monthly.
Video-On-Demand: No
Internet Service
Operational: Yes, DSL.
Telephone Service
None
Assistant Manager: Tyler Kilde.
Ownership: MLGC (MSO).

KULM—Dickey Rural Networks. Formerly served by Oakes, ND [ND0226]. This cable system has converted to IPTV, 9628 Hwy 281, PO Box 69, Ellendale, ND 58436-0069. Phones: 877-559-4692; 701-344-5000. Fax: 701-344-4300. Web Site: http://www.drtel.net. ICA: ND5026.
Channel capacity: N.A. Channels available but not in use: N.A.
Pay Service 1
Pay Units: N.A.
Fee: $11.00 monthly (HBO), $14.95 monthly (Showtime/TMC).
Internet Service
Operational: Yes.
Fee: $59.95 monthly.
Telephone Service
Digital: Operational
Fee: monthly (installation; $15.75 monthly
General Manager: Jeff Wilson. Engineering Manager: James Byerley. Marketing Manager: Janell Hauck. Plant Manager: Kent Schimke.

KULM—Formerly served by Cable Services Inc. No longer in operation. ICA: ND0108.

LA MOURE—Midcontinent Communications, PO Box 5010, Sioux Falls, SD 57117. Phones: 800-456-0564; 605-229-1775. Fax: 605-229-0478. Web Site: http://www.midcocomm.com. ICA: ND0051.
TV Market Ranking: Outside TV Markets (LA MOURE). Franchise award date: April 23, 1990. Franchise expiration date: November 2, 2012. Began: October 1, 1982.
Channel capacity: N.A. Channels available but not in use: N.A.
Basic Service
Subscribers: 320.
Programming (received off-air): KFME (PBS) Fargo; KJRR (FOX) Jamestown; KVLY-TV (NBC) Fargo; KXJB-TV (CBS) Valley City; WDAY-TV (ABC, CW) Fargo.
Programming (via satellite): A&E Networks; ABC Family Channel; AMC; Cartoon Network; CNBC; CNN; Country Music TV; C-SPAN; Discovery Channel; Disney Channel; ESPN; ESPN 2; ESPNews; Fox Sports Net North; FX; Headline News; HGTV; History Channel; INSP; Lifetime; Nickelodeon; QVC; Spike TV; TBS Superstation; The Learning Channel; The Weather Channel; Turner Network TV; TV Guide Network; TV Land; USA Network; VH1; WGN America.
Fee: $50.00 installation; $26.50 monthly.
Pay Service 1
Pay Units: 24.
Programming (via satellite): Showtime.
Fee: $20.00 installation; $11.00 monthly.

Pay Service 2
Pay Units: 9.
Programming (via satellite): HBO.
Fee: $20.00 installation; $11.00 monthly.
Pay Service 3
Pay Units: 5.
Programming (via satellite): The Movie Channel.
Fee: $20.00 installation; $11.00 monthly.
Video-On-Demand: No
Internet Service
Operational: Yes.
Fee: $35.00 installation; $19.95 monthly.
Telephone Service
Digital: Operational
Fee: $18.00 monthly
Miles of Plant: 7.0 (coaxial); None (fiber optic).
Manager: Darrell Wrege. Marketing Director: Fred Jamieson. Customer Service Manager: Kathy Fuhrmann.
Ownership: Midcontinent Media Inc. (MSO).; Comcast Cable Communications Inc. (MSO).

LAKOTA—Polar Cablevision, 110 4th St E, PO Box 270, Park River, ND 58270. Phones: 800-284-7222; 701-284-7221. Fax: 701-284-7205. Web Site: http://www.polarcomm.com. ICA: ND0058.
TV Market Ranking: Below 100 (LAKOTA). Franchise award date: N.A. Franchise expiration date: N.A. Began: November 1, 1979.
Channel capacity: N.A. Channels available but not in use: N.A.
Basic Service
Subscribers: N.A. Included in Pembina
Programming (received off-air): KGFE (PBS) Grand Forks; KNRR (FOX) Pembina; KVLY-TV (NBC) Fargo; KXJB-TV (CBS) Valley City; WDAZ-TV (ABC, CW) Devils Lake.
Programming (via satellite): ABC Family Channel; CNN; Discovery Channel; TBS Superstation; WGN America.
Fee: $38.27 installation; $41.95 monthly; $19.14 additional installation.
Expanded Basic Service 1
Subscribers: N.A.
Programming (via satellite): AMC; ESPN; truTV; Turner Network TV; USA Network.
Fee: $3.00 monthly.
Pay Service 1
Pay Units: 82.
Programming (via satellite): Encore; HBO.
Fee: $10.20 monthly (HBO).
Video-On-Demand: No
Internet Service
Operational: No, DSL.
Telephone Service
None
Miles of Plant: 9.0 (coaxial); None (fiber optic).
Chief Executive Officer & General Manager: David Dunning. Regulatory Affairs Manager: Shari Flanders.
Ownership: Polar Communications (MSO).

LANGDON—Midcontinent Communications, PO Box 5010, Sioux Falls, SD 57117. Phones: 800-456-0564; 605-229-1775. Fax: 605-229-0478. E-mail: darrell_wrege@mmi.net. Web Site: http://www.midcocomm.com. Also serves Walhalla. ICA: ND0022.
TV Market Ranking: Below 100 (Walhalla); Outside TV Markets (LANGDON). Franchise award date: April 19, 1990. Franchise expiration date: September 9, 2011. Began: January 1, 1971.
Channel capacity: N.A. Channels available but not in use: N.A.
Basic Service
Subscribers: 1,246.
Programming (received off-air): KBRR (FOX) Thief River Falls; KGFE (PBS) Grand Forks; KVLY-TV (NBC) Fargo; KXJB-TV (CBS) Valley City; WDAZ-TV (ABC, CW) Devils Lake; allband FM.
Programming (via satellite): CNN; C-SPAN; CW+; TBS Superstation; The Weather Channel; TV Guide Network; various Canadian stations; WGN America.
Programming (via translator): KVLY-TV (NBC) Fargo.
Fee: $25.00 installation; $38.95 monthly.
Expanded Basic Service 1
Subscribers: N.A.
Programming (via satellite): A&E Networks; ABC Family Channel; AMC; Animal Planet; Cartoon Network; CNBC; Comedy Central; Country Music TV; C-SPAN 2; Discovery Channel; Discovery Health Channel; Disney Channel; E! Entertainment Television; ESPN; ESPN 2; Eternal Word TV Network; Food Network; Fox News Channel; Fox Sports Net North; FX; G4; Great American Country; Hallmark Channel; Headline News; HGTV; History Channel; INSP; ION Television; Lifetime; MSNBC; MTV; Nickelodeon; Outdoor Channel; QVC; Speed; Spike TV; Syfy; The Learning Channel; Travel Channel; truTV; Turner Network TV; TV Land; USA Network; Versus; VH1; WE tv.
Digital Basic Service
Subscribers: N.A.
Programming (via satellite): 3 Angels Broadcasting Network; A&E HD; ABC Family HD; AmericanLife TV Network; Animal Planet HD; BBC America; Bio; Boomerang; Bravo; BTN; Canal Sur; CBS Sports Network; Cine Latino; Cine Mexicano; CMT Pure Country; CNN en Espanol; CNN HD; Cooking Channel; C-SPAN 3; Current; Discovery Channel HD; Discovery en Espanol; Discovery Fit & Health; Discovery Health Channel; Discovery Kids Channel; Disney Channel HD; DIY Network; ESPN 2 HD; ESPN Classic Sports; ESPN Deportes; ESPN HD; ESPNews; EWTN en Espanol; Food Network HD; Fox Business Channel; Fox College Sports Atlantic; Fox College Sports Central; Fox College Sports Pacific; Fox Deportes; Fox Movie Channel; Fox Soccer; FSN HD; Fuse; G4; Golf Channel; GolTV; Great American Country; GSN; Halogen Network; HD Theater; HDNet; HDNet Movies; HGTV HD; History Channel en Espanol; History Channel HD; History Channel International; ID Investigation Discovery; Independent Film Channel; ION Life; ION Television; JCTV; Lifetime Movie Network; Military Channel; MTV Hits; MTV

Jams; MTV2; mun2 television; Music Choice; National Geographic Channel; National Geographic Channel HD Network; NFL Network; NHL Network; Nick Jr.; Nick Too; NickToons TV; Outdoor Channel; Palladia; PBS HD; PBS Kids Sprout; Pentagon Channel; Planet Green; Qubo; ReelzChannel; RFD-TV; Science Television; SoapNet; Style Network; Sundance Channel; Syfy HD; TBS in HD; TeenNick; Telemundo; Tennis Channel; TLC HD; Toon Disney; Toon Disney en Espanol; Tr3s; Trinity Broadcasting Network; Turner Classic Movies; Turner Network TV HD; TV One; TVE Internacional; TVG Network; Universal HD; USA Network HD; Versus; Versus HD; VH1 Classic; VH1 Soul; WE tv.
Fee: $47.95 monthly.

Digital Pay Service 1
Pay Units: N.A.
Programming (via satellite): Cinemax (multiplexed); Cinemax HD; Encore (multiplexed); Flix; HBO (multiplexed); HBO HD; HBO Latino; Showtime (multiplexed); Showtime HD; Starz (multiplexed); Starz HDTV; The Movie Channel (multiplexed); The Movie Channel HD.

Video-On-Demand: No

Pay-Per-View
iN DEMAND (delivered digitally); ESPN (delivered digitally); NHL Center Ice (delivered digitally); MLB Extra Innings (delivered digitally).

Internet Service
Operational: Yes.
Broadband Service: MidcoNet.
Fee: $35.00 installation; $19.95 monthly; $8.00 modem lease; $39.00 modem purchase.

Telephone Service
Digital: Operational
Fee: $18.00 monthly

Miles of Plant: 32.0 (coaxial); None (fiber optic).
Manager: Darrell Wrege. Marketing Director: Fred Jamieson. Customer Service Manager: Kathy Fuhrmann.
Ownership: Midcontinent Media Inc. (MSO).; Comcast Cable Communications Inc. (MSO).

LARIMORE—Midcontinent Communications, PO Box 5010, Sioux Falls, SD 57117. Phones: 800-456-0564; 605-229-1775. Fax: 605-229-0478. E-mail: butch_motenberg@mmi.net. Web Site: http://www.midcocomm.com. ICA: ND0048.
TV Market Ranking: Below 100 (LARIMORE). Franchise award date: N.A. Franchise expiration date: N.A. Began: October 1, 1979.
Channel capacity: 33 (not 2-way capable). Channels available but not in use: N.A.

Basic Service
Subscribers: 357.
Programming (received off-air): KBRR (FOX) Thief River Falls; KGFE (PBS) Grand Forks; KVLY-TV (NBC) Fargo; KXJB-TV (CBS) Valley City; WDAZ-TV (ABC, CW) Devils Lake.
Programming (via satellite): ABC Family Channel; CityTV; CNN; Discovery Channel; TBS Superstation; Turner Network TV.
Fee: $25.00 installation; $19.35 monthly; $19.02 additional installation.

Expanded Basic Service 1
Subscribers: N.A.
Programming (via satellite): A&E Networks; AMC; Animal Planet; Cartoon Network; Country Music TV; C-SPAN; ESPN; ESPN 2; Fox News Channel; Fox Sports Net North; FX; HGTV; History Channel; Spike TV; The Weather Channel; truTV; TV Land; USA Network.
Fee: $28.95 monthly.

Pay Service 1
Pay Units: 166.
Programming (via satellite): Encore; HBO; Starz.
Fee: $9.75 monthly (HBO).

Video-On-Demand: No

Internet Service
Operational: No.

Telephone Service
None

Miles of Plant: 9.0 (coaxial); None (fiber optic).
Manager: Butch Motenberg. Chief Technician: Jeff Wilde.
Ownership: Midcontinent Media Inc. (MSO).; Comcast Cable Communications Inc. (MSO).

LEEDS—Midcontinent Communications, PO Box 5010, Sioux Falls, SD 57117. Phones: 800-456-0564; 605-229-1775. Fax: 605-229-0478. Web Site: http://www.midcocomm.com. ICA: ND0081.
TV Market Ranking: Below 100 (LEEDS). Franchise award date: December 1, 1986. Franchise expiration date: December 1, 2011. Began: October 1, 1974.
Channel capacity: 41 (not 2-way capable). Channels available but not in use: N.A.

Basic Service
Subscribers: 202.
Programming (received off-air): KGFE (PBS) Grand Forks; KMOT (NBC) Minot; KVLY-TV (NBC) Fargo; KXMC-TV (CBS) Minot; WDAZ-TV (ABC, CW) Devils Lake.
Programming (via satellite): A&E Networks; ABC Family Channel; AMC; Cartoon Network; CNBC; CNN; Country Music TV; C-SPAN; Discovery Channel; Disney Channel; ESPN; ESPN 2; FX; Headline News; INSP; Lifetime; Nickelodeon; QVC; Spike TV; TBS Superstation; The Learning Channel; The Weather Channel; Turner Network TV; TV Guide Network; TV Land; USA Network; VH1; WGN America.
Fee: $50.00 installation; $26.50 monthly.

Pay Service 1
Pay Units: 16.
Programming (via satellite): Showtime.
Fee: $20.00 installation; $11.00 monthly.

Pay Service 2
Pay Units: N.A.
Programming (via satellite): HBO.
Fee: $20.00 installation; $12.00 monthly.

Pay Service 3
Pay Units: 6.
Programming (via satellite): The Movie Channel.
Fee: $20.00 installation; $11.00 monthly.

Internet Service
Operational: No.

Telephone Service
None

Miles of Plant: 6.0 (coaxial); None (fiber optic).
Manager: Darrell Wrege. Marketing Director: Fred Jamieson. Customer Service Manager: Kathy Fuhrmann.
Ownership: Midcontinent Media Inc. (MSO).; Comcast Cable Communications Inc. (MSO).

LISBON—Cable Services Inc., PO Box 1995, Jamestown, ND 58402-1995. Phones: 701-845-4383; 701-252-5281. Fax: 701-252-1105. E-mail: info@csicable.com. Web Site: http://www.csicable.com. ICA: ND0040.
TV Market Ranking: Outside TV Markets (LISBON). Franchise award date: N.A. Franchise expiration date: N.A. Began: January 1, 1981.
Channel capacity: N.A. Channels available but not in use: N.A.

Basic Service
Subscribers: 708.
Programming (received off-air): KFME (PBS) Fargo; KVLY-TV (NBC) Fargo; KVRR (FOX) Fargo; KXJB-TV (CBS) Valley City; WDAY-TV (ABC, CW) Fargo; allband FM.
Programming (via satellite): ABC Family Channel; CNN; CW+; Discovery Channel; Disney Channel; ESPN; Fox News Channel; Headline News; MSNBC; Nickelodeon; QVC; Spike TV; TBS Superstation; The Learning Channel; Turner Network TV; USA Network; WGN America.
Fee: $22.00 installation; $20.83 monthly.

Pay Service 1
Pay Units: 130.
Programming (via satellite): Showtime.
Fee: $8.95 monthly.

Video-On-Demand: No

Internet Service
Operational: No.

Telephone Service
None

Miles of Plant: 10.0 (coaxial); None (fiber optic). Additional miles planned: 2.0 (coaxial).
Manager: Roy Sheppard. Chief Technician: Roger Nelson. Marketing Manager: Chris Sheppard.
Ownership: Cable Services Inc. (MSO).

LISBON—Dickey Rural Networks. Formerly [ND0225] & formerly served by Oakes, ND [ND0226]. These cable systems have converted to IPTV, 9628 Hwy 281, PO Box 69, Ellendale, ND 58436-0069. Phones: 877-559-4692; 701-344-5000. Fax: 701-344-4300. Web Site: http://www.drtel.net. ICA: ND5028.
Channel capacity: N.A. Channels available but not in use: N.A.

Pay Service 1
Pay Units: N.A.
Fee: $11.00 monthly (HBO), $14.95 monthly (Showtime/TMC).

Internet Service
Operational: Yes.
Fee: $59.95 monthly.

Telephone Service
Digital: Operational
Fee: monthly (installation; $18.00 monthly

General Manager: Jeff Wilson. Engineering Manager: James Byerley. Marketing Manager: Janell Hauck. Plant Manager: Kent Schimke.

LISBON—Dickey Rural Networks. This cable system has converted to IPTV. See Lisbon, ND [ND5028]. ICA: ND0225.

LITCHVILLE—Dickey Rural Networks. Formerly [ND0135]. This cable system has converted to IPTV, 9628 Hwy 281, PO Box 69, Ellendale, ND 58436-0069. Phones: 877-559-4692; 701-344-5000. Fax: 701-344-4300. Web Site: http://www.drtel.net. ICA: ND5029.
Channel capacity: N.A. Channels available but not in use: N.A.

Pay Service 1
Pay Units: N.A.
Fee: $11.00 monthly (HBO), $14.95 monthly (Showtime/TMC).

Internet Service
Operational: Yes.
Fee: $59.95 monthly.

Telephone Service
Digital: Operational
Fee: monthly (installation; $15.75 monthly

General Manager: Jeff Wilson. Engineering Manager: James Byerley. Marketing Manager: Janell Hauck. Plant Manager: Kent Schimke.

LITCHVILLE—Dickey Rural Networks. This cable system has converted to IPTV. See listings for Litchville, ND [ND5029] & Marion, ND [ND5030]. ICA: ND0135.

MADDOCK—Maddock Cable TV, PO Box 368, Maddock, ND 58348-0368. Phone: 701-438-2541. ICA: ND0087.
TV Market Ranking: Below 100 (MADDOCK). Franchise award date: N.A. Franchise expiration date: N.A. Began: February 1, 1983.
Channel capacity: N.A. Channels available but not in use: N.A.

Basic Service
Subscribers: 140.
Programming (received off-air): KARE (NBC) Minneapolis; KMOT (NBC) Minot; KNRR (FOX) Pembina; KXMC-TV (CBS) Minot; WDAZ-TV (ABC, CW) Devils Lake; allband FM.
Programming (via satellite): A&E Networks; ABC Family Channel; CNN; Country Music TV; C-SPAN; Discovery Channel; Disney Channel; ESPN; ESPN 2; Fox News Channel; Fox Sports Net; Hallmark Channel; Hallmark Movie Channel; History Channel; MTV; National Geographic Channel; Nickelodeon; TBS Superstation; The Learning Channel; Turner Network TV; TV Land; VH1; WGN America.
Programming (via translator): KGFE (PBS) Grand Forks.
Fee: $28.00 monthly.

Digital Basic Service
Subscribers: N.A.
Programming (via satellite): BBC America; Bio; Bloomberg Television; cloo; CMT Pure Country; Current; Discovery Fit & Health; Discovery Health Channel; Discovery Kids Channel; ESPN 2; ESPN Classic Sports; ESPNews; Fox College Sports Atlantic; Fox College Sports Central; Fox College Sports Pacific; Fox Movie Channel; Fox Soccer; Fuse; G4; GMC; Golf Channel; Great American Country; GSN; Halogen Network; HGTV; History Channel International; ID Investigation Discovery; Independent Film Channel; Military Channel; MTV Hits; MTV2; National Geographic Channel; Nick Jr.; NickToons TV; Outdoor Channel; Ovation; Planet Green; Science; Speed; Style Network; Sundance Channel; TeenNick; The Word Network; Toon Disney; Trinity Broadcasting Network; Turner Classic Movies; Versus; VH1 Classic; VH1 Soul; WE tv.

Pay Service 1
Pay Units: 127.
Programming (via satellite): HBO.
Fee: $7.00 monthly.

Digital Pay Service 1
Pay Units: N.A.
Programming (via satellite): Encore (multiplexed); Flix; Showtime (multiplexed); Starz (multiplexed); The Movie Channel (multiplexed).

Video-On-Demand: No

Internet Service
Operational: No.

Telephone Service
None

Miles of Plant: 5.0 (coaxial); None (fiber optic).
Manager: Byron Ellingson.
Ownership: Maddock Area Development Corp.

MANDAN—Midcontinent Communications, 719 Memorial Hwy, Bismarck, ND 58504-5330. Phones: 701-224-0897; 800-888-1300; 605-229-1775 (Administrative office). Fax: 701-258-8751. Web Site: http://www.midcocomm.com. Also serves Acres-A-Plenty, Bismarck & Lincoln. ICA: ND0002.

TV Market Ranking: Below 100 (Acres-A-Plenty, Bismarck, Lincoln, MANDAN). Franchise award date: January 1, 1967. Franchise expiration date: N.A. Began: December 1, 1967.

Channel capacity: 66 (operating 2-way). Channels available but not in use: N.A.

Basic Service

Subscribers: 24,659.

Programming (received off-air): KBME-TV (PBS) Bismarck; KBMY (ABC) Bismarck; KFYR-TV (NBC) Bismarck; KNDX (FOX) Bismarck; KXMB-TV (CBS) Bismarck.

Programming (via satellite): A&E Networks; ABC Family Channel; AMC; Animal Planet; BET Networks; Bravo; Cartoon Network; Celebrity Shopping Network; CNBC; CNN; Comedy Central; Country Music TV; C-SPAN; C-SPAN 2; CW+; Discovery Channel; Discovery Health Channel; Disney Channel; E! Entertainment Television; ESPN; ESPN 2; Eternal Word TV Network; Food Network; Fox News Channel; Fox Sports Net North; FX; G4; Hallmark Channel; Headline News; HGTV; History Channel; INSP; Lifetime; MSNBC; MTV; Nickelodeon; Outdoor Channel; Oxygen; QVC; Radar Channel; Speed; Spike TV; Syfy; TBS Superstation; The Learning Channel; The Weather Channel; Travel Channel; Trinity Broadcasting Network; truTV; Turner Classic Movies; Turner Network TV; TV Guide Network; TV Land; USA Network; Versus; VH1; WE tv; WGN America.

Fee: $5.02 monthly.

Digital Basic Service

Subscribers: 3,521.

Programming (via satellite): 3 Angels Broadcasting Network; A&E HD; ABC Family HD; AmericanLife TV Network; Animal Planet HD; BBC America; Bio; Bloomberg Television; Boomerang; BTN; Canal Sur; CBS Sports Network; Cine Latino; Cine Mexicano; CMT Pure Country; CNN en Espanol; CNN HD; Cooking Channel; C-SPAN 3; Current; Discovery Channel HD; Discovery en Espanol; Discovery Fit & Health; Discovery Health Channel; Discovery Kids Channel; Disney Channel HD; DIY Network; ESPN 2 HD; ESPN Classic Sports; ESPN Deportes; ESPN HD; ESPNews; EWTN en Espanol; Food Network HD; Fox Business Channel; Fox College Sports Atlantic; Fox College Sports Central; Fox College Sports Pacific; Fox Deportes; Fox Soccer; FSN HD; Fuse; G4; Golf Channel; GolTV; Great American Country; GSN; Halogen Network; HD Theater; HDNet; HDNet Movies; HGTV HD; History Channel en Espanol; History Channel HD; History Channel International; ID Investigation Discovery; Independent Film Channel; ION Life; ION Television; JCTV; Lifetime Movie Network; Military Channel; MTV Hits; MTV Jams; MTV2; mun2 television; Music Choice; National Geographic Channel; National Geographic Channel HD Network; NFL Network; NHL Network; Nick Jr.; Nick Too; NickToons TV; Outdoor Channel; Palladia; PBS Kids Sprout; Pentagon Channel; Planet Green; Qubo; ReelzChannel; RFD-TV; Science; SoapNet; Style Network; Sundance Channel; Syfy HD; TBS in HD; TeenNick; Telemundo; Tennis Channel; TLC HD; Toon Disney; Toon Disney en Espanol; Tr3s; Trinity Broadcasting Network; Turner Classic Movies; Turner Network TV HD; TV One; TVE Internacional; TVG Network; Universal HD; Versus; Versus HD; VH1 Classic; VH1 Soul; WE tv.

Digital Pay Service 1

Pay Units: N.A.

Programming (via satellite): Cinemax (multiplexed); Cinemax HD; Encore (multiplexed); Flix; HBO (multiplexed); HBO HD; HBO Latino; Showtime (multiplexed); Showtime HD; Starz (multiplexed); Starz HDTV; The Movie Channel (multiplexed); The Movie Channel HD.

Video-On-Demand: No

Pay-Per-View

Addressable homes: 18,418.

iN DEMAND (delivered digitally); Sports PPV (delivered digitally).

Internet Service

Operational: Yes. Began: January 1, 1996.

Subscribers: 8,404.

Broadband Service: MidcoNet.

Fee: $35.00 installation; $19.95 monthly; $10.00 modem lease; $50.00 modem purchase.

Telephone Service

Digital: Operational

Fee: $18.00 monthly

Miles of Plant: 641.0 (coaxial); 8.0 (fiber optic).

Manager: Darrel Wrege.

Ownership: Midcontinent Media Inc. (MSO).; Comcast Cable Communications Inc. (MSO).

MANVEL—Midcontinent Communications, PO Box 5010, Sioux Falls, SD 57117. Phones: 800-456-0564; 605-229-1775. Fax: 605-229-0478. Web Site: http://www.midcocomm.com. ICA: ND0127.

TV Market Ranking: Below 100 (MANVEL). Franchise award date: N.A. Franchise expiration date: N.A. Began: February 1, 1984.

Channel capacity: N.A. Channels available but not in use: N.A.

Basic Service

Subscribers: 66.

Programming (received off-air): KBRR (FOX) Thief River Falls; KGFE (PBS) Grand Forks; KVLY-TV (NBC) Fargo; KXJB-TV (CBS) Valley City; WDAZ-TV (ABC, CW) Devils Lake.

Programming (via satellite): ABC Family Channel; CNN; Discovery Channel; ESPN; TBS Superstation; Turner Network TV.

Fee: $39.29 installation; $18.01 monthly; $19.65 additional installation.

Pay Service 1

Pay Units: 57.

Programming (via satellite): HBO.

Fee: $10.20 monthly.

Video-On-Demand: No

Internet Service

Operational: No.

Telephone Service

None

Miles of Plant: 4.0 (coaxial); None (fiber optic).

Manager: Butch Motenberg. Chief Technician: Jeff Wilde.

Ownership: Midcontinent Media Inc. (MSO).; Comcast Cable Communications Inc. (MSO).

MARION—Dickey Rural Networks. Formerly served by Litchville, ND [ND0135]. This cable system has converted to IPTV, 9628 Hwy 281, PO Box 69, Ellendale, ND 58436-0069. Phones: 877-559-4692; 701-344-5000. Fax: 701-344-4300. Web Site: http://www.drtel.net. ICA: ND5030.

Channel capacity: N.A. Channels available but not in use: N.A.

Pay Service 1

Pay Units: N.A.

Fee: $11.00 monthly (HBO), $14.95 monthly (Showtime/TMC).

Internet Service

Operational: Yes.

Fee: $59.95 monthly.

Telephone Service

Digital: Operational

Fee: monthly (installation; $15.75 monthly

General Manager: Jeff Wilson. Engineering Manager: James Byerley. Marketing Manager: Janell Hauck. Plant Manager: Kent Schimke.

MAX—Reservation Telephone Cooperative, 24 Main St N, PO Box 68, Parshall, ND 58770-0068. Phones: 888-862-3115; 701-862-3115. Fax: 701-862-3008. E-mail: kristin@rtc.coop. Web Site: http://www.reservationtelephone.com. ICA: ND0109.

TV Market Ranking: Below 100 (MAX). Franchise award date: December 2, 1986. Franchise expiration date: December 2, 2011. Began: October 1, 1983.

Channel capacity: 41 (not 2-way capable). Channels available but not in use: N.A.

Basic Service

Subscribers: 86.

Programming (received off-air): KMCY (ABC) Minot; KMOT (NBC) Minot; KSRE (PBS) Minot; KXMC-TV (CBS) Minot; KXND (FOX) Minot.

Programming (via satellite): A&E Networks; ABC Family Channel; AMC; Animal Planet; Cartoon Network; CNBC; CNN; Country Music TV; C-SPAN; Discovery Channel; ESPN; ESPN 2; Fox Sports Net; Headline News; HGTV; History Channel; INSP; Lifetime; Nickelodeon; QVC; Spike TV; Syfy; TBS Superstation; The Learning Channel; The Weather Channel; Turner Classic Movies; Turner Network TV; TV Land; USA Network; VH1; WE tv; WGN America.

Fee: $20.00 installation; $32.95 monthly.

Pay Service 1

Pay Units: 6.

Programming (via satellite): Showtime; The Movie Channel.

Fee: $10.00 monthly (Showtime & TMC).

Pay Service 2

Pay Units: N.A.

Programming (via satellite): HBO.

Fee: $10.00 monthly.

Video-On-Demand: Planned

Internet Service

Operational: No.

Telephone Service

None

Miles of Plant: 4.0 (coaxial); None (fiber optic).

General Manager: Royce S. Aslakson. Marketing Manager: Kristin Jaeger. Office Manager: Jan Boschee.

Ownership: Reservation Telephone Cooperative (MSO).

MCCLUSKY—Midcontinent Communications, PO Box 5010, Sioux Falls, SD 57117. Phones: 800-456-0564; 605-229-1775. Fax: 605-229-0478. Web Site: http://www.midcocomm.com. Also serves Goodrich. ICA: ND0092.

TV Market Ranking: Outside TV Markets (Goodrich, MCCLUSKY). Franchise award date: April 5, 1988. Franchise expiration date: April 5, 2011. Began: January 15, 1983.

Channel capacity: 41 (operating 2-way). Channels available but not in use: N.A.

Basic Service

Subscribers: 226.

Programming (received off-air): KBME-TV (PBS) Bismarck; KBMY (ABC) Bismarck; KFYR-TV (NBC) Bismarck; KNDX (FOX) Bismarck; KXMC-TV (CBS) Minot.

Programming (via satellite): A&E Networks; ABC Family Channel; AMC; Animal Planet; Cartoon Network; CNBC; CNN; Country Music TV; C-SPAN; Discovery Channel; Disney Channel; ESPN; ESPN 2; Fox Sports Net North; Headline News; HGTV; History Channel; INSP; Lifetime; Nickelodeon; QVC; Spike TV; Syfy; TBS Superstation; The Learning Channel; The Weather Channel; Turner Network TV; TV Land; USA Network; VH1; WE tv; WGN America.

Fee: $50.00 installation; $26.50 monthly.

Pay Service 1

Pay Units: 14.

Programming (via satellite): HBO.

Fee: $20.00 installation; $12.00 monthly.

Pay Service 2

Pay Units: 18.

Programming (via satellite): Showtime.

Fee: $20.00 installation; $11.00 monthly.

Pay Service 3

Pay Units: 18.

Programming (via satellite): The Movie Channel.

Fee: $20.00 installation; $11.00 monthly.

Video-On-Demand: No

Internet Service

Operational: Yes.

Fee: $35.00 installation; $19.95 monthly.

Telephone Service

Digital: Operational

Fee: $18.00 monthly

Miles of Plant: 5.0 (coaxial); None (fiber optic).

Manager: Darrell Wrege. Marketing Director: Fred Jamieson. Customer Service Manager: Kathy Fuhrmann.

Ownership: Midcontinent Media Inc. (MSO).; Comcast Cable Communications Inc. (MSO).

MEDINA—Formerly served by Cable Services Inc. No longer in operation. ICA: ND0101.

METIGOSHE—SRT Communications. Now served by VELVA, ND [ND0059]. ICA: ND0198.

MILNOR—Dickey Rural Networks. See Wyndmere, ND [ND0086]. ICA: ND0067.

MINNEWAUKAN—Midcontinent Communications, PO Box 5010, Sioux Falls, SD 57117. Phones: 800-456-0564; 605-229-1775. Fax: 605-229-0478. Web Site: http://www.midcocomm.com. ICA: ND0102.

TV Market Ranking: Below 100 (MINNEWAUKAN). Franchise award date: January 1, 1987. Franchise expiration date: January 1, 2011. Began: January 10, 1975.

Channel capacity: 41 (not 2-way capable). Channels available but not in use: N.A.

Basic Service

Subscribers: 117.

Programming (received off-air): KGFE (PBS) Grand Forks; KNRR (FOX) Pembina; KVLY-TV (NBC) Fargo; KXJB-TV (CBS) Valley City; WDAZ-TV (ABC, CW) Devils Lake; allband FM.

Programming (via satellite): A&E Networks; ABC Family Channel; AMC; Animal Planet; Cartoon Network; CNBC; CNN; Country Music TV; C-SPAN; Discovery Channel; Disney Channel; ESPN; ESPN 2; Fox Sports Net North; Headline News; HGTV; History Channel; INSP; Lifetime; Nickelodeon; QVC; Spike TV; Syfy; TBS Superstation; The Learning Channel; The Weather Channel; Turner Classic Movies; Turner Network TV; TV Land; USA Network; VH1; WE tv; WGN America.

Fee: $50.00 installation; $26.50 monthly.

Pay Service 1

Pay Units: 14.

Programming (via satellite): Showtime.

Fee: $20.00 installation; $11.00 monthly.

Pay Service 2

Pay Units: N.A.

Programming (via satellite): HBO.

Fee: $20.00 installation; $12.00 monthly.

Pay Service 3

Pay Units: 6.

Programming (via satellite): The Movie Channel.

Fee: $20.00 installation; $11.00 monthly.

Video-On-Demand: No

Internet Service

Operational: No.

Telephone Service

None

Miles of Plant: 3.0 (coaxial); None (fiber optic).

Manager: Darrell Wrege. Marketing Director: Fred Jamieson. Customer Service Manager: Kathy Fuhrmann.

Ownership: Midcontinent Media Inc. (MSO).; Comcast Cable Communications Inc. (MSO).

MINOT—Formerly served by Microwave Communication Services. No longer in operation. ICA: ND0219.

MINOT—Formerly served by Vision Systems. No longer in operation. ICA: ND0210.

MINOT—Midcontinent Communications, 717 20th Ave SE, Minot, ND 58702. Phones: 701-852-0376; 800-888-1300 (Customer service); 605-229-1775 (Administrative office). Fax: 605-229-0478. Web Site: http://www.midcocomm.com. Also serves Burlington, Glenburn, Lansford, Minot AFB, Mohall, Ruthville, Surrey & Ward County (portions). ICA: ND0004.

TV Market Ranking: Below 100 (Burlington, Glenburn, Lansford, MINOT, Minot AFB, Ruthville, Surrey, Ward County (portions)); Outside TV Markets (Mohall, Ward County (portions)). Franchise award date: N.A. Franchise expiration date: N.A. Began: December 1, 1974.

Channel capacity: 76 (operating 2-way). Channels available but not in use: N.A.

Basic Service

Subscribers: 14,421.

Programming (received off-air): KMCY (ABC) Minot; KMOT (NBC) Minot; KSRE (PBS) Minot; KXMC-TV (CBS) Minot; KXND (FOX) Minot; 4 FMs.

Programming (via satellite): A&E Networks; ABC Family Channel; AMC; Animal Planet; BET Networks; Bravo; Cartoon Network; CNBC; CNN; Comedy Central; Country Music TV; C-SPAN; C-SPAN 2; CW+; Discovery Channel; Discovery Fit & Health; Discovery Health Channel; Disney Channel; E! Entertainment Television; ESPN; ESPN 2; Eternal Word TV Network; Food Network; Fox Movie Channel; Fox News Channel; Fox Sports Net North; FX; Great American Country; Hallmark Channel; Headline News; HGTV; History Channel; INSP; Lifetime; MSNBC; MTV; MTV2; Nickelodeon; Oxygen; QVC; Speed; Spike TV; Syfy; TBS Superstation; The Learning Channel; The Weather Channel; Travel Channel; Trinity Broadcasting Network; truTV; Turner Classic Movies; Turner Network TV; TV Guide Network; TV Land; Univision Studios; USA Network; Versus; VH1; WE tv; WGN America.

Fee: $36.86 installation; $12.95 monthly.

Digital Basic Service

Subscribers: 4,089.

Programming (via satellite): 3 Angels Broadcasting Network; A&E HD; ABC Family HD; AmericanLife TV Network; Animal Planet HD; BBC America; Bio; Bloomberg Television; Boomerang; BTN; Canal Sur; CBS Sports Network; Cine Latino; Cine Mexicano; CMT Pure Country; CNN en Espanol; CNN HD; Cooking Channel; C-SPAN 3; Current; Discovery en Espanol; Discovery Fit & Health; Discovery Health Channel; Discovery Kids Channel; Disney Channel HD; DIY Network; ESPN Classic Sports; ESPN Deportes; ESPN HD; ESPNews; EWTN en Espanol; Food Network HD; Fox Business Channel; Fox College Sports Atlantic; Fox College Sports Central; Fox College Sports Pacific; Fox Deportes; Fox Movie Channel; Fox Soccer; Fuse; G4; Golf Channel; GolTV; Great American Country; GSN; Halogen Network; HD Theater; HDNet; HDNet Movies; HGTV HD; History Channel en Espanol; History Channel HD; History Channel International; ID Investigation Discovery; Independent Film Channel; ION Life; ION Television; JCTV; Lifetime Movie Network; Military Channel; MTV Hits; MTV Jams; MTV2; mun2 television; Music Choice; National Geographic Channel; National Geographic Channel HD Network; NFL Network; NHL Network; Nick Jr.; Nick Too; NickToons TV; Outdoor Channel; Palladia; PBS Kids Sprout; Pentagon Channel; Planet Green; Qubo; ReelzChannel; RFD-TV; Science; SoapNet; Style Network; Sundance Channel; Syfy HD; TBS in HD; TeenNick; Telemundo; Tennis Channel; TLC HD; Toon Disney; Toon Disney en Espanol; Tr3s; Trinity Broadcasting Network; Turner Classic Movies; Turner Network TV HD; TV One; TVE Internacional; TVG Network; Universal HD; USA Network HD; Versus; Versus HD; VH1 Classic; VH1 Soul; WE tv.

Digital Pay Service 1

Pay Units: 5,180.

Programming (via satellite): Cinemax (multiplexed); Cinemax HD; Encore (multiplexed); Flix; HBO (multiplexed); HBO Latino; Showtime (multiplexed); Starz (multiplexed); Starz HDTV; The Movie Channel (multiplexed); The Movie Channel HD.

Video-On-Demand: No

Pay-Per-View

Addressable homes: 2,149.

iN DEMAND (delivered digitally); Hot Choice (delivered digitally); Fresh (delivered digitally).

Internet Service

Operational: Yes.

Subscribers: 4,506.

Broadband Service: MidcoNet.

Fee: $19.95 monthly.

Telephone Service

Digital: Operational

Fee: $18.00 monthly

Miles of Plant: 272.0 (coaxial); 34.0 (fiber optic).

Manager: Todd Jensen. Chief Technician: Brad Nixon.

Ownership: Midcontinent Media Inc. (MSO).; Comcast Cable Communications Inc. (MSO).

MINTO—Midcontinent Communications, PO Box 5010, Sioux Falls, SD 57117. Phones: 800-456-0564; 605-229-1775. Fax: 605-229-0478. Web Site: http://www.midcocomm.com. ICA: ND0082.

TV Market Ranking: Below 100 (MINTO). Franchise award date: N.A. Franchise expiration date: N.A. Began: June 1, 1983.

Channel capacity: 12 (not 2-way capable). Channels available but not in use: N.A.

Basic Service

Subscribers: 135.

Programming (received off-air): KGFE (PBS) Grand Forks; KNRR (FOX) Pembina; WDAZ-TV (ABC, CW) Devils Lake.

Programming (via satellite): ABC Family Channel; CNN; Disney Channel; ESPN; TBS Superstation.

Programming (via translator): KVLY-TV (NBC) Fargo; KXJB-TV (CBS) Valley City.

Fee: $36.53 installation; $16.22 monthly; $18.76 additional installation.

Pay Service 1

Pay Units: 10.

Programming (via satellite): HBO.

Fee: $10.20 monthly.

Video-On-Demand: No

Internet Service

Operational: No.

Telephone Service

None

Miles of Plant: 5.0 (coaxial); None (fiber optic).

Manager: Butch Motenberg. Chief Technician: Jeff Wilde.

Ownership: Midcontinent Media Inc. (MSO).; Comcast Cable Communications Inc. (MSO).

MOTT—Midcontinent Communications, PO Box 5010, Sioux Falls, SD 57117. Phones: 800-456-0564; 605-229-1775. Fax: 605-229-0478. Web Site: http://www.midcocomm.com. ICA: ND0052.

TV Market Ranking: Outside TV Markets (MOTT). Franchise award date: March 2, 1992. Franchise expiration date: March 2, 2007. Began: June 15, 1980.

Channel capacity: N.A. Channels available but not in use: N.A.

Basic Service

Subscribers: 307.

Programming (received off-air): KBMY (ABC) Bismarck; KDSE (PBS) Dickinson; KFYR-TV (NBC) Bismarck; KXMA-TV (CBS) Dickinson; KXMB-TV (CBS) Bismarck.

Programming (via satellite): A&E Networks; ABC Family Channel; AMC; Animal Planet; Cartoon Network; CNBC; CNN; Country Music TV; C-SPAN; Discovery Channel; Disney Channel; ESPN; ESPN 2; Fox News Channel; Headline News; HGTV; History Channel; INSP; Lifetime; Nickelodeon; Outdoor Channel; QVC; Spike TV; Syfy; TBS Superstation; The Learning Channel; The Weather Channel; Turner Network TV; TV Land; USA Network; VH1; WE tv; WGN America.

Fee: $50.00 installation; $26.50 monthly.

Pay Service 1

Pay Units: 40.

Programming (via satellite): HBO.

Fee: $20.00 installation; $12.00 monthly.

Pay Service 2

Pay Units: 22.

Programming (via satellite): Showtime.

Fee: $20.00 installation; $11.00 monthly.

Pay Service 3

Pay Units: 22.

Programming (via satellite): The Movie Channel.

Fee: $20.00 installation; $11.00 monthly.

Video-On-Demand: No

Internet Service

Operational: Yes.

Fee: $35.00 installation; $19.95 monthly.

Telephone Service

Digital: Operational

Fee: $18.00 monthly

Miles of Plant: 8.0 (coaxial); None (fiber optic).

Manager: Darrell Wrege. Marketing Director: Fred Jamieson. Customer Service Manager: Kathy Fuhrmann.

Ownership: Midcontinent Media Inc. (MSO).; Comcast Cable Communications Inc. (MSO).

MUNICH—United Telephone Mutual Aid Corp., 411 7th Ave, Langdon, ND 58249-2517. Phones: 800-844-9708; 701-256-5156. Fax: 701-256-5150. E-mail: info@utma.com. Web Site: http://www.utma.com. Also serves Rock Lake. ICA: ND0091.

TV Market Ranking: Outside TV Markets (MUNICH, Rock Lake). Franchise award date: N.A. Franchise expiration date: N.A. Began: April 1, 1968.

Channel capacity: 18 (2-way capable). Channels available but not in use: N.A.

Basic Service

Subscribers: 97.

Programming (received off-air): KNRR (FOX) Pembina; WDAZ-TV (ABC, CW) Devils Lake.

Programming (via satellite): A&E Networks; ABC Family Channel; CNN; Discovery Channel; Disney Channel; ESPN; Spike TV; TBS Superstation; Turner Network TV; USA Network; various Canadian stations; WGN America.

Programming (via translator): KFME (PBS) Fargo; KVLY-TV (NBC) Fargo; KXJB-TV (CBS) Valley City.

Fee: $28.00 installation; $20.00 monthly.

Pay Service 1

Pay Units: 10.

Programming (via satellite): Showtime.

Fee: $10.00 monthly.

Video-On-Demand: No

Internet Service

Operational: No, DSL & dial-up.

Telephone Service

None

Miles of Plant: 5.0 (coaxial); None (fiber optic).

Manager: Kenneth Carlson. Assistant General Manager: Dennis Hansel. Office Manager: Perry Oster.
Ownership: United Telephone Mutual Aid Corp.

NEW ENGLAND—Formerly served by New England Cablevision Inc. No longer in operation. ICA: ND0075.

NEW LEIPZIG—Formerly served by Northland Communications. No longer in operation. ICA: ND0113.

NEWBURG—SRT Communications. Now served by VELVA, ND [ND0059]. ICA: ND0175.

NORTHWOOD—MLGC, 301 Dewey St, Enderlin, ND 58027. Phone: 701-437-3300. Fax: 701-437-3022. E-mail: mandl@mlgc.com. Web Site: http://www.mlgc.com. ICA: ND0224.
TV Market Ranking: Outside TV Markets (NORTHWOOD). Franchise award date: N.A. Franchise expiration date: N.A. Began: N.A.
Channel capacity: N.A. Channels available but not in use: N.A.
Basic Service
Subscribers: 341.
Programming (received off-air): KFME (PBS) Fargo; KVLY-TV (NBC) Fargo; KVRR (FOX) Fargo; KXJB-TV (CBS) Valley City; WDAY-TV (ABC, CW) Fargo.
Programming (via satellite): A&E Networks; ABC Family Channel; CNN; Country Music TV; Discovery Channel; Disney Channel; ESPN; ESPN 2; Fox Sports Net; History Channel; Nickelodeon; QVC; Spike TV; Syfy; TBS Superstation; The Weather Channel; Turner Network TV; USA Network; WGN America.
Fee: $40.00 installation; $26.50 monthly.
Pay Service 1
Pay Units: N.A.
Programming (via satellite): HBO.
Fee: $11.00 monthly.
Video-On-Demand: No
Internet Service
Operational: Yes.
Telephone Service
None
Assistant Manager: Tyler Kilde.
Ownership: MLGC (MSO).

OAKES—Cable Services Inc., PO Box 1995, Jamestown, ND 58402-1995. Phones: 701-845-4383; 701-252-5281. Fax: 701-252-1105. E-mail: info@csicable.com. Web Site: http://www.csicable.com. ICA: ND0038.
TV Market Ranking: Outside TV Markets (OAKES). Franchise award date: N.A. Franchise expiration date: N.A. Began: December 27, 1974.
Channel capacity: N.A. Channels available but not in use: N.A.
Basic Service
Subscribers: 682.
Programming (received off-air): KABY-TV (ABC) Aberdeen; KDLO-TV (CBS, MNT) Florence; KDSD-TV (PBS) Aberdeen; KFME (PBS) Fargo; KJRR (FOX) Jamestown; KVLY-TV (NBC) Fargo; KXJB-TV (CBS) Valley City; WDAY-TV (ABC, CW) Fargo; 4 FMs.
Programming (via satellite): ABC Family Channel; CNN; Discovery Channel; Disney Channel; ESPN; Fox News Channel; Headline News; MSNBC; Nickelodeon; Spike TV; TBS Superstation; The Weather Channel; Turner Classic Movies; Turner Network TV; USA Network; WGN America.
Fee: $10.00 installation; $20.00 monthly.
Pay Service 1
Pay Units: 110.
Programming (via satellite): Showtime.
Fee: $8.95 monthly.
Video-On-Demand: No
Internet Service
Operational: No.
Telephone Service
None
Miles of Plant: 14.0 (coaxial); None (fiber optic).
Manager: Roy Sheppard. Chief Technician: Roger Nelson. Marketing Manager: Chris Sheppard.
Ownership: Cable Services Inc. (MSO).

OAKES—Dickey Rural Networks. Formerly [ND0226]. This cable system has converted to IPTV, 9628 Hwy 281, PO Box 69, Ellendale, ND 58436-0069. Phones: 877-559-4692; 701-344-5000. Fax: 701-344-4300. Web Site: http://www.drtel.net. ICA: ND5032.
Channel capacity: N.A. Channels available but not in use: N.A.
Internet Service
Operational: Yes.
Fee: $59.95 monthly.
Telephone Service
Digital: Operational
Fee: monthly (installation; $15.75 monthly
General Manager: Jeff Wilson. Engineering Manager: James Byerley. Marketing Manager: Janell Hauck. Plant Manager: Kent Schimke.

OAKES—Dickey Rural Networks. This cable system has converted to IPTV. See listings for Ellendale, ND [ND5021], Forman, ND [ND5022], Kulm, ND [ND5026], Lisbon, ND [ND5028] & Oakes, ND [ND5032]. ICA: ND0226.

PARK RIVER—Polar Cablevision. Now served by PEMBINA, ND [ND0078]. ICA: ND0026.

PARSHALL—Reservation Telephone Cooperative, 24 Main St N, PO Box 68, Parshall, ND 58770-0068. Phones: 701-862-3115; 888-862-3115. Fax: 701-862-3008. E-mail: kristin@rtc.coop. Web Site: http://www.reservationtelephone.com. Also serves Makoti, New Town, Plaza & Ryder. ICA: ND0020.
TV Market Ranking: Below 100 (Makoti, Plaza, Ryder); Outside TV Markets (New Town, PARSHALL). Franchise award date: N.A. Franchise expiration date: N.A. Began: November 1, 1981.
Channel capacity: 19 (not 2-way capable). Channels available but not in use: N.A.
Basic Service
Subscribers: 980.
Programming (received off-air): KMCY (ABC) Minot; KMOT (NBC) Minot; KSRE (PBS) Minot; KXMC-TV (CBS) Minot; KXND (FOX) Minot.
Programming (via satellite): A&E Networks; ABC Family Channel; Animal Planet; CNBC; CNN; Country Music TV; Discovery Channel; Disney Channel; E! Entertainment Television; ESPN; ESPN 2; Eternal Word TV Network; Food Network; Fox News Channel; Fox Sports Net; Great American Country; Hallmark Channel; HGTV; History Channel; MSNBC; MTV; Nickelodeon; Spike TV; Syfy; TBS Superstation; The Learning Channel; The Weather Channel; Turner Classic Movies; Turner Network TV; TV Land; USA Network; Versus; VH1; WGN America.
Fee: $20.00 installation; $27.95 monthly.
Pay Service 1
Pay Units: 623.
Programming (via satellite): HBO.
Fee: $10.00 monthly.
Video-On-Demand: Planned
Internet Service
Operational: No.
Telephone Service
None
Miles of Plant: 21.0 (coaxial); None (fiber optic).
General Manager: Royce S. Aslakson. Marketing Manager: Kristin Jaeger. Office Manager: Jan Boschee.
Ownership: Reservation Telephone Cooperative.

PEMBINA—Polar Cablevision, 110 4th St E, PO Box 270, Park River, ND 58270. Phones: 701-284-7221; 800-284-7222. Fax: 701-284-7205. Web Site: http://www.thinkpolar.com. Also serves Adams, Cavalier, Cavalier Air Force Station, Crystal, Edinburg, Fordville, Gilby, Hensel, Hoople, Mayville, Michigan, Mountain, Neche, Park River, Petersburg, Pisek, Portland & St. Thomas. ICA: ND0078.
TV Market Ranking: Below 100 (Cavalier, Cavalier Air Force Station, Crystal, Gilby, Hensel, Mountain, Neche, PEMBINA, St. Thomas); Outside TV Markets (Adams, Edinburg, Fordville, Hoople, Mayville, Michigan, Park River, Petersburg, Pisek, Portland). Franchise award date: January 1, 1983. Franchise expiration date: N.A. Began: August 1, 1983.
Channel capacity: N.A. Channels available but not in use: N.A.
Basic Service
Subscribers: 2,942 Includes Lakota.
Programming (received off-air): KGFE (PBS) Grand Forks; KNRR (FOX) Pembina; KVLY-TV (NBC) Fargo; KXJB-TV (CBS) Valley City; various Canadian stations; WDAY-TV (ABC, CW) Fargo; WDAZ-TV (ABC, CW) Devils Lake.
Programming (via satellite): A&E Networks; ABC Family Channel; AMC; Animal Planet; CNBC; CNN; Comedy Central; Country Music TV; C-SPAN; CW+; Discovery Channel; Disney Channel; ESPN; ESPN 2; ESPN Classic Sports; Food Network; Fox News Channel; Fox Sports Net; FX; Headline News; HGTV; History Channel; INSP; Lifetime; LWS Local Weather Station; MSNBC; MTV; NFL Network; Nickelodeon; Outdoor Channel; Spike TV; Syfy; TBS Superstation; The Learning Channel; The Weather Channel; Toon Disney; Travel Channel; Turner Classic Movies; Turner Network TV; TV Land; USA Network; Versus; VH1; WGN America.
Fee: $20.00 installation; $41.95 monthly.
Digital Basic Service
Subscribers: N.A.
Programming (via satellite): BBC America; Bio; Bloomberg Television; Bravo; cloo; CMT Pure Country; Discovery Fit & Health; Discovery Health Channel; Discovery Kids Channel; DIY Network; DMX Music; ESPN U; ESPNews; Eternal Word TV Network; Fox Movie Channel; G4; Golf Channel; Great American Country; GSN; Hallmark Channel; History Channel International; ID Investigation Discovery; Lifetime Movie Network; Lifetime Real Women; Military Channel; MTV Hits; MTV2; National Geographic Channel; Nick Jr.; NickToons TV; Planet Green; QVC; RFD-TV; Science; SoapNet; Speed; Style Network; TeenNick; Trinity Broadcasting Network; VH1 Classic; VH1 Soul; WE tv.
Fee: $7.00 monthly.
Digital Pay Service 1
Pay Units: N.A.
Programming (via satellite): Cinemax (multiplexed); Encore (multiplexed); HBO (multiplexed); Showtime (multiplexed); Starz (multiplexed); The Movie Channel (multiplexed).
Fee: $5.95 monthly (Encore), $7.95 monthly (Cinemax), $10.95 monthly (Starz/Encore), $ 11.95 monthly (HBO).
Video-On-Demand: No
Pay-Per-View
iN DEMAND (delivered digitally); Playboy TV (delivered digitally); Club Jenna (delivered digitally).
Internet Service
Operational: No, DSL.
Telephone Service
None
Miles of Plant: 6.0 (coaxial); None (fiber optic).
Chief Executive Officer & General Manager: David L. Dunning. Chief Financial Officer: Shari Flanders. Cable TV Special Projects Supervisor: Russ Ramsey.
Ownership: Polar Communications.

RAY—Northwest Communications Cooperative, 111 Railroad Ave, PO Box 38, Ray, ND 58849. Phones: 800-245-5884; 701-568-3331. Fax: 701-568-7777. E-mail: ncc@nccray.com. Web Site: http://www.nccray.com. Also serves Bowbells, Columbus, Crosby, Flaxton, Grenora, Lignite, Noonan, Powers Lake, Tioga & Wildrose. ICA: ND0069.
TV Market Ranking: Below 100 (Grenora, RAY); Outside TV Markets (Bowbells, Columbus, Crosby, Flaxton, Lignite, Noonan, Powers Lake, Tioga, Wildrose). Franchise award date: N.A. Franchise expiration date: N.A. Began: March 1, 1981.
Channel capacity: N.A. Channels available but not in use: N.A.
Basic Service
Subscribers: 1,600.
Programming (received off-air): KMCY (ABC) Minot; KMOT (NBC) Minot; KNDX (FOX) Bismarck; KSRE (PBS) Minot; KUMV-TV (NBC) Williston; KXMC-TV (CBS) Minot; KXMD-TV (CBS) Williston; allband FM.
Programming (via satellite): A&E Networks; ABC Family Channel; AMC; Animal Planet; BTN; CNBC; CNN; Comedy Central; C-SPAN; CW+; Discovery Channel; Disney Channel; DIY Network; ESPN; ESPN

2; ESPN Classic Sports; ESPNews; Eternal Word TV Network; FamilyNet; Food Network; Fox News Channel; Fox Sports Net North; FX; Great American Country; Hallmark Channel; Headline News; HGTV; History Channel; INSP; Lifetime; MTV; National Geographic Channel; NFL Network; Nickelodeon; Outdoor Channel; QVC; RFD-TV; TBS Superstation; The Learning Channel; The Weather Channel; Toon Disney; Travel Channel; truTV; Turner Classic Movies; Turner Network TV; TV Land; USA Network; Versus; VH1; WGN America.

Fee: $25.00 installation; $28.45 monthly; $4.95 converter.

Digital Basic Service

Subscribers: N.A.

Programming (via satellite): A&E HD; BBC America; Bio; Bloomberg Television; Bravo; BTN HD; cloo; Cooking Channel; Discovery Channel HD; Discovery Fit & Health; Discovery Health Channel; Discovery Home Channel; Discovery Kids Channel; Discovery Times Channel; DMX Music; ESPN HD; Fox College Sports Atlantic; Fox College Sports Central; Fox College Sports Pacific; Fox Movie Channel; Fox Soccer; FSN HD; G4; Golf Channel; GSN; HDNet; History Channel HD; History Channel International; Independent Film Channel; Lifetime Movie Network; Military Channel; MTV Hits; MTV2; NFL Network HD; Nick Jr.; NickToons TV; Science; SoapNet; Speed; TeenNick; Turner Network TV HD; VH1 Classic; VH1 Country; VH1 Soul; WE tv; WealthTV HD.

Digital Pay Service 1

Pay Units: N.A.

Programming (via satellite): Cinemax (multiplexed); Cinemax HD; Encore (multiplexed); Flix; HBO (multiplexed); HBO HD; Showtime (multiplexed); Showtime HD; Starz (multiplexed); Starz HDTV; The Movie Channel (multiplexed).

Video-On-Demand: No

Internet Service

Operational: No, DSL.

Telephone Service

None

Miles of Plant: 41.0 (coaxial); None (fiber optic).

Manager: Dwight Schmitt. Office Manager: Michael Steffan. Operations Manager: Dean Rustad.

Ownership: Northwest Communications Cooperative (MSO).

REGENT—Consolidated Telecommunications Co. Now served by DICKINSON, ND [ND0005]. ICA: ND0201.

ROLETTE—Midcontinent Communications, PO Box 5010, Sioux Falls, SD 57117. Phones: 800-456-0564; 605-229-1775. Fax: 605-229-0478. Web Site: http://www.midcocomm.com. Also serves Bisbee, Bottineau, Dunseith, Rolla, St. John & Willow City. ICA: ND0094.

TV Market Ranking: Outside TV Markets (Bisbee, Bottineau, Dunseith, ROLETTE, Rolla, St. John, Willow City). Franchise award date: January 7, 1987. Franchise expiration date: January 7, 2011. Began: January 1, 1977.

Channel capacity: N.A. Channels available but not in use: N.A.

Basic Service

Subscribers: 1,838.

Programming (received off-air): KMCY (ABC) Minot; KMOT (NBC) Minot; KSRE (PBS) Minot; KXMC-TV (CBS) Minot; KXND (FOX) Minot; allband FM.

Programming (via satellite): A&E Networks; ABC Family Channel; AMC; Animal Planet; BET Networks; Bravo; Cartoon Network; CNBC; CNN; Comedy Central; Country Music TV; C-SPAN; C-SPAN 2; CW+; Discovery Channel; Discovery Health Channel; Disney Channel; E! Entertainment Television; ESPN; ESPN 2; Eternal Word TV Network; Food Network; Fox News Channel; Fox Sports Net North; FX; G4; Great American Country; Hallmark Channel; Headline News; HGTV; History Channel; INSP; Lifetime; MSNBC; MTV; Nickelodeon; Outdoor Channel; Oxygen; QVC; Speed; Spike TV; Syfy; TBS Superstation; The Learning Channel; The Weather Channel; Travel Channel; Trinity Broadcasting Network; truTV; Turner Classic Movies; Turner Network TV; TV Guide Network; TV Land; USA Network; Versus; VH1; WE tv; WGN America.

Fee: $50.00 installation; $26.50 monthly.

Digital Basic Service

Subscribers: N.A.

Programming (received off-air): KSRE (PBS) Minot.

Programming (via satellite): 3 Angels Broadcasting Network; A&E HD; ABC Family HD; AmericanLife TV Network; Animal Planet HD; BBC America; Bio; Bloomberg Television; Boomerang; BTN; Canal Sur; CBS Sports Network; Cine Latino; Cine Mexicano; CMT Pure Country; CNN en Espanol; CNN HD; Cooking Channel; C-SPAN 3; Current; Discovery Channel HD; Discovery en Espanol; Discovery Fit & Health; Discovery Health Channel; Discovery Kids Channel; Disney Channel HD; DIY Network; ESPN 2 HD; ESPN Classic Sports; ESPN Deportes; ESPN HD; ESPNews; EWTN en Espanol; Food Network HD; Fox Business Channel; Fox College Sports Atlantic; Fox College Sports Central; Fox College Sports Pacific; Fox Deportes; Fox Movie Channel; Fox Soccer; FSN HD; Fuse; G4; Golf Channel; GolTV; Great American Country; GSN; Halogen Network; HD Theater; HDNet; HDNet Movies; HGTV HD; History Channel en Espanol; History Channel HD; History Channel International; ID Investigation Discovery; Independent Film Channel; ION Life; ION Television; JCTV; Lifetime Movie Network; Military Channel; MTV Hits; MTV Jams; MTV2; mun2 television; Music Choice; National Geographic Channel; National Geographic Channel HD Network; NFL Network; NHL Network; Nick Jr.; Nick Too; NickToons TV; Outdoor Channel; Palladia; PBS Kids Sprout; Pentagon Channel; Planet Green; Qubo; ReelzChannel; RFD-TV; Science; SoapNet; Style Network; Sundance Channel; Syfy HD; TBS in HD; TeenNick; Telemundo; Tennis Channel; TLC HD; Toon Disney; Toon Disney en Espanol; Tr3s; Trinity Broadcasting Network; Turner Classic Movies; Turner Network TV HD; TV One; TVE Internacional; TVG Network; Universal HD; USA Network HD; Versus; Versus HD; VH1 Classic; VH1 Soul; WE tv.

Digital Pay Service 1

Pay Units: N.A.

Programming (via satellite): Cinemax (multiplexed); Cinemax HD; Encore (multiplexed); Flix; HBO (multiplexed); HBO HD; HBO Latino; Showtime (multiplexed); Showtime HD; Starz (multiplexed); Starz HDTV; The Movie Channel (multiplexed); The Movie Channel HD.

Video-On-Demand: No

Pay-Per-View

iN DEMAND (delivered digitally); MLS Direct Kick (delivered digitally); NBA League Pass (delivered digitally); NHL Center Ice (delivered digitally); MLB Extra Innings (delivered digitally); ESPN (delivered digitally).

Internet Service

Operational: Yes.

Fee: $35.00 installation; $19.95 monthly.

Telephone Service

None

Miles of Plant: 49.0 (coaxial); None (fiber optic).

Manager: Darrell Wrege. Marketing Director: Fred Jamieson. Customer Service Manager: Kathy Fuhrmann.

Ownership: Midcontinent Media Inc. (MSO).; Comcast Cable Communications Inc. (MSO).

RUGBY—Midcontinent Communications, PO Box 5010, Sioux Falls, SD 57117. Phones: 800-456-0564; 605-229-1775. Fax: 605-330-4089. E-mail: darrell_wrege@mmi.net. Web Site: http://www.midcocomm.com. Also serves Towner. ICA: ND0018.

TV Market Ranking: Outside TV Markets (RUGBY, Towner). Franchise award date: April 4, 1988. Franchise expiration date: April 4, 2011. Began: March 1, 1973.

Channel capacity: 59 (operating 2-way). Channels available but not in use: N.A.

Basic Service

Subscribers: 1,309.

Programming (received off-air): KMCY (ABC) Minot; KXND (FOX) Minot; allband FM.

Programming (via satellite): ABC Family Channel; C-SPAN; Fox News Channel; TBS Superstation; The Learning Channel; The Weather Channel; Univision Studios; WGN America.

Fee: $25.00 installation; $38.95 monthly.

Expanded Basic Service 1

Subscribers: N.A.

Programming (via satellite): A&E Networks; AMC; Animal Planet; BET Networks; Bravo; Cartoon Network; CNBC; CNN; Comedy Central; Country Music TV; C-SPAN 2; Discovery Channel; Discovery Health Channel; Disney Channel; E! Entertainment Television; ESPN; ESPN 2; Eternal Word TV Network; Food Network; Fox Sports Net North; FX; Great American Country; Hallmark Channel; Headline News; HGTV; History Channel; INSP; ION Television; Lifetime; MSNBC; MTV; NFL Network; Nickelodeon; Outdoor Channel; Oxygen; QVC; Speed; Spike TV; Syfy; Travel Channel; Trinity Broadcasting Network; Turner Classic Movies; Turner Network TV; TV Guide Network; TV Land; USA Network; Versus; VH1; WE tv.

Digital Basic Service

Subscribers: N.A.

Programming (via satellite): AmericanLife TV Network; BBC America; Bio; Bloomberg Television; Boomerang; CBS Sports Network; Cooking Channel; C-SPAN 3; Current; Discovery Fit & Health; Discovery Health Channel; Discovery Home Channel; Discovery Kids Channel; Discovery Times Channel; DIY Network; DMX Music; ESPN Classic Sports; ESPNews; Fox College Sports Atlantic; Fox College Sports Central; Fox College Sports Pacific; Fox Movie Channel; Fox Soccer; Fuse; G4; GAS; Golf Channel; GolTV; Great American Country; GSN; Halogen Network; History Channel International; Independent Film Channel; Lifetime Movie Network; MTV Networks Digital Suite; National Geographic Channel; Nick Jr.; Nick Too; NickToons TV; Outdoor Channel; Science Television; Style Network; Sundance Channel; Tennis Channel; Toon Disney; Trinity Broadcasting Network; Turner Classic Movies; TV One; WE tv.

Fee: $47.95 monthly.

Digital Pay Service 1

Pay Units: N.A.

Programming (via satellite): Canales N; Cinemax (multiplexed); Encore (multiplexed); Flix; HBO (multiplexed); Showtime (multiplexed); Starz (multiplexed); The Movie Channel (multiplexed).

Video-On-Demand: No

Internet Service

Operational: Yes.

Broadband Service: MidcoNet.

Fee: $35.00 installation; $19.95 monthly; $8.00 modem lease; $39.00 modem purchase.

Telephone Service

Digital: Operational

Fee: $18.00 monthly

Miles of Plant: 22.0 (coaxial); None (fiber optic).

General Manager: Darrell Wrege. Marketing Director: Fred Jamieson. Customer Service Manager: Kathy Fuhrmann.

Ownership: Midcontinent Media Inc. (MSO).; Comcast Cable Communications Inc. (MSO).

SANBORN—Formerly served by Cable Services Inc. No longer in operation. ICA: ND0204.

SAWYER—Formerly served by Sawyer CATV. No longer in operation. ICA: ND0134.

SELFRIDGE—West River Cable Television, 801 Coleman Ave, PO Box 39, Bison, SD 57620. Phones: 888-411-5651; 605-244-5236. Fax: 605-244-7288. E-mail: westriver@sdplains.com. Web Site: http://www.westrivercatv.com. ICA: ND0056.

TV Market Ranking: Outside TV Markets (SELFRIDGE). Franchise award date: December 12, 1988. Franchise expiration date: December 12, 2011. Began: N.A.

Channel capacity: 36 (not 2-way capable). Channels available but not in use: N.A.

Basic Service

Subscribers: 26.

Programming (received off-air): KBME-TV (PBS) Bismarck; KBMY (ABC) Bismarck; KFYR-TV (NBC) Bismarck; KNDX (FOX) Bismarck; KXMB-TV (CBS) Bismarck.

Programming (via satellite): A&E Networks; ABC Family Channel; AMC; Cartoon Network; CNBC; CNN; Country Music TV; C-SPAN; Discovery Channel; Disney Channel; ESPN; ESPN 2; Headline News; HGTV; History Channel; INSP; Lifetime; Nickelodeon; QVC; Spike TV; TBS Superstation; The Learning Channel; The Weather Channel; Turner Network TV; TV Land; USA Network; VH1; WGN America.

Fee: $50.00 installation; $32.95 monthly.

Pay Service 1

Pay Units: N.A.

Programming (via satellite): HBO; Showtime; The Movie Channel.

Fee: $20.00 installation; $10.00 monthly (Showtime), $10.95 monthly (HBO).

Video-On-Demand: No

Internet Service

Operational: No.

Telephone Service

None

Miles of Plant: 1.0 (coaxial); None (fiber optic).

General Manager: Jerry Reisenauer. Assistant Manager: Colgan Huber.

Ownership: West River Cooperative Telephone Co. (MSO).

SHERWOOD—SRT Communications. Now served by VELVA, ND [ND0059]. ICA: ND0117.

SHEYENNE—Dakota Central Telecommunications, 630 Fifth St N, PO Box 299, Carrington, ND 58421. Phones: 701-674-8121; 701-652-3184. E-mail: customerservice@daktel.com. Web Site: http://www.daktel.com. ICA: ND0130.

TV Market Ranking: Below 100 (SHEYENNE). Franchise award date: N.A. Franchise expiration date: N.A. Began: December 1, 1984.

Channel capacity: 28 (not 2-way capable). Channels available but not in use: N.A.

Digital Basic Service

Subscribers: 76.

Programming (via satellite): CW+; ION Television; JCTV; Superstation WGN; TBS Superstation; This TV.

Fee: $13.95 monthly.

Digital Expanded Basic Service

Subscribers: N.A.

Programming (received off-air): KFME (PBS) Fargo; KJRR (FOX) Jamestown; KVLY-TV (NBC) Fargo; KXJB-TV (CBS) Valley City; WDAZ-TV (ABC, CW) Devils Lake.

Programming (via satellite): 3 Angels Broadcasting Network; A&E HD; A&E Networks; ABC Family Channel; American Movie Classics; AmericanLife TV Network; Animal Planet; Animal Planet HD; BBC America; Big Ten Network; Bio; Bloomberg Television; Boomerang; Bravo; Bravo HD; Cartoon Network; CBS Sports Network; Chiller; CNBC; CNBC HD+; CNN; CNN International; Comedy Central; Cooking Channel; Country Music TV; C-SPAN; C-SPAN 2; C-SPAN 3; Discovery Channel; Discovery Channel HD; Discovery Fit & Health; Discovery Kids Channel; Disney Channel; Disney XD; DIY Network; E! Entertainment Television; ESPN; ESPN 2; ESPN 2 HD; ESPN Classic Sports; ESPN HD; ESPN U; ESPNews; ESPNews HD; ESPNU HD; Eternal Word TV Network; Food Network; Food Network HD; Fox College Sports Atlantic; Fox College Sports Central; Fox College Sports Pacific; Fox Movie Channel; Fox News Channel; Fox Soccer; FSN Digital; FSN HD; Fuel TV; Fuse; FX; G4; Golf Channel; Golf Channel HD; GolTV; Great American Country; GSN; Hallmark Channel; Halogen Network; HD Theater; HDNet; HDNet Movies; Headline News; HGTV; HGTV HD; History Channel; History Channel International; Home Shopping Network; HorseTV Channel; ID Investigation Discovery; INSP; Jewelry Television; Lifetime; Lifetime Movie Network; Lifetime Television HD; Military Channel; MSNBC; MTV; MTV Hits; MTV2; Music Choice; National Geographic Channel; National Geographic Channel HD Network; NFL Network; NFL Network HD; NFL RedZone; Nick Jr.; Nickelodeon; NickToons TV; Outdoor Channel; Ovation; OWN: Oprah Winfrey Network; Oxygen; Palladia; Planet Green; Planet Green HD; QVC; RFD-TV; Science; Science HD; SoapNet; Speed; Spike TV; Style Network; Syfy; Syfy HD; TeenNick; Tennis Channel; The Learning Channel; The Sportsman Channel; The Weather Channel; TLC HD; Travel Channel; Trinity Broadcasting Network; truTV; Turner Classic Movies; Turner Network TV; TV Land; TVG Network; Universal HD; USA Network; USA Network HD; Versus; VH1; VH1 Classic; VH1 Country; WE tv; World Fishing Network.

Digital Pay Service 1

Pay Units: N.A.

Programming (via satellite): Cinemax (multiplexed); Encore (multiplexed); Flix; HBO (multiplexed); Showtime (multiplexed); Showtime HD; Starz (multiplexed); Starz HDTV; Sundance Channel; The Movie Channel (multiplexed).

Video-On-Demand: No

Internet Service

Operational: No, DSL.

Telephone Service

None

Miles of Plant: 3.0 (coaxial); None (fiber optic).

General Manager: Keith Carson. Marketing Manager: Robin Anderson. Chief Technician: Paul Berg. Sales & Customer Service Manager: Holly Topp.

Ownership: Dakota Central Telecommunications.

SOLEN—Formerly served by Midcontinent Communications. No longer in operation. ICA: ND0055.

SOURIS—United Telephone Mutual Aid Corp., 411 7th Ave, Langdon, ND 58249-2517. Phone: 701-256-5156. Fax: 701-256-5150, 701-256-5150. E-mail: info@utma.com. Web Site: http://www.utma.com. ICA: ND0179.

TV Market Ranking: Outside TV Markets (SOURIS). Franchise award date: N.A. Franchise expiration date: N.A. Began: July 1, 1985.

Channel capacity: 21 (not 2-way capable). Channels available but not in use: N.A.

Basic Service

Subscribers: 20.

Programming (received off-air): KMCY (ABC) Minot; KMOT (NBC) Minot; KNDX (FOX) Bismarck; KSRE (PBS) Minot; KXMC-TV (CBS) Minot.

Programming (via satellite): ABC Family Channel; CNN; ESPN; TBS Superstation; Turner Network TV.

Fee: $20.00 installation; $20.00 monthly.

Pay Service 1

Pay Units: N.A.

Programming (via satellite): HBO.

Fee: $20.00 installation; $11.00 monthly.

Video-On-Demand: No

Internet Service

Operational: No.

Telephone Service

None

Miles of Plant: 1.0 (coaxial); None (fiber optic).

General Manager: Kenneth Carlson. Assistant Manager: Dennis Hansel. Office Manager: Perry Oster.

Ownership: United Telephone Mutual Aid Corp. (MSO).

SOUTH HEART—Midcontinent Communications, PO Box 5010, Sioux Falls, SD 57117. Phones: 800-456-0564; 605-229-1775. Fax: 605-229-0478. Web Site: http://www.midcocomm.com. Also serves Belfield. ICA: ND0013.

TV Market Ranking: Below 100 (Belfield, SOUTH HEART). Franchise award date: December 12, 1988. Franchise expiration date: December 12, 2011. Began: N.A.

Channel capacity: 40 (not 2-way capable). Channels available but not in use: N.A.

Basic Service

Subscribers: 286.

Programming (received off-air): KDSE (PBS) Dickinson; KQCD-TV (NBC) Dickinson; KXMA-TV (CBS) Dickinson.

Programming (via satellite): A&E Networks; ABC Family Channel; AMC; Animal Planet; Cartoon Network; CNBC; CNN; Country Music TV; C-SPAN; Discovery Channel; Disney Channel; ESPN; ESPN 2; Hallmark Channel; Headline News; HGTV; History Channel; INSP; KMGH-TV (ABC) Denver; Lifetime; Nickelodeon; Outdoor Channel; QVC; Spike TV; Syfy; TBS Superstation; The Learning Channel; The Weather Channel; Turner Network TV; TV Land; USA Network; VH1; WE tv; WGN America.

Fee: $50.00 installation; $26.50 monthly.

Pay Service 1

Pay Units: 37.

Programming (via satellite): Showtime.

Fee: $20.00 installation; $11.00 monthly.

Pay Service 2

Pay Units: 27.

Programming (via satellite): HBO.

Fee: $12.00 monthly.

Pay Service 3

Pay Units: 37.

Programming (via satellite): The Movie Channel.

Fee: $11.00 monthly.

Internet Service

Operational: No.

Telephone Service

None

Miles of Plant: 13.0 (coaxial); 3.0 (fiber optic).

Manager: Darrell Wrege. Marketing Director: Fred Jamieson. Customer Service Manager: Kathy Fuhrmann.

Ownership: Midcontinent Media Inc. (MSO).; Comcast Cable Communications Inc. (MSO).

STANLEY—Stanley Cablevision Inc., 215 Main St, PO Box 400, Stanley, ND 58784-0400. Phones: 701-628-2522; 701-628-3333. Fax: 701-628-3737. E-mail: Servicedept@midstatetel.com. Web Site: http://www.midstatetel.com. Also serves Portal. ICA: ND0049.

TV Market Ranking: Outside TV Markets (Portal, STANLEY). Franchise award date: N.A. Franchise expiration date: N.A. Began: February 1, 1979.

Channel capacity: 60 (operating 2-way). Channels available but not in use: N.A.

Basic Service

Subscribers: 650.

Programming (received off-air): KMCY (ABC) Minot; KMOT (NBC) Minot; KSRE (PBS) Minot; KXMC-TV (CBS) Minot.

Programming (via satellite): A&E Networks; ABC Family Channel; AMC; Animal Planet; Cartoon Network; CNBC; CNN; Comedy Central; Country Music TV; C-SPAN 2; CW+; Discovery Channel; E! Entertainment Television; Encore; ESPN; ESPN 2; ESPN Classic Sports; Eternal Word TV Network; Food Network; Fox Movie Channel; Fox News Channel; Fox Sports Net; FX; Hallmark Channel; Hallmark Movie Channel; Headline News; HGTV; INSP; Lifetime Movie Network; MTV; National Geographic Channel; Nickelodeon; Outdoor Channel; QVC; Radar Channel; RFD-TV; Spike TV; Syfy; TBS Superstation; The Learning Channel; The Weather Channel; Travel Channel; Trinity Broadcasting Network; Turner Network TV; TV Land; USA Network; VH1; WGN America.

Fee: $20.00 installation; $27.00 monthly.

Digital Basic Service

Subscribers: 90.

Programming (via satellite): AmericanLife TV Network; BBC America; Bio; Bloomberg Television; Current; Discovery Fit & Health; Discovery Health Channel; Discovery Kids Channel; DMX Music; ESPN Classic Sports; ESPNews; Fox Movie Channel; Fox Soccer; FSN Digital Atlantic; FSN Digital Central; FSN Digital Pacific; G4; Great American Country; GSN; History Channel; ID Investigation Discovery; INSP; Lifetime Movie Network; Military Channel; MTV Hits; MTV Jams; MTV2; National Geographic Channel; Nick Jr.; NickToons TV; Outdoor Channel; Planet Green; Science; Speed; Style Network; Sundance Channel; Syfy; TeenNick; Turner Classic Movies; VH1 Classic; VH1 Country; VH1 Soul; WE tv.

Fee: $17.50 monthly.

Pay Service 1

Pay Units: 111.

Programming (via satellite): HBO.

Fee: $11.00 monthly.

Digital Pay Service 1

Pay Units: N.A.

Programming (via satellite): Cinemax (multiplexed); Encore (multiplexed); Flix; HBO (multiplexed); Showtime (multiplexed); Starz (multiplexed); Sundance Channel; The Movie Channel (multiplexed).

Fee: $9.00 monthly (Cinemax, Starz or Encore), $11.00 monthly (HBO), $12.00 monthly (Showtime/TMC/Flix/Sundance).

Internet Service

Operational: No.

Telephone Service

None

Miles of Plant: 12.0 (coaxial); None (fiber optic).

Manager: Mark Wilhelmi. Chief Technician & Marketing Director: Larry Fritel. Program Director: Deb Beehler.

Ownership: Stanley Cablevision Inc.

SYKESON—Dakota Central Telecommunications. This cable system has converted to IPTV. See Sykeston, ND [ND5010]. ICA: ND0152.

SYKESTON—Dakota Central Telecommunications. Formerly [ND0152]. This cable system has converted to IPTV, 630 Fifth St N, PO Box 299, Carrington, ND 58421. Phones: 800-771-0974; 701-652-3184. Fax: 701-674-8121. E-mail: customerservice@daktel.com. Web Site: http://www.daktel.com. ICA: ND5010.

TV Market Ranking: Outside TV Markets (SYKESTON). Franchise award date: N.A. Franchise expiration date: N.A. Began: N.A.

Channel capacity: N.A. Channels available but not in use: N.A.

Internet Service

Operational: Yes.

Telephone Service
Digital: Operational
Chief Executive Officer & General Manager: Keith Larson.

TAYLOR—Consolidated Telecommunications Co. Now served by DICKINSON, ND [ND0005]. ICA: ND0166.

UPHAM—RAE Cable. Now served by NEWBURG, ND [ND0059]. ICA: ND0150.

VALLEY CITY—Cable Services Inc., PO Box 1995, Jamestown, ND 58402-1995. Phones: 701-845-4383; 701-252-5281. Fax: 701-252-1105. E-mail: info@csicable.com. Web Site: http://www.csicable.com. ICA: ND0012.
TV Market Ranking: 98 (VALLEY CITY). Franchise award date: N.A. Franchise expiration date: N.A. Began: January 1, 1979.
Channel capacity: N.A. Channels available but not in use: N.A.
Basic Service
Subscribers: 2,232.
Programming (received off-air): KFME (PBS) Fargo; KJRR (FOX) Jamestown; KVLY-TV (NBC) Fargo; KXJB-TV (CBS) Valley City; WDAY-TV (ABC, CW) Fargo.
Programming (via satellite): 3 Angels Broadcasting Network; A&E Networks; ABC Family Channel; Animal Planet; Bloomberg Television; Boomerang; BTN; Cartoon Network; CNBC; CNN; Comedy Central; Country Music TV; C-SPAN; C-SPAN 2; C-SPAN 3; CW+; Discovery Channel; Disney Channel; E! Entertainment Television; ESPN; ESPN 2; Eternal Word TV Network; Food Network; Fox News Channel; Fox Sports Net; FX; Great American Country; Hallmark Channel; Hallmark Movie Channel; Headline News; HGTV; History Channel; INSP; Lifetime; MSNBC; MTV; NASA TV; Nickelodeon; Outdoor Channel; QVC; Spike TV; Syfy; TBS Superstation; The Learning Channel; The Weather Channel; Travel Channel; Trinity Broadcasting Network; Turner Classic Movies; Turner Network TV; TV Land; USA Network; various Canadian stations; Versus; VH1; WGN America.
Fee: $20.00 installation; $29.99 monthly.
Pay Service 1
Pay Units: 65.
Programming (via satellite): Showtime; The Movie Channel.
Fee: $20.00 installation; $10.00 monthly.
Video-On-Demand: No
Internet Service
Operational: Yes. Began: December 31, 1999.
Broadband Service: In-house.
Fee: $30.00 installation; $29.99 monthly.
Telephone Service
Digital: Planned
Miles of Plant: 47.0 (coaxial); None (fiber optic).
Manager: Roy Sheppard. Chief Technician: Roger Nelson. Marketing Manager: Chris Sheppard.
Ownership: Cable Services Inc. (MSO).

VELVA—SRT Communications, 3615 N Broadway, PO Box 2027, Minot, ND 58702-2027. Phones: 701-858-5252; 800-737-9130; 701-858-1200. Fax: 701-858-1428. E-mail: email@srt.com. Web Site: http://www.srt.com. Also serves Antler, Berthold, Butte, Carpio, Deering, Des Lacs, Donnybrook, Granville, Karlsruhe, Maxbass, Metigoshe, Newburg, Sawyer, Sherwood, Tolley, Upham & Westhope. ICA: ND0059.
TV Market Ranking: Below 100 (Berthold, Carpio, Deering, Des Lacs, Granville, Karlsruhe, Maxbass, Sawyer, VELVA); Outside TV Markets (Antler, Butte, Donnybrook, Metigoshe, Newburg, Sherwood, Tolley, Upham, Westhope). Franchise award date: N.A. Franchise expiration date: N.A. Began: September 6, 1980.
Channel capacity: 78 (not 2-way capable). Channels available but not in use: N.A.
Basic Service
Subscribers: 1,400.
Programming (received off-air): KMCY (ABC) Minot; KMOT (NBC) Minot; KSRE (PBS) Minot; KXMC-TV (CBS) Minot; KXND (FOX) Minot.
Programming (via satellite): C-SPAN; TBS Superstation; The Weather Channel; WGN America.
Fee: $39.00 installation; $16.99 monthly.
Expanded Basic Service 1
Subscribers: 1,300.
Programming (via satellite): A&E Networks; ABC Family Channel; AMC; CNBC; CNN; Comedy Central; Country Music TV; Discovery Channel; Disney Channel; ESPN; ESPN 2; Fox News Channel; Fox Sports Net; FX; Headline News; HGTV; History Channel; Lifetime; MTV; NFL Network; Nickelodeon; Outdoor Channel; Spike TV; Syfy; The Learning Channel; Toon Disney; Turner Classic Movies; Turner Network TV; TV Land; USA Network; VH1.
Fee: $31.95 monthly.
Digital Basic Service
Subscribers: 8.
Fee: $39.00 installation; $54.95 monthly; $35.00 additional installation.
Pay Service 1
Pay Units: 108.
Programming (via satellite): HBO.
Fee: $12.00 monthly.
Pay Service 2
Pay Units: 132.
Programming (via satellite): Encore; Starz.
Fee: $10.00 monthly.
Video-On-Demand: No
Internet Service
Operational: No, DSL & dial-up.
Telephone Service
None
Miles of Plant: 70.0 (coaxial); None (fiber optic).
Chief Executive Officer & General Manager: Steve D. Lysne. Chief Operations Officer & Assistant General Manager: John A. Reiser. Chief Financial Officer: Perry G. Erdmann. Sales & Marketing Director: Jamie Hogarth.
Ownership: SRT Communications Inc.

WAHPETON—Midcontinent Communications, 635 8th Ave S, Wahpeton, ND 58075-4845. Phones: 800-888-1300 (Customer service); 605-229-1775 (Customer service). Fax: 605-229-0478; 701-642-9033. Web Site: http://www.midcocomm.com. Also serves Breckenridge. ICA: ND0007.
TV Market Ranking: Outside TV Markets (Breckenridge, WAHPETON). Franchise award date: N.A. Franchise expiration date: N.A. Began: July 1, 1969.
Channel capacity: 56 (operating 2-way). Channels available but not in use: N.A.
Basic Service
Subscribers: 3,771.
Programming (received off-air): KCCO-TV (CBS) Alexandria; KFME (PBS) Fargo; KVLY-TV (NBC) Fargo; KVRR (FOX) Fargo; KXJB-TV (CBS) Valley City; WDAY-TV (ABC, CW) Fargo; allband FM.
Programming (via satellite): A&E Networks; ABC Family Channel; AMC; Animal Planet; Bravo; Cartoon Network; CNBC; CNN; Comedy Central; C-SPAN; C-SPAN 2; CW+; Discovery Channel; Discovery Fit & Health; Disney Channel; E! Entertainment Television; ESPN; ESPN 2; Eternal Word TV Network; Food Network; Fox News Channel; Fox Sports Net North; FX; Hallmark Channel; Headline News; HGTV; History Channel; INSP; ION Television; Lifetime; MSNBC; MTV; Nickelodeon; Oxygen; QVC; Speed; Spike TV; Syfy; TBS Superstation; The Learning Channel; The Weather Channel; Travel Channel; truTV; Turner Network TV; TV Guide Network; TV Land; USA Network; VH1; WGN America.
Fee: $44.95 installation; $11.66 monthly; $3.00 converter.
Digital Basic Service
Subscribers: 450.
Programming (via satellite): 3 Angels Broadcasting Network; A&E HD; ABC Family HD; AmericanLife TV Network; Animal Planet HD; BBC America; Bio; Bloomberg Television; Boomerang; BTN; Canal Sur; CBS Sports Network; Cine Latino; Cine Mexicano; CMT Pure Country; CNN en Espanol; CNN HD; Cooking Channel; C-SPAN 3; Current; Discovery Channel HD; Discovery en Espanol; Discovery Fit & Health; Discovery Health Channel; Discovery Kids Channel; Disney Channel HD; DIY Network; ESPN 2 HD; ESPN Classic Sports; ESPN Deportes; ESPN HD; ESPNews; Eternal Word TV Network; Food Network HD; Fox Business Channel; Fox College Sports Atlantic; Fox College Sports Central; Fox College Sports Pacific; Fox Deportes; Fox Movie Channel; Fox Soccer; Fuse; G4; Golf Channel; GolTV; Great American Country; GSN; Halogen Network; HD Theater; HDNet; HDNet Movies; HGTV HD; History Channel en Espanol; History Channel HD; History Channel International; ID Investigation Discovery; Independent Film Channel; ION Life; ION Television; JCTV; Lifetime Movie Network; Military Channel; MTV Hits; MTV Jams; MTV2; mun2 television; Music Choice; National Geographic Channel; National Geographic Channel HD Network; NFL Network; Nick Jr.; Nick Too; NickToons TV; Outdoor Channel; Palladia; PBS Kids Sprout; Pentagon Channel; Planet Green; Qubo; ReelzChannel; RFD-TV; Science Television; SoapNet; Style Network; Sundance Channel; Syfy HD; TBS in HD; TeenNick; Telemundo; Tennis Channel; TLC HD; Toon Disney en Espanol; Tr3s; Trinity Broadcasting Network; Turner Classic Movies; Turner Network TV HD; TV One; TVE Internacional; TVG Network; Universal HD; USA Network HD; Versus; Versus HD; VH1 Classic; VH1 Soul; WE tv.
Digital Pay Service 1
Pay Units: N.A.
Programming (via satellite): Cinemax; Cinemax HD; Encore (multiplexed); Flix; HBO (multiplexed); HBO Latino; Showtime (multiplexed); Showtime HD; Starz (multiplexed); Starz HDTV; The Movie Channel (multiplexed); The Movie Channel HD.
Video-On-Demand: No
Pay-Per-View
iN DEMAND (delivered digitally); NHL Center Ice (delivered digitally); MLB Extra Innings (delivered digitally); ESPN (delivered digitally); NBA League Pass (delivered digitally); MLS Direct Kick (delivered digitally).
Internet Service
Operational: Yes.
Fee: $35.00 installation; $19.95 monthly.
Telephone Service
Digital: Operational
Fee: $18.00 monthly
Miles of Plant: 48.0 (coaxial); None (fiber optic).
Manager: Steve Schirber. Office Manager: Avis Althoff. Chief Technician: Raymond Olson.
Ownership: Midcontinent Media Inc. (MSO).; Comcast Cable Communications Inc. (MSO).

WATFORD CITY—Reservation Telephone Cooperative, 24 Main St N, PO Box 68, Parshall, ND 58770-0068. Phones: 888-862-3115; 701-862-3115. Fax: 701-832-3008. E-mail: kristin@rtc.coop. Web Site: http://www.reservationtelephone.com. Also serves Alexander & Arnegard. ICA: ND0024.
TV Market Ranking: Below 100 (Alexander, Arnegard, WATFORD CITY). Franchise award date: May 21, 1986. Franchise expiration date: May 21, 2011. Began: November 1, 1979.
Channel capacity: 47 (not 2-way capable). Channels available but not in use: N.A.
Basic Service
Subscribers: 603.
Programming (received off-air): KUMV-TV (NBC) Williston; KWSE (PBS) Williston; KXMD-TV (CBS) Williston.
Programming (via satellite): A&E Networks; ABC Family Channel; AMC; Animal Planet; Cartoon Network; CNBC; CNN; Country Music TV; C-SPAN; Discovery Channel; Disney Channel; E! Entertainment Television; ESPN; ESPN 2; Fox News Channel; Fox Sports Net; FX; Headline News; HGTV; History Channel; INSP; Lifetime; Nickelodeon; Outdoor Channel; QVC; Spike TV; TBS Superstation; The Learning Channel; The Weather Channel; truTV; Turner Classic Movies; Turner Network TV; TV Land; USA Network; VH1; WE tv; WGN America.
Programming (via translator): KMCY (ABC) Minot; KXND (FOX) Minot.
Fee: $20.00 installation; $32.95 monthly.
Pay Service 1
Pay Units: 32.
Programming (via satellite): HBO.
Fee: $10.00 monthly.
Pay Service 2
Pay Units: 106.
Programming (via satellite): Showtime; The Movie Channel.
Fee: $20.00 installation; $10.00 monthly (Showtime & TMC).
Video-On-Demand: Planned
Internet Service
Operational: No.
Telephone Service
None
Miles of Plant: 20.0 (coaxial); None (fiber optic).
General Manager: Royce S. Aslakson. Marketing Manager: Kristin Jaeger. Office Manager: Jan Boschee.
Ownership: Reservation Telephone Cooperative (MSO).

WESTHOPE—SRT Communications. Now served by VELVA, ND [ND0059]. ICA: ND0074.

WILLISTON—Midcontinent Communications, PO Box 5010, Sioux Falls, SD 57117. Phones: 800-456-0564; 605-229-1775. Fax: 605-229-0478; 701-572-9615. Web Site: http://www.midcocomm.com. Also serves Williston Twp. (portions). ICA: ND0006.
TV Market Ranking: Below 100 (WILLISTON, Williston Twp. (portions)). Franchise

award date: N.A. Franchise expiration date: N.A. Began: June 1, 1967.

Channel capacity: 32 (not 2-way capable). Channels available but not in use: N.A.

Basic Service

Subscribers: 3,366.

Programming (received off-air): KUMV-TV (NBC) Williston; KWSE (PBS) Williston; KXMD-TV (CBS) Williston.

Programming (via satellite): A&E Networks; ABC Family Channel; AMC; Animal Planet; Cartoon Network; CNBC; CNN; Comedy Central; Country Music TV; C-SPAN; C-SPAN 2; Discovery Channel; Disney Channel; E! Entertainment Television; Encore Action; ESPN; ESPN 2; Eternal Word TV Network; Food Network; Fox News Channel; Fox Sports Net North; FX; Hallmark Channel; Headline News; HGTV; History Channel; INSP; ION Television; Lifetime; MSNBC; MTV; Nickelodeon; QVC; Spike TV; TBS Superstation; The Learning Channel; The Weather Channel; Travel Channel; Trinity Broadcasting Network; truTV; Turner Classic Movies; Turner Network TV; TV Guide Network; USA Network; VH1; WGN America.

Fee: $29.60 installation; $10.16 monthly; $14.80 additional installation.

Digital Basic Service

Subscribers: 440.

Programming (via satellite): BBC America; Bio; Bravo; Discovery Digital Networks; DMX Music; ESPN Classic Sports; ESPNews; Fox Movie Channel; Fox Sports World; Fuse; G4; GAS; Golf Channel; GSN; Halogen Network; History Channel International; Independent Film Channel; Lifetime Movie Network; MTV Hits; MTV2; National Geographic Channel; Nick Jr.; NickToons TV; Outdoor Channel; Speed; Style Network; Syfy; Toon Disney; TV Land; Versus; VH1 Classic; VH1 Country; VH1 Soul; WE tv.

Digital Pay Service 1

Pay Units: N.A.

Programming (via satellite): Cinemax (multiplexed); Encore; HBO (multiplexed); Showtime (multiplexed); The Movie Channel (multiplexed).

Video-On-Demand: No

Pay-Per-View

Hot Choice (delivered digitally); Playboy TV (delivered digitally); NBA TV (delivered digitally); Sports PPV (delivered digitally); iN DEMAND (delivered digitally).

Internet Service

Operational: Yes.

Fee: $35.00 installation; $19.95 monthly.

Telephone Service

Digital: Operational

Fee: $18.00 monthly

Miles of Plant: 82.0 (coaxial); None (fiber optic). Additional miles planned: 2.0 (coaxial).

Manager: Todd Jensen. Chief Technician: Steve Peterson.

Ownership: Midcontinent Media Inc. (MSO).; Comcast Cable Communications Inc. (MSO).

WISHEK—Midcontinent Communications, PO Box 5010, Sioux Falls, SD 57117. Phones: 800-456-0564; 605-229-1775. Fax: 605-229-0478. Web Site: http://www.midcocomm.com. Also serves Lehr, Linton, Napoleon & Zeeland. ICA: ND0044.

TV Market Ranking: Outside TV Markets (Lehr, Linton, Napoleon, WISHEK, Zeeland). Franchise award date: April 6, 1992. Franchise expiration date: April 6, 2011. Began: April 1, 1980.

Channel capacity: N.A. Channels available but not in use: N.A.

Basic Service

Subscribers: 1,409.

Programming (received off-air): KBME-TV (PBS) Bismarck; KBMY (ABC) Bismarck; KFYR-TV (NBC) Bismarck; KNDX (FOX) Bismarck; KXMB-TV (CBS) Bismarck.

Programming (via satellite): A&E Networks; ABC Family Channel; AMC; Animal Planet; BET Networks; Bravo; Cartoon Network; CNBC; CNN; Comedy Central; Country Music TV; C-SPAN; C-SPAN 2; CW+; Discovery Channel; Disney Channel; E! Entertainment Television; ESPN; ESPN 2; Eternal Word TV Network; Food Network; Fox News Channel; Fox Sports Net North; FX; Hallmark Channel; Headline News; HGTV; History Channel; INSP; Lifetime; MSNBC; MTV; Nickelodeon; Outdoor Channel; Oxygen; QVC; Speed; Spike TV; Syfy; TBS Superstation; The Learning Channel; The Weather Channel; Travel Channel; Trinity Broadcasting Network; truTV; Turner Classic Movies; Turner Network TV; TV Guide Network; TV Land; USA Network; VH1; WE tv; WGN America.

Fee: $50.00 installation; $26.50 monthly.

Digital Basic Service

Subscribers: N.A.

Programming (via satellite): 3 Angels Broadcasting Network; A&E HD; ABC Family HD; AmericanLife TV Network; Animal Planet HD; BBC America; Bio; Boomerang; BTN; Canal Sur; CBS Sports Network; Cine Latino; Cine Mexicano; CMT Pure Country; CNN en Espanol; CNN HD; Cooking Channel; C-SPAN 3; Current; Discovery Channel HD; Discovery en Espanol; Discovery Fit & Health; Discovery Health Channel; Discovery Kids Channel; Disney Channel HD; DIY Network; ESPN 2 HD; ESPN Classic Sports; ESPN Deportes; ESPN HD; ESPNews; EWTN en Espanol; Food Network HD; Fox Business Channel; Fox College Sports Atlantic; Fox College Sports Central; Fox College Sports Pacific; Fox Deportes; Fox Soccer; Fuse; G4; Golf Channel; GolTV; Great American Country; GSN; Halogen Network; HD Theater; HDNet; HDNet Movies; HGTV HD; History Channel en Espanol; History Channel HD; History Channel International; ID Investigation Discovery; Independent Film Channel; JCTV; Lifetime Movie Network; Military Channel; MTV Hits; MTV Jams; MTV2; mun2 television; Music Choice; National Geographic Channel; National Geographic Channel HD Network; NFL Network; NHL Network; Nick Jr.; Nick Too; NickToons TV; Outdoor Channel; Palladia; PBS Kids Sprout; Pentagon Channel; Planet Green; ReelzChannel; RFD-TV; Science; SoapNet; Style Network; Sundance Channel; Syfy HD; TBS in HD; TeenNick; Telemundo; Tennis Channel; TLC HD; Toon Disney; Tr3s; Trinity Broadcasting Network; Turner Classic Movies; Turner Network TV HD; TV One; TVE Internacional; TVG Network; Universal HD; USA Network HD; Versus; Versus HD; VH1 Classic; VH1 Soul; WE tv.

Digital Pay Service 1

Pay Units: N.A.

Programming (via satellite): Cinemax (multiplexed); Cinemax HD; Encore (multiplexed); Flix; HBO (multiplexed); HBO HD; HBO Latino; Showtime (multiplexed); Showtime HD; Starz (multiplexed); Starz HDTV; The Movie Channel (multiplexed); The Movie Channel HD.

Video-On-Demand: No

Pay-Per-View

iN DEMAND (delivered digitally); MLS Direct Kick (delivered digitally); NBA League Pass (delivered digitally); NHL Center Ice (delivered digitally); MLB Extra Innings (delivered digitally).

Internet Service

Operational: Yes.

Fee: $35.00 installation; $19.95 monthly.

Telephone Service

Digital: Operational

Fee: $18.00 monthly

Miles of Plant: 35.0 (coaxial); None (fiber optic).

Manager: Darrell Wrege. Marketing Director: Fred Jamieson. Customer Service Manager: Kathy Fuhrmann.

Ownership: Midcontinent Media Inc. (MSO).; Comcast Cable Communications Inc. (MSO).

WOODWORTH—Dakota Central Telecommunications. Formerly [ND0168]. This cable system has converted to IPTV, 630 Fifth St N, PO Box 299, Carrington, ND 58421. Phones: 800-771-0974; 701-652-3184. Fax: 701-674-8121. E-mail: customerservice@daktel.com. Web Site: http://www.daktel.com. ICA: ND5013.

TV Market Ranking: Below 100 (WOODWORTH). Franchise award date: N.A. Franchise expiration date: N.A. Began: N.A.

Channel capacity: N.A. Channels available but not in use: N.A.

Internet Service

Operational: Yes.

Telephone Service

Digital: Operational

Chief Executive Officer & General Manager: Keith Larson.

WOODWORTH—Dakota Central Telecommunications. This cable system has converted to IPTV. See Woodworth, ND [ND5013]. ICA: ND0168.

WYNDMERE—Dickey Rural Networks, 9628 Hwy 281, PO Box 69, Ellendale, ND 58436-0069. Phones: 877-559-4692; 701-344-5000. Fax: 701-344-4300. E-mail: drtc@drtel.net. Web Site: http://www.drtel.net. Also serves Milnor. ICA: ND0086.

TV Market Ranking: Outside TV Markets (WYNDMERE). Franchise award date: March 1, 1982. Franchise expiration date: N.A. Began: November 1, 1982.

Channel capacity: N.A. Channels available but not in use: N.A.

Basic Service

Subscribers: 254.

Programming (received off-air): KFME (PBS) Fargo; KSFY-TV (ABC) Sioux Falls; KVLY-TV (NBC) Fargo; KVRR (FOX) Fargo; KXJB-TV (CBS) Valley City; WDAY-TV (ABC, CW) Fargo.

Programming (via satellite): A&E Networks; ABC Family Channel; AMC; Animal Planet; Bravo; Cartoon Network; CNBC; CNN; C-SPAN; C-SPAN 2; Discovery Channel; Discovery Health Channel; Disney Channel; DIY Network; ESPN; ESPN 2; ESPN Classic Sports; ESPNews; Eternal Word TV Network; Fox News Channel; Fox Sports Net North; Headline News; HGTV; History Channel; INSP; Jewelry Television; Lifetime; MSNBC; MTV; NASA TV; National Geographic Channel; Nickelodeon; Outdoor Channel; QVC; Spike TV; TBS Superstation; The Learning Channel; The Weather Channel; Travel Channel; Trinity Broadcasting Network; Turner Classic Movies; Turner Network TV; TV Guide Network; TV Land; USA Network; VH1; WGN America.

Fee: $20.00 installation; $19.95 monthly.

Pay Service 1

Pay Units: 206.

Programming (via satellite): HBO.

Fee: $11.00 monthly.

Video-On-Demand: No

Internet Service

Operational: Yes.

Telephone Service

None

Miles of Plant: 17.0 (coaxial); 51.0 (fiber optic).

General Manager: Jeff Wilson. Marketing Manager: Janell Hauck. Engineering Manager: James Byerley. Plant Manager: Kent Shimke.

Ownership: Dickey Rural Services Inc. (MSO).

YPSILANTI—Dakota Central Telecommunications. Formerly [ND0169]. This cable system has converted to IPTV, 630 Fifth St N, PO Box 299, Carrington, ND 58421. Phones: 800-771-0974; 701-652-3184. Fax: 701-674-8121. E-mail: customerservice@daktel.com. Web Site: http://www.daktel.com. ICA: ND5104.

TV Market Ranking: 98 (YPSILANTI). Franchise award date: N.A. Franchise expiration date: N.A. Began: N.A.

Channel capacity: N.A. Channels available but not in use: N.A.

Internet Service

Operational: Yes.

Telephone Service

Digital: Operational

Chief Executive Officer & General Manager: Keith A. Larson.

YPSILANTI—Dakota Central Telecommunications. This cable system has converted to IPTV. See Ypsilanti, ND [ND5104]. ICA: ND0169.

OHIO

Total Systems: **168**
Total Communities Served: **1,814**
Franchises Not Yet Operating: **0**
Applications Pending: **0**
Communities with Applications: **0**
Number of Basic Subscribers: **3,168,698**
Number of Expanded Basic Subscribers: **528,845**
Number of Pay Units: **368,658**

Top 100 Markets Represented: Pittsburgh (10); Cincinnati, OH-Newport, KY (17); Columbus-Chillicothe (27); Charleston-Huntington, WV (36); Dayton-Kettering (41); Toledo (52); Youngstown (79); Fort Wayne-Roanoke, IN (82); Cleveland-Lorain-Akron (8); Wheeling, WV-Steubenville, OH (90).

For a list of cable communities in this section, see the Cable Community Index located in the back of Cable Volume 2.
For explanation of terms used in cable system listings, see p. D-11.

ADA—Time Warner Cable. Now served by KENTON, OH [OH0128]. ICA: OH0313.

ADENA—Comcast Cable. Now served by WHEELING, WV [WV0004]. ICA: OH0181.

AKRON—Time Warner Cable, 530 S Main St, Ste 1751, Akron, OH 44311-1090. Phones: 330-747-2555; 330-633-9203. Fax: 330-633-7970. Web Site: http://www.timewarnercable.com/northeastohio. Also serves Barberton, Boston Twp. (Summit County), Chippewa Twp. (Wayne County), Copley, Coventry Twp. (Summit County), Cuyahoga Falls, Doylestown, Fairlawn, Lakemore, Mogadore, Munroe Falls, Norton, Silver Lake, Springfield Twp. (Summit County), Stow, Tallmadge, Wadsworth & Willows Mobile Home Park. ICA: OH0005.

TV Market Ranking: 8 (AKRON, Barberton, Boston Twp. (Summit County), Chippewa Twp. (Wayne County), Copley, Coventry Twp. (Summit County), Cuyahoga Falls, Doylestown, Fairlawn, Lakemore, Mogadore, Munroe Falls, Norton, Silver Lake, Springfield Twp. (Summit County), Stow, Tallmadge, Wadsworth, Willows Mobile Home Park). Franchise award date: N.A. Franchise expiration date: August 10, 2008. Began: August 1, 1969.

Channel capacity: N.A. Channels available but not in use: N.A.

Basic Service

Subscribers: 114,115.

Programming (received off-air): WAOH-LP Akron; WBNX-TV (CW) Akron; WDLI-TV (TBN) Canton; WEAO (PBS) Akron; WEWS-TV (ABC) Cleveland; WJW (FOX) Cleveland; WKYC (NBC) Cleveland; WNEO (PBS) Alliance; WOIO (CBS) Shaker Heights; WQHS-DT (UNV) Cleveland; WUAB (MNT) Lorain; WVIZ (PBS) Cleveland; WVPX-TV (ION) Akron.

Programming (via satellite): WGN America.

Fee: $29.95 installation; $11.50 monthly.

Expanded Basic Service 1

Subscribers: N.A.

Programming (via satellite): A&E Networks; ABC Family Channel; AMC; Animal Planet; BET Networks; Bravo; CNBC; CNN; C-SPAN; C-SPAN 2; Discovery Channel; Discovery Fit & Health; Discovery Health Channel; Disney Channel; E! Entertainment Television; ESPN; ESPN 2; Eternal Word TV Network; Food Network; Fox News Channel; Fox Sports Net Ohio; FX; Golf Channel; Great American Country; GSN; Hallmark Channel; Headline News; HGTV; INSP; Lifetime; Lifetime Movie Network; MSNBC; MTV; Nickelodeon; OpenTV; Oxygen; QVC; SoapNet; Spike TV; TBS Superstation; The Learning Channel; The Weather Channel; Travel Channel; Turner Classic Movies; Turner Network TV; TV Land; USA Network; Versus; VH1; WE tv.

Fee: $45.49 monthly.

Digital Basic Service

Subscribers: N.A.

Programming (via satellite): AmericanLife TV Network; America's Store; BBC America; Bloomberg Television; CNN International; Cooking Channel; Country Music TV; C-SPAN 3; Discovery Digital Networks; DIY Network; DMX Music; ESPNews; Fox Movie Channel; Fox Sports World; Fuse; G4; GAS; Independent Film Channel; Jewelry Television; Lifetime Real Women; MTV2; Music Choice; National Geographic Channel; Nick Jr.; Ohio News Network; Outdoor Channel; Ovation; Science Television; Speed; Style Network; The Word Network; Toon Disney; VH1 Classic.

Fee: $11.00 monthly.

Digital Expanded Basic Service

Subscribers: N.A.

Programming (via satellite): ART America; Bio; Boomerang; Canales N; Discovery Kids Channel; Fox Sports World; FSN Digital Atlantic; FSN Digital Central; FSN Digital Pacific; Fuel TV; History Channel International; NBA TV; Nick Jr.; RAI International; Speed; Tennis Channel; Toon Disney; TV Asia; Zee TV USA.

Digital Pay Service 1

Pay Units: N.A.

Programming (via satellite): Cinemax; Encore; HBO; Showtime; Showtime (multiplexed); The Movie Channel.

Fee: $12.00 monthly (each).

Video-On-Demand: Yes

Pay-Per-View

iN DEMAND (delivered digitally).

Internet Service

Operational: Yes. Began: December 1, 1994.

Broadband Service: EarthLink, Road Runner.

Fee: $99.00 installation; $44.95 monthly.

Telephone Service

Digital: Operational

Fee: $44.95 monthly

Miles of Plant: 1,527.0 (coaxial); None (fiber optic).

Division President: Stephen R. Fry. Area Vice President: Scott Miller. Vice President, Engineering: Al Costanzi. Vice President, Marketing: Patrick Burke. Vice President, Sales: Woody E. Woodward. Vice President, Public Affairs: William G. Jasso. Vice President, Customer Care: Donald Jensen. Marketing Director: Liz Watson. Government & Media Relations Director: Chris Thomas.

Ownership: Time Warner Cable (MSO).

ALBANY—Time Warner Cable. Now served by JACKSON, OH [OH0098]. ICA: OH0314.

AMELIA—Formerly served by Adelphia Communications. No longer in operation. ICA: OH0041.

AMESVILLE—Formerly served by Riley Video Services. No longer in operation. ICA: OH0307.

AMSTERDAM—Windjammer Cable, 4400 PGA Blvd, Ste 902, Palm Beach Gardens, FL 33410. Phones: 877-450-5558; 561-775-1208. Fax: 561-775-7811. Web Site: http://www.windjammercable.com. Also serves Bergholz & Springfield Twp. (portions). ICA: OH0230.

TV Market Ranking: 90 (AMSTERDAM, Bergholz, Springfield Twp. (portions)). Franchise award date: N.A. Franchise expiration date: N.A. Began: February 1, 1969.

Channel capacity: 57 (not 2-way capable). Channels available but not in use: N.A.

Basic Service

Subscribers: 600.

Programming (received off-air): KDKA-TV (CBS) Pittsburgh; WNEO (PBS) Alliance; WPGH-TV (FOX) Pittsburgh; WPXI (IND, NBC) Pittsburgh; WQED (PBS) Pittsburgh; WTAE-TV (ABC) Pittsburgh; WTOV-TV (IND, NBC) Steubenville; WTRF-TV (CBS) Wheeling; WYTV (ABC, MNT) Youngstown; allband FM.

Programming (via satellite): AMC; QVC; TBS Superstation.

Fee: $44.95 installation; $13.86 monthly; $19.95 additional installation.

Expanded Basic Service 1

Subscribers: 591.

Programming (via satellite): A&E Networks; ABC Family Channel; Animal Planet; Cartoon Network; CNBC; CNN; Comedy Central; C-SPAN; C-SPAN 2; Discovery Channel; Disney Channel; ESPN; Fox News Channel; Fox Sports Net Ohio; FX; Hallmark Channel; HGTV; ION Television; Lifetime; MoviePlex; MTV; Nickelodeon; Spike TV; SportsTime Ohio; The Learning Channel; Travel Channel; Turner Network TV; USA Network.

Fee: $28.64 monthly.

Digital Basic Service

Subscribers: N.A.

Programming (via satellite): BBC America; Bravo; Discovery Health Channel; Discovery Home Channel; Discovery Kids Channel; Discovery Times Channel; ESPN 2; ESPN Classic Sports; ESPNews; Fox Soccer; Golf Channel; GSN; History Channel; Independent Film Channel; Military Channel; Music Choice; National Geographic Channel; Nick Jr.; Science; Speed; Turner Classic Movies; Versus; WE tv.

Fee: $11.00 monthly.

Digital Pay Service 1

Pay Units: N.A.

Programming (via satellite): Cinemax (multiplexed); Encore (multiplexed); HBO (multiplexed); Showtime (multiplexed); Starz (multiplexed); The Movie Channel (multiplexed).

Fee: $12.00 monthly (each).

Video-On-Demand: No

Pay-Per-View

Playboy TV (delivered digitally); iN DEMAND (delivered digitally).

Internet Service

Operational: No.

Telephone Service

None

Miles of Plant: 16.0 (coaxial); None (fiber optic).

Ownership: Windjammer Communications LLC (MSO).

ANDOVER—Formerly served by Cebridge Connections. Now served by MEADVILLE, PA [PA0062]. ICA: OH0258.

ASHLAND—Armstrong Cable Services, 100 E 2nd St, Ashland, OH 44805-2304. Phones: 877-277-5711; 419-289-0161; 419-894-3886. Fax: 419-289-3508. Web Site: http://cable.armstrongonewire.com. Also serves Blooming Grove Twp. (Richland County), Butler Twp. (Richland County), Hayesville, Mifflin Twp. (Ashland County), Milton Twp. (Ashland County), Montgomery Twp. (Ashland County), Nankin, Olivesburg, Orange Twp. (Ashland County), Sullivan Twp., Troy Twp. (Ashland County) & Weller Twp. (Richland County). ICA: OH0079.

TV Market Ranking: 8 (Sullivan Twp.); Below 100 (ASHLAND, Blooming Grove Twp. (Richland County), Butler Twp. (Richland County), Hayesville, Mifflin Twp. (Ashland County), Milton Twp. (Ashland County), Montgomery Twp. (Ashland County), Nankin, Olivesburg, Orange Twp. (Ashland County), Troy Twp. (Ashland County), Weller Twp. (Richland County)). Franchise award date: December 1, 1968. Franchise expiration date: December 1, 2009. Began: August 20, 1969.

Channel capacity: N.A. Channels available but not in use: N.A.

Digital Basic Service

Subscribers: 1,772.

Programming (via satellite): A&E HD; ABC Family Channel; AMC; Animal Planet; Bravo; Cartoon Network; CNBC; CNN; Comedy Central; Country Music TV; C-SPAN; Discovery Channel; Disney Channel; E! Entertainment Television; ESPN; ESPN 2; ESPN Classic Sports; Food Network; Fox News Channel; Fox Sports Net Ohio; FX; Headline News; HGTV; History Channel; INSP; Lifetime; MSNBC; MTV; Music Choice; MyNetworkTV Inc.; Nickelodeon;

NickToons TV; Outdoor Channel; Pentagon Channel; QVC; ShopNBC; Spike TV; SportsTime Ohio; Syfy; TBS Superstation; The Learning Channel; The Weather Channel; Travel Channel; truTV; Turner Classic Movies; Turner Network TV; TV Guide Network; TV Land; TVN Entertainment; USA Network; VH1.
Fee: $35.00 installation; $51.40 monthly.

Digital Expanded Basic Service
Subscribers: N.A.
Programming (via satellite): AmericanLife TV Network; BBC America; Bio; Bloomberg Television; Boomerang; Chiller; cloo; CMT Pure Country; Cooking Channel; Discovery Fit & Health; Discovery Health Channel; Discovery Kids Channel; DIY Network; ESPN Classic Sports; ESPN U; ESPNews; Fox Soccer; G4; Golf Channel; Great American Country; GSN; Hallmark Channel; Hallmark Movie Channel; History Channel International; HRTV; ID Investigation Discovery; Jewelry Television; Lifetime Movie Network; Military Channel; MTV Hits; MTV Jams; MTV2; mun2 television; National Geographic Channel; NFL Network; NHL Network; Nick Jr.; Nick Too; Ohio News Network; Outdoor Channel; Oxygen; PBS Kids Sprout; Pentagon Channel; Planet Green; RFD-TV; Science; SoapNet; Speed; TeenNick; Tennis Channel; Toon Disney; Tr3s; Versus; VH1 Classic; VH1 Soul; WE tv.
Fee: $12.00 monthly.

Digital Expanded Basic Service 2
Subscribers: N.A.
Programming (received off-air): WEWS-TV (ABC) Cleveland; WJW (FOX) Cleveland; WKYC (NBC) Cleveland; WOIO (CBS) Shaker Heights.
Programming (via satellite): A&E HD; Animal Planet HD; Bravo HD; CNN HD; Discovery Channel HD; Disney Channel HD; ESPN 2 HD; ESPN HD; Food Network HD; Fox News HD; FSN HD; FX HD; Golf Channel HD; Hallmark Movie Channel HD; HD Theater; HDNet; HDNet Movies; HGTV HD; History Channel HD; MGM HD; National Geographic Channel HD Network; NFL Network HD; Outdoor Channel 2 HD; PBS HD; QVC HD; Science HD; Syfy HD; TBS in HD; The Weather Channel HD; TLC HD; Turner Network TV HD; Universal HD; USA Network HD; Versus HD; WealthTV HD.
Fee: $9.00 monthly.

Digital Pay Service 1
Pay Units: 781.
Programming (via satellite): Cinemax (multiplexed); Cinemax HD; Encore (multiplexed); Flix; HBO (multiplexed); HBO HD; RAI USA; Showtime (multiplexed); Showtime HD; Starz (multiplexed); Starz HDTV; The Movie Channel (multiplexed); TV5 USA.
Fee: $13.95 monthly (HBO, Cinemax, Showtime/TMC/Flix or Starz/Encore.

Video-On-Demand: Yes

Pay-Per-View
Hot Choice (delivered digitally); iN DEMAND; Sports PPV (delivered digitally); ESPN Extra (delivered digitally).

Internet Service
Operational: Yes. Began: January 1, 2002.
Subscribers: 4,712.
Broadband Service: Armstrong Zoom.
Fee: 26.95-$39.95 monthly.

Telephone Service
Digital: Operational
Fee: $49.95 monthly

Miles of Plant: 265.0 (coaxial); None (fiber optic).

General Manager: Dex R. Sedwick. Chief Technician: Bill Stauffer. Marketing Director: Jud D. Stewart.

Ownership: Armstrong Group of Companies (MSO).

ASHLEY CORNER—Time Warner Cable, 1266 Dublin Rd, Columbus, OH 43215-1008. Phone: 614-481-5000. Fax: 614-481-5052. Web Site: http://www.timewarnercable.com/midohio. ICA: OH0377.

TV Market Ranking: Below 100 (ASHLEY CORNER). Franchise award date: N.A. Franchise expiration date: N.A. Began: N.A.

Channel capacity: N.A. Channels available but not in use: N.A.

Basic Service
Subscribers: 516.
Programming (received off-air): WBNS-TV (CBS) Columbus; WCHS-TV (ABC) Charleston; WOWK-TV (CBS) Huntington; WPBO (PBS) Portsmouth; WQCW (CW) Portsmouth; WSAZ-TV (MNT, NBC) Huntington; WVAH-TV (FOX) Charleston.
Programming (via satellite): C-SPAN; QVC; The Weather Channel; Trinity Broadcasting Network; WGN America.
Fee: $47.50 installation; $12.94 monthly.

Expanded Basic Service 1
Subscribers: 483.
Programming (via satellite): A&E Networks; ABC Family Channel; AMC; CNN; Country Music TV; Discovery Channel; Disney Channel; ESPN; ESPN 2; Fox Sports Net Ohio; FX; Headline News; HGTV; Lifetime; Nickelodeon; Ohio News Network; Spike TV; TBS Superstation; The Learning Channel; Turner Network TV; TV Land; USA Network.

Digital Basic Service
Subscribers: N.A.
Programming (via satellite): BBC America; Bravo; Discovery Health Channel; Discovery Kids Channel; ESPN Classic Sports; ESPNews; Fox Soccer; Golf Channel; GSN; History Channel; Independent Film Channel; Music Choice; Nick Jr.; Science; Syfy; Versus; WE tv.
Fee: $52.40 monthly.

Digital Pay Service 1
Pay Units: N.A.
Programming (via satellite): Cinemax (multiplexed); Encore (multiplexed); HBO (multiplexed); Showtime (multiplexed); Starz (multiplexed); The Movie Channel (multiplexed).

Video-On-Demand: No

Pay-Per-View
iN DEMAND (delivered digitally); Playboy TV (delivered digitally); Club Jenna (delivered digitally).

Internet Service
Operational: No.

Telephone Service
None

Miles of Plant: 44.0 (coaxial); None (fiber optic).

President: Rhonda Fraas. Vice President & General Manager: David Kreiman. Vice President, Marketing: Mark Psigoda. Vice President, Engineering: Randy Hall. Vice President, Government & Public Affairs: Mary Jo Green. Technical Operations Director: Jim Cavender. Government Affairs Director: Steve Cuckler.

Ownership: Time Warner Cable (MSO).

ASHTABULA—Time Warner Cable, 530 S Main St, Ste 1751, Akron, OH 44311-1090. Phone: 330-633-9203. Fax: 330-633-7970. Web Site: http://www.timewarnercable.com/northeastohio. Also serves Ashtabula Twp. (Ashtabula County), Austinburg Twp., Conneaut, Geneva, Geneva Twp. (Ashtabula County), Geneva-on-the-Lake, Harpersfield Twp. (Ashtabula County), Jefferson, Jefferson Twp. (Ashtabula County), Kingsville, Lenox Twp., Madison, Madison Twp. (Lake County), North Kingsville, Plymouth Twp. (Ashtabula County), Saybrook Twp. (Ashtabula County) & Sheffield Twp. (Ashtabula County). ICA: OH0093.

TV Market Ranking: Below 100 (Conneaut, Kingsville, Madison, Madison Twp. (Lake County), North Kingsville); Outside TV Markets (ASHTABULA, Ashtabula Twp. (Ashtabula County), Austinburg Twp., Geneva, Geneva Twp. (Ashtabula County), Geneva-on-the-Lake, Harpersfield Twp. (Ashtabula County), Jefferson, Jefferson Twp. (Ashtabula County), Lenox Twp., Plymouth Twp. (Ashtabula County), Saybrook Twp. (Ashtabula County), Sheffield Twp. (Ashtabula County)). Franchise award date: N.A. Franchise expiration date: N.A. Began: November 1, 1969.

Channel capacity: N.A. Channels available but not in use: N.A.

Basic Service
Subscribers: N.A. Included in Warren OH
Programming (received off-air): WBNX-TV (CW) Akron; WEWS-TV (ABC) Cleveland; WFXP (FOX) Erie; WICU-TV (NBC) Erie; WJET-TV (ABC) Erie; WJW (FOX) Cleveland; WKYC (NBC) Cleveland; WNEO (PBS) Alliance; WOIO (CBS) Shaker Heights; WQHS-DT (UNV) Cleveland; WQLN (PBS) Erie; WRLM (IND) Canton; WSEE-TV (CBS, CW) Erie; WUAB (MNT) Lorain; WVIZ (PBS) Cleveland; WVPX-TV (ION) Akron; allband FM.
Programming (via microwave): WEWS-TV (ABC) Cleveland; WJW (FOX) Cleveland; WKYC (NBC) Cleveland.
Programming (via satellite): WGN America.
Fee: $44.95 installation; $10.34 monthly; $2.00 converter.

Expanded Basic Service 1
Subscribers: 25,500.
Programming (via satellite): A&E Networks; ABC Family Channel; AMC; Animal Planet; BET Networks; Bravo; Cartoon Network; CNBC; CNN; Comedy Central; Country Music TV; C-SPAN; C-SPAN 2; Discovery Channel; Disney Channel; E! Entertainment Television; ESPN; ESPN 2; Eternal Word TV Network; Food Network; Fox News Channel; Fox Sports Net Ohio; FX; Golf Channel; Hallmark Channel; Headline News; HGTV; History Channel; INSP; Lifetime; MSNBC; MTV; Nickelodeon; Ohio News Network; Oxygen; Product Information Network; QVC; ShopNBC; Spike TV; Style Network; Syfy; TBS Superstation; The Learning Channel; The Weather Channel; Travel Channel; truTV; Turner Classic Movies; Turner Network TV; TV Guide Network; TV Land; USA Network; VH1.
Fee: $42.66 monthly.

Digital Basic Service
Subscribers: N.A.
Programming (via satellite): AmericanLife TV Network; BBC America; Bio; Bloomberg Television; Canal 52MX; CBS Sports Network; Cine Latino; CMT Pure Country; CNN en Espanol; Cooking Channel; C-SPAN 3; Current; Discovery Fit & Health; Discovery Health Channel; Discovery Home Channel; Discovery Kids Channel; DIY Network; Encore (multiplexed); ESPN 2 HD; ESPN Classic Sports; ESPN Deportes; ESPN HD; ESPNews; Familyland Television Network; Fox College Sports Atlantic; Fox College Sports Central; Fox College Sports Pacific; Fox Deportes; Fox Movie Channel; Fox Reality Channel; Fox Soccer; Fuel TV; Fuse; G4; GAS; Great American Country; GSN; HD Theater; HDNet; HDNet Movies; History Channel en Espanol; History Channel International; ID Investigation Discovery; Independent Film Channel; INHD; INSP; Lifetime Movie Network; LOGO; Military Channel; MTV Jams; MTV2; Music Choice; National Geographic Channel; NBA TV; Nick Jr.; Nick Too; NickToons TV; Ohio Channel; Outdoor Channel; Science; SoapNet; Speed; SportsTime Ohio; Sundance Channel; Tennis Channel; The Word Network; Toon Disney; Toon Disney en Espanol; Trinity Broadcasting Network; Turner Network TV HD; TV One; TVG Network; Versus; VH1 Classic; VH1 Soul; WE tv.
Fee: $11.00 monthly.

Pay Service 1
Pay Units: 6,410.
Programming (via satellite): HBO; Starz.
Fee: $20.00 installation; $8.00 monthly (each).

Digital Pay Service 1
Pay Units: N.A.
Programming (via satellite): Cinemax (multiplexed); Cinemax HD; Cinemax On Demand; Flix; HBO (multiplexed); HBO HD; HBO On Demand; Showtime (multiplexed); Showtime HD; Showtime On Demand; Starz (multiplexed); Starz HDTV; Starz On Demand; The Movie Channel (multiplexed); The Movie Channel On Demand.
Fee: $12.00 monthly (each).

Video-On-Demand: Yes

Pay-Per-View
iN DEMAND (delivered digitally); Playboy TV (delivered digitally); Fresh (delivered digitally); Club Jenna (delivered digitally); Hot Choice (delivered digitally); Shorteez (delivered digitally).

Internet Service
Operational: Yes.
Broadband Service: EarthLink, Road Runner.
Fee: $45.95 monthly.

Telephone Service
Digital: Operational
Fee: $44.95 monthly

Miles of Plant: 886.0 (coaxial); None (fiber optic).

President: Stephen Fry. Area Vice President: Rick Whaley. Vice President, Engineering: Al Costanzi. Vice President, Marketing: Patrick Burke. Vice President, Public Affairs: William Jasso. Government & Media Relations Director: Chris Thomas.

Ownership: Time Warner Cable (MSO).

ATHENS—Time Warner Cable, 1266 Dublin Rd, Columbus, OH 43215-1008. Phone: 614-481-5000. Fax: 614-481-5052. Web Site: http://www.timewarnercable.com/midohio. Also serves Albany, Alexander Twp. & New Marshfield. ICA: OH0448.

TV Market Ranking: Below 100 (Alexander Twp., ATHENS (portions)); Outside TV Markets (Albany, ATHENS (portions), New Marshfield).

Channel capacity: N.A. Channels available but not in use: N.A.

Basic Service
Subscribers: N.A.
Programming (received off-air): WBNS-TV (CBS) Columbus; WCHS-TV (ABC) Charleston; WCMH-TV (NBC) Columbus; WOUB-TV (PBS) Athens; WOWK-TV (CBS) Huntington; WPBY-TV (PBS) Huntington; WQCW (CW) Portsmouth; WSAZ-TV (MNT,

NBC) Huntington; WSYX (ABC, MNT) Columbus; WTTE (FOX) Columbus.
Programming (via satellite): Animal Planet; C-SPAN; Disney Channel; Hallmark Channel; QVC; WGN America.

Expanded Basic Service 1
Subscribers: N.A.
Programming (via satellite): ABC Family Channel; Cartoon Network; CNN; Country Music TV; Discovery Channel; ESPN; ESPN 2; Headline News; MTV; Nickelodeon; Spike TV; TBS Superstation; Turner Classic Movies; Turner Network TV; USA Network; VH1.

Digital Basic Service
Subscribers: N.A.
Programming (via satellite): BBC America; Bravo; Discovery Health Channel; Discovery Kids Channel; ESPN Classic Sports; ESPNews; Fox Soccer; Golf Channel; GSN; HGTV; History Channel; Independent Film Channel; Music Choice; Nick Jr.; Science; Syfy; Versus; WE tv.

Digital Pay Service 1
Pay Units: N.A.
Programming (via satellite): Cinemax (multiplexed); Encore (multiplexed); HBO (multiplexed); Showtime (multiplexed); Starz (multiplexed); The Movie Channel (multiplexed).

Video-On-Demand: No

Pay-Per-View
iN DEMAND (delivered digitally); Playboy TV (delivered digitally); Club Jenna (delivered digitally).

Internet Service
Operational: Yes.
Broadband Service: Road Runner.
Fee: $44.95 monthly.

Telephone Service
None

President: Rhonda Fraas. Vice President & General Manager: David Kreiman. Vice President, Marketing: Mark Psigoda. Vice President, Engineering: Randy Hall. Vice President, Government & Public Affairs: Mary Jo Green. Technical Operations Director: Jim Cavender. Government Affairs Director: Steve Cuckler.
Ownership: Time Warner Cable (MSO).

ATHENS—Time Warner Cable, 1266 Dublin Rd, Columbus, OH 43215-1008. Phone: 614-481-5000. Fax: 614-481-5052. Web Site: http://www.timewarnercable.com/midohio. Also serves Athens Twp., Canaan Twp. (Athens County), Dover Twp. (Athens County), Nelsonville & The Plains. ICA: OH0074.

TV Market Ranking: Below 100 (ATHENS, Athens Twp., Canaan Twp. (Athens County), Dover Twp. (Athens County), The Plains); Outside TV Markets (Nelsonville).
Channel capacity: N.A. Channels available but not in use: N.A.

Basic Service
Subscribers: N.A.
Programming (received off-air): WBNS-TV (CBS) Columbus; WCHS-TV (ABC) Charleston; WCMH-TV (NBC) Columbus; WLPX-TV (ION) Charleston; WOUB-TV (PBS) Athens; WOWK-TV (CBS) Huntington; WQCW (CW) Portsmouth; WSAZ-TV (MNT, NBC) Huntington; WSYX (ABC, MNT) Columbus; WTTE (FOX) Columbus; WWHO (CW) Chillicothe.
Programming (via satellite): C-SPAN; C-SPAN 2; Headline News; History Channel; QVC; Radar Channel; ShopNBC; TBS Superstation; The Learning Channel; TV Guide Network; WGN America.

Expanded Basic Service 1
Subscribers: N.A.
Programming (via satellite): A&E Networks; ABC Family Channel; AMC; Animal Planet; BBC America; BET Networks; Bravo; Cartoon Network; CNBC; CNN; Comedy Central; Country Music TV; Discovery Channel; Discovery Health Channel; Disney Channel; E! Entertainment Television; ESPN; ESPN 2; Food Network; Fox News Channel; Fox Sports Net Ohio; FX; Golf Channel; HGTV; Jewelry Television; Lifetime; Lifetime Movie Network; MSNBC; MTV; MTV2; National Geographic Channel; Nick Jr.; Nickelodeon; Oxygen; Spike TV; SportsTime Ohio; Syfy; The Weather Channel; Travel Channel; truTV; Turner Classic Movies; Turner Network TV; TV Land; Univision Studios; USA Network; Versus; VH1; WE tv.

Digital Basic Service
Subscribers: N.A.
Programming (via satellite): AmericanLife TV Network; BBC America On Demand; Bio; Bloomberg Television; Boomerang; Canal Sur; Cine Latino; cloo; CNN en Espanol; CNN International; College Sports Television; Cooking Channel; C-SPAN 3; Current; Discovery en Espanol; Discovery Fit & Health; Discovery Kids Channel; Disney Channel; DIY Network; Encore (multiplexed); ESPN 2 HD; ESPN Classic Sports; ESPN HD; ESPN U; ESPNews; Eternal Word TV Network; Exercise TV; Food Network; Fox Business Channel; Fox College Sports Atlantic; Fox College Sports Central; Fox College Sports Pacific; Fox Deportes; Fox Movie Channel; Fox Reality Channel; Fox Soccer; FSN HD; Fuel TV; Fuse; G4; Great American Country; GSN; HD Theater; HDNet; HDNet Movies; HGTV; History Channel International; ID Investigation Discovery; Independent Film Channel; INSP; Jewelry Television; La Familia Network; Lifetime Real Women; LOGO; Military Channel; Mojo Mix; MTV Hits; mun2 television; Music Choice; National Geographic Channel On Demand; NBA TV; NHL Network; NickToons TV; Ohio News Network; Outdoor Channel; Ovation; Oxygen On Demand; Planet Green; Science; SoapNet; Speed; Speed On Demand; Style Network; Sundance Channel; TBS in HD; TeenNick; Tennis Channel; The Weather Channel; The Word Network; Toon Disney; Tr3s; Turner Network TV HD; TV One; Universal HD; Versus HD; VH1 Classic; VHUNO; Video Rola.

Digital Pay Service 1
Pay Units: N.A.
Programming (via satellite): Cinemax (multiplexed); Cinemax On Demand; Encore; HBO (multiplexed); HBO HD; HBO Latino; HBO On Demand; Showtime (multiplexed); Showtime HD; Starz (multiplexed); The Movie Channel (multiplexed).

Pay-Per-View
iN DEMAND (delivered digitally); Playboy TV (delivered digitally); NBA League Pass (delivered digitally); MLS Direct Kick (delivered digitally); NHL Center Ice (delivered digitally); MLB Extra Innings (delivered digitally); ESPN Gameplan (delivered digitally).

Internet Service
Operational: Yes.
Broadband Service: Road Runner.

Telephone Service
Digital: Operational
Fee: $44.95 monthly

President: Rhonda Fraas. Vice President & General Manager: David Kreiman. Vice President, Marketing: Mark Psigoda. Vice President, Engineering: Randy Hall. Vice President, Government & Public Affairs: Mary Jo Green. Technical Operations Director: Jim Cavender. Government Affairs Director: Steve Cuckler.
Ownership: Time Warner Cable (MSO).

ATTICA—Time Warner Cable. Now served by SYCAMORE, OH [OH0215]. ICA: OH0315.

ATWATER TWP.—Time Warner Cable, 530 S Main St, Ste 1751, Akron, OH 44311-1090. Phone: 330-633-9203. Fax: 330-633-7970. Web Site: http://www.timewarnercable.com/northeastohio. Also serves Charlestown Twp., Deerfield Twp. (Portage County), Edinburg Twp., Marlboro Twp. (Stark County), Palmyra Twp. (portions), Randolph Twp. (Portage County) & Smith Twp. (Mahoning County). ICA: OH0111.

TV Market Ranking: 8,79 (ATWATER TWP., Charlestown Twp., Deerfield Twp. (Portage County), Edinburg Twp., Marlboro Twp. (Stark County), Palmyra Twp. (portions), Randolph Twp. (Portage County), Smith Twp. (Mahoning County)). Franchise award date: October 1, 1989. Franchise expiration date: N.A. Began: October 1, 1989.
Channel capacity: N.A. Channels available but not in use: N.A.

Basic Service
Subscribers: 1,897.
Programming (received off-air): WBNX-TV (CW) Akron; WDLI-TV (TBN) Canton; WEAO (PBS) Akron; WEWS-TV (ABC) Cleveland; WJW (FOX) Cleveland; WKYC (NBC) Cleveland; WNEO (PBS) Alliance; WOIO (CBS) Shaker Heights; WQHS-DT (UNV) Cleveland; WRLM (IND) Canton; WUAB (MNT) Lorain; WVIZ (PBS) Cleveland; WVPX-TV (ION) Akron.
Programming (via satellite): TV Guide Network; WGN America.
Fee: $44.95 installation; $17.66 monthly.

Expanded Basic Service 1
Subscribers: N.A.
Programming (via satellite): A&E Networks; ABC Family Channel; AMC; Animal Planet; BET Networks; Bravo; Cartoon Network; CNBC; CNN; Comedy Central; C-SPAN; C-SPAN 2; Discovery Channel; Discovery Fit & Health; Discovery Health Channel; Disney Channel; E! Entertainment Television; ESPN; ESPN 2; ESPN Classic Sports; Eternal Word TV Network; Food Network; Fox News Channel; Fox Sports Net Ohio; FX; Golf Channel; Great American Country; GSN; Hallmark Channel; Headline News; HGTV; History Channel; INSP; Lifetime; Lifetime Movie Network; MSNBC; MTV; Nickelodeon; Oxygen; QVC; ShopNBC; SoapNet; Spike TV; Syfy; TBS Superstation; The Learning Channel; The Weather Channel; Travel Channel; truTV; Turner Classic Movies; Turner Network TV; TV Land; USA Network; Versus; VH1; WE tv.
Fee: $39.33 monthly.

Digital Basic Service
Subscribers: N.A.
Programming (via satellite): AmericanLife TV Network; America's Store; ART America; BBC America; Bio; Bloomberg Television; Boomerang; Canales N; CBS Sports Network; cloo; CNN International; Cooking Channel; Country Music TV; C-SPAN 3; Current; Daystar TV Network; Disney Channel; DIY Network; DMX Music; ESPN; ESPNews; Fox College Sports Atlantic; Fox College Sports Central; Fox College Sports Pacific; Fox Movie Channel; Fox Soccer; Fuel TV; Fuse; G4; GAS; HD Theater; HDNet; HDNet Movies; History Channel International; Independent Film Channel; INHD (multiplexed); Lifetime Real Women; MTV2; National Geographic Channel; NBA TV; Nick Jr.; NickToons TV; Ohio News Network; Outdoor Channel; RAI International; Speed; Style Network; Tennis Channel; The Word Network; Toon Disney; Turner Network TV HD; TV Asia; TVG Network; VH1 Classic; Zee TV USA.
Fee: $11.00 monthly.

Digital Pay Service 1
Pay Units: N.A.
Programming (via satellite): Cinemax (multiplexed); Encore (multiplexed); HBO (multiplexed); Showtime (multiplexed); Starz (multiplexed); The Movie Channel (multiplexed).
Fee: $12.00 monthly (HBO, Cinemax, Showtime/TMC, or Starz).

Video-On-Demand: Yes

Internet Service
Operational: Yes.
Broadband Service: EarthLink, Road Runner.
Fee: $99.00 installation; $44.95 monthly.

Telephone Service
Digital: Operational
Fee: $44.95 monthly

Miles of Plant: 250.0 (coaxial); None (fiber optic).
President: Stephen Fry. Area Vice President: Scott Miller. Vice President, Engineering: Al Costanzi. Vice President, Marketing: Patrick Burke. Vice President, Sales: Woody E. Woodward. Vice President, Public Affairs: William Jasso. Vice President, Customer Care: Donald Jenson. Government & Media Relations Director: Chris Thomas.
Ownership: Time Warner Cable (MSO).

AUBURN TWP.—Formerly served by Cebridge Connections. Now served by NELSON TWP., OH [OH0160]. ICA: OH0198.

AVA—Formerly served by Cebridge Connections. No longer in operation. ICA: OH0309.

BAINBRIDGE—Time Warner Cable, 1266 Dublin Rd, Columbus, OH 43215-1008. Phone: 614-481-5000. Fax: 614-481-5052. Web Site: http://www.timewarnercable.com/midohio. Also serves Bourneville, Paxton Twp. & Twin Twp. (Ross County). ICA: OH0221.

TV Market Ranking: 27 (BAINBRIDGE, Bourneville, Paxton Twp., Twin Twp. (Ross County)). Franchise award date: June 3, 1974. Franchise expiration date: N.A. Began: February 15, 1974.
Channel capacity: 34 (not 2-way capable). Channels available but not in use: N.A.

Basic Service
Subscribers: 669.
Programming (received off-air): WBNS-TV (CBS) Columbus; WCMH-TV (NBC) Columbus; WCPO-TV (ABC) Cincinnati; WHIO-TV (CBS) Dayton; WOSU-TV (PBS) Columbus; WSYX (ABC, MNT) Columbus; WXIX-TV (FOX) Newport; allband FM.
Programming (via satellite): A&E Networks; ABC Family Channel; AMC; Animal Planet; CNN; Country Music TV; Discovery Channel; Disney Channel; ESPN; ESPN 2; Lifetime; MTV; Nickelodeon; QVC; Spike TV; TBS Superstation; The Learning Channel; The Weather Channel; Turner Network TV; USA Network; VH1; WGN America.
Fee: $44.95 installation; $9.45 monthly; $15.12 additional installation.

Pay Service 1
Pay Units: N.A.
Programming (via satellite): Encore; HBO; Showtime; Starz; The Movie Channel.
Video-On-Demand: No
Internet Service
Operational: Yes.
Broadband Service: RoadRunner.
Fee: $24.95 monthly.
Telephone Service
Digital: Operational
Fee: $24.99 monthly
Miles of Plant: 45.0 (coaxial); None (fiber optic).
President: Rhonda Fraas. Vice President & General Manager: David Kreiman. Vice President, Engineering: Randy Hall. Vice President, Marketing: Mark Psigoda. Vice President, Government & Public Affairs: Mary Jo Green. Technical Operations Director: Jim Cavender. Government Affairs Director: Steve Cuckler.
Ownership: Time Warner Cable (MSO).

BALTIMORE—Time Warner Cable. Now served by LANCASTER, OH [OH0039]. ICA: OH0159.

BARTON—Powhatan Point Cable Co., PO Box 67, Powhatan Point, OH 43942-0067. Phone: 740-795-5005. Also serves Crescent & Maynard. ICA: OH0212.
TV Market Ranking: 90 (BARTON, Crescent, Maynard). Franchise award date: N.A. Franchise expiration date: N.A. Began: December 1, 1965.
Channel capacity: 53 (not 2-way capable). Channels available but not in use: N.A.
Basic Service
Subscribers: 308.
Programming (received off-air): WFMJ-TV (CW, NBC) Youngstown; WKBN-TV (CBS) Youngstown; WOUC-TV (PBS) Cambridge; WPGH-TV (FOX) Pittsburgh; WPMY (MNT) Pittsburgh; WQED (PBS) Pittsburgh; WTAE-TV (ABC) Pittsburgh; WTOV-TV (IND, NBC) Steubenville; WTRF-TV (CBS) Wheeling; allband FM.
Programming (via satellite): A&E Networks; ABC Family Channel; Animal Planet; Cartoon Network; CNN; Comedy Central; Country Music TV; CW+; Discovery Channel; ESPN; ESPN 2; Eternal Word TV Network; Food Network; Fox News Channel; Fox Sports Net Ohio; FX; Golf Channel; Great American Country; Hallmark Channel; HGTV; History Channel; Lifetime; Local Cable Weather; MTV; Nickelodeon; Outdoor Channel; QVC; Speed; Spike TV; Syfy; TBS Superstation; The Learning Channel; Travel Channel; truTV; Turner Classic Movies; Turner Network TV; TV Land; USA Network; VH1; WGN America.
Fee: $33.00 monthly.
Pay Service 1
Pay Units: N.A.
Programming (via satellite): Encore; HBO (multiplexed).
Fee: $12.00 monthly (HBO), $5.00 monthly (Encore).
Video-On-Demand: No
Internet Service
Operational: Yes.
Fee: $40.00 monthly.
Telephone Service
None
Miles of Plant: 11.0 (coaxial); None (fiber optic).
Manager: Kasmir Majewski.
Ownership: Walter Matkovich (MSO).; Kasmir Majewski (MSO).

BAZETTA TWP.—Comcast Cable. Now served by WARREN, OH [OH0013]. ICA: OH0082.

BELLEFONTAINE—Time Warner Cable, 1266 Dublin Rd, Columbus, OH 43215. Phone: 614-481-5050. Web Site: http://www.timewarnercable.com. Also serves Huntsville (village), Lakeview (Logan County), Russells Point, Stokes Twp. (Logan County) & Zanesfield (village). ICA: OH0117.
TV Market Ranking: Below 100 (BELLEFONTAINE, Huntsville (village), Lakeview (Logan County), Russells Point, Stokes Twp. (Logan County), Zanesfield (village)). Franchise award date: N.A. Franchise expiration date: N.A. Began: September 1, 1966.
Channel capacity: N.A. Channels available but not in use: N.A.
Basic Service
Subscribers: 5,885.
Programming (received off-air): WBDT (CW) Springfield; WBGU-TV (PBS) Bowling Green; WBNS-TV (CBS) Columbus; WDTN (NBC) Dayton; WHIO-TV (CBS) Dayton; WKEF (ABC) Dayton; WLIO (CW, NBC) Lima; WOSU-TV (PBS) Columbus; WSYX (ABC, MNT) Columbus; WTLW (IND) Lima; WTTE (FOX) Columbus; 1 FM.
Programming (via satellite): C-SPAN; C-SPAN 2; Eternal Word TV Network; INSP; ION Television; QVC; ShopNBC; Trinity Broadcasting Network; TV Guide Network; WGN America.
Fee: $35.95 installation; $1.04 converter.
Expanded Basic Service 1
Subscribers: 6,627.
Programming (via satellite): A&E Networks; ABC Family Channel; AMC; Animal Planet; BET Networks; Cartoon Network; CNBC; CNN; Comedy Central; Country Music TV; Discovery Channel; Disney Channel; E! Entertainment Television; ESPN; ESPN 2; Food Network; Fox News Channel; Fox Sports Net Ohio; FX; G4; Golf Channel; GSN; Hallmark Channel; Headline News; HGTV; History Channel; Lifetime; MSNBC; MTV; National Geographic Channel; Nickelodeon; Ohio News Network; Oxygen; Speed; Spike TV; Style Network; Syfy; TBS Superstation; The Learning Channel; The Weather Channel; Travel Channel; truTV; Turner Classic Movies; Turner Network TV; TV Land; USA Network; Versus; VH1.
Fee: $45.00 monthly.
Digital Basic Service
Subscribers: N.A.
Programming (via satellite): BBC America; Bio; Bloomberg Television; Discovery Digital Networks; DIY Network; ESPNews; Fox College Sports Atlantic; Fox College Sports Central; Fox College Sports Pacific; Fox Deportes; Fox Movie Channel; Fox Soccer; Fuel TV; Fuse; GAS; History Channel International; Independent Film Channel; Lifetime Movie Network; MTV Networks Digital Suite; Music Choice; Nick Jr.; NickToons TV; Science Television; SoapNet; Sundance Channel; Toon Disney; WE tv.
Digital Pay Service 1
Pay Units: N.A.
Programming (via satellite): Cinemax (multiplexed); HBO (multiplexed); Starz (multiplexed).
Video-On-Demand: No
Pay-Per-View
Playboy TV (delivered digitally); Fresh (delivered digitally); Shorteez (delivered digitally).
Internet Service
Operational: Yes.
Broadband Service: Charter Pipeline.
Fee: $29.99 monthly.
Telephone Service
None
Miles of Plant: 144.0 (coaxial); None (fiber optic). Additional miles planned: 3.0 (coaxial).
President: Rhonda Fraas.
Ownership: Time Warner Cable (MSO).

BELLEVUE—Time Warner Cable, 205 Crystal Ave, Findlay, OH 45840. Phones: 614-481-5000 (Columbus office); 419-429-7474. Fax: 419-429-7402. Web Site: http://www.timewarnercable.com/midohio. Also serves Adams Twp. (Seneca County), Ballville Twp., Clyde, Fremont, Green Creek Twp. (Sandusky County), Green Springs, Lyme Twp. (Huron County), Pleasant Twp. (Seneca County), Riley Twp. (Sandusky County), Sandusky Twp., Sherman Twp. (Huron County), Thompson Twp. (Seneca County), Townsend Twp. (Sandusky County), Vickery & York Twp. (Sandusky County). ICA: OH0086.
TV Market Ranking: 52 (Fremont, Vickery); Below 100 (Adams Twp. (Seneca County), Ballville Twp., BELLEVUE, Clyde, Green Creek Twp. (Sandusky County), Green Springs, Lyme Twp. (Huron County), Pleasant Twp. (Seneca County), Riley Twp. (Sandusky County), Sandusky Twp. (Sandusky County), Sherman Twp. (Huron County), Thompson Twp. (Seneca County), Townsend Twp. (Sandusky County), York Twp. (Sandusky County)). Franchise award date: August 29, 1969. Franchise expiration date: N.A. Began: September 1, 1970.
Channel capacity: N.A. Channels available but not in use: N.A.
Basic Service
Subscribers: 12,285.
Programming (received off-air): WBGU-TV (PBS) Bowling Green; WEWS-TV (ABC) Cleveland; WGGN-TV (TBN) Sandusky; WGTE-TV (PBS) Toledo; WJW (FOX) Cleveland; WKBD-TV (CW) Detroit; WKYC (NBC) Cleveland; WNWO-TV (NBC) Toledo; WTOL (CBS) Toledo; WTVG (ABC) Toledo; WUAB (MNT) Lorain; WUPW (FOX) Toledo; WVPX-TV (ION) Akron; 14 FMs.
Programming (via satellite): QVC; TV Guide Network.
Fee: $45.86 installation; $10.47 monthly.
Expanded Basic Service 1
Subscribers: N.A.
Programming (via satellite): A&E Networks; ABC Family Channel; AMC; Animal Planet; BET Networks; Bravo; Cartoon Network; CNBC; CNN; Comedy Central; Country Music TV; C-SPAN; C-SPAN 2; Discovery Channel; Disney Channel; E! Entertainment Television; ESPN; ESPN 2; ESPN Classic Sports; Eternal Word TV Network; Food Network; Fox News Channel; Fox Sports Net Ohio; Fuse; FX; Golf Channel; Hallmark Channel; Headline News; HGTV; History Channel; INSP; Lifetime; Lifetime Movie Network; MSNBC; MTV; National Geographic Channel; Nickelodeon; Oxygen; ShopNBC; Spike TV; Syfy; TBS Superstation; The Learning Channel; The Weather Channel; Travel Channel; truTV; Turner Classic Movies; Turner Network TV; TV Land; USA Network; Versus; VH1; WE tv.
Fee: $30.47 monthly.
Digital Basic Service
Subscribers: 1,556.
Programming (via satellite): AmericanLife TV Network; America's Store; BBC America; Bio; Bloomberg Television; Boomerang; Canales N; CBS Sports Network; CNN International; Cooking Channel; C-SPAN 3; Deutsche Welle TV; Discovery Fit & Health; DIY Network; ESPN; ESPNews; Fox Movie Channel; Fox Sports World; FSN Digital Atlantic; FSN Digital Central; FSN Digital Pacific; Fuel TV; G4; GAS; Great American Country; GSN; HD Theater; HDNet; HDNet Movies; Independent Film Channel; INHD; Lifetime Real Women; MTV2; Music Choice; NBA TV; Nick Jr.; Ohio News Network; Outdoor Channel; Ovation; SoapNet; Sorpresa; Speed; Style Network; Sundance Channel; Tennis Channel; Toon Disney; Turner Network TV; TV Asia; VH1 Classic; WAM! America's Kidz Network; Zee TV USA.
Fee: $9.90 monthly.
Digital Pay Service 1
Pay Units: 3,979.
Programming (via satellite): Cinemax (multiplexed); Encore Action; Flix; HBO (multiplexed); Showtime (multiplexed); Starz (multiplexed); The Movie Channel (multiplexed).
Fee: $15.00 installation; $11.95 monthly (Cinemax, HBO, Showtime, Starz/Encore, or Flix/TMC).
Video-On-Demand: Yes
Pay-Per-View
Addressable homes: 1,556.
iN DEMAND (delivered digitally); Fresh (delivered digitally); Sports PPV (delivered digitally).
Internet Service
Operational: Yes.
Subscribers: 933.
Broadband Service: Road Runner.
Fee: $69.95 installation; $44.95 monthly.
Telephone Service
Digital: Operational
Miles of Plant: 195.0 (coaxial); 54.0 (fiber optic).
President: Rhonda Fraas. Vice President, Operations: Brad Wakely. Vice President, Engineering: Randy Hall. Vice President, Marketing: Mark Psigoda. Technical Operations Director: John Ellingson. Public Affairs Director: Brian Young. Public Affairs Manager: Patrick McCauley.
Ownership: Time Warner Cable (MSO).

BENTON RIDGE—B. R. Cablevision Co., 3225 W Elm St, Lima, OH 45805-2520. Phone: 419-227-2266. Fax: 419-999-2140. E-mail: info@watchtv.net. Web Site: http://www.watchtv.net. Also serves Blanchard Twp. (Hancock County), Liberty Twp. (Hancock County) & Union Twp. (Hancock County). ICA: OH0287.
TV Market Ranking: Below 100 (BENTON RIDGE, Blanchard Twp. (Hancock County), Liberty Twp. (Hancock County), Union Twp. (Hancock County)). Franchise award date: N.A. Franchise expiration date: N.A. Began: December 1, 1983.
Channel capacity: N.A. Channels available but not in use: N.A.
Digital Basic Service
Subscribers: 138.
Programming (via satellite): A&E Networks; ABC Family Channel; AMC; Animal Planet; BBC America; Bio; Cartoon Network; CNN; Comedy Central; Country Music TV; C-SPAN; CW+; Discovery Channel; Discovery Digital Networks; Disney Channel; E! Entertainment Television; ESPN; ESPN 2; ESPN Classic Sports; ESPNews; Eternal Word TV Network; Food Network; Fox News Channel; Fox Soccer; Fox Sports Net Ohio; FX; G4; Golf Channel; Great American Country; GSN; Headline

News; HGTV; History Channel; INSP; ION Television; Lifetime; MSNBC; MTV; Nickelodeon; Outdoor Channel; QVC; Speed; Spike TV; Syfy; TBS Superstation; The Learning Channel; The Weather Channel; Toon Disney; Travel Channel; Trinity Broadcasting Network; truTV; Turner Classic Movies; Turner Network TV; TV Land; USA Network; VH1; WGN America.
Fee: $29.95 installation; $35.97 monthly.

Digital Pay Service 1
Pay Units: 15.
Programming (via satellite): HBO (multiplexed).
Fee: $25.00 installation; $12.99 monthly.

Digital Pay Service 2
Pay Units: 8.
Programming (via satellite): Showtime (multiplexed); The Movie Channel (multiplexed).
Fee: $25.00 installation; $12.99 monthly.

Digital Pay Service 3
Pay Units: 6.
Programming (via satellite): Cinemax (multiplexed).
Fee: $25.00 installation; $7.99 monthly.

Digital Pay Service 4
Pay Units: N.A.
Programming (via satellite): Encore; Starz (multiplexed).

Video-On-Demand: No

Pay-Per-View
Addressable homes: 200.

Internet Service
Operational: Yes.

Telephone Service
None

Miles of Plant: 11.0 (coaxial); None (fiber optic).
President & Chief Executive Officer: Ken Wiliams. General Manager: Thomas Knippen. Installation Manager: Jim Hardin. Engineer: Mike Birkemeier.
Ownership: W.A.T.C.H. TV.

BERLIN TWP. (Mahoning County)—Shentel, 106 S Main St, Edinburg, VA 22824. Phones: 800-743-6835; 540-984-5224. Web Site: http://www.shentel.net. Also serves Beaver Twp. (Mahoning County), Canfield Twp., Ellsworth Twp., Goshen Twp. (Mahoning County), Green Twp. (Mahoning County), Jackson Twp. (Mahoning County), Milton Twp. (Mahoning County) & Smith Twp. (portions) (Mahoning County). ICA: OH0161.
TV Market Ranking: 79 (Beaver Twp. (Mahoning County), BERLIN TWP., Canfield Twp., Ellsworth Twp., Goshen Twp. (Mahoning County), Green Twp. (Mahoning County), Jackson Twp. (Mahoning County), Milton Twp. (Mahoning County), Smith Twp. (portions) (Mahoning County)). Franchise award date: N.A. Franchise expiration date: N.A. Began: May 1, 1990.
Channel capacity: 62 (not 2-way capable). Channels available but not in use: N.A.

Basic Service
Subscribers: 1,322.
Programming (received off-air): WBNX-TV (CW) Akron; WFMJ-TV (CW, NBC) Youngstown; WJW (FOX) Cleveland; WKBN-TV (CBS) Youngstown; WNEO (PBS) Alliance; WOIO (CBS) Shaker Heights; WUAB (MNT) Lorain; WYTV (ABC, MNT) Youngstown.
Programming (via satellite): QVC; TBS Superstation.
Fee: $29.95 installation; $19.95 monthly; $1.95 converter.

Expanded Basic Service 1
Subscribers: N.A.
Programming (via satellite): A&E Networks; ABC Family Channel; AMC; Cartoon Network; CNBC; CNN; Country Music TV; C-SPAN; Discovery Channel; Disney Channel; ESPN; ESPN 2; Fox News Channel; Fox Sports Net Ohio; Headline News; HGTV; History Channel; Lifetime; MTV; Nickelodeon; Root Sports Pittsburgh; Spike TV; Syfy; The Learning Channel; The Weather Channel; Turner Network TV; TV Land; USA Network; VH1.
Fee: $20.00 monthly.

Pay Service 1
Pay Units: 148.
Programming (via satellite): Cinemax.
Fee: $11.00 monthly.

Pay Service 2
Pay Units: 231.
Programming (via satellite): HBO.
Fee: $11.00 monthly.

Pay Service 3
Pay Units: 212.
Programming (via satellite): Showtime; The Movie Channel.
Fee: $12.95 monthly (Showtime or TMC).

Video-On-Demand: No

Internet Service
Operational: No.

Telephone Service
None

Miles of Plant: 137.0 (coaxial); None (fiber optic).
General Manager: Robert Harold. Chief Technician: Steve Adkins.
Ownership: Shenandoah Telecommunications Inc. (MSO).

BETTSVILLE—Time Warner Cable. Now served by CLAY CENTER/GIBSONBURG (formerly Allen Twp.), OH [OH0071]. ICA: OH0179.

BEVERLY—Time Warner Cable, 1266 Dublin Rd, Columbus, OH 43215-1008. Phone: 614-481-5000. Fax: 614-481-5052. Web Site: http://www.timewarnercable.com/midohio. Also serves Adams Twp. (Washington County), Barlow Twp., Belpre Twp. (Washington County), Chester Twp., Coal Run, Coolville, Guysville, Hockingport, Little Hocking, Malta, McConnelsville, Olive Twp. (Meigs County), Reedsville, Rome Twp. (Athens County), Stewart, Stockport, Torch, Troy Twp. (Athens County), Tuppers Plains, Vincent, Waterford Twp. & Watertown. ICA: OH0175.
TV Market Ranking: Below 100 (Adams Twp. (Washington County), Barlow Twp., Belpre Twp. (Washington County), BEVERLY, Chester Twp., Coal Run, Coolville, Guysville, Hockingport, Little Hocking, Malta, McConnelsville, Olive Twp. (Meigs County), Reedsville, Rome Twp. (Athens County), Stewart, Stockport, Torch, Troy Twp. (Athens County), Tuppers Plains, Vincent, Waterford Twp., Watertown). Franchise award date: N.A. Franchise expiration date: N.A. Began: June 29, 1963.
Channel capacity: N.A. Channels available but not in use: N.A.

Basic Service
Subscribers: N.A.
Programming (received off-air): WBNS-TV (CBS) Columbus; WCHS-TV (ABC) Charleston; WHIZ-TV (NBC) Zanesville; WOUB-TV (PBS) Athens; WSYX (ABC, MNT) Columbus; WTAP-TV (FOX, MNT, NBC) Parkersburg; WVAH-TV (FOX) Charleston; allband FM.
Programming (via satellite): QVC; TBS Superstation; The Weather Channel; TV Guide Network; WGN America.
Fee: $29.95 installation; $10.57 monthly.

Expanded Basic Service 1
Subscribers: N.A.
Programming (via satellite): A&E Networks; ABC Family Channel; AMC; Animal Planet; BET Networks; Bravo; Cartoon Network; CNBC; CNN; Comedy Central; Country Music TV; C-SPAN; Discovery Channel; Disney Channel; E! Entertainment Television; ESPN; ESPN 2; Food Network; Fox News Channel; Fox Sports Net Ohio; FX; Golf Channel; Hallmark Channel; Headline News; HGTV; History Channel; INSP; Lifetime; MSNBC; MTV; Nick Jr.; Nickelodeon; Spike TV; SportsTime Ohio; Syfy; The Learning Channel; Toon Disney; Travel Channel; Trinity Broadcasting Network; truTV; Turner Network TV; TV Land; USA Network; VH1.
Fee: $15.60 monthly.

Digital Basic Service
Subscribers: N.A.
Programming (via satellite): BBC America; Bloomberg Television; CMT Pure Country; Current; Discovery Fit & Health; Discovery Health Channel; Discovery Home Channel; Discovery Kids Channel; Discovery Times Channel; DIY Network; ESPN Classic Sports; ESPN U; ESPNews; Fox Business Channel; Fox Movie Channel; Fox Reality Channel; Fox Soccer; Fuse; G4; GAS; GMC; Great American Country; GSN; INSP; Lifetime Movie Network; LOGO; Military Channel; MTV Hits; MTV Jams; MTV2; Music Choice; National Geographic Channel; Nick Too; NickToons TV; Ohio News Network; Science; SoapNet; Speed; The Word Network; Turner Classic Movies; VH1 Classic; WE tv.
Fee: $52.40 monthly.

Digital Expanded Basic Service
Subscribers: N.A.
Programming (via satellite): Bio; Flix; Fox College Sports Atlantic; Fox College Sports Central; Fox College Sports Pacific; History Channel International; Independent Film Channel; Outdoor Channel; Sundance Channel; Versus.

Digital Pay Service 1
Pay Units: N.A.
Programming (via satellite): Cinemax (multiplexed); Encore (multiplexed); HBO (multiplexed); Showtime (multiplexed); Starz (multiplexed); The Movie Channel (multiplexed).

Video-On-Demand: Yes

Pay-Per-View
iN DEMAND (delivered digitally); Playboy TV (delivered digitally); Fresh (delivered digitally); Club Jenna (delivered digitally); Hot Choice (delivered digitally).

Internet Service
Operational: Yes.
Broadband Service: Road Runner.
Fee: $42.95 monthly.

Telephone Service
Digital: Operational
Fee: $44.95 monthly

Miles of Plant: 76.0 (coaxial); None (fiber optic).
President: Rhonda Fraas. Vice President & General Manager: David Kreiman. Vice President, Engineering: Randy Hall. Vice President, Marketing: Mark Psigoda. Vice President, Government & Public Affairs: Mary Jo Green. Technical Operations Director: David Bowen. Government Affairs Director: Steve Cuckler.
Ownership: Time Warner Cable (MSO).

BIG ISLAND TWP.—Now served by MARION, OH [OH0040]. ICA: OH0317.

BLOOMINGDALE—Suddenlink Communications, 12444 Powerscourt Dr, Saint Louis, MO 63131-3660. Phone: 314-965-2020. Web Site: http://www.suddenlink.com. Also serves German (village), Ross Twp. (Jefferson County), Salem Twp. (Jefferson County), Springfield Twp. (Jefferson County) & Wayne Twp. (Jefferson County). ICA: OH0203.
TV Market Ranking: 10 (German (village)); 90 (BLOOMINGDALE, Ross Twp. (Jefferson County), Salem Twp. (Jefferson County), Springfield Twp. (Jefferson County), Wayne Twp. (Jefferson County)). Franchise award date: N.A. Franchise expiration date: N.A. Began: March 1, 1990.
Channel capacity: 62 (not 2-way capable). Channels available but not in use: N.A.

Basic Service
Subscribers: 935.
Programming (received off-air): KDKA-TV (CBS) Pittsburgh; WINP-TV (IND, ION) Pittsburgh; WPGH-TV (FOX) Pittsburgh; WPMY (MNT) Pittsburgh; WPXI (IND, NBC) Pittsburgh; WQED (PBS) Pittsburgh; WTAE-TV (ABC) Pittsburgh; WTOV-TV (IND, NBC) Steubenville; WTRF-TV (CBS) Wheeling.
Programming (via satellite): QVC; TBS Superstation.
Fee: $30.00 installation; $19.95 monthly; $1.95 converter.

Expanded Basic Service 1
Subscribers: 904.
Programming (via satellite): A&E Networks; ABC Family Channel; AMC; CNBC; CNN; C-SPAN; Discovery Channel; Disney Channel; ESPN; Headline News; History Channel; Lifetime; MTV; Nickelodeon; Root Sports Pittsburgh; Spike TV; Syfy; The Weather Channel; Turner Network TV; TV Land; USA Network; VH1.
Fee: $22.00 monthly.

Pay Service 1
Pay Units: 83.
Programming (via satellite): Cinemax.
Fee: $11.00 monthly.

Pay Service 2
Pay Units: 118.
Programming (via satellite): HBO.
Fee: $11.00 monthly.

Pay Service 3
Pay Units: 97.
Programming (via satellite): Showtime; The Movie Channel.
Fee: $12.95 monthly.

Internet Service
Operational: No.

Telephone Service
None

Miles of Plant: 56.0 (coaxial); None (fiber optic).
Manager: Peter Brown.
Ownership: Cequel Communications LLC (MSO).

BLUFFTON—Time Warner Cable. Now served by LIMA, OH [OH0020]. ICA: OH0214.

BOARDMAN—Armstrong Cable Services, 9328 Woodworth Rd, North Lima, OH 44452. Phones: 877-277-5711; 330-726-0115. Fax: 330-726-0117. E-mail: info@zoominternet.net. Web Site: http://cable.armstrongonewire.com. Also serves Austintown Twp., Beaver Twp. (Mahoning County), Campbell, Canfield, Canfield Twp., Mahoning County (portions), McDonald, Mineral Ridge, New Springfield (portions), North Lima, Poland, Poland Twp. (Mahoning County), Springfield Twp. (Mahoning County), Trumbull County (southern portion) & Weathersfield Twp. (Trumbull County). ICA: OH0024.

TV Market Ranking: 79 (Austintown Twp., Beaver Twp. (Mahoning County), BOARDMAN, Campbell, Canfield, Canfield Twp., Mahoning County (portions), McDonald, Mineral Ridge, New Springfield (portions), North Lima, Poland, Poland Twp. (Mahoning County), Springfield Twp. (Mahoning County), Weathersfield Twp. (Trumbull County)); 8,79 (Trumbull County (portions)). Franchise award date: December 4, 1972. Franchise expiration date: January 1, 2007. Began: October 1, 1974.

Channel capacity: N.A. Channels available but not in use: N.A.

Digital Basic Service

Subscribers: 12,220.

Programming (via satellite): A&E Networks; ABC Family Channel; AMC; Animal Planet; BET Networks; Bravo; Cartoon Network; CNBC; CNN; Comedy Central; Country Music TV; C-SPAN; C-SPAN 2; CW+; Discovery Channel; Disney Channel; E! Entertainment Television; ESPN; ESPN 2; ESPN Classic Sports; ETC; Food Network; Fox News Channel; Fox Sports Net Ohio; FX; Headline News; HGTV; History Channel; Lifetime; MSNBC; MTV; Music Choice; MyNetworkTV Inc.; Nickelodeon; NickToons TV; QVC; Root Sports Pittsburgh; ShopNBC; Speed; Spike TV; SportsTime Ohio; Syfy; TBS Superstation; Telemundo; The Learning Channel; The Weather Channel; Travel Channel; truTV; Turner Classic Movies; Turner Network TV; TV Guide Network; TV Land; USA Network; VH1.

Fee: $12.00 monthly.

Digital Expanded Basic Service

Subscribers: N.A.

Programming (via satellite): AmericanLife TV Network; BBC America; Bio; Bloomberg Television; Boomerang; Chiller; cloo; CMT Pure Country; Cooking Channel; Discovery Fit & Health; Discovery Health Channel; Discovery Kids Channel; DIY Network; ESPN Classic Sports; ESPNews; G4; Golf Channel; Great American Country; GSN; Hallmark Channel; Hallmark Movie Channel; History Channel International; HRTV; ID Investigation Discovery; Jewelry Television; Lifetime Movie Network; Military Channel; MTV Hits; MTV Jams; MTV2; mun2 television; National Geographic Channel; NFL Network; NHL Network; Nick Jr.; Nick Too; Ohio News Network; Outdoor Channel; Oxygen; PBS Kids Sprout; Pentagon Channel; Planet Green; RFD-TV; Science; SoapNet; TeenNick; Tennis Channel; Toon Disney; Tr3s; Versus; VH1 Classic; VH1 Soul; WE tv.

Fee: $12.00 monthly.

Digital Expanded Basic Service 2

Subscribers: N.A.

Programming (received off-air): WFMJ-TV (CW, NBC) Youngstown; WKBN-TV (CBS) Youngstown; WQED (PBS) Pittsburgh; WYFX-LP Youngstown; WYTV (ABC, MNT) Youngstown.

Programming (via satellite): A&E HD; Animal Planet HD; Bravo HD; CNN HD; Discovery Channel HD; Disney Channel HD; ESPN 2 HD; ESPN HD; Food Network HD; Fox News HD; FSN HD; FX HD; Golf Channel HD; Hallmark Movie Channel HD; HD Theater; HDNet; HDNet Movies; HGTV HD; History Channel HD; MGM HD; National Geographic Channel HD Network; NFL Network HD; NHL Network HD; Outdoor Channel 2 HD; Palladia; Science HD; Syfy HD; TBS in HD; The Weather Channel HD; TLC HD; Turner Network TV HD; Universal HD; USA Network HD; Versus HD; WealthTV HD.

Fee: $9.00 monthly.

Digital Pay Service 1

Pay Units: N.A.

Programming (via satellite): Cinemax (multiplexed); Cinemax HD; Encore (multiplexed); Flix; HBO (multiplexed); HBO HD; RAI USA; Showtime (multiplexed); Showtime HD; Starz (multiplexed); Starz HDTV; The Movie Channel (multiplexed); TV5 USA.

Fee: $13.95 monthly (HBO, Cinemax, Showtime/TMC/Flix or Starz/Encore).

Video-On-Demand: Yes

Pay-Per-View

Addressable homes: 21,852.

ESPN Now (delivered digitally); Hot Choice (delivered digitally); iN DEMAND (delivered digitally); NHL/MLB (delivered digitally); ESPN Extra (delivered digitally).

Internet Service

Operational: Yes. Began: June 1, 1999.

Subscribers: 19,876.

Broadband Service: Armstrong Zoom.

Fee: $26.95-$39.95 monthly.

Telephone Service

Digital: Operational

Fee: $49.99 monthly

Miles of Plant: 842.0 (coaxial); 145.0 (fiber optic).

General Manager: Dan McGahagan. Technical Operations Manager: Joe Battista. Marketing Coordinator: Krista White.

Ownership: Armstrong Group of Companies (MSO).

BOLIVAR—Now served by NEW PHILADELPHIA, OH [OH0030]. ICA: OH0168.

BOWLING GREEN—Time Warner Cable, 205 Crystal Ave, Findlay, OH 45840. Phones: 419-429-7474; 614-481-5000 (Columbus office). Fax: 419-429-7402. Web Site: http://www.timewarnercable.com. Also serves Bairdstown, Bloom Twp. (Wood County), Bloomdale, Center Twp. (Wood County), Custar (village), Cygnet, Dunbridge, Henry Twp. (Wood County), Jerry City, Liberty Twp. (Wood County), McClure, Milton Center (village), Milton Twp. (Wood County), NORTH BALTIMORE, Plain Twp. (Wood County), Portage, Webster Twp. (Wood County) & Weston. ICA: OH0054.

TV Market Ranking: 52 (Bairdstown, Bloom Twp. (Wood County), Bloomdale, BOWLING GREEN, Center Twp. (Wood County), Custar (village), Cygnet, Dunbridge, Henry Twp. (Wood County), Jerry City, Liberty Twp. (Wood County), McClure, Milton Center (village), Milton Twp. (Wood County), North Baltimore, Plain Twp. (Wood County), Portage, Webster Twp. (Wood County), Weston). Franchise award date: N.A. Franchise expiration date: N.A. Began: December 1, 1965.

Channel capacity: N.A. Channels available but not in use: N.A.

Basic Service

Subscribers: 6,740.

Programming (received off-air): various Canadian stations; WBGU-TV (PBS) Bowling Green; WGTE-TV (PBS) Toledo; WKBD-TV (CW) Detroit; WLMB (IND) Toledo; WNWO-TV (NBC) Toledo; WTOL (CBS) Toledo; WTVG (ABC) Toledo; WUAB (MNT) Lorain; WUPW (FOX) Toledo; 1 FM.

Programming (via satellite): QVC; TV Guide Network.

Fee: $45.86 installation; $10.21 monthly; $31.81 additional installation.

Expanded Basic Service 1

Subscribers: N.A.

Programming (via satellite): A&E Networks; ABC Family Channel; AMC; Animal Planet; BET Networks; Bravo; Cartoon Network; CNBC; CNN; Comedy Central; Country Music TV; C-SPAN; C-SPAN 2; Discovery Channel; Disney Channel; E! Entertainment Television; ESPN; ESPN 2; ESPN Classic Sports; Eternal Word TV Network; Food Network; Fox News Channel; Fox Sports Net Ohio; FX; Golf Channel; Hallmark Channel; Headline News; HGTV; History Channel; INSP; Lifetime; Lifetime Movie Network; MSNBC; MTV; National Geographic Channel; Nickelodeon; Oxygen; ShopNBC; Spike TV; Syfy; TBS Superstation; The Learning Channel; The Weather Channel; Travel Channel; truTV; Turner Classic Movies; Turner Network TV; TV Land; Univision Studios; USA Network; Versus; VH1; WE tv.

Fee: $30.74 monthly.

Digital Basic Service

Subscribers: 2,022.

Programming (via satellite): AmericanLife TV Network; America's Store; BBC America; Bloomberg Television; CNN International; Cooking Channel; C-SPAN 3; Discovery Fit & Health; DIY Network; DMX Music; ESPNews; Fox Sports World; FSN Digital Atlantic; FSN Digital Central; FSN Digital Pacific; Fuse; G4; GAS; Great American Country; GSN; Lifetime Real Women; MTV2; Nick Jr.; Ohio News Network; Outdoor Channel; Ovation; SoapNet; Sorpresa; Speed; Style Network; Toon Disney; VH1 Classic.

Fee: $9.90 monthly.

Digital Expanded Basic Service

Subscribers: N.A.

Programming (via satellite): Encore Action.

Fee: $8.95 monthly.

Digital Pay Service 1

Pay Units: 375.

Programming (via satellite): Cinemax (multiplexed); Flix; HBO (multiplexed); Showtime (multiplexed); Starz (multiplexed); The Movie Channel (multiplexed).

Fee: $15.00 installation; $10.95 monthly (Cinemax, HBO, ShowtimeTMC/Flix, or Starz).

Video-On-Demand: Yes

Pay-Per-View

Addressable homes: 2,022.

iN DEMAND (delivered digitally); Fresh (delivered digitally); Sports PPV (delivered digitally).

Internet Service

Operational: Yes.

Subscribers: 1,213.

Broadband Service: AOL for Broadband; EarthLink; Road Runner; WCoil.

Fee: $69.95 installation; $44.95 monthly.

Telephone Service

Digital: Operational

Fee: $44.95 monthly

Miles of Plant: 170.0 (coaxial); None (fiber optic).

President: Rhonda Fraas. Senior Engineering Director: Larry Bryan. Technical Operations Director: James Gerhard. Affairs Director: Brian Young.

Ownership: Time Warner Cable (MSO).

BROOKFIELD TWP. (Trumbull County)—Northeast Cable TV, PO Box 4177, Youngstown, OH 44515-0177. Phone: 330-793-7434. Fax: 330-793-7434. ICA: OH0382.

TV Market Ranking: 79 (BROOKFIELD TWP.). Franchise award date: N.A. Franchise expiration date: N.A. Began: May 1, 1987.

Channel capacity: 60 (not 2-way capable). Channels available but not in use: N.A.

Basic Service

Subscribers: N.A.

Programming (received off-air): WBNX-TV (CW) Akron; WFMJ-TV (CW, NBC) Youngstown; WKBN-TV (CBS) Youngstown; WNEO (PBS) Alliance; WOIO (CBS) Shaker Heights; WPGH-TV (FOX) Pittsburgh; WUAB (MNT) Lorain; WYTV (ABC, MNT) Youngstown.

Programming (via satellite): A&E Networks; ABC Family Channel; AMC; CNN; Discovery Channel; ESPN; Fox Sports Net Ohio; Lifetime; MTV; Nickelodeon; Spike TV; Syfy; TBS Superstation; The Learning Channel; The Weather Channel; Turner Network TV; USA Network; WGN America.

Programming (via translator): WPCB-TV (IND) Greensburg.

Fee: $54.95 installation; $32.95 monthly.

Pay Service 1

Pay Units: N.A.

Programming (via satellite): HBO.

Fee: $9.95 monthly.

Internet Service

Operational: No.

Telephone Service

None

Miles of Plant: 11.0 (coaxial); None (fiber optic).

Manager & Chief Technician: Al Pezzenti.

Ownership: Northeast Cable TV (MSO).

BRUNSWICK—Time Warner Cable, 530 S Main St, Ste 1751, Akron, OH 44311-1090. Phone: 330-633-9203. Fax: 330-633-7970. Web Site: http://www.timewarnercable.com/northeastohio. Also serves Brunswick Hills. ICA: OH0059.

TV Market Ranking: 8 (BRUNSWICK, Brunswick Hills).

Channel capacity: N.A. Channels available but not in use: N.A.

Basic Service

Subscribers: N.A. Included in Akron,OH

Programming (received off-air): WBNX-TV (CW) Akron; WEAO (PBS) Akron; WEWS-TV (ABC) Cleveland; WJW (FOX) Cleveland; WKYC (NBC) Cleveland; WNEO (PBS) Alliance; WOIO (CBS) Shaker Heights; WQHS-DT (UNV) Cleveland; WRLM (IND) Canton; WUAB (MNT) Lorain; WVIZ (PBS) Cleveland; WVPX-TV (ION) Akron.

Programming (via satellite): Eternal Word TV Network; QVC; SportsTime Ohio; TV Guide Network; WGN America.

Fee: $44.95 installation; $9.45 monthly.

Expanded Basic Service 1
Subscribers: N.A.
Programming (via satellite): A&E Networks; ABC Family Channel; AMC; Animal Planet; BET Networks; Bravo; Cartoon Network; CNBC; CNN; Comedy Central; Country Music TV; C-SPAN; Discovery Channel; Disney Channel; E! Entertainment Television; ESPN; ESPN 2; Food Network; Fox News Channel; Fox Sports Net Ohio; FX; Golf Channel; Headline News; HGTV; History Channel; Lifetime; MSNBC; MTV; MTV2; Nickelodeon; Oxygen; ShopNBC; Speed; Spike TV; Style Network; Syfy; TBS Superstation; Telemundo; The Learning Channel; The Weather Channel; Travel Channel; truTV; Turner Network TV; TV Land; TV One; USA Network; VH1; VH1 Classic.
Fee: $43.55 monthly.

Digital Basic Service
Subscribers: 11.
Programming (via satellite): AmericanLife TV Network; BBC America; Bloomberg Television; Canal 52MX; CCTV News; Cine Latino; CMT Pure Country; CNN en Espanol; C-SPAN 2; C-SPAN 3; Current; Discovery en Espanol; Discovery Fit & Health; Discovery Health Channel; Discovery Home Channel; Discovery Kids Channel; DIY Network; ESPN 2 HD; ESPN Classic Sports; ESPN Deportes; ESPN HD; ESPN U; ESPNews; Familyland Television Network; Fox Business Channel; Fox Deportes; Fox Movie Channel; Fox Reality Channel; Fox Soccer; Fuse; G4; GAS; GMC; Great American Country; GSN; Hallmark Channel; Halogen Network; HD Theater; HDNet; HDNet Movies; here! On Demand; History Channel en Espanol; Howard TV; ID Investigation Discovery; Lifetime Movie Network; LOGO; Military Channel; MTV Hits; MTV Jams; Music Choice; National Geographic Channel; Nick Jr.; Nick Too; NickToons TV; Ohio News Network; Science; SoapNet; SportsTime Ohio; TBS in HD; The Word Network; Toon Disney; Toon Disney en Espanol; Tr3s; Trinity Broadcasting Network; Turner Classic Movies; Turner Network TV HD; TV One; TVG Network; Universal HD; VH1 Soul; WE tv.

Digital Expanded Basic Service
Subscribers: N.A.
Programming (via satellite): Bio; CBS Sports Network; Cooking Channel; Flix; FSN Digital Atlantic; FSN Digital Central; FSN Digital Pacific; Fuel TV; History Channel International; Independent Film Channel; NBA TV; Outdoor Channel; Sundance Channel; Tennis Channel; Versus.
Fee: $10.00 monthly.

Digital Pay Service 1
Pay Units: N.A.
Programming (via satellite): Arabic Channel; CCTV-4; Cinemax (multiplexed); Cinemax HD; Cinemax On Demand; Encore (multiplexed); Filipino Channel; HBO (multiplexed); HBO HD; HBO On Demand; RAI International; Russian Television Network; Showtime (multiplexed); Showtime HD; Showtime On Demand; Starz (multiplexed); Starz HDTV; Starz On Demand; The Movie Channel (multiplexed); The Movie Channel On Demand; TV Asia; TV Japan; TV5, La Television International; Zhong Tian Channel.
Fee: $12.00 monthly (HBO, Showtime/TMC/Flix, Starz/Encore or Cinemax), $14.95 monthly (TV Russia, CCTV4, TV Asia, TV5 Monde, Filipino Channel, RAI or ART), $25.00 monthly (TV Japan).

Video-On-Demand: Yes

Pay-Per-View
iN DEMAND (delivered digitally); ESPN Gameplan (delivered digitally); ESPN Full Court (delivered digitally); NBA League Pass (delivered digitally); MLS Direct Kick (delivered digitally); MLB Extra Innings (delivered digitally); NHL Center Ice (delivered digitally).

Internet Service
Operational: Yes.
Broadband Service: Road Runner.
Fee: $45.95 monthly.

Telephone Service
Digital: Operational
Fee: $44.95 monthly

President: Stephen Fry. Area Vice President: Scott Miller. Vice President, Engineering: Al Costanzi. Vice President, Marketing: Patrick Burke. Vice President, Sales: Woody Woodward. Vice President, Government & Media Affairs: William Jasso. Government & Media Relations Director: Chris Thomas.
Ownership: Time Warner Cable (MSO).

BRYAN—Bryan Municipal Utilities, 841 E Edgerton St, Bryan, OH 43506-1413. Phone: 419-633-6130. Fax: 419-633-6105. E-mail: communications@cityofbryan.com. Web Site: http://www.cityofbryan.net. ICA: OH0439. **Note:** This system is an overbuild.
TV Market Ranking: Below 100 (BRYAN).
Channel capacity: 116 (operating 2-way). Channels available but not in use: N.A.

Basic Service
Subscribers: 2,533.
Programming (received off-air): WANE-TV (CBS) Fort Wayne; WBGU-TV (PBS) Bowling Green; WDFM-LP (IND) Defiance; WFFT-TV (IND) Fort Wayne; WFWA (PBS) Fort Wayne; WGTE-TV (PBS) Toledo; WINM (IND) Angola; WISE-TV (FOX, MNT, NBC) Fort Wayne; WLMB (IND) Toledo; WNWO-TV (NBC) Toledo; WPTA (ABC, CW) Fort Wayne; WTOL (CBS) Toledo; WTVG (ABC) Toledo; WUPW (FOX) Toledo.
Programming (via satellite): C-SPAN; C-SPAN 2; Eternal Word TV Network; INSP; QVC; The Weather Channel; Trinity Broadcasting Network; WGN America.
Fee: $13.50 monthly.

Expanded Basic Service 1
Subscribers: N.A.
Programming (via satellite): A&E Networks; ABC Family Channel; AMC; Animal Planet; Bio; Cartoon Network; CNBC; CNN; Comedy Central; Country Music TV; Discovery Channel; Discovery Fit & Health; Discovery Health Channel; Disney Channel; E! Entertainment Television; ESPN; ESPN 2; ESPN Classic Sports; ESPNews; Food Network; Fox News Channel; Fox Sports Net Detroit; Fuse; FX; G4; Golf Channel; GSN; Hallmark Channel; Headline News; HGTV; History Channel; Lifetime; Lifetime Movie Network; MSNBC; MTV; MTV2; National Geographic Channel; Nickelodeon; Outdoor Channel; Speed; Spike TV; SportsTime Ohio; Syfy; TBS Superstation; The Learning Channel; Toon Disney; Travel Channel; truTV; Turner Classic Movies; Turner Network TV; TV Land; Univision Studios; USA Network; Versus; VH1.
Fee: $22.50 monthly.

Digital Basic Service
Subscribers: N.A.
Programming (via satellite): A&E HD; AmericanLife TV Network; BBC America; Bloomberg Television; Chiller; cloo; CMT Pure Country; Cooking Channel; Discovery Channel HD; Discovery Kids Channel; Disney Channel HD; DMX Music; ESPN 2 HD; ESPN HD; ESPN U; Food Network HD; Fox Business Channel; Fox College Sports Atlantic; Fox College Sports Central; Fox College Sports Pacific; Fox News HD; Fox Soccer; FX HD; Halogen Network; HD Theater; HDNet; HDNet Movies; HGTV HD; History Channel HD; History Channel International; ID Investigation Discovery; Military Channel; MTV Hits; National Geographic Channel HD Network; NickToons TV; Noggin; Outdoor Channel 2 HD; PBS Kids Sprout; Planet Green; Planet Green HD; RFD-TV; Science; Science HD; SoapNet; Speed HD; Style Network; Syfy HD; TLC HD; Travel Channel HD; USA Network HD; VH1 Classic.
Fee: $10.00 monthly.

Digital Pay Service 1
Pay Units: N.A.
Programming (via satellite): Cinemax (multiplexed); Cinemax HD; Encore (multiplexed); HBO (multiplexed); HBO HD; Showtime (multiplexed); Showtime HD; Starz (multiplexed); Starz HDTV; The Movie Channel.
Fee: $12.95 monthly (Cinemax), $14.25 monthly (Showtime/TMC or Starz/Encore), $14.95 monthly (HBO).

Pay-Per-View
iN DEMAND (delivered digitally).

Internet Service
Operational: Yes.
Broadband Service: In-house.
Fee: $28.00 monthly; $125.00 modem purchase.

Telephone Service
None

Cable Communications Superintendent: Joe Ferrell. Chief Technician: Tracy Goodwin.
Ownership: Bryan Municipal Utilities.

BRYAN—Time Warner Cable, 310 Jefferson Ave, Defiance, OH 43512. Phones: 614-481-5000 (Columbus office); 419-784-1992. Fax: 419-782-2640. Web Site: http://www.timewarnercable.com. Also serves Archbold, Brady Twp. (Williams County), Center Twp. (Williams County), Edgerton, German Twp. (Fulton County), Montpelier, Pulaski Twp. (Williams County), St. Joseph Twp. (Williams County), Stryker & West Unity. ICA: OH0078.
TV Market Ranking: 82 (Edgerton); Below 100 (Archbold, Brady Twp. (Williams County), BRYAN, Center Twp. (Williams County), German Twp. (Fulton County), Montpelier, St. Joseph Twp. (Williams County), Stryker, West Unity). Franchise award date: N.A. Franchise expiration date: N.A. Began: August 1, 1974.
Channel capacity: N.A. Channels available but not in use: N.A.

Basic Service
Subscribers: 6,438.
Programming (received off-air): WANE-TV (CBS) Fort Wayne; WBGU-TV (PBS) Bowling Green; WDFM-LP (IND) Defiance; WFFT-TV (IND) Fort Wayne; WFWA (PBS) Fort Wayne; WGTE-TV (PBS) Toledo; WINM (IND) Angola; WISE-TV (FOX, MNT, NBC) Fort Wayne; WLMB (IND) Toledo; WNWO-TV (NBC) Toledo; WPTA (ABC, CW) Fort Wayne; WTOL (CBS) Toledo; WTVG (ABC) Toledo; WUPW (FOX) Toledo; allband FM.
Programming (via satellite): C-SPAN; C-SPAN 2; Product Information Network; QVC; ShopNBC; TBS Superstation; The Weather Channel; TV Guide Network; WGN America.
Fee: $60.00 installation; $10.22 monthly; $30.00 additional installation.

Expanded Basic Service 1
Subscribers: 6,256.
Programming (via satellite): A&E Networks; ABC Family Channel; AMC; Animal Planet; Bio; Bravo; Cartoon Network; CNBC; CNN; Comedy Central; Country Music TV; Discovery Channel; Discovery Fit & Health; Disney Channel; E! Entertainment Television; ESPN; ESPN 2; ESPN Classic Sports; ESPNews; Food Network; Fox Movie Channel; Fox News Channel; Fox Sports Net Detroit; Fox Sports Net Ohio; Fuse; FX; G4; Golf Channel; Great American Country; Hallmark Channel; Headline News; HGTV; History Channel; INSP; Lifetime; Lifetime Movie Network; MSNBC; MTV; Nickelodeon; Ohio News Network; Outdoor Channel; Speed; Spike TV; Syfy; The Learning Channel; Toon Disney; Travel Channel; Trinity Broadcasting Network; truTV; Turner Classic Movies; Turner Network TV; TV Land; USA Network; VH1.
Fee: $11.49 monthly.

Digital Basic Service
Subscribers: 1,631.
Programming (via satellite): BBC America; Bloomberg Television; Discovery Digital Networks; Fox Sports World; GSN; History Channel International; Independent Film Channel; Style Network; Versus; WE tv.

Digital Expanded Basic Service
Subscribers: N.A.
Programming (via satellite): Canales N; FSN Digital Atlantic; FSN Digital Central; FSN Digital Pacific; MTV2; Music Choice; National Geographic Channel; Nick Jr.; VH1 Classic; VH1 Country.

Pay Service 1
Pay Units: 653.
Programming (via satellite): Cinemax.
Fee: $15.00 installation; $9.95 monthly.

Pay Service 2
Pay Units: 1,880.
Programming (via satellite): Encore.

Pay Service 3
Pay Units: 1,107.
Programming (via satellite): HBO.
Fee: $15.00 installation; $9.95 monthly.

Pay Service 4
Pay Units: 404.
Programming (via satellite): The Movie Channel.
Fee: $15.00 installation; $9.95 monthly.

Pay Service 5
Pay Units: 798.
Programming (via satellite): Starz.

Digital Pay Service 1
Pay Units: N.A.
Programming (via satellite): Cinemax (multiplexed); Encore (multiplexed); HBO (multiplexed); Showtime (multiplexed); Starz (multiplexed); The Movie Channel (multiplexed).

Video-On-Demand: No

Pay-Per-View
HITS PPV 1-30 (delivered digitally); Urban Extra (delivered digitally); Hot Choice (delivered digitally); Fresh (delivered digitally); Playboy TV (delivered digitally).

Internet Service
Operational: Yes.
Subscribers: 1,767.
Broadband Service: Road Runner.
Fee: $42.95 monthly.

Telephone Service
None

Miles of Plant: 240.0 (coaxial); None (fiber optic).
President: Rhonda Fraas.; Rhonda Fraas. Area Manager: Brad Wakely. Manager: John Ellingson. Customer Service Manager: Cindy Sierra.
Ownership: Time Warner Cable (MSO).

BUCYRUS—Time Warner Cable, 205 Crystal Ave, Findlay, OH 45840. Phone: 419-429-7474. Fax: 419-429-7402. Web Site: http://

www.timewarnercable.com/midohio. Also serves Holmes Twp., Liberty Twp. (Crawford County), Lykens Twp. (Crawford County) & Sulphur Springs. ICA: OH0105.

TV Market Ranking: Below 100 (BUCYRUS, Holmes Twp., Liberty Twp. (Crawford County), Lykens Twp. (Crawford County), Sulphur Springs).

Channel capacity: N.A. Channels available but not in use: N.A.

Basic Service

Subscribers: N.A. Included in Columbus

Programming (received off-air): WBNS-TV (CBS) Columbus; WCMH-TV (NBC) Columbus; WEWS-TV (ABC) Cleveland; WJW (FOX) Cleveland; WOSU-TV (PBS) Columbus; WSFJ-TV (TBN) Newark; WSYX (ABC, MNT) Columbus; WTOL (CBS) Toledo; WTTE (FOX) Columbus; WUAB (MNT) Lorain; WWHO (CW) Chillicothe.

Programming (via satellite): C-SPAN; C-SPAN 3; Hallmark Channel; Headline News; History Channel; LWS Local Weather Station; QVC; ShopNBC; TBS Superstation; The Learning Channel; Travel Channel; WGN America.

Expanded Basic Service 1

Subscribers: N.A.

Programming (via satellite): A&E Networks; ABC Family Channel; AMC; Animal Planet; BET Networks; Bravo; BTN; Cartoon Network; CNBC; CNN; Comedy Central; Country Music TV; C-SPAN 2; C-SPAN 3; Discovery Channel; Disney Channel; E! Entertainment Television; ESPN; ESPN 2; Food Network; Fox News Channel; Fox Sports Net Ohio; FX; Golf Channel; HGTV; Lifetime; Lifetime Movie Network; MSNBC; MTV; MTV2; National Geographic Channel; Nick Jr.; Nickelodeon; Oxygen; Spike TV; SportsTime Ohio; Syfy; The Weather Channel; truTV; Turner Classic Movies; Turner Network TV; TV Land; Univision Studios; USA Network; Versus; VH1; WE tv.

Digital Basic Service

Subscribers: N.A. Included in Columbus

Programming (via satellite): A&E HD; AmericanLife TV Network; Animal Planet HD; Auction TV; BBC America; BBC America On Demand; Bio; Bloomberg Television; Boomerang; BTN (multiplexed); BTN HD; Canal Sur; CBS Sports Network; Cine Latino; cloo; CNN en Espanol; CNN International; Cooking Channel; C-SPAN 3; Current; Discovery Channel HD; Discovery en Espanol; Discovery Fit & Health; Discovery Health Channel; Discovery Kids Channel; Disney Channel; Disney Channel HD; DIY Network; Encore (multiplexed); ESPN 2 HD; ESPN Classic Sports; ESPN Deportes; ESPN HD; ESPN U; ESPNews; Eternal Word TV Network; Exercise TV; Food Network; Food Network HD; Fox Business Channel; Fox College Sports Atlantic; Fox College Sports Central; Fox College Sports Pacific; Fox Deportes; Fox Movie Channel; Fox Reality Channel; Fox Soccer; FSN HD; Fuel TV; Fuse; G4; Great American Country; GSN; HD Theater; HDNet; HDNet Movies; here! TV; HGTV; HGTV HD; History Channel en Espanol; History Channel HD; History Channel International; Howard TV; ID Investigation Discovery; Independent Film Channel; INSP; Jewelry Television; La Familia Network; Lifetime Real Women; LOGO; Military Channel; MTV Hits; mun2 television; Music Choice; National Geographic Channel HD Network; National Geographic Channel On Demand; NBA TV; NHL Network; NickToons TV; Ohio News Network; Outdoor Channel; Ovation; Oxygen On Demand; Palladia; Planet Green; Product Information Network; Science; SoapNet; Speed; Style Network; Sundance Channel; TBS in HD; TeenNick; Tennis Channel; The Weather Channel; The Word Network; Toon Disney; Tr3s; Turner Network TV HD; TV One; Universal HD; Versus HD; VH1 Classic; Video Rola.

Fee: $4.95 monthly (Latino or Sports Plus), $10.40 monthly (Movies or Variety), $14.60 monthly (Premier Digital).

Digital Pay Service 1

Pay Units: N.A.

Programming (via satellite): Cinemax (multiplexed); Cinemax On Demand; Encore; HBO (multiplexed); HBO HD; HBO Latino; HBO On Demand; Showtime (multiplexed); Showtime HD; Showtime On Demand; Starz (multiplexed); Starz On Demand; The Movie Channel (multiplexed); The Movie Channel On Demand.

Fee: $11.95 monthly (HBO, Cinemax, Starz/ Encore or Showtime/TMC).

Video-On-Demand: Yes

Pay-Per-View

iN DEMAND (delivered digitally); Playboy TV (delivered digitally); Sports PPV (delivered digitally).

Internet Service

Operational: Yes.

Broadband Service: Road Runner.

Fee: $44.95 monthly.

Telephone Service

Digital: Operational

Fee: $44.95 monthly

Miles of plant included in Columbus

President: Rhonda Fraas. Vice President & General Manager: Brad Wakely. Vice President, Engineering: Randy Hall. Technical Operations Director: John Ellingson. Vice President, Marketing: Mark Psigoda. Government Affairs Manager: Brian Young.; Patrick McCauley.

Ownership: Time Warner Cable (MSO).

CADIZ—Time Warner Cable, 530 S Main St, Ste 1751, Akron, OH 44311-1090. Phone: 330-633-9203. Fax: 330-633-7970. Web Site: http://www.timewarnercable.com/northeastohio. ICA: OH0200.

TV Market Ranking: 90 (CADIZ). Franchise award date: N.A. Franchise expiration date: N.A. Began: June 1, 1970.

Channel capacity: 57 (not 2-way capable). Channels available but not in use: N.A.

Basic Service

Subscribers: 1,100.

Programming (received off-air): KDKA-TV (CBS) Pittsburgh; WDLI-TV (TBN) Canton; WNPB-TV (PBS) Morgantown; WOUC-TV (PBS) Cambridge; WPGH-TV (FOX) Pittsburgh; WPXI (IND, NBC) Pittsburgh; WQED (PBS) Pittsburgh; WTAE-TV (ABC) Pittsburgh; WTOV-TV (IND, NBC) Steubenville; WTRF-TV (CBS) Wheeling.

Programming (via satellite): C-SPAN; CW+; Discovery Channel; QVC; SportsTime Ohio; TBS Superstation.

Fee: $44.95 installation; $14.00 monthly.

Expanded Basic Service 1

Subscribers: 1,016.

Programming (via satellite): A&E Networks; ABC Family Channel; AMC; Animal Planet; BET Networks; Cartoon Network; CNBC; CNN; Country Music TV; Disney Channel; E! Entertainment Television; ESPN; ESPN 2; Fox News Channel; Fox Sports Net Ohio; FX; Hallmark Channel; Lifetime; MoviePlex; MTV; Nickelodeon; Root Sports Pittsburgh; Spike TV; The Weather Channel; Travel Channel; truTV; Turner Network TV; TVG Network; USA Network.

Fee: $29.75 monthly.

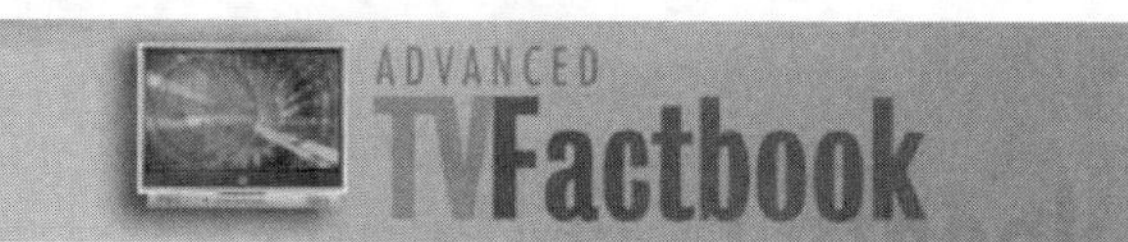

Digital Basic Service

Subscribers: N.A.

Programming (via satellite): BBC America; Bravo; Discovery Health Channel; Discovery Home Channel; Discovery Kids Channel; ESPN Classic Sports; ESPNews; Fox Soccer; Golf Channel; GSN; HGTV; History Channel; ID Investigation Discovery; Independent Film Channel; Military History Channel; Music Choice; National Geographic Channel; Nick Jr.; Science; Speed; Turner Classic Movies; Versus; WE tv.

Fee: $10.50 monthly.

Digital Pay Service 1

Pay Units: N.A.

Programming (via satellite): Cinemax (multiplexed); Encore (multiplexed); HBO (multiplexed); Showtime (multiplexed); Starz (multiplexed); The Movie Channel (multiplexed).

Fee: $12.00 monthly (each).

Video-On-Demand: No

Pay-Per-View

iN DEMAND (delivered digitally); Playboy TV (delivered digitally); Club Jenna (delivered digitally).

Internet Service

Operational: No.

Telephone Service

None

Miles of Plant: 26.0 (coaxial); None (fiber optic).

President: Stephen Fry. Area Vice President: Scott Miller. Vice President, Engineering: Al Costanzi. Vice President, Marketing: Patrick Burke. Vice President, Public Affairs: William Jasso. Government & Media Relations Director: Chris Thomas.

Ownership: Time Warner Cable (MSO).

CALEDONIA—Now served by MARION, OH [OH0040]. ICA: OH0257.

CAMBRIDGE—Time Warner Cable. Now served by NEWARK, OH [OH0019]. ICA: OH0088.

CAMERON—Formerly served by Cebridge Connections. No longer in operation. ICA: OH0310.

CANAAN TWP. (Madison County)—Time Warner Cable. Now served by COLUMBUS, OH [OH0002]. ICA: OH0131.

CANTON—Time Warner Cable, 530 S Main St, Ste 1751, Akron, OH 44311-1090. Phone: 330-633-9203. Fax: 330-633-7970. Web Site: http://www.timewarnercable.com/northeastohio. Also serves Alliance, Brown Twp. (Carroll County), East Canton, East Sparta, Hartville, Hills & Dales (village), Jackson Twp. (Stark County), Lake Twp. (Stark County), Lexington Twp., Limaville, Louisville, Magnolia, Marlboro Twp. (Stark County), Meyers Lake, Mineral City, Nimishillen Twp. (Stark County), North Canton, Osnaburg Twp. (Stark County), Paris Twp. (Stark County), Perry Twp. (Stark County), Pike Twp. (Stark County), Plain Twp. (Stark County), Sandy Twp. (Stark County), Sandy Twp. (Tuscarawas County), Stark County (portions), Washington Twp. (Stark County) & Waynesburg (village). ICA: OH0008.

TV Market Ranking: 8 (Brown Twp. (Carroll County), CANTON, East Canton, East Sparta, Hartville, Hills & Dales (village), Jackson Twp. (Stark County), Lake Twp. (Stark County), Limaville, Louisville, Magnolia, Meyers Lake, Mineral City, Nimishillen Twp. (Stark County), North Canton, Osnaburg Twp. (Stark County), Paris Twp. (Stark County), Perry Twp. (Stark County), Pike Twp. (Stark County), Plain Twp. (Stark County), Sandy Twp. (Stark County), Sandy Twp. (Tuscarawas County), Waynesburg (village)); 8,79 (Alliance, Lexington Twp., Marlboro Twp. (Stark County), Stark County (portions) (portions), Washington Twp. (Stark County)). Franchise award date: October 26, 1965. Franchise expiration date: N.A. Began: June 1, 1966.

Channel capacity: N.A. Channels available but not in use: N.A.

Basic Service

Subscribers: 80,225.

Programming (received off-air): WBNX-TV (CW) Akron; WDLI-TV (TBN) Canton; WEAO (PBS) Akron; WEWS-TV (ABC) Cleveland; WIVM-LD Canton; WJW (FOX) Cleveland; WKYC (NBC) Cleveland; WNEO (PBS) Alliance; WOIO (CBS) Shaker Heights; WQHS-DT (UNV) Cleveland; WRLM (IND) Canton; WUAB (MNT) Lorain; WVIZ (PBS) Cleveland; WVPX-TV (ION) Akron; allband FM.

Programming (via satellite): TV Guide Network.

Fee: $29.95 installation; $13.09 monthly.

Expanded Basic Service 1

Subscribers: N.A.

Programming (via satellite): A&E Networks; ABC Family Channel; AMC; Animal Planet; BET Networks; Bravo; Cartoon Network; CNBC; CNN; Comedy Central; C-SPAN; C-SPAN 2; Discovery Channel; Discovery Fit & Health; Disney Channel; E! Entertainment Television; ESPN; ESPN 2; ESPN Classic Sports; Eternal Word TV Network; Food Network; Fox News Channel; Fox Sports Net Ohio; FX; Golf Channel; Great American Country; GSN; Hallmark Channel; Headline News; HGTV; History Channel; INSP; Lifetime; Lifetime Movie Network; MSNBC; MTV; Nickelodeon; Oxygen; QVC; ShopNBC; SoapNet; Spike TV; Syfy; TBS Superstation; The Learning Channel; The Weather Channel; Travel Channel; truTV; Turner Classic Movies; Turner Network TV; TV Land; USA Network; Versus; VH1; WE tv; WGN America.

Fee: $43.90 monthly.

Digital Basic Service

Subscribers: N.A.

Programming (via satellite): A&E Networks; AmericanLife TV Network; America's Store; ART America; BBC America; Bio; Bloomberg Television; Boomerang; Canales N; CBS Sports Network; CNN; CNN International; Cooking Channel; Coun-

try Music TV; C-SPAN 3; Current; Daystar TV Network; Deutsche Welle TV; Disney Channel; DIY Network; Encore (multiplexed); ESPN; ESPNews; Fox College Sports Atlantic; Fox College Sports Central; Fox College Sports Pacific; Fox Movie Channel; Fox News Channel; Fox Soccer; Fuel TV; Fuse; G4; GAS; HD Theater; HDNet; HDNet Movies; Headline News; History Channel International; Independent Film Channel; INHD (multiplexed); Jewelry Television; Lifetime; Lifetime Real Women; MTV2; Music Choice; National Geographic Channel; NBA TV; Nick Jr.; NickToons TV; Ohio News Network; Outdoor Channel; RAI International; Speed; Style Network; Tennis Channel; The Weather Channel; The Word Network; Toon Disney; Trinity Broadcasting Network; Trio; Turner Network TV; Turner Network TV HD; TV Asia; TVG Network; USA Network; VH1 Classic; Zee TV USA.
Fee: $11.00 monthly.

Digital Pay Service 1
Pay Units: N.A.
Programming (via satellite): Cinemax (multiplexed); HBO (multiplexed); Showtime (multiplexed); Starz (multiplexed); Sundance Channel; The Movie Channel (multiplexed).
Fee: $12.00 monthly (each).

Video-On-Demand: Yes

Pay-Per-View
iN DEMAND (delivered digitally); Playboy TV (delivered digitally); MLB Extra Innings (delivered digitally); Spice Live (delivered digitally); Pleasure (delivered digitally); NASCAR In Car (delivered digitally); NBA League Pass (delivered digitally); MLS Direct Kick (delivered digitally); ESPN (delivered digitally); NHL Center Ice (delivered digitally).

Internet Service
Operational: Yes.
Broadband Service: EarthLink, Road Runner.
Fee: $99.00 installation; $44.95 monthly.

Telephone Service
Digital: Operational
Fee: $44.95 monthly

Miles of Plant: 1,318.0 (coaxial); None (fiber optic). Additional miles planned: 60.0 (coaxial).

President: Stephen Fry. Area Vice President: Scott Miller. Vice President, Engineering: Al Costanzi. Vice President, Marketing: Patrick Burke. Vice President, Public Affairs: William Jasso. Vice President, Customer Care: Donald Jenson. Government & Media Relations Director: Chris Thomas.

Ownership: Time Warner Cable (MSO).

CAREY—Time Warner Cable. Now served by SYCAMORE, OH [OH0215]. ICA: OH0210.

CARROLLTON—Time Warner Cable. Now served by MINERVA, OH [OH0132]. ICA: OH0201.

CELINA—Time Warner Cable, 205 Crystal Ave, Findlay, OH 45840. Phone: 614-481-5000 (Columbus office). Fax: 419-429-7402. Web Site: http://www.timewarnercable.com/midohio. Also serves Butler Twp. (Mercer County), Carthagena, Coldwater, Franklin Twp. (Mercer County), Granville Twp. (Mercer County), Hopewell Twp. (Mercer County), Montezuma & St. Henry. ICA: OH0092.

TV Market Ranking: Below 100 (Carthagena, CELINA, Coldwater, Franklin Twp. (Mercer County), Hopewell Twp. (Mercer County), Montezuma); Outside TV Markets (Butler Twp. (Mercer County), Granville Twp. (Mercer County), St. Henry). Franchise award date: N.A. Franchise expiration date: N.A. Began: September 1, 1978.

Channel capacity: N.A. Channels available but not in use: N.A.

Basic Service
Subscribers: 6,504.
Programming (received off-air): WANE-TV (CBS) Fort Wayne; WBDT (CW) Springfield; WBGU-TV (PBS) Bowling Green; WDTN (NBC) Dayton; WFFT-TV (IND) Fort Wayne; WHIO-TV (CBS) Dayton; WISE-TV (FOX, MNT, NBC) Fort Wayne; WLIO (CW, NBC) Lima; WPTA (ABC, CW) Fort Wayne; WPTD (PBS) Dayton; WRGT-TV (FOX, MNT) Dayton; WTLW (IND) Lima; allband FM.
Programming (via satellite): ABC Family Channel; QVC; TBS Superstation; TV Guide Network; WGN America.
Fee: $60.00 installation; $11.55 monthly.

Expanded Basic Service 1
Subscribers: 5,892.
Programming (via satellite): A&E Networks; AMC; Animal Planet; BET Networks; Bravo; Cartoon Network; CNBC; CNN; Comedy Central; Country Music TV; C-SPAN; C-SPAN 2; Discovery Channel; Disney Channel; E! Entertainment Television; ESPN; ESPN 2; Eternal Word TV Network; Food Network; Fox News Channel; Fox Sports Net Detroit; Fox Sports Net Ohio; FX; Great American Country; Hallmark Channel; Headline News; HGTV; History Channel; Lifetime; MSNBC; MTV; Nickelodeon; Ohio News Network; Oxygen; Product Information Network; ShopNBC; Spike TV; Syfy; Telemundo; The Learning Channel; The Weather Channel; Travel Channel; Trinity Broadcasting Network; truTV; Turner Network TV; TV Land; USA Network; VH1.
Fee: $26.40 monthly.

Digital Basic Service
Subscribers: 1,231.
Programming (via satellite): AmericanLife TV Network; BBC America; Bio; Black Family Channel; Bloomberg Television; Discovery Fit & Health; DIY Network; ESPN Classic Sports; ESPNews; Fox Sports World; Fuse; G4; GAS; Golf Channel; GSN; History Channel International; Independent Film Channel; INSP; MTV Networks Digital Suite; Music Choice; National Geographic Channel; Nick Jr.; Nick Too; Outdoor Channel; SoapNet; Speed; Style Network; Sundance Channel; Toon Disney; Turner Classic Movies; Versus; WE tv; Weatherscan.
Fee: $11.95 monthly.

Digital Expanded Basic Service
Subscribers: N.A.
Programming (via satellite): ART America; Canales N; Filipino Channel; RAI International; Russian Television Network; TV Asia; TV Japan; TV5, La Television International.
Fee: $6.95 monthly.

Digital Pay Service 1
Pay Units: N.A.
Programming (via satellite): Cinemax (multiplexed); Encore (multiplexed); Flix (multiplexed); HBO (multiplexed); Showtime (multiplexed); Starz (multiplexed); The Movie Channel (multiplexed).
Fee: $11.95 monthly (each).

Video-On-Demand: No

Pay-Per-View
Addressable homes: 1,268.
iN DEMAND (delivered digitally); NBA League Pass, NBA Season Pass, NHL Center Ice & MLB (delivered digitally); ESPN (delivered digitally).

Internet Service
Operational: Yes.
Subscribers: 1,321.
Broadband Service: Road Runner.
Fee: $44.95 monthly.

Telephone Service
Digital: Operational
Fee: $44.95 monthly

Miles of Plant: 145.0 (coaxial); None (fiber optic).

President: Rhonda Fraas. Vice President & General Manager: Brad Wakely. Vice President, Engineering: Randy Hall. Vice President, Marketing: Mark Psigoda. Manager: John Ellingson. Government Affairs Director: Brian Young. Government Affairs Manager: Patrick McCauley.

Ownership: Time Warner Cable (MSO).

CHANDLERSVILLE—Now served by NEWARK, OH [OH0019]. ICA: OH0400.

CHILLICOTHE—Time Warner Cable, 1266 Dublin Rd, Columbus, OH 43215-1008. Phones: 614-481-5000 (Columbus office); 740-775-4288 (Chillicothe office). Fax: 614-481-5044. Web Site: http://www.timewarnercable.com. Also serves Adelphi, Amanda Twp. (Fairfield County), Beaver, Benton Twp. (Pike County), Clearcreek Twp. (Fairfield County), Colerain Twp. (Ross County), Frankfort, Hallsville, Hocking Twp. (Fairfield County), Huntington Twp. (Ross County), Jefferson Twp. (Ross County), Kingston, Lake White, Laurelville, Liberty Twp. (Fairfield County), Liberty Twp. (Ross County), Mifflin Twp. (Pike County), Newton Twp. (Pike County), Pebble Twp. (Pike County), Pee Pee Twp. (Pike County), Pickaway Twp. (Pickaway County), Pike County, Richmond Dale, Ross County (portions), Salt Creek Twp. (Pickaway County), Saltcreek Twp. (Pickaway County), Scioto Twp. (Ross County), South Salem, Stoutsville, Sunfish Twp., Tarlton & Waverly. ICA: OH0033.

TV Market Ranking: 27 (Adelphi, Amanda Twp. (Fairfield County), Beaver, Benton Twp. (Pike County), CHILLICOTHE, Clearcreek Twp. (Fairfield County), Colerain Twp. (Ross County), Frankfort, Hallsville, Hocking Twp. (Fairfield County), Huntington Twp. (Ross County), Jefferson Twp. (Ross County), Kingston, Lake White, Laurelville, Liberty Twp. (Fairfield County), Liberty Twp. (Ross County), Mifflin Twp. (Pike County), Newton Twp. (Pike County), Pebble Twp. (Pike County), Pee Pee Twp. (Pike County), Pickaway Twp. (Pickaway County), Pike County, Richmond Dale, Ross County (portions), Saltcreek Twp. (Pickaway County), Saltcreek Twp. (Pickaway County), Scioto Twp. (Pike County), South Salem, Stoutsville, Sunfish Twp., Tarlton, Waverly). Franchise award date: N.A. Franchise expiration date: N.A. Began: September 11, 1964.

Channel capacity: 77 (operating 2-way). Channels available but not in use: N.A.

Basic Service
Subscribers: 15,355.
Programming (received off-air): WBNS-TV (CBS) Columbus; WCMH-TV (NBC) Columbus; WHIO-TV (CBS) Dayton; WOSU-TV (PBS) Columbus; WOUB-TV (PBS) Athens; WSYX (ABC, MNT) Columbus; WTTE (FOX) Columbus; WWHO (CW) Chillicothe; 14 FMs.
Programming (via satellite): ABC Family Channel; C-SPAN; C-SPAN 2; Eternal Word TV Network; Gospel Music TV; INSP; QVC; TBS Superstation; The Weather Channel; TV Guide Network; WGN America.
Fee: $50.00 installation; $24.94 monthly.

Expanded Basic Service 1
Subscribers: N.A.
Programming (via satellite): A&E Networks; AMC; Animal Planet; BET Networks; Bio; Bravo; Cartoon Network; CNBC; CNN; Comedy Central; Country Music TV; Discovery Channel; Disney Channel; E! Entertainment Television; ESPN; ESPN 2; Food Network; Fox News Channel; Fox Sports Net Ohio; FX; Golf Channel; Great American Country; Hallmark Channel; Headline News; HGTV; History Channel; Lifetime; MSNBC; MTV; National Geographic Channel; Nickelodeon; Ohio News Network; Outdoor Channel; Oxygen; Product Information Network; ShopNBC; Speed; Spike TV; Syfy; The Learning Channel; Toon Disney; Travel Channel; truTV; Turner Network TV; TV Land; USA Network; VH1; WE tv.

Digital Basic Service
Subscribers: N.A.
Programming (via satellite): AmericanLife TV Network; BBC America; Bloomberg Television; Discovery Fit & Health; DIY Network; Encore Action; ESPN Classic Sports; ESPNews; Fox Movie Channel; Fox Sports World; Fuse; G4; GSN; History Channel International; SoapNet; Trinity Broadcasting Network; Turner Classic Movies; Versus.

Digital Expanded Basic Service
Subscribers: N.A.
Programming (via satellite): Canales N; Music Choice; Nick Jr.; NickToons TV; Style Network; VH1 Classic; VH1 Country.

Digital Pay Service 1
Pay Units: 2,400.
Programming (via satellite): ART America; CCTV-4; Cinemax (multiplexed); Filipino Channel; Flix; HBO (multiplexed); RAI International; Showtime (multiplexed); Starz (multiplexed); Sundance Channel; The Movie Channel (multiplexed); TV Asia; TV Japan; TV5, La Television International; Zee TV USA; Zhong Tian Channel.
Fee: $11.95 monthly (each).

Video-On-Demand: No

Pay-Per-View
HITS PPV 1-30 (delivered digitally).

Internet Service
Operational: Yes. Began: December 1, 2000.
Broadband Service: Road Runner.
Fee: $42.95 monthly.

Telephone Service
None

President: Rhonda Fraas. Vice President & General Manager: David Kreiman. Vice President, Engineering: Randy Hall. Vice President, Sales & Marketing: Mark Psigoda. Plant Manager: Jim Cavender. Engineering Director: Bill Ricker. Marketing Director: Thomas Smith. Marketing Coordinator: Bonita Yeager.

Ownership: Time Warner Cable (MSO).

CHIPPEWA TWP.—Time Warner Cable. Now served by AKRON, OH [OH0005]. ICA: OH0173.

CINCINNATI—Time Warner Cable, 11252 Cornell Park Dr, Cincinnati, OH 45242. Phone: 513-489-5000. Fax: 513-489-5991. Web Site: http://www.timewarnercable.com/cincinnati. Also serves Adams County (portions), Adams Twp. (Clinton County), Amberley, Anderson Twp. (Hamilton County), Arlington Heights, Bentonville, Blanchester, Blue Ash, Bowersville, Butler County (portions), Butlerville, Caesars Creek Twp., Carlisle, Cherry Fork, Cheviot, Clark Twp. (Brown County), Clark Twp. (Clinton County),

Clermont County (portions), Clinton County (portions), Colerain Twp. (Hamilton County), Columbia Twp. (Hamilton County), Crosby Twp. (Hamilton County), Darrtown, Deer Park, Deerfield Twp. (Warren County), Dodson Twp., Elmwood Place, Evendale, Fairfax, Fairfield, Fayetteville, Forest Park, Franklin, Glendale, Golf Manor, Goshen Twp. (Clermont County), Green Twp. (Brown County), Green Twp. (Hamilton County), Greenhills, Hamer Twp., Hamilton, Hamilton Twp. (Warren County), Hanover Twp., Harlan Twp., Harrison, Highland, Hillsboro, Indian Hill, Indian Springs, Jacksonburg (village), Lebanon, Leesburg, Lemon Twp., Liberty Twp. (Butler County), Liberty Twp. (Clinton County), Liberty Twp. (Highland County), Lincoln Heights, Lindale, Lockland, Loveland, Lynchburg, Madeira, Maineville, Manchester, Mariemont, Marion Twp. (Clinton County), Marshall Twp. (Clinton County), Martinsville, Mason, Meigs Twp. (Adams County), Middletown, Midland, Milford, Milford Twp. (Butler County), Millville, Monroe, Montgomery, Morgan Twp. (Butler County), Morrow, Mount Healthy, Mowrystown, New Market Twp., New Miami, New Vienna, Newtonsville, Newtown, North College Hill, Norwood, Owensville, Oxford Twp. (Butler County), Peebles, Penn Twp., Pike Twp. (Brown County), Pleasant Plain, Port William, Reading, Reily Twp., Ripley, Ross Twp. (Butler County), Sardinia, Seaman, Seven Mile, Sharonville, Silverton, Somerville, South Lebanon, Springdale, Springfield Twp. (Hamilton County), St. Bernard, St. Clair Twp., St. Martin, Sterling Twp. (Brown County), Stonelick Twp., Sycamore Twp. (Hamilton County), Symmes Twp. (Hamilton County), Terrace Park, Trenton, Turtle Creek Twp. (Warren County), Warren County (portions), West Chester Twp. (Butler County), West Union, Westboro, White Oak Twp., Wilmington, Winchester, Woodlawn & Wyoming. ICA: OH0001.

TV Market Ranking: 17 (Adams Twp. (Clinton County), Amberley, Anderson Twp. (Hamilton County), Arlington Heights, Blanchester, Butlerville, Carlisle, CINCINNATI, Clermont County (portions), Clinton County (portions), Colerain Twp. (Hamilton County), Columbia Twp. (Hamilton County), Darrtown, Deer Park, Elmwood Place, Fairfax, Fairfield, Fayetteville, Franklin, Golf Manor, Green Twp. (Brown County), Green Twp. (Hamilton County), Green Twp. (Highland County), Greenhills, Hamilton, Hanover Twp., Hanover Twp., Harlan Twp., Harrison, Indian Hill, Jacksonburg (village), Lemon Twp., Liberty Twp. (Butler County), Lincoln Heights, Lockland, Loveland, Madeira, Mariemont, Marion Twp. (Clinton County), Martinsville, Middletown, Midland, Milford Twp. (Butler County), Millville, Monroe, Morgan Twp. (Butler County), Morrow, Mount Healthy, New Miami, Newtonsville, Newtown, North College Hill, Norwood, Owensville, Oxford Twp. (Butler County), Pleasant Plain, Reading, Reily Twp., Ross Twp. (Butler County), Seven Mile, Silverton, Somerville, St. Bernard, St. Clair Twp., St. Martin, Stonelick Twp., Terrace Park, Trenton, Wayne Twp., Westboro, Wyoming); 17,41 (Blue Ash, Butler County (portions), Crosby Twp. (Hamilton County), Deerfield Twp. (Warren County), Evendale, Forest Park, Glendale, Goshen Twp. (Clermont County), Hamilton Twp. (Warren County), Indian Springs, Lebanon, Maineville, Mason, Montgomery, Sharonville, South Lebanon, Springdale, Springfield Twp. (Hamilton County), Sycamore Twp. (Hamilton County), Symmes Twp. (Hamilton County), Warren County (portions), Woodlawn); 27 (Highland, Hillsboro, Leesburg, Liberty Twp. (Highland County) (portions), Meigs Twp. (Adams County) (portions), Peebles, Penn Twp. (portions)); 41 (Bowersville, Caesars Creek Twp., Liberty Twp. (Clinton Twp.), Marshall Twp. (Clinton County), New Vienna, Port William, Wilmington); Below 100 (Adams County (portions), Bentonville, West Union, Liberty Twp. (Highland County) (portions), Meigs Twp. (Adams County) (portions)); Outside TV Markets (Cherry Fork, Dodson Twp., Hamer Twp., Lynchburg, Manchester, Mowrystown, New Market Twp., Ripley, Sardinia, Seaman, White Oak Twp., Winchester, Penn Twp. (portions)). Franchise award date: July 17, 1979. Franchise expiration date: June 17, 2011. Began: August 1, 1980.

Channel capacity: N.A. Channels available but not in use: N.A.

Basic Service

Subscribers: 350,000.

Programming (received off-air): WCPO-TV (ABC) Cincinnati; WCVN-TV (PBS) Covington; WKRC-TV (CBS, CW) Cincinnati; WLWT (NBC) Cincinnati; WOTH-CA (IND) Cincinnati; WPTD (PBS) Dayton; WPTO (PBS) Oxford; WSTR-TV (MNT) Cincinnati; WXIX-TV (FOX) Newport; allband FM.

Programming (via satellite): C-SPAN; C-SPAN 2; Eternal Word TV Network; ION Television; QVC; Trinity Broadcasting Network; TV Guide Network; WGN America.

Fee: $28.95 installation; $44.40 monthly.

Expanded Basic Service 1

Subscribers: N.A.

Programming (via satellite): A&E Networks; ABC Family Channel; AMC; Animal Planet; BET Networks; Bravo!; Cartoon Network; CNBC; CNN; Comedy Central; Discovery Channel; Discovery Health Channel; Disney Channel; E! Entertainment Television; ESPN; ESPN 2; ESPN Classic Sports; Food Network; Fox News Channel; Fox Sports Net Ohio; FX; Golf Channel; Great American Country; Headline News; HGTV; History Channel; Lifetime; Lifetime Movie Network; MSNBC; MTV; National Geographic Channel; Nickelodeon; Oxygen; SoapNet; Spike TV; Syfy; TBS Superstation; The Learning Channel; The Weather Channel; Travel Channel; truTV; Turner Classic Movies; Turner Network TV; TV Land; USA Network; VH1; WE tv.

Digital Basic Service

Subscribers: 185,000.

Programming (via satellite): AmericanLife TV Network; America's Store; BBC America; Bio; Black Family Channel; Bloomberg Television; Boomerang; Canales N; CBS Sports Network; CNN International; Cooking Channel; Country Music TV; C-SPAN 3; Discovery Fit & Health; DIY Network; ESPNews; Eternal Word TV Network; Fox College Sports Atlantic; Fox College Sports Central; Fox College Sports Pacific; Fox Sports World; Fuel TV; Fuse; G4; GAS; GSN; Hallmark Channel; History Channel International; Independent Film Channel; INSP; International Television (ITV); Lifetime Real Women; MTV Networks Digital Suite; NBA TV; Nick Jr.; NickToons TV; Ohio News Network; Outdoor Channel; Ovation; Science Television; ShopNBC; Speed; Tennis Channel; The Word Network; Toon Disney; Trinity Broadcasting Network.

Digital Pay Service 1

Pay Units: N.A.

Programming (via satellite): Cinemax (multiplexed); Deutsche Welle TV; Encore (multiplexed); Fox Movie Channel; HBO (multiplexed); Showtime (multiplexed); Starz (multiplexed); Sundance Channel; WAM! America's Kidz Network; Zee TV USA.

Video-On-Demand: Yes

Pay-Per-View

iN DEMAND; Movies.

Internet Service

Operational: Yes. Began: July 1, 1999.

Subscribers: 130,000.

Broadband Service: Road Runner.

Fee: $44.95 monthly.

Telephone Service

Digital: Operational

Subscribers: 100,000.

Miles of Plant: 6,925.0 (coaxial); None (fiber optic).

President: Kevin G. Kidd. Vice President, Marketing: Rob Fordham. Vice President, Operations: Vin Zachariah. Vice President, Public Affairs & Government Relations: Pamela McDonald. Public Affairs Director: Karen Baxter.

Ownership: Time Warner Cable (MSO).

CIRCLEVILLE—Time Warner Cable, 1266 Dublin Rd, Columbus, OH 43215-1008. Phone: 614-481-5000. Fax: 614-481-5052. Web Site: http://www.timewarnercable.com/midohio. Also serves Ashville, South Bloomfield & Walnut Twp. ICA: OH0320.

TV Market Ranking: 27 (Ashville, CIRCLEVILLE, South Bloomfield, Walnut Twp.). Franchise award date: September 1, 1989. Franchise expiration date: N.A. Began: September 1, 1989.

Channel capacity: N.A. Channels available but not in use: N.A.

Basic Service

Subscribers: 7,436.

Programming (received off-air): WBNS-TV (CBS) Columbus; WCMH-TV (NBC) Columbus; WOSU-TV (PBS) Columbus; WSFJ-TV (TBN) Newark; WSYX (ABC, MNT) Columbus; WTTE (FOX) Columbus; WUAB (MNT) Lorain; WWHO (CW) Chillicothe.

Programming (via satellite): AmericanLife TV Network; C-SPAN; C-SPAN 2; Hallmark Channel; Headline News; History Channel; International Television (ITV); QVC; Radar Channel; ShopNBC; TBS Superstation; The Learning Channel; TV Guide Network; WGN America.

Fee: $50.00 installation; $9.30 monthly.

Expanded Basic Service 1

Subscribers: N.A.

Programming (via satellite): A&E Networks; ABC Family Channel; AMC; Animal Planet; BBC America; BET Networks; Bravo; Cartoon Network; CNBC; CNN; Comedy Central; Country Music TV; Discovery Channel; Discovery Health Channel; Disney Channel; E! Entertainment Television; ESPN; ESPN 2; Food Network; Fox News Channel; Fox Sports Net Ohio; FX; Golf Channel; HGTV; Jewelry Television; Lifetime; Lifetime Movie Network; MSNBC; MTV; MTV2; National Geographic Channel; Nick Jr.; Nickelodeon; Oxygen; Spike TV; SportsTime Ohio; Syfy; The Weather Channel; Travel Channel; truTV; Turner Classic Movies; Turner Network TV; TV Land; Univision Studios; USA Network; Versus; VH1; WE tv.

Digital Basic Service

Subscribers: N.A.

Programming (via satellite): AmericanLife TV Network; BBC America On Demand; Bio; Bloomberg Television; Boomerang; Canal Sur; Cine Latino; cloo; CNN en Espanol; CNN International; College Sports Television; Cooking Channel; C-SPAN 3; Current; Discovery en Espanol; Discovery Fit & Health; Discovery Home Channel; Discovery Kids Channel; Disney Channel; DIY Network; Encore (multiplexed); ESPN 2 HD; ESPN Classic Sports; ESPN HD; ESPN U; ESPNews; Eternal Word TV Network; Exercise TV; Expo TV; Food Network; Fox Business Channel; Fox College Sports Atlantic; Fox College Sports Central; Fox College Sports Pacific; Fox Deportes; Fox Movie Channel; Fox Reality Channel; Fox Soccer; Fuel TV; Fuse; G4; Great American Country; GSN; HD Theater; HDNet; here! On Demand; History Channel International; Howard TV; ID Investigation Discovery; Independent Film Channel; INSP; Jewelry Television; La Familia Network; Lifetime Real Women; LOGO; Military Channel; MTV Hits; mun2 television; Music Choice; National Geographic Channel On Demand; NBA TV; NHL Network; NickToons TV; Ohio News Network; Outdoor Channel; Ovation; Oxygen On Demand; Science; SoapNet; Speed; Speed On Demand; Style Network; Sundance Channel; TBS in HD; TeenNick; Tennis Channel; The Weather Channel; The Word Network; Toon Disney; Tr3s; Turner Network TV HD; TV Guide SPOT; TV One; Universal HD; VH1 Classic; VHUNO; Video Rola.

Fee: $52.40 monthly.

Digital Pay Service 1

Pay Units: N.A.

Programming (via satellite): Cinemax (multiplexed); Cinemax On Demand; HBO (multiplexed); HBO On Demand; Showtime (multiplexed); Showtime On Demand; Starz (multiplexed); Starz On Demand; The Movie Channel (multiplexed); The Movie Channel On Demand.

Fee: $11.95 monthly (HBO, Cinemax, Starz or Showtime/TMC).

Video-On-Demand: Yes

Pay-Per-View

NBA League Pass (delivered digitally); MLS Direct Kick (delivered digitally); NHL Center Ice (delivered digitally); MLB Extra Innings (delivered digitally); ESPN Gameplan (delivered digitally).

Internet Service

Operational: Yes.

Broadband Service: Road Runner.

Fee: $44.95 monthly.

Telephone Service

Digital: Operational

Fee: $44.95 monthly

President: Rhonda Fraas. Vice President & General Manager: David Kreiman. Vice President, Engineering: Randy Hall. Vice President, Marketing: Mark Psigoda. Vice President, Government & Public Affairs:

Mary Jo Green. Technical Operations Director: Jim Cavendar. Government Affairs Director: Steve Cuckler.
Ownership: Time Warner Cable (MSO).

CIRCLEVILLE—Time Warner Communications. Now served by COLUMBUS, OH [OH0002]. ICA: OH0087.

CLAY CENTER/GIBSONBURG—Time Warner Cable, 205 Crystal Ave, Findlay, OH 45840. Phones: 419-429-7474; 614-481-5000 (Columbus office). Fax: 419-429-7402. Web Site: http://www.timewarnercable.com/midohio. Also serves Allen Twp. (Ottawa County), Bettsville, Bradner, Burgoon (village), Clay Twp. (Ottawa County), Curtice, Elmore, Fort Seneca, Genoa, Gibsonburg, Harris Twp. (Ottawa County), Helena (village), Hessville, Lake Twp. (Wood County), Liberty Twp. (Seneca County), Lindsey, Millbury, Montgomery Twp. (Wood County), Old Fort, Pemberville, Perrysburg Twp. (Wood County), Rising Sun, Walbridge, Wayne, West Millgrove, Williston & Woodville. ICA: OH0071.

TV Market Ranking: 52 (Allen Twp., Bettsville, Bradner, Burgoon (village), CLAY CENTER, Clay Twp. (Ottawa County), Curtice, Elmore, Genoa, GIBSONBURG, Harris Twp. (Ottawa County), Helena (village), Lake Twp. (Wood County), Liberty Twp. (Seneca County), Lindsey, Millbury, Montgomery Twp. (Wood County), Pemberville, Perrysburg Twp. (Wood County), Rising Sun, Walbridge, Wayne, West Millgrove, Williston, Woodville); Below 100 (Fort Seneca, Old Fort). Franchise award date: January 1, 1981. Franchise expiration date: N.A. Began: January 1, 1981.

Channel capacity: N.A. Channels available but not in use: N.A.

Basic Service

Subscribers: 5,911.

Programming (received off-air): WBGU-TV (PBS) Bowling Green; WGTE-TV (PBS) Toledo; WKBD-TV (CW) Detroit; WNWO-TV (NBC) Toledo; WTOL (CBS) Toledo; WTVG (ABC) Toledo; WUAB (MNT) Lorain; WUPW (FOX) Toledo.

Programming (via satellite): QVC; TV Guide Network.

Fee: $45.86 installation; $10.21 monthly.

Expanded Basic Service 1

Subscribers: N.A.

Programming (via satellite): A&E Networks; ABC Family Channel; AMC; Animal Planet; BET Networks; Bravo; Cartoon Network; CNBC; CNN; Comedy Central; Country Music TV; C-SPAN; C-SPAN 2; Discovery Channel; Disney Channel; E! Entertainment Television; ESPN; ESPN 2; ESPN Classic Sports; Eternal Word TV Network; Food Network; Fox News Channel; Fox Sports Net Ohio; FX; Golf Channel; Hallmark Channel; Headline News; HGTV; History Channel; INSP; Lifetime; Lifetime Movie Network; MSNBC; MTV; National Geographic Channel; Nickelodeon; Oxygen; ShopNBC; Spike TV; Syfy; TBS Superstation; The Learning Channel; The Weather Channel; Travel Channel; truTV; Turner Classic Movies; Turner Network TV; TV Land; Univision Studios; USA Network; Versus; VH1; WE tv.

Fee: $30.74 monthly.

Digital Basic Service

Subscribers: 1,733.

Programming (via satellite): AmericanLife TV Network; America's Store; BBC America; Bloomberg Television; CNN International; Cooking Channel; C-SPAN 3; Discovery Fit & Health; DIY Network; DMX Music; ESPNews; Fox Sports World; FSN Digital Atlantic; FSN Digital Central; FSN Digital Pacific; Fuse; G4; GAS; Great American Country; GSN; Lifetime Real Women; MTV2; Nick Jr.; Ohio News Network; Outdoor Channel; Ovation; SoapNet; Sorpresa; Speed; Style Network; Toon Disney; VH1 Classic.

Fee: $8.95 monthly.

Digital Pay Service 1

Pay Units: 3,602.

Programming (via satellite): Cinemax (multiplexed); Encore (multiplexed); Flix; HBO (multiplexed); Showtime (multiplexed); Starz (multiplexed); The Movie Channel (multiplexed).

Fee: $10.50 monthly (Cinemax, HBO, Showtime, Starz/Encore, or Flix/TMC).

Video-On-Demand: Yes

Pay-Per-View

Addressable homes: 1,733.

iN DEMAND (delivered digitally); Fresh (delivered digitally); Sports PPV (delivered digitally).

Internet Service

Operational: Yes.

Subscribers: 1,064.

Broadband Service: Road Runner.

Fee: $69.95 installation; $44.95 monthly.

Telephone Service

Analog: Not Operational

Digital: Operational

Fee: $44.95 monthly

Miles of Plant: 250.0 (coaxial); None (fiber optic).

President: Rhonda Fraas. Vice President & General Manager: Brad Wakely. Vice President, Engineering: Randy Hall. Vice President, Marketing: Mark Psigoda. Technical Operations Director: John Ellingson. Government Affairs Director: Brian Young. Government Affairs Manager: Patrick McCauley.

Ownership: Time Warner Cable (MSO).

CLEVELAND—Time Warner Cable (formerly Adelphia Cable). Now served by CLEVELAND HEIGHTS, OH [OH0006]. ICA: OH0003.

CLEVELAND—WOW! Internet Cable & Phone, 7887 E Belleview Ave, Ste 1000, Englewood, CO 80111. Phones: 720-479-3500 (Corporate office); 866-496-9669 (Customer service). Fax: 720-479-3585. Web Site: http://www1.wowway.com. Also serves Berea, Brecksville, Brook Park, Brooklyn, Cleveland Heights (portions), Cuyahoga Heights, Fairview Park, Garfield Heights, Independence, Linndale, Maple Heights, Middleburg Heights, North Olmsted, North Royalton, Shaker Heights, Strongsville, Valley View & Westlake. ICA: OH0418. **Note:** This system is an overbuild.

TV Market Ranking: 8 (Berea, Brecksville, Brook Park, Brooklyn, CLEVELAND, Cleveland Heights (portions), Cuyahoga Heights, Fairview Park, Garfield Heights, Independence, Linndale, Maple Heights, Middleburg Heights, North Olmsted, North Royalton, Shaker Heights, Strongsville, Valley View, Westlake). Franchise award date: April 1, 1996. Franchise expiration date: N.A. Began: N.A.

Channel capacity: N.A. Channels available but not in use: N.A.

Basic Service

Subscribers: N.A. Included in Chicago, IL

Programming (received off-air): WBNX-TV (CW) Akron; WEAO (PBS) Akron; WEWS-TV (ABC) Cleveland; WJW (FOX) Cleveland; WKYC (NBC) Cleveland; WOIO (CBS) Shaker Heights; WQHS-DT (UNV) Cleveland; WUAB (MNT) Lorain; WVIZ (PBS) Cleveland; WVPX-TV (ION) Akron.

Programming (via satellite): Eternal Word TV Network; Fox News Channel; INSP; QVC; TBS Superstation; USA Network; WGN America.

Fee: $39.95 installation; $16.99 monthly.

Expanded Basic Service 1

Subscribers: N.A.

Programming (received off-air): WRLM (IND) Canton.

Programming (via satellite): A&E Networks; ABC Family Channel; AMC; Animal Planet; BET Networks; Bravo; BTN; Cartoon Network; CNBC; CNN; Comedy Central; Country Music TV; C-SPAN; C-SPAN 2; Discovery Channel; Discovery Health Channel; Disney Channel; E! Entertainment Television; ESPN; ESPN 2; ESPN Classic Sports; Food Network; Fox Sports Net Ohio; FX; Golf Channel; GSN; Hallmark Channel; Headline News; HGTV; History Channel; Lifetime; MSNBC; MTV; MTV2; National Geographic Channel; Nickelodeon; NickToons TV; ShopNBC; Speed; Spike TV; SportsTime Ohio; Syfy; The Learning Channel; The Weather Channel; Toon Disney; Travel Channel; truTV; Turner Classic Movies; Turner Network TV; TV Land; Versus; VH1.

Fee: $32.01 monthly.

Digital Basic Service

Subscribers: N.A.

Programming (via satellite): A&E HD; ABC News Now; Animal Planet HD; BBC America; Bio; Bloomberg Television; BTN; BTN HD; CMT Pure Country; Cooking Channel; Daystar TV Network; Discovery Channel HD; Discovery Kids Channel; DIY Network; DMX Music; Encore (multiplexed); ESPN HD; ESPNews; Food Network HD; Fox Business Channel; Fox College Sports Atlantic; Fox College Sports Central; Fox College Sports Pacific; Fox HD; Fox Movie Channel; Fox News HD; Fox Reality Channel; Fox Soccer; FSN HD; FX HD; G4; HD Theater; HDNet; HDNet Movies; HGTV HD; History Channel HD; History Channel International; ID Investigation Discovery; Jewelry Television; Lifetime Movie Network; Lifetime Real Women; Military Channel; MTV Hits; National Geographic Channel HD Network; NFL Network; NFL Network HD; Nick Jr.; Nick Too; Outdoor Channel 2 HD; Oxygen; PBS HD; PBS Kids Sprout; Planet Green; Science; SoapNet; Starz (multiplexed); Style Network; Sundance Channel; TeenNick; Tennis Channel; TLC HD; Trinity Broadcasting Network; Turner Network TV HD; VH1 Classic; WealthTV HD; WWE 24/7.

Fee: $44.97 monthly.

Digital Pay Service 1

Pay Units: N.A.

Programming (via satellite): Cinemax (multiplexed); Cinemax HD; Cinemax On Demand; Flix; HBO (multiplexed); HBO HD; HBO On Demand; Showtime (multiplexed); Showtime HD; Showtime On Demand; Starz HDTV; The Movie Channel (multiplexed); The Movie Channel On Demand.

Fee: $15.00 monthly (HBO, Cinemax, Starz or Showtime/TMC/Flix).

Video-On-Demand: Yes

Pay-Per-View

Hot Choice (delivered digitally); iN DEMAND (delivered digitally); Special events (delivered digitally); Playboy TV (delivered digitally); ESPN (delivered digitally).

Internet Service

Operational: Yes.

Broadband Service: WOW! Internet.

Fee: $40.99-$72.99 monthly; $2.50 modem lease.

Telephone Service

Digital: Operational

Vice President & General Manager: Scott Neesley. Vice President, Sales & Marketing: Cathy Kuo. Regional General Manager: Scott Schup. Chief Technician: Cash Hagen.

Ownership: WideOpenWest LLC (MSO).

CLEVELAND HEIGHTS—Time Warner Cable, 3400 Lakeside Ave E, Cleveland, OH 44114-3754. Phones: 330-633-9203 (Akron regional office); 216-575-8016. Fax: 216-575-0212. Web Site: http://www.timewarnercable.com/northeastohio. Also serves Amherst, Amherst Twp., Aquilla, Avon, Avon Lake, Bainbridge Twp., Bath Twp. (Summit County), Bay Village, Beachwood, Bedford, Bedford Heights, Bentleyville, Berea, Berlin Heights, Berlinville, Bratenahl, Brecksville, Brook Park, Brooklyn, Brownhelm Twp., Burton, Burton Twp., Carlisle Twp. (Lorain County), Chagrin Falls, Chardon, Chardon Twp., Chesterland, Claridon, Cleveland, Collins, Concord Twp. (Lake County), Copley Twp., Cuyahoga Falls, Cuyahoga Heights, Eastlake, Elyria, Elyria Twp. (Lorain County), Euclid, Fairpoint Harbor, Florence Twp. (Erie County), Garfield Heights, Gates Mills, Glenwillow, Grand River, Granger Twp., Hambden Twp., Highland Heights, Highland Hills, Hinckley Twp., Hunting Valley, Independence, Kirtland, Kirtland Hills, Lakeline, Lakewood, Leroy Twp. (Lake County), Linndale, Lorain, Lyndhurst, Maple Heights, Mayfield Heights, Mayfield Village, Mentor, Mentor-on-the-Lake, Middleburg Heights, Middlefield, Moreland Hills, Munson Twp., Munson Twp. (Geauga County), New Russia Twp., Newburgh Heights, Newbury, North Olmsted, North Perry (village), North Randall, North Ridgeville, North Royalton, Oakwood, Orange, Painesville, Painesville Twp. (Lake County), Pepper Pike, Perry, Richfield (village), Richfield Twp. (Summit County), Richmond Heights, Russell Twp., Shaker Heights, Sharon Twp. (Medina County), Sheffield, Sheffield Lake, Sheffield Twp. (Lorain County), Solon, South Amherst, South Euclid, South Russell, Strongsville, Timberlake, University Heights, Valley View, Vermilion, Vermilion Twp., Waite Hill, Wakeman, Walton Hills, Warrensville Heights, Westlake, Wickliffe, Willoughby, Willoughby Hills, Willowick & Woodmere. ICA: OH0006. **Note:** This system is an overbuild.

TV Market Ranking: 8 (Amherst, Amherst Twp., Aquilla, Avon, Avon, Avon Lake, Bainbridge Twp., Bath Twp. (Summit County), Bay Village, Bay Village, Beachwood, Bedford, Bedford Heights, Bentleyville, Berea, Berlin Heights, Berlinville, Bratenahl, Brecksville, Brook Park, Brooklyn, Brownhelm Twp., Brunswick, Brunswick Hills Twp., Burton, Burton Twp., Carlisle Twp. (Lorain County), Chagrin Falls, Chardon, Chardon Twp., Chesterland, Claridon, Cleveland, CLEVELAND HEIGHTS, Collins, Concord Twp. (Lake County), Copley Twp., Cuyahoga Falls, Cuyahoga Heights, Eastlake, Elyria, Elyria Twp. (Lorain County), Euclid, Fairpoint Harbor, Florence Twp. (Erie County), Garfield Heights, Gates Mills, Glenwillow, Grand River, Granger Twp., Hambden Twp., Highland Heights, Highland Hills, Hinckley Twp., Hunting Valley, Independence, Kirtland, Kirtland Hills, Lakeline, Lakewood, Leroy Twp. (Lake

County), Linndale, Lorain, Lyndhurst, Maple Heights, Mayfield Heights, Mayfield Village, Mentor, Mentor-on-the-Hill, Middleburg Heights, Middlefield, Moreland Hills, Munson Twp., Munson Twp. (Geauga County), New Russia Twp., Newburgh Heights, Newbury, North Olmsted, North Randall, North Ridgeville, North Royalton, Oakwood, Orange, Painesville, Painesville Twp. (Lake County), Pepper Pike, Perry, Richfield (village), Richfield Twp. (Summit County), Richmond Heights, Russell Twp., Shaker Heights, Sharon Twp. (Medina County), Sheffield, Sheffield Lake, Sheffield Twp. (Loraine County), Solon, South Amherst, South Euclid, South Russell, Strongsville, Timberlake, University Heights, Valley View, Vermilion, Vermilion Twp., Waite Hill, Wakeman, Walton Hills, Warrensville Heights, Westlake, Wickliffe, Willoughby, Willoughby Hills, Willowick, Woodmere); Below 100 (North Perry (village)). Franchise award date: May 25, 1965. Franchise expiration date: N.A. Began: January 1, 1966.

Channel capacity: N.A. Channels available but not in use: N.A.

Basic Service

Subscribers: 400,000.

Programming (received off-air): WBNX-TV (CW) Akron; WEAO (PBS) Akron; WEWS-TV (ABC) Cleveland; WJW (FOX) Cleveland; WKYC (NBC) Cleveland; WNEO (PBS) Alliance; WOIO (CBS) Shaker Heights; WQHS-DT (UNV) Cleveland; WRLM (IND) Canton; WUAB (MNT) Lorain; WVIZ (PBS) Cleveland; WVPX-TV (ION) Akron.

Programming (via satellite): Eternal Word TV Network; QVC; Scola; TV Guide Network; WGN America.

Fee: $44.95 installation; $6.95 monthly.

Expanded Basic Service 1

Subscribers: N.A.

Programming (via satellite): A&E Networks; ABC Family Channel; AMC; Animal Planet; BET Networks; Bravo; Cartoon Network; CNBC; CNN; Comedy Central; C-SPAN; C-SPAN 2; Discovery Channel; Disney Channel; E! Entertainment Television; ESPN; ESPN 2; Food Network; Fox News Channel; Fox Sports Net Ohio; FX; Golf Channel; Headline News; HGTV; History Channel; Lifetime; MSNBC; MTV; MTV2; Nickelodeon; ShopNBC; Speed; Spike TV; Style Network; Syfy; TBS Superstation; Telemundo; The Learning Channel; The Weather Channel; Travel Channel; truTV; Turner Network TV; TV Land; USA Network; VH1; VH1 Classic.

Fee: $46.50 monthly.

Digital Basic Service

Subscribers: 81,500.

Programming (via satellite): AmericanLife TV Network; BBC America; Bloomberg Television; Canal 52MX; Cine Latino; CMT Pure Country; CNN en Espanol; C-SPAN 3; Current; Discovery en Espanol; Discovery Fit & Health; Discovery Health Channel; Discovery Home Channel; Discovery Kids Channel; Discovery Times Channel; DIY Network; ESPN 2 HD; ESPN Classic Sports; ESPN Deportes; ESPN HD; ESPN U; ESPNews; Familyland Television Network; Fox Business Channel; Fox Deportes; Fox Movie Channel; Fox Reality Channel; Fox Soccer; Fuse; G4; GAS; GMC; Great American Country; GSN; Hallmark Channel; Halogen Network; HD Theater; HDNet; HDNet Movies; History Channel en Espanol; Lifetime Movie Network; LOGO; Military Channel; MTV Hits; MTV Jams; Music Choice; National Geographic Channel; Nick Jr.; Nick Too; NickToons TV; Ohio News Network; Science; SoapNet; SportsTime Ohio; TBS in HD; The Word Network; Toon Disney; Toon Disney en Espanol; Tr3s; Trinity Broadcasting Network; Turner Classic Movies; Turner Network TV HD; TV One; TVG Network; Universal HD; VH1 Soul; WE tv.

Fee: $11.00 monthly.

Digital Expanded Basic Service

Subscribers: N.A.

Programming (via satellite): Bio; Cooking Channel; Flix; FSN Digital Atlantic; FSN Digital Central; FSN Digital Pacific; Fuel TV; History Channel International; Independent Film Channel; NBA TV; Outdoor Channel; Sundance Channel; Tennis Channel; Versus.

Fee: $10.00 monthly.

Digital Pay Service 1

Pay Units: 108,000.

Programming (via satellite): ART America; CCTV-4; Cinemax (multiplexed); Cinemax HD; Cinemax On Demand; Encore (multiplexed); Filipino Channel; Flix; HBO (multiplexed); HBO HD; HBO On Demand; RAI International; Russian Television Network; Showtime (multiplexed); Showtime HD; Showtime On Demand; Starz (multiplexed); Starz HDTV; Starz On Demand; The Movie Channel (multiplexed); The Movie Channel On Demand; TV Asia; TV Japan; TV5, La Television International; Zhong Tian Channel.

Fee: $12.00 monthly (HBO, Cinemax, Showtime/TMC/Flix, or Showtime/Encore).

Video-On-Demand: Yes

Pay-Per-View

Addressable homes: 81,500.

iN DEMAND; Sports PPV.

Internet Service

Operational: Yes. Began: February 14, 2001.

Broadband Service: EarthLink, Road Runner.

Fee: $45.95 monthly.

Telephone Service

Digital: Operational

Fee: $44.95 monthly

Miles of Plant: 9,049.0 (coaxial); 49.0 (fiber optic).

President: Stephen Fry. Vice President & General Manager: Darrel Hegar. Operations Manager: Derrick Moore. Chief Technician: Jim Farone. Marketing Manager: Dana Olden. Government & Media Relations Director: Chris Thomas.

Ownership: Time Warner Cable (MSO).

COITSVILLE TWP.—Shentel, 106 S Main St, Edinburg, VA 22824. Phones: 800-743-6835; 540-984-5224. Web Site: http://www.shentel.net. Also serves Hubbard Twp. (Trumbull County). ICA: OH0233.

TV Market Ranking: 79 (COITSVILLE TWP., Hubbard Twp. (Trumbull County)). Franchise award date: N.A. Franchise expiration date: N.A. Began: N.A.

Channel capacity: 62 (not 2-way capable). Channels available but not in use: N.A.

Basic Service

Subscribers: 310.

Programming (received off-air): WFMJ-TV (CW, NBC) Youngstown; WKBN-TV (CBS) Youngstown; WNEO (PBS) Alliance; WOIO (CBS) Shaker Heights; WPGH-TV (FOX) Pittsburgh; WUAB (MNT) Lorain; WYTV (ABC, MNT) Youngstown.

Programming (via satellite): QVC; TBS Superstation.

Fee: $29.95 installation; $19.95 monthly; $1.95 converter.

Expanded Basic Service 1

Subscribers: N.A.

Programming (via satellite): A&E Networks; ABC Family Channel; AMC; CNBC; CNN; C-SPAN; Discovery Channel; Disney Channel; ESPN; Fox Sports Net Ohio; Headline News; History Channel; Lifetime; MTV; Nickelodeon; Root Sports Pittsburgh; Spike TV; Syfy; The Learning Channel; The Weather Channel; Turner Network TV; TV Land; USA Network; VH1.

Fee: $25.00 monthly.

Pay Service 1

Pay Units: 48.

Programming (via satellite): Cinemax.

Fee: $11.00 monthly.

Pay Service 2

Pay Units: 83.

Programming (via satellite): HBO.

Fee: $11.00 monthly.

Pay Service 3

Pay Units: 51.

Programming (via satellite): Showtime; The Movie Channel.

Fee: $12.95 monthly (each).

Internet Service

Operational: No.

Telephone Service

None

Miles of Plant: 32.0 (coaxial); None (fiber optic).

General Manager: Robert Harold. Chief Technician: Steve Adkins.

Ownership: Shenandoah Telecommunications Inc. (MSO).

COLLINSVILLE—Formerly served by Time Warner Cable. No longer in operation. ICA: OH0172.

COLUMBUS—Formerly served by Sprint Corp. No longer in operation. ICA: OH0390.

COLUMBUS—Insight Communications, 3770 E Livingston Ave, Columbus, OH 43227-2246. Phones: 800-686-2200; 614-236-1200; 614-236-1292. Fax: 614-238-7023. Web Site: http://www.myinsight.com. Also serves Amanda Twp. (Fairfield County), Berkshire Twp. (Delaware County), Blacklick, Blendon Twp. (Franklin County), Bloom Twp. (Fairfield County), Brice, Brown Twp. (Delaware County), Canal Winchester, Clinton Twp. (Franklin County), Delaware Twp. (Delaware County), Etna Twp., Gahanna (Franklin County), Genoa Twp. (Delaware County), Greenfield Twp. (Fairfield County), Hamilton Twp. (Franklin County), Harlem Twp. (Delaware County), Harrison Twp. (Pickaway County), Jefferson Twp. (Franklin County), Jersey Twp., Kilbourne, Lewis Center, Liberty Twp. (Fairfield County), Lithopolis, Lockbourne Village, Madison Twp. (Franklin County), Madison Twp. (Pickaway County), Mifflin Twp. (Franklin County), New Albany, Orange Twp. (Delaware County), Pickerington, Plain Twp. (Franklin County), Reynoldsburg, Sharon Twp. (Franklin County), St. Albans Twp. (Licking County), Violet Twp., Westerville (Delaware & Franklin Counties) & Whitehall. ICA: OH0007.

TV Market Ranking: 27 (Amanda Twp. (Fairfield County), Berkshire Twp. (Delaware County), Blacklick, Blendon Twp. (Franklin County), Bloom Twp. (Fairfield County), Brice, Brown Twp. (Delaware County), Canal Winchester, Clinton Twp. (Franklin County), COLUMBUS, Delaware Twp. (Delaware County), Etna Twp., Gahanna (Franklin County), Genoa Twp. (Delaware County), Greenfield Twp. (Franklin County), Hamilton Twp. (Franklin County), Harlem Twp. (Delaware County), Harrison Twp. (Pickaway County), Jefferson Twp. (Franklin County), Jersey Twp., Kilbourne, Lewis Center, Liberty Twp. (Fairfield County), Lithopolis, Lockbourne Village, Madison Twp. (Franklin County), Madison Twp. (Pickaway County), Mifflin Twp. (Franklin County), New Albany, Orange Twp. (Delaware County), Pickerington, Plain Twp. (Franklin County), Reynoldsburg, Sharon Twp. (Franklin County), St. Albans Twp. (Licking County), Violet Twp., Westerville (Delaware & Franklin Counties), Whitehall). Franchise award date: May 1, 1973. Franchise expiration date: N.A. Began: May 1, 1973.

Channel capacity: N.A. Channels available but not in use: N.A.

Basic Service

Subscribers: 94,400.

Programming (received off-air): WBNS-TV (CBS) Columbus; WCMH-TV (NBC) Columbus; WOSU-TV (PBS) Columbus; WSFJ-TV (TBN) Newark; WSYX (ABC, MNT) Columbus; WTTE (FOX) Columbus; WWHO (CW) Chillicothe; 28 FMs.

Programming (via satellite): QVC; ShopNBC; TBS Superstation; The Weather Channel; WGN America.

Fee: $35.00 installation.

Expanded Basic Service 1

Subscribers: N.A.

Programming (via satellite): A&E Networks; ABC Family Channel; AMC; Animal Planet; BET Networks; Bravo; BTN; Cartoon Network; CNBC; CNN; Comedy Central; Country Music TV; C-SPAN; C-SPAN 2; Discovery Channel; Disney Channel; E! Entertainment Television; ESPN; ESPN 2; Food Network; Fox News Channel; Fox Sports Net Ohio; FX; G4; Golf Channel; Great American Country; Hallmark Channel; Headline News; HGTV; History Channel; Lifetime; MoviePlex; MSNBC; MTV; Nickelodeon; Ohio News Network; Oxygen; Speed; Spike TV; SportsTime Ohio; Style Network; Syfy; The Learning Channel; Travel Channel; truTV; Turner Classic Movies; Turner Network TV; TV Guide Network; TV Land; TV One; USA Network; VH1; WE tv.

Fee: $40.00 monthly.

Digital Basic Service

Subscribers: 36,500.

Programming (via satellite): AmericanLife TV Network; BBC America; Bio; Bloomberg Television; Boomerang; BTN; Canales N; CBS Sports Network; Church Channel; cloo; CMT Pure Country; CNN International; Cooking Channel; C-SPAN 3; Daystar TV Network; DIY Network; Encore

(multiplexed); ESPN 2 HD; ESPN Classic Sports; ESPN HD; ESPN U; ESPNews; Eternal Word TV Network; Fox College Sports Atlantic; Fox College Sports Central; Fox College Sports Pacific; Fox Movie Channel; Fox Reality Channel; Fox Soccer; Fuel TV; Fuse; GMC; GSN; Halogen Network; HD Theater; HDNet; HDNet Movies; History Channel International; HRTV; Independent Film Channel; Lifetime Movie Network; Lifetime Real Women; MTV Networks Digital Suite; Music Choice; National Geographic Channel; NFL Network; Nick Jr.; Nick Too; NickToons TV; Outdoor Channel; Ovation; Palladia; PBS Kids Sprout; SoapNet; Sundance Channel; TeenNick; Tennis Channel; The Word Network; Toon Disney; Trinity Broadcasting Network; Turner Network TV HD; TVG Network; Universal HD; Versus.
Fee: $17.00 monthly.

Digital Pay Service 1
Pay Units: 11,930.
Programming (via satellite): Cinemax (multiplexed).
Fee: $10.00 monthly.

Digital Pay Service 2
Pay Units: N.A.
Programming (via satellite): CCTV-4; Filipino Channel; Korean Channel; Saigon Broadcasting Television Network; Starz (multiplexed); TV Asia; TV Japan; Zee TV USA.
Fee: $10.00 monthly (Starz).

Digital Pay Service 3
Pay Units: 36,750.
Programming (via satellite): HBO (multiplexed); HBO HD.
Fee: $13.00 monthly.

Digital Pay Service 4
Pay Units: 2,153.
Programming (via satellite): Flix (multiplexed); Showtime (multiplexed); Showtime HD; The Movie Channel (multiplexed).
Fee: $13.00 monthly.

Video-On-Demand: Yes

Pay-Per-View
iN DEMAND (delivered digitally); ESPN (delivered digitally).

Internet Service
Operational: Yes.
Subscribers: 26,700.
Broadband Service: In-house.
Fee: $99.95 installation; $40.00 monthly.

Telephone Service
Digital: Operational
Fee: $40.00 monthly

Miles of Plant: 2,635.0 (coaxial); 115.0 (fiber optic). Additional miles planned: 60.0 (coaxial).

President & Chief Operating Officer: Dinni Jain. Senior Vice President, Operations: John Hutton. District Vice President: Patrick Eltzroth. Chief Technician: Greg Piper. Marketing Manager: Denise Keefe.

Ownership: Insight Communications Co. (MSO).

COLUMBUS—Time Warner Cable, 1266 Dublin Rd, Columbus, OH 43215-1008. Phone: 614-481-5000. Fax: 614-481-5052. Web Site: http://www.timewarnercable.com/midohio. Also serves Berkshire Twp., Bexley, Bokescreek Twp., Canaan Twp. (Madison County), Concord Twp., Crystal Lake Mobile Home Park, Darby Twp. (Pickaway County), Deer Creek Twp., Dublin, East Liberty, Galena, Grandview Heights, Grove City, Groveport, Hamilton Twp. (Franklin County), Harlem Twp. (Delaware County), Harrisburg, Jerome Twp., Leesburg Twp., Leesville, Liberty Twp. (Delaware County), Liberty Twp. (Union County), London, Magnetic Springs, Marble Cliff, Marysville, Middleburg, Mifflin Twp. (Franklin County), Milford Center, Minerva Park, Monroe Twp., Mount Sterling, North Lewisburg Village, Oak Run Twp., Obetz, Orient, Perry Twp. (Franklin County), Perry Twp. (Logan County), Pickaway County, Plain City, Pleasant Twp. (Franklin County), Porter Twp. (Delaware County), Powell (village), Prairie Twp. (Franklin County), Raymond, Reese Station, Richwood, Riverlea, Sharon Twp., Shawnee Hills, South Bloomfield, Sunbury, Taylor Twp., Unionville Center, Upper Arlington, Urbancrest, Valley Hi, Valleyview, West Jefferson, West Mansfield, Worthington & Zane Twp. (Logan County). ICA: OH0002.

TV Market Ranking: 27 (Berkshire Twp., Bexley, Canaan Twp. (Madison County), COLUMBUS, Concord Twp., Crystal Lake Mobile Home Park, Darby Twp. (Pickaway County), Deer Creek Twp., Dublin, Galena, Grandview Heights, Grove City, Groveport, Hamilton Twp. (Franklin County), Harlem Twp. (Delaware County), Harrisburg, Jerome Twp., Leesburg Twp., Liberty Twp. (Delaware County), Liberty Twp. (Union County), London, Magnetic Springs, Marble Cliff, Marysville, Mifflin Twp. (Franklin County), Milford Center, Minerva Park, Mount Sterling, North Lewisburg Village, Oak Run Twp., Obetz, Orient, Perry Twp. (Franklin County), Pickaway County, Plain City, Pleasant Twp. (Franklin County), Porter Twp. (Delaware County), Powell (village), Prairie Twp. (Franklin County), Raymond, Reese Station, Richwood, Riverlea, Sharon Twp., Shawnee Hills, South Bloomfield, Sunbury, Taylor Twp., Unionville Center, Upper Arlington, Urbancrest, Valleyview, West Jefferson, Worthington); Below 100 (Bokescreek Twp., Leesville, Middleburg, Monroe Twp. (Logan County), Perry Twp. (Logan County), West MansfieldOHIO, Zane Twp. (Logan County)); Outside TV Markets (East Liberty, Valley Hi). Franchise award date: N.A. Franchise expiration date: November 30, 2009. Began: December 1, 1971.

Channel capacity: N.A. Channels available but not in use: N.A.

Basic Service
Subscribers: 325,189.
Programming (received off-air): WBNS-TV (CBS) Columbus; WCMH-TV (NBC) Columbus; WOSU-TV (PBS) Columbus; WSFJ-TV (TBN) Newark; WSYX (ABC, MNT) Columbus; WTTE (FOX) Columbus; WUAB (MNT) Lorain; WWHO (CW) Chillicothe.
Programming (via satellite): C-SPAN; C-SPAN 2; Hallmark Channel; Headline News; History Channel; LWS Local Weather Station; QVC; ShopNBC; TBS Superstation; The Learning Channel; TV Guide Network; WGN America.
Fee: $39.90 installation; $9.95 monthly.

Expanded Basic Service 1
Subscribers: 175,000.
Programming (via satellite): A&E Networks; ABC Family Channel; AMC; Animal Planet; BBC America; BET Networks; Bravo; Cartoon Network; CNBC; CNN; Comedy Central; Country Music TV; Discovery Channel; Discovery Fit & Health; Discovery Health Channel; Disney Channel; E! Entertainment Television; ESPN; ESPN 2; Food Network; Fox News Channel; Fox Sports Net Ohio; FX; Golf Channel; HGTV; Jewelry Television; Lifetime; Lifetime Movie Network; MTV; MTV2; National Geographic Channel; Nickelodeon; Oxygen; Spike TV; SportsTime Ohio; Syfy; The Weather Channel; Travel Channel; truTV; Turner Classic Movies; Turner Network TV; TV Land; Univision Studios; USA Network; VH1; WE tv.
Fee: $26.95 monthly.

Digital Basic Service
Subscribers: 159,166.
Programming (via satellite): AmericanLife TV Network; America's Store; Bio; Bloomberg Television; Boomerang; Canales N; CBS Sports Network; cloo; CNN International; Cooking Channel; C-SPAN 3; Current; Disney Channel; DIY Network; Encore (multiplexed); ESPN Classic Sports; ESPNews; Eternal Word TV Network; Food Network; Fox College Sports Atlantic; Fox College Sports Central; Fox College Sports Pacific; Fox Movie Channel; Fox Soccer; Fuel TV; Fuse; G4; GAS; Great American Country; GSN; HD Theater; HDNet; HDNet Movies; Healthy Living Channel; HGTV; History Channel International; Independent Film Channel; INHD; INHD2; INSP; La Familia Network; Lifetime Real Women; MTV Hits; Music Choice; NBA TV; Nick Jr.; NickToons TV; Ohio News Network; Outdoor Channel; Ovation; SoapNet; Speed; Style Network; Sundance Channel; Tennis Channel; The Weather Channel; The Word Network; Toon Disney; Turner Network TV HD; TV One; Universal HD; VH1 Classic.
Fee: $7.15 monthly.

Digital Pay Service 1
Pay Units: N.A.
Programming (via satellite): Cinemax (multiplexed); Encore; HBO (multiplexed); Showtime (multiplexed); Showtime HD; Starz; The Movie Channel (multiplexed).
Fee: $11.95 monthly (each).

Video-On-Demand: Yes

Pay-Per-View
iN DEMAND (delivered digitally); NBA League Pass (delivered digitally); NHL Center Ice (delivered digitally); MLB Extra Innings (delivered digitally); ESPN Gameplan (delivered digitally); NASCAR In Car (delivered digitally); MLS Direct Kick (delivered digitally).

Internet Service
Operational: Yes.
Subscribers: 137,737.
Broadband Service: Road Runner.
Fee: $69.95 installation; $44.95 monthly.

Telephone Service
Digital: Operational
Fee: $44.95 monthly

Miles of Plant: 7,425.0 (coaxial); 2,945.0 (fiber optic).

President: Rhonda Fraas. Vice President, Operations: Paul Schonewolf. Vice President, Engineering: Randy Hall. Vice President, Marketing: Mark Psigoda. Vice President, Public Affairs: Mary Jo Green. Vice President, Customer Service: Kathy Chamberlin. Government Affairs Director: Steve Cuckler.

Ownership: Time Warner Cable (MSO).

COLUMBUS—WOW! Internet Cable & Phone, 7887 E Belleview Ave, Ste 1000, Englewood, CO 80111. Phones: 720-479-3500 (Corporate office); 866-496-9669 (Customer service). Fax: 720-479-3585. Web Site: http://www1.wowway.com. Also serves Bexley, Blendon Twp., Brice, Canal Winchester, Clinton Twp., Dublin, Franklin Twp., Gahanna, Grandview Heights, Grove City, Hilliard, Jackson Twp., Madison Twp., Marble Cliff, Mifflin Twp., Minerva Park, New Rome, Norwich Twp., Obetz, Perry Twp., Prairie Twp., Reynoldsburg, Riverlea, Sharon Twp., Upper Arlington, Urbancrest, Valleyview, Westerville, Whitehall & Worthington. ICA: OH0426.
Note: This system is an overbuild.

TV Market Ranking: 27 (Bexley, Blendon Twp., Brice, Canal Winchester, Clinton Twp., COLUMBUS, Dublin, Franklin Twp., Gahanna, Grandview Heights, Grove City, Hilliard, Jackson Twp., Madison Twp., Marble Cliff, Mifflin Twp., Minerva Park, New Rome, Norwich Twp., Obetz, Perry Twp., Prairie Twp., Reynoldsburg, Riverlea, Sharon Twp., Upper Arlington, Urbancrest, Valleyview, Westerville, Whitehall, Worthington). Franchise award date: April 1, 1996. Franchise expiration date: N.A. Began: N.A.

Channel capacity: N.A. Channels available but not in use: N.A.

Basic Service
Subscribers: N.A. Included in Chicago, IL
Programming (received off-air): WBNS-TV (CBS) Columbus; WCMH-TV (NBC) Columbus; WOSU-TV (PBS) Columbus; WSFJ-TV (TBN) Newark; WSYX (ABC, MNT) Columbus; WTTE (FOX) Columbus; WWHO (CW) Chillicothe.
Programming (via satellite): C-SPAN; INSP; Ohio News Network; TBS Superstation; WGN America.
Fee: $39.95 installation; $16.99 monthly.

Expanded Basic Service 1
Subscribers: N.A.
Programming (via satellite): A&E Networks; ABC Family Channel; AMC; Animal Planet; BET Networks; Bravo; BTN; Cartoon Network; CNBC; CNN; Comedy Central; Country Music TV; C-SPAN 2; Discovery Channel; Discovery Health Channel; Disney Channel; E! Entertainment Television; ESPN; ESPN 2; ESPN Classic Sports; Food Network; Fox News Channel; Fox Sports Net Ohio; FX; Golf Channel; GSN; Hallmark Channel; Headline News; HGTV; History Channel; Lifetime; MSNBC; MTV; MTV2; National Geographic Channel; Nick Jr.; Nickelodeon; NickToons TV; QVC; ShopNBC; Speed; Spike TV; SportsTime Ohio; Syfy; Telemundo; The Learning Channel; The Weather Channel; Toon Disney; Travel Channel; truTV; Turner Classic Movies; Turner Network TV; TV Land; USA Network; Versus; VH1.
Fee: $33.01 monthly.

Digital Basic Service
Subscribers: N.A.
Programming (via satellite): A&E HD; ABC News Now; Animal Planet HD; BBC America; Bio; Bloomberg Television; Bridges TV; BTN; BTN HD; CMT Pure Country; Cooking Channel; Daystar TV Network; Discovery Channel HD; Discovery Kids Channel; DIY Network; DMX Music; Encore (multiplexed); ESPN HD; ESPNews; Eternal Word TV Network; Food Network HD; Fox Business Channel; Fox College Sports Atlantic; Fox College Sports Central; Fox College Sports Pacific; Fox HD; Fox Movie Channel; Fox News HD; Fox Reality Channel; Fox Soccer; FSN HD; FX HD; G4; HD Theater; HDNet; HDNet Movies; here! On Demand; HGTV HD; History Channel HD; History Channel International; ID Investigation Discovery; Jewelry Television; Lifetime Movie Network; Lifetime Real Women; Military Channel; MTV Hits; National Geographic Channel HD Network; NFL Network; NFL Network HD; Nick Too; Oxygen; PBS HD; PBS Kids Sprout; Planet Green; Science; SoapNet; Starz (multiplexed); Style Network; Sundance Channel; TeenNick; The Word Network; TLC HD; Turner Network TV HD; VH1 Classic; WealthTV HD; WWE 24/7.
Fee: $26.98 monthly.

Digital Pay Service 1
Pay Units: N.A.
Programming (via satellite): Cinemax (multiplexed); Cinemax HD; Cinemax On Demand; Flix; HBO (multiplexed); HBO HD; HBO On Demand; Showtime (multiplexed); Showtime HD; Showtime On Demand; Starz HDTV; The Movie Channel (multiplexed); The Movie Channel On Demand.
Fee: $15.00 monthly (HBO, Cinemax, Starz/Encore or Showtime/TMC/Flix).
Video-On-Demand: Yes
Pay-Per-View
Hot Choice; iN DEMAND (delivered digitally); Special events (delivered digitally); Playboy TV (delivered digitally); ESPN.
Internet Service
Operational: Yes.
Broadband Service: WOW! Internet.
Fee: $40.99-$72.99 monthly; $2.50 modem lease.
Telephone Service
Digital: Operational
Vice President & General Manager: Scott Neesley. Vice President, Sales & Marketing: Cathy Kuo. Regional General Manager: Scott Schup. Chief Technician: Cash Hagen.
Ownership: WideOpenWest LLC (MSO).

COLUMBUS GROVE (village)—FairPoint Communications, PO Box 36, Columbus Grove, OH 45830. Phones: 800-400-5588 (Customer Service); 419-659-2199 (Internet Technical Support). Fax: 419-659-5701. Web Site: http://www.fairpoint.com. Also serves Continental, Gilboa, Leipsic, Melrose, Miller City, Oakwood (Paulding County), Pandora & West Leipsic (village). ICA: OH0402. **Note:** This system is an overbuild.
TV Market Ranking: Below 100 (COLUMBUS GROVE (VILLAGE), Continental, Gilboa, Leipsic, Melrose, Miller City, Oakwood (Paulding County), Pandora, West Leipsic (village)). Franchise award date: September 9, 1996. Franchise expiration date: N.A. Began: May 1, 1997.
Channel capacity: N.A. Channels available but not in use: N.A.
Basic Service
Subscribers: 2,500.
Programming (received off-air): WBGU-TV (PBS) Bowling Green; WLIO (CW, NBC) Lima; WLMB (IND) Toledo; WNWO-TV (NBC) Toledo; WOHL-CD (FOX) Lima; WTLW (IND) Lima; WTOL (CBS) Toledo; WTVG (ABC) Toledo.
Programming (via satellite): Discovery Channel; Disney Channel; Fox News Channel; TBS Superstation; The Learning Channel; The Weather Channel; Univision Studios.
Fee: $13.75 monthly.
Expanded Basic Service 1
Subscribers: N.A.
Programming (via satellite): ABC Family Channel; CNBC; Country Music TV; ESPN; ESPN 2; Eternal Word TV Network; Food Network; Fox Sports Net Ohio; HGTV; Syfy; Toon Disney; TV Guide Network; TV Land; USA Network.
Fee: $8.20 monthly.
Expanded Basic Service 2
Subscribers: N.A.
Programming (received off-air): WBNS-TV (CBS) Columbus; WFFT-TV (IND) Fort Wayne; WISE-TV (FOX, MNT, NBC) Fort Wayne; WLQP-LP Lima; WPTA (ABC, CW) Fort Wayne.
Programming (via satellite): 3 Angels Broadcasting Network; A&E Networks; AMC; Animal Planet; Cartoon Network; CNN; Comedy Central; C-SPAN; Current; FX; G4; Golf Channel; GSN; Hallmark Channel; Headline News; History Channel; Lifetime; MTV; Nickelodeon; Outdoor Channel; QVC; SoapNet; Speed; Spike TV; Travel Channel; truTV; Turner Classic Movies; Turner Network TV; VH1; WE tv; WGN America.
Fee: $14.55 monthly.
Pay Service 1
Pay Units: N.A.
Programming (via satellite): Cinemax; Encore; HBO; Playboy TV; Starz.
Fee: $7.95 monthly (Cinemax), $9.95 monthly (HBO), $6.95 monthly (Encore/Starz), $12.95 monthly (Playboy).
Video-On-Demand: No
Pay-Per-View
iN DEMAND; Playboy TV.
Internet Service
Operational: Yes. Began: January 1, 1999.
Broadband Service: Qone.net.
Fee: $39.95 monthly.
Telephone Service
None
Miles of Plant: 25.0 (coaxial); 7.0 (fiber optic).
Ownership: FairPoint Communications Inc.

COMMERCIAL POINT—Time Warner Cable, 1266 Dublin Rd, Columbus, OH 43215-1008. Phones: 740-345-4329 (Newark office); 614-481-5000 (Columbus office). Fax: 614-481-5052. Web Site: http://www.timewarnercable.com/midohio. Also serves Darbyville, Muhlenberg Twp. & Scioto Twp. (Pickaway County). ICA: OH0213.
TV Market Ranking: 27 (COMMERCIAL POINT, Darbyville, Muhlenberg Twp., Scioto Twp. (Pickaway County)). Franchise award date: July 14, 1988. Franchise expiration date: N.A. Began: October 1, 1989.
Channel capacity: 48 (not 2-way capable). Channels available but not in use: N.A.
Basic Service
Subscribers: 453.
Programming (received off-air): WBNS-TV (CBS) Columbus; WCMH-TV (NBC) Columbus; WOSU-TV (PBS) Columbus; WSYX (ABC, MNT) Columbus; WTTE (FOX) Columbus; WWHO (CW) Chillicothe.
Programming (via satellite): TBS Superstation.
Expanded Basic Service 1
Subscribers: N.A.
Programming (via satellite): A&E Networks; ABC Family Channel; AMC; Animal Planet; Cartoon Network; CNN; Country Music TV; Discovery Channel; Disney Channel; E! Entertainment Television; ESPN; ESPN 2; Fox News Channel; Fox Sports Net Ohio; FX; Headline News; HGTV; History Channel; INSP; Lifetime; MSNBC; MTV; Nickelodeon; QVC; Spike TV; Syfy; The Learning Channel; The Weather Channel; Travel Channel; truTV; Turner Network TV; TV Land; USA Network; VH1; WGN America.
Digital Basic Service
Subscribers: N.A.
Programming (via satellite): BBC America; Bloomberg Television; Discovery Fit & Health; ESPN Classic Sports; ESPNews; Fox Movie Channel; Fox Soccer; G4; Golf Channel; GSN; Halogen Network; Music Choice; NickToons TV; Outdoor Channel; Science Television; Trinity Broadcasting Network; Versus; WE tv.
Fee: $52.40 monthly.
Digital Pay Service 1
Pay Units: N.A.
Programming (via satellite): Cinemax (multiplexed); Encore (multiplexed); HBO (multiplexed); Showtime (multiplexed); Starz (multiplexed); The Movie Channel (multiplexed).
Fee: $11.95 monthly (each).
Video-On-Demand: No
Pay-Per-View
HITS PPV 1-14 (delivered digitally); Fresh (delivered digitally); Playboy TV (delivered digitally).
Internet Service
Operational: Yes.
Broadband Service: RoadRunner.
Fee: $24.95 monthly.
Telephone Service
Digital: Operational
Fee: $24.99 monthly
Miles of Plant: 101.0 (coaxial); None (fiber optic).
President: Rhonda Fraas. Vice President & General Manager: David Kreiman. Vice President, Engineering: Randy Hall. Vice President, Marketing: Mark Psigoda. Vice President, Government & Public Affairs: Mary Jo Green. Technical Operations Director: Jim Cavender. Government Affairs Director: Steve Cuckler.
Ownership: Time Warner Cable (MSO).

CONCORD TWP. (Lake County)—Time Warner Cable. Now served by CLEVELAND HEIGHTS, OH [OH0006]. ICA: OH0042.

CONGRESS TWP.—Time Warner Cable, 530 S Main St, Ste 1751, Akron, OH 44311-1090. Phone: 330-633-9203. Fax: 330-633-7970. Web Site: http://www.timewarnercable.com/northeastohio. ICA: OH0305.
TV Market Ranking: 8 (CONGRESS TWP.). Franchise award date: November 1, 1983. Franchise expiration date: N.A. Began: July 1, 1984.
Channel capacity: 35 (not 2-way capable). Channels available but not in use: N.A.
Basic Service
Subscribers: N.A. Included in Mansfield
Programming (received off-air): WEWS-TV (ABC) Cleveland; WJW (FOX) Cleveland; WKYC (NBC) Cleveland; WOIO (CBS) Shaker Heights; WQHS-DT (UNV) Cleveland; WRLM (IND) Canton; WUAB (MNT) Lorain; WVPX-TV (ION) Akron.
Programming (via satellite): TBS Superstation; Turner Network TV.
Fee: $44.95 installation; $18.45 monthly; $2.50 converter.
Pay Service 1
Pay Units: 15.
Programming (via satellite): The Movie Channel.
Fee: $10.50 monthly.
Internet Service
Operational: Yes.
Broadband Service: RoadRunner.
Fee: $24.95 monthly.
Telephone Service
Digital: Operational
Fee: $24.99 monthly
Miles of Plant: 1.0 (coaxial); None (fiber optic).
President: Stephen Fry. Area Vice President: Scott Miller. Vice President, Engineering: Al Costanzi. Vice President, Marketing: Patrick Burke. Vice President, Sales: Woody Woodward. Vice President, Public Affairs: William Jasso. Area Manager: Carol Jagger. Government & Media Relations Director: Chris Thomas.
Ownership: Time Warner Cable (MSO).

CONVOY—Comcast Cable, 720 Taylor St, Fort Wayne, IN 46802-5144. Phones: 317-275-6370 (Indianapolis office); 260-458-5103. Fax: 260-458-5138. Web Site: http://www.comcast.com. ICA: OH0444.
TV Market Ranking: 82 (CONVOY).
Channel capacity: N.A. Channels available but not in use: N.A.
Basic Service
Subscribers: N.A. Included in Indianapolis
Programming (received off-air): W07CL Auburn; WANE-TV (CBS) Fort Wayne; WFFT-TV (IND) Fort Wayne; WFWA (PBS) Fort Wayne; WINM (IND) Angola; WISE-TV (FOX, MNT, NBC) Fort Wayne; WPTA (ABC, CW) Fort Wayne.
Programming (via satellite): ABC Family Channel; CityTV; C-SPAN; CW+; QVC; Radar Channel; WGN America.
Fee: $32.48 monthly.
Expanded Basic Service 1
Subscribers: N.A.
Programming (via satellite): A&E Networks; AMC; Animal Planet; BET Networks; Cartoon Network; CNBC; CNN; Comcast SportsNet Chicago; Comedy Central; Country Music TV; Discovery Channel; Disney Channel; E! Entertainment Television; ESPN; ESPN 2; Food Network; Fox News Channel; FX; Golf Channel; Great American Country; Headline News; HGTV; History Channel; Lifetime; MSNBC; MTV; Nickelodeon; Speed; Spike TV; Style Network; Syfy; TBS Superstation; The Learning Channel; The Weather Channel; Travel Channel; truTV; Turner Classic Movies; Turner Network TV; TV Land; Univision Studios; USA Network; Versus; VH1.
Digital Basic Service
Subscribers: N.A.
Programming (via satellite): A&E HD; ABC Family HD; Animal Planet HD; BBC America; Bio; Cine Latino; Cine Mexicano; CMT Pure Country; CNN en Espanol; CNN HD; College Sports Television; Cooking Channel; C-SPAN 2; C-SPAN 3; Current; Discovery Channel HD; Discovery en Espanol; Discovery Home Channel; Discovery Kids Channel; Disney Channel HD; DIY Network; Encore (multiplexed); ESPN 2 HD; ESPN Classic Sports; ESPN Deportes; ESPN HD; ESPNews; Eternal Word TV Network; Exercise TV; FEARnet; Flix; Food Network HD; Fox Business Channel; Fox Deportes; Fox Reality Channel; Fox Soccer; G4; GalaVision; GolTV; GSN; Hallmark Channel; Halogen Network; HD Theater; Headline News; HGTV HD; History Channel en Espanol; History Channel HD; History Channel International; ID Investigation Discovery; Lifetime Movie Network; LOGO; Military Channel; MoviePlex; MTV Jams; MTV2; mun2 television; National Geographic Channel; National Geographic Channel HD Network;

NBA TV; NFL Network; NFL Network HD; NHL Network; Nick Jr.; Nick Too; NickToons TV; Oxygen; Palladia; PBS Kids Sprout; Qubo; Science; Science HD; SoapNet; Sundance Channel; Syfy HD; TBS in HD; TeenNick; Telefutura; Tennis Channel; The Word Network; Toon Disney; Tr3s; Turner Network TV HD; TV One; TVG Network; Universal HD; USA Network HD; VeneMovies; Versus HD; VH1 Classic; VH1 Soul; Weatherscan.

Digital Pay Service 1
Pay Units: N.A.
Programming (via satellite): Cinemax (multiplexed); Cinemax HD; HBO (multiplexed); HBO HD; Playboy TV; Showtime (multiplexed); Showtime HD; Starz (multiplexed); Starz HDTV; The Movie Channel (multiplexed).

Pay-Per-View
iN DEMAND (delivered digitally); Playboy TV (delivered digitally); NBA League Pass (delivered digitally); NHL Center Ice (delivered digitally); MLB Extra Innings (delivered digitally); Fresh (delivered digitally); Shorteez (delivered digitally); Spice: Xcess (delivered digitally).

Internet Service
Operational: Yes.
Broadband Service: Comcast High Speed Internet.

Telephone Service
None

Miles of plant included in Fort Wayne

Regional Vice President: Scott Tenney. Vice President, Marketing: Aaron Geisel. Vice President, Communications: Mark Apple. Technical Operations Director: Bennie Logan. Engineering Manager: Tom Stuckholz. Marketing Manager: Marci Hefley.

Ownership: Comcast Cable Communications Inc. (MSO).

CORNING—Zito Media, 611 Vader Hill Rd, Coudersport, PA 16915. Phone: 814-260-9575. Web Site: http://www.zitomedia.com. Also serves Coal Twp. (Perry County), Hemlock, Hocking County, Monroe Twp. (Perry County), Moxahala, New Lexington (Perry County), New Straitsville, Oakfield, Pleasant Twp. (Perry County), Rendville, Salt Lick Twp. & Shawnee. ICA: OH0193.

TV Market Ranking: 27 (Hocking County (portions)); Below 100 (Coal Twp. (Perry County), CORNING, Hemlock, Monroe Twp. (Perry County), Moxahala, New Lexington (Perry County), New Straitsville, Oakfield, Pleasant Twp. (Perry County), Rendville, Salt Lick Twp., Shawnee, Hocking County (portions)); Outside TV Markets (Hocking County (portions)). Franchise award date: N.A. Franchise expiration date: N.A. Began: November 1, 1975.

Channel capacity: 37 (not 2-way capable). Channels available but not in use: N.A.

Basic Service
Subscribers: 368.
Programming (received off-air): WBNS-TV (CBS) Columbus; WCMH-TV (NBC) Columbus; WHIZ-TV (NBC) Zanesville; WOSU-TV (PBS) Columbus; WOUB-TV (PBS) Athens; WSFJ-TV (TBN) Newark; WSYX (ABC, MNT) Columbus; WTTE (FOX) Columbus.
Programming (via satellite): C-SPAN; C-SPAN 2; INSP; The Weather Channel; Trinity Broadcasting Network; WGN America.
Fee: $29.95 installation; $19.95 monthly; $1.24 converter.

Expanded Basic Service 1
Subscribers: N.A.
Programming (via satellite): A&E Networks; ABC Family Channel; AMC; Animal Planet; Cartoon Network; CNN; Comedy Central; Discovery Channel; Disney Channel; DIY Network; E! Entertainment Television; ESPN; ESPN 2; Food Network; Fox News Channel; Fox Sports Net Ohio; FX; Great American Country; GSN; Hallmark Channel; Headline News; HGTV; History Channel; Lifetime; Lifetime Movie Network; MSNBC; MTV; Nickelodeon; ShopNBC; Speed; Spike TV; Syfy; TBS Superstation; The Learning Channel; Turner Network TV; TV Land; USA Network; VH1.
Fee: $22.00 monthly.

Pay Service 1
Pay Units: 138.
Fee: $17.50 installation; $3.99 monthly (Encore), $7.95 monthly (Cinemax), $11.95 monthly (HBO, Showtime or TMC).

Video-On-Demand: No

Pay-Per-View
iN DEMAND (delivered digitally); Playboy TV (delivered digitally); Fresh (delivered digitally).

Internet Service
Operational: No.

Telephone Service
None

Miles of Plant: 46.0 (coaxial); None (fiber optic).

Public Relations Manager: Mark Laver.

Ownership: Zito Media (MSO).

COSHOCTON—Formerly served by Time Warner Cable. No longer in operation. ICA: OH0083.

CRAIG BEACH—Time Warner Cable, 530 S Main St, Ste 1751, Akron, OH 44311-1090. Phone: 330-633-9203. Fax: 330-633-7970. Web Site: http://www.timewarnercable.com/northeastohio. Also serves Milton Twp. (Mahoning County) & Palmyra Twp. (portions). ICA: OH0231.

TV Market Ranking: 79 (Palmyra Twp. (portions)); 8,79 (CRAIG BEACH, Milton Twp. (Mahoning County)). Franchise award date: March 9, 1981. Franchise expiration date: July 22, 2014. Began: July 1, 1987.

Channel capacity: N.A. Channels available but not in use: N.A.

Basic Service
Subscribers: N.A. Included in Warren
Programming (received off-air): WFMJ-TV (CW, NBC) Youngstown; WJW (FOX) Cleveland; WKBN-TV (CBS) Youngstown; WKYC (NBC) Cleveland; WNEO (PBS) Alliance; WOIO (CBS) Shaker Heights; WUAB (MNT) Lorain; WYTV (ABC, MNT) Youngstown.
Programming (via satellite): TV Guide Network; WGN America.
Fee: $19.95 installation; $19.54 monthly; $1.50 converter.

Expanded Basic Service 1
Subscribers: 910.
Programming (via satellite): A&E Networks; ABC Family Channel; AMC; Animal Planet; BET Networks; Bravo; Cartoon Network; CNBC; CNN; Comedy Central; C-SPAN; C-SPAN 2; Discovery Channel; Disney Channel; E! Entertainment Television; ESPN; ESPN 2; ESPN Classic Sports; Food Network; Fox News Channel; Fox Sports Net Ohio; FX; Golf Channel; Great American Country; Headline News; HGTV; History Channel; ION Television; Lifetime; MSNBC; MTV; Nickelodeon; Oxygen; QVC; SoapNet; Spike TV; Syfy; TBS Superstation; The Learning Channel; The Weather Channel; Travel Channel; truTV; Turner Classic Movies; Turner Network TV; TV Land; USA Network; VH1; WE tv.
Fee: $35.45 monthly.

Digital Basic Service
Subscribers: N.A.
Programming (via satellite): AmericanLife TV Network; America's Store; BBC America; Bloomberg Television; Cooking Channel; Country Music TV; C-SPAN 3; Discovery Fit & Health; DIY Network; DMX Music; ESPNews; Fox Sports World; G4; GSN; Lifetime Movie Network; MTV2; MuchMusic Network; National Geographic Channel; Nick Jr.; Ohio News Network; Outdoor Channel; Ovation; Speed; Style Network; Toon Disney; Versus; VH1 Classic.
Fee: $13.00 monthly.

Digital Pay Service 1
Pay Units: N.A.
Programming (via satellite): Cinemax (multiplexed); HBO (multiplexed); Showtime (multiplexed); Starz (multiplexed); The Movie Channel (multiplexed).
Fee: $12.00 monthly (HBO, Cinemax, Starz or Showtime/TMC).

Video-On-Demand: Yes

Pay-Per-View
Sports PPV (delivered digitally).

Internet Service
Operational: Yes.
Broadband Service: EarthLink, Road Runner.
Fee: $99.00 installation; $44.95 monthly.

Telephone Service
Digital: Operational
Fee: $44.95 monthly

Miles of Plant: 44.0 (coaxial); None (fiber optic). Additional miles planned: 3.0 (coaxial).

President: Stephen Fry. Area Vice President: Rick Whaley. Vice President, Engineering: Al Costanzi. Vice President, Marketing: Patrick Burke. Vice President, Sales: Woody Woodward. Vice President, Public Affairs: William Jasso. Area Manager: Daryl Morrison. Government & Media Relations Director: Chris Thomas.

Ownership: Time Warner Cable (MSO).

CRIDERSVILLE—Time Warner Cable. Now served by LIMA, OH [OH0020]. ICA: OH0120.

CROOKSVILLE—Time Warner Cable. Now served by ZANESVILLE, OH [OH0037]. ICA: OH0153.

CROWN CITY—Windjammer Cable, 4400 PGA Blvd, Ste 902, Palm Beach Gardens, FL 33410. Phones: 877-450-5558; 561-775-1208. Fax: 561-775-7811. Web Site: http://www.windjammercable.com. Also serves Athalia, Clay Twp. & Gallia County (unincorporated areas). ICA: OH0260.

TV Market Ranking: 36 (Clay Twp., CROWN CITY, Gallia County (unincorporated areas) (portions)); Below 100 (Gallia County (unincorporated areas) (portions)); Outside TV Markets (Athalia, Gallia County (unincorporated areas) (portions)). Franchise award date: N.A. Franchise expiration date: N.A. Began: January 1, 1983.

Channel capacity: 32 (not 2-way capable). Channels available but not in use: N.A.

Basic Service
Subscribers: 208.
Programming (received off-air): WCHS-TV (ABC) Charleston; WOWK-TV (CBS) Huntington; WPBY-TV (PBS) Huntington; WSAZ-TV (MNT, NBC) Huntington; WVAH-TV (FOX) Charleston.
Programming (via satellite): A&E Networks; ABC Family Channel; AMC; CNN; Country Music TV; Discovery Channel; Disney Channel; E! Entertainment Television; ESPN; ESPN 2; Headline News; Lifetime; Nickelodeon; QVC; Spike TV; Syfy; TBS Superstation; The Learning Channel; The Weather Channel; Turner Network TV; USA Network; WGN America.
Fee: $29.95 installation; $43.23 monthly.

Digital Basic Service
Subscribers: N.A.
Programming (via satellite): BBC America; Bravo; Discovery Health Channel; Discovery Kids Channel; ESPN Classic Sports; ESPNews; Fox Soccer; Golf Channel; GSN; HGTV; History Channel; Independent Film Channel; Nick Jr.; Science; Versus; WE tv.
Fee: $11.45 monthly.

Digital Pay Service 1
Pay Units: N.A.
Programming (via satellite): Cinemax (multiplexed); Encore (multiplexed); HBO (multiplexed); Showtime (multiplexed); Starz (multiplexed); The Movie Channel (multiplexed).
Fee: $16.95 monthly (each).

Video-On-Demand: No

Pay-Per-View
iN DEMAND (delivered digitally); Playboy TV (delivered digitally); Fresh (delivered digitally).

Internet Service
Operational: No.

Telephone Service
None

Miles of Plant: 18.0 (coaxial); None (fiber optic).

General Manager: Timothy Evard. Operations Director: Belinda Graham. Engineering Director: Mike Earehart. Finance & Accounting Director: Cindy Johnson.

Ownership: Windjammer Communications LLC (MSO).

CRYSTAL LAKE MOBILE HOME PARK—Time Warner Cable. Now served by COLUMBUS, OH [OH0002]. ICA: OH0435.

CUMBERLAND—Formerly served by Almega Cable. No longer in operation. ICA: OH0294.

DAYTON—Time Warner Cable, 11252 Cornell Park Dr, Cincinnati, OH 45242. Phones: 513-489-5000; 937-294-6800. Fax: 513-489-5991. Web Site: http://www.timewarnercable.com/Dayton. Also serves College Corner, Harrisville & Union City, IN; Adams Twp., Adams Twp. (Darke County), Allen Twp. (Darke County), Anna, Ansonia, Arcanum, Beavercreek, Bellbrook, Botkins, Bradford, Brookville, Brown Twp. (Darke County), Burketsville, Camden, Casstown, Castine, Catawba (village), Cedarville, Centerville, Champaign County (portions), Christiansburg, Clay Twp. (Montgomery County), Clayton, Clifton (village), Corwin (village), De Graff, Dinsmore Twp., Donnelsville, Eaton, Eldorado, Elizabeth Twp. (Miami County), Englewood, Enon, Fairborn, Farmersville, Fletcher, German Twp., German Twp. (Montgomery County), Germantown, Gettysburg, Gordon, Gratis, Green Meadows, Green Twp. (Clark County), Greenville, Harmony Twp., Hillgrove, Hollansburg, Huber Heights, Ithaca, Jackson Center, Jamestown (village), Kettering, Lawrenceville, Lewisburg, Liberty Twp., Liberty Twp. (Darke County), Lockington (village), Logan County (portions), Lostcreek Twp., Mad River Twp. (Clark County), Maplewood, Mechanicsburg, Miamisburg, Moorefield Twp., Moraine, Mutual, Naeve Twp. (Darke County), New Carlisle, New Jasper Twp., New Lebanon, New Madison, New Paris, New Weston, Newberry Twp., Newton Twp., North Hampton, Oakwood, Oxford, Palestine, Phillipsburg, Pike

Twp., Pitsburg, Pleasant Twp., Port Jefferson, Quincy, Riverside, Rosewood (village), Rossburg, Sidney, Silvercreek Twp., South Charleston, South Solon, South Vienna, South Vinemont, Spring Valley, Springboro, Springcreek Twp., Springfield, Springfield Twp., St. Paris, Staunton Twp., Stokes Twp., Tipp City, Tremont City, Trotwood, Troy, Union, Union City, Urbana, Vandalia, Verona, Washington Twp. (Darke County), Washington Twp. (Montgomery County), Washington Twp. (Shelby County), Wayne Lakes (village), Waynesville, West Alexandria, West Carrollton, West Elkton, West Liberty, West Manchester, West Milton Twp., Wilberforce, Woodstock, Wright-Patterson, Xenia & Yellow Springs, OH. ICA: OH0011.

TV Market Ranking: 17 (College Corner, Oxford); 27 (Catawba (village), Champaign County (portions), Harmony Twp., Pleasant Twp., South Solon, South Vienna, Springfield Twp., Woodstock); 41 (Adams Twp. (Darke County), Allen Twp. (Darke County), Arcanum, Beavercreek, Bellbrook, Bradford, Brookville, Camden, Casstown, Castine, Cedarville, Centerville, Clay Twp. (Montgomery County), Clayton, Clifton (village), Corwin (village), DAYTON, Donnelsville, Eaton, Eldorado, Elizabeth Twp. (Miami County), Englewood, Enon, Fairborn, Farmersville, Fletcher, German Twp., German Twp. (Montgomery County), Germantown, Gettysburg, Gordon, Gratis, Green Meadows, Green Twp. (Clark County), Greenville, Huber Heights, Ithaca, Jamestown (village), Kettering, Lawrenceville, Lewisburg, Liberty Twp. (Darke County), Lostcreek Twp., Mad River Twp. (Clark County), Mechanicsburg, Miamisburg, Moorefield Twp., Moraine, Mutual, Naeve Twp. (Darke County), New Carlisle, New Jasper Twp., New Lebanon, New Madison, New Paris, Newberry Twp., Newton Twp., North Hampton, Oakwood, Palestine, Phillipsburg, Pike Twp., Pitsburg, Riverside, Rosewood (village), Silvercreek Twp., South Charleston, Spring Valley, Springboro, Springcreek Twp., Springfield, St. Paris, Staunton Twp., Stokes Twp., Tipp City, Tremont City, Trotwood, Troy, Union, Urbana, Vandalia, Verona, Verona, Washington Twp. (Darke County), Washington Twp. (Montgomery County), Wayne Lakes (village), Waynesville, West Alexandria, West Carrollton, West Elkton, West Manchester, West Milton Twp., Wilberforce, Wright-Patterson, Xenia, Yellow Springs); Below 100 (Adams Twp., Anna, Ansonia, Botkins, Brown Twp. (Darke County), Burketsville, Burketsville, Christiansburg, De Graff, Dinsmore Twp., Harrisville, Hillgrove, Hollansburg, Jackson Center, Liberty Twp. (Logan County), Lockington (village), Logan County (portions), Maplewood, Port Jefferson, Quincy, Rossburg, Sidney, Union City, Union City, Washington Twp. (Shelby County), West Liberty, Champaign County (portions)); Outside TV Markets (New Weston). Franchise award date: N.A. Franchise expiration date: August 31, 2006. Began: September 24, 1976.

Channel capacity: 75 (operating 2-way). Channels available but not in use: N.A.

Basic Service

Subscribers: 29,000 Includes Williamsburg IN.

Programming (received off-air): WBDT (CW) Springfield; WDTN (NBC) Dayton; WHIO-TV (CBS) Dayton; WKEF (ABC) Dayton; WKOI-TV (TBN) Richmond; WPTD (PBS) Dayton; WPTO (PBS) Oxford; WRGT-TV (FOX, MNT) Dayton; WXIX-TV (FOX) Newport; 18 FMs.

Programming (via satellite): Eternal Word TV Network; QVC; ShopNBC; WGN America.

Fee: $28.95 installation; $9.14 monthly; $3.45 converter; $31.81 additional installation.

Expanded Basic Service 1

Subscribers: N.A.

Programming (via satellite): A&E Networks; ABC Family Channel; AMC; Animal Planet; BET Networks; Bravo; Cartoon Network; CNBC; CNN; Comedy Central; Country Music TV; C-SPAN; C-SPAN 2; Discovery Channel; Disney Channel; E! Entertainment Television; ESPN; ESPN 2; ESPN Classic Sports; Food Network; Fox News Channel; Fox Sports Net Ohio; FX; Golf Channel; Hallmark Channel; Headline News; HGTV; History Channel; Lifetime; Lifetime Movie Network; MSNBC; MTV; National Geographic Channel; Nickelodeon; Oxygen; Spike TV; Style Network; Syfy; TBS Superstation; The Learning Channel; The Weather Channel; Travel Channel; truTV; Turner Classic Movies; Turner Network TV; TV Guide Network; TV Land; USA Network; Versus; VH1; WE tv.

Fee: $45.99 monthly.

Digital Basic Service

Subscribers: 120,000.

Programming (via satellite): AmericanLife TV Network; America's Store; BBC America; Bio; Bloomberg Television; Boomerang; Canales N; CBS Sports Network; CNN International; Cooking Channel; C-SPAN 3; Discovery Fit & Health; DIY Network; DMX Music; ESPNews; Fox Movie Channel; Fox Sports World; FSN Digital Atlantic; FSN Digital Central; FSN Digital Pacific; Fuel TV; Fuse; G4; GAS; Great American Country; GSN; History Channel; Independent Film Channel; Lifetime Real Women; MTV Hits; MTV2; NBA TV; Nick Jr.; Ohio News Network; Outdoor Channel; SoapNet; Sorpresa; Speed; Sundance Channel; Tennis Channel; Toon Disney; TV Asia; TV One; VH1 Classic; Zee TV USA.

Fee: $9.90 monthly.

Digital Expanded Basic Service

Subscribers: N.A.

Programming (via satellite): Encore Action.

Fee: $7.95 monthly.

Digital Pay Service 1

Pay Units: 45,600.

Programming (via satellite): Cinemax (multiplexed); Flix; HBO (multiplexed); Showtime (multiplexed); Starz (multiplexed); The Movie Channel (multiplexed).

Fee: $20.00 installation; $10.95 monthly (Cinemax, HBO, Showtime, Starz or Flix & TMC).

Video-On-Demand: Yes

Pay-Per-View

Addressable homes: 13,800.

iN DEMAND (delivered digitally); Fresh (delivered digitally); Sports PPV (delivered digitally).

Internet Service

Operational: Yes.

Subscribers: 105,000.

Broadband Service: AOL for Broadband, BigSpeed, EarthLink, Road Runner, WCOIL Express.

Fee: $69.95 installation; $44.95 monthly.

Telephone Service

Digital: Operational

Fee: $44.95 monthly

Miles of Plant: 6,133.0 (coaxial); 652.0 (fiber optic). Miles of plant (coax & fiber) include Williamsburg IN

President: Kevin G. Kidd. Vice President, Operations: Mark Dunford. Vice President, Marketing: Rob Fordham. Vice President, Public & Government Affairs: Pamela McDonald. Public Affairs Director: Karen Baxter.

Ownership: Time Warner Cable (MSO).

DEFIANCE—Time Warner Cable, 310 Jefferson Ave, Defiance, OH 43512. Phones: 614-481-5000; 419-784-1992. Fax: 419-782-2640. Web Site: http://www.timewarnercable.com. Also serves Brunersburg, Defiance County (portions), Dover Twp. (Fulton County), Florida, Liberty Center, Liberty Twp. (Henry County), Ney, Pettisville & Richland Twp. (Defiance County). ICA: OH0047.

TV Market Ranking: 52 (Dover Twp. (Fulton County), Liberty Center, Liberty Twp. (Henry County), Pettisville); 82 (Defiance County (portions) (portions)); Below 100 (Ney, Defiance County (portions) (portions)); Outside TV Markets (Brunersburg, DEFIANCE, Florida, Richland Twp. (Defiance County), Defiance County (portions) (portions)). Franchise award date: May 1, 1964. Franchise expiration date: N.A. Began: May 1, 1964.

Channel capacity: N.A. Channels available but not in use: N.A.

Basic Service

Subscribers: 7,015.

Programming (received off-air): WBGU-TV (PBS) Bowling Green; WGTE-TV (PBS) Toledo; WLIO (CW, NBC) Lima; WNWO-TV (NBC) Toledo; WPTA (ABC, CW) Fort Wayne; WTOL (CBS) Toledo; WTVG (ABC) Toledo; WUPW (FOX) Toledo; 17 FMs.

Programming (via satellite): C-SPAN; QVC; truTV; TV5 USA; WGN America.

Fee: $45.35 installation; $14.95 monthly; $28.33 additional installation.

Expanded Basic Service 1

Subscribers: N.A.

Programming (received off-air): WDFM-LP (IND) Defiance.

Programming (via satellite): A&E Networks; ABC Family Channel; Animal Planet; BET Networks; CNBC; CNN; Comedy Central; Disney Channel; E! Entertainment Television; ESPN; ESPN 2; Fox Sports Net; Fox Sports Net Ohio; FX; Golf Channel; Headline News; HGTV; History Channel; Lifetime; MSNBC; MTV; Nickelodeon; Outdoor Channel; Syfy; TBS Superstation; The Learning Channel; The Weather Channel; Travel Channel; TV Guide Network; USA Network.

Fee: $16.30 monthly.

Expanded Basic Service 2

Subscribers: N.A.

Programming (via satellite): Turner Network TV.

Fee: $2.00 monthly.

Digital Basic Service

Subscribers: 1,851.

Programming (via satellite): AmericanLife TV Network; BBC America; Bloomberg Television; Discovery Fit & Health; ESPN Classic Sports; ESPNews; Fox Sports World; G4; GSN; Independent Film Channel; INSP; National Geographic Channel; Nick Jr.; Outdoor Channel; Speed; Trinity Broadcasting Network; VH1 Classic; VH1 Country; WE tv.

Fee: $11.95 monthly.

Digital Expanded Basic Service

Subscribers: N.A.

Programming (via satellite): Canales N.

Fee: $6.95 monthly.

Pay Service 1

Pay Units: 736.

Programming (via satellite): HBO.

Fee: $15.49 monthly.

Digital Pay Service 1

Pay Units: N.A.

Programming (via satellite): Cinemax (multiplexed); Encore (multiplexed); HBO (multiplexed); Showtime (multiplexed); Starz (multiplexed); The Movie Channel (multiplexed).

Fee: $17.95 monthly (each).

Video-On-Demand: No

Pay-Per-View

Addressable homes: 1,762.

iN DEMAND (delivered digitally).

Internet Service

Operational: Yes.

Subscribers: 972.

Broadband Service: Road Runner.

Fee: $42.95 monthly.

Telephone Service

None

Miles of Plant: 169.0 (coaxial); None (fiber optic). Additional miles planned: 3.0 (coaxial).

President: Rhonda Fraas. Area Manager: Brad Wakely. Manager: John Ellingson. Customer Service Manager: Cindy Sierra.

Ownership: Time Warner Cable (MSO).

DELHI TWP.—Formerly served by Adelphia Communications. No longer in operation. ICA: OH0053.

DELLROY—Now served by NEW PHILADELPHIA, OH [OH0030]. ICA: OH0238.

DELPHOS—Time Warner Cable, 205 Crystal Ave, Findlay, OH 45840. Phones: 614-481-5000 (Columbus office); 419-429-7474. Fax: 419-429-7402. Web Site: http://www.timewarnercable.com/midohio. ICA: OH0143.

TV Market Ranking: Below 100 (DELPHOS). Franchise award date: N.A. Franchise expiration date: October 26, 2010. Began: January 1, 1968.

Channel capacity: N.A. Channels available but not in use: N.A.

Basic Service

Subscribers: 2,480.

Programming (received off-air): WANE-TV (CBS) Fort Wayne; WBGU-TV (PBS) Bowling Green; WFFT-TV (IND) Fort Wayne; WFWA (PBS) Fort Wayne; WHIO-TV (CBS) Dayton; WLIO (CW, NBC) Lima; WLQP-LP Lima; WOHL-CD (FOX) Lima; WPTA (ABC, CW) Fort Wayne; WTLW (IND) Lima; allband FM.

Programming (via satellite): Discovery Channel; TBS Superstation; WGN America.

Fee: $45.86 installation; $10.12 monthly.

Expanded Basic Service 1

Subscribers: N.A.

Programming (via satellite): A&E Networks; ABC Family Channel; AMC; Animal Planet; Bravo; Cartoon Network; CNBC;

CNN; Comedy Central; Country Music TV; C-SPAN; Disney Channel; E! Entertainment Television; ESPN; ESPN 2; ESPN Classic Sports; Eternal Word TV Network; Food Network; Fox News Channel; Fox Sports Net Ohio; FX; Golf Channel; Hallmark Channel; Headline News; HGTV; History Channel; Lifetime; Lifetime Movie Network; MSNBC; MTV; National Geographic Channel; Nickelodeon; Oxygen; QVC; ShopNBC; Spike TV; Syfy; The Learning Channel; The Weather Channel; Travel Channel; truTV; Turner Classic Movies; Turner Network TV; TV Guide Network; TV Land; USA Network; Versus; VH1; WE tv.
Fee: $30.83 monthly.

Digital Basic Service
Subscribers: 744.
Programming (via satellite): AmericanLife TV Network; America's Store; BBC America; Bloomberg Television; CNN International; Cooking Channel; C-SPAN 3; Discovery Fit & Health; DIY Network; DMX Music; ESPNews; Fox Sports World; FSN Digital Atlantic; FSN Digital Central; FSN Digital Pacific; Fuse; G4; GAS; Great American Country; GSN; Lifetime Real Women; MTV2; Nick Jr.; Ohio News Network; Outdoor Channel; Ovation; SoapNet; Sorpresa; Speed; Style Network; Toon Disney; VH1 Classic.
Fee: $9.90 monthly.

Digital Pay Service 1
Pay Units: 615.
Programming (via satellite): Cinemax (multiplexed); Encore (multiplexed); Flix; HBO (multiplexed); Showtime (multiplexed); Starz (multiplexed); The Movie Channel (multiplexed).
Fee: $11.95 monthly (Cinemax, HBO, Showtime/Flix/TMC or Starz/Encore).

Video-On-Demand: Yes

Pay-Per-View
Addressable homes: 744.
iN DEMAND (delivered digitally); Fresh (delivered digitally); Sports PPV (delivered digitally).

Internet Service
Operational: Yes.
Subscribers: 446.
Broadband Service: Road Runner.
Fee: $69.95 installation; $44.95 monthly.

Telephone Service
Digital: Operational
Fee: $44.95 monthly

Miles of Plant: 55.0 (coaxial); None (fiber optic).
President: Rhonda Fraas. Vice President, Engineering: Randy Hall. Vice President, Marketing: Mark Psigoda. Technical Operations Director: John Ellingson. Government Affairs Director: Brian Young. Government Affairs Manager: Patrick McCauley.
Ownership: Time Warner Cable (MSO).

DENMARK TWP.—Zito Media, 611 Vader Hill Rd, Coudersport, PA 16915. Phone: 814-260-9575. Web Site: http://www.zitomedia.com. Also serves Ashtabula County (eastern portion), Dorset Twp., Jefferson Twp. (Ashtabula County), Monroe Twp. (Ashtabula County), Pierpont Twp., Plymouth Twp. (Ashtabula County) & Sheffield Twp. (Ashtabula County). ICA: OH0228.
TV Market Ranking: 79 (Ashtabula County (eastern portion) (portions)); Below 100 (Monroe Twp. (Ashtabula County), Ashtabula County (eastern portion) (portions)); Outside TV Markets (DENMARK TWP., Dorset Twp., Jefferson Twp. (Ashtabula County), Pierpont Twp., Plymouth Twp. (Ashtabula County), Sheffield Twp. (Ashtabula County), Ashtabula County (eastern portion) (portions)). Franchise award date: N.A. Franchise expiration date: N.A. Began: January 24, 1992.
Channel capacity: 36 (not 2-way capable). Channels available but not in use: N.A.

Basic Service
Subscribers: 271.
Programming (received off-air): WEWS-TV (ABC) Cleveland; WICU-TV (NBC) Erie; WJET-TV (ABC) Erie; WJW (FOX) Cleveland; WKYC (NBC) Cleveland; WOIO (CBS) Shaker Heights; WQLN (PBS) Erie; WSEE-TV (CBS, CW) Erie; WUAB (MNT) Lorain.
Programming (via satellite): A&E Networks; ABC Family Channel; AMC; CNN; Discovery Channel; Disney Channel; ESPN; Fox Sports Net Ohio; Nickelodeon; QVC; Spike TV; TBS Superstation; The Weather Channel; Turner Classic Movies; Turner Network TV; USA Network; VH1.
Fee: $29.95 installation; $19.95 monthly; $3.00 converter.

Pay Service 1
Pay Units: 53.
Programming (via satellite): Cinemax.
Fee: $11.00 monthly.

Pay Service 2
Pay Units: 96.
Programming (via satellite): HBO.
Fee: $11.50 monthly.

Pay Service 3
Pay Units: 79.
Programming (via satellite): Showtime; The Movie Channel.
Fee: $12.95 monthly.

Video-On-Demand: No

Internet Service
Operational: No.

Telephone Service
None

Miles of Plant: 53.0 (coaxial); None (fiber optic). Additional miles planned: 15.0 (coaxial).
Public Relations Manager: Mark Laver.
Ownership: Zito Media (MSO).

DESHLER—Time Warner Cable, 205 Crystal Ave, Findlay, OH 45840. Phone: 614-481-5000 (Columbus office). Fax: 419-429-7402. Web Site: http://www.timewarnercable.com/midohio. Also serves Bartlow Twp., Hamler, Holgate & Pleasant Twp. (Henry County). ICA: OH0191.
TV Market Ranking: Below 100 (Bartlow Twp., DESHLER, Hamler, Holgate, Pleasant Twp. (Henry County)). Franchise award date: N.A. Franchise expiration date: N.A. Began: June 1, 1983.
Channel capacity: N.A. Channels available but not in use: N.A.

Basic Service
Subscribers: 712.
Programming (received off-air): WBGU-TV (PBS) Bowling Green; WDFM-LP (IND) Defiance; WFFT-TV (IND) Fort Wayne; WGTE-TV (PBS) Toledo; WKBD-TV (CW) Detroit; WLIO (CW, NBC) Lima; WLMB (IND) Toledo; WMNT-CA (MNT) Toledo; WNWO-TV (NBC) Toledo; WTOL (CBS) Toledo; WTVG (ABC) Toledo; WUPW (FOX) Toledo.
Programming (via satellite): ABC Family Channel; QVC; TV Guide Network; WGN America.
Fee: $42.50 installation; $15.00 monthly.

Expanded Basic Service 1
Subscribers: N.A.
Programming (via satellite): A&E Networks; AMC; Animal Planet; BET Networks; Bravo; Cartoon Network; CNBC; CNN; Country Music TV; C-SPAN; C-SPAN 2; Discovery Channel; Disney Channel; E! Entertainment Television; ESPN; ESPN 2; Eternal Word TV Network; Food Network; Fox News Channel; Fox Sports Net Detroit; Fox Sports Net Ohio; FX; Golf Channel; Great American Country; Hallmark Channel; Headline News; HGTV; History Channel; Lifetime; MSNBC; MTV; Nickelodeon; Ohio News Network; Oxygen; Product Information Network; ShopNBC; Spike TV; Syfy; TBS Superstation; The Learning Channel; The Weather Channel; Travel Channel; Trinity Broadcasting Network; truTV; Turner Network TV; TV Land; Univision Studios; USA Network; Versus; VH1.
Fee: $22.95 monthly.

Digital Basic Service
Subscribers: 150.
Programming (via satellite): AmericanLife TV Network; BBC America; Bio; Black Family Channel; Bloomberg Television; Discovery Fit & Health; DIY Network; ESPN Classic Sports; ESPNews; Fox Sports World; G4; GAS; GSN; History Channel International; Independent Film Channel; INSP; MTV Networks Digital Suite; MuchMusic Network; Music Choice; National Geographic Channel; Nick Jr.; Nick Too; Outdoor Channel; SoapNet; Speed; Style Network; Sundance Channel; Toon Disney; Turner Classic Movies; WE tv.
Fee: $11.95 monthly.

Digital Expanded Basic Service
Subscribers: N.A.
Programming (via satellite): ART America; Canales N; CCTV-4; Filipino Channel; Fox Deportes; RAI International; Rio de la Plata; Russian Television Network; Telemundo; TV Asia; TV Japan; TV5, La Television International.
Fee: $6.95 monthly.

Digital Pay Service 1
Pay Units: N.A.
Programming (via satellite): Cinemax (multiplexed); Encore (multiplexed); Flix (multiplexed); HBO (multiplexed); Showtime (multiplexed); Starz (multiplexed); The Movie Channel (multiplexed).
Fee: $11.95 each.

Video-On-Demand: No

Pay-Per-View
Addressable homes: 127.
iN DEMAND (delivered digitally); NBA 1, NBA 2, NHL Center Ice & MLB (delivered digitally); ESPN (delivered digitally).

Internet Service
Operational: Yes.
Subscribers: 49.
Broadband Service: Road Runner.
Fee: $44.95 monthly.

Telephone Service
Digital: Operational
Fee: $44.95 monthly

Miles of Plant: 43.0 (coaxial); None (fiber optic).
President: Rhonda Fraas. Vice President & General Manager: Brad Wakely. Vice President, Engineering: Randy Hall. Vice President, Marketing: Mark Psigoda. Technical Operations Director: John Ellingson. Public Affairs Director: Brian Young. Public Affairs Manager: Patrick McCauley.
Ownership: Time Warner Cable (MSO).

DOYLESTOWN—Doylestown Communications, 18 N Portage St, Doylestown, OH 44230. Phone: 330-658-2121. Fax: 330-658-2272. E-mail: info@doylestowntelephone.com. Web Site: http://www.doylestowncommunications.com. Also serves Chippewa Twp. ICA: OH0447. **Note:** This system is an overbuild.
TV Market Ranking: 8 (Chippewa Twp., DOYLESTOWN). Franchise award date: N.A. Franchise expiration date: N.A. Began: June 1, 1997.
Channel capacity: N.A. Channels available but not in use: N.A.

Basic Service
Subscribers: 1,500.
Programming (received off-air): WAOH-LP Akron; WBNX-TV (CW) Akron; WCPO-TV (ABC) Cincinnati; WEAO (PBS) Akron; WJW (FOX) Cleveland; WKRC-TV (CBS, CW) Cincinnati; WKYC (NBC) Cleveland; WQHS-DT (UNV) Cleveland; WRLM (IND) Canton; WUAB (MNT) Lorain; WVIZ (PBS) Cleveland; WVPX-TV (ION) Akron.
Programming (via satellite): TV Guide Network.
Fee: $17.95 monthly.

Expanded Basic Service 1
Subscribers: N.A.
Programming (via satellite): A&E Networks; ABC Family Channel; AMC; Animal Planet; Bravo; Cartoon Network; CNBC; CNN; Comedy Central; Country Music TV; C-SPAN; C-SPAN 2; Discovery Channel; Discovery Fit & Health; Disney Channel; E! Entertainment Television; ESPN; ESPN 2; ESPN Classic Sports; Eternal Word TV Network; Food Network; Fox News Channel; Fox Sports Net Ohio; FX; G4; Great American Country; GSN; Headline News; HGTV; History Channel; Lifetime; MSNBC; MTV; National Geographic Channel; Nickelodeon; QVC; Speed; Spike TV; SportsTime Ohio; Syfy; TBS Superstation; The Learning Channel; The Weather Channel; Toon Disney; Travel Channel; Trinity Broadcasting Network; truTV; Turner Classic Movies; Turner Network TV; TV Land; USA Network; VH1; WE tv; WGN America.
Fee: $42.95 monthly.

Digital Basic Service
Subscribers: N.A.
Programming (via satellite): BBC America; Bio; Bloomberg Television; Cooking Channel; DIY Network; DMX Music; ESPNews; Fox Movie Channel; GAS; Golf Channel; Hallmark Channel; Halogen Network; History Channel International; Lifetime Movie Network; MTV Networks Digital Suite; NFL Network; Nick Jr.; NickToons TV; Outdoor Channel; SoapNet; Style Network; Trio.
Fee: $14.95 monthly.

Digital Pay Service 1
Pay Units: N.A.
Programming (via satellite): Cinemax (multiplexed); Encore (multiplexed); Flix; HBO (multiplexed); Showtime (multiplexed); Starz (multiplexed); Sundance Channel; The Movie Channel (multiplexed).
Fee: $10.95 monthly (HBO, Cinemax, Showtime/TMC/Flix/Sundance or Starz/Encore).

Video-On-Demand: No

Internet Service
Operational: Yes.
Fee: $24.95 monthly.

Telephone Service
Digital: Operational

Manager: Barb Webb. Technical Operations Manager: Dennis Hartman.
Ownership: Doylestown Communications Inc.

DRESDEN—Time Warner Cable. Now served by ZANESVILLE, OH [OH0037]. ICA: OH0218.

DUNKIRK—Time Warner Cable. Now served by KENTON, OH [OH0128]. ICA: OH0276.

EAST CLEVELAND—East Cleveland Cable TV & Communications LLC, 1395 Hayden Ave, East Cleveland, OH 44112-1850. Phone: 216-851-2215. Fax: 216-851-0231. E-mail: info@ecctv.tv. Web Site: http://www.ecctv.tv. Also serves Bratenahl. ICA: OH0066.

TV Market Ranking: 8 (Bratenahl, EAST CLEVELAND). Franchise award date: January 1, 1981. Franchise expiration date: January 1, 2008. Began: November 20, 1981.

Channel capacity: 46 (not 2-way capable). Channels available but not in use: N.A.

Basic Service

Subscribers: 3,100.

Programming (received off-air): WBNX-TV (CW) Akron; WEWS-TV (ABC) Cleveland; WJW (FOX) Cleveland; WKYC (NBC) Cleveland; WOIO (CBS) Shaker Heights; WQHS-DT (UNV) Cleveland; WUAB (MNT) Lorain.

Programming (via satellite): A&E Networks; ABC Family Channel; AMC; Animal Planet; BET Networks; Cartoon Network; CNBC; CNN; Comedy Central; Discovery Channel; Disney Channel; E! Entertainment Television; ESPN; Fox Sports Net Ohio; Headline News; History Channel; Lifetime; MTV; Nickelodeon; Syfy; TBS Superstation; The Learning Channel; The Weather Channel; Trinity Broadcasting Network; truTV; Turner Network TV; TV Guide Network; USA Network; VH1; WGN America.

Fee: $25.00 installation; $35.40 monthly; $1.75 converter; $25.00 additional installation.

Pay Service 1

Pay Units: 350.

Programming (via satellite): Cinemax.

Fee: $7.95 monthly.

Pay Service 2

Pay Units: 950.

Programming (via satellite): HBO.

Fee: $11.95 monthly.

Pay Service 3

Pay Units: 550.

Programming (via satellite): Showtime; The Movie Channel.

Fee: $10.95 monthly.

Video-On-Demand: No

Pay-Per-View

Addressable homes: 1,882.

iN DEMAND.

Internet Service

Operational: Yes.

Fee: $39.95-$64.95 monthly.

Telephone Service

None

Miles of Plant: 50.0 (coaxial); None (fiber optic). Additional miles planned: 43.0 (coaxial).

General Manager: James Gruttadaurio. Chief Technician & Plant Manager: Ron Kessler. Customer Service Manager: Wayne Barnes.

Ownership: East Cleveland Cable TV LLC.

EAST LIVERPOOL—Comcast Cable, 15 Summit Park Dr, Pittsburgh, PA 15275. Phone: 412-747-6400. Fax: 412-747-6401. Web Site: http://www.comcast.com. Also serves Liverpool Twp., Madison Twp. (Columbiana County), St. Clair Twp. (Columbiana County), Wellsville & Yellow Creek. ICA: OH0062.

TV Market Ranking: 10,79 (EAST LIVERPOOL, Madison Twp. (Columbiana County)); 79,10 (Liverpool Twp. (portions)); 79,90 (St. Clair Twp. (Columbiana County), Wellsville, Yellow Creek). Franchise award date: N.A. Franchise expiration date: N.A. Began: May 1, 1966.

Channel capacity: N.A. Channels available but not in use: N.A.

Basic Service

Subscribers: N.A. Included in Pittsburgh

Programming (received off-air): KDKA-TV (CBS) Pittsburgh; WFMJ-TV (CW, NBC) Youngstown; WINP-TV (IND, ION) Pittsburgh; WKBN-TV (CBS) Youngstown; WNEO (PBS) Alliance; WPGH-TV (FOX) Pittsburgh; WPMY (MNT) Pittsburgh; WPXI (IND, NBC) Pittsburgh; WQED (PBS) Pittsburgh; WTAE-TV (ABC) Pittsburgh; WTOV-TV (IND, NBC) Steubenville; WYTV (ABC, MNT) Youngstown; allband FM.

Programming (via satellite): BET Networks; C-SPAN; Discovery Channel; Ecumenical TV Channel; Hallmark Channel; QVC; The Weather Channel.

Fee: $14.00 monthly.

Expanded Basic Service 1

Subscribers: 8,842.

Programming (via satellite): A&E Networks; ABC Family Channel; AMC; Animal Planet; Cartoon Network; CNBC; CNN; Comedy Central; C-SPAN 2; Disney Channel; E! Entertainment Television; ESPN; ESPN 2; Eternal Word TV Network; Fox News Channel; FX; Headline News; HGTV; History Channel; ION Television; Lifetime; MSNBC; MTV; Nickelodeon; Oxygen; Root Sports Pittsburgh; Shop at Home; ShopNBC; Spike TV; TBS Superstation; The Learning Channel; Travel Channel; truTV; Turner Network TV; TV Guide Network; TV Land; USA Network; VH1.

Fee: $37.99 monthly.

Digital Basic Service

Subscribers: N.A.

Programming (via satellite): BBC America; Bravo; Discovery Digital Networks; ESPN Classic Sports; Fox Sports World; Golf Channel; GSN; Independent Film Channel; Nick Jr.; Syfy; Turner Classic Movies; Versus; WE tv.

Fee: $10.95 monthly.

Digital Pay Service 1

Pay Units: N.A.

Programming (via satellite): Cinemax (multiplexed); Encore (multiplexed); HBO (multiplexed); Showtime (multiplexed); Starz (multiplexed); The Movie Channel (multiplexed).

Video-On-Demand: Yes

Pay-Per-View

Hot Choice (delivered digitally); iN DEMAND; Fresh (delivered digitally); Shorteez (delivered digitally).

Internet Service

Operational: Yes. Began: October 1, 2001.

Broadband Service: Comcast High Speed Internet.

Fee: $42.95 monthly.

Telephone Service

Analog: Not Operational

Digital: Operational

Fee: $44.95 monthly

Miles of Plant: 175.0 (coaxial); None (fiber optic).

Regional Vice President: Linda Hossinger. Vice President, Technical Operations: Randy Bender. Vice President, Marketing: Donna Corning. Vice President, Public Affairs: Jody Doherty.

Ownership: Comcast Cable Communications Inc. (MSO).

EAST PALESTINE—Comcast Cable. Now served by NEW MIDDLETOWN, OH (formerly Springfield Twp.) [OH0145]. ICA: OH0099.

EATON—Time Warner Cable. Now served by DAYTON, OH [OH0011]. ICA: OH0045.

EDON—Windjammer Cable, 4400 PGA Blvd, Ste 902, Palm Beach Gardens, FL 33410. Phones: 877-450-5558; 561-775-1208. Fax: 561-775-7811. Web Site: http://www.windjammercable.com. ICA: OH0240.

TV Market Ranking: Below 100 (EDON). Franchise award date: N.A. Franchise expiration date: N.A. Began: May 1, 1985.

Channel capacity: 37 (not 2-way capable). Channels available but not in use: N.A.

Basic Service

Subscribers: 156.

Programming (received off-air): WANE-TV (CBS) Fort Wayne; WBGU-TV (PBS) Bowling Green; WFFT-TV (IND) Fort Wayne; WISE-TV (FOX, MNT, NBC) Fort Wayne; WNWO-TV (NBC) Toledo; WPTA (ABC, CW) Fort Wayne; WTOL (CBS) Toledo; WTVG (ABC) Toledo; WUPW (FOX) Toledo.

Programming (via satellite): TBS Superstation; WGN America.

Fee: $42.50 installation; $13.00 monthly.

Expanded Basic Service 1

Subscribers: 34.

Programming (via satellite): A&E Networks; ABC Family Channel; CNN; C-SPAN; Discovery Channel; Disney Channel; ESPN; Headline News; History Channel; Lifetime; MTV; Nickelodeon; Spike TV; The Weather Channel; Turner Network TV; USA Network; VH1.

Fee: $19.38 monthly.

Digital Basic Service

Subscribers: 28.

Programming (via satellite): BBC America; Bloomberg Television; Bravo; Discovery Fit & Health; Discovery Health Channel; Discovery Kids Channel; ESPN Classic Sports; ESPNews; Fox Movie Channel; Fox Soccer; G4; Golf Channel; GSN; Halogen Network; HGTV; Independent Film Channel; Music Choice; Nick Jr.; NickToons TV; Outdoor Channel; Science; Syfy; Trinity Broadcasting Network; Versus; WE tv.

Fee: $11.98 monthly.

Pay Service 1

Pay Units: 21.

Programming (via satellite): Cinemax.

Fee: $10.49 monthly.

Pay Service 2

Pay Units: 25.

Programming (via satellite): HBO.

Fee: $14.49 monthly.

Digital Pay Service 1

Pay Units: N.A.

Programming (via satellite): Cinemax (multiplexed); Encore (multiplexed); HBO (multiplexed); Showtime (multiplexed); The Movie Channel (multiplexed).

Fee: $11.95 monthly (each).

Video-On-Demand: No

Pay-Per-View

iN DEMAND (delivered digitally).

Internet Service

Operational: No.

Telephone Service

None

Miles of Plant: 10.0 (coaxial); None (fiber optic).

General Manager: Timothy Evard. Operations Director: Belinda Graham. Engineering Director: Mike Earehart. Finance & Accounting Director: Cindy Johnson.

Ownership: Windjammer Communications LLC (MSO).

ELYRIA—Time Warner Cable. Now served by CLEVELAND HEIGHTS, OH [OH0006]. ICA: OH0026.

EUREKA—Windjammer Cable, 4400 PGA Blvd, Ste 902, Palm Beach Gardens, FL 33410. Phones: 877-450-5558; 561-775-1208. Fax: 561-775-7811. Web Site: http://www.windjammercable.com. ICA: OH0378.

TV Market Ranking: 36 (EUREKA). Franchise award date: N.A. Franchise expiration date: N.A. Began: N.A.

Channel capacity: 29 (not 2-way capable). Channels available but not in use: N.A.

Basic Service

Subscribers: 261.

Programming (received off-air): WCHS-TV (ABC) Charleston; WOWK-TV (CBS) Huntington; WPBY-TV (PBS) Huntington; WSAZ-TV (MNT, NBC) Huntington; WVAH-TV (FOX) Charleston.

Programming (via satellite): A&E Networks; ABC Family Channel; AMC; CNN; Country Music TV; Discovery Channel; Disney Channel; ESPN; ESPN 2; Headline News; HGTV; Lifetime; Nickelodeon; QVC; Spike TV; TBS Superstation; The Learning Channel; The Weather Channel; Trinity Broadcasting Network; Turner Network TV; TV Land; USA Network; WGN America.

Fee: $39.17 monthly.

Pay Service 1

Pay Units: 24.

Programming (via satellite): HBO.

Digital Pay Service 1

Pay Units: N.A.

Programming (via satellite): Cinemax (multiplexed); Encore (multiplexed); HBO (multiplexed); Showtime (multiplexed); Starz (multiplexed); The Movie Channel (multiplexed).

Fee: $15.95 monthly (each).

Video-On-Demand: No

Internet Service

Operational: No.

Telephone Service

None

Miles of Plant: 28.0 (coaxial); None (fiber optic).

General Manager: Timothy Evard. Operations Director: Belinda Graham. Engineering Director: Mike Earehart. Finance & Accounting Director: Cindy Johnson.

Ownership: Windjammer Communications LLC (MSO).

FAIRBORN—Time Warner Cable. Now served by DAYTON, OH [OH0011]. ICA: OH0432.

FAIRFIELD (Butler County)—Formerly served by Adelphia Communications. Now served by CINCINNATI, OH [OH0001]. ICA: OH0376.

FAYETTE—Formerly served by Adelphia Communications. Now served by WAUSEON, OH [OH0106]. ICA: OH0194.

FINDLAY—Time Warner Cable, 205 Crystal Ave, Findlay, OH 45840. Phone: 419-429-7474. Fax: 419-429-7402. Web Site: http://www.timewarnercable.com/midohio. Also serves Allen Twp. (Hancock County), Arlington, Biglick Twp., Blanchard Twp. (Hancock County), Cass Twp. (Hancock County), Eagle Twp. (Hancock County), Jenera, Liberty Twp. (Hancock County), McComb, Mount Blanchard, Mount Cory, Pleasant Twp. (Hancock County), Rawson, Van Buren & Vanlue. ICA: OH0036.

TV Market Ranking: Below 100 (Allen Twp. (Hancock County), Arlington, Biglick Twp. (portions), Blanchard Twp. (Hancock County), Cass Twp. (Hancock County), Eagle Twp. (Hancock County), FINDLAY, Jenera, Liberty Twp. (Hancock County), McComb, Mount Blanchard, Mount Cory, Pleasant Twp. (Hancock County), Rawson); Outside TV Markets (Biglick Twp. (portions), Van Buren, Vanlue). Franchise award date: August 1, 1963. Franchise expiration date: September 3, 2013. Began: February 8, 1965.

Channel capacity: N.A. Channels available but not in use: N.A.

Basic Service

Subscribers: 17,827.

Programming (received off-air): WBGU-TV (PBS) Bowling Green; WGTE-TV (PBS) Toledo; WLIO (CW, NBC) Lima; WNWO-TV (NBC) Toledo; WTLW (IND) Lima; WTOL (CBS) Toledo; WTVG (ABC) Toledo; WUPW (FOX) Toledo; 17 FMs.

Programming (via microwave): WBNS-TV (CBS) Columbus; WEWS-TV (ABC) Cleveland; WKBD-TV (CW) Detroit; WUAB (MNT) Lorain.

Programming (via satellite): QVC; TVG Network.

Fee: $45.86 installation; $11.13 monthly; $31.81 additional installation.

Expanded Basic Service 1

Subscribers: N.A.

Programming (via satellite): A&E Networks; ABC Family Channel; AMC; AmericanLife TV Network; Animal Planet; BET Networks; Bravo; Cartoon Network; CNBC; CNN; Comedy Central; Country Music TV; C-SPAN; C-SPAN 2; Discovery Channel; Disney Channel; E! Entertainment Television; ESPN; ESPN 2; ESPN Classic Sports; Eternal Word TV Network; Food Network; Fox News Channel; Fox Sports Net Ohio; Fuse; FX; Golf Channel; GSN; Hallmark Channel; Headline News; HGTV; History Channel; INSP; Lifetime; Lifetime Movie Network; MSNBC; MTV; National Geographic Channel; Nickelodeon; Outdoor Channel; Oxygen; ShopNBC; Speed; Spike TV; Syfy; TBS Superstation; The Learning Channel; The Weather Channel; Travel Channel; truTV; Turner Classic Movies; Turner Network TV; TV Land; USA Network; Versus; VH1; WE tv.

Fee: $29.82 monthly.

Digital Basic Service

Subscribers: 5,348.

Programming (received off-air): WBGU-TV (PBS) Bowling Green; WNWO-TV (NBC) Toledo; WTOL (CBS) Toledo; WTVG (ABC) Toledo; WUPW (FOX) Toledo.

Programming (via satellite): America's Store; BBC America; Bio; Bloomberg Television; Boomerang; CNN International; Cooking Channel; C-SPAN 3; Current; Discovery Fit & Health; DIY Network; ESPN; Fox Soccer; GAS; Great American Country; HD Theater; HDNet Movies; INHD (multiplexed); Lifetime Real Women; MTV Hits; MTV2; Nick Jr.; Ohio News Network; SoapNet; Sorpresa; Toon Disney; Trio; Turner Network TV HD; TV One; VH1 Classic.

Fee: $8.95 monthly.

Digital Expanded Basic Service

Subscribers: N.A.

Programming (via satellite): Canales N; CBS Sports Network; Deutsche Welle TV; Encore Action; Fox Movie Channel; FSN Digital Atlantic; FSN Digital Central; FSN Digital Pacific; Fuel TV; Independent Film Channel; NBA TV; Sundance Channel; Tennis Channel; TV Asia; WAM! America's Kidz Network; Zee TV USA.

Digital Pay Service 1

Pay Units: 13,129.

Programming (via satellite): Cinemax (multiplexed); Flix; HBO (multiplexed); Showtime (multiplexed); Starz (multiplexed); The Movie Channel (multiplexed).

Fee: $11.95 monthly (Cinemax, HBO, Showtime or Starz & TMC).

Video-On-Demand: Yes

Pay-Per-View

Addressable homes: 5,348.

iN DEMAND (delivered digitally); Fresh (delivered digitally); Sports PPV (delivered digitally).

Internet Service

Operational: Yes.

Subscribers: 3,209.

Broadband Service: Road Runner.

Fee: $69.95 installation; $44.95 monthly.

Telephone Service

Digital: Operational

Fee: $44.95 monthly

Miles of Plant: 242.0 (coaxial); 29.0 (fiber optic).

President: Rhonda Fraas. Vice President, Operations: Brad Wakely. Vice President, Engineering: Randy Hall. Vice President, Marketing: Mark Psigoda. Technical Operations Director: John Ellingson. Government Affairs Director: Brian Young. Government Affairs Manager: Patrick McCauley.

Ownership: Time Warner Cable (MSO).

FLUSHING—Comcast Cable. Now served by WHEELING, WV [WV0004]. ICA: OH0243.

FOREST—Time Warner Cable. Now served by KENTON, OH [OH0128]. ICA: OH0222.

FORT JENNINGS—Fort Jennings Telephone Co., 65 W 3rd St, PO Box 146, Fort Jennings, OH 45844-0146. Phones: 800-362-2764; 419-286-2181. Fax: 419-286-2193. E-mail: fjtc@bright.net. Web Site: http://www.fjtelephone.com. ICA: OH0253.

TV Market Ranking: Below 100 (FORT JENNINGS). Franchise award date: N.A. Franchise expiration date: N.A. Began: September 1, 1987.

Channel capacity: 78 (not 2-way capable). Channels available but not in use: N.A.

Basic Service

Subscribers: 462.

Programming (received off-air): WANE-TV (CBS) Fort Wayne; WBGU-TV (PBS) Bowling Green; WBNS-TV (CBS) Columbus; WLIO (CW, NBC) Lima; WLQP-LP Lima; WNWO-TV (NBC) Toledo; WOHL-CD (FOX) Lima; WPTA (ABC, CW) Fort Wayne; WTLW (IND) Lima; WTOL (CBS) Toledo; WTVG (ABC) Toledo; WUPW (FOX) Toledo.

Programming (via satellite): A&E Networks; ABC Family Channel; BTN; Cartoon Network; CNN; CW+; Discovery Channel; Disney Channel; ESPN; ESPN 2; ESPN Classic Sports; Eternal Word TV Network; Food Network; Fox News Channel; Fox Sports Net Ohio; FX; Hallmark Channel; Lifetime; MSNBC; MTV; National Geographic Channel; SportsTime Ohio; TBS Superstation; The Learning Channel; The Weather Channel; Travel Channel; Turner Classic Movies; Turner Network TV; TV Land; USA Network; VH1; WGN America.

Fee: $24.50 installation; $25.95 monthly.

Expanded Basic Service 1

Subscribers: 298.

Programming (via satellite): Comedy Central; Country Music TV; History Channel; Nickelodeon; Spike TV.

Fee: $6.00 monthly.

Digital Basic Service

Subscribers: N.A.

Programming (via satellite): BBC America; Bloomberg Television; Discovery Health Channel; Discovery Home Channel; Discovery Kids Channel; DMX Music; ESPN Classic Sports; Fox Sports Net; GAS; Golf Channel; HGTV; ID Investigation Discovery; Independent Film Channel; Lifetime Movie Network; Military Channel; MTV2; National Geographic Channel; Nick Jr.; NickToons TV; Science; Speed; Toon Disney; Versus; VH1 Classic; VH1 Country; WE tv.

Fee: $13.50 monthly.

Digital Expanded Basic Service

Subscribers: N.A.

Programming (via satellite): Bio; Discovery Fit & Health; ESPNews; Fox Movie Channel; Fuse; G4; GSN; History Channel International; Outdoor Channel.

Pay Service 1

Pay Units: 47.

Programming (via satellite): HBO.

Fee: $11.95 monthly.

Pay Service 2

Pay Units: 107.

Programming (via satellite): Showtime.

Fee: $9.95 monthly.

Pay Service 3

Pay Units: 73.

Programming (via satellite): The Movie Channel.

Fee: $9.95 monthly.

Digital Pay Service 1

Pay Units: N.A.

Programming (via satellite): Cinemax (multiplexed); Encore (multiplexed); HBO (multiplexed); Showtime (multiplexed); Starz (multiplexed); The Movie Channel (multiplexed).

Video-On-Demand: No

Internet Service

Operational: No, DSL.

Telephone Service

None

Miles of Plant: 57.0 (coaxial); None (fiber optic).

General Manager: Michael Metzger. Secretary-Treasurer: Randy Wieging. Chief Technician: David Will.

Ownership: Fort Jennings Telephone Co.

FORT RECOVERY (village)—Comcast Cable, 5330 E 65th St, Indianapolis, IN 46220. Phone: 317-275-6370. Fax: 317-275-6340. Web Site: http://www.comcast.com. ICA: OH0324.

TV Market Ranking: Outside TV Markets (FORT RECOVERY (VILLAGE)). Franchise award date: N.A. Franchise expiration date: N.A. Began: May 1, 1987.

Channel capacity: N.A. Channels available but not in use: N.A.

Basic Service

Subscribers: N.A. Included in Anderson IN

Programming (received off-air): WANE-TV (CBS) Fort Wayne; WDTN (NBC) Dayton; WFFT-TV (IND) Fort Wayne; WFYI (PBS) Indianapolis; WHIO-TV (CBS) Dayton; WIPB (PBS) Muncie; WISE-TV (FOX, MNT, NBC) Fort Wayne; WLIO (CW, NBC) Lima; WNDY-TV (MNT) Marion; WPTA (ABC, CW) Fort Wayne; WRGT-TV (FOX, MNT) Dayton; WTTK (CW) Kokomo.

Programming (via satellite): C-SPAN; C-SPAN 2; QVC; Trinity Broadcasting Network; WGN America.

Expanded Basic Service 1

Subscribers: N.A.

Programming (via satellite): A&E Networks; ABC Family Channel; AMC; Animal Planet; BET Networks; Bravo; Cartoon Network; CNBC; CNN; Comedy Central; Country Music TV; Discovery Channel; Disney Channel; E! Entertainment Television; ESPN; ESPN 2; Eternal Word TV Network; Food Network; Fox News Channel; Fox Sports Net Ohio; FX; Golf Channel; Headline News; HGTV; History Channel; Lifetime; MSNBC; MTV; National Geographic Channel; Nickelodeon; Oxygen; Speed; Spike TV; Syfy; TBS Superstation; The Learning Channel; The Weather Channel; Travel Channel; truTV; Turner Network TV; TV Guide Network; TV Land; USA Network; VH1.

Fee: $51.74 monthly.

Digital Basic Service

Subscribers: N.A.

Programming (via satellite): BBC America; Bio; Bloomberg Television; CBS Sports Network; CNBC; Cooking Channel; C-SPAN 3; DIY Network; DMX Music; Encore (multiplexed); ESPN Classic Sports; ESPN HD; ESPNews; Fox College Sports Atlantic; Fox College Sports Central; Fox College Sports Pacific; Fox Movie Channel; Fox Soccer; G4; GAS; GSN; Halogen Network; HD Theater; HDNet; HDNet Movies; History Channel International; Independent Film Channel; Lifetime Movie Network; Lifetime Real Women; MTV2; NFL Network; Nick Jr.; Nick Too; Outdoor Channel; Ovation; SoapNet; Style Network; Sundance Channel; Toon Disney; Turner Classic Movies; Universal HD; Versus; WE tv.

Fee: $17.00 monthly.

Digital Pay Service 1

Pay Units: N.A.

Programming (via satellite): Cinemax (multiplexed); Flix; HBO (multiplexed); HBO HD; Showtime (multiplexed); Showtime HD; Starz (multiplexed); The Movie Channel.

Fee: $10.00 monthly (Cinemax or Starz), $13.00 monthly (HBO or Showtime).

Video-On-Demand: Yes

Internet Service

Operational: Yes.

Broadband Service: Comcast High Speed Internet.

Fee: $99.95 installation; $44.95 monthly; $15.00 modem lease; $99.95 modem purchase.

Telephone Service

Digital: Operational

Fee: $39.95 monthly

Miles of Plant: 13.0 (coaxial); 19.0 (fiber optic).

Regional Vice President: Scott Tenney. Regional Vice President, Technical Operations: Max Woolsey. Regional Vice President, Marketing: Aaron Geisel. Regional Vice President, Communications: Mark Apple.

Ownership: Comcast Cable Communications Inc. (MSO).

FOSTORIA—Time Warner Cable, 205 Crystal Ave, Findlay, OH 45840. Phones: 614-481-5000 (Columbus office); 419-429-7474. Fax: 419-429-7402. Web Site: http://www.

timewarnercable.com/midohio. Also serves Arcadia, Bascom, Eden Twp. (Seneca County), Hopewell Twp. (Seneca County), Loudon Twp. (Seneca County) & Tiffin. ICA: OH0050.

TV Market Ranking: Below 100 (Bascom, Tiffin); Outside TV Markets (Arcadia, Eden Twp. (Seneca County), FOSTORIA, Hopewell Twp. (Seneca County), Loudon Twp. (Seneca County)). Franchise award date: N.A. Franchise expiration date: December 18, 2008. Began: December 1, 1964.

Channel capacity: N.A. Channels available but not in use: N.A.

Basic Service

Subscribers: 13,593.

Programming (received off-air): WBGU-TV (PBS) Bowling Green; WEWS-TV (ABC) Cleveland; WGGN-TV (TBN) Sandusky; WGTE-TV (PBS) Toledo; WKBD-TV (CW) Detroit; WKYC (NBC) Cleveland; WLMB (IND) Toledo; WNWO-TV (NBC) Toledo; WTOL (CBS) Toledo; WTVG (ABC) Toledo; WUAB (MNT) Lorain; WUPW (FOX) Toledo; allband FM.

Programming (via satellite): QVC; TV Guide Network.

Fee: $45.86 installation; $8.20 monthly; $2.95 converter.

Expanded Basic Service 1

Subscribers: N.A.

Programming (via satellite): A&E Networks; ABC Family Channel; AMC; Animal Planet; BET Networks; Bravo; Cartoon Network; CNBC; CNN; Comedy Central; Country Music TV; C-SPAN; C-SPAN 2; Discovery Channel; Disney Channel; E! Entertainment Television; ESPN; ESPN 2; ESPN Classic Sports; Eternal Word TV Network; Food Network; Fox News Channel; Fox Sports Net Ohio; FX; Golf Channel; Hallmark Channel; Headline News; HGTV; History Channel; INSP; Lifetime; Lifetime Movie Network; MSNBC; MTV; National Geographic Channel; Nickelodeon; Oxygen; ShopNBC; Spike TV; Syfy; TBS Superstation; The Learning Channel; The Weather Channel; Travel Channel; truTV; Turner Classic Movies; Turner Network TV; TV Land; USA Network; Versus; VH1; WE tv.

Fee: $32.75 monthly.

Digital Basic Service

Subscribers: 4,078.

Programming (via satellite): AmericanLife TV Network; America's Store; BBC America; Bloomberg Television; CNN International; Cooking Channel; C-SPAN 3; Discovery Fit & Health; DIY Network; DMX Music; ESPNews; Fox Sports World; FSN Digital Atlantic; FSN Digital Central; FSN Digital Pacific; Fuse; G4; GAS; Great American Country; GSN; Lifetime Real Women; MTV2; Nick Jr.; Ohio News Network; Outdoor Channel; Ovation; SoapNet; Sorpresa; Speed; Style Network; Toon Disney; VH1 Classic.

Fee: $9.90 monthly.

Digital Pay Service 1

Pay Units: 999.

Programming (via satellite): Cinemax (multiplexed); Encore (multiplexed); Flix; HBO (multiplexed); Showtime (multiplexed); Starz (multiplexed); The Movie Channel (multiplexed).

Fee: $11.95 monthly (Cinemax, HBO, Showtime/Flix/TMC or Starz/Encore).

Video-On-Demand: Yes

Pay-Per-View

Addressable homes: 4,078.

iN DEMAND (delivered digitally); Fresh (delivered digitally); Sports PPV (delivered digitally).

Internet Service

Operational: Yes.

Subscribers: 2,447.

Broadband Service: Road Runner.

Fee: $69.95 installation; $44.95 monthly.

Telephone Service

Digital: Operational

Fee: $44.95 monthly

President: Rhonda Fraas. Vice President & General Manager: Brad Wakely. Vice President, Engineering: Randy Hall. Vice President, Marketing: Mark Psigoda. Technical Operations Director: John Ellingson. Government Affairs Director: Brian Young. Government Affairs Manager: Patrick McCauley.

Ownership: Time Warner Cable (MSO).

FRANKFORT—Formerly served by Adelphia Communications. Now served by CHILLICOTHE, OH [OH0033]. ICA: OH0227.

FRANKLIN FURNACE—Formerly served by Adelphia Communications. Now served by ASHLAND, KY [KY0326]. ICA: OH0325.

FRAZEYBURG—Time Warner Cable. Now served by ZANESVILLE, OH [OH0037]. ICA: OH0271.

FREDERICKTOWN—Time Warner Cable. Now served by MOUNT VERNON, OH [OH0095]. ICA: OH0326.

FREEPORT TWP.—Windjammer Cable, 4400 PGA Blvd, Ste 902, Palm Beach Gardens, FL 33410. Phones: 877-450-5558; 561-775-1208. Fax: 561-775-7811. Web Site: http://www.windjammercable.com. Also serves Freeport. ICA: OH0295.

TV Market Ranking: 90 (Freeport, FREEPORT TWP.). Franchise award date: N.A. Franchise expiration date: N.A. Began: June 1, 1972.

Channel capacity: 81 (not 2-way capable). Channels available but not in use: N.A.

Basic Service

Subscribers: 95.

Programming (received off-air): KMGH-TV (ABC) Denver; WBDT (CW) Springfield; WOUC-TV (PBS) Cambridge; WTOV-TV (IND, NBC) Steubenville; WTRF-TV (CBS) Wheeling.

Programming (via satellite): ABC Family Channel; AMC; Animal Planet; Cartoon Network; CNBC; CNN; Discovery Channel; ESPN; Fox News Channel; Hallmark Channel; HGTV; History Channel; Nickelodeon; QVC; Spike TV; TBS Superstation; Turner Network TV; USA Network.

Fee: $31.95 monthly; $3.40 converter.

Pay Service 1

Pay Units: 16.

Programming (via satellite): Showtime.

Fee: $14.95 monthly.

Pay Service 2

Pay Units: 29.

Programming (via satellite): Encore.

Fee: $4.00 monthly.

Pay Service 3

Pay Units: 22.

Programming (via satellite): Starz.

Fee: $8.95 monthly.

Video-On-Demand: No

Internet Service

Operational: No.

Telephone Service

None

Miles of Plant: 4.0 (coaxial); None (fiber optic).

General Manager: Timothy Evard. Operations Director: Belinda Graham. Engineering Director: Mike Earehart. Finance & Accounting Director: Cindy Johnson.

Ownership: Windjammer Communications LLC (MSO).

FREMONT—Time Warner Cable. Now served by BELLEVUE, OH [OH0086]. ICA: OH0085.

FRIENDSHIP—Time Warner Cable, 1266 Dublin Rd, Columbus, OH 43215-1008. Phone: 614-481-5000. Fax: 614-481-5052. Web Site: http://www.timewarnercable.com/midohio. Also serves Nile Twp. ICA: OH0224.

TV Market Ranking: Below 100 (FRIENDSHIP, Nile Twp.). Franchise award date: December 5, 1981. Franchise expiration date: N.A. Began: August 1, 1982.

Channel capacity: N.A. Channels available but not in use: N.A.

Basic Service

Subscribers: 504.

Programming (received off-air): WCHS-TV (ABC) Charleston; WOWK-TV (CBS) Huntington; WPBO (PBS) Portsmouth; WSAZ-TV (MNT, NBC) Huntington; WVAH-TV (FOX) Charleston.

Programming (via satellite): ABC Family Channel; CNN; Country Music TV; Discovery Channel; Disney Channel; ESPN; MTV; Nickelodeon; QVC; Spike TV; TBS Superstation; Turner Network TV; USA Network; WGN America.

Fee: $19.95 installation; $16.99 monthly.

Pay Service 1

Pay Units: 47.

Programming (via satellite): Cinemax; HBO.

Fee: $10.95 monthly (each).

Internet Service

Operational: Yes.

Broadband Service: RoadRunner.

Fee: $24.95 monthly.

Telephone Service

Digital: Operational

Fee: $24.99 monthly

Miles of Plant: 32.0 (coaxial); None (fiber optic).

President: Rhonda Fraas. Vice President & General Manager: David Kreiman. Vice President, Engineering: Randy Hall. Vice President, Marketing: Mark Psigoda. Vice President, Government & Public Affairs: Mary Jo Green. Government Affairs Director: Steve Cuckler.

Ownership: Time Warner Cable (MSO).

FULTON TWP.—Formerly served by Adelphia Communications. Now served by WAUSEON, OH [OH0106]. ICA: OH0327.

GALION—Time Warner Cable, 205 Crystal Ave, Findlay, OH 45840. Phone: 419-429-7474. Fax: 419-429-7402. Web Site: http://www.timewarnercable.com/midohio. Also serves Crestline, Iberia, North Robinson, Polk Twp. & Whetstone Twp. ICA: OH0077.

Channel capacity: N.A. Channels available but not in use: N.A.

Basic Service

Subscribers: N.A. Included in Columbus

Programming (received off-air): WBNS-TV (CBS) Columbus; WCMH-TV (NBC) Columbus; WEWS-TV (ABC) Cleveland; WJW (FOX) Cleveland; WOSU-TV (PBS) Columbus; WSFJ-TV (TBN) Newark; WSYX (ABC, MNT) Columbus; WTOL (CBS) Toledo; WTTE (FOX) Columbus; WUAB (MNT) Lorain; WWHO (CW) Chillicothe.

Programming (via satellite): C-SPAN; C-SPAN 3; Hallmark Channel; Headline News; History Channel; LWS Local Weather Station; QVC; ShopNBC; TBS Superstation; The Learning Channel; Travel Channel; WGN America.

Expanded Basic Service 1

Subscribers: N.A.

Programming (via satellite): A&E Networks; ABC Family Channel; AMC; Animal Planet; BET Networks; Bravo; BTN; Cartoon Network; CNBC; CNN; Comedy Central; Country Music TV; Discovery Channel; Disney Channel; E! Entertainment Television; ESPN; ESPN 2; Food Network; Fox News Channel; Fox Sports Net Ohio; FX; Golf Channel; HGTV; Lifetime; Lifetime Movie Network; MSNBC; MTV; MTV2; National Geographic Channel; Nick Jr.; Nickelodeon; Oxygen; Spike TV; SportsTime Ohio; Syfy; The Weather Channel; truTV; Turner Classic Movies; Turner Network TV; TV Land; Univision Studios; USA Network; Versus; VH1; WE tv.

Digital Basic Service

Subscribers: N.A. Included in Columbus

Programming (via satellite): A&E HD; AmericanLife TV Network; Animal Planet HD; Auction TV; BBC America; BBC America On Demand; Bio; Bloomberg Television; Boomerang; BTN (multiplexed); BTN HD; Canal Sur; CBS Sports Network; Cine Latino; cloo; CNN en Espanol; CNN International; Cooking Channel; C-SPAN 3; Current; Discovery Channel HD; Discovery en Espanol; Discovery Fit & Health; Discovery Health Channel; Discovery Kids Channel; Disney Channel; Disney Channel HD; DIY Network; Encore (multiplexed); ESPN 2 HD; ESPN Classic Sports; ESPN Deportes; ESPN HD; ESPN U; ESPNews; Eternal Word TV Network; Exercise TV; Food Network; Food Network HD; Fox Business Channel; Fox College Sports Atlantic; Fox College Sports Central; Fox College Sports Pacific; Fox Deportes; Fox Movie Channel; Fox Reality Channel; Fox Soccer; FSN HD; Fuel TV; Fuse; G4; Great American Country; GSN; HD Theater; HDNet; HDNet Movies; here! TV; HGTV; HGTV HD; History Channel en Espanol; History Channel HD; History Channel International; Howard TV; ID Investigation Discovery; Independent Film Channel; INSP; Jewelry Television; La Familia Network; Lifetime Real Women; LOGO; Military Channel; MTV Hits; mun2 television; Music Choice; National Geographic Channel HD Network;

National Geographic Channel On Demand; NBA TV; NHL Network; NickToons TV; Ohio News Network; Outdoor Channel; Ovation; Oxygen On Demand; Palladia; Planet Green; Product Information Network; Science; SoapNet; Speed; Style Network; Sundance Channel; TBS in HD; TeenNick; Tennis Channel; The Weather Channel; The Word Network; Toon Disney; Tr3s; Turner Network TV HD; TV One; Universal HD; Versus HD; VH1 Classic; Video Rola.

Fee: $4.95 monthly (Latino or Sports Plus), $10.40 monthly (Movies or Variety), $14.60 monthly (Premier Digital).

Digital Pay Service 1

Pay Units: N.A.

Programming (via satellite): Cinemax (multiplexed); Cinemax On Demand; Encore; HBO (multiplexed); HBO HD; HBO Latino; HBO On Demand; Showtime (multiplexed); Showtime HD; Showtime On Demand; Starz (multiplexed); Starz On Demand; The Movie Channel (multiplexed); The Movie Channel On Demand.

Fee: $11.95 monthly (HBO, Cinemax, Starz/Encore or Showtime/TMC).

Video-On-Demand: Yes

Pay-Per-View

iN DEMAND (delivered digitally); Playboy TV (delivered digitally); Sports PPV (delivered digitally).

Internet Service

Operational: Yes.

Broadband Service: Road Runner.

Fee: $44.95 monthly.

Telephone Service

Digital: Operational

Fee: $44.95 monthly

Miles of plant included in Columbus

President: Rhonda Fraas. Vice President & General Manager: Brad Wakely. Vice President, Engineering: Randy Hall. Vice President, Marketing: Mark Psigoda. Technical Operations Director: John Ellingson. Government Affairs Director: Brian Young. Government Affairs Manager: Patrick McCauley.

Ownership: Time Warner Cable (MSO).

GALLIPOLIS—Zito Media, 106 S Main St, Edinburg, VA 22824. Phone: 814-260-9575. Web Site: http://www.zitomedia.com. ICA: OH0178.

TV Market Ranking: 36 (GALLIPOLIS). Franchise award date: N.A. Franchise expiration date: N.A. Began: January 1, 1984.

Channel capacity: 36 (not 2-way capable). Channels available but not in use: N.A.

Basic Service

Subscribers: 391.

Programming (received off-air): WCHS-TV (ABC) Charleston; WLPX-TV (ION) Charleston; WOUB-TV (PBS) Athens; WOWK-TV (CBS) Huntington; WPBY-TV (PBS) Huntington; WQCW (CW) Portsmouth; WSAZ-TV (MNT, NBC) Huntington; WVAH-TV (FOX) Charleston.

Programming (via satellite): A&E Networks; ABC Family Channel; AMC; Cartoon Network; CNN; Country Music TV; Discovery Channel; Disney Channel; ESPN; ESPN 2; FX; Headline News; History Channel; Lifetime; MTV; Nickelodeon; QVC; Spike TV; Syfy; TBS Superstation; The Weather Channel; Trinity Broadcasting Network; Turner Network TV; USA Network; VH1; WGN America.

Fee: $29.95 installation; $39.95 monthly.

Pay Service 1

Pay Units: 37.

Programming (via satellite): HBO.

Fee: $11.95 monthly.

Pay Service 2

Pay Units: 10.

Programming (via satellite): Showtime.

Fee: $10.95 monthly.

Pay Service 3

Pay Units: 14.

Programming (via satellite): Cinemax.

Fee: $10.95 monthly.

Video-On-Demand: No

Internet Service

Operational: No.

Telephone Service

None

Miles of Plant: 43.0 (coaxial); None (fiber optic).

Public Relations Manager: Mark Laver.

Ownership: Zito Media (MSO).

GERMANTOWN—Time Warner Cable. Now served by DAYTON, OH [OH0011]. ICA: OH0158.

GLENCOE—Comcast Cable. Now served by WHEELING, WV [WV0004]. ICA: OH0298.

GLENMONT—Now served by NEW PHILADELPHIA, OH [OH0030]. ICA: OH0300.

GOSHEN TWP. (Clermont County)—Time Warner Cable. Now served by CINCINNATI, OH [OH0001]. ICA: OH0129.

GRAFTON—Grafton Cable Communications. Now served by WELLINGTON, OH [OH0189]. ICA: OH0133.

GREEN—Time Warner Cable, 530 S Main St, Ste 1751, Akron, OH 44311-1090. Phone: 330-633-9203. Fax: 330-633-7970. Web Site: http://www.timewarnercable.com/northeastohio. Also serves Clinton, Coventry Twp. (Summit County) & Franklin Twp. (Summit County). ICA: OH0031.

TV Market Ranking: 8 (Clinton, Coventry Twp. (Summit County), Franklin Twp. (Summit County), GREEN). Franchise award date: October 15, 1981. Franchise expiration date: N.A. Began: October 15, 1981.

Channel capacity: N.A. Channels available but not in use: N.A.

Basic Service

Subscribers: 17,288.

Programming (received off-air): WAOH-LP Akron; WBNX-TV (CW) Akron; WDLI-TV (TBN) Canton; WEAO (PBS) Akron; WEWS-TV (ABC) Cleveland; WJW (FOX) Cleveland; WKYC (NBC) Cleveland; WOIO (CBS) Shaker Heights; WQHS-DT (UNV) Cleveland; WRLM (IND) Canton; WUAB (MNT) Lorain; WVIZ (PBS) Cleveland; WVPX-TV (ION) Akron; 18 FMs.

Programming (via satellite): TV Guide Network.

Fee: $29.95 installation; $12.55 monthly.

Expanded Basic Service 1

Subscribers: N.A.

Programming (via satellite): A&E Networks; ABC Family Channel; AMC; Animal Planet; BET Networks; Bravo; Cartoon Network; CNBC; CNN; Comedy Central; C-SPAN; C-SPAN 2; Discovery Channel; Discovery Fit & Health; Discovery Health Channel; Disney Channel; E! Entertainment Television; ESPN; ESPN 2; ESPN Classic Sports; Eternal Word TV Network; Food Network; Fox News Channel; Fox Sports Net Ohio; FX; Golf Channel; Great American Country; GSN; Hallmark Channel; Headline News; HGTV; History Channel; INSP; Lifetime; Lifetime Movie Network; MSNBC; MTV; Nickelodeon; Oxygen; QVC; ShopNBC; SoapNet; Spike TV; Syfy; TBS Superstation; The Learning Channel; The Weather Channel; Travel Channel; truTV; Turner Classic Movies; Turner Network TV; TV Land; USA Network; Versus; VH1; WE tv; WGN America.

Fee: $44.44 monthly.

Digital Basic Service

Subscribers: N.A.

Programming (via satellite): A&E Networks; AmericanLife TV Network; America's Store; ART America; BBC America; Bio; Bloomberg Television; Boomerang; Canales N; CBS Sports Network; cloo; CNN; CNN International; Cooking Channel; Country Music TV; C-SPAN 3; Current; Daystar TV Network; Disney Channel; DIY Network; ESPN; ESPNews; Fox College Sports Atlantic; Fox College Sports Central; Fox College Sports Pacific; Fox Movie Channel; Fox News Channel; Fox Soccer; Fuel TV; Fuse; G4; GAS; HD Theater; HDNet; HDNet Movies; Headline News; History Channel International; Independent Film Channel; INHD (multiplexed); Jewelry Television; Lifetime; Lifetime Real Women; MTV2; Music Choice; National Geographic Channel; NBA TV; Nick Jr.; NickToons TV; Ohio News Network; Outdoor Channel; RAI International; Speed; Style Network; TBS Superstation; Tennis Channel; The Weather Channel; The Word Network; Toon Disney; Turner Network TV; Turner Network TV HD; TV Asia; TVG Network; USA Network; VH1 Classic; Zee TV USA.

Fee: $11.00 monthly.

Digital Pay Service 1

Pay Units: N.A.

Programming (via satellite): Cinemax (multiplexed); Encore (multiplexed); HBO (multiplexed); Showtime (multiplexed); Starz (multiplexed); Sundance Channel; The Movie Channel (multiplexed).

Fee: $12.00 monthly (HBO, Cinemax, Showtime/TMC, or Encore/Starz).

Video-On-Demand: Yes

Pay-Per-View

iN DEMAND (delivered digitally); Playboy TV (delivered digitally); MLB Extra Innings (delivered digitally); Spice Live (delivered digitally); Pleasure (delivered digitally); NASCAR In Car (delivered digitally); NBA League Pass (delivered digitally); MLS Direct Kick (delivered digitally); ESPN (delivered digitally); NHL Center Ice (delivered digitally).

Internet Service

Operational: Yes.

Broadband Service: EarthLink, Road Runner.

Fee: $99.00 installation; $44.95 monthly.

Telephone Service

Digital: Operational

Fee: $44.95 monthly

Miles of Plant: 465.0 (coaxial); 57.0 (fiber optic). Additional miles planned: 10.0 (coaxial).

President: Stephen Fry. Area Vice President: Scott Miller. Vice President, Engineering: Al Costanzi. Vice President, Sales: Woody E. Woodward. Vice President, Public Affairs: William Jasso.

Ownership: Time Warner Cable (MSO).

GREEN MEADOWS—Time Warner Entertainment Co. LP. Now served by DAYTON, OH [OH0011]. ICA: OH0286.

GREEN TWP. (Hamilton County)—Time Warner Cable. Now served by CINCINNATI, OH [OH0001]. ICA: OH0032.

GREENFIELD—Formerly served by Adelphia Communications. Now served by WASHINGTON COURT HOUSE, OH [OH0070]. ICA: OH0157.

GREENFIELD ESTATES—Formerly served by World Cable. No longer in operation. ICA: OH0328.

GREENVILLE—Time Warner Cable. Now served by DAYTON, OH [OH0011]. ICA: OH0076.

GREENWOOD (village)—Formerly served by Adelphia Communications. No longer in operation. ICA: OH0329.

GUERNSEY COUNTY (portions)—Now served by NEWARK, OH [OH0019]. ICA: OH0396.

GUILFORD LAKE—Time Warner Cable. Now served by SALEM, OH [OH0096]. ICA: OH0220.

GUYSVILLE—Formerly served by Adelphia Communications. Now served by WATERTOWN, OH [OH0175]. ICA: OH0265.

HAMILTON—Time Warner Cable. Now served by CINCINNATI, OH [OH0001]. ICA: OH0022.

HANNIBAL—Windjammer Cable, 4400 PGA Blvd, Ste 902, Palm Beach Gardens, FL 33410. Phones: 877-450-5558; 561-775-1208. Fax: 561-775-7811. Web Site: http://www.windjammercable.com. Also serves Clarington, Lee Twp. (Monroe County), New Matamoras, Ohio Twp. (Monroe County) & Sardis. ICA: OH0251.

TV Market Ranking: 90 (Clarington, HANNIBAL, Lee Twp. (Monroe County), Ohio Twp. (Monroe County), Sardis); Below 100 (New Matamoras). Franchise award date: N.A. Franchise expiration date: N.A. Began: September 1, 1959.

Channel capacity: N.A. Channels available but not in use: N.A.

Basic Service

Subscribers: 1,229.

Programming (received off-air): KDKA-TV (CBS) Pittsburgh; WBOY-TV (NBC) Clarksburg; WNPB-TV (PBS) Morgantown; WOUC-TV (PBS) Cambridge; WPMY (MNT) Pittsburgh; WPXI (IND, NBC) Pittsburgh; WTAE-TV (ABC) Pittsburgh; WTOV-TV (IND, NBC) Steubenville; WTRF-TV (CBS) Wheeling; allband FM.

Programming (via satellite): QVC; TBS Superstation; WGN America.

Fee: $47.50 installation; $11.21 monthly; $.73 converter.

Expanded Basic Service 1

Subscribers: 1,090.

Programming (received off-air): WVFX (CW, FOX) Clarksburg.

Programming (via satellite): A&E Networks; ABC Family Channel; AMC; Animal Planet; CNN; Country Music TV; Discovery Channel; Disney Channel; ESPN; ESPN 2; Fox News Channel; Fox Sports Net Ohio; FX; HGTV; History Channel; Lifetime; MSNBC; MTV; Nick Jr.; Nickelodeon; Root Sports Pittsburgh; Speed; Spike TV; The Learning Channel; The Weather Channel; Turner Network TV; TV Land; USA Network; VH1.

Fee: $8.56 monthly.

Digital Basic Service

Subscribers: N.A.

Programming (via satellite): BBC America; Bloomberg Television; CMT Pure Country; Current; Discovery Fit & Health; Discovery Health Channel; Discovery Home Channel;

Discovery Kids Channel; Discovery Times Channel; ESPN Classic Sports; ESPNews; Fox Movie Channel; Fox Soccer; Fuse; G4; GAS; Golf Channel; Halogen Network; Lifetime Movie Network; LOGO; Military Channel; MTV Hits; MTV Jams; MTV2; Music Choice; National Geographic Channel; Nick Too; NickToons TV; Ohio News Network; Science; Style Network; Toon Disney; Tr3s; Trinity Broadcasting Network; Turner Classic Movies; VH1 Classic; VH1 Soul; WE tv.

Digital Expanded Basic Service

Subscribers: N.A.

Programming (via satellite): Bio; GSN; History Channel International; Independent Film Channel; Outdoor Channel; Versus.

Digital Pay Service 1

Pay Units: N.A.

Programming (via satellite): Cinemax (multiplexed); Encore (multiplexed); HBO (multiplexed); Showtime (multiplexed); Starz (multiplexed); The Movie Channel (multiplexed).

Fee: $11.95 monthly (HBO, Cinemax, Showtime/TMC or Starz/Encore).

Video-On-Demand: No

Pay-Per-View

iN DEMAND (delivered digitally); Playboy TV (delivered digitally); Club Jenna (delivered digitally); Fresh (delivered digitally).

Internet Service

Operational: Yes.

Broadband Service: Road Runner.

Fee: $44.95 monthly.

Telephone Service

None

Miles of Plant: 39.0 (coaxial); 15.0 (fiber optic).

General Manager: Timothy Evard. Operations Director: Belinda Graham. Engineering Director: Mike Earehart. Finance & Accounting Director: Cindy Johnson.

Ownership: Windjammer Communications LLC (MSO).

HARRISON TWP. (Carroll County)—Time Warner Cable. Now served by NEW PHILADELPHIA, OH [OH0030]. ICA: OH0249.

HAYDEN HEIGHTS—Formerly served by Time Warner Cable. No longer in operation. ICA: OH0301.

HICKSVILLE—Mediacom, 109 E 5th St, Ste A, Auburn, IN 46706. Phone: 260-927-3015. Fax: 260-347-4433. Web Site: http://www.mediacomcable.com. Also serves Antwerp. ICA: OH0169.

TV Market Ranking: 82 (Antwerp, HICKSVILLE). Franchise award date: N.A. Franchise expiration date: November 1, 2010. Began: March 4, 1981.

Channel capacity: N.A. Channels available but not in use: N.A.

Basic Service

Subscribers: 1,115.

Programming (received off-air): WANE-TV (CBS) Fort Wayne; WBGU-TV (PBS) Bowling Green; WFFT-TV (IND) Fort Wayne; WFWA (PBS) Fort Wayne; WINM (IND) Angola; WISE-TV (FOX, MNT, NBC) Fort Wayne; WLIO (CW, NBC) Lima; WNWO-TV (NBC) Toledo; WPTA (ABC, CW) Fort Wayne; WTVG (ABC) Toledo.

Programming (via satellite): TBS Superstation.

Fee: $45.00 installation; $20.95 monthly.

Expanded Basic Service 1

Subscribers: 966.

Programming (via satellite): A&E Networks; ABC Family Channel; AMC; Animal Planet; Bio; Bloomberg Television; Cartoon Network; CNBC; CNN; Comedy Central; Country Music TV; C-SPAN; Discovery Channel; Disney Channel; E! Entertainment Television; ESPN; ESPN 2; Fox Movie Channel; Fox Sports Net Midwest; FX; G4; Hallmark Channel; Headline News; HGTV; History Channel; Lifetime; Lifetime Movie Network; MSNBC; MTV; Nickelodeon; QVC; Radar Channel; Speed; Spike TV; Style Network; Syfy; The Learning Channel; The Weather Channel; Travel Channel; Turner Network TV; TV Guide Network; TV Land; USA Network; VH1; WGN America.

Fee: $34.00 monthly.

Digital Basic Service

Subscribers: 29.

Programming (via satellite): BBC America; Discovery Digital Networks; DMX Music; ESPN Classic Sports; Fox Soccer; Golf Channel; GSN; Independent Film Channel; Turner Classic Movies.

Fee: $9.00 monthly.

Digital Pay Service 1

Pay Units: 21.

Programming (via satellite): Cinemax (multiplexed); Encore (multiplexed); HBO (multiplexed); Showtime (multiplexed); Starz (multiplexed); The Movie Channel (multiplexed).

Fee: $11.95 monthly (HBO, Cinemax, Showtime/TMC or Starz/Encore).

Video-On-Demand: Yes

Pay-Per-View

iN DEMAND (delivered digitally); Playboy TV (delivered digitally); Pleasure (delivered digitally); Fresh (delivered digitally); Shorteez (delivered digitally).

Internet Service

Operational: Yes.

Broadband Service: Mediacom High Speed Internet.

Fee: $59.95 installation; $40.95 monthly.

Telephone Service

Digital: Operational

Fee: $39.95 monthly

Miles of Plant: 40.0 (coaxial); 10.0 (fiber optic).

Operations Director: Joe Poffenberger. Technical Operations Manager: Craig Grey.

Ownership: Mediacom LLC (MSO).

HIDE-A-WAY HILLS—Time Warner Cable, 1266 Dublin Rd, Columbus, OH 43215-1008. Phones: 740-345-4329 (Newark office); 614-481-5000 (Columbus office). Fax: 614-481-5052. Web Site: http://www.timewarnercable.com/midohio. Also serves Berne Twp. & Rush Creek Twp. ICA: OH0229.

TV Market Ranking: 27 (Berne Twp., HIDE-A-WAY HILLS, Rush Creek Twp.). Franchise award date: December 9, 1986. Franchise expiration date: N.A. Began: October 1, 1989.

Channel capacity: N.A. Channels available but not in use: N.A.

Basic Service

Subscribers: 627.

Programming (received off-air): WBNS-TV (CBS) Columbus; WCMH-TV (NBC) Columbus; WOSU-TV (PBS) Columbus; WSYX (ABC, MNT) Columbus; WTTE (FOX) Columbus; WWHO (CW) Chillicothe.

Programming (via satellite): QVC; WGN America.

Fee: $20.99 installation; $22.95 monthly.

Expanded Basic Service 1

Subscribers: N.A.

Programming (via satellite): A&E Networks; ABC Family Channel; AMC; Animal Planet; CNN; Country Music TV; Discovery Channel; Disney Channel; ESPN; ESPN 2; Fox News Channel; FX; HGTV; History Channel; Lifetime; MSNBC; Nickelodeon; Spike TV; TBS Superstation; The Learning Channel; The Weather Channel; Travel Channel; Turner Classic Movies; Turner Network TV; TV Land; USA Network.

Digital Basic Service

Subscribers: N.A.

Programming (via satellite): BBC America; Bravo; Discovery Health Channel; Discovery Kids Channel; ESPN Classic Sports; ESPNews; Fox Sports World; Golf Channel; GSN; Independent Film Channel; Music Choice; Nick Jr.; Science; Syfy; Versus; WE tv.

Digital Pay Service 1

Pay Units: N.A.

Programming (via satellite): Cinemax (multiplexed); Encore (multiplexed); HBO (multiplexed); Showtime (multiplexed); Starz (multiplexed); The Movie Channel (multiplexed).

Fee: $11.95 monthly (each).

Video-On-Demand: No

Pay-Per-View

Hits Movies & Events (delivered digitally); Playboy TV (delivered digitally).

Internet Service

Operational: No.

Telephone Service

None

Miles of Plant: 65.0 (coaxial); None (fiber optic).

President: Rhonda Fraas. Vice President & General Manager: David Kreiman. Vice President, Engineering: Randy Hall. Vice President, Marketing: Mark Psigoda. Vice President, Government & Public Affairs: Mary Jo Green. Technical Operations Director: Jim Cavender. Government Affairs Director: Steve Cuckler.

Ownership: Time Warner Cable (MSO).

HILLSBORO—Time Warner Cable. Now served by CINCINNATI, OH [OH0001]. ICA: OH0110.

HOPEDALE—Time Warner Cable, 530 S Main St, Ste 1751, Akron, OH 44311-1090. Phone: 330-633-9203. Fax: 330-633-7970. Web Site: http://www.timewarnercable.com/northeastohio. ICA: OH0281.

TV Market Ranking: 90 (HOPEDALE). Franchise award date: N.A. Franchise expiration date: N.A. Began: April 1, 1975.

Channel capacity: 40 (not 2-way capable). Channels available but not in use: N.A.

Basic Service

Subscribers: 250.

Programming (received off-air): KDKA-TV (CBS) Pittsburgh; WOUC-TV (PBS) Cambridge; WPGH-TV (FOX) Pittsburgh; WPXI (IND, NBC) Pittsburgh; WQED (PBS) Pittsburgh; WTAE-TV (ABC) Pittsburgh; WTOV-TV (IND, NBC) Steubenville; WTRF-TV (CBS) Wheeling; WVPX-TV (ION) Akron.

Programming (via satellite): ABC Family Channel; Discovery Channel; Hallmark Channel; TBS Superstation.

Fee: $44.95 installation; $16.89 monthly; $3.40 converter.

Expanded Basic Service 1

Subscribers: 224.

Programming (via satellite): A&E Networks; AMC; Animal Planet; Cartoon Network; CNBC; CNN; Disney Channel; ESPN; ESPN 2; Fox News Channel; Headline News; MoviePlex; Spike TV; Turner Network TV; USA Network.

Fee: $18.36 monthly.

Pay Service 1

Pay Units: 45.

Programming (via satellite): HBO.

Fee: $14.95 monthly.

Pay Service 2

Pay Units: 30.

Programming (via satellite): Showtime.

Fee: $14.95 monthly.

Pay Service 3

Pay Units: 66.

Programming (via satellite): Encore.

Fee: $4.00 monthly.

Pay Service 4

Pay Units: 34.

Programming (via satellite): Starz.

Fee: $8.95 monthly.

Video-On-Demand: No

Internet Service

Operational: Yes.

Broadband Service: RoadRunner.

Telephone Service

None

Miles of Plant: 8.0 (coaxial); None (fiber optic).

President: Stephen Fry. Area Vice President: Scot Miller. Vice President, Engineering: Al Costanzi. Vice President, Marketing: Patrick Burke. Vice President, Public Affairs: William Jasso. Government & Media Relations Director: Chris Thomas.

Ownership: Time Warner Cable (MSO).

HOWARD—Formerly served by Adelphia Communications. Now served by NEWARK, OH [OH0019]. ICA: OH0397.

HUBBARD TWP. (Trumbull County)—Northeast Cable TV, PO Box 4177, Youngstown, OH 44515-0177. Phone: 330-793-7434. Fax: 330-793-7434. ICA: OH0383.

TV Market Ranking: 79 (HUBBARD TWP.). Franchise award date: N.A. Franchise expiration date: N.A. Began: May 1, 1985.

Channel capacity: N.A. Channels available but not in use: N.A.

Basic Service

Subscribers: N.A.

Programming (received off-air): WBNX-TV (CW) Akron; WEWS-TV (ABC) Cleveland; WFMJ-TV (CW, NBC) Youngstown; WJW (FOX) Cleveland; WKBN-TV (CBS) Youngstown; WKYC (NBC) Cleveland; WNEO (PBS) Alliance; WOIO (CBS) Shaker Heights; WUAB (MNT) Lorain; WYTV (ABC, MNT) Youngstown.

Programming (via satellite): CNN; Discovery Channel; ESPN; Fox Sports Net Ohio; History Channel; Lifetime; Nickelodeon; Spike TV; Syfy; TBS Superstation; The Weather Channel; Turner Network TV; USA Network; WGN America.

Fee: $54.95 installation; $32.95 monthly.

Pay Service 1
Pay Units: N.A.
Programming (via satellite): HBO.
Fee: $9.95 monthly.
Internet Service
Operational: No.
Telephone Service
None
Miles of Plant: 5.0 (coaxial); None (fiber optic).
Manager & Chief Technician: Al Pezzenti.
Ownership: Northeast Cable TV (MSO).

HUNTINGTON TWP.—Formerly served by Adelphia Communications. Now served by CHILLICOTHE, OH [OH0033]. ICA: OH0174.

IRONDALE—Comcast Cable. Now served by WHEELING, WV [WV0004]. ICA: OH0285.

IRONTON—Formerly served by Adelphia Communications. Now served by HUNTINGTON, WV [WV0002]. ICA: OH0073.

JACKSON—Time Warner Cable, 1266 Dublin Rd, Columbus, OH 43215-1008. Phone: 614-481-5000. Fax: 614-481-5052. Web Site: http://www.timewarnercable.com/midohio. Also serves Albany, Coal Twp. (Jackson County), Coalton, Hamden, Jackson County (portions), Liberty Twp. (Jackson County), Lick Twp. (Jackson County), McArthur, Oak Hill, Wellston & Zaleski. ICA: OH0098.
TV Market Ranking: 27 (Coal Twp. (Jackson County), Coalton, Hamden, JACKSON, Liberty Twp. (Jackson County), Lick Twp. (Jackson County), McArthur, Oak Hill, Wellston, Zaleski); 27,36 (Jackson County (portions)); Below 100 (Jackson County (portions)); Outside TV Markets (Albany). Franchise award date: June 9, 1968. Franchise expiration date: N.A. Began: March 1, 1969.
Channel capacity: N.A. Channels available but not in use: N.A.
Basic Service
Subscribers: 9,780.
Programming (received off-air): WBNS-TV (CBS) Columbus; WCHS-TV (ABC) Charleston; WCMH-TV (NBC) Columbus; WOUB-TV (PBS) Athens; WOWK-TV (CBS) Huntington; WSAZ-TV (MNT, NBC) Huntington; WVAH-TV (FOX) Charleston; WWHO (CW) Chillicothe; 16 FMs.
Programming (via satellite): ABC Family Channel; C-SPAN; C-SPAN 2; Eternal Word TV Network; INSP; TBS Superstation; TV Guide Network; WGN America; WQCW (CW) Portsmouth.
Fee: $22.21 installation; $23.50 monthly.
Expanded Basic Service 1
Subscribers: N.A.
Programming (via satellite): A&E Networks; AMC; Animal Planet; BET Networks; Bio; Bravo; Cartoon Network; CNBC; CNN; Comedy Central; Country Music TV; Discovery Channel; Disney Channel; E! Entertainment Television; ESPN; ESPN 2; Food Network; Fox News Channel; Fox Sports Net Ohio; FX; Golf Channel; Great American Country; Hallmark Channel; Headline News; HGTV; History Channel; Lifetime; MSNBC; MTV; National Geographic Channel; Nickelodeon; Ohio News Network; Outdoor Channel; Oxygen; Product Information Network; QVC; ShopNBC; Speed; Spike TV; Syfy; The Learning Channel; The Weather Channel; Toon Disney; Travel Channel; truTV; Turner Network TV; TV Land; Univision Studios; USA Network; VH1; WE tv.
Digital Basic Service
Subscribers: N.A.
Programming (via satellite): AmericanLife TV Network; BBC America; Bloomberg Television; CNBC; Discovery Fit & Health; DIY Network; ESPN Classic Sports; ESPNews; Fox Movie Channel; Fox Sports World; Fuse; G4; GSN; History Channel International; Music Choice; SoapNet; Trinity Broadcasting Network; Turner Classic Movies; Versus.
Digital Expanded Basic Service
Subscribers: N.A.
Programming (via satellite): Nick Jr.; NickToons TV; Style Network; VH1 Classic; VH1 Country.
Digital Pay Service 1
Pay Units: N.A.
Programming (via satellite): ART America; Canales N; CCTV-4; Cinemax (multiplexed); Encore (multiplexed); Filipino Channel; Flix; HBO (multiplexed); RAI Internctional; Showtime (multiplexed); Starz (multiplexed); Sundance Channel; The Movie Channel (multiplexed); TV Asia; TV Japan; TV5, La Television International; Zee TV USA; Zhong Tian Channel.
Fee: $11.95 monthly (each).
Video-On-Demand: Yes
Pay-Per-View
Urban Xtra (delivered digitally); Hot Choice (delivered digitally); Fresh (delivered digitally); Playboy TV (delivered digitally); Movies (delivered digitally).
Internet Service
Operational: Yes. Began: June 1, 2002.
Broadband Service: Road Runner.
Fee: $44.95 monthly.
Telephone Service
Digital: Operational
Fee: $44.95 monthly
Miles of Plant: 198.0 (coaxial); None (fiber optic).
President: Rhonda Fraas. Vice President & General Manager: David Kreiman. Vice President, Engineering: Randy Hall. Vice President, Marketing: Mark Psigoda. Vice President, Public Affairs: Mary Jo Green. Technical Operations Director: Jim Cavender. Government Affairs Director: Steve Cuckler.
Ownership: Time Warner Cable (MSO).

JASPER—Time Warner Cable, 1266 Dublin Rd, Columbus, OH 43215-1008. Phone: 614-481-5000. Fax: 614-481-5052. Web Site: http://www.timewarnercable.com/midohio. ICA: OH0442.
TV Market Ranking: 27 (JASPER).
Channel capacity: N.A. Channels available but not in use: N.A.
Basic Service
Subscribers: N.A.
Programming (received off-air): WBNS-TV (CBS) Columbus; WCHS-TV (ABC) Charleston; WCMH-TV (NBC) Columbus; WOWK-TV (CBS) Huntington; WPBO (PBS) Portsmouth; WSAZ-TV (MNT, NBC) Huntington; WVAH-TV (FOX) Charleston; WWHO (CW) Chillicothe.
Programming (via satellite): QVC; WGN America.
Expanded Basic Service 1
Subscribers: N.A.
Programming (via satellite): ABC Family Channel; AMC; Cartoon Network; CNN; Country Music TV; Discovery Channel; Disney Channel; ESPN; ESPN 2; Fox News Channel; HBO; History Channel; Lifetime; MSNBC; Nickelodeon; Spike TV; Syfy; TBS Superstation; The Weather Channel; Turner Network TV; USA Network; VH1.
Digital Basic Service
Subscribers: N.A.
Programming (via satellite): BBC America; Bloomberg Television; Bravo!; Discovery Fit & Health; Discovery Health Channel; Discovery Kids Channel; ESPN Classic Sports; ESPNews; Fox Movie Channel; Fox Sports World; G4; Golf Channel; GSN; HGTV; Independent Film Channel; INSP; Music Choice; Nick Jr.; NickToons TV; Outdoor Channel; Science; Trinity Broadcasting Network; Versus; WE tv.
Fee: $52.40 monthly.
Digital Pay Service 1
Pay Units: N.A.
Programming (via satellite): Cinemax (multiplexed); Encore (multiplexed); HBO (multiplexed); Showtime (multiplexed).
Fee: $11.95 monthly (each).
Video-On-Demand: No
Pay-Per-View
HITS 1 (delivered digitally); Fresh (delivered digitally).
Internet Service
Operational: No.
Telephone Service
None
Miles of Plant: 89.0 (coaxial); None (fiber optic).
President: Rhonda Fraas. Vice President & General Manager: David Kreiman. Vice President, Engineering: Randy Hall. Vice President, Marketing: Mark Psigoda. Vice President, Government & Public Relations: Mary Jo Green. Technical Operations Director: Jim Cavender. Government Affairs Director: Steve Cuckler.
Ownership: Time Warner Cable (MSO).

JEROMESVILLE—Time Warner Cable, 530 S Main St, Ste 1751, Akron, OH 44311-1090. Phone: 330-633-9203. Fax: 330-633-7970. Web Site: http://www.timewarnercable.com/northeastohio. Also serves Big Prairie, Lakeville, Loudonville, Nashville, Perrysville, Rowsburg & Shreve. ICA: OH0266.
TV Market Ranking: Below 100 (Big Prairie, JEROMESVILLE, Lakeville, Loudonville, Nashville, Perrysville, Rowsburg, Shreve). Franchise award date: N.A. Franchise expiration date: N.A. Began: June 1, 1978.
Channel capacity: N.A. Channels available but not in use: N.A.
Basic Service
Subscribers: N.A. Included in Mansfield
Programming (received off-air): WBNS-TV (CBS) Columbus; WBNX-TV (CW) Akron; WCMH-TV (NBC) Columbus; WEWS-TV (ABC) Cleveland; WGGN-TV (TBN) Sandusky; WJW (FOX) Cleveland; WKYC (NBC) Cleveland; WMFD-TV (IND) Mansfield; WOIO (CBS) Shaker Heights; WOSU-TV (PBS) Columbus; WQHS-DT (UNV) Cleveland; WRLM (IND) Canton; WSYX (ABC, MNT) Columbus; WUAB (MNT) Lorain; WVIZ (PBS) Cleveland; WVPX-TV (ION) Akron.
Programming (via satellite): A&E Networks; AMC; Cartoon Network; INSP; QVC.
Fee: $44.95 installation; $16.19 monthly; $2.50 converter.
Expanded Basic Service 1
Subscribers: N.A.
Programming (via satellite): ABC Family Channel; Animal Planet; BET Networks; Bravo!; CNBC; CNN; Comedy Central; C-SPAN; C-SPAN 2; Discovery Channel; Discovery Fit & Health; Discovery Health Channel; Disney Channel; E! Entertainment Television; ESPN; ESPN 2; ESPN Classic Sports; Eternal Word TV Network; Food Network; Fox News Channel; Fox Sports Net Ohio; FX; Golf Channel; Great American Country; GSN; Hallmark Channel; Headline News; HGTV; History Channel; Lifetime; Lifetime Movie Network; MSNBC; MTV; Nickelodeon; Oxygen; ShopNBC; SoapNet; Spike TV; Syfy; TBS Superstation; The Learning Channel; The Weather Channel; Travel Channel; truTV; Turner Classic Movies; Turner Network TV; TV Land; USA Network; Versus; VH1; WE tv; WGN America.
Fee: $32.31 monthly.
Digital Basic Service
Subscribers: N.A.
Programming (via satellite): A&E Networks; AmericanLife TV Network; America's Store; BBC America; Bio; Bloomberg Television; Boomerang; Canales N; CBS Sports Network; CNN; CNN International; Cooking Channel; Country Music TV; C-SPAN 3; Current; Daystar TV Network; Disney Channel; DIY Network; DMX Music; ESPN; ESPNews; Fox College Sports Atlantic; Fox College Sports Central; Fox College Sports Pacific; Fox Movie Channel; Fox News Channel; Fox Soccer; Fuel TV; Fuse; G4; GAS; HD Theater; HDNet; HDNet Movies; Headline News; History Channel International; Independent Film Channel; INHD (multiplexed); International Television (ITV); Jewelry Television; Lifetime; Lifetime Real Women; MTV2; National Geographic Channel; NBA TV; Nick Jr.; NickToons TV; Ohio News Network; Outdoor Channel; Speed; Style Network; TBS Superstation; Tennis Channel; The Weather Channel; Toon Disney; Trio; Turner Network TV; Turner Network TV HD; USA Network; VH1 Classic.
Fee: $19.49 monthly.
Digital Pay Service 1
Pay Units: 59.
Programming (via satellite): Cinemax (multiplexed); Encore (multiplexed); HBO (multiplexed); Showtime (multiplexed); Starz (multiplexed); Sundance Channel; The Movie Channel (multiplexed).
Fee: $12.00 monthly (each).
Video-On-Demand: Yes
Pay-Per-View
Movies (delivered digitally); iN DEMAND (delivered digitally); MLB Extra Innings (delivered digitally); Playboy TV (delivered digitally); Fresh (delivered digitally); Pleasure (delivered digitally); NASCAR In Car (delivered digitally); NBA League Pass (delivered digitally); ESPN (delivered digitally); NHL Center Ice (delivered digitally).
Internet Service
Operational: Yes.
Broadband Service: EarthLink, Road Runner.
Fee: $99.00 installation; $44.95 monthly.
Telephone Service
Analog: Not Operational
Digital: Operational
Fee: $44.95 monthly
Miles of Plant: 56.0 (coaxial); None (fiber optic).
President: Stephen Fry. Area Vice President: Scott Miller. Vice President, Engineering: Al Costanzi. Vice President, Marketing: Patrick Burke. Vice President, Sales: Woody Woodward. Vice President, Public Affairs: William Jasso. Area Manager: Carol Jagger. Government & Media Relations Director: Chris Thomas.
Ownership: Time Warner Cable (MSO).

JEWETT—Time Warner Cable, 530 S Main St, Ste 1751, Akron, OH 44311-1090. Phone: 330-633-9203. Fax: 330-633-7970.

Web Site: http://www.timewarnercable.com/northeastohio. ICA: OH0283.

TV Market Ranking: 90 (JEWETT). Franchise award date: N.A. Franchise expiration date: N.A. Began: August 1, 1971.

Channel capacity: 40 (not 2-way capable). Channels available but not in use: N.A.

Basic Service

Subscribers: 233.

Programming (received off-air): KDKA-TV (CBS) Pittsburgh; WOUC-TV (PBS) Cambridge; WPGH-TV (FOX) Pittsburgh; WPXI (IND, NBC) Pittsburgh; WQED (PBS) Pittsburgh; WTAE-TV (ABC) Pittsburgh; WTOV-TV (IND, NBC) Steubenville; WTRF-TV (CBS) Wheeling; WVPX-TV (ION) Akron; WYTV (ABC, MNT) Youngstown.

Programming (via satellite): Discovery Channel; QVC; TBS Superstation.

Fee: $44.95 installation; $14.79 monthly; $3.40 converter.

Expanded Basic Service 1

Subscribers: 208.

Programming (via satellite): A&E Networks; ABC Family Channel; AMC; Animal Planet; Cartoon Network; CNBC; CNN; C-SPAN; E! Entertainment Television; ESPN; ESPN 2; Fox News Channel; HGTV; ION Television; Lifetime; MoviePlex; MTV; Nickelodeon; Spike TV; Trinity Broadcasting Network; Turner Network TV; USA Network.

Fee: $22.46 monthly.

Pay Service 1

Pay Units: 36.

Programming (via satellite): HBO.

Fee: $14.95 monthly.

Pay Service 2

Pay Units: 16.

Programming (via satellite): Showtime.

Fee: $14.95 monthly.

Pay Service 3

Pay Units: 69.

Programming (via satellite): Encore.

Fee: $4.00 monthly.

Pay Service 4

Pay Units: 27.

Programming (via satellite): Starz.

Fee: $14.95 monthly.

Video-On-Demand: No

Internet Service

Operational: No.

Telephone Service

None

Miles of Plant: 5.0 (coaxial); None (fiber optic).

President: Stephen Fry. Area Vice President: Scott Miller. Vice President, Engineering: Al Costanzi. Vice President, Marketing: Patrick Burke. Vice President, Public Affairs: William Jasso. Government & Media Relations Director: Chris Thomas.

Ownership: Time Warner Cable (MSO).

KALIDA—Kalida Telephone Co., 121 E Main St, PO Box 267, Kalida, OH 45853. Phone: 419-532-3218. Fax: 419-532-3300. E-mail: ktc@kalidatel.com. Web Site: http://www.kalidatel.com. Also serves Greensburg Twp., Jackson Twp. (Putnam County), Sugar Creek Twp. (Putnam County) & Union Twp. (Putnam County). ICA: OH0277.

TV Market Ranking: Below 100 (Greensburg Twp., Jackson Twp. (Putnam County), KALIDA, Sugar Creek Twp. (Putnam County), Union Twp. (Putnam County)). Franchise award date: December 7, 1981. Franchise expiration date: N.A. Began: May 1, 1985.

Channel capacity: 45 (operating 2-way). Channels available but not in use: N.A.

Basic Service

Subscribers: 940.

Programming (received off-air): WANE-TV (CBS) Fort Wayne; WBGU-TV (PBS) Bowling Green; WBNS-TV (CBS) Columbus; WLIO (CW, NBC) Lima; WNWO-TV (NBC) Toledo; WOHL-CD (FOX) Lima; WPTA (ABC, CW) Fort Wayne; WTLW (IND) Lima; WTOL (CBS) Toledo; WTVG (ABC) Toledo; WUPW (FOX) Toledo; 1 FM.

Programming (via satellite): A&E Networks; ABC Family Channel; BTN; Cartoon Network; CNN; CW+; Discovery Channel; Disney Channel; ESPN; ESPN 2; ESPN Classic Sports; Eternal Word TV Network; Food Network; Fox News Channel; Fox Sports Net Ohio; FX; Hallmark Channel; Lifetime; MSNBC; MTV; National Geographic Channel; SportsTime Ohio; TBS Superstation; The Learning Channel; The Weather Channel; Travel Channel; Turner Classic Movies; Turner Network TV; TV Land; USA Network; VH1; WGN America.

Fee: $24.50 installation; $30.95 monthly.

Expanded Basic Service 1

Subscribers: 200.

Programming (via satellite): Comedy Central; Country Music TV; History Channel; Nickelodeon; Spike TV.

Fee: $6.00 monthly.

Digital Basic Service

Subscribers: N.A.

Programming (via satellite): BBC America; Bloomberg Television; CMT Pure Country; Discovery Health Channel; Discovery Kids Channel; DMX Music; ESPN Classic Sports; Fox Soccer; Golf Channel; HGTV; ID Investigation Discovery; Independent Film Channel; Lifetime Movie Network; Military Channel; MTV2; National Geographic Channel; Nick Jr.; NickToons TV; Planet Green; Science; Speed; TeenNick; Toon Disney; Versus; VH1 Classic; WE tv.

Fee: $13.50 monthly.

Digital Expanded Basic Service

Subscribers: N.A.

Programming (via satellite): Bio; Discovery Fit & Health; ESPNews; Fox Movie Channel; Fuse; G4; GSN; History Channel International; Outdoor Channel.

Fee: $3.50 monthly.

Pay Service 1

Pay Units: 164.

Programming (via satellite): The Movie Channel.

Fee: $9.95 monthly.

Pay Service 2

Pay Units: 211.

Programming (via satellite): Showtime.

Fee: $9.95 monthly.

Pay Service 3

Pay Units: N.A.

Programming (via satellite): HBO.

Fee: $11.95 monthly.

Digital Pay Service 1

Pay Units: N.A.

Programming (via satellite): Cinemax (multiplexed); Encore (multiplexed); HBO (multiplexed); Showtime (multiplexed); Starz (multiplexed); The Movie Channel (multiplexed).

Fee: $5.95 monthly (Encore), $8.95 monthly (Cinemax), $9.95 monthly (Showtime or TMC), $11.95 monthly (HBO), $12.95 monthly (Starz/Encore), $13.95 monthly (Showtime/TMC).

Video-On-Demand: No

Internet Service

Operational: No, DSL & dial-up.

Telephone Service

None

Miles of Plant: 35.0 (coaxial); None (fiber optic).

Manager: Chris J. Phillips. Chief Technician: Chris Hoffman. Business Manager: Sue Gerdeman.

Ownership: Kalida Telephone Co.

KENT—Time Warner Cable, 530 S Main St, Ste 1751, Akron, OH 44311-1090. Phone: 330-633-9203. Fax: 330-633-7970. Web Site: http://www.timewarnercable.com/northeastohio. Also serves Brady Lake Village, Brimfield Twp. (Portage County), Franklin Twp. (Portage County), Ravenna, Robin Mobile Home Park, Rootstown Twp. (Portage County), Spring Lakes Mobile Home Park, Streetsboro, Suffield Twp. & Sugar Bush Knolls. ICA: OH0034.

TV Market Ranking: 79 (Robin Mobile Home Park); 8 (Brimfield Twp. (Portage County), Franklin Twp. (Portage County), KENT, Streetsboro, Suffield Twp., Sugar Bush Knolls); 8,79 (Brady Lake Village, Ravenna, Rootstown Twp. (Portage County), Spring Lakes Mobile Home Park). Franchise award date: N.A. Franchise expiration date: March 20, 2010. Began: March 1, 1972.

Channel capacity: N.A. Channels available but not in use: N.A.

Basic Service

Subscribers: 20,458.

Programming (received off-air): WAOH-LP Akron; WBNX-TV (CW) Akron; WDLI-TV (TBN) Canton; WEAO (PBS) Akron; WEWS-TV (ABC) Cleveland; WJW (FOX) Cleveland; WKYC (NBC) Cleveland; WOIO (CBS) Shaker Heights; WQHS-DT (UNV) Cleveland; WRLM (IND) Canton; WUAB (MNT) Lorain; WVIZ (PBS) Cleveland; WVPX-TV (ION) Akron; 3 FMs.

Programming (via satellite): WGN America.

Fee: $29.95 installation; $13.60 monthly; $1.50 converter.

Expanded Basic Service 1

Subscribers: 14,878.

Programming (via satellite): A&E Networks; ABC Family Channel; AMC; Animal Planet; BET Networks; Bravo!; Cartoon Network; CNBC; CNN; Comedy Central; C-SPAN; C-SPAN 2; Discovery Channel; Discovery Fit & Health; Discovery Health Channel; Disney Channel; E! Entertainment Television; ESPN; ESPN 2; ESPN Classic Sports; Eternal Word TV Network; Food Network; Fox News Channel; Fox Sports Net Ohio; FX; Golf Channel; Great American Country; GSN; Hallmark Channel; Headline News; HGTV; History Channel; INSP; Lifetime; Lifetime Movie Network; MSNBC; MTV; Nickelodeon; Oxygen; QVC; ShopNBC; SoapNet; Spike TV; Syfy; TBS Superstation; The Learning Channel; The Weather Channel; Travel Channel; truTV; Turner Classic Movies; Turner Network TV; TV Land; USA Network; Versus; VH1; WE tv.

Fee: $43.39 monthly.

Digital Basic Service

Subscribers: N.A.

Programming (via satellite): AmericanLife TV Network; America's Store; ART America; BBC America; Bio; Bloomberg Television; Boomerang; CBS Sports Network; CNN International; Cooking Channel; Country Music TV; C-SPAN 3; Current; Daystar TV Network; Disney Channel; DIY Network; DMX Music; Do-It-Yourself On Demand; ESPN; ESPNews; Food Network On Demand; Fox College Sports Atlantic; Fox College Sports Central; Fox College Sports Pacific; Fox Movie Channel; Fox Soccer; Fuel TV; Fuse; G4; GAS; Great American Country On Demand; HBO (multiplexed); HD Theater; HDNet; HDNet Movies; HGTV On Demand; History Channel International; Independent Film Channel; INHD; Jewelry Television; Lifetime Real Women; MTV2; National Geographic Channel; NBA TV; Nick Jr.; NickToons TV; Ohio News Network; Outdoor Channel; RAI International; Showtime (multiplexed); Speed; Tennis Channel; The Learning Channel; The Word Network; Toon Disney; Trio; TV Asia; TVG Network; various Mexican stations; VH1 Classic; Zee TV USA.

Fee: $11.00 monthly.

Digital Pay Service 1

Pay Units: 920.

Programming (via satellite): Cinemax (multiplexed); Encore (multiplexed); HBO (multiplexed); HBO On Demand; Showtime (multiplexed); Showtime On Demand; Starz (multiplexed); The Movie Channel (multiplexed); The Movie Channel On Demand.

Fee: $12.00 monthly (each).

Video-On-Demand: Yes

Pay-Per-View

Movies (delivered digitally); ESPN (delivered digitally); NHL Center Ice - MLB Extra Innings (delivered digitally); iN DEMAND (delivered digitally); Playboy TV (delivered digitally); Spice Live (delivered digitally); Ten Clips (delivered digitally); Pleasure (delivered digitally); NASCAR In Car (delivered digitally); NBA League Pass (delivered digitally).

Internet Service

Operational: Yes.

Broadband Service: EarthLink, Road Runner.

Fee: $99.00 installation; $44.95 monthly.

Telephone Service

Digital: Operational

Fee: $44.95 monthly

Miles of Plant: 415.0 (coaxial); None (fiber optic).

President: Stephen Fry. Area Vice President: Scott Miller. Vice President, Engineering: Al Costanzi. Vice President, Marketing: Patrick Burke. Vice President, Sales: Woody E. Woodward. Vice President, Customer Care: Donald A. Jensen. Vice President, Public Affairs: William Jasso. Government & Media Relations Director: Chris Thomas.

Ownership: Time Warner Cable (MSO).

KENTON—Time Warner Cable, 205 Crystal Ave, Findlay, OH 45840. Phone: 419-429-7474. Fax: 419-429-7402. Web Site: http://www.timewarnercable.com/midohio. Also serves Ada, Alger, Belle Center, Dunkirk, Forest, Hale Twp., La Rue, Liberty Twp. (Hardin County), McGuffey, Mount Victory, New Bloomington, Patterson, Pleasant Twp. (Hardin County), Richland Twp. (Logan

County), Richland Twp. (Wyandot County), Ridgeway, Rush Creek Twp. (Logan County), Rushsylvania & Wharton. ICA: OH0128.

TV Market Ranking: Below 100 (Ada, Alger, Belle Center, Dunkirk, Forest, Hale Twp. (portions), Liberty Twp. (Hardin County), McGuffey, Mount Victory, Patterson, Pleasant Twp. (Hardin County), Richland Twp. (Logan County), Richland Twp. (Wyandot County) (portions), Ridgeway, Rush Creek Twp. (Logan County), Rushsylvania, Wharton); Outside TV Markets (Hale Twp. (portions), KENTON, La Rue, New Bloomington, Richland Twp. (Wyandot County) (portions)).

Channel capacity: N.A. Channels available but not in use: N.A.

Basic Service

Subscribers: N.A. Included in Columbus

Programming (received off-air): WBNS-TV (CBS) Columbus; WCMH-TV (NBC) Columbus; WOSU-TV (PBS) Columbus; WSFJ-TV (TBN) Newark; WSYX (ABC, MNT) Columbus; WTLW (IND) Lima; WTTE (FOX) Columbus; WUAB (MNT) Lorain; WWHO (CW) Chillicothe.

Programming (via satellite): C-SPAN; C-SPAN 2; Hallmark Channel; Headline News; History Channel; LWS Local Weather Station; QVC; ShopNBC; SoapNet; TBS Superstation; The Learning Channel; TV Guide Network; WGN America.

Expanded Basic Service 1

Subscribers: N.A.

Programming (via satellite): A&E Networks; ABC Family Channel; AMC; Animal Planet; BBC America; BET Networks; Bravo; Cartoon Network; CNBC; CNN; Comedy Central; Country Music TV; Discovery Channel; Discovery Health Channel; Disney Channel; E! Entertainment Television; ESPN; ESPN 2; Food Network; Fox News Channel; Fox Sports Net Ohio; FX; Golf Channel; HGTV; Lifetime; Lifetime Movie Network; MSNBC; MTV; MTV2; National Geographic Channel; Nick Jr.; Nickelodeon; Oxygen; Spike TV; SportsTime Ohio; Syfy; The Weather Channel; Travel Channel; truTV; Turner Classic Movies; Turner Network TV; TV Land; Univision Studios; USA Network; Versus; VH1; WE tv.

Digital Basic Service

Subscribers: N.A. Included in Columbus

Programming (received off-air): WBNS-TV (CBS) Columbus.

Programming (via satellite): AmericanLife TV Network; BBC America On Demand; Bio; Bloomberg Television; Boomerang; Canal Sur; CBS Sports Network; Cine Latino; cloo; CNN en Espanol; CNN International; Cooking Channel; C-SPAN 3; Current; Discovery en Espanol; Discovery Fit & Health; Discovery Kids Channel; Disney Channel; DIY Network; Encore (multiplexed); ESPN 2 HD; ESPN Classic Sports; ESPN HD; ESPN U; ESPNews; Eternal Word TV Network; Exercise TV; Food Network; Fox Business Channel; Fox College Sports Atlantic; Fox College Sports Central; Fox College Sports Pacific; Fox Deportes; Fox Movie Channel (multiplexed); Fox Reality Channel; Fox Soccer; FSN HD; Fuel TV; Fuse; G4; Great American Country; GSN; HD Theater; HDNet; HDNet Movies; HGTV; History Channel International; ID Investigation Discovery; Independent Film Channel; INSP; La Familia Network; Lifetime Real Women; LOGO; Military Channel; MTV Hits; mun2 television; Music Choice; National Geographic Channel HD Network; NBA TV; NHL Network; NickToons TV; Ohio News Network; Outdoor Channel; Ovation; Oxygen On Demand; Planet Green; Science; SoapNet; Speed; Speed On Demand; Style Network; Sundance Channel; TBS in HD; TeenNick; Tennis Channel; The Weather Channel; The Word Network; Toon Disney; Tr3s; Turner Network TV HD; TV One; Universal HD; VH1 Classic; VHUNO; Video Rola.

Fee: $4.95 monthly (Latino or Sports Plus), $10.40 monthly (Movies or Variety), $14.60 monthly (Premier Digital).

Digital Pay Service 1

Pay Units: N.A.

Programming (via satellite): Cinemax (multiplexed); Cinemax On Demand; Encore; HBO (multiplexed); HBO HD; HBO Latino; HBO On Demand; Showtime (multiplexed); Showtime HD; Showtime On Demand; Starz (multiplexed); Starz On Demand; The Movie Channel (multiplexed); The Movie Channel On Demand.

Fee: $11.95 monthly (HBO, Cinemax, Showtime/TMC or Starz/Encore).

Video-On-Demand: Yes

Pay-Per-View

iN DEMAND (delivered digitally); Playboy TV (delivered digitally); Sports PPV (delivered digitally).

Internet Service

Operational: Yes.

Fee: $44.95 monthly.

Telephone Service

Digital: Operational

Fee: $44.95 monthly

Miles of plant included in Columbus

President: Rhonda Fraas. Vice President & General Manager: Brad Wakely. Vice President, Engineering: Randy Hall. Vice President, Marketing: Mark Psigoda. Technical Operations Director: John Ellingson. Government Affairs Director: Brian Young. Government Affairs Manager: Patrick McCauley.

Ownership: Time Warner Cable (MSO).

KETTERING—Time Warner Cable. Now served by DAYTON, OH [OH0011]. ICA: OH0010.

KEY—Comcast Cable. Now served by WHEELING, WV [WV0004]. ICA: OH0441.

KINGSTON—Formerly served by Adelphia Communications. Now served by CHILLICOTHE, OH [OH0033]. ICA: OH0185.

KINSMAN—Formerly served by Cebridge Connections. Now served by MEADVILLE, PA [PA0062]. ICA: OH0282.

KIRKERSVILLE—Time Warner Cable. Now served by MOUNT VERNON, OH [OH0095]. ICA: OH0170.

KNOXVILLE—Suddenlink Communications, 12444 Powerscourt Dr, Saint Louis, MO 63131-3660. Phone: 314-965-2020. Web Site: http://www.suddenlink.com. Also serves Island Creek Twp. (Jefferson County), Knox Twp. (Jefferson County) & Saline Twp. ICA: OH0239.

TV Market Ranking: 10,90 (Island Creek Twp. (Jefferson County), Knox Twp. (Jefferson County), KNOXVILLE, Saline Twp.). Franchise award date: N.A. Franchise expiration date: N.A. Began: March 1, 1990.

Channel capacity: 62 (not 2-way capable). Channels available but not in use: N.A.

Basic Service

Subscribers: 529.

Programming (received off-air): KDKA-TV (CBS) Pittsburgh; WPGH-TV (FOX) Pittsburgh; WPMY (MNT) Pittsburgh; WPXI (IND, NBC) Pittsburgh; WQED (PBS) Pittsburgh; WTAE-TV (ABC) Pittsburgh; WTOV-TV (IND, NBC) Steubenville; WTRF-TV (CBS) Wheeling.

Programming (via satellite): QVC; TBS Superstation.

Fee: $30.00 installation; $10.50 monthly; $1.95 converter.

Expanded Basic Service 1

Subscribers: 505.

Programming (via satellite): A&E Networks; ABC Family Channel; AMC; CNBC; CNN; C-SPAN; Discovery Channel; Disney Channel; ESPN; Headline News; History Channel; Lifetime; MTV; Nickelodeon; Root Sports Pittsburgh; Spike TV; Syfy; The Weather Channel; Turner Network TV; TV Land; USA Network; VH1.

Fee: $20.00 monthly.

Pay Service 1

Pay Units: 43.

Programming (via satellite): Cinemax.

Fee: $11.00 monthly.

Pay Service 2

Pay Units: 76.

Programming (via satellite): HBO.

Fee: $11.00 monthly.

Pay Service 3

Pay Units: 64.

Programming (via satellite): Showtime; The Movie Channel.

Fee: $12.95 monthly.

Internet Service

Operational: No.

Telephone Service

None

Miles of Plant: 33.0 (coaxial); None (fiber optic).

Manager: Terry Dickerhoof. Chief Technician: Tom Beat.

Ownership: Cequel Communications LLC (MSO).

LA RUE—Time Warner Cable. Now served by KENTON, OH [OH0128]. ICA: OH0242.

LANCASTER—Time Warner Cable, 1266 Dublin Rd, Columbus, OH 43215-1008. Phone: 614-481-5000. Fax: 614-481-5052. Web Site: http://www.timewarnercable.com/midohio. Also serves Baltimore, Breman, Buckeye Lake, Carroll, Millersport, Pleasant Twp. (Fairfield County), Pleasantville, Rush Creek Twp. (Fairfield County), Sugar Grove, Thurston & Walnut Twp. (Fairfield County). ICA: OH0039.

TV Market Ranking: 27 (Baltimore, Buckeye Lake, Carroll, LANCASTER, Millersport, Pleasant Twp. (Fairfield County), Pleasantville, Sugar Grove, Thurston, Walnut Twp. (Fairfield County)); Below 100 (Breman, Rush Creek Twp. (Fairfield County)).

Channel capacity: N.A. Channels available but not in use: N.A.

Basic Service

Subscribers: N.A.

Programming (received off-air): WBNS-TV (CBS) Columbus; WCMH-TV (NBC) Columbus; WOSU-TV (PBS) Columbus; WSFJ-TV (TBN) Newark; WSYX (ABC, MNT) Columbus; WTTE (FOX) Columbus; WUAB (MNT) Lorain; WWHO (CW) Chillicothe.

Programming (via satellite): AmericanLife TV Network; C-SPAN; C-SPAN 2; Hallmark Channel; Headline News; History Channel; QVC; Radar Channel; ShopNBC; TBS Superstation; The Learning Channel; TV Guide Network; WGN America.

Expanded Basic Service 1

Subscribers: N.A.

Programming (via satellite): A&E Networks; ABC Family Channel; AMC; Animal Planet; BBC America; BET Networks; Bravo; Cartoon Network; CNBC; CNN; Comedy Central; Country Music TV; Discovery Channel; Discovery Health Channel; Disney Channel; E! Entertainment Television; ESPN; ESPN 2; Food Network; Fox News Channel; Fox Sports Net Ohio; FX; Golf Channel; HGTV; Jewelry Television; Lifetime; Lifetime Movie Network; MSNBC; MTV; MTV2; National Geographic Channel; Nick Jr.; Nickelodeon; Oxygen; Spike TV; SportsTime Ohio; Syfy; The Weather Channel; Travel Channel; truTV; Turner Classic Movies; Turner Network TV; TV Land; Univision Studios; USA Network; Versus; VH1; WE tv.

Digital Basic Service

Subscribers: N.A.

Programming (via satellite): AmericanLife TV Network; BBC America On Demand; Bio; Bloomberg Television; Boomerang; Canal Sur; Cine Latino; cloo; CNN en Espanol; CNN International; College Sports Television; Cooking Channel; C-SPAN 3; Current; Discovery en Espanol; Discovery Fit & Health; Discovery Kids Channel; Disney Channel; DIY Network; Encore (multiplexed); ESPN 2 HD; ESPN Classic Sports; ESPN HD; ESPN U; ESPNews; Eternal Word TV Network; Exercise TV; Food Network; Fox Business Channel; Fox College Sports Atlantic; Fox College Sports Central; Fox College Sports Pacific; Fox Deportes; Fox Movie Channel; Fox Reality Channel; Fox Soccer; FSN HD; Fuel TV; Fuse; G4; Great American Country; GSN; HD Theater; HDNet; HDNet Movies; here! TV; HGTV; History Channel International; Howard TV; ID Investigation Discovery; Independent Film Channel; INSP; Jewelry Television; La Familia Network; Lifetime Real Women; LOGO; Military Channel; Mojo Mix; MTV Hits; mun2 television; Music Choice; National Geographic Channel On Demand; NBA TV; NHL Network; NickToons TV; Ohio News Network; Outdoor Channel; Ovation; Oxygen On Demand; Planet Green; Science; SoapNet; Speed; Speed On Demand; Style Network; Sundance Channel; TBS in HD; TeenNick; Tennis Channel; The Weather Channel; The Word Network; Toon Disney; Tr3s; Turner Network TV HD; TV One; Universal HD; VH1 Classic; VHUNO; Video Rola.

Digital Pay Service 1

Pay Units: N.A.

Programming (via satellite): Cinemax (multiplexed); Cinemax On Demand; Encore; HBO (multiplexed); HBO HD; HBO Latino; HBO On Demand; Showtime (multiplexed); Showtime HD; Showtime On Demand; Starz (multiplexed); Starz On Demand; The Movie Channel (multiplexed); The Movie Channel On Demand.

Video-On-Demand: Yes

Pay-Per-View

iN DEMAND (delivered digitally); NBA League Pass (delivered digitally); MLS Direct Kick (delivered digitally); NHL Center Ice (delivered digitally); MLB Extra Innings (delivered digitally); ESPN Gameplan (delivered digitally).

Internet Service

Operational: Yes.

Broadband Service: Road Runner.

Fee: $44.95 monthly.

Telephone Service

Digital: Operational

Fee: $44.95 monthly

President: Rhonda Fraas. Vice President & General Manager: David Kreiman. Vice President, Engineering: Randy Hall. Vice President, Marketing: Mark Psigoda. Vice President, Government: Mary Jo

Green. Government Affairs Director: Steve Cuckler.
Ownership: Time Warner Cable (MSO).

LEBANON—Cincinnati Bell Extended Territories, 125 S Sycamore St, Lebanon, OH 45036. Phones: 513-228-3299; 513-933-7201. Fax: 513-933-7208. E-mail: charlie.lloyd@cinbell.com. Web Site: http://www.cincinnatibell.com. ICA: OH0438. **Note:** This system is an overbuild.
TV Market Ranking: 17,41 (LEBANON). Franchise award date: N.A. Franchise expiration date: N.A. Began: N.A.
Channel capacity: 80 (operating 2-way). Channels available but not in use: N.A.
Basic Service
Subscribers: 2,730.
Programming (received off-air): WCET (PBS) Cincinnati; WCPO-TV (ABC) Cincinnati; WHIO-TV (CBS) Dayton; WKEF (ABC) Dayton; WKRC-TV (CBS, CW) Cincinnati; WLWT (NBC) Cincinnati; WOTH-CA (IND) Cincinnati; WPTD (PBS) Dayton; WPTO (PBS) Oxford; WRGT-TV (FOX, MNT) Dayton; WSTR-TV (MNT) Cincinnati; WXIX-TV (FOX) Newport.
Programming (via satellite): C-SPAN; C-SPAN 2; Eternal Word TV Network; ION Television; Ohio News Network; QVC; The Weather Channel; Trinity Broadcasting Network; TV Guide Network; TVW; WGN America.
Fee: $40.00 installation; $9.99 monthly.
Expanded Basic Service 1
Subscribers: N.A.
Programming (via satellite): A&E Networks; ABC Family Channel; AMC; Animal Planet; BET Networks; Bravo; Cartoon Network; CNBC; CNN; Comedy Central; Cooking Channel; Country Music TV; Discovery Channel; Discovery Health Channel; Disney Channel; DIY Network; E! Entertainment Television; ESPN; ESPN 2; ESPN Classic Sports; ESPNews; Food Network; Fox News Channel; Fox Sports Net; FX; Golf Channel; Great American Country; Hallmark Channel; Headline News; HGTV; History Channel; Lifetime; MSNBC; MTV; National Geographic Channel; Nickelodeon; Oxygen; SoapNet; Speed; Spike TV; Syfy; TBS Superstation; The Learning Channel; Toon Disney; Travel Channel; truTV; Turner Classic Movies; Turner Network TV; TV Land; USA Network; VH1.
Fee: $33.96 monthly.
Digital Basic Service
Subscribers: 479.
Programming (via satellite): AmericanLife TV Network; BBC America; Bio; Black Family Channel; Bloomberg Television; Discovery Fit & Health; DMX Music; ESPN; ESPN 2; ESPN U; Fox College Sports Atlantic; Fox College Sports Central; Fox College Sports Pacific; Fox Movie Channel; Fox Soccer; G4; GAS; GSN; Halogen Network; HD Theater; HDNet; HDNet Movies; History Channel International; INHD; Lifetime Movie Network; MTV Networks Digital Suite; Nick Jr.; NickToons TV; Outdoor Channel; Ovation; ShopNBC; Trio; Versus; Weatherscan.
Fee: $19.50 monthly.
Digital Pay Service 1
Pay Units: N.A.
Programming (via satellite): Cinemax (multiplexed); Encore (multiplexed); HBO (multiplexed); Showtime (multiplexed); Starz (multiplexed); The Movie Channel (multiplexed).
Fee: $11.49 monthly (Cinemax or Starz), $12.49 monthly (HBO or Showtime & TMC).
Video-On-Demand: No
Pay-Per-View
iN DEMAND (delivered digitally); Playboy TV (delivered digitally); Hot Choice (delivered digitally); Fresh (delivered digitally); Shorteez (delivered digitally).
Internet Service
Operational: Yes.
Subscribers: 600.
Broadband Service: GO Concepts Inc..
Fee: $39.99 monthly.
Telephone Service
None
Miles of Plant: 105.0 (coaxial); 40.0 (fiber optic).
Video Operations Manager: Charlie Lloyd. Controller: Kurt Freyberger.
Ownership: Cincinnati Bell Extended Territories.

LEBANON—Formerly served by Adelphia Communications. Now served by CINCINNATI, OH [OH0001]. ICA: OH0171.

LEESBURG—Time Warner Cable. Now served by CINCINNATI, OH [OH0001]. ICA: OH0205.

LEESVILLE—Time Warner Cable, 530 S Main St, Ste 1751, Akron, OH 44311-1090. Phone: 330-633-9203. Fax: 330-633-7970. Web Site: http://www.timewarnercable.com/northeastohio. Also serves Bowerston. ICA: OH0404.
TV Market Ranking: 10 (Bowerston, LEESVILLE). Franchise award date: February 6, 1989. Franchise expiration date: N.A. Began: N.A.
Channel capacity: 42 (not 2-way capable). Channels available but not in use: N.A.
Basic Service
Subscribers: 200.
Programming (received off-air): WDLI-TV (TBN) Canton; WEWS-TV (ABC) Cleveland; WJW (FOX) Cleveland; WKYC (NBC) Cleveland; WNEO (PBS) Alliance; WOIO (CBS) Shaker Heights; WRLM (IND) Canton; WTOV-TV (IND, NBC) Steubenville; WTRF-TV (CBS) Wheeling; WUAB (MNT) Lorain; WVPX-TV (ION) Akron.
Fee: $44.95 installation; $13.24 monthly.
Expanded Basic Service 1
Subscribers: 173.
Programming (via satellite): A&E Networks; ABC Family Channel; Animal Planet; Cartoon Network; CNN; Disney Channel; ESPN; Headline News; MTV; Nickelodeon; Spike TV; TBS Superstation; Turner Network TV; USA Network.
Fee: $19.75 monthly.
Pay Service 1
Pay Units: 32.
Programming (via satellite): Encore.
Fee: $4.00 monthly.
Pay Service 2
Pay Units: 23.
Programming (via satellite): HBO.
Fee: $14.95 monthly.
Pay Service 3
Pay Units: 15.
Programming (via satellite): Showtime.
Fee: $14.95 monthly.
Pay Service 4
Pay Units: 22.
Programming (via satellite): Starz.
Fee: $14.95 monthly.
Video-On-Demand: No
Internet Service
Operational: Yes.
Telephone Service
Digital: Operational
Miles of Plant: 18.0 (coaxial); None (fiber optic).

President: Stephen Fry. Area Vice President: Scott Miller. Vice President, Engineering: Al Costanzi. Vice President, Marketing: Patrick Burke. Vice President, Public Affairs: William Jasso. Government & Media Relations Director: Chris Thomas.
Ownership: Time Warner Cable (MSO).

LEIPSIC—Orwell Cable TV Co. Now served by COLUMBUS GROVE, OH [OH0402]. ICA: OH0163.

LIBERTY TWP. (Butler County)—Time Warner Cable. Now served by CINCINNATI, OH [OH0001]. ICA: OH0142.

LICKING COUNTY—Now served by NEWARK, OH [OH0019]. ICA: OH0436.

LIMA—Time Warner Cable, 205 Crystal Ave, Findlay, OH 45840. Phones: 614-481-5000 (Columbus office); 419-429-7474. Fax: 419-429-7402. Web Site: http://www.timewarnercable.com/midohio. Also serves Allen County (portions), American Twp. (Allen County), Auglaize County (portions), Auglaize Twp. (Allen County), Bath Twp. (Allen County), Beaverdam, Bluffton, Cairo, Cridersville, Elida, Fort Shawnee, Gomer, Harrod, Jackson Twp. (Allen County), Lafayette, Richland Twp. (Allen County), Shawnee Twp. (Allen County), Spencer Twp. (Allen County), Spencerville, Sugar Creek Twp., Sugar Creek Twp. (Allen County) & Vaughnsville. ICA: OH0020.
TV Market Ranking: Below 100 (Allen County (portions), American Twp. (Allen County), Auglaize County (portions), Auglaize Twp. (Allen County), Bath Twp. (Allen County), Beaverdam, Bluffton, Cairo, Cridersville, Elida, Fort Shawnee, Gomer, Harrod, Jackson Twp. (Allen County), Lafayette, LIMA, Richland Twp. (Allen County), Shawnee Twp. (Allen County), Spencer Twp. (Allen County), Spencerville, Sugar Creek Twp., Sugar Creek Twp. (Allen County), Vaughnsville). Franchise award date: December 19, 1965. Franchise expiration date: January 5, 2011. Began: September 1, 1966.
Channel capacity: N.A. Channels available but not in use: N.A.
Basic Service
Subscribers: 27,486.
Programming (received off-air): WANE-TV (CBS) Fort Wayne; WBGU-TV (PBS) Bowling Green; WBNS-TV (CBS) Columbus; WHIO-TV (CBS) Dayton; WLIO (CW, NBC) Lima; WLQP-LP Lima; WOHL-CD (FOX) Lima; WTLW (IND) Lima; WTVG (ABC) Toledo.
Programming (via satellite): ION Television.
Fee: $45.86 installation; $11.35 monthly.
Expanded Basic Service 1
Subscribers: N.A.
Programming (via satellite): A&E Networks; ABC Family Channel; AMC; Animal Planet; BET Networks; Bravo; Cartoon Network; CNBC; CNN; Comedy Central; Country Music TV; C-SPAN; C-SPAN 2; Discovery Channel; Disney Channel; E! Entertainment Television; Encore Action; ESPN; ESPN 2; ESPN Classic Sports; Eternal Word TV Network; Food Network; Fox News Channel; Fox Sports Net Ohio; FX; Golf Channel; Hallmark Channel; Headline News; HGTV; History Channel; Lifetime; Lifetime Movie Network; MSNBC; MTV; National Geographic Channel; Nickelodeon; Oxygen; QVC; ShopNBC; Spike TV; Syfy; TBS Superstation; The Learning Channel; The Weather Channel; Travel Channel; truTV; Turner Classic Movies; Turner Network TV; TV Guide Network; TV Land; USA Network; Versus; VH1; WE tv.
Fee: $45.99 monthly.
Digital Basic Service
Subscribers: 8,246.
Programming (via satellite): AmericanLife TV Network; America's Store; BBC America; Bloomberg Television; CNN International; Cooking Channel; C-SPAN 3; Discovery Fit & Health; DIY Network; DMX Music; ESPNews; Fox Sports World; FSN Digital Atlantic; FSN Digital Central; FSN Digital Pacific; Fuse; G4; GAS; Great American Country; GSN; Lifetime Real Women; MTV2; Nick Jr.; Ohio News Network; Outdoor Channel; Ovation; SoapNet; Sorpresa; Speed; Style Network; Toon Disney; VH1 Classic.
Fee: $9.90 monthly.
Digital Pay Service 1
Pay Units: 2,343.
Programming (via satellite): Cinemax (multiplexed); Encore (multiplexed); Flix; HBO (multiplexed); Showtime (multiplexed); Starz (multiplexed); The Movie Channel (multiplexed).
Fee: $10.00 installation; $11.95 monthly (Cinemax, HBO, Showtime/Flix/TMC or Starz/Encore).
Video-On-Demand: Yes
Pay-Per-View
Addressable homes: 8,246.
iN DEMAND (delivered digitally); Fresh (delivered digitally); Sports PPV (delivered digitally).
Internet Service
Operational: Yes. Began: January 1, 1999.
Subscribers: 4,948.
Broadband Service: Road Runner.
Fee: $69.95 installation; $44.95 monthly.
Telephone Service
Digital: Operational
Fee: $44.95 monthly
Miles of Plant: 441.0 (coaxial); None (fiber optic). Additional miles planned: 9.0 (coaxial).
President: Rhonda Fraas. Vice President & General Manager: Brad Wakely. Vice President, Engineering: Randy Hall. Vice President, Marketing: Mark Psigoda. Technical Operations Director: John Ellingson. Government Affairs Manager: Patrick McCauley. Government Affairs Director: Brian Young.
Ownership: Time Warner Cable (MSO).

LINDSEY (Sandusky County)—Tiime Warner Cable. Now served by CLAY CENTER/GIBSONBURG (formerly Allen Twp.), OH [OH0071]. ICA: OH0333.

LISBON—Time Warner Cable. Now served by SALEM, OH [OH0096]. ICA: OH0182.

LODI—Time Warner Cable, 530 S Main St, Ste 1751, Akron, OH 44311-1090. Phone: 330-633-9203. Fax: 330-633-7970. Web Site: http://www.timewarnercable.com/northeastohio. Also serves Briarwood Beach, Burbank, Canaan Twp. (Wayne County), Chatham Twp., Chippewa Lake, Creston, Gloria Glens, Guilford Twp., Homer Twp. (Medina County), Lafayette Twp. (Medina County), Milton Twp. (Wayne County), Montville Twp. (Medina County), Rittman, Seville, Spencer, Sterling, West Salem & Westfield Center. ICA: OH0068.

TV Market Ranking: 8 (Briarwood Beach, Burbank, Canaan Twp. (Wayne County), Chatham Twp., Chippewa Lake, Creston, Gloria Glens, Guilford Twp., Homer Twp. (Medina County), Lafayette Twp. (Medina County), LODI, Milton Twp. (Wayne County), Montville Twp. (Medina County), Rittman, Seville, Spencer, Sterling, West Salem, Westfield Center, Westfield Twp. (Medina County)). Franchise award date: N.A. Franchise expiration date: N.A. Began: November 1, 1970.

Channel capacity: N.A. Channels available but not in use: N.A.

Basic Service

Subscribers: N.A. Included in Mansfield

Programming (received off-air): WBNX-TV (CW) Akron; WDLI-TV (TBN) Canton; WEAO (PBS) Akron; WEWS-TV (ABC) Cleveland; WGGN-TV (TBN) Sandusky; WJW (FOX) Cleveland; WKYC (NBC) Cleveland; WMFD-TV (IND) Mansfield; WNEO (PBS) Alliance; WOIO (CBS) Shaker Heights; WQHS-DT (UNV) Cleveland; WRLM (IND) Canton; WUAB (MNT) Lorain; WVIZ (PBS) Cleveland; WVPX-TV (ION) Akron; 9 FMs.

Programming (via satellite): A&E Networks; ABC Family Channel; AMC; CNBC; CNN; C-SPAN; Discovery Channel; Disney Channel; ESPN; Headline News; INSP; Lifetime; MTV; Nickelodeon; Spike TV; TBS Superstation; The Weather Channel; Turner Network TV; USA Network; WGN America.

Fee: $44.95 installation; $14.61 monthly.

Expanded Basic Service 1

Subscribers: N.A.

Programming (via satellite): Animal Planet; BET Networks; Bravo; Cartoon Network; Comedy Central; C-SPAN 2; Discovery Fit & Health; Discovery Health Channel; E! Entertainment Television; ESPN 2; ESPN Classic Sports; Eternal Word TV Network; Food Network; Fox News Channel; Fox Sports Net Ohio; FX; Golf Channel; Great American Country; GSN; Hallmark Channel; HGTV; History Channel; Lifetime Movie Network; MSNBC; Oxygen; QVC; ShopNBC; SoapNet; Syfy; The Learning Channel; Travel Channel; truTV; Turner Classic Movies; TV Land; Versus; VH1; WE tv.

Fee: $33.89 monthly.

Digital Basic Service

Subscribers: N.A.

Programming (via satellite): A&E HD; AmericanLife TV Network; America's Store; ART America; BBC America; Bio; Bloomberg Television; Boomerang; Canales N; CBS Sports Network; CNN; CNN International; Cooking Channel; Country Music TV; C-SPAN 3; Daystar TV Network; Deutsche Welle TV; DIY Network; ESPNews; Fox College Sports Atlantic; Fox College Sports Central; Fox College Sports Pacific; Fox HD; Fox Movie Channel; Fox Soccer; Fuel TV; Fuse; G4; GAS; HD Theater; HDNet; HDNet Movies; Headline News; History Channel International; Independent Film Channel; INHD; INHD2; Jewelry Television; Lifetime; Lifetime Real Women; MTV Networks Digital Suite; Music Choice; National Geographic Channel; NBA TV; Nick Jr.; NickToons TV; Ohio News Network; Outdoor Channel; RAI International; Speed; TBS Superstation; Tennis Channel; The Weather Channel; The Word Network; Toon Disney; Trio; Turner Network TV HD; TV Asia; TVG Network; USA Network; Zee TV USA.

Fee: $19.50 monthly.

Digital Pay Service 1

Pay Units: 1,037.

Programming (via satellite): Cinemax (multiplexed); HBO (multiplexed); HBO HD; Showtime (multiplexed); Showtime HD; Starz (multiplexed); The Movie Channel (multiplexed).

Fee: $9.95 monthly (Cinemax, HBO, Showtime or TMC), $12.95 monthly (Starz).

Video-On-Demand: Yes

Pay-Per-View

iN DEMAND (delivered digitally); Playboy TV (delivered digitally); NHL Center Ice (delivered digitally); MLB Extra Innings (delivered digitally); Spice Live (delivered digitally); Ten Clips (delivered digitally); Pleasure (delivered digitally); NASCAR In Car (delivered digitally); NBA League Pass (delivered digitally); MLS Direct Kick (delivered digitally); ESPN (delivered digitally).

Internet Service

Operational: Yes.

Broadband Service: EarthLink, Road Runner.

Fee: $99.00 installation; $44.95 monthly.

Telephone Service

Digital: Operational

Miles of Plant: 255.0 (coaxial); 10.0 (fiber optic).

President: Stephen Fry. Area Vice President: Scott Miller. Vice President, Engineering: Al Costanzi. Vice President, Marketing: Patrick Burke. Vice President, Sales: Woody Woodward. Vice President, Public Affairs: William Jasso. Government & Media Relations Director: Chris Thomas.

Ownership: Time Warner Cable (MSO).

LOGAN—Time Warner Cable, 1266 Dublin Rd, Columbus, OH 43215-1008. Phone: 614-481-5000. Fax: 614-481-5052. Web Site: http://www.timewarnercable.com/midohio. Also serves Falls Twp. (Hocking County), Good Hope Twp. & Rockbridge. ICA: OH0232.

TV Market Ranking: 27 (Falls Twp. (Hocking County) (portions), Good Hope Twp., LOGAN, Rockbridge); Below 100 (Falls Twp. (Hocking County) (portions)). Franchise award date: N.A. Franchise expiration date: N.A. Began: October 1, 1989.

Channel capacity: N.A. Channels available but not in use: N.A.

Basic Service

Subscribers: 664.

Programming (received off-air): WBNS-TV (CBS) Columbus; WCMH-TV (NBC) Columbus; WOUB-TV (PBS) Athens; WSFJ-TV (TBN) Newark; WSYX (ABC, MNT) Columbus; WTTE (FOX) Columbus.

Programming (via satellite): WGN America.

Fee: $20.99 installation; $23.70 monthly.

Expanded Basic Service 1

Subscribers: N.A.

Programming (via satellite): A&E Networks; ABC Family Channel; CNN; Country Music TV; Discovery Channel; Disney Channel; ESPN; ESPN 2; Fox Sports Net Ohio; HGTV; History Channel; Lifetime; MTV; Nickelodeon; Spike TV; TBS Superstation; The Weather Channel; Turner Classic Movies; Turner Network TV; USA Network.

Digital Basic Service

Subscribers: N.A.

Programming (via satellite): BBC America; Bravo; Discovery Digital Networks; ESPN Classic Sports; ESPNews; Fox Sports World; Golf Channel; GSN; Independent Film Channel; Nick Jr.; Syfy; Versus; WE tv.

Digital Pay Service 1

Pay Units: N.A.

Programming (via satellite): Cinemax (multiplexed); Encore (multiplexed); HBO (multiplexed); Showtime (multiplexed); Starz (multiplexed); The Movie Channel (multiplexed).

Fee: $11.95 monthly (each).

Video-On-Demand: No

Pay-Per-View

Playboy TV (delivered digitally); Hits Movies & Events (delivered digitally).

Internet Service

Operational: Yes.

Broadband Service: Road Runner.

Fee: $44.95 monthly.

Telephone Service

None

Miles of Plant: 48.0 (coaxial); None (fiber optic).

President: Rhonda Fraas. Vice President & General Manager: David Kreiman. Vice President, Engineering: Randy Hall. Vice President, Marketing: Mark Psigoda. Vice President, Government & Public Affairs: Mary Jo Green. Technical Operations Director: Jim Cavender. Government Affairs Director: Steve Cuckler.

Ownership: Time Warner Cable (MSO).

LONDON—Time Warner Cable. Now served by COLUMBUS, OH [OH0002]. ICA: OH0089.

LORAIN—Time Warner Cable. Now served by CLEVELAND HEIGHTS, OH [OH0006]. ICA: OH0025.

LOUDONVILLE—Time Warner Cable. Now served by JEROMESVILLE, OH [OH0266]. ICA: OH0334.

LOWELL—Lowell Community TV Corp., 364 Water St, PO Box 364, Lowell, OH 45744. Phone: 740-896-2626. ICA: OH0335.

TV Market Ranking: Below 100 (LOWELL). Franchise award date: N.A. Franchise expiration date: N.A. Began: September 1, 1954.

Channel capacity: 12 (not 2-way capable). Channels available but not in use: N.A.

Basic Service

Subscribers: 300.

Programming (received off-air): WHIZ-TV (NBC) Zanesville; WKRN-TV (ABC) Nashville; WOUB-TV (PBS) Athens; WOWK-TV (CBS) Huntington; WTAP-TV (FOX, MNT, NBC) Parkersburg; WTRF-TV (CBS) Wheeling; allband FM.

Programming (via satellite): ESPN; TBS Superstation; Turner Network TV; WABC-TV (ABC) New York; WGN America.

Fee: $45.00 installation; $8.33 monthly.

Internet Service

Operational: No.

Telephone Service

None

Miles of Plant: 5.0 (coaxial); None (fiber optic).

Manager: Debbie Cline. Chief Technician: Steve Weckbacher.

Ownership: Lowell Community TV Corp.

LUCASVILLE—Time Warner Cable, 1266 Dublin Rd, Columbus, OH 43215-1008. Phone: 614-481-5000. Fax: 614-481-5052. Web Site: http://www.timewarnercable.com/midohio. Also serves Clay Twp. (Scioto County), Jefferson Twp. (Scioto County), Minford, Morgan Twp. (Scioto County), Rush Twp. (Scioto County), Scioto County (portions) & Valley Twp. (Scioto County). ICA: OH0113.

TV Market Ranking: 27 (Clay Twp. (Scioto County) (portions), LUCASVILLE, Minford, Morgan Twp. (Scioto County), Rush Twp. (Scioto County), Valley Twp. (Scioto County)); 27,36 (Scioto County (portions) (portions)); Below 100 (Jefferson Twp. (Scioto County), Clay Twp. (Scioto County) (portions), Scioto County (portions) (portions)). Franchise award date: May 24, 1976. Franchise expiration date: N.A. Began: January 1, 1974.

Channel capacity: N.A. Channels available but not in use: N.A.

Basic Service

Subscribers: 2,589.

Programming (received off-air): WBNS-TV (CBS) Columbus; WCHS-TV (ABC) Charleston; WCMH-TV (NBC) Columbus; WLWT (NBC) Cincinnati; WOWK-TV (CBS) Huntington; WPBO (PBS) Portsmouth; WSAZ-TV (MNT, NBC) Huntington; WSYX (ABC, MNT) Columbus; WVAH-TV (FOX) Charleston.

Programming (via satellite): A&E Networks; ABC Family Channel; AMC; Animal Planet; BET Networks; Bravo; Cartoon Network; CNBC; CNN; Comedy Central; C-SPAN; C-SPAN 2; Discovery Channel; Discovery Health Channel; Disney Channel; E! Entertainment Television; ESPN; ESPN 2; ESPN Classic Sports; Eternal Word TV Network; Food Network; Fox News Channel; Fox Sports Net Ohio; FX; Golf Channel; Great American Country; Hallmark Channel; Headline News; HGTV; History Channel; Lifetime; Lifetime Movie Network; MSNBC; MTV; National Geographic Channel; Nickelodeon; Outdoor Channel; Oxygen; QVC; SoapNet; Speed; Spike TV; Style Network; Syfy; TBS Superstation; The Learning Channel; The Weather Channel; Travel Channel; Trinity Broadcasting Network; truTV; Turner Classic Movies; Turner Network TV; TV Guide Network; TV Land; USA Network; VH1; WE tv; WGN America; WQCW (CW) Portsmouth.

Fee: $25.00 installation; $12.00 monthly.

Digital Basic Service

Subscribers: N.A.

Programming (via satellite): AmericanLife TV Network; BBC America; Bio; Bloomberg Television; CNN en Espanol; Current; Discovery Digital Networks; Encore (multiplexed); ESPNews; Fox Movie Channel; Fox Soccer; Fuse; G4; GAS; GSN; History Channel International; Independent Film Channel; MTV Hits; MTV2; Nick Jr.; NickToons TV; Outdoor Channel; Ovation; ShopNBC; Sorpresa; Speed; Sundance Channel; The Word Network; Toon Disney; Trinity Broadcasting Network; VH1 Classic.

Fee: $11.95 monthly (each).

Digital Pay Service 1

Pay Units: N.A.

Programming (via satellite): Cinemax (multiplexed); HBO (multiplexed); Showtime (multiplexed); Starz (multiplexed); The Movie Channel (multiplexed).

Video-On-Demand: No

Pay-Per-View
iN DEMAND (delivered digitally); Fresh (delivered digitally); Shorteez (delivered digitally).
Internet Service
Operational: Yes.
Telephone Service
None
Miles of Plant: 90.0 (coaxial); None (fiber optic). Additional miles planned: 2.0 (coaxial).
President: Rhonda Fraas. Vice President & General Manager: David Kreiman. Vice President, Engineering: Randy Hall. Vice President, Marketing: Mark Psigoda. Vice President, Government & Public Affairs: Mary Jo Green. Government Affairs Director: Steve Cuckler.
Ownership: Time Warner Cable (MSO).

LUCKEY—Now served by WATERVILLE, OH [OH0072]. ICA: OH0216.

LYNCHBURG—Time Warner Cable. Now served by CINCINNATI, OH [OH0001]. ICA: OH0268.

MACEDONIA—Time Warner Cable, 530 S Main St, Ste 1751, Akron, OH 44311-1090. Phone: 330-633-9203. Fax: 330-633-7970. Web Site: http://www.timewarnercable.com/northeastohio. Also serves Aurora, Boston Heights, Hiram, Hudson, Hudson Twp. (Summit County), Hudson Village, Mantua, Mantua Twp., Northfield, Northfield Center Twp. (Summit County), Reminderville, Sagamore Hills Twp. (Summit County), Shalersville Twp., Twinsburg & Twinsburg Twp. (Summit County). ICA: OH0043.
TV Market Ranking: 8 (Aurora, Boston Heights, Hiram, Hudson, Hudson Twp. (Summit County), Hudson Village, MACEDONIA, Mantua, Mantua Twp., Northfield, Northfield Center Twp. (Summit County), Reminderville, Sagamore Hills Twp. (Summit County), Shalersville Twp., Twinsburg, Twinsburg Twp. (Summit County)). Franchise award date: N.A. Franchise expiration date: N.A. Began: April 1, 1982.
Channel capacity: N.A. Channels available but not in use: N.A.
Basic Service
Subscribers: 25,000.
Programming (received off-air): WAOH-LP Akron; WBNX-TV (CW) Akron; WDLI-TV (TBN) Canton; WEAO (PBS) Akron; WEWS-TV (ABC) Cleveland; WJW (FOX) Cleveland; WKYC (NBC) Cleveland; WNEO (PBS) Alliance; WOIO (CBS) Shaker Heights; WQHS-DT (UNV) Cleveland; WRLM (IND) Canton; WUAB (MNT) Lorain; WVIZ (PBS) Cleveland; WVPX-TV (ION) Akron.
Programming (via satellite): QVC; SportsTime Ohio; WGN America.
Fee: $44.95 installation; $12.60 monthly.
Expanded Basic Service 1
Subscribers: N.A.
Programming (via satellite): A&E Networks; ABC Family Channel; AMC; Animal Planet; BET Networks; Bravo; Cartoon Network; CNBC; CNN; Comedy Central; Country Music TV; C-SPAN; C-SPAN 2; Discovery Channel; Disney Channel; E! Entertainment Television; ESPN; ESPN 2; Eternal Word TV Network; Food Network; Fox News Channel; Fox Sports Net Ohio; FX; Golf Channel; Headline News; HGTV; History Channel; Lifetime; MSNBC; MTV; MTV2; Nickelodeon; Oxygen; Product Information Network; Spike TV; Style Network; Syfy; TBS Superstation; The Learning Channel; The Weather Channel; Travel Channel; truTV; Turner Network TV; TV Land; USA Network; VH1; VH1 Classic.
Fee: $40.40 monthly.
Digital Basic Service
Subscribers: N.A.
Programming (via satellite): AmericanLife TV Network; BBC America; Bloomberg Television; Canal 52MX; CCTV News; CCTV-4; Cine Latino; CMT Pure Country; CNN en Espanol; Current; Discovery en Espanol; Discovery Fit & Health; Discovery Health Channel; Discovery Home Channel; Discovery Kids Channel; Discovery Times Channel; DIY Network; ESPN 2 HD; ESPN Classic Sports; ESPN Deportes; ESPN HD; ESPN U; ESPNews; Fox Business Channel; Fox Deportes; Fox Movie Channel; Fox Reality Channel; Fox Soccer; Fuse; G4; GAS; GMC; Great American Country; GSN; Hallmark Channel; Halogen Network; HD Theater; HDNet; HDNet Movies; History Channel en Espanol; Lifetime Movie Network; LOGO; Military Channel; MTV Hits; MTV Jams; Music Choice; Nick Jr.; Nick Too; NickToons TV; Ohio News Network; Science; SoapNet; Speed; SportsTime Ohio; TBS in HD; The Word Network; Toon Disney; Toon Disney en Espanol; Tr3s; Trinity Broadcasting Network; Turner Classic Movies; Turner Network TV HD; TV One; TVG Network; Universal HD; VH1 Soul; WE tv.
Fee: $11.00 monthly.
Digital Expanded Basic Service
Subscribers: N.A.
Programming (via satellite): Bio; CBS Sports Network; Cooking Channel; Flix; FSN Digital Atlantic; FSN Digital Central; FSN Digital Pacific; Fuel TV; History Channel International; Independent Film Channel; National Geographic Channel; NBA TV; Outdoor Channel; Sundance Channel; Tennis Channel; Versus.
Fee: $10.00 monthly.
Digital Pay Service 1
Pay Units: N.A.
Programming (via satellite): ART America; Cinemax (multiplexed); Cinemax HD; Cinemax On Demand; Encore (multiplexed); Filipino Channel; Flix; HBO (multiplexed); HBO HD; HBO On Demand; RAI USA; Russian Television Network; Showtime (multiplexed); Showtime HD; Showtime On Demand; Starz (multiplexed); Starz HDTV; Starz On Demand; The Movie Channel (multiplexed); The Movie Channel On Demand; TV Asia; TV Japan; TV5, La Television International; Zhong Tian Channel.
Fee: $12.00 monthly (HBO, Cinemax, Starz/Encore or Showtime/TMC/Flix).
Video-On-Demand: Yes
Pay-Per-View
iN DEMAND (delivered digitally); Playboy TV (delivered digitally); Shorteez (delivered digitally); Fresh (delivered digitally); Club Jenna (delivered digitally); Hot Choice (delivered digitally); Spice: Xcess (delivered digitally); ESPN (delivered digitally); MLB Extra Innings (delivered digitally); NHL Center Ice (delivered digitally).
Internet Service
Operational: Yes. Began: January 1, 2002.
Broadband Service: EarthLink, Road Runner.
Fee: $44.95 monthly.
Telephone Service
Digital: Operational
Fee: $44.95 monthly
Miles of Plant: 871.0 (coaxial); 10.0 (fiber optic).
President: Stephen Fry. Area Vice President: Scott Miller. Vice President, Engineering: Al Costanzi. Vice President, Manager: Patrick Burke. Vice President, Sales: Wody Woodward. Vice President, Government & Media Affairs: William Jasso. Government & Media Relations Director: Chris Thomas.
Ownership: Time Warner Cable (MSO).

MALAGA TWP.—Richards TV Cable, PO Box 2, Jerusalem, OH 43747-0002. Phone: 740-926-1742. Fax: 740-926-1800. Also serves Beallsville, Jerusalem & Wilson. ICA: OH0270.
TV Market Ranking: 90 (Beallsville, Jerusalem, MALAGA TWP., Wilson). Franchise award date: N.A. Franchise expiration date: N.A. Began: October 15, 1977.
Channel capacity: N.A. Channels available but not in use: N.A.
Basic Service
Subscribers: 400 includes Middlebourne, New Athens.
Programming (received off-air): KDKA-TV (CBS) Pittsburgh; WHIZ-TV (NBC) Zanesville; WOUC-TV (PBS) Cambridge; WPGH-TV (FOX) Pittsburgh; WPMY (MNT) Pittsburgh; WTAE-TV (ABC) Pittsburgh; WTOV-TV (IND, NBC) Steubenville; WTRF-TV (CBS) Wheeling; allband FM.
Programming (via satellite): A&E Networks; ABC Family Channel; Cartoon Network; CNN; Country Music TV; Discovery Channel; Disney Channel; ESPN; ESPN 2; Headline News; History Channel; Lifetime; Spike TV; TBS Superstation; The Learning Channel; The Weather Channel; Turner Network TV; TV Land; USA Network.
Fee: $15.00 installation; $25.00 monthly.
Pay Service 1
Pay Units: N.A.
Programming (via satellite): HBO; The Movie Channel.
Internet Service
Operational: No.
Telephone Service
None
Miles of Plant: 26.0 (coaxial); None (fiber optic).
Manager: Paul E. Richards. Chief Technician: Mark Richards.
Ownership: Paul E. Richards (MSO).

MANCHESTER—Formerly served by Adelphia Communications. Now served by CINCINNATI, OH [OH0001]. ICA: OH0209.

MANSFIELD—Time Warner Cable, 530 S Main St, Ste 1751, Akron, OH 44311-1090. Phone: 330-633-9203. Fax: 330-633-7970. Web Site: http://www.timewarnercable.com/northeastohio. Also serves Ashland, Bellville, Butler, Lexington (Richland County), Lucas, Madison Twp. (Richland County), Mifflin, Mifflin Twp. (Ashland & Richland Counties), Ontario, Perry Twp. (Richland County), Richland County, Sandusky Twp. (Richland County), Springfield Twp. (Richland County), Tiro, Troy Twp. (Richland County) & Washington Twp. (Richland County). ICA: OH0023.
TV Market Ranking: 27 (Monroe Twp. (Richland County)); Below 100 (Ashland, Bellville, Butler, Lexington (Richland County), Lucas, Madison Twp. (Richland County), MANSFIELD, Mifflin, Mifflin Twp. (Ashland & Richland Counties), Ontario, Perry Twp. (Richland County), Richland County, Sandusky Twp. (Richland County), Springfield Twp. (Richland County), Tiro, Troy Twp. (Richland County), Washington Twp. (Richland County)). Franchise award date: January 1, 1965. Franchise expiration date: N.A. Began: June 1, 1965.
Channel capacity: N.A. Channels available but not in use: N.A.
Basic Service
Subscribers: 65,000 Includes Congress, Jeromesville, Lodi, Loudonville, New London, Norwalk, Polk, Shelby, Shreve & Willard.
Programming (received off-air): WBNS-TV (CBS) Columbus; WBNX-TV (CW) Akron; WCMH-TV (NBC) Columbus; WEWS-TV (ABC) Cleveland; WGGN-TV (TBN) Sandusky; WJW (FOX) Cleveland; WKYC (NBC) Cleveland; WMFD-TV (IND) Mansfield; WOHZ-CA (IND) Mansfield; WOIO (CBS) Shaker Heights; WOSU-TV (PBS) Columbus; WQHS-DT (UNV) Cleveland; WRLM (IND) Canton; WSYX (ABC, MNT) Columbus; WUAB (MNT) Lorain; WVIZ (PBS) Cleveland; WVPX-TV (ION) Akron.
Programming (via satellite): WGN America.
Fee: $29.95 installation; $13.05 monthly.
Expanded Basic Service 1
Subscribers: N.A.
Programming (via satellite): A&E Networks; ABC Family Channel; AMC; Animal Planet; BET Networks; Bravo; Cartoon Network; CNBC; CNN; Comedy Central; C-SPAN; C-SPAN 2; Discovery Channel; Discovery Fit & Health; Discovery Health Channel; Disney Channel; E! Entertainment Television; ESPN; ESPN 2; ESPN Classic Sports; Eternal Word TV Network; Food Network; Fox News Channel; Fox Sports Net Ohio; FX; Golf Channel; Great American Country; GSN; Hallmark Channel; Headline News; HGTV; History Channel; INSP; Lifetime; Lifetime Movie Network; MSNBC; MTV; Nickelodeon; Oxygen; QVC; SoapNet; Spike TV; Syfy; TBS Superstation; The Learning Channel; The Weather Channel; Travel Channel; truTV; Turner Classic Movies; Turner Network TV; TV Land; USA Network; Versus; VH1; WE tv.
Fee: $42.45 monthly.
Digital Basic Service
Subscribers: N.A.
Programming (via satellite): AmericanLife TV Network; America's Store; BBC America; BBC America On Demand; Bio; Bloomberg Television; Boomerang; Canales N; CBS Sports Network; cloo; CNN International; Cooking Channel; Country Music TV; C-SPAN 3; Current; Daystar TV Network; Disney Channel; DIY Network; ESPN; ESPNews; Fox College Sports Atlantic; Fox College Sports Central; Fox College Sports Pacific; Fox Movie Channel; Fox Soccer; Fuel TV; Fuse; G4; GAS; HD Theater; HDNet; HDNet Movies; History Channel International; Independent Film Channel; INHD; INHD2; Jewelry Television; Lifetime Real Women; MTV2; Music

Choice; National Geographic Channel; NBA TV; Nick Jr.; NickToons TV; Ohio News Network; Outdoor Channel; Speed; Style Network; Tennis Channel; The Word Network; Toon Disney; Turner Network TV HD; TVG Network; VH1 Classic.
Fee: $12.49 monthly.
Digital Pay Service 1
Pay Units: N.A.
Programming (via satellite): ART America; Cinemax (multiplexed); Cinemax On Demand; Deutsche Welle TV; Encore (multiplexed); HBO (multiplexed); HBO On Demand; RAI International; Showtime (multiplexed); Showtime HD; Showtime On Demand; Starz (multiplexed); Sundance Channel; The Movie Channel (multiplexed); The Movie Channel On Demand; TV Asia; Zee TV USA.
Fee: $12.00 monthly (HBO, Cinemax, Starz or Showtime/TMC), $14.95 monthly (Deutsche Welle, ART, TV Asia, Zee TV or RAI International).
Video-On-Demand: Yes
Pay-Per-View
iN DEMAND (delivered digitally); Playboy TV (delivered digitally); ESPN (delivered digitally); NHL Center Ice (delivered digitally); MLB Extra Innings (delivered digitally); Spice Live (delivered digitally); Ten Clips (delivered digitally); Pleasure (delivered digitally); Movies (delivered digitally); NASCAR In Car (delivered digitally); NBA League Pass (delivered digitally); MLS Direct Kick (delivered digitally).
Internet Service
Operational: Yes.
Broadband Service: EarthLink, Road Runner.
Fee: $99.00 installation; $44.95 monthly.
Telephone Service
Digital: Operational
Fee: $44.95 monthly
Miles of Plant: 477.0 (coaxial); None (fiber optic).
President: Stephen Fry. Area Vice President: Scott Miller. Vice President, Engineering: Al Costanzi. Vice President, Marketing: Patrick Burke. Vice President, Sales: Woody Woodward. Vice President, Public Affairs: William Jasso. Area Manager: Carol Jagger. Government & Media Relations Director: Chris Thomas.
Ownership: Time Warner Cable (MSO).

MANTUA—Now served by MACEDONIA, OH [OH0043]. ICA: OH0337.

MARGARETTA TWP.—Now served by PORT CLINTON, OH [OH0060]. ICA: OH0338.

MARIETTA—Charter Communications. Now served by PARKERSBURG, WV [WV0003]. ICA: OH0339.

MARION—Time Warner Cable, 160 N Greenwood St, Marion, OH 43302-3163. Phones: 740-387-3187; 419-784-1992 (Defiance office). Fax: 740-387-4891. Web Site: http://www.timewarnercable.com. Also serves Big Island Twp., Caledonia, Claridon Twp., Fountain Place, Grand Prairie Twp., Green Camp, Marion County, Marion Twp. (Marion County), Morral, Pleasant Twp. (Marion County), Prospect Twp. (Marion County), Richland Twp., Waldo, Wood Valley & Wood Valley Mobile Home Park. ICA: OH0040.
TV Market Ranking: 27 (Prospect Twp. (Marion County), Waldo); Below 100 (Big Island Twp., Caledonia, Claridon Twp., Fountain Place, Grand Prairie Twp., MARION, Marion County (portions), Marion Twp. (Marion County), Pleasant Twp. (Marion County), Richland Twp., Wood Valley, Wood Valley Mobile Home Park); Outside TV Markets (Green Camp, Marion County (portions), Morral). Franchise award date: N.A. Franchise expiration date: N.A. Began: September 19, 1966.
Channel capacity: N.A. Channels available but not in use: N.A.
Basic Service
Subscribers: 15,342.
Programming (received off-air): WBNS-TV (CBS) Columbus; WCMH-TV (NBC) Columbus; WOCB-CD (TBN) Marion; WOSU-TV (PBS) Columbus; WSYX (ABC, MNT) Columbus; WWHO (CW) Chillicothe.
Programming (via satellite): QVC; The Learning Channel; TV Guide Network; WGN America.
Fee: $43.00 installation; $14.05 monthly; $3.25 converter; $21.00 additional installation.
Expanded Basic Service 1
Subscribers: 14,689.
Programming (via satellite): A&E Networks; ABC Family Channel; AMC; Animal Planet; BET Networks; Bravo; Cartoon Network; CNBC; CNN; Comedy Central; Country Music TV; C-SPAN; C-SPAN 2; Discovery Channel; Disney Channel; E! Entertainment Television; ESPN; ESPN 2; Eternal Word TV Network; Food Network; Fox News Channel; Fox Sports Net Ohio; FX; Hallmark Channel; Headline News; HGTV; History Channel; ION Television; Lifetime; MSNBC; MTV; Nick Jr.; Nickelodeon; Oxygen; Product Information Network; ShopNBC; Speed; Spike TV; Syfy; TBS Superstation; The Weather Channel; Travel Channel; truTV; Turner Network TV; TV Land; Univision Studios; USA Network; VH1; WPIX (CW, IND) New York.
Fee: $20.51 monthly.
Digital Basic Service
Subscribers: 75.
Programming (via satellite): AmericanLife TV Network; BBC America; Bio; Bloomberg Television; Canal 52MX; Cine Latino; CMT Pure Country; CNN en Espanol; Current; Discovery en Espanol; Discovery Fit & Health; Discovery Health Channel; Discovery Home Channel; Discovery Kids Channel; DIY Network; DMX Music; ESPN Classic Sports; ESPN Deportes; ESPNews; Fox College Sports Atlantic; Fox College Sports Central; Fox College Sports Pacific; Fox Deportes; Fox Movie Channel; Fox Reality Channel; Fox Soccer; Fuel TV; Fuse; G4; GMC; Golf Channel; Great American Country; GSN; Halogen Network; History Channel en Espanol; History Channel International; ID Investigation Discovery; Independent Film Channel; Lifetime Movie Network; LOGO; Military Channel; MTV Hits; MTV Jams; MTV2; National Geographic Channel; Nick Jr.; Nick Too; NickToons TV; Ohio News Network; Outdoor Channel; Science; SoapNet; Style Network; Sundance Channel; TeenNick; The Word Network; Toon Disney; Tr3s; Trinity Broadcasting Network; Turner Classic Movies; TVG Network; Versus; VH1 Classic; VH1 Soul; WE tv.
Fee: $14.95 monthly.
Digital Pay Service 1
Pay Units: N.A.
Programming (via satellite): Arabic Channel; CCTV-4; Chinese Television Network; Cinemax (multiplexed); Encore (multiplexed); Filipino Channel; Flix; HBO (multiplexed); RAI International; Russian Television Network; Showtime (multiplexed); Starz (multiplexed); TV Asia; TV Japan; TV5, La Television International.
Video-On-Demand: No
Pay-Per-View
Playboy TV (delivered digitally); Fresh (delivered digitally); Shorteez; Hot Choice (delivered digitally); ESPN (delivered digitally); NHL Center Ice (delivered digitally); MLB Extra Innings (delivered digitally); iN DEMAND (delivered digitally).
Internet Service
Operational: Yes.
Broadband Service: Road Runner.
Fee: $42.95 monthly.
Telephone Service
None
Miles of Plant: 215.0 (coaxial); 215.0 (fiber optic).
President: Rhonda Fraas. Vice President, Engineering: Randy Hall. Vice President, Sales & Marketing: Mark Psigoda. Area Manager: Brad Wakely. General Manager: John Ellingson.
Ownership: Time Warner Cable (MSO).

MARTINS FERRY—Comcast Cable. Now served by WHEELING, WV [WV0004]. ICA: OH0102.

MARTINSBURG (village)—Formerly served by National Cable Inc. No longer in operation. ICA: OH0341.

MARYSVILLE—Time Warner Cable. Now served by COLUMBUS, OH [OH0002]. ICA: OH0097.

MASSILLON—Massillon Cable TV Inc., 814 Cable Ct NW, PO Box 1000, Massillon, OH 44648-1000. Phone: 330-833-4134. Fax: 330-833-9775. E-mail: rbgessner@massilloncabletv.com. Web Site: http://www.massilloncabletv.com. Also serves Bethlehem Twp. (Stark County), Brewster, Canal Fulton, Jackson Twp. (Stark County), Lawrence Twp. (Stark County), Mount Eaton, Mount Hope, Navarre, Perry Twp. (Stark County), Richville, Sugar Creek Twp. (Stark County), Summit County (southwestern portion), Tuscarawas Twp. (Stark County) & Wayne County (eastern portion). ICA: OH0021.
TV Market Ranking: 8 (Bethlehem Twp. (Stark County), Brewster, Canal Fulton, Jackson Twp. (Stark County), Lawrence Twp. (Stark County), MASSILLON, Mount Eaton, Navarre, Perry Twp. (Stark County), Richville, Sugar Creek Twp. (Stark County), Summit County (southwestern portion), Tuscarawas Twp. (Stark County), Wayne County (eastern portion)); Below 100 (Mount Hope). Franchise award date: October 1, 1966. Franchise expiration date: N.A. Began: October 1, 1966.
Channel capacity: 110 (operating 2-way). Channels available but not in use: N.A.
Basic Service
Subscribers: 45,801 Includes Wooster.
Programming (received off-air): WBNX-TV (CW) Akron; WDLI-TV (TBN) Canton; WEWS-TV (ABC) Cleveland; WJW (FOX) Cleveland; WKYC (NBC) Cleveland; WNEO (PBS) Alliance; WOIO (CBS) Shaker Heights; WQHS-DT (UNV) Cleveland; WRLM (IND) Canton; WUAB (MNT) Lorain; WVIZ (PBS) Cleveland; WVPX-TV (ION) Akron.
Programming (via satellite): A&E Networks; ABC Family Channel; AMC; Animal Planet; BET Networks; Boomerang; Bravo; BTN; Cartoon Network; CNBC; CNN; Comedy Central; Country Music TV; C-SPAN; C-SPAN 2; Discovery Channel; Discovery Health Channel; Disney Channel; E! Entertainment Television; ESPN; ESPN 2; ESPN Classic Sports; ESPN U; Eternal Word TV Network; Food Network; Fox News Channel; Fox Sports Net Ohio; FX; Golf Channel; Great American Country; GSN; Hallmark Channel; Headline News; HGTV; History Channel; INSP; ION Life; Lifetime; MSNBC; MTV; National Geographic Channel; Nickelodeon; Oxygen; Qubo; QVC; ReelzChannel; SoapNet; Speed; Spike TV; SportsTime Ohio; Syfy; TBS Superstation; The Learning Channel; The Weather Channel; Travel Channel; truTV; Turner Classic Movies; Turner Network TV; TV Land; USA Network; VH1; Weatherscan; WGN America; zap2it Program Guide.
Fee: $30.00 installation; $52.75 monthly; $3.00 converter; $20.00 additional installation.
Digital Basic Service
Subscribers: 35,080.
Programming (via satellite): A&E HD; AmericanLife TV Network; BBC America; Bio; Bloomberg Television; Bravo HD; BTN HD; CBS Sports Network; Chiller; CMT Pure Country; CNBC HD+; CNN HD; Cooking Channel; Discovery Fit & Health; Discovery Kids Channel; Disney XD; DIY Network; DMX Music; ESPN 2 HD; ESPN HD; ESPNews; Fox Business Channel; Fox Movie Channel; Fox Soccer; G4; GMC; Halogen Network; HD Theater; HDNet; HDNet Movies; History Channel HD; History Channel International; ID Investigation Discovery; Lifetime Movie Network; MGM HD; Military History Channel; MLB Network; MTV Hits; MTV2; NHL Network; Nick Jr.; NickToons TV; Outdoor Channel; PBS Kids Sprout; Planet Green; Science; SportsTime Ohio; Syfy HD; TBS in HD; TeenNick; Tennis Channel; Turner Network TV HD; TV One; Universal HD; USA Network HD; Versus; VH1 Classic; VH1 Soul; WE tv.
Fee: $7.50 monthly; $4.50 converter.
Digital Pay Service 1
Pay Units: 4,121.
Programming (via satellite): HBO (multiplexed); HBO HD.
Fee: $10.00 installation; $14.25 monthly.
Digital Pay Service 2
Pay Units: 1,846.
Programming (via satellite): Flix; Showtime (multiplexed); Showtime HD; Sundance Channel; The Movie Channel.
Fee: $14.00 monthly.
Digital Pay Service 3
Pay Units: 1,592.
Programming (via satellite): Encore (multiplexed); Starz (multiplexed).
Fee: $11.50 monthly.
Digital Pay Service 4
Pay Units: 1,480.
Programming (via satellite): Cinemax (multiplexed).
Fee: $10.75 monthly.
Video-On-Demand: Yes
Pay-Per-View
Addressable homes: 21,964.
MLB Extra Innings (delivered digitally); NHL Center Ice (delivered digitally); iN DEMAND (delivered digitally).
Internet Service
Operational: Yes. Began: January 1, 1999.
Subscribers: 34,062.
Broadband Service: In-house.
Fee: $30.00 installation; $25.00-$40.00 monthly.
Telephone Service
Digital: Operational
Subscribers: 14,608.
Fee: $33.20-$47.95 monthly

Miles of Plant: 1,200.0 (coaxial); 121.0 (fiber optic). Additional miles planned: 25.0 (coaxial).
President: Robert Gessner. Chief Operating Officer: David Hoffer. Chief Technician: Tom Mogus. Marketing Director: Shannon Delaney. Customer Service Manager: Brenda Murphy.
Ownership: Massillon Cable TV Inc. (MSO).

McCONNELSVILLE—Formerly served by Adelphia Communications. Now served by WATERTOWN, OH [OH0175]. ICA: OH0177.

MEDINA—Armstrong Cable Services, 1141 Lafayette Rd, Medina, OH 44256-2421. Phones: 877-277-5711; 330-722-3141. Fax: 330-725-3366. E-mail: info@zoominternet.net. Web Site: http://cable.armstrongonewire.com. Also serves Litchfield Twp. (portions), Liverpool Twp., Medina Twp., Montville Twp. & York Twp. ICA: OH0067.
TV Market Ranking: 8 (Litchfield Twp. (portions), Liverpool Twp., MEDINA, Medina Twp., Montville Twp., York Twp.). Franchise award date: September 24, 1979. Franchise expiration date: April 10, 2010. Began: January 1, 1982.
Channel capacity: N.A. Channels available but not in use: N.A.

Digital Basic Service
Subscribers: 6,710 Includes Orrville.
Programming (via satellite): A&E Networks; ABC Family Channel; AMC; Animal Planet; Bravo; Cartoon Network; CNBC; CNN; Comedy Central; Country Music TV; C-SPAN; Discovery Channel; Disney Channel; E! Entertainment Television; ESPN; ESPN 2; Eternal Word TV Network; Food Network; Fox News Channel; Fox Sports Net Ohio; FX; Headline News; HGTV; History Channel; INSP; Lifetime; MSNBC; MTV; Music Choice; MyNetworkTV Inc.; Nickelodeon; NickToons TV; Pentagon Channel; QVC; ShopNBC; SoapNet; Speed; Spike TV; SportsTime Ohio; Syfy; TBS Superstation; The Learning Channel; The Weather Channel; Travel Channel; truTV; Turner Classic Movies; Turner Network TV; TV Guide Network; TV Land; USA Network; VH1.
Fee: $35.00 installation; $52.40 monthly.

Digital Expanded Basic Service
Subscribers: N.A.
Programming (via satellite): AmericanLife TV Network; BBC America; Bio; Bloomberg Television; Boomerang; Chiller; cloo; CMT Pure Country; Cooking Channel; Discovery Fit & Health; Discovery Health Channel; Discovery Kids Channel; DIY Network; ESPN Classic Sports; ESPNews; Fox Soccer; G4; Golf Channel; Great American Country; GSN; Hallmark Channel; Hallmark Movie Channel; History Channel International; HRTV; ID Investigation Discovery; Jewelry Television; Lifetime Movie Network; Military Channel; MTV Hits; MTV Jams; MTV2; mun2 television; National Geographic Channel; NFL Network; NHL Network; Nick Jr.; Nick Too; Ohio News Network; Outdoor Channel; Oxygen; PBS Kids Sprout; Pentagon Channel; Planet Green; RFD-TV; Science; SoapNet; Speed; TeenNick; Tennis Channel; Toon Disney; Tr3s; Versus; VH1 Classic; VH1 Soul; WE tv.
Fee: $12.00 monthly.

Digital Expanded Basic Service 2
Subscribers: N.A.
Programming (received off-air): WEWS-TV (ABC) Cleveland; WJW (FOX) Cleveland; WKYC (NBC) Cleveland; WOIO (CBS) Shaker Heights; WVIZ (PBS) Cleveland.
Programming (via satellite): A&E HD; Animal Planet HD; Bravo HD; CNN HD; Discovery Channel HD; Disney Channel HD; ESPN 2 HD; ESPN HD; Food Network HD; Fox News HD; FSN HD; FX HD; Golf Channel HD; Hallmark Movie Channel HD; HD Theater; HDNet; HDNet Movies; HGTV HD; History Channel HD; MGM HD; National Geographic Channel HD Network; NFL Network HD; NHL Network HD; Outdoor Channel 2 HD; QVC HD; Science HD; Syfy HD; TBS in HD; The Weather Channel HD; TLC HD; Turner Network TV HD; Universal HD; USA Network HD; Versus HD; WealthTV HD.
Fee: $9.00 monthly.

Digital Pay Service 1
Pay Units: N.A.
Programming (via satellite): Cinemax (multiplexed); Cinemax HD; Encore (multiplexed); Flix; HBO (multiplexed); HBO HD; RAI USA; Showtime (multiplexed); Showtime HD; Starz (multiplexed); Starz HDTV; The Movie Channel (multiplexed); TV5 USA.
Fee: $13.95 monthly (HBO, Cinemax, Showtime/TMC/Flix or Starz/Encore).

Video-On-Demand: Yes

Pay-Per-View
Addressable homes: 3,623.
ESPN Now (delivered digitally); Hot Choice (delivered digitally); iN DEMAND (delivered digitally); MLB Extra Innings (delivered digitally); NHL Center Ice (delivered digitally).

Internet Service
Operational: Yes. Began: November 1, 2000.
Subscribers: 12,653.
Broadband Service: Armstrong Zoom.
Fee: $26.95-$39.95 monthly.

Telephone Service
Analog: Not Operational
Digital: Operational
Fee: $49.95 monthly
Miles of Plant: 368.0 (coaxial); None (fiber optic).
General Manager: Karen Wolff. Chief Technician: Mike Bricker. Marketing Director: Jud D. Stewart.
Ownership: Armstrong Group of Companies (MSO).

MENTOR—Time Warner Cable. Now served by CLEVELAND HEIGHTS, OH [OH0006]. ICA: OH0015.

METAMORA—Formerly served by Adelphia Communications. Now served by WAUSEON, OH [OH0106]. ICA: OH0255.

MIDDLEBURG (Noble County)—Formerly served by Cebridge Connections. No longer in operation. ICA: OH0312.

MIDDLETOWN—Time Warner Cable. Now served by CINCINNATI, OH [OH0001]. ICA: OH0018.

MILLERSBURG—Now served by NEW PHILADELPHIA, OH [OH0030]. ICA: OH0144.

MINERVA—Time Warner Cable, 530 S Main St, Ste 1751, Akron, OH 44311-1090. Phone: 330-633-9203. Fax: 330-633-7970. Web Site: http://www.timewarnercable.com/northeastohio. Also serves Beloit, Brown Twp. (Carroll County), Carrollton, Knox Twp. (Columbiana County), Malvern, Sebring, Smith Twp. (Mahoning County) & West Twp. ICA: OH0132.
TV Market Ranking: 8 (Beloit, Brown Twp. (Carroll County), Malvern, Sebring, Smith Twp. (Mahoning County)); 8,79 (Knox Twp. (Columbiana County), MINERVA, West Twp.); 90 (Carrollton). Franchise award date: N.A. Franchise expiration date: August 3, 2006. Began: May 1, 1971.
Channel capacity: N.A. Channels available but not in use: N.A.

Basic Service
Subscribers: 5,804.
Programming (received off-air): WBNX-TV (CW) Akron; WDLI-TV (TBN) Canton; WEWS-TV (ABC) Cleveland; WFMJ-TV (CW, NBC) Youngstown; WJW (FOX) Cleveland; WKYC (NBC) Cleveland; WNEO (PBS) Alliance; WOIO (CBS) Shaker Heights; WRLM (IND) Canton; WUAB (MNT) Lorain; WVPX-TV (ION) Akron.
Programming (via satellite): Discovery Channel; QVC; TBS Superstation.
Fee: $44.95 installation; $15.00 monthly; $3.40 converter; $19.95 additional installation.

Expanded Basic Service 1
Subscribers: 5,282.
Programming (via satellite): A&E Networks; ABC Family Channel; AMC; Cartoon Network; CNBC; CNN; C-SPAN; C-SPAN 2; Disney Channel; ESPN; Fox News Channel; Fox Sports Net Ohio; FX; Lifetime; MTV; Nickelodeon; Root Sports Pittsburgh; Spike TV; The Learning Channel; The Weather Channel; Turner Network TV; USA Network.
Fee: $38.00 monthly.

Digital Basic Service
Subscribers: N.A.
Programming (via satellite): BBC America; Bravo; Discovery Digital Networks; ESPN Classic Sports; GSN; HGTV; History Channel International; Speed; Syfy; WE tv.
Fee: $12.49 monthly.

Digital Expanded Basic Service
Subscribers: N.A.
Programming (via satellite): ESPNews; Fox Sports World; Golf Channel; Independent Film Channel; Music Choice; National Geographic Channel; Nick Jr.; Turner Classic Movies; Versus; VH1 Classic; VH1 Country.
Fee: $10.00 monthly.

Digital Pay Service 1
Pay Units: N.A.
Programming (via satellite): ART America; CCTV-4; Cinemax (multiplexed); Encore (multiplexed); Filipino Channel; HBO (multiplexed); RAI USA; Russian Television Network; Showtime (multiplexed); Starz (multiplexed); The Movie Channel (multiplexed); TV Asia; TV Japan; TV5 USA.
Fee: $10.00 monthly (CCTV, TV Asia, TV5, Filipino, RAI, or ART), $15.00 monthly (TV Russia), $15.95 monthly (HBO, Cinemax, Starz, or Showtime), $25.00 monthly (TV Japan).

Video-On-Demand: Yes

Pay-Per-View
Playboy TV (delivered digitally).

Internet Service
Operational: Yes.
Broadband Service: EarthLink, Road Runner.
Fee: $44.95 monthly.

Telephone Service
Digital: Operational
Fee: $44.95 monthly
Miles of Plant: 162.0 (coaxial); None (fiber optic).
President: Stephen Fry. Area Vice President: Scott Miller. Vice President, Engineering: Al Costanzi. Vice President, Marketing: Patrick Burke. Vice President, Public Affairs: William Jasso. Government & Media Relations Director: Chris Thomas.
Ownership: Time Warner Cable (MSO).

MINSTER—Time Warner Cable, 310 Jefferson Ave, Defiance, OH 43512. Phone: 419-784-1992. Fax: 419-782-2640. Web Site: http://www.timewarnercable.com. Also serves Chickasaw, Cynthian Twp., Fort Loramie, German Twp. (Auglaize County), Kettlersville, McLean Twp. (Shelby County), New Bremen & New Knoxville. ICA: OH0164.
TV Market Ranking: Below 100 (Chickasaw, Cynthian Twp., Fort Loramie, German Twp. (Auglaize County), Kettlersville, McLean Twp. (Shelby County), MINSTER, New Bremen, New Knoxville). Franchise award date: N.A. Franchise expiration date: N.A. Began: March 1, 1971.
Channel capacity: N.A. Channels available but not in use: N.A.

Basic Service
Subscribers: 2,292.
Programming (received off-air): WANE-TV (CBS) Fort Wayne; WBDT (CW) Springfield; WBGU-TV (PBS) Bowling Green; WBNS-TV (CBS) Columbus; WDTN (NBC) Dayton; WFFT-TV (IND) Fort Wayne; WHIO-TV (CBS) Dayton; WISE-TV (FOX, MNT, NBC) Fort Wayne; WKEF (ABC) Dayton; WLIO (CW, NBC) Lima; WOHL-CD (FOX) Lima; WPTA (ABC, CW) Fort Wayne; WPTD (PBS) Dayton; WRGT-TV (FOX, MNT) Dayton; WTLW (IND) Lima; allband FM.
Programming (via satellite): QVC; TBS Superstation; WGN America.
Fee: $50.00 installation; $10.50 monthly.

Expanded Basic Service 1
Subscribers: N.A.
Programming (via satellite): A&E Networks; ABC Family Channel; AMC; Animal Planet; BET Networks; Bravo; Cartoon Network; CNBC; CNN; Comedy Central; Country Music TV; C-SPAN; C-SPAN 2; Discovery Channel; Disney Channel; E! Entertainment Television; ESPN; ESPN 2; ESPN Classic Sports; Eternal Word TV Network; Food Network; Fox News Channel; Fox Sports Net Detroit; Fox Sports Net Ohio; FX; Great American Country; Hallmark Channel; Headline News; HGTV; History Channel; Lifetime; MSNBC; MTV; Nickelodeon; Ohio News Network; Oxygen; Product Information Network; Spike TV; Syfy; Telemundo; The Learning Channel; The Weather Channel; Travel Channel; Trinity Broadcasting Network; truTV; Turner Classic Movies; Turner Network TV; TV Guide Network; TV Land; USA Network; VH1; WE tv.
Fee: $12.45 monthly.

Digital Basic Service
Subscribers: 567.
Programming (via satellite): AmericanLife TV Network; BBC America; Bio; Black Family Channel; Bloomberg Television; Discovery Fit & Health; DIY Network; ESPNews; Fox Sports World; Fuse; G4; GAS; Golf Channel; GSN; History Channel International; Independent Film Channel; INSP; MTV Networks Digital Suite; National Geographic Channel; Nick Jr.; Nick Too; Outdoor Channel; SoapNet; Speed; Style Network; Sundance Channel; Toon Disney; Versus.
Digital Expanded Basic Service
Subscribers: N.A.
Programming (via satellite): ART America; Canales N; CCTV-4; Filipino Channel; Fox Deportes; RAI International; Rio de la Plata; Russian Television Network; Telemundo; TV Asia; TV Japan; TV5 USA.
Fee: $6.95 monthly.
Digital Pay Service 1
Pay Units: N.A.
Programming (via satellite): Cinemax (multiplexed); Encore (multiplexed); HBO (multiplexed); Showtime (multiplexed); Starz (multiplexed).
Fee: $17.95 monthly (each).
Video-On-Demand: No
Pay-Per-View
Addressable homes: 563.
iN DEMAND (delivered digitally); NBA 1, NBA 2, NHL & MBL (delivered digitally); ESPN (delivered digitally).
Internet Service
Operational: Yes.
Subscribers: 652.
Broadband Service: Road Runner.
Fee: $42.95 monthly.
Telephone Service
None
Miles of Plant: 113.0 (coaxial); None (fiber optic).
President: Rhonda Fraas. Area Manager: Brad Wakely. Manager: John Ellingson. Customer Service Manager: Cindy Sierra.
Ownership: Time Warner Cable (MSO).

MORROW—Formerly served by Adelphia Communications. Now served by CINCINNATI, OH [OH0001]. ICA: OH0115.

MOUNT EATON—Clear Picture Inc. Now served by WOOSTER, OH [OH0061]. ICA: OH0344.

MOUNT GILEAD—Time Warner Cable, 205 Crystal Ave, Findlay, OH 45840. Phone: 419-429-7474. Fax: 419-429-7402. Web Site: http://www.timewarnercable.com/midohio. Also serves Cardington, Chesterville, Edison, Fulton, Gilead Twp., Harmony Twp., Lincoln Twp., Marengo, North Bloomfield Twp., Peru Twp. & Sparta. ICA: OH0166.
TV Market Ranking: 27 (Fulton, Harmony Twp. (portions), Lincoln Twp., Marengo, Peru Twp., Sparta); Below 100 (Cardington, Chesterville, Edison, Gilead Twp., MOUNT GILEAD, North Bloomfield Twp., Harmony Twp. (portions)).
Channel capacity: N.A. Channels available but not in use: N.A.
Basic Service
Subscribers: N.A. Included in Columbus
Programming (received off-air): WBNS-TV (CBS) Columbus; WCMH-TV (NBC) Columbus; WMFD-TV (IND) Mansfield; WOSU-TV (PBS) Columbus; WSFJ-TV (TBN) Newark; WSYX (ABC, MNT) Columbus; WTTE (FOX) Columbus; WUAB (MNT) Lorain; WWHO (CW) Chillicothe.
Programming (via satellite): AmericanLife TV Network; C-SPAN; Hallmark Channel; Headline News; History Channel; LWS Local Weather Station; QVC; ShopNBC; SoapNet; TBS Superstation; The Learning Channel; Travel Channel; TV Guide Network; WGN America.
Expanded Basic Service 1
Subscribers: N.A.
Programming (via satellite): A&E Networks; ABC Family Channel; AMC; Animal Planet; BET Networks; Bravo; BTN; Cartoon Network; CNBC; CNN; Comedy Central; Country Music TV; C-SPAN 2; C-SPAN 3; Discovery Channel; Disney Channel; E! Entertainment Television; ESPN; ESPN 2; Food Network; Fox News Channel; Fox Sports Net Ohio; FX; Golf Channel; HGTV; Lifetime; Lifetime Movie Network; MSNBC; MTV; MTV2; National Geographic Channel; Nick Jr.; Nickelodeon; Oxygen; Spike TV; SportsTime Ohio; Syfy; The Weather Channel; truTV; Turner Classic Movies; Turner Network TV; TV Land; Univision Studios; USA Network; Versus; VH1; WE tv.
Digital Basic Service
Subscribers: N.A. Included in Columbus
Programming (via satellite): A&E HD; AmericanLife TV Network; Animal Planet HD; Auction TV; BBC America; BBC America On Demand; Bio; Bloomberg Television; Boomerang; BTN (multiplexed); BTN HD; Canal Sur; CBS Sports Network; Cine Latino; cloo; CNN en Espanol; CNN International; Cooking Channel; C-SPAN 3; Current; Discovery Channel HD; Discovery en Espanol; Discovery Fit & Health; Discovery Health Channel; Discovery Kids Channel; Disney Channel; Disney Channel HD; DIY Network; Encore (multiplexed); ESPN 2 HD; ESPN Classic Sports; ESPN Deportes; ESPN HD; ESPN U; ESPNews; Eternal Word TV Network; Exercise TV; Food Network; Food Network HD; Fox Business Channel; Fox College Sports Atlantic; Fox College Sports Central; Fox College Sports Pacific; Fox Deportes; Fox Movie Channel; Fox Reality Channel; Fox Soccer; FSN HD; Fuel TV; Fuse; G4; Great American Country; GSN; HD Theater; HDNet; HDNet Movies; here! TV; HGTV; HGTV HD; History Channel en Espanol; History Channel HD; History Channel International; Howard TV; ID Investigation Discovery; Independent Film Channel; INSP; Jewelry Television; La Familia Network; Lifetime Real Women; LOGO; Military Channel; MTV Hits; mun2 television; Music Choice; National Geographic Channel HD Network; National Geographic Channel On Demand; NBA TV; NHL Network; NickToons TV; Ohio News Network; Outdoor Channel; Ovation; Oxygen On Demand; Palladia; Planet Green; Product Information Network; Science; SoapNet; Speed; Style Network; Sundance Channel; TBS in HD; TeenNick; Tennis Channel; The Weather Channel; The Word Network; Toon Disney; Tr3s; Turner Network TV HD; TV One; Universal HD; Versus HD; VH1 Classic; Video Rola.
Fee: $4.95 monthly (Latino or Sports), $10.40 monthly (Variety or Movies), $14.60 monthly (Premier).
Digital Pay Service 1
Pay Units: N.A.
Programming (via satellite): Cinemax (multiplexed); Cinemax On Demand; Encore; HBO (multiplexed); HBO HD; HBO Latino; HBO On Demand; Showtime (multiplexed); Showtime HD; Showtime On Demand; Starz (multiplexed); Starz On Demand; The Movie Channel (multiplexed); The Movie Channel On Demand.
Fee: $11.95 monthly (HBO, Cinemax, Showtime/TMC or Starz/Encore).
Pay-Per-View
iN DEMAND (delivered digitally); Playboy TV (delivered digitally); Sports PPV (delivered digitally).
Internet Service
Operational: Yes.
Broadband Service: Road Runner.
Fee: $44.95 monthly.
Telephone Service
Digital: Operational
Fee: $44.95 monthly
Miles of plant included in Columbus
President: Rhonda Fraas. Vice President & General Manager: Brad Wakely. Vice President, Engineering: Randy Hall. Vice President, Marketing: Mark Psigoda. Technical Operations Director: John Ellingson. Government Affairs Director: Brian Young. Government Affairs Manager: Patrick McCauley.
Ownership: Time Warner Cable (MSO).

MOUNT ORAB—S. Bryer Cable TV Corp., PO Box 226, Kinsman, OH 44428. Phone: 330-876-0294. Fax: 330-876-0294. ICA: OH0345.
TV Market Ranking: 17 (MOUNT ORAB). Franchise award date: N.A. Franchise expiration date: N.A. Began: January 1, 1988.
Channel capacity: N.A. Channels available but not in use: N.A.
Basic Service
Subscribers: 452.
Programming (received off-air): WCET (PBS) Cincinnati; WCPO-TV (ABC) Cincinnati; WHIO-TV (CBS) Dayton; WKEF (ABC) Dayton; WKRC-TV (CBS, CW) Cincinnati; WLWT (NBC) Cincinnati; WPTD (PBS) Dayton; WSTR-TV (MNT) Cincinnati; WXIX-TV (FOX) Newport.
Programming (via satellite): Trinity Broadcasting Network; WGN America.
Fee: $37.45 installation; $19.95 monthly.
Expanded Basic Service 1
Subscribers: N.A.
Programming (via satellite): A&E Networks; ABC Family Channel; AMC; AmericanLife TV Network; Animal Planet; Bloomberg Television; Boomerang; Cartoon Network; Classic Arts Showcase; CNBC; CNN; Comedy Central; Cooking Channel; Country Music TV; Crime & Investigation Network; C-SPAN; Discovery Channel; Discovery Health Channel; Disney Channel; DIY Network; E! Entertainment Television; ESPN; ESPN 2; Food Network; Fox News Channel; Fox Sports Net Ohio; Great American Country; Hallmark Channel; Hallmark Movie Channel; Halogen Network; Headline News; HGTV; History Channel; Lifetime; Lifetime Movie Network; Military History Channel; MTV; Nick Jr.; Nickelodeon; QVC; RFD-TV; ShopNBC; SoapNet; Speed; Spike TV; Syfy; TBS Superstation; The Learning Channel; The Weather Channel; Toon Disney; Travel Channel; truTV; Turner Classic Movies; Turner Network TV; TV Guide Network; TV Land; USA Network; VH1; WE tv.
Fee: $17.00 monthly.
Pay Service 1
Pay Units: 24.
Programming (via satellite): Cinemax; HBO; Showtime; The Movie Channel.
Fee: $12.95 monthly (each).
Video-On-Demand: No
Internet Service
Operational: Yes.
Subscribers: 154.
Telephone Service
Digital: Operational
Miles of Plant: 54.0 (coaxial); None (fiber optic). Miles of plant (coax) includes fiber
Manager: Scott Bryer. Chief Technician: Dave Pollard.
Ownership: SBC-Tele (MSO).

MOUNT PLEASANT TWP.—Comcast Cable (formerly Community TV Systems Cable Co.). Now served by WHEELING, WV [WV0004]. ICA: OH0346.

MOUNT STERLING (Muskingum County)—Time Warner Cable. Now served by ZANESVILLE, OH [OH0037]. ICA: OH0237.

MOUNT VERNON—Time Warner Cable, 1266 Dublin Rd, Columbus, OH 43215-1008. Phone: 614-481-5000. Fax: 614-481-5052. Web Site: http://www.timewarnercable.com/midohio. Also serves Alexandria, Ashley, Centerburg, Clay Twp. (Knox County), College Twp. (Knox County), Croton, Danville, Etna Twp., Fredericktown, Gambier, Hilliar Twp. (Knox County), Howard Twp. (Knox County), Johnstown, Kirkersville, Liberty Twp. (Knox County), Martinsburg, Middlebury Twp. (Knox County), Morris Twp. (Knox County), Pataskala, Pleasant Twp. (Knox County), St. Albans Twp. & Utica. ICA: OH0095.
TV Market Ranking: 27 (Alexandria, Ashley, Centerburg, Croton, Etna Twp., Hilliar, Johnstown, Kirkersville, Liberty Twp. (Knox County) (portions), Patalaska, Utica); Below 100 (Clay Twp. (Knox County), College Twp. (Knox County), Danville, Fredericktown, Gambier, Howard Twp. (Knox County), Martinsburg, Middlebury Twp. (Knox County), Morris Twp. (Knox County), MOUNT VERNON, Pleasant Twp., St. Albans Twp., Liberty Twp. (Knox County) (portions)).
Channel capacity: N.A. Channels available but not in use: N.A.
Basic Service
Subscribers: N.A. Included in Columbus
Programming (received off-air): WBNS-TV (CBS) Columbus; WCMH-TV (NBC) Columbus; WOSU-TV (PBS) Columbus; WSFJ-TV (TBN) Newark; WSYX (ABC, MNT) Columbus; WTTE (FOX) Columbus; WUAB (MNT) Lorain; WWHO (CW) Chillicothe.
Programming (via satellite): AmericanLife TV Network; C-SPAN; C-SPAN 3; Hallmark Channel; Headline News; History Channel; LWS Local Weather Station; QVC; ShopNBC; SoapNet; TBS Superstation; The Learning Channel; Travel Channel; TV Guide Network; WGN America.
Expanded Basic Service 1
Subscribers: N.A.
Programming (via satellite): A&E Networks; ABC Family Channel; AMC; Animal Planet; BET Networks; Bravo; BTN; Cartoon Network; CNBC; CNN; Comedy Central; Country Music TV; Discovery Channel; Disney Channel; E! Entertainment Television; ESPN; ESPN 2; Food Network; Fox News Channel; Fox Sports Net Ohio; FX; Golf Channel; HGTV; Lifetime; Lifetime Movie Network; MSNBC; MTV; MTV2; National Geographic Channel; Nick Jr.; Nickelodeon; Oxygen; Spike TV; SportsTime Ohio; Syfy; The Weather Channel; truTV; Turner Classic Movies; Turner Network TV; TV Land; Univision Studios; USA Network; Versus; VH1; WE tv.

Digital Basic Service
Subscribers: N.A. Included in Columbus
Programming (via satellite): A&E HD; AmericanLife TV Network; Animal Planet HD; Auction TV; BBC America; BBC America On Demand; Bio; Bloomberg Television; Boomerang; BTN; BTN HD; Canal Sur; CBS Sports Network; Cine Latino; cloo; CNN en Espanol; CNN International; Cooking Channel; C-SPAN 2; C-SPAN 3; Current; Discovery Channel HD; Discovery en Espanol; Discovery Fit & Health; Discovery Health Channel; Discovery Kids Channel; Disney Channel; Disney Channel HD; DIY Network; Encore (multiplexed); ESPN 2 HD; ESPN Classic Sports; ESPN Deportes; ESPN HD; ESPN U; ESPNews; Eternal Word TV Network; Exercise TV; Food Network; Food Network HD; Fox Business Channel; Fox College Sports Atlantic; Fox College Sports Central; Fox College Sports Pacific; Fox Deportes; Fox Movie Channel; Fox Reality Channel; Fox Soccer; FSN HD; Fuel TV; Fuse; G4; Great American Country; GSN; HD Theater; HDNet; HDNet Movies; HGTV; HGTV HD; History Channel en Espanol; History Channel HD; History Channel International; ID Investigation Discovery; Independent Film Channel; INSP; Jewelry Television; La Familia Network; Lifetime Real Women; LOGO; Military Channel; MTV Hits; mun2 television; Music Choice; National Geographic Channel HD Network; National Geographic Channel On Demand; NHL Network; NickToons TV; Ohio News Network; Outdoor Channel; Ovation; Oxygen On Demand; Palladia; Planet Green; Product Information Network; Science; SoapNet; Speed; Style Network; Sundance Channel; TBS in HD; TeenNick; Tennis Channel; The Weather Channel; The Word Network; Toon Disney; Tr3s; Turner Network TV HD; TV One; Universal HD; Versus HD; VH1 Classic; Video Rola.
Fee: $4.95 monthly (Latino or Sports Plus), $10.40 monthly (Movies or Variety), $14.60 monthly (Premier Digital).

Digital Pay Service 1
Pay Units: N.A.
Programming (via satellite): Cinemax On Demand; Encore; HBO (multiplexed); HBO HD; HBO Latino; HBO On Demand; Showtime (multiplexed); Showtime HD; Showtime On Demand; Starz (multiplexed); Starz On Demand; The Movie Channel (multiplexed); The Movie Channel On Demand.
Fee: $11.95 monthly (HBO, Cinemax, Starz/Encore or Showtime/TMC).

Video-On-Demand: Yes

Pay-Per-View
iN DEMAND (delivered digitally); Playboy TV (delivered digitally); Sports PPV (delivered digitally).

Internet Service
Operational: Yes.
Fee: $44.95 monthly.

Telephone Service
Digital: Operational
Fee: $44.95 monthly

Miles of plant included in Columbus

President: Rhonda Fraas. Vice President & General Manager: Brad Wakely. Vice President, Engineering: Randy Hall.; Mark Psigoda. Technical Operations Director: John Ellingson. Government Affairs Director: Brian Young. Government Affairs Manager: Patrick McCauley.

Ownership: Time Warner Cable (MSO).

MURRAY CITY—Time Warner Cable, 1266 Dublin Rd, Columbus, OH 43215-1008. Phone: 614-481-5000. Fax: 614-481-5052. Web Site: http://www.timewarnercable.com/midohio. Also serves Hocking County (unincorporated areas) & Ward Twp. ICA: OH0284.

TV Market Ranking: 27 (Hocking County (unincorporated areas) (portions)); Below 100 (MURRAY CITY, Ward Twp., Hocking County (unincorporated areas) (portions)); Outside TV Markets (Hocking County (unincorporated areas) (portions)). Franchise award date: N.A. Franchise expiration date: N.A. Began: November 1, 1951.

Channel capacity: N.A. Channels available but not in use: N.A.

Basic Service
Subscribers: 204.
Programming (received off-air): WBNS-TV (CBS) Columbus; WCHS-TV (ABC) Charleston; WCMH-TV (NBC) Columbus; WHIZ-TV (NBC) Zanesville; WOUB-TV (PBS) Athens; WOWK-TV (CBS) Huntington; WSAZ-TV (MNT, NBC) Huntington; WSFJ-TV (TBN) Newark; WSYX (ABC, MNT) Columbus; WTTE (FOX) Columbus; WVAH-TV (FOX) Charleston; allband FM.
Programming (via satellite): WGN America.
Fee: $47.50 installation; $10.94 monthly; $2.00 converter.

Expanded Basic Service 1
Subscribers: 197.
Programming (via satellite): A&E Networks; Animal Planet; CNN; Country Music TV; Discovery Channel; ESPN; Fox News Channel; Lifetime; Nickelodeon; Spike TV; TBS Superstation; Turner Network TV; USA Network.
Fee: $5.01 monthly.

Digital Basic Service
Subscribers: N.A.
Programming (via satellite): BBC America; Bloomberg Television; Discovery Fit & Health; ESPN Classic Sports; ESPNews; Fox Movie Channel; Fox Sports World; G4; Golf Channel; GSN; Halogen Network; HGTV; History Channel; Independent Film Channel; Music Choice; Nick Jr.; NickToons TV; Outdoor Channel; Syfy; Trinity Broadcasting Network; Versus; WE tv.

Digital Pay Service 1
Pay Units: N.A.
Programming (via satellite): Cinemax (multiplexed); Encore (multiplexed); HBO (multiplexed); Showtime (multiplexed); Starz (multiplexed); The Movie Channel (multiplexed).
Fee: $11.95 monthly (each).

Video-On-Demand: No

Pay-Per-View
Hits Movies & Events (delivered digitally); Fresh (delivered digitally); Playboy TV (delivered digitally).

Internet Service
Operational: Yes.

Telephone Service
None

Miles of Plant: 3.0 (coaxial); None (fiber optic).

President: Rhonda Fraas. Vice President & General Manager: David Kreiman. Vice President, Engineering: Randy Hall. Vice President, Marketing: Mark Psigoda. Vice President, Government & Public Affairs: Mary Jo Green. Technical Operations Director: Jim Cavender. Government Affairs Director: Steve Cuckler.

Ownership: Time Warner Cable (MSO).

NAPOLEON—Time Warner Cable, 310 Jefferson Ave, Defiance, OH 43512. Phones: 614-481-5000 (Columbus office); 419-784-1992 (Administrative office). Fax: 419-782-2640. Web Site: http://www.timewarnercable.com. Also serves Flatrock Twp., Florida & Malinta. ICA: OH0121.

TV Market Ranking: 52 (Malinta, NAPOLEON); Outside TV Markets (Flatrock Twp., Florida). Franchise award date: January 1, 1964. Franchise expiration date: N.A. Began: January 1, 1964.

Channel capacity: N.A. Channels available but not in use: N.A.

Basic Service
Subscribers: 3,368.
Programming (received off-air): WBGU-TV (PBS) Bowling Green; WDFM-LP (IND) Defiance; WDIV-TV (NBC) Detroit; WGTE-TV (PBS) Toledo; WKBD-TV (CW) Detroit; WLMB (IND) Toledo; WMNT-CA (MNT) Toledo; WNWO-TV (NBC) Toledo; WTOL (CBS) Toledo; WTVG (ABC) Toledo; WUPW (FOX) Toledo; 16 FMs.
Programming (via satellite): ABC Family Channel; ION Television; QVC; TV Guide Network; WGN America.
Fee: $45.35 installation; $15.00 monthly; $28.33 additional installation.

Expanded Basic Service 1
Subscribers: N.A.
Programming (via satellite): A&E Networks; AMC; Animal Planet; BET Networks; Bravo; Cartoon Network; CNBC; CNN; Comedy Central; Country Music TV; C-SPAN; C-SPAN 2; Discovery Channel; Disney Channel; E! Entertainment Television; ESPN; ESPN 2; Eternal Word TV Network; Food Network; Fox News Channel; Fox Sports Net Detroit; Fox Sports Net Ohio; FX; Golf Channel; Great American Country; Hallmark Channel; Headline News; HGTV; History Channel; Lifetime; MSNBC; MTV; Nickelodeon; Ohio News Network; Oxygen; Product Information Network; ShopNBC; Spike TV; Syfy; TBS Superstation; The Learning Channel; The Weather Channel; Travel Channel; Trinity Broadcasting Network; truTV; Turner Network TV; TV Land; Univision Studios; USA Network; Versus; VH1.
Fee: $22.95 monthly.

Digital Basic Service
Subscribers: 777.
Programming (via satellite): AmericanLife TV Network; BBC America; Bio; Black Family Channel; Bloomberg Television; Discovery Fit & Health; DIY Network; ESPN Classic Sports; ESPNews; Fox Sports World; G4; GAS; GSN; History Channel International; Independent Film Channel; INSP; MTV Networks Digital Suite; MuchMusic Network; National Geographic Channel; Nick Jr.; Nick Too; Outdoor Channel; SoapNet; Speed; Style Network; Sundance Channel; Toon Disney; Turner Classic Movies; WE tv.

Digital Expanded Basic Service
Subscribers: N.A.
Programming (via satellite): ART America; CCTV-4; Filipino Channel; Fox Deportes; MTV Networks Digital Suite; RAI International; Rio de la Plata; Russian Television Network; Telemundo; TV Asia; TV Japan; TV5 USA.

Digital Pay Service 1
Pay Units: N.A.
Programming (via satellite): Cinemax (multiplexed); Encore (multiplexed); HBO (multiplexed); Showtime (multiplexed).
Fee: $11.95 monthly (each).

Video-On-Demand: Planned

Pay-Per-View
Addressable homes: 707.
iN DEMAND (delivered digitally); Sports PPV (delivered digitally).

Internet Service
Operational: Yes.
Subscribers: 638.
Broadband Service: Road Runner.
Fee: $42.95 monthly.

Telephone Service
None

Miles of Plant: 89.0 (coaxial); None (fiber optic).

President: Rhonda Fraas. Area Manager: Brad Wakely. Manager: John Ellingson. Customer Service Manager: Cindy Sierra.

Ownership: Time Warner Cable (MSO).

NASHPORT—Time Warner Cable. Now served by ZANESVILLE, OH [OH0037]. ICA: OH0247.

NELSON MOBILE HOME PARK—Time Warner Cable, 530 S Main St, Ste 1751, Akron, OH 44311-1090. Phone: 330-633-9203. Fax: 330-633-7970. Web Site: http://www.timewarnercable.com/northeastohio. ICA: OH0306.

TV Market Ranking: 79 (NELSON MOBILE HOME PARK). Franchise award date: December 1, 1988. Franchise expiration date: N.A. Began: December 1, 1988.

Channel capacity: N.A. Channels available but not in use: N.A.

Basic Service
Subscribers: N.A.
Programming (received off-air): WBNX-TV (CW) Akron; WDLI-TV (TBN) Canton; WEAO (PBS) Akron; WEWS-TV (ABC) Cleveland; WFMJ-TV (CW, NBC) Youngstown; WJW (FOX) Cleveland; WKBN-TV (CBS) Youngstown; WKYC (NBC) Cleveland; WNEO (PBS) Alliance; WOIO (CBS) Shaker Heights; WQHS-DT (UNV) Cleveland; WRLM (IND) Canton; WUAB (MNT) Lorain; WVPX-TV (ION) Akron; WYTV (ABC, MNT) Youngstown.
Programming (via satellite): TV Guide Network.
Fee: $44.95 installation; $17.66 monthly.

Expanded Basic Service 1
Subscribers: N.A.
Programming (via satellite): A&E Networks; ABC Family Channel; AMC; Animal Planet; BET Networks; Bravo; Cartoon Network; CNBC; CNN; Comedy Central; Country Music TV; C-SPAN; C-SPAN 2; Discovery Channel; Discovery Fit & Health; Discovery Health Channel; Disney Channel; E! Entertainment Television; ESPN; ESPN 2; ESPN Classic Sports; Food Network; Fox News Channel; Fox Sports Net Ohio; FX; Golf Channel; Great American Country; GSN; Hallmark Channel; Headline News; HGTV; History Channel; INSP; Lifetime; Lifetime Movie Network; MSNBC; MTV; MTV2; Nickelodeon; Oxygen; QVC; ShopNBC; SoapNet; Spike TV; Syfy; TBS Superstation; The Learning Channel; The Weather Channel; Travel Channel; truTV;

Turner Classic Movies; Turner Network TV; TV Land; USA Network; Versus; VH1; WE tv.
Fee: $34.33 monthly.

Digital Basic Service
Subscribers: N.A.
Programming (received off-air): WJW (FOX) Cleveland.
Programming (via satellite): American-Life TV Network; America's Store; BBC America; Bio; Bloomberg Television; Boomerang; Canales N; CBS Sports Network; cloo; CNN International; Cooking Channel; Country Music TV; C-SPAN 3; Current; Daystar TV Network; Disney Channel; DIY Network; DMX Music; Encore (multiplexed); ESPNews; Fox College Sports Atlantic; Fox College Sports Central; Fox College Sports Pacific; Fox Movie Channel; Fox Soccer; Fuel TV; Fuse; G4; GAS; HD Theater; HDNet; HDNet Movies; History Channel International; Independent Film Channel; INHD (multiplexed); Lifetime Real Women; MTV2; National Geographic Channel; NBA TV; Nick Jr.; NickToons TV; Ohio News Network; Outdoor Channel; Speed; Style Network; Tennis Channel; The Word Network; Toon Disney; Turner Network TV HD; TVG Network; VH1 Classic.
Fee: $16.00 monthly.

Digital Pay Service 1
Pay Units: N.A.
Programming (via satellite): ART America; Cinemax (multiplexed); HBO (multiplexed); RAI International; Showtime (multiplexed); Starz (multiplexed); The Movie Channel (multiplexed); TV Asia; Zee TV USA.
Fee: $12.00 monthly (each).

Video-On-Demand: Yes

Internet Service
Operational: Yes.
Broadband Service: EarthLink, Road Runner.
Fee: $99.00 installation; $44.95 monthly.

Telephone Service
Digital: Operational
Fee: $44.95 monthly

Miles of Plant: 1.0 (coaxial); None (fiber optic).
President: Stephen Fry. Area Vice President: Scott Miller. Vice President, Engineering: Al Costanzi. Vice President, Marketing: Patrick Burke.; Woody Woodward. Vice President, Public Affairs: William Jasso. Government & Media Relations Director: Chris Thomas.
Ownership: Time Warner Cable (MSO).

NELSON TWP.—Suddenlink Communications, 12444 Powerscourt Dr, Saint Louis, MO 63131-3660. Phone: 314-965-2020. Web Site: http://www.suddenlink.com. Also serves Auburn Twp., Blue Water Manor, Farmington, Freedom Twp. (Portage County), Geauga County (portions), Mesopotamia, Mesopotamia Twp., Newton Twp., Paris Twp. (Portage County), Parkman, Parkman Twp., Rogers, Windham (Portage County) & Windham Twp. ICA: OH0160.
TV Market Ranking: 79 (Farmington); 8 (Auburn Twp., Geauga County (portions)); 8,79 (Blue Water Manor, Freedom Twp. (Portage County), Mesopotamia, Mesopotamia Twp., NELSON TWP., Newton Twp., Paris Twp. (Portage County), Parkman, Parkman Twp., Rogers, Windham (Portage County), Windham Twp.). Franchise award date: June 25, 1988. Franchise expiration date: N.A. Began: November 1, 1989.
Channel capacity: 62 (operating 2-way). Channels available but not in use: N.A.

Basic Service
Subscribers: 3,083.
Programming (received off-air): WBNX-TV (CW) Akron; WDLI-TV (TBN) Canton; WEWS-TV (ABC) Cleveland; WFMJ-TV (CW, NBC) Youngstown; WJW (FOX) Cleveland; WKBN-TV (CBS) Youngstown; WKYC (NBC) Cleveland; WNEO (PBS) Alliance; WOIO (CBS) Shaker Heights; WRLM (IND) Canton; WUAB (MNT) Lorain; WVIZ (PBS) Cleveland; WVPX-TV (ION) Akron; WYTV (ABC, MNT) Youngstown.
Fee: $25.00 installation; $17.95 monthly; $1.95 converter.

Expanded Basic Service 1
Subscribers: 1,637.
Programming (via satellite): A&E Networks; ABC Family Channel; AMC; Animal Planet; Cartoon Network; CNBC; CNN; Comedy Central; C-SPAN; Discovery Channel; Disney Channel; E! Entertainment Television; ESPN; ESPN 2; Food Network; Fox News Channel; Fox Sports Net Ohio; FX; Great American Country; Headline News; HGTV; History Channel; Lifetime; MTV; Nickelodeon; QVC; Root Sports Pittsburgh; Spike TV; SportsTime Ohio; Syfy; TBS Superstation; The Learning Channel; The Weather Channel; Turner Classic Movies; Turner Network TV; TV Land; USA Network; VH1.
Fee: $25.00 monthly.

Digital Basic Service
Subscribers: N.A.
Programming (via satellite): BBC America; Bio; Bloomberg Television; cloo; Country Music TV; Discovery Digital Networks; DMX Music; ESPN Classic Sports; ESPNews; Fuse; G4; GAS; Golf Channel; GSN; History Channel International; Independent Film Channel; Lifetime Movie Network; MTV Networks Digital Suite; Nick Jr.; NickToons TV; Speed; Style Network; Toon Disney; Trinity Broadcasting Network; Versus; WE tv.

Pay Service 1
Pay Units: 184.
Programming (via satellite): Cinemax.
Fee: $11.00 monthly.

Pay Service 2
Pay Units: 260.
Programming (via satellite): HBO.
Fee: $11.00 monthly.

Pay Service 3
Pay Units: 256.
Programming (via satellite): Showtime; The Movie Channel.
Fee: $12.95 monthly.

Digital Pay Service 1
Pay Units: N.A.
Programming (via satellite): Cinemax (multiplexed); Encore (multiplexed); HBO (multiplexed); Showtime (multiplexed); Starz; The Movie Channel (multiplexed).

Pay-Per-View
iN DEMAND (delivered digitally); Playboy TV (delivered digitally); Fresh (delivered digitally).

Internet Service
Operational: Yes. Began: October 4, 2004.
Broadband Service: Suddenlink High Speed Internet.
Fee: $20.00 installation; $20.95 monthly.

Telephone Service
None

Miles of Plant: 187.0 (coaxial); None (fiber optic).
Manager: Peter Brown. Chief Technician: Tom Beat.
Ownership: Cequel Communications LLC (MSO).

NELSONVILLE—Nelsonville TV Cable, 1 W Columbus St, Nelsonville, OH 45764. Phones: 740-594-2860; 740-753-2686. E-mail: oldcableman74@yahoo.com. Also serves Athens County, Buchtel, Carbon Hill, Chauncey, Glouster, Haydenville, Jacksonville, Millfield, The Plains, Trimble & Union Furnace. ICA: OH0347.
TV Market Ranking: Below 100 (Athens County (portions), Buchtel, Carbon Hill, Chauncey, Glouster, Jacksonville, Millfield, The Plains, Trimble); Outside TV Markets (Athens County (portions), Haydenville, NELSONVILLE, Union Furnace). Franchise award date: N.A. Franchise expiration date: N.A. Began: December 8, 1952.
Channel capacity: 36 (not 2-way capable). Channels available but not in use: N.A.

Basic Service
Subscribers: 6,800.
Programming (received off-air): WBNS-TV (CBS) Columbus; WCHS-TV (ABC) Charleston; WCMH-TV (NBC) Columbus; WHIZ-TV (NBC) Zanesville; WOUB-TV (PBS) Athens; WOWK-TV (CBS) Huntington; WQCW (CW) Portsmouth; WSAZ-TV (MNT, NBC) Huntington; WSFJ-TV (TBN) Newark; WTTE (FOX) Columbus; WVAH-TV (FOX) Charleston; allband FM.
Programming (via satellite): A&E Networks; ABC Family Channel; AMC; Animal Planet; BET Networks; Cartoon Network; CNBC; CNN; Comedy Central; Discovery Channel; Disney Channel; E! Entertainment Television; ESPN; ESPN 2; ESPN Classic Sports; Food Network; Fox Movie Channel; Fox News Channel; Fox Sports Net Ohio; FSN Digital Atlantic; FSN Digital Central; FSN Digital Pacific; FX; Gospel Music TV; Great American Country; GSN; Headline News; HGTV; History Channel; Lifetime; MSNBC; MTV; MTV2; National Geographic Channel; Nickelodeon; Ohio News Network; Outdoor Channel; Speed; Spike TV; Syfy; TBS Superstation; The Learning Channel; The Weather Channel; Travel Channel; truTV; Turner Classic Movies; Turner Network TV; TV Land; VH1; WGN America.
Fee: $21.50 installation; $18.50 monthly.

Pay Service 1
Pay Units: 2,427.
Programming (via satellite): HBO (multiplexed); Showtime (multiplexed).
Fee: $20.00 installation; $7.00 monthly (Showtime), $8.00 monthly (HBO).

Pay Service 2
Pay Units: N.A.
Programming (via satellite): Cinemax (multiplexed); Encore (multiplexed); Flix; Starz (multiplexed); Sundance Channel; The Movie Channel.

Digital Pay Service 1
Pay Units: N.A.
Programming (via satellite): Cinemax (multiplexed); Encore (multiplexed); Flix; HBO (multiplexed); Showtime (multiplexed); Starz (multiplexed); Sundance Channel; The Movie Channel (multiplexed).

Video-On-Demand: No

Pay-Per-View
iN DEMAND.

Internet Service
Operational: Yes.
Fee: $12.00 installation; $59.95 monthly.

Telephone Service
None

Miles of Plant: 150.0 (coaxial); None (fiber optic). Additional miles planned: 5.0 (coaxial).
Manager: Eugene R. Edwards.
Ownership: Nelsonville TV Cable Inc.

NEW ATHENS—Richards TV Cable, PO Box 2, Jerusalem, OH 43747-0002. Phone: 740-926-1742. Fax: 740-926-1800. Also serves Lloydsville. ICA: OH0348.
TV Market Ranking: 90 (Lloydsville, NEW ATHENS). Franchise award date: N.A. Franchise expiration date: N.A. Began: N.A.
Channel capacity: N.A. Channels available but not in use: N.A.

Basic Service
Subscribers: N.A. Included in Malaga Twp.
Programming (received off-air): KDKA-TV (CBS) Pittsburgh; WPGH-TV (FOX) Pittsburgh; WPMY (MNT) Pittsburgh; WQED (PBS) Pittsburgh; WTAE-TV (ABC) Pittsburgh; WTOV-TV (IND, NBC) Steubenville; WTRF-TV (CBS) Wheeling.
Programming (via satellite): TBS Superstation; Turner Network TV.
Fee: $15.00 installation; $20.00 monthly.

Internet Service
Operational: No.

Telephone Service
None

Miles of plant included in Malaga Twp.
Manager: Paul E. Richards. Chief Technician: Mark Richards.
Ownership: Paul E. Richards (MSO).

NEW CONCORD—Time Warner Cable. Now served by ZANESVILLE, OH [OH0037]. ICA: OH0226.

NEW HOLLAND—Time Warner Cable, 1266 Dublin Rd, Columbus, OH 43215-1008. Phone: 614-481-5000. Fax: 614-481-5052. Web Site: http://www.timewarnercable.com/midohio. Also serves Clarksburg, Deercreek Twp. (Pickaway County), Perry Twp. (Pickaway County) & Williamsport. ICA: OH0207.
TV Market Ranking: 27 (Clarksburg, Deercreek Twp. (Pickaway County), NEW HOLLAND, Perry Twp. (Pickaway County), Williamsport). Franchise award date: December 8, 1986. Franchise expiration date: N.A. Began: December 8, 1987.
Channel capacity: N.A. Channels available but not in use: N.A.

Basic Service
Subscribers: 486.
Programming (received off-air): WBNS-TV (CBS) Columbus; WCMH-TV (NBC) Columbus; WOSU-TV (PBS) Columbus; WSYX (ABC, MNT) Columbus; WTTE (FOX) Columbus; WWHO (CW) Chillicothe.
Programming (via satellite): QVC; The Learning Channel; The Weather Channel; WGN America.
Fee: $20.99 installation; $23.70 monthly.

Expanded Basic Service 1
Subscribers: N.A.
Programming (via satellite): A&E Networks; ABC Family Channel; Animal Planet; CNN; Country Music TV; Discovery Channel; Disney Channel; ESPN; ESPN 2; Fox News Channel; FX; HGTV; History Channel; INSP; Lifetime; MSNBC; MTV; Nickelodeon; Ohio News Network; Spike TV; TBS Superstation; Turner Network TV; USA Network.

Digital Basic Service
Subscribers: N.A.
Programming (via satellite): BBC America; Bravo; Discovery Digital Networks; ESPN Classic Sports; ESPNews; Fox Soccer; Golf Channel; GSN; Independent Film Channel; Nick Jr.; Turner Classic Movies; Versus; WE tv.

Digital Pay Service 1
Pay Units: N.A.
Programming (via satellite): Cinemax (multiplexed); Encore (multiplexed); HBO

(multiplexed); Showtime (multiplexed); Starz (multiplexed); The Movie Channel (multiplexed).
Fee: $11.95 monthly (each).

Video-On-Demand: No

Pay-Per-View

Hits Movies & Events (delivered digitally); HITS 2 (delivered digitally); HITS 3 (delivered digitally); HITS 4 (delivered digitally); Playboy TV (delivered digitally).

Internet Service

Operational: Yes.

Telephone Service

None

Miles of Plant: 38.0 (coaxial); None (fiber optic).

President: Rhonda Fraas. Vice President & General Manager: David Kreiman. Vice President, Engineering: Randy Hall. Vice President, Marketing: Mark Psigoda. Vice President, Government & Public Affairs: Mary Jo Green. Technical Operations Director: Jim Cavender. Government Affairs Director: Steve Cuckler.

Ownership: Time Warner Cable (MSO).

NEW KNOXVILLE—NKTelco Services, 301 W South St, PO Box 219, New Knoxville, OH 45871-0219. Phones: 888-658-3526; 419-753-5000. Fax: 419-753-2950. E-mail: info@nktelco.net. Web Site: http://www.nktelco.net. Also serves Fort Loramie, Minster & New Bremen. ICA: OH0275. **Note:** This system is an overbuild.

TV Market Ranking: Below 100 (Fort Loramie, Minster, New Bremen, NEW KNOXVILLE). Franchise award date: May 5, 1985. Franchise expiration date: N.A. Began: February 1, 1986.

Channel capacity: 77 (operating 2-way). Channels available but not in use: N.A.

Basic Service

Subscribers: 2,090.

Programming (received off-air): WBGU-TV (PBS) Bowling Green; WBNS-TV (CBS) Columbus; WDTN (NBC) Dayton; WHIO-TV (CBS) Dayton; WKEF (ABC) Dayton; WLIO (CW, NBC) Lima; WLMO-LP Lima; WLQP-LP Lima; WOHL-CD (FOX) Lima; WPTA (ABC, CW) Fort Wayne; WPTD (PBS) Dayton; WRGT-TV (FOX, MNT) Dayton; WTLW (IND) Lima.

Programming (via satellite): America One Television; CW+; QVC; ShopNBC.

Fee: $24.95 installation; $9.95 monthly.

Expanded Basic Service 1

Subscribers: 2,017.

Programming (via satellite): A&E Networks; ABC Family Channel; AMC; Animal Planet; Boomerang; Bravo; Cartoon Network; CNBC; CNN; Comedy Central; Country Music TV; C-SPAN; C-SPAN 2; Discovery Channel; Disney Channel; E! Entertainment Television; ESPN; ESPN 2; ESPN Classic Sports; Eternal Word TV Network; Food Network; Fox News Channel; Fox Sports Net Ohio; FX; G4; Golf Channel; GSN; Hallmark Channel; Headline News; HGTV; History Channel; HRTV; ION Television; Lifetime; MSNBC; MTV; National Geographic Channel; NFL Network; Nickelodeon; Ohio News Network; Speed; Spike TV; SportsTime Ohio; Syfy; TBS Superstation; The Learning Channel; The Weather Channel; Toon Disney; Travel Channel; Trinity Broadcasting Network; truTV; Turner Classic Movies; Turner Network TV; TV Guide Network; TV Land; USA Network; Versus; VH1; WE tv; WGN America.

Fee: $14.00 monthly.

Digital Basic Service

Subscribers: N.A.

Programming (via satellite): AmericanLife TV Network; BBC America; Bio; Bloomberg Television; cloo; CMT Pure Country; Discovery Digital Networks; DMX Music; ESPNews; Fox College Sports Atlantic; Fox College Sports Central; Fox College Sports Pacific; Fox Movie Channel; Fox Soccer; GAS; Great American Country; Halogen Network; History Channel International; Lifetime Movie Network; MTV Networks Digital Suite; Nick Jr.; NickToons TV; Outdoor Channel; Ovation; Style Network.

Fee: $14.00 monthly.

Digital Pay Service 1

Pay Units: N.A.

Programming (via satellite): Cinemax (multiplexed); Encore (multiplexed); Flix; HBO (multiplexed); Showtime (multiplexed); Starz (multiplexed); Sundance Channel; The Movie Channel (multiplexed).

Fee: $9.50 monthly (Cinemax), $9.95 monthly (HBO), $10.95 monthly (Showtime, Sundance, Flix, & TMC), $13.50 monthly (Starz & Encore).

Video-On-Demand: No

Pay-Per-View

Playboy TV (delivered digitally); Fresh (delivered digitally); Shorteez (delivered digitally).

Internet Service

Operational: Yes, DSL.

Subscribers: 1,600.

Broadband Service: nktelco.net.

Fee: $59.95 installation; $19.95-$39.95 monthly; $10.00 modem lease; $200.00 modem purchase.

Telephone Service

Analog: Not Operational

Digital: Operational

Fee: $21.74 monthly

Miles of Plant: 40.0 (coaxial); 15.0 (fiber optic).

General Manager: Preston Meyer. Project Manager: Clint Conover. Sales & Marketing Manager: Erin Brown. Controller: Susan Quellhorst.

Ownership: New Knoxville Telephone & Cable Co.

NEW LEXINGTON (Perry County)—Time Warner Communications. Now served by THORNVILLE, OH [OH0154]. ICA: OH0148.

NEW LONDON—Time Warner Cable, 530 S Main St, Ste 1751, Akron, OH 44311-1090. Phone: 330-633-9203. Fax: 330-633-7970. Web Site: http://www.timewarnercable.com/northeastohio. Also serves Bailey Lakes, Clarksfield, New London Twp. & Savannah. ICA: OH0202.

TV Market Ranking: 8 (Clarksfield, NEW LONDON, New London Twp., Savannah); Below 100 (Bailey Lakes). Franchise award date: N.A. Franchise expiration date: June 6, 2010. Began: March 1, 1973.

Channel capacity: N.A. Channels available but not in use: N.A.

Basic Service

Subscribers: N.A. Included in Mansfield

Programming (received off-air): WBNX-TV (CW) Akron; WEAO (PBS) Akron; WEWS-TV (ABC) Cleveland; WGGN-TV (TBN) Sandusky; WJW (FOX) Cleveland; WKYC (NBC) Cleveland; WMFD-TV (IND) Mansfield; WNEO (PBS) Alliance; WOIO (CBS) Shaker Heights; WQHS-DT (UNV) Cleveland; WRLM (IND) Canton; WTOL (CBS) Toledo; WTVG (ABC) Toledo; WUAB (MNT) Lorain; WVIZ (PBS) Cleveland; WVPX-TV (ION) Akron.

Fee: $44.95 installation; $17.67 monthly; $.94 converter.

Expanded Basic Service 1

Subscribers: N.A.

Programming (via satellite): A&E Networks; ABC Family Channel; AMC; Animal Planet; BET Networks; Bravo; Cartoon Network; CNBC; CNN; Comedy Central; C-SPAN; C-SPAN 2; Discovery Channel; Discovery Fit & Health; Discovery Health Channel; Disney Channel; E! Entertainment Television; ESPN; ESPN 2; ESPN Classic Sports; Eternal Word TV Network; Food Network; Fox News Channel; Fox Sports Net Ohio; FX; Golf Channel; Great American Country; GSN; Hallmark Channel; Headline News; HGTV; History Channel; INSP; Lifetime; Lifetime Movie Network; MSNBC; MTV; Nickelodeon; Oxygen; QVC; ShopNBC; SoapNet; Spike TV; Syfy; TBS Superstation; The Learning Channel; The Weather Channel; Travel Channel; truTV; Turner Classic Movies; Turner Network TV; TV Land; USA Network; Versus; VH1; WE tv; WGN America.

Fee: $30.83 monthly.

Digital Basic Service

Subscribers: N.A.

Programming (via satellite): A&E HD; AmericanLife TV Network; America's Store; ART America; BBC America; Bio; Bloomberg Television; Boomerang; Canales N; CBS Sports Network; CNN; CNN International; Cooking Channel; Country Music TV; C-SPAN 3; Daystar TV Network; Deutsche Welle TV; DIY Network; ESPN; ESPNews; Fox College Sports Atlantic; Fox College Sports Central; Fox College Sports Pacific; Fox HD; Fox Movie Channel; Fox Soccer; Fuel TV; Fuse; G4; GAS; HD Theater; Headline News; History Channel International; Independent Film Channel; INHD; INHD2; Jewelry Television; Lifetime; Lifetime Real Women; MTV Networks Digital Suite; Music Choice; National Geographic Channel; NBA TV; Nick Jr.; NickToons TV; Ohio News Network; Outdoor Channel; RAI International; Speed; TBS Superstation; Tennis Channel; The Weather Channel; The Word Network; Toon Disney; Trio; Turner Network TV HD; TV Asia; TVG Network; USA Network; Zee TV USA.

Fee: $19.49 monthly.

Digital Pay Service 1

Pay Units: N.A.

Programming (via satellite): Cinemax (multiplexed); HBO (multiplexed); HBO HD; Showtime (multiplexed); Showtime HD; Starz (multiplexed); The Movie Channel (multiplexed).

Fee: $12.00 monthly (each).

Video-On-Demand: Yes

Pay-Per-View

iN DEMAND (delivered digitally); Playboy TV (delivered digitally); NHL Center Ice (delivered digitally); MLB Extra Innings (delivered digitally); Spice Live (delivered digitally); Ten Clips (delivered digitally); Pleasure (delivered digitally); NASCAR In Car (delivered digitally); NBA League Pass (delivered digitally); MLS Direct Kick (delivered digitally); ESPN (delivered digitally).

Internet Service

Operational: Yes.

Broadband Service: EarthLink, Road Runner.

Fee: $99.00 installation; $44.95 monthly.

Telephone Service

Digital: Operational

Fee: $44.95 monthly

Miles of Plant: 25.0 (coaxial); None (fiber optic).

President: Stephen Fry. Area Vice President: Scott Miller. Area Manager: Carol Jagger. Vice President, Marketing: Patrick Burke. Vice President, Sales: Woody Woodward. Vice President, Engineering: Al Costanzi. Government & Media Relations Director: Chris Thomas. Vice President, Public Affairs: William Jasso.

Ownership: Time Warner Cable (MSO).

NEW MATAMORAS—Formerly served by Adelphia Communications. Now served by HANNIBAL, OH [OH0251]. ICA: OH0245.

NEW MIDDLETOWN—Comcast Cable, 15 Summit Park Dr, Pittsburgh, PA 15275. Phones: 724-656-8230 (New Castle office); 412-747-6400. Fax: 412-747-6401. Web Site: http://www.comcast.com. Also serves East Palestine & Petersburg, OH; Bessemer, Edinburg, Hillsville, Mahoning Twp. (Lawrence County), Neshannock Twp., New Castle, North Beaver Twp. (Lawrence County), Plain Grove Twp., Scott Twp. (Lawrence County), South New Castle, Union Twp. (Lawrence County) & Wilmington Twp. (Lawrence County), PA. ICA: OH0145.

TV Market Ranking: 79 (Bessemer, East Palestine, Edinburg, Hillsville, Mahoning Twp. (Lawrence County), Neshannock Twp., New Castle, NEW MIDDLETOWN, North Beaver Twp. (Lawrence County), Petersburg, Plain Grove Twp., Scott Twp. (Lawrence County), South New Castle, Union Twp. (Lawrence County), Wilmington Twp. (Lawrence County)). Franchise award date: N.A. Franchise expiration date: N.A. Began: March 1, 1983.

Channel capacity: N.A. Channels available but not in use: N.A.

Basic Service

Subscribers: 29,622.

Programming (received off-air): KDKA-TV (CBS) Pittsburgh; WFMJ-TV (CW, NBC) Youngstown; WKBN-TV (CBS) Youngstown; WNEO (PBS) Alliance; WPGH-TV (FOX) Pittsburgh; WUAB (MNT) Lorain; WYFX-LP Youngstown; WYTV (ABC, MNT) Youngstown; allband FM.

Programming (via satellite): BET Networks; CNBC; C-SPAN; Discovery Channel; Hallmark Channel; QVC; The Weather Channel.

Fee: $43.99 installation; $14.00 monthly.

Expanded Basic Service 1

Subscribers: 2,393.

Programming (via satellite): A&E Networks; ABC Family Channel; AMC; Animal Planet; Cartoon Network; CNN; Comedy Central; Country Music TV; C-SPAN; C-SPAN 2;

Disney Channel; E! Entertainment Television; ESPN; ESPN 2; Eternal Word TV Network; Food Network; Fox News Channel; Fox Sports Net; FX; Headline News; HGTV; History Channel; Lifetime; MSNBC; MTV; Nickelodeon; Oxygen; Pennsylvania Cable Network; Root Sports Pittsburgh; Spike TV; TBS Superstation; The Learning Channel; Travel Channel; truTV; Turner Classic Movies; Turner Network TV; TV Land; USA Network; Versus; VH1.
Fee: $37.99 monthly.

Digital Basic Service
Subscribers: N.A.
Programming (via satellite): AmericanLife TV Network; BBC America; Bio; Black Family Channel; Bloomberg Television; Bravo; Cooking Channel; C-SPAN 3; Discovery Fit & Health; Discovery Kids Channel; DIY Network; DMX Music; ESPN Classic Sports; ESPNews; Fox Movie Channel; Fox Sports World; FSN Digital Atlantic; FSN Digital Central; FSN Digital Pacific; Fuse; G4; GAS; Golf Channel; Great American Country; GSN; Halogen Network; History Channel International; Independent Film Channel; International Television (ITV); Lifetime Movie Network; Lime; MTV Networks Digital Suite; MTV2; Music Choice; National Geographic Channel; Nick Jr.; NickToons TV; Outdoor Channel; Ovation; ShopNBC; Speed; Style Network; Sundance Channel; Syfy; The Word Network; Toon Disney; Trinity Broadcasting Network; WE tv; Weatherscan.
Fee: $10.95 monthly.

Digital Pay Service 1
Pay Units: N.A.
Programming (via satellite): Cinemax (multiplexed); Encore; Flix; HBO (multiplexed); Russian Television Network; Showtime (multiplexed); Starz (multiplexed); The Movie Channel (multiplexed); TV Asia; Zee TV USA.

Video-On-Demand: Yes

Pay-Per-View
NBA TV (delivered digitally); NHL/MLB (delivered digitally); iN DEMAND (delivered digitally); Urban American Television Network (delivered digitally); Barker (delivered digitally); Fresh (delivered digitally); Shorteez (delivered digitally); Playboy TV (delivered digitally); Hot Choice (delivered digitally); Sports PPV (delivered digitally).

Internet Service
Operational: Yes.
Broadband Service: Comcast High Speed Internet.
Fee: $42.95 monthly.

Telephone Service
Digital: Operational

Miles of Plant: 900.0 (coaxial); 300.0 (fiber optic).
Regional Vice President: Linda Hossinger. Vice President, Technical Operations: Randy Bender. Vice President, Marketing: Donna Corning. Vice President, Public Affairs: Jody Doherty.
Ownership: Comcast Cable Communications Inc. (MSO).

NEW PHILADELPHIA—Time Warner Cable, 530 S Main St, Ste 1751, Akron, OH 44311-1090. Phone: 330-633-9203. Fax: 330-633-7970. Web Site: http://www.timewarnercable.com/northeastohio. Also serves Baltic, Barnhill, Beach City, Berlin Twp., Bolivar, Clark Twp. (Holmes County), Columbia, Dellroy, Dennison, Dover, Fredericksburg, Glenmont, Gnadenhutton, Harrison Twp. (Carroll County), Holmesville, Killbuck, Lake Buckhorn, Lawrence Twp., Loudon Twp. (Carroll County), Midvale, Millersburg, New Cumberland, Newcomerstown, Oxford Twp. (Tuscarawas County), Parral, Port Washington, Richland Twp., Roswell, Sherrodsville, Strasburg, Sugarcreek, Tuscarawas, Uhrichsville, Wainwright Twp., Walnut Creek Twp., Wilmot & Zoar. ICA: OH0030.

TV Market Ranking: 8 (Beach City, Bolivar, Lawrence Twp., Strasburg, Wilmot, Zoar); 90 (Dellroy, Harrison Twp. (Carroll County), Loudon Twp. (Carroll County), New Cumberland, Sherrodsville); Below 100 (Baltic, Barnhill, Berlin Twp., Clark Twp. (Holmes County), Columbia, Dennison, Dover, Fredericksburg, Glenmont, Gnadenhutton, Holmesville, Killbuck, Lake Buckhorn, Midvale, Millersburg, NEW PHILADELPHIA, Newcomerstown, Oxford Twp. (Tuscarawas County), Parral, Port Washington, Richland Twp., Roswell, Sugarcreek, Tuscarawas, Uhrichsville, Wainwright Twp., Walnut Creek Twp.). Franchise award date: January 1, 1951. Franchise expiration date: N.A. Began: May 1, 1982.

Channel capacity: 70 (operating 2-way). Channels available but not in use: N.A.

Basic Service
Subscribers: 27,196.
Programming (received off-air): WBNX-TV (CW) Akron; WDLI-TV (TBN) Canton; WEAO (PBS) Akron; WEWS-TV (ABC) Cleveland; WJW (FOX) Cleveland; WKYC (NBC) Cleveland; WOIO (CBS) Shaker Heights; WOUC-TV (PBS) Cambridge; WQHS-DT (UNV) Cleveland; WRLM (IND) Canton; WTOV-TV (IND, NBC) Steubenville; WTRF-TV (CBS) Wheeling; WUAB (MNT) Lorain; WVPX-TV (ION) Akron.
Programming (via microwave): WCMH-TV (NBC) Columbus.
Programming (via satellite): QVC; TBS Superstation; TV Guide Network.
Fee: $44.95 installation; $17.69 monthly.

Expanded Basic Service 1
Subscribers: 25,728.
Programming (via satellite): A&E Networks; ABC Family Channel; AMC; Animal Planet; BET Networks; Bravo; Cartoon Network; CNBC; CNN; Comedy Central; Country Music TV; C-SPAN; C-SPAN 2; Discovery Channel; Disney Channel; E! Entertainment Television; ESPN; ESPN 2; Food Network; Fox News Channel; Fox Sports Net Ohio; FX; Golf Channel; Headline News; HGTV; History Channel; Lifetime; MSNBC; MTV; Nickelodeon; Ohio News Network; Oxygen; ShopNBC; Spike TV; Syfy; The Learning Channel; The Weather Channel; Travel Channel; truTV; Turner Classic Movies; Turner Network TV; TV Land; USA Network; VH1.
Fee: $33.31 monthly.

Digital Basic Service
Subscribers: N.A.
Programming (via satellite): AmericanLife TV Network; BBC America; Bloomberg Television; Discovery Fit & Health; ESPN Classic Sports; ESPNews; Fox Sports World; G4; GSN; Independent Film Channel; INSP; Music Choice; National Geographic Channel; Nick Jr.; Outdoor Channel; Trinity Broadcasting Network; VH1 Classic; VH1 Country; WE tv.
Fee: $12.49 monthly.

Digital Pay Service 1
Pay Units: 5,682.
Programming (via satellite): Canales N; Cinemax (multiplexed); Encore (multiplexed); Flix; HBO (multiplexed); Showtime (multiplexed); Starz (multiplexed); The Movie Channel (multiplexed).
Fee: $12.00 monthly (each).

Video-On-Demand: Yes

Pay-Per-View
NHL Center Ice/MLB Exta Innings (delivered digitally); iN DEMAND.

Internet Service
Operational: Yes.
Broadband Service: EarthLink, Road Runner.
Fee: $49.95 installation; $44.95 monthly.

Telephone Service
Analog: Not Operational
Digital: Operational

Miles of Plant: 689.0 (coaxial); None (fiber optic).
President: Stephen Fry. Area Vice President: Scott Miller. Vice President, Engineering: Al Costanzi. Vice President, Marketing: Patrick Burke. Vice President, Public Affairs: William Jasso. Government & Media Relations Director: Chris Thomas.
Ownership: Time Warner Cable (MSO).

NEWARK—Time Warner Cable, 111 N 11th St, Newark, OH 43055. Phones: 614-481-5000 (Columbus office); 740-345-4329. Fax: 740-349-0823. Web Site: http://www.timewarnercable.com/midohio. Also serves Adams Twp. (Guernsey County), Belle Valley, Bennington Twp., Bethlehem Twp. (Coshocton County), Burlington Twp., Caldwell, Cambridge, Center Twp., Chandlersville, Conesville, Eden Twp., Granville, Guernsey County (portions), Hanover, Heath, Howard, Keene Twp., Kimbolton, Liberty Twp., Liberty Twp. (Guernsey County), Licking County, Linton Twp., Mary Ann Twp., Newton Twp., Noble County (portions), Olive Twp. (Noble County), Plainfield, Salt Creek Twp., St. Louisville, West Lafayette & Wheeling Twp. (Guernsey County). ICA: OH0019.

TV Market Ranking: 27 (Bennington Twp., Burlington Twp., Granville, Heath, Hebron, Liberty Twp., Licking County, Mary Ann Twp. (portions), NEWARK, Newark Twp., St. Louisville); Below 100 (Adams Twp. (Guernsey County), Belle Valley, Bethlehem Twp. (Coshocton Twp.), Caldwell, Cambridge, Center Twp., Chandlersville, Conesville, Eden Twp., Guernsey County (portions), Hanover, Howard, Keene Twp., Kimbolton, Liberty Twp. (Guernsey County), Linton Twp., Noble County (portions), Olive Twp. (Noble County), Plainfield, Salt Creek Twp., West Lafayette, Wheeling Twp. (Guernsey County), Mary Ann Twp. (portions)). Franchise award date: N.A. Franchise expiration date: N.A. Began: July 19, 1976.

Channel capacity: N.A. Channels available but not in use: N.A.

Basic Service
Subscribers: 45,236.
Programming (received off-air): WBNS-TV (CBS) Columbus; WCMH-TV (NBC) Columbus; WHIZ-TV (NBC) Zanesville; WOSU-TV (PBS) Columbus; WOUC-TV (PBS) Cambridge; WSFJ-TV (TBN) Newark; WSYX (ABC, MNT) Columbus; WTTE (FOX) Columbus; WWHO (CW) Chillicothe; 19 FMs.
Programming (via satellite): C-SPAN; C-SPAN 2; QVC; ShopNBC; TBS Superstation; The Weather Channel; TV Guide Network; WGN America.
Fee: $43.00 installation; $18.80 monthly.

Expanded Basic Service 1
Subscribers: 27,625.
Programming (via satellite): A&E Networks; ABC Family Channel; AMC; Animal Planet; BET Networks; Bravo; Cartoon Network; CNBC; CNN; Comedy Central; Country Music TV; Discovery Channel; Disney Channel; E! Entertainment Television; ESPN; ESPN 2; Eternal Word TV Network; Food Network; Fox News Channel; Fox Sports Net Ohio; FX; Hallmark Channel; Headline News; HGTV; History Channel; Lifetime; MSNBC; MTV; MTV2; Nickelodeon; Ohio News Network; Oxygen; Speed; Spike TV; Syfy; The Learning Channel; Travel Channel; truTV; Turner Classic Movies; Turner Network TV; TV Land; USA Network; VH1.
Fee: $22.32 monthly.

Digital Basic Service
Subscribers: N.A.
Programming (via satellite): AmericanLife TV Network; BBC America; Black Family Channel; Bloomberg Television; C-SPAN 3; Discovery Fit & Health; DIY Network; ESPN Classic Sports; ESPNews; Fox Movie Channel; Fox Sports World; Fuse; G4; GAS; Great American Country; GSN; Halogen Network; Lifetime Movie Network; Lime; MTV Networks Digital Suite; Music Choice; National Geographic Channel; Nick Jr.; Nick Too; NickToons TV; Outdoor Channel; SoapNet; Style Network; The Word Network; Toon Disney; Trinity Broadcasting Network; WE tv.
Fee: $14.95 monthly.

Digital Expanded Basic Service
Subscribers: N.A.
Programming (via satellite): Bio; CBS Sports Network; FSN Digital Atlantic; FSN Digital Central; FSN Digital Pacific; Fuel TV; Golf Channel; History Channel International; Independent Film Channel; Sundance Channel; Tennis Channel; Versus.

Digital Pay Service 1
Pay Units: 978.
Programming (via satellite): Flix (multiplexed); Showtime (multiplexed); The Movie Channel (multiplexed).
Fee: $8.95 monthly.

Digital Pay Service 2
Pay Units: 1,185.
Programming (via satellite): Encore (multiplexed); Starz (multiplexed).
Fee: $8.95 monthly.

Digital Pay Service 3
Pay Units: 2,489.
Programming (via satellite): HBO (multiplexed).
Fee: $8.95 monthly.

Digital Pay Service 4
Pay Units: 3,060.
Programming (via satellite): Cinemax (multiplexed).
Fee: $8.95 monthly.

Digital Pay Service 5
Pay Units: N.A.
Programming (via satellite): ART America; Canales N; CCTV-4; Filipino Channel; RAI International; Russian Television Network; TV Asia; TV Japan; TV5, La Television International; Zhong Tian Channel.

Video-On-Demand: Yes

Pay-Per-View
Hot Choice (delivered digitally); iN DEMAND (delivered digitally); Playboy TV (delivered digitally); Fresh (delivered digitally).

Internet Service
Operational: Yes. Began: August 1, 2001.
Broadband Service: Road Runner.
Fee: $44.95 monthly; $5.00 modem lease.

Telephone Service
Analog: Not Operational
Digital: Operational
Fee: $44.95 monthly

Miles of Plant: 986.0 (coaxial); None (fiber optic).
President: Rhonda Fraas. Vice President & General Manager: David Kreiman. Vice President, Engineering: Randy Hall. Vice

President, Marketing: Mark Psigoda. Vice President, Public Affairs: Mary Jo Green. Technical Operations Manager: David Bowen. Marketing Coordinator: Sandra Tilton. Government Affairs Coordinator: Steve Cuckler.

Ownership: Time Warner Cable (MSO).

NEWPORT—Windjammer Cable, 4400 PGA Blvd, Ste 902, Palm Beach Gardens, FL 33410. Phones: 877-450-5558; 561-775-1208. Fax: 561-775-7811. Web Site: http://www.windjammercable.com. ICA: OH0264.

TV Market Ranking: Below 100 (NEWPORT). Franchise award date: N.A. Franchise expiration date: N.A. Began: November 1, 1965.

Channel capacity: N.A. Channels available but not in use: N.A.

Basic Service

Subscribers: 360.

Programming (received off-air): WCHS-TV (ABC) Charleston; WHIZ-TV (NBC) Zanesville; WOUB-TV (PBS) Athens; WOWK-TV (CBS) Huntington; WSAZ-TV (MNT, NBC) Huntington; WTAP-TV (FOX, MNT, NBC) Parkersburg; WTRF-TV (CBS) Wheeling; allband FM.

Programming (via satellite): ABC Family Channel; C-SPAN.

Fee: $29.95 installation; $11.21 monthly; $.73 converter.

Expanded Basic Service 1

Subscribers: 342.

Programming (via satellite): CNN; Country Music TV; Discovery Channel; Disney Channel; ESPN; ESPN 2; Lifetime; Spike TV; TBS Superstation; USA Network; WGN America.

Fee: $8.56 monthly.

Digital Basic Service

Subscribers: N.A.

Programming (via satellite): Bravo; ESPN Classic Sports; HGTV; History Channel; Syfy; Versus; WE tv.

Digital Pay Service 1

Pay Units: N.A.

Programming (via satellite): Cinemax (multiplexed); Encore (multiplexed); HBO (multiplexed); Showtime (multiplexed); Starz (multiplexed); The Movie Channel (multiplexed).

Fee: $11.95 monthly (each).

Video-On-Demand: No

Pay-Per-View

Club Jenna (delivered digitally).

Internet Service

Operational: No.

Telephone Service

None

Miles of Plant: 12.0 (coaxial); None (fiber optic).

General Manager: Timothy Evard. Operations Director: Belinda Graham. Engineering Director: Mike Earehart. Finance & Accounting Director: Cindy Johnson.

Ownership: Windjammer Communications LLC (MSO).

NEWTON FALLS—Time Warner Cable. Now served by WARREN, OH [OH0013]. ICA: OH0114.

NORTH BALTIMORE—Time Warner Cable. Now served by BOWLING GREEN, OH [OH0054]. ICA: OH0349.

NORTHWOOD—Now served by WATERVILLE, OH [OH0072]. ICA: OH0141.

NORWALK—Time Warner Cable, 530 S Main St, Ste 1751, Akron, OH 44311-1090. Phone: 330-633-9203. Fax: 330-633-7970. Web Site: http://www.timewarnercable.com/northeastohio. Also serves Bronson Twp., Hartland Twp., Milan, Milan Twp. (Erie County), Monroeville, Norwalk Twp. (Huron County), Oxford Twp. (Erie County), Peru Twp. (Huron County) & Ridgefield Twp. (Huron County). ICA: OH0075.

TV Market Ranking: 8 (Bronson Twp., Hartland Twp., Milan, Milan Twp. (Erie County), Monroeville, NORWALK, Norwalk Twp. (Huron County), Oxford Twp. (Erie County), Peru Twp. (Huron County), Ridgefield Twp. (Huron County)). Franchise award date: July 1, 1969. Franchise expiration date: May 1, 2011. Began: September 1, 1970.

Channel capacity: N.A. Channels available but not in use: N.A.

Basic Service

Subscribers: N.A. Included in Mansfield

Programming (received off-air): WBNX-TV (CW) Akron; WEWS-TV (ABC) Cleveland; WGGN-TV (TBN) Sandusky; WGTE-TV (PBS) Toledo; WJW (FOX) Cleveland; WKYC (NBC) Cleveland; WMFD-TV (IND) Mansfield; WNWO-TV (NBC) Toledo; WOIO (CBS) Shaker Heights; WQHS-DT (UNV) Cleveland; WTOL (CBS) Toledo; WTVG (ABC) Toledo; WUAB (MNT) Lorain; WVIZ (PBS) Cleveland; WVPX-TV (ION) Akron; 14 FMs.

Fee: $45.99 installation; $13.18 monthly.

Expanded Basic Service 1

Subscribers: N.A.

Programming (via satellite): A&E Networks; ABC Family Channel; AMC; Animal Planet; BET Networks; Bravo; Cartoon Network; CNBC; CNN; Comedy Central; C-SPAN; C-SPAN 2; Discovery Channel; Discovery Fit & Health; Disney Channel; E! Entertainment Television; ESPN; ESPN 2; ESPN Classic Sports; Eternal Word TV Network; Food Network; Fox News Channel; Fox Sports Net Ohio; FX; Golf Channel; Great American Country; GSN; Hallmark Channel; Headline News; HGTV; History Channel; INSP; Lifetime; Lifetime Movie Network; MSNBC; MTV; Nickelodeon; Oxygen; QVC; SoapNet; Spike TV; SportsTime Ohio; Syfy; TBS Superstation; The Learning Channel; The Weather Channel; Travel Channel; truTV; Turner Classic Movies; Turner Network TV; TV Land; USA Network; Versus; VH1; WE tv.

Fee: $41.81 monthly.

Digital Basic Service

Subscribers: N.A.

Programming (via satellite): A&E Networks; AmericanLife TV Network; BBC America; BBC America On Demand; Beauty and Fashion Channel; Bio; Bloomberg Television; Boomerang; Canales N; CBS Sports Network; Celebrity Shopping Network; cloo; CNN; CNN International; Cooking Channel; Country Music TV; C-SPAN 3; Current; Daystar TV Network; Disney Channel; DIY Network; ESPN 2 HD; ESPN HD; ESPNews; Exercise TV; Fox College Sports Atlantic; Fox College Sports Central; Fox College Sports Pacific; Fox Movie Channel; Fox Reality Channel; Fox Soccer; Fuel TV; Fuse; G4; GAS; HD Theater; HDNet; HDNet Movies; Headline News; Healthy Living Channel; History Channel International; Howard TV; Independent Film Channel; Jewelry Television; Lifetime; Lifetime Real Women; LOGO; Men's Channel; MTV2; Music Choice; National Geographic Channel; National Geographic Channel On Demand; NBA TV; Nick Jr.; NickToons TV; Ohio News Network; Outdoor Channel; Speed; Speed On Demand; Style Network; TBS Superstation; Tennis Channel; The Weather Channel; The Word Network; Toon Disney; Turner Network TV; Turner Network TV HD; TV One; TVG Network; Universal HD; USA Network; VH1 Classic.

Fee: $13.00 monthly.

Digital Pay Service 1

Pay Units: N.A.

Programming (via satellite): ART America; Cinemax (multiplexed); Cinemax On Demand; Deutsche Welle TV; Encore (multiplexed); HBO (multiplexed); HBO HD; HBO On Demand; RAI International; Showtime (multiplexed); Showtime HD; Showtime On Demand; Starz (multiplexed); Starz On Demand; The Movie Channel (multiplexed); The Movie Channel On Demand; TV Asia; Zee TV USA.

Fee: $12.00 monthly (HBO, Showtime/TMC, Starz or Cinemax).

Video-On-Demand: Yes

Pay-Per-View

Movies (delivered digitally); iN DEMAND (delivered digitally); Playboy TV (delivered digitally); Fresh (delivered digitally); Pleasure (delivered digitally); NASCAR In Car (delivered digitally); NBA League Pass (delivered digitally); ESPN (delivered digitally); NHL Center Ice (delivered digitally).

Internet Service

Operational: Yes.

Broadband Service: EarthLink, Road Runner.

Fee: $44.95 monthly.

Telephone Service

Digital: Operational

Fee: $44.95 monthly

Miles of Plant: 115.0 (coaxial); 25.0 (fiber optic).

President: Stephen Fry. Area Vice President: Scott Miller. Vice President, Engineering: Al Costanzi. Vice President, Marketing: Patrick Burke. Vice President, Sales: Woody Woodward. Vice President, Public Affairs: William Jasso. Area Manager: Carol Jagger. Government & Media Relations Director: Chris Thomas.

Ownership: Time Warner Cable (MSO).

NORWICH—Time Warner Cable. Now served by ZANESVILLE, OH [OH0037]. ICA: OH0225.

OAK HARBOR—Now served by PORT CLINTON, OH [OH0060]. ICA: OH0351.

OAK HILL—Time Warner Cable. Now served by JACKSON, OH [OH0098]. ICA: OH0219.

OAKLAND—Time Warner Cable, 1266 Dublin Rd, Columbus, OH 43215-1008. Phone: 614-481-5000. Fax: 614-481-5052. Web Site: http://www.timewarnercable.com/midohio. Also serves Amanda & Fairfield County (portions). ICA: OH0352.

TV Market Ranking: 27 (Amanda, Fairfield County (portions), OAKLAND). Franchise award date: N.A. Franchise expiration date: N.A. Began: N.A.

Channel capacity: N.A. Channels available but not in use: N.A.

Basic Service

Subscribers: 1,990.

Programming (received off-air): WBNS-TV (CBS) Columbus; WCMH-TV (NBC) Columbus; WOSU-TV (PBS) Columbus; WOUB-TV (PBS) Athens; WSFJ-TV (TBN) Newark; WSYX (ABC, MNT) Columbus; WTTE (FOX) Columbus; WWHO (CW) Chillicothe.

Programming (via satellite): AMC; Nickelodeon; QVC; TBS Superstation; WGN America.

Fee: $40.00 installation; $16.45 monthly.

Expanded Basic Service 1

Subscribers: N.A.

Programming (via satellite): A&E Networks; ABC Family Channel; CNN; Country Music TV; Discovery Channel; Disney Channel; ESPN; ESPN 2; Fox News Channel; FX; HGTV; Lifetime; MSNBC; MTV; Spike TV; The Learning Channel; The Weather Channel; Turner Network TV; USA Network; WGN America.

Digital Basic Service

Subscribers: N.A.

Programming (via satellite): BBC America; Bloomberg Television; Bravo; Discovery Fit & Health; ESPN Classic Sports; ESPNews; Fox Movie Channel; Fox Sports World; G4; Golf Channel; GSN; Halogen Network; History Channel International; Independent Film Channel; Music Choice; Nick Jr.; NickToons TV; Outdoor Channel; Syfy; Trinity Broadcasting Network; Versus; WE tv.

Digital Pay Service 1

Pay Units: N.A.

Programming (via satellite): Cinemax (multiplexed); Encore (multiplexed); HBO (multiplexed); Showtime (multiplexed); Starz (multiplexed); The Movie Channel (multiplexed).

Fee: $11.95 monthly (each).

Video-On-Demand: No

Pay-Per-View

HITS PPV 1-6 (delivered digitally); Fresh (delivered digitally); Playboy TV (delivered digitally).

Internet Service

Operational: No.

Telephone Service

Digital: Operational

Miles of Plant: 175.0 (coaxial); None (fiber optic).

President: Rhonda Fraas. Vice President & General Manager: David Kreiman. Vice President, Engineering: Randy Hall. Vice President, Marketing: Mark Psigoda. Vice President, Government & Public Affairs: Mary Jo Green. Technical Operations Director: Jim Cavender. Government Affairs Director: Steve Cuckler.

Ownership: Time Warner Cable (MSO).

OBERLIN—Cable Co-op Inc., 27 E College St, Oberlin, OH 44074-1612. Phone: 440-775-4001. Fax: 440-775-1635. E-mail: support@oberlin.net. Web Site: http://www.oberlin.net. ICA: OH0147.

TV Market Ranking: 8 (OBERLIN). Franchise award date: June 27, 1986. Franchise expiration date: N.A. Began: January 25, 1988.
Channel capacity: 71 (operating 2-way). Channels available but not in use: N.A.

Basic Service
Subscribers: 1,926.
Programming (received off-air): WBNX-TV (CW) Akron; WEAO (PBS) Akron; WEWS-TV (ABC) Cleveland; WGGN-TV (TBN) Sandusky; WJW (FOX) Cleveland; WKYC (NBC) Cleveland; WOIO (CBS) Shaker Heights; WQHS-DT (UNV) Cleveland; WUAB (MNT) Lorain; WVIZ (PBS) Cleveland; WVPX-TV (ION) Akron; 20 FMs.
Programming (via satellite): A&E Networks; ABC Family Channel; AMC; Animal Planet; BET Networks; Bravo; Cartoon Network; CNBC; CNN; Comedy Central; Country Music TV; C-SPAN; C-SPAN 2; Discovery Channel; Discovery Fit & Health; Disney Channel; DIY Network; E! Entertainment Television; ESPN; ESPN 2; ESPN Classic Sports; Food Network; Fox News Channel; Fox Sports Net Ohio; FX; Hallmark Channel; Headline News; HGTV; History Channel; Lifetime; MSNBC; MTV; National Geographic Channel; Nickelodeon; Ovation; Oxygen; QVC; Spike TV; Syfy; TBS Superstation; The Learning Channel; The Weather Channel; Travel Channel; truTV; Turner Classic Movies; Turner Network TV; TV Guide Network; TV Land; TV One; USA Network; VH1; WGN America.
Fee: $25.00 installation; $31.00 monthly; $15.00 converter; $25.00 additional installation.

Digital Basic Service
Subscribers: N.A.
Programming (via satellite): American-Life TV Network; BBC America; Bio; Black Family Channel; Bloomberg Television; cloo; Cooking Channel; Current; Discovery Health Channel; DMX Music; ESPN Classic Sports; ESPNews; Fox Movie Channel; Fox Soccer; FSN Digital Atlantic; FSN Digital Central; FSN Digital Pacific; Fuse; G4; Golf Channel; Great American Country; Halogen Network; History Channel International; Independent Film Channel; Lifetime Movie Network; Lime; MTV Networks Digital Suite; National Geographic Channel; Nick Jr.; NickToons TV; Outdoor Channel; Speed; Style Network; TeenNick; Toon Disney; Trinity Broadcasting Network; Versus; WE tv.

Pay Service 1
Pay Units: 368.
Programming (via satellite): HBO.
Fee: $10.95 monthly.

Digital Pay Service 1
Pay Units: N.A.
Programming (via satellite): Cinemax (multiplexed); Encore (multiplexed); Flix; HBO (multiplexed); Showtime (multiplexed); Starz (multiplexed); Sundance Channel; The Movie Channel (multiplexed).
Video-On-Demand: No

Pay-Per-View
Movies & Events (delivered digitally); Playboy TV (delivered digitally); Fresh (delivered digitally); Shorteez (delivered digitally); Hot Choice (delivered digitally); NBA League Pass (delivered digitally); MLB Extra Innings (delivered digitally).

Internet Service
Operational: Yes.
Broadband Service: In-house.
Fee: $25.00 installation; $19.95-$71.45 monthly.

Telephone Service
None
Miles of Plant: 45.0 (coaxial); None (fiber optic).
Manager: Ralph L. Potts. Chief Technician: Engel Smit III. Customer Service Manager: Rita Casey.
Ownership: Cable Cooperative Inc.

OLMSTED TWP.—Olmsted Cable Co. Corp. Now served by PARMA, OH [OH0009]. ICA: OH0223.

ORRVILLE—Armstrong Cable Services, 1141 Lafayette Rd, Medina, OH 44256-2421. Phones: 877-277-5711; 330-722-3141. Fax: 330-725-3366. E-mail: info@zoominternet.net. Web Site: http://cable.armstrongonewire.com. Also serves Baughman Twp., Burton City (portions), Dalton, Green Twp. (Wayne County), Marshallville & Sugar Creek Twp. (Wayne County). ICA: OH0109.
TV Market Ranking: 8 (Baughman Twp., Burton City (portions), Dalton, Green Twp. (Wayne County), Marshallville, ORRVILLE, Sugar Creek Twp. (Wayne County)). Franchise award date: September 7, 1965. Franchise expiration date: N.A. Began: March 1, 1967.
Channel capacity: N.A. Channels available but not in use: N.A.

Digital Basic Service
Subscribers: N.A. Included in Medina
Programming (via satellite): A&E Networks; ABC Family Channel; AMC; Animal Planet; Bravo; Cartoon Network; CNBC; CNN; Comedy Central; Country Music TV; C-SPAN; Discovery Channel; Disney Channel; E! Entertainment Television; ESPN; ESPN 2; Eternal Word TV Network; Food Network; Fox News Channel; Fox Sports Net Ohio; FX; Headline News; HGTV; History Channel; INSP; Lifetime; MSNBC; MTV; Music Choice; MyNetworkTV Inc.; Nickelodeon; NickToons TV; Pentagon Channel; QVC; ShopNBC; Spike TV; SportsTime Ohio; Syfy; TBS Superstation; The Learning Channel; The Weather Channel; Travel Channel; truTV; Turner Classic Movies; Turner Network TV; TV Guide Network; TV Land; USA Network; VH1.
Fee: $51.40 monthly.

Digital Expanded Basic Service
Subscribers: N.A.
Programming (via satellite): AmericanLife TV Network; BBC America; Bio; Bloomberg Television; Boomerang; Chiller; cloo; CMT Pure Country; Cooking Channel; Discovery Fit & Health; Discovery Health Channel; Discovery Kids Channel; DIY Network; ESPN Classic Sports; ESPNews; Fox Soccer; G4; Golf Channel; Great American Country; GSN; Hallmark Channel; Hallmark Movie Channel; History Channel International; HRTV; ID Investigation Discovery; Jewelry Television; Lifetime Movie Network; Military Channel; MTV Hits; MTV Jams; MTV2; mun2 television; National Geographic Channel; NFL Network; NHL Network; Nick Jr.; Nick Too; Ohio News Network; Outdoor Channel; Oxygen; PBS Kids Sprout; Pentagon Channel; Planet Green; RFD-TV; Science; SoapNet; Speed; TeenNick; Tennis Channel; Toon Disney; Tr3s; Versus; VH1 Classic; VH1 Soul; WE tv.
Fee: $12.00 monthly.

Digital Expanded Basic Service 2
Subscribers: N.A.
Programming (received off-air): WEWS-TV (ABC) Cleveland; WJW (FOX) Cleveland; WKYC (NBC) Cleveland; WOIO (CBS) Shaker Heights; WVIZ (PBS) Cleveland.
Programming (via satellite): A&E HD; Animal Planet HD; Bravo HD; CNN HD; Discovery Channel HD; ESPN 2 HD; ESPN HD; Food Network HD; Fox News HD; FSN HD; FX HD; Golf Channel HD; Hallmark Movie Channel HD; HD Theater; HDNet; HDNet Movies; HGTV HD; History Channel HD; MGM HD; National Geographic Channel HD Network; NFL Network HD; NHL Network HD; Outdoor Channel 2 HD; QVC HD; Science HD; Syfy HD; TBS in HD; The Weather Channel HD; TLC HD; Turner Network TV HD; Universal HD; USA Network HD; Versus HD; WealthTV HD.
Fee: $9.00 monthly.

Digital Pay Service 1
Pay Units: N.A.
Programming (via satellite): Cinemax (multiplexed); Cinemax HD; Encore (multiplexed); Flix; HBO (multiplexed); HBO HD; RAI USA; Showtime (multiplexed); Showtime HD; Starz (multiplexed); Starz HDTV; The Movie Channel (multiplexed); TV5 USA.
Fee: $13.95 monthly (HBO, Cinemax, Showtime/TMC/Flix or Starz/Encore).
Video-On-Demand: Yes

Pay-Per-View
Addressable homes: 220.
iN DEMAND (delivered digitally); Hot Choice (delivered digitally); ESPN Now (delivered digitally); ESPN Extra (delivered digitally); NHL/MLB (delivered digitally).

Internet Service
Operational: Yes. Began: November 1, 2000.
Broadband Service: Armstrong Zoom.
Fee: $26.95-$39.95 monthly.

Telephone Service
Digital: Operational
Fee: $49.95 monthly
Miles of Plant: 118.0 (coaxial); None (fiber optic).
General Manager: Karen Wolff. Chief Technician: Mike Bricker. Marketing Director: Jud D. Stewart.
Ownership: Armstrong Group of Companies (MSO).

ORWELL—FairPoint Communications, 70 S Maple St, PO Box 337, Orwell, OH 44076-0337. Phones: 800-824-3620; 440-437-6111. Fax: 440-437-1000. Web Site: http://www.fairpoint.com. Also serves Colebrook, North Bloomfield Twp., Rome Twp. & Windsor. ICA: OH0195.
TV Market Ranking: 79 (Colebrook, North Bloomfield Twp., ORWELL, Rome Twp., Windsor). Franchise award date: N.A. Franchise expiration date: N.A. Began: October 1, 1982.
Channel capacity: N.A. Channels available but not in use: N.A.

Basic Service
Subscribers: 1,150.
Programming (received off-air): WBNX-TV (CW) Akron; WEWS-TV (ABC) Cleveland; WFMJ-TV (CW, NBC) Youngstown; WNEO (PBS) Alliance; WOIO (CBS) Shaker Heights; WUAB (MNT) Lorain; WVIZ (PBS) Cleveland; WYTV (ABC, MNT) Youngstown; allband FM.
Programming (via satellite): A&E Networks; ABC Family Channel; Animal Planet; Cartoon Network; CNN; Comedy Central; Country Music TV; C-SPAN; Discovery Channel; Discovery Fit & Health; Disney Channel; DIY Network; ESPN; ESPN 2; ESPN Classic Sports; Food Network; Fox News Channel; Fox Sports Net; FX; G4; Hallmark Channel; Headline News; HGTV; History Channel; Lifetime; MTV; National Geographic Channel; Nickelodeon; Outdoor Channel; QVC; Shop at Home; Speed; Syfy; TBS Superstation; The Learning Channel; The Weather Channel; Trinity Broadcasting Network; Turner Classic Movies; Turner Network TV; TV Land; Univision Studios; USA Network; VH1.
Fee: $25.00 installation; $30.95 monthly; $25.00 additional installation.

Pay Service 1
Pay Units: 352.
Programming (via satellite): HBO.
Fee: $25.00 installation; $9.00 monthly.

Pay Service 2
Pay Units: 404.
Programming (via satellite): Showtime; Spike TV.
Fee: $25.00 installation; $9.00 monthly.
Video-On-Demand: No

Internet Service
Operational: Yes.
Subscribers: 214.
Broadband Service: In-house.
Fee: $25.00 installation; $39.95 monthly; $10.00 modem lease; $200.00 modem purchase.

Telephone Service
Digital: Planned
Miles of Plant: 62.0 (coaxial); 14.0 (fiber optic). Additional miles planned: 5.0 (coaxial).
Manager: John Campbell. Chief Technician: Paul Place.
Ownership: FairPoint Communications Inc.

OTTAWA—Time Warner Cable, 205 Crystal Ave, Findlay, OH 45840. Phone: 419-523-4600. Fax: 419-429-7402. Web Site: http://www.timewarnercable.com/midohio. Also serves Blanchard Twp. (Putnam County), Columbus Grove, Glandorf (village) & Pleasant Twp. (Putnam County). ICA: OH0137.
TV Market Ranking: Below 100 (Blanchard Twp. (Putnam County), Columbus Grove, Glandorf (village), OTTAWA, Pleasant Twp. (Putnam County)). Franchise award date: September 1, 1970. Franchise expiration date: N.A. Began: August 15, 1971.
Channel capacity: N.A. Channels available but not in use: N.A.

Basic Service
Subscribers: 3,036.
Programming (received off-air): WBGU-TV (PBS) Bowling Green; WLIO (CW, NBC) Lima; WNWO-TV (NBC) Toledo; WOHL-CD (FOX) Lima; WPTA (ABC, CW) Fort Wayne; WTLW (IND) Lima; WTOL (CBS) Toledo; WTVG (ABC) Toledo; WUPW (FOX) Toledo; 14 FMs.
Programming (via satellite): WGN America.
Fee: $45.86 installation; $11.42 monthly.

Expanded Basic Service 1
Subscribers: N.A.
Programming (via satellite): A&E Networks; ABC Family Channel; AMC; Animal Planet; Bravo; Cartoon Network; CNBC; CNN; Comedy Central; Country Music TV; C-SPAN; C-SPAN 2; Discovery Channel; Disney Channel; E! Entertainment Television; Encore Action; ESPN; ESPN 2; ESPN Classic Sports; Eternal Word TV Network; Food Network; Fox News Channel; Fox Sports Net Ohio; FX; Golf Channel; Hallmark Channel; Headline News; HGTV; History Channel; Lifetime; Lifetime Movie Network; MSNBC; MTV; National Geographic Channel; Nickelodeon; Oxygen; QVC; ShopNBC; Spike TV; Syfy; TBS Superstation; The Learning Channel; The Weather Channel; Travel Channel; truTV; Turner Classic Movies; Turner Network TV; TV Guide Network; TV Land; USA Network; Versus; VH1; WE tv.
Fee: $29.53 monthly.

Digital Basic Service
Subscribers: 911.
Programming (via satellite): AmericanLife TV Network; America's Store; BBC America; Bloomberg Television; CNN International; Cooking Channel; C-SPAN 3; Discovery Fit & Health; DIY Network; DMX Music; ESPNews; Fox Sports World; FSN Digital Atlantic; FSN Digital Central; FSN Digital Pacific; Fuse; G4; GAS; Great American Country; GSN; Lifetime Real Women; MTV2; Nick Jr.; Ohio News Network; Outdoor Channel; Ovation; SoapNet; Sorpresa; Speed; Style Network; Toon Disney; VH1 Classic.
Fee: $9.90 monthly.
Digital Pay Service 1
Pay Units: 132.
Programming (via satellite): Cinemax (multiplexed); Encore (multiplexed); Flix; HBO (multiplexed); Showtime (multiplexed); Starz (multiplexed); The Movie Channel (multiplexed).
Fee: $10.00 installation; $11.95 monthly (Cinemax, HBO, Showtime/Flix/TMC or Starz/Encore).
Video-On-Demand: Yes
Pay-Per-View
Addressable homes: 911.
iN DEMAND (delivered digitally); Fresh (delivered digitally); Sports PPV (delivered digitally).
Internet Service
Operational: Yes.
Subscribers: 547.
Broadband Service: Road Runner.
Fee: $69.95 installation; $44.95 monthly.
Telephone Service
Digital: Operational
Fee: $44.95 monthly
Miles of Plant: 60.0 (coaxial); None (fiber optic).
President: Rhonda Fraas. Vice President & General Manager: Brad Wakely. Vice President, Engineering: Randy Hall. Vice President, Marketing: Mark Psigoda. Technical Operations Director: John Ellingson. Public Affairs Director: Brian Young. Government Affairs Manager: Patrick McCauley.
Ownership: Time Warner Cable (MSO).

OTTOVILLE—OTEC Communication Co., 245 W Third St, PO Box 427, Ottoville, OH 45876. Phone: 419-453-3324. Fax: 419-453-2468. E-mail: tomtc@bright.net. Web Site: http://www.ottovillemutual.com. Also serves Cloverdale, Grover Hill, Hoaglin Twp. (Van Wert County), Jackson Twp. (Putnam County), Jackson Twp. (Van Wert County), Jennings Twp. (Putnam County), Latty Twp., Monterey Twp. (Putnam County), Perry Twp. (Putnam County) & Washington Twp. (Paulding County). ICA: OH0211.
TV Market Ranking: 82 (Grover Hill, Latty Twp.); Below 100 (Cloverdale, Hoaglin Twp. (Van Wert County), Jackson Twp. (Putnam County), Jackson Twp. (Van Wert County), Jennings Twp. (Putnam County), Monterey Twp. (Putnam County), OTTOVILLE, Perry Twp. (Putnam County), Washington Twp. (Paulding County), Grover Hill). Franchise award date: April 7, 1980. Franchise expiration date: N.A. Began: October 1, 1983.
Channel capacity: N.A. Channels available but not in use: N.A.
Basic Service
Subscribers: 950.
Programming (received off-air): WANE-TV (CBS) Fort Wayne; WBGU-TV (PBS) Bowling Green; WBNS-TV (CBS) Columbus; WLIO (CW, NBC) Lima; WLQP-LP Lima; WNWO-TV (NBC) Toledo; WOHL-CD (FOX) Lima; WPTA (ABC, CW) Fort Wayne; WTLW (IND) Lima; WTOL (CBS) Toledo; WTVG (ABC) Toledo; WUPW (FOX) Toledo; allband FM.
Programming (via satellite): A&E Networks; ABC Family Channel; Cartoon Network; CNN; CW+; Discovery Channel; Disney Channel; ESPN; ESPN 2; ESPN Classic Sports; Eternal Word TV Network; Food Network; Fox News Channel; Fox Sports Net Ohio; FX; Hallmark Channel; Lifetime; MSNBC; MTV; National Geographic Channel; SportsTime Ohio; TBS Superstation; The Learning Channel; The Weather Channel; Travel Channel; Turner Classic Movies; Turner Network TV; TV Land; USA Network; VH1; WGN America.
Fee: $24.50 installation; $28.95 monthly; $5.00 additional installation.
Expanded Basic Service 1
Subscribers: N.A.
Programming (via satellite): Comedy Central; Country Music TV; History Channel; Nickelodeon; Spike TV.
Fee: $6.00 monthly.
Digital Basic Service
Subscribers: 30.
Programming (via satellite): BBC America; Bloomberg Television; CMT Pure Country; Discovery Health Channel; Discovery Kids Channel; DMX Music; ESPN Classic Sports; Fox Soccer; Golf Channel; HGTV; ID Investigation Discovery; Independent Film Channel; Lifetime Movie Network; Military Channel; MTV2; National Geographic Channel; Nick Jr.; NickToons TV; Planet Green; Science; Speed; TeenNick; Toon Disney; Versus; VH1 Classic; WE tv.
Fee: $13.50 monthly.
Digital Expanded Basic Service
Subscribers: N.A.
Programming (via satellite): Bio; ESPNews; Fox Movie Channel; Fuse; G4; GSN; History Channel International; Outdoor Channel; WebMD Television.
Fee: $3.50 monthly.
Pay Service 1
Pay Units: 40.
Programming (via satellite): HBO.
Fee: $11.95 monthly.
Pay Service 2
Pay Units: 137.
Programming (via satellite): The Movie Channel.
Fee: $9.95 monthly.
Pay Service 3
Pay Units: 132.
Programming (via satellite): Showtime.
Fee: $9.95 monthly.
Digital Pay Service 1
Pay Units: N.A.
Programming (via satellite): Cinemax (multiplexed); Encore (multiplexed); HBO (multiplexed); Showtime (multiplexed); Starz (multiplexed); The Movie Channel (multiplexed).
Fee: $8.95 monthly (Cinemax), $9.95 monthly (Showtime or TMC), $11.95 monthly (HBO), $12.95 monthly (Starz/Encore), $13.95 monthly (Showtime & TMC).
Pay-Per-View
Playboy TV (delivered digitally); Fresh (delivered digitally); Club Jenna (delivered digitally).
Internet Service
Operational: No, DSL & dial-up.
Telephone Service
None
Miles of Plant: 93.0 (coaxial); None (fiber optic).
Manager: Don Hoersten. Chief Technician: Bill Honigford.
Ownership: OTEC Communication Co.

OWENSVILLE—Time Warner Cable. Now served by CINCINNATI, OH [OH0001]. ICA: OH0368.

OXFORD—Time Warner Cable. Now served by DAYTON, OH [OH0011]. ICA: OH0101.

PARMA—Cox Communications, 12221 Plaza Dr, Parma, OH 44130-1059. Phones: 216-535-3500; 216-676-8100 (Customer service); 216-676-8300. Fax: 216-676-8689. Web Site: http://www.cox.com/cleveland. Also serves Broadview Heights, Brooklyn Heights, Fairview Park, Lakewood (Cuyahoga County), Olmsted Falls, Olmsted Twp., Parma Heights, Rocky River & Seven Hills. ICA: OH0009.
TV Market Ranking: 8 (Broadview Heights, Brooklyn Heights, Fairview Park, Lakewood (Cuyahoga County), Olmsted Falls, Olmsted Twp., PARMA, Parma Heights, Rocky River, Seven Hills). Franchise award date: March 12, 1973. Franchise expiration date: N.A. Began: May 1, 1980.
Channel capacity: N.A. Channels available but not in use: N.A.
Basic Service
Subscribers: 76,000.
Programming (received off-air): WBNX-TV (CW) Akron; WEAO (PBS) Akron; WEWS-TV (ABC) Cleveland; WJW (FOX) Cleveland; WKYC (NBC) Cleveland; WOIO (CBS) Shaker Heights; WQHS-DT (UNV) Cleveland; WRLM (IND) Canton; WUAB (MNT) Lorain; WVIZ (PBS) Cleveland; WVPX-TV (ION) Akron; 3 FMs.
Programming (via satellite): Fox Sports Net Ohio; WGN America.
Fee: $23.85 installation; $8.30 monthly; $.50 converter; $10.50 additional installation.
Expanded Basic Service 1
Subscribers: N.A.
Programming (via satellite): A&E Networks; ABC Family Channel; AMC; Animal Planet; Cartoon Network; CNBC; CNN; Comedy Central; Country Music TV; C-SPAN; C-SPAN 2; Discovery Channel; Discovery Health Channel; Disney Channel; E! Entertainment Television; ESPN; ESPN 2; Eternal Word TV Network; Food Network; Fox News Channel; FX; Hallmark Channel; Headline News; HGTV; History Channel; INSP; Lifetime; MSNBC; MTV; Nickelodeon; Oxygen; Product Information Network; QVC; Scola; Speed; Spike TV; Syfy; TBS Superstation; The Learning Channel; The Weather Channel; Travel Channel; Trinity Broadcasting Network; truTV; Turner Classic Movies; Turner Network TV; TV Guide Network; TV Land; USA Network; VH1.
Fee: $37.65 monthly.
Digital Basic Service
Subscribers: N.A.
Programming (via satellite): BBC America; Bio; Bloomberg Television; Discovery Digital Networks; DIY Network; ESPN Classic Sports; ESPNews; Flix; G4; Golf Channel; History Channel International; Independent Film Channel; Lifetime Movie Network; MuchMusic Network; Music Choice; Nick Too; Ovation; SoapNet; Sundance Channel; Toon Disney; Weatherscan.
Fee: $8.99 monthly.
Digital Pay Service 1
Pay Units: N.A.
Programming (via satellite): Cinemax (multiplexed); Encore (multiplexed); HBO (multiplexed); Showtime (multiplexed); Starz (multiplexed); The Movie Channel (multiplexed).
Fee: $11.00 monthly (each).
Video-On-Demand: Yes
Pay-Per-View
Addressable homes: 13,500.
ESPN Full Court (delivered digitally); ESPN Now (delivered digitally); Fresh (delivered digitally); Shorteez (delivered digitally); Hot Choice (delivered digitally); iN DEMAND (delivered digitally); Playboy TV (delivered digitally).
Internet Service
Operational: Yes.
Broadband Service: Cox High Speed Internet.
Fee: $9.99 installation; $26.95 monthly; $15.00 modem lease; $49.00 modem purchase.
Telephone Service
Digital: Operational
Fee: $8.00 monthly
Miles of Plant: 775.0 (coaxial); 50.0 (fiber optic). Additional miles planned: 8.0 (coaxial); 150.0 (fiber optic).
Vice President & General Manager: Kevin Haynes. Network Operations Director: Tim Yanda. Marketing & Sales Director: Laura Morabito. Public Relations & Government Affairs Director: Christy Bykowski.
Ownership: Cox Communications Inc. (MSO).

PATASKALA—Time Warner Cable. Now served by MOUNT VERNON, OH [OH0095]. ICA: OH0165.

PAULDING—Time Warner Cable, 205 Crystal Ave, Findlay, OH 45840. Phones: 614-481-5000 (Columbus office); 419-429-7402. Fax: 419-429-7402. Web Site: http://www.timewarnercable.com/midohio. Also serves Cecil, Emerald Twp., Latty & Paulding Twp. (Paulding County). ICA: OH0186.
TV Market Ranking: 82 (Cecil, Emerald Twp. (portions), Latty, PAULDING, Paulding Twp. (Paulding County)); Outside TV Markets (Emerald Twp. (portions)). Franchise award date: N.A. Franchise expiration date: N.A. Began: October 1, 1976.
Channel capacity: N.A. Channels available but not in use: N.A.
Basic Service
Subscribers: 1,055.
Programming (received off-air): WANE-TV (CBS) Fort Wayne; WBGU-TV (PBS) Bowling Green; WDFM-LP (IND) Defiance; WFFT-TV (IND) Fort Wayne; WGTE-TV (PBS) Toledo; WISE-TV (FOX, MNT, NBC) Fort Wayne; WLIO (CW, NBC) Lima; WLMB (IND) Toledo; WNWO-TV (NBC) Toledo; WPTA (ABC, CW) Fort Wayne; WTOL (CBS) Toledo; WTVG (ABC) Toledo; WUPW (FOX) Toledo; allband FM.

Programming (via satellite): ABC Family Channel; QVC; TV Guide Network; WGN America.
Fee: $60.00 installation; $13.95 monthly.

Expanded Basic Service 1
Subscribers: 1,017.
Programming (received off-air): WINM (IND) Angola.
Programming (via satellite): A&E Networks; AMC; Animal Planet; BET Networks; Bravo; Cartoon Network; CNBC; CNN; Comedy Central; Country Music TV; C-SPAN; C-SPAN 2; Discovery Channel; Disney Channel; E! Entertainment Television; ESPN; ESPN 2; Eternal Word TV Network; Food Network; Fox News Channel; Fox Sports Net Detroit; Fox Sports Net Ohio; FX; Hallmark Channel; Headline News; HGTV; History Channel; Lifetime; MSNBC; MTV; Nickelodeon; Ohio News Network; Oxygen; Product Information Network; ShopNBC; Spike TV; Syfy; TBS Superstation; The Learning Channel; The Weather Channel; Travel Channel; truTV; Turner Network TV; TV Land; Univision Studios; USA Network; VH1.
Fee: $17.84 monthly.

Digital Basic Service
Subscribers: 140.
Programming (via satellite): AmericanLife TV Network; BBC America; Black Family Channel; Bloomberg Television; Canales N; Discovery Fit & Health; DIY Network; DMX Music; Fox Movie Channel; Fox Sports World; Fuse; G4; GAS; Great American Country; GSN; Halogen Network; Lifetime Movie Network; MTV Networks Digital Suite; National Geographic Channel; Nick Jr.; Nick Too; NickToons TV; SoapNet; Speed; Style Network; The Word Network; Toon Disney; Trinity Broadcasting Network; Turner Classic Movies; WE tv.

Digital Expanded Basic Service
Subscribers: N.A.
Programming (via satellite): Arabic Channel; Bio; CCTV-4; ESPN Classic Sports; ESPNews; Filipino Channel; Flix; FSN Digital Atlantic; FSN Digital Central; FSN Digital Pacific; Golf Channel; History Channel International; Independent Film Channel; Outdoor Channel; RAI International; Russian Television Network; Sundance Channel; TV Asia; TV Japan; TV5, La Television International; Versus; Zhong Tian Channel.

Digital Pay Service 1
Pay Units: N.A.
Programming (via satellite): Cinemax (multiplexed); Encore (multiplexed); HBO; Showtime (multiplexed); Starz (multiplexed); The Movie Channel (multiplexed).

Video-On-Demand: No

Pay-Per-View
ESPN Now (delivered digitally); NHL Center Ice (delivered digitally); MLB Extra Innings (delivered digitally); Playboy TV (delivered digitally); Fresh (delivered digitally); Shorteez (delivered digitally); Hot Choice (delivered digitally); Urban American Television Network (delivered digitally); ESPN (delivered digitally); Movies & Events (delivered digitally).

Internet Service
Operational: Yes.
Subscribers: 104.
Broadband Service: Road Runner.
Fee: $44.95 monthly.

Telephone Service
Digital: Operational
Fee: $44.95 monthly

Miles of Plant: 57.0 (coaxial); None (fiber optic).
President: Rhonda Fraas. Vice President & General Manager: Brad Wakely. Vice President, Engineering: Randy Hall. Vice President, Marketing: Mark Psigoda. Technical Operations Director: John Ellingson. Government Affairs Director: Brian Young. Government Affairs Manager: Patrick McCauley.
Ownership: Time Warner Cable (MSO).

PAYNE—Comcast Cable, 720 Taylor St, Fort Wayne, IN 46802-5144. Phones: 317-275-6370 (Indianapolis office); 260-458-5103. Fax: 260-458-5138. Web Site: http://www.comcast.com. ICA: OH0445.
TV Market Ranking: 82 (PAYNE).
Channel capacity: N.A. Channels available but not in use: N.A.

Basic Service
Subscribers: N.A. Included in Indianapolis
Programming (received off-air): W07CL Auburn; WANE-TV (CBS) Fort Wayne; WFFT-TV (IND) Fort Wayne; WFWA (PBS) Fort Wayne; WINM (IND) Angola; WISE-TV (FOX, MNT, NBC) Fort Wayne; WPTA (ABC, CW) Fort Wayne.
Programming (via satellite): ABC Family Channel; Animal Planet; C-SPAN; Discovery Health Channel; ESPN Classic Sports; Golf Channel; Local Cable Weather; QVC; TBS Superstation; The Learning Channel; Turner Classic Movies; Turner Network TV; TV Guide Network; TV Land; USA Network; WGN America.
Fee: $32.48 monthly.

Expanded Basic Service 1
Subscribers: N.A.
Programming (via satellite): A&E Networks; AMC; BET Networks; Cartoon Network; CNBC; CNN; Comcast SportsNet Chicago; Comedy Central; Country Music TV; C-SPAN 2; Discovery Channel; Disney Channel; E! Entertainment Television; ESPN; ESPN 2; Eternal Word TV Network; Food Network; Fox News Channel; FX; Great American Country; GSN; Headline News; HGTV; History Channel; ION Television; Lifetime; MSNBC; MTV; MTV2; Nickelodeon; Speed; Spike TV; Style Network; Syfy; The Weather Channel; Travel Channel; truTV; Univision Studios; Versus; VH1.

Pay Service 1
Pay Units: N.A.
Programming (via satellite): Cinemax; HBO; Showtime.

Pay-Per-View
iN DEMAND (delivered digitally); Playboy TV (delivered digitally); NBA League Pass (delivered digitally); NHL Center Ice (delivered digitally); MLB Extra Innings (delivered digitally).

Internet Service
Operational: Yes.

Telephone Service
Digital: Operational

Miles of plant included in Fort Wayne
Regional Vice President: Scott Tenney. Vice President, Marketing: Aaron Geisel. Vice President, Communications: Mark Apple. Technical Operations Director: Bennie Logan. Engineering Manager: Tom Stuckholz. Marketing Manager: Marci Hefley.
Ownership: Comcast Cable Communications Inc. (MSO).

PEDRO—Windjammer Cable, 4400 PGA Blvd, Ste 902, Palm Beach Gardens, FL 33410. Phones: 877-450-5558; 561-775-1208. Fax: 561-775-7811. Web Site: http://www.windjammercable.com. Also serves Decatur Twp. (Lawrence County) & Elizabeth Twp. (Lawrence County). ICA: OH0244.
TV Market Ranking: 36 (Decatur Twp. (Lawrence County), Elizabeth Twp. (Lawrence County), PEDRO). Franchise award date: February 1, 1989. Franchise expiration date: N.A. Began: N.A.
Channel capacity: 32 (not 2-way capable). Channels available but not in use: N.A.

Basic Service
Subscribers: 375.
Programming (received off-air): WCHS-TV (ABC) Charleston; WOWK-TV (CBS) Huntington; WPBY-TV (PBS) Huntington; WSAZ-TV (MNT, NBC) Huntington; WTSF (IND) Ashland; WVAH-TV (FOX) Charleston.
Programming (via satellite): A&E Networks; ABC Family Channel; Cartoon Network; CNN; Country Music TV; Discovery Channel; Disney Channel; ESPN; Headline News; History Channel; Lifetime; Nickelodeon; QVC; Spike TV; Syfy; TBS Superstation; Trinity Broadcasting Network; Turner Classic Movies; Turner Network TV; USA Network; WGN America; WQCW (CW) Portsmouth.
Fee: $42.17 monthly.

Digital Basic Service
Subscribers: N.A.
Programming (via satellite): Bravo; ESPN Classic Sports; HGTV; Versus; WE tv.
Fee: $54.17 monthly.

Digital Pay Service 1
Pay Units: N.A.
Programming (via satellite): Cinemax (multiplexed); Encore (multiplexed); HBO (multiplexed); Showtime (multiplexed); Starz (multiplexed); The Movie Channel (multiplexed).
Fee: $15.95 monthly (each).

Video-On-Demand: No

Pay-Per-View
Movies (delivered digitally).

Internet Service
Operational: No.

Telephone Service
None

Miles of Plant: 31.0 (coaxial); None (fiber optic).
General Manager: Timothy Evard. Operations Director: Belinda Graham. Engineering Director: Mike Earehart. Finance & Accounting Director: Cindy Johnson.
Ownership: Windjammer Communications LLC (MSO).

PEEBLES—Time Warner Cable. Now served by CINCINNATI, OH [OH0001]. ICA: OH0197.

PHILO (portions)—Time Warner Cable. Now served by ZANESVILLE, OH [OH0037]. ICA: OH0354.

PIKETON—Time Warner Cable, 1266 Dublin Rd, Columbus, OH 43215-1008. Phone: 614-481-5000. Fax: 614-481-5052. Web Site: http://www.timewarnercable.com/midohio. Also serves Seal Twp. (Pike County). ICA: OH0199.
TV Market Ranking: 27 (PIKETON, Seal Twp. (Pike County)). Franchise award date: May 30, 1978. Franchise expiration date: May 17, 2008. Began: October 1, 1958.
Channel capacity: N.A. Channels available but not in use: N.A.

Basic Service
Subscribers: 703.
Programming (received off-air): WBNS-TV (CBS) Columbus; WCHS-TV (ABC) Charleston; WCMH-TV (NBC) Columbus; WOWK-TV (CBS) Huntington; WPBO (PBS) Portsmouth; WSAZ-TV (MNT, NBC) Huntington; WSYX (ABC, MNT) Columbus; WVAH-TV (FOX) Charleston.
Programming (via satellite): A&E Networks; ABC Family Channel; Disney Channel; ESPN; MTV; Nickelodeon; QVC; TBS Superstation; Turner Network TV; WGN America.
Fee: $19.95 installation; $16.99 monthly; $25.00 additional installation.

Pay Service 1
Pay Units: 95.
Programming (via satellite): Cinemax; HBO.
Fee: $25.00 installation; $10.95 monthly (each).

Internet Service
Operational: Yes.

Telephone Service
Digital: Operational

Miles of Plant: 25.0 (coaxial); None (fiber optic).
President: Rhonda Fraas. Vice President & General Manager: David Kreiman. Vice President, Engineering: Randy Hall. Vice President, Marketing: Mark Rsigoda. Vice President, Government & Public Affairs: Mary Jo Green. Government Affairs Director: Steve Cuckler.
Ownership: Time Warner Cable (MSO).

PINE LAKE TRAILER PARK—Formerly served by Marshall County Cable. No longer in operation. ICA: OH0355.

PIONEER—Formerly served by Windjammer Cable. No longer in operation. ICA: OH0273.

PIQUA—Time Warner Cable. No longer in operation. ICA: OH0065.

POLK—Time Warner Cable, 530 S Main St, Ste 1751, Akron, OH 44311-1090. Phone: 330-633-9203. Fax: 330-633-7970. Web Site: http://www.timewarnercable.com/northeastohio. Also serves Ashland County (portions). ICA: OH0304.
TV Market Ranking: 8 (Ashland County (portions), POLK). Franchise award date: November 1, 1984. Franchise expiration date: N.A. Began: September 1, 1985.
Channel capacity: N.A. Channels available but not in use: N.A.

Basic Service
Subscribers: N.A. Included in Mansfield
Programming (received off-air): WBNX-TV (CW) Akron; WDLI-TV (TBN) Canton; WEAO (PBS) Akron; WEWS-TV (ABC) Cleveland; WJW (FOX) Cleveland; WKYC (NBC) Cleveland; WMFD-TV (IND) Mansfield; WNEO (PBS) Alliance; WOIO (CBS) Shaker Heights; WQHS-DT (UNV) Cleveland; WRLM (IND) Canton; WUAB (MNT) Lorain; WVIZ (PBS) Cleveland; WVPX-TV (ION) Akron.
Programming (via satellite): CNN; ESPN; Headline News; Spike TV; TBS Superstation; Turner Network TV.
Fee: $29.95 installation; $14.14 monthly; $2.50 converter.

Expanded Basic Service 1
Subscribers: N.A.
Programming (via satellite): A&E Networks; ABC Family Channel; AMC; Animal Planet; BET Networks; Bravo; Cartoon Network; CNBC; Comedy Central; C-SPAN; C-SPAN 2; Discovery Channel; Discovery Fit & Health; Discovery Health Channel; Disney Channel; E! Entertainment Television; ESPN 2; ESPN Classic Sports; Eternal Word TV Network; Food Network; Fox News Channel; Fox Sports Net Ohio; FX; Golf Channel; Great American Country; GSN; Hallmark Channel; HGTV; History Channel; INSP; Lifetime; Lifetime Movie Network; MSNBC; MTV; Nickelodeon; Oxygen; QVC; ShopNBC; SoapNet; Syfy; The Learning Channel; The Weather Channel; Travel Channel; truTV; Turner Classic

Movies; TV Guide Network; TV Land; USA Network; Versus; VH1; WE tv; WGN America.
Fee: $34.36 monthly.

Digital Basic Service
Subscribers: N.A.
Programming (via satellite): A&E HD; AmericanLife TV Network; America's Store; ART America; BBC America; Bio; Bloomberg Television; Boomerang; Canales N; CBS Sports Network; CNN; CNN International; Cooking Channel; Country Music TV; C-SPAN 3; Daystar TV Network; Deutsche Welle TV; DIY Network; ESPN; ESPNews; Fox College Sports Atlantic; Fox College Sports Central; Fox College Sports Pacific; Fox HD; Fox Movie Channel; Fox Soccer; Fuel TV; Fuse; G4; GAS; HD Theater; Headline News; History Channel International; Independent Film Channel; INHD; INHD2; Jewelry Television; Lifetime; Lifetime Real Women; MTV Networks Digital Suite; Music Choice; National Geographic Channel; NBA TV; Nick Jr.; NickToons TV; Ohio News Network; Outdoor Channel; RAI International; Speed; TBS Superstation; Tennis Channel; The Weather Channel; The Word Network; Toon Disney; Trio; Turner Network TV HD; TV Asia; TVG Network; USA Network; Zee TV USA.
Fee: $19.49 monthly.

Digital Pay Service 1
Pay Units: N.A.
Programming (via satellite): Cinemax (multiplexed); HBO (multiplexed); HBO HD; Showtime (multiplexed); Showtime HD; Starz (multiplexed); The Movie Channel (multiplexed).
Fee: $12.00 monthly (HBO, Showtime/TMC, Cinemax, or Starz).

Video-On-Demand: Yes

Pay-Per-View
iN DEMAND (delivered digitally); Playboy TV (delivered digitally); NHL Center Ice (delivered digitally); MLB Extra Innings (delivered digitally); Spice Live (delivered digitally); Ten Clips (delivered digitally); Pleasure (delivered digitally); NASCAR In Car (delivered digitally); NBA League Pass (delivered digitally); MLS Direct Kick (delivered digitally); ESPN (delivered digitally).

Internet Service
Operational: Yes.
Broadband Service: EarthLink, Road Runner.
Fee: $99.00 installation; $44.95 monthly.

Telephone Service
Digital: Operational
Fee: $44.95 monthly

Miles of Plant: 2.0 (coaxial); None (fiber optic).

President: Stephen Fry. Area Vice President: Scott Miller. Vice President, Engineering: Al Costanzi. Vice President, Marketing: Patrick Burke. Vice President, Sales: Woody Woodward. Vice President, Public Affairs: William Jasso. Area Manager: Carol Jagger. Government & Media Relations Director: Chris Thomas.

Ownership: Time Warner Cable.

PORT CLINTON—Time Warner Cable, 530 S Main St, Ste 1751, Akron, OH 44311-1090. Phones: 330-633-9203 (regional office); 419-734-5905 (Port Clinton office). Fax: 330-633-7970. Web Site: http://www.timewarnercable.com/northeastohio. Also serves Bay Twp. (Ottawa County), Benton Twp. (Ottawa County), Carroll Twp. (Ottawa County), Catawba Island Twp. (Ottawa County), Danbury Twp. (Ottawa County), Erie Twp. (Ottawa County), Graytown, Lacarne, Lakeside, Marblehead, Oak Harbor, Portage Twp. (Ottawa County), Rice Twp., Rocky Ridge, Salem Twp. (Ottawa County) & Sandusky Twp. (Sandusky County). ICA: OH0060.

TV Market Ranking: 52 (Bay Twp. (Ottawa County), Benton Twp. (Ottawa County), Carroll Twp. (Ottawa County), Erie Twp. (Ottawa County), Graytown, Lacarne, Lakeside, Marblehead, Oak Harbor, PORT CLINTON, Portage Twp. (Ottawa County), Rice Twp., Rocky Ridge, Salem Twp. (Ottawa County), Sandusky Twp. (Sandusky County)); Below 100 (Catawba Island Twp. (Ottawa County), Danbury Twp. (Ottawa County)). Franchise award date: N.A. Franchise expiration date: N.A. Began: N.A.

Channel capacity: N.A. Channels available but not in use: N.A.

Basic Service
Subscribers: 10,155.
Programming (received off-air): WBGU-TV (PBS) Bowling Green; WEWS-TV (ABC) Cleveland; WGGN-TV (TBN) Sandusky; WGTE-TV (PBS) Toledo; WJW (FOX) Cleveland; WKBD-TV (CW) Detroit; WLMB (IND) Toledo; WNWO-TV (NBC) Toledo; WTOL (CBS) Toledo; WTVG (ABC) Toledo; WUAB (MNT) Lorain; WUPW (FOX) Toledo.
Programming (via satellite): QVC; SportsTime Ohio; various Canadian stations; WGN America.
Fee: $44.95 installation; $15.75 monthly.

Expanded Basic Service 1
Subscribers: 8,862.
Programming (via satellite): A&E Networks; ABC Family Channel; AMC; Animal Planet; Bravo; Cartoon Network; CNBC; CNN; Comedy Central; Country Music TV; C-SPAN; C-SPAN 2; Discovery Channel; Disney Channel; E! Entertainment Television; ESPN; ESPN 2; Eternal Word TV Network; Food Network; Fox News Channel; Fox Sports Net Detroit; Fox Sports Net Ohio; FX; Golf Channel; Hallmark Channel; Headline News; HGTV; History Channel; ION Television; Lifetime; MSNBC; MTV; Nickelodeon; Oxygen; Product Information Network; ShopNBC; Spike TV; Syfy; TBS Superstation; The Learning Channel; The Weather Channel; Travel Channel; truTV; Turner Classic Movies; Turner Network TV; TV Guide Network; TV Land; Univision Studios; USA Network; VH1.
Fee: $37.25 monthly.

Digital Basic Service
Subscribers: 1,694.
Programming (via satellite): AmericanLife TV Network; BBC America; Bloomberg Television; Canal 52MX; Cine Latino; CMT Pure Country; CNN en Espanol; C-SPAN 3; Current; Discovery en Espanol; Discovery Fit & Health; Discovery Health Channel; Discovery Home Channel; Discovery Kids Channel; Discovery Times Channel; DIY Network; ESPN 2 HD; ESPN Classic Sports; ESPN Deportes; ESPN HD; ESPN U; ESPNews; Fox Business Channel; Fox Deportes; Fox Movie Channel; Fox Reality Channel; Fox Soccer; Fuse; G4; GAS; GMC; Great American Country; GSN; Halogen Network; HD Theater; HDNet; HDNet Movies; History Channel en Espanol; Lifetime Movie Network; LOGO; Military Channel; MTV Hits; MTV Jams; MTV2; Music Choice; National Geographic Channel; Nick Jr.; Nick Too; NickToons TV; Ohio News Network; Science; SoapNet; Speed; SportsTime Ohio; Style Network; TBS in HD; The Word Network; Toon Disney; Toon Disney en Espanol; Tr3s; Trinity Broadcasting Network; Turner Network TV HD; TV Guide Network; TV One; Universal HD; VH1 Classic; VH1 Soul; WE tv.
Fee: $11.00 monthly.

Digital Expanded Basic Service
Subscribers: N.A.
Programming (via satellite): Bio; CBS Sports Network; Cooking Channel; Flix; FSN Digital Atlantic; FSN Digital Central; FSN Digital Pacific; Fuel TV; History Channel International; Independent Film Channel; NBA TV; Outdoor Channel; Sundance Channel; Tennis Channel; Versus.
Fee: $10.00 monthly.

Digital Pay Service 1
Pay Units: N.A.
Programming (via satellite): Cinemax (multiplexed); Cinemax HD; Encore (multiplexed); Flix; HBO (multiplexed); HBO HD; Showtime (multiplexed); Showtime HD; Starz (multiplexed); Starz HDTV; The Movie Channel (multiplexed).
Fee: $12.00 monthly (HBO, Cinemax, Showtime/TMC/Flix, or Starz/Encore).

Video-On-Demand: No

Pay-Per-View
Addressable homes: 1,694.
iN DEMAND (delivered digitally); Playboy TV (delivered digitally); Fresh (delivered digitally); Shorteez (delivered digitally); Hot Choice (delivered digitally); ESPN (delivered digitally); MLB Extra Innings (delivered digitally); NHL Network (delivered digitally).

Internet Service
Operational: Yes.
Broadband Service: EarthLink, Road Runner.
Fee: $45.95 monthly.

Telephone Service
None

Miles of Plant: 408.0 (coaxial); None (fiber optic).

President: Stephen Fry. Area Vice President: Scott Miller. Vice President, Engineering: Al Costanzi. Vice President, Marketing: Patrick Burke. Vice President, Public Affairs: William Jasso. Area Manager: Carol Jagger. Government & Media Relations Director: Chris Thomas.

Ownership: Time Warner Cable (MSO).

PORT WILLIAM—Time Warner Cable. Now served by CINCINNATI, OH [OH0001]. ICA: OH0259.

PORTERFIELD—Formerly served by Adelphia Communications. No longer in operation. ICA: OH0372.

PORTSMOUTH—Time Warner Cable, 1266 Dublin Rd, Columbus, OH 43215-1008. Phone: 614-481-5000. Fax: 614-481-5052. Web Site: http://www.timewarnercable.com/midohio. Also serves Greenup County, Lewis County (portions), South Portsmouth & South Shore, KY; Bloom Twp. (Scioto County), Clay Twp. (Scioto County), New Boston, Porter Twp. (Scioto County), Sciotoville, South Webster (village), Valley Twp. (Scioto County) & Wheelersburg, OH. ICA: OH0035.

TV Market Ranking: 27 (Clay Twp. (Scioto County) (portions), PORTSMOUTH (portions), Valley Twp. (Scioto County)); 27,36 (Bloom Twp. (Scioto County) (portions)); 36 (Greenup County (portions), New Boston, Porter Twp. (Scioto County), Sciotoville, South Shore, South Webster (village), Wheelersburg); Below 100 (Lewis County (portions) (portions), South Portsmouth, Clay Twp. (Scioto County) (portions), PORTSMOUTH (portions), Greenup County (portions)); Outside TV Markets (Lewis County (portions) (portions)). Franchise award date: N.A. Franchise expiration date: N.A. Began: December 18, 1962.

Channel capacity: N.A. Channels available but not in use: N.A.

Basic Service
Subscribers: 17,001.
Programming (received off-air): WBNS-TV (CBS) Columbus; WCHS-TV (ABC) Charleston; WKMR (PBS) Morehead; WLPX-TV (ION) Charleston; WLWT (NBC) Cincinnati; WOWK-TV (CBS) Huntington; WPBO (PBS) Portsmouth; WQCW (CW) Portsmouth; WSAZ-TV (MNT, NBC) Huntington; WSYX (ABC, MNT) Columbus; WTSF (IND) Ashland; WVAH-TV (FOX) Charleston; 12 FMs.
Programming (via satellite): ABC Family Channel; C-SPAN; Eternal Word TV Network; QVC; TBS Superstation; The Weather Channel; TV Guide Network; WGN America.
Fee: $25.00 installation; $12.95 monthly.

Expanded Basic Service 1
Subscribers: N.A.
Programming (via satellite): A&E Networks; AMC; Animal Planet; BET Networks; Bio; Bravo; Cartoon Network; CNBC; CNN; Comedy Central; Country Music TV; Discovery Channel; Disney Channel; E! Entertainment Television; ESPN; ESPN 2; Food Network; Fox News Channel; Fox Sports Net Ohio; FX; Golf Channel; Great American Country; Hallmark Channel; Headline News; HGTV; History Channel; Lifetime; MSNBC; MTV; National Geographic Channel; Nick Jr.; Nickelodeon; Outdoor Channel; Oxygen; Product Information Network; ShopNBC; Speed; Spike TV; SportsTime Ohio; Syfy; The Learning Channel; Toon Disney; Travel Channel; truTV; Turner Network TV; TV Land; Univision Studios; USA Network; VH1; WE tv.

Digital Basic Service
Subscribers: N.A.
Programming (via satellite): AmericanLife TV Network; BBC America; Bloomberg Television; Cine Latino; CMT Pure Country; CNN en Espanol; Current; Discovery en Espanol; Discovery Fit & Health; Discovery Health Channel; Discovery Home Channel; Discovery Kids Channel; Discovery Times Channel; DIY Network; ESPN 2 HD; ESPN Classic Sports; ESPN Deportes; ESPN HD; ESPN U; ESPNews; Fox Business Channel; Fox Deportes; Fox Movie Channel; Fox Reality Channel; Fox Soccer; FSN HD; Fuse; G4; GAS; GMC; GSN; HD Theater; HDNet; HDNet Movies; History Channel en Espanol; History Channel International; Independent Film Channel; INSP; Lifetime Movie Net-

work; LOGO; Military Channel; MTV Hits; MTV Jams; MTV2; Music Choice; Nick Too; NickToons TV; Ohio News Network; Science; SoapNet; Style Network; TBS in HD; The Word Network; Tr3s; Trinity Broadcasting Network; Turner Classic Movies; Turner Network TV HD; TVG Network; Universal HD; Versus; Versus HD; VH1 Classic; VH1 Soul.

Digital Expanded Basic Service
Subscribers: N.A.
Programming (via satellite): CBS Sports Network; Fox College Sports Atlantic; Fox College Sports Central; Fox College Sports Pacific; Fuel TV; Tennis Channel.

Digital Pay Service 1
Pay Units: N.A.
Programming (via satellite): ART America; CCTV-4; Cinemax (multiplexed); Cinemax HD; Encore (multiplexed); Filipino Channel; Flix; HBO (multiplexed); HBO HD; RAI International; Showtime (multiplexed); Showtime HD; Starz (multiplexed); Starz HDTV; Sundance Channel; The Movie Channel (multiplexed); TV Asia; TV Japan; TV5, La Television International; Zhong Tian Channel.

Video-On-Demand: Yes

Pay-Per-View
iN DEMAND (delivered digitally); Playboy TV (delivered digitally); Fresh (delivered digitally); Club Jenna (delivered digitally); Hot Choice (delivered digitally); ESPN (delivered digitally); NHL Center Ice (delivered digitally); MLB Extra Innings (delivered digitally); NBA League Pass (delivered digitally).

Internet Service
Operational: Yes.
Broadband Service: Road Runner.
Fee: $44.95 monthly.

Telephone Service
Digital: Operational
Fee: $44.95 monthly

Miles of Plant: 629.0 (coaxial); None (fiber optic).

President: Rhonda Fraas. Vice President & General Manager: David Kreiman. Vice President, Engineering: Randy Hall. Vice President, Marketing: Mark Psigoda. Vice President, Government & Public Affairs: Mary Jo Green. Technical Operations Director: Jim Cavender. Government Affairs Director: Steve Cuckler.

Ownership: Time Warner Cable (MSO).

POWHATAN POINT—Powhatan Point Cable Co., PO Box 67, Powhatan Point, OH 43942-0067. Phone: 740-795-5005. ICA: OH0356.

TV Market Ranking: 90 (POWHATAN POINT). Franchise award date: N.A. Franchise expiration date: N.A. Began: June 1, 1970.

Channel capacity: 54 (not 2-way capable). Channels available but not in use: N.A.

Basic Service
Subscribers: 896.
Programming (received off-air): KDKA-TV (CBS) Pittsburgh; WFMJ-TV (CW, NBC) Youngstown; WKBN-TV (CBS) Youngstown; WOUC-TV (PBS) Cambridge; WQED (PBS) Pittsburgh; WTAE-TV (ABC) Pittsburgh; WTOV-TV (IND, NBC) Steubenville; WTRF-TV (CBS) Wheeling.
Programming (via satellite): A&E Networks; ABC Family Channel; Animal Planet; Cartoon Network; CNN; Comedy Central; Country Music TV; Discovery Channel; ESPN; ESPN 2; Food Network; Fox News Channel; FX; Great American Country; Hallmark Channel; HGTV; Lifetime; MTV; Nickelodeon; Outdoor Channel; Root Sports Pittsburgh; Speed; Spike TV; Syfy; TBS Superstation; The Learning Channel; The Weather Channel; Travel Channel; Trinity Broadcasting Network; truTV; Turner Classic Movies; Turner Network TV; TV Land; USA Network; VH1; WABC-TV (ABC) New York; WGN America.
Fee: $33.00 monthly.

Pay Service 1
Pay Units: N.A.
Programming (via satellite): Encore; HBO (multiplexed).
Fee: $5.00 monthly (Encore), $12.00 monthly (HBO).

Video-On-Demand: No

Internet Service
Operational: Yes.
Fee: $35.00 monthly.

Telephone Service
None

Manager & Chief Technician: Kasmir Majewski.

Ownership: Kasmir Majewski (MSO).; Walter Matkovich (MSO).

PROCTORVILLE—Formerly served by Lycom Communications. No longer in operation. ICA: OH0291.

PUT IN BAY—Time Warner Cable, 530 S Main St, Ste 1751, Akron, OH 44311-1090. Phones: 419-734-5905 (Port Clinton office); 330-633-9203 (Regional office). Fax: 330-633-7970. Web Site: http://www.timewarnercable.com. ICA: OH0357.

TV Market Ranking: Below 100 (PUT IN BAY). Franchise award date: N.A. Franchise expiration date: N.A. Began: April 8, 1989.

Channel capacity: N.A. Channels available but not in use: N.A.

Basic Service
Subscribers: 97.
Programming (received off-air): WGTE-TV (PBS) Toledo; WNWO-TV (NBC) Toledo; WTOL (CBS) Toledo; WTVG (ABC) Toledo; WUAB (MNT) Lorain; WUPW (FOX) Toledo.
Programming (via satellite): QVC; WGN America.
Fee: $44.95 installation; $15.75 monthly.

Expanded Basic Service 1
Subscribers: N.A.
Programming (via satellite): A&E Networks; ABC Family Channel; AMC; CNN; Country Music TV; Discovery Channel; ESPN; History Channel; MTV; Nickelodeon; Spike TV; TBS Superstation; The Weather Channel; Turner Network TV; USA Network.
Fee: $18.50 monthly.

Pay Service 1
Pay Units: 13.
Programming (via satellite): Cinemax.
Fee: $15.95 monthly.

Pay Service 2
Pay Units: 19.
Programming (via satellite): HBO.
Fee: $15.95 monthly.

Video-On-Demand: No

Internet Service
Operational: No.

Telephone Service
None

Miles of Plant: 20.0 (coaxial); None (fiber optic).

President: Stephen Fry. Area Vice President: Scott Miller. Vice President, Engineering: Al Costanzi. Vice President, Marketing: Patrick Burke. Vice President, Public Affairs: William Jasso. Area Manager: Carol Jagger. Government & Media Relations Director: Chris Thomas.

Ownership: Time Warner Cable (MSO).

RAINSBORO—Formerly served by Adelphia Communications. Now served by WASHINGTON COURT HOUSE, OH [OH0070]. ICA: OH0196.

RICHMOND DALE—Formerly served by Adelphia Communications. Now served by CHILLICOTHE, OH [OH0033]. ICA: OH0262.

RIDGEVILLE TWP.—RTEC Communications, 105 E Holland St, PO Box 408, Archibold, OH 43502. Phone: 419-267-8800. Fax: 419-267-8808. E-mail: info@rtecexpress.net. Web Site: http://www.rtecexpress.net. ICA: OH0358.

TV Market Ranking: Outside TV Markets (RIDGEVILLE TWP.). Franchise award date: N.A. Franchise expiration date: N.A. Began: August 1, 1990.

Channel capacity: N.A. Channels available but not in use: N.A.

Basic Service
Subscribers: 1,166.
Programming (received off-air): WANE-TV (CBS) Fort Wayne; WGTE-TV (PBS) Toledo; WISE-TV (FOX, MNT, NBC) Fort Wayne; WKGB-TV (PBS) Bowling Green; WLIO (CW, NBC) Lima; WLMB (IND) Toledo; WNWO-TV (NBC) Toledo; WPTA (ABC, CW) Fort Wayne; WTOL (CBS) Toledo; WTVG (ABC) Toledo; WUPW (FOX) Toledo.
Programming (via satellite): CNN; C-SPAN; C-SPAN 2; Fox News Channel; INSP; NASA TV; TV Guide Network; WGN America.
Fee: $19.95 installation; $14.75 monthly.

Expanded Basic Service 1
Subscribers: 1,071.
Programming (received off-air): WBNS-TV (CBS) Columbus.
Programming (via satellite): A&E Networks; ABC Family Channel; AMC; Animal Planet; Cartoon Network; Discovery Channel; Disney Channel; ESPN; ESPN 2; ESPN Classic Sports; ESPNews; History Channel; Nickelodeon; QVC; TBS Superstation; The Learning Channel; Toon Disney; Turner Classic Movies; Turner Network TV; TV Land.
Fee: $43.75 monthly.

Expanded Basic Service 2
Subscribers: N.A.
Programming (received off-air): WDFM-LP (IND) Defiance.
Programming (via satellite): Bio; Bloomberg Television; Boomerang; CNBC; CNN International; Comedy Central; Country Music TV; Discovery Health Channel; DIY Network; E! Entertainment Television; Food Network; Fox Movie Channel; Fox Sports Net Detroit; Fox Sports Net Ohio; FX; G4; GalaVision; Golf Channel; Great American Country; GSN; Hallmark Channel; Headline News; HGTV; Lifetime; Lifetime Movie Network; MSNBC; MTV; National Geographic Channel; Ohio News Network; Outdoor Channel; SoapNet; Speed; Spike TV; SportsTime Ohio; Syfy; The Weather Channel; Travel Channel; Trinity Broadcasting Network; truTV; Univision Studios; USA Network; Versus; VH1.
Fee: $8.50 monthly.

Pay Service 1
Pay Units: 26.
Programming (via satellite): Showtime.
Fee: $8.95 monthly.

Pay Service 2
Pay Units: 23.
Programming (via satellite): The Movie Channel.
Fee: $8.95 monthly.

Pay Service 3
Pay Units: 33.
Programming (via satellite): Encore; Starz (multiplexed).
Fee: $8.95 monthly.

Pay Service 4
Pay Units: 131.
Programming (via satellite): HBO (multiplexed).
Fee: $8.95 monthly.

Pay Service 5
Pay Units: 21.
Programming (via satellite): Cinemax.
Fee: $8.95 monthly.

Internet Service
Operational: No, DSL.

Telephone Service
None

General Manager: Ken Miller. Assistant Manager: Dave Gobrogge. Office Manager: Marcia Bruns. Outside Plant Manager: Brian Miller. Marketing Manager: Jayma Gobrogge.

Ownership: RTEC Communications Division.

RIO GRANDE—Time Warner Cable, 1266 Dublin Rd, Columbus, OH 43215-1008. Phone: 614-481-5000. Fax: 614-481-5052. Web Site: http://www.timewarnercable.com/midohio. Also serves Raccoon Twp. ICA: OH0379.

TV Market Ranking: 36 (Raccoon Twp., RIO GRANDE). Franchise award date: N.A. Franchise expiration date: N.A. Began: N.A.

Channel capacity: N.A. Channels available but not in use: N.A.

Basic Service
Subscribers: 193.
Programming (received off-air): WCHS-TV (ABC) Charleston; WOUB-TV (PBS) Athens; WOWK-TV (CBS) Huntington; WQCW (CW) Portsmouth; WSAZ-TV (MNT, NBC) Huntington; WVAH-TV (FOX) Charleston.
Programming (via satellite): A&E Networks; ABC Family Channel; Animal Planet; CNN; Country Music TV; Discovery Channel; Disney Channel; ESPN; Headline News; History Channel; Lifetime; Nickelodeon; QVC; Spike TV; Syfy; TBS Superstation; The Learning Channel; The Weather Channel; Turner Classic Movies; Turner Network TV; USA Network; VH1; WGN America.
Fee: $22.00 monthly.

Digital Basic Service
Subscribers: N.A.
Programming (via satellite): BBC America; Bloomberg Television; Bravo; Discovery Fit & Health; ESPN Classic Sports; ESPNews; Fox Movie Channel; Fox Sports World; G4; Golf Channel; GSN; Halogen Network; HGTV; Independent Film Channel; Music Choice; Outdoor Channel; Trinity Broadcasting Network; Versus; WE tv.

Digital Expanded Basic Service
Subscribers: N.A.
Programming (via satellite): Nick Jr.; NickToons TV.

Pay Service 1
Pay Units: 17.
Programming (via satellite): HBO.
Fee: $10.95 monthly.

Digital Pay Service 1
Pay Units: N.A.
Programming (via satellite): Cinemax (multiplexed); Encore (multiplexed); HBO (multiplexed); Showtime (multiplexed); Starz (multiplexed); The Movie Channel (multiplexed).
Fee: $11.95 monthly (each).

Video-On-Demand: No

Pay-Per-View
Fresh (delivered digitally); Playboy TV (delivered digitally); HITS PPV 1-6 (delivered digitally).
Internet Service
Operational: Yes.
Telephone Service
Digital: Operational
Miles of Plant: 6.0 (coaxial); None (fiber optic).
President: Rhonda Fraas. Vice President & General Manager: David Kreiman. Vice President, Engineering: Randy Hall. Vice President, Marketing: Mark Psigoda. Vice President, Public Affairs: Mary Jo Green. Technical Operations Director: Jim Cavender. Government Affairs Director: Steve Cuckler.
Ownership: Time Warner Cable (MSO).

RIPLEY (Brown County)—Formerly served by Adelphia Communications. Now served by CINCINNATI, OH [OH0001]. ICA: OH0167.

RISING SUN—Time Warner Cable. Now served by CLAY CENTER/GIBSONBURG (formerly Allen Twp.), OH [OH0071]. ICA: OH0359.

RIVERSIDE—Now served by DAYTON, OH [OH0011]. ICA: OH0437.

ROBBINS MOBILE HOME PARK—Time Warner Cable. Now served by KENT, OH [OH0034]. ICA: OH0293.

ROCK CREEK—Zito Media, 611 Vader Hill Rd, Coudersport, PA 16915. Phone: 814-260-9575. Web Site: http://www.zitomedia.com. Also serves Ashtabula County (portions) & Roaming Shores. ICA: OH0427.
TV Market Ranking: 79 (Ashtabula County (portions) (portions)); Below 100 (Ashtabula County (portions) (portions)); Outside TV Markets (Roaming Shores, ROCK CREEK, Ashtabula County (portions) (portions)). Franchise award date: N.A. Franchise expiration date: N.A. Began: N.A.
Channel capacity: N.A. Channels available but not in use: N.A.
Basic Service
Subscribers: 435.
Programming (received off-air): WBNX-TV (CW) Akron; WEWS-TV (ABC) Cleveland; WJW (FOX) Cleveland; WKYC (NBC) Cleveland; WOIO (CBS) Shaker Heights; WQHS-DT (UNV) Cleveland; WRLM (IND) Canton; WUAB (MNT) Lorain; WVIZ (PBS) Cleveland.
Programming (via satellite): A&E Networks; ABC Family Channel; AMC; Animal Planet; BET Networks; Cartoon Network; CNBC; CNN; Comedy Central; C-SPAN; Discovery Channel; Disney Channel; E! Entertainment Television; ESPN; ESPN 2; Food Network; Fox News Channel; Fox Sports Net Ohio; FX; Great American Country; Headline News; HGTV; History Channel; ION Television; MSNBC; MTV; Nickelodeon; QVC; Spike TV; Syfy; TBS Superstation; The Learning Channel; The Weather Channel; Turner Classic Movies; Turner Network TV; TV Land; USA Network; VH1.
Fee: $19.95 monthly; $1.95 converter.
Digital Basic Service
Subscribers: N.A.
Programming (via satellite): BBC America; Bio; Bloomberg Television; cloo; Discovery Health Channel; Discovery Kids Channel; ESPN Classic Sports; ESPNews; Fox College Sports Atlantic; Fox College Sports Central; Fox College Sports Pacific; Fox Soccer; Fuse; G4; Golf Channel; GSN; History Channel International; ID Investigation Discovery; Independent Film Channel; Military Channel; Outdoor Channel; Planet Green; Science; ShopNBC; Speed; Style Network; Sundance Channel; Toon Disney; Trinity Broadcasting Network; Versus; WE tv.
Pay Service 1
Pay Units: 149.
Programming (via satellite): HBO.
Fee: $11.50 monthly.
Pay Service 2
Pay Units: 141.
Programming (via satellite): Showtime.
Fee: $12.95 monthly.
Pay Service 3
Pay Units: N.A.
Programming (via satellite): Cinemax; The Movie Channel.
Digital Pay Service 1
Pay Units: N.A.
Programming (via satellite): Cinemax (multiplexed); Encore (multiplexed); Flix; HBO (multiplexed); Showtime (multiplexed); Starz (multiplexed); The Movie Channel (multiplexed).
Video-On-Demand: No
Pay-Per-View
iN DEMAND (delivered digitally); Playboy TV (delivered digitally); Club Jenna (delivered digitally); Fresh (delivered digitally); Shorteez (delivered digitally).
Internet Service
Operational: No.
Telephone Service
None
Miles of Plant: 50.0 (coaxial); None (fiber optic).
Public Relations Manager: Mark Laver.
Ownership: Zito Media (MSO).

ROCKFORD—Time Warner Cable, 205 Crystal Ave, Findlay, OH 45840. Phones: 614-481-5000 (Columbus office); 419-429-7474. Fax: 416-429-7402. Web Site: http://www.timewarnercable.com. Also serves Blackcreek Twp., Jennings Twp., Mendon, Venedocia, Willshire & Wren. ICA: OH0204.
TV Market Ranking: 82 (Vendocia, Willshire, Wren); Below 100 (Blackcreek Twp., Jennings Twp., Mendon, ROCKFORD). Franchise award date: July 1, 1984. Franchise expiration date: N.A. Began: November 1, 1985.
Channel capacity: N.A. Channels available but not in use: N.A.
Basic Service
Subscribers: 729.
Programming (received off-air): WANE-TV (CBS) Fort Wayne; WBDT (CW) Springfield; WBGU-TV (PBS) Bowling Green; WFFT-TV (IND) Fort Wayne; WFWA (PBS) Fort Wayne; WHIO-TV (CBS) Dayton; WLIO (CW, NBC) Lima; WOHL-CD (FOX) Lima; WPTA (ABC, CW) Fort Wayne; WTLW (IND) Lima.
Programming (via satellite): WGN America.
Fee: $45.86 installation; $10.31 monthly; $4.50 converter; $31.81 additional installation.
Expanded Basic Service 1
Subscribers: N.A.
Programming (via satellite): A&E Networks; ABC Family Channel; Animal Planet; Bravo; Cartoon Network; CNBC; CNN; Comedy Central; Country Music TV; C-SPAN; C-SPAN 2; Discovery Channel; Disney Channel; E! Entertainment Television; Encore Action; ESPN; ESPN 2; ESPN Classic Sports; Eternal Word TV Network; Food Network; Fox News Channel; Fox Sports Net Ohio; Golf Channel; Hallmark Channel; Headline News; HGTV; History Channel; Lifetime; Lifetime Movie Network; MSNBC; MTV; National Geographic Channel; Nickelodeon; Oxygen; QVC; ShopNBC; Spike TV; Syfy; TBS Superstation; The Learning Channel; The Weather Channel; Travel Channel; truTV; Turner Classic Movies; Turner Network TV; TV Guide Network; TV Land; USA Network; Versus; VH1; WE tv.
Fee: $30.64 monthly.
Digital Basic Service
Subscribers: 219.
Programming (via satellite): AmericanLife TV Network; America's Store; BBC America; Bloomberg Television; CNN International; Cooking Channel; C-SPAN 3; Discovery Fit & Health; DIY Network; DMX Music; ESPNews; Fox Sports World; FSN Digital Atlantic; FSN Digital Central; FSN Digital Pacific; Fuse; G4; GAS; Great American Country; GSN; Lifetime Real Women; MTV2; Nick Jr.; Ohio News Network; Outdoor Channel; Ovation; SoapNet; Sorpresa; Speed; Style Network; Toon Disney; VH1 Classic.
Fee: $9.90 monthly.
Digital Expanded Basic Service
Subscribers: N.A.
Programming (via satellite): Encore Action.
Fee: $8.95 monthly.
Digital Pay Service 1
Pay Units: 55.
Programming (via satellite): Cinemax (multiplexed); Flix; HBO (multiplexed); Showtime (multiplexed); Starz (multiplexed); The Movie Channel (multiplexed).
Fee: $18.00 installation; $10.95 monthly (Cinemax, HBO, Showtime, Starz, or Flix/TMC).
Video-On-Demand: Yes
Pay-Per-View
Addressable homes: 219.
iN DEMAND (delivered digitally); Fresh (delivered digitally); Sports PPV (delivered digitally).
Internet Service
Operational: Yes.
Subscribers: 131.
Broadband Service: AOL for Broadband, BigSpeed, EarthLink, Road Runner, WCOIL Express.
Fee: $69.95 installation; $44.95 monthly.
Telephone Service
Digital: Operational
Fee: $44.95 monthly
Miles of Plant: 45.0 (coaxial); None (fiber optic).
President: Rhonda Fraas. Public Affairs Director: Brian Young. Senior Engineering Director: Larry Bryan. Technical Operations Director: James Gerhard.
Ownership: Time Warner Cable (MSO).

ROSS TWP. (Butler County)—Formerly served by Adelphia Communications. Now served by CINCINNATI, OH [OH0001]. ICA: OH0127.

RUSH RUN—Jefferson County Cable Inc., 116 S 4th St, Toronto, OH 43964-1368. Phone: 740-537-2214. Fax: 740-537-2802. Web Site: http://www.voiceflight.biz. ICA: OH0360.
TV Market Ranking: 10,90 (RUSH RUN). Franchise award date: N.A. Franchise expiration date: N.A. Began: N.A.
Channel capacity: 12 (not 2-way capable). Channels available but not in use: N.A.
Basic Service
Subscribers: 324.
Programming (received off-air): KDKA-TV (CBS) Pittsburgh; WPGH-TV (FOX) Pittsburgh; WPXI (IND, NBC) Pittsburgh; WQED (PBS) Pittsburgh; WTAE-TV (ABC) Pittsburgh; WTOV-TV (IND, NBC) Steubenville; WTRF-TV (CBS) Wheeling.
Programming (via satellite): ABC Family Channel; ESPN; TBS Superstation; WGN America.
Fee: $25.00 installation; $9.32 monthly.
Pay Service 1
Pay Units: 62.
Programming (via satellite): HBO.
Fee: $11.95 monthly.
Video-On-Demand: Planned
Internet Service
Operational: No.
Telephone Service
Digital: Operational
Fee: $36.00 monthly
Miles of Plant: 4.0 (coaxial); None (fiber optic).
Manager: David Bates. Office Manager: Joanne Conner.
Ownership: Jefferson County Cable Inc. (MSO).

SALEM—Time Warner Cable, 530 S Main St, Ste 1751, Akron, OH 44311-1090. Phones: 330-633-9203; 330-332-9607 (Salem office). Fax: 330-633-7970. Web Site: http://www.timewarnercable.com/northeastohio. Also serves Butler Twp. (Columbiana County), Center Twp. (Columbiana County), Green Twp. (Mahoning County), Guilford Lake, Hanover Twp. (Columbiana County), Hanoverton, Lisbon, New Garden, Perry Twp. (Columbiana County), Salem Twp. (Columbiana County) & Winona. ICA: OH0096.
TV Market Ranking: 79 (Butler Twp. (Columbiana County), Center Twp. (Columbiana County), Green Twp. (Mahoning County), Guilford Lake, Hanover Twp., Hanoverton, Lisbon, New Garden, Salem Twp. (Columbiana County), Winona); 8 (Perry Twp. (Columbiana County)); 8,79 (SALEM). Franchise award date: April 15, 1986. Franchise expiration date: N.A. Began: February 7, 1970.
Channel capacity: N.A. Channels available but not in use: N.A.
Basic Service
Subscribers: N.A. Included in Warren
Programming (received off-air): KDKA-TV (CBS) Pittsburgh; WEAO (PBS) Akron; WFMJ-TV (CW, NBC) Youngstown; WJW (FOX) Cleveland; WKBN-TV (CBS) Youngstown; WNEO (PBS) Alliance; WPGH-TV (FOX) Pittsburgh; WUAB (MNT)

Lorain; WYFX-LP Youngstown; WYTV (ABC, MNT) Youngstown; 1 FM.
Programming (via satellite): Ecumenical TV Channel; Trinity Broadcasting Network; TV Guide Network; WGN America.
Fee: $44.95 installation; $17.96 monthly; $1.82 converter.
Expanded Basic Service 1
Subscribers: N.A.
Programming (via satellite): A&E Networks; ABC Family Channel; AMC; Animal Planet; BET Networks; Bravo; Cartoon Network; CNBC; CNN; Comedy Central; C-SPAN; C-SPAN 2; Discovery Channel; Discovery Fit & Health; Discovery Health Channel; Disney Channel; E! Entertainment Television; ESPN; ESPN 2; ESPN Classic Sports; Food Network; Fox News Channel; Fox Sports Net Ohio; FX; Golf Channel; Great American Country; GSN; Hallmark Channel; Headline News; HGTV; History Channel; INSP; Lifetime; Lifetime Movie Network; MSNBC; MTV; MTV2; Nickelodeon; Oxygen; Paxson Communications Corp.; QVC; ShopNBC; SoapNet; Spike TV; Syfy; TBS Superstation; The Learning Channel; The Weather Channel; Travel Channel; truTV; Turner Classic Movies; Turner Network TV; TV Land; USA Network; Versus; VH1; WE tv.
Fee: $37.03 monthly.
Digital Basic Service
Subscribers: N.A.
Programming (via satellite): AmericanLife TV Network; America's Store; ART America; BBC America; Bio; Bloomberg Television; Boomerang; Canales N; CBS Sports Network; CNN International; Cooking Channel; Country Music TV; C-SPAN 3; Current; Daystar TV Network; Deutsche Welle TV; Disney Channel; DIY Network; Do-It-Yourself On Demand; Encore; ESPN; ESPNews; Food Network On Demand; Fox College Sports Atlantic; Fox College Sports Central; Fox College Sports Pacific; Fox Movie Channel; Fox Soccer; Fuel TV; Fuse; G4; GAS; Great American Country On Demand; HD Theater; HDNet; HDNet Movies; HGTV On Demand; History Channel International; Independent Film Channel; INHD; INHD2; Jewelry Television; Lifetime Real Women; MTV2; Music Choice; National Geographic Channel; NBA TV; Nick Jr.; NickToons TV; Ohio News Network; Outdoor Channel; RAI International; Speed; Style Network; Tennis Channel; The Word Network; Toon Disney; Trio; Turner Network TV HD; TV Asia; TVG Network; VH1 Classic; Zee TV USA.
Fee: $13.00 monthly.
Digital Pay Service 1
Pay Units: N.A.
Programming (via satellite): Cinemax (multiplexed); HBO (multiplexed); HBO HD (multiplexed); HBO On Demand; Showtime (multiplexed); Showtime HD; Showtime On Demand; Starz (multiplexed); The Movie Channel (multiplexed); The Movie Channel On Demand.
Fee: $12.00 monthly (each).
Video-On-Demand: Yes
Internet Service
Operational: Yes.
Broadband Service: EarthLink, Road Runner.
Fee: $44.95 monthly.
Telephone Service
Digital: Operational
Miles of Plant: 125.0 (coaxial); None (fiber optic).
Area Vice President: Rick Whales. Vice President, Engineering: Al Costanzi. Vice President, Marketing: Patrick Burke. Vice President, Sales: Woody Woodward. Vice President, Customer Care: Donald A. Jensen. Vice President, Public Affairs: William Jasso. Area Manager: Daryl Morrison. Government & Media Relations Director: Chris Thomas.
Ownership: Time Warner Cable (MSO).

SALINEVILLE—Windjammer Cable, 4400 PGA Blvd, Ste 902, Palm Beach Gardens, FL 33410. Phones: 877-450-5558; 561-775-1208. Fax: 561-775-7811. Web Site: http://www.windjammercable.com. ICA: OH0254.
TV Market Ranking: 79,90 (SALINEVILLE). Franchise award date: N.A. Franchise expiration date: N.A. Began: September 1, 1968.
Channel capacity: 65 (not 2-way capable). Channels available but not in use: N.A.
Basic Service
Subscribers: N.A. Included in Warren
Programming (received off-air): KDKA-TV (CBS) Pittsburgh; WFMJ-TV (CW, NBC) Youngstown; WKBN-TV (CBS) Youngstown; WNEO (PBS) Alliance; WPGH-TV (FOX) Pittsburgh; WPMY (MNT) Pittsburgh; WPXI (IND, NBC) Pittsburgh; WQED (PBS) Pittsburgh; WTAE-TV (ABC) Pittsburgh; WTOV-TV (IND, NBC) Steubenville; WYTV (ABC, MNT) Youngstown.
Programming (via satellite): Discovery Channel; TBS Superstation.
Fee: $44.95 installation; $13.20 monthly.
Expanded Basic Service 1
Subscribers: 435.
Programming (via satellite): A&E Networks; ABC Family Channel; AMC; Animal Planet; Cartoon Network; CNBC; CNN; C-SPAN; C-SPAN 2; Disney Channel; Encore Action; ESPN; ESPN 2; Fox News Channel; Fox Sports Net Ohio; Hallmark Channel; HGTV; ION Television; Lifetime; MTV; Nickelodeon; QVC; Spike TV; The Learning Channel; Travel Channel; Turner Network TV; USA Network.
Fee: $21.75 monthly.
Digital Basic Service
Subscribers: N.A.
Programming (via satellite): BBC America; Bravo; Discovery Digital Networks; DMX Music; ESPN Classic Sports; ESPNews; Fox Sports World; Golf Channel; GSN; History Channel; Independent Film Channel; National Geographic Channel; Nick Jr.; Speed; Turner Classic Movies; WE tv.
Fee: $9.00 monthly.
Digital Pay Service 1
Pay Units: N.A.
Programming (via satellite): Cinemax; Encore; HBO (multiplexed); Showtime (multiplexed); The Movie Channel (multiplexed).
Fee: $10.00 monthly (each).
Video-On-Demand: No
Pay-Per-View
iN DEMAND (delivered digitally).
Internet Service
Operational: No.
Telephone Service
None
Miles of Plant: 11.0 (coaxial); None (fiber optic).
General Manager: Timothy Evard. Operations Director: Belinda Evard. Engineering Director: Mike Earehart. Finance & Accounting Director: Cindy Johnson.
Ownership: Windjammer Communications LLC (MSO).

SANDUSKY—Buckeye Cable System, 409 E Market St, PO Box 5800, Sandusky, OH 44871. Phones: 419-627-1371; 419-627-0800 (Customer service). Fax: 419-627-0180. E-mail: customerservice@eriecable.com. Web Site: http://www.buckeyecablesystem.com. Also serves Bay View, Berlin Twp. (Erie County), Castalia, Groton Twp. (Erie County), Huron, Huron Twp. (Erie County), Margaretta Twp., Milan Twp. (Erie County), Oxford Twp. (Erie County), Perkins Twp. (Erie County) & Townsend Twp. ICA: OH0029.
TV Market Ranking: 52 (Townsend Twp.); 8 (Bay View, Berlin Twp. (Erie County), Castalia, Groton Twp. (Erie County), Huron, Huron Twp. (Erie County), Margaretta Twp., Milan Twp. (Erie County), Oxford Twp. (Erie County), Perkins Twp. (Erie County), SANDUSKY). Franchise award date: January 1, 1970. Franchise expiration date: N.A. Began: September 1, 1970.
Channel capacity: 64 (operating 2-way). Channels available but not in use: N.A.
Basic Service
Subscribers: 20,000.
Programming (received off-air): WBNX-TV (CW) Akron; WEWS-TV (ABC) Cleveland; WGGN-TV (TBN) Sandusky; WGTE-TV (PBS) Toledo; WJW (FOX) Cleveland; WKYC (NBC) Cleveland; WNWO-TV (NBC) Toledo; WOIO (CBS) Shaker Heights; WQHS-DT (UNV) Cleveland; WTOL (CBS) Toledo; WTVG (ABC) Toledo; WUAB (MNT) Lorain; WUPW (FOX) Toledo; WVIZ (PBS) Cleveland; WVPX-TV (ION) Akron.
Programming (via satellite): A&E Networks; ABC Family Channel; AMC; Animal Planet; BET Networks; Bravo; Cartoon Network; CNBC; CNN; Comedy Central; Country Music TV; C-SPAN; C-SPAN 2; Discovery Channel; Discovery Health Channel; Disney Channel; E! Entertainment Television; ESPN; ESPN 2; Eternal Word TV Network; Food Network; Fox News Channel; Fox Sports Net Ohio; FX; Great American Country; Hallmark Channel; Headline News; HGTV; History Channel; Jewelry Television; Lifetime; MTV; Nickelodeon; QVC; Shop at Home; ShopNBC; Spike TV; Syfy; TBS Superstation; The Learning Channel; The Weather Channel; Travel Channel; truTV; Turner Network TV; TV Land; USA Network; VH1.
Fee: $20.00 installation; $33.15 monthly; $1.50 converter; $18.00 additional installation.
Digital Basic Service
Subscribers: N.A.
Programming (via satellite): BBC America; CCTV-4; Daystar TV Network; ESPN; ESPN Classic Sports; ESPNews; Fox College Sports Atlantic; Fox College Sports Central; Fox College Sports Pacific; Fox Deportes; Fox Soccer; GAS; Golf Channel; HD Theater; HDNet; HDNet Movies; INSP; Lifetime Movie Network; MTV Networks Digital Suite; Music Choice; NBA TV; Nick Jr.; NickToons TV; Style Network; Trinity Broadcasting Network; Turner Network TV; WE tv.
Digital Pay Service 1
Pay Units: N.A.
Programming (via satellite): Cinemax (multiplexed); Encore (multiplexed); Flix (multiplexed); HBO (multiplexed); Showtime (multiplexed); Starz (multiplexed); Sundance Channel; The Movie Channel.
Video-On-Demand: Yes
Pay-Per-View
NBA League Pass (delivered digitally); NHL Center Ice (delivered digitally); MLB Extra Innings (delivered digitally); ESPN College Sports (delivered digitally); NASCAR In Car (delivered digitally); iN DEMAND (delivered digitally); Hot Choice (delivered digitally); Playboy TV (delivered digitally); Fresh (delivered digitally).
Internet Service
Operational: Yes. Began: August 1, 2001.
Subscribers: 6,365.
Broadband Service: Buckeye Express.
Fee: $19.00 installation; $29.99 monthly.
Telephone Service
Digital: Operational
Fee: $13.75 monthly
Miles of Plant: 370.0 (coaxial); 33.0 (fiber optic).
President: Patrick Deville. Government Affairs Director: Tom Dawson.
Ownership: Block Communications Inc. (MSO).

SARAHSVILLE—Formerly served by Cebridge Connections. No longer in operation. ICA: OH0362.

SARDINIA—Formerly served by Crystal Broadband Networks. No longer in operation. ICA: OH0267.

SCIO—Time Warner Cable, 530 S Main St, Ste 1751, Akron, OH 44311-1090. Phones: 330-633-9203; 330-868-5413 (Local office). Fax: 330-633-7970. Web Site: http://www.timewarnercable.com/northeastohio. ICA: OH0269.
TV Market Ranking: 90 (SCIO). Franchise award date: N.A. Franchise expiration date: March 9, 2010. Began: December 1, 1976.
Channel capacity: 40 (not 2-way capable). Channels available but not in use: N.A.
Basic Service
Subscribers: N.A. Included in Warren
Programming (received off-air): KDKA-TV (CBS) Pittsburgh; WNEO (PBS) Alliance; WPGH-TV (FOX) Pittsburgh; WPXI (IND, NBC) Pittsburgh; WTOV-TV (IND, NBC) Steubenville; WTRF-TV (CBS) Wheeling; WVPX-TV (ION) Akron; WYTV (ABC, MNT) Youngstown.
Programming (via satellite): C-SPAN; QVC; TBS Superstation; The Learning Channel.
Fee: $44.95 installation; $14.79 monthly; $3.40 converter.
Expanded Basic Service 1
Subscribers: 276.
Programming (via satellite): A&E Networks; ABC Family Channel; AMC; Animal Planet; Cartoon Network; CNBC; CNN; Disney Channel; ESPN; Fox News Channel; Fox Sports Net Ohio; Hallmark Channel; Lifetime; MoviePlex; Nickelodeon; Spike TV; The Weather Channel; truTV; Turner Network TV; USA Network.
Fee: $24.96 monthly.
Pay Service 1
Pay Units: 92.
Programming (via satellite): Encore.
Fee: $4.00 monthly.
Pay Service 2
Pay Units: 23.
Programming (via satellite): HBO.
Fee: $14.95 monthly.
Pay Service 3
Pay Units: 26.
Programming (via satellite): Showtime.
Fee: $14.95 monthly.
Pay Service 4
Pay Units: 39.
Programming (via satellite): Starz.
Fee: $8.95 monthly.
Video-On-Demand: No
Internet Service
Operational: Yes.
Telephone Service
Digital: Operational
Miles of Plant: 10.0 (coaxial); None (fiber optic).
President: Stephen Fry. Area Vice President: Rick Whaley. Vice President, Engineering:

Al Costanzi. Vice President, Marketing: Patrick Burke. Vice President, Public Affairs: William Jasso. Government & Media Relations Director: Chris Thomas.
Ownership: Time Warner Cable (MSO).

SCIPIO TWP. (Meigs County)—Time Warner Cable, 1266 Dublin Rd, Columbus, OH 43215-1008. Phone: 614-481-5000. Fax: 614-481-5052. Web Site: http://www.timewarnercable.com/midohio. Also serves Bedford Twp., Lodi Twp., Rutland & Salisbury Twp. ICA: OH0274.
TV Market Ranking: Below 100 (Bedford Twp., Lodi Twp., Rutland, Salisbury Twp., SCIPIO TWP.). Franchise award date: March 4, 1989. Franchise expiration date: N.A. Began: January 1, 1990.
Channel capacity: N.A. Channels available but not in use: N.A.
Basic Service
Subscribers: 226.
Programming (received off-air): WCHS-TV (ABC) Charleston; WOUB-TV (PBS) Athens; WOWK-TV (CBS) Huntington; WQCW (CW) Portsmouth; WSAZ-TV (MNT, NBC) Huntington; WVAH-TV (FOX) Charleston.
Programming (via satellite): WGN America.
Fee: $20.99 installation; $22.70 monthly.
Expanded Basic Service 1
Subscribers: N.A.
Programming (via satellite): A&E Networks; ABC Family Channel; CNN; Country Music TV; Discovery Channel; ESPN; ESPN 2; History Channel; MTV; Nickelodeon; Spike TV; TBS Superstation; The Weather Channel; Turner Classic Movies; Turner Network TV; USA Network.
Digital Basic Service
Subscribers: N.A.
Programming (via satellite): BBC America; Bloomberg Television; Bravo; Discovery Fit & Health; ESPN Classic Sports; ESPNews; Fox Movie Channel; Fox Sports World; G4; Golf Channel; Halogen Network; HGTV; Independent Film Channel; Outdoor Channel; Syfy; Trinity Broadcasting Network; Versus; WE tv.
Digital Expanded Basic Service
Subscribers: N.A.
Programming (via satellite): Music Choice; Nick Jr.; NickToons TV.
Digital Pay Service 1
Pay Units: N.A.
Programming (via satellite): Cinemax (multiplexed); Encore; HBO (multiplexed); Showtime (multiplexed); Starz (multiplexed); The Movie Channel (multiplexed).
Video-On-Demand: No
Pay-Per-View
Hits Movies & Events (delivered digitally); Fresh (delivered digitally); Playboy TV (delivered digitally).
Internet Service
Operational: No.
Telephone Service
None
Miles of Plant: 33.0 (coaxial); None (fiber optic).
President: Rhonda Fraas. Vice President & General Manager: David Kreiman. Vice President, Engineering: Randy Hall. Vice President, Marketing: Mark Psigoda. Vice President, Government & Public Affairs: Mary Jo Green. Technical Operations Director: Jim Cavender. Government Affairs Director: Steve Cuckler.
Ownership: Time Warner Cable (MSO).

SCOTT (village)—Formerly served by CableDirect. No longer in operation. ICA: OH0363.

SEAMAN—Time Warner Cable. Now served by CINCINNATI, OH [OH0001]. ICA: OH0208.

SEBRING—Time Warner Cable. Now served by MINERVA, OH [OH0132]. ICA: OH0126.

SENECAVILLE—Suddenlink Communications, 12444 Powerscourt Dr, Saint Louis, MO 63131-3660. Phones: 314-965-2020; 304-472-4193. Fax: 304-472-0756. Web Site: http://www.suddenlink.com. Also serves Buffalo, Byesville, Derwent, Jackson Twp. (Guernsey County), Kipling, Lore City, Millwood Twp., Old Washington, Pleasant City, Quaker City, Richland Twp. (Guernsey County), Salesville, Valley Twp. (Guernsey County) & Wills Twp. ICA: OH0124.
TV Market Ranking: 90 (Millwood Twp., Quaker City, Salesville); Below 100 (Buffalo, Byesville, Derwent, Jackson Twp. (Guernsey County), Kipling, Lore City, Old Washington, Pleasant City, Richland Twp. (Guernsey County), SENECAVILLE, Valley Twp. (Guernsey County), Wills Twp.). Franchise award date: N.A. Franchise expiration date: N.A. Began: N.A.
Channel capacity: 36 (operating 2-way). Channels available but not in use: N.A.
Basic Service
Subscribers: 2,723.
Programming (received off-air): WBNS-TV (CBS) Columbus; WHIZ-TV (NBC) Zanesville; WOUC-TV (PBS) Cambridge; WSYX (ABC, MNT) Columbus; WTOV-TV (IND, NBC) Steubenville; WTRF-TV (CBS) Wheeling; WTTE (FOX) Columbus.
Programming (via satellite): C-SPAN; C-SPAN 2; INSP; The Weather Channel; Trinity Broadcasting Network; WABC-TV (ABC) New York; WGN America.
Fee: $61.25 installation; $17.95 monthly; $1.24 converter.
Expanded Basic Service 1
Subscribers: 2,549.
Programming (via satellite): A&E Networks; ABC Family Channel; AMC; Animal Planet; Cartoon Network; CNN; Comedy Central; Discovery Channel; Disney Channel; E! Entertainment Television; ESPN; ESPN 2; ESPN Classic Sports; Fox News Channel; Fox Sports Net Ohio; FX; G4; Great American Country; GSN; Hallmark Channel; Headline News; HGTV; History Channel; ION Television; Lifetime; MSNBC; MTV; National Geographic Channel; Nickelodeon; Outdoor Channel; SoapNet; Speed; Spike TV; Syfy; TBS Superstation; The Learning Channel; Toon Disney; Travel Channel; Turner Network TV; TV Guide Network; TV Land; USA Network; VH1; WE tv.
Fee: $17.50 installation; $25.00 monthly.
Digital Basic Service
Subscribers: N.A.
Programming (via satellite): BBC America; Bio; Bloomberg Television; cloo; Discovery Digital Networks; DMX Music; ESPNews; Fox College Sports Atlantic; Fox College Sports Central; Fox College Sports Pacific; Fox Movie Channel; Fox Soccer; Fuse; Golf Channel; History Channel International; Independent Film Channel; Lifetime Movie Network; ShopNBC; Style Network; Turner Classic Movies; Versus.
Fee: $13.95 monthly.
Pay Service 1
Pay Units: 296.
Programming (via satellite): Cinemax; Encore; HBO; Showtime; The Movie Channel.
Fee: $3.99 monthly (Encore), $7.95 monthly (Cinemax).

Digital Pay Service 1
Pay Units: N.A.
Programming (via satellite): Cinemax (multiplexed); Encore (multiplexed); Flix; HBO (multiplexed); Showtime (multiplexed); Starz (multiplexed); The Movie Channel (multiplexed).
Pay-Per-View
iN DEMAND (delivered digitally); Playboy TV (delivered digitally); Fresh (delivered digitally).
Internet Service
Operational: Yes. Began: August 15, 2004.
Broadband Service: Suddenlink High Speed Internet.
Fee: $20.00 installation; $20.95 monthly.
Telephone Service
None
Miles of Plant: 109.0 (coaxial); None (fiber optic).
Manager: Peter Brown. Regional Engineer: Gene Wuchner.
Ownership: Cequel Communications LLC (MSO).

SHELBY—Time Warner Cable, 530 S Main St, Ste 1751, Akron, OH 44311-1090. Phone: 330-633-9203. Fax: 330-633-7970. Web Site: http://www.timewarnercable.com/northeastohio. ICA: OH0125.
TV Market Ranking: Below 100 (SHELBY). Franchise award date: N.A. Franchise expiration date: October 5, 2007. Began: January 1, 1968.
Channel capacity: N.A. Channels available but not in use: N.A.
Basic Service
Subscribers: N.A. Included in Mansfield
Programming (received off-air): WBNS-TV (CBS) Columbus; WBNX-TV (CW) Akron; WCMH-TV (NBC) Columbus; WEWS-TV (ABC) Cleveland; WGGN-TV (TBN) Sandusky; WJW (FOX) Cleveland; WKYC (NBC) Cleveland; WMFD-TV (IND) Mansfield; WOIO (CBS) Shaker Heights; WOSU-TV (PBS) Columbus; WQHS-DT (UNV) Cleveland; WRLM (IND) Canton; WSYX (ABC, MNT) Columbus; WUAB (MNT) Lorain; WVIZ (PBS) Cleveland; WVPX-TV (ION) Akron; 14 FMs.
Programming (via satellite): TBS Superstation; WGN America.
Fee: $29.95 installation; $12.45 monthly.
Expanded Basic Service 1
Subscribers: N.A.
Programming (via satellite): A&E Networks; ABC Family Channel; AMC; Animal Planet; Bravo; Cartoon Network; CNBC; CNN; Comedy Central; C-SPAN; C-SPAN 2; Discovery Channel; Discovery Fit & Health; Discovery Health Channel; Disney Channel; E! Entertainment Television; ESPN; ESPN 2; ESPN Classic Sports; Eternal Word TV Network; Food Network; Fox News Channel; Fox Sports Net Ohio; FX; Golf Channel; Great American Country; GSN; Hallmark Channel; Headline News; HGTV; History Channel; INSP; Lifetime; Lifetime Movie Network; MSNBC; MTV; Nickelodeon; Oxygen; QVC; SoapNet; Spike TV; SportsTime Ohio; Syfy; The Learning Channel; The Weather Channel; Travel Channel; truTV; Turner Classic Movies; Turner Network TV; TV Land; USA Network; Versus; VH1; WE tv.
Fee: $43.05 monthly.
Digital Basic Service
Subscribers: N.A.
Programming (via satellite): AmericanLife TV Network; BBC America; BBC America On Demand; Bio; Bloomberg Television; Boomerang; Canales N; CBS Sports Network; cloo; CNN International; Cooking Channel; Country Music TV; C-SPAN 3; Current; Daystar TV Network; Disney Channel; DIY Network; ESPN 2 HD; ESPN HD; ESPNews; Fox College Sports Atlantic; Fox College Sports Central; Fox College Sports Pacific; Fox Movie Channel; Fox Soccer; Fuel TV; Fuse; G4; GAS; HD Theater; HDNet; HDNet Movies; History Channel International; Howard TV; Independent Film Channel; Jewelry Television; Lifetime Real Women; MTV2; Music Choice; National Geographic Channel; National Geographic Channel On Demand; NBA TV; Nick Jr.; NickToons TV; Ohio News Network; Outdoor Channel; Speed; Speed On Demand; SportsTime Ohio; Style Network; Tennis Channel; The Word Network; Toon Disney; Turner Network TV HD; TVG Network; Universal HD; VH1 Classic.
Fee: $12.49 monthly.
Digital Pay Service 1
Pay Units: N.A.
Programming (via satellite): ART America; Cinemax (multiplexed); Cinemax On Demand; Deutsche Welle TV; Encore (multiplexed); HBO (multiplexed); HBO HD; HBO On Demand; RAI International; Showtime (multiplexed); Showtime HD; Showtime On Demand; Starz (multiplexed); Sundance Channel; The Movie Channel (multiplexed); The Movie Channel On Demand; TV Asia; Zee TV USA.
Fee: $12.00 monthly (HBO, Showtime/TMC, Starz, or Cinemax), $14.95 monthly (Deutsch Welle, RAI, Zee TV, Art, or TV Asia).
Video-On-Demand: Yes
Pay-Per-View
iN DEMAND (delivered digitally); Movies (delivered digitally); ESPN (delivered digitally); NHL Center Ice (delivered digitally); MLB Extra Innings (delivered digitally); Playboy TV (delivered digitally); Spice Live (delivered digitally); Ten Clips (delivered digitally); Pleasure (delivered digitally); NASCAR In Car (delivered digitally); NBA League Pass (delivered digitally); MLS Direct Kick (delivered digitally).
Internet Service
Operational: Yes.
Broadband Service: EarthLink, Road Runner.
Fee: $99.00 installation; $44.95 monthly.
Telephone Service
Digital: Operational
Fee: $44.95 monthly
Miles of Plant: 89.0 (coaxial); None (fiber optic).
President: Stephen Fry. Area Vice President: Scott Miller. Vice President, Engineering: Al Costanzi. Vice President, Marketing: Patrick

Burke. Vice President, Sales: Woody Woodward. Vice President, Public Affairs: William Jasso. Area Manager: Carol Jagger. Government & Media Relations Director: Chris Thomas.

Ownership: Time Warner Cable (MSO).

SHERWOOD—Formerly served by Shertel Cable [OH0365]. This cable system has converted to IPTV, 105 W Vine St, Sherwood, OH 43556. Phone: 419-899-2121. E-mail: shertele@bright.net. Web Site: http://www.smta.cc. ICA: OH5191.

Channel capacity: N.A. Channels available but not in use: N.A.

Basic Service

Subscribers: N.A.

Fee: $25.00 installation; $34.95 monthly.

Expanded Basic Service 1

Subscribers: N.A.

Fee: $44.95 monthly.

Pay Service 1

Pay Units: N.A.

Fee: $11.95 monthly (Encore/Starz!); $12.99 monthly (HBO or Showtime).

Internet Service

Operational: Yes.

Fee: $39.95 monthly.

Telephone Service

Digital: Operational

General Manager: Michael Woodring.

SHERWOOD—Shertel Cable. This cable system has converted to IPTV. See Sherwood, OH [OH5191]. ICA: OH0365.

SHREVE—Time Warner Cable. Now served by JEROMESVILLE, OH [OH0266]. ICA: OH0366.

SIDNEY—Time Warner Cable. Now served by DAYTON, OH [OH0011]. ICA: OH0080.

SOMERSET—Time Warner Communications. Now served by THORNVILLE, OH [OH0154]. ICA: OH0290.

SOUTH POINT—Armstrong Cable Services, 9651 County Rd 1, South Point, OH 45680-8438. Phones: 877-277-5711; 740-894-6357; 740-894-3886 (Customer service). Fax: 740-894-0875. E-mail: info@zoominternet.net. Web Site: http://cable.armstrongonewire.com. Also serves Ashland (portions), Boyd County, Catlettsburg, Flatwoods, Greenup, Greenup County (eastern portion), Ironville, Lloyd, Rockdale & Wurtland, KY; Burlington, Chesapeake, Fayette Twp., Perry Twp. (Lawrence County), Proctorville (portions), Rome Twp. (Lawrence County), Sybene & Union Twp. (Lawrence County), OH; Ceredo, Kenova, Shoals, Spring Valley & Wayne County (northern portion), WV. ICA: WV0011.

TV Market Ranking: 36 (Ashland (portions), Boyd County, Burlington, Catlettsburg, Ceredo, Chesapeake, Fayette Twp., Flatwoods, Greenup, Greenup County (eastern portion), Ironville, Kenova, Lloyd, Perry Twp. (Lawrence County), Proctorville (portions), Rome Twp. (Lawrence County), Shoals, SOUTH POINT, Spring Valley, Sybene, Union Twp. (Lawrence County), Wayne County (northern portion), Wurtland). Franchise award date: N.A. Franchise expiration date: N.A. Began: June 1, 1974.

Channel capacity: N.A. Channels available but not in use: N.A.

Digital Basic Service

Subscribers: 5,053.

Programming (via satellite): A&E Networks; ABC Family Channel; AMC; Animal Planet; Bravo; Cartoon Network; CNBC; CNN; Comedy Central; Country Music TV; C-SPAN; Discovery Channel; Disney Channel; E! Entertainment Television; ESPN; ESPN 2; ESPN Classic Sports; Eternal Word TV Network; Food Network; Fox News Channel; Fox Sports Net Ohio; FX; Headline News; HGTV; History Channel; INSP; Lifetime; MSNBC; MTV; Music Choice; Nickelodeon; NickToons TV; QVC; Root Sports Pittsburgh; ShopNBC; Spike TV; Syfy; TBS Superstation; The Learning Channel; The Weather Channel; Travel Channel; truTV; Turner Classic Movies; Turner Network TV; TV Guide Network; TV Land; USA Network; VH1.

Fee: $51.40 monthly.

Digital Expanded Basic Service

Subscribers: N.A.

Programming (via satellite): AmericanLife TV Network; BBC America; Bio; Bloomberg Television; Boomerang; CBS Sports Network; Chiller; cloo; CMT Pure Country; Cooking Channel; Discovery Fit & Health; Discovery Health Channel; Discovery Kids Channel; DIY Network; ESPN Classic Sports; ESPNews; G4; Golf Channel; Great American Country; GSN; Hallmark Channel; Hallmark Movie Channel; History Channel International; HRTV; ID Investigation Discovery; Jewelry Television; Lifetime Movie Network; Military Channel; MTV Hits; MTV Jams; MTV2; mun2 television; National Geographic Channel; NFL Network; NHL Network; Nick Jr.; Nick Too; Outdoor Channel; Oxygen; PBS Kids Sprout; Pentagon Channel; Planet Green; RFD-TV; Science; SoapNet; Speed; TeenNick; Tennis Channel; Toon Disney; Tr3s; Versus; VH1 Classic; VH1 Soul; WE tv.

Fee: $12.00 monthly.

Digital Expanded Basic Service 2

Subscribers: N.A.

Programming (received off-air): WOWK-TV (CBS) Huntington; WSAZ-TV (MNT, NBC) Huntington.

Programming (via satellite): A&E HD; Animal Planet HD; Bravo HD; CNN HD; Discovery Channel HD; Disney Channel HD; ESPN 2 HD; ESPN HD; Food Network HD; Fox News HD; FX HD; Golf Channel HD; Hallmark Movie Channel HD; HD Theater; HDNet; HDNet Movies; HGTV HD; History Channel HD; MGM HD; National Geographic Channel HD Network; NFL Network HD; NHL Network HD; Outdoor Channel 2 HD; Palladia; PBS HD; QVC HD; Science HD; Syfy HD; TBS in HD; The Weather Channel HD; TLC HD; Turner Network TV HD; Universal HD; USA Network HD; Versus HD; WealthTV HD.

Fee: $9.00 monthly.

Digital Pay Service 1

Pay Units: N.A.

Programming (via satellite): Cinemax (multiplexed); Cinemax HD; Encore (multiplexed); Flix; HBO (multiplexed); HBO HD; RAI USA; Showtime (multiplexed); Showtime HD; Starz (multiplexed); Starz HDTV; The Movie Channel (multiplexed); TV5 USA.

Fee: $13.95 monthly (HBO, Cinemax, Showtime/TMC/Flix or Starz/Encore).

Video-On-Demand: Yes

Pay-Per-View

iN DEMAND (delivered digitally); Hot Choice (delivered digitally); ESPN (delivered digitally); Sports PPV (delivered digitally).

Internet Service

Operational: Yes. Began: March 1, 2000.

Subscribers: 8,616.

Broadband Service: Armstrong Zoom.

Fee: $26.95-$39.95 monthly.

Telephone Service

Digital: Operational

Fee: $49.95 monthly

Miles of Plant: 397.0 (coaxial); 16.0 (fiber optic).

General Manager: Gordon Waters. Operations Manager: Richard Hagley. Chief Technician: Greg Little.

Ownership: Armstrong Group of Companies (MSO).

SPRINGFIELD—Time Warner Cable. Now served by DAYTON, OH [OH0011]. ICA: OH0433.

ST. MARY'S—Time Warner Cable, 205 Crystal Ave, Findlay, OH 45840. Phones: 614-481-5000 (Columbus office); 419-429-7474. Fax: 419-429-7402. Web Site: http://www.timewarnercable.com/midohio. ICA: OH0123.

TV Market Ranking: Below 100 (ST. MARY'S). Franchise award date: N.A. Franchise expiration date: May 27, 2007. Began: December 14, 1968.

Channel capacity: N.A. Channels available but not in use: N.A.

Basic Service

Subscribers: 3,633.

Programming (received off-air): WBDT (CW) Springfield; WBGU-TV (PBS) Bowling Green; WBNS-TV (CBS) Columbus; WDTN (NBC) Dayton; WHIO-TV (CBS) Dayton; WKEF (ABC) Dayton; WLIO (CW, NBC) Lima; WLQP-LP Lima; WOHL-CD (FOX) Lima; WPTA (ABC, CW) Fort Wayne; WRGT-TV (FOX, MNT) Dayton; WTLW (IND) Lima.

Fee: $45.86 installation; $10.15 monthly.

Expanded Basic Service 1

Subscribers: N.A.

Programming (via satellite): A&E Networks; ABC Family Channel; AMC; Animal Planet; Bravo; Cartoon Network; CNBC; CNN; Comedy Central; Country Music TV; C-SPAN; C-SPAN 2; Discovery Channel; Disney Channel; E! Entertainment Television; Encore Action; ESPN; ESPN 2; ESPN Classic Sports; Eternal Word TV Network; Food Network; Fox News Channel; Fox Sports Net Ohio; FX; Golf Channel; Hallmark Channel; Headline News; HGTV; History Channel; Lifetime; Lifetime Movie Network; MSNBC; MTV; National Geographic Channel; Nickelodeon; Oxygen; QVC; ShopNBC; Spike TV; Syfy; TBS Superstation; The Learning Channel; The Weather Channel; Travel Channel; truTV; Turner Classic Movies; Turner Network TV; TV Guide Network; TV Land; USA Network; Versus; VH1; WE tv.

Fee: $30.80 monthly.

Digital Basic Service

Subscribers: 1,090.

Programming (via satellite): AmericanLife TV Network; America's Store; BBC America; Bloomberg Television; CNN International; Cooking Channel; C-SPAN 3; Discovery Fit & Health; DIY Network; DMX Music; ESPNews; Fox Sports World; FSN Digital Atlantic; FSN Digital Central; FSN Digital Pacific; Fuse; G4; GAS; Great American Country; GSN; Lifetime Real Women; MTV2; Nick Jr.; Ohio News Network; Outdoor Channel; Ovation; SoapNet; Sorpresa; Speed; Style Network; Toon Disney; VH1 Classic.

Fee: $9.90 monthly.

Digital Pay Service 1

Pay Units: 1,238.

Programming (via satellite): Cinemax (multiplexed); Encore (multiplexed); Flix; HBO (multiplexed); Showtime (multiplexed); Starz (multiplexed); The Movie Channel (multiplexed).

Fee: $9.95 installation; $10.95 monthly (Cinemax, HBO, Showtime/Flix/TMC or Starz/Encore).

Video-On-Demand: Yes

Pay-Per-View

Addressable homes: 1,090.

iN DEMAND (delivered digitally); Fresh (delivered digitally); Sports PPV (delivered digitally).

Internet Service

Operational: Yes.

Subscribers: 654.

Broadband Service: Road Runner.

Fee: $69.95 installation; $44.95 monthly.

Telephone Service

Digital: Operational

Fee: $44.95 monthly

Miles of Plant: 127.0 (coaxial); None (fiber optic).

President: Rhonda Fraas. Vice President, Engineering: Randy Hall. Vice President, Marketing: Mark Psigoda. Technical Operations Director: John Ellingson. Public Affairs Director: Brian Young. Government Affairs Manager: Patrick McCauley.

Ownership: Time Warner Cable (MSO).

ST. PARIS—Time Warner Communications. Now served by DAYTON, OH [OH0011]. ICA: OH0176.

STEUBENVILLE—Comcast Cable. Now served by WHEELING, WV [WV0004]. ICA: OH0048.

STRUTHERS—Time Warner Cable, 530 S Main St, Ste 1751, Akron, OH 44311-1090. Phone: 330-633-9203. Fax: 330-633-7970. Web Site: http://www.timewarnercable.com/northeastohio. Also serves Cortsville Twp. (portions), Lowellville (village) & Poland Twp. (Mahoning County). ICA: OH0116.

TV Market Ranking: 79 (Cortsville Twp. (portions), Lowellville (village), Poland Twp. (Mahoning County), STRUTHERS). Franchise award date: January 1, 1973. Franchise expiration date: December 20, 2007. Began: January 1, 1974.

Channel capacity: N.A. Channels available but not in use: N.A.

Basic Service

Subscribers: N.A. Included in Warren

Programming (received off-air): WFMJ-TV (CW, NBC) Youngstown; WKBN-TV (CBS) Youngstown; WNEO (PBS) Alliance; WOHZ-CA (IND) Mansfield; WPGH-TV (FOX) Pittsburgh; WPMY (MNT) Pittsburgh; WQED (PBS) Pittsburgh; WUAB (MNT) Lorain; WYFX-LP Youngstown; WYTV (ABC, MNT) Youngstown.

Programming (via satellite): C-SPAN; C-SPAN 2; Ecumenical TV Channel; ION Television; Ohio News Network; Pittsburgh Cable News Channel; QVC; ShopNBC; TV Guide Network.

Fee: $44.95 installation; $15.09 monthly; $.31 converter.

Expanded Basic Service 1

Subscribers: N.A.

Programming (via satellite): A&E Networks; ABC Family Channel; AMC; Animal Planet; BET Networks; Cartoon Network; CNBC; CNN; Comedy Central; Country Music TV; Discovery Channel; Disney Channel; E! Entertainment Television; ESPN; ESPN 2; Food

Network; Fox News Channel; Fox Sports Net Ohio; FX; Headline News; HGTV; History Channel; Lifetime; MSNBC; MTV; Nickelodeon; Oxygen; Root Sports Pittsburgh; Spike TV; Style Network; Syfy; TBS Superstation; The Learning Channel; The Weather Channel; Travel Channel; truTV; Turner Network TV; TV Land; USA Network; VH1.
Fee: $38.90 monthly.

Digital Basic Service
Subscribers: 1,400.
Programming (via satellite): American-Life TV Network; BBC America; Black Family Channel; Bloomberg Television; Bravo; Discovery Fit & Health; DIY Network; ESPN Classic Sports; ESPNews; Fox Sports World; Fuse; G4; Golf Channel; Great American Country; GSN; Hallmark Channel; Halogen Network; Music Choice; Outdoor Channel; Speed; The Word Network; Trinity Broadcasting Network; WE tv.
Fee: $12.95 monthly.

Digital Expanded Basic Service
Subscribers: N.A.
Programming (via satellite): Bio; Fox Movie Channel; FSN Digital Atlantic; FSN Digital Central; FSN Digital Pacific; GAS; History Channel International; Independent Film Channel; MTV Networks Digital Suite; Nick Jr.; Nick Too; NickToons TV; SoapNet; Sundance Channel; Toon Disney; Turner Classic Movies; Versus.
Fee: $10.00 monthly.

Digital Pay Service 1
Pay Units: N.A.
Programming (via satellite): ART America; Canales N; CCTV-4; Cinemax (multiplexed); Encore (multiplexed); Filipino Channel; Flix; HBO (multiplexed); RAI International; Russian Television Network; Showtime (multiplexed); Starz (multiplexed); The Movie Channel (multiplexed); TV Asia; TV Japan; TV5, La Television International; Zee TV USA; Zhong Tian Channel.
Fee: $12.00 monthly (each).

Video-On-Demand: Yes

Pay-Per-View
Playboy TV (delivered digitally); Urban American Television Network (delivered digitally); Hot Choice (delivered digitally); Shorteez (delivered digitally); Fresh (delivered digitally); Playboy TV (delivered digitally); HITS PPV (delivered digitally).

Internet Service
Operational: Yes. Began: January 1, 2002.
Subscribers: 700.
Broadband Service: Road Runner.
Fee: $45.95 monthly.

Telephone Service
Digital: Operational
Fee: $44.95 monthly

Miles of Plant: 69.0 (coaxial); None (fiber optic).

President: Stephen Fry. Area Vice President: Rick Whaley. Vice President, Engineering: Al Costanzi. Vice President, Marketing: Patrick Burke. Vice President, Public Affairs: William Jasso. Area Manager: Daryl Morrison. Government & Media Relations Director: Chris Thomas.

Ownership: Time Warner Cable (MSO).

SUMMERFIELD (village)—Formerly served by Almega Cable. No longer in operation. ICA: OH0303.

SUNBURY—Time Warner Cable. Now served by COLUMBUS, OH [OH0002]. ICA: OH0370.

SYCAMORE—Time Warner Cable, 205 Crystal Ave, Findlay, OH 45840. Phones: 614-481-5000 (Columbus office); 419-429-7474. Fax: 419-429-7402. Web Site: http://www.timewarnercable.com/midohio. Also serves Adrian, Attica, Big Spring Twp., Bloom Twp. (Seneca County), Bloomville, Carey, Caroline, Carrothers, Chatfield, Cranberry Twp., Crawford Twp., McCutchenville, Melmore, New Riegel, New Washington, Reed Twp., Republic, Scipio Twp. (Seneca County), Seneca Twp. (Seneca County), Siam, Tymochtee Twp. & Venice Twp. ICA: OH0215.

TV Market Ranking: Below 100 (Attica, Bloomville, Caroline, Carrothers, Chatfield, Cranberry Twp., New Washington, Reed Twp., Republic, Scipio Twp. (Seneca County), Siam, Venice Twp.); Outside TV Markets (Adrian, Big Spring Twp., Bloom Twp., Carey, Crawford Twp., McCutchenville, Melmore, New Riegel, Seneca Twp. (Seneca County), SYCAMORE, Tymochtee Twp.). Franchise award date: N.A. Franchise expiration date: N.A. Began: August 1, 1984.

Channel capacity: N.A. Channels available but not in use: N.A.

Basic Service
Subscribers: 10,127.
Programming (received off-air): WBGU-TV (PBS) Bowling Green; WBNS-TV (CBS) Columbus; WCMH-TV (NBC) Columbus; WEWS-TV (ABC) Cleveland; WGTE-TV (PBS) Toledo; WLMB (IND) Toledo; WNWO-TV (NBC) Toledo; WTOL (CBS) Toledo; WTVG (ABC) Toledo; WUAB (MNT) Lorain; WUPW (FOX) Toledo.
Programming (via satellite): C-SPAN; CW+; QVC; TV Guide Network; various Canadian stations.
Fee: $45.86 installation; $10.02 monthly.

Expanded Basic Service 1
Subscribers: N.A.
Programming (via satellite): A&E Networks; ABC Family Channel; AMC; Animal Planet; BET Networks; Bravo; Cartoon Network; CNBC; CNN; Comedy Central; Country Music TV; C-SPAN 2; Discovery Channel; Disney Channel; E! Entertainment Television; ESPN; ESPN 2; Food Network; Fox News Channel; Fox Sports Net Ohio; FX; Golf Channel; Hallmark Channel; Headline News; HGTV; History Channel; Lifetime; Lifetime Movie Network; MSNBC; MTV; National Geographic Channel; Nick Jr.; Nickelodeon; Oxygen; Radar Channel; ShopNBC; Spike TV; SportsTime Ohio; Style Network; Syfy; TBS Superstation; The Learning Channel; The Weather Channel; Travel Channel; truTV; Turner Classic Movies; Turner Network TV; TV Land; Univision Studios; USA Network; Versus; VH1; WE tv.
Fee: $30.93 monthly.

Digital Basic Service
Subscribers: 2,472.
Programming (via satellite): AmericanLife TV Network; BBC America; BBC America On Demand; Bio; Bloomberg Television; Boomerang; CBS Sports Network; Cine Latino; cloo; CNBC; CNN International; Cooking Channel; C-SPAN 2; C-SPAN 3; Current; Discovery en Espanol; Discovery Fit & Health; Discovery Health Channel; Discovery Home Channel; Discovery Kids Channel; Discovery Times Channel; Disney Channel; DIY Network; Encore (multiplexed); ESPN 2 HD; ESPN Classic Sports; ESPN HD; ESPN U; ESPNews; Eternal Word TV Network; Exercise TV; Food Network; Fox Business Channel; Fox College Sports Atlantic; Fox College Sports Central; Fox College Sports Pacific; Fox Deportes; Fox Movie Channel; Fox Reality Channel; Fox Soccer; Fuel TV; Fuse; G4; GAS; Great American Country; Great American Country On Demand; GSN; Halogen Network; HD Theater; HDNet; HDNet Movies; Headline News; HGTV; History Channel International; Howard TV; Independent Film Channel; INSP; La Familia Network; Lifetime Real Women; Military Channel; MTV Hits; MTV2; Music Choice; National Geographic Channel On Demand; NBA TV; Ohio News Network; Outdoor Channel; Oxygen On Demand; Puma TV; Science; Sorpresa; Speed; Speed On Demand; Sundance Channel; Sur Network; Tennis Channel; The Weather Channel; Toon Disney; Turner Network TV HD; TV Guide SPOT; TV One; Universal HD; VH1 Classic; Video Rola.
Fee: $9.90 monthly.

Digital Pay Service 1
Pay Units: 8,818.
Programming (via satellite): Cinemax (multiplexed); Cinemax On Demand; HBO (multiplexed); HBO HD; HBO On Demand; Showtime (multiplexed); Showtime HD; Showtime On Demand; Starz (multiplexed); Starz On Demand; The Movie Channel (multiplexed); The Movie Channel On Demand.
Fee: $11.95 monthly (Cinemax, HBO, Showtime, Starz or Flix & TMC).

Video-On-Demand: Yes

Pay-Per-View
Addressable homes: 2,472.
iN DEMAND (delivered digitally); Fresh (delivered digitally); sports (delivered digitally).

Internet Service
Operational: Yes.
Subscribers: 1,483.
Broadband Service: Road Runner.
Fee: $69.95 installation; $44.95 monthly.

Telephone Service
Analog: Not Operational
Digital: Operational

Miles of Plant: 301.0 (coaxial); None (fiber optic).

President: Rhonda Fraas. Vice President & General Manager: Brad Wakely. Vice President, Engineering: Randy Hall. Vice President, Marketing: Mark Psigoda. Technical Operations Director: John Ellingson. Government Affairs Director: Brian Young. Government Affairs Manager: Patrick McCauley.

Ownership: Time Warner Cable (MSO).

THOMPSON TWP. (Geauga County)—Zito Media, 611 Vader Hill Rd, Coudersport, PA 16915. Phone: 814-260-9575. Web Site: http://www.zitomedia.com. Also serves Claridon, Hambden Twp. (Geauga County), Hartsgrove, Huntsburg Twp., Leroy Twp. (Lake County), Montville, Trumbull Twp. & Windsor. ICA: OH0162.

TV Market Ranking: 79 (Montville); 8 (Hambden Twp. (Geauga County), Huntsburg Twp., Leroy Twp. (Lake County), Trumbull Twp.); 8,79 (Claridon, THOMPSON TWP., Windsor); Outside TV Markets (Hartsgrove). Franchise award date: N.A. Franchise expiration date: N.A. Began: N.A.

Channel capacity: 62 (not 2-way capable). Channels available but not in use: N.A.

Basic Service
Subscribers: 963.
Programming (received off-air): WBNX-TV (CW) Akron; WEWS-TV (ABC) Cleveland; WJW (FOX) Cleveland; WKYC (NBC) Cleveland; WOIO (CBS) Shaker Heights; WQHS-DT (UNV) Cleveland; WRLM (IND) Canton; WUAB (MNT) Lorain; WVIZ (PBS) Cleveland.
Programming (via satellite): ION Television; QVC.
Fee: $40.00 installation; $22.00 monthly; $1.95 converter.

Expanded Basic Service 1
Subscribers: N.A.
Programming (via satellite): A&E Networks; ABC Family Channel; AMC; Animal Planet; BET Networks; Cartoon Network; CNBC; CNN; Comedy Central; C-SPAN; Discovery Channel; Disney Channel; E! Entertainment Television; ESPN; ESPN 2; Food Network; Fox News Channel; Fox Sports Net Ohio; FX; Great American Country; Headline News; HGTV; History Channel; MSNBC; MTV; Nickelodeon; Spike TV; Syfy; TBS Superstation; The Learning Channel; The Weather Channel; Turner Classic Movies; Turner Network TV; TV Land; USA Network; VH1.
Fee: $20.00 monthly.

Digital Basic Service
Subscribers: N.A.
Programming (via satellite): BBC America; Bio; Bloomberg Television; cloo; Discovery Health Channel; Discovery Kids Channel; DMX Music; ESPN Classic Sports; ESPNews; Fox College Sports Atlantic; Fox College Sports Central; Fox College Sports Pacific; Fox Soccer; Fuse; G4; Golf Channel; GSN; History Channel International; ID Investigation Discovery; Independent Film Channel; Military Channel; Outdoor Channel; Planet Green; Science; ShopNBC; Speed; Style Network; Sundance Channel; Toon Disney; Trinity Broadcasting Network; Versus; WE tv.

Pay Service 1
Pay Units: 172.
Programming (via satellite): Cinemax.
Fee: $11.00 monthly.

Pay Service 2
Pay Units: 296.
Programming (via satellite): HBO.
Fee: $11.00 monthly.

Pay Service 3
Pay Units: 251.
Programming (via satellite): Showtime; The Movie Channel.
Fee: $12.95 monthly.

Digital Pay Service 1
Pay Units: N.A.
Programming (via satellite): Cinemax (multiplexed); Encore (multiplexed); Flix; HBO (multiplexed); Showtime (multiplexed); Starz (multiplexed); The Movie Channel (multiplexed).

Video-On-Demand: No

Pay-Per-View
iN DEMAND (delivered digitally); Playboy TV (delivered digitally); Club Jenna (delivered digitally); Fresh (delivered digitally); Shorteez (delivered digitally).

Internet Service
Operational: No.
Telephone Service
None
Miles of Plant: 137.0 (coaxial); None (fiber optic).
Public Relations Manager: Mark Laver.
Ownership: Zito Media (MSO).

THORNVILLE—Time Warner Cable, 1266 Dublin Rd, Columbus, OH 43215-1008. Phone: 614-481-5000. Fax: 614-481-5052. Web Site: http://www.timewarnercable.com/midohio. Also serves Clayton Twp., Glenford, Jacksontown, Junction City, New Lexington, Pike Twp. (Perry County), Richland Twp. (Fairfield County), Rushville, Somerset, Thorn Twp. & West Rushville. ICA: OH0154.
TV Market Ranking: 27 (Jacksontown, Richland Twp. (Fairfield County), Rushville, Thorn Twp., THORNVILLE, West Rushville); Below 100 (Clayton Twp., Glenford, Junction City, New Lexington, Pike Twp. (Perry County), Somerset).
Channel capacity: N.A. Channels available but not in use: N.A.
Basic Service
Subscribers: N.A. Included in Columbus
Programming (received off-air): WBNS-TV (CBS) Columbus; WCMH-TV (NBC) Columbus; WHIZ-TV (NBC) Zanesville; WOSU-TV (PBS) Columbus; WOUB-TV (PBS) Athens; WSFJ-TV (TBN) Newark; WSYX (ABC, MNT) Columbus; WTTE (FOX) Columbus; WUAB (MNT) Lorain; WWHO (CW) Chillicothe.
Programming (via satellite): C-SPAN; Hallmark Channel; Headline News; History Channel; LWS Local Weather Station; Nick Jr.; QVC; ShopNBC; SoapNet; TBS Superstation; The Learning Channel; Travel Channel; TV Guide Network; Univision Studios; WGN America.
Expanded Basic Service 1
Subscribers: N.A.
Programming (via satellite): A&E Networks; ABC Family Channel; AMC; Animal Planet; BET Networks; Bravo; BTN; Cartoon Network; CNBC; CNN; Comedy Central; Country Music TV; Discovery Channel; Disney Channel; E! Entertainment Television; ESPN; ESPN 2; Food Network; Fox News Channel; Fox Sports Net Ohio; FX; Golf Channel; HGTV; Lifetime; Lifetime Movie Network; MSNBC; MTV; National Geographic Channel; Nickelodeon; Oxygen; Spike TV; SportsTime Ohio; Syfy; The Weather Channel; truTV; Turner Classic Movies; Turner Network TV; TV Land; USA Network; Versus; VH1; WE tv.
Digital Basic Service
Subscribers: N.A. Included in Columbus
Programming (via satellite): A&E HD; AmericanLife TV Network; Animal Planet HD; Auction TV; BBC America; BBC America On Demand; Bio; Bloomberg Television; Boomerang; BTN (multiplexed); BTN HD; Canal Sur; CBS Sports Network; Cine Latino; cloo; CNN en Espanol; CNN International; Cooking Channel; C-SPAN 3; Current; Discovery Channel HD; Discovery en Espanol; Discovery Fit & Health; Discovery Health Channel; Discovery Kids Channel; Disney Channel; Disney Channel HD; DIY Network; Encore (multiplexed); ESPN 2 HD; ESPN Classic Sports; ESPN Deportes; ESPN HD; ESPN U; ESPNews; Eternal Word TV Network; Exercise TV; Food Network; Food Network HD; Fox Business Channel; Fox College Sports Atlantic; Fox College Sports Central; Fox College Sports Pacific; Fox Deportes; Fox Movie Channel; Fox Reality Channel; Fox Soccer; FSN HD; Fuel TV; Fuse; G4; Great American Country; GSN; HD Theater; HDNet; HDNet Movies; HGTV; HGTV HD; History Channel en Espanol; History Channel HD; History Channel International; ID Investigation Discovery; Independent Film Channel; INSP; Jewelry Television; La Familia Network; Lifetime Real Women; LOGO; Military Channel; MTV Hits; mun2 television; Music Choice; National Geographic Channel HD Network; National Geographic Channel On Demand; NBA TV; NHL Network; NickToons TV; Ohio News Network; Outdoor Channel; Ovation; Oxygen On Demand; Palladia; Planet Green; Product Information Network; Science; SoapNet; Speed; Style Network; Sundance Channel; TBS in HD; TeenNick; Tennis Channel; The Weather Channel; The Word Network; Toon Disney; Tr3s; Turner Network TV HD; TV One; Universal HD; Versus HD; VH1 Classic; Video Rola.
Fee: $4.95 monthly (Latino or Sports Plus), $10.40 monthly (Movies or Variety), $14.60 monthly (Premier Digital).
Digital Pay Service 1
Pay Units: N.A.
Programming (via satellite): Cinemax (multiplexed); Cinemax On Demand; Encore; HBO (multiplexed); HBO HD; HBO Latino; HBO On Demand; Showtime (multiplexed); Showtime HD; Showtime On Demand; Starz (multiplexed); Starz On Demand; The Movie Channel (multiplexed); The Movie Channel On Demand.
Fee: $11.95 monthly (HBO, Cinemax, Showtime/TMC or Starz/Encore).
Video-On-Demand: Yes
Pay-Per-View
iN DEMAND (delivered digitally); Playboy TV (delivered digitally); Sports PPV (delivered digitally).
Internet Service
Operational: Yes.
Fee: $44.95 monthly.
Telephone Service
Digital: Operational
Fee: $44.95 monthly
Miles of plant included in Columbus
President: Rhonda Fraas. Vice President & General Manager: Brad Wakely. Vice President, Engineering: Randy Hall. Vice President, Marketing: Mark Psigoda. Technical Operations Director: John Ellingson. Government Affairs Director: Brian Young. Government Affairs Manager: Patrick McCauley.
Ownership: Time Warner Cable (MSO).

TOLEDO—Buckeye Cable System Inc, 5566 Southwyck Blvd, Toledo, OH 43614-1536. Phones: 419-724-9802; 419-724-9800. Fax: 419-724-7074. E-mail: askus@cablesystem.com. Web Site: http://www.buckeyecablesystem.com. Also serves Erie Twp. (portions), Lambertville, Lost Peninsula, Ottawa Lake, Riga Twp. (portions), Temperance, Whiteford & Whiteford Twp., MI; Harbor View, Holland, Maumee, Middleton Twp., Monclova Twp. (Lucas County), Northwood, Oregon, Ottawa Hills, Perrysburg Twp., Rossford, Sylvania, Sylvania Twp. (Lucas County), Waterville & Waterville Twp. (Lucas County), OH. ICA: OH0004. **Note:** This system is an overbuild.
TV Market Ranking: 52 (Erie Twp. (portions), Harbor View, Holland, Lambertville, Lost Peninsula, Maumee, Middleton Twp., Monclova Twp. (Lucas County), Northwood, Oregon, Ottawa Hills, Ottawa Lake, Perrysburg, Perrysburg Twp., Riga Twp. (portions), Rossford, Sylvania, Sylvania Twp. (Lucas County), Temperence, TOLEDO, Waterville, Waterville Twp. (Lucas County), Whiteford, Whiteford Twp.). Franchise award date: May 17, 1965. Franchise expiration date: July 31, 2017. Began: March 15, 1966.
Channel capacity: N.A. Channels available but not in use: N.A.
Basic Service
Subscribers: 128,000.
Programming (received off-air): WBGU-TV (PBS) Bowling Green; WCWG (CW) Lexington; WDIV-TV (NBC) Detroit; WGTE-TV (PBS) Toledo; WJBK (FOX) Detroit; WKBD-TV (CW) Detroit; WLMB (IND) Toledo; WMNT-CA (MNT) Toledo; WNWO-TV (NBC) Toledo; WTOL (CBS) Toledo; WTVG (ABC) Toledo; WUPW (FOX) Toledo; WXYZ-TV (ABC) Detroit.
Programming (via satellite): C-SPAN; C-SPAN 2; Eternal Word TV Network; Shop at Home; The Learning Channel.
Fee: $13.00 installation; $11.65 monthly; $2.02 converter.
Expanded Basic Service 1
Subscribers: 122,880.
Programming (via satellite): A&E Networks; ABC Family Channel; AMC; Animal Planet; BET Networks; Black Family Channel; Bravo; Cartoon Network; CNBC; CNN; Comedy Central; Discovery Channel; Disney Channel; E! Entertainment Television; Encore; ESPN; ESPN 2; ESPN Classic Sports; Fox News Channel; Fox Sports Net Detroit; Fox Sports Net Ohio; Fox Sports World; FX; Golf Channel; Hallmark Channel; Headline News; HGTV; History Channel; History Channel International; Lifetime; MTV; National Geographic Channel; Nickelodeon; QVC; ShopNBC; Spike TV; Syfy; TBS Superstation; Telemundo; The Weather Channel; Travel Channel; Turner Network TV; TV Land; USA Network; VH1; WGN America.
Fee: $28.34 monthly.
Digital Basic Service
Subscribers: 36,694.
Programming (via satellite): AmericanLife TV Network; BBC America; Bio; Bloomberg Television; Boomerang; Discovery Digital Networks; DIY Network; DMX Music; Food Network; Fox Sports World; FSN Digital Atlantic; FSN Digital Central; FSN Digital Pacific; G4; Great American Country; GSN; History Channel International; MSNBC; Speed; Style Network; Trinity Broadcasting Network; Turner Classic Movies; Versus; WE tv.
Fee: $6.95 monthly.
Pay Service 1
Pay Units: N.A. Included in Digital Pay Service 1
Programming (via satellite): HBO (multiplexed).
Fee: $5.00 installation; $12.95 monthly.
Pay Service 2
Pay Units: N.A. Included in Digital Pay Service 2
Programming (via satellite): Showtime (multiplexed).
Fee: $5.00 installation; $10.50 monthly.
Pay Service 3
Pay Units: N.A. Included in Digital Pay Service 3
Programming (via satellite): The Movie Channel (multiplexed).
Fee: $5.00 installation; $10.50 monthly.
Pay Service 4
Pay Units: N.A. Included in Digital Pay Service 4
Programming (via satellite): Cinemax (multiplexed).
Fee: $9.95 monthly.
Digital Pay Service 1
Pay Units: 21,500.
Programming (via satellite): HBO (multiplexed).
Fee: $12.95 monthly.
Digital Pay Service 2
Pay Units: 14,799.
Programming (via satellite): Showtime (multiplexed).
Fee: $12.95 monthly.
Digital Pay Service 3
Pay Units: 13,294.
Programming (via satellite): Flix; The Movie Channel (multiplexed).
Fee: $12.95 monthly.
Digital Pay Service 4
Pay Units: 11,635.
Programming (via satellite): Cinemax (multiplexed).
Fee: $9.95 monthly.
Digital Pay Service 5
Pay Units: 6,007.
Programming (via satellite): Encore (multiplexed); Starz (multiplexed).
Fee: $12.95 monthly.
Digital Pay Service 6
Pay Units: 410.
Programming (via satellite): Playboy TV.
Digital Pay Service 7
Pay Units: N.A.
Programming (via satellite): ART America.
Fee: $12.95 monthly.
Video-On-Demand: Yes
Pay-Per-View
Addressable homes: 28,750.
ESPN Now (delivered digitally); Hot Choice (delivered digitally); iN DEMAND (delivered digitally); NBA League Pass (delivered digitally); Playboy TV (delivered digitally); Fresh (delivered digitally).
Internet Service
Operational: Yes.
Subscribers: 28,750.
Broadband Service: In-house.
Fee: $19.00 installation; $29.99 monthly.
Telephone Service
Digital: Operational
Fee: $13.75 monthly
Miles of Plant: 2,721.0 (coaxial); 2,214.0 (fiber optic).
President & General Manager: W. H. Carstensen. Vice President & Marketing Director: Florence Buchanan. Government Affairs Director: Tom Dawson. Chief Technician: Joseph Jensen. Customer Service Manager: Bonnie Ash.
Ownership: Block Communications Inc. (MSO).

TOLEDO—Formerly served by American Telecasting/WanTV. No longer in operation. ICA: OH0392.

TORONTO—Jefferson County Cable Inc., 116 S 4th St, Toronto, OH 43964-1368. Phone: 740-537-2214. Fax: 740-537-2802. Also serves Costonia, Empire, Pleasant Hill (Jefferson County), Pottery Addition, Smithfield, Stratton & Taylortown. ICA: OH0371.
TV Market Ranking: 10,90 (Costonia, Empire, Pleasant Hill (Jefferson County), Pottery Addition, Taylortown, TORONTO); 90 (Smithfield, Stratton). Franchise award date: N.A. Franchise expiration date: N.A. Began: December 1, 1984.
Channel capacity: 36 (not 2-way capable). Channels available but not in use: N.A.
Basic Service
Subscribers: 2,857.
Programming (received off-air): KDKA-TV (CBS) Pittsburgh; WKBN-TV (CBS) Youngstown; WPGH-TV (FOX) Pittsburgh; WPXI (IND, NBC) Pittsburgh; WQED (PBS)

Pittsburgh; WTAE-TV (ABC) Pittsburgh; WTOV-TV (IND, NBC) Steubenville; WTRF-TV (CBS) Wheeling; WYTV (ABC, MNT) Youngstown.
Programming (via satellite): ESPN.
Fee: $25.00 installation; $9.67 monthly.
Expanded Basic Service 1
Subscribers: 1,582.
Programming (via satellite): ABC Family Channel; CNBC; CNN; Disney Channel; Lifetime; MTV; Nickelodeon; TBS Superstation; Turner Network TV; USA Network; WGN America.
Fee: $31.50 monthly.
Pay Service 1
Pay Units: N.A.
Programming (via satellite): Cinemax; HBO; The Movie Channel.
Fee: $8.60 monthly (Cinemax), $9.60 monthly (TMC), $11.00 monthly (HBO).
Video-On-Demand: Planned
Internet Service
Operational: Yes.
Fee: $25.00 installation; $41.95 monthly.
Telephone Service
None
Miles of Plant: 15.0 (coaxial); None (fiber optic).
Manager: David Bates. Office Manager: Joanne Conner.
Ownership: Jefferson County Cable Inc. (MSO).

TROY—Time Warner Cable. Now served by DAYTON, OH [OH0011]. ICA: OH0069.

UPPER SANDUSKY—Time Warner Cable, 205 Crystal Ave, Findlay, OH 45840. Phones: 419-352-8424; 419-429-7400; 800-425-2225. Fax: 419-429-7402. Web Site: http://www.timewarnercable.com. Also serves Antrim Twp., Crane Twp. (Wyandot County), Eden Twp. (Wyandot County), Harpster, Marseilles, Nevada & Pitt Twp. ICA: OH0138.
TV Market Ranking: Below 100 (Antrim Twp. (portions), Crane Twp. (Wyandot County) (portions), Eden Twp. (Wyandot County) (portions), Nevada); Outside TV Markets (Antrim Twp. (portions), Crane Twp. (Wyandot County) (portions), Eden Twp. (Wyandot County) (portions), Harpster, Marseilles, Pitt Twp., UPPER SANDUSKY). Franchise award date: January 1, 1967. Franchise expiration date: N.A. Began: September 1, 1967.
Channel capacity: N.A. Channels available but not in use: N.A.
Basic Service
Subscribers: 2,792.
Programming (received off-air): WBGU-TV (PBS) Bowling Green; WBNS-TV (CBS) Columbus; WCMH-TV (NBC) Columbus; WEWS-TV (ABC) Cleveland; WGGN-TV (TBN) Sandusky; WJW (FOX) Cleveland; WLMB (IND) Toledo; WMFD-TV (IND) Mansfield; WNWO-TV (NBC) Toledo; WOSU-TV (PBS) Columbus; WTOL (CBS) Toledo; WTVG (ABC) Toledo; WUPW (FOX) Toledo; 12 FMs.
Programming (via microwave): WUAB (MNT) Lorain.
Programming (via satellite): QVC; TV Guide Network.
Fee: $45.86 installation; $11.37 monthly; $31.81 additional installation.
Expanded Basic Service 1
Subscribers: N.A.
Programming (via satellite): A&E Networks; ABC Family Channel; AMC; Animal Planet; BET Networks; Bravo; Cartoon Network; CNBC; CNN; Comedy Central; Country Music TV; C-SPAN; C-SPAN 2; Discovery Channel; Disney Channel; E! Entertainment Television; ESPN; ESPN 2; ESPN Classic Sports; Eternal Word TV Network; Food Network; Fox News Channel; Fox Sports Net Ohio; FX; Golf Channel; Hallmark Channel; Headline News; HGTV; History Channel; INSP; Lifetime; Lifetime Movie Network; MSNBC; MTV; National Geographic Channel; Nickelodeon; Oxygen; ShopNBC; Spike TV; Syfy; TBS Superstation; The Learning Channel; The Weather Channel; Travel Channel; truTV; Turner Classic Movies; Turner Network TV; TV Land; USA Network; Versus; VH1; WE tv.
Fee: $29.58 monthly.
Digital Basic Service
Subscribers: 838.
Programming (via satellite): AmericanLife TV Network; America's Store; BBC America; Bloomberg Television; CNN International; Cooking Channel; C-SPAN 3; Discovery Fit & Health; DIY Network; DMX Music; ESPNews; Fox Sports World; FSN Digital Atlantic; FSN Digital Central; FSN Digital Pacific; Fuse; G4; GAS; Great American Country; GSN; Lifetime Real Women; MTV2; Nick Jr.; Ohio News Network; Outdoor Channel; Ovation; SoapNet; Sorpresa; Speed; Style Network; Toon Disney; VH1 Classic.
Fee: $9.90 monthly.
Digital Expanded Basic Service
Subscribers: N.A.
Programming (via satellite): Encore Action.
Fee: $8.95 monthly.
Digital Pay Service 1
Pay Units: 1,685.
Programming (via satellite): Cinemax (multiplexed); Flix; HBO (multiplexed); Showtime (multiplexed); Starz (multiplexed); The Movie Channel (multiplexed).
Fee: $12.00 installation; $10.95 monthly (Cinemax, HBO, Showtime, Starz or Flix & TMC).
Video-On-Demand: Yes
Pay-Per-View
Addressable homes: 838.
iN DEMAND (delivered digitally); Fresh (delivered digitally); Sports PPV (delivered digitally).
Internet Service
Operational: Yes.
Subscribers: 503.
Broadband Service: AOL for Broadband, BigSpeed, EarthLink, Road Runner, WCOIL Express.
Fee: $69.95 installation; $44.95 monthly.
Telephone Service
Digital: Operational
Fee: $44.95 monthly
Miles of Plant: 44.0 (coaxial); 7.0 (fiber optic).
President: Rhonda Fraas. Public Affairs Director: Brian Young. Senior Engineering Director: Larry Bryan. Technical Operations Director: James Garhard.
Ownership: Time Warner Cable (MSO).

URBANA—Champaign Telephone Co. Formerly [OH0443]. This cable system has converted to IPTV, 126 Scioto St, Urbana, OH 43078. Phones: 937-653-2227; 937-653-4000. Fax: 937-652-1952. E-mail: customerservice@ctcommunications.com. Web Site: http://www.ctcn.net. ICA: OH5029.
TV Market Ranking: 41 (URBANA).
Channel capacity: N.A. Channels available but not in use: N.A.
Internet Service
Operational: Yes, Both DSL & dial-up.

Telephone Service
Digital: Operational
President & Chief Executive Officer: Mike Conrad. Sales & Marketing Director: Brian Strunk. Chief Technician: John Ridder.

URBANA—Champaign Telephone Co. This cable system has converted to IPTV. See Urbana, OH [OH5029]. ICA: OH0443.

URBANA—Time Warner Cable. Now served by DAYTON, OH [OH0011]. ICA: OH0094.

VAN WERT—Time Warner Cable, 205 Crystal Ave, Findlay, OH 45840. Phone: 614-481-5000 (Columbus office). Fax: 419-429-7402. Web Site: http://www.timewarnercable.com/midohio. Also serves Crane Twp. (Paulding County), Hoaglin Twp. (Van Wert County), Liberty Twp. (Van Wert County), Ohio City, Pleasant Twp. (Van Wert County) & Ridge Twp. (Van Wert County). ICA: OH0104.
TV Market Ranking: 82 (Ohio City, VAN WERT); Below 100 (Crane Twp. (Paulding County), Hoaglin Twp. (Van Wert County), Liberty Twp. (Van Wert County), Pleasant Twp. (Van Wert County), Ridge Twp. (Van Wert County)). Franchise award date: N.A. Franchise expiration date: N.A. Began: October 1, 1974.
Channel capacity: N.A. Channels available but not in use: N.A.
Basic Service
Subscribers: 3,706.
Programming (received off-air): WANE-TV (CBS) Fort Wayne; WBDT (CW) Springfield; WBGU-TV (PBS) Bowling Green; WFFT-TV (IND) Fort Wayne; WFWA (PBS) Fort Wayne; WHIO-TV (CBS) Dayton; WINM (IND) Angola; WISE-TV (FOX, MNT, NBC) Fort Wayne; WLIO (CW, NBC) Lima; WOHL-CD (FOX) Lima; WPTA (ABC, CW) Fort Wayne; WPTD (PBS) Dayton; WTLW (IND) Lima.
Programming (via satellite): ABC Family Channel; QVC; TBS Superstation; TV Guide Network; WGN America.
Fee: $29.95 installation; $12.00 monthly; $14.95 additional installation.
Expanded Basic Service 1
Subscribers: 3,679.
Programming (via satellite): A&E Networks; AMC; Animal Planet; BET Networks; Bravo; Cartoon Network; CNBC; CNN; Comedy Central; Country Music TV; C-SPAN; C-SPAN 2; Discovery Channel; Disney Channel; E! Entertainment Television; ESPN; ESPN 2; Eternal Word TV Network; Fox News Channel; Fox Sports Net Detroit; Fox Sports Net Ohio; FX; Great American Country; Hallmark Channel; Headline News; HGTV; History Channel; Lifetime; MSNBC; MTV; Nickelodeon; Ohio News Network; Oxygen; Product Information Network; ShopNBC; Spike TV; Syfy; Telemundo; The Learning Channel; The Weather Channel; Travel Channel; Trinity Broadcasting Network; truTV; Turner Network TV; TV Land; USA Network; VH1.
Fee: $40.76 monthly.
Digital Basic Service
Subscribers: 755.
Programming (via satellite): AmericanLife TV Network; BBC America; Bio; Black Family Channel; Bloomberg Television; Discovery Fit & Health; DIY Network; ESPN Classic Sports; ESPNews; Fox Sports World; Fuse; G4; Golf Channel; GSN; Halogen Network; History Channel International; Independent Film Channel; Music Choice; National Geographic Channel; Outdoor Channel; SoapNet; Speed; Toon Disney; Turner Classic Movies; Versus; WE tv.
Fee: $5.00 monthly (each tier).
Digital Expanded Basic Service
Subscribers: N.A.
Programming (via satellite): Fox Movie Channel; FSN Digital Atlantic; FSN Digital Central; FSN Digital Pacific; GAS; MTV Networks Digital Suite; Nick Jr.; Nick Too; Style Network.
Fee: $5.00 monthly.
Digital Pay Service 1
Pay Units: N.A.
Programming (via satellite): ART America; Canales N; CCTV-4; Cinemax (multiplexed); Encore (multiplexed); Filipino Channel; Flix; HBO (multiplexed); RAI International; Showtime (multiplexed); Starz (multiplexed); Sundance Channel; The Movie Channel (multiplexed); TV Asia; TV Japan; TV5, La Television International; Zee TV USA; Zhong Tian Channel.
Fee: $11.95 monthly (Zhong Tian, TFC, ART, or SBTN), $14.95 monthly (TV Asia, TV5, RAI, MBC, or RTN), $15.00 monthly (HBO, Cinemax, Showtime/TMC, or Starz), $24.95 monthly (TV Japan).
Video-On-Demand: No
Pay-Per-View
Addressable homes: 646.
HITS PPV (delivered digitally); Hot Choice (delivered digitally); Playboy TV (delivered digitally); Fresh (delivered digitally); Shorteez (delivered digitally); Urban American Television Network (delivered digitally).
Internet Service
Operational: Yes.
Subscribers: 409.
Broadband Service: Road Runner.
Fee: $44.95 monthly.
Telephone Service
Digital: Operational
Fee: $44.95 monthly
Miles of Plant: 115.0 (coaxial); None (fiber optic).
President: Rhonda Fraas. Vice President & General Manager: Brad Wakely. Vice President, Marketing: Randy Hall.; Mark Psigoda. Technical Operations Director: John Ellingson. Government Affairs Director: Brian Young. Government Affairs Manager: Patrick McCauley.
Ownership: Time Warner Cable (MSO).

VANDALIA—Time Warner Cable. Now served by DAYTON, OH [OH0011]. ICA: OH0434.

VERNON—S. Bryer Cable TV Corp., PO Box 226, Kinsman, OH 44428. Phone: 330-876-0294. Fax: 330-876-0294. Also serves Andover Twp. (portions), Pymatuning State Park, Vernon Twp. (Trumbull County) & Williamsfield. ICA: OH0246.

TV Market Ranking: 79 (Andover Twp. (portions), Pymatuning State Park, VERNON, Vernon Twp. (Trumbull County), Williamsfield). Franchise award date: July 13, 1989. Franchise expiration date: N.A. Began: July 1, 1990.

Channel capacity: 62 (not 2-way capable). Channels available but not in use: N.A.

Basic Service

Subscribers: 266.

Programming (received off-air): WBNX-TV (CW) Akron; WEWS-TV (ABC) Cleveland; WFMJ-TV (CW, NBC) Youngstown; WJW (FOX) Cleveland; WKBN-TV (CBS) Youngstown; WKYC (NBC) Cleveland; WOIO (CBS) Shaker Heights; WUAB (MNT) Lorain; WVIZ (PBS) Cleveland; WYTV (ABC, MNT) Youngstown.

Programming (via satellite): RFD-TV; TBS Superstation.

Fee: $19.95 monthly; $1.95 converter.

Expanded Basic Service 1

Subscribers: N.A.

Programming (received off-air): WYFX-LP Youngstown.

Programming (via satellite): A&E Networks; ABC Family Channel; AMC; Animal Planet; CNN; Comedy Central; Cooking Channel; Country Music TV; C-SPAN; Discovery Channel; Disney Channel; ESPN; ESPN 2; Food Network; Fox News Channel; Fox Sports Net Ohio; Great American Country; Hallmark Channel; Hallmark Movie Channel; Headline News; HGTV; History Channel; INSP; Lifetime; Lifetime Movie Network; MTV; National Geographic Channel; Nickelodeon; QVC; Speed; Spike TV; Syfy; The Learning Channel; The Weather Channel; Travel Channel; truTV; Turner Classic Movies; Turner Network TV; TV Land; USA Network; VH1.

Fee: $17.00 monthly.

Pay Service 1

Pay Units: 53.

Programming (via satellite): Cinemax.

Fee: $11.00 monthly.

Pay Service 2

Pay Units: 71.

Programming (via satellite): HBO.

Fee: $11.00 monthly.

Pay Service 3

Pay Units: 56.

Programming (via satellite): Showtime; The Movie Channel.

Fee: $11.00 monthly (each).

Video-On-Demand: No

Internet Service

Operational: No.

Telephone Service

Digital: Planned

Miles of Plant: 45.0 (coaxial); None (fiber optic).

Manager & Chief Technician: Scott Bryer. Customer Service Manager: Cathy Hyde.

Ownership: SBC-Tele (MSO).

VERSAILLES—Time Warner Cable, 310 Jefferson Ave, Defiance, OH 43512. Phones: 614-481-5000 (Columbus office); 419-784-1992. Fax: 419-782-2640. Web Site: http://www.timewarnercable.com. Also serves Loramie Twp., North Star, Osgood, Russia, Wabash & Yorkshire. ICA: OH0190.

TV Market Ranking: 41 (Loramie Twp., Russia); Below 100 (Osgood, VERSAILLES); Outside TV Markets (North Star, Wabash Twp., Yorkshire). Franchise award date: N.A. Franchise expiration date: N.A. Began: October 1, 1975.

Channel capacity: N.A. Channels available but not in use: N.A.

Basic Service

Subscribers: 1,421.

Programming (received off-air): WANE-TV (CBS) Fort Wayne; WBDT (CW) Springfield; WBGU-TV (PBS) Bowling Green; WBNS-TV (CBS) Columbus; WDTN (NBC) Dayton; WFFT-TV (IND) Fort Wayne; WHIO-TV (CBS) Dayton; WISE-TV (FOX, MNT, NBC) Fort Wayne; WKEF (ABC) Dayton; WKOI-TV (TBN) Richmond; WLIO (CW, NBC) Lima; WPTA (ABC, CW) Fort Wayne; WPTD (PBS) Dayton; WRGT-TV (FOX, MNT) Dayton; WTLW (IND) Lima; allband FM.

Programming (via satellite): ABC Family Channel; QVC; TBS Superstation; WGN America.

Fee: $31.90 installation; $11.59 monthly.

Expanded Basic Service 1

Subscribers: N.A.

Programming (via satellite): A&E Networks; AMC; Animal Planet; BET Networks; Bravo; Cartoon Network; CNBC; CNN; Country Music TV; C-SPAN; C-SPAN 2; Discovery Channel; Disney Channel; E! Entertainment Television; ESPN; ESPN 2; Eternal Word TV Network; Food Network; Fox News Channel; Fox Sports Net Detroit; Fox Sports Net Ohio; FX; Great American Country; Hallmark Channel; Headline News; HGTV; History Channel; Lifetime; MSNBC; MTV; Nickelodeon; Ohio News Network; Oxygen; Product Information Network; ShopNBC; Telemundo; The Learning Channel; The Weather Channel; Travel Channel; Trinity Broadcasting Network; truTV; Turner Network TV; TV Guide Network; TV Land; USA Network; VH1.

Digital Basic Service

Subscribers: 280.

Programming (via satellite): AmericanLife TV Network; BBC America; Bio; Black Family Channel; Bloomberg Television; Discovery Fit & Health; DIY Network; ESPN Classic Sports; ESPNews; Fox Sports World; Fuse; G4; Golf Channel; GSN; Halogen Network; History Channel International; Independent Film Channel; Music Choice; Outdoor Channel; SoapNet; Toon Disney; truTV; Turner Classic Movies; Versus; WE tv.

Digital Expanded Basic Service

Subscribers: N.A.

Programming (via satellite): Canales N; Fox Movie Channel; FSN Digital Atlantic; FSN Digital Central; GAS; MTV Networks Digital Suite; Nick Jr.; NickToons TV; Sundance Channel.

Digital Pay Service 1

Pay Units: N.A.

Programming (via satellite): ART America; CCTV-4; Cinemax (multiplexed); Encore (multiplexed); Filipino Channel; HBO (multiplexed); RAI International; Russian Television Network; Showtime (multiplexed); Starz (multiplexed); The Movie Channel (multiplexed); TV Asia; TV Japan; TV5, La Television International; Zee TV USA; Zhong Tian Channel.

Video-On-Demand: No

Pay-Per-View

Addressable homes: 300.

Movies (delivered digitally); Urban American Television Network (delivered digitally); Playboy TV (delivered digitally); Hot Choice (delivered digitally); Fresh (delivered digitally); Shorteez (delivered digitally).

Internet Service

Operational: Yes.

Subscribers: 269.

Broadband Service: Road Runner.

Fee: $42.95 monthly.

Telephone Service

None

Miles of Plant: 58.0 (coaxial); None (fiber optic).

President: Rhonda Fraas. Area Manager: Brad Wakely. Manager: John Ellingson. Customer Service Manager: Cindy Sierra.

Ownership: Time Warner Cable (MSO).

WADSWORTH—Wadsworth Cable TV, 120 Maple St, Wadsworth, OH 44281-1825. Phone: 330-335-2888. Fax: 330-335-2829. E-mail: tvsupport@wadsnet.com. Web Site: http://tv.wadsnet.com. ICA: OH0440. **Note:** This system is an overbuild.

TV Market Ranking: 8 (WADSWORTH).

Channel capacity: 75 (operating 2-way). Channels available but not in use: N.A.

Basic Service

Subscribers: 3,652.

Programming (received off-air): WAOH-LP Akron; WBNX-TV (CW) Akron; WDLI-TV (TBN) Canton; WEWS-TV (ABC) Cleveland; WJW (FOX) Cleveland; WKYC (NBC) Cleveland; WNEO (PBS) Alliance; WOIO (CBS) Shaker Heights; WQHS-DT (UNV) Cleveland; WUAB (MNT) Lorain; WVIZ (PBS) Cleveland; WVPX-TV (ION) Akron.

Programming (via satellite): C-SPAN; C-SPAN 2; Eternal Word TV Network; INSP; QVC; Shop at Home; The Weather Channel; TV Guide Network.

Fee: $12.50 monthly.

Expanded Basic Service 1

Subscribers: 3,204.

Programming (via satellite): A&E Networks; ABC Family Channel; AMC; Animal Planet; Bravo; BTN; Cartoon Network; CNBC; CNN; Comedy Central; Country Music TV; Discovery Channel; Discovery Fit & Health; Disney Channel; E! Entertainment Television; ESPN; ESPN 2; ESPN Classic Sports; Food Network; Fox News Channel; Fox Sports Net Ohio; FX; G4; Golf Channel; Hallmark Channel; Headline News; HGTV; History Channel; Lifetime; MSNBC; MTV; National Geographic Channel; Nickelodeon; Speed; Spike TV; Syfy; TBS Superstation; The Learning Channel; Travel Channel; truTV; Turner Classic Movies; Turner Network TV; TV Land; USA Network; VH1; WE tv; WGN America.

Fee: $23.50 monthly.

Digital Basic Service

Subscribers: N.A.

Programming (via satellite): BBC America; Bio; Cooking Channel; Discovery Channel HD; Discovery Health Channel; DIY Network; DMX Music; ESPN 2 HD; ESPN HD; ESPN U; ESPNews; Fox College Sports Atlantic; Fox College Sports Central; Fox College Sports Pacific; Fox Soccer; HDNet; HDNet Movies; History Channel International; ID Investigation Discovery; Independent Film Channel; Military Channel; MTV Hits; MTV2; National Geographic Channel; Nick Jr.; NickToons TV; Outdoor Channel; Oxygen; Planet Green; Science; SoapNet; Style Network; TeenNick; Toon Disney; Versus; VH1 Classic; VH1 Country; VH1 Soul.

Fee: $6.75 monthly.

Pay Service 1

Pay Units: N.A.

Programming (via satellite): Cinemax; Encore; HBO; Starz.

Fee: $12.75 monthly (Cinemax, HBO or Starz/Encore).

Digital Pay Service 1

Pay Units: N.A.

Programming (via satellite): Cinemax (multiplexed); Encore (multiplexed); Flix; HBO (multiplexed); Showtime (multiplexed); Starz (multiplexed); The Movie Channel (multiplexed).

Fee: $10.75 monthly (HBO, Cinemax, Starz/Encore or Showtime/TMC/Flix).

Pay-Per-View

iN DEMAND (delivered digitally); ESPN Gameplan (delivered digitally).

Internet Service

Operational: Yes.

Subscribers: 2,229.

Broadband Service: WadsNet.com.

Fee: $18.95-$28.95 monthly; $7.00 modem lease.

Telephone Service

None

Ownership: Wadsworth Communications.

WAKEMAN—Now served by CLEVELAND HEIGHTS, OH [OH0006]. ICA: OH0373.

WAPAKONETA—Time Warner Cable, 205 Crystal Ave, Findlay, OH 45840. Phones: 614-481-5000 (Columbus office); 419-429-7474. Fax: 419-429-7402. Web Site: http://www.timewarnercable.com/midohio. Also serves Auglaize County, Duchoquet Twp. (southern portion), Moulton Twp. & Pusheta Twp. ICA: OH0119.

TV Market Ranking: Below 100 (Auglaize County, Duchoquet Twp. (southern portion), Moulton Twp., Pusheta Twp., WAPAKONETA). Franchise award date: N.A. Franchise expiration date: N.A. Began: January 20, 1967.

Channel capacity: N.A. Channels available but not in use: N.A.

Basic Service

Subscribers: 4,457.

Programming (received off-air): WBDT (CW) Springfield; WBGU-TV (PBS) Bowling Green; WBNS-TV (CBS) Columbus; WDTN (NBC) Dayton; WHIO-TV (CBS) Dayton; WKEF (ABC) Dayton; WLIO (CW, NBC) Lima; WLQP-LP Lima; WOHL-CD (FOX) Lima; WPTA (ABC, CW) Fort Wayne; WRGT-TV (FOX, MNT) Dayton; WTLW (IND) Lima; allband FM.

Fee: $45.86 installation; $7.23 monthly; $2.71 converter.

Expanded Basic Service 1

Subscribers: 3,792.

Programming (via satellite): A&E Networks; ABC Family Channel; Animal Planet; Bravo; Cartoon Network; CNBC; CNN; Comedy Central; Country Music TV; C-SPAN; C-SPAN 2; Discovery Channel; Disney Channel; E! Entertainment Television; ESPN; ESPN 2; ESPN Classic Sports; Eternal Word TV Network; Food Network; Fox News Channel; Fox Sports Net Ohio; FX; Golf Channel; Hallmark Channel; Headline News; HGTV; History Channel; ION Television; Lifetime; Lifetime Movie Network; MSNBC; MTV; National Geographic Channel; Nickelodeon; Ohio News Network; Oxygen; QVC; Spike TV; Syfy; TBS Superstation; The Learning Channel; The Weather Channel; Travel Channel; truTV; Turner Classic Movies; Turner Network TV; TV Guide Network; TV Land; USA Network; Versus; VH1; WE tv.

Fee: $20.60 monthly.

Digital Basic Service

Subscribers: 1,337.

Programming (via satellite): AmericanLife TV Network; America's Store; BBC America; Bloomberg Television; CNN International; Cooking Channel; C-SPAN 3; Discovery Fit & Health; DIY Network; DMX Music; ESPNews; Fox Sports World; FSN Digital Atlantic; FSN Digital Central; FSN Dig-

ital Pacific; Fuse; G4; GAS; Great American Country; GSN; Lifetime Real Women; MTV2; Nick Jr.; Outdoor Channel; Ovation; SoapNet; Sorpresa; Speed; Style Network; Toon Disney; VH1 Classic.
Fee: $9.90 monthly.
Digital Pay Service 1
Pay Units: 204.
Programming (via satellite): Cinemax (multiplexed).
Fee: $11.95 monthly.
Digital Pay Service 2
Pay Units: 201.
Programming (via satellite): Encore (multiplexed); Starz (multiplexed).
Fee: $11.95 monthly.
Digital Pay Service 3
Pay Units: 375.
Programming (via satellite): Flix; The Movie Channel (multiplexed).
Fee: $11.95 monthly.
Digital Pay Service 4
Pay Units: 402.
Programming (via satellite): HBO (multiplexed).
Fee: $11.95 monthly.
Digital Pay Service 5
Pay Units: 374.
Programming (via satellite): Showtime.
Fee: $11.95 monthly.
Video-On-Demand: Yes
Pay-Per-View
Addressable homes: 1,337.
iN DEMAND (delivered digitally); Fresh (delivered digitally); Sports PPV (delivered digitally).
Internet Service
Operational: Yes.
Subscribers: 802.
Broadband Service: Road Runner.
Fee: $69.95 installation; $44.95 monthly.
Telephone Service
Digital: Operational
Fee: $44.95 monthly
Miles of Plant: 91.0 (coaxial); None (fiber optic).
President: Rhonda Fraas. Vice President & General Manager: Brad Wakely. Vice President, Engineering: Randy Hall.; Mark Psigoda. Technical Operations Director: John Ellingson. Government Affairs Director: Brian Young.
Ownership: Time Warner Cable (MSO).

WARNER—Zito Media, 611 Vader Hill Rd, Coudersport, PA 16915. Phone: 814-260-9575. Web Site: http://www.zitomedia.com. Also serves Aurelius Twp., Dexter City, Dudley, Elba, Jackson Twp. (Noble County), Lower Salem, Macksburg, Salem Twp. (Washington County) & Whipple. ICA: OH0248.
TV Market Ranking: Below 100 (Aurelius Twp., Dexter City, Dudley, Elba, Jackson Twp. (Noble County), Lower Salem, Macksburg, Salem Twp. (Washington County), WARNER, Whipple). Franchise award date: April 3, 1985. Franchise expiration date: N.A. Began: N.A.
Channel capacity: 31 (not 2-way capable). Channels available but not in use: N.A.
Basic Service
Subscribers: 216.
Programming (received off-air): WCHS-TV (ABC) Charleston; WDTV (CBS) Weston; WHIZ-TV (NBC) Zanesville; WKRN-TV (ABC) Nashville; WOUB-TV (PBS) Athens; WOWK-TV (CBS) Huntington; WSAZ-TV (MNT, NBC) Huntington; WTAP-TV (FOX, MNT, NBC) Parkersburg; WTOV-TV (IND, NBC) Steubenville; WTRF-TV (CBS) Wheeling.
Programming (via satellite): ABC Family Channel; AMC; Animal Planet; CNN; Discovery Channel; Disney Channel; ESPN; Great American Country; Lifetime; Nickelodeon; Spike TV; TBS Superstation; Trinity Broadcasting Network; Turner Network TV; USA Network; VH1; WGN America.
Fee: $61.25 installation; $36.95 monthly; $1.24 converter; $17.50 additional installation.
Pay Service 1
Pay Units: 72.
Programming (via satellite): Cinemax; HBO; Showtime; The Movie Channel.
Fee: $17.50 installation; $7.95 monthly (Cinemax), $11.95 monthly (Showtime or TMC), $11.99 monthly (HBO).
Video-On-Demand: No
Internet Service
Operational: No.
Telephone Service
None
Miles of Plant: 29.0 (coaxial); None (fiber optic).
Public Relations Manager: Mark Laver.
Ownership: Zito Media (MSO).

WARREN—Time Warner Cable, 530 S Main St, Ste 1751, Akron, OH 44311-1090. Phones: 330-633-9203; 330-369-7107. Fax: 330-633-7970. Web Site: http://www.timewarnercable.com/northeastohio. Also serves Bazetta Twp., Braceville Twp. (Trumbull County), Bristol Twp., Champion Twp. (Trumbull County), Cortland, Farmington Twp., Fowler Twp., Garrettsville, Girard, Howland Twp. (Trumbull County), Hubbard, Hubbard Twp. (Trumbull County), Johnston Twp., Leavittsburg, Liberty Twp. (Trumbull County), Lordstown, Mecca Twp., Nelson Twp., Newton Falls, Niles, North Jackson, Portage County (portions), Southington Twp., Trumbull County (portions), Vienna Twp., Warren Twp. (Trumbull County), Weathersfield Twp. (Trumbull County), West Farmington & Windham. ICA: OH0013.
TV Market Ranking: 79 (Bazetta Twp., Bristol Twp., Champion Twp. (Trumbull County), Cortland, Farmington Twp., Fowler Twp., Girard, Howland Twp. (Trumbull County), Hubbard, Hubbard Twp. (Trumbull County), Johnston Twp., Liberty Twp. (Trumbull County), Niles, North Jackson, Portage County (portions), Trumbull County (portions), Vienna Twp., WARREN, Weathersfield Twp. (Trumbull County), West Farmington); 79,8 (Warren Twp. (Trumbull County)); 8 (Braceville Twp. (Trumbull County), Garrettsville, Leavittsburg, Lordstown, Mecca Twp., Nelson Twp., Newton Falls, Southington Twp., Windham). Franchise award date: N.A. Franchise expiration date: N.A. Began: January 1, 1974.
Channel capacity: N.A. Channels available but not in use: N.A.
Basic Service
Subscribers: 220,000 Includes Ashtabula, Craig Beach, Salem, Salineville, Scio, Struthers, Youngstown, Corry PA, Erie PA, Franklin PA, Greenville PA, & Sharon PA.
Programming (received off-air): WEWS-TV (ABC) Cleveland; WFMJ-TV (CW, NBC) Youngstown; WJW (FOX) Cleveland; WKBN-TV (CBS) Youngstown; WKYC (NBC) Cleveland; WNEO (PBS) Alliance; WOIO (CBS) Shaker Heights; WUAB (MNT) Lorain; WYTV (ABC, MNT) Youngstown; 4 FMs.
Programming (via satellite): Discovery Channel; Ecumenical TV Channel; QVC; Sneak Prevue; TBS Superstation; truTV.
Fee: $44.95 installation; $13.35 monthly; $3.50 converter; $9.95 additional installation.

Expanded Basic Service 1
Subscribers: 41,032.
Programming (via satellite): A&E Networks; ABC Family Channel; AMC; Animal Planet; BET Networks; Cartoon Network; CNBC; CNN; Country Music TV; C-SPAN; C-SPAN 2; Disney Channel; E! Entertainment Television; ESPN; ESPN 2; Fox News Channel; Fox Sports Net Ohio; FX; Hallmark Channel; Headline News; HGTV; ION Television; Lifetime; MoviePlex; MSNBC; MTV; Nickelodeon; Ohio News Network; Root Sports Pittsburgh; Spike TV; The Learning Channel; The Weather Channel; Turner Network TV; TV Guide Network; USA Network.
Fee: $13.95 installation; $42.13 monthly.
Digital Basic Service
Subscribers: N.A.
Programming (via satellite): BBC America; Bravo; Discovery Digital Networks; ESPN Classic Sports; Fox Sports World; Golf Channel; GSN; History Channel; Independent Film Channel; Speed; Syfy; Turner Classic Movies; Versus; WE tv.
Fee: $12.49 monthly.
Digital Pay Service 1
Pay Units: N.A.
Programming (via satellite): Cinemax (multiplexed); DMX Music; HBO (multiplexed); Showtime; Starz; The Movie Channel.
Fee: $12.00 monthly (each).
Video-On-Demand: Yes
Pay-Per-View
iN DEMAND (delivered digitally); Fresh (delivered digitally).
Internet Service
Operational: Yes. Began: August 1, 2001.
Broadband Service: EarthLink, Road Runner.
Fee: $99.00 installation; $45.95 monthly.
Telephone Service
Digital: Operational
Fee: $44.95 monthly
Miles of Plant: 1,172.0 (coaxial); 176.0 (fiber optic).
President: Stephen Fry. Area Vice President: Rick Whaley. Vice President, Engineering: Al Constanzi. Vice President, Marketing: Patrick Burke. Vice President, Sales: Woody Woodward. Vice President, Public Affairs: William Jasso. Area Manager: Daryl Morrison. Government & Media Relations Director: Chris Thomas.
Ownership: Time Warner Cable (MSO).

WARREN TWP. (Trumbull County)—Northeast Cable TV, PO Box 4177, Youngstown, OH 44515-0177. Phone: 330-793-7434. Fax: 330-793-7434. ICA: OH0380.
TV Market Ranking: 79 (WARREN TWP.). Franchise award date: N.A. Franchise expiration date: N.A. Began: May 1, 1991.
Channel capacity: N.A. Channels available but not in use: N.A.
Basic Service
Subscribers: N.A.
Programming (received off-air): WBNX-TV (CW) Akron; WDLI-TV (TBN) Canton; WEAO (PBS) Akron; WEWS-TV (ABC) Cleveland; WFMJ-TV (CW, NBC) Youngstown; WJW (FOX) Cleveland; WKBN-TV (CBS) Youngstown; WKYC (NBC) Cleveland; WOIO (CBS) Shaker Heights; WRLM (IND) Canton; WUAB (MNT) Lorain; WVIZ (PBS) Cleveland; WVPX-TV (ION) Akron; WYFX-LP Youngstown; WYTV (ABC, MNT) Youngstown.
Programming (via satellite): A&E Networks; ABC Family Channel; AMC; Catholic Television Network; CNN; Discovery Channel; ESPN; Fox Sports Net Ohio; History Channel; Lifetime; Spike TV; Syfy; TBS Superstation; The Weather Channel; Turner Network TV; USA Network; WGN America.
Programming (via translator): WPCB-TV (IND) Greensburg.
Fee: $54.95 installation; $32.95 monthly.
Pay Service 1
Pay Units: N.A.
Programming (via satellite): HBO.
Fee: $9.95 monthly.
Internet Service
Operational: No.
Telephone Service
None
Miles of Plant: 11.0 (coaxial); None (fiber optic).
Manager: Al Pezzenti.
Ownership: Northeast Cable TV (MSO).

WASHINGTON COURT HOUSE—Time Warner Cable, 1266 Dublin Rd, Columbus, OH 43215-1008. Phone: 614-481-5000. Fax: 614-481-5052. Web Site: http://www.timewarnercable.com/midohio. Also serves Bloomingburg, Greenfield, Jasper Twp. (Fayette County), Jefferson Twp. (Fayette County), Jeffersonville, Milledgeville, Octa, Paint Twp. (Fayette County), Paint Twp. (Highland County), Rainsboro, Richland Twp. (Clinton County) & Sabina. ICA: OH0070.
TV Market Ranking: 27 (Bloomingburg, Greenfield, Paint Twp. (Fayette County), Paint Twp. (Highland County), Rainsboro, WASHINGTON COURT HOUSE); 27,41 (Jasper Twp. (Fayette County) (portions), Richland Twp. (Clinton County) (portions)); 41 (Jefferson Twp. (Fayette County), Jeffersonville, Milledgeville, Octa, Sabina). Franchise award date: N.A. Franchise expiration date: N.A. Began: December 15, 1968.
Channel capacity: 80 (operating 2-way). Channels available but not in use: N.A.
Basic Service
Subscribers: 7,690.
Programming (received off-air): WBNS-TV (CBS) Columbus; WCMH-TV (NBC) Columbus; WDTN (NBC) Dayton; WHIO-TV (CBS) Dayton; WOSU-TV (PBS) Columbus; WPTD (PBS) Dayton; WSYX (ABC, MNT) Columbus; WTTE (FOX) Columbus; WWHO (CW) Chillicothe; allband FM.
Programming (via satellite): C-SPAN; INSP; QVC; TBS Superstation; TV Guide Network; VH1; WGN America.
Fee: $29.95 installation; $11.02 monthly.
Expanded Basic Service 1
Subscribers: 7,142.
Programming (via satellite): A&E Networks; ABC Family Channel; AMC; Animal Planet; Cartoon Network; CNN; Comedy Central; Country Music TV; Discovery

Channel; Disney Channel; E! Entertainment Television; ESPN; ESPN 2; Fox News Channel; Fox Sports Net Ohio; FX; Great American Country; Hallmark Channel; Headline News; HGTV; History Channel; Lifetime; MSNBC; MTV; Nickelodeon; Ohio News Network; Spike TV; Syfy; The Learning Channel; The Weather Channel; Toon Disney; Travel Channel; Turner Network TV; TV Land; USA Network.
Fee: $41.48 monthly.

Digital Basic Service
Subscribers: 1,025.
Programming (via satellite): BBC America; Bio; Bloomberg Television; Discovery Digital Networks; DIY Network; ESPN Classic Sports; ESPNews; Fox Movie Channel; Fox Sports World; Fuse; G4; Golf Channel; GSN; Halogen Network; History Channel International; Music Choice; Outdoor Channel; SoapNet; Speed; Trinity Broadcasting Network; Turner Classic Movies; Versus; WE tv.
Fee: $12.49 monthly.

Digital Expanded Basic Service
Subscribers: N.A.
Programming (via satellite): Independent Film Channel; National Geographic Channel; Nick Jr.; NickToons TV; Style Network; Sundance Channel; VH1 Classic; VH1 Country.

Digital Pay Service 1
Pay Units: N.A.
Programming (via satellite): Cinemax (multiplexed); Encore (multiplexed); Flix; HBO (multiplexed); Showtime (multiplexed); Starz (multiplexed); The Movie Channel (multiplexed).
Fee: $12.00 monthly (each).

Video-On-Demand: No

Pay-Per-View
Addressable homes: 1,025.
HITS PPV (delivered digitally); Playboy TV (delivered digitally); Fresh (delivered digitally).

Internet Service
Operational: Yes.
Broadband Service: Road Runner.
Fee: $44.95 monthly.

Telephone Service
None

Miles of Plant: 226.0 (coaxial); 9.0 (fiber optic).
President: Rhonda Fraas. Vice President & General Manager: David Kreiman. Vice President, Engineering: Randy Hall. Vice President, Marketing: Mark Psigoda. Vice President, Government & Public Affairs: Mary Jo Gree. Technical Operations Director: Jim Cavender. Government Affairs Director: Steve Cuckler.
Ownership: Time Warner Cable (MSO).

WATERVILLE—Time Warner Cable, 205 Crystal Ave, Findlay, OH 45840. Phone: 614-481-5000 (Columbus office). Fax: 419-429-7402. Web Site: http://www.timewarnercable.com/midohio. Also serves Grand Rapids, Haskins, Lemoyne, Luckey, Middleton Twp. (Wood County), Monclova Twp., Northwood, Perrysburg, Spencer Twp. (Lucas County), Stony Ridge, Tontogany, Troy Twp., Walbridge & Whitehouse. ICA: OH0072.
TV Market Ranking: 52 (Grand Rapids, Haskins, Lemoyne, Luckey, Middleton Twp. (Wood County), Monclova Twp., Perrysburg, Spencer Twp. (Lucas County), Stony Ridge, Tontogany, Troy Twp., Walbridge, WATERVILLE, Whitehouse). Franchise award date: N.A. Franchise expiration date: July 2, 2015. Began: January 1, 1983.
Channel capacity: N.A. Channels available but not in use: N.A.

Basic Service
Subscribers: 10,391.
Programming (received off-air): WBGU-TV (PBS) Bowling Green; WGTE-TV (PBS) Toledo; WKBD-TV (CW) Detroit; WLMB (IND) Toledo; WMNT-CA (MNT) Toledo; WNWO-TV (NBC) Toledo; WTOL (CBS) Toledo; WTVG (ABC) Toledo; WUPW (FOX) Toledo.
Programming (via satellite): ABC Family Channel; C-SPAN; C-SPAN 2; ION Television; QVC; Spike TV; The Weather Channel; Turner Network TV; TV Guide Network; WGN America.
Fee: $42.50 installation; $9.21 monthly.

Expanded Basic Service 1
Subscribers: N.A.
Programming (via satellite): A&E Networks; AMC; Animal Planet; BET Networks; Bravo; Cartoon Network; CNBC; CNN; Comedy Central; Country Music TV; Discovery Channel; Disney Channel; E! Entertainment Television; ESPN; ESPN 2; Eternal Word TV Network; Food Network; Fox News Channel; Fox Sports Net Detroit; Fox Sports Net Ohio; FX; Great American Country; Hallmark Channel; Headline News; HGTV; History Channel; Lifetime; MSNBC; MTV; Nickelodeon; Oxygen; Product Information Network; ShopNBC; Syfy; TBS Superstation; The Learning Channel; Travel Channel; Trinity Broadcasting Network; truTV; TV Land; Univision Studios; USA Network; VH1.
Fee: $19.28 monthly.

Digital Basic Service
Subscribers: 4,280.
Programming (via satellite): AmericanLife TV Network; ART America; BBC America; Bio; Black Family Channel; Bloomberg Television; CCTV-4; Discovery Digital Networks; DIY Network; ESPN Classic Sports; ESPNews; Filipino Channel; Fox Sports World; Fuse; G4; GAS; Golf Channel; GSN; Halogen Network; History Channel International; Independent Film Channel; MTV Networks Digital Suite; Music Choice; National Geographic Channel; Nick Jr.; Nick Too; Outdoor Channel; RAI USA; Russian Television Network; SoapNet; Speed; Style Network; Toon Disney; Turner Classic Movies; TV Asia; TV Japan; TV5 USA; Versus; WE tv.
Fee: $8.45 monthly.

Digital Expanded Basic Service
Subscribers: N.A.
Programming (via satellite): Sundance Channel.
Fee: $4.95 monthly.

Digital Pay Service 1
Pay Units: 2,804.
Programming (via satellite): Canales N; Cinemax (multiplexed); Encore (multiplexed); HBO (multiplexed); Showtime (multiplexed); Starz (multiplexed); The Movie Channel (multiplexed).
Fee: $6.95 monthly (Canales N), $11.95 monthly (Cinemax, HBO, Showtime, Starz, TMC or Encore).

Video-On-Demand: No

Pay-Per-View
Addressable homes: 3,787.
iN DEMAND (delivered digitally); sports (delivered digitally).

Internet Service
Operational: Yes.
Subscribers: 2,995.
Broadband Service: Road Runner.
Fee: $44.95 monthly.

Telephone Service
Digital: Operational
Fee: $44.95 monthly

Miles of Plant: 267.0 (coaxial); None (fiber optic).
President: Rhonda Fraas. Vice President & General Manager: Brad Wakely. Vice President, Engineering: Randy Hall. Vice President, Marketing: Mark Psigoda. Technical Operations Director: John Ellingson. Government Affairs Director: Brian Young. Government Affairs Manager: Patrick McCauley.
Ownership: Time Warner Cable (MSO).

WAUSEON—Time Warner Cable, 205 Crystal Ave, Findlay, OH 45840. Phone: 614-481-5000 (Columbus office). Fax: 419-429-7402. Web Site: http://www.timewarnercable.com/midohio. Also serves Morenci, MI; Amboy Twp., Delta, Fayette, Fulton Twp., Harding Twp., Lyons, Metamora, Neapolis, Pike Twp., Providence Twp., Royalton, Swan Creek Twp., Swanton & York Twp. (Fulton County), OH. ICA: OH0106.
TV Market Ranking: 52 (Amboy Twp., Delta, Fulton Twp., Harding Twp., Lyons, Metamora, Neapolis, Pike Twp. (Fulton County), Providence, Royalton, Swan Creek Twp., Swanton, WAUSEON, York Twp. (Fulton County)); Below 100 (Fayette); Outside TV Markets (Morenci). Franchise award date: N.A. Franchise expiration date: N.A. Began: December 31, 1979.
Channel capacity: N.A. Channels available but not in use: N.A.

Basic Service
Subscribers: 6,109.
Programming (received off-air): WANE-TV (CBS) Fort Wayne; WBGU-TV (PBS) Bowling Green; WDFM-LP (IND) Defiance; WGTE-TV (PBS) Toledo; WKBD-TV (CW) Detroit; WLMB (IND) Toledo; WNWO-TV (NBC) Toledo; WPTA (ABC, CW) Fort Wayne; WTOL (CBS) Toledo; WTVG (ABC) Toledo; WUPW (FOX) Toledo; allband FM.
Programming (via satellite): C-SPAN; C-SPAN 2; ION Television; QVC; Spike TV; The Weather Channel; Turner Network TV; WGN America.
Fee: $42.50 installation; $11.87 monthly.

Expanded Basic Service 1
Subscribers: N.A.
Programming (via satellite): A&E Networks; ABC Family Channel; AMC; Animal Planet; BET Networks; Bravo; Cartoon Network; CNBC; CNN; Comedy Central; Country Music TV; Discovery Channel; Disney Channel; E! Entertainment Television; ESPN; ESPN 2; Eternal Word TV Network; Food Network; Fox News Channel; Fox Sports Net Detroit; Fox Sports Net Ohio; FX; Hallmark Channel; Headline News; HGTV; History Channel; Lifetime; MSNBC; MTV; Nick Jr.; Nickelodeon; Oxygen; ShopNBC; SportsTime Ohio; Syfy; TBS Superstation; Telemundo; The Learning Channel; Travel Channel; truTV; TV Guide Network; TV Land; Univision Studios; USA Network; VH1.
Fee: $19.90 monthly.

Digital Basic Service
Subscribers: 1,376.
Programming (via satellite): AmericanLife TV Network; BBC America; Bio; Bloomberg Television; CMT Pure Country; CNBC; Current; Discovery Fit & Health; Discovery Health Channel; Discovery Home Channel; Discovery Kids Channel; Discovery Times Channel; DIY Network; ESPN Classic Sports; ESPN U; ESPNews; Flix; Fox Business Channel; Fox Movie Channel; Fox Reality Channel; Fox Soccer; Fuel TV; Fuse; G4; GMC; Golf Channel; GSN; History Channel International; Independent Film Channel; INSP; Lifetime Movie Network; LOGO; Military Channel; MTV Hits; MTV Jams; MTV2; National Geographic Channel; Nick Too; NickToons TV; Ohio News Network; Outdoor Channel; Science; SoapNet; Speed; Style Network; Sundance Channel; TeenNick; Toon Disney; Tr3s; Trinity Broadcasting Network; Turner Classic Movies; TVG Network; Versus; VH1 Classic; VH1 Soul; WE tv.
Fee: $11.95 monthly.

Digital Pay Service 1
Pay Units: N.A.
Programming (via satellite): Cinemax (multiplexed); Encore (multiplexed); HBO (multiplexed); Showtime (multiplexed); Starz (multiplexed); The Movie Channel (multiplexed).
Fee: $11.95 monthly (Cinemax, HBO, Flix/Showtime/TMC, or Starz/Encore).

Video-On-Demand: No

Pay-Per-View
iN DEMAND (delivered digitally); Playboy TV (delivered digitally); Club Jenna (delivered digitally); Fresh (delivered digitally).

Internet Service
Operational: Yes. Began: November 4, 2004.
Subscribers: 545.
Broadband Service: Road Runner.
Fee: $44.95 monthly.

Telephone Service
Analog: Not Operational
Digital: Operational
Fee: $44.95 monthly

Miles of Plant: 150.0 (coaxial); None (fiber optic).
President: Rhonda Fraas. Vice President & General Manager: Brad Wakely. Vice President, Engineering: Randy Hall. Vice President, Marketing: Mark Psigoda. Technical Operations Director: John Ellingson. Government Affairs Director: Brian Young. Government Affairs Manager: Patrick McCauley.
Ownership: Time Warner Cable (MSO).

WAVERLY—Formerly served by Adelphia Communications. Now served by CHILLICOTHE, OH [OH0033]. ICA: OH0139.

WAYNESFIELD—Time Warner Cable, 205 Crystal Ave, Findlay, OH 45840. Phones: 614-481-5000 (Columbus office); 419-331-3333. Fax: 419-429-7474. Web Site: http://www.timewarnercable.com/midohio. Also serves Auglaize County (portions), Clay Twp. (Auglaize County), Lakeview (Logan County), New Hampshire, Roundhead Twp., St. Johns, Stokes Twp. (Logan County) & Uniopolis. ICA: OH0146.
TV Market Ranking: Below 100 (Auglaize County (portions), Clay Twp. (Auglaize County), Lakeview (Logan County), New Hampshire, Roundhead Twp., St. Johns, Stokes Twp. (Logan County), Uniopolis, WAYNESFIELD). Franchise award date: April 3, 1984. Franchise expiration date: N.A. Began: N.A.
Channel capacity: N.A. Channels available but not in use: N.A.

Basic Service
Subscribers: 1,806.
Programming (received off-air): WBDT (CW) Springfield; WBGU-TV (PBS) Bowling Green; WBNS-TV (CBS) Columbus; WDTN (NBC) Dayton; WHIO-TV (CBS) Dayton; WKEF (ABC) Dayton; WLIO (CW, NBC) Lima; WLQP-LP Lima; WOHL-CD (FOX) Lima; WRGT-TV (FOX, MNT) Day-

ton; WSYX (ABC, MNT) Columbus; WTLW (IND) Lima.
Fee: $45.86 installation; $8.94 monthly.

Expanded Basic Service 1
Subscribers: N.A.
Programming (via satellite): A&E Networks; ABC Family Channel; AMC; Animal Planet; Bravo; Cartoon Network; CNBC; CNN; Comedy Central; Country Music TV; C-SPAN; C-SPAN 2; Discovery Channel; Disney Channel; E! Entertainment Television; Encore Action; ESPN; ESPN 2; ESPN Classic Sports; Eternal Word TV Network; Food Network; Fox News Channel; Fox Sports Net Ohio; FX; Golf Channel; Hallmark Channel; Headline News; HGTV; History Channel; Lifetime; Lifetime Movie Network; MSNBC; MTV; National Geographic Channel; Nickelodeon; Oxygen; QVC; ShopNBC; Spike TV; Syfy; TBS Superstation; The Learning Channel; The Weather Channel; Travel Channel; truTV; Turner Classic Movies; Turner Network TV; TV Guide Network; TV Land; USA Network; Versus; VH1; WE tv.
Fee: $32.01 monthly.

Digital Basic Service
Subscribers: 542.
Programming (via satellite): AmericanLife TV Network; America's Store; BBC America; Bloomberg Television; CNN International; Cooking Channel; C-SPAN 3; Discovery Fit & Health; DIY Network; DMX Music; ESPNews; Fox Sports World; FSN Digital Atlantic; FSN Digital Central; FSN Digital Pacific; Fuse; G4; GAS; Great American Country; GSN; Lifetime Real Women; MTV2; Nick Jr.; Ohio News Network; Outdoor Channel; Ovation; SoapNet; Sorpresa; Speed; Style Network; Toon Disney; VH1 Classic.
Fee: $9.90 monthly.

Digital Pay Service 1
Pay Units: 80.
Programming (via satellite): Cinemax (multiplexed); Encore (multiplexed); Flix; HBO (multiplexed); Showtime (multiplexed); Starz (multiplexed); The Movie Channel (multiplexed).
Fee: $18.00 installation; $11.95 monthly (Cinemax, HBO, Showtime, Starz/ Encore, or Flix/TMC).

Video-On-Demand: Yes

Pay-Per-View
Addressable homes: 542.
iN DEMAND (delivered digitally); Fresh (delivered digitally); Sports PPV (delivered digitally).

Internet Service
Operational: Yes.
Subscribers: 325.
Broadband Service: Road Runner.
Fee: $69.95 installation; $44.95 monthly.

Telephone Service
Digital: Operational
Fee: $44.95 monthly

Miles of Plant: 59.0 (coaxial); None (fiber optic).
President: Rhonda Fraas. Vice President & General Manager: Brad Wakely. Vice President, Engineering: Randy Hall. Vice President, Marketing: Mark Psigoda. Technical Operations Director: John Ellingdson. Government Affairs Director: Brian Young. Government Affairs Manager: Patrick McCauley.
Ownership: Time Warner Cable (MSO).

WEATHERSFIELD TWP.—Northeast Cable TV, PO Box 4177, Youngstown, OH 44515-0177. Phone: 330-793-7434. Fax: 330-793-7434. ICA: OH0446.
TV Market Ranking: 79 (WEATHERSFIELD TWP.).
Channel capacity: N.A. Channels available but not in use: N.A.

Basic Service
Subscribers: N.A.
Programming (received off-air): WBNX-TV (CW) Akron; WEWS-TV (ABC) Cleveland; WFMJ-TV (CW, NBC) Youngstown; WJW (FOX) Cleveland; WKBN-TV (CBS) Youngstown; WNEO (PBS) Alliance; WOIO (CBS) Shaker Heights; WUAB (MNT) Lorain; WYTV (ABC, MNT) Youngstown.
Programming (via satellite): ABC Family Channel; Discovery Channel; ESPN; TBS Superstation; Turner Network TV; USA Network; WGN America.
Fee: $54.95 installation; $32.95 monthly.

Pay Service 1
Pay Units: N.A.
Programming (via satellite): HBO.
Fee: $9.95 monthly.

Internet Service
Operational: No.

Telephone Service
None

Manager: Albert Pezzenti.
Ownership: Northeast Cable TV (MSO).

WELLINGTON—GLW Broadband, 993 Commerce Dr, PO Box 67, Grafton, OH 44044. Phones: 440-816-0033; 440-926-3230. Fax: 440-926-2889. E-mail: support@glwb.net. Web Site: http://www.glwb.net. Also serves Brighton Twp., Brownhelm Twp., Camden Twp., Eaton Twp. (Lorain County), Grafton, Grafton Twp., Henrietta Twp., Kipton (village), Lagrange, Lagrange (village), Lagrange Twp., Penfield Twp., Pittsfield Twp., Rochester (village), Rochester Twp., Wellington (village) & Wellington Twp. ICA: OH0189.
TV Market Ranking: 8 (Brighton Twp., Brownhelm Twp., Camden Twp., Eaton Twp. (Lorain County), Grafton, Grafton Twp., Henrietta Twp., Kipton (village), Lagrange, Lagrange (village), Lagrange Twp., Penfield Twp., Pittsfield Twp., Rochester (village), Rochester Twp., WELLINGTON, Wellington (village), Wellington Twp.). Franchise award date: N.A. Franchise expiration date: N.A. Began: November 1, 1983.
Channel capacity: 52 (operating 2-way). Channels available but not in use: N.A.

Basic Service
Subscribers: 3,085.
Programming (received off-air): WBNX-TV (CW) Akron; WEWS-TV (ABC) Cleveland; WJW (FOX) Cleveland; WKYC (NBC) Cleveland; WNEO (PBS) Alliance; WOIO (CBS) Shaker Heights; WQHS-DT (UNV) Cleveland; WRLM (IND) Canton; WUAB (MNT) Lorain; WVIZ (PBS) Cleveland; WVPX-TV (ION) Akron; allband FM.
Programming (via satellite): A&E Networks; AMC; BTN; Country Music TV; History Channel; Lifetime; Nickelodeon; TBS Superstation; The Learning Channel; The Weather Channel; TV Guide Network; VH1.
Fee: $30.00 installation; $13.00 monthly; $2.83 converter.

Expanded Basic Service 1
Subscribers: N.A.
Programming (via satellite): ABC Family Channel; Animal Planet; Cartoon Network; CNBC; CNN; Comedy Central; C-SPAN; Discovery Channel; Discovery Health Channel; Disney Channel; E! Entertainment Television; ESPN; ESPN 2; ESPN Classic Sports; Food Network; Fox News Channel; Fox Sports Net Ohio; FX; Hallmark Channel; Headline News; HGTV; INSP; MSNBC; MTV; National Geographic Channel; NFL Network; Ohio News Network; QVC; SoapNet; Speed; Spike TV; SportsTime Ohio; Syfy; Toon Disney; Travel Channel; truTV; Turner Network TV; TV Land; USA Network; WGN America.
Fee: $29.55 monthly.

Digital Basic Service
Subscribers: N.A.
Programming (via satellite): AmericanLife TV Network; BBC America; Bio; Bloomberg Television; Bravo; Discovery Fit & Health; Discovery Health Channel; Discovery Home Channel; Discovery Kids Channel; Discovery Times Channel; DMX Music; ESPN; ESPN 2; ESPN Classic Sports; ESPNews; Fox Movie Channel; Fox Soccer; Fuse; G4; GAS; Golf Channel; GSN; Halogen Network; HGTV; History Channel International; Independent Film Channel; Lifetime Movie Network; Military Channel; MTV2; Nick Jr.; Outdoor Channel; Science; Speed; Syfy; Trinity Broadcasting Network; Trio; Turner Classic Movies; Versus; VH1 Classic; VH1 Country; WE tv.
Fee: $14.30 monthly.

Pay Service 1
Pay Units: N.A.
Programming (via satellite): HBO.
Fee: $12.90 monthly.

Digital Pay Service 1
Pay Units: N.A.
Programming (via satellite): Cinemax (multiplexed); Encore (multiplexed); HBO (multiplexed); Showtime (multiplexed); The Movie Channel (multiplexed).
Fee: $4.95 monthly (Encore), $12.90 monthly (HBO, Cinemax or Showtime/ TMC).

Video-On-Demand: Planned

Internet Service
Operational: Yes.
Broadband Service: GLW Broadband.
Fee: $19.99 monthly.

Telephone Service
Digital: Operational

Miles of Plant: 23.0 (coaxial); None (fiber optic). Additional miles planned: 3.0 (coaxial).
Manager: Joel Large.
Ownership: GLW Broadband Inc.

WEST LAFAYETTE—Time Warner Cable. Now served by NEWARK, OH [OH0019]. ICA: OH0374.

WEST LIBERTY (village)—Champaign Telephone Co. Formerly served by Urbana, OH [OH0443]. This cable system has converted to IPTV, 126 Scioto St, Urbana, OH 43078. Fax: 937-652-1952. E-mail: customerservice@ctcommunications.com. Web Site: http://www.ctcn.net. ICA: OH5030.
TV Market Ranking: Below 100 (WEST LIBERTY (village)).
Channel capacity: N.A. Channels available but not in use: N.A.

Internet Service
Operational: Yes, Both DSL & dial-up.

Telephone Service
Digital: Operational

WEST MANSFIELD—Time Warner Cable. Now served by COLUMBUS, OH [OH0002]. ICA: OH0236.

WEST UNION—Time Warner Cable. Now served by CINCINNATI, OH [OH0001]. ICA: OH0152.

WILLARD—Time Warner Cable, 530 S Main St, Ste 1751, Akron, OH 44311-1090. Phone: 330-633-9203. Fax: 330-633-7970. Web Site: http://www.timewarnercable.com/northeastohio. Also serves Cass Twp., Fairfield Twp. (Huron County), Greenfield Twp. (Huron County), Greenwich, New Haven, North Fairfield, Norwich Twp. (Huron County), Plymouth, Ripley Twp. (portions) & Shiloh. ICA: OH0108.
TV Market Ranking: 8 (Fairfield Twp. (Huron County), Greenwich, North Fairfield); Below 100 (Cass Twp., Greenfield Twp. (Huron County), New Haven, Norwich Twp. (Huron County), Plymouth, Ripley Twp. (portions), Shiloh, WILLARD). Franchise award date: N.A. Franchise expiration date: N.A. Began: December 13, 1968.
Channel capacity: N.A. Channels available but not in use: N.A.

Basic Service
Subscribers: N.A. Included in Mansfield
Programming (received off-air): WBNX-TV (CW) Akron; WEWS-TV (ABC) Cleveland; WGGN-TV (TBN) Sandusky; WGTE-TV (PBS) Toledo; WJW (FOX) Cleveland; WKYC (NBC) Cleveland; WMFD-TV (IND) Mansfield; WNWO-TV (NBC) Toledo; WOIO (CBS) Shaker Heights; WQHS-DT (UNV) Cleveland; WTOL (CBS) Toledo; WTVG (ABC) Toledo; WUAB (MNT) Lorain; WVIZ (PBS) Cleveland; WVPX-TV (ION) Akron; 12 FMs.
Programming (via satellite): A&E Networks; ABC Family Channel; CNBC; CNN; C-SPAN; C-SPAN 2; Discovery Channel; Disney Channel; ESPN; Eternal Word TV Network; Lifetime; MTV; Nickelodeon; Spike TV; TBS Superstation; The Learning Channel; The Weather Channel; Turner Network TV; USA Network; VH1.
Fee: $44.95 installation; $13.05 monthly; $2.75 converter.

Expanded Basic Service 1
Subscribers: N.A.
Programming (via satellite): AMC; Animal Planet; BET Networks; Bravo; Cartoon Network; Comedy Central; Discovery Fit & Health; Discovery Health Channel; E! Entertainment Television; ESPN 2; ESPN Classic Sports; Food Network; Fox News Channel; Fox Sports Net Ohio; FX; Golf Channel; Great American Country; GSN; Hallmark Channel; Headline News; HGTV; History Channel; INSP; Lifetime Movie Network; MSNBC; Oxygen; QVC; ShopNBC; SoapNet; Syfy; Travel Channel; truTV; Turner Classic Movies; TV Land; Versus; WE tv.
Fee: $41.95 monthly.

Digital Basic Service
Subscribers: N.A.
Programming (via satellite): A&E HD; AmericanLife TV Network; America's Store; ART America; BBC America;

Bio; Bloomberg Television; Boomerang; Canales N; CBS Sports Network; CNN HD; CNN International; Cooking Channel; Country Music TV; C-SPAN 3; Daystar TV Network; Deutsche Welle TV; DIY Network; ESPN HD; ESPNews; Fox College Sports Atlantic; Fox College Sports Central; Fox College Sports Pacific; Fox HD; Fox Movie Channel; Fox Soccer; Fuel TV; Fuse; G4; GAS; HD Theater; HDNet; HDNet Movies; Headline News; History Channel International; Independent Film Channel; INHD; INHD2; Jewelry Television; Lifetime; Lifetime Real Women; MTV Networks Digital Suite; Music Choice; National Geographic Channel; NBA TV; Nick Jr.; NickToons TV; Ohio News Network; Outdoor Channel; RAI International; Speed; TBS in HD; Tennis Channel; The Word Network; Toon Disney; Trio; Turner Network TV HD; TV Asia; TVG Network; USA Network HD; Zee TV USA.

Fee: $13.00 monthly.

Digital Pay Service 1

Pay Units: 3,393.

Programming (via satellite): Cinemax (multiplexed); HBO (multiplexed); HBO HD; Showtime (multiplexed); Showtime HD; Starz (multiplexed); The Movie Channel (multiplexed).

Fee: $12.00 monthly (each).

Video-On-Demand: Yes

Pay-Per-View

iN DEMAND (delivered digitally); Playboy TV (delivered digitally); NHL Center Ice (delivered digitally); MLB Extra Innings (delivered digitally); Spice Live (delivered digitally); Ten Clips (delivered digitally); Pleasure (delivered digitally); NASCAR In Car (delivered digitally); NBA League Pass (delivered digitally); MLS Direct Kick (delivered digitally); ESPN (delivered digitally).

Internet Service

Operational: Yes. Began: December 31, 2000.

Broadband Service: EarthLink, Road Runner.

Fee: $99.00 installation; $44.95 monthly.

Telephone Service

Digital: Operational

Fee: $44.95 monthly

Miles of Plant: 158.0 (coaxial); 6.0 (fiber optic).

President: Stephen Fry. Area Vice President: Scott Miller. Vice President, Engineering: Al Costanzi. Vice President, Marketing: Patrick Burke. Vice President, Sales: Woody Woodward. Vice President, Public Affairs: William Jasso. Area Manager: Carol Jagger. Government & Media Relations Director: Chris Thomas.

Ownership: Time Warner Cable (MSO).

WILLOWS MOBILE HOME PARK—Time Warner Cable. Now served by AKRON, OH [OH0005]. ICA: OH0302.

WILMINGTON—Time Warner Cable. Now served by CINCINNATI, OH [OH0001]. ICA: OH0112.

WINESBURG—Formerly served by National Cable Inc. No longer in operation. ICA: OH0375.

WOODSFIELD—City of Woodsfield, 221 S Main St, Woodsfield, OH 43793. Phone: 740-472-1865. Also serves Lewisville. ICA: OH0206.

TV Market Ranking: 90 (Lewisville, WOODSFIELD). Franchise award date: N.A. Franchise expiration date: N.A. Began: October 1, 1966.

Channel capacity: 43 (operating 2-way). Channels available but not in use: N.A.

Basic Service

Subscribers: 1,096.

Programming (received off-air): KDKA-TV (CBS) Pittsburgh; WHIZ-TV (NBC) Zanesville; WOUC-TV (PBS) Cambridge; WTAE-TV (ABC) Pittsburgh; WTOV-TV (IND, NBC) Steubenville; WTRF-TV (CBS) Wheeling; allband FM.

Programming (via satellite): CNN; Discovery Channel; Fox Sports Net; TBS Superstation; The Learning Channel; The Weather Channel; Trinity Broadcasting Network; Turner Network TV; USA Network; WABC-TV (ABC) New York.

Fee: $61.25 installation; $47.99 monthly; $1.24 converter; $17.50 additional installation.

Expanded Basic Service 1

Subscribers: 817.

Programming (via satellite): A&E Networks; ABC Family Channel; AMC; Cartoon Network; Comedy Central; C-SPAN; Disney Channel; ESPN; ESPN 2; Great American Country; GSN; Headline News; HGTV; History Channel; INSP; Lifetime; MSNBC; MTV; National Geographic Channel; Nickelodeon; SoapNet; Speed; Spike TV; Syfy; Toon Disney; TV Land; Versus; VH1; WE tv.

Fee: $23.00 monthly.

Digital Basic Service

Subscribers: N.A.

Programming (via satellite): BBC America; Bio; Black Family Channel; Bloomberg Television; cloo; Discovery Digital Networks; ESPN Classic Sports; ESPNews; Fox College Sports Atlantic; Fox College Sports Central; Fox College Sports Pacific; Fox Movie Channel; Fox Soccer; Golf Channel; Halogen Network; History Channel International; Independent Film Channel; Lifetime Movie Network; Lime; Military History Channel; Outdoor Channel; Science Television; ShopNBC; Turner Classic Movies.

Fee: $13.95 monthly.

Pay Service 1

Pay Units: 601.

Programming (via satellite): Cinemax; Encore; HBO; Showtime; The Movie Channel.

Fee: $3.99 monthly (Encore), $13.95 monthly (Cinemax), $13.95 monthly (Showtime or TMC), $11.99 monthly (HBO).

Digital Pay Service 1

Pay Units: N.A.

Programming (via satellite): Cinemax (multiplexed); Encore (multiplexed); Flix; HBO (multiplexed); Showtime (multiplexed); Starz (multiplexed); The Movie Channel (multiplexed).

Pay-Per-View

iN DEMAND (delivered digitally); Playboy TV (delivered digitally); Fresh (delivered digitally).

Internet Service

Operational: Yes. Began: November 1, 2004.

Broadband Service: In-house.

Fee: $20.00 installation; $30.95 monthly.

Telephone Service

None

Miles of Plant: 23.0 (coaxial); None (fiber optic).

General Manager: Sam McPeak. Office Manager: Krystal Boon.

Ownership: City of Woodsfield, OH (MSO).

WOOSTER—Clear Picture Inc., 444 W Milltown Rd, PO Box 917, Wooster, OH 44691-0917. Phone: 330-345-8114. Fax: 330-345-5265. Web Site: http://www.cpiwooster.com. Also serves Apple Creek, Canaan Twp. (Wayne County), Chester Twp. (Wayne County), Clinton Twp. (Wayne County), East Union Twp. (Wayne County), Franklin Twp. (Wayne County), Plain Twp. (Wayne County), Smithville, Sugar Creek Twp. (Wayne County), Wayne County (southeastern portion), Wayne Twp. (Wayne County) & Wooster Twp. (Wayne County). ICA: OH0061.

TV Market Ranking: 8 (Apple Creek, Canaan Twp. (Wayne County), Chester Twp. (Wayne County), Clinton Twp. (Wayne County), East Union Twp. (Wayne County), Franklin Twp. (Wayne County), Plain Twp. (Wayne County), Smithville, Sugar Creek Twp. (Wayne County), Wayne Twp. (Wayne County), WOOSTER, Wooster Twp. (Wayne County)); Below 100 (Wayne County (southeastern portion)). Franchise award date: November 1, 1967. Franchise expiration date: N.A. Began: November 1, 1967.

Channel capacity: 182 (operating 2-way). Channels available but not in use: N.A.

Basic Service

Subscribers: N.A. Included in Massillon

Programming (received off-air): WBNX-TV (CW) Akron; WDLI-TV (TBN) Canton; WEWS-TV (ABC) Cleveland; WJW (FOX) Cleveland; WKYC (NBC) Cleveland; WMFD-TV (IND) Mansfield; WNEO (PBS) Alliance; WOIO (CBS) Shaker Heights; WQHS-DT (UNV) Cleveland; WRLM (IND) Canton; WUAB (MNT) Lorain; WVIZ (PBS) Cleveland; WVPX-TV (ION) Akron.

Programming (via satellite): A&E Networks; ABC Family Channel; AMC; Animal Planet; BET Networks; Boomerang; Bravo; BTN; Cartoon Network; CNBC; CNN; Comedy Central; Country Music TV; C-SPAN; C-SPAN 2; Discovery Channel; Discovery Health Channel; Disney Channel; E! Entertainment Television; ESPN; ESPN 2; ESPN Classic Sports; ESPN U; Eternal Word TV Network; Food Network; Fox News Channel; Fox Sports Net Ohio; FX; Golf Channel; Great American Country; GSN; Hallmark Channel; Headline News; HGTV; History Channel; INSP; ION Life; Lifetime; MLB Network; MSNBC; MTV; National Geographic Channel; Nickelodeon; Oxygen; Qubo; QVC; ReelzChannel; SoapNet; Speed; Spike TV; SportsTime Ohio; Syfy; TBS Superstation; The Learning Channel; The Weather Channel; Travel Channel; truTV; Turner Classic Movies; Turner Network TV; TV Guide Network; TV Land; USA Network; VH1; Weatherscan; WGN America.

Fee: $30.00 installation; $52.75 monthly; $20.00 additional installation.

Digital Basic Service

Subscribers: N.A.

Programming (via satellite): A&E HD; AmericanLife TV Network; BBC America; Bio; Bloomberg Television; Bravo HD; BTN HD; CBS Sports Network; Chiller; CMT Pure Country; CNBC HD+; CNN HD; Cooking Channel; Discovery Fit & Health; Discovery Kids Channel; Disney XD; DIY Network; DMX Music; ESPN 2 HD; ESPN HD; ESPNews; Fox Business Channel; Fox Movie Channel; Fox Soccer; G4; GMC; Halogen Network; HD Theater; HDNet; HDNet Movies; History Channel HD; History Channel International; ID Investigation Discovery; Lifetime Movie Network; MGM HD; Military History Channel; MLB Network; MTV Hits; MTV2; NHL Network; Nick Jr.; NickToons TV; Outdoor Channel; PBS Kids Sprout; Planet Green; Science; SportsTime Ohio; Style Network; Syfy HD; TBS in HD; TeenNick; Tennis Channel; Turner Network TV HD; TV One; Universal HD; USA Network HD; Versus; VH1 Classic; VH1 Soul; WE tv; Weatherscan.

Fee: $7.50 monthly.

Digital Pay Service 1

Pay Units: N.A.

Programming (via satellite): Cinemax (multiplexed); Encore (multiplexed); Flix; HBO (multiplexed); HBO HD; Showtime (multiplexed); Showtime HD; Starz (multiplexed); Sundance Channel; The Movie Channel (multiplexed).

Fee: $10.75 monthly (Cinemax), $11.50 monthly (Starz/Encore), $14.00 monthly (Showtime Pkg.), $14.25 monthly (HBO).

Video-On-Demand: Yes

Pay-Per-View

iN DEMAND (delivered digitally); MLB Extra Innings (delivered digitally); NHL Center Ice (delivered digitally).

Internet Service

Operational: Yes. Began: May 1, 1999.

Broadband Service: Super Net.

Fee: $35.00 installation; $25.00-$40.00 monthly.

Telephone Service

Digital: Operational

Fee: $33.20-$47.95 monthly

Miles of Plant: 528.0 (coaxial); 2.0 (fiber optic). Additional miles planned: 10.0 (coaxial).

General Manager: Keith Chambers. Chief Technician: Kelly Rehm. Customer Service Manager: Susan Bicker.

Ownership: Massillon Cable TV Inc. (MSO).

YELLOW SPRINGS—Time Warner Cable Communications Inc. Now served by DAYTON, OH [OH0011]. ICA: OH0103.

YOUNGSTOWN—Formerly served by Sprint Corp. No longer in operation. ICA: OH0389.

YOUNGSTOWN—Northeast Cable TV, PO Box 4177, Youngstown, OH 44515-0177. Phone: 330-793-7434. Fax: 330-793-7434. Also serves Hubbard Twp. & Warren Twp. ICA: OH0384.

TV Market Ranking: 79 (Hubbard Twp., Warren Twp., YOUNGSTOWN). Franchise award date: N.A. Franchise expiration date: N.A. Began: May 1, 1987.

Channel capacity: N.A. Channels available but not in use: N.A.

Basic Service

Subscribers: N.A.

Programming (received off-air): WBNX-TV (CW) Akron; WEWS-TV (ABC) Cleveland; WFMJ-TV (CW, NBC) Youngstown; WJW (FOX) Cleveland; WKBN-TV (CBS) Youngstown; WNEO (PBS) Alliance; WOIO (CBS) Shaker Heights; WUAB (MNT) Lorain; WYTV (ABC, MNT) Youngstown.

Programming (via satellite): ABC Family Channel; Discovery Channel; ESPN; TBS Superstation; Turner Network TV; USA Network; WGN America.

Fee: $54.95 installation; $32.95 monthly.

Pay Service 1

Pay Units: N.A.

Programming (via satellite): HBO.

Fee: $9.95 monthly.

Internet Service

Operational: No.

Telephone Service

None

Miles of Plant: 20.0 (coaxial); None (fiber optic).

Manager: Albert F. Pezzenti.

Ownership: Northeast Cable TV (MSO).

YOUNGSTOWN—Time Warner Cable, 530 S Main St, Ste 1751, Akron, OH 44311-1090. Phone: 330-633-9203. Fax: 330-633-7970. Web Site: http://www.timewarnercable.com/northeastohio. ICA: OH0017.

TV Market Ranking: 79 (YOUNGSTOWN). Franchise award date: October 18, 1978. Franchise expiration date: June 21, 2008. Began: January 2, 1980.

Channel capacity: N.A. Channels available but not in use: N.A.

Basic Service

Subscribers: N.A. Included in Warren

Programming (received off-air): WEAO (PBS) Akron; WFMJ-TV (CW, NBC) Youngstown; WKBN-TV (CBS) Youngstown; WNEO (PBS) Alliance; WOIO (CBS) Shaker Heights; WUAB (MNT) Lorain; WYFX-LP Youngstown; WYTV (ABC, MNT) Youngstown.

Programming (via satellite): CNBC; Eternal Word TV Network; ShopNBC; TV Guide Network.

Fee: $29.95 installation; $14.18 monthly; $9.99 additional installation.

Expanded Basic Service 1

Subscribers: N.A.

Programming (via satellite): A&E Networks; ABC Family Channel; AMC; Animal Planet; BET Networks; Bravo; Cartoon Network; CNN; Comedy Central; C-SPAN; C-SPAN 2; Discovery Channel; Discovery Fit & Health; Discovery Health Channel; Disney Channel; E! Entertainment Television; ESPN; ESPN 2; ESPN Classic Sports; Food Network; Fox News Channel; Fox Sports Net Ohio; FX; Golf Channel; Great American Country; GSN; Hallmark Channel; Headline News; HGTV; History Channel; Independent Film Channel; INSP; Lifetime; Lifetime Movie Network; MSNBC; MTV; MTV2; Nickelodeon; Oxygen; QVC; ShopNBC; SoapNet; Spike TV; Syfy; TBS Superstation; The Learning Channel; The Weather Channel; Travel Channel; truTV; Turner Classic Movies; Turner Network TV; TV Land; Univision Studios; USA Network; Versus; VH1; WE tv.

Fee: $41.32 monthly.

Digital Basic Service

Subscribers: N.A.

Programming (received off-air): WUAB (MNT) Lorain.

Programming (via satellite): AmericanLife TV Network; America's Store; ART America; BBC America; Bio; Bloomberg Television; Boomerang; Canales N; CBS Sports Network; cloo; CNN International; Cooking Channel; Country Music TV; C-SPAN 3; Current; Daystar TV Network; Deutsche Welle TV; Disney Channel; DIY Network; DMX Music; ESPN; ESPNews; Fox College Sports Atlantic; Fox College Sports Central; Fox College Sports Pacific; Fox Movie Channel; Fox Soccer; Fuel TV; Fuse; G4; GAS; HD Theater; HDNet; HDNet Movies; History Channel International; Independent Film Channel; INHD (multiplexed); Lifetime Real Women; MTV2; National Geographic Channel; NBA TV; Nick Jr.; NickToons TV; Ohio News Network; Outdoor Channel; RAI International; Speed; Style Network; Tennis Channel; The Word Network; Toon Disney; Turner Network TV HD; TV Asia; TVG Network; VH1 Classic; Zee TV USA.

Fee: $12.49 monthly.

Digital Pay Service 1

Pay Units: N.A.

Programming (via satellite): Cinemax (multiplexed); Encore (multiplexed); HBO (multiplexed); Showtime (multiplexed); Starz (multiplexed); The Movie Channel (multiplexed).

Fee: $12.00 monthly (each).

Video-On-Demand: Yes

Pay-Per-View

iN DEMAND.

Internet Service

Operational: Yes.

Broadband Service: EarthLink, Road Runner.

Fee: $99.00 installation; $44.95 monthly.

Telephone Service

Digital: Operational

Fee: $44.95 monthly

Miles of Plant: 348.0 (coaxial); None (fiber optic).

President: Stephen Fry. Area Vice President: Rick Whaley. Vice President, Engineering: Al Costanzi. Vice President, Marketing: Patrick Burke. Vice President, Public Affairs: William Jasso. Area Manager: Daryl Morrison. Government & Media Relations Director: Chris Thomas.

Ownership: Time Warner Cable (MSO).

ZANESVILLE—Time Warner Cable, 1266 Dublin Rd, Columbus, OH 43215-1008. Phone: 614-481-5000. Fax: 614-481-5052. Web Site: http://www.timewarnercable.com/midohio. Also serves Adamsville, Bloom Twp. (Morgan County), Bowling Green Twp. (Licking County), Brownsville, Bushcreek Twp. (Muskingum County), Crooksville, Dresden, Duncan Falls, East Fultonham, Frazeyburg, Fultonham, Gratiot, Hopewell Twp. (Muskingum County), Jacksontown, Licking Twp. (Muskingum County), Morgan County (portions), Mount Sterling (village), Muskingum Twp. (Muskingum County), Nashport, New Concord, Newton Twp. (Muskingum County), Norwich, Perry County (portions), Philo, Rich Hill Twp., Roseville, Sonora, South Zanesville, Trinway, Washington Twp. (Muskingum County), White Cottage & York Twp. (Muskingum County). ICA: OH0037.

TV Market Ranking: 27 (Jacksontown); Below 100 (Adamsville, Bloom Twp. (Morgan County), Bowling Green Twp. (Licking County), Bushcreek Twp. (Muskingum County), Crooksville, Dresden, Duncan Falls, East Fultonham, Frazeyburg, Fultonham, Gratiot, Hopewell Twp. (Muskingum County), Licking Twp. (Muskingum County), Morgan County (portions), Mount Sterling (village), Muskingum Twp. (Muskingum County), Nashport, New Concord, Newton Twp. (Muskingum County),

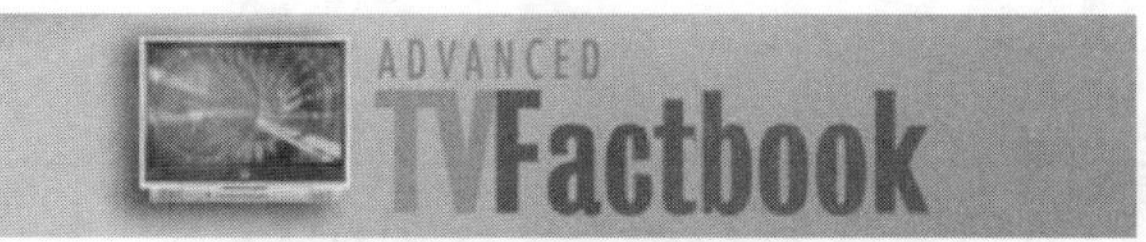

Norwich, Perry County (portions), Philo, Rich Hill Twp., Roseville, Sonora, South Zanesville, Trinway, Washington Twp. (Muskingum County), White Cottage, York Twp. (Morgan County), ZANESVILLE); Outside TV Markets (Brownsville).

Channel capacity: N.A. Channels available but not in use: N.A.

Basic Service

Subscribers: N.A.

Programming (received off-air): WBNS-TV (CBS) Columbus; WCMH-TV (NBC) Columbus; WHIZ-TV (NBC) Zanesville; WOSU-TV (PBS) Columbus; WOUC-TV (PBS) Cambridge; WSFJ-TV (TBN) Newark; WSYX (ABC, MNT) Columbus; WTTE (FOX) Columbus; WUAB (MNT) Lorain; WWHO (CW) Chillicothe.

Programming (via satellite): C-SPAN; C-SPAN 2; CW+; Hallmark Channel; Headline News; History Channel; QVC; Radar Channel; ShopNBC; SoapNet; TBS Superstation; The Learning Channel; TV Guide Network; WGN America.

Expanded Basic Service 1

Subscribers: N.A.

Programming (via satellite): A&E Networks; ABC Family Channel; AMC; Animal Planet; BBC America; BET Networks; Bravo; Cartoon Network; CNBC; CNN; Comedy Central; Country Music TV; Discovery Channel; Discovery Health Channel; Disney Channel; E! Entertainment Television; ESPN; ESPN 2; Food Network; Fox News Channel; Fox Sports Net Ohio; FX; Golf Channel; HGTV; Jewelry Television; Lifetime; Lifetime Movie Network; MSNBC; MTV; MTV2; National Geographic Channel; Nick Jr.; Nickelodeon; Oxygen; Spike TV; SportsTime Ohio; Syfy; The Weather Channel; Travel Channel; truTV; Turner Classic Movies; Turner Network TV; TV Land; Univision Studios; USA Network; Versus; VH1; WE tv.

Digital Basic Service

Subscribers: N.A.

Programming (via satellite): AmericanLife TV Network; BBC America On Demand; Bio; Bloomberg Television; Boomerang; Canal Sur; Cine Latino; cloo; CNN en Espanol; CNN International; College Sports Television; Cooking Channel; C-SPAN 3; Current; Discovery en Espanol; Discovery Fit & Health; Discovery Kids Channel; Disney Channel; DIY Network; Encore; ESPN 2 HD; ESPN Classic Sports; ESPN HD; ESPN U; ESPNews; Eternal Word TV Network; Exercise TV; Food Network; Fox Business Channel; Fox College Sports Atlantic; Fox College Sports Central; Fox College Sports Pacific; Fox Deportes; Fox Movie Channel; Fox Reality Channel; Fox Soccer; FSN HD; Fuel TV; Fuse; G4; Great American Country; GSN; HD Theater; HDNet; HDNet Movies; here! TV; HGTV; History Channel International; Howard TV; ID Investigation Discovery; Independent Film Channel; INSP; Jewelry Television; La Familia Network; Lifetime Real Women; LOGO; Military Channel; Mojo Mix; MTV Hits; mun2 television; Music Choice; National Geographic Channel On Demand; NBA TV; NHL Network; NickToons TV; Ohio News Network; Outdoor Channel; Ovation; Oxygen On Demand; Planet Green; Science; SoapNet; Speed; Speed On Demand; Style Network; Sundance Channel; TBS in HD; TeenNick; Tennis Channel; The Weather Channel; The Word Network; Toon Disney; Tr3s; Turner Network TV HD; TV One; Universal HD; VH1 Classic; VHUNO; Video Rola.

Digital Pay Service 1

Pay Units: N.A.

Programming (via satellite): Cinemax (multiplexed); Cinemax On Demand; Encore; HBO (multiplexed); HBO HD; HBO Latino; HBO On Demand; Showtime (multiplexed); Showtime HD; Showtime On Demand; Starz (multiplexed); Starz On Demand; The Movie Channel (multiplexed); The Movie Channel On Demand.

Video-On-Demand: Yes

Pay-Per-View

iN DEMAND (delivered digitally); iN DEMAND (delivered digitally); NBA League Pass (delivered digitally); MLS Direct Kick (delivered digitally); NHL Center Ice (delivered digitally); MLB Extra Innings (delivered digitally); ESPN Gameplan (delivered digitally).

Internet Service

Operational: Yes.

Broadband Service: Road Runner.

Fee: $44.95 monthly.

Telephone Service

Digital: Operational

President: Rhonda Fraas. Vice President & General Manager: David Kreiman. Vice President, Marketing: Mark Psigoda. Vice President, Engineering: Randy Hall. Vice President, Government & Public Affairs: Mary Jo Green. Technical Operations Manager: David Bowen. Government Affairs Director: Steve Cuckler.

Ownership: Time Warner Cable (MSO).

OKLAHOMA

Total Systems: 230
Total Communities Served: 411
Franchises Not Yet Operating: 0
Applications Pending: 0
Communities with Applications: 0
Number of Basic Subscribers: 724,901
Number of Expanded Basic Subscribers: 457,828
Number of Pay Units: 212,992

Top 100 Markets Represented: Oklahoma City (39); Tulsa (54).

**For a list of cable communities in this section, see the Cable Community Index located in the back of Cable Volume 2.
For explanation of terms used in cable system listings, see p. D-11.**

ACHILLE—CommuniComm Services. Now served by TISHOMINGO, OK [OK0064]. ICA: OK0342.

ADA—Cable One, 1610 Arlington St, Ada, OK 74820-2640. Phone: 580-332-8333. Fax: 580-332-4005. Web Site: http://www.cableone.net. Also serves Byng, Davis, Elmore City, Francis, Pontotoc County, Roff & Sulphur. ICA: OK0018.
TV Market Ranking: Below 100 (ADA, Byng, Davis, Francis, Pontotoc County, Roff, Sulphur); Outside TV Markets (Elmore City). Franchise award date: N.A. Franchise expiration date: N.A. Began: June 1, 1965.
Channel capacity: 52 (operating 2-way). Channels available but not in use: N.A.

Basic Service
Subscribers: 10,000.
Programming (received off-air): KAUT-TV (MNT) Oklahoma City; KETA-TV (PBS) Oklahoma City; KFOR-TV (NBC) Oklahoma City; KOCO-TV (ABC) Oklahoma City; KOKH-TV (FOX) Oklahoma City; KSBI (IND) Oklahoma City; KTEN (ABC, CW, NBC) Ada; KWTV-DT (CBS) Oklahoma City; KXII (CBS, FOX, MNT) Sherman; 10 FMs.
Programming (via satellite): CW+; Trinity Broadcasting Network; TV Guide Network.
Fee: $40.00 installation; $46.00 monthly.

Expanded Basic Service 1
Subscribers: N.A.
Programming (via satellite): A&E Networks; ABC Family Channel; AMC; Animal Planet; BET Networks; Cartoon Network; CNBC; CNN; Country Music TV; C-SPAN; Discovery Channel; Disney Channel; E! Entertainment Television; ESPN; ESPN 2; Food Network; Fox News Channel; Fox Sports Southwest; FX; Headline News; HGTV; History Channel; Lifetime; MSNBC; MTV; Nickelodeon; QVC; Spike TV; Syfy; TBS Superstation; The Learning Channel; The Weather Channel; Travel Channel; Turner Classic Movies; Turner Network TV; TV Land; USA Network; VH1.
Fee: $42.50 monthly.

Digital Basic Service
Subscribers: 3,766.
Programming (via satellite): 3 Angels Broadcasting Network; Bio; Boomerang; BYU Television; Canales N; Discovery Digital Networks; DMX Music; ESPN Classic Sports; ESPNews; FamilyNet; Fox College Sports Atlantic; Fox College Sports Central; Fox College Sports Pacific; Fox HD; Fox Movie Channel; Fox Soccer; Fuel TV; G4; Golf Channel; Great American Country; Hallmark Channel; History Channel International; INSP; National Geographic Channel; Outdoor Channel; SoapNet; Speed; Toon Disney; Trinity Broadcasting Network; truTV; Turner Network TV HD; TVG Network; Universal HD.

Digital Pay Service 1
Pay Units: N.A.
Programming (via satellite): Cinemax (multiplexed); Encore (multiplexed); Flix; HBO (multiplexed); Showtime (multiplexed); Showtime HD; Starz (multiplexed); Sundance Channel; The Movie Channel (multiplexed); The Movie Channel HD.
Fee: $15.00 monthly (each).

Video-On-Demand: No

Pay-Per-View
iN DEMAND (delivered digitally); Pleasure (delivered digitally); Ten Clips (delivered digitally); Ten Blox (delivered digitally); Ten Blue (delivered digitally); ESPN (delivered digitally).

Internet Service
Operational: Yes. Began: April 1, 2000.
Subscribers: 3,437.
Broadband Service: CableONE.net.
Fee: $75.00 installation; $43.00 monthly; $5.00 modem lease.

Telephone Service
Digital: Operational
Fee: $39.95 monthly
Miles of Plant: 266.0 (coaxial); 133.0 (fiber optic).
Manager: Bill W. Dalton. Marketing Manager: David Cobb. Technical Operations Manager: Stanley Barnes. Chief Technician: Darren Flowers.
Ownership: Cable ONE Inc. (MSO).

ADAIR—Allegiance Communications, 707 W Saratoga St, Shawnee, OK 74804. Phones: 405-275-6923; 405-395-1131. Web Site: http://www.allegiance.tv. ICA: OK0219.
TV Market Ranking: Outside TV Markets (ADAIR). Franchise award date: June 1, 1981. Franchise expiration date: N.A. Began: January 1, 1983.
Channel capacity: 35 (not 2-way capable). Channels available but not in use: N.A.

Basic Service
Subscribers: N.A.
Programming (received off-air): KDOR-TV (TBN) Bartlesville; KJRH-TV (NBC) Tulsa; KMYT-TV (MNT) Tulsa; KOED-TV (PBS) Tulsa; KOKI-TV (FOX) Tulsa; KOTV-DT (CBS) Tulsa; KQCW-DT (CW) Muskogee; KRSC-TV (ETV) Claremore; KTPX-TV (ION) Okmulgee; KTUL (ABC) Tulsa; KWHB (IND) Tulsa.
Programming (via satellite): A&E Networks; ABC Family Channel; AMC; CNBC; CNN; Discovery Channel; ESPN; ESPN 2; Lifetime; Nickelodeon; Spike TV; Syfy; TBS Superstation; Turner Network TV; USA Network; WGN America.
Fee: $30.00 installation; $21.95 monthly; $20.00 additional installation.

Pay Service 1
Pay Units: 30.
Programming (via satellite): Cinemax; HBO; Showtime.
Fee: $20.00 installation; $10.95 monthly (Showtime or TMC), $11.95 monthly (HBO).

Video-On-Demand: No

Pay-Per-View
Hot Choice (delivered digitally); Playboy TV (delivered digitally); Fresh (delivered digitally); Shorteez (delivered digitally); iN DEMAND (delivered digitally).

Internet Service
Operational: No.

Telephone Service
None
Miles of Plant: 6.0 (coaxial); None (fiber optic).
Chief Executive Officer: Bill Haggarty. Regional Vice President: Andrew Dearth. Vice President, Marketing: Tracy Bass.
Ownership: Allegiance Communications (MSO).

AGRA—Formerly served by Allegiance Communications. No longer in operation. ICA: OK0260.

ALEX—Southern Plains Cable, PO Box 165, Medicine Park, OK 73557. Phones: 800-218-1856; 580-529-5000. Fax: 580-529-5556. E-mail: office@wichitaonline.net. Web Site: http://www.southernplainscommunications.com. ICA: OK0334.
TV Market Ranking: Below 100 (ALEX). Franchise award date: N.A. Franchise expiration date: N.A. Began: January 1, 1992.
Channel capacity: N.A. Channels available but not in use: N.A.

Basic Service
Subscribers: 26.
Programming (received off-air): KAUT-TV (MNT) Oklahoma City; KETA-TV (PBS) Oklahoma City; KFOR-TV (NBC) Oklahoma City; KOCB (CW) Oklahoma City; KOCO-TV (ABC) Oklahoma City; KOKH-TV (FOX) Oklahoma City; KOPX-TV (ION) Oklahoma City; KTBO-TV (TBN) Oklahoma City; KWTV-DT (CBS) Oklahoma City; Local Cable Weather.
Programming (via satellite): A&E Networks; ABC Family Channel; AMC; Animal Planet; CNN; Country Music TV; Discovery Channel; ESPN; ESPN 2; History Channel; Lifetime; Nickelodeon; PBS Kids Channel; ShopNBC; Spike TV; Syfy; TBS Superstation; The Learning Channel; The Weather Channel; Turner Network TV; TV Land; USA Network; WGN America.
Fee: $45.00 installation; $32.45 monthly.

Pay Service 1
Pay Units: N.A.
Programming (via satellite): Showtime; The Movie Channel.
Fee: $10.00 monthly (each).

Video-On-Demand: No

Internet Service
Operational: Yes.

Telephone Service
Analog: Not Operational
Digital: Planned
Miles of Plant: 6.0 (coaxial); None (fiber optic).
President: Dustin Hilliary.
Ownership: Southern Plains Cable (MSO).

ALINE (town)—Formerly served by Blue Sky Cable LLC. No longer in operation. ICA: OK0387.

ALLEN (town)—Allegiance Communications, 707 W Saratoga St, Shawnee, OK 74804. Phones: 405-275-6923; 405-395-1131. Web Site: http://www.allegiance.tv. ICA: OK0351.
TV Market Ranking: Below 100 (ALLEN (TOWN)). Franchise award date: N.A. Franchise expiration date: N.A. Began: N.A.
Channel capacity: 40 (not 2-way capable). Channels available but not in use: N.A.

Basic Service
Subscribers: 228.
Programming (received off-air): KAUT-TV (MNT) Oklahoma City; KFOR-TV (NBC) Oklahoma City; KOCB (CW) Oklahoma City; KOCO-TV (ABC) Oklahoma City; KOKH-TV (FOX) Oklahoma City; KTEN (ABC, CW, NBC) Ada; KTUL (ABC) Tulsa; KWTV-DT (CBS) Oklahoma City.
Programming (via satellite): A&E Networks; ABC Family Channel; AMC; Animal Planet; CNN; Country Music TV; C-SPAN; Discovery Channel; Disney Channel; ESPN; Fox Sports Southwest; History Channel; Lifetime; Nickelodeon; Spike TV; Syfy; TBS Superstation; The Weather Channel; Trinity Broadcasting Network; Turner Network TV; TV Land; USA Network; WGN America.
Fee: $21.95 monthly.

Digital Basic Service
Subscribers: N.A.
Programming (via satellite): AmericanLife TV Network; BBC America; Black Family Channel; Bloomberg Television; Bravo; Discovery Digital Networks; DMX Music; Encore Action; ESPN 2; ESPN Classic Sports; ESPNews; Fox Movie Channel; Fox Sports World; Fuse; G4; Golf Channel; Great American Country; GSN; Halogen Network; HGTV; Independent Film Channel; Lifetime Movie Network; Outdoor Channel; ShopNBC; Speed; Sundance Channel; The Word Network; Toon Disney; Turner Classic Movies; Versus.

Digital Pay Service 1
Pay Units: N.A.
Programming (via satellite): Cinemax (multiplexed); Encore (multiplexed); HBO (multiplexed); Showtime (multiplexed); Starz (multiplexed); The Movie Channel (multiplexed).

Pay-Per-View
ESPN Now (delivered digitally); Hot Choice (delivered digitally); iN DEMAND (delivered digitally).

Internet Service
Operational: No.
Telephone Service
None
Chief Executive Officer: Bill Haggarty. Regional Vice President: Andrew Dearth. Vice President, Marketing: Tracy Bass.
Ownership: Allegiance Communications (MSO).

ALTUS—Cable One, 618 N Main, Altus, OK 73521. Phone: 580-482-0523. Fax: 580-477-0911. E-mail: robin.graham@cableone.net. Web Site: http://www.cableone.net. Also serves Altus AFB, Frederick & Jackson County. ICA: OK0017.
TV Market Ranking: Outside TV Markets (ALTUS, Altus AFB, Frederick, Jackson County). Franchise award date: July 30, 1956. Franchise expiration date: May 22, 2007. Began: September 1, 1957.
Channel capacity: 64 (operating 2-way). Channels available but not in use: N.A.
Basic Service
Subscribers: 8,080.
Programming (received off-air): KAUZ-TV (CBS, CW) Wichita Falls; KFDX-TV (NBC) Wichita Falls; KFOR-TV (NBC) Oklahoma City; KJTL (FOX) Wichita Falls; KOCB (CW) Oklahoma City; KOCO-TV (ABC) Oklahoma City; KOKH-TV (FOX) Oklahoma City; KSWO-TV (ABC, TMO) Lawton; KWET (PBS) Cheyenne; KWTV-DT (CBS) Oklahoma City.
Programming (via satellite): 24/7 News Channel; A&E Networks; ABC Family Channel; AMC; Animal Planet; BET Networks; Bravo; Cartoon Network; CNBC; CNN; Country Music TV; C-SPAN; C-SPAN 2; Discovery Channel; Disney Channel; DMX Music; E! Entertainment Television; ESPN; ESPN 2; ESPN Classic Sports; Food Network; Fox News Channel; Fox Sports Southwest; FX; Headline News; HGTV; History Channel; INSP; ION Television; Lifetime; MSNBC; MTV; Nickelodeon; QVC; ShopNBC; Spike TV; Syfy; TBS Superstation; Telemundo; The Learning Channel; The Weather Channel; Trinity Broadcasting Network; Turner Classic Movies; Turner Network TV; TV Guide Network; TV Land; Univision Studios; USA Network; VH1; WGN America.
Fee: $35.00 installation; $46.00 monthly; $1.50 converter; $25.00 additional installation.
Digital Basic Service
Subscribers: 2,447.
Programming (via satellite): 3 Angels Broadcasting Network; Bio; Boomerang; BYU Television; Canales N; Discovery Digital Networks; ESPN Classic Sports; ESPNews; FamilyNet; Fox College Sports Atlantic; Fox College Sports Central; Fox College Sports Pacific; Fox Movie Channel; Fox Soccer; Fuel TV; G4; Golf Channel; Great American Country; Hallmark Channel; History Channel International; INSP; National Geographic Channel; Outdoor Channel; SoapNet; Speed; Toon Disney; Trinity Broadcasting Network; truTV; Turner Network TV HD; TVG Network; Universal HD.
Fee: $8.95 monthly.
Digital Pay Service 1
Pay Units: N.A.
Programming (via satellite): Cinemax (multiplexed); Encore (multiplexed); Flix; HBO (multiplexed); Showtime (multiplexed); Showtime HD; Starz (multiplexed); Sundance Channel; The Movie Channel (multiplexed); The Movie Channel HD.
Fee: $15.00 monthly.
Video-On-Demand: No
Pay-Per-View
Addressable homes: 2,991.
Movies (delivered digitally); Pleasure (delivered digitally); Ten Clips (delivered digitally); Ten Blox (delivered digitally); Ten Blue (delivered digitally).
Internet Service
Operational: Yes. Began: January 1, 2003.
Subscribers: 2,300.
Broadband Service: CableONE.net.
Fee: $75.00 installation; $43.00 monthly.
Telephone Service
Digital: Operational
Fee: $39.95 monthly
Miles of Plant: 165.0 (coaxial); 55.0 (fiber optic).
Manager: George Wilburn. Marketing Director: Robin Graham. Technical Operations Manager: Ted Ramsey.
Ownership: Cable ONE Inc. (MSO).

ALVA—Suddenlink Communications, 603 College Ave, Alva, OK 73717. Phones: 580-327-1664; 580-237-7373. Fax: 580-242-4801. Web Site: http://www.suddenlink.com. Also serves Woods County (eastern portion). ICA: OK0063.
TV Market Ranking: Outside TV Markets (ALVA, Woods County (eastern portion)). Franchise award date: N.A. Franchise expiration date: N.A. Began: May 1, 1957.
Channel capacity: 78 (operating 2-way). Channels available but not in use: N.A.
Basic Service
Subscribers: N.A.
Programming (received off-air): KAUT-TV (MNT) Oklahoma City; KETA-TV (PBS) Oklahoma City; KFOR-TV (NBC) Oklahoma City; KOCB (CW) Oklahoma City; KOCO-TV (ABC) Oklahoma City; KOKH-TV (FOX) Oklahoma City; KSBI (IND) Oklahoma City; KTUZ-TV (TMO) Shawnee; KWTV-DT (CBS) Oklahoma City.
Programming (via satellite): A&E Networks; ABC Family Channel; AMC; Animal Planet; Cartoon Network; CNBC; CNN; Comedy Central; Country Music TV; C-SPAN; Discovery Channel; Disney Channel; ESPN; ESPN 2; Food Network; Fox News Channel; Fox Sports Southwest; FX; Hallmark Channel; HGTV; History Channel; Lifetime; MSNBC; MTV; Nickelodeon; Spike TV; Syfy; TBS Superstation; The Learning Channel; The Weather Channel; Travel Channel; Trinity Broadcasting Network; truTV; Turner Network TV; TV Guide Network; TV Land; USA Network; WGN America.
Fee: $37.50 installation; $35.06 monthly; $18.75 additional installation.
Digital Basic Service
Subscribers: N.A.
Programming (via satellite): BBC America; Bloomberg Television; Bravo; CMT Pure Country; Discovery Health Channel; Discovery Home Channel; Discovery Kids Channel; DMX Music; ESPNews; Fox College Sports Atlantic; Fox College Sports Central; Fox College Sports Pacific; Fox Movie Channel; Fox Soccer; Fuse; G4; Golf Channel; Great American Country; GSN; Halogen Network; ID Investigation Discovery; Independent Film Channel; Lifetime Movie Network; Military Channel; MTV Hits; National Geographic Channel; Outdoor Channel; Science Television; ShopNBC; Speed; Sundance Channel; Toon Disney; Turner Classic Movies; Versus.
Digital Pay Service 1
Pay Units: N.A.
Programming (via satellite): Cinemax (multiplexed); Encore (multiplexed); HBO (multiplexed); Showtime (multiplexed); Starz (multiplexed); The Movie Channel.
Pay-Per-View
Addressable homes: 200.
iN DEMAND (delivered digitally); Fresh (delivered digitally); Spice: Xcess (delivered digitally).
Internet Service
Operational: Yes.
Broadband Service: Suddenlink High Speed Internet.
Fee: $45.95 installation; $24.95 monthly.
Telephone Service
Digital: Operational
Fee: $49.95 monthly
Miles of Plant: 43.0 (coaxial); 4.0 (fiber optic).
Manager: Byron Mahaffey. Marketing Manager: Heather Eastwood. Chief Technician: Dave Lyon.
Ownership: Cequel Communications LLC (MSO).

AMES—Pioneer Telephone Coop. Formerly [OK0370]. This cable system has converted to IPTV, PO Box 539, Kingfisher, OK 73750. Phones: 888-782-2667; 405-375-4111. E-mail: website@pldi.net. Web Site: http://www.ptci.com. ICA: OK5062.
Channel capacity: N.A. Channels available but not in use: N.A.
Internet Service
Operational: No.
Telephone Service
Digital: Operational
General Manager: Richard Ruhl.

AMES—Pioneer Telephone Coop. This cable system has converted to IPTV. See Ames, OK [OK5062]. ICA: OK0370.

ANADARKO—Suddenlink Communications, 12444 Powerscourt Dr, Saint Louis, MO 63131-3660. Phones: 800-999-6845 (Customer service); 314-315-9346; 314-965-2020. Web Site: http://www.suddenlink.com. ICA: OK0052.
TV Market Ranking: Below 100 (ANADARKO). Franchise award date: N.A. Franchise expiration date: N.A. Began: March 6, 1977.
Channel capacity: 41 (operating 2-way). Channels available but not in use: N.A.
Basic Service
Subscribers: 1,936.
Programming (received off-air): KAUT-TV (MNT) Oklahoma City; KETA-TV (PBS) Oklahoma City; KFOR-TV (NBC) Oklahoma City; KOCB (CW) Oklahoma City; KOCM (IND) Norman; KOCO-TV (ABC) Oklahoma City; KOKH-TV (FOX) Oklahoma City; KOPX-TV (ION) Oklahoma City; KSWO-TV (ABC, TMO) Lawton; KTBO-TV (TBN) Oklahoma City; KWTV-DT (CBS) Oklahoma City; allband FM.
Fee: $35.00 installation; $19.95 monthly.
Expanded Basic Service 1
Subscribers: N.A.
Programming (via satellite): A&E Networks; ABC Family Channel; AMC; Animal Planet; BET Networks; Cartoon Network; CNBC; CNN; Comedy Central; C-SPAN; Discovery Channel; Disney Channel; E! Entertainment Television; ESPN; ESPN 2; Food Network; Fox News Channel; Fox Sports Southwest; FX; Great American Country; Headline News; HGTV; History Channel; Lifetime; MTV; National Geographic Channel; Nickelodeon; QVC; Shopping Channel; Spike TV; Syfy; TBS Superstation; The Learning Channel; The Weather Channel; Turner Classic Movies; Turner Network TV; TV Land; Univision Studios; USA Network; VH1.
Fee: $24.00 monthly.
Digital Basic Service
Subscribers: N.A.
Programming (via satellite): BBC America; Bio; Bloomberg Television; cloo; Discovery Digital Networks; ESPN Classic Sports; ESPNews; Fox College Sports Atlantic; Fox College Sports Central; Fox College Sports Pacific; Fox Soccer; Fuse; G4; Golf Channel; GSN; History Channel International; Independent Film Channel; Outdoor Channel; ShopNBC; Speed; Toon Disney; Versus; WE tv.
Pay Service 1
Pay Units: 283.
Programming (via satellite): HBO.
Fee: $10.95 monthly.
Pay Service 2
Pay Units: 232.
Programming (via satellite): Showtime.
Fee: $9.95 monthly.
Pay Service 3
Pay Units: 246.
Programming (via satellite): The Movie Channel.
Fee: $5.95 monthly.
Digital Pay Service 1
Pay Units: N.A.
Programming (via satellite): Cinemax (multiplexed); Encore (multiplexed); Flix; HBO (multiplexed); Showtime (multiplexed); Starz (multiplexed); The Movie Channel (multiplexed).
Video-On-Demand: No
Pay-Per-View
iN DEMAND (delivered digitally).
Internet Service
Operational: Yes. Began: December 17, 2002.
Broadband Service: Suddenlink High Speed Internet.
Fee: $45.95 installation; $24.95 monthly.
Telephone Service
Digital: Operational
Fee: $49.95 monthly
Miles of Plant: 65.0 (coaxial); None (fiber optic).
Regional Manager: Todd Cruthird. Marketing Director: Beverly Gambell. Chief Technician: Roger Campbell.
Ownership: Cequel Communications LLC (MSO).

ANTLERS—Alliance Communications, 6125 Paluxy Dr, Tyler, TX 75703. Phones: 800-842-8160; 501-679-6619. Fax: 501-679-5694. Web Site: http://www.alliancecable.net. ICA: OK0101.
TV Market Ranking: Outside TV Markets (ANTLERS). Franchise award date: N.A. Franchise expiration date: December 4, 2010. Began: November 1, 1963.
Channel capacity: 36 (not 2-way capable). Channels available but not in use: N.A.
Basic Service
Subscribers: 281.
Programming (received off-air): KHBS (ABC, CW) Fort Smith; KMSS-TV (FOX) Shreveport; KOET (PBS) Eufaula; KTEN (ABC, CW, NBC) Ada; KXII (CBS, FOX, MNT) Sherman; allband FM.
Programming (via satellite): A&E Networks; ABC Family Channel; AMC; Bio; CNN; Country Music TV; Discovery Channel; Disney Channel; ESPN; ESPN 2; Fox News Channel; Fox Sports Net; INSP; Lifetime; Nickelodeon; QVC; Spike TV; Syfy;

TBS Superstation; The Weather Channel; Turner Classic Movies; Turner Network TV; USA Network; VH1; WGN America.
Fee: $54.95 installation; $44.05 monthly.

Pay Service 1
Pay Units: N.A.
Programming (via satellite): Encore; HBO; Showtime; Starz; The Movie Channel.
Video-On-Demand: No

Internet Service
Operational: No.

Telephone Service
None
Miles of Plant: 15.0 (coaxial); None (fiber optic).
Vice President & General Manager: John Brinker. Vice President, Programming: Julie Newman.
Ownership: Buford Media Group LLC (MSO).

APACHE—Southern Plains Cable, PO Box 165, Medicine Park, OK 73557. Phones: 800-218-1856; 580-529-5000. Fax: 580-529-5556. E-mail: office@wichitaonline.net. Web Site: http://www.southernplainscommunications.com. ICA: OK0139.
TV Market Ranking: Below 100 (APACHE). Franchise award date: N.A. Franchise expiration date: N.A. Began: April 1, 1982.
Channel capacity: N.A. Channels available but not in use: N.A.

Basic Service
Subscribers: 175.
Programming (received off-air): KAUT-TV (MNT) Oklahoma City; KETA-TV (PBS) Oklahoma City; KFOR-TV (NBC) Oklahoma City; KJTL (FOX) Wichita Falls; KOCO-TV (ABC) Oklahoma City; KOKH-TV (FOX) Oklahoma City; KSWO-TV (ABC, TMO) Lawton; KWTV-DT (CBS) Oklahoma City.
Programming (via satellite): Trinity Broadcasting Network.
Fee: $45.00 installation; $13.95 monthly.

Expanded Basic Service 1
Subscribers: N.A.
Programming (via satellite): A&E Networks; ABC Family Channel; AMC; Animal Planet; Cartoon Network; CNBC; CNN; Comedy Central; Country Music TV; C-SPAN; C-SPAN 2; Discovery Channel; Disney Channel; E! Entertainment Television; ESPN; ESPN 2; ESPN Classic Sports; ESPNews; Fox News Channel; FX; Headline News; HGTV; History Channel; INSP; Lifetime; Local Cable Weather; MTV; Nickelodeon; Outdoor Channel; QVC; RFD-TV; ShopNBC; Spike TV; Syfy; TBS Superstation; Telemundo; The Learning Channel; The Weather Channel; Turner Classic Movies; Turner Network TV; TV Land; USA Network; WGN America.
Fee: $31.83 monthly.

Pay Service 1
Pay Units: N.A.
Programming (via satellite): Showtime; The Movie Channel.
Fee: $10.00 monthly (each).
Video-On-Demand: No

Internet Service
Operational: Yes.
Fee: $24.95 monthly.

Telephone Service
Digital: Planned
Miles of Plant: 12.0 (coaxial); None (fiber optic).
President: Dustin Hilliary.
Ownership: Southern Plains Cable (MSO).

ARAPAHO—Full Circle Communications, PO Box 56, Rockey, OK 73661. Phone: 580-562-3521. Fax: 580-666-2252. ICA: OK0187.
TV Market Ranking: Outside TV Markets (ARAPAHO). Franchise award date: N.A. Franchise expiration date: N.A. Began: July 1, 1976.
Channel capacity: 43 (not 2-way capable). Channels available but not in use: N.A.
Basic Service
Subscribers: 110 Includes Burns Flat & Canute.
Programming (received off-air): KFOR-TV (NBC) Oklahoma City; KOCB (CW) Oklahoma City; KOCO-TV (ABC) Oklahoma City; KOKH-TV (FOX) Oklahoma City; KWET (PBS) Cheyenne; KWTV-DT (CBS) Oklahoma City; allband FM.
Programming (via satellite): A&E Networks; ABC Family Channel; Cartoon Network; CNN; Country Music TV; Discovery Channel; Disney Channel; E! Entertainment Television; ESPN; Headline News; HGTV; History Channel; Outdoor Channel; QVC; Spike TV; Syfy; TBS Superstation; The Learning Channel; Trinity Broadcasting Network; Turner Network TV; TV Land; USA Network; WGN America.
Fee: $35.00 installation; $29.95 monthly; $2.00 converter.
Pay Service 1
Pay Units: 19.
Programming (via satellite): HBO.
Fee: $9.95 monthly.
Pay Service 2
Pay Units: 8.
Programming (via satellite): Showtime.
Fee: $9.95 monthly.
Pay Service 3
Pay Units: 10.
Programming (via satellite): The Movie Channel.
Fee: $9.95 monthly.
Video-On-Demand: No
Internet Service
Operational: No.
Telephone Service
None
Miles of Plant: 9.0 (coaxial); None (fiber optic).
Technical Manager: Buster Perette.
Ownership: Full Circle Communications (MSO).

ARDMORE/LONE GROVE—Cable One, 811 W Broadway St, Ardmore, OK 73401-4526. Phone: 580-223-9600. Fax: 580-226-4472. E-mail: dwall@cableone.net. Web Site: http://www.cableone.net. Also serves Carter County, Dickson, Lone Grove, Madill, Marietta, Marshall County (northern portion) & Oakland. ICA: OK0012.
TV Market Ranking: Below 100 (Madill, Oakland); Outside TV Markets (ARDMORE, Carter County, Dickson, LONE GROVE, Marietta, Marshall County (northern portion)). Franchise award date: February 1, 1952. Franchise expiration date: N.A. Began: May 1, 1951.
Channel capacity: 62 (operating 2-way). Channels available but not in use: N.A.
Basic Service
Subscribers: 11,259.
Programming (received off-air): KETA-TV (PBS) Oklahoma City; KOKT-LP (UNV) Sulphur; KTEN (ABC, CW, NBC) Ada; KXII (CBS, FOX, MNT) Sherman; WFAA (ABC) Dallas; 7 FMs.
Programming (via microwave): KFOR-TV (NBC) Oklahoma City; KWTV-DT (CBS) Oklahoma City; WFAA (ABC) Dallas.
Programming (via satellite): A&E Networks; ABC Family Channel; AMC; Animal Planet; BET Networks; Bravo; Cartoon Network; CNBC; CNN; Comedy Central; Country Music TV; C-SPAN; C-SPAN 2; Discovery Channel; Disney Channel; E! Entertainment Television; ESPN; ESPN 2; ESPN Classic Sports; Food Network; Fox News Channel; Fox Sports Southwest; FX; Headline News; HGTV; History Channel; Lifetime; MSNBC; MTV; Nickelodeon; QVC; ShopNBC; Spike TV; Syfy; TBS Superstation; The Learning Channel; The Weather Channel; Trinity Broadcasting Network; Turner Classic Movies; Turner Network TV; TV Guide Network; TV Land; USA Network; VH1.
Fee: $45.00 installation; $46.00 monthly; $20.24 additional installation.
Digital Basic Service
Subscribers: 4,386.
Programming (via satellite): 3 Angels Broadcasting Network; Bio; Boomerang; BYU Television; Canales N; Discovery Digital Networks; DMX Music; ESPN Classic Sports; ESPNews; FamilyNet; Fox College Sports Atlantic; Fox College Sports Central; Fox College Sports Pacific; Fox HD; Fox Movie Channel; Fox Soccer; Fuel TV; G4; Great American Country; Hallmark Channel; History Channel International; INSP; National Geographic Channel; Outdoor Channel; SoapNet; Speed; Toon Disney; Trinity Broadcasting Network; truTV; Turner Network TV HD; Universal HD.
Fee: $8.95 monthly.
Digital Pay Service 1
Pay Units: N.A.
Programming (via satellite): Cinemax (multiplexed); Encore (multiplexed); Flix (multiplexed); HBO (multiplexed); Showtime (multiplexed); Showtime HD; Starz (multiplexed); Sundance Channel; The Movie Channel (multiplexed); The Movie Channel HD.
Fee: $15.00 monthly (each).
Video-On-Demand: No
Pay-Per-View
Addressable homes: 4,386.
iN DEMAND (delivered digitally); Pleasure (delivered digitally); Ten Clips (delivered digitally); Ten Blox (delivered digitally); Ten Blue (delivered digitally); ESPN (delivered digitally).
Internet Service
Operational: Yes. Began: March 1, 2002.
Subscribers: 3,200.
Broadband Service: CableONE.net.
Fee: $75.00 installation; $43.00 monthly.
Telephone Service
Digital: Operational
Fee: $39.95 monthly
Miles of Plant: 360.0 (coaxial); 8.0 (fiber optic).
Manager: David H. Wall Jr. Chief Technician: Bill Reynolds.
Ownership: Cable ONE Inc. (MSO).

ARNETT—Pioneer Telephone Coop. Formerly [OK0261]. This cable system has converted to IPTV, PO Box 539, Kingfisher, OK 73750. Phones: 888-782-2667; 405-375-4111. E-mail: website@pldi.net. Web Site: http://www.ptci.com. ICA: OK5012.
TV Market Ranking: Outside TV Markets (ARNETT). Franchise award date: N.A. Franchise expiration date: N.A. Began: September 28, 2005.
Channel capacity: N.A. Channels available but not in use: N.A.
Internet Service
Operational: Yes.
Telephone Service
Digital: Operational
General Manager: Richard Ruhl.

ARNETT—Pioneer Telephone Coop. This cable system has converted to IPTV. See Arnett, OK [OK5012]. ICA: OK0261.

ASHER—Formerly served by CableDirect. No longer in operation. ICA: OK0230.

ATOKA—CommuniComm Services. Now served by COALGATE, OK [OK0120]. ICA: OK0378.

AVANT—Community Cablevision Co., 1550 W Rogers Blvd, PO Box 307, Skiatook, OK 74070-0307. Phone: 918-396-3019. Fax: 918-396-2081. E-mail: info@communitycablevision.com. Web Site: http://www.communitycablebroadband.com. ICA: OK0239.
TV Market Ranking: 54 (AVANT). Franchise award date: January 25, 1988. Franchise expiration date: January 25, 2013. Began: August 15, 1988.
Channel capacity: 35 (not 2-way capable). Channels available but not in use: N.A.
Basic Service
Subscribers: 57.
Programming (received off-air): KDOR-TV (TBN) Bartlesville; KJRH-TV (NBC) Tulsa; KOED-TV (PBS) Tulsa; KOKI-TV (FOX) Tulsa; KOTV-DT (CBS) Tulsa; KQCW-DT (CW) Muskogee; KRSC-TV (ETV) Claremore; KTUL (ABC) Tulsa; KWHB (IND) Tulsa.
Programming (via microwave): KTFO-CD (TEL) Austin.
Programming (via satellite): ABC Family Channel; Cartoon Network; CNN; Country Music TV; Discovery Channel; Disney Channel; ESPN; ESPN 2; Headline News; HGTV; Nickelodeon; QVC; Spike TV; Syfy; TBS Superstation; Turner Classic Movies; Turner Network TV; USA Network; WGN America.
Fee: $29.95 installation; $32.95 monthly.
Pay Service 1
Pay Units: 7.
Programming (via satellite): HBO.
Fee: $11.50 monthly.
Pay Service 2
Pay Units: 6.
Programming (via satellite): Cinemax.
Fee: $11.50 monthly.
Video-On-Demand: No
Internet Service
Operational: Yes.
Fee: $44.95 installation.
Telephone Service
Digital: Operational
Fee: $39.95 monthly
Miles of Plant: 3.0 (coaxial); None (fiber optic).
President & General Manager: Dennis Soule.
Ownership: Community Cablevision Co. (MSO).

BARNSDALL—Community Cablevision Co., 1550 W Rogers Blvd, PO Box 307, Skiatook, OK 74070-0307. Phone: 918-396-3019. Fax: 918-396-2081. E-mail: info@communitycablevision.com. Web Site: http://www.communitycablebroadband.com. ICA: OK0118.
TV Market Ranking: 54 (BARNSDALL). Franchise award date: April 6, 1982. Franchise expiration date: April 6, 2007. Began: May 1, 1983.
Channel capacity: N.A. Channels available but not in use: N.A.
Basic Service
Subscribers: 402.
Programming (received off-air): KDOR-TV (TBN) Bartlesville; KGEB (IND) Tulsa;

KJRH-TV (NBC) Tulsa; KOED-TV (PBS) Tulsa; KOKI-TV (FOX) Tulsa; KOTV-DT (CBS) Tulsa; KRSC-TV (ETV) Claremore; KTUL (ABC) Tulsa; KWHB (IND) Tulsa.
Programming (via microwave): KTFO-CD (TEL) Austin.
Programming (via satellite): A&E Networks; ABC Family Channel; AMC; Animal Planet; BET Networks; Cartoon Network; CNN; Comedy Central; Country Music TV; C-SPAN; CW+; Discovery Channel; Discovery Health Channel; Disney Channel; ESPN; ESPN 2; ESPN Classic Sports; Food Network; Fox News Channel; Fox Sports Southwest; FX; Hallmark Channel; HGTV; History Channel; ION Television; Lifetime; MoviePlex; MTV; National Geographic Channel; Nickelodeon; Outdoor Channel; Oxygen; QVC; Spike TV; Syfy; TBS Superstation; The Learning Channel; The Weather Channel; Travel Channel; truTV; Turner Classic Movies; Turner Network TV; TV Land; USA Network; VH1; WE tv; WGN America.
Fee: $29.95 installation; $32.95 monthly; $10.00 additional installation.

Digital Basic Service
Subscribers: N.A.
Programming (via satellite): AmericanLife TV Network; BBC America; Bio; Bloomberg Television; Bravo; Church Channel; Current; Discovery Fit & Health; Discovery Health Channel; Discovery Home Channel; Discovery Kids Channel; Discovery Times Channel; DMX Music; ESPN 2; ESPN Classic Sports; ESPNews; Fox College Sports Atlantic; Fox College Sports Central; Fox College Sports Pacific; Fox Movie Channel; Fox Soccer; Fuse; G4; GAS; Golf Channel; Great American Country; GSN; Halogen Network; HGTV; History Channel; History Channel International; Independent Film Channel; JCTV; Lifetime Movie Network; Lime; MBC America; Military Channel; MTV Hits; MTV Jams; MTV2; National Geographic Channel; Nick Jr.; NickToons TV; Outdoor Channel; Ovation; Science; ShopNBC; Speed; Style Network; Syfy; The Word Network; Toon Disney; Trinity Broadcasting Network; Trio; Turner Classic Movies; Versus; VH1 Classic; VH1 Country; VH1 Soul; WE tv.
Fee: $24.00 monthly.

Digital Pay Service 1
Pay Units: N.A.
Programming (via satellite): Cinemax (multiplexed); Encore (multiplexed); Flix; HBO (multiplexed); Showtime (multiplexed); Starz (multiplexed); Sundance Channel; The Movie Channel (multiplexed).
Fee: $11.50 monthly (HBO, Cinemax, Starz/Encore, or Showtime/TMC/Sundance/Flix).

Video-On-Demand: No

Pay-Per-View
iN DEMAND (delivered digitally).

Internet Service
Operational: Yes.
Broadband Service: In-house.
Fee: $44.95 monthly.

Telephone Service
Digital: Operational

President & General Manager: Dennis Soule.
Ownership: Community Cablevision Co. (MSO).

BARTLESVILLE—Cable One, 4127 SE Nowata Rd, Bartlesville, OK 74006-5120. Phone: 918-335-0123. Fax: 918-333-6757. Web Site: http://www.cableone.net. Also serves Dewey, Nowata & Nowata County. ICA: OK0010.
TV Market Ranking: Below 100 (BARTLESVILLE, Dewey, Nowata, Nowata County). Franchise award date: N.A. Franchise expiration date: April 13, 2010. Began: September 1, 1972.
Channel capacity: 78 (operating 2-way). Channels available but not in use: N.A.

Basic Service
Subscribers: 14,127.
Programming (received off-air): KDOR-TV (TBN) Bartlesville; KJRH-TV (NBC) Tulsa; KMYT-TV (MNT) Tulsa; KOED-TV (PBS) Tulsa; KOKI-TV (FOX) Tulsa; KOTV-DT (CBS) Tulsa; KQCW-DT (CW) Muskogee; KRSC-TV (ETV) Claremore; KTPX-TV (ION) Okmulgee; KTUL (ABC) Tulsa; KWHB (IND) Tulsa; 14 FMs.
Programming (via satellite): A&E Networks; ABC Family Channel; AMC; Animal Planet; BET Networks; Cartoon Network; CNBC; CNN; Comedy Central; Country Music TV; C-SPAN; C-SPAN 2; Discovery Channel; Disney Channel; ESPN; ESPN 2; Food Network; Fox News Channel; Fox Sports Southwest; FX; Headline News; HGTV; History Channel; Lifetime; MSNBC; MTV; Nickelodeon; QVC; Spike TV; Syfy; TBS Superstation; The Learning Channel; The Weather Channel; Turner Classic Movies; Turner Network TV; TV Guide Network; TV Land; USA Network; VH1; WGN America.
Fee: $30.00 installation; $46.00 monthly; $1.00 converter; $30.00 additional installation.

Digital Basic Service
Subscribers: 4,000.
Programming (via satellite): 3 Angels Broadcasting Network; Bio; Boomerang; BYU Television; Canales N; Discovery Digital Networks; DMX Music; ESPN Classic Sports; ESPNews; FamilyNet; Fox College Sports Atlantic; Fox College Sports Central; Fox College Sports Pacific; Fox Movie Channel; Fox Soccer; Fuel TV; G4; Golf Channel; Hallmark Channel; History Channel International; INSP; National Geographic Channel; Outdoor Channel; SoapNet; Speed; Toon Disney; Trinity Broadcasting Network; truTV; Turner Network TV HD.
Fee: $9.95 monthly.

Digital Pay Service 1
Pay Units: N.A.
Programming (via satellite): Cinemax (multiplexed); Encore (multiplexed); Flix; HBO (multiplexed); Showtime (multiplexed); Showtime HD; Starz (multiplexed); Sundance Channel; The Movie Channel (multiplexed); The Movie Channel HD.
Fee: $15.00 monthly (each).

Video-On-Demand: No

Pay-Per-View
iN DEMAND (delivered digitally); Pleasure (delivered digitally); Ten Clips (delivered digitally); Ten Blox (delivered digitally); Ten Blue (delivered digitally).

Internet Service
Operational: Yes. Began: February 1, 2001.
Broadband Service: CableONE.net.
Fee: $75.00 installation; $43.00 monthly; $5.00 modem lease.

Telephone Service
Digital: Operational
Fee: $39.95 monthly

Miles of Plant: 270.0 (coaxial); None (fiber optic).
Manager: Dick Marnell. Chief Technician: Dennis Anderson. Marketing Director: Brett Dugan.
Ownership: Cable ONE Inc. (MSO).

BEAVER—Panhandle Telephone Coop. Inc., 2222 NW Hwy 64, Guymon, OK 73942. Phones: 580-338-2556; 800-562-2556. Fax: 580-338-8260. E-mail: support@ptsi.net. Web Site: http://www.ptsi.net. Also serves Forgan. ICA: OK0114.
TV Market Ranking: Outside TV Markets (BEAVER). Franchise award date: N.A. Franchise expiration date: N.A. Began: April 19, 1962.
Channel capacity: N.A. Channels available but not in use: N.A.

Basic Service
Subscribers: N.A.
Programming (received off-air): KAMR-TV (NBC) Amarillo; KBSD-DT (CBS) Ensign; KCIT (FOX) Amarillo; KETA-TV (PBS) Oklahoma City; KFDA-TV (CBS) Amarillo; KPTF-DT (IND) Farwell; KUPK (ABC) Garden City; KVII-TV (ABC, CW) Amarillo.
Programming (via satellite): The Weather Channel.
Fee: $18.99 monthly.

Expanded Basic Service 1
Subscribers: N.A.
Programming (via satellite): A&E Networks; ABC Family Channel; American Movie Classics; Animal Planet; Bravo; Cartoon Network; CNN; Comedy Central; CW+; Discovery Channel; Disney Channel; E! Entertainment Television; ESPN; ESPN 2; Food Network; Fox News Channel; Fox Sports Southwest; FX; GalaVision; Great American Country; Hallmark Channel; HGTV; History Channel; Lifetime; MSNBC; MTV; National Geographic Channel; Nickelodeon; Outdoor Channel; QVC; Spike TV; Syfy; TBS Superstation; TLC; TNT; Trinity Broadcasting Network; Turner Classic Movies; TV Land; Univision Studios; USA Network; VH1.
Fee: $25.00 monthly.

Pay Service 1
Pay Units: 105.
Programming (via satellite): HBO.
Fee: $14.00 monthly.

Pay Service 2
Pay Units: 106.
Programming (via satellite): Showtime.
Fee: $13.95 monthly.

Pay Service 3
Pay Units: 108.
Programming (via satellite): The Movie Channel.
Fee: $13.95 monthly.

Internet Service
Operational: Yes.
Broadband Service: In-house.
Fee: $22.95 monthly.

Telephone Service
None

Miles of Plant: 20.0 (coaxial); None (fiber optic).
President: Charles Russell.
Ownership: Panhandle Telephone Cooperative Inc. (MSO).

BEGGS—Allegiance Communications, 707 W Saratoga St, Shawnee, OK 74804. Phones: 405-395-1131; 405-275-6923. Web Site: http://www.allegiance.tv. ICA: OK0154.
TV Market Ranking: 54 (BEGGS). Franchise award date: February 1, 1980. Franchise expiration date: N.A. Began: October 1, 1982.
Channel capacity: N.A. Channels available but not in use: N.A.

Basic Service
Subscribers: 275.
Programming (received off-air): KGEB (IND) Tulsa; KJRH-TV (NBC) Tulsa; KMYT-TV (MNT) Tulsa; KOED-TV (PBS) Tulsa; KOKI-TV (FOX) Tulsa; KOTV-DT (CBS) Tulsa; KQCW-DT (CW) Muskogee; KTPX-TV (ION) Okmulgee; KTUL (ABC) Tulsa; KWHB (IND) Tulsa.
Programming (via satellite): A&E Networks; ABC Family Channel; AMC; Animal Planet; BET Networks; Cartoon Network; CNBC; CNN; Country Music TV; Discovery Channel; Disney Channel; ESPN; ESPN 2; Fox Sports Southwest; HGTV; History Channel; Lifetime; Nickelodeon; Oxygen; Product Information Network; Speed; Spike TV; TBS Superstation; The Learning Channel; The Weather Channel; Travel Channel; Trinity Broadcasting Network; Turner Classic Movies; Turner Network TV; USA Network; WGN America.
Fee: $30.00 installation; $21.95 monthly.

Digital Basic Service
Subscribers: N.A.
Programming (via satellite): BBC America; Bio; Bloomberg Television; Bravo; Discovery Fit & Health; DMX Music; ESPN Classic Sports; Fox Movie Channel; Fuse; G4; GAS; Golf Channel; GSN; Halogen Network; History Channel International; Independent Film Channel; Lifetime Movie Network; MTV Networks Digital Suite; Nick Jr.; Outdoor Channel; ShopNBC; Style Network; Syfy; Toon Disney; Versus; WE tv.

Pay Service 1
Pay Units: 23.
Programming (via satellite): Cinemax; HBO.
Fee: $20.00 installation; $8.95 monthly (each).

Digital Pay Service 1
Pay Units: N.A.
Programming (via satellite): Cinemax (multiplexed); Encore (multiplexed); HBO (multiplexed); Showtime (multiplexed); Starz (multiplexed); The Movie Channel (multiplexed).

Video-On-Demand: No

Pay-Per-View
Hot Choice (delivered digitally); Playboy TV (delivered digitally); Fresh (delivered digitally); Shorteez (delivered digitally); iN DEMAND (delivered digitally).

Internet Service
Operational: No.

Telephone Service
None

Miles of Plant: 13.0 (coaxial); None (fiber optic).
Chief Executive Officer: Bill Haggarty. Regional Vice President: Andrew Dearth. Vice President, Marketing: Tracy Bass.
Ownership: Allegiance Communications (MSO).

BENNINGTON—Formerly served by Allegiance Communications. No longer in operation. ICA: OK0352.

BESSIE—Formerly served by Cebridge Connections. No longer in operation. ICA: OK0380.

BILLINGS—Formerly served by Cebridge Connections. No longer in operation. ICA: OK0235.

BINGER—Cable West, 314 W Main St, PO Box 237, Mountain View, OK 73062. Phones: 800-980-7912; 580-347-3220. Fax: 580-347-2143. ICA: OK0262.

TV Market Ranking: Outside TV Markets (BINGER). Franchise award date: N.A. Franchise expiration date: N.A. Began: N.A.

Channel capacity: 36 (2-way capable). Channels available but not in use: N.A.

Basic Service

Subscribers: 207.

Programming (received off-air): KAUT-TV (MNT) Oklahoma City; KETA-TV (PBS) Oklahoma City; KFOR-TV (NBC) Oklahoma City; KOCB (CW) Oklahoma City; KOCO-TV (ABC) Oklahoma City; KOKH-TV (FOX) Oklahoma City; KSBI (IND) Oklahoma City; KTBO-TV (TBN) Oklahoma City; KWTV-DT (CBS) Oklahoma City.

Programming (via satellite): ABC Family Channel; CNN; Country Music TV; Discovery Channel; Disney Channel; E! Entertainment Television; ESPN; History Channel; Nickelodeon; Spike TV; TBS Superstation; The Weather Channel; Turner Network TV; TV Land; USA Network; WGN America.

Fee: $35.00 installation; $27.95 monthly.

Pay Service 1

Pay Units: 34.

Programming (via satellite): HBO.

Fee: $10.95 monthly.

Pay Service 2

Pay Units: 17.

Programming (via satellite): Showtime.

Fee: $9.95 monthly.

Internet Service

Operational: No.

Telephone Service

None

Miles of Plant: 7.0 (coaxial); None (fiber optic).

Manager & Chief Technician: Mickey Davis.

Ownership: Mickey Davis (MSO).

BLACKWELL—Suddenlink Communications, 1105 N 9th St, Blackwell, OK 74631. Phone: 580-363-1870. Fax: 580-363-5242. Web Site: http://www.suddenlink.com. ICA: OK0036.

TV Market Ranking: Outside TV Markets (BLACKWELL). Franchise award date: October 1, 1964. Franchise expiration date: September 8, 2007. Began: October 1, 1964.

Channel capacity: N.A. Channels available but not in use: N.A.

Basic Service

Subscribers: 1,772.

Programming (received off-air): KAUT-TV (MNT) Oklahoma City; KETA-TV (PBS) Oklahoma City; KFOR-TV (NBC) Oklahoma City; KOCO-TV (ABC) Oklahoma City; KOKH-TV (FOX) Oklahoma City; KSNW (NBC) Wichita; KWTV-DT (CBS) Oklahoma City.

Programming (via satellite): ION Television; LWS Local Weather Station; TBS Superstation; WGN America.

Fee: $38.00 installation; $6.88 monthly.

Expanded Basic Service 1

Subscribers: 1,715.

Programming (via satellite): A&E Networks; ABC Family Channel; AMC; American-Life TV Network; Animal Planet; Cartoon Network; CNN; Comedy Central; C-SPAN; Discovery Channel; Discovery Health Channel; Disney Channel; ESPN; ESPN 2; Food Network; Fox News Channel; Fox Sports Southwest; FX; Golf Channel; Great American Country; GSN; Headline News; HGTV; History Channel; INSP; Lifetime; Lifetime Movie Network; MoviePlex; MTV; Nickelodeon; Outdoor Channel; SoapNet; Speed; Spike TV; Syfy; The Weather Channel; Trinity Broadcasting Network; Turner Classic Movies; Turner Network TV; TV Guide Network; TV Land; Univision Studios; USA Network; VH1; WE tv.

Fee: $19.00 monthly.

Digital Basic Service

Subscribers: N.A.

Programming (via satellite): BBC America; Black Family Channel; Bloomberg Television; Bravo; Discovery Digital Networks; DMX Music; Encore Action; ESPN 2; ESPN Classic Sports; ESPNews; Fox Movie Channel; Fox Sports World; Fuse; G4; Independent Film Channel; ShopNBC; Sundance Channel; The Word Network; Toon Disney; Versus.

Pay Service 1

Pay Units: 608.

Programming (via satellite): Cinemax.

Fee: $10.95 monthly.

Pay Service 2

Pay Units: 146.

Programming (via satellite): Encore; Starz.

Fee: $4.95 monthly.

Pay Service 3

Pay Units: 701.

Programming (via satellite): HBO.

Fee: $10.95 monthly.

Pay Service 4

Pay Units: 134.

Programming (via satellite): The Movie Channel.

Fee: $11.00 monthly.

Pay Service 5

Pay Units: 191.

Programming (via satellite): Showtime.

Fee: $7.95 monthly.

Digital Pay Service 1

Pay Units: N.A.

Programming (via satellite): Cinemax (multiplexed); Encore (multiplexed); HBO (multiplexed); Showtime (multiplexed); Starz (multiplexed); The Movie Channel (multiplexed).

Video-On-Demand: No

Pay-Per-View

ESPN Now (delivered digitally); Hot Choice (delivered digitally); iN DEMAND (delivered digitally).

Internet Service

Operational: No.

Telephone Service

None

Miles of Plant: 51.0 (coaxial); 6.0 (fiber optic).

Manager: Byron Mahaffey. Marketing Director: Heather Eastwood. Chief Technician: Richard Kindred.

Ownership: Cequel Communications LLC (MSO).

BLAIR—LakeView Cable, Hwy 115, PO Box 460, Cache, OK 73527-0460. Phone: 580-429-8800. Fax: 580-429-6599. Web Site: http://www.lvcisp.com. ICA: OK0181.

TV Market Ranking: Outside TV Markets (BLAIR). Franchise award date: N.A. Franchise expiration date: September 22, 2007. Began: January 1, 1972.

Channel capacity: 77 (operating 2-way). Channels available but not in use: N.A.

Basic Service

Subscribers: 125.

Programming (received off-air): KAUZ-TV (CBS, CW) Wichita Falls; KETA-TV (PBS) Oklahoma City; KFDX-TV (NBC) Wichita Falls; KFOR-TV (NBC) Oklahoma City; KJBO-LP (MNT) Wichita Falls; KJTL (FOX) Wichita Falls; KSWO-TV (ABC, TMO) Lawton; KWTV-DT (CBS) Oklahoma City; allband FM.

Programming (via satellite): A&E Networks; ABC Family Channel; AMC; Animal Planet; BET Networks; Cartoon Network; CNN; Comedy Central; C-SPAN; Discovery Channel; Disney Channel; E! Entertainment Television; ESPN; ESPN 2; FamilyNet; Food Network; Fox News Channel; Great American Country; Headline News; HGTV; History Channel; INSP; Lifetime; MSNBC; Nickelodeon; Outdoor Channel; QVC; Syfy; TBS Superstation; The Learning Channel; The Weather Channel; Travel Channel; Trinity Broadcasting Network; Turner Network TV; USA Network; WGN America.

Fee: $50.00 installation; $17.98 monthly; $3.95 converter.

Digital Basic Service

Subscribers: 150 Includes Mountain Park & Tipton.

Programming (via satellite): AmericanLife TV Network; BBC America; Bio; Bloomberg Television; Discovery Digital Networks; DMX Music; Encore (multiplexed); ESPN Classic Sports; ESPNews; Fox Movie Channel; Fox Soccer; G4; Golf Channel; GSN; Halogen Network; History Channel International; Lifetime Movie Network; Speed; Style Network; Toon Disney; Turner Classic Movies.

Fee: $17.00 monthly.

Pay Service 1

Pay Units: 21.

Programming (via satellite): Cinemax; HBO; Showtime; The Movie Channel.

Fee: $8.95 monthly (TMC), $10.95 monthly (Showtime or Cinemax), $12.95 monthly (HBO).

Digital Pay Service 1

Pay Units: N.A.

Programming (via satellite): Cinemax (multiplexed); Flix; HBO (multiplexed); Showtime (multiplexed); Starz (multiplexed); The Movie Channel (multiplexed).

Fee: $8.95 monthly (TMC), $10.95 monthly (Showtime or Cinemax), $12.95 monthly (HBO).

Video-On-Demand: No

Pay-Per-View

iN DEMAND (delivered digitally); Hot Choice (delivered digitally); Playboy TV (delivered digitally); Fresh (delivered digitally); Shorteez (delivered digitally).

Internet Service

Operational: Yes.

Subscribers: 600.

Broadband Service: IBBS.

Fee: $29.95 monthly.

Telephone Service

Digital: Planned

Miles of Plant: 16.0 (coaxial); None (fiber optic).

Manager: Bill Rowell. Chief Technician: Mike Rowell.

Ownership: Lakeview Cable Inc. (MSO).

BLANCHARD—Pioneer Telephone Coop. Formerly [OK0391]. This cable system has converted to IPTV, PO Box 539, Kingfisher, OK 73750. Phones: 888-782-2667; 405-375-4111. E-mail: website@pldi.net. Web Site: http://www.ptci.com. ICA: OK5015.

TV Market Ranking: 39 (BLANCHARD). Franchise award date: N.A. Franchise expiration date: N.A. Began: January 12, 2005.

Channel capacity: N.A. Channels available but not in use: N.A.

Internet Service

Operational: Yes.

Telephone Service

Digital: Operational

General Manager: Richard Ruhl.

BLANCHARD—Pioneer Telephone Coop. This cable system has converted to IPTV. See Blanchard, OK [OK5015]. ICA: OK0391.

BOISE CITY—Panhandle Telephone Coop. Inc., 2222 NW Hwy 64, Guymon, OK 73942. Phones: 580-338-2556; 800-562-2556. Fax: 580-338-8260. E-mail: support@ptsi.net. Web Site: http://www.ptsi.net. ICA: OK0119.

TV Market Ranking: Outside TV Markets (BOISE CITY). Franchise award date: January 1, 1988. Franchise expiration date: January 1, 2013. Began: October 1, 1962.

Channel capacity: N.A. Channels available but not in use: N.A.

Basic Service

Subscribers: N.A.

Programming (received off-air): KPTF-DT (IND) Farwell; KWET (PBS) Cheyenne.

Programming (via satellite): CW Television Network; QVC; The Weather Channel; Trinity Broadcasting Network.

Programming (via translator): KAMR-TV (NBC) Amarillo; KCIT (FOX) Amarillo; KFDA-TV (CBS) Amarillo; KVII-TV (ABC, CW) Amarillo.

Fee: $18.99 monthly.

Expanded Basic Service 1

Subscribers: N.A.

Programming (via satellite): A&E Networks; ABC Family Channel; American Movie Classics; CNN; Comedy Central; C-SPAN; Discovery Channel; Disney Channel; ESPN; ESPN 2; Fox Deportes; Fox News Channel; Fox Sports Southwest; FX; Great American Country; Home & Garden Television; Lifetime; MSNBC; National Geographic Channel; Nickelodeon; Outdoor Channel; Spike TV; Syfy; TBS Superstation; TLC; TNT; TV Land; Univision Studios; USA Network; VH1.

Fee: $29.50 monthly.

Pay Service 1

Pay Units: 144.

Programming (via satellite): HBO.

Fee: $14.00 monthly.

Pay Service 2

Pay Units: N.A.

Programming (via satellite): Showtime; The Movie Channel.

Fee: $13.95 monthly.

Video-On-Demand: No

Internet Service

Operational: Yes.

Broadband Service: In-house.

Fee: $22.95 monthly.

Telephone Service

None

Miles of Plant: 11.0 (coaxial); None (fiber optic).

President: Charles Russell.

Ownership: Panhandle Telephone Cooperative Inc. (MSO).

BOSHOKE—Formerly served by Cebridge Connections. No longer in operation. ICA: OK0263.

BOSWELL—Allegiance Communications, 707 W Saratoga St, Shawnee, OK 74804. Phones: 405-395-1131; 405-275-6923.

Web Site: http://www.allegiance.tv. Also serves Choctaw County (unincorporated areas). ICA: OK0199.

TV Market Ranking: Outside TV Markets (BOSWELL, Choctaw County (unincorporated areas) (portions)). Franchise award date: N.A. Franchise expiration date: N.A. Began: March 1, 1984.

Channel capacity: 25 (not 2-way capable). Channels available but not in use: N.A.

Basic Service

Subscribers: 197.

Programming (received off-air): KOED-TV (PBS) Tulsa; KTEN (ABC, CW, NBC) Ada; KXII (CBS, FOX, MNT) Sherman.

Programming (via satellite): ABC Family Channel; AMC; CMT Pure Country; CNN; Discovery Channel; Disney Channel; ESPN; Headline News; KMGH-TV (ABC) Denver; Nickelodeon; Spike TV; TBS Superstation; Trinity Broadcasting Network; USA Network; WGN America.

Fee: $25.00 installation; $21.95 monthly.

Pay Service 1

Pay Units: N.A.

Programming (via satellite): Cinemax; HBO.

Fee: $10.00 monthly (each).

Pay-Per-View

iN DEMAND (delivered digitally); Hot Choice (delivered digitally); Playboy TV (delivered digitally); Fresh (delivered digitally); Shorteez (delivered digitally).

Internet Service

Operational: No.

Telephone Service

None

Miles of Plant: 9.0 (coaxial); None (fiber optic).

Chief Executive Officer: Bill Haggarty. Regional Vice President: Andrew Dearth. Vice President, Marketing: Tracy Bass.

Ownership: Allegiance Communications (MSO).

BOYNTON—Formerly served by Allegiance Communications. No longer in operation. ICA: OK0245.

BRAGGS—Allegiance Communications, 707 W Saratoga St, Shawnee, OK 74804. Phones: 405-395-1131; 405-275-6923. Web Site: http://www.allegiance.tv. ICA: OK0264.

TV Market Ranking: Below 100 (BRAGGS). Franchise award date: N.A. Franchise expiration date: N.A. Began: May 15, 1990.

Channel capacity: 36 (not 2-way capable). Channels available but not in use: N.A.

Basic Service

Subscribers: 106.

Programming (received off-air): KGEB (IND) Tulsa; KHBS (ABC, CW) Fort Smith; KJRH-TV (NBC) Tulsa; KOED-TV (PBS) Tulsa; KOET (PBS) Eufaula; KOKI-TV (FOX) Tulsa; KOTV-DT (CBS) Tulsa; KTUL (ABC) Tulsa.

Programming (via satellite): ABC Family Channel; AMC; CNN; Country Music TV; Discovery Channel; Disney Channel; ESPN; Headline News; MTV; Nickelodeon; Spike TV; TBS Superstation; The Weather Channel; Turner Network TV; USA Network; WGN America.

Fee: $35.00 installation; $21.95 monthly.

Pay Service 1

Pay Units: 70.

Programming (via satellite): HBO.

Fee: $10.00 monthly.

Pay-Per-View

iN DEMAND (delivered digitally); Hot Choice (delivered digitally); Fresh (delivered digitally); Shorteez (delivered digitally); ESPN Now (delivered digitally); ESPN Gameplan (delivered digitally).

Internet Service

Operational: No.

Telephone Service

None

Chief Executive Officer: Bill Haggarty. Regional Vice President: Andrew Dearth. Vice President, Marketing: Tracy Bass.

Ownership: Allegiance Communications (MSO).

BRECKINRIDGE—Formerly served by Cebridge Connections. No longer in operation. ICA: OK0265.

BRISTOW—Allegiance Communications, 707 W Saratoga St, Shawnee, OK 74804. Phones: 405-395-1131; 405-275-6923. Web Site: http://www.allegiance.tv. ICA: OK0394.

TV Market Ranking: 54 (BRISTOW).

Channel capacity: N.A. Channels available but not in use: N.A.

Basic Service

Subscribers: N.A.

Programming (received off-air): KDOR-TV (TBN) Bartlesville; KJRH-TV (NBC) Tulsa; KMYT-TV (MNT) Tulsa; KOED-TV (PBS) Tulsa; KOKI-TV (FOX) Tulsa; KOTV-DT (CBS) Tulsa; KQCW-DT (CW) Muskogee; KTUL (ABC) Tulsa; KWHB (IND) Tulsa.

Programming (via satellite): CNN; C-SPAN; Paxson Communications Corp.; QVC; The Weather Channel; TV Guide Network.

Fee: $21.95 monthly.

Expanded Basic Service 1

Subscribers: N.A.

Programming (via satellite): A&E Networks; ABC Family Channel; AMC; Animal Planet; BET Networks; Bravo; Cartoon Network; CNBC; Country Music TV; Discovery Channel; Disney Channel; ESPN; ESPN 2; ESPN Classic Sports; Fox News Channel; Fox Sports Southwest; FX; Hallmark Channel; Headline News; HGTV; History Channel; Lifetime; MTV; NFL Network; Nickelodeon; Spike TV; Syfy; TBS Superstation; The Learning Channel; Turner Network TV; USA Network; VH1.

Digital Basic Service

Subscribers: N.A.

Programming (via satellite): AmericanLife TV Network; BBC America; Bio; Black Family Channel; Bloomberg Television; Bravo; Canales N; Church Channel; Current; Discovery Fit & Health; DMX Music; Encore (multiplexed); ESPN 2; ESPN Classic Sports; ESPNews; Flix; Fox Movie Channel; Fox Soccer; FSN Digital Atlantic; FSN Digital Central; FSN Digital Pacific; Fuse; G4; GAS; Golf Channel; Great American Country; GSN; Halogen Network; HGTV; History Channel; History Channel International; Independent Film Channel; JCTV; Lifetime Movie Network; Lime; MTV Networks Digital Suite; National Geographic Channel; Nick Jr.; NickToons TV; Outdoor Channel; Ovation; ShopNBC; Speed; Style Network; Sundance Channel; Syfy; The Word Network; Toon Disney; Trinity Broadcasting Network; Trio; Turner Classic Movies; Versus; WE tv.

Pay Service 1

Pay Units: N.A.

Programming (via satellite): Cinemax; Encore; HBO; Showtime; Starz.

Digital Pay Service 1

Pay Units: N.A.

Programming (via satellite): Cinemax (multiplexed); HBO (multiplexed); Showtime (multiplexed); Starz (multiplexed); The Movie Channel (multiplexed).

Pay-Per-View

iN DEMAND (delivered digitally); Hot Choice (delivered digitally); Playboy TV (delivered digitally); Fresh (delivered digitally); Shorteez (delivered digitally).

Internet Service

Operational: Yes.

Fee: $24.95 installation; $39.95 monthly.

Telephone Service

None

Chief Executive Officer: Bill Haggarty. Regional Vice President: Andrew Dearth. Vice President, Marketing: Tracy Bass.

Ownership: Allegiance Communications (MSO).

BROKEN BOW—Broken Bow TV Cable Co. Inc., 108 N Park Dr, PO Box 817, Broken Bow, OK 74728-0817. Phone: 580-584-3340. Fax: 580-584-3338. Also serves Eagletown, Haworth, Hochatowa, Idabel (Shultz Community), Lukfata, McCurtain County (portions) & Oak Hill. ICA: OK0070.

TV Market Ranking: Outside TV Markets (BROKEN BOW, Eagletown, Haworth, Hochatowa, Idabel (Shultz Community), Lukfata, McCurtain County (portions), Oak Hill). Franchise award date: N.A. Franchise expiration date: N.A. Began: February 15, 1964.

Channel capacity: N.A. Channels available but not in use: N.A.

Basic Service

Subscribers: 3,000.

Programming (received off-air): KETA-TV (PBS) Oklahoma City; KETG (PBS) Arkadelphia; KHBS (ABC, CW) Fort Smith; KSLA (CBS) Shreveport; KTAL-TV (NBC) Texarkana; KTBS-TV (ABC) Shreveport; KTEN (ABC, CW, NBC) Ada.

Programming (via microwave): KTUL (ABC) Tulsa; WFAA (ABC) Dallas.

Programming (via satellite): ABC Family Channel; CNN; ESPN; Lifetime; MTV; Nickelodeon; TBS Superstation; The Weather Channel; Turner Network TV; USA Network; WGN America; WPIX (CW, IND) New York.

Fee: $40.70 installation; $25.91 monthly; $3.00 converter.

Pay Service 1

Pay Units: 519.

Programming (via satellite): Cinemax; HBO; Showtime; The Movie Channel.

Fee: $20.00 installation; $11.25 monthly (HBO or Cinemax), $11.95 monthly (Showtime or TMC).

Internet Service

Operational: No.

Telephone Service

None

Miles of Plant: 350.0 (coaxial); None (fiber optic).

Manager: Dale Fitzsimmons. Chief Technician: Jerry Whisenhunt.

Ownership: Jewel B. Callaham Revocable Trust.

BUFFALO—Pioneer Telephone Coop. Formerly [OK0151]. This cable system has converted to IPTV, PO Box 539, Kingfisher, OK 73750. Phones: 888-782-2667; 405-375-4111. E-mail: website@pldi.net. Web Site: http://www.ptci.com. ICA: OK5091.

TV Market Ranking: Outside TV Markets (BUFFALO). Franchise award date: N.A. Franchise expiration date: N.A. Began: September 28, 2005.

Channel capacity: N.A. Channels available but not in use: N.A.

Internet Service

Operational: Yes.

Telephone Service

Digital: Operational

General Manager: Richard Ruhl.

BUFFALO—Pioneer Telephone Coop. This cable system has converted to IPTV. See Buffalo, OK [OK5091]. ICA: OK0151.

BURNS FLAT—Full Circle Communications, PO Box 56, Rockey, OK 73661. Phone: 580-562-3521. Fax: 580-666-2252. ICA: OK0098.

TV Market Ranking: Outside TV Markets (BURNS FLAT). Franchise award date: N.A. Franchise expiration date: N.A. Began: N.A.

Channel capacity: 36 (not 2-way capable). Channels available but not in use: N.A.

Basic Service

Subscribers: N.A. Included in Arapaho

Programming (received off-air): KAUT-TV (MNT) Oklahoma City; KFOR-TV (NBC) Oklahoma City; KOCB (CW) Oklahoma City; KOCO-TV (ABC) Oklahoma City; KOKH-TV (FOX) Oklahoma City; KWET (PBS) Cheyenne; KWTV-DT (CBS) Oklahoma City.

Programming (via satellite): ABC Family Channel; AMC; CNN; Country Music TV; Discovery Channel; Disney Channel; E! Entertainment Television; ESPN; Headline News; History Channel; Lifetime; Nickelodeon; QVC; Spike TV; Syfy; TBS Superstation; The Learning Channel; The Weather Channel; Travel Channel; Trinity Broadcasting Network; Turner Network TV; TV Land; USA Network; WGN America.

Fee: $39.95 installation; $29.95 monthly.

Pay Service 1

Pay Units: N.A.

Programming (via satellite): HBO; The Movie Channel.

Fee: $7.95 monthly (TMC), $9.95 monthly (HBO).

Video-On-Demand: No

Internet Service

Operational: No.

Telephone Service

None

Miles of Plant: 11.0 (coaxial); None (fiber optic).

Technical Manager: Buster Perette.

Ownership: Full Circle Communications (MSO).

BUTLER—Formerly served by Basic Cable Services Inc. No longer in operation. ICA: OK0240.

BYARS—Formerly served by Cebridge Connections. No longer in operation. ICA: OK0268.

CACHE—LakeView Cable, Hwy 115, PO Box 460, Cache, OK 73527-0460. Phone: 580-429-8800. Fax: 580-429-6599. Web Site: http://www.lvcisp.com. Also serves Indiahoma. ICA: OK0105.

TV Market Ranking: Below 100 (CACHE, Indiahoma). Franchise award date: N.A. Franchise expiration date: N.A. Began: January 1, 1987.

Channel capacity: N.A. Channels available but not in use: N.A.

Basic Service
Subscribers: 615.
Programming (received off-air): KAUT-TV (MNT) Oklahoma City; KAUZ-TV (CBS, CW) Wichita Falls; KETA-TV (PBS) Oklahoma City; KFDX-TV (NBC) Wichita Falls; KFOR-TV (NBC) Oklahoma City; KJTL (FOX) Wichita Falls; KSWO-TV (ABC, TMO) Lawton; KWTV-DT (CBS) Oklahoma City.
Programming (via satellite): A&E Networks; ABC Family Channel; AMC; American-Life TV Network; CNN; Country Music TV; C-SPAN; Discovery Channel; Disney Channel; E! Entertainment Television; ESPN; Fox News Channel; Fox Sports Southwest; Headline News; History Channel; Lifetime; Nickelodeon; QVC; Spike TV; Syfy; TBS Superstation; The Learning Channel; The Weather Channel; Trinity Broadcasting Network; Turner Network TV; TV Land; USA Network; WGN America.
Fee: $39.95 installation; $31.75 monthly.
Pay Service 1
Pay Units: 141.
Programming (via satellite): HBO.
Fee: $10.95 monthly.
Pay Service 2
Pay Units: 79.
Programming (via satellite): Showtime.
Fee: $9.95 monthly.
Pay Service 3
Pay Units: 79.
Programming (via satellite): The Movie Channel.
Fee: $7.95 monthly.
Internet Service
Operational: Yes.
Broadband Service: In-house.
Telephone Service
None
Miles of Plant: 63.0 (coaxial); None (fiber optic). Mies of plant includes Comanche County (unincorporated areas), Geronimo, Lake Ellsworth & Lake Lawtonka
Manager: Bill Rowell. Chief Technician: Mike Rowell.
Ownership: Lakeview Cable Inc. (MSO).

CALUMET—Pioneer Telephone Coop. Formerly [OK0238]. This cable system has converted to IPTV, PO Box 539, Kingfisher, OK 73750. Phones: 888-782-2667; 405-375-4111. E-mail: website@pldi.net. Web Site: http://www.ptci.com. ICA: OK5063.
Channel capacity: N.A. Channels available but not in use: N.A.
Internet Service
Operational: Yes.
Telephone Service
Digital: Operational
General Manager: Richard Ruhl.

CALUMET—Pioneer Telephone Coop. This cable system has converted to IPTV. See Calumet, OK [OK5063]. ICA: OK0238.

CALVIN—Allegiance Communications, 707 W Saratoga St, Shawnee, OK 74804. Phones: 405-395-1131; 405-275-6923. Web Site: http://www.allegiance.tv. ICA: OK0254.
TV Market Ranking: Below 100 (CALVIN). Franchise award date: N.A. Franchise expiration date: June 1, 2010. Began: January 1, 1985.
Channel capacity: 36 (not 2-way capable). Channels available but not in use: N.A.
Basic Service
Subscribers: 41.
Programming (received off-air): KAUT-TV (MNT) Oklahoma City; KETA-TV (PBS) Oklahoma City; KFOR-TV (NBC) Oklahoma City; KOCB (CW) Oklahoma City; KOKH-TV (FOX) Oklahoma City; KTEN (ABC, CW, NBC) Ada; KTUL (ABC) Tulsa; KWTV-DT (CBS) Oklahoma City.
Programming (via satellite): A&E Networks; ABC Family Channel; CNN; Country Music TV; C-SPAN; Discovery Channel; ESPN; Fox Sports Southwest; Nickelodeon; Spike TV; TBS Superstation; Trinity Broadcasting Network; Turner Network TV.
Fee: $20.00 installation; $25.52 monthly.
Pay Service 1
Pay Units: N.A.
Programming (via satellite): Encore; Showtime; Starz.
Fee: $1.75 monthly (Encore), $6.75 monthly (Starz), $11.00 monthly (Showtime).
Pay-Per-View
iN DEMAND (delivered digitally); Hot Choice (delivered digitally); Playboy TV (delivered digitally); Fresh (delivered digitally); Shorteez (delivered digitally).
Internet Service
Operational: No.
Telephone Service
None
Miles of Plant: 4.0 (coaxial); None (fiber optic).
Chief Executive Officer: Bill Haggarty. Regional Vice President: Andrew Dearth. Vice President, Marketing: Tracy Bass.
Ownership: Allegiance Communications (MSO).

CAMARGO—Formerly served by Cebridge Connections. No longer in operation. ICA: OK0371.

CAMERON—Allegiance Communications, 707 W Saratoga St, Shawnee, OK 74804. Phones: 405-275-6923; 405-395-1131. Web Site: http://www.allegiance.tv. ICA: OK0252.
TV Market Ranking: Below 100 (CAMERON). Franchise award date: January 1, 1989. Franchise expiration date: January 1, 2014. Began: September 1, 1989.
Channel capacity: N.A. Channels available but not in use: N.A.
Basic Service
Subscribers: N.A.
Programming (received off-air): KFSM-TV (CBS) Fort Smith; KHBS (ABC, CW) Fort Smith; KOET (PBS) Eufaula; WBFS-TV (MNT) Miami.
Programming (via satellite): A&E Networks; ABC Family Channel; CNBC; CNN; Country Music TV; Discovery Channel; Disney Channel; ESPN; ESPN 2; Headline News; Lifetime; MTV; Nickelodeon; Spike TV; Syfy; TBS Superstation; Travel Channel; Turner Network TV; USA Network; WGN America.
Fee: $30.00 installation; $21.95 monthly.
Pay Service 1
Pay Units: N.A.
Programming (via satellite): HBO.
Fee: $10.00 monthly.
Video-On-Demand: No
Pay-Per-View
Hot Choice (delivered digitally); Playboy TV (delivered digitally); Fresh (delivered digitally); Shorteez (delivered digitally); iN DEMAND (delivered digitally).
Internet Service
Operational: No.
Telephone Service
None
Miles of Plant: 3.0 (coaxial); None (fiber optic).
Chief Executive Officer: Bill Haggarty. Regional Vice President: Andrew Dearth. Vice President, Marketing: Tracy Bass.
Ownership: Allegiance Communications (MSO).

CANADIAN—Lakeland Cable TV Inc., PO Box 321, Crowder, OK 74430-0321. Phone: 918-334-6200. Fax: 918-334-3202. Also serves Crowder & Indianola. ICA: OK0269.
TV Market Ranking: Below 100 (Indianola); Outside TV Markets (CANADIAN, Crowder). Franchise award date: N.A. Franchise expiration date: N.A. Began: April 1, 1982.
Channel capacity: N.A. Channels available but not in use: N.A.
Basic Service
Subscribers: 616.
Programming (received off-air): KGEB (IND) Tulsa; KJRH-TV (NBC) Tulsa; KMYT-TV (MNT) Tulsa; KOET (PBS) Eufaula; KOKI-TV (FOX) Tulsa; KOTV-DT (CBS) Tulsa; KQCW-DT (CW) Muskogee; KTPX-TV (ION) Okmulgee; KTUL (ABC) Tulsa; KWHB (IND) Tulsa.
Programming (via satellite): C-SPAN; C-SPAN 2; Outdoor Channel; TBS Superstation; The Weather Channel; WGN America.
Fee: $60.00 installation; $12.96 monthly.
Expanded Basic Service 1
Subscribers: N.A.
Programming (via satellite): A&E Networks; ABC Family Channel; AMC; Animal Planet; CNN; Country Music TV; Discovery Channel; Disney Channel; ESPN; ESPN 2; ESPN Classic Sports; Food Network; Fox News Channel; Fox Sports Southwest; HGTV; History Channel; Lifetime; Nickelodeon; Spike TV; Syfy; The Learning Channel; Turner Network TV; TV Land; USA Network; Versus.
Fee: $20.40 monthly.
Pay Service 1
Pay Units: 39.
Programming (via satellite): Encore; Encore Westerns; Starz.
Fee: $3.06 monthly (Encore), $9.70 monthly (Starz & Encore).
Video-On-Demand: Yes
Internet Service
Operational: Yes.
Telephone Service
Digital: Operational
Miles of Plant: 10.0 (coaxial); None (fiber optic).
Manager: Charles O. Smith. Chief Technician: Gary Brooks.
Ownership: Lakeland Cable TV Inc.

CANEY—Formerly served by Allegiance Communications. No longer in operation. ICA: OK0353.

CANTON—Formerly served by Blue Sky Cable LLC. No longer in operation. ICA: OK0236.

CANUTE—Full Circle Communications, PO Box 56, Rockey, OK 73661. Phone: 580-562-3521. Fax: 580-666-2252. ICA: OK0215.
TV Market Ranking: Outside TV Markets (CANUTE). Franchise award date: N.A. Franchise expiration date: N.A. Began: January 1, 1975.
Channel capacity: 36 (not 2-way capable). Channels available but not in use: N.A.
Basic Service
Subscribers: N.A. Included in Arapaho
Programming (received off-air): KFOR-TV (NBC) Oklahoma City; KOCO-TV (ABC) Oklahoma City; KOKH-TV (FOX) Oklahoma City; KWET (PBS) Cheyenne; KWTV-DT (CBS) Oklahoma City; allband FM.
Programming (via satellite): ABC Family Channel; CNN; Discovery Channel; Disney Channel; E! Entertainment Television; ESPN; Headline News; History Channel; Nickelodeon; QVC; Spike TV; Syfy; TBS Superstation; The Learning Channel; Trinity Broadcasting Network; Turner Network TV; TV Land; USA Network; WGN America.
Fee: $39.95 installation; $31.75 monthly.
Pay Service 1
Pay Units: 31.
Programming (via satellite): HBO.
Fee: $9.95 monthly.
Pay Service 2
Pay Units: 12.
Programming (via satellite): Showtime.
Fee: $9.95 monthly.
Pay Service 3
Pay Units: 17.
Programming (via satellite): The Movie Channel.
Fee: $9.95 monthly.
Video-On-Demand: No
Internet Service
Operational: No.
Telephone Service
None
Miles of Plant: 12.0 (coaxial); None (fiber optic).
Technical Manager: Buster Perette.
Ownership: Full Circle Communications (MSO).

CARMEN—Pioneer Telephone Coop. Formerly [OK0234]. This cable system has converted to IPTV, PO Box 539, Kingfisher, OK 73750. Phones: 888-782-2667; 405-375-4111. E-mail: website@pldi.net. Web Site: http://www.ptci.com. ICA: OK5092.
TV Market Ranking: Franchise award date: N.A. Franchise expiration date: N.A. Began: January 5, 2006.
Channel capacity: N.A. Channels available but not in use: N.A.
Internet Service
Operational: Yes.
Telephone Service
Digital: Operational
General Manager: Richard Ruhl.

CARMEN—Pioneer Telephone Coop. This cable system has converted to IPTV. See CARMEN, OK [OK5092]. ICA: OK0234.

CARNEGIE—Carnegie Cable, 25 S Colorado St, PO Box 96, Carnegie, OK 73015-0096. Phone: 580-654-1002. Fax: 580-654-2699. E-mail: info@carnegiecable.com. Web Site: http://www.carnegietelephone.com. ICA: OK0107.
TV Market Ranking: Outside TV Markets (CARNEGIE). Franchise award date: N.A. Franchise expiration date: N.A. Began: July 1, 1974.
Channel capacity: 84 (not 2-way capable). Channels available but not in use: N.A.
Basic Service
Subscribers: 626.
Programming (received off-air): KAUT-TV (MNT) Oklahoma City; KETA-TV (PBS) Oklahoma City; KFOR-TV (NBC) Oklahoma City; KOCB (CW) Oklahoma City; KOCM (IND) Norman; KOCO-TV (ABC) Oklahoma City; KOKH-TV (FOX) Oklahoma City; KOPX-TV (ION) Oklahoma City; KSBI (IND) Oklahoma City; KSWO-TV (ABC, TMO) Lawton; KTBO-TV (TBN) Oklahoma City; KWTV-DT (CBS) Oklahoma City; allband FM.
Programming (via satellite): A&E Networks; ABC Family Channel; Animal Planet; Boomerang; Cartoon Network; Comedy Central; Country Music TV; C-SPAN;

C-SPAN 2; Discovery Channel; Disney Channel; DIY Network; ESPN; Food Network; Fox News Channel; Fox Sports Southwest; FX; Golf Channel; Great American Country; Hallmark Channel; HGTV; INSP; Lifetime; MSNBC; National Geographic Channel; QVC; Shop at Home; ShopNBC; Spike TV; TBS Superstation; The Learning Channel; truTV; Turner Network TV; Univision Studios; USA Network.
Fee: $32.50 monthly.

Digital Basic Service
Subscribers: 100.
Programming (via satellite): BBC America; Bio; Bloomberg Television; DMX Music; ESPN 2; ESPN Classic Sports; ESPNews; Fox Movie Channel; Fuse; G4; Golf Channel; GSN; Halogen Network; History Channel; History Channel International; Independent Film Channel; Lifetime Movie Network; National Geographic Channel; Outdoor Channel; Science Television; Speed; Style Network; Toon Disney; Trinity Broadcasting Network; Trio; Turner Classic Movies; Versus; WE tv.
Fee: $15.95 monthly.

Pay Service 1
Pay Units: 150.
Programming (via satellite): Cinemax; HBO.
Fee: $9.00 monthly.

Digital Pay Service 1
Pay Units: 190.
Programming (via satellite): Cinemax (multiplexed); Encore (multiplexed); Flix; HBO; Showtime (multiplexed); Starz (multiplexed); The Movie Channel (multiplexed).
Fee: $4.95 monthly (Encore), $5.95 monthly (Starz), $9.00 monthly (Cinemax), $11.00 monthly (HBO) $11.99 monthly (Showtime/TMC/Flix).

Internet Service
Operational: No.

Telephone Service
None

Miles of Plant: 25.0 (coaxial); None (fiber optic).
President: Lyn Johnson. Vice President & Chief Operating Officer: Gary Woodruff. Operations Manager: James Powers. Outside Plant Manager: Travis Ridgeway.
Ownership: Carnegie Cable.

CARNEY—Formerly served by Allegiance Communications. No longer in operation. ICA: OK0270.

CARTER—Formerly served by CableDirect. No longer in operation. ICA: OK0242.

CASHION—Formerly served by Cebridge Connections. No longer in operation. ICA: OK0233.

CATOOSA—Pine River Cable, PO Box 96, McBain, MI 49657. Phone: 888-244-2288. Fax: 918-825-8008. E-mail: info@pinerivercable.com. Web Site: http://www.pinerivercable.com. Also serves Rogers County (portions) & Wagoner County (portions). ICA: OK0271.
TV Market Ranking: 54 (CATOOSA, Rogers County (portions), Wagoner County (portions)). Franchise award date: N.A. Franchise expiration date: N.A. Began: May 1, 1990.
Channel capacity: N.A. Channels available but not in use: N.A.

Basic Service
Subscribers: 194.
Programming (received off-air): KDOR-TV (TBN) Bartlesville; KGEB (IND) Tulsa; KJRH-TV (NBC) Tulsa; KMYT-TV (MNT) Tulsa; KOED-TV (PBS) Tulsa; KOKI-TV (FOX) Tulsa; KOTV-DT (CBS) Tulsa; KQCW-DT (CW) Muskogee; KTPX-TV (ION) Okmulgee; KTUL (ABC) Tulsa; KWHB (IND) Tulsa.
Programming (via satellite): WGN America.
Fee: $29.95 installation; $11.30 monthly.

Expanded Basic Service 1
Subscribers: 172.
Programming (via satellite): A&E Networks; ABC Family Channel; AMC; Animal Planet; Cartoon Network; CNBC; CNN; Comedy Central; Country Music TV; C-SPAN; Discovery Channel; Discovery Fit & Health; Disney Channel; Encore; ESPN; ESPN 2; ESPN Classic Sports; Food Network; Fox News Channel; Fox Sports Southwest; FX; Hallmark Channel; Headline News; HGTV; History Channel; INSP; Lifetime; MTV; National Geographic Channel; Nickelodeon; Outdoor Channel; QVC; Speed; Spike TV; Syfy; TBS Superstation; The Learning Channel; The Weather Channel; truTV; Turner Classic Movies; Turner Network TV; TV Land; USA Network; Versus; VH1.
Fee: $31.65 monthly.

Pay Service 1
Pay Units: 46.
Programming (via satellite): HBO; Showtime; The Movie Channel.
Fee: $10.95 monthly.

Pay-Per-View
ESPN Now (delivered digitally); ESPN Extra (delivered digitally); iN DEMAND (delivered digitally); Sports PPV (delivered digitally).

Internet Service
Operational: No.

Telephone Service
None

Miles of Plant: 39.0 (coaxial); None (fiber optic).
President & General Manager: John Hetzler. Chief Technician: John Miller.
Ownership: Pine River Cable (MSO).

CEMENT—Southern Plains Cable, PO Box 165, Medicine Park, OK 73557. Phones: 800-218-1856; 580-529-5000. Fax: 580-529-5556. E-mail: office@wichitaonline.net. Web Site: http://www.southernplainscommunications.com. ICA: OK0195.
TV Market Ranking: Below 100 (CEMENT). Franchise award date: N.A. Franchise expiration date: N.A. Began: December 1, 1981.
Channel capacity: N.A. Channels available but not in use: N.A.

Basic Service
Subscribers: 60.
Programming (received off-air): KAUT-TV (MNT) Oklahoma City; KETA-TV (PBS) Oklahoma City; KFOR-TV (NBC) Oklahoma City; KJTL (FOX) Wichita Falls; KOCB (CW) Oklahoma City; KOCO-TV (ABC) Oklahoma City; KOKH-TV (FOX) Oklahoma City; KSWO-TV (ABC, TMO) Lawton; KWTV-DT (CBS) Oklahoma City.
Programming (via satellite): A&E Networks; ABC Family Channel; AMC; Cartoon Network; CNN; Comedy Central; Country Music TV; Discovery Channel; Disney Channel; E! Entertainment Television; ESPN; ESPN 2; Eternal Word TV Network; Fox News Channel; Headline News; History Channel; INSP; ION Television; Lifetime; Local Cable Weather; Nickelodeon; ShopNBC; Spike TV; Syfy; TBS Superstation; The Learning Channel; The Weather Channel; Trinity Broadcasting Network; Turner Network TV; TV Land; USA Network; WGN America.
Fee: $45.00 installation; $31.83 monthly.

Pay Service 1
Pay Units: N.A.
Programming (via satellite): The Movie Channel.
Fee: $10.00 monthly.

Video-On-Demand: No

Internet Service
Operational: Yes.

Telephone Service
Analog: Not Operational
Digital: Planned

Miles of Plant: 6.0 (coaxial); None (fiber optic).
President: Dustin Hilliary.
Ownership: Southern Plains Cable (MSO).

CHANDLER—Allegiance Communications, 707 W Saratoga St, Shawnee, OK 74804. Phones: 405-395-1131; 405-275-6923. Web Site: http://www.allegiance.tv. ICA: OK0112.
TV Market Ranking: Outside TV Markets (CHANDLER). Franchise award date: N.A. Franchise expiration date: N.A. Began: May 1, 1981.
Channel capacity: 41 (not 2-way capable). Channels available but not in use: N.A.

Basic Service
Subscribers: 533.
Programming (received off-air): KAUT-TV (MNT) Oklahoma City; KETA-TV (PBS) Oklahoma City; KFOR-TV (NBC) Oklahoma City; KOCB (CW) Oklahoma City; KOCO-TV (ABC) Oklahoma City; KOKH-TV (FOX) Oklahoma City; KOPX-TV (ION) Oklahoma City; KTBO-TV (TBN) Oklahoma City; KWTV-DT (CBS) Oklahoma City.
Programming (via satellite): A&E Networks; ABC Family Channel; AMC; Animal Planet; Cartoon Network; CNBC; CNN; Discovery Channel; Disney Channel; ESPN; Fox News Channel; Fox Sports Southwest; FX; Headline News; HGTV; Lifetime; Nickelodeon; Spike TV; TBS Superstation; The Learning Channel; The Weather Channel; Turner Network TV; USA Network; WGN America.
Fee: $50.00 installation; $30.82 monthly; $3.30 converter; $30.00 additional installation.

Digital Basic Service
Subscribers: N.A.
Programming (via satellite): AmericanLife TV Network; BBC America; Bloomberg Television; Bravo; Discovery Digital Networks; DMX Music; ESPN 2; ESPN Classic Sports; ESPNews; Fox Movie Channel; Fox Sports World; Fuse; G4; Golf Channel; Great American Country; GSN; Halogen Network; Independent Film Channel; Lifetime Movie Network; MBC America; Outdoor Channel; ShopNBC; Speed; Sundance Channel; Syfy; The Word Network; Toon Disney; Turner Classic Movies; Versus.

Pay Service 1
Pay Units: 139.
Programming (via satellite): Encore; HBO; Showtime; Starz.
Fee: $10.00 installation; $14.19 monthly.

Digital Pay Service 1
Pay Units: N.A.
Programming (via satellite): Cinemax (multiplexed); Encore (multiplexed); HBO (multiplexed); Showtime (multiplexed); Starz (multiplexed); The Movie Channel (multiplexed).

Video-On-Demand: No

Pay-Per-View
iN DEMAND (delivered digitally); Hot Choice (delivered digitally); Fresh (delivered digitally); Shorteez (delivered digitally); ESPN Now (delivered digitally); ESPN Gameplan (delivered digitally).

Internet Service
Operational: Yes.
Fee: $24.95 installation; $39.95 monthly.

Telephone Service
None

Miles of Plant: 31.0 (coaxial); None (fiber optic).
Chief Executive Officer: Bill Haggarty. Regional Vice President: Andrew Dearth. Vice President, Marketing: Tracy Bass.
Ownership: Allegiance Communications (MSO).

CHATTANOOGA—Formerly served by Southern Plains Cable. No longer in operation. ICA: OK0272.

CHELSEA—Charter Communications. Now served by KETCHUM, OK [OK0179]. ICA: OK0127.

CHEROKEE—Formerly served by Alliance Communications Network. No longer in operation. ICA: OK0110.

CHEYENNE—James Mogg TV, PO Box 328, Cheyenne, OK 73628-0328. Phone: 580-497-2182. ICA: OK0147.
TV Market Ranking: Outside TV Markets (CHEYENNE). Franchise award date: N.A. Franchise expiration date: N.A. Began: N.A.
Channel capacity: N.A. Channels available but not in use: N.A.

Basic Service
Subscribers: 240.
Programming (received off-air): KJTL (FOX) Wichita Falls; KOCB (CW) Oklahoma City; KOCO-TV (ABC) Oklahoma City; KOKH-TV (FOX) Oklahoma City; KOMI-CD Woodward; KWET (PBS) Cheyenne; 1 FM.
Programming (via microwave): KFOR-TV (NBC) Oklahoma City; KWTV-DT (CBS) Oklahoma City.
Programming (via satellite): ABC Family Channel; CNN; Discovery Channel; ESPN; Spike TV; TBS Superstation; Trinity Broadcasting Network; Turner Network TV; USA Network; WGN America.
Fee: $17.00 monthly.

Internet Service
Operational: No.

Telephone Service
None

Miles of Plant: 6.0 (coaxial); None (fiber optic).
Ownership: James Mogg TV.

CHICKASHA—Suddenlink Communications, 12444 Powerscourt Dr, Saint Louis, MO 63131-3660. Phone: 405-224-0110. Fax: 405-224-3760. Web Site: http://www.suddenlink.com. Also serves Grady County (portions). ICA: OK0023.
TV Market Ranking: 39 (Grady County (portions)); Below 100 (CHICKASHA, Grady County (portions)); Outside TV Markets (Grady County (portions)). Franchise award date: N.A. Franchise expiration date: November 18, 2006. Began: March 1, 1978.
Channel capacity: 81 (operating 2-way). Channels available but not in use: N.A.

Basic Service
Subscribers: 4,860.
Programming (received off-air): KAUT-TV (MNT) Oklahoma City; KETA-TV (PBS) Oklahoma City; KFOR-TV (NBC) Oklahoma City; KOCB (CW) Oklahoma City; KOCM (IND) Norman; KOCO-TV (ABC) Oklahoma City; KOKH-TV (FOX) Oklahoma City; KOPX-TV (ION) Oklahoma City; KSBI (IND) Okla-

homa City; KTBO-TV (TBN) Oklahoma City; KWTV-DT (CBS) Oklahoma City; 18 FMs.
Programming (via satellite): C-SPAN; C-SPAN 2; QVC; Turner Classic Movies; TV Guide Network; WGN America.
Fee: $20.47 installation; $21.91 monthly.

Expanded Basic Service 1
Subscribers: 4,557.
Programming (via satellite): A&E Networks; ABC Family Channel; AMC; Animal Planet; BET Networks; Cartoon Network; CNBC; CNN; Comedy Central; Country Music TV; Discovery Channel; Disney Channel; E! Entertainment Television; ESPN; ESPN 2; Food Network; Fox News Channel; Fox Sports Southwest; FX; Golf Channel; Headline News; HGTV; History Channel; Lifetime; MSNBC; MTV; Nickelodeon; Spike TV; TBS Superstation; The Learning Channel; The Weather Channel; Travel Channel; truTV; Turner Classic Movies; Turner Network TV; TV Land; USA Network; VH1.
Fee: $4.95 monthly.

Digital Basic Service
Subscribers: N.A.
Programming (via satellite): BBC America; Bio; Canales N; Cooking Channel; Country Music TV; DIY Network; Encore (multiplexed); ESPN Classic Sports; ESPN HD; ESPNews; Eternal Word TV Network; Fox Soccer; GAS; GSN; Hallmark Channel; HD Theater; HDNet; HDNet Movies; History Channel International; Lifetime Movie Network; MTV Networks Digital Suite; Music Choice; National Geographic Channel; Nick Jr.; NickToons TV; Outdoor Channel; SoapNet; Sundance Channel; Toon Disney; Universal HD.

Digital Pay Service 1
Pay Units: N.A.
Programming (via satellite): Cinemax (multiplexed); HBO (multiplexed); HBO HD; Showtime (multiplexed); Showtime HD; Starz (multiplexed); The Movie Channel.

Video-On-Demand: No

Pay-Per-View
iN DEMAND (delivered digitally), Addressable: No; Playboy TV (delivered digitally).

Internet Service
Operational: Yes.
Broadband Service: Suddenlink High Speed Internet.
Fee: $45.95 installation; $24.95 monthly.

Telephone Service
Digital: Operational
Miles of Plant: 89.0 (coaxial); None (fiber optic).
Manager: R. C. Lewis. Marketing Director: Heather Eastwood.
Ownership: Cequel Communications LLC (MSO).

CHICKEN CREEK—Formerly served by Eagle Media. No longer in operation. ICA: OK0368.

CHOUTEAU—Charter Communications. Now served by KETCHUM, OK [OK0179]. ICA: OK0358.

CLAREMORE—Zoom Media, PO Box 2126, Flint, TX 75762. Phone: 855-261-5304. Web Site: http://www.zoommediallc.com. ICA: OK0451.
TV Market Ranking: 54 (CLAREMORE).
Channel capacity: N.A. Channels available but not in use: N.A.

Basic Service
Subscribers: 596.
Programming (received off-air): KDOR-TV (TBN) Bartlesville; KGEB (IND) Tulsa; KJRH-TV (NBC) Tulsa; KMYT-TV (MNT) Tulsa; KOED-TV (PBS) Tulsa; KOKI-TV (FOX) Tulsa; KOTV-DT (CBS) Tulsa; KQCW-DT (CW) Muskogee; KRSC-TV (ETV) Claremore; KTPX-TV (ION) Okmulgee; KTUL (ABC) Tulsa; KWHB (IND) Tulsa.
Programming (via satellite): C-SPAN; C-SPAN 2; Home Shopping Network; QVC; The Weather Channel; TV Guide Network; WGN America.

Digital Basic Service
Subscribers: 504.
Programming (via satellite): A&E Networks; ABC Family Channel; AMC; Animal Planet; Bio; Cartoon Network; CNBC; CNN; Comedy Central; Country Music TV; Discovery Channel; Discovery Fit & Health; Disney Channel; Disney XD; DMX Music; E! Entertainment Television; ESPN; ESPN 2; Food Network; Fox Business Channel; Fox College Sports Atlantic; Fox College Sports Central; Fox College Sports Pacific; Fox News Channel; Fox Soccer; Fox Sports Net; Fuel TV; FX; Great American Country; Hallmark Channel; Halogen Network; Headline News; HGTV; History Channel; History Channel International; Lifetime; MSNBC; MTV; Nat Geo WILD; National Geographic Channel; Nick Jr.; Nickelodeon; SoapNet; Speed; Spike TV; Syfy; TBS Superstation; The Learning Channel; Travel Channel; Trinity Broadcasting Network; truTV; Turner Classic Movies; Turner Network TV; TV Land; USA Network; VH1; VH1 Soul.

Digital Expanded Basic Service
Subscribers: N.A.
Programming (via satellite): BBC America; Bloomberg Television; Bravo; CMT Pure Country; Discovery Health Channel; ESPN Classic Sports; ESPN U; ESPNews; Fox Movie Channel; Fuse; G4; Golf Channel; GSN; ID Investigation Discovery; Independent Film Channel; Lifetime Movie Network; Military Channel; MLB Network; MTV2; NickToons TV; Outdoor Channel; Planet Green; Science; Style Network; Sundance Channel; TeenNick; The Hub; Versus; VH1 Classic; WE tv.

Digital Expanded Basic Service 2
Subscribers: N.A.
Programming (received off-air): KJRH-TV (NBC) Tulsa; KOTV-DT (CBS) Tulsa; KQCW-DT (CW) Muskogee; KTUL (ABC) Tulsa.
Programming (via satellite): A&E HD; Animal Planet HD; Discovery Channel HD; Disney Channel HD; ESPN 2 HD; ESPN HD; Fox News HD; FX HD; HD Theater; HGTV HD; History Channel HD; MLB Network HD; National Geographic Channel HD Network; Science HD; Travel Channel HD; Turner Network TV HD.

Digital Pay Service 1
Pay Units: N.A.
Programming (via satellite): Cinemax (multiplexed); Encore (multiplexed); HBO (multiplexed); HBO HD; Showtime (multiplexed); Showtime HD; Starz (multiplexed); The Movie Channel (multiplexed).

Pay-Per-View
iN DEMAND (delivered digitally); Playboy TV (delivered digitally); Club Jenna (delivered digitally).
Chief Executive Officer: Steve Houston.
Ownership: Zoom Media LLC (MSO).

CLAYTON (town)—Allegiance Communications, 707 W Saratoga St, Shawnee, OK 74804. Phones: 405-395-1131; 405-275-6923. Web Site: http://www.allegiance.tv. ICA: OK0273.
TV Market Ranking: Outside TV Markets (CLAYTON (TOWN)). Franchise award date: N.A. Franchise expiration date: December 11, 2010. Began: July 1, 1977.
Channel capacity: 36 (not 2-way capable). Channels available but not in use: N.A.

Basic Service
Subscribers: 123.
Programming (received off-air): KFSM-TV (CBS) Fort Smith; KFTA-TV (FOX, NBC) Fort Smith; KJRH-TV (NBC) Tulsa; KOET (PBS) Eufaula; KTEN (ABC, CW, NBC) Ada; KTUL (ABC) Tulsa; KXII (CBS, FOX, MNT) Sherman.
Programming (via satellite): A&E Networks; ABC Family Channel; CMT Pure Country; CNN; Discovery Channel; Discovery Kids Channel; Disney Channel; ESPN; MTV; Nickelodeon; Spike TV; Syfy; TBS Superstation; The Learning Channel; The Weather Channel; Trinity Broadcasting Network; Turner Network TV; USA Network; VH1; WGN America.
Fee: $21.95 monthly.

Pay Service 1
Pay Units: N.A.
Programming (via satellite): HBO; Showtime; The Movie Channel.
Fee: $10.00 monthly (each).

Pay-Per-View
iN DEMAND (delivered digitally); Hot Choice (delivered digitally); Playboy TV (delivered digitally); Fresh (delivered digitally); Shorteez (delivered digitally).

Internet Service
Operational: No.

Telephone Service
None
Miles of Plant: 11.0 (coaxial); None (fiber optic).
Chief Executive Officer: Bill Haggarty. Regional Vice President: Andrew Dearth. Vice President, Marketing: Tracy Bass.
Ownership: Allegiance Communications (MSO).

CLEO SPRINGS—Formerly served by Blue Sky Cable LLC. No longer in operation. ICA: OK0227.

COALGATE—CommuniComm Services, 1501 W Mississippi St, PO Box 597, Durant, OK 74701. Phones: 800-752-4992; 580-924-2367. Fax: 580-924-5970. Web Site: http://www.netcommander.com. Also serves Atoka, Cottonwood, Stonewall, Tupelo & Tushka. ICA: OK0120.
TV Market Ranking: Below 100 (COALGATE, Cottonwood, Stonewall, Tupelo); Outside TV Markets (Atoka, Tushka). Franchise award date: N.A. Franchise expiration date: N.A. Began: February 1, 1974.
Channel capacity: N.A. Channels available but not in use: N.A.

Basic Service
Subscribers: N.A. Included in Durant
Programming (received off-air): KETA-TV (PBS) Oklahoma City; KOCO-TV (ABC) Oklahoma City; KTEN (ABC, CW, NBC) Ada; KWTV-DT (CBS) Oklahoma City; KXII (CBS, FOX, MNT) Sherman; allband FM.
Programming (via satellite): C-SPAN; C-SPAN 2; CW+; MyNetworkTV Inc.; Trinity Broadcasting Network; WXYZ-TV (ABC) Detroit.
Fee: $49.95 installation; $10.75 monthly.

Expanded Basic Service 1
Subscribers: N.A.
Programming (via satellite): A&E Networks; ABC Family Channel; AMC; Animal Planet; BET Networks; Bravo; Cartoon Network; CNBC; CNN; Comedy Central; Country Music TV; Discovery Channel; Disney Channel; E! Entertainment Television; ESPN; ESPN 2; Food Network; Fox News Channel; Fox Sports Southwest; FX; Hallmark Channel; Headline News; HGTV; History Channel; Lifetime; Local Cable Weather; MSNBC; MTV; Nick Jr.; Nickelodeon; QVC; ShopNBC; Spike TV; Syfy; TBS Superstation; The Learning Channel; The Weather Channel; Travel Channel; truTV; Turner Classic Movies; Turner Network TV; TV Guide Network; TV Land; USA Network; VH1; WE tv.
Fee: $49.95 installation; $20.25 monthly.

Digital Basic Service
Subscribers: N.A.
Programming (via satellite): AmericanLife TV Network; BBC America; Bio; Bloomberg Television; Bravo; Church Channel; cloo; CMT Pure Country; Current; Discovery Fit & Health; Discovery Health Channel; Discovery Home Channel; Discovery Kids Channel; Discovery Times Channel; DMX Music; ESPN 2; ESPN Classic Sports; ESPNews; Fox Movie Channel; Fox Soccer; Fuse; G4; Golf Channel; Great American Country; GSN; Halogen Network; HGTV; History Channel; History Channel International; Independent Film Channel; JCTV; Lifetime Movie Network; LOGO; Men's Channel; Military Channel; MTV Hits; MTV Jams; MTV2; National Geographic Channel; Nick Jr.; NickToons TV; Outdoor Channel; Ovation; RFD-TV; Science; ShopNBC; SoapNet; Speed; Style Network; TeenNick; The Word Network; Toon Disney; Trinity Broadcasting Network; Turner Classic Movies; Versus; VH1 Classic; VH1 Soul; WE tv.

Pay Service 1
Pay Units: 108.
Programming (via satellite): Cinemax; Encore; HBO (multiplexed); Starz.
Fee: $20.00 installation; $9.95 monthly (Starz/Encore), $10.95 monthly (Cinemax), $12.95 monthly (HBO).

Digital Pay Service 1
Pay Units: N.A.
Programming (via satellite): Cinemax (multiplexed); Encore (multiplexed); Flix; HBO (multiplexed); Showtime (multiplexed); Starz (multiplexed); Sundance Channel; The Movie Channel (multiplexed).

Video-On-Demand: No

Pay-Per-View
iN DEMAND (delivered digitally); Hot Choice (delivered digitally); Playboy TV (delivered digitally); Fresh (delivered digitally); Spice: Xcess (delivered digitally); Club Jenna (delivered digitally).

Internet Service
Operational: Yes.
Broadband Service: Net Commander.
Fee: $39.95 installation; $51.95 monthly.

Telephone Service
None
Miles of Plant: 139.0 (coaxial); None (fiber optic).
General Manager: Jeff Beck. Customer Service Manager: Lisa Hamill.
Ownership: James Cable LLC (MSO).

COLBERT—CommuniComm Services. Now served by TISHOMINGO, OK [OK0064]. ICA: OK0068.

COLCORD—Allegiance Communications, 707 W Saratoga St, Shawnee, OK 74804. Phones: 405-275-6923; 405-395-1131. Web Site: http://www.allegiance.tv. ICA: OK0204.

TV Market Ranking: Below 100 (COLCORD). Franchise award date: N.A. Franchise expiration date: N.A. Began: January 1, 1983.
Channel capacity: 35 (not 2-way capable). Channels available but not in use: N.A.

Basic Service

Subscribers: 114.
Programming (received off-air): KJRH-TV (NBC) Tulsa; KMYT-TV (MNT) Tulsa; KOED-TV (PBS) Tulsa; KOKI-TV (FOX) Tulsa; KOTV-DT (CBS) Tulsa; KQCW-DT (CW) Muskogee; KTUL (ABC) Tulsa; KWHB (IND) Tulsa.
Programming (via satellite): A&E Networks; ABC Family Channel; AMC; CNBC; CNN; Country Music TV; Discovery Channel; Disney Channel; ESPN; ESPN 2; Headline News; Lifetime; MTV; Nickelodeon; Speed; Spike TV; TBS Superstation; Travel Channel; Turner Network TV; USA Network; WGN America.
Fee: $40.00 installation; $21.95 monthly; $1.96 converter; $19.95 additional installation.

Pay Service 1

Pay Units: 11.
Programming (via satellite): Cinemax; HBO; Showtime.
Fee: $9.95 monthly (each).

Video-On-Demand: No

Pay-Per-View

Hot Choice (delivered digitally); Playboy TV (delivered digitally); Fresh (delivered digitally); Shorteez (delivered digitally); iN DEMAND (delivered digitally).

Internet Service

Operational: No.

Telephone Service

None

Miles of Plant: 6.0 (coaxial); None (fiber optic).
Chief Executive Officer: Bill Haggarty. Regional Vice President: Andrew Dearth. Vice President, Marketing: Tracy Bass.
Ownership: Allegiance Communications (MSO).

COLLINSVILLE—Community Cablevision Co., 1550 W Rogers Blvd, PO Box 307, Skiatook, OK 74070-0307. Phone: 918-396-3019. Fax: 918-396-2081. Web Site: http://www.communitycablebroadband.com. ICA: OK0069.
TV Market Ranking: 54 (COLLINSVILLE). Franchise award date: April 2, 1980. Franchise expiration date: N.A. Began: January 1, 1980.
Channel capacity: N.A. Channels available but not in use: N.A.

Basic Service

Subscribers: 1,201.
Programming (received off-air): KDOR-TV (TBN) Bartlesville; KGEB (IND) Tulsa; KJRH-TV (NBC) Tulsa; KOED-TV (PBS) Tulsa; KOKI-TV (FOX) Tulsa; KOTV-DT (CBS) Tulsa; KRSC-TV (ETV) Claremore; KTPX-TV (ION) Okmulgee; KTUL (ABC) Tulsa; KWHB (IND) Tulsa; allband FM.
Programming (via microwave): KTFO-CD (TEL) Austin.
Programming (via satellite): A&E Networks; ABC Family Channel; AMC; Animal Planet; BET Networks; Cartoon Network; CNN; Comedy Central; Country Music TV; C-SPAN; CW+; Discovery Channel; Discovery Health Channel; Disney Channel; ESPN; ESPN 2; ESPN Classic Sports; Food Network; Fox News Channel; Fox Sports Southwest; FX; Hallmark Channel; HGTV; History Channel; Lifetime; MoviePlex; MTV; National Geographic Channel; Nickelodeon; Outdoor Channel; Oxygen; QVC; Spike TV; Syfy; TBS Superstation; The Learning Channel; The Weather Channel; Travel Channel; truTV; Turner Classic Movies; Turner Network TV; TV Land; USA Network; VH1; WE tv; WGN America.
Fee: $29.95 installation; $32.95 monthly; $10.00 additional installation.

Digital Basic Service

Subscribers: N.A.
Programming (via satellite): AmericanLife TV Network; BBC America; Bio; Bloomberg Television; Bravo; Church Channel; Current; Discovery Fit & Health; Discovery Health Channel; Discovery Home Channel; Discovery Kids Channel; Discovery Times Channel; DMX Music; ESPN 2; ESPN Classic Sports; ESPNews; Fox College Sports Atlantic; Fox College Sports Central; Fox College Sports Pacific; Fox Movie Channel; Fox Soccer; Fuse; G4; GAS; Golf Channel; Great American Country; GSN; Halogen Network; HGTV; History Channel; History Channel International; Independent Film Channel; JCTV; Lifetime Movie Network; Lime; MBC America; Military Channel; MTV Hits; MTV Jams; MTV2; National Geographic Channel; Nick Jr.; NickToons TV; Outdoor Channel; Ovation; Science; ShopNBC; Speed; Style Network; Syfy; The Word Network; Toon Disney; Trinity Broadcasting Network; Trio; Turner Classic Movies; Versus; VH1 Classic; VH1 Country; VH1 Soul; WE tv.
Fee: $24.00 monthly.

Digital Pay Service 1

Pay Units: N.A.
Programming (via satellite): Cinemax (multiplexed); Encore (multiplexed); Flix; HBO (multiplexed); Showtime (multiplexed); Starz (multiplexed); Sundance Channel; The Movie Channel (multiplexed).
Fee: $11.50 monthly (HBO, Cinemax, Starz/Encore, or Showtime/TMC/Flix/Sundance).

Video-On-Demand: Yes

Pay-Per-View

iN DEMAND (delivered digitally).

Internet Service

Operational: Yes.
Broadband Service: In-house.
Fee: $29.95 installation; $34.95 monthly.

Telephone Service

None

Miles of Plant: 33.0 (coaxial); None (fiber optic).
President & General Manager: Dennis Soule.
Ownership: Community Cablevision Co. (MSO).

COMANCHE—Pioneer Telephone Coop. Formerly [OK0177]. This cable system has converted to IPTV, PO Box 539, Kingfisher, OK 73750. Phones: 888-782-2667; 405-375-4111. E-mail: website@pldi.net. Web Site: http://www.ptci.com. ICA: OK5022.
TV Market Ranking: 39 (COMANCHE (portions)); Below 100 (COMANCHE (portions)). Franchise award date: N.A. Franchise expiration date: N.A. Began: March 31, 2005.
Channel capacity: N.A. Channels available but not in use: N.A.

Internet Service

Operational: Yes.

Telephone Service

Digital: Operational

General Manager: Richard Ruhl.

COMANCHE—Pioneer Telephone Coop. This cable system has converted to IPTV. See Comanche, OK [OK5022]. ICA: OK0177.

COMANCHE COUNTY (unincorporated area)—LakeView Cable, Hwy 115, PO Box 460, Cache, OK 73527-0460. Phone: 580-429-8800. Fax: 580-429-6599. Web Site: http://www.lvcisp.com. ICA: OK0396.
TV Market Ranking: Below 100 (COMANCHE COUNTY (UNINCORPORATED AREA)).
Channel capacity: N.A. Channels available but not in use: N.A.

Basic Service

Subscribers: 275.
Programming (received off-air): KAUT-TV (MNT) Oklahoma City; KAUZ-TV (CBS, CW) Wichita Falls; KETA-TV (PBS) Oklahoma City; KFDX-TV (NBC) Wichita Falls; KFOR-TV (NBC) Oklahoma City; KJTL (FOX) Wichita Falls; KSWO-TV (ABC, TMO) Lawton; KWTV-DT (CBS) Oklahoma City.
Programming (via satellite): A&E Networks; ABC Family Channel; AMC; American-Life TV Network; CNN; Country Music TV; C-SPAN; Discovery Channel; Disney Channel; E! Entertainment Television; ESPN; Fox News Channel; Fox Sports Southwest; Headline News; History Channel; Lifetime; Nickelodeon; QVC; Spike TV; Syfy; TBS Superstation; The Learning Channel; The Weather Channel; Trinity Broadcasting Network; Turner Network TV; TV Land; USA Network; WGN America.
Fee: $39.95 installation; $31.75 monthly.

Pay Service 1

Pay Units: N.A.
Programming (via satellite): HBO; Showtime; The Movie Channel.
Fee: $7.95 monthly (TMC), $9.95 monthly (Showtime), $10.95 monthly (HBO).

Internet Service

Operational: No.

Manager: Bill Rowell. Chief Technician: Mike Rowell.
Ownership: Lakeview Cable Inc. (MSO).

COOKSON—Formerly served by Eagle Media. No longer in operation. ICA: OK0367.

COPAN—Community Cablevision Co., 1550 W Rogers Blvd, PO Box 307, Skiatook, OK 74070-0307. Phone: 918-396-3019. Fax: 918-396-2081. E-mail: info@communitycablevision.com. Web Site: http://www.communitycablebroadband.com. ICA: OK0168.
TV Market Ranking: Below 100 (COPAN). Franchise award date: N.A. Franchise expiration date: N.A. Began: N.A.
Channel capacity: 35 (not 2-way capable). Channels available but not in use: N.A.

Basic Service

Subscribers: 234.
Programming (received off-air): KDOR-TV (TBN) Bartlesville; KGEB (IND) Tulsa; KJRH-TV (NBC) Tulsa; KOED-TV (PBS) Tulsa; KOKI-TV (FOX) Tulsa; KOTV-DT (CBS) Tulsa; KQCW-DT (CW) Muskogee; KRSC-TV (ETV) Claremore; KTPX-TV (ION) Okmulgee; KTUL (ABC) Tulsa; KWHB (IND) Tulsa.
Programming (via satellite): A&E Networks; ABC Family Channel; Cartoon Network; CNN; Country Music TV; C-SPAN; Discovery Channel; Disney Channel; ESPN; ESPN 2; Fox News Channel; Fox Sports Southwest; Headline News; Lifetime; MTV; Nickelodeon; QVC; Spike TV; Syfy; TBS Superstation; The Learning Channel; The Weather Channel; Turner Classic Movies; Turner Network TV; USA Network; WGN America.
Fee: $29.95 installation; $19.95 monthly; $7.50 additional installation.

Video-On-Demand: No

Internet Service

Operational: Yes.
Fee: $44.95 monthly.

Telephone Service

None

Miles of Plant: 12.0 (coaxial); None (fiber optic).
President & General Manager: Dennis Soule.
Ownership: Community Cablevision Co. (MSO).

CORN—Cable West, 314 W Main St, PO Box 237, Mountain View, OK 73062. Phones: 800-980-7912; 580-347-3220. Fax: 580-347-2143. ICA: OK0274.
TV Market Ranking: Outside TV Markets (CORN). Franchise award date: November 1, 1979. Franchise expiration date: N.A. Began: N.A.
Channel capacity: 36 (2-way capable). Channels available but not in use: N.A.

Basic Service

Subscribers: 123.
Programming (received off-air): KAUT-TV (MNT) Oklahoma City; KETA-TV (PBS) Oklahoma City; KFOR-TV (NBC) Oklahoma City; KOCB (CW) Oklahoma City; KOCO-TV (ABC) Oklahoma City; KOKH-TV (FOX) Oklahoma City; KTBO-TV (TBN) Oklahoma City; KWTV-DT (CBS) Oklahoma City.
Programming (via satellite): ABC Family Channel; CNN; Discovery Channel; Disney Channel; E! Entertainment Television; ESPN; Nickelodeon; Spike TV; TBS Superstation; The Weather Channel; Turner Network TV; TV Land; USA Network; WGN America.
Fee: $39.95 installation; $31.75 monthly.

Pay Service 1

Pay Units: 5.
Programming (via satellite): HBO.
Fee: $10.95 monthly.

Pay Service 2

Pay Units: 6.
Programming (via satellite): Showtime.
Fee: $9.95 monthly.

Internet Service

Operational: No.

Telephone Service

None

Miles of Plant: 4.0 (coaxial); None (fiber optic).
Manager & Chief Technician: Mickey Davis.
Ownership: Mickey Davis (MSO).

COVINGTON—Pioneer Telephone Coop. Formerly [OK0203]. This cable system has converted to IPTV, PO Box 539, Kingfisher, OK 73750. Phones: 888-782-2667; 405-375-

MediaPrints
Map a Winning Business Strategy
Digital Cable and TV Coverage Maps.
Visit www.warren-news.com/mediaprints.htm

4111. E-mail: website@pldi.net. Web Site: http://www.ptci.com. ICA: OK5064.
Channel capacity: N.A. Channels available but not in use: N.A.
Internet Service
Operational: Yes.
Telephone Service
Digital: Operational
General Manager: Richard Ruhl.

COVINGTON—Pioneer Telephone Coop. This cable system has converted to IPTV. See Covington, OK [OK5064]. ICA: OK0203.

CRESCENT—Suddenlink Communications, 12444 Powerscourt Dr, Saint Louis, MO 63131-3660. Phone: 580-237-7373. Fax: 316-262-2309. Web Site: http://www.suddenlink.com. ICA: OK0124.
TV Market Ranking: 39 (CRESCENT). Franchise award date: March 16, 1980. Franchise expiration date: N.A. Began: October 19, 1981.
Channel capacity: 37 (not 2-way capable). Channels available but not in use: N.A.
Basic Service
Subscribers: 195.
Programming (received off-air): KAUT-TV (MNT) Oklahoma City; KETA-TV (PBS) Oklahoma City; KFOR-TV (NBC) Oklahoma City; KOCB (CW) Oklahoma City; KOCO-TV (ABC) Oklahoma City; KOKH-TV (FOX) Oklahoma City; KSBI (IND) Oklahoma City; KTBO-TV (TBN) Oklahoma City; KWTV-DT (CBS) Oklahoma City.
Programming (via satellite): A&E Networks; AMC; Animal Planet; C-SPAN; Discovery Channel; ESPN; Food Network; Fox Sports Southwest; HGTV; Lifetime; MSNBC; Nickelodeon; The Learning Channel; The Weather Channel; TV Land; USA Network.
Fee: $16.78 installation; $20.00 monthly; $13.10 additional installation.
Expanded Basic Service 1
Subscribers: N.A.
Programming (via satellite): ABC Family Channel; CNN; Disney Channel; Headline News; Spike TV; TBS Superstation; Turner Network TV; WGN America.
Fee: $3.91 monthly.
Pay Service 1
Pay Units: N.A.
Programming (via satellite): Cinemax; HBO; Showtime.
Internet Service
Operational: No.
Telephone Service
None
Miles of Plant: 39.0 (coaxial); None (fiber optic).
Manager: Byron Mahaffey. Marketing Manager: Heather Eastwood. Chief Technician: Richard Kindred.
Ownership: Cequel Communications LLC (MSO).

CROMWELL—Allegiance Communications, 707 W Saratoga St, Shawnee, OK 74804. Phones: 405-275-6923; 405-395-1131. Web Site: http://www.allegiance.tv. ICA: OK0258.
TV Market Ranking: Below 100 (CROMWELL). Franchise award date: January 1, 1989. Franchise expiration date: January 1, 2014. Began: September 1, 1989.
Channel capacity: N.A. Channels available but not in use: N.A.
Basic Service
Subscribers: N.A.
Programming (received off-air): KAUT-TV (MNT) Oklahoma City; KETA-TV (PBS) Oklahoma City; KFOR-TV (NBC) Oklahoma City; KOCB (CW) Oklahoma City; KOCO-TV (ABC) Oklahoma City; KOKH-TV (FOX) Oklahoma City; KOPX-TV (ION) Oklahoma City; KTBO-TV (TBN) Oklahoma City; KWTV-DT (CBS) Oklahoma City.
Programming (via satellite): A&E Networks; ABC Family Channel; AMC; Animal Planet; CNBC; CNN; Country Music TV; Discovery Channel; Disney Channel; ESPN; ESPN 2; Lifetime; MTV; Nickelodeon; Spike TV; Syfy; TBS Superstation; Travel Channel; Turner Network TV; USA Network; WGN America.
Fee: $30.00 installation; $21.95 monthly.
Pay Service 1
Pay Units: N.A.
Programming (via satellite): HBO.
Fee: $10.00 monthly.
Video-On-Demand: No
Pay-Per-View
Hot Choice (delivered digitally); Playboy TV (delivered digitally); Fresh (delivered digitally); Shorteez (delivered digitally); iN DEMAND (delivered digitally).
Internet Service
Operational: No.
Telephone Service
None
Miles of Plant: 3.0 (coaxial); None (fiber optic).
Chief Executive Officer: Bill Haggarty. Regional Vice President: Andrew Dearth. Vice President, Marketing: Tracy Bass.
Ownership: Allegiance Communications (MSO).

CUSHING—Suddenlink Communications, 12444 Powerscourt Dr, Saint Louis, MO 63131-3660. Phone: 918-225-0130. Fax: 405-372-3980. Web Site: http://www.suddenlink.com. ICA: OK0037.
TV Market Ranking: Outside TV Markets (CUSHING). Franchise award date: August 28, 1978. Franchise expiration date: N.A. Began: March 5, 1980.
Channel capacity: 116 (operating 2-way). Channels available but not in use: N.A.
Basic Service
Subscribers: 2,754.
Programming (received off-air): KAUT-TV (MNT) Oklahoma City; KETA-TV (PBS) Oklahoma City; KFOR-TV (NBC) Oklahoma City; KOCB (CW) Oklahoma City; KOCO-TV (ABC) Oklahoma City; KOKH-TV (FOX) Oklahoma City; KOPX-TV (ION) Oklahoma City; KSBI (IND) Oklahoma City; KTBO-TV (TBN) Oklahoma City; KTUL (ABC) Tulsa; KWTV-DT (CBS) Oklahoma City.
Programming (via satellite): C-SPAN; Jewelry Television; QVC; The Weather Channel; TV Guide Network; WGN America.
Fee: $50.00 installation; $13.98 monthly.
Expanded Basic Service 1
Subscribers: 2,396.
Programming (via satellite): A&E Networks; ABC Family Channel; AMC; Animal Planet; BET Networks; Bravo; Cartoon Network; CNBC; CNN; Comedy Central; Country Music TV; C-SPAN 2; Discovery Channel; Discovery Health Channel; Disney Channel; E! Entertainment Television; ESPN; ESPN 2; ESPN Classic Sports; Eternal Word TV Network; Food Network; Fox News Channel; Fox Sports Southwest; FX; Hallmark Channel; Headline News; HGTV; History Channel; Lifetime; Lifetime Movie Network; MSNBC; MTV; MTV2; Nickelodeon; Oxygen; Spike TV; Syfy; TBS Superstation; The Learning Channel; Travel Channel; truTV; Turner Network TV; TV Land; Univision Studios; USA Network; VH1.
Fee: $19.52 monthly.
Digital Basic Service
Subscribers: 245.
Programming (via satellite): A&E HD; BBC America; Bio; Bloomberg Television; CBS Sports Network; CMT Pure Country; Discovery Home Channel; Discovery Kids Channel; DMX Music; Encore (multiplexed); ESPN HD; ESPN U; ESPNews; Food Network HD; Fox Movie Channel; Fox Soccer; Fuse; G4; Golf Channel; GSN; HD Theater; HDNet; HDNet Movies; HGTV HD; History Channel HD; History Channel International; ID Investigation Discovery; Independent Film Channel; Lifetime Movie Network; Military Channel; MTV Hits; National Geographic Channel; National Geographic Channel HD Network; Nick Jr.; NickToons TV; Science; SoapNet; Speed; TeenNick; Toon Disney; Turner Classic Movies; Turner Network TV HD; Versus; VH1 Classic; VH1 Soul.
Fee: $20.00 installation; $17.00 monthly.
Pay Service 1
Pay Units: 788.
Programming (via satellite): HBO.
Fee: $10.00 installation; $12.95 monthly.
Pay Service 2
Pay Units: 409.
Programming (via satellite): Cinemax.
Fee: $12.95 monthly.
Pay Service 3
Pay Units: 89.
Programming (via satellite): Starz.
Fee: $10.00 installation; $12.95 monthly.
Pay Service 4
Pay Units: 790.
Programming (via satellite): Encore.
Fee: $10.00 installation; $6.75 monthly.
Pay Service 5
Pay Units: 805.
Programming (via satellite): Showtime.
Fee: $10.00 installation; $1.75 monthly.
Digital Pay Service 1
Pay Units: N.A.
Programming (via satellite): Cinemax (multiplexed); HBO (multiplexed); HBO HD; Showtime (multiplexed); Showtime HD; Starz (multiplexed); The Movie Channel (multiplexed).
Video-On-Demand: No
Pay-Per-View
iN DEMAND (delivered digitally); Fresh (delivered digitally); Shorteez (delivered digitally); Playboy TV (delivered digitally); ESPN Now (delivered digitally); sports (delivered digitally).
Internet Service
Operational: Yes. Began: January 15, 2003.
Broadband Service: Suddenlink High Speed Internet.
Fee: $45.95 installation; $24.95 monthly; $10.00 modem lease; $99.95 modem purchase.
Telephone Service
Analog: Not Operational
Digital: Operational
Fee: $49.95 monthly
Miles of Plant: 63.0 (coaxial); 13.0 (fiber optic).
Manager: Nicloe Evans. Marketing Manager: Heather Eastwood. Chief Technician: Johnny Stanley.
Ownership: Cequel Communications LLC (MSO).

CUSTER CITY—Pioneer Telephone Coop. Formerly [OK0277]. This cable system has converted to IPTV, PO Box 539, Kingfisher, OK 73750. Phones: 888-782-2667; 405-375-4111. E-mail: website@pldi.net. Web Site: http://www.ptci.com. ICA: OK5066.
Channel capacity: N.A. Channels available but not in use: N.A.
Internet Service
Operational: Yes.
Telephone Service
Digital: Operational
General Manager: Richard Ruhl.

CUSTER CITY—Pioneer Telephone Coop. This cable system has converted to IPTV. See Custer City, OK [OK5066]. ICA: OK0277.

CYRIL—Alliance Cable Network, 290 S Broadview, Greenbrier, AR 72058. Phones: 800-842-8160; 501-679-6619. Web Site: http://www.alliancecable.net. ICA: OK0372.
TV Market Ranking: Below 100 (CYRIL). Franchise award date: N.A. Franchise expiration date: N.A. Began: N.A.
Channel capacity: 36 (not 2-way capable). Channels available but not in use: N.A.
Basic Service
Subscribers: 100.
Programming (received off-air): KAUT-TV (MNT) Oklahoma City; KETA-TV (PBS) Oklahoma City; KFOR-TV (NBC) Oklahoma City; KJTL (FOX) Wichita Falls; KOCB (CW) Oklahoma City; KOCO-TV (ABC) Oklahoma City; KOKH-TV (FOX) Oklahoma City; KSBI (IND) Oklahoma City; KSWO-TV (ABC, TMO) Lawton; KTBO-TV (TBN) Oklahoma City; KWTV-DT (CBS) Oklahoma City.
Programming (via satellite): A&E Networks; ABC Family Channel; AMC; CNN; C-SPAN; Discovery Channel; Disney Channel; ESPN; Fox Sports Southwest; Great American Country; History Channel; National Geographic Channel; Nickelodeon; QVC; Spike TV; TBS Superstation; The Learning Channel; The Weather Channel; Turner Network TV; TV Land; USA Network.
Fee: $29.95 installation; $38.00 monthly.
Pay Service 1
Pay Units: 47.
Programming (via satellite): HBO.
Fee: $10.95 monthly.
Pay Service 2
Pay Units: 21.
Programming (via satellite): Showtime.
Fee: $9.95 monthly.
Video-On-Demand: Yes
Internet Service
Operational: No.
Telephone Service
None
Miles of Plant: 17.0 (coaxial); None (fiber optic).
Ownership: Alliance Communications Network (MSO).

DACOMA—Pioneer Telephone Coop. Formerly [OK0278]. This cable system has converted to IPTV, PO Box 539, Kingfisher, OK 73750. Phones: 888-782-2667; 405-

375-4111. E-mail: website@pldi.net. Web Site: http://www.ptci.com. ICA: OK5093.
TV Market Ranking: Franchise award date: N.A. Franchise expiration date: N.A. Began: January 15, 2006.
Channel capacity: N.A. Channels available but not in use: N.A.
Internet Service
Operational: Yes.
Telephone Service
Digital: Operational
General Manager: Richard Ruhl.

DACOMA—Pioneer Telephone Coop. This cable system has converted to IPTV. See Dacoma, OK [OK5093]. ICA: OK0278.

DAVENPORT—Vi-Tel Inc., 223 Broadway, PO Box 789, Davenport, OK 74026-0789. Phones: 800-252-8854; 918-377-2241; 918-377-2347. Fax: 918-377-2506. E-mail: staff@cotc.net. Web Site: http://www.cotc.net. ICA: OK0182.
TV Market Ranking: Below 100 (DAVENPORT). Franchise award date: N.A. Franchise expiration date: N.A. Began: April 1, 1983.
Channel capacity: 61 (not 2-way capable). Channels available but not in use: N.A.
Basic Service
Subscribers: 194.
Programming (received off-air): KAUT-TV (MNT) Oklahoma City; KETA-TV (PBS) Oklahoma City; KFOR-TV (NBC) Oklahoma City; KJRH-TV (NBC) Tulsa; KOCB (CW) Oklahoma City; KOCO-TV (ABC) Oklahoma City; KOKH-TV (FOX) Oklahoma City; KOPX-TV (ION) Oklahoma City; KSBI (IND) Oklahoma City; KTBO-TV (TBN) Oklahoma City; KWTV-DT (CBS) Oklahoma City.
Programming (via satellite): A&E Networks; ABC Family Channel; AMC; Animal Planet; Cartoon Network; CNN; Comedy Central; Country Music TV; C-SPAN; Discovery Channel; Disney Channel; ESPN; ESPN 2; Fox Sports Southwest; Headline News; HGTV; History Channel; Lifetime; Nickelodeon; Spike TV; Syfy; TBS Superstation; The Learning Channel; The Weather Channel; truTV; Turner Classic Movies; Turner Network TV; TV Land; USA Network; WGN America.
Fee: $17.50 installation; $25.95 monthly.
Pay Service 1
Pay Units: 37.
Programming (via satellite): HBO.
Fee: $10.95 monthly.
Pay Service 2
Pay Units: 15.
Programming (via satellite): Showtime.
Fee: $10.95 monthly.
Internet Service
Operational: No.
Telephone Service
None
Miles of Plant: 13.0 (coaxial); None (fiber optic).
Manager: Steve Guest.
Ownership: Vi-Tel Inc.

DAVIDSON—Formerly served by CableDirect. No longer in operation. ICA: OK0279.

DEER CREEK—Formerly served by CableDirect. No longer in operation. ICA: OK0280.

DELAWARE—Allegiance Communications, 707 W Saratoga St, Shawnee, OK 74804. Phones: 405-275-6923; 405-395-1131. Web Site: http://www.allegiance.tv. Also serves Lenapah. ICA: OK0189.
TV Market Ranking: Below 100 (DELAWARE, Lenapah). Franchise award date: December 1, 1983. Franchise expiration date: N.A. Began: January 1, 1984.
Channel capacity: 35 (not 2-way capable). Channels available but not in use: N.A.
Basic Service
Subscribers: 106.
Programming (received off-air): KDOR-TV (TBN) Bartlesville; KJRH-TV (NBC) Tulsa; KMYT-TV (MNT) Tulsa; KOED-TV (PBS) Tulsa; KOKI-TV (FOX) Tulsa; KOTV-DT (CBS) Tulsa; KQCW-DT (CW) Muskogee; KRSC-TV (ETV) Claremore; KTUL (ABC) Tulsa; KWHB (IND) Tulsa.
Programming (via satellite): A&E Networks; ABC Family Channel; AMC; Animal Planet; BET Networks; CNBC; CNN; Country Music TV; Discovery Channel; Disney Channel; E! Entertainment Television; ESPN; ESPN 2; Headline News; Lifetime; MTV; Nickelodeon; Spike TV; Syfy; TBS Superstation; The Learning Channel; Travel Channel; Turner Network TV; USA Network; WGN America.
Fee: $30.00 installation; $22.95 monthly.
Pay Service 1
Pay Units: N.A.
Programming (via satellite): Cinemax; HBO; Showtime.
Fee: $20.00 installation; $9.95 monthly (each).
Video-On-Demand: No
Pay-Per-View
iN DEMAND (delivered digitally); Hot Choice (delivered digitally); Playboy TV (delivered digitally); Fresh (delivered digitally); Shorteez (delivered digitally).
Internet Service
Operational: No.
Telephone Service
None
Miles of Plant: 14.0 (coaxial); None (fiber optic).
Chief Executive Officer: Bill Haggarty. Regional Vice President: Andrew Dearth. Vice President, Marketing: Tracy Bass.
Ownership: Allegiance Communications (MSO).

DEPEW—Allegiance Communications, 707 W Saratoga St, Shawnee, OK 74804. Phones: 405-275-6923; 405-395-1131. Web Site: http://www.allegiance.tv. ICA: OK0212.
TV Market Ranking: Below 100 (DEPEW). Franchise award date: January 1, 1989. Franchise expiration date: January 1, 2014. Began: September 1, 1989.
Channel capacity: N.A. Channels available but not in use: N.A.
Basic Service
Subscribers: 89.
Programming (received off-air): KAUT-TV (MNT) Oklahoma City; KJRH-TV (NBC) Tulsa; KMYT-TV (MNT) Tulsa; KOED-TV (PBS) Tulsa; KOKH-TV (FOX) Oklahoma City; KOTV-DT (CBS) Tulsa; KQCW-DT (CW) Muskogee; KSBI (IND) Oklahoma City; KTPX-TV (ION) Okmulgee; KTUL (ABC) Tulsa; KWHB (IND) Tulsa.
Programming (via satellite): A&E Networks; ABC Family Channel; CNBC; CNN; Discovery Channel; Disney Channel; ESPN; ESPN 2; Headline News; Lifetime; MTV; Nickelodeon; Spike TV; Syfy; TBS Superstation; Travel Channel; Turner Network TV; USA Network; WGN America.
Fee: $40.00 installation; $22.95 monthly; $1.96 converter; $19.95 additional installation.
Pay Service 1
Pay Units: 22.
Programming (via satellite): HBO.

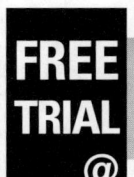

Fee: $20.00 installation; $9.95 monthly.
Video-On-Demand: No
Pay-Per-View
iN DEMAND (delivered digitally); Hot Choice (delivered digitally); Playboy TV (delivered digitally); Fresh (delivered digitally); Shorteez (delivered digitally).
Internet Service
Operational: No.
Telephone Service
None
Miles of Plant: 4.0 (coaxial); None (fiber optic).
Chief Executive Officer: Bill Haggarty. Regional Vice President: Andrew Dearth. Vice President, Marketing: Tracy Bass.
Ownership: Allegiance Communications (MSO).

DILL CITY—Cable West, 314 W Main St, PO Box 237, Mountain View, OK 73062. Phones: 800-980-7912; 580-347-3220. Fax: 580-347-2143. ICA: OK0188.
TV Market Ranking: Outside TV Markets (DILL CITY). Franchise award date: N.A. Franchise expiration date: N.A. Began: June 1, 1970.
Channel capacity: 41 (2-way capable). Channels available but not in use: N.A.
Basic Service
Subscribers: 149.
Programming (received off-air): KAUT-TV (MNT) Oklahoma City; KFOR-TV (NBC) Oklahoma City; KOCB (CW) Oklahoma City; KOCO-TV (ABC) Oklahoma City; KOKH-TV (FOX) Oklahoma City; KSWO-TV (ABC, TMO) Lawton; KWET (PBS) Cheyenne; KWTV-DT (CBS) Oklahoma City.
Programming (via satellite): ABC Family Channel; AMC; CNN; Country Music TV; Discovery Channel; Disney Channel; ESPN; Nickelodeon; Spike TV; Syfy; TBS Superstation; Trinity Broadcasting Network; Turner Network TV; USA Network; WGN America.
Fee: $39.95 installation; $29.95 monthly.
Pay Service 1
Pay Units: 35.
Programming (via satellite): HBO.
Fee: $9.95 monthly.
Internet Service
Operational: No.
Telephone Service
None
Miles of Plant: 6.0 (coaxial); None (fiber optic).
Manager & Chief Technician: Mickey Davis.
Ownership: Mickey Davis (MSO).

DISNEY—Omni III Cable TV Inc., 226 S 4th St, PO Box 308, Jay, OK 74346-0308. Phone: 918-253-4545. Fax: 918-253-3400. Also serves Jay. ICA: OK0216.
TV Market Ranking: Outside TV Markets (DISNEY, Jay). Franchise award date: N.A. Franchise expiration date: N.A. Began: March 1, 1983.
Channel capacity: 34 (not 2-way capable). Channels available but not in use: N.A.
Basic Service
Subscribers: 1,005.
Programming (received off-air): KDOR-TV (TBN) Bartlesville; KJRH-TV (NBC) Tulsa; KOAM-TV (CBS) Pittsburg; KOKI-TV (FOX) Tulsa; KOTV-DT (CBS) Tulsa; KSNF (NBC) Joplin; KTUL (ABC) Tulsa.
Programming (via satellite): A&E Networks; ABC Family Channel; AMC; Cartoon Network; CNN; Country Music TV; C-SPAN; Discovery Channel; Disney Channel; ESPN; Headline News; History Channel; Nickelodeon; QVC; Spike TV; TBS Superstation; The Weather Channel; Turner Classic Movies; Turner Network TV; USA Network; WGN America.
Fee: $20.00 installation; $15.00 monthly.
Pay Service 1
Pay Units: 104.
Programming (via satellite): HBO.
Fee: $10.00 installation; $13.00 monthly.
Pay Service 2
Pay Units: 21.
Programming (via satellite): Cinemax.
Fee: $10.00 installation; $13.00 monthly.
Pay Service 3
Pay Units: 24.
Programming (via satellite): Showtime.
Fee: $10.00 installation; $13.00 monthly.
Video-On-Demand: No
Internet Service
Operational: No.
Telephone Service
None
Miles of Plant: 7.0 (coaxial); 15.0 (fiber optic).
Manager: Rex Brixey.
Ownership: Omni III Cable TV Inc.

DOVER—Pioneer Telephone Coop. Formerly [OK0250]. This cable system has converted to IPTV, PO Box 539, Kingfisher, OK 73750. Phones: 888-782-2667; 405-375-4111. E-mail: website@pldi.net. Web Site: http://www.ptci.com. ICA: OK5099.
Channel capacity: N.A. Channels available but not in use: N.A.
Internet Service
Operational: Yes.
Telephone Service
Digital: Operational
General Manager: Richard Ruhl.

DOVER—Pioneer Telephone Coop. This cable system has converted to IPTV. See Dover, OK [OK5099]. ICA: OK0250.

DRUMMOND—Pioneer Telephone Coop. Formerly [OK0281]. This cable system has converted to IPTV, PO Box 539, Kingfisher, OK 73750. Phones: 888-782-2667; 405-375-4111. E-mail: website@pldi.net. Web Site: http://www.ptci.com. ICA: OK5094.
TV Market Ranking: Franchise award date: N.A. Franchise expiration date: N.A. Began: September 30, 2004.
Channel capacity: N.A. Channels available but not in use: N.A.
Internet Service
Operational: Yes.

Telephone Service
Digital: Operational
General Manager: Richard Ruhl.

DRUMMOND—Pioneer Telephone Coop. This cable system has converted to IPTV. See Drummond, OK [OK5094]. ICA: OK0281.

DRUMRIGHT—Suddenlink Communications, 12444 Powerscourt Dr, Saint Louis, MO 63131-3660. Phone: 918-225-0130. Fax: 405-372-3980. Web Site: http://www.suddenlink.com. ICA: OK0393.
TV Market Ranking: Outside TV Markets (DRUMRIGHT).
Channel capacity: N.A. Channels available but not in use: N.A.
Basic Service
Subscribers: N.A.
Programming (received off-air): KDOR-TV (TBN) Bartlesville; KFOR-TV (NBC) Oklahoma City; KJRH-TV (NBC) Tulsa; KMYT-TV (MNT) Tulsa; KOCO-TV (ABC) Oklahoma City; KOED-TV (PBS) Tulsa; KOKI-TV (FOX) Tulsa; KOTV-DT (CBS) Tulsa; KQCW-DT (CW) Muskogee; KTPX-TV (ION) Okmulgee; KTUL (ABC) Tulsa; KWHB (IND) Tulsa; KWTV-DT (CBS) Oklahoma City.
Programming (via satellite): C-SPAN; QVC; The Weather Channel; TV Guide Network; WGN America.
Expanded Basic Service 1
Subscribers: N.A.
Programming (via satellite): A&E Networks; ABC Family Channel; AMC; Animal Planet; BET Networks; Bravo; Cartoon Network; CNBC; CNN; Comedy Central; Country Music TV; C-SPAN 2; Discovery Channel; Discovery Health Channel; Disney Channel; E! Entertainment Television; ESPN; ESPN 2; ESPN Deportes; Eternal Word TV Network; Food Network; Fox News Channel; Fox Sports Southwest; FX; Headline News; HGTV; History Channel; Lifetime; MSNBC; MTV; MTV2; News Now 53; Nickelodeon; Oxygen; Spike TV; Syfy; TBS Superstation; The Learning Channel; Travel Channel; truTV; Turner Network TV; TV Land; Univision Studios; USA Network; VH1.
Digital Basic Service
Subscribers: N.A.
Programming (via satellite): BBC America; Bio; Bloomberg Television; Discovery Fit & Health; DMX Music; Encore (multiplexed); ESPN Classic Sports; ESPNews; Fox Movie Channel; Fox Soccer; Fuse; G4; GAS; Golf Channel; GSN; HD Theater; History Channel International; Independent Film Channel; INHD; INHD2; Lifetime Movie Network; MTV Networks Digital Suite; National Geographic Channel; Nick Jr.; NickToons TV; Outdoor Channel; Speed; Toon Disney; Turner Classic Movies; Versus.
Digital Pay Service 1
Pay Units: N.A.
Programming (via satellite): Cinemax (multiplexed); HBO (multiplexed); Showtime (multiplexed); Showtime HD; Starz (multiplexed); The Movie Channel (multiplexed).
Video-On-Demand: No
Pay-Per-View
iN DEMAND (delivered digitally); Hot Choice (delivered digitally); Fresh (delivered digitally); Shorteez (delivered digitally); Playboy TV (delivered digitally).
Internet Service
Operational: Yes.
Broadband Service: Suddenlink High Speed Internet.
Fee: $45.95 installation; $24.95 monthly.
Telephone Service
Digital: Operational
Fee: $49.95 monthly
Miles of Plant: 31.0 (coaxial); 3.0 (fiber optic).
Manager: Nicole Evans. Marketing Manager: Heather Eastwood. Chief Technician: Johnny Stanley.
Ownership: Cequel Communications LLC (MSO).

DUKE—Formerly served by CableDirect. No longer in operation. ICA: OK0224.

DUNCAN—Cable One, 1206 N Hwy 81, Ste 30, Duncan, OK 73533-1795. Phone: 580-252-0992. Fax: 580-252-9488. E-mail: lthompson@cableone.net. Web Site: http://www.cableone.net. Also serves Marlow. ICA: OK0013.
TV Market Ranking: Below 100 (DUNCAN, Marlow). Franchise award date: January 1, 1970. Franchise expiration date: January 1, 2020. Began: July 1, 1971.
Channel capacity: 78 (operating 2-way). Channels available but not in use: N.A.
Basic Service
Subscribers: 8,991.
Programming (received off-air): KAUZ-TV (CBS, CW) Wichita Falls; KETA-TV (PBS) Oklahoma City; KFDX-TV (NBC) Wichita Falls; KFOR-TV (NBC) Oklahoma City; KJTL (FOX) Wichita Falls; KOCO-TV (ABC) Oklahoma City; KOKH-TV (FOX) Oklahoma City; KSWO-TV (ABC, TMO) Lawton; KWTV-DT (CBS) Oklahoma City; 6 FMs.
Programming (via satellite): C-SPAN; C-SPAN 2; CW+; QVC; Telemundo; TV Guide Network.
Fee: $75.00 installation; $46.00 monthly; $1.60 converter.
Expanded Basic Service 1
Subscribers: N.A.
Programming (via satellite): A&E Networks; ABC Family Channel; AMC; Animal Planet; BET Networks; Cartoon Network; CNBC; CNN; Country Music TV; Discovery Channel; Disney Channel; ESPN; ESPN 2; Food Network; Fox News Channel; Fox Sports Southwest; FX; Headline News; HGTV; History Channel; INSP; Lifetime; MSNBC; MTV; Nickelodeon; Spike TV; Syfy; TBS Superstation; The Learning Channel; The Weather Channel; Travel Channel; Trinity Broadcasting Network; Turner Classic Movies; Turner Network TV; TV Land; USA Network; VH1.
Fee: $46.00 monthly.
Digital Basic Service
Subscribers: 1,800.
Programming (received off-air): KWTV-DT (CBS) Oklahoma City.
Programming (via satellite): 3 Angels Broadcasting Network; Bio; Boomerang; BYU Television; Canales N; Discovery Digital Networks; DMX Music; ESPN Classic Sports; ESPNews; FamilyNet; Fox College Sports Atlantic; Fox College Sports Central; Fox College Sports Pacific; Fox HD; Fox Movie Channel; Fox Soccer; Fuel TV; G4; Golf Channel; Great American Country; Hallmark Channel; History Channel International; INSP; National Geographic Channel; Outdoor Channel; SoapNet; Speed; Toon Disney; Trinity Broadcasting Network; truTV; Turner Network TV HD; TVG Network; Universal HD.
Digital Pay Service 1
Pay Units: 3,412.
Programming (via satellite): Cinemax (multiplexed); Encore (multiplexed); Flix; HBO (multiplexed); Showtime (multiplexed); Showtime HD; Starz (multiplexed); Sundance Channel; The Movie Channel (multiplexed); The Movie Channel HD.
Fee: $15.00 monthly (each).
Video-On-Demand: No
Pay-Per-View
Addressable homes: 1,800.
iN DEMAND (delivered digitally); Pleasure (delivered digitally); Ten Clips (delivered digitally); Ten Blox (delivered digitally); Ten Blue (delivered digitally).
Internet Service
Operational: Yes. Began: March 1, 2001.
Subscribers: 2,675.
Broadband Service: CableONE.net.
Fee: $75.00 installation; $43.00 monthly.
Telephone Service
Digital: Operational
Fee: $39.95 monthly
Miles of Plant: 249.0 (coaxial); None (fiber optic).
Manager: Deron Lindsay. Marketing Director: Steve Sutton. Chief Technician: Darrel Massie. Office Manager: Lita Thompson.
Ownership: Cable ONE Inc. (MSO).

DURANT—CommuniComm Services, 1501 W Mississippi St, PO Box 597, Durant, OK 74701. Phones: 800-752-4992; 580-924-2367. Fax: 580-924-5970. Web Site: http://www.communicomm.com. Also serves Armstrong, Bryan County & Calera. ICA: OK0022.
TV Market Ranking: Below 100 (Armstrong, Bryan County, Calera, DURANT). Franchise award date: November 10, 1980. Franchise expiration date: N.A. Began: September 1, 1958.
Channel capacity: N.A. Channels available but not in use: N.A.
Basic Service
Subscribers: 10,000 Includes Coalgate, Sandpoint, Stringtown, Tishomingo, & Wapanucka.
Programming (received off-air): KETA-TV (PBS) Oklahoma City; KTEN (ABC, CW, NBC) Ada; KWTV-DT (CBS) Oklahoma City; KXII (CBS, FOX, MNT) Sherman; WFAA (ABC) Dallas; allband FM.
Programming (via satellite): CW+; Fox Business Channel.
Fee: $49.95 installation; $34.95 monthly.
Expanded Basic Service 1
Subscribers: N.A.
Programming (via satellite): A&E Networks; ABC Family Channel; AMC; Animal Planet; BET Networks; Bravo; BYU Television; Cartoon Network; CNBC; CNN; Comedy Central; Country Music TV; C-SPAN; C-SPAN 2; Discovery Channel; Disney Channel; E! Entertainment Television; ESPN; ESPN 2; ESPN Classic Sports; ESPNews; Eternal Word TV Network; Food Network; Fox News Channel; Fox Sports Southwest; FX; Hallmark Channel; Headline News; HGTV; History Channel; ION Television; Lifetime; MSNBC; MTV; MyNetworkTV Inc.; Nickelodeon; Outdoor Channel; QVC; ShopNBC; Spike TV; Syfy; TBS Superstation; The Learning Channel; The Weather Channel; Travel Channel; Trinity Broadcasting Network; truTV; Turner Network TV; TV Guide Network; TV Land; USA Network; VH1; WE tv.
Digital Basic Service
Subscribers: N.A.
Programming (via satellite): A&E HD; AmericanLife TV Network; BBC America; Bio; Bloomberg Television; Bravo; Church Channel; CMT Pure Country; Current; Daystar TV Network; Discovery Fit & Health; Discovery Health Channel; Discovery Home Channel; Discovery Kids Channel; Discovery Times Channel; DMX Music; ESPN 2; ESPN 2 HD; ESPN Classic Sports; ESPN HD; ESPNews; Fox Movie Channel; Fox Soccer; Fuse; G4; Golf Channel; Great American Country; GSN; Halogen Network; HD Theater; HGTV; History Channel; History Channel International; Independent Film Channel; JCTV; Lifetime Movie Network; Military Channel; MTV Hits; MTV Jams; MTV2; National Geographic Channel; Nick Jr.; NickToons TV; Outdoor Channel; Ovation; RFD-TV; Science; ShopNBC; SoapNet; Speed; Style Network; TeenNick; The Word Network; Toon Disney; Trinity Broadcasting Network; Turner Classic Movies; Turner Network TV HD; Universal HD; Versus; VH1 Classic; VH1 Soul; WE tv.
Pay Service 1
Pay Units: 505.
Programming (via satellite): Cinemax (multiplexed).
Fee: $9.95 monthly.
Pay Service 2
Pay Units: 780.
Programming (via satellite): HBO (multiplexed).
Fee: $12.95 monthly.
Pay Service 3
Pay Units: 270.
Programming (via satellite): Encore; Starz (multiplexed).
Fee: $9.95 monthly.
Digital Pay Service 1
Pay Units: N.A.
Programming (via satellite): Cinemax (multiplexed); Encore (multiplexed); Flix; HBO (multiplexed); Showtime (multiplexed); Starz (multiplexed); Starz HDTV; The Movie Channel (multiplexed).
Video-On-Demand: No
Pay-Per-View
iN DEMAND (delivered digitally); Hot Choice (delivered digitally); Playboy TV (delivered digitally); Fresh (delivered digitally); Spice: Xcess (delivered digitally); Club Jenna (delivered digitally).
Internet Service
Operational: Yes. Began: December 1, 1997.
Subscribers: 150.
Broadband Service: Net Commander.
Fee: $39.95 installation; $51.95 monthly.
Telephone Service
None
Miles of Plant: 150.0 (coaxial); 30.0 (fiber optic).
General Manager & Chief Technician: Jeff Beck. Customer Service Manager: Lisa Hamill.
Ownership: James Cable LLC (MSO).

DUSTIN—Allegiance Communications, 707 W Saratoga St, Shawnee, OK 74804. Phones: 405-275-9623; 405-395-1131. Web Site: http://www.allegiance.tv. ICA: OK0237.
TV Market Ranking: Outside TV Markets (DUSTIN). Franchise award date: January 1, 1989. Franchise expiration date: January 1, 2014. Began: September 1, 1989.
Channel capacity: 45 (not 2-way capable). Channels available but not in use: N.A.
Basic Service
Subscribers: N.A.
Programming (received off-air): KJRH-TV (NBC) Tulsa; KMYT-TV (MNT) Tulsa; KOED-TV (PBS) Tulsa; KOKI-TV (FOX) Tulsa; KOPX-TV (ION) Oklahoma City; KOTV-DT (CBS) Tulsa; KQCW-DT (CW) Muskogee; KTUL (ABC) Tulsa; KWHB (IND) Tulsa.
Programming (via satellite): A&E Networks; ABC Family Channel; CNBC; CNN; Country Music TV; Discovery Channel; Disney Channel; ESPN; ESPN 2; Headline News; Lifetime; MTV; Nickelodeon; Spike TV; TBS

Superstation; Travel Channel; Turner Network TV; USA Network; WGN America.
Fee: $40.00 installation; $22.00 monthly; $1.96 converter; $19.95 additional installation.
Video-On-Demand: No
Pay-Per-View
iN DEMAND (delivered digitally); Hot Choice (delivered digitally); Playboy TV (delivered digitally); Fresh (delivered digitally); Shorteez (delivered digitally).
Internet Service
Operational: No.
Telephone Service
None
Miles of Plant: 6.0 (coaxial); None (fiber optic).
Chief Executive Officer: Bill Haggarty. Regional Vice President: Andrew Dearth. Vice President, Marketing: Tracy Bass.
Ownership: Allegiance Communications (MSO).

EAKLY—Hinton CATV Co. Now served by HINTON, OK [OK0140]. ICA: OK0282.

ELDORADO—Formerly served by Cable West. No longer in operation. ICA: OK0383.

ELK CITY—Cable One, 310 N Van Buren St, Elk City, OK 73644. Phone: 580-225-3244. Fax: 580-225-5011. Web Site: http://www.cableone.net. Also serves Clinton, Cordell, Mangum & Sayre. ICA: OK0032.
TV Market Ranking: Below 100 (ELK CITY, Sayre); Outside TV Markets (Clinton, Cordell, Mangum). Franchise award date: March 1, 1953. Franchise expiration date: August 2, 2009. Began: March 1, 1953.
Channel capacity: 78 (operating 2-way). Channels available but not in use: N.A.
Basic Service
Subscribers: 9,500.
Programming (received off-air): KFOR-TV (NBC) Oklahoma City; KOCB (CW) Oklahoma City; KOCO-TV (ABC) Oklahoma City; KOKH-TV (FOX) Oklahoma City; KSBI (IND) Oklahoma City; KUOK-DT (UNV) Woodward; KWET (PBS) Cheyenne; KWTV-DT (CBS) Oklahoma City.
Programming (via satellite): C-SPAN; ION Television; LWS Local Weather Station; QVC; TBS Superstation; TV Guide Network; WGN America.
Fee: $35.00 installation; $46.00 monthly; $3.25 converter; $20.00 additional installation.
Expanded Basic Service 1
Subscribers: 8,350.
Programming (via satellite): A&E Networks; ABC Family Channel; AMC; Animal Planet; BET Networks; Cartoon Network; CNBC; CNN; Country Music TV; C-SPAN 2; Discovery Channel; Disney Channel; E! Entertainment Television; ESPN; ESPN 2; Food Network; Fox News Channel; Fox Sports Southwest; FX; Headline News; HGTV; History Channel; Lifetime; MSNBC; MTV; Nickelodeon; Spike TV; Syfy; The Learning Channel; The Weather Channel; Trinity Broadcasting Network; Turner Classic Movies; Turner Network TV; TV Land; USA Network; VH1.
Fee: $35.00 installation; $46.00 monthly.
Digital Basic Service
Subscribers: 2,350.
Programming (via satellite): 3 Angels Broadcasting Network; Bio; Boomerang; BYU Television; Canales N; Discovery Digital Networks; DMX Music; ESPN Classic Sports; ESPNews; FamilyNet; Fox College Sports Atlantic; Fox College Sports Central; Fox College Sports Pacific; Fox HD; Fox Movie Channel; Fox Soccer; Fuel TV; G4; Golf Channel; Great American Country; Hallmark Channel; History Channel International; INSP; National Geographic Channel; Outdoor Channel; SoapNet; Speed; Toon Disney; Trinity Broadcasting Network; truTV; Turner Network TV HD; TVG Network; Universal HD.
Digital Pay Service 1
Pay Units: 2,308.
Programming (via satellite): Cinemax (multiplexed); Encore (multiplexed); Flix; HBO (multiplexed); Showtime (multiplexed); Showtime HD; Starz (multiplexed); Sundance Channel; The Movie Channel (multiplexed); The Movie Channel HD.
Fee: $15.00 monthly each package.
Video-On-Demand: No
Pay-Per-View
iN DEMAND (delivered digitally); Pleasure (delivered digitally); Ten Clips (delivered digitally); Ten Blox (delivered digitally); Ten Blue (delivered digitally).
Internet Service
Operational: Yes. Began: October 1, 2001.
Subscribers: 2,270.
Broadband Service: CableONE.net.
Fee: $75.00 installation; $43.00 monthly.
Telephone Service
Digital: Operational
Fee: $39.95 monthly
Miles of Plant: 240.0 (coaxial); 32.0 (fiber optic).
Manager: Brook McDonald. Office Manager: Melissa Briscoe. Chief Technician: Tom Leistner.
Ownership: Cable ONE Inc. (MSO).

ELK CREEK—Formerly served by Eagle Media. No longer in operation. ICA: OK0364.

ENID—Suddenlink Communications, 12444 Powerscourt Dr, Saint Louis, MO 63131-3660. Phone: 580-237-7373. Fax: 580-242-4801. Web Site: http://www.suddenlink.com. Also serves Garfield County, North Enid & Vance AFB. ICA: OK0006.
TV Market Ranking: Outside TV Markets (ENID, Garfield County, North Enid, Vance AFB). Franchise award date: N.A. Franchise expiration date: N.A. Began: March 1, 1966.
Channel capacity: 111 (operating 2-way). Channels available but not in use: N.A.
Basic Service
Subscribers: 16,366.
Programming (received off-air): KAUT-TV (MNT) Oklahoma City; KETA-TV (PBS) Oklahoma City; KFOR-TV (NBC) Oklahoma City; KOCB (CW) Oklahoma City; KOCO-TV (ABC) Oklahoma City; KOKH-TV (FOX) Oklahoma City; KOPX-TV (ION) Oklahoma City; KTBO-TV (TBN) Oklahoma City; KWTV-DT (CBS) Oklahoma City.
Programming (via satellite): Discovery Channel; FX; TBS Superstation.
Fee: $44.95 installation; $14.53 monthly; $1.50 converter; $12.50 additional installation.
Expanded Basic Service 1
Subscribers: 14,455.
Programming (via satellite): A&E Networks; ABC Family Channel; AMC; Animal Planet; BET Networks; Cartoon Network; CNBC; CNN; Comedy Central; Country Music TV; C-SPAN; Disney Channel; ESPN; ESPN 2; Fox News Channel; Fox Sports Southwest; Headline News; HGTV; History Channel; INSP; Lifetime; MTV; Nickelodeon; QVC; Spike TV; Syfy; The Learning Channel; The Weather Channel; Turner Network TV; USA Network; VH1; WGN America.
Fee: $20.97 monthly.
Digital Basic Service
Subscribers: N.A.
Programming (via satellite): BBC America; Bravo; Discovery Digital Networks; ESPN Classic Sports; Fox Sports World; Golf Channel; GSN; Independent Film Channel; Turner Classic Movies; Versus; WE tv.
Fee: $9.00 monthly.
Pay Service 1
Pay Units: 1,524.
Programming (via satellite): Cinemax; Encore; HBO; Showtime; Starz.
Fee: $1.67 monthly (Encore), $6.75 monthly (Starz), $13.00 monthly (Cinemax), $13.51 monthly (HBO or Showtime).
Digital Pay Service 1
Pay Units: N.A.
Programming (via satellite): DMX Music; Encore (multiplexed); HBO (multiplexed); Showtime (multiplexed); Starz (multiplexed); The Movie Channel.
Fee: $1.67 monthly (Encore), $6.75 monthly (Starz) $12.95 monthly (HBO or Showtime).
Video-On-Demand: No
Pay-Per-View
Addressable homes: 1,800.
iN DEMAND (delivered digitally); Fresh (delivered digitally).
Internet Service
Operational: Yes.
Broadband Service: Suddenlink High Speed Internet.
Fee: $45.95 installation; $24.95 monthly.
Telephone Service
Digital: Operational
Fee: $49.95 monthly
Miles of Plant: 274.0 (coaxial); 53.0 (fiber optic).
Manager: Byron Mahaffey. Marketing Manager: Heather Eastwood. Chief Technician: Tom Richie.
Ownership: Cequel Communications LLC (MSO).

ERICK—Reach Broadband, 515 E Longview St, Arp, TX 75750. Phone: 800-687-1258. Web Site: http://www.reachbroadband.net. ICA: OK0150.
TV Market Ranking: Below 100 (ERICK). Franchise award date: N.A. Franchise expiration date: N.A. Began: January 1, 1955.
Channel capacity: 41 (not 2-way capable). Channels available but not in use: N.A.
Basic Service
Subscribers: 207.
Programming (received off-air): KETA-TV (PBS) Oklahoma City; KOCO-TV (ABC) Oklahoma City; KOKH-TV (FOX) Oklahoma City; KVII-TV (ABC, CW) Amarillo.
Programming (via microwave): KFOR-TV (NBC) Oklahoma City; KWTV-DT (CBS) Oklahoma City.
Programming (via satellite): A&E Networks; ABC Family Channel; AMC; Animal Planet; Cartoon Network; CNN; C-SPAN; Discovery Channel; Disney Channel; E! Entertainment Television; ESPN; ESPN 2; Fox Sports Net; FX; Great American Country; Headline News; HGTV; History Channel; Lifetime; National Geographic Channel; Nickelodeon; Outdoor Channel; QVC; Spike TV; TBS Superstation; The Learning Channel; The Weather Channel; Travel Channel; Trinity Broadcasting Network; Turner Network TV; TV Land; USA Network.
Fee: $29.95 installation; $38.00 monthly.
Digital Basic Service
Subscribers: N.A.
Programming (via satellite): BBC America; Bio; Bloomberg Television; cloo; Discovery Kids Channel; DMX Music; ESPN Classic Sports; ESPNews; Fox College Sports Atlantic; Fox College Sports Central; Fox College Sports Pacific; Fox Soccer; Fuse; G4; Golf Channel; GSN; History Channel International; ID Investigation Discovery; Independent Film Channel; Military Channel; Planet Green; Science; ShopNBC; Speed; Style Network; Sundance Channel; Toon Disney; Turner Classic Movies; Versus; WE tv.
Pay Service 1
Pay Units: 24.
Programming (via satellite): Showtime.
Fee: $20.00 installation; $9.95 monthly.
Pay Service 2
Pay Units: 85.
Programming (via satellite): HBO.
Fee: $20.00 installation; $10.95 monthly.
Digital Pay Service 1
Pay Units: N.A.
Programming (via satellite): Cinemax (multiplexed); Encore (multiplexed); Flix; HBO (multiplexed); Showtime (multiplexed); Starz (multiplexed); The Movie Channel (multiplexed).
Video-On-Demand: No
Pay-Per-View
iN DEMAND; Playboy TV (delivered digitally).
Internet Service
Operational: No.
Telephone Service
None
Miles of Plant: 13.0 (coaxial); None (fiber optic).
Ownership: RB3 LLC (MSO).

EUFAULA—Reach Broadband, 515 E Longview St, Arp, TX 75750. Phones: 800-842-8160; 501-679-6619. E-mail: support@reachbroadband.net. Web Site: http://www.reachbroadband.net. Also serves Checotah & McIntosh County (portions). ICA: OK0054.
TV Market Ranking: Below 100 (Checotah, EUFAULA); Outside TV Markets (McIntosh County (portions)). Franchise award date: N.A. Franchise expiration date: N.A. Began: July 1, 1973.
Channel capacity: 44 (2-way capable). Channels available but not in use: N.A.
Basic Service
Subscribers: 1,061.
Programming (received off-air): KGEB (IND) Tulsa; KJRH-TV (NBC) Tulsa; KMYT-TV (MNT) Tulsa; KOED-TV (PBS) Tulsa; KOKI-TV (FOX) Tulsa; KOTV-DT (CBS)

Tulsa; KQCW-DT (CW) Muskogee; KTUL (ABC) Tulsa; KWHB (IND) Tulsa.
Programming (via satellite): A&E Networks; ABC Family Channel; AMC; BET Networks; Cartoon Network; CNBC; CNN; C-SPAN; Discovery Channel; Disney Channel; E! Entertainment Television; ESPN; ESPN 2; Fox News Channel; Fox Sports Southwest; FX; Great American Country; Headline News; History Channel; Lifetime; National Geographic Channel; Nickelodeon; Outdoor Channel; QVC; Spike TV; TBS Superstation; The Learning Channel; The Weather Channel; Turner Network TV; TV Guide Network; TV Land; USA Network.
Fee: $54.95 installation; $44.05 monthly.

Digital Basic Service
Subscribers: N.A.
Programming (via satellite): AmericanLife TV Network; BBC America; Bio; Bloomberg Television; Discovery Fit & Health; Discovery Health Channel; Discovery Kids Channel; DMX Music; ESPN 2; ESPN Classic Sports; ESPNews; Fox College Sports Atlantic; Fox College Sports Central; Fox College Sports Pacific; Fox Soccer; Fuse; G4; Golf Channel; GSN; Halogen Network; HGTV; History Channel; History Channel International; ID Investigation Discovery; Lifetime Movie Network; Military Channel; Outdoor Channel; Ovation; Planet Green; Science; ShopNBC; Speed; Style Network; Syfy; Trinity Broadcasting Network; Turner Classic Movies; Versus; WE tv.

Pay Service 1
Pay Units: 209.
Programming (via satellite): HBO.
Fee: $12.95 monthly.

Pay Service 2
Pay Units: 218.
Programming (via satellite): The Movie Channel.
Fee: $12.95 monthly.

Pay Service 3
Pay Units: 228.
Programming (via satellite): Showtime.
Fee: $12.95 monthly.

Digital Pay Service 1
Pay Units: N.A.
Programming (via satellite): Cinemax (multiplexed); Encore (multiplexed); Flix; HBO (multiplexed); Showtime (multiplexed); Starz (multiplexed); The Movie Channel (multiplexed).

Video-On-Demand: Yes

Pay-Per-View
iN DEMAND (delivered digitally); Playboy TV (delivered digitally); ESPN Now (delivered digitally); Sports PPV (delivered digitally); Men's Channel (delivered digitally).

Internet Service
Operational: No.

Telephone Service
None

Miles of Plant: 75.0 (coaxial); None (fiber optic).
Ownership: RB3 LLC (MSO).

FAIRFAX—Cim Tel Cable Inc. Now served by MANNFORD, OK [OK0296]. ICA: OK0133.

FAIRVIEW—Suddenlink Communications, 12444 Powerscourt Dr, Saint Louis, MO 63131-3660. Phones: 800-999-6845; 314-315-9346; 314-965-2020. Web Site: http://www.suddenlink.com. ICA: OK0089.
TV Market Ranking: Outside TV Markets (FAIRVIEW). Franchise award date: N.A. Franchise expiration date: N.A. Began: July 1, 1967.
Channel capacity: N.A. Channels available but not in use: N.A.

Basic Service
Subscribers: 844.
Programming (received off-air): KAUT-TV (MNT) Oklahoma City; KETA-TV (PBS) Oklahoma City; KFOR-TV (NBC) Oklahoma City; KOCB (CW) Oklahoma City; KOCO-TV (ABC) Oklahoma City; KOKH-TV (FOX) Oklahoma City; KOMI-CD Woodward; KTBO-TV (TBN) Oklahoma City; KWTV-DT (CBS) Oklahoma City.
Programming (via satellite): A&E Networks; ABC Family Channel; AMC; CNN; Country Music TV; C-SPAN; Discovery Channel; Disney Channel; E! Entertainment Television; ESPN; Fox News Channel; Fox Sports Southwest; Headline News; HGTV; History Channel; Lifetime; MTV; Nickelodeon; Outdoor Channel; QVC; Spike TV; Syfy; TBS Superstation; The Learning Channel; The Weather Channel; truTV; Turner Network TV; TV Land; USA Network; VH1; WGN America.
Fee: $39.95 installation; $19.95 monthly.

Pay Service 1
Pay Units: 132.
Programming (via satellite): HBO.
Fee: $10.95 monthly.

Pay Service 2
Pay Units: 42.
Programming (via satellite): Showtime.
Fee: $9.95 monthly.

Pay Service 3
Pay Units: 35.
Programming (via satellite): Cinemax.
Fee: $9.95 monthly.

Pay Service 4
Pay Units: 46.
Programming (via satellite): The Movie Channel.
Fee: $7.95 monthly.

Video-On-Demand: No

Internet Service
Operational: Yes. Began: May 26, 2003.
Broadband Service: Suddenlink High Speed Internet.
Fee: $45.95 installation; $24.95 monthly.

Telephone Service
Digital: Operational
Fee: $49.95 monthly

Miles of Plant: 30.0 (coaxial); None (fiber optic).
Regional Manager: Todd Cruthird. Regional Marketing Manager: Beverly Gambell. Plant Manager: Roger Campbell.
Ownership: Cequel Communications LLC (MSO).

FARGO—Pioneer Telephone Coop. Formerly [OK0345]. This cable system has converted to IPTV, PO Box 539, Kingfisher, OK 73750. Phones: 888-782-2667; 405-375-4111. E-mail: website@pldi.net. Web Site: http://www.ptci.com. ICA: OK5096.
TV Market Ranking: Franchise award date: N.A. Franchise expiration date: N.A. Began: September 28, 2005.
Channel capacity: N.A. Channels available but not in use: N.A.

Internet Service
Operational: Yes.

Telephone Service
Digital: Operational

General Manager: Richard Ruhl.

FARGO—Pioneer Telephone Coop. This cable system has converted to IPTV. See Fargo, OK [OK5096]. ICA: OK0345.

FLETCHER—Reach Broadband, 515 E Longview St, Arp, TX 75750. Phones: 800-842-8160; 501-679-6619. E-mail: support@reachbroadband.net. Web Site: http://www.reachbroadband.net. Also serves Elgin. ICA: OK0284.
TV Market Ranking: Below 100 (Elgin, FLETCHER). Franchise award date: January 6, 1977. Franchise expiration date: N.A. Began: N.A.
Channel capacity: 22 (not 2-way capable). Channels available but not in use: N.A.

Basic Service
Subscribers: 296.
Programming (received off-air): KAUT-TV (MNT) Oklahoma City; KETA-TV (PBS) Oklahoma City; KFDX-TV (NBC) Wichita Falls; KFOR-TV (NBC) Oklahoma City; KJTL (FOX) Wichita Falls; KOCB (CW) Oklahoma City; KOCO-TV (ABC) Oklahoma City; KOKH-TV (FOX) Oklahoma City; KSBI (IND) Oklahoma City; KSWO-TV (ABC, TMO) Lawton; KTBO-TV (TBN) Oklahoma City; KWTV-DT (CBS) Oklahoma City.
Programming (via satellite): A&E Networks; ABC Family Channel; AMC; CNN; C-SPAN; Discovery Channel; Disney Channel; ESPN; Fox Sports Southwest; Great American Country; History Channel; National Geographic Channel; Nickelodeon; QVC; Spike TV; TBS Superstation; The Learning Channel; The Weather Channel; Turner Network TV; TV Land; USA Network.
Fee: $29.95 installation; $38.00 monthly.

Pay Service 1
Pay Units: 107.
Programming (via satellite): HBO.
Fee: $10.95 monthly.

Pay Service 2
Pay Units: 45.
Programming (via satellite): Showtime.
Fee: $9.95 monthly.

Video-On-Demand: No

Internet Service
Operational: No.

Telephone Service
None

Miles of Plant: 35.0 (coaxial); None (fiber optic).
Ownership: RB3 LLC (MSO).

FORT COBB—Cable West, 314 W Main St, PO Box 237, Mountain View, OK 73062. Phones: 800-960-7912; 580-347-3220. Fax: 580-347-2143. ICA: OK0285.
TV Market Ranking: Below 100 (FORT COBB). Franchise award date: June 2, 1980. Franchise expiration date: N.A. Began: N.A.
Channel capacity: N.A. Channels available but not in use: N.A.

Basic Service
Subscribers: 27.
Programming (received off-air): KAUT-TV (MNT) Oklahoma City; KETA-TV (PBS) Oklahoma City; KFOR-TV (NBC) Oklahoma City; KOCB (CW) Oklahoma City; KOCO-TV (ABC) Oklahoma City; KOKH-TV (FOX) Oklahoma City; KSWO-TV (ABC, TMO) Lawton; KWTV-DT (CBS) Oklahoma City.
Programming (via satellite): A&E Networks; ABC Family Channel; CNN; Country Music TV; Discovery Channel; Disney Channel; ESPN; Headline News; HGTV; Lifetime; Nickelodeon; Syfy; TBS Superstation; The Weather Channel; Trinity Broadcasting Network; Turner Network TV; TV Land; USA Network; WGN America.
Fee: $29.95 installation; $27.95 monthly; $2.95 converter.

Pay Service 1
Pay Units: 16.
Programming (via satellite): Cinemax.
Fee: $9.00 monthly.

Pay Service 2
Pay Units: 23.
Programming (via satellite): HBO.
Fee: $10.00 monthly.

Video-On-Demand: No

Internet Service
Operational: No.

Telephone Service
None

Miles of Plant: 6.0 (coaxial); None (fiber optic).
Manager & Chief Technician: Mickey Davis.
Ownership: Mickey Davis (MSO).

FORT GIBSON—Allegiance Communications, 707 W Saratoga St, Shawnee, OK 74804. Phones: 405-275-6923; 405-395-1131. Web Site: http://www.allegiance.tv. ICA: OK0090.
TV Market Ranking: Below 100 (FORT GIBSON). Franchise award date: November 1, 1971. Franchise expiration date: N.A. Began: April 1, 1977.
Channel capacity: N.A. Channels available but not in use: N.A.

Basic Service
Subscribers: 1,150.
Programming (received off-air): KDOR-TV (TBN) Bartlesville; KGEB (IND) Tulsa; KJRH-TV (NBC) Tulsa; KMYT-TV (MNT) Tulsa; KOED-TV (PBS) Tulsa; KOKI-TV (FOX) Tulsa; KOTV-DT (CBS) Tulsa; KQCW-DT (CW) Muskogee; KRSC-TV (ETV) Claremore; KTPX-TV (ION) Okmulgee; KTUL (ABC) Tulsa; KWHB (IND) Tulsa.
Programming (via satellite): C-SPAN; INSP; QVC; TV Guide Network; WGN America.
Fee: $40.00 installation; $24.95 monthly; $1.96 converter; $19.95 additional installation.

Expanded Basic Service 1
Subscribers: N.A.
Programming (via satellite): A&E Networks; ABC Family Channel; AMC; Animal Planet; Bravo; Cartoon Network; CNBC; CNN; Comedy Central; Country Music TV; Discovery Channel; Disney Channel; E! Entertainment Television; ESPN; ESPN 2; Food Network; Fox News Channel; Fox Sports Southwest; FX; G4; Golf Channel; Hallmark Channel; Headline News; HGTV; History Channel; Lifetime; MSNBC; MTV; National Geographic Channel; Nickelodeon; Outdoor Channel; Oxygen; SoapNet; Speed; Spike TV; Syfy; TBS Superstation; The Learning Channel; The Weather Channel; Travel Channel; truTV; Turner Classic Movies; Turner Network TV; TV Land; USA Network; VH1.

Digital Basic Service
Subscribers: N.A.
Programming (via satellite): BBC America; Discovery Digital Networks; ESPN Classic Sports; Music Choice; Style Network; Sundance Channel; Toon Disney; WE tv.

Digital Pay Service 1
Pay Units: N.A.
Programming (via satellite): Cinemax (multiplexed); Encore (multiplexed); HBO (multiplexed); Showtime (multiplexed); Starz (multiplexed); The Movie Channel (multiplexed).

Video-On-Demand: No

Pay-Per-View
iN DEMAND (delivered digitally); Fox Sports Net (delivered digitally); Hot Choice (delivered digitally).

Internet Service
Operational: Yes. Began: December 31, 2005.
Fee: $24.95 installation; $39.95 monthly.

Telephone Service
None

Miles of Plant: 21.0 (coaxial); None (fiber optic). Additional miles planned: 15.0 (coaxial).

Chief Executive Officer: Bill Haggarty. Regional Vice President: Andrew Dearth. Vice President, Marketing: Tracy Bass.
Ownership: Allegiance Communications (MSO).

FORT SILL—Suddenlink Communications, 930 NW Fort Sill Blvd, Fort Sill, OK 73503. Phones: 580-248-2060; 314-965-2020. Web Site: http://www.suddenlink.com. ICA: OK0031.
TV Market Ranking: Below 100 (FORT SILL). Franchise award date: January 1, 1980. Franchise expiration date: N.A. Began: September 1, 1980.
Channel capacity: 38 (operating 2-way). Channels available but not in use: N.A.
Basic Service
Subscribers: 1,778.
Programming (received off-air): KAUZ-TV (CBS, CW) Wichita Falls; KETA-TV (PBS) Oklahoma City; KFDX-TV (NBC) Wichita Falls; KJTL (FOX) Wichita Falls; KSWO-TV (ABC, TMO) Lawton; KWTV-DT (CBS) Oklahoma City.
Programming (via satellite): C-SPAN; TV Guide Network.
Fee: $16.08 installation; $19.95 monthly; $1.43 converter; $16.08 additional installation.
Expanded Basic Service 1
Subscribers: 1,713.
Programming (via satellite): A&E Networks; ABC Family Channel; AMC; Animal Planet; BET Networks; Bravo; Cartoon Network; CNBC; CNN; Comedy Central; Discovery Channel; Disney Channel; E! Entertainment Television; ESPN; ESPN 2; Eternal Word TV Network; Food Network; Fox News Channel; Fox Sports Southwest; FX; Great American Country; Hallmark Channel; Headline News; HGTV; History Channel; Lifetime; MSNBC; MTV; National Geographic Channel; Nickelodeon; Outdoor Channel; QVC; Shopping Channel; Speed; Spike TV; Syfy; TBS Superstation; The Learning Channel; The Weather Channel; truTV; Turner Classic Movies; Turner Network TV; TV Land; Univision Studios; USA Network; VH1.
Fee: $21.00 monthly.
Digital Basic Service
Subscribers: N.A.
Programming (via satellite): BBC America; Bio; Bloomberg Television; cloo; Discovery Digital Networks; DMX Music; ESPN Classic Sports; ESPNews; Fox Movie Channel; Fox Soccer; Fuse; G4; Golf Channel; GSN; History Channel International; Independent Film Channel; Toon Disney; Trinity Broadcasting Network; Versus; WE tv.
Fee: $3.99 monthly.
Pay Service 1
Pay Units: 309.
Programming (via satellite): Cinemax.
Pay Service 2
Pay Units: 709.
Programming (via satellite): HBO.
Pay Service 3
Pay Units: 262.
Programming (via satellite): Showtime.
Pay Service 4
Pay Units: 168.
Programming (via satellite): The Movie Channel.
Digital Pay Service 1
Pay Units: N.A.
Programming (via satellite): Cinemax (multiplexed); Encore (multiplexed); HBO (multiplexed); Showtime (multiplexed); Starz (multiplexed); The Movie Channel (multiplexed).
Video-On-Demand: No
Pay-Per-View
iN DEMAND (delivered digitally); Playboy TV (delivered digitally); Fresh (delivered digitally).
Internet Service
Operational: Yes. Began: November 29, 2004.
Broadband Service: Suddenlink High Speed Internet.
Fee: $45.95 installation; $24.95 monthly.
Telephone Service
Digital: Operational
Fee: $49.95 monthly
Miles of Plant: 60.0 (coaxial); None (fiber optic).
Regional Manager: Todd Cruthird. Marketing Director: Beverly Gambell.
Ownership: Cequel Communications LLC (MSO).

FORT SUPPLY—Formerly served by CableDirect. No longer in operation. ICA: OK0376.

FREDERICK—Cable One. Now served by ALTUS, OK [OK0017]. ICA: OK0062.

FREEDOM—Formerly served by Pioneer Telephone Coop. No longer in operation. ICA: OK0247.

GAGE—Pioneer Telephone Coop. Formerly served by Shattuck, OK [OK0135]. This cable system has converted to IPTV, PO Box 539, Kingfisher, OK 73750. Phones: 405-375-4111; 888-782-2667. E-mail: website@pldi.net. Web Site: http://www.ptci.com. ICA: OK5029.
TV Market Ranking: Outside TV Markets (GAGE). Franchise award date: N.A. Franchise expiration date: N.A. Began: September 28, 2005.
Channel capacity: N.A. Channels available but not in use: N.A.
Internet Service
Operational: Yes.
Telephone Service
Digital: Operational
General Manager: Richard Ruhl.

GANS—Allegiance Communications, 707 W Saratoga St, Shawnee, OK 74804. Phones: 405-275-6923; 405-395-1131. Web Site: http://www.allegiance.tv. Also serves Sequoyah County (unincorporated areas). ICA: OK0172.
TV Market Ranking: Below 100 (GANS, Sequoyah County (unincorporated areas)). Franchise award date: October 18, 1988. Franchise expiration date: N.A. Began: November 1, 1989.
Channel capacity: N.A. Channels available but not in use: N.A.
Basic Service
Subscribers: 350.
Programming (received off-air): KFSM-TV (CBS) Fort Smith; KHBS (ABC, CW) Fort Smith; KJRH-TV (NBC) Tulsa; KOET (PBS) Eufaula; KOTV-DT (CBS) Tulsa; KPBI-CA (FOX) Fort Smith; KTUL (ABC) Tulsa.
Programming (via satellite): A&E Networks; ABC Family Channel; AMC; Animal Planet; Cartoon Network; CNN; Country Music TV; C-SPAN; Discovery Channel; Disney Channel; ESPN; ESPN 2; Fox News Channel; Fox Sports Southwest; Headline News; History Channel; Lifetime; Nickelodeon; Outdoor Channel; QVC; Spike TV; Syfy; TBS Superstation; The Learning Channel; The Weather Channel; Trinity Broadcasting Network; Turner Classic Movies; Turner Network TV; USA Network; WGN America.
Fee: $30.00 installation; $21.95 monthly.
Pay Service 1
Pay Units: 52.
Programming (via satellite): Cinemax.
Pay Service 2
Pay Units: 66.
Programming (via satellite): HBO.
Fee: $10.00 installation; $9.50 monthly.
Pay Service 3
Pay Units: 69.
Programming (via satellite): Showtime.
Fee: $10.00 installation; $6.95 monthly.
Video-On-Demand: No
Pay-Per-View
iN DEMAND (delivered digitally); Hot Choice (delivered digitally); Playboy TV (delivered digitally); Fresh (delivered digitally); Shorteez (delivered digitally).
Internet Service
Operational: No.
Telephone Service
None
Miles of Plant: 25.0 (coaxial); None (fiber optic).
Chief Executive Officer: Bill Haggarty. Regional Vice President: Andrew Dearth. Vice President, Marketing: Tracy Bass.
Ownership: Allegiance Communications (MSO).

GARBER—Formerly served by Longview Communications. No longer in operation. ICA: OK0169.

GEARY—Formerly served by Cebridge Connections. No longer in operation. ICA: OK0145.

GERONIMO—Formerly served by CableDirect. No longer in operation. ICA: OK0197.

GERONIMO—LakeView Cable, Hwy 115, PO Box 460, Cache, OK 73527-0460. Phone: 304-429-8800. Fax: 580-429-6599. Web Site: http://www.lvcisp.com. ICA: OK0395.
TV Market Ranking: Below 100 (GERONIMO).
Channel capacity: N.A. Channels available but not in use: N.A.
Basic Service
Subscribers: 100.
Programming (received off-air): KAUZ-TV (CBS, CW) Wichita Falls; KETA-TV (PBS) Oklahoma City; KFDX-TV (NBC) Wichita Falls; KJTL (FOX) Wichita Falls; KSWO-TV (ABC, TMO) Lawton.
Programming (via satellite): A&E Networks; Animal Planet; CNN; C-SPAN; Discovery Channel; Disney Channel; ESPN; ESPN 2; Fuse; Great American Country; HGTV; History Channel; Lifetime Movie Network; National Geographic Channel; QVC; Speed; Syfy; TBS Superstation; The Learning Channel; The Weather Channel; Travel Channel; Trinity Broadcasting Network; Turner Classic Movies; Turner Network TV; WGN America.
Fee: $39.95 installation; $31.75 monthly.
Pay Service 1
Pay Units: N.A.
Programming (via satellite): HBO; Showtime (multiplexed).
Video-On-Demand: No
Internet Service
Operational: Yes.
Broadband Service: In-house.
Telephone Service
Digital: Planned
Miles of plant included in Cache
Manager: Bill Rowell. Chief Technician: Mike Rowell.
Ownership: Lakeview Cable Inc. (MSO).

GLENCOE—Allegiance Communications, 707 W Saratoga St, Shawnee, OK 74804. Phones: 405-275-6923; 405-395-1131. Web Site: http://www.allegiance.tv. ICA: OK0221.
TV Market Ranking: Outside TV Markets (GLENCOE). Franchise award date: December 1, 1985. Franchise expiration date: N.A. Began: March 1, 1988.
Channel capacity: 35 (not 2-way capable). Channels available but not in use: N.A.
Basic Service
Subscribers: 114.
Programming (received off-air): KAUT-TV (MNT) Oklahoma City; KETA-TV (PBS) Oklahoma City; KFOR-TV (NBC) Oklahoma City; KOCB (CW) Oklahoma City; KOCO-TV (ABC) Oklahoma City; KOKH-TV (FOX) Oklahoma City; KOKI-TV (FOX) Tulsa; KTBO-TV (TBN) Oklahoma City; KWHB (IND) Tulsa; KWTV-DT (CBS) Oklahoma City.
Programming (via satellite): A&E Networks; ABC Family Channel; CMT Pure Country; CNBC; CNN; C-SPAN; Discovery Channel; Disney Channel; ESPN; ESPN 2; Lifetime; MSNBC; MTV; Nickelodeon; Spike TV; TBS Superstation; Travel Channel; Turner Network TV; WGN America.
Fee: $40.00 installation; $22.00 monthly; $1.96 converter; $19.95 additional installation.
Video-On-Demand: No
Pay-Per-View
Movies (delivered digitally); Special events (delivered digitally); Hot Choice (delivered digitally); Playboy TV (delivered digitally); Fresh (delivered digitally); Shorteez (delivered digitally).
Internet Service
Operational: No.
Telephone Service
None
Miles of Plant: 3.0 (coaxial); None (fiber optic).
Chief Executive Officer: Bill Haggarty. Regional Vice President: Andrew Dearth. Vice President, Marketing: Tracy Bass.
Ownership: Allegiance Communications (MSO).

GLENPOOL (southern portion)—Formerly served by Titan Broadband Services. No longer in operation. ICA: OK0388.

GOLTRY—Formerly served by Cebridge Connections. No longer in operation. ICA: OK0286.

GOODWELL—Allegiance Communications, 707 W Saratoga St, Shawnee, OK 74804. Phones: 405-275-6923; 405-395-1131. Fax: 620-873-2238. Web Site: http://www.allegiance.tv. ICA: OK0183.

TV Market Ranking: Outside TV Markets (GOODWELL). Franchise award date: N.A. Franchise expiration date: N.A. Began: May 1, 1983.

Channel capacity: N.A. Channels available but not in use: N.A.

Basic Service

Subscribers: N.A.

Programming (received off-air): KCIT (FOX) Amarillo; KETA-TV (PBS) Oklahoma City; KPTF-DT (IND) Farwell.

Programming (via microwave): KAMR-TV (NBC) Amarillo; KFDA-TV (CBS) Amarillo; KVII-TV (ABC, CW) Amarillo.

Programming (via satellite): A&E Networks; ABC Family Channel; AMC; Animal Planet; Cartoon Network; CNN; Comedy Central; Country Music TV; Discovery Channel; Disney Channel; E! Entertainment Television; ESPN; ESPN 2; Food Network; Hallmark Channel; Headline News; HGTV; History Channel; Lifetime; MTV; Nickelodeon; Oxygen; QVC; Speed; Spike TV; Syfy; TBS Superstation; The Learning Channel; The Weather Channel; Travel Channel; Turner Network TV; TV Land; Univision Studios; USA Network; VH1.

Fee: $20.00 installation; $21.95 monthly.

Pay-Per-View

Hot Choice (delivered digitally); Playboy TV (delivered digitally); Fresh (delivered digitally); Shorteez (delivered digitally); iN DEMAND (delivered digitally).

Internet Service

Operational: No.

Telephone Service

None

Miles of Plant: 6.0 (coaxial); None (fiber optic).

Chief Executive Officer: Bill Haggarty. Regional Vice President: Andrew Dearth. Vice President, Marketing: Tracy Bass.

Ownership: Allegiance Communications (MSO).

GORE—Allegiance Communications, 707 W Saratoga St, Shawnee, OK 74804. Phones: 405-275-6923; 405-395-1131. Web Site: http://www.allegiance.tv. Also serves Webbers Falls. ICA: OK0164.

TV Market Ranking: Below 100 (GORE, Webbers Falls). Franchise award date: N.A. Franchise expiration date: N.A. Began: N.A.

Channel capacity: N.A. Channels available but not in use: N.A.

Basic Service

Subscribers: 308.

Programming (received off-air): KFSM-TV (CBS) Fort Smith; KHBS (ABC, CW) Fort Smith; KJRH-TV (NBC) Tulsa; KOET (PBS) Eufaula; KOKI-TV (FOX) Tulsa; KOTV-DT (CBS) Tulsa; KTUL (ABC) Tulsa.

Programming (via satellite): A&E Networks; ABC Family Channel; AMC; Animal Planet; Cartoon Network; CNBC; CNN; Country Music TV; C-SPAN; Discovery Channel; Disney Channel; ESPN; ESPN 2; Fox News Channel; Fox Sports Southwest; Headline News; HGTV; History Channel; Lifetime; Nickelodeon; Outdoor Channel; QVC; Spike TV; Syfy; TBS Superstation; The Learning Channel; The Weather Channel; Travel Channel; Trinity Broadcasting Network; Turner Classic Movies; Turner Network TV; USA Network; WGN America.

Fee: $30.00 installation; $21.95 monthly.

Digital Basic Service

Subscribers: N.A.

Programming (via satellite): AmericanLife TV Network; BBC America; Bio; Bloomberg Television; Bravo; Discovery Fit & Health; DMX Music; ESPN Classic Sports; ESPNews; Fox Movie Channel; Fox Soccer; Fuse; G4; GAS; Golf Channel; GSN; Halogen Network; History Channel International; Independent Film Channel; Lifetime Movie Network; MTV Networks Digital Suite; Nick Jr.; ShopNBC; Speed; Style Network; Toon Disney; TV Guide Network; Versus; WE tv.

Pay Service 1

Pay Units: 139.

Programming (via satellite): Cinemax; HBO; Showtime.

Fee: $9.50 monthly (Cinemax), $10.95 monthly (HBO).

Digital Pay Service 1

Pay Units: N.A.

Programming (via satellite): Cinemax (multiplexed); Encore (multiplexed); Flix; HBO (multiplexed); Showtime (multiplexed); Starz (multiplexed); The Movie Channel (multiplexed).

Video-On-Demand: No

Pay-Per-View

iN DEMAND (delivered digitally); Hot Choice (delivered digitally); Playboy TV (delivered digitally); Fresh (delivered digitally); Shorteez (delivered digitally).

Internet Service

Operational: No.

Telephone Service

None

Miles of Plant: 17.0 (coaxial); None (fiber optic).

Chief Executive Officer: Bill Haggarty. Regional Vice President: Andrew Dearth. Vice President, Marketing: Tracy Bass.

Ownership: Allegiance Communications (MSO).

GOTEBO—Formerly served by Basic Cable Services Inc. No longer in operation. ICA: OK0228.

GOULD—Pioneer Telephone Coop. Formerly served by Hollis, OK [OK0087]. This cable system has converted to IPTV, PO Box 539, Kingfisher, OK 73750. Phones: 405-375-4111; 888-782-2667. E-mail: website@pldi.net. Web Site: http://www.ptci.com. ICA: OK5030.

TV Market Ranking: Outside TV Markets (GOULD). Franchise award date: N.A. Franchise expiration date: N.A. Began: March 31, 2005.

Channel capacity: N.A. Channels available but not in use: N.A.

Internet Service

Operational: Yes.

Telephone Service

Digital: Operational

General Manager: Richard Ruhl.

GRACEMONT—Cable West, 314 W Main St, PO Box 237, Mountain View, OK 73062. Phones: 800-960-7912; 580-347-3220. Fax: 580-347-2143. ICA: OK0287.

TV Market Ranking: Outside TV Markets (GRACEMONT). Franchise award date: January 3, 1983. Franchise expiration date: N.A. Began: N.A.

Channel capacity: 36 (not 2-way capable). Channels available but not in use: N.A.

Basic Service

Subscribers: 28.

Programming (received off-air): KAUT-TV (MNT) Oklahoma City; KETA-TV (PBS) Oklahoma City; KFOR-TV (NBC) Oklahoma City; KOCB (CW) Oklahoma City; KOCO-TV (ABC) Oklahoma City; KOKH-TV (FOX) Oklahoma City; KWTV-DT (CBS) Oklahoma City.

Programming (via satellite): ABC Family Channel; CNN; Country Music TV; Discovery Channel; Disney Channel; ESPN; Nickelodeon; Spike TV; TBS Superstation; The Weather Channel; Trinity Broadcasting Network; Turner Network TV; TV Land; USA Network; WGN America.

Fee: $29.95 installation; $24.95 monthly; $3.95 converter.

Pay Service 1

Pay Units: 14.

Programming (via satellite): Cinemax; HBO; Showtime; The Movie Channel.

Fee: $10.95 monthly (Cinemax or Showtime), $12.95 monthly (HBO), $8.95 monthly (TMC).

Video-On-Demand: No

Internet Service

Operational: No.

Telephone Service

None

Miles of Plant: 5.0 (coaxial); None (fiber optic).

Manager & Chief Technician: Mickey Davis.

Ownership: Mickey Davis (MSO).

GRANDFIELD—Southern Plains Cable, PO Box 165, Medicine Park, OK 73557. Phones: 800-218-1856; 580-529-5000. Fax: 580-529-5556. E-mail: office@wichitaonline.net. Web Site: http://www.southernplainscommunications.com. ICA: OK0143.

TV Market Ranking: Below 100 (GRANDFIELD). Franchise award date: N.A. Franchise expiration date: N.A. Began: October 1, 1982.

Channel capacity: 41 (operating 2-way). Channels available but not in use: N.A.

Basic Service

Subscribers: 96.

Programming (received off-air): KAUZ-TV (CBS, CW) Wichita Falls; KETA-TV (PBS) Oklahoma City; KFDX-TV (NBC) Wichita Falls; KJTL (FOX) Wichita Falls; KSWO-TV (ABC, TMO) Lawton.

Programming (via satellite): Local Cable Weather; Telemundo; Trinity Broadcasting Network.

Fee: $45.00 installation; $13.95 monthly.

Expanded Basic Service 1

Subscribers: N.A.

Programming (via satellite): A&E Networks; ABC Family Channel; AMC; Animal Planet; BET Networks; CNBC; CNN; Comedy Central; Country Music TV; Discovery Channel; Disney Channel; E! Entertainment Television; ESPN; ESPN 2; Fox News Channel; Fox Sports Net; FX; Headline News; HGTV; History Channel; Lifetime; Nickelodeon; RFD-TV; Speed; Spike TV; Syfy; TBS Superstation; The Learning Channel; The Weather Channel; Turner Network TV; TV Land; USA Network.

Fee: $31.83 monthly.

Digital Basic Service

Subscribers: N.A.

Programming (via satellite): Alterna'TV; AZ TV; BBC America; Bio; Black Family Channel; Blackbelt TV; Bloomberg Television; Bravo; Church Channel; cloo; CMT Pure Country; Cooking Channel; Current; Daystar TV Network; Discovery Health Channel; Discovery Home Channel; Discovery Kids Channel; Discovery Times Channel; Fox College Sports Atlantic; Fox College Sports Central; Fox College Sports Pacific; Fox Movie Channel; Fox Reality Channel; Fox Soccer; Fuse; G4; Golf Channel; Great American Country; GSN; History Channel International; Independent Film Channel; INSP; JCTV; Lifetime Movie Network; Lime; Men's Channel; Military Channel; MTV Hits; MTV Jams; National Geographic Channel; Nick Jr.; NickToons TV; Ovation; PBS Kids Sprout; Science; Style Network; Sundance Channel; TeenNick; The Word Network; Toon Disney; TVG Network; Versus; VH1 Classic; VH1 Soul; WE tv.

Fee: $23.95 monthly.

Digital Expanded Basic Service

Subscribers: N.A.

Programming (via satellite): Canal 52MX; Cine Latino; Cine Mexicano; CNN en Espanol; Discovery en Espanol; ESPN Deportes; Fox Deportes; HBO Latino; History Channel en Espanol; Tr3s; VeneMovies.

Pay Service 1

Pay Units: N.A.

Programming (via satellite): Showtime; The Movie Channel.

Fee: $7.00 monthly (each).

Digital Pay Service 1

Pay Units: N.A.

Programming (via satellite): Cinemax (multiplexed); Encore (multiplexed); Flix (multiplexed); HBO (multiplexed); Showtime (multiplexed); Starz (multiplexed); The Movie Channel (multiplexed).

Fee: $12.00 monthly (each).

Video-On-Demand: No

Pay-Per-View

iN DEMAND (delivered digitally); Hot Choice (delivered digitally); Playboy TV (delivered digitally); Fresh (delivered digitally); Spice: Xcess (delivered digitally).

Internet Service

Operational: No.

Telephone Service

Analog: Not Operational

Digital: Planned

Miles of Plant: 13.0 (coaxial); None (fiber optic).

President: Dustin Hilliary.

Ownership: Southern Plains Cable (MSO).

GRANITE—Cable West, 314 W Main St, PO Box 237, Mountain View, OK 73062. Phones: 800-960-7912; 580-347-3220. Fax: 703-476-9107. ICA: OK0134.

TV Market Ranking: Outside TV Markets (GRANITE). Franchise award date: March 12, 1979. Franchise expiration date: N.A. Began: January 1, 1958.

Channel capacity: 36 (not 2-way capable). Channels available but not in use: N.A.

Basic Service

Subscribers: 88.

Programming (received off-air): KAUZ-TV (CBS, CW) Wichita Falls; KETA-TV (PBS) Oklahoma City; KFDX-TV (NBC) Wichita Falls; KFOR-TV (NBC) Oklahoma City; KJTL (FOX) Wichita Falls; KOCB (CW) Oklahoma City; KOCO-TV (ABC) Oklahoma City; KOKH-TV (FOX) Oklahoma City; KSWO-TV (ABC, TMO) Lawton; KWTV-DT (CBS) Oklahoma City; 1 FM.

Programming (via satellite): A&E Networks; ABC Family Channel; CNN; Country Music TV; C-SPAN; Discovery Channel; Disney Channel; ESPN; ESPN 2; Fox News Channel; Fox Sports Southwest; HGTV; Nickelodeon; QVC; Spike TV; TBS Superstation; The Weather Channel; Trinity Broadcast-

ing Network; Turner Classic Movies; Turner Network TV; TV Land; USA Network; WGN America.
Fee: $29.95 installation; $24.95 monthly; $3.95 converter.

Pay Service 1
Pay Units: 21.
Programming (via satellite): Showtime; The Movie Channel.
Fee: $10.95 monthly (Showtime), $8.95 monthly (TMC).

Video-On-Demand: No

Internet Service
Operational: No.

Telephone Service
None
Miles of Plant: 18.0 (coaxial); None (fiber optic).
Manager & Chief Technician: Mickey Davis.
Ownership: Mickey Davis (MSO).

GROVE—Suddenlink Communications, 12444 Powerscourt Dr, Saint Louis, MO 63131-3660. Phones: 800-999-6845 (Customer service); 918-786-5131. Fax: 918-786-3810. Web Site: http://www.suddenlink.com. Also serves Delaware County (northern portion). ICA: OK0039.
TV Market Ranking: Below 100 (Delaware County (northern portion) (portions)); Outside TV Markets (Delaware County (northern portion) (portions), GROVE). Franchise award date: November 1, 1972. Franchise expiration date: N.A. Began: July 1, 1973.
Channel capacity: 42 (not 2-way capable). Channels available but not in use: N.A.

Basic Service
Subscribers: 2,891.
Programming (received off-air): KDOR-TV (TBN) Bartlesville; KELF-LP (IND) Miami; KJRH-TV (NBC) Tulsa; KOED-TV (PBS) Tulsa; KOKI-TV (FOX) Tulsa; KOTV-DT (CBS) Tulsa; KQCW-DT (CW) Muskogee; KTPX-TV (ION) Okmulgee; KTUL (ABC) Tulsa; allband FM.
Programming (via satellite): A&E Networks; ABC Family Channel; AMC; Animal Planet; Cartoon Network; CNN; Country Music TV; Discovery Channel; Disney Channel; ESPN; ESPN 2; Food Network; Fox News Channel; Fox Sports Southwest; FX; Headline News; HGTV; MoviePlex; Nickelodeon; QVC; Spike TV; TBS Superstation; The Learning Channel; The Weather Channel; Turner Network TV; TV Guide Network; USA Network; WGN America.
Fee: $18.75 installation; $23.44 monthly; $1.50 converter; $12.50 additional installation.

Digital Basic Service
Subscribers: N.A.
Programming (via satellite): BBC America; Bio; Discovery Digital Networks; DMX Music; Encore; ESPN Classic Sports; ESPNews; Fox Soccer; Fuse; Golf Channel; GSN; History Channel; History Channel International; Independent Film Channel; Lifetime Movie Network; Military History Channel; Speed; Toon Disney; Versus.

Digital Pay Service 1
Pay Units: N.A.
Programming (via satellite): Cinemax (multiplexed); HBO (multiplexed); Showtime (multiplexed); Starz (multiplexed); The Movie Channel (multiplexed).

Video-On-Demand: No

Pay-Per-View
iN DEMAND (delivered digitally); Playboy TV (delivered digitally).

Internet Service
Operational: Yes.
Broadband Service: Suddenlink High Speed Internet.

Telephone Service
Digital: Operational
Miles of Plant: 102.0 (coaxial); None (fiber optic).
Manager: Billy Jowell. Chief Technician: Allan Popp. Marketing Manager: Heather Eastwood. Office Manager: Bondy Giger.
Ownership: Cequel Communications LLC (MSO).

GUYMON—Allegiance Communications, 707 W Saratoga St, Shawnee, OK 74804. Phones: 405-275-6923; 405-395-1131. Fax: 620-873-2238. Web Site: http://www.allegiance.tv. ICA: OK0053.
TV Market Ranking: Outside TV Markets (GUYMON). Franchise award date: N.A. Franchise expiration date: N.A. Began: July 15, 1955.
Channel capacity: N.A. Channels available but not in use: N.A.

Basic Service
Subscribers: 2,763.
Programming (received off-air): KCIT (FOX) Amarillo; KPTF-DT (IND) Farwell; 5 FMs.
Programming (via microwave): KAMR-TV (NBC) Amarillo; KETA-TV (PBS) Oklahoma City; KFDA-TV (CBS) Amarillo; KVII-TV (ABC, CW) Amarillo.
Programming (via satellite): C-SPAN; C-SPAN 2; CW+; GalaVision; Telefutura; Telemundo; The Weather Channel; Univision Studios; WGN America.
Fee: $8.00 installation; $21.95 monthly.

Expanded Basic Service 1
Subscribers: N.A.
Programming (via satellite): A&E Networks; ABC Family Channel; AMC; Animal Planet; Cartoon Network; CNN; Country Music TV; Discovery Channel; Disney Channel; ESPN; ESPN 2; Fox News Channel; Fox Sports Southwest; Headline News; Lifetime; MTV; Nickelodeon; Spike TV; Syfy; TBS Superstation; The Learning Channel; Turner Network TV; TV Land; USA Network; VH1.

Digital Basic Service
Subscribers: N.A.
Programming (via satellite): BBC America; Bio; Bloomberg Television; Bravo; Cinemax; Discovery Health Channel; Discovery Home Channel; Discovery Kids Channel; Discovery Times Channel; ESPN Classic Sports; ESPNews; Fox Movie Channel; Fox Sports World; Fuse; G4; Golf Channel; Great American Country; GSN; Halogen Network; HBO; HGTV; History Channel; History Channel International; Independent Film Channel; Lifetime Movie Network; MBC America; Military Channel; Outdoor Channel; Science Television; ShopNBC; Showtime; Speed; Starz; Sundance Channel; The Movie Channel; Toon Disney; Trinity Broadcasting Network; Turner Classic Movies; Versus.

Pay Service 1
Pay Units: N.A.
Programming (via satellite): HBO.

Digital Pay Service 1
Pay Units: 430.
Programming (via satellite): Encore (multiplexed).
Fee: $9.95 monthly (Cinemax), $10.95 monthly (HBO, Showtime, Starz, or TMC).

Video-On-Demand: No

Internet Service
Operational: Yes.
Fee: $24.95 installation; $39.95 monthly.

Telephone Service
None
Miles of Plant: 40.0 (coaxial); None (fiber optic).
Chief Executive Officer: Bill Haggarty. Regional Vice President: Andrew Dearth. Vice President, Marketing: Tracy Bass.
Ownership: Allegiance Communications (MSO).

HAMMON—Formerly served by Rapid Cable. No longer in operation. ICA: OK0220.

HARDESTY—Panhandle Telephone Coop. Inc. Formerly [OK0373]. This cable system has converted to IPTV, 2222 NW Hwy 64, Guymon, OK 73942. Phones: 580-338-2556; 800-562-2556. Fax: 580-338-8260. E-mail: support@ptsi.net. Web Site: http://www.ptsi.net. ICA: OK5032.
TV Market Ranking: Outside TV Markets (HARDESTY). Franchise award date: N.A. Franchise expiration date: N.A. Began: N.A.
Channel capacity: N.A. Channels available but not in use: N.A.

Internet Service
Operational: Yes.
Broadband Service: In-house.

Telephone Service
Digital: Operational
President: Charles Russell.

HARDESTY—Panhandle Telephone Coop. Inc. This cable system has converted to IPTV. See Hardesty, OK [OK5032]. ICA: OK0373.

HARTSHORNE—Allegiance Communications, 707 W Saratoga St, Shawnee, OK 74804. Phones: 405-275-6923; 405-395-1131. Web Site: http://www.allegiance.tv. Also serves Haileyville. ICA: OK0083.
TV Market Ranking: Outside TV Markets (Haileyville, HARTSHORNE). Franchise award date: N.A. Franchise expiration date: N.A. Began: July 1, 1965.
Channel capacity: N.A. Channels available but not in use: N.A.

Basic Service
Subscribers: N.A.
Programming (received off-air): KJRH-TV (NBC) Tulsa; KMYT-TV (MNT) Tulsa; KOET (PBS) Eufaula; KOKI-TV (FOX) Tulsa; KOTV-DT (CBS) Tulsa; KQCW-DT (CW) Muskogee; KTEN (ABC, CW, NBC) Ada; KTUL (ABC) Tulsa; KWHB (IND) Tulsa; allband FM.
Programming (via satellite): C-SPAN; QVC; Trinity Broadcasting Network; WGN America.
Fee: $29.95 installation; $24.95 monthly; $1.96 converter; $19.95 additional installation.

Expanded Basic Service 1
Subscribers: N.A.
Programming (via satellite): A&E Networks; ABC Family Channel; AMC; Animal Planet; Cartoon Network; CNBC; CNN; Comedy Central; Country Music TV; Discovery Channel; Disney Channel; E! Entertainment Television; ESPN; ESPN 2; Food Network; Fox News Channel; Fox Sports Southwest; FX; G4; Headline News; HGTV; History Channel; Lifetime; MTV; Nickelodeon; Outdoor Channel; Oxygen; Speed; Spike TV; Syfy; TBS Superstation; The Learning Channel; The Weather Channel; Travel Channel; truTV; Turner Classic Movies; Turner Network TV; TV Land; USA Network; VH1.

Digital Basic Service
Subscribers: N.A.
Programming (via satellite): BBC America; Bio; Bloomberg Television; Discovery Fit & Health; DIY Network; DMX Music; ESPN Classic Sports; ESPNews; GAS; GSN; History Channel International; Independent Film Channel; Lifetime Movie Network; MTV Networks Digital Suite; Nick Jr.; Nick Too; NickToons TV; SoapNet; Style Network; Sundance Channel; Toon Disney; TV Guide Interactive Inc.; WE tv.

Digital Pay Service 1
Pay Units: N.A.
Programming (via satellite): Cinemax (multiplexed); Encore (multiplexed); Flix; HBO (multiplexed); Showtime (multiplexed); Starz (multiplexed); The Movie Channel (multiplexed).

Video-On-Demand: No

Pay-Per-View
iN DEMAND (delivered digitally); Hot Choice (delivered digitally); Playboy TV (delivered digitally); Fresh (delivered digitally); Shorteez (delivered digitally).

Internet Service
Operational: No.

Telephone Service
None
Miles of Plant: 45.0 (coaxial); None (fiber optic).
Chief Executive Officer: Bill Haggarty. Regional Vice President: Andrew Dearth. Vice President, Marketing: Tracy Bass.
Ownership: Allegiance Communications (MSO).

HASKELL—Allegiance Communications, 707 W Saratoga St, Shawnee, OK 74804. Phones: 405-275-6923; 405-395-1131. Web Site: http://www.allegiance.tv. Also serves Wagoner County (portions). ICA: OK0096.
TV Market Ranking: 54 (HASKELL, Wagoner County (portions)); Below 100 (Wagoner County (portions)). Franchise award date: N.A. Franchise expiration date: N.A. Began: February 1, 1982.
Channel capacity: 35 (not 2-way capable). Channels available but not in use: N.A.

Basic Service
Subscribers: 237.
Programming (received off-air): KDOR-TV (TBN) Bartlesville; KJRH-TV (NBC) Tulsa; KMYT-TV (MNT) Tulsa; KOED-TV (PBS) Tulsa; KOKI-TV (FOX) Tulsa; KOTV-DT (CBS) Tulsa; KRSC-TV (ETV) Claremore; KTUL (ABC) Tulsa; KWHB (IND) Tulsa.
Programming (via satellite): ABC Family Channel; AMC; Animal Planet; BET Networks; Cartoon Network; CMT Pure Country; CNBC; CNN; CW+; Discovery Channel; ESPN; Food Network; Fox News Channel; Headline News; Lifetime; Nickelodeon;

MediaPrints™
Map a Winning Business Strategy
Digital Cable and TV Coverage Maps.
Visit www.warren-news.com/mediaprints.htm

QVC; Spike TV; TBS Superstation; Turner Network TV; USA Network.
Fee: $60.00 installation; $28.22 monthly; $6.27 additional installation.

Digital Basic Service
Subscribers: N.A.
Programming (via satellite): American-Life TV Network; BBC America; Black Family Channel; Bloomberg Television; Bravo; Discovery Health Channel; Discovery Home Channel; Discovery Kids Channel; Discovery Times Channel; DMX Music; ESPN 2; ESPN Classic Sports; ESPNews; Fox Movie Channel; Fox Sports World; Fuse; G4; GAS; Golf Channel; Great American Country; GSN; Halogen Network; HGTV; Independent Film Channel; Lifetime Movie Network; MTV Hits; MTV2; Nick Jr.; NickToons TV; Outdoor Channel; Science; ShopNBC; Speed; Sundance Channel; Syfy; The Word Network; Trinity Broadcasting Network; Turner Classic Movies; Versus; VH1 Classic.

Pay Service 1
Pay Units: 30.
Programming (via satellite): Cinemax; Encore; HBO; Showtime; Starz.

Digital Pay Service 1
Pay Units: N.A.
Programming (via satellite): Cinemax (multiplexed); Encore (multiplexed); HBO (multiplexed); Showtime (multiplexed); Starz (multiplexed); The Movie Channel (multiplexed).

Pay-Per-View
iN DEMAND (delivered digitally); Hot Choice (delivered digitally); Playboy TV (delivered digitally); Fresh (delivered digitally); Shorteez (delivered digitally).

Internet Service
Operational: No.

Telephone Service
None

Miles of Plant: 13.0 (coaxial); None (fiber optic).
Chief Executive Officer: Bill Haggarty. Regional Vice President: Andrew Dearth. Vice President, Marketing: Tracy Bass.
Ownership: Allegiance Communications (MSO).

HEALDTON—Suddenlink Communications, 12444 Powerscourt Dr, Saint Louis, MO 63131-3660. Phones: 800-999-6845 (Customer service); 314-315-9346; 314-965-2020. Web Site: http://www.suddenlink.com. Also serves Cornish, Ringling & Wilson. ICA: OK0055.
TV Market Ranking: Outside TV Markets (Cornish, HEALDTON, Ringling, Wilson). Franchise award date: N.A. Franchise expiration date: N.A. Began: September 1, 1974.
Channel capacity: 41 (2-way capable). Channels available but not in use: N.A.

Basic Service
Subscribers: 1,299.
Programming (received off-air): KAUZ-TV (CBS, CW) Wichita Falls; KETA-TV (PBS) Oklahoma City; KFDX-TV (NBC) Wichita Falls; KFOR-TV (NBC) Oklahoma City; KJTL (FOX) Wichita Falls; KOCO-TV (ABC) Oklahoma City; KOKH-TV (FOX) Oklahoma City; KTEN (ABC, CW, NBC) Ada; KWTV-DT (CBS) Oklahoma City; KXII (CBS, FOX, MNT) Sherman.
Programming (via satellite): A&E Networks; ABC Family Channel; CNN; Country Music TV; Discovery Channel; Disney Channel; ESPN; Fox Sports Southwest; Headline News; History Channel; Lifetime; Nickelodeon; QVC; Spike TV; TBS Superstation; The Weather Channel; Trinity Broadcasting Network; Turner Classic Movies; Turner Network TV; TV Land; USA Network; WGN America.
Fee: $39.95 installation; $12.00 monthly.

Pay Service 1
Pay Units: 131.
Programming (via satellite): HBO.
Fee: $10.95 monthly.

Pay Service 2
Pay Units: 126.
Programming (via satellite): Showtime.
Fee: $9.95 monthly.

Pay Service 3
Pay Units: 141.
Programming (via satellite): The Movie Channel.
Fee: $7.95 monthly.

Video-On-Demand: No

Internet Service
Operational: Yes.
Broadband Service: Suddenlink High Speed Internet.

Telephone Service
None

Miles of Plant: 56.0 (coaxial); None (fiber optic).
Regional Manager: Todd Cruthird. Regional Marketing Manager: Beverly Gambell. Plant Manager: Kriss Miller.
Ownership: Cequel Communications LLC (MSO).

HEAVENER—Suddenlink Communications, 12444 Powerscourt Dr, Saint Louis, MO 63131-3660. Phones: 800-999-6845; 314-315-9346; 314-965-2020. Web Site: http://www.suddenlink.com. ICA: OK0103.
TV Market Ranking: Outside TV Markets (HEAVENER). Franchise award date: N.A. Franchise expiration date: September 1, 2014. Began: March 1, 1965.
Channel capacity: N.A. Channels available but not in use: N.A.

Basic Service
Subscribers: 617.
Programming (received off-air): KAFT (PBS) Fayetteville; KFSM-TV (CBS) Fort Smith; KFTA-TV (FOX, NBC) Fort Smith; KHBS (ABC, CW) Fort Smith; KOKI-TV (FOX) Tulsa; KOTV-DT (CBS) Tulsa; KTUL (ABC) Tulsa; allband FM.
Programming (via microwave): KETA-TV (PBS) Oklahoma City.
Programming (via satellite): A&E Networks; ABC Family Channel; CNN; Country Music TV; C-SPAN; Discovery Channel; Disney Channel; ESPN; Fox Sports Southwest; Headline News; HGTV; History Channel; Lifetime; Nickelodeon; QVC; Spike TV; TBS Superstation; The Weather Channel; Turner Classic Movies; Turner Network TV; TV Land; USA Network; WGN America.
Fee: $39.95 installation; $19.95 monthly.

Pay Service 1
Pay Units: 108.
Programming (via satellite): HBO.
Fee: $35.00 installation; $10.95 monthly.

Pay Service 2
Pay Units: 57.
Programming (via satellite): Showtime.
Fee: $35.00 installation; $9.95 monthly.

Pay Service 3
Pay Units: 51.
Programming (via satellite): The Movie Channel.
Fee: $35.00 installation; $7.95 monthly.

Video-On-Demand: No

Internet Service
Operational: Yes. Began: March 24, 2004.
Broadband Service: Suddenlink High Speed Internet.
Fee: $45.95 installation; $24.95 monthly.

Telephone Service
Digital: Operational
Fee: $49.95 monthly

Miles of Plant: 25.0 (coaxial); None (fiber optic).
Regional Manager: Todd Cruthird. Regional Marketing Manager: Beverly Gambell. Plant Manager: Danny Keith.
Ownership: Cequel Communications LLC (MSO).

HECTORVILLE—Quality Cablevision of Oklahoma Inc. No longer in operation. ICA: OK0336.

HELENA—Pioneer Telephone Coop. Formerly [OK0153]. This cable system has converted to IPTV, PO Box 539, Kingfisher, OK 73750. Phones: 888-782-2667; 405-375-4111. E-mail: website@pldi.net. Web Site: http://www.ptci.com. ICA: OK5072.
TV Market Ranking: Outside TV Markets (HELENA).
Channel capacity: N.A. Channels available but not in use: N.A.

Internet Service
Operational: Yes.

Telephone Service
Digital: Operational

General Manager: Richard Ruhl.

HELENA—Pioneer Telephone Coop. This cable system has converted to IPTV. See Helena, OK [OK5072]. ICA: OK0153.

HENNESSEY—Pioneer Telephone Coop. Formerly [OK0113]. This cable system has converted to IPTV, PO Box 539, Kingfisher, OK 73750. Phones: 888-782-2667; 405-375-4111. E-mail: website@pldi.net. Web Site: http://www.ptci.com. ICA: OK5087.
TV Market Ranking: Outside TV Markets (HENNESSEY). Franchise award date: N.A. Franchise expiration date: N.A. Began: September 30, 2004.
Channel capacity: N.A. Channels available but not in use: N.A.

Internet Service
Operational: Yes.

Telephone Service
Digital: Operational

General Manager: Richard Ruhl.

HENNESSEY—Pioneer Telephone Coop. This cable system has converted to IPTV. See Hennessey, OK [OK5087]. ICA: OK0113.

HENRYETTA—Suddenlink Communications. Now served by OKMULGEE, OK [OK0026]. ICA: OK0049.

HINTON—Hinton CATV Co., 120 W Main St, PO Box 70, Hinton, OK 73047-0070. Phone: 405-542-3211. Fax: 405-542-3131. E-mail: hintoncatv@hintonet.net. Web Site: http://www.hintonet.net. Also serves Bridgeport, Cedar Lake, Colony, Eakly, Lookeba & Sickles. ICA: OK0140.
TV Market Ranking: Outside TV Markets (Bridgeport, Cedar Lake, Colony, Eakly, HINTON, Lookeba, Sickles). Franchise award date: N.A. Franchise expiration date: N.A. Began: July 1, 1983.
Channel capacity: N.A. Channels available but not in use: N.A.

Basic Service
Subscribers: 730.
Programming (received off-air): KAUT-TV (MNT) Oklahoma City; KETA-TV (PBS) Oklahoma City; KFOR-TV (NBC) Oklahoma City; KOCB (CW) Oklahoma City; KOCO-TV (ABC) Oklahoma City; KOKH-TV (FOX) Oklahoma City; KTBO-TV (TBN) Oklahoma City; KWTV-DT (CBS) Oklahoma City.
Programming (via satellite): CNN; Disney Channel; ESPN; Hallmark Channel; TBS Superstation; Turner Network TV; WGN America.
Fee: $25.00 installation; $23.24 monthly.

Pay Service 1
Pay Units: 275.
Programming (via satellite): Cinemax; HBO; Showtime.
Fee: $10.99 monthly (Cinemax or Showtime), $13.99 monthly (HBO).

Video-On-Demand: No

Internet Service
Operational: Yes, DSL.
Broadband Service: Hinton Net.
Fee: $27.95-$64.95 monthly.

Telephone Service
None

Miles of Plant: 27.0 (coaxial); None (fiber optic).
Manager & Chief Technician: Kenneth Doughty. Secretary & Treasurer: Jason Doughty.
Ownership: Hinton CATV Co.

HOBART—Cable One, 315 S Washington St, PO Box 720, Hobart, OK 73651-0720. Phone: 580-726-2523. Fax: 580-726-5818. E-mail: rick.iliff@cableone.net. Web Site: http://www.cableone.net. Also serves Kiowa County (portions). ICA: OK0067.
TV Market Ranking: Below 100 (Kiowa County (portions) (portions)); Outside TV Markets (HOBART, Kiowa County (portions) (portions)). Franchise award date: April 1, 1985. Franchise expiration date: February 25, 2016. Began: April 1, 1956.
Channel capacity: 76 (operating 2-way). Channels available but not in use: N.A.

Basic Service
Subscribers: 1,300.
Programming (received off-air): KAUT-TV (MNT) Oklahoma City; KFOR-TV (NBC) Oklahoma City; KOCB (CW) Oklahoma City; KOCO-TV (ABC) Oklahoma City; KOKH-TV (FOX) Oklahoma City; KSBI (IND) Oklahoma City; KWET (PBS) Cheyenne; KWTV-DT (CBS) Oklahoma City; allband FM.
Programming (via satellite): A&E Networks; ABC Family Channel; AMC; Animal Planet; BET Networks; Cartoon Network; CNBC; CNN; Country Music TV; C-SPAN; C-SPAN 2; Discovery Channel; Disney Channel; E! Entertainment Television; ESPN; ESPN 2; Food Network; Fox News Channel; Fox Sports Southwest; FX; Headline News; HGTV; History Channel; ION Television; Lifetime; LWS Local Weather Station; MSNBC; MTV; Nickelodeon; QVC; Spike TV; Syfy; TBS Superstation; The

Learning Channel; The Weather Channel; Trinity Broadcasting Network; Turner Classic Movies; Turner Network TV; TV Guide Network; TV Land; Univision Studios; USA Network; VH1; WGN America.

Fee: $20.00 installation; $46.00 monthly; $.69 converter; $25.00 additional installation.

Digital Basic Service

Subscribers: 450.

Programming (via satellite): 3 Angels Broadcasting Network; Bio; Boomerang; BYU Television; Canales N; Discovery Digital Networks; ESPN Classic Sports; ESPN HD; ESPNews; FamilyNet; Fox College Sports Atlantic; Fox College Sports Central; Fox College Sports Pacific; Fox Movie Channel; Fox Soccer; Fuel TV; Golf Channel; Great American Country; GSN; Hallmark Channel; History Channel International; INSP; Music Choice; National Geographic Channel; Outdoor Channel; SoapNet; Speed; Toon Disney; Trinity Broadcasting Network; truTV; Turner Network TV HD; TVG Network; Universal HD; WE tv.

Fee: $9.95 monthly.

Digital Pay Service 1

Pay Units: N.A.

Programming (via satellite): Cinemax (multiplexed); Encore (multiplexed); Flix; HBO (multiplexed); HBO HD; Showtime (multiplexed); Showtime HD; Starz (multiplexed); Sundance Channel; The Movie Channel (multiplexed); The Movie Channel HD.

Fee: $20.00 installation; $15.00 monthly for first premium channel, $7.00 for each additional premium channel.

Video-On-Demand: No

Pay-Per-View

iN DEMAND (delivered digitally); Pleasure (delivered digitally); Ten Clips (delivered digitally); Ten Blox (delivered digitally); Ten Blue (delivered digitally).

Internet Service

Operational: Yes.

Subscribers: 300.

Broadband Service: CableONE.net.

Fee: $75.00 installation; $43.00 monthly.

Telephone Service

Digital: Operational

Fee: $39.95 monthly

Miles of Plant: 29.0 (coaxial); None (fiber optic).

Manager & Chief Engineer: Rick Iliff. Office Manager: Peggy Miller.

Ownership: Cable ONE Inc. (MSO).

HOLDENVILLE—Allegiance Communications, 707 W Saratoga St, Shawnee, OK 74804. Phones: 405-395-1131; 405-275-6923. Web Site: http://www.allegiance.tv. ICA: OK0061.

TV Market Ranking: Below 100 (HOLDENVILLE). Franchise award date: N.A. Franchise expiration date: N.A. Began: September 1, 1967.

Channel capacity: 36 (not 2-way capable). Channels available but not in use: N.A.

Basic Service

Subscribers: 1,310.

Programming (received off-air): KETA-TV (PBS) Oklahoma City; KFOR-TV (NBC) Oklahoma City; KOCO-TV (ABC) Oklahoma City; KOKI-TV (FOX) Tulsa; KOPX-TV (ION) Oklahoma City; KOTV-DT (CBS) Tulsa; KTBO-TV (TBN) Oklahoma City; KTEN (ABC, CW, NBC) Ada; KWTV-DT (CBS) Oklahoma City; allband FM.

Programming (via satellite): A&E Networks; ABC Family Channel; AMC; Animal Planet; Cartoon Network; CMT Pure Country; CNBC; CNN; Comedy Central; Discovery Channel; Disney Channel; ESPN; ESPN 2; ESPN Classic Sports; Food Network; Fox News Channel; Fox Sports Southwest; FX; Hallmark Channel; HGTV; History Channel; Lifetime; MTV; NFL Network; QVC; Spike TV; Syfy; TBS Superstation; The Learning Channel; The Weather Channel; Turner Network TV; TV Land; USA Network; VH1.

Fee: $21.75 installation; $25.77 monthly; $14.50 additional installation.

Digital Basic Service

Subscribers: N.A.

Programming (via satellite): AmericanLife TV Network; BBC America; Bio; Black Family Channel; Bloomberg Television; Bravo; Canal 52MX; Cine Latino; Cine Mexicano; cloo; CMT Pure Country; CNN en Espanol; Current; Discovery en Espanol; Discovery Fit & Health; Discovery Health Channel; Discovery Home Channel; Discovery Kids Channel; Discovery Times Channel; DMX Music; Encore (multiplexed); ESPN 2; ESPN Classic Sports; ESPNews; Flix; Fox College Sports Atlantic; Fox College Sports Central; Fox College Sports Pacific; Fox Deportes; Fox Movie Channel; Fox Soccer; Fuse; G4; GAS; Golf Channel; Great American Country; GSN; Halogen Network; HGTV; History Channel; History Channel en Espanol; History Channel International; Independent Film Channel; Lifetime Movie Network; Military Channel; MTV Hits; MTV2; National Geographic Channel; Nick Jr.; NickToons TV; Outdoor Channel; Ovation; Science; ShopNBC; Speed; Style Network; Sundance Channel; Syfy; The Word Network; Toon Disney; Tr3s; Trinity Broadcasting Network; Turner Classic Movies; Versus; VH1 Classic; VH1 Soul; WE tv.

Pay Service 1

Pay Units: 345.

Programming (via satellite): Encore.

Fee: $1.75 monthly.

Pay Service 2

Pay Units: 213.

Programming (via satellite): HBO.

Fee: $12.95 monthly.

Pay Service 3

Pay Units: 121.

Programming (via satellite): Showtime.

Fee: $12.95 monthly.

Pay Service 4

Pay Units: 131.

Programming (via satellite): Starz.

Fee: $6.75 monthly.

Digital Pay Service 1

Pay Units: N.A.

Programming (via satellite): Cinemax (multiplexed); HBO (multiplexed); HBO Latino; Showtime (multiplexed); Starz (multiplexed); The Movie Channel (multiplexed).

Video-On-Demand: No

Pay-Per-View

iN DEMAND (delivered digitally); Hot Choice (delivered digitally); Playboy TV (delivered digitally); Fresh (delivered digitally); Shorteez (delivered digitally).

Internet Service

Operational: Yes.

Fee: $24.95 installation; $39.95 monthly.

Telephone Service

Digital: Operational

Miles of Plant: 24.0 (coaxial); None (fiber optic). Additional miles planned: 3.0 (coaxial).

Chief Executive Officer: Bill Haggarty. Regional Vice President: Andrew Dearth. Vice President, Marketing: Tracy Bass.

Ownership: Allegiance Communications (MSO).

FREE
TRIAL
@
Access the most current data instantly.
ADVANCED
TVFactbook
www.warren-news.com/factbook.htm

HOLLIS—Pioneer Telephone Coop. Formerly [OK0087]. This cable system has converted to IPTV, PO Box 539, Kingfisher, OK 73750. Phones: 888-782-2667; 405-375-4111. E-mail: website@pldi.net. Web Site: http://www.ptci.com. ICA: OK5086.

TV Market Ranking: Outside TV Markets (HOLLIS). Franchise award date: N.A. Franchise expiration date: N.A. Began: March 31, 2005.

Channel capacity: N.A. Channels available but not in use: N.A.

Internet Service

Operational: Yes.

Telephone Service

Digital: Operational

General Manager: Richard Ruhl.

HOLLIS—Pioneer Telephone Coop. This cable system has converted to IPTV. See Hollis, OK [OK5086]. ICA: OK0087.

HOMINY—Community Cablevision Co., 1550 W Rogers Blvd, PO Box 307, Skiatook, OK 74070-0307. Phone: 918-396-3019. Fax: 918-396-2081. E-mail: info@communitycablevision.com. Web Site: http://www.communitycablebroadband.com. ICA: OK0085.

TV Market Ranking: 54 (HOMINY). Franchise award date: June 20, 1979. Franchise expiration date: N.A. Began: January 1, 1980.

Channel capacity: N.A. Channels available but not in use: N.A.

Basic Service

Subscribers: 839.

Programming (received off-air): KDOR-TV (TBN) Bartlesville; KGEB (IND) Tulsa; KJRH-TV (NBC) Tulsa; KOED-TV (PBS) Tulsa; KOKI-TV (FOX) Tulsa; KOTV-DT (CBS) Tulsa; KTPX-TV (ION) Okmulgee; KTUL (ABC) Tulsa; KWHB (IND) Tulsa; allband FM.

Programming (via microwave): KTFO-CD (TEL) Austin.

Programming (via satellite): A&E Networks; ABC Family Channel; AMC; Animal Planet; BET Networks; Cartoon Network; CNN; Comedy Central; Country Music TV; C-SPAN; CW+; Discovery Channel; Discovery Health Channel; Disney Channel; ESPN; ESPN 2; ESPN Classic Sports; Food Network; Fox News Channel; Fox Sports Southwest; FX; Hallmark Channel; HGTV; History Channel; Lifetime; MoviePlex; MTV; National Geographic Channel; Nickelodeon; Outdoor Channel; Oxygen; QVC; Spike TV; Syfy; TBS Superstation; The Learning Channel; The Weather Channel; Travel Channel; truTV; Turner Classic Movies; Turner Network TV; TV Land; USA Network; VH1; WE tv; WGN America.

Fee: $29.95 installation; $32.95 monthly; $10.00 additional installation.

Digital Basic Service

Subscribers: N.A.

Programming (via satellite): AmericanLife TV Network; BBC America; Bio; Bloomberg Television; Bravo; Church Channel; Current; Discovery Fit & Health; Discovery Health Channel; Discovery Home Channel; Discovery Kids Channel; Discovery Times Channel; DMX Music; ESPN 2; ESPN Classic Sports; ESPNews; Fox College Sports Atlantic; Fox College Sports Central; Fox College Sports Pacific; Fox Movie Channel; Fox Soccer; Fuse; G4; GAS; Golf Channel; Great American Country; GSN; Halogen Network; HGTV; History Channel; History Channel International; Independent Film Channel; JCTV; Lifetime Movie Network; Lime; MBC America; Military Channel; MTV Hits; MTV Jams; MTV2; National Geographic Channel; Nick Jr.; NickToons TV; Outdoor Channel; Ovation; Science; ShopNBC; Speed; Style Network; Syfy; The Word Network; Toon Disney; Trinity Broadcasting Network; Trio; Turner Classic Movies; Versus; VH1 Classic; VH1 Country; VH1 Soul; WE tv.

Fee: $21.00 monthly.

Digital Pay Service 1

Pay Units: N.A.

Programming (via satellite): Cinemax (multiplexed); Encore (multiplexed); Flix; HBO (multiplexed); Showtime (multiplexed); Starz (multiplexed); Sundance Channel; The Movie Channel (multiplexed).

Fee: $11.50 monthly (HBO, Cinemax, Starz/Encore, or Showtime/TMC/Flix/Sundance).

Internet Service

Operational: Yes.

Broadband Service: In-house.

Fee: $44.95 monthly.

Telephone Service

Digital: Operational

Miles of Plant: 12.0 (coaxial); None (fiber optic). Additional miles planned: 4.0 (coaxial).

President & General Manager: Dennis Soule.

Ownership: Community Cablevision Co. (MSO).

HOOKER—Panhandle Telephone Coop. Inc., 2222 NW Hwy 64, Guymon, OK 73942. Phones: 580-338-2556; 800-562-2556. Fax: 580-338-8260. E-mail: support@ptsi.net. Web Site: http://www.ptsi.net. ICA: OK0125.

TV Market Ranking: Outside TV Markets (HOOKER).

Channel capacity: N.A. Channels available but not in use: N.A.

Basic Service

Subscribers: N.A.

Programming (received off-air): KBSD-DT (CBS) Ensign; KETA-TV (PBS) Oklahoma City; KSNG (NBC) Garden City; KUPK (ABC) Garden City.

Programming (via satellite): CW Television Network; The Weather Channel.

Programming (via translator): KAMR-TV (NBC) Amarillo; KCIT (FOX) Amarillo; KFDA-TV (CBS) Amarillo; KVII-TV (ABC, CW) Amarillo.

Fee: $18.99 monthly.

Expanded Basic Service 1

Subscribers: N.A.

Programming (via satellite): A&E Networks; ABC Family Channel; Cartoon Network; CNN; C-SPAN; Discovery Channel; Disney Channel; E! Entertainment Television; ESPN; ESPN 2; Fox News Channel; Fox Sports Southwest; FX; Great American Country; History Channel; Home

& Garden Television; Lifetime; National Geographic Channel; Nickelodeon; QVC; Spike TV; Syfy; TBS Superstation; TNT; Trinity Broadcasting Network; TV Land; USA Network.
Fee: $25.00 monthly.

Pay Service 1
Pay Units: N.A.
Programming (via satellite): HBO; Showtime; The Movie Channel.
Fee: $13.95 monthly (Showtime/The Movie Channel); $14.00 monthly (HBO).

Video-On-Demand: No

Telephone Service
None

Miles of Plant: 10.0 (coaxial); None (fiber optic).
President: Charles Russell.
Ownership: Panhandle Telephone Cooperative Inc. (MSO).

HOWE—Allegiance Communications, 707 W Saratoga St, Shawnee, OK 74804. Phones: 405-395-1131; 405-275-6923. Web Site: http://www.allegiance.tv. ICA: OK0243.
TV Market Ranking: Below 100 (HOWE). Franchise award date: N.A. Franchise expiration date: October 1, 2009. Began: January 1, 1985.
Channel capacity: 36 (not 2-way capable). Channels available but not in use: N.A.

Basic Service
Subscribers: 107.
Programming (received off-air): KAFT (PBS) Fayetteville; KFDF-CA Fort Smith; KFSM-TV (CBS) Fort Smith; KFTA-TV (FOX, NBC) Fort Smith; KHBS (ABC, CW) Fort Smith; KNWA-TV (FOX, NBC) Rogers; KTUL (ABC) Tulsa.
Programming (via satellite): ABC Family Channel; CMT Pure Country; CNN; Discovery Channel; Disney Channel; ESPN; Spike TV; TBS Superstation; Trinity Broadcasting Network; Turner Network TV; USA Network; WGN America.
Fee: $25.00 installation; $21.95 monthly.

Pay Service 1
Pay Units: 31.
Programming (via satellite): Showtime.
Fee: $25.00 installation; $11.00 monthly.

Pay Service 2
Pay Units: 27.
Programming (via satellite): HBO.
Fee: $13.00 monthly.

Pay-Per-View
Urban American Television Network (delivered digitally); iN DEMAND (delivered digitally); Playboy TV (delivered digitally); Fresh (delivered digitally); Shorteez (delivered digitally).

Internet Service
Operational: No.

Telephone Service
None

Miles of Plant: 5.0 (coaxial); None (fiber optic).
Chief Executive Officer: Bill Haggarty. Regional Vice President: Andrew Dearth. Vice President, Marketing: Tracy Bass.
Ownership: Allegiance Communications (MSO).

HUGO—Suddenlink Communications, 12444 Powerscourt Dr, Saint Louis, MO 63131-3660. Phones: 314-315-9346; 314-965-2020. Web Site: http://www.suddenlink.com. Also serves Choctaw County (portions). ICA: OK0050.
TV Market Ranking: Outside TV Markets (Choctaw County (portions), HUGO). Franchise award date: June 1, 1976. Franchise expiration date: N.A. Began: August 1, 1976.
Channel capacity: N.A. Channels available but not in use: N.A.

Basic Service
Subscribers: 2,219.
Programming (received off-air): KETA-TV (PBS) Oklahoma City; KTEN (ABC, CW, NBC) Ada; KXII (CBS, FOX, MNT) Sherman; WFAA (ABC) Dallas; allband FM.
Programming (via satellite): ABC Family Channel; AMC; BET Networks; Cartoon Network; CNBC; CNN; Country Music TV; Discovery Channel; Disney Channel; ESPN; Fox News Channel; Fox Sports Southwest; FX; Hallmark Channel; Headline News; Lifetime; MTV; Nickelodeon; QVC; Spike TV; TBS Superstation; The Weather Channel; Trinity Broadcasting Network; truTV; Turner Classic Movies; Turner Network TV; USA Network; WGN America.
Programming (via translator): KDFW-DT (FOX) Dallas; KTVT (CBS) Fort Worth; KXAS-TV (NBC) Fort Worth.
Fee: $35.23 installation; $19.95 monthly; $1.24 converter; $16.12 additional installation.

Pay Service 1
Pay Units: 307.
Programming (via satellite): Cinemax.

Pay Service 2
Pay Units: 245.
Programming (via satellite): HBO.

Pay Service 3
Pay Units: 147.
Programming (via satellite): Showtime.

Pay-Per-View
Special events.

Internet Service
Operational: Yes. Began: December 22, 2003.
Broadband Service: Suddenlink High Speed Internet.
Fee: $45.95 installation; $24.95 monthly.

Telephone Service
Digital: Operational
Fee: $49.95 monthly

Miles of Plant: 59.0 (coaxial); None (fiber optic).
Regional Manager: Todd Cruthird. Manager & Chief Technician: Lindy Loftin. Marketing Director: Beverly Gambell.
Ownership: Cequel Communications LLC (MSO).

HULBERT—Allegiance Communications, 707 W Saratoga St, Shawnee, OK 74804. Phones: 405-395-1131; 405-275-6923. Web Site: http://www.allegiance.tv. ICA: OK0202.
TV Market Ranking: Below 100 (HULBERT). Franchise award date: January 1, 1989. Franchise expiration date: January 1, 2014. Began: September 1, 1989.
Channel capacity: N.A. Channels available but not in use: N.A.

Basic Service
Subscribers: 102.
Programming (received off-air): KJRH-TV (NBC) Tulsa; KMYT-TV (MNT) Tulsa; KOED-TV (PBS) Tulsa; KOKI-TV (FOX) Tulsa; KOTV-DT (CBS) Tulsa; KRSC-TV (ETV) Claremore; KTUL (ABC) Tulsa; KWHB (IND) Tulsa.
Programming (via satellite): A&E Networks; ABC Family Channel; CNN; Country Music TV; Discovery Channel; ESPN; Lifetime; Nickelodeon; Spike TV; TBS Superstation; Turner Network TV; USA Network; WGN America.
Fee: $40.00 installation; $21.95 monthly; $1.96 converter; $19.95 additional installation.

Pay Service 1
Pay Units: N.A.
Programming (via satellite): HBO.
Fee: $9.95 monthly.

Video-On-Demand: No

Internet Service
Operational: No.

Telephone Service
None

Miles of Plant: 5.0 (coaxial); None (fiber optic).
Chief Executive Officer: Bill Haggarty. Vice President, Marketing: Tracy Bass. General Manager: Andrew Dearth.
Ownership: Allegiance Communications (MSO).

HUNTER—Formerly served by Pioneer Telephone Coop. No longer in operation. ICA: OK0288.

IDABEL—Suddenlink Communications, 12444 Powerscourt Dr, Saint Louis, MO 63131-3660. Phone: 314-965-2020. Web Site: http://www.suddenlink.com. ICA: OK0056.
TV Market Ranking: Outside TV Markets (IDABEL). Franchise award date: January 17, 1961. Franchise expiration date: N.A. Began: October 10, 1961.
Channel capacity: 40 (operating 2-way). Channels available but not in use: N.A.

Basic Service
Subscribers: 2,400.
Programming (received off-air): KOET (PBS) Eufaula; KTAL-TV (NBC) Texarkana; KTBS-TV (ABC) Shreveport; KTEN (ABC, CW, NBC) Ada.
Programming (via satellite): C-SPAN; Trinity Broadcasting Network; TV Guide Network.
Programming (via translator): KDFW-DT (FOX) Dallas; KSLA (CBS) Shreveport; KTVT (CBS) Fort Worth.
Fee: $15.31 installation; $17.95 monthly; $2.22 converter.

Expanded Basic Service 1
Subscribers: 2,350.
Programming (via satellite): A&E Networks; ABC Family Channel; AMC; Animal Planet; BET Networks; Cartoon Network; CNBC; CNN; Comedy Central; Discovery Channel; Disney Channel; E! Entertainment Television; ESPN; ESPN 2; Food Network; Fox News Channel; Fox Sports Southwest; FX; Great American Country; Headline News; HGTV; History Channel; Lifetime; MSNBC; MTV; National Geographic Channel; Nickelodeon; Outdoor Channel; Spike TV; Syfy; TBS Superstation; The Learning Channel; The Weather Channel; Turner Classic Movies; Turner Network TV; TV Land; Univision Studios; USA Network; VH1.
Fee: $15.31 installation; $18.00 monthly.

Digital Basic Service
Subscribers: N.A.
Programming (via satellite): BBC America; Bio; Bloomberg Television; cloo; Discovery Digital Networks; DMX Music; ESPN Classic Sports; ESPNews; Fox College Sports Atlantic; Fox College Sports Central; Fox College Sports Pacific; Fox Soccer; Fuse; G4; Golf Channel; GSN; History Channel International; Independent Film Channel; Military History Channel; Science Television; ShopNBC; Speed; Toon Disney; Versus; WE tv.

Pay Service 1
Pay Units: 300.
Programming (via satellite): Cinemax; HBO (multiplexed); Showtime; The Movie Channel.
Fee: $15.31 installation; $13.95 monthly (each).

Pay-Per-View
iN DEMAND (delivered digitally); Playboy TV (delivered digitally); Fresh (delivered digitally).

Internet Service
Operational: Yes. Began: May 19, 2003.
Broadband Service: Suddenlink High Speed Internet.
Fee: $45.95 installation; $24.95 monthly.

Telephone Service
Digital: Operational
Fee: $49.95 monthly

Miles of Plant: 49.0 (coaxial); None (fiber optic). Additional miles planned: 10.0 (coaxial).
Regional Manager: Todd Cruthird. Manager: Marianne Bogy. Chief Technician: Sonny Myers. Customer Service Manager: Jeanie Acker.
Ownership: Cequel Communications LLC (MSO).

INOLA—Allegiance Communications, 707 W Saratoga St, Shawnee, OK 74804. Phones: 405-275-6923; 405-395-1131. Web Site: http://www.allegiance.tv. ICA: OK0129.
TV Market Ranking: 54 (INOLA). Franchise award date: December 2, 1980. Franchise expiration date: N.A. Began: February 1, 1982.
Channel capacity: N.A. Channels available but not in use: N.A.

Basic Service
Subscribers: 402.
Programming (received off-air): KDOR-TV (TBN) Bartlesville; KELF-LP (IND) Miami; KJRH-TV (NBC) Tulsa; KMYT-TV (MNT) Tulsa; KOAM-TV (CBS) Pittsburg; KODE-TV (ABC) Joplin; KOED-TV (PBS) Tulsa; KOKI-TV (FOX) Tulsa; KOTV-DT (CBS) Tulsa; KQCW-DT (CW) Muskogee; KRSC-TV (ETV) Claremore; KTPX-TV (ION) Okmulgee; KTUL (ABC) Tulsa; KWHB (IND) Tulsa.
Programming (via satellite): C-SPAN; INSP; QVC; WGN America.
Programming (via translator): KSNF (NBC) Joplin.
Fee: $40.00 installation; $24.95 monthly; $1.96 converter; $19.95 additional installation.

Expanded Basic Service 1
Subscribers: N.A.
Programming (via satellite): A&E Networks; ABC Family Channel; AMC; Animal Planet; Bravo; Cartoon Network; CNBC; CNN; Comedy Central; Country Music TV; Discovery Channel; Disney Channel; E! Entertainment Television; ESPN; ESPN 2; Food Network; Fox News Channel; Fox Sports Southwest; FX; G4; Hallmark Channel; Headline News; HGTV; History Channel; Lifetime; MSNBC; MTV; Nickelodeon; Outdoor Channel; Oxygen; Spike TV; Syfy; TBS Superstation; The Learning Channel; The Weather Channel; Travel Channel; Turner Network TV; TV Land; USA Network; VH1.

Digital Basic Service
Subscribers: N.A.
Programming (via satellite): BBC America; Bloomberg Television; Discovery Digital Networks; ESPN Classic Sports; ESPNews; Golf Channel; GSN; Independent Film Channel; Music Choice; Nick Jr.; SoapNet;

Style Network; Toon Disney; Turner Classic Movies; TV Guide Interactive Inc.; Versus; WE tv.

Digital Pay Service 1

Pay Units: N.A.

Programming (via satellite): Cinemax (multiplexed); Encore (multiplexed); Flix; HBO (multiplexed); Showtime (multiplexed); Starz (multiplexed); The Movie Channel (multiplexed).

Video-On-Demand: No

Pay-Per-View

iN DEMAND (delivered digitally); Fox Sports Net (delivered digitally).

Internet Service

Operational: Yes.

Fee: $24.95 installation; $39.95 monthly.

Telephone Service

None

Miles of Plant: 25.0 (coaxial); None (fiber optic).

Chief Executive Officer: Bill Haggarty. Regional Vice President: Andrew Dearth. Vice President, Marketing: Tracy Bass.

Ownership: Allegiance Communications (MSO).

JET—Formerly served by Cebridge Connections. No longer in operation. ICA: OK0290.

JONES—Formerly served by Almega Cable. No longer in operation. ICA: OK0291.

KANSAS—Allegiance Communications, 707 W Saratoga St, Shawnee, OK 74804. Phones: 405-275-6923; 405-395-1131. Web Site: http://www.allegiance.tv. ICA: OK0292.

TV Market Ranking: Outside TV Markets (KANSAS). Franchise award date: January 1, 1989. Franchise expiration date: January 1, 2014. Began: June 1, 1989.

Channel capacity: N.A. Channels available but not in use: N.A.

Basic Service

Subscribers: N.A.

Programming (received off-air): KJRH-TV (NBC) Tulsa; KMYT-TV (MNT) Tulsa; KOED-TV (PBS) Tulsa; KOKI-TV (FOX) Tulsa; KOTV-DT (CBS) Tulsa; KQCW-DT (CW) Muskogee; KRSC-TV (ETV) Claremore; KTUL (ABC) Tulsa; KWHB (IND) Tulsa.

Programming (via satellite): A&E Networks; ABC Family Channel; AMC; CNBC; CNN; Country Music TV; Discovery Channel; Disney Channel; ESPN; ESPN 2; Headline News; Lifetime; Nickelodeon; Speed; Spike TV; TBS Superstation; Travel Channel; Turner Network TV; USA Network; WGN America.

Fee: $40.00 installation; $22.95 monthly; $1.96 converter; $19.95 additional installation.

Pay Service 1

Pay Units: N.A.

Programming (via satellite): HBO.

Fee: $9.95 monthly.

Video-On-Demand: No

Pay-Per-View

iN DEMAND (delivered digitally); Hot Choice (delivered digitally); Playboy TV (delivered digitally); Fresh (delivered digitally); Shorteez (delivered digitally).

Internet Service

Operational: No.

Telephone Service

None

Miles of Plant: 4.0 (coaxial); None (fiber optic).

Chief Executive Officer: Bill Haggarty. Regional Vice President: Andrew Dearth. Vice President, Marketing: Tracy Bass.

Ownership: Allegiance Communications (MSO).

KAW CITY—Community Cablevision Co., 1550 W Rogers Blvd, PO Box 307, Skiatook, OK 74070-0307. Phone: 918-396-3019. Fax: 918-396-2081. E-mail: info@communitycablevision.com. Web Site: http://www.communitycablebroadband.com. ICA: OK0231.

TV Market Ranking: Outside TV Markets (KAW CITY). Franchise award date: N.A. Franchise expiration date: N.A. Began: N.A.

Channel capacity: 35 (not 2-way capable). Channels available but not in use: N.A.

Basic Service

Subscribers: 107.

Programming (received off-air): KDOR-TV (TBN) Bartlesville; KFOR-TV (NBC) Oklahoma City; KJRH-TV (NBC) Tulsa; KOED-TV (PBS) Tulsa; KOKI-TV (FOX) Tulsa; KOTV-DT (CBS) Tulsa; KQCW-DT (CW) Muskogee; KTPX-TV (ION) Okmulgee; KTUL (ABC) Tulsa.

Programming (via satellite): ABC Family Channel; Cartoon Network; CNN; Country Music TV; C-SPAN; Discovery Channel; Disney Channel; ESPN; ESPN 2; Fox Sports Southwest; Headline News; QVC; Spike TV; Syfy; TBS Superstation; The Learning Channel; The Weather Channel; Turner Classic Movies; Turner Network TV; USA Network; WGN America.

Fee: $29.95 installation; $18.00 monthly.

Video-On-Demand: No

Internet Service

Operational: Yes.

Fee: $44.95 monthly.

Telephone Service

None

Miles of Plant: 6.0 (coaxial); None (fiber optic).

President & General Manager: Dennis Soule.

Ownership: Community Cablevision Co. (MSO).

KELLYVILLE—Allegiance Communications, 707 W Saratoga St, Shawnee, OK 74804. Phones: 405-275-6923; 405-395-1131. Web Site: http://www.allegiance.tv. ICA: OK0171.

TV Market Ranking: 54 (KELLYVILLE). Franchise award date: June 13, 1983. Franchise expiration date: N.A. Began: April 1, 1985.

Channel capacity: N.A. Channels available but not in use: N.A.

Basic Service

Subscribers: 181.

Programming (received off-air): KDOR-TV (TBN) Bartlesville; KGEB (IND) Tulsa; KJRH-TV (NBC) Tulsa; KMYT-TV (MNT) Tulsa; KOED-TV (PBS) Tulsa; KOKI-TV (FOX) Tulsa; KOTV-DT (CBS) Tulsa; KQCW-DT (CW) Muskogee; KTPX-TV (ION) Okmulgee; KTUL (ABC) Tulsa; KWHB (IND) Tulsa.

Programming (via satellite): A&E Networks; ABC Family Channel; AMC; Animal Planet; CNBC; CNN; Country Music TV; Discovery Channel; Disney Channel; E! Entertainment Television; ESPN; ESPN 2; G4; History Channel; Lifetime; MTV; Nickelodeon; Oxygen; Product Information Network; Speed; Spike TV; Syfy; TBS Superstation; The Weather Channel; Travel Channel; Turner Network TV; USA Network; WGN America.

Fee: $30.00 installation; $22.95 monthly.

Digital Basic Service

Subscribers: N.A.

Programming (via satellite): AmericanLife TV Network; BBC America; Bio; Bloomberg Television; Bravo; Discovery Fit & Health; DMX Music; ESPN Classic Sports; Fox Movie Channel; Fox Soccer; Fuse; GAS; Golf Channel; GSN; Halogen Network; HGTV; History Channel International; Independent Film Channel; Lifetime Movie Network; MTV Networks Digital Suite; Nick Jr.; Outdoor Channel; ShopNBC; Style Network; The Learning Channel; Toon Disney; Turner Classic Movies; TV Guide Network; Versus; WE tv.

Pay Service 1

Pay Units: N.A.

Programming (via satellite): Cinemax; HBO; Showtime.

Fee: $10.95 monthly (Showtime), $11.95 monthly (HBO).

Digital Pay Service 1

Pay Units: N.A.

Programming (via satellite): Cinemax (multiplexed); Encore (multiplexed); Flix; HBO (multiplexed); Showtime (multiplexed); Starz (multiplexed); The Movie Channel (multiplexed).

Video-On-Demand: No

Pay-Per-View

iN DEMAND (delivered digitally); Hot Choice (delivered digitally); Playboy TV (delivered digitally); Fresh (delivered digitally); Shorteez (delivered digitally).

Internet Service

Operational: No.

Telephone Service

None

Miles of Plant: 7.0 (coaxial); None (fiber optic).

Chief Executive Officer: Bill Haggarty. Regional Vice President: Andrew Dearth. Vice President, Marketing: Tracy Bass.

Ownership: Allegiance Communications (MSO).

KEOTA—Allegiance Communications, 707 W Saratoga St, Shawnee, OK 74804. Phones: 405-275-6923; 405-395-1131. Web Site: http://www.allegiance.tv. ICA: OK0218.

TV Market Ranking: Below 100 (KEOTA). Franchise award date: April 1, 1982. Franchise expiration date: N.A. Began: April 15, 1982.

Channel capacity: N.A. Channels available but not in use: N.A.

Basic Service

Subscribers: 154.

Programming (received off-air): KFSM-TV (CBS) Fort Smith; KHBS (ABC, CW) Fort Smith; KOET (PBS) Eufaula; KOKI-TV (FOX) Tulsa; KQCW-DT (CW) Muskogee; KTUL (ABC) Tulsa; KWHB (IND) Tulsa.

Programming (via satellite): A&E Networks; ABC Family Channel; Animal Planet; CNBC; CNN; Country Music TV; Discovery Channel; Disney Channel; E! Entertainment Television; ESPN; ESPN 2; G4; History Channel; Lifetime; MSNBC; MTV; Nickelodeon; QVC; Spike TV; Syfy; TBS Superstation; Travel Channel; Trinity Broadcasting Network; Turner Classic Movies; Turner Network TV; USA Network; WGN America.

Fee: $30.00 installation; $22.95 monthly; $1.00 converter.

Pay Service 1

Pay Units: 47.

Programming (via satellite): Cinemax; HBO.

Fee: $9.00 monthly (HBO).

Video-On-Demand: No; No

Pay-Per-View

iN DEMAND (delivered digitally); Hot Choice (delivered digitally); Playboy TV (delivered digitally); Fresh (delivered digitally); Shorteez (delivered digitally).

Internet Service

Operational: No.

Telephone Service

None

Miles of Plant: 7.0 (coaxial); None (fiber optic).

Chief Executive Officer: Bill Haggarty. Regional Vice President: Andrew Dearth. Vice President, Marketing: Tracy Bass.

Ownership: Allegiance Communications (MSO).

KETCHUM—Allegiance Communications, 707 W Saratoga St, Shawnee, OK 74804. Phones: 405-275-6923; 405-395-1131. Web Site: http://www.allegiance.tv. Also serves Afton, Bernice, Chelsea, Chouteau, Fairland, Grand Lake, Grove, Langley, Monkey Island & Spavinaw. ICA: OK0179.

TV Market Ranking: 54 (Chouteau); Below 100 (Chelsea, Fairland); Outside TV Markets (Afton, Bernice, Grand Lake, Grove, KETCHUM, Langley, Monkey Island, Spavinaw). Franchise award date: October 4, 1979. Franchise expiration date: N.A. Began: January 1, 1983.

Channel capacity: N.A. Channels available but not in use: N.A.

Basic Service

Subscribers: 3,011.

Programming (received off-air): KDOR-TV (TBN) Bartlesville; KELF-LP (IND) Miami; KJRH-TV (NBC) Tulsa; KMYT-TV (MNT) Tulsa; KOAM-TV (CBS) Pittsburg; KODE-TV (ABC) Joplin; KOED-TV (PBS) Tulsa; KOKI-TV (FOX) Tulsa; KOTV-DT (CBS) Tulsa; KQCW-DT (CW) Muskogee; KRSC-TV (ETV) Claremore; KSNF (NBC) Joplin; KTPX-TV (ION) Okmulgee; KTUL (ABC) Tulsa; KWHB (IND) Tulsa.

Programming (via satellite): C-SPAN; QVC; WGN America.

Fee: $40.00 installation; $24.95 monthly; $1.96 converter.

Expanded Basic Service 1

Subscribers: N.A.

Programming (via satellite): A&E Networks; ABC Family Channel; AMC; Animal Planet; Bravo; Cartoon Network; CNBC; CNN; Comedy Central; Country Music TV; Discovery Channel; Disney Channel; E! Entertainment Television; ESPN; ESPN 2; Food Network; Fox News Channel; Fox Sports Southwest; FX; G4; Hallmark Channel; Headline News; HGTV; History Channel; Lifetime; Lifetime Movie Network; MSNBC; MTV; Nickelodeon; Outdoor Channel; Oxygen; RFD-TV; Spike TV; Syfy;

TBS Superstation; The Learning Channel; The Weather Channel; Travel Channel; Turner Network TV; TV Land; USA Network; VH1.

Digital Basic Service

Subscribers: N.A.

Programming (via satellite): A&E HD; BBC America; Bio; Bloomberg Television; Chiller; cloo; CMT Pure Country; Current; Discovery Fit & Health; Discovery Health Channel; Discovery Kids Channel; Encore (multiplexed); ESPN 2 HD; ESPN Classic Sports; ESPN HD; ESPN U; ESPNews; Flix; Food Network HD; Fox College Sports Atlantic; Fox College Sports Central; Fox College Sports Pacific; Fox Movie Channel; Fox Soccer; Fuse; Golf Channel; Great American Country; GSN; HD Theater; HDNet; HDNet Movies; HGTV HD; History Channel International; ID Investigation Discovery; Independent Film Channel; Military Channel; MTV Hits; MTV2; Music Choice; National Geographic Channel; National Geographic Channel HD Network; Nick Jr.; NickToons TV; Outdoor Channel 2 HD; Planet Green; Science; ShopNBC; SoapNet; Speed; Style Network; Sundance Channel; TeenNick; The Word Network; Toon Disney; Turner Classic Movies; Universal HD; Versus; VH1 Classic; VH1 Soul; WE tv.

Digital Pay Service 1

Pay Units: 2,069.

Programming (via satellite): Cinemax (multiplexed); Encore (multiplexed); Flix; HBO (multiplexed); HBO HD; Showtime (multiplexed); Showtime HD; Starz (multiplexed); Starz HDTV; The Movie Channel (multiplexed).

Fee: $20.00 installation; $9.95 monthly (each).

Video-On-Demand: Yes

Pay-Per-View

iN DEMAND (delivered digitally); Club Jenna (delivered digitally); Spice: Xcess (delivered digitally); Playboy TV (delivered digitally); Fresh (delivered digitally).

Internet Service

Operational: Yes.

Fee: $24.95 installation; $39.95 monthly.

Telephone Service

None

Miles of Plant: 1,360.0 (coaxial); None (fiber optic).

Chief Executive Officer: Bill Haggarty. Regional Vice President: Andrew Dearth. Vice President, Marketing: Tracy Bass.

Ownership: Allegiance Communications (MSO).

KINGFISHER—Pioneer Telephone Coop. Formerly [OK0800]. This cable system has converted to IPTV, PO Box 539, Kingfisher, OK 73750. Phones: 888-782-2667; 405-375-4111. E-mail: website@pldi.net. Web Site: http://www.ptci.com. ICA: OK5074.

TV Market Ranking: Outside TV Markets (KINGFISHER). Franchise award date: N.A. Franchise expiration date: N.A. Began: N.A.

Channel capacity: N.A. Channels available but not in use: N.A.

Internet Service

Operational: Yes.

Telephone Service

Digital: Operational

General Manager: Richard Ruhl.

KINGFISHER—Pioneer Telephone Coop. This cable system has converted to IPTV. See Kingfisher, OK [OK5074]. ICA: OK0800.

KINGSTON—CommuniComm Services. Now served by TISHOMINGO, OK [OK0064]. ICA: OK0343.

KONAWA—Allegiance Communications, 707 W Saratoga St, Shawnee, OK 74804. Phones: 405-275-6923; 405-395-1131. Web Site: http://www.allegiance.tv. Also serves Seminole County (southern portion). ICA: OK0131.

TV Market Ranking: Below 100 (KONAWA, Seminole County (southern portion)). Franchise award date: N.A. Franchise expiration date: N.A. Began: January 1, 1981.

Channel capacity: 36 (not 2-way capable). Channels available but not in use: N.A.

Basic Service

Subscribers: 328.

Programming (received off-air): KETA-TV (PBS) Oklahoma City; KFOR-TV (NBC) Oklahoma City; KOCB (CW) Oklahoma City; KOCO-TV (ABC) Oklahoma City; KOKH-TV (FOX) Oklahoma City; KTEN (ABC, CW, NBC) Ada; KWTV-DT (CBS) Oklahoma City.

Programming (via satellite): A&E Networks; ABC Family Channel; AMC; Animal Planet; Cartoon Network; CNBC; CNN; Country Music TV; Discovery Channel; Disney Channel; ESPN; Fox News Channel; Fox Sports Southwest; FX; Headline News; HGTV; MTV; Nickelodeon; Spike TV; TBS Superstation; The Learning Channel; The Weather Channel; Turner Network TV; USA Network.

Fee: $21.75 installation; $21.95 monthly; $14.50 additional installation.

Pay Service 1

Pay Units: N.A.

Programming (via satellite): Cinemax; Encore; HBO; Starz.

Pay-Per-View

iN DEMAND (delivered digitally); Hot Choice (delivered digitally); Fresh (delivered digitally); Shorteez (delivered digitally); ESPN Now (delivered digitally); ESPN Gameplan (delivered digitally).

Internet Service

Operational: No.

Telephone Service

None

Miles of Plant: 9.0 (coaxial); None (fiber optic).

Chief Executive Officer: Bill Haggarty. Regional Vice President: Andrew Dearth. Vice President, Marketing: Tracy Bass.

Ownership: Allegiance Communications (MSO).

KREMLIN—Formerly served by Cebridge Connections. No longer in operation. ICA: OK0293.

LAHOMA—Pioneer Telephone Coop. Formerly [OK0298]. This cable system has converted to IPTV, PO Box 539, Kingfisher, OK 73750. Phones: 888-782-2667; 405-375-4111. E-mail: website@pldi.net. Web Site: http://www.ptci.com. ICA: OK5097.

TV Market Ranking: Franchise award date: N.A. Franchise expiration date: N.A. Began: September 30, 2004.

Channel capacity: N.A. Channels available but not in use: N.A.

Internet Service

Operational: Yes.

Telephone Service

Digital: Operational

General Manager: Richard Ruhl.

LAHOMA—Pioneer Telephone Coop. This cable system has converted to IPTV. See Lahoma, OK [OK5097]. ICA: OK0382.

LAKE ELLSWORTH—LakeView Cable, Hwy 115, PO Box 460, Cache, OK 73527-0460. Phone: 580-429-8800. Fax: 580-429-6599. Web Site: http://www.lvcisp.com. ICA: OK0385.

TV Market Ranking: Below 100 (LAKE ELLSWORTH). Franchise award date: N.A. Franchise expiration date: N.A. Began: N.A.

Channel capacity: N.A. Channels available but not in use: N.A.

Basic Service

Subscribers: 100.

Programming (received off-air): KAUT-TV (MNT) Oklahoma City; KAUZ-TV (CBS, CW) Wichita Falls; KETA-TV (PBS) Oklahoma City; KFOR-TV (NBC) Oklahoma City; KJTL (FOX) Wichita Falls; KOCB (CW) Oklahoma City; KOCO-TV (ABC) Oklahoma City; KOKH-TV (FOX) Oklahoma City; KSWO-TV (ABC, TMO) Lawton; KWTV-DT (CBS) Oklahoma City.

Programming (via satellite): A&E Networks; ABC Family Channel; Cartoon Network; CNN; Country Music TV; C-SPAN; Discovery Channel; Disney Channel; ESPN; Headline News; History Channel; Spike TV; Syfy; TBS Superstation; The Learning Channel; The Weather Channel; Travel Channel; Trinity Broadcasting Network; Turner Classic Movies; Turner Network TV; TV Land; USA Network; WGN America.

Fee: $35.00 installation; $26.75 monthly.

Pay Service 1

Pay Units: N.A.

Programming (via satellite): HBO; Showtime (multiplexed).

Fee: $8.50 monthly (Showtime), $10.00 monthly (HBO).

Video-On-Demand: No

Internet Service

Operational: No.

Telephone Service

None

Manager: Bill Rowell. Chief Technician: Mike Rowell.

Ownership: Lakeview Cable Inc. (MSO).

LAKE LAWTONKA—LakeView Cable, Hwy 115, PO Box 460, Cache, OK 73527-0460. Phone: 580-429-8800. Fax: 580-429-6599. Web Site: http://www.lvcisp.com. ICA: OK0386.

TV Market Ranking: Below 100 (LAKE LAWTONKA). Franchise award date: N.A. Franchise expiration date: N.A. Began: N.A.

Channel capacity: 42 (2-way capable). Channels available but not in use: N.A.

Basic Service

Subscribers: 125.

Programming (received off-air): KAUT-TV (MNT) Oklahoma City; KAUZ-TV (CBS, CW) Wichita Falls; KETA-TV (PBS) Oklahoma City; KFDX-TV (NBC) Wichita Falls; KFOR-TV (NBC) Oklahoma City; KJTL (FOX) Wichita Falls; KOCB (CW) Oklahoma City; KOCO-TV (ABC) Oklahoma City; KOKH-TV (FOX) Oklahoma City; KSWO-TV (ABC, TMO) Lawton; KWTV-DT (CBS) Oklahoma City.

Programming (via satellite): A&E Networks; ABC Family Channel; Cartoon Network; CNN; Country Music TV; C-SPAN; Discovery Channel; Disney Channel; ESPN; Headline News; History Channel; Spike TV; Syfy; TBS Superstation; The Learning Channel; The Weather Channel; Travel Channel; Trinity Broadcasting Network; Turner Classic Movies; Turner Network TV; TV Land; USA Network; WGN America.

Fee: $35.00 installation; $28.75 monthly.

Pay Service 1

Pay Units: N.A.

Programming (via satellite): HBO; Showtime (multiplexed).

Fee: $8.50 monthly (Showtime), $10.00 monthly (HBO).

Video-On-Demand: No

Internet Service

Operational: Yes.

Telephone Service

None

Miles of plant included in Cache

Manager: Bill Rowell. Chief Technician: Mike Rowell.

Ownership: Lakeview Cable Inc. (MSO).

LAKE TENKILLER—Formerly served by Cox Communications. No longer in operation. ICA: OK0328.

LAMONT—Formerly served by Blue Sky Cable LLC. No longer in operation. ICA: OK0211.

LANGSTON—Allegiance Communications, 707 W Saratoga St, Shawnee, OK 74804. Phones: 405-275-6923; 405-395-1131. Web Site: http://www.allegiance.tv. Also serves Coyle. ICA: OK0275.

TV Market Ranking: Outside TV Markets (Coyle, LANGSTON). Franchise award date: December 27, 1988. Franchise expiration date: December 27, 2013. Began: March 1, 1989.

Channel capacity: 35 (not 2-way capable). Channels available but not in use: N.A.

Basic Service

Subscribers: N.A.

Programming (received off-air): KAUT-TV (MNT) Oklahoma City; KETA-TV (PBS) Oklahoma City; KFOR-TV (NBC) Oklahoma City; KOCB (CW) Oklahoma City; KOCO-TV (ABC) Oklahoma City; KOKH-TV (FOX) Oklahoma City; KTBO-TV (TBN) Oklahoma City; KWTV-DT (CBS) Oklahoma City.

Programming (via microwave): KOPX-TV (ION) Oklahoma City.

Programming (via satellite): A&E Networks; ABC Family Channel; AMC; BET Networks; Black Family Channel; CNBC; CNN; Comedy Central; Country Music TV; C-SPAN; Discovery Channel; Disney Channel; E! Entertainment Television; ESPN; ESPN 2; History Channel; Lifetime; MTV; Nickelodeon; Oxygen; QVC; Speed; Spike TV; Syfy; TBS Superstation; The Learning Channel; The Weather Channel; Travel Channel; Turner Network TV; USA Network; WGN America.

Fee: $40.00 installation; $22.95 monthly; $1.96 converter; $19.95 additional installation.

Video-On-Demand: No

Pay-Per-View

Hot Choice (delivered digitally); Playboy TV (delivered digitally); Fresh (delivered digitally); Shorteez (delivered digitally); iN DEMAND (delivered digitally).

Internet Service

Operational: No.

Telephone Service

None

Miles of Plant: 9.0 (coaxial); None (fiber optic).

Chief Executive Officer: Bill Haggarty. Regional Vice President: Andrew Dearth. Vice President, Marketing: Tracy Bass.

Ownership: Allegiance Communications (MSO).

LAVERNE—Panhandle Telephone Coop. Inc., 2222 NW Hwy 64, Guymon, OK 73942. Phones: 580-338-2556; 800-562-2556. Fax: 580-338-8260. E-mail: support@ptsi.net. Web Site: http://www.ptsi.net. ICA: OK0132.

TV Market Ranking: Outside TV Markets (LAVERNE). Franchise award date: N.A. Franchise expiration date: N.A. Began: February 15, 1962.
Channel capacity: N.A. Channels available but not in use: N.A.
Basic Service
Subscribers: N.A.
Programming (received off-air): KETA-TV (PBS) Oklahoma City; KFOR-TV (NBC) Oklahoma City; KOCO-TV (ABC) Oklahoma City; KOKH-TV (FOX) Oklahoma City; KWTV-DT (CBS) Oklahoma City.
Programming (via satellite): QVC; The Weather Channel; Trinity Broadcasting Network.
Fee: $18.99 monthly.
Expanded Basic Service 1
Subscribers: N.A.
Programming (via satellite): A&E Networks; ABC Family Channel; Cartoon Network; CNN; Discovery Channel; Disney Channel; ESPN; ESPN 2; Fox News Channel; Fox Sports Southwest; FX; Great American Country; History Channel; Home & Garden Television; National Geographic Channel; Nickelodeon; Spike TV; Syfy; TBS Superstation; TLC; TNT; TV Land; Univision Studios; USA Network.
Fee: $25.20 monthly.
Pay Service 1
Pay Units: N.A.
Programming (via satellite): Cinemax; HBO; Showtime; The Movie Channel.
Fee: $13.49 monthly (Cinemax), $13.95 monthly (Showtime/TMC), $14.00 monthly (HBO).
Internet Service
Operational: Yes.
Telephone Service
None
Miles of Plant: 15.0 (coaxial); None (fiber optic).
President: Charles Russell.
Ownership: Panhandle Telephone Cooperative Inc. (MSO).

LAWTON—Fidelity Communications, 64 N Clark St, Sullivan, MO 63080. Phones: 800-392-8070; 573-468-8081. Fax: 573-468-5440. E-mail: custserv@fidelitycommunications.com. Web Site: http://www.fidelitycommunications.com. Also serves Comanche County. ICA: OK0004.
TV Market Ranking: Below 100 (Comanche County, LAWTON). Franchise award date: N.A. Franchise expiration date: January 1, 2015. Began: March 20, 1968.
Channel capacity: 100 (operating 2-way). Channels available but not in use: N.A.
Basic Service
Subscribers: 24,000.
Programming (received off-air): KAUZ-TV (CBS, CW) Wichita Falls; KETA-TV (PBS) Oklahoma City; KFDX-TV (NBC) Wichita Falls; KFOR-TV (NBC) Oklahoma City; KJTL (FOX) Wichita Falls; KSWO-TV (ABC, TMO) Lawton; KWTV-DT (CBS) Oklahoma City.
Programming (via satellite): TBS Superstation; The Weather Channel; WGN America.
Fee: $25.00 installation; $12.90 monthly; $11.00 additional installation.
Expanded Basic Service 1
Subscribers: 9,300.
Programming (via satellite): A&E Networks; ABC Family Channel; AMC; Animal Planet; BET Networks; Boomerang; Cartoon Network; Classic Arts Showcase; CNBC; CNN; Comedy Central; Country Music TV; C-SPAN; C-SPAN 2; Discovery Channel; Discovery Health Channel; Disney Channel; DIY Network; E! Entertainment Television; ESPN; ESPN 2; Fox Movie Channel; Fox News Channel; Fox Sports Southwest; FX; G4; Golf Channel; GSN; Headline News; HGTV; History Channel; INSP; Lifetime; Lifetime Movie Network; MTV; MTV2; National Geographic Channel; Nickelodeon; Outdoor Channel; QVC; SoapNet; Speed; Spike TV; Style Network; Syfy; Telemundo; The Learning Channel; Toon Disney; Travel Channel; Trinity Broadcasting Network; truTV; Turner Network TV; TV Guide Network; TV Land; USA Network; VH1.
Fee: $11.00 installation; $36.05 monthly.
Digital Basic Service
Subscribers: N.A.
Programming (via satellite): DMX Music; ESPN 2 HD; ESPN HD; Food Network HD; HD Theater; HDNet; HDNet Movies; HGTV HD; National Geographic Channel HD Network; Universal HD.
Fee: $13.95 monthly.
Digital Pay Service 1
Pay Units: N.A.
Programming (via satellite): Cinemax (multiplexed); Encore (multiplexed); Flix; HBO (multiplexed); Playboy TV; Showtime (multiplexed); Starz (multiplexed); Sundance Channel; The Movie Channel (multiplexed).
Fee: $20.00 installation; $10.00 monthly (Cinemax or Starz/Encore), $12.00 monthly (Showtime/TMC), $13.50 monthly (HBO), $14.95 monthly (Playboy).
Video-On-Demand: No
Internet Service
Operational: Yes.
Subscribers: 300.
Broadband Service: Lawton Cablevision.
Fee: $35.00 installation; $21.95 monthly.
Telephone Service
None
Miles of Plant: 320.0 (coaxial); 101.0 (fiber optic).
President: John T. Davis. Senior Vice President: John Colbert. Marketing Director: Robert Trottmann. Public Relations Manager: Craig Montgomery.
Ownership: Fidelity Communications Co. (MSO).

LEEDEY—Formerly served by Rapid Cable. No longer in operation. ICA: OK0381.

LINDSAY—Suddenlink Communications, 12444 Powerscourt Dr, Saint Louis, MO 63131-3660. Phone: 405-224-0110. Fax: 405-224-3760. Web Site: http://www.suddenlink.com. Also serves Erin Springs. ICA: OK0073.
TV Market Ranking: Below 100 (Erin Springs, LINDSAY). Franchise award date: September 1, 1977. Franchise expiration date: January 11, 2008. Began: March 15, 1979.
Channel capacity: 81 (not 2-way capable). Channels available but not in use: N.A.
Basic Service
Subscribers: 1,225.
Programming (received off-air): KAUT-TV (MNT) Oklahoma City; KETA-TV (PBS) Oklahoma City; KFOR-TV (NBC) Oklahoma City; KOCB (CW) Oklahoma City; KOCO-TV (ABC) Oklahoma City; KOKH-TV (FOX) Oklahoma City; KOPX-TV (ION) Oklahoma City; KSBI (IND) Oklahoma City; KTBO-TV (TBN) Oklahoma City; KWTV-DT (CBS) Oklahoma City.
Programming (via satellite): A&E Networks; ABC Family Channel; AMC; Animal Planet; Cartoon Network; CNN; Country Music TV; C-SPAN; Discovery Channel;

Disney Channel; E! Entertainment Television; ESPN; ESPN 2; Food Network; Fox News Channel; Fox Sports Southwest; Headline News; HGTV; History Channel; Lifetime; MSNBC; MTV; Nickelodeon; QVC; Spike TV; Syfy; TBS Superstation; The Learning Channel; The Weather Channel; Travel Channel; truTV; Turner Network TV; TV Land; Univision Studios; USA Network; VH1; WGN America.
Fee: $27.50 installation; $21.50 monthly; $22.40 additional installation.
Digital Basic Service
Subscribers: N.A.
Programming (via satellite): AmericanLife TV Network; BBC America; Black Family Channel; Bloomberg Television; Bravo; Discovery Fit & Health; ESPN Classic Sports; ESPNews; Fox Movie Channel; Fox Soccer; Fuse; G4; Golf Channel; Great American Country; GSN; Halogen Network; Independent Film Channel; Lifetime Movie Network; Music Choice; National Geographic Channel HD Network; Outdoor Channel; ShopNBC; Speed; Sundance Channel; The Word Network; Toon Disney; Turner Classic Movies; Versus.
Pay Service 1
Pay Units: 255.
Programming (via satellite): HBO.
Fee: $12.95 monthly.
Digital Pay Service 1
Pay Units: N.A.
Programming (via satellite): Cinemax (multiplexed); Encore (multiplexed); HBO (multiplexed); Showtime (multiplexed); Starz (multiplexed); The Movie Channel (multiplexed).
Video-On-Demand: No
Pay-Per-View
ESPN Gameplan (delivered digitally); Shorteez (delivered digitally); Fresh (delivered digitally); Playboy TV (delivered digitally); Hot Choice (delivered digitally); iN DEMAND (delivered digitally).
Internet Service
Operational: Yes.
Broadband Service: Suddenlink High Speed Internet.
Telephone Service
Digital: Operational
Miles of Plant: 29.0 (coaxial); None (fiber optic).
Manager: R. C. Lewis. Marketing Manager: Heather Eastwood.
Ownership: Cequel Communications LLC (MSO).

LONE WOLF—Formerly served by Cable West. No longer in operation. ICA: OK0377.

LONGDALE—LongView Communications. No longer in operation. ICA: OK0257.

LONGTOWN—Allegiance Communications, 707 W Saratoga St, Shawnee, OK 74804. Phones: 405-275-6923; 405-395-1131. Web Site: http://www.allegiance.tv. Also serves Brooken & Enterprise. ICA: OK0294.
TV Market Ranking: Outside TV Markets (Brooken, Enterprise, LONGTOWN). Franchise award date: N.A. Franchise expiration date: N.A. Began: February 1, 1984.
Channel capacity: 35 (not 2-way capable). Channels available but not in use: N.A.
Basic Service
Subscribers: 641.
Programming (received off-air): KJRH-TV (NBC) Tulsa; KMYT-TV (MNT) Tulsa; KOET (PBS) Eufaula; KOKI-TV (FOX) Tulsa; KOTV-DT (CBS) Tulsa; KQCW-DT (CW) Muskogee; KTPX-TV (ION) Okmulgee; KTUL (ABC) Tulsa; KWHB (IND) Tulsa.
Programming (via satellite): C-SPAN; QVC; Trinity Broadcasting Network; WGN America.
Fee: $40.00 installation; $24.95 monthly; $1.96 converter; $19.95 additional installation.
Expanded Basic Service 1
Subscribers: N.A.
Programming (via satellite): A&E Networks; ABC Family Channel; AMC; Animal Planet; Cartoon Network; CNBC; CNN; Comedy Central; Country Music TV; Discovery Channel; Disney Channel; E! Entertainment Television; ESPN; ESPN 2; Food Network; Fox News Channel; Fox Sports Southwest; FX; G4; Headline News; HGTV; History Channel; Lifetime; MTV; Nickelodeon; Outdoor Channel; Oxygen; Speed; Spike TV; Syfy; TBS Superstation; The Learning Channel; The Weather Channel; Travel Channel; truTV; Turner Classic Movies; Turner Network TV; TV Land; USA Network; VH1.
Digital Basic Service
Subscribers: N.A.
Programming (via satellite): BBC America; Bio; Bloomberg Television; Chiller; CMT Pure Country; Discovery Fit & Health; Discovery Health Channel; Discovery Kids Channel; ESPN Classic Sports; ESPNews; Golf Channel; GSN; History Channel International; ID Investigation Discovery; Lifetime Movie Network; Military Channel; MTV Hits; MTV2; Music Choice; National Geographic Channel; Nick Jr.; NickToons TV; Planet Green; RFD-TV; Science; Style Network; TeenNick; Toon Disney; VH1 Classic; VH1 Soul; WE tv.
Digital Expanded Basic Service
Subscribers: N.A.
Programming (via satellite): Encore (multiplexed); Flix; Independent Film Channel; Sundance Channel.
Digital Pay Service 1
Pay Units: N.A.
Programming (via satellite): Cinemax (multiplexed); Encore (multiplexed); HBO (multiplexed); Showtime (multiplexed); Starz (multiplexed); The Movie Channel (multiplexed).
Video-On-Demand: No
Pay-Per-View
iN DEMAND (delivered digitally); Fresh (delivered digitally); Playboy TV (delivered digitally); Club Jenna (delivered digitally); Spice: Xcess (delivered digitally).
Internet Service
Operational: No.

Telephone Service
None
Miles of Plant: 61.0 (coaxial); None (fiber optic).
Chief Executive Officer: Bill Haggarty. Regional Vice President: Andrew Dearth. Vice President, Marketing: Tracy Bass.
Ownership: Allegiance Communications (MSO).

LUTHER—Allegiance Communications, 707 W Saratoga St, Shawnee, OK 74804. Phones: 405-275-6923; 405-395-1131. Web Site: http://www.allegiance.tv. ICA: OK0225.
TV Market Ranking: 39 (LUTHER). Franchise award date: January 1, 1988. Franchise expiration date: January 1, 2013. Began: June 1, 1988.
Channel capacity: 35 (not 2-way capable). Channels available but not in use: N.A.
Basic Service
Subscribers: 93.
Programming (received off-air): KAUT-TV (MNT) Oklahoma City; KETA-TV (PBS) Oklahoma City; KFOR-TV (NBC) Oklahoma City; KOCB (CW) Oklahoma City; KOCO-TV (ABC) Oklahoma City; KOKH-TV (FOX) Oklahoma City; KOPX-TV (ION) Oklahoma City; KTBO-TV (TBN) Oklahoma City; KWTV-DT (CBS) Oklahoma City.
Programming (via satellite): A&E Networks; ABC Family Channel; BET Networks; Cartoon Network; CNBC; CNN; Discovery Channel; Disney Channel; ESPN; ESPN 2; Headline News; MSNBC; Spike TV; Syfy; TBS Superstation; Turner Network TV; USA Network; WGN America.
Fee: $29.95 installation; $22.95 monthly; $1.96 converter; $19.95 additional installation.
Video-On-Demand: No
Pay-Per-View
Hot Choice (delivered digitally); Playboy TV (delivered digitally); Fresh (delivered digitally); Shorteez (delivered digitally); iN DEMAND (delivered digitally).
Internet Service
Operational: No.
Telephone Service
None
Miles of Plant: 5.0 (coaxial); None (fiber optic).
Chief Executive Officer: Bill Haggarty. Regional Vice President: Andrew Dearth. Vice President, Marketing: Tracy Bass.
Ownership: Allegiance Communications (MSO).

MANGUM—Cable One. Now served by ELK CITY, OK [OK0032]. ICA: OK0079.

MANNFORD—Cim Tel Cable Inc., 103-D Cimarron St, Mannford, OK 74044. Phones: 918-865-3311; 918-865-3314. Fax: 918-865-7786. E-mail: staff@cimtel.net. Web Site: http://www.cimtel.net. Also serves Cleveland, Fairfax, Jennings, Osage, Pawnee, Prue & Westport. ICA: OK0296.
TV Market Ranking: 54 (Cleveland, MANNFORD, Osage, Prue, Westport); Outside TV Markets (Fairfax, Jennings, Pawnee). Franchise award date: N.A. Franchise expiration date: N.A. Began: January 1, 1982.
Channel capacity: 35 (not 2-way capable). Channels available but not in use: N.A.
Basic Service
Subscribers: 4,400.
Programming (received off-air): KDOR-TV (TBN) Bartlesville; KGEB (IND) Tulsa; KJRH-TV (NBC) Tulsa; KMYT-TV (MNT) Tulsa; KOED-TV (PBS) Tulsa; KOKI-TV (FOX) Tulsa; KOTV-DT (CBS) Tulsa; KQCW-DT (CW) Muskogee; KRSC-TV (ETV) Claremore; KTPX-TV (ION) Okmulgee; KTUL (ABC) Tulsa; KWHB (IND) Tulsa.
Programming (via satellite): A&E Networks; ABC Family Channel; AMC; CNN; Country Music TV; C-SPAN; Discovery Channel; Disney Channel; ESPN; ESPN 2; Fox News Channel; Fox Sports Net; FX; Headline News; History Channel; Lifetime; Nickelodeon; QVC; Spike TV; Syfy; TBS Superstation; The Learning Channel; The Weather Channel; Travel Channel; Turner Network TV; TV Guide Network; USA Network; VH1; WGN America.
Fee: $30.00 installation; $21.99 monthly.
Digital Basic Service
Subscribers: 550.
Programming (via satellite): Animal Planet; Bravo; Cartoon Network; CNBC; Comedy Central; C-SPAN 2; DMX Music; E! Entertainment Television; ESPN Classic Sports; ESPNews; Food Network; Golf Channel; Great American Country; GSN; Hallmark Channel; HGTV; MSNBC; MTV; National Geographic Channel; Outdoor Channel; Oxygen; Speed; Turner Classic Movies; TV Land; WE tv.
Fee: $39.99 monthly.
Pay Service 1
Pay Units: 385.
Programming (via satellite): HBO.
Fee: $10.99 monthly.
Pay Service 2
Pay Units: 112.
Programming (via satellite): Cinemax.
Fee: $10.99 monthly.
Digital Pay Service 1
Pay Units: N.A.
Programming (via satellite): Cinemax (multiplexed); Encore (multiplexed); Flix; HBO (multiplexed); Showtime (multiplexed); Starz (multiplexed); Sundance Channel; The Movie Channel (multiplexed).
Fee: $10.99 monthly (HBO, Cinemax or Encore), $17.99 (Showtime/Starz/Flix/Sundance/TMC).
Video-On-Demand: No
Internet Service
Operational: Yes.
Broadband Service: DSL service only.
Telephone Service
None
Manager & Chief Technician: Robert Berryman.
Ownership: Cim Tel Cable Inc. (MSO).

MARLAND—Formerly served by Allegiance Communications. No longer in operation. ICA: OK0297.

MARSHALL—Pioneer Telephone Coop. Formerly [OK0298]. This cable system has converted to IPTV, PO Box 539, Kingfisher, OK 73750. Phones: 888-782-2667; 405-375-4111. E-mail: website@pldi.net. Web Site: http://www.ptci.com. ICA: OK5076.
Channel capacity: N.A. Channels available but not in use: N.A.
Internet Service
Operational: Yes.
Telephone Service
Digital: Operational
General Manager: Richard Ruhl.

MARSHALL—Pioneer Telephone Coop. This cable system has converted to IPTV. See Marshall, OK [OK5076]. ICA: OK0298.

MARTHA—Formerly served by CableDirect. No longer in operation. ICA: OK0299.

MAUD—Allegiance Communications, 707 W Saratoga St, Shawnee, OK 74804. Phones: 405-395-1131; 405-275-6923. Web Site: http://www.allegiance.tv. ICA: OK0178.
TV Market Ranking: Below 100 (MAUD). Franchise award date: N.A. Franchise expiration date: N.A. Began: January 1, 1982.
Channel capacity: 35 (not 2-way capable). Channels available but not in use: N.A.
Basic Service
Subscribers: 242.
Programming (received off-air): KETA-TV (PBS) Oklahoma City; KFOR-TV (NBC) Oklahoma City; KOCB (CW) Oklahoma City; KOCO-TV (ABC) Oklahoma City; KOKH-TV (FOX) Oklahoma City; KTEN (ABC, CW, NBC) Ada; KWTV-DT (CBS) Oklahoma City.
Programming (via satellite): ABC Family Channel; Animal Planet; Cartoon Network; CMT Pure Country; CNBC; CNN; C-SPAN; Discovery Channel; Disney Channel; Fox News Channel; FX; Headline News; HGTV; MTV; Nickelodeon; TBS Superstation; The Learning Channel; The Weather Channel; Turner Network TV.
Fee: $60.00 installation; $29.73 monthly; $20.00 additional installation.
Pay Service 1
Pay Units: N.A.
Programming (via satellite): Cinemax; Encore; HBO; Starz.
Fee: $20.00 installation; $10.00 monthly (each).
Pay-Per-View
iN DEMAND (delivered digitally); Hot Choice (delivered digitally); Playboy TV (delivered digitally); Fresh (delivered digitally); Shorteez (delivered digitally).
Internet Service
Operational: No.
Telephone Service
None
Miles of Plant: 11.0 (coaxial); None (fiber optic).
Chief Executive Officer: Bill Haggarty. Regional Vice President: Andrew Dearth. Vice President, Marketing: Tracy Bass.
Ownership: Allegiance Communications (MSO).

McALESTER—Allegiance Communications, 707 W Saratoga St, Shawnee, OK 74804. Phones: 405-395-1131; 405-275-6923. Web Site: http://www.allegiance.tv. Also serves Alderson & Krebs. ICA: OK0019.
TV Market Ranking: Outside TV Markets (Alderson, Krebs, MCALESTER). Franchise award date: August 26, 1961. Franchise expiration date: N.A. Began: February 1, 1963.
Channel capacity: 70 (operating 2-way). Channels available but not in use: N.A.
Basic Service
Subscribers: 6,682.
Programming (received off-air): KJRH-TV (NBC) Tulsa; KMYT-TV (MNT) Tulsa; KOED-TV (PBS) Tulsa; KOKI-TV (FOX) Tulsa; KOTV-DT (CBS) Tulsa; KQCW-DT (CW) Muskogee; KTEN (ABC, CW, NBC) Ada; KTPX-TV (ION) Okmulgee; KTUL (ABC) Tulsa; KWHB (IND) Tulsa; 12 FMs.
Programming (via microwave): KFOR-TV (NBC) Oklahoma City; KWTV-DT (CBS) Oklahoma City.
Programming (via satellite): C-SPAN; C-SPAN 2; QVC; The Weather Channel; TV Guide Network; WGN America.
Fee: $60.00 installation; $21.95 monthly; $2.00 converter.
Expanded Basic Service 1
Subscribers: N.A.
Programming (via satellite): A&E Networks; ABC Family Channel; AMC; Animal Planet; BET Networks; Bravo; Cartoon Network; CNBC; CNN; Comedy Central; Country Music TV; Discovery Channel; Disney Channel; E! Entertainment Television; ESPN; ESPN 2; ESPN Classic Sports; ESPN U; Eternal Word TV Network; Food Network; Fox News Channel; Fox Sports Southwest; FX; Hallmark Channel; Headline News; HGTV; History Channel; Lifetime; Lifetime Movie Network; MoviePlex; MSNBC; MTV; National Geographic Channel; NFL Network; Nickelodeon; RFD-TV; ShopNBC; SoapNet; Spike TV; Syfy; TBS Superstation; The Learning Channel; Travel Channel; Trinity Broadcasting Network; truTV; Turner Network TV; TV Land; Univision Studios; USA Network; VH1.
Fee: $13.28 monthly.
Digital Basic Service
Subscribers: N.A.
Programming (via satellite): 3 Angels Broadcasting Network; A&E HD; AmericanLife TV Network; BBC America; Bio; Bloomberg Television; Bravo; BYU Television; Church Channel; Cine Latino; Cine Mexicano; cloo; CMT Pure Country; CNN en Espanol; Colours; Daystar TV Network; Discovery en Espanol; Discovery Fit & Health; Discovery Health Channel; Discovery Kids Channel; DMX Music; Encore (multiplexed); ESPN 2 HD; ESPN Classic Sports; ESPN Deportes; ESPN HD; ESPNews; FamilyNet; Flix; Food Network HD; Fox College Sports Atlantic; Fox College Sports Central; Fox College Sports Pacific; Fox Deportes; Fox Movie Channel; Fox Soccer; Fuse; G4; GMC; Golden Eagle Broadcasting; Golf Channel; Great American Country; GSN; Halogen Network; HD Theater; HDNet; HDNet Movies; HGTV HD; History Channel; History Channel en Espanol; History Channel International; ID Investigation Discovery; Independent Film Channel; JCTV; La Familia Network; Latin Television (LTV); Lifetime Movie Network; Military Channel; MTV Hits; MTV2; mun2 television; National Geographic Channel; National Geographic Channel HD Network; Nick Jr.; NickToons TV; Outdoor Channel; Outdoor Channel 2 HD; Planet Green; Science; ShopNBC; Speed; Style Network; Sundance Channel; Syfy; TeenNick; The Word Network; Toon Disney; Tr3s; Trinity Broadcasting Network; Turner Classic Movies; TV Chile; TV Colombia; Universal HD; Versus; VH1 Classic; WE tv; World Harvest Television.
Pay Service 1
Pay Units: N.A.
Programming (via satellite): Cinemax; Encore; HBO; Showtime; Starz.
Fee: $6.75 monthly.
Digital Pay Service 1
Pay Units: N.A.
Programming (via satellite): Cinemax (multiplexed); HBO (multiplexed); HBO HD; HBO Latino; Showtime (multiplexed); Showtime HD; Starz (multiplexed); Starz HDTV; The Movie Channel (multiplexed).
Video-On-Demand: No
Pay-Per-View
Hot Choice (delivered digitally); iN DEMAND (delivered digitally); Fresh (delivered digitally); Playboy TV (delivered digitally); Spice: Xcess (delivered digitally); Club Jenna (delivered digitally).

Internet Service
Operational: Yes. Began: December 31, 2002.
Broadband Service: Cox High Speed Internet.
Fee: $24.95 installation; $39.95 monthly.
Telephone Service
None
Miles of Plant: 161.0 (coaxial); None (fiber optic).
Chief Executive Officer: Bill Haggarty. Regional Vice President: Andrew Dearth. Vice President, Marketing: Tracy Bass.
Ownership: Allegiance Communications (MSO).

McCURTAIN—Allegiance Communications, 707 W Saratoga St, Shawnee, OK 74804. Phones: 405-275-6923; 405-395-1131. Web Site: http://www.allegiance.tv. ICA: OK0244.
TV Market Ranking: Outside TV Markets (MCCURTAIN). Franchise award date: N.A. Franchise expiration date: September 11, 2010. Began: N.A.
Channel capacity: N.A. Channels available but not in use: N.A.
Basic Service
Subscribers: 103.
Programming (received off-air): KHBS (ABC, CW) Fort Smith; KOET (PBS) Eufaula; KOKI-TV (FOX) Tulsa; KQCW-DT (CW) Muskogee; KTUL (ABC) Tulsa; KWHB (IND) Tulsa.
Programming (via satellite): A&E Networks; ABC Family Channel; Country Music TV; Discovery Channel; Disney Channel; ESPN; Spike TV; Syfy; TBS Superstation; Trinity Broadcasting Network; Turner Network TV; USA Network; WGN America.
Fee: $21.95 monthly.
Pay Service 1
Pay Units: N.A.
Programming (via satellite): HBO.
Pay-Per-View
ESPN Now (delivered digitally); Hot Choice (delivered digitally); iN DEMAND (delivered digitally).
Internet Service
Operational: No.
Telephone Service
None
Miles of Plant: 3.0 (coaxial); None (fiber optic).
Chief Executive Officer: Bill Haggarty. Regional Vice President: Andrew Dearth. Vice President, Marketing: Tracy Bass.
Ownership: Allegiance Communications (MSO).

MEDICINE PARK—LakeView Cable, Hwy 115, PO Box 460, Cache, OK 73527-0460. Phone: 580-429-8800. Fax: 580-429-6599. Web Site: http://www.lvcisp.com. ICA: OK0116.
TV Market Ranking: Below 100 (MEDICINE PARK). Franchise award date: N.A. Franchise expiration date: N.A. Began: September 1, 1977.
Channel capacity: N.A. Channels available but not in use: N.A.
Basic Service
Subscribers: 354.
Programming (received off-air): KAUT-TV (MNT) Oklahoma City; KAUZ-TV (CBS, CW) Wichita Falls; KETA-TV (PBS) Oklahoma City; KFDX-TV (NBC) Wichita Falls; KFOR-TV (NBC) Oklahoma City; KJTL (FOX) Wichita Falls; KOCB (CW) Oklahoma City; KOKH-TV (FOX) Oklahoma City; KSWO-TV (ABC, TMO) Lawton; KWTV-DT (CBS) Oklahoma City; allband FM.
Programming (via satellite): A&E Networks; ABC Family Channel; CNN; Country Music TV; C-SPAN; Discovery Channel; Disney Channel; ESPN; Headline News; History Channel; Nickelodeon; Spike TV; Syfy; TBS Superstation; The Learning Channel; The Weather Channel; Travel Channel; Trinity Broadcasting Network; Turner Classic Movies; Turner Network TV; TV Land; USA Network; WGN America.
Fee: $35.00 installation; $29.20 monthly.
Pay Service 1
Pay Units: N.A.
Programming (via satellite): HBO; Showtime (multiplexed).
Fee: $9.95 monthly (Showtime), $10.95 monthly (HBO).
Video-On-Demand: No
Internet Service
Operational: No.
Telephone Service
None
Miles of Plant: 15.0 (coaxial); None (fiber optic).
Manager: Bill Rowell. Chief Technician: Mike Rowell.
Ownership: Lakeview Cable Inc. (MSO).

MENO—Formerly served by CableDirect. No longer in operation. ICA: OK0255.

MIAMI—Cable One, 136 D Northeast, Miami, OK 74354. Phones: 918-542-1568; 918-542-1811 (Customer service). Fax: 918-542-6745. E-mail: mslyman@cableone.net. Web Site: http://www.cableone.net. Also serves Commerce, North Miami & Ottawa County. ICA: OK0021.
TV Market Ranking: Below 100 (Commerce, MIAMI, North Miami, Ottawa County (portions)); Outside TV Markets (Ottawa County (portions)). Franchise award date: March 15, 1965. Franchise expiration date: N.A. Began: July 5, 1968.
Channel capacity: 62 (operating 2-way). Channels available but not in use: N.A.
Basic Service
Subscribers: 5,266.
Programming (received off-air): KFJX (FOX) Pittsburg; KJRH-TV (NBC) Tulsa; KODE-TV (ABC) Joplin; KOED-TV (PBS) Tulsa; KOTV-DT (CBS) Tulsa; KOZJ (PBS) Joplin; KSNF (NBC) Joplin; KTUL (ABC) Tulsa; 10 FMs.
Programming (via satellite): C-SPAN; C-SPAN 2; CW+; Eternal Word TV Network; QVC; TBS Superstation; Trinity Broadcasting Network; TV Guide Network; WGN America.
Fee: $75.00 installation; $46.00 monthly; $15.00 additional installation.
Expanded Basic Service 1
Subscribers: N.A.
Programming (via satellite): A&E Networks; ABC Family Channel; AMC; Animal Planet; Cartoon Network; CNBC; CNN; Comedy Central; Country Music TV; Discovery Channel; Disney Channel; ESPN; ESPN 2; Food Network; Fox News Channel; Fox Sports Southwest; FX; Headline News; HGTV; History Channel; Lifetime; MSNBC; MTV; Nickelodeon; Spike TV; Syfy; The Learning Channel; The Weather Channel; Turner Classic Movies; Turner Network TV; TV Land; USA Network; VH1.
Fee: $42.50 monthly.
Digital Basic Service
Subscribers: 1,822.
Programming (via satellite): 3 Angels Broadcasting Network; Bio; Boomerang; BYU Television; Canales N; Discovery Digital Networks; DMX Music; ESPN Classic Sports; ESPNews; FamilyNet; Fox College Sports Atlantic; Fox College Sports Central; Fox College Sports Pacific; Fox Movie Channel; Fox Soccer; Fuel TV; G4; Golf Channel; Great American Country; Hallmark Channel; History Channel International; INSP; National Geographic Channel; Outdoor Channel; SoapNet; Speed; Toon Disney; Trinity Broadcasting Network; truTV; Turner Network TV HD; TVG Network; Universal HD.
Digital Pay Service 1
Pay Units: N.A.
Programming (via satellite): Cinemax (multiplexed); Encore (multiplexed); Flix; HBO (multiplexed); Showtime (multiplexed); Showtime HD; Starz (multiplexed); Sundance Channel; The Movie Channel (multiplexed); The Movie Channel HD.
Fee: $15.00 monthly (each).
Video-On-Demand: No
Pay-Per-View
iN DEMAND (delivered digitally); Pleasure (delivered digitally); Ten Clips (delivered digitally); Ten Blox (delivered digitally); Ten Blue (delivered digitally).
Internet Service
Operational: Yes. Began: November 1, 2001.
Subscribers: 1,280.
Broadband Service: CableONE.net.
Fee: $75.00 installation; $43.00 monthly; $5.00 modem lease.
Telephone Service
Digital: Operational
Fee: $39.95 monthly
Miles of Plant: 156.0 (coaxial); None (fiber optic).
Manager: Mike Slyman. Chief Technician: Danny Douthit.
Ownership: Cable ONE Inc. (MSO).

MILBURN—Formerly served by Allegiance Communications. No longer in operation. ICA: OK0253.

MOORELAND—Pioneer Telephone Coop. Formerly [OK0392]. This cable system has converted to IPTV, PO Box 539, Kingfisher, OK 73750. Phones: 888-782-2667; 405-375-4111. E-mail: website@pldi.net. Web Site: http://www.ptci.com. ICA: OK5043.
TV Market Ranking: Outside TV Markets (MOORELAND). Franchise award date: N.A. Franchise expiration date: N.A. Began: September 30, 2004.
Channel capacity: N.A. Channels available but not in use: N.A.
Internet Service
Operational: Yes.
Telephone Service
Digital: Operational
General Manager: Richard Ruhl.

MOORELAND—Pioneer Telephone Coop. This cable system has converted to IPTV. See Mooreland, OK [OK5043]. ICA: OK0392.

MORRIS—Allegiance Communications, 707 W Saratoga St, Shawnee, OK 74804. Phones: 405-395-1131; 405-275-6923. Web Site: http://www.allegiance.tv. ICA: OK0152.
TV Market Ranking: Below 100 (MORRIS). Franchise award date: N.A. Franchise expiration date: N.A. Began: March 1, 1982.
Channel capacity: 42 (not 2-way capable). Channels available but not in use: N.A.
Basic Service
Subscribers: 337.
Programming (received off-air): KDOR-TV (TBN) Bartlesville; KJRH-TV (NBC) Tulsa; KMYT-TV (MNT) Tulsa; KOED-TV (PBS) Tulsa; KOKI-TV (FOX) Tulsa; KOTV-DT (CBS) Tulsa; KQCW-DT (CW) Muskogee; KTPX-TV (ION) Okmulgee; KTUL (ABC) Tulsa; KWHB (IND) Tulsa.
Programming (via satellite): A&E Networks; ABC Family Channel; AMC; Animal Planet; Cartoon Network; CNN; Country Music TV; Discovery Channel; Disney Channel; E! Entertainment Television; ESPN; ESPN 2; Fox News Channel; Fox Sports Southwest; Headline News; HGTV; History Channel; INSP; Lifetime; Nickelodeon; Outdoor Channel; QVC; Spike TV; Syfy; TBS Superstation; The Learning Channel; The Weather Channel; Travel Channel; Turner Classic Movies; Turner Network TV; USA Network; WGN America.
Fee: $40.00 installation; $24.95 monthly; $1.96 converter; $19.95 additional installation.
Pay Service 1
Pay Units: 101.
Programming (via satellite): Cinemax; HBO.
Fee: $15.00 installation; $9.95 monthly (each).
Video-On-Demand: No
Pay-Per-View
iN DEMAND (delivered digitally); Hot Choice (delivered digitally); Playboy TV (delivered digitally); Fresh (delivered digitally); Shorteez (delivered digitally).
Internet Service
Operational: No.
Telephone Service
None
Miles of Plant: 13.0 (coaxial); None (fiber optic).
Chief Executive Officer: Bill Haggarty. Regional Vice President: Andrew Dearth. Vice President, Marketing: Tracy Bass.
Ownership: Allegiance Communications (MSO).

MORRISON—Allegiance Communications, 707 W Saratoga St, Shawnee, OK 74804. Phones: 405-275-6923; 405-395-1131. Web Site: http://www.allegiance.tv. ICA: OK0357.
TV Market Ranking: Outside TV Markets (MORRISON). Franchise award date: N.A. Franchise expiration date: N.A. Began: N.A.
Channel capacity: N.A. Channels available but not in use: N.A.
Basic Service
Subscribers: 135.
Programming (received off-air): KAUT-TV (MNT) Oklahoma City; KETA-TV (PBS) Oklahoma City; KFOR-TV (NBC) Oklahoma City; KOCB (CW) Oklahoma City; KOCO-TV (ABC) Oklahoma City; KOKH-TV (FOX) Oklahoma City; KOKI-TV (FOX) Tulsa;

MediaPrints
Map a Winning Business Strategy
Digital Cable and TV Coverage Maps.
Visit www.warren-news.com/mediaprints.htm

KTBO-TV (TBN) Oklahoma City; KWHB (IND) Tulsa; KWTV-DT (CBS) Oklahoma City.

Programming (via satellite): A&E Networks; ABC Family Channel; AMC; Cartoon Network; CNBC; CNN; Country Music TV; Discovery Channel; ESPN; ESPN 2; Fox Sports Southwest; History Channel; Nickelodeon; Oxygen; Product Information Network; SoapNet; Speed; Spike TV; TBS Superstation; The Weather Channel; Turner Network TV; USA Network; WGN America.

Fee: $40.00 installation; $22.95 monthly; $1.96 converter; $19.95 additional installation.

Video-On-Demand: No

Pay-Per-View

Hot Choice (delivered digitally); Playboy TV (delivered digitally); Fresh (delivered digitally); Shorteez (delivered digitally); iN DEMAND (delivered digitally).

Internet Service

Operational: No.

Telephone Service

None

Chief Executive Officer: Bill Haggarty. Regional Vice President: Andrew Dearth. Vice President, Marketing: Tracy Bass.

Ownership: Allegiance Communications (MSO).

MOUNDS—Allegiance Communications, 707 W Saratoga St, Shawnee, OK 74804. Phones: 405-275-6923; 405-395-1131. Web Site: http://www.allegiance.tv. ICA: OK0175.

TV Market Ranking: 54 (MOUNDS). Franchise award date: February 1, 1980. Franchise expiration date: February 1, 2010. Began: January 1, 1983.

Channel capacity: N.A. Channels available but not in use: N.A.

Basic Service

Subscribers: N.A.

Programming (received off-air): KGEB (IND) Tulsa; KJRH-TV (NBC) Tulsa; KMYT-TV (MNT) Tulsa; KOED-TV (PBS) Tulsa; KOKI-TV (FOX) Tulsa; KOTV-DT (CBS) Tulsa; KQCW-DT (CW) Muskogee; KTPX-TV (ION) Okmulgee; KTUL (ABC) Tulsa; KWHB (IND) Tulsa.

Programming (via satellite): A&E Networks; ABC Family Channel; AMC; Animal Planet; BET Networks; Cartoon Network; CNBC; CNN; Country Music TV; C-SPAN; Discovery Channel; Disney Channel; E! Entertainment Television; ESPN; ESPN 2; Food Network; Fox News Channel; FX; Headline News; History Channel; Lifetime; MTV; Nickelodeon; Oxygen; QVC; Speed; Spike TV; Syfy; TBS Superstation; The Learning Channel; The Weather Channel; Travel Channel; Turner Network TV; USA Network; VH1; WGN America.

Fee: $30.00 installation; $21.95 monthly.

Digital Basic Service

Subscribers: N.A.

Programming (via satellite): BBC America; Bio; Bloomberg Television; Bravo; Chiller; cloo; CMT Pure Country; Current; Discovery Fit & Health; Discovery Health Channel; Discovery Kids Channel; DMX Music; Encore (multiplexed); ESPN Classic Sports; Flix; Fox College Sports Atlantic; Fox College Sports Central; Fox College Sports Pacific; Fox Movie Channel; Fuse; G4; Golf Channel; Great American Country; GSN; HGTV; History Channel International; ID Investigation Discovery; Independent Film Channel; Lifetime Movie Network; Military Channel; MTV Hits; MTV2; National Geographic Channel; Nick Jr.; NickToons TV; Outdoor Channel; Planet Green; RFD-TV; Science; ShopNBC; SoapNet; Style Network; Sundance Channel; TeenNick; Toon Disney; Trinity Broadcasting Network; Turner Classic Movies; Versus; VH1 Classic; VH1 Soul; WE tv.

Pay Service 1

Pay Units: 20.

Programming (via satellite): Cinemax; HBO.

Fee: $20.00 installation; $10.00 monthly (each).

Digital Pay Service 1

Pay Units: N.A.

Programming (via satellite): Cinemax (multiplexed); HBO (multiplexed); Showtime (multiplexed); Starz (multiplexed); The Movie Channel (multiplexed).

Video-On-Demand: No

Pay-Per-View

iN DEMAND (delivered digitally); Spice: Xcess (delivered digitally); Playboy TV (delivered digitally); Fresh (delivered digitally); Club Jenna (delivered digitally).

Internet Service

Operational: No.

Telephone Service

None

Miles of Plant: 7.0 (coaxial); None (fiber optic).

Chief Executive Officer: Bill Haggarty. Regional Vice President: Andrew Dearth. Vice President, Marketing: Tracy Bass.

Ownership: Allegiance Communications (MSO).

MOUNTAIN PARK—LakeView Cable, Hwy 115, PO Box 460, Cache, OK 73527-0460. Phone: 580-429-8800. Fax: 580-429-6599. Web Site: http://www.lvcisp.com. Also serves Snyder. ICA: OK0300.

TV Market Ranking: Below 100 (MOUNTAIN PARK, Snyder). Franchise award date: N.A. Franchise expiration date: N.A. Began: N.A.

Channel capacity: N.A. Channels available but not in use: N.A.

Basic Service

Subscribers: 260.

Programming (received off-air): KAUZ-TV (CBS, CW) Wichita Falls; KETA-TV (PBS) Oklahoma City; KFDX-TV (NBC) Wichita Falls; KFOR-TV (NBC) Oklahoma City; KJBO-LP (MNT) Wichita Falls; KJTL (FOX) Wichita Falls; KOCO-TV (ABC) Oklahoma City; KSWO-TV (ABC, TMO) Lawton.

Programming (via satellite): INSP; QVC; Trinity Broadcasting Network.

Fee: $50.00 installation; $17.98 monthly.

Expanded Basic Service 1

Subscribers: N.A.

Programming (received off-air): KSWO-TV (ABC, TMO) Lawton.

Programming (via satellite): A&E Networks; ABC Family Channel; AMC; Animal Planet; BET Networks; Cartoon Network; CNN; Comedy Central; C-SPAN; Discovery Channel; Disney Channel; E! Entertainment Television; ESPN; ESPN 2; FamilyNet; Food Network; Fox News Channel; Great American Country; Headline News; HGTV; History Channel; Lifetime; MSNBC; Outdoor Channel; Syfy; TBS Superstation; Telemundo; The Learning Channel; The Weather Channel; Toon Disney; Travel Channel; Turner Network TV; USA Network; WGN America.

Fee: $21.97 monthly.

Digital Basic Service

Subscribers: N.A. Included in Blair

Programming (via satellite): AmericanLife TV Network; BBC America; Bio; Bloomberg Television; Discovery Fit & Health; DMX Music; Encore (multiplexed); ESPN Classic Sports; ESPNews; Fox Movie Channel; Fox Soccer; G4; Golf Channel; GSN; Halogen Network; History Channel International; Lifetime Movie Network; Speed; Toon Disney; Turner Classic Movies.

Fee: $17.00 monthly.

Pay Service 1

Pay Units: 68.

Programming (via satellite): Cinemax.

Fee: $10.95 monthly.

Pay Service 2

Pay Units: N.A.

Programming (via satellite): HBO; Showtime; The Movie Channel.

Fee: $8.95 monthly (TMC), $10.95 monthly (Showtime), $12.95 monthly (HBO).

Digital Pay Service 1

Pay Units: N.A.

Programming (via satellite): Cinemax (multiplexed); Flix; HBO (multiplexed); Showtime (multiplexed); Starz (multiplexed); The Movie Channel (multiplexed).

Fee: $8.95 monthly (TMC), $10.95 monthly (Showtime or Cinemax), $12.95 monthly (HBO).

Video-On-Demand: No

Pay-Per-View

iN DEMAND (delivered digitally); Hot Choice (delivered digitally); Playboy TV (delivered digitally); Fresh (delivered digitally); Shorteez (delivered digitally).

Internet Service

Operational: Yes.

Broadband Service: In-house.

Fee: $29.95 monthly.

Telephone Service

Digital: Planned

Miles of Plant: 22.0 (coaxial); None (fiber optic).

Manager: Bill Rowell. Chief Technician: Mike Rowell.

Ownership: Lakeview Cable Inc. (MSO).

MOUNTAIN VIEW—Mountain View Cable TV, 314 W Main St, PO Box 237, Mountain View, OK 73062. Phone: 800-980-7912. Fax: 580-347-2143. ICA: OK0166.

TV Market Ranking: Outside TV Markets (MOUNTAIN VIEW). Franchise award date: March 19, 1969. Franchise expiration date: N.A. Began: May 1, 1969.

Channel capacity: 48 (not 2-way capable). Channels available but not in use: N.A.

Basic Service

Subscribers: 138.

Programming (received off-air): KAUT-TV (MNT) Oklahoma City; KETA-TV (PBS) Oklahoma City; KFOR-TV (NBC) Oklahoma City; KOCB (CW) Oklahoma City; KOCO-TV (ABC) Oklahoma City; KOKH-TV (FOX) Oklahoma City; KSWO-TV (ABC, TMO) Lawton; KWTV-DT (CBS) Oklahoma City; 20 FMs.

Programming (via satellite): ESPN; TBS Superstation.

Fee: $20.00 installation; $29.95 monthly.

Pay Service 1

Pay Units: 5.

Programming (via satellite): Cinemax.

Fee: $15.00 installation; $9.00 monthly.

Pay Service 2

Pay Units: 17.

Programming (via satellite): HBO.

Fee: $9.00 monthly.

Video-On-Demand: No

Internet Service

Operational: No.

Telephone Service

None

Miles of Plant: 9.0 (coaxial); None (fiber optic).

Manager & Chief Technician: Mickey Davis.

Ownership: Mickey Davis.

MUSKOGEE—Suddenlink Communications, 2510 Elliott, Muskogee, OK 74403. Phone: 918-687-7511 (Customer service). Fax: 918-687-3291. Web Site: http://www.suddenlink.com. Also serves Muskogee County, Wagoner & Wagoner County (eastern portion). ICA: OK0009.

TV Market Ranking: 54 (Muskogee County (portions), Wagoner, Wagoner County (eastern portion)); Below 100 (MUSKOGEE, Muskogee County (portions), Wagoner County (eastern portion)). Franchise award date: January 1, 1969. Franchise expiration date: July 1, 2010. Began: July 1, 1971.

Channel capacity: 40 (operating 2-way). Channels available but not in use: N.A.

Basic Service

Subscribers: 14,935.

Programming (received off-air): KDOR-TV (TBN) Bartlesville; KJRH-TV (NBC) Tulsa; KMYT-TV (MNT) Tulsa; KOED-TV (PBS) Tulsa; KOKI-TV (FOX) Tulsa; KOTV-DT (CBS) Tulsa; KQCW-DT (CW) Muskogee; KRSC-TV (ETV) Claremore; KTPX-TV (ION) Okmulgee; KTUL (ABC) Tulsa; KWHB (IND) Tulsa.

Programming (via satellite): C-SPAN 2; Discovery Channel; FX; TBS Superstation; TV Guide Network; WGN America.

Fee: $60.00 installation; $18.45 monthly; $.74 converter; $6.94 additional installation.

Expanded Basic Service 1

Subscribers: 10,710.

Programming (via satellite): A&E Networks; ABC Family Channel; AMC; Animal Planet; BET Networks; Bravo; Cartoon Network; CNBC; CNN; Comedy Central; Country Music TV; C-SPAN; Disney Channel; E! Entertainment Television; ESPN; ESPN 2; Eternal Word TV Network; Food Network; Fox News Channel; Fox Sports Southwest; Headline News; HGTV; History Channel; Lifetime; MoviePlex; MSNBC; MTV; MTV2; Nickelodeon; QVC; Spike TV; Syfy; The Learning Channel; The Weather Channel; Travel Channel; truTV; Turner Network TV; TV Land; Univision Studios; USA Network; VH1.

Digital Basic Service

Subscribers: N.A.

Programming (via satellite): BBC America; Bio; Bloomberg Television; Discovery Digital Networks; Encore Action; ESPN Classic Sports; ESPNews; Fox Sports World; Fuse; G4; GAS; Golf Channel; GSN; History Channel International; Independent Film Channel; Lifetime Movie Network; MTV Networks Digital Suite; Music Choice; Nick Jr.; NickToons TV; Speed; Toon Disney; Turner Classic Movies; Versus.

Pay Service 1
Pay Units: 961.
Programming (via satellite): Cinemax (multiplexed).
Fee: $12.59 monthly.

Pay Service 2
Pay Units: 354.
Programming (via satellite): Starz.

Pay Service 3
Pay Units: 3,613.
Programming (via satellite): Encore.

Pay Service 4
Pay Units: 1,875.
Programming (via satellite): HBO.
Fee: $12.59 monthly.

Pay Service 5
Pay Units: 981.
Programming (via satellite): Showtime.
Fee: $12.59 monthly.

Digital Pay Service 1
Pay Units: N.A.
Programming (via satellite): Cinemax (multiplexed); HBO (multiplexed); Showtime (multiplexed); Starz (multiplexed); The Movie Channel (multiplexed).

Video-On-Demand: No

Pay-Per-View
ESPN Gameplan (delivered digitally); ESPN Now (delivered digitally); Playboy TV (delivered digitally); Shorteez (delivered digitally); Fresh (delivered digitally); Hot Choice (delivered digitally); iN DEMAND (delivered digitally).

Internet Service
Operational: Yes. Began: December 1, 2002.
Subscribers: 12,000.
Broadband Service: Suddenlink High Speed Internet.
Fee: $45.95 installation; $24.95 monthly.

Telephone Service
Digital: Operational
Fee: $49.95 monthly

Miles of Plant: 335.0 (coaxial); 55.0 (fiber optic).
Manager: Billy Jewell. Marketing Manager: Heather Eastwood.
Ownership: Cequel Communications LLC (MSO).

NASH—Pioneer Telephone Coop. Formerly [OK0301]. This cable system has converted to IPTV, PO Box 539, Kingfisher, OK 73750. Phones: 888-782-2667; 405-375-4111. E-mail: website@pldi.net. Web Site: http://www.ptci.com. ICA: OK5100.
Channel capacity: N.A. Channels available but not in use: N.A.

Internet Service
Operational: Yes.

Telephone Service
Digital: Operational

General Manager: Richard Ruhl.

NASH—Pioneer Telephone Coop. This cable system has converted to IPTV. See Nash, OK [OK5100]. ICA: OK0301.

NEWCASTLE—Pioneer Telephone Coop. Formerly [OK0302]. This cable system has converted to IPTV, PO Box 539, Kingfisher, OK 73750. Phones: 888-782-2667; 405-375-4111. E-mail: website@pldi.net. Web Site: http://www.ptci.com. ICA: OK5095.
TV Market Ranking: 39 (NEWCASTLE (VILLAGE)). Franchise award date: N.A. Franchise expiration date: N.A. Began: January 12, 2005.
Channel capacity: N.A. Channels available but not in use: N.A.

Internet Service
Operational: Yes.

Telephone Service
Digital: Operational

General Manager: Richard Ruhl.

NEWCASTLE—Pioneer Telephone Coop. This cable system has converted to IPTV. See Newcastle, OK [OK5095]. ICA: OK0302.

NEWKIRK—Allegiance Communications, 707 W Saratoga St, Shawnee, OK 74804. Phones: 405-395-1131; 405-275-6923. Web Site: http://www.allegiance.tv. ICA: OK0303.
TV Market Ranking: Outside TV Markets (NEWKIRK). Franchise award date: N.A. Franchise expiration date: N.A. Began: N.A.
Channel capacity: N.A. Channels available but not in use: N.A.

Basic Service
Subscribers: 892.
Programming (received off-air): KETA-TV (PBS) Oklahoma City; KFOR-TV (NBC) Oklahoma City; KOCO-TV (ABC) Oklahoma City; KOTV-DT (CBS) Tulsa; KSAS-TV (FOX) Wichita; KSNW (NBC) Wichita; KWTV-DT (CBS) Oklahoma City.
Programming (via satellite): CNN; C-SPAN; C-SPAN 2; CW+; QVC; ShopNBC; The Weather Channel; Trinity Broadcasting Network; TV Guide Network; WGN America.
Fee: $36.80 installation; $21.95 monthly.

Expanded Basic Service 1
Subscribers: 837.
Programming (via satellite): A&E Networks; ABC Family Channel; AMC; Animal Planet; CMT Pure Country; CNBC; Discovery Channel; Disney Channel; ESPN; ESPN 2; Food Network; Fox News Channel; Fox Sports Southwest; FX; Headline News; HGTV; History Channel; Lifetime; MSNBC; MTV; Nickelodeon; Spike TV; Syfy; TBS Superstation; The Learning Channel; truTV; Turner Classic Movies; Turner Network TV; TV Land; USA Network; VH1.
Fee: $11.18 monthly.

Digital Basic Service
Subscribers: N.A.
Programming (via satellite): AmericanLife TV Network; BBC America; Bio; Black Family Channel; Bloomberg Television; Bravo; Canal 52MX; Cine Latino; Cine Mexicano; cloo; CMT Pure Country; CNN en Espanol; Current; Discovery en Espanol; Discovery Fit & Health; Discovery Health Channel; Discovery Home Channel; Discovery Kids Channel; Discovery Times Channel; DMX Music; Encore (multiplexed); ESPN 2; ESPN Classic Sports; ESPNews; Flix; Fox College Sports Atlantic; Fox College Sports Central; Fox College Sports Pacific; Fox Deportes; Fox Movie Channel; Fox Soccer; Fuse; G4; GAS; Golf Channel; Great American Country; GSN; Halogen Network; HGTV; History Channel; History Channel en Espanol; History Channel International; Independent Film Channel; Lifetime Movie Network; Military Channel; MTV Hits; MTV2; National Geographic Channel; Nick Jr.; NickToons TV; Outdoor Channel; Ovation; Science; ShopNBC; Speed; Style Network; Sundance Channel; Syfy; The Word Network; Toon Disney; Toon Disney en Espanol; Tr3s; Trinity Broadcasting Network; Turner Classic Movies; Versus; VH1 Classic; VH1 Soul; WE tv.

FREE
TRIAL
@

Access the most current data instantly.
ADVANCED
TVFactbook
www.warren-news.com/factbook.htm

Pay Service 1
Pay Units: 257.
Programming (via satellite): Encore.
Fee: $1.70 monthly.

Pay Service 2
Pay Units: 147.
Programming (via satellite): HBO.
Fee: $10.00 installation; $13.34 monthly.

Pay Service 3
Pay Units: 103.
Programming (via satellite): Showtime.
Fee: $10.00 installation; $13.34 monthly.

Digital Pay Service 1
Pay Units: N.A.
Programming (via satellite): Cinemax (multiplexed); HBO (multiplexed); HBO Latino; Showtime (multiplexed); Starz (multiplexed); The Movie Channel (multiplexed).

Pay-Per-View
iN DEMAND (delivered digitally); Hot Choice (delivered digitally); Playboy TV (delivered digitally); Fresh (delivered digitally); Shorteez (delivered digitally).

Internet Service
Operational: Yes.
Fee: $24.95 installation; $39.95 monthly.

Telephone Service
None

Miles of Plant: 19.0 (coaxial); None (fiber optic).
Chief Executive Officer: Bill Haggarty. Regional Vice President: Andrew Dearth. Vice President, Marketing: Tracy Bass.
Ownership: Allegiance Communications (MSO).

NINNEKAH—Formerly served by Cable West. No longer in operation. ICA: OK0163.

NOBLE—Formerly served by Cebridge Connections. Now served by PURCELL, OK [OK0048]. ICA: OK0084.

NOWATA—Cable One. Now served by BARTLESVILLE, OK [OK0010]. ICA: OK0075.

OCHELATA—Community Cablevision Co., 1550 W Rogers Blvd, PO Box 307, Skiatook, OK 74070-0307. Phone: 918-396-3019. Fax: 918-396-2081. E-mail: info@communitycablevision.com. Web Site: http://www.communitycablebroadband.com. ICA: OK0148.
TV Market Ranking: 54 (OCHELATA). Franchise award date: October 1, 1983. Franchise expiration date: N.A. Began: December 31, 1983.
Channel capacity: 35 (not 2-way capable). Channels available but not in use: N.A.

Basic Service
Subscribers: 233.
Programming (received off-air): KDOR-TV (TBN) Bartlesville; KJRH-TV (NBC) Tulsa; KOED-TV (PBS) Tulsa; KOKI-TV (FOX) Tulsa; KOTV-DT (CBS) Tulsa; KQCW-DT (CW) Muskogee; KRSC-TV (ETV) Claremore; KTPX-TV (ION) Okmulgee; KTUL (ABC) Tulsa; KWHB (IND) Tulsa.
Programming (via satellite): A&E Networks; ABC Family Channel; Cartoon Network; CNN; Country Music TV; C-SPAN; Discovery Channel; Disney Channel; ESPN; ESPN 2; Headline News; HGTV; History Channel; MTV; Nickelodeon; QVC; Spike TV; Syfy; TBS Superstation; The Learning Channel; The Weather Channel; Turner Classic Movies; Turner Network TV; USA Network; WGN America.
Programming (via translator): KTFO-CD (TEL) Austin.
Fee: $29.95 installation; $19.00 monthly.

Video-On-Demand: No

Internet Service
Operational: Yes.
Fee: $44.95 monthly.

Telephone Service
None

Miles of Plant: 21.0 (coaxial); None (fiber optic).
President & General Manager: Dennis Soule.
Ownership: Community Cablevision Co. (MSO).

OILTON—Community Cablevision Co., 1550 W Rogers Blvd, PO Box 307, Skiatook, OK 74070-0307. Phone: 918-396-3019. Fax: 918-396-2081. E-mail: info@communitycablevision.com. Web Site: http://www.communitycablebroadband.com. ICA: OK0162.
TV Market Ranking: Outside TV Markets (OILTON). Franchise award date: April 1, 1987. Franchise expiration date: April 1, 2012. Began: July 1, 1983.
Channel capacity: 42 (not 2-way capable). Channels available but not in use: N.A.

Basic Service
Subscribers: 251.
Programming (received off-air): KDOR-TV (TBN) Bartlesville; KFOR-TV (NBC) Oklahoma City; KGEB (IND) Tulsa; KJRH-TV (NBC) Tulsa; KOED-TV (PBS) Tulsa; KOKI-TV (FOX) Tulsa; KOTV-DT (CBS) Tulsa; KQCW-DT (CW) Muskogee; KRSC-TV (ETV) Claremore; KTFO-CD (TEL) Austin; KTPX-TV (ION) Okmulgee; KTUL (ABC) Tulsa; KWHB (IND) Tulsa.
Programming (via satellite): A&E Networks; ABC Family Channel; Cartoon Network; CNN; Country Music TV; C-SPAN; Discovery Channel; Disney Channel; ESPN; ESPN 2; Fox Sports Southwest; Headline News; MTV; Nickelodeon; QVC; Spike TV; Syfy; TBS Superstation; The Learning Channel; The Weather Channel; Turner Classic Movies; Turner Network TV; USA Network; VH1; WGN America.
Fee: $29.95 installation; $24.95 monthly; $25.00 additional installation.

Pay Service 1
Pay Units: 36.
Programming (via satellite): HBO.
Fee: $11.50 monthly.

Pay Service 2
Pay Units: 31.
Programming (via satellite): Cinemax.
Fee: $11.50 monthly.

Video-On-Demand: No

Internet Service
Operational: Yes.
Fee: $44.95 monthly.

Telephone Service
Digital: Operational
Fee: $39.95 monthly
Miles of Plant: 9.0 (coaxial); None (fiber optic).
President & General Manager: Dennis Soule.
Ownership: Community Cablevision Co. (MSO).

OKARCHE—Pioneer Telephone Coop. Formerly [OK0176]. This cable system has converted to IPTV, PO Box 539, Kingfisher, OK 73750. Phones: 888-782-2667; 405-375-4111. E-mail: website@pldi.net. Web Site: http://www.ptci.net. ICA: OK5079.
Channel capacity: N.A. Channels available but not in use: N.A.
Internet Service
Operational: Yes.
Telephone Service
Digital: Operational
General Manager: Richard Ruhl.

OKARCHE—Pioneer Telephone Coop. This cable system has converted to IPTV. See Okarche, OK [OK5079]. ICA: OK0176.

OKAY—Allegiance Communications, 707 W Saratoga St, Shawnee, OK 74804. Phone: 405-395-1131. Fax: 405-275-0276. Web Site: http://www.allegiance.tv. ICA: OK0161.
TV Market Ranking: Below 100 (OKAY). Franchise award date: N.A. Franchise expiration date: N.A. Began: June 1, 1986.
Channel capacity: N.A. Channels available but not in use: N.A.
Basic Service
Subscribers: N.A.
Programming (received off-air): KJRH-TV (NBC) Tulsa; KMYT-TV (MNT) Tulsa; KOED-TV (PBS) Tulsa; KOKI-TV (FOX) Tulsa; KOTV-DT (CBS) Tulsa; KTPX-TV (ION) Okmulgee; KTUL (ABC) Tulsa; KWHB (IND) Tulsa.
Programming (via satellite): C-SPAN; QVC; Trinity Broadcasting Network; WGN America.
Fee: $30.00 installation; $19.95 monthly; $15.00 additional installation.
Expanded Basic Service 1
Subscribers: N.A.
Programming (via satellite): A&E Networks; ABC Family Channel; AMC; Animal Planet; Cartoon Network; CNBC; CNN; Comedy Central; Country Music TV; Discovery Channel; Disney Channel; E! Entertainment Television; ESPN; ESPN 2; Food Network; Fox News Channel; Fox Sports Southwest; FX; G4; Headline News; HGTV; History Channel; Lifetime; MTV; Nickelodeon; Outdoor Channel; Oxygen; Speed; Spike TV; Syfy; TBS Superstation; The Learning Channel; The Weather Channel; Travel Channel; truTV; Turner Classic Movies; Turner Network TV; TV Land; USA Network; VH1.
Digital Basic Service
Subscribers: N.A.
Programming (via satellite): BBC America; Bio; Bloomberg Television; Discovery Digital Networks; DIY Network; ESPN Classic Sports; GAS; GSN; History Channel International; Independent Film Channel; MTV Networks Digital Suite; Music Choice; Nick Jr.; Nick Too; NickToons TV; SoapNet; Style Network; Sundance Channel; Toon Disney; TV Guide Interactive Inc.; WE tv.
Digital Pay Service 1
Pay Units: N.A.
Programming (via satellite): Cinemax (multiplexed); Encore; Flix; HBO (multiplexed); Showtime (multiplexed); Starz (multiplexed); The Movie Channel (multiplexed).
Video-On-Demand: No
Pay-Per-View
iN DEMAND (delivered digitally); Hot Choice (delivered digitally); Playboy TV (delivered digitally); Fresh (delivered digitally); Shorteez (delivered digitally).
Internet Service
Operational: Yes.
Telephone Service
Digital: Operational
Miles of Plant: 12.0 (coaxial); None (fiber optic).
Vice President, Marketing: Rory Erchul. General Manager: Andrew Dearth.
Ownership: Allegiance Communications (MSO).

OKEENE—Pioneer Telephone Coop. Formerly [OK0146]. This cable system has converted to IPTV, PO Box 539, Kingfisher, OK 73750. Phones: 888-782-2667; 405-375-4111. E-mail: website@pldi.net. Web Site: http://www.ptci.com. ICA: OK5090.
TV Market Ranking: Outside TV Markets (OKEENE). Franchise award date: N.A. Franchise expiration date: N.A. Began: January 12, 2005.
Channel capacity: N.A. Channels available but not in use: N.A.
Internet Service
Operational: Yes.
Telephone Service
Digital: Operational
General Manager: Richard Ruhl.

OKEENE—Pioneer Telephone Coop. This cable system has converted to IPTV. See Okeene, OK [OK5090]. ICA: OK0146.

OKEMAH—Allegiance Communications, 707 W Saratoga St, Shawnee, OK 74804. Phones: 405-275-6923; 405-395-1131. Web Site: http://www.allegiance.tv. ICA: OK0111.
TV Market Ranking: Below 100 (OKEMAH). Franchise award date: N.A. Franchise expiration date: N.A. Began: February 11, 1979.
Channel capacity: N.A. Channels available but not in use: N.A.
Basic Service
Subscribers: 728.
Programming (received off-air): KETA-TV (PBS) Oklahoma City; KFOR-TV (NBC) Oklahoma City; KJRH-TV (NBC) Tulsa; KMYT-TV (MNT) Tulsa; KOCB (CW) Oklahoma City; KOKI-TV (FOX) Tulsa; KOTV-DT (CBS) Tulsa; KTBO-TV (TBN) Oklahoma City; KTPX-TV (ION) Okmulgee; KTUL (ABC) Tulsa; KWTV-DT (CBS) Oklahoma City.
Programming (via satellite): CNBC; CNN; C-SPAN; Fox News Channel; Fox Sports Southwest; QVC; The Learning Channel; The Weather Channel.
Fee: $60.00 installation; $21.95 monthly; $5.03 additional installation.
Expanded Basic Service 1
Subscribers: N.A.
Programming (via satellite): A&E Networks; ABC Family Channel; AMC; Animal Planet; Cartoon Network; Comedy Central; Country Music TV; Discovery Channel; Disney Channel; ESPN; ESPN 2; Food Network; FX; Hallmark Channel; History Channel; Lifetime; MTV; NFL Network; Nickelodeon; Spike TV; TBS Superstation; Turner Network TV; TV Land; USA Network.
Fee: $17.05 monthly.
Digital Basic Service
Subscribers: N.A.
Programming (via satellite): AmericanLife TV Network; BBC America; Bio; Bloomberg Television; Bravo; Cine Latino; Cine Mexicano; cloo; CMT Pure Country; CNN en Espanol; Current; Discovery en Espanol; Discovery Fit & Health; Discovery Health Channel; Discovery Kids Channel; DMX Music; Encore (multiplexed); ESPN 2; ESPN Classic Sports; ESPN Deportes; ESPNews; Flix; Fox College Sports Atlantic; Fox College Sports Central; Fox College Sports Pacific; Fox Deportes; Fox Movie Channel; Fox Soccer; Fuse; G4; GMC; Golf Channel; Great American Country; GSN; Halogen Network; HGTV; History Channel; History Channel en Espanol; History Channel International; ID Investigation Discovery; Independent Film Channel; Lifetime Movie Network; Lime; Military Channel; MTV Hits; MTV2; mun2 television; National Geographic Channel; Nick Jr.; NickToons TV; Outdoor Channel; Planet Green; Science; ShopNBC; Speed; Style Network; Sundance Channel; Syfy; TeenNick; The Word Network; Toon Disney; Tr3s; Trinity Broadcasting Network; Turner Classic Movies; VeneMovies; Versus; VH1 Classic; VH1 Soul; WE tv.
Pay Service 1
Pay Units: N.A.
Programming (via satellite): Encore; Showtime; Starz.
Digital Pay Service 1
Pay Units: N.A.
Programming (via satellite): Cinemax (multiplexed); HBO (multiplexed); HBO Latino; Showtime (multiplexed); Starz (multiplexed); The Movie Channel (multiplexed).
Pay-Per-View
iN DEMAND (delivered digitally); Hot Choice (delivered digitally); Fresh (delivered digitally); Playboy TV (delivered digitally); Spice: Xcess (delivered digitally); Club Jenna (delivered digitally).
Internet Service
Operational: Yes.
Fee: $24.95 installation; $39.95 monthly.
Telephone Service
None
Miles of Plant: 22.0 (coaxial); None (fiber optic).
Chief Executive Officer: Bill Haggarty. Regional Vice President: Andrew Dearth. Vice President, Marketing: Tracy Bass.
Ownership: Allegiance Communications (MSO).

OKLAHOMA CITY—Cox Communications, 6301 Waterford Blvd, Ste 200, Oklahoma City, OK 73118. Phone: 405-286-5381. Fax: 405-286-5260. Web Site: http://www.cox.com/oklahoma. Also serves Bethany, Choctaw, Del City, Edmond, El Reno, Forest Park, Guthrie, Harrah, Midwest City, Moore, Mustang, Nichols Hills, Norman, Spencer, The Village, Valley Brook, Warr Acres & Yukon. ICA: OK0002.
TV Market Ranking: 39 (Bethany, Choctaw, Del City, Edmond, El Reno, Forest Park, Guthrie, Harrah, Midwest City, Moore, Mustang, Nichols Hills, Norman, OKLAHOMA CITY, Spencer, The Village, Valley Brook, Warr Acres, Yukon). Franchise award date: May 4, 1980. Franchise expiration date: December 31, 2011. Began: May 4, 1980.
Channel capacity: N.A. Channels available but not in use: N.A.
Basic Service
Subscribers: 233,004.
Programming (received off-air): KAUT-TV (MNT) Oklahoma City; KETA-TV (PBS) Oklahoma City; KFOR-TV (NBC) Oklahoma City; KOCB (CW) Oklahoma City; KOCO-TV (ABC) Oklahoma City; KOKH-TV (FOX) Oklahoma City; KOPX-TV (ION) Oklahoma City; KSBI (IND) Oklahoma City; KTBO-TV (TBN) Oklahoma City; KWTV-DT (CBS) Oklahoma City.
Programming (via satellite): C-SPAN; TBS Superstation; TV Guide Network; WGN America.
Fee: $21.60 installation; $6.16 monthly.
Expanded Basic Service 1
Subscribers: 216,858.
Programming (via satellite): A&E Networks; ABC Family Channel; AMC; Animal Planet; BET Networks; Bravo; Cartoon Network; CNBC; CNN; Comedy Central; Country Music TV; Discovery Channel; Disney Channel; E! Entertainment Television; ESPN; ESPN 2; Food Network; Fox News Channel; Fox Sports Southwest; FX; Golf Channel; Headline News; HGTV; History Channel; INSP; Lifetime; MSNBC; MTV; Nickelodeon; Product Information Network; QVC; Speed; Spike TV; Syfy; The Learning Channel; The Weather Channel; Travel Channel; truTV; Turner Classic Movies; Turner Network TV; TV Land; USA Network; Versus; VH1.
Fee: $21.60 installation; $25.79 monthly.
Digital Basic Service
Subscribers: N.A.
Programming (via satellite): BBC America; Bloomberg Television; Discovery Digital Networks; Encore; ESPN Classic Sports; Eternal Word TV Network; G4; GSN; Independent Film Channel; MTV Networks Digital Suite; MuchMusic Network; Nick Jr.; Sundance Channel; Toon Disney; Weatherscan.
Fee: $16.00 monthly.
Pay Service 1
Pay Units: 29,328.
Programming (via satellite): Cinemax.
Fee: $11.00 monthly.
Pay Service 2
Pay Units: 72,394.
Programming (via satellite): HBO (multiplexed).
Fee: $11.00 monthly.
Pay Service 3
Pay Units: 4,994.
Programming (via satellite): The Movie Channel.
Fee: $11.00 monthly.
Pay Service 4
Pay Units: 41,711.
Programming (via satellite): Showtime (multiplexed).
Fee: $11.00 monthly.
Digital Pay Service 1
Pay Units: N.A.
Programming (via satellite): Canales N; Cinemax (multiplexed); HBO (multiplexed); Showtime (multiplexed); Starz (multiplexed); The Movie Channel (multiplexed).
Fee: $6.95 monthly (Canales N), $12.00 monthly (Cinemax/HBO), $16.00 monthly (Showtime/Starz/TMC).
Video-On-Demand: Yes
Pay-Per-View
Addressable homes: 69,295.
ESPN Extra (delivered digitally); ESPN Full Court (delivered digitally); ESPN Now (delivered digitally); Hot Choice; iN DEMAND; iN DEMAND (delivered digitally).
Internet Service
Operational: Yes.
Broadband Service: Cox High Speed Internet.
Fee: $149.00 installation; $54.95 monthly; $199.95 modem purchase.

Telephone Service
Digital: Operational
Fee: $29.95 monthly
Miles of Plant: 4,349.0 (coaxial); 511.0 (fiber optic). Additional miles planned: 15.0 (coaxial).
President & General Manager: David Bialis. Vice President, Operations: John Bowen. Vice President, Marketing: Mollie Andrews.
Ownership: Cox Communications Inc. (MSO).

OKLAHOMA CITY—Formerly served by WANTV of OKC. No longer in operation. ICA: OK0333.

OKMULGEE—Suddenlink Communications, 2510 Elliott, Muskogee, OK 74403. Phone: 918-687-7511. Fax: 918-687-3291. Web Site: http://www.suddenlink.com. Also serves Dewar, Henryetta & Okmulgee County (central portion). ICA: OK0026.
TV Market Ranking: 54 (OKMULGEE, Okmulgee County (central portion) (portions)); Below 100 (Dewar, Henryetta, Okmulgee County (central portion) (portions)). Franchise award date: January 1, 1977. Franchise expiration date: N.A. Began: January 1, 1974.
Channel capacity: 40 (operating 2-way). Channels available but not in use: N.A.

Basic Service
Subscribers: 4,404.
Programming (received off-air): KDOR-TV (TBN) Bartlesville; KGEB (IND) Tulsa; KJRH-TV (NBC) Tulsa; KMYT-TV (MNT) Tulsa; KOED-TV (PBS) Tulsa; KOKI-TV (FOX) Tulsa; KOTV-DT (CBS) Tulsa; KQCW-DT (CW) Muskogee; KTPX-TV (ION) Okmulgee; KTUL (ABC) Tulsa; KWHB (IND) Tulsa; allband FM.
Programming (via satellite): C-SPAN; C-SPAN 2; Eternal Word TV Network; QVC; The Weather Channel; TV Guide Network; WGN America.
Fee: $34.82 installation; $12.96 monthly; $.98 converter; $17.41 additional installation.

Expanded Basic Service 1
Subscribers: N.A.
Programming (via satellite): A&E Networks; ABC Family Channel; AMC; Animal Planet; BET Networks; Bravo; Cartoon Network; CNBC; CNN; Comedy Central; Country Music TV; Discovery Channel; Disney Channel; E! Entertainment Television; ESPN; ESPN 2; Food Network; Fox News Channel; Fox Sports Southwest; FX; Headline News; HGTV; History Channel; Lifetime; MSNBC; MTV; MTV2; News Now 53; Nickelodeon; Spike TV; Syfy; TBS Superstation; The Learning Channel; Travel Channel; truTV; Turner Network TV; TV Land; USA Network; VH1.
Fee: $25.04 monthly.

Digital Basic Service
Subscribers: N.A.
Programming (via satellite): BBC America; Bio; Bloomberg Television; Discovery Fit & Health; ESPN Classic Sports; ESPNews; Fox Soccer; Fuse; G4; GAS; Golf Channel; GSN; History Channel International; Independent Film Channel; Lifetime Movie Network; MTV Networks Digital Suite; Music Choice; National Geographic Channel; Nick Jr.; NickToons TV; Outdoor Channel; Speed; Toon Disney; Turner Classic Movies; Versus.

Digital Pay Service 1
Pay Units: N.A.
Programming (via satellite): Cinemax (multiplexed); Encore; HBO (multiplexed); Showtime (multiplexed); Starz (multiplexed); The Movie Channel (multiplexed).
Video-On-Demand: No

Pay-Per-View
ESPN Gameplan (delivered digitally); Playboy TV (delivered digitally); Shorteez (delivered digitally); Fresh (delivered digitally); Hot Choice (delivered digitally); iN DEMAND (delivered digitally).

Internet Service
Operational: Yes.
Fee: $45.95 installation; $24.95 monthly.

Telephone Service
Digital: Operational
Fee: $49.95 monthly
Miles of Plant: 170.0 (coaxial); 29.0 (fiber optic).
Manager: Billy Jewell. Marketing Manager: Heather Eastwood.
Ownership: Cequel Communications LLC (MSO).

OLUSTEE—Formerly served by Basic Cable Services Inc. No longer in operation. ICA: OK0223.

OOLOGAH—Allegiance Communications, 707 W Saratoga St, Shawnee, OK 74804. Phones: 405-275-6923; 405-395-1131. Web Site: http://www.allegiance.tv. ICA: OK0144.
TV Market Ranking: 54 (OOLOGAH). Franchise award date: June 1, 1980. Franchise expiration date: N.A. Began: May 1, 1982.
Channel capacity: 42 (not 2-way capable). Channels available but not in use: N.A.

Basic Service
Subscribers: 290.
Programming (received off-air): KDOR-TV (TBN) Bartlesville; KJRH-TV (NBC) Tulsa; KMYT-TV (MNT) Tulsa; KOED-TV (PBS) Tulsa; KOKI-TV (FOX) Tulsa; KOTV-DT (CBS) Tulsa; KQCW-DT (CW) Muskogee; KRSC-TV (ETV) Claremore; KTPX-TV (ION) Okmulgee; KTUL (ABC) Tulsa; KWHB (IND) Tulsa.
Programming (via satellite): A&E Networks; ABC Family Channel; AMC; Animal Planet; Cartoon Network; CNBC; CNN; Country Music TV; Discovery Channel; Disney Channel; ESPN; ESPN 2; Fox News Channel; Fox Sports Southwest; Headline News; HGTV; History Channel; Lifetime; Nickelodeon; Oxygen; QVC; Spike TV; TBS Superstation; The Learning Channel; The Weather Channel; Travel Channel; Turner Classic Movies; Turner Network TV; USA Network; VH1; WGN America.
Fee: $30.00 installation; $23.45 monthly.

Pay Service 1
Pay Units: N.A.
Programming (via satellite): Cinemax; HBO; Showtime.
Fee: $10.95 monthly (Showtime), $11.95 monthly (HBO).
Video-On-Demand: No

Pay-Per-View
iN DEMAND (delivered digitally); Hot Choice (delivered digitally); Playboy TV (delivered digitally); Fresh (delivered digitally); Shorteez (delivered digitally).

Internet Service
Operational: No.

Telephone Service
None
Miles of Plant: 20.0 (coaxial); None (fiber optic).
Chief Executive Officer: Bill Haggarty. Regional Vice President: Andrew Dearth. Vice President, Marketing: Tracy Bass.
Ownership: Allegiance Communications (MSO).

ORLANDO—Formerly served by CableDirect. No longer in operation. ICA: OK0256.

PANAMA—Allegiance Communications, 707 W Saratoga St, Shawnee, OK 74804. Phones: 405-395-1131; 405-275-6923. Web Site: http://www.allegiance.tv. Also serves Le Flore County (unincorporated areas) & Shady Point. ICA: OK0109.
TV Market Ranking: Below 100 (Le Flore County (unincorporated areas) (portions), PANAMA, Shady Point); Outside TV Markets (Le Flore County (unincorporated areas) (portions)). Franchise award date: N.A. Franchise expiration date: October 22, 2010. Began: November 1, 1979.
Channel capacity: 36 (operating 2-way). Channels available but not in use: N.A.

Basic Service
Subscribers: 460.
Programming (received off-air): KFDF-CA Fort Smith; KFSM-TV (CBS) Fort Smith; KFTA-TV (FOX, NBC) Fort Smith; KHBS (ABC, CW) Fort Smith; KNWA-TV (FOX, NBC) Rogers; KOET (PBS) Eufaula; KTUL (ABC) Tulsa.
Programming (via satellite): A&E Networks; ABC Family Channel; AMC; Animal Planet; Cartoon Network; CMT Pure Country; CNN; Comedy Central; Discovery Channel; Disney Channel; ESPN; ESPN 2; Food Network; Fox News Channel; Fox Sports Southwest; FX; Hallmark Channel; Headline News; HGTV; History Channel; MTV; NFL Network; Nickelodeon; QVC; Spike TV; Syfy; TBS Superstation; The Weather Channel; Trinity Broadcasting Network; Turner Network TV; TV Land; USA Network; WGN America.
Fee: $25.00 installation; $21.95 monthly.

Digital Basic Service
Subscribers: N.A.
Programming (via satellite): AmericanLife TV Network; BBC America; Bio; Bloomberg Television; Bravo; Canal 52MX; Cine Latino; Cine Mexicano; cloo; CMT Pure Country; CNN en Espanol; Current; Discovery en Espanol; Discovery Fit & Health; Discovery Health Channel; Discovery Kids Channel; DMX Music; Encore (multiplexed); ESPN 2; ESPN Classic Sports; ESPNews; Flix; Fox College Sports Atlantic; Fox College Sports Central; Fox College Sports Pacific; Fox Deportes; Fox Movie Channel; Fox Soccer; Fuse; G4; GAS; GMC; Golf Channel; Great American Country; GSN; Halogen Network; HGTV; History Channel; History Channel en Espanol; History Channel International; ID Investigation Discovery; Independent Film Channel; Lifetime Movie Network; Military Channel; MTV Hits; MTV2; National Geographic Channel; Nick Jr.; NickToons TV; Outdoor Channel; Ovation; Planet Green; Science; ShopNBC; Speed; Style Network; Sundance Channel; Syfy; The Word Network; Toon Disney; Toon Disney en Espanol; Tr3s; Trinity Broadcasting Network; Turner Classic Movies; Versus; VH1 Classic; VH1 Soul; WE tv.

Pay Service 1
Pay Units: N.A.
Programming (via satellite): Encore; HBO; Showtime; Starz; The Movie Channel.
Fee: $10.00 monthly (each).

Digital Pay Service 1
Pay Units: N.A.
Programming (via satellite): Cinemax (multiplexed); HBO (multiplexed); HBO Latino; Showtime (multiplexed); Starz (multiplexed); The Movie Channel (multiplexed).

Pay-Per-View
iN DEMAND (delivered digitally); Hot Choice (delivered digitally); Playboy TV (delivered digitally); Fresh (delivered digitally); Shorteez (delivered digitally).

Internet Service
Operational: Yes.
Fee: $24.95 installation; $39.95 monthly.

Telephone Service
None
Miles of Plant: 25.0 (coaxial); None (fiber optic).
Chief Executive Officer: Bill Haggarty. Regional Vice President: Andrew Dearth. Vice President, Marketing: Tracy Bass.
Ownership: Allegiance Communications (MSO).

PAOLI—Formerly served by Cebridge Connections. No longer in operation. ICA: OK0210.

PARADISE HILL—Formerly served by Eagle Media. No longer in operation. ICA: OK0366.

PARK HILL—Formerly served by Eagle Media. No longer in operation. ICA: OK0350.

PAULS VALLEY—Suddenlink Communications, 12444 Powerscourt Dr, Saint Louis, MO 63131-3660. Phone: 405-238-7476. Fax: 405-238-3066. Web Site: http://www.suddenlink.com. Also serves Garvin County (unincorporated areas) & Wynnewood. ICA: OK0033.
TV Market Ranking: Below 100 (Garvin County (unincorporated areas) (portions), PAULS VALLEY, Wynnewood); Outside TV Markets (Garvin County (unincorporated areas) (portions)). Franchise award date: N.A. Franchise expiration date: N.A. Began: October 20, 1969.
Channel capacity: N.A. Channels available but not in use: N.A.

Basic Service
Subscribers: 3,097.
Programming (received off-air): KAUT-TV (MNT) Oklahoma City; KETA-TV (PBS) Oklahoma City; KFOR-TV (NBC) Oklahoma City; KOCB (CW) Oklahoma City; KOCO-TV (ABC) Oklahoma City; KOKH-TV (FOX) Oklahoma City; KOPX-TV (ION) Oklahoma City; KTEN (ABC, CW, NBC) Ada; KWTV-DT (CBS) Oklahoma City; KXII (CBS, FOX, MNT) Sherman; 20 FMs.
Programming (via satellite): C-SPAN; C-SPAN 2; TV Guide Network; WGN America.
Fee: $20.47 installation; $22.50 monthly; $8.12 additional installation.

Expanded Basic Service 1
Subscribers: 2,760.
Programming (received off-air): KSBI (IND) Oklahoma City; KTBO-TV (TBN) Oklahoma City.
Programming (via satellite): A&E Networks; ABC Family Channel; AMC; Animal Planet; BET Networks; Cartoon Network; CNBC; CNN; Comedy Central; Country Music TV; Discovery Channel; Disney Channel; E! Entertainment Television; ESPN; ESPN 2; Food Network; Fox News Channel; Fox Sports Net; FX; Golf Channel; Headline News; HGTV; History Channel; Lifetime; MSNBC; MTV; MTV2; Nickelodeon; Oxygen; QVC; Spike TV; Syfy; TBS Superstation; The Learning Channel; The Weather Channel; Travel Channel; truTV; Turner Classic Movies; Turner Network TV; TV Land; Univision Studios; USA Network; VH1.
Fee: $39.96 monthly.

Digital Basic Service
Subscribers: N.A.
Programming (via satellite): BBC America; Bio; Bloomberg Television; Canales N; Cooking Channel; Discovery Fit & Health; DIY Network; ESPN Classic Sports; ESPNews; Eternal Word TV Network; Fox Soccer; G4; GAS; GSN; Hallmark Channel; History Channel International; Independent Film Channel; Lifetime Movie Network; MTV Networks Digital Suite; Music Choice; National Geographic Channel; Nick Jr.; Nick Too; NickToons TV; Outdoor Channel; SoapNet; Sundance Channel; Toon Disney; WAM! America's Kidz Network.

Pay Service 1
Pay Units: N.A.
Programming (via satellite): HBO.
Fee: $13.95 monthly.

Digital Pay Service 1
Pay Units: N.A.
Programming (via satellite): Cinemax (multiplexed); Encore (multiplexed); HBO (multiplexed); Showtime (multiplexed); Starz; The Movie Channel (multiplexed).

Video-On-Demand: No

Pay-Per-View
iN DEMAND (delivered digitally); Playboy TV (delivered digitally); Fresh (delivered digitally); Shorteez (delivered digitally); Hot Choice (delivered digitally); ESPN (delivered digitally); NBA League Pass (delivered digitally); NHL Center Ice (delivered digitally); MLB Extra Innings (delivered digitally).

Internet Service
Operational: Yes.
Broadband Service: Suddenlink High Speed Internet.
Fee: $45.95 installation; $24.95 monthly.

Telephone Service
Analog: Not Operational
Digital: Operational

Miles of Plant: 85.0 (coaxial); None (fiber optic).
Manager: Eugene Biller. Marketing Manager: Heather Eastwood. Chief Technician: Gene Reed.
Ownership: Cequel Communications LLC (MSO).

PAWHUSKA—Allegiance Communications, 707 W Saratoga St, Shawnee, OK 74804. Phones: 405-395-1131; 405-275-6923. Web Site: http://www.allegiance.tv. ICA: OK0060.
TV Market Ranking: Below 100 (PAWHUSKA). Franchise award date: N.A. Franchise expiration date: N.A. Began: September 1, 1974.
Channel capacity: N.A. Channels available but not in use: N.A.

Basic Service
Subscribers: 1,320.
Programming (received off-air): KDOR-TV (TBN) Bartlesville; KGEB (IND) Tulsa; KJRH-TV (NBC) Tulsa; KMYT-TV (MNT) Tulsa; KOED-TV (PBS) Tulsa; KOKI-TV (FOX) Tulsa; KOTV-DT (CBS) Tulsa; KQCW-DT (CW) Muskogee; KRSC-TV (ETV) Claremore; KTPX-TV (ION) Okmulgee; KTUL (ABC) Tulsa; KWHB (IND) Tulsa; allband FM.
Programming (via satellite): A&E Networks; ABC Family Channel; AMC; Animal Planet; Cartoon Network; CMT Pure Country; CNBC; CNN; C-SPAN; Discovery Channel; Disney Channel; ESPN; ESPN 2; ESPN Classic Sports; Food Network; Fox News Channel; Fox Sports Southwest; FX; Hallmark Channel; HGTV; History Channel; Lifetime; MoviePlex; MSNBC; MTV; Nickelodeon; Outdoor Channel; QVC; Spike TV; Syfy; TBS Superstation; The Learning Channel; The Weather Channel; truTV; Turner Network TV; USA Network; VH1; WGN America.
Fee: $60.00 installation; $21.95 monthly; $10.00 additional installation.

Digital Basic Service
Subscribers: N.A.
Programming (via satellite): AmericanLife TV Network; BBC America; Bio; Black Family Channel; Bloomberg Television; Bravo; Canal 52MX; Cine Latino; Cine Mexicano; cloo; CMT Pure Country; CNN en Espanol; Current; Discovery en Espanol; Discovery Fit & Health; Discovery Health Channel; Discovery Home Channel; Discovery Kids Channel; Discovery Times Channel; DMX Music; Encore (multiplexed); ESPN 2; ESPN Classic Sports; ESPNews; Flix; Fox College Sports Atlantic; Fox College Sports Central; Fox College Sports Pacific; Fox Deportes; Fox Movie Channel; Fox Soccer; Fuse; G4; Golf Channel; Great American Country; GSN; Halogen Network; HGTV; History Channel; History Channel en Espanol; History Channel International; Independent Film Channel; Lifetime Movie Network; Military Channel; MTV Hits; MTV2; National Geographic Channel; Nick Jr.; NickToons TV; Outdoor Channel; Ovation; Science; ShopNBC; Speed; Style Network; Sundance Channel; Syfy; TeenNick; The Word Network; Toon Disney; Toon Disney en Espanol; Tr3s; Trinity Broadcasting Network; Turner Classic Movies; Versus; VH1 Classic; VH1 Soul; WE tv.

Pay Service 1
Pay Units: 58.
Programming (via satellite): Encore; HBO; Showtime; Starz.
Fee: $11.50 monthly (each).

Digital Pay Service 1
Pay Units: N.A.
Programming (via satellite): Cinemax (multiplexed); HBO (multiplexed); Showtime (multiplexed); Starz (multiplexed); The Movie Channel (multiplexed).

Video-On-Demand: No

Pay-Per-View
iN DEMAND (delivered digitally); Hot Choice (delivered digitally); Playboy TV (delivered digitally); Fresh (delivered digitally); Shorteez (delivered digitally).

Internet Service
Operational: Yes.
Fee: $24.95 installation; $39.95 monthly.

Telephone Service
None

Miles of Plant: 37.0 (coaxial); None (fiber optic).
Chief Executive Officer: Bill Haggarty. Regional Vice President: Andrew Dearth. Vice President, Marketing: Tracy Bass.
Ownership: Allegiance Communications (MSO).

PAWNEE—Now served by MANNFORD, OK [OK0296]. ICA: OK0117.

PERRY—Suddenlink Communications, 12444 Powerscourt Dr, Saint Louis, MO 63131-3660. Phone: 405-377-7785. Fax: 405-372-3920. Web Site: http://www.suddenlink.com. Also serves Noble County (portions). ICA: OK0057.
TV Market Ranking: Outside TV Markets (Noble County (portions), PERRY). Franchise award date: September 1, 1977. Franchise expiration date: N.A. Began: January 1, 1979.
Channel capacity: 78 (not 2-way capable). Channels available but not in use: N.A.

Basic Service
Subscribers: 1,800.
Programming (received off-air): KAUT-TV (MNT) Oklahoma City; KETA-TV (PBS) Oklahoma City; KFOR-TV (NBC) Oklahoma City; KOCB (CW) Oklahoma City; KOCO-TV (ABC) Oklahoma City; KOKH-TV (FOX) Oklahoma City; KOPX-TV (ION) Oklahoma City; KSBI (IND) Oklahoma City; KTBO-TV (TBN) Oklahoma City; KWTV-DT (CBS) Oklahoma City; 10 FMs.
Programming (via satellite): Daystar TV Network; TBS Superstation; The Weather Channel; WGN America.
Fee: $50.00 installation; $14.27 monthly; $3.30 converter.

Expanded Basic Service 1
Subscribers: 1,523.
Programming (via satellite): A&E Networks; ABC Family Channel; AMC; Animal Planet; Cartoon Network; CNBC; CNN; Comedy Central; Country Music TV; C-SPAN; Discovery Channel; Disney Channel; ESPN; ESPN 2; Fox News Channel; Fox Sports Southwest; Headline News; HGTV; History Channel; Lifetime; MoviePlex; Nickelodeon; QVC; Spike TV; Syfy; The Learning Channel; Turner Network TV; TV Land; USA Network; VH1.
Fee: $17.85 monthly.

Digital Basic Service
Subscribers: 56.
Programming (via satellite): AmericanLife TV Network; BBC America; Black Family Channel; Bloomberg Television; Bravo!; Discovery Fit & Health; ESPN 2; ESPN Classic Sports; ESPNews; Fox Movie Channel; Fox Soccer; Fuse; G4; Golf Channel; Great American Country; GSN; Halogen Network; Independent Film Channel; Music Choice; National Geographic Channel; Outdoor Channel; ShopNBC; Speed; Sundance Channel; The Word Network; Toon Disney; Versus.
Fee: $13.95 monthly.

Pay Service 1
Pay Units: 453.
Programming (via satellite): Cinemax.
Fee: $10.00 installation; $10.68 monthly.

Pay Service 2
Pay Units: 323.
Programming (via satellite): HBO.
Fee: $10.00 installation; $10.68 monthly.

Pay Service 3
Pay Units: 454.
Programming (via satellite): Encore.
Fee: $10.00 installation; $6.75 monthly.

Pay Service 4
Pay Units: 458.
Programming (via satellite): Starz.
Fee: $10.00 installation; $1.75 monthly.

Digital Pay Service 1
Pay Units: N.A.
Programming (via satellite): Cinemax (multiplexed); Encore (multiplexed); HBO (multiplexed); Showtime (multiplexed); Starz (multiplexed); The Movie Channel (multiplexed).

Video-On-Demand: No

Pay-Per-View
iN DEMAND (delivered digitally); Hot Choice (delivered digitally); Adult PPV (delivered digitally); ESPN Now (delivered digitally); ESPN (delivered digitally); ESPN Extra (delivered digitally).

Internet Service
Operational: Yes.
Broadband Service: Suddenlink High Speed Internet.

Telephone Service
Digital: Operational

Miles of Plant: 49.0 (coaxial); 5.0 (fiber optic).
Manager: Nicole Evans. Marketing Manager: Heather Eastwood. Chief Technician: Johnny Stanley.
Ownership: Cequel Communications LLC (MSO).

PICHER—Formerly served by Mediacom. No longer in operation. ICA: OK0093.

PIEDMONT—Formerly served by Almega Cable. No longer in operation. ICA: OK0374.

POCASSET—Formerly served by CableDirect. No longer in operation. ICA: OK0305.

POCOLA—Cox Communications. Now served by FORT SMITH, AR [AR0003]. ICA: OK0099.

PONCA CITY—Cable One, 303 N 4th St, PO Box 2149, Ponca City, OK 74602-2149. Phone: 580-762-6684. Fax: 580-762-0312. E-mail: danny.thompson@cableone.net. Web Site: http://www.cableone.net. Also serves Kay County (portions), Osage County (portions) & Tonkawa. ICA: OK0014.
TV Market Ranking: 54 (Osage County (portions)); Below 100 (Osage County (portions)); Outside TV Markets (Kay County (portions), PONCA CITY, Tonkawa, Osage County (portions)). Franchise award date: N.A. Franchise expiration date: N.A. Began: March 1, 1967.
Channel capacity: 70 (operating 2-way). Channels available but not in use: N.A.

Basic Service
Subscribers: 9,400.
Programming (received off-air): KAUT-TV (MNT) Oklahoma City; KETA-TV (PBS) Oklahoma City; KFOR-TV (NBC) Oklahoma City; KJRH-TV (NBC) Tulsa; KOCB (CW) Oklahoma City; KOCO-TV (ABC) Oklahoma City; KOKH-TV (FOX) Oklahoma City; KOKI-TV (FOX) Tulsa; KOTV-DT (CBS) Tulsa; KSBI (IND) Oklahoma City; KSNW (NBC) Wichita; KTEW-LD Ponca City; KTUL (ABC) Tulsa; KWTV-DT (CBS) Oklahoma City.
Programming (via satellite): A&E Networks; ABC Family Channel; AMC; BET Networks; Cartoon Network; CNBC; CNN; Country Music TV; C-SPAN; C-SPAN 2; Discovery Channel; Disney Channel; ESPN; ESPN 2; Fox News Channel; Fox Sports Southwest; FX; Headline News; HGTV; History Channel; Lifetime; MSNBC; MTV; Nickelodeon; QVC; Spike TV; Syfy; TBS Superstation; The

Learning Channel; The Weather Channel; Travel Channel; Trinity Broadcasting Network; Turner Network TV; TV Guide Network; TV Land; Univision Studios; USA Network; VH1.
Fee: $75.00 installation; $39.50 monthly.

Digital Basic Service
Subscribers: 3,500.
Programming (via satellite): 3 Angels Broadcasting Network; Bio; Boomerang; BYU Television; Canales N; Discovery Digital Networks; DMX Music; ESPN Classic Sports; ESPNews; FamilyNet; Fox College Sports Atlantic; Fox College Sports Central; Fox College Sports Pacific; Fox Movie Channel; Fox Soccer; Fuel TV; G4; Golf Channel; Hallmark Channel; History Channel International; INSP; National Geographic Channel; Outdoor Channel; SoapNet; Speed; Toon Disney; Trinity Broadcasting Network; truTV; Turner Network TV HD; Universal HD.
Fee: $48.95 monthly.

Digital Pay Service 1
Pay Units: N.A.
Programming (via satellite): Cinemax (multiplexed); Encore (multiplexed); Flix; HBO (multiplexed); Showtime (multiplexed); Showtime HD; Starz (multiplexed); Sundance Channel; The Movie Channel (multiplexed); The Movie Channel HD.
Fee: $15.00 monthly (each).

Video-On-Demand: No

Pay-Per-View
iN DEMAND (delivered digitally); Pleasure (delivered digitally); Ten Clips (delivered digitally); Ten Blox (delivered digitally); Ten Blue (delivered digitally).

Internet Service
Operational: Yes. Began: December 1, 2000.
Subscribers: 3,147.
Broadband Service: CableONE.net.
Fee: $75.00 installation; $43.00 monthly; $5.00 modem lease.

Telephone Service
Digital: Operational
Fee: $39.95 monthly

Miles of Plant: 235.0 (coaxial); 44.0 (fiber optic).
Manager: Danny Thompson. Marketing Director: Terry Bush. Office Manager: Vicki Hardesty. Plant Manager: Ray Snider.
Ownership: Cable ONE Inc. (MSO).

POND CREEK—Pioneer Telephone Coop. Formerly [OK0185]. This cable system has converted to IPTV, PO Box 539, Kingfisher, OK 73750. Phones: 405-375-4111; 888-782-2667. E-mail: website@pldi.net. Web Site: http://www.ptci.com. ICA: OK5081.
TV Market Ranking: Outside TV Markets (POND CREEK). Franchise award date: N.A. Franchise expiration date: N.A. Began: N.A.
Channel capacity: N.A. Channels available but not in use: N.A.

Internet Service
Operational: Yes.

Telephone Service
Digital: Operational

General Manager: Richard Ruhl.

POND CREEK—Pioneer Telephone Coop. This cable system has converted to IPTV. See Pond Creek, OK [OK5081]. ICA: OK0185.

PORTER—Allegiance Communications, 707 W Saratoga St, Shawnee, OK 74804. Phones: 405-275-6923; 405-395-1131. Web Site: http://www.allegiance.tv. ICA: OK0306.
TV Market Ranking: 54 (PORTER). Franchise award date: January 1, 1989. Franchise expiration date: January 1, 2014. Began: September 1, 1989.
Channel capacity: N.A. Channels available but not in use: N.A.

Basic Service
Subscribers: N.A.
Programming (received off-air): KDOR-TV (TBN) Bartlesville; KJRH-TV (NBC) Tulsa; KMYT-TV (MNT) Tulsa; KOED-TV (PBS) Tulsa; KOKI-TV (FOX) Tulsa; KOTV-DT (CBS) Tulsa; KQCW-DT (CW) Muskogee; KRSC-TV (ETV) Claremore; KTUL (ABC) Tulsa; KWHB (IND) Tulsa.
Programming (via satellite): A&E Networks; ABC Family Channel; CNBC; CNN; Comedy Central; Country Music TV; C-SPAN; Discovery Channel; Disney Channel; ESPN; ESPN 2; Lifetime; MTV; Nickelodeon; Spike TV; TBS Superstation; Travel Channel; Turner Network TV; WGN America.
Fee: $30.00 installation; $21.95 monthly.

Pay Service 1
Pay Units: N.A.
Programming (via satellite): HBO.
Fee: $10.95 monthly.

Video-On-Demand: No

Internet Service
Operational: No.

Telephone Service
None

Miles of Plant: 6.0 (coaxial); None (fiber optic).
Chief Executive Officer: Bill Haggarty. Regional Vice President: Andrew Dearth. Vice President, Marketing: Tracy Bass.
Ownership: Allegiance Communications (MSO).

PORUM—Allegiance Communications, 707 W Saratoga St, Shawnee, OK 74804. Phones: 405-275-6923; 405-395-1131. Web Site: http://www.allegiance.tv. ICA: OK0196.
TV Market Ranking: Below 100 (PORUM). Franchise award date: July 1, 1981. Franchise expiration date: N.A. Began: January 1, 1982.
Channel capacity: N.A. Channels available but not in use: N.A.

Basic Service
Subscribers: N.A.
Programming (received off-air): KJRH-TV (NBC) Tulsa; KMYT-TV (MNT) Tulsa; KOET (PBS) Eufaula; KOKI-TV (FOX) Tulsa; KOTV-DT (CBS) Tulsa; KQCW-DT (CW) Muskogee; KTUL (ABC) Tulsa; KWHB (IND) Tulsa.
Programming (via satellite): A&E Networks; ABC Family Channel; AMC; Animal Planet; CNBC; CNN; Country Music TV; Discovery Channel; Disney Channel; E! Entertainment Television; ESPN; ESPN 2; Headline News; History Channel; Lifetime; MSNBC; Nickelodeon; QVC; Spike TV; Syfy; TBS Superstation; The Learning Channel; Travel Channel; Turner Network TV; USA Network; WGN America.
Fee: $30.00 installation; $21.95 monthly.

Pay Service 1
Pay Units: 26.
Programming (via satellite): Cinemax; HBO.
Fee: $9.00 monthly (HBO).

Video-On-Demand: No

Pay-Per-View
iN DEMAND (delivered digitally); Hot Choice (delivered digitally); Playboy TV (delivered digitally); Fresh (delivered digitally); Shorteez (delivered digitally).

Internet Service
Operational: No.

Telephone Service
None

Miles of Plant: 6.0 (coaxial); None (fiber optic).
Chief Executive Officer: Bill Haggarty. Regional Vice President: Andrew Dearth. Vice President, Marketing: Tracy Bass.
Ownership: Allegiance Communications (MSO).

PORUM LANDING—Allegiance Communications, 707 W Saratoga St, Shawnee, OK 74804. Phones: 405-395-1131; 405-275-6923. Web Site: http://www.allegiance.tv. ICA: OK0307.
TV Market Ranking: Outside TV Markets (PORUM LANDING). Franchise award date: N.A. Franchise expiration date: N.A. Began: June 1, 1990.
Channel capacity: 36 (not 2-way capable). Channels available but not in use: N.A.

Basic Service
Subscribers: 222.
Programming (received off-air): KJRH-TV (NBC) Tulsa; KMYT-TV (MNT) Tulsa; KOED-TV (PBS) Tulsa; KOKI-TV (FOX) Tulsa; KOTV-DT (CBS) Tulsa; KQCW-DT (CW) Muskogee; KTUL (ABC) Tulsa.
Programming (via satellite): A&E Networks; ABC Family Channel; AMC; CMT Pure Country; CNN; Discovery Channel; Disney Channel; ESPN; History Channel; Lifetime; Nickelodeon; QVC; Spike TV; TBS Superstation; The Weather Channel; Turner Network TV; USA Network; WGN America.
Fee: $25.00 installation; $21.95 monthly.

Pay Service 1
Pay Units: N.A.
Programming (via satellite): HBO; Showtime.
Fee: $10.00 monthly (each).

Pay-Per-View
iN DEMAND (delivered digitally); Hot Choice (delivered digitally); Playboy TV (delivered digitally); Fresh (delivered digitally); Shorteez (delivered digitally).

Internet Service
Operational: No.

Telephone Service
None

Miles of Plant: 25.0 (coaxial); None (fiber optic).
Chief Executive Officer: Bill Haggarty. Regional Vice President: Andrew Dearth. Vice President, Marketing: Tracy Bass.
Ownership: Allegiance Communications (MSO).

POTEAU—Suddenlink Communications, 12444 Powerscourt Dr, Saint Louis, MO 63131-3660. Phones: 800-999-8876; 314-965-2020. Web Site: http://www.suddenlink.com. ICA: OK0308.
TV Market Ranking: Below 100 (POTEAU). Franchise award date: July 1, 1962. Franchise expiration date: July 1, 2010. Began: July 1, 1962.
Channel capacity: 41 (operating 2-way). Channels available but not in use: N.A.

Basic Service
Subscribers: 2,218.
Programming (received off-air): KAFT (PBS) Fayetteville; KFSM-TV (CBS) Fort Smith; KHBS (ABC, CW) Fort Smith; KMYT-TV (MNT) Tulsa; KNWA-TV (FOX, NBC) Rogers; KOET (PBS) Eufaula; KPBI-CA (FOX) Fort Smith; KTUL (ABC) Tulsa; allband FM.
Programming (via satellite): INSP; QVC; Trinity Broadcasting Network.
Fee: $39.95 installation; $19.95 monthly.

Expanded Basic Service 1
Subscribers: N.A.
Programming (via satellite): A&E Networks; ABC Family Channel; AMC; Animal Planet; Cartoon Network; CNBC; CNN; Comedy Central; C-SPAN; Discovery Channel; Disney Channel; E! Entertainment Television; ESPN; ESPN 2; Food Network; Fox News Channel; Fox Sports Southwest; FX; Great American Country; Hallmark Channel; Headline News; HGTV; History Channel; Lifetime; MSNBC; MTV; National Geographic Channel; Nickelodeon; Outdoor Channel; Shopping Channel; Spike TV; Syfy; TBS Superstation; The Learning Channel; The Weather Channel; Travel Channel; Turner Classic Movies; Turner Network TV; TV Land; USA Network; VH1.
Fee: $23.00 monthly.

Digital Basic Service
Subscribers: N.A.
Programming (via satellite): BBC America; Bio; Bloomberg Television; Bravo; cloo; Discovery Digital Networks; DMX Music; ESPN Classic Sports; ESPNews; Fox Soccer; Fuse; G4; Golf Channel; GSN; History Channel International; Independent Film Channel; Speed; Toon Disney; Versus; WE tv.
Fee: $3.99 monthly.

Pay Service 1
Pay Units: 320.
Programming (via satellite): HBO.
Fee: $10.95 monthly.

Pay Service 2
Pay Units: 185.
Programming (via satellite): The Movie Channel.
Fee: $7.95 monthly.

Pay Service 3
Pay Units: 196.
Programming (via satellite): Showtime.
Fee: $9.95 monthly.

Digital Pay Service 1
Pay Units: N.A.
Programming (via satellite): Cinemax (multiplexed); Encore (multiplexed); HBO (multiplexed); Showtime (multiplexed); Starz (multiplexed); The Movie Channel (multiplexed).

Video-On-Demand: No

Pay-Per-View
iN DEMAND (delivered digitally); Playboy TV (delivered digitally); Fresh (delivered digitally).

Internet Service
Operational: Yes. Began: June 23, 2002.
Broadband Service: Suddenlink High Speed Internet.
Fee: $45.95 installation; $24.95 monthly.

Telephone Service
Digital: Operational
Fee: $49.95 monthly
Miles of Plant: 125.0 (coaxial); None (fiber optic).
Area Manager: Carl Miller. Regional Manager: Todd Cruthird. Regional Marketing Manager: Beverly Gambell. Plant Manager: Danny Keith.
Ownership: Cequel Communications LLC (MSO).

PRESTON—Formerly served by Quality Cablevision of Oklahoma Inc. No longer in operation. ICA: OK0338.

PRYOR—Alliance Communications, 6125 Paluxy Dr, Tyler, TX 75703. Phones: 800-842-8160; 501-679-6619. Fax: 501-679-5694. Web Site: http://www.alliancecable.net. Also serves Mayes County (portions). ICA: OK0046.
TV Market Ranking: 54 (Mayes County (portions)); Outside TV Markets (PRYOR, Mayes County (portions)). Franchise award date: August 5, 1972. Franchise expiration date: December 3, 2012. Began: November 22, 1974.
Channel capacity: N.A. Channels available but not in use: N.A.
Basic Service
Subscribers: 1,313.
Programming (received off-air): KDOR-TV (TBN) Bartlesville; KGEB (IND) Tulsa; KJRH-TV (NBC) Tulsa; KMYT-TV (MNT) Tulsa; KOED-TV (PBS) Tulsa; KOKI-TV (FOX) Tulsa; KOTV-DT (CBS) Tulsa; KQCW-DT (CW) Muskogee; KRSC-TV (ETV) Claremore; KTPX-TV (ION) Okmulgee; KTUL (ABC) Tulsa; KWHB (IND) Tulsa; allband FM.
Programming (via satellite): ABC Family Channel.
Fee: $35.80 installation; $21.52 monthly; $10.00 additional installation.
Expanded Basic Service 1
Subscribers: 1,167.
Programming (via satellite): A&E Networks; AMC; AmericanLife TV Network; Animal Planet; Cartoon Network; CNN; Comedy Central; Country Music TV; C-SPAN; Discovery Channel; Discovery Fit & Health; Discovery Health Channel; Disney Channel; ESPN; ESPN 2; ESPN Classic Sports; Food Network; Fox News Channel; Fox Sports Southwest; FX; Headline News; HGTV; History Channel; INSP; Lifetime; MSNBC; MTV; National Geographic Channel; Nickelodeon; Oxygen; ShopNBC; Spike TV; Syfy; TBS Superstation; The Learning Channel; The Weather Channel; Travel Channel; Turner Network TV; TV Guide Network; TV Land; USA Network; WE tv; WGN America.
Fee: $28.16 monthly.
Digital Basic Service
Subscribers: 319.
Programming (via satellite): BBC America; Bio; Bloomberg Television; Current; Discovery Digital Networks; ESPNews; Fox Soccer; G4; GAS; Golf Channel; GSN; Halogen Network; History Channel International; Lifetime Movie Network; MTV Hits; MTV2; Music Choice; Nick Jr.; NickToons TV; Outdoor Channel; Ovation; Speed; Style Network; Toon Disney; Turner Classic Movies; Versus; VH1 Classic.
Fee: $25.49 monthly.
Digital Pay Service 1
Pay Units: N.A.
Programming (via satellite): Cinemax (multiplexed); Encore (multiplexed); Fox Movie Channel; HBO (multiplexed); HBO; Independent Film Channel; Showtime (multiplexed); Showtime; Starz; Sundance Channel; The Movie Channel (multiplexed).
Fee: $13.00 monthly (each).
Video-On-Demand: No
Pay-Per-View
Movies (delivered digitally); Fresh (delivered digitally); Shorteez (delivered digitally); Hot Choice (delivered digitally).
Internet Service
Operational: No.
Telephone Service
None
Vice President & General Manager: John Brinker. Vice President, Programming: Julie Newman.
Ownership: Buford Media Group LLC (MSO).

PRYOR (outside areas)—Formerly served by Time Warner Cable. No longer in operation. ICA: OK0354.

PURCELL—Suddenlink Communications, 2206 North Green Ave, Purcell, OK 73080. Phones: 800-999-6845; 405-527-5651. Fax: 405-527-5392. Web Site: http://www.suddenlink.com. Also serves Lexington, Maysville, McClain County, Noble & Wayne. ICA: OK0048.
TV Market Ranking: 39 (Lexington, McClain County (portions), Noble, PURCELL); Below 100 (Maysville, Wayne, McClain County (portions)); Outside TV Markets (McClain County (portions)). Franchise award date: N.A. Franchise expiration date: N.A. Began: November 1, 1976.
Channel capacity: 40 (operating 2-way). Channels available but not in use: N.A.
Basic Service
Subscribers: 3,497.
Programming (received off-air): KAUT-TV (MNT) Oklahoma City; KETA-TV (PBS) Oklahoma City; KFOR-TV (NBC) Oklahoma City; KOCB (CW) Oklahoma City; KOCM (IND) Norman; KOCO-TV (ABC) Oklahoma City; KOKH-TV (FOX) Oklahoma City; KOPX-TV (ION) Oklahoma City; KSBI (IND) Oklahoma City; KTBO-TV (TBN) Oklahoma City; KWTV-DT (CBS) Oklahoma City; allband FM.
Fee: $44.95 installation; $19.95 monthly; $24.95 additional installation.
Expanded Basic Service 1
Subscribers: N.A.
Programming (via satellite): A&E Networks; ABC Family Channel; AMC; Animal Planet; Cartoon Network; CNBC; CNN; Comedy Central; C-SPAN; Discovery Channel; Disney Channel; E! Entertainment Television; ESPN; ESPN 2; Food Network; Fox News Channel; Fox Sports Southwest; FX; Great American Country; Hallmark Channel; Headline News; HGTV; History Channel; Lifetime; MTV; Nickelodeon; Outdoor Channel; QVC; Spike TV; Syfy; TBS Superstation; The Learning Channel; The Weather Channel; Turner Classic Movies; Turner Network TV; TV Land; Univision Studios; USA Network; VH1.
Digital Basic Service
Subscribers: N.A.
Programming (via satellite): BBC America; Bio; Bloomberg Television; cloo; Discovery Digital Networks; DMX Music; ESPN Classic Sports; ESPNews; Fox College Sports Atlantic; Fox College Sports Central; Fox College Sports Pacific; Fox Soccer; Fuse; G4; Golf Channel; GSN; History Channel International; Independent Film Channel; ShopNBC; Speed; Style Network; Toon Disney; Versus; WE tv.
Pay Service 1
Pay Units: 736.
Programming (via satellite): HBO.
Pay Service 2
Pay Units: 249.
Programming (via satellite): The Movie Channel.
Pay Service 3
Pay Units: 413.
Programming (via satellite): Cinemax.
Pay Service 4
Pay Units: N.A.
Programming (via satellite): Showtime.
Digital Pay Service 1
Pay Units: N.A.
Programming (via satellite): Cinemax (multiplexed); Encore (multiplexed); HBO (multiplexed); Showtime (multiplexed); Starz (multiplexed); The Movie Channel (multiplexed).
Video-On-Demand: No
Pay-Per-View
iN DEMAND (delivered digitally); Playboy TV (delivered digitally); Fresh (delivered digitally).
Internet Service
Operational: Yes. Began: January 21, 2003.
Broadband Service: Suddenlink High Speed Internet.
Fee: $45.95 installation; $24.95 monthly.
Telephone Service
Digital: Operational
Fee: $49.95 monthly
Miles of Plant: 85.0 (coaxial); None (fiber optic).
General Manager: Charles Hembree. Regional Manager: Todd Cruthird. Chief Technician: Kurt Widmer.
Ownership: Cequel Communications LLC (MSO).

QUINTON—Allegiance Communications, 707 W Saratoga St, Shawnee, OK 74804. Phones: 405-275-6923; 405-395-1131. Web Site: http://www.allegiance.tv. Also serves Kinta. ICA: OK0156.
TV Market Ranking: Outside TV Markets (Kinta, QUINTON). Franchise award date: N.A. Franchise expiration date: N.A. Began: January 1, 1977.
Channel capacity: 45 (not 2-way capable). Channels available but not in use: N.A.
Basic Service
Subscribers: 443.
Programming (received off-air): KJRH-TV (NBC) Tulsa; KMYT-TV (MNT) Tulsa; KOET (PBS) Eufaula; KOKI-TV (FOX) Tulsa; KOTV-DT (CBS) Tulsa; KQCW-DT (CW) Muskogee; KTUL (ABC) Tulsa; KWHB (IND) Tulsa.
Programming (via satellite): A&E Networks; ABC Family Channel; AMC; Animal Planet; Cartoon Network; CNBC; CNN; Country Music TV; C-SPAN; Discovery Channel; Disney Channel; E! Entertainment Television; ESPN; ESPN 2; Fox News Channel; Fox Sports Southwest; Headline News; HGTV; History Channel; Lifetime; Nickelodeon; Outdoor Channel; Spike TV; Syfy; TBS Superstation; The Learning Channel; The Weather Channel; Travel Channel; Turner Classic Movies; Turner Network TV; USA Network; WGN America.
Fee: $30.00 installation; $23.45 monthly.
Digital Basic Service
Subscribers: N.A.
Programming (via satellite): BBC America; Bio; Bloomberg Television; Bravo; Chiller; cloo; CMT Pure Country; Current; Discovery Fit & Health; Discovery Health Channel; Discovery Kids Channel; DMX Music; Encore (multiplexed); ESPN Classic Sports; ESPNews; Flix; Fox Movie Channel; Fox Soccer; Fuse; G4; Golf Channel; GSN; History Channel International; ID Investigation Discovery; Independent Film Channel; Lifetime Movie Network; Military Channel; MTV Hits; MTV2; National Geographic Channel; Nick Jr.; NickToons TV; Planet Green; RFD-TV; Science; SoapNet; Style Network; TeenNick; Toon Disney; Trinity Broadcasting Network; Versus; VH1 Classic; VH1 Soul; WE tv.
Pay Service 1
Pay Units: N.A.
Programming (via satellite): Cinemax; HBO; Showtime.
Fee: $9.00 monthly (HBO).
Digital Pay Service 1
Pay Units: N.A.
Programming (via satellite): Cinemax (multiplexed); HBO (multiplexed); Showtime (multiplexed); Starz (multiplexed); The Movie Channel (multiplexed).
Video-On-Demand: No
Pay-Per-View
iN DEMAND (delivered digitally); Club Jenna (delivered digitally); Spice: Xcess (delivered digitally); Playboy TV (delivered digitally); Fresh (delivered digitally).
Internet Service
Operational: No.
Telephone Service
None
Miles of Plant: 22.0 (coaxial); None (fiber optic).
Chief Executive Officer: Bill Haggarty. Regional Vice President: Andrew Dearth. Vice President, Marketing: Tracy Bass.
Ownership: Allegiance Communications (MSO).

RALSTON—Allegiance Communications, 707 W Saratoga St, Shawnee, OK 74804. Phones: 405-275-6923; 405-395-1131. Web Site: http://www.allegiance.tv. ICA: OK0241.
TV Market Ranking: Outside TV Markets (RALSTON). Franchise award date: January 1, 1988. Franchise expiration date: January 1, 2013. Began: April 1, 1988.
Channel capacity: 35 (not 2-way capable). Channels available but not in use: N.A.
Basic Service
Subscribers: N.A.
Programming (received off-air): KJRH-TV (NBC) Tulsa; KOED-TV (PBS) Tulsa; KOKI-TV (FOX) Tulsa; KOTV-DT (CBS) Tulsa; KQCW-DT (CW) Muskogee; KTUL (ABC) Tulsa; KWHB (IND) Tulsa.
Programming (via satellite): A&E Networks; ABC Family Channel; CNBC; CNN; Country Music TV; Discovery Channel; Disney Channel; ESPN; ESPN 2; Headline News; Lifetime; MTV; Nickelodeon; Speed; Spike TV; TBS Superstation; Travel Channel; Turner Network TV; USA Network; WGN America.
Fee: $30.00 installation; $21.95 monthly.
Video-On-Demand: No
Pay-Per-View
Hot Choice (delivered digitally); Playboy TV (delivered digitally); Fresh (delivered digitally); Shorteez (delivered digitally); iN DEMAND (delivered digitally).
Internet Service
Operational: No.
Telephone Service
None
Miles of Plant: 3.0 (coaxial); None (fiber optic).
Chief Executive Officer: Bill Haggarty. Regional Vice President: Andrew Dearth. Vice President, Marketing: Tracy Bass.
Ownership: Allegiance Communications (MSO).

RAMONA—Community Cablevision Co., 1550 W Rogers Blvd, PO Box 307, Skiatook, OK 74070-0307. Phone: 918-396-3019. Fax: 918-396-2081. E-mail: info@communitycablevision.com. Web Site: http://www.communitycablebroadband.com. ICA: OK0206.

TV Market Ranking: 54 (RAMONA). Franchise award date: N.A. Franchise expiration date: January 1, 2009. Began: January 1, 1984.

Channel capacity: 40 (not 2-way capable). Channels available but not in use: N.A.

Basic Service

Subscribers: 139.

Programming (received off-air): KDOR-TV (TBN) Bartlesville; KGEB (IND) Tulsa; KJRH-TV (NBC) Tulsa; KOED-TV (PBS) Tulsa; KOKI-TV (FOX) Tulsa; KOTV-DT (CBS) Tulsa; KQCW-DT (CW) Muskogee; KRSC-TV (ETV) Claremore; KTPX-TV (ION) Okmulgee; KTUL (ABC) Tulsa; KWHB (IND) Tulsa.

Programming (via microwave): KTFO-CD (TEL) Austin.

Programming (via satellite): A&E Networks; ABC Family Channel; Cartoon Network; CNN; Country Music TV; C-SPAN; Discovery Channel; Disney Channel; ESPN; ESPN 2; Fox News Channel; Fox Sports Southwest; Headline News; Lifetime; MTV; Nickelodeon; QVC; Spike TV; Syfy; TBS Superstation; The Learning Channel; The Weather Channel; Turner Classic Movies; Turner Network TV; USA Network; WGN America.

Fee: $29.95 installation; $19.00 monthly.

Video-On-Demand: No

Internet Service

Operational: Yes.

Fee: $44.95 monthly.

Telephone Service

None

Miles of Plant: 8.0 (coaxial); None (fiber optic).

President & General Manager: Dennis Soule.

Ownership: Community Cablevision Co. (MSO).

RANDLETT—Formerly served by Cable Television Inc. No longer in operation. ICA: OK0335.

RATTAN—Allegiance Communications, 707 W Saratoga St, Shawnee, OK 74804. Phones: 405-395-1131; 405-275-6923. Web Site: http://www.allegiance.tv. ICA: OK0450.

TV Market Ranking: Outside TV Markets (RATTAN). Franchise award date: N.A. Franchise expiration date: N.A. Began: N.A.

Channel capacity: 20 (not 2-way capable). Channels available but not in use: N.A.

Basic Service

Subscribers: 83.

Programming (received off-air): KOET (PBS) Eufaula; KTEN (ABC, CW, NBC) Ada; KXII (CBS, FOX, MNT) Sherman.

Programming (via satellite): ABC Family Channel; CNN; Discovery Channel; Disney Channel; ESPN; KMGH-TV (ABC) Denver; Spike TV; TBS Superstation; USA Network; WGN America.

Fee: $35.00 installation; $22.98 monthly.

Pay Service 1

Pay Units: N.A.

Programming (via satellite): HBO; Showtime.

Pay-Per-View

iN DEMAND (delivered digitally); Hot Choice (delivered digitally); Playgirl TV (delivered digitally); Fresh (delivered digitally); Shorteez (delivered digitally).

Internet Service

Operational: No.

Telephone Service

None

Chief Executive Officer: Bill Haggarty. Regional Vice President: Andrew Dearth. Vice President, Marketing: Tracy Bass.

Ownership: Allegiance Communications (MSO).

RED ROCK—Formerly served by Blue Sky Cable LLC. No longer in operation. ICA: OK0251.

RINGWOOD—Pioneer Telephone Coop. Formerly [OK0375]. This cable system has converted to IPTV, PO Box 539, Kingfisher, OK 73750. Phones: 888-782-2667; 405-375-4111. E-mail: website@pldi.net. Web Site: http://www.ptci.com. ICA: OK5082.

Channel capacity: N.A. Channels available but not in use: N.A.

Internet Service

Operational: Yes.

Telephone Service

Digital: Operational

General Manager: Richard Ruhl.

RINGWOOD—Pioneer Telephone Coop. This cable system has converted to IPTV. See Ringwood, OK [OK5082]. ICA: OK0375.

RIPLEY—Formerly served by CableDirect. No longer in operation. ICA: OK0232.

ROCKY—Formerly served by CableDirect. No longer in operation. ICA: OK0249.

ROGERS COUNTY (northern portion)—Time Warner Cable, 16021 S Highway 66, Claremore, OK 74017. Phone: 918-342-9482. Fax: 918-341-8443. Web Site: http://www.timewarnercable.com. Also serves Mayes County (western portion) & Tulsa (northwestern portion). ICA: OK0104.

TV Market Ranking: 54 (Mayes County (western portion) (portions), ROGERS COUNTY (NORTHERN PORTION) (portions), Tulsa (northwestern portion)); Below 100 (ROGERS COUNTY (NORTHERN PORTION) (portions)); Outside TV Markets (Mayes County (western portion) (portions), ROGERS COUNTY (NORTHERN PORTION) (portions)). Franchise award date: N.A. Franchise expiration date: N.A. Began: July 6, 1992.

Channel capacity: 77 (2-way capable). Channels available but not in use: N.A.

Basic Service

Subscribers: N.A.

Programming (received off-air): KDOR-TV (TBN) Bartlesville; KGEB (IND) Tulsa; KJRH-TV (NBC) Tulsa; KOET (PBS) Eufaula; KOKI-TV (FOX) Tulsa; KOTV-DT (CBS) Tulsa; KTFO-CD (TEL) Austin; KTPX-TV (ION) Okmulgee; KTUL (ABC) Tulsa; KWHB (IND) Tulsa.

Programming (via satellite): CNN; C-SPAN; KQCW-DT (CW) Muskogee; QVC; The Weather Channel; TV Guide Network; WGN America.

Fee: $35.95 installation; $16.99 monthly.

Digital Basic Service

Subscribers: N.A.

Programming (via satellite): A&E Networks; ABC Family Channel; AMC; Animal Planet; Bio; Cartoon Network; CNBC; Comedy Central; Country Music TV; C-SPAN 2; Discovery Channel; Discovery Fit & Health; Disney Channel; E! Entertainment Television; ESPN; ESPN 2; Food Network; Fox News Channel; Fox Soccer; Fox Sports Southwest; FX; Great American Country; Hallmark Channel; Halogen Network; Headline News; HGTV; History Channel; History Channel International; Lifetime; MSNBC; MTV Networks Digital Suite; National Geographic Channel; Nick Jr.; Nickelodeon; SoapNet; Speed; Spike TV; Syfy; TBS Superstation; The Learning Channel; Toon Disney; Travel Channel; Trinity Broadcasting Network; truTV; Turner Classic Movies; Turner Network TV; TV Land; USA Network.

Fee: $21.74 monthly.

Digital Expanded Basic Service

Subscribers: N.A.

Programming (via satellite): BBC America; Bloomberg Television; Bravo; Discovery Health Channel; Discovery Home Channel; Discovery Kids Channel; Discovery Times Channel; DMX Music; ESPN Classic Sports; ESPNews; Fox Movie Channel; Fuse; G4; Golf Channel; GSN; Independent Film Channel; Lifetime Movie Network; Military Channel; MTV2; NickToons TV; Outdoor Channel; Ovation; Science; Style Network; Sundance Channel; TeenNick; Versus; VH1 Classic; WE tv.

Fee: $15.95 monthly.

Digital Pay Service 1

Pay Units: N.A.

Programming (via satellite): Cinemax (multiplexed); Encore (multiplexed); HBO (multiplexed); HD Theater; Showtime (multiplexed); Starz (multiplexed); The Movie Channel (multiplexed).

Fee: $15.95 monthly (each).

Video-On-Demand: No

Pay-Per-View

iN DEMAND (delivered digitally); Playboy TV (delivered digitally).

Internet Service

Operational: Yes.

Telephone Service

Digital: Operational

General Manager: Mike Miller. Chief Technician: Paul Stanley.

Ownership: Time Warner Cable (MSO).

ROOSEVELT TWP.—Cable West, 314 W Main St, PO Box 237, Mountain View, OK 73062. Phones: 800-980-7912; 580-347-3220. Fax: 580-347-2143. ICA: OK0246.

TV Market Ranking: Outside TV Markets (ROOSEVELT TWP.). Franchise award date: N.A. Franchise expiration date: N.A. Began: February 1, 1980.

Channel capacity: 36 (2-way capable). Channels available but not in use: N.A.

Basic Service

Subscribers: 91.

Programming (received off-air): KAUZ-TV (CBS, CW) Wichita Falls; KETA-TV (PBS) Oklahoma City; KFDX-TV (NBC) Wichita Falls; KFOR-TV (NBC) Oklahoma City; KJTL (FOX) Wichita Falls; KOKH-TV (FOX) Oklahoma City; KSWO-TV (ABC, TMO) Lawton; KWTV-DT (CBS) Oklahoma City.

Programming (via satellite): A&E Networks; ABC Family Channel; AMC; CNN; Country Music TV; Discovery Channel; Disney Channel; ESPN; Lifetime; Spike TV; Syfy; TBS Superstation; Turner Network TV; USA Network.

Fee: $35.00 installation; $28.45 monthly.

Pay Service 1

Pay Units: 11.

Programming (via satellite): HBO.

Fee: $30.00 installation; $9.95 monthly.

Internet Service

Operational: No.

Telephone Service

None

Miles of Plant: 10.0 (coaxial); None (fiber optic).

Manager & Chief Technician: Mickey Davis.

Ownership: Mickey Davis (MSO).

RUSH SPRINGS—Reach Broadband, 515 E Longview St, Arp, TX 75750. Phones: 800-842-8160; 501-679-6619. E-mail: support@reachbroadband.net. Web Site: http://www.reachbroadband.net. ICA: OK0121.

TV Market Ranking: Below 100 (RUSH SPRINGS). Franchise award date: N.A. Franchise expiration date: N.A. Began: November 1, 1982.

Channel capacity: 41 (not 2-way capable). Channels available but not in use: N.A.

Basic Service

Subscribers: 131.

Programming (received off-air): KAUT-TV (MNT) Oklahoma City; KETA-TV (PBS) Oklahoma City; KFOR-TV (NBC) Oklahoma City; KOCB (CW) Oklahoma City; KOCO-TV (ABC) Oklahoma City; KOKH-TV (FOX) Oklahoma City; KSWO-TV (ABC, TMO) Lawton; KTBO-TV (TBN) Oklahoma City; KWTV-DT (CBS) Oklahoma City.

Programming (via satellite): A&E Networks; ABC Family Channel; AMC; CNN; C-SPAN; Discovery Channel; Disney Channel; E! Entertainment Television; ESPN; Great American Country; Headline News; History Channel; National Geographic Channel; Nickelodeon; QVC; Spike TV; Syfy; TBS Superstation; The Learning Channel; Turner Network TV; TV Land; USA Network.

Fee: $29.95 installation; $38.00 monthly.

Pay Service 1

Pay Units: 66.

Programming (via satellite): HBO.

Fee: $9.95 monthly.

Pay Service 2

Pay Units: 21.

Programming (via satellite): Showtime.

Fee: $9.95 monthly.

Video-On-Demand: No

Internet Service

Operational: No.

Telephone Service

None

Miles of Plant: 20.0 (coaxial); None (fiber optic).

Ownership: RB3 LLC (MSO).

RYAN—Formerly served by Almega Cable. No longer in operation. ICA: OK0184.

SALINA—Allegiance Communications, 707 W Saratoga St, Shawnee, OK 74804. Phone: 405-395-1131. Fax: 405-275-0276. Web Site: http://www.allegiance.tv. Also serves Locust Grove. ICA: OK0071.

TV Market Ranking: Below 100 (Locust Grove); Outside TV Markets (SALINA).

MediaPrints™
Map a Winning Business Strategy
Digital Cable and TV Coverage Maps.
Visit www.warren-news.com/mediaprints.htm

Franchise award date: April 1, 1980. Franchise expiration date: N.A. Began: May 1, 1983.

Channel capacity: N.A. Channels available but not in use: N.A.

Basic Service

Subscribers: 774.

Programming (received off-air): KDOR-TV (TBN) Bartlesville; KELF-LP (IND) Miami; KJRH-TV (NBC) Tulsa; KMYT-TV (MNT) Tulsa; KOAM-TV (CBS) Pittsburg; KODE-TV (ABC) Joplin; KOED-TV (PBS) Tulsa; KOKI-TV (FOX) Tulsa; KOTV-DT (CBS) Tulsa; KQCW-DT (CW) Muskogee; KRSC-TV (ETV) Claremore; KSNF (NBC) Joplin; KTPX-TV (ION) Okmulgee; KTUL (ABC) Tulsa; KWHB (IND) Tulsa.

Programming (via satellite): C-SPAN; QVC; WGN America.

Fee: $30.00 installation; $21.95 monthly.

Expanded Basic Service 1

Subscribers: N.A.

Programming (via satellite): A&E Networks; ABC Family Channel; AMC; Animal Planet; Bravo; Cartoon Network; CNBC; CNN; Comedy Central; Country Music TV; Discovery Channel; Disney Channel; E! Entertainment Television; ESPN; ESPN 2; Food Network; Fox News Channel; Fox Sports Southwest; FX; G4; Hallmark Channel; Headline News; HGTV; History Channel; Lifetime; Lifetime Movie Network; MSNBC; MTV; Nickelodeon; Outdoor Channel; Oxygen; RFD-TV; Spike TV; Syfy; TBS Superstation; The Learning Channel; The Weather Channel; Travel Channel; Turner Network TV; TV Land; USA Network; VH1.

Digital Basic Service

Subscribers: N.A.

Programming (via satellite): A&E HD; BBC America; Bio; Bloomberg Television; Chiller; cloo; CMT Pure Country; Current; Discovery Fit & Health; Discovery Health Channel; Discovery Kids Channel; DMX Music; Encore (multiplexed); ESPN 2 HD; ESPN Classic Sports; ESPN HD; ESPN U; ESPNews; Flix; Food Network HD; Fox College Sports Atlantic; Fox College Sports Central; Fox College Sports Pacific; Fox Movie Channel; Fox Soccer; Fuse; Golf Channel; Great American Country; GSN; HD Theater; HDNet; HDNet Movies; HGTV HD; History Channel International; ID Investigation Discovery; Independent Film Channel; Military Channel; MTV Hits; MTV2; National Geographic Channel; National Geographic Channel HD Network; Nick Jr.; NickToons TV; Outdoor Channel 2 HD; Planet Green; Science; ShopNBC; SoapNet; Speed; Style Network; Sundance Channel; TeenNick; The Word Network; Toon Disney; Turner Classic Movies; Universal HD; Versus; VH1 Classic; VH1 Soul; WE tv.

Digital Pay Service 1

Pay Units: N.A.

Programming (via satellite): Cinemax (multiplexed); Encore (multiplexed); Flix; HBO (multiplexed); HBO HD; Showtime (multiplexed); Showtime HD; Starz (multiplexed); Starz HDTV; The Movie Channel (multiplexed).

Video-On-Demand: No

Pay-Per-View

iN DEMAND (delivered digitally); Club Jenna (delivered digitally); Spice: Xcess (delivered digitally); Playboy TV (delivered digitally); Fresh (delivered digitally).

Internet Service

Operational: Yes.

Fee: $24.95 installation; $39.95 monthly.

Telephone Service

None

Miles of Plant: 43.0 (coaxial); None (fiber optic).

Chief Executive Officer: Bill Haggarty. Regional Vice President: Andrew Dearth. Vice President, Marketing: Tracy Bass.

Ownership: Allegiance Communications (MSO).

SALLISAW—Suddenlink Communications, 410 E Cherokee, Sallisaw, OK 74955. Phones: 314-315-9346; 314-965-2020. Web Site: http://www.suddenlink.com. ICA: OK0043.

TV Market Ranking: Below 100 (SALLISAW). Franchise award date: N.A. Franchise expiration date: N.A. Began: June 1, 1966.

Channel capacity: 40 (operating 2-way). Channels available but not in use: N.A.

Basic Service

Subscribers: 2,490.

Programming (received off-air): KETA-TV (PBS) Oklahoma City; KFSM-TV (CBS) Fort Smith; KHBS (ABC, CW) Fort Smith; KJRH-TV (NBC) Tulsa; KNWA-TV (FOX, NBC) Rogers; KOKI-TV (FOX) Tulsa; KOTV-DT (CBS) Tulsa; KTUL (ABC) Tulsa.

Programming (via satellite): C-SPAN; QVC; The Weather Channel; TV Guide Network; WGN America.

Fee: $16.54 installation; $11.00 monthly; $1.34 converter; $20.00 additional installation.

Expanded Basic Service 1

Subscribers: 2,340.

Programming (via satellite): A&E Networks; ABC Family Channel; AMC; Animal Planet; Cartoon Network; CNBC; CNN; Comedy Central; Discovery Channel; Disney Channel; E! Entertainment Television; ESPN; ESPN 2; Food Network; Fox News Channel; Fox Sports Southwest; FX; Great American Country; Headline News; HGTV; History Channel; INSP; Lifetime; MSNBC; MTV; National Geographic Channel; Nickelodeon; Outdoor Channel; Spike TV; Syfy; TBS Superstation; The Learning Channel; Turner Network TV; TV Land; Univision Studios; USA Network; VH1.

Fee: $16.54 installation; $19.95 monthly.

Digital Basic Service

Subscribers: N.A.

Programming (via satellite): BBC America; Bio; cloo; Discovery Digital Networks; DMX Music; ESPN Classic Sports; ESPNews; Fox Soccer; Fuse; Golf Channel; GSN; History Channel International; Independent Film Channel; Speed; Toon Disney; Turner Classic Movies; Versus; WE tv.

Fee: $3.99 monthly.

Pay Service 1

Pay Units: 216.

Programming (via satellite): Cinemax.

Fee: $12.39 monthly.

Pay Service 2

Pay Units: 628.

Programming (via satellite): Starz.

Fee: $4.75 monthly.

Pay Service 3

Pay Units: 820.

Programming (via satellite): Encore.

Fee: $1.75 monthly.

Pay Service 4

Pay Units: 583.

Programming (via satellite): HBO.

Fee: $10.00 installation; $12.83 monthly.

Pay Service 5

Pay Units: 213.

Programming (via satellite): Showtime.

Fee: $10.00 installation; $12.82 monthly.

Digital Pay Service 1

Pay Units: N.A.

Programming (via satellite): Cinemax (multiplexed); Encore (multiplexed); HBO (multiplexed); Showtime (multiplexed); Starz (multiplexed); The Movie Channel (multiplexed).

Video-On-Demand: No

Pay-Per-View

iN DEMAND (delivered digitally); Playboy TV (delivered digitally).

Internet Service

Operational: Yes. Began: November 24, 2003.

Broadband Service: Suddenlink High Speed Internet.

Fee: $45.95 installation; $24.95 monthly.

Telephone Service

Digital: Operational

Fee: $49.95 monthly

Miles of Plant: 90.0 (coaxial); None (fiber optic).

Regional Manager: Todd Cruthird. Manager & Chief Technician: Danny Keith. Marketing Director: Beverly Gambell.

Ownership: Cequel Communications LLC (MSO).

SAND POINT—CommuniComm Services, 1501 W Mississippi St, PO Box 597, Durant, OK 74701. Phones: 800-752-4992; 580-924-2367. Fax: 580-924-5970. Web Site: http://www.netcommander.com. ICA: OK0344.

TV Market Ranking: Below 100 (SAND POINT). Franchise award date: N.A. Franchise expiration date: N.A. Began: N.A.

Channel capacity: 35 (not 2-way capable). Channels available but not in use: N.A.

Basic Service

Subscribers: N.A. Included in Durant

Programming (received off-air): KETA-TV (PBS) Oklahoma City; KTEN (ABC, CW, NBC) Ada; KXII (CBS, FOX, MNT) Sherman.

Programming (via satellite): CNN; ESPN; Spike TV; TBS Superstation.

Fee: $39.95 installation; $22.00 monthly.

Video-On-Demand: No

Internet Service

Operational: No.

Telephone Service

None

Miles of Plant: 7.0 (coaxial); None (fiber optic).

General Manager: Jeff Beck. Customer Service Manager: Lisa Hamill.

Ownership: James Cable LLC (MSO).

SAVANNA—Allegiance Communications, 707 W Saratoga St, Shawnee, OK 74804. Phones: 405-275-6923; 405-395-1131. Web Site: http://www.allegiance.tv. Also serves Kiowa & McAlester Army Ammunition Plant. ICA: OK0310.

TV Market Ranking: Outside TV Markets (Kiowa, McAlester Army Ammunition Plant, SAVANNA). Franchise award date: N.A. Franchise expiration date: N.A. Began: January 1, 1988.

Channel capacity: 45 (not 2-way capable). Channels available but not in use: N.A.

Basic Service

Subscribers: 519.

Programming (received off-air): KJRH-TV (NBC) Tulsa; KOET (PBS) Eufaula; KOTV-DT (CBS) Tulsa; KTEN (ABC, CW, NBC) Ada; KTUL (ABC) Tulsa; KXII (CBS, FOX, MNT) Sherman.

Programming (via satellite): A&E Networks; ABC Family Channel; AMC; Animal Planet; Cartoon Network; CNN; Country Music TV; C-SPAN; Discovery Channel; Disney Channel; ESPN; ESPN 2; Fox News Channel; Fox Sports Net; Fox Sports Southwest; Headline News; HGTV; History Channel; INSP; Lifetime; Nickelodeon; Outdoor Channel; QVC; Spike TV; Syfy; TBS Superstation; The Learning Channel; The Weather Channel; Travel Channel; Turner Classic Movies; Turner Network TV; USA Network; WGN America.

Fee: $30.00 installation; $21.95 monthly.

Pay Service 1

Pay Units: N.A.

Programming (via satellite): Cinemax; Showtime.

Pay Service 2

Pay Units: 141.

Programming (via satellite): HBO.

Fee: $9.00 monthly.

Video-On-Demand: No

Pay-Per-View

iN DEMAND (delivered digitally); Hot Choice; Playboy TV (delivered digitally); Fresh (delivered digitally); Shorteez (delivered digitally).

Internet Service

Operational: No.

Telephone Service

None

Miles of Plant: 36.0 (coaxial); None (fiber optic).

Chief Executive Officer: Bill Haggarty. Regional Vice President: Andrew Dearth. Vice President, Marketing: Tracy Bass.

Ownership: Allegiance Communications (MSO).

SCHULTER—Allegiance Communications, 707 W Saratoga St, Shawnee, OK 74804. Phones: 405-275-6923; 405-395-1131. Web Site: http://www.allegiance.tv. ICA: OK0311.

TV Market Ranking: Below 100 (SCHULTER). Franchise award date: January 1, 1989. Franchise expiration date: January 1, 2014. Began: September 1, 1989.

Channel capacity: 45 (not 2-way capable). Channels available but not in use: N.A.

Basic Service

Subscribers: N.A.

Programming (received off-air): KJRH-TV (NBC) Tulsa; KMYT-TV (MNT) Tulsa; KOED-TV (PBS) Tulsa; KOKI-TV (FOX) Tulsa; KOTV-DT (CBS) Tulsa; KQCW-DT (CW) Muskogee; KTPX-TV (ION) Okmulgee; KTUL (ABC) Tulsa; KWHB (IND) Tulsa.

Programming (via satellite): ABC Family Channel; Animal Planet; CNBC; CNN; Country Music TV; Discovery Channel; Disney Channel; ESPN; ESPN 2; MTV; Nickelodeon; Spike TV; Syfy; TBS Super-

station; Travel Channel; Turner Network TV; USA Network; WGN America.
Fee: $40.00 installation; $21.95 monthly; $1.96 converter.

Pay Service 1
Pay Units: N.A.
Programming (via satellite): HBO.
Fee: $10.00 monthly.

Video-On-Demand: No

Pay-Per-View
iN DEMAND (delivered digitally); Hot Choice (delivered digitally); Playboy TV (delivered digitally); Fresh (delivered digitally); Shorteez (delivered digitally).

Internet Service
Operational: No.

Telephone Service
None

Miles of Plant: 7.0 (coaxial); None (fiber optic).
Chief Executive Officer: Bill Haggarty. Regional Vice President: Andrew Dearth. Vice President, Marketing: Tracy Bass.
Ownership: Allegiance Communications (MSO).

SEILING—Pioneer Telephone Coop. Formerly [OK0122]. This cable system has converted to IPTV, PO Box 539, Kingfisher, OK 73750. Phones: 888-782-2667; 405-375-4111. E-mail: website@pldi.net. Web Site: http://www.ptci.com. ICA: OK5088.
TV Market Ranking: Outside TV Markets (SEILING). Franchise award date: N.A. Franchise expiration date: N.A. Began: September 30, 2004.
Channel capacity: N.A. Channels available but not in use: N.A.

Internet Service
Operational: Yes.

Telephone Service
Digital: Operational

General Manager: Richard Ruhl.

SEILING—Pioneer Telephone Coop. This cable system has converted to IPTV. See Seiling, OK [OK5088]. ICA: OK0122.

SEMINOLE—Suddenlink Communications, 12444 Powerscourt Dr, Saint Louis, MO 63131-3660. Phone: 405-382-2880. Fax: 405-382-6119. Web Site: http://www.suddenlink.com. Also serves Wewoka. ICA: OK0042.
TV Market Ranking: Below 100 (SEMINOLE, Wewoka). Franchise award date: N.A. Franchise expiration date: N.A. Began: November 17, 1975.
Channel capacity: 37 (operating 2-way). Channels available but not in use: N.A.

Basic Service
Subscribers: 3,517.
Programming (received off-air): KAUT-TV (MNT) Oklahoma City; KETA-TV (PBS) Oklahoma City; KFOR-TV (NBC) Oklahoma City; KOCB (CW) Oklahoma City; KOCO-TV (ABC) Oklahoma City; KOKH-TV (FOX) Oklahoma City; KOPX-TV (ION) Oklahoma City; KTBO-TV (TBN) Oklahoma City; KTEN (ABC, CW, NBC) Ada; KWTV-DT (CBS) Oklahoma City; allband FM.
Programming (via satellite): A&E Networks; ABC Family Channel; Animal Planet; Cartoon Network; CNBC; CNN; Country Music TV; C-SPAN; C-SPAN 2; Discovery Channel; Disney Channel; Fox News Channel; FX; Headline News; HGTV; Lifetime; MTV; Nickelodeon; QVC; Syfy; TBS Superstation; The Learning Channel; The Weather Channel; truTV; Turner Network TV; TV Guide Network; TV Land; Univision Studios; WGN America.
Fee: $60.00 installation; $11.51 monthly; $20.00 additional installation.

Expanded Basic Service 1
Subscribers: 2,829.
Programming (via satellite): AMC; BET Networks; Bravo; Comedy Central; E! Entertainment Television; ESPN; Eternal Word TV Network; Food Network; Fox Sports Southwest; History Channel; MSNBC; Spike TV; Travel Channel; USA Network; VH1.
Fee: $21.99 monthly.

Digital Basic Service
Subscribers: N.A.
Programming (via satellite): BBC America; Bio; Bloomberg Television; Discovery Digital Networks; DMX Music; Encore Action; ESPN Classic Sports; ESPNews; Fox Sports World; Fuse; G4; Golf Channel; GSN; History Channel International; Independent Film Channel; Lifetime Movie Network; Speed; Toon Disney; Turner Classic Movies; Versus.

Pay Service 1
Pay Units: 182.
Programming (via satellite): Cinemax; HBO; Showtime; Starz.
Fee: $20.00 installation; $10.00 monthly (Cinemax or HBO).

Digital Pay Service 1
Pay Units: N.A.
Programming (via satellite): Cinemax (multiplexed); HBO (multiplexed); Showtime (multiplexed); Starz (multiplexed); The Movie Channel (multiplexed).

Video-On-Demand: No

Pay-Per-View
ESPN Gameplan (delivered digitally); ESPN Now (delivered digitally); Playboy TV (delivered digitally); Shorteez (delivered digitally); Fresh (delivered digitally); Hot Choice (delivered digitally); iN DEMAND.

Internet Service
Operational: Yes.
Broadband Service: Suddenlink High Speed Internet.
Fee: $45.95 installation; $24.95 monthly.

Telephone Service
Digital: Operational
Fee: $49.95 monthly

Miles of Plant: 105.0 (coaxial); 31.0 (fiber optic).
Manager: Eugene Biller. Marketing Manager: Heather Eastwood. Chief Technician: Gene Reed.
Ownership: Cequel Communications LLC (MSO).

SENTINEL—Cable West, 314 W Main St, PO Box 237, Mountain View, OK 73062. Phones: 800-960-7912; 580-347-3220. Fax: 580-347-2143. ICA: OK0157.
TV Market Ranking: Outside TV Markets (SENTINEL). Franchise award date: January 2, 1979. Franchise expiration date: N.A. Began: June 1, 1955.
Channel capacity: 36 (not 2-way capable). Channels available but not in use: N.A.

Basic Service
Subscribers: 57.
Programming (received off-air): KETA-TV (PBS) Oklahoma City; KFOR-TV (NBC) Oklahoma City; KOCB (CW) Oklahoma City; KOCO-TV (ABC) Oklahoma City; KOKH-TV (FOX) Oklahoma City; KSWO-TV (ABC, TMO) Lawton; KWTV-DT (CBS) Oklahoma City.
Programming (via satellite): ABC Family Channel; CNN; Country Music TV; Discovery Channel; Disney Channel; ESPN; Fox News Channel; Headline News; Lifetime; Syfy; TBS Superstation; The Weather Channel; Trinity Broadcasting Network; Turner Network TV; USA Network; WGN America.
Fee: $29.95 installation; $15.98 monthly; $3.95 converter.

Pay Service 1
Pay Units: 9.
Programming (via satellite): Cinemax.
Fee: $9.00 monthly.

Pay Service 2
Pay Units: 15.
Programming (via satellite): HBO.
Fee: $10.00 monthly.

Video-On-Demand: No

Internet Service
Operational: No.

Telephone Service
None

Miles of Plant: 8.0 (coaxial); None (fiber optic).
Manager & Chief Technician: Mickey Davis.
Ownership: Mickey Davis (MSO).

SHATTUCK—Pioneer Telephone Coop. Formerly [OK0135]. This cable system has converted to IPTV, PO Box 539, Kingfisher, OK 73750. Phones: 888-782-2667; 405-375-4111. E-mail: website@pldi.net. Web Site: http://www.ptci.com. ICA: OK5089.
TV Market Ranking: Outside TV Markets (SHATTUCK). Franchise award date: N.A. Franchise expiration date: N.A. Began: September 28, 2005.
Channel capacity: N.A. Channels available but not in use: N.A.

Internet Service
Operational: Yes.

Telephone Service
Digital: Operational

General Manager: Richard Ruhl.

SHATTUCK—Pioneer Telephone Coop. This cable system has converted to IPTV. See Shattuck, OK [OK5089]. ICA: OK0135.

SHAWNEE—Allegiance Communications, 707 W Saratoga St, Shawnee, OK 74804. Phones: 405-275-6923; 405-395-1131. Fax: 405-275-0276. Web Site: http://www.allegiance.tv. Also serves Bethel Acres, Dale, Earlsboro, McLoud, Meeker, Prague & Tecumseh. ICA: OK0016.
TV Market Ranking: 39 (Bethel Acres, Dale, McLoud, Meeker, SHAWNEE, Tecumseh); Below 100 (Earlsboro, Prague). Franchise award date: October 1, 1978. Franchise expiration date: N.A. Began: October 1, 1979.
Channel capacity: N.A. Channels available but not in use: N.A.

Basic Service
Subscribers: 10,369.
Programming (received off-air): KAUT-TV (MNT) Oklahoma City; KETA-TV (PBS) Oklahoma City; KFOR-TV (NBC) Oklahoma City; KOCB (CW) Oklahoma City; KOCO-TV (ABC) Oklahoma City; KOKH-TV (FOX) Oklahoma City; KOPX-TV (ION) Oklahoma City; KSBI (IND) Oklahoma City; KTBO-TV (TBN) Oklahoma City; KTUZ-TV (TMO) Shawnee; KUOK-DT (UNV) Woodward; KWTV-DT (CBS) Oklahoma City; 14 FMs.
Programming (via satellite): A&E Networks; AMC; CNBC; CNN; Country Music TV; C-SPAN; Daystar TV Network; Discovery Channel; E! Entertainment Television; Fox News Channel; Headline News; INSP; Lifetime; MTV; Nickelodeon; QVC; Syfy; The Weather Channel; TV Land; USA Network; WGN America.
Fee: $20.00 installation; $21.95 monthly.

Expanded Basic Service 1
Subscribers: 10,211.
Programming (via satellite): ABC Family Channel; Animal Planet; BET Networks; Bravo; Cartoon Network; Comedy Central; C-SPAN 2; Disney Channel; ESPN; ESPN 2; ESPN U; Food Network; Fox Movie Channel; Fox Sports Southwest; FX; G4; Golf Channel; GSN; Hallmark Channel; HGTV; History Channel; MSNBC; National Geographic Channel; Outdoor Channel; Oxygen; RFD-TV; SoapNet; Speed; Spike TV; TBS Superstation; The Learning Channel; Travel Channel; truTV; Turner Classic Movies; Turner Network TV; Versus; VH1; WE tv.
Fee: $19.68 monthly.

Digital Basic Service
Subscribers: N.A.
Programming (via satellite): A&E HD; BBC America; Bio; Bloomberg Television; CMT Pure Country; Discovery en Espanol; Discovery Health Channel; Discovery Kids Channel; DIY Network; Encore (multiplexed); ESPN 2 HD; ESPN Classic Sports; ESPN Deportes; ESPN HD; ESPNews; Flix; Food Network HD; Fox College Sports Atlantic; Fox College Sports Central; Fox College Sports Pacific; Fox Deportes; Fox Soccer; Fuel TV; Great American Country; HD Theater; HDNet; HDNet Movies; HGTV HD; History Channel International; ID Investigation Discovery; Independent Film Channel; Lifetime Movie Network; Military Channel; MTV Hits; MTV Jams; MTV2; mtvU; Music Choice; National Geographic Channel HD Network; Nick Jr.; NickToons TV; Outdoor Channel 2 HD; Planet Green; Science; Sundance Channel; TeenNick; Toon Disney; Tr3s; Universal HD; VH1 Classic; VH1 Soul.

Digital Pay Service 1
Pay Units: 649.
Programming (via satellite): Cinemax (multiplexed); HBO HD; Showtime HD; Starz HDTV.
Fee: $20.00 installation; $10.45 monthly.

Digital Pay Service 2
Pay Units: N.A.
Programming (via satellite): Encore (multiplexed); Starz (multiplexed).

Digital Pay Service 3
Pay Units: 3,078.
Programming (via satellite): HBO (multiplexed).
Fee: $20.00 installation; $10.45 monthly.

Digital Pay Service 4
Pay Units: 466.
Programming (via satellite): Showtime (multiplexed).
Fee: $20.00 installation; $10.45 monthly.

Digital Pay Service 5
Pay Units: 267.
Programming (via satellite): The Movie Channel (multiplexed).
Fee: $10.45 monthly.
Video-On-Demand: No
Pay-Per-View
Hot Choice (delivered digitally); Special events (delivered digitally); Club Jenna (delivered digitally); iN DEMAND (delivered digitally); Fresh (delivered digitally); Shorteez (delivered digitally); Spice: Xcess (delivered digitally).
Internet Service
Operational: Yes.
Broadband Service: ISP Alliance.
Fee: $24.95 installation; $39.95 monthly.
Telephone Service
None
Miles of Plant: 532.0 (coaxial); None (fiber optic). Miles of plant (coax) includes miles of plant (fiber)
Chief Executive Officer: Bill Haggarty. Regional Vice President: Andrew Dearth. Vice President, Marketing: Tracy Bass.
Ownership: Allegiance Communications (MSO).

SHIDLER—Community Cablevision Co., 1550 W Rogers Blvd, PO Box 307, Skiatook, OK 74070-0307. Phone: 918-396-3019. Fax: 918-396-2081. E-mail: info@communitycablevision.com. Web Site: http://www.communitycablebroadband.com. ICA: OK0390.
TV Market Ranking: Outside TV Markets (SHIDLER). Franchise award date: N.A. Franchise expiration date: N.A. Began: N.A.
Channel capacity: 32 (not 2-way capable). Channels available but not in use: N.A.
Basic Service
Subscribers: 116.
Programming (received off-air): KDOR-TV (TBN) Bartlesville; KFOR-TV (NBC) Oklahoma City; KJRH-TV (NBC) Tulsa; KOED-TV (PBS) Tulsa; KOKI-TV (FOX) Tulsa; KOTV-DT (CBS) Tulsa; KQCW-DT (CW) Muskogee; KTPX-TV (ION) Okmulgee; KTUL (ABC) Tulsa.
Programming (via satellite): ABC Family Channel; Cartoon Network; CNN; Country Music TV; C-SPAN; Discovery Channel; Disney Channel; ESPN; ESPN 2; Fox Sports Southwest; Headline News; QVC; Spike TV; Syfy; TBS Superstation; The Learning Channel; The Weather Channel; Turner Classic Movies; Turner Network TV; USA Network; WGN America.
Fee: $29.95 installation; $18.00 monthly.
Video-On-Demand: No
Internet Service
Operational: Yes.
Fee: $44.95 monthly.
Telephone Service
None
President & General Manager: Dennis Soule.
Ownership: Community Cablevision Co. (MSO).

SKIATOOK—Community Cablevision Co., 1550 W Rogers Blvd, PO Box 307, Skiatook, OK 74070-0307. Phone: 918-396-3019. Fax: 918-396-2081. E-mail: info@communitycablevision.com. Web Site: http://www.communitycablebroadband.com. Also serves Sperry. ICA: OK0065.
TV Market Ranking: 54 (SKIATOOK, Sperry). Franchise award date: September 6, 1979. Franchise expiration date: N.A. Began: January 1, 1980.
Channel capacity: N.A. Channels available but not in use: N.A.
Basic Service
Subscribers: 1,542.
Programming (received off-air): KDOR-TV (TBN) Bartlesville; KGEB (IND) Tulsa; KJRH-TV (NBC) Tulsa; KOED-TV (PBS) Tulsa; KOKI-TV (FOX) Tulsa; KOTV-DT (CBS) Tulsa; KRSC-TV (ETV) Claremore; KTPX-TV (ION) Okmulgee; KTUL (ABC) Tulsa; KWHB (IND) Tulsa; allband FM.
Programming (via microwave): KTFO-CD (TEL) Austin.
Programming (via satellite): A&E Networks; ABC Family Channel; AMC; Animal Planet; BET Networks; Cartoon Network; CNN; Comedy Central; Country Music TV; C-SPAN; Discovery Channel; Discovery Health Channel; Disney Channel; ESPN; ESPN 2; ESPN Classic Sports; Food Network; Fox News Channel; Fox Sports Southwest; FX; Hallmark Channel; HGTV; History Channel; Lifetime; MoviePlex; MTV; National Geographic Channel; Nickelodeon; Outdoor Channel; Oxygen; QVC; Spike TV; Syfy; TBS Superstation; The Learning Channel; The Weather Channel; Travel Channel; truTV; Turner Classic Movies; Turner Network TV; TV Land; USA Network; VH1; WGN America.
Fee: $29.95 installation; $32.95 monthly; $10.00 additional installation.
Digital Basic Service
Subscribers: 103.
Programming (via satellite): AmericanLife TV Network; BBC America; Bio; Bloomberg Television; Bravo!; Church Channel; cloo; Current; Discovery Fit & Health; Discovery Health Channel; Discovery Home Channel; Discovery Kids Channel; Discovery Times Channel; DMX Music; ESPN 2; ESPN Classic Sports; ESPNews; Flix; Fox College Sports Atlantic; Fox College Sports Central; Fox College Sports Pacific; Fox Movie Channel; Fox Soccer; Fuse; G4; Golf Channel; Great American Country; GSN; Halogen Network; HGTV; History Channel; History Channel International; Independent Film Channel; International Television (ITV); JCTV; Lifetime Movie Network; Lime; MBC America; Military Channel; MTV Hits; MTV Jams; MTV2; National Geographic Channel; Nick Jr.; NickToons TV; Outdoor Channel; Ovation; Science Television; ShopNBC; Speed; Sundance Channel; Syfy; TeenNick; The Word Network; Toon Disney; Trinity Broadcasting Network; Turner Classic Movies; Versus; VH1 Classic; VH1 Country; VH1 Soul; WE tv.
Fee: $24.00 monthly.
Digital Pay Service 1
Pay Units: N.A.
Programming (via satellite): Cinemax (multiplexed); Encore (multiplexed); HBO (multiplexed); Showtime (multiplexed); Starz (multiplexed); The Movie Channel (multiplexed).
Fee: $11.50 monthly (HBO, Cinemax, Starz/Encore or Showtime/TMC/Flix/Sundance).
Video-On-Demand: No
Pay-Per-View
iN DEMAND (delivered digitally).
Internet Service
Operational: Yes.
Subscribers: 168.
Broadband Service: In-house.
Fee: $29.95 installation; $44.95 monthly.
Telephone Service
Digital: Operational
Fee: $39.95 monthly
Miles of Plant: 24.0 (coaxial); None (fiber optic).
President & General Manager: Dennis Soule.
Ownership: Community Cablevision Co. (MSO).

SNYDER—LongView Communications. Now served by MOUNTAIN PARK, OK [OK0300]. ICA: OK0158.

SOPER—Soper Cable TV, PO Box 222, Soper, OK 74759-0222. Phone: 580-345-2898. ICA: OK0312.
TV Market Ranking: Outside TV Markets (SOPER). Franchise award date: N.A. Franchise expiration date: N.A. Began: April 1, 1988.
Channel capacity: 22 (not 2-way capable). Channels available but not in use: N.A.
Basic Service
Subscribers: 80.
Programming (received off-air): KETA-TV (PBS) Oklahoma City; KTEN (ABC, CW, NBC) Ada; KXII (CBS, FOX, MNT) Sherman.
Programming (via satellite): ABC Family Channel; Discovery Channel; ESPN; Fox Sports Net; Spike TV; TBS Superstation; Trinity Broadcasting Network; Turner Network TV; USA Network; WGN America; WXIA-TV (NBC) Atlanta.
Programming (via translator): KTVT (CBS) Fort Worth.
Fee: $17.00 monthly.
Internet Service
Operational: No.
Telephone Service
None
Manager: Mary S. Loar.
Ownership: Mary S. Loar.

SPIRO—Suddenlink Communications, 12444 Powerscourt Dr, Saint Louis, MO 63131-3660. Phones: 800-999-6845; 314-315-9346; 314-965-2020. Web Site: http://www.suddenlink.com. ICA: OK0313.
TV Market Ranking: Below 100 (SPIRO). Franchise award date: August 1, 1969. Franchise expiration date: N.A. Began: August 1, 1969.
Channel capacity: N.A. Channels available but not in use: N.A.
Basic Service
Subscribers: 595.
Programming (received off-air): KAFT (PBS) Fayetteville; KETA-TV (PBS) Oklahoma City; KFSM-TV (CBS) Fort Smith; KFTA-TV (FOX, NBC) Fort Smith; KHBS (ABC, CW) Fort Smith; KJRH-TV (NBC) Tulsa; KOKI-TV (FOX) Tulsa; KPBI-CA (FOX) Fort Smith; KTUL (ABC) Tulsa; allband FM.
Programming (via satellite): A&E Networks; ABC Family Channel; CNN; Country Music TV; Discovery Channel; Disney Channel; ESPN; Headline News; History Channel; Nickelodeon; Spike TV; TBS Superstation; The Weather Channel; Turner Classic Movies; Turner Network TV; TV Land; USA Network; WGN America.
Fee: $35.00 installation; $19.95 monthly.
Pay Service 1
Pay Units: 71.
Programming (via satellite): HBO.
Fee: $11.00 monthly.
Pay Service 2
Pay Units: 44.
Programming (via satellite): Showtime.
Fee: $6.95 monthly.
Pay Service 3
Pay Units: 18.
Programming (via satellite): The Movie Channel.
Fee: $11.00 monthly.
Video-On-Demand: No
Internet Service
Operational: Yes. Began: October 6, 2003.
Broadband Service: Suddenlink High Speed Internet.
Fee: $45.95 installation; $24.95 monthly.
Telephone Service
Digital: Operational
Fee: $49.95 monthly
Miles of Plant: 38.0 (coaxial); None (fiber optic).
Regional Manager: Todd Cruthird. Manager: Dave Walker. Chief Technician: Carl Miller. Marketing Director: Beverly Gambell.
Ownership: Cequel Communications LLC (MSO).

STERLING—Southern Plains Cable, PO Box 165, Medicine Park, OK 73557. Phones: 800-218-1856; 580-365-4235. Fax: 580-365-4126. E-mail: office@wichitaonline.net. Web Site: http://www.southernplainscommunications.com. ICA: OK0208.
TV Market Ranking: Below 100 (STERLING). Franchise award date: N.A. Franchise expiration date: N.A. Began: October 1, 1982.
Channel capacity: N.A. Channels available but not in use: N.A.
Basic Service
Subscribers: 125.
Programming (received off-air): KAUT-TV (MNT) Oklahoma City; KAUZ-TV (CBS, CW) Wichita Falls; KETA-TV (PBS) Oklahoma City; KFDX-TV (NBC) Wichita Falls; KFOR-TV (NBC) Oklahoma City; KJTL (FOX) Wichita Falls; KOCB (CW) Oklahoma City; KOCO-TV (ABC) Oklahoma City; KOKH-TV (FOX) Oklahoma City; KSWO-TV (ABC, TMO) Lawton; KTBO-TV (TBN) Oklahoma City; KWTV-DT (CBS) Oklahoma City.
Programming (via satellite): A&E Networks; ABC Family Channel; AMC; Animal Planet; Cartoon Network; CNN; Country Music TV; C-SPAN; Discovery Channel; ESPN; ESPN 2; Eternal Word TV Network; Fox News Channel; HGTV; History Channel; Lifetime; Local Cable Weather; Nickelodeon; Outdoor Channel; ShopNBC; Spike TV; Syfy; TBS Superstation; The Learning Channel; The Weather Channel; Turner Classic Movies; Turner Network TV; TV Land; USA Network; WGN America.
Fee: $45.00 installation; $33.89 monthly.
Pay Service 1
Pay Units: N.A.
Programming (via satellite): Cinemax; HBO; Showtime; The Movie Channel.
Fee: $10.00 monthly (each).
Video-On-Demand: No
Internet Service
Operational: Yes.
Telephone Service
Analog: Not Operational
Digital: Planned
Miles of Plant: 6.0 (coaxial); None (fiber optic).
President: Dustin Hilliary.
Ownership: Southern Plains Cable (MSO).

STIGLER—Allegiance Communications, 707 W Saratoga St, Shawnee, OK 74804. Phones: 405-395-1131; 405-275-6923. Web Site: http://www.allegiance.tv. Also serves Haskell County & Whitefield. ICA: OK0081.
TV Market Ranking: Below 100 (Haskell County (portions)); Outside TV Markets (Haskell County (portions), STIGLER, Whitefield). Franchise award date: November 18, 1968. Franchise expiration date: N.A. Began: August 1, 1970.
Channel capacity: N.A. Channels available but not in use: N.A.

Basic Service
Subscribers: 1,082.
Programming (received off-air): KFSM-TV (CBS) Fort Smith; KJRH-TV (NBC) Tulsa; KMYT-TV (MNT) Tulsa; KOET (PBS) Eufaula; KOKI-TV (FOX) Tulsa; KOTV-DT (CBS) Tulsa; KQCW-DT (CW) Muskogee; KTUL (ABC) Tulsa; allband FM.
Programming (via satellite): A&E Networks; ABC Family Channel; AMC; Cartoon Network; CMT Pure Country; CNBC; CNN; C-SPAN; Discovery Channel; Disney Channel; ESPN; ESPN 2; ESPN Classic Sports; Food Network; Fox News Channel; Fox Sports Southwest; FX; Hallmark Channel; HGTV; History Channel; Lifetime; NFL Network; Nickelodeon; QVC; Spike TV; TBS Superstation; The Weather Channel; truTV; Turner Network TV; TV Land; USA Network; VH1.
Fee: $25.00 installation; $24.97 monthly.

Digital Basic Service
Subscribers: N.A.
Programming (via satellite): AmericanLife TV Network; Animal Planet; BBC America; Bio; Black Family Channel; Bloomberg Television; Bravo; Canal 52MX; Cine Latino; Cine Mexicano; cloo; CMT Pure Country; CNN en Espanol; Current; Discovery en Espanol; Discovery Fit & Health; Discovery Health Channel; Discovery Kids Channel; DMX Music; Encore (multiplexed); ESPN 2; ESPN Classic Sports; ESPNews; Flix; Fox College Sports Atlantic; Fox College Sports Central; Fox College Sports Pacific; Fox Deportes; Fox Movie Channel; Fox Soccer; Fuse; G4; Golf Channel; Great American Country; GSN; Halogen Network; HGTV; History Channel; History Channel en Espanol; History Channel International; ID Investigation Discovery; Independent Film Channel; Lifetime Movie Network; Military Channel; MTV Hits; MTV2; National Geographic Channel; Nick Jr.; NickToons TV; Outdoor Channel; Ovation; Planet Green; Science; ShopNBC; Speed; Style Network; Sundance Channel; Syfy; TeenNick; The Word Network; Toon Disney; Toon Disney en Espanol; Tr3s; Trinity Broadcasting Network; Turner Classic Movies; Versus; VH1 Classic; VH1 Soul; WE tv.

Pay Service 1
Pay Units: 68.
Programming (via satellite): Cinemax.
Fee: $7.95 monthly.

Pay Service 2
Pay Units: 278.
Programming (via satellite): Encore; Starz.

Pay Service 3
Pay Units: 77.
Programming (via satellite): HBO.
Fee: $10.50 monthly.

Pay Service 4
Pay Units: 46.
Programming (via satellite): Showtime.
Fee: $10.00 installation; $9.95 monthly.

Digital Pay Service 1
Pay Units: N.A.
Programming (via satellite): Cinemax (multiplexed); HBO (multiplexed); Showtime (multiplexed); Starz (multiplexed); The Movie Channel (multiplexed).

Video-On-Demand: No

Pay-Per-View
iN DEMAND (delivered digitally); Hot Choice (delivered digitally); Playboy TV (delivered digitally); Fresh (delivered digitally); Shorteez (delivered digitally).

Internet Service
Operational: Yes.
Fee: $24.95 installation; $39.95 monthly.

Telephone Service
None

Miles of Plant: 39.0 (coaxial); None (fiber optic).
Chief Executive Officer: Bill Haggarty. Regional Vice President: Andrew Dearth. Vice President, Marketing: Tracy Bass.
Ownership: Allegiance Communications (MSO).

STILLWATER—Suddenlink Communications, 12444 Powerscourt Dr, Saint Louis, MO 63131-3660. Phone: 405-377-7785. Fax: 405-372-3980. Web Site: http://www.suddenlink.com. Also serves Perkins. ICA: OK0008.
TV Market Ranking: Outside TV Markets (Perkins, STILLWATER). Franchise award date: January 27, 2000. Franchise expiration date: January 27, 2010. Began: November 1, 1971.
Channel capacity: 116 (operating 2-way). Channels available but not in use: N.A.

Basic Service
Subscribers: 14,487.
Programming (received off-air): KAUT-TV (MNT) Oklahoma City; KETA-TV (PBS) Oklahoma City; KFOR-TV (NBC) Oklahoma City; KOCB (CW) Oklahoma City; KOCO-TV (ABC) Oklahoma City; KOKH-TV (FOX) Oklahoma City; KOPX-TV (ION) Oklahoma City; KOTV-DT (CBS) Tulsa; KSBI (IND) Oklahoma City; KTBO-TV (TBN) Oklahoma City; KTUL (ABC) Tulsa; KWTV-DT (CBS) Oklahoma City; 39 FMs.
Programming (via satellite): C-SPAN; Daystar TV Network; NASA TV; QVC; The Weather Channel; TV Guide Network; WGN America.
Fee: $50.00 installation; $10.63 monthly; $.78 converter; $30.00 additional installation.

Expanded Basic Service 1
Subscribers: 12,167.
Programming (via satellite): A&E Networks; ABC Family Channel; AMC; Animal Planet; BET Networks; Bravo; Cartoon Network; CNBC; CNN; Comedy Central; Country Music TV; C-SPAN 2; Discovery Channel; Discovery Health Channel; Disney Channel; E! Entertainment Television; ESPN; ESPN 2; Eternal Word TV Network; Food Network; Fox News Channel; Fox Sports Southwest; FX; Headline News; HGTV; History Channel; Lifetime; MoviePlex; MSNBC; MTV; MTV2; News Now 53; Nickelodeon; Oxygen; Spike TV; Syfy; TBS Superstation; The Learning Channel; Travel Channel; truTV; Turner Network TV; TV Land; Univision Studios; USA Network; VH1.
Fee: $36.00 monthly.

Digital Basic Service
Subscribers: 2,856.
Programming (via satellite): BBC America; Bio; Bloomberg Television; DMX Music; ESPN; ESPN Classic Sports; ESPNews; Fox Movie Channel; Fox Sports World; Fuse; G4; GAS; Golf Channel; GSN; HD Theater; History Channel International; Independent Film Channel; Lifetime Movie Network; Nick Jr.; NickToons TV; Speed; Toon Disney; Turner Classic Movies; Versus.
Fee: $20.00 installation; $16.00 monthly.

Pay Service 1
Pay Units: 3,585.
Programming (via satellite): Cinemax.
Fee: $10.00 installation; $12.95 monthly.

Pay Service 2
Pay Units: 1,148.
Programming (via satellite): HBO.
Fee: $10.00 installation; $12.95 monthly.

Pay Service 3
Pay Units: 1,164.
Programming (via satellite): Showtime.
Fee: $10.00 installation; $12.95 monthly.

Pay Service 4
Pay Units: 3,644.
Programming (via satellite): Starz.
Fee: $10.00 installation; $6.75 monthly.

Pay Service 5
Pay Units: 3,696.
Programming (via satellite): Encore.
Fee: $10.00 installation; $1.75 monthly.

Digital Pay Service 1
Pay Units: N.A.
Programming (via satellite): Encore (multiplexed); HBO (multiplexed); HBO; Showtime (multiplexed); Showtime; Starz (multiplexed); The Movie Channel.

Video-On-Demand: No

Pay-Per-View
iN DEMAND (delivered digitally); Hot Choice (delivered digitally); Fresh (delivered digitally); Shorteez (delivered digitally); Playboy TV (delivered digitally).

Internet Service
Operational: Yes. Began: August 31, 2001.
Broadband Service: Suddenlink High Speed Internet.
Fee: $45.95 installation; $24.95 monthly.

Telephone Service
Digital: Operational
Fee: $49.95 monthly

Miles of Plant: 281.0 (coaxial); 53.0 (fiber optic).
Manager: Nicole Evans. Marketing Manager: Heather Eastwood. Chief Technician: Johnny Stanley.
Ownership: Cequel Communications LLC (MSO).

STILWELL—Allegiance Communications, 707 W Saratoga St, Shawnee, OK 74804. Phones: 405-275-6923; 405-395-1131. Web Site: http://www.allegiance.tv. ICA: OK0314.
TV Market Ranking: Below 100 (STILWELL). Franchise award date: N.A. Franchise expiration date: N.A. Began: July 1, 1982.
Channel capacity: N.A. Channels available but not in use: N.A.

Basic Service
Subscribers: 818.
Programming (received off-air): KFSM-TV (CBS) Fort Smith; KJRH-TV (NBC) Tulsa; KMYT-TV (MNT) Tulsa; KOED-TV (PBS) Tulsa; KOKI-TV (FOX) Tulsa; KOTV-DT (CBS) Tulsa; KQCW-DT (CW) Muskogee; KTUL (ABC) Tulsa.
Programming (via satellite): A&E Networks; ABC Family Channel; AMC; Animal Planet; Cartoon Network; CNBC; CNN; Comedy Central; Country Music TV; C-SPAN; Discovery Channel; Disney Channel; E! Entertainment Television; ESPN; ESPN 2; Fox News Channel; Fox Sports Southwest; FX; Headline News; HGTV; History Channel; Lifetime; MTV; Nickelodeon; Oxygen; QVC; SoapNet; Speed; Spike TV; Syfy; TBS Superstation; The Learning Channel; The Weather Channel; Travel Channel; Trinity Broadcasting Network; truTV; Turner Classic Movies; Turner Network TV; TV Guide Network; TV Land; USA Network; VH1; WGN America.
Fee: $30.00 installation; $21.95 monthly.

Digital Basic Service
Subscribers: N.A.
Programming (via satellite): BBC America; Bio; Bloomberg Television; Bravo; Chiller; cloo; CMT Pure Country; Current; Discovery Fit & Health; Discovery Health Channel; Discovery Kids Channel; DMX Music; Encore (multiplexed); ESPN Classic Sports; ESPNews; Flix; Fox Movie Channel; Fox Soccer; Fuse; G4; Golf Channel; GSN; History Channel International; ID Investigation Discovery; Independent Film Channel; Lifetime Movie Network; Military Channel; MTV Hits; MTV2; National Geographic Channel; Nick Jr.; NickToons TV; Outdoor Channel; Planet Green; RFD-TV; Science; Style Network; Sundance Channel; TeenNick; Toon Disney; Trinity Broadcasting Network; Versus; VH1 Classic; VH1 Soul; WE tv.

Digital Pay Service 1
Pay Units: N.A.
Programming (via satellite): Cinemax (multiplexed); HBO (multiplexed); Showtime (multiplexed); Starz (multiplexed); The Movie Channel.

Video-On-Demand: No

Pay-Per-View
iN DEMAND (delivered digitally); Club Jenna (delivered digitally); Playboy TV (delivered digitally); Fresh (delivered digitally); Spice: Xcess (delivered digitally).

Internet Service
Operational: No.

Telephone Service
None

Miles of Plant: 36.0 (coaxial); None (fiber optic).
Chief Executive Officer: Bill Haggarty. Regional Vice President: Andrew Dearth. Vice President, Marketing: Tracy Bass.
Ownership: Allegiance Communications (MSO).

STONEWALL—CommuniComm Services. Now served by COALGATE, OK [OK0120]. ICA: OK0379.

STRANG—Allegiance Communications, 707 W Saratoga St, Shawnee, OK 74804. Phone: 405-395-1131. Fax: 405-275-0276. Web Site: http://www.allegiance.tv. ICA: OK0259.
TV Market Ranking: Outside TV Markets (STRANG). Franchise award date: November 1, 1991. Franchise expiration date: November 1, 2016. Began: November 28, 1991.
Channel capacity: 35 (operating 2-way). Channels available but not in use: N.A.

Basic Service
Subscribers: N.A.
Programming (received off-air): KDOR-TV (TBN) Bartlesville; KELF-LP (IND) Miami; KJRH-TV (NBC) Tulsa; KMYT-TV (MNT) Tulsa; KOAM-TV (CBS) Pittsburg; KODE-TV (ABC) Joplin; KOED-TV (PBS) Tulsa; KOKI-TV (FOX) Tulsa; KOTV-DT (CBS) Tulsa; KQCW-DT (CW) Muskogee; KRSC-TV (ETV) Claremore; KSNF (NBC) Joplin;

KTPX-TV (ION) Okmulgee; KTUL (ABC) Tulsa; KWHB (IND) Tulsa.
Programming (via satellite): C-SPAN; QVC; WGN America.
Fee: $40.00 installation; $21.95 monthly; $1.96 converter; $19.95 additional installation.

Expanded Basic Service 1
Subscribers: N.A.
Programming (via satellite): A&E Networks; ABC Family Channel; AMC; Animal Planet; Bravo; Cartoon Network; CNBC; CNN; Comedy Central; Country Music TV; Discovery Channel; Disney Channel; E! Entertainment Television; ESPN; ESPN 2; Food Network; Fox News Channel; Fox Sports Southwest; FX; G4; Hallmark Channel; Headline News; HGTV; History Channel; Lifetime; Lifetime Movie Network; MSNBC; MTV; Nickelodeon; Outdoor Channel; Oxygen; RFD-TV; Spike TV; Syfy; TBS Superstation; The Learning Channel; The Weather Channel; Travel Channel; Turner Network TV; TV Land; USA Network; VH1.

Digital Basic Service
Subscribers: N.A.
Programming (via satellite): A&E HD; BBC America; Bio; Bloomberg Television; Chiller; cloo; CMT Pure Country; Current; Discovery Fit & Health; Discovery Health Channel; Discovery Kids Channel; Encore (multiplexed); ESPN 2 HD; ESPN Classic Sports; ESPN HD; ESPN U; ESPNews; Flix; Food Network HD; Fox College Sports Atlantic; Fox College Sports Central; Fox College Sports Pacific; Fox Movie Channel; Fox Soccer; Fuse; Golf Channel; Great American Country; GSN; HD Theater; HDNet; HDNet Movies; HGTV HD; History Channel International; ID Investigation Discovery; Independent Film Channel; Military Channel; MTV Hits; MTV2; Music Choice; National Geographic Channel; National Geographic Channel HD Network; Nick Jr.; NickToons TV; Outdoor Channel 2 HD; Planet Green; Science; ShopNBC; SoapNet; Speed; Style Network; Sundance Channel; TeenNick; The Word Network; Toon Disney; Turner Classic Movies; Universal HD; Versus; VH1 Classic; VH1 Soul; WE tv.

Digital Pay Service 1
Pay Units: N.A.
Programming (via satellite): Cinemax (multiplexed); Encore (multiplexed); Flix; HBO (multiplexed); HBO HD; Showtime (multiplexed); Showtime HD; Starz (multiplexed); Starz HDTV; The Movie Channel (multiplexed).

Video-On-Demand: No

Pay-Per-View
iN DEMAND (delivered digitally); Club Jenna (delivered digitally); Spice: Xcess (delivered digitally); Playboy TV (delivered digitally); Fresh (delivered digitally).

Internet Service
Operational: Yes.
Fee: $24.95 installation; $39.95 monthly.

Telephone Service
None

Miles of Plant: 4.0 (coaxial); None (fiber optic).

Chief Executive Officer: Bill Haggarty. Regional Vice President: Andrew Dearth. Vice President, Marketing: Tracy Bass.

Ownership: Allegiance Communications (MSO).

STRATFORD—Allegiance Communications, 707 W Saratoga St, Shawnee, OK 74804. Phones: 405-395-1131; 405-275-6923. Web Site: http://www.allegiance.tv. ICA: OK0315.

TV Market Ranking: Below 100 (STRATFORD). Franchise award date: June 3, 1980. Franchise expiration date: N.A. Began: June 1, 1981.

Channel capacity: 54 (operating 2-way). Channels available but not in use: N.A.

Basic Service
Subscribers: 228.
Programming (received off-air): KAUT-TV (MNT) Oklahoma City; KETA-TV (PBS) Oklahoma City; KFOR-TV (NBC) Oklahoma City; KOCB (CW) Oklahoma City; KOCO-TV (ABC) Oklahoma City; KOKH-TV (FOX) Oklahoma City; KTEN (ABC, CW, NBC) Ada; KWTV-DT (CBS) Oklahoma City.
Programming (via satellite): C-SPAN; QVC; Trinity Broadcasting Network; WGN America.
Fee: $21.95 monthly.

Expanded Basic Service 1
Subscribers: N.A.
Programming (via satellite): A&E Networks; ABC Family Channel; AMC; Animal Planet; CNBC; CNN; Comedy Central; Country Music TV; C-SPAN 2; Discovery Channel; Disney Channel; E! Entertainment Television; ESPN; Fox News Channel; Fox Sports Southwest; Headline News; History Channel; Lifetime; MTV; Nickelodeon; SoapNet; Spike TV; Syfy; TBS Superstation; The Learning Channel; The Weather Channel; Travel Channel; Turner Network TV; TV Land; USA Network; WE tv.

Digital Basic Service
Subscribers: N.A.
Programming (via satellite): BBC America; Bio; Bloomberg Television; Bravo; Chiller; cloo; CMT Pure Country; Current; Discovery Fit & Health; Discovery Health Channel; Discovery Kids Channel; DMX Music; Encore (multiplexed); ESPN Classic Sports; ESPNews; Flix; Fox College Sports Atlantic; Fox College Sports Central; Fox College Sports Pacific; Fox Movie Channel; Fox Soccer; Fuse; G4; Golf Channel; Great American Country; GSN; HGTV; History Channel International; ID Investigation Discovery; Independent Film Channel; Lifetime Movie Network; Military Channel; MTV Hits; MTV2; National Geographic Channel; Nick Jr.; NickToons TV; Planet Green; RFD-TV; Science; ShopNBC; Speed; Style Network; Sundance Channel; TeenNick; Toon Disney; Turner Classic Movies; Versus; VH1 Classic; VH1 Soul.

Digital Pay Service 1
Pay Units: N.A.
Programming (via satellite): Cinemax (multiplexed); HBO (multiplexed); Showtime (multiplexed); Starz (multiplexed); The Movie Channel (multiplexed).

Video-On-Demand: No

Pay-Per-View
iN DEMAND (delivered digitally); Spice: Xcess (delivered digitally); Fresh (delivered digitally); Playboy TV (delivered digitally); Club Jenna (delivered digitally).

Internet Service
Operational: No.
Fee: $24.95 installation; $39.95 monthly.

Telephone Service
None

Miles of Plant: 13.0 (coaxial); None (fiber optic).

Chief Executive Officer: Bill Haggarty. Regional Vice President: Andrew Dearth. Vice President, Marketing: Tracy Bass.

Ownership: Allegiance Communications (MSO).

STRINGTOWN—CommuniComm Services, 1501 W Mississippi St, PO Box 597, Durant, OK 74701. Phones: 781-356-8701 (administrative office); 800-752-4992; 580-924-2367. Fax: 580-924-5970. Web Site: http://www.netcommander.com. ICA: OK0339.

TV Market Ranking: Outside TV Markets (STRINGTOWN). Franchise award date: N.A. Franchise expiration date: N.A. Began: January 1, 1988.

Channel capacity: 62 (not 2-way capable). Channels available but not in use: N.A.

Basic Service
Subscribers: N.A. Included in Durant
Programming (received off-air): KETA-TV (PBS) Oklahoma City; KFOR-TV (NBC) Oklahoma City; KOCO-TV (ABC) Oklahoma City; KTEN (ABC, CW, NBC) Ada; KWTV-DT (CBS) Oklahoma City; KXII (CBS, FOX, MNT) Sherman.
Programming (via satellite): C-SPAN; C-SPAN 2; Trinity Broadcasting Network.
Fee: $49.95 installation; $22.00 monthly.

Expanded Basic Service 1
Subscribers: N.A.
Programming (via satellite): A&E Networks; ABC Family Channel; American Movie Classics; Animal Planet; BET Networks; Bravo; Cartoon Network; CNBC; CNN; Comedy Central; Country Music TV; Discovery Channel; Disney Channel; E! Entertainment Television; ESPN; ESPN 2; Food Network; Fox News Channel; Fox Sports Net; FX; Hallmark Channel; Headline News; HGTV; History Channel; Lifetime; MSNBC; MTV; Nickelodeon; Noggin; QVC; ShopNBC; Spike TV; Syfy; TBS Superstation; The Learning Channel; The Weather Channel; Travel Channel; truTV; Turner Classic Movies; Turner Network TV; TV Guide Network; TV Land; USA Network; VH1; WE tv.

Digital Basic Service
Subscribers: N.A.
Programming (via satellite): BBC America; Bio; Bloomberg Television; Bravo; Chiller; Church Channel; cloo; CMT Pure Country; Current; Discovery Fit & Health; Discovery Health Channel; Discovery Kids Channel; Disney XD; DMX Music; ESPN 2; ESPN Classic Sports; ESPNews; Fox Business Channel; Fox Movie Channel; Fox Soccer; Fuse; G4; Golf Channel; Great American Country; GSN; Halogen Network; HGTV; History Channel; History Channel International; ID Investigation Discovery; Independent Film Channel; JCTV; Lifetime Movie Network; Military Channel; MTV Hits; MTV Jams; MTV2; National Geographic Channel; Nick Jr.; NickToons TV; Outdoor Channel; PBS Kids Sprout; Planet Green; RFD-TV; Science; ShopNBC; SoapNet; Speed; Style Network; Sundance Channel; Syfy; TeenNick; The Word Network; Trinity Broadcasting Network; Turner Classic Movies; Versus; VH1 Classic; VH1 Soul; WE tv.

Pay Service 1
Pay Units: N.A.
Programming (via satellite): Cinemax; Encore; HBO (multiplexed); Starz.

Digital Pay Service 1
Pay Units: N.A.
Programming (via satellite): Cinemax; Encore; Flix; HBO (multiplexed); Showtime (multiplexed); Starz (multiplexed); The Movie Channel (multiplexed).

Video-On-Demand: No

Internet Service
Operational: No.

Telephone Service
None

Miles of Plant: 6.0 (coaxial); None (fiber optic).

General Manager: Jeff Beck. Customer Service Manager: Lisa Hamill.

Ownership: James Cable LLC (MSO).

STROUD—Allegiance Communications, 707 W Saratoga St, Shawnee, OK 74804. Phones: 405-395-1131; 405-275-6923. Web Site: http://www.allegiance.tv. ICA: OK0100.

TV Market Ranking: Outside TV Markets (STROUD). Franchise award date: July 12, 1994. Franchise expiration date: N.A. Began: May 1, 1981.

Channel capacity: N.A. Channels available but not in use: N.A.

Basic Service
Subscribers: 664.
Programming (received off-air): KAUT-TV (MNT) Oklahoma City; KETA-TV (PBS) Oklahoma City; KFOR-TV (NBC) Oklahoma City; KOCB (CW) Oklahoma City; KOCO-TV (ABC) Oklahoma City; KOKH-TV (FOX) Oklahoma City; KOTV-DT (CBS) Tulsa; KTBO-TV (TBN) Oklahoma City; KWTV-DT (CBS) Oklahoma City.
Programming (via satellite): A&E Networks; ABC Family Channel; AMC; Animal Planet; Bravo; Cartoon Network; CMT Pure Country; CNBC; CNN; C-SPAN; C-SPAN 2; Discovery Channel; Disney Channel; ESPN; ESPN 2; ESPN Classic Sports; Food Network; Fox News Channel; Fox Sports Southwest; FX; Hallmark Channel; Headline News; HGTV; History Channel; Lifetime; MTV; NFL Network; Nickelodeon; QVC; Spike TV; Syfy; TBS Superstation; The Learning Channel; The Weather Channel; Turner Network TV; USA Network; WGN America.
Fee: $50.00 installation; $29.94 monthly; $3.30 converter; $30.00 additional installation.

Digital Basic Service
Subscribers: 48.
Programming (via satellite): AmericanLife TV Network; BBC America; Bio; Black Family Channel; Bloomberg Television; Bravo!; Canal 52MX; Cine Latino; Cine Mexicano; CMT Pure Country; CNN en Espanol; Current; Discovery en Espanol; Discovery Fit & Health; Discovery Health Channel; Discovery Home Channel; DMX Music; Encore (multiplexed); ESPN 2; ESPN Classic Sports; ESPNews; Flix; Fox College Sports Atlantic; Fox College Sports Central; Fox College Sports Pacific; Fox Deportes; Fox Movie Channel; Fox Soccer; Fuse; G4; GAS; Golf Channel; Great American Country; GSN; Halogen Network; HGTV; History Channel; History Channel en Espanol; History Channel International; ID Investigation Discovery; Independent Film Channel; Lifetime Movie Network; Lime; Military Channel; MTV2; mtvU; National Geographic Channel; Nick Jr.; NickToons TV; Outdoor Channel; Ovation; Science; ShopNBC; Speed; Style Network; Sundance Channel; Syfy; The Word Network; Toon Disney; Toon Disney en Espanol; Tr3s; Trinity Broadcasting Network; Trio; Turner Classic Movies; TV Land; Versus; VH1 Classic; VH1 Soul; WE tv.
Fee: $13.95 monthly.

Pay Service 1
Pay Units: 158.
Programming (via satellite): Encore; HBO; Showtime; Starz.
Fee: $10.00 installation; $14.19 monthly.

Digital Pay Service 1
Pay Units: N.A.
Programming (via satellite): Cinemax (multiplexed); HBO (multiplexed); Showtime (multiplexed); Starz (multiplexed); The Movie Channel (multiplexed).

Pay-Per-View
iN DEMAND (delivered digitally); Hot Choice (delivered digitally); Fresh (delivered digitally); Spice: Xcess (delivered digitally); Club Jenna (delivered digitally); Playboy TV (delivered digitally).

Internet Service
Operational: No.

Telephone Service
None

Miles of Plant: 26.0 (coaxial); None (fiber optic).

Chief Executive Officer: Bill Haggarty. Regional Vice President: Andrew Dearth. Vice President, Marketing: Tracy Bass.

Ownership: Allegiance Communications (MSO).

STUART—Allegiance Communications, 707 W Saratoga St, Shawnee, OK 74804. Phones: 405-395-1131; 405-275-6923. Web Site: http://www.allegiance.tv. Also serves Arpelar & Haywood. ICA: OK0356.

TV Market Ranking: Below 100 (STUART); Outside TV Markets (Arpelar, Haywood). Franchise award date: N.A. Franchise expiration date: October 10, 2009. Began: N.A.

Channel capacity: 36 (not 2-way capable). Channels available but not in use: N.A.

Basic Service
Subscribers: 254.
Programming (received off-air): KFOR-TV (NBC) Oklahoma City; KOED-TV (PBS) Tulsa; KOKI-TV (FOX) Tulsa; KOTV-DT (CBS) Tulsa; KQCW-DT (CW) Muskogee; KTEN (ABC, CW, NBC) Ada; KTUL (ABC) Tulsa.
Programming (via satellite): A&E Networks; ABC Family Channel; AMC; Animal Planet; CMT Pure Country; CNN; Discovery Channel; Disney Channel; ESPN; Fox Sports Southwest; History Channel; Lifetime; Nickelodeon; Spike TV; Syfy; TBS Superstation; The Weather Channel; Turner Network TV; TV Land; USA Network; WGN America.
Fee: $21.95 monthly.

Pay Service 1
Pay Units: N.A.
Programming (via satellite): Encore; HBO; Showtime; Starz.
Fee: $10.00 monthly (each).

Pay-Per-View
iN DEMAND (delivered digitally); Hot Choice (delivered digitally); Playboy TV (delivered digitally); Fresh (delivered digitally); Shorteez (delivered digitally).

Internet Service
Operational: No.

Telephone Service
None

Miles of Plant: 31.0 (coaxial); None (fiber optic).

Chief Executive Officer: Bill Haggarty. Regional Vice President: Andrew Dearth. Vice President, Marketing: Tracy Bass.

Ownership: Allegiance Communications (MSO).

TAHLEQUAH—Tahlequah Cable TV Inc., 110 E Keetoowah St, PO Box 1689, Tahlequah, OK 74465-1689. Phone: 918-456-1102. Fax: 918-456-1172. E-mail: tahlequahcabletvcs@cablelynx.com. Web Site: http://www.tahlequahcabletv.com. Also serves Park Hill. ICA: OK0034.

TV Market Ranking: Below 100 (Park Hill, TAHLEQUAH). Franchise award date: May 7, 2002. Franchise expiration date: May 7, 2027. Began: July 1, 1980.

Channel capacity: 78 (operating 2-way). Channels available but not in use: N.A.

Basic Service
Subscribers: 4,260.
Programming (received off-air): KDOR-TV (TBN) Bartlesville; KGEB (IND) Tulsa; KJRH-TV (NBC) Tulsa; KMYT-TV (MNT) Tulsa; KOED-TV (PBS) Tulsa; KOKI-TV (FOX) Tulsa; KOTV-DT (CBS) Tulsa; KRSC-TV (ETV) Claremore; KTPX-TV (ION) Okmulgee; KTUL (ABC) Tulsa; KWHB (IND) Tulsa; allband FM.
Programming (via satellite): A&E Networks; ABC Family Channel; AMC; Animal Planet; Cartoon Network; CNN; Comedy Central; Country Music TV; C-SPAN; C-SPAN 2; Discovery Channel; Disney Channel; DIY Network; ESPN; ESPN 2; Food Network; Fox News Channel; Fox Sports Southwest; FX; GalaVision; Hallmark Channel; Headline News; HGTV; History Channel; Lifetime; MTV; Nickelodeon; ShopNBC; Spike TV; Syfy; TBS Superstation; The Learning Channel; The Weather Channel; Travel Channel; Turner Classic Movies; Turner Network TV; TV Guide Network; TV Land; Univision Studios; USA Network; VH1; WGN America.
Fee: $40.00 installation; $54.45 monthly; $20.00 additional installation.

Digital Basic Service
Subscribers: 433.
Programming (via satellite): AmericanLife TV Network; BBC America; Bio; CMT Pure Country; Discovery Fit & Health; Discovery Health Channel; Discovery Kids Channel; DMX Music; ESPNews; Fox Soccer; FSN Digital Atlantic; FSN Digital Central; FSN Digital Pacific; G4; Golf Channel; Great American Country; GSN; Halogen Network; History Channel International; ID Investigation Discovery; Lifetime Movie Network; Military Channel; MTV Hits; MTV Jams; MTV2; National Geographic Channel; Nick Jr.; Nick Too; NickToons TV; Outdoor Channel; Planet Green; Science; SoapNet; Speed; TeenNick; Toon Disney; Tr3s; VH1 Classic; VH1 Soul; WE tv.
Fee: $10.00 monthly.

Digital Pay Service 1
Pay Units: 961.
Programming (via satellite): Cinemax (multiplexed); Encore (multiplexed); HBO (multiplexed); Showtime (multiplexed); Starz (multiplexed).
Fee: $12.95 monthly (Cinemax), $14.95 monthly (HBO or Starz/Encore).

Video-On-Demand: No

Pay-Per-View
iN DEMAND (delivered digitally); special events.

Internet Service
Operational: Yes. Began: January 1, 2000.
Subscribers: 663.
Broadband Service: Cablelynx.
Fee: $24.95-$44.95 monthly.

Telephone Service
Analog: Not Operational
Digital: Operational
Fee: $45.70 monthly

Miles of Plant: 186.0 (coaxial); None (fiber optic). Additional miles planned: 3.0 (coaxial).

General Manager: Robert Sluptick. Chief Technician: Steve Crone. Office Manager: Shirley Little.

Ownership: WEHCO Video Inc. (MSO).

TALALA—Formerly served by Quality Cablevision of Oklahoma Inc. No longer in operation. ICA: OK0340.

TALIHINA—Allegiance Communications, 707 W Saratoga St, Shawnee, OK 74804. Phones: 405-395-1131; 405-275-6923. Web Site: http://www.allegiance.tv. ICA: OK0136.

TV Market Ranking: Outside TV Markets (TALIHINA). Franchise award date: N.A. Franchise expiration date: N.A. Began: February 1, 1972.

Channel capacity: 36 (not 2-way capable). Channels available but not in use: N.A.

Basic Service
Subscribers: 619.
Programming (received off-air): KFDF-CA Fort Smith; KFSM-TV (CBS) Fort Smith; KFTA-TV (FOX, NBC) Fort Smith; KHBS (ABC, CW) Fort Smith; KJRH-TV (NBC) Tulsa; KOET (PBS) Eufaula; KOTV-DT (CBS) Tulsa; KTUL (ABC) Tulsa; 1 FM.
Programming (via satellite): ABC Family Channel; AMC; CMT Pure Country; CNN; C-SPAN; Discovery Channel; Disney Channel; ESPN; ESPN 2; Nickelodeon; QVC; Spike TV; TBS Superstation; The Learning Channel; The Weather Channel; Trinity Broadcasting Network; Turner Network TV; USA Network; WGN America.
Fee: $21.95 monthly.

Pay Service 1
Pay Units: N.A.
Programming (via satellite): Encore; HBO; Showtime; Starz; The Movie Channel.
Fee: $10.00 monthly (each).

Pay-Per-View
iN DEMAND (delivered digitally); Hot Choice (delivered digitally); Playboy TV (delivered digitally); Fresh (delivered digitally); Shorteez (delivered digitally).

Internet Service
Operational: No.

Telephone Service
None

Miles of Plant: 21.0 (coaxial); None (fiber optic).

Chief Executive Officer: Bill Haggarty. Regional Vice President: Andrew Dearth. Vice President, Marketing: Tracy Bass.

Ownership: Allegiance Communications (MSO).

TALOGA—Taloga Cable TV, 114A S Broadway, PO Box 218, Taloga, OK 73667-0218. Phone: 580-328-5262. Fax: 580-328-5262. E-mail: support@talogatv.com. ICA: OK0222.

TV Market Ranking: Outside TV Markets (TALOGA). Franchise award date: March 1, 1980. Franchise expiration date: N.A. Began: March 1, 1980.

Channel capacity: N.A. Channels available but not in use: N.A.

Basic Service
Subscribers: 62.
Programming (received off-air): KAUT-TV (MNT) Oklahoma City; KFOR-TV (NBC) Oklahoma City; KOCB (CW) Oklahoma City; KOCO-TV (ABC) Oklahoma City; KOKH-TV (FOX) Oklahoma City; KWET (PBS) Cheyenne; KWTV-DT (CBS) Oklahoma City.
Programming (via satellite): A&E Networks; Comedy Central; Country Music TV; C-SPAN; C-SPAN 2; Discovery Channel; ESPN; Food Network; Fox News Channel; Fox Sports Southwest; G4; Hallmark Channel; History Channel; ION Television; Lifetime; Nickelodeon; QVC; Spike TV; Syfy; TBS Superstation; The Learning Channel; The Weather Channel; Travel Channel; Trinity Broadcasting Network; Turner Classic Movies; Turner Network TV; USA Network.
Fee: $30.00 installation; $34.00 monthly; $3.00 converter.

Pay Service 1
Pay Units: 50.
Programming (via satellite): Cinemax; HBO; Showtime; Starz; The Movie Channel.
Fee: $12.00 monthly (each).

Video-On-Demand: No

Internet Service
Operational: Yes. Began: January 1, 2000.
Subscribers: 60.
Broadband Service: InterTECH.
Fee: $150.00 installation; $35.00 monthly.

Telephone Service
None

Miles of Plant: 9.0 (coaxial); None (fiber optic).

Manager & Chief Technician: Glenn Gore.

Ownership: Taloga Cable TV.

TERRAL—Formerly served by Almega Cable. No longer in operation. ICA: OK0229.

THOMAS—Pioneer Telephone Coop. Formerly served by [OK0155]. This cable system has converted to IPTV., PO Box 539, Kingfisher, OK 73750. Phones: 405-375-4111; 888-782-2667. E-mail: website@pldi.net. Web Site: http://www.ptci.com. ICA: OK5083.

TV Market Ranking: Outside TV Markets (THOMAS). Franchise award date: N.A. Franchise expiration date: N.A. Began: N.A.

Channel capacity: N.A. Channels available but not in use: N.A.

Internet Service
Operational: Yes.

Telephone Service
Digital: Operational

General Manager: Richard Ruhl.

THOMAS—Pioneer Telephone Coop. This cable system has converted to IPTV. See Thomas, OK [OK5083]. ICA: OK0155.

TIPTON—LakeView Cable, Hwy 115, PO Box 460, Cache, OK 73527-0460. Phone: 580-429-8800. Fax: 580-429-6599. Web Site: http://www.lvcisp.com. ICA: OK0191.

TV Market Ranking: Outside TV Markets (TIPTON). Franchise award date: May 5, 1980. Franchise expiration date: N.A. Began: August 1, 1981.

Channel capacity: 77 (operating 2-way). Channels available but not in use: N.A.

Basic Service
Subscribers: 200.
Programming (received off-air): KAUZ-TV (CBS, CW) Wichita Falls; KETA-TV (PBS) Oklahoma City; KFDX-TV (NBC) Wichita Falls; KJBO-LP (MNT) Wichita Falls; KJTL (FOX) Wichita Falls; KSWO-TV (ABC, TMO) Lawton; KWTV-DT (CBS) Oklahoma City.

Programming (via satellite): C-SPAN 2; INSP; QVC; Trinity Broadcasting Network.
Fee: $50.00 installation; $17.98 monthly; $3.95 converter.

Expanded Basic Service 1
Subscribers: N.A.
Programming (received off-air): KSMO-TV (MNT) Kansas City.
Programming (via satellite): A&E Networks; ABC Family Channel; AMC; Animal Planet; BET Networks; Cartoon Network; CNN; Comedy Central; C-SPAN; Discovery Channel; Disney Channel; E! Entertainment Television; ESPN; ESPN 2; FamilyNet; Food Network; Fox News Channel; Great American Country; Headline News; HGTV; History Channel; Lifetime; MSNBC; Nickelodeon; Outdoor Channel; Syfy; TBS Superstation; Telemundo; The Learning Channel; The Weather Channel; Toon Disney; Travel Channel; Turner Network TV; USA Network; WGN America.
Fee: $21.97 monthly.

Digital Basic Service
Subscribers: N.A. Included in Blair
Programming (via satellite): AmericanLife TV Network; BBC America; Bio; Bloomberg Television; Discovery Digital Networks; DMX Music; Encore (multiplexed); ESPN Classic Sports; ESPNews; Fox Movie Channel; Fox Soccer; G4; Golf Channel; GSN; Halogen Network; History Channel International; Lifetime Movie Network; Speed; Style Network; Toon Disney; Turner Classic Movies.
Fee: $17.00 monthly.

Pay Service 1
Pay Units: N.A.
Programming (via satellite): Cinemax; HBO; Showtime; The Movie Channel.
Fee: $8.95 monthly (TMC), $10.95 monthly (Showtime or Cinemax), $12.95 monthly (HBO).

Digital Pay Service 1
Pay Units: 16.
Programming (via satellite): Cinemax (multiplexed); Flix; HBO (multiplexed); Showtime (multiplexed); Starz (multiplexed); The Movie Channel (multiplexed).
Fee: $8.95 monthly (TMC), $10.95 monthly (Showtime or Cinemax), $12.95 monthly (HBO).

Video-On-Demand: No

Pay-Per-View
iN DEMAND (delivered digitally); Hot Choice (delivered digitally); Playboy TV (delivered digitally); Fresh (delivered digitally); Shorteez (delivered digitally).

Internet Service
Operational: Yes.
Broadband Service: In-house.
Fee: $29.95 monthly.

Telephone Service
Digital: Planned

Miles of Plant: 9.0 (coaxial); None (fiber optic).
Manager: Bill Rowell. Chief Technician: Mike Rowell.
Ownership: Lakeview Cable Inc. (MSO).

TISHOMINGO—CommuniComm Services, 1501 W Mississippi St, PO Box 597, Durant, OK 74701. Phones: 800-752-4992; 580-924-2367. Fax: 580-924-5970. Web Site: http://www.netcommander.com. Also serves Achille, Bokchito, Buncombe Creek, Colbert, Johnston County (portions), Kingston & Ravia. ICA: OK0064.
TV Market Ranking: Below 100 (Achille, Buncombe Creek, Colbert, Johnston County (portions), Kingston); Outside TV Markets (Bokchito, Johnston County (portions), Ravia, TISHOMINGO). Franchise award date: N.A. Franchise expiration date: N.A. Began: March 15, 1972.
Channel capacity: N.A. Channels available but not in use: N.A.

Basic Service
Subscribers: N.A. Included in Durant
Programming (received off-air): KETA-TV (PBS) Oklahoma City; KTEN (ABC, CW, NBC) Ada; KWTV-DT (CBS) Oklahoma City; KXII (CBS, FOX, MNT) Sherman; WFAA (ABC) Dallas; allband FM.
Programming (via satellite): CW+; Local Cable Weather; QVC; Telemundo.
Fee: $49.95 installation; $31.00 monthly.

Expanded Basic Service 1
Subscribers: N.A.
Programming (via satellite): A&E Networks; ABC Family Channel; AMC; Animal Planet; BET Networks; Bravo; Cartoon Network; CNBC; CNN; Comedy Central; Country Music TV; C-SPAN; Discovery Channel; Disney Channel; E! Entertainment Television; ESPN; ESPN 2; ESPN Classic Sports; ESPNews; Food Network; Fox News Channel; Fox Sports Southwest; FX; Hallmark Channel; Headline News; HGTV; History Channel; ION Television; Lifetime; MSNBC; MTV; MyNetworkTV Inc.; Nick Jr.; Nickelodeon; Outdoor Channel; ShopNBC; Spike TV; Syfy; TBS Superstation; The Learning Channel; The Weather Channel; Travel Channel; Trinity Broadcasting Network; truTV; Turner Network TV; TV Guide Network; TV Land; USA Network; VH1; WE tv.

Digital Basic Service
Subscribers: N.A.
Programming (via satellite): AmericanLife TV Network; BBC America; Bio; Bloomberg Television; Bravo; Church Channel; CMT Pure Country; Current; Daystar TV Network; Discovery Fit & Health; Discovery Health Channel; Discovery Home Channel; Discovery Kids Channel; Discovery Times Channel; DMX Music; ESPN Classic Sports; Fox Movie Channel; Fox Soccer; Fuse; G4; Golf Channel; Great American Country; GSN; Halogen Network; HGTV; History Channel; History Channel International; Independent Film Channel; JCTV; Lifetime Movie Network; Military Channel; MTV Hits; MTV Jams; MTV2; National Geographic Channel; Nick Jr.; NickToons TV; Outdoor Channel; Ovation; RFD-TV; Science; ShopNBC; SoapNet; Speed; Style Network; TeenNick; The Word Network; Toon Disney; Trinity Broadcasting Network; Turner Classic Movies; Versus; VH1 Classic; VH1 Soul; WE tv.

Digital Pay Service 1
Pay Units: N.A.
Programming (via satellite): Cinemax (multiplexed); Encore (multiplexed); Flix; HBO (multiplexed); Showtime (multiplexed); Starz (multiplexed); The Movie Channel (multiplexed).

Video-On-Demand: No

Pay-Per-View
iN DEMAND (delivered digitally); Hot Choice (delivered digitally); Playboy TV (delivered digitally); Fresh (delivered digitally); Spice: Xcess (delivered digitally); Club Jenna (delivered digitally).

Internet Service
Operational: Yes.
Broadband Service: Net Commander.
Fee: $39.95 installation; $51.95 monthly.

Telephone Service
None

Miles of Plant: 121.0 (coaxial); None (fiber optic).
General Manager: Jeff Beck. Customer Service Manager: Lisa Hamill.
Ownership: James Cable LLC (MSO).

TRYON—Allegiance Communications, 707 W Saratoga St, Shawnee, OK 74804. Phones: 405-275-6923; 405-395-1131. Web Site: http://www.allegiance.tv. ICA: OK0316.
TV Market Ranking: Outside TV Markets (TRYON). Franchise award date: N.A. Franchise expiration date: N.A. Began: N.A.
Channel capacity: N.A. Channels available but not in use: N.A.

Basic Service
Subscribers: N.A.
Programming (received off-air): KAUT-TV (MNT) Oklahoma City; KETA-TV (PBS) Oklahoma City; KFOR-TV (NBC) Oklahoma City; KOCB (CW) Oklahoma City; KOCO-TV (ABC) Oklahoma City; KOKH-TV (FOX) Oklahoma City; KOPX-TV (ION) Oklahoma City; KTBO-TV (TBN) Oklahoma City; KWTV-DT (CBS) Oklahoma City.
Programming (via satellite): A&E Networks; ABC Family Channel; CNBC; CNN; Country Music TV; Discovery Channel; Disney Channel; ESPN; ESPN 2; Lifetime; MTV; Nickelodeon; Spike TV; Syfy; TBS Superstation; Travel Channel; Turner Network TV; USA Network; WGN America.
Fee: $30.00 installation; $21.95 monthly.

Video-On-Demand: No

Pay-Per-View
Hot Choice (delivered digitally); Playboy TV (delivered digitally); Fresh (delivered digitally); Shorteez (delivered digitally); iN DEMAND (delivered digitally).

Internet Service
Operational: No.

Telephone Service
None

Miles of Plant: 5.0 (coaxial); None (fiber optic).
Chief Executive Officer: Bill Haggarty. Regional Vice President: Andrew Dearth. Vice President, Marketing: Tracy Bass.
Ownership: Allegiance Communications (MSO).

TULSA—Cox Communications, 6301 Waterford Blvd, Ste 200, Oklahoma City, OK 73118. Phones: 405-286-5381; 918-459-3500; 918-665-0200. Fax: 405-286-5260. Web Site: http://www.cox.com/oklahoma. Also serves Bixby, Broken Arrow, Catoosa, Claremore, Coweta, Creek County (portions), Glenpool, Jenks, Kiefer, Osage County (portions), Owasso, Rogers County (portions), Rolling Hills, Sand Springs, Sapulpa & Wagoner County (portions). ICA: OK0001.
TV Market Ranking: 54 (Bixby, Broken Arrow, Catoosa, Claremore, Coweta, Creek County (portions), Glenpool, Jenks, Kiefer, Osage County (portions), Owasso, Rogers County (portions), Rolling Hills, Sand Springs, Sapulpa, TULSA, Wagoner County (portions)); Below 100 (Osage County (portions), Rogers County (portions)); Outside TV Markets (Creek County (portions), Osage County (portions), Rogers County (portions), Wagoner County (portions)). Franchise award date: June 1, 1971. Franchise expiration date: N.A. Began: January 18, 1974.
Channel capacity: N.A. Channels available but not in use: N.A.

Basic Service
Subscribers: 172,000.
Programming (received off-air): KDOR-TV (TBN) Bartlesville; KGEB (IND) Tulsa; KJRH-TV (NBC) Tulsa; KMYT-TV (MNT) Tulsa; KOED-TV (PBS) Tulsa; KOKI-TV (FOX) Tulsa; KOTV-DT (CBS) Tulsa; KQCW-DT (CW) Muskogee; KRSC-TV (ETV) Claremore; KTUL (ABC) Tulsa; KWHB (IND) Tulsa.
Programming (via satellite): ION Television; Product Information Network; QVC; TV Guide Network; Univision Studios; WGN America.
Fee: $30.00 installation; $11.75 monthly; $20.00 additional installation.

Expanded Basic Service 1
Subscribers: 150,359.
Programming (via satellite): A&E Networks; ABC Family Channel; AMC; Animal Planet; BET Networks; Bravo; Cartoon Network; CNBC; CNN; Comedy Central; Country Music TV; C-SPAN; C-SPAN 2; Discovery Channel; Discovery Health Channel; Disney Channel; E! Entertainment Television; ESPN; ESPN 2; Food Network; Fox News Channel; Fox Sports Southwest; FX; Headline News; HGTV; History Channel; Lifetime; MSNBC; MTV; Nickelodeon; Spike TV; TBS Superstation; The Learning Channel; The Weather Channel; Travel Channel; truTV; Turner Network TV; TV Land; USA Network; VH1.
Fee: $32.24 monthly.

Digital Basic Service
Subscribers: N.A.
Programming (via satellite): BBC America; Bio; Bloomberg Television; Canales N; Cooking Channel; Discovery Fit & Health; DIY Network; Encore (multiplexed); Encore Family; ESPN; ESPN Classic Sports; ESPNews; Eternal Word TV Network; FamilyNet; Fox Soccer; G4; GAS; Golf Channel; Great American Country; GSN; Hallmark Channel; HD Theater; History Channel International; Independent Film Channel; INHD (multiplexed); Lifetime Movie Network; MTV Networks Digital Suite; Music Choice; National Geographic Channel; NBA TV; NFL Network; Nick Jr.; Nick Too; NickToons TV; Outdoor Channel; Oxygen; PBS Kids Sprout; SoapNet; Speed; Sundance Channel; Syfy; Toon Disney; Turner Classic Movies; TV One; Universal HD; Versus; WE tv.
Fee: $13.50 monthly.

Digital Pay Service 1
Pay Units: N.A.
Programming (via satellite): Cinemax (multiplexed); HBO (multiplexed); Showtime (multiplexed); Starz (multiplexed); Starz HDTV; The Movie Channel.
Fee: $12.00 monthly (each package).

Video-On-Demand: No

Pay-Per-View
Addressable homes: 42,263.
ESPN Extra (delivered digitally); Hot Choice (delivered digitally); iN DEMAND (delivered digitally); Playboy TV (delivered digitally); Fresh (delivered digitally); Shorteez (delivered digitally); NBA League Pass (delivered digitally); NHL Center Ice (delivered digitally); MLB Extra Innings (delivered digitally).

Internet Service
Operational: Yes.
Subscribers: 11,903.
Broadband Service: Cox High Speed Internet.
Fee: $99.95 installation; $34.95 monthly; $10.00 modem lease.

Telephone Service
Digital: Operational
Fee: $12.36 monthly

Miles of Plant: 3,173.0 (coaxial); 70.0 (fiber optic). Additional miles planned: 15.0 (fiber optic).

President & General Manager: Dave Bialis. Vice President, Operations: John Bowen. Vice President, Marketing: Mollie Andrews. Communications Director: Cristine Martin.
Ownership: Cox Communications Inc. (MSO).

TULSA COUNTY (western portion)—Pine River Cable, PO Box 96, McBain, MI 49657. Phone: 888-244-2288. Fax: 918-825-8008. E-mail: info@pinerivercable.com. Web Site: http://www.pinerivercable.com. Also serves Creek County (portions) & Osage County (portions). ICA: OK0341.
TV Market Ranking: 54 (Creek County (portions), Osage County (portions), TULSA COUNTY). Franchise award date: N.A. Franchise expiration date: N.A. Began: May 1, 1990.
Channel capacity: 63 (not 2-way capable). Channels available but not in use: N.A.
Basic Service
Subscribers: 774.
Programming (received off-air): KDOR-TV (TBN) Bartlesville; KGEB (IND) Tulsa; KJRH-TV (NBC) Tulsa; KMYT-TV (MNT) Tulsa; KOED-TV (PBS) Tulsa; KOKI-TV (FOX) Tulsa; KOTV-DT (CBS) Tulsa; KQCW-DT (CW) Muskogee; KTPX-TV (ION) Okmulgee; KTUL (ABC) Tulsa; KWHB (IND) Tulsa.
Programming (via satellite): WGN America.
Fee: $29.95 installation; $11.35 monthly.
Expanded Basic Service 1
Subscribers: 711.
Programming (via satellite): A&E Networks; ABC Family Channel; AMC; Animal Planet; Cartoon Network; CNBC; CNN; Comedy Central; Country Music TV; C-SPAN; Discovery Channel; Discovery Fit & Health; Disney Channel; Encore; ESPN; ESPN 2; ESPN Classic Sports; Food Network; Fox News Channel; Fox Sports Southwest; FX; Hallmark Channel; Headline News; HGTV; History Channel; INSP; Lifetime; MTV; National Geographic Channel; Nickelodeon; Outdoor Channel; QVC; Speed; Spike TV; Syfy; TBS Superstation; The Learning Channel; The Weather Channel; truTV; Turner Classic Movies; Turner Network TV; TV Land; USA Network; Versus; VH1.
Fee: $29.95 installation; $31.65 monthly.
Pay Service 1
Pay Units: 206.
Programming (via satellite): HBO (multiplexed); Showtime; The Movie Channel.
Fee: $10.95 monthly.
Video-On-Demand: No
Pay-Per-View
Addressable homes: 30.
ESPN Extra (delivered digitally); ESPN Now (delivered digitally); iN DEMAND (delivered digitally); Sports PPV (delivered digitally).
Internet Service
Operational: No.
Telephone Service
None
Miles of Plant: 138.0 (coaxial); None (fiber optic).
General Manager: John Metzler. Chief Technician: John Miller.
Ownership: Pine River Cable (MSO).

TURPIN—Allegiance Communications, 707 W Saratoga St, Shawnee, OK 74804. Phones: 405-275-6923; 405-395-1131. Web Site: http://www.allegiance.tv. ICA: OK0317.
TV Market Ranking: Outside TV Markets (TURPIN). Franchise award date: N.A. Franchise expiration date: N.A. Began: N.A.
Channel capacity: 42 (not 2-way capable). Channels available but not in use: N.A.
Basic Service
Subscribers: 219.
Programming (received off-air): KBSD-DT (CBS) Ensign; KETA-TV (PBS) Oklahoma City; KPTF-DT (IND) Farwell; KSNG (NBC) Garden City; KUPK (ABC) Garden City.
Programming (via microwave): KAMR-TV (NBC) Amarillo; KCIT (FOX) Amarillo; KFDA-TV (CBS) Amarillo; KVII-TV (ABC, CW) Amarillo.
Programming (via satellite): A&E Networks; ABC Family Channel; AMC; Animal Planet; Cartoon Network; CNN; Comedy Central; Country Music TV; Discovery Channel; Disney Channel; E! Entertainment Television; ESPN; ESPN 2; Food Network; Headline News; HGTV; History Channel; Lifetime; MTV; Nickelodeon; Oxygen; QVC; Speed; Spike TV; Syfy; TBS Superstation; The Learning Channel; The Weather Channel; Travel Channel; Turner Network TV; TV Land; USA Network.
Fee: $39.95 installation; $25.45 monthly.
Video-On-Demand: No
Pay-Per-View
Hot Choice (delivered digitally); Playboy TV (delivered digitally); Fresh (delivered digitally); Shorteez (delivered digitally); iN DEMAND (delivered digitally).
Internet Service
Operational: No.
Telephone Service
None
Miles of Plant: 16.0 (coaxial); None (fiber optic).
Chief Executive Officer: Bill Haggarty. Regional Vice President: Andrew Dearth. Vice President, Marketing: Tracy Bass.
Ownership: Allegiance Communications (MSO).

TUTTLE—Formerly served by Vidia Communications. No longer in operation. ICA: OK0137.

TYRONE—Allegiance Communications, 707 W Saratoga St, Shawnee, OK 74804. Phones: 405-275-6923; 405-395-1131. Fax: 620-873-2238. Web Site: http://www.allegiance.tv. ICA: OK0318.
TV Market Ranking: Outside TV Markets (TYRONE). Franchise award date: N.A. Franchise expiration date: N.A. Began: September 1, 1982.
Channel capacity: 42 (not 2-way capable). Channels available but not in use: N.A.
Basic Service
Subscribers: 236.
Programming (received off-air): KBSD-DT (CBS) Ensign; KETA-TV (PBS) Oklahoma City; KSNG (NBC) Garden City; KUPK (ABC) Garden City.
Programming (via microwave): KAMR-TV (NBC) Amarillo; KCIT (FOX) Amarillo; KFDA-TV (CBS) Amarillo; KVII-TV (ABC, CW) Amarillo.
Programming (via satellite): A&E Networks; ABC Family Channel; AMC; Animal Planet; Cartoon Network; CNN; Comedy Central; Country Music TV; Discovery Channel; Disney Channel; E! Entertainment Television; ESPN; ESPN 2; Food Network; Headline News; HGTV; History Channel; Lifetime; MTV; Nickelodeon; Oxygen; QVC; Speed; Spike TV; Syfy; TBS Superstation; The Learning Channel; The Weather Channel; Travel Channel; Turner Network TV; TV Land; USA Network; WGN America.
Fee: $19.95 installation; $23.50 monthly.
Video-On-Demand: No

Pay-Per-View
Hot Choice (delivered digitally); Playboy TV (delivered digitally); Fresh (delivered digitally); Shorteez (delivered digitally); iN DEMAND (delivered digitally).
Internet Service
Operational: No.
Telephone Service
None
Miles of Plant: 11.0 (coaxial); None (fiber optic).
Chief Executive Officer: Bill Haggarty. Regional Vice President: Andrew Dearth. Vice President, Marketing: Tracy Bass.
Ownership: Allegiance Communications (MSO).

UNION CITY—Formerly served by Vidia Communications. No longer in operation. ICA: OK0319.

VALLIANT—Allegiance Communications, 707 W Saratoga St, Shawnee, OK 74804. Phones: 405-395-1131; 405-275-6923. Web Site: http://www.allegiance.tv. ICA: OK0167.
TV Market Ranking: Outside TV Markets (VALLIANT). Franchise award date: July 1, 1968. Franchise expiration date: N.A. Began: July 1, 1968.
Channel capacity: 35 (not 2-way capable). Channels available but not in use: N.A.
Basic Service
Subscribers: 385.
Programming (received off-air): KFSM-TV (CBS) Fort Smith; KHBS (ABC, CW) Fort Smith; KOET (PBS) Eufaula; KTAL-TV (NBC) Texarkana; KTEN (ABC, CW, NBC) Ada; KXII (CBS, FOX, MNT) Sherman.
Programming (via satellite): AMC; CMT Pure Country; CNBC; CNN; C-SPAN; Discovery Channel; Disney Channel; ESPN; Headline News; Lifetime; Nickelodeon; Outdoor Channel; QVC; Spike TV; TBS Superstation; The Weather Channel; Trinity Broadcasting Network; Turner Network TV; TV Land; USA Network; VH1; WGN America.
Fee: $25.00 installation; $21.95 monthly.
Pay Service 1
Pay Units: 40.
Programming (via satellite): Starz.
Pay Service 2
Pay Units: 80.
Programming (via satellite): Encore.
Fee: $1.75 monthly.
Pay Service 3
Pay Units: 98.
Programming (via satellite): HBO.
Fee: $12.20 monthly.
Pay-Per-View
iN DEMAND (delivered digitally); Hot Choice (delivered digitally); Playboy TV (delivered digitally); Fresh (delivered digitally); Shorteez (delivered digitally).
Internet Service
Operational: No.
Telephone Service
None
Miles of Plant: 18.0 (coaxial); None (fiber optic).
Chief Executive Officer: Bill Haggarty. Regional Vice President: Andrew Dearth. Vice President, Marketing: Tracy Bass.
Ownership: Allegiance Communications (MSO).

VELMA—Reach Broadband, 515 E Longview St, Arp, TX 75750. Phones: 800-842-8160; 501-679-6619. E-mail: support@reachbroadband.net. Web Site: http://www.reachbroadband.net. Also serves Alma, Countyline, Fox, Pruitt City & Ratliff City. ICA: OK0320.
TV Market Ranking: Outside TV Markets (Alma, Countyline, Fox, Pruitt City, Ratliff City, VELMA). Franchise award date: N.A. Franchise expiration date: N.A. Began: February 1, 1983.
Channel capacity: 41 (not 2-way capable). Channels available but not in use: N.A.
Basic Service
Subscribers: 313.
Programming (received off-air): KAUT-TV (MNT) Oklahoma City; KETA-TV (PBS) Oklahoma City; KFOR-TV (NBC) Oklahoma City; KJTL (FOX) Wichita Falls; KOCB (CW) Oklahoma City; KOCO-TV (ABC) Oklahoma City; KOKH-TV (FOX) Oklahoma City; KSWO-TV (ABC, TMO) Lawton; KWTV-DT (CBS) Oklahoma City; KXII (CBS, FOX, MNT) Sherman.
Programming (via satellite): A&E Networks; ABC Family Channel; AMC; CNN; Discovery Channel; Disney Channel; E! Entertainment Television; ESPN; ESPN 2; Fox Sports Southwest; FX; Headline News; HGTV; History Channel; Lifetime; National Geographic Channel; Nickelodeon; Outdoor Channel; QVC; Spike TV; Syfy; TBS Superstation; The Learning Channel; The Weather Channel; Travel Channel; Trinity Broadcasting Network; truTV; Turner Network TV; TV Land; USA Network.
Fee: $29.95 installation; $38.00 monthly.
Pay Service 1
Pay Units: 89.
Programming (via satellite): HBO.
Fee: $20.00 installation; $9.95 monthly.
Pay Service 2
Pay Units: 45.
Programming (via satellite): Showtime.
Fee: $9.95 monthly.
Pay Service 3
Pay Units: 76.
Programming (via satellite): The Movie Channel.
Fee: $9.95 monthly.
Video-On-Demand: No
Internet Service
Operational: No.
Telephone Service
None
Miles of Plant: 63.0 (coaxial); None (fiber optic).
Ownership: RB3 LLC (MSO).

VERDEN—Cable West, 314 W Main St, PO Box 237, Mountain View, OK 73062. Phones: 800-960-7912; 580-347-3220. Fax: 580-347-2143. ICA: OK0321.
TV Market Ranking: Outside TV Markets (VERDEN). Franchise award date: December 6,

MediaPrints
Map a Winning Business Strategy
Digital Cable and TV Coverage Maps.
Visit www.warren-news.com/mediaprints.htm

1982. Franchise expiration date: December 6, 2007. Began: March 1, 1986.
Channel capacity: 36 (not 2-way capable). Channels available but not in use: N.A.
Basic Service
Subscribers: 52.
Programming (received off-air): KAUT-TV (MNT) Oklahoma City; KETA-TV (PBS) Oklahoma City; KFOR-TV (NBC) Oklahoma City; KOCB (CW) Oklahoma City; KOCO-TV (ABC) Oklahoma City; KOKH-TV (FOX) Oklahoma City; KWTV-DT (CBS) Oklahoma City.
Programming (via satellite): ABC Family Channel; CNN; Country Music TV; Discovery Channel; Disney Channel; ESPN; Headline News; Spike TV; TBS Superstation; The Weather Channel; Trinity Broadcasting Network; Turner Network TV; USA Network; WGN America.
Fee: $29.95 installation; $24.95 monthly; $3.95 converter.
Pay Service 1
Pay Units: 19.
Programming (via satellite): Cinemax.
Fee: $9.00 monthly.
Pay Service 2
Pay Units: 25.
Programming (via satellite): HBO.
Fee: $10.00 monthly.
Video-On-Demand: No
Internet Service
Operational: No.
Telephone Service
None
Miles of Plant: 4.0 (coaxial); None (fiber optic).
Manager & Chief Technician: Mickey Davis.
Ownership: Mickey Davis (MSO).

VERDIGRIS—Allegiance Communications, 707 W Saratoga St, Shawnee, OK 74804. Phones: 405-275-6923; 405-395-1131. Web Site: http://www.allegiance.tv. ICA: OK0094.
TV Market Ranking: 54 (VERDIGRIS). Franchise award date: April 1, 1982. Franchise expiration date: N.A. Began: July 1, 1983.
Channel capacity: N.A. Channels available but not in use: N.A.
Basic Service
Subscribers: 710.
Programming (received off-air): KDOR-TV (TBN) Bartlesville; KJRH-TV (NBC) Tulsa; KMYT-TV (MNT) Tulsa; KOED-TV (PBS) Tulsa; KOKI-TV (FOX) Tulsa; KOTV-DT (CBS) Tulsa; KQCW-DT (CW) Muskogee; KRSC-TV (ETV) Claremore; KTPX-TV (ION) Okmulgee; KTUL (ABC) Tulsa; KWHB (IND) Tulsa.
Programming (via satellite): C-SPAN; INSP; QVC; WGN America.
Fee: $60.00 installation; $21.95 monthly.
Expanded Basic Service 1
Subscribers: N.A.
Programming (via satellite): A&E Networks; ABC Family Channel; AMC; Animal Planet; Cartoon Network; CNBC; CNN; Comedy Central; Country Music TV; Discovery Channel; Disney Channel; E! Entertainment Television; ESPN; ESPN 2; Food Network; Fox News Channel; Fox Sports Southwest; FX; Headline News; HGTV; History Channel; Lifetime; MTV; Nickelodeon; Outdoor Channel; Oxygen; Speed; Spike TV; Syfy; TBS Superstation; The Learning Channel; The Weather Channel; Travel Channel; truTV; Turner Classic Movies; Turner Network TV; TV Land; USA Network; VH1.
Digital Basic Service
Subscribers: N.A.
Programming (via satellite): BBC America; Bio; Bloomberg Television; CMT Pure Country; Discovery en Espanol; Discovery Health Channel; Discovery Kids Channel; DIY Network; Encore; ESPN Classic Sports; ESPN U; Flix; GSN; History Channel International; ID Investigation Discovery; Independent Film Channel; LOGO; Military Channel; MTV Hits; MTV Jams; MTV2; Music Choice; Nick Jr.; Nick Too; NickToons TV; Planet Green; Science; SoapNet; Style Network; Sundance Channel; TeenNick; Toon Disney; Tr3s; VH1 Classic; VH1 Soul; WE tv.
Digital Pay Service 1
Pay Units: N.A.
Programming (via satellite): Cinemax (multiplexed); HBO (multiplexed); Showtime (multiplexed); Starz (multiplexed); The Movie Channel (multiplexed).
Video-On-Demand: No
Pay-Per-View
iN DEMAND (delivered digitally); Shorteez (delivered digitally); Fresh (delivered digitally); Playboy TV (delivered digitally); Club Jenna (delivered digitally); Spice: Xcess (delivered digitally).
Internet Service
Operational: No.
Telephone Service
None
Miles of Plant: 47.0 (coaxial); None (fiber optic).
Chief Executive Officer: Bill Haggarty. Regional Vice President: Andrew Dearth. Vice President, Marketing: Tracy Bass.
Ownership: Allegiance Communications (MSO).

VIAN—Allegiance Communications, 707 W Saratoga St, Shawnee, OK 74804. Phones: 405-275-6923; 405-395-1131. Web Site: http://www.allegiance.tv. ICA: OK0130.
TV Market Ranking: Below 100 (VIAN). Franchise award date: January 28, 1980. Franchise expiration date: N.A. Began: N.A.
Channel capacity: N.A. Channels available but not in use: N.A.
Basic Service
Subscribers: 442.
Programming (received off-air): KFSM-TV (CBS) Fort Smith; KGEB (IND) Tulsa; KHBS (ABC, CW) Fort Smith; KJRH-TV (NBC) Tulsa; KOET (PBS) Eufaula; KOKI-TV (FOX) Tulsa; KQCW-DT (CW) Muskogee; KTUL (ABC) Tulsa; KWHB (IND) Tulsa.
Programming (via satellite): A&E Networks; ABC Family Channel; AMC; Animal Planet; Cartoon Network; CNBC; CNN; Comedy Central; Country Music TV; C-SPAN; Discovery Channel; Disney Channel; E! Entertainment Television; ESPN; ESPN 2; Food Network; Fox News Channel; Fox Sports Southwest; FX; Hallmark Channel; Headline News; HGTV; History Channel; INSP; Lifetime; MSNBC; Nickelodeon; Outdoor Channel; Oxygen; QVC; Speed; Spike TV; Syfy; TBS Superstation; The Learning Channel; The Weather Channel; Travel Channel; truTV; Turner Classic Movies; Turner Network TV; USA Network; WGN America.
Fee: $30.00 installation; $23.45 monthly.
Digital Basic Service
Subscribers: N.A.
Programming (via satellite): BBC America; Bio; Bloomberg Television; Bravo; Chiller; cloo; CMT Pure Country; Current; Discovery Fit & Health; Discovery Health Channel; Discovery Kids Channel; DMX Music; Encore (multiplexed); ESPN Classic Sports; ESPNews; Flix; Fox College Sports Atlantic; Fox College Sports Central; Fox College Sports Pacific; Fox Movie Channel; Fox Soccer; Fuse; G4; Golf Channel; GSN; History Channel International; ID Investigation Discovery; Independent Film Channel; Lifetime Movie Network; Military Channel; MTV Hits; MTV2; National Geographic Channel; Nick Jr.; NickToons TV; Planet Green; RFD-TV; Science; ShopNBC; SoapNet; Style Network; Sundance Channel; TeenNick; Toon Disney; Trinity Broadcasting Network; Versus; VH1 Classic; VH1 Soul; WE tv.
Pay Service 1
Pay Units: 54.
Programming (via satellite): Cinemax; HBO; Showtime.
Fee: $9.00 monthly (HBO).
Digital Pay Service 1
Pay Units: N.A.
Programming (via satellite): Cinemax (multiplexed); HBO (multiplexed); Showtime (multiplexed); Starz (multiplexed); The Movie Channel (multiplexed).
Video-On-Demand: No
Pay-Per-View
iN DEMAND (delivered digitally); Club Jenna (delivered digitally); Playboy TV (delivered digitally); Fresh (delivered digitally); Spice: Xcess (delivered digitally).
Internet Service
Operational: No.
Telephone Service
None
Miles of Plant: 16.0 (coaxial); None (fiber optic).
Chief Executive Officer: Bill Haggarty. Regional Vice President: Andrew Dearth. Vice President, Marketing: Tracy Bass.
Ownership: Allegiance Communications (MSO).

VICI—Formerly served by Rapid Cable. No longer in operation. ICA: OK0174.

VINITA—Cable One, 105 W Delaware Ave, PO Box 309, Vinita, OK 74301-0309. Phone: 918-256-7871. Fax: 918-256-8275. E-mail: mslyman@cableone.net. Web Site: http://www.cableone.net. Also serves Craig County. ICA: OK0322.
TV Market Ranking: Below 100 (Craig County (portions)); Outside TV Markets (Craig County (portions), VINITA). Franchise award date: November 18, 1975. Franchise expiration date: N.A. Began: July 1, 1979.
Channel capacity: 58 (operating 2-way). Channels available but not in use: N.A.
Basic Service
Subscribers: 1,762.
Programming (received off-air): KGEB (IND) Tulsa; KJRH-TV (NBC) Tulsa; KOAM-TV (CBS) Pittsburg; KODE-TV (ABC) Joplin; KOED-TV (PBS) Tulsa; KOKI-TV (FOX) Tulsa; KOTV-DT (CBS) Tulsa; KQCW-DT (CW) Muskogee; KRSC-TV (ETV) Claremore; KSNF (NBC) Joplin; KTPX-TV (ION) Okmulgee; KTUL (ABC) Tulsa; KWHB (IND) Tulsa; 2 FMs.
Programming (via satellite): A&E Networks; ABC Family Channel; AMC; Animal Planet; Cartoon Network; CNN; Country Music TV; C-SPAN; Discovery Channel; Disney Channel; ESPN; ESPN 2; Food Network; Fox News Channel; Fox Sports Southwest; FX; Headline News; HGTV; History Channel; ION Television; Lifetime; MSNBC; MTV; Nickelodeon; QVC; Spike TV; Syfy; TBS Superstation; The Learning Channel; The Weather Channel; Turner Classic Movies; Turner Network TV; TV Guide Network; TV Land; USA Network; VH1.
Fee: $75.00 installation; $46.00 monthly; $1.56 converter; $9.04 additional installation.
Digital Basic Service
Subscribers: 650.
Programming (via satellite): Bio; Boomerang; BYU Television; Canales N; Discovery Digital Networks; DMX Music; ESPN Classic Sports; ESPNews; FamilyNet; Fox Movie Channel; Fox Soccer; FSN Digital Atlantic; FSN Digital Central; FSN Digital Pacific; Fuel TV; G4; Golf Channel; Great American Country; Hallmark Channel; History Channel International; INSP; Military History Channel; National Geographic Channel; Outdoor Channel; SoapNet; Speed; Toon Disney; truTV; TVG Network.
Fee: $46.00 monthly.
Digital Pay Service 1
Pay Units: N.A.
Programming (via satellite): Cinemax (multiplexed); Encore (multiplexed); Flix; HBO (multiplexed); Showtime (multiplexed); Starz (multiplexed); Sundance Channel; The Movie Channel (multiplexed).
Fee: $7.00 monthly (each).
Video-On-Demand: No
Pay-Per-View
Addressable homes: 2,000.
Hot Choice; iN DEMAND; Fresh; iN DEMAND (delivered digitally); Pleasure (delivered digitally); Sports PPV (delivered digitally).
Internet Service
Operational: Yes. Began: December 1, 2001.
Subscribers: 427.
Broadband Service: CableONE.net.
Fee: $75.00 installation; $43.00 monthly; $5.00 modem lease.
Telephone Service
Digital: Operational
Fee: $39.95 monthly
Miles of Plant: 61.0 (coaxial); None (fiber optic). Additional miles planned: 10.0 (coaxial).
Manager: Mike Slyman. Chief Technician: Bob Young. Marketing & Office Director: Sandy Shultz.
Ownership: Cable ONE Inc. (MSO).

WAKITA—Pioneer Telephone Coop. Formerly served by [OK0226]. This cable system has converted to IPTV., PO Box 539, Kingfisher, OK 73750. Phones: 405-375-4111; 888-782-2667. E-mail: website@pldi.net. Web Site: http://www.ptci.com. ICA: OK5084.
TV Market Ranking: Outside TV Markets (WAKITA). Franchise award date: N.A.

Franchise expiration date: N.A. Began: N.A.
Channel capacity: N.A. Channels available but not in use: N.A.
Internet Service
Operational: Yes.
Telephone Service
Digital: Operational
General Manager: Richard Ruhl.

WAKITA—Pioneer Telephone Coop. This cable system has converted to IPTV. See Wakita, OK [OK5084]. ICA: OK0226.

WALTERS—Alliance Communications, 6125 Paluxy Dr, Tyler, TX 75703. Phones: 800-842-8160; 501-679-6619. Fax: 501-679-5694. Web Site: http://www.alliancecable.net. Also serves Temple. ICA: OK0108.
TV Market Ranking: Below 100 (Temple, WALTERS). Franchise award date: N.A. Franchise expiration date: N.A. Began: January 1, 1978.
Channel capacity: 46 (not 2-way capable). Channels available but not in use: N.A.
Basic Service
Subscribers: 235.
Programming (received off-air): KAUZ-TV (CBS, CW) Wichita Falls; KETA-TV (PBS) Oklahoma City; KFDX-TV (NBC) Wichita Falls; KFOR-TV (NBC) Oklahoma City; KJTL (FOX) Wichita Falls; KSWO-TV (ABC, TMO) Lawton; KWTV-DT (CBS) Oklahoma City.
Programming (via satellite): A&E Networks; ABC Family Channel; Animal Planet; Cartoon Network; CNBC; CNN; C-SPAN; Discovery Channel; Disney Channel; E! Entertainment Television; ESPN; ESPN 2; Fox News Channel; Fox Sports Southwest; Great American Country; Headline News; HGTV; History Channel; Lifetime; MSNBC; MTV; National Geographic Channel; Nickelodeon; QVC; Spike TV; Syfy; TBS Superstation; The Learning Channel; The Weather Channel; Trinity Broadcasting Network; truTV; Turner Network TV; TV Land; USA Network.
Fee: $29.95 installation; $38.00 monthly.
Expanded Basic Service 1
Subscribers: 201.
Programming (via satellite): The Movie Channel.
Pay Service 1
Pay Units: N.A.
Programming (via satellite): HBO; Showtime.
Fee: $10.95 monthly.
Video-On-Demand: No
Pay-Per-View
iN DEMAND (delivered digitally); Playboy TV (delivered digitally); Shorteez (delivered digitally).
Internet Service
Operational: No.
Telephone Service
None
Miles of Plant: 35.0 (coaxial); None (fiber optic).
Vice President & General Manager: John Brinker. Vice President, Programming: Julie Newman.
Ownership: Buford Media Group LLC (MSO).

WANETTE—Formerly served by Cebridge Connections. No longer in operation. ICA: OK0323.

WAPANUCKA—CommuniComm Services, 1501 W Mississippi St, PO Box 597, Durant, OK 74701. Phones: 800-752-4992; 580-924-2367. Fax: 580-924-5970. Web Site: http://www.netcommander.com. ICA: OK0337.
TV Market Ranking: Below 100 (WAPANUCKA). Franchise award date: N.A. Franchise expiration date: N.A. Began: January 1, 1988.
Channel capacity: 62 (not 2-way capable). Channels available but not in use: N.A.
Basic Service
Subscribers: N.A. Included in Durant
Programming (received off-air): KTEN (ABC, CW, NBC) Ada; KXII (CBS, FOX, MNT) Sherman.
Programming (via satellite): ABC Family Channel; CNN; ESPN; Headline News; TBS Superstation.
Fee: $49.95 installation; $22.00 monthly.
Video-On-Demand: No
Internet Service
Operational: No.
Telephone Service
None
Miles of Plant: 6.0 (coaxial); None (fiber optic).
General Manager: Jeff Beck. Customer Service Manager: Lisa Hamill.
Ownership: James Cable LLC (MSO).

WARNER—Cross Cable TV, 704 3rd Ave, PO Box 9, Warner, OK 74469-0509. Phone: 918-463-2921. Fax: 918-463-2551. E-mail: staff@crosstel.net. Web Site: http://www.crosstel.net. ICA: OK0160.
TV Market Ranking: Below 100 (WARNER). Franchise award date: January 1, 1984. Franchise expiration date: January 1, 2009. Began: January 1, 1984.
Channel capacity: N.A. Channels available but not in use: N.A.
Digital Basic Service
Subscribers: N.A.
Programming (via satellite): A&E Networks; ABC Family Channel; AMC; Animal Planet; BBC America; BET Networks; Bio; Bloomberg Television; BYU Television; CNN; Country Music TV; C-SPAN; C-SPAN 2; CW+; Discovery Channel; Discovery Health Channel; Discovery Kids Channel; Disney Channel; DIY Network; DMX Music; ESPN; ESPN 2; ESPN Classic Sports; ESPNews; Eternal Word TV Network; Fox News Channel; Fox Sports Southwest; FX; G4; Hallmark Channel; Headline News; HGTV; History Channel; History Channel International; ID Investigation Discovery; Independent Film Channel; INSP; Lifetime; Lifetime Movie Network; Lifetime Real Women; Military Channel; MSNBC; MTV; MTV Hits; MTV2; National Geographic Channel; Nick Jr.; Nickelodeon; NickToons TV; Oxygen; Planet Green; QVC; RFD-TV; Science; Spike TV; Syfy; TBS Superstation; TeenNick; The Learning Channel; The Weather Channel; Toon Disney; Travel Channel; truTV; Turner Classic Movies; Turner Network TV; TV Land; USA Network; VH1; VH1 Classic; WE tv; WGN America.
Digital Expanded Basic Service
Subscribers: N.A.
Programming (via satellite): Bravo; Cartoon Network; CNBC; Comedy Central; Cooking Channel; E! Entertainment Television; Food Network; Fox Movie Channel; Fox Soccer; Golf Channel; Great American Country; GSN; Outdoor Channel; Speed; Versus.
Digital Pay Service 1
Pay Units: N.A.
Programming (via satellite): Cinemax (multiplexed); Encore (multiplexed); HBO (multiplexed); Starz (multiplexed).
Video-On-Demand: Planned
Internet Service
Operational: No.

Telephone Service
None
Miles of Plant: 30.0 (coaxial); None (fiber optic).
General Manager: R. David Right. Chief Technician & Program Director: Troy Duncan. Marketing Director: Ashley Thompson. Customer Service Manager: Dale Wiggins.
Ownership: V. David & Billie Lynn Miller.

WASHINGTON—Formerly served by Cebridge Connections. No longer in operation. ICA: OK0248.

WATONGA—Pioneer Telephone Coop. Formerly served by [OK0082]. This cable system has converted to IPTV., PO Box 539, Kingfisher, OK 73750. Phones: 405-375-4111; 888-782-2667. E-mail: website@pldi.net. Web Site: http://www.ptci.com. ICA: OK5085.
TV Market Ranking: Outside TV Markets (WATONGA). Franchise award date: N.A. Franchise expiration date: N.A. Began: N.A.
Channel capacity: N.A. Channels available but not in use: N.A.
Internet Service
Operational: Yes.
Telephone Service
Digital: Operational
General Manager: Richard Ruhl.

WATONGA—Pioneer Telephone Coop. This cable system has converted to IPTV. See Watonga, OK [OK5085]. ICA: OK0082.

WAUKOMIS—Formerly served by Adelphia Cable. No longer in operation. ICA: OK0369.

WAURIKA—Alliance Communications, 6125 Paluxy Dr, Tyler, TX 75703. Phones: 800-842-8160; 501-679-6619. Fax: 501-679-5694. Web Site: http://www.alliancecable.net. ICA: OK0106.
TV Market Ranking: Below 100 (WAURIKA). Franchise award date: June 5, 1978. Franchise expiration date: N.A. Began: September 1, 1981.
Channel capacity: 41 (not 2-way capable). Channels available but not in use: N.A.
Basic Service
Subscribers: 147.
Programming (received off-air): KAUZ-TV (CBS, CW) Wichita Falls; KETA-TV (PBS) Oklahoma City; KFDX-TV (NBC) Wichita Falls; KFOR-TV (NBC) Oklahoma City; KJTL (FOX) Wichita Falls; KOCO-TV (ABC) Oklahoma City; KOKH-TV (FOX) Oklahoma City; KSWO-TV (ABC, TMO) Lawton; KWTV-DT (CBS) Oklahoma City.
Programming (via satellite): A&E Networks; ABC Family Channel; CNBC; CNN; C-SPAN; Discovery Channel; Disney Channel; ESPN; ESPN 2; Fox News Channel; Fox Sports Net; FX; Great American Country; Headline News; HGTV; History Channel; INSP; Lifetime; National Geographic Channel; Nickelodeon; QVC; Spike TV; The Learning Channel; The Weather Channel; Trinity Broadcasting Network; Turner Classic Movies; Turner Network TV; USA Network.
Fee: $29.95 installation; $38.00 monthly.
Expanded Basic Service 1
Subscribers: 147.
Fee: $9.95 monthly.
Pay Service 1
Pay Units: N.A.
Programming (via satellite): HBO; Showtime; The Movie Channel.
Fee: $10.95 monthly.
Video-On-Demand: No
Internet Service
Operational: No.
Telephone Service
None
Miles of Plant: 16.0 (coaxial); None (fiber optic).
Vice President & General Manager: John Brinker. Vice President, Programming: Julie Newman.
Ownership: Buford Media Group LLC (MSO).

WAYNOKA—Formerly served by Waynoka Community TV. No longer in operation. ICA: OK0149.

WEATHERFORD—Suddenlink Communications, 201 S Broadway, Weatherford, OK 73096. Phones: 877-423-2743 (Customer service); 314-965-2020. Web Site: http://www.suddenlink.com. Also serves Hydro. ICA: OK0045.
TV Market Ranking: Outside TV Markets (Hydro, WEATHERFORD). Franchise award date: July 1, 1967. Franchise expiration date: July 1, 2008. Began: July 1, 1967.
Channel capacity: 45 (operating 2-way). Channels available but not in use: N.A.
Basic Service
Subscribers: 3,811.
Programming (received off-air): KAUT-TV (MNT) Oklahoma City; KETA-TV (PBS) Oklahoma City; KFOR-TV (NBC) Oklahoma City; KOCB (CW) Oklahoma City; KOCO-TV (ABC) Oklahoma City; KOKH-TV (FOX) Oklahoma City; KOPX-TV (ION) Oklahoma City; KSBI (IND) Oklahoma City; KWTV-DT (CBS) Oklahoma City; allband FM.
Fee: $35.00 installation; $19.95 monthly.
Expanded Basic Service 1
Subscribers: N.A.
Programming (via satellite): A&E Networks; ABC Family Channel; AMC; Animal Planet; BET Networks; Bravo; Cartoon Network; CNBC; CNN; Comedy Central; C-SPAN; Discovery Channel; Disney Channel; E! Entertainment Television; ESPN; ESPN 2; Eternal Word TV Network; Food Network; Fox News Channel; Fox Sports Southwest; FX; Golf Channel; Great American Country; Hallmark Channel; Headline News; HGTV; History Channel; INSP; Lifetime; MSNBC; MTV; National Geographic Channel; Nickelodeon; Outdoor Channel; QVC; Shop at Home; Shopping Channel; Speed; Spike TV; Syfy; TBS Superstation; The Learning Channel; The Weather Channel; Travel Channel; Trinity Broadcasting Network; Turner Classic Movies; Turner Network TV; TV Guide Net-

work; TV Land; Univision Studios; USA Network; VH1.
Fee: $24.00 monthly.

Digital Basic Service
Subscribers: N.A.
Programming (via satellite): BBC America; Bio; Bloomberg Television; cloo; Discovery Digital Networks; ESPN Classic Sports; ESPNews; Fox Soccer; Fuse; G4; GSN; History Channel International; Independent Film Channel; Sundance Channel; Toon Disney; Versus; WE tv.
Fee: $3.99 monthly.

Pay Service 1
Pay Units: 624.
Programming (via satellite): HBO.
Fee: $35.00 installation; $10.95 monthly.

Pay Service 2
Pay Units: 267.
Programming (via satellite): Showtime.
Fee: $35.00 installation; $9.95 monthly.

Pay Service 3
Pay Units: 290.
Programming (via satellite): The Movie Channel.
Fee: $35.00 installation; $5.95 monthly.

Digital Pay Service 1
Pay Units: N.A.
Programming (via satellite): Cinemax (multiplexed); Encore (multiplexed); HBO (multiplexed); Showtime (multiplexed); Starz (multiplexed); The Movie Channel (multiplexed).

Video-On-Demand: No

Pay-Per-View
iN DEMAND (delivered digitally); Playboy TV (delivered digitally).

Internet Service
Operational: Yes. Began: June 23, 2002.
Broadband Service: Suddenlink High Speed Internet.
Fee: $45.95 installation; $24.95 monthly.

Telephone Service
Digital: Operational
Fee: $49.95 monthly

Miles of Plant: 89.0 (coaxial); None (fiber optic).
Regional Manager: Todd Cruthird. Manager: Dave Walker. Chief Technician: Roger Campbell. Marketing Director: Beverly Gambell.
Ownership: Cequel Communications LLC (MSO).

WELCH—Allegiance Communications, 707 W Saratoga St, Shawnee, OK 74804. Phones: 405-275-6923; 405-395-1131. Web Site: http://www.allegiance.tv. ICA: OK0190.
TV Market Ranking: Outside TV Markets (WELCH). Franchise award date: October 4, 1988. Franchise expiration date: October 4, 2013. Began: September 1, 1990.
Channel capacity: 35 (not 2-way capable). Channels available but not in use: N.A.

Basic Service
Subscribers: N.A.
Programming (received off-air): KFJX (FOX) Pittsburg; KMYT-TV (MNT) Tulsa; KOAM-TV (CBS) Pittsburg; KODE-TV (ABC) Joplin; KOED-TV (PBS) Tulsa; KRSC-TV (ETV) Claremore; KSNF (NBC) Joplin; KTUL (ABC) Tulsa; KWHB (IND) Tulsa.
Programming (via satellite): A&E Networks; ABC Family Channel; Animal Planet; CNBC; CNN; Country Music TV; C-SPAN; Discovery Channel; Disney Channel; E! Entertainment Television; ESPN; ESPN 2; Headline News; History Channel; Lifetime; Nickelodeon; Oxygen; Product Information Network; Spike TV; Syfy; TBS Superstation; The Learning Channel; The Weather Channel; Travel Channel; Turner Network TV; USA Network; VH1; WGN America.
Fee: $40.00 installation; $22.00 monthly; $1.96 converter; $19.95 additional installation.

Pay Service 1
Pay Units: 42.
Programming (via satellite): HBO.
Fee: $9.95 monthly.

Video-On-Demand: No

Pay-Per-View
iN DEMAND (delivered digitally); Hot Choice (delivered digitally); Playboy TV (delivered digitally); Fresh (delivered digitally); Shorteez (delivered digitally).

Internet Service
Operational: No.

Telephone Service
None

Miles of Plant: 6.0 (coaxial); None (fiber optic).
Chief Executive Officer: Bill Haggarty. Regional Vice President: Andrew Dearth. Vice President, Marketing: Tracy Bass.
Ownership: Allegiance Communications (MSO).

WELEETKA—Allegiance Communications, 707 W Saratoga St, Shawnee, OK 74804. Phones: 405-275-6923; 405-395-1131. Web Site: http://www.allegiance.tv. ICA: OK0165.
TV Market Ranking: Outside TV Markets (WELEETKA). Franchise award date: N.A. Franchise expiration date: N.A. Began: January 1, 1982.
Channel capacity: N.A. Channels available but not in use: N.A.

Basic Service
Subscribers: N.A.
Programming (received off-air): KJRH-TV (NBC) Tulsa; KMYT-TV (MNT) Tulsa; KOED-TV (PBS) Tulsa; KOKI-TV (FOX) Tulsa; KOPX-TV (ION) Oklahoma City; KOTV-DT (CBS) Tulsa; KQCW-DT (CW) Muskogee; KTUL (ABC) Tulsa; KWHB (IND) Tulsa.
Programming (via satellite): A&E Networks; ABC Family Channel; AMC; Animal Planet; Cartoon Network; CNN; Country Music TV; Discovery Channel; Disney Channel; ESPN; ESPN 2; Fox News Channel; Fox Sports Southwest; HGTV; History Channel; INSP; Lifetime; Nickelodeon; Oxygen; Product Information Network; QVC; SoapNet; Speed; Spike TV; Syfy; TBS Superstation; The Learning Channel; The Weather Channel; Turner Classic Movies; Turner Network TV; USA Network; WGN America.
Fee: $30.00 installation; $21.95 monthly.

Pay Service 1
Pay Units: N.A.
Programming (via satellite): Cinemax; HBO.
Fee: $9.00 monthly (HBO).

Video-On-Demand: No

Pay-Per-View
iN DEMAND (delivered digitally); Hot Choice (delivered digitally); Playboy TV (delivered digitally); Fresh (delivered digitally); Shorteez (delivered digitally).

Internet Service
Operational: No.

Telephone Service
None

Miles of Plant: 11.0 (coaxial); None (fiber optic).
Chief Executive Officer: Bill Haggarty. Regional Vice President: Andrew Dearth. Vice President, Marketing: Tracy Bass.
Ownership: Allegiance Communications (MSO).

WELLSTON—Allegiance Communications, 707 W Saratoga St, Shawnee, OK 74804. Phones: 405-395-1131; 405-275-6923. Web Site: http://www.allegiance.tv. ICA: OK0192.
TV Market Ranking: Below 100 (WELLSTON). Franchise award date: N.A. Franchise expiration date: N.A. Began: January 1, 1981.
Channel capacity: N.A. Channels available but not in use: N.A.

Basic Service
Subscribers: 120.
Programming (received off-air): KAUT-TV (MNT) Oklahoma City; KETA-TV (PBS) Oklahoma City; KFOR-TV (NBC) Oklahoma City; KOCB (CW) Oklahoma City; KOCO-TV (ABC) Oklahoma City; KOKH-TV (FOX) Oklahoma City; KTBO-TV (TBN) Oklahoma City; KWTV-DT (CBS) Oklahoma City.
Programming (via satellite): ABC Family Channel; AMC; Animal Planet; Cartoon Network; CNBC; CNN; Discovery Channel; Disney Channel; ESPN; Fox News Channel; Fox Sports Southwest; Headline News; HGTV; MTV; Spike TV; TBS Superstation; The Learning Channel; The Weather Channel; Turner Network TV; USA Network.
Fee: $50.00 installation; $29.38 monthly; $3.30 converter; $30.00 additional installation.

Pay Service 1
Pay Units: 35.
Programming (via satellite): HBO.
Fee: $10.00 installation; $13.00 monthly.

Pay Service 2
Pay Units: 27.
Programming (via satellite): Cinemax.
Fee: $10.00 installation; $12.75 monthly.

Pay Service 3
Pay Units: 53.
Programming (via satellite): Encore.
Fee: $10.00 installation; $1.75 monthly.

Video-On-Demand: Yes

Pay-Per-View
iN DEMAND (delivered digitally); Hot Choice (delivered digitally); Playboy TV (delivered digitally); Fresh (delivered digitally); Shorteez (delivered digitally).

Internet Service
Operational: Yes.
Fee: $24.95 installation; $39.95 monthly.

Telephone Service
None

Miles of Plant: 7.0 (coaxial); None (fiber optic).
Chief Executive Officer: Bill Haggarty. Regional Vice President: Andrew Dearth. Vice President, Marketing: Tracy Bass.
Ownership: Allegiance Communications (MSO).

WESTVILLE—Allegiance Communications, 707 W Saratoga St, Shawnee, OK 74804. Phones: 405-275-6923; 405-395-1131. Web Site: http://www.allegiance.tv. Also serves Watts. ICA: OK0138.
TV Market Ranking: Below 100 (Watts, WESTVILLE). Franchise award date: N.A. Franchise expiration date: N.A. Began: August 1, 1974.
Channel capacity: N.A. Channels available but not in use: N.A.

Basic Service
Subscribers: 567.
Programming (received off-air): KFSM-TV (CBS) Fort Smith; KJRH-TV (NBC) Tulsa; KMYT-TV (MNT) Tulsa; KOED-TV (PBS) Tulsa; KOKI-TV (FOX) Tulsa; KOTV-DT (CBS) Tulsa; KQCW-DT (CW) Muskogee; KTUL (ABC) Tulsa; allband FM.
Programming (via satellite): A&E Networks; ABC Family Channel; AMC; Animal Planet; Cartoon Network; CMT Pure Country; CNBC; CNN; C-SPAN; Discovery Channel; Disney Channel; E! Entertainment Television; ESPN; ESPN 2; Fox News Channel; Fox Sports Southwest; History Channel; Lifetime; Nickelodeon; Outdoor Channel; QVC; Spike TV; Syfy; TBS Superstation; The Learning Channel; The Weather Channel; Travel Channel; Trinity Broadcasting Network; Turner Classic Movies; Turner Network TV; USA Network; WGN America.
Fee: $30.00 installation; $21.95 monthly.

Digital Basic Service
Subscribers: N.A.
Programming (via satellite): AmericanLife TV Network; BBC America; Bio; Bloomberg Television; Bravo; Discovery Fit & Health; Discovery Health Channel; Discovery Home Channel; Discovery Kids Channel; Discovery Times Channel; DMX Music; ESPN Classic Sports; ESPNews; Fox Movie Channel; Fox Soccer; Fuse; G4; GAS; Golf Channel; GSN; Halogen Network; HGTV; History Channel International; Independent Film Channel; Lifetime Movie Network; Military Channel; MTV Hits; MTV2; Nick Jr.; Outdoor Channel; Science; ShopNBC; Speed; Style Network; Toon Disney; TV Guide Network; Versus; VH1 Classic; VH1 Country; VH1 Soul; WE tv.

Pay Service 1
Pay Units: N.A.
Programming (via satellite): Cinemax; HBO; Showtime.
Fee: $10.00 installation; $10.00 monthly (each).

Digital Pay Service 1
Pay Units: N.A.
Programming (via satellite): Cinemax (multiplexed); Encore (multiplexed); Flix; HBO (multiplexed); Showtime (multiplexed); Starz (multiplexed); The Movie Channel (multiplexed).

Video-On-Demand: No

Pay-Per-View
iN DEMAND (delivered digitally); Hot Choice (delivered digitally); Playboy TV (delivered digitally); Fresh (delivered digitally); Shorteez (delivered digitally).

Internet Service
Operational: Yes.
Fee: $24.95 installation; $39.95 monthly.

Telephone Service
None

Miles of Plant: 26.0 (coaxial); None (fiber optic).
Chief Executive Officer: Bill Haggarty. Regional Vice President: Andrew Dearth. Vice President, Marketing: Tracy Bass.
Ownership: Allegiance Communications (MSO).

WETUMKA—Allegiance Communications, 707 W Saratoga St, Shawnee, OK 74804. Phones: 405-395-1131; 405-275-6923. Web Site: http://www.allegiance.tv. ICA: OK0325.
TV Market Ranking: Below 100 (WETUMKA). Franchise award date: N.A. Franchise expiration date: N.A. Began: June 1, 1981.
Channel capacity: 36 (not 2-way capable). Channels available but not in use: N.A.

Basic Service
Subscribers: 388.
Programming (received off-air): KAUT-TV (MNT) Oklahoma City; KETA-TV (PBS) Oklahoma City; KFOR-TV (NBC) Oklahoma City; KOCB (CW) Oklahoma City; KOKH-TV (FOX) Oklahoma City; KOTV-DT (CBS) Tulsa; KTEN (ABC, CW, NBC) Ada; KTUL (ABC) Tulsa; KWHB (IND) Tulsa; KWTV-DT (CBS) Oklahoma City.

Programming (via satellite): A&E Networks; ABC Family Channel; AMC; CMT Pure Country; CNN; Discovery Channel; Disney Channel; ESPN; Fox Sports Southwest; Lifetime; Nickelodeon; QVC; Spike TV; TBS Superstation; The Weather Channel; Trinity Broadcasting Network; Turner Network TV; TV Land; USA Network; WGN America.
Fee: $23.45 monthly.

Digital Basic Service
Subscribers: N.A.
Programming (via satellite): AMC; BBC America; Black Family Channel; Bloomberg Television; Bravo; Discovery Health Channel; Discovery Home Channel; Discovery Kids Channel; Discovery Times Channel; DMX Music; ESPN 2; ESPN Classic Sports; ESPNews; Fox Movie Channel; Fox Sports World; Fuse; G4; Golf Channel; Great American Country; GSN; Halogen Network; HGTV; Independent Film Channel; Lifetime Movie Network; Outdoor Channel; Science; ShopNBC; Speed; Sundance Channel; Syfy; The Word Network; Toon Disney; Turner Classic Movies; Versus.

Digital Pay Service 1
Pay Units: N.A.
Programming (via satellite): Cinemax (multiplexed); Encore (multiplexed); HBO (multiplexed); Showtime (multiplexed); Starz (multiplexed); The Movie Channel (multiplexed).

Pay-Per-View
iN DEMAND (delivered digitally); Playboy TV (delivered digitally); Playboy TV (delivered digitally); Fresh (delivered digitally); Shorteez (delivered digitally).

Internet Service
Operational: No.

Telephone Service
None

Miles of Plant: 16.0 (coaxial); None (fiber optic).
Chief Executive Officer: Bill Haggarty. Regional Vice President: Andrew Dearth. Vice President, Marketing: Tracy Bass.
Ownership: Allegiance Communications (MSO).

WEWOKA—Formerly served by Cebridge Connections. Now served by SEMINOLE, OK [OK0042]. ICA: OK0077.

WHITE HORN COVE—Formerly served by Lake Area TV Cable. No longer in operation. ICA: OK0095.

WILBURTON—Allegiance Communications, 707 W Saratoga St, Shawnee, OK 74804. Phones: 405-275-6923; 405-395-1131. Web Site: http://www.allegiance.tv. Also serves Red Oak. ICA: OK0088.
TV Market Ranking: Outside TV Markets (Red Oak, WILBURTON). Franchise award date: N.A. Franchise expiration date: N.A. Began: October 1, 1962.
Channel capacity: N.A. Channels available but not in use: N.A.

Basic Service
Subscribers: 1,500.
Programming (received off-air): KJRH-TV (NBC) Tulsa; KMYT-TV (MNT) Tulsa; KOET (PBS) Eufaula; KOKI-TV (FOX) Tulsa; KOTV-DT (CBS) Tulsa; KQCW-DT (CW) Muskogee; KTEN (ABC, CW, NBC) Ada; KTPX-TV (ION) Okmulgee; KTUL (ABC) Tulsa; KWHB (IND) Tulsa; allband FM.
Programming (via satellite): C-SPAN; QVC; Trinity Broadcasting Network; WGN America.
Fee: $29.95 installation; $24.95 monthly; $1.96 converter; $19.95 additional installation.

Expanded Basic Service 1
Subscribers: N.A.
Programming (via satellite): A&E Networks; ABC Family Channel; AMC; Animal Planet; Cartoon Network; CNBC; CNN; Comedy Central; Country Music TV; Discovery Channel; Disney Channel; E! Entertainment Television; ESPN; ESPN 2; Food Network; Fox News Channel; Fox Sports Southwest; FX; Headline News; HGTV; History Channel; Lifetime; MTV; Nickelodeon; Outdoor Channel; Oxygen; Speed; Spike TV; Syfy; TBS Superstation; The Learning Channel; The Weather Channel; Travel Channel; truTV; Turner Classic Movies; Turner Network TV; TV Land; USA Network; VH1.

Digital Basic Service
Subscribers: N.A.
Programming (via satellite): BBC America; Bio; Bloomberg Television; CMT Pure Country; Discovery en Espanol; Discovery Health Channel; Discovery Kids Channel; DIY Network; Encore (multiplexed); ESPN Classic Sports; ESPN U; Flix; GSN; History Channel International; ID Investigation Discovery; Independent Film Channel; LOGO; Military Channel; MTV Hits; MTV Jams; MTV2; Music Choice; Nick Jr.; Nick Too; NickToons TV; Planet Green; Science; SoapNet; Style Network; Sundance Channel; TeenNick; Toon Disney; Tr3s; Turner Classic Movies; VH1 Classic; VH1 Soul; WE tv.

Digital Pay Service 1
Pay Units: N.A.
Programming (via satellite): Cinemax (multiplexed); Encore (multiplexed); HBO (multiplexed); Showtime (multiplexed); Starz (multiplexed); The Movie Channel (multiplexed).

Video-On-Demand: No

Pay-Per-View
iN DEMAND (delivered digitally); Spice: Xcess (delivered digitally); Club Jenna (delivered digitally); Playboy TV (delivered digitally); Fresh (delivered digitally); Shorteez (delivered digitally).

Internet Service
Operational: No.

Telephone Service
None

Miles of Plant: 80.0 (coaxial); None (fiber optic). Additional miles planned: 6.0 (coaxial).
Chief Executive Officer: Bill Haggarty. Regional Vice President: Andrew Dearth. Vice President, Marketing: Tracy Bass.
Ownership: Allegiance Communications (MSO).

WISTER—Allegiance Communications, 707 W Saratoga St, Shawnee, OK 74804. Phones: 405-275-6923; 405-395-1131. Web Site: http://www.allegiance.tv. ICA: OK0193.
TV Market Ranking: Below 100 (WISTER). Franchise award date: N.A. Franchise expiration date: N.A. Began: July 1, 1980.
Channel capacity: 36 (not 2-way capable). Channels available but not in use: N.A.

Basic Service
Subscribers: 300.
Programming (received off-air): KFSM-TV (CBS) Fort Smith; KHBS (ABC, CW) Fort Smith; KOET (PBS) Eufaula; KPBI-CA (FOX) Fort Smith; KTUL (ABC) Tulsa.
Programming (via satellite): AMC; CNN; Country Music TV; Discovery Channel;

Disney Channel; ESPN; ESPN 2; Headline News; Nickelodeon; QVC; Spike TV; TBS Superstation; The Weather Channel; Trinity Broadcasting Network; Turner Network TV; USA Network; WGN America.
Fee: $21.95 monthly.

Pay Service 1
Pay Units: N.A.
Programming (via satellite): Encore; HBO; Showtime; Starz; The Movie Channel.

Internet Service
Operational: No.

Telephone Service
None

Miles of Plant: 15.0 (coaxial); None (fiber optic).
Chief Executive Officer: Bill Haggarty. Regional Vice President: Andrew Dearth. Vice President, Marketing: Tracy Bass.
Ownership: Allegiance Communications (MSO).

WOODALL—Formerly served by Eagle Media. No longer in operation. ICA: OK0365.

WOODWARD—Suddenlink Communications, 1904 Main St, Woodward, OK 73801. Phones: 800-999-6845; 314-315-9346; 314-965-2020. Fax: 580-254-3426. Web Site: http://www.suddenlink.com. ICA: OK0029.
TV Market Ranking: Outside TV Markets (WOODWARD). Franchise award date: March 18, 1956. Franchise expiration date: N.A. Began: April 1, 1956.
Channel capacity: N.A. Channels available but not in use: N.A.

Basic Service
Subscribers: 4,165.
Programming (received off-air): KETA-TV (PBS) Oklahoma City; KOCB (CW) Oklahoma City; KOMI-CD Woodward; KUOK-DT (UNV) Woodward.
Programming (via microwave): KFOR-TV (NBC) Oklahoma City; KOCO-TV (ABC) Oklahoma City; KOKH-TV (FOX) Oklahoma City; KWTV-DT (CBS) Oklahoma City.
Programming (via satellite): QVC; The Weather Channel.
Fee: $35.00 installation; $19.95 monthly.

Expanded Basic Service 1
Subscribers: N.A.
Programming (received off-air): KVDA (TMO) San Antonio.
Programming (via satellite): A&E Networks; ABC Family Channel; AMC; Animal Planet; Cartoon Network; CNBC; CNN; Comedy Central; C-SPAN; Discovery Channel; Disney Channel; E! Entertainment Television; ESPN; ESPN 2; Food Network; Fox News Channel; Fox Sports Southwest; FX; Great American Country; Hallmark Channel; Headline News; HGTV; History Channel; Independent Film Channel; Lifetime; MSNBC; MTV; National Geographic Channel; Nickelodeon; Outdoor Channel; Spike TV; Syfy; TBS Superstation; The Learning Channel; Toon Disney; Travel Channel; Trinity Broadcasting Network; Turner Classic Movies; Turner Network TV; TV Land; USA Network; VH1.
Fee: $24.00 monthly.

Digital Basic Service
Subscribers: N.A.
Programming (via satellite): BBC America; Bio; cloo; Discovery Digital Networks; DMX Music; ESPN Classic Sports; ESPNews; Fox Soccer; Fuse; Golf Channel; GSN; History Channel International; Speed; Style Network; Versus; WE tv.
Fee: $3.99 monthly.

Pay Service 1
Pay Units: 128.
Programming (via satellite): Cinemax.
Fee: $10.00 installation; $9.95 monthly.

Pay Service 2
Pay Units: 859.
Programming (via satellite): HBO.
Fee: $10.95 monthly.

Pay Service 3
Pay Units: 381.
Programming (via satellite): Showtime.
Fee: $9.95 monthly.

Pay Service 4
Pay Units: 368.
Programming (via satellite): The Movie Channel.
Fee: $5.95 monthly.

Digital Pay Service 1
Pay Units: N.A.
Programming (via satellite): Cinemax (multiplexed); Encore (multiplexed); HBO (multiplexed); Showtime (multiplexed); Starz; The Movie Channel (multiplexed).

Video-On-Demand: No

Pay-Per-View
iN DEMAND (delivered digitally); Playboy TV (delivered digitally); Fresh (delivered digitally).

Internet Service
Operational: Yes. Began: October 1, 2002.
Broadband Service: Suddenlink High Speed Internet.
Fee: $45.95 installation; $24.95 monthly.

Telephone Service
Digital: Operational
Fee: $49.95 monthly

Miles of Plant: 130.0 (coaxial); None (fiber optic).
Manager: Dave Walker. Marketing Director: Beverly Gambell. Chief Technician: Jeff Smith.
Ownership: Cequel Communications LLC (MSO).

WRIGHT CITY—Allegiance Communications, 707 W Saratoga St, Shawnee, OK 74804. Phones: 405-275-6923; 405-395-1131. Web Site: http://www.allegiance.tv. ICA: OK0198.
TV Market Ranking: Outside TV Markets (WRIGHT CITY). Franchise award date: N.A. Franchise expiration date: N.A. Began: December 1, 1965.
Channel capacity: N.A. Channels available but not in use: N.A.

Basic Service
Subscribers: 235.
Programming (received off-air): KOET (PBS) Eufaula; KSLA (CBS) Shreveport; KTAL-TV (NBC) Texarkana; KTBS-TV (ABC) Shreveport; KTEN (ABC, CW, NBC) Ada; KXII (CBS, FOX, MNT) Sherman.

Programming (via satellite): AMC; CNBC; CNN; Country Music TV; Discovery Channel; Disney Channel; ESPN; Headline News; Lifetime; Nickelodeon; Outdoor Channel; QVC; Spike TV; TBS Superstation; The Weather Channel; Trinity Broadcasting Network; Turner Network TV; TV Land; USA Network; VH1; WGN America.
Fee: $25.00 installation; $21.95 monthly.

Pay Service 1
Pay Units: N.A.
Programming (via satellite): Encore; HBO; Starz.

Pay-Per-View
iN DEMAND (delivered digitally); Hot Choice (delivered digitally); Fresh (delivered digitally); Shorteez (delivered digitally); ESPN Now (delivered digitally); ESPN Gameplan (delivered digitally).

Internet Service
Operational: Yes.
Fee: $24.95 installation; $39.95 monthly.

Telephone Service
None

Miles of Plant: 7.0 (coaxial); None (fiber optic).
Chief Executive Officer: Bill Haggarty. Regional Vice President: Andrew Dearth. Vice President, Marketing: Tracy Bass.
Ownership: Allegiance Communications (MSO).

WYANDOTTE—Allegiance Communications, 707 W Saratoga St, Shawnee, OK 74804. Phones: 405-275-6923; 405-395-1131. Web Site: http://www.allegiance.tv. ICA: OK0327.
TV Market Ranking: Below 100 (WYANDOTTE). Franchise award date: January 1, 1989. Franchise expiration date: N.A. Began: September 1, 1989.
Channel capacity: N.A. Channels available but not in use: N.A.

Basic Service
Subscribers: N.A.
Programming (received off-air): KFJX (FOX) Pittsburg; KOAM-TV (CBS) Pittsburg; KODE-TV (ABC) Joplin; KOED-TV (PBS) Tulsa; KSNF (NBC) Joplin; KTUL (ABC) Tulsa.
Programming (via satellite): A&E Networks; ABC Family Channel; CNBC; CNN; Country Music TV; Discovery Channel; Disney Channel; E! Entertainment Television; ESPN; ESPN 2; Headline News; Lifetime; Nickelodeon; Spike TV; Syfy; TBS Superstation; Travel Channel; Trinity Broadcasting Network; Turner Network TV; USA Network; WGN America.
Fee: $30.00 installation; $21.95 monthly.

Video-On-Demand: No

Pay-Per-View
iN DEMAND (delivered digitally); Hot Choice (delivered digitally); Playboy TV (delivered digitally); Fresh (delivered digitally); Shorteez (delivered digitally).

Internet Service
Operational: No.

Telephone Service
None

Miles of Plant: 2.0 (coaxial); None (fiber optic).
Chief Executive Officer: Bill Haggarty. Regional Vice President: Andrew Dearth. Vice President, Marketing: Tracy Bass.
Ownership: Allegiance Communications (MSO).

WYNONA—Community Cablevision Co., 1550 W Rogers Blvd, PO Box 307, Skiatook, OK 74070-0307. Phone: 918-396-3019. Fax: 918-396-2081. E-mail: info@communitycablevision.com. Web Site: http://www.communitycablebroadband.com. ICA: OK0214.
TV Market Ranking: Below 100 (WYNONA). Franchise award date: October 15, 1986. Franchise expiration date: October 15, 2011. Began: February 1, 1987.
Channel capacity: 35 (not 2-way capable). Channels available but not in use: N.A.

Basic Service
Subscribers: 118.
Programming (received off-air): KDOR-TV (TBN) Bartlesville; KJRH-TV (NBC) Tulsa; KOED-TV (PBS) Tulsa; KOKI-TV (FOX) Tulsa; KOTV-DT (CBS) Tulsa; KQCW-DT (CW) Muskogee; KRSC-TV (ETV) Claremore; KTFO-CD (TEL) Austin; KTPX-TV (ION) Okmulgee; KTUL (ABC) Tulsa; KWHB (IND) Tulsa.
Programming (via satellite): ABC Family Channel; Cartoon Network; CNN; Country Music TV; Discovery Channel; Disney Channel; ESPN; ESPN 2; Fox Sports Southwest; Headline News; HGTV; QVC; Spike TV; Syfy; TBS Superstation; Turner Classic Movies; Turner Network TV; USA Network; WGN America.
Fee: $29.95 installation; $18.50 monthly.

Video-On-Demand: No

Internet Service
Operational: Yes.
Fee: $44.95 monthly.

Telephone Service
None

Miles of Plant: 4.0 (coaxial); None (fiber optic).
President & General Manager: Dennis Soule.
Ownership: Community Cablevision Co. (MSO).

YALE—Community Cablevision Co., 1550 W Rogers Blvd, PO Box 307, Skiatook, OK 74070-0307. Phone: 918-396-3019. Fax: 918-396-2081. E-mail: info@communitycablevision.com. Web Site: http://www.communitycablebroadband.com. ICA: OK0141.
TV Market Ranking: Outside TV Markets (YALE). Franchise award date: March 24, 1987. Franchise expiration date: March 24, 2012. Began: April 20, 1983.
Channel capacity: 39 (not 2-way capable). Channels available but not in use: N.A.

Basic Service
Subscribers: 270.
Programming (received off-air): KFOR-TV (NBC) Oklahoma City; KJRH-TV (NBC) Tulsa; KOCB (CW) Oklahoma City; KOCO-TV (ABC) Oklahoma City; KOED-TV (PBS) Tulsa; KOKH-TV (FOX) Oklahoma City; KQCW-DT (CW) Muskogee; KTBO-TV (TBN) Oklahoma City; KTFO-CD (TEL) Austin; KTPX-TV (ION) Okmulgee; KTUL (ABC) Tulsa; KWHB (IND) Tulsa; KWTV-DT (CBS) Oklahoma City.
Programming (via satellite): A&E Networks; ABC Family Channel; Cartoon Network; CNN; Country Music TV; C-SPAN; Discovery Channel; Disney Channel; ESPN; ESPN 2; Fox Sports Southwest; Headline News; MTV; Nickelodeon; QVC; Spike TV; Syfy; TBS Superstation; The Learning Channel; The Weather Channel; Turner Classic Movies; Turner Network TV; USA Network; VH1; WGN America.
Fee: $29.95 installation; $24.95 monthly.

Video-On-Demand: No

Internet Service
Operational: Yes.
Fee: $44.95 monthly.

Telephone Service
None

Miles of Plant: 10.0 (coaxial); None (fiber optic).
President & General Manager: Dennis Soule.
Ownership: Community Cablevision Co. (MSO).

OREGON

Total Systems: **82**
Total Communities Served: **359**
Franchises Not Yet Operating: **0**
Applications Pending: **0**
Communities with Applications: **0**
Number of Basic Subscribers: **1,085,846**
Number of Expanded Basic Subscribers: **425,128**
Number of Pay Units: **132,552**

Top 100 Markets Represented: Portland (29).

For a list of cable communities in this section, see the Cable Community Index located in the back of Cable Volume 2.
For explanation of terms used in cable system listings, see p. D-11.

ARLINGTON—Arlington TV Cooperative Inc., 120 On The Mall, PO Box 184, Arlington, OR 97812-0184. Phone: 541.454.2707. Fax: 541-454-2707. E-mail: arlingtontv@yahoo.com. ICA: OR0106.

TV Market Ranking: Outside TV Markets (ARLINGTON). Franchise award date: N.A. Franchise expiration date: N.A. Began: December 1, 1955.

Channel capacity: 36 (2-way capable). Channels available but not in use: N.A.

Basic Service

Subscribers: 75.

Programming (received off-air): KATU (ABC) Portland; KEPR-TV (CBS) Pasco; KGW (NBC) Portland; KNDU (NBC) Richland; KOIN (CBS) Portland; KPDX (MNT) Vancouver; KPTV (FOX) Portland; KVEW (ABC, MNT) Kennewick.

Programming (via satellite): ABC Family Channel; Cartoon Network; CNN; Discovery Channel; Disney Channel; ESPN; ESPN 2; Golf Channel; HGTV; QVC; TBS Superstation; Turner Network TV.

Fee: $25.00 installation; $29.50 monthly.

Pay Service 1

Pay Units: 13.

Programming (via satellite): HBO.

Fee: $12.50 monthly.

Video-On-Demand: No

Internet Service

Operational: No.

Telephone Service

None

Miles of Plant: 8.0 (coaxial); None (fiber optic).

Vice President: Judith Hughes. Office Manager & Chief Technician: John Neys.

Ownership: Arlington TV Cooperative Inc.

ASHLAND—Ashland TV. This cable system has converted to IPTV. See Ashland, OR [OR5023]. ICA: OR0174.

ASHLAND—Formerly served by Ashland TV [OR0174]. This cable system has converted to IPTV, 607 Siskiyou Blvd, Ashland, OR 97520. Phone: 541-488-9207. Web Site: http://www.ashlandtv.com. ICA: OR5023.

Channel capacity: N.A. Channels available but not in use: N.A.

Internet Service

Operational: Yes.

ASTORIA—Charter Communications, 521 NE 136th Ave, Vancouver, WA 98684. Phone: 360-828-6600. Fax: 360-828-6795. Web Site: http://www.charter.com. Also serves Arch Cape, Cannon Beach, Clatskanie, Clatsop County, Columbia County (northern portion), Gearhart, Hammond, Seaside & Warrenton, OR; Cathlamet, Ilwaco, Long Beach, Nahcotta, Naselle, Ocean Park, Oysterville, Pacific County & Seaview, WA. ICA: OR0012.

TV Market Ranking: Outside TV Markets (Arch Cape, ASTORIA, Cannon Beach, Cathlamet, Clatskanie, Clatsop County, Columbia County (northern portion), Gearhart, Hammond, Ilwaco, Long Beach, Nahcotta, Naselle, Ocean Park, Oysterville, Pacific County, Seaside, Seaview, Warrenton). Franchise award date: January 1, 1971. Franchise expiration date: N.A. Began: November 25, 1948.

Channel capacity: 76 (operating 2-way). Channels available but not in use: N.A.

Basic Service

Subscribers: 14,801.

Programming (received off-air): KATU (ABC) Portland; KGW (NBC) Portland; KING-TV (NBC) Seattle; KOIN (CBS) Portland; KOMO-TV (ABC) Seattle; KOPB-TV (PBS) Portland; KPDX (MNT) Vancouver; KPTV (FOX) Portland; KRCW-TV (CW) Salem; 13 FMs.

Programming (via satellite): A&E Networks; AmericanLife TV Network; CNN; C-SPAN; Fox Movie Channel; Fox News Channel; FX; G4; HGTV; INSP; MTV; Nickelodeon; QVC; TBS Superstation; The Learning Channel; Trinity Broadcasting Network; TV Guide Network; USA Network.

Fee: $29.95 installation.

Expanded Basic Service 1

Subscribers: 11,059.

Programming (via satellite): ABC Family Channel; AMC; Animal Planet; Bravo; Cartoon Network; CNBC; Comedy Central; Country Music TV; C-SPAN 2; Discovery Channel; Disney Channel; E! Entertainment Television; ESPN; ESPN 2; Food Network; Golf Channel; Hallmark Channel; Headline News; History Channel; Lifetime; MSNBC; National Geographic Channel; Northwest Cable News; Oxygen; SoapNet; Speed; Spike TV; Syfy; The Weather Channel; Toon Disney; Travel Channel; truTV; Turner Classic Movies; Turner Network TV; TV Land; Versus; VH1.

Fee: $42.99 monthly.

Digital Basic Service

Subscribers: 4,597.

Programming (via satellite): BBC America; Bio; Discovery Digital Networks; DIY Network; GAS; History Channel International; Independent Film Channel; Lifetime Movie Network; MTV Networks Digital Suite; Music Choice; Nick Jr.; Sundance Channel.

Fee: $6.95 monthly.

Digital Pay Service 1

Pay Units: 751.

Programming (via satellite): Cinemax (multiplexed).

Fee: $10.00 installation; $10.95 monthly.

Digital Pay Service 2

Pay Units: 1,906.

Programming (via satellite): HBO (multiplexed).

Fee: $10.00 installation; $11.95 monthly.

Digital Pay Service 3

Pay Units: 1,107.

Programming (via satellite): Flix; Showtime (multiplexed).

Fee: $10.00 installation; $10.95 monthly.

Digital Pay Service 4

Pay Units: 675.

Programming (via satellite): The Movie Channel (multiplexed).

Fee: $10.95 monthly.

Digital Pay Service 5

Pay Units: 1,467.

Programming (via satellite): Encore (multiplexed); Starz (multiplexed).

Video-On-Demand: Yes

Pay-Per-View

Addressable homes: 4,597.

Hot Choice (delivered digitally); iN DEMAND (delivered digitally); Playboy TV (delivered digitally); Fresh (delivered digitally); Shorteez (delivered digitally).

Internet Service

Operational: Yes. Began: November 30, 2001.

Subscribers: 1,500.

Broadband Service: Charter Pipeline.

Fee: $29.99 monthly.

Telephone Service

Digital: Operational

Miles of Plant: 625.0 (coaxial); None (fiber optic).

Vice President: Frank Antonovich. General Manager: Linda Kimberly. Technical Operations Director: Brian Lindholme. Marketing Director: Diane Long.

Ownership: Charter Communications Inc. (MSO).

BEAVERCREEK—Beaver Creek Telephone Co., 15223 S Henrici Rd, PO Box 1390, Oregon City, OR 97045. Phone: 503-632-3113. Fax: 503-632-4159. E-mail: support@bctonline.com. Web Site: http://www.bctelco.com. Also serves Clackamas County (portions), Mulino & Oregon City. ICA: OR0167. **Note:** This system is an overbuild.

TV Market Ranking: 29 (BEAVERCREEK, Clackamas County (portions), Mulino, Oregon City). Franchise award date: N.A. Franchise expiration date: N.A. Began: April 15, 1994.

Channel capacity: 78 (not 2-way capable). Channels available but not in use: N.A.

Basic Service

Subscribers: 2,700.

Programming (received off-air): KATU (ABC) Portland; KGW (NBC) Portland; KNMT (TBN) Portland; KOIN (CBS) Portland; KOPB-TV (PBS) Portland; KPDX (MNT) Vancouver; KPTV (FOX) Portland; KPXG-TV (ION) Salem.

Programming (via satellite): ABC Family Channel; C-SPAN; Disney Channel; Headline News; Northwest Cable News; TV Guide Network.

Fee: $39.95 installation; $14.50 monthly.

Expanded Basic Service 1

Subscribers: 2,300.

Programming (received off-air): KRCW-TV (CW) Salem.

Programming (via satellite): A&E Networks; AMC; Animal Planet; Cartoon Network; CNBC; CNN; Comedy Central; Country Music TV; Discovery Channel; E! Entertainment Television; ESPN; Food Network; FX; HGTV; History Channel; Lifetime; MTV; Nickelodeon; Spike TV; Syfy; TBS Superstation; The Learning Channel; The Weather Channel; Turner Classic Movies; Turner Network TV; USA Network; VH1; WGN America.

Fee: $19.95 monthly.

Digital Basic Service

Subscribers: 250.

Programming (via satellite): BBC America; Bio; Bloomberg Television; Discovery Digital Networks; DIY Network; ESPN Classic Sports; ESPNews; G4; GAS; Golf Channel; History Channel International; Independent Film Channel; Lifetime Movie Network; MTV2; National Geographic Channel; Nick Jr.; NickToons TV; Outdoor Channel; Speed; Style Network; TV Land; Versus; WE tv.

Fee: $7.05 monthly.

Pay Service 1

Pay Units: 167.

Programming (via satellite): Cinemax (multiplexed).

Fee: $9.95 monthly.

Pay Service 2

Pay Units: 417.

Programming (via satellite): HBO (multiplexed).

Fee: $10.95 monthly.

Pay Service 3

Pay Units: 80.

Programming (via satellite): Showtime.

Fee: $9.95 monthly.

Pay Service 4

Pay Units: 220.

Programming (via satellite): Encore; Starz.

Fee: $7.95 monthly.

Digital Pay Service 1

Pay Units: N.A.

Programming (via satellite): Cinemax (multiplexed); Encore (multiplexed); HBO (multiplexed); Showtime (multiplexed); The Movie Channel (multiplexed).

Fee: $8.95 monthly (Starz), 10.95 monthly (HBO, TMC, Showtime, or Cinemax).

Video-On-Demand: No

Pay-Per-View

iN DEMAND.

Internet Service

Operational: No, DSL.

Telephone Service

None

Miles of Plant: 217.0 (coaxial); 1.0 (fiber optic).

President & Chief Executive Officer: Tom Linstrom. Executive Vice President: Paul Hauer. Vice President, Operations: Mark

Beaudry. Assistant Operations Manager: Roselle Potts. Marketing Director: Tangee Summerhill-Bishop. Chief Technician: Chris Stewart.
Ownership: Beaver Creek Cooperative Telephone Co. (MSO).

BEAVERTON—Comcast Cable, 9605 SW Nimbus Ave, Beaverton, OR 97008-7198. Phones: 503-605-6000; 503-605-4895. Fax: 503-605-6226. Web Site: http://www.comcast.com. Also serves Aloha, Banks, Columbia City, Columbia County (portions), Cornelius, Durham, Forest Grove, Gaston, Hillsboro, King City, Lake Oswego, North Plains, Rivergrove, Scappoose, Sherwood, St. Helens, Tigard, Tualatin, Warren, Washington County & Wilsonville. ICA: OR0002.
TV Market Ranking: 29 (Aloha, Banks, BEAVERTON, Columbia City, Cornelius, Durham, Forest Grove, Gaston, Hillsboro, King City, Lake Oswego, North Plains, Rivergrove, Scappoose, Sherwood, St. Helens, Tigard, Tualatin, Warren, Washington County, Wilsonville); Below 100 (Columbia County (portions)); Outside TV Markets (Columbia County (portions)). Franchise award date: N.A. Franchise expiration date: N.A. Began: December 1, 1982.
Channel capacity: N.A. Channels available but not in use: N.A.
Basic Service
Subscribers: 594,726 Includes Corvallis, Eugene, Portland, Salem, Longview WA, & Vancouver WA.
Programming (received off-air): KATU (ABC) Portland; KGW (NBC) Portland; KNMT (TBN) Portland; KOIN (CBS) Portland; KOPB-TV (PBS) Portland; KPDX (MNT) Vancouver; KPTV (FOX) Portland; KPXG-TV (ION) Salem; KRCW-TV (CW) Salem.
Programming (via satellite): C-SPAN; C-SPAN 2; Discovery Channel; Hallmark Channel; Product Information Network; QVC; ShopNBC; TV Guide Network; Univision Studios; WGN America.
Fee: $44.99 installation; $8.15 monthly.
Expanded Basic Service 1
Subscribers: N.A.
Programming (via satellite): A&E Networks; ABC Family Channel; AMC; Animal Planet; BET Networks; Cartoon Network; CNBC; CNN; Comedy Central; Country Music TV; Disney Channel; E! Entertainment Television; ESPN; ESPN 2; Food Network; Fox News Channel; FX; Golf Channel; Headline News; HGTV; History Channel; Lifetime; MSNBC; MTV; Nickelodeon; Northwest Cable News; Oxygen; Spike TV; Syfy; TBS Superstation; The Learning Channel; The Weather Channel; Travel Channel; truTV; Turner Network TV; TV Land; USA Network; VH1.
Fee: $43.74 monthly.
Digital Basic Service
Subscribers: 31,085.
Programming (via satellite): AmericanLife TV Network; BBC America; Bio; Black Family Channel; Bloomberg Television; Bravo; Canales N; Discovery Fit & Health; DMX Music; Encore Action; ESPN Classic Sports; ESPNews; Eternal Word TV Network; Fox Movie Channel; Fox Sports World; FSN Digital Atlantic; FSN Digital Central; FSN Digital Pacific; Fuse; G4; GAS; Great American Country; GSN; Halogen Network; History Channel International; Independent Film Channel; Lifetime Movie Network; Lime; MTV Networks Digital Suite; National Geographic Channel; Nick Jr.; NickToons TV; Nuvo TV; Outdoor Channel; Ovation; Speed; Style Network; Sundance Channel; The Word Network; Toon Disney; Turner Classic Movies; Versus; WE tv; Weatherscan.
Fee: $10.95 monthly; $3.25 converter.
Digital Pay Service 1
Pay Units: N.A.
Programming (via satellite): CCTV-4; Cinemax (multiplexed); Filipino Channel; Flix; HBO (multiplexed); Russian Television Network; Showtime (multiplexed); Starz (multiplexed); The Movie Channel (multiplexed).
Fee: $18.15 monthly (each).
Video-On-Demand: Yes
Pay-Per-View
Addressable homes: 31,085.
iN DEMAND (delivered digitally); Fresh (delivered digitally); Sports PPV (delivered digitally); Urban Xtra (delivered digitally); Shorteez (delivered digitally); Playboy TV (delivered digitally).
Internet Service
Operational: Yes.
Subscribers: 33,028.
Broadband Service: Comcast High Speed Internet.
Fee: $42.95 monthly; $3.00 modem lease.
Telephone Service
None
Miles of Plant: 15,837.0 (coaxial); None (fiber optic). Miles of plant (coax & fiber combined) includes Corvallis, Eugene, Portland, Salem, Longview WA, & Vancouver WA
Senior Vice President: Curt Henninger. Vice President, Technical Operations: Mike Mason. Vice President, Marketing: Lars Lofas. Marketing Director: Brad Nosler. Sales Director: Mike Williams. Public Relations Director: Theressa Davis.
Ownership: Comcast Cable Communications Inc. (MSO).

BEND—Bend Broadband, 63090 Sherman Rd, Bend, OR 97701-5750. Phones: 541-388-5820 (Administrative office); 541-549-1911; 541-382-5551. Fax: 541-385-3271. Web Site: http://www.bendcable.com. Also serves Black Butte Ranch, Prineville, Redmond, Sisters, Terrebonne & Tumalo. ICA: OR0013.
TV Market Ranking: Below 100 (BEND, Black Butte Ranch, Prineville, Redmond, Sisters, Terrebonne, Tumalo). Franchise award date: January 1, 1955. Franchise expiration date: N.A. Began: September 1, 1955.
Channel capacity: N.A. Channels available but not in use: N.A.
Digital Basic Service
Subscribers: 37,000.
Programming (via satellite): A&E HD; A&E Networks; ABC Family Channel; ABC Family HD; AMC; AmericanLife TV Network; Animal Planet; Animal Planet HD; Bio; Bio HD; Bloomberg Television; BlueHighways TV; Boomerang; Bravo; Bravo HD; BTN; BTN HD; BYU Television; Cartoon Network; Cartoon Network HD; CBS Sports Network; CNBC; CNBC HD+; CNN; CNN HD; Comcast SportsNet California; Comedy Central; Country Music TV; C-SPAN; C-SPAN 2; Current; CW+; Discovery Channel HD; Discovery Kids Channel; Disney Channel; Disney Channel HD; DIY Network; E! Entertainment Television; ESPN; ESPN 2; ESPN 2 HD; ESPN Classic Sports; ESPN HD; ESPN U; Eternal Word TV Network; Food Network; Food Network HD; Fox Business Channel; Fox Business Channel HD; Fox News Channel; Fox News HD; FSN HD; FX; FX HD; Golf Channel; Hallmark Channel; Halogen Network; Headline News; here! TV; HGTV; HGTV HD; History Channel; History Channel HD; ID Investigation Discovery; Lifetime; Lifetime Television HD; MSNBC; MTV; Music Choice; NASA TV; National Geographic Channel; National Geographic Channel HD Network; Nick Jr.; Nickelodeon; NickToons TV; Odyssey Television Network; Outdoor Channel; Outdoor Channel 2 HD; Oxygen; PBS Kids Sprout; QVC; ReelzChannel; RLTV; Science; SoapNet; Spike TV; Syfy; Syfy HD; TBS in HD; TBS Superstation; TeenNick; Telemundo; The Learning Channel; The Weather Channel; The Weather Channel HD; TLC HD; Toon Disney; Toon Disney HD; Travel Channel; Travel Channel HD; Trinity Broadcasting Network; truTV; Turner Classic Movies; Turner Network TV; Turner Network TV HD; TV Land; USA Network; USA Network HD; Versus; Versus HD; VH1.
Fee: $39.50 installation; $34.95 (Limited, Family, Essentials, & Preferred).
Digital Expanded Basic Service
Subscribers: N.A.
Programming (via satellite): Africa Channel; BBC America; CBS Sports Network HD; Chiller; cloo; CMT Pure Country; Cooking Channel; Crime & Investigation Network; Discovery Fit & Health; Discovery Health Channel; Encore (multiplexed); ESPNews; ESPNews HD; Fox College Sports Atlantic; Fox College Sports Central; Fox College Sports Pacific; Fox Movie Channel; Fox Soccer; Fuel TV; Fuse; G4; GSN; Hallmark Movie Channel; Hallmark Movie Channel HD; HD Theater; HDNet; HDNet Movies; History Channel International; Independent Film Channel; MGM HD; Military Channel; Military History Channel; MTV Hits; MTV2; Palladia; Planet Green; RFD-TV; Science HD; Smithsonian Channel HD; Speed; Speed HD; Style Network; Tennis Channel; Tennis Channel HD; Universal HD; VH1 Classic; WE tv.
Digital Pay Service 1
Pay Units: 2,880.
Programming (via satellite): Cinemax (multiplexed); Cinemax HD; HBO (multiplexed); HBO HD; Showtime (multiplexed); Showtime HD; Starz (multiplexed); Starz HDTV; The Movie Channel (multiplexed); The Movie Channel HD.
Fee: $15.25 monthly (HBO, Cinemax, Starz or Showtime/TMC).
Video-On-Demand: Yes
Pay-Per-View
Playboy TV (delivered digitally); Fresh (delivered digitally).
Internet Service
Operational: Yes. Began: April 1, 1998.
Subscribers: 30,000.
Broadband Service: InstaNet.
Fee: $39.50 installation; $26.95-$89.99 monthly; $10.00 modem lease; $99.00 modem purchase.
Telephone Service
Analog: Not Operational
Digital: Operational
Subscribers: 11,500.
Fee: $14.95-$29.95 monthly
Miles of Plant: 1,300.0 (coaxial); 315.0 (fiber optic).
President & Chief Executive Officer: Amy C. Tykeson. Vice President, Business Operations: John Farwell. Chief Technology Officer: Frank Miller.
Ownership: Tykeson & Associates.

BEND—Formerly served by WANTV. No longer in operation. ICA: OR0164.

BLY—Formerly served by Bly Cable Co. No longer in operation. ICA: OR0110.

BOARDMAN—Rapid Cable, 1750 S Hwy 10, Price, UT 84501-4364. Phone: 435-637-6823. Fax: 435-637-9755. ICA: OR0070.
TV Market Ranking: Outside TV Markets (BOARDMAN). Franchise award date: N.A. Franchise expiration date: N.A. Began: October 8, 1979.
Channel capacity: 61 (not 2-way capable). Channels available but not in use: N.A.
Basic Service
Subscribers: 160.
Programming (received off-air): KATU (ABC) Portland; KEPR-TV (CBS) Pasco; KFFX-TV (FOX, IND) Pendleton; KGW (NBC) Portland; KNDU (NBC) Richland; KOIN (CBS) Portland; KOPB-TV (PBS) Portland; KPTV (FOX) Portland; KVEW (ABC, MNT) Kennewick; allband FM.
Programming (via satellite): A&E Networks; ABC Family Channel; AMC; Animal Planet; CNBC; CNN; C-SPAN; Discovery Channel; Disney Channel; E! Entertainment Television; ESPN; ESPN 2; Fox Movie Channel; Fox News Channel; FX; GalaVision; Great American Country; Headline News; HGTV; History Channel; INSP; Lifetime; MoviePlex; MTV; Nickelodeon; Spike TV; Style Network; TBS Superstation; The Weather Channel; Toon Disney; Trinity Broadcasting Network; Turner Network TV; TV Guide Network; Univision Studios; USA Network; VH1; WGN America.
Fee: $29.95 installation; $19.95 monthly.
Pay Service 1
Pay Units: N.A.
Programming (via satellite): Encore; HBO (multiplexed); Starz.
Video-On-Demand: No
Pay-Per-View
Movies; special events (delivered digitally).
Internet Service
Operational: No.
Telephone Service
None
Miles of Plant: 18.0 (coaxial); None (fiber optic).
Regional Manager: Shane Baggs. Engineering Director: Richard O'Neill. Chief Technician: David Ramsey.
Ownership: Rapid Communications LLC (MSO).

BONANZA—Formerly served by Almega Cable. No longer in operation. ICA: OR0109.

BORING—Formerly served by Community Cable Inc. No longer in operation. ICA: OR0125.

BROOKINGS—Charter Communications, 1286 Northcrest Dr, Crescent City, CA 95531-2321. Phones: 360-828-6600 (Vancouver office); 707-464-5722. Fax: 707-464-4849. Web Site: http://www.charter.com. Also serves Curry County (portions). ICA: OR0173.
TV Market Ranking: Outside TV Markets (BROOKINGS, Curry County (portions)). Franchise award date: N.A. Franchise expiration date: N.A. Began: N.A.
Channel capacity: N.A. Channels available but not in use: N.A.
Basic Service
Subscribers: 3,678.
Programming (received off-air): KBLN (IND) Grants Pass; KBSC-LP (IND) Brookings; KBVU (FOX) Eureka; KDRV (ABC) Medford; KIEM-TV (NBC) Eureka; KOBI (NBC) Medford; KSYS (PBS) Medford; KTVL (CBS, CW) Medford.
Programming (via satellite): C-SPAN; C-SPAN 2; Eternal Word TV Network; INSP; QVC; ShopNBC; Telemundo; The Weather

Channel; Trinity Broadcasting Network; Univision Studios; WGN America.
Fee: $29.95 installation.

Expanded Basic Service 1
Subscribers: 3,671.
Programming (via satellite): A&E Networks; ABC Family Channel; AMC; Animal Planet; Bravo; Cartoon Network; CNBC; CNN; Comedy Central; Country Music TV; Discovery Channel; Disney Channel; DIY Network; E! Entertainment Television; ESPN; ESPN 2; Food Network; Fox News Channel; FX; G4; Golf Channel; Great American Country; GSN; Hallmark Channel; Headline News; HGTV; History Channel; Lifetime; MSNBC; MTV; MTV2; National Geographic Channel; Nickelodeon; Northwest Cable News; Oxygen; Speed; Spike TV; Style Network; Syfy; TBS Superstation; The Learning Channel; Toon Disney; Travel Channel; truTV; Turner Classic Movies; Turner Network TV; TV Land; USA Network; Versus; VH1; WE tv.
Fee: $42.99 monthly.

Digital Basic Service
Subscribers: N.A.
Programming (via satellite): BBC America; Bio; Boomerang; CNN en Espanol; CNN International; Discovery Digital Networks; ESPN Classic Sports; ESPNews; Fox College Sports Atlantic; Fox College Sports Central; Fox College Sports Pacific; Fox Deportes; Fox Movie Channel; Fox Soccer; GAS; History Channel International; Independent Film Channel; Lifetime Movie Network; MTV Networks Digital Suite; Music Choice; NFL Network; Nick Jr.; NickToons TV; SoapNet; Sundance Channel; TV Guide Interactive Inc.

Digital Pay Service 1
Pay Units: N.A.
Programming (via satellite): Cinemax (multiplexed); Encore (multiplexed); Flix; HBO (multiplexed); Showtime (multiplexed); Starz (multiplexed); The Movie Channel (multiplexed).

Video-On-Demand: Yes

Pay-Per-View
iN DEMAND (delivered digitally); NASCAR In Car (delivered digitally); Hot Choice (delivered digitally); Playboy TV (delivered digitally); Fresh (delivered digitally); Shorteez (delivered digitally).

Internet Service
Operational: Yes.
Broadband Service: Charter Pipeline.
Fee: $29.99 monthly.

Telephone Service
Digital: Operational

Miles of Plant: 202.0 (coaxial); None (fiber optic).
Vice President: Frank Antonovich. General Manager: Linda Kimberly. Plant Manager: Earl DeSomber. Chief Technician: Dennis Putnam. Marketing Director: Diane Long. Office Manager: Sandra Milunich.
Ownership: Charter Communications Inc. (MSO).

BROOKS—Formerly served by Country Cablevision Ltd. No longer in operation. ICA: OR0088.

BROWNSVILLE—Rapid Cable, 1750 S Hwy 10, Price, UT 84501-4364. Phone: 435-637-6823. Fax: 435-637-9755. ICA: OR0079.
TV Market Ranking: Below 100 (BROWNSVILLE). Franchise award date: N.A. Franchise expiration date: N.A. Began: January 1, 1971.
Channel capacity: 40 (not 2-way capable). Channels available but not in use: N.A.

Basic Service
Subscribers: 548.
Programming (received off-air): KATU (ABC) Portland; KEZI (ABC) Eugene; KGW (NBC) Portland; KLSR-TV (FOX) Eugene; KMTR (CW, NBC) Eugene; KOAC-TV (PBS) Corvallis; KOIN (CBS) Portland; KPTV (FOX) Portland; KVAL-TV (CBS, IND) Eugene; allband FM.
Programming (via satellite): ABC Family Channel; AMC; Animal Planet; Bravo; Cartoon Network; C-SPAN; ESPN; ESPN 2; Food Network; Fox Sports Net; Headline News; HGTV; INSP; Nickelodeon; QVC; Speed; TBS Superstation; The Learning Channel; Travel Channel; Trinity Broadcasting Network; truTV.
Fee: $29.95 installation; $19.95 monthly.

Expanded Basic Service 1
Subscribers: 483.
Programming (via satellite): A&E Networks; Lifetime; Syfy; USA Network.
Fee: $4.57 monthly.

Expanded Basic Service 2
Subscribers: 269.
Programming (via satellite): CNN; Country Music TV; Discovery Channel; Disney Channel; Spike TV; Turner Network TV.
Fee: $5.35 monthly.

Pay Service 1
Pay Units: 60.
Programming (via satellite): HBO.
Fee: $11.95 monthly.

Pay Service 2
Pay Units: 68.
Programming (via satellite): Showtime.
Fee: $10.95 monthly.

Pay Service 3
Pay Units: 50.
Programming (via satellite): The Movie Channel.
Fee: $10.95 monthly.

Pay Service 4
Pay Units: N.A.
Programming (via satellite): Cinemax.

Video-On-Demand: No

Internet Service
Operational: No.

Telephone Service
None

Miles of Plant: 50.0 (coaxial); None (fiber optic).
Regional Manager: Shane Baggs. Engineering Director: Richard O'Neill. Chief Technician: David Ramsey.
Ownership: Rapid Communications LLC (MSO).

BURNS—Charter Communications, 639 N Kellogg St, Kennewick, WA 99336. Phones: 509-222-2500; 509-783-0132. Fax: 509-735-3795. Web Site: http://www.charter.com. Also serves Harney County (portions) & Hines. ICA: OR0045.
TV Market Ranking: Outside TV Markets (BURNS, Harney County (portions), Hines). Franchise award date: N.A. Franchise expiration date: N.A. Began: June 1, 1956.
Channel capacity: N.A. Channels available but not in use: N.A.

Basic Service
Subscribers: 1,248.
Programming (received off-air): KOPB-TV (PBS) Portland; KPDX (MNT) Vancouver; KTVZ (CW, NBC) Bend.
Programming (via microwave): KATU (ABC) Portland; KOIN (CBS) Portland.
Programming (via satellite): C-SPAN; C-SPAN 2; Eternal Word TV Network; INSP; ION Television; KCNC-TV (CBS) Denver; KUSA (NBC) Denver; QVC; Trinity Broadcasting Network; TV Guide Network; WGN America.
Fee: $29.99 installation.

Expanded Basic Service 1
Subscribers: N.A.
Programming (via satellite): A&E Networks; ABC Family Channel; AMC; Animal Planet; Bravo; Cartoon Network; CNBC; CNN; Comedy Central; Country Music TV; Discovery Channel; Disney Channel; DIY Network; E! Entertainment Television; ESPN; ESPN 2; Food Network; Fox News Channel; FX; GSN; Hallmark Channel; Headline News; HGTV; History Channel; Lifetime; MSNBC; MTV; Nickelodeon; Northwest Cable News; Outdoor Channel; Oxygen; Spike TV; Syfy; TBS Superstation; The Learning Channel; The Weather Channel; Travel Channel; truTV; Turner Network TV; Univision Studios; USA Network; VH1; WE tv.
Fee: $50.99 monthly.

Digital Basic Service
Subscribers: N.A.
Programming (via satellite): BBC America; Bloomberg Television; Discovery Fit & Health; DMX Music; ESPN Classic Sports; ESPNews; Fox Movie Channel; Fox Soccer; G4; Golf Channel; Independent Film Channel; National Geographic Channel; Nick Jr.; Speed; Turner Classic Movies; TV Guide Interactive Inc.; Versus; VH1 Classic; VH1 Country.

Digital Pay Service 1
Pay Units: 143.
Programming (via satellite): Cinemax (multiplexed); Encore (multiplexed); HBO (multiplexed).
Fee: $20.00 installation; $7.95 monthly.

Digital Pay Service 2
Pay Units: N.A.
Programming (via satellite): Showtime (multiplexed); Starz (multiplexed); The Movie Channel (multiplexed).

Video-On-Demand: No

Pay-Per-View
iN DEMAND (delivered digitally); Playboy TV (delivered digitally); Fresh (delivered digitally).

Internet Service
Operational: No.

Telephone Service
None

Miles of plant included in Kennewick, WA
General Manager: Linda Kimberly. Technical Operations Manager: Jeff Hopkins. Marketing Director: Diane Long. Program Director: Lloyd Swain.
Ownership: Charter Communications Inc. (MSO).

BUTTE FALLS—Almega Cable, 4016 W Airport Freeway, Ste 545, Bedford, TX 76021. Phones: 877-725-6342; 817-685-9588. Fax: 817-685-6488. Web Site: http://almegacable.com. ICA: OR0127.
TV Market Ranking: Below 100 (BUTTE FALLS). Franchise award date: N.A. Franchise expiration date: N.A. Began: January 1, 1980.
Channel capacity: 40 (not 2-way capable). Channels available but not in use: N.A.

Basic Service
Subscribers: 57.
Programming (received off-air): KDRV (ABC) Medford; KMVU-DT (FOX) Medford; KOBI (NBC) Medford; KSYS (PBS) Medford; KTVL (CBS, CW) Medford.
Programming (via satellite): A&E Networks; ABC Family Channel; AMC; Bravo; CNBC; CNN; Comedy Central; Country Music TV; Discovery Channel; Disney Channel; ESPN; HGTV; History Channel; Lifetime; MSNBC; Spike TV; TBS Superstation; The Learning Channel; The Weather Channel; Turner Network TV; USA Network; WGN America.
Fee: $29.95 installation; $28.45 monthly.

Pay Service 1
Pay Units: 7.
Programming (via satellite): Cinemax.
Fee: $11.55 monthly.

Pay Service 2
Pay Units: 13.
Programming (via satellite): HBO.
Fee: $11.55 monthly.

Video-On-Demand: No

Internet Service
Operational: No.

Telephone Service
None

Miles of Plant: 3.0 (coaxial); None (fiber optic).
President: Thomas Kurien.
Ownership: Almega Cable (MSO).

CANBY—Wave Broadband. Now served by WOODBURN, OR [OR0023]. ICA: OR0017.

CASCADE LOCKS—City of Cascade Locks Cable TV, 140 SW WaNaPa, PO Box 308, Cascade Locks, OR 97014. Phone: 541-374-8484. Fax: 541-374-8752. E-mail: thupp@cascade-locks.or.us. Web Site: http://www.cascade-locks.or.us. ICA: OR0087.
TV Market Ranking: Below 100 (CASCADE LOCKS). Franchise award date: N.A. Franchise expiration date: N.A. Began: January 1, 1971.
Channel capacity: N.A. Channels available but not in use: N.A.

Basic Service
Subscribers: 290.
Programming (received off-air): KATU (ABC) Portland; KGW (NBC) Portland; KOIN (CBS) Portland; KOPB-TV (PBS) Portland; KPDX (MNT) Vancouver; KPTV (FOX) Portland; allband FM.
Programming (via satellite): A&E Networks; CNN; Discovery Channel; Disney Channel; ESPN; HGTV; History Channel; Lifetime; Nickelodeon; Spike TV; Syfy; TBS Superstation; Turner Network TV; TV Land; USA Network; WGN America.
Fee: $35.00 installation; $24.00 monthly.

Pay Service 1
Pay Units: 87.
Programming (via satellite): HBO.
Fee: $8.75 monthly.

Video-On-Demand: No

Internet Service
Operational: Yes. Began: March 21, 2002.
Subscribers: 110.
Broadband Service: In-house.
Fee: $25.00 installation; $25.00 monthly.

Telephone Service
None

Miles of Plant: 15.0 (coaxial); None (fiber optic).
Manager: Tracy Hupp. Chief Technician: Ed Winnett.
Ownership: City of Cascade Locks Cable TV.

CAVE JUNCTION—Formerly served by Almega Cable. No longer in operation. ICA: OR0054.

CHILOQUIN—Almega Cable, 4013 W Airport Freeway, Ste 542, Bedford, TX 76021. Phones: 877-725-6342; 817-685-9588. Fax: 817-685-6488. Web Site: http://almegacable.com. ICA: OR0090.
TV Market Ranking: Below 100 (CHILOQUIN). Franchise award date: N.A. Franchise ex-

piration date: December 31, 2012. Began: October 15, 1981.

Channel capacity: 45 (not 2-way capable). Channels available but not in use: N.A.

Basic Service

Subscribers: 113.

Programming (received off-air): KDRV (ABC) Medford; KOTI (NBC) Klamath Falls; KTVL (CBS, CW) Medford.

Programming (via satellite): A&E Networks; ABC Family Channel; Bravo; Cartoon Network; CNBC; CNN; Comedy Central; Discovery Channel; Disney Channel; ESPN; ESPN 2; Food Network; HGTV; History Channel; MSNBC; National Geographic Channel; Spike TV; Syfy; TBS Superstation; Turner Classic Movies; Turner Network TV; USA Network; WE tv; WGN America.

Fee: $29.95 installation; $26.45 monthly.

Pay Service 1

Pay Units: 30.

Programming (via satellite): HBO.

Fee: $15.00 installation; $10.95 monthly.

Video-On-Demand: No

Internet Service

Operational: No.

Telephone Service

None

Miles of Plant: 20.0 (coaxial); None (fiber optic).

Ownership: Almega Cable (MSO).

COLTON—ColtonTel, 20983 S Hwy 211, PO Box 68, Colton, OR 97017-0068. Phone: 503-824-3211. Fax: 503-824-9944. E-mail: customercare@coltontel.com. Web Site: http://www.coltontel.com. ICA: OR0176.

TV Market Ranking: 29 (COLTON).

Channel capacity: 48 (not 2-way capable). Channels available but not in use: N.A.

Basic Service

Subscribers: 440.

Programming (received off-air): KATU (ABC) Portland; KGW (NBC) Portland; KNMT (TBN) Portland; KOIN (CBS) Portland; KOPB-TV (PBS) Portland; KPDX (MNT) Vancouver; KPTV (FOX) Portland; KPXG-TV (ION) Salem; KRCW-TV (CW) Salem.

Programming (via satellite): C-SPAN; Northwest Cable News; QVC; The Weather Channel; TV Guide Network.

Fee: $19.75 monthly.

Expanded Basic Service 1

Subscribers: 264.

Programming (via satellite): A&E Networks; ABC Family Channel; AMC; Animal Planet; Cartoon Network; CNBC; CNN; Comedy Central; Country Music TV; Discovery Channel; Disney Channel; E! Entertainment Television; ESPN; ESPN 2; Food Network; Fox News Channel; Fox Sports Net; FX; GalaVision; Hallmark Channel; Headline News; HGTV; History Channel; Lifetime; MTV; Nickelodeon; Outdoor Channel; RFD-TV; Speed; Spike TV; Syfy; TBS Superstation; The Learning Channel; Travel Channel; truTV; Turner Classic Movies; Turner Network TV; TV Land; USA Network; Versus; VH1; WGN America.

Fee: $18.20 monthly.

Digital Basic Service

Subscribers: 142.

Programming (via satellite): 3 Angels Broadcasting Network; BBC America; Bio; BYU Television; Chiller; CMT Pure Country; Cooking Channel; Discovery Fit & Health; Discovery Health Channel; Discovery Home Channel; Discovery Kids Channel; Discovery Times Channel; Disney XD; DIY Network; ESPN Classic Sports; ESPN U; ESPNews; Estrella TV; G4; Golf Channel; Great American Country; GSN; Hallmark Channel; Hallmark Movie Channel; History Channel International; Lifetime Movie Network; Lifetime Real Women; Military Channel; MTV Hits; MTV Jams; MTV2; Music Choice; National Geographic Channel; Nick Jr.; Nick Too; NickToons TV; Oxygen; Science; SoapNet; Sundance Channel; The N; Tr3s; VH1 Classic; VH1 Soul; WE tv.

Fee: $29.74 monthly.

Digital Pay Service 1

Pay Units: 124.

Programming (via satellite): Cinemax (multiplexed); Encore (multiplexed); Flix; HBO (multiplexed); Showtime (multiplexed); Starz (multiplexed); The Movie Channel (multiplexed).

Video-On-Demand: No

Pay-Per-View

TVN Entertainment (delivered digitally).

Internet Service

Operational: Yes.

Fee: $95.00 installation; $34.95-$49.95 monthly.

Telephone Service

None

Miles of Plant: 64.0 (coaxial); None (fiber optic).

General Manager: Peggy Turner.

Ownership: ColtonTel.

CONDON—J & N Cable, 614 S Columbus Ave, Goldendale, WA 98620-9006. Phone: 509-773-5359. Fax: 509-773-7090. E-mail: john@jncable.com. Web Site: http://www.jncable.com. ICA: OR0093.

TV Market Ranking: Outside TV Markets (CONDON). Franchise award date: N.A. Franchise expiration date: N.A. Began: January 1, 1955.

Channel capacity: N.A. Channels available but not in use: N.A.

Basic Service

Subscribers: 200.

Programming (received off-air): KATU (ABC) Portland; KGW (NBC) Portland; KOIN (CBS) Portland; KOPB-TV (PBS) Portland; KPDX (MNT) Vancouver; KPTV (FOX) Portland; KRCW-TV (CW) Salem; allband FM.

Programming (via satellite): 3 Angels Broadcasting Network; A&E Networks; ABC Family Channel; AMC; AmericanLife TV Network; Animal Planet; Cartoon Network; CNBC; CNN; C-SPAN; C-SPAN 2; Discovery Channel; Disney Channel; DIY Network; ESPN; ESPN 2; ESPN Classic Sports; ESPNews; Eternal Word TV Network; Food Network; Fox News Channel; Fox Sports Net; G4; Golf Channel; Great American Country; Hallmark Channel; Headline News; HGTV; History Channel; ION Television; Lifetime; MSNBC; Northwest Cable News; Outdoor Channel; QVC; ShopNBC; Speed; Style Network; Syfy; TBS Superstation; The Weather Channel; TLC; Travel Channel; Trinity Broadcasting Network; truTV; Turner Classic Movies; Turner Network TV; USA Network; Versus.

Fee: $20.00 installation; $11.95 monthly.

Pay Service 1

Pay Units: 40.

Programming (via satellite): HBO (multiplexed).

Fee: $12.95 monthly.

Pay Service 2

Pay Units: 5.

Programming (via satellite): Showtime (multiplexed).

Fee: $12.95 monthly.

Pay Service 3

Pay Units: N.A.

Programming (via satellite): Cinemax (multiplexed); The Movie Channel.

Video-On-Demand: No

Internet Service

Operational: Yes. Began: December 31, 2001.

Subscribers: 100.

Broadband Service: InterTECH.

Fee: $39.95 monthly.

Telephone Service

None

Miles of Plant: 14.0 (coaxial); None (fiber optic).

Manager: John Kusky. Marketing Manager: Nancy Kusky.

Ownership: J & N Cable Systems Inc. (MSO).

COOS BAY—Charter Communications, 521 NE 136th Ave, Vancouver, WA 98684. Phone: 360-828-6600. Fax: 360-828-6795. Web Site: http://www.charter.com. Also serves Bandon, Coos County (northern portion), Coquille, Gardiner, Lakeside, Myrtle Point, North Bend, Port Orford, Reedsport & Winchester Bay. ICA: OR0015.

TV Market Ranking: Below 100 (Bandon, COOS BAY, Coos County (northern portion), Coquille, Gardiner, Lakeside, Myrtle Point, North Bend, Reedsport, Winchester Bay); Outside TV Markets (Port Orford). Franchise award date: N.A. Franchise expiration date: N.A. Began: October 1, 1954.

Channel capacity: 78 (operating 2-way). Channels available but not in use: N.A.

Basic Service

Subscribers: 17,383.

Programming (received off-air): KCBY-TV (CBS) Coos Bay; KEZI (ABC) Eugene; KLSR-TV (FOX) Eugene; KMCB (NBC) Coos Bay; KOAC-TV (PBS) Corvallis; KOBI (NBC) Medford; KPTV (FOX) Portland; 14 FMs.

Programming (via satellite): C-SPAN; C-SPAN 2; INSP; MTV; QVC; ShopNBC; The Weather Channel; Trinity Broadcasting Network; WGN America.

Fee: $29.95 installation.

Expanded Basic Service 1

Subscribers: 16,916.

Programming (via satellite): A&E Networks; ABC Family Channel; AMC; Animal Planet; Bravo; Cartoon Network; CNBC; CNN; Comedy Central; Country Music TV; Discovery Channel; Disney Channel; E! Entertainment Television; ESPN; ESPN 2; Food Network; Fox Movie Channel; Fox News Channel; FX; G4; Golf Channel; Great American Country; GSN; Hallmark Channel; Headline News; HGTV; History Channel; Lifetime; MSNBC; National Geographic Channel; Nickelodeon; Northwest Cable News; Outdoor Channel; Oxygen; SoapNet; Speed; Spike TV; Syfy; TBS Superstation; Telemundo; The Learning Channel; The Weather Channel; Toon Disney; Travel Channel; truTV; Turner Classic Movies; Turner Network TV; TV Land; USA Network; Versus; VH1; WE tv.

Fee: $42.99 monthly.

Digital Basic Service

Subscribers: 4,279.

Programming (via satellite): BBC America; Bio; Bloomberg Television; Boomerang; CNN en Espanol; Discovery Digital Networks; DIY Network; ESPN Classic Sports; Fox Sports World; GAS; History Channel International; Independent Film Channel; Lifetime Movie Network; MTV Networks Digital Suite; Music Choice; Nick Jr.; Nick Too; Style Network; Sundance Channel.

Digital Pay Service 1

Pay Units: 656.

Programming (via satellite): Cinemax (multiplexed).

Fee: $10.00 monthly.

Digital Pay Service 2

Pay Units: 1,543.

Programming (via satellite): HBO (multiplexed).

Fee: $10.00 monthly.

Digital Pay Service 3

Pay Units: 1,310.

Programming (via satellite): Flix; Showtime (multiplexed).

Fee: $10.00 monthly.

Digital Pay Service 4

Pay Units: 649.

Programming (via satellite): The Movie Channel (multiplexed).

Fee: $10.00 monthly.

Digital Pay Service 5

Pay Units: 1,542.

Programming (via satellite): Encore (multiplexed); Starz.

Fee: $10.00 monthly.

Video-On-Demand: Yes

Pay-Per-View

Addressable homes: 4,279.

Hot Choice (delivered digitally); Fresh (delivered digitally); Playboy TV (delivered digitally); iN DEMAND (delivered digitally).

Internet Service

Operational: Yes. Began: November 1, 2001.

Subscribers: 2,566.

Broadband Service: Charter Pipeline.

Fee: $29.99 monthly; $4.95 modem lease.

Telephone Service

Digital: Operational

Miles of Plant: 444.0 (coaxial); None (fiber optic).

Vice President: Frank Antonovich. General Manager: Linda Kimberly. Technical Operations Director: Brian Lindholme. Marketing Director: Diane Long.

Ownership: Charter Communications Inc. (MSO).

CORVALLIS—Comcast Cable, 9605 SW Nimbus Ave, Beaverton, OR 97008-7198. Phone: 503-605-6000. Fax: 503-605-6226. Web Site: http://www.comcast.com. Also serves Adair Village, Albany, Benton County, Lebanon, Linn County (western portion), Millersburg, North Albany, Oakville, Philomath, Sodaville, Sweet Home, Tangent & Waterloo. ICA: OR0008.

TV Market Ranking: Below 100 (Adair Village, Albany, Benton County, CORVALLIS,

Lebanon, Linn County (western portion), Millersburg, North Albany, Oakville, Philomath, Sodaville, Sweet Home, Tangent, Waterloo). Franchise award date: N.A. Franchise expiration date: N.A. Began: October 1, 1964.

Channel capacity: N.A. Channels available but not in use: N.A.

Basic Service

Subscribers: N.A. Included in Beaverton

Programming (received off-air): KATU (ABC) Portland; KEVU-CD (MNT) Eugene; KEZI (ABC) Eugene; KGW (NBC) Portland; KLSR-TV (FOX) Eugene; KMTR (CW, NBC) Eugene; KOAC-TV (PBS) Corvallis; KOIN (CBS) Portland; KOPB-TV (PBS) Portland; KPDX (MNT) Vancouver; KPTV (FOX) Portland; KPXG-TV (ION) Salem; KRCW-TV (CW) Salem; KTVC (IND) Roseburg; KVAL-TV (CBS, IND) Eugene; 18 FMs.

Programming (via satellite): C-SPAN; C-SPAN 2; Discovery Channel; Hallmark Channel; Jewelry Television; QVC; ShopNBC; Telemundo; TV Guide Network; Versus HD.

Fee: $43.99 installation; $12.25 monthly; $14.99 additional installation.

Expanded Basic Service 1

Subscribers: 35,321.

Programming (via satellite): A&E Networks; ABC Family Channel; AMC; Animal Planet; BET Networks; Cartoon Network; CNBC; CNN; Comcast SportsNet California; Comedy Central; Country Music TV; Disney Channel; E! Entertainment Television; ESPN; ESPN 2; Food Network; Fox News Channel; Fox Sports Net; FX; Golf Channel; Headline News; HGTV; History Channel; Lifetime; MTV; Nickelodeon; Northwest Cable News; Oxygen; Spike TV; Syfy; TBS Superstation; The Learning Channel; The Weather Channel; Travel Channel; truTV; Turner Network TV; TV Land; Univision Studios; USA Network; Versus; VH1.

Fee: $28.97 monthly.

Digital Basic Service

Subscribers: 14,162.

Programming (via microwave): Turner Network TV HD.

Programming (via satellite): A&E HD; ABC Family HD; Animal Planet HD; Azteca America; BBC America; Bio; Bloomberg Television; Bravo; BTN; BYU Television; Canal Sur; CBS Sports Network; Cine Latino; CNN HD; Cooking Channel; Current; Daystar TV Network; Discovery Channel HD; Discovery en Espanol; Discovery Fit & Health; Discovery Health Channel; Discovery Kids Channel; Disney Channel HD; Disney XD; DIY Network; ESPN 2 HD; ESPN Classic Sports; ESPN HD; ESPN U; ESPNews; Eternal Word TV Network; FEARnet; Food Network HD; Fox Business Channel; Fox College Sports Atlantic; Fox College Sports Central; Fox College Sports Pacific; Fox Deportes; Fox Movie Channel; Fox News HD; Fox Reality Channel; Fox Soccer; Fuse; FX HD; G4; GalaVision; GMC; Golf Channel HD; GolTV; Great American Country; GSN; Hallmark Channel; Halogen Network; HD Theater; HGTV HD; History Channel en Espanol; History Channel HD; History Channel International; ID Investigation Discovery; Independent Film Channel; Latele Novela Network; Lifetime Movie Network; LOGO; Military Channel; MoviePlex; MSNBC; MTV Hits; MTV Jams; MTV2; mun2 television; Music Choice; National Geographic Channel; National Geographic Channel HD Network; NBA TV; NFL Network; NFL Network HD; Nick Jr.; Nick Too; NickToons TV; Nuvo TV; Outdoor Channel; Oxygen; Palladia; PBS Kids Sprout; Planet Green; Science; Science HD; ShopNBC; SoapNet; Sorpresa; Speed; Speed HD; Starz IndiePlex; Starz RetroPlex; Style Network; Sundance Channel; Syfy HD; TBS in HD; TeenNick; Tennis Channel; The Word Network; TLC HD; Tr3s; Trinity Broadcasting Network; Turner Classic Movies; TV One; TVG Network; Universal HD; USA Network HD; VeneMovies; VH1 Classic; VH1 Soul; WE tv; Weatherscan.

Fee: $14.95 monthly.

Digital Pay Service 1

Pay Units: 10,133.

Programming (via satellite): Cinemax (multiplexed); Cinemax HD; Encore (multiplexed); Filipino Channel; Flix; HBO (multiplexed); HBO HD; Russian Television Network; Showtime (multiplexed); Showtime HD; Starz (multiplexed); Starz HDTV; The Movie Channel (multiplexed).

Fee: $11.49 monthly (each).

Video-On-Demand: Yes

Pay-Per-View

Addressable homes: 14,162.

iN DEMAND (delivered digitally); Sports PPV (delivered digitally); Playboy TV (delivered digitally).

Internet Service

Operational: Yes.

Subscribers: 15,048.

Broadband Service: Comcast High Speed Internet.

Fee: $42.95 monthly; $3.00 modem lease.

Telephone Service

Digital: Operational

Miles of plant included in Beaverton

Senior Vice President: Curt Henninger. Vice President, Technical Operations: Mike Mason. Vice President, Marketing: Lars Lofas. Sales Director: Mike Williams. Marketing Director: Brad Nosler. Public Relations Director: Theressa Davis.

Ownership: Comcast Cable Communications Inc. (MSO).

COTTAGE GROVE—Charter Communications, 521 NE 136th Ave, Vancouver, WA 98684. Phone: 360-828-6600. Fax: 360-828-6795. Web Site: http://www.charter.com. Also serves Coburg, Creswell, Dexter, Douglas County (northern portion), Drain, Elmira, Jasper, Lane County (portions), Leaburg, Lowell, Marcola, McKenzie, Noti, Oakridge, Pleasant Hill, Veneta, Walterville, Westfir & Yoncalla. ICA: OR0073.

TV Market Ranking: Below 100 (Coburg, COTTAGE GROVE, Creswell, Dexter, Douglas County (Portions), Drain, Elmira, Jasper, Lane County (Portions), Leaburg, Lowell, Marcola, Mckenzie, Noti, Pleasant Hill, Veneta, Walterville, Yoncalla); Outside TV Markets (Oakridge, Westfir). Franchise award date: N.A. Franchise expiration date: N.A. Began: July 1, 1983.

Channel capacity: 52 (not 2-way capable). Channels available but not in use: N.A.

Basic Service

Subscribers: 10,653.

Programming (received off-air): KEVU-CD (MNT) Eugene; KEZI (ABC) Eugene; KLSR-TV (FOX) Eugene; KMTR (CW, NBC) Eugene; KOAC-TV (PBS) Corvallis; KOBI (NBC) Medford; KVAL-TV (CBS, IND) Eugene.

Programming (via satellite): A&E Networks; AMC; Comedy Central; C-SPAN; Disney Channel; INSP; ION Television; MTV; QVC; TBS Superstation; The Weather Channel; TV Guide Network; USA Network; VH1.

Fee: $29.95 installation.

Expanded Basic Service 1

Subscribers: 9,399.

Programming (via satellite): ABC Family Channel; Animal Planet; Bravo; Cartoon Network; CNN; Country Music TV; Discovery Channel; E! Entertainment Television; ESPN; Food Network; Fox News Channel; FX; Headline News; HGTV; History Channel; Lifetime; MSNBC; Nickelodeon; Speed; Spike TV; Syfy; The Learning Channel; Travel Channel; truTV; Turner Classic Movies; Turner Network TV; TV Land.

Fee: $42.99 monthly.

Digital Basic Service

Subscribers: 2,366.

Programming (via satellite): BBC America; Bio; Bloomberg Television; DIY Network; G4; Lifetime Movie Network; MTV Networks Digital Suite; MuchMusic Network; Music Choice; Nick Jr.; Style Network.

Fee: $7.62 monthly.

Digital Pay Service 1

Pay Units: 492.

Programming (via satellite): Cinemax (multiplexed).

Fee: $10.00 monthly.

Digital Pay Service 2

Pay Units: 1,186.

Programming (via satellite): HBO (multiplexed).

Fee: $10.00 monthly.

Digital Pay Service 3

Pay Units: 894.

Programming (via satellite): Flix; Showtime (multiplexed).

Fee: $10.00 monthly.

Digital Pay Service 4

Pay Units: 465.

Programming (via satellite): The Movie Channel (multiplexed).

Fee: $10.00 monthly.

Digital Pay Service 5

Pay Units: 1,134.

Programming (via satellite): Encore (multiplexed); Starz.

Video-On-Demand: No

Pay-Per-View

Addressable homes: 2,366.

Shorteez (delivered digitally); Fresh (delivered digitally); Playboy TV (delivered digitally); iN DEMAND (delivered digitally).

Internet Service

Operational: No.

Telephone Service

None

Miles of Plant: 531.0 (coaxial); None (fiber optic).

Vice President: Frank Antonovich. General Manager: Linda Kimberly. Technical Operations Director: Brian Lindholme. Marketing Director: Diane Long.

Ownership: Charter Communications Inc. (MSO).

COVE—Formerly served by Almega Cable. No longer in operation. ICA: OR0099.

DALLAS—Charter Communications, 521 NE 136th Ave, Vancouver, WA 98684. Phone: 360-828-6600. Fax: 360-828-6795. Web Site: http://www.charter.com. Also serves Falls City, Independence, Jefferson, Marion County (southwestern portion), Monmouth, Polk County (portions) & Rickreall. ICA: OR0039.

TV Market Ranking: Below 100 (DALLAS, Falls City, Independence, Jefferson, Marion County (southwestern portion), Monmouth, Polk County (portions), Rickreall). Franchise award date: N.A. Franchise expiration date: N.A. Began: April 1, 1966.

Channel capacity: 39 (operating 2-way). Channels available but not in use: N.A.

Basic Service

Subscribers: 5,920.

Programming (received off-air): KATU (ABC) Portland; KGW (NBC) Portland; KOAC-TV (PBS) Corvallis; KOIN (CBS) Portland; KPDX (MNT) Vancouver; KPTV (FOX) Portland; KPXG-TV (ION) Salem; KRCW-TV (CW) Salem; allband FM.

Programming (via satellite): A&E Networks; CNBC; C-SPAN; Eternal Word TV Network; HGTV; MTV; QVC; TBS Superstation; Trinity Broadcasting Network; TV Guide Network; USA Network; WGN America.

Fee: $29.99 installation.

Expanded Basic Service 1

Subscribers: 5,233.

Programming (via satellite): ABC Family Channel; AMC; Animal Planet; CNN; Comedy Central; Discovery Channel; Discovery Fit & Health; Disney Channel; E! Entertainment Television; ESPN; ESPN 2; Food Network; Fox News Channel; FX; Headline News; History Channel; Lifetime; MSNBC; Nickelodeon; Northwest Cable News; SoapNet; Speed; Spike TV; Syfy; The Learning Channel; The Weather Channel; Toon Disney; Travel Channel; Turner Network TV; TV Land; Univision Studios; Versus; WE tv.

Fee: $42.99 monthly.

Digital Basic Service

Subscribers: N.A.

Programming (via satellite): BBC America; Bio; Bloomberg Television; Bravo; Discovery Digital Networks; DIY Network; ESPN Classic Sports; ESPNews; Fox College Sports Atlantic; Fox College Sports Central; Fox College Sports Pacific; Fox Movie Channel; Fuel TV; Fuse; G4; GAS; GSN; History Channel International; Independent Film Channel; Lifetime Movie Network; MTV Networks Digital Suite; Music Choice; NFL Network; Nick Jr.; NickToons TV; Outdoor Channel; TV Guide Interactive Inc.

Digital Pay Service 1

Pay Units: 431.

Programming (via satellite): Cinemax (multiplexed).

Fee: $25.00 installation; $11.95 monthly.

Digital Pay Service 2

Pay Units: 947.

Programming (via satellite): HBO (multiplexed).

Fee: $25.00 installation; $11.95 monthly.

Digital Pay Service 3

Pay Units: 947.

Programming (via satellite): Encore (multiplexed).

Fee: $5.95 monthly.

Digital Pay Service 4

Pay Units: 602.

Programming (via satellite): Showtime (multiplexed).

Fee: $25.00 installation; $11.95 monthly.

Digital Pay Service 5

Pay Units: 406.

Programming (via satellite): The Movie Channel (multiplexed).

Fee: $25.00 installation; $11.95 monthly.

Digital Pay Service 6

Pay Units: N.A.

Programming (via satellite): Flix; Starz (multiplexed).

Fee: $11.95 monthly.

Video-On-Demand: Yes

Pay-Per-View

iN DEMAND (delivered digitally); Hot Choice (delivered digitally); Playboy TV (delivered digitally); Fresh (delivered digitally); Shorteez (delivered digitally).

Internet Service
Operational: Yes. Began: October 1, 2007.
Broadband Service: Charter Pipeline.
Fee: $29.99 monthly.
Telephone Service
Digital: Operational
Miles of Plant: 180.0 (coaxial); 8.0 (fiber optic).
Vice President: Frank Antonovich. General Manager: Linda Kimberly. Technical Operations Director: Brian Lindholme. Marketing Director: Diane Long.
Ownership: Charter Communications Inc. (MSO).

DAYVILLE—Blue Mountain TV Cable Co., 300 Highlan Terrace, PO Box 267, Mount Vernon, OR 97865-0267. Phone: 541-932-4613. Fax: 541-932-4613. E-mail: bmtv@bluemountaindigital.com. Web Site: http://www.bmtvcable.com. ICA: OR0120.
TV Market Ranking: Outside TV Markets (DAYVILLE). Franchise award date: N.A. Franchise expiration date: N.A. Began: October 1, 1956.
Channel capacity: 16 (not 2-way capable). Channels available but not in use: N.A.
Basic Service
Subscribers: 17.
Programming (via microwave): KOIN (CBS) Portland; KPTV (FOX) Portland.
Programming (via satellite): 3 Angels Broadcasting Network; Discovery Channel; KATU (ABC) Portland; KGW (NBC) Portland; KOPB-TV (PBS) Portland; Northwest Cable News; QVC; The Learning Channel.
Fee: $20.00 installation; $14.50 monthly.
Video-On-Demand: No
Internet Service
Operational: No.
Telephone Service
None
Miles of Plant: 3.0 (coaxial); None (fiber optic).
Manager: Chuck McKenna.
Ownership: Blue Mountain TV Cable Co. (MSO).

DEPOE BAY—Broadstripe, 41 Spring St, PO Box 367, Depoe Bay, WA. Phones: 800-829-2225; 425-747-4600. Fax: 425-644-4621. E-mail: contact_nw@broadstripe.com. Web Site: http://www.broadstripe.com. Also serves Gleneden Beach, Kernville, Lincoln Beach, Lincoln County (portions), Rose Lodge, Salmon River, Seal Rock, Siletz, Siletz River & South Beach. ICA: OR0134.
TV Market Ranking: Outside TV Markets (DEPOE BAY, Gleneden Beach, Kernville, Lincoln Beach, Lincoln County (portions), Rose Lodge, Salmon River, Seal Rock, Siletz, Siletz River, South Beach). Franchise award date: N.A. Franchise expiration date: N.A. Began: June 1, 1956.
Channel capacity: 35 (operating 2-way). Channels available but not in use: N.A.
Basic Service
Subscribers: 3,499.
Programming (received off-air): KATU (ABC) Portland; KGW (NBC) Portland; KOIN (CBS) Portland; KOPB-TV (PBS) Portland; KPDX (MNT) Vancouver; KPTV (FOX) Portland; allband FM.
Programming (via satellite): A&E Networks; ABC Family Channel; AMC; Animal Planet; Bravo; CNBC; CNN; Comedy Central; C-SPAN; Discovery Channel; Disney Channel; E! Entertainment Television; ESPN; ESPN 2; Food Network; Fox News Channel; FX; G4; Headline News; HGTV; History Channel; Lifetime; National Geographic Channel; Nickelodeon; Northwest Cable News; QVC; Spike TV; Syfy; TBS Superstation; The Learning Channel; The Weather Channel; Travel Channel; Trinity Broadcasting Network; Turner Network TV; TV Guide Network; TV Land; USA Network; WGN America.
Fee: $29.95 installation; $45.99 monthly.
Digital Basic Service
Subscribers: N.A.
Programming (via satellite): BBC America; Bio; Discovery Kids Channel; DMX Music; ESPNews; Fox Soccer; Golf Channel; GSN; History Channel International; Independent Film Channel; Lifetime Movie Network; Speed; Style Network; Versus.
Fee: $17.40 monthly.
Digital Pay Service 1
Pay Units: N.A.
Programming (via satellite): Cinemax (multiplexed); Encore (multiplexed); HBO (multiplexed); Showtime (multiplexed); Starz (multiplexed); The Movie Channel (multiplexed).
Fee: $10.00 monthly (each).
Video-On-Demand: No
Pay-Per-View
Playboy TV (delivered digitally); iN DEMAND (delivered digitally).
Internet Service
Operational: Yes.
Broadband Service: Millennium CableSpeed.
Fee: $49.95 installation; $37.95 monthly.
Telephone Service
Digital: Operational
Miles of Plant: 122.0 (coaxial); None (fiber optic).
President & Chief Executive Officer: Bill Shreffler. Vice President, Programming: Frank Scotello. Business Manager: Bob Lam.
Ownership: Broadstripe (MSO).

DUFUR—Northstate Cablevision, 180 NE 2nd St, PO Box 297, Dufur, OR 97021. Phone: 541-467-2409. ICA: OR0097.
TV Market Ranking: Outside TV Markets (DUFUR). Franchise award date: April 16, 1984. Franchise expiration date: N.A. Began: June 1, 1955.
Channel capacity: 35 (not 2-way capable). Channels available but not in use: N.A.
Basic Service
Subscribers: 180.
Programming (received off-air): KATU (ABC) Portland; KGW (NBC) Portland; KOIN (CBS) Portland; KOPB-TV (PBS) Portland; KPDX (MNT) Vancouver; KPTV (FOX) Portland; KRHP-LD (IND) The Dalles; allband FM.
Programming (via satellite): ABC Family Channel; Discovery Channel; Disney Channel; Spike TV; TBS Superstation.
Fee: $30.00 installation; $13.50 monthly.
Pay Service 1
Pay Units: 45.
Programming (via satellite): HBO.
Fee: $10.00 installation; $9.95 monthly.
Internet Service
Operational: No, DSL.
Miles of Plant: 5.0 (coaxial); None (fiber optic).
Manager: Gary E. Miller. Network Technician: Herb Watts.
Ownership: Northstate Cablevision Co.

ELGIN—Elgin TV Assn. Inc., 830 Alder St, PO Box 246, Elgin, OR 97827-0246. Phone: 541-437-4575. ICA: OR0076.
TV Market Ranking: Outside TV Markets (ELGIN). Franchise award date: N.A. Franchise expiration date: N.A. Began: October 1, 1955.
Channel capacity: N.A. Channels available but not in use: N.A.
Basic Service
Subscribers: 483.
Programming (received off-air): KATU (ABC) Portland; KGW (NBC) Portland; KHQ-TV (NBC) Spokane; KOIN (CBS) Portland; KPDX (MNT) Vancouver; KPTV (FOX) Portland; KREM (CBS) Spokane; KTVB (NBC) Boise; KTVR (PBS) La Grande; KXLY-TV (ABC, MNT) Spokane.
Programming (via satellite): A&E Networks; ABC Family Channel; AMC; CNN; Country Music TV; C-SPAN; Discovery Channel; Disney Channel; ESPN; HGTV; Northwest Cable News; Outdoor Channel; Spike TV; Syfy; TBS Superstation; The Learning Channel; Turner Network TV; TV Land; USA Network; WGN America.
Fee: $28.00 monthly.
Pay Service 1
Pay Units: 78.
Programming (via satellite): HBO; Showtime.
Fee: $10.00 installation; $10.00 monthly (each).
Internet Service
Operational: Yes.
Broadband Service: ParaSun Technologies (ISP & Tech support) and SBC to Net.
Fee: $50.00 installation; $43.95 monthly.
Telephone Service
None
Miles of Plant: 20.0 (coaxial); None (fiber optic).
Chief Technician: Michael McCants. Office Manager: Coral Rose.
Ownership: Elgin TV Assn. Inc.

ENTERPRISE—Almega Cable, 4011 W Airport Freeway, Ste 540, Bedford, TX 76021. Phones: 800-285-2330; 541-426-3636; 541-447-4342. Web Site: http://www.almega.com. Also serves Joseph, Lostine, Wallowa & Wallowa Lake. ICA: OR0048.
TV Market Ranking: Outside TV Markets (ENTERPRISE, Joseph, Lostine, Wallowa, Wallowa Lake). Franchise award date: N.A. Franchise expiration date: N.A. Began: June 1, 1955.
Channel capacity: N.A. Channels available but not in use: N.A.
Basic Service
Subscribers: 1,200.
Programming (received off-air): KATU (ABC) Portland; KEZI (ABC) Eugene; KFXO-LP (FOX) Bend; KOAB-TV (PBS) Bend; KOIN (CBS) Portland; KPDX (MNT) Vancouver; KTVZ (CW, NBC) Bend; 14 FMs.
Programming (via satellite): C-SPAN.
Fee: $30.50 installation; $14.95 monthly; $1.00 converter; $10.00 additional installation.
Expanded Basic Service 1
Subscribers: 1,179.
Programming (via satellite): A&E Networks; ABC Family Channel; CNBC; CNN; Country Music TV; Discovery Channel; Disney Channel; ESPN; ESPN 2; Fox News Channel; Hallmark Channel; Headline News; HGTV; History Channel; Lifetime; Nickelodeon; QVC; Spike TV; Syfy; The Learning Channel; Turner Classic Movies; Turner Network TV; USA Network; VH1; WPCH-TV (IND) Atlanta.
Fee: $12.95 monthly.
Pay Service 1
Pay Units: 97.
Programming (via satellite): Cinemax.
Fee: $10.00 installation; $10.00 monthly.
Pay Service 2
Pay Units: 147.
Programming (via satellite): HBO.
Fee: $10.00 monthly.
Video-On-Demand: No
Internet Service
Operational: No, DSL.
Telephone Service
None
Miles of Plant: 100.0 (coaxial); None (fiber optic).
Ownership: Almega Cable (MSO).

ESTACADA—Reliance Connects, 301 S Broadway St, PO Box 1283, Estacada, OR 97023. Phones: 503-630-4213; 503-630-3545. Fax: 503-630-8944. Web Site: http://www.relianceconnects.com. Also serves Clackamas County, Colton, Corbett & Eagle Creek. ICA: OR0068.
TV Market Ranking: 29 (Clackamas County, ESTACADA). Franchise award date: February 1, 1983. Franchise expiration date: N.A. Began: March 10, 1983.
Channel capacity: 60 (not 2-way capable). Channels available but not in use: N.A.
Basic Service
Subscribers: 830.
Programming (received off-air): KATU (ABC) Portland; KGW (NBC) Portland; KNMT (TBN) Portland; KOIN (CBS) Portland; KOPB-TV (PBS) Portland; KPDX (MNT) Vancouver; KPTV (FOX) Portland; KPXG-TV (ION) Salem; KRCW-TV (CW) Salem; KUNP-LP (UNV) Portland.
Programming (via satellite): A&E Networks; ABC Family Channel; AMC; Animal Planet; Cartoon Network; CNBC; CNN; Comedy Central; Country Music TV; C-SPAN; Discovery Channel; Disney Channel; E! Entertainment Television; ESPN; ESPN 2; Food Network; Fox News Channel; FX; GalaVision; Hallmark Channel; Headline News; HGTV; History Channel; Lifetime; MTV; Nickelodeon; Northwest Cable News; Outdoor Channel; QVC; RFD-TV; Speed; Spike TV; Syfy; TBS Superstation; The Learning Channel; The Weather Channel; Travel Channel; truTV; Turner Classic Movies; Turner Network TV; TV Guide Network; TV Land; USA Network; VH1; WGN America.
Fee: $35.00 installation; $19.95 monthly; $20.00 additional installation.
Digital Basic Service
Subscribers: N.A.
Programming (via satellite): BBC America; Cooking Channel; Discovery Digital Networks; DMX Music; GAS; MTV Networks

Digital Suite; Nick Jr.; Nick Too; NickToons TV.
Fee: $6.95 monthly.

Digital Pay Service 1
Pay Units: N.A.
Programming (via satellite): Cinemax (multiplexed); Encore (multiplexed); Flix; HBO (multiplexed); Showtime (multiplexed); Starz (multiplexed); Sundance Channel; The Movie Channel (multiplexed).
Fee: $13.99 monthly (Starz/Encore, HBO, Cinemax, or Showtime/TMC/Flix).

Pay-Per-View
iN DEMAND; TVN Entertainment (delivered digitally); ETC (delivered digitally); Pleasure (delivered digitally); Playboy TV.

Internet Service
Operational: No, DSL.

Telephone Service
None

Miles of Plant: 77.0 (coaxial); None (fiber optic).
Manager: Steven Crosby. Engineering Manager: Dennis Anderson. Chief Technician: Steve Valiant.
Ownership: Reliance Connects.

EUGENE—Comcast Cable, 9605 SW Nimbus Ave, Beaverton, OR 97008-7198. Phone: 503-605-6000. Fax: 503-605-6226. Web Site: http://www.comcast.com. Also serves Alvadore, Glenwood, Harrisburg, Junction City, Lane County, Santa Clara & Springfield. ICA: OR0004.
TV Market Ranking: Below 100 (Alvadore, EUGENE, Glenwood, Harrisburg, Junction City, Lane County (portions), Santa Clara, Springfield); Outside TV Markets (Lane County (portions)). Franchise award date: N.A. Franchise expiration date: June 1, 2008. Began: June 1, 1954.
Channel capacity: N.A. Channels available but not in use: N.A.

Basic Service
Subscribers: N.A. Included in Beaverton
Programming (received off-air): KEPB-TV (PBS) Eugene; KEVU-CD (MNT) Eugene; KEZI (ABC) Eugene; KLSR-TV (FOX) Eugene; KMTR (CW, NBC) Eugene; KTVC (IND) Roseburg; KVAL-TV (CBS, IND) Eugene.
Programming (via satellite): C-SPAN; C-SPAN 2; Discovery Channel; Hallmark Channel; ION Television; Product Information Network; QVC; ShopNBC; TV Guide Network.
Fee: $44.99 installation; $14.12 monthly; $14.99 additional installation.

Expanded Basic Service 1
Subscribers: 54,500.
Programming (via satellite): A&E Networks; ABC Family Channel; AMC; Animal Planet; BET Networks; Cartoon Network; CNBC; CNN; Comedy Central; Country Music TV; Disney Channel; E! Entertainment Television; ESPN; ESPN 2; Food Network; Fox News Channel; FX; Golf Channel; Headline News; HGTV; History Channel; Lifetime; MSNBC; MTV; Nickelodeon; Northwest Cable News; Oxygen; Spike TV; Syfy; TBS Superstation; The Learning Channel; The Weather Channel; Travel Channel; truTV; Turner Network TV; TV Land; Univision Studios; USA Network; VH1.
Fee: $37.77 monthly.

Digital Basic Service
Subscribers: 20,036.
Programming (via satellite): AmericanLife TV Network; BBC America; Bio; Black Family Channel; Bloomberg Television; Bravo; Canales N; Discovery Fit & Health; DMX Music; Encore Action; ESPN Classic Sports; ESPNews; Eternal Word TV Network; Fox Movie Channel; Fox Sports World; FSN Digital Atlantic; FSN Digital Central; FSN Digital Pacific; Fuse; G4; GAS; Great American Country; GSN; Halogen Network; History Channel International; Independent Film Channel; Lifetime Movie Network; Lime; MTV Networks Digital Suite; National Geographic Channel; Nick Jr.; NickToons TV; Nuvo TV; Outdoor Channel; Ovation; Speed; Style Network; Sundance Channel; The Word Network; Toon Disney; Trinity Broadcasting Network; Turner Classic Movies; Versus; WE tv.
Fee: $10.95 monthly.

Digital Pay Service 1
Pay Units: 6,000.
Programming (via satellite): CCTV-4; Cinemax (multiplexed); Filipino Channel; Flix; Russian Television Network.
Fee: $18.15 monthly.

Digital Pay Service 2
Pay Units: 20,000.
Programming (via satellite): The Movie Channel (multiplexed).
Fee: $11.49 monthly (CCTV-4, Filipino or RTN), $15.99 monthly (Flix & TMC).

Digital Pay Service 3
Pay Units: 10,000.
Programming (via satellite): HBO (multiplexed).
Fee: $18.15 monthly.

Digital Pay Service 4
Pay Units: 7,000.
Programming (via satellite): Showtime (multiplexed).
Fee: $18.15 monthly.

Digital Pay Service 5
Pay Units: 16,000.
Programming (via satellite): Starz (multiplexed).
Fee: $18.15 monthly.

Video-On-Demand: Yes

Pay-Per-View
Addressable homes: 20,036.
iN DEMAND (delivered digitally); Sports PPV (delivered digitally); Urban Xtra (delivered digitally); Fresh (delivered digitally); Shorteez (delivered digitally); Playboy TV (delivered digitally).

Internet Service
Operational: Yes.
Subscribers: 21,288.
Broadband Service: Comcast High Speed Internet.
Fee: $42.95 monthly; $3.00 modem lease.

Telephone Service
Digital: Operational
Fee: $44.95 monthly

Miles of plant included in Beaverton
Senior Vice President: Curt Henninger. Vice President, Technical Operations: Mike Mason. Vice President, Marketing: Lars Lofas. Sales Director: Mike Williams. Marketing Director: Brad Nosler. Public Relations Director: Theressa Davis.
Ownership: Comcast Cable Communications Inc. (MSO).

FLORENCE—Charter Communications, 521 NE 136th Ave, Vancouver, WA 98684. Phone: 360-828-6600. Fax: 360-828-6795. Web Site: http://www.charter.com. Also serves Dunes City & Lane County (portions). ICA: OR0030.
TV Market Ranking: Below 100 (Lane County (portions) (portions)); Outside TV Markets (Dunes City, FLORENCE, Lane County (portions) (portions)). Franchise award date: May 1, 1965. Franchise expiration date: N.A. Began: July 1, 1965.
Channel capacity: N.A. Channels available but not in use: N.A.

MediaPrints™
Map a Winning Business Strategy
Digital Cable and TV Coverage Maps.
Visit www.warren-news.com/mediaprints.htm

Basic Service
Subscribers: 3,715.
Programming (received off-air): KEVU-CD (MNT) Eugene; KEZI (ABC) Eugene; KLSR-TV (FOX) Eugene; KMTR (CW, NBC) Eugene; KOAC-TV (PBS) Corvallis; KTVC (IND) Roseburg; KVAL-TV (CBS, IND) Eugene; allband FM.
Programming (via satellite): C-SPAN; INSP; QVC; ShopNBC; The Weather Channel; Trinity Broadcasting Network; TV Guide Network; WGN America.
Fee: $29.95 installation.

Expanded Basic Service 1
Subscribers: 3,466.
Programming (via satellite): A&E Networks; ABC Family Channel; AMC; Animal Planet; Bravo; Cartoon Network; CNBC; CNN; Comedy Central; Country Music TV; Discovery Channel; Disney Channel; DIY Network; E! Entertainment Television; ESPN; ESPN 2; Food Network; Fox Movie Channel; Fox News Channel; FX; G4; Golf Channel; Great American Country; GSN; Hallmark Channel; Headline News; HGTV; History Channel; Lifetime; MSNBC; MTV; MTV2; National Geographic Channel; Nickelodeon; Northwest Cable News; Outdoor Channel; Oxygen; SoapNet; Speed; Spike TV; Syfy; TBS Superstation; Telemundo; The Learning Channel; Toon Disney; Travel Channel; truTV; Turner Classic Movies; Turner Network TV; TV Land; USA Network; Versus; VH1; WE tv.
Fee: $42.99 monthly.

Digital Basic Service
Subscribers: N.A.
Programming (via satellite): BBC America; Bio; Bloomberg Television; Boomerang; CNN en Espanol; CNN International; Discovery Digital Networks; ESPN Classic Sports; ESPNews; Fox College Sports Atlantic; Fox College Sports Central; Fox College Sports Pacific; Fox Soccer; Fuel TV; GAS; History Channel International; Independent Film Channel; Lifetime Movie Network; MTV Networks Digital Suite; Music Choice; NFL Network; Nick Jr.; NickToons TV; Sundance Channel.

Digital Pay Service 1
Pay Units: N.A.
Programming (via satellite): Cinemax (multiplexed); Encore (multiplexed); Flix; HBO (multiplexed); Showtime (multiplexed); Starz (multiplexed); The Movie Channel (multiplexed).

Video-On-Demand: Yes

Pay-Per-View
iN DEMAND; Spice; Spice2.

Internet Service
Operational: Yes.
Broadband Service: Charter Pipeline.
Fee: $29.99 monthly.

Telephone Service
Digital: Operational

Miles of Plant: 130.0 (coaxial); None (fiber optic). Additional miles planned: 1.0 (coaxial).
Vice President: Frank Antonovich. General Manager: Linda Kimberly. Technical Operations Director: Brian Lindholme. Marketing Director: Diane Long.
Ownership: Charter Communications Inc. (MSO).

FOSSIL—Fossil Community TV Inc., PO Box 209, Fossil, OR 97830-0209. Phone: 540-763-2698. ICA: OR0104.
TV Market Ranking: Outside TV Markets (FOSSIL). Franchise award date: N.A. Franchise expiration date: N.A. Began: May 1, 1955.
Channel capacity: 12 (not 2-way capable). Channels available but not in use: N.A.

Basic Service
Subscribers: 137.
Programming (received off-air): KATU (ABC) Portland; KEPR-TV (CBS) Pasco; KGW (NBC) Portland; KNDU (NBC) Richland; KOIN (CBS) Portland; KOPB-TV (PBS) Portland; KPTV (FOX) Portland; KVEW (ABC, MNT) Kennewick; allband FM.
Programming (via satellite): A&E Networks; ABC Family Channel; AMC; CNN; Discovery Channel; Disney Channel; History Channel; TBS Superstation; Turner Network TV.
Fee: $25.00 installation; $20.00 monthly.

Pay Service 1
Pay Units: 14.
Programming (via satellite): Showtime.
Fee: $10.00 monthly.

Video-On-Demand: No

Internet Service
Operational: No.

Telephone Service
None

Miles of Plant: 9.0 (coaxial); None (fiber optic).
Manager: Ron Deluca. Chief Technician: Steve Conlee.
Ownership: Fossil Community TV Inc.

GILCHRIST—Country Cablevision Ltd., 2003 25th St SE, PO Box 12038, Salem, OR 97309-0038. Phone: 503-588-8247. Fax: 503-588-0544. Also serves Crescent. ICA: OR0137.
TV Market Ranking: Outside TV Markets (Crescent, GILCHRIST). Franchise award date: January 1, 1988. Franchise expiration date: N.A. Began: January 1, 1990.
Channel capacity: 42 (2-way capable). Channels available but not in use: N.A.

Basic Service
Subscribers: 275.
Programming (received off-air): KATU (ABC) Portland; KOAB-TV (PBS) Bend; KOTI (NBC) Klamath Falls; KPDX (MNT) Vancouver; KTVL (CBS, CW) Medford; KTVZ (CW, NBC) Bend.
Programming (via satellite): ABC Family Channel; CNN; Country Music TV; Discovery Channel; Disney Channel; ESPN; Headline News; Lifetime; Spike TV; TBS Superstation; Turner Network TV; USA Network; WGN America.
Fee: $49.95 installation; $28.50 monthly.

Pay Service 1
Pay Units: N.A.
Programming (via satellite): Encore; HBO; Showtime; The Movie Channel.

Fee: $19.95 installation; $4.95 monthly (Encore), $10.95 monthly (TMC or Showtime), $13.60 monthly (HBO).
Video-On-Demand: No
Internet Service
Operational: No.
Telephone Service
None
Miles of Plant: 12.0 (coaxial); None (fiber optic).
President: John P. Johnson. Systems Manager: Robie Robinson.
Ownership: Country Cablevision Ltd. (MSO).

GLENDALE—Almega Cable, 4017 W Airport Freeway, Ste 546, Bedford, TX 76021. Phones: 877-725-6342; 817-685-9588. Fax: 817-685-6488. Web Site: http://almegacable.com. ICA: OR0138.
TV Market Ranking: Below 100 (GLENDALE). Franchise award date: August 1, 1981. Franchise expiration date: October 4, 2013. Began: January 1, 1985.
Channel capacity: 45 (not 2-way capable). Channels available but not in use: N.A.
Basic Service
Subscribers: 297.
Programming (received off-air): KOBI (NBC) Medford; KPIC (CBS) Roseburg; KSYS (PBS) Medford.
Programming (via satellite): A&E Networks; ABC Family Channel; Cartoon Network; CNN; Country Music TV; Discovery Channel; Disney Channel; ESPN; ESPN 2; HGTV; History Channel; Lifetime; Spike TV; Syfy; TBS Superstation; The Learning Channel; The Weather Channel; Travel Channel; Trinity Broadcasting Network; Turner Classic Movies; Turner Network TV; USA Network; WGN America.
Fee: $29.95 installation; $24.89 monthly.
Pay Service 1
Pay Units: 27.
Programming (via satellite): Cinemax.
Fee: $15.00 installation; $11.55 monthly.
Pay Service 2
Pay Units: 47.
Programming (via satellite): HBO.
Fee: $15.00 installation; $11.55 monthly.
Video-On-Demand: No
Internet Service
Operational: No.
Telephone Service
None
Miles of Plant: 20.0 (coaxial); None (fiber optic).
President: Thomas Kurien.
Ownership: Almega Cable (MSO).

GLIDE—Glide Cablevision, 19181 N Umpqua Hwy, PO Box 609, Glide, OR 97443-0609. Phone: 541-496-0515. Fax: 541-496-0515. Web Site: http://www.glidecable.com. Also serves Idleyld Park. ICA: OR0139.
TV Market Ranking: Below 100 (GLIDE, Idleyld Park). Franchise award date: N.A. Franchise expiration date: N.A. Began: January 1, 1988.
Channel capacity: N.A. Channels available but not in use: N.A.
Basic Service
Subscribers: 290.
Programming (received off-air): KEZI (ABC) Eugene; KMTR (CW, NBC) Eugene; KOBI (NBC) Medford; KPIC (CBS) Roseburg; KSYS (PBS) Medford.
Programming (via satellite): A&E Networks; ABC Family Channel; Animal Planet; Cartoon Network; CNBC; CNN; Country Music TV; Discovery Channel; Disney Channel; ESPN; ESPN 2; FX; Hallmark Channel; HGTV; History Channel; Lifetime; MTV; Nickelodeon; Outdoor Channel; Spike TV; Syfy; TBS Superstation; The Learning Channel; Travel Channel; Turner Classic Movies; Turner Network TV; TV Land; USA Network; VH1; WGN America; WPIX (CW, IND) New York.
Fee: $25.00 installation; $39.95 monthly.
Pay Service 1
Pay Units: 42.
Programming (via satellite): HBO.
Fee: $10.50 monthly.
Pay Service 2
Pay Units: 14.
Programming (via satellite): Showtime.
Fee: $9.00 monthly.
Video-On-Demand: No
Internet Service
Operational: Yes.
Subscribers: 11.
Broadband Service: ISPA.
Fee: $25.00 installation; $22.00 monthly; $60.00 modem purchase.
Telephone Service
None
Miles of Plant: 11.0 (coaxial); None (fiber optic).
Manager: Sheryln Arwood. Chief Technician: Rick Arwood.
Ownership: Glide Cablevision.

GOLD BEACH—Charter Communications, 1286 Northcrest Dr, Crescent City, CA 95531-2321. Phones: 260-828-6600 (Vancouver office); 707-464-5722. Fax: 707-464-4849. Web Site: http://www.charter.com. ICA: OR0044.
TV Market Ranking: Outside TV Markets (GOLD BEACH). Franchise award date: N.A. Franchise expiration date: January 31, 2014. Began: March 1, 1964.
Channel capacity: N.A. Channels available but not in use: N.A.
Basic Service
Subscribers: 1,130.
Programming (received off-air): KBLN (IND) Grants Pass; KBSC-LP (IND) Brookings; KBVU (FOX) Eureka; KDRV (ABC) Medford; KIEM-TV (NBC) Eureka; KOBI (NBC) Medford; KSYS (PBS) Medford; KTVL (CBS, CW) Medford; 5 FMs.
Programming (via satellite): C-SPAN; C-SPAN 2; Eternal Word TV Network; INSP; QVC; ShopNBC; Telemundo; The Weather Channel; Trinity Broadcasting Network; Univision Studios; WGN America.
Fee: $29.95 installation.
Expanded Basic Service 1
Subscribers: 1,122.
Programming (received off-air): KCBY-TV (CBS) Coos Bay.
Programming (via satellite): A&E Networks; ABC Family Channel; AMC; Animal Planet; Bravo; Cartoon Network; CNBC; CNN; Comedy Central; Country Music TV; Discovery Channel; Disney Channel; DIY Network; E! Entertainment Television; ESPN; ESPN 2; Food Network; Fox News Channel; FX; G4; Golf Channel; Great American Country; GSN; Hallmark Channel; Headline News; HGTV; History Channel; Lifetime; MSNBC; MTV; MTV2; National Geographic Channel; Nickelodeon; Northwest Cable News; Oxygen; Speed; Spike TV; Style Network; Syfy; TBS Superstation; The Learning Channel; Toon Disney; Travel Channel; truTV; Turner Classic Movies; Turner Network TV; TV Land; USA Network; Versus; VH1; WE tv.
Fee: $42.99 monthly.
Digital Basic Service
Subscribers: N.A.
Programming (via satellite): BBC America; Bio; Boomerang; CNN en Espanol; CNN International; Discovery Digital Networks; ESPN Classic Sports; ESPNews; Fox College Sports Atlantic; Fox College Sports Central; Fox College Sports Pacific; Fox Deportes; Fox Movie Channel; Fox Soccer; Fuel TV; GAS; History Channel International; Independent Film Channel; Lifetime Movie Network; MTV Networks Digital Suite; Music Choice; NFL Network; Nick Jr.; NickToons TV; SoapNet; Sundance Channel; TV Guide Interactive Inc.
Digital Pay Service 1
Pay Units: N.A.
Programming (via satellite): Cinemax (multiplexed); Encore (multiplexed); Flix; HBO (multiplexed); Showtime (multiplexed); Starz (multiplexed); The Movie Channel (multiplexed).
Video-On-Demand: Yes
Pay-Per-View
iN DEMAND (delivered digitally); NASCAR In Car (delivered digitally); Hot Choice (delivered digitally); Playboy TV (delivered digitally); Fresh (delivered digitally); Shorteez (delivered digitally).
Internet Service
Operational: Yes.
Broadband Service: Charter Pipeline.
Fee: $29.99 monthly.
Telephone Service
Digital: Operational
Miles of Plant: 59.0 (coaxial); None (fiber optic). Additional miles planned: 5.0 (coaxial).
Vice President: Frank Antonovich. General Manager: Linda Kimberly. Plant Manager: Earl DeSomber. Chief Technician: Dennis Putman. Marketing Director: Diane Long. Office Manager: Sandra Milunich.
Ownership: Charter Communications Inc. (MSO).

GOVERNMENT CAMP—CharlieVision, PO Box 10, Government Camp, OR 97028-0010. Phone: 503-272-3333. Fax: 503-272-3800. ICA: OR0168.
TV Market Ranking: Outside TV Markets (GOVERNMENT CAMP). Franchise award date: N.A. Franchise expiration date: N.A. Began: N.A.
Channel capacity: 36 (not 2-way capable). Channels available but not in use: N.A.
Basic Service
Subscribers: 90.
Programming (received off-air): KATU (ABC) Portland; KGW (NBC) Portland; KOIN (CBS) Portland; KOPB-TV (PBS) Portland; KPTV (FOX) Portland.
Programming (via satellite): A&E Networks; Cartoon Network; CNN; Discovery Channel; ESPN; ESPN 2; Spike TV; TBS Superstation; Turner Network TV; WGN America.
Fee: $25.00 monthly.
Pay Service 1
Pay Units: 65.
Programming (via satellite): HBO.
Fee: $2.50 monthly.
Video-On-Demand: No
Internet Service
Operational: No.
Telephone Service
None
Miles of Plant: 7.0 (coaxial); None (fiber optic).
Manager: Charlie Sperr. Chief Technician: Mike Beckman.
Ownership: Government Camp Cable.

GRANTS PASS—Charter Communications, 521 NE 136th Ave, Vancouver, WA 98684. Phone: 360-828-6600. Fax: 360-828-6795. Web Site: http://www.charter.com. Also serves Josephine County, Merlin & Rogue River. ICA: OR0010.
TV Market Ranking: Below 100 (GRANTS PASS, Josephine County, Merlin, Rogue River). Franchise award date: November 20, 1957. Franchise expiration date: N.A. Began: January 1, 1954.
Channel capacity: N.A. Channels available but not in use: N.A.
Basic Service
Subscribers: 13,104.
Programming (received off-air): KBLN (IND) Grants Pass; KDRV (ABC) Medford; KMVU-DT (FOX) Medford; KOBI (NBC) Medford; KSYS (PBS) Medford; KTVL (CBS, CW) Medford; 13 FMs.
Programming (via satellite): C-SPAN; C-SPAN 2; Eternal Word TV Network; INSP; QVC; TBS Superstation; Trinity Broadcasting Network; TV Guide Network.
Fee: $29.99 installation; $2.00 converter.
Expanded Basic Service 1
Subscribers: 12,838.
Programming (via satellite): A&E Networks; ABC Family Channel; AMC; Animal Planet; Bravo; Cartoon Network; CNBC; CNN; Comedy Central; Country Music TV; Discovery Channel; Disney Channel; DIY Network; E! Entertainment Television; ESPN; ESPN 2; Food Network; Fox Deportes; Fox News Channel; FX; G4; GalaVision; Golf Channel; Great American Country; GSN; Hallmark Channel; Headline News; HGTV; History Channel; Lifetime; MSNBC; MTV; National Geographic Channel; Nickelodeon; Northwest Cable News; Oxygen; SoapNet; Speed; Spike TV; Style Network; Syfy; Telemundo; The Learning Channel; The Weather Channel; Toon Disney; Travel Channel; truTV; Turner Classic Movies; Turner Network TV; TV Land; Univision Studios; USA Network; Versus; VH1; WE tv.
Fee: $50.99 monthly.
Digital Basic Service
Subscribers: N.A.
Programming (via satellite): BBC America; Bio; Bloomberg Television; CNN en Espanol; Discovery Fit & Health; ESPN; ESPN Classic Sports; ESPNews; Fox College Sports Atlantic; Fox College Sports Central; Fox College Sports Pacific; Fox Movie Channel; Fox Soccer; Fuel TV; GAS; HD Theater; HDNet; HDNet Movies; History Channel International; Independent Film Channel; Lifetime Movie Network; MTV Networks Digital Suite; Music Choice; NFL Network; Nick Jr.; NickToons TV; Outdoor Channel; Sundance Channel; Turner Network TV; TV Guide Interactive Inc.
Digital Pay Service 1
Pay Units: N.A.
Programming (via satellite): Cinemax (multiplexed); Cinemax HD; Encore (multiplexed); HBO (multiplexed); HBO HD; Showtime (multiplexed); Showtime HD; Starz (multiplexed); Starz; The Movie Channel (multiplexed); The Movie Channel HD.
Video-On-Demand: Yes
Pay-Per-View
iN DEMAND (delivered digitally); NASCAR In Car (delivered digitally); Playboy TV (delivered digitally); Fresh (delivered digitally); Shorteez (delivered digitally).
Internet Service
Operational: Yes.
Broadband Service: Charter Pipeline.
Fee: $29.99 monthly.
Telephone Service
Digital: Operational
Fee: $29.99 monthly

Miles of Plant: 350.0 (coaxial); 18.0 (fiber optic).
Vice President: Frank Antonovich. General Manager: Linda Kimberly. Technical Operations Director: Greg Lemming. Marketing Manager: Dolly Brock. Office Manager: Kelly Williams.
Ownership: Charter Communications Inc. (MSO).

GREEN ACRES—Greenacres TV Cable, 93688 Cordell Ln, Coos Bay, OR 97420. ICA: OR0163.
TV Market Ranking: Below 100 (GREEN ACRES). Franchise award date: N.A. Franchise expiration date: N.A. Began: August 1, 1993.
Channel capacity: 13 (2-way capable). Channels available but not in use: N.A.
Basic Service
Subscribers: 50.
Programming (received off-air): KCBY-TV (CBS) Coos Bay; KEZI (ABC) Eugene; KLSR-TV (FOX) Eugene; KMCB (NBC) Coos Bay; KOAC-TV (PBS) Corvallis; KOBI (NBC) Medford.
Fee: $100.00 installation; $11.50 monthly.
Expanded Basic Service 1
Subscribers: N.A.
Programming (via satellite): CNN; Discovery Channel; ESPN; TBS Superstation; Trinity Broadcasting Network; Turner Network TV; WGN America.
Fee: $8.50 monthly.
Internet Service
Operational: No.
Miles of Plant: 5.0 (coaxial); None (fiber optic).
Manager: Wayne Morgan.
Ownership: Wayne E. Morgan.

HAINES—Formerly served by Almega Cable. No longer in operation. ICA: OR0108.

HALFWAY—Formerly served by Charter Communications. No longer in operation. ICA: OR0140.

HALSEY—Roome Telecommunications Inc., 705 W 2nd St, PO Box 227, Halsey, OR 97348-0227. Phones: 800-343-2211; 541-369-2211. Fax: 541-369-2233. E-mail: rti@rtinet.com. Web Site: http://www.rtinet.com. ICA: OR0100.
TV Market Ranking: Below 100 (HALSEY). Franchise award date: July 22, 1981. Franchise expiration date: N.A. Began: October 1, 1983.
Channel capacity: 43 (not 2-way capable). Channels available but not in use: N.A.
Basic Service
Subscribers: 109.
Programming (received off-air): KEVU-CD (MNT) Eugene; KEZI (ABC) Eugene; KLSR-TV (FOX) Eugene; KMTR (CW, NBC) Eugene; KOAC-TV (PBS) Corvallis; KVAL-TV (CBS, IND) Eugene.
Programming (via satellite): A&E Networks; ABC Family Channel; Animal Planet; Cartoon Network; CNN; Comedy Central; Country Music TV; Discovery Channel; Disney Channel; ESPN; Fox Movie Channel; G4; Headline News; HGTV; History Channel; INSP; KTLA (CW) Los Angeles; Lifetime; MTV; Nickelodeon; Outdoor Channel; QVC; Spike TV; Syfy; TBS Superstation; The Learning Channel; Travel Channel; Turner Classic Movies; Turner Network TV; TV Land; USA Network; VH1; WGN America.
Fee: $29.00 installation; $29.95 monthly.
Pay Service 1
Pay Units: 18.
Programming (via satellite): HBO; Showtime.
Fee: $10.00 monthly (each).
Video-On-Demand: No
Internet Service
Operational: No, DSL & dial-up.
Telephone Service
None
Manager: Randal L. Roome. Chief Technician: Tim Wolford.
Ownership: Roome Telecommunications Inc.

HELIX—Helix Communications, 200 Concord St, PO Box 326, Helix, OR 97835. Phones: 541-457-2385; 541-457-6000. Fax: 541-457-2111. E-mail: support@helixtel.com. Web Site: http://www.helixtel.com. ICA: OR0119.
TV Market Ranking: Below 100 (HELIX). Franchise award date: N.A. Franchise expiration date: N.A. Began: December 1, 1977.
Channel capacity: 10 (not 2-way capable). Channels available but not in use: N.A.
Basic Service
Subscribers: 45.
Programming (received off-air): KEPR-TV (CBS) Pasco; KGW (NBC) Portland; KNDU (NBC) Richland; KPDX (MNT) Vancouver; KPTV (FOX) Portland; KTVR (PBS) La Grande; KVEW (ABC, MNT) Kennewick.
Programming (via satellite): A&E Networks; ABC Family Channel; AMC; Animal Planet; BBC America; Bravo; Cartoon Network; CNBC; CNN; CNN International; Comedy Central; Country Music TV; C-SPAN; C-SPAN 2; Discovery Channel; Discovery Health Channel; Disney Channel; Dominion Sky Angel; E! Entertainment Television; ESPN; ESPN 2; ESPN Classic Sports; ESPNews; Eternal Word TV Network; Food Network; Fox News Channel; Fuse; FX; G4; GSN; Headline News; HGTV; History Channel; Independent Film Channel; ION Television; Lifetime; Lifetime Movie Network; MSNBC; MTV; MTV2; NASA TV; Nick At Nite; Nick Jr.; Nickelodeon; QVC; RFD-TV; Speed; Spike TV; Syfy; TBS Superstation; The Learning Channel; The Weather Channel; Toon Disney; Travel Channel; Trinity Broadcasting Network; truTV; Turner Classic Movies; Turner Network TV; TV Land; USA Network; VH1; WE tv; WGN America.
Fee: $35.00 installation; $35.00 monthly.
Pay Service 1
Pay Units: 6.
Programming (via satellite): HBO.
Fee: $9.00 monthly.
Pay Service 2
Pay Units: N.A.
Programming (via satellite): Cinemax.
Fee: $9.00 monthly.
Video-On-Demand: No
Internet Service
Operational: No, DSL & dial-up.
Telephone Service
None
Miles of Plant: 2.0 (coaxial); None (fiber optic).
President & General Manager: James A. Smith.
Ownership: Helix Communications.

HEPPNER—Heppner TV Inc., 162 N Main St, PO Box 815, Heppner, OR 97836-0587. Phone: 541-676-9663. Fax: 541-676-9655. E-mail: windtech@windwave.org. Web Site: http://www.windwave.org. Also serves Ione & Lexington. ICA: OR0077.

TV Market Ranking: Outside TV Markets (HEPPNER, Ione, Lexington). Franchise award date: March 1, 1955. Franchise expiration date: N.A. Began: June 1, 1955.
Channel capacity: 35 (not 2-way capable). Channels available but not in use: N.A.
Basic Service
Subscribers: 420.
Programming (received off-air): KEPR-TV (CBS) Pasco; KNDU (NBC) Richland; KOPB-TV (PBS) Portland; KVEW (ABC, MNT) Kennewick; allband FM.
Programming (via microwave): KATU (ABC) Portland; KGW (NBC) Portland; KOIN (CBS) Portland; KPTV (FOX) Portland.
Programming (via satellite): A&E Networks; ABC Family Channel; CNN; Discovery Channel; Disney Channel; ESPN; Spike TV; Syfy; TBS Superstation; The Learning Channel; Turner Network TV; USA Network; VH1; WGN America.
Programming (via translator): KPDX (MNT) Vancouver.
Fee: $20.00 installation; $35.50 monthly.
Pay Service 1
Pay Units: 55.
Programming (via satellite): HBO.
Fee: $12.50 installation; $11.00 monthly.
Video-On-Demand: No
Internet Service
Operational: No.
Fee: $75.00 installation.
Telephone Service
None
Miles of Plant: 17.0 (coaxial); 4.0 (fiber optic).
President: Nate Arbogast. Vice President: Don Russel. Office Manager: Sandy Matthews. Chief Technician: Thomas Rawlins.
Ownership: WindWave Communications.

IDANHA—Formerly served by Wave Broadband. No longer in operation. ICA: OR0101.

IMBLER—Formerly served by Almega Cable. No longer in operation. ICA: OR0116.

IONE—Ione TV Co-op. Now served by HEPPNER, OR [OR0077]. ICA: OR0114.

KLAMATH FALLS—Charter Communications, 521 NE 136th Ave, Vancouver, WA 98684. Phone: 360-828-6600. Fax: 360-828-6795. Web Site: http://www.charter.com. Also serves Keno, Klamath County (unincorporated areas) & Midland. ICA: OR0011.
TV Market Ranking: Below 100 (Keno, Klamath County (unincorporated areas), KLAMATH FALLS, Midland). Franchise award date: N.A. Franchise expiration date: N.A. Began: January 1, 1953.
Channel capacity: N.A. Channels available but not in use: N.A.
Basic Service
Subscribers: 12,471.
Programming (received off-air): KDKF (ABC) Klamath Falls; KFTS (PBS) Klamath Falls; KMVU-DT (FOX) Medford; KOTI (NBC) Klamath Falls; 11 FMs.
Programming (via satellite): C-SPAN; C-SPAN 2; INSP; QVC; Telemundo; Trinity Broadcasting Network; WGN America.
Fee: $29.99 installation.
Expanded Basic Service 1
Subscribers: 12,314.
Programming (via satellite): A&E Networks; ABC Family Channel; AMC; Animal Planet; Bravo; Cartoon Network; CNBC; CNN; Comedy Central; Country Music TV; Discovery Channel; Disney Channel; DIY Network; E! Entertainment Television; ESPN; ESPN 2; Food Network; Fox News Channel; Fox Soccer; FX; G4; GalaVision; Golf Channel; GSN; Hallmark Channel; Headline News; HGTV; History Channel; Lifetime; MSNBC; MTV; MTV2; National Geographic Channel; Nickelodeon; Northwest Cable News; Outdoor Channel; Oxygen; SoapNet; Speed; Spike TV; Style Network; Syfy; TBS Superstation; The Learning Channel; The Weather Channel; Toon Disney; Travel Channel; truTV; Turner Classic Movies; Turner Network TV; TV Land; Univision Studios; USA Network; Versus; VH1; WE tv.
Fee: $50.99 monthly.
Digital Basic Service
Subscribers: N.A.
Programming (via satellite): BBC America; Bio; Bloomberg Television; CNN en Espanol; CNN International; Discovery Fit & Health; ESPN Classic Sports; ESPNews; Fox College Sports Atlantic; Fox College Sports Central; Fox College Sports Pacific; Fox Deportes; Fox Movie Channel; Fuel TV; Fuse; GAS; History Channel International; Independent Film Channel; Lifetime Movie Network; MTV Networks Digital Suite; Music Choice; NFL Network; Nick Jr.; NickToons TV; Sundance Channel; TV Guide Interactive Inc.
Digital Pay Service 1
Pay Units: N.A.
Programming (via satellite): Cinemax (multiplexed); Encore; Flix; HBO (multiplexed); Showtime (multiplexed); Starz (multiplexed); The Movie Channel (multiplexed).
Video-On-Demand: Yes
Pay-Per-View
iN DEMAND (delivered digitally); NASCAR In Car (delivered digitally); Hot Choice (delivered digitally); Playboy TV (delivered digitally); Fresh (delivered digitally); Shorteez (delivered digitally).
Internet Service
Operational: Yes.
Broadband Service: Charter Pipeline.
Fee: $29.99 monthly.
Telephone Service
Digital: Operational
Fee: $29.99 monthly
Miles of Plant: 242.0 (coaxial); None (fiber optic).
Vice President: Frank Antonovich. General Manager: Linda Kimberly. Technical Operations Director: Greg Lemming. Marketing Manager: Dolly Brock. Office Manager: Kelly Williams.
Ownership: Charter Communications Inc. (MSO).

KNAPPA—Rapid Cable, 1750 S Hwy 10, Price, UT 84501-4364. Phone: 435-637-6823. Fax: 435-637-9755. Also serves Svensen. ICA: OR0071.

TV Market Ranking: Outside TV Markets (KNAPPA, Svensen). Franchise award date: N.A. Franchise expiration date: N.A. Began: January 1, 1965.

Channel capacity: 61 (not 2-way capable). Channels available but not in use: N.A.

Basic Service

Subscribers: 257.

Programming (received off-air): KATU (ABC) Portland; KGW (NBC) Portland; KOIN (CBS) Portland; KOPB-TV (PBS) Portland; KPTV (FOX) Portland; allband FM.

Programming (via satellite): A&E Networks; ABC Family Channel; CNN; Discovery Channel; Disney Channel; ESPN; Lifetime; MTV; Nickelodeon; Spike TV; TBS Superstation; Turner Network TV; VH1; WGN America.

Fee: $29.95 installation; $19.95 monthly.

Pay Service 1

Pay Units: 27.

Programming (via satellite): HBO.

Fee: $15.00 installation; $8.95 monthly.

Video-On-Demand: No

Internet Service

Operational: No.

Telephone Service

None

Miles of Plant: 30.0 (coaxial); None (fiber optic).

Regional Manager: Shane Baggs. Engineering Director: Richard O'Neill. Chief Technician: David Ramsey.

Ownership: Rapid Communications LLC (MSO).

LA GRANDE—Charter Communications, 639 N Kellogg St, Kennewick, WA 99336. Phones: 509-222-2500; 509-783-0132. Fax: 509-735-3795. Web Site: http://www.charter.com. Also serves Baker City, Baker County (northern portion), Island City, Union & Union County. ICA: OR0028.

TV Market Ranking: Outside TV Markets (Baker City, Baker County (northern portion), Island City, LA GRANDE, Union, Union County). Franchise award date: January 1, 1954. Franchise expiration date: N.A. Began: September 29, 1954.

Channel capacity: 36 (not 2-way capable). Channels available but not in use: N.A.

Basic Service

Subscribers: 7,820.

Programming (received off-air): KTVB (NBC) Boise; KTVR (PBS) La Grande; KUNP-LP (UNV) Portland.

Programming (via microwave): KATU (ABC) Portland; KGW (NBC) Portland; KOIN (CBS) Portland; KPDX (MNT) Vancouver; KPTV (FOX) Portland.

Programming (via satellite): A&E Networks; ABC Family Channel; AMC; Animal Planet; CNBC; CNN; C-SPAN; Discovery Channel; Disney Channel; E! Entertainment Television; ESPN; Fox News Channel; FX; Hallmark Channel; Headline News; Lifetime; MTV; Nickelodeon; Northwest Cable News; QVC; Spike TV; TBS Superstation; The Learning Channel; The Weather Channel; Toon Disney; Travel Channel; truTV; Turner Network TV; USA Network; VH1.

Fee: $29.99 installation; $50.99 monthly.

Digital Basic Service

Subscribers: 1,350.

Programming (via satellite): BBC America; Bloomberg Television; Bravo; Discovery Fit & Health; DMX Music; ESPN 2; ESPN Classic Sports; ESPNews; Fox Movie Channel; Fox Soccer; G4; Golf Channel; GSN; Halogen Network; HGTV; History Channel; Independent Film Channel; National Geographic Channel; Nick Jr.; Outdoor Channel; Speed; Syfy; Trinity Broadcasting Network; Turner Classic Movies; TV Guide Interactive Inc.; Versus; VH1 Classic; VH1 Country; WE tv.

Digital Pay Service 1

Pay Units: 297.

Programming (via satellite): Cinemax (multiplexed); Encore (multiplexed); HBO (multiplexed); Showtime (multiplexed); Starz (multiplexed).

Digital Pay Service 2

Pay Units: N.A.

Programming (via satellite): The Movie Channel (multiplexed).

Video-On-Demand: No

Pay-Per-View

Addressable homes: 1,350.

iN DEMAND (delivered digitally); Fresh (delivered digitally); Playboy TV (delivered digitally).

Internet Service

Operational: Yes.

Fee: $19.99 monthly.

Telephone Service

Digital: Operational

Fee: $14.99 monthly

Miles of plant included in Kennewick, WA

General Manager: Linda Kimberly. Technical Operations Manager: Jeff Hopkins. Marketing Director: Diane Long. Program Director: Lloyd Swain.

Ownership: Charter Communications Inc. (MSO).

LA PINE—Crestview Cable TV, 350 NE Dunham St, Prineville, OR 97754-1955. Phones: 800-285-2330; 541-447-4342. Fax: 541-447-5987. E-mail: customerservice@crestviewcable.com. Web Site: http://www.crestviewcable.com. ICA: OR0142.

TV Market Ranking: Below 100 (LA PINE). Franchise award date: N.A. Franchise expiration date: N.A. Began: October 1, 1988.

Channel capacity: N.A. Channels available but not in use: N.A.

Basic Service

Subscribers: 1,891.

Programming (received off-air): KATU (ABC) Portland; KBNZ-LD Bend; KEZI (ABC) Eugene; KFXO-LP (FOX) Bend; KOAB-TV (PBS) Bend; KOHD (ABC) Bend; KOIN (CBS) Portland; KPDX (MNT) Vancouver; KTVZ (CW, NBC) Bend.

Programming (via satellite): C-SPAN.

Fee: $30.50 installation; $15.99 monthly; $14.80 additional installation.

Expanded Basic Service 1

Subscribers: 1,754.

Programming (via satellite): A&E Networks; ABC Family Channel; CNBC; CNN; Country Music TV; Discovery Channel; Disney Channel; ESPN; ESPN 2; Fox News Channel; Hallmark Channel; Headline News; HGTV; History Channel; Lifetime; Nickelodeon; QVC; Spike TV; Syfy; TBS Superstation; The Learning Channel; Turner Classic Movies; Turner Network TV; USA Network; VH1.

Fee: $20.94 monthly.

Digital Basic Service

Subscribers: N.A.

Programming (via satellite): A&E HD; ABC Family HD; BBC America; Bio; Bloomberg Television; Chiller; cloo; CMT Pure Country; CNN HD; Discovery Fit & Health; Disney Channel HD; Disney XD; DMX Music; ESPN 2 HD; ESPN HD; ESPN U; ESPNews; Food Network HD; Fox Business Channel; Fox College Sports Atlantic; Fox College Sports Central; Fox College Sports Pacific; Fox Movie Channel; Fox Soccer; FSN HD; Fuse; G4; Golf Channel; History Channel HD; History Channel International; ID Investigation Discovery; Lifetime Movie Network; Military Channel; MTV2; Nick Jr.; NickToons TV; Northwest Cable News; Outdoor Channel; OWN: Oprah Winfrey Network; Planet Green; QVC HD; Science; SoapNet; Speed; TBS in HD; TeenNick; The Hub; Travel Channel HD; Turner Network TV HD; USA Network HD; Versus; VH1 Classic; WE tv.

Fee: $17.82 monthly.

Digital Pay Service 1

Pay Units: N.A.

Programming (via satellite): Cinemax (multiplexed); Encore (multiplexed); HBO (multiplexed); Starz (multiplexed).

Fee: $10.00 monthly (Cinemax), $12.00 monthly (Starz/Encore), $12.99 monthly (HBO).

Video-On-Demand: No

Internet Service

Operational: Yes.

Subscribers: 205.

Fee: $19.20 installation; $44.95 monthly.

Telephone Service

None

Miles of Plant: 100.0 (coaxial); None (fiber optic).

Manager: Tony Ashcraft. Office Manager: Audrey Gautney.

Ownership: California-Oregon Broadcasting Inc. (MSO).

LACOMBE—Wave Broadband, 277 N 3rd Ave, Stayton, OR 97383-1723. Phone: 888-222-5314. Fax: 503-848-1134. Web Site: http://www.wbcable.com. Also serves Lebanon. ICA: OR0078.

TV Market Ranking: Below 100 (LACOMBE, Lebanon). Franchise award date: N.A. Franchise expiration date: N.A. Began: August 1, 1992.

Channel capacity: N.A. Channels available but not in use: N.A.

Basic Service

Subscribers: 220.

Programming (received off-air): KATU (ABC) Portland; KGW (NBC) Portland; KOIN (CBS) Portland; KOPB-TV (PBS) Portland; KPDX (MNT) Vancouver; KPTV (FOX) Portland; KPXG-TV (ION) Salem.

Programming (via satellite): A&E Networks; ABC Family Channel; AMC; Cartoon Network; CNN; Country Music TV; C-SPAN; Discovery Channel; Disney Channel; ESPN; ESPN 2; Headline News; HGTV; Lifetime; MTV; Nickelodeon; Northwest Cable News; Spike TV; Syfy; TBS Superstation; The Learning Channel; Trinity Broadcasting Network; Turner Network TV; USA Network; VH1; WE tv; WGN America.

Fee: $35.00 installation; $32.99 monthly.

Pay Service 1

Pay Units: 202.

Programming (via satellite): HBO.

Fee: $9.95 monthly.

Internet Service

Operational: No.

Telephone Service

None

Miles of Plant: 26.0 (coaxial); None (fiber optic).

Manager: Janice Wilcox. Chief Technician: Dan Guthrie.

Ownership: WaveDivision Holdings LLC (MSO).

LAKEVIEW—Charter Communications, 521 NE 136th Ave, Vancouver, WA 98684. Phone: 360-828-6600. Fax: 360-828-6795. Web Site: http://www.charter.com. Also serves Lake County (portions). ICA: OR0051.

TV Market Ranking: Outside TV Markets (Lake County (portions), LAKEVIEW). Franchise award date: N.A. Franchise expiration date: N.A. Began: August 1, 1956.

Channel capacity: N.A. Channels available but not in use: N.A.

Basic Service

Subscribers: 1,016.

Programming (received off-air): KOTI (NBC) Klamath Falls; KPDX (MNT) Vancouver; KTVL (CBS, CW) Medford; KTVZ (CW, NBC) Bend; 7 FMs.

Programming (via microwave): KDKF (ABC) Klamath Falls; KOIN (CBS) Portland; KOPB-TV (PBS) Portland.

Programming (via satellite): C-SPAN; C-SPAN 2; Discovery Channel; Hallmark Channel; WGN America.

Fee: $29.99 installation; $2.00 converter.

Expanded Basic Service 1

Subscribers: 1,006.

Programming (via satellite): A&E Networks; ABC Family Channel; AMC; Animal Planet; Bravo; Cartoon Network; CNN; Country Music TV; Discovery Fit & Health; Disney Channel; E! Entertainment Television; ESPN; ESPN 2; Food Network; Fox News Channel; FX; Headline News; HGTV; History Channel; Lifetime; MTV; Nickelodeon; Spike TV; Syfy; TBS Superstation; The Learning Channel; The Weather Channel; truTV; Turner Network TV; Univision Studios; USA Network; Versus.

Fee: $47.99 monthly.

Digital Basic Service

Subscribers: N.A.

Programming (via satellite): AmericanLife TV Network; BBC America; Bio; Bloomberg Television; Bravo; Discovery Digital Networks; DMX Music; Fox Movie Channel; Fox Soccer; Fuse; G4; GAS; Golf Channel; GSN; Halogen Network; History Channel International; Independent Film Channel; Lifetime Movie Network; MTV Networks Digital Suite; Nick Jr.; Outdoor Channel; Speed; Style Network; Toon Disney; Trinity Broadcasting Network; Turner Classic Movies; TV Guide Network; WAM! America's Kidz Network; WE tv.

Pay Service 1

Pay Units: 183.

Programming (via satellite): Cinemax; Encore; HBO; Starz.

Digital Pay Service 1

Pay Units: N.A.

Programming (via satellite): Cinemax (multiplexed); Encore (multiplexed); Flix; HBO (multiplexed); Showtime (multiplexed); Starz (multiplexed); The Movie Channel (multiplexed).

Video-On-Demand: No

Pay-Per-View

iN DEMAND (delivered digitally).

Internet Service

Operational: Yes.

Fee: $19.99 monthly.

Telephone Service

None

Miles of Plant: 25.0 (coaxial); None (fiber optic).

Vice President: Frank Antonovich. General Manager: Linda Kimberly. Technical Operations Director: Greg Lemming. Marketing Manager: Dolly Brock. Office Manager: Kelly Williams.

Ownership: Charter Communications Inc. (MSO).

LEBANON—Comcast Cable. Now served by CORVALLIS, OR [OR0008]. ICA: OR0024.

LINCOLN CITY—Charter Communications, 521 NE 136th Ave, Vancouver, WA 98684. Phone: 360-828-6600. Fax: 360-828-6795. Web Site: http://www.charter.com. Also serves Bay City, Beaver, Cape Meares, Cloverdale, Garibaldi, Hebo, Lincoln County (portions), Manzanita, Nehalem, Neotsu, Neskowin, Netarts, Newport, Oceanside, Otter Rock, Pacific City, Rockaway Beach, Tillamook, Tillamook County (portions), Toledo, Wheeler & Yachats. ICA: OR0020.

TV Market Ranking: Below 100 (Lincoln County (portions) (portions), Tillamook (portions)); Outside TV Markets (Bay City, Beaver, Cape Meares, Cloverdale, Garibaldi, Hebo, LINCOLN CITY, Lincoln County (portions) (portions), Manzanita, Nehalem, Neotsu, Neskowin, Netarts, Newport, Oceanside, Otter Rock, Pacific City, Rockaway Beach, Tillamook, Tillamook (portions), Toledo, Wheeler, Yachats). Franchise award date: January 1, 1955. Franchise expiration date: November 13, 2010. Began: October 22, 1954.

Channel capacity: 80 (operating 2-way). Channels available but not in use: N.A.

Basic Service

Subscribers: 17,667.

Programming (received off-air): KATU (ABC) Portland; KGW (NBC) Portland; KOIN (CBS) Portland; KOPB-TV (PBS) Portland; KPDX (MNT) Vancouver; KPTV (FOX) Portland; KRCW-TV (CW) Salem; allband FM.

Programming (via satellite): C-SPAN; C-SPAN 2; INSP; QVC; Trinity Broadcasting Network; TV Guide Network; WGN America.

Fee: $29.95 installation.

Expanded Basic Service 1

Subscribers: 16,000.

Programming (via satellite): A&E Networks; ABC Family Channel; AMC; Animal Planet; Bravo; Cartoon Network; CNBC; CNN; Comedy Central; Country Music TV; Discovery Channel; Discovery Fit & Health; Disney Channel; DIY Network; E! Entertainment Television; ESPN; ESPN 2; Food Network; Fox Movie Channel; FX; G4; Golf Channel; GSN; Hallmark Channel; Headline News; HGTV; ION Television; Lifetime; MSNBC; MTV; National Geographic Channel; Nickelodeon; Northwest Cable News; Outdoor Channel; Oxygen; ShopNBC; SoapNet; Speed; Spike TV; Syfy; TBS Superstation; The Learning Channel; The Weather Channel; Toon Disney; Travel Channel; truTV; Turner Classic Movies; Turner Network TV; TV Land; Univision Studios; USA Network; Versus; VH1.

Fee: $42.99 monthly.

Digital Basic Service

Subscribers: 12,000.

Programming (via satellite): BBC America; Bio; Bloomberg Television; Boomerang; CMT Pure Country; CNN en Espanol; CNN International; Discovery Digital Networks; ESPN Classic Sports; ESPNews; Fox College Sports Atlantic; Fox College Sports Central; Fox College Sports Pacific; Fox Soccer; Fuel TV; GAS; GSN; History Channel International; Independent Film Channel; Lifetime Movie Network; MTV Networks Digital Suite; Music Choice; NFL Network; Nick Jr.; Nick Too; Style Network; Sundance Channel; WE tv.

Fee: $6.95 monthly.

Digital Pay Service 1

Pay Units: 282.

Programming (via satellite): Cinemax (multiplexed).

Fee: $11.95 monthly.

Digital Pay Service 2

Pay Units: 518.

Programming (via satellite): HBO (multiplexed).

Fee: $11.95 monthly.

Digital Pay Service 3

Pay Units: 359.

Programming (via satellite): Flix; Showtime (multiplexed).

Fee: $11.95 monthly.

Digital Pay Service 4

Pay Units: 205.

Programming (via satellite): The Movie Channel (multiplexed).

Fee: $11.95 monthly.

Digital Pay Service 5

Pay Units: N.A.

Programming (via satellite): Encore (multiplexed); Starz (multiplexed).

Fee: $11.95 monthly.

Video-On-Demand: Yes

Pay-Per-View

Addressable homes: 12,000.

Hot Choice (delivered digitally); iN DEMAND (delivered digitally); Playboy TV (delivered digitally); Fresh (delivered digitally); Shorteez (delivered digitally).

Internet Service

Operational: Yes. Began: March 1, 2001.

Subscribers: 2,634.

Broadband Service: Charter Pipeline.

Fee: $29.99 monthly.

Telephone Service

Digital: Operational

Miles of Plant: 1,100.0 (coaxial); 300.0 (fiber optic).

Vice President: Frank Antonovich. General Manager: Linda Kimberly. Technical Operations Director: Brian Lindholme. Marketing Director: Diane Long.

Ownership: Charter Communications Inc. (MSO).

MACLEAY—Country Cablevision Ltd., 2003 25th St SE, PO Box 12038, Salem, OR 97309-0038. Phone: 503-588-8247. Fax: 503-588-0544. Also serves Marion, Marion County (portions), Shaw & West Stayton. ICA: OR0064.

TV Market Ranking: 29 (Marion (portions)); Below 100 (MACLEAY, Marion, Shaw, West Stayton, Marion (portions)); Outside TV Markets (Marion (portions)). Franchise award date: January 1, 1987. Franchise expiration date: N.A. Began: August 1, 1987.

Channel capacity: 42 (2-way capable). Channels available but not in use: N.A.

Basic Service

Subscribers: 930.

Programming (received off-air): KATU (ABC) Portland; KGW (NBC) Portland; KOIN (CBS) Portland; KOPB-TV (PBS) Portland; KPDX (MNT) Vancouver; KPTV (FOX) Portland.

Programming (via satellite): A&E Networks; ABC Family Channel; AMC; CNN; Country Music TV; Discovery Channel; Disney Channel; ESPN; Headline News; Lifetime; MTV; Nickelodeon; QVC; Spike TV; TBS Superstation; Turner Network TV; USA Network; VH1; WGN America.

Fee: $49.95 installation; $32.50 monthly.

Pay Service 1

Pay Units: 350.

Programming (via satellite): Encore; HBO; Showtime; The Movie Channel.

Fee: $5.20 monthly (Encore), $11.50 monthly (Showtime & TMC), $13.60 monthly (HBO).

Video-On-Demand: No

Internet Service

Operational: Yes.

Setting the industry standard...
Communications Daily
Warren Communications News
FREE 30-day trial–call 800-771-9202 or visit www.warren-news.com

Telephone Service

None

Miles of Plant: 65.0 (coaxial); None (fiber optic).

President: John P. Johnson. Systems Manager: Robie Robinson.

Ownership: Country Cablevision Ltd. (MSO).

MADRAS—Crestview Cable TV, 35 C St, Ste E, Madras, OR 97741. Phones: 541-475-2969 (Madras office); 541-447-4342 (Prineville office). Fax: 541-447-5987. E-mail: customerservice@crestviewcable.com. Web Site: http://www.crestviewcable.com. Also serves Culver & Metolius. ICA: OR0146.

TV Market Ranking: Below 100 (Culver); Outside TV Markets (MADRAS, Metolius). Franchise award date: January 1, 1955. Franchise expiration date: N.A. Began: June 1, 1955.

Channel capacity: 78 (operating 2-way). Channels available but not in use: N.A.

Basic Service

Subscribers: 6,136.

Programming (received off-air): KATU (ABC) Portland; KFXO-LP (FOX) Bend; KGW (NBC) Portland; KOAB-TV (PBS) Bend; KOIN (CBS) Portland; KPDX (MNT) Vancouver; KTVZ (CW, NBC) Bend; 14 FMs.

Programming (via satellite): C-SPAN; QVC; TV Guide Network; Univision Studios.

Fee: $32.00 installation; $17.80 monthly; $.86 converter; $10.00 additional installation.

Expanded Basic Service 1

Subscribers: 5,169.

Programming (via satellite): A&E Networks; ABC Family Channel; AMC; Animal Planet; CNBC; CNN; Comedy Central; Country Music TV; C-SPAN 2; Discovery Channel; Disney Channel; ESPN; ESPN 2; ESPNews; Food Network; Fox News Channel; Hallmark Channel; Headline News; HGTV; History Channel; Lifetime; MSNBC; MTV; Nickelodeon; Northwest Cable News; Spike TV; Syfy; TBS Superstation; The Learning Channel; Toon Disney; Travel Channel; Trinity Broadcasting Network; Turner Classic Movies; Turner Network TV; TV Land; USA Network; Versus; VH1; WE tv.

Fee: $23.05 monthly.

Digital Basic Service

Subscribers: N.A.

Programming (via satellite): BBC America; Bio; Bloomberg Television; Canales N; cloo; Discovery Fit & Health; DMX Music; Fox College Sports Atlantic; Fox College Sports Central; Fox College Sports Pacific; Fox Movie Channel; Fox Soccer; Fuse; G4; Golf Channel; Halogen Network; History Channel International; Outdoor Channel; Speed.

Fee: $4.55 monthly.

Digital Pay Service 1

Pay Units: N.A.

Programming (via satellite): Cinemax (multiplexed); Encore (multiplexed); HBO (multiplexed); Starz (multiplexed).

Fee: $10.00 monthly (Cinemax), $12.00 monthly (HBO or Starz/Encore).

Video-On-Demand: No

Pay-Per-View

iN DEMAND (delivered digitally); Playboy TV (delivered digitally); Fresh (delivered digitally).

Internet Service

Operational: Yes. Began: December 1, 2000.

Subscribers: 940.

Broadband Service: In-house.

Fee: $69.95 installation; $44.95 monthly; $10.00 modem lease.

Telephone Service

Analog: Not Operational

Digital: Operational

Fee: $34.95 monthly

Miles of Plant: 59.0 (coaxial); None (fiber optic).

Manager: Tony Ashcraft. Office Manager: Audrey Gautney.

Ownership: California-Oregon Broadcasting Inc. (MSO).

MALIN—Almega Cable, 4014 W Airport Freeway, Ste 543, Bedford, TX 76021. Phones: 877-725-6342; 817-685-9588. Fax: 817-685-6488. Web Site: http://almegacable.com. ICA: OR0092.

TV Market Ranking: Below 100 (MALIN). Franchise award date: N.A. Franchise expiration date: June 9, 2010. Began: May 1, 1981.

Channel capacity: 45 (not 2-way capable). Channels available but not in use: N.A.

Basic Service

Subscribers: 103.

Programming (received off-air): KDKF (ABC) Klamath Falls; KMVU-DT (FOX) Medford; KOTI (NBC) Klamath Falls; KSYS (PBS) Medford; KTVL (CBS, CW) Medford.

Programming (via satellite): A&E Networks; ABC Family Channel; Bravo; Cartoon Network; CNBC; CNN; Discovery Channel; Disney Channel; ESPN; ESPN 2; HGTV; MSNBC; Spike TV; Syfy; TBS Superstation; Trinity Broadcasting Network; Turner Classic Movies; Turner Network TV; Univision Studios; USA Network; WGN America.

Fee: $29.95 installation; $26.45 monthly.

Pay Service 1

Pay Units: 12.

Programming (via satellite): HBO.

Fee: $15.00 installation; $10.95 monthly.

Video-On-Demand: No

Internet Service

Operational: No.

Telephone Service

None

Miles of Plant: 4.0 (coaxial); None (fiber optic).

President: Thomas Kurien.

Ownership: Almega Cable (MSO).

MAPLETON—Rapid Cable, 1750 S Hwy 10, Price, UT 84501-4364. Phone: 435-637-6823. Fax: 435-637-9755. ICA: OR0161.

TV Market Ranking: Outside TV Markets (MAPLETON). Franchise award date: N.A.

Franchise expiration date: N.A. Began: N.A.
Channel capacity: N.A. Channels available but not in use: N.A.
Basic Service
Subscribers: 152.
Programming (received off-air): KATU (ABC) Portland; KEVU-CD (MNT) Eugene; KEZI (ABC) Eugene; KMTR (CW, NBC) Eugene; KOAC-TV (PBS) Corvallis; KVAL-TV (CBS, IND) Eugene.
Programming (via satellite): ABC Family Channel; Country Music TV; Discovery Channel; Disney Channel; ESPN; QVC; Syfy; TBS Superstation; USA Network; WGN America.
Fee: $29.95 installation; $19.95 monthly.
Pay Service 1
Pay Units: 44.
Programming (via satellite): HBO.
Fee: $11.95 monthly.
Video-On-Demand: No
Internet Service
Operational: No.
Telephone Service
None
Miles of Plant: 7.0 (coaxial); None (fiber optic).
Regional Manager: Shane Baggs. Engineering Director: Richard O'Neill. Chief Technician: David Ramsey.
Ownership: Rapid Communications LLC (MSO).

MEDFORD—Charter Communications, 521 NE 136th Ave, Vancouver, WA 98684. Phone: 360-828-6600. Fax: 360-828-6795. Web Site: http://www.charter.com. Also serves Applegate, Ashland, Central Point, Eagle Point, Gold Hill, Jackson County, Jacksonville, Phoenix, Talent & White City. ICA: OR0006.
TV Market Ranking: Below 100 (Applegate, Ashland, Central Point, Eagle Point, Gold Hill, Jackson County, Jacksonville, MEDFORD, Phoenix, Talent, White City). Franchise award date: N.A. Franchise expiration date: N.A. Began: January 1, 1958.
Channel capacity: N.A. Channels available but not in use: N.A.
Basic Service
Subscribers: 38,741.
Programming (received off-air): KBLN (IND) Grants Pass; KMVU-DT (FOX) Medford; KOBI (NBC) Medford; KSYS (PBS) Medford; KTVL (CBS, CW) Medford; allband FM.
Programming (via satellite): C-SPAN; C-SPAN 2; Discovery Channel; Fox News Channel; Hallmark Channel; INSP; MTV; Northwest Cable News; QVC; TBS Superstation; The Learning Channel; Trinity Broadcasting Network; TV Guide Network.
Fee: $29.99 installation.
Expanded Basic Service 1
Subscribers: 35,532.
Programming (via satellite): A&E Networks; ABC Family Channel; AMC; Animal Planet; Bravo; Cartoon Network; CNBC; CNN; Comedy Central; Country Music TV; Discovery Fit & Health; Disney Channel; E! Entertainment Television; ESPN; ESPN 2; Eternal Word TV Network; Food Network; FX; G4; Golf Channel; Headline News; HGTV; History Channel; Lifetime; National Geographic Channel; Nickelodeon; Oxygen; SoapNet; Speed; Spike TV; Style Network; Syfy; The Weather Channel; Toon Disney; Travel Channel; truTV; Turner Network TV; TV Land; USA Network; Versus; VH1; WE tv.
Fee: $50.99 monthly.
Digital Basic Service
Subscribers: 6,333.
Programming (via satellite): BBC America; Bio; Bloomberg Television; Discovery Digital Networks; DIY Network; ESPN Classic Sports; ESPNews; Fox Movie Channel; Fox Sports World; GAS; GSN; History Channel International; Independent Film Channel; Lifetime Movie Network; MSNBC; MTV Networks Digital Suite; Music Choice; Nick Jr.; NickToons TV; Outdoor Channel; Turner Classic Movies.
Digital Pay Service 1
Pay Units: 1,038.
Programming (via satellite): Cinemax (multiplexed).
Fee: $12.95 monthly.
Digital Pay Service 2
Pay Units: 1,154.
Programming (via satellite): DMX Music.
Fee: $12.95 monthly.
Digital Pay Service 3
Pay Units: 3,494.
Programming (via satellite): HBO (multiplexed).
Fee: $12.95 monthly.
Digital Pay Service 4
Pay Units: 1,797.
Programming (via satellite): Flix; Showtime (multiplexed); Sundance Channel; The Movie Channel (multiplexed).
Fee: $12.95 monthly.
Video-On-Demand: Yes
Pay-Per-View
Addressable homes: 6,333.
iN DEMAND (delivered digitally); Fresh (delivered digitally); Shorteez (delivered digitally).
Internet Service
Operational: Yes. Began: December 1, 2000.
Broadband Service: Charter Pipeline.
Fee: $29.99 monthly.
Telephone Service
Digital: Operational
Fee: $29.99 monthly
Miles of Plant: 728.0 (coaxial); 92.0 (fiber optic). Additional miles planned: 14.0 (coaxial); 2.0 (fiber optic).
Vice President: Frank Antonovich. General Manager: Linda Kimberly. Technical Operations Director: Greg Lemming. Marketing Manager: Dolly Brock. Office Manager: Kelly Williams.
Ownership: Charter Communications Inc. (MSO).

MERRILL—Almega Cable, 4012 W Airport Freeway, Ste 541, Bedford, TX 76021. Phones: 877-725-6342; 817-685-9588. Fax: 817-685-6488. Web Site: http://almegacable.com. ICA: OR0081.
TV Market Ranking: Below 100 (MERRILL). Franchise award date: N.A. Franchise expiration date: N.A. Began: May 1, 1981.
Channel capacity: 45 (not 2-way capable). Channels available but not in use: N.A.
Basic Service
Subscribers: 156.
Programming (received off-air): KDKF (ABC) Klamath Falls; KMVU-DT (FOX) Medford; KOTI (NBC) Klamath Falls; KSYS (PBS) Medford; KTVL (CBS, CW) Medford.
Programming (via satellite): A&E Networks; ABC Family Channel; Bravo; Cartoon Network; CNBC; CNN; Discovery Channel; Disney Channel; ESPN; Food Network; HGTV; INSP; MSNBC; National Geographic Channel; Spike TV; Syfy; TBS Superstation; Turner Classic Movies; Turner Network TV; Univision Studios; WE tv; WGN America.
Fee: $29.95 installation; $26.45 monthly.
Pay Service 1
Pay Units: 23.
Programming (via satellite): HBO.
Fee: $15.00 installation; $10.95 monthly.
Video-On-Demand: No
Internet Service
Operational: No.
Telephone Service
None
Miles of Plant: 6.0 (coaxial); None (fiber optic).
Ownership: Almega Cable (MSO).

MILTON-FREEWATER—Charter Communications. Now served by WALLA WALLA, WA [WA0016]. ICA: OR0043.

MILWAUKIE—Comcast Cable. Now served by PORTLAND, OR [OR0001]. ICA: OR0018.

MONROE—Monroe Telephone Co. This cable system has converted to IPTV. See Monroe, OR [OR5001]. ICA: OR0105.

MONROE—Monroe Telephone. Formerly [OR0105]. This cable system has converted to IPTV, 575 Commercial St, PO Box 130, Monroe, OR 97456-0130. Phone: 541-847-5135. Fax: 541-847-9997. E-mail: telco@monroetel.com. Web Site: http://www.monroetel.com. ICA: OR5001.
TV Market Ranking: Below 100 (MONROE). Franchise award date: N.A. Franchise expiration date: N.A. Began: N.A.
Channel capacity: N.A. Channels available but not in use: N.A.
Basic Service
Subscribers: N.A.
Fee: $34.95 monthly; $4.95 converter.
Expanded Basic Service 1
Subscribers: N.A.
Fee: $44.90 monthly.
Pay Service 1
Pay Units: N.A.
Programming (via satellite): HBO.
Fee: $9.95 monthly (Cinemax or Encore/Starz!); $14.95 monthly (Showtime); $18.95 monthly (HBO).
Internet Service
Operational: Yes.
Fee: $34.45 monthly.
Telephone Service
Digital: Operational

MORO—J & N Cable, 614 S Columbus Ave, Goldendale, WA 98620-9006. Phone: 509-773-5359. Fax: 509-773-7090. E-mail: john@jncable.com. Web Site: http://www.jncable.com. ICA: OR0111.
TV Market Ranking: Outside TV Markets (MORO). Franchise award date: November 3, 1954. Franchise expiration date: N.A. Began: January 1, 1955.
Channel capacity: N.A. Channels available but not in use: N.A.
Basic Service
Subscribers: 88.
Programming (received off-air): KEPR-TV (CBS) Pasco; KNDU (NBC) Richland; KRCW-TV (CW) Salem; KVEW (ABC, MNT) Kennewick.
Programming (via microwave): KATU (ABC) Portland; KGW (NBC) Portland; KOIN (CBS) Portland; KOPB-TV (PBS) Portland; KPDX (MNT) Vancouver; KPTV (FOX) Portland.
Programming (via satellite): A&E Networks; ABC Family Channel; AMC; Cartoon Network; CNN; C-SPAN; C-SPAN 2; Discovery Channel; Disney Channel; ESPN; ESPN 2; Fox News Channel; Fox Sports Net; Hallmark Channel; Headline News; HGTV; History Channel; Northwest Cable News; QVC; Syfy; TBS Superstation; The Learning Channel; Trinity Broadcasting Network; Turner Classic Movies; Turner Network TV; USA Network; WGN America.
Fee: $25.00 installation; $24.95 monthly; $15.00 converter.
Pay Service 1
Pay Units: N.A.
Programming (via satellite): HBO.
Video-On-Demand: No
Internet Service
Operational: No.
Telephone Service
None
Miles of Plant: 9.0 (coaxial); None (fiber optic). Additional miles planned: 1.0 (coaxial).
General Manager: John Kusky. Marketing Manager: Nancy Kusky.
Ownership: J & N Cable Systems Inc.

MOUNT VERNON—Blue Mountain TV Cable Co., 300 Highlan Terrace, PO Box 267, Mount Vernon, OR 97865-0267. Phone: 541-932-4613. Fax: 541-932-4613. E-mail: bmtv@bluemountaindigital.com. Web Site: http://www.bmtvcable.com. Also serves Canyon City & John Day. ICA: OR0061.
TV Market Ranking: Outside TV Markets (Canyon City, John Day, MOUNT VERNON). Franchise award date: N.A. Franchise expiration date: N.A. Began: October 1, 1954.
Channel capacity: 25 (not 2-way capable). Channels available but not in use: N.A.
Basic Service
Subscribers: 493.
Programming (received off-air): KPDX (MNT) Vancouver; 4 FMs.
Programming (via microwave): KOIN (CBS) Portland; KPTV (FOX) Portland.
Programming (via satellite): 3 Angels Broadcasting Network; ABC Family Channel; CW+; Discovery Channel; Disney Channel; ESPN; ESPN 2; Fox News Channel; HGTV; KATU (ABC) Portland; KGW (NBC) Portland; KOPB-TV (PBS) Portland; Outdoor Channel; QVC; Syfy; TBS Superstation; WGN America.
Fee: $20.00 installation; $20.50 monthly.
Video-On-Demand: No
Internet Service
Operational: Yes.
Subscribers: 60.
Fee: $24.95 monthly.
Telephone Service
None
Miles of Plant: 30.0 (coaxial); None (fiber optic).
Manager: Chuck McKenna.
Ownership: Blue Mountain TV Cable Co. (MSO).

MYRTLE CREEK—Charter Communications. Now served by ROSEBURG, OR [OR0016]. ICA: OR0021.

NEWBERG—Comcast Cable. Now served by SALEM, OR [OR0005]. ICA: OR0014.

NORTH POWDER—Formerly served by Almega Cable. No longer in operation. ICA: OR0107.

ODELL—Valley TV Co-op Inc., 614 S Columbus Ave, Goldendale, WA 98620-9006. Phone: 541-352-7278. Fax: 541-352-7277. ICA: OR0102.
TV Market Ranking: Outside TV Markets (ODELL). Franchise award date: N.A.

Franchise expiration date: N.A. Began: April 1, 1955.
Channel capacity: 52 (not 2-way capable). Channels available but not in use: N.A.

Basic Service
Subscribers: N.A. Included in Parkdale
Programming (received off-air): KATU (ABC) Portland; KGW (NBC) Portland; KOIN (CBS) Portland; KOPB-TV (PBS) Portland; KPTV (FOX) Portland.
Programming (via satellite): A&E Networks; ABC Family Channel; Discovery Channel; Disney Channel; ESPN; Great American Country; National Geographic Channel; Outdoor Channel; Spike TV; Syfy; TBS Superstation; The Learning Channel; Turner Network TV; Univision Studios; WGN America.
Fee: $25.00 installation; $27.50 monthly.

Pay Service 1
Pay Units: 30.
Programming (via satellite): HBO; The Movie Channel.
Fee: $10.00 monthly.

Internet Service
Operational: No.
Miles of plant included in Parkdale
Chief Technician: John Kusky.
Ownership: Valley TV Co-op Inc. (MSO).

OREGON CITY (unincorporated areas)—Clear Creek Telephone & TeleVision, 18238 S Fischers Mill Rd, Oregon City, OR 97045-9612. Phone: 503-631-2101. Fax: 503-631-2098. E-mail: info@clearcreek.coop. Web Site: http://www.ccmtc.com. Also serves Redland. ICA: OR0180.
TV Market Ranking: 29 (OREGON CITY, Redland).
Channel capacity: N.A. Channels available but not in use: N.A.

Basic Service
Subscribers: 1,700.
Programming (received off-air): KATU (ABC) Portland; KGW (NBC) Portland; KNMT (TBN) Portland; KOIN (CBS) Portland; KOPB-TV (PBS) Portland; KPDX (MNT) Vancouver; KPTV (FOX) Portland; KPXG-TV (ION) Salem; KRCW-TV (CW) Salem.
Programming (via satellite): ABC Family Channel; CNN; C-SPAN; C-SPAN 2; Lifetime; QVC; TV Guide Network.
Fee: $16.00 monthly.

Expanded Basic Service 1
Subscribers: N.A.
Programming (via satellite): A&E Networks; AMC; Animal Planet; Cartoon Network; CNBC; Comedy Central; Country Music TV; Discovery Channel; Discovery Fit & Health; Discovery Health Channel; Disney Channel; ESPN; ESPN 2; Food Network; Fox News Channel; G4; Headline News; HGTV; History Channel; INSP; MTV; Nickelodeon; Northwest Cable News; Spike TV; Syfy; TBS Superstation; The Learning Channel; The Weather Channel; Travel Channel; Turner Classic Movies; Turner Network TV; TV Land; Univision Studios; USA Network; VH1; WGN America.
Fee: $19.95 monthly.

Digital Basic Service
Subscribers: N.A.
Programming (via satellite): BBC America; Discovery Digital Networks; ESPNews; Fox Sports World; Golf Channel; GSN; Independent Film Channel; Music Choice; Speed.
Fee: $55.00 monthly.

Pay Service 1
Pay Units: N.A.
Programming (via satellite): Cinemax; HBO (multiplexed); Showtime (multiplexed); The Movie Channel.
Fee: $10.50 monthly (Cinemax or TMC), $12 monthly (HBO or Showtime).

Digital Pay Service 1
Pay Units: N.A.
Programming (via satellite): Cinemax (multiplexed); Flix; HBO (multiplexed); Showtime (multiplexed); Sundance Channel; The Movie Channel (multiplexed).
Fee: $10.50 monthly (Cinemax or Flix/Sundance/TMC), $11.75 monthly (HBO or Showtime).
Video-On-Demand: No
Pay-Per-View
iN DEMAND (delivered digitally); Playboy TV (delivered digitally); Fresh (delivered digitally).

Internet Service
Operational: Yes.
Subscribers: 900.
Broadband Service: ccwebster.net.
Fee: $50.00 installation; $44.95 monthly.

Telephone Service
None
President: Mitchell Moore.
Ownership: Clear Creek Telephone & Television.

OTIS—Broadstripe, 40 Spring St, PO Box 367, Depoe Bay, OR 97341-0367. Phone: 425-747-4600. Fax: 425-644-4621. E-mail: contact_nw@broadstripe.com. Web Site: http://www.broadstripe.com. ICA: OR0175.
TV Market Ranking: Outside TV Markets (OTIS).
Channel capacity: N.A. Channels available but not in use: N.A.

Basic Service
Subscribers: N.A.
Programming (received off-air): KPDX (MNT) Vancouver.
Programming (via microwave): KOIN (CBS) Portland; KPTV (FOX) Portland.
Programming (via satellite): A&E Networks; ABC Family Channel; AMC; Animal Planet; CNBC; CNN; C-SPAN; Discovery Channel; Disney Channel; ESPN; Fox News Channel; Fox Sports Net; Hallmark Channel; HBO; Headline News; HGTV; KATU (ABC) Portland; KGW (NBC) Portland; KOPB-TV (PBS) Portland; Lifetime; Nickelodeon; Northwest Cable News; QVC; Showtime; Spike TV; Syfy; TBN Enlace USA; TBS Superstation; The Learning Channel; The Movie Channel; Travel Channel; Turner Network TV; USA Network; WGN America.
Fee: $37.39 monthly.

Digital Basic Service
Subscribers: N.A.
Programming (via satellite): DMX Music.
Fee: $49.39 monthly.

Digital Expanded Basic Service
Subscribers: N.A.
Programming (via satellite): BBC America; Bio; Bravo; Discovery Digital Networks; ESPN 2; ESPNews; Fox Movie Channel; Fox Soccer; Golf Channel; GSN; Independent Film Channel; INSP; Lifetime Movie Network; National Geographic Channel; ShopNBC; Speed; Style Network; Toon Disney; Turner Classic Movies; Versus; W Network.

Digital Pay Service 1
Pay Units: N.A.
Programming (via satellite): Cinemax (multiplexed); Encore (multiplexed); HBO (multiplexed); Showtime (multiplexed); Starz (multiplexed); The Movie Channel (multiplexed).
Fee: $13.95 monthly (Showtime or Cinemax), $14.95 monthly (HBO).

Pay-Per-View
Movies (delivered digitally).

Internet Service
Operational: Yes.
Fee: $49.95 installation; $37.95 monthly.

Telephone Service
Digital: Operational
Fee: $39.99 monthly
Miles of Plant: 27.0 (coaxial); None (fiber optic).
President & Chief Executive Officer: Bill Shreffler. Vice President, Programming: Frank Scotello. Business Manager: Bob Lam.
Ownership: Broadstripe (MSO).

PARKDALE—Valley TV Co-op Inc., 614 S Columbus Ave, Goldendale, WA 98620-9006. Phone: 541-352-7278. Fax: 541-352-7277. Also serves Mount Hood. ICA: OR0147.
TV Market Ranking: Outside TV Markets (Mount Hood, PARKDALE). Franchise award date: N.A. Franchise expiration date: N.A. Began: January 1, 1955.
Channel capacity: N.A. Channels available but not in use: N.A.

Basic Service
Subscribers: 185 Includes Odell.
Programming (received off-air): KATU (ABC) Portland; KGW (NBC) Portland; KOIN (CBS) Portland; KOPB-TV (PBS) Portland; KPTV (FOX) Portland.
Programming (via satellite): A&E Networks; ABC Family Channel; Discovery Channel; Disney Channel; ESPN; Great American Country; National Geographic Channel; Outdoor Channel; Spike TV; Syfy; TBS Superstation; The Learning Channel; Turner Network TV; Univision Studios; WGN America.
Fee: $27.50 monthly.

Pay Service 1
Pay Units: 20.
Programming (via satellite): HBO; The Movie Channel.
Fee: $10.00 monthly.

Internet Service
Operational: No.
Miles of Plant: 130.0 (coaxial); None (fiber optic). Miles of plant include Odell
Chief Technician: John Kusky.
Ownership: Valley TV Co-op Inc. (MSO).

PENDLETON—Charter Communications, 639 N Kellogg St, Kennewick, WA 99336. Phone: 509-222-2500. Fax: 509-735-3795. Web Site: http://www.charter.com. Also serves Echo, Hermiston, Pilot Rock, Rieth, Stanfield & Umatilla County (portions). ICA: OR0019.
TV Market Ranking: Below 100 (Echo, Hermiston, PENDLETON, Pilot Rock, Rieth, Stanfield); Outside TV Markets (Umatilla County (portions)). Franchise award date: N.A. Franchise expiration date: N.A. Began: October 1, 1954.
Channel capacity: 36 (not 2-way capable). Channels available but not in use: N.A.

Basic Service
Subscribers: 9,260.
Programming (received off-air): K42IT-D Pendleton; KATU (ABC) Portland; KEPR-TV (CBS) Pasco; KFFX-TV (FOX, IND) Pendleton; KGW (NBC) Portland; KNDU (NBC) Richland; KOIN (CBS) Portland; KPTV (FOX) Portland; KVEW (ABC, MNT) Kennewick; 9 FMs.
Programming (via satellite): C-SPAN; QVC.
Fee: $30.00 installation.

Expanded Basic Service 1
Subscribers: N.A.
Programming (via satellite): A&E Networks; ABC Family Channel; AMC; Animal Planet; CNBC; CNN; Discovery Channel; Disney Channel; ESPN; Fox News Channel; FX; MTV; Nickelodeon; Northwest Cable News; Spike TV; TBS Superstation; The Learning Channel; The Weather Channel; Toon Disney; Travel Channel; truTV; Turner Network TV; Univision Studios; USA Network; VH1.
Fee: $50.99 monthly.

Digital Basic Service
Subscribers: 1,450.
Programming (via satellite): BBC America; Bloomberg Television; Bravo; Discovery Fit & Health; DMX Music; ESPN 2; ESPN Classic Sports; ESPNews; Fox Movie Channel; Fox Soccer; G4; Golf Channel; GSN; Halogen Network; HGTV; History Channel; Independent Film Channel; National Geographic Channel; Nick Jr.; Outdoor Channel; Speed; Syfy; Trinity Broadcasting Network; Turner Classic Movies; TV Guide Interactive Inc.; Versus; VH1 Classic; VH1 Country; WE tv.

Digital Pay Service 1
Pay Units: N.A.
Programming (via satellite): Cinemax (multiplexed); Encore (multiplexed); HBO (multiplexed); Showtime (multiplexed); Starz (multiplexed); The Movie Channel (multiplexed).
Video-On-Demand: Yes
Pay-Per-View
iN DEMAND (delivered digitally); Fresh (delivered digitally); Playboy TV (delivered digitally).

Internet Service
Operational: Yes.
Broadband Service: Charter Pipeline.
Fee: $29.99 monthly.

Telephone Service
Digital: Operational
Miles of plant included in Kennewick, WA
General Manager: Linda Kimberly. Technical Operations Manager: Jeff Hopkins. Marketing Director: Diane Long. Program Director: Lloyd Swain.
Ownership: Charter Communications Inc. (MSO).

PORTLAND—Comcast Cable, 9605 SW Nimbus Ave, Beaverton, OR 97008-7198. Phone: 503-605-6000. Fax: 503-605-6226. Web Site: http://www.comcast.com. Also serves Clackamas County, Corbett, Dunthorpe, Eagle Creek, Fairview, Gladstone, Gresham, Happy Valley, Johnson City, Linnton, Maywood Park, Milwaukie, Multnomah County (unincorporated areas), Oregon City, Orient, Riverdale, Springdale, Sylvan, Troutdale, Washington County, West Linn & Wood Village. ICA: OR0001.

TV Market Ranking: 29 (Clackamas County, Corbett, Dunthorpe, Eagle Creek, Fairview, Gladstone, Gresham, Happy Valley, Johnson City, Linnton, Maywood Park, Milwaukie, Multnomah County (unincorporated areas), Oregon City, Orient, PORTLAND, Riverdale, Springdale, Sylvan, Troutdale, Washington County, West Linn, Wood Village). Franchise award date: May 1, 1981. Franchise expiration date: December 31, 2010. Began: February 1, 1982.

Channel capacity: N.A. Channels available but not in use: N.A.

Basic Service

Subscribers: N.A. Included in Beaverton

Programming (received off-air): KATU (ABC) Portland; KGW (NBC) Portland; KNMT (TBN) Portland; KOIN (CBS) Portland; KOPB-TV (PBS) Portland; KPDX (MNT) Vancouver; KPTV (FOX) Portland; KPXG-TV (ION) Salem; KRCW-TV (CW) Salem.

Programming (via satellite): C-SPAN; C-SPAN 2; Discovery Channel; Hallmark Channel; QVC; ShopNBC; TV Guide Network; Univision Studios; WGN America.

Fee: $44.99 installation; $12.37 monthly.

Expanded Basic Service 1

Subscribers: 176,000.

Programming (via satellite): A&E Networks; ABC Family Channel; AMC; Animal Planet; BET Networks; Cartoon Network; CNBC; CNN; Comedy Central; Country Music TV; Disney Channel; E! Entertainment Television; ESPN; ESPN 2; Food Network; Fox News Channel; FX; Golf Channel; Headline News; HGTV; History Channel; Lifetime; MSNBC; MTV; Nickelodeon; Northwest Cable News; Oxygen; Spike TV; Syfy; TBS Superstation; The Learning Channel; The Weather Channel; Travel Channel; truTV; Turner Network TV; TV Land; USA Network; VH1.

Fee: $39.52 monthly.

Digital Basic Service

Subscribers: 99,000.

Programming (via satellite): American-Life TV Network; BBC America; Bio; Black Family Channel; Bloomberg Television; Bravo; Canales N; Discovery Fit & Health; DMX Music; Encore Action; ESPN Classic Sports; ESPNews; Eternal Word TV Network; Fox Movie Channel; Fox Sports World; FSN Digital Atlantic; FSN Digital Central; FSN Digital Pacific; Fuse; G4; GAS; Great American Country; GSN; Halogen Network; History Channel International; Independent Film Channel; Lifetime Movie Network; Lime; MTV Networks Digital Suite; National Geographic Channel; Nick Jr.; NickToons TV; Nuvo TV; Outdoor Channel; Ovation; Speed; Style Network; Sundance Channel; The Word Network; Toon Disney; Turner Classic Movies; Versus; WE tv; Weatherscan.

Fee: $10.95 monthly.

Digital Pay Service 1

Pay Units: N.A.

Programming (via satellite): CCTV-4; Cinemax; Filipino Channel; Flix; HBO (multiplexed); Russian Television Network; Showtime (multiplexed); Starz (multiplexed); The Movie Channel (multiplexed).

Fee: $14.99 monthly (CCTV4, Filipino Channel, Russian TV Network & Starz); $18.15 monthly (Cinemax, Starz, HBO, Showtime & TMC).

Video-On-Demand: Yes

Pay-Per-View

Addressable homes: 99,000.

iN DEMAND (delivered digitally); Sports PPV (delivered digitally); Urban Xtra (delivered digitally); Fresh (delivered digitally); Shorteez (delivered digitally); Playboy TV (delivered digitally).

Internet Service

Operational: Yes.

Subscribers: 123,000.

Broadband Service: Comcast High Speed Internet.

Fee: $99.95 installation; $52.95 monthly; $3.00 modem lease.

Telephone Service

Digital: Operational

Fee: $44.95 monthly

Miles of plant included in Beaverton

Senior Vice President: Curt Henninger. Vice President, Technical Operations: Mike Mason. Vice President, Marketing: Lars Lofas. Sales Director: Mike Williams. Marketing Director: Brad Nosler. Public Relations Director: Theressa Davis.

Ownership: Comcast Cable Communications Inc. (MSO).

PORTLAND (western portion)—Comcast Cable. Now served by PORTLAND, OR [OR0001]. ICA: OR0009.

POWERS—Formerly served by Charter Communications. No longer in operation. ICA: OR0094.

PRAIRIE CITY—Blue Mountain TV Cable Co., 300 Highlan Terrace, PO Box 267, Mount Vernon, OR 97865-0267. Phone: 541-932-4613. Fax: 541-932-4613. E-mail: bmtv@bluemountaindigital.com. Web Site: http://www.bmtvcable.com. ICA: OR0084.

TV Market Ranking: Outside TV Markets (PRAIRIE CITY). Franchise award date: N.A. Franchise expiration date: N.A. Began: October 1, 1962.

Channel capacity: 23 (not 2-way capable). Channels available but not in use: N.A.

Basic Service

Subscribers: 150.

Programming (via microwave): KOIN (CBS) Portland; KOPB-TV (PBS) Portland; KPTV (FOX) Portland.

Programming (via satellite): 3 Angels Broadcasting Network; ABC Family Channel; CW+; Discovery Channel; Disney Channel; ESPN; ESPN 2; Fox News Channel; HGTV; KATU (ABC) Portland; KGW (NBC) Portland; Northwest Cable News; Outdoor Channel; QVC; Syfy; TBS Superstation; WGN America.

Fee: $20.00 installation; $20.50 monthly.

Pay Service 1

Pay Units: 13.

Programming (via satellite): HBO.

Fee: $10.50 installation; $13.00 monthly.

Video-On-Demand: No

Internet Service

Operational: No.

Telephone Service

None

Miles of Plant: 10.0 (coaxial); None (fiber optic).

Manager: Chuck McKenna.

Ownership: Blue Mountain TV Cable Co. (MSO).

PRINEVILLE—Crestview Cable TV, 350 NE Dunham St, Prineville, OR 97754-1955. Phones: 800-285-2330; 541-447-4342. Fax: 541-447-5987. E-mail: customerservice@crestviewcable.com. Web Site: http://www.crestviewcable.com. ICA: OR0038.

TV Market Ranking: Below 100 (PRINEVILLE). Franchise award date: N.A. Franchise expiration date: N.A. Began: June 1, 1971.

Channel capacity: 78 (operating 2-way). Channels available but not in use: N.A.

Basic Service

Subscribers: 3,634.

Programming (received off-air): KATU (ABC) Portland; KFXO-LP (FOX) Bend; KGW (NBC) Portland; KOAB-TV (PBS) Bend; KOIN (CBS) Portland; KPDX (MNT) Vancouver; KTVZ (CW, NBC) Bend; 14 FMs.

Programming (via satellite): C-SPAN; QVC; TV Guide Network; Univision Studios.

Fee: $32.00 installation; $18.23 monthly; $.86 converter; $10.40 additional installation.

Expanded Basic Service 1

Subscribers: 3,374.

Programming (via satellite): A&E Networks; ABC Family Channel; AMC; Animal Planet; CNBC; CNN; Comedy Central; Country Music TV; C-SPAN 2; Discovery Channel; Disney Channel; ESPN; ESPN 2; ESPNews; Food Network; Fox News Channel; Hallmark Channel; Headline News; HGTV; History Channel; Lifetime; MSNBC; MTV; Nickelodeon; Northwest Cable News; Spike TV; Syfy; TBS Superstation; The Learning Channel; Toon Disney; Travel Channel; Trinity Broadcasting Network; Turner Classic Movies; Turner Network TV; TV Land; USA Network; Versus; VH1; WE tv.

Fee: $26.31 monthly.

Digital Basic Service

Subscribers: N.A.

Programming (via satellite): BBC America; Bio; Bloomberg Television; Canales N; cloo; Discovery Fit & Health; DMX Music; Fox College Sports Atlantic; Fox College Sports Central; Fox College Sports Pacific; Fox Movie Channel; Fox Soccer; Fuse; G4; Golf Channel; Halogen Network; History Channel International; Outdoor Channel; Speed.

Fee: $20.17 monthly.

Digital Pay Service 1

Pay Units: N.A.

Programming (via satellite): Cinemax (multiplexed); Encore (multiplexed); HBO (multiplexed); Starz (multiplexed).

Fee: $10.00 monthly (Cinemax), $12.00 monthly (Starz/Encore), $12.99 monthly (HBO).

Video-On-Demand: No

Pay-Per-View

iN DEMAND (delivered digitally); Playboy TV (delivered digitally); Fresh (delivered digitally).

Internet Service

Operational: Yes. Began: December 1, 2000.

Subscribers: 600.

Broadband Service: In-house.

Fee: $19.20 installation; $44.95 monthly; $10.00 modem lease.

Telephone Service

Analog: Not Operational

Digital: Operational

Miles of Plant: 80.0 (coaxial); None (fiber optic).

Manager: Tony Ashcroft.

Ownership: California-Oregon Broadcasting Inc. (MSO).

PRINEVILLE—Formerly served by Central Vision. No longer in operation. ICA: OR0169.

PROSPECT—Almega Cable, 4015 W Airport Freeway, Ste 544, Bedford, TX 76021. Phones: 877-725-6342; 817-685-9588. Fax: 817-685-6488. Web Site: http://almegacable.com. ICA: OR0096.

TV Market Ranking: Below 100 (PROSPECT). Franchise award date: January 1, 1980. Franchise expiration date: N.A. Began: January 1, 1982.

Channel capacity: 45 (not 2-way capable). Channels available but not in use: N.A.

Basic Service

Subscribers: 122.

Programming (received off-air): KOBI (NBC) Medford; KSYS (PBS) Medford; KTVL (CBS, CW) Medford.

Programming (via satellite): A&E Networks; ABC Family Channel; CNN; Country Music TV; Discovery Channel; Disney Channel; ESPN; ESPN 2; HGTV; History Channel; Lifetime; Spike TV; Syfy; TBS Superstation; The Learning Channel; The Weather Channel; Turner Classic Movies; Turner Network TV; USA Network; WGN America.

Fee: $29.95 installation; $25.50 monthly.

Pay Service 1

Pay Units: 13.

Programming (via satellite): Cinemax.

Fee: $15.00 installation; $11.55 monthly.

Pay Service 2

Pay Units: 21.

Programming (via satellite): HBO.

Fee: $15.00 installation; $7.95 monthly.

Video-On-Demand: No

Internet Service

Operational: No.

Telephone Service

None

Miles of Plant: 15.0 (coaxial); None (fiber optic).

Ownership: Almega Cable (MSO).

RAINIER—J & N Cable, 614 S Columbus Ave, Goldendale, WA 98620-9006. Phone: 435-637-6823. Fax: 509-773-7090. Web Site: http://www.jncable.com. ICA: OR0058.

TV Market Ranking: Below 100 (RAINIER). Franchise award date: January 1, 1958. Franchise expiration date: N.A. Began: January 1, 1958.

Channel capacity: 61 (not 2-way capable). Channels available but not in use: N.A.

Basic Service

Subscribers: 235.

Programming (received off-air): KATU (ABC) Portland; KGPX-TV (ION) Spokane; KGW (NBC) Portland; KOIN (CBS) Portland; KOPB-TV (PBS) Portland; KPDX (MNT) Vancouver; KPTV (FOX) Portland; allband FM.

Programming (via satellite): A&E Networks; ABC Family Channel; AMC; Animal Planet; Cartoon Network; CNBC; CNN; Comedy Central; Discovery Channel; Disney Channel; E! Entertainment Television; ESPN; ESPN 2; Fox News Channel; Fox Sports Net; FX; Great American Country; Hallmark Channel; Headline News; HGTV; History Channel; Lifetime; MSNBC; MTV; Nickelodeon; QVC; ShopNBC; Spike TV; Syfy; TBS Superstation; The Learning Channel; Toon Disney; Trinity Broadcasting Network; Turner Network TV; TV Land; USA Network; VH1; WGN America.

Fee: $25.00 installation; $14.95 monthly.

Digital Basic Service

Subscribers: N.A.

Programming (via satellite): BBC America; Bio; Bravo; CMT Pure Country; Discovery Health Channel; Discovery Kids Channel; DMX Music; Fuse; GSN; History Channel International; ID Investigation Discovery; Mil-

itary Channel; MTV2; National Geographic Channel; Nick Jr.; Planet Green; Science; ShopNBC; Style Network; TeenNick; Trinity Broadcasting Network; VH1 Classic; WE tv.
Fee: $15.95 monthly.

Digital Expanded Basic Service
Subscribers: N.A.
Programming (via satellite): ESPN Classic Sports; ESPNews; Fox College Sports Atlantic; Fox College Sports Central; Fox College Sports Pacific; Fox Soccer; Golf Channel; Independent Film Channel; Lifetime Movie Network; Speed; Versus.
Fee: $15.95 monthly.

Pay Service 1
Pay Units: N.A.
Programming (via satellite): HBO.
Fee: $10.00 installation; $9.95 monthly.

Digital Pay Service 1
Pay Units: N.A.
Programming (via satellite): Cinemax (multiplexed); Encore; HBO (multiplexed); Showtime (multiplexed); Starz (multiplexed); The Movie Channel.
Fee: $10.95 monthly (Cinemax), $12.00 monthly (Showtime & TMC), $12.95 monthly (HBO).

Video-On-Demand: Planned

Pay-Per-View
special events (delivered digitally); Playboy TV (delivered digitally).

Internet Service
Operational: No.

Telephone Service
None

Miles of Plant: 36.0 (coaxial); None (fiber optic).
General Manager: John Kusky.
Ownership: J & N Cable Systems Inc. (MSO).

REDMOND—Formerly served by Central Vision. No longer in operation. ICA: OR0166.

RICHLAND—Eagle Valley Communications, 349 1st St, PO Box 180, Richland, OR 97870. Phones: 800-366-0795; 541-893-6116. Fax: 541-893-6903. Web Site: http://www.eagletelephone.com/services_eaglevalley.shtml. Also serves New Bridge. ICA: OR0113.
TV Market Ranking: Outside TV Markets (New Bridge, RICHLAND). Franchise award date: N.A. Franchise expiration date: N.A. Began: N.A.
Channel capacity: N.A. Channels available but not in use: N.A.

Basic Service
Subscribers: 95.
Programming (received off-air): KBOI-TV (CBS, CW) Boise; KIVI-TV (ABC) Nampa; KTRV-TV (IND) Nampa; KTVB (NBC) Boise; WKRN-TV (ABC) Nashville; WSEE-TV (CBS, CW) Erie.
Programming (via satellite): A&E Networks; ABC Family Channel; AMC; Animal Planet; CNBC; CNN; Country Music TV; C-SPAN; Discovery Channel; Disney Channel; Encore; ESPN; ESPN 2; Fox News Channel; Headline News; History Channel; Lifetime; MTV; Nickelodeon; Northwest Cable News; Spike TV; Syfy; TBS Superstation; The Learning Channel; The Weather Channel; Turner Network TV; USA Network; WNBC (NBC) New York.
Fee: $10.00 installation; $31.95 monthly.

Pay Service 1
Pay Units: 20.
Programming (via satellite): HBO.
Fee: $15.00 installation; $10.00 monthly.

Pay Service 2
Pay Units: 20.
Programming (via satellite): Cinemax.
Fee: $4.50 monthly.

Video-On-Demand: No

Internet Service
Operational: No, DSL.
Broadband Service: DSL service only.

Telephone Service
None

Chief Technician & Program Director: Gary Fehrenbach. Plant Manager: Mike Lattin. Marketing Director: Marcia Lincoln.
Ownership: Eagle Valley Communications (MSO).

ROSE LODGE—Millennium Digital Media. Now served by DEPOE BAY, OR [OR0134]. ICA: OR0150.

ROSEBURG—Charter Communications, 521 NE 136th Ave, Vancouver, WA 98684. Phone: 360-828-6600. Fax: 360-828-6795. Web Site: http://www.charter.com. Also serves Canyonville, Dillard, Douglas County (portions), Myrtle Creek, Oakland, Riddle, Sutherlin, Tri-City & Winston. ICA: OR0016.
TV Market Ranking: Below 100 (Canyonville, Dillard, Douglas County (portions), Myrtle Creek, Oakland, Riddle, ROSEBURG, Sutherlin, Tri-City, Winston). Franchise award date: November 1, 1973. Franchise expiration date: N.A. Began: January 1, 1954.
Channel capacity: N.A. Channels available but not in use: N.A.

Basic Service
Subscribers: 16,010.
Programming (received off-air): KEVU-CD (MNT) Eugene; KEZI (ABC) Eugene; KLSR-TV (FOX) Eugene; KOBI (NBC) Medford; KPIC (CBS) Roseburg; KSYS (PBS) Medford; KTCW (NBC) Roseburg; KTVC (IND) Roseburg; 12 FMs.
Programming (via satellite): C-SPAN; INSP; QVC; ShopNBC; Trinity Broadcasting Network; WGN America.
Fee: $29.99 installation; $24.78 monthly; $15.00 additional installation.

Expanded Basic Service 1
Subscribers: 8,742.
Programming (via satellite): A&E Networks; ABC Family Channel; AMC; Animal Planet; Bravo; Cartoon Network; CNBC; CNN; Comedy Central; Country Music TV; Discovery Channel; Disney Channel; E! Entertainment Television; ESPN; ESPN 2; Food Network; Fox Movie Channel; Fox News Channel; FX; G4; Golf Channel; GSN; Hallmark Channel; Headline News; HGTV; History Channel; Lifetime; MSNBC; MTV; National Geographic Channel; Nickelodeon; Northwest Cable News; Speed; Spike TV; Syfy; TBS Superstation; The Learning Channel; The Weather Channel; Toon Disney; Travel Channel; truTV; Turner Classic Movies; Turner Network TV; TV Land; USA Network; Versus; VH1; WE tv.
Fee: $50.99 monthly.

Digital Basic Service
Subscribers: 2,579.
Programming (via satellite): BBC America; Bio; Bloomberg Television; Boomerang; DIY Network; Lifetime Movie Network; MTV Networks Digital Suite; Music Choice; Nick Jr.; SoapNet; Style Network.
Fee: $8.55 monthly.

Digital Pay Service 1
Pay Units: 837.
Programming (via satellite): HBO (multiplexed).
Fee: $25.00 installation; $5.00 monthly.

Digital Pay Service 2
Pay Units: 574.
Programming (via satellite): Flix; Showtime (multiplexed).
Fee: $25.00 installation; $5.00 monthly.

Digital Pay Service 3
Pay Units: 414.
Programming (via satellite): The Movie Channel (multiplexed).
Fee: $25.00 installation; $5.00 monthly.

Digital Pay Service 4
Pay Units: 440.
Programming (via satellite): Cinemax (multiplexed).
Fee: $5.00 monthly.

Digital Pay Service 5
Pay Units: 857.
Programming (via satellite): Encore; Starz.
Fee: $5.00 monthly.

Video-On-Demand: Yes

Pay-Per-View
Addressable homes: 2,579.
Hot Choice (delivered digitally); Shorteez (delivered digitally); Fresh (delivered digitally); Playboy TV (delivered digitally); iN DEMAND (delivered digitally).

Internet Service
Operational: Yes.
Broadband Service: Charter Pipeline.
Fee: $29.99 monthly.

Telephone Service
Digital: Operational

Miles of Plant: 413.0 (coaxial); None (fiber optic).
Vice President: Frank Antonovich. General Manager: Mike O'Herron. Technical Operations Director: Greg Lemming. Marketing Manager: Dolly Brock. Office Manager: Kelly Williams.
Ownership: Charter Communications Inc. (MSO).

SALEM—Comcast Cable, 9605 SW Nimbus Ave, Beaverton, OR 97008-7198. Phone: 503-605-6000. Fax: 503-605-6226. Web Site: http://www.comcast.com. Also serves Amity, Carlton, Dayton, Dundee, Keizer, Lafayette, Marion County (portions), McMinnville, Newberg, Polk County (portions) & Yamhill. ICA: OR0005.
TV Market Ranking: 29 (Carlton, Dayton, Dundee, Lafayette, Marion County (portions), McMinnville, Newberg, Yamhill); Below 100 (Amity, Keizer, Polk County (portions), SALEM, Marion County (portions)); Outside TV Markets (Polk County (portions), Marion County (portions)). Franchise award date: March 14, 1967. Franchise expiration date: N.A. Began: November 1, 1969.
Channel capacity: N.A. Channels available but not in use: N.A.

Basic Service
Subscribers: N.A. Included in Beaverton
Programming (received off-air): KATU (ABC) Portland; KGW (NBC) Portland; KNMT (TBN) Portland; KOIN (CBS) Portland; KOPB-TV (PBS) Portland; KPDX (MNT) Vancouver; KPTV (FOX) Portland; KPXG-TV (ION) Salem; KRCW-TV (CW) Salem; 20 FMs.
Programming (via satellite): C-SPAN; C-SPAN 2; Discovery Channel; Hallmark Channel; Product Information Network; QVC; ShopNBC; TV Guide Network; Univision Studios; WGN America.
Fee: $44.99 installation; $14.57 monthly.

Expanded Basic Service 1
Subscribers: N.A.
Programming (via satellite): A&E Networks; ABC Family Channel; AMC; Animal Planet; BET Networks; Cartoon Network; CNBC; CNN; Comedy Central; Country Music TV; Disney Channel; E! Entertainment Television; ESPN; ESPN 2; Food Network; Fox News Channel; FX; GalaVision; Golf Channel; Headline News; HGTV; History Channel; Lifetime; MSNBC; MTV; Nickelodeon; Northwest Cable News; Oxygen; Spike TV; Syfy; TBS Superstation; The Learning Channel; The Weather Channel; Travel Channel; truTV; Turner Network TV; TV Land; USA Network; VH1.
Fee: $37.32 monthly.

Digital Basic Service
Subscribers: 17,388.
Programming (via satellite): American-Life TV Network; BBC America; Bio; Black Family Channel; Bloomberg Television; Bravo; Canales N; Discovery Fit & Health; DMX Music; Encore Action; ESPN Classic Sports; ESPNews; Eternal Word TV Network; Fox Movie Channel; Fox Sports World; FSN Digital Atlantic; FSN Digital Central; FSN Digital Pacific; Fuse; G4; GAS; Great American Country; GSN; Halogen Network; History Channel International; Independent Film Channel; Lifetime Movie Network; Lime; MTV Networks Digital Suite; National Geographic Channel; Nick Jr.; NickToons TV; Nuvo TV; Outdoor Channel; Ovation; Speed; Style Network; Sundance Channel; The Word Network; Toon Disney; Turner Classic Movies; Versus; WE tv; Weatherscan.
Fee: $10.95 monthly.

Digital Pay Service 1
Pay Units: 19,532.
Programming (via satellite): CCTV-4; Cinemax; Filipino Channel; Flix; HBO (multiplexed); Russian Television Network; Showtime (multiplexed); Starz (multiplexed); The Movie Channel (multiplexed).
Fee: $14.99 monthly (CCTV-4, Filipino or RTN), $18.15 monthly (Cinemax, HBO, Showtime, Starz or TMC).

Video-On-Demand: Planned

Pay-Per-View
Addressable homes: 17,388.
iN DEMAND (delivered digitally); Sports PPV (delivered digitally); Urban Xtra (delivered digitally); Fresh (delivered digitally); Shorteez (delivered digitally); Playboy TV (delivered digitally).

Internet Service
Operational: Yes.
Subscribers: 18,475.
Broadband Service: Comcast High Speed Internet.
Fee: $99.95 installation; $42.95 monthly; $3.00 modem lease.

Telephone Service
Digital: Operational
Miles of plant included in Beaverton
Senior Vice President: Curt Henninger. Vice President, Technical Operations: Mike Mason. Vice President, Marketing: Lars Lofas. Marketing Director: Brad Nosler. Sales Director: Mike Williams. Public Relations Director: Theressa Davis.
Ownership: Comcast Cable Communications Inc. (MSO).

SALEM (southeastern portion)—Formerly served by Mill Creek Cable TV Inc. No longer in operation. ICA: OR0086.

SANDY—Wave Broadband, 401 Kirkland Parkplace, Ste 500, Kirkland, WA 98033. Phones: 888-222-5314; 425-576-8200. Fax: 425-576-8221. Web Site: http://www.wavebroadband.com. Also serves Clackamas County (portions) & Wemme. ICA: OR0063.
TV Market Ranking: 29 (Clackamas County (portions) (portions), SANDY); Below 100 (Clackamas County (portions) (portions)); Outside TV Markets (Wemme, Clackamas County (portions) (portions)). Franchise award date: N.A. Franchise expiration date: N.A. Began: December 1, 1980.
Channel capacity: 42 (not 2-way capable). Channels available but not in use: N.A.
Basic Service
Subscribers: 4,000 Includes subscribers for Silverton, OR.
Programming (received off-air): KATU (ABC) Portland; KGW (NBC) Portland; KNMT (TBN) Portland; KOIN (CBS) Portland; KOPB-TV (PBS) Portland; KPDX (MNT) Vancouver; KPTV (FOX) Portland; KRCW-TV (CW) Salem; KUNP (UNV) La Grande; 15 FMs.
Programming (via satellite): A&E Networks; ABC Family Channel; Comedy Central; C-SPAN; ESPN; ESPN 2; HGTV; MTV; MyNetworkTV Inc.; Nickelodeon; QVC; TBS Superstation; TV Guide Network; USA Network; VH1; WGN America.
Fee: $29.95 installation; $21.62 monthly.
Expanded Basic Service 1
Subscribers: N.A.
Programming (via satellite): AMC; Animal Planet; Bravo; Cartoon Network; CNBC; CNN; Country Music TV; C-SPAN 2; Discovery Channel; Discovery Fit & Health; Disney Channel; E! Entertainment Television; Food Network; Fox Movie Channel; Fox News Channel; FX; Golf Channel; Headline News; History Channel; Lifetime; MSNBC; National Geographic Channel; Northwest Cable News; Oxygen; SoapNet; Speed; Spike TV; Style Network; Syfy; The Learning Channel; The Weather Channel; Travel Channel; truTV; Turner Classic Movies; Turner Network TV; TV Land; Versus.
Fee: $4.39 monthly.
Digital Basic Service
Subscribers: N.A.
Programming (via satellite): BBC America; Bio; Discovery en Espanol; Discovery Health Channel; Discovery Kids Channel; History Channel International; ID Investigation Discovery; Independent Film Channel; Military Channel; Music Choice; Planet Green; Science; TV Guide Interactive Inc.
Digital Expanded Basic Service
Subscribers: N.A.
Programming (via satellite): CMT Pure Country; DIY Network; Lifetime Movie Network; MTV Jams; MTV2; Nick Jr.; NickToons TV; TeenNick; Tr3s; VH1 Classic; VH1 Soul.
Digital Expanded Basic Service 2
Subscribers: N.A.
Programming (via satellite): ESPN Classic Sports; ESPNews; Fox College Sports Atlantic; Fox College Sports Central; Fox College Sports Pacific; Fox Soccer; Fuel TV.
Digital Pay Service 1
Pay Units: N.A.
Programming (via satellite): Cinemax (multiplexed); Flix; HBO (multiplexed); Showtime (multiplexed); The Movie Channel (multiplexed).
Fee: $29.95 installation.
Video-On-Demand: No
Pay-Per-View
iN DEMAND; Hot Choice (delivered digitally); Playboy TV (delivered digitally); iN DEMAND (delivered digitally); Fresh (delivered digitally); Shorteez (delivered digitally).
Internet Service
Operational: Yes.
Fee: $29.95-$74.95 monthly.
Telephone Service
Digital: Operational
Fee: $29.95 monthly
Miles of Plant: 148.0 (coaxial); 20.0 (fiber optic).
General Manager: Tim Peters. Marketing Director: Adam Lazara.
Ownership: WaveDivision Holdings LLC (MSO).

SCIO—Scio Cablevision Inc., 38982 SE 2nd Ave, PO Box 1100, Scio, OR 97374-1100. Phone: 503-394-2995. Fax: 503-394-3999. E-mail: scv@smt-net.com. Web Site: http://www.smt-net.com. ICA: OR0151.
TV Market Ranking: Below 100 (SCIO). Franchise award date: January 1, 1982. Franchise expiration date: January 1, 2008. Began: December 1, 1982.
Channel capacity: 62 (operating 2-way). Channels available but not in use: N.A.
Basic Service
Subscribers: 700.
Programming (received off-air): KATU (ABC) Portland; KGW (NBC) Portland; KOIN (CBS) Portland; KOPB-TV (PBS) Portland; KPDX (MNT) Vancouver; KPTV (FOX) Portland; KPXG-TV (ION) Salem; KRCW-TV (CW) Salem.
Programming (via satellite): A&E Networks; ABC Family Channel; AMC; Animal Planet; Cartoon Network; CNBC; CNN; Comedy Central; Country Music TV; C-SPAN; Discovery Channel; Disney Channel; ESPN; ESPN 2; Food Network; Fox News Channel; FX; Hallmark Channel; Headline News; HGTV; History Channel; Lifetime; MSNBC; MTV; National Geographic Channel; Nickelodeon; Northwest Cable News; Outdoor Channel; RFD-TV; Spike TV; Syfy; TBS Superstation; The Learning Channel; The Weather Channel; Travel Channel; Trinity Broadcasting Network; truTV; Turner Network TV; TV Land; USA Network; VH1; WE tv; WGN America.
Fee: $36.00 monthly.
Digital Basic Service
Subscribers: 150.
Programming (via satellite): BBC America; Bio; Bloomberg Television; Bravo; cloo; CMT Pure Country; Daystar TV Network; Discovery Fit & Health; Discovery Health Channel; Discovery Kids Channel; DMX Music; ESPN 2; ESPN Classic Sports; ESPNews; Fox College Sports Atlantic; Fox College Sports Central; Fox College Sports Pacific; Fox Movie Channel; Fox Soccer; Fuse; G4; GMC; Golf Channel; Great American Country; GSN; Halogen Network; HGTV; History Channel; History Channel International; ID Investigation Discovery; Independent Film Channel; Lifetime Movie Network; Military Channel; MTV2; National Geographic Channel; Nick Jr.; NickToons TV; Outdoor Channel; Planet Green; Science; SoapNet; Speed; Style Network; Syfy; TeenNick; The Word Network; Toon Disney; Trinity Broadcasting Network; Turner Classic Movies; Versus; VH1 Classic; WE tv.
Fee: $17.00 monthly.
Digital Pay Service 1
Pay Units: N.A.
Programming (via satellite): Cinemax (multiplexed); Encore (multiplexed); Flix; HBO (multiplexed); Showtime (multiplexed); Starz (multiplexed); The Movie Channel (multiplexed).
Video-On-Demand: No
Internet Service
Operational: No, DSL.
Telephone Service
None
Miles of Plant: 60.0 (coaxial); 30.0 (fiber optic).
Manager: Tom Barth.
Ownership: Scio Cablevision Inc.

SENECA—Blue Mountain TV Cable Co., 300 Highlan Terrace, PO Box 267, Mount Vernon, OR 97865-0267. Phone: 541-932-4613. Fax: 541-932-4613. E-mail: bmtv@bluemountaindigital.com. Web Site: http://www.bmtvcable.com. ICA: OR0122.
TV Market Ranking: Outside TV Markets (SENECA). Franchise award date: N.A. Franchise expiration date: N.A. Began: October 1, 1956.
Channel capacity: 16 (not 2-way capable). Channels available but not in use: N.A.
Basic Service
Subscribers: 20.
Programming (received off-air): KOPB-TV (PBS) Portland; KPDX (MNT) Vancouver.
Programming (via microwave): KOIN (CBS) Portland.
Programming (via satellite): 3 Angels Broadcasting Network; KATU (ABC) Portland; KGW (NBC) Portland; Northwest Cable News; QVC; Syfy; WGN America.
Fee: $20.00 installation; $14.50 monthly.
Video-On-Demand: No
Internet Service
Operational: No.
Telephone Service
None
Miles of Plant: 2.0 (coaxial); None (fiber optic).
Manager: Chuck McKenna.
Ownership: Blue Mountain TV Cable Co. (MSO).

SHADY COVE—Almega Cable, 4018 W Airport Freeway, Ste 547, Bedford, TX 76021. Phones: 877-725-6342; 817-685-9588. Fax: 817-685-6488. Web Site: http://almegacable.com. Also serves Trail. ICA: OR0152.
TV Market Ranking: Below 100 (SHADY COVE, Trail). Franchise award date: N.A. Franchise expiration date: N.A. Began: November 1, 1980.
Channel capacity: N.A. Channels available but not in use: N.A.
Basic Service
Subscribers: 1,037.
Programming (received off-air): KMVU-DT (FOX) Medford; KOBI (NBC) Medford; KSYS (PBS) Medford; KTVL (CBS, CW) Medford; 1 FM.
Programming (via satellite): Country Music TV; C-SPAN; Headline News; WGN America.
Fee: $29.95 installation; $15.00 monthly.
Expanded Basic Service 1
Subscribers: 670.
Programming (via satellite): A&E Networks; ABC Family Channel; AmericanLife TV Network; Animal Planet; Cartoon Network; CNBC; CNN; Comedy Central; Discovery Channel; Disney Channel; E! Entertainment Television; ESPN; ESPN 2; Fox News Channel; History Channel; KTLA (CW) Los Angeles; Lifetime; MTV; Nickelodeon; Spike TV; Syfy; TBS Superstation; The Learning Channel; The Weather Channel; Travel Channel; Turner Classic Movies; Turner Network TV; TV Land; USA Network; VH1; WPIX (CW, IND) New York.
Fee: $14.45 monthly.
Digital Basic Service
Subscribers: N.A.
Programming (via satellite): AmericanLife TV Network; BBC America; Bloomberg Television; Bravo; Discovery Digital Networks; Fox Movie Channel; Fox Sports World; G4; Golf Channel; GSN; Halogen Network; HGTV; History Channel; History Channel International; Independent Film Channel; Lifetime Movie Network; MuchMusic Network; Outdoor Channel; Ovation; Speed; Style Network; Sundance Channel; Syfy; Trinity Broadcasting Network; Turner Classic Movies; Versus.
Pay Service 1
Pay Units: 21.
Programming (via satellite): Cinemax.
Fee: $15.00 installation; $13.95 monthly.
Pay Service 2
Pay Units: 47.
Programming (via satellite): HBO.
Fee: $15.00 installation; $13.00 monthly.
Digital Pay Service 1
Pay Units: N.A.
Programming (via satellite): Cinemax (multiplexed); Encore (multiplexed); HBO (multiplexed); Showtime (multiplexed); Starz (multiplexed); The Movie Channel (multiplexed).
Video-On-Demand: No
Pay-Per-View
iN DEMAND (delivered digitally); Playboy TV (delivered digitally); Fresh (delivered digitally); ESPN Extra (delivered digitally); ESPN Now (delivered digitally).
Internet Service
Operational: Yes.
Fee: $29.95 monthly.
Telephone Service
None
Miles of Plant: 20.0 (coaxial); None (fiber optic).
President: Thomas Kurien.
Ownership: Almega Cable (MSO).

SHERIDAN—Wave Broadband, 128 N Bridge St, Sheridan, OR 97378-1802. Phones: 866-928-3123; 503-981-1891 (Woodburn administrative office); 888-222-5314. Fax: 503-848-1134. Web Site: http://www.wavebroadband.com. Also serves Grand Ronde & Willamina. ICA: OR0052.
TV Market Ranking: Below 100 (Grand Ronde, SHERIDAN, Willamina). Franchise award date: N.A. Franchise expiration date: N.A. Began: June 1, 1955.
Channel capacity: 69 (operating 2-way). Channels available but not in use: N.A.
Basic Service
Subscribers: 1,025.
Programming (received off-air): KATU (ABC) Portland; KGW (NBC) Portland; KOAC-TV (PBS) Corvallis; KOIN (CBS) Portland; KOPB-TV (PBS) Portland; KPDX (MNT) Vancouver; KPTV (FOX) Portland; KPXG-TV (ION) Salem; KRCW-TV (CW) Salem; allband FM.

Programming (via satellite): C-SPAN; Northwest Cable News; QVC; ShopNBC; TV Guide Network; Univision Studios; WGN America.
Fee: $60.00 installation; $21.95 monthly; $35.00 additional installation.

Expanded Basic Service 1
Subscribers: 500.
Programming (via satellite): A&E Networks; ABC Family Channel; AMC; Animal Planet; Bravo; Cartoon Network; CNN; Comedy Central; Cooking Channel; Country Music TV; Discovery Channel; Discovery Health Channel; Disney Channel; DIY Network; ESPN; ESPN 2; ESPN Classic Sports; Food Network; Fox News Channel; FX; G4; Great American Country; Hallmark Channel; Headline News; HGTV; History Channel; INSP; Jewelry Television; Lifetime; MSNBC; MTV; National Geographic Channel; Nickelodeon; Outdoor Channel; SoapNet; Speed; Spike TV; Syfy; TBS Superstation; The Learning Channel; The Weather Channel; Travel Channel; Turner Network TV; TV Land; USA Network; Versus; VH1.
Fee: $24.54 monthly.

Digital Basic Service
Subscribers: 350.
Programming (via satellite): BBC America; Bio; Bravo; cloo; Country Music TV; DMX Music; ESPN Classic Sports; ESPNews; Fox Soccer; Fuse; Golf Channel; GSN; History Channel International; ID Investigation Discovery; Independent Film Channel; Military Channel; MTV2; Nick Jr.; Planet Green; Science; Style Network; TeenNick; Toon Disney; Turner Classic Movies; VH1 Classic; WE tv.
Fee: $30.00 installation; $9.00 monthly; $8.00 converter.

Digital Pay Service 1
Pay Units: N.A.
Programming (via satellite): Cinemax (multiplexed); Encore (multiplexed); Flix; HBO (multiplexed); Showtime (multiplexed); Starz; The Movie Channel (multiplexed).
Fee: $13.99 monthly (HBO, Cinemax, Starz/Encore or Showtime/TMC/Flix).

Pay-Per-View
iN DEMAND (delivered digitally); Playboy TV (delivered digitally).

Internet Service
Operational: Yes.
Subscribers: 450.
Fee: $27.99 monthly.

Telephone Service
Digital: Operational
Fee: $29.95 monthly

Miles of Plant: 32.0 (coaxial); None (fiber optic).
Manager: Janice Wilcox. Chief Technician: Dan Gutherie.
Ownership: WaveDivision Holdings LLC (MSO).

SILETZ—Millennium Digital Media. Now served by DEPOE BAY, OR [OR0134]. ICA: OR0080.

SILVERTON—Wave Broadband, 669 Glatt Circle, Woodburn, OR 97071. Phones: 503-981-1891; 866-928-3123; 503-982-4085. Web Site: http://www.wavebroadband.com. Also serves Marion County (portions) & Mount Angel. ICA: OR0047.
TV Market Ranking: 29 (Marion County (portions), Mount Angel); Below 100 (SILVERTON, Marion County (portions)); Outside TV Markets (Marion County (portions)). Franchise award date: March 3, 1980. Franchise expiration date: N.A. Began: September 1, 1980.
Channel capacity: N.A. Channels available but not in use: N.A.

Basic Service
Subscribers: 1,580.
Programming (received off-air): KATU (ABC) Portland; KGW (NBC) Portland; KNMT (TBN) Portland; KOIN (CBS) Portland; KOPB-TV (PBS) Portland; KPDX (MNT) Vancouver; KPTV (FOX) Portland; KPXG-TV (ION) Salem; KRCW-TV (CW) Salem.
Programming (via satellite): C-SPAN; C-SPAN 2; Eternal Word TV Network; INSP; Jewelry Television; QVC; TV Guide Network; Univision Studios.
Fee: $65.00 installation; $19.85 monthly; $1.61 converter; $65.00 additional installation.

Expanded Basic Service 1
Subscribers: 1,268.
Programming (via satellite): A&E Networks; ABC Family Channel; AMC; Animal Planet; Bravo; Cartoon Network; CNN; Comedy Central; Discovery Fit & Health; DIY Network; E! Entertainment Television; ESPN; ESPN 2; Food Network; Fox News Channel; FX; G4; GalaVision; Golf Channel; Hallmark Channel; Headline News; HGTV; History Channel; Lifetime; MSNBC; MTV; National Geographic Channel; Nickelodeon; Northwest Cable News; Oxygen; SoapNet; Speed; Syfy; TBS Superstation; Telemundo; The Learning Channel; The Weather Channel; Toon Disney; Travel Channel; TV Land; Versus; VH1; WE tv.
Fee: $5.37 monthly.

Expanded Basic Service 2
Subscribers: 860.
Programming (via satellite): Country Music TV; Discovery Channel; Disney Channel; Spike TV; Turner Network TV; USA Network.
Fee: $8.80 monthly.

Digital Basic Service
Subscribers: N.A.
Programming (via satellite): BBC America; Bio; Bloomberg Television; Discovery Digital Networks; ESPN Classic Sports; ESPNews; Fox College Sports Atlantic; Fox College Sports Central; Fox College Sports Pacific; Fox Deportes; Fox Movie Channel; Fox Soccer; Fuel TV; Fuse; GAS; GSN; History Channel International; Independent Film Channel; Lifetime Movie Network; MTV Networks Digital Suite; Music Choice; NFL Network; Nick Jr.; NickToons TV; Outdoor Channel; Science Television; Sundance Channel; truTV; Turner Classic Movies; TV Guide Interactive Inc.

Digital Pay Service 1
Pay Units: 131.
Programming (via satellite): Cinemax (multiplexed).
Fee: $25.00 installation; $11.95 monthly.

Digital Pay Service 2
Pay Units: 260.
Programming (via satellite): HBO (multiplexed).
Fee: $25.00 installation; $11.95 monthly.

Digital Pay Service 3
Pay Units: 180.
Programming (via satellite): Showtime (multiplexed).
Fee: $25.00 installation; $11.95 monthly.

Digital Pay Service 4
Pay Units: 117.
Programming (via satellite): The Movie Channel (multiplexed).
Fee: $11.95 monthly.

Digital Pay Service 5
Pay Units: N.A.
Programming (via satellite): Encore (multiplexed); Flix; Starz (multiplexed).

Video-On-Demand: No

Pay-Per-View
iN DEMAND (delivered digitally); Hot Choice (delivered digitally); Playboy TV (delivered digitally); Fresh (delivered digitally); Shorteez (delivered digitally).

Internet Service
Operational: Yes.

Telephone Service
None

Miles of Plant: 58.0 (coaxial); None (fiber optic). Additional miles planned: 5.0 (coaxial).
General Manager: Ross Waggoner. Technical Operations Manager: Lynn Tussing.
Ownership: WaveDivision Holdings LLC (MSO).

SOUTH SALEM—Formerly served by Country Cablevision Ltd. No longer in operation. ICA: OR0160.

SOUTHBEACH—Millennium Digital Media. Now served by DEPOE BAY, OR [OR0134]. ICA: OR0153.

ST. HELENS—Comcast Cable. Now served by BEAVERTON, OR [OR0002]. ICA: OR0027.

ST. PAUL (town)—Formerly served by St. Paul Cooperative Telephone Assoc. No longer in operation. ICA: OR0154.

STAYTON—Wave Broadband, 277 3rd Ave, Stayton, OR 97383-1723. Phones: 503-981-1891 (Woodburn administrative office); 888-222-5314. Fax: 503-848-1134. Web Site: http://www.wbcable.com. Also serves Aumsville, Gates, Lyons, Mehama, Mill City, Sublimity & Turner. ICA: OR0065.
TV Market Ranking: Below 100 (Aumsville, Gates, Lyons, Mehama, Mill City, STAYTON, Sublimity, Turner). Franchise award date: October 1, 1981. Franchise expiration date: N.A. Began: February 2, 1982.
Channel capacity: 71 (operating 2-way). Channels available but not in use: N.A.

Basic Service
Subscribers: 5,090.
Programming (received off-air): KATU (ABC) Portland; KGW (NBC) Portland; KNMT (TBN) Portland; KOAC-TV (PBS) Corvallis; KOIN (CBS) Portland; KOPB-TV (PBS) Portland; KPDX (MNT) Vancouver; KPTV (FOX) Portland; KPXG-TV (ION) Salem; KRCW-TV (CW) Salem.
Programming (via satellite): Northwest Cable News; QVC; ShopNBC; TV Guide Network; Univision Studios; WGN America.
Fee: $60.00 installation; $23.95 monthly; $3.75 converter; $30.00 additional installation.

Expanded Basic Service 1
Subscribers: N.A.
Programming (via satellite): A&E Networks; ABC Family Channel; AMC; Animal Planet; Bravo; Cartoon Network; CNBC; CNN; Comedy Central; Cooking Channel; Country Music TV; C-SPAN; Discovery Channel; Discovery Health Channel; Disney Channel; DIY Network; ESPN; ESPN 2; ESPN Classic Sports; Eternal Word TV Network; Food Network; Fox News Channel; FX; G4; Great American Country; Hallmark Channel; Headline News; HGTV; History Channel; INSP; Jewelry Television; Lifetime; Military Channel; MSNBC; MTV; National Geographic Channel; Nickelodeon; Outdoor Channel; Speed; Spike TV; Syfy; TBS Superstation; The Learning Channel; The Weather Channel; Travel Channel; truTV; Turner Network TV; TV Land; USA Network; Versus; VH1.
Fee: $51.95 monthly.

Digital Basic Service
Subscribers: N.A.
Programming (via satellite): BBC America; Bio; Bravo; cloo; CMT Pure Country; Discovery Kids Channel; DMX Music; ESPN 2; ESPNews; Fox Soccer; Fuse; Golf Channel; GSN; History Channel International; ID Investigation Discovery; Independent Film Channel; MTV2; Nick Jr.; Planet Green; Science; Style Network; TeenNick; Toon Disney; Turner Classic Movies; VH1 Classic; WE tv.
Fee: $33.95 monthly.

Digital Pay Service 1
Pay Units: 1,750.
Programming (via satellite): Cinemax (multiplexed); Encore (multiplexed); Flix; HBO (multiplexed); Showtime (multiplexed); Starz (multiplexed); The Movie Channel (multiplexed).
Fee: $16.00 monthly (HBO, Cinemax, Showtime/TMC/Flix, or Starz/Encore).

Video-On-Demand: No

Pay-Per-View
iN DEMAND (delivered digitally); Playboy TV (delivered digitally).

Internet Service
Operational: Yes. Began: October 1, 2002.
Subscribers: 1,300.
Broadband Service: Cable Rocket.
Fee: $24.95-$74.95 monthly; $6.00 modem lease.

Telephone Service
None

Miles of Plant: 180.0 (coaxial); 6.0 (fiber optic).
General Manager: Ross Waggoner. Technical Operations Manager: Lynn Tussing. Marketing Manager: Elizabeth Regan.
Ownership: WaveDivision Holdings LLC (MSO).

SUMPTER—Formerly served by Almega Cable. No longer in operation. ICA: OR0112.

SUNRIVER—Chambers Cable of Sunriver Inc., 2 Venture Ln, PO Box 3275, Sunriver, OR 97707-0275. Phone: 541-593-1296. Fax: 541-593-1001. E-mail: support@chamberscable.com. Web Site: http://www.chamberscable.com. Also serves Spring River. ICA: OR0155.
TV Market Ranking: Below 100 (Spring River, SUNRIVER). Franchise award date: N.A.

Franchise expiration date: N.A. Began: October 1, 1969.
Channel capacity: 59 (operating 2-way). Channels available but not in use: N.A.
Basic Service
Subscribers: 3,600.
Programming (received off-air): KEZI (ABC) Eugene; KFXO-LP (FOX) Bend; KOAB-TV (PBS) Bend; KOIN (CBS) Portland; KPTV (FOX) Portland; KTVZ (CW, NBC) Bend; 30 DMX.
Programming (via satellite): A&E Networks; ABC Family Channel; Cartoon Network; CNBC; CNN; Country Music TV; C-SPAN; Discovery Channel; Discovery Fit & Health; Discovery Health Channel; Disney Channel; E! Entertainment Television; ESPN; ESPN 2; Eternal Word TV Network; Food Network; Fox News Channel; G4; Golf Channel; Headline News; HGTV; History Channel; Lifetime; Nickelodeon; Outdoor Channel; ShopNBC; Spike TV; Syfy; TBS Superstation; The Learning Channel; The Weather Channel; Travel Channel; Trinity Broadcasting Network; Turner Classic Movies; Turner Network TV; TV Guide Network; USA Network; Versus; VH1.
Fee: $37.50 installation; $46.70 monthly; $4.95 converter; $10.00 additional installation.
Digital Basic Service
Subscribers: N.A.
Programming (via satellite): BBC America; Bio; Bloomberg Television; Chiller; cloo; CMT Pure Country; Comedy Central; Cooking Channel; Discovery Fit & Health; Disney XD; DMX Music; ESPN Classic Sports; ESPN U; ESPNews; Fox Business Channel; Fox Movie Channel; Fuse; Hallmark Channel; Hallmark Movie Channel; History Channel International; ID Investigation Discovery; Independent Film Channel; Military Channel; MSNBC; MTV2; National Geographic Channel; Nick Jr.; NickToons TV; Planet Green; Science; Speed; Style Network; Syfy; TeenNick; Telemundo; Trinity Broadcasting Network; Turner Classic Movies; VH1 Classic; WE tv.
Fee: $14.95 monthly.
Digital Expanded Basic Service
Subscribers: N.A.
Programming (received off-air): KBNZ-LD Bend; KFXO-LP (FOX) Bend; KOHD (ABC) Bend; KOPB-TV (PBS) Portland; KTVZ (CW, NBC) Bend.
Programming (via satellite): A&E HD; ESPN 2 HD; ESPN HD; Food Network HD; HD Theater; HGTV HD; National Geographic Channel HD Network; Syfy HD; Universal HD; USA Network HD.
Fee: $10.95 monthly.
Digital Pay Service 1
Pay Units: N.A.
Programming (via satellite): Encore (multiplexed); HBO (multiplexed); Showtime (multiplexed); Starz (multiplexed); Starz HDTV; The Movie Channel (multiplexed).
Fee: $11.95 monthly (Starz/Encore), $14.95 monthly (Showtime/TMC), $15.25 monthly (HBO).
Video-On-Demand: No
Pay-Per-View
Addressable homes: 400.
Playboy TV; iN DEMAND (delivered digitally).
Internet Service
Operational: Yes, Dial-up.
Subscribers: 1,500.
Fee: $50.00 installation; $39.95 monthly.
Telephone Service
None
Miles of Plant: 82.0 (coaxial); None (fiber optic).
Manager: Michael McLain. Office Manager: Tonya Moore. Sales Manager: Ramona Davis.
Ownership: Chambers Communications Corp.

THE DALLES—Charter Communications, 521 NE 136th Ave, Vancouver, WA 98684. Phone: 360-828-6600. Fax: 360-828-6795. Web Site: http://www.charter.com. Also serves Brightwood, Hood River, Hood River County, Rhododendron, Wasco County & Welches, OR; Bingen, Dallesport, Klickitat, Klickitat County (portions) & White Salmon, WA. ICA: OR0025.
TV Market Ranking: Outside TV Markets (Bingen, Brightwood, Dallesport, Hood River, Hood River County, Klickitat, Klickitat County (portions), Rhododendron, THE DALLES, Wasco County, Welches, White Salmon). Franchise award date: January 1, 1954. Franchise expiration date: N.A. Began: June 1, 1954.
Channel capacity: 78 (operating 2-way). Channels available but not in use: N.A.
Basic Service
Subscribers: 5,550.
Programming (received off-air): KATU (ABC) Portland; KGW (NBC) Portland; KOAC-TV (PBS) Corvallis; KOIN (CBS) Portland; KOPB-TV (PBS) Portland; KPDX (MNT) Vancouver; KPTV (FOX) Portland; 10 FMs.
Programming (via satellite): ABC Family Channel; Animal Planet; C-SPAN; C-SPAN 2; ESPN; ESPN 2; Fox News Channel; FX; HGTV; INSP; MTV; QVC; ShopNBC; TBS Superstation; Travel Channel; TV Guide Network; USA Network; VH1.
Fee: $29.95 installation.
Expanded Basic Service 1
Subscribers: N.A.
Programming (via satellite): A&E Networks; AMC; Bravo; Cartoon Network; CNBC; CNN; Comedy Central; Country Music TV; Discovery Channel; Discovery Health Channel; Disney Channel; E! Entertainment Television; Food Network; Fox Movie Channel; G4; GalaVision; Golf Channel; GSN; Hallmark Channel; Headline News; History Channel; Lifetime; MSNBC; National Geographic Channel; Nickelodeon; Northwest Cable News; SoapNet; Speed; Spike TV; Syfy; The Learning Channel; The Weather Channel; Toon Disney; Trinity Broadcasting Network; truTV; Turner Classic Movies; Turner Network TV; TV Land; Versus; WE tv; WGN America.
Fee: $42.99 monthly.
Digital Basic Service
Subscribers: 2,279.
Programming (via satellite): BBC America; Bio; Discovery Digital Networks; DIY Network; GAS; History Channel International; Independent Film Channel; Lifetime Movie Network; MTV Networks Digital Suite; Music Choice; Nick Jr.; Nick Too.
Fee: $9.00 monthly.
Digital Pay Service 1
Pay Units: 425.
Programming (via satellite): Cinemax (multiplexed).
Fee: $10.00 installation; $10.95 monthly.
Digital Pay Service 2
Pay Units: 867.
Programming (via satellite): HBO (multiplexed).
Fee: $10.00 installation; $11.95 monthly.
Digital Pay Service 3
Pay Units: 674.
Programming (via satellite): Flix; Showtime (multiplexed).
Fee: $10.00 installation; $10.95 monthly.
Digital Pay Service 4
Pay Units: 399.
Programming (via satellite): The Movie Channel (multiplexed).
Fee: $10.95 monthly.
Digital Pay Service 5
Pay Units: 636.
Programming (via satellite): Encore (multiplexed); Starz (multiplexed).
Fee: $10.95 monthly.
Video-On-Demand: Yes
Pay-Per-View
iN DEMAND; Fresh; Hot Choice (delivered digitally); iN DEMAND (delivered digitally); Playboy TV (delivered digitally); Fresh (delivered digitally); Shorteez (delivered digitally).
Internet Service
Operational: Yes.
Subscribers: 887.
Broadband Service: Charter Pipeline.
Fee: $29.99 monthly.
Telephone Service
Digital: Operational
Miles of Plant: 253.0 (coaxial); 80.0 (fiber optic).
Vice President: Frank Antonovich. General Manager: Linda Kimberly. Technical Operations Director: Brian Lindholme. Marketing Director: Diane Long.
Ownership: Charter Communications Inc. (MSO).

TYGH VALLEY—Formerly served by J & N Cable. No longer in operation. ICA: OR0117.

UMATILLA—Rapid Cable, 1750 S Hwy 10, Price, UT 84501-4364. Phone: 435-637-6823. Fax: 435-637-9755. Also serves Irrigon & Umatilla County (unincorporated areas). ICA: OR0053.
TV Market Ranking: Below 100 (Irrigon, UMATILLA, Umatilla County (unincorporated areas) (portions)); Outside TV Markets (Umatilla County (unincorporated areas) (portions)). Franchise award date: N.A. Franchise expiration date: N.A. Began: February 1, 1981.
Channel capacity: 61 (not 2-way capable). Channels available but not in use: N.A.
Basic Service
Subscribers: 1,002.
Programming (received off-air): KEPR-TV (CBS) Pasco; KNDU (NBC) Richland; KVEW (ABC, MNT) Kennewick; allband FM.
Programming (via microwave): KATU (ABC) Portland; KGW (NBC) Portland; KOIN (CBS) Portland; KOPB-TV (PBS) Portland; KPTV (FOX) Portland.
Programming (via satellite): A&E Networks; ABC Family Channel; Animal Planet; CNBC; CNN; C-SPAN; Discovery Channel; Disney Channel; E! Entertainment Television; ESPN; ESPN 2; Fox News Channel; FX; GalaVision; Great American Country; Headline News; HGTV; History Channel; Lifetime; MSNBC; MTV; Nickelodeon; Northwest Cable News; QVC; Style Network; Syfy; TBS Superstation; The Weather Channel; Toon Disney; Trinity Broadcasting Network; Turner Classic Movies; TV Land; USA Network; VH1; WGN America; WPIX (CW, IND) New York.
Fee: $35.00 installation; $17.95 monthly.
Digital Basic Service
Subscribers: N.A.
Programming (via satellite): BBC America; Bravo; Discovery Digital Networks; DMX Music; ESPN Classic Sports; ESPNews; Fox Sports World; Golf Channel; GSN; Nick Jr.; Speed; Versus; VH1 Classic; VH1 Country.
Digital Expanded Basic Service
Subscribers: N.A.
Programming (via satellite): Encore (multiplexed); Independent Film Channel; Starz (multiplexed); WE tv.
Pay Service 1
Pay Units: 575.
Programming (via satellite): HBO.
Fee: $10.95 monthly.
Digital Pay Service 1
Pay Units: N.A.
Programming (via satellite): Cinemax (multiplexed); HBO (multiplexed); Showtime (multiplexed); The Movie Channel (multiplexed).
Video-On-Demand: No
Pay-Per-View
iN DEMAND.
Internet Service
Operational: No.
Telephone Service
None
Miles of Plant: 83.0 (coaxial); None (fiber optic). Additional miles planned: 1.0 (coaxial).
Regional Manager: Shane Baggs. Engineering Director: Richard O'Neill. Chief Technician: David Ramsey.
Ownership: Rapid Communications LLC (MSO).

VERNONIA—Vernonia CATV Inc., 536 1st Ave, Vernonia, OR 97064-1115. Phone: 503-429-5103. ICA: OR0083.
TV Market Ranking: 29 (VERNONIA). Franchise award date: N.A. Franchise expiration date: N.A. Began: March 1, 1969.
Channel capacity: N.A. Channels available but not in use: N.A.
Basic Service
Subscribers: 100.
Programming (received off-air): KATU (ABC) Portland; KGW (NBC) Portland; KOIN (CBS) Portland; KOPB-TV (PBS) Portland; KPDX (MNT) Vancouver; KPTV (FOX) Portland; allband FM.
Programming (via satellite): A&E Networks; Animal Planet; Cartoon Network; CNBC; CNN; Country Music TV; C-SPAN; Discovery Channel; Food Network; Great American Country; HGTV; History Channel; ION Television; Lifetime; Military History Channel; MSNBC; MTV; National Geographic Channel; Nickelodeon; Speed; Spike TV; Syfy; TBS Superstation; The Learning Channel; The Weather Channel; Turner Classic Movies; Turner Network TV; TV Land; USA Network; Versus; VH1; WGN America.
Fee: $40.00 installation; $36.00 monthly.
Pay Service 1
Pay Units: N.A.
Programming (via satellite): HBO.
Fee: $12.55 monthly.
Pay Service 2
Pay Units: N.A.
Programming (via satellite): Cinemax.
Fee: $9.45 monthly.
Internet Service
Operational: No.
Telephone Service
None
Miles of Plant: 7.0 (coaxial); None (fiber optic).
Owner: Mike Seager.
Ownership: Vernonia CATV Inc.

WALDPORT—Alsea River Cable Co., 222 Northwest Spring St, PO Box 386, Waldport, OR 97394-0386. Phone: 541-563-4807. Fax: 541-563-7341. Also serves Lincoln County (portions). ICA: OR0069.
TV Market Ranking: Outside TV Markets (Lincoln County (portions), WALDPORT).

Franchise award date: January 1, 1996. Franchise expiration date: N.A. Began: January 1, 1969.

Channel capacity: 36 (2-way capable). Channels available but not in use: N.A.

Basic Service

Subscribers: 960.

Programming (received off-air): KATU (ABC) Portland; KEZI (ABC) Eugene; KGW (NBC) Portland; KOAC-TV (PBS) Corvallis; KOIN (CBS) Portland; KPDX (MNT) Vancouver; KPTV (FOX) Portland; KVAL-TV (CBS, IND) Eugene.

Programming (via satellite): A&E Networks; ABC Family Channel; CNBC; CNN; C-SPAN 2; Discovery Channel; Disney Channel; ESPN; Lifetime; MTV; Nickelodeon; QVC; Spike TV; TBS Superstation; The Learning Channel; Turner Classic Movies; Turner Network TV; USA Network; WGN America.

Fee: $15.00 installation; $22.00 monthly.

Pay Service 1

Pay Units: N.A.

Programming (via satellite): Cinemax; HBO.

Fee: $9.50 monthly (each).

Video-On-Demand: No

Internet Service

Operational: No.

Telephone Service

None

Miles of Plant: 15.0 (coaxial); None (fiber optic).

Manager & Chief Technician: James Dale Haslett.

Ownership: James Dale Haslett.

WARM SPRINGS—Formerly served by American Telecasting. No longer in operation. ICA: OR0085.

WASCO—J & N Cable, 614 S Columbus Ave, Goldendale, WA 98620-9006. Phone: 509-773-5359. Fax: 509-773-7090. E-mail: john@jncable.com. Web Site: http://www.jncable.com. ICA: OR0159.

TV Market Ranking: Outside TV Markets (WASCO). Franchise award date: N.A. Franchise expiration date: N.A. Began: January 1, 1989.

Channel capacity: N.A. Channels available but not in use: N.A.

Basic Service

Subscribers: 120.

Programming (via satellite): 3 Angels Broadcasting Network; A&E Networks; ABC Family Channel; AMC; AmericanLife TV Network; Animal Planet; Cartoon Network; CNBC; CNN; C-SPAN; C-SPAN 2; Discovery Channel; Disney Channel; DIY Network; ESPN; ESPN 2; ESPNews; Eternal Word TV Network; Food Network; Fox News Channel; Fox Sports Net; G4; Great American Country; Hallmark Channel; Headline News; HGTV; History Channel; Lifetime; MSNBC; Northwest Cable News; Outdoor Channel; QVC; ShopNBC; Speed; Syfy; TBS Superstation; The Learning Channel; Travel Channel; Trinity Broadcasting Network; Turner Classic Movies; Turner Network TV; USA Network; WE tv; WGN America.

Programming (via translator): KATU (ABC) Portland; KGW (NBC) Portland; KOIN (CBS) Portland; KOPB-TV (PBS) Portland; KPDX (MNT) Vancouver; KPTV (FOX) Portland.

Fee: $25.00 installation; $11.95 monthly.

Pay Service 1

Pay Units: 12.

Programming (via satellite): HBO (multiplexed); Showtime (multiplexed); The Movie Channel.

Fee: $12.95 monthly (HBO), $9.95 monthly (Showtime).

Video-On-Demand: No

Internet Service

Operational: No.

Telephone Service

None

Manager: John Kusky. Marketing Director: Nancy Kusky.

Ownership: J & N Cable Systems Inc. (MSO).

WESTON—Rapid Cable, 1750 S Hwy 10, Price, UT 84501-4364. Phone: 435-637-6823. Fax: 435-647-9755. Also serves Adams & Athena. ICA: OR0075.

TV Market Ranking: Below 100 (Adams, Athena, WESTON). Franchise award date: N.A. Franchise expiration date: N.A. Began: October 1, 1955.

Channel capacity: 30 (not 2-way capable). Channels available but not in use: N.A.

Basic Service

Subscribers: 671.

Programming (received off-air): KEPR-TV (CBS) Pasco; KFFX-TV (FOX, IND) Pendleton; KNDU (NBC) Richland; KPTV (FOX) Portland; KTVR (PBS) La Grande; KVEW (ABC, MNT) Kennewick.

Programming (via satellite): A&E Networks; ABC Family Channel; CNN; Discovery Channel; Disney Channel; ESPN; Fox News Channel; Fox Sports Net; FX; Nickelodeon; QVC; Spike TV; TBS Superstation; Turner Network TV; USA Network.

Fee: $29.95 installation; $19.95 monthly.

Pay Service 1

Pay Units: 68.

Programming (via satellite): Encore; HBO; Starz.

Video-On-Demand: No

Internet Service

Operational: No.

Telephone Service

None

Miles of Plant: 22.0 (coaxial); None (fiber optic).

Regional Manager: Shane Baggs. Engineering Director: Richard O'Neill. Chief Technician: David Ramsey.

Ownership: Rapid Communications LLC (MSO).

WESTPORT—Formerly served by Almega Cable. No longer in operation. ICA: OR0170.

WOODBURN—Wave Broadband, 669 Glatt Circle, Woodburn, OR 97071. Phones: 888-222-5314; 503-981-1891; 503-982-4085. Fax: 503-982-4804. Web Site: http://www.wavebroadband.com. Also serves Aurora, Barlow, Canby, Clackamas, Clackamas County (portions), Donald, Gervais, Hubbard, Marion County (portions), Molalla, Mulino, Needy & Oregon City (portions). ICA: OR0023.

TV Market Ranking: 29 (Aurora, Barlow, Canby, Clackamas, Clackamas County (portions) (portions), Donald, Gervais, Hubbard, Marion County (portions), Molalla, Molalla, Mulino, Needy, Oregon City (portions), WOODBURN); Below 100 (Clackamas County (portions) (portions), Marion County (portions)); Outside TV Markets (Clackamas County (portions) (portions), Marion County (portions)). Franchise award date: October 12, 1992. Franchise expiration date: N.A. Began: March 7, 1983.

Channel capacity: 61 (operating 2-way). Channels available but not in use: N.A.

Basic Service

Subscribers: 5,200.

Programming (received off-air): KATU (ABC) Portland; KGW (NBC) Portland; KNMT (TBN) Portland; KOIN (CBS) Portland; KOPB-TV (PBS) Portland; KPDX (MNT) Vancouver; KPTV (FOX) Portland; KPXG-TV (ION) Salem; KRCW-TV (CW) Salem.

Programming (via satellite): C-SPAN; C-SPAN 2; Eternal Word TV Network; INSP; QVC; The Weather Channel; TV Guide Network; Univision Studios; WGN America.

Fee: $60.00 installation; $23.95 monthly.

Expanded Basic Service 1

Subscribers: 3,919.

Programming (via satellite): 3 Angels Broadcasting Network; A&E Networks; ABC Family Channel; AMC; Animal Planet; Bravo; BYU Television; Cartoon Network; CNBC; CNN; Comedy Central; Country Music TV; Discovery Channel; Disney Channel; E! Entertainment Television; ESPN; ESPN 2; ESPN Classic Sports; ESPN Deportes; Food Network; Fox Movie Channel; Fox News Channel; FX; GalaVision; Great American Country; Hallmark Channel; Headline News; HGTV; History Channel; Lifetime; MSNBC; MTV; National Geographic Channel; Nickelodeon; Northwest Cable News; Oxygen; SoapNet; Speed; Spike TV; Syfy; TBS Superstation; Telefutura; Telemundo; The Learning Channel; Travel Channel; truTV; Turner Network TV; TV Land; USA Network; Versus; VH1.

Fee: $28.00 monthly.

Digital Basic Service

Subscribers: N.A.

Programming (via satellite): A&E HD; Animal Planet HD; Azteca America; Bandamax; BBC America; Bio; Bloomberg Television; Boomerang; CBS Sports Network; Channel One; Cine Latino; Cine Mexicano; cloo; CMT Pure Country; CNN en Espanol; Colours; Cooking Channel; Current; De Pelicula; De Pelicula Clasico; Discovery Channel HD; Discovery en Espanol; Discovery Familia; Discovery Fit & Health; Discovery Health Channel; Discovery Kids Channel; Disney Channel HD; DIY Network; ESPN 2 HD; ESPN Deportes; ESPN HD; ESPN U; ESPNews; Filipino Channel; Food Network HD; Fox Business Channel; Fox College Sports Atlantic; Fox College Sports Central; Fox College Sports Pacific; Fox Deportes; Fox Soccer; FSN HD; Fuel TV; Fuse; G4; GMA Pinoy TV; Golf Channel; GolTV; GSN; Hallmark Movie Channel; Halogen Network; HD Theater; HDNet; HDNet Movies; HGTV HD; History Channel en Espanol; History Channel HD; History Channel International; ID Investigation Discovery; Independent Film Channel; Jewelry Television; La Familia Network; Latele Novela Network; Lifetime Movie Network; Lifetime Real Women; MGM HD; Military Channel; MTV Hits; MTV Jams; MTV2; mun2 television; Music Choice; National Geographic Channel HD Network; NFL Network; NFL Network HD; Nick Jr.; NickToons TV; Outdoor Channel; Ovation; PBS Kids Sprout; Planet Green; RFD-TV; Russian Television Network; Science; Science HD; ShopNBC; Sorpresa; Style Network; Sundance Channel; TBN Enlace USA; TBS in HD; TeenNick; Tennis Channel; TLC HD; Toon Disney; Toon Disney en Espanol; Tr3s; Travel Channel HD; Turner Classic Movies; Turner Network TV HD; TV Chile; Universal HD; VeneMovies; VH1 Classic; VH1 Soul; WE tv.

Fee: $24.00 monthly.

Digital Pay Service 1

Pay Units: 312.

Programming (via satellite): Cinemax (multiplexed); Cinemax HD; Encore (multiplexed); Flix; HBO (multiplexed); HBO HD; here! TV; MoviePlex; Showtime (multiplexed); Showtime HD; Starz (multiplexed); Starz HDTV; The Movie Channel (multiplexed); The Movie Channel HD.

Fee: $30.00 installation; $5.00 monthly (MoviePlex), $7.00 monthly (Here) $15.00 monthly (Starz/Encore) $16.00 monthly (HBO, Cinemax or Showtime/TMC/Flix).

Video-On-Demand: No

Pay-Per-View

iN DEMAND (delivered digitally); Special events (delivered digitally); ESPN (delivered digitally).

Internet Service

Operational: Yes.

Broadband Service: Wave Broadband.

Fee: 24.95-$74.95 monthly; $59.95 modem purchase.

Telephone Service

None

Miles of Plant: 116.0 (coaxial); None (fiber optic). Additional miles planned: 5.0 (coaxial).

General Manager: Ross Waggoner. Technical Operations Manager: Lynn Tussing. Marketing Manager: Elizabeth Regan.

Ownership: WaveDivision Holdings LLC (MSO).

PENNSYLVANIA

Total Systems: 274
Total Communities Served: 2,582
Franchises Not Yet Operating: 0
Applications Pending: 0
Communities with Applications: 0
Number of Basic Subscribers: 3,900,520
Number of Expanded Basic Subscribers: 1,350,957
Number of Pay Units: 136,574

Top 100 Markets Represented: Pittsburgh (10); Baltimore (14); Wilkes Barre-Scranton (49); Philadelphia, PA-Burlington, NJ (4); Harrisburg-Lancaster-York (57); Johnstown-Altoona (74); Youngstown, OH (79); Wheeling, WV-Steubenville, OH (90).

**For a list of cable communities in this section, see the Cable Community Index located in the back of Cable Volume 2.
For explanation of terms used in cable system listings, see p. D-11.**

ADAMS TWP. (Cambria County)—Comcast Cable, 15 Summit Park Dr, Pittsburgh, PA 15275. Phones: 412-747-6400; 814-344-8055 (Carrolltown office). Fax: 412-747-6401. Web Site: http://www.comcast.com. Also serves Beaverdale, Black Lick Twp., Ehrenfeld, Elton, Lloydell, Nanty Glo, Ogle Twp., Paint, Portage (borough), Salix, Scalp Level, Sidman, South Fork, St. Michael, Summerhill, Twin Rocks, Vintondale, Wilmore & Windber. ICA: PA0133.

TV Market Ranking: 74 (ADAMS TWP. (CAMBRIA COUNTY), Beaverdale, Blacklick Twp., Ehrenfeld, Elton, Lloydell, Nanty Glo, Ogle Twp., Paint, Portage (borough), Salix, Scalp Level, Sidman, South Fork, St. Michael, Summerhill, Twin Rocks, Vintondale, Wilmore, Windber).

Channel capacity: N.A. Channels available but not in use: N.A.

Basic Service

Subscribers: N.A. Included in Bensalem Twp.

Programming (received off-air): KDKA-TV (CBS) Pittsburgh; WATM-TV (ABC) Altoona; WBGN-LD Pittsburgh; WINP-TV (IND, ION) Pittsburgh; WJAC-TV (NBC) Johnstown; WPCB-TV (IND) Greensburg; WPCW (CW) Jeannette; WPMY (MNT) Pittsburgh; WPSU-TV (PBS) Clearfield; WPXI (IND, NBC) Pittsburgh; WQED (PBS) Pittsburgh; WTAE-TV (ABC) Pittsburgh; WTAJ-TV (CBS) Altoona; WWCP-TV (FOX) Johnstown.

Programming (via satellite): C-SPAN; C-SPAN 2; QVC; WGN America.

Fee: $39.95 installation; $17.80 monthly.

Expanded Basic Service 1

Subscribers: N.A.

Programming (via satellite): A&E Networks; ABC Family Channel; AMC; Animal Planet; BET Networks; Bravo; Cartoon Network; CNBC; CNN; Comedy Central; Country Music TV; Discovery Channel; Disney Channel; E! Entertainment Television; ESPN; ESPN 2; Eternal Word TV Network; Food Network; Fox News Channel; FX; Golf Channel; Hallmark Channel; Headline News; HGTV; History Channel; HRTV; Lifetime; MSNBC; MTV; Nickelodeon; Outdoor Channel; Oxygen; Pennsylvania Cable Network; Pittsburgh Cable News Channel; Product Information Network; Spike TV; Style Network; Syfy; TBS Superstation; The Learning Channel; The Weather Channel; Travel Channel; truTV; Turner Network TV; TV Guide Network; TV Land; USA Network; VH1.

Fee: $32.19 monthly.

Digital Basic Service

Subscribers: N.A.

Programming (via satellite): AmericanLife TV Network; BBC America; Black Family Channel; Bloomberg Television; Discovery Fit & Health; DIY Network; ESPN; ESPN Classic Sports; ESPN U; ESPNews; Fox Movie Channel; Fox Soccer; Fuse; G4; GAS; Great American Country; GSN; Halogen Network; HDNet; HDNet Movies; INHD (multiplexed); Lifetime Movie Network; LOGO; MTV Networks Digital Suite; Music Choice; National Geographic Channel; NFL Network; Nick Jr.; Nick Too; NickToons TV; SoapNet; Speed; The Word Network; Toon Disney; Trinity Broadcasting Network; Turner Classic Movies; WE tv.

Fee: $15.95 monthly.

Digital Expanded Basic Service

Subscribers: N.A.

Programming (via satellite): Bio; FSN Digital Atlantic; FSN Digital Central; FSN Digital Pacific; History Channel International; Independent Film Channel; Sundance Channel; Versus.

Fee: $6.95 monthly.

Digital Pay Service 1

Pay Units: N.A.

Programming (via satellite): Cinemax (multiplexed); Cinemax HD; Encore (multiplexed); Flix; HBO (multiplexed); HBO HD; Showtime (multiplexed); Showtime HD; Starz (multiplexed); Starz HDTV; The Movie Channel (multiplexed).

Fee: $15.95 monthly (each).

Video-On-Demand: Yes

Pay-Per-View

Movies (delivered digitally); Special events (delivered digitally); Playboy TV (delivered digitally); Fresh (delivered digitally); Shorteez (delivered digitally); Hot Choice (delivered digitally); Sports PPV (delivered digitally).

Internet Service

Operational: Yes.

Broadband Service: Comcast High Speed Internet.

Fee: $42.95 monthly.

Telephone Service

Digital: Operational

Regional Vice President: Linda Hossinger. Vice President, Technical Operations: Randy Bender. Vice President, Marketing: Donna Corning. Vice President, Public Affairs: Jody Doherty. Manager: Diane Kirsch.

Ownership: Comcast Cable Communications Inc. (MSO).

ADDISON TWP. (southern portion)—Somerfield Cable TV Co., 6511 National Pike, Addison, PA 15411-2153. Phones: 800-344-3084; 814-395-3084. Fax: 814-395-5037. E-mail: sc-tv@sc-tv.net. Web Site: http://www.sc-tv.net. Also serves Accident (unincorporated areas), Friendsville (unincorporated areas), Garrett County (portions) & Grantsville (unincorporated areas), MD; Addison, PA. ICA: PA0307.

TV Market Ranking: Outside TV Markets (Accident (unincorporated areas), Addison, ADDISON TWP., Friendsville, Garrett County (portions), Grantsville). Franchise award date: N.A. Franchise expiration date: N.A. Began: April 1, 1989.

Channel capacity: 50 (operating 2-way). Channels available but not in use: N.A.

Basic Service

Subscribers: 684.

Programming (received off-air): KDKA-TV (CBS) Pittsburgh; Local Cable Weather; WGPT (PBS) Oakland; WJAC-TV (NBC) Johnstown; WPCW (CW) Jeannette; WPMY (MNT) Pittsburgh; WPXI (IND, NBC) Pittsburgh; WQED (PBS) Pittsburgh; WTAE-TV (ABC) Pittsburgh; WWCP-TV (FOX) Johnstown.

Programming (via satellite): Cornerstone Television; Hallmark Channel; ION Television; Outdoor Channel; QVC; TBS Superstation; The Weather Channel; Trinity Broadcasting Network; TV Guide Network; WGN America.

Fee: $25.00 installation; $25.00 monthly; $3.00 converter; $8.00 additional installation.

Digital Basic Service

Subscribers: 400.

Programming (received off-air): WGPT (PBS) Oakland; WQED (PBS) Pittsburgh.

Programming (via satellite): 3 Angels Broadcasting Network; A&E HD; A&E Networks; ABC Family Channel; ABC Family HD; ABC News Now; AMC; Animal Planet; Animal Planet HD; BBC America; BET Gospel; BET Networks; BETSoundz; Bio; Boomerang; Bravo; Bravo HD; BTN; Cartoon Network; Church Channel; cloo; CMT Pure Country; CNBC; CNN; Comedy Central; Cooking Channel; Country Music TV; C-SPAN; C-SPAN 2; C-SPAN 3; Daystar TV Network; Discovery Channel; Discovery Channel HD; Discovery Fit & Health; Discovery Health Channel; Discovery Home Channel; Discovery Kids Channel; Disney Channel; Disney Channel HD; DIY Network; DMX Music; E! Entertainment Television; ESPN; ESPN 2; ESPN 2 HD; ESPN Classic Sports; ESPN HD; ESPN U; ESPNews; Eternal Word TV Network; FamilyNet; Food Network; Food Network HD; Fox Business Channel; Fox Business Channel HD; Fox College Sports Atlantic; Fox College Sports Central; Fox College Sports Pacific; Fox Movie Channel; Fox News Channel; Fox Soccer; FX; FX HD; G4; GalaVision; GAS; Golden Eagle Broadcasting; Golf Channel; Gospel Music TV; Great American Country; GSN; Hallmark Movie Channel; Halogen Network; HDNet; HDNet Movies; Headline News; HGTV; HGTV HD; History Channel; History Channel HD; History Channel International; ID Investigation Discovery; Independent Film Channel; INSP; JCTV; Lifetime; Lifetime Movie Network; Lifetime Movie Network HD; Lifetime Real Women; Military Channel; Military History Channel; Mojo Mix; MSNBC; MTV; MTV Hits; MTV Jams; MTV2; National Geographic Channel; NFL Network; Nick Jr.; Nick Too; Nickelodeon; NickToons TV; Outdoor Channel 2 HD; RFD HD; RFD-TV; Root Sports Pittsburgh; Science; Science HD; Smile of a Child; SoapNet; Speed; Speed HD; Spike TV; Style Network; Syfy; Syfy HD; The Learning Channel; Toon Disney; Toon Disney HD; Travel Channel; truTV; Turner Classic Movies; Turner Network TV; Turner Network TV HD; TV Land; Universal HD; Univision Studios; USA Network; USA Network HD; Versus; VH1; VH1 Classic; V-me TV; WE tv; WealthTV; WealthTV HD.

Fee: $55.00 monthly.

Digital Pay Service 1

Pay Units: 43.

Programming (via satellite): HBO (multiplexed).

Fee: $12.00 monthly.

Digital Pay Service 2

Pay Units: 27.

Programming (via satellite): Cinemax (multiplexed).

Fee: $8.00 monthly.

Digital Pay Service 3

Pay Units: 35.

Programming (via satellite): Encore (multiplexed); Starz.

Fee: $7.25 monthly (Encore), $8.00 monthly (Starz).

Digital Pay Service 4

Pay Units: 26.

Programming (via satellite): Flix; The Movie Channel (multiplexed).

Fee: $8.00 monthly.

Digital Pay Service 5

Pay Units: 7.

Programming (via satellite): Showtime (multiplexed).

Fee: $8.00 monthly.

Video-On-Demand: No

Pay-Per-View

Addressable homes: 129.

iN DEMAND (delivered digitally); ESPN (delivered digitally); Adult (delivered digitally).

Internet Service

Operational: Yes. Began: December 31, 2000.

Broadband Service: QCOL.

Fee: $25.00 monthly.

Telephone Service

None

Miles of Plant: 85.0 (coaxial); 30.0 (fiber optic). Additional miles planned: 5.0 (coaxial).

Manager & Chief Technician: Michael J. Diehl.

Ownership: Somerfield Cable TV Co.

ALLEN TWP.—RCN Corp. Formerly served by NORTHAMPTON BOROUGH, PA [PA0008]. This cable system has converted to IPTV, 196 Van Buren St, Herndon, VA 20170.

Phone: 703-434-8200. Web Site: http://www.rcn.com. ICA: PA5200.
TV Market Ranking: Below 100 (ALLEN TWP.).
Channel capacity: N.A. Channels available but not in use: N.A.
Internet Service
Operational: Yes.
Telephone Service
Digital: Operational
Chairman: Steven J. Simmons. Chief Executive Officer: Jim Holanda.

ALLENSVILLE—Formerly served by Valley Cable Systems. No longer in operation. ICA: PA0285.

ALLENTOWN—RCN Corp. Formerly served by NORTHAMPTON BOROUGH, PA [PA0008]. This cable system has converted to IPTV, 196 Van Buren St, Herndon, VA 20170. Phone: 703-434-8200. Web Site: http://www.rcn.com. ICA: PA5201.
TV Market Ranking: Below 100 (ALLENTOWN).
Channel capacity: N.A. Channels available but not in use: N.A.
Internet Service
Operational: Yes.
Telephone Service
Digital: Operational
Chairman: Steven J. Simmons. Chief Executive Officer: Jim Holanda.

ALTOONA—Atlantic Broadband, 120 Southmont Blvd, Johnstown, PA 15905. Phones: 888-536-9600; 814-539-8971; 814-946-5491. Fax: 814-535-7749. E-mail: info@atlanticbb.com. Web Site: http://www.atlanticbb.com. Also serves Allegheny Twp. (Blair County), Antis Twp., Bellwood, Birmingham Borough, Blair Twp. (Blair County), Bloomfield Twp., Canoe Creek, Catherine Twp., Claysburg, Curryville, Duncansville, Frankstown, Frankstown Twp., Frankstown Twp. (Blair County), Freedom Twp. (Blair County), Gallitzin, Greenfield Twp. (Blair County), Hollidaysburg, Huston Twp. (Blair County), Imler, Juniata Twp. (Blair County), Kimmell Twp., Logan Twp. (Blair County), Martinsburg, Newry, North Woodbury Twp., Pavia Twp., Queen, Roaring Spring, Snyder, Sproul, Taylor Twp. (Blair County), Tyrone, Tyrone Twp. (Blair County), Warriors Mark & Woodbury Twp. ICA: PA0018.
TV Market Ranking: 74 (Allegheny Twp. (Blair County), ALTOONA, Antis Twp., Bellwood, Birmingham Borough, Blair Twp. (Blair County), Bloomfield Twp., Canoe Creek, Catherine Twp., Claysburg, Curryville, Duncansville, Frankstown, Frankstown Twp., Frankstown Twp. (Blair County), Freedom Twp. (Blair County), Gallitzin, Greenfield Twp. (Blair County), Hollidaysburg, Huston Twp. (Blair County), Imler, Juniata Twp. (Blair County), Kimmell Twp., Logan Twp. (Blair County), Martinsburg, Newry, North Woodbury Twp., Pavia Twp., Queen, Roaring Spring, Snyder, Sproul, Taylor Twp. (Blair County), Tyrone, Tyrone Twp. (Blair County), Warriors Mark, Woodbury Twp.). Franchise award date: April 1, 1962. Franchise expiration date: N.A. Began: April 21, 1962.
Channel capacity: 116 (operating 2-way). Channels available but not in use: N.A.
Basic Service
Subscribers: 31,959.
Programming (received off-air): KDKA-TV (CBS) Pittsburgh; WATM-TV (ABC) Altoona; WHVL-LP State College, etc.; WJAC-TV (NBC) Johnstown; WKBS-TV (IND) Altoona; WPCW (CW) Jeannette; WPSU-TV (PBS) Clearfield; WTAE-TV (ABC) Pittsburgh; WTAJ-TV (CBS) Altoona; WWCP-TV (FOX) Johnstown; allband FM.
Programming (via satellite): C-SPAN; C-SPAN 2; Eternal Word TV Network; HRTV; ION Television; Jewelry Television; MyNetworkTV Inc.; PBS World; Pennsylvania Cable Network; QVC; ShopNBC; TV Guide Network.
Fee: $45.24 installation; $18.72 monthly; $.67 converter.
Expanded Basic Service 1
Subscribers: N.A.
Programming (via satellite): A&E Networks; ABC Family Channel; AMC; Animal Planet; BET Networks; Bravo; Cartoon Network; CNBC; CNN; Comedy Central; Country Music TV; Discovery Channel; Disney Channel; E! Entertainment Television; ESPN; ESPN 2; ESPN Classic Sports; Food Network; Fox News Channel; FX; G4; Golf Channel; GSN; Hallmark Channel; Headline News; HGTV; History Channel; INSP; Lifetime; MSNBC; MTV; National Geographic Channel; Nickelodeon; NickToons TV; Outdoor Channel; Oxygen; Root Sports Pittsburgh; Speed; Spike TV; Syfy; TBS Superstation; The Learning Channel; The Weather Channel; Toon Disney; Travel Channel; truTV; Turner Classic Movies; Turner Network TV; TV Land; USA Network; Versus; VH1.
Fee: $39.04 monthly.
Digital Basic Service
Subscribers: 10,500.
Programming (via satellite): A&E HD; Animal Planet HD; BBC America; Bio; Bloomberg Television; Boomerang; CCTV-4; Chiller; CMT Pure Country; Discovery Channel HD; Discovery Health Channel; Discovery Kids Channel; Disney Channel HD; DIY Network; DMX Music; Encore; ESPN 2 HD; ESPN HD; ESPN U; ESPNews; Fox News HD; Fuel TV; Fuse; Great American Country; HD Theater; History Channel HD; History Channel International; ID Investigation Discovery; Independent Film Channel; Lifetime Movie Network; Lifetime Real Women; Military Channel; MTV Hits; MTV Jams; MTV2; NFL Network; Nick Jr.; Nick Too; Outdoor Channel 2 HD; Planet Green; Root Sports Pittsburgh; RTN; Science; Science HD; SoapNet; Starz; Starz HDTV; Syfy HD; TBS in HD; TeenNick; TLC HD; Tr3s; Turner Network TV HD; TVG Network; USA Network HD; VH1 Classic; VH1 Soul; WE tv.
Fee: $18.95 monthly.
Digital Pay Service 1
Pay Units: 2,419.
Programming (via satellite): Cinemax (multiplexed); Cinemax HD.
Fee: $15.95 monthly.
Digital Pay Service 2
Pay Units: 5,829.
Programming (via satellite): HBO (multiplexed); HBO HD.
Fee: $15.95 monthly.
Digital Pay Service 3
Pay Units: 2,284.
Programming (via satellite): Flix; Showtime (multiplexed); Showtime HD; The Movie Channel (multiplexed).
Fee: $15.95 monthly.
Video-On-Demand: Yes
Pay-Per-View
Addressable homes: 11,169.
Hot Choice (delivered digitally); iN DEMAND (delivered digitally).
Internet Service
Operational: Yes.
Subscribers: 4,000.
Broadband Service: Atlantic Broadband High-Speed Internet.
Fee: $24.95-$57.95 monthly.
Telephone Service
Digital: Operational
Fee: $44.95 monthly
Miles of Plant: 818.0 (coaxial); 188.0 (fiber optic).
Vice President: David Dane. General Manager: Mike Papasergi. Technical Operations Director: Charles Sorchilla. Marketing & Customer Service Director: Dara Leslie. Marketing Director: Natalie Kurchak.
Ownership: Atlantic Broadband (MSO).

ARMAGH—Comcast Cable, 15 Summit Park Dr, Pittsburgh, PA 15275. Phones: 814-344-8055 (Carolltown office); 412-747-6400. Fax: 412-747-6401. Web Site: http://www.comcast.com. Also serves East Wheatfield Twp., New Florence, Seward & West Wheatfield Twp. ICA: PA0153.
TV Market Ranking: 74 (ARMAGH, East Wheatfield Twp., New Florence, Seward, West Wheatfield Twp.). Franchise award date: N.A. Franchise expiration date: N.A. Began: October 1, 1982.
Channel capacity: N.A. Channels available but not in use: N.A.
Basic Service
Subscribers: N.A. Included in Pittsburgh
Programming (received off-air): KDKA-TV (CBS) Pittsburgh; WBGN-LD Pittsburgh; WINP-TV (IND, ION) Pittsburgh; WJAC-TV (NBC) Johnstown; WPCB-TV (IND) Greensburg; WPCW (CW) Jeannette; WPGH-TV (FOX) Pittsburgh; WPMY (MNT) Pittsburgh; WPSU-TV (PBS) Clearfield; WPXI (IND, NBC) Pittsburgh; WQED (PBS) Pittsburgh; WTAE-TV (ABC) Pittsburgh; WTAJ-TV (CBS) Altoona; WWCP-TV (FOX) Johnstown.
Programming (via satellite): QVC; WGN America.
Fee: $39.95 installation; $12.15 monthly; $1.60 converter.
Expanded Basic Service 1
Subscribers: N.A.
Programming (via satellite): A&E Networks; ABC Family Channel; AMC; Animal Planet; Cartoon Network; CNBC; CNN; Comedy Central; Country Music TV; C-SPAN; C-SPAN 2; Discovery Channel; Disney Channel; E! Entertainment Television; ESPN; ESPN 2; Eternal Word TV Network; Food Network; Fox News Channel; FX; Headline News; HGTV; History Channel; HRTV; Lifetime; MSNBC; MTV; Nickelodeon; Oxygen; Pennsylvania Cable Network; Pittsburgh Cable News Channel; Root Sports Pittsburgh; Spike TV; Style Network; Syfy; TBS Superstation; The Learning Channel; The Weather Channel; Travel Channel; truTV; Turner Network TV; TV Land; USA Network; VH1.
Fee: $17.15 monthly.
Digital Basic Service
Subscribers: N.A.
Programming (via satellite): AmericanLife TV Network; BBC America; Black Family Channel; Bloomberg Television; Discovery Fit & Health; DIY Network; DMX Music; Fox Movie Channel; Fox Sports World; Fuse; G4; GAS; Golf Channel; Great American Country; GSN; Halogen Network; Lifetime Movie Network; MTV Networks Digital Suite; National Geographic Channel; Nick Jr.; Nick Too; NickToons TV; SoapNet; Speed; The Word Network; Toon Disney; Trinity Broadcasting Network; Turner Classic Movies; WE tv.
Fee: $10.95 monthly.
Digital Expanded Basic Service
Subscribers: N.A.
Programming (via satellite): Bio; ESPN Classic Sports; ESPNews; Flix; FSN Digital Atlantic; FSN Digital Central; FSN Digital Pacific; History Channel International; Independent Film Channel; International Television (ITV); Outdoor Channel; Sundance Channel; Versus.
Digital Pay Service 1
Pay Units: 105.
Programming (via satellite): Cinemax (multiplexed); Encore (multiplexed); HBO (multiplexed); Showtime (multiplexed); Starz (multiplexed).
Fee: $15.95 monthly (each).
Video-On-Demand: No
Pay-Per-View
Playboy TV (delivered digitally); Fresh (delivered digitally); Shorteez (delivered digitally); Hot Choice (delivered digitally); HITS (Headend In The Sky) (delivered digitally).
Internet Service
Operational: Yes.
Broadband Service: Comcast High Speed Internet.
Fee: $42.95 monthly.
Telephone Service
Digital: Operational
Miles of Plant: 63.0 (coaxial); None (fiber optic).
Regional Vice President: Linda Hossinger. Vice President, Technical Operations: Randy Bender. Vice President, Marketing: Donna Corning. Vice President, Public Affairs: Jody Doherty. Manager: Diane Kirsh.
Ownership: Comcast Cable Communications Inc. (MSO).

ARNOT—Blue Ridge Communications, 613 3rd St, PO Box 215, Palmerton, PA 18071-0215. Phones: 610-826-2551; 570-724-4516 (Customer service). Web Site: http://www.brctv.com. ICA: PA0308.
TV Market Ranking: Below 100 (ARNOT). Franchise award date: N.A. Franchise expiration date: N.A. Began: N.A.
Channel capacity: N.A. Channels available but not in use: N.A.
Basic Service
Subscribers: N.A.
Programming (received off-air): WBNG-TV (CBS, CW) Binghamton; WENY-TV (ABC, CW) Elmira; WETM-TV (NBC) Elmira; WPIX (CW, IND) New York; WSKG-TV (PBS) Binghamton; WVIA-TV (PBS) Scranton; WYDC (FOX, MNT) Corning; WYOU (CBS) Scranton.
Programming (via satellite): C-SPAN; C-SPAN 2; WGN America.
Fee: $22.50 installation; $16.05 monthly.
Expanded Basic Service 1
Subscribers: N.A.
Programming (via satellite): A&E Networks; ABC Family Channel; AMC; Animal Planet; BET Networks; Cartoon Network; CNBC; CNN; Comedy Central; Country Music TV; Discovery Channel; Disney Channel; E! Entertainment Television; ESPN; ESPN 2; Eternal Word TV Network; Food Network; Fox News Channel; FX; Hallmark Channel; Headline News; HGTV; History Channel; Lifetime; Lifetime Movie Network; MSNBC; MTV; Nickelodeon; Pennsylvania Cable Network; QVC; Root Sports Pittsburgh; SoapNet; Speed; Spike TV; Syfy; TBS Superstation; The Learning Channel; The Weather Channel; Travel Channel; Trinity Broadcasting Network; truTV; Turner Classic Movies; Turner Network TV; TV Land; USA Network; Versus; VH1.
Fee: $27.99 monthly.

Digital Basic Service
Subscribers: N.A.
Programming (via satellite): Discovery Digital Networks; DMX Music; ESPN Classic Sports; ESPNews; Fox Movie Channel; GAS; GSN; Halogen Network; MTV Networks Digital Suite; National Geographic Channel; Nick Jr.; Outdoor Channel; Toon Disney.
Fee: $35.00 installation; $9.95 monthly.
Digital Expanded Basic Service
Subscribers: N.A.
Programming (via satellite): BBC America; Bio; Bloomberg Television; G4; Golf Channel; History Channel International; Style Network.
Fee: $5.00 monthly.
Pay Service 1
Pay Units: N.A.
Programming (via satellite): Cinemax; HBO; Showtime.
Fee: $12.50 monthly.
Digital Pay Service 1
Pay Units: N.A.
Programming (via satellite): Cinemax (multiplexed); Encore (multiplexed); Flix; Starz (multiplexed); Sundance Channel; The Movie Channel (multiplexed).
Fee: $12.50 monthly (Cinemax, Showtime or TMC), $12.95 monthly (Starz), $13.50 monthly (HBO).
Pay-Per-View
iN DEMAND (delivered digitally); iN DEMAND; Sports PPV (delivered digitally).
Internet Service
Operational: Yes.
Broadband Service: ProLog Express.
Fee: $34.95 monthly; $10.00 modem lease; $59.95 modem purchase.
Telephone Service
None
Vice President, Operations: Richard Semmel. General Manager: Mark Masonheimer. Fiber Manager: Randy Semmel. Chief Technician: Garry Woods.
Ownership: Pencor Services Inc. (MSO).

AUBURN—Comcast Cable, 1 E Uwchlan Ave, Ste 411, Exton, PA 19341. Phone: 717-960-3100. Web Site: http://www.comcast.com. Also serves Lake Wynonah. ICA: PA0448.
TV Market Ranking: Below 100 (AUBURN, Lake Wynonah). Franchise award date: N.A. Franchise expiration date: N.A. Began: N.A.
Channel capacity: N.A. Channels available but not in use: N.A.
Basic Service
Subscribers: 1,000.
Programming (received off-air): WBRE-TV (NBC) Wilkes-Barre; WFMZ-TV (IND) Allentown; WGAL (NBC) Lancaster; WLYH-TV (CW) Lancaster; WNEP-TV (ABC) Scranton; WOLF-TV (CW, FOX, MNT) Hazleton; WPHL-TV (MNT, IND) Philadelphia; WPIX (CW, IND) New York; WPVI-TV (ABC) Philadelphia; WVIA-TV (PBS) Scranton; WYOU (CBS) Scranton.
Programming (via satellite): A&E Networks; ABC Family Channel; AMC; AmericanLife TV Network; Animal Planet; Cartoon Network; CNBC; CNN; Comcast SportsNet Philadelphia; Comedy Central; Country Music TV; C-SPAN; Discovery Channel; Disney Channel; E! Entertainment Television; ESPN; ESPN 2; Eternal Word TV Network; Food Network; Fox News Channel; FX; Hallmark Channel; Headline News; HGTV; Lifetime; MSNBC; MTV; National Geographic Channel; Nickelodeon; Pennsylvania Cable Network; QVC; Spike TV; Syfy; TBS Superstation; The Learning Channel; The Weather Channel; Travel Channel; truTV; Turner Network TV; TV Land; USA Network; Versus; VH1; WGN America.
Fee: $36.75 monthly.
Digital Basic Service
Subscribers: N.A.
Programming (via satellite): BBC America; Bravo; Discovery Digital Networks; DMX Music; ESPN Classic Sports; ESPNews; Fox Sports World; Golf Channel; GSN; History Channel; Independent Film Channel; Speed; Turner Classic Movies.
Fee: $41.61 monthly.
Pay Service 1
Pay Units: N.A.
Programming (via satellite): Cinemax; HBO.
Fee: $12.19 monthly (each).
Digital Pay Service 1
Pay Units: N.A.
Programming (via satellite): Cinemax (multiplexed); Encore (multiplexed); HBO (multiplexed); Showtime (multiplexed); Starz (multiplexed); The Movie Channel (multiplexed).
Fee: $10.50 monthly (each).
Pay-Per-View
TVN Entertainment (delivered digitally).
Internet Service
Operational: Yes.
Broadband Service: Comcast High Speed Internet.
Fee: $50.00 installation; $39.95 monthly.
Telephone Service
None
Miles of Plant: 80.0 (coaxial); None (fiber optic).
Manager: George Uritis. Chief Technician: Tom Lewis.
Ownership: Comcast Cable Communications Inc.

AULTMAN—Formerly served by Adelphia Communications. Now served by BLAIRSVILLE, PA [PA0320]. ICA: PA0309.

AVELLA—Blue Devil Cable TV Inc., 116 S 4th St, Toronto, OH 43964-1368. Phone: 800-931-9392. Fax: 740-537-2802. ICA: PA0310.
TV Market Ranking: 10,90 (AVELLA). Franchise award date: N.A. Franchise expiration date: N.A. Began: October 1, 1976.
Channel capacity: N.A. Channels available but not in use: N.A.
Basic Service
Subscribers: 1,475.
Programming (received off-air): KDKA-TV (CBS) Pittsburgh; WPGH-TV (FOX) Pittsburgh; WPMY (MNT) Pittsburgh; WPXI (IND, NBC) Pittsburgh; WQED (PBS) Pittsburgh; WTAE-TV (ABC) Pittsburgh; WTOV-TV (IND, NBC) Steubenville; WTRF-TV (CBS) Wheeling.
Programming (via satellite): ABC Family Channel; ESPN; WGN America.
Fee: $25.00 installation; $8.95 monthly.
Pay Service 1
Pay Units: 153.
Programming (via satellite): HBO; The Movie Channel.
Fee: $10.60 monthly (TMC); $11.66 monthly (HBO).
Video-On-Demand: No
Internet Service
Operational: No.
Telephone Service
None
Miles of Plant: 6.0 (coaxial); None (fiber optic).
Manager: David Bates. Office Manager: Joanne Conner.
Ownership: Blue Devil Cable TV Inc. (MSO).

BANGOR BOROUGH—RCN Corp. Formerly served by NORTHAMPTON BOROUGH, PA [PA0008]. This cable system has converted to IPTV, 196 Van Buren St, Herndon, VA 20170. Phone: 703-434-8200. Web Site: http://www.rcn.com. ICA: PA5202.
TV Market Ranking: Below 100 (BANGOR BOROUGH).
Channel capacity: N.A. Channels available but not in use: N.A.
Internet Service
Operational: Yes.
Telephone Service
Digital: Operational
Chairman: Steven J. Simmons. Chief Executive Officer: Jim Holanda.

BASTRESS TWP.—Formerly served by Bastress TV Cable Association. No longer in operation. ICA: PA0313.

BATH BOROUGH—Formerly served by NORTHAMPTON BOROUGH, PA [PA0008]. RCN Corp. This cable system has converted to IPTV, 196 Van Buren St, Herndon, VA 20170. Phone: 703-434-8200. Web Site: http://www.rcn.com. ICA: PA5203.
TV Market Ranking: Below 100 (BATH BOROUGH).
Channel capacity: N.A. Channels available but not in use: N.A.
Internet Service
Operational: Yes.
Telephone Service
Digital: Operational
Chairman: Steven J. Simmons. Chief Executive Officer: Jim Holanda.

BEACH LAKE—Blue Ridge Communications, 613 3rd St, PO Box 215, Palmerton, PA 18071-0215. Phone: 610-826-2551. Web Site: http://www.brctv.com. Also serves Berlin Twp. (Wayne County) & Damascus Twp. ICA: PA0314.
TV Market Ranking: 49 (BEACH LAKE, Berlin Twp. (Wayne County), Damascus Twp.). Franchise award date: N.A. Franchise expiration date: N.A. Began: January 1, 1971.
Channel capacity: 42 (operating 2-way). Channels available but not in use: N.A.
Basic Service
Subscribers: N.A.
Programming (received off-air): WABC-TV (ABC) New York; WCBS-TV (CBS) New York; WNBC (NBC) New York; WNEP-TV (ABC) Scranton; WNET (PBS) Newark; WNYW (FOX) New York; WOLF-TV (CW, FOX, MNT) Hazleton; WPIX (CW, IND) New York; WPVI-TV (ABC) Philadelphia; WQPX-TV (ION) Scranton; WSKG-TV (PBS) Binghamton; WSWB (CW) Scranton; WVIA-TV (PBS) Scranton; WWOR-TV (MNT) Secaucus; WYOU (CBS) Scranton.
Programming (via satellite): Headline News; WGN America.
Fee: $22.50 installation; $14.68 monthly.
Expanded Basic Service 1
Subscribers: N.A.
Programming (via satellite): A&E Networks; ABC Family Channel; AMC; Animal Planet; CNBC; CNN; Comedy Central; Country Music TV; C-SPAN; Discovery Channel; Discovery Health Channel; Disney Channel; E! Entertainment Television; ESPN; ESPN 2; Eternal Word TV Network; Food Network; Fox News Channel; FX; Golf Channel; HGTV; History Channel; Home Shopping Network 2; Lifetime; Lifetime Movie Network; MSG; MSNBC; MTV; Nickelodeon; Pennsylvania Cable Network; QVC; Speed; Spike TV; Syfy; TBS Superstation; The Learning Channel; The Weather Channel; Travel Channel; Trinity Broadcasting Network; truTV; Turner Classic Movies; Turner Network TV; TV Guide Network; TV Land; USA Network; Versus; VH1; WE tv; Yankees Entertainment & Sports.
Fee: $25.66 monthly.
Digital Basic Service
Subscribers: N.A.
Programming (via satellite): Concert TV; Discovery Digital Networks; Fox Movie Channel; FSN Digital Atlantic; FSN Digital Central; FSN Digital Pacific; GAS; Halogen Network; Meadows Racing Network; MTV Networks Digital Suite; Music Choice; National Geographic Channel; NBA TV; Nick Jr.; Nick Too; NickToons TV; Outdoor Channel; PBS Kids Channel; SoapNet; Toon Disney.
Fee: $35.00 installation; $9.95 monthly.
Digital Expanded Basic Service
Subscribers: N.A.
Programming (via satellite): BBC America; Bio; Bloomberg Television; Boomerang; Cooking Channel; DIY Network; G4; Hallmark Channel; History Channel International; Lifetime Real Women; LWS Local Weather Station; Style Network.
Fee: $5.00 monthly.
Pay Service 1
Pay Units: N.A.
Programming (via satellite): Cinemax; HBO; Showtime.
Fee: $11.50 monthly (Cinemax or Showtime), $12.50 monthly (HBO).
Digital Pay Service 1
Pay Units: N.A.
Programming (via satellite): Cinemax (multiplexed); Encore (multiplexed); Flix; HBO (multiplexed); Showtime (multiplexed); Starz (multiplexed); Sundance Channel; The Movie Channel (multiplexed).
Fee: $12.50 monthly (Cinemax, Showtime or TMC), $12.95 monthly (Starz), $13.50 monthly (HBO).
Video-On-Demand: No
Pay-Per-View
iN DEMAND; iN DEMAND (delivered digitally); sports (delivered digitally); Adult PPV (delivered digitally); Barker (delivered digitally).
Internet Service
Operational: No.
Telephone Service
None
Vice President, Operations: Richard Semmel. General Manager: Mark Masonheimer. Fiber Manager: Randy Semmel. Chief Technician: Garry Woods.
Ownership: Pencor Services Inc. (MSO).

BEAVER FALLS—Comcast Cable, 15 Summit Park Dr, Pittsburgh, PA 15275. Phone: 412-747-6400. Fax: 412-747-6401. Web Site: http://www.comcast.com. Also serves Big Beaver, Brighton Twp., Chippewa Twp., Darlington, Darlington Twp. (Beaver County), Daugherty Twp., Eastvale, Enon Valley, Fallston, Glasgow, Industry, Midland, New Beaver, New Brighton, New Galilee, Ohioville, Patterson Heights, Patterson Twp., Shippingport Borough, South Beaver Twp. & West Mayfield. ICA: PA0065.
TV Market Ranking: 10 (Brighton Twp., Darlington Twp. (Beaver County), Glasgow, Ohioville); 10,79 (BEAVER FALLS, Chippewa Twp., Daugherty Twp., Eastvale, Fallston, New Brighton, Patterson Heights, Patterson Twp., West Mayfield). Franchise award date: N.A. Franchise expiration date: N.A. Began: January 1, 1957.
Channel capacity: N.A. Channels available but not in use: N.A.

Basic Service
Subscribers: 18,700.
Programming (received off-air): KDKA-TV (CBS) Pittsburgh; WFMJ-TV (CW, NBC) Youngstown; WINP-TV (IND, ION) Pittsburgh; WKBN-TV (CBS) Youngstown; WNEO (PBS) Alliance; WPCB-TV (IND) Greensburg; WPCW (CW) Jeannette; WPGH-TV (FOX) Pittsburgh; WPMY (MNT) Pittsburgh; WPXI (IND, NBC) Pittsburgh; WQED (PBS) Pittsburgh; WTAE-TV (ABC) Pittsburgh; WTOV-TV (IND, NBC) Steubenville; WYTV (ABC, MNT) Youngstown.
Programming (via satellite): C-SPAN; C-SPAN 2; QVC; The Weather Channel; TV Guide Network.
Fee: $43.99 installation; $14.00 monthly.
Expanded Basic Service 1
Subscribers: 16,109.
Programming (via microwave): Pittsburgh Cable News Channel.
Programming (via satellite): A&E Networks; ABC Family Channel; AMC; Animal Planet; BET Networks; Cartoon Network; CNBC; CNN; Comedy Central; Country Music TV; Discovery Channel; Disney Channel; E! Entertainment Television; ESPN; ESPN 2; Eternal Word TV Network; Fox News Channel; FX; Hallmark Channel; Headline News; HGTV; History Channel; ION Television; Lifetime; MSNBC; MTV; Nickelodeon; Oxygen; Pennsylvania Cable Network; Root Sports Pittsburgh; Spike TV; TBS Superstation; The Learning Channel; Travel Channel; truTV; Turner Classic Movies; Turner Network TV; TV Land; USA Network; Versus; VH1.
Fee: $36.49 monthly.
Digital Basic Service
Subscribers: 531.
Programming (via satellite): AmericanLife TV Network; BBC America; Bio; Black Family Channel; Bloomberg Television; Bravo; C-SPAN 3; Discovery Channel; Discovery Fit & Health; DMX Music; ESPN; ESPN Classic Sports; ESPNews; Food Network; Fox College Sports Atlantic; Fox College Sports Central; Fox College Sports Pacific; Fox Movie Channel; Fuse; G4; GAS; Golf Channel; Great American Country; GSN; Halogen Network; History Channel International; iN DEMAND; Independent Film Channel; Lifetime Movie Network; Lime; MTV Networks Digital Suite; National Geographic Channel; Nick Jr.; NickToons TV; Outdoor Channel; Ovation; ShopNBC; Speed; Style Network; Sundance Channel; Syfy; The Word Network; Toon Disney; Trinity Broadcasting Network; Turner Classic Movies; WE tv; Weatherscan.
Fee: $10.95 monthly.
Pay Service 1
Pay Units: 1,584.
Fee: $9.95 monthly (Cinemax), $10.95 monthly (Showtime), $11.95 monthly (HBO).
Digital Pay Service 1
Pay Units: N.A.
Programming (via satellite): Cinemax (multiplexed); Cinemax; Encore (multiplexed); Flix; HBO (multiplexed); HBO HD; Showtime (multiplexed); Showtime HD; Starz (multiplexed); Starz; The Movie Channel (multiplexed).
Video-On-Demand: Yes
Pay-Per-View
Addressable homes: 531.
NBA TV (delivered digitally); NASCAR In Car (delivered digitally); Hot Choice (delivered digitally); Zee TV USA (delivered digitally); RAI International (delivered digitally); Sports PPV (delivered digitally); NHL Center Ice (delivered digitally); MLB Extra Innings (delivered digitally); Russian Television Network (delivered digitally); TV Asia (delivered digitally); iN DEMAND (delivered digitally); Urban Xtra (delivered digitally); Fresh (delivered digitally); Shorteez (delivered digitally); Playboy TV (delivered digitally).
Internet Service
Operational: Yes.
Broadband Service: Comcast High Speed Internet.
Fee: $42.95 monthly.
Telephone Service
Digital: Operational
Miles of Plant: 405.0 (coaxial); 5.0 (fiber optic).
Regional Vice President: Linda Hossinger. Vice President, Technical Operations: Randy Bender. Vice President, Marketing: Donna Corning. Vice President, Public Relations: Jody Doherty.
Ownership: Comcast Cable Communications Inc. (MSO).

BEAVER SPRINGS—Service Electric Cable TV & Communications. Now served by SUNBURY, PA [PA0029]. ICA: PA0259.

BEAVER VALLEY—Comcast Cable, 15 Summit Park Dr, Pittsburgh, PA 15275. Phones: 412-747-6400; 724-775-2813 (Rochester office). Fax: 412-747-6401. Web Site: http://www.comcast.com. Also serves Greene Twp. (Beaver County), Hookstown, Potter Twp. (Beaver County) & Raccoon Twp. (southern portion). ICA: PA0157.
TV Market Ranking: 10 (Potter Twp. (Beaver County)); 10,90 (BEAVER VALLEY, Greene Twp. (Beaver County), Hookstown, Raccoon Twp. (southern portion)). Franchise award date: N.A. Franchise expiration date: N.A. Began: April 1, 1983.
Channel capacity: N.A. Channels available but not in use: N.A.
Basic Service
Subscribers: N.A. Included in Bensalem Twp.
Programming (received off-air): KDKA-TV (CBS) Pittsburgh; WINP-TV (IND, ION) Pittsburgh; WPCB-TV (IND) Greensburg; WPCW (CW) Jeannette; WPGH-TV (FOX) Pittsburgh; WPMY (MNT) Pittsburgh; WPXI (IND, NBC) Pittsburgh; WQED (PBS) Pittsburgh; WTAE-TV (ABC) Pittsburgh.
Programming (via satellite): QVC; The Weather Channel.
Fee: $43.99 installation; $12.70 monthly.
Expanded Basic Service 1
Subscribers: 549.
Programming (via satellite): A&E Networks; ABC Family Channel; AMC; Animal Planet; CNBC; CNN; Comedy Central; Country Music TV; C-SPAN; Discovery Channel; Discovery Fit & Health; Disney Channel; E! Entertainment Television; ESPN; ESPN 2; Eternal Word TV Network; Fox News Channel; FX; Headline News; HGTV; History Channel; Lifetime; MSNBC; MTV; Nickelodeon; Root Sports Pittsburgh; Spike TV; Syfy; TBS Superstation; The Learning Channel; Travel Channel; truTV; Turner Network TV; TV Land; USA Network; VH1.
Fee: $31.14 monthly.
Pay Service 1
Pay Units: N.A.
Programming (via satellite): Cinemax; HBO; Showtime; The Movie Channel.
Video-On-Demand: No
Pay-Per-View
Playboy TV (delivered digitally); Fresh (delivered digitally); Hot Choice (delivered digitally).
Internet Service
Operational: Yes.
Broadband Service: Comcast High Speed Internet.
Telephone Service
None
Miles of Plant: 130.0 (coaxial); None (fiber optic).
Regional Vice President: Linda Hossinger. Vice President, Technical Operations: Randy Bender. Vice President, Marketing: Donna Corning. Vice President, Public Affairs: Jody Doherty.
Ownership: Comcast Cable Communications Inc. (MSO).

BEAVERTOWN—Formerly served by Nittany Media Inc. No longer in operation. ICA: PA0315.

BEDFORD—Comcast Cable, 15 Summit Park Dr, Pittsburgh, PA 15275. Phones: 412-747-6400; 814-344-8055 (Carrolltown office). Fax: 412-747-6401. Web Site: http://www.comcast.com. Also serves Alum Bank, Breezewood, East Providence Twp., East St. Clair Twp. (Bedford County), Everett, Fishertown, Manns Choice, Napier Twp. (Bedford County), New Paris, Rainsburg, Schellsburg, Snake Spring Valley Twp., West Providence Twp. & West St. Clair. ICA: PA0082.
TV Market Ranking: 74 (Alum Bank, BEDFORD, Breezewood, East Providence Twp., East St. Clair Twp. (Bedford County), Everett, Fishertown, Manns Choice, Napier Twp. (Bedford County), New Paris, Schellsburg, Snake Spring Valley Twp., West Providence Twp., West St. Clair); Outside TV Markets (Rainsburg). Franchise award date: N.A. Franchise expiration date: N.A. Began: October 1, 1958.
Channel capacity: N.A. Channels available but not in use: N.A.
Basic Service
Subscribers: N.A.
Programming (received off-air): KDKA-TV (CBS) Pittsburgh; WATM-TV (ABC) Altoona; WIVB-TV (CBS) Buffalo; WJAC-TV (NBC) Johnstown; WKBS-TV (IND) Altoona; WPCB-TV (IND) Greensburg; WPCW (CW) Jeannette; WPSU-TV (PBS) Clearfield; WQED (PBS) Pittsburgh; WTAE-TV (ABC) Pittsburgh; WTAJ-TV (CBS) Altoona; WWCP-TV (FOX) Johnstown; 10 FMs.
Programming (via satellite): Discovery Channel; QVC; TBS Superstation; The Weather Channel; TV Guide Network; WGN America.
Fee: $39.95 installation; $18.99 monthly; $4.00 converter.
Expanded Basic Service 1
Subscribers: 6,756.
Programming (via satellite): A&E Networks; ABC Family Channel; AMC; Animal Planet; Bravo; Cartoon Network; CNBC; CNN; Comedy Central; Country Music TV; C-SPAN; Discovery Channel; Disney Channel; E! Entertainment Television; ESPN; ESPN 2; Eternal Word TV Network; Food Network; Fox News Channel; FX; Hallmark Channel; Headline News; HGTV; History Channel; Lifetime; MoviePlex; MSNBC; MTV; Nickelodeon; Outdoor Channel; Root Sports Pittsburgh; Spike TV; Syfy; The Learning Channel; Travel Channel; Trinity Broadcasting Network; truTV; Turner Classic Movies; Turner Network TV; TV Land; USA Network; VH1.
Fee: $36.00 monthly.
Digital Basic Service
Subscribers: N.A.
Programming (via satellite): BBC America; Bio; Bloomberg Television; CMT Pure Country; Cooking Channel; C-SPAN 3; Discovery Fit & Health; Discovery Health Channel; Discovery Kids Channel; Disney XD; DIY Network; DMX Music; ESPN Classic Sports; ESPNews; Fox College Sports Atlantic; Fox College Sports Central; Fox College Sports Pacific; Fox Movie Channel; Fox Reality Channel; Fox Soccer; Fuse; G4; GMC; Golf Channel; Great American Country; GSN; Halogen Network; History Channel International; HRTV; ID Investigation Discovery; Independent Film Channel; ION Life; ION Television; Lifetime Movie Network; Military Channel; MTV Hits; MTV2; National Geographic Channel; NFL Network; Nick Jr.; Nick Too; NickToons TV; Nuvo TV; Outdoor Channel; Oxygen; PBS Kids Sprout; Planet Green; Qubo; Science; Speed; Starz IndiePlex; Starz RetroPlex; Style Network; Sundance Channel; TeenNick; The Comcast Network; The Word Network; Versus; VH1 Classic; VH1 Soul; WE tv; Weatherscan.
Fee: $10.95 monthly; $3.40 converter.
Digital Pay Service 1
Pay Units: N.A.
Programming (via satellite): Cinemax (multiplexed); Encore (multiplexed); Flix; HBO (multiplexed); Showtime (multiplexed); Starz (multiplexed); The Movie Channel (multiplexed).
Fee: $15.95 monthly (each).
Video-On-Demand: No
Pay-Per-View
Club Jenna (delivered digitally); Sports PPV; Playboy TV (delivered digitally); Fresh (delivered digitally); Movies (delivered digitally); Spice: Xcess.
Internet Service
Operational: Yes.
Broadband Service: Comcast High Speed Internet.
Fee: $42.95 monthly.
Telephone Service
Digital: Operational
Miles of Plant: 241.0 (coaxial); 20.0 (fiber optic).
Regional Vice President: Linda Hossinger. Vice President, Technical Operations: Randy Bender. Vice President, Marketing: Donna Corning. Vice President, Public Affairs: Jody Doherty. Manager: Diane Kirsh.
Ownership: Comcast Cable Communications Inc. (MSO).

BELLEVILLE—Zampelli Electronics, PO Box 830, Lewistown, PA 17044-0830. Phone: 717-248-1544. ICA: PA0316.
TV Market Ranking: Outside TV Markets (BELLEVILLE). Franchise award date: N.A. Franchise expiration date: N.A. Began: N.A.
Channel capacity: 14 (not 2-way capable). Channels available but not in use: N.A.
Basic Service
Subscribers: N.A.
Programming (received off-air): WGAL (NBC) Lancaster; WHP-TV (CBS, MNT) Harrisburg; WHTM-TV (ABC) Harrisburg; WJAC-TV (NBC) Johnstown; WLYH-TV (CW) Lancaster; WNEP-TV (ABC) Scranton; WPSU-TV (PBS) Clearfield; WTAJ-TV (CBS) Altoona; WVIA-TV (PBS) Scranton; 1 FM.
Programming (via satellite): Disney Channel; ESPN; TBS Superstation; WGN America.
Fee: $25.00 installation; $10.75 monthly.

Pay Service 1
Pay Units: N.A.
Programming (via satellite): The Movie Channel.
Fee: $10.95 monthly.
Video-On-Demand: No
Internet Service
Operational: No.
Telephone Service
None
Manager & Chief Technician: Joe Zampelli.
Ownership: Zampelli TV (MSO).

BENSALEM TWP.—Comcast Cable, 3220 Tillman Dr, Bensalem, PA 19010. Phone: 215-642-6400. Fax: 215-638-6510. Web Site: http://www.comcast.com. Also serves Falls Twp. (Bucks County), Lower Southampton, Morrisville, Tullytown, Upper Southampton & Warminster. ICA: PA0027.
TV Market Ranking: 4 (BENSALEM TWP., Falls Twp. (Bucks County), Lower Southampton, Morrisville, Tullytown, Upper Southampton, Warminster). Franchise award date: January 1, 1979. Franchise expiration date: N.A. Began: January 1, 1979.
Channel capacity: N.A. Channels available but not in use: N.A.
Basic Service
Subscribers: 1,125,000 Includes entire Philadelphia metro area.
Programming (received off-air): KYW-TV (CBS) Philadelphia; WCAU (NBC) Philadelphia; WFMZ-TV (IND) Allentown; WGTW-TV (TBN) Burlington; WHYY-TV (PBS) Wilmington; WMCN-TV (IND) Atlantic City; WNJT (PBS) Trenton; WPHL-TV (MNT, IND) Philadelphia; WPIX (CW, IND) New York; WPPX-TV (ION) Wilmington; WPSG (CW) Philadelphia; WPVI-TV (ABC) Philadelphia; WTVE (IND) Reading; WTXF-TV (FOX) Philadelphia; WUVP-DT (UNV) Vineland; WYBE (ETV, IND) Philadelphia.
Programming (via satellite): CNBC; QVC; TBS Superstation; The Comcast Network.
Fee: $14.10 monthly.
Expanded Basic Service 1
Subscribers: 45,886.
Programming (received off-air): WBPH-TV (IND) Bethlehem; WWSI (TMO) Atlantic City.
Programming (via satellite): A&E Networks; ABC Family Channel; AMC; Animal Planet; BET Networks; Bravo; Cartoon Network; CNN; Comcast SportsNet Philadelphia; Comedy Central; Country Music TV; C-SPAN; C-SPAN 2; Discovery Channel; Discovery Health Channel; Disney Channel; E! Entertainment Television; ESPN; ESPN 2; Eternal Word TV Network; Food Network; Fox News Channel; FX; Golf Channel; GSN; Headline News; HGTV; History Channel; Lifetime; MSNBC; MTV; MTV2; Nickelodeon; Pennsylvania Cable Network; Philadelphia Park Live; Speed; Spike TV; Style Network; Syfy; The Learning Channel; The Weather Channel; truTV; Turner Classic Movies; Turner Network TV; TV Guide Network; TV Land; USA Network; Versus; VH1.
Fee: $38.10 monthly.
Digital Basic Service
Subscribers: N.A.
Programming (via satellite): BBC America; Bio; Comcast SportsNet Philadelphia; Cooking Channel; C-SPAN 3; DIY Network; DMX Music; ESPN; ESPNews; Eternal Word TV Network; Flix (multiplexed); Fox College Sports Atlantic; Fox College Sports Central; Fox College Sports Pacific; Fox Soccer; G4; GAS; GolTV; HD Theater; History Channel International; Independent Film Channel; INHD; MTV Networks Digital Suite; National Geographic Channel; NBA TV; NFL Network; Nick Jr.; Nick Too; NickToons TV; ShopNBC; SoapNet; Sundance Channel (multiplexed); Toon Disney; Weatherscan.
Fee: $14.95 monthly.
Digital Pay Service 1
Pay Units: N.A.
Programming (via satellite): Cinemax (multiplexed); HBO (multiplexed); Showtime (multiplexed); Starz (multiplexed); The Movie Channel (multiplexed).
Video-On-Demand: Yes
Pay-Per-View
Playboy TV (delivered digitally); Fresh (delivered digitally); Shorteez (delivered digitally); Pleasure (delivered digitally); Sports PPV (delivered digitally).
Internet Service
Operational: Yes. Began: July 12, 1999.
Broadband Service: Comcast High Speed Internet.
Fee: $149.95 installation; $42.95 monthly; $9.95 modem lease; $299.00 modem purchase.
Telephone Service
Digital: Operational
Fee: $44.95 monthly
Miles of Plant: 450.0 (coaxial); None (fiber optic).
Senior Regional Vice President: Amy Smith. Vice President, Technical Operations: Rich Massi. Vice President, Marketing: Chip Goodman. Public Relations Director: Gabriel Weissman.
Ownership: Comcast Cable Communications Inc. (MSO).

BENTLEY CREEK—Blue Ridge Communications, 613 3rd St, PO Box 215, Palmerton, PA 18071-0215. Phone: 610-826-2551. Web Site: http://www.brctv.com. Also serves Bradford County, Centerville (Bradford County) & Fassett. ICA: PA0317.
TV Market Ranking: Below 100 (BENTLEY CREEK, Bradford County, Centerville (Bradford County), Fassett). Franchise award date: N.A. Franchise expiration date: N.A. Began: January 1, 1975.
Channel capacity: 12 (not 2-way capable). Channels available but not in use: N.A.
Basic Service
Subscribers: N.A.
Programming (received off-air): WBNG-TV (CBS, CW) Binghamton; WENY-TV (ABC, CW) Elmira; WETM-TV (NBC) Elmira; WICZ-TV (FOX) Binghamton; WSKG-TV (PBS) Binghamton; WSWB (CW) Scranton; WVIA-TV (PBS) Scranton; WYOU (CBS) Scranton; allband FM.
Programming (via satellite): A&E Networks; ABC Family Channel; Disney Channel; Lifetime; Pennsylvania Cable Network; QVC; Speed; Syfy; The Learning Channel; The Weather Channel.
Fee: $22.50 installation; $15.30 monthly.
Expanded Basic Service 1
Subscribers: N.A.
Programming (via satellite): AMC; Animal Planet; CNN; Discovery Channel; ESPN; ESPN 2; FX; HGTV; History Channel; MTV; Nickelodeon; SoapNet; Spike TV; TBS Superstation; Trinity Broadcasting Network; Turner Network TV; USA Network; Versus; VH1; WPIX (CW, IND) New York.
Fee: $24.91 monthly.
Digital Basic Service
Subscribers: N.A.
Programming (via satellite): BBC America; Bio; Bloomberg Television; Discovery Kids Channel; ESPN Classic Sports; ESPNews; Fox Sports World; G4; GAS; Golf Channel; GSN; Halogen Network; History Channel International; Lifetime Movie Network; MTV Networks Digital Suite; Music Choice; National Geographic Channel; Nick Jr.; Outdoor Channel; Speed; Style Network; Sundance Channel; The Word Network; Toon Disney; Turner Classic Movies; Versus.
Fee: $35.00 installation; $18.90 monthly.
Pay Service 1
Pay Units: N.A.
Programming (via satellite): HBO; The Movie Channel.
Fee: $15.00 installation; $9.00 monthly (each).
Digital Pay Service 1
Pay Units: N.A.
Programming (via satellite): Cinemax (multiplexed); Encore (multiplexed); HBO (multiplexed); Showtime (multiplexed); Starz (multiplexed); The Movie Channel (multiplexed).
Fee: $12.50 monthly (Cinemax, Showtime or TMC), $12.95 monthly (Starz), $13.50 monthly (HBO).
Video-On-Demand: No
Pay-Per-View
Sports PPV (delivered digitally); ESPN Now (delivered digitally); iN DEMAND (delivered digitally).
Internet Service
Operational: No.
Miles of Plant: 14.0 (coaxial); None (fiber optic).
Vice President, Operations: Richard Semmel. General Manager: Mark Masonheimer. Fiber Manager: Randy Semmel. Chief Technician: Garry Woods.
Ownership: Pencor Services Inc. (MSO).

BENTLEYVILLE—FairPoint Communications, 608 Main St, Bentleyville, PA 15314-1539. Phone: 724-239-2501. Fax: 724-239-1000. Web Site: http://www.fairpoint.com. Also serves Amwell Twp., Ellsworth, Fallowfield Twp., North Bethlehem Twp., Scenery Hill, Somerset Twp. (Washington County), South Strabane Twp. & West Pike Run Twp. ICA: PA0442. **Note:** This system is an overbuild.
TV Market Ranking: 10 (BENTLEYVILLE, Ellsworth, Fallowfield Twp., Scenery Hill, Somerset Twp. (Washington County), South Strabane Twp., West Pike Run Twp.); 10,90 (Amwell Twp., North Bethlehem Twp.). Franchise award date: January 1, 1992. Franchise expiration date: N.A. Began: N.A.
Channel capacity: N.A. Channels available but not in use: N.A.
Basic Service
Subscribers: 1,368.
Programming (received off-air): KDKA-TV (CBS) Pittsburgh; WINP-TV (IND, ION) Pittsburgh; WPCB-TV (IND) Greensburg; WPCW (CW) Jeannette; WPGH-TV (FOX) Pittsburgh; WPMY (MNT) Pittsburgh; WPXI (IND, NBC) Pittsburgh; WQED (PBS) Pittsburgh; WTAE-TV (ABC) Pittsburgh.
Programming (via satellite): A&E Networks; ABC Family Channel; AMC; Animal Planet; Cartoon Network; CNBC; CNN; Comedy Central; Country Music TV; C-SPAN; Discovery Channel; Disney Channel; E! Entertainment Television; ESPN; ESPN 2; Eternal Word TV Network; Food Network; Fox News Channel; FX; Golf Channel; Hallmark Channel; Headline News; HGTV; History Channel; ION Television; Lifetime; Lifetime Movie Network; MSNBC; MTV; Nickelodeon; Outdoor Channel; Pennsylvania Cable Network; QVC; Root Sports Pittsburgh; Speed; Spike TV; Syfy; TBS Superstation; The Learning Channel; The Weather Channel; Toon Disney; Trinity Broadcasting Network; Turner Classic Movies; Turner Network TV; TV Guide Online; TV Land; TVN Entertainment; USA Network; VH1; WE tv; WGN America.
Fee: $22.00 installation; $37.50 monthly; $3.00 converter.
Pay Service 1
Pay Units: 40.
Programming (via satellite): Cinemax.
Fee: $12.50 monthly.
Pay Service 2
Pay Units: 59.
Programming (via satellite): The Movie Channel.
Fee: $11.00 monthly.
Pay Service 3
Pay Units: 100.
Programming (via satellite): HBO.
Fee: $14.25 monthly.
Pay Service 4
Pay Units: 18.
Programming (via satellite): Playboy TV.
Fee: $12.00 monthly.
Pay Service 5
Pay Units: 72.
Programming (via satellite): Showtime.
Fee: $11.75 monthly.
Video-On-Demand: No
Pay-Per-View
Addressable homes: 1,350.
iN DEMAND; Playboy TV.
Internet Service
Operational: Yes. Began: March 1, 1995.
Subscribers: 412.
Broadband Service: Nauticaus.
Fee: $40.50 installation; $44.95 monthly; $80.00 modem purchase.
Telephone Service
Digital: Operational
Fee: $39.95 monthly
Miles of Plant: 93.0 (coaxial); 15.0 (fiber optic).
Plant Manager: Walter R. Ziemba. Chief Technician: John B. Conkle. Marketing Director: Pam Joy.
Ownership: FairPoint Communications Inc.

BERWICK—MetroCast Communications, 1059 E 10th St, Hazleton, PA 18201-3421. Phones: 800-633-8578; 570-455-4251 (Administrative office); 570-759-6898 (Customer service). Fax: 570-455-0963. Web Site: http://www.metrocastcommunications.com. Also serves Beach Haven, Benton, Bloomsburg, Dallas, Dorrance, Edwardsville, Fern Glen, Glen Lyon, Hunlock Creek, Jackson Twp. (Columbia County), Larksville, Mifflinville, Millville, Mocanaqua, Mountain Top, Nanticoke, Nescopeck, Newport Twp., Nuangola, Nuremberg, Orangeville, Plymouth Twp. (Luzerne County), Rock Glen, Shavertown, Shickshinny, Stillwater, Sugarloaf, Sugarloaf Twp., Wapwallopen, West Nanticoke, Weston & Zion Grove. ICA: PA0094.
TV Market Ranking: 49 (Beach Haven, Benton, BERWICK, Bloomsburg, Dallas, Dorrance, Edwardsville, Fern Glen, Glen Lyon, Hunlock Creek, Jackson Twp. (Columbia County), Larksville, Mifflinville, Millville, Mocanaqua, Mountain Top, Nanticoke, Nescopeck, Newport Twp., Nuangola, Nuremberg, Orangeville, Plymouth Twp. (Luzerne County), Rock Glen, Shavertown, Shickshinny, South Centre Twp. (Columbia County), Stillwater, Sugarloaf, Sugarloaf Twp., Wapwallopen, West Nanticoke, Weston, Zion Grove). Franchise award date: January 1, 1947. Franchise expiration date: May 31, 2007. Began: December 1, 1950.
Channel capacity: 60 (operating 2-way). Channels available but not in use: N.A.

Basic Service

Subscribers: 13,215.

Programming (received off-air): WBRE-TV (NBC) Wilkes-Barre; WNEP-TV (ABC) Scranton; WOLF-TV (CW, FOX, MNT) Hazleton; WQMY (MNT) Williamsport; WQPX-TV (ION) Scranton; WSWB (CW) Scranton; WVIA-TV (PBS) Scranton; WYLN-LP (IND) Hazleton; WYOU (CBS) Scranton; allband FM.

Programming (via microwave): WWOR-TV (MNT) Secaucus.

Programming (via satellite): Catalog TV; QVC; TV Guide Network; WPIX (CW, IND) New York.

Fee: $60.00 installation; $10.90 monthly; $1.35 converter; $25.92 additional installation.

Expanded Basic Service 1

Subscribers: 11,746.

Programming (via satellite): A&E Networks; ABC Family Channel; AMC; Animal Planet; Bravo; Cartoon Network; CNBC; CNN; Comcast SportsNet Philadelphia; Comedy Central; Country Music TV; C-SPAN; Discovery Channel; Disney Channel; E! Entertainment Television; ESPN; ESPN 2; Food Network; Fox Movie Channel; Fox News Channel; FX; G4; Hallmark Channel; Hallmark Movie Channel; Headline News; HGTV; History Channel; Lifetime; MSNBC; MTV; National Geographic Channel; Nickelodeon; Outdoor Channel; Pennsylvania Cable Network; Root Sports Pittsburgh; SoapNet; Speed; Spike TV; Syfy; TBS Superstation; The Learning Channel; The Weather Channel; Travel Channel; Trinity Broadcasting Network; truTV; Turner Network TV; TV Land; USA Network; Versus; VH1; WE tv.

Fee: $25.92 installation; $28.74 monthly.

Digital Basic Service

Subscribers: 1,762.

Programming (via satellite): BBC America; Bio; Bloomberg Television; Boomerang; Country Music TV; DMX Music; ESPN 2 HD; ESPN HD; ESPN U; Fuse; GAS; GMC; GSN; HD Theater; HDNet; HDNet Movies; History Channel International; Lifetime Movie Network; MTV2; National Geographic Channel HD Network; NFL Network; NFL Network HD; Nick Jr.; NickToons TV; Outdoor Channel 2 HD; Toon Disney; Turner Network TV HD; Universal HD; VH1 Classic; WealthTV.

Fee: $7.95 monthly.

Digital Expanded Basic Service

Subscribers: N.A.

Programming (via satellite): ESPN Classic Sports; ESPNews; Fox College Sports Atlantic; Fox College Sports Central; Fox College Sports Pacific; Fox Soccer; Fuel TV; Golf Channel; Independent Film Channel; Starz HDTV; Turner Classic Movies.

Fee: $9.95 monthly.

Digital Pay Service 1

Pay Units: N.A.

Programming (via satellite): Cinemax (multiplexed); Cinemax HD; Flix; HBO (multiplexed); HBO HD; Showtime (multiplexed); Showtime HD; The Movie Channel (multiplexed).

Fee: $9.95 monthly (Cinemax), $10.95 monthly (HBO or Showtime/TMC).

Video-On-Demand: No

Pay-Per-View

Addressable homes: 924.

ESPN Now (delivered digitally); iN DEMAND (delivered digitally); Sports PPV (delivered digitally).

Internet Service

Operational: Yes.

Subscribers: 234.

Broadband Service: MetroCast Internet.

Fee: $41.95 monthly; $9.95 modem lease; $199.95 modem purchase.

Telephone Service

None

Miles of Plant: 396.0 (coaxial); 71.0 (fiber optic).

General Manager: Danny Jobe. Chief Technician: Joe Kutchi. Programming Director: Linda Stuchell.

Ownership: Harron Communications LP (MSO).

BETHEL PARK—Comcast Cable, 15 Summit Park Dr, Pittsburgh, PA 15275. Phone: 412-851-2600. Fax: 412-747-6401. Web Site: http://www.comcast.com. Also serves Dravosburg, Duquesne, Homestead, Lowber, McDonald, Midway, Mount Lebanon Twp., Mount Oliver, Munhall, Peters Twp., Robinson Twp. (Washington County), South Huntingdon Twp., Sutersville, Union Twp. (Washington County), Upper St. Clair Twp., West Homestead, West Mifflin, West Newton & Whitaker. ICA: PA0318.

TV Market Ranking: 10 (Dravosburg, Duquesne, Homestead, Lowber, McDonald, Midway, Mount Oliver, Munhall, Robinson Twp. (Washington County), South Huntingdon Twp., Sutersville, West Homestead, West Mifflin, West Newton, Whitaker); 10,90 (BETHEL PARK, Mount Lebanon Twp., Union Twp. (Washington County), Upper St. Clair Twp.). Franchise award date: N.A. Franchise expiration date: N.A. Began: March 31, 1972.

Channel capacity: N.A. Channels available but not in use: N.A.

Basic Service

Subscribers: N.A. Included in Bensalem Twp.

Programming (received off-air): KDKA-TV (CBS) Pittsburgh; WINP-TV (IND, ION) Pittsburgh; WPCB-TV (IND) Greensburg; WPCW (CW) Jeannette; WPGH-TV (FOX) Pittsburgh; WPMY (MNT) Pittsburgh; WPXI (IND, NBC) Pittsburgh; WQED (PBS) Pittsburgh; WTAE-TV (ABC) Pittsburgh.

Programming (via satellite): QVC; TV Guide Network; WGN America.

Fee: $43.99 installation; $8.00 monthly.

Expanded Basic Service 1

Subscribers: N.A.

Programming (via satellite): A&E Networks; ABC Family Channel; AMC; Animal Planet; BET Networks; Bravo; Cartoon Network; CNBC; CNN; Comedy Central; Country Music TV; C-SPAN; C-SPAN 2; Discovery Channel; Disney Channel; E! Entertainment Television; ESPN; ESPN 2; Eternal Word TV Network; Food Network; Fox News Channel; FX; Golf Channel; Hallmark Channel; Headline News; HGTV; History Channel; HRTV; ION Television; Lifetime; MSNBC; MTV; Nickelodeon; Oxygen; Pennsylvania Cable Network; Pittsburgh Cable News Channel; Root Sports Pittsburgh; ShopNBC; Spike TV; Style Network; Syfy; TBS Superstation; The Learning Channel; The Weather Channel; Travel Channel; truTV; Turner Network TV; TV Land; USA Network; Versus; VH1.

Fee: $44.40 monthly.

Digital Basic Service

Subscribers: 22,600.

Programming (via satellite): BBC America; Bio; Bloomberg Television; CMT Pure Country; Cooking Channel; Current; DIY Network; Encore (multiplexed); ESPN 2 HD; ESPN Classic Sports; ESPN HD; ESPNews; Flix; Fox College Sports Atlantic; Fox College Sports Central; Fox College Sports Pacific; Fox Movie Channel; Fox Soccer; Fuse; G4; GAS; GMC; Great American Country; GSN; Halogen Network; HD Theater; History Channel International; Independent Film Channel; Lifetime Movie Network; LOGO; MTV Networks Digital Suite; Music Choice; National Geographic Channel; NFL Network; Nick Jr.; Nick Too; NickToons TV; Outdoor Channel; SoapNet; Speed; Sundance Channel; The Word Network; Toon Disney; Trinity Broadcasting Network; Turner Classic Movies; Turner Network TV HD; WE tv.

Fee: $10.95 monthly.

Digital Pay Service 1

Pay Units: 10,515.

Programming (via satellite): Cinemax (multiplexed); Cinemax HD; HBO (multiplexed); HBO HD; Showtime (multiplexed); Showtime HD; Starz (multiplexed); Starz HDTV; The Movie Channel.

Fee: $8.00 monthly (each).

Video-On-Demand: Yes

Pay-Per-View

Addressable homes: 22,600.

ESPN Extra (delivered digitally); iN DEMAND; iN DEMAND (delivered digitally); Hot Choice (delivered digitally); Playboy TV (delivered digitally).

Internet Service

Operational: Yes. Began: January 1, 2002.

Subscribers: 4,000.

Broadband Service: Comcast High Speed Internet.

Fee: $42.95 monthly; $3.00 modem lease.

Telephone Service

Digital: Operational

Fee: $44.95 monthly

Miles of Plant: 930.0 (coaxial); None (fiber optic).

Regional Vice President: Linda Hossinger. Vice President, Technical Operations: Randy Bender. Vice President, Marketing: Donna Corning. Vice President, Public Affairs: Jody Doherty.

Ownership: Comcast Cable Communications Inc. (MSO).

BETHLEHEM—Formerly served by NORTHAMPTON BOROUGH, PA [PA0008]. RCN Corp. This cable system has converted to IPTV, 196 Van Buren St, Herndon, VA 20170. Phone: 703-434-8200. Web Site: http://www.rcn.com. ICA: PA5204.

TV Market Ranking: Below 100 (BETHLEHEM).

Channel capacity: N.A. Channels available but not in use: N.A.

Internet Service

Operational: Yes.

Telephone Service

Digital: Operational

Chairman: Steven J. Simmons. Chief Executive Officer: Jim Holanda.

BETHLEHEM TWP.—Formerly served by NORTHAMPTON BOROUGH, PA [PA0008]. RCN Corp. This cable system has converted to IPTV, 196 Van Buren St, Herndon, VA 20170. Phone: 703-434-8200. Web Site: http://www.rcn.com. ICA: PA5205.

TV Market Ranking: Below 100 (BETHLEHEM TWP.).

Channel capacity: N.A. Channels available but not in use: N.A.

Internet Service

Operational: Yes.

Telephone Service

Digital: Operational

Chairman: Steven J. Simmons. Chief Executive Officer: Jim Holanda.

BIG POND—Formerly served by Barrett's TV Cable System. No longer in operation. ICA: PA0319.

BIGLER TWP.—Comcast Cable. Now served by PHILLIPSBURG, PA [PA0109]. ICA: PA0159.

BIRDSBORO—Service Electric Cablevision, 6400 Perkiomen Ave, PO Box 8, Birdsboro, PA 19508. Phones: 800-344-0347; 610-582-5317. Fax: 610-582-3094. E-mail: corporateoffice@secv.com. Web Site: http://www.secv.com. Also serves Amity Twp. (Berks County), Brecknock Twp. (Berks County), Caernarvon Twp. (Berks County), Caernarvon Twp. (Lancaster County), Cumru, District Twp., Earl Twp. (Lancaster County), East Nantheal Twp., Elverson Borough, Exeter Twp. (Berks County), Fleetwood, Honey Brook Borough, Honeybrook Twp. (Chester County), Kutztown, Longswamp Twp., Lyon Station, Maidencreek, Maidencreek Twp., Maxatawny Twp., Oley, Pike Twp., Richmond Twp., Robeson Twp., Rockland Twp., Ruscombmanor Twp., St. Lawrence, Topton, Union Twp. (Berks County), Warwick, Warwick Twp. (Berks County) & Warwick Twp. (Chester County). ICA: PA0070.

TV Market Ranking: 4 (Maidencreek, Oley, Warwick); 4,57 (Warwick Twp. (Chester County)); 57 (Amity Twp. (Berks County), BIRDSBORO, Brecknock Twp. (Berks County), Caernarvon Twp. (Berks County), Caernarvon Twp. (Lancaster County), Cumru, Earl Twp. (Lancaster County), East Nantheal Twp., Elverson Borough, Exeter Twp. (Berks County), Honey Brook Borough, Honeybrook Twp. (Chester County), Robeson Twp., St. Lawrence, Union Twp. (Berks County), Warwick Twp. (Berks County)); Below 100 (District Twp., Fleetwood, Kutztown, Longswamp Twp., Lyon Station, Maidencreek Twp., Maxatawny Twp., Pike Twp., Richmond Twp., Rockland Twp., Ruscombmanor Twp., Topton). Franchise award date: N.A. Franchise expiration date: N.A. Began: January 1, 1956.

Channel capacity: 75 (operating 2-way). Channels available but not in use: N.A.

Basic Service

Subscribers: 31,000.

Programming (received off-air): KYW-TV (CBS) Philadelphia; WCAU (NBC) Philadelphia; WFMZ-TV (IND) Allentown; WGAL (NBC) Lancaster; WGTW-TV (TBN) Burlington; WHYY-TV (PBS) Wilmington; WLVT-TV (PBS) Allentown; WLYH-TV (CW) Lancaster; WPHL-TV (MNT, IND) Philadelphia; WPMT (FOX) York; WPPX-TV (ION) Wilmington; WPSG (CW) Philadelphia; WPVI-TV (ABC) Philadelphia; WTVE (IND) Reading; WTXF-TV (FOX) Philadelphia; WUVP-DT (UNV) Vineland; allband FM.

Programming (via satellite): C-SPAN; Eternal Word TV Network; Headline News; Pennsylvania Cable Network; QVC; ShopNBC; The Weather Channel; Travel Channel.

Fee: $61.00 installation; $19.95 monthly.

Expanded Basic Service 1

Subscribers: 29,700.

Programming (via satellite): A&E Networks; ABC Family Channel; AMC; AmericanLife TV Network; Animal Planet; BET Networks; Bravo; Cartoon Network; CNBC; CNN; Comcast SportsNet Philadelphia; Comedy Central; Country Music TV; Discovery Channel; Discovery Fit & Health; Disney Channel; E! Entertainment Televi-

sion; ESPN; ESPN 2; ESPN Classic Sports; Food Network; Fox News Channel; FX; HGTV; History Channel; Lifetime; MSNBC; MTV; National Geographic Channel; NFL Network; Nickelodeon; Outdoor Channel; Speed; Spike TV; Syfy; TBS Superstation; The Learning Channel; Toon Disney; truTV; Turner Network TV; TV Land; USA Network; VH1; WE tv.
Fee: $26.95 monthly.

Digital Basic Service
Subscribers: N.A.
Programming (via satellite): 3 Angels Broadcasting Network; BBC America; Bio; Bloomberg Television; Boomerang; BYU Television; CBS Sports Network; Church Channel; CMT Pure Country; Colours; Cooking Channel; Current; Daystar TV Network; Discovery Health Channel; Discovery Home Channel; Discovery Kids Channel; Discovery Times Channel; DIY Network; ESPN 2 HD; ESPN HD; ESPN U; ESPNews; FamilyNet; Food Network HD; Fox College Sports Atlantic; Fox College Sports Central; Fox College Sports Pacific; Fox Movie Channel; Fox Reality Channel; Fox Soccer; Fox Sports World; Fuel TV; Fuse; G4; GAS; Golden Eagle Broadcasting; Golf Channel; Great American Country; Hallmark Channel; Hallmark Movie Channel; HD Theater; HDNet; HDNet Movies; HGTV HD; History Channel International; Independent Film Channel; INSP; JCTV; Lifetime Movie Network; Military Channel; MTV Hits; MTV Jams; MTV2; Music Choice; National Geographic Channel HD Network; NFL Network HD; NHL Network; Nick Jr.; Nick Too; NickToons TV; Outdoor Channel 2 HD; Ovation; Palladia; PBS Kids Sprout; Penn National Racing Alive; Science; Smile of a Child; SoapNet; Style Network; TBS in HD; Tennis Channel; Tr3s; Trinity Broadcasting Network; Turner Classic Movies; Turner Network TV HD; Universal HD; Versus; VH1 Classic; VH1 Soul; WealthTV HD.
Fee: $25.05 monthly.

Digital Pay Service 1
Pay Units: 21,648.
Programming (via satellite): Cinemax (multiplexed); Cinemax HD; Encore (multiplexed); Flix; HBO (multiplexed); HBO HD; Showtime (multiplexed); Showtime HD; Starz (multiplexed); Starz HDTV; The Movie Channel (multiplexed); The Movie Channel HD.
Fee: $31.00 installation; $11.50 monthly (Cinemax), $12.45 monthly (Starz/Encore), $14.45 monthly (HBO or Flix/Showtime//TMC).

Video-On-Demand: No

Pay-Per-View
Sports PPV (delivered digitally); iN DEMAND (delivered digitally).

Internet Service
Operational: Yes. Began: August 1, 2001.
Subscribers: 14,711.
Broadband Service: ProLog Express.
Fee: $61.00 installation; $22.95-$52.95 monthly; $4.95 modem lease; $99.95 modem purchase.

Telephone Service
Analog: Not Operational
Digital: Operational
Subscribers: 1,416.
Fee: $44.95 monthly

Miles of Plant: 1,146.0 (coaxial); 2,975.0 (fiber optic).

Manager: Karl Kowatch. Engineering Director: Jim Dorsa. Regulatory Affairs Director: Arlean Lilly. Customer Service Manager: Barb Fazekas.

Ownership: Service Electric Cable TV Inc. (MSO).

BLAIRSVILLE—Comcast Cable, 15 Summit Park Dr, Pittsburgh, PA 15275. Phones: 412-747-6400; 724-459-9042 (Blairsville office). Fax: 412-747-6401. Web Site: http://www.comcast.com. Also serves Aultman, Banks Twp., Barr Twp., Black Lick Twp., Bolivar, Buffington Twp., Burrell Twp. (Indiana County), Cambria Twp., Canoe Twp., Carrolltown Borough, Cherry Tree, Cherryhill Twp., Clarksburg, Clymer, Commodore (Indiana County), Creekside, Derry, Dixonville (Indiana County), East Carroll Twp., East Conemaugh, Ebensburg, Ernest, Glen Campbell, Green Twp. (Indiana County), Hastings, Homer City, Indiana, Latrobe, Laurel Mountain, Ligonier Twp., Loyalhanna Twp. (Westmoreland County), Marion Center, McIntyre, Monroeville, Patton, Pine Twp. (Indiana County), Rayne Twp. (portions), Saltsburg, South Fork, Starford, Unity Twp. (Westmoreland County), West Carroll Twp., West Wheatfield Twp. (Indiana County), Young Twp. (Indiana County) & Youngstown. ICA: PA0320.

TV Market Ranking: 10 (Latrobe, Loyalhanna Twp. (Westmoreland County), Monroeville); 10,74 (Saltsburg); 74 (Aultman, Banks Twp., Barr Twp., Black Lick Twp., BLAIRSVILLE, Bolivar, Buffington Twp., Burrell Twp. (Indiana County), Cambria Twp., Carrolltown Borough, Cherry Tree, Cherryhill Twp., Clarksburg, Clymer, Commodore (Indiana County), Creekside, Derry, Dixonville (Indiana County), East Carroll Twp., East Conemaugh, Ebensburg, Ernest, Glen Campbell, Green Twp. (Indiana County), Hastings, Homer City, Indiana, Laurel Mountain, Ligonier Twp., Marion Center, McIntyre, Patton, Pine Twp. (Indiana County), Rayne Twp. (portions), South Fork, Starford, Unity Twp. (Westmoreland County), West Carroll Twp., West Wheatfield Twp. (Indiana County), Young Twp. (Indiana County), Youngstown); Outside TV Markets (Canoe Twp.). Franchise award date: N.A. Franchise expiration date: N.A. Began: March 1, 1965.

Channel capacity: N.A. Channels available but not in use: N.A.

Basic Service
Subscribers: 48,711.
Programming (received off-air): KDKA-TV (CBS) Pittsburgh; WBGN-LD Pittsburgh; WINP-TV (IND, ION) Pittsburgh; WJAC-TV (NBC) Johnstown; WPCB-TV (IND) Greensburg; WPCW (CW) Jeannette; WPGH-TV (FOX) Pittsburgh; WPMY (MNT) Pittsburgh; WPSU-TV (PBS) Clearfield; WPXI (IND, NBC) Pittsburgh; WQED (PBS) Pittsburgh; WTAE-TV (ABC) Pittsburgh; WTAJ-TV (CBS) Altoona; allband FM.
Programming (via satellite): Fuse; QVC; TBS Superstation; WGN America.
Fee: $39.95 installation; $13.90 monthly.

Expanded Basic Service 1
Subscribers: 35,500.
Programming (via microwave): Pittsburgh Cable News Channel.
Programming (via satellite): A&E Networks; ABC Family Channel; AMC; Animal Planet; BET Networks; Bravo; Cartoon Network; CNBC; CNN; Comedy Central; Country Music TV; C-SPAN; C-SPAN 2; Discovery Channel; Disney Channel; E! Entertainment Television; ESPN; ESPN 2; Eternal Word TV Network; Food Network; Fox News Channel; FX; Golf Channel; Headline News; HGTV; History Channel; HRTV; ION Television; Lifetime; MSNBC; MTV; Nickelodeon; Oxygen; Pennsylvania Cable Network; Product Information Network; Root Sports Pittsburgh; Spike TV; Style Network; Syfy; The Learning Channel; The Weather Channel; Travel Channel; truTV; Turner Network TV; TV Guide Network; TV Land; USA Network; VH1.
Fee: $38.50 monthly.

Digital Basic Service
Subscribers: 9,000.
Programming (via satellite): AmericanLife TV Network; BBC America; Black Family Channel; Bloomberg Television; Discovery Fit & Health; Discovery Health Channel; Discovery Home Channel; Discovery Kids Channel; Discovery Times Channel; DIY Network; Fox Movie Channel; Fox Sports World; G4; GAS; Great American Country; GSN; INSP; Lifetime Movie Network; Military Channel; MTV Networks Digital Suite; National Geographic Channel; Nick Jr.; Nick Too; NickToons TV; Science; SoapNet; Speed; The Word Network; Toon Disney; Trinity Broadcasting Network; Turner Classic Movies; WE tv.
Fee: $15.95 monthly.

Digital Pay Service 1
Pay Units: 6,902.
Programming (via satellite): Cinemax (multiplexed); Encore (multiplexed); HBO (multiplexed); Music Choice; Showtime (multiplexed); Starz (multiplexed); The Movie Channel (multiplexed).
Fee: $15.95 monthly (each).

Video-On-Demand: Yes

Pay-Per-View
Addressable homes: 6,933.
HITS (Headend In The Sky) (delivered digitally); Hot Choice (delivered digitally); iN DEMAND; iN DEMAND (delivered digitally); Playboy TV (delivered digitally); Fresh (delivered digitally).

Internet Service
Operational: Yes.
Subscribers: 8,800.
Broadband Service: Comcast High Speed Internet.
Fee: $42.95 monthly.

Telephone Service
Digital: Operational
Fee: $44.95 monthly

Miles of Plant: 1,963.0 (coaxial); 930.0 (fiber optic).

Regional Vice President: Linda Hossinger. Vice President, Technical Operations: Randy Bender. Vice President, Marketing: Donna Corning. Vice President, Public Affairs: Jody Doherty.

Ownership: Comcast Cable Communications Inc. (MSO).

BLOOMSBURG—Service Electric Cable TV & Communications. Now served by SUNBURY, PA [PA0029]. ICA: PA0088.

BLOSSBURG—Formerly served by Williamson Road TV Co. Inc. No longer in operation. ICA: PA0321.

BOYERS—Formerly served by Cebridge Connections. Now served by GROVE CITY, PA [PA0089]. ICA: PA0276.

BRADFORD—Atlantic Broadband, 24 Main St, Bradford, PA 16701. Phones: 888-536-9600; 814-368-8590. Fax: 814-362-2190. E-mail: info@atlanticbb.com. Web Site: http://www.atlanticbb.com. Also serves Bradford Twp. (McKean County), Foster Twp. (McKean County) & Lewis Run. ICA: PA0085.

TV Market Ranking: Below 100 (BRADFORD, Bradford Twp. (McKean County), Foster Twp. (McKean County), Lewis Run). Franchise award date: April 16, 1954. Franchise expiration date: N.A. Began: April 16, 1954.

Channel capacity: N.A. Channels available but not in use: N.A.

Basic Service
Subscribers: 4,850.
Programming (received off-air): WGRZ (NBC) Buffalo; WICU-TV (NBC) Erie; WIVB-TV (CBS) Buffalo; WKBW-TV (ABC) Buffalo; WNYB (IND) Jamestown; WPSU-TV (PBS) Clearfield; WSEE-TV (CBS, CW) Erie; WUTV (FOX) Buffalo; allband FM.
Programming (via satellite): C-SPAN; Eternal Word TV Network; INSP; Jewelry Television; PBS World; Pennsylvania Cable Network; Product Information Network; QVC; TV Guide Network; WGN America.
Fee: $25.00 installation; $18.98 monthly; $1.60 converter.

Expanded Basic Service 1
Subscribers: N.A.
Programming (via satellite): A&E Networks; ABC Family Channel; AMC; Animal Planet; Bravo; Cartoon Network; CNBC; CNN; Comedy Central; Country Music TV; Discovery Channel; Discovery Health Channel; Disney Channel; E! Entertainment Television; ESPN; ESPN 2; ESPN Classic Sports; Food Network; Fox News Channel; FX; G4; Golf Channel; Hallmark Channel; Headline News; HGTV; History Channel; Lifetime; Lifetime Movie Network; MSG; MSNBC; MTV; National Geographic Channel; Nickelodeon; Outdoor Channel; Oxygen; Root Sports Pittsburgh; Speed; Spike TV; Style Network; Syfy; TBS Superstation; The Learning Channel; The Weather Channel; Travel Channel; truTV; Turner Classic Movies; Turner Network TV; TV Land; USA Network; VH1.
Fee: $37.47 monthly.

Digital Basic Service
Subscribers: N.A.
Programming (via satellite): A&E HD; Animal Planet HD; BBC America; Bio; Bloomberg Television; Boomerang; Chiller; CMT Pure Country; Discovery Channel HD; Discovery Kids Channel; Disney Channel HD; DIY Network; Encore (multiplexed); ESPN 2 HD; ESPN HD; ESPN U; ESPNews; Fuel TV; HD Theater; History Channel International; ID Investigation Discovery; Independent Film Channel; Military Channel; MTV Hits; MTV Jams; MTV2; Music Choice; NFL Network; NFL Network HD; Nick Jr.; Nick Too; NickToons TV; Planet Green; Root Sports Pittsburgh; Science; SoapNet; Starz (multiplexed); Syfy HD; TBS in HD; TeenNick; TLC HD; Toon Disney; Tr3s; Turner Network TV HD; USA Network HD; VH1 Classic; VH1 Soul; WE tv; Weatherscan.
Fee: $18.95 monthly.

Digital Pay Service 1
Pay Units: 400.
Programming (via satellite): HBO (multiplexed).
Fee: $15.95 monthly.

Digital Pay Service 2
Pay Units: 215.
Programming (via satellite): Cinemax (multiplexed).
Fee: $15.95 monthly.

Digital Pay Service 3
Pay Units: N.A.
Programming (via satellite): Flix; Showtime (multiplexed); The Movie Channel (multiplexed).
Fee: $15.95 monthly.

Video-On-Demand: No

Pay-Per-View
iN DEMAND (delivered digitally); Hot Choice (delivered digitally); Spice: Xcess (delivered digitally); Club Jenna (delivered digitally); Fresh (delivered digitally); Shorteez (delivered digitally); Playboy TV (delivered digitally).

Internet Service
Operational: Yes.
Broadband Service: Atlantic Broadband High-Speed Internet.
Fee: $24.95-$57.95 monthly.

Telephone Service
Digital: Operational
Fee: $44.95 monthly

Miles of Plant: 143.0 (coaxial); None (fiber optic).
Vice President: David Dane. General Manager: Mike Papasergi. Technical Operations Director: Charles Sorchilla. Chief Technician: Richard C. Himes. Marketing & Customer Service Director: Dara Leslie. Marketing Manager: Natalie Kurchak.
Ownership: Atlantic Broadband (MSO).

BRAVE—Zito Media, 611 Vader Hill Rd, Coudersport, PA 16915. Phone: 814-260-9575. Web Site: http://www.zitomedia.com. Also serves Spraggs (Greene County) & Wayne Twp., PA; Blacksville, Daybrook, Mooresville, Pentress, Wadestown & Wana, WV. ICA: PA0201.
TV Market Ranking: 90 (BRAVE, Spraggs (Greene County), Wadestown, Wana, Wayne Twp.); Below 100 (Blacksville, Daybrook, Mooresville, Pentress). Franchise award date: N.A. Franchise expiration date: N.A. Began: N.A.
Channel capacity: 39 (not 2-way capable). Channels available but not in use: N.A.

Basic Service
Subscribers: 407.
Programming (received off-air): KDKA-TV (CBS) Pittsburgh; WBOY-TV (NBC) Clarksburg; WDTV (CBS) Weston; WNPB-TV (PBS) Morgantown; WPGH-TV (FOX) Pittsburgh; WPMY (MNT) Pittsburgh; WPXI (IND, NBC) Pittsburgh; WQED (PBS) Pittsburgh; WTAE-TV (ABC) Pittsburgh; WTRF-TV (CBS) Wheeling.
Programming (via satellite): WGN America.
Fee: $29.95 installation; $19.95 monthly; $1.24 converter.

Expanded Basic Service 1
Subscribers: N.A.
Programming (via satellite): ABC Family Channel; AMC; Animal Planet; Cartoon Network; CNN; C-SPAN; Discovery Channel; Disney Channel; E! Entertainment Television; ESPN; ESPN 2; Fox News Channel; FX; Golf Channel; Great American Country; GSN; HGTV; History Channel; Lifetime; Nickelodeon; Outdoor Channel; Root Sports Pittsburgh; Speed; Spike TV; Syfy; TBS Superstation; The Learning Channel; The Weather Channel; Trinity Broadcasting Network; Turner Network TV; USA Network; WE tv.
Fee: $16.93 monthly.

Digital Basic Service
Subscribers: N.A.
Programming (via satellite): Bio; Bloomberg Television; cloo; Discovery Digital Networks; DMX Music; ESPN Classic Sports; ESPNews; Fox College Sports Atlantic; Fox College Sports Central; Fox College Sports Pacific; Fox Movie Channel; Fox Soccer; Fuse; G4; History Channel International; Independent Film Channel; Lifetime Movie Network; National Geographic Channel; ShopNBC; Style Network; Turner Classic Movies; Versus.

Pay Service 1
Pay Units: 574.
Programming (via satellite): Cinemax; HBO; Showtime.
Fee: $7.95 monthly (Cinemax), $11.95 monthly (HBO or Showtime).

Pay Service 2
Pay Units: N.A.
Programming (via satellite): Encore; The Movie Channel.
Fee: $3.99 monthly (Encore), $11.95 monthly (TMC).

Digital Pay Service 1
Pay Units: N.A.
Programming (via satellite): Cinemax (multiplexed); Encore (multiplexed); Flix; HBO (multiplexed); Showtime (multiplexed); Starz (multiplexed); The Movie Channel (multiplexed).

Video-On-Demand: No

Pay-Per-View
iN DEMAND (delivered digitally); Playboy TV (delivered digitally); Fresh (delivered digitally).

Internet Service
Operational: No.

Telephone Service
None

Miles of Plant: 45.0 (coaxial); None (fiber optic).
Public Relations Manager: Mark Laver.
Ownership: Zito Media (MSO).

BROAD TOP CITY—Formerly served by Adelphia Communications. Now served by HUNTINGDON, PA [PA0107]. ICA: PA0224.

BROCKWAY—Brockway TV Inc., 501 Main St, Brockway, PA 15824-1326. Phone: 814-268-6565. Fax: 814-265-1300. Also serves Horton Twp. (Elk County), Snyder Twp. (Jefferson County) & Washington Twp. (Jefferson County). ICA: PA0182.
TV Market Ranking: Outside TV Markets (BROCKWAY, Horton Twp. (Elk County), Snyder Twp. (Jefferson County), Washington Twp. (Jefferson County)). Franchise award date: N.A. Franchise expiration date: N.A. Began: April 1, 1952.
Channel capacity: 60 (operating 2-way). Channels available but not in use: N.A.

Basic Service
Subscribers: 1,900.
Programming (received off-air): KDKA-TV (CBS) Pittsburgh; WATM-TV (ABC) Altoona; WJAC-TV (NBC) Johnstown; WKBS-TV (IND) Altoona; WPCW (CW) Jeannette; WPGH-TV (FOX) Pittsburgh; WPMY (MNT) Pittsburgh; WPSU-TV (PBS) Clearfield; WPXI (IND, NBC) Pittsburgh; WQED (PBS) Pittsburgh; WTAE-TV (ABC) Pittsburgh; WTAJ-TV (CBS) Altoona; WWCP-TV (FOX) Johnstown; 18 FMs.
Programming (via satellite): A&E Networks; ABC Family Channel; AMC; Cartoon Network; CNN; Country Music TV; Discovery Channel; ESPN; ESPN 2; Eternal Word TV Network; Fox Movie Channel; FX; Headline News; History Channel; Lifetime; National Geographic Channel; Nickelodeon; Outdoor Channel; Pennsylvania Cable Network; QVC; Root Sports Pittsburgh; Spike TV; TBS Superstation; The Learning Channel; The Weather Channel; Turner Classic Movies; Turner Network TV; USA Network; VH1; WGN America.
Fee: $28.00 monthly.

Digital Basic Service
Subscribers: N.A.
Programming (via satellite): AmericanLife TV Network; BBC America; Bio; Black Family Channel; Bloomberg Television; cloo; Current; Discovery Fit & Health; DMX Music; Fox Movie Channel; Fuse; G4; GAS; Great American Country; GSN; Halogen Network; HGTV; History Channel; History Channel International; Lifetime Movie Network; Lime; MTV Networks Digital Suite; National Geographic Channel; Nick Jr.; NickToons TV; Ovation; Style Network; Sundance Channel; Syfy; The Word Network; Trinity Broadcasting Network; Turner Classic Movies; WE tv.
Fee: $12.95 monthly; $6.25 converter.

Digital Expanded Basic Service
Subscribers: N.A.
Programming (via satellite): ESPN 2; ESPN Classic Sports; ESPNews; Fox Soccer; FSN Digital Atlantic; FSN Digital Central; FSN Digital Pacific; Golf Channel; Outdoor Channel; Speed; Versus.
Fee: $4.95 monthly.

Digital Pay Service 1
Pay Units: N.A.
Programming (via satellite): Cinemax (multiplexed); Encore (multiplexed); Flix; HBO (multiplexed); Showtime (multiplexed); Starz (multiplexed); Sundance Channel; The Movie Channel (multiplexed).
Fee: $11.50 monthly (Showtime, Cinemax, or Starz/Encore), $14.00 monthly (HBO).

Video-On-Demand: No

Internet Service
Operational: Yes.
Broadband Service: In-house.
Fee: $20.00 installation; $24.95 monthly.

Telephone Service
None

Miles of Plant: 55.0 (coaxial); None (fiber optic).
Manager: Laurie Wayne. Chief Technician: Howard Olay.
Ownership: Brockway TV Inc.

BRUSH VALLEY TWP.—Formerly served by Brush Valley Cablevision. No longer in operation. ICA: PA0322.

BURGETTSTOWN—Blue Devil Cable TV Inc., 116 S 4th St, Toronto, OH 43964-1368. Phone: 800-931-9392. Fax: 740-537-2802. Also serves Atlasburg, Bulger, Joffre, Langeloth, Slovan & Smith Twp. (Washington County). ICA: PA0323.
TV Market Ranking: 10,90 (Atlasburg, Bulger, BURGETTSTOWN, Joffre, Langeloth, Slovan, Smith Twp. (Washington County)). Franchise award date: N.A. Franchise expiration date: N.A. Began: October 1, 1974.
Channel capacity: 22 (not 2-way capable). Channels available but not in use: N.A.

Basic Service
Subscribers: 2,700.
Programming (received off-air): KDKA-TV (CBS) Pittsburgh; WPGH-TV (FOX) Pittsburgh; WPMY (MNT) Pittsburgh; WPXI (IND, NBC) Pittsburgh; WQED (PBS) Pittsburgh; WTAE-TV (ABC) Pittsburgh; WTOV-TV (IND, NBC) Steubenville; WTRF-TV (CBS) Wheeling.
Programming (via satellite): ABC Family Channel; CNN; ESPN; Lifetime; MTV; Nickelodeon; TBS Superstation; Turner Network TV; USA Network; WGN America.
Fee: $25.00 installation; $8.19 monthly.

Pay Service 1
Pay Units: 221.
Programming (via satellite): HBO; The Movie Channel.
Fee: $10.60 monthly (TMC), $11.66 monthly (HBO).

Video-On-Demand: No

Internet Service
Operational: No.

Telephone Service
None

Miles of Plant: 23.0 (coaxial); None (fiber optic). Additional miles planned: 15.0 (coaxial).
Vice President: David Bates. General Manager: Robert Loveridge. Office Manager: Joanne Conner.
Ownership: Blue Devil Cable TV Inc. (MSO).

BUSHKILL TWP.—Formerly served by NORTHAMPTON BOROUGH, PA [PA0008]. RCN Corp. This cable system has converted to IPTV, 196 Van Buren St, Herndon, VA 20170. Phone: 703-434-8200. Web Site: http://www.rcn.com. ICA: PA5206.
TV Market Ranking: Below 100 (BUSHKILL TWP.).
Channel capacity: N.A. Channels available but not in use: N.A.

Internet Service
Operational: Yes.

Telephone Service
Digital: Operational

Chairman: Steven J. Simmons. Chief Executive Officer: Jim Holanda.

BUTLER—Armstrong Cable Services, 660 S Benbrook Rd, Butler, PA 16001. Phones: 877-277-5711; 724-482-4885; 724-283-0925 (Corporate office). Fax: 724-482-4884. E-mail: info@zoominternet.net. Web Site: http://cable.armstrongonewire.com. Also serves Brady Twp., Bradys Bend Twp., Bruin, Buffalo Twp. (Butler County), Butler Twp. (Butler County), Center Twp. (Butler County), Cherry Twp., Chicora, Connoquenessing Twp. (Butler County), East Brady, East Butler, Forward Twp., Karns City, Parker Twp., Petrolia, Prospect, Saxonburg & W. Sunbury. ICA: PA0044. **Note:** This system is an overbuild.
TV Market Ranking: 10 (Buffalo Twp. (Butler County), BUTLER, Butler Twp. (Butler County), Center Twp. (Butler County), Connoquenessing Twp. (Butler County), East Butler, Forward Twp., Prospect, Saxonburg); Below 100 (Brady Twp., Cherry Twp., W. Sunbury); Outside TV Markets (Bradys Bend Twp., Bruin, Chicora, East Brady, Karns City, Parker Twp., Petrolia). Franchise award date: October 21, 1963. Franchise expiration date: N.A. Began: April 1, 1964.
Channel capacity: N.A. Channels available but not in use: N.A.

Digital Basic Service
Subscribers: 7,564.
Programming (via satellite): A&E Networks; ABC Family Channel; AMC; Animal Planet; Bravo; Cartoon Network; CNBC; CNN; Comedy Central; Country Music TV; C-SPAN; Discovery Channel; Disney Channel; E! Entertainment Television; ESPN; ESPN 2; Eternal Word TV Network; Food Network; Fox News Channel; FX; Headline News; HGTV; History Channel; INSP; Lifetime; MSNBC; MTV; Music Choice; Nickelodeon; NickToons TV; Pennsylvania Cable Network; Pentagon Channel; Pittsburgh Cable News Channel; QVC; Root Sports Pittsburgh; ShopNBC; Spike TV; Syfy; TBS Superstation; The Learning Channel; The Weather Channel; Travel Channel; truTV; Turner Classic Movies; Turner Network TV; TV Guide Network; TV Land; USA Network; VH1.
Fee: $35.00 installation; $51.40 monthly.

Digital Expanded Basic Service
Subscribers: N.A.
Programming (via satellite): AmericanLife TV Network; BBC America; Bio; Bloomberg Television; Boomerang; Chiller; cloo; CMT

Pure Country; Cooking Channel; Discovery Fit & Health; Discovery Health Channel; Discovery Kids Channel; DIY Network; ESPN Classic Sports; ESPN U; ESPNews; G4; Golf Channel; Great American Country; GSN; Hallmark Channel; Hallmark Movie Channel; History Channel International; HRTV; ID Investigation Discovery; Jewelry Television; Lifetime Movie Network; Military Channel; MTV Hits; MTV Jams; MTV2; mun2 television; National Geographic Channel; NFL Network; NHL Network; Nick Jr.; Nick Too; Outdoor Channel; Oxygen; PBS Kids Sprout; Pentagon Channel; Planet Green; RFD-TV; RTN; Science; SoapNet; Speed; TeenNick; Tennis Channel; Toon Disney; Tr3s; Versus; VH1 Classic; VH1 Soul; WE tv.
Fee: $12.00 monthly.

Digital Expanded Basic Service 2
Subscribers: N.A.
Programming (received off-air): KDKA-TV (CBS) Pittsburgh; WPCW (CW) Jeannette; WPGH-TV (FOX) Pittsburgh; WPXI (IND, NBC) Pittsburgh; WQED (PBS) Pittsburgh; WTAE-TV (ABC) Pittsburgh.
Programming (via satellite): A&E HD; Animal Planet HD; Bravo HD; CNN HD; Discovery Channel HD; Disney Channel HD; ESPN 2 HD; ESPN HD; Food Network HD; Fox News HD; FSN HD; FX HD; Golf Channel HD; Hallmark Movie Channel HD; HD Theater; HDNet; HDNet Movies; HGTV HD; History Channel HD; MGM HD; National Geographic Channel HD Network; NFL Network HD; NHL Network HD; Outdoor Channel 2 HD; QVC HD; Science HD; Syfy HD; TBS in HD; The Weather Channel HD; TLC HD; Turner Network TV HD; Universal HD; USA Network HD; Versus HD; WealthTV HD.
Fee: $9.00 monthly.

Digital Pay Service 1
Pay Units: N.A.
Programming (via satellite): Cinemax (multiplexed); Cinemax HD; Encore (multiplexed); Flix; HBO (multiplexed); HBO HD; RAI USA; Showtime (multiplexed); Showtime HD; Starz (multiplexed); Starz HDTV; The Movie Channel (multiplexed); TV5 USA.
Fee: $13.95 monthly (HBO, Cinemax, Showtime/TMC/Flix or Starz/Encore).

Video-On-Demand: Yes

Pay-Per-View
Addressable homes: 2,661.
ESPN Sports (delivered digitally); ESPN Now (delivered digitally); Hot Choice (delivered digitally); iN DEMAND (delivered digitally); NHL/MLB (delivered digitally).

Internet Service
Operational: Yes. Began: April 1, 1998.
Subscribers: 15,219.
Broadband Service: Armstrong Zoom.
Fee: $26.95-$39.95 monthly.

Telephone Service
Digital: Operational
Fee: $49.95 monthly

Miles of Plant: 856.0 (coaxial); None (fiber optic). Additional miles planned: 217.0 (coaxial); 15.0 (fiber optic).
Vice President, Marketing: Jud Stewart. General Manager: Joe Taylor. Chief Engineer: Barry Osche. Marketing Manager: Andrea Lucas. Program Director: Matt Lutz. Customer Service Manager: Connie Swartzfeger.
Ownership: Armstrong Group of Companies (MSO).

CALIFORNIA—Armstrong Communications Inc. Now served by CONNELLSVILLE, PA [PA0046]. ICA: PA0099.

CALLENSBURG—Formerly served by Cebridge Connections. Now served by MEADVILLE, PA [PA0062]. ICA: PA0258.

CAMP HILL CORRECTIONAL INSTITUTE—Suddenlink Communications, 12444 Powerscourt Dr, Saint Louis, MO 63131-3660. Phone: 314-965-2020. Web Site: http://www.suddenlink.com. ICA: PA0324.
TV Market Ranking: 57 (CAMP HILL CORRECTIONAL). Franchise award date: October 1, 1985. Franchise expiration date: N.A. Began: October 1, 1985.
Channel capacity: 12 (not 2-way capable). Channels available but not in use: N.A.

Basic Service
Subscribers: 450.
Programming (received off-air): WGAL (NBC) Lancaster; WHP-TV (CBS, MNT) Harrisburg; WHTM-TV (ABC) Harrisburg; WITF-TV (PBS) Harrisburg; WLYH-TV (CW) Lancaster.
Programming (via satellite): ABC Family Channel; BET Networks; ESPN; TBS Superstation.
Fee: $10.45 monthly.

Internet Service
Operational: No.

Telephone Service
None

Miles of Plant: 3.0 (coaxial); None (fiber optic).
Ownership: Cequel Communications LLC (MSO).

CANADOHTA LAKE—Master Vision, 25167 Weed Rd, Union City, PA 16438. Phones: 888-827-2259; 814-694-3682. ICA: PA0446.
TV Market Ranking: Below 100 (CANADOHTA LAKE). Franchise award date: N.A. Franchise expiration date: N.A. Began: N.A.
Channel capacity: N.A. Channels available but not in use: N.A.

Basic Service
Subscribers: 280.
Programming (received off-air): WFMJ-TV (CW, NBC) Youngstown; WFXP (FOX) Erie; WICU-TV (NBC) Erie; WJET-TV (ABC) Erie; WKBN-TV (CBS) Youngstown; WQLN (PBS) Erie; WSEE-TV (CBS, CW) Erie.
Programming (via satellite): A&E Networks; ABC Family Channel; CNN; Discovery Channel; ESPN; ESPN 2; Great American Country; Headline News; History Channel; Lifetime; MTV; Nickelodeon; QVC; Root Sports Pittsburgh; Spike TV; Syfy; TBS Superstation; The Learning Channel; The Weather Channel; Turner Classic Movies; Turner Network TV; TV Land; USA Network; WGN America.
Fee: $50.00 installation; $36.00 monthly; $8.75 additional installation.

Pay Service 1
Pay Units: 45.
Programming (via satellite): HBO.
Fee: $11.50 monthly.

Pay Service 2
Pay Units: 25.
Programming (via satellite): Showtime.
Fee: $11.50 monthly.

Internet Service
Operational: Yes.

Telephone Service
None

: Chris Wright.
Ownership: Master Vision Cable (MSO).

CANOE CREEK—Atlantic Broadband. Now served by ALTOONA, PA [PA0018]. ICA: PA0439.

CANONSBURG—Comcast Cable. Now served by PITTSBURGH, PA [PA0001]. ICA: PA0057.

CANTON—Zito Media, 611 Vader Hill Rd, Coudersport, PA 16915. Phone: 570-673-5326. Web Site: http://www.zitomedia.com. Also serves Alba, Canton Twp. (Bradford County), East Canton & Grover. ICA: PA0184.
TV Market Ranking: Below 100 (Alba, CANTON, Canton Twp. (Bradford County), East Canton, Grover). Franchise award date: N.A. Franchise expiration date: N.A. Began: May 1, 1956.
Channel capacity: N.A. Channels available but not in use: N.A.

Basic Service
Subscribers: 1,400.
Programming (received off-air): WBRE-TV (NBC) Wilkes-Barre; WNEP-TV (ABC) Scranton; WOLF-TV (CW, FOX, MNT) Hazleton; WQMY (MNT) Williamsport; WSKG-TV (PBS) Binghamton; WSWB (CW) Scranton; WVIA-TV (PBS) Scranton; WYOU (CBS) Scranton; allband FM.
Programming (via satellite): Discovery Channel; ESPN; Hallmark Channel; Lifetime.
Fee: $23.00 monthly.

Expanded Basic Service 1
Subscribers: N.A.
Programming (via satellite): ABC Family Channel; CNBC; Disney Channel; HGTV; MTV; Nickelodeon; TBS Superstation; Turner Network TV; USA Network.
Fee: $14.00 monthly.

Expanded Basic Service 2
Subscribers: N.A.
Programming (received off-air): WETM-TV (NBC) Elmira.
Programming (via satellite): A&E Networks; Animal Planet; CNN; Comedy Central; ESPN 2; Food Network; Fox News Channel; FX; Great American Country; Headline News; History Channel; Outdoor Channel; QVC; Speed; Spike TV; Syfy; The Learning Channel; The Weather Channel; Trinity Broadcasting Network; Turner Classic Movies; TV Land; VH1; WGN America.
Fee: $11.00 monthly.

Pay Service 1
Pay Units: 200.
Programming (via satellite): HBO.
Fee: $11.00 monthly.

Video-On-Demand: No

Internet Service
Operational: No.

Telephone Service
None

Miles of Plant: 41.0 (coaxial); 70.0 (fiber optic). Additional miles planned: 3.0 (coaxial).
Manager: Terry W. Hughes.
Ownership: Zito Media (MSO).

CARBONDALE—Adams Digital Cable, 19 N Main St, Carbondale, PA 18407-2303. Phones: 888-222-0077; 570-282-6121. Fax: 570-282-3787. E-mail: frontdesk@echoes.net. Web Site: http://www.adamscable.com. Also serves Afton (southwestern portion), Colesville, Deposit, Kirkwood (portions), Sanford, Windsor (Broome County) & Windsor (village), NY; Aldenville, Ararat Twp., Browndale, Canaan Twp. (Lackawanna County), Carbondale Twp. (Lackawanna County), Clifford Twp. (Susquehanna County), Clinton Twp. (Wayne County), Coxton Lake, Dyberry Twp., Farview State Hospital, Fell Twp. (Lackawanna County), Forest City, Gibson Twp., Great Bend, Great Bend Borough, Great Bend Twp., Greenfield Twp. (Lackawanna County), Hallstead, Hallstead (Susquehanna County), Hamlin, Harmony Twp., Herrick Twp., Hollisterville, Independent Lake, Jackson Twp., Jefferson Twp. (Lackawanna County), Jermyn, Lake Ariel, Lake Lorain, Lake Twp. (Wayne County), Lakeville, Lanesboro, Lenox Twp. (Susquehanna County), Madison Twp. (Lackawanna County), Mayfield, Mount Pleasant Twp. (Wayne County), New Milford (Susquehanna County), New Milford Borough, New Milford Twp., Oakland Borough, Oakland Twp., Orson, Paupack Twp. (Wayne County), Pleasant Mount, Poyntelle, Preston Twp., Prompton, Richmondale Village, Salem Twp. (Wayne County), Scott Twp. (Wayne County), Seelyville (Wayne County), Simpson, South Canaan Twp., South Sterling, Spruce Lake, Starrucca, Sterling, Sterling Twp. (Wayne County), Summit Lake, Susquehanna Depot Borough, The Hideout, Thompson Borough, Thompson Twp., Uniondale, Vandling, Wallenpaupack Lake Estates, Waymart & Wrighter Lake, PA. ICA: PA0067.
TV Market Ranking: 49 (Aldenville, Browndale, Canaan Twp. (Lackawanna County), CARBONDALE, Carbondale Twp. (Lackawanna County), Clifford Twp. (Susquehanna County), Clinton Twp. (Wayne County), Coxton Lake, Dyberry Twp., Farview State Hospital, Fell Twp. (Lackawanna County), Forest City, Gibson Twp., Greenfield Twp. (Lackawanna County), Hamlin, Herrick Twp., Hollisterville, Independent Lake, Jackson Twp., Jefferson Twp. (Lackawanna County), Jermyn, Lake Ariel, Lake Lorain, Lake Twp. (Wayne County), Lakeville, Lenox Twp. (Susquehanna County), Madison Twp. (Lackawanna County), Mayfield, Mount Pleasant Twp. (Wayne County), New Milford (Susquehanna County), New Milford Borough, New Milford Twp., Orson, Paupack Twp. (Wayne County), Pleasant Mount, Poyntelle, Preston Twp., Prompton, Richmondale Village, Salem Twp. (Wayne County), Scott Twp. (Wayne County), Seelyville (Wayne County), Simpson, South Canaan Twp., South Sterling, Spruce Lake, Starrucca, Sterling, Sterling Twp. (Wayne County), Summit Lake, Susquehanna Depot Borough, The Hideout, Thompson Borough, Uniondale, Vandling, Wallenpaupack Lake Estates, Waymart); Below 100 (Afton (southwestern portion), Ararat Twp., Colesville, Deposit, Great Bend, Great Bend Borough, Great Bend Twp., Hallstead, Hallstead (Susquehanna County), Harmony Twp., Kirkwood (portions), Lanesboro, Oakland Borough, Oakland Twp., Sanford, Windsor (Broome County), Windsor (village)). Franchise award date: February 1, 1965. Franchise expiration date: N.A. Began: July 1, 1962.
Channel capacity: 110 (operating 2-way). Channels available but not in use: N.A.

Basic Service
Subscribers: 22,300.
Programming (received off-air): WBRE-TV (NBC) Wilkes-Barre; WNEP-TV (ABC) Scranton; WOLF-TV (CW, FOX, MNT) Hazleton; WQMY (MNT) Williamsport; WQPX-TV (ION) Scranton; WSWB (CW) Scranton; WVIA-TV (PBS) Scranton; WYOU (CBS) Scranton.
Programming (via satellite): C-SPAN; Eternal Word TV Network; Pennsylvania Cable Network; QVC; The Weather Channel; TV Guide Network.
Fee: $40.00 installation; $16.99 monthly.

Expanded Basic Service 1
Subscribers: N.A.
Programming (via satellite): A&E Networks; ABC Family Channel; AMC; Animal Planet; Bravo; Cartoon Network; CNBC; CNN;

Comcast SportsNet Philadelphia; Comedy Central; Country Music TV; Discovery Channel; Disney Channel; E! Entertainment Television; ESPN; ESPN 2; ESPN Classic Sports; Food Network; Fox News Channel; FX; Golf Channel; GSN; Hallmark Channel; Headline News; HGTV; History Channel; Lifetime; Lifetime Movie Network; MSNBC; MTV; National Geographic Channel; NFL Network; Nickelodeon; Speed; Spike TV; Syfy; TBS Superstation; The Learning Channel; Travel Channel; truTV; Turner Classic Movies; Turner Network TV; TV Land; USA Network; Versus; VH1; WE tv; Yankees Entertainment & Sports.
Fee: $27.00 monthly.

Digital Basic Service
Subscribers: N.A.
Programming (via satellite): ABC News Now; AmericanLife TV Network; Bio; Boomerang; cloo; CNN International; Discovery Health Channel; Discovery Kids Channel; DIY Network; Fox Movie Channel; Fuse; Great American Country; Halogen Network; History Channel International; ID Investigation Discovery; ION Life; Military Channel; MTV2; NASA TV; Nick Jr.; Nick Too; NickToons TV; Outdoor Channel; Ovation; Oxygen; PBS Kids Sprout; Planet Green; Qubo; RFD-TV; Science; SoapNet; Style Network; TeenNick; Telemundo; Toon Disney; Worship Network.
Fee: $8.00 monthly.

Digital Expanded Basic Service
Subscribers: N.A.
Programming (via satellite): BBC America; Bloomberg Television; CBS Sports Network; CMT Pure Country; CNBC World; Cooking Channel; Crime & Investigation Network; Current; Discovery Fit & Health; ESPN U; ESPNews; Fox College Sports Atlantic; Fox College Sports Central; Fox College Sports Pacific; Fox Soccer; Fuel TV; G4; Hallmark Channel; Hallmark Movie Channel; HRTV; Lifetime Movie Network; Lifetime Real Women; LOGO; Military History Channel; MTV Hits; MTV Jams; NBA TV; Nuvo TV; Tennis Channel; VH1 Classic; VH1 Soul; WealthTV; WGN America.
Fee: $8.00 monthly.

Pay Service 1
Pay Units: N.A.
Programming (via satellite): HBO (multiplexed).
Fee: $15.00 installation; $12.00 monthly.

Digital Pay Service 1
Pay Units: N.A.
Programming (via satellite): Cinemax (multiplexed); Encore (multiplexed); Flix; HBO (multiplexed); Showtime (multiplexed); Starz (multiplexed); The Movie Channel (multiplexed).
Fee: $14.99 monthly (Starz/Encore), $16.99 monthly (Showtime/TMC/Flix), $19.99 monthly (HBO/Showtime).

Video-On-Demand: No

Pay-Per-View
iN DEMAND (delivered digitally); Playboy TV (delivered digitally); Club Jenna (delivered digitally); Spice: Xcess (delivered digitally); Shorteez (delivered digitally); Hustler TV (delivered digitally); Hot Choice (delivered digitally).

Internet Service
Operational: Yes. Began: June 1, 1998.
Subscribers: 50,000.
Broadband Service: Adams CATV.
Fee: $40.00 installation; $24.99-$59.99 monthly.

Telephone Service
Digital: Operational
Fee: $29.99 monthly

Miles of Plant: 900.0 (coaxial); 175.0 (fiber optic).
President: Doug Adams. General Manager: Wendy Hartman. Chief Technician: John Wallis. Collections Manager: Ed Burell. Office Manager: Becky Oakley.
Ownership: Adams CATV Inc. (MSO).

CARLISLE—Comcast Cable. Now served by SHIPPENSBURG, PA [PA0066]. ICA: PA0047.

CARNEGIE—Comcast Cable. Now served by PITTSBURGH, PA [PA0001]. ICA: PA0045.

CARROLLTOWN—Formerly served by Adelphia Communications. Now served by BLAIRSVILLE, PA [PA0320]. ICA: PA0461.

CARROLLTOWN BOROUGH—Formerly served by Adelphia Communications. Now served by BLAIRSVILLE, PA [PA0320]. ICA: PA0078.

CASTLE SHANNON—Comcast Cable. Now served by PITTSBURGH, PA [PA0001]. ICA: PA0457.

CATASAUQUA BOROUGH—Formerly served by NORTHAMPTON BOROUGH, PA [PA0008]. RCN Corp. This cable system has converted to IPTV, 196 Van Buren St, Herndon, VA 20170. Phone: 703-434-8200. Web Site: http://www.rcn.com. ICA: PA5207.
TV Market Ranking: Below 100 (CATASAUQUA BOROUGH).
Channel capacity: N.A. Channels available but not in use: N.A.

Internet Service
Operational: Yes.

Telephone Service
Digital: Operational
Chairman: Steven J. Simmons. Chief Executive Officer: Jim Holanda.

CENTRAL CITY BOROUGH—Comcast Cable, 15 Summit Park Dr, Pittsburgh, PA 15275. Phones: 412-747-6400; 814-344-8055 (Carrolltown office). Fax: 412-747-6401. Web Site: http://www.comcast.com. Also serves Berlin Borough, Black Twp., Boswell, Brothersvalley Twp., Casselman, Central City, Hooversville, Hyndman Borough, Indian Lake, Jenners, Jennerstown, Lincoln, Paint Twp. (Somerset County), Quemahoning Twp. (Somerset County), Rockwood, Shade Twp. (Somerset County), Somerset Borough, Stonycreek Twp. (Somerset County) & Stoystown. ICA: PA0132.
TV Market Ranking: 74 (Berlin Borough, Black Twp., Boswell, Brothersvalley Twp., Casselman, Central City, CENTRAL CITY BOROUGH, Hooversville, Indian Lake, Jenners, Jennerstown, Lincoln, Paint Twp. (Somerset County), Quemahoning Twp. (Somerset County), Rockwood, Shade Twp. (Somerset County), Shanksville, Somerset, Somerset Borough, Stonycreek Twp. (Somerset County), Stoystown); Outside TV Markets (Hyndman Borough). Franchise award date: N.A. Franchise expiration date: N.A. Began: June 1, 1973.
Channel capacity: N.A. Channels available but not in use: N.A.

Basic Service
Subscribers: N.A. Included in Bensalem Twp.
Programming (received off-air): KDKA-TV (CBS) Pittsburgh; WATM-TV (ABC) Altoona; WJAC-TV (NBC) Johnstown; WPCB-TV (IND) Greensburg; WPSU-TV (PBS) Clearfield; WTAE-TV (ABC) Pittsburgh; WTAJ-TV (CBS) Altoona; WWCP-TV (FOX) Johnstown; allband FM.
Programming (via satellite): Discovery Channel; FX; QVC; TBS Superstation; The Weather Channel; TV Guide Network.
Fee: $39.95 installation; $11.65 monthly; $1.60 converter.

Expanded Basic Service 1
Subscribers: 2,347.
Programming (via satellite): A&E Networks; ABC Family Channel; AMC; Animal Planet; Cartoon Network; CNN; Country Music TV; C-SPAN; Disney Channel; ESPN; Eternal Word TV Network; Fox News Channel; Hallmark Channel; Headline News; HGTV; ION Television; Lifetime; MoviePlex; MTV; Nickelodeon; Root Sports Pittsburgh; Spike TV; The Learning Channel; truTV; Turner Classic Movies; Turner Network TV; USA Network.
Fee: $18.34 monthly.

Digital Basic Service
Subscribers: N.A.
Programming (via satellite): BBC America; Bravo; Discovery Digital Networks; DMX Music; Encore (multiplexed); ESPN 2; ESPN Classic Sports; Fox Soccer; Golf Channel; GSN; History Channel; Independent Film Channel; Nick Jr.; Outdoor Channel; Speed; Syfy; TV Land; Versus; VH1 Country; WE tv.
Fee: $10.95 monthly; $3.40 converter.

Digital Pay Service 1
Pay Units: N.A.
Programming (via satellite): HBO (multiplexed); Showtime (multiplexed); Starz (multiplexed); The Movie Channel (multiplexed).
Fee: $15.95 monthly (each).

Video-On-Demand: Yes

Pay-Per-View
Hot Choice; Playboy TV; Spice; Movies.

Internet Service
Operational: Yes.
Broadband Service: Comcast High Speed Internet.
Fee: $42.95 monthly.

Telephone Service
None
Miles of Plant: 111.0 (coaxial); None (fiber optic).
Regional Vice President: Linda Hossinger. Vice President, Technical Operations: Randy Bender. Vice President, Marketing: Donna Corning. Vice President, Public Affairs: Jody Doherty. Manager: Diane Kirsh.
Ownership: Comcast Cable Communications Inc. (MSO).

CHAPMAN BOROUGH—Formerly served by NORTHAMPTON BOROUGH, PA [PA0008]. RCN Corp. This cable system has converted to IPTV, 196 Van Buren St, Herndon, VA 20170. Phone: 703-434-8200. Web Site: http://www.rcn.com. ICA: PA5208.
TV Market Ranking: Below 100 (CHAPMAN BOROUGH).
Channel capacity: N.A. Channels available but not in use: N.A.

Internet Service
Operational: Yes.

Telephone Service
Digital: Operational
Chairman: Steven J. Simmons. Chief Executive Officer: Jim Holanda.

CHICORA—Armstrong Cable Services. Now served by BUTLER, PA [PA0044]. ICA: PA0206.

CLARENDON—Clarendon TV Association, PO Box 315, Clarendon, PA 16313-0315. Phones: 814-723-6011; 814-726-3972 (Administrative office). Also serves Clarendon Heights & Stoneham. ICA: PA0240.
TV Market Ranking: Below 100 (CLARENDON, Clarendon Heights, Stoneham). Franchise award date: N.A. Franchise expiration date: N.A. Began: January 1, 1955.
Channel capacity: 36 (not 2-way capable). Channels available but not in use: N.A.

Basic Service
Subscribers: 400.
Programming (received off-air): WFXP (FOX) Erie; WICU-TV (NBC) Erie; WIVB-TV (CBS) Buffalo; WJET-TV (ABC) Erie; WPSU-TV (PBS) Clearfield; allband FM.
Programming (via satellite): Discovery Channel; ESPN; Nickelodeon; Spike TV; TBS Superstation; Turner Network TV; USA Network; WGN America.
Fee: $22.50 installation; $8.33 monthly.

Video-On-Demand: No

Internet Service
Operational: No.

Telephone Service
None
Miles of Plant: 10.0 (coaxial); None (fiber optic).
President: Brian Mealy.
Ownership: Clarendon TV Association.

CLARION BOROUGH—Comcast Cable, 15 Summit Park Dr, Pittsburgh, PA 15275. Phones: 412-747-6400; 814-226-6350 (Clarion office). Fax: 412-747-6401. Web Site: http://www.comcast.com. Also serves Brookville, Corsica, East Brady, Eldred Twp. (Jefferson County), Emlenton, Foxburg, Hovey Twp., Huey, Marion Twp. (Clarion County), Parker, Piney Twp., Rimersburg, Rose Twp., Sligo, St. Petersburg, Strattanville, Toby Twp. & Union Twp. (Jefferson County). ICA: PA0137.
TV Market Ranking: Outside TV Markets (Brookville, CLARION BOROUGH, Corsica, East Brady, Eldred Twp. (Jefferson County), Emlenton, Foxburg, Hovey Twp., Huey, Marion Twp. (Clarion County), Parker, Piney Twp., Rimersburg, Rose Twp., Sligo, St. Petersburg, Strattanville, Toby Twp., Union Twp. (Jefferson County)). Franchise award date: January 1, 1966. Franchise expiration date: N.A. Began: September 1, 1966.
Channel capacity: N.A. Channels available but not in use: N.A.

Basic Service
Subscribers: N.A. Included in Bensalem Twp.
Programming (received off-air): KDKA-TV (CBS) Pittsburgh; WJAC-TV (NBC) Johnstown; WNPB-TV (PBS) Morgantown; WPCB-TV (IND) Greensburg; WPCW (CW) Jeannette; WPGH-TV (FOX) Pittsburgh; WPMY (MNT) Pittsburgh; WPSU-TV (PBS) Clearfield; WPXI (IND, NBC) Pittsburgh; WQED (PBS) Pittsburgh; WTAE-TV (ABC) Pittsburgh; WWCP-TV (FOX) Johnstown; allband FM.
Programming (via satellite): C-SPAN; C-SPAN 2; QVC; TBS Superstation.
Fee: $39.95 installation; $10.15 monthly; $2.00 converter.

Expanded Basic Service 1
Subscribers: 2,291.
Programming (via satellite): A&E Networks; ABC Family Channel; AMC; Animal Planet; Cartoon Network; CNBC; CNN; Comedy Central; Country Music TV; Discovery Channel; Disney Channel; E! Entertainment Television; ESPN; ESPN 2; Eternal Word TV Network; Food Network; Fox News

Channel; FX; Hallmark Channel; Headline News; HGTV; History Channel; ION Television; Lifetime; MoviePlex; MSNBC; MTV; Nickelodeon; Outdoor Channel; Oxygen; Pennsylvania Cable Network; Root Sports Pittsburgh; Spike TV; Syfy; The Learning Channel; The Weather Channel; Travel Channel; truTV; Turner Network TV; TV Guide Network; TV Land; USA Network; VH1.
Fee: $12.06 monthly.

Digital Basic Service
Subscribers: 1,400.
Programming (via satellite): BBC America; Bio; Black Family Channel; Bloomberg Television; Bravo; CMT Pure Country; Discovery Digital Networks; Encore (multiplexed); ESPNews; Flix; Fox College Sports Atlantic; Fox College Sports Central; Fox College Sports Pacific; Fox Movie Channel; Fox Soccer; Fuse; G4; GAS; Golf Channel; Great American Country; GSN; Halogen Network; History Channel International; Independent Film Channel; Lifetime Movie Network; MTV Networks Digital Suite; Music Choice; National Geographic Channel; Nick Jr.; NickToons TV; Outdoor Channel; Speed; Style Network; Sundance Channel; The Word Network; Toon Disney; Trinity Broadcasting Network; Turner Classic Movies; Versus; WE tv.

Digital Pay Service 1
Pay Units: N.A.
Programming (via satellite): Cinemax (multiplexed); Flix; HBO (multiplexed); Showtime (multiplexed); Starz (multiplexed); The Movie Channel (multiplexed).
Fee: $15.95 monthly (HBO, Cinemax, Showtime/TMC or Starz).

Video-On-Demand: No

Pay-Per-View
Playboy TV (delivered digitally); Fresh (delivered digitally); Hot Choice (delivered digitally); Movies & Events (delivered digitally).

Internet Service
Operational: Yes.
Subscribers: 900.
Broadband Service: Comcast High Speed Internet.
Fee: $42.95 monthly.

Telephone Service
None

Miles of Plant: 206.0 (coaxial); None (fiber optic).
Regional Vice President: LInda Hossinger. Vice President, Technical Operations: Randy Bender. Vice President, Marketing: Donna Corning. Vice President, Public Affairs: Jody Doherty.
Ownership: Comcast Cable Communications Inc. (MSO).

CLAYSVILLE—Blue Devil Cable TV Inc., 116 S 4th St, Toronto, OH 43964-1368. Phone: 800-931-9392. ICA: PA0265.
TV Market Ranking: 10,90 (CLAYSVILLE). Franchise award date: N.A. Franchise expiration date: N.A. Began: March 1, 1978.
Channel capacity: N.A. Channels available but not in use: N.A.

Basic Service
Subscribers: 179.
Programming (received off-air): KDKA-TV (CBS) Pittsburgh; WNPB-TV (PBS) Morgantown; WPGH-TV (FOX) Pittsburgh; WPMY (MNT) Pittsburgh; WPXI (IND, NBC) Pittsburgh; WQED (PBS) Pittsburgh; WTAE-TV (ABC) Pittsburgh; WTOV-TV (IND, NBC) Steubenville; WTRF-TV (CBS) Wheeling.
Programming (via satellite): ABC Family Channel; ESPN; WGN America.
Fee: $25.00 installation; $15.00 monthly.

Pay Service 1
Pay Units: 45.
Programming (via satellite): HBO.
Fee: $10.60 monthly.

Internet Service
Operational: No.

Telephone Service
None

Miles of Plant: 6.0 (coaxial); None (fiber optic).
Manager: David Bates. Office Manager: Joanne Conner.
Ownership: Blue Devil Cable TV Inc. (MSO).

CLEARFIELD—Atlantic Broadband, 120 Southmont Blvd, Johnstown, PA 15905. Phones: 888-536-9600; 814-539-8971. Fax: 814-535-7749. E-mail: info@atlanticbb.com. Web Site: http://www.atlanticbb.com. Also serves Bloomington, Boggs Twp. (Clearfield County), Bradford Twp. (Clearfield County), Curwensville (Clearfield County), Glen Richey, Hyde, Knox Twp., Lawrence Twp. (Clearfield County), Olanta, Oshanter & Pike Twp. (Clearfield County). ICA: PA0084.
TV Market Ranking: 74 (Bloomington, Boggs Twp. (Clearfield County), Curwensville (Clearfield County), Glen Richey, Hyde, Olanta, Oshanter); Outside TV Markets (Bradford Twp. (Clearfield County), CLEARFIELD, Knox Twp., Lawrence Twp. (Clearfield County), Pike Twp. (Clearfield County)). Franchise award date: N.A. Franchise expiration date: N.A. Began: February 1, 1952.
Channel capacity: N.A. Channels available but not in use: N.A.

Basic Service
Subscribers: 5,400.
Programming (received off-air): KDKA-TV (CBS) Pittsburgh; WATM-TV (ABC) Altoona; WJAC-TV (NBC) Johnstown; WKBS-TV (IND) Altoona; WPSU-TV (PBS) Clearfield; WTAE-TV (ABC) Pittsburgh; WTAJ-TV (CBS) Altoona; WWCP-TV (FOX) Johnstown; 11 FMs.
Programming (via satellite): C-SPAN; C-SPAN 2; Eternal Word TV Network; Pennsylvania Cable Network; Product Information Network; QVC; ShopNBC; TV Guide Network; WPIX (CW, IND) New York.
Fee: $25.00 installation; $18.95 monthly; $1.60 converter.

Expanded Basic Service 1
Subscribers: N.A.
Programming (via satellite): A&E Networks; ABC Family Channel; AMC; Animal Planet; Bravo; Cartoon Network; CNBC; CNN; Comedy Central; Country Music TV; Discovery Channel; Discovery Health Channel; Disney Channel; E! Entertainment Television; ESPN; ESPN 2; Food Network; Fox News Channel; FX; Golf Channel; Hallmark Channel; Headline News; HGTV; History Channel; ION Television; Lifetime; MSNBC; MTV; National Geographic Channel; Nickelodeon; NickToons TV; Oxygen; Root Sports Pittsburgh; Speed; Spike TV; Syfy; TBS Superstation; The Learning Channel; The Weather Channel; Travel Channel; truTV; Turner Classic Movies; Turner Network TV; TV Land; USA Network; Versus; VH1.
Fee: $35.54 monthly.

Digital Basic Service
Subscribers: N.A.
Programming (via satellite): A&E HD; Animal Planet HD; BBC America; Bio; Bloomberg Television; Boomerang; CMT Pure Country; Discovery Channel HD; Discovery Kids Channel; DIY Network; DMX Music; Encore; ESPN 2 HD; ESPN Classic Sports; ESPN HD; ESPNews; Fuel TV; G4; HD Theater; History Channel International; ID Investigation Discovery; Independent Film Channel; INSP; Lifetime Movie Network; Lifetime Real Women; Military Channel; MTV Hits; MTV Jams; MTV2; NFL Network; Nick Jr.; Nick Too; Planet Green; Root Sports Pittsburgh; Science; SoapNet; Starz; Style Network; TBS in HD; TeenNick; Toon Disney; Tr3s; Turner Network TV HD; VH1 Classic; VH1 Soul; WE tv.
Fee: $18.95 monthly.

Digital Pay Service 1
Pay Units: 310.
Programming (via satellite): HBO (multiplexed).
Fee: $15.95 monthly.

Digital Pay Service 2
Pay Units: 150.
Programming (via satellite): Cinemax (multiplexed).
Fee: $15.95 monthly.

Digital Pay Service 3
Pay Units: N.A.
Programming (via satellite): Flix; Showtime (multiplexed); The Movie Channel (multiplexed).
Fee: $15.95 monthly.

Video-On-Demand: No

Pay-Per-View
iN DEMAND (delivered digitally); Hot Choice (delivered digitally); Spice: Xcess (delivered digitally); Club Jenna (delivered digitally); Fresh (delivered digitally); Shorteez (delivered digitally); Playboy TV (delivered digitally).

Internet Service
Operational: Yes.
Broadband Service: Atlantic Broadband High-Speed Internet.
Fee: $24.95 monthly.

Telephone Service
Digital: Operational
Fee: $44.95-$57.95 monthly

Miles of Plant: 195.0 (coaxial); None (fiber optic).
Vice President: David Dane. General Manager: Mike Papasergi. Technical Operations Director: Charles Serchilla. Marketing & Customer Service Director: Dara Leslie. Marketing Manager: Natalie Kurchak.
Ownership: Atlantic Broadband (MSO).

CLIFTON HEIGHTS—RCN Corp. Formerly served by Philadelphia (suburbs), PA [PA0447]. This cable system has converted to IPTV, 196 Van Buren St, Herndon, VA 20170. Phone: 703-434-8200. Web Site: http://www.rcn.com. ICA: PA5246.
Channel capacity: N.A. Channels available but not in use: N.A.

Internet Service
Operational: Yes.

Chairman: Steven J. Simmons. Chief Executive Officer: Jim Holanda.

CLINTONVILLE—Armstrong Utilities Inc. Now served by GROVE CITY, PA [PA0089]. ICA: PA0325.

COALPORT—Comcast Cable, 15 Summit Park Dr, Pittsburgh, PA 15275. Phones: 412-747-6400; 814-344-8055 (Carrolltown office). Fax: 412-747-6401. Web Site: http://www.comcast.com. Also serves Beccaria Twp., Dean Twp. (Cambria County), Glen Hope, Irvona, Reade Twp. (Cambria County) & White Twp. (Cambria County). ICA: PA0158.
TV Market Ranking: 74 (Beccaria Twp., COALPORT, Dean Twp. (Cambria County), Glen Hope, Irvona, Reade Twp. (Cambria County), White Twp. (Cambria County)). Franchise award date: N.A. Franchise expiration date: N.A. Began: December 1, 1968.
Channel capacity: 36 (not 2-way capable). Channels available but not in use: N.A.

Basic Service
Subscribers: N.A. Included in Bensalem Twp.
Programming (received off-air): WATM-TV (ABC) Altoona; WJAC-TV (NBC) Johnstown; WKBS-TV (IND) Altoona; WPMY (MNT) Pittsburgh; WPSU-TV (PBS) Clearfield; WPXI (IND, NBC) Pittsburgh; WTAJ-TV (CBS) Altoona; WWCP-TV (FOX) Johnstown.
Programming (via satellite): A&E Networks; ABC Family Channel; AMC; CNN; Country Music TV; C-SPAN; Discovery Channel; Disney Channel; ESPN; ESPN 2; HGTV; History Channel; ION Television; Lifetime; Nickelodeon; Outdoor Channel; QVC; Root Sports Pittsburgh; Spike TV; Syfy; TBS Superstation; The Learning Channel; The Weather Channel; Turner Network TV; TV Land; USA Network; WGN America.
Fee: $25.99 monthly; $1.06 converter.

Pay Service 1
Pay Units: 198.
Programming (via satellite): The Movie Channel.
Fee: $9.95 monthly.

Pay Service 2
Pay Units: 245.
Programming (via satellite): HBO.
Fee: $11.95 monthly.

Video-On-Demand: No

Internet Service
Operational: No.

Telephone Service
None

Miles of Plant: 99.0 (coaxial); None (fiber optic).
Regional Vice President: Linda Hossinger. Vice President, Technical Operations: Randy Bender. Vice President, Marketing: Donna Corning. Vice President, Public Affairs: Jody Doherty. Manager: Diane Kirsh.
Ownership: Comcast Cable Communications Inc. (MSO).

COATESVILLE—Comcast Cable, 3220 Tillman Dr, Bensalem, PA 19010. Phone: 215-642-6400. Fax: 215-638-6510. Web Site: http://www.comcast.com. Also serves Atglen (Chester County), Caln Twp. (Chester County), Charlestown Twp., Chester County, Downingtown, East Bradford Twp. (Chester County), East Brandywine Twp., East Caln Twp., East Fallowfield Twp. (Chester County), East Goshen Twp., East Goshen Twp. (Chester County), East Nantmeal Twp., East Whiteland Twp., Easttown Twp., Edgemont Twp., Exton, Malvern, Malvern Borough, Modena, Newtown Twp., Parkesburg, Pocopson Twp., Sadsbury Twp. (Chester County), South Coatesville, Thornbury Twp. (Chester County), Thornbury Twp. (Delaware County), Tredyffrin Twp., Upper Uwchlan Twp. (Chester County), Uwchlan Twp., Valley Twp. (Chester County), Wallace Twp., West Bradford Twp., West Brandywine Twp., West Caln Twp., West Chester, West Goshen, West Nantmeal, West Pikeland Twp. (portions), West Sadsbury Twp. (Chester County), West Vincent Twp., West Whitehead Twp. (Chester County), West

Whiteland Twp., Westtown Twp. & Willistown Twp. ICA: PA0014.

TV Market Ranking: 4 (Charlestown Twp., East Goshen Twp., East Nantmeal Twp., East Whiteland Twp., Edgemont Twp., Exton, Malvern, Malvern Borough, Newtown Twp., Thornbury Twp. (Chester County), Thornbury Twp. (Delaware County), Tredyffrin Twp., West Vincent Twp., West Whiteland Twp., Willistown Twp.); 4,57 (Caln Twp. (Chester County), Chester County (portions), COATESVILLE, Downingtown, East Bradford Twp. (Chester County), East Brandywine Twp., East Caln Twp., East Fallowfield Twp. (Chester County), East Goshen Twp. (Chester County), Wallace Twp.); 57 (Atglen (Chester County), Modena, Parkesburg, Pocopson Twp., Sadsbury Twp. (Chester County), South Coatesville, Upper Uwchlan Twp. (Chester County), Uwchlan Twp., Valley Twp. (Chester County), West Bradford Twp., West Brandywine Twp., West Caln Twp., West Chester, West Goshen, West Nantmeal, West Pikeland Twp. (portions), West Sadsbury Twp. (Chester County), West Whitehead Twp. (Chester County), Westtown Twp.). Franchise award date: January 1, 1965. Franchise expiration date: N.A. Began: November 1, 1968.

Channel capacity: N.A. Channels available but not in use: N.A.

Basic Service

Subscribers: N.A. Included in Bensalem Twp.

Programming (received off-air): KYW-TV (CBS) Philadelphia; WCAU (NBC) Philadelphia; WFMZ-TV (IND) Allentown; WGAL (NBC) Lancaster; WGTW-TV (TBN) Burlington; WHYY-TV (PBS) Wilmington; WNJS (PBS) Camden; WPHL-TV (MNT, IND) Philadelphia; WPPX-TV (ION) Wilmington; WPSG (CW) Philadelphia; WPVI-TV (ABC) Philadelphia; WTVE (IND) Reading; WTXF-TV (FOX) Philadelphia; 1 FM.

Programming (via satellite): C-SPAN; MarketConnect Network; MSNBC; QVC; The Comcast Network; Univision Studios.

Fee: $45.10 installation; $12.30 monthly.

Expanded Basic Service 1

Subscribers: 57,397.

Programming (via satellite): A&E Networks; ABC Family Channel; AMC; Animal Planet; BET Networks; Bravo; Cartoon Network; CNBC; CNN; Comcast SportsNet Philadelphia; Comedy Central; Country Music TV; Discovery Channel; Discovery Health Channel; Disney Channel; E! Entertainment Television; ESPN; ESPN 2; ESPN Classic Sports; Eternal Word TV Network; Food Network; Fox News Channel; FX; Golf Channel; Hallmark Channel; Headline News; HGTV; History Channel; Lifetime; MTV; Nickelodeon; Philadelphia Park Live; Speed; Spike TV; Style Network; Syfy; TBS Superstation; The Learning Channel; The Weather Channel; Travel Channel; truTV; Turner Classic Movies; Turner Network TV; TV Land; USA Network; Versus; VH1.

Fee: $39.90 monthly.

Digital Basic Service

Subscribers: 35,888.

Programming (via satellite): BBC America; Bio; Cooking Channel; C-SPAN 3; Discovery Digital Networks; DIY Network; ESPNews; Flix (multiplexed); G4; GAS; History Channel International; Independent Film Channel; MTV Networks Digital Suite; Music Choice; National Geographic Channel; Nick Jr.; Nick Too; ShopNBC; SoapNet; Sundance Channel (multiplexed); Toon Disney; WAM! America's Kidz Network; Weatherscan.

Digital Pay Service 1

Pay Units: N.A.

Programming (via satellite): Cinemax (multiplexed); HBO (multiplexed); Showtime (multiplexed); Starz; The Movie Channel (multiplexed).

Fee: $18.95 monthly (each).

Video-On-Demand: Yes

Pay-Per-View

Pleasure (delivered digitally); Shorteez (delivered digitally); iN DEMAND (delivered digitally); Playboy TV (delivered digitally); Fresh (delivered digitally).

Internet Service

Operational: Yes. Began: January 1, 2001.

Broadband Service: Comcast High Speed Internet.

Fee: $42.95 monthly.

Telephone Service

Digital: Operational

Fee: $44.95 monthly

Miles of Plant: 1,640.0 (coaxial); 400.0 (fiber optic).

Senior Regional Vice President: Amy Smith. Vice President, Technical Operations: Rich Massi. Vice President, Marketing: Chip Goodman.

Ownership: Comcast Cable Communications Inc. (MSO).

COGAN STATION—Zito Media, 611 Vader Hill Rd, Coudersport, PA 16915. Phone: 570-673-5326. Web Site: http://www.zitomedia.com. Also serves Hepburnville, Perryville, Quiggleville & Trout Run. ICA: PA0207.

TV Market Ranking: Below 100 (COGAN STATION, Hepburnville, Perryville, Quiggleville, Trout Run). Franchise award date: N.A. Franchise expiration date: N.A. Began: June 1, 1953.

Channel capacity: N.A. Channels available but not in use: N.A.

Basic Service

Subscribers: 800.

Programming (received off-air): WBRE-TV (NBC) Wilkes-Barre; WNEP-TV (ABC) Scranton; WSWB (CW) Scranton; WVIA-TV (PBS) Scranton; WYOU (CBS) Scranton; allband FM.

Programming (via satellite): A&E Networks; ABC Family Channel; Animal Planet; CNBC; CNN; Comedy Central; CTV Inc.; Discovery Channel; ESPN; ESPN 2; Fox News Channel; FX; Hallmark Channel; Headline News; History Channel; Lifetime; MTV; Nickelodeon; Outdoor Channel; QVC; Speed; Spike TV; Syfy; TBS Superstation; The Learning Channel; The Weather Channel; Trinity Broadcasting Network; Turner Network TV; TV Land; USA Network; VH1; WGN America.

Fee: $50.00 installation; $39.00 monthly.

Pay Service 1

Pay Units: 300.

Programming (via satellite): Showtime.

Fee: $15.00 installation; $11.00 monthly.

Video-On-Demand: No

Internet Service

Operational: No.

Telephone Service

None

Miles of Plant: 35.0 (coaxial); 70.0 (fiber optic). Additional miles planned: 3.0 (coaxial).

Public Relations Manager: Mark Laver.

Ownership: Zito Media (MSO).

COLLINGDALE—RCN Corp. Formerly served by Philadelphia (suburbs), PA [PA5259]. This cable system has converted to IPTV, 196 Van Buren St, Herndon, VA 20170. Phone: 703-434-8200. Web Site: http://www.rcn.com. ICA: PA5247.

Channel capacity: N.A. Channels available but not in use: N.A.

Internet Service

Operational: Yes.

Chairman: Steven J. Simmons. Chief Executive Officer: Jim Holanda.

COLWYN—RCN Corp. Formerly served by Philadelphia (suburbs), PA [PA5259]. This cable system has converted to IPTV, 196 Van Buren St, Herndon, VA 20170. Phone: 703-434-8200. Web Site: http://www.rcn.com. ICA: PA5248.

Channel capacity: N.A. Channels available but not in use: N.A.

Internet Service

Operational: Yes.

Chairman: Steven J. Simmons. Chief Executive Officer: Jim Holanda.

CONNELLSVILLE—Armstrong Cable Services, 259 E Crawford Ave, Connellsville, PA 15425. Phones: 877-277-5711; 724-628-5462; 724-628-6600. E-mail: info@zoominternet.net. Web Site: http://cable.armstrongonewire.com. Also serves Acme, Acosta, Allenport, California, Coal Center, Connellsville Twp. (Fayette County), Daisytown, Dunbar, Dunbar Twp., Dunlevy, East Huntingdon Twp., Elco, Everson, Friedens, Gray, Hidden Valley, Listie, Long Branch, Markleton, Mount Pleasant Twp. (Westmoreland County), Newell, Norvelt, Pioneer Park Campground, Quecreek, Rockwood Borough, Roscoe, Saltlick Twp. (Fayette County), Scottdale, Sipesville, Somerset County, Somerset Twp. (Somerset County), South Connellsville Twp. (Fayette County), South Huntingdon Twp. (portions), Stockdale, Trent, Vanderbilt, West Brownsville & West Pike Run Twp. ICA: PA0046. **Note:** This system is an overbuild.

TV Market Ranking: 10 (Allenport, California, Coal Center, Daisytown, Dunlevy, East Huntingdon Twp., Elco, Everson, Long Branch, Mount Pleasant Twp. (Westmoreland County), Newell, Roscoe, Scottdale, South Huntingdon Twp. (portions), Stockdale, Vanderbilt, West Brownsville, West Pike Run Twp.); 74 (Acosta, Friedens, Gray, Hidden Valley, Listie, Pioneer Park Campground, Quecreek, Rockwood Borough, Saltlick Twp. (Fayette County), Sipesville, Somerset County (portions), Somerset Twp. (Somerset County), Trent); Below 100 (Acme, CONNELLSVILLE, Connellsville Twp. (Fayette County), Dunbar, Dunbar Twp., Markleton, Norvelt, South Connellsville Twp. (Fayette County), Somerset County (portions)); Outside TV Markets (Somerset County (portions)). Franchise award date: July 1, 1967. Franchise expiration date: April 1, 2010. Began: July 1, 1967.

Channel capacity: N.A. Channels available but not in use: N.A.

Digital Basic Service

Subscribers: 5,288.

Programming (via satellite): A&E Networks; ABC Family Channel; AMC; Animal Planet; Bravo; Cartoon Network; CNBC; CNN; Comedy Central; Country Music TV; C-SPAN; Discovery Channel; Disney Channel; E! Entertainment Television; ESPN; ESPN 2; ESPN Classic Sports; Eternal Word TV Network; Food Network; Fox News Channel; FX; Headline News; HGTV; History Channel; Lifetime; MSNBC; MTV; Music Choice; Nickelodeon; NickToons TV; Pennsylvania Cable Network; Pentagon Channel; Pittsburgh Cable News Channel; QVC; Root Sports Pittsburgh; ShopNBC; Spike TV; Syfy; TBS Superstation; The Learning Channel; The Weather Channel; Travel Channel; truTV; Turner Classic Movies; Turner Network TV; TV Guide Network; TV Land; USA Network; VH1.

Fee: $35.00 installation; $51.40 monthly.

Digital Expanded Basic Service

Subscribers: N.A.

Programming (via satellite): AmericanLife TV Network; BBC America; Bio; Bloomberg Television; Boomerang; Chiller; cloo; CMT Pure Country; Cooking Channel; Discovery Fit & Health; Discovery Health Channel; Discovery Kids Channel; DIY Network; ESPN Classic Sports; ESPNews; G4; Golf Channel; Great American Country; GSN; Hallmark Channel; Hallmark Movie Channel; History Channel International; HRTV; ID Investigation Discovery; Jewelry Television; Lifetime Movie Network; Military Channel; MTV Hits; MTV Jams; MTV2; mun2 television; National Geographic Channel; NFL Network; NHL Network; Nick Jr.; Nick Too; Outdoor Channel; Oxygen; PBS Kids Sprout; Pentagon Channel; Planet Green; RFD-TV; RTN; Science; SoapNet; Speed; TeenNick; Tennis Channel; Toon Disney; Tr3s; Versus; VH1 Classic; VH1 Soul; WE tv.

Fee: $12.00 monthly.

Digital Expanded Basic Service 2

Subscribers: N.A.

Programming (received off-air): KDKA-TV (CBS) Pittsburgh; WPCW (CW) Jeannette; WPGH-TV (FOX) Pittsburgh; WPXI (IND, NBC) Pittsburgh; WQED (PBS) Pittsburgh; WTAE-TV (ABC) Pittsburgh.

Programming (via satellite): A&E HD; Animal Planet HD; Bravo HD; CNN HD; Discovery Channel HD; Disney Channel HD; ESPN 2 HD; ESPN HD; Food Network HD; Fox News HD; FSN HD; FX HD; Golf Channel HD; Hallmark Movie Channel HD; HD Theater; HDNet; HDNet Movies; HGTV HD; History Channel HD; MGM HD; National Geographic Channel HD Network; NFL Network HD; NHL Network HD; Outdoor Channel 2 HD; Palladia; Science HD; Syfy HD; TBS in HD; The Weather Channel HD; TLC HD; Turner Network TV HD; Universal HD; USA Network HD; Versus HD; WealthTV HD.

Fee: $9.00 monthly.

Digital Pay Service 1

Pay Units: 490.

Programming (via satellite): Cinemax (multiplexed); Cinemax HD; Encore (multiplexed); Flix; HBO (multiplexed); HBO HD; RAI USA; Showtime (multiplexed); Showtime HD; Starz (multiplexed); Starz HDTV;

The Movie Channel (multiplexed); The Movie Channel HD; TV5 USA.
Fee: $13.95 monthly (HBO, Cinemax, Showtime/TMC/Flix, or Starz/Encore).
Video-On-Demand: Yes
Pay-Per-View
Addressable homes: 1,185.
ESPN Now (delivered digitally); Hot Choice (delivered digitally); iN DEMAND (delivered digitally); NHL/MLB (delivered digitally); ESPN Extra (delivered digitally).
Internet Service
Operational: Yes. Began: April 1, 1998.
Subscribers: 11,566.
Broadband Service: Armstrong Zoom.
Fee: $26.95-$39.95 monthly.
Telephone Service
Digital: Operational
Fee: $49.95 monthly
Miles of Plant: 723.0 (coaxial); 234.0 (fiber optic).
Manager: Carl Rose. Chief Technician: Jack Thornton. Marketing Director: Lori Kaczmarek. Program Director: Jenn Areford. Customer Service Manager: Karen Brooks.
Ownership: Armstrong Group of Companies (MSO).

COOPERSTOWN—Formerly served by Cebridge Connections. Now served by MEADVILLE, PA [PA0062]. ICA: PA0214.

COPLAY BOROUGH—Formerly served by NORTHAMPTON BOROUGH, PA [PA0008]. RCN Corp. This cable system has converted to IPTV, 196 Van Buren St, Herndon, VA 20170. Phone: 703-434-8200. Web Site: http://www.rcn.com. ICA: PA5209.
TV Market Ranking: Below 100 (COPLAY BOROUGH).
Channel capacity: N.A. Channels available but not in use: N.A.
Internet Service
Operational: Yes.
Telephone Service
Digital: Operational
Chairman: Steven J. Simmons. Chief Executive Officer: Jim Holanda.

CORAOPOLIS—Comcast Cable. Now served by PITTSBURGH, PA [PA0001]. ICA: PA0061.

CORRY—Time Warner Cable, 3627 Zimmerman Rd, Erie, PA 16510-2642. Phones: 330-633-9203 (Akron office); 814-898-1656. Fax: 814-456-5162. Web Site: http://www.timewarnercable.com. Also serves Columbus Twp. (Warren County), Concord Twp. (Erie County), Elgin, Union City, Union Twp. (Erie County) & Wayne Twp. (Erie County). ICA: PA0113.
TV Market Ranking: Below 100 (Columbus Twp. (Warren County), Concord Twp. (Erie County), CORRY, Elgin, Union City, Union Twp. (Erie County), Wayne Twp. (Erie County)). Franchise award date: September 1, 1957. Franchise expiration date: N.A. Began: September 1, 1957.
Channel capacity: N.A. Channels available but not in use: N.A.
Basic Service
Subscribers: N.A. Included in Warren, OH
Programming (received off-air): WFXP (FOX) Erie; WICU-TV (NBC) Erie; WJET-TV (ABC) Erie; WQLN (PBS) Erie; WSEE-TV (CBS, CW) Erie; 13 FMs.
Programming (via satellite): C-SPAN; C-SPAN 2; QVC; ShopNBC; TV Guide Network.
Fee: $39.95 installation; $11.14 monthly; $9.95 additional installation.
Expanded Basic Service 1
Subscribers: 3,891.
Programming (via satellite): A&E Networks; ABC Family Channel; AMC; AmericanLife TV Network; Animal Planet; BET Networks; Bravo; Cartoon Network; CNBC; CNN; Comedy Central; Country Music TV; Discovery Channel; Discovery Fit & Health; Discovery Health Channel; Disney Channel; E! Entertainment Television; ESPN; ESPN 2; ESPN Classic Sports; Eternal Word TV Network; Food Network; Fox News Channel; FX; Golf Channel; Great American Country; Hallmark Channel; Headline News; HGTV; History Channel; INSP; ION Television; Lifetime; Lifetime Movie Network; MSNBC; MTV; MTV2; Nickelodeon; Oxygen; Root Sports Pittsburgh; SoapNet; Spike TV; Syfy; TBS Superstation; The Learning Channel; The Weather Channel; Travel Channel; Trinity Broadcasting Network; truTV; Turner Classic Movies; Turner Network TV; TV Land; Univision Studios; USA Network; VH1; WE tv.
Fee: $31.36 monthly.
Digital Basic Service
Subscribers: N.A.
Programming (via satellite): AmericanLife TV Network; America's Store; BBC America; Bio; Bloomberg Television; cloo; CNN International; Cooking Channel; Country Music TV; C-SPAN 3; Current; Disney Channel; DIY Network; DMX Music; ESPN; ESPNews; Fox Movie Channel; Fox Soccer; Fuse; G4; GAS; GSN; HD Theater; HDNet; HDNet Movies; History Channel International; Independent Film Channel; INHD (multiplexed); Lifetime Real Women; MTV2; National Geographic Channel; Nick Jr.; NickToons TV; Outdoor Channel; Speed; Style Network; The Word Network; Toon Disney; Turner Network TV HD; TVG Network; VH1 Classic.
Fee: $20.00 monthly.
Digital Expanded Basic Service
Subscribers: N.A.
Programming (via satellite): Boomerang; Canales N; CBS Sports Network; Daystar TV Network; Discovery Kids Channel; Encore (multiplexed); Fox College Sports Atlantic; Fox College Sports Central; Fox College Sports Pacific; Fox Soccer; Fuel TV; GAS; NBA TV; Nick Jr.; Speed; Sundance Channel; Tennis Channel; Toon Disney.
Digital Pay Service 1
Pay Units: N.A.
Programming (via satellite): ART America; Cinemax (multiplexed); HBO (multiplexed); RAI International; Showtime (multiplexed); Starz (multiplexed); The Movie Channel (multiplexed); TV Asia; Zee TV USA.
Fee: $9.95 monthly (HBO, Cinemax, or Showtime/TMC), $12.95 monthly (Starz). $14.95 monthly (Foreign Language Channels).
Video-On-Demand: Yes
Internet Service
Operational: Yes.
Broadband Service: Road Runner.
Fee: $99.00 installation; $44.95 monthly.
Telephone Service
Digital: Operational
Fee: $44.95 monthly
Miles of Plant: 98.0 (coaxial); 13.0 (fiber optic).
President: Stephen Fry. Area Vice President: Rick Whaley. Vice President, Engineering: Al Costanzi. Vice President, Marketing: Patrick Burke. Vice President, Government & Media Relations: William Jasso. General Manager: Brian Frederick.
Ownership: Time Warner Cable (MSO).

COUDERSPORT—Zito Media, 611 Vader Hill Rd, Coudersport, PA 16915. Phones: 814-260-9570; 814-260-9569; 814-260-9575. Fax: 814-260-9580. E-mail: rigas@zitomedia.com. Web Site: http://www.zitomedia.com. Also serves Annin Twp., Austin Borough, Emporium, Port Allegany, Roulette Twp., Shippen & Shippen Twp. (Cameron County). ICA: PA0121.
TV Market Ranking: Outside TV Markets (Annin Twp., Austin Borough, COUDERSPORT, Emporium, Port Allegany, Roulette Twp., Shippen, Shippen Twp. (Cameron County)). Franchise award date: January 1, 1952. Franchise expiration date: N.A. Began: March 1, 1953.
Channel capacity: N.A. Channels available but not in use: N.A.
Basic Service
Subscribers: 6,000.
Programming (received off-air): WGRZ (NBC) Buffalo; WIVB-TV (CBS) Buffalo; WJAC-TV (NBC) Johnstown; WKBW-TV (ABC) Buffalo; WNED-TV (PBS) Buffalo; WPSU-TV (PBS) Clearfield; WTAJ-TV (CBS) Altoona; WWCP-TV (FOX) Johnstown.
Programming (via satellite): TV Guide Network; WGN America; WPIX (CW, IND) New York.
Fee: $29.95 installation; $17.55 monthly; $4.50 converter.
Expanded Basic Service 1
Subscribers: N.A.
Programming (via satellite): A&E Networks; ABC Family Channel; AMC; Animal Planet; Cartoon Network; CNBC; CNN; Comedy Central; Country Music TV; C-SPAN; C-SPAN 2; Discovery Channel; Disney Channel; E! Entertainment Television; ESPN; ESPN 2; ESPN Classic Sports; Eternal Word TV Network; Food Network; Fox News Channel; FX; Hallmark Channel; Headline News; HGTV; History Channel; INSP; Lifetime; MSG; MSNBC; MTV; NFL Network; Nickelodeon; Outdoor Channel; Oxygen; Pennsylvania Cable Network; QVC; Root Sports Pittsburgh; Speed; Spike TV; Syfy; TBS Superstation; The Learning Channel; The Weather Channel; Travel Channel; Trinity Broadcasting Network; truTV; Turner Classic Movies; Turner Network TV; TV Land; USA Network; VH1.
Fee: $31.90 monthly.
Digital Basic Service
Subscribers: 2,200.
Programming (via satellite): A&E HD; ABC Family HD; AmericanLife TV Network; BBC America; Bio HD; Bloomberg Television; Boomerang; Cartoon Network HD; CNN HD; Discovery Channel HD; Discovery Fit & Health; Discovery Health Channel; Discovery Kids Channel; Disney Channel HD; ESPN 2 HD; ESPN HD; ESPNews; ESPNews HD; Familyland Television Network; Food Network HD; Fox Movie Channel; Fox Soccer; FSN HD; FX HD; Golf Channel; Great American Country; GSN; HD Theater; HGTV HD; HRTV; ID Investigation Discovery; INSP; Lifetime Movie Network; Lifetime Movie Network HD; Lifetime Real Women; Lifetime Television HD; Military Channel; MTV Hits; MTV Jams; MTV2; Music Choice; NFL Network HD; NHL Network; NHL Network HD; Nick Jr.; Nick Too; NickToons TV; Outdoor Channel 2 HD; Planet Green; RFD-TV; Science; Science HD; SoapNet; Speed; Speed HD; TBS in HD; TeenNick; The Word Network; TLC HD; Toon Disney; Trinity Broadcasting Network; Turner Network TV HD; VH1 Classic; VH1 Country; VH1 Soul; WAM! America's Kidz Network; WE tv.
Fee: $11.95 monthly.
Digital Expanded Basic Service
Subscribers: N.A.
Programming (via satellite): Bio; DIY Network; Flix; FSN Digital Atlantic; FSN Digital Central; FSN Digital Pacific; History Channel International; Independent Film Channel; Outdoor Channel; Sundance Channel; Versus.
Fee: $10.00 monthly.
Digital Pay Service 1
Pay Units: N.A.
Programming (via satellite): Cinemax (multiplexed); Cinemax HD; Encore (multiplexed); Flix; HBO (multiplexed); HBO HD; Showtime (multiplexed); Showtime HD; Starz (multiplexed); Starz HDTV; The Movie Channel (multiplexed).
Fee: $8.00 monthly (Cinemax or Starz/Encore), $10.00 monthly (HBO or Showtime/TMC/Flix).
Video-On-Demand: Yes
Pay-Per-View
iN DEMAND (delivered digitally); NHL Center Ice (delivered digitally); MLB Extra Innings (delivered digitally).
Internet Service
Operational: Yes.
Subscribers: 2,700.
Fee: $42.95 monthly.
Telephone Service
Digital: Operational
Fee: $35.00 monthly
Miles of Plant: 380.0 (coaxial); 120.0 (fiber optic).
Manager: James Rigas. Marketing Director: Kathy Fox.
Ownership: Zito Media.

CRESSON—Comcast Cable, 15 Summit Park Dr, Pittsburgh, PA 15275. Phones: 412-747-6400; 814-344-8055 (Carroltown office). Fax: 412-747-6401. Web Site: http://www.comcast.com. Also serves Ashville, Cambria County, Cassandra, Clearfield County, Dean Twp. (Cambria County), Gallitzin Borough, Lilly, Loretto, Sankertown & Tunnelhill. ICA: PA0118.
TV Market Ranking: 74 (Ashville, Cambria County, Cassandra, Clearfield County (portions), CRESSON, Dean Twp. (Cambria County), Gallitzin Borough, Lilly, Loretto, Sankertown, Tunnelhill); Outside TV Markets (Clearfield County (portions)). Franchise award date: N.A. Franchise expiration date: N.A. Began: October 1, 1970.
Channel capacity: N.A. Channels available but not in use: N.A.
Basic Service
Subscribers: N.A. Included in Bensalem Twp.
Programming (received off-air): KDKA-TV (CBS) Pittsburgh; WATM-TV (ABC) Altoona; WJAC-TV (NBC) Johnstown; WKBS-TV (IND) Altoona; WPCW (CW) Jeannette; WPSU-TV (PBS) Clearfield; WPXI (IND, NBC) Pittsburgh; WQED (PBS) Pittsburgh; WTAE-TV (ABC) Pittsburgh; WTAJ-TV (CBS) Altoona; WWCP-TV (FOX) Johnstown; allband FM.
Programming (via satellite): C-SPAN; C-SPAN 2; Eternal Word TV Network; QVC; TBS Superstation; The Weather Channel; TV Guide Network; WGN America.
Fee: $39.95 installation; $10.74 monthly; $1.60 converter.
Expanded Basic Service 1
Subscribers: 3,310.
Programming (via satellite): A&E Networks; ABC Family Channel; AMC; Animal Planet; BET Networks; Cartoon Network; CNBC; CNN; Comedy Central; Country Music TV; Discovery Channel; Disney

Channel; E! Entertainment Television; ESPN; ESPN 2; Food Network; Fox News Channel; FX; Hallmark Channel; Headline News; HGTV; History Channel; Lifetime; MoviePlex; MSNBC; MTV; Nickelodeon; Root Sports Pittsburgh; Spike TV; Syfy; The Learning Channel; Travel Channel; truTV; Turner Network TV; TV Land; USA Network; VH1.
Fee: $19.85 monthly.

Digital Basic Service
Subscribers: N.A.
Programming (via satellite): BBC America; Bio; Bloomberg Television; Bravo; CMT Pure Country; Discovery Fit & Health; Discovery Health Channel; Discovery Kids Channel; DMX Music; ESPN Classic Sports; ESPNews; Fox College Sports Atlantic; Fox College Sports Central; Fox College Sports Pacific; Fox Movie Channel; Fuse; G4; GMC; Golf Channel; GSN; History Channel International; ID Investigation Discovery; Independent Film Channel; INSP; Lifetime Movie Network; Military Channel; MTV2; National Geographic Channel; NFL Network; Nick Jr.; NickToons TV; Planet Green; Science; Speed; Style Network; Sundance Channel; TeenNick; The Word Network; Toon Disney; Trinity Broadcasting Network; Turner Classic Movies; TVG Network; Versus; VH1 Classic; VH1 Soul; WE tv.
Fee: $10.95 monthly; $3.50 converter.

Digital Pay Service 1
Pay Units: N.A.
Programming (via satellite): Cinemax (multiplexed); Encore (multiplexed); Flix; HBO (multiplexed); Showtime (multiplexed); Starz (multiplexed); The Movie Channel (multiplexed).
Fee: $15.95 monthly (each).

Video-On-Demand: No

Pay-Per-View
iN DEMAND (delivered digitally); Playboy TV (delivered digitally).

Internet Service
Operational: Yes.
Broadband Service: Comcast High Speed Internet.
Fee: $42.95 monthly.

Telephone Service
Digital: Operational

Miles of Plant: 85.0 (coaxial); None (fiber optic).
Regional Vice President: Linda Hossinger. Vice President, Technical Operations: Randy Bender. Vice President, Marketing: Donna Corning. Vice President, Public Affairs: Jody Doherty. Manager: Diane Kirsh.
Ownership: Comcast Cable Communications Inc. (MSO).

CROSBY—Formerly served by GMP-County Cable. No longer operating. ICA: PA0301.

CURTIN TWP.—Formerly served by Adelphia Communications. Now served by STATE COLLEGE, PA [PA0037]. ICA: PA0215.

DALLAS—Comcast Cable, 1 E Uwchlan Ave, Ste 411, Exton, PA 19341. Phones: 570-451-4311 (Dryea office); 484-288-6500. Web Site: http://www.comcast.com. Also serves Harveys Lake Borough, Kingston Twp., Lehman Twp. (Luzerne County) & Northmoreland Twp. ICA: PA0087.
TV Market Ranking: 49 (DALLAS, Harveys Lake Borough, Kingston Twp., Lehman Twp. (Luzerne County), Northmoreland Twp.). Franchise award date: N.A. Franchise expiration date: N.A. Began: August 31, 1976.
Channel capacity: N.A. Channels available but not in use: N.A.

Basic Service
Subscribers: N.A. Included in Harrisburg
Programming (received off-air): WNEP-TV (ABC) Scranton; WOLF-TV (CW, FOX, MNT) Hazleton; WQPX-TV (ION) Scranton; WSWB (CW) Scranton; WVIA-TV (PBS) Scranton; WYOU (CBS) Scranton; allband FM.
Programming (via satellite): Disney Channel; QVC; TBS Superstation; The Learning Channel; USA Network; VH1; WPIX (CW, IND) New York.
Fee: $45.10 installation; $12.45 monthly.

Expanded Basic Service 1
Subscribers: 6,829.
Programming (via satellite): A&E Networks; ABC Family Channel; AMC; Cartoon Network; CNBC; CNN; Comcast SportsNet Philadelphia; Comedy Central; Country Music TV; C-SPAN; Discovery Channel; ESPN; ESPN 2; FX; HGTV; History Channel; Lifetime; MTV; Nickelodeon; Pennsylvania Cable Network; Spike TV; Syfy; The Weather Channel; Turner Network TV; TV Land.
Fee: $41.55 monthly.

Digital Basic Service
Subscribers: N.A.
Programming (via satellite): AmericanLife TV Network; BBC America; Bloomberg Television; Discovery Digital Networks; ESPN Classic Sports; Fox Sports World; G4; GSN; Halogen Network; Outdoor Channel; Trinity Broadcasting Network; Turner Classic Movies; Weatherscan.
Fee: $14.95 monthly.

Digital Pay Service 1
Pay Units: N.A.
Programming (via satellite): Cinemax (multiplexed); Encore (multiplexed); HBO (multiplexed); Starz (multiplexed); The Movie Channel (multiplexed).

Video-On-Demand: Yes

Pay-Per-View
ESPN Extra; ESPN Now; TVN Digital Cable Television (delivered digitally); movies.

Internet Service
Operational: Yes.
Broadband Service: Comcast High Speed Internet.
Fee: $99.00 installation; $39.95 monthly.

Telephone Service
Digital: Operational

Miles of Plant: 231.0 (coaxial); None (fiber optic). Additional miles planned: 8.0 (coaxial).
Area Vice President: Jim Samaha. Vice President, Marketing: Larry Goldman.
Ownership: Comcast Cable Communications Inc. (MSO).

DALLAS CORRECTIONAL INSTITUTE—Suddenlink Communications, 12444 Powerscourt Dr, Saint Louis, MO 63131-3660. Phones: 800-874-2915; 314-965-2020. Web Site: http://www.suddenlink.com. ICA: PA0200.
TV Market Ranking: 49 (DALLAS CORRECTIONAL INSTITUTE). Franchise award date: November 1, 1983. Franchise expiration date: December 1, 2008. Began: May 1, 1983.
Channel capacity: 30 (not 2-way capable). Channels available but not in use: N.A.

Basic Service
Subscribers: 800.
Programming (received off-air): WNEP-TV (ABC) Scranton; WVIA-TV (PBS) Scranton; WYOU (CBS) Scranton.
Programming (via satellite): BET Networks; CNN; Comedy Central; Discovery Channel; ESPN; ESPN 2; MTV; Syfy; TBS Superstation; Turner Classic Movies; Turner Network TV; USA Network; WGN America.
Fee: $12.95 monthly.

Pay Service 1
Pay Units: 180.
Programming (via satellite): HBO.
Fee: $9.95 monthly.

Video-On-Demand: No

Internet Service
Operational: No.

Telephone Service
None

Miles of Plant: 3.0 (coaxial); None (fiber optic).
Ownership: Cequel Communications LLC (MSO).

DANVILLE—CATV Service Inc., 115 Mill St, PO Box 198, Danville, PA 17821-0198. Phones: 570-275-3101 (Customer service); 570-275-8410. Fax: 570-275-3888. E-mail: catvserv@ptd.net. Web Site: http://www.catvservice.com. Also serves East Buffalo Twp., Kelly Twp. (Union County), Lewisburg, Liberty Twp. (Montour County), Limestone Twp. (Montour County), Mahoning Twp. (Montour County), Mayberry Twp. (Montour County), McEwensville, Milton, Montour County, New Columbia Twp., Riverside (Northumberland County), Turbot Twp. (Northumberland County), Turbotville, Valley Twp. (Montour County), Washingtonville, Watsontown, West Chillisquaque Twp. (portions), West Hemlock Twp. & White Deer Twp. ICA: PA0054.
TV Market Ranking: Below 100 (DANVILLE, East Buffalo Twp., Kelly Twp. (Union County), Lewisburg, Liberty Twp. (Montour County), Limestone Twp. (Montour County), Mahoning Twp. (Montour County), Mayberry Twp. (Montour County), McEwensville, Milton, Montour County, New Columbia Twp., Riverside (Northumberland County), Turbot Twp. (Northumberland County), Turbotville, Valley Twp. (Montour County), Washingtonville, Watsontown, West Chillisquaque Twp. (portions), West Hemlock Twp., White Deer Twp.). Franchise award date: N.A. Franchise expiration date: N.A. Began: May 1, 1953.
Channel capacity: 78 (operating 2-way). Channels available but not in use: N.A.

Basic Service
Subscribers: 15,000.
Programming (received off-air): WHTM-TV (ABC) Harrisburg; WITF-TV (PBS) Harrisburg; WNEP-TV (ABC) Scranton; WSWB (CW) Scranton; WVIA-TV (PBS) Scranton; WYOU (CBS) Scranton; allband FM.
Programming (via microwave): WPHL-TV (MNT, IND) Philadelphia; WPIX (CW, IND) New York; WTXF-TV (FOX) Philadelphia.
Programming (via satellite): ABC Family Channel; CNBC; Eternal Word TV Network; TBS Superstation.
Fee: $50.00 installation; $16.95 monthly.

Expanded Basic Service 1
Subscribers: 14,400.
Programming (via satellite): A&E Networks; AMC; CNN; C-SPAN; Discovery Channel; ESPN; Food Network; FX; Headline News; Lifetime; MTV; Nickelodeon; QVC; Spike TV; The Weather Channel; Turner Network TV; USA Network; VH1.
Fee: $39.95 monthly.

Digital Basic Service
Subscribers: 475.
Fee: $11.95 monthly.

Pay Service 1
Pay Units: 1,800.
Programming (via satellite): Cinemax (multiplexed).
Fee: $35.00 installation; $10.00 monthly.

Pay Service 2
Pay Units: 2,500.
Programming (via satellite): HBO (multiplexed).
Fee: $35.00 installation; $11.00 monthly.

Video-On-Demand: No

Pay-Per-View
iN DEMAND (delivered digitally), Addressable: No.

Internet Service
Operational: Yes. Began: December 31, 2001.
Subscribers: 153.
Broadband Service: ProLog Express.
Fee: $39.95-$59.95 monthly; $9.95 modem lease.

Telephone Service
Analog: Not Operational
Digital: Operational
Fee: $44.95 monthly

Miles of Plant: 450.0 (coaxial); 60.0 (fiber optic).
Manager: Sam Haulman. Chief Technician: Matt Kujat. Marketing & Program Director: Dave Skelton.
Ownership: CATV Service Inc.

DARBY—RCN Corp. Formerly served by Philadelphia (suburbs), PA [PA5259]. This cable system has converted to IPTV, 196 Van Buren St, Herndon, VA 20170. Phone: 703-434-8200. Web Site: http://www.rcn.com. ICA: PA5249.
Channel capacity: N.A. Channels available but not in use: N.A.

Internet Service
Operational: Yes.

Telephone Service
Digital: Operational

Chairman: Steven J. Simmons. Chief Executive Officer: Jim Holanda.

DARBY TWP.—RCN Corp. Formerly served by Philadelphia (suburbs), PA [PA5259]. This cable system has converted to IPTV, 196 Van Buren St, Herndon, VA 20170. Phone: 703-434-8200. Web Site: http://www.rcn.com. ICA: PA5250.
Channel capacity: N.A. Channels available but not in use: N.A.

Internet Service
Operational: Yes.

Chairman: Steven J. Simmons. Chief Executive Officer: Jim Holanda.

DARLINGTON TWP. (Beaver County)—Comcast Cable. Now served by BEAVER FALLS, PA [PA0065]. ICA: PA0144.

DERRY/DECATUR—Atlantic Broadband, 120 Southmont Blvd, Johnstown, PA 15905. Phones: 888-536-9600; 814-539-8971. Fax: 814-535-7749. E-mail: info@atlanticbb.com. Web Site: http://www.atlanticbb.com. Also serves Decatur, Lewistown & McClure. ICA: PA0175.

TV Market Ranking: Outside TV Markets (DECATUR TWP. (MIFFLIN COUNTY), DERRY TWP. (MIFFLIN COUNTY), Lewistown, McClure). Franchise award date: January 1, 1972. Franchise expiration date: N.A. Began: January 1, 1956.

Channel capacity: 40 (not 2-way capable). Channels available but not in use: N.A.

Basic Service

Subscribers: 1,218.

Programming (received off-air): WGAL (NBC) Lancaster; WHP-TV (CBS, MNT) Harrisburg; WHTM-TV (ABC) Harrisburg; WITF-TV (PBS) Harrisburg; WLYH-TV (CW) Lancaster; WPIX (CW, IND) New York; WPMT (FOX) York; WTAJ-TV (CBS) Altoona; WVIA-TV (PBS) Scranton; allband FM.

Programming (via satellite): C-SPAN; QVC.

Fee: $25.00 installation; $16.95 monthly.

Expanded Basic Service 1

Subscribers: 1,207.

Programming (via satellite): A&E Networks; ABC Family Channel; AMC; Animal Planet; Bravo; Cartoon Network; CNN; Comedy Central; Country Music TV; Discovery Channel; Discovery Health Channel; Disney Channel; E! Entertainment Television; ESPN; ESPN 2; Food Network; Fox News Channel; FX; Hallmark Channel; Headline News; HGTV; History Channel; INSP; Lifetime; MSNBC; MTV; National Geographic Channel; Nickelodeon; Oxygen; Root Sports Pittsburgh; Speed; Spike TV; Syfy; TBS Superstation; The Learning Channel; The Weather Channel; Travel Channel; truTV; Turner Network TV; TV Land; USA Network; VH1.

Fee: $58.60 installation; $31.04 monthly.

Digital Basic Service

Subscribers: N.A.

Programming (via satellite): BBC America; Bio; Bloomberg Television; CMT Pure Country; Cooking Channel; Discovery Fit & Health; Discovery Kids Channel; DMX Music; Encore (multiplexed); ESPN Classic Sports; ESPNews; Fuse; G4; Golf Channel; GSN; Halogen Network; History Channel International; ID Investigation Discovery; Independent Film Channel; Lifetime Movie Network; Military Channel; MTV2; Nick Jr.; NickToons TV; Outdoor Channel; Planet Green; Science; Speed; Starz (multiplexed); Style Network; TeenNick; Toon Disney; Trinity Broadcasting Network; VH1 Classic.

Fee: $21.90 monthly.

Digital Pay Service 1

Pay Units: N.A.

Programming (via satellite): Cinemax (multiplexed); HBO (multiplexed); Showtime (multiplexed); The Movie Channel (multiplexed).

Video-On-Demand: No

Pay-Per-View

iN DEMAND (delivered digitally).

Internet Service

Operational: No.

Telephone Service

None

Miles of Plant: 50.0 (coaxial); None (fiber optic).

Vice President: David Dane. General Manager: Mike Papasergi. Technical Operations Director: Charles Sorchilla. Marketing & Customer Service Director: Dara Leslie. Marketing Manager: Natalie Kurchak.

Ownership: Atlantic Broadband (MSO).

DILLSBURG—Formerly served by Adelphia Communications. Now served by HIGHROCK, PA [PA0106]. ICA: PA0326.

DOYLESBURG—Valley Cable Systems, 21700 Path Valley Rd, PO Box 1078, Doylesburg, PA 17219. Phone: 717-349-7717. Also serves Blairs Mills, Fannett Twp. (Franklin County) & Tell Twp. ICA: PA0286.

TV Market Ranking: 74 (Fannett Twp. (Franklin County), Tell Twp.); Outside TV Markets (Blairs Mills, DOYLESBURG, Fannett Twp. (Franklin County)). Franchise award date: January 1, 1982. Franchise expiration date: N.A. Began: February 1, 1981.

Channel capacity: 60 (not 2-way capable). Channels available but not in use: N.A.

Basic Service

Subscribers: 52.

Programming (received off-air): WATM-TV (ABC) Altoona; WGAL (NBC) Lancaster; WHAG-TV (NBC) Hagerstown; WJAC-TV (NBC) Johnstown; WJAL (IND) Hagerstown; WJZ-TV (CBS) Baltimore; WMPB (PBS) Baltimore; WPMT (FOX) York; WTAJ-TV (CBS) Altoona; WTTG (FOX) Washington.

Programming (via satellite): ABC Family Channel; Country Music TV; C-SPAN; Discovery Channel; ESPN; QVC; Syfy; TBS Superstation; Trinity Broadcasting Network; Turner Network TV.

Fee: $40.00 installation; $17.95 monthly.

Internet Service

Operational: No.

Miles of Plant: 20.0 (coaxial); None (fiber optic).

Manager: Barry L. Kepner.

Ownership: Valley Cable Systems (MSO).

DU BOIS—Formerly served by Adelphia Communications. Now served by PUNXSUTAWNEY, PA [PA0397]. ICA: PA0093.

DUNCANNON—Blue Ridge Communications, 613 3rd St, PO Box 215, Palmerton, PA 18071-0215. Phones: 717-834-5715 (Customer service); 800-232-2273; 610-826-2551. Web Site: http://www.brctv.com. Also serves Carroll Twp. (Perry County), Miller Twp. (Perry County), New Buffalo (portions), Reed Twp. (Perry County), Rye Twp., Watts Twp. & Wheatfield Twp. ICA: PA0117.

TV Market Ranking: 57 (Carroll Twp. (Perry County), DUNCANNON, Miller Twp. (Perry County), New Buffalo (portions), Reed Twp. (Perry County), Rye Twp., Watts Twp., Wheatfield Twp.). Franchise award date: N.A. Franchise expiration date: N.A. Began: January 1, 1971.

Channel capacity: 53 (not 2-way capable). Channels available but not in use: N.A.

Basic Service

Subscribers: 3,500.

Programming (received off-air): WGAL (NBC) Lancaster; WGCB-TV (IND) Red Lion; WHP-TV (CBS, MNT) Harrisburg; WHTM-TV (ABC) Harrisburg; WITF-TV (PBS) Harrisburg; WLYH-TV (CW) Lancaster; WPHL-TV (MNT, IND) Philadelphia; WPMT (FOX) York; WTXF-TV (FOX) Philadelphia.

Programming (via satellite): Pennsylvania Cable Network.

Fee: $22.50 installation; $12.98 monthly.

Expanded Basic Service 1

Subscribers: 3,200.

Programming (via satellite): A&E Networks; ABC Family Channel; AMC; Animal Planet; Bravo; Cartoon Network; CNBC; CNN; Comcast SportsNet Mid-Atlantic; Comcast SportsNet Philadelphia; Comedy Central; Country Music TV; C-SPAN; Discovery Channel; Discovery Health Channel; Disney Channel; E! Entertainment Television; ESPN; ESPN 2; ESPN Classic Sports; Eternal Word TV Network; Food Network; Fox News Channel; FX; Golf Channel; GSN; Hallmark Channel; Headline News; HGTV; History Channel; INSP; Lifetime; Lifetime Movie Network; MSNBC; MTV; National Geographic Channel; NFL Network; Nickelodeon; QVC; Root Sports Pittsburgh; SoapNet; Speed; Spike TV; Syfy; TBS Superstation; The Learning Channel; The Weather Channel; Travel Channel; Trinity Broadcasting Network; truTV; Turner Classic Movies; Turner Network TV; TV Land; USA Network; Versus; VH1; WE tv.

Fee: $30.81 monthly.

Digital Basic Service

Subscribers: N.A.

Programming (via satellite): America's Store; BBC America; Bio; Bloomberg Television; Boomerang; Canales N; CCTV-4; CMT Pure Country; Cooking Channel; DIY Network; ESPN 2 HD; ESPN HD; ESPN U; Fox College Sports Atlantic; Fox College Sports Central; Fox College Sports Pacific; Fox Movie Channel; Fox Soccer; G4; GAS; GMC; Great American Country; Halogen Network; HD Theater; HDNet; HDNet Movies; History Channel International; HRTV; Independent Film Channel; Lifetime Real Women; MTV Networks Digital Suite; Music Choice; NBA TV; Nick Jr.; Nick Too; NickToons TV; Outdoor Channel; Oxygen; PBS Kids Sprout; ShopNBC; Style Network; Tennis Channel; Toon Disney; Turner Network TV HD; Universal HD.

Fee: $14.95 monthly.

Digital Pay Service 1

Pay Units: N.A.

Programming (via satellite): Cinemax (multiplexed); Encore (multiplexed); Flix; HBO (multiplexed); HBO HD; HBO On Demand; Showtime (multiplexed); Showtime HD; Starz (multiplexed); Starz HDTV; Starz On Demand; Sundance Channel; The Movie Channel (multiplexed).

Fee: $12.50 monthly (Cinemax, Showtime or TMC), $12.95 monthly (Starz), $13.50 monthly (HBO).

Video-On-Demand: No

Pay-Per-View

iN DEMAND.

Internet Service

Operational: Yes.

Broadband Service: ProLog Express.

Telephone Service

None

Miles of Plant: 181.0 (coaxial); None (fiber optic). Additional miles planned: 6.0 (coaxial).

Vice President, Operations: Richard Semmel. General Manager: Mark Masonheimer. Chief Technician: Randy Semmel.

Ownership: Pencor Services Inc. (MSO).

DUNMORE—Comcast Cable, 1 E Uwchlan Ave, Ste 411, Exton, PA 19341. Phone: 570-451-4300. Web Site: http://www.comcast.com. Also serves Archbald, Blakely, Chinchilla, Clarks Green, Clarks Summit, Dalton, Dupont, Elmhurst Twp., Exeter Borough (portions), Eynon, Factoryville, Falls Twp. (Wyoming County), Glenburn Twp. (Lackawanna County), Hughestown, Jenkins Twp. (Luzerne County), Jessup, La Plume, Laflin Borough, Moscow (Lackawanna County), Newton Twp. (Lackawanna County), Nicholson Borough, North Abington Twp., Olyphant, Peckville, Pittston, Pittston Twp., Roaring Brook Twp., Scott Twp. (Lackawanna County), South Abington Twp., Springbrook Twp. (Lackawanna County), West Pittston & Yatesville. ICA: PA0022.

TV Market Ranking: 49 (Archbald, Blakely, Chinchilla, Clarks Green, Clarks Summit, Dalton, DUNMORE, Dupont, Elmhurst Twp., Exeter Borough (portions), Eynon, Factoryville, Falls Twp. (Wyoming County), Glenburn Twp. (Lackawanna County), Hughestown, Jenkins Twp. (Luzerne County), Jessup, La Plume, Laflin Borough, Moscow (Lackawanna County), Newton Twp. (Lackawanna County), Nicholson Borough, North Abington Twp., Olyphant, Peckville, Pittston, Pittston Twp., Roaring Brook Twp., Scott Twp. (Lackawanna County), South Abington Twp., Springbrook Twp. (Lackawanna County), West Pittston, Yatesville). Franchise award date: N.A. Franchise expiration date: N.A. Began: March 1, 1970.

Channel capacity: N.A. Channels available but not in use: N.A.

Basic Service

Subscribers: N.A. Included in Harrisburg

Programming (received off-air): WNEP-TV (ABC) Scranton; WOLF-TV (CW, FOX, MNT) Hazleton; WPSG (CW) Philadelphia; WQPX-TV (ION) Scranton; WSWB (CW) Scranton; WVIA-TV (PBS) Scranton; WYOU (CBS) Scranton.

Programming (via satellite): Catholic Television Network; TBS Superstation; TV Guide Network.

Fee: $45.10 installation; $12.45 monthly; $15.00 additional installation.

Expanded Basic Service 1

Subscribers: N.A.

Programming (via satellite): A&E Networks; ABC Family Channel; AMC; Animal Planet; Bravo; Cartoon Network; CNBC; CNN; Comcast SportsNet Philadelphia; Comedy Central; Country Music TV; C-SPAN; C-SPAN 2; Discovery Channel; Discovery Fit & Health; Disney Channel; E! Entertainment Television; ESPN; ESPN 2; Food Network; Fox News Channel; FX; GSN; Hallmark Channel; Headline News; HGTV; History Channel; Lifetime; MSG; MSNBC; MTV; Nickelodeon; Pennsylvania Cable Network; QVC; Root Sports Pittsburgh; ShopNBC; Spike TV; Syfy; The Learning Channel; The Weather Channel; Travel Channel; Trinity Broadcasting Network; truTV; Turner Network TV; TV Land; USA Network; VH1; WE tv; Yankees Entertainment & Sports.

Fee: $41.55 monthly.

Digital Basic Service

Subscribers: 4,720.

Programming (via satellite): AmericanLife TV Network; BBC America; Bio; Black Family Channel; Bloomberg Television; Canales N; Discovery Fit & Health; DIY Network; ESPN Classic Sports; ESPNews; Fox Movie Channel; Fox Sports World; FSN Digital Atlantic; FSN Digital Central; FSN Digital Pacific; Fuse; G4; GAS; Golf Channel; History Channel International; Independent Film Channel; MTV Networks Digital Suite; Music Choice; National Geographic Channel; Nick Jr.; Nick Too; NickToons TV; Outdoor Channel; SoapNet; Speed; Style Network; Sundance Channel; Trinity Broadcasting Network; Versus.

Fee: $14.00 monthly.

Digital Pay Service 1
Pay Units: N.A.
Programming (via satellite): ART America; CCTV-4; Cinemax (multiplexed); Encore (multiplexed); Filipino Channel; Flix; HBO (multiplexed); RAI International; Russian Television Network; Showtime (multiplexed); Starz (multiplexed); The Movie Channel (multiplexed); TV Asia; TV Japan; TV5, La Television International; Zee TV USA; Zhong Tian Channel.
Video-On-Demand: Yes
Pay-Per-View
Addressable homes: 4,720.
iN DEMAND.
Internet Service
Operational: Yes.
Broadband Service: Comcast High Speed Internet.
Fee: $42.95 monthly.
Telephone Service
Analog: Not Operational
Digital: Operational
Miles of Plant: 913.0 (coaxial); 140.0 (fiber optic).
Area Vice President: Jim Samaha. Vice President, Marketing: Larry Goldman.
Ownership: Comcast Cable Communications Inc. (MSO).

DUSHORE—Blue Ridge Communications, 613 3rd St, PO Box 215, Palmerton, PA 18071-0215. Phones: 610-826-2551; 800-275-0724 (Customer service); 570-836-5422. Web Site: http://www.brctv.com. Also serves Cherry Twp. (Sullivan County), Colley Twp. (Sullivan County), Jonestown (Columbia County), Muncy Valley, New Albany & Sonestown. ICA: PA0327.
TV Market Ranking: 49 (Cherry Twp. (Sullivan County), Colley Twp. (Sullivan County), DUSHORE, Jonestown (Columbia County), Sonestown); Below 100 (Muncy Valley); Outside TV Markets (New Albany). Franchise award date: N.A. Franchise expiration date: N.A. Began: June 1, 1960.
Channel capacity: 42 (operating 2-way). Channels available but not in use: N.A.
Basic Service
Subscribers: 853.
Programming (received off-air): WBNG-TV (CBS, CW) Binghamton; WICZ-TV (FOX) Binghamton; WNEP-TV (ABC) Scranton; WOLF-TV (CW, FOX, MNT) Hazleton; WPIX (CW, IND) New York; WQPX-TV (ION) Scranton; WSKG-TV (PBS) Binghamton; WSWB (CW) Scranton; WVIA-TV (PBS) Scranton; WYOU (CBS) Scranton; allband FM.
Programming (via satellite): ShopNBC; WGN America.
Fee: $22.50 installation; $15.28 monthly.
Expanded Basic Service 1
Subscribers: N.A.
Programming (via satellite): A&E Networks; ABC Family Channel; AMC; Animal Planet; Bravo; Cartoon Network; CNBC; CNN; Comedy Central; Country Music TV; C-SPAN; Discovery Channel; Discovery Health Channel; Disney Channel; E! Entertainment Television; ESPN; ESPN 2; Food Network; Fox News Channel; FX; GSN; Hallmark Channel; Headline News; HGTV; History Channel; INSP; Lifetime; Lifetime Movie Network; MSG; MSNBC; MTV; Nickelodeon; Pennsylvania Cable Network; QVC; Root Sports Pittsburgh; SoapNet; Spike TV; Syfy; TBS Superstation; The Learning Channel; The Weather Channel; Travel Channel; truTV; Turner Classic Movies; Turner Network TV; TV Land; USA Network; Versus; VH1; WE tv; Yankees Entertainment & Sports.
Fee: $25.59 monthly.
Digital Basic Service
Subscribers: N.A.
Programming (via satellite): Discovery Digital Networks; ESPN Classic Sports; ESPNews; Fox Movie Channel; GAS; Halogen Network; MTV Networks Digital Suite; Music Choice; National Geographic Channel; Nick Jr.; Outdoor Channel; Speed; Toon Disney.
Fee: $35.00 installation; $13.95 monthly.
Digital Expanded Basic Service
Subscribers: N.A.
Programming (via satellite): BBC America; Bio; Bloomberg Television; G4; Golf Channel; History Channel International; Style Network.
Fee: $4.95 monthly.
Pay Service 1
Pay Units: 59.
Programming (via satellite): Cinemax; HBO; Showtime.
Fee: $11.50 monthly (Showtime or Cinemax), $12.50 monthly (HBO).
Digital Pay Service 1
Pay Units: N.A.
Programming (via satellite): Cinemax (multiplexed); Encore (multiplexed); Flix; HBO (multiplexed); Showtime (multiplexed); Starz (multiplexed); Sundance Channel; The Movie Channel (multiplexed).
Fee: $12.50 monthly (Cinemax, Showtime or TMC), $12.95 monthly (Starz), $13.50 monthly (HBO).
Video-On-Demand: No
Pay-Per-View
iN DEMAND; iN DEMAND (delivered digitally); Adult PPV (delivered digitally); sports (delivered digitally).
Internet Service
Operational: No.
Telephone Service
None
Vice President, Operations: Richard Semmel. General Manager: Mark Masonheimer. Chief Technician: Garry Woods. Fiber Manager: Randy Semmel.
Ownership: Pencor Services Inc. (MSO).

EAST ALLEN TWP.—Formerly served by NORTHAMPTON BOROUGH, PA [PA0008]. RCN Corp. This cable system has converted to IPTV, 196 Van Buren St, Herndon, VA 20170. Phone: 703-434-8200. Web Site: http://www.rcn.com. ICA: PA5210.
TV Market Ranking: Below 100 (EAST ALLEN TWP.).
Channel capacity: N.A. Channels available but not in use: N.A.
Internet Service
Operational: Yes.
Telephone Service
Digital: Operational
Chairman: Steven J. Simmons. Chief Executive Officer: Jim Holanda.

EAST CONEMAUGH—Formerly served by Adelphia Communications. Now served by BLAIRSVILLE, PA [PA0320]. ICA: PA0217.

EAST LANSDOWNE—RCN Corp. Formerly served by Philadelphia (suburbs), PA [PA5259]. This cable system has converted to IPTV, 196 Van Buren St, Herndon, VA 20170. Phone: 703-434-8200. Web Site: http://www.rcn.com. ICA: PA5251.
Channel capacity: N.A. Channels available but not in use: N.A.

Internet Service
Operational: Yes.
Chairman: Steven J. Simmons. Chief Executive Officer: Jim Holanda.

EAST SMITHFIELD—Community Cable Corp., 4145 Rt 549, Mansfield, PA 16933-9238. Phone: 570-549-4788. Fax: 570-549-2500. E-mail: nptinfo@npacc.net. Web Site: http://www.northpenntelephone.com. ICA: PA0280.
TV Market Ranking: Below 100 (EAST SMITHFIELD). Franchise award date: N.A. Franchise expiration date: N.A. Began: October 15, 1965.
Channel capacity: N.A. Channels available but not in use: N.A.
Basic Service
Subscribers: 258.
Programming (received off-air): ION Television; WBNG-TV (CBS, CW) Binghamton; WBRE-TV (NBC) Wilkes-Barre; WENY-TV (ABC, CW) Elmira; WETM-TV (NBC) Elmira; WICZ-TV (FOX) Binghamton; WNEP-TV (ABC) Scranton; WSKG-TV (PBS) Binghamton; WSWB (CW) Scranton; WVIA-TV (PBS) Scranton.
Programming (via satellite): C-SPAN; Pennsylvania Cable Network; QVC.
Fee: $25.00 installation; $14.95 monthly.
Expanded Basic Service 1
Subscribers: N.A.
Programming (via satellite): A&E Networks; ABC Family Channel; AMC; Animal Planet; BTN; Cartoon Network; CNBC; CNN; Comedy Central; Country Music TV; Discovery Channel; Disney Channel; E! Entertainment Television; ESPN; ESPN 2; Eternal Word TV Network; Food Network; Fox News Channel; FX; Great American Country; GSN; Hallmark Channel; Headline News; HGTV; History Channel; Lifetime; MSNBC; MTV; National Geographic Channel; Nickelodeon; Outdoor Channel; RFD-TV; Root Sports Pittsburgh; Science; Speed; Spike TV; Syfy; TBS Superstation; The Learning Channel; The Weather Channel; Travel Channel; Trinity Broadcasting Network; truTV; Turner Classic Movies; Turner Network TV; TV Land; USA Network; VH1; WGN America; Yankees Entertainment & Sports.
Fee: $23.00 monthly.
Internet Service
Operational: No, DSL.
Telephone Service
None
Miles of Plant: 8.0 (coaxial); None (fiber optic).
President: Robert Wagner. Vice President: Pete McClure. Engineer: Frank Pilling.
Ownership: Community Cable Corp. of Pennsylvania.

EAST WATERFORD—Formerly served by Valley Cable Systems. No longer in operation. ICA: PA0290.

EASTON—Formerly served by NORTHAMPTON BOROUGH, PA [PA0008]. RCN Corp. This cable system has converted to IPTV, 196 Van Buren St, Herndon, VA 20170. Phone: 703-434-8200. Web Site: http://www.rcn.com. ICA: PA5211.
TV Market Ranking: Below 100 (EASTON).
Channel capacity: N.A. Channels available but not in use: N.A.
Internet Service
Operational: Yes.
Telephone Service
Digital: Operational
Chairman: Steven J. Simmons. Chief Executive Officer: Jim Holanda.

EASTON—Service Electric Cable TV & Communcations. Now served by LEHIGH VALLEY, PA [PA0006]. ICA: PA0035.

EASTVILLE—Eastville TV Cable. No longer in operation. ICA: PA0306.

EAU CLAIRE—Formerly served by Cebridge Connections. Now served by GROVE CITY, PA [PA0089]. ICA: PA0269.

EDDYSTONE—RCN Corp. Formerly served by Philadelphia (suburbs), PA [PA0447]. This cable system has converted to IPTV, 196 Van Buren St, Herndon, VA 20170. Phone: 703-434-8200. Web Site: http://www.rcn.com. ICA: PA5252.
Channel capacity: N.A. Channels available but not in use: N.A.
Internet Service
Operational: Yes.
Chairman: Steven J. Simmons. Chief Executive Officer: Jim Holanda.

EDINBORO—Coaxial Cable TV Corp., 105 Walker Dr, Edinboro, PA 16412-2237. Phones: 800-684-1681; 814-734-1424. Fax: 814-734-8898. E-mail: info@coaxpa.com. Web Site: http://www.coaxialcabletv.com. Also serves Cambridge Springs, Cambridge Twp. (Crawford County), Franklin Twp. (Erie County), Richmond Twp. (Crawford County), Rockdale Twp. (Crawford County), Townville, Venango, Venango Twp. (Crawford County), Washington Twp. (Erie County) & Woodcock Borough. ICA: PA0115.
TV Market Ranking: Below 100 (Cambridge Springs, Cambridge Twp. (Crawford County), EDINBORO, Franklin Twp. (Erie County), Richmond Twp. (Crawford County), Rockdale Twp. (Crawford County), Townville, Venango, Venango Twp. (Crawford County), Washington Twp. (Erie County), Woodcock Borough). Franchise award date: July 1, 1967. Franchise expiration date: N.A. Began: July 1, 1967.
Channel capacity: N.A. Channels available but not in use: N.A.
Digital Basic Service
Subscribers: N.A.
Programming (via satellite): Bio; Bloomberg Television; Bravo; Discovery Digital Networks; DMX Music; ESPN Classic Sports; G4; GAS; Halogen Network; History Channel International; Lifetime Movie Network; MTV2; MuchMusic Network; National Geographic Channel; Speed; Style Network; VH1 Classic; VH1 Country; WE tv.
Fee: $25.95 monthly.

Digital Pay Service 1
Pay Units: N.A.
Programming (via satellite): Cinemax (multiplexed); Encore (multiplexed); Flix; Fox Movie Channel; HBO (multiplexed); Showtime (multiplexed); Starz (multiplexed); The Movie Channel (multiplexed).
Fee: $11.95 monthly (each).
Video-On-Demand: No
Pay-Per-View
iN DEMAND (delivered digitally); Fresh (delivered digitally).
Internet Service
Operational: Yes.
Subscribers: 300.
Broadband Service: Stargate Ind..
Fee: free installation; $25.95-$45.95 monthly.
Telephone Service
Analog: Not Operational
Digital: Operational
Fee: $34.95 monthly
Miles of Plant: 200.0 (coaxial); 60.0 (fiber optic). Additional miles planned: 10.0 (coaxial); 15.0 (fiber optic).
General Manager: Chris Lovell.
Ownership: Coaxial Cable TV Corp.

ELDERTON BOROUGH—Comcast Cable. Now served by KISKIMINETAS TWP., PA [PA0074]. ICA: PA0229.

ELDRED TWP.—Herr Cable Co., Box 108, RR 2, Paxinos, PA 17860. Phone: 570-672-2496. Also serves Barbours & Hillsgrove. ICA: PA0389.
TV Market Ranking: Below 100 (Barbours, ELDRED TWP., Hillsgrove).
Channel capacity: N.A. Channels available but not in use: N.A.
Basic Service
Subscribers: 1,300.
Programming (received off-air): WBRE-TV (NBC) Wilkes-Barre; WNEP-TV (ABC) Scranton; WOLF-TV (CW, FOX, MNT) Hazleton; WQMY (MNT) Williamsport; WSWB (CW) Scranton; WVIA-TV (PBS) Scranton; WYOU (CBS) Scranton.
Programming (via satellite): A&E Networks; ABC Family Channel; AMC; Animal Planet; Bravo; CNBC; CNN; C-SPAN; Discovery Channel; Discovery Fit & Health; Disney Channel; ESPN; ESPN 2; Eternal Word TV Network; Food Network; Fox News Channel; FX; Great American Country; Hallmark Channel; Headline News; HGTV; History Channel; INSP; Lifetime; National Geographic Channel; Outdoor Channel; QVC; RFD-TV; ShopNBC; Speed; Syfy; TBS Superstation; The Learning Channel; The Weather Channel; Turner Classic Movies; Turner Network TV; TV Land; USA Network.
Pay Service 1
Pay Units: N.A.
Programming (via satellite): HBO (multiplexed).
Internet Service
Operational: No.
Telephone Service
None
Miles of Plant: 100.0 (coaxial); None (fiber optic).
Manager & Chief Technician: Al Herr.
Ownership: Herr Cable Co.

ELIZABETHTOWN—Comcast Cable, 1 E Uwchlan Ave, Ste 411, Exton, PA 19341. Phone: 484-288-6500. Web Site: http://www.comcast.com. Also serves Buffalo Twp., Conoy Twp., East Donegal Twp., Greenwood Twp. (Perry County), Howe Twp., Juniata Twp. (Perry County), Marietta, Maytown, Millerstown, Rapho Twp. (Lancaster County) & West Donegal Twp. ICA: PA0068.
TV Market Ranking: 57 (Buffalo Twp., Conoy Twp., East Donegal Twp., ELIZABETHTOWN, Greenwood Twp. (Perry County), Howe Twp., Juniata Twp. (Perry County), Marietta, Maytown, Millerstown, Mount Joy (Lancaster County), Rapho Twp. (Lancaster County), West Donegal Twp.). Franchise award date: N.A. Franchise expiration date: N.A. Began: June 1, 1967.
Channel capacity: N.A. Channels available but not in use: N.A.
Basic Service
Subscribers: N.A. Included in Harrisburg
Programming (received off-air): KYW-TV (CBS) Philadelphia; WBAL-TV (NBC) Baltimore; WCAU (NBC) Philadelphia; WGAL (NBC) Lancaster; WGCB-TV (IND) Red Lion; WHP-TV (CBS, MNT) Harrisburg; WHTM-TV (ABC) Harrisburg; WITF-TV (PBS) Harrisburg; WLYH-TV (CW) Lancaster; WMAR-TV (ABC) Baltimore; WPHL-TV (MNT, IND) Philadelphia; WPMT (FOX) York; WPSG (CW) Philadelphia; WPVI-TV (ABC) Philadelphia; WTXF-TV (FOX) Philadelphia; allband FM.
Programming (via satellite): Discovery Channel; TBS Superstation; The Comcast Network; TV Guide Network.
Fee: $45.10 installation; $12.74 monthly.
Expanded Basic Service 1
Subscribers: N.A.
Programming (via satellite): A&E Networks; ABC Family Channel; AMC; Animal Planet; BET Networks; Bravo; Cartoon Network; CNBC; CNN; Comcast SportsNet Philadelphia; Comedy Central; Country Music TV; C-SPAN; C-SPAN 2; Discovery Health Channel; Disney Channel; E! Entertainment Television; ESPN; ESPN 2; Food Network; Fox News Channel; FX; Golf Channel; GSN; Headline News; HGTV; History Channel; ION Television; Lifetime; MarketConnect Network; MSNBC; MTV; Nickelodeon; Pennsylvania Cable Network; QVC; Root Sports Pittsburgh; Speed; Spike TV; Style Network; Syfy; The Learning Channel; The Weather Channel; Travel Channel; Turner Network TV; TV Land; USA Network; Versus; VH1.
Fee: $38.05 monthly.
Digital Basic Service
Subscribers: 6,215.
Programming (via satellite): BBC America; C-SPAN 3; Discovery Digital Networks; DMX Music; Encore (multiplexed); ESPNews; Flix; G4; GAS; Mid-Atlantic Sports Network; MTV Networks Digital Suite; National Geographic Channel; Nick Jr.; Nick Too; SoapNet; Sundance Channel; Toon Disney; Weatherscan.
Fee: $14.95 monthly.
Digital Pay Service 1
Pay Units: N.A.
Programming (via satellite): Cinemax (multiplexed); HBO (multiplexed); Showtime (multiplexed); Starz (multiplexed); The Movie Channel (multiplexed).
Video-On-Demand: Yes
Pay-Per-View
Addressable homes: 10,891.
iN DEMAND; iN DEMAND (delivered digitally); Playboy TV (delivered digitally); Fresh (delivered digitally); Shorteez (delivered digitally); Pleasure (delivered digitally); ESPN Now (delivered digitally); ESPN Extra (delivered digitally); NBA TV (delivered digitally).
Internet Service
Operational: Yes.
Subscribers: 4,440.
Broadband Service: Comcast High Speed Internet.
Fee: $42.95 monthly; $3.00 modem lease.
Telephone Service
Digital: Operational
Miles of Plant: 520.0 (coaxial); 16.0 (fiber optic). Additional miles planned: 28.0 (coaxial).
Area Vice President: Jim Samah. Vice President, Marketing: Larry Goldman.
Ownership: Comcast Cable Communications Inc. (MSO).

ELKLAND—Time Warner Cable. Now served by ELMIRA/CORNING, NY [NY0057]. ICA: PA0160.

EMMAUS—Service Electric Cable TV & Communications. Now served by LEHIGH VALLEY, PA [PA0006]. ICA: PA0081.

EPHRATA—Blue Ridge Communications, 613 3rd St, PO Box 215, Palmerton, PA 18071-0215. Phones: 610-826-2551; 717-484-2266 (Customer service); 717-733-4111. Web Site: http://www.brctv.com. Also serves Adamstown, Akron, Brecknock Twp. (Lancaster County), Caernarvon Twp. (Lancaster County), Clay Twp. (Lancaster County), Denver, Earl Twp. (Lancaster County), East Cocalico Twp., East Earl Twp. (portions), Elizabeth Twp. (Lancaster County), Ephrata Twp. (Lancaster County), Lititz, Manheim, Penn Twp. (Lancaster County), Rapho Twp. (Lancaster County), South Heidelberg Twp. (Berks County), Spring Twp. (Berks County), Terre Hill, Warwick Twp. (Lancaster County), West Cocalico Twp. & West Earl Twp. (northern portion). ICA: PA0031.
TV Market Ranking: 57 (Adamstown, Akron, Brecknock Twp. (Lancaster County), Caernarvon Twp. (Lancaster County), Clay Twp. (Lancaster County), Denver, Earl Twp. (Lancaster County), East Cocalico Twp., East Earl Twp. (portions), Elizabeth Twp. (Lancaster County), EPHRATA, Ephrata Twp. (Lancaster County), Lititz, Manheim, Penn Twp. (Lancaster County), Rapho Twp. (Lancaster County), South Heidelberg Twp. (Berks County), Spring Twp. (Berks County), Terre Hill, Warwick Twp. (Lancaster County), West Cocalico Twp., West Earl Twp. (northern portion)). Franchise award date: N.A. Franchise expiration date: N.A. Began: November 11, 1965.
Channel capacity: 62 (operating 2-way). Channels available but not in use: N.A.
Basic Service
Subscribers: 33,000.
Programming (received off-air): KYW-TV (CBS) Philadelphia; WCAU (NBC) Philadelphia; WGAL (NBC) Lancaster; WGCB-TV (IND) Red Lion; WHP-TV (CBS, MNT) Harrisburg; WHTM-TV (ABC) Harrisburg; WITF-TV (PBS) Harrisburg; WLYH-TV (CW) Lancaster; WPHL-TV (MNT, IND) Philadelphia; WPMT (FOX) York; WPSG (CW) Philadelphia; WPVI-TV (ABC) Philadelphia; WTXF-TV (FOX) Philadelphia; allband FM.
Programming (via satellite): C-SPAN; C-SPAN 2; WGN America.
Fee: $22.50 installation; $16.06 monthly.
Expanded Basic Service 1
Subscribers: 29,106.
Programming (via satellite): A&E Networks; ABC Family Channel; AMC; Animal Planet; Bravo; Cartoon Network; CNBC; CNN; Comcast SportsNet Mid-Atlantic; Comcast SportsNet Philadelphia; Comedy Central; Country Music TV; Discovery Channel; Discovery Health Channel; Disney Channel; E! Entertainment Television; ESPN; ESPN 2; ESPN Classic Sports; Eternal Word TV Network; Food Network; Fox News Channel; FX; Golf Channel; GSN; Hallmark Channel; Headline News; HGTV; History Channel; INSP; ION Television; Lifetime; Lifetime Movie Network; MSNBC; MTV; Nickelodeon; Pennsylvania Cable Network; Praise Television; QVC; Speed; Spike TV; Syfy; TBS Superstation; The Learning Channel; The Weather Channel; Travel Channel; Trinity Broadcasting Network; truTV; Turner Classic Movies; Turner Network TV; TV Land; USA Network; Versus; VH1; WE tv.
Fee: $31.24 monthly.
Digital Basic Service
Subscribers: N.A.
Programming (via satellite): Discovery Digital Networks; Fox Movie Channel; FSN Digital Atlantic; FSN Digital Central; FSN Digital Pacific; GAS; Halogen Network; Meadows Racing Network; MTV Networks Digital Suite; Music Choice; National Geographic Channel; Nick Jr.; Nick Too; NickToons TV; Outdoor Channel; PBS Kids Channel; SoapNet; Toon Disney.
Fee: $35.00 installation; $9.95 monthly.
Digital Expanded Basic Service
Subscribers: N.A.
Programming (via satellite): BBC America; Bio; Bloomberg Television; Boomerang; Cooking Channel; DIY Network; G4; History Channel International; Lifetime Real Women; LWS Local Weather Station; Style Network.
Fee: $5.00 monthly.
Digital Pay Service 1
Pay Units: N.A.
Programming (via satellite): Cinemax (multiplexed); Encore (multiplexed); Flix; HBO (multiplexed); Showtime (multiplexed); Starz (multiplexed); Sundance Channel; The Movie Channel (multiplexed).
Fee: $12.50 monthly (Cinemax or Showtime/Flix/Sundance/TMC), $12.95 monthly (Starz/Encore), $13.50 monthly (HBO).
Video-On-Demand: Yes
Pay-Per-View
Addressable homes: 7,000.
iN DEMAND; iN DEMAND (delivered digitally); Sports PPV (delivered digitally); Barker (delivered digitally); adult PPV (delivered digitally).
Internet Service
Operational: Yes.
Broadband Service: ProLog Express.
Fee: $50.00 installation; $36.95 monthly; $10.00 modem lease; $59.95 modem purchase.
Telephone Service
None
Miles of Plant: 627.0 (coaxial); 10.0 (fiber optic). Additional miles planned: 12.0 (coaxial); 50.0 (fiber optic).
Vice President, Operations: Richard Semmel. General Manager: Mark Masonheimer. Chief Technician: Randy Semmel.
Ownership: Pencor Services Inc. (MSO).

ERIE—Time Warner Cable, 3627 Zimmerman Rd, Erie, PA 16510-2642. Phones: 330-633-9203 (Akron office); 814-898-1656. Fax: 814-456-5162. Web Site: http://www.timewarnercable.com. ICA: PA0019.
TV Market Ranking: Below 100 (ERIE). Franchise award date: N.A. Franchise expiration date: N.A. Began: December 14, 1981.
Channel capacity: N.A. Channels available but not in use: N.A.

Basic Service
Subscribers: N.A. Included in Warren, OH
Programming (received off-air): WFXP (FOX) Erie; WICU-TV (NBC) Erie; WJET-TV (ABC) Erie; WQLN (PBS) Erie; WSEE-TV (CBS, CW) Erie; allband FM.
Programming (via satellite): C-SPAN; C-SPAN 2; QVC; ShopNBC; WGN America.
Fee: $39.95 installation; $11.14 monthly; $.57 converter.

Expanded Basic Service 1
Subscribers: N.A.
Programming (via satellite): A&E Networks; ABC Family Channel; AMC; AmericanLife TV Network; Animal Planet; BET Networks; Bravo; Cartoon Network; CNBC; CNN; Comedy Central; Country Music TV; Discovery Channel; Discovery Fit & Health; Discovery Health Channel; Disney Channel; E! Entertainment Television; ESPN; ESPN 2; ESPN Classic Sports; Eternal Word TV Network; Food Network; Fox News Channel; Fox Sports Net Ohio; FX; Golf Channel; Great American Country; Hallmark Channel; Headline News; HGTV; History Channel; INSP; ION Television; Lifetime; Lifetime Movie Network; MSNBC; MTV; MTV2; Nickelodeon; Oxygen; Root Sports Pittsburgh; SoapNet; Spike TV; Syfy; TBS Superstation; The Learning Channel; The Weather Channel; Travel Channel; Trinity Broadcasting Network; truTV; Turner Classic Movies; Turner Network TV; TV Guide Network; TV Land; Univision Studios; USA Network; Versus; VH1; WE tv.
Fee: $35.89 monthly.

Digital Basic Service
Subscribers: N.A.
Programming (via satellite): AmericanLife TV Network; America's Store; BBC America; Bio; Bloomberg Television; Boomerang; Canales N; CBS Sports Network; CNN International; Cooking Channel; Country Music TV; C-SPAN 3; Daystar TV Network; Discovery Kids Channel; Disney Channel; DIY Network; ESPN; ESPNews; Fox College Sports Atlantic; Fox College Sports Central; Fox College Sports Pacific; Fox Movie Channel; Fox Soccer; Fuel TV; Fuse; G4; GAS; GSN; HD Theater; HDNet; HDNet Movies; History Channel International; Independent Film Channel; INHD (multiplexed); Lifetime Real Women; MTV2; Music Choice; National Geographic Channel; NBA TV; Nick Jr.; NickToons TV; Outdoor Channel; Speed; Style Network; Tennis Channel; The Word Network; Toon Disney; Turner Network TV; TVG Network; VH1.
Fee: $15.51 monthly.

Digital Pay Service 1
Pay Units: N.A.
Programming (via satellite): ART America; Cinemax (multiplexed); Deutsche Welle TV; Encore (multiplexed); HBO (multiplexed); RAI International; Showtime (multiplexed); Starz (multiplexed); Sundance Channel; The Movie Channel (multiplexed); TV Asia; Zee TV USA.

Video-On-Demand: Yes

Pay-Per-View
Hot Choice; iN DEMAND; Playboy TV; Spice.

Internet Service
Operational: Yes. Began: September 1, 2002.
Broadband Service: Road Runner.
Fee: $99.00 installation; $44.95 monthly.

Telephone Service
Digital: Operational
Fee: $44.95 monthly

Miles of Plant: 269.0 (coaxial); None (fiber optic). Additional miles planned: 40.0 (fiber optic).
President: Stephen Fry. Area Vice President: Rick Whaley. Vice President, Engineering: Al Costanzi. Vice President, Marketing: Patrick Burke. Vice President, Public Affairs: William Jasso. General Manager: Brian Frederick. Office Manager: Dana Bachman.
Ownership: Time Warner Cable (MSO).

FANNETTSBURG—Fannettsburg Cable TV Co. No longer in operation. ICA: PA0331.

FAWN GROVE—Formerly served by Armstrong Cable Services. No longer in operation. ICA: PA0152.

FOLCROFT—RCN Corp. Formerly served by Philadelphia (suburbs), PA [PA0447]. This cable system has converted to IPTV, 196 Van Buren St, Herndon, VA 20170. Phone: 703-434-8200. Web Site: http://www.rcn.com. ICA: PA5253.
Channel capacity: N.A. Channels available but not in use: N.A.

Internet Service
Operational: Yes.

Chairman: Steven J. Simmons. Chief Executive Officer: Jim Holanda.

FOREST CITY—Formerly served by Adams Cable Service. Now served by CARBONDALE, PA [PA0067]. ICA: PA0179.

FORKS TWP.—Formerly served by NORTHAMPTON BOROUGH, PA [PA0008]. RCN Corp. This cable system has converted to IPTV, 196 Van Buren St, Herndon, VA 20170. Phone: 703-434-8200. Web Site: http://www.rcn.com. ICA: PA5212.
TV Market Ranking: Below 100 (FORKS TWP.).
Channel capacity: N.A. Channels available but not in use: N.A.

Internet Service
Operational: Yes.

Telephone Service
Digital: Operational

Chairman: Steven J. Simmons. Chief Executive Officer: Jim Holanda.

FORT INDIANTOWN GAP—Gap Cable TV Inc., 1 Washington Rd, Annville, PA 17003. Phone: 717-865-0511. E-mail: sales@gapbroadband.com. Web Site: http://www.gapbroadband.com. Also serves East Hanover Twp. (Lebanon County) & Union Twp. (Lebanon County). ICA: PA0332.
TV Market Ranking: 57 (East Hanover Twp. (Lebanon County), FORT INDIANTOWN GAP, Union Twp. (Lebanon County)). Franchise award date: December 5, 1991. Franchise expiration date: N.A. Began: August 15, 1992.
Channel capacity: N.A. Channels available but not in use: N.A.

Basic Service
Subscribers: 300.
Programming (received off-air): WGAL (NBC) Lancaster; WGCB-TV (IND) Red Lion; WHP-TV (CBS, MNT) Harrisburg; WHTM-TV (ABC) Harrisburg; WITF-TV (PBS) Harrisburg; WLYH-TV (CW) Lancaster; WPMT (FOX) York.
Programming (via satellite): A&E Networks; ABC Family Channel; AMC; BET Networks; Cartoon Network; CNBC; CNN; Comedy Central; C-SPAN; C-SPAN 2; Discovery Channel; Disney Channel; ESPN; ESPN 2; Headline News; Lifetime; MTV; Nickelodeon; Spike TV; Syfy; TBS Superstation; The Learning Channel; The Weather Channel; Turner Network TV; USA Network; VH1; WGN America; WPIX (CW, IND) New York.
Fee: $30.00 installation; $28.00 monthly; $3.40 converter.

Pay Service 1
Pay Units: 12.
Programming (via satellite): Cinemax; HBO; Showtime; The Movie Channel.
Fee: $11.00 monthly (each).

Video-On-Demand: No

Internet Service
Operational: Yes, DSL.
Subscribers: 100.
Broadband Service: In-house.
Fee: $35.00 installation; $46.40 monthly.

Telephone Service
None

Miles of Plant: 18.0 (coaxial); None (fiber optic).
Manager & Chief Technician: George Bryce.
Ownership: Gap Cable TV Inc. (MSO).

FORT LOUDON—Comcast Cable. Now served by CHAMBERSBURG, PA [PA0066]. ICA: PA0333.

FOUNTAIN HILL BOROUGH—Formerly served by NORTHAMPTON BOROUGH, PA [PA0008]. RCN Corp. This cable system has converted to IPTV, 196 Van Buren St, Herndon, VA 20170. Phone: 703-434-8200. Web Site: http://www.rcn.com. ICA: PA5213.
TV Market Ranking: Below 100 (FOUNTAIN HILL BOROUGH).
Channel capacity: N.A. Channels available but not in use: N.A.

Internet Service
Operational: Yes.

Telephone Service
Digital: Operational

Chairman: Steven J. Simmons. Chief Executive Officer: Jim Holanda.

FRANKLIN (Venango County)—Time Warner Cable, 3627 Zimmerman Rd, Erie, PA 16510-2642. Phone: 814-898-1656. Fax: 814-456-5162. Web Site: http://www.timewarnercable.com. Also serves Cranberry Twp. (Venango County), Frenchcreek Twp. (Venango County), Mineral Twp., Polk, Reno, Sandy Creek Twp. (Venango County) & Sugarcreek (Venango County). ICA: PA0100.
TV Market Ranking: Outside TV Markets (Cranberry Twp. (Venango County), FRANKLIN (VENANGO COUNTY), Frenchcreek Twp. (Venango County), Mineral Twp., Polk, Reno, Sandy Creek Twp. (Venango County), Sugarcreek (Venango County)). Franchise award date: N.A. Franchise expiration date: N.A. Began: October 1, 1954.
Channel capacity: N.A. Channels available but not in use: N.A.

Basic Service
Subscribers: N.A. Included in Warren, OH
Programming (received off-air): KDKA-TV (CBS) Pittsburgh; WICU-TV (NBC) Erie; WJET-TV (ABC) Erie; WPCB-TV (IND) Greensburg; WPGH-TV (FOX) Pittsburgh; WPMY (MNT) Pittsburgh; WPXI (IND, NBC) Pittsburgh; WQED (PBS) Pittsburgh; WQLN (PBS) Erie; WSEE-TV (CBS, CW) Erie; WTAE-TV (ABC) Pittsburgh; allband FM.
Programming (via satellite): ABC Family Channel; BET Networks; C-SPAN; Disney Channel; ESPN; Lifetime; QVC; TBS Superstation; The Learning Channel; The Weather Channel; Turner Network TV; TV Guide Network; USA Network.
Fee: $41.80 installation; $17.38 monthly.

Expanded Basic Service 1
Subscribers: N.A.
Programming (via satellite): A&E Networks; AMC; Animal Planet; Bravo; Cartoon Network; CNBC; CNN; Comedy Central; Country Music TV; Discovery Channel; Discovery Health Channel; E! Entertainment Television; ESPN 2; ESPN Classic Sports; Eternal Word TV Network; Food Network; Fox News Channel; FX; Great American Country; Hallmark Channel; Headline News; HGTV; History Channel; MSNBC; MTV; Nickelodeon; Oxygen; Pennsylvania Cable Network; Philadelphia Park Live; Root Sports Pittsburgh; ShopNBC; Spike TV; Syfy; Travel Channel; truTV; TV Land; Versus; VH1; WE tv.
Fee: $27.12 monthly.

Digital Basic Service
Subscribers: N.A.
Programming (via satellite): AmericanLife TV Network; BBC America; Bloomberg Television; Discovery Digital Networks; ESPNews; Fox Soccer; Fuse; G4; GAS; Golf Channel; GSN; Lifetime Movie Network; MTV2; Music Choice; National Geographic Channel; Nick Jr.; Outdoor Channel; Ovation; Speed; Toon Disney; Trio; Turner Classic Movies; VH1 Classic.
Fee: $16.62 monthly.

Digital Expanded Basic Service
Subscribers: N.A.
Programming (via satellite): Encore; Fox Movie Channel; Independent Film Channel; Sundance Channel.
Fee: $4.95 monthly.

Digital Pay Service 1
Pay Units: 2,297.
Programming (via satellite): Cinemax; HBO; Showtime (multiplexed); Starz (multiplexed); The Movie Channel (multiplexed).
Fee: $10.00 monthly (each).

Video-On-Demand: No

Pay-Per-View
iN DEMAND (delivered digitally); Fresh (delivered digitally); Shorteez (delivered digitally); Hot Choice (delivered digitally).

Internet Service
Operational: Yes.
Broadband Service: Road Runner.

Telephone Service
Digital: Operational

Miles of Plant: 106.0 (coaxial); None (fiber optic).
President: Stephen Fry. Area Vice President: Rick Whaley. Vice President, Engineering: Al Costanzi. Vice President, Marketing: Patrick Burke. Vice President, Government & Media Relations: Bill Jasso. General

Manager: Brian Frederick. Office Manager: Dana Bachman.
Ownership: Time Warner Cable (MSO).

FREEMANSBURG BOROUGH—Formerly served by NORTHAMPTON BOROUGH, PA [PA0008]. RCN Corp. This cable system has converted to IPTV, 196 Van Buren St, Herndon, VA 20170. Phone: 703-434-8200. Web Site: http://www.rcn.com. ICA: PA5214.
TV Market Ranking: Below 100 (FREEMANSBURG BOROUGH).
Channel capacity: N.A. Channels available but not in use: N.A.
Internet Service
Operational: Yes.
Telephone Service
Digital: Operational
Chairman: Steven J. Simmons. Chief Executive Officer: Jim Holanda.

FREEPORT—Formerly served by Adelphia Communications. Now served by KISKIMINETAS TWP., PA [PA0074]. ICA: PA0334.

GAINES—Gaines-Watrous TV Inc., 55 Chestnut St, Gaines, PA 16921-9554. Phone: 814-435-6578. Fax: 814-435-6578. Also serves Gaines Twp. (Tioga County) & Pike Twp. (Potter County). ICA: PA0266.
TV Market Ranking: Outside TV Markets (GAINES, Gaines Twp. (Tioga County), Pike Twp. (Potter County)). Franchise award date: N.A. Franchise expiration date: N.A. Began: January 1, 1954.
Channel capacity: 36 (not 2-way capable). Channels available but not in use: N.A.
Basic Service
Subscribers: 125.
Programming (received off-air): WBNG-TV (CBS, CW) Binghamton; WENY-TV (ABC, CW) Elmira; WETM-TV (NBC) Elmira; WIVB-TV (CBS) Buffalo; WVIA-TV (PBS) Scranton; WYDC (FOX, MNT) Corning; WYOU (CBS) Scranton.
Programming (via satellite): ABC Family Channel; AMC; CNN; Country Music TV; C-SPAN; Discovery Channel; Disney Channel; ESPN; ESPN 2; Hallmark Channel; Outdoor Channel; QVC; Spike TV; Syfy; TBS Superstation; The Learning Channel; The Weather Channel; Trinity Broadcasting Network; Turner Network TV; TV Land; USA Network; WGN America.
Fee: $35.00 installation; $15.00 monthly.
Pay Service 1
Pay Units: 60.
Programming (via satellite): Showtime.
Fee: $8.50 monthly.
Video-On-Demand: No
Internet Service
Operational: No.
Telephone Service
None
Miles of Plant: 20.0 (coaxial); None (fiber optic).
Chief Technician: Melvin Lowrey.
Ownership: Gaines Watrous TV Association Inc.

GALETON—Blue Ridge Communications, 613 3rd St, PO Box 215, Palmerton, PA 18071-0215. Phones: 610-826-2551; 800-543-8128 (Customer service); 570-662-2369. Web Site: http://www.brctv.com. Also serves Pike Twp. (Potter County) & West Branch Twp. (Potter County). ICA: PA0222.
TV Market Ranking: Outside TV Markets (GALETON, Pike Twp. (Potter County), West Branch Twp. (Potter County)). Franchise award date: N.A. Franchise expiration date: N.A. Began: January 1, 1953.
Channel capacity: 35 (not 2-way capable). Channels available but not in use: N.A.
Basic Service
Subscribers: 574.
Programming (received off-air): WBNG-TV (CBS, CW) Binghamton; WENY-TV (ABC, CW) Elmira; WETM-TV (NBC) Elmira; WPIX (CW, IND) New York; WSKG-TV (PBS) Binghamton; WVIA-TV (PBS) Scranton; WYDC (FOX, MNT) Corning; WYOU (CBS) Scranton; allband FM.
Programming (via satellite): C-SPAN; C-SPAN 2; WGN America.
Fee: $22.50 installation; $16.05 monthly.
Expanded Basic Service 1
Subscribers: N.A.
Programming (via satellite): A&E Networks; ABC Family Channel; AMC; Animal Planet; BET Networks; Cartoon Network; CNBC; CNN; Comedy Central; Country Music TV; Discovery Channel; Disney Channel; E! Entertainment Television; ESPN; ESPN 2; Eternal Word TV Network; Food Network; Fox News Channel; FX; Hallmark Channel; Headline News; HGTV; History Channel; Lifetime; Lifetime Movie Network; MSNBC; MTV; Nickelodeon; Pennsylvania Cable Network; QVC; Root Sports Pittsburgh; SoapNet; Speed; Spike TV; Syfy; TBS Superstation; The Learning Channel; The Weather Channel; Travel Channel; Trinity Broadcasting Network; truTV; Turner Classic Movies; Turner Network TV; TV Land; USA Network; Versus; VH1.
Fee: $27.99 monthly.
Digital Basic Service
Subscribers: N.A.
Programming (via satellite): Discovery Digital Networks; ESPN Classic Sports; ESPNews; Fox Movie Channel; GAS; GSN; Halogen Network; MTV Networks Digital Suite; Music Choice; National Geographic Channel; Nick Jr.; Outdoor Channel; Toon Disney.
Fee: $13.95 monthly.
Digital Expanded Basic Service
Subscribers: N.A.
Programming (via satellite): BBC America; Bio; Bloomberg Television; G4; Golf Channel; History Channel International; Style Network.
Fee: $5.00 monthly.
Pay Service 1
Pay Units: 71.
Programming (via satellite): Cinemax; HBO; Showtime.
Fee: $11.50 monthly (Showtime), $12.50 monthly (HBO).
Digital Pay Service 1
Pay Units: N.A.
Programming (via satellite): Cinemax (multiplexed); Encore (multiplexed); Flix; HBO (multiplexed); Showtime (multiplexed); Starz (multiplexed); Sundance Channel; The Movie Channel (multiplexed).
Fee: $12.50 monthly (Cinemax, Showtime or TMC), $12.95 monthly (Starz), $13.50 monthly (HBO).
Video-On-Demand: No
Pay-Per-View
iN DEMAND (delivered digitally); Sports PPV (delivered digitally); iN DEMAND; adult PPV (delivered digitally).
Internet Service
Operational: No.
Telephone Service
None
Miles of Plant: 12.0 (coaxial); None (fiber optic).
Vice President, Operations: Richard Semmel. General Manager: Mark Masonheimer. Chief Technician: Randy Semmel.
Ownership: Pencor Services Inc. (MSO).

GARLAND—Formerly served by Cebridge Connections. No longer in operation. ICA: PA0291.

GETTYSBURG—Comcast Cable, 1 E Uwchlan Ave, Ste 411, Exton, PA 19341. Phones: 484-288-6500; 717-337-1630 (Gettysburg office). Web Site: http://www.comcast.com. Also serves Arendtsville, Bendersville, Biglerville, Bonneauville, Carroll Twp., Carroll Valley, Codorus Twp., Cumberland Twp., Dillsburg, Dover Twp., East Berlin, Fairfield, Franklintown, Germany Twp., Glen Rock, Hamiltonban Twp., Highrock, Latimore Twp, Littlestown, Menallen Twp., Monaghan Twp., New Freedom, New Oxford, North Codorus Twp., Railroad, Seven Valleys, Shrewsbury, Shrewsbury Twp., Spring Grove, Straban Twp., Warrington Twp., West Manheim Twp. & York Springs. ICA: PA0106.
TV Market Ranking: 57 (Arendtsville, Bendersville, Biglerville, Bonneauville, Carroll Twp., Carroll Valley, Codorus Twp., Cumberland Twp., Dillsburg, Dover Twp., East Berlin, Fairfield, Franklintown, Germany Twp., GETTYSBURG, Glen Rock, Hamiltonban Twp., Highrock, Latimore Twp., Littlestown, Menallen Twp., Monaghan Twp., New Freedom, New Oxford, North Codorus Twp., Railroad, Seven Valleys, Shrewsbury, Shrewsbury Twp., Spring Grove, Straban Twp., Warrington Twp., West Manheim Twp., York Springs).
Channel capacity: N.A. Channels available but not in use: N.A.
Basic Service
Subscribers: N.A. Included in Harrisburg
Programming (received off-air): WBAL-TV (NBC) Baltimore; WDCW (CW) Washington; WGAL (NBC) Lancaster; WGCB-TV (IND) Red Lion; WHP-TV (CBS, MNT) Harrisburg; WHTM-TV (ABC) Harrisburg; WITF-TV (PBS) Harrisburg; WJAL (IND) Hagerstown; WJZ-TV (CBS) Baltimore; WLYH-TV (CW) Lancaster; WMAR-TV (ABC) Baltimore; WMPB (PBS) Baltimore; WPMT (FOX) York.
Programming (via satellite): C-SPAN; C-SPAN 2; Eternal Word TV Network; INSP; Pennsylvania Cable Network; QVC; The Comcast Network; Trinity Broadcasting Network; TV Guide Network.
Fee: $45.10 installation; $17.45 monthly.
Expanded Basic Service 1
Subscribers: N.A.
Programming (via satellite): A&E Networks; ABC Family Channel; AMC; Animal Planet; BET Networks; Bravo; Cartoon Network; CNBC; CNN; Comcast SportsNet Mid-Atlantic; Comedy Central; Discovery Channel; Disney Channel; E! Entertainment Television; ESPN; ESPN 2; Food Network; Fox News Channel; FX; Headline News; HGTV; History Channel; Lifetime; Mid-Atlantic Sports Network; MSNBC; MTV; Nickelodeon; Spike TV; Syfy; TBS Superstation; The Learning Channel; The Weather Channel; Travel Channel; Turner Network TV; TV Land; Univision Studios; USA Network; VH1.
Fee: $33.45 monthly.
Digital Basic Service
Subscribers: N.A.
Programming (via satellite): BBC America; Bio; Bloomberg Television; Canales N; CMT Pure Country; Cooking Channel; Country Music TV; C-SPAN 2; C-SPAN 3; DIY Network; Encore (multiplexed); ESPN 2 HD; ESPN Classic Sports; ESPN HD; ESPNews; Flix; Fox College Sports Atlantic; Fox College Sports Central; Fox College Sports Pacific; Fox Movie Channel; Fox Reality Channel; Fox Soccer; Fuse; G4; GAS; GMC; Golf Channel; GolTV; Great American Country; GSN; Hallmark Channel; Halogen Network; HD Theater; History Channel International; Independent Film Channel; INSP; Jewelry Television; Lifetime Movie Network; LOGO; MoviePlex; MTV Networks Digital Suite; Music Choice; National Geographic Channel; Nick Jr.; Nick Too; NickToons TV; Outdoor Channel; Oxygen; PBS Kids Sprout; ShopNBC; SoapNet; Speed; Style Network; Sundance Channel; The Word Network; Toon Disney; Trinity Broadcasting Network; truTV; Turner Classic Movies; Turner Network TV HD; TV One; Universal HD; Versus; Versus HD; WE tv.
Fee: $14.95 monthly.
Digital Pay Service 1
Pay Units: N.A.
Programming (via satellite): Cinemax (multiplexed); Cinemax HD; HBO (multiplexed); HBO HD; Showtime (multiplexed); Showtime HD; Starz (multiplexed); Starz HDTV; The Movie Channel (multiplexed).
Video-On-Demand: No
Pay-Per-View
iN DEMAND; iN DEMAND (delivered digitally); Playboy TV (delivered digitally); Fresh (delivered digitally).
Internet Service
Operational: Yes.
Broadband Service: Comcast High Speed Internet.
Fee: $42.95 monthly.
Miles of Plant: 15.0 (coaxial); None (fiber optic).
Area Vice President: Jim Samaha. Vice President, Marketing: Larry Goldman. Technical Operations Manager: Lloyd Mayhew.
Ownership: Comcast Cable Communications Inc. (MSO).

GLEN ROCK—Formerly served by Adelphia Communications. Now served by HIGHROCK, PA [PA0106]. ICA: PA0336.

GLENOLDEN—RCN Corp. Formerly served by Philadelphia (suburbs), PA [PA0447]. This cable system has converted to IPTV, 196 Van Buren St, Herndon, VA 20170. Phone: 703-434-8200. Web Site: http://www.rcn.com. ICA: PA5254.
Channel capacity: N.A. Channels available but not in use: N.A.
Internet Service
Operational: Yes.
Chairman: Steven J. Simmons. Chief Executive Officer: Jim Holanda.

GRAHAM TWP.—Tele-Media. Now served by SNOW SHOE, PA [PA0188]. ICA: PA0251.

GRAMPIAN—Atlantic Broadband, 120 Southmont Blvd, Johnstown, PA 15905. Phones: 888-536-9600; 814-539-8971. Fax: 814-535-7749. E-mail: info@atlanticbb.com. Web Site: http://www.atlanticbb.com. ICA: PA0236.
TV Market Ranking: 74 (GRAMPIAN). Franchise award date: N.A. Franchise expiration date: N.A. Began: January 1, 1982.
Channel capacity: N.A. Channels available but not in use: N.A.
Basic Service
Subscribers: 342.
Programming (received off-air): KDKA-TV (CBS) Pittsburgh; WATM-TV (ABC)

Altoona; WJAC-TV (NBC) Johnstown; WKBS-TV (IND) Altoona; WPIX (CW, IND) New York; WPSU-TV (PBS) Clearfield; WTAE-TV (ABC) Pittsburgh; WTAJ-TV (CBS) Altoona; WWCP-TV (FOX) Johnstown.

Programming (via satellite): C-SPAN; C-SPAN 2; Eternal Word TV Network; Pennsylvania Cable Network; Product Information Network; QVC; ShopNBC; TV Guide Network.

Fee: $25.00 installation; $18.95 monthly; $1.24 converter; $17.50 additional installation.

Expanded Basic Service 1

Subscribers: N.A.

Programming (via satellite): A&E Networks; ABC Family Channel; AMC; Animal Planet; Bravo; Cartoon Network; CNBC; CNN; Comedy Central; Country Music TV; Discovery Channel; Discovery Health Channel; Disney Channel; E! Entertainment Television; ESPN; ESPN 2; Food Network; Fox News Channel; FX; Golf Channel; Hallmark Channel; Headline News; HGTV; History Channel; ION Television; Lifetime; MSNBC; MTV; National Geographic Channel; Nickelodeon; NickToons TV; Oxygen; Root Sports Pittsburgh; Speed; Spike TV; Syfy; TBS Superstation; The Learning Channel; The Weather Channel; Travel Channel; truTV; Turner Classic Movies; Turner Network TV; TV Land; USA Network; Versus; VH1.

Fee: $35.54 monthly.

Digital Basic Service

Subscribers: N.A.

Programming (via satellite): A&E HD; Animal Planet HD; BBC America; Bio; Bloomberg Television; Boomerang; CMT Pure Country; Discovery Channel HD; Discovery Kids Channel; DIY Network; Encore (multiplexed); ESPN 2 HD; ESPN Classic Sports; ESPN HD; ESPNews; Fuel TV; G4; HD Theater; History Channel International; ID Investigation Discovery; Independent Film Channel; INSP; Lifetime Movie Network; Lifetime Real Women; Military Channel; MTV Hits; MTV Jams; MTV2; Music Choice; NFL Network; Nick Jr.; Nick Too; Planet Green; Root Sports Pittsburgh; Science; SoapNet; Starz (multiplexed); Style Network; TBS in HD; TeenNick; Toon Disney; Tr3s; Turner Network TV HD; VH1 Classic; VH1 Soul; WE tv.

Fee: $18.95 monthly.

Digital Pay Service 1

Pay Units: N.A.

Programming (via satellite): Cinemax (multiplexed); Flix; HBO (multiplexed); Showtime (multiplexed); The Movie Channel.

Fee: $15.95 monthly (HBO, Cinemax or Showtime/TMC/Flix).

Pay-Per-View

iN DEMAND (delivered digitally); Hot Choice (delivered digitally); Club Jenna (delivered digitally); Spice: Xcess (delivered digitally); Fresh (delivered digitally); Shorteez (delivered digitally); Playboy TV (delivered digitally).

Internet Service

Operational: Yes.

Broadband Service: Atlantic Broadband High-Speed Internet.

Fee: $24.95-$57.95 monthly.

Telephone Service

Digital: Operational

Fee: $44.95 monthly

Miles of Plant: 28.0 (coaxial); None (fiber optic).

Vice President: David Dane. General Manager: Mike Papasergi. Technical Operations Director: Charles Sorchilla. Marketing & Customer Service Director: Dara Leslie. Marketing Manager: Natalie Kurchak.

Ownership: Atlantic Broadband (MSO).

GRANVILLE TWP.—Nittany Media Inc. Now served by LEWISTOWN (formerly McAlisterville), PA [PA0365]. ICA: PA0337.

GREEN TWP. (Indiana County)—Formerly served by Adelphia Communications. Now served by BLAIRSVILLE, PA [PA0320]. ICA: PA0338.

GREENBURR—Formerly served by Greenburr TV Cable. No longer in operation. ICA: PA0339.

GREENE COUNTY—Formerly served by DuCom Cable TV. No longer in operation. ICA: PA0437.

GREENSBURG—Comcast Cable, 15 Summit Park Dr, Pittsburgh, PA 15275. Phones: 724-845-1338; 412-771-8100; 412-875-1100. Fax: 412-747-6401. Web Site: http://www.comcast.com. Also serves Adamsburg, Arona, Derry Twp. (Westmoreland County), East Huntingdon Twp. (portions), Hempfield Twp. (Westmoreland County), Hunker, Irwin, Jeannette, Madison, Manor, Mount Pleasant, New Alexandria, New Stanton, North Huntingdon Twp. (Westmoreland County), North Irwin, Penn, Salem Twp. (Westmoreland County), South Greensburg, South Versailles, South Versailles Twp. (portions), Southwest Greensburg, Westmoreland City & Youngwood. ICA: PA0015.

TV Market Ranking: 10 (Adamsburg, Arona, Derry Twp. (Westmoreland County), East Huntingdon Twp. (portions), Hempfield Twp. (Westmoreland County), Hunker, Irwin, Jeannette, Madison, Manor, Mount Pleasant, New Alexandria, New Stanton, North Huntingdon Twp. (Westmoreland County), North Irwin, Penn, Salem Twp. (Westmoreland County), South Versailles Twp. (portions), Southwest Greensburg, Westmoreland City); 10,74 (GREENSBURG, South Greensburg, Youngwood). Franchise award date: January 1, 1966. Franchise expiration date: N.A. Began: March 1, 1966.

Channel capacity: N.A. Channels available but not in use: N.A.

Basic Service

Subscribers: N.A. Included in Bensalem Twp.

Programming (received off-air): KDKA-TV (CBS) Pittsburgh; WINP-TV (IND, ION) Pittsburgh; WJAC-TV (NBC) Johnstown; WPCB-TV (IND) Greensburg; WPCW (CW) Jeannette; WPGH-TV (FOX) Pittsburgh; WPMY (MNT) Pittsburgh; WPXI (IND, NBC) Pittsburgh; WQED (PBS) Pittsburgh; WTAE-TV (ABC) Pittsburgh; 19 FMs.

Programming (via satellite): C-SPAN; Discovery Channel; QVC; TBS Superstation.

Fee: $43.99 installation; $12.16 monthly; $1.85 converter.

Expanded Basic Service 1

Subscribers: N.A.

Programming (via satellite): A&E Networks; ABC Family Channel; AMC; Animal Planet; BET Networks; Cartoon Network; CNBC; CNN; Comedy Central; Country Music TV; C-SPAN 2; Disney Channel; E! Entertainment Television; ESPN; ESPN 2; Eternal Word TV Network; Food Network; Fox News Channel; FX; Golf Channel; Hallmark Channel; Headline News; HGTV; History Channel; ION Television; Lifetime; MSNBC; MTV; Nickelodeon; Oxygen; Pennsylvania Cable Network; Pittsburgh Cable News Channel; Root Sports Pittsburgh; Shop at Home; ShopNBC; Spike TV; Syfy; The Learning Channel; The Weather Channel; Travel Channel; truTV; Turner Network TV; TV Guide Network; TV Land; USA Network; VH1; WGN America.

Fee: $39.85 monthly.

Digital Basic Service

Subscribers: 12,338.

Programming (via satellite): American-Life TV Network; BBC America; Bio; Black Family Channel; Bravo; Discovery Digital Networks; DMX Music; ESPN Classic Sports; ESPNews; Fox Movie Channel; Fox Sports World; FSN Digital Atlantic; FSN Digital Central; FSN Digital Pacific; Fuse; G4; GAS; Great American Country; GSN; Halogen Network; History Channel International; Independent Film Channel; Lifetime Movie Network; Lime; MTV Networks Digital Suite; Music Choice; National Geographic Channel; Nick Jr.; NickToons TV; Outdoor Channel; Ovation; Speed; Style Network; Sundance Channel; The Word Network; Toon Disney; Trinity Broadcasting Network; Turner Classic Movies; Versus; WE tv; Weatherscan.

Fee: $10.95 monthly; $4.60 converter.

Digital Pay Service 1

Pay Units: N.A.

Programming (via satellite): Cinemax (multiplexed); Encore (multiplexed); Flix; HBO (multiplexed); Showtime (multiplexed); Starz (multiplexed); The Movie Channel (multiplexed).

Fee: $8.00 monthly (each).

Video-On-Demand: Yes

Pay-Per-View

Addressable homes: 12,338.

ESPN Now (delivered digitally); Sports PPV (delivered digitally); Hot Choice (delivered digitally); NBA TV (delivered digitally); iN DEMAND (delivered digitally); Barker (delivered digitally); Urban Xtra (delivered digitally); Fresh (delivered digitally); Shorteez (delivered digitally); Playboy TV (delivered digitally).

Internet Service

Operational: Yes.

Broadband Service: Comcast High Speed Internet.

Fee: $42.95 monthly.

Telephone Service

Digital: Operational

Fee: $44.95 monthly

Miles of Plant: 645.0 (coaxial); None (fiber optic).

Regional Vice President: Linda Hossinger. Vice President, Technical Operations: Randy Bender. Vice President, Marketing: Donna Corning. Vice President, Public Affairs: Jody Doherty.

Ownership: Comcast Cable Communications Inc. (MSO).

GREENTOWN—Blue Ridge Communications, 613 3rd St, PO Box 215, Palmerton, PA 18071-0215. Phones: 610-826-2551; 800-426-0606 (Customer service); 570-226-4914. Web Site: http://www.brctv.com. Also serves Cherry Ridge Twp. (Wayne County), Greene Twp. (Pike County) & Palmyra Twp. (Pike County). ICA: PA0177.

TV Market Ranking: 49 (Cherry Ridge Twp. (Wayne County), Greene Twp. (Pike County), GREENTOWN, Palmyra Twp. (Pike County)). Franchise award date: N.A. Franchise expiration date: N.A. Began: January 1, 1981.

Channel capacity: 42 (operating 2-way). Channels available but not in use: N.A.

Basic Service

Subscribers: N.A.

Programming (received off-air): WABC-TV (ABC) New York; WBRE-TV (NBC) Wilkes-Barre; WCBS-TV (CBS) New York; WNBC (NBC) New York; WNEP-TV (ABC) Scranton; WNET (PBS) Newark; WNYW (FOX) New York; WOLF-TV (CW, FOX, MNT) Hazleton; WPIX (CW, IND) New York; WPVI-TV (ABC) Philadelphia; WQPX-TV (ION) Scranton; WSKG-TV (PBS) Binghamton; WSWB (CW) Scranton; WVIA-TV (PBS) Scranton; WWOR-TV (MNT) Secaucus; WYOU (CBS) Scranton.

Programming (via satellite): Headline News; WGN America.

Fee: $22.50 installation; $16.49 monthly.

Expanded Basic Service 1

Subscribers: N.A.

Programming (via satellite): A&E Networks; ABC Family Channel; AMC; Animal Planet; Bravo; Cartoon Network; CNBC; CNN; Comedy Central; Country Music TV; C-SPAN; Discovery Channel; Discovery Health Channel; Disney Channel; E! Entertainment Television; ESPN; ESPN 2; Eternal Word TV Network; Food Network; Fox News Channel; FX; Golf Channel; HGTV; History Channel; Lifetime; Lifetime Movie Network; MSG; MSG Plus; MSNBC; MTV; National Geographic Channel; NFL Network; Nickelodeon; Pennsylvania Cable Network; QVC; Speed; Spike TV; Syfy; TBS Superstation; The Learning Channel; The Weather Channel; Travel Channel; Trinity Broadcasting Network; truTV; Turner Classic Movies; Turner Network TV; TV Land; USA Network; Versus; VH1; WE tv; Yankees Entertainment & Sports.

Fee: $28.09 monthly.

Digital Basic Service

Subscribers: N.A.

Programming (via satellite): America's Store; Canales N; CCTV-4; ESPN 2 HD; ESPN HD; ESPN U; Fox College Sports Atlantic; Fox College Sports Central; Fox College Sports Pacific; Fox Movie Channel; Fox Soccer; GAS; GMC; Halogen Network; HD Theater; HDNet; HDNet Movies; HRTV; Independent Film Channel; Lifetime Real Women; MTV Networks Digital Suite; Music Choice; Nick Jr.; Nick Too; NickToons TV; Outdoor Channel; Oxygen; PBS Kids Channel; ShopNBC; SoapNet; Toon Disney; Turner Network TV HD; Universal HD.

Fee: $9.95 monthly.

Digital Expanded Basic Service

Subscribers: N.A.

Programming (via satellite): BBC America; Bio; Bloomberg Television; Boomerang; CMT Pure Country; Cooking Channel; DIY Network; G4; Great American Country;

GSN; Hallmark Channel; History Channel International; LWS Local Weather Station; NBA TV; Style Network; Tennis Channel.
Fee: $5.00 monthly.

Pay Service 1
Pay Units: 150.
Programming (via satellite): Cinemax; HBO; Showtime.
Fee: $12.50 installation; $11.50 monthly (Showtime or Cinemax), $12.50 monthly (HBO).

Digital Pay Service 1
Pay Units: N.A.
Programming (via satellite): Cinemax (multiplexed); Encore (multiplexed); Flix; HBO (multiplexed); HBO HD; Showtime (multiplexed); Showtime HD; Starz (multiplexed); Starz HDTV; Sundance Channel; The Movie Channel (multiplexed).
Fee: $12.50 monthly (Cinemax, Showtime or TMC), $12.95 monthly (Starz), $13.50 monthly (HBO).

Video-On-Demand: Yes

Pay-Per-View
iN DEMAND; sports (delivered digitally); iN DEMAND (delivered digitally); adult PPV (delivered digitally); Barker (delivered digitally).

Internet Service
Operational: Yes.
Broadband Service: ProLog Express.
Fee: $34.95 monthly; $10.00 modem lease; $59.95 modem purchase.

Telephone Service
None

Miles of Plant: 51.0 (coaxial); None (fiber optic).

Vice President, Operations: Richard Semmel. General Manager: Mark Masonheimer. Chief Technician: Garry Woods. Fiber Manager: Randy Semmel.

Ownership: Pencor Services Inc. (MSO).

GREENVILLE—Time Warner Cable, 530 S Main St, Ste 1751, Akron, OH 44311-1090. Phone: 330-633-9203. Fax: 330-633-7970. Web Site: http://www.timewarnercable.com/northeastohio. Also serves Delaware Twp. (Mercer County), Fredonia, Greenville Twp., Hempfield Twp. (Mercer County), Sugar Grove Twp. & West Salem Twp. ICA: PA0116.

TV Market Ranking: 79 (Delaware Twp. (Mercer County), Fredonia, GREENVILLE, Greenville Twp., Hempfield Twp. (Mercer County), Sugar Grove Twp., West Salem Twp.). Franchise award date: N.A. Franchise expiration date: December 31, 2007. Began: November 1, 1968.

Channel capacity: N.A. Channels available but not in use: N.A.

Basic Service
Subscribers: N.A. Included in Warren, OH
Programming (received off-air): KDKA-TV (CBS) Pittsburgh; WEAO (PBS) Akron; WFMJ-TV (CW, NBC) Youngstown; WKBN-TV (CBS) Youngstown; WPGH-TV (FOX) Pittsburgh; WQLN (PBS) Erie; WUAB (MNT) Lorain; WYFX-LP Youngstown; WYTV (ABC, MNT) Youngstown; allband FM.
Programming (via satellite): ABC Family Channel; C-SPAN; Eternal Word TV Network; Fox Sports Net Ohio; MTV2; QVC; ShopNBC; TV Guide Network.
Fee: $44.95 installation; $14.91 monthly.

Expanded Basic Service 1
Subscribers: 3,966.
Programming (via satellite): A&E Networks; AMC; Animal Planet; BET Networks; Bravo; Cartoon Network; CNBC; CNN; Comedy Central; C-SPAN 2; Discovery Channel; Discovery Fit & Health; Discovery Health Channel; Disney Channel; E! Entertainment Television; ESPN; ESPN 2; ESPN Classic Sports; Food Network; Fox News Channel; FX; Golf Channel; Great American Country; GSN; Hallmark Channel; Headline News; HGTV; History Channel; INSP; ION Television; Lifetime; Lifetime Movie Network; MSNBC; MTV; Nickelodeon; Oxygen; Root Sports Pittsburgh; SoapNet; Spike TV; Syfy; TBS Superstation; The Learning Channel; The Weather Channel; Travel Channel; truTV; Turner Classic Movies; Turner Network TV; TV Land; USA Network; Versus; VH1; WE tv.
Fee: $38.34 monthly.

Digital Basic Service
Subscribers: N.A.
Programming (via satellite): A&E Networks; AmericanLife TV Network; America's Store; ART America; BBC America; Bloomberg Television; Boomerang; Canales N; CBS Sports Network; CNN; CNN International; Cooking Channel; Country Music TV; C-SPAN 3; Current; Daystar TV Network; Deutsche Welle TV; Disney Channel; DIY Network; ESPN; ESPNews; Fox College Sports Atlantic; Fox College Sports Central; Fox College Sports Pacific; Fox Movie Channel; Fox News Channel; Fox Soccer; Fuel TV; Fuse; G4; GAS; HD Theater; HDNet; HDNet Movies; Headline News; History Channel International; Independent Film Channel; INHD; Jewelry Television; Lifetime; Lifetime Real Women; MTV2; Music Choice; National Geographic Channel; NBA TV; Nick Jr.; NickToons TV; Outdoor Channel; RAI International; Speed; Style Network; TBS Superstation; Tennis Channel; The Weather Channel; The Word Network; Toon Disney; Trio; Turner Network TV; Turner Network TV HD; TV Asia; TVG Network; USA Network; VH1 Classic; Zee TV USA.
Fee: $14.74 monthly.

Digital Pay Service 1
Pay Units: N.A.
Programming (via satellite): Cinemax (multiplexed); Encore (multiplexed); HBO (multiplexed); Showtime (multiplexed); Starz (multiplexed); Sundance Channel; The Movie Channel (multiplexed).
Fee: $12.00 monthly (each).

Video-On-Demand: Yes

Pay-Per-View
iN DEMAND (delivered digitally); Playboy TV (delivered digitally); MLB Extra Innings (delivered digitally); Spice Live (delivered digitally); Pleasure (delivered digitally); NASCAR In Car (delivered digitally); NBA League Pass (delivered digitally); MLS Direct Kick (delivered digitally); ESPN (delivered digitally); NHL Center Ice (delivered digitally).

Internet Service
Operational: Yes.
Broadband Service: EarthLink, Road Runner.
Fee: $99.00 installation; $44.95 monthly.

Telephone Service
Digital: Operational
Fee: $44.95 monthly

Miles of Plant: 81.0 (coaxial); None (fiber optic).

President: Stephen Fry. Area Vice President: Rick Whaley. Vice President, Engineering: Al Costanzi. Vice President, Marketing: Patrick Burke. Vice President, Public Affairs: William Jasso. Government & Media Relations Director: Chris Thomas.

Ownership: Time Warner Cable (MSO).

GROVE CITY—Armstrong Cable Services, 660 S Benbrook Rd, Butler, PA 16001. Phones: 877-277-5711; 724-482-4885; 724-283-0925 (Corporate office); 740-894-3886 (Customer service). Fax: 724-482-4884. E-mail: info@zoominternet.net. Web Site: http://cable.armstrongonewire.com. Also serves Barkeyville, Boyers, Clinton Twp. (Venango County), Clintonville, Concord Twp. (Butler County), Coolspring Twp. (portions), East Lackawannock Twp. (portions), Eau Claire, Findley Twp. (Mercer County), Harrisville, Hilliards, Irwin Twp. (Venango County), Jackson Center, Jackson Center Borough, Jackson Twp. (Butler County), Kennerdell, Lake Latonka Borough, Lake Twp. (Mercer County), Liberty Twp. (Mercer County), Mercer, Mercer Twp. (portions), Pine Twp. (Mercer County), Rockland Twp. (Venango County), Sandy Lake, Sandy Lake Twp., Slippery Rock (Butler County), Slippery Rock Twp. (Butler County), Springfield Twp. (Mercer County), Stoneboro, Venango Twp. (Butler County), Volant Borough, Washington Twp. (Lawrence County) & Wolf Creek Twp. ICA: PA0089. **Note:** This system is an overbuild.

TV Market Ranking: 10 (Jackson Twp. (Butler County)); 79 (Coolspring Twp. (portions), East Lackawannock Twp. (portions), Findley Twp. (Mercer County), GROVE CITY, Jackson Center, Jackson Center Borough, Lake Latonka Borough, Lake Twp. (Mercer County), Liberty Twp. (Mercer County), Mercer, Mercer Twp. (portions), Pine Twp. (Mercer County) (portions), Sandy Lake Twp. (portions), Slippery Rock (Butler County), Slippery Rock Twp. (Butler County), Springfield Twp. (Mercer County), Stoneboro, Volant Borough, Washington Twp. (Lawrence County), Wolf Creek Twp. (portions)); Below 100 (Concord Twp. (Butler County)); Outside TV Markets (Barkeyville, Boyers, Clinton Twp. (Venango County), Clintonville, Eau Claire, Harrisville, Hilliards, Irwin Twp. (Venango County), Kennerdell, Rockland Twp. (Venango County), Sandy Lake, Venango Twp. (Butler County), Pine Twp. (Mercer County) (portions), Sandy Lake Twp. (portions)). Franchise award date: January 1, 1975. Franchise expiration date: N.A. Began: May 1, 1976.

Channel capacity: N.A. Channels available but not in use: N.A.

Digital Basic Service
Subscribers: 2,573.
Programming (via satellite): A&E Networks; ABC Family Channel; AMC; Animal Planet; Bravo; Cartoon Network; CNBC; CNN; Comedy Central; Country Music TV; C-SPAN; Discovery Channel; Disney Channel; E! Entertainment Television; ESPN; ESPN 2; ESPN Classic Sports; Eternal Word TV Network; Food Network; Fox News Channel; FX; Headline News; HGTV; History Channel; INSP; Lifetime; MSNBC; MTV; Music Choice; Nickelodeon; NickToons TV; Pennsylvania Cable Network; Pittsburgh Cable News Channel; QVC; Root Sports Pittsburgh; Spike TV; Syfy; TBS Superstation; The Learning Channel; The Weather Channel; Travel Channel; truTV; Turner Classic Movies; Turner Network TV; TV Guide Network; TV Land; TVN Entertainment; USA Network; VH1.
Fee: $51.40 monthly.

Digital Expanded Basic Service
Subscribers: N.A.
Programming (via satellite): AmericanLife TV Network; BBC America; Bio; Bloomberg Television; Boomerang; Chiller; cloo; CMT Pure Country; Cooking Channel; Discovery Fit & Health; Discovery Health Channel; Discovery Kids Channel; DIY Network; ESPN U; ESPNews; G4; Golf Channel; Great American Country; GSN; Hallmark Channel; Hallmark Movie Channel; History Channel International; HRTV; ID Investigation Discovery; Jewelry Television; Lifetime Movie Network; Military Channel; MTV Hits; MTV Jams; MTV2; mun2 television; National Geographic Channel; NFL Network; NHL Network; Nick Jr.; Nick Too; Outdoor Channel; Oxygen; PBS Kids Sprout; Pentagon Channel; Planet Green; RFD-TV; RTN; Science; ShopNBC; SoapNet; Speed; TeenNick; Tennis Channel; Toon Disney; Tr3s; Versus; VH1 Classic; VH1 Soul; WE tv.
Fee: $12.00 monthly.

Digital Expanded Basic Service 2
Subscribers: N.A.
Programming (received off-air): KDKA-TV (CBS) Pittsburgh; WPGH-TV (FOX) Pittsburgh; WPXI (IND, NBC) Pittsburgh; WQED (PBS) Pittsburgh; WTAE-TV (ABC) Pittsburgh.
Programming (via satellite): A&E HD; Animal Planet HD; Bravo HD; CNN HD; Discovery Channel HD; Disney Channel HD; ESPN 2 HD; ESPN HD; Food Network HD; Fox News HD; FSN HD; FX HD; Golf Channel HD; Hallmark Movie Channel HD; HD Theater; HDNet; HDNet Movies; HGTV HD; History Channel HD; MGM HD; National Geographic Channel HD Network; NFL Network HD; NHL Network HD; Outdoor Channel 2 HD; Palladia; QVC HD; Science HD; Syfy HD; TBS in HD; The Weather Channel HD; TLC HD; Turner Network TV HD; Universal HD; USA Network HD; Versus HD; WealthTV HD.
Fee: $9.00 monthly.

Digital Pay Service 1
Pay Units: N.A.
Programming (via satellite): Cinemax (multiplexed); Cinemax HD; Encore (multiplexed); Flix; HBO (multiplexed); HBO HD; RAI USA; Showtime (multiplexed); Showtime HD; Starz (multiplexed); Starz HDTV; The Movie Channel (multiplexed); TV5 USA.
Fee: $35.00 installation; $13.95 monthly (Starz/Encore, Cinemax, HBO or Showtime/TMC/Flix).

Video-On-Demand: Yes

Pay-Per-View
ESPN Now (delivered digitally); Hot Choice (delivered digitally); iN DEMAND (delivered digitally); NHL/MLB (delivered digitally); ESPN Extra (delivered digitally).

Internet Service
Operational: Yes. Began: October 1, 2001.
Subscribers: 5,493.
Broadband Service: Armstrong Zoom.
Fee: $39.95 monthly.

Telephone Service
Digital: Operational
Fee: $49.95 monthly

Miles of Plant: 382.0 (coaxial); 45.0 (fiber optic).

Vice President, Marketing: Jud Stewart. General Manager: Joe Taylor. Chief Technician: Barry Osche. Marketing Manager: Andrea Lucas. Program Director: Matt Lutz. Customer Service Manager: Connie Swartzfegger.

Ownership: Armstrong Group of Companies (MSO).

HAMBURG—Comcast Cable. Now served by READING, PA [PA0012]. ICA: PA0102.

HAMPTON TWP.—Comcast Cable. Now served by TARENTUM BOROUGH, PA [PA0424]. ICA: PA0455.

HANOVER TWP. (Lehigh County)—Formerly served by NORTHAMPTON BOROUGH, PA [PA0008]. RCN Corp. This cable system has converted to IPTV, 196 Van Buren St, Herndon, VA 20170. Phone: 703-434-8200. Web Site: http://www.rcn.com. ICA: PA5215.
TV Market Ranking: Below 100 (HANOVER TWP. (LEHIGH COUNTY)).
Channel capacity: N.A. Channels available but not in use: N.A.
Internet Service
Operational: Yes.
Telephone Service
Digital: Operational
Chairman: Steven J. Simmons. Chief Executive Officer: Jim Holanda.

HANOVER TWP. (Northampton County)—Formerly served by NORTHAMPTON BOROUGH, PA [PA0008]. RCN Corp. This cable system has converted to IPTV, 196 Van Buren St, Herndon, VA 20170. Phone: 703-434-8200. Web Site: http://www.rcn.com. ICA: PA5216.
TV Market Ranking: Below 100 (HANOVER TWP. (NORTHAMPTON COUNTY)).
Channel capacity: N.A. Channels available but not in use: N.A.
Internet Service
Operational: Yes.
Telephone Service
Digital: Operational
Chairman: Steven J. Simmons. Chief Executive Officer: Jim Holanda.

HARBORCREEK TWP.—Time Warner Cable, 3627 Zimmerman Rd, Erie, PA 16510-2642. Phones: 330-633-9203 (Akron office); 814-898-1656. Fax: 814-456-5162. Web Site: http://www.timewarnercable.com. Also serves Albion, Conneat Twp., Conneautville, Cranesville, Elk Creek Twp., Fairview (Erie County), Fairview Twp. (Erie County), Girard Borough, Girard Twp. (Erie County), Greene Twp. (Erie County), Lake City, Lundys Lane, McKean Borough, McKean Twp. (Erie County), North East, Northeast Twp. (Erie County), Platea Boro, Spring Twp., Springboro, Springfield Twp., Summit Twp. (Erie County), Waterford (Erie County), Waterford Twp. (Erie County) & Wesleyville. ICA: PA0025.
TV Market Ranking: Below 100 (Albion, Conneat Twp., Conneautville, Cranesville, Elk Creek Twp., Fairview (Erie County), Fairview Twp. (Erie County), Girard Borough, Girard Twp. (Erie County), Greene Twp. (Erie County), HARBORCREEK TWP., Lake City, Lundys Lane, McKean Borough, McKean Twp. (Erie County), North East, Northeast Twp. (Erie County), Platea Boro, Spring Twp., Springboro, Springfield Twp., Summit Twp. (Erie County), Waterford (Erie County), Waterford Twp. (Erie County), Wesleyville). Franchise award date: N.A. Franchise expiration date: N.A. Began: April 1, 1976.
Channel capacity: 78 (operating 2-way). Channels available but not in use: N.A.
Basic Service
Subscribers: 37,522.
Programming (received off-air): WFXP (FOX) Erie; WICU-TV (NBC) Erie; WJET-TV (ABC) Erie; WQLN (PBS) Erie; WSEE-TV (CBS, CW) Erie; allband FM.
Programming (via microwave): WUAB (MNT) Lorain.
Programming (via satellite): C-SPAN; Discovery Channel; QVC; TBS Superstation.
Fee: $29.95 installation; $19.60 monthly; $3.00 converter.
Expanded Basic Service 1
Subscribers: 33,230.
Programming (via satellite): A&E Networks; ABC Family Channel; AMC; America's Store; Animal Planet; Cartoon Network; CNBC; CNN; Comedy Central; Country Music TV; C-SPAN 2; Discovery Fit & Health; Disney Channel; E! Entertainment Television; ESPN; ESPN 2; Eternal Word TV Network; Food Network; Fox News Channel; Fox Sports Net; Fox Sports Net Ohio; FX; Hallmark Channel; Headline News; HGTV; ION Television; Lifetime; MSNBC; MTV; Nickelodeon; Pennsylvania Cable Network; Root Sports Pittsburgh; Spike TV; The Learning Channel; The Weather Channel; Travel Channel; truTV; Turner Network TV; TV Guide Network; TV Land; USA Network; VH1.
Fee: $30.65 monthly.
Digital Basic Service
Subscribers: N.A.
Programming (via satellite): AmericanLife TV Network; BBC America; Black Family Channel; Bloomberg Television; Bravo; Discovery Digital Networks; DIY Network; DMX Music; Fox Movie Channel; Fox Sports World; Fuse; G4; GAS; Golf Channel; GSN; Halogen Network; History Channel; Lifetime Movie Network; MTV Networks Digital Suite; National Geographic Channel; Nick Jr.; Nick Too; NickToons TV; SoapNet; Speed; Style Network; Syfy; The Word Network; Toon Disney; Trinity Broadcasting Network; Turner Classic Movies; WE tv.
Fee: $11.95 monthly.
Digital Expanded Basic Service
Subscribers: N.A.
Programming (via satellite): Bio; Canales N; ESPN Classic Sports; ESPNews; Flix; FSN Digital Atlantic; FSN Digital Central; FSN Digital Pacific; History Channel International; Independent Film Channel; International Television (ITV); Outdoor Channel; Sundance Channel; Versus.
Digital Pay Service 1
Pay Units: N.A.
Programming (via satellite): Cinemax; Encore (multiplexed); HBO (multiplexed); Showtime (multiplexed); Starz (multiplexed); The Movie Channel.
Fee: $12.00 monthly (each).
Video-On-Demand: Yes
Pay-Per-View
iN DEMAND (delivered digitally); Playboy TV (delivered digitally); Fresh.
Internet Service
Operational: Yes.
Broadband Service: Road Runner.
Fee: $45.95 monthly.
Telephone Service
Digital: Operational
Fee: $44.95 monthly
Miles of Plant: 1,057.0 (coaxial); 1,057.0 (fiber optic).
President: Stephen Fry. Area Vice President: Rick Whaley. Vice President, Engineering: Al Costanzi. Vice President, Marketing: Patrick Burke. Vice President, Government & Media Relations: Bill Jasso. General Manager: Brian Frederick. Office Manager: Dana Bachman.
Ownership: Time Warner Cable (MSO).

HARRISBURG—Comcast Cable, 1 E Uwchlan Ave, Ste 411, Exton, PA 19341. Phones: 717-960-3100 (Harrisburg office); 484-288-6500. Web Site: http://www.comcast.com. Also serves Camp Hill, Dauphin, East Pennsboro Twp. (Cumberland County), Hampden Twp. (Cumberland County), Highspire, Lemoyne, Lower Allen Twp., Lower Paxton Twp. (Dauphin County), Lower Swatara Twp., Marysville, Mechanicsburg, Middle Paxton, Middletown, New Cumberland, Paxtang, Penbrook, Royalton, Shiremanstown, Steelton, Swatara, Upper Allen Twp., West Fairview, West Hanover Twp. (Dauphin County) & Wormleysburg. ICA: PA0009.
TV Market Ranking: 57 (Camp Hill, Dauphin, East Pennsboro Twp. (Cumberland County), Hampden Twp. (Cumberland County), HARRISBURG, Highspire, Lemoyne, Lower Allen Twp., Lower Paxton Twp. (Dauphin County), Lower Swatara Twp., Marysville, Mechanicsburg, Middle Paxton, Middletown, New Cumberland, Paxtang, Penbrook, Royalton, Shiremanstown, Steelton, Swatara, Upper Allen Twp., West Fairview, West Hanover Twp. (Dauphin County), Wormleysburg). Franchise award date: December 1, 1965. Franchise expiration date: N.A. Began: December 1, 1965.
Channel capacity: N.A. Channels available but not in use: N.A.
Basic Service
Subscribers: 720,000 Includes all of central Pennsylvania.
Programming (received off-air): WGAL (NBC) Lancaster; WGCB-TV (IND) Red Lion; WHP-TV (CBS, MNT) Harrisburg; WHTM-TV (ABC) Harrisburg; WITF-TV (PBS) Harrisburg; WLYH-TV (CW) Lancaster; WPHL-TV (MNT, IND) Philadelphia; WPMT (FOX) York.
Programming (via satellite): C-SPAN; QVC; The Comcast Network; TV Guide Network; WPIX (CW, IND) New York.
Fee: $45.10 installation; $16.90 monthly; $1.02 converter.
Expanded Basic Service 1
Subscribers: N.A.
Programming (via satellite): A&E Networks; ABC Family Channel; AMC; Animal Planet; BET Networks; Box; Bravo; Cartoon Network; CNBC; CNN; Comcast SportsNet Mid-Atlantic; Comcast SportsNet Philadelphia; Comedy Central; Country Music TV; C-SPAN 2; Discovery Channel; Discovery Health Channel; Disney Channel; E! Entertainment Television; ESPN; ESPN 2; ESPN Classic Sports; Food Network; Fox News Channel; FX; Golf Channel; GSN; Headline News; HGTV; History Channel; INSP; ION Television; Lifetime; MSNBC; MTV; MTV2; Nickelodeon; Pennsylvania Cable Network; Speed; Spike TV; Style Network; Syfy; TBS Superstation; The Learning Channel; The Weather Channel; truTV; Turner Classic Movies; Turner Network TV; TV Land; Univision Studios; USA Network; Versus; VH1.
Fee: $33.90 monthly.
Digital Basic Service
Subscribers: 30,389.
Programming (via satellite): BBC America; C-SPAN 3; Discovery Digital Networks; DMX Music; Encore; ESPNews; Flix; G4; GAS; Independent Film Channel; MTV Networks Digital Suite; National Geographic Channel; Nick Jr.; Nick Too; ShopNBC; SoapNet; Sundance Channel; Toon Disney; Weatherscan.
Fee: $14.95 monthly.
Digital Pay Service 1
Pay Units: 370.
Programming (via satellite): Cinemax (multiplexed); HBO (multiplexed); Showtime (multiplexed); Starz (multiplexed); The Movie Channel (multiplexed).
Video-On-Demand: Yes
Pay-Per-View
Addressable homes: 38,955.
iN DEMAND; iN DEMAND (delivered digitally); NBA TV (delivered digitally); Hot Choice (delivered digitally); Playboy TV (delivered digitally); Fresh (delivered digitally); Shorteez (delivered digitally); Pleasure (delivered digitally); ESPN Now (delivered digitally); Sports PPV (delivered digitally).
Internet Service
Operational: Yes. Began: December 6, 1999.
Subscribers: 21,706.
Broadband Service: Comcast High Speed Internet.
Fee: $42.95 monthly; $3.00 modem lease; $299.00 modem purchase.
Telephone Service
Digital: Operational
Miles of Plant: 1,623.0 (coaxial); 60.0 (fiber optic).
Regional Vice President: Jim Samaha. Vice President, Marketing: Larry Goldman. Technical Operations Director: William Mays. Marketing Manager: Jason Wicht. Public Relations Director: Gabe Weissman.
Ownership: Comcast Cable Communications Inc. (MSO).

HARRISBURG—Formerly served by Gap Cable TV. No longer in operation. ICA: PA0406.

HARTSLOG—Formerly served by Milestone Communications LP. No longer in operation. ICA: PA0440.

HAWLEY—Blue Ridge Communications, 613 3rd St, PO Box 215, Palmerton, PA 18071-0215. Phones: 610-826-2551; 800-426-0606 (Customer service); 570-226-4914. Web Site: http://www.brctv.com. Also serves Dreher Twp., Palmyra Twp. (Wayne County) & Paupack Twp. (Wayne County). ICA: PA0342.
TV Market Ranking: 49 (Dreher Twp., HAWLEY, Palmyra Twp. (Wayne County), Paupack Twp. (Wayne County)). Franchise award date: N.A. Franchise expiration date: N.A. Began: June 1, 1955.
Channel capacity: 42 (operating 2-way). Channels available but not in use: N.A.
Basic Service
Subscribers: N.A.
Programming (received off-air): WABC-TV (ABC) New York; WCBS-TV (CBS) New York; WNBC (NBC) New York; WNEP-TV (ABC) Scranton; WNET (PBS) Newark; WNYW (FOX) New York; WOLF-TV (CW, FOX, MNT) Hazleton; WPIX (CW, IND) New York; WPVI-TV (ABC) Philadelphia; WQPX-TV (ION) Scranton; WSKG-TV (PBS) Binghamton; WSWB (CW) Scran-

ton; WVIA-TV (PBS) Scranton; WWOR-TV (MNT) Secaucus; WYOU (CBS) Scranton.
Programming (via satellite): Headline News; WGN America.
Fee: $22.50 installation; $15.22 monthly.

Digital Basic Service
Subscribers: N.A.
Programming (via satellite): America's Store; Canales N; CCTV-4; CMT Pure Country; ESPN 2 HD; ESPN HD; ESPN U; Fox College Sports Atlantic; Fox College Sports Central; Fox College Sports Pacific; Fox Movie Channel; Fox Soccer; GAS; Great American Country; GSN; Halogen Network; HD Theater; HDNet; HDNet Movies; HRTV; Independent Film Channel; Lifetime Real Women; MTV Networks Digital Suite; Music Choice; NBA TV; Nick Jr.; Nick Too; NickToons TV; Outdoor Channel; Oxygen; PBS Kids Channel; ShopNBC; SoapNet; Tennis Channel; Toon Disney; Turner Network TV HD; Universal HD.
Fee: $35.00 installation; $9.95 monthly.

Digital Expanded Basic Service
Subscribers: N.A.
Programming (via satellite): BBC America; Bio; Bloomberg Television; Boomerang; Cooking Channel; DIY Network; G4; Hallmark Channel; History Channel International; LWS Local Weather Station; Style Network.
Fee: $5.00 monthly.

Pay Service 1
Pay Units: N.A.
Programming (via satellite): Cinemax; HBO; Showtime.
Fee: $11.50 monthly (Cinemax or Showtime), $12.50 monthly (HBO).

Digital Pay Service 1
Pay Units: N.A.
Programming (via satellite): Cinemax (multiplexed); Encore (multiplexed); Flix; HBO (multiplexed); HBO HD; Showtime (multiplexed); Showtime HD; Starz (multiplexed); Starz HDTV; Sundance Channel; The Movie Channel (multiplexed).
Fee: $12.50 monthly (Cinemax or Showtime/Flix/Sundance/TMC), $12.95 monthly (Starz/Encore), $13.50 monthly (HBO).

Video-On-Demand: Yes

Pay-Per-View
iN DEMAND; iN DEMAND (delivered digitally); sports (delivered digitally); Barker (delivered digitally); adult PPV (delivered digitally).

Internet Service
Operational: Yes.
Broadband Service: ProLog Express.
Fee: $34.95 monthly; $10.00 modem lease; $59.95 modem purchase.

Telephone Service
None

Miles of Plant: 16.0 (coaxial); None (fiber optic).
Vice President, Operations: Richard Semmel. General Manager: Mark Masonheimer. Chief Technician: Garry Woods. Fiber Manager: Randy Semmel.
Ownership: Pencor Services Inc. (MSO).

HAZEN—Zito Media, 611 Vader Hill Rd, Coudersport, PA 16915. Phones: 866-879-6235; 814-260-9570; 814-260-9575. Fax: 814-260-9580. E-mail: rigas@zitomedia.com. Web Site: http://www.zitomedia.com. Also serves Pinecreek, Polk Twp. (Jefferson County), Warsaw Twp. & Washington Twp. (Jefferson County). ICA: PA0223.
TV Market Ranking: Outside TV Markets (HAZEN, Pinecreek, Polk Twp. (Jefferson County), Warsaw Twp., Washington Twp. (Jefferson County)). Franchise award date: November 12, 1989. Franchise expiration date: N.A. Began: August 1, 1990.
Channel capacity: 60 (not 2-way capable). Channels available but not in use: N.A.

Basic Service
Subscribers: 420.
Programming (received off-air): WATM-TV (ABC) Altoona; WJAC-TV (NBC) Johnstown; WKBS-TV (IND) Altoona; WPMY (MNT) Pittsburgh; WPSU-TV (PBS) Clearfield; WTAE-TV (ABC) Pittsburgh; WTAJ-TV (CBS) Altoona; WWCP-TV (FOX) Johnstown.
Programming (via satellite): A&E Networks; ABC Family Channel; Cartoon Network; CNN; Comedy Central; Country Music TV; C-SPAN; CW+; Discovery Channel; Disney Channel; ESPN; ESPN 2; Eternal Word TV Network; Fox News Channel; FX; Headline News; HGTV; History Channel; Lifetime; MSNBC; MTV; Nickelodeon; QVC; Root Sports Pittsburgh; Speed; Spike TV; Syfy; TBS Superstation; The Learning Channel; The Weather Channel; Trinity Broadcasting Network; Turner Classic Movies; Turner Network TV; TV Land; USA Network; VH1; WGN America.
Fee: $39.95 installation; $37.95 monthly.

Pay Service 1
Pay Units: 6.
Programming (via satellite): Showtime.
Fee: $11.95 monthly.

Pay Service 2
Pay Units: 29.
Programming (via satellite): HBO.
Fee: $12.95 monthly.

Pay Service 3
Pay Units: N.A.
Programming (via satellite): Cinemax.
Fee: $9.00 monthly.

Internet Service
Operational: No.

Telephone Service
None

Miles of Plant: 105.0 (coaxial); None (fiber optic).
Manager: James Rigas. Marketing Director: Kathy Fox.
Ownership: Zito Media (MSO).

HAZLETON—Service Electric Cablevision, 16 Maplewood Dr, PO Box R, Hazleton, PA 18201. Phones: 610-432-2210 (Corporate office); 570-454-3841. Fax: 570-454-3652. E-mail: corporateoffice@secv.com. Web Site: http://www.secv.com. Also serves Banks Twp. (Carbon County), Beaver Meadows, Butler Twp. (Luzerne County), Conyngham Borough, Dorrance Twp., Foster Twp. (Luzerne County), Freeland, Hazle Twp., Jeddo Borough, Kline Twp., McAdoo Borough, Sugarloaf Twp. & West Hazleton Borough. ICA: PA0050.
TV Market Ranking: 49 (Banks Twp. (Carbon County), Beaver Meadows, Butler Twp. (Luzerne County), Conyngham Borough, Dorrance Twp., Foster Twp. (Luzerne County), Freeland, Hazle Twp., HAZLETON, Jeddo Borough, Kline Twp., McAdoo Borough, Sugarloaf Twp., West Hazleton Borough). Franchise award date: January 1, 1952. Franchise expiration date: N.A. Began: January 1, 1952.
Channel capacity: 71 (operating 2-way). Channels available but not in use: N.A.

Basic Service
Subscribers: 18,200.
Programming (received off-air): KYW-TV (CBS) Philadelphia; WBRE-TV (NBC) Wilkes-Barre; WNEP-TV (ABC) Scranton; WOLF-TV (CW, FOX, MNT) Hazleton; WPVI-TV (ABC) Philadelphia; WQMY (MNT) Williamsport; WQPX-TV (ION) Scranton; WSWB (CW) Scranton; WVIA-TV (PBS) Scranton; WWOR-TV (MNT) Secaucus; WYLN-LP (IND) Hazleton; WYOU (CBS) Scranton; allband FM.
Programming (via microwave): WPIX (CW, IND) New York.
Programming (via satellite): AmericanLife TV Network; C-SPAN; Disney Channel; Eternal Word TV Network; Pennsylvania Cable Network; QVC; ShopNBC; Univision Studios.
Fee: $61.00 installation; $19.95 monthly; $2.56 converter.

Expanded Basic Service 1
Subscribers: 17,400.
Programming (via satellite): A&E Networks; ABC Family Channel; AMC; Animal Planet; Bravo; Cartoon Network; CNBC; CNN; Comcast SportsNet Philadelphia; Comedy Central; Country Music TV; Discovery Channel; Discovery Fit & Health; E! Entertainment Television; ESPN; ESPN 2; ESPN Classic Sports; Food Network; Fox News Channel; FX; Headline News; HGTV; History Channel; Lifetime; MSNBC; MTV; National Geographic Channel; NFL Network; Nickelodeon; Outdoor Channel; Root Sports Pittsburgh; Speed; Spike TV; Syfy; TBS Superstation; The Learning Channel; The Weather Channel; Toon Disney; Travel Channel; truTV; Turner Network TV; TV Land; USA Network; VH1; WE tv; Yankees Entertainment & Sports.
Fee: $54.95 monthly.

Digital Basic Service
Subscribers: 9,203.
Programming (via satellite): 3 Angels Broadcasting Network; BBC America; Bio; Bloomberg Television; Boomerang; BYU Television; Canal 52MX; CBS Sports Network; Church Channel; Cine Mexicano; CMT Pure Country; CNN en Espanol; Colours; Cooking Channel; Daystar TV Network; Discovery en Espanol; Discovery Health Channel; Discovery Home Channel; Discovery Kids Channel; Discovery Times Channel; ESPN 2 HD; ESPN Deportes; ESPN HD; ESPNews; FamilyNet; Food Network HD; Fox College Sports Atlantic; Fox College Sports Central; Fox College Sports Pacific; Fox Deportes; Fox Movie Channel; Fox Reality Channel; Fox Soccer; Fuel TV; Fuse; GalaVision; GAS; Golden Eagle Broadcasting; Golf Channel; Great American Country; GSN; Hallmark Channel; Hallmark Movie Channel; HD Theater; HDNet; HDNet Movies; HGTV HD; History Channel International; HRTV; Independent Film Channel; INSP; JCTV; La Familia Network; Latele Novela Network; Lifetime Movie Network; Military Channel; MTV Hits; MTV Jams; MTV2; mun2 television; Music Choice; National Geographic Channel HD Network; NFL Network HD; NHL Network; Nick Jr.; Nick Too; NickToons TV; Outdoor Channel 2 HD; Ovation; Palladia; PBS Kids Sprout; Science; Smile of a Child; SoapNet; Sorpresa; Style Network; TBN Enlace USA; TBS in HD; Telefutura; Telemundo; Tennis Channel; Tr3s; Trinity Broadcasting Network; Turner Classic Movies; Turner Network TV HD; TV Chile; TV Colombia; Universal HD; Versus; VH1 Classic; VH1 Soul; WealthTV HD; YES HD.
Fee: $19.00 monthly.

Digital Pay Service 1
Pay Units: 6,594.
Programming (via satellite): Cinemax (multiplexed); Encore (multiplexed); Flix; HBO (multiplexed); HBO HD; Showtime (multiplexed); Showtime HD; Starz (multiplexed); Starz HDTV; The Movie Channel (multiplexed); The Movie Channel HD.
Fee: $35.00 installation; $11.50 monthly (Cinemax), $12.45 monthly (Starz & Encore), $14.45 monthly (HBO or Flix, Showtime & TMC).

Video-On-Demand: No

Pay-Per-View
iN DEMAND (delivered digitally); MLB Extra Innings (delivered digitally); NHL Center Ice (delivered digitally); NBA League Pass (delivered digitally); ESPN (delivered digitally).

Internet Service
Operational: Yes.
Subscribers: 7,350.
Broadband Service: ProLog Express.
Fee: $61.00 installation; $22.95-$52.95 monthly; $4.95 modem lease; $99.95 modem purchase.

Telephone Service
Analog: Not Operational
Digital: Operational
Subscribers: 1,413.
Fee: $44.95 monthly

Miles of Plant: 299.0 (coaxial); 92.0 (fiber optic).
Manager: Timothy M. Trently. Regulatory Affairs Director: Arlean Lilly. Customer Service & Office Manager: Suzanne Matuella.
Ownership: Service Electric Cable TV Inc. (MSO).

HEIDELBERG TWP.—Formerly served by NORTHAMPTON BOROUGH, PA [PA0008]. RCN Corp. This cable system has converted to IPTV, 196 Van Buren St, Herndon, VA 20170. Phone: 703-434-8200. Web Site: http://www.rcn.com. ICA: PA5217.
TV Market Ranking: Below 100 (HEIDELBERG TWP.).
Channel capacity: N.A. Channels available but not in use: N.A.

Internet Service
Operational: Yes.

Telephone Service
Digital: Operational

Chairman: Steven J. Simmons. Chief Executive Officer: Jim Holanda.

HELLERTOWN BOROUGH—Formerly served by NORTHAMPTON BOROUGH, PA [PA0008]. RCN Corp. This cable system has converted to IPTV, 196 Van Buren St, Herndon, VA 20170. Phone: 703-434-8200. Web Site: http://www.rcn.com. ICA: PA5218.
TV Market Ranking: Below 100 (HELLERTOWN BOROUGH).
Channel capacity: N.A. Channels available but not in use: N.A.

Internet Service
Operational: Yes.

Telephone Service
Digital: Operational

Chairman: Steven J. Simmons. Chief Executive Officer: Jim Holanda.

HEMLOCK FARMS DEVELOPMENT—Blue Ridge Communications, 613 3rd St, PO Box 215, Palmerton, PA 18071-0215. Phone: 610-826-2551. Web Site: http://www.brctv.com. ICA: PA0343.
TV Market Ranking: Below 100 (HEMLOCK FARMS DEVELOPMENT). Franchise award date: N.A. Franchise expiration date: N.A. Began: November 1, 1978.
Channel capacity: 36 (operating 2-way). Channels available but not in use: N.A.

Basic Service
Subscribers: N.A.
Programming (received off-air): WCAU (NBC) Philadelphia; WFMZ-TV (IND) Allen-

town; WLVT-TV (PBS) Allentown; WNEP-TV (ABC) Scranton; WNYW (FOX) New York; WOLF-TV (CW, FOX, MNT) Hazleton; WPIX (CW, IND) New York; WPSG (CW) Philadelphia; WPVI-TV (ABC) Philadelphia; WQPX-TV (ION) Scranton; WSWB (CW) Scranton; WTXF-TV (FOX) Philadelphia; WVIA-TV (PBS) Scranton; WWOR-TV (MNT) Secaucus; WYOU (CBS) Scranton.

Programming (via satellite): Headline News; KYW-TV (CBS) Philadelphia.

Fee: $22.50 installation; $16.49 monthly.

Expanded Basic Service 1

Subscribers: N.A.

Programming (via satellite): A&E Networks; ABC Family Channel; AMC; Animal Planet; Bravo; Cartoon Network; CNBC; CNN; Comcast SportsNet Philadelphia; Comedy Central; Country Music TV; C-SPAN; Discovery Channel; Discovery Fit & Health; Disney Channel; E! Entertainment Television; ESPN; ESPN 2; ESPN Classic Sports; ESPNews; Eternal Word TV Network; Food Network; Fox News Channel; FX; Golf Channel; GSN; Hallmark Channel; HGTV; History Channel; INSP; Lifetime; Lifetime Movie Network; MSG; MSNBC; MTV; Nickelodeon; Pennsylvania Cable Network; QVC; ShopNBC; Speed; Spike TV; Syfy; TBS Superstation; The Learning Channel; The Weather Channel; Travel Channel; truTV; Turner Classic Movies; Turner Network TV; TV Land; Univision Studios; USA Network; Versus; VH1; WE tv; Yankees Entertainment & Sports.

Fee: $29.68 monthly.

Digital Basic Service

Subscribers: N.A.

Programming (via satellite): Bloomberg Television; Discovery Digital Networks; Fox Movie Channel; FSN Digital Atlantic; FSN Digital Central; FSN Digital Pacific; GAS; Halogen Network; Meadows Racing Network; MTV Networks Digital Suite; Music Choice; National Geographic Channel; Nick Jr.; Nick Too; NickToons TV; Outdoor Channel; PBS Kids Channel; SoapNet; Toon Disney.

Fee: $35.00 installation; $9.95 monthly.

Digital Expanded Basic Service

Subscribers: N.A.

Programming (via satellite): BBC America; Bio; Boomerang; Cooking Channel; DIY Network; G4; History Channel International; Lifetime Real Women; LWS Local Weather Station; Style Network.

Fee: $5.00 monthly.

Pay Service 1

Pay Units: N.A.

Programming (via satellite): Cinemax; HBO; Showtime; The Movie Channel.

Fee: $11.50 monthly (Cinemax or Showtime), $12.50 monthly (HBO).

Digital Pay Service 1

Pay Units: N.A.

Programming (via satellite): Cinemax (multiplexed); Encore (multiplexed); Flix; HBO (multiplexed); Showtime (multiplexed); Starz (multiplexed); Sundance Channel; The Movie Channel (multiplexed).

Fee: $12.50 monthly (Cinemax or Showtime/Flix/Sundance/TMC), $12.95 monthly (Starz/Encore), $13.50 monthly (HBO).

Pay-Per-View

iN DEMAND; iN DEMAND (delivered digitally); Sports PPV (delivered digitally); Barker (delivered digitally); adult PPV (delivered digitally).

Internet Service

Operational: Yes.

Broadband Service: ProLog Express.

Fee: $34.95 monthly; $10.00 modem lease; $59.95 modem purchase.

Telephone Service

None

Miles of Plant: 69.0 (coaxial); None (fiber optic).

Vice President, Operations: Richard Semmel. General Manager: Mark Masonheimer. Chief Technician: Randy Semmel.

Ownership: Pencor Services Inc. (MSO).

HERNDON—Formerly served by Pike's Peak TV Association. No longer in operation. ICA: PA0344.

HERSHEY—Comcast Cable. Now served by LEBANON, PA [PA0024]. ICA: PA0052.

HOLLAND—Comcast Cable. Now served by JAMISON, PA [PA0033]. ICA: PA0345.

HONESDALE—Blue Ridge Communications, 613 3rd St, PO Box 215, Palmerton, PA 18071-0215. Phones: 610-826-2551; 800-426-0606 (Customer service); 570-226-4914. Web Site: http://www.brctv.com. Also serves Berlin Twp. (Wayne County), Bethany, Cherry Ridge Twp. (Wayne County), Indian Orchard, Palmyra Twp. (Wayne County), Texas Twp. (Wayne County) & White Mills. ICA: PA0346.

TV Market Ranking: 49 (Berlin Twp. (Wayne County), Bethany, Cherry Ridge Twp. (Wayne County), HONESDALE, Indian Orchard, Palmyra Twp. (Wayne County), Texas Twp. (Wayne County), White Mills). Franchise award date: N.A. Franchise expiration date: N.A. Began: January 1, 1950.

Channel capacity: 67 (operating 2-way). Channels available but not in use: N.A.

Basic Service

Subscribers: 3,295.

Programming (received off-air): WABC-TV (ABC) New York; WCBS-TV (CBS) New York; WNBC (NBC) New York; WNEP-TV (ABC) Scranton; WNET (PBS) Newark; WNYW (FOX) New York; WOLF-TV (CW, FOX, MNT) Hazleton; WPIX (CW, IND) New York; WPVI-TV (ABC) Philadelphia; WQPX-TV (ION) Scranton; WSKG-TV (PBS) Binghamton; WSWB (CW) Scranton; WVIA-TV (PBS) Scranton; WWOR-TV (MNT) Secaucus; WYOU (CBS) Scranton; allband FM.

Programming (via satellite): Headline News; WGN America.

Fee: $22.50 installation; $16.49 monthly.

Expanded Basic Service 1

Subscribers: 650.

Programming (via satellite): A&E Networks; ABC Family Channel; AMC; Animal Planet; Cartoon Network; CNBC; CNN; Comedy Central; Country Music TV; C-SPAN; Discovery Channel; Discovery Health Channel; Disney Channel; E! Entertainment Television; ESPN; ESPN 2; Eternal Word TV Network; Food Network; Fox News Channel; FX; Golf Channel; HGTV; History Channel; Home Shopping Network 2; Lifetime; Lifetime Movie Network; MSG; MSNBC; MTV; Nickelodeon; Pennsylvania Cable Network; QVC; Speed; Spike TV; Syfy; TBS Superstation; The Learning Channel; The Weather Channel; Travel Channel; Trinity Broadcasting Network; truTV; Turner Classic Movies; Turner Network TV; TV Land; USA Network; Versus; VH1; WE tv; Yankees Entertainment & Sports.

Fee: $21.16 monthly.

Digital Basic Service

Subscribers: N.A.

Programming (via satellite): Discovery Digital Networks; Fox Movie Channel; FSN Digital Atlantic; FSN Digital Central; FSN Digital Pacific; GAS; Halogen Network; Meadows Racing Network; MTV Networks Digital Suite; Music Choice; National Geographic Channel; NBA TV; Nick Jr.; Nick Too; NickToons TV; Outdoor Channel; PBS Kids Channel; SoapNet; Toon Disney.

Fee: $35.00 installation; $9.95 monthly.

Digital Expanded Basic Service

Subscribers: N.A.

Programming (via satellite): BBC America; Bio; Bloomberg Television; Boomerang; Cooking Channel; DIY Network; G4; Hallmark Channel; History Channel International; Lifetime Real Women; LWS Local Weather Station; Style Network.

Fee: $5.00 monthly.

Pay Service 1

Pay Units: N.A.

Programming (via satellite): Cinemax; HBO; Showtime.

Fee: $35.00 installation; $11.50 monthly (Cinemax or Showtime), $12.50 monthly (HBO).

Digital Pay Service 1

Pay Units: N.A.

Programming (via satellite): Cinemax (multiplexed); Encore (multiplexed); Flix; HBO (multiplexed); Showtime (multiplexed); Starz (multiplexed); Sundance Channel; The Movie Channel (multiplexed).

Fee: $12.50 monthly (Cinemax or Showtime/Flix/Sundance/TMC), $12.95 monthly (Starz/Encore), $13.50 monthly (HBO).

Video-On-Demand: Yes

Pay-Per-View

iN DEMAND; Barker (delivered digitally); iN DEMAND (delivered digitally); Sports PPV (delivered digitally); adult PPV (delivered digitally).

Internet Service

Operational: Yes.

Broadband Service: ProLog Express.

Fee: $34.95 monthly; $10.00 modem lease; $59.95 modem purchase.

Telephone Service

None

Miles of Plant: 30.0 (coaxial); None (fiber optic). Additional miles planned: 5.0 (coaxial).

Vice President, Operations: Richard Semmel. General Manager: Mark Masonheimer. Fiber Manager: Randy Semmel. Chief Technician: Garry Woods.

Ownership: Pencor Services Inc. (MSO).

HONEY GROVE—Formerly served by Nittany Media. No longer in operation. ICA: PA0347.

HUNTINGDON—Comcast Cable, 1 E Uwchlan Ave, Ste 411, Exton, PA 19341. Phones: 484-288-6500; 814-238-5050 (State College office). Web Site: http://www.comcast.com. Also serves Alexandria, Broad Top City, Broad Top Twp., Carbon Twp., Catherine Twp., Coalmont, Dudley, Henderson Twp. (Huntingdon County), Hopewell, Juniata Twp. (Huntingdon County), Liberty Twp. (Bedford County), Logan Twp. (Huntingdon County), Marklesburg, Mill Creek, Miller Twp. (Huntingdon County), Morris Twp., Petersburg, Saxton, Todd Twp., Union Twp., Wells Twp., Williamsburg, Wood Twp. & Woodbury Twp. ICA: PA0107.

TV Market Ranking: 74 (Alexandria, Broad Top City, Broad Top Twp., Carbon Twp., Catherine Twp., Coalmont, Dudley, Frankstown Twp., Henderson Twp. (Huntingdon County), Hopewell, HUNTINGDON, Juniata Twp. (Huntingdon County), Liberty Twp. (Bedford County), Lincoln Twp., Logan Twp. (Huntingdon County), Marklesburg, Mill Creek, Mill Creek Borough, Miller Twp. (Huntingdon County), Morris Twp., Petersburg, Robertsdale, Saxton, Todd Twp., Union Twp., Wells Twp., Williamsburg, Wood, Woodbury Twp.). Franchise award date: N.A. Franchise expiration date: N.A. Began: March 24, 1962.

Channel capacity: N.A. Channels available but not in use: N.A.

Basic Service

Subscribers: N.A. Included in Harrisburg

Programming (received off-air): WATM-TV (ABC) Altoona; WJAC-TV (NBC) Johnstown; WKBS-TV (IND) Altoona; WPSU-TV (PBS) Clearfield; WTAJ-TV (CBS) Altoona; WWCP-TV (FOX) Johnstown; allband FM.

Programming (via satellite): C-SPAN; C-SPAN 2; Eternal Word TV Network; HTV Musica; INSP; Pennsylvania Cable Network; Product Information Network; QVC; ShopNBC; TV Guide Network; WPIX (CW, IND) New York.

Fee: $45.10 installation; $15.85 monthly.

Expanded Basic Service 1

Subscribers: N.A.

Programming (via satellite): A&E Networks; ABC Family Channel; AMC; AmericanLife TV Network; Animal Planet; Bravo; Cartoon Network; CNBC; CNN; Comedy Central; Country Music TV; Discovery Channel; Discovery Kids Channel; Disney Channel; E! Entertainment Television; ESPN; ESPN 2; ESPN Classic Sports; Food Network; Fox News Channel; FX; GSN; Hallmark Channel; Headline News; HGTV; History Channel; ION Television; Lifetime; MSNBC; MTV; Nickelodeon; Outdoor Channel; Oxygen; Root Sports Pittsburgh; Spike TV; Syfy; TBS Superstation; The Learning Channel; The Weather Channel; Travel Channel; truTV; Turner Network TV; TV Land; USA Network; VH1.

Fee: $30.15 monthly.

Digital Basic Service

Subscribers: N.A.

Programming (via satellite): BBC America; Bio; Black Family Channel; Bloomberg Television; Discovery Fit & Health; DIY Network; ESPN U; ESPNews; Fox Movie Channel; Fox Soccer; Fuse; G4; GAS; Golf Channel; Great American Country; Halogen Network; Lifetime Movie Network; LOGO; Military History Channel; MTV Hits; MTV Jams; MTV2; National Geographic Channel; Nick Jr.; Nick Too; NickToons TV; Speed; The Word Network; Toon Disney; Trinity Broadcasting Network; Turner Classic Movies; VH1; VH1 Country; VH1 Soul; WE tv.

Fee: $14.95 monthly.

Digital Pay Service 1
Pay Units: N.A.
Programming (via satellite): Cinemax (multiplexed); Encore (multiplexed); HBO (multiplexed); Showtime (multiplexed); Starz (multiplexed); The Movie Channel (multiplexed).
Video-On-Demand: Yes
Internet Service
Operational: Yes.
Subscribers: 950.
Broadband Service: Comcast High Speed Internet.
Fee: $42.95 monthly.
Telephone Service
Digital: Operational
Miles of Plant: 293.0 (coaxial); 186.0 (fiber optic).
Area Vice President: Jim Samaha. Vice President, Marketing: Larry Goldman. Technical Operations Manager: Dan Cramer.
Ownership: Comcast Cable Communications Inc. (MSO).

HUNTINGTON TWP. (Luzerne County)—Formerly served by Comcast Cable. No longer in operation. ICA: PA0300.

HYNDMAN BOROUGH—Formerly served by Adelphia Communications. Now served by CENTRAL CITY BOROUGH, PA [PA0132]. ICA: PA0227.

ICKESBURG—Nittany Media Inc. Now served by LEWISTOWN (formerly McAlisterville), PA [PA0365]. ICA: PA0275.

INDIAN CREEK—Laurel Highland Television Co., 4157 Main St, PO Box 168, Stahlstown, PA 15687-0168. Phone: 724-593-2411. Fax: 724-593-2423. E-mail: jstough@lhtot.com. Web Site: http://www.lhtot.com. Also serves Champion, Cook Twp., Donegal, Donegal Twp. (Westmoreland County), Indian Head, Melcroft, Mill Run, Normalville, Saltlick Twp. (Fayette County) & Stahlstown. ICA: PA0348.
TV Market Ranking: 74 (Champion, Cook Twp., Donegal, Donegal Twp. (Westmoreland County), INDIAN CREEK, Indian Head, Melcroft, Mill Run, Normalville, Saltlick Twp. (Fayette County), Stahlstown). Franchise award date: N.A. Franchise expiration date: N.A. Began: January 1, 1967.
Channel capacity: 37 (not 2-way capable). Channels available but not in use: N.A.
Basic Service
Subscribers: 3,759.
Programming (received off-air): KDKA-TV (CBS) Pittsburgh; WJAC-TV (NBC) Johnstown; WPCB-TV (IND) Greensburg; WPGH-TV (FOX) Pittsburgh; WPMY (MNT) Pittsburgh; WPXI (IND, NBC) Pittsburgh; WQED (PBS) Pittsburgh; WTAE-TV (ABC) Pittsburgh.
Programming (via satellite): A&E Networks; ABC Family Channel; AMC; America's Store; Animal Planet; Bloomberg Television; Boomerang; Bravo; Cartoon Network; CNN; Comedy Central; Country Music TV; C-SPAN; Discovery Channel; Disney Channel; E! Entertainment Television; ESPN; ESPN 2; ESPN Classic Sports; Eternal Word TV Network; FamilyNet; Food Network; Fox Movie Channel; Fox News Channel; FX; G4; Golf Channel; Great American Country; Hallmark Channel; Hallmark Movie Channel; Headline News; HGTV; History Channel; Lifetime; Lifetime Movie Network; MSNBC; National Geographic Channel; Nickelodeon; Outdoor Channel; Paramount Network (UPN); Pennsylvania Cable Network; QVC; Root Sports Pittsburgh; SoapNet; Speed; Spike TV; Syfy; TBS Superstation; The Learning Channel; The Weather Channel; Travel Channel; Trinity Broadcasting Network; truTV; Turner Network TV; TV Land; USA Network; VH1.
Fee: $20.00 installation; $44.95 monthly.
Pay Service 1
Pay Units: 849.
Programming (via satellite): Cinemax; HBO; Showtime; The Movie Channel.
Fee: $8.00 monthly (Cinemax), $15.00 monthly (HBO), $15.95 monthly (Showtime/TMC).
Internet Service
Operational: No, DSL & dial-up.
Telephone Service
None
Miles of Plant: 322.0 (coaxial); 60.0 (fiber optic).
President & Chief Executive Officer: James J. Kail. Plant Manager: Jeffrey A. Stough.
Ownership: Laurel Highland Total Communications.

INDIANA—Formerly served by Adelphia Communications. Now served by BLAIRSVILLE, PA [PA0320]. ICA: PA0463.

JAMESTOWN—Formerly served by Cebridge Connections. Now served by MEADVILLE, PA [PA0062]. ICA: PA0202.

JAMISON—Comcast Cable, 3220 Tillman Dr, Bensalem, PA 19010. Phone: 215-642-6400. Fax: 215-638-6510. Web Site: http://www.comcast.com. Also serves Buckingham Twp. (Bucks County), Chalfont, Doylestown, Holland, Ivyland (portions), Mechanicsville, New Britain, Richboro, Solebury Twp., Warrington Twp. (Bucks County) & Warwick Twp. (Bucks County). ICA: PA0033.
TV Market Ranking: 4 (Buckingham Twp. (Bucks County), Chalfont, Doylestown, Holland, Ivyland (portions), JAMISON, Mechanicsville, New Britain, Richboro, Solebury Twp., Warrington Twp. (Bucks County), Warwick Twp. (Bucks County)). Franchise award date: May 24, 1982. Franchise expiration date: N.A. Began: July 1, 1982.
Channel capacity: N.A. Channels available but not in use: N.A.
Basic Service
Subscribers: N.A. Included in Bensalem Twp.
Programming (received off-air): KYW-TV (CBS) Philadelphia; WCAU (NBC) Philadelphia; WFMZ-TV (IND) Allentown; WGTW-TV (TBN) Burlington; WHYY-TV (PBS) Wilmington; WLVT-TV (PBS) Allentown; WMCN-TV (IND) Atlantic City; WNET (PBS) Newark; WNJT (PBS) Trenton; WPHL-TV (MNT, IND) Philadelphia; WPPX-TV (ION) Wilmington; WPSG (CW) Philadelphia; WPVI-TV (ABC) Philadelphia; WTVE (IND) Reading; WTXF-TV (FOX) Philadelphia; WUVP-DT (UNV) Vineland; WWSI (TMO) Atlantic City; WYBE (ETV, IND) Philadelphia; allband FM.
Programming (via satellite): C-SPAN; C-SPAN 2; QVC; TBS Superstation; The Comcast Network; TV Land.
Fee: $15.50 monthly.
Expanded Basic Service 1
Subscribers: 52,667.
Programming (received off-air): WBPH-TV (IND) Bethlehem.
Programming (via satellite): A&E Networks; ABC Family Channel; AMC; Animal Planet; Bravo; Cartoon Network; CNBC; CNN; Comcast SportsNet Philadelphia; Comedy Central; Country Music TV; Discovery Channel; Discovery Health Channel; Disney Channel; E! Entertainment Television; ESPN; ESPN 2; Food Network; Fox News Channel; FX; Golf Channel; GSN; Headline News; HGTV; History Channel; Lifetime; MSNBC; MTV; MTV2; Nickelodeon; Philadelphia Park Live; Speed; Spike TV; Style Network; Syfy; The Learning Channel; The Weather Channel; Travel Channel; truTV; Turner Classic Movies; Turner Network TV; USA Network; Versus; VH1.
Fee: $36.70 monthly.
Digital Basic Service
Subscribers: N.A.
Programming (via satellite): BBC America; Bio; Comcast SportsNet Philadelphia; Cooking Channel; C-SPAN 3; DIY Network; DMX Music; Encore; ESPN; ESPNews; Eternal Word TV Network; Flix; Fox College Sports Atlantic; Fox College Sports Central; Fox College Sports Pacific; Fox Soccer; G4; GAS; GolTV; Great American Country; Hallmark Channel; HD Theater; History Channel International; Independent Film Channel; INHD (multiplexed); Lifetime Movie Network; LOGO; MTV Networks Digital Suite; National Geographic Channel; NBA TV; NFL Network; Nick Jr.; Nick Too; NickToons TV; Oxygen; PBS Kids Sprout; Pennsylvania Cable Network; ShopNBC; SoapNet; Sundance Channel; Toon Disney; TV One; WAM! America's Kidz Network; Weatherscan.
Fee: $15.00 monthly.
Digital Pay Service 1
Pay Units: N.A.
Programming (via satellite): Cinemax (multiplexed); Cinemax HD; HBO (multiplexed); HBO HD; Showtime (multiplexed); Showtime HD; Starz (multiplexed); Starz HDTV; The Movie Channel (multiplexed).
Video-On-Demand: Yes
Pay-Per-View
Special events (delivered digitally); Movies (delivered digitally); NBA TV (delivered digitally); NBA League Pass (delivered digitally); NHL Center Ice (delivered digitally); MLB Extra Innings (delivered digitally); Playboy TV (delivered digitally); Fresh (delivered digitally); Shorteez (delivered digitally); Pleasure (delivered digitally); Canal 52MX (delivered digitally); Russian Television Network (delivered digitally); ESPN (delivered digitally).
Internet Service
Operational: Yes.
Broadband Service: Comcast High Speed Internet.
Fee: $49.00 installation; $42.95 monthly.
Telephone Service
Digital: Operational
Miles of Plant: 1,000.0 (coaxial); 16.0 (fiber optic).
Senior Regional Vice President: Amy Smith. Vice President, Technical Operations: Rich Massi. Vice President, Marketing: Chip Goodman.
Ownership: Comcast Cable Communications Inc. (MSO).

JOHNSONBURG—Johnsonburg Community TV Co., 424 Center St, Johnsonburg, PA 15845-1305. Phone: 814-965-4888. Fax: 814-965-4040. ICA: PA0174.
TV Market Ranking: Outside TV Markets (JOHNSONBURG). Franchise award date: October 1, 1953. Franchise expiration date: N.A. Began: October 1, 1953.
Channel capacity: 36 (not 2-way capable). Channels available but not in use: N.A.
Basic Service
Subscribers: 1,020.
Programming (received off-air): KDKA-TV (CBS) Pittsburgh; WICU-TV (NBC) Erie; WJAC-TV (NBC) Johnstown; WKBW-TV (ABC) Buffalo; WPSU-TV (PBS) Clearfield; WTAJ-TV (CBS) Altoona; WWCP-TV (FOX) Johnstown; allband FM.
Programming (via satellite): A&E Networks; ABC Family Channel; AMC; CNN; Discovery Channel; ESPN; Eternal Word TV Network; Headline News; Lifetime; Nickelodeon; Spike TV; TBS Superstation; The Weather Channel; Turner Network TV; USA Network; WGN America.
Fee: $125.00 installation; $16.00 monthly; $25.00 additional installation.
Pay Service 1
Pay Units: 386.
Programming (via satellite): Cinemax.
Fee: $25.00 installation; $7.00 monthly.
Pay Service 2
Pay Units: 575.
Programming (via satellite): HBO.
Fee: $13.90 monthly.
Pay Service 3
Pay Units: 244.
Programming (via satellite): Showtime.
Fee: $12.25 monthly.
Video-On-Demand: Planned
Internet Service
Operational: No.
Telephone Service
None
Miles of Plant: 30.0 (coaxial); None (fiber optic).
Manager, Marketing & Program Director: Harry Horne. Chief Technician: Jerry Muroski.
Ownership: Johnsonburg Community TV Co. Inc.

JOHNSONBURG—Zito Media, 611 Vader Hill Rd, Coudersport, PA 16915. Fax: 814-260-9580. E-mail: rigas@zitomedia.com. Web Site: http://www.zitomedia.com. ICA: PA0472.
TV Market Ranking: Outside TV Markets (JOHNSONBURG).
Channel capacity: N.A. Channels available but not in use: N.A.
Basic Service
Subscribers: N.A.
Programming (received off-air): WATM-TV (ABC) Altoona; WGRZ (NBC) Buffalo; WIVB-TV (CBS) Buffalo; WJAC-TV (NBC) Johnstown; WKBW-TV (ABC) Buffalo; WNED-TV (PBS) Buffalo; WPSU-TV (PBS) Clearfield; WTAE-TV (ABC) Pittsburgh; WTAJ-TV (CBS) Altoona; WWCP-TV (FOX) Johnstown.
Programming (via satellite): A&E Networks; ABC Family Channel; AMC; Animal Planet; Bravo; Cartoon Network; CNBC; CNN; Comedy Central; Country Music TV; C-SPAN; Discovery Channel; Disney Channel; E! Entertainment Television; ESPN; ESPN 2; ESPN Classic Sports; ESPNews; Eternal Word TV Network; Food Network; Fox News Channel; FX; Hallmark Channel; Headline News; HGTV; History Channel; INSP; Lifetime; MSNBC; MTV; NFL Network; Nickelodeon; Outdoor Channel; Pennsylvania Cable Network; QVC; Root Sports Pittsburgh; Speed; Spike TV; Superstation WGN; Syfy; TBS Superstation; The Learning Channel; The Weather Channel; Travel Channel; Trinity Broadcasting Network; truTV; Turner Classic Movies; Turner Network TV; TV Guide; TV Land; USA Network; VH1; WPIX (CW, IND) New York.
Fee: $39.95 installation; $42.64 monthly.

Digital Basic Service
Subscribers: N.A.
Programming (via satellite): A&E HD; ABC Family HD; AMC; Bio HD; Cartoon Network HD; CNN HD; C-SPAN 2; Discovery Channel HD; Disney Channel HD; ESPN 2 HD; ESPN HD; ESPNews HD; Food Network HD; FX HD; HD Theater; HGTV HD; Independent Film Channel; Lifetime Movie Network; Lifetime Movie Network HD; Lifetime Real Women; Lifetime Television HD; National Geographic Channel; NFL Network HD; NHL Network HD; Outdoor Channel 2 HD; Planet Green; Root Sports Pittsburgh; Science HD; Speed HD; TBS in HD; TLC HD; Turner Network TV HD; WE tv.

Digital Pay Service 1
Pay Units: N.A.
Programming (via satellite): Cinemax HD; HBO HD; Showtime HD; Starz HDTV.
Video-On-Demand: Yes

Pay-Per-View
NHL Center Ice (delivered digitally); MLB Extra Innings (delivered digitally).

Internet Service
Operational: Yes.
Fee: $30.51 monthly.

Telephone Service
Digital: Operational
Fee: $20.00-$35.00 monthly
Manager: James Rigas.
Ownership: Zito Media.

JOHNSTOWN—Atlantic Broadband, 120 Southmont Blvd, Johnstown, PA 15905. Phones: 814-539-8971; 888-536-9600 (Customer service). Fax: 814-535-7749. E-mail: info@atlanticbb.com. Web Site: http://www.atlanticbb.com. Also serves Benson, Boswell, Brownstown (Cambria County), Conemaugh Twp. (Cambria County), Conemaugh Twp. (Somerset County), Daisytown (Cambria County), Dale (Cambria County), Davidsville, East Taylor Twp., Ferndale (Cambria County), Franklin (Cambria County), Geistown, Hollsopple, Jackson Twp. (Cambria County), Jenner Twp. (Somerset County), Jerome, Lorain, Lower Yoder Twp., Middle Taylor Twp., Mineral Point, Nanty-Glo (portions), Paint Twp. (Somerset County), Quemahoning Twp. (Somerset County), Richland Twp. (Cambria County), Southmont, Stonycreek Twp. (Cambria County), Summerhill (portions), Tire Hill, Upper Yoder Twp., West Taylor Twp., Westmont (Cambria County) & Windber. ICA: PA0026.
TV Market Ranking: 74 (Benson, Boswell, Brownstown (Cambria County), Conemaugh Twp. (Cambria County), Conemaugh Twp. (Somerset County), Daisytown (Cambria County), Dale (Cambria County), Davidsville, East Taylor Twp., Ferndale (Cambria County), Franklin (Cambria County), Geistown, Hollsopple, Jackson Twp. (Cambria County), Jenner Twp. (Somerset County), Jerome, JOHNSTOWN, Lorain, Lower Yoder Twp., Middle Taylor Twp., Mineral Point, Nanty-Glo (portions), Paint Twp. (Somerset County), Quemahoning Twp. (Somerset County), Richland Twp. (Cambria County), Southmont, Stonycreek Twp. (Cambria County), Summerhill (portions), Tire Hill, Upper Yoder Twp., West Taylor Twp., Westmont (Cambria County), Windber). Franchise award date: February 23, 1983. Franchise expiration date: N.A. Began: August 1, 1960.
Channel capacity: N.A. Channels available but not in use: N.A.

Basic Service
Subscribers: 29,865.
Programming (received off-air): KDKA-TV (CBS) Pittsburgh; WATM-TV (ABC) Altoona; WHVL-LP State College, etc.; WJAC-TV (NBC) Johnstown; WKBS-TV (IND) Altoona; WPCW (CW) Jeannette; WPSU-TV (PBS) Clearfield; WQED (PBS) Pittsburgh; WTAE-TV (ABC) Pittsburgh; WTAJ-TV (CBS) Altoona; WWCP-TV (FOX) Johnstown.
Programming (via satellite): C-SPAN; C-SPAN 2; Eternal Word TV Network; HRTV; ION Television; Jewelry Television; PBS World; Pennsylvania Cable Network; QVC; ShopNBC; TV Guide Network.
Fee: $25.00 installation; $18.95 monthly.

Expanded Basic Service 1
Subscribers: 25,419.
Programming (via satellite): A&E Networks; ABC Family Channel; AMC; Animal Planet; BET Networks; Bravo; Cartoon Network; CNBC; CNN; Comedy Central; Country Music TV; Discovery Channel; Disney Channel; E! Entertainment Television; ESPN; ESPN 2; ESPN Classic Sports; Food Network; Fox News Channel; FX; G4; Golf Channel; GSN; Hallmark Channel; Headline News; HGTV; History Channel; INSP; Lifetime; MSNBC; MTV; National Geographic Channel; Nickelodeon; Nick-Toons TV; Outdoor Channel; Oxygen; Root Sports Pittsburgh; Speed; Spike TV; Style Network; Syfy; TBS Superstation; The Learning Channel; The Weather Channel; Toon Disney; Travel Channel; truTV; Turner Classic Movies; Turner Network TV; TV Land; USA Network; Versus; VH1; World Shopping Network.
Fee: $25.00 installation; $39.04 monthly.

Digital Basic Service
Subscribers: N.A.
Programming (via satellite): A&E HD; Animal Planet HD; BBC America; Bio; Bloomberg Television; Boomerang; CCTV-4; Chiller; Cinemax HD; CMT Pure Country; Discovery Health Channel; Discovery Kids Channel; Disney Channel HD; DIY Network; Encore; ESPN 2 HD; ESPN HD; ESPN U; ESPNews; Fox News HD; Fuel TV; Fuse; GAS; Great American Country; HBO HD; HD Theater; History Channel HD; History Channel International; ID Investigation Discovery; Independent Film Channel; Lifetime Movie Network; Lifetime Real Women; Military Channel; MTV Hits; MTV Jams; MTV2; Music Choice; NFL Network; NFL Network HD; Nick Jr.; Nick Too; Outdoor Channel 2 HD; Planet Green; Root Sports Pittsburgh; RTN; Science; Science HD; Showtime HD; SoapNet; Starz (multiplexed); Starz HDTV; Syfy HD; TBS in HD; TLC HD; Tr3s; Turner Network TV HD; TVG Network; USA Network HD; VH1 Classic; VH1 Soul; WE tv.
Fee: $18.95 monthly.

Digital Pay Service 1
Pay Units: N.A.
Programming (via satellite): Cinemax (multiplexed); Flix; HBO (multiplexed); Showtime (multiplexed); The Movie Channel (multiplexed).
Fee: $15.95 monthly (HBO, Cinemax or Showtime/TMC/Flix).
Video-On-Demand: No

Pay-Per-View
iN DEMAND (delivered digitally); Hot Choice (delivered digitally).

Internet Service
Operational: Yes.
Broadband Service: Atlantic Broadband High-Speed Internet.
Fee: $24.95-$57.95 monthly.

Telephone Service
Analog: Not Operational
Digital: Operational
Fee: $44.95 monthly
Miles of Plant: 578.0 (coaxial); 140.0 (fiber optic).
Vice President: David Dane. General Manager: Mike Papasergi. Technical Operations Director: Charles Sorchilla. Marketing & Customer Service Director: Dara Leslie. Marketing Manager: Natalie Kurchak.
Ownership: Atlantic Broadband (MSO).

KANE—Comcast Cable, 15 Summit Park Dr, Pittsburgh, PA 15275. Phones: 412-747-6400; 814-226-6350 (Clarion office). Fax: 412-747-6401. Web Site: http://www.comcast.com. Also serves East Kane, Hamlin Twp., Hazel Hurst, Highland Twp. (Elk County), James City, Mount Jewett & Wetmore Twp. ICA: PA0125.
TV Market Ranking: Outside TV Markets (East Kane, Hamlin Twp., Hazel Hurst, Highland Twp. (Elk County), James City, KANE, Mount Jewett, Wetmore Twp.). Franchise award date: N.A. Franchise expiration date: N.A. Began: November 1, 1959.
Channel capacity: N.A. Channels available but not in use: N.A.

Basic Service
Subscribers: N.A. Included in Bensalem Twp.
Programming (received off-air): WICU-TV (NBC) Erie; WIVB-TV (CBS) Buffalo; WJAC-TV (NBC) Johnstown; WJET-TV (ABC) Erie; WKBW-TV (ABC) Buffalo; WNYB (IND) Jamestown; WPSU-TV (PBS) Clearfield; WTAJ-TV (CBS) Altoona; allband FM.
Programming (via satellite): Hallmark Channel; QVC; TBS Superstation; The Weather Channel; WPIX (CW, IND) New York.
Fee: $39.95 installation; $17.80 monthly; $2.00 converter.

Expanded Basic Service 1
Subscribers: N.A.
Programming (via satellite): A&E Networks; ABC Family Channel; AMC; Animal Planet; Cartoon Network; CNBC; CNN; Comedy Central; Country Music TV; C-SPAN; C-SPAN 2; Discovery Channel; Disney Channel; E! Entertainment Television; ESPN; Eternal Word TV Network; Fox News Channel; FX; Headline News; History Channel; ION Television; Lifetime; MoviePlex; MSNBC; MTV; Nickelodeon; Oxygen; Pennsylvania Cable Network; Root Sports Pittsburgh; Spike TV; The Learning Channel; Travel Channel; truTV; Turner Network TV; TV Land; USA Network; VH1.
Fee: $11.34 monthly.

Digital Basic Service
Subscribers: 45.
Programming (via satellite): AmericanLife TV Network; BBC America; Bio; Bloomberg Television; Bravo; Discovery Fit & Health; ESPN 2; ESPN Classic Sports; ESPNews; Fox Movie Channel; Fox Sports World; Fuse; G4; Golf Channel; GSN; Halogen Network; HGTV; History Channel International; Independent Film Channel; Lifetime Movie Network; Outdoor Channel; Ovation; Speed; Sundance Channel; Syfy; Toon Disney; Trinity Broadcasting Network; Turner Classic Movies; Versus; WE tv.
Fee: $10.95 monthly.

Digital Expanded Basic Service
Subscribers: N.A.
Programming (via satellite): GAS; MTV Networks Digital Suite; MTV2; National Geographic Channel; Nick Jr.; Style Network.
Fee: $5.00 monthly.

Digital Pay Service 1
Pay Units: N.A.
Programming (via satellite): Cinemax (multiplexed); Encore (multiplexed); HBO (multiplexed); Showtime (multiplexed); Starz (multiplexed); The Movie Channel (multiplexed).
Fee: $15.95 monthly (each).
Video-On-Demand: No

Pay-Per-View
Playboy TV (delivered digitally); Shorteez (delivered digitally); Fresh (delivered digitally); Hot Choice (delivered digitally); HITS (delivered digitally).

Internet Service
Operational: Yes.
Subscribers: 70.
Broadband Service: Comcast High Speed Internet.
Fee: $42.95 monthly.

Telephone Service
Digital: Operational
Miles of Plant: 60.0 (coaxial); None (fiber optic).
Regional Vice President: Linda Hossinger. Vice President, Technical Operations: Randy Bender. Vice President, Marketing: Donna Corning. Vice President, Public Affairs: Jody Doherty.
Ownership: Comcast Cable Communications Inc. (MSO).

KELLETTVILLE—Formerly served by Cebridge Connections. No longer in operation. ICA: PA0270.

KENNETT SQUARE—Comcast Cable, 3220 Tillman Dr, Bensalem, PA 19010. Phone: 215-642-6400. Fax: 215-638-6510. Web Site: http://www.comcast.com. Also serves Avondale, Chadds Ford Twp., East Marlborough Twp., Kennett Twp., London Britain Twp., London Grove Twp., New Garden Twp., New London Twp., Pennsbury Twp. (Chester County), Pocopson Twp., Upper Oxford Twp. & West Grove. ICA: PA0071.
TV Market Ranking: 4 (Chadds Ford Twp., Pennsbury Twp. (Chester County), Pocopson Twp.); 4,57 (Avondale, East Marlborough Twp., KENNETT SQUARE, London Britain Twp., London Grove Twp., New Garden Twp., Upper Oxford Twp.); 57 (Kennett Twp., New London Twp., West Grove). Franchise award date: N.A. Franchise expiration date: December 3, 2010. Began: December 3, 1980.
Channel capacity: N.A. Channels available but not in use: N.A.

Basic Service
Subscribers: N.A. Included in Bensalem Twp.
Programming (received off-air): KYW-TV (CBS) Philadelphia; WCAU (NBC) Philadelphia; WFMZ-TV (IND) Allentown; WGAL (NBC) Lancaster; WGTW-TV (TBN) Burlington; WHYY-TV (PBS) Wilmington; WPHL-TV (MNT, IND) Philadelphia; WPPX-TV (ION) Wilmington; WPSG (CW) Philadelphia; WPVI-TV (ABC) Philadelphia; WTVE (IND) Reading; WTXF-TV (FOX) Philadelphia; WUVP-DT (UNV) Vineland; WYBE (ETV, IND) Philadelphia.
Programming (via satellite): C-SPAN; Eternal Word TV Network; MarketConnect Network; QVC; TBS Superstation; Telemundo; The Comcast Network.
Fee: $12.50 monthly.

Expanded Basic Service 1
Subscribers: 12,717.
Programming (via satellite): A&E Networks; ABC Family Channel; AMC; Animal Planet; BET Networks; Bravo; Cartoon Network; CNBC; CNN; Comcast SportsNet Philadelphia; Comedy Central; Country Music TV; C-SPAN 2; Discovery Channel; Discovery Health Channel; Disney Channel; E! Entertainment Television; ESPN; ESPN 2; ESPN Classic Sports; Food Network; Fox News Channel; FX; Golf Channel; GSN; Hallmark Channel; Headline News; HGTV; History Channel; Lifetime; MSNBC; MTV; Nickelodeon; Pennsylvania Cable Network; Philadelphia Park Live; Speed; Spike TV; Style Network; Syfy; The Learning Channel; The Weather Channel; Travel Channel; truTV; Turner Classic Movies; Turner Network TV; TV Land; USA Network; Versus; VH1.
Fee: $39.70 monthly.

Digital Basic Service
Subscribers: N.A.
Programming (via satellite): BBC America; Bio; Canales N; Comcast SportsNet Philadelphia; Cooking Channel; C-SPAN 3; DIY Network; DMX Music; ESPN; ESPNews; Fox Sports World; FSN Digital Atlantic; FSN Digital Central; FSN Digital Pacific; G4; GAS; GolTV; HD Theater; History Channel International; Independent Film Channel; INHD; MTV Networks Digital Suite; Music Choice; National Geographic Channel; NBA TV; NFL Network; Nick Jr.; Nick Too; NickToons TV; ShopNBC; SoapNet; Toon Disney; WAM! America's Kidz Network; Weatherscan.
Fee: $24.95 monthly.

Digital Pay Service 1
Pay Units: N.A.
Programming (via satellite): Cinemax (multiplexed); Cinemax HD; Encore; Flix (multiplexed); HBO (multiplexed); HBO HD; Showtime (multiplexed); Showtime HD; Starz (multiplexed); Starz HDTV; Sundance Channel (multiplexed); The Movie Channel (multiplexed).

Video-On-Demand: Yes

Pay-Per-View
Playboy TV (delivered digitally); iN DEMAND (delivered digitally); Fresh (delivered digitally); Shorteez (delivered digitally); Pleasure (delivered digitally).

Internet Service
Operational: Yes.
Broadband Service: Comcast High Speed Internet.
Fee: $42.95 monthly.

Telephone Service
Digital: Operational
Fee: $44.95 monthly

Miles of Plant: 455.0 (coaxial); 27.0 (fiber optic). Additional miles planned: 5.0 (coaxial).
Senior Regional Vice President: Amy Smith. Vice President, Technical Operations: Rich Massi. Vice President, Marketing: Chip Goodman.
Ownership: Comcast Cable Communications Inc. (MSO).

KING OF PRUSSIA—Comcast Cable, 3220 Tillman Dr, Bensalem, PA 19010. Phone: 215-642-6400. Fax: 215-638-6510. Web Site: http://www.comcast.com. Also serves Graterford, Perkiomen, Rahns, Upper Merion Twp. & Wayne. ICA: PA0059.
TV Market Ranking: 4 (Graterford, KING OF PRUSSIA, Perkiomen, Rahns, Upper Merion Twp., Upper Providence Twp. (Delaware County), Wayne). Franchise award date: N.A. Franchise expiration date: N.A. Began: November 1, 1981.
Channel capacity: N.A. Channels available but not in use: N.A.

Basic Service
Subscribers: N.A. Included in Bensalem Twp.
Programming (received off-air): KYW-TV (CBS) Philadelphia; WBPH-TV (IND) Bethlehem; WCAU (NBC) Philadelphia; WFMZ-TV (IND) Allentown; WGTW-TV (TBN) Burlington; WHYY-TV (PBS) Wilmington; WLVT-TV (PBS) Allentown; WNJT (PBS) Trenton; WPHL-TV (MNT, IND) Philadelphia; WPPX-TV (ION) Wilmington; WPSG (CW) Philadelphia; WPVI-TV (ABC) Philadelphia; WTVE (IND) Reading; WTXF-TV (FOX) Philadelphia; WUVP-DT (UNV) Vineland; WYBE (ETV, IND) Philadelphia.
Programming (via satellite): ABC Family Channel; C-SPAN; Eternal Word TV Network; MSNBC; MTV2; QVC; TBS Superstation; Telemundo; The Comcast Network.
Fee: $16.10 monthly.

Expanded Basic Service 1
Subscribers: 17,138.
Programming (via satellite): A&E Networks; AMC; Animal Planet; BET Networks; Bravo; Cartoon Network; CNBC; CNN; Comcast SportsNet Philadelphia; Comedy Central; Country Music TV; Discovery Channel; Discovery Health Channel; Disney Channel; E! Entertainment Television; Encore Action; ESPN; ESPN 2; Food Network; Fox News Channel; FX; Golf Channel; GSN; Headline News; HGTV; History Channel; Home Shopping Network 2; Lifetime; MTV; Nickelodeon; Philadelphia Park Live; Speed; Spike TV; Style Network; Syfy; The Learning Channel; The Weather Channel; Travel Channel; truTV; Turner Classic Movies; Turner Network TV; TV Land; USA Network; VH1.
Fee: $34.30 monthly.

Digital Basic Service
Subscribers: N.A.
Programming (via satellite): BBC America; Bio; Cooking Channel; C-SPAN 3; Discovery Digital Networks; DIY Network; DMX Music; ESPNews; G4; GAS; History Channel International; Independent Film Channel; MTV Networks Digital Suite; National Geographic Channel; Nick Jr.; Nick Too; Science Television; ShopNBC; SoapNet; Toon Disney; WAM! America's Kidz Network; Weatherscan.
Fee: $15.00 monthly.

Digital Pay Service 1
Pay Units: N.A.
Programming (via satellite): Cinemax (multiplexed); HBO (multiplexed); Showtime (multiplexed); Starz (multiplexed); The Movie Channel (multiplexed).
Fee: $18.95 monthly (each).

Video-On-Demand: Yes

Pay-Per-View
Addressable homes: 2,300.
iN DEMAND; Playboy TV (delivered digitally); Spice (delivered digitally); Pleasure (delivered digitally); iN DEMAND (delivered digitally); ESPN (delivered digitally); NBA League (delivered digitally); NHL/MLB (delivered digitally).

Internet Service
Operational: Yes. Began: June 1, 2002.
Broadband Service: Comcast High Speed Internet.
Fee: $42.95 monthly.

Telephone Service
Digital: Operational
Fee: $44.95 monthly

Miles of Plant: 250.0 (coaxial); None (fiber optic). Additional miles planned: 6.0 (coaxial).
Senior Regional Vice President: Amy Smith. Vice President, Technical Operations: Rich Massi. Vice President, Marketing: Chip Goodman.
Ownership: Comcast Cable Communications Inc. (MSO).

KISKIMINETAS TWP.—Comcast Cable, 15 Summit Park Dr, Pittsburgh, PA 15275. Phone: 412-747-6400. Fax: 412-747-6401. Web Site: http://www.comcast.com. Also serves Adrian, Apollo, Applewold, Avonmore, Beyer, Cowanshannock Twp., Cowansville, Dayton Borough, Distant, East Vandergrift, Edmon, Elderton, Elderton Borough, Ford City, Freeport, Gilpin Twp., Home, Hyde Park, Kittanning, Leechburg, Loyalhanna Twp., Manorville, McGrann, North Apollo, North Buffalo Twp., Nu Mine, Parks Twp., Penn Hills, Pine Twp., Plumcreek Twp., Plumville, Rural Valley, Sagamore, Salina, Saltsburg, Sarver, Seminole, Shelocta, South Buffalo Twp., South Mahoning Twp., Spring Church, Templeton, Vandergrift, West Kittanning, West Leechburg, Widnoon, Worthington & Yatesboro. ICA: PA0074.
TV Market Ranking: 10 (Apollo, Applewold, East Vandergrift, Edmon, Freeport, Gilpin Twp., Hyde Park, KISKIMINETAS TWP., Leechburg, Loyalhanna Twp., Manorville, McGrann, North Apollo, North Buffalo Twp., Parks Twp., Penn Hills, Sarver, South Buffalo Twp., Vandergrift, West Leechburg); 10,74 (Avonmore, Salina, Spring Church); 74 (Plumville, Shelocta); 74,10 (Saltsburg); Below 100 (Ford City, Kittanning, West Kittanning, Worthington); Outside TV Markets (Adrian, Beyer, Cowanshannock Twp., Cowansville, Dayton Borough, Distant, Home, Nu Mine, Pine Twp., Rural Valley, Sagamore, Seminole, Templeton, Widnoon, Yatesboro). Franchise award date: N.A. Franchise expiration date: N.A. Began: February 1, 1967.
Channel capacity: N.A. Channels available but not in use: N.A.

Basic Service
Subscribers: 17,635.
Programming (received off-air): KDKA-TV (CBS) Pittsburgh; WINP-TV (IND, ION) Pittsburgh; WPCB-TV (IND) Greensburg; WPCW (CW) Jeannette; WPGH-TV (FOX) Pittsburgh; WPMY (MNT) Pittsburgh; WPXI (IND, NBC) Pittsburgh; WQED (PBS) Pittsburgh; WTAE-TV (ABC) Pittsburgh; allband FM.
Programming (via satellite): C-SPAN; C-SPAN 2; Eternal Word TV Network; QVC; The Weather Channel; TV Guide Network; WGN America; WPCH-TV (IND) Atlanta.
Fee: $43.99 installation; $14.00 monthly; $1.85 converter; $19.99 additional installation.

Expanded Basic Service 1
Subscribers: 10,916.
Programming (via satellite): A&E Networks; ABC Family Channel; AMC; Animal Planet; BET Networks; Cartoon Network; CNBC; CNN; Comedy Central; Country Music TV; Discovery Channel; Disney Channel; E! Entertainment Television; ESPN; ESPN 2; Food Network; Fox News Channel; FX; Golf Channel; GSN; Hallmark Channel; Headline News; HGTV; History Channel; ION Television; Lifetime; MSNBC; MTV; Nickelodeon; Oxygen; Pennsylvania Cable Network; Pittsburgh Cable News Channel; Root Sports Pittsburgh; Spike TV; The Learning Channel; Travel Channel; truTV; Turner Classic Movies; Turner Network TV; TV Land; USA Network; Versus; VH1.
Fee: $37.99 monthly.

Digital Basic Service
Subscribers: N.A.
Programming (via satellite): AmericanLife TV Network; BBC America; Bio; Black Family Channel; Bloomberg Television; Bravo; CBS Sports Network; Cooking Channel; C-SPAN 3; Discovery Fit & Health; DIY Network; DMX Music; Encore; ESPN; ESPN Classic Sports; ESPNews; Flix; Fox College Sports Atlantic; Fox College Sports Central; Fox College Sports Pacific; Fox Movie Channel; Fox Sports World; Fuse; G4; GAS; GolTV; Great American Country; Halogen Network; HD Theater; History Channel International; HRTV; iN DEMAND; Independent Film Channel; International Television (ITV); Jewelry Television; Lifetime Movie Network; Lime; MTV Networks Digital Suite; National Geographic Channel; NBA TV; NFL Network; Nick Jr.; Nick Too; NickToons TV; Outdoor Channel; Ovation; RAI International; Russian Television Network; ShopNBC; Speed; Style Network; Sundance Channel; Syfy; The Word Network; Toon Disney; Trinity Broadcasting Network; TV Asia; TVG Network; WAM! America's Kidz Network; WE tv; Weatherscan; Zee TV USA.
Fee: $10.95 monthly; $4.60 converter.

Digital Pay Service 1
Pay Units: N.A.
Programming (via satellite): Cinemax (multiplexed); HBO (multiplexed); HBO HD; Showtime (multiplexed); Showtime HD; Starz (multiplexed); Starz HDTV; The Movie Channel (multiplexed).

Video-On-Demand: Yes

Pay-Per-View
Hot Choice (delivered digitally); iN DEMAND (delivered digitally); MLB Extra Innings (delivered digitally); Playboy TV (delivered digitally); Movies (delivered digitally); Fresh (delivered digitally); Shorteez (delivered digitally); Sports PPV (delivered digitally); NBA TV (delivered digitally); NHL Center Ice (delivered digitally).

Internet Service
Operational: Yes.
Broadband Service: Comcast High Speed Internet.
Fee: $42.95 monthly.

Telephone Service
Digital: Operational

Miles of Plant: 605.0 (coaxial); None (fiber optic).
Regional Vice President: Linda Hossinger. Vice President, Technical Operations: Randy Bender. Vice President, Marketing: Donna Corning. Vice President, Public Affairs: Jody Doherty.
Ownership: Comcast Cable Communications Inc. (MSO).

KITTANNING—Comcast Cable. Now served by KISKIMINETAS TWP., PA [PA0074]. ICA: PA0351.

KUTZTOWN—Hometown Utilicom. Formerly [PA0452]. This cable system has converted to IPTV, 45 Railroad St, Kutztown, PA 19530-1112. Phone: 610-683-5722. Fax: 610-683-6729. E-mail: huservices@kutztownboro.org. Web Site: http://www.hometownu.com. ICA: PA5144.

Channel capacity: N.A. Channels available but not in use: N.A.

Internet Service

Operational: Yes.

Miles of Plant: None (coaxial); 27.0 (fiber optic).

KUTZTOWN—Hometown Utilicom. This cable system has converted to IPTV. See Kutztown, PA [PA5144]. ICA: PA0452.

KYLERTOWN—Tele-Media. Now served by SNOWSHOE, PA [PA0188]. ICA: PA0449.

LA PORTE BOROUGH—Comcast Cable, 400 Riverfront Dr, Reading, PA 19602. Phone: 610-790-8838. Fax: 610-378-4668. Web Site: http://www.comcast.com. Also serves Eagles Mere Borough, Laporte Twp. (Sullivan County) & Shrewsbury Twp. (Sullivan County). ICA: PA0413.

TV Market Ranking: 49 (LA PORTE BOROUGH, Laporte Twp. (Sullivan County)); Below 100 (Eagles Mere Borough, Shrewsbury Twp. (Sullivan County)). Franchise award date: June 1, 1988. Franchise expiration date: June 1, 2018. Began: November 1, 1988.

Channel capacity: 40 (not 2-way capable). Channels available but not in use: N.A.

Basic Service

Subscribers: 1,339.

Programming (received off-air): WBNG-TV (CBS, CW) Binghamton; WHTM-TV (ABC) Harrisburg; WITF-TV (PBS) Harrisburg; WNEP-TV (ABC) Scranton; WSKG-TV (PBS) Binghamton; WSWB (CW) Scranton; WVIA-TV (PBS) Scranton; WYOU (CBS) Scranton.

Programming (via satellite): A&E Networks; ABC Family Channel; AMC; Animal Planet; CNBC; CNN; Country Music TV; C-SPAN; C-SPAN 2; Discovery Channel; Disney Channel; ESPN; ESPN 2; Fox News Channel; FX; Headline News; History Channel; Lifetime; MTV; Nickelodeon; Pennsylvania Cable Network; QVC; Spike TV; TBS Superstation; The Learning Channel; The Weather Channel; Turner Network TV; USA Network; VH1; WGN America.

Fee: $50.00 installation; $31.90 monthly.

Pay Service 1

Pay Units: 40.

Programming (via satellite): HBO; Showtime; The Movie Channel.

Fee: $11.95 monthly (each).

Video-On-Demand: No

Telephone Service

None

Miles of Plant: 38.0 (coaxial); None (fiber optic).

General Manager: Greg Wells.

Ownership: Comcast Cable Communications Inc. (MSO).

LAIRDSVILLE—Formerly served by Ralph Herr TV. No longer in operation. ICA: PA0305.

LAKEWOOD—Hancock Video, 34 Read St, PO Box 608, Hancock, NY 13783-0608. Phones: 800-360-4664; 607-637-2568. Fax: 607-637-9999. E-mail: telco@hancock.net. Web Site: http://www.hancockvideo.com. Also serves Lake Como (village), Preston Park (village) & Starlight (village). ICA: PA0282.

TV Market Ranking: 49 (Lake Como (village), LAKEWOOD, Preston Park (village), Starlight (village)). Franchise award date: N.A. Franchise expiration date: N.A. Began: November 1, 1989.

Channel capacity: 31 (not 2-way capable). Channels available but not in use: N.A.

Basic Service

Subscribers: 190.

Programming (received off-air): WBNG-TV (CBS, CW) Binghamton; WICZ-TV (FOX) Binghamton; WIVT (ABC) Binghamton; WNEP-TV (ABC) Scranton; WSKG-TV (PBS) Binghamton; WSWB (CW) Scranton; WVIA-TV (PBS) Scranton; 15 FMs.

Programming (via satellite): Disney Channel; TBS Superstation; Toon Disney; WGN America.

Fee: $150.50 installation; $15.00 monthly.

Expanded Basic Service 1

Subscribers: 148.

Programming (received off-air): WYOU (CBS) Scranton.

Programming (via satellite): CNN; Discovery Channel; ESPN; ESPN 2; QVC; Spike TV; Turner Network TV; WPIX (CW, IND) New York.

Fee: $8.50 monthly.

Expanded Basic Service 2

Subscribers: 91.

Programming (via satellite): ABC Family Channel; AMC; CNBC; History Channel; Nickelodeon; Syfy; The Weather Channel.

Fee: $6.95 monthly.

Pay Service 1

Pay Units: 60.

Programming (via satellite): HBO.

Fee: $9.50 monthly.

Video-On-Demand: No

Internet Service

Operational: No, DSL & dial-up.

Telephone Service

None

Miles of Plant: 7.0 (coaxial); None (fiber optic).

President: Robert C. Wrighter, Sr. Vice President & Treasurer: Donald C. Wrighter, Sr. Manager: Beth Millar. Chief Technician: Gary Schoonmaker. Customer Service Manager: Mary Lynn Smith.

Ownership: Hancel Inc. (MSO).

LANCASTER—Comcast Cable, 1 E Uwchlan Ave, Ste 411, Exton, PA 19341. Phone: 484-288-6500. Web Site: http://www.comcast.com. Also serves Bareville, Bart Twp., Blue Ball, Caernarvon Twp. (Lancaster County), Christiana Borough, Columbia Borough, Drumore Twp., Earl Twp. (Lancaster County), East Drumore Twp., East Earl Twp. (southern portion), East Hempfield Twp. (Lancaster County), East Lampeter Twp. (Lancaster County), East Petersburg, Eden Twp., Fulton Twp., Gap, Hellam (York County), Hellam Twp. (York County), Kinzers, Leacock Twp. (Lancaster County), Leola, Little Britain Twp., Martic Twp., Millersville, Mountville, Narvon, New Holland, Paradise Twp. (Lancaster County), Pequea Twp. (Lancaster County), Providence Twp. (Lancaster County), Quarryville, Sadsbury Twp. (Lancaster County), Salisbury Twp. (Lancaster County), Strasburg, Upper Leacock Twp., Washington Twp. (York County), West Earl Twp., West Hempfield Twp. (Lancaster County), West Lampeter Twp. & Wrightsville. ICA: PA0010.

TV Market Ranking: 57 (Bareville, Bart Twp., Blue Ball, Caernarvon Twp. (Lancaster County), Christiana Borough, Columbia Borough, Drumore Twp., Earl Twp. (Lancaster County), East Drumore Twp., East Earl Twp. (southern portion), East Hempfield Twp. (Lancaster County), East Lampeter Twp. (Lancaster County), East Petersburg, Eden Twp., Fulton Twp., Gap, Hellam (York County), Hellam Twp. (York County), Kinzers, LANCASTER, Leacock Twp. (Lancaster County), Leola, Little Britain Twp., Martic Twp., Millersville, Mountville, Narvon, New Holland, Paradise Twp. (Lancaster County), Pequea Twp. (Lancaster County), Providence Twp. (Lancaster County), Quarryville, Sadsbury Twp. (Lancaster County), Salisbury Twp. (Lancaster County), Strasburg, Upper Leacock Twp., Washington Twp. (York County), West Earl Twp., West Hempfield Twp. (Lancaster County), West Lampeter Twp., Wrightsville). Franchise award date: October 1, 1966. Franchise expiration date: N.A. Began: October 12, 1966.

Channel capacity: 76 (operating 2-way). Channels available but not in use: N.A.

Basic Service

Subscribers: N.A. Included in Harrisburg

Programming (received off-air): WCAU (NBC) Philadelphia; WGAL (NBC) Lancaster; WGCB-TV (IND) Red Lion; WHP-TV (CBS, MNT) Harrisburg; WHTM-TV (ABC) Harrisburg; WITF-TV (PBS) Harrisburg; WLYH-TV (CW) Lancaster; WPHL-TV (MNT, IND) Philadelphia; WPMT (FOX) York; WPVI-TV (ABC) Philadelphia; WTVE (IND) Reading; WTXF-TV (FOX) Philadelphia.

Programming (via satellite): C-SPAN; MarketConnect Network; Pennsylvania Cable Network; QVC; The Comcast Network; WGN America.

Fee: $45.10 installation; $16.00 monthly.

Expanded Basic Service 1

Subscribers: 77,807.

Programming (via satellite): A&E Networks; ABC Family Channel; AMC; Animal Planet; BET Networks; Bravo; Cartoon Network; CNBC; CNN; Comcast SportsNet Philadelphia; Comedy Central; Country Music TV; Discovery Channel; Discovery Health Channel; Disney Channel; E! Entertainment Television; ESPN; ESPN 2; ESPN Classic Sports; Food Network; Fox News Channel; FX; Golf Channel; GSN; Headline News; HGTV; History Channel; Lifetime; MSNBC; MTV; MTV2; Nickelodeon; Speed; Spike TV; Style Network; Syfy; TBS Superstation; The Learning Channel; The Weather Channel; Travel Channel; truTV; Turner Classic Movies; Turner Network TV; TV Guide Network; TV Land; Univision Studios; USA Network; Versus; VH1.

Fee: $34.80 monthly.

Digital Basic Service

Subscribers: 24,630.

Programming (via satellite): BBC America; Bio; C-SPAN 3; Discovery Digital Networks; DMX Music; Encore; ESPN Classic Sports; Eternal Word TV Network; Flix; G4; GAS; History Channel International; Independent Film Channel; Mid-Atlantic Sports Network; MTV Networks Digital Suite; National Geographic Channel; Nick Jr.; Nick Too; ShopNBC; SoapNet; Sundance Channel; Toon Disney; Weatherscan.

Fee: $14.95 monthly.

Digital Pay Service 1

Pay Units: N.A.

Programming (via satellite): Cinemax (multiplexed); HBO (multiplexed); Showtime (multiplexed); Starz (multiplexed); The Movie Channel (multiplexed).

Video-On-Demand: Yes

Pay-Per-View

Playboy TV (delivered digitally); Fresh (delivered digitally); Shorteez (delivered digitally); Pleasure (delivered digitally); iN DEMAND (delivered digitally); ESPN Now (delivered digitally); ESPN Extra (delivered digitally); NBA TV (delivered digitally).

Internet Service

Operational: Yes. Began: December 31, 2002.

Subscribers: 16,608.

Broadband Service: Comcast High Speed Internet.

Fee: $42.95 monthly; $3.00 modem lease.

Telephone Service

Digital: Operational

Fee: $44.95 monthly

Miles of Plant: 1,422.0 (coaxial); 145.0 (fiber optic).

Area Vice President: Jim Samaha. Vice President, Marketing: Larry Goldman.

Ownership: Comcast Cable Communications Inc. (MSO).

LANSDALE—Comcast Cable, 3220 Tillman Dr, Bensalem, PA 19010. Phone: 215-642-6400. Fax: 215-638-6510. Web Site: http://www.comcast.com. Also serves Ambler, Broomall, Erdenheim, Flourtown, Hatboro, Haverford Twp., Horsham Twp., Laverock, Lower Gwynedd Twp. (Montgomery County), Marple Twp. (Delaware County), Montgomeryville, North Wales, Oreland, Penllyn, Plymouth Meeting, Towamencin, Upper Dublin Twp., Upper Gwynedd Twp., Whitemarsh Twp., Whitpain Twp. (portions) & Wyndmoor. ICA: PA0352.

TV Market Ranking: 4 (Ambler, Broomall, Erdenheim, Flourtown, Hatboro, Haverford Twp., Horsham Twp., LANSDALE, Laverock, Lower Gwynedd Twp. (Montgomery County), Marple Twp. (Delaware County), Montgomeryville, North Wales, Oreland, Penllyn, Plymouth Meeting, Towamencin, Upper Dublin Twp., Upper Gwynedd Twp., Whitemarsh Twp., Whitpain Twp. (portions), Wyndmoor). Franchise award date: November 1, 1978. Franchise expiration date: N.A. Began: September 1, 1979.

Channel capacity: N.A. Channels available but not in use: N.A.

Basic Service

Subscribers: N.A. Included in Bensalem Twp.

Programming (received off-air): KYW-TV (CBS) Philadelphia; WBPH-TV (IND) Bethlehem; WCAU (NBC) Philadelphia; WFMZ-TV (IND) Allentown; WGTW-TV (TBN) Burlington; WHYY-TV (PBS) Wilmington; WLVT-TV (PBS) Allentown; WNJS (PBS) Camden; WPHL-TV (MNT, IND) Philadelphia; WPPX-TV (ION) Wilmington; WPSG (CW) Philadelphia; WPVI-TV (ABC) Philadelphia; WTVE (IND) Reading; WTXF-TV (FOX) Philadelphia; WUVP-DT (UNV) Vineland; WWSI (TMO) Atlantic City; WYBE (ETV, IND) Philadelphia.

Programming (via satellite): TBS Superstation.

Fee: $15.15 monthly.

Expanded Basic Service 1

Subscribers: N.A.

Programming (via satellite): A&E Networks; ABC Family Channel; AMC; Animal Planet; BET Networks; Bravo; Cartoon Network; CNBC; CNN; Comcast SportsNet Philadelphia; Comedy Central; Country Music TV; C-SPAN; Discovery Channel; Discovery Health Channel; Disney Channel;

E! Entertainment Television; ESPN; ESPN 2; Eternal Word TV Network; Food Network; Fox News Channel; FX; Golf Channel; GSN; Headline News; HGTV; History Channel; Lifetime; MSNBC; MTV; Nickelodeon; Pennsylvania Cable Network; Philadelphia Park Live; Product Information Network; QVC; Speed; Spike TV; Syfy; The Comcast Network; The Learning Channel; The Weather Channel; Travel Channel; truTV; Turner Classic Movies; Turner Network TV; TV Land; USA Network; VH1.
Fee: $35.00 installation; $35.25 monthly.

Digital Basic Service
Subscribers: N.A.
Programming (via satellite): BBC America; Bio; Cooking Channel; C-SPAN 3; Discovery Digital Networks; DIY Network; DMX Music; ESPNews; G4; GAS; History Channel International; Independent Film Channel; MTV Networks Digital Suite; National Geographic Channel; Nick Jr.; Nick Too; Science Television; ShopNBC; SoapNet; Toon Disney; WAM! America's Kidz Network; Weatherscan.
Fee: $14.95 monthly.

Digital Pay Service 1
Pay Units: N.A.
Programming (via satellite): Cinemax (multiplexed); HBO (multiplexed); Showtime (multiplexed); Starz (multiplexed); The Movie Channel (multiplexed).
Fee: $18.95 monthly (each).

Video-On-Demand: Yes

Pay-Per-View
iN DEMAND (delivered digitally); Playboy TV (delivered digitally); Fresh (delivered digitally); Pleasure (delivered digitally); ESPN (delivered digitally); NBA (delivered digitally); NHL/MLB (delivered digitally).

Internet Service
Operational: Yes. Began: January 1, 2001.
Broadband Service: Comcast High Speed Internet.
Fee: $42.95 monthly.

Telephone Service
Digital: Operational
Fee: $44.95 monthly

Miles of Plant: 571.0 (coaxial); None (fiber optic). Additional miles planned: 35.0 (coaxial).
Senior Regional Vice President: Amy Smith. Vice President, Technical Operations: Rich Massi. Vice President, Marketing: Chip Goodman.
Ownership: Comcast Cable Communications Inc. (MSO).

LANSDOWNE—RCN Corp. Formerly served by Philadelphia (suburbs), PA [PA0447]. This cable system has converted to IPTV, 196 Van Buren St, Herndon, VA 20170. Phone: 703-434-8200. Web Site: http://www.rcn.com. ICA: PA5255.
Channel capacity: N.A. Channels available but not in use: N.A.

Internet Service
Operational: Yes.

Chairman: Steven J. Simmons. Chief Executive Officer: Jim Holanda.
Ownership: RCN Corp.

LATROBE—Comcast Cable. Now served by BLAIRSVILLE, PA [PA0320]. ICA: PA0470.

LAURELTON—Formerly served by D&E Communications. No longer in operation. ICA: PA5282.

LAWRENCEVILLE—Formerly served by Time Warner Cable. No longer in operation. ICA: PA0354.

LEBANON—Comcast Cable, 1 E Uwchlan Ave, Ste 411, Exton, PA 19341. Phones: 484-288-6500; 717-960-8100 (Harrisburg office). Web Site: http://www.comcast.com. Also serves Annville Twp., Bethel Twp. (Berks County), Cleona, Cornwall, Dalmatia, East Hanover Twp. (Dauphin County), East Hanover Twp. (Lebanon County), Halifax, Hershey, Hummelstown, Jonestown (Lebanon County), Londonderry Twp. (Dauphin County), Millcreek Twp. (Lebanon County), Millersburg, Mount Gretna, Myerstown, North Annville Twp., North Cornwall Twp., North Lebanon Twp., North Londonderry Twp., Palmyra, Reed Twp. (Dauphin County), Richland (Lebanon County), Robesonia, South Annville Twp., South Hanover Twp., South Lebanon Twp., South Londonderry Twp. (Lebanon County), Tulpehocken Twp., Union Twp. (Lebanon County), Upper Paxton Twp. (Dauphin County), West Cornwall Twp. & Womelsdorf. ICA: PA0024.
TV Market Ranking: 57 (Annville Twp., Bethel Twp. (Berks County), Cleona, Cornwall, Dalmatia, East Hanover Twp. (Dauphin County), East Hanover Twp. (Lebanon County), Halifax, Hummelstown, Jonestown (Lebanon County), LEBANON, Londerry Twp. (Dauphin County), Millcreek Twp. (Lebanon County), Millersburg, Mount Gretna, Myerstown, North Annville Twp., North Cornwall Twp., North Lebanon Twp., North Londonderry Twp., Palmyra, Reed Twp. (Dauphin County), Richland (Lebanon County), Robesonia, South Annville Twp., South Hanover Twp., South Lebanon Twp., South Londonderry Twp. (Lebanon County), Tulpehocken Twp., Union Twp. (Lebanon County), Upper Paxton Twp. (Dauphin County), West Cornwall Twp., Womelsdorf). Franchise award date: January 1, 1967. Franchise expiration date: N.A. Began: January 1, 1967.
Channel capacity: 78 (operating 2-way). Channels available but not in use: N.A.

Basic Service
Subscribers: N.A. Included in Harrisburg
Programming (received off-air): KYW-TV (CBS) Philadelphia; WGAL (NBC) Lancaster; WGCB-TV (IND) Red Lion; WHP-TV (CBS, MNT) Harrisburg; WHTM-TV (ABC) Harrisburg; WITF-TV (PBS) Harrisburg; WLYH-TV (CW) Lancaster; WPHL-TV (MNT, IND) Philadelphia; WPMT (FOX) York; WPSG (CW) Philadelphia; WPVI-TV (ABC) Philadelphia; WVIA-TV (PBS) Scranton; allband FM.
Programming (via satellite): ION Television; QVC; ShopNBC; The Comcast Network.
Fee: $45.10 installation; $16.90 monthly; $18.95 additional installation.

Expanded Basic Service 1
Subscribers: 28,380.
Programming (via satellite): A&E Networks; ABC Family Channel; AMC; Animal Planet; BET Networks; Bravo; Cartoon Network; CNBC; CNN; Comcast SportsNet Philadelphia; Comedy Central; Country Music TV; C-SPAN; Discovery Channel; Discovery Health Channel; Disney Channel; E! Entertainment Television; ESPN; ESPN 2; Eternal Word TV Network; Food Network; Fox News Channel; FX; Golf Channel; GSN; Hallmark Channel; Headline News; HGTV; History Channel; Lifetime; MSNBC; MTV; Nickelodeon; Oxygen; Pennsylvania Cable Network; Speed; Spike TV; Style Network; Syfy; TBS Superstation; The Learning Channel; The Weather Channel; Travel Channel; truTV; Turner Classic Movies; Turner Network TV; TV Land; Univision Studios; USA Network; Versus; VH1.
Fee: $21.50 installation; $33.90 monthly.

Digital Basic Service
Subscribers: 8,568.
Programming (via satellite): BBC America; Bio; Canales N; CBS Sports Network; CMT Pure Country; Cooking Channel; C-SPAN 3; Current; DIY Network; Encore (multiplexed); ESPN 2 HD; ESPN Classic Sports; ESPN HD; ESPNews; Exercise TV; Flix; Fox College Sports Atlantic; Fox College Sports Central; Fox College Sports Pacific; Fox Reality Channel; Fox Soccer; G4; GAS; GolTV; Great American Country; HD Theater; History Channel International; Jewelry Television; Lifetime Movie Network; LOGO; MTV Networks Digital Suite; Music Choice; National Geographic Channel; NBA TV; NFL Network; Nick Jr.; Nick Too; NickToons TV; Outdoor Channel; Palladia; PBS Kids Sprout; SoapNet; Sundance Channel; Toon Disney; Turner Network TV HD; TV One; Universal HD; Versus HD; Weatherscan.
Fee: $14.95 monthly.

Digital Pay Service 1
Pay Units: 10,608.
Programming (via satellite): Cinemax (multiplexed); Cinemax HD; HBO (multiplexed); HBO HD; Showtime (multiplexed); Showtime HD; Starz (multiplexed); Starz HDTV; The Movie Channel (multiplexed).

Video-On-Demand: Yes

Pay-Per-View
Addressable homes: 15,020.
iN DEMAND; iN DEMAND (delivered digitally); MLB Extra Innings (delivered digitally); Playboy TV (delivered digitally); Fresh (delivered digitally); NHL Center Ice (delivered digitally); MLS Direct Kick (delivered digitally); ESPN Full Court (delivered digitally); ESPN Gameplan (delivered digitally); NBA TV (delivered digitally).

Internet Service
Operational: Yes.
Broadband Service: Comcast High Speed Internet.
Fee: $42.95 monthly; $3.00 modem lease.

Telephone Service
Digital: Operational

Miles of Plant: 1,318.0 (coaxial); 253.0 (fiber optic).
Regional Vice President: Jim Samaha. Vice President, Marketing: Larry Goldman. Technical Operations Director: William Mays.
Ownership: Comcast Cable Communications Inc. (MSO).

LEHIGH TWP.—Formerly served by NORTHAMPTON BOROUGH, PA [PA0008]. RCN Corp. This cable system has converted to IPTV, 196 Van Buren St, Herndon, VA 20170. Phone: 703-434-8200. Web Site: http://www.rcn.com. ICA: PA5219.
TV Market Ranking: Below 100 (LEHIGH TWP.).
Channel capacity: N.A. Channels available but not in use: N.A.

Internet Service
Operational: Yes.

Telephone Service
Digital: Operational

Chairman: Steven J. Simmons. Chief Executive Officer: Jim Holanda.

LEHIGH VALLEY—Service Electric Cable TV & Communications, 2260 Ave A, Bethlehem, PA 18017-2170. Phones: 610-841-4100 (Customer service for phone services); 800-232-9100; 610-865-9100. Fax: 610-865-5031. E-mail: office@secv.com. Web Site: http://www.sectv.com. Also serves Alburtis, Allen Twp., Allentown, Bangor Boro, Bath Boro, Bethelem Twp., Bethlehem, Bridgeton Twp., Bushkill Twp., Catasauqua Boro, Chapman Boro, Coopersburg Boro, Coplay Boro, Durham Twp., East Allen Twp., East Bangor Boro, Easton, Emmaus, Forks Twp., Fountain Hill Boro, Freemansburg Boro, Glendon, Greenwich Twp., Hanover Twp., Haycock Twp., Hellertown Boro, Hereford Twp. (Berks County), Longswamp Twp., Lower Macungie Twp., Lower Mount Bethel Twp., Lower Nazareth Twp., Lower Saucon Twp., Lowhill Twp., Macungie, Moore Twp., Nazareth Boro, North Catasauqua Boro, Palmer Twp., Pen Argyl Boro, Plainfield Twp., Portland Boro, Richland Twp., Riegelsville Boro, Roseto Boro, Salisbury Twp., Springfield Twp., Stockertown, Tatamy Boro, Tinicum Twp., Upper Macungie Twp., Upper Milford Twp., Upper Mount Bethel Twp., Upper Nazareth Twp., Upper Saucon Twp., Washington Twp., Weisenberg Twp., West Easton, Whitehall Twp., Williams Twp., Wilson & Wind Gap Boro. ICA: PA0006.
TV Market Ranking: 4 (Haycock Twp., Upper Mount Bethel Twp.); Below 100 (Alburtis, Allen Twp., Allentown, Bangor Boro, Bath Boro, Bethlehem, Bridgeton Twp., Bushkill Twp., Catasauqua Boro, Chapman Boro, Coopersburg Boro, Coplay Boro, East Allen Twp., East Bangor Boro, Easton, Emmaus, Forks Twp., Fountain Hill Boro, Freemansburg Boro, Glendon, Greenwich Twp., Hanover Twp., Hellertown Boro, Hereford Twp. (Berks County), LEHIGH VALLEY, Longswamp Twp., Lower Macungie Twp., Lower Mount Bethel Twp., Lower Nazareth Twp., Lower Saucon Twp., Lowhill Twp., Macungie, Moore Twp., Nazareth Boro, North Catasauqua Boro, Palmer Twp., Palmer Twp., Pen Argyl Boro, Plainfield Twp., Portland Boro, Richland Twp., Roseto Boro, Springfield Twp., Stockertown, Tatamy Boro, Upper Macungie Twp., Upper Milford Twp., Upper Nazareth Twp., Upper Saucon Twp., Washington Twp., Weisenberg Twp., West Easton, Whitehall Twp., Williams Twp., Wilson, Wind Gap Boro); Outside TV Markets (Durham Twp., Riegelsville Boro). Franchise award date: January 1, 1955. Franchise expiration date: N.A. Began: January 1, 1951.
Channel capacity: 90 (not 2-way capable). Channels available but not in use: N.A.

Basic Service
Subscribers: 88,087.
Programming (received off-air): KYW-TV (CBS) Philadelphia; WBPH-TV (IND) Bethlehem; WCAU (NBC) Philadelphia; WFMZ-TV (IND) Allentown; WGTW-TV (TBN) Burlington; WLVT-TV (PBS) Allentown; WNBC (NBC) New York; WNEP-TV (ABC) Scranton; WNYW (FOX) New York; WPHL-TV (MNT, IND) Philadelphia; WPIX (CW, IND) New York; WPPX-TV (ION) Wilmington; WPSG (CW) Philadelphia; WPVI-TV (ABC) Philadelphia; WTVE (IND) Reading; WTXF-TV (FOX) Philadelphia; WWOR-TV (MNT) Secaucus; allband FM.
Programming (via satellite): C-SPAN; Eternal Word TV Network; INSP; Pennsylvania Cable Network; QVC; ShopNBC; TV Guide Network.
Fee: $49.95 installation; $18.99 monthly; $4.95 converter; $29.95 additional installation.

Expanded Basic Service 1
Subscribers: 8,235.
Programming (received off-air): Local Cable Weather.
Programming (via satellite): A&E Networks; ABC Family Channel; AMC; AmericanLife TV Network; Animal Planet; BBC America;

BET Networks; Bravo!; Cartoon Network; CNBC; CNN; Comcast SportsNet Philadelphia; Comedy Central; Country Music TV; C-SPAN 2; Discovery Channel; Disney Channel; E! Entertainment Television; ESPN; ESPN 2; ESPN Classic Sports; ESPNews; Food Network; Fox News Channel; FX; Golf Channel; GSN; Hallmark Channel; Headline News; HGTV; History Channel; Lifetime; MSNBC; MTV; Nickelodeon; Outdoor Channel; Oxygen; Portuguese Channel; SoapNet; Speed; Spike TV; Syfy; TBS Superstation; The Learning Channel; The Weather Channel; Toon Disney; Travel Channel; truTV; Turner Classic Movies; Turner Network TV; TV Land; USA Network; Versus; VH1; WE tv.
Fee: $46.24 monthly; $4.95 converter; $29.95 additional installation.

Digital Basic Service
Subscribers: 33,599.
Fee: $8.99 monthly.

Digital Pay Service 1
Pay Units: 11,268.
Programming (via satellite): Cinemax (multiplexed); Encore (multiplexed); Flix; HBO (multiplexed); Playboy TV; RAI International; Showtime (multiplexed); Starz (multiplexed); The Movie Channel (multiplexed); Zee TV USA.
Fee: $10.95 monthly (Cinemax or Starz), $11.05 monthly (Filipino or Playboy), $12.95 monthly (HBO or Showtime & TMC), $14.99 monthly (Zee TV).

Video-On-Demand: Yes

Pay-Per-View
Sports PPV (delivered digitally); Movies, Special Events (delivered digitally).

Internet Service
Operational: Yes. Began: January 1, 1995.
Subscribers: 48,767.
Broadband Service: ProLog Express.
Fee: $39.95 installation; $24.95-$49.95 monthly.

Telephone Service
Analog: Not Operational
Digital: Operational
Subscribers: 15,631.
Fee: $29.95 monthly

Miles of Plant: 3,180.0 (coaxial); None (fiber optic).
Manager: John J. Capparell. Marketing Director: Steve Salash. Program Director: Andy Himmelwright. Chief Technician: Jeffrey Kelly. Regulatory Affairs Director: Arlean Lilly. Customer Service Manager: John Ritter.
Ownership: Service Electric Cable TV Inc. (MSO).

LEROY TWP.—Blue Ridge Communications, 613 3rd St, PO Box 215, Palmerton, PA 18071-0215. Phone: 610-826-2551. Web Site: http://www.brctv.com. ICA: PA0302.
TV Market Ranking: Below 100 (LEROY TWP.). Franchise award date: N.A. Franchise expiration date: N.A. Began: July 1, 1977.
Channel capacity: 54 (2-way capable). Channels available but not in use: N.A.

Basic Service
Subscribers: 41.
Programming (received off-air): CW11 New York; WBNG-TV (CBS, CW) Binghamton; WENY-TV (ABC, CW) Elmira; WETM-TV (NBC) Elmira; WSKG-TV (PBS) Binghamton; WVIA-TV (PBS) Scranton; WYDC (FOX, MNT) Corning; WYOU (CBS) Scranton; allband FM.
Programming (via satellite): C-SPAN; C-SPAN 2; WGN America.
Fee: $22.50 installation; $14.16 monthly.

Expanded Basic Service 1
Subscribers: 39.
Programming (via satellite): A&E Networks; ABC Family Channel; AMC; Animal Planet; BET Networks; Cartoon Network; CNBC; CNN; Comedy Central; Country Music TV; Discovery Channel; Disney Channel; E! Entertainment Television; ESPN; ESPN 2; Eternal Word TV Network; Food Network; Fox News Channel; FX; Hallmark Channel; Headline News; HGTV; History Channel; Lifetime; Lifetime Movie Network; MSNBC; MTV; Nickelodeon; Pennsylvania Cable Network; QVC; Root Sports Pittsburgh; SoapNet; Speed; Spike TV; Syfy; TBS Superstation; The Learning Channel; The Weather Channel; Travel Channel; Trinity Broadcasting Network; truTV; Turner Classic Movies; Turner Network TV; TV Land; USA Network; Versus; VH1.
Fee: $38.84 monthly.

Pay Service 1
Pay Units: N.A.
Programming (via satellite): Cinemax; HBO; Showtime.
Fee: $11.50 monthly (Cinemax or Showtime), $12.50 monthly (HBO).

Pay-Per-View
iN DEMAND.

Internet Service
Operational: No.

Telephone Service
None

Miles of Plant: 3.0 (coaxial); None (fiber optic). Additional miles planned: 1.0 (coaxial).
Vice President, Operations: Richard Semmel. General Manager: Mark Masonheimer. Fiber Manager: Randy Semmel. Chief Technician: Garry Woods.
Ownership: Pencor Services Inc. (MSO).

LEVITTOWN—Comcast Cable, 3220 Tillman Dr, Bensalem, PA 19010. Phone: 215-642-6400. Fax: 215-638-6510. Web Site: http://www.comcast.com. Also serves Bristol, Hulmeville, Langhorne, Langhorne Manor, Lower Makefield Twp., Middletown Twp. (Bucks County), Penndel & Yardley. ICA: PA0016.
TV Market Ranking: 4 (Bristol, Hulmeville, Langhorne, Langhorne Manor, LEVITTOWN, Lower Makefield Twp., Middletown Twp. (Bucks County), Penndel, Yardley). Franchise award date: December 1, 1965. Franchise expiration date: N.A. Began: April 10, 1967.
Channel capacity: N.A. Channels available but not in use: N.A.

Basic Service
Subscribers: N.A. Included in Bensalem Twp.
Programming (received off-air): KYW-TV (CBS) Philadelphia; WBPH-TV (IND) Bethlehem; WCAU (NBC) Philadelphia; WFMZ-TV (IND) Allentown; WGTW-TV (TBN) Burlington; WHYY-TV (PBS) Wilmington; WLVT-TV (PBS) Allentown; WMCN-TV (IND) Atlantic City; WNJN (PBS) Montclair; WPHL-TV (MNT, IND) Philadelphia; WPPX-TV (ION) Wilmington; WPSG (CW) Philadelphia; WPVI-TV (ABC) Philadelphia; WTVE (IND) Reading; WTXF-TV (FOX) Philadelphia; WUVP-DT (UNV) Vineland; WWSI (TMO) Atlantic City; WYBE (ETV, IND) Philadelphia.
Programming (via satellite): C-SPAN 2; Eternal Word TV Network; The Comcast Network.
Fee: $14.10 monthly.

Expanded Basic Service 1
Subscribers: 41,000.
Programming (via satellite): A&E Networks; ABC Family Channel; AMC; Animal Planet; Bravo; Cartoon Network; CNBC; CNN; Comcast SportsNet Philadelphia; Country Music TV; Discovery Channel; Disney Channel; E! Entertainment Television; ESPN; ESPN 2; Food Network; Fox News Channel; FX; Headline News; HGTV; History Channel; Lifetime; MSNBC; MTV; Nickelodeon; Philadelphia Park Live; QVC; Speed; Spike TV; Style Network; TBS Superstation; The Learning Channel; The Weather Channel; Travel Channel; Turner Network TV; TV Land; USA Network; Versus; VH1.
Fee: $44.80 monthly.

Expanded Basic Service 2
Subscribers: 40,700.
Programming (via satellite): BET Networks; Comedy Central; ESPN Classic Sports; Golf Channel; GSN; Syfy; truTV; Turner Classic Movies.
Fee: $7.33 monthly.

Digital Basic Service
Subscribers: 5,000.
Programming (via satellite): BBC America; Bio; Cooking Channel; C-SPAN 3; Discovery Digital Networks; DIY Network; ESPNews; Eternal Word TV Network; Flix; G4; GAS; GolTV; History Channel International; Independent Film Channel; MTV Networks Digital Suite; Music Choice; National Geographic Channel; NBA TV; NFL Network; Nick Jr.; Nick Too; NickToons TV; Pennsylvania Cable Network; Science Television; ShopNBC; SoapNet; Sundance Channel; Toon Disney; WAM! America's Kidz Network; Weatherscan.
Fee: $35.87 installation; $14.95 monthly.

Digital Pay Service 1
Pay Units: N.A.
Programming (via satellite): Cinemax (multiplexed); Encore (multiplexed); HBO (multiplexed); Showtime (multiplexed); Starz (multiplexed); The Movie Channel (multiplexed).

Video-On-Demand: Yes

Pay-Per-View
Addressable homes: 21,700.
iN DEMAND; Playboy TV; NHL Center Ice (delivered digitally); MLB Extra Innings (delivered digitally); Pleasure; Spice; Spice2; Russian Television Network (delivered digitally); ESPN (delivered digitally); NBA TV (delivered digitally); NBA League Pass (delivered digitally).

Internet Service
Operational: Yes.
Broadband Service: Comcast High Speed Internet.
Fee: $42.95 monthly.

Telephone Service
Digital: Operational
Fee: $44.95 monthly

Miles of Plant: 632.0 (coaxial); None (fiber optic). Additional miles planned: 5.0 (coaxial).
Senior Regional Vice President: Amy Smith. Vice President, Technical Operations: Rich Massi. Vice President, Marketing: Chip Goodman.
Ownership: Comcast Cable Communications Inc. (MSO).

LEWIS TWP.—Eagles Mere & La Porte Cablevision Inc., 513 Jordan Ave, Montoursville, PA 17754-2309. Phones: 800-464-3000; 570-368-3266. Fax: 570-368-8154. Also serves Anthony Twp., Delaware Twp. (Northumberland County), Limestone Twp. (Montour County), Madison Twp. (Columbia County), Northumberland County (portions) & Turbot Twp. (Northumberland County). ICA: PA0375.
TV Market Ranking: Below 100 (Anthony Twp., Limestone Twp. (Montour County), Madison Twp. (Columbia County), Northumberland County (portions), Turbot Twp. (Northumberland County)); Outside TV Markets (Delaware Twp. (Northumberland County), LEWIS TWP., Northumberland County (portions)). Franchise award date: July 1, 1989. Franchise expiration date: July 1, 2019. Began: N.A.
Channel capacity: 40 (not 2-way capable). Channels available but not in use: N.A.

Basic Service
Subscribers: 650.
Programming (received off-air): WITF-TV (PBS) Harrisburg; WNEP-TV (ABC) Scranton; WSWB (CW) Scranton; WVIA-TV (PBS) Scranton; WYOU (CBS) Scranton.
Programming (via satellite): A&E Networks; ABC Family Channel; AMC; Animal Planet; CNBC; CNN; Country Music TV; C-SPAN; C-SPAN 2; Discovery Channel; Disney Channel; ESPN; ESPN 2; Fox News Channel; FX; Headline News; History Channel; Lifetime; MTV; Nickelodeon; Pennsylvania Cable Network; QVC; Spike TV; TBS Superstation; The Learning Channel; The Weather Channel; Trinity Broadcasting Network; Turner Network TV; USA Network; VH1; WGN America.

Pay Service 1
Pay Units: N.A.
Programming (via satellite): HBO; Showtime; The Movie Channel.
Fee: $9.95 monthly (TMC), $10.95 monthly (Showtime), $11.95 monthly (HBO).

Video-On-Demand: No

Internet Service
Operational: No.

Telephone Service
None

Miles of Plant: 81.0 (coaxial); 2.0 (fiber optic).
Manager: Roxanne Y. Criswell. Chief Technician: Timothy J. Criswell.
Ownership: Eagles Mere & La Porte Cablevision Inc.

LEWISBURG—Lewisburg CATV. Now served by DANVILLE, PA [PA0054]. ICA: PA0356.

LEWISBURG—Windstream (formerly D&E Communications.) This cable system has converted to IPTV. See Lewisburg, PA [PA5118]. ICA: PA0390.

LEWISBURG—Windstream. Formerly [PA0390]. This cable system has converted to IPTV, 4001 Rodney Parham Rd, Little Rock, AR 17522. Phones: 800-347-1991; 501-748-7000. Fax: 877-807-9463. Web Site: http://www.windstream.com. ICA: PA5118.

TV Market Ranking: Below 100 (LEWISBURG).
Channel capacity: N.A. Channels available but not in use: N.A.
Video-On-Demand: No
Internet Service
Operational: Yes.
Telephone Service
Digital: Operational
President & Chief Executive Officer: Jeff Gardner. Chief Operating Officer: Brent Whittington.

LEWISTOWN—Comcast Cable, 1 E Uwchlan Ave, Ste 411, Exton, PA 19341. Phones: 814-238-5050 (State College office); 484-288-6500. Web Site: http://www.comcast.com. Also serves Burnham, Derry Twp. (Mifflin County), Granville Twp. & Juniata Terrace. ICA: PA0092.
TV Market Ranking: Outside TV Markets (Burnham, Derry Twp. (Mifflin County), Granville Twp., Juniata Terrace, LEWISTOWN). Franchise award date: N.A. Franchise expiration date: N.A. Began: January 1, 1951.
Channel capacity: N.A. Channels available but not in use: N.A.
Basic Service
Subscribers: N.A. Included in Harrisburg
Programming (received off-air): WGAL (NBC) Lancaster; WHP-TV (CBS, MNT) Harrisburg; WHTM-TV (ABC) Harrisburg; WKBS-TV (IND) Altoona; WLYH-TV (CW) Lancaster; WPSU-TV (PBS) Clearfield; WTAJ-TV (CBS) Altoona; WWCP-TV (FOX) Johnstown; allband FM.
Programming (via satellite): C-SPAN; Eternal Word TV Network; Hallmark Channel; QVC; TBS Superstation; TV Guide Network.
Fee: $45.10 installation; $11.25 monthly.
Expanded Basic Service 1
Subscribers: 5,822.
Programming (via satellite): A&E Networks; ABC Family Channel; AMC; Animal Planet; Cartoon Network; CNBC; CNN; Comedy Central; Country Music TV; C-SPAN 2; Discovery Channel; Disney Channel; E! Entertainment Television; ESPN; ESPN 2; Fox News Channel; FX; Headline News; History Channel; ION Television; Lifetime; MSNBC; MTV; Nickelodeon; Oxygen; Pennsylvania Cable Network; Root Sports Pittsburgh; Spike TV; The Learning Channel; The Weather Channel; Travel Channel; truTV; Turner Network TV; TV Land; USA Network; VH1.
Fee: $35.75 monthly.
Digital Basic Service
Subscribers: N.A.
Programming (via satellite): BBC America; Bio; Bloomberg Television; Bravo; Discovery Fit & Health; ESPN Classic Sports; ESPNews; Fox Movie Channel; Fox Sports World; Fuse; G4; Golf Channel; GSN; Halogen Network; HGTV; History Channel International; Independent Film Channel; Lifetime; Outdoor Channel; Ovation; Speed; Sundance Channel; Syfy; Toon Disney; Trinity Broadcasting Network; Turner Classic Movies; Versus; WE tv.
Fee: $14.95 monthly.
Digital Expanded Basic Service
Subscribers: N.A.
Programming (via satellite): GAS; MTV Networks Digital Suite; National Geographic Channel; Nick Jr.; NickToons TV; Style Network.
Digital Pay Service 1
Pay Units: N.A.
Programming (via satellite): Cinemax (multiplexed); Encore (multiplexed); HBO (multiplexed); Showtime (multiplexed); Starz (multiplexed); The Movie Channel (multiplexed).
Video-On-Demand: No
Pay-Per-View
HITS PPV 1-6 (delivered digitally); Playboy TV (delivered digitally); Shorteez (delivered digitally); Fresh (delivered digitally); Hot Choice (delivered digitally).
Internet Service
Operational: Yes. Began: June 1, 2004.
Broadband Service: Comcast High Speed Internet.
Fee: $42.95 monthly.
Telephone Service
None
Miles of Plant: 91.0 (coaxial); None (fiber optic).
Area Vice President: Jim Samah. Vice President, Marketing: Larry Goldman. Technical Operations Manager: Dan Cramer.
Ownership: Comcast Cable Communications Inc. (MSO).

LEWISTOWN—Nittany Media Inc., 18 Juniata St, PO Box 111, Lewistown, PA 17044. Phones: 800-692-7401; 717-248-3733. Fax: 717-248-3732. E-mail: info@nittanymedia.com. Web Site: http://www.nittanymedia.com. Also serves Fermanagh Twp., Granville Twp., Ickesburg, McAlisterville, Mifflin, Mifflintown, Milford Twp., New Bloomfield, Old Port, Oliver Twp., Port Royal, Richfield, Thompsontown & Turbett Twp. ICA: PA0365.
TV Market Ranking: 57 (Ickesburg, New Bloomfield, Old Port, Port Royal, Richfield, Thompsontown); Outside TV Markets (Fermanagh Twp., Granville Twp., LEWISTOWN, McAlisterville, Mifflin, Mifflintown, Milford Twp., Oliver Twp., Turbett Twp.). Franchise award date: N.A. Franchise expiration date: N.A. Began: N.A.
Channel capacity: N.A. Channels available but not in use: N.A.
Basic Service
Subscribers: N.A.
Programming (received off-air): WGAL (NBC) Lancaster; WHP-TV (CBS, MNT) Harrisburg; WHTM-TV (ABC) Harrisburg; WHVL-LP State College, etc.; WITF-TV (PBS) Harrisburg; WLYH-TV (CW) Lancaster; WNEP-TV (ABC) Scranton; WOLF-TV (CW, FOX, MNT) Hazleton; WPMT (FOX) York; WPSU-TV (PBS) Clearfield; WTAJ-TV (CBS) Altoona; WVIA-TV (PBS) Scranton.
Programming (via satellite): Bloomberg Television; C-SPAN; La Familia Network; Pennsylvania Cable Network; QVC.
Fee: $17.40 monthly.
Expanded Basic Service 1
Subscribers: N.A.
Programming (via satellite): A&E Networks; ABC Family Channel; AMC; Animal Planet; Boomerang; Bravo; Cartoon Network; CNBC; CNN; Comedy Central; Cornerstone Television; Country Music TV; C-SPAN 2; Discovery Channel; Discovery Fit & Health; Disney Channel; ESPN; ESPN 2; Food Network; Fox News Channel; Fox Sports Net; FX; Great American Country; Hallmark Channel; Headline News; HGTV; History Channel; INSP; ION Television; Lifetime; MSNBC; MTV; Nickelodeon; Outdoor Channel; Sorpresa; Speed; Spike TV; Syfy; TBS Superstation; The Learning Channel; The Weather Channel; Travel Channel; Trinity Broadcasting Network; Turner Network TV; TV Land; USA Network; VH1; WGN America.
Fee: $27.10 monthly.
Digital Basic Service
Subscribers: N.A.
Programming (via satellite): BBC America; Bio; Bloomberg Television; Bravo; cloo; CMT Pure Country; Cooking Channel; DMX Music; ESPN 2; ESPN HD; Fox Movie Channel; Fuse; G4; GAS; GSN; Halogen Network; HD Theater; HDNet; HDNet Movies; HGTV; History Channel; History Channel International; Lifetime Movie Network; MTV Networks Digital Suite; Nick Jr.; NickToons TV; Outdoor Channel; SoapNet; Speed; Style Network; Syfy; Toon Disney; Trinity Broadcasting Network; TV Land; WE tv.
Fee: $15.99 monthly.
Digital Expanded Basic Service
Subscribers: N.A.
Programming (via satellite): ESPN 2; ESPN Classic Sports; Fox Soccer; Golf Channel; Versus.
Fee: $3.99 monthly.
Digital Expanded Basic Service 2
Subscribers: N.A.
Programming (via satellite): Independent Film Channel; Turner Classic Movies.
Fee: $1.99 monthly.
Digital Pay Service 1
Pay Units: N.A.
Programming (via satellite): Cinemax (multiplexed); Encore (multiplexed); Flix; HBO (multiplexed); Showtime (multiplexed); Starz (multiplexed); The Movie Channel (multiplexed).
Fee: $12.99 monthly (each).
Video-On-Demand: No
Pay-Per-View
iN DEMAND (delivered digitally).
Internet Service
Operational: Yes. Began: January 1, 2001.
Broadband Service: NMAX.
Fee: $40.00 installation; $34.99 monthly.
Telephone Service
None
Manager: Anna H. Hain. Chief Technician: Michael Hain.
Ownership: Nittany Media Inc. (MSO).

LIGONIER—Formerly served by Adelphia Communications. Now served by BLAIRSVILLE, PA [PA0320]. ICA: PA0462.

LIMESTONE—Atlantic Broadband, 120 Southmont Blvd, Johnstown, PA 15905. Phone: 814-539-8971. Fax: 814-535-7747. E-mail: info@atlanticbb.com. Web Site: http://www.atlanticbb.com. Also serves Corsica, Curllsville, Fairmont City, Mayport, Monroe (Clarion County), New Bethlehem, Piney, Porter Twp. (Clarion County), Redbank Twp. (Clarion County), Sligo, Strattonville & Summerville. ICA: PA0197.
TV Market Ranking: Outside TV Markets (Corsica, Curllsville, Fairmont City, LIMESTONE, Mayport, Monroe (Clarion County), New Bethlehem, Piney, Porter Twp. (Clarion County), Redbank Twp. (Clarion County), Sligo, Strattonville, Summerville). Franchise award date: N.A. Franchise expiration date: N.A. Began: January 1, 1986.
Channel capacity: 59 (not 2-way capable). Channels available but not in use: N.A.
Basic Service
Subscribers: 608.
Programming (received off-air): KDKA-TV (CBS) Pittsburgh; WKBN-TV (CBS) Youngstown; WPCB-TV (IND) Greensburg; WPCW (CW) Jeannette; WPGH-TV (FOX) Pittsburgh; WPMY (MNT) Pittsburgh; WPXI (IND, NBC) Pittsburgh; WQED (PBS) Pittsburgh; WTAE-TV (ABC) Pittsburgh.
Programming (via satellite): A&E Networks; ABC Family Channel; AMC; Animal Planet; Bravo; CNN; Comedy Central; Country Music TV; C-SPAN; Discovery Channel; Disney Channel; E! Entertainment Television; ESPN; ESPN 2; Food Network; Fox Movie Channel; Fox News Channel; FX; Hallmark Channel; Headline News; HGTV; History Channel; Lifetime; MSNBC; MTV; Nickelodeon; Outdoor Channel; QVC; Root Sports Pittsburgh; Speed; Spike TV; Syfy; TBS Superstation; The Learning Channel; The Weather Channel; Travel Channel; truTV; Turner Classic Movies; Turner Network TV; TV Land; USA Network; VH1; WE tv.
Fee: $30.00 installation; $37.99 monthly; $3.00 converter; $20.00 additional installation.
Pay Service 1
Pay Units: 24.
Programming (via satellite): HBO.
Fee: $10.00 installation; $11.95 monthly.
Pay Service 2
Pay Units: 15.
Programming (via satellite): Showtime.
Fee: $10.00 installation; $12.95 monthly.
Pay Service 3
Pay Units: N.A.
Programming (via satellite): The Movie Channel.
Fee: $10.00 installation; $12.95 monthly.
Video-On-Demand: No
Internet Service
Operational: Yes.
Fee: $19.95 installation; $45.95 monthly.
Telephone Service
Digital: Operational
Fee: $29.95 monthly
Miles of Plant: 72.0 (coaxial); None (fiber optic).
Vice President: David Dane. General Manager: Dan Feiertag. Technical Operations Director: Charles Sorchilla. Marketing & Customer Service Director: Dara Leslie. Marketing Manager: Natalie Kurchak.
Ownership: Atlantic Broadband (MSO).

LIMESTONE TWP. (Lycoming County)—Comcast Cable. Now served by WILLIAMSPORT, PA [PA0040]. ICA: PA0247.

LINESVILLE—Formerly served by Cebridge Connections. No longer in operation. ICA: PA0196.

LIVERPOOL—Zampelli Electronics, PO Box 830, Lewistown, PA 17044-0830. Phone: 717-248-1544. ICA: PA0359.
TV Market Ranking: 57 (LIVERPOOL). Franchise award date: N.A. Franchise expiration date: N.A. Began: N.A.
Channel capacity: N.A. Channels available but not in use: N.A.
Basic Service
Subscribers: N.A.
Programming (received off-air): WGAL (NBC) Lancaster; WHP-TV (CBS, MNT) Harrisburg; WHTM-TV (ABC) Harrisburg; WPMT (FOX) York.
Video-On-Demand: No
Internet Service
Operational: No.
Telephone Service
None
Manager & Chief Technician: Joe Zampelli.
Ownership: Zampelli TV (MSO).

LOCK HAVEN—Comcast Cable, 1 E Uwchlan Ave, Ste 411, Exton, PA 19341. Phones: 814-238-5050 (State College office); 484-288-6500. Web Site: http://www.comcast.com. Also serves Bald Eagle Twp. (Clinton County),

Castanea Twp., Dunnstable Twp. (eastern portion) & Flemington. ICA: PA0111.

TV Market Ranking: Below 100 (Bald Eagle Twp. (Clinton County), Castanea Twp., Dunnstable Twp. (eastern portion), Flemington, LOCK HAVEN). Franchise award date: N.A. Franchise expiration date: N.A. Began: January 1, 1950.

Channel capacity: N.A. Channels available but not in use: N.A.

Basic Service

Subscribers: N.A. Included in Harrisburg

Programming (received off-air): WNEP-TV (ABC) Scranton; WOLF-TV (CW, FOX, MNT) Hazleton; WPSU-TV (PBS) Clearfield; WTAJ-TV (CBS) Altoona; WVIA-TV (PBS) Scranton; WYOU (CBS) Scranton.

Programming (via satellite): ABC Family Channel; C-SPAN; Discovery Channel; QVC; TBS Superstation; TV Guide Network.

Fee: $45.10 installation; $10.77 monthly.

Expanded Basic Service 1

Subscribers: 1,458.

Programming (via satellite): A&E Networks; AMC; Animal Planet; Cartoon Network; CNBC; CNN; Comedy Central; Country Music TV; C-SPAN 2; Disney Channel; E! Entertainment Television; ESPN; ESPN 2; Eternal Word TV Network; Fox News Channel; FX; Hallmark Channel; Headline News; HGTV; History Channel; ION Television; Lifetime; MSNBC; MTV; Nickelodeon; Oxygen; Pennsylvania Cable Network; Root Sports Pittsburgh; Spike TV; The Learning Channel; The Weather Channel; Travel Channel; truTV; Turner Network TV; TV Land; USA Network; VH1.

Fee: $38.78 monthly.

Digital Basic Service

Subscribers: 1,450.

Programming (via satellite): BBC America; Bravo; Discovery Digital Networks; ESPN Classic Sports; ESPNews; Fox Movie Channel; Fox Sports World; Golf Channel; GSN; Independent Film Channel; Outdoor Channel; Speed; Syfy; Turner Classic Movies; Versus; WE tv.

Fee: $14.95 monthly.

Digital Expanded Basic Service

Subscribers: N.A.

Programming (via satellite): National Geographic Channel; Nick Jr.; NickToons TV; VH1 Classic; VH1 Country.

Digital Pay Service 1

Pay Units: N.A.

Programming (via satellite): Cinemax (multiplexed); Encore (multiplexed); HBO (multiplexed); Showtime (multiplexed); Starz (multiplexed); The Movie Channel (multiplexed).

Video-On-Demand: No

Pay-Per-View

HITS PPV 1-6 (delivered digitally); Playboy TV (delivered digitally); Fresh (delivered digitally); Hot Choice (delivered digitally).

Internet Service

Operational: Yes.

Broadband Service: Comcast High Speed Internet.

Fee: $42.95 monthly.

Telephone Service

None

Miles of Plant: 84.0 (coaxial); None (fiber optic).

Area Vice President: Jim Samaha. Technical Operations Manager: Dan Cramer. Vice President, Marketing: Larry Goldman.

Ownership: Comcast Cable Communications Inc. (MSO).

LOGANTON—TV Cable Associates Inc., 110 W Main St, Loganton, PA 17747. Phone: 570-725-3602. ICA: PA0271.

TV Market Ranking: Below 100 (LOGANTON). Franchise award date: N.A. Franchise expiration date: N.A. Began: February 1, 1960.

Channel capacity: N.A. Channels available but not in use: N.A.

Basic Service

Subscribers: 106.

Programming (received off-air): WGAL (NBC) Lancaster; WHTM-TV (ABC) Harrisburg; WITF-TV (PBS) Harrisburg; WJAC-TV (NBC) Johnstown; WLYH-TV (CW) Lancaster; WNEP-TV (ABC) Scranton; WSWB (CW) Scranton; WTAJ-TV (CBS) Altoona; WVIA-TV (PBS) Scranton; WYOU (CBS) Scranton; allband FM.

Programming (via satellite): Disney Channel; TBS Superstation; Turner Network TV.

Fee: $20.00 monthly.

Pay Service 1

Pay Units: 27.

Programming (via satellite): HBO.

Fee: $12.00 monthly.

Video-On-Demand: No

Internet Service

Operational: No.

Telephone Service

None

Miles of Plant: 2.0 (coaxial); None (fiber optic).

President: Art Grieb. Chief Technician: Brian Dowdy.

Ownership: TV Cable Associates Inc.

LONDONDERRY TWP. (Bedford County)—Leap Cable TV, PO Box 703, Hyndman, PA 15545-0703. Phone: 814-842-3370. ICA: PA0360.

TV Market Ranking: Outside TV Markets (LONDONDERRY TWP.). Franchise award date: N.A. Franchise expiration date: N.A. Began: July 1, 1981.

Channel capacity: 30 (not 2-way capable). Channels available but not in use: N.A.

Basic Service

Subscribers: 130.

Programming (received off-air): KDKA-TV (CBS) Pittsburgh; WJAC-TV (NBC) Johnstown; WPSU-TV (PBS) Clearfield; WTAE-TV (ABC) Pittsburgh; WTAJ-TV (CBS) Altoona.

Programming (via satellite): ABC Family Channel; TBS Superstation; Turner Network TV.

Fee: $21.00 monthly.

Pay Service 1

Pay Units: 30.

Programming (via satellite): HBO.

Fee: $10.99 monthly.

Video-On-Demand: No

Internet Service

Operational: No.

Telephone Service

None

Manager: Don T. Leap.

Ownership: Don T. Leap.

LOOMIS LAKE—Adams Digital Cable, 19 N Main St, Carbondale, PA 18407-2303. Phones: 888-222-0077; 570-282-6121. Fax: 570-282-3787. E-mail: frontdesk@echoes.net. Web Site: http://www.adamscable.com. Also serves Acre Lake, Brooklyn Twp., Harford, Harford Twp., Hop Bottom, Kingsley, Lathrop Twp. & Tingley Lake. ICA: PA0361.

TV Market Ranking: 49 (Acre Lake, Brooklyn Twp., Harford, Harford Twp., Hop Bottom, Kingsley, Lathrop Twp., LOOMIS LAKE, Tingley Lake). Franchise award date: N.A. Franchise expiration date: N.A. Began: May 1, 1966.

Channel capacity: 40 (2-way capable). Channels available but not in use: N.A.

Basic Service

Subscribers: 380.

Programming (received off-air): WBNG-TV (CBS, CW) Binghamton; WBRE-TV (NBC) Wilkes-Barre; WNEP-TV (ABC) Scranton; WOLF-TV (CW, FOX, MNT) Hazleton; WQPX-TV (ION) Scranton; WSKG-TV (PBS) Binghamton; WSWB (CW) Scranton; WVIA-TV (PBS) Scranton; WYOU (CBS) Scranton; allband FM.

Programming (via satellite): A&E Networks; ABC Family Channel; CNBC; CNN; Country Music TV; Discovery Channel; Disney Channel; ESPN; ESPN 2; FX; Headline News; HGTV; History Channel; Lifetime; MTV; Nickelodeon; QVC; Spike TV; Syfy; TBS Superstation; The Learning Channel; Travel Channel; Turner Classic Movies; Turner Network TV; USA Network; VH1; Yankees Entertainment & Sports.

Fee: $40.00 installation; $20.04 monthly.

Pay Service 1

Pay Units: 55.

Programming (via satellite): HBO (multiplexed).

Fee: $15.00 installation; $21.00 monthly.

Video-On-Demand: No

Internet Service

Operational: No.

Telephone Service

None

Miles of Plant: 25.0 (coaxial); 12.0 (fiber optic).

President: Doug Adams. Manager: Wendy Hartman. Chief Technician: John Wallis. Collections Manager: Ed Burrell. Office Manager: Becky Oakley.

Ownership: Adams CATV Inc. (MSO).

LOWER MACUNGIE TWP.—Formerly served by NORTHAMPTON BOROUGH, PA [PA0008]. RCN Corp. This cable system has converted to IPTV, 196 Van Buren St, Herndon, VA 20170. Phone: 703-434-8200. Web Site: http://www.rcn.com. ICA: PA5221.

TV Market Ranking: Below 100 (LOWER MACUNGIE TWP.).

Channel capacity: N.A. Channels available but not in use: N.A.

Internet Service

Operational: Yes.

Telephone Service

Digital: Operational

Chairman: Steven J. Simmons. Chief Executive Officer: Jim Holanda.

LOWER MERION TWP.—Comcast Cable, 3220 Tillman Dr, Bensalem, PA 19010. Phone: 215-642-6400. Fax: 215-638-6510. Web Site: http://www.comcast.com. Also serves Bala Cynwyd, Gladwyne & Narberth Borough. ICA: PA0048.

TV Market Ranking: 4 (Bala Cynwyd, Gladwyne, LOWER MERION TWP., Narberth Borough). Franchise award date: N.A. Franchise expiration date: N.A. Began: June 1, 1981.

Channel capacity: N.A. Channels available but not in use: N.A.

Basic Service

Subscribers: N.A. Included in Bensalem Twp.

Programming (received off-air): KYW-TV (CBS) Philadelphia; WBPH-TV (IND) Bethlehem; WCAU (NBC) Philadelphia; WFMZ-TV (IND) Allentown; WGTW-TV (TBN) Burlington; WHYY-TV (PBS) Wilmington; WLVT-TV (PBS) Allentown; WMCN-TV (IND) Atlantic City; WNJN (PBS) Montclair; WPHL-TV (MNT, IND) Philadelphia; WPPX-TV (ION) Wilmington; WPSG (CW) Philadelphia; WPVI-TV (ABC) Philadelphia; WTVE (IND) Reading; WTXF-TV (FOX) Philadelphia; WUVP-DT (UNV) Vineland; WWSI (TMO) Atlantic City; WYBE (ETV, IND) Philadelphia.

Programming (via satellite): QVC; The Comcast Network; TV Guide Network.

Fee: $10.65 monthly.

Expanded Basic Service 1

Subscribers: N.A.

Programming (via satellite): A&E Networks; ABC Family Channel; AMC; Animal Planet; BET Networks; Bravo; Cartoon Network; CNBC; CNN; Comcast SportsNet Philadelphia; Comedy Central; C-SPAN; C-SPAN 2; Discovery Channel; Disney Channel; E! Entertainment Television; ESPN; ESPN 2; Eternal Word TV Network; Food Network; Fox News Channel; FX; G4; Golf Channel; GSN; Hallmark Channel; Headline News; HGTV; History Channel; Lifetime; MSNBC; MTV; Nickelodeon; Philadelphia Park Live; Speed; Spike TV; Style Network; Syfy; TBS Superstation; The Learning Channel; The Weather Channel; truTV; Turner Classic Movies; Turner Network TV; TV Land; USA Network; Versus.

Fee: $41.90 monthly.

Digital Basic Service

Subscribers: N.A.

Programming (via satellite): BBC America; Bio; Canal 52MX; Canales N; CBS Sports Network; Cooking Channel; Country Music TV; C-SPAN 3; Current; DIY Network; Encore (multiplexed); ESPN 2 HD; ESPN Classic Sports; ESPN HD; ESPNews; FEARnet; Flix (multiplexed); Fox College Sports Atlantic; Fox College Sports Central; Fox College Sports Pacific; Fox Reality Channel; Fox Soccer; G4; GAS; GolTV; Great American Country; Hallmark Channel; HD Theater; History Channel International; INHD; Jewelry Television; Lifetime Movie Network; LOGO; Mid-Atlantic Sports Network; MTV Networks Digital Suite; Music Choice; National Geographic Channel; NBA TV; NFL Network; Nick Jr.; Nick Too; NickToons TV; Oxygen; Palladia; PBS Kids Sprout; Pennsylvania Cable Network; ShopNBC; SoapNet; Sundance Channel (multiplexed); Tennis Channel; Toon Disney; Travel Channel; Turner Network TV HD; TV One; Universal HD; Versus HD; WAM! America's Kidz Network; Weatherscan.

Digital Pay Service 1
Pay Units: N.A.
Programming (via satellite): Cinemax (multiplexed); Cinemax HD; HBO (multiplexed); HBO HD; Playboy TV; Showtime (multiplexed); Showtime HD; Starz (multiplexed); Starz HDTV; The Movie Channel (multiplexed).
Fee: $18.95 monthly (each).
Video-On-Demand: Yes
Pay-Per-View
Playboy TV (delivered digitally); Fresh (delivered digitally); iN DEMAND (delivered digitally); ESPN Full Court (delivered digitally); ESPN Gameplan (delivered digitally); NBA League Pass (delivered digitally); MLS Direct Kick (delivered digitally); NHL Center Ice (delivered digitally).
Internet Service
Operational: Yes.
Broadband Service: Comcast High Speed Internet.
Fee: $42.95 monthly.
Telephone Service
Digital: Operational
Fee: $44.95 monthly
Senior Regional Vice President: Amy Smith. Vice President, Technical Operations: Rich Massi. Vice President, Marketing: Chip Goodman.
Ownership: Comcast Cable Communications Inc. (MSO).

LOWER NAZARETH TWP.—Formerly served by NORTHAMPTON BOROUGH, PA [PA0008]. RCN Corp. This cable system has converted to IPTV, 196 Van Buren St, Herndon, VA 20170. Phone: 703-434-8200. Web Site: http://www.rcn.com. ICA: PA5222.
TV Market Ranking: Below 100 (LOWER NAZARETH TWP.).
Channel capacity: N.A. Channels available but not in use: N.A.
Internet Service
Operational: Yes.
Telephone Service
Digital: Operational
Chairman: Steven J. Simmons. Chief Executive Officer: Jim Holanda.

LOWER SAUCON TWP.—Formerly served by NORTHAMPTON BOROUGH, PA [PA0008]. RCN Corp. This cable system has converted to IPTV, 196 Van Buren St, Herndon, VA 20170. Phone: 703-434-8200. Web Site: http://www.rcn.com. ICA: PA5220.
TV Market Ranking: Below 100 (LOWER SAUCON TWP.).
Channel capacity: N.A. Channels available but not in use: N.A.
Internet Service
Operational: Yes.
Telephone Service
Digital: Operational
Chairman: Steven J. Simmons. Chief Executive Officer: Jim Holanda.

LOWHILL TWP.—Formerly served by NORTHAMPTON BOROUGH, PA [PA0008]. RCN Corp. This cable system has converted to IPTV, 196 Van Buren St, Herndon, VA 20170. Phone: 703-434-8200. Web Site: http://www.rcn.com. ICA: PA5223.
TV Market Ranking: Below 100 (LOWHILL TWP.).
Channel capacity: N.A. Channels available but not in use: N.A.
Internet Service
Operational: Yes.
Telephone Service
Digital: Operational
Chairman: Steven J. Simmons. Chief Executive Officer: Jim Holanda.

LYKENS—Comcast Cable, 1 E Uwchlan Ave, Ste 411, Exton, PA 19341. Phones: 484-288-6500; 717-960-3100 (Harrisburg office). Web Site: http://www.comcast.com. Also serves Berrysburg, Elizabethville, Gratz, Hegins Twp., Hubley Twp., Lykens Twp., Pillow, Porter Twp. (Schuylkill County), Tower City, Upper Mahantango Twp., Upper Paxton Twp. (Dauphin County), Wiconisco Twp., Williams Twp. (Dauphin County) & Williamstown (Dauphin County). ICA: PA0096.
TV Market Ranking: 57 (Berrysburg, Elizabethville, Gratz, Hegins Twp., Hubley Twp., LYKENS, Lykens Twp., Pillow, Porter Twp. (Schuylkill County), Tower City, Upper Mahantango Twp., Upper Paxton Twp. (Dauphin County), Wiconisco Twp., Williams Twp. (Dauphin County), Williamstown (Dauphin County)). Franchise award date: N.A. Franchise expiration date: N.A. Began: June 6, 1951.
Channel capacity: N.A. Channels available but not in use: N.A.
Basic Service
Subscribers: N.A. Included in Harrisburg
Programming (received off-air): WGAL (NBC) Lancaster; WHP-TV (CBS, MNT) Harrisburg; WHTM-TV (ABC) Harrisburg; WITF-TV (PBS) Harrisburg; WLYH-TV (CW) Lancaster; WPHL-TV (MNT, IND) Philadelphia; WPMT (FOX) York; 20 FMs.
Programming (via satellite): C-SPAN; C-SPAN 2; FX; Pennsylvania Cable Network; Product Information Network; QVC; ShopNBC; TV Guide Network; WGN America.
Fee: $45.10 installation; $17.60 monthly.
Expanded Basic Service 1
Subscribers: N.A.
Programming (via satellite): A&E Networks; ABC Family Channel; AMC; Animal Planet; Bravo; Cartoon Network; CNBC; CNN; Comcast SportsNet Philadelphia; Comedy Central; Country Music TV; Discovery Channel; Disney Channel; E! Entertainment Television; ESPN; ESPN 2; Eternal Word TV Network; Food Network; Fox News Channel; Great American Country; Hallmark Channel; Headline News; HGTV; History Channel; INSP; ION Television; Lifetime; MSNBC; MTV; Nickelodeon; Oxygen; Spike TV; Syfy; TBS Superstation; The Learning Channel; The Weather Channel; Toon Disney; Travel Channel; truTV; Turner Network TV; TV Land; USA Network; VH1.
Fee: $30.90 monthly.
Digital Basic Service
Subscribers: N.A.
Programming (via satellite): AmericanLife TV Network; BBC America; Bio; Black Family Channel; Bloomberg Television; Discovery Fit & Health; DIY Network; ESPN Classic Sports; ESPNews; Fox Sports World; Fuse; G4; Golf Channel; GSN; Halogen Network; History Channel International; Music Choice; Outdoor Channel; Speed; Trinity Broadcasting Network; Versus; WE tv.
Fee: $14.95 monthly.
Digital Expanded Basic Service
Subscribers: N.A.
Programming (via satellite): Fox Movie Channel; GAS; Independent Film Channel; MTV Networks Digital Suite; National Geographic Channel; Nick Jr.; Nick Too; NickToons TV; SoapNet; Style Network; Sundance Channel.
Digital Pay Service 1
Pay Units: N.A.
Programming (via satellite): ART America; Canales N; CCTV-4; Cinemax (multiplexed); Encore (multiplexed); Filipino Channel; Flix; HBO (multiplexed); RAI International; Russian Television Network; Showtime (multiplexed); Starz (multiplexed); The Movie Channel (multiplexed); TV Asia; TV Japan; TV5, La Television International; Zee TV USA; Zhong Tian Channel.
Video-On-Demand: No
Pay-Per-View
Urban Xtra (delivered digitally); Hot Choice (delivered digitally); Shorteez (delivered digitally); Fresh (delivered digitally); Playboy TV (delivered digitally); HITS (delivered digitally).
Internet Service
Operational: Yes.
Broadband Service: Comcast High Speed Internet.
Fee: $42.95 monthly.
Telephone Service
None
Miles of Plant: 172.0 (coaxial); 19.0 (fiber optic).
Area Vice President: Jim Samaha.
Ownership: Comcast Cable Communications Inc. (MSO).

MAHAFFEY—Formerly served by Adelphia Communications. Now served by PUNXSUTAWNEY, PA [PA0397]. ICA: PA0363.

MAHANOY CITY—Service Electric Cable Company, 201 W Centre St, Mahanoy City, PA 17948-2505. Phones: 800-242-3707; 570-874-1010; 570-773-2585. Fax: 570-773-0276. E-mail: fmseco@ptd.net. Web Site: http://www.secable.com/mahanoycity. Also serves Ashland, Barry Twp., Delano, East Brunswick Twp., Frackville, Gilberton, Girardville, Gordon, Mahanoy Twp., New Ringgold, Ringtown, Rush Twp. (Schuylkill County), St. Clair (Schuylkill County), Tamaqua, West Mahanoy & West Penn Twp. (northwestern portion). ICA: PA0055.
TV Market Ranking: 49 (Delano, MAHANOY CITY, Mahanoy Twp., Rush Twp. (Schuylkill County), Tamaqua); Below 100 (Ashland, Barry Twp., East Brunswick Twp., Frackville, Gilberton, Girardville, Gordon, New Ringgold, Ringtown, St. Clair (Schuylkill County), West Mahanoy, West Penn Twp. (northwestern portion)). Franchise award date: N.A. Franchise expiration date: N.A. Began: June 1, 1948.
Channel capacity: N.A. Channels available but not in use: N.A.
Basic Service
Subscribers: 13,500.
Programming (received off-air): KYW-TV (CBS) Philadelphia; WBRE-TV (NBC) Wilkes-Barre; WCAU (NBC) Philadelphia; WNEP-TV (ABC) Scranton; WOLF-TV (CW, FOX, MNT) Hazleton; WPVI-TV (ABC) Philadelphia; WQPX-TV (ION) Scranton; WSWB (CW) Scranton; WTXF-TV (FOX) Philadelphia; WVIA-TV (PBS) Scranton; WYOU (CBS) Scranton; allband FM.
Programming (via microwave): WNYW (FOX) New York; WPIX (CW, IND) New York.
Programming (via satellite): C-SPAN; Eternal Word TV Network; QVC; WWOR-TV (MNT) Secaucus.
Fee: $36.00 installation; $19.99 monthly.
Expanded Basic Service 1
Subscribers: N.A.
Programming (via satellite): A&E Networks; ABC Family Channel; AMC; AmericanLife TV Network; Animal Planet; Bravo; Cartoon Network; CNBC; CNN; Comcast SportsNet Philadelphia; Comedy Central; Country Music TV; Discovery Channel; Discovery Fit & Health; E! Entertainment Television; ESPN; ESPN 2; ESPN Classic Sports; ESPNews; Food Network; Fox Movie Channel; Fox News Channel; FX; Hallmark Channel; Headline News; HGTV; History Channel; Lifetime; MSNBC; MTV; NASA TV; National Geographic Channel; Nickelodeon; Pennsylvania Cable Network; ShopNBC; SoapNet; Speed; Spike TV; Syfy; TBS Superstation; The Learning Channel; The Weather Channel; Travel Channel; truTV; Turner Classic Movies; Turner Network TV; TV Land; USA Network; Versus; VH1; WE tv.
Fee: $29.96 monthly.
Digital Basic Service
Subscribers: 9,000.
Programming (via satellite): BBC America; Bio; Boomerang; Country Music TV; C-SPAN 2; DIY Network; Fox Soccer; FSN Digital Atlantic; FSN Digital Central; FSN Digital Pacific; Fuel TV; G4; Golf Channel; HD Theater; HDNet; HDNet Movies; History Channel International; Independent Film Channel; MTV Networks Digital Suite; Music Choice; Nick Jr.; Nick Too; Outdoor Channel; PBS Kids Sprout; TeenNick; Turner Network TV HD; TVG Network; WALN Cable Radio.
Fee: $5.99 monthly.
Digital Pay Service 1
Pay Units: N.A.
Programming (via satellite): Cinemax (multiplexed); Encore (multiplexed); HBO (multiplexed); Showtime (multiplexed); Showtime HD; Starz (multiplexed); The Movie Channel (multiplexed).
Fee: $5.99 monthly (Showtime), $11.00 monthly (Cinemax), $13.00 monthly (HBO).
Video-On-Demand: Planned
Pay-Per-View
iN DEMAND.
Internet Service
Operational: Yes.
Subscribers: 2,500.
Broadband Service: ProLog Express.
Fee: $19.95 monthly.
Telephone Service
None
Miles of Plant: 350.0 (coaxial); None (fiber optic).
Manager: William Brayford. Chief Technician: Robert Jais. Regulatory Affairs Director: Arlean Lilly.
Ownership: Service Electric Cable TV Inc. (MSO).

MALVERN—Comcast Cable. Now served by COATESVILLE (formerly Chester County), PA [PA0014]. ICA: PA0034.

MAMMOTH—Citizens Cable Communications. Formerly [PA0400]. This cable system has converted to IPTV, Rte 982, PO Box 135, Mammoth, PA 15664. Phone: 724-423-3000. Fax: 724-423-3003. E-mail: cable@wpa.net. Web Site: http://cable.wpa.net. ICA: PA5000.
TV Market Ranking: 10 (MAMMOTH).
Channel capacity: N.A. Channels available but not in use: N.A.
Telephone Service
Digital: Operational

MAMMOTH—Citizens Cable Communications. This cable system has converted to IPTV. See Mammoth, PA [PA5000]. ICA: PA0400.

MARIENVILLE—Formerly served by Cebridge Connections. Now served by MEADVILLE, PA [PA0062]. ICA: PA0221.

MARKLEYSBURG—Comcast Cable, 15 Summit Park Dr, Pittsburgh, PA 15275. Phones: 412-747-6400; 301-895-4375 (Grantsville, MD office). Fax: 412-747-6401. Web Site: http://www.comcast.com. Also serves Chalk Hill, Confluence, Fayette County (unincorporated areas), Henry Clay Twp., Lower Turkeyfoot Twp., Ohiopyle, Ursina & Wharton Twp., PA; Bruceton Mills, WV. ICA: PA0129.

TV Market Ranking: 10,74 (Fayette County (unincorporated areas) (portions)); Below 100 (Chalk Hill, Lower Turkeyfoot Twp., Ursina, Fayette County (unincorporated areas) (portions)); Outside TV Markets (Bruceton Mills, Confluence, Henry Clay Twp., MARKLEYSBURG, Ohiopyle, Wharton Twp., Fayette County (unincorporated areas) (portions)). Franchise award date: N.A. Franchise expiration date: N.A. Began: November 1, 1977.

Channel capacity: 42 (not 2-way capable). Channels available but not in use: N.A.

Basic Service

Subscribers: 1,986.

Programming (received off-air): KDKA-TV (CBS) Pittsburgh; WDTV (CBS) Weston; WJAC-TV (NBC) Johnstown; WKBS-TV (IND) Altoona; WNPB-TV (PBS) Morgantown; WPGH-TV (FOX) Pittsburgh; WPMY (MNT) Pittsburgh; WPXI (IND, NBC) Pittsburgh; WQED (PBS) Pittsburgh; WTAE-TV (ABC) Pittsburgh; WWCP-TV (FOX) Johnstown.

Programming (via satellite): TBS Superstation.

Fee: $39.95 installation; $10.27 monthly; $3.50 converter.

Expanded Basic Service 1

Subscribers: N.A.

Programming (via satellite): A&E Networks; ABC Family Channel; AMC; CNN; Country Music TV; Discovery Channel; Disney Channel; E! Entertainment Television; ESPN; ESPN 2; Headline News; MTV; Nickelodeon; Spike TV; Syfy; The Weather Channel; Trinity Broadcasting Network; Turner Network TV; USA Network.

Fee: $38.00 monthly.

Pay Service 1

Pay Units: 506.

Programming (via satellite): Cinemax; HBO; Showtime.

Fee: $29.95 installation; $8.95 monthly (Cinemax), $11.95 monthly (Showtime), $11.99 monthly (HBO).

Pay Service 2

Pay Units: N.A.

Programming (via satellite): Encore; The Movie Channel.

Fee: $3.99 monthly (Encore), $11.95 monthly (TMC).

Video-On-Demand: No

Internet Service

Operational: Yes.

Telephone Service

None

Miles of Plant: 160.0 (coaxial); None (fiber optic).

Regional Vice President: Linda Hossinger. Vice President, Technical Operations: Randy Bender. Vice President, Marketing: Donna Corning. Vice President, Public Affairs: Jody Doherty. Manager: Barry Savage.

Ownership: Comcast Cable Communications Inc. (MSO).

MATAMORAS—Cablevision Systems Corp., 683 Route 10 E, Randolph, NJ 7869. Phones: 516-803-2300 (Corporate office); 973-659-2200. Fax: 973-659-2266. Web Site: http://www.cablevision.com. Also serves Layton, Montague Twp. & Sandyston Twp., NJ; Milford (portions), Millrift & Westfall Twp. (portions), PA. ICA: PA0168.

TV Market Ranking: 1 (Milford (portions), Millrift); Below 100 (Layton, MATAMORAS, Montague Twp., Westfall Twp. (portions)); Outside TV Markets (Sandyston Twp.). Franchise award date: N.A. Franchise expiration date: N.A. Began: October 6, 1966.

Channel capacity: N.A. Channels available but not in use: N.A.

Basic Service

Subscribers: 1,550.

Programming (received off-air): WABC-TV (ABC) New York; WCBS-TV (CBS) New York; WFME-TV (ETV) West Milford; WFUT-DT (TEL) Newark; WMBC-TV (IND) Newton; WNBC (NBC) New York; WNET (PBS) Newark; WNJN (PBS) Montclair; WNJU (TMO) Linden; WNYE-TV (PBS) New York; WNYW (FOX) New York; WPIX (CW, IND) New York; WPXN-TV (ION) New York; WRNN-TV (IND) Kingston; WTBY-TV (TBN) Poughkeepsie; WWOR-TV (MNT) Secaucus; WXTV-DT (UNV) Paterson; 24 FMs.

Fee: $49.95 installation; $49.95 monthly.

Digital Basic Service

Subscribers: N.A.

Programming (via satellite): Azteca America; BBC World News; Bio; Bloomberg Television; Canal Sur; Caracol TV; Cartoon Network Tambien en Espanol; Cine Latino; CNN en Espanol; CNN HD; Country Music TV; C-SPAN 3; Discovery en Espanol; Discovery Home Channel; Discovery Kids Channel; Discovery Times Channel; Docu TVE; Ecuavisia Internacional; ESPN 2 HD; ESPN Classic Sports; ESPN Deportes; ESPN HD; ESPNews; EuroNews; EWTN en Espanol; Food Network HD; Fox College Sports Atlantic; Fox College Sports Central; Fox College Sports Pacific; Fox Deportes; Fox Movie Channel; Fox Soccer; Fuel TV; G4; Golf Channel; GolTV; Great American Country; Hallmark Channel; HD Theater; here! On Demand; HGTV HD; History Channel en Espanol; History Channel International; Howard TV; HTV Musica; Infinito; Jewelry Television; La Familia Network; Latele Novela Network; LOGO; Mag Rack; Mariavision; Military Channel; Momentum TV; MTV Hits; mun2 television; Music Choice; National Geographic Channel; National Geographic Channel HD Network; NBA TV; NDTV The Dominican Channel; NHL Network; Nick Jr.; NickToons TV; Outdoor Channel; Oxygen; Science Television; Sorpresa; Sundance Channel; Supercanal Caribe; TBS in HD; Telefe Internacional; Toon Disney; Toon Disney en Espanol; Tr3s; Turner Network TV HD; TV Chile; TV Colombia; TVE Internacional; TVG Network; Universal HD; Utilisima; VeneMovies; Versus; Versus HD; VH1 Classic; VH1 Soul; V-me TV; WAPA America; World Cinema HD; WWE 24/7; YES HD.

Fee: $10.95 monthly.

Pay Service 1

Pay Units: N.A.

Programming (via satellite): Cinemax; Flix; HBO (multiplexed); Independent Film Channel; Showtime (multiplexed); The Movie Channel.

Fee: $9.95 monthly (Cinemax, Showtime, Starz or TMC), $11.95 monthly (HBO).

Digital Pay Service 1

Pay Units: N.A.

Programming (via satellite): CCTV-4; Channel One; Chinese Television Network; Cinemax (multiplexed); Cinemax HD; Cinemax On Demand; Encore (multiplexed); HBO (multiplexed); HBO HD; HBO On Demand; Korean Channel; MBC America; Portuguese Channel; RAI International; Russian Television Network; Showtime (multiplexed); Showtime HD; Showtime On Demand; Starz (multiplexed); Starz HDTV; The Movie Channel (multiplexed); TV Asia; TV Japan; TV Polonia; TV5, La Television International; Zee TV USA.

Fee: $9.95 monthly (Showtime, Cinemax, TMC, Starz/Encore, Playboy, RAI, SPT, TV5, or TV Polonia), $11.95 monthly (HBO), $14.95 monthly (Korean Package or Chinese Package), $19.95 monthly (South Asian Package), $24.95 monthly (TV Japan), $29.95 monthly (Russian Pack.

Video-On-Demand: Yes

Pay-Per-View

iN DEMAND; Playboy TV; Sports PPV (delivered digitally); NBA TV (delivered digitally); iN DEMAND (delivered digitally); Playboy TV (delivered digitally).

Internet Service

Operational: Yes.

Broadband Service: Optimum Online.

Fee: $46.95 installation; $34.95 monthly; $299.00 modem purchase.

Telephone Service

Digital: Operational

Fee: $34.95 monthly

Miles of Plant: 30.0 (coaxial); None (fiber optic).

Vice President, Field Operations: Frank Dagliere. Operations Manager: Laura Cavazzi.

Ownership: Cablevision Systems Corp. (MSO).

McALEVYS FORT—Atlantic Broadband, 120 Southmont Blvd, Johnstown, PA 15905. Phones: 888-536-9600; 814-539-8971. Fax: 814-535-7749. E-mail: info@atlanticbb.com. Web Site: http://www.atlanticbb.com. Also serves Huntingdon & Petersburg. ICA: PA0441.

TV Market Ranking: 74 (Huntingdon, MCALEVYS FORT, Petersburg). Franchise award date: N.A. Franchise expiration date: March 5, 2015. Began: N.A.

Channel capacity: 29 (not 2-way capable). Channels available but not in use: N.A.

Basic Service

Subscribers: 183.

Programming (received off-air): WATM-TV (ABC) Altoona; WJAC-TV (NBC) Johnstown; WKBS-TV (IND) Altoona; WPSU-TV (PBS) Clearfield; WTAJ-TV (CBS) Altoona; WWCP-TV (FOX) Johnstown.

Programming (via satellite): A&E Networks; ABC Family Channel; AMC; Animal Planet; CNN; Comedy Central; Country Music TV; Discovery Channel; ESPN; ESPN 2; Fox News Channel; FX; Headline News; History Channel; Lifetime; Nickelodeon; QVC; Root Sports Pittsburgh; Spike TV; Syfy; TBS Superstation; The Learning Channel; The Weather Channel; Trinity Broadcasting Network; Turner Network TV; TV Land; USA Network; WGN America.

Fee: $25.00 installation; $30.99 monthly; $2.50 converter; $20.00 additional installation.

Pay Service 1

Pay Units: 17.

Programming (via satellite): Showtime; The Movie Channel.

Fee: $13.95 monthly (each).

Internet Service

Operational: No.

Telephone Service

None

Miles of Plant: 21.0 (coaxial); None (fiber optic).

Vice President: David Dane. General Manager: Mike Papasergi. Technical Operations Director: Charles Sorchilla. Marketing & Customer Service Director: Dara Leslie. Marketing Manager: Natalie Kurchak.

Ownership: Atlantic Broadband (MSO).

McCLURE—Nittany Media Inc., 18 Juniata St, PO Box 111, Lewistown, PA 17044. Phones: 800-692-7401; 717-248-3733. Fax: 717-248-3732. E-mail: info@nittanymedia.com. Web Site: http://www.nittanymedia.com. ICA: PA0255.

TV Market Ranking: Outside TV Markets (MCCLURE). Franchise award date: N.A. Franchise expiration date: N.A. Began: May 1, 1953.

Channel capacity: N.A. Channels available but not in use: N.A.

Basic Service

Subscribers: 350.

Programming (received off-air): WGAL (NBC) Lancaster; WHP-TV (CBS, MNT) Harrisburg; WHTM-TV (ABC) Harrisburg; WHVL-LP State College, etc.; WITF-TV (PBS) Harrisburg; WLYH-TV (CW) Lancaster; WNEP-TV (ABC) Scranton; WOLF-TV (CW, FOX, MNT) Hazleton; WPMT (FOX) York; WPSU-TV (PBS) Clearfield; WTAJ-TV (CBS) Altoona; WVIA-TV (PBS) Scranton; allband FM.

Programming (via satellite): Bloomberg Television; C-SPAN; La Familia Network; Pennsylvania Cable Network; QVC.

Fee: $25.00 installation; $17.40 monthly.

Expanded Basic Service 1

Subscribers: N.A.

Programming (via satellite): A&E Networks; ABC Family Channel; AMC; Animal Planet; Boomerang; Bravo; Cartoon Network; CNBC; CNN; Comedy Central; Cornerstone Television; Country Music TV; C-SPAN 2; Discovery Channel; Discovery Fit & Health; Disney Channel; ESPN; ESPN 2; Food Network; Fox News Channel; Fox Sports Net; FX; Great American Country; Hallmark Channel; Headline News; HGTV; History Channel; INSP; ION Television; Lifetime; MSNBC; MTV; Nickelodeon; Outdoor Channel; Sorpresa; Speed; Spike TV; Syfy; TBS Superstation; The Learning Channel; The Weather Channel; Travel Channel; Trinity Broadcasting Network; Turner Network TV; TV Land; USA Network; VH1; WGN America.

Fee: $27.10 monthly.

Digital Basic Service
Subscribers: N.A.
Programming (via satellite): BBC America; Bio; Bloomberg Television; Bravo; cloo; CMT Pure Country; Cooking Channel; DMX Music; ESPN 2; ESPN HD; Fox Movie Channel; Fuse; G4; GAS; GSN; Halogen Network; HD Theater; HDNet; HDNet Movies; HGTV; History Channel; History Channel International; Lifetime Movie Network; MTV Networks Digital Suite; Nick Jr.; NickToons TV; Outdoor Channel; SoapNet; Speed; Style Network; Syfy; Toon Disney; Trinity Broadcasting Network; TV Land; WE tv.
Fee: $15.99 monthly.

Digital Expanded Basic Service
Subscribers: N.A.
Programming (via satellite): ESPN 2; ESPN Classic Sports; Fox Soccer; Golf Channel; Versus.
Fee: $3.99 monthly.

Digital Expanded Basic Service 2
Subscribers: N.A.
Programming (via satellite): Independent Film Channel; Turner Classic Movies.
Fee: $1.99 monthly.

Digital Pay Service 1
Pay Units: N.A.
Programming (via satellite): Cinemax (multiplexed); Encore (multiplexed); Flix; HBO (multiplexed); Showtime (multiplexed); Starz (multiplexed); The Movie Channel (multiplexed).
Fee: $12.99 monthly (each).

Video-On-Demand: No

Pay-Per-View
iN DEMAND.

Internet Service
Operational: Yes.
Fee: $39.95 monthly.

Telephone Service
None

Miles of Plant: 3.0 (coaxial); None (fiber optic). Additional miles planned: 1.0 (coaxial).
Chief Technician: Michael Hain.
Ownership: Nittany Media Inc. (MSO).

McCONNELLSBURG—Comcast Cable. Now served by SHIPPENSBURG, PA [PA0066]. ICA: PA0148.

McVEYTOWN—Zampelli Electronics, PO Box 830, Lewistown, PA 17044-0830. Phone: 717-248-1544. Also serves Mattawana. ICA: PA0366.
TV Market Ranking: 74 (Mattawana, MCVEYTOWN). Franchise award date: N.A. Franchise expiration date: N.A. Began: N.A.
Channel capacity: 5 (not 2-way capable). Channels available but not in use: N.A.

Basic Service
Subscribers: N.A.
Programming (received off-air): WGAL (NBC) Lancaster; WHP-TV (CBS, MNT) Harrisburg; WHTM-TV (ABC) Harrisburg; WTAJ-TV (CBS) Altoona.

Video-On-Demand: No

Internet Service
Operational: No.

Telephone Service
None

Manager & Chief Technician: Joe Zampelli.
Ownership: Zampelli TV (MSO).

MEADVILLE—Armstrong Cable Services, 160 Westview Dr, Meadville, PA 16335-7904. Phones: 877-277-5711; 877-486-4666; 814-333-8442. Fax: 814-337-2510. E-mail: info@zoominternet.net. Web Site: http://cable.armstrongonewire.com. Also serves Andover, Andover Boro, Andover Twp. (Ashtabula County), Andover Village, Kinsman & Kinsman Twp., OH; Blooming Valley, Callensburg, Centerville (Crawford County), Cochranton, Conneaut Lake, Cooperstown, Cornplanter Twp. (Venango County), East Hickory, Franklin (Venango County), Guys Mills, Hydetown, Jamestown, Lowville, Marienville, Mill Village, Pleasantville, Saegertown, Sheakleyville Twp., Shenango Twp. (Mercer County), South Shenango Twp., Sugarcreek (Venango County), Titusville, Townville, Utica, Wattsburg, West Hickory, West Mead Twp. & West Shenango Twp., PA. ICA: PA0062. **Note:** This system is an overbuild.
TV Market Ranking: 79 (Andover Twp. (Ashtabula County), Andover Village, Jamestown, Kinsman, Kinsman Twp., Shenango Twp. (Mercer County), South Shenango Twp., West Shenango Twp.); Below 100 (Andover Boro, Blooming Valley, Guys Mills, Lowville, MEADVILLE, Mill Village, Saegertown, Sheakleyville Twp., Townville, Wattsburg, West Mead Twp.); Outside TV Markets (Callensburg, Centerville (Crawford County), Cochranton, Conneaut Lake, Cooperstown, Cornplanter Twp. (Venango County), East HIckory, Franklin (Venango County), Hydetown, Marienville, Pleasantville, Sugarcreek (Venango County), Titusville, Utica, West HIckory). Franchise award date: January 1, 1953. Franchise expiration date: N.A. Began: July 1, 1953.
Channel capacity: N.A. Channels available but not in use: N.A.

Digital Basic Service
Subscribers: 3,970.
Programming (via satellite): A&E Networks; ABC Family Channel; AMC; Animal Planet; Bravo; Cartoon Network; CNBC; CNN; Comedy Central; Country Music TV; C-SPAN; CW+; Discovery Channel; Disney Channel; E! Entertainment Television; ESPN; ESPN 2; ESPN Classic Sports; Eternal Word TV Network; Food Network; Fox News Channel; FX; Headline News; HGTV; History Channel; INSP; Lifetime; MSNBC; MTV; Music Choice; Nickelodeon; Nick-Toons TV; Pennsylvania Cable Network; Pentagon Channel; QVC; Root Sports Pittsburgh; Spike TV; SportsTime Ohio; Syfy; TBS Superstation; The Learning Channel; The Weather Channel; Travel Channel; truTV; Turner Classic Movies; Turner Network TV; TV Guide Network; TV Land; TVN Entertainment; USA Network; VH1.
Fee: $35.00 installation; $51.40 monthly.

Digital Expanded Basic Service
Subscribers: N.A.
Programming (via satellite): AmericanLife TV Network; BBC America; Bio; Bloomberg Television; Boomerang; Chiller; cloo; CMT Pure Country; Cooking Channel; Discovery Fit & Health; Discovery Health Channel; Discovery Kids Channel; DIY Network; ESPN Classic Sports; ESPNews; G4; Golf Channel; Great American Country; GSN; Hallmark Channel; Hallmark Movie Channel; History Channel International; HRTV; ID Investigation Discovery; Jewelry Television; Lifetime Movie Network; Military Channel; MTV Hits; MTV Jams; MTV2; mun2 television; National Geographic Channel; NFL Network; NHL Network; Nick Jr.; Nick Too; Outdoor Channel; Oxygen; PBS Kids Sprout; Pentagon Channel; Planet Green; RFD-TV; Science; ShopNBC; SoapNet; Speed; TeenNick; Tennis Channel; Toon Disney; Tr3s; Versus; VH1 Classic; VH1 Soul; WE tv.
Fee: $12.00 monthly.

Digital Expanded Basic Service 2
Subscribers: N.A.
Programming (received off-air): WFXP (FOX) Erie; WICU-TV (NBC) Erie; WJET-TV (ABC) Erie; WQED (PBS) Pittsburgh; WSEE-TV (CBS, CW) Erie.
Programming (via satellite): A&E HD; Animal Planet HD; Bravo HD; CNN HD; Disney Channel HD; ESPN 2 HD; ESPN HD; Food Network HD; Fox News HD; FSN HD; FX HD; Golf Channel HD; Hallmark Movie Channel HD; HD Theater; HDNet; HDNet Movies; HGTV HD; History Channel HD; MGM HD; National Geographic Channel HD Network; NFL Network HD; NHL Network HD; Outdoor Channel 2 HD; Palladia; QVC HD; Syfy HD; TBS in HD; The Weather Channel HD; Turner Network TV HD; Universal HD; USA Network HD; Versus HD; WealthTV HD.
Fee: $9.00 monthly.

Digital Pay Service 1
Pay Units: 502.
Programming (via satellite): Encore (multiplexed); Starz (multiplexed); Starz HDTV.
Fee: $13.95 monthly.

Digital Pay Service 2
Pay Units: 620.
Programming (via satellite): HBO (multiplexed); HBO HD.
Fee: $13.95 monthly.

Digital Pay Service 3
Pay Units: 322.
Programming (via satellite): Cinemax (multiplexed); Cinemax HD.
Fee: $13.95 monthly.

Digital Pay Service 4
Pay Units: 250.
Programming (via satellite): Flix; Showtime (multiplexed); Showtime HD; The Movie Channel (multiplexed).
Fee: $13.95 monthly.

Digital Pay Service 5
Pay Units: N.A.
Programming (via satellite): RAI USA; TV5 USA.

Video-On-Demand: Yes

Pay-Per-View
ESPN Now (delivered digitally); Hot Choice (delivered digitally); iN DEMAND; iN DEMAND (delivered digitally); NBA TV (delivered digitally); ESPN Sports (delivered digitally).

Internet Service
Operational: Yes.
Subscribers: 7,258.
Broadband Service: Armstrong Zoom.
Fee: $39.95 monthly.

Telephone Service
Digital: Operational
Fee: $39.95 monthly

Miles of Plant: 667.0 (coaxial); 35.0 (fiber optic). Additional miles planned: 25.0 (coaxial).
Manager: Scott Brush. Chief Technician: Pat Gladis. Marketing Director: Joan Kocan.
Ownership: Armstrong Group of Companies (MSO).

MERCER COUNTY—Time Warner Cable, 4352 Youngstown Rd SE, Warren, OH 44484. Phone: 330-633-9203. Fax: 330-633-2599. Web Site: http://www.timewarnercable.com/northeastohio. Also serves Brookfield Twp., Hartford Twp., Hubbard Twp., Orangeville & Yankee Lake, OH; Clark, Farrell, Hermitage, Pymatuning Twp., Sharon, Sharpsville, Shenango Twp., South Pymatuning Twp., West Middlesex, Wheatland & Wilmington Twp. (Mercer County), PA. ICA: PA0471.
TV Market Ranking: 79 (Brookfield Twp., Clark, Farrell, Hartford Twp., Hermitage, Hubbard Twp., MERCER COUNTY, Orangeville, Pymatuning Twp., Sharon, Sharpsville, Shenango Twp., South Pymatuning Twp., West Middlesex, Wheatland, Wilmington Twp. (Mercer County), Yankee Lake).
Channel capacity: N.A. Channels available but not in use: N.A.

Basic Service
Subscribers: N.A.
Programming (received off-air): KDKA-TV (CBS) Pittsburgh; W29CO (IND) Sharon; WFMJ-TV (CW, NBC) Youngstown; WKBN-TV (CBS) Youngstown; WNEO (PBS) Alliance; WPGH-TV (FOX) Pittsburgh; WPMY (MNT) Pittsburgh; WQED (PBS) Pittsburgh; WUAB (MNT) Lorain; WYFX-LP Youngstown; WYTV (ABC, MNT) Youngstown.
Programming (via satellite): C-SPAN; C-SPAN 2; ION Television; MyNetworkTV Inc.; Ohio News Network; QVC; ShopNBC; TV Guide Network.
Fee: $29.95 installation; $14.37 monthly; $19.95 additional installation.

Expanded Basic Service 1
Subscribers: N.A.
Programming (via satellite): A&E Networks; ABC Family Channel; AMC; Animal Planet; BET Networks; Bravo; Cartoon Network; CNBC; CNN; Comedy Central; Country Music TV; Court TV; Discovery Channel; Disney Channel; E! Entertainment Television; ESPN; ESPN 2; Food Network; Fox News Channel; Fox Sports Net Ohio; FX; Hallmark Channel; Headline News; HGTV; History Channel; Lifetime; MSNBC; MTV; Nickelodeon; Outdoor Channel; Oxygen; Pennsylvania Cable Network; Root Sports Pittsburgh; Speed; Spike TV; SportsTime Ohio; Style Network; Syfy; TBS Superstation; The Learning Channel; The Weather Channel; Travel Channel; Turner Classic Movies; Turner Network TV; TV Land; USA Network; VH1.
Fee: $37.13 monthly.

Digital Basic Service
Subscribers: N.A.
Programming (via satellite): AmericanLife TV Network; BBC America; BBC America On Demand; Bloomberg Television; CMT Pure Country; C-SPAN 3; Current; Discovery Channel HD; Discovery Fit & Health; Discovery Health Channel; Discovery Kids Channel; DIY Network; Do-It-Yourself On Demand; ESPN 2 HD; ESPN Classic Sports; ESPN HD; ESPNews; Exercise TV; Fox Movie Channel; Fox Soccer; Fuse; G4; GMC; Golf Channel; Great American Country; GSN; Halogen Network; HDNet; HDNet Movies; HGTV On Demand; ID Investigation Discovery; Lifetime Movie Network; LOGO; Military Channel; Mojo Mix; MTV Hits; MTV Jams; MTV2; Music Choice; National Geographic Channel; Nick Jr.; Nick Too; NickToons TV; Oxygen On Demand; Planet Green; Science; SoapNet; Speed On Demand; TeenNick; The Word Network; Toon Disney; Trinity Broadcasting Network; Turner Network TV HD; TV Guide SPOT; VH1 Classic; VH1 Soul; WE tv.
Fee: $11.95 monthly.

Digital Expanded Basic Service
Subscribers: N.A.
Programming (via satellite): Bio; Cooking Channel; Encore; Flix; Fox College Sports Atlantic; Fox College Sports Central; Fox College Sports Pacific; Fox Reality Channel; Fuel TV; History Channel International; Independent Film Channel; NBA TV; Sundance Channel; Versus.
Fee: $10.00 monthly.

Digital Pay Service 1
Pay Units: N.A.
Programming (via satellite): Cinemax (multiplexed); Cinemax HD; Cinemax On Demand; Encore (multiplexed); Flix; HBO (multiplexed); HBO HD; HBO Latino; HBO On Demand; Showtime (multiplexed); Showtime HD; Showtime On Demand; Starz (multiplexed); Starz HDTV; Starz On Demand; The Movie Channel (multiplexed); The Movie Channel On Demand.
Fee: $15.95 monthly (HBO, Showtime/TMC/Flix, Starz/Encore, Cinemax or Playboy).
Video-On-Demand: Yes
Pay-Per-View
Playboy TV (delivered digitally); Club Jenna (delivered digitally); Fresh (delivered digitally); Shorteez (delivered digitally); Hot Choice (delivered digitally); ESPN (delivered digitally); NBA League Pass (delivered digitally); NHL Center Ice (delivered digitally); MLB Extra Innings (delivered digitally).
Internet Service
Operational: Yes.
Broadband Service: Road Runner.
President: Stephen Fry. Vice President, Operations: Ken Fuchs. Vice President, Engineering: Al Costanzi. Vice President, Marketing: Patrick Burke. Vice President, Public Affairs: William Jasso. Manager: Daryl Morrison.
Ownership: Time Warner Cable (MSO).

MESHOPPEN—Blue Ridge Communications, 613 3rd St, PO Box 215, Palmerton, PA 18071-0215. Phones: 610-826-2551; 800-275-0724 (Customer service); 570-836-5422. Web Site: http://www.brctv.com. Also serves Albany Twp., Braintrim Twp., Camptown, Dallas, Dallas Twp., Eaton Twp., Eatonville, Falls Twp. (Wyoming County), Forkston Twp., Hunlock Creek, Kunkle, Laceyville, Lake Carey, Lake Winola, Lemon Twp., Mehoopany, Meshoppen Borough, Meshoppen Twp., Monroe Twp., Muhlenberg, Newton Twp. (Lackawanna County), Noxen, Overfield Twp., Sweet Valley, Terry Twp., Tunkhannock Borough, Tunkhannock Twp. (Wyoming County), Tuscarora Twp. (Bradford County), Union Twp., Washington Twp. (Wyoming County), Wilmot Twp., Windham Twp., Wyalusing Borough, Wyalusing Twp. & Wyoming County. ICA: PA0367.
TV Market Ranking: 49 (Braintrim Twp., Dallas, Dallas Twp., Eaton Twp., Eatonville, Falls Twp. (Wyoming County), Forkston Twp., Hunlock Creek, Kunkle, Laceyville, Lake Carey, Lake Winola, Lemon Twp., Mehoopany, MESHOPPEN, Meshoppen Borough, Meshoppen Twp., Monroe Twp., Muhlenberg, Newton Twp. (Lackawanna County), Noxen, Overfield Twp., Sweet Valley, Terry Twp., Tunkhannock Borough, Tunkhannock Twp. (Wyoming County), Tuscarora Twp. (Bradford County), Union Twp., Washington Twp. (Wyoming County), Wilmot Twp., Windham Twp., Wyoming County); Below 100 (Camptown, Wyalusing Borough, Wyalusing Twp.); Outside TV Markets (Albany Twp.). Franchise award date: N.A. Franchise expiration date: N.A. Began: September 1, 1966.
Channel capacity: 42 (operating 2-way). Channels available but not in use: N.A.
Basic Service
Subscribers: 7,556.
Programming (received off-air): WBNG-TV (CBS, CW) Binghamton; WBRE-TV (NBC) Wilkes-Barre; WICZ-TV (FOX) Binghamton; WNEP-TV (ABC) Scranton; WOLF-TV (CW, FOX, MNT) Hazleton; WPIX (CW, IND) New York; WQMY (MNT) Williamsport; WQPX-TV (ION) Scranton; WSKG-TV (PBS) Binghamton; WSWB (CW) Scranton; WVIA-TV (PBS) Scranton; WYOU (CBS) Scranton.
Programming (via satellite): WGN America.
Fee: $22.50 installation; $17.43 monthly.
Expanded Basic Service 1
Subscribers: N.A.
Programming (via satellite): A&E Networks; ABC Family Channel; AMC; Animal Planet; Bravo; Cartoon Network; CNBC; CNN; Comedy Central; Country Music TV; C-SPAN; Discovery Channel; Discovery Health Channel; Disney Channel; E! Entertainment Television; ESPN; ESPN 2; Eternal Word TV Network; Food Network; Fox News Channel; FX; GSN; Hallmark Channel; Headline News; HGTV; History Channel; INSP; Lifetime; Lifetime Movie Network; MSG; MSNBC; MTV; National Geographic Channel; NFL Network; Nickelodeon; Pennsylvania Cable Network; QVC; Root Sports Pittsburgh; SoapNet; Speed; Spike TV; SportsNet New York; Syfy; TBS Superstation; The Learning Channel; The Weather Channel; Travel Channel; truTV; Turner Classic Movies; Turner Network TV; TV Land; USA Network; Versus; VH1; WE tv; Yankees Entertainment & Sports.
Fee: $31.95 monthly.
Digital Basic Service
Subscribers: N.A.
Programming (via satellite): BBC America; Bio; Bloomberg Television; CMT Pure Country; Discovery Fit & Health; Discovery Home Channel; Discovery Kids Channel; Discovery Times Channel; ESPN Classic Sports; ESPNews; Fox College Sports Atlantic; Fox College Sports Central; Fox College Sports Pacific; Fox Movie Channel; Fox Soccer; G4; Golf Channel; Great American Country; Halogen Network; History Channel International; Independent Film Channel; Military Channel; MTV Hits; MTV2; Music Choice; Nick Jr.; Outdoor Channel; PBS Kids Sprout; RFD-TV; Science; ShopNBC; Style Network; TeenNick; Toon Disney; Trinity Broadcasting Network; VH1 Classic; VH1 Soul.
Fee: $35.00 installation; $14.95 monthly.
Digital Pay Service 1
Pay Units: N.A.
Programming (via satellite): Cinemax (multiplexed); Encore (multiplexed); Flix; HBO (multiplexed); Showtime (multiplexed); Starz (multiplexed); Sundance Channel; The Movie Channel (multiplexed).
Fee: $12.50 monthly (Cinemax, TMC or Showtime/Flix/Sundance), $12.95 monthly (Starz/Encore), $13.50 monthly (HBO).
Video-On-Demand: No
Pay-Per-View
iN DEMAND; iN DEMAND (delivered digitally); Sports PPV (delivered digitally); Adult PPV (delivered digitally).
Internet Service
Operational: Yes.
Broadband Service: ProLog Express.
Fee: $50.00 installation; $36.95 monthly; $10.00 modem lease; $59.95 modem purchase.
Telephone Service
None
Miles of Plant: 178.0 (coaxial); None (fiber optic).
Vice President, Operations: Richard Semmel. General Manager: Mark Masonheimer. Chief Technician: Randy Semmel.
Ownership: Pencor Services Inc. (MSO).

MediaPrints™
Map a Winning Business Strategy

METAL TWP.—Valley Cable Systems, 21700 Path Valley Rd, PO Box 1078, Doylesburg, PA 17219. Phone: 717-349-7717. ICA: PA0330.
TV Market Ranking: Below 100 (METAL TWP.). Franchise award date: January 1, 1987. Franchise expiration date: January 1, 2007. Began: January 1, 1987.
Channel capacity: N.A. Channels available but not in use: N.A.
Basic Service
Subscribers: 100.
Programming (received off-air): WDCA (MNT) Washington; WGAL (NBC) Lancaster; WHAG-TV (NBC) Hagerstown; WHP-TV (CBS, MNT) Harrisburg; WHTM-TV (ABC) Harrisburg; WITF-TV (PBS) Harrisburg; WJAC-TV (NBC) Johnstown; WJAL (IND) Hagerstown; WJLA-TV (ABC) Washington; WLYH-TV (CW) Lancaster; WMPT (PBS) Annapolis; WPMT (FOX) York; WTAJ-TV (CBS) Altoona; WTTG (FOX) Washington.
Programming (via satellite): ABC Family Channel; CNBC; CNN; Country Music TV; Discovery Channel; Disney Channel; ESPN; ESPN 2; MTV; Nickelodeon; QVC; Spike TV; TBS Superstation; The Weather Channel; Turner Network TV; USA Network; VH1; WGN America.
Fee: $40.00 installation; $17.95 monthly.
Pay Service 1
Pay Units: 14.
Programming (via satellite): The Movie Channel.
Fee: $9.54 monthly.
Internet Service
Operational: No.
Miles of Plant: 10.0 (coaxial); None (fiber optic). Additional miles planned: 5.0 (coaxial).
Manager & Chief Technician: Barry L. Kepner.
Ownership: Valley Cable Systems (MSO).

MEYERSDALE—Comcast Cable, 15 Summit Park Dr, Pittsburgh, PA 15275. Phones: 301-895-4375 (Grantsville, MD office); 412-747-6400. Fax: 412-747-6401. Web Site: http://www.comcast.com. Also serves Summit Twp. (Somerset County). ICA: PA0192.
TV Market Ranking: Outside TV Markets (MEYERSDALE, Summit Twp. (Somerset County)). Franchise award date: N.A. Franchise expiration date: N.A. Began: January 1, 1951.
Channel capacity: 30 (operating 2-way). Channels available but not in use: N.A.
Basic Service
Subscribers: 1,418.
Programming (received off-air): WGRZ (NBC) Buffalo; WIVB-TV (CBS) Buffalo; WJAC-TV (NBC) Johnstown; WKBW-TV (ABC) Buffalo; WPSU-TV (PBS) Clearfield; WQED (PBS) Pittsburgh; WTAJ-TV (CBS) Altoona; WWCP-TV (FOX) Johnstown.
Programming (via satellite): TV Guide Network; WGN America; WPIX (CW, IND) New York.
Fee: $39.95 installation; $39.95 monthly; $2.00 converter.
Expanded Basic Service 1
Subscribers: 1,286.
Programming (via satellite): A&E Networks; ABC Family Channel; AMC; Animal Planet; Cartoon Network; CNBC; CNN; Comedy Central; Country Music TV; C-SPAN; C-SPAN 2; Discovery Channel; Disney Channel; E! Entertainment Television; ESPN; ESPN 2; Eternal Word TV Network; Food Network; Fox News Channel; FX; Hallmark Channel; Headline News; HGTV; History Channel; INSP; Lifetime; MSNBC; MTV; Nickelodeon; Oxygen; Pennsylvania Cable Network; QVC; Root Sports Pittsburgh; ShopNBC; Spike TV; Syfy; TBS Superstation; The Learning Channel; The Weather Channel; Travel Channel; Trinity Broadcasting Network; truTV; Turner Classic Movies; Turner Network TV; TV Land; USA Network; VH1.
Fee: $39.30 installation; $38.00 monthly.
Digital Basic Service
Subscribers: N.A.
Programming (via satellite): AmericanLife TV Network; BBC America; Black Family Channel; Bloomberg Television; Discovery Fit & Health; ESPNews; Fox Movie Channel; Fox Sports World; Fuse; G4; GAS; Golf Channel; Great American Country; GSN; Halogen Network; Lifetime Movie Network; MTV; MTV Networks Digital Suite; MTV2; National Geographic Channel; Nick Jr.; Nick Too; NickToons TV; SoapNet; Speed; Style Network; The Word Network; Toon Disney; Trinity Broadcasting Network; WE tv.
Fee: $15.95 monthly.
Pay Service 1
Pay Units: 110.
Programming (via satellite): HBO.
Fee: $9.45 monthly.
Digital Pay Service 1
Pay Units: N.A.
Programming (via satellite): Cinemax (multiplexed); Encore; HBO (multiplexed); Showtime (multiplexed).
Video-On-Demand: No
Pay-Per-View
Movies & Events (delivered digitally); Sports PPV (delivered digitally).
Telephone Service
None
Miles of Plant: 36.0 (coaxial); None (fiber optic).
Regional Vice President: Linda Hossinger. Vice President, Marketing: Donna Corning. Vice President, Technical Operations: Randy Bender. Vice President, Public Affairs: Jody Doherty. Manager: Barry Savage.
Ownership: Comcast Cable Communications Inc. (MSO).

MIDLAND—Comcast Cable. Now served by BEAVER FALLS, PA [PA0065]. ICA: PA0456.

MIDWAY—Formerly served by Adelphia Communications. Now served by BETHEL PARK, PA [PA0318]. ICA: PA0187.

MIFFLINBURG—Atlantic Broadband, 120 Southmont Blvd, Johnstown, PA 15905. Phones: 888-536-9600; 814-539-8971. Fax: 814-539-7749. E-mail: info@atlanticbb.com. Web Site: http://www.atlanticbb.com. Also serves Buffalo Twp. (Union County), Decatur Twp. (Mifflin County), Gleniron,

Hartleton, Hartley Twp., Laurelton, Lewis Twp. (Union County), Limestone Twp. (Union County), Millmont, Swengel, Union County, Weikert & West Buffalo Twp. (portions). ICA: PA0131.

TV Market Ranking: Below 100 (Buffalo Twp. (Union County), Gleniron, Hartleton, Hartley Twp., Laurelton, Lewis Twp. (Union County), Limestone Twp. (Union County), MIFFLINBURG, Millmont, Swengel, Union County, Weikert, West Buffalo Twp. (portions)); Outside TV Markets (Decatur Twp. (Mifflin County), Lewis Twp. (Union County)). Franchise award date: N.A. Franchise expiration date: N.A. Began: October 17, 1962.

Channel capacity: N.A. Channels available but not in use: N.A.

Basic Service

Subscribers: 1,249.

Programming (received off-air): WBRE-TV (NBC) Wilkes-Barre; WGAL (NBC) Lancaster; WHTM-TV (ABC) Harrisburg; WITF-TV (PBS) Harrisburg; WLYH-TV (CW) Lancaster; WNEP-TV (ABC) Scranton; WOLF-TV (CW, FOX, MNT) Hazleton; WVIA-TV (PBS) Scranton; WYOU (CBS) Scranton; allband FM.

Programming (via satellite): QVC; WPIX (CW, IND) New York.

Fee: $25.00 installation; $18.45 monthly.

Expanded Basic Service 1

Subscribers: 1,221.

Programming (via satellite): A&E Networks; ABC Family Channel; AMC; Animal Planet; Bravo; Cartoon Network; CNN; Comedy Central; Country Music TV; C-SPAN; Discovery Channel; Discovery Health Channel; Disney Channel; E! Entertainment Television; ESPN; ESPN 2; Eternal Word TV Network; Food Network; Fox News Channel; FX; Hallmark Channel; Headline News; HGTV; History Channel; Lifetime; MSNBC; MTV; National Geographic Channel; Nickelodeon; Outdoor Channel; Oxygen; Root Sports Pittsburgh; Speed; Spike TV; Syfy; TBS Superstation; The Learning Channel; The Weather Channel; Travel Channel; truTV; Turner Network TV; TV Land; USA Network; VH1.

Fee: $31.04 monthly.

Digital Basic Service

Subscribers: N.A.

Programming (via satellite): BBC America; Bio; CMT Pure Country; Discovery Home Channel; Discovery Kids Channel; Discovery Times Channel; DMX Music; Encore (multiplexed); ESPNews; Fuse; GAS; History Channel International; Independent Film Channel; MTV2; Nick Jr.; Science; Starz; Toon Disney; VH1 Classic; WE tv.

Fee: $18.95 monthly.

Digital Pay Service 1

Pay Units: N.A.

Programming (via satellite): Cinemax (multiplexed); HBO (multiplexed); Showtime (multiplexed); The Movie Channel (multiplexed).

Fee: $14.95 monthly (HBO, Cinemax or Showtime/TMC).

Video-On-Demand: No

Pay-Per-View

iN DEMAND (delivered digitally); Club Jenna (delivered digitally); Playboy TV (delivered digitally).

Internet Service

Operational: Yes.

Broadband Service: Atlantic Broadband High-Speed Internet.

Fee: $23.95-$30.95 monthly.

Telephone Service

None

Miles of Plant: 137.0 (coaxial); None (fiber optic).

Vice President: David Dane. General Manager: Mike Papasergi. Technical Operations Director: Charles Sorchilla. Marketing & Customer Service Director: Dara Leslie. Marketing Manager: Natalie Kurchak.

Ownership: Atlantic Broadband (MSO).

MIFFLINBURG (portions)—Windstream. Formerly served by Lewisburg, PA [PA0390]. This cable system has converted to IPTV, 4001 Rodney Parham Rd, Little Rock, AR 17522. Phones: 800-347-1991; 501-748-7000. Fax: 877-807-9463. Web Site: http://www.windstream.com. ICA: PA5139.

TV Market Ranking: Below 100 (MIFFLINBURG (PORTIONS)).

Channel capacity: N.A. Channels available but not in use: N.A.

Internet Service

Operational: Yes.

Telephone Service

Digital: Operational

President & Chief Executive Officer: Jeff Gardner. Chief Operating Officer: Brent Whittington.

MIFFLINTOWN—Nittany Media Inc. Now served by LEWISTOWN (formerly McAlisterville), PA [PA0365]. ICA: PA0368.

MILFORD—Blue Ridge Communications, 613 3rd St, PO Box 215, Palmerton, PA 18071-0215. Phones: 610-826-2551; 570-296-8200. Web Site: http://www.brctv.com. Also serves Dingman Twp., Lackawaxen Twp., Milford Twp. (Pike County), Rowland & Shohola Twp. ICA: PA0369.

TV Market Ranking: 49 (Lackawaxen Twp., Rowland, Shohola Twp.); Below 100 (Dingman Twp., MILFORD, Milford Twp. (Pike County)). Franchise award date: N.A. Franchise expiration date: N.A. Began: December 1, 1965.

Channel capacity: 42 (operating 2-way). Channels available but not in use: N.A.

Basic Service

Subscribers: 13,010.

Programming (received off-air): WABC-TV (ABC) New York; WCBS-TV (CBS) New York; WMBC-TV (IND) Newton; WNBC (NBC) New York; WNEP-TV (ABC) Scranton; WNET (PBS) Newark; WNYW (FOX) New York; WOLF-TV (CW, FOX, MNT) Hazleton; WPHL-TV (MNT, IND) Philadelphia; WPIX (CW, IND) New York; WSKG-TV (PBS) Binghamton; WTBY-TV (TBN) Poughkeepsie; WVIA-TV (PBS) Scranton; WWOR-TV (MNT) Secaucus; WYOU (CBS) Scranton; allband FM.

Programming (via satellite): Pennsylvania Cable Network.

Fee: $22.50 installation; $16.49 monthly.

Expanded Basic Service 1

Subscribers: N.A.

Programming (via satellite): A&E Networks; ABC Family Channel; AMC; Animal Planet; Cartoon Network; CNBC; CNN; Comedy Central; Country Music TV; C-SPAN; Discovery Channel; Discovery Health Channel; Disney Channel; E! Entertainment Television; ESPN; ESPN 2; Eternal Word TV Network; Food Network; Fox News Channel; FX; Golf Channel; Headline News; HGTV; History Channel; Lifetime; Lifetime Movie Network; MSG; MSNBC; MTV; Nickelodeon; QVC; Speed; Spike TV; Syfy; TBS Superstation; The Learning Channel; The Weather Channel; Travel Channel; truTV; Turner Classic Movies; Turner Network TV; TV Guide Network; TV Land; USA Network; Versus; VH1; WE tv; Yankees Entertainment & Sports.

Fee: $28.09 monthly.

Digital Basic Service

Subscribers: N.A.

Programming (via satellite): Concert TV; Discovery Digital Networks; Fox Movie Channel; FSN Digital Atlantic; FSN Digital Central; FSN Digital Pacific; GAS; Halogen Network; Meadows Racing Network; MTV Networks Digital Suite; Music Choice; National Geographic Channel; Nick Jr.; Nick Too; NickToons TV; Outdoor Channel; PBS Kids Channel; SoapNet; Toon Disney.

Fee: $35.00 installation; $9.95 monthly.

Digital Expanded Basic Service

Subscribers: N.A.

Programming (via satellite): BBC America; Bio; Bloomberg Television; Boomerang; Cooking Channel; DIY Network; G4; Hallmark Channel; History Channel International; Lifetime Real Women; Style Network.

Fee: $5.00 monthly.

Pay Service 1

Pay Units: 344.

Programming (via satellite): Cinemax; HBO; Showtime.

Fee: $11.50 monthly (Cinemax or Showtime), $12.50 monthly (HBO).

Digital Pay Service 1

Pay Units: N.A.

Programming (via satellite): Cinemax (multiplexed); Encore (multiplexed); Flix; HBO (multiplexed); Showtime (multiplexed); Starz (multiplexed); Sundance Channel; The Movie Channel (multiplexed).

Fee: $12.50 monthly (Cinemax or Showtime/Flix/Sundance/TMC), $12.95 monthly (Starz/Encore), $13.50 monthly (HBO).

Video-On-Demand: Yes

Pay-Per-View

iN DEMAND; iN DEMAND (delivered digitally); adult (delivered digitally); Barker (delivered digitally); sports (delivered digitally).

Internet Service

Operational: Yes.

Broadband Service: ProLog Express.

Fee: $34.95 monthly; $10.00 modem lease; $59.95 modem purchase.

Telephone Service

None

Miles of Plant: 18.0 (coaxial); None (fiber optic). Additional miles planned: 20.0 (coaxial).

Vice President, Operations: Richard Semmel. General Manager: Mark Masonheimer. Fiber Manager: Randy Semmel. Chief Technician: Garry Woods.

Ownership: Pencor Services Inc. (MSO).

MILL VILLAGE—Formerly served by Cebridge Connections. Now served by MEADVILLE, PA [PA0062]. ICA: PA0277.

MILLBOURNE—RCN Corp. Formerly served by Philadelphia (suburbs), PA [PA0447]. This cable system has converted to IPTV, 196 Van Buren St, Herndon, VA 20170. Phone: 703-434-8200. Web Site: http://www.rcn.com. ICA: PA5256.

Channel capacity: N.A. Channels available but not in use: N.A.

Internet Service

Operational: Yes.

Chairman: Steven J. Simmons. Chief Executive Officer: Jim Holanda.

MILLERSBURG—Comcast Cable. Now served by LEBANON, PA [PA0024]. ICA: PA0373.

MILLHEIM—Millheim TV Transmission Co., PO Box 365, Millheim, PA 16854-0365. Phone: 814-349-4837. Fax: 814-349-5857. Also serves Aaronsburg, Coburn & Spring Mills. ICA: PA0216.

TV Market Ranking: Below 100 (Aaronsburg, Coburn, MILLHEIM, Spring Mills). Franchise award date: January 1, 1996. Franchise expiration date: N.A. Began: January 1, 1962.

Channel capacity: 36 (not 2-way capable). Channels available but not in use: N.A.

Basic Service

Subscribers: 951.

Programming (received off-air): WBRE-TV (NBC) Wilkes-Barre; WHTM-TV (ABC) Harrisburg; WJAC-TV (NBC) Johnstown; WKBS-TV (IND) Altoona; WNEP-TV (ABC) Scranton; WOLF-TV (CW, FOX, MNT) Hazleton; WSWB (CW) Scranton; WTAJ-TV (CBS) Altoona; WVIA-TV (PBS) Scranton; allband FM.

Programming (via satellite): A&E Networks; ABC Family Channel; AMC; Animal Planet; CNN; Country Music TV; Discovery Channel; Disney Channel; ESPN; ESPN 2; Fox News Channel; FX; History Channel; Nickelodeon; Outdoor Channel; QVC; Root Sports Pittsburgh; Spike TV; TBS Superstation; The Learning Channel; Turner Network TV; TV Land; USA Network; WGN America; WPIX (CW, IND) New York.

Fee: $135.00 installation; $25.00 monthly.

Pay Service 1

Pay Units: 410.

Programming (via satellite): HBO.

Fee: $10.00 installation; $10.00 monthly.

Video-On-Demand: No

Internet Service

Operational: No.

Telephone Service

None

Miles of Plant: 32.0 (coaxial); None (fiber optic).

Manager: Wayne Rishel. Technical Engineer: David McClintick. Office Manager: Vickie Saserman.

Ownership: Millheim TV Transmission Co.

MILLMONT—Formerly served by D&E Communications. No longer in operation. ICA: PA5283.

MONROEVILLE—Comcast Cable, 15 Summit Park Dr, Pittsburgh, PA 15275. Phones: 412-747-6400; 412-856-4288. Fax: 412-747-6401. Web Site: http://www.comcast.com. Also serves Braddock, Churchill, East McKeesport, East Pittsburgh, North Braddock, North Versailles Twp., Plum, Rankin, Swissvale, Trafford, Turtle Creek, Upper Burrell Twp. & Wilkins Twp. ICA: PA0023.

TV Market Ranking: 10 (Braddock, Churchill, East McKeesport, East Pittsburgh, MONROEVILLE, North Braddock, North Versailles Twp., Plum, Rankin, Swissvale, Trafford, Turtle Creek, Upper Burrell Twp., Wilkins Twp.). Franchise award date: N.A. Franchise expiration date: N.A. Began: January 1, 1966.

Channel capacity: 110 (operating 2-way). Channels available but not in use: N.A.

Basic Service

Subscribers: 27,173.

Programming (received off-air): KDKA-TV (CBS) Pittsburgh; WINP-TV (IND, ION) Pittsburgh; WPCB-TV (IND) Greensburg;

WPCW (CW) Jeannette; WPGH-TV (FOX) Pittsburgh; WPMY (MNT) Pittsburgh; WPXI (IND, NBC) Pittsburgh; WQED (PBS) Pittsburgh; WTAE-TV (ABC) Pittsburgh.
Programming (via satellite): C-SPAN; C-SPAN 2; Eternal Word TV Network; QVC; The Weather Channel; TV Guide Network; WGN America.
Fee: $43.99 installation; $11.99 monthly; $19.95 additional installation.

Expanded Basic Service 1
Subscribers: N.A.
Programming (via microwave): Pittsburgh Cable News Channel.
Programming (via satellite): A&E Networks; ABC Family Channel; AMC; Animal Planet; BET Networks; Cartoon Network; CNBC; CNN; Comedy Central; Discovery Channel; Disney Channel; E! Entertainment Television; ESPN; ESPN 2; Food Network; Fox News Channel; FX; G4; Golf Channel; GSN; Hallmark Channel; Headline News; HGTV; History Channel; ION Television; Lifetime; MSNBC; MTV; Nickelodeon; Oxygen; Pennsylvania Cable Network; Root Sports Pittsburgh; Spike TV; Style Network; TBS Superstation; The Learning Channel; Travel Channel; truTV; Turner Classic Movies; Turner Network TV; TV Land; USA Network; Versus; VH1.
Fee: $40.41 monthly.

Digital Basic Service
Subscribers: N.A.
Programming (via satellite): A&E HD; BBC America; Bio; Bloomberg Television; Bravo; CMT Pure Country; Cooking Channel; Country Music TV; C-SPAN 3; Current; Daystar TV Network; DIY Network; Encore (multiplexed); ESPN 2 HD; ESPN Classic Sports; ESPN HD; Flix; Fox Reality Channel; Fox Soccer; Fuse; GAS; GMC; Great American Country; Halogen Network; HD Theater; History Channel International; HRTV; Independent Film Channel; Jewelry Television; Lifetime Movie Network; LOGO; MTV Networks Digital Suite; Music Choice; National Geographic Channel; National Geographic Channel HD Network; Nick Jr.; Nick Too; NickToons TV; Outdoor Channel; Palladia; PBS Kids Sprout; ShopNBC; SoapNet; Speed; Sundance Channel; Syfy; The Comcast Network; The Word Network; Toon Disney; Trinity Broadcasting Network; Turner Network TV HD; TV One; Universal HD; WE tv; Weatherscan.
Fee: $10.99 monthly.

Digital Pay Service 1
Pay Units: N.A.
Programming (via satellite): Cinemax (multiplexed); Cinemax HD; HBO (multiplexed); HBO HD; Playboy TV; RAI International; Russian Television Network; Showtime (multiplexed); Showtime HD; Starz (multiplexed); Starz HDTV; The Movie Channel (multiplexed); TV Asia; Zee TV USA.
Fee: $8.00 monthly (each).

Video-On-Demand: Yes

Pay-Per-View
Hot Choice (delivered digitally); Playgirl TV (delivered digitally); MLB Extra Innings (delivered digitally); iN DEMAND; iN DEMAND (delivered digitally); Fresh (delivered digitally); Sports PPV (delivered digitally); NBA League Pass (delivered digitally); NHL Center Ice (delivered digitally).

Internet Service
Operational: Yes.
Broadband Service: Comcast High Speed Internet.
Fee: $42.95 monthly.

Telephone Service
Digital: Operational
Fee: $44.95 monthly

Miles of Plant: 347.0 (coaxial); None (fiber optic).
Regional Vice President: Linda Hossinger. Vice President, Technical Operations: Randy Bender. Vice President, Marketing: Donna Corning. Vice President, Public Affairs: Jody Doherty.
Ownership: Comcast Cable Communications Inc. (MSO).

MONTGOMERY—Comcast Cable. Now served by WILLIAMSPORT, PA [PA0040]. ICA: PA0056.

MONTROSE—Time Warner Cable, 120 Plaza Dr, Vestal, NY 13850-3658. Phone: 607-644-0646. Fax: 607-644-1501. Web Site: http://www.timewarnercable.com. Also serves Bridgewater Twp., Dimock Twp. & Springville. ICA: PA0171.
TV Market Ranking: 49 (Bridgewater Twp., Dimock Twp., MONTROSE, Springville). Franchise award date: N.A. Franchise expiration date: N.A. Began: December 1, 1984.
Channel capacity: N.A. Channels available but not in use: N.A.

Basic Service
Subscribers: N.A. Included in Binghamton
Programming (received off-air): WBNG-TV (CBS, CW) Binghamton; WICZ-TV (FOX) Binghamton; WIVT (ABC) Binghamton; WNEP-TV (ABC) Scranton; WOLF-TV (CW, FOX, MNT) Hazleton; WQPX-TV (ION) Scranton; WSKG-TV (PBS) Binghamton; WSWB (CW) Scranton; WVIA-TV (PBS) Scranton; WYOU (CBS) Scranton.
Programming (via satellite): QVC; TBS Superstation.
Fee: $47.21 installation; $10.00 monthly.

Expanded Basic Service 1
Subscribers: N.A.
Programming (via satellite): A&E Networks; ABC Family Channel; AMC; Animal Planet; BET Networks; Bravo; Cartoon Network; CNBC; CNN; Comedy Central; Country Music TV; C-SPAN; Discovery Channel; Discovery Fit & Health; Disney Channel; E! Entertainment Television; ESPN; ESPN 2; ESPN Classic Sports; Eternal Word TV Network; Food Network; Fox News Channel; Fuse; FX; Golf Channel; GSN; Hallmark Channel; Headline News; HGTV; History Channel; Lifetime; Lifetime Movie Network; MoviePlex; MSG; MSG Plus; MSNBC; MTV; MTV2; National Geographic Channel; Nickelodeon; Oxygen; SoapNet; Speed; Spike TV; Style Network; Syfy; The Learning Channel; The Weather Channel; Travel Channel; truTV; Turner Classic Movies; Turner Network TV; TV Land; USA Network; Versus; VH1; WE tv; Yesterday USA.
Fee: $29.36 monthly.

Digital Basic Service
Subscribers: N.A. Included in Binghamton
Programming (via satellite): American-Life TV Network; America's Store; BBC America; Bio; Bloomberg Television; Cooking Channel; C-SPAN 3; Discovery Kids Channel; DIY Network; Encore Action; ESPNews; Fox Movie Channel; Fox Sports World; G4; GAS; Great American Country; History Channel International; Independent Film Channel; Lifetime Real Women; Music Choice; Nick Jr.; Outdoor Channel; Ovation; Sundance Channel; Toon Disney; Trinity Broadcasting Network; VH1 Classic; WAM! America's Kidz Network.
Fee: $8.45 monthly.

Digital Expanded Basic Service
Subscribers: N.A.
Programming (via satellite): ESPNews; Fox Sports Net; Fox Sports World; Fuel TV; NBA TV; Tennis Channel.
Fee: $4.95 monthly.

Digital Pay Service 1
Pay Units: 865.
Programming (via satellite): Canales N; Cinemax (multiplexed); Flix; HBO (multiplexed); Showtime (multiplexed); Starz; TV Asia; Zee TV USA.
Fee: $11.25 monthly (Cinemax, HBO, Starz, or Showtime/TMC), $19.95 monthly (TV Asia or Zee TV).

Video-On-Demand: Yes

Pay-Per-View
Addressable homes: 412.
iN DEMAND (delivered digitally); Pleasure (delivered digitally); Shorteez (delivered digitally); Fresh (delivered digitally); Playboy TV (delivered digitally); Hot Choice (delivered digitally).

Internet Service
Operational: Yes.
Broadband Service: Road Runner.
Fee: $39.95 installation; $44.95 monthly.

Telephone Service
Digital: Operational
Fee: $39.95 monthly

Miles of plant included in Binghamton
President: Mary Cotter. Vice President & General Manager: Chris Strahm. Vice President, Marketing: John Melvany. Vice President, Public Affairs: Dave Whalen. Technical Operations Director: Bruce Tomkins.
Ownership: Time Warner Cable (MSO).; Advance/Newhouse Partnership (MSO).

MONUMENT—Formerly served by Monument TV. No longer in operation. ICA: PA0376.

MOORE TWP.—Formerly served by NORTHAMPTON BOROUGH, PA [PA0008]. RCN Corp. This cable system has converted to IPTV, 196 Van Buren St, Herndon, VA 20170. Phone: 703-434-8200. Web Site: http://www.rcn.com. ICA: PA5224.
TV Market Ranking: Below 100 (MOORE TWP.).
Channel capacity: N.A. Channels available but not in use: N.A.

Internet Service
Operational: Yes.

Telephone Service
Digital: Operational

Chairman: Steven J. Simmons. Chief Executive Officer: Jim Holanda.

MORTON—RCN Corp. Formerly served by Philadelphia (suburbs), PA [PA0447]. This cable system has converted to IPTV, 196 Van Buren St, Herndon, VA 20170. Phone: 703-434-8200. Web Site: http://www.rcn.com. ICA: PA5257.
Channel capacity: N.A. Channels available but not in use: N.A.

Internet Service
Operational: Yes.

Chairman: Steven J. Simmons. Chief Executive Officer: Jim Holanda.

MOUNT MORRIS—Comcast Cable. Now served by WAYNESBURG, PA [PA0134]. ICA: PA0254.

MOUNT OLIVER—Mount Oliver TV Cable/Adelphia Cable. Now served by BETHEL PARK, PA [PA0318]. ICA: PA0162.

MOUNT PLEASANT MILLS—Zampelli Electronics, PO Box 830, Lewistown, PA 17044-0830. Phone: 717-248-1544. Also serves Monroe, Port Trevorton & West Perry Twp. ICA: PA0377.
TV Market Ranking: 57 (Monroe (Juniata County), MOUNT PLEASANT MILLS, West Perry Twp.); Outside TV Markets (Port Trevorton). Franchise award date: N.A. Franchise expiration date: N.A. Began: January 1, 1965.
Channel capacity: 18 (not 2-way capable). Channels available but not in use: N.A.

Basic Service
Subscribers: N.A.
Programming (received off-air): WBRE-TV (NBC) Wilkes-Barre; WGAL (NBC) Lancaster; WGCB-TV (IND) Red Lion; WHP-TV (CBS, MNT) Harrisburg; WHTM-TV (ABC) Harrisburg; WITF-TV (PBS) Harrisburg; WLYH-TV (CW) Lancaster; WNEP-TV (ABC) Scranton; WOLF-TV (CW, FOX, MNT) Hazleton; WPHL-TV (MNT, IND) Philadelphia; WPMT (FOX) York; WTXF-TV (FOX) Philadelphia; WVIA-TV (PBS) Scranton.
Programming (via satellite): Discovery Channel; ESPN; Spike TV; TBS Superstation; USA Network; WGN America.

Video-On-Demand: No

Internet Service
Operational: No.

Telephone Service
None

Miles of Plant: 25.0 (coaxial); None (fiber optic).
Manager & Chief Technician: Joe Zampelli.
Ownership: Zampelli TV (MSO).

MURRYSVILLE—Formerly served by Adelphia Communications. No longer in operation. ICA: PA0378.

NANTY GLO—Formerly served by Adelphia Communications. Now served by ADAMS TWP. (Cambria County), PA [PA0133]. ICA: PA0145.

NAZARETH BOROUGH—Formerly served by NORTHAMPTON BOROUGH, PA [PA0008]. RCN Corp. This cable system has converted to IPTV, 196 Van Buren St, Herndon, VA 20170. Phone: 703-434-8200. Web Site: http://www.rcn.com. ICA: PA5225.
TV Market Ranking: Below 100 (NAZARETH BOROUGH).
Channel capacity: N.A. Channels available but not in use: N.A.

Internet Service
Operational: Yes.

Telephone Service
Digital: Operational

Chairman: Steven J. Simmons. Chief Executive Officer: Jim Holanda.

NEELYTON—Formerly served by Valley Cable Systems. No longer in operation. ICA: PA0298.

NEW BALTIMORE—Laurel Cable LP, PO Box 125, Berlin, PA 15530-0125. Phones: 800-732-5604; 814-443-6250. Fax: 814-445-1896. Also serves Allegheny Twp. (Somerset County). ICA: PA0292.

TV Market Ranking: 74 (Allegheny Twp. (Somerset County), NEW BALTIMORE). Franchise award date: N.A. Franchise expiration date: N.A. Began: July 1, 1979.

Channel capacity: 40 (not 2-way capable). Channels available but not in use: N.A.

Basic Service

Subscribers: 150.

Programming (received off-air): KDKA-TV (CBS) Pittsburgh; WATM-TV (ABC) Altoona; WHAG-TV (NBC) Hagerstown; WJAC-TV (NBC) Johnstown; WKBS-TV (IND) Altoona; WPCW (CW) Jeannette; WPSU-TV (PBS) Clearfield; WTAE-TV (ABC) Pittsburgh; WTAJ-TV (CBS) Altoona; WWCP-TV (FOX) Johnstown; WWPB (PBS) Hagerstown.

Programming (via satellite): A&E Networks; ABC Family Channel; CNN; Country Music TV; C-SPAN; Discovery Channel; Disney Channel; ESPN; ESPN 2; Headline News; HGTV; Lifetime; Root Sports Pittsburgh; Spike TV; TBS Superstation; The Learning Channel; The Weather Channel; Turner Classic Movies; Turner Network TV; USA Network.

Fee: $29.50 monthly.

Pay Service 1

Pay Units: 15.

Programming (via satellite): HBO.

Fee: $10.50 monthly.

Video-On-Demand: No

Internet Service

Operational: No.

Telephone Service

None

Miles of Plant: 4.0 (coaxial); None (fiber optic).

Manager: Angela Miller. Chief Technician: Kevin Custer.

Ownership: Laurel Cable LP.

NEW BETHLEHEM—Formerly served by Adelphia Communications. Now served by PUNXSUTAWNEY, PA [PA0397]. ICA: PA0167.

NEW BLOOMFIELD—Nittany Media Inc. Now served by LEWISTOWN (formerly McAlisterville), PA [PA0365]. ICA: PA0380.

NEW CASTLE—Comcast Cable. Now served by NEW MIDDLETOWN, OH [OH0145]. ICA: PA0041.

NEW COLUMBIA—Formerly served by D&E Communications. No longer in operation. ICA: PA5285.

NEW MILFORD TWP.—Formerly served by Adams Cable Service. Now served by CARBONDALE, PA [PA0067]. ICA: PA0381.

NEW WILMINGTON—Armstrong Cable Services, 660 S Benbrook Rd, Butler, PA 16001. Phones: 877-277-5711; 724-482-4885. Fax: 724-482-4884. E-mail: info@zoominternet.net. Web Site: http://www.cable.armstrongonewire.com. ICA: PA0382.

TV Market Ranking: 79 (NEW WILMINGTON). Franchise award date: N.A. Franchise expiration date: N.A. Began: June 1, 1979.

Channel capacity: N.A. Channels available but not in use: N.A.

Basic Service

Subscribers: 900.

Programming (received off-air): KDKA-TV (CBS) Pittsburgh; WFMJ-TV (CW, NBC) Youngstown; WKBN-TV (CBS) Youngstown; WNEO (PBS) Alliance; WPCB-TV (IND) Greensburg; WPCW (CW) Jeannette; WPGH-TV (FOX) Pittsburgh; WPMY (MNT) Pittsburgh; WPXI (IND, NBC) Pittsburgh; WQED (PBS) Pittsburgh; WTAE-TV (ABC) Pittsburgh; WYFX-LP Youngstown; WYTV (ABC, MNT) Youngstown.

Programming (via satellite): A&E Networks; ABC Family Channel; AMC; Animal Planet; Bravo; Cartoon Network; CNBC; CNN; Comedy Central; Country Music TV; C-SPAN; Discovery Channel; Discovery Health Channel; Disney Channel; ESPN; ESPN 2; ESPN Classic Sports; Food Network; Fox News Channel; FX; Headline News; HGTV; History Channel; Lifetime; MSNBC; MTV; Nickelodeon; QVC; Root Sports Pittsburgh; Speed; Spike TV; Syfy; TBS Superstation; The Learning Channel; The Weather Channel; Travel Channel; truTV; Turner Classic Movies; Turner Network TV; TV Guide Network; TV Land; USA Network; VH1; WGN America.

Fee: $25.00 installation; $29.99 monthly; $25.00 additional installation.

Video-On-Demand: No

Internet Service

Operational: Yes.

Subscribers: 155.

Broadband Service: Armstrong Zoom.

Fee: $25.00 installation; $39.95 monthly.

Telephone Service

None

Miles of Plant: 8.0 (coaxial); 8.0 (fiber optic).

General Manager: Joe Taylor.

Ownership: Armstrong Group of Companies (MSO).

NEWBERRY TWP.—Blue Ridge Communications, 613 3rd St, PO Box 215, Palmerton, PA 18071-0215. Phones: 610-826-2551; 800-232-2273 (Customer service); 717-938-6501. Web Site: http://www.brctv.com. Also serves Fairview Twp. (York County), Lewisberry, Warrington Twp. (York County), Wellsville & York Haven (York County). ICA: PA0105.

TV Market Ranking: 57 (Fairview Twp. (York County), Lewisberry, NEWBERRY TWP., Warrington Twp. (York County), Wellsville, York Haven (York County)). Franchise award date: N.A. Franchise expiration date: N.A. Began: May 1, 1982.

Channel capacity: 63 (operating 2-way). Channels available but not in use: N.A.

Basic Service

Subscribers: 5,700.

Programming (received off-air): WGAL (NBC) Lancaster; WGCB-TV (IND) Red Lion; WHP-TV (CBS, MNT) Harrisburg; WHTM-TV (ABC) Harrisburg; WITF-TV (PBS) Harrisburg; WLYH-TV (CW) Lancaster; WPHL-TV (MNT, IND) Philadelphia; WPMT (FOX) York; WTXF-TV (FOX) Philadelphia.

Fee: $22.50 installation; $11.65 monthly.

Expanded Basic Service 1

Subscribers: 5,100.

Programming (via satellite): A&E Networks; ABC Family Channel; AMC; Animal Planet; Bravo; Cartoon Network; CNBC; CNN; Comcast SportsNet Mid-Atlantic; Comcast SportsNet Philadelphia; Comedy Central; Country Music TV; C-SPAN; Discovery Channel; Discovery Health Channel; Disney Channel; E! Entertainment Television; ESPN; ESPN 2; Eternal Word TV Network; Food Network; Fox News Channel; FX; Golf Channel; GSN; Hallmark Channel; Headline News; HGTV; History Channel; INSP; Lifetime; Lifetime Movie Network; MSNBC; MTV; National Geographic Channel; Nickelodeon; QVC; Root Sports Pittsburgh; SoapNet; Speed; Spike TV; Syfy; TBS Superstation; The Learning Channel; The Weather Channel; Travel Channel; Trinity Broadcasting Network; truTV; Turner Classic Movies; Turner Network TV; TV Land; USA Network; Versus; VH1; WE tv.

Fee: $32.14 monthly.

Digital Basic Service

Subscribers: N.A.

Programming (via satellite): America's Store; Bio; Bloomberg News Radio; Boomerang; CCTV-4; Comcast SportsNet Philadelphia; Cooking Channel; Discovery Fit & Health; DIY Network; ESPN; Fox College Sports Atlantic; Fox College Sports Central; Fox College Sports Pacific; Fox Movie Channel; G4; GAS; Great American Country; Halogen Network; HDNet; HDNet Movies; History Channel International; HRTV; Independent Film Channel; Lifetime Real Women; MTV Networks Digital Suite; MTV2; NBA TV; NFL Network; Nick Jr.; Nick Too; NickToons TV; Outdoor Channel; Oxygen; PBS Kids Channel; Science Television; ShopNBC; Style Network; Tennis Channel; Toon Disney; VH1 Classic.

Fee: $14.95 monthly.

Digital Pay Service 1

Pay Units: N.A.

Programming (via satellite): Cinemax (multiplexed); Encore (multiplexed); Flix; HBO (multiplexed); HBO HD; Showtime (multiplexed); Showtime HD; Starz; Sundance Channel; The Movie Channel (multiplexed).

Fee: $12.50 monthly (Cinemax, Showtime or TMC), $12.95 monthly (Starz), $13.50 monthly (HBO).

Video-On-Demand: Yes

Pay-Per-View

Addressable homes: 350.

iN DEMAND.

Internet Service

Operational: Yes.

Broadband Service: ProLog Express.

Fee: $36.95 monthly.

Telephone Service

None

Miles of Plant: 173.0 (coaxial); 11.0 (fiber optic). Additional miles planned: 6.0 (coaxial).

Vice President, Operations: Richard Semmel. General Manager: Mark Masonheimer. Chief Technician: Randy Semmel.

Ownership: Pencor Services Inc. (MSO).

NEWBURG—Kuhn Communications. Now served by WALNUT BOTTOM, PA [PA0220]. ICA: PA0272.

NEWPORT—Comcast Cable, 1 E Uwchlan Ave, Ste 411, Exton, PA 19341. Phones: 484-288-6500; 814-238-5050 (State College office). Web Site: http://www.comcast.com. ICA: PA0454.

TV Market Ranking: 57 (NEWPORT).

Channel capacity: N.A. Channels available but not in use: N.A.

Basic Service

Subscribers: 2,100.

Programming (received off-air): W12CA Elliottsburg; WGAL (NBC) Lancaster; WGCB-TV (IND) Red Lion; WHP-TV (CBS, MNT) Harrisburg; WHTM-TV (ABC) Harrisburg; WITF-TV (PBS) Harrisburg; WLYH-TV (CW) Lancaster; WPMT (FOX) York.

Programming (via satellite): A&E Networks; ABC Family Channel; AMC; Animal Planet; Bravo; Cartoon Network; CNBC; CNN; Comedy Central; Country Music TV; C-SPAN; Discovery Channel; Disney Channel; E! Entertainment Television; ESPN; ESPN 2; Food Network; Fox News Channel; FX; Golf Channel; GSN; Hallmark Channel; HGTV; History Channel; ION Television; Lifetime; MSNBC; MTV; Nickelodeon; Oxygen; Pennsylvania Cable Network; QVC; Root Sports Pittsburgh; Speed; Spike TV; Style Network; Syfy; TBS Superstation; The Learning Channel; The Weather Channel; Travel Channel; truTV; Turner Classic Movies; Turner Network TV; TV Guide Network; TV Land; USA Network; Versus; VH1.

Pay Service 1

Pay Units: N.A.

Programming (via satellite): Cinemax (multiplexed); Encore; HBO (multiplexed); Showtime; Starz; The Movie Channel.

Pay-Per-View

iN DEMAND; Hot Choice.

Internet Service

Operational: No.

Telephone Service

None

Miles of Plant: 214.0 (coaxial); None (fiber optic). Miles of plant (coax) includes Reedsville

Area Vice President: Jim Samaha. Vice President, Marketing: Larry Goldman.

Ownership: Comcast Cable Communications Inc. (MSO).

NEWTOWN—Comcast Cable, 3220 Tillman Dr, Bensalem, PA 19010. Phone: 215-642-6400. Fax: 215-638-6510. Web Site: http://www.comcast.com. Also serves Milford Square, New Hope (Bucks County), Penns Park, Pineville, Pipersville, Upper Makefield Twp. & Wrightstown Twp. ICA: PA0083.

TV Market Ranking: 4 (Milford Square, New Hope (Bucks County), NEWTOWN (BOROUGH), Penns Park, Pineville, Pipersville, Upper Makefield Twp., Wrightstown Twp.). Franchise award date: N.A. Franchise expiration date: N.A. Began: October 26, 1983.

Channel capacity: N.A. Channels available but not in use: N.A.

Basic Service

Subscribers: N.A. Included in Bensalem Twp.

Programming (received off-air): KYW-TV (CBS) Philadelphia; WCAU (NBC) Philadelphia; WFMZ-TV (IND) Allentown; WGTW-TV (TBN) Burlington; WHYY-TV (PBS) Wilmington; WLVT-TV (PBS) Allentown; WMCN-TV (IND) Atlantic City; WNET (PBS) Newark; WNJT (PBS) Trenton; WPHL-TV (MNT, IND) Philadelphia; WPPX-TV (ION) Wilmington; WPSG (CW) Philadelphia; WPVI-TV (ABC) Philadelphia; WTVE (IND) Reading; WTXF-TV (FOX) Philadelphia; WUVP-DT (UNV) Vineland; WWSI (TMO) Atlantic City; WYBE (ETV, IND) Philadelphia.

Programming (via satellite): Animal Planet; C-SPAN; C-SPAN 2; MTV2; QVC; TBS Superstation.

Fee: $11.60 monthly.

Expanded Basic Service 1

Subscribers: N.A.

Programming (received off-air): WBPH-TV (IND) Bethlehem.

Programming (via satellite): A&E Networks; ABC Family Channel; AMC; Bravo; Cartoon Network; CNBC; CNN; Comcast

SportsNet Philadelphia; Comedy Central; Country Music TV; Discovery Channel; Discovery Health Channel; Disney Channel; E! Entertainment Television; ESPN; ESPN 2; Food Network; Fox News Channel; FX; Golf Channel; GSN; Headline News; HGTV; History Channel; Lifetime; MSNBC; MTV; Nickelodeon; Philadelphia Park Live; Speed; Spike TV; Style Network; Syfy; The Comcast Network; The Learning Channel; The Weather Channel; Travel Channel; truTV; Turner Classic Movies; Turner Network TV; TV Land; USA Network; Versus; VH1.
Fee: $40.65 monthly.

Digital Basic Service
Subscribers: N.A.
Programming (via satellite): BBC America; Bio; Cooking Channel; C-SPAN 3; Discovery Kids Channel; DIY Network; DMX Music; ESPNews; Eternal Word TV Network; Flix; FSN Digital Atlantic; FSN Digital Central; FSN Digital Pacific; G4; GAS; GolTV; History Channel International; Independent Film Channel; MTV Networks Digital Suite; National Geographic Channel; NBA TV; NFL Network; Nick Jr.; Nick Too; NickToons TV; Pennsylvania Cable Network; Science Television; ShopNBC; SoapNet; Sundance Channel; Toon Disney; WAM! America's Kidz Network; Weatherscan.

Digital Pay Service 1
Pay Units: N.A.
Programming (via satellite): Cinemax; Encore (multiplexed); HBO (multiplexed); Showtime (multiplexed); The Movie Channel (multiplexed).
Fee: $18.95 monthly (each).

Video-On-Demand: Yes

Pay-Per-View
Playboy TV (delivered digitally); Fresh (delivered digitally); Shorteez (delivered digitally); Pleasure (delivered digitally); NTV International Corp. (delivered digitally); ESPN Sports/MLS (delivered digitally); NBA TV (delivered digitally); NBA League Pass (delivered digitally); NHL Center Ice (delivered digitally); MLB Extra Innings (delivered digitally); iN DEMAND (delivered digitally).

Internet Service
Operational: Yes. Began: February 1, 2002.
Broadband Service: Comcast High Speed Internet.
Fee: $49.00 installation; $42.95 monthly.

Telephone Service
Digital: Operational
Fee: $44.95 monthly

Miles of Plant: 167.0 (coaxial); None (fiber optic).
Senior Regional Vice President: Amy Smith. Vice President, Technical Operations: Rich Massi. Vice President, Marketing: Chip Goodman.
Ownership: Comcast Cable Communications Inc. (MSO).

NORRISTOWN—Comcast Cable, 3220 Tillman Dr, Bensalem, PA 19010. Phone: 215-642-6400. Fax: 215-638-6510. Web Site: http://www.comcast.com. Also serves Bridgeport, Conshohocken, East Norriton Twp., Lower Gwynedd Twp. (Montgomery County), Lower Providence Twp., West Conshohocken, West Norriton Twp., Whitemarsh Twp. (southern portion), Whitpain Twp. & Worcester Twp. (Montgomery County). ICA: PA0028.
TV Market Ranking: 4 (Bridgeport, Conshohocken, East Norriton Twp., Lower Gwynedd Twp. (Montgomery County), Lower Providence Twp., NORRISTOWN, West Conshohocken, West Norriton Twp., Whitemarsh Twp. (southern portion), Whitpain Twp., Worcester Twp. (Montgomery County)). Franchise award date: N.A. Franchise expiration date: N.A. Began: October 6, 1975.
Channel capacity: N.A. Channels available but not in use: N.A.

Basic Service
Subscribers: N.A. Included in Bensalem Twp.
Programming (received off-air): KYW-TV (CBS) Philadelphia; WBPH-TV (IND) Bethlehem; WCAU (NBC) Philadelphia; WFMZ-TV (IND) Allentown; WHYY-TV (PBS) Wilmington; WLVT-TV (PBS) Allentown; WMCN-TV (IND) Atlantic City; WPHL-TV (MNT, IND) Philadelphia; WPSG (CW) Philadelphia; WPVI-TV (ABC) Philadelphia; WTXF-TV (FOX) Philadelphia; WUVP-DT (UNV) Vineland.
Programming (via satellite): C-SPAN; QVC; TBS Superstation; The Comcast Network; Versus.
Fee: $16.10 monthly.

Expanded Basic Service 1
Subscribers: 33,380.
Programming (received off-air): WGTW-TV (TBN) Burlington; WNJT (PBS) Trenton; WPPX-TV (ION) Wilmington; WTVE (IND) Reading; WWSI (TMO) Atlantic City; WYBE (ETV, IND) Philadelphia.
Programming (via satellite): A&E Networks; ABC Family Channel; AMC; Animal Planet; BET Networks; Bravo; Cartoon Network; CNBC; CNN; Comcast/Charter Sports Southeast (CSS); Comedy Central; Country Music TV; Discovery Channel; Discovery Health Channel; Disney Channel; E! Entertainment Television; Encore; ESPN; ESPN 2; Eternal Word TV Network; Food Network; Fox News Channel; FX; Golf Channel; GSN; Headline News; HGTV; History Channel; Lifetime; MSNBC; MTV; MTV2; Nickelodeon; Philadelphia Park Live; Speed; Spike TV; Style Network; Syfy; The Learning Channel; The Weather Channel; Travel Channel; truTV; Turner Classic Movies; Turner Network TV; TV Land; USA Network; VH1.
Fee: $34.30 monthly.

Digital Basic Service
Subscribers: N.A.
Programming (via satellite): BBC America; Bio; Comcast SportsNet Philadelphia; Cooking Channel; C-SPAN 3; DIY Network; DMX Music; ESPN; ESPNews; Eternal Word TV Network; Fox College Sports Atlantic; Fox College Sports Central; Fox College Sports Pacific; Fox Soccer; G4; GAS; GolTV; HD Theater; History Channel International; Independent Film Channel; INHD (multiplexed); MTV Networks Digital Suite; National Geographic Channel; NBA TV; NFL Network; Nick Jr.; Nick Too; NickToons TV; Pennsylvania Cable Network; ShopNBC; SoapNet; Toon Disney; WAM! America's Kidz Network; Weatherscan.

Digital Pay Service 1
Pay Units: N.A.
Programming (via satellite): Cinemax (multiplexed); Cinemax; HBO; Showtime; Starz (multiplexed); Starz; The Movie Channel (multiplexed).
Fee: $18.95 monthly (each).

Video-On-Demand: Yes

Pay-Per-View
iN DEMAND; Playboy TV (delivered digitally); Spice; Shorteez (delivered digitally); Pleasure (delivered digitally); ESPN (delivered digitally).

Internet Service
Operational: Yes.
Broadband Service: Comcast High Speed Internet.
Fee: $99.95 installation; $42.95 monthly; $9.95 modem lease; $299.00 modem purchase.

Telephone Service
Digital: Operational
Fee: $44.95 monthly

Miles of Plant: 450.0 (coaxial); None (fiber optic). Additional miles planned: 50.0 (coaxial).
Senior Regional Vice President: Amy Smith. Vice President, Technical Operations: Rich Massi. Vice President, Marketing: Chip Goodman.
Ownership: Comcast Cable Communications Inc. (MSO).

NORTH CATASAUQUA BOROUGH—Formerly served by NORTHAMPTON BOROUGH, PA [PA0008]. RCN Corp. This cable system has converted to IPTV, 196 Van Buren St, Herndon, VA 20170. Phone: 703-434-8200. Web Site: http://www.rcn.com. ICA: PA5226.
TV Market Ranking: Below 100 (NORTH CATASAUQUA BOROUGH).
Channel capacity: N.A. Channels available but not in use: N.A.

Internet Service
Operational: Yes.

Telephone Service
Digital: Operational

Chairman: Steven J. Simmons. Chief Executive Officer: Jim Holanda.

NORTH CLARION—Armstrong Cable Services, 160 Westview Dr, Meadville, PA 16335-7904. Phones: 877-277-5711; 814-333-8442. Fax: 814-337-2510. E-mail: info@zoominternet.net. Web Site: http://cable.armstrongonewire.com. Also serves Crown, Farmington Twp. (Clarion County), Fryburg, Huefner, Leeper, Lickingville, Lucinda, Marble, Rockmere, Snydersburg, Tionesta, Tionesta Twp., Tylersburg, Venus, Vowinckel & Washington Twp. (Clarion County). ICA: PA0142.
TV Market Ranking: Outside TV Markets (Crown, Farmington Twp. (Clarion County), Fryburg, Huefner, Leeper, Lickingville, Lucinda, Marble, NORTH CLARION, Rockmere, Snydersburg, Tionesta, Tionesta Twp., Tylersburg, Venus, Vowinckel, Washington Twp. (Clarion County)). Franchise award date: N.A. Franchise expiration date: N.A. Began: May 1, 1957.
Channel capacity: N.A. Channels available but not in use: N.A.

Digital Basic Service
Subscribers: N.A.
Programming (via satellite): A&E Networks; ABC Family Channel; AMC; Cartoon Network; CNBC; CNN; Comedy Central; Country Music TV; C-SPAN; Discovery Channel; Disney Channel; E! Entertainment Television; ESPN; ESPN 2; Food Network; Fox News Channel; FX; Headline News; HGTV; History Channel; INSP; Lifetime; MSNBC; MTV; Music Choice; Nickelodeon; QVC; Root Sports Pittsburgh; Spike TV; Syfy; TBS Superstation; The Learning Channel; The Weather Channel; Turner Network TV; TV Land; USA Network; VH1.
Fee: $51.40 monthly.

Digital Expanded Basic Service
Subscribers: N.A.
Programming (via satellite): AmericanLife TV Network; BBC America; Bio; Bloomberg Television; Boomerang; Chiller; cloo; CMT Pure Country; Cooking Channel; Discovery Fit & Health; Discovery Health Channel; Discovery Kids Channel; DIY Network; ESPN Classic Sports; ESPNews; G4; Golf Channel; Great American Country; GSN; Hallmark Channel; Hallmark Movie Channel; History Channel International; HRTV; ID Investigation Discovery; Jewelry Television; Lifetime Movie Network; Military Channel; MTV Hits; MTV Jams; MTV2; mun2 television; National Geographic Channel; NFL Network; NHL Network; Nick Jr.; Nick Too; Outdoor Channel; Oxygen; PBS Kids Sprout; Pentagon Channel; Planet Green; RFD-TV; Science; SoapNet; Speed; TeenNick; Tennis Channel; Toon Disney; Tr3s; Versus; VH1 Classic; VH1 Soul; WE tv.
Fee: $12.00 monthly.

Digital Expanded Basic Service 2
Subscribers: N.A.
Programming (received off-air): KDKA-TV (CBS) Pittsburgh; WPGH-TV (FOX) Pittsburgh; WPXI (IND, NBC) Pittsburgh; WTAE-TV (ABC) Pittsburgh.
Programming (via satellite): ESPN 2 HD; ESPN HD; HD Theater; HDNet; HDNet Movies; National Geographic Channel HD Network; Syfy HD; The Weather Channel HD; Turner Network TV HD; Universal HD; USA Network HD.
Fee: $9.00 monthly.

Digital Pay Service 1
Pay Units: N.A.
Programming (via satellite): Cinemax (multiplexed); Cinemax HD; Encore (multiplexed); Flix; HBO (multiplexed); HBO HD; RAI International; Showtime (multiplexed); Showtime HD; Starz (multiplexed); Starz HDTV; The Movie Channel (multiplexed); TV5, La Television International.
Fee: $13.95 monthly (HBO, Showtime/TMC/Flix, Cinemax or Starz/Encore).

Video-On-Demand: Yes

Pay-Per-View
iN DEMAND (delivered digitally); Hot Choice (delivered digitally); ESPN (delivered digitally); MLB Extra Innings (delivered digitally); NHL Center Ice (delivered digitally).

Internet Service
Operational: Yes.
Broadband Service: Armstrong Zoom.
Fee: $26.95 monthly.

Telephone Service
Digital: Operational
Fee: $49.95 monthly

Miles of Plant: 98.0 (coaxial); None (fiber optic).
Manager: Scott Brush. Marketing Director: Joan Kocan. Chief Technician: Pat Gladis.
Ownership: Armstrong Group of Companies (MSO).

NORTH WHITEHALL TWP.—Formerly served by NORTHAMPTON BOROUGH, PA [PA0008]. RCN Corp. This cable system has converted to IPTV, 196 Van Buren St, Herndon, VA 20170. Phone: 703-434-8200. Web Site: http://www.rcn.com. ICA: PA5227.
TV Market Ranking: Below 100 (NORTH WHITEHALL TWP.).
Channel capacity: N.A. Channels available but not in use: N.A.

Internet Service
Operational: Yes.

Telephone Service
Digital: Operational

Chairman: Steven J. Simmons. Chief Executive Officer: Jim Holanda.

NORTHAMPTON—RCN Corp. This cable system has converted to IPTV. See Northampton Borough, PA [PA5228]. ICA: PA0008.

NORTHAMPTON BOROUGH—Formerly [PA0008]. RCN Corp. This cable system has converted to IPTV, 196 Van Buren St, Herndon, VA 20170. Phone: 703-434-8200. Web Site: http://www.rcn.com. ICA: PA5228.

TV Market Ranking: Below 100 (NORTHAMPTON BOROUGH).

Channel capacity: N.A. Channels available but not in use: N.A.

Internet Service

Operational: Yes.

Telephone Service

Digital: Operational

Chairman: Steven J. Simmons. Chief Executive Officer: Jim Holanda.

NORWOOD—RCN Corp. Formerly served by Philadelphia (suburbs), PA [PA0447]. This cable system has converted to IPTV, 196 Van Buren St, Herndon, VA 20170. Phone: 703-434-8200. Web Site: http://www.rcn.com. ICA: PA5258.

Channel capacity: N.A. Channels available but not in use: N.A.

Internet Service

Operational: Yes.

Chairman: Steven J. Simmons. Chief Executive Officer: Jim Holanda.

OIL CITY—Comcast Cable, 219 N Findley St, Punxsutawney, PA 15767-2020. Phone: 814-938-6130. Fax: 514-938-7622. Web Site: http://www.comcast.com. Also serves Cornplanter Twp. (Venango County), Cranberry Twp. (Venango County), Rouseville & Sugarcreek (Venango County). ICA: PA0086.

TV Market Ranking: Outside TV Markets (Cornplanter Twp. (Venango County), Cranberry Twp. (Venango County), OIL CITY, Rouseville, Sugarcreek (Venango County)). Franchise award date: October 1, 1951. Franchise expiration date: N.A. Began: October 1, 1951.

Channel capacity: N.A. Channels available but not in use: N.A.

Basic Service

Subscribers: 6,180.

Programming (received off-air): KDKA-TV (CBS) Pittsburgh; WICU-TV (NBC) Erie; WJET-TV (ABC) Erie; WPCB-TV (IND) Greensburg; WPGH-TV (FOX) Pittsburgh; WPXI (IND, NBC) Pittsburgh; WQED (PBS) Pittsburgh; WQLN (PBS) Erie; WSEE-TV (CBS, CW) Erie; WTAE-TV (ABC) Pittsburgh; allband FM.

Programming (via satellite): ABC Family Channel; C-SPAN; C-SPAN 2; ESPN; Hallmark Channel; TBS Superstation; TV Guide Network.

Fee: $35.00 installation; $11.60 monthly; $3.00 converter; $15.00 additional installation.

Expanded Basic Service 1

Subscribers: 840.

Programming (via satellite): A&E Networks; AMC; Animal Planet; Cartoon Network; CNN; Discovery Channel; Disney Channel; Fox News Channel; FX; Headline News; HGTV; Lifetime; MSNBC; MTV; Nickelodeon; Pennsylvania Cable Network; QVC; Root Sports Pittsburgh; Spike TV; The Learning Channel; The Weather Channel; truTV; Turner Network TV; TV Land; USA Network; VH1.

Fee: $20.00 installation; $3.00 monthly.

Digital Basic Service

Subscribers: 1,300.

Programming (via satellite): BBC America; Bravo; Discovery Health Channel; Discovery Home Channel; Discovery Kids Channel; Discovery Times Channel; ESPN 2; ESPN Classic Sports; ESPNews; Fox Sports World; Golf Channel; GSN; History Channel; Independent Film Channel; Military Channel; Outdoor Channel; Science; Syfy; Turner Classic Movies; Versus; WE tv.

Fee: $15.95 monthly.

Digital Expanded Basic Service

Subscribers: N.A.

Programming (via satellite): National Geographic Channel; Nick Jr.; VH1 Country.

Pay Service 1

Pay Units: 534.

Programming (via satellite): Cinemax; Encore Action; HBO; Starz.

Fee: $20.00 installation; $10.20 monthly (Cinemax), $11.40 monthly (Showtime), $11.80 monthly (HBO).

Digital Pay Service 1

Pay Units: N.A.

Programming (via satellite): Cinemax; Encore Action; HBO; Showtime; Starz; The Movie Channel.

Video-On-Demand: No

Pay-Per-View

Hot Choice (delivered digitally); Fresh (delivered digitally); Playboy TV (delivered digitally).

Internet Service

Operational: Yes.

Subscribers: 250.

Broadband Service: Comcast High Speed Internet.

Fee: $42.95 monthly.

Telephone Service

None

Miles of Plant: 118.0 (coaxial); 118.0 (fiber optic).

Manager: Scott Brush. Marketing Manager: David Smith. Office Manager: Suzanne Smith. Technical Operations Manager: Bob Brush.

Ownership: Comcast Cable Communications Inc. (MSO).

OLD PORT—Nittany Media Inc. Now served by LEWISTOWN (formerly McAlisterville), PA [PA0365]. ICA: PA0287.

ORRSTOWN—Kuhn Communications. Now served by WALNUT BOTTOM, PA [PA0220]. ICA: PA0218.

ORVISTON—Formerly served by Orviston TV. No longer in operation. ICA: PA0385.

OSWAYO—Zito Media, 611 Vader Hill Rd, Coudersport, PA 16915. Phones: 814-260-9570; 866-879-6235; 814-260-9575. Fax: 814-260-9580. E-mail: rigas@zitomedia.com. Web Site: http://www.zitomedia.com. Also serves Genesee. ICA: PA0386.

TV Market Ranking: Outside TV Markets (Genesee, OSWAYO). Franchise award date: January 1, 1989. Franchise expiration date: N.A. Began: January 1, 1989.

Channel capacity: N.A. Channels available but not in use: N.A.

Basic Service

Subscribers: 65.

Programming (received off-air): WGRZ (NBC) Buffalo; WIVB-TV (CBS) Buffalo; WJAC-TV (NBC) Johnstown; WKBW-TV (ABC) Buffalo; WNED-TV (PBS) Buffalo; WPSU-TV (PBS) Clearfield; WTAJ-TV (CBS) Altoona; WWCP-TV (FOX) Johnstown.

Programming (via satellite): WGN America; WPIX (CW, IND) New York.

Fee: $29.95 installation; $16.95 monthly.

Expanded Basic Service 1

Subscribers: N.A.

Programming (via satellite): A&E Networks; ABC Family Channel; AMC; Animal Planet; Cartoon Network; CNBC; CNN; Country Music TV; C-SPAN; C-SPAN 2; Discovery Channel; Disney Channel; E! Entertainment Television; ESPN; ESPN 2; ESPN Classic Sports; Eternal Word TV Network; Food Network; Fox News Channel; FX; Hallmark Channel; Headline News; HGTV; History Channel; INSP; Lifetime; MSG; MSNBC; MTV; NFL Network; Nickelodeon; QVC; Root Sports Pittsburgh; Spike TV; Syfy; TBS Superstation; The Learning Channel; The Weather Channel; Trinity Broadcasting Network; Turner Classic Movies; Turner Network TV; TV Land; USA Network; VH1.

Fee: $18.05 monthly.

Digital Basic Service

Subscribers: N.A.

Programming (via satellite): AmericanLife TV Network; BBC America; Bloomberg Television; Boomerang; C-SPAN 3; Discovery Fit & Health; Discovery Health Channel; Discovery Kids Channel; ESPN 2 HD; ESPN HD; ESPNews; Familyland Television Network; Fox Movie Channel; Fox Soccer; Golf Channel; Great American Country; GSN; HRTV; ID Investigation Discovery; INSP; Lifetime Movie Network; Military Channel; MTV Hits; MTV Jams; MTV2; Music Choice; Nick Too; NickToons TV; Planet Green; RFD-TV; Science; SoapNet; Speed; TeenNick; The Word Network; Toon Disney; Trinity Broadcasting Network; VH1 Classic; VH1 Country; VH1 Soul; WE tv.

Fee: $15.95 monthly.

Digital Expanded Basic Service

Subscribers: N.A.

Programming (via satellite): Bio; DIY Network; Flix; FSN Digital Atlantic; FSN Digital Central; FSN Digital Pacific; History Channel International; Independent Film Channel; Outdoor Channel; Sundance Channel; Versus.

Fee: $10.00 monthly.

Digital Pay Service 1

Pay Units: N.A.

Programming (via satellite): Cinemax (multiplexed); Cinemax HD; Encore (multiplexed); Flix; HBO (multiplexed); HBO HD; Showtime (multiplexed); Showtime HD; Starz (multiplexed); Starz HDTV; The Movie Channel (multiplexed).

Fee: $8.00 monthly (Cinemax or Starz/Encore), $10.00 monthly (HBO or Showtime/TMC/Flix).

Video-On-Demand: Planned

Pay-Per-View

iN DEMAND (delivered digitally); NHL Center Ice (delivered digitally); MLB Extra Innings (delivered digitally).

Internet Service

Operational: Yes.

Fee: $42.95 monthly.

Telephone Service

Digital: Operational

Fee: $35.00 monthly

Miles of Plant: 23.0 (coaxial); None (fiber optic).

Manager: James Rigas. Marketing Director: Kathy Fox.

Ownership: Zito Media (MSO).

OXFORD—Armstrong Cable Services, 122 S Queen St, PO Box 709, Rising Sun, MD 21911-0709. Phones: 410-658-3500; 877-277-5711; 410-658-5511. Fax: 410-658-4777. E-mail: info@zoominternet.net. Web Site: http://cable.armstrongonewire.com. Also serves Cecil County (portions) & Rising Sun, MD; East Nottingham Twp., Elk Twp. (Chester County), Highland Twp. (Chester County), Londonderry Twp. (Chester County), Lower Oxford Twp., Upper Oxford Twp., West Fallowfield Twp. & West Nottingham Twp., PA. ICA: PA0098.

TV Market Ranking: 57 (Cecil County (portions), East Nottingham Twp., Elk Twp. (Chester County), Highland Twp. (Chester County), Londonderry Twp. (Chester County), Lower Oxford Twp., OXFORD, Rising Sun, Upper Oxford Twp., West Fallowfield Twp., West Nottingham Twp.). Franchise award date: N.A. Franchise expiration date: N.A. Began: June 1, 1982.

Channel capacity: N.A. Channels available but not in use: N.A.

Digital Basic Service

Subscribers: 4,829.

Programming (via satellite): A&E Networks; ABC Family Channel; AMC; Animal Planet; Bravo; Cartoon Network; CNBC; CNN; Comedy Central; Country Music TV; C-SPAN; Discovery Channel; Discovery Fit & Health; Disney Channel; E! Entertainment Television; ESPN; ESPN 2; ESPN Classic Sports; Eternal Word TV Network; Food Network; Fox News Channel; FX; Headline News; HGTV; History Channel; INSP; Lifetime; Mid-Atlantic Sports Network; MSNBC; MTV; Music Choice; Nickelodeon; Pennsylvania Cable Network; Pentagon Channel; QVC; ShopNBC; Spike TV; Syfy; TBS Superstation; Telemundo; The Learning Channel; The Weather Channel; Travel Channel; truTV; Turner Classic Movies; Turner Network TV; TV Guide Network; TV Land; VH1.

Fee: $51.40 monthly.

Digital Expanded Basic Service

Subscribers: N.A.

Programming (via satellite): AmericanLife TV Network; BBC America; Bio; Bloomberg Television; Boomerang; Chiller; cloo; CMT Pure Country; Cooking Channel; Discovery Fit & Health; Discovery Health Channel; Discovery Kids Channel; DIY Network; ESPN Classic Sports; ESPNews; G4; Golf Channel; Great American Country; GSN; Hallmark Channel; Hallmark Movie Channel; History Channel International; HRTV; ID Investigation Discovery; Jewelry Television; Lifetime Movie Network; Military Channel; MTV Hits; MTV Jams; MTV2; mun2 television; National Geographic Channel; NFL Network; NHL Network; Nick Jr.; Nick Too; Outdoor Channel; Oxygen; PBS Kids Sprout; Pentagon Channel; Planet Green; RFD-TV; Science; SoapNet; Speed; TeenNick; Tennis Channel; Toon Disney; Tr3s; Versus; VH1 Classic; VH1 Soul; WE tv.

Fee: $12.00 monthly.

Digital Expanded Basic Service 2

Subscribers: N.A.

Programming (received off-air): KYW-TV (CBS) Philadelphia; WCAU (NBC) Philadelphia; WJZ-TV (CBS) Baltimore; WPHL-TV (MNT, IND) Philadelphia; WPSG (CW) Philadelphia; WPVI-TV (ABC) Philadelphia; WTXF-TV (FOX) Philadelphia.

Programming (via satellite): A&E HD; Animal Planet HD; Bravo HD; CNN HD; Discovery Channel HD; Disney Channel HD; Food Network HD; Fox News HD; FX HD; Golf Channel HD; Hallmark Movie Channel HD; HD Theater; HDNet; HDNet Movies; HGTV HD; History Channel HD; MGM HD; National Geographic Channel HD Network; NFL Network HD; NHL Network HD; Outdoor Channel 2 HD; Palladia; PBS HD; QVC HD; Science HD; Syfy HD; TBS in HD; The Weather Channel HD; TLC HD; Turner Network TV HD; Universal HD; USA Network HD; Versus HD; WealthTV HD.

Fee: $9.00 monthly.

Digital Pay Service 1
Pay Units: N.A.
Programming (via satellite): Cinemax (multiplexed); Cinemax HD; Encore (multiplexed); Flix; HBO (multiplexed); HBO HD; RAI USA; Showtime (multiplexed); Showtime HD; Starz (multiplexed); Starz HDTV; The Movie Channel (multiplexed); TV5 USA.
Fee: $13.95 monthly (HBO, Cinemax, Showtime/TMC/Flix or Starz/Encore).
Video-On-Demand: Yes
Pay-Per-View
ESPN Extra (delivered digitally); ESPN Now (delivered digitally); Hot Choice (delivered digitally); iN DEMAND (delivered digitally); NHL/MLB (delivered digitally).
Internet Service
Operational: Yes. Began: November 1, 2001.
Subscribers: 8,329.
Broadband Service: Armstrong Zoom.
Fee: $26.95-$39.95 monthly.
Telephone Service
Digital: Operational
Subscribers: 300.
Fee: $49.95 monthly
Miles of Plant: 645.0 (coaxial); 200.0 (fiber optic).
General Manager: James Culver. Marketing & Program Director: Jud D. Stewart. Technical Operations Director: Ken Goodman.
Ownership: Armstrong Group of Companies (MSO).

PALMER TWP.—Formerly served by NORTHAMPTON BOROUGH, PA [PA0008]. RCN Corp. This cable system has converted to IPTV, 196 Van Buren St, Herndon, VA 20170. Phone: 703-434-8200. Web Site: http://www.rcn.com. ICA: PA5229.
TV Market Ranking: Below 100 (PALMER TWP.).
Channel capacity: N.A. Channels available but not in use: N.A.
Internet Service
Operational: Yes.
Telephone Service
Digital: Operational
Chairman: Steven J. Simmons. Chief Executive Officer: Jim Holanda.

PALMERTON—Blue Ridge Communications, 613 3rd St, PO Box 215, Palmerton, PA 18071-0215. Phone: 610-826-2551 (Administrative office). Fax: 610-826-7626. Web Site: http://www.brctv.com. Also serves Albrightsville, Bowmanstown, Coaldale, East Penn Twp., Eldred Twp. (Schuylkill County), Franklin Twp. (Carbon County), Heidelberg Twp. (Lehigh County), Jim Thorpe, Kidder Twp. (Carbon County), Lansford, Lehigh Twp. (Northampton County), Lehighton, Lower Towamensing Twp., Lynn Twp. (Lehigh County), Mahoning Twp. (Carbon County), Nesquehoning, Parryville, Penn Forest Twp. (Carbon County), Reynolds, Rush Twp., Slatington, Summit Hill, Towamensing Twp., Walker Twp. (Schuylkill County), Walnutport, Washington Twp. (Carbon County), Weissport & West Penn Twp. (southeastern portion). ICA: PA0042.
TV Market Ranking: 49 (Albrightsville, Bowmanstown, Coaldale, East Penn Twp., Franklin Twp. (Carbon County), Jim Thorpe, Kidder Twp. (Carbon County), Lansford, Lehighton, Lower Towamensing Twp., Mahoning Twp. (Carbon County), Nesquehoning, PALMERTON, Parryville, Penn Forest Twp. (Carbon County), Rush Twp., Summit Hill, Towamensing Twp., Washington Twp. (Carbon County), Weissport); Below 100 (Eldred Twp. (Schuylkill County), Heidelberg Twp. (Lehigh County), Lehigh Twp. (Northampton County), Lynn Twp. (Lehigh County), Reynolds, Slatington, Walker Twp. (Schuylkill County), Walnutport, West Penn Twp. (southeastern portion)). Franchise award date: N.A. Franchise expiration date: N.A. Began: September 14, 1951.
Channel capacity: 54 (operating 2-way). Channels available but not in use: N.A.
Basic Service
Subscribers: 30,748.
Programming (received off-air): KYW-TV (CBS) Philadelphia; WCAU (NBC) Philadelphia; WFMZ-TV (IND) Allentown; WLVT-TV (PBS) Allentown; WNEP-TV (ABC) Scranton; WNYW (FOX) New York; WOLF-TV (CW, FOX, MNT) Hazleton; WPIX (CW, IND) New York; WPSG (CW) Philadelphia; WPVI-TV (ABC) Philadelphia; WQPX-TV (ION) Scranton; WSWB (CW) Scranton; WTXF-TV (FOX) Philadelphia; WVIA-TV (PBS) Scranton; WWOR-TV (MNT) Secaucus; WYOU (CBS) Scranton; allband FM.
Programming (via satellite): Headline News.
Fee: $22.50 installation; $16.54 monthly.
Expanded Basic Service 1
Subscribers: N.A.
Programming (via satellite): A&E Networks; ABC Family Channel; AMC; Animal Planet; Bravo; Cartoon Network; CNBC; CNN; Comcast SportsNet Philadelphia; Comedy Central; Country Music TV; C-SPAN; Discovery Channel; Discovery Fit & Health; Disney Channel; E! Entertainment Television; ESPN; ESPN 2; ESPN Classic Sports; ESPNews; Eternal Word TV Network; Food Network; Fox News Channel; FX; Golf Channel; GSN; Hallmark Channel; HGTV; History Channel; INSP; Lifetime; Lifetime Movie Network; MSG; MSNBC; MTV; Nickelodeon; Pennsylvania Cable Network; QVC; ShopNBC; Speed; Spike TV; Syfy; TBS Superstation; The Learning Channel; The Weather Channel; Travel Channel; truTV; Turner Classic Movies; Turner Network TV; TV Land; Univision Studios; USA Network; Versus; VH1; WE tv; Yankees Entertainment & Sports.
Fee: $31.69 monthly.
Digital Basic Service
Subscribers: N.A.
Programming (via satellite): Discovery Digital Networks; Fox Movie Channel; FSN Digital Atlantic; FSN Digital Central; FSN Digital Pacific; GAS; Halogen Network; Meadows Racing Network; MTV Networks Digital Suite; Music Choice; National Geographic Channel; Nick Jr.; Nick Too; NickToons TV; Outdoor Channel; PBS Kids Channel; SoapNet; Toon Disney.
Fee: $9.95 monthly.
Digital Expanded Basic Service
Subscribers: N.A.
Programming (via satellite): BBC America; Bio; Bloomberg Television; Boomerang; Cooking Channel; DIY Network; G4; History Channel International; Lifetime Real Women; LWS Local Weather Station; Style Network.
Fee: $5.00 monthly.
Digital Pay Service 1
Pay Units: N.A.
Programming (via satellite): Cinemax (multiplexed); Encore (multiplexed); Flix; HBO (multiplexed); Showtime (multiplexed); Starz (multiplexed); Sundance Channel; The Movie Channel (multiplexed).
Fee: $12.50 monthly (Cinemax or Showtime/Flix/Sundance/TMC), $12.95 monthly (Starz/Encore), $13.50 monthly (HBO).
Video-On-Demand: Yes
Pay-Per-View
Addressable homes: 10,967.
iN DEMAND; iN DEMAND (delivered digitally); Barker (delivered digitally); adult PPV (delivered digitally); sports (delivered digitally).
Internet Service
Operational: Yes.
Broadband Service: ProLog Express.
Fee: $36.95 monthly; $10.00 modem lease; $59.95 modem purchase.
Telephone Service
None
Miles of Plant: 865.0 (coaxial); 50.0 (fiber optic). Additional miles planned: 20.0 (coaxial).
Vice President, Operations: Richard Semmel. General Manager: Mark Masonheimer. Chief Technician: Randy Semmel.
Ownership: Pencor Services Inc. (MSO).

PARKS TWP.—Comcast Cable. Now served by KISKIMINETAS TWP., PA [PA0074]. ICA: PA0388.

PEN ARGYL BOROUGH—Formerly served by NORTHAMPTON BOROUGH, PA [PA0008]. RCN Corp. This cable system has converted to IPTV, 196 Van Buren St, Herndon, VA 20170. Phone: 703-434-8200. Web Site: http://www.rcn.com. ICA: PA5230.
TV Market Ranking: Below 100 (PEN ARGYL BOROUGH).
Channel capacity: N.A. Channels available but not in use: N.A.
Internet Service
Operational: Yes.
Telephone Service
Digital: Operational
Chairman: Steven J. Simmons. Chief Executive Officer: Jim Holanda.

PENN HILLS—Comcast Cable. Now served by KISKIMINETAS TWP., PA [PA0074]. ICA: PA0458.

PERRY COUNTY—Kuhn Communications, PO Box 277, Walnut Bottom, PA 17266. Phone: 717-532-8857. Fax: 717-532-5563. E-mail: kuhncom1@kuhncom.net. Web Site: http://www.kuhncom.net. Also serves Elliottsburg, Landisburg & Loysville. ICA: PA0393.
TV Market Ranking: 57 (Elliottsburg, Landisburg, Loysville, PERRY COUNTY).
Channel capacity: N.A. Channels available but not in use: N.A.
Basic Service
Subscribers: N.A.
Programming (received off-air): WGAL (NBC) Lancaster; WHP-TV (CBS, MNT) Harrisburg; WHTM-TV (ABC) Harrisburg; WITF-TV (PBS) Harrisburg; WLYH-TV (CW) Lancaster; WPMT (FOX) York.
Programming (via satellite): Animal Planet; Barker; ESPN; Spike TV.
Expanded Basic Service 1
Subscribers: N.A.
Programming (via satellite): ABC Family Channel; CNN; Country Music TV; MTV; TBS Superstation; Turner Network TV; USA Network; WGN America.
Expanded Basic Service 2
Subscribers: N.A.
Programming (received off-air): WPIX (CW, IND) New York.
Programming (via satellite): A&E Networks; Bravo; Cartoon Network; Comcast SportsNet Philadelphia; Discovery Channel; Disney Channel; ESPN 2; Fox News Channel; Fox Sports Net; FX; Headline News; HGTV; History Channel; Nickelodeon; Outdoor Channel; Speed; Syfy; The Learning Channel; The Weather Channel; Trinity Broadcasting Network; Turner Classic Movies; TV Land; VH1.
Digital Basic Service
Subscribers: N.A.
Programming (via satellite): BBC America; Bio; Black Family Channel; Bloomberg Television; Bravo; cloo; Daystar TV Network; Discovery Digital Networks; DMX Music; ESPN Classic Sports; ESPNews; Fox Movie Channel; Fox Soccer; FSN Digital Atlantic; FSN Digital Central; FSN Digital Pacific; Fuse; G4; GAS; Golf Channel; Great American Country; GSN; Halogen Network; HDNet; HDNet Movies; HGTV; History Channel; History Channel International; Independent Film Channel; Lifetime Movie Network; Lime; MTV Networks Digital Suite; National Geographic Channel; Nick Jr.; NickToons TV; Outdoor Channel; ShopNBC; Speed; Style Network; Syfy; The Word Network; Trinity Broadcasting Network; Turner Classic Movies; Versus; WE tv.
Pay Service 1
Pay Units: N.A.
Programming (via satellite): HBO; The Movie Channel.
Digital Pay Service 1
Pay Units: N.A.
Programming (via satellite): Cinemax (multiplexed); Encore (multiplexed); HBO (multiplexed); Showtime (multiplexed); Starz (multiplexed); The Movie Channel (multiplexed).
Video-On-Demand: No
Pay-Per-View
iN DEMAND (delivered digitally); Playboy TV (delivered digitally); Fresh (delivered digitally).
Internet Service
Operational: Yes.
Broadband Service: kuhncom.net.
Fee: $50.00 installation; $24.95 monthly.
Telephone Service
None
Manager: Earl Kuhn. Office Manager: Tracy Reath.
Ownership: Kuhn Communications (MSO).

PHILADELPHIA (area 1)—Comcast of Philadelphia. Now served by PHILADELPHIA (areas 3 & 4), PA [PA0005]. ICA: PA0003.

PHILADELPHIA (area 2)—Comcast Cable, 3220 Tillman Dr, Bensalem, PA 19010. Phone: 215-642-6400. Fax: 215-638-6510. Web Site: http://www.comcast.com. ICA: PA0004.

TV Market Ranking: 4 (PHILADELPHIA (AREA 2)). Franchise award date: November 1, 1984. Franchise expiration date: August 2, 2015. Began: December 15, 1987.

Channel capacity: 200 (operating 2-way). Channels available but not in use: N.A.

Basic Service

Subscribers: 65,000.

Programming (received off-air): KYW-TV (CBS) Philadelphia; WBPH-TV (IND) Bethlehem; WCAU (NBC) Philadelphia; WFMZ-TV (IND) Allentown; WGTW-TV (TBN) Burlington; WHYY-TV (PBS) Wilmington; WLVT-TV (PBS) Allentown; WMCN-TV (IND) Atlantic City; WNJS (PBS) Camden; WPHL-TV (MNT, IND) Philadelphia; WPPX-TV (ION) Wilmington; WPSG (CW) Philadelphia; WPVI-TV (ABC) Philadelphia; WTVE (IND) Reading; WTXF-TV (FOX) Philadelphia; WUVP-DT (UNV) Vineland; WWSI (TMO) Atlantic City; WYBE (ETV, IND) Philadelphia.

Programming (via satellite): A&E Networks; ABC Family Channel; AMC; Animal Planet; BET Networks; Bravo; Cartoon Network; CNBC; CNN; Comcast SportsNet Philadelphia; Comedy Central; C-SPAN; C-SPAN 2; Discovery Channel; Disney Channel; E! Entertainment Television; ESPN; ESPN 2; Eternal Word TV Network; Food Network; Fox News Channel; FX; Headline News; HGTV; History Channel; Lifetime; MSNBC; MTV; Nickelodeon; Pennsylvania Cable Network; QVC; Spike TV; Syfy; TBS Superstation; The Comcast Network; The Learning Channel; The Weather Channel; truTV; Turner Classic Movies; Turner Network TV; TV Guide Network; TV One; USA Network; Versus; VH1.

Fee: $57.00 installation; $35.60 monthly.

Digital Basic Service

Subscribers: N.A.

Programming (via satellite): BBC America; Bio; Bloomberg Television; Canales N; CBS Sports Network; CMT Pure Country; Cooking Channel; Country Music TV; C-SPAN 3; Current; DIY Network; Encore (multiplexed); ESPN 2 HD; ESPN Classic Sports; ESPN HD; ESPNews; Exercise TV; FEARnet; Flix; Fox College Sports Atlantic; Fox College Sports Central; Fox College Sports Pacific; Fox Reality Channel; Fox Soccer; G4; GAS; GMC; GolTV; Great American Country; Hallmark Channel; HD Theater; History Channel International; Independent Film Channel; Jewelry Television; Lifetime Movie Network; LOGO; MoviePlex; MTV Networks Digital Suite; Music Choice; National Geographic Channel; NBA TV; NFL Network; Nick Jr.; Nick Too; NickToons TV; Oxygen; Palladia; PBS Kids Sprout; Pennsylvania Cable Network; Philadelphia Park Live; ShopNBC; SoapNet; Sundance Channel; Tennis Channel; The Word Network; Toon Disney; Turner Network TV HD; TV One; Universal HD; Versus HD; Weatherscan.

Fee: $14.95 monthly.

Digital Pay Service 1

Pay Units: N.A.

Programming (via satellite): Cinemax (multiplexed); Cinemax HD; HBO (multiplexed); HBO HD; HBO On Demand; Showtime (multiplexed); Showtime HD; Starz (multiplexed); Starz HDTV; The Movie Channel (multiplexed).

Fee: $18.95 monthly (each).

Video-On-Demand: Yes

Pay-Per-View

Barker (delivered digitally); Hot Choice (delivered digitally); Pleasure (delivered digitally); Shorteez (delivered digitally); ESPN Extra (delivered digitally); iN DEMAND (delivered digitally); Sports PPV (delivered digitally); Fresh (delivered digitally).

Internet Service

Operational: Yes. Began: February 1, 2002.

Broadband Service: Comcast High Speed Internet.

Fee: $42.95 monthly.

Telephone Service

Analog: Not Operational

Digital: Operational

Fee: $44.95 monthly

Miles of Plant: 600.0 (coaxial); None (fiber optic). Additional miles planned: 1.0 (coaxial).

Senior Regional Vice President: Amy Smith. Vice President, Technical Operations: Rich Massi. Vice President, Marketing: Chip Goodman.

Ownership: Comcast Cable Communications Inc. (MSO).

PHILADELPHIA (areas 1, 3 & 4)—Comcast Cable, 3220 Tillman Dr, Bensalem, PA 19010. Phone: 215-642-6400. Fax: 215-638-6510. Web Site: http://www.comcast.com. ICA: PA0005.

TV Market Ranking: 4 (PHILADELPHIA). Franchise award date: November 1, 1984. Franchise expiration date: N.A. Began: September 1, 1986.

Channel capacity: 83 (operating 2-way). Channels available but not in use: N.A.

Basic Service

Subscribers: N.A. Included in Bensalem Twp.

Programming (received off-air): KYW-TV (CBS) Philadelphia; WBPH-TV (IND) Bethlehem; WCAU (NBC) Philadelphia; WFMZ-TV (IND) Allentown; WFPA-CA (TEL) Philadelphia; WGTW-TV (TBN) Burlington; WHYY-TV (PBS) Wilmington; WLVT-TV (PBS) Allentown; WMCN-TV (IND) Atlantic City; WNJS (PBS) Camden; WPHL-TV (MNT, IND) Philadelphia; WPPX-TV (ION) Wilmington; WPSG (CW) Philadelphia; WPVI-TV (ABC) Philadelphia; WTVE (IND) Reading; WTXF-TV (FOX) Philadelphia; WUVP-DT (UNV) Vineland; WYBE (ETV, IND) Philadelphia.

Programming (via satellite): A&E Networks; ABC Family Channel; AMC; Animal Planet; BET Networks; Bravo; Cartoon Network; CNBC; CNN; Comcast SportsNet Philadelphia; Comedy Central; C-SPAN; C-SPAN 2; Discovery Channel; Disney Channel; E! Entertainment Television; ESPN; ESPN 2; Eternal Word TV Network; Food Network; Fox News Channel; FX; Golf Channel; GSN; Hallmark Channel; Headline News; HGTV; History Channel; Lifetime; MSNBC; MTV; Nickelodeon; Pennsylvania Cable Network; Philadelphia Park Live; QVC; Speed; Spike TV; Style Network; Syfy; TBS Superstation; The Comcast Network; The Learning Channel; The Weather Channel; truTV; Turner Classic Movies; Turner Network TV; TV Guide Network; TV Land; TV One; USA Network; Versus; VH1.

Fee: $15.55 monthly.

Digital Basic Service

Subscribers: 140,000.

Programming (via satellite): Action 36 Cable 6; BBC America; Comcast SportsNet Philadelphia; DMX Music; Encore; ESPN 2 HD; ESPN HD; Flix; GAS; HD Theater; Mid-Atlantic Sports Network; MTV Networks Digital Suite; NBA TV; Nick Jr.; Palladia; Sundance Channel; Turner Network TV HD; Universal HD; Versus HD; Weatherscan; WeatherVision.

Fee: $6.15 monthly.

Digital Pay Service 1

Pay Units: N.A.

Programming (via satellite): Cinemax (multiplexed); Cinemax HD; HBO (multiplexed); HBO HD; Showtime (multiplexed); Showtime HD; Starz (multiplexed); Starz HDTV; The Movie Channel (multiplexed).

Fee: $15.35 monthly (each).

Video-On-Demand: Yes

Pay-Per-View

iN DEMAND (delivered digitally); Fresh; Shorteez; Sports PPV (delivered digitally).

Internet Service

Operational: Yes. Began: March 1, 2002.

Subscribers: 12,916.

Broadband Service: Comcast High Speed Internet.

Fee: $42.95 monthly.

Telephone Service

Digital: Operational

Fee: $44.95 monthly

Senior Regional Vice President: Amy Smith. Vice President, Technical Operations: Rich Massi. Vice President, Marketing: Chip Goodman.

Ownership: Comcast Cable Communications Inc. (MSO).

PHILADELPHIA (suburbs)—RCN Corp. Formerly [PA0447]. This cable system has converted to IPTV, 196 Van Buren St, Herndon, VA 20170. Phone: 703-434-8200. Web Site: http://www.rcn.com. ICA: PA5259.

Channel capacity: N.A. Channels available but not in use: N.A.

Internet Service

Operational: Yes.

Chairman: Steven J. Simmons. Chief Executive Officer: Jim Holanda.

PHILIPSBURG BOROUGH—Comcast Cable, 1 E Uwchlan Ave, Ste 411, Exton, PA 19341. Phones: 484-288-6500; 814-238-5050 (State College office). Web Site: http://www.comcast.com. Also serves Bigler Twp., Brisbin, Chester Hill, Gulich Twp., Houtzdale, Kistler, Mount Union, Newton Hamilton, Osceola Mills, Philipsburg, Ramey, Shirley Twp., Shirleysburg & South Philipsburg. ICA: PA0109.

TV Market Ranking: 74 (Bigler Twp., Brisbin, Chester Hill, Guilich Twp., Houtzdale, Kistler, Mount Union, Newton Hamilton, Osceola Mills, Philipsburg, PHILIPSBURG BOROUGH, Ramey, Shirley Twp., Shirleysburg, South Philipsburg). Franchise award date: N.A. Franchise expiration date: N.A. Began: December 1, 1958.

Channel capacity: N.A. Channels available but not in use: N.A.

Basic Service

Subscribers: N.A. Included in Harrisburg

Programming (received off-air): WATM-TV (ABC) Altoona; WJAC-TV (NBC) Johnstown; WKBS-TV (IND) Altoona; WPSU-TV (PBS) Clearfield; WTAE-TV (ABC) Pittsburgh; WTAJ-TV (CBS) Altoona; WWCP-TV (FOX) Johnstown; 14 FMs.

Programming (via satellite): CNN; C-SPAN; TV Guide Network.

Fee: $45.10 installation; $13.60 monthly; $49.99 additional installation.

Expanded Basic Service 1

Subscribers: 5,078.

Programming (via satellite): A&E Networks; ABC Family Channel; AMC; Animal Planet; Cartoon Network; CNBC; Country Music TV; C-SPAN 2; Discovery Channel; Disney Channel; ESPN; ESPN 2; Eternal Word TV Network; Food Network; Fox News Channel; FX; Hallmark Channel; Headline News; HGTV; History Channel; ION Television; Lifetime; MSNBC; MTV; Nickelodeon; Oxygen; Pennsylvania Cable Network; QVC; Root Sports Pittsburgh; Spike TV; Syfy; TBS Superstation; The Learning Channel; The Weather Channel; Travel Channel; truTV; Turner Network TV; TV Land; USA Network; VH1.

Fee: $35.95 monthly.

Digital Basic Service

Subscribers: N.A.

Programming (via satellite): BBC America; Black Family Channel; Bloomberg Television; Bravo; Discovery Fit & Health; ESPNews; Fox Movie Channel; Fox Sports World; Fuse; G4; GAS; Great American Country; GSN; Halogen Network; Lifetime Movie Network; MTV Networks Digital Suite; MTV2; National Geographic Channel; Nick Jr.; NickToons TV; Ovation; Speed; Style Network; The Word Network; Toon Disney; Trinity Broadcasting Network; Turner Classic Movies; WE tv.

Fee: $14.95 monthly.

Digital Expanded Basic Service

Subscribers: N.A.

Programming (via satellite): Bio; ESPN Classic Sports; ESPNews; FSN Digital Atlantic; FSN Digital Central; FSN Digital Pacific; Golf Channel; History Channel International; Independent Film Channel; Outdoor Channel; Sundance Channel; Versus.

Digital Pay Service 1

Pay Units: N.A.

Programming (via satellite): Cinemax (multiplexed); Encore; HBO (multiplexed); Showtime (multiplexed).

Video-On-Demand: No

Pay-Per-View

Playboy TV (delivered digitally); Shorteez (delivered digitally); Fresh (delivered digitally); Hot Choice (delivered digitally); Movies & Events (delivered digitally).

Internet Service

Operational: Yes.

Broadband Service: Comcast High Speed Internet.

Fee: $42.95 monthly.

Telephone Service

None

Miles of Plant: 209.0 (coaxial); None (fiber optic).

Area Vice President: Jim Samaha. Vice President, Marketing: Larry Goldman. Technical Operations Manager: Dan Cramer.

Ownership: Comcast Cable Communications Inc. (MSO).

PINOAK—Formerly served by Cebridge Connections. Now served by MEADVILLE, PA [PA0062]. ICA: PA0284.

PITCAIRN—Pitcairn Community Cable System, 582 6th St, Pitcairn, PA 15140-1200. Phone: 412-372-6500. Fax: 412-373-1464. ICA: PA0166.

TV Market Ranking: 10 (PITCAIRN). Franchise award date: N.A. Franchise expiration date: N.A. Began: November 1, 1952.

Channel capacity: 40 (not 2-way capable). Channels available but not in use: N.A.

Basic Service

Subscribers: 1,554.

Programming (received off-air): KDKA-TV (CBS) Pittsburgh; WINP-TV (IND, ION) Pittsburgh; WPCB-TV (IND) Greensburg; WPGH-TV (FOX) Pittsburgh; WPMY (MNT) Pittsburgh; WPXI (IND, NBC) Pittsburgh; WQED (PBS) Pittsburgh; WTAE-TV (ABC) Pittsburgh.

Programming (via satellite): A&E Networks; ABC Family Channel; AMC; CNN; Country Music TV; Discovery Channel; Disney Channel; ESPN; ESPN 2; Eternal Word TV Network; Lifetime; MTV; Nickelodeon; QVC; Root Sports Pittsburgh; Spike TV; TBS Superstation; Turner Network TV; USA Network; WGN America.
Fee: $35.00 installation; $28.00 monthly.

Pay Service 1
Pay Units: 500.
Programming (via satellite): HBO.
Fee: $12.84 monthly.

Pay Service 2
Pay Units: 255.
Programming (via satellite): Showtime.
Fee: $12.84 monthly.

Video-On-Demand: No

Internet Service
Operational: No.

Telephone Service
None

Miles of Plant: 10.0 (coaxial); None (fiber optic).
Borough Manager: Gary Parks.
Ownership: Pitcairn Community Antenna System.

PITTSBURGH—Comcast Cable, 15 Summit Park Dr, Pittsburgh, PA 15275. Phone: 412-747-6400. Fax: 412-747-6401. Web Site: http://www.comcast.com. Also serves Aliquippa, Allegheny County, Ambridge, Amity, Amwell Twp., Aspinwall, Avalon, Baden, Baldwin, Bell Acres, Belle Vernon, Bellevue, Ben Avon, Ben Avon Heights, Blaine Twp., Braddock Hills, Brentwood, Bridgeville, Buffalo Twp. (Washington County), Canonsburg, Carnegie, Carroll Twp. (Washington County), Castle Shannon, Center Twp. (Beaver County), Chalfant, Charleroi, Chartiers Twp. (Washington County), Clairton, Collier Twp., Conway, Coraopolis, Crafton, Crescent Twp., Cuddy, Donora, Dormont, East Washington, Economy, Edgewood, Edgeworth, Emsworth, Etna, Fallowfield Twp., Findlay Twp. (Allegheny County), Forest Hills, Forward Twp. (Allegheny County), Fox Chapel, Franklin Park, Glassport, Glenfield, Green Tree, Haysville, Heidelburg, Ingram, Kilbuck, Leet Twp., Leetsdale, Liberty, McCandless, McDonald, McKees Rocks, McKeesport, Millvale, Monessen, Monongahela, Moon Twp., Morgan, Neville Twp., New Eagle, New Sewickley Twp., North Belle Vernon, North Charleroi, North Fayette Twp. (Allegheny County), North Franklin Twp., Oakdale, O'Hara Twp., Ohio Twp., Osborne, Pennsbury Village, Pleasant Hills, Port Vue, Presto, Reserve Twp. (Allegheny County), Ross Twp. (Allegheny County), Rosslyn Farms, Rostraver Twp., Scott Twp. (Allegheny Twp.), Sewickley, Sewickley Heights, Sewickley Hills, Shaler Twp., Sharpsburg, South Fayette Twp., South Franklin Twp., South Heights, South Park, South Strabane Twp., Speers, Thornburg, Twilight, Versailles, Washington, West Elizabeth, West View, Whitehall & Wilkinsburg. ICA: PA0001.

TV Market Ranking: 10 (Aliquippa, Ambridge, Amity, Amwell Twp., Aspinwall, Avalon, Baden, Baldwin, Bell Acres, Belle Vernon, Bellevue, Ben Avon, Ben Avon Heights, Blaine Twp., Braddock Hills, Brentwood, Bridgeville, Buffalo Twp. (Washington County), Canonsburg, Carnegie, Carroll Twp. (Washington County), Castle Shannon, Center Twp. (Beaver County), Chalfant, Charleroi, Chartiers Twp. (Washington County), Clairton, Collier Twp., Conway, Coraopolis, Crafton, Crescent Twp., Cuddy, Donora, Dormont, East Washington, Economy, Edgewood, Edgeworth, Emsworth, Etna, Fallowfield Twp., Findlay Twp. (Allegheny County), Forest Hills, Forward Twp. (Allegheny County), Fox Chapel, Franklin Park, Glassport, Glenfield, Green Tree, Haysville, Heidelburg, Ingram, Kilbuck, Leet Twp., Leetsdale, Liberty, Lincoln (Allegheny County), McCandless, McDonald, McKees Rocks, McKeesport, Millvale, Monessen, Monongahela, Moon Twp., Morgan, Neville Twp., New Eagle, New Sewickley Twp., North Belle Vernon, North Charleroi, North Fayette Twp. (Allegheny County), North Franklin Twp., Oakdale, O'Hara Twp., Ohio Twp., Osborne, Pennsbury Village, PITTSBURGH, Pleasant Hills, Port Vue, Presto, Reserve Twp. (Allegheny County), Ross Twp., Rosslyn Farms, Rostraver Twp., Scott Twp. (Allegheny County), Sewickley, Sewickley Heights, Sewickley Hills, Shaler Twp., Sharpsburg, South Fayette Twp. (Allegheny County), South Franklin Twp., South Heights, South Park, South Strabane Twp., Speers, Thornburg, Twilight, Versailles, Washington, West Elizabeth, West View, Whitehall, Wilkinsburg). Franchise award date: N.A. Franchise expiration date: December 31, 2009. Began: December 1, 1980.

Channel capacity: 77 (operating 2-way). Channels available but not in use: N.A.

Basic Service
Subscribers: 475,249.
Programming (received off-air): KDKA-TV (CBS) Pittsburgh; WINP-TV (IND, ION) Pittsburgh; WPCB-TV (IND) Greensburg; WPCW (CW) Jeannette; WPGH-TV (FOX) Pittsburgh; WPMY (MNT) Pittsburgh; WPXI (IND, NBC) Pittsburgh; WQED (PBS) Pittsburgh; WTAE-TV (ABC) Pittsburgh.
Programming (via satellite): C-SPAN; C-SPAN 2; Eternal Word TV Network; QVC; Radar Channel; The Weather Channel; TV Guide Network; WGN America.
Fee: $43.99 installation; $12.15 monthly.

Expanded Basic Service 1
Subscribers: 94,744.
Programming (via satellite): A&E Networks; ABC Family Channel; AMC; Animal Planet; BET Networks; Cartoon Network; CNBC; CNN; Comedy Central; Country Music TV; Discovery Channel; Disney Channel; E! Entertainment Television; ESPN; ESPN 2; Food Network; Fox News Channel; FX; G4; Golf Channel; GSN; Hallmark Channel; Headline News; HGTV; History Channel; ION Television; Lifetime; MSNBC; MTV; Nickelodeon; Oxygen; Pennsylvania Cable Network; Pittsburgh Cable News Channel; Root Sports Pittsburgh; Spike TV; Style Network; TBS Superstation; The Learning Channel; Travel Channel; truTV; Turner Classic Movies; Turner Network TV; TV Land; USA Network; Versus; VH1.
Fee: $39.84 monthly.

Digital Basic Service
Subscribers: 151,355.
Programming (via satellite): BBC America; Bio; Black Family Channel; Bloomberg Television; Bravo; CBS Sports Network; Cooking Channel; Country Music TV; C-SPAN 3; Current; Daystar TV Network; DIY Network; Encore (multiplexed); ESPN 2 HD; ESPN Classic Sports; ESPN HD; ESPNews; Flix; Fox College Sports Atlantic; Fox College Sports Central; Fox College Sports Pacific; Fox Movie Channel; Fox Reality Channel; Fox Soccer; Fuse; GAS; GolTV; Great American Country; Halogen Network; HD Theater; History Channel International; HRTV; Independent Film Channel; INHD; Jewelry Television; Lifetime Movie Network; Lime; LOGO; MoviePlex; MTV Networks Digital Suite; Music Choice; National Geographic Channel; NBA TV; NFL Network; Nick Jr.; Nick Too; NickToons TV; Outdoor Channel; Palladia; PBS Kids Sprout; ShopNBC; SoapNet; Speed; Sundance Channel; Syfy; Tennis Channel; The Comcast Network; The Word Network; Toon Disney; Trinity Broadcasting Network; Turner Network TV HD; TV One; TVG Network; Universal HD; WE tv; Weatherscan.
Fee: $10.95 monthly.

Digital Pay Service 1
Pay Units: N.A.
Programming (via satellite): Cinemax (multiplexed); Cinemax HD; HBO (multiplexed); HBO HD; Playboy TV; RAI International; Russian Television Network; Showtime (multiplexed); Showtime HD; Starz (multiplexed); Starz HDTV; The Movie Channel (multiplexed); TV Asia; Zee TV USA.
Fee: $8.00 monthly (each).

Video-On-Demand: Yes

Pay-Per-View
Addressable homes: 151,355.
iN DEMAND (delivered digitally); Playboy TV (delivered digitally); Fresh (delivered digitally); Hot Choice (delivered digitally); NBA League Pass (delivered digitally); NHL Center Ice (delivered digitally); MLB Extra Innings (delivered digitally).

Internet Service
Operational: Yes.
Subscribers: 48,083.
Broadband Service: Comcast High Speed Internet.
Fee: $42.95 monthly.

Telephone Service
Digital: Operational
Subscribers: 75,615.
Fee: $44.95 monthly

Miles of Plant: 6,447.0 (coaxial); None (fiber optic).
Regional Vice President: Linda Hossinger. Vice President, Technical Operations: Randy Bender. Vice President, Marketing: Donna Coming. Vice President, Public Affairs: Jody Doherty.
Ownership: Comcast Cable Communications Inc. (MSO).

PLAINFIELD TWP.—Formerly served by NORTHAMPTON BOROUGH, PA [PA0008]. RCN Corp. This cable system has converted to IPTV, 196 Van Buren St, Herndon, VA 20170. Phone: 703-434-8200. Web Site: http://www.rcn.com. ICA: PA5231.
TV Market Ranking: Below 100 (PLAINFIELD TWP.).
Channel capacity: N.A. Channels available but not in use: N.A.

Internet Service
Operational: Yes.

Telephone Service
Digital: Operational

Chairman: Steven J. Simmons. Chief Executive Officer: Jim Holanda.

PLUM—Comcast Cable. Now served by MONROEVILLE, PA [PA0023]. ICA: PA0465.

PLUMER—Formerly served by Cebridge Connections. No longer in operation. ICA: PA0238.

POCONO—MetroCast Communications, 1059 E 10th St, Hazleton, PA 18201-3421. Phone: 570-455-4251. Fax: 570-455-4251. Web Site: http://www.metrocastcommunications.com. Also serves Albrightsville, Blakeslee, East Side, Freeland, Lake Harmony, Long Pond, Weatherly & White Haven. ICA: PA0141.
TV Market Ranking: 49 (Albrightsville, Blakeslee, East Side, Freeland, Lake Harmony, Long Pond, POCONO, Weatherly, White Haven). Franchise award date: January 1, 1972. Franchise expiration date: N.A. Began: March 22, 1973.
Channel capacity: 100 (operating 2-way). Channels available but not in use: N.A.

Basic Service
Subscribers: 4,954.
Programming (received off-air): KYW-TV (CBS) Philadelphia; WBRE-TV (NBC) Wilkes-Barre; WCAU (NBC) Philadelphia; WLVT-TV (PBS) Allentown; WNEP-TV (ABC) Scranton; WOLF-TV (CW, FOX, MNT) Hazleton; WPHL-TV (MNT, IND) Philadelphia; WPIX (CW, IND) New York; WSWB (CW) Scranton; WVIA-TV (PBS) Scranton; WYLN-LP (IND) Hazleton; WYOU (CBS) Scranton; allband FM.
Programming (via satellite): Eternal Word TV Network; QVC; TV Guide Network; WWOR-TV (MNT) Secaucus.
Fee: $60.00 installation; $15.26 monthly; $1.35 converter; $25.92 additional installation.

Expanded Basic Service 1
Subscribers: 4,355.
Programming (via satellite): A&E Networks; ABC Family Channel; AMC; Animal Planet; Bloomberg Television; Bravo; Cartoon Network; CNBC; CNN; Comcast SportsNet Philadelphia; Comedy Central; Country Music TV; C-SPAN; Discovery Channel; Disney Channel; E! Entertainment Television; ESPN; ESPN 2; Food Network; Fox Movie Channel; Fox News Channel; FX; G4; Headline News; HGTV; History Channel; Lifetime; MSNBC; MTV; National Geographic Channel; Nickelodeon; Outdoor Channel; Pennsylvania Cable Network; Spike TV; Syfy; TBS Superstation; The Learning Channel; The Weather Channel; Travel Channel; Trinity Broadcasting Network; truTV; Turner Network TV; TV Land; USA Network; Versus; VH1; WE tv.
Fee: $24.38 monthly.

Digital Basic Service
Subscribers: 918.
Programming (via satellite): BBC America; Bio; Country Music TV; DMX Music; Fuse; GAS; GSN; HD Theater; HDNet; HDNet Movies; Lifetime Movie Network; MTV2; NFL Network; Nick Jr.; NickToons TV; Outdoor Channel 2 HD; Speed; Toon Disney; Turner Network TV HD; Universal HD; VH1 Classic; WealthTV.
Fee: $25.92 installation; $7.95 monthly.

Digital Expanded Basic Service
Subscribers: N.A.
Programming (via satellite): Encore (multiplexed); ESPN Classic Sports; ESPNews; Fox Soccer; Golf Channel; History Chan-

nel International; Independent Film Channel; Starz (multiplexed); Turner Classic Movies.
Fee: $9.95 monthly.

Digital Pay Service 1
Pay Units: N.A.
Programming (via satellite): Cinemax (multiplexed); HBO (multiplexed); Showtime (multiplexed); Showtime HD; Starz HDTV; The Movie Channel (multiplexed).
Fee: $12.95 monthly (Cinemax, HBO, or Showtime/TMC).

Video-On-Demand: No

Pay-Per-View
iN DEMAND.

Internet Service
Operational: Yes. Began: April 1, 2002.
Broadband Service: MetroCast Internet.
Fee: $39.95 monthly.

Telephone Service
None

Miles of Plant: 112.0 (coaxial); 6.0 (fiber optic).

General Manager: Danny Jobe. Programming Director: Linda Stuchell.

Ownership: Harron Communications LP (MSO).

PORT ROYAL—Nittany Media Inc. Now served by LEWISTOWN (formerly McAlisterville), PA [PA0365]. ICA: PA0392.

PORTAGE—Formerly served by Adelphia Communications. Now served by ADAMS TWP. (Cambria County), PA [PA0133]. ICA: PA0146.

POTTSTOWN—Comcast Cable, 3220 Tillman Dr, Bensalem, PA 19010. Phone: 215-642-6400. Fax: 215-638-6510. Web Site: http://www.comcast.com. Also serves Bally, Bechtelsville, Boyertown, Colebrookdale Twp., Douglass Twp. (Montgomery County), Earl Twp. (Berks County), East Coventry Twp., East Greenville, East Pikeland Twp., East Vincent Twp., Hereford Twp. (Berks County), Limerick Twp., Lower Pottsgrove Twp., New Hanover Twp. (Montgomery County), North Coventry Twp., Oley Twp. (Berks County), Pennsburg, Phoenixville, Red Hill, Royersford, Schuylkill Twp. (Chester County), South Coventry Twp., Spring City, Upper Hanover Twp., Upper Pottsgrove, West Pottsgrove Twp. & Worcester. ICA: PA0394.

TV Market Ranking: 4 (Boyertown, Colebrookdale Twp., Douglass Twp. (Montgomery County), East Coventry Twp., East Greenville, East Pikeland Twp., East Vincent Twp., Limerick Twp., Lower Pottsgrove Twp., New Hanover Twp. (Montgomery County), North Coventry Twp., Pennsburg, Phoenixville, POTTSTOWN, Red Hill, Royersford, Schuylkill Twp. (Chester County), South Coventry Twp., Spring City, Upper Hanover Twp., Upper Pottsgrove, West Pottsgrove Twp., Worcester); Below 100 (Bally, Bechtelsville, Earl Twp. (Berks County), Hereford Twp. (Berks County), Oley Twp. (Berks County)). Franchise award date: May 1, 1977. Franchise expiration date: N.A. Began: February 14, 1979.

Channel capacity: N.A. Channels available but not in use: N.A.

Basic Service
Subscribers: N.A. Included in Bensalem Twp.
Programming (received off-air): KYW-TV (CBS) Philadelphia; WBPH-TV (IND) Bethlehem; WCAU (NBC) Philadelphia; WFMZ-TV (IND) Allentown; WGTW-TV (TBN) Burlington; WHYY-TV (PBS) Wilmington; WLVT-TV (PBS) Allentown; WMCN-TV (IND) Atlantic City; WNJT (PBS) Trenton; WPHL-TV (MNT, IND) Philadelphia; WPPX-TV (ION) Wilmington; WPSG (CW) Philadelphia; WPVI-TV (ABC) Philadelphia; WTVE (IND) Reading; WTXF-TV (FOX) Philadelphia; WUVP-DT (UNV) Vineland; WWSI (TMO) Atlantic City; WYBE (ETV, IND) Philadelphia.
Programming (via satellite): C-SPAN; Pennsylvania Cable Network; Philadelphia Park Live; QVC; The Comcast Network.
Fee: $16.10 monthly.

Expanded Basic Service 1
Subscribers: 49,508.
Programming (via satellite): A&E Networks; ABC Family Channel; AMC; Animal Planet; BET Networks; Bravo; Cartoon Network; CNBC; CNN; Comcast SportsNet Philadelphia; Comedy Central; Discovery Channel; Discovery Health Channel; Disney Channel; E! Entertainment Television; ESPN; ESPN 2; Food Network; Fox News Channel; FX; Golf Channel; GSN; Headline News; HGTV; History Channel; Lifetime; MSNBC; MTV; MTV2; Nickelodeon; Speed; Spike TV; Style Network; Syfy; TBS Superstation; The Learning Channel; The Weather Channel; Travel Channel; truTV; Turner Classic Movies; Turner Network TV; TV Land; USA Network; Versus; VH1.
Fee: $34.30 monthly.

Digital Basic Service
Subscribers: N.A.
Programming (via satellite): BBC America; Bio; Canales N; CBS Sports Network; CMT Pure Country; Cooking Channel; Country Music TV; C-SPAN 2; C-SPAN 3; Current; DIY Network; Encore; ESPN 2 HD; ESPN HD; ESPNews; Eternal Word TV Network; FEARnet; Flix; Fox College Sports Atlantic; Fox College Sports Central; Fox College Sports Pacific; Fox Reality Channel; Fox Soccer; G4; GAS; GolTV; Great American Country; Hallmark Channel; HD Theater; History Channel International; Independent Film Channel; INHD; Jewelry Television; Lifetime Movie Network; LOGO; MTV Networks Digital Suite; Music Choice; National Geographic Channel; NBA TV; NFL Network; Nick Jr.; Nick Too; NickToons TV; Oxygen; Palladia; PBS Kids Sprout; Pennsylvania Cable Network; ShopNBC; SoapNet; Sundance Channel; Telefutura; Tennis Channel; Toon Disney; Travel Channel; Turner Network TV HD; TV One; Universal HD; Versus HD; Weatherscan.
Fee: $14.95 monthly.

Digital Pay Service 1
Pay Units: N.A.
Programming (via satellite): Cinemax (multiplexed); Cinemax HD; HBO (multiplexed); HBO HD; Showtime (multiplexed); Showtime HD; Starz (multiplexed); Starz HDTV; The Movie Channel (multiplexed).

Video-On-Demand: Yes

Pay-Per-View
iN DEMAND (delivered digitally); Playboy TV (delivered digitally); Fresh (delivered digitally); MLS Direct Kick (delivered digitally); MLB Extra Innings (delivered digitally); ESPN (delivered digitally); NBA TV (delivered digitally); NHL Center Ice (delivered digitally); NBA League Pass (delivered digitally).

Internet Service
Operational: Yes.
Broadband Service: Comcast High Speed Internet.
Fee: $42.95 monthly.

Telephone Service
Digital: Operational
Fee: $44.95 monthly

Miles of Plant: 916.0 (coaxial); 60.0 (fiber optic).

Senior Regional Vice President: Amy Smith. Vice President, Technical Operations: Rich Massi. Vice President, Marketing: Chip Goodman.

Ownership: Comcast Cable Communications Inc. (MSO).

POTTSVILLE—Comcast Cable, 1 E Uwchlan Ave, Ste 411, Exton, PA 19341. Phone: 484-288-6500. Web Site: http://www.comcast.com. Also serves Branch Twp., Cass Twp. (Schuylkill County), Cressona, East Norwegian Twp. (Schuylkill County), Friedensburg, Landingville, Llewellyn, Mar Lin, Minersville, Mount Carbon, North Manheim Twp., Norwegian Twp. (Schuylkill County), Orwigsburg, Pine Grove (Schuylkill County), Schuylkill County, Schuylkill Haven, Seltzer, South Manheim Twp., Tremont Twp. & West Brunswick Twp. ICA: PA0060.

TV Market Ranking: 49,57 (Schuylkill County (portions)); 57 (Mount Carbon, Pine Grove (Schuylkill County), Tremont Twp.); Below 100 (Branch Twp., Cass Twp. (Schuylkill County), Cressona, East Norwegian Twp. (Schuylkill County), Friedensburg, Landingville, Llewellyn, Mar Lin, Minersville, North Manheim Twp., Norwegian Twp. (Schuylkill County), Orwigsburg, POTTSVILLE, Schuylkill Haven, Seltzer, South Manheim Twp., West Brunswick Twp., Schuylkill County (portions)). Franchise award date: N.A. Franchise expiration date: N.A. Began: February 1, 1951.

Channel capacity: 60 (operating 2-way). Channels available but not in use: N.A.

Basic Service
Subscribers: N.A. Included in Harrisburg
Programming (received off-air): WBRE-TV (NBC) Wilkes-Barre; WGAL (NBC) Lancaster; WLYH-TV (CW) Lancaster; WNEP-TV (ABC) Scranton; WOLF-TV (CW, FOX, MNT) Hazleton; WPHL-TV (MNT, IND) Philadelphia; WPVI-TV (ABC) Philadelphia; WSWB (CW) Scranton; WTXF-TV (FOX) Philadelphia; WVIA-TV (PBS) Scranton; WYOU (CBS) Scranton; allband FM.
Programming (via satellite): C-SPAN; ION Television; The Comcast Network.
Fee: $45.10 installation; $11.25 monthly.

Expanded Basic Service 1
Subscribers: N.A.
Programming (via satellite): A&E Networks; ABC Family Channel; AMC; Animal Planet; Bravo; Cartoon Network; CNBC; CNN; Comcast SportsNet Philadelphia; Comedy Central; Country Music TV; C-SPAN 2; Discovery Channel; Discovery Health Channel; Disney Channel; E! Entertainment Television; ESPN; ESPN 2; Eternal Word TV Network; Food Network; Fox News Channel; FX; Golf Channel; GSN; Hallmark Channel; Headline News; HGTV; History Channel; INSP; Lifetime; MSNBC; MTV; Nickelodeon; Pennsylvania Cable Network; QVC; ShopNBC; Speed; Spike TV; Style Network; Syfy; TBS Superstation; The Learning Channel; The Weather Channel; Travel Channel; truTV; Turner Classic Movies; Turner Network TV; TV Guide Network; TV Land; USA Network; Versus; VH1; WWOR-TV (MNT) Secaucus.
Fee: $35.75 monthly.

Digital Basic Service
Subscribers: N.A.
Programming (via satellite): BBC America; Bio; CBS Sports Network; CMT Pure Country; Cooking Channel; C-SPAN 3; Current; DIY Network; Encore (multiplexed); ESPN 2 HD; ESPN HD; ESPNews; FEARnet; Flix; Fox College Sports Atlantic; Fox College Sports Central; Fox College Sports Pacific; Fox Reality Channel; Fox Soccer; G4; GAS; GolTV; HD Theater; History Channel International; INHD; Jewelry Television; Lifetime Movie Network; LOGO; MTV Networks Digital Suite; Music Choice; National Geographic Channel; NBA TV; NFL Network; Nick Jr.; Nick Too; NickToons TV; Outdoor Channel; Oxygen; Palladia; PBS Kids Sprout; SoapNet; Sundance Channel; Toon Disney; Turner Network TV HD; TV One; Universal HD; Versus HD; Weatherscan.
Fee: $14.95 monthly.

Digital Pay Service 1
Pay Units: N.A.
Programming (via satellite): Cinemax (multiplexed); Cinemax HD; Great American Country; HBO (multiplexed); HBO HD; Showtime (multiplexed); Showtime HD; Starz HDTV; The Movie Channel (multiplexed).

Video-On-Demand: Yes

Pay-Per-View
iN DEMAND (delivered digitally); Playboy TV (delivered digitally); Fresh (delivered digitally); NBA TV (delivered digitally); MLS Direct Kick; NBA League Pass (delivered digitally); NHL Center Ice (delivered digitally); ESPN Gameplan (delivered digitally); ESPN Full Court (delivered digitally).

Internet Service
Operational: Yes.
Broadband Service: Comcast High Speed Internet.
Fee: $42.95 monthly.

Telephone Service
Analog: Not Operational
Digital: Operational

Miles of Plant: 388.0 (coaxial); 25.0 (fiber optic). Additional miles planned: 16.0 (coaxial).

Area Vice President: Jim Samaha. Vice President, Marketing: Larry Goldman.

Ownership: Comcast Cable Communications Inc. (MSO).

POTTSVILLE—Wire Television Corp., 603 E Market St, Pottsville, PA 17901-2718. Phone: 570-622-4501. Fax: 570-622-8340. E-mail: customerservice@wtvaccess.com. Web Site: http://www.wtvaccess.com. Also serves Palo Alto & Port Carbon. ICA: PA0123.

TV Market Ranking: Below 100 (Palo Alto, Port Carbon, POTTSVILLE). Franchise award date: N.A. Franchise expiration date: N.A. Began: June 11, 1951.

Channel capacity: 65 (operating 2-way). Channels available but not in use: N.A.

Basic Service
Subscribers: 2,247.
Programming (received off-air): KYW-TV (CBS) Philadelphia; WCAU (NBC) Philadelphia; WFMZ-TV (IND) Allentown; WGAL (NBC) Lancaster; WHP-TV (CBS, MNT) Harrisburg; WHTM-TV (ABC) Harrisburg; WITF-TV (PBS) Harrisburg; WNEP-TV (ABC) Scranton; WOLF-TV (CW, FOX, MNT) Hazleton; WPIX (CW, IND) New York; WPSG (CW) Philadelphia; WSWB (CW) Scranton; WTXF-TV (FOX) Philadelphia; WVIA-TV (PBS) Scranton; allband FM.
Programming (via satellite): A&E Networks; ABC Family Channel; AMC; AmericanLife TV Network; Animal Planet; Bloomberg Television; Cartoon Network; CNN; Comcast SportsNet Philadelphia; Comedy Central; Country Music TV; C-SPAN 2; Discovery Channel; Disney Channel; ESPN; ESPN 2; Eternal Word TV Network; Food Network; Fox News Channel; Fox Sports Net Philadelphia; FX; Hallmark Channel; HGTV; History Channel; INSP; ION Television; Lifetime; Lifetime Movie Network; MTV; National Geographic Channel; Nickelodeon; Pennsylvania Cable Network;

QVC; Spike TV; Syfy; TBS Superstation; The Learning Channel; The Weather Channel; Travel Channel; truTV; Turner Network TV; TV Land; USA Network; VH1; WGN America.

Fee: $37.50 installation; $44.55 monthly.

Digital Basic Service

Subscribers: N.A.

Programming (via satellite): BBC America; Bravo; Daystar TV Network; Discovery Fit & Health; Discovery Health Channel; Discovery Kids Channel; DMX Music; ESPN Classic Sports; ESPNews; Fox College Sports Atlantic; Fox College Sports Central; Fox College Sports Pacific; Fox Movie Channel; Fox Soccer; G4; GMC; Golf Channel; Great American Country; GSN; Halogen Network; HGTV; History Channel; ID Investigation Discovery; Independent Film Channel; Military Channel; National Geographic Channel; Nick Jr.; NickToons TV; Outdoor Channel; Planet Green; Science; ShopNBC; SoapNet; Speed; The Word Network; Trinity Broadcasting Network; Turner Classic Movies; Versus; VH1 Classic; VH1 Country; WE tv.

Fee: $20.95 monthly.

Pay Service 1

Pay Units: 155.

Programming (via satellite): HBO.

Fee: $15.00 installation; $15.95 monthly.

Pay Service 2

Pay Units: 86.

Programming (via satellite): Cinemax.

Fee: $15.00 installation; $15.95 monthly.

Digital Pay Service 1

Pay Units: N.A.

Programming (via satellite): Cinemax (multiplexed); Encore (multiplexed); Flix; HBO (multiplexed); Playboy TV; Showtime (multiplexed); Starz (multiplexed); The Movie Channel.

Fee: $15.95 monthly (HBO, Cinemax, Showtime/TMC/Flix or Starz/Encore).

Pay-Per-View

iN DEMAND (delivered digitally); Fresh (delivered digitally); Club Jenna (delivered digitally).

Internet Service

Operational: Yes. Began: March 1, 2001.

Subscribers: 112.

Broadband Service: Wtvaccess.

Fee: $49.95 installation; $24.95 monthly; $10.00 modem lease; $150.00 modem purchase.

Telephone Service

None

Miles of Plant: 33.0 (coaxial); None (fiber optic).

Manager: Margaret Davenport. Chief Technician: Brian Brennan.

Ownership: Wire Tele-View Corp. (MSO).

PRIMROSE—J. B. Cable, PO Box 268, Minersville, PA 17954-0268. Phone: 570-544-5582. Also serves Branch Twp., Cass Twp. (Schuylkill County), Foster Twp. (Schuylkill County) & Reilly Twp. ICA: PA0395.

TV Market Ranking: Below 100 (Branch Twp., Cass Twp. (Schuylkill County), Foster Twp. (Schuylkill County), PRIMROSE, Reilly Twp.). Franchise award date: N.A. Franchise expiration date: N.A. Began: January 1, 1950.

Channel capacity: 36 (not 2-way capable). Channels available but not in use: N.A.

Basic Service

Subscribers: 620.

Programming (received off-air): KYW-TV (CBS) Philadelphia; WCAU (NBC) Philadelphia; WFMZ-TV (IND) Allentown; WGAL (NBC) Lancaster; WNEP-TV (ABC) Scranton; WOLF-TV (CW, FOX, MNT) Hazleton; WPHL-TV (MNT, IND) Philadelphia; WPMT (FOX) York; WPVI-TV (ABC) Philadelphia; WTXF-TV (FOX) Philadelphia; WVIA-TV (PBS) Scranton; WYOU (CBS) Scranton.

Programming (via satellite): CNN; Country Music TV; Discovery Channel; ESPN; TBS Superstation; Turner Network TV; USA Network.

Fee: $40.00 installation; $35.00 monthly.

Video-On-Demand: No

Internet Service

Operational: No.

Telephone Service

None

Miles of Plant: 34.0 (coaxial); None (fiber optic).

Manager: Thomas O'Brien. Chief Technician: Edward Goodman.

Ownership: J. B. Cable.

PROSPECT PARK—RCN Corp. Formerly served by Philadelphia (suburbs), PA [PA0447]. This cable system has converted to IPTV, 196 Van Buren St, Herndon, VA 20170. Phone: 703-434-8200. Web Site: http://www.rcn.com. ICA: PA5260.

Channel capacity: N.A. Channels available but not in use: N.A.

Internet Service

Operational: Yes.

Chairman: Steven J. Simmons. Chief Executive Officer: Jim Holanda.

PULASKI—Comcast Cable, 15 Summit Park Dr, Pittsburgh, PA 15275. Phones: 800-527-2222; 800-266-2278. Fax: 412-747-6401. Web Site: http://www.comcast.com. Also serves Mahoning Twp. (Lawrence County) & Pulaski Twp. (Lawrence County). ICA: PA0396.

TV Market Ranking: 79 (Mahoning Twp. (Lawrence County), PULASKI, Pulaski Twp. (Lawrence County)). Franchise award date: N.A. Franchise expiration date: N.A. Began: May 1, 1988.

Channel capacity: 54 (operating 2-way). Channels available but not in use: N.A.

Basic Service

Subscribers: 265.

Programming (received off-air): KDKA-TV (CBS) Pittsburgh; WFMJ-TV (CW, NBC) Youngstown; WKBN-TV (CBS) Youngstown; WNEO (PBS) Alliance; WPGH-TV (FOX) Pittsburgh; WPXI (IND, NBC) Pittsburgh; WQED (PBS) Pittsburgh; WTAE-TV (ABC) Pittsburgh; WYTV (ABC, MNT) Youngstown.

Programming (via satellite): A&E Networks; ABC Family Channel; AMC; Cartoon Network; CNN; Comedy Central; Country Music TV; Discovery Channel; ESPN; Headline News; HGTV; History Channel; Lifetime; MTV; Nickelodeon; QVC; Root Sports Pittsburgh; Spike TV; Syfy; TBS Superstation; The Learning Channel; The Weather Channel; Travel Channel; Turner Network TV; USA Network; WGN America.

Fee: $35.00 installation; $41.75 monthly; $35.00 additional installation.

Digital Basic Service

Subscribers: N.A.

Programming (via satellite): AmericanLife TV Network; Bio; Black Family Channel; Bloomberg Television; cloo; Discovery Fit & Health; DMX Music; ESPN 2; ESPN Classic Sports; ESPNews; Fox Movie Channel; Fox Sports World; FSN Digital Atlantic; FSN Digital Central; FSN Digital Pacific; Fuse; G4; GAS; Golf Channel; Great American Country; GSN; Halogen Network; HGTV; History Channel; History Channel International; MTV Networks Digital Suite; National Geographic Channel; Nick Jr.; NickToons TV; Outdoor Channel; Ovation; Speed; Style Network; Syfy; Toon Disney; Trinity Broadcasting Network; Turner Classic Movies; Versus; WE tv.

Fee: $40.00 installation; $12.95 monthly (Digital Basic), $3.95 monthly (Sports Tier).

Digital Pay Service 1

Pay Units: N.A.

Programming (via satellite): Cinemax (multiplexed); Encore (multiplexed); HBO (multiplexed); Showtime (multiplexed); Starz (multiplexed); Sundance Channel; The Movie Channel (multiplexed).

Fee: $11.99 monthly (Cinemax, Showtime/TMC, or Starz/Encore), $12.99 monthly (HBO).

Video-On-Demand: No

Internet Service

Operational: Yes. Began: May 24, 2003.

Subscribers: 52.

Broadband Service: Comcast High Speed Internet.

Fee: $27.95-$55.95 monthly; $7.95 modem lease.

Telephone Service

Analog: Not Operational

Digital: Operational

Fee: $44.95 monthly

Miles of Plant: 55.0 (coaxial); None (fiber optic).

Regional Vice President: Linda Hossinger.

Ownership: Comcast Cable Communications Inc.

PUNXSUTAWNEY—Comcast Cable, 15 Summit Park Dr, Pittsburgh, PA 15275. Phones: 814-938-6130 (Punxsutawny office); 412-747-6400. Fax: 412-747-6401. Web Site: http://www.comcast.com. Also serves Bell Twp. (Clearfield County), Bell Twp. (Jefferson County), Big Run, Brockport, Burnside, Canoe Twp., Clearfield County (portions), Clover Twp., Du Bois, Fairmount City, Falls Creek, Gaskill Twp., Hawthorn, Henderson Twp. (Jefferson County), Horton Twp. (Elk County), Jefferson County, Knox Twp., Limestone Twp., Mahaffey, McCalmont Twp., New Bethlehem, Oak Ridge, Redbank Twp., Reynoldsville, Ridgway Borough, Ringgold Twp., Rose Twp., Rossiter, Sandy Twp., Snyder Twp. (Jefferson County), South Bethlehem, Summerville, Sykesville, Timblin, Troutville, Union Twp., Walston, Winslow Twp. (portions), Worthville & Young Twp. (Jefferson County). ICA: PA0397.

TV Market Ranking: Outside TV Markets (Bell Twp. (Clearfield County), Bell Twp. (Jefferson County), Big Run, Brockport, Burnside, Canoe Twp., Clearfield County (portions), Clover Twp., Du Bois, Fairmount City, Falls Creek, Gaskill Twp., Hawthorn, Henderson Twp. (Jefferson County), Horton Twp. (Elk County), Jefferson County, Knox Twp., Limestone Twp., Mahaffey, McCalmont Twp., New Bethlehem, Oak Ridge, PUNXSUTAWNEY, Redbank Twp., Reynoldsville, Ridgway Borough, Ringgold Twp., Rose Twp., Rossiter, Sandy Twp., Snyder Twp. (Jefferson County), South Bethlehem, Summerville, Sykesville, Timblin, Troutville, Union Twp., Walston, Winslow Twp. (portions), Worthville, Young Twp. (Jefferson County)). Franchise award date: N.A. Franchise expiration date: N.A. Began: December 1, 1964.

Channel capacity: 82 (operating 2-way). Channels available but not in use: N.A.

Basic Service

Subscribers: N.A. Included in Bensalem Twp.

Programming (received off-air): KDKA-TV (CBS) Pittsburgh; WATM-TV (ABC) Altoona; WJAC-TV (NBC) Johnstown; WPCB-TV (IND) Greensburg; WPCW (CW) Jeannette; WPMY (MNT) Pittsburgh; WPSU-TV (PBS) Clearfield; WPXI (IND, NBC) Pittsburgh; WQED (PBS) Pittsburgh; WTAE-TV (ABC) Pittsburgh; WTAJ-TV (CBS) Altoona; WWCP-TV (FOX) Johnstown; 20 FMs.

Programming (via satellite): Product Information Network; QVC; ShopNBC; TV Guide Network; WGN America.

Fee: $39.95 installation; $17.80 monthly; $2.00 converter.

Expanded Basic Service 1

Subscribers: 15,568.

Programming (via satellite): A&E Networks; ABC Family Channel; AMC; Animal Planet; Bravo; Cartoon Network; CNBC; CNN; Comedy Central; Country Music TV; C-SPAN; C-SPAN 2; Discovery Channel; Disney Channel; E! Entertainment Television; ESPN; ESPN 2; Eternal Word TV Network; Food Network; Fox News Channel; FX; Hallmark Channel; Headline News; HGTV; History Channel; Lifetime; Meadows Racing Network; MSNBC; MTV; Nickelodeon; Oxygen; Pennsylvania Cable Network; Root Sports Pittsburgh; Spike TV; Style Network; Syfy; TBS Superstation; The Learning Channel; The Weather Channel; Travel Channel; truTV; Turner Classic Movies; Turner Network TV; TV Land; USA Network; VH1.

Fee: $34.60 monthly.

Digital Basic Service

Subscribers: 3,600.

Programming (via satellite): AmericanLife TV Network; BBC America; Bloomberg Television; Discovery Fit & Health; ESPNews; Fox Movie Channel; Fox Sports World; G4; Golf Channel; GSN; Halogen Network; Outdoor Channel; Speed; Trinity Broadcasting Network; Versus.

Fee: $10.95 monthly.

Digital Expanded Basic Service

Subscribers: N.A.

Programming (via satellite): GAS; MTV Networks Digital Suite; Music Choice; National Geographic Channel; Nick Jr.; Nick Too; NickToons TV.

Fee: $5.00 monthly.

Digital Pay Service 1

Pay Units: 6,662.

Programming (via satellite): Cinemax (multiplexed); Encore (multiplexed); HBO (multiplexed); Showtime (multiplexed); Starz (multiplexed); The Movie Channel (multiplexed).

Video-On-Demand: Yes

Pay-Per-View
HITS PPV 1-30 (delivered digitally); Hot Choice (delivered digitally); Fresh (delivered digitally); Playboy TV (delivered digitally).
Internet Service
Operational: Yes.
Subscribers: 3,400.
Broadband Service: Comcast High Speed Internet.
Fee: $42.95 monthly.
Telephone Service
None
Miles of Plant: 504.0 (coaxial); 23.0 (fiber optic).
Regional Vice President: Linda Hossinger. Vice President, Technical Operations: Randy Bender. Vice President, Public Affairs: Jody Doherty. Marketing Manager: Donna Corning.
Ownership: Comcast Cable Communications Inc. (MSO).

RALSTON—Zito Media, 611 Vader Hill Rd, Coudersport, PA 16915. Phone: 570-673-5326. Web Site: http://www.zitomedia.com. Also serves Roaring Branch. ICA: PA0253.
TV Market Ranking: Below 100 (RALSTON, Roaring Branch). Franchise award date: N.A. Franchise expiration date: N.A. Began: January 1, 1952.
Channel capacity: N.A. Channels available but not in use: N.A.
Basic Service
Subscribers: 120.
Programming (received off-air): WBRE-TV (NBC) Wilkes-Barre; WNEP-TV (ABC) Scranton; WSWB (CW) Scranton; WVIA-TV (PBS) Scranton; WYOU (CBS) Scranton; allband FM.
Programming (via satellite): A&E Networks; ABC Family Channel; Animal Planet; CNBC; CNN; Comedy Central; CTV Inc.; Discovery Channel; ESPN; ESPN 2; Fox News Channel; FX; Hallmark Channel; Headline News; History Channel; Lifetime; MTV; Nickelodeon; Outdoor Channel; QVC; Speed; Spike TV; Syfy; TBS Superstation; The Learning Channel; The Weather Channel; Trinity Broadcasting Network; Turner Network TV; TV Land; USA Network; VH1; WGN America.
Fee: $39.00 monthly.
Pay Service 1
Pay Units: 38.
Programming (via satellite): Showtime.
Fee: $11.00 monthly.
Video-On-Demand: No
Internet Service
Operational: No.
Telephone Service
None
Miles of Plant: 15.0 (coaxial); None (fiber optic). Additional miles planned: 1.0 (coaxial).
Public Relations Manager: Mark Laver.
Ownership: Zito Media (MSO).

RAYNE TWP.—Formerly served by Satterlee Leasing Inc. No longer in operation. ICA: PA0399.

READING—Comcast Cable, 400 Riverfront Dr, Reading, PA 19602. Phone: 800-266-2278 (Customer service). Web Site: http://www.comcast.com. Also serves Alsace Twp., Bern Twp. (Berks County), Bernville, Brecknock Twp. (Lancaster County), Centerport, Centre Twp., Cumru Twp., Greenwich Twp., Hamburg, Kenhorst, Laureldale, Leesport, Lenhartsville, Lower Alsace Twp., Lower Heidelberg Twp. (Berks County), Maidencreek Twp. (Berks County), Mohnton, Mount Penn, Muhlenberg Twp., North Heidelberg, Ontelaunee Twp., Perry Twp., Port Clinton, Ruscombmanor Twp. (Berks County), Shartlesville, Shillington, Shoemakersville, Sinking Spring, South Heidelberg Twp. (Berks County), Spring Twp. (Berks County), Strausstown, Temple, Tilden Twp., Upper Bern Twp., Wernersville, West Lawn, West Reading, Wyomissing & Wyomissing Hills. ICA: PA0012.
TV Market Ranking: 57 (Alsace Twp., Bern Twp. (Berks County), Bernville, Brecknock Twp. (Lancaster County), Centerport, Centre Twp. (Berks County), Cumru Twp., Kenhorst, Laureldale, Leesport, Lower Alsace Twp., Lower Heidelberg Twp. (Berks County), Maidencreek Twp. (Berks County), Mohnton, Mount Penn, Muhlenberg Twp., North Heidelberg, Ontelaunee Twp. (Berks County), READING, Ruscombmanor Twp. (Berks County), Shartlesville, Shillington, Sinking Spring, South Heidelberg Twp. (Berks County), Spring Twp. (Berks County), Strausstown, Temple, Tilden Twp., Upper Bern Twp., Wernersville, West Lawn, West Reading, Wyomissing, Wyomissing Hills); Below 100 (Greenwich Twp. (Berks County), Hamburg, Lenhartsville, Perry Twp. (Berks County), Port Clinton, Shoemakersville). Franchise award date: January 1, 1963. Franchise expiration date: N.A. Began: May 1, 1964.
Channel capacity: N.A. Channels available but not in use: N.A.
Basic Service
Subscribers: N.A. Included in Harrisburg
Programming (received off-air): KYW-TV (CBS) Philadelphia; WCAU (NBC) Philadelphia; WFMZ-TV (IND) Allentown; WGAL (NBC) Lancaster; WGTW-TV (TBN) Burlington; WHYY-TV (PBS) Wilmington; WITF-TV (PBS) Harrisburg; WLVT-TV (PBS) Allentown; WMCN-TV (IND) Atlantic City; WPHL-TV (MNT, IND) Philadelphia; WPMT (FOX) York; WPSG (CW) Philadelphia; WPVI-TV (ABC) Philadelphia; WTVE (IND) Reading; WTXF-TV (FOX) Philadelphia; WUVP-DT (UNV) Vineland; WVIA-TV (PBS) Scranton; WWSI (TMO) Atlantic City; WYBE (ETV, IND) Philadelphia.
Programming (via satellite): ION Television.
Fee: $45.50 installation; $11.25 monthly; $15.00 additional installation.
Expanded Basic Service 1
Subscribers: N.A.
Programming (via satellite): A&E Networks; ABC Family Channel; Animal Planet; BET Networks; Bravo; Cartoon Network; CNBC; Comcast SportsNet Philadelphia; Comedy Central; Country Music TV; C-SPAN; C-SPAN 2; Discovery Health Channel; Disney Channel; E! Entertainment Television; ESPN; ESPN 2; Eternal Word TV Network; Food Network; Fox News Channel; FX; GalaVision; Golf Channel; GSN; Hallmark Channel; Headline News; HGTV; History Channel; Lifetime; MSNBC; MTV; Nickelodeon; Oxygen; Pennsylvania Cable Network; QVC; Speed; Spike TV; Syfy; The Comcast Network; The Learning Channel; The Weather Channel; Travel Channel; truTV; Turner Classic Movies; Turner Network TV; TV Land; USA Network; Versus; VH1.
Fee: $41.15 monthly.
Digital Basic Service
Subscribers: N.A.
Programming (via satellite): BBC America; Bio; Cooking Channel; C-SPAN 3; Discovery Digital Networks; DIY Network; DMX Music; ESPNews; Flix; G4; GAS; History Channel International; MTV Networks Digital Suite; National Geographic Channel; Nick Jr.; Nick Too; Science Television; SoapNet; Sundance Channel; Toon Disney; WAM! America's Kidz Network; Weatherscan.
Fee: $14.95 monthly.
Digital Pay Service 1
Pay Units: N.A.
Programming (via satellite): Cinemax (multiplexed); Encore; HBO (multiplexed); Showtime (multiplexed); The Movie Channel (multiplexed).
Video-On-Demand: Yes
Pay-Per-View
Addressable homes: 22,009.
Hot Choice (delivered digitally); iN DEMAND (delivered digitally); Spice (delivered digitally); Playboy TV (delivered digitally); Pleasure (delivered digitally); ESPN (delivered digitally); NBA (delivered digitally); NHL/MLB (delivered digitally).
Internet Service
Operational: Yes.
Broadband Service: Comcast High Speed Internet.
Fee: $42.95 monthly.
Telephone Service
Digital: Operational
Fee: $44.95 monthly
Miles of Plant: 3,637.0 (coaxial); 143.0 (fiber optic).
Area Vice President: Jim Samaha. Vice President, Marketing: Larry Goldman.
Ownership: Comcast Cable Communications Inc. (MSO).

READING—Formerly served by Digital Wireless Systems. No longer in operation. ICA: PA0430.

REEDSVILLE—Comcast Cable, 1 E Uwchlan Ave, Ste 411, Exton, PA 19341. Phone: 484-288-6500. Web Site: http://www.comcast.com. Also serves Brown Twp. (Mifflin County) & Milroy. ICA: PA0150.
TV Market Ranking: Outside TV Markets (Brown Twp. (Mifflin County), Milroy, REEDSVILLE). Franchise award date: N.A. Franchise expiration date: N.A. Began: December 1, 1953.
Channel capacity: 71 (not 2-way capable). Channels available but not in use: N.A.
Basic Service
Subscribers: N.A. Included in Harrisburg
Programming (received off-air): WATM-TV (ABC) Altoona; WGAL (NBC) Lancaster; WHP-TV (CBS, MNT) Harrisburg; WHTM-TV (ABC) Harrisburg; WJAC-TV (NBC) Johnstown; WKBS-TV (IND) Altoona; WLYH-TV (CW) Lancaster; WPMT (FOX) York; WPSU-TV (PBS) Clearfield; WTAJ-TV (CBS) Altoona; allband FM.
Programming (via satellite): ABC Family Channel; AMC; CNN; C-SPAN; ESPN; QVC; TV Guide Network.
Fee: $25.00 installation; $12.74 monthly.
Expanded Basic Service 1
Subscribers: N.A.
Programming (via satellite): A&E Networks; Animal Planet; Bravo; Cartoon Network; CNBC; Comedy Central; Country Music TV; C-SPAN 2; Discovery Channel; Disney Channel; E! Entertainment Television; ESPN 2; Eternal Word TV Network; Food Network; Fox News Channel; FX; Golf Channel; GSN; Hallmark Channel; Headline News; HGTV; History Channel; ION Television; Lifetime; MSNBC; MTV; Nickelodeon; Outdoor Channel; Pennsylvania Cable Network; Root Sports Pittsburgh; Speed; Spike TV; Style Network; Syfy; TBS Superstation; The Learning Channel; The Weather Channel; Travel Channel; truTV; Turner Classic Movies; Turner Network TV; TV Land; USA Network; Versus; VH1.
Fee: $25.91 monthly.
Pay Service 1
Pay Units: 75.
Programming (via satellite): Cinemax (multiplexed); Encore; HBO (multiplexed); Showtime; Starz; The Movie Channel.
Fee: $15.00 installation; $11.77 monthly (each).
Pay-Per-View
Addressable homes: 590.
iN DEMAND; Hot Choice.
Internet Service
Operational: No.
Telephone Service
None
Miles of plant (coax) included in Newport
Area Vice President: Jim Samaha. Vice President, Marketing: Larry Goldman. Technical Operations Manager: Dan Cramer.
Ownership: Comcast Cable Communications Inc. (MSO).

RENO—Time Warner Cable. Now served by FRANKLIN (Venango County), PA [PA0100]. ICA: PA0273.

RETREAT CORRECTIONAL INSTITUTION—Suddenlink Communications, 12444 Powerscourt Dr, Saint Louis, MO 63131-3660. Phone: 341-965-2020. Web Site: http://www.suddenlink.com. ICA: PA0445.
TV Market Ranking: 49 (RETREAT CORRECTIONAL). Franchise award date: January 1, 1989. Franchise expiration date: N.A. Began: N.A.
Channel capacity: 12 (not 2-way capable). Channels available but not in use: N.A.
Basic Service
Subscribers: 386.
Programming (received off-air): WNEP-TV (ABC) Scranton; WVIA-TV (PBS) Scranton; WYOU (CBS) Scranton.
Programming (via satellite): BET Networks; ESPN; TBS Superstation; Turner Network TV; WGN America.
Fee: $9.70 monthly.
Internet Service
Operational: No.
Telephone Service
None
Miles of Plant: 3.0 (coaxial); None (fiber optic).
Ownership: Cequel Communications LLC (MSO).

RICHFIELD—Zampelli Electronics. Now served by MOUNT PLEASANT MILLS [PA0377]. ICA: PA0225.

RIDGWAY BOROUGH—Formerly served by Adelphia Communications. Now served by PUNXSUTAWNEY, PA [PA0397]. ICA: PA0124.

RIDLEY PARK—RCN Corp. Formerly served by Philadelphia (suburbs), PA [PA0447]. This cable system has converted to IPTV, 196 Van Buren St, Herndon, VA 20170. Phone: 703-434-8200. Web Site: http://www.rcn.com. ICA: PA5261.
Channel capacity: N.A. Channels available but not in use: N.A.
Internet Service
Operational: Yes.
Chairman: Steven J. Simmons. Chief Executive Officer: Jim Holanda.

RIDLEY TWP.—RCN Corp. Formerly served by Philadelphia (suburbs), PA [PA0447]. This cable system has converted to IPTV, 196 Van Buren St, Herndon, VA 20170. Phone: 703-

434-8200. Web Site: http://www.rcn.com. ICA: PA5262.

Channel capacity: N.A. Channels available but not in use: N.A.

Internet Service

Operational: Yes.

Chairman: Steven J. Simmons. Chief Executive Officer: Jim Holanda.

ROBINSON TWP. (Allegheny County)—Formerly served by Adelphia Communications. Now served by BETHEL PARK, PA [PA0318]. ICA: PA0401.

ROCHESTER—Comcast Cable, 15 Summit Park Dr, Pittsburgh, PA 15275. Phones: 412-771-1300; 412-771-8100; 412-747-6400. Fax: 412-747-6401. Web Site: http://www.comcast.com. Also serves Beaver, East Rochester, Freedom, Monaca, Rochester Borough & Vanport Twp. ICA: PA0076.

TV Market Ranking: 10,79 (Beaver, East Rochester, Freedom, Monaca, ROCHESTER, Rochester Borough, Vanport Twp.). Franchise award date: N.A. Franchise expiration date: N.A. Began: November 1, 1967.

Channel capacity: N.A. Channels available but not in use: N.A.

Basic Service

Subscribers: N.A. Included in Bensalem Twp.

Programming (received off-air): KDKA-TV (CBS) Pittsburgh; WINP-TV (IND, ION) Pittsburgh; WKBN-TV (CBS) Youngstown; WNEO (PBS) Alliance; WPCB-TV (IND) Greensburg; WPCW (CW) Jeannette; WPGH-TV (FOX) Pittsburgh; WPMY (MNT) Pittsburgh; WPXI (IND, NBC) Pittsburgh; WQED (PBS) Pittsburgh; WTAE-TV (ABC) Pittsburgh; WTOV-TV (IND, NBC) Steubenville; WYTV (ABC, MNT) Youngstown.

Programming (via satellite): CNN; ESPN; Headline News; QVC; TBS Superstation; The Weather Channel.

Fee: $43.99 installation; $8.56 monthly; $2.00 converter.

Expanded Basic Service 1

Subscribers: N.A.

Programming (via satellite): A&E Networks; ABC Family Channel; AMC; Animal Planet; BET Networks; CNBC; Country Music TV; C-SPAN; C-SPAN 2; Discovery Channel; Disney Channel; ESPN 2; Eternal Word TV Network; Food Network; Fox News Channel; FX; HGTV; Lifetime; MSNBC; MTV; Nickelodeon; Philadelphia Park Live; Product Information Network; Root Sports Pittsburgh; Spike TV; Syfy; The Learning Channel; Turner Network TV; TV Guide Network; TV Land; USA Network; VH1.

Fee: $43.03 monthly.

Digital Basic Service

Subscribers: N.A.

Programming (via satellite): AmericanLife TV Network; BBC America; Bloomberg Television; Discovery Digital Networks; DMX Music; ESPN Classic Sports; G4; Golf Channel; GSN; Halogen Network; MuchMusic Network; Outdoor Channel; SoapNet; Style Network; The Weather Channel; Toon Disney; Trinity Broadcasting Network; truTV; Versus; WE tv.

Fee: $10.95 monthly.

Digital Pay Service 1

Pay Units: N.A.

Programming (via satellite): Cinemax (multiplexed); Encore (multiplexed); HBO (multiplexed); Showtime (multiplexed); Starz (multiplexed); The Movie Channel (multiplexed).

Video-On-Demand: No

Pay-Per-View

iN DEMAND; iN DEMAND (delivered digitally); special events.

Internet Service

Operational: Yes. Began: January 1, 2001.

Subscribers: 3,400.

Broadband Service: Comcast High Speed Internet.

Fee: $42.95 monthly; $3.00 modem lease.

Telephone Service

None

Miles of Plant: 115.0 (coaxial); None (fiber optic).

Regional Vice President: Linda Hossinger. Vice President, Technical Operations: Randy Bender. Vice President, Marketing: Donna Corning. Vice President, Public Affairs: Jody Doherty.

Ownership: Comcast Cable Communications Inc. (MSO).

ROCKMERE—Formerly served by Cebridge Connections. Now served by NORTH CLARION, PA [PA0142]. ICA: PA0237.

ROCKWOOD—Formerly served by Adelphia Communications. Now served by CENTRAL CITY BOROUGH, PA [PA0132]. ICA: PA0402.

ROME—Beaver Valley Cable Co., RR 2 Box 60D, Rome, PA 18837-9802. Phones: 800-391-9615; 570-247-2512. Fax: 570-247-2494. E-mail: bvc@cableracer.com. Web Site: http://www.beavervalleycable.com. Also serves Estella, Le Raysville, Le Raysville Borough, Lincoln Falls, Little Meadows, Little Meadows Borough, Millview, North Orwell, North Rome, Potterville, Rome Borough, Ulster & Warren Center Twp. ICA: PA0403.

TV Market Ranking: 49 (Little Meadows); Below 100 (Le Raysville, Le Raysville Borough, Lincoln Falls, Little Meadows Borough, Millview, North Orwell, North Rome, Potterville, ROME, Rome Borough, Ulster, Warren Center Twp.); Outside TV Markets (Estella). Franchise award date: N.A. Franchise expiration date: N.A. Began: N.A.

Channel capacity: 54 (operating 2-way). Channels available but not in use: N.A.

Basic Service

Subscribers: 1,200.

Programming (received off-air): WBNG-TV (CBS, CW) Binghamton; WBRE-TV (NBC) Wilkes-Barre; WENY-TV (ABC, CW) Elmira; WETM-TV (NBC) Elmira; WNEP-TV (ABC) Scranton; WOLF-TV (CW, FOX, MNT) Hazleton; WQPX-TV (ION) Scranton; WSKG-TV (PBS) Binghamton; WSWB (CW) Scranton; WVIA-TV (PBS) Scranton; WYOU (CBS) Scranton.

Programming (via satellite): 3 Angels Broadcasting Network; A&E Networks; ABC Family Channel; AMC; Animal Planet; Bravo; Cartoon Network; CNBC; CNN; Comedy Central; Country Music TV; Discovery Channel; Disney Channel; ESPN; ESPN 2; ESPN Classic Sports; Eternal Word TV Network; Fox News Channel; FX; G4; Great American Country; Lifetime; MTV; National Geographic Channel; Nickelodeon; Outdoor Channel; Root Sports Pittsburgh; Speed; Spike TV; Syfy; TBS Superstation; The Learning Channel; The Weather Channel; Toon Disney; Trinity Broadcasting Network; truTV; Turner Network TV; TV Guide Network; TV Land; USA Network; Versus; VH1; WGN America.

Fee: $30.00 installation; $44.00 monthly.

Digital Basic Service

Subscribers: 70.

Programming (via satellite): BBC America; Discovery Digital Networks; ESPNews; Fox College Sports Atlantic; Fox College Sports Central; Fox College Sports Pacific; Fox Soccer; Golf Channel; GSN; HGTV; History Channel; Independent Film Channel; Nick Jr.; Turner Classic Movies.

Fee: $30.00 installation; $14.95 monthly.

Digital Pay Service 1

Pay Units: 60.

Programming (via satellite): HBO (multiplexed).

Fee: $12.19 monthly.

Digital Pay Service 2

Pay Units: N.A.

Programming (via satellite): Cinemax (multiplexed); Encore; Showtime (multiplexed); The Movie Channel (multiplexed).

Fee: $10.60 monthly (Cinemax or Starz/Encore), $12.19 monthly (Showtime/TMC).

Video-On-Demand: No

Pay-Per-View

iN DEMAND (delivered digitally); Hot Choice (delivered digitally); Pleasure (delivered digitally).

Internet Service

Operational: Yes. Began: November 1, 2002.

Subscribers: 425.

Broadband Service: Cableracer.

Fee: $50.00 installation; $41.00 monthly.

Telephone Service

None

Miles of Plant: 46.0 (coaxial); 34.0 (fiber optic).

Manager & Owner: Doug Soden. Chief Technician: Gary Powers. IT Technician & Office Manager: Bonnie Gray.

Ownership: Beaver Valley Cable Inc.

ROSE TWP.—Formerly served by Adelphia Communications. Now served by CLARION BOROUGH, PA [PA0137]. ICA: PA0135.

ROSETO BOROUGH—Formerly served by NORTHAMPTON BOROUGH, PA [PA0008]. RCN Corp. This cable system has converted to IPTV, 196 Van Buren St, Herndon, VA 20170. Phone: 703-434-8200. Web Site: http://www.rcn.com. ICA: PA5232.

TV Market Ranking: Below 100 (ROSETO BOROUGH).

Channel capacity: N.A. Channels available but not in use: N.A.

Internet Service

Operational: Yes.

Telephone Service

Digital: Operational

Chairman: Steven J. Simmons. Chief Executive Officer: Jim Holanda.

ROSS TWP. (Allegheny County)—Comcast Cable. Now served by PITTSBURGH, PA [PA0001]. ICA: PA0032.

RURAL VALLEY—Comcast Cable. Now served by KISKIMINETAS TWP., PA [PA0074]. ICA: PA0199.

RUTLEDGE—RCN Corp. Formerly served by Philadelphia (suburbs), PA [PA0447]. This cable system has converted to IPTV, 196 Van Buren St, Herndon, VA 20170. Phone: 703-434-8200. Web Site: http://www.rcn.com. ICA: PA5263.

Channel capacity: N.A. Channels available but not in use: N.A.

Internet Service

Operational: Yes.

Chairman: Steven J. Simmons. Chief Executive Officer: Jim Holanda.

SABULA—Zito Media, 611 Vader Hill Rd, Coudersport, PA 16915. Phones: 866-879-6235; 814-260-9270; 814-260-9575. Fax: 814-260-9580. E-mail: rigas@zitomedia.com. Web Site: http://www.zitomedia.com. Also serves Huston Twp. (Clearfield County). ICA: PA0249.

TV Market Ranking: Outside TV Markets (Huston Twp. (Clearfield County), SABULA). Franchise award date: August 1, 1989. Franchise expiration date: N.A. Began: August 1, 1990.

Channel capacity: 60 (not 2-way capable). Channels available but not in use: N.A.

Basic Service

Subscribers: N.A. Included in Treasure Lake

Programming (received off-air): WATM-TV (ABC) Altoona; WJAC-TV (NBC) Johnstown; WKBS-TV (IND) Altoona; WPMY (MNT) Pittsburgh; WPSU-TV (PBS) Clearfield; WTAE-TV (ABC) Pittsburgh; WTAJ-TV (CBS) Altoona; WWCP-TV (FOX) Johnstown.

Programming (via satellite): A&E Networks; ABC Family Channel; AMC; Animal Planet; Cartoon Network; CNBC; CNN; Country Music TV; C-SPAN; CW+; Discovery Channel; Disney Channel; ESPN; ESPN 2; ESPN Classic Sports; Eternal Word TV Network; Fox News Channel; FX; Headline News; HGTV; History Channel; INSP; Lifetime; MSNBC; MTV; Nickelodeon; QVC; Root Sports Pittsburgh; Spike TV; TBS Superstation; The Learning Channel; The Weather Channel; Trinity Broadcasting Network; Turner Classic Movies; Turner Network TV; TV Land; USA Network; VH1; WGN America.

Fee: $29.95 installation; $44.50 monthly; $7.95 converter.

Digital Basic Service

Subscribers: N.A.

Programming (via satellite): AmericanLife TV Network; BBC America; Bloomberg Television; Boomerang; C-SPAN 3; Discovery Fit & Health; Discovery Health Channel; Discovery Kids Channel; ESPN 2 HD; ESPN HD; ESPNews; Familyland Television Network; Fox Movie Channel; Fox Soccer; Golf Channel; Great American Country; GSN; HRTV; ID Investigation Discovery; INSP; Lifetime Movie Network; Military Channel; MTV Hits; MTV Jams; MTV2; Music Choice; Nick Jr.; Nick Too; NickToons TV; Planet Green; RFD-TV; Science; SoapNet; Speed; TeenNick; The Word Network; Toon Disney; Trinity Broadcasting Network; VH1 Classic; VH1 Country; VH1 Soul; WAM! America's Kidz Network; WE tv.

Fee: $15.95 monthly.

Digital Expanded Basic Service
Subscribers: N.A.
Programming (via satellite): Bio; DIY Network; Flix; FSN Digital Atlantic; FSN Digital Central; FSN Digital Pacific; History Channel International; Independent Film Channel; Outdoor Channel; Sundance Channel; Versus.
Fee: $10.00 monthly.
Digital Pay Service 1
Pay Units: N.A.
Programming (via satellite): Cinemax (multiplexed); Cinemax HD; Encore (multiplexed); HBO (multiplexed); HBO HD; Showtime (multiplexed); Showtime HD; Starz (multiplexed); Starz HDTV; The Movie Channel (multiplexed).
Fee: $8.00 monthly (Cinemax or Starz/Encore), $10.00 monthly (HBO or Showtime/TMC/Flix).
Video-On-Demand: Yes
Pay-Per-View
iN DEMAND (delivered digitally); NHL Center Ice (delivered digitally); MLB Extra Innings (delivered digitally).
Internet Service
Operational: Yes.
Fee: $49.95 monthly.
Telephone Service
Digital: Operational
Fee: $35.00 monthly
Miles of plant (coax) included in Treasure Lake
Manager: James Rigas. Marketing Director: Kathy Fox.
Ownership: Zito Media (MSO).

SALISBURY TWP.—Formerly served by NORTHAMPTON BOROUGH, PA [PA0008]. RCN Corp. This cable system has converted to IPTV, 196 Van Buren St, Herndon, VA 20170. Phone: 703-434-8200. Web Site: http://www.rcn.com. ICA: PA5233.
TV Market Ranking: Below 100 (SALISBURY TWP.).
Channel capacity: N.A. Channels available but not in use: N.A.
Internet Service
Operational: Yes.
Telephone Service
Digital: Operational
Chairman: Steven J. Simmons. Chief Executive Officer: Jim Holanda.

SALTILLO—Saltillo TV Cable Corp., PO Box 89, Saltillo, PA 17253-0089. Phone: 814-448-2443. Fax: 814-448-9182. ICA: PA0404.
TV Market Ranking: 74 (SALTILLO). Franchise award date: N.A. Franchise expiration date: N.A. Began: January 1, 1964.
Channel capacity: 47 (not 2-way capable). Channels available but not in use: N.A.
Basic Service
Subscribers: 161.
Programming (received off-air): WBAL-TV (NBC) Baltimore; WGAL (NBC) Lancaster; WHTM-TV (ABC) Harrisburg; WJAC-TV (NBC) Johnstown; WJZ-TV (CBS) Baltimore; WMAR-TV (ABC) Baltimore; WPMT (FOX) York; WPSU-TV (PBS) Clearfield; WTAJ-TV (CBS) Altoona; WTTG (FOX) Washington.
Programming (via satellite): ABC Family Channel; Cartoon Network; CNN; Country Music TV; Discovery Channel; Disney Channel; ESPN; ESPN 2; Hallmark Channel; History Channel; QVC; Spike TV; TBS Superstation; Trinity Broadcasting Network; Turner Classic Movies; Turner Network TV; TV Land; USA Network; VH1; WGN America.
Fee: $100.00 installation; $32.00 monthly.
Pay Service 1
Pay Units: 45.
Programming (via satellite): HBO.
Fee: $13.00 monthly.
Video-On-Demand: No
Internet Service
Operational: No.
Telephone Service
None
Ownership: Saltillo TV Cable Corp.

SANDY LAKE—Formerly served by Cebridge Connections. Now served by GROVE CITY, PA [PA0089]. ICA: PA0176.

SANDY TWP. (Clearfield County)—Formerly served by Satterlee Leasing Inc. No longer in operation. ICA: PA0405.

SAYRE—Time Warner Cable, 120 Plaza Dr, Vestal, NY 13850-3658. Phones: 607-644-0646; 570-888-8071 (Sayre office). Fax: 607-644-1501. Web Site: http://www.timewarnercable.com. ICA: PA0079.
TV Market Ranking: Below 100 (SAYRE). Franchise award date: N.A. Franchise expiration date: August 18, 2007. Began: November 1, 1958.
Channel capacity: N.A. Channels available but not in use: N.A.
Basic Service
Subscribers: N.A. Included in Binghamton
Programming (received off-air): WBNG-TV (CBS, CW) Binghamton; WENY-TV (ABC, CW) Elmira; WETM-TV (NBC) Elmira; WICZ-TV (FOX) Binghamton; WIVT (ABC) Binghamton; WSKG-TV (PBS) Binghamton; WVIA-TV (PBS) Scranton; WYOU (CBS) Scranton; allband FM.
Programming (via satellite): C-SPAN; ION Television; QVC; TV Guide Network; WGN America.
Fee: $47.21 installation; $8.15 monthly.
Expanded Basic Service 1
Subscribers: N.A.
Programming (via satellite): A&E Networks; ABC Family Channel; AMC; Animal Planet; Bravo; Cartoon Network; CNBC; CNN; Comedy Central; Country Music TV; Discovery Channel; Discovery Fit & Health; Disney Channel; E! Entertainment Television; ESPN; ESPN 2; ESPN Classic Sports; Eternal Word TV Network; Food Network; Fox News Channel; Fuse; FX; Golf Channel; GSN; Headline News; HGTV; History Channel; Lifetime; Lifetime Movie Network; MoviePlex; MSG; MSNBC; MTV; MTV2; National Geographic Channel; Nickelodeon; Oxygen; ShopNBC; SoapNet; Speed; Spike TV; Style Network; Syfy; TBS Superstation; The Learning Channel; The Weather Channel; Travel Channel; truTV; Turner Classic Movies; Turner Network TV; TV Land; USA Network; Versus; VH1; WE tv; Yankees Entertainment & Sports.
Fee: $35.42 monthly.
Digital Basic Service
Subscribers: N.A. Included in Binghamton
Programming (via satellite): AmericanLife TV Network; America's Store; BBC America; Bio; Bloomberg Television; Cooking Channel; C-SPAN 3; Discovery Digital Networks; DIY Network; Encore Action; ESPNews; Fox Movie Channel; Fox Sports World; G4; GAS; Great American Country; History Channel International; Independent Film Channel; Lifetime Real Women; Music Choice; Nick Jr.; Outdoor Channel; Ovation; Sundance Channel; Toon Disney; Trinity Broadcasting Network; VH1 Classic.
Fee: $8.45 monthly.
Digital Expanded Basic Service
Subscribers: N.A.
Programming (via satellite): Fox Deportes; FSN Digital Atlantic; FSN Digital Central; FSN Digital Pacific; Fuel TV; NBA TV; Tennis Channel.
Fee: $4.95 monthly.
Digital Pay Service 1
Pay Units: 5,811.
Programming (via satellite): Canales N; Cinemax (multiplexed); Flix; HBO (multiplexed); Showtime (multiplexed); Starz (multiplexed); The Movie Channel (multiplexed); TV Asia; Zee TV USA.
Fee: $4.95 monthly (Canales n), $11.25 monthly (Cinemax, HBO, Starz, or Flix/Showtime/TMC), $19.95 monthly (TV Asia & Zee TV).
Video-On-Demand: Yes
Pay-Per-View
iN DEMAND (delivered digitally); Hot Choice (delivered digitally); Playboy TV (delivered digitally); Fresh (delivered digitally); Shorteez (delivered digitally); Pleasure (delivered digitally); ESPN Full Court (delivered digitally); ESPN Gameplan (delivered digitally); Sports PPV (delivered digitally).
Internet Service
Operational: Yes. Began: June 1, 2000.
Broadband Service: Road Runner.
Fee: $39.95 installation; $44.95 monthly.
Telephone Service
Digital: Operational
Fee: $29.95 monthly
Miles of plant included in Binghamton
President: Mary Cotter. Vice President & General Manager: Chris Strahm. Vice President, Marketing: John Melvany. Vice President, Public Affairs: Dave Whalen. Technical Operations Director: Bruce Tomkins.
Ownership: Time Warner Cable (MSO).; Advance/Newhouse Partnership (MSO).Day-to-day operations are managed by Time Warner Cable.

SCHUYLKILL TWP.—MetroCast Communications, 1059 E 10th St, Hazleton, PA 18201-3421. Phone: 570-455-4251. Fax: 570-459-0963. Web Site: http://www.metrocastcommunications.com. Also serves Brockton, Cumbola, Kaska, Mary D, Middleport, New Philadelphia, Tamaqua & Tuscarora. ICA: PA0450.
TV Market Ranking: 49 (SCHUYLKILL TWP.); Below 100 (Brockton, Cumbola, Kaska, Mary D, Middleport, New Philadelphia, Tamaqua, Tuscarora). Franchise award date: N.A. Franchise expiration date: June 1, 2009. Began: N.A.
Channel capacity: 46 (operating 2-way). Channels available but not in use: N.A.
Basic Service
Subscribers: 1,307.
Programming (received off-air): WBRE-TV (NBC) Wilkes-Barre; WITF-TV (PBS) Harrisburg; WLYH-TV (CW) Lancaster; WNEP-TV (ABC) Scranton; WOLF-TV (CW, FOX, MNT) Hazleton; WVIA-TV (PBS) Scranton; WYLN-LP (IND) Hazleton; WYOU (CBS) Scranton.
Programming (via satellite): C-SPAN; Eternal Word TV Network; QVC; TBS Superstation; WGN America.
Programming (via translator): KYW-TV (CBS) Philadelphia; WCAU (NBC) Philadelphia; WPHL-TV (MNT, IND) Philadelphia; WPIX (CW, IND) New York; WPSG (CW) Philadelphia; WTXF-TV (FOX) Philadelphia.
Fee: $60.00 installation; $15.26 monthly.
Expanded Basic Service 1
Subscribers: 1,228.
Programming (via satellite): A&E Networks; ABC Family Channel; Animal Planet; Bloomberg Television; Cartoon Network; CNBC; CNN; Comcast SportsNet Philadelphia; Comedy Central; Country Music TV; C-SPAN 2; Discovery Channel; Disney Channel; ESPN; ESPN 2; Food Network; Fox Movie Channel; Fox News Channel; FX; G4; Headline News; HGTV; History Channel; Lifetime; MSNBC; MTV; Nickelodeon; Outdoor Channel; Pennsylvania Cable Network; Speed; Spike TV; Syfy; The Learning Channel; The Weather Channel; Turner Classic Movies; Turner Network TV; TV Land; USA Network; Versus; VH1.
Fee: $26.99 monthly.
Digital Basic Service
Subscribers: N.A.
Programming (via satellite): BBC America; Bio; Discovery Digital Networks; DMX Music; Fuse; GAS; GSN; Lifetime Movie Network; MTV Networks Digital Suite; National Geographic Channel; Nick Jr.; NickToons TV; Toon Disney; Trio.
Fee: $8.95 monthly.
Digital Expanded Basic Service
Subscribers: N.A.
Programming (via satellite): Bravo; Encore (multiplexed); ESPN Classic Sports; ESPNews; Fox Soccer; Golf Channel; History Channel International; Independent Film Channel; Starz (multiplexed); WE tv.
Fee: $9.95 monthly.
Digital Pay Service 1
Pay Units: N.A.
Programming (via satellite): Cinemax (multiplexed); Flix; HBO (multiplexed); Showtime (multiplexed); The Movie Channel (multiplexed).
Fee: $9.95 monthly (Cinemax), $10.95 monthly (HBO or Showtime/TMC).
Pay-Per-View
iN DEMAND (delivered digitally).
Internet Service
Operational: No.
Telephone Service
None
General Manager: Danny Jobe. Programming Director: Linda Stuchell.
Ownership: Harron Communications LP (MSO).

SCRANTON—Comcast Cable, 1 E Uwchlan Ave, Ste 411, Exton, PA 19341. Phone: 484-288-6500. Web Site: http://www.comcast.com. Also serves Avoca, Dickson City, Duryea, Edwardsville, Forty Fort, Luzerne, Moosic, Nanticoke, Old Forge, Plains Twp. (Luzerne County), Plymouth, Swoyersville, Taylor, Throop, West Wyoming & Wyoming. ICA: PA0011.
TV Market Ranking: 49 (Avoca, Dickson City, Duryea, Edwardsville, Forty Fort, Luzerne, Moosic, Nanticoke, Old Forge, Plains Twp. (Luzerne County), Plymouth, SCRANTON, Swoyersville, Taylor, Throop, West Wyoming, Wyoming). Franchise award date: June 1, 1973. Franchise expiration date: December 31, 2010. Began: October 7, 1973.
Channel capacity: 82 (operating 2-way). Channels available but not in use: N.A.
Basic Service
Subscribers: N.A. Included in Harrisburg
Programming (received off-air): WNEP-TV (ABC) Scranton; WPSG (CW) Philadelphia; WQPX-TV (ION) Scranton; WSWB (CW) Scranton; WVIA-TV (PBS) Scranton; WYOU (CBS) Scranton.
Programming (via microwave): Catholic Television Network; WOLF-TV (CW, FOX, MNT) Hazleton; WPIX (CW, IND) New York.
Programming (via satellite): Pennsylvania Cable Network; Product Information Network; QVC; ShopNBC; Style Network; TBS

Superstation; Trinity Broadcasting Network; TV Guide Network; WGN America.
Fee: $45.10 installation; $12.45 monthly; $15.00 additional installation.

Expanded Basic Service 1
Subscribers: 57,650.
Programming (via satellite): A&E Networks; ABC Family Channel; AMC; Animal Planet; Bravo; Cartoon Network; CNBC; CNN; Comcast SportsNet Philadelphia; Comedy Central; Country Music TV; C-SPAN; C-SPAN 2; Discovery Channel; Disney Channel; E! Entertainment Television; ESPN; ESPN 2; ESPN Classic Sports; Food Network; Fox News Channel; FX; GSN; Hallmark Channel; Headline News; HGTV; History Channel; Lifetime; MSG; MSNBC; MTV; Nickelodeon; Root Sports Pittsburgh; Speed; Spike TV; Syfy; The Learning Channel; The Weather Channel; Toon Disney; Travel Channel; truTV; Turner Classic Movies; Turner Network TV; TV Land; USA Network; Versus; VH1; WE tv; Yankees Entertainment & Sports.
Fee: $41.55 monthly.

Digital Basic Service
Subscribers: N.A. Included in Towanda
Programming (via satellite): AmericanLife TV Network; BBC America; Bio; Black Family Channel; Bloomberg Television; Discovery Fit & Health; DIY Network; ESPN Classic Sports; ESPNews; Fox Movie Channel; Fox Sports World; Fuse; G4; Golf Channel; Great American Country; GSN; Halogen Network; History Channel International; Outdoor Channel; Speed; Toon Disney; Trinity Broadcasting Network; Versus; WE tv.
Fee: $14.95 monthly.

Digital Expanded Basic Service
Subscribers: N.A.
Programming (via satellite): Canales N; FSN Digital Atlantic (multiplexed); FSN Digital Central; FSN Digital Pacific; GAS; Independent Film Channel; MTV Networks Digital Suite; Music Choice; National Geographic Channel; Nick Jr.; Nick Too; NickToons TV; SoapNet; Style Network; Sundance Channel; Turner Classic Movies.
Fee: $5.00 monthly.

Digital Pay Service 1
Pay Units: N.A.
Programming (via satellite): Cinemax (multiplexed); Encore (multiplexed); Flix; HBO (multiplexed); Showtime (multiplexed); Starz (multiplexed); The Movie Channel (multiplexed).

Video-On-Demand: Yes

Pay-Per-View
Addressable homes: 3,800.
iN DEMAND (delivered digitally); iN DEMAND.

Internet Service
Operational: Yes.
Broadband Service: Comcast High Speed Internet.
Fee: $42.95 monthly.

Telephone Service
Analog: Not Operational
Digital: Operational

Miles of Plant: 1,704.0 (coaxial); 429.0 (fiber optic).
Area Vice President: Jim Samaha. Vice President, Marketing: Larry Goldman.
Ownership: Comcast Cable Communications Inc. (MSO).

SELLERSVILLE—Comcast Cable, 3220 Tillman Dr, Bensalem, PA 19010. Phone: 215-642-6400 (Philadelphia office). Fax: 215-638-6510. Web Site: http://www.comcast.com. Also serves Bedminster Twp., Dublin Borough, East Rockhill Twp., Franconia, Green Lane Borough, Hatfield, Hilltown Twp., Lower Frederick, Lower Salford, Marlborough Twp., Perkasie, Quakertown, Richlandtown, Salford, Silverdale, Souderton, Telford, Trumbauersville, Upper Frederick Twp., Upper Salford & West Rockhill Twp. ICA: PA0017.
TV Market Ranking: 4 (Bedminster Twp., Dublin Borough, East Rockhill Twp., Franconia, Green Lane Borough, Hatfield, Hilltown Twp., Lower Frederick, Lower Salford, Marlborough Twp., Perkasie, Quakertown, Richlandtown, Salford, SELLERSVILLE, Silverdale, Souderton, Telford, Trumbauersville, Upper Frederick Twp., Upper Salford, West Rockhill Twp.). Franchise award date: N.A. Franchise expiration date: N.A. Began: February 1, 1975.
Channel capacity: N.A. Channels available but not in use: N.A.

Basic Service
Subscribers: N.A. Included in Bensalem Twp.
Programming (received off-air): KYW-TV (CBS) Philadelphia; WBPH-TV (IND) Bethlehem; WCAU (NBC) Philadelphia; WFMZ-TV (IND) Allentown; WGTW-TV (TBN) Burlington; WHYY-TV (PBS) Wilmington; WLVT-TV (PBS) Allentown; WMCN-TV (IND) Atlantic City; WNJT (PBS) Trenton; WPHL-TV (MNT, IND) Philadelphia; WPPX-TV (ION) Wilmington; WPSG (CW) Philadelphia; WPVI-TV (ABC) Philadelphia; WTVE (IND) Reading; WTXF-TV (FOX) Philadelphia; WUVP-DT (UNV) Vineland; WWSI (TMO) Atlantic City; WYBE (ETV, IND) Philadelphia; allband FM.
Programming (via satellite): ABC Family Channel; Bravo; C-SPAN; MSNBC; MTV2; QVC; TBS Superstation; The Comcast Network.
Fee: $15.65 monthly.

Expanded Basic Service 1
Subscribers: 37,585.
Programming (via satellite): A&E Networks; AMC; Animal Planet; Cartoon Network; CNBC; CNN; Comcast SportsNet Philadelphia; Comedy Central; Country Music TV; Discovery Channel; Discovery Health Channel; Disney Channel; E! Entertainment Television; ESPN; ESPN 2; Food Network; Fox News Channel; FX; Golf Channel; GSN; Headline News; HGTV; History Channel; Lifetime; MTV; Nickelodeon; Philadelphia Park Live; Speed; Spike TV; Syfy; The Learning Channel; The Weather Channel; Travel Channel; truTV; Turner Classic Movies; Turner Network TV; TV Land; USA Network; Versus; VH1.
Fee: $36.65 monthly.

Digital Basic Service
Subscribers: N.A.
Programming (via satellite): BBC America; Bio; Comcast SportsNet Philadelphia; Cooking Channel; C-SPAN 3; DIY Network; DMX Music; Encore (multiplexed); ESPN; ESPNews; Eternal Word TV Network; Flix (multiplexed); Fox College Sports Atlantic; Fox College Sports Central; Fox College Sports Pacific; Fox Soccer; G4; GAS; GolTV; Great American Country; Hallmark Channel; HD Theater; History Channel International; Independent Film Channel; INHD (multiplexed); Lifetime Movie Network; LOGO; MTV Networks Digital Suite; National Geographic Channel; NBA TV; NFL Network; Nick Jr.; Nick Too; NickToons TV; Oxygen; PBS Kids Sprout; Pennsylvania Cable Network; ShopNBC; SoapNet; Sundance Channel (multiplexed); Toon Disney; Turner Network TV HD; TV One; WAM! America's Kidz Network; Weatherscan.
Fee: $14.95 monthly.

Digital Pay Service 1
Pay Units: N.A.
Programming (via satellite): Cinemax (multiplexed); Cinemax HD; HBO (multiplexed); HBO HD; Showtime (multiplexed); Showtime HD; Starz (multiplexed); Starz HDTV; The Movie Channel (multiplexed).
Fee: $18.95 monthly (each).

Video-On-Demand: Yes

Pay-Per-View
iN DEMAND (delivered digitally); Playboy TV (delivered digitally); MLB Extra Innings (delivered digitally); Fresh (delivered digitally); Shorteez (delivered digitally); Pleasure (delivered digitally); Canal 52MX (delivered digitally); ESPN (delivered digitally); NBA League Pass (delivered digitally); NHL Center Ice (delivered digitally).

Internet Service
Operational: Yes.
Broadband Service: Comcast High Speed Internet.
Fee: $99.95 installation; $42.95 monthly; $7.00 modem lease.

Telephone Service
Digital: Operational
Fee: $44.95 monthly

Miles of Plant: 1,009.0 (coaxial); 43.0 (fiber optic). Additional miles planned: 20.0 (coaxial).
Senior Regional Vice President: Amy Smith. Vice President, Technical Operations: Rich Massi. Vice President, Marketing: Chip Goodman. Regional Vice President: Jim Samaha.
Ownership: Comcast Cable Communications Inc. (MSO).

SHADE GAP—Shade Gap TV Assn., HC 83 Box 398, Shade Gap, PA 17255-9317. Phone: 814-259-3415. Also serves Dublin Twp. (Huntingdon County). ICA: PA0283.
TV Market Ranking: Outside TV Markets (Dublin Twp. (Huntingdon County), SHADE GAP). Franchise award date: N.A. Franchise expiration date: N.A. Began: January 1, 1953.
Channel capacity: 19 (not 2-way capable). Channels available but not in use: N.A.

Basic Service
Subscribers: 66.
Programming (received off-air): WGAL (NBC) Lancaster; WHAG-TV (NBC) Hagerstown; WHTM-TV (ABC) Harrisburg; WJAC-TV (NBC) Johnstown; WPMT (FOX) York; WPSU-TV (PBS) Clearfield; WTAJ-TV (CBS) Altoona; allband FM.
Programming (via satellite): ABC Family Channel; AMC; Country Music TV; Discovery Channel; Disney Channel; ESPN; Food Network; Hallmark Channel; Nickelodeon; Spike TV; TBS Superstation; Trinity Broadcasting Network; Turner Network TV; USA Network; WGN America.
Fee: $18.00 monthly.

Pay Service 1
Pay Units: 10.
Programming (via satellite): Cinemax.
Fee: $6.00 monthly.

Video-On-Demand: No

Internet Service
Operational: No.

Telephone Service
None

Miles of Plant: 4.0 (coaxial); None (fiber optic).
Manager: Donald E. Naugle. Secretary-Treasurer: Mary McMullen.
Ownership: Shade Gap TV Assn.

SHARON—Time Warner Cable, 530 S Main St, Ste 1751, Akron, OH 44311-1090. Phone: 330-633-9203. Fax: 330-633-7970. Web Site: http://www.timewarnercable.com. Also serves Hartford Twp., Orangeville & Yankee Lake, OH; Clark, Farrell, Hermitage, Jefferson Twp., Lackawonnock Twp., Pymatuning Twp., Sharpsville, Shenango Twp., South Pymatuning Twp., West Middlesex, Wheatland & Wilmington Twp., PA. ICA: PA0038.
TV Market Ranking: 79 (Clark, Farrell, Hartford Twp., Hermitage, Jefferson Twp., Lackawonnock Twp., Orangeville, Pymatuning Twp., SHARON, Sharpsville, Shenango Twp., South Pymatuning Twp., West Middlesex, Wheatland, Wilmington Twp., Yankee Lake).
Channel capacity: N.A. Channels available but not in use: N.A.

Basic Service
Subscribers: N.A. Included in Warren, OH
Programming (received off-air): KDKA-TV (CBS) Pittsburgh; W29CO (IND) Sharon; WEAO (PBS) Akron; WFMJ-TV (CW, NBC) Youngstown; WKBN-TV (CBS) Youngstown; WNEO (PBS) Alliance; WPGH-TV (FOX) Pittsburgh; WQED (PBS) Pittsburgh; WUAB (MNT) Lorain; WYFX-LP Youngstown; WYTV (ABC, MNT) Youngstown.
Programming (via satellite): C-SPAN; C-SPAN 2; CW+; QVC; ShopNBC; TV Guide Network; TVG Network.
Fee: $44.95 installation; $15.09 monthly.

Expanded Basic Service 1
Subscribers: N.A.
Programming (via satellite): A&E Networks; ABC Family Channel; AMC; Animal Planet; BET Networks; Bravo; Cartoon Network; CNBC; CNN; Comedy Central; Country Music TV; Discovery Channel; Disney Channel; E! Entertainment Television; ESPN; ESPN 2; Food Network; Fox News Channel; Fox Sports Net Ohio; FX; Hallmark Channel; Headline News; HGTV; History Channel; Lifetime; MSNBC; MTV; Nickelodeon; Outdoor Channel; Oxygen; Pennsylvania Cable Network; Root Sports Pittsburgh; Speed; Spike TV; SportsTime Ohio; Style Network; Syfy; TBS Superstation; The Learning Channel; The Weather Channel; Travel Channel; truTV; Turner Classic Movies; Turner Network TV; TV Land; USA Network; VH1.
Fee: $38.90 monthly.

Digital Basic Service
Subscribers: N.A.
Programming (via satellite): AmericanLife TV Network; BBC America; BBC America On Demand; Bloomberg Television; CMT Pure Country; C-SPAN 3; Current; Discovery Channel HD; Discovery Fit & Health; Discovery Health Channel; Dis-

covery Home Channel; Discovery Kids Channel; DIY Network; ESPN 2 HD; ESPN Classic Sports; ESPN HD; ESPN U; ESPNews; Exercise TV; Fox Business Channel; Fox Movie Channel; Fox Reality Channel; Fox Soccer; Fuse; G4; GAS; GMC; Golf Channel; Great American Country; GSN; Halogen Network; HDNet; HDNet Movies; Howard TV; ID Investigation Discovery; Lifetime Movie Network; LOGO; Military Channel; MTV Hits; MTV Jams; MTV2; Music Choice; National Geographic Channel; National Geographic Channel On Demand; Nick Jr.; Nick Too; NickToons TV; Ohio News Network; Oxygen On Demand; Science; SoapNet; Speed On Demand; TBS in HD; The Word Network; Toon Disney; Trinity Broadcasting Network; Turner Network TV HD; TV Guide SPOT; TV One; Universal HD; VH1 Classic; VH1 Soul; WE tv.
Fee: $12.95 monthly.

Digital Expanded Basic Service
Subscribers: N.A.
Programming (via satellite): Bio; Cooking Channel; Encore (multiplexed); Flix; Fox College Sports Atlantic; Fox College Sports Central; Fox College Sports Pacific; Fuel TV; History Channel International; Independent Film Channel; NBA TV; Sundance Channel; Versus.
Fee: $10.00 monthly.

Digital Pay Service 1
Pay Units: N.A.
Programming (via satellite): Cinemax (multiplexed); Cinemax HD; Cinemax On Demand; Encore (multiplexed); Flix; HBO (multiplexed); HBO HD; HBO On Demand; Showtime (multiplexed); Showtime HD; Showtime On Demand; Starz (multiplexed); Starz HDTV; Starz On Demand; The Movie Channel (multiplexed); The Movie Channel On Demand.
Fee: $12.00 monthly (HBO, Cinemax, Starz/Encore or Showtime/TMC/Flix).

Video-On-Demand: Yes

Pay-Per-View
iN DEMAND (delivered digitally); ESPN (delivered digitally); NHL Center Ice (delivered digitally); MLB Extra Innings (delivered digitally); Playboy TV (delivered digitally); Club Jenna (delivered digitally); Fresh (delivered digitally); Shorteez (delivered digitally); Hot Choice (delivered digitally).

Internet Service
Operational: Yes.
Broadband Service: EarthLink, Road Runner.
Fee: $45.95 monthly.

Telephone Service
Digital: Operational
Fee: $44.95 monthly

President: Stephen Fry. Area Vice President: Rick Whaley. Vice President, Engineering: Al Costanzi. Vice President, Marketing: Patrick Burke. Vice President, Sales: Woody Woodward. Vice President, Government & Media Affairs: William Jasso. Government & Media Relations Director: Chris Thomas.
Ownership: Time Warner Cable (MSO).

SHARON HILL—RCN Corp. Formerly served by Philadelphia (suburbs), PA [PA0447]. This cable system has converted to IPTV, 196 Van Buren St, Herndon, VA 20170. Phone: 703-434-8200. Web Site: http://www.rcn.com. ICA: PA5264.
Channel capacity: N.A. Channels available but not in use: N.A.

Internet Service
Operational: Yes.

Chairman: Steven J. Simmons. Chief Executive Officer: Jim Holanda.

SHEFFIELD—South Side TV Assn. Now served by SHEFFIELD, PA [PA0242]. ICA: PA0246.

SHEFFIELD—WestPA.net Inc., 216 Pennsylvania Ave W, PO Box 703, Warren, PA 16365. Phones: 877-726-9462; 814-726-9462. Fax: 814-723-9585. E-mail: info@westpa.net. Web Site: http://www.westpa.net. Also serves Barnes, Ludlow, Saybrook, Tiona & Weldbank. ICA: PA0473.
TV Market Ranking: Below 100 (Barnes, Ludlow, Saybrook, SHEFFIELD, Tiona, Weldbank).
Channel capacity: N.A. Channels available but not in use: N.A.

Internet Service
Operational: Yes.
Fee: $24.95 monthly.

Telephone Service
Digital: Operational
Fee: $29.95 monthly

General Manager: Elaine Bailey.
Ownership: WestPA.net Inc.

SHEFFIELD—WestPA.net Inc., 216 Pennsylvania Ave W, Warren, PA 16365. Phone: 814-726-9462. Fax: 814-726-9462. E-mail: info@westpa.net. Web Site: http://www.westpa.net. Also serves Saybrook. ICA: PA0242.
TV Market Ranking: Below 100 (Saybrook, SHEFFIELD). Franchise award date: N.A. Franchise expiration date: N.A. Began: December 1, 1953.
Channel capacity: 20 (not 2-way capable). Channels available but not in use: N.A.

Basic Service
Subscribers: 650.
Programming (received off-air): KDKA-TV (CBS) Pittsburgh; WICU-TV (NBC) Erie; WIVB-TV (CBS) Buffalo; WJAC-TV (NBC) Johnstown; WJET-TV (ABC) Erie; WKBW-TV (ABC) Buffalo; WPSU-TV (PBS) Clearfield; WTAJ-TV (CBS) Altoona; allband FM.
Fee: $30.00 installation; $28.00 monthly.

Video-On-Demand: No

Internet Service
Operational: Yes.
Broadband Service: In-house.
Fee: $24.95-$36.95 monthly.

Telephone Service
Digital: Operational
Fee: $29.95 monthly

Miles of Plant: 12.0 (coaxial); None (fiber optic).
Ownership: WestPA.net Inc.

SHENANDOAH—Shen-Heights TV Assoc. Inc., 38 N Main St, Shenandoah, PA 17976-1777. Phone: 570-462-1911. Fax: 570-462-1948. Web Site: http://www.shenhgts.net. Also serves Brandonville, East Union Twp., Oneida, Sheppton, Union Twp. (Schuylkill County) & West Mahanoy Twp. ICA: PA0114.
TV Market Ranking: 49 (Brandonville, East Union Twp., Oneida, SHENANDOAH, Sheppton, Union Twp. (Schuylkill County), West Mahanoy Twp.). Franchise award date: October 1, 1951. Franchise expiration date: N.A. Began: October 1, 1950.
Channel capacity: 60 (not 2-way capable). Channels available but not in use: N.A.

Basic Service
Subscribers: 4,000.
Programming (received off-air): KYW-TV (CBS) Philadelphia; WCAU (NBC) Philadelphia; WNEP-TV (ABC) Scranton; WOLF-TV (CW, FOX, MNT) Hazleton; WPSG (CW) Philadelphia; WPVI-TV (ABC) Philadelphia; WQMY (MNT) Williamsport; WSWB (CW) Scranton; WVIA-TV (PBS) Scranton; WYLN-LP (IND) Hazleton; allband FM.
Programming (via satellite): Pennsylvania Cable Network; QVC; TV Guide Network; WGN America; WPIX (CW, IND) New York.
Fee: $45.00 installation; $19.95 monthly.

Expanded Basic Service 1
Subscribers: 3,000.
Programming (via satellite): A&E Networks; ABC Family Channel; AMC; Animal Planet; Cartoon Network; CNBC; CNN; Comcast SportsNet Philadelphia; Comedy Central; Country Music TV; C-SPAN; Discovery Channel; Disney Channel; E! Entertainment Television; ESPN; ESPN 2; Eternal Word TV Network; Food Network; Fox News Channel; FX; HGTV; History Channel; Lifetime; MSNBC; MTV; NFL Network; Nickelodeon; Speed; Spike TV; Syfy; TBS Superstation; The Learning Channel; The Weather Channel; Travel Channel; Trinity Broadcasting Network; truTV; Turner Network TV; USA Network; Versus; VH1.
Fee: $34.00 monthly.

Digital Basic Service
Subscribers: 250.
Programming (via satellite): American-Life TV Network; BBC America; Bloomberg Television; Bravo; Discovery Fit & Health; Discovery Health Channel; Discovery Kids Channel; DMX Music; ESPN 2 HD; ESPN Classic Sports; ESPN HD; ESPN Now; ESPNews; Fox Movie Channel; Fox Soccer; FSN Digital Atlantic; FSN Digital Central; FSN Digital Pacific; Fuse; G4; Golf Channel; GSN; Independent Film Channel; Nick Jr.; Outdoor Channel; Science; Style Network; TBS in HD; Toon Disney; Turner Classic Movies; Turner Network TV HD; TV Guide Interactive Inc.; WE tv.
Fee: $25.00 installation; $12.95 monthly.

Digital Pay Service 1
Pay Units: N.A.
Programming (via satellite): Cinemax (multiplexed); Encore (multiplexed); HBO (multiplexed); Showtime (multiplexed); Starz (multiplexed).
Fee: $23.95 monthly (HBO & Cinemax), $31.95 monthly (Showtime and Starz/Encore).

Video-On-Demand: No

Pay-Per-View
iN DEMAND (delivered digitally); Playboy TV (delivered digitally); Fresh (delivered digitally); Club Jenna (delivered digitally); Spice (delivered digitally); ESPN Now (delivered digitally).

Internet Service
Operational: Yes.
Fee: $24.95-$69.95 monthly.

Telephone Service
None

Miles of Plant: 42.0 (coaxial); None (fiber optic). Additional miles planned: 5.0 (coaxial).
Manager: Martin Brophy. Chief Technician: Anthony Brophy.
Ownership: Shen-Heights TV Assn. Inc.

SHIPPENSBURG—Comcast Cable, 1 E Uwchlan Ave, Ste 411, Exton, PA 19341. Phones: 484-288-6500; 717-960-3100 (Harrisburg office). Web Site: http://www.comcast.com. Also serves Cascade, Pen-Mar & Washington County, MD; Antrim Twp., Ayr Twp., Blue Ridge Summit, Boiling Springs, Carlisle, Carlisle Barracks, Carroll Twp. (Perry County), Chambersburg, Cumberland County, Cumberland Twp. (Adams County), Dickinson Twp. (Cumberland County), Fort Loudon, Franklin County, Fulton County (portions), Greencastle, Greene Twp. (Franklin County), Guilford Twp., Letterkenny Twp. (Franklin County), Lower Frankford Twp., Lower Mifflin Twp., Mainsville, McConnellsburg, Mercersburg, Middlesex Twp. (Cumberland County), Mont Alto, Mount Holly Springs, Newville, North Middleton Twp. (Cumberland County), North Newton Twp., Peters Twp., Quinoy Twp., Rouzerville, Shady Grove, Shermans Dale, South Middleton Twp. (Cumberland County), St. Thomas Twp. (Franklin County), State Line, Wayne Heights, Waynesboro, West Pennsboro Twp. (Cumberland County) & Zulinger, PA. ICA: PA0066.
TV Market Ranking: 57 (Boiling Springs, Carlisle, Carlisle Barracks, Carroll Twp. (Perry County), Cumberland County (portions), Dickinson Twp. (Cumberland County), Lower Frankford Twp., Lower Mifflin Twp., Middlesex Twp. (Cumberland County), Mount Holly Springs, Newville, North Middleton Twp. (Cumberland County), Shermans Dale, South Middleton Twp. (Cumberland County), West Pennsboro Twp. (Cumberland County)); 74 (Fulton County (portions)); Below 100 (Antrim Twp., Ayr Twp., Blue Ridge Summit, Cascade, Chambersburg, Cumberland Twp. (Adams County), Fort Loudon, Franklin County (portions), Greencastle, Greene Twp. (Franklin County), Guilford Twp., Letterkenny Twp. (Franklin County), Mainsville, McConnellsburg, Mercersburg, Mont Alto, North Newton Twp., Pen-Mar, Peters Twp., Quinoy Twp., Rouzerville, Shady Grove, SHIPPENSBURG, St. Thomas Twp. (Franklin County), State Line, Washington County, Wayne Heights, Waynesboro, Zulinger, Fulton County (portions)); Outside TV Markets (Franklin County (portions), Cumberland County (portions)). Franchise award date: N.A. Franchise expiration date: N.A. Began: November 1, 1964.
Channel capacity: N.A. Channels available but not in use: N.A.

Basic Service
Subscribers: N.A. Included in Harrisburg
Programming (received off-air): WDCA (MNT) Washington; WDCW (CW) Washington; WGAL (NBC) Lancaster; WHAG-TV (NBC) Hagerstown; WHP-TV (CBS, MNT) Harrisburg; WHTM-TV (ABC) Harrisburg; WITF-TV (PBS) Harrisburg; WJAL (IND) Hagerstown; WJLA-TV (ABC) Washington; WLYH-TV (CW) Lancaster; WPMT (FOX) York; WRC-TV (NBC) Washington; WTTG (FOX) Washington; WUSA (CBS) Washington; WWPX-TV (ION) Martinsburg.
Programming (via satellite): C-SPAN; Pennsylvania Cable Network; QVC; TBS Superstation; The Comcast Network.
Fee: $45.10 installation; $16.90 monthly; $1.94 converter.

Expanded Basic Service 1
Subscribers: 38,000.
Programming (via satellite): A&E Networks; ABC Family Channel; AMC; Animal Planet; BET Networks; Bravo; Cartoon Network; CNBC; CNN; Comcast SportsNet Philadelphia; Comedy Central; Country Music TV; C-SPAN 2; Discovery Channel; Discovery Health Channel; E! Entertainment Television; ESPN; ESPN 2; ESPN Classic Sports; Food Network; Fox News Channel; FX; Golf Channel; GSN; Hallmark Channel; Headline News; HGTV; History Channel; Lifetime; MSNBC; MTV; Nickelodeon; Outdoor Channel; Root Sports Pittsburgh; ShopNBC; Speed; Spike TV; Style Network; Syfy; The Learning Channel; The Weather Channel; Travel Channel; Trinity Broadcasting Network; truTV; Turner

Classic Movies; Turner Network TV; TV Guide Network; TV Land; USA Network; Versus; VH1.
Fee: $33.90 monthly.

Digital Basic Service
Subscribers: N.A.
Programming (via satellite): BBC America; Bio; Cooking Channel; C-SPAN 3; Discovery Digital Networks; Disney Channel; DIY Network; DMX Music; Encore (multiplexed); ESPNews; Flix; G4; GAS; History Channel International; Independent Film Channel; Mid-Atlantic Sports Network; MTV Networks Digital Suite; National Geographic Channel; NFL Network; Nick Jr.; Nick Too; NickToons TV; SoapNet; Sundance Channel; Toon Disney; WAM! America's Kidz Network; Weatherscan.
Fee: $14.95 monthly.

Digital Pay Service 1
Pay Units: N.A.
Programming (via satellite): Cinemax (multiplexed); HBO (multiplexed); Showtime (multiplexed); Starz (multiplexed); The Movie Channel (multiplexed).

Video-On-Demand: Yes

Pay-Per-View
Fresh (delivered digitally); iN DEMAND (delivered digitally); NHL Center Ice (delivered digitally); MLB Extra Innings (delivered digitally); NASCAR In Car (delivered digitally); Playboy TV (delivered digitally); Shorteez (delivered digitally); Pleasure (delivered digitally); ESPN (delivered digitally); NBA TV (delivered digitally); NBA League Pass.

Internet Service
Operational: Yes.
Broadband Service: Comcast High Speed Internet.
Fee: $42.95 monthly.

Telephone Service
Digital: Operational

Miles of Plant: 1,088.0 (coaxial); 200.0 (fiber optic). Additional miles planned: 100.0 (coaxial).

Regional Vice President: Jim Samaha. Vice President, Marketing: Larry Goldman. Technical Operations Director: William Mays.

Ownership: Comcast Cable Communications Inc. (MSO).

SHIPPENVILLE—Atlantic Broadband, 120 Southmont Blvd, Johnstown, PA 15905. Phones: 888-536-9600; 814-539-8971. Fax: 814-535-7749. E-mail: info@atlanticbb.com. Web Site: http://www.atlanticbb.com. Also serves Cranberry, Elk Twp. (Clarion County), Emlenton, Knox Twp. (Clarion County), Kossuth, Lamartine, Nineveh, Salem Twp. (Clarion County) & Turkey City. ICA: PA0198.

TV Market Ranking: Below 100 (Knox Twp. (Clarion County) (portions)); Outside TV Markets (Cranberry, Elk Twp. (Clarion County), Emlenton, Knox Twp. (Clarion County) (portions), Kossuth, Lamartine, Salem Twp. (Clarion County), Turkey City, Nineveh, SHIPPENVILLE). Franchise award date: N.A. Franchise expiration date: N.A. Began: January 1, 1988.

Channel capacity: 59 (not 2-way capable). Channels available but not in use: N.A.

Basic Service
Subscribers: 417.
Programming (received off-air): KDKA-TV (CBS) Pittsburgh; WJAC-TV (NBC) Johnstown; WKBN-TV (CBS) Youngstown; WPCB-TV (IND) Greensburg; WPCW (CW) Jeannette; WPGH-TV (FOX) Pittsburgh; WPMY (MNT) Pittsburgh; WPSU-TV (PBS) Clearfield; WPXI (IND, NBC) Pittsburgh; WQED (PBS) Pittsburgh; WTAE-TV (ABC) Pittsburgh; WYTV (ABC, MNT) Youngstown.
Programming (via satellite): C-SPAN; Meadows Racing Network; Pennsylvania Cable Network; QVC; Trinity Broadcasting Network.
Fee: $25.00 installation; $19.39 monthly; $3.00 converter; $10.00 additional installation.

Expanded Basic Service 1
Subscribers: N.A.
Programming (via satellite): A&E Networks; ABC Family Channel; AMC; Animal Planet; Bravo; Cartoon Network; CNBC; CNN; Comedy Central; Country Music TV; Discovery Channel; Discovery Health Channel; Disney Channel; E! Entertainment Television; ESPN; ESPN 2; Food Network; Fox News Channel; FX; Hallmark Channel; Headline News; HGTV; History Channel; Lifetime; Lifetime Movie Network; MSNBC; MTV; Nickelodeon; Outdoor Channel; Root Sports Pittsburgh; Speed; Spike TV; Syfy; TBS Superstation; The Learning Channel; The Weather Channel; Travel Channel; truTV; Turner Classic Movies; Turner Network TV; TV Land; USA Network; VH1.
Fee: $37.06 monthly.

Digital Basic Service
Subscribers: N.A.
Programming (via satellite): BBC America; Bio; Bloomberg Television; CMT Pure Country; Discovery Kids Channel; Discovery Times Channel; DMX Music; ESPN Classic Sports; ESPNews; Fuel TV; GSN; History Channel International; Lifetime Real Women; Military Channel; MTV Hits; MTV2; NFL Network; Nick Jr.; NickToons TV; Planet Green; Science; SoapNet; TeenNick; Toon Disney; VH1 Classic; VH1 Soul; WE tv; Weatherscan.
Fee: $18.95 monthly.

Digital Pay Service 1
Pay Units: N.A.
Programming (via satellite): Cinemax (multiplexed); Encore (multiplexed); Flix; HBO (multiplexed); Showtime (multiplexed); Starz (multiplexed); The Movie Channel (multiplexed).
Fee: $15.95 monthly (HBO, Cinemax, Starz, Encore or Showtime/TMC/Flix).

Pay-Per-View
iN DEMAND (delivered digitally); Hot Choice (delivered digitally); Playboy TV (delivered digitally); Club Jenna (delivered digitally); Spice: Xcess (delivered digitally); Fresh (delivered digitally).

Internet Service
Operational: Yes.
Fee: $24.95-$57.95 monthly.

Telephone Service
None

Miles of Plant: 62.0 (coaxial); None (fiber optic).

Vice President: David Dane. General Manager: Mike Papasergi. Technical Operations Director: Charles Sorchilla. Marketing & Customer Service Director: Dara Leslie. Marketing Manager: Natalie Kurchak.

Ownership: Atlantic Broadband (MSO).

SHIPPENVILLE—Atlantic Broadband, 120 Southmont Blvd, Johnstown, PA 15905. Phones: 888-536-9600; 814-539-8971. Fax: 814-535-7749. E-mail: info@atlanticbb.com. Web Site: http://www.atlanticbb.com. Also serves Elk Twp. (Clarion County), Knox, Ninevah & Paint Twp. (Clarion County). ICA: PA0387.

TV Market Ranking: Outside TV Markets (Elk Twp. (Clarion County), Knox, Ninevah, Paint Twp. (Clarion County), SHIPPENVILLE). Franchise award date: N.A. Franchise expiration date: N.A. Began: April 1, 1973.

Channel capacity: 61 (operating 2-way). Channels available but not in use: N.A.

Basic Service
Subscribers: 1,026.
Programming (received off-air): KDKA-TV (CBS) Pittsburgh; WJAC-TV (NBC) Johnstown; WKBN-TV (CBS) Youngstown; WPCB-TV (IND) Greensburg; WPCW (CW) Jeannette; WPGH-TV (FOX) Pittsburgh; WPMY (MNT) Pittsburgh; WPSU-TV (PBS) Clearfield; WPXI (IND, NBC) Pittsburgh; WQED (PBS) Pittsburgh; WTAE-TV (ABC) Pittsburgh; WYTV (ABC, MNT) Youngstown.
Programming (via satellite): C-SPAN; Meadows Racing Network; Pennsylvania Cable Network; QVC; Trinity Broadcasting Network.
Fee: $25.00 installation; $19.39 monthly.

Expanded Basic Service 1
Subscribers: 998.
Programming (via satellite): A&E Networks; ABC Family Channel; AMC; Animal Planet; Bravo; Cartoon Network; CNBC; CNN; Comedy Central; Country Music TV; Discovery Channel; Discovery Health Channel; Disney Channel; E! Entertainment Television; ESPN; ESPN 2; Food Network; Fox News Channel; FX; Hallmark Channel; Headline News; HGTV; History Channel; Lifetime; Lifetime Movie Network; MSNBC; MTV; Nickelodeon; Outdoor Channel; Root Sports Pittsburgh; Speed; Spike TV; Syfy; TBS Superstation; The Learning Channel; The Weather Channel; Travel Channel; truTV; Turner Classic Movies; Turner Network TV; TV Land; USA Network; VH1.
Fee: $37.06 monthly.

Digital Basic Service
Subscribers: N.A.
Programming (via satellite): BBC America; Bio; Bloomberg Television; CMT Pure Country; Discovery Kids Channel; Discovery Times Channel; Encore (multiplexed); ESPN Classic Sports; ESPNews; Fuel TV; GSN; History Channel International; Lifetime Real Women; Military Channel; MTV Hits; MTV2; Music Choice; NFL Network; Nick Jr.; NickToons TV; Planet Green; Science; SoapNet; Starz (multiplexed); TeenNick; Toon Disney; VH1 Classic; VH1 Soul; WE tv; WeatherVision.
Fee: $18.95 monthly.

Digital Pay Service 1
Pay Units: N.A.
Programming (via satellite): Cinemax (multiplexed); Flix; HBO (multiplexed); Showtime (multiplexed); The Movie Channel (multiplexed).
Fee: $15.95 monthly (HBO, Cinemax or Showime/TMC/Flix).

Video-On-Demand: No

Pay-Per-View
iN DEMAND (delivered digitally); Hot Choice (delivered digitally); Fresh (delivered digitally); Playboy TV (delivered digitally); Club Jenna (delivered digitally); Spice: Xcess (delivered digitally).

Internet Service
Operational: Yes.
Broadband Service: Atlantic Broadband High-Speed Internet.
Fee: 24.95-$57.95 monthly.

Telephone Service
None

Miles of Plant: 47.0 (coaxial); 140.0 (fiber optic). Additional miles planned: 10.0 (fiber optic).

Vice President: David Dane. General Manager: Mike Papasergi. Technical Operations Director: Charles Sorchilla. Marketing & Customer Service Director: Dara Leslie. Marketing Manager: Natalie Kurchak.

Ownership: Atlantic Broadband (MSO).

SHIPPINGPORT BOROUGH—Comcast Cable. Now served by BEAVER FALLS, PA [PA0065]. ICA: PA0296.

SHIRLEY TWP.—Formerly served by Adelphia Communications. Now served by PHILIPSBURG BOROUGH, PA [PA0109]. ICA: PA0139.

SIX MILE RUN—Six Mile Run TV Assn., 1171 Six Mile Run Rd, Six Mile Run, PA 16679-9260. Phone: 814-928-4093. ICA: PA0295.

TV Market Ranking: 74 (SIX MILE RUN). Franchise award date: January 1, 1950. Franchise expiration date: N.A. Began: April 20, 1951.

Channel capacity: 14 (not 2-way capable). Channels available but not in use: N.A.

Basic Service
Subscribers: 16.
Programming (received off-air): WATM-TV (ABC) Altoona; WJAC-TV (NBC) Johnstown; WPSU-TV (PBS) Clearfield; WTAJ-TV (CBS) Altoona; WWCP-TV (FOX) Johnstown; allband FM.
Programming (via satellite): BET Networks; Cartoon Network; CNN; ESPN; TBS Superstation; Turner Classic Movies; USA Network; WGN America.
Fee: $40.00 installation; $20.00 monthly.

Pay Service 1
Pay Units: N.A.
Programming (via satellite): HBO.
Fee: $8.50 monthly.

Video-On-Demand: No

Internet Service
Operational: No.

Telephone Service
None

Miles of Plant: 3.0 (coaxial); None (fiber optic).

Manager: Richard W. White. Chief Technician: Harold Colbert.

Ownership: Six Mile Run TV Association.

SMETHPORT—Comcast Cable, 15 Summit Park Dr, Pittsburgh, PA 15275. Phone: 412-747-6400. Fax: 412-747-6401. Web Site: http://www.comcast.com. Also serves Duke Center, Eldred, Foster Twp. (McKean County), Otto Twp. & Rixford. ICA: PA0147.

TV Market Ranking: Outside TV Markets (Duke Center, Eldred, Foster Twp. (McKean County), Otto Twp., Rixford, SMETHPORT). Franchise award date: N.A. Franchise expiration date: N.A. Began: June 1, 1953.

Channel capacity: N.A. Channels available but not in use: N.A.

Basic Service
Subscribers: N.A. Included in Bensalem Twp.
Programming (received off-air): WGRZ (NBC) Buffalo; WICU-TV (NBC) Erie; WIVB-TV (CBS) Buffalo; WKBW-TV (ABC) Buffalo; WPSU-TV (PBS) Clearfield; WTAJ-TV (CBS) Altoona; allband FM.
Programming (via satellite): C-SPAN; C-SPAN 2; QVC; TBS Superstation; The Weather Channel; TV Guide Network; WGN America.
Fee: $39.95 installation; $10.25 monthly; $2.00 converter.

Expanded Basic Service 1
Subscribers: N.A.
Programming (via satellite): A&E Networks; ABC Family Channel; AMC; Animal Planet; BET Networks; Bravo!; Cartoon Network;

CNBC; CNN; Comedy Central; Discovery Channel; Discovery Fit & Health; E! Entertainment Television; ESPN; ESPN 2; Eternal Word TV Network; Flix; Fox News Channel; FX; GSN; Hallmark Channel; Headline News; HGTV; History Channel; Lifetime; MSNBC; MTV; Nickelodeon; Oxygen; Product Information Network; Root Sports Pittsburgh; ShopNBC; Spike TV; Syfy; TBS Superstation; The Learning Channel; Travel Channel; truTV; Turner Classic Movies; Turner Network TV; TV Land; USA Network; VH1; Yankees Entertainment & Sports.
Fee: $11.42 monthly.

Digital Basic Service
Subscribers: 45.
Programming (via satellite): AmericanLife TV Network; BBC America; Bloomberg Television; CNN en Espanol; Discovery Fit & Health; DMX Music; ESPNews; Fox Deportes; Fox Movie Channel; Fox Sports World; Fuse; G4; GAS; Golf Channel; Great American Country; History Channel en Espanol; INSP; Lifetime Movie Network; MTV Networks Digital Suite; MTV2; National Geographic Channel; Nick Jr.; Nick Too; NickToons TV; SoapNet; Speed; The Word Network; Toon Disney; Trinity Broadcasting Network; TVE Internacional; WE tv.

Digital Expanded Basic Service
Subscribers: N.A.
Programming (via satellite): Bio; ESPN Classic Sports; Fox Sports Net (multiplexed); History Channel International; Independent Film Channel; International Television (ITV); Outdoor Channel; Sundance Channel; Versus.

Digital Pay Service 1
Pay Units: N.A.
Programming (via satellite): Cinemax (multiplexed); Encore; HBO (multiplexed); Showtime (multiplexed); Starz; The Movie Channel (multiplexed).

Video-On-Demand: Yes

Pay-Per-View
special events; ESPN Pak; NHL/MLB Pak; iN DEMAND (delivered digitally); Playboy TV (delivered digitally); Fresh (delivered digitally); Shorteez (delivered digitally); Spice Live (delivered digitally); Spice Platinum (delivered digitally); Spice Hot (delivered digitally).

Internet Service
Operational: Yes.
Subscribers: 70.
Broadband Service: Comcast High Speed Internet.
Fee: $42.95 monthly.

Telephone Service
None

Miles of Plant: 77.0 (coaxial); None (fiber optic).
Regional Vice President: Linda Hossinger. Vice President, Technical Operations: Randy Bender. Vice President, Marketing: Donna Corning. Vice President, Public Affairs: Jody Doherty.
Ownership: Comcast Cable Communications Inc. (MSO).

SNOW SHOE—Tele-Media, 804 Jacksonville Rd, PO Box 39, Bellefonte, PA 16823-0039. Phone: 814-353-2025. Fax: 814-353-2072. Web Site: http://www.tele-media.com. Also serves Boggs Twp. (Clearfield County), Clarence, Cooper Twp., Cooper Twp. (Clearfield County), Drifting, Graham Twp., Grassflat, Karthaus Twp., Kylertown, Lanse, Lecontes Mills, Morrisdale, Wallaceton & Winburne. ICA: PA0188.
TV Market Ranking: 74 (Boggs Twp. (Clearfield County), Cooper Twp. (portions), Kylertown, Lanse, Morrisdale, Wallaceton, Winburne); Outside TV Markets (Clarence, Cooper Twp. (Clearfield County), Drifting, Graham Twp., Lecontes Mills, SNOW SHOE, Cooper Twp. (portions)). Franchise award date: N.A. Franchise expiration date: N.A. Began: May 1, 1957.
Channel capacity: N.A. Channels available but not in use: N.A.

Basic Service
Subscribers: 1,582 Included in Zion.
Programming (received off-air): WATM-TV (ABC) Altoona; WHVL-LP State College, etc.; WJAC-TV (NBC) Johnstown; WKBS-TV (IND) Altoona; WPSU-TV (PBS) Clearfield; WTAJ-TV (CBS) Altoona; WWCP-TV (FOX) Johnstown; allband FM.
Programming (via satellite): C-SPAN; C-SPAN 2; QVC; The Weather Channel; WGN America.
Fee: $18.95 monthly; $1.24 converter.

Expanded Basic Service 1
Subscribers: N.A.
Programming (via satellite): A&E Networks; ABC Family Channel; Animal Planet; Celebrity Shopping Network; CNN; Comedy Central; Discovery Channel; Disney Channel; ESPN; ESPN 2; Eternal Word TV Network; Food Network; Fox News Channel; FX; G4; Great American Country; GSN; Hallmark Channel; Headline News; HGTV; History Channel; Lifetime; MSNBC; MTV; National Geographic Channel; Nickelodeon; Outdoor Channel; Root Sports Pittsburgh; SoapNet; Speed; Spike TV; Syfy; TBS Superstation; The Learning Channel; Toon Disney; Turner Classic Movies; Turner Network TV; TV Land; USA Network; Versus; VH1; WE tv.
Fee: $25.85 monthly.

Digital Basic Service
Subscribers: 76 Included in Zion.
Programming (via satellite): BBC America; Bio; Bloomberg Television; cloo; Discovery Health Channel; Discovery Kids Channel; DMX Music; ESPN Classic Sports; ESPNews; Fox College Sports Atlantic; Fox College Sports Central; Fox College Sports Pacific; Fox Movie Channel; Fox Soccer; Golf Channel; Great American Country; Halogen Network; History Channel International; ID Investigation Discovery; Independent Film Channel; Lifetime Movie Network; Military Channel; Planet Green; Science; ShopNBC; Style Network; Trinity Broadcasting Network.
Fee: $10.00 monthly.

Digital Pay Service 1
Pay Units: N.A.
Programming (via satellite): Cinemax (multiplexed); Encore (multiplexed); Flix; HBO (multiplexed); Showtime (multiplexed); Starz (multiplexed); The Movie Channel (multiplexed).
Fee: $9.45 monthly (Cinemax), $11.00 monthly (Starz/Encore), $12.50 monthly (HBO or Showtime/TMC/Flix).

Video-On-Demand: No

Internet Service
Operational: Yes.
Subscribers: 610.
Broadband Service: In-house.
Fee: $27.95 monthly.

Telephone Service
None

Miles of plant included in Zion
Senior Vice President, Finance: Bob Stemler. General Manager: Lesley Strouse. Chief Technician: Dean Colbert.
Ownership: Tele-Media Corp. (MSO).

SOMERSET—Formerly served by Cebridge Connections. Now served by CONNELLSVILLE, PA [PA0046]. ICA: PA0128.

SOMERSET TWP.—Formerly served by Adelphia Communications. Now served by CENTRAL CITY BOROUGH, PA [PA0132]. ICA: PA0091.

SOUTH BUFFALO TWP.—South Buffalo Cablevision. Now served by KISKIMINETAS TWP., OH [OH0074]. ICA: PA0257.

SOUTH FORK—Formerly served by Adelphia Communications. Now served by ADAMS TWP. (Cambria County), PA [PA0133]. ICA: PA0189.

SOUTH WHITEHALL TWP.—Formerly served by NORTHAMPTON BOROUGH, PA [PA0008]. RCN Corp. This cable system has converted to IPTV, 196 Van Buren St, Herndon, VA 20170. Phone: 703-434-8200. Web Site: http://www.rcn.com. ICA: PA5234.
TV Market Ranking: Below 100 (SOUTH WHITEHALL TWP.).
Channel capacity: N.A. Channels available but not in use: N.A.

Internet Service
Operational: Yes.

Telephone Service
Digital: Operational

Chairman: Steven J. Simmons. Chief Executive Officer: Jim Holanda.

SPARTANSBURG—Zito Media, 611 Vader Hill Rd, Coudersport, PA 16915. Phones: 866-879-6235; 814-260-9570; 814-260-9575. Fax: 814-260-9580. E-mail: rigas@zitomedia.com. Web Site: http://www.zitomedia.com. Also serves Sparta Twp. (Crawford County). ICA: PA0438.
TV Market Ranking: Below 100 (Sparta Twp. (Crawford County), SPARTANSBURG). Franchise award date: N.A. Franchise expiration date: N.A. Began: N.A.
Channel capacity: 41 (not 2-way capable). Channels available but not in use: N.A.

Basic Service
Subscribers: 50.
Programming (received off-air): WFXP (FOX) Erie; WICU-TV (NBC) Erie; WJET-TV (ABC) Erie; WQLN (PBS) Erie; WSEE-TV (CBS, CW) Erie.
Programming (via satellite): ABC Family Channel; Animal Planet; Cartoon Network; CNN; C-SPAN 2; Discovery Channel; Disney Channel; ESPN; ESPN 2; Headline News; Lifetime; MTV; Nickelodeon; QVC; Syfy; TBS Superstation; Travel Channel; Trinity Broadcasting Network; Turner Network TV; USA Network; VH1; WGN America.
Fee: $39.95 installation; $29.95 monthly; $2.50 converter.

Pay Service 1
Pay Units: N.A.
Programming (via satellite): HBO.
Fee: $12.95 monthly.

Internet Service
Operational: No.

Telephone Service
None

Miles of Plant: 5.0 (coaxial); None (fiber optic).
Manager: James Rigas. Marketing Director: Kathy Fox.
Ownership: Zito Media (MSO).

SPRING MILLS—Spring Mills TV Co. Now served by MILLHEIM, PA [PA0216]. ICA: PA0268.

SPRING TWP. (Crawford County)—Formerly served by Adelphia Communications. Now served by HARBORCREEK TWP., PA [PA0025]. ICA: PA0230.

SPRUCE CREEK TWP.—MetroCast Communications, 1059 E 10th St, Hazleton, PA 18201-3421. Phones: 800-633-8578; 570-455-6851. Fax: 570-459-0963. Web Site: http://www.metrocastcommunications.com. Also serves Franklin Twp. (Huntingdon County). ICA: PA0274.
TV Market Ranking: 74 (Franklin Twp. (Huntingdon County), SPRUCE CREEK TWP.). Franchise award date: N.A. Franchise expiration date: N.A. Began: November 1, 1984.
Channel capacity: 42 (not 2-way capable). Channels available but not in use: N.A.

Basic Service
Subscribers: 100.
Programming (received off-air): WATM-TV (ABC) Altoona; WJAC-TV (NBC) Johnstown; WKBS-TV (IND) Altoona; WPSU-TV (PBS) Clearfield; WTAJ-TV (CBS) Altoona; allband FM.
Programming (via satellite): ABC Family Channel; AMC; Animal Planet; CNN; Discovery Channel; Disney Channel; ESPN; ESPN 2; FX; Headline News; History Channel; Lifetime; Nickelodeon; QVC; Speed; Spike TV; Syfy; The Learning Channel; The Weather Channel; Turner Network TV; TV Land; USA Network.
Fee: $42.95 installation; $31.80 monthly.

Digital Basic Service
Subscribers: N.A.
Programming (via satellite): Bio; Discovery Digital Networks; DMX Music; Fox Sports World; Golf Channel; GSN; Independent Film Channel; Lifetime; Turner Classic Movies; WE tv.
Fee: $25.92 installation; $7.95 monthly.

Pay Service 1
Pay Units: 12.
Programming (via satellite): HBO.
Fee: $12.95 monthly.

Pay Service 2
Pay Units: 19.
Programming (via satellite): Cinemax.
Fee: $12.95 monthly.

Digital Pay Service 1
Pay Units: N.A.
Programming (via satellite): Cinemax (multiplexed); HBO (multiplexed); Showtime (multiplexed).
Fee: $12.95 monthly (each).

Pay-Per-View
ESPN Now (delivered digitally); ESPN Extra (delivered digitally); Hot Choice (delivered digitally); Fresh (delivered digitally); Sports PPV (delivered digitally).

Internet Service
Operational: No.

Telephone Service
None

Miles of Plant: 11.0 (coaxial); None (fiber optic).
Manager: Joseph Gans III. Marketing Director: Lori A. Warg.
Ownership: Harron Communications LP (MSO).

ST. MARY'S—Zito Media, 611 Vader Hill Rd, Coudersport, PA 16915. Phone: 814-260-9575. Fax: 814-260-9580. E-mail: rigas@zitomedia.com. Web Site: http://www.zitomedia.com. Also serves Benzinger Twp., Daguscahonda, Fox Twp. (Elk County), Kersey & Toby. ICA: PA0101.
TV Market Ranking: Outside TV Markets (Benzinger Twp., Daguscahonda, Fox Twp. (Elk County), Kersey, ST. MARY'S, Toby). Fran-

chise award date: N.A. Franchise expiration date: N.A. Began: May 1, 1953.
Channel capacity: 65 (operating 2-way). Channels available but not in use: N.A.

Basic Service
Subscribers: 4,501.
Programming (received off-air): WATM-TV (ABC) Altoona; WJAC-TV (NBC) Johnstown; WPCB-TV (IND) Greensburg; WPSU-TV (PBS) Clearfield; WTAE-TV (ABC) Pittsburgh; WTAJ-TV (CBS) Altoona; WWCP-TV (FOX) Johnstown.
Programming (via satellite): C-SPAN; C-SPAN 2; Eternal Word TV Network; INSP; Pennsylvania Cable Network; QVC; Trinity Broadcasting Network; TV Guide Network; WGN America; WPIX (CW, IND) New York.
Fee: $39.95 installation; $1.75 converter.

Expanded Basic Service 1
Subscribers: 4,119.
Programming (via satellite): A&E Networks; ABC Family Channel; AMC; Animal Planet; Bravo; Cartoon Network; CNBC; CNN; Comedy Central; Country Music TV; Discovery Channel; Disney Channel; E! Entertainment Television; ESPN; ESPN 2; ESPN Classic Sports; ESPNews; Food Network; Fox News Channel; FX; Hallmark Channel; Headline News; HGTV; History Channel; Lifetime; Lifetime Movie Network; Lifetime Real Women; MSNBC; MTV; NFL Network; Nickelodeon; Outdoor Channel; Root Sports Pittsburgh; Speed; Spike TV; Syfy; TBS Superstation; The Learning Channel; The Weather Channel; Travel Channel; truTV; Turner Classic Movies; Turner Network TV; TV Land; USA Network; VH1.
Fee: $43.48 monthly.

Digital Basic Service
Subscribers: N.A.
Programming (via satellite): A&E HD; ABC Family HD; BBC America; Bio; Bio HD; Bloomberg Television; Cartoon Network HD; CNN HD; Discovery Channel HD; Discovery Fit & Health; Discovery Health Channel; Discovery Kids Channel; Disney Channel HD; DMX Music; ESPN 2 HD; ESPN HD; ESPNews HD; Food Network HD; Fox College Sports Atlantic; Fox College Sports Central; Fox College Sports Pacific; Fox Soccer; FSN HD; Fuel TV; Fuse; FX HD; G4; GSN; HD Theater; HGTV HD; History Channel International; ID Investigation Discovery; Independent Film Channel; Lifetime Movie Network; Lifetime Movie Network HD; Lifetime Television HD; MTV Hits; MTV2; NFL Network HD; NHL Network HD; Nick Jr.; NickToons TV; Outdoor Channel 2 HD; Planet Green; Science; Science HD; Speed; Speed HD; Style Network; TBS in HD; TeenNick; TLC HD; Turner Network TV HD; VH1 Classic; VH1 Country; WE tv.
Fee: $5.60 monthly.

Digital Pay Service 1
Pay Units: N.A.
Programming (via satellite): Cinemax (multiplexed); Cinemax HD; Encore (multiplexed); Flix; HBO (multiplexed); HBO HD; Showtime (multiplexed); Showtime HD; Starz (multiplexed); Starz HDTV; Sundance Channel; The Movie Channel (multiplexed).
Fee: $6.54 monthly (Cinemax), $10.25 monthly (Starz/Encore), $11.45 monthly (Showtime, TMC, Flix & Sundance), $16.66 monthly (HBO).

Video-On-Demand: No

Pay-Per-View
iN DEMAND (delivered digitally); Playboy TV (delivered digitally).

Internet Service
Operational: Yes.
Fee: $30.51 monthly.

Telephone Service
Digital: Operational
Fee: $20.00 monthly
Miles of Plant: 308.0 (coaxial); 8.0 (fiber optic). Additional miles planned: 12.0 (fiber optic).
Manager: James Rigas.
Ownership: Zito Media (MSO).

STATE COLLEGE—Comcast Cable, 1 E Uwchlan Ave, Ste 411, Exton, PA 19341. Phone: 484-288-6500. Web Site: http://www.comcast.com. Also serves Bellefonte, Benner Twp., Boggs Twp. (Centre County), Centre Hall, College Twp. (Centre County), Curtin Twp., Ferguson Twp., Halfmoon Twp., Harris Twp. (Centre County), Howard, Milesburg, Port Matilda, Potter Twp. (Centre County), Snyder Twp. (Blair County), Spring Twp. (Centre County), Tyrone & Worth Twp. ICA: PA0037.
TV Market Ranking: 74 (College Twp. (Centre County), Ferguson Twp., Halfmoon Twp., Harris Twp. (Centre County) (portions), Port Matilda, Snyder Twp. (Blair County), STATE COLLEGE, Tyrone, Worth Twp.); Outside TV Markets (Bellefonte, Benner Twp. (portions), Boggs Twp. (Centre County), Centre Hall, Curtin Twp., Howard, Milesburg, Potter Twp. (Centre County), Spring Twp. (Centre County), Harris Twp. (Centre County) (portions)). Franchise award date: N.A. Franchise expiration date: N.A. Began: February 1, 1952.
Channel capacity: N.A. Channels available but not in use: N.A.

Basic Service
Subscribers: N.A. Included in Harrisburg
Programming (received off-air): WATM-TV (ABC) Altoona; WKBS-TV (IND) Altoona; WTAJ-TV (CBS) Altoona; WWCP-TV (FOX) Johnstown.
Programming (via microwave): WJAC-TV (NBC) Johnstown; WNEP-TV (ABC) Scranton; WPIX (CW, IND) New York; WPSU-TV (PBS) Clearfield.
Programming (via satellite): C-SPAN; Discovery Channel; Hallmark Channel; Pennsylvania Cable Network; QVC; TBS Superstation; TV Guide Network.
Fee: $45.10 installation; $13.60 monthly.

Expanded Basic Service 1
Subscribers: N.A.
Programming (via satellite): A&E Networks; ABC Family Channel; AMC; Animal Planet; BET Networks; Bravo; Cartoon Network; CNBC; CNN; Comedy Central; Country Music TV; C-SPAN 2; Disney Channel; E! Entertainment Television; ESPN; ESPN 2; Eternal Word TV Network; Food Network; Fox News Channel; FX; Golf Channel; Headline News; HGTV; History Channel; ION Television; Lifetime; MSNBC; MTV; Nickelodeon; Outdoor Channel; Oxygen; Root Sports Pittsburgh; Speed; Spike TV; Syfy; The Learning Channel; The Weather Channel; Travel Channel; truTV; Turner Classic Movies; Turner Network TV; TV Land; USA Network; VH1.
Fee: $32.85 monthly.

Digital Basic Service
Subscribers: 9,000.
Programming (via satellite): BBC America; Black Family Channel; Bloomberg Television; CBS Sports Network; Discovery Fit & Health; DIY Network; ESPN U; ESPNews; Fox Movie Channel; Fox Soccer; Fuse; Gaming Entertainment Television; GAS; Great American Country; GSN; INSP; Lifetime; Military History Channel; MTV Hits; MTV Networks Digital Suite; MTV2; National Geographic Channel; NFL Network; Nick Jr.; NickToons TV; Ovation; SoapNet; Style Network; The Word Network; Toon Disney; Trinity Broadcasting Network; TVG Network; VH1 Classic; VH1 Country; VH1 Soul; WE tv.
Fee: $14.95 monthly.

Digital Pay Service 1
Pay Units: N.A.
Programming (via satellite): Cinemax (multiplexed); HBO (multiplexed); Showtime (multiplexed); Starz (multiplexed).

Video-On-Demand: Yes

Internet Service
Operational: Yes.
Subscribers: 10,000.
Broadband Service: Comcast High Speed Internet.
Fee: $42.95 monthly.

Telephone Service
Digital: Operational
Miles of Plant: 664.0 (coaxial); 150.0 (fiber optic).
Area Vice President: Jim Samaha. Vice President, Marketing: Larry Goldman. Technical Operations Manager: Dan Cramer.
Ownership: Comcast Cable Communications Inc. (MSO).

STATE COLLEGE—Formerly served by D&E Communications. No longer in operation. ICA: PA5280.

STATE COLLEGE—Windstream (formerly D&E Communications.) This cable system has converted to IPTV. See State College, PA [PA5280]. ICA: PA0391.

STOCKERTOWN BOROUGH—Formerly served by NORTHAMPTON BOROUGH, PA [PA0008]. RCN Corp. This cable system has converted to IPTV, 196 Van Buren St, Herndon, VA 20170. Phone: 703-434-8200. Web Site: http://www.rcn.com. ICA: PA5235.
TV Market Ranking: Below 100 (STOCKERTOWN BOROUGH).
Channel capacity: N.A. Channels available but not in use: N.A.

Internet Service
Operational: Yes.

Telephone Service
Digital: Operational
Chairman: Steven J. Simmons. Chief Executive Officer: Jim Holanda.

STROUDSBURG—Blue Ridge Communications, 613 3rd St, PO Box 215, Palmerton, PA 18071-0215. Phones: 610-826-2551; 800-622-8925 (Customer service); 570-421-0780. Web Site: http://www.brctv.com. Also serves Barrett Twp., Buck Hill Falls, Bushkill, Chestnut Hill Twp., Coolbaugh Twp., Delaware Water Gap, East Stroudsburg, Hamilton Twp. (Monroe County), Jackson Twp. (Monroe County), Lehman Twp. (Pike County), Middle Smithfield, Middle Smithfield Twp., Mount Pocono, Paradise Twp. (Monroe County), Pine Ridge, Pocono Lake, Pocono Twp., Polk Twp. (Monroe County), Price Twp. (Monroe County), Ross Twp. (Monroe County), Saw Creek, Saw Creek Estates, Smithfield Twp. (Monroe County), Stroud Twp. (Monroe County), The Falls, Timothy Lake, Tobyhanna Twp. (Monroe County) & Winona Lakes (Monroe & Pike Counties). ICA: PA0411.
TV Market Ranking: 49 (Barrett Twp., Buck Hill Falls, Chestnut Hill Twp., Coolbaugh Twp., Jackson Twp. (Monroe County), Middle Smithfield, Mount Pocono, Paradise Twp. (Monroe County), Pine Ridge, Pocono Lake, Pocono Twp., Polk Twp. (Monroe County), Price Twp. (Monroe County), Saw Creek, Smithfield Twp. (Monroe County), Stroud Twp. (Monroe County), STROUDSBURG, The Falls, Timothy Lake, Tobyhanna Twp. (Monroe County)); Below 100 (Delaware Water Gap, East Stroudsburg, Hamilton Twp. (Monroe County), Ross Twp. (Monroe County)); Outside TV Markets (Bushkill, Lehman Twp. (Pike County), Middle Smithfield Twp., Saw Creek Estates, Winona Lakes (Monroe & Pike Counties)). Franchise award date: N.A. Franchise expiration date: N.A. Began: March 31, 1952.
Channel capacity: 54 (operating 2-way). Channels available but not in use: N.A.

Basic Service
Subscribers: 41,559.
Programming (received off-air): KYW-TV (CBS) Philadelphia; WCAU (NBC) Philadelphia; WCBS-TV (CBS) New York; WFMZ-TV (IND) Allentown; WLVT-TV (PBS) Allentown; WNBC (NBC) New York; WNEP-TV (ABC) Scranton; WNYW (FOX) New York; WOLF-TV (CW, FOX, MNT) Hazleton; WPIX (CW, IND) New York; WPSG (CW) Philadelphia; WPVI-TV (ABC) Philadelphia; WQPX-TV (ION) Scranton; WSWB (CW) Scranton; WVIA-TV (PBS) Scranton; WWOR-TV (MNT) Secaucus; WYOU (CBS) Scranton; allband FM.
Programming (via satellite): Headline News.
Fee: $22.50 installation; $16.54 monthly.

Expanded Basic Service 1
Subscribers: N.A.
Programming (via satellite): A&E Networks; ABC Family Channel; AMC; Animal Planet; BET Networks; Bravo; Cartoon Network; CNBC; CNN; Comcast SportsNet Philadelphia; Comedy Central; Country Music TV; C-SPAN; Discovery Channel; Discovery Health Channel; Disney Channel; E! Entertainment Television; ESPN; ESPN 2; ESPN Classic Sports; ESPNews; Eternal Word TV Network; Food Network; Fox News Channel; FX; Golf Channel; HGTV; History Channel; Lifetime; Lifetime Movie Network; MSG; MSNBC; MTV; Nickelodeon; Pennsylvania Cable Network; QVC; ShopNBC; Speed; Spike TV; Syfy; TBS Superstation; The Learning Channel; The Weather Channel; Travel Channel; Trinity Broadcasting Network; truTV; Turner Classic Movies; Turner Network TV; TV Land; Univision Studios; USA Network; Versus; VH1; WE tv; Yankees Entertainment & Sports.
Fee: $31.69 monthly.

Digital Basic Service
Subscribers: N.A.
Programming (via satellite): Bio; Discovery Digital Networks; Fox Movie Channel; FSN Digital Atlantic; FSN Digital Central; FSN Digital Pacific; GAS; Halogen Network; Lifetime Real Women; Meadows Racing Network; MTV Networks Digital Suite; Music Choice; National Geographic Channel; Nick Jr.; Nick Too; NickToons TV; Outdoor Channel; PBS Kids Channel; SoapNet; Toon Disney.
Fee: $35.00 installation; $9.95 monthly.
Digital Expanded Basic Service
Subscribers: N.A.
Programming (via satellite): BBC America; Bloomberg Television; Boomerang; Cooking Channel; DIY Network; G4; Hallmark Channel; History Channel International; LWS Local Weather Station; Style Network.
Fee: $5.00 monthly.
Digital Pay Service 1
Pay Units: N.A.
Programming (via satellite): Cinemax (multiplexed); Encore (multiplexed); Flix; HBO (multiplexed); Showtime (multiplexed); Starz (multiplexed); Sundance Channel; The Movie Channel (multiplexed).
Fee: $12.50 monthly (Cinemax or Showtime/Flix/Sundance/TMC), $12.95 monthly (Starz/Encore), $13.50 monthly (HBO).
Video-On-Demand: Yes
Pay-Per-View
iN DEMAND; iN DEMAND (delivered digitally); adult PPV (delivered digitally); Barker (delivered digitally); sports (delivered digitally).
Internet Service
Operational: Yes.
Broadband Service: ProLog Express.
Fee: $34.95 monthly; $10.00 modem lease; $59.95 modem purchase.
Telephone Service
None
Miles of Plant: 150.0 (coaxial); 13.0 (fiber optic). Additional miles planned: 15.0 (coaxial).
Vice President, Operations: Richard Semmel. General Manager: Mark Masonheimer. Fiber Manager: Randy Semmel. Chief Technician: Garry Woods.
Ownership: Pencor Services Inc. (MSO).

SUGAR GROVE—MetroCast Communications, 1059 E 10th St, Hazleton, PA 18201-3421. Phones: 800-633-8578; 570-455-6851. Fax: 570-459-0963. Web Site: http://www.metrocastcommunications.com. ICA: PA0412.
TV Market Ranking: Below 100 (SUGAR GROVE). Franchise award date: N.A. Franchise expiration date: N.A. Began: October 1, 1977.
Channel capacity: 42 (not 2-way capable). Channels available but not in use: N.A.
Basic Service
Subscribers: 146.
Programming (received off-air): WFXP (FOX) Erie; WGRZ (NBC) Buffalo; WICU-TV (NBC) Erie; WIVB-TV (CBS) Buffalo; WJET-TV (ABC) Erie; WKBW-TV (ABC) Buffalo; WNED-TV (PBS) Buffalo; WSEE-TV (CBS, CW) Erie.
Programming (via satellite): ABC Family Channel; AMC; Animal Planet; CNN; Country Music TV; Discovery Channel; Disney Channel; ESPN; ESPN 2; Headline News; Lifetime; Nickelodeon; QVC; Speed; Spike TV; Syfy; TBS Superstation; The Learning Channel; The Weather Channel; Turner Network TV; TV Land; USA Network.
Fee: $42.95 installation; $33.07 monthly.
Digital Basic Service
Subscribers: N.A.
Programming (via satellite): Bio; Discovery Digital Networks; DMX Music; Fox Sports World; Golf Channel; GSN; Independent Film Channel; Lifetime Movie Network; Turner Classic Movies; WE tv.
Fee: $25.92 installation; $7.95 monthly.
Pay Service 1
Pay Units: N.A.
Programming (via satellite): The Movie Channel.
Fee: $12.95 monthly.
Pay Service 2
Pay Units: 11.
Programming (via satellite): HBO.
Fee: $12.95 monthly.
Digital Pay Service 1
Pay Units: N.A.
Programming (via satellite): Cinemax (multiplexed); HBO (multiplexed); Showtime (multiplexed).
Fee: $12.95 monthly (each).
Pay-Per-View
Addressable homes: 1,367.
ESPN Extra (delivered digitally); ESPN Now (delivered digitally); Hot Choice (delivered digitally); iN DEMAND (delivered digitally); Fresh (delivered digitally); Sports PPV (delivered digitally).
Internet Service
Operational: No.
Telephone Service
None
Miles of Plant: 6.0 (coaxial); None (fiber optic).
Manager: Joseph Gans III. Marketing Director: Lori A. Warg.
Ownership: Harron Communications LP (MSO).

SUGARLOAF TWP.—MetroCast Communications. Now served by BERWICK, PA [PA0094]. ICA: PA0256.

SUMMERVILLE—Formerly served by Adelphia Communications. Now served by PUNXSUTAWNEY, PA [PA0397]. ICA: PA0232.

SUNBURY—Service Electric Cablevision, 500 Grant St, Sunbury, PA 17801-2500. Phone: 570-286-5951. Fax: 570-286-9710. E-mail: sunburyoffice@secv.com. Web Site: http://www.secv.com. Also serves Aristes, Beaver Twp. (Snyder County), Beavertown Borough, Bloomsburg, Catawissa Borough, Catawissa Twp., Center Twp. (Snyder County), Cleveland Twp., Coal, Coal Twp. (Northumberland County), East Cameron Twp., Elysburg, Franklin Twp. (Columbia County), Franklin Twp. (Northumberland County), Franklin Twp. (Snyder County), Freeburg, Hemlock Twp., Jackson Twp. (Northumberland County), Jackson Twp. (Snyder County), Kreamer, Kulpmont (Northumberland County), Limestone Twp. (Union County), Little Mahanoy Twp., Locust Twp., Lower Mahanoy Twp., Main Twp., Marion Heights, Middleburg, Middleburg Borough, Middlecreek Twp., Monroe Twp. (Snyder County), Montour Twp. (Columbia County), Mount Carmel Borough, Mount Carmel Twp. (Northumberland County), Mount Pleasant Twp. (Columbia County), New Berlin, North Centre (portions), Northumberland, Orange Twp. (Columbia County), Paxinos, Paxtonville, Penn Twp. (Snyder County), Penns Creek, Point Twp. (Montour County), Ralpho Twp., Roaring Creek Twp., Rockefeller Twp., Scott Twp. (Columbia County), Selinsgrove, Shamokin, Shamokin Dam, Shamokin Twp., Snydertown (Northumberland County), South Centre Twp. (Columbia County), Strong, Union Twp. (Union County), Upper Augusta Twp., Upper Mahanoy Twp., Washington Twp. (Northumberland County), Washington Twp. (Snyder County), West Cameron Twp. & Zerbe Twp. ICA: PA0029.
TV Market Ranking: 49 (BLOOMSBURG, Hemlock Twp., Main Twp., Montour Twp. (Columbia County), Mount Pleasant Twp. (Columbia County), North Centre (portions), Orange Twp. (Columbia County), Scott Twp. (Columbia County), South Centre Twp. (Columbia County)); 57 (Lower Mahanoy Twp.); Below 100 (Aristes, Beavertown Borough, Catawissa Borough, Catawissa Twp. (portions), Center Twp. (Snyder County), Cleveland Twp., Coal, Coal Twp. (Northumberland County), East Cameron Twp., Elysburg, Franklin Twp. (Columbia County), Franklin Twp. (Northumberland County), Franklin Twp. (Snyder County), Freeburg, Jackson Twp. (Northumberland County), Jackson Twp. (Snyder County), Kreamer, Kulpmont (Northumberland County), Limestone Twp. (Union County), Locust Twp., Marion Heights, Middleburg, Middleburg Borough, Middlecreek Twp., Monroe Twp. (Snyder County), Mount Carmel Borough, Mount Carmel Twp. (Northumberland County), New Berlin, Northumberland, Penn Twp. (Snyder County), Penns Creek, Point Twp. (Montour County), Ralpho Twp., Roaring Creek Twp., Rockefeller Twp., Selinsgrove, Shamokin, Shamokin Dam, Shamokin Twp., Snydertown (Northumberland County), Strong, SUNBURY, Upper Mahanoy Twp., Washington Twp. (Northumberland County), Washington Twp. (Snyder County), West Cameron Twp., Zerbe Twp.); Outside TV Markets (Beaver Twp. (Snyder County), Catawissa Twp. (portions), Little Mahanoy Twp., Paxinos, Paxtonville, SUNBURY, Union Twp. (Union County), Upper Augusta Twp.). Franchise award date: N.A. Franchise expiration date: N.A. Began: May 1, 1953.
Channel capacity: 74 (operating 2-way). Channels available but not in use: N.A.
Basic Service
Subscribers: 34,384.
Programming (received off-air): WBRE-TV (NBC) Wilkes-Barre; WGAL (NBC) Lancaster; WHP-TV (CBS, MNT) Harrisburg; WHTM-TV (ABC) Harrisburg; WITF-TV (PBS) Harrisburg; WLYH-TV (CW) Lancaster; WNEP-TV (ABC) Scranton; WOLF-TV (CW, FOX, MNT) Hazleton; WPIX (CW, IND) New York; WPVI-TV (ABC) Philadelphia; WQMY (MNT) Williamsport; WQPX-TV (ION) Scranton; WSWB (CW) Scranton; WVIA-TV (PBS) Scranton; WWOR-TV (MNT) Secaucus; WYOU (CBS) Scranton; allband FM.
Programming (via satellite): C-SPAN; Eternal Word TV Network; INSP; Pennsylvania Cable Network; QVC; The Weather Channel.
Fee: $61.00 installation; $19.95 monthly.
Expanded Basic Service 1
Subscribers: 32,844.
Programming (via satellite): A&E Networks; ABC Family Channel; AMC; Animal Planet; BBC America; BET Networks; Bravo; Cartoon Network; CNBC; CNN; Comcast SportsNet Philadelphia; Comedy Central; Country Music TV; Discovery Channel; Discovery Fit & Health; Disney Channel; E! Entertainment Television; ESPN; ESPN 2; ESPN Classic Sports; Food Network; Fox News Channel; FX; Hallmark Channel; Headline News; HGTV; History Channel; Lifetime; MSNBC; MTV; National Geographic Channel; NFL Network; Nickelodeon; Outdoor Channel; Root Sports Pittsburgh; Speed; Spike TV; Syfy; TBS Superstation; The Learning Channel; Toon Disney; Travel Channel; truTV; Turner Network TV; TV Land; Univision Studios; USA Network; VH1.
Fee: $54.95 monthly.
Digital Basic Service
Subscribers: 14,460.
Programming (via satellite): 3 Angels Broadcasting Network; ABC News Now; Bio; Bloomberg Television; Boomerang; BYU Television; CBS Sports Network; Church Channel; CMT Pure Country; Colours; Cooking Channel; Daystar TV Network; Discovery Health Channel; Discovery Kids Channel; DIY Network; ESPN U; ESPNews; FamilyNet; Fox College Sports Atlantic; Fox College Sports Central; Fox College Sports Pacific; Fox Movie Channel; Fox Reality Channel; Fox Soccer; Fuel TV; Fuse; G4; Golden Eagle Broadcasting; Golf Channel; Great American Country; GSN; Hallmark Movie Channel; Halogen Network; History Channel International; HRTV; ID Investigation Discovery; Independent Film Channel; JCTV; Lifetime Movie Network; Military Channel; MTV Hits; MTV Jams; MTV2; Music Choice; NHL Network; Nick Jr.; Nick Too; NickToons TV; Ovation; PBS Kids Sprout; Planet Green; Science; Smile of a Child; SoapNet; Style Network; Tennis Channel; Trinity Broadcasting Network; Turner Classic Movies; Versus; VH1 Classic; VH1 Soul; WE tv.
Fee: $54.45 monthly; $2.95 converter.
Digital Expanded Basic Service
Subscribers: N.A.
Programming (via satellite): Cine Mexicano; CNN en Espanol; Discovery en Espanol; Discovery Familia; ESPN Deportes; Fox Deportes; GalaVision; La Familia Network; Latele Novela Network; mun2 television; Sorpresa; TBN Enlace USA; Telefutura; Telemundo; Tr3s; TV Chile; TV Colombia.
Fee: $3.95 monthly.
Digital Expanded Basic Service 2
Subscribers: N.A.
Programming (received off-air): WBRE-TV (NBC) Wilkes-Barre; WHP-TV (CBS, MNT) Harrisburg; WNEP-TV (ABC) Scranton; WOLF-TV (CW, FOX, MNT) Hazleton; WSWB (CW) Scranton; WVIA-TV (PBS) Scranton; WYOU (CBS) Scranton.
Programming (via satellite): A&E HD; ABC Family HD; Animal Planet HD; CNN HD; Discovery Channel HD; Disney Channel HD; ESPN 2 HD; ESPN HD; Food Network HD; Fox News HD; FX HD; Hallmark Movie Channel HD; HD Theater; HDNet; HDNet Movies; HGTV HD; History Channel HD; National Geographic Channel HD Network; NFL Network HD; NHL Network HD; Outdoor Channel 2 HD; Palladia; Science HD; Speed HD; TBS in HD; The Weather Channel HD; TLC HD; Turner Network TV HD; Universal HD; Versus HD; WealthTV HD.
Fee: $11.00 monthly.
Digital Pay Service 1
Pay Units: 8,912.
Programming (via satellite): Cinemax (multiplexed); Cinemax HD; Encore (multiplexed); Flix; HBO (multiplexed); HBO HD; Showtime (multiplexed); Showtime HD; Starz (multiplexed); Starz HDTV; The Movie Channel (multiplexed); The Movie Channel HD.
Fee: $61.00 installation; $11.50 monthly (Cinemax), $12.45 monthly (Starz/En-

core), $14.45 monthly (HBO or Showtime/TMC/Flix); $2.95 converter.

Video-On-Demand: No

Pay-Per-View

iN DEMAND (delivered digitally); Sports PPV (delivered digitally).

Internet Service

Operational: Yes. Began: January 1, 2001.
Subscribers: 13,375.
Broadband Service: ProLog Express.
Fee: $61.00 installation; $22.95-$52.95 monthly; $4.95 modem lease; $59.95 modem purchase.

Telephone Service

Analog: Not Operational
Digital: Operational
Subscribers: 2,264.
Fee: $44.95 monthly

Miles of Plant: 912.0 (coaxial); 345.0 (fiber optic).
Manager: Dwight Walter. Field Manager: John Kurtz. Regulatory Affairs Director: Arlean Lilly. Office Manager: Lindy Mannello.
Ownership: Service Electric Cable TV Inc. (MSO).

SWENGEL—Formerly served by D&E Communications. No longer in operation. ICA: PA5286.

TARENTUM BOROUGH—Comcast Cable, 5211 Brownsville Rd, Pittsburgh, PA 15238. Phone: 800-532-3779. Fax: 724-335-6648. Web Site: http://www.comcast.com. Also serves Arnold, Bairdford, Blawnox Borough, Brackenridge Borough, Buffalo Twp. (Butler County), Cheswick, Clinton Twp., Creighton, East Deer Twp., Fawn Twp. (Allegheny County), Hampton Twp., Hampton Twp. (Allegheny County), Harmar Twp., Harwick, Indianola, Lower Burrell, Natrona Heights, New Kensington, Oakmont, Rural Ridge, Russellton, Springdale Borough, Verona Borough & West Deer Twp. ICA: PA0424.

TV Market Ranking: 10 (Arnold, Bairdford, Blawnox Borough, Brackenridge Borough, Buffalo Twp. (Butler County), Cheswick, Clinton Twp., Creighton, East Deer Twp., Fawn Twp. (Allegheny County), Hampton Twp., Hampton Twp. (Allegheny County), Harmar Twp., Harwick, Indianola, Lower Burrell, Natrona Heights, New Kensington, Oakmont, Rural Ridge, Russellton, Springdale Borough, TARENTUM BOROUGH, Verona Borough, West Deer Twp.). Franchise award date: N.A. Franchise expiration date: N.A. Began: September 1, 1966.
Channel capacity: N.A. Channels available but not in use: N.A.

Basic Service

Subscribers: 42,996.
Programming (received off-air): KDKA-TV (CBS) Pittsburgh; WINP-TV (IND, ION) Pittsburgh; WPCB-TV (IND) Greensburg; WPCW (CW) Jeannette; WPGH-TV (FOX) Pittsburgh; WPMY (MNT) Pittsburgh; WPXI (IND, NBC) Pittsburgh; WQED (PBS) Pittsburgh; WTAE-TV (ABC) Pittsburgh.
Programming (via satellite): C-SPAN; C-SPAN 2; Eternal Word TV Network; QVC; The Weather Channel; TV Guide Network; WGN America.
Fee: $43.99 installation; $12.15 monthly; $15.49 additional installation.

Expanded Basic Service 1

Subscribers: 41,600.
Programming (via satellite): A&E Networks; ABC Family Channel; AMC; Animal Planet; BET Networks; Cartoon Network; CNBC; CNN; Comedy Central; Country Music TV; Discovery Channel; Disney Channel; E! Entertainment Television; ESPN; ESPN 2; Food Network; Fox News Channel; FX; Golf Channel; GSN; Hallmark Channel; Headline News; HGTV; History Channel; ION Television; Lifetime; MSNBC; MTV; Nickelodeon; Oxygen; Pennsylvania Cable Network; Pittsburgh Cable News Channel; Root Sports Pittsburgh; Spike TV; The Learning Channel; Travel Channel; truTV; Turner Classic Movies; Turner Network TV; TV Land; USA Network; Versus; VH1; WPCH-TV (IND) Atlanta.
Fee: $45.34 installation; $39.84 monthly.

Digital Basic Service

Subscribers: 21,200.
Programming (received off-air): WTAE-TV (ABC) Pittsburgh.
Programming (via satellite): BBC America; Black Family Channel; Bravo; C-SPAN 3; Discovery Channel; Discovery Digital Networks; ESPN; ESPN Classic Sports; ESPNews; G4; GAS; Independent Film Channel; INHD; Jewelry Television; Lime; MTV Networks Digital Suite; Music Choice; National Geographic Channel; Nick Jr.; NickToons TV; ShopNBC; Style Network; Syfy; The Word Network; Trinity Broadcasting Network; WE tv; Weatherscan.
Fee: $10.95 monthly.

Digital Pay Service 1

Pay Units: 5,491.
Programming (via satellite): Cinemax (multiplexed); HBO (multiplexed); RAI International; Russian Television Network; Showtime (multiplexed); Starz (multiplexed); The Movie Channel (multiplexed); TV Asia; Zee TV USA.
Fee: $8.00 monthly (each).

Video-On-Demand: Yes

Pay-Per-View

Addressable homes: 21,200.
Movies (delivered digitally); NASCAR In Car (delivered digitally); Hot Choice (delivered digitally); NBA TV (delivered digitally); NHL Center Ice (delivered digitally); MLB Extra Innings (delivered digitally); iN DEMAND (delivered digitally); Playboy TV (delivered digitally); Fresh (delivered digitally); Shorteez (delivered digitally).

Internet Service

Operational: Yes.
Broadband Service: Comcast High Speed Internet.
Fee: $42.95 monthly.

Telephone Service

Digital: Operational

Miles of Plant: 681.0 (coaxial); 30.0 (fiber optic).
Regional Vice President: Linda Hossinger. Vice President, Technical Operations: Randy Bender. Vice President, Marketing: Donna Corning. Vice President, Public Affairs: Jody Doherty.
Ownership: Comcast Cable Communications Inc. (MSO).

TATAMY BOROUGH—Formerly served by NORTHAMPTON BOROUGH, PA [PA0008]. RCN Corp. This cable system has converted to IPTV, 196 Van Buren St, Herndon, VA 20170. Phone: 703-434-8200. Web Site: http://www.rcn.com. ICA: PA5236.

TV Market Ranking: Below 100 (TATAMY BOROUGH).
Channel capacity: N.A. Channels available but not in use: N.A.

Internet Service

Operational: Yes.

Telephone Service

Digital: Operational

Chairman: Steven J. Simmons. Chief Executive Officer: Jim Holanda.

THOMPSON TWP.—Adams Cable Service. Now served by Carbondale, PA [PA0067]. ICA: PA0414.

THOMPSONTOWN—Nittany Media Inc. Now served by LEWISTOWN (formerly McAlisterville), PA [PA0365]. ICA: PA0415.

THREE SPRINGS—MetroCast Communications, 1059 E 10th St, Hazleton, PA 18201-3421. Phones: 800-633-8578; 570-455-6851. Fax: 570-459-0963. Web Site: http://www.metrocastcommunications.com. Also serves Clay Twp. (Huntingdon County) & Cromwell. ICA: PA0233.

TV Market Ranking: 74 (Clay Twp. (Huntingdon County), Cromwell, THREE SPRINGS). Franchise award date: N.A. Franchise expiration date: N.A. Began: November 1, 1984.
Channel capacity: 42 (operating 2-way). Channels available but not in use: N.A.

Basic Service

Subscribers: 246.
Programming (received off-air): WATM-TV (ABC) Altoona; WHAG-TV (NBC) Hagerstown; WJAL (IND) Hagerstown; WPSU-TV (PBS) Clearfield; WTAJ-TV (CBS) Altoona; WWPX-TV (ION) Martinsburg; allband FM.
Programming (via satellite): A&E Networks; ABC Family Channel; AMC; Animal Planet; CNN; Country Music TV; Discovery Channel; Disney Channel; ESPN; ESPN 2; Eternal Word TV Network; Lifetime; Nickelodeon; QVC; Speed; Syfy; TBS Superstation; The Learning Channel; The Weather Channel; Trinity Broadcasting Network; Turner Network TV; TV Land; USA Network.
Fee: $42.95 installation; $33.65 monthly.

Digital Basic Service

Subscribers: N.A.
Programming (via satellite): Bio; Discovery Digital Networks; DMX Music; Fox Sports World; Golf Channel; GSN; Independent Film Channel; Lifetime; Turner Classic Movies; WE tv.
Fee: $25.92 installation; $7.95 monthly.

Pay Service 1

Pay Units: N.A.
Programming (via satellite): HBO (multiplexed).
Fee: $12.95 monthly.

Pay Service 2

Pay Units: 13.
Programming (via satellite): Cinemax.
Fee: $12.95 monthly.

Digital Pay Service 1

Pay Units: N.A.
Programming (via satellite): Cinemax (multiplexed); HBO (multiplexed); Showtime (multiplexed).
Fee: $12.95 monthly (each).

Pay-Per-View

ESPN Extra (delivered digitally); ESPN Now (delivered digitally); Hot Choice (delivered digitally); iN DEMAND (delivered digitally); Fresh (delivered digitally); Sports PPV (delivered digitally).

Internet Service

Operational: No.

Telephone Service

None

Miles of Plant: 30.0 (coaxial); None (fiber optic).
Manager: Joseph Gans. Marketing Director: Lori A. Warg.
Ownership: Harron Communications LP (MSO).

TIDIOUTE—Formerly served by Cebridge Connections. No longer in operation. ICA: PA0183.

TIMBLIN BOROUGH—Formerly served by Adelphia Communications. Now served by PUNXSUTAWNEY, PA [PA0397]. ICA: PA0349.

TINICUM—RCN Corp. Formerly served by Philadelphia (suburbs), PA [PA0447]. This cable system has converted to IPTV, 196 Van Buren St, Herndon, PA 20170. Phone: 703-434-8200. Web Site: http://www.rcn.com. ICA: PA5265.

Channel capacity: N.A. Channels available but not in use: N.A.

Internet Service

Operational: Yes.

Chairman: Steven J. Simmons. Chief Executive Officer: Jim Holanda.

TITUSVILLE—Formerly served by Cebridge Connections. Now served by MEADVILLE, PA [PA0062]. ICA: PA0416.

TOBY TWP.—Formerly served by Adelphia Communications. Now served by CLARION BOROUGH, PA [PA0137]. ICA: PA0186.

TOWANDA—Comcast Cable, 1 E Uwchlan Ave, Ste 411, Exton, PA 19341. Phone: 484-288-6500. Web Site: http://www.comcast.com. Also serves Asylum Twp., Monroeton Borough, North Towanda Twp. & Wysox Twp. ICA: PA0138.

TV Market Ranking: Below 100 (Asylum Twp., Monroeton Borough, North Towanda Twp., TOWANDA, Wysox Twp.). Franchise award date: N.A. Franchise expiration date: N.A. Began: April 1, 1961.
Channel capacity: 119 (operating 2-way). Channels available but not in use: N.A.

Basic Service

Subscribers: N.A. Included in Harrisburg
Programming (received off-air): WBNG-TV (CBS, CW) Binghamton; WENY-TV (ABC, CW) Elmira; WETM-TV (NBC) Elmira; WICZ-TV (FOX) Binghamton; WIVT (ABC) Binghamton; WNEP-TV (ABC) Scranton; WOLF-TV (CW, FOX, MNT) Hazleton; WQPX-TV (ION) Scranton; WSKG-TV (PBS) Binghamton; WSWB (CW) Scranton; WVIA-TV (PBS) Scranton; WYOU (CBS) Scranton; allband FM.
Programming (via satellite): Discovery Channel; TBS Superstation.
Fee: $45.10 installation; $15.55 monthly; $3.25 converter.

Expanded Basic Service 1

Subscribers: N.A.
Programming (via satellite): A&E Networks; ABC Family Channel; AMC; Animal Planet;

Cartoon Network; CNBC; CNN; C-SPAN; Disney Channel; ESPN; Fox News Channel; Headline News; Lifetime; MTV; Nickelodeon; QVC; Spike TV; The Weather Channel; Turner Network TV; USA Network.
Fee: $32.20 monthly.

Digital Basic Service
Subscribers: 22,359 Includes Scranton.
Programming (via satellite): BBC America; Bravo; Discovery Digital Networks; ESPN 2; ESPN Classic Sports; ESPNews; Fox Sports World; Golf Channel; GSN; HGTV; History Channel; Independent Film Channel; National Geographic Channel; Nick Jr.; Speed; Syfy; Turner Classic Movies; TV Land; Versus; VH1 Country; WE tv.
Fee: $14.95 monthly; $3.25 converter.

Digital Pay Service 1
Pay Units: N.A.
Programming (via satellite): Cinemax (multiplexed); Encore (multiplexed); HBO (multiplexed); Showtime (multiplexed); Starz (multiplexed); The Movie Channel (multiplexed).

Video-On-Demand: Yes

Pay-Per-View
Hot Choice (delivered digitally); Playboy TV (delivered digitally).

Internet Service
Operational: Yes.
Subscribers: 17,247.
Broadband Service: Comcast High Speed Internet.
Fee: $42.95 monthly.

Telephone Service
Analog: Not Operational
Digital: Operational

Miles of Plant: 69.0 (coaxial); 16.0 (fiber optic).
Area Vice President: Jim Samaha.
Ownership: Comcast Cable Communications Inc. (MSO).

TOWNVILLE—Formerly served by Cebridge Connections. Now served by MEADVILLE, PA [PA0062]. ICA: PA0278.

TRAPPE—Comcast Cable, 3220 Tillman Dr, Bensalem, PA 19010. Phone: 215-642-6400. Fax: 215-638-6510. Web Site: http://www.comcast.com. Also serves Collegeville, Schwenksville & Skippack Twp. ICA: PA0453.
TV Market Ranking: 4 (Collegeville, Schwenksville, Skippack Twp., TRAPPE).
Channel capacity: N.A. Channels available but not in use: N.A.

Basic Service
Subscribers: N.A. Included in Bensalem Twp.
Programming (received off-air): KYW-TV (CBS) Philadelphia; WCAU (NBC) Philadelphia; WFMZ-TV (IND) Allentown; WGTW-TV (TBN) Burlington; WHYY-TV (PBS) Wilmington; WLVT-TV (PBS) Allentown; WNJT (PBS) Trenton; WPHL-TV (MNT, IND) Philadelphia; WPPX-TV (ION) Wilmington; WPSG (CW) Philadelphia; WPVI-TV (ABC) Philadelphia; WTVE (IND) Reading; WTXF-TV (FOX) Philadelphia; WWSI (TMO) Atlantic City.
Programming (via satellite): A&E Networks; ABC Family Channel; AMC; BET Networks; Bravo; Cartoon Network; CNBC; CNN; Comcast SportsNet Philadelphia; Comedy Central; Country Music TV; C-SPAN; Discovery Channel; Discovery Health Channel; Disney Channel; E! Entertainment Television; ESPN; ESPN 2; Eternal Word TV Network; Food Network; Fox News Channel; FX; Golf Channel; GSN; Headline News; HGTV; History Channel; Lifetime; MSNBC; MTV; MTV2; Nickelodeon; Philadelphia Park Live; QVC; Speed; Spike TV; Style Network; Syfy; TBS Superstation; The Comcast Network; The Learning Channel; The Weather Channel; Travel Channel; truTV; Turner Classic Movies; Turner Network TV; TV Land; Univision Studios; USA Network; VH1.
Fee: $16.10 monthly.

Digital Basic Service
Subscribers: N.A.
Programming (via satellite): BBC America; Bio; Cooking Channel; C-SPAN 3; Discovery Digital Networks; DIY Network; ESPNews; G4; History Channel International; Independent Film Channel; MTV Networks Digital Suite; Music Choice; National Geographic Channel; Nick Jr.; Nick Too; ShopNBC; SoapNet; TeenNick; Toon Disney; WAM! America's Kidz Network; Weatherscan.
Fee: $14.95 monthly.

Digital Pay Service 1
Pay Units: N.A.
Programming (via satellite): Cinemax (multiplexed); Encore (multiplexed); Flix; HBO (multiplexed); Showtime (multiplexed); Sundance Channel; The Movie Channel (multiplexed).
Fee: $18.95 monthly (each).

Video-On-Demand: Yes

Pay-Per-View
iN DEMAND (delivered digitally); Playboy TV (delivered digitally); Fresh (delivered digitally); Shorteez (delivered digitally); Pleasure (delivered digitally); ESPN (delivered digitally).

Internet Service
Operational: Yes.
Broadband Service: Comcast High Speed Internet.
Fee: $42.95 monthly.

Telephone Service
Digital: Operational
Fee: $44.95 monthly

Senior Regional Vice President: Amy Smith. Regional Vice President: Jim Samaha. Vice President, Technical Operations: Rich Massi. Vice President, Marketing: Chip Goodman.
Ownership: Comcast Cable Communications Inc. (MSO).

TREASURE LAKE—Zito Media, 611 Vader Hill Rd, Coudersport, PA 16915. Phones: 866-879-6235; 814-260-9570; 814-260-9575. Fax: 814-260-9580. E-mail: rigas@zitomedia.com. Web Site: http://www.zitomedia.com. ICA: PA0451.
TV Market Ranking: Outside TV Markets (TREASURE LAKE). Franchise award date: January 1, 1986. Franchise expiration date: N.A. Began: N.A.
Channel capacity: N.A. Channels available but not in use: N.A.

Basic Service
Subscribers: 2,200 Includes Sabula & Weedville.
Programming (received off-air): WATM-TV (ABC) Altoona; WJAC-TV (NBC) Johnstown; WKBS-TV (IND) Altoona; WPMY (MNT) Pittsburgh; WPSU-TV (PBS) Clearfield; WTAE-TV (ABC) Pittsburgh; WTAJ-TV (CBS) Altoona; WWCP-TV (FOX) Johnstown.
Programming (via satellite): CW+.
Fee: $29.95 installation; $16.95 monthly.

Expanded Basic Service 1
Subscribers: N.A.
Programming (via satellite): A&E Networks; ABC Family Channel; AMC; Animal Planet; Bravo; Cartoon Network; CNBC; CNN; Comedy Central; Country Music TV; C-SPAN; C-SPAN 2; Discovery Channel; Disney Channel; E! Entertainment Television; ESPN; ESPN 2; ESPN Classic Sports; Eternal Word TV Network; Food Network; Fox News Channel; FX; Golf Channel; Hallmark Channel; Headline News; HGTV; History Channel; INSP; Lifetime; MSNBC; MTV; NFL Network; Nickelodeon; Outdoor Channel; Pennsylvania Cable Network; QVC; Root Sports Pittsburgh; Speed; Spike TV; Syfy; TBS Superstation; The Learning Channel; The Weather Channel; Travel Channel; Trinity Broadcasting Network; truTV; Turner Classic Movies; Turner Network TV; TV Land; USA Network; VH1; WGN America.
Fee: $32.00 monthly.

Digital Basic Service
Subscribers: N.A.
Programming (via satellite): AmericanLife TV Network; BBC America; Bloomberg Television; Boomerang; C-SPAN 3; Discovery Fit & Health; Discovery Health Channel; Discovery Kids Channel; ESPN 2 HD; ESPN HD; ESPNews; Familyland Television Network; Fox HD; Fox Movie Channel; Fox Soccer; Golf Channel; Great American Country; GSN; HRTV; ID Investigation Discovery; INSP; Lifetime Movie Network; Military Channel; MTV Hits; MTV Jams; MTV2; Music Choice; Nick Jr.; Nick Too; NickToons TV; Planet Green; RFD-TV; Science; SoapNet; Speed; TeenNick; The Word Network; Toon Disney; Trinity Broadcasting Network; VH1 Classic; VH1 Country; VH1 Soul; WE tv.
Fee: $11.95 monthly.

Digital Expanded Basic Service
Subscribers: N.A.
Programming (via satellite): Bio; DIY Network; Flix; FSN Digital Atlantic; FSN Digital Central; FSN Digital Pacific; History Channel International; Independent Film Channel; Outdoor Channel; Sundance Channel; Versus.
Fee: $10.00 monthly.

Digital Pay Service 1
Pay Units: N.A.
Programming (via satellite): Cinemax (multiplexed); Cinemax HD; Encore (multiplexed); Flix; HBO (multiplexed); HBO HD; Showtime (multiplexed); Showtime HD; Starz (multiplexed); Starz HDTV; The Movie Channel (multiplexed).
Fee: $8.00 monthly (Cinemax or Starz/Encore), $10.00 monthly (HBO or Showtime/TMC).

Video-On-Demand: Yes

Pay-Per-View
iN DEMAND (delivered digitally); NHL Center Ice (delivered digitally); MLB Extra Innings (delivered digitally).

Internet Service
Operational: Yes.
Subscribers: 418.
Broadband Service: In-house.
Fee: $49.95 monthly.

Telephone Service
Digital: Operational
Fee: $35.00 monthly

Miles of Plant: 140.0 (coaxial); None (fiber optic). Miles of plant (coax) include Sabula & Weedville
Manager: James Rigas. Marketing Director: Kathy Fox.
Ownership: Zito Media (MSO).

TREMONT—Wire Television Corp., 603 E Market St, Pottsville, PA 17901-2718. Phone: 570-622-4501. Fax: 570-622-8340. E-mail: customerservice@wtvaccess.com. Web Site: http://www.wtvaccess.com. Also serves Frailey Twp. & Zerbe. ICA: PA0204.
TV Market Ranking: Below 100 (Frailey Twp., TREMONT, Zerbe). Franchise award date: N.A. Franchise expiration date: N.A. Began: June 18, 1952.
Channel capacity: 65 (operating 2-way). Channels available but not in use: N.A.

Basic Service
Subscribers: 732.
Programming (received off-air): KYW-TV (CBS) Philadelphia; WGAL (NBC) Lancaster; WHP-TV (CBS, MNT) Harrisburg; WHTM-TV (ABC) Harrisburg; WHYY-TV (PBS) Wilmington; WITF-TV (PBS) Harrisburg; WLYH-TV (CW) Lancaster; WNEP-TV (ABC) Scranton; WPMT (FOX) York; WPSG (CW) Philadelphia; WSWB (CW) Scranton; WTXF-TV (FOX) Philadelphia; allband FM.
Programming (via satellite): A&E Networks; ABC Family Channel; AMC; AmericanLife TV Network; Animal Planet; Bloomberg Television; Cartoon Network; CNN; Comcast SportsNet Philadelphia; Comedy Central; Country Music TV; C-SPAN 2; Discovery Channel; Disney Channel; ESPN; ESPN 2; ESPN Classic Sports; Eternal Word TV Network; Food Network; Fox News Channel; Fox Sports Net Philadelphia; FX; Hallmark Channel; HGTV; History Channel; INSP; ION Television; Lifetime; Lifetime Movie Network; MTV; National Geographic Channel; Nickelodeon; Pennsylvania Cable Network; QVC; Spike TV; Syfy; TBS Superstation; The Learning Channel; The Weather Channel; Travel Channel; truTV; Turner Network TV; TV Land; USA Network; VH1; WGN America; WPIX (CW, IND) New York.
Fee: $37.50 installation; $44.55 monthly.

Digital Basic Service
Subscribers: N.A.
Programming (via satellite): BBC America; Bravo; Daystar TV Network; Discovery Fit & Health; Discovery Health Channel; Discovery Kids Channel; DMX Music; ESPN Classic Sports; ESPNews; Fox College Sports Atlantic; Fox College Sports Central; Fox College Sports Pacific; Fox Movie Channel; Fox Soccer; G4; GMC; Golf Channel; Great American Country; GSN; Halogen Network; HGTV; History Channel; ID Investigation Discovery; Independent Film Channel; Military Channel; National Geographic Channel; Nick Jr.; NickToons TV; Outdoor Channel; Planet Green; Science; ShopNBC; SoapNet; Speed; The Word Network; Trinity Broadcasting Network; Turner Classic Movies; Versus; VH1 Classic; VH1 Country; WE tv.
Fee: $20.95 monthly.

Pay Service 1
Pay Units: 90.
Programming (via satellite): HBO.
Fee: $15.00 installation; $15.95 monthly.

Pay Service 2
Pay Units: 46.
Programming (via satellite): Cinemax.
Fee: $15.00 installation; $15.95 monthly.

Digital Pay Service 1
Pay Units: N.A.
Programming (via satellite): Cinemax (multiplexed); Encore (multiplexed); Flix; HBO (multiplexed); Playboy TV; Showtime (multiplexed); Starz (multiplexed); The Movie Channel.
Fee: $15.95 monthly (HBO, Cinemax, Starz/Encore, Showtime/TMC/Flix or Playboy).

Pay-Per-View
iN DEMAND (delivered digitally); Fresh (delivered digitally); Club Jenna (delivered digitally); Sports PPV (delivered digitally).

Internet Service
Operational: Yes. Began: November 1, 2001.
Subscribers: 13.
Broadband Service: Wtvaccess.
Fee: $49.95 installation; $24.95 monthly; $10.00 modem lease; $150.00 modem purchase.
Telephone Service
None
Miles of Plant: 14.0 (coaxial); None (fiber optic).
General Manager: Darlene Mills. Chief Technician: Brian Brennan.
Ownership: Wire Tele-View Corp. (MSO).

TROY—Blue Ridge Communications, 613 3rd St, PO Box 215, Palmerton, PA 18071-0215. Phone: 610-826-2551. Web Site: http://www.brctv.com. Also serves Austinville Twp., Burlington, Burlington Borough, Columbia Crossroads, Columbia Crossroads Twp., Columbia Twp. (Bradford County), East Troy, Franklindale Twp., Powell, Powell Twp., Sylvania, Sylvania Borough & Troy Twp. ICA: PA0165.
TV Market Ranking: Below 100 (Austinville Twp., Burlington, Burlington Borough, Columbia Crossroads, Columbia Crossroads Twp., Columbia Twp. (Bradford County), East Troy, Franklindale Twp., Powell Twp., Sylvania, Sylvania Borough, TROY, Troy Twp.); Outside TV Markets (Powell). Franchise award date: N.A. Franchise expiration date: N.A. Began: June 1, 1958.
Channel capacity: 35 (operating 2-way). Channels available but not in use: N.A.
Basic Service
Subscribers: N.A.
Programming (received off-air): WBNG-TV (CBS, CW) Binghamton; WENY-TV (ABC, CW) Elmira; WETM-TV (NBC) Elmira; WSKG-TV (PBS) Binghamton; WVIA-TV (PBS) Scranton; WYDC (FOX, MNT) Corning; WYOU (CBS) Scranton; allband FM.
Programming (via satellite): C-SPAN; C-SPAN 2; WGN America; WPIX (CW, IND) New York.
Fee: $22.50 installation; $16.05 monthly.
Expanded Basic Service 1
Subscribers: N.A.
Programming (via satellite): A&E Networks; ABC Family Channel; AMC; Animal Planet; BET Networks; Cartoon Network; CNBC; CNN; Comedy Central; Country Music TV; Discovery Channel; Disney Channel; E! Entertainment Television; ESPN; ESPN 2; Eternal Word TV Network; Food Network; Fox News Channel; FX; Hallmark Channel; Headline News; HGTV; History Channel; Lifetime; Lifetime Movie Network; MSNBC; MTV; Nickelodeon; Pennsylvania Cable Network; QVC; Root Sports Pittsburgh; SoapNet; Speed; Spike TV; Syfy; TBS Superstation; The Learning Channel; The Weather Channel; Travel Channel; Trinity Broadcasting Network; truTV; Turner Classic Movies; Turner Network TV; TV Land; USA Network; Versus; VH1.
Fee: $27.99 monthly.
Digital Basic Service
Subscribers: N.A.
Programming (via satellite): DMX Music; ESPN Classic Sports; ESPNews; Fox Movie Channel; GAS; GSN; Halogen Network; MTV Networks Digital Suite; National Geographic Channel; Nick Jr.; Outdoor Channel; Speed; Toon Disney; Versus.
Fee: $13.95 monthly.
Digital Expanded Basic Service
Subscribers: N.A.
Programming (via satellite): BBC America; Bio; Bloomberg Television; Discovery Digital Networks; G4; Golf Channel; History Channel International; Style Network.
Fee: $5.00 monthly.
Pay Service 1
Pay Units: 341.
Programming (via satellite): Cinemax; HBO; Showtime.
Fee: $11.50 monthly (Showtime or Cinemax), $12.50 monthly (HBO).
Digital Pay Service 1
Pay Units: N.A.
Programming (via satellite): Cinemax (multiplexed); Encore (multiplexed); Flix; HBO (multiplexed); Showtime (multiplexed); Starz (multiplexed); Sundance Channel; The Movie Channel (multiplexed).
Fee: $12.50 monthly (Cinemax, Showtime or TMC), $12.95 monthly (Starz), $13.50 monthly (HBO).
Video-On-Demand: No
Pay-Per-View
iN DEMAND; Movies (delivered digitally); Sports PPV (delivered digitally); iN DEMAND (delivered digitally).
Internet Service
Operational: No.
Telephone Service
None
Miles of Plant: 25.0 (coaxial); None (fiber optic).
Vice President, Operations: Richard Semmel. General Manager: Mark Masonheimer. Fiber Manager: Randy Semmel. Chief Technician: Garry Woods.
Ownership: Pencor Services Inc. (MSO).

TYLERSVILLE—Tylersville Community TV Cable Assoc., 1133 Summer Mountain Rd, Loganton, PA 17747. Phone: 570-725-3865. ICA: PA0417.
TV Market Ranking: Below 100 (TYLERSVILLE). Franchise award date: N.A. Franchise expiration date: N.A. Began: January 1, 1972.
Channel capacity: 37 (not 2-way capable). Channels available but not in use: N.A.
Basic Service
Subscribers: 115.
Programming (received off-air): WBRE-TV (NBC) Wilkes-Barre; WNEP-TV (ABC) Scranton; WOLF-TV (CW, FOX, MNT) Hazleton; WPSU-TV (PBS) Clearfield; WSWB (CW) Scranton; WTAJ-TV (CBS) Altoona; WVIA-TV (PBS) Scranton; WYOU (CBS) Scranton.
Programming (via satellite): A&E Networks; ABC Family Channel; CNN; ESPN; Hallmark Channel; History Channel; RFD-TV; Spike TV; Starz; TBS Superstation; Turner Network TV; TV Land.
Fee: $17.00 monthly.
Pay Service 1
Pay Units: N.A.
Programming (via satellite): Encore; Starz.
Internet Service
Operational: No.
Telephone Service
None
Miles of Plant: 6.0 (coaxial); None (fiber optic).
President & Chief Technician: Jim Breon.
Ownership: Tylersville Community TV Association Inc.

TYRONE—Formerly served by Adelphia Communications. Now served by STATE COLLEGE, PA [PA0037]. ICA: PA0418.

ULYSSES—Time Warner Cable, 120 Plaza Dr, Vestal, NY 13850-3658. Phone: 607-644-0646. Fax: 607-644-1501. Web Site: http://www.timewarnercable.com. ICA: PA0419.

TV Market Ranking: Outside TV Markets (ULYSSES). Franchise award date: N.A. Franchise expiration date: N.A. Began: July 1, 1982.
Channel capacity: 61 (not 2-way capable). Channels available but not in use: N.A.
Basic Service
Subscribers: N.A. Included in Binghamton
Programming (received off-air): WENY-TV (ABC, CW) Elmira; WETM-TV (NBC) Elmira; WGRZ (NBC) Buffalo; WIVB-TV (CBS) Buffalo; WKBW-TV (ABC) Buffalo; WPSU-TV (PBS) Clearfield.
Programming (via satellite): A&E Networks; ABC Family Channel; AMC; Animal Planet; CNN; Country Music TV; C-SPAN; Discovery Channel; E! Entertainment Television; ESPN; ESPN 2; Hallmark Channel; Headline News; History Channel; Lifetime; Nickelodeon; Spike TV; Syfy; TBS Superstation; The Learning Channel; The Weather Channel; Travel Channel; truTV; Turner Network TV; TV Land; USA Network; WGN America.
Fee: $47.00 installation; $28.00 monthly; $.88 converter.
Pay Service 1
Pay Units: 115.
Programming (via satellite): HBO; Showtime.
Fee: $9.50 monthly (each).
Internet Service
Operational: Yes.
Telephone Service
None
Miles of plant included in Binghamton
President: Mary Cotter. Vice President & General Manager: Chris Strahm. Vice President, Marketing: John Melvany. Vice President, Public Affairs: Dave Whalen. Technical Operations Director: Bruce Tompkins.
Ownership: Time Warner Cable (MSO).; Advance/Newhouse Partnership (MSO).

UNION TWP. (Centre County)—Country Cable, 196 S Main St, Pleasant Gap, PA 16823-3221. Phone: 814-359-3161. Fax: 814-359-2145. Also serves Fleming Borough, Huston Twp. (Centre County) & Julian. ICA: PA0209.
TV Market Ranking: Outside TV Markets (Fleming Borough, Huston Twp. (Centre County), Julian, UNION TWP.). Franchise award date: N.A. Franchise expiration date: N.A. Began: June 1, 1974.
Channel capacity: 36 (not 2-way capable). Channels available but not in use: N.A.
Basic Service
Subscribers: 830.
Programming (received off-air): WATM-TV (ABC) Altoona; WJAC-TV (NBC) Johnstown; WKBS-TV (IND) Altoona; WNEP-TV (ABC) Scranton; WPSU-TV (PBS) Clearfield; WTAJ-TV (CBS) Altoona; WVIA-TV (PBS) Scranton; WWCP-TV (FOX) Johnstown.
Programming (via satellite): A&E Networks; ABC Family Channel; Animal Planet; Cartoon Network; CNN; Discovery Channel; Disney Channel; ESPN; ESPN 2; Nickelodeon; Outdoor Channel; Root Sports Pittsburgh; Spike TV; TBS Superstation; Turner Classic Movies; Turner Network TV; TV Guide Network; TV Land; USA Network; WGN America.
Fee: $50.00 installation; $25.50 monthly.
Pay Service 1
Pay Units: 120.
Programming (via satellite): HBO.
Fee: $20.00 installation; $13.86 monthly.
Video-On-Demand: No
Internet Service
Operational: No.
Telephone Service
None
Miles of Plant: 70.0 (coaxial); None (fiber optic).
Manager & Chief Technician: Lee Dorman.
Ownership: Country Cable TV.

UNION TWP. (Huntingdon County)—Atlantic Broadband, 120 Southmont Blvd, Johnstown, PA 15905. Phones: 888-536-9600; 814-539-8971; 814-946-5491. Fax: 814-535-7749. E-mail: info@atlanticbb.com. Web Site: http://www.atlanticbb.com. Also serves Calvin, Cass Twp. (Huntingdon County), Cassville Borough, Todd & Todd Twp. (Huntingdon County). ICA: PA0208.
TV Market Ranking: 74 (Calvin, Cass Twp. (Huntingdon County), Cassville Borough, Todd, Todd Twp., UNION TWP.). Franchise award date: N.A. Franchise expiration date: N.A. Began: November 1, 1984.
Channel capacity: 43 (not 2-way capable). Channels available but not in use: N.A.
Basic Service
Subscribers: 936.
Programming (received off-air): WATM-TV (ABC) Altoona; WJAC-TV (NBC) Johnstown; WJAL (IND) Hagerstown; WKBS-TV (IND) Altoona; WLYH-TV (CW) Lancaster; WPSU-TV (PBS) Clearfield; WTAJ-TV (CBS) Altoona; WWCP-TV (FOX) Johnstown.
Programming (via satellite): A&E Networks; ABC Family Channel; Animal Planet; Cartoon Network; CNN; Country Music TV; Discovery Channel; Disney Channel; ESPN; Fox News Channel; FX; Hallmark Channel; Headline News; HGTV; History Channel; ION Television; Lifetime; National Geographic Channel; Outdoor Channel; QVC; Root Sports Pittsburgh; Spike TV; Syfy; TBS Superstation; The Learning Channel; The Weather Channel; Trinity Broadcasting Network; truTV; Turner Network TV; USA Network.
Fee: $25.00 installation; $29.69 monthly.
Expanded Basic Service 1
Subscribers: 313.
Programming (via satellite): ESPN 2; MTV; Nickelodeon.
Fee: $5.00 monthly.
Pay Service 1
Pay Units: 732.
Programming (via satellite): Cinemax; Encore; HBO.
Fee: $5.50 monthly (Encore), $8.00 monthly (Cinemax), $10.00 monthly (HBO).
Video-On-Demand: No
Internet Service
Operational: No.

Telephone Service
None
Miles of Plant: 100.0 (coaxial); None (fiber optic).
Vice President: David Lane. General Manager: Mike Papasergi. Technical Operations Director: Charles Sorchilla. Marketing Director: Natalie Kurchak. Marketing & Customer Service Director: Dara Leslie.
Ownership: Atlantic Broadband (MSO).

UNIONTOWN—Atlantic Broadband, 120 Southmont Blvd, Johnstown, PA 15905. Phones: 888-536-9600; 814-539-8971. Fax: 814-535-7749. E-mail: info@atlanticbb.com. Web Site: http://www.atlanticbb.com. Also serves Beallsville, Bentleyville, Bobtown, Brownsville, Carmichaels, Clarksville, Cokeburg, Crucible, Cumberland Twp. (Greene County), Dawson, Deemston, Dunkard Twp., East Bethlehem Twp. (Washington County), Ellsworth, Fairbank, Fairchance, Fayette City (Fayette County), Fredericktown, Georges Twp. (Fayette County), German Twp. (Fayette County), Greensboro, Grindstone, Jefferson (Greene County), Keisterville, La Belle, Lower Tyrone Twp., Marianna, Masontown, Mather, McClellandtown, Menallen Twp. (Fayette County), Merrittstown, Millsboro, Monongahela Twp., Nemacolin, North Bethlehem Twp. (portions), Perryopolis, Point Marion, Redstone Twp. (Fayette County), Republic, Rices Landing, Rostraver (Westmoreland County), Smithfield, Smithton, Smock (portions), South Union Twp., Springhill Twp. (Fayette County), Springhill Twp. (Greene County), Vestaburg & West Bethlehem Twp. ICA: PA0020.
TV Market Ranking: 10 (Beallsville, Bentleyville, Brownsville, Crucible, Dawson, Deemston, East Bethlehem Twp. (Washington County), Ellsworth, Fairbank, Fairchance, Fayette City (Fayette County), Fredericktown, Georges Twp. (Fayette County), German Twp. (Fayette County), Grindstone, Keisterville, La Belle, Lower Tyrone Twp., Marianna, Masontown, Mather, McClellandtown, Menallen Twp. (Fayette County), Merrittstown, Millsboro, North Bethlehem Twp. (portions), Perryopolis, Point Marion, Redstone Twp. (Fayette County), Republic, Rices Landing, Rostraver (Westmoreland County), Smithton, Smock (portions), Vestaburg, West Bethlehem Twp.); 10,90 (Cokeburg); 90 (Clarksville, Jefferson (Greene County)); Below 100 (Bobtown, Dunkard Twp., South Union Twp.); Outside TV Markets (Carmichaels, Cumberland Twp. (Greene County), Greensboro, Monongahela Twp., Nemacolin, Smithfield, Springhill Twp. (Fayette County), Springhill Twp. (Greene County)). Franchise award date: January 1, 1966. Franchise expiration date: N.A. Began: January 1, 1966.
Channel capacity: N.A. Channels available but not in use: N.A.

Basic Service
Subscribers: 28,969.
Programming (received off-air): KDKA-TV (CBS) Pittsburgh; WNPB-TV (PBS) Morgantown; WPCB-TV (IND) Greensburg; WPCW (CW) Jeannette; WPGH-TV (FOX) Pittsburgh; WPMY (MNT) Pittsburgh; WPXI (IND, NBC) Pittsburgh; WQED (PBS) Pittsburgh; WTAE-TV (ABC) Pittsburgh.
Planned programming (received off-air): WWCP-TV (FOX) Johnstown.
Programming (via satellite): C-SPAN; C-SPAN 2; Eternal Word TV Network; Pennsylvania Cable Network; QVC; Trinity Broadcasting Network; TV Guide Network.
Fee: $25.00 installation; $19.16 monthly.

Expanded Basic Service 1
Subscribers: 27,230.
Programming (via satellite): A&E Networks; ABC Family Channel; AMC; Animal Planet; BET Networks; Bravo; Cartoon Network; CNBC; CNN; Comedy Central; Country Music TV; Discovery Channel; Discovery Fit & Health; Disney Channel; E! Entertainment Television; ESPN; ESPN 2; ESPNews; Food Network; Fox News Channel; FX; Golf Channel; Hallmark Channel; Headline News; HGTV; History Channel; Lifetime; Meadows Racing Network; MSNBC; MTV; National Geographic Channel; Nickelodeon; Oxygen; Pittsburgh Cable News Channel; Root Sports Pittsburgh; Speed; Spike TV; Syfy; TBS Superstation; The Learning Channel; The Weather Channel; Toon Disney; Travel Channel; truTV; Turner Network TV; TV Land; USA Network; Versus; VH1.
Fee: $38.61 monthly.

Digital Basic Service
Subscribers: 8,400.
Programming (via satellite): A&E HD; BBC America; Bio; Bloomberg Television; Boomerang; CMT Pure Country; Discovery Health Channel; Discovery Kids Channel; DIY Network; Encore Action; ESPN Classic Sports; ESPN HD; Fuel TV; G4; GAS; Great American Country; HD Theater; History Channel International; ID Investigation Discovery; Independent Film Channel; Lifetime Movie Network; Lifetime Real Women; Military Channel; MTV Hits; MTV Jams; MTV2; Music Choice; NFL Network; Nick Jr.; Nick Too; NickToons TV; Planet Green; Root Sports Pittsburgh; RTN; Science; SoapNet; Starz; Starz HDTV; Style Network; Tr3s; Turner Network TV HD; VH1 Classic; VH1 Soul; WE tv; WeatherVision.
Fee: $18.95 monthly.

Digital Pay Service 1
Pay Units: 822.
Programming (via satellite): Cinemax (multiplexed); Cinemax HD.
Fee: $20.00 installation; $15.95 monthly.

Digital Pay Service 2
Pay Units: 3,338.
Programming (via satellite): Flix; Showtime (multiplexed); The Movie Channel (multiplexed).
Fee: $20.00 installation; $15.95 monthly.

Digital Pay Service 3
Pay Units: 3,187.
Programming (via satellite): HBO (multiplexed); HBO HD.
Fee: $20.00 installation; $15.95 monthly.

Video-On-Demand: No

Pay-Per-View
Addressable homes: 8,400.
iN DEMAND (delivered digitally); Fresh (delivered digitally); Club Jenna (delivered digitally); Playboy TV (delivered digitally); Hot Choice (delivered digitally).

Internet Service
Operational: Yes.
Broadband Service: Atlantic Broadband High-Speed Internet.
Fee: $24.95-$57.95 monthly.

Telephone Service
Digital: Operational
Fee: $44.95 monthly
Miles of Plant: 1,017.0 (coaxial); 231.0 (fiber optic). Additional miles planned: 4.0 (fiber optic).
Vice President: David Dane. General Manager: Mike Papasergi. Technical Operations Director: Charles Sorchilla. Marketing & Customer Service Director: Dara Leslie. Marketing Manager: Natalie Kurchak.
Ownership: Atlantic Broadband (MSO).

UPPER DARBY—RCN Corp. Formerly served by Philadelphia (suburbs), PA [PA0447]. This cable system has converted to IPTV, 196 Van Buren St, Herndon, VA 20170. Phone: 703-434-8200. Web Site: http://www.rcn.com. ICA: PA5266.
Channel capacity: N.A. Channels available but not in use: N.A.

Internet Service
Operational: Yes.
Chairman: Steven J. Simmons. Chief Executive Officer: Jim Holanda.

UPPER MACUNGIE TWP.—Formerly served by NORTHAMPTON BOROUGH, PA [PA0008]. RCN Corp. This cable system has converted to IPTV, 196 Van Buren St, Herndon, VA 20170. Phone: 703-434-8200. Web Site: http://www.rcn.com. ICA: PA5237.
TV Market Ranking: Below 100 (UPPER MACUNGIE TWP.).
Channel capacity: N.A. Channels available but not in use: N.A.

Internet Service
Operational: Yes.

Telephone Service
Digital: Operational
Chairman: Steven J. Simmons. Chief Executive Officer: Jim Holanda.

UPPER NAZARETH TWP.—Formerly served by NORTHAMPTON BOROUGH, PA [PA0008]. RCN Corp. This cable system has converted to IPTV, 196 Van Buren St, Herndon, VA 20170. Phone: 703-434-8200. Web Site: http://www.rcn.com. ICA: PA5238.
TV Market Ranking: Below 100 (UPPER NAZARETH TWP.).
Channel capacity: N.A. Channels available but not in use: N.A.

Internet Service
Operational: Yes.

Telephone Service
Digital: Operational
Chairman: Steven J. Simmons. Chief Executive Officer: Jim Holanda.

UPPER SAUCON TWP.—Formerly served by NORTHAMPTON BOROUGH, PA [PA0008]. RCN Corp. This cable system has converted to IPTV, 196 Van Buren St, Herndon, VA 20170. Phone: 703-434-8200. Web Site: http://www.rcn.com. ICA: PA5239.
TV Market Ranking: Below 100 (UPPER SAUCON TWP.).
Channel capacity: N.A. Channels available but not in use: N.A.

Internet Service
Operational: Yes.

Telephone Service
Digital: Operational
Chairman: Steven J. Simmons. Chief Executive Officer: Jim Holanda.

VICKSBURG—Formerly served by D&E Communications. No longer in operation. ICA: PA5287.

WALLINGFORD—Comcast Cable, 3220 Tillman Dr, Bensalem, PA 19010. Phone: 215-642-6400. Fax: 215-638-6510. Web Site: http://www.comcast.com. Also serves Aldan, Aston Twp., Brookhaven, Chester, Chester Heights, Chester Twp. (Delaware County), Clifton Heights, Collingdale, Colwyn, Concordville, Darby, Darby Twp., East Lansdowne, Eddystone (Delaware County), Folcroft, Glenolden, Lansdowne, Lower Chichester Twp., Marcus Hook, Media (Delaware County), Millbourne (Delaware County), Morton Twp., Nether Providence Twp., Norwood, Parkside, Prospect Park, Ridley Park (Delaware County), Rose Valley, Rutledge (Delaware County), Sharon Hill, Springfield Twp. (Delaware County), Swarthmore, Tinicum Twp. (Delaware County), Trainer, Upland, Upper Chichester Twp., Upper Darby Twp., Upper Providence Twp. (Delaware County) & Yeadon. ICA: PA0002.
TV Market Ranking: 4 (Aldan, Aston Twp., Brookhaven, Chester, Chester Heights, Chester Twp. (Delaware County), Clifton Heights, Collingdale, Colwyn, Concordville, Darby, Darby Twp., East Lansdowne, Eddystone (Delaware County), Folcroft, Glenolden, Lansdowne, Lower Chichester Twp., Marcus Hook, Media (Delaware County), Millbourne (Delaware County), Morton, Nether Providence Twp., Norwood, Parkside, Prospect Park, Ridley Park (Delaware County), Rose Valley, Rutledge (Delaware County), Sharon Hill, Springfield Twp. (Delaware County), Swarthmore, Tinicum Twp. (Delaware County), Trainer, Upland, Upper Chichester Twp., Upper Darby Twp., Upper Providence Twp. (Delaware County), WALLINGFORD, Yeadon). Franchise award date: N.A. Franchise expiration date: N.A. Began: November 1, 1979.
Channel capacity: 82 (operating 2-way). Channels available but not in use: N.A.

Basic Service
Subscribers: N.A. Included in Bensalem Twp.
Programming (received off-air): KYW-TV (CBS) Philadelphia; WCAU (NBC) Philadelphia; WFMZ-TV (IND) Allentown; WGTW-TV (TBN) Burlington; WHYY-TV (PBS) Wilmington; WLVT-TV (PBS) Allentown; WNJS (PBS) Camden; WPHL-TV (MNT, IND) Philadelphia; WPPX-TV (ION) Wilmington; WPSG (CW) Philadelphia; WPVI-TV (ABC) Philadelphia; WTVE (IND) Reading; WTXF-TV (FOX) Philadelphia; WUVP-DT (UNV) Vineland; WWSI (TMO) Atlantic City; WYBE (ETV, IND) Philadelphia.
Programming (via satellite): C-SPAN 2; TBS Superstation; The Comcast Network.
Fee: $15.85 monthly.

Expanded Basic Service 1
Subscribers: 128,401.
Programming (via satellite): A&E Networks; ABC Family Channel; AMC; Animal Planet; BET Networks; Bravo; Cartoon Network; CNBC; CNN; Comcast SportsNet Philadelphia; Comedy Central; Country Music TV; Discovery Channel; Discovery Health Channel; Disney Channel; E! Entertainment Television; ESPN; ESPN 2; Eternal Word TV Network; Food Network; Fox News Channel; FX; Golf Channel; GSN; Headline News; HGTV; History Channel; Lifetime; MarketConnect Network; MSNBC; MTV; MTV2; Nickelodeon; Philadelphia Park Live; QVC; Speed; Style Network; Syfy; The Learning Channel; The Weather Channel; Travel Channel; truTV; Turner Classic Movies; Turner Network TV; TV Guide Network; TV Land; USA Network; Versus; VH1.
Fee: $33.90 monthly.

Digital Basic Service
Subscribers: 51,857.
Programming (via satellite): BBC America; Bio; Cooking Channel; C-SPAN 3; Discovery Digital Networks; DIY Network; DMX Music; ESPNews; G4; GAS; History Channel International; Independent Film Channel; MTV Networks Digital Suite; National Geographic Channel; Nick Jr.; Nick Too; Science Television; ShopNBC; SoapNet; Toon Disney; WAM! America's Kidz Network; Weatherscan.
Fee: $14.95 monthly.

Digital Pay Service 1
Pay Units: N.A.
Programming (via satellite): Cinemax (multiplexed); Encore (multiplexed); Flix (multiplexed); HBO (multiplexed); Showtime (multiplexed); Sundance Channel (multiplexed); The Movie Channel (multiplexed).
Fee: $18.95 monthly (each).
Video-On-Demand: Yes
Pay-Per-View
Addressable homes: 58,700.
Playboy TV (delivered digitally); Spice (delivered digitally); Pleasure (delivered digitally); iN DEMAND (delivered digitally); ESPN (delivered digitally); NBA (delivered digitally); NHL?MLB (delivered digitally).
Internet Service
Operational: Yes.
Broadband Service: Comcast High Speed Internet.
Fee: $42.95 monthly; $9.95 modem lease.
Telephone Service
Digital: Operational
Fee: $44.95 monthly
Miles of Plant: 1,737.0 (coaxial); 329.0 (fiber optic).
Senior Regional Vice President: Amy Smith. Regional Vice President: Jim Samaha. Vice President, Technical Operations: Rich Massi. Vice President, Marketing: Chip Goodman.
Ownership: Comcast Cable Communications Inc. (MSO).

WALNUT—Formerly served by Penn CATV of Walnut. No longer in operation. ICA: PA0281.

WALNUT BOTTOM—Kuhn Communications, PO Box 277, Walnut Bottom, PA 17266. Phone: 717-532-8857. Fax: 717-532-5563. E-mail: kuhncom1@kuhncom.net. Web Site: http://www.kuhncom.net. Also serves Hopewell Twp., Letterkenny Twp., Newburg, Orrstown, Penn Twp. (Cumberland County) & Southampton Twp. ICA: PA0220.
TV Market Ranking: 57 (Penn Twp. (Cumberland County), WALNUT BOTTOM); Below 100 (Letterkenny Twp., Orrstown, Southampton Twp.); Outside TV Markets (Hopewell Twp., Newburg). Franchise award date: N.A. Franchise expiration date: N.A. Began: January 1, 1978.
Channel capacity: N.A. Channels available but not in use: N.A.
Basic Service
Subscribers: N.A.
Programming (received off-air): WGAL (NBC) Lancaster; WHAG-TV (NBC) Hagerstown; WHP-TV (CBS, MNT) Harrisburg; WHTM-TV (ABC) Harrisburg; WITF-TV (PBS) Harrisburg; WLYH-TV (CW) Lancaster; WPIX (CW, IND) New York; WPMT (FOX) York.
Programming (via satellite): ESPN; Headline News; Spike TV.
Fee: $20.00 installation; $6.75 monthly.
Expanded Basic Service 1
Subscribers: N.A.
Programming (via satellite): A&E Networks; ABC Family Channel; Animal Planet; CNN; C-SPAN; Discovery Channel; Disney Channel; ESPN 2; Food Network; Outdoor Channel; Pennsylvania Cable Network; QVC; TBS Superstation; The Weather Channel; Travel Channel; TV Land; USA Network.
Expanded Basic Service 2
Subscribers: N.A.
Programming (via satellite): AMC; Cartoon Network; CNBC; Comcast SportsNet Philadelphia; Comedy Central; Country Music TV; E! Entertainment Television; Fox News Channel; Fox Sports Net; FX; Hallmark Channel; HGTV; History Channel; Lifetime; MSNBC; MTV; Nickelodeon; The Learning Channel; Trinity Broadcasting Network; Turner Classic Movies; Turner Network TV; VH1; WGN America.
Digital Basic Service
Subscribers: N.A.
Programming (via satellite): BBC America; Bio; Black Family Channel; Bloomberg Television; Bravo; Daystar TV Network; Discovery Fit & Health; DMX Music; ESPN Classic Sports; ESPNews; Fox College Sports Atlantic; Fox College Sports Central; Fox College Sports Pacific; Fox Movie Channel; Fox Soccer; Fuse; G4; GAS; Golf Channel; Great American Country; GSN; Halogen Network; HGTV; History Channel; History Channel International; Independent Film Channel; Lifetime Movie Network; Lime; MTV2; National Geographic Channel; Nick Jr.; NickToons TV; Outdoor Channel; ShopNBC; Speed; Style Network; Syfy; The Word Network; Toon Disney; Trinity Broadcasting Network; Turner Classic Movies; TV Land; Versus; VH1 Classic; VH1 Country; WE tv.
Pay Service 1
Pay Units: 180.
Programming (via satellite): Cinemax; HBO; Starz; The Movie Channel.
Fee: $9.60 monthly (each).
Digital Pay Service 1
Pay Units: N.A.
Programming (via satellite): Cinemax (multiplexed); Encore (multiplexed); HBO (multiplexed); Showtime (multiplexed); Starz (multiplexed); The Movie Channel (multiplexed).
Video-On-Demand: No
Pay-Per-View
Movies (delivered digitally).
Internet Service
Operational: Yes. Began: January 1, 2001.
Broadband Service: kuhncom.net.
Fee: $50.00 installation; $29.95 monthly.
Telephone Service
None
Miles of Plant: 37.0 (coaxial); None (fiber optic).
Manager: Earl Kuhn. Office Manager: Tracy Reath.
Ownership: Kuhn Communications (MSO).

WARREN—Atlantic Broadband, 120 Southmont Blvd, Johnstown, PA 15905. Phones: 888-536-9600; 814-539-8971. Fax: 814-535-7749. E-mail: info@atlanticbb.com. Web Site: http://www.atlanticbb.com. Also serves Conewango Twp. (Warren County), Glade Twp. (Warren County), Mead Twp. (Warren County), Pine Grove Twp. (Warren County), Pleasant Twp. (Warren County) & Warren County. ICA: PA0090.
TV Market Ranking: Below 100 (Conewango Twp. (Warren County), Glade Twp. (Warren County), Mead Twp. (Warren County), Pine Grove Twp. (Warren County), Pleasant Twp. (Warren County), WARREN, Warren County). Franchise award date: March 1, 1952. Franchise expiration date: N.A. Began: February 1, 1953.
Channel capacity: N.A. Channels available but not in use: N.A.
Basic Service
Subscribers: 6,000.
Programming (received off-air): WFXP (FOX) Erie; WGRZ (NBC) Buffalo; WICU-TV (NBC) Erie; WJET-TV (ABC) Erie; WKBW-TV (ABC) Buffalo; WPSU-TV (PBS) Clearfield; WSEE-TV (CBS, CW) Erie; allband FM.
Programming (via satellite): C-SPAN; C-SPAN 2; Eternal Word TV Network; INSP; Jewelry Television; PBS World; Pennsylvania Cable Network; Product Information Network; QVC; Trinity Broadcasting Network; TV Guide Network.
Fee: $25.00 installation; $15.07 monthly; $1.77 converter; $18.10 additional installation.
Expanded Basic Service 1
Subscribers: N.A.
Programming (via satellite): A&E Networks; ABC Family Channel; AMC; Animal Planet; Bravo; Cartoon Network; CNBC; CNN; Comedy Central; Country Music TV; Discovery Channel; Discovery Health Channel; Disney Channel; E! Entertainment Television; ESPN; ESPN 2; ESPN Classic Sports; Food Network; Fox News Channel; FX; G4; Golf Channel; Hallmark Channel; Headline News; HGTV; History Channel; Lifetime; MSNBC; MTV; National Geographic Channel; Nickelodeon; Outdoor Channel; Oxygen; Root Sports Pittsburgh; Speed; Spike TV; Syfy; TBS Superstation; The Learning Channel; The Weather Channel; Travel Channel; truTV; Turner Classic Movies; Turner Network TV; TV Land; USA Network; VH1.
Fee: $41.38 monthly.
Digital Basic Service
Subscribers: N.A.
Programming (via satellite): A&E HD; Animal Planet HD; BBC America; Bio; Bloomberg Television; Boomerang; Chiller; CMT Pure Country; Discovery Channel HD; Discovery Kids Channel; Disney Channel HD; DIY Network; DMX Music; Encore (multiplexed); ESPN 2 HD; ESPN HD; ESPN U; ESPNews; Fuel TV; GAS; HD Theater; History Channel International; ID Investigation Discovery; Independent Film Channel; Lifetime Movie Network; Lifetime Real Women; Military Channel; MTV Hits; MTV Jams; MTV2; NFL Network; NFL Network HD; Nick Jr.; Nick Too; NickToons TV; Planet Green; Root Sports Pittsburgh; Science; SoapNet; Starz (multiplexed); Syfy HD; TBS in HD; TLC HD; Toon Disney; Tr3s; Turner Network TV HD; USA Network HD; VH1 Classic; VH1 Soul; WE tv.
Fee: $18.95 monthly.
Digital Pay Service 1
Pay Units: 400.
Programming (via satellite): HBO (multiplexed).
Fee: $15.95 monthly.
Digital Pay Service 2
Pay Units: 210.
Programming (via satellite): Cinemax (multiplexed).
Fee: $15.95 monthly.
Digital Pay Service 3
Pay Units: N.A.
Programming (via satellite): Flix; Showtime (multiplexed); The Movie Channel (multiplexed).
Fee: $15.95 monthly.
Video-On-Demand: No
Pay-Per-View
iN DEMAND (delivered digitally); Playboy TV (delivered digitally); Fresh (delivered digitally); Shorteez (delivered digitally); Club Jenna (delivered digitally); Spice Hot (delivered digitally); Hot Choice (delivered digitally).
Internet Service
Operational: Yes. Began: February 1, 2002.
Broadband Service: Atlantic Broadband High-Speed Internet.
Fee: $24.95-$57.95 monthly.
Telephone Service
Digital: Operational
Fee: $44.95 monthly
Miles of Plant: 130.0 (coaxial); None (fiber optic).
Vice President: David Dane. General Manager: Mike Papasergi. Technical Operations Director: Charles Sorchilla. Marketing & Customer Service Director: Dara Leslie. Marketing Manager: Natalie Kurchak.
Ownership: Atlantic Broadband (MSO).

WARRIORS MARK—Atlantic Broadband. Now served by ALTOONA, PA [PA0018]. ICA: PA0434.

WASHINGTON—Comcast Cable. Now served by PITTSBURGH, PA [PA0001]. ICA: PA0058.

WASHINGTON TWP.—Formerly served by NORTHAMPTON BOROUGH, PA [PA0008]. RCN Corp. This cable system has converted to IPTV, 196 Van Buren St, Herndon, VA 20170. Phone: 703-434-8200. Web Site: http://www.rcn.com. ICA: PA5240.
TV Market Ranking: Below 100 (WASHINGTON TWP.).
Channel capacity: N.A. Channels available but not in use: N.A.
Internet Service
Operational: Yes.
Telephone Service
Digital: Operational
Chairman: Steven J. Simmons. Chief Executive Officer: Jim Holanda.

WATERFALL—Waterfall Community TV, PO Box 3, Waterfall, PA 16689-0003. Phone: 814-685-3464. Fax: 814-685-3447. Also serves New Grenada & Wells Tannery. ICA: PA0260.
TV Market Ranking: 74 (New Grenada, WATERFALL, Wells Tannery). Franchise award date: N.A. Franchise expiration date: N.A. Began: January 1, 1973.
Channel capacity: 21 (not 2-way capable). Channels available but not in use: N.A.
Basic Service
Subscribers: 160.
Programming (received off-air): WDCA (MNT) Washington; WGAL (NBC) Lancaster; WLYH-TV (CW) Lancaster; WPMT (FOX) York; WPSU-TV (PBS) Clearfield; WTTG (FOX) Washington.
Programming (via satellite): ABC Family Channel; Cartoon Network; CNN; Country Music TV; Discovery Channel; ESPN; TBS Superstation; Turner Classic Movies; Turner Network TV.
Fee: $50.00 installation; $25.00 monthly.

Pay Service 1
Pay Units: 16.
Programming (via satellite): HBO.
Fee: $10.00 monthly.
Pay Service 2
Pay Units: 19.
Programming (via satellite): Cinemax.
Fee: $10.00 monthly.
Video-On-Demand: No
Internet Service
Operational: No.
Telephone Service
None
Miles of Plant: 15.0 (coaxial); None (fiber optic).
Manager: Tom Newman.
Ownership: Tom Newman.

WATTSBURG—Formerly served by Cebridge Connections. Now served by MEADVILLE, PA [PA0062]. ICA: PA0248.

WAYNESBURG—Comcast Cable, 15 Summit Park Dr, Pittsburgh, PA 15275. Phone: 412-747-6400. Fax: 412-747-6401. Web Site: http://www.comcast.com. Also serves Center Twp., Greene County, Mount Morris & Rogersville. ICA: PA0134.
TV Market Ranking: 90 (Center Twp., Rogersville, WAYNESBURG); 90,10 (Greene County (portions)); Below 100 (Mount Morris, Greene County (portions)); Outside TV Markets (Greene County (portions)). Franchise award date: N.A. Franchise expiration date: N.A. Began: November 1, 1963.
Channel capacity: N.A. Channels available but not in use: N.A.
Basic Service
Subscribers: 3,192.
Programming (received off-air): KDKA-TV (CBS) Pittsburgh; WPCB-TV (IND) Greensburg; WPCW (CW) Jeannette; WPGH-TV (FOX) Pittsburgh; WPMY (MNT) Pittsburgh; WPXI (IND, NBC) Pittsburgh; WQED (PBS) Pittsburgh; WTAE-TV (ABC) Pittsburgh; allband FM.
Programming (via satellite): BET Networks; C-SPAN; C-SPAN 2; Hallmark Channel; QVC; The Weather Channel; WGN America.
Fee: $43.99 installation; $16.79 monthly; $19.99 additional installation.
Expanded Basic Service 1
Subscribers: 2,911.
Programming (via satellite): A&E Networks; ABC Family Channel; AMC; Animal Planet; Cartoon Network; CNBC; CNN; Comedy Central; Country Music TV; Disney Channel; E! Entertainment Television; ESPN; ESPN 2; Eternal Word TV Network; Food Network; Fox News Channel; FX; Golf Channel; Headline News; HGTV; History Channel; ION Television; Lifetime; MSNBC; MTV; Nickelodeon; Oxygen; Pennsylvania Cable Network; Pittsburgh Cable News Channel; Root Sports Pittsburgh; Shop at Home; ShopNBC; Spike TV; Syfy; TBS Superstation; The Learning Channel; Travel Channel; truTV; Turner Network TV; TV Guide Network; TV Land; USA Network; VH1.
Fee: $33.70 monthly.
Digital Basic Service
Subscribers: N.A.
Programming (via satellite): AmericanLife TV Network; BBC America; Bio; Black Family Channel; Bloomberg Television; Bravo; Discovery Channel; Discovery Digital Networks; DMX Music; ESPN Classic Sports; ESPNews; Fox Movie Channel; Fox Sports World; FSN Digital Atlantic; FSN Digital Central; FSN Digital Pacific; Fuse; G4; GAS; Great American Country; GSN; History Channel International; Independent Film Channel; Lifetime Movie Network; Lime; MTV Networks Digital Suite; Music Choice; National Geographic Channel; Nick Jr.; NickToons TV; Outdoor Channel; Ovation; Style Network; Sundance Channel; Syfy; The Word Network; Toon Disney; Trinity Broadcasting Network; Turner Classic Movies; Versus; WE tv; Weatherscan.
Fee: $10.95 monthly; $4.35 converter.
Digital Pay Service 1
Pay Units: N.A.
Programming (via satellite): Cinemax (multiplexed); Encore (multiplexed); Flix; HBO (multiplexed); Showtime (multiplexed); Starz (multiplexed); The Movie Channel (multiplexed).
Video-On-Demand: Yes
Pay-Per-View
ESPN Now (delivered digitally); Hot Choice (delivered digitally); Urban Xtra (delivered digitally); iN DEMAND (delivered digitally); Playboy TV (delivered digitally); Fresh (delivered digitally); Sports PPV (delivered digitally); Shorteez (delivered digitally); NBA TV (delivered digitally); Barker (delivered digitally).
Internet Service
Operational: Yes.
Broadband Service: Comcast High Speed Internet.
Fee: $42.95 monthly.
Telephone Service
Digital: Operational
Miles of Plant: 51.0 (coaxial); None (fiber optic).
Regional Vice President: Linda Hossinger. Vice President, Technical Operations: Randy Bender. Vice President, Marketing: Donna Corning. Public Affairs Director: Jody Doherty.
Ownership: Comcast Cable Communications Inc. (MSO).

WEEDVILLE—Zito Media, 611 Vader Hill Rd, Coudersport, PA 16915. Phones: 814-260-9570; 814-260-9575. Fax: 814-260-9580. E-mail: rigas@zitomedia.com. Web Site: http://www.zitomedia.com. Also serves Caledonia & Jay Twp. ICA: PA0234.
TV Market Ranking: Outside TV Markets (Caledonia, Jay Twp., WEEDVILLE). Franchise award date: N.A. Franchise expiration date: N.A. Began: January 1, 1959.
Channel capacity: N.A. Channels available but not in use: N.A.
Basic Service
Subscribers: N.A. Included in Treasure Lake
Programming (received off-air): WATM-TV (ABC) Altoona; WJAC-TV (NBC) Johnstown; WKBS-TV (IND) Altoona; WPMY (MNT) Pittsburgh; WPSU-TV (PBS) Clearfield; WTAE-TV (ABC) Pittsburgh; WTAJ-TV (CBS) Altoona; WWCP-TV (FOX) Johnstown.
Programming (via satellite): CW+; WGN America.
Fee: $29.95 installation; $16.95 monthly.
Expanded Basic Service 1
Subscribers: N.A.
Programming (via satellite): A&E Networks; ABC Family Channel; AMC; Animal Planet; Cartoon Network; CNBC; CNN; Comedy Central; Country Music TV; C-SPAN; Discovery Channel; Disney Channel; E! Entertainment Television; ESPN; ESPN 2; ESPN Classic Sports; Eternal Word TV Network; Food Network; Fox News Channel; FX; Hallmark Channel; Headline News; HGTV; History Channel; INSP; Lifetime; MSNBC; MTV; NFL Network; Nickelodeon; QVC; Root Sports Pittsburgh; Spike TV; Syfy; TBS Superstation; The Learning Channel; The Weather Channel; Trinity Broadcasting Network; Turner Classic Movies; Turner Network TV; TV Land; USA Network; VH1.
Fee: $21.55 monthly.
Digital Basic Service
Subscribers: N.A.
Programming (via satellite): AmericanLife TV Network; BBC America; Bloomberg Television; Boomerang; C-SPAN 3; Discovery Fit & Health; Discovery Health Channel; Discovery Kids Channel; ESPN 2 HD; ESPN HD; ESPNews; Familyland Television Network; Fox Movie Channel; Fox Soccer; Golf Channel; Great American Country; GSN; HRTV; ID Investigation Discovery; INSP; Lifetime Movie Network; Military Channel; MTV Hits; MTV Jams; MTV2; Music Choice; Nick Jr.; Nick Too; NickToons TV; Planet Green; RFD-TV; Science; SoapNet; Speed; TeenNick; The Word Network; Toon Disney; Trinity Broadcasting Network; VH1 Classic; VH1 Country; VH1 Soul; WAM! America's Kidz Network; WE tv.
Fee: $15.95 monthly.
Digital Expanded Basic Service
Subscribers: N.A.
Programming (via satellite): Bio; DIY Network; Flix; FSN Digital Atlantic; FSN Digital Central; FSN Digital Pacific; History Channel International; Independent Film Channel; Outdoor Channel; Sundance Channel; Versus.
Fee: $10.00 monthly.
Digital Pay Service 1
Pay Units: N.A.
Programming (via satellite): Cinemax (multiplexed); Cinemax HD; Encore (multiplexed); Flix; HBO (multiplexed); HBO HD; Showtime (multiplexed); Showtime HD; Starz (multiplexed); Starz HDTV; The Movie Channel (multiplexed).
Fee: $8.00 monthly (Cinemax or Starz/Encore), $10.00 monthly (HBO or Showtime/TMC/Flix).
Video-On-Demand: Planned
Pay-Per-View
iN DEMAND (delivered digitally).
Internet Service
Operational: Yes.
Fee: $49.95 monthly.
Telephone Service
Digital: Operational
Fee: $35.00 monthly
Miles of plant (coax) included in Treasure Lake
Manager: James Rigas. Marketing Director: Kathy Fox.
Ownership: Zito Media (MSO).

WELLSBORO—Blue Ridge Communications, 613 3rd St, PO Box 215, Palmerton, PA 18071-0215. Phone: 610-826-2551. Web Site: http://www.brctv.com. Also serves Catlin Hollow, Covington Twp., Kennedyville, Lambs Creek, Mainesburg, Mansfield, Middlebury, Putnam Twp., Richmond Twp., Shippen Twp. (Tioga County) & Sullivan Twp. ICA: PA0421.
TV Market Ranking: Below 100 (Covington Twp., Lambs Creek, Mainesburg, Mansfield, Putnam Twp., Richmond Twp., Sullivan Twp.); Outside TV Markets (Catlin Hollow, Kennedyville, Middlebury, Shippen Twp. (Tioga County), WELLSBORO). Franchise award date: N.A. Franchise expiration date: N.A. Began: October 1, 1951.
Channel capacity: N.A. Channels available but not in use: N.A.
Basic Service
Subscribers: 4,698.
Programming (received off-air): WBNG-TV (CBS, CW) Binghamton; WENY-TV (ABC, CW) Elmira; WETM-TV (NBC) Elmira; WSKG-TV (PBS) Binghamton; WVIA-TV (PBS) Scranton; WYDC (FOX, MNT) Corning; WYOU (CBS) Scranton; 2 FMs.
Programming (via microwave): WPIX (CW, IND) New York.
Programming (via satellite): C-SPAN; C-SPAN 2; WGN America.
Fee: $22.50 installation; $16.05 monthly.
Expanded Basic Service 1
Subscribers: N.A.
Programming (via satellite): A&E Networks; ABC Family Channel; AMC; Animal Planet; BET Networks; Cartoon Network; CNBC; CNN; Comedy Central; Country Music TV; Discovery Channel; Disney Channel; E! Entertainment Television; ESPN; ESPN 2; Eternal Word TV Network; Food Network; Fox News Channel; FX; Hallmark Channel; Headline News; HGTV; History Channel; Lifetime; Lifetime Movie Network; MSNBC; MTV; Nickelodeon; Pennsylvania Cable Network; QVC; Root Sports Pittsburgh; SoapNet; Speed; Spike TV; Syfy; TBS Superstation; The Learning Channel; The Weather Channel; Travel Channel; Trinity Broadcasting Network; truTV; Turner Classic Movies; Turner Network TV; TV Land; USA Network; Versus; VH1.
Fee: $27.99 monthly.
Digital Basic Service
Subscribers: N.A.
Programming (via satellite): Discovery Digital Networks; ESPN Classic Sports; ESPNews; Fox Movie Channel; GAS; GSN; Halogen Network; MTV Networks Digital Suite; Music Choice; National Geographic Channel; Nick Jr.; Outdoor Channel; Toon Disney.
Fee: $35.00 installation; $9.95 monthly.
Digital Expanded Basic Service
Subscribers: N.A.
Programming (via satellite): BBC America; Bio; Bloomberg Television; G4; Golf Channel; History Channel International; Style Network.
Fee: $5.00 monthly.
Digital Pay Service 1
Pay Units: N.A.
Programming (via satellite): Cinemax (multiplexed); Encore (multiplexed); Flix; HBO (multiplexed); Showtime (multiplexed); Starz (multiplexed); Sundance Channel; The Movie Channel (multiplexed).
Fee: $12.50 monthly (Cinemax or Showtime/Flix/Sundance/TMC), $12.95 monthly (Starz/Encore), $13.50 monthly (HBO).
Video-On-Demand: No
Pay-Per-View
iN DEMAND; iN DEMAND (delivered digitally); Adult PPV (delivered digitally); Sports PPV (delivered digitally).
Internet Service
Operational: Yes.
Broadband Service: ProLog Express.
Fee: $36.95 monthly; $10.00 modem lease; $59.95 modem purchase.
Telephone Service
None
Miles of Plant: 154.0 (coaxial); None (fiber optic).
Vice President, Operations: Richard Semmel. General Manager: Mark Masonheimer. Fiber Manager: Randy Semmel. Chief Technician: Garry Wood.
Ownership: Pencor Services Inc. (MSO).

WEST ALEXANDER—Comcast Cable, 300 Carliss St, Pittsburgh, PA 15220. Phone: 412-747-6400. Fax: 412-747-6111. Web Site: http://www.comcast.com. Also serves Donegal Twp. (Washington County). ICA: PA0235.

TV Market Ranking: 10,90 (Donegal Twp. (Washington County), WEST ALEXANDER). Franchise award date: August 1, 1988. Franchise expiration date: N.A. Began: January 1, 1989.

Channel capacity: 60 (not 2-way capable). Channels available but not in use: N.A.

Basic Service

Subscribers: 403.

Programming (received off-air): KDKA-TV (CBS) Pittsburgh; WINP-TV (IND, ION) Pittsburgh; WPCB-TV (IND) Greensburg; WPCW (CW) Jeannette; WPGH-TV (FOX) Pittsburgh; WPMY (MNT) Pittsburgh; WPXI (IND, NBC) Pittsburgh; WQED (PBS) Pittsburgh; WTAE-TV (ABC) Pittsburgh.

Programming (via satellite): C-SPAN; QVC; The Weather Channel.

Fee: $25.00 installation; $24.00 monthly.

Expanded Basic Service 1

Subscribers: N.A.

Programming (via satellite): A&E Networks; ABC Family Channel; AMC; Animal Planet; BET Networks; BTN; Cartoon Network; CNBC; CNN; Comedy Central; Discovery Channel; Disney Channel; E! Entertainment Television; ESPN; ESPN 2; Food Network; Fox News Channel; FX; Golf Channel; Headline News; HGTV; History Channel; Lifetime; MTV; Nickelodeon; Pennsylvania Cable Network; Pittsburgh Cable News Channel; Root Sports Pittsburgh; Spike TV; Style Network; TBS Superstation; The Learning Channel; Travel Channel; Turner Classic Movies; Turner Network TV; TV Land; USA Network; Versus; VH1.

Digital Basic Service

Subscribers: N.A.

Programming (via satellite): A&E HD; Animal Planet HD; BBC America; Bio; Bloomberg Television; Bravo; BTN; CBS Sports Network; CMT Pure Country; CNN HD; Comcast SportsNet Philadelphia; Cooking Channel; Country Music TV; C-SPAN 2; C-SPAN 3; Current; Daystar TV Network; Discovery Channel HD; Discovery Fit & Health; Discovery Health Channel; Discovery Kids Channel; Disney XD; DIY Network; Encore (multiplexed); ESPN 2 HD; ESPN Classic Sports; ESPN HD; ESPNews; Eternal Word TV Network; Flix; Food Network HD; Fox Business Channel; Fox College Sports Atlantic; Fox College Sports Central; Fox College Sports Pacific; Fox Movie Channel; Fox News HD; Fox Reality Channel; Fox Soccer; Fuse; FX HD; G4; GMC; Golf Channel HD; GolTV; GSN; Hallmark Channel; Halogen Network; HD Theater; HGTV HD; History Channel HD; History Channel International; HRTV; ID Investigation Discovery; Independent Film Channel; ION Life; ION Television; Jewelry Television; Lifetime Movie Network; LOGO; Military Channel; MLB Network; MoviePlex; MSNBC; MTV Hits; MTV Jams; MTV2; Music Choice; National Geographic Channel; National Geographic Channel HD Network; NBA TV; NFL Network; NFL Network HD; NHL Network; Nick Jr.; Nick Too; NickToons TV; Nuvo TV; Outdoor Channel; Oxygen; Palladia; PBS Kids Sprout; Planet Green; Qubo; Root Sports Pittsburgh; RTN; Science; ShopNBC; SoapNet; Speed; Speed HD; Starz IndiePlex; Starz RetroPlex; Sundance Channel; Syfy; Syfy HD; TBS in HD; TeenNick; Tennis Channel; The Word Network; TLC HD; Toon Disney; Tr3s; Trinity Broadcasting Network; truTV; Turner Network TV HD; TV Guide Network; TV One; TVG Network; Universal HD; USA Network HD; Versus HD; VH1 Classic; VH1 Soul; WE tv; Weatherscan.

Digital Pay Service 1

Pay Units: N.A.

Programming (via satellite): Cinemax (multiplexed); Cinemax HD; HBO (multiplexed); HBO HD; RAI USA; Russian Television Network; Showtime (multiplexed); Showtime HD; Starz (multiplexed); Starz HDTV; The Movie Channel (multiplexed); TV Asia; Zee TV USA.

Video-On-Demand: No

Pay-Per-View

Sports PPV (delivered digitally); NBA League Pass (delivered digitally); NHL Center Ice (delivered digitally); MLB Extra Innings (delivered digitally).

Internet Service

Operational: Yes.

Telephone Service

Digital: Operational

Miles of Plant: 27.0 (coaxial); None (fiber optic).

Regional Vice President: Linda Hossinger. Vice President, Technical Operations: Randy Bender. Vice President, Marketing: Donna Corning. Vice President, Public Affairs: Jody Doherty.

Ownership: Comcast Cable Communications Inc. (MSO).

WEST BURLINGTON TWP.—Formerly served by Barrett's TV Cable System. No longer in operation. ICA: PA0303.

WEST DEER TWP.—Comcast Cable. Now served by TARENTUM BOROUGH, PA [PA0424]. ICA: PA0459.

WEST EASTON BOROUGH—Formerly served by NORTHAMPTON BOROUGH, PA [PA0008]. RCN Corp. This cable system has converted to IPTV, 196 Van Buren St, Herndon, VA 20170. Phone: 703-434-8200. Web Site: http://www.rcn.com. ICA: PA5241.

TV Market Ranking: Below 100 (WEST EASTON BOROUGH).

Channel capacity: N.A. Channels available but not in use: N.A.

Internet Service

Operational: Yes.

Telephone Service

Digital: Operational

Chairman: Steven J. Simmons. Chief Executive Officer: Jim Holanda.

WEST MIFFLIN—Formerly served by Adelphia Communications. Now served by BETHEL PARK, PA [PA0318]. ICA: PA0422.

WEST NEWTON—Formerly served by Adelphia Communications. Now served by BETHEL PARK, PA [PA0318]. ICA: PA0423.

WESTFIELD—Westfield Community Antenna, 121 Strang St, Westfield, PA 16950-1313. Phone: 814-367-5190. Fax: 814-367-5586. Also serves Cowanesque & Westfield Twp. ICA: PA0185.

TV Market Ranking: Outside TV Markets (Cowanesque, WESTFIELD, Westfield Twp.). Franchise award date: N.A. Franchise expiration date: N.A. Began: September 1, 1952.

Channel capacity: 45 (not 2-way capable). Channels available but not in use: N.A.

Basic Service

Subscribers: 980.

Programming (received off-air): WENY-TV (ABC, CW) Elmira; WETM-TV (NBC) Elmira; WIVB-TV (CBS) Buffalo; WKBW-TV (ABC) Buffalo; WPSU-TV (PBS) Clearfield; WSKG-TV (PBS) Binghamton; allband FM.

Programming (via satellite): 3 Angels Broadcasting Network; A&E Networks; ABC Family Channel; Cartoon Network; CNN; Country Music TV; C-SPAN 2; Discovery Channel; ESPN; ESPN 2; FX; Great American Country; Hallmark Channel; Headline News; HGTV; History Channel; KTLA (CW) Los Angeles; Lifetime; Nickelodeon; Outdoor Channel; QVC; RFD-TV; Root Sports Pittsburgh; Speed; Spike TV; Syfy; TBS Superstation; The Weather Channel; Trinity Broadcasting Network; Turner Classic Movies; Turner Network TV; TV Land; USA Network; WGN America; WPIX (CW, IND) New York.

Fee: free installation; $28.00 monthly.

Pay Service 1

Pay Units: 85.

Programming (via satellite): HBO.

Fee: $12.72 monthly.

Video-On-Demand: No

Internet Service

Operational: No.

Telephone Service

None

Miles of Plant: 23.0 (coaxial); None (fiber optic).

Manager: Marlo Kroeck. Chief Technician: Stan Taft.

Ownership: Westfield Community Antenna Assn. Inc.

WESTLINE—Keystone Wilcox Cable TV Inc., PO Box 431, DuBois, PA 15801-0431. Phone: 814-371-2939. Fax: 814-371-2939. ICA: PA0427.

TV Market Ranking: Below 100 (WESTLINE). Franchise award date: N.A. Franchise expiration date: N.A. Began: June 1, 1990.

Channel capacity: 30 (not 2-way capable). Channels available but not in use: N.A.

Basic Service

Subscribers: 24.

Programming (received off-air): WGRZ (NBC) Buffalo; WICU-TV (NBC) Erie; WIVB-TV (CBS) Buffalo; WJAC-TV (NBC) Johnstown; WKBW-TV (ABC) Buffalo; WPSU-TV (PBS) Clearfield; WTAJ-TV (CBS) Altoona; WWCP-TV (FOX) Johnstown; allband FM.

Programming (via satellite): CNN; TBS Superstation; Turner Network TV; USA Network.

Fee: $20.00 installation; $18.00 monthly.

Internet Service

Operational: No.

Telephone Service

None

Miles of Plant: 4.0 (coaxial); None (fiber optic).

Manager: Shirley W. McCoy. Chief Technician: Edward Hulings.

Ownership: Keystone Wilcox Cable TV Inc.

WHITEHALL TWP.—Formerly served by NORTHAMPTON BOROUGH, PA [PA0008]. RCN Corp. This cable system has converted to IPTV, 196 Van Buren St, Herndon, VA 20170. Phone: 703-434-8200. Web Site: http://www.rcn.com. ICA: PA5242.

TV Market Ranking: Below 100 (WHITEHALL TWP.).

Channel capacity: N.A. Channels available but not in use: N.A.

Internet Service

Operational: Yes.

Telephone Service

Digital: Operational

Chairman: Steven J. Simmons. Chief Executive Officer: Jim Holanda.

WILCOX—Zito Media, 611 Vader Hill Rd, Coudersport, PA 16915. Phones: 814-260-9570; 814-260-9575. Fax: 814-260-9580. E-mail: rigas@zitomedia.com. Web Site: http://www.zitomedia.com. ICA: PA0241.

TV Market Ranking: Outside TV Markets (WILCOX). Franchise award date: October 1, 1978. Franchise expiration date: N.A. Began: October 1, 1978.

Channel capacity: 36 (operating 2-way). Channels available but not in use: N.A.

Basic Service

Subscribers: 300.

Programming (received off-air): WATM-TV (ABC) Altoona; WGRZ (NBC) Buffalo; WIVB-TV (CBS) Buffalo; WJAC-TV (NBC) Johnstown; WKBW-TV (ABC) Buffalo; WNED-TV (PBS) Buffalo; WPSU-TV (PBS) Clearfield; WTAJ-TV (CBS) Altoona; WWCP-TV (FOX) Johnstown; allband FM.

Programming (via satellite): WGN America.

Fee: $29.95 installation; $17.55 monthly.

Expanded Basic Service 1

Subscribers: N.A.

Programming (via satellite): A&E Networks; ABC Family Channel; AMC; Animal Planet; Cartoon Network; CNBC; CNN; Country Music TV; C-SPAN 2; Discovery Channel; Disney Channel; E! Entertainment Television; ESPN; ESPN 2; Eternal Word TV Network; Food Network; Fox News Channel; FX; Hallmark Channel; Headline News; HGTV; History Channel; INSP; Lifetime; MSNBC; MTV; NFL Network; Nickelodeon; Outdoor Channel; Oxygen; QVC; Root Sports Pittsburgh; Speed; Spike TV; Syfy; TBS Superstation; The Learning Channel; The Weather Channel; Trinity Broadcasting Network; truTV; Turner Classic Movies; Turner Network TV; TV Land; USA Network; VH1.

Fee: $30.00 monthly.

Digital Basic Service

Subscribers: N.A.

Programming (via satellite): A&E HD; ABC Family HD; AmericanLife TV Network; Animal Planet HD; BBC America; Bio HD; Bloomberg Television; Boomerang; Cartoon Network HD; CMT Pure Country; CNN HD; C-SPAN 3; Discovery Channel HD; Discovery Fit & Health; Discovery Health Channel; Discovery Kids Channel; Disney Channel HD; ESPN 2 HD; ESPN HD; ESPNews; ESPNews HD; ESPNU HD; Familyland Television Network; Food Network HD; Fox HD; Fox Movie Channel; Fox Soccer; FSN HD; FX HD; Golf Channel; Great American Country; GSN; HD Theater; HGTV HD; History Channel HD; HRTV;

ID Investigation Discovery; INSP; Lifetime Movie Network; Lifetime Movie Network HD; Lifetime Real Women; Lifetime Television HD; Military Channel; MTV Hits; MTV Jams; MTV2; Music Choice; NFL Network HD; NHL Network; NHL Network HD; Nick Jr.; Nick Too; Nickelodeon; Outdoor Channel 2 HD; Planet Green; RFD-TV; Science; Science HD; SoapNet; Speed; Speed HD; TBS in HD; TeenNick; The Word Network; TLC HD; Toon Disney; Trinity Broadcasting Network; Turner Network TV HD; VH1 Classic; VH1 Soul; WE tv.
Fee: $31.90 monthly.

Digital Expanded Basic Service
Subscribers: N.A.
Programming (via satellite): Bio; DIY Network; Flix; Fox College Sports Atlantic; Fox College Sports Central; Fox College Sports Pacific; History Channel International; Independent Film Channel; Outdoor Channel; Sundance Channel; Versus.
Fee: $10.00 monthly.

Digital Pay Service 1
Pay Units: N.A.
Programming (via satellite): Cinemax (multiplexed); Cinemax HD; Encore (multiplexed); Flix; HBO (multiplexed); HBO HD; Showtime (multiplexed); Showtime HD; Starz (multiplexed); The Movie Channel (multiplexed).
Fee: $8.00 monthly (Cinemax or Starz/Encore), $10.00 monthly (HBO or Showtime/TMC/Flix).

Video-On-Demand: Yes

Internet Service
Operational: Yes.
Fee: $42.95 monthly.

Telephone Service
Analog: Not Operational
Digital: Operational
Fee: $35.00 monthly

Miles of Plant: 30.0 (coaxial); None (fiber optic).
Manager: James Rigas. Marketing Director: Kathy Fox.
Ownership: Zito Media (MSO).

WILKES-BARRE—Service Electric Cable Company, 15 J Campbell Collins Dr, Wilkes Barre, PA 18702. Phone: 570-825-8508. Fax: 570-822-2601. E-mail: corporateoffice@secv.com. Web Site: http://www.secable.com/wilkes-barre. Also serves Ashley, Bear Creek Twp., Buck Twp., Courtdale, Fairview Twp. (Luzerne County), Hanover Twp. (Luzerne County), Kingston (Luzerne County), Laurel Run, Mountain Top, Pringle, Rice Twp., Sugar Notch, Warrior Run Borough, Wilkes-Barre Twp. & Wright Twp. ICA: PA0036.
TV Market Ranking: 49 (Ashley, Bear Creek Twp., Buck Twp., Courtdale, Fairview Twp. (Luzerne County), Hanover Twp. (Luzerne County), Kingston (Luzerne County), Laurel Run, Mountain Top, Pringle, Rice Twp., Sugar Notch, Warrior Run Borough, WILKES-BARRE, Wilkes-Barre Twp., Wright Twp.). Franchise award date: N.A. Franchise expiration date: N.A. Began: January 1, 1951.
Channel capacity: N.A. Channels available but not in use: N.A.

Basic Service
Subscribers: 22,000.
Programming (received off-air): KYW-TV (CBS) Philadelphia; WBRE-TV (NBC) Wilkes-Barre; WCAU (NBC) Philadelphia; WNEP-TV (ABC) Scranton; WQPX-TV (ION) Scranton; WSWB (CW) Scranton; WTXF-TV (FOX) Philadelphia; WVIA-TV (PBS) Scranton; WWOR-TV (MNT) Secaucus; WYOU (CBS) Scranton; allband FM.
Programming (via satellite): C-SPAN; Eternal Word TV Network; Food Network; Ovation; Pennsylvania Cable Network; QVC; ShopNBC; TV Guide Network; WPIX (CW, IND) New York.
Fee: $36.00 installation; $19.99 monthly.

Expanded Basic Service 1
Subscribers: N.A.
Programming (via satellite): A&E Networks; ABC Family Channel; AMC; AmericanLife TV Network; Animal Planet; Bravo; Cartoon Network; CNBC; CNN; Comcast SportsNet Philadelphia; Comedy Central; Discovery Channel; Discovery Fit & Health; Discovery Health Channel; E! Entertainment Television; ESPN; ESPN 2; ESPN Classic Sports; ESPNews; Fox Movie Channel; Fox News Channel; FX; Hallmark Channel; Headline News; HGTV; History Channel; Lifetime; Lifetime Movie Network; MTV; National Geographic Channel; Nickelodeon; Outdoor Channel; Penn National Racing Alive; SoapNet; Speed; Spike TV; Syfy; TBS Superstation; The Learning Channel; The Weather Channel; Travel Channel; truTV; Turner Classic Movies; Turner Network TV; TV Land; USA Network; Versus; VH1; WE tv.
Fee: $29.96 monthly.

Digital Basic Service
Subscribers: 15,000.
Programming (via satellite): Bio; Boomerang; Country Music TV; C-SPAN 2; DIY Network; Fox Soccer; FSN Digital Atlantic; FSN Digital Central; FSN Digital Pacific; Fuel TV; G4; GAS; Golf Channel; HD Theater; HDNet; HDNet Movies; History Channel International; Independent Film Channel; Lifetime Movie Network; MTV; Music Choice; Nick Jr.; Nick Too; Outdoor Channel; PBS Kids Channel; Turner Network TV HD; TVG Network; WALN Cable Radio.
Fee: $5.99 monthly.

Digital Pay Service 1
Pay Units: N.A.
Programming (via satellite): Cinemax (multiplexed); Encore (multiplexed); HBO (multiplexed); Showtime (multiplexed); Showtime HD; Starz (multiplexed); Starz HDTV; The Movie Channel (multiplexed).
Fee: $13.00 monthly (HBO), $11.00 monthly (Cinemax), $5.99 monthly (Showtime), $10.00 monthly (Starz/Encore).

Video-On-Demand: Planned

Internet Service
Operational: Yes. Began: December 31, 1996.
Subscribers: 4,000.
Broadband Service: ProLog Express.
Fee: $50.00 installation; $32.95 monthly; $100.00 modem purchase.

Telephone Service
None

Miles of Plant: 640.0 (coaxial); 46.0 (fiber optic).
Manager: William Brayford. Chief Technician: Robert Jais. Regulatory Affairs Director: Arlean Lilly.
Ownership: Service Electric Cable TV Inc. (MSO).

WILLIAMS TWP.—Formerly served by NORTHAMPTON BOROUGH, PA [PA0008]. RCN Corp. This cable system has converted to IPTV, 196 Van Buren St, Herndon, VA 20170. Phone: 703-434-8200. Web Site: http://www.rcn.com. ICA: PA5243.
TV Market Ranking: Below 100 (WILLIAMS TWP.).
Channel capacity: N.A. Channels available but not in use: N.A.

Internet Service
Operational: Yes.

Telephone Service
Digital: Operational

Chairman: Steven J. Simmons. Chief Executive Officer: Jim Holanda.

WILLIAMSBURG (Blair County)—Formerly served by Adelphia Communications. Now served by HUNTINGDON, PA [PA0107]. ICA: PA0205.

WILLIAMSPORT—Comcast Cable, 330 Basin St, Williamsport, PA 17701-5216. Phones: 570-326-3384; 570-326-3387. Fax: 570-326-2783. Web Site: http://www.comcast.com. Also serves Allenwood, Armstrong Twp. (Lycoming County), Avis, Bald Eagle Twp. (Clinton County), Beech Creek, Brady Twp. (Lycoming County), Collomsville, Cummings Twp., Curtin Twp., Delaware Twp. (Northumberland County), Duboistown, Dunnstable Twp., Elimsport, Greene Twp. (Clinton County), Gregg Twp. (Union County), Hepburn Twp., Hughesville, Jersey Shore, Lamar Twp. (Clinton County), Limestone Twp., Loganton, Loyalsock Twp., Lycoming Twp., Mill Hall, Montgomery, Montoursville, Muncy, Muncy Creek Twp., Nippenose Twp., North Bend, Noyes Twp., Old Lycoming Twp., Piatt Twp. (Lycoming County), Picture Rocks, Pine Creek Twp., Rauchtown, Renovo, Salladasburg, South Renovo, South Williamsport, Watson Twp., Wolf Twp. & Woodward Twp. (Lycoming County). ICA: PA0040.
TV Market Ranking: Below 100 (Allenwood, Armstrong Twp. (Lycoming County), Avis, Bald Eagle Twp. (Clinton County), Beech Creek, Brady Twp. (Lycoming County), Collomsville, Cummings Twp., Curtin Twp., Delaware Twp. (Northumberland County), Duboistown, Dunnstable Twp., Elimsport, Greene Twp. (Clinton County), Gregg Twp. (Union County), Hepburn Twp., Hughesville, Jersey Shore, Lamar Twp. (Clinton County), Limestone Twp., Loganton, Loyalsock Twp., Lycoming Twp., Mill Hall, Montgomery, Montoursville, Muncy, Muncy Creek Twp., Nippenose Twp., North Bend, Old Lycoming Twp., Piatt Twp. (Lycoming County), Picture Rocks, Pine Creek Twp., Rauchtown, Salladasburg, South Williamsport, Watson Twp., WILLIAMSPORT, Wolf Twp., Woodward Twp. (Lycoming County)); Outside TV Markets (Noyes Twp., Renovo, South Renovo). Franchise award date: N.A. Franchise expiration date: N.A. Began: April 1, 1952.
Channel capacity: N.A. Channels available but not in use: N.A.

Basic Service
Subscribers: N.A. Included in Harrisburg
Programming (received off-air): WNEP-TV (ABC) Scranton; WOLF-TV (CW, FOX, MNT) Hazleton; WPSU-TV (PBS) Clearfield; WSWB (CW) Scranton; WVIA-TV (PBS) Scranton; WWOR-TV (MNT) Secaucus; WYOU (CBS) Scranton; 14 FMs.
Programming (via microwave): WPHL-TV (MNT, IND) Philadelphia; WPIX (CW, IND) New York.
Programming (via satellite): C-SPAN; C-SPAN 2; Eternal Word TV Network; ION Television; Pennsylvania Cable Network; QVC; ShopNBC; Spike TV; Trinity Broadcasting Network; Turner Network TV; TV Guide Network; WGN America.
Fee: $45.10 installation; $17.00 monthly.

Expanded Basic Service 1
Subscribers: 34,500.
Programming (via satellite): A&E Networks; ABC Family Channel; AMC; Animal Planet; BET Networks; Bravo; Cartoon Network; CNBC; CNN; Comcast SportsNet Philadelphia; Comedy Central; Country Music TV; Discovery Channel; Discovery Health Channel; Disney Channel; E! Entertainment Television; ESPN; ESPN 2; Food Network; Fox News Channel; G4; Golf Channel; GSN; Hallmark Channel; Headline News; HGTV; History Channel; Lifetime; MSNBC; MTV; Nickelodeon; Outdoor Channel; SoapNet; Syfy; TBS Superstation; The Learning Channel; The Weather Channel; Toon Disney; Travel Channel; truTV; TV Land; USA Network; VH1; WE tv.
Fee: $32.00 monthly.

Digital Basic Service
Subscribers: 7,745.
Programming (received off-air): WNEP-TV (ABC) Scranton; WVIA-TV (PBS) Scranton.
Programming (via satellite): Discovery Channel; Discovery Digital Networks; ESPN; GAS; HDNet; HDNet Movies; Lifetime Movie Network; MTV Networks Digital Suite; Music Choice; NFL Network; Nick Jr.; Nick Too.
Fee: $14.95 monthly.

Digital Pay Service 1
Pay Units: N.A.
Programming (via satellite): Cinemax (multiplexed); Encore (multiplexed); HBO (multiplexed); Showtime (multiplexed); Starz (multiplexed); The Movie Channel (multiplexed).

Video-On-Demand: Yes

Pay-Per-View
iN DEMAND (delivered digitally); Sports PPV (delivered digitally).

Internet Service
Operational: Yes.
Subscribers: 18,480.
Broadband Service: Comcast High Speed Internet.
Fee: $42.95 monthly.

Telephone Service
Digital: Operational

Miles of Plant: 1,065.0 (coaxial); None (fiber optic).
Manager: Carol Rosebrough. Chief Technician: Bill Reilly. Marketing Director: Michael Loeh. Customer Service Manager: Lorrie Howe.
Ownership: Comcast Cable Communications Inc. (MSO).

WILLOW GROVE—Comcast Cable, 3220 Tillman Dr, Bensalem, PA 19010. Phone: 215-642-6400. Fax: 215-638-6510. Web Site: http://www.comcast.com. Also serves Abington Twp. (Montgomery County), Bryn Athyn Borough, Cheltenham Twp., Jenkintown Borough, Lower Moreland Twp., Rockledge Borough & Upper Moreland Twp. ICA: PA0425.
TV Market Ranking: 4 (Abington Twp. (Montgomery County), Bryn Athyn Borough, Cheltenham Twp., Jenkintown Borough, Lower Moreland Twp., Rockledge Borough, Upper Moreland Twp., WILLOW GROVE). Franchise award date: N.A. Franchise expiration date: N.A. Began: July 1, 1979.
Channel capacity: N.A. Channels available but not in use: N.A.

Basic Service
Subscribers: N.A. Included in Bensalem Twp.
Programming (received off-air): KYW-TV (CBS) Philadelphia; WBPH-TV (IND) Bethlehem; WCAU (NBC) Philadelphia; WFMZ-TV (IND) Allentown; WGTW-TV (TBN) Burlington; WHYY-TV (PBS) Wilmington; WLVT-TV (PBS) Allentown; WMCN-TV (IND) Atlantic City; WPHL-TV (MNT, IND) Philadelphia;

WPPX-TV (ION) Wilmington; WPSG (CW) Philadelphia; WPVI-TV (ABC) Philadelphia; WTVE (IND) Reading; WTXF-TV (FOX) Philadelphia; WUVP-DT (UNV) Vineland; WWSI (TMO) Atlantic City; WYBE (ETV, IND) Philadelphia.

Programming (via satellite): A&E Networks; ABC Family Channel; AMC; Animal Planet; BET Networks; Bravo; Cartoon Network; CNBC; CNN; Comcast SportsNet Philadelphia; Comedy Central; Country Music TV; C-SPAN; C-SPAN 2; Discovery Channel; Disney Channel; E! Entertainment Television; ESPN; ESPN 2; Eternal Word TV Network; Food Network; Fox News Channel; FX; Golf Channel; GSN; Headline News; HGTV; History Channel; Lifetime; MSNBC; MTV; MTV2; Nickelodeon; Philadelphia Park Live; QVC; Speed; Spike TV; Style Network; Syfy; TBS Superstation; The Comcast Network; The Learning Channel; The Weather Channel; truTV; Turner Network TV; TV Guide Network; TV Land; USA Network; Versus; VH1.

Fee: $50.85 monthly.

Digital Basic Service

Subscribers: N.A.

Programming (via satellite): BBC America; Bio; Cooking Channel; C-SPAN 3; Discovery Digital Networks; DIY Network; ESPNews; G4; GAS; History Channel International; MTV Networks Digital Suite; MTV2; Music Choice; National Geographic Channel; Nick Jr.; Nick Too; ShopNBC; SoapNet; Toon Disney; WAM! America's Kidz Network; Weatherscan.

Fee: $9.95 monthly.

Digital Pay Service 1

Pay Units: N.A.

Programming (via satellite): Cinemax (multiplexed); Encore (multiplexed); Flix; HBO (multiplexed); Showtime (multiplexed); Starz (multiplexed); Sundance Channel (multiplexed).

Fee: $18.95 monthly (each).

Video-On-Demand: Yes

Pay-Per-View

iN DEMAND (delivered digitally).

Internet Service

Operational: Yes. Began: March 1, 2002.

Subscribers: 9,472.

Broadband Service: Comcast High Speed Internet.

Fee: $42.95 monthly.

Telephone Service

Digital: Operational

Fee: $44.95 monthly

Miles of Plant: 472.0 (coaxial); None (fiber optic).

Senior Regional Vice President: Amy Smith. Vice President, Technical Operations: Rich Massi. Vice President, Marketing: Chip Goodman.

Ownership: Comcast Cable Communications Inc. (MSO).

WILSON BOROUGH—Formerly served by NORTHAMPTON BOROUGH, PA [PA0008]. RCN Corp. This cable system has converted to IPTV, 196 Van Buren St, Herndon, VA 20170. Phone: 703-434-8200. Web Site: http://www.rcn.com. ICA: PA5244.

TV Market Ranking: Below 100 (WILSON BOROUGH).

Channel capacity: N.A. Channels available but not in use: N.A.

Internet Service

Operational: Yes.

Telephone Service

Digital: Operational

Chairman: Steven J. Simmons. Chief Executive Officer: Jim Holanda.

WIND GAP BOROUGH—Formerly served by NORTHAMPTON BOROUGH, PA [PA0008]. RCN Corp. This cable system has converted to IPTV, 196 Van Buren St, Herndon, VA 20170. Phone: 703-434-8200. Web Site: http://www.rcn.com. ICA: PA5245.

TV Market Ranking: Below 100 (WIND GAP BOROUGH).

Channel capacity: N.A. Channels available but not in use: N.A.

Internet Service

Operational: Yes.

Telephone Service

Digital: Operational

Chairman: Steven J. Simmons. Chief Executive Officer: Jim Holanda.

WINFIELD—Formerly served by D&E Communications. No longer in operation. ICA: PA5290.

WOODBURY—Atlantic Broadband, 120 Southmont Blvd, Johnstown, PA 15905. Phones: 888-536-9600 (Customer service); 814-539-8971. Fax: 814-535-7749. E-mail: info@atlanticbb.com. Web Site: http://www.atlanticbb.com. Also serves East St. Clair Twp. (Bedford County), King Twp., South Woodbury Twp., St. Clair (Bedford County), St. Clairsville & Woodbury Twp. (Bedford County). ICA: PA0426.

TV Market Ranking: 74 (East St. Clair Twp. (Bedford County), King Twp., South Woodbury Twp., St. Clair (Bedford County), St. Clairsville, WOODBURY, Woodbury Twp. (Bedford County)). Franchise award date: January 1, 1977. Franchise expiration date: January 1, 2007. Began: June 1, 1977.

Channel capacity: 35 (not 2-way capable). Channels available but not in use: N.A.

Basic Service

Subscribers: 720.

Programming (received off-air): KDKA-TV (CBS) Pittsburgh; WATM-TV (ABC) Altoona; WJAC-TV (NBC) Johnstown; WKBS-TV (IND) Altoona; WPCW (CW) Jeannette; WPSU-TV (PBS) Clearfield; WTAE-TV (ABC) Pittsburgh; WTAJ-TV (CBS) Altoona; WWCP-TV (FOX) Johnstown.

Programming (via satellite): A&E Networks; ABC Family Channel; AMC; Animal Planet; Cartoon Network; CNN; Country Music TV; C-SPAN; Discovery Channel; Disney Channel; ESPN; ESPN 2; Fox News Channel; FX; Hallmark Channel; Headline News; HGTV; History Channel; INSP; ION Television; Lifetime; Nickelodeon; Outdoor Channel; Pennsylvania Cable Network; QVC; RFD-TV; Root Sports Pittsburgh; Speed; Spike TV; Syfy; TBS Superstation; The Learning Channel; The Weather Channel; Travel Channel; Turner Network TV; TV Guide Network; TV Land; USA Network; VH1; WGN America.

Fee: $25.00 installation; $34.00 monthly.

Pay Service 1

Pay Units: 70.

Programming (via satellite): HBO.

Fee: $10.00 monthly.

Video-On-Demand: No

Internet Service

Operational: No.

Telephone Service

None

Miles of Plant: 60.0 (coaxial); None (fiber optic).

Vice President: David Dane. General Manager: Mike Papasergi. Technical Operations Director: Charles Sorchilla. Marketing & Customer Service Director: Dara Leslie. Marketing Manager: Natalie Kurchak.

Ownership: Atlantic Broadband (MSO).

YEADON—RCN Corp. Formerly served by Philadelphia (suburbs), PA [PA0447]. This cable system has converted to IPTV, 196 Van Buren St, Herndon, VA 20170. Phone: 703-434-8200. Web Site: http://www.rcn.com. ICA: PA5267.

Channel capacity: N.A. Channels available but not in use: N.A.

Internet Service

Operational: Yes.

Chairman: Steven J. Simmons. Chief Executive Officer: Jim Holanda.

YORK—Comcast Cable, 1 E Uwchlan Ave, Ste 411, Exton, PA 19341. Phones: 484-288-6500; 717-854-1912 (York office). Web Site: http://www.comcast.com. Also serves Abbottstown, Conewago Twp. (York County), Dallastown, Dover, East Manchester Twp. (York County), East Prospect, Felton, Goldsboro, Hallam Borough, Hanover, Heidelberg Twp. (York County), Hellam Twp. (York County), Jacobus, Littlestown, Loganville, Lower Windsor Twp. (York County), Manchester, McSherrystown, Mount Wolf, North York, Red Lion, Spring Garden Twp., Springettsbury Twp., Union Twp., West Manchester Twp., West Manheim Twp., West York, Windsor, Yoe, York Haven (York County) & Yorkana. ICA: PA0013.

TV Market Ranking: 57 (Abbottstown, Conewago Twp. (York County), Dallastown, Dover, East Manchester Twp. (York County), East Prospect, Felton, Goldsboro, Hallam Borough, Hanover, Heidelberg Twp. (York County), Hellam Twp. (York County), Jacobus, Littlestown, Loganville, Lower Windsor Twp. (York County), Manchester, McSherrystown, Mount Wolf, North York, Red Lion, Spring Garden Twp., Springettsbury Twp., Union Twp., West Manchester Twp., West Manheim Twp., West York, Windsor, Yoe, YORK, York Haven (York County), Yorkana). Franchise award date: N.A. Franchise expiration date: N.A. Began: N.A.

Channel capacity: N.A. Channels available but not in use: N.A.

Basic Service

Subscribers: N.A. Included in Harrisburg

Programming (received off-air): WBAL-TV (NBC) Baltimore; WDCW (CW) Washington; WGAL (NBC) Lancaster; WGCB-TV (IND) Red Lion; WHP-TV (CBS, MNT) Harrisburg; WHTM-TV (ABC) Harrisburg; WITF-TV (PBS) Harrisburg; WJZ-TV (CBS) Baltimore; WLYH-TV (CW) Lancaster; WMAR-TV (ABC) Baltimore; WMPB (PBS) Baltimore; WPMT (FOX) York.

Programming (via satellite): C-SPAN; C-SPAN 2; Eternal Word TV Network; INSP; Pennsylvania Cable Network; QVC; The Comcast Network; Trinity Broadcasting Network; TV Guide Network.

Fee: $45.10 installation; $17.75 monthly.

Expanded Basic Service 1

Subscribers: 81,491.

Programming (via satellite): A&E Networks; ABC Family Channel; AMC; Animal Planet; BET Networks; Bravo; Cartoon Network; CNBC; CNN; Comcast SportsNet Philadelphia; Comedy Central; Discovery Channel; Disney Channel; E! Entertainment Television; ESPN; ESPN 2; Food Network; Fox News Channel; FX; Headline News; HGTV; History Channel; Lifetime; Mid-Atlantic Sports Network; MSNBC; MTV; Nickelodeon; Spike TV; Syfy; TBS Superstation; The Learning Channel; The Weather Channel; Travel Channel; Turner Network TV; TV Land; USA Network; VH1.

Fee: $30.85 monthly.

Digital Basic Service

Subscribers: 23,717.

Programming (via satellite): BBC America; Bio; Bloomberg Television; Canales N; CMT Pure Country; Cooking Channel; Country Music TV; C-SPAN 2; C-SPAN 3; DIY Network; Encore (multiplexed); ESPN 2 HD; ESPN Classic Sports; ESPN HD; ESPNews; Flix; Fox College Sports Atlantic; Fox College Sports Central; Fox College Sports Pacific; Fox Movie Channel; Fox Reality Channel; Fox Soccer; Fuse; G4; GAS; GMC; Golf Channel; GolTV; Great American Country; GSN; Hallmark Channel; Halogen Network; HD Theater; History Channel International; Independent Film Channel; INSP; Jewelry Television; Lifetime Movie Network; LOGO; MoviePlex; MTV Networks Digital Suite; Music Choice; National Geographic Channel; Nick Jr.; Nick Too; NickToons TV; Outdoor Channel; Oxygen; PBS Kids Sprout; ShopNBC; SoapNet; Speed; Style Network; Sundance Channel; The Word Network; Toon Disney; Trinity Broadcasting Network; truTV; Turner Classic Movies; Turner Network TV HD; TV One; Universal HD; Versus; Versus HD; WE tv.

Fee: $14.95 monthly.

Digital Pay Service 1

Pay Units: N.A.

Programming (via satellite): Cinemax (multiplexed); Cinemax HD; HBO (multiplexed); HBO HD; Showtime (multiplexed); Showtime HD; Starz (multiplexed); Starz HDTV.

Video-On-Demand: Yes

Pay-Per-View

iN DEMAND; Playboy TV; Fresh.

Internet Service

Operational: Yes. Began: February 1, 1997.

Subscribers: 28,716.

Broadband Service: Comcast High Speed Internet.

Fee: $42.95 monthly.

Telephone Service

Digital: Operational

Fee: $44.95 monthly

Miles of Plant: 1,850.0 (coaxial); 245.0 (fiber optic).

Area Vice President: Jim Samaha. Vice President, Marketing: Larry Goldman.

Ownership: Comcast Cable Communications Inc. (MSO).

YOUNGSVILLE—Youngsville TV Corp., 3 W Main St, Youngsville, PA 16371-1420. Phone: 814-563-3336. Fax: 814-563-7299. E-mail: ytv@eaglezip.net. Web Site: http://youngsvilletv.com. Also serves Brokenstraw Twp., Irvine & Pittsfield. ICA: PA0190.

TV Market Ranking: Below 100 (Brokenstraw Twp., Irvine, Pittsfield, YOUNGSVILLE, YOUNGSVILLE). Franchise award date: N.A. Franchise expiration date: N.A. Began: N.A.

Channel capacity: N.A. Channels available but not in use: N.A.

Basic Service

Subscribers: 1,209.

Programming (received off-air): KDKA-TV (CBS) Pittsburgh; WFPX-TV (ION) Fayetteville; WGRZ (NBC) Buffalo; WICU-TV (NBC) Erie; WJET-TV (ABC) Erie; WKBW-TV (ABC) Buffalo; WPSU-TV (PBS) Clearfield; WQLN (PBS) Erie; WSEE-TV (CBS, CW) Erie; allband FM.

Programming (via satellite): A&E Networks; ABC Family Channel; AMC; AmericanLife TV Network; Animal Planet; Bloomberg Television; CNN; Country Music TV; C-SPAN; C-SPAN 2; CW+; Discovery Channel; Disney Channel; DIY Network;

ESPN; ESPN 2; ESPN Classic Sports; Eternal Word TV Network; Food Network; Fox News Channel; FX; Golf Channel; Great American Country; Hallmark Channel; Headline News; HGTV; History Channel; Lifetime; MTV; NASA TV; National Geographic Channel; Nickelodeon; Outdoor Channel; Pennsylvania Cable Network; Root Sports Pittsburgh; RTN; Speed; Spike TV; Syfy; TBS Superstation; The Learning Channel; Travel Channel; Trinity Broadcasting Network; Turner Network TV; TV Land; USA Network; VH1; WGN America.
Fee: $150.00 installation; $30.00 monthly.

Pay Service 1
Pay Units: 196.
Programming (via satellite): HBO.
Fee: $12.00 monthly.

Video-On-Demand: No

Internet Service
Operational: Yes.
Subscribers: 164.
Broadband Service: In-house.
Fee: $29.95 monthly.

Telephone Service
Digital: Operational

Miles of Plant: 28.0 (coaxial); 28.0 (fiber optic).
General Manager: Scott D. Barber Sr.
Ownership: Youngsville TV Corp.

ZELIENOPLE—Armstrong Cable Services, 660 S Benbrook Rd, Butler, PA 16001. Phones: 877-277-5711; 724-452-5213 (Customer service); 724-452-5695. Fax: 724-452-8008. E-mail: info@zoominternet.net. Web Site: http://cable.armstrongonewire.com. Also serves Adams Twp. (Butler County), Big Beaver, Bradford Woods, Callery, Clinton Twp. (Butler County), Cranberry Twp. (Butler County), Daugherty Twp., Ellport, Ellwood City, Evans City, Forward, Franklin Twp. (Beaver County), Hampton Twp. (Allegheny County), Harmony, Homewood, Jackson Twp. (Butler County), Koppel, Lancaster Twp. (Butler County), Lawrence County (southern portion), Marion Twp. (Butler County), Mars, Marshall Twp., Muddycreek Twp., New Beaver, New Sewickley Twp., North Beaver Twp. (Lawrence County), North Sewickley Twp., Perry Twp. (Lawrence County), Pine Twp. (Allegheny County), Pine Twp. (Butler County), Portersville, Richland Twp. (Allegheny County), Seven Fields, Shenango Twp. (Lawrence County), Slippery Rock Twp. (Lawrence County), Taylor Twp. (Lawrence County), Treesdale, Valencia, Wampum, Wayne Twp. (Lawrence County), West Deer Twp. (portions) & Worth Twp. ICA: PA0053. **Note:** This system is an overbuild.

TV Market Ranking: 10 (Adams Twp. (Butler County), Bradford Woods, Callery, Clinton Twp. (Butler County), Cranberry Twp. (Butler County), Daugherty Twp., Ellwood City, Evans City, Forward, Hampton Twp. (Allegheny County), Harmony, Jackson Twp. (Butler County), Lancaster Twp. (Butler County), Marion Twp. (Butler County), Mars, Marshall Twp., Muddycreek Twp., Pine Twp. (Allegheny County), Pine Twp. (Butler County), Portersville, Richland Twp. (Allegheny County), Seven Fields, Slippery Rock Twp. (Lawrence County), Treesdale, Valencia, West Deer Twp. (portions), ZELIENOPLE); 10,79 (Big Beaver, Ellport, Franklin Twp. (Beaver County), Homewood, Koppel, Lawrence County (portions), New Beaver, North Beaver Twp. (Lawrence County), North Sewickley Twp., Perry Twp. (Lawrence County), Taylor Twp. (Lawrence County), Wampum, Wayne Twp. (Lawrence County)); 79 (New Sewickley Twp., Shenango Twp. (Lawrence County), Worth Twp.). Franchise award date: February 1, 1983. Franchise expiration date: February 1, 2008. Began: January 1, 1969.

Channel capacity: N.A. Channels available but not in use: N.A.

Digital Basic Service
Subscribers: N.A.
Programming (via satellite): A&E Networks; ABC Family Channel; AMC; Animal Planet; Bravo; Cartoon Network; CNBC; CNN; Comedy Central; Country Music TV; C-SPAN; Discovery Channel; Disney Channel; E! Entertainment Television; ESPN; ESPN 2; Eternal Word TV Network; Food Network; Fox News Channel; FX; Headline News; HGTV; History Channel; Lifetime; MSNBC; MTV; Music Choice; Nickelodeon; NickToons TV; Pennsylvania Cable Network; Pentagon Channel; Pittsburgh Cable News Channel; QVC; Root Sports Pittsburgh; ShopNBC; Spike TV; Syfy; TBS Superstation; The Learning Channel; The Weather Channel; Travel Channel; truTV; Turner Classic Movies; Turner Network TV; TV Guide Network; TV Land; USA Network; VH1.
Fee: $51.40 monthly.

Digital Expanded Basic Service
Subscribers: N.A.
Programming (via satellite): AmericanLife TV Network; BBC America; Bio; Bloomberg Television; Boomerang; Chiller; cloo; CMT Pure Country; Cooking Channel; Discovery Fit & Health; Discovery Health Channel; Discovery Kids Channel; DIY Network; ESPN Classic Sports; ESPN U; ESPNews; G4; Golf Channel; Great American Country; GSN; Hallmark Channel; Hallmark Movie Channel; History Channel International; HRTV; ID Investigation Discovery; Jewelry Television; Lifetime Movie Network; Military Channel; MTV Hits; MTV Jams; MTV2; mun2 television; National Geographic Channel; NFL Network; NHL Network; Nick Jr.; Nick Too; Outdoor Channel; Oxygen; PBS Kids Sprout; Pentagon Channel; Planet Green; RFD-TV; RTN; Science; SoapNet; Speed; TeenNick; Tennis Channel; Toon Disney; Tr3s; Versus; VH1 Classic; VH1 Soul; WE tv.
Fee: $12.00 monthly.

Digital Expanded Basic Service 2
Subscribers: N.A.
Programming (received off-air): KDKA-TV (CBS) Pittsburgh; WPCW (CW) Jeannette; WPGH-TV (FOX) Pittsburgh; WPXI (IND, NBC) Pittsburgh; WQED (PBS) Pittsburgh; WTAE-TV (ABC) Pittsburgh.
Programming (via satellite): A&E HD; Animal Planet HD; Bravo HD; CNN HD; Discovery Channel HD; Disney Channel HD; ESPN 2 HD; ESPN HD; Food Network HD; Fox News HD; FSN HD; FX HD; Golf Channel HD; Hallmark Movie Channel HD; HD Theater; HDNet; HDNet Movies; HGTV HD; History Channel HD; MGM HD; National Geographic Channel HD Network; NFL Network HD; NHL Network HD; Outdoor Channel 2 HD; Palladia; QVC HD; Science HD; Syfy HD; TBS in HD; The Weather Channel HD; TLC HD; Turner Network TV HD; Universal HD; USA Network HD; Versus HD; WealthTV HD.
Fee: $9.00 monthly.

Digital Pay Service 1
Pay Units: N.A.
Programming (via satellite): Cinemax (multiplexed); Cinemax HD; Encore (multiplexed); Flix; HBO (multiplexed); HBO HD; RAI USA; Showtime (multiplexed); Showtime HD; Starz (multiplexed); Starz HDTV; The Movie Channel (multiplexed); TV5 USA.
Fee: $13.95 monthly (HBO, Cinemax, Starz/Encore or Showtime/TMC/Flix).

Video-On-Demand: Yes

Pay-Per-View
Addressable homes: 2,142.
ESPN Now (delivered digitally); Hot Choice (delivered digitally); iN DEMAND (delivered digitally); Sports PPV (delivered digitally); ESPN Extra (delivered digitally).

Internet Service
Operational: Yes. Began: April 1, 1998.
Subscribers: 22,417.
Broadband Service: Armstrong Zoom.
Fee: $39.95 monthly.

Telephone Service
Digital: Operational
Fee: $34.95 monthly

Miles of Plant: 1,384.0 (coaxial); 500.0 (fiber optic).
Vice President, Marketing: Jud Stewart. General Manager: Joe Taylor. Chief Engineer: Barry Osche. Marketing Manager: Andrea Lucas. Program Director: Matt Lutz. Customer Service Manager: Connie Swartfegger.
Ownership: Armstrong Group of Companies (MSO).

ZION—Tele-Media, 804 Jacksonville Rd, PO Box 39, Bellefonte, PA 16823-0039. Phone: 814-353-2025. Fax: 814-353-2072. E-mail: tmilligan@tele-media.com. Web Site: http://www.tele-media.com. Also serves Hublersburg, Mingoville & Spring Twp. (Centre County). ICA: PA0193.

TV Market Ranking: Outside TV Markets (Hublersburg, Mingoville, Spring Twp. (Centre County), ZION). Franchise award date: N.A. Franchise expiration date: N.A. Began: January 1, 1974.

Channel capacity: 61 (operating 2-way). Channels available but not in use: N.A.

Basic Service
Subscribers: 922 Includes Snow Shoe.
Programming (received off-air): WATM-TV (ABC) Altoona; WJAC-TV (NBC) Johnstown; WKBS-TV (IND) Altoona; WPMT (FOX) York; WPSU-TV (PBS) Clearfield; WTAJ-TV (CBS) Altoona; allband FM.
Programming (via satellite): CNN; Headline News; History Channel; QVC; TBS Superstation; The Weather Channel; TV Land; WGN America.
Fee: $48.40 installation; $16.70 monthly.

Expanded Basic Service 1
Subscribers: N.A.
Programming (via satellite): A&E Networks; ABC Family Channel; AMC; Cartoon Network; Comedy Central; Country Music TV; Discovery Channel; Disney Channel; ESPN; Food Network; Fox News Channel; Fox Sports Net; FX; HGTV; Lifetime; MTV; Nickelodeon; Outdoor Channel; Spike TV; The Learning Channel; Turner Network TV; USA Network; VH1.
Fee: $26.25 monthly.

Digital Basic Service
Subscribers: 223 Includes Snow Shoe.
Programming (via satellite): AmericanLife TV Network; BBC America; Bio; Bloomberg Television; DMX Music; Fox Sports World; G4; Golf Channel; GSN; History Channel; INSP; Outdoor Channel; Syfy; Trinity Broadcasting Network; Turner Classic Movies; Versus.
Fee: $12.27 monthly.

Digital Pay Service 1
Pay Units: 350.
Programming (via satellite): Cinemax (multiplexed); Encore (multiplexed); HBO (multiplexed); Showtime (multiplexed); Starz (multiplexed); The Movie Channel.
Fee: $7.00 monthly (Cinemax), $9.00 monthly (Starz/Encore), $12.00 monthly (HBO), $12.50 monthly (Showtime/TMC).

Video-On-Demand: No

Pay-Per-View
Movies (delivered digitally); special events (delivered digitally).

Internet Service
Operational: Yes.
Subscribers: 540.
Broadband Service: In-house.
Fee: $99.95 installation; $27.95 monthly; $9.95 modem lease.

Telephone Service
Digital: Operational

Miles of Plant: 251.0 (coaxial); None (fiber optic). Miles of plant include Snow Shoe
Senior Vice President, Finance: Bob Stemler. General Manager: Lesley Strouse. Chief Technician: Dean Colbert.
Ownership: Tele-Media Corp. (MSO).

RHODE ISLAND

Total Systems: 3
Total Communities Served: 45
Franchises Not Yet Operating: 0
Applications Pending: 0
Communities with Applications: 0
Number of Basic Subscribers: 317,024
Number of Expanded Basic Subscribers: 272,375
Number of Pay Units: 7,000

Top 100 Markets Represented: Hartford-New Haven-New Britain-Waterbury-New London, CT (19); Providence, RI-New Bedford, MA (33); Boston-Cambridge-Worcester-Lawrence (6).

For a list of cable communities in this section, see the Cable Community Index located in the back of Cable Volume 2.
For explanation of terms used in cable system listings, see p. D-11.

BURRILLVILLE (town)—Cox Communications. Now served by PROVIDENCE, RI [RI0001]. ICA: RI0016.

CRANSTON—Cox Communications. Now served by PROVIDENCE, RI [RI0001]. ICA: RI0004.

NEW SHOREHAM—Formerly served by Block Island Cable TV. No longer in operation. ICA: RI0013.

NEWPORT—Cox Communications, 9 James P. Murphy Hwy, West Warwick, RI 2893. Phones: 401-383-1919 (Administrative office); 401-821-1919. Web Site: http://www.cox.com/newengland. Also serves Bristol, Little Compton, Middletown & Newport Naval Base. ICA: RI0011.

TV Market Ranking: 33 (Bristol, Little Compton, Middletown, NEWPORT, Newport Naval Base). Franchise award date: N.A. Franchise expiration date: N.A. Began: December 1, 1986.

Channel capacity: 62 (operating 2-way). Channels available but not in use: N.A.

Basic Service

Subscribers: N.A.

Programming (received off-air): WGBH-TV (PBS) Boston; WGBX-TV (PBS) Boston; WHPX-TV (ION) New London; WJAR (NBC) Providence; WLNE-TV (ABC) New Bedford; WLWC (CW) New Bedford; WNAC-TV (FOX) Providence; WPRI-TV (CBS) Providence; WSBE-TV (PBS) Providence; WUNI (UNV) Worcester.

Programming (via satellite): Cox Sports Television; Eternal Word TV Network; QVC; Rhode Island News Channel; Rhode Island Statewide Interconnect; RTP-USA; TV Guide Network.

Fee: $55.99 installation; $12.30 monthly; $1.50 converter.

Expanded Basic Service 1

Subscribers: N.A.

Programming (via satellite): A&E Networks; ABC Family Channel; AMC; Animal Planet; BET Networks; Bravo; Cartoon Network; CNBC; CNN; Comcast SportsNet Mid-Atlantic; Comedy Central; Country Music TV; C-SPAN; C-SPAN 2; Discovery Channel; Discovery Health Channel; Disney Channel; ESPN; ESPN 2; Food Network; Fox News Channel; FX; Headline News; HGTV; History Channel; Lifetime; MSNBC; MTV; MTV2; New England Sports Network; Nickelodeon; Portuguese Channel; ShopNBC; Spike TV; Syfy; TBS Superstation; Telemundo; The Learning Channel; The Weather Channel; Travel Channel; truTV; Turner Network TV; TV Land; USA Network; VH1.

Digital Basic Service

Subscribers: N.A.

Programming (via satellite): A&E HD; Animal Planet HD; AZ TV; BBC America; Bio; Bloomberg Television; Boomerang; Canales N; CMT Pure Country; CNN HD; CNN International; College Sports Television; Comcast SportsNet Mid-Atlantic; Cooking Channel; Discovery Channel HD; Discovery Fit & Health; DIY Network; ESPN 2 HD; ESPN Classic Sports; ESPN HD; ESPN U; ESPNews; Food Network HD; Fox Soccer; Fuel TV; Fuse; G4; Golf Channel; GoScout Homes; GSN; Hallmark Channel; Halogen Network; HD Theater; HGTV HD; History Channel HD; History Channel International; Independent Film Channel; INSP; Lifetime Movie Network; Military History Channel; MTV Hits; Music Choice; National Geographic Channel; National Geographic Channel HD Network; NBA TV; New England Sports Network; NFL Network; NFL Network HD; NHL Network; NHL Network HD; Nick Jr.; NickToons TV; Oxygen; Palladia; PBS Kids Sprout; Science; Science HD; SoapNet; Speed; Style Network; Sundance Channel; TBS in HD; TeenNick; The Learning Channel; Toon Disney; Travel Channel HD; Trinity Broadcasting Network; Turner Classic Movies; Turner Network TV HD; TV One; Universal HD; Versus; Versus HD; VH1 Classic; WE tv; Weatherscan; WeatherVision.

Digital Pay Service 1

Pay Units: N.A.

Programming (via satellite): Cinemax (multiplexed); Cinemax HD; Encore (multiplexed); HBO (multiplexed); HBO HD; RAI International; Showtime (multiplexed); Showtime HD; Starz (multiplexed); Starz HDTV; The Movie Channel (multiplexed); TV5, La Television International.

Video-On-Demand: No

Pay-Per-View

iN DEMAND (delivered digitally); ESPN Gameplan (delivered digitally); Spice: Xcess (delivered digitally); ESPN Full Court (delivered digitally); NBA League Pass (delivered digitally); MLS Direct Kick (delivered digitally); MLB Extra Innings (delivered digitally); NHL Center Ice (delivered digitally); Club Jenna (delivered digitally); Playboy TV (delivered digitally); Shorteez (delivered digitally).

Internet Service

Operational: Yes.

Broadband Service: Cox High Speed Internet.

Telephone Service

Digital: Operational

Miles of Plant: 634.0 (coaxial); None (fiber optic).

Vice President & Regional Manager: Paul Cronin. Vice President, Marketing: Doreen Studley. Vice President, Government & Public Affairs: John Wolfe. Vice President, Network Services: Allan Gardiner. Public Relations Director: Leigh Ann Woisard.

Ownership: Cox Communications Inc. (MSO).

NEWPORT & LINCOLN—Cox Communications. Now served by PROVIDENCE, RI [RI0001]. ICA: RI0002.

PROVIDENCE—Cox Communications, 9 James P. Murphy Hwy, West Warwick, RI 2893. Phones: 401-383-1919 (Administrative office); 401-821-1919 (Customer service). Web Site: http://www.cox.com/newengland. Also serves Ashaway, Barrington, Bradford, Bristol County, Burrillville (town), Central Falls, Charlestown, Coventry, Cranston, Cumberland, East Greenwich, East Providence, Exeter (town), Glocester (town), Hopkinton, Jamestown, Johnston, Lincoln, Narragansett, Newport, Newport County, North Kingstown, North Providence, North Smithfield, Pawtucket, Providence County, Richmond, Scituate (town), Smithfield, South Kingstown, Tiverton, Warwick, West Greenwich, West Warwick, Westerly & Woonsocket. ICA: RI0001.

TV Market Ranking: 19 (Ashaway, Bradford, Charlestown, Hopkinton, West Greenwich, Westerly); 19,33 (Exeter (town), Narragansett, Richmond, South Kingstown); 33 (Barrington, Bristol County, Burillville (town), Coventry, Cranston, East Greenwich, East Providence, Glocester (town), Jamestown, Johnston, Lincoln, Newport, North Kingstown, PROVIDENCE, Scituate (town), Tiverton, Warwick, West Warwick, Woonsocket); 6 (Central Falls, Cumberland, Providence County); 6,33 (North Providence, North Smithfield, Pawtucket, Smithfield). Franchise award date: November 1, 1974. Franchise expiration date: N.A. Began: August 18, 1982.

Channel capacity: N.A. Channels available but not in use: N.A.

Basic Service

Subscribers: 308,944.

Programming (received off-air): WGBH-TV (PBS) Boston; WGBX-TV (PBS) Boston; WJAR (NBC) Providence; WLNE-TV (ABC) New Bedford; WLWC (CW) New Bedford; WNAC-TV (FOX) Providence; WPRI-TV (CBS) Providence; WSBE-TV (PBS) Providence; WUNI (UNV) Worcester.

Programming (via satellite): Cox Sports Television; Eternal Word TV Network; ION Television; QVC; Rhode Island News Channel; TV Guide Network.

Fee: $29.99 installation; $12.50 monthly.

Expanded Basic Service 1

Subscribers: 272,375.

Programming (via satellite): A&E Networks; ABC Family Channel; AMC; Animal Planet; BET Networks; Bravo; Cartoon Network; CNBC; CNN; Comcast SportsNet New England; Comedy Central; Country Music TV; C-SPAN; C-SPAN 2; Discovery Channel; Discovery Health Channel; Disney Channel; E! Entertainment Television; ESPN; ESPN 2; Food Network; Fox News Channel; FX; Headline News; HGTV; History Channel; Lifetime; MSNBC; MTV; MTV2; New England Sports Network; Nickelodeon; Portuguese Channel; ShopNBC; Spike TV; Syfy; TBS Superstation; Telemundo; The Learning Channel; The Weather Channel; Travel Channel; truTV; Turner Network TV; TV Land; USA Network; VH1.

Fee: $50.11 installation; $33.45 monthly.

Digital Basic Service

Subscribers: N.A.

Programming (received off-air): WJAR (NBC) Providence.

Programming (via satellite): BBC America; Bio; Bloomberg Television; Boomerang; Canales N; CNN International; Cooking Channel; Country Music TV; Discovery Fit & Health; DIY Network; ESPN Classic Sports; ESPNews; Fox Soccer; Fuel TV; G4; GAS; Golf Channel; GolTV; GSN; Hallmark Channel; Halogen Network; HD Theater; History Channel International; Independent Film Channel; INHD; INHD2; INSP; Lifetime Movie Network; MTV Networks Digital Suite; Music Choice; National Geographic Channel; NBA TV; NFL Network; Nick Jr.; NickToons TV; Oxygen; Palladia; PBS Kids Sprout; RAI International; SoapNet; Speed; Style Network; Toon Disney; Trinity Broadcasting Network; Turner Classic Movies; Turner Network TV HD; TV One; TV5, La Television International; Universal HD; Versus.

Fee: $12.95 monthly.

Digital Pay Service 1

Pay Units: N.A.

Programming (via satellite): Cinemax (multiplexed); Encore (multiplexed); HBO (multiplexed); Showtime (multiplexed); Showtime HD; Starz (multiplexed); Sundance Channel; The Movie Channel (multiplexed).

Fee: $10.95 monthly.

Video-On-Demand: Yes

Pay-Per-View

iN DEMAND (delivered digitally); Movies (delivered digitally); Playboy TV (delivered digitally); Shorteez (delivered digitally).

Internet Service

Operational: Yes. Began: February 1, 1998.

Broadband Service: Cox High Speed Internet.

Fee: $99.95 installation; $39.95 monthly; $15.00 modem lease; $299.00 modem purchase.

Telephone Service

Digital: Operational

Fee: $11.95 monthly

Miles of Plant: 3,009.0 (coaxial); 164.0 (fiber optic). Additional miles planned: 27.0 (fiber optic).

Vice President & Regional Manager: Paul Cronin. Vice President, Network Services: Allan Gardiner. Vice President, Government & Public Affairs: John Wolfe. Vice President, Marketing: Doreen Studley. Marketing Director: Mark Cameron. Public Relations Director: Leigh Ann Woisard.
Ownership: Cox Communications Inc. (MSO).

WARREN—Full Channel TV Inc., 57 Everett St, Warren, RI 02885-1909. Phones: 401-247-1250; 401-247-2250. Fax: 401-247-0191. Web Site: http://www.fullchannel.com. Also serves Barrington, Bristol & Bristol County. ICA: RI0009.
TV Market Ranking: 33 (Barrington, Bristol, Bristol County, WARREN). Franchise award date: November 1, 1974. Franchise expiration date: N.A. Began: February 2, 1984.
Channel capacity: N.A. Channels available but not in use: N.A.

Basic Service
Subscribers: 6,880.
Programming (received off-air): WFXT (FOX) Boston; WGBH-TV (PBS) Boston; WGBX-TV (PBS) Boston; WHDH (NBC) Boston; WJAR (NBC) Providence; WLNE-TV (ABC) New Bedford; WLWC (CW) New Bedford; WNAC-TV (FOX) Providence; WPRI-TV (CBS) Providence; WPXQ-TV (ION) Block Island; WSBE-TV (PBS) Providence; WSBK-TV (CBS, MNT) Boston; WUNI (UNV) Worcester; allband FM.
Programming (via satellite): A&E Networks; ABC Family Channel; AMC; AmericanLife TV Network; Animal Planet; Bloomberg Television; Boomerang; Cartoon Network; CNBC; CNN; Comcast SportsNet New England; Comedy Central; C-SPAN; C-SPAN 2; Discovery Channel; Discovery Health Channel; DIY Network; E! Entertainment Television; ESPN; ESPN 2; Eternal Word TV Network; Food Network; Fox News Channel; G4; Golf Channel; Hallmark Channel; Headline News; HGTV; History Channel; Lifetime; MSNBC; MTV; MTV2; NASA TV; National Geographic Channel; New England Sports Network; Nickelodeon; Portuguese Channel; QVC; ShopNBC; Speed; Spike TV; Syfy; TBS Superstation; The Learning Channel; The Weather Channel; Travel Channel; Trinity Broadcasting Network; truTV; Turner Network TV; TV Guide Network; TV Land; USA Network; Versus; VH1.
Fee: $59.95 installation; $43.55 monthly; $3.00 converter.

Digital Basic Service
Subscribers: 1,200.
Programming (via satellite): BBC America; Bio; Bravo; Discovery Digital Networks; ESPN Classic Sports; ESPNews; Fox Movie Channel; Fox Sports World; GAS; GSN; History Channel International; Independent Film Channel; Lifetime Movie Network; MTV Networks Digital Suite; MuchMusic Network; Music Choice; Nick Jr.; Outdoor Channel; Style Network; Turner Classic Movies; WE tv.
Fee: $4.95 monthly.

Pay Service 1
Pay Units: 7,000.
Programming (via satellite): Cinemax; HBO (multiplexed); Showtime; The Movie Channel.
Fee: $10.00 installation; $12.95 monthly (Cinemax, HBO, or Showtime/TMC).

Digital Pay Service 1
Pay Units: N.A.
Programming (via satellite): Cinemax (multiplexed); Encore (multiplexed); Flix; HBO (multiplexed); Showtime (multiplexed); Starz (multiplexed); Sundance Channel; The Movie Channel (multiplexed).
Fee: $12.95 monthly (Starz/Encore, Showtime/TMC/Flix, HBO or Cinemax).

Video-On-Demand: No

Pay-Per-View
iN DEMAND; ESPN Now (delivered digitally); Hot Choice (delivered digitally); iN DEMAND (delivered digitally); Playboy TV (delivered digitally); Fresh (delivered digitally); Shorteez (delivered digitally); sports (delivered digitally).

Internet Service
Operational: Yes.
Subscribers: 3,100.
Broadband Service: In-house.
Fee: $59.95 installation; $25.99-$33.99 monthly; $9.95 modem lease; $79.95 modem purchase.

Telephone Service
Digital: Operational
Fee: $25.99-$34.99 monthly
Miles of Plant: 483.0 (coaxial); None (fiber optic).
President & Chief Executive Officer: Linda Jones Maaia. Chief Technician: Richard Adams. Vice President: Levi C. Maaia.
Ownership: Full Channel TV Inc.

WESTERLY—Cox Communications. Now served by PROVIDENCE, RI [RI0001]. ICA: RI0008.

SOUTH CAROLINA

Total Systems: 45
Total Communities Served: 365
Franchises Not Yet Operating: 0
Applications Pending: 0
Communities with Applications: 0
Number of Basic Subscribers: 1,147,027
Number of Expanded Basic Subscribers: 628,522
Number of Pay Units: 131,170

Top 100 Markets Represented: Columbia (100); Charlotte (42); Greenville-Spartanburg-Anderson, SC-Asheville, NC (46).

**For a list of cable communities in this section, see the Cable Community Index located in the back of Cable Volume 2.
For explanation of terms used in cable system listings, see p. D-11.**

ABBEVILLE—Charter Communications. Now served by GREENVILLE/SPARTANBURG, SC [SC0003]. ICA: SC0041.

AIKEN—Atlantic Broadband, 520 E Pine Log, Aiken, SC 29803. Phones: 888-301-8649; 803-648-8362. Fax: 803-642-9241. E-mail: info@atlanticbb.com. Web Site: http://www.atlanticbb.com. Also serves Bath, Burnettown, Gloverville, Graniteville, Jackson, Langley, Montmorenci, New Ellenton, Vaucluse & Warrenville. ICA: SC0106.

TV Market Ranking: Below 100 (AIKEN, Bath, Burnettown, Gloverville, Graniteville, Jackson, Langley, Montmorenci, New Ellenton, Vaucluse, Warrenville). Franchise award date: June 7, 1977. Franchise expiration date: July 1, 2008. Began: December 1, 1968.

Channel capacity: 151 (operating 2-way). Channels available but not in use: N.A.

Basic Service

Subscribers: 20,500 Includes Allendale, Bamburg, & Barnwell.

Programming (received off-air): WAGT (CW, NBC) Augusta; WCES-TV (PBS) Wrens; WEBA-TV (PBS) Allendale; WFXG (FOX) Augusta; WIS (NBC) Columbia; WJBF (ABC) Augusta; WOLO-TV (ABC) Columbia; WRDW-TV (CBS, MNT) Augusta.

Programming (via satellite): C-SPAN; C-SPAN 2; CW+; MyNetworkTV Inc.; QVC; The Weather Channel; TV Guide Network.

Fee: $25.00 installation; $20.64 monthly.

Expanded Basic Service 1

Subscribers: 15,644.

Programming (via satellite): A&E Networks; ABC Family Channel; AMC; Animal Planet; BET Networks; Bravo; Cartoon Network; CNBC; CNN; Comedy Central; Country Music TV; Discovery Channel; Disney Channel; E! Entertainment Television; ESPN; ESPN 2; ESPN Classic Sports; Food Network; Fox Movie Channel; Fox News Channel; Fox Sports South; FX; Golf Channel; Great American Country; GSN; Hallmark Channel; Headline News; HGTV; History Channel; INSP; Lifetime; MSNBC; MTV; National Geographic Channel; Nickelodeon; SoapNet; Speed; Spike TV; SportSouth; Syfy; TBS Superstation; The Learning Channel; Travel Channel; Trinity Broadcasting Network; truTV; Turner Classic Movies; Turner Network TV; TV Land; USA Network; VH1.

Fee: $29.96 monthly.

Digital Basic Service

Subscribers: 2,520.

Programming (via satellite): 3 Angels Broadcasting Network; A&E HD; AmericanLife TV Network; Animal Planet HD; BBC America; Bio; Bloomberg Television; Boomerang; BYU Television; Chiller; Church Channel; cloo; CMT Pure Country; Cooking Channel; Daystar TV Network; Discovery Channel HD; Discovery Fit & Health; Discovery Home Channel; Discovery Kids Channel; Disney Channel HD; DIY Network; Encore (multiplexed); ESPN 2 HD; ESPN HD; ESPN U; ESPNews; Eternal Word TV Network; Fox College Sports Atlantic; Fox College Sports Central; Fox College Sports Pacific; Fox Reality Channel; Fox Sports South; Fuel TV; Fuse; G4; GMC; Golden Eagle Broadcasting; Halogen Network; HD Theater; HDNet; HDNet Movies; History Channel International; ID Investigation Discovery; Independent Film Channel; ION Television; JCTV; Lifetime Movie Network; Lifetime Real Women; Military Channel; MTV Hits; MTV Jams; MTV2; Music Choice; NFL Network; NFL Network HD; Nick Jr.; NickToons TV; Outdoor Channel; Oxygen; RLTV; Science; Starz (multiplexed); Starz HDTV; Style Network; Syfy HD; TBS in HD; TeenNick; Tennis Channel; TLC HD; Toon Disney; Turner Network TV HD; TVG Network; USA Network HD; Versus; VH1 Classic; VH1 Soul; WE tv; Weatherscan.

Fee: $17.95 monthly.

Digital Pay Service 1

Pay Units: 774.

Programming (via satellite): Cinemax (multiplexed); Cinemax HD.

Fee: $14.95 monthly.

Digital Pay Service 2

Pay Units: 761.

Programming (via satellite): Flix; Showtime (multiplexed); Showtime HD; The Movie Channel (multiplexed).

Fee: $14.95 monthly.

Digital Pay Service 3

Pay Units: 1,874.

Programming (via satellite): HBO (multiplexed); HBO HD.

Fee: $14.95 monthly.

Video-On-Demand: Yes

Pay-Per-View

iN DEMAND (delivered digitally); Playboy TV (delivered digitally); Fresh (delivered digitally); Club Jenna (delivered digitally); Shorteez (delivered digitally); Spice: Xcess (delivered digitally).

Internet Service

Operational: Yes. Began: January 18, 2004.

Subscribers: 306.

Broadband Service: Atlantic Broadband High-Speed Internet.

Fee: $21.95-$55.95 monthly; $5.00 modem lease.

Telephone Service

Digital: Operational

Fee: $44.95 monthly

Miles of Plant: 1,200.0 (coaxial); 19.0 (fiber optic). Additional miles planned: 20.0 (coaxial); 20.0 (fiber optic).

Vice President & General Manager: Sam McGill. Technical Supervisor: Jim Walker.

Ownership: Atlantic Broadband (MSO).

ALLENDALE—Atlantic Broadband, 520 E Pine Log, Aiken, SC 29803. Phone: 888-301-8649 (Customer service). Fax: 803-642-9241. E-mail: info@atlanticbb.com. Web Site: http://www.atlanticbb.com. Also serves Allendale County & Fairfax. ICA: SC0166.

TV Market Ranking: Below 100 (Allendale County); Outside TV Markets (ALLENDALE, Allendale County, Fairfax).

Channel capacity: N.A. Channels available but not in use: N.A.

Basic Service

Subscribers: N.A. Included in Aiken

Programming (received off-air): WAGT (CW, NBC) Augusta; WCES-TV (PBS) Wrens; WEBA-TV (PBS) Allendale; WFXG (FOX) Augusta; WIS (NBC) Columbia; WJBF (ABC) Augusta; WOLO-TV (ABC) Columbia; WRDW-TV (CBS, MNT) Augusta.

Programming (via satellite): C-SPAN; C-SPAN 2; CW+; MyNetworkTV Inc.; QVC; The Weather Channel; TV Guide Network.

Fee: $25.00 installation; $20.64 monthly.

Expanded Basic Service 1

Subscribers: 1,138.

Programming (via satellite): A&E Networks; ABC Family Channel; AMC; Animal Planet; BET Networks; Bravo; Cartoon Network; CNBC; CNN; Comedy Central; Country Music TV; Discovery Channel; Disney Channel; E! Entertainment Television; ESPN; ESPN 2; ESPN Classic Sports; Food Network; Fox Movie Channel; Fox News Channel; Fox Sports South; FX; Golf Channel; Great American Country; GSN; Hallmark Channel; Headline News; HGTV; History Channel; INSP; Lifetime; MSNBC; MTV; National Geographic Channel; Nickelodeon; SoapNet; Speed; Spike TV; SportSouth; Syfy; TBS Superstation; The Learning Channel; Travel Channel; Trinity Broadcasting Network; truTV; Turner Classic Movies; Turner Network TV; TV Land; USA Network; VH1.

Fee: $29.96 monthly.

Digital Basic Service

Subscribers: N.A.

Programming (via satellite): 3 Angels Broadcasting Network; A&E HD; AmericanLife TV Network; Animal Planet HD; BBC America; Bio; Bloomberg Television; Boomerang; BYU Television; Chiller; Church Channel; cloo; CMT Pure Country; Cooking Channel; Daystar TV Network; Discovery Channel HD; Discovery Fit & Health; Discovery Home Channel; Discovery Kids Channel; Disney Channel HD; DIY Network; Encore (multiplexed); ESPN 2 HD; ESPN HD; ESPN U; ESPNews; Eternal Word TV Network; Fox Reality Channel; Fox Sports South; Fuse; G4; GMC; Golden Eagle Broadcasting; Halogen Network; HD Theater; HDNet; HDNet Movies; History Channel International; ID Investigation Discovery; Independent Film Channel; ION Television; JCTV; Lifetime Movie Network; Lifetime Real Women; Military Channel; MTV Hits; MTV Jams; MTV2; Music Choice; NFL Network; NFL Network HD; Nick Jr.; NickToons TV; Outdoor Channel; Oxygen; RLTV; Science; Starz (multiplexed); Starz HDTV; Style Network; TBS in HD; TeenNick; TLC HD; Toon Disney; Turner Network TV HD; TVG Network; Versus; VH1 Classic; VH1 Soul; WE tv; Weatherscan.

Fee: $17.95 monthly.

Digital Pay Service 1

Pay Units: N.A.

Programming (via satellite): Cinemax (multiplexed); Cinemax HD; Flix; HBO (multiplexed); HBO HD; Showtime (multiplexed); Showtime HD; The Movie Channel (multiplexed).

Fee: $14.95 monthly (HBO, Cinemax or Showtime/TMC/Flix).

Video-On-Demand: Planned

Pay-Per-View

iN DEMAND (delivered digitally); Playboy TV (delivered digitally); Fresh (delivered digitally); Shorteez (delivered digitally); Spice: Xcess (delivered digitally); Club Jenna (delivered digitally).

Internet Service

Operational: Yes.

Broadband Service: Atlantic Broadband High-Speed Internet.

Fee: $21.95-$55.95 monthly.

Telephone Service

Digital: Operational

Fee: $49.95 monthly

Vice President & General Manager: Sam McGill. Technical Supervisor: Jim Walker.

Ownership: Atlantic Broadband.

ANCHOR POINT—Charter Communications, 2 Digital Place, Simpsonville, SC 29681. Phone: 864-254-7260. Fax: 864-254-7345. Web Site: http://www.charter.com. Also serves Anderson County (unincorporated areas), La France, Sandy Springs & Townville. ICA: SC0107.

TV Market Ranking: 46 (ANCHOR POINT, Anderson County (unincorporated areas), La France, Sandy Springs, Townville). Franchise award date: N.A. Franchise expiration date: N.A. Began: N.A.

Channel capacity: N.A. Channels available but not in use: N.A.

Basic Service

Subscribers: 1,629.

Programming (received off-air): WHNS (FOX) Greenville; WLOS (ABC) Asheville; WNTV (PBS) Greenville; WSPA-TV (CBS) Spartanburg; WYFF (NBC) Greenville.

Programming (via satellite): ABC Family Channel; ESPN; QVC; TBS Superstation; The Weather Channel; WGN America.

Fee: $40.00 installation; $9.86 monthly.

Expanded Basic Service 1
Subscribers: 1,608.
Programming (via satellite): AmericanLife TV Network; CNN; Country Music TV; Discovery Channel; Disney Channel; Fox Sports South; Headline News; MTV; Nickelodeon; Spike TV; Turner Network TV; USA Network; VH1.
Fee: $11.76 monthly.
Pay Service 1
Pay Units: 177.
Programming (via satellite): Cinemax.
Fee: $9.95 monthly.
Pay Service 2
Pay Units: 235.
Programming (via satellite): HBO.
Fee: $11.95 monthly.
Pay Service 3
Pay Units: 131.
Programming (via satellite): Showtime.
Fee: $9.95 monthly.
Video-On-Demand: Planned
Internet Service
Operational: Yes.
Fee: $19.99 monthly.
Telephone Service
Digital: Operational
Fee: $14.99 monthly
Miles of Plant: 174.0 (coaxial); None (fiber optic).
Vice President & General Manager: Anthony Pope. Operations Manager: Pat Hayes. Marketing Director: Brroke Sinclair.
Ownership: Charter Communications Inc. (MSO).

ANDERSON—Charter Communications. Now served by GREENVILLE/SPARTANBURG, SC [SC0003]. ICA: SC0011.

AWENDAW—US Cable of Coastal Texas LP. Now served by CHARLESTON, SC [SC0001]. ICA: SC0094.

BAMBERG—Atlantic Broadband, 520 E Pine Log, Aiken, SC 29803. Phone: 888-301-8649 (Customer service). Fax: 803-642-9241. E-mail: info@atlanticbb.com. Web Site: http://www.atlanticbb.com. Also serves Bamberg County. ICA: SC0167.
TV Market Ranking: Outside TV Markets (BAMBERG, Bamberg County).
Channel capacity: N.A. Channels available but not in use: N.A.
Basic Service
Subscribers: N.A. Included in Aiken
Programming (received off-air): WAGT (CW, NBC) Augusta; WCES-TV (PBS) Wrens; WEBA-TV (PBS) Allendale; WFXG (FOX) Augusta; WIS (NBC) Columbia; WJBF (ABC) Augusta; WOLO-TV (ABC) Columbia; WRDW-TV (CBS, MNT) Augusta.
Programming (via satellite): C-SPAN; C-SPAN 2; CW+; MyNetworkTV Inc.; QVC; The Weather Channel; TV Guide Network.
Fee: $25.00 installation; $20.64 monthly.
Expanded Basic Service 1
Subscribers: 1,773.
Programming (via satellite): A&E Networks; ABC Family Channel; AMC; Animal Planet; BET Networks; Bravo; Cartoon Network; CNBC; CNN; Comedy Central; Country Music TV; Discovery Channel; Disney Channel; E! Entertainment Television; ESPN; ESPN 2; ESPN Classic Sports; Food Network; Fox Movie Channel; Fox News Channel; Fox Sports South; FX; Golf Channel; Great American Country; GSN; Hallmark Channel; Headline News; HGTV; History Channel; INSP; Lifetime; MSNBC; MTV; National Geographic Channel; Nickelodeon; SoapNet; Speed; Spike TV; SportSouth; Syfy; TBS Superstation; The Learning Channel; Travel Channel; Trinity Broadcasting Network; truTV; Turner Classic Movies; Turner Network TV; TV Land; USA Network; VH1.
Fee: $29.96 monthly.
Digital Basic Service
Subscribers: N.A.
Programming (via satellite): 3 Angels Broadcasting Network; A&E HD; AmericanLife TV Network; Animal Planet HD; BBC America; Bio; Bloomberg Television; Boomerang; BYU Television; Chiller; Church Channel; cloo; CMT Pure Country; Cooking Channel; Daystar TV Network; Discovery Channel HD; Discovery Fit & Health; Discovery Home Channel; Discovery Kids Channel; Disney Channel HD; DIY Network; Encore (multiplexed); ESPN 2 HD; ESPN HD; ESPN U; ESPNews; Eternal Word TV Network; Fox Reality Channel; Fox Sports South; Fuse; G4; Golden Eagle Broadcasting; Gospel Music TV; Halogen Network; HD Theater; HDNet; HDNet Movies; History Channel International; ID Investigation Discovery; Independent Film Channel; ION Television; JCTV; Lifetime Movie Network; Lifetime Real Women; Military Channel; MTV Hits; MTV Jams; MTV2; Music Choice; NFL Network; NFL Network HD; Nick Jr.; NickToons TV; Outdoor Channel; Oxygen; RLTV; Science; Starz (multiplexed); Starz HDTV; Style Network; TBS in HD; TeenNick; TLC HD; Toon Disney; Turner Network TV HD; TVG Network; Versus; VH1 Classic; VH1 Soul; WE tv; Weatherscan.
Fee: $17.95 monthly.
Digital Pay Service 1
Pay Units: N.A.
Programming (via satellite): Cinemax (multiplexed); Cinemax HD; Flix; HBO (multiplexed); HBO HD; Showtime (multiplexed); Showtime HD; The Movie Channel (multiplexed).
Fee: $14.95 monthly (HBO, Cinemax or Showtime/TMC/Flix).
Video-On-Demand: Planned
Pay-Per-View
iN DEMAND (delivered digitally); Fresh (delivered digitally); Spice: Xcess (delivered digitally); Shorteez (delivered digitally); Club Jenna (delivered digitally); Playboy TV (delivered digitally).
Internet Service
Operational: Yes.
Broadband Service: Atlantic Broadband High-Speed Internet.
Fee: $21.95-$55.95 monthly.
Telephone Service
Digital: Operational
Fee: $49.95 monthly
Vice President & General Manager: Sam McGill. Technical Supervisor: Jim Walker.
Ownership: Atlantic Broadband (MSO).

BARNWELL—Atlantic Broadband, 520 E Pine Log, Aiken, SC 29803. Phone: 888-301-8649 (Customer service). Fax: 803-644-1952. E-mail: info@atlanticbb.com. Web Site: http://www.atlanticbb.com. Also serves Barnwell County, Blackville, Denmark, Elko, Snelling & Williston. ICA: SC0018.
TV Market Ranking: Below 100 (Barnwell County (portions), Snelling, Williston); Outside TV Markets (BARNWELL, Barnwell County (portions), Blackville, Denmark, Elko). Franchise award date: December 14, 1965. Franchise expiration date: October 1, 2006. Began: December 1, 1966.
Channel capacity: 151 (operating 2-way). Channels available but not in use: N.A.
Basic Service
Subscribers: N.A. Included in Aiken
Programming (received off-air): WAGT (CW, NBC) Augusta; WCES-TV (PBS) Wrens; WEBA-TV (PBS) Allendale; WFXG (FOX) Augusta; WIS (NBC) Columbia; WJBF (ABC) Augusta; WOLO-TV (ABC) Columbia; WRDW-TV (CBS, MNT) Augusta; allband FM.
Programming (via satellite): C-SPAN; C-SPAN 2; CW+; MyNetworkTV Inc.; QVC; The Weather Channel; TV Guide Network.
Fee: $25.00 installation; $20.64 monthly.
Expanded Basic Service 1
Subscribers: 2,027.
Programming (via satellite): A&E Networks; ABC Family Channel; AMC; Animal Planet; BET Networks; Bravo; Cartoon Network; CNBC; CNN; Comedy Central; Country Music TV; Discovery Channel; Disney Channel; E! Entertainment Television; ESPN; ESPN 2; ESPN Classic Sports; Food Network; Fox Movie Channel; Fox News Channel; Fox Sports South; FX; Golf Channel; Great American Country; GSN; Hallmark Channel; Headline News; HGTV; History Channel; INSP; Lifetime; MSNBC; MTV; National Geographic Channel; Nickelodeon; SoapNet; Speed; Spike TV; SportSouth; Syfy; TBS Superstation; The Learning Channel; Travel Channel; Trinity Broadcasting Network; truTV; Turner Classic Movies; Turner Network TV; TV Land; USA Network; VH1.
Fee: $29.96 monthly.
Digital Basic Service
Subscribers: N.A.
Programming (via satellite): 3 Angels Broadcasting Network; A&E HD; AmericanLife TV Network; Animal Planet HD; BBC America; Bio; Bloomberg Television; Boomerang; BYU Television; Chiller; Church Channel; cloo; CMT Pure Country; Cooking Channel; Daystar TV Network; Discovery Channel HD; Discovery Fit & Health; Discovery Home Channel; Discovery Kids Channel; Disney Channel HD; DIY Network; Encore (multiplexed); ESPN 2 HD; ESPN HD; ESPN U; ESPNews; Eternal Word TV Network; Fox Reality Channel; Fox Sports South; Fuse; G4; Golden Eagle Broadcasting; Gospel Music TV; Halogen Network; HD Theater; HDNet; HDNet Movies; History Channel International; ID Investigation Discovery; Independent Film Channel; ION Television; JCTV; Lifetime Movie Network; Lifetime Real Women; Military Channel; MTV Hits; MTV Jams; MTV2; Music Choice; NFL Network; NFL Network HD; Nick Jr.; NickToons TV; Outdoor Channel; Oxygen; RLTV; Science; Starz (multiplexed); Starz HDTV; Style Network; TBS in HD; TeenNick; TLC HD; Toon Disney; Turner Network TV HD; TVG Network; Versus; VH1 Classic; VH1 Soul; WE tv; Weatherscan.
Fee: $17.95 monthly.
Digital Pay Service 1
Pay Units: N.A.
Programming (via satellite): Cinemax (multiplexed); Cinemax HD; Flix; HBO (multiplexed); HBO HD; Showtime (multiplexed); Showtime HD; The Movie Channel (multiplexed).
Fee: $14.95 monthly (HBO, Cinemax or Showtime/TMC/Flix).
Video-On-Demand: Planned
Pay-Per-View
iN DEMAND (delivered digitally); Playboy TV (delivered digitally); Fresh (delivered digitally); Spice: Xcess (delivered digitally); Shorteez (delivered digitally); Club Jenna (delivered digitally).
Internet Service
Operational: Yes.
Broadband Service: Atlantic Broadband High-Speed Internet.
Fee: $21.95-$55.95 monthly.
Telephone Service
Digital: Operational
Fee: $49.95 monthly
Miles of Plant: 338.0 (coaxial); None (fiber optic). Additional miles planned: 12.0 (coaxial).
Vice President & General Manager: Sam McGill. Technical Supervisor: Jim Walker.
Ownership: Atlantic Broadband (MSO).

BEAUFORT—Hargray, PO Box 5986, Hilton Head, SC 29938. Phone: 843-686-5000. Fax: 843-842-8559. Web Site: http://www.hargray.com. Also serves Beaufort County, Lady's Island, Parris Island & Port Royal. ICA: SC0020. **Note:** This system is an overbuild.
TV Market Ranking: Below 100 (BEAUFORT, Beaufort County, Lady's Island, Parris Island, Port Royal). Franchise award date: N.A. Franchise expiration date: N.A. Began: June 1, 1979.
Channel capacity: N.A. Channels available but not in use: N.A.
Basic Service
Subscribers: 10,452.
Programming (received off-air): WCBD-TV (CW, NBC) Charleston; WCIV (ABC) Charleston; WGSA (CW) Baxley; WJCL (ABC) Savannah; WJWJ-TV (PBS) Beaufort; WSAV-TV (MNT, NBC) Savannah; WTGS (FOX) Hardeeville; WTOC-TV (CBS) Savannah; WVAN-TV (PBS) Savannah.
Programming (via satellite): A&E Networks; ABC Family Channel; AMC; Animal Planet; BET Networks; Bravo; Cartoon Network; CNBC; CNN; Comedy Central; Country Music TV; C-SPAN; Discovery Channel; Discovery Fit & Health; Disney Channel; E! Entertainment Television; ESPN; ESPN 2; ESPN Classic Sports; Eternal Word TV Network; Food Network; Fox News Channel; Fox Sports South; FX; Golf Channel; Headline News; HGTV; History Channel; Lifetime; MSNBC; MTV; National Geographic Channel; Nickelodeon; Oxygen; QVC; Speed; Spike TV; SportSouth; Syfy; TBS Superstation; The Learning Channel; The Weather Channel; Toon Disney; Travel Channel; Trinity Broadcasting Network; truTV; Turner Classic Movies; Turner Network TV; TV Guide Network; TV Land; Univision Studios; USA Network; Versus; VH1; WE tv; WGN America.
Fee: $53.00 installation; $47.99 monthly; $2.95 converter.
Digital Basic Service
Subscribers: N.A.
Programming (via satellite): BBC America; Bio; Boomerang; Canales N; DIY Network; ESPN Classic Sports; ESPNews; Fox College Sports Atlantic; Fox College Sports Central; Fox College Sports Pacific; Fox Soccer; Fuel TV; G4; GAS; Great American Country; GSN; Hallmark Channel; HD Theater; History Channel International; Independent Film Channel; ION Television; Lifetime Movie Network; MTV Networks Digital Suite; Music Choice; MyNetworkTV Inc.; NFL Network; Nick Jr.; Nick Too; Outdoor Channel; Tennis Channel.
Digital Pay Service 1
Pay Units: 1,445.
Programming (via satellite): Cinemax (multiplexed).
Fee: $20.00 installation; $11.95 monthly.

Digital Pay Service 2
Pay Units: 2,669.
Programming (via satellite): HBO (multiplexed).
Fee: $20.00 installation; $11.95 monthly.
Digital Pay Service 3
Pay Units: 2,042.
Programming (via satellite): Flix; Showtime (multiplexed); Sundance Channel; The Movie Channel (multiplexed).
Fee: $20.00 installation; $11.95 monthly.
Digital Pay Service 4
Pay Units: N.A.
Programming (via satellite): Encore (multiplexed); Starz (multiplexed).
Video-On-Demand: Yes
Pay-Per-View
iN DEMAND (delivered digitally).
Internet Service
Operational: Yes.
Fee: $39.95 monthly.
Telephone Service
Digital: Operational
Miles of plant (coax & fiber combined) included in Bluffton
Operations Manager: Mark Reinhardt. Marketing Director: Karen Ehrhardt. Media Relations Manager: Tray Hunter.
Ownership: Hargray Communications Group Inc. (MSO).

BEAUFORT USMC AIR STATION—Comcast Cable, 4400 Belle Oaks Dr, North Charleston, SC 29405. Phone: 843-747-1403. Fax: 843-266-3272. Web Site: http://www.comcast.com. ICA: SC0168.
TV Market Ranking: Below 100 (BEAUFORT USMC AIR STATION).
Channel capacity: N.A. Channels available but not in use: N.A.
Basic Service
Subscribers: 600.
Programming (received off-air): WCIV (ABC) Charleston; WCSC-TV (CBS) Charleston; WJCL (ABC) Savannah; WJWJ-TV (PBS) Beaufort; WSAV-TV (MNT, NBC) Savannah; WTGS (FOX) Hardeeville; WTOC-TV (CBS) Savannah.
Programming (via satellite): CW+; QVC; TBS Superstation.
Fee: $61.25 installation; $6.90 monthly.
Expanded Basic Service 1
Subscribers: N.A.
Programming (via satellite): A&E Networks; ABC Family Channel; AMC; Animal Planet; BET Networks; Bravo; Cartoon Network; CNBC; CNN; Comcast/Charter Sports Southeast (CSS); Comedy Central; Country Music TV; C-SPAN; C-SPAN 2; Discovery Channel; Disney Channel; E! Entertainment Television; ESPN; ESPN 2; Food Network; Fox News Channel; Fox Sports South; FX; Golf Channel; Great American Country; GSN; Headline News; HGTV; History Channel; Lifetime; MSNBC; MTV; Nickelodeon; Speed; Spike TV; Style Network; Syfy; The Learning Channel; The Weather Channel; truTV; Turner Network TV; TV Land; USA Network; Versus; VH1; WGN America.
Fee: $21.95 monthly.
Digital Basic Service
Subscribers: N.A.
Programming (via satellite): Encore (multiplexed); Flix; Music Choice; Sundance Channel.
Fee: $9.95 monthly.
Digital Pay Service 1
Pay Units: N.A.
Programming (via satellite): Cinemax (multiplexed); HBO (multiplexed); Showtime (multiplexed); The Movie Channel (multiplexed).
Fee: $13.95 monthly (each).
Video-On-Demand: No
Pay-Per-View
iN DEMAND (delivered digitally); Playboy TV (delivered digitally); Fresh (delivered digitally); Shorteez (delivered digitally).
Internet Service
Operational: Yes.
Broadband Service: Comcast High Speed Internet.
Fee: $42.95 monthly.
Telephone Service
None
General Manager: Bill Watson. Technical Operations Director: Anthony Douglas. Chief Technician: Bob Bradshaw. Marketing Director: Sean O'Connell. Marketing Manager: Audrey Jones.
Ownership: Comcast Cable Communications Inc. (MSO).

BELTON—Charter Communications. Now served by GREENVILLE/SPARTANBURG, SC [SC0003]. ICA: SC0028.

BENNETTSVILLE—MetroCast Communications, 404C Cheraw St, PO Box 1073, Bennettsville, SC 29512-1073. Phone: 843-479-4063. Fax: 843-479-7115. Web Site: http://www.metrocastcommunications.com. Also serves Clio, Marlboro County, McColl & Tatum. ICA: SC0037.
TV Market Ranking: Below 100 (BENNETTSVILLE, Clio, Marlboro County (portions), Tatum); Outside TV Markets (Marlboro County (portions), McColl). Franchise award date: September 1, 1990. Franchise expiration date: N.A. Began: May 15, 1991.
Channel capacity: N.A. Channels available but not in use: N.A.
Basic Service
Subscribers: 3,825.
Programming (received off-air): WBTW (CBS, MNT) Florence; WECT (NBC) Wilmington; WFXB (FOX) Myrtle Beach; WIS (NBC) Columbia; WJPM-TV (PBS) Florence; WPDE-TV (ABC) Florence; WSOC-TV (ABC) Charlotte; WWMB (CW) Florence.
Programming (via satellite): A&E Networks; ABC Family Channel; Animal Planet; BET Networks; Cartoon Network; CNBC; CNN; Comedy Network; Country Music TV; C-SPAN; CW+; Discovery Channel; Disney Channel; E! Entertainment Television; ESPN; ESPN 2; Food Network; Fox News Channel; Fox Sports South; FX; Gospel Music TV; Great American Country; Hallmark Channel; Headline News; HGTV; History Channel; INSP; Lifetime; MTV; National Geographic Channel; Nickelodeon; Outdoor Channel; QVC; Speed; Spike TV; SportSouth; Syfy; TBS Superstation; The Learning Channel; The Weather Channel; Travel Channel; Trinity Broadcasting Network; truTV; Turner Classic Movies; Turner Network TV; TV Land; USA Network; VH1.
Fee: $55.00 installation; $27.99 monthly; $47.99 converter.
Digital Basic Service
Subscribers: 225.
Programming (via satellite): BBC America; Bloomberg Television; Bravo; CMT Pure Country; Discovery Fit & Health; Discovery Health Channel; Discovery Kids Channel; DMX Music; ESPNews; Fox Soccer; G4; Golf Channel; ID Investigation Discovery; Independent Film Channel; Lifetime Movie Network; Military Channel; MTV2; Nick Jr.; NickToons TV; Planet Green; Science; VH1 Classic; WE tv.
Fee: $5.00 monthly.
Digital Pay Service 1
Pay Units: N.A.
Programming (via satellite): Cinemax (multiplexed); Encore (multiplexed); Flix; HBO (multiplexed); Showtime (multiplexed); Starz (multiplexed); The Movie Channel (multiplexed).
Video-On-Demand: No
Pay-Per-View
iN DEMAND (delivered digitally); Playboy TV (delivered digitally); Fresh (delivered digitally).
Internet Service
Operational: Yes.
Subscribers: 650.
Broadband Service: MetroCast Internet.
Fee: $42.99 monthly.
Telephone Service
None
Miles of Plant: 138.0 (coaxial); 25.0 (fiber optic).
General Manager: Andy Hanson. Chief Technician: Leroy Hendricks.
Ownership: Harron Communications LP (MSO).

BETHUNE—Formerly served by Pine Tree Cablevision. No longer in operation. ICA: SC0110.

BISHOPVILLE—Time Warner. Now served by COLUMBIA, SC [SC0002]. ICA: SC0111.

BLUFFTON—Hargray, PO Box 5986, Hilton Head, SC 29938. Phone: 843-686-5000. Fax: 843-842-8559. Web Site: http://www.hargray.com. Also serves Beaufort County (southern portion) & Okatie. ICA: SC0042.
TV Market Ranking: Below 100 (Beaufort County (southern portion), BLUFFTON, Okatie). Franchise award date: March 1, 1984. Franchise expiration date: N.A. Began: August 1, 1984.
Channel capacity: 36 (operating 2-way). Channels available but not in use: N.A.
Basic Service
Subscribers: N.A.
Programming (received off-air): WCSC-TV (CBS) Charleston; WJCL (ABC) Savannah; WJWJ-TV (PBS) Beaufort; WSAV-TV (MNT, NBC) Savannah; WTOC-TV (CBS) Savannah.
Programming (via satellite): A&E Networks; ABC Family Channel; AMC; Animal Planet; BET Networks; Bio; Bravo; Cartoon Network; CNBC; CNN; Comedy Central; Country Music TV; C-SPAN; Discovery Channel; Discovery Fit & Health; Disney Channel; E! Entertainment Television; ESPN; ESPN 2; Eternal Word TV Network; Food Network; Fox Movie Channel; Fox News Channel; Fox Sports South; FX; Golf Channel; Headline News; HGTV; History Channel; Lifetime; MSNBC; MTV; National Geographic Channel; Nickelodeon; Oxygen; QVC; Speed; Spike TV; SportSouth; Sundance Channel; Syfy; TBS Superstation; The Learning Channel; The Weather Channel; Toon Disney; Travel Channel; Trinity Broadcasting Network; truTV; Turner Classic Movies; Turner Network TV; TV Guide Network; TV Land; Univision Studios; USA Network; Versus; VH1; WE tv; WGN America.
Fee: $25.00 installation; $47.99 monthly.
Digital Basic Service
Subscribers: N.A.
Programming (via satellite): BBC America; Boomerang; Canales N; Discovery Digital Networks; DIY Network; DMX Music; ESPN Classic Sports; ESPNews; Fox Sports World; Fuel TV; G4; GAS; Great American Country; GSN; Hallmark Channel; History Channel International; Independent Film Channel; ION Television; Lifetime Movie Network; MTV Networks Digital Suite; Nick Jr.; NickToons TV; Outdoor Channel; Tennis Channel.
Fee: $47.99 monthly.
Digital Pay Service 1
Pay Units: N.A.
Programming (via satellite): Cinemax (multiplexed); Encore (multiplexed); Flix; HBO (multiplexed); Showtime (multiplexed); Starz (multiplexed); The Movie Channel (multiplexed).
Video-On-Demand: Yes
Pay-Per-View
iN DEMAND (delivered digitally).
Internet Service
Operational: No, DSL.
Telephone Service
None
Miles of Plant: 1,000.0 (coaxial); None (fiber optic). Miles of plant (coax & fiber combined) includes Beaufort, Estill, Hardeeville, Ridgeland, & Pooler
Operations Manager: Mark Reinhardt. Marketing Director: Karen Ehrhardt. Media Relations Manager: Tray Hunter.
Ownership: Hargray Communications Group Inc. (MSO).

BOWMAN—Almega Cable, 4022 W Airport Freeway, Ste 551, Bedford, TX 76021. Phones: 817-685-9588; 877-725-6342. Fax: 817-685-6488. Web Site: http://almegacable.com. Also serves Branchville & Orangeburg County. ICA: SC0112.
TV Market Ranking: Below 100 (Orangeburg County (portions)); Outside TV Markets (BOWMAN, Branchville, Orangeburg County (portions)). Franchise award date: April 1, 1982. Franchise expiration date: N.A. Began: January 1, 1985.
Channel capacity: 65 (not 2-way capable). Channels available but not in use: N.A.
Basic Service
Subscribers: 394.
Programming (received off-air): WACH (FOX) Columbia; WCBD-TV (CW, NBC) Charleston; WCIV (ABC) Charleston; WIS (NBC) Columbia; WLTX (CBS) Columbia; WOLO-TV (ABC) Columbia; WRJA-TV (PBS) Sumter.
Programming (via satellite): ABC Family Channel; BET Networks; CNBC; CNN; Country Music TV; Discovery Channel; Disney Channel; ESPN; Fox News Channel; Fox Sports Net; Headline News; Lifetime; Nickelodeon; QVC; Spike TV; Syfy; TBS Superstation; The Movie Channel; The Weather Channel; Trinity Broadcasting Network; Turner Classic Movies; Turner Network TV; TV Land; USA Network; WGN America.
Fee: $29.95 installation; $27.95 monthly.
Pay Service 1
Pay Units: 62.
Programming (via satellite): HBO; Showtime; The Movie Channel.
Fee: $10.95 monthly.
Video-On-Demand: No
Internet Service
Operational: Yes.
Fee: $29.95 monthly.
Telephone Service
None
Miles of Plant: 65.0 (coaxial); None (fiber optic).
General Manager: Thomas Kurien.
Ownership: Almega Cable (MSO).

BRIARCLIFF ACRES—Cablevision Industries Inc. Now served by MYRTLE BEACH, SC [SC0007]. ICA: SC0027.

BRISSEY ROCK—Formerly served by KLiP Interactive. No longer in operation. ICA: SC0165.

BROWNS FERRY—Time Warner Cable. Now served by MYRTLE BEACH, SC [SC0007]. ICA: SC0089.

CALHOUN FALLS—Comcast Cable, 105 River Shoals Pkwy, Augusta, GA 30909. Phone: 706-738-0091. Fax: 706-738-1871. Web Site: http://www.comcast.com. Also serves Abbeville County (portions). ICA: SC0075.

TV Market Ranking: 46 (Abbeville County (portions), CALHOUN FALLS). Franchise award date: February 8, 1982. Franchise expiration date: N.A. Began: September 1, 1982.

Channel capacity: N.A. Channels available but not in use: N.A.

Basic Service

Subscribers: 475.

Programming (received off-air): WHNS (FOX) Greenville; WLOS (ABC) Asheville; WMYA-TV (MNT) Anderson; WNTV (PBS) Greenville; WRDW-TV (CBS, MNT) Augusta; WSPA-TV (CBS) Spartanburg; WYCW (CW) Asheville; WYFF (NBC) Greenville.

Programming (via satellite): A&E Networks; ABC Family Channel; AMC; Animal Planet; BET Networks; Cartoon Network; CNBC; CNN; Comcast/Charter Sports Southeast (CSS); Comedy Central; Country Music TV; Discovery Channel; Disney Channel; E! Entertainment Television; ESPN; ESPN 2; Food Network; Fox News Channel; Fox Sports Net; FX; G4; Golf Channel; Great American Country; GSN; Hallmark Channel; Headline News; HGTV; History Channel; INSP; Lifetime; MSNBC; MTV; Nickelodeon; QVC; Speed; Spike TV; SportSouth; Syfy; TBS Superstation; The Learning Channel; The Weather Channel; Trinity Broadcasting Network; truTV; Turner Network TV; TV Guide Network; TV Land; USA Network; Versus; VH1; WGN America.

Fee: $50.00 installation; $15.95 monthly.

Pay Service 1

Pay Units: 119.

Programming (via satellite): Cinemax; HBO.

Fee: $9.95 monthly (Cinemax), $10.95 monthly (HBO).

Video-On-Demand: No

Internet Service

Operational: No.

Telephone Service

None

Miles of Plant: 20.0 (coaxial); None (fiber optic).

Engineering Director: Harry Hess. Technical Operations Director: Butch Jernigan. Area Marketing Director: Joey Fortier.

Ownership: Comcast Cable Communications Inc. (MSO).

CAMDEN—TruVista Communications, 112 York St, PO Box 160, Chester, SC 29706. Phone: 803-385-2191. Fax: 803-581-2226. Web Site: http://www.truvista.net. Also serves Cassatt, Kershaw County & Lugoff. ICA: SC0113.

TV Market Ranking: 100 (CAMDEN, Cassatt, Kershaw County (portions), Lugoff); Below 100 (Kershaw County (portions)); Outside TV Markets (Kershaw County (portions)). Franchise award date: N.A. Franchise expiration date: N.A. Began: December 15, 1978.

Channel capacity: N.A. Channels available but not in use: N.A.

Basic Service

Subscribers: N.A. Included in Chester

Programming (received off-air): WACH (FOX) Columbia; WIS (NBC) Columbia; WKTC (IND, MNT, TMO) Sumter; WLTX (CBS) Columbia; WOLO-TV (ABC) Columbia; WRJA-TV (PBS) Sumter.

Programming (via satellite): INSP; QVC; Trinity Broadcasting Network; TV Guide Network; WGN America.

Fee: $35.00 installation; $48.99 monthly; $1.45 converter.

Expanded Basic Service 1

Subscribers: 4,830.

Programming (via satellite): A&E Networks; ABC Family Channel; AMC; Animal Planet; BET Networks; Bravo; Cartoon Network; CNBC; CNN; Comcast/Charter Sports Southeast (CSS); Comedy Central; Country Music TV; C-SPAN; Discovery Channel; Disney Channel; DIY Network; E! Entertainment Television; ESPN; ESPN 2; ESPN Classic Sports; Food Network; Fox News Channel; Fox Sports South; FX; G4; GMC; Golf Channel; GSN; Hallmark Channel; Headline News; HGTV; History Channel; Lifetime; MTV; National Geographic Channel; Nickelodeon; Outdoor Channel; Oxygen; ShopNBC; SoapNet; Speed; Spike TV; SportSouth; Style Network; Syfy; TBS Superstation; The Learning Channel; The Weather Channel; Toon Disney; Travel Channel; truTV; Turner Classic Movies; Turner Network TV; TV Land; USA Network; VH1; WE tv; WGN America.

Fee: $15.00 installation; $31.30 monthly.

Digital Basic Service

Subscribers: N.A.

Programming (via satellite): A&E HD; BBC America; Bio; Bloomberg Television; Boomerang; CBS Sports Network; Church Channel; cloo; CMT Pure Country; CNN en Espanol; CNN International; Cooking Channel; Discovery Channel HD; Discovery en Espanol; Discovery Health Channel; Discovery Kids Channel; ESPN 2 HD; ESPN HD; ESPN U; ESPNews; Fox Deportes; Fox Movie Channel; FSN Digital Atlantic; FSN Digital Central; FSN Digital Pacific; Fuel TV; Fuse; Hallmark Movie Channel; HD Theater; HDNet; HDNet Movies; History Channel International; ID Investigation Discovery; Independent Film Channel; INSP; ION Television; Lifetime Movie Network; Lifetime Movie Network HD; Military Channel; MSNBC; MTV Hits; MTV Jams; MTV2; Music Choice; Nick Jr.; Nick Too; NickToons TV; Ovation; PBS HD; Science; Speed HD; Sundance Channel; Syfy HD; TBS in HD; TeenNick; TLC HD; Tr3s; Turner Network TV HD; TV Guide Interactive Inc.; Universal HD; USA Network HD; Versus; VH1 Classic; VH1 Soul.

Digital Pay Service 1

Pay Units: 172.

Programming (via satellite): Cinemax (multiplexed); Cinemax HD; Flix; HBO (multiplexed); HBO HD; Showtime (multiplexed); Showtime HD; The Movie Channel (multiplexed).

Fee: $11.45 monthly (HBO, Cinemax or Showtime/TMC/Flix.

Digital Pay Service 2

Pay Units: N.A.

Programming (via satellite): Encore (multiplexed); Starz (multiplexed); Starz HDTV.

Video-On-Demand: No

Pay-Per-View

Addressable homes: 500.

iN DEMAND (delivered digitally); ESPN Gameplan (delivered digitally); Ten Xtsy (delivered digitally); Playboy TV (delivered digitally); Fresh (delivered digitally); Shorteez (delivered digitally); Club Jenna (delivered digitally); Spice: Xcess (delivered digitally); Playboy en Espanol (delivered digitally).

Internet Service

Operational: Yes.

Broadband Service: In-house.

Telephone Service

Digital: Operational

Miles of Plant: 200.0 (coaxial); None (fiber optic).

President & Chief Executive Officer: Brian Singleton. Vice President, Sales & Marketing: Allison Johnson. Marketing Manager: Bob Wilkinson. Video Services Manager: Tony Helms.

Ownership: TruVista Communications (MSO).

CAMERON—Formerly served by Almega Cable. No longer in operation. ICA: SC0159.

CHARLESTON—Comcast Cable, 4400 Belle Oaks Dr, North Charleston, SC 29405. Phone: 843-747-1403. Fax: 843-266-3272. Web Site: http://www.comcast.com. Also serves Awendaw, Berkeley County, Charleston County (northern portion), Folly Beach, Goose Creek, Hanahan, Hollywood, Isle of Palms, James Island, Johns Island, Kiawah Island, Mount Pleasant, North Charleston, Ravenel, Seabrook Island, Sullivan's Island, Summerville & Wadmalaw Island. ICA: SC0001.

TV Market Ranking: Below 100 (Awendaw, Berkeley County (portions), CHARLESTON, Charleston County (northern portion), Folly Beach, Goose Creek, Hanahan, Hollywood, Isle of Palms, James Island, Johns Island, Kiawah Island, Mount Pleasant, North Charleston, Ravenel, Seabrook Island, Sullivan's Island, Summerville, Wadmalaw Island); Outside TV Markets (Berkeley County (portions)). Franchise award date: N.A. Franchise expiration date: N.A. Began: January 1, 1973.

Channel capacity: N.A. Channels available but not in use: N.A.

Basic Service

Subscribers: 93,000.

Programming (received off-air): WCBD-TV (CW, NBC) Charleston; WCIV (ABC) Charleston; WCSC-TV (CBS) Charleston; WIS (NBC) Columbia; WITV (PBS) Charleston; WJWJ-TV (PBS) Beaufort; WMMP (MNT) Charleston; WTAT-TV (FOX) Charleston.

Fee: $45.75 installation; $5.80 monthly; $.74 converter.

Expanded Basic Service 1

Subscribers: 66,450.

Programming (via satellite): A&E Networks; ABC Family Channel; Animal Planet; BET Networks; Cartoon Network; CNN; Comcast SportsNet Philadelphia; Comedy Central; Country Music TV; C-SPAN; Disney Channel; E! Entertainment Television; ESPN; ESPN 2; Food Network; Fox News Channel; Fox Sports South; FX; Golf Channel; Hallmark Channel; Headline News; HGTV; History Channel; INSP; Lifetime; Nickelodeon; QVC; Speed; Style Network; Syfy; The Learning Channel; The Weather Channel; truTV; Turner Network TV; TV Land; Versus; VH1.

Fee: $42.90 monthly.

Expanded Basic Service 2

Subscribers: N.A.

Programming (via satellite): AMC; Discovery Channel; Spike TV; TBS Superstation.

Fee: $2.48 monthly.

Digital Basic Service

Subscribers: 28,000.

Programming (via satellite): BBC America; Cinemax; Discovery Home Channel; Discovery Kids Channel; Discovery Times Channel; Encore; ESPNews; Flix; GAS; HBO; Military Channel; MTV Networks Digital Suite; Music Choice; Nick Jr.; Nick Too; Science Television; Showtime; SoapNet; The Movie Channel; Toon Disney.

Fee: $14.95 monthly.

Video-On-Demand: Yes

Pay-Per-View

Hot Choice; iN DEMAND; Shorteez; Playboy TV; Pleasure; special events; Fresh.

Internet Service

Operational: Yes.

Subscribers: 35,000.

Broadband Service: Comcast High Speed Internet.

Fee: $42.95 monthly; $7.00 modem lease; $199.00 modem purchase.

Telephone Service

Digital: Operational

Miles of Plant: 1,583.0 (coaxial); None (fiber optic). Additional miles planned: 28.0 (coaxial).

General Manager: Bill Watson. Technical Operations Director: Anthony Douglas. Chief Technician: Bob Bradshaw. Marketing Director: Sean O'Connell. Marketing Assistant: Audrey Jones.

Ownership: Comcast Cable Communications Inc. (MSO).

CHARLESTON—Knology, 4506 Dorchester Rd, North Charleston, SC 29405. Phones: 706-645-8553 (Corporate office); 843-225-1000 (Customer service). Fax: 845-740-1919. Web Site: http://www.knology.com. Also serves Ladson, Mount Pleasant, North Charleston & Summerville. ICA: SC0158. **Note:** This system is an overbuild.

TV Market Ranking: Below 100 (CHARLESTON, Ladson, Mount Pleasant, North Charleston, Summerville). Franchise award date: April 28, 1998. Franchise expiration date: April 28, 2013. Began: January 1, 1991.

Channel capacity: N.A. Channels available but not in use: N.A.

Basic Service

Subscribers: 4,935.

Programming (received off-air): WAZS-LP North Charleston; WCBD-TV (CW, NBC) Charleston; WCIV (ABC) Charleston; WCSC-TV (CBS) Charleston; WITV (PBS) Charleston; WJNI-LP North Charleston; WLCN-CD Charleston; WMMP (MNT) Charleston; WTAT-TV (FOX) Charleston.

Programming (via satellite): A&E Networks; ABC Family Channel; AMC; Animal Planet; BET Networks; Bloomberg Television; Bravo; Cartoon Network; CNBC; CNN; Comedy Central; Country Music TV; C-SPAN; C-SPAN 2; CW+; Discovery Channel; Discovery Health Channel; Disney Channel; E! Entertainment Television; ESPN; ESPN 2; Food Network; Fox News Channel; Fox Sports South; FX; G4; Golf Channel; Great American Country; GSN; Hallmark Channel; Headline News; HGTV; History Channel; INSP; Lifetime; Lifetime Movie Network; MSNBC; MTV; MTV2; Nick At Nite; Nickelodeon; Outdoor Channel; Oxygen; QVC; ShopNBC; Speed; Spike TV; SportSouth; Syfy; TBS Superstation;

The Learning Channel; The Weather Channel; Toon Disney; Travel Channel; Trinity Broadcasting Network; truTV; Turner Classic Movies; Turner Network TV; TV Guide Network; TV Land; Univision Studios; USA Network; VH1; WE tv; WGN America.
Fee: $50.60 monthly.

Digital Basic Service
Subscribers: N.A. Included in Valley AL
Programming (via satellite): BBC America; Boomerang; CBS Sports Network; Church Channel; CMT Pure Country; C-SPAN 3; Discovery Fit & Health; Discovery Health Channel; Discovery Kids Channel; DIY Network; ESPN 2 HD; ESPN HD; ESPN U; ESPNews; Eternal Word TV Network; Fox College Sports Atlantic; Fox College Sports Central; Fox College Sports Pacific; Fox Soccer; Fuel TV; GMC; Hallmark Movie Channel; HD Theater; HDNet; HD-Net Movies; ID Investigation Discovery; Independent Film Channel; JCTV; Jewelry Television; Lifetime Real Women; Military Channel; MTV Hits; MTV Jams; Music Choice; NFL Network; Nick Jr.; Nick Too; NickToons TV; Ovation; Pentagon Channel; Planet Green; Science; SoapNet; TeenNick; Tennis Channel; Tr3s; Turner Network TV HD; Universal HD; Versus; VH1 Classic; VH1 Soul; VHUNO.

Pay Service 1
Pay Units: N.A.
Programming (via satellite): HBO; Showtime.

Digital Pay Service 1
Pay Units: N.A.
Programming (via satellite): Cinemax (multiplexed); Encore (multiplexed); Flix; HBO (multiplexed); HBO HD; Showtime (multiplexed); Starz (multiplexed); Starz HDTV; The Movie Channel (multiplexed).

Video-On-Demand: Yes

Pay-Per-View
iN DEMAND (delivered digitally); ESPN Extra (delivered digitally); Spice: Xcess (delivered digitally); Club Jenna (delivered digitally); Playboy TV (delivered digitally); Fresh (delivered digitally); Shorteez (delivered digitally); Hot Choice (delivered digitally); ESPN Now (delivered digitally).

Internet Service
Operational: Yes.
Broadband Service: Knology.Net.
Fee: $29.95 installation; $59.95 monthly; $9.00 modem lease; $249.00 modem purchase.

Telephone Service
Analog: Not Operational
Digital: Operational

General Manager: Lee Endicott. Technical Operations Manager: Richard Henslee. Marketing Manager: Todd Trevillian.
Ownership: Knology Inc. (MSO).

CHERAW—Time Warner Cable. Now served by MYRTLE BEACH, SC [SC0007]. ICA: SC0038.

CHESTER—TruVista Communications, 112 York St, PO Box 160, Chester, SC 29706. Phone: 803-385-2191. Fax: 803-581-2226. Web Site: http://www.truvista.net. Also serves Chester County (unincorporated areas). ICA: SC0034.

TV Market Ranking: Below 100 (CHESTER, Chester County (unincorporated areas)). Franchise award date: December 4, 1978. Franchise expiration date: N.A. Began: October 1, 1978.

Channel capacity: N.A. Channels available but not in use: N.A.

Basic Service
Subscribers: 10,000 Includes Camden & Winnsboro.
Programming (received off-air): WAXN-TV (IND) Kannapolis; WBTV (CBS) Charlotte; WCCB (FOX) Charlotte; WCNC-TV (NBC) Charlotte; WIS (NBC) Columbia; WJZY (CW) Belmont; WMYT-TV (MNT) Rock Hill; WNSC-TV (PBS) Rock Hill; WSOC-TV (ABC) Charlotte; WSPA-TV (CBS) Spartanburg.
Programming (via satellite): QVC; Trinity Broadcasting Network; TV Guide Network.
Fee: $47.07 installation; $46.99 monthly; $3.50 converter.

Expanded Basic Service 1
Subscribers: N.A.
Programming (via satellite): A&E Networks; ABC Family Channel; AMC; Animal Planet; BET Networks; Bravo; Cartoon Network; CNBC; CNN; Comcast/Charter Sports Southeast (CSS); Comedy Central; Country Music TV; C-SPAN; C-SPAN 2; Discovery Channel; Disney Channel; DIY Network; E! Entertainment Television; ESPN; ESPN 2; ESPN Classic Sports; Food Network; Fox News Channel; Fox Sports South; FX; G4; GMC; Golf Channel; GSN; Hallmark Channel; Headline News; HGTV; History Channel; Lifetime; MTV; National Geographic Channel; Nickelodeon; Outdoor Channel; Oxygen; ShopNBC; SoapNet; Speed; Spike TV; SportSouth; Style Network; Syfy; TBS Superstation; The Learning Channel; The Weather Channel; Toon Disney; Travel Channel; truTV; Turner Classic Movies; Turner Network TV; TV Land; USA Network; VH1; WE tv; WGN America.
Fee: $9.00 monthly.

Digital Basic Service
Subscribers: N.A.
Programming (via satellite): A&E HD; BBC America; Bio; Bloomberg Television; Boomerang; CBS Sports Network; Church Channel; cloo; CMT Pure Country; CNN en Espanol; CNN International; Discovery Channel HD; Discovery en Espanol; Discovery Health Channel; Discovery Kids Channel; ESPN 2 HD; ESPN HD; ESPN U; ESPNews; Fox Deportes; Fox Movie Channel; FSN Digital Atlantic; FSN Digital Central; FSN Digital Pacific; Fuel TV; Fuse; Hallmark Movie Channel; HD Theater; HDNet; HDNet Movies; History Channel International; ID Investigation Discovery; Independent Film Channel; INSP; ION Television; Lifetime Movie Network; Lifetime Movie Network HD; Military Channel; MSNBC; MTV Hits; MTV Jams; MTV2; Music Choice; Nick Jr.; Nick Too; NickToons TV; Ovation; PBS HD; Planet Green; Science; Speed HD; Sundance Channel; Syfy HD; TBS in HD; TeenNick; TLC HD; Tr3s; Turner Network TV HD; Universal HD; USA Network HD; Versus; VH1 Classic; VH1 Soul.

Digital Pay Service 1
Pay Units: 264.
Programming (via satellite): Cinemax (multiplexed); Cinemax HD.
Fee: $15.69 installation; $9.95 monthly.

Digital Pay Service 2
Pay Units: 389.
Programming (via satellite): HBO (multiplexed); HBO HD.
Fee: $15.69 installation; $11.95 monthly.

Digital Pay Service 3
Pay Units: 384.
Programming (via satellite): Flix; Showtime (multiplexed); Showtime HD; The Movie Channel (multiplexed).
Fee: $15.69 installation; $11.95 monthly.

Digital Pay Service 4
Pay Units: N.A.
Programming (via satellite): Encore (multiplexed); Starz (multiplexed); Starz HDTV.

Video-On-Demand: No

Pay-Per-View
Ten Xtsy (delivered digitally); Club Jenna (delivered digitally); iN DEMAND (delivered digitally); Spice: Xcess (delivered digitally); Playboy en Espanol (delivered digitally); Fresh (delivered digitally); Playboy TV (delivered digitally); Shorteez (delivered digitally).

Internet Service
Operational: Yes.
Broadband Service: In-house.

Telephone Service
Digital: Operational

Miles of Plant: 95.0 (coaxial); None (fiber optic).

President & Chief Executive Officer: Brian Singleton. Vice President, Sales & Marketing: Allison Johnson. Marketing Manager: Bob Wilkinson. Video Services Manager: Tony Helms.

Ownership: TruVista Communications (MSO).

CHESTERFIELD (town)—NewWave Communications, 122 N Maple St, PO Box 86, Pageland, SC 29728-0086. Phone: 843-672-5929. Fax: 843-672-5373. Web Site: http://www.newwavecom.com. Also serves Chesterfield County (portions) & Ruby. ICA: SC0087.

TV Market Ranking: Below 100 (Chesterfield County (portions)); Outside TV Markets (CHESTERFIELD (TOWN), Chesterfield County (portions), Ruby). Franchise award date: N.A. Franchise expiration date: N.A. Began: January 1, 1984.

Channel capacity: 37 (not 2-way capable). Channels available but not in use: N.A.

Basic Service
Subscribers: 276.
Programming (received off-air): WAXN-TV (IND) Kannapolis; WBTV (CBS) Charlotte; WBTW (CBS, MNT) Florence; WCCB (FOX) Charlotte; WCNC-TV (NBC) Charlotte; WIS (NBC) Columbia; WJPM-TV (PBS) Florence; WJZY (CW) Belmont; WMYT-TV (MNT) Rock Hill; WPDE-TV (ABC) Florence; WSOC-TV (ABC) Charlotte; WUNG-TV (PBS) Concord.
Programming (via satellite): QVC; WGN America.
Fee: $29.95 installation; $12.95 monthly.

Expanded Basic Service 1
Subscribers: 245.
Programming (via satellite): A&E Networks; ABC Family Channel; AMC; Animal Planet; BET Networks; Bravo; Cartoon Network; CNBC; CNN; Comedy Central; Country Music TV; C-SPAN; Discovery Channel; Disney Channel; E! Entertainment Television; ESPN; ESPN 2; ESPN Classic Sports; Food Network; Fox News Channel; FX; GSN; Hallmark Channel; Headline News; HGTV; History Channel; INSP; Lifetime; MTV; Nickelodeon; Outdoor Channel; SoapNet; Speed; Spike TV; Syfy; TBS Superstation; The Learning Channel; The Weather Channel; Turner Network TV; TV Land; USA Network; VH1.
Fee: $38.95 monthly.

Digital Basic Service
Subscribers: 21.
Programming (via satellite): BBC America; Bio; Black Family Channel; Bloomberg Television; cloo; Discovery Digital Networks; DMX Music; ESPNews; Fox Movie Channel; G4; GAS; Great American Country; Halogen Network; History Channel International; Independent Film Channel; Lifetime Movie Network; MTV Networks Digital Suite; Nick Jr.; NickToons TV; ShopNBC; Style Network; The Word Network; Toon Disney; Trinity Broadcasting Network; Turner Classic Movies.

Digital Pay Service 1
Pay Units: 60.
Programming (via satellite): Cinemax (multiplexed); Encore (multiplexed); Flix; HBO (multiplexed); Showtime (multiplexed); Starz (multiplexed); The Movie Channel (multiplexed).

Video-On-Demand: No

Pay-Per-View
Shorteez (delivered digitally); Fresh (delivered digitally); Playboy TV (delivered digitally); Hot Choice (delivered digitally); iN DEMAND (delivered digitally).

Internet Service
Operational: No.

Telephone Service
Analog: Not Operational
Digital: Planned

Miles of Plant: 36.0 (coaxial); None (fiber optic).

General Manager: Mark Bookout. Chief Technician: Bobby Thurman. Office Manager: Brenda Thurman.

Ownership: NewWave Communications LLC (MSO).

COLUMBIA—Time Warner Cable, 3347 Platt Springs Rd, West Columbia, SC 29170. Phone: 803-251-5300. Fax: 803-251-5345. Web Site: http://www.timewarnercable.com/carolinas. Also serves Arcadia Lakes, Batesburg, Bishopville, Blythewood, Calhoun County (portions), Cayce, Chapin, Clarendon County, Cordova (southwestern portion), Dalzell, Eastover, Elgin, Forest Acres, Fort Jackson, Harbison, Irmo, Lake Murray, Lee County, Leesville, Lexington, Lexington County, Little Mountain, Manning, Mayesville, Orangeburg, Orangeburg County (portions), Pelion, Pineridge, Pinewood, Ravenwood, Richland County, Saluda County (portions), Shaw AFB, South Congaree, Springdale, St. Matthews, Summerton, Sumter, Sumter County & West Columbia. ICA: SC0002.

TV Market Ranking: 100 (Arcadia Lakes, Blythewood, Calhoun County (portions), Cayce, Chapin, COLUMBIA, Dalzell, Eastover, Forest Acres, Fort Jackson, Harbison, Irmo, Lake Murray, Lexington, Lexington County (portions), Little Mountain, Orangeburg County (portions), Pelion, Pineridge, Pinewood, Ravenwood, Richland County, Saluda County (portions), Shaw AFB, South Congaree, Springdale, St. Matthews, Sumter, Sumter County (portions), West

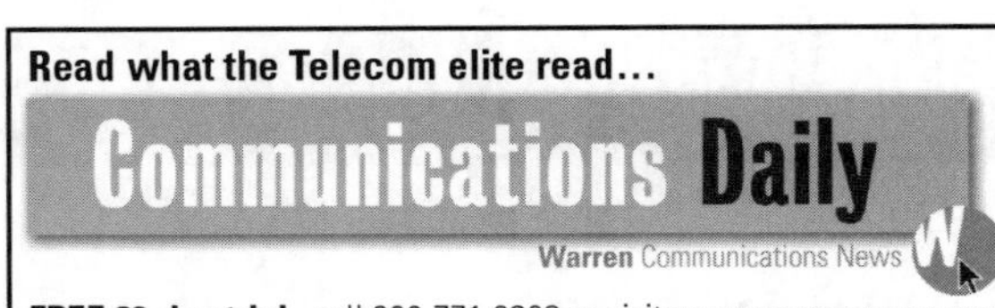
Read what the Telecom elite read...
Communications Daily
Warren Communications News
FREE 30-day trial–call 800-771-9202 or visit www.warren-news.com

Columbia); Below 100 (Bishopville, Clarendon County, Elgin, Lee County, Manning, Mayesville, Summerton, Calhoun County (portions), Orangeburg County (portions), Sumter County (portions)); Outside TV Markets (Batesburg, Cordova, Leesville, Orangeburg, Lexington County (portions), Saluda County (portions)). Franchise award date: November 2, 1977. Franchise expiration date: N.A. Began: December 1, 1977.

Channel capacity: N.A. Channels available but not in use: N.A.

Basic Service

Subscribers: 400,785 Includes McClellanville & Myrtle Beach.

Programming (received off-air): WACH (FOX) Columbia; WIS (NBC) Columbia; WKTC (IND, MNT, TMO) Sumter; WLTX (CBS) Columbia; WOLO-TV (ABC) Columbia; WRLK-TV (PBS) Columbia.

Programming (via satellite): C-SPAN; QVC; TV Guide Network; WGN America.

Fee: $51.00 installation; $8.15 monthly; $2.63 converter; $17.00 additional installation.

Expanded Basic Service 1

Subscribers: 380,000 Includes Myrtle Beach.

Programming (via satellite): A&E Networks; ABC Family Channel; AMC; AmericanLife TV Network; Animal Planet; BET Networks; Bravo; Cartoon Network; CNBC; CNN; Comedy Central; Country Music TV; C-SPAN 2; Discovery Channel; Discovery Fit & Health; Discovery Health Channel; Disney Channel; E! Entertainment Television; ESPN; ESPN 2; ESPN Classic Sports; Food Network; Fox News Channel; Fox Sports South; Golf Channel; Hallmark Channel; Headline News; HGTV; History Channel; INSP; ION Television; Lifetime; Lifetime Movie Network; MSNBC; MTV; National Geographic Channel; Nickelodeon; Oxygen; Spike TV; SportSouth; Style Network; Syfy; TBS Superstation; The Learning Channel; The Weather Channel; Travel Channel; truTV; Turner Classic Movies; Turner Network TV; TV Land; USA Network; Versus; VH1; WE tv.

Fee: $27.01 monthly.

Digital Basic Service

Subscribers: 183,800 Includes Myrtle Beach.

Programming (via satellite): America's Store; BBC America; Bio; Black Family Channel; Bloomberg Television; Boomerang; Canales N; Cooking Channel; C-SPAN 3; Discovery Digital Networks; DIY Network; ESPNews; FamilyNet; Fox Movie Channel; Fox Sports World; FSN Digital Atlantic; FSN Digital Central; FSN Digital Pacific; Fuel TV; Fuse; G4; GAS; Great American Country; GSN; History Channel International; Jewelry Television; Lifetime Real Women; MTV Networks Digital Suite; Music Choice; NBA TV; Nick Jr.; NickToons TV; Outdoor Channel; Ovation; SoapNet; Speed; Tennis Channel; Toon Disney; Trinity Broadcasting Network.

Fee: $4.95 monthly (movie, sports or Canales N), $5.95 monthly (variety).

Digital Pay Service 1

Pay Units: 79,000 Includes Myrtle Beach.

Programming (via satellite): Cinemax (multiplexed); Encore (multiplexed); Flix (multiplexed); HBO (multiplexed); Independent Film Channel; Showtime (multiplexed); Sundance Channel (multiplexed); The Movie Channel (multiplexed).

Fee: $10.95 monthly (each).

Video-On-Demand: Yes

Pay-Per-View

NBA League Pass (delivered digitally); NHL Center Ice (delivered digitally); MLB Extra Innings (delivered digitally); ESPN Full Court (delivered digitally); ESPN Gameplan (delivered digitally); NASCAR In Car (delivered digitally).

Internet Service

Operational: Yes.

Subscribers: 204,000.

Broadband Service: AOL for Broadband; EarthLink; Road Runner.

Fee: $49.95 monthly; $7.00 modem lease.

Telephone Service

Digital: Operational

Subscribers: 68,000.

Fee: $44.95 monthly

Miles of Plant: 10,770.0 (coaxial); 2,851.0 (fiber optic). Miles of plant include McClellanville & Myrtle Beach

President, Network Operations & Engineering: Mike Munley. Vice President & General Manager: Chris Whitaker. Vice President, Operations & Voice: Charlene Keyes. Vice President, Marketing: Dan Santelle. Vice President, Public Affairs: Dan E Jones. Technical Operations Director: David Sykes. Regional Vice President, Communications: Susan Leepson.

Ownership: Time Warner Cable (MSO).; Advance/Newhouse Partnership (MSO).

COTTAGEVILLE—Formerly served by Pine Tree Cablevision. No longer in operation. ICA: SC0114.

CROSS—Formerly served by Pine Tree Cablevision. No longer in operation. ICA: SC0115.

CROSS HILL—Formerly served by KLiP Interactive. No longer in operation. ICA: SC0040.

DANIEL ISLAND—Home Telecom. See North Charleston, SC [SC5008]. ICA: SC5004.

DAUFUSKIE ISLAND—Resorts Cable TV, 2190 S Hwy 27, Somerset, KY 42501. Phone: 606-679-3427. Fax: 606-678-4178. ICA: SC0116.

TV Market Ranking: Below 100 (DAUFUSKIE ISLAND). Franchise award date: N.A. Franchise expiration date: N.A. Began: September 1, 1989.

Channel capacity: 36 (not 2-way capable). Channels available but not in use: N.A.

Basic Service

Subscribers: 120.

Programming (received off-air): WJCL (ABC) Savannah; WSAV-TV (MNT, NBC) Savannah; WTGS (FOX) Hardeeville; WTOC-TV (CBS) Savannah; WVAN-TV (PBS) Savannah.

Programming (via satellite): A&E Networks; ABC Family Channel; AMC; Animal Planet; Bravo; CNBC; CNN; C-SPAN; Discovery Channel; Disney Channel; ESPN; ESPN 2; Fox News Channel; Golf Channel; Headline News; History Channel; Lifetime; Syfy; TBS Superstation; The Learning Channel; The Weather Channel; Travel Channel; Turner Network TV; USA Network; WE tv; WGN America.

Fee: $35.00 monthly.

Pay Service 1

Pay Units: 21.

Programming (via satellite): Showtime.

Fee: $10.00 monthly.

Pay Service 2

Pay Units: 50.

Programming (via satellite): HBO.

Fee: $12.00 monthly.

Video-On-Demand: No

Internet Service

Operational: No.

Telephone Service

None

Chief Technician: George Lawson. Office Manager: Beth Wright.

Ownership: Resorts Cable TV.

DEBORDIEU COLONY—Time Warner Cable. Now served by MYRTLE BEACH, SC [SC0007]. ICA: SC0047.

DILLON—Formerly served by Adelphia Communications. Now served by MYRTLE BEACH, SC [SC0007]. ICA: SC0036.

EHRHARDT—Formerly served by Almega Cable. No longer in operation. ICA: SC0160.

ELLOREE—Formerly served by Pine Tree Cablevision. No longer in operation. ICA: SC0099.

ESTILL—Hargray, PO Box 5986, Hilton Head, SC 29938. Phone: 843-686-5000. Fax: 843-842-8559. Web Site: http://www.hargray.com. ICA: SC0118.

TV Market Ranking: Below 100 (ESTILL). Franchise award date: N.A. Franchise expiration date: N.A. Began: August 1, 1984.

Channel capacity: N.A. Channels available but not in use: N.A.

Basic Service

Subscribers: N.A.

Programming (received off-air): WCSC-TV (CBS) Charleston; WJCL (ABC) Savannah; WJWJ-TV (PBS) Beaufort; WSAV-TV (MNT, NBC) Savannah; WTOC-TV (CBS) Savannah.

Programming (via satellite): A&E Networks; ABC Family Channel; AMC; BET Networks; CNBC; CNN; Comedy Central; Country Music TV; C-SPAN; Discovery Channel; Discovery Fit & Health; Disney Channel; E! Entertainment Television; ESPN; ESPN 2; Fox Movie Channel; Fox News Channel; Fox Sports South; FX; Headline News; HGTV; History Channel; Lifetime; MTV; Nickelodeon; Oxygen; QVC; Speed; Spike TV; Syfy; TBS Superstation; The Learning Channel; The Weather Channel; Toon Disney; Travel Channel; Trinity Broadcasting Network; truTV; Turner Classic Movies; Turner Network TV; TV Guide Network; TV Land; USA Network; VH1; WGN America.

Fee: $33.50 installation; $26.95 monthly.

Pay Service 1

Pay Units: N.A.

Programming (via satellite): Cinemax; Encore; Flix; HBO; Showtime; Sundance Channel; The Movie Channel.

Fee: $3.95 monthly (Encore), $12.95 monthly (HBO or Cinemax), $17.00 monthly (Showtime, TMC, Flix and Sundance).

Video-On-Demand: No

Internet Service

Operational: No, DSL.

Telephone Service

None

Miles of plant (coax & fiber combined) included in Bluffton

Operations Manager: Mark Reinhardt. Marketing Director: Karen Ehrhardt. Media Relations Manager: Tray Hunter.

Ownership: Hargray Communications Group Inc. (MSO).

FIVE POINTS—Northland Cable Television, 615 N Pine St, PO Box 833, Seneca, SC 29679-0833. Phone: 864-882-0002. Fax: 864-882-4490. E-mail: seneca@northlandcabletv.com. Web Site: http://www.northlandcabletv.com. Also serves Oconee County (portions), Walhalla & Westminster. ICA: SC0081.

TV Market Ranking: 46 (FIVE POINTS, Oconee County (portions), Walhalla, Westminster).

Channel capacity: 28 (not 2-way capable). Channels available but not in use: N.A.

Basic Service

Subscribers: 98.

Programming (received off-air): WGGS-TV (IND) Greenville; WHNS (FOX) Greenville; WLOS (ABC) Asheville; WMYA-TV (MNT) Anderson; WNTV (PBS) Greenville; WSPA-TV (CBS) Spartanburg; WUNF-TV (PBS) Asheville; WYFF (NBC) Greenville.

Programming (via satellite): A&E Networks; Animal Planet; BET Networks; Cartoon Network; CNBC; CNN; C-SPAN; Discovery Channel; ESPN; ESPN 2; Food Network; Fox Movie Channel; Fox News Channel; Fox Sports South; FX; Great American Country; Headline News; History Channel; Lifetime; MTV; Nickelodeon; QVC; ShopNBC; Spike TV; SportSouth; TBS Superstation; The Learning Channel; The Weather Channel; Trinity Broadcasting Network; Turner Network TV; USA Network; WGN America.

Fee: $55.00 installation; $29.95 monthly.

Digital Basic Service

Subscribers: N.A.

Programming (via satellite): BBC America; Bloomberg Television; Bravo; Discovery Fit & Health; DMX Music; ESPNews; Fox Soccer; G4; Golf Channel; GSN; Halogen Network; HGTV; Independent Film Channel; Lifetime Movie Network; National Geographic Channel; Outdoor Channel; ShopNBC; Speed; Syfy; Trinity Broadcasting Network; Turner Classic Movies; Versus; WE tv.

Fee: $13.00 monthly.

Pay Service 1

Pay Units: 68.

Programming (via satellite): Cinemax; HBO.

Fee: $10.50 monthly (Cinemax), $12.50 monthly (HBO).

Digital Pay Service 1

Pay Units: N.A.

Programming (via satellite): Cinemax (multiplexed); Encore (multiplexed); Flix; HBO (multiplexed); Showtime (multiplexed); Starz (multiplexed); The Movie Channel (multiplexed).

Fee: $14.75 monthly (HBO, Cinemax, Starz/Encore or Showtime/TMC/Flix).

Pay-Per-View
iN DEMAND (delivered digitally); Hot Choice (delivered digitally); Playboy TV (delivered digitally); Fresh (delivered digitally).
Internet Service
Operational: Yes.
Telephone Service
None
Miles of Plant: 34.0 (coaxial); None (fiber optic).
Manager: Bill Staley. Marketing Manager: Melinda Harbin. Office Manager: Sharon Martin. Plant Manager: Travis Blakely.
Ownership: Northland Communications Corp. (MSO).

FLORENCE—Time Warner Cable. Now served by MYRTLE BEACH, SC [SC0007]. ICA: SC0005.

FOLLY BEACH—US Cable of Coastal Texas LP. Now served by CHARLESTON, SC [SC0001]. ICA: SC0052.

FORT MILL—Comporium Communications. Now served by ROCK HILL, SC [SC0138]. ICA: SC0120.

GAFFNEY—Charter Communications. Now served by GREENVILLE/SPARTANBURG, SC [SC0003]. ICA: SC0021.

GASTON—Formerly served by Pine Tree Cablevision. No longer in operation. ICA: SC0080.

GILBERT—Comporium Cable, 1660 Juniper Springs Rd, Gilbert, SC 29054. Phone: 803-894-3121. Fax: 803-892-2123. E-mail: cabletv@comporium.net. Web Site: http://www.pbtcomm.net. Also serves Aiken County (portions), Lake Murray, Lexington County (northwestern portion), Ridge Spring, Saluda County (eastern portion) & Summit. ICA: SC0148.
TV Market Ranking: 100 (Aiken County (portions), GILBERT, Lake Murray, Lexington County (northwestern portion), Saluda County (eastern portion), Summit); Below 100 (Ridge Spring, Aiken County (portions)). Franchise award date: N.A. Franchise expiration date: N.A. Began: November 29, 1991.
Channel capacity: N.A. Channels available but not in use: N.A.
Basic Service
Subscribers: 2,070.
Programming (received off-air): WACH (FOX) Columbia; WIS (NBC) Columbia; WKTC (IND, MNT, TMO) Sumter; WLTX (CBS) Columbia; WOLO-TV (ABC) Columbia; WRLK-TV (PBS) Columbia.
Programming (via satellite): TBS Superstation; TV Guide Network.
Fee: $25.00 installation; $11.45 monthly.
Expanded Basic Service 1
Subscribers: 1,000.
Programming (via satellite): A&E Networks; ABC Family Channel; Cartoon Network; CNN; Country Music TV; Discovery Channel; ESPN; ESPN 2; Fox Sports South; Hallmark Channel; Lifetime; Nickelodeon; Spike TV; The Learning Channel; The Weather Channel; Turner Network TV; Turner South.
Digital Basic Service
Subscribers: 1,200.
Programming (via satellite): AMC; Animal Planet; BBC America; BET Networks; Bio; Bloomberg Television; CMT Pure Country; CNBC; CNN; Comedy Central; C-SPAN; C-SPAN 2; Discovery Digital Networks; Disney Channel; DMX Music; ESPN 2 HD; ESPN Classic Sports; ESPN HD; ESPN U; ESPNews; Food Network; Fox News Channel; Fox Sports Net; FX; G4; GSN; Halogen Network; Headline News; HGTV; History Channel; ION Television; MSNBC; MTV Networks Digital Suite; National Geographic Channel; National Geographic Channel HD Network; NickToons TV; QVC; RFD-TV; SoapNet; Syfy; Travel Channel; truTV; Turner Classic Movies; TV Land; USA Network; Versus.
Fee: $26.50 monthly.
Digital Expanded Basic Service
Subscribers: N.A.
Programming (via satellite): Bravo; cloo; Cooking Channel; DIY Network; Fox Movie Channel; Fox Soccer; Fuse; GAS; Golf Channel; History Channel International; Independent Film Channel; Lifetime Movie Network; Nick Jr.; Outdoor Channel; Oxygen; Speed; Style Network; Toon Disney; WE tv.
Fee: $5.00 monthly.
Digital Pay Service 1
Pay Units: 300.
Programming (via satellite): HBO (multiplexed).
Fee: $10.99 monthly.
Digital Pay Service 2
Pay Units: 300.
Programming (via satellite): Cinemax (multiplexed).
Fee: $10.99 monthly.
Digital Pay Service 3
Pay Units: N.A.
Programming (via satellite): Encore (multiplexed); Flix; Starz (multiplexed).
Fee: $9.95 monthly.
Digital Pay Service 4
Pay Units: 134.
Programming (via satellite): Showtime (multiplexed); The Movie Channel (multiplexed).
Fee: $10.99 monthly.
Video-On-Demand: No
Pay-Per-View
iN DEMAND (delivered digitally).
Internet Service
Operational: No, DSL & dial-up.
Telephone Service
None
Miles of Plant: 40.0 (coaxial); None (fiber optic).
Manager: Al Harman. Chief Technician: William Spruell. Repair Manager: Tom Fink.
Ownership: Comporium Communications.

GRAY COURT—Charter Communications. Now served by GREENVILLE/SPARTANBURG, SC [SC0003]. ICA: SC0013.

GREENVILLE COUNTY—Formerly served by KLiP Interactive. No longer in operation. ICA: SC0164.

GREENWOOD—Northland Cable Television, 235 N Creek Blvd, PO Box 8069, Greenwood, SC 29649-8069. Phones: 800-248-5421; 864-229-5421. Fax: 864-229-6609. Web Site: http://www.northlandcabletv.com. Also serves Abbeville County (unincorporated areas), Edgefield, Edgefield County (portions), Greenwood County, Hodges, Johnston, Laurens County (portions), Ninety-Six, Saluda, Saluda County (portions) & Ware Shoals. ICA: SC0014.
TV Market Ranking: 46 (Abbeville County (unincorporated areas), Greenwood County (portions), Hodges, Laurens County (portions), Ware Shoals); Below 100 (Edgefield, Edgefield County (portions), Johnston); Outside TV Markets (GREENWOOD, Ninety-Six, Saluda, Saluda County (portions), Greenwood County (portions), Laurens County (portions)). Franchise award date: N.A. Franchise expiration date: N.A. Began: March 1, 1968.
Channel capacity: 139 (operating 2-way). Channels available but not in use: N.A.
Basic Service
Subscribers: 14,900.
Programming (received off-air): WGGS-TV (IND) Greenville; WHNS (FOX) Greenville; WIS (NBC) Columbia; WLOS (ABC) Asheville; WMYA-TV (MNT) Anderson; WNEH (PBS) Greenwood; WSPA-TV (CBS) Spartanburg; WYCW (CW) Asheville; WYFF (NBC) Greenville; allband FM.
Programming (via satellite): A&E Networks; Animal Planet; BET Networks; Cartoon Network; CNBC; CNN; Comedy Central; C-SPAN; C-SPAN 2; Discovery Channel; Disney Channel; ESPN; ESPN 2; Food Network; Fox Movie Channel; Fox News Channel; Fox Sports South; FX; Golf Channel; Great American Country; Hallmark Channel; Headline News; HGTV; History Channel; INSP; Lifetime; MTV; National Geographic Channel; NFL Network; Nickelodeon; QVC; Spike TV; SportSouth; Syfy; TBS Superstation; The Learning Channel; The Weather Channel; truTV; Turner Classic Movies; Turner Network TV; TV Land; USA Network; VH1; WGN America.
Fee: $35.95 installation; $49.99 monthly; $1.03 converter.
Digital Basic Service
Subscribers: 2,300.
Programming (via satellite): BBC America; Bloomberg Television; Bravo; Cine Mexicano; CNN en Espanol; Discovery en Espanol; Discovery Fit & Health; Discovery Kids Channel; DMX Music; ESPN 2 HD; ESPN Deportes; ESPNews; Food Network HD; Fox Deportes; Fox Soccer; G4; HGTV HD; History Channel en Espanol; ID Investigation Discovery; Independent Film Channel; Military Channel; mun2 television; Planet Green; Science; Speed; Tr3s; Trinity Broadcasting Network; Turner Network TV HD; VeneMovies; Versus HD; WE tv.
Fee: $1.00 monthly.
Digital Expanded Basic Service
Subscribers: N.A.
Programming (via satellite): ESPN HD; HD Theater; HDNet; HDNet Movies; National Geographic Channel HD Network; Universal HD.
Fee: $5.99 monthly.
Pay Service 1
Pay Units: 1,200.
Programming (via satellite): HBO (multiplexed).
Fee: $14.95 installation; $13.00 monthly.
Digital Pay Service 1
Pay Units: 4,000.
Programming (via satellite): Cinemax (multiplexed); Encore (multiplexed); Flix; HBO (multiplexed); Showtime (multiplexed); Starz (multiplexed); The Movie Channel (multiplexed).

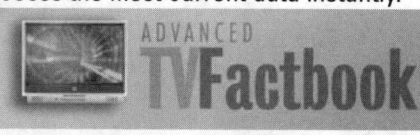

Fee: $14.75 monthly (HBO, Cinemax, Starz/Encore or Showtime/TMC/Flix).
Video-On-Demand: Planned
Pay-Per-View
Addressable homes: 1,495.
iN DEMAND (delivered digitally); Playboy TV (delivered digitally); Fresh (delivered digitally); Hot Choice (delivered digitally).
Internet Service
Operational: Yes.
Subscribers: 3,100.
Broadband Service: Northland Express.
Fee: $42.99 monthly.
Telephone Service
Digital: Operational
Fee: $29.99 monthly
Miles of Plant: 629.0 (coaxial); None (fiber optic).
General Manager: Bill Staley. Marketing Coordinator: Derquis Mitchell. Plant Manager: Cliff Jackson.
Ownership: Northland Communications Corp. (MSO).

GREER—Charter Communications. Now served by GREENVILLE/SPARTANBURG, SC [SC0003]. ICA: SC0030.

HAMPTON—Comcast Cable, 4400 Belle Oaks Dr, North Charleston, SC 29405. Phone: 843-747-1403. Fax: 843-266-3272. Web Site: http://www.comcast.com. Also serves Brunson, Hampton County (portions) & Varnville. ICA: SC0154.
TV Market Ranking: Outside TV Markets (Brunson, HAMPTON, Hampton County (portions), Varnville). Franchise award date: N.A. Franchise expiration date: N.A. Began: N.A.
Channel capacity: N.A. Channels available but not in use: N.A.
Basic Service
Subscribers: 1,622.
Programming (received off-air): WCIV (ABC) Charleston; WCSC-TV (CBS) Charleston; WIS (NBC) Columbia; WJBF (ABC) Augusta; WJCL (ABC) Savannah; WJWJ-TV (PBS) Beaufort; WSAV-TV (MNT, NBC) Savannah; WTGS (FOX) Hardeeville; WTOC-TV (CBS) Savannah.
Programming (via satellite): E! Entertainment Television; QVC; truTV.
Fee: $34.95 installation; $11.00 monthly.
Expanded Basic Service 1
Subscribers: 1,484.
Programming (via satellite): A&E Networks; ABC Family Channel; Animal Planet; BET Networks; Cartoon Network; CNBC; CNN; Comcast/Charter Sports Southeast (CSS); Comedy Central; C-SPAN; Discovery Health Channel; Disney Channel; ESPN; ESPN 2; Food Network; Fox News Channel; Fox Sports South; FX; Great American Country; GSN; Headline News; HGTV; History Channel; ION Television; Lifetime; Nickelodeon; Spike TV; The Learning Channel; The Weather Channel; Trinity Broadcasting Network; Turner Network TV; TV Land; USA Network; Versus; VH1.
Fee: $37.70 monthly.

Expanded Basic Service 2
Subscribers: N.A.
Programming (via satellite): AMC; Discovery Channel; TBS Superstation.
Fee: $3.50 monthly.
Digital Basic Service
Subscribers: N.A.
Programming (via satellite): Encore; Flix; GAS; MTV Networks Digital Suite; Music Choice; Nick Jr.; Nick Too; WAM! America's Kidz Network.
Digital Pay Service 1
Pay Units: N.A.
Programming (via satellite): Cinemax (multiplexed); HBO (multiplexed); Showtime (multiplexed); Starz (multiplexed); The Movie Channel (multiplexed).
Video-On-Demand: Yes
Pay-Per-View
iN DEMAND (delivered digitally); Hot Choice (delivered digitally).
Internet Service
Operational: Yes.
Broadband Service: Comcast High Speed Internet.
Fee: $42.95 monthly.
Telephone Service
Digital: Operational
Miles of Plant: 70.0 (coaxial); None (fiber optic).
General Manager: Bill Watson. Technical Operations Director: Anthony Douglas. Marketing Director: Sean O'Connell. Marketing Manager: Audrey Jones.
Ownership: Comcast Cable Communications Inc. (MSO).

HARDEEVILLE—Hargray, PO Box 5986, Hilton Head, SC 29938. Phones: 843-686-5000; 800-800-7988. Fax: 843-842-8559. Web Site: http://www.hargray.com. ICA: SC0122.
TV Market Ranking: Below 100 (HARDEEVILLE). Franchise award date: N.A. Franchise expiration date: N.A. Began: April 1, 1983.
Channel capacity: N.A. Channels available but not in use: N.A.
Basic Service
Subscribers: N.A.
Programming (received off-air): WCSC-TV (CBS) Charleston; WJCL (ABC) Savannah; WJWJ-TV (PBS) Beaufort; WSAV-TV (MNT, NBC) Savannah; WTOC-TV (CBS) Savannah.
Programming (via satellite): A&E Networks; ABC Family Channel; AMC; Animal Planet; BET Networks; Bio; Bravo; Cartoon Network; CNBC; CNN; Comedy Central; Country Music TV; C-SPAN; Discovery Channel; Discovery Fit & Health; Disney Channel; E! Entertainment Television; ESPN; ESPN 2; Eternal Word TV Network; Food Network; Fox News Channel; Fox Sports South; FX; Golf Channel; Headline News; HGTV; History Channel; Lifetime; MSNBC; MTV; National Geographic Channel; Nickelodeon; Oxygen; QVC; Speed; Spike TV; SportSouth; Syfy; TBS Superstation; The Learning Channel; The Weather Channel; Toon Disney; Travel Channel; Trinity Broadcasting Network; truTV; Turner Classic Movies; Turner Network TV; TV Guide Network; TV Land; Univision Studios; USA Network; Versus; VH1; WE tv; WGN America.
Fee: $39.95 monthly.
Digital Basic Service
Subscribers: N.A.
Programming (via satellite): BBC America; Boomerang; Canales N; DIY Network; ESPN Classic Sports; ESPN HD; ESPNews; Fox Sports World; FSN Digital Atlantic; FSN Digital Central; FSN Digital Pacific; Fuel TV; G4; GAS; Great American Country; GSN; Hallmark Channel; HD Theater; Independent Film Channel; ION Television; Lifetime Movie Network; MTV Networks Digital Suite; Music Choice; Nick Jr.; NickToons TV; Outdoor Channel; Style Network; Tennis Channel.
Fee: $47.99 monthly.
Digital Pay Service 1
Pay Units: N.A.
Programming (via satellite): Cinemax (multiplexed); Cinemax HD; Encore (multiplexed); Flix; Fox Movie Channel; HBO (multiplexed); HBO HD; Showtime (multiplexed); Starz (multiplexed); Sundance Channel; The Movie Channel (multiplexed).
Video-On-Demand: Yes
Internet Service
Operational: Yes.
Broadband Service: In-house.
Fee: $39.95 monthly.
Telephone Service
Digital: Operational
Miles of plant (coax & fiber combined) included in Bluffton
Operations Manager: Mark Reinhardt. Marketing Director: Karen Ehrhardt. Media Relations Manager: Tray Hunter.
Ownership: Hargray Communications Group Inc. (MSO).

HARTSVILLE—Time Warner Cable. Now served by MYRTLE BEACH, SC [SC0007]. ICA: SC0025.

HARTWELL VILLAS—Charter Communications, 2 Digital Place, Simpsonville, SC 29681. Phone: 864-254-7260. Fax: 864-254-7345. Web Site: http://www.charter.com. ICA: SC0123.
TV Market Ranking: 46 (HARTWELL VILLAS). Franchise award date: N.A. Franchise expiration date: N.A. Began: N.A.
Channel capacity: N.A. Channels available but not in use: N.A.
Basic Service
Subscribers: 65.
Programming (received off-air): WGGS-TV (IND) Greenville; WHNS (FOX) Greenville; WLOS (ABC) Asheville; WNTV (PBS) Greenville; WSPA-TV (CBS) Spartanburg; WYFF (NBC) Greenville.
Programming (via satellite): CNN; ESPN; TBS Superstation; Turner Network TV; USA Network.
Fee: $40.00 installation; $15.95 monthly.
Pay Service 1
Pay Units: 19.
Programming (via satellite): HBO.
Fee: $11.95 monthly.
Video-On-Demand: No
Internet Service
Operational: Yes.
Fee: $19.99 monthly.
Telephone Service
Digital: Operational
Fee: $14.99 monthly
Miles of Plant: 1.0 (coaxial); None (fiber optic).
Vice President & General Manager: Anthony Pope. Operations Manager: Pat Hayes. Marketing Director: Brooke Sinclair.
Ownership: Charter Communications Inc. (MSO).

HILDA—Formerly served by Pine Tree Cablevision. No longer in operation. ICA: SC0091.

HILTON HEAD ISLAND—Time Warner Cable. Now served by MYRTLE BEACH, SC [SC0007]. ICA: SC0010.

HOLLY HILL—Almega Cable, 4021 W Airport Freeway, Ste 550, Bedford, TX 76021. Phones: 817-685-9588; 877-725-6342. Fax: 817-685-6488. Web Site: http://almegacable.com. Also serves Eutawville & Orangeburg County (unincorporated areas). ICA: SC0088.
TV Market Ranking: 100 (Orangeburg County (unincorporated areas) (portions)); Outside TV Markets (Eutawville, HOLLY HILL, Orangeburg County (unincorporated areas) (portions)). Franchise award date: January 1, 1981. Franchise expiration date: N.A. Began: January 1, 1983.
Channel capacity: 65 (not 2-way capable). Channels available but not in use: N.A.
Basic Service
Subscribers: 793.
Programming (received off-air): WCBD-TV (CW, NBC) Charleston; WCIV (ABC) Charleston; WCSC-TV (CBS) Charleston; WIS (NBC) Columbia; WITV (PBS) Charleston; WLTX (CBS) Columbia; WMMP (MNT) Charleston; WOLO-TV (ABC) Columbia; WTAT-TV (FOX) Charleston.
Programming (via satellite): A&E Networks; ABC Family Channel; AMC; Animal Planet; BET Networks; CNBC; CNN; Discovery Channel; Disney Channel; ESPN; ESPN 2; Great American Country; Headline News; HGTV; History Channel; Lifetime; National Geographic Channel; Nickelodeon; QVC; Spike TV; TBS Superstation; The Learning Channel; The Weather Channel; Travel Channel; Trinity Broadcasting Network; Turner Classic Movies; Turner Network TV; USA Network; WGN America.
Fee: $34.95 installation; $34.95 monthly.
Pay Service 1
Pay Units: 69.
Programming (via satellite): Cinemax.
Fee: $10.95 monthly.
Pay Service 2
Pay Units: 109.
Programming (via satellite): HBO.
Fee: $10.95 monthly.
Pay Service 3
Pay Units: 14.
Programming (via satellite): The Movie Channel.
Fee: $10.95 monthly.
Pay Service 4
Pay Units: 54.
Programming (via satellite): Showtime.
Fee: $10.95 monthly.
Video-On-Demand: No
Internet Service
Operational: No.
Telephone Service
None
Miles of Plant: 84.0 (coaxial); None (fiber optic).
Vice President, Marketing & Programming: Lori Dunn. General Manager: Thomas Kurien.
Ownership: Almega Cable (MSO).

HOLLYWOOD—US Cable of Coastal Texas LP. Now served by CHARLESTON, SC [SC0001]. ICA: SC0061.

HOMEWOOD—Horry Telephone Coop., 3480 Hwy 701 N, PO Box 1820, Conway, SC 29528-1820. Phones: 843-365-2154; 843-365-2151. Fax: 843-365-1111. Web Site: http://www.htcinc.net. Also serves Aynor, Bucksport, Conway, Georgetown County (portions), Horry County (portions), Longs, Loris, Murrells Inlet, North Myrtle Beach (portions), Socastee & Wampee. ICA: SC0016.
TV Market Ranking: Below 100 (Aynor, Bucksport, Conway, Georgetown County (portions), HOMEWOOD, Horry Count (portions), Longs, Loris, Murrells Inlet, North Myrtle Beach (portions), Socastee, Wampee). Franchise award date: January 1, 1980. Franchise expiration date: N.A. Began: October 11, 1983.
Channel capacity: N.A. Channels available but not in use: N.A.
Basic Service
Subscribers: 36,000.
Programming (received off-air): WBTW (CBS, MNT) Florence; WCSC-TV (CBS) Charleston; WECT (NBC) Wilmington; WFXB (FOX) Myrtle Beach; WHMC (PBS) Conway; WIS (NBC) Columbia; WPDE-TV (ABC) Florence; WWMB (CW) Florence.
Programming (via satellite): ABC Family Channel; Headline News; QVC; TBS Superstation; TV Guide Network; WGN America.
Fee: $35.00 installation; $12.95 monthly; $2.50 converter.
Expanded Basic Service 1
Subscribers: 34,000.
Programming (via satellite): A&E Networks; AMC; AmericanLife TV Network; Animal Planet; BET Networks; Cartoon Network; CNBC; CNN; Comedy Central; Country Music TV; C-SPAN; Discovery Channel; Discovery Health Channel; Disney Channel; E! Entertainment Television; ESPN; ESPN 2; Fox News Channel; Fox Sports South; FX; Golf Channel; HGTV; History Channel; Lifetime; MTV; Nickelodeon; Speed; Spike TV; Syfy; The Learning Channel; The Weather Channel; Travel Channel; Trinity Broadcasting Network; truTV; Turner Classic Movies; Turner Network TV; TV Land; USA Network; VH1.
Fee: $23.50 monthly.
Digital Basic Service
Subscribers: 6,000.
Programming (via satellite): BBC America; Bio; Bloomberg Television; Discovery Digital Networks; DIY Network; Fox Sports World; G4; GAS; History Channel International; Independent Film Channel; ION Television; MTV2; National Geographic Channel; Nick Jr.; Outdoor Channel; VH1 Classic; VH1 Country.
Fee: $6.95 monthly; $6.95 converter.
Digital Pay Service 1
Pay Units: N.A.
Programming (via satellite): Cinemax; Flix; HBO; Showtime (multiplexed); Sundance Channel; The Movie Channel.
Fee: $12.95 monthly (each).
Video-On-Demand: Yes
Pay-Per-View
Addressable homes: 11,700.
Hot Choice; iN DEMAND; movies; special events.
Internet Service
Operational: Yes, Both DSL & dial-up.
Subscribers: 2,000.
Broadband Service: In-house.
Fee: $24.95 monthly; $10.00 modem lease.
Telephone Service
Analog: Operational
Fee: $10.00 monthly
Miles of Plant: 1,500.0 (coaxial); None (fiber optic). Additional miles planned: 70.0 (coaxial).
Chief Executive Officer & General Manager: Curley Huggins. Chief Operating Officer: Mike Hagg. Chief Technician: Jim Morgan. Marketing Director: Tom Vitt.
Ownership: Horry Telephone Cooperative Inc.

HOPKINS—Formerly served by Pine Tree Cablevision. No longer in operation. ICA: SC0156.

IVA—Charter Communications. Now served by GREENVILLE/SPARTANBURG, SC [SC0003]. ICA: SC0125.

JEFFERSON—Formerly served by Pine Tree Cablevision. No longer in operation. ICA: SC0126.

JOHNS ISLAND—US Cable of Coastal Texas LP. Now served by CHARLESTON, SC [SC0001]. ICA: SC0054.

JOHNSONVILLE—Time Warner Cable. Now served by MYRTLE BEACH, SC [SC0007]. ICA: SC0057.

LADY'S ISLAND—Comcast Cable, 4400 Belle Oaks Dr, North Charleston, SC 29405. Phone: 843-747-1403. Fax: 843-266-3272. Web Site: http://www.comcast.com. Also serves Dataw Island, Fripp Island & St. Helena Island. ICA: SC0056.

TV Market Ranking: Below 100 (Dataw Island, Fripp Island, LADY'S ISLAND, St. Helena Island). Franchise award date: N.A. Franchise expiration date: N.A. Began: N.A.

Channel capacity: N.A. Channels available but not in use: N.A.

Basic Service

Subscribers: 5,656.

Programming (received off-air): WCBD-TV (CW, NBC) Charleston; WCIV (ABC) Charleston; WCSC-TV (CBS) Charleston; WITV (PBS) Charleston; WMMP (MNT) Charleston; WTAT-TV (FOX) Charleston.

Programming (via satellite): AMC; Discovery Channel; FX; ION Television; TBS Superstation; Turner Network TV; WGN America.

Fee: $61.25 installation; $13.22 monthly.

Expanded Basic Service 1

Subscribers: 4,572.

Programming (via satellite): A&E Networks; ABC Family Channel; Animal Planet; BET Networks; Bravo; Cartoon Network; CNBC; CNN; Comcast/Charter Sports Southeast (CSS); Comedy Central; C-SPAN; C-SPAN 2; Discovery Health Channel; Disney Channel; E! Entertainment Television; ESPN; ESPN 2; ESPN Classic Sports; Food Network; Fox News Channel; Fox Sports South; Golf Channel; Great American Country; GSN; Hallmark Channel; Headline News; HGTV; History Channel; INSP; Lifetime; MSNBC; MTV; Nickelodeon; QVC; Speed; Spike TV; Style Network; Syfy; The Learning Channel; The Weather Channel; Travel Channel; Trinity Broadcasting Network; truTV; Turner Classic Movies; Turner South; TV Guide Network; TV Land; Univision Studios; USA Network; Versus; VH1.

Fee: $21.52 monthly.

Digital Basic Service

Subscribers: 307.

Programming (via satellite): BBC America; Bio; Cooking Channel; Country Music TV; C-SPAN 3; Current; DIY Network; Encore (multiplexed); ESPN HD; ESPNews; Eternal Word TV Network; Flix (multiplexed); G4; GAS; HD Theater; History Channel International; Jewelry Television; Lifetime Movie Network; LOGO; MoviePlex; MTV Networks Digital Suite; Music Choice; National Geographic Channel; NFL Network; Nick Jr.; Nick Too; PBS Kids Sprout; ShopNBC; SoapNet; Sundance Channel (multiplexed); Toon Disney; Turner Network TV HD; TV One; Weatherscan.

Fee: $9.95 monthly.

Digital Pay Service 1

Pay Units: 132.

Programming (via satellite): HBO (multiplexed); HBO HD.

Fee: $13.95 monthly.

Digital Pay Service 2

Pay Units: 46.

Programming (via satellite): Cinemax (multiplexed); Cinemax HD.

Fee: $13.95 monthly.

Digital Pay Service 3

Pay Units: 57.

Programming (via satellite): Showtime (multiplexed); Showtime HD.

Fee: $13.95 monthly.

Digital Pay Service 4

Pay Units: 7.

Programming (via satellite): The Movie Channel (multiplexed).

Fee: $13.95 monthly.

Digital Pay Service 5

Pay Units: 35.

Programming (via satellite): Starz (multiplexed); Starz HDTV.

Fee: $13.95 monthly.

Digital Pay Service 6

Pay Units: N.A.

Programming (via satellite): Playboy TV.

Video-On-Demand: No

Pay-Per-View

Addressable homes: 307.

iN DEMAND (delivered digitally); iN DEMAND; Playboy TV (delivered digitally); Hot Choice (delivered digitally); Fresh (delivered digitally); Pleasure (delivered digitally); Shorteez (delivered digitally); ESPN (delivered digitally); NBA League Pass (delivered digitally); NHL Center Ice (delivered digitally); MLB Extra Innings (delivered digitally).

Internet Service

Operational: Yes.

Broadband Service: Comcast High Speed Internet.

Fee: $42.95 monthly.

Telephone Service

None

Miles of Plant: 311.0 (coaxial); None (fiber optic).

General Manager: Bill Watson. Technical Operations Director: Anthony Douglas. Chief Technician: Bob Bradshaw. Marketing Director: Sean O'Connell. Marketing Manager: Audrey Jones.

Ownership: Comcast Cable Communications Inc. (MSO).

LAKE CITY—Time Warner Cable. Now served by MYRTLE BEACH, SC [SC0007]. ICA: SC0128.

LAKE VIEW—Time Warner Cable. Now served by MYRTLE BEACH, SC [SC0007]. ICA: SC0066.

LAMAR—Formerly served by Pine Tree Cablevision. No longer in operation. ICA: SC0129.

LANCASTER—Comporium Communications. Now served by ROCK HILL, SC [SC0138]. ICA: SC0023.

LANE—Time Warner Cable. Now served by MYRTLE BEACH, SC [SC0007]. ICA: SC0155.

LAURENS—Charter Communications. Now served by GREENVILLE/SPARTANBURG, SC [SC0003]. ICA: SC0022.

LITTLE RIVER—Time Warner Cable. Now served by MYRTLE BEACH, SC [SC0007]. ICA: SC0130.

LOCKHART—Charter Communications. Now served by GREENVILLE/SPARTANBURG, SC [SC0003]. ICA: SC0098.

LUGOFF—Formerly served by Pine Tree Cablevision. No longer in operation. ICA: SC0076.

McCLELLANVILLE—Windjammer Cable, 8500 W 110th St, Ste 600, Overland Park, KS 66210. Phone: 888-495-2881. Fax: 913-563-5454. Web Site: http://www.windjammercable.com. Also serves Charleston County (unincorporated areas) & South Santee. ICA: SC0101.

TV Market Ranking: Below 100 (Charleston County (unincorporated areas), MCCLELLANVILLE, South Santee). Franchise award date: January 1, 1988. Franchise expiration date: N.A. Began: January 1, 1988.

Channel capacity: 36 (not 2-way capable). Channels available but not in use: N.A.

Basic Service

Subscribers: N.A. Included in Columbia

Programming (received off-air): WCBD-TV (CW, NBC) Charleston; WCIV (ABC) Charleston; WCSC-TV (CBS) Charleston; WITV (PBS) Charleston; WMMP (MNT) Charleston; WTAT-TV (FOX) Charleston.

Programming (via satellite): A&E Networks; ABC Family Channel; AMC; Animal Planet; BET Networks; Cartoon Network; CNN; Discovery Channel; Disney Channel; ESPN; Fox News Channel; Headline News; MTV; Nickelodeon; QVC; Spike TV; Syfy; TBS Superstation; The Weather Channel; Trinity Broadcasting Network; Turner Network TV; USA Network; VH1; WGN America.

Fee: $25.00 installation; $24.92 monthly; $2.00 converter.

Pay Service 1

Pay Units: 22.

Programming (via satellite): Cinemax; HBO.

Fee: $9.95 monthly (each).

Video-On-Demand: No

Internet Service

Operational: No.

Telephone Service

None

Miles of plant included in Myrtle Beach

Ownership: Windjammer Communications LLC (MSO).

McCORMICK—Formerly served by McCormick Cable. No longer in operation. ICA: SC0079.

McCORMICK COUNTY—Formerly served by KLiP Interactive. No longer in operation. ICA: SC0100.

MONCKS CORNER—Home Telecom, 579 Stoney Landing Rd, PO Box 1194, Moncks Corner, SC 29461. Phones: 843-471-2200; 843-761-9101 (Customer service). Fax: 843-761-9199. Web Site: http://www.HomeSC.com. Also serves Berkeley County (unincorporated areas), Bonneau, Cross & Harleyville. ICA: SC0132.

TV Market Ranking: Below 100 (Berkeley County (unincorporated areas) (portions), Cross, MONCKS CORNER); Outside TV Markets (Berkeley County (unincorporated areas) (portions), Bonneau, Harleyville). Franchise award date: N.A. Franchise expiration date: December 31, 2050. Began: October 1, 1980.

Channel capacity: 70 (operating 2-way). Channels available but not in use: N.A.

Basic Service

Subscribers: 6,644.

Programming (received off-air): WCBD-TV (CW, NBC) Charleston; WCIV (ABC) Charleston; WCSC-TV (CBS) Charleston; WITV (PBS) Charleston; WMMP (MNT) Charleston; WTAT-TV (FOX) Charleston.

Programming (via satellite): A&E Networks; ABC Family Channel; AMC; Animal Planet; BET Networks; Bloomberg Television; Bravo; Cartoon Network; CNBC; CNN; Comedy Central; Country Music TV; C-SPAN; Discovery Channel; Disney Channel; E! Entertainment Television; ESPN; ESPN 2; ESPN Classic Sports; Food Network; Fox News Channel; Fox Sports South; FX; Great American Country; Headline News; HGTV; History Channel; Lifetime; MTV; National Geographic Channel; Nickelodeon; QVC; SportSouth; Syfy; TBS Superstation; The Learning Channel; The Weather Channel; Travel Channel; Trinity Broadcasting Network; truTV; Turner Classic Movies; TV Guide Network; TV Land; USA Network; VH1; WGN America.

Fee: $35.00 installation; $27.00 monthly; $2.25 converter; $25.00 additional installation.

Digital Basic Service

Subscribers: 1,800.

Programming (via satellite): BBC America; Bio; cloo; C-SPAN 2; DMX Music; ESPNews; Fox Soccer; G4; GAS; Golf Channel; GSN; Hallmark Channel; HD Theater; HDNet; HDNet Movies; History Channel International; Independent Film Channel; INSP; Lifetime Movie Network; MSNBC; MTV Networks Digital Suite; Nick Jr.; NickToons TV; Outdoor Channel; PBS HD; Speed; Versus; WE tv.

Fee: $42.00 monthly.

Digital Pay Service 1

Pay Units: 580.

Programming (via satellite): Cinemax (multiplexed); Encore (multiplexed); Flix; HBO (multiplexed); Showtime (multiplexed); Showtime HD; Starz (multiplexed); The Movie Channel; The Movie Channel HD.

Fee: $9.95 monthly (Cinemax), $11.50 monthly (HBO, Showtime, or Starz/Encore).

Video-On-Demand: No

Pay-Per-View

Addressable homes: 6,644.

iN DEMAND (delivered digitally).

Internet Service

Operational: Yes.

Subscribers: 1,117.

Read what the Telecom elite read...
Communications Daily
Warren Communications News
FREE 30-day trial—call 800-771-9202 or visit www.warren-news.com

Broadband Service: HomeExpress.
Fee: $99.00 installation; $44.95 monthly.
Telephone Service
None
Miles of Plant: 296.0 (coaxial); 250.0 (fiber optic).
President & Chief Operating Officer: William S. Helmly. Chief Executive Officer: Robert L. Helmly, Sr. Support Operations Director: Robert L. Helmly, Jr. Engineering Director: Robert P. Abbott, Jr. Customer Operations Director: Julie Forte. Marketing Manager: Gina Austin. Cable Product Coordinator: Dewey Ford.
Ownership: Berkeley Cable TV Co. Inc. (MSO).

MOUNT PLEASANT (portions)—Comcast Cable. Now served by CHARLESTON, SC [SC0001]. ICA: SC0149.

MULLINS—Time Warner Cable. Now served by MYRTLE BEACH, SC [SC0007]. ICA: SC0032.

MYRTLE BEACH—Time Warner Cable, 3347 Platt Springs Rd, West Columbia, SC 29170. Phones: 843-251-5300; 843-913-7940 (myrtle Beach). Fax: 843-251-5345. Web Site: http://www.timewarnercable.com/carolinas. Also serves East Laurinburg, Gibson, Laurinburg, Maxton, Robeson County, Rowland & Scotland County, NC; Andrews, Atlantic Beach, Beaufort County, Berkeley County (portions), Briarcliff Acres, Browns Ferry, Cheraw, Chesterfield County, Choppee, Conway, Darlington, Darlington County, Debordieu Colony, Dillon, Dillon County, Dorchester County (portions), Dunbar, Florence, Florence County, Forestbrook, Garden City Beach, Georgetown, Georgetown County, Hartsville, Hemingway, Hilton Head Island, Horry County, Johnsonville, Kellytown, Kingstree, Lake City, Lake View, Lambertown, Lane, Latta, Litchfield Beach, Little River, Marion, Marion County, Mullins, Murrells Inlet, North Charleston, North Myrtle Beach, North Santee, North Stone, Paplico, Pawley's Island, Pineridge, Quinby, Ridgeville, Sampit, Scranton, Socastee, Summerville, Surfside Beach, Timmonsville & Williamsburg County, SC. ICA: SC0007. **Note:** This system is an overbuild.
TV Market Ranking: 73 (Maxton, Robeson County (portions), Scotland County (portions)); Below 100 (Atlantic Beach, Beaufort County, Berkeley County (portions) (portions), Briarcliff Acres, Browns Ferry, Chesterfield County (portions), Choppee, Conway, Darlington, Darlington County, Debordieu Colony, Dillon, Dillon County, Dorchester County (portions) (portions), Dunbar, Florence, Forestbrook, Garden City Beach, Georgetown (portions), Georgetown County, Hartsville, Hemingway, Hilton Head Island, Horry County, Johnsonville, Kellytown, Lake City, Lake View, Lambertown, Latta, Litchfield Beach, Little River, Marion, Marion County (portions), Mullins, Murrells Inlet, MYRTLE BEACH, North Charleston, North Myrtle Beach, North Stone, Pamplico, Pawley's Island, Pineridge, Quinby, Ridgeville, Sampit, Scranton, Socastee, Summerville, Surfside Beach, Timmonsville, Williamsburg County, Williamsburg County (portions), Robeson County (portions), Scotland County (portions)); Outside TV Markets (Andrews, Berkeley County (portions) (portions), Cheraw, Chesterfield County (portions), Dorchester County (portions) (portions), East Laurinburg, Georgetown (portions), Georgetown County, Gibson, Kingstree, Lane, Laurinburg, Laurinburg, North Santee, Rowland, Williamsburg County, Williamsburg County (portions), Robeson County (portions), Scotland County (portions)). Franchise award date: January 1, 1961. Franchise expiration date: N.A. Began: September 17, 1962.
Channel capacity: N.A. Channels available but not in use: N.A.
Basic Service
Subscribers: N.A. Included in Columbia
Programming (received off-air): LWS Local Weather Station; WBTW (CBS, MNT) Florence; WECT (NBC) Wilmington; WFXB (FOX) Myrtle Beach; WHMC (PBS) Conway; WIS (NBC) Columbia; WPDE-TV (ABC) Florence; WTAT-TV (FOX) Charleston; WUNJ-TV (PBS) Wilmington; WWMB (CW) Florence.
Programming (via satellite): C-SPAN; ION Television; TBS Superstation; WGN America.
Fee: $27.00 installation; $9.65 monthly; $18.00 additional installation.
Expanded Basic Service 1
Subscribers: N.A. Included in Columbia
Programming (via satellite): A&E Networks; ABC Family Channel; AMC; Animal Planet; BET Networks; Bravo; Cartoon Network; CNBC; CNN; Comedy Central; Country Music TV; Discovery Channel; Disney Channel; E! Entertainment Television; ESPN; ESPN 2; Eternal Word TV Network; Food Network; Fox News Channel; Fox Sports South; FX; Golf Channel; Hallmark Channel; Headline News; HGTV; History Channel; Lifetime; Lifetime Movie Network; MSNBC; MTV; National Geographic Channel; Nickelodeon; Oxygen; QVC; Speed; Spike TV; Syfy; The Learning Channel; The Weather Channel; Travel Channel; Trinity Broadcasting Network; truTV; Turner Classic Movies; Turner Network TV; TV Guide Network; TV Land; USA Network; Versus; VH1; WE tv.
Fee: $28.00 installation; $21.45 monthly.
Digital Basic Service
Subscribers: N.A. Included in Columbia
Programming (via satellite): AmericanLife TV Network; America's Store; BBC America; Bio; Black Family Channel; Bloomberg Television; Canales N; Cooking Channel; C-SPAN 3; Discovery Digital Networks; DIY Network; Encore (multiplexed); ESPN Classic Sports; ESPNews; Flix; Fox Movie Channel; Fox Sports World; FSN Digital Atlantic; FSN Digital Central; FSN Digital Pacific; Fuse; G4; Great American Country; GSN; History Channel International; Independent Film Channel; Jewelry Television; Lifetime Real Women; MTV Networks Digital Suite; Music Choice; Nick Jr.; Outdoor Channel; Ovation; Style Network; Sundance Channel; Toon Disney.
Fee: $4.95 monthly (movie, sports or Canales N), $5.95 monthly (variety).
Pay Service 1
Pay Units: 3,806.
Programming (via satellite): Cinemax (multiplexed).
Fee: $9.95 monthly.
Pay Service 2
Pay Units: 10,815.
Programming (via satellite): HBO (multiplexed).
Fee: $10.95 monthly.
Pay Service 3
Pay Units: 4,266.
Programming (via satellite): Showtime (multiplexed).
Fee: $9.95 monthly.
Digital Pay Service 1
Pay Units: N.A. Included in Columbia
Programming (via satellite): Cinemax (multiplexed); HBO (multiplexed); Showtime (multiplexed); Starz (multiplexed); The Movie Channel (multiplexed); The Movie Channel.
Fee: $10.95 monthly (each).
Video-On-Demand: Yes
Pay-Per-View
Fresh; Hot Choice (delivered digitally); iN DEMAND (delivered digitally); Playboy TV (delivered digitally); Fresh (delivered digitally); Sports PPV (delivered digitally).
Internet Service
Operational: Yes. Began: January 1, 1999.
Broadband Service: Road Runner.
Fee: $99.00 installation; $39.95 monthly.
Telephone Service
Digital: Operational
Fee: $44.95 monthly
Miles of plant included in Columbia
Vice President & General Manager: Chris Whitaker. President, Network Operations & Engineering: Mike Munley. Vice President, Public Affairs: Dan E Jones. Vice President, Operations: Michael Smith. Vice President, Marketing: Dan Santelle. Regional Vice President, Communications: Susan Leepson.
Ownership: Time Warner Cable (MSO).; Advance/Newhouse Partnership (MSO).

NEWBERRY—Comcast Cable, 105 River Shoals Pkwy, Augusta, GA 30909. Phone: 706-738-0091. Fax: 706-739-1871. Web Site: http://www.comcast.com. Also serves Newberry County & Prosperity. ICA: SC0035.
TV Market Ranking: 100 (Newberry County (portions)); Outside TV Markets (NEWBERRY, Prosperity, Newberry County (portions)). Franchise award date: March 9, 1968. Franchise expiration date: N.A. Began: June 1, 1968.
Channel capacity: N.A. Channels available but not in use: N.A.
Basic Service
Subscribers: 4,748.
Programming (received off-air): WACH (FOX) Columbia; WIS (NBC) Columbia; WJZY (CW) Belmont; WLOS (ABC) Asheville; WLTX (CBS) Columbia; WOLO-TV (ABC) Columbia; WRLK-TV (PBS) Columbia; WSPA-TV (CBS) Spartanburg; WYFF (NBC) Greenville; 17 FMs.
Programming (via satellite): QVC; WGN America.
Fee: $50.00 installation; $14.95 monthly; $2.00 converter.
Expanded Basic Service 1
Subscribers: N.A.
Programming (via satellite): A&E Networks; ABC Family Channel; AMC; AmericanLife TV Network; Animal Planet; BET Networks; Cartoon Network; CNBC; CNN; Comcast/Charter Sports Southeast (CSS); Comedy Central; Country Music TV; C-SPAN; C-SPAN 2; Disney Channel; E! Entertainment Television; ESPN; ESPN 2; Food Network; Fox News Channel; Fox Sports South; FX; Golf Channel; GSN; Headline News; HGTV; History Channel; ION Television; Lifetime; MTV; Nickelodeon; Speed; SportSouth; Style Network; Syfy; The Learning Channel; The Weather Channel; Travel Channel; Trinity Broadcasting Network; truTV; Turner Classic Movies; TV Guide Network; TV Land; USA Network; Versus.
Fee: $30.04 monthly.
Digital Basic Service
Subscribers: N.A.
Programming (via satellite): BBC America; Discovery Digital Networks; Encore (multiplexed); Flix (multiplexed); GAS; MTV Networks Digital Suite; Music Choice; Nick Jr.; Nick Too; Sundance Channel (multiplexed); WAM! America's Kidz Network.
Fee: $12.95 monthly.
Pay Service 1
Pay Units: 715.
Programming (via satellite): HBO.
Fee: $10.00 installation; $12.95 monthly.
Digital Pay Service 1
Pay Units: N.A.
Programming (via satellite): Cinemax (multiplexed); HBO (multiplexed); Showtime (multiplexed); The Movie Channel (multiplexed).
Video-On-Demand: No
Pay-Per-View
iN DEMAND (delivered digitally); Hot Choice (delivered digitally).
Internet Service
Operational: Yes.
Broadband Service: Comcast High Speed Internet.
Fee: $42.95 monthly.
Telephone Service
Digital: Operational
Miles of Plant: 181.0 (coaxial); None (fiber optic).
Engineering Director: Harry Hess. Technical Operations Director: Butch Jernigan. Area Marketing Director: Joey Fortier.
Ownership: Comcast Cable Communications Inc. (MSO).

NORTH—Formerly served by Pine Tree Cablevision. No longer in operation. ICA: SC0092.

NORWAY—Formerly served by Almega Cable. No longer in operation. ICA: SC0161.

OLANTA—FTC Vision. Formerly served by Turbeville, SC [SC0085]. This cable system has converted to IPTV, 1101 E Main St, Kingstree, SC 29556. Phones: 888-218-5050; 843-382-1387. Web Site: http://www.ftcvision.com. ICA: SC5027.
Channel capacity: N.A. Channels available but not in use: N.A.
Internet Service
Operational: Yes.
Telephone Service
Digital: Operational
Chief Executive Officer: Brad Erwin.

PAGELAND—NewWave Communications, 122 N Maple St, PO Box 86, Pageland, SC 29728. Phone: 843-672-5929. Fax: 843-672-5373. E-mail: info@newwavecom.com. Web Site: http://www.newwavecom.com. ICA: SC0082.
TV Market Ranking: Outside TV Markets (PAGELAND). Franchise award date: N.A.

Franchise expiration date: N.A. Began: July 1, 1983.
Channel capacity: 35 (operating 2-way). Channels available but not in use: None.

Basic Service

Subscribers: 525.

Programming (received off-air): WAXN-TV (IND) Kannapolis; WBTV (CBS) Charlotte; WCCB (FOX) Charlotte; WCNC-TV (NBC) Charlotte; WIS (NBC) Columbia; WJPM-TV (PBS) Florence; WJZY (CW) Belmont; WMYT-TV (MNT) Rock Hill; WPDE-TV (ABC) Florence; WSOC-TV (ABC) Charlotte; WUNG-TV (PBS) Concord.

Programming (via satellite): QVC; WGN America.

Fee: $29.95 installation.

Expanded Basic Service 1

Subscribers: 475.

Programming (via satellite): A&E Networks; ABC Family Channel; AMC; Animal Planet; Bravo; Cartoon Network; CNBC; CNN; Comedy Central; Country Music TV; C-SPAN; Discovery Channel; Disney Channel; E! Entertainment Television; ESPN; ESPN 2; ESPN Classic Sports; Food Network; Fox News Channel; FX; GSN; Hallmark Channel; Headline News; HGTV; History Channel; INSP; Lifetime; MTV; Nickelodeon; Outdoor Channel; SoapNet; Speed; Spike TV; Syfy; TBS Superstation; The Learning Channel; The Weather Channel; Turner Network TV; TV Land; USA Network; VH1.

Fee: $42.99 monthly.

Digital Basic Service

Subscribers: 43.

Programming (via satellite): BBC America; Bio; Black Family Channel; Bloomberg Television; cloo; Discovery Digital Networks; DMX Music; ESPNews; Fox Movie Channel; G4; GAS; Great American Country; Halogen Network; History Channel International; Independent Film Channel; Lifetime Movie Network; MTV Networks Digital Suite; Nick Jr.; NickToons TV; ShopNBC; Style Network; The Word Network; Toon Disney; Trinity Broadcasting Network; Turner Classic Movies.

Digital Pay Service 1

Pay Units: 62.

Programming (via satellite): Cinemax (multiplexed); Encore (multiplexed); Flix; HBO (multiplexed); Showtime (multiplexed); Starz (multiplexed); The Movie Channel (multiplexed).

Video-On-Demand: No

Pay-Per-View

iN DEMAND (delivered digitally); Hot Choice (delivered digitally); Playboy TV (delivered digitally); Fresh (delivered digitally); Shorteez (delivered digitally).

Internet Service

Operational: No.

Telephone Service

None

Miles of Plant: 69.0 (coaxial); None (fiber optic).

General Manager: Mark Bookout. Lead Technician: Bobby Thurman. Office Manager: Brenda Thurman.

Ownership: NewWave Communications LLC (MSO).

PICKENS—Charter Communications. Now served by GREENVILLE/SPARTANBURG, SC [SC0003]. ICA: SC0135.

REGENT PARK—Comporium Communications. Now served by ROCK HILL, SC [SC0138]. ICA: SC0150.

RIDGELAND—Hargray, PO Box 5986, Hilton Head, SC 29938. Phone: 843-686-5000. Fax: 843-842-8559. Web Site: http://www.hargray.com. ICA: SC0137.

TV Market Ranking: Below 100 (RIDGELAND). Franchise award date: N.A. Franchise expiration date: N.A. Began: March 1, 1983.

Channel capacity: N.A. Channels available but not in use: N.A.

Basic Service

Subscribers: N.A.

Programming (received off-air): WCSC-TV (CBS) Charleston; WGSA (CW) Baxley; WJCL (ABC) Savannah; WJWJ-TV (PBS) Beaufort; WSAV-TV (MNT, NBC) Savannah; WTOC-TV (CBS) Savannah.

Programming (via satellite): A&E Networks; ABC Family Channel; AMC; Animal Planet; BET Networks; Bio; Bravo; Cartoon Network; CNBC; CNN; Comedy Central; Country Music TV; C-SPAN; Discovery Channel; Discovery Fit & Health; Disney Channel; E! Entertainment Television; ESPN; ESPN 2; ESPN Classic Sports; Food Network; Fox News Channel; Fox Sports South; FX; Golf Channel; Headline News; HGTV; History Channel; Lifetime; MSNBC; MTV; National Geographic Channel; NFL Network; Nickelodeon; Oxygen; QVC; Speed; Spike TV; SportSouth; Syfy; TBS Superstation; The Learning Channel; The Weather Channel; Toon Disney; Travel Channel; truTV; Turner Classic Movies; Turner Network TV; TV Guide Network; TV Land; Univision Studios; USA Network; Versus; VH1; WE tv; WGN America.

Fee: $47.99 monthly.

Digital Basic Service

Subscribers: N.A.

Programming (via satellite): BBC America; Boomerang; Canales N; Discovery Channel HD; Discovery Digital Networks; DIY Network; ESPN HD; ESPNews; Eternal Word TV Network; Fox College Sports Atlantic; Fox College Sports Central; Fox College Sports Pacific; Fox Soccer; Fuel TV; G4; GAS; Great American Country; GSN; Hallmark Channel; HDNet; HDNet Movies; History Channel International; Independent Film Channel; ION Television; MTV Networks Digital Suite; Music Choice; MyNetworkTV Inc.; Nick Jr.; NickToons TV; Outdoor Channel; SoapNet; Style Network; Tennis Channel; Trinity Broadcasting Network; Universal HD.

Digital Pay Service 1

Pay Units: N.A.

Programming (via satellite): Cinemax (multiplexed); Cinemax HD; Encore (multiplexed); Flix; Fox Movie Channel; HBO (multiplexed); HBO HD; Showtime (multiplexed); Starz (multiplexed); Sundance Channel; The Movie Channel (multiplexed).

Video-On-Demand: Yes

Internet Service

Operational: Yes.

Broadband Service: In-house.

Fee: $39.95 monthly.

Telephone Service

Digital: Operational

Miles of plant (coax & fiber combined) included in Bluffton

Operations Manager: Mark Reinhardt. Marketing Director: Karen Ehrhardt. Media Relations Manager: Tray Hunter.

Ownership: Hargray Communications Group Inc. (MSO).

RIDGEVILLE—Time Warner Cable. Now served by MYRTLE BEACH, SC [SC0007]. ICA: SC0151.

ROCK HILL—Comporium Communications, 332 East Main St, Rock Hill, SC 29730. Phones: 803-283-1000 (Customer service); 803-324-9011 (Residence service); 803-326-6011 (Business service). Fax: 803-326-5708. Web Site: http://www.comporium.com. Also serves Brevard, NC; Chester County (unincorporated areas), Fairfield County (northern portion), Fort Lawn, Fort Mill, Great Falls, Heath Springs, Hickory Grove, Kershaw, Lake Wylie Woods, Lancaster, Lancaster County (portions), Regent Park, Richburg, River Hills, Sharon, Tega Cay, York & York County, SC. ICA: SC0138.

TV Market Ranking: 42 (Fort Lawn, Fort Mill, Lake Wylie Woods, Lancaster, Lancaster County (portions), Regent Park, Richburg, River Hills, ROCK HILL, Tega Cay, York); 42,46 (Chester County (unincorporated areas) (portions), York County (portions)); 46 (Hickory Grove, Sharon); Below 100 (Fairfield County (northern portion), Great Falls, Heath Springs, Richburg, Chester County (unincorporated areas) (portions), York County (portions)); Outside TV Markets (Kershaw). Franchise award date: January 1, 1965. Franchise expiration date: March 1, 2007. Began: January 1, 1967.

Channel capacity: N.A. Channels available but not in use: N.A.

Basic Service

Subscribers: 54,800.

Programming (received off-air): WAXN-TV (IND) Kannapolis; WBTV (CBS) Charlotte; WCCB (FOX) Charlotte; WCNC-TV (NBC) Charlotte; WJZY (CW) Belmont; WNSC-TV (PBS) Rock Hill; WSOC-TV (ABC) Charlotte; WTVI (PBS) Charlotte; allband FM.

Programming (via satellite): C-SPAN; C-SPAN 2; QVC; Trinity Broadcasting Network; TV Guide Network.

Fee: $45.00 installation; $9.95 monthly; $2.10 converter.

Expanded Basic Service 1

Subscribers: 46,605.

Programming (via satellite): A&E Networks; ABC Family Channel; AMC; Animal Planet; BET Networks; Cartoon Network; CNBC; CNN; Comedy Central; Country Music TV; Discovery Channel; Disney Channel; ESPN; ESPN 2; ESPN Classic Sports; Food Network; Fox News Channel; Fox Sports South; FX; Golf Channel; Headline News; HGTV; History Channel; Lifetime; MSNBC; MTV; Nickelodeon; Spike TV; Syfy; TBS Superstation; The Learning Channel; The Weather Channel; Turner Classic Movies; Turner Network TV; TV Land; USA Network; VH1.

Fee: $32.35 monthly.

Digital Basic Service

Subscribers: 19,107.

Programming (via satellite): BBC America; Bio; CNN en Espanol; Discovery Digital Networks; DIY Network; DMX Music; G4; GSN; History Channel International; ION Television; Lifetime Movie Network; MTV Networks Digital Suite; National Geographic Channel; Nick Jr.; Nick Too; Outdoor Channel; Ovation; SoapNet; Speed; The Weather Channel; Toon Disney.

Fee: $12.95 monthly.

Pay Service 1

Pay Units: 13,182.

Programming (via satellite): Cinemax; HBO; Showtime; Starz; The Movie Channel.

Fee: $12.95 monthly (HBO, Cinemax, Showtime/TMC or Starz/Encore).

Digital Pay Service 1

Pay Units: N.A.

Programming (via satellite): Encore (multiplexed); HBO (multiplexed); Showtime (multiplexed); Starz (multiplexed).

Fee: $12.95 monthly (HBO, Cinemax, Showtime/TMC or Starz/Encore).

Video-On-Demand: No

Pay-Per-View

Addressable homes: 14,000.

iN DEMAND (delivered digitally).

Internet Service

Operational: Yes.

Subscribers: 24,800.

Broadband Service: InfoAve.net.

Fee: $49.95 installation; $44.95 monthly; $7.00 modem lease.

Telephone Service

None

Miles of Plant: 837.0 (coaxial); None (fiber optic). Additional miles planned: 100.0 (coaxial).

Executive Vice President, Cable TV & Affiliate Relations: William C. Beaty Jr. Executive Vice President, Marketing: John Barnes Jr. Broadband Engineering Manager: Brian Bendt. Video Content Director: Karl Skroban.

Ownership: Comporium Communications.

ROWESVILLE—Formerly served by Almega Cable. No longer in operation. ICA: SC0162.

SALEM—Charter Communications. Now served by GREENVILLE/SPARTANBURG, SC [SC0003]. ICA: SC0139.

SAMPIT—Time Warner Cable. Now served by MYRTLE BEACH, SC [SC0007]. ICA: SC0090.

SANTEE—Almega Cable, 4023 W Airport Freeway, Ste 552, Bedford, TX 76021. Phones: 817-685-9588; 877-725-6342. Fax: 817-685-6488. Web Site: http://almegacable.com. Also serves Orangeburg County & Vance. ICA: SC0140.

TV Market Ranking: Below 100 (Orangeburg County, SANTEE); Outside TV Markets (Orangeburg County, Vance). Franchise award date: April 1, 1982. Franchise expiration date: N.A. Began: January 1, 1985.

Channel capacity: N.A. Channels available but not in use: N.A.

Basic Service

Subscribers: 876.

Programming (received off-air): KPDX (MNT) Vancouver; WCBD-TV (CW, NBC) Charleston; WCSC-TV (CBS) Charleston; WIS (NBC) Columbia; WOLO-TV (ABC) Columbia.

Programming (via satellite): A&E Networks; ABC Family Channel; Animal Planet; BET Networks; Cartoon Network; CNN; Country Music TV; Discovery Channel; Disney Channel; E! Entertainment Televi-

sion; ESPN; ESPN 2; Fox News Channel; Fox Sports South; FX; Golf Channel; Hallmark Channel; Headline News; HGTV; History Channel; Lifetime; National Geographic Channel; QVC; Spike TV; Syfy; TBS Superstation; The Learning Channel; The Weather Channel; Trinity Broadcasting Network; truTV; Turner Classic Movies; Turner Network TV; TV Land; USA Network; WGN America.
Fee: $34.95 installation; $34.95 monthly.

Pay Service 1
Pay Units: 33.
Programming (via satellite): Cinemax.
Fee: $10.95 monthly.

Pay Service 2
Pay Units: 93.
Programming (via satellite): HBO.
Fee: $10.95 monthly.

Pay Service 3
Pay Units: 46.
Programming (via satellite): Showtime.
Fee: $10.95 monthly.

Pay Service 4
Pay Units: 44.
Programming (via satellite): The Movie Channel.
Fee: $10.95 monthly.

Video-On-Demand: No

Internet Service
Operational: No.

Telephone Service
None

Miles of Plant: 79.0 (coaxial); None (fiber optic).
General Manager: Thomas Kurien.
Ownership: Almega Cable (MSO).

SENECA—Northland Cable Television, 615 N Pine St, PO Box 833, Seneca, SC 29679-0833. Phone: 864-882-0002. Fax: 864-882-4490. E-mail: seneca@northlandcabletv.com. Web Site: http://www.northlandcabletv.com. Also serves Central, Clemson, Liberty, Norris, Oconee County (portions), Pendleton, Pickens, Pickens County, Six Mile & West Union. ICA: SC0019.
TV Market Ranking: 46 (Central, Clemson, Liberty, Norris, Oconee County (portions), Pendleton, Pickens, Pickens County, SENECA, Six Mile, West Union). Franchise award date: April 11, 1977. Franchise expiration date: September 22, 2017. Began: June 1, 1979.
Channel capacity: 64 (operating 2-way). Channels available but not in use: N.A.

Basic Service
Subscribers: 13,000.
Programming (received off-air): WGGS-TV (IND) Greenville; WHNS (FOX) Greenville; WLOS (ABC) Asheville; WMYA-TV (MNT) Anderson; WNTV (PBS) Greenville; WSPA-TV (CBS) Spartanburg; WUGA-TV (PBS) Toccoa; WYCW (CW) Asheville; WYFF (NBC) Greenville.
Programming (via satellite): A&E Networks; Animal Planet; BET Networks; CNBC; CNN; C-SPAN; Discovery Channel; ESPN; Food Network; Fox News Channel; Great American Country; QVC; SportSouth; TBS Superstation; The Learning Channel; The Weather Channel; Turner Network TV; TV Guide Network; WGN America.
Fee: $55.00 installation; $31.99 monthly.

Expanded Basic Service 1
Subscribers: 10,000.
Programming (via satellite): Cartoon Network; Comedy Central; ESPN 2; Fox Movie Channel; Fox Sports South; FX; Golf Channel; Headline News; HGTV; History Channel; Lifetime; MTV; National Geographic Channel; Nickelodeon; Spike TV; Syfy; Travel Channel; Turner Classic Movies; TV Land; USA Network; VH1.
Fee: $11.30 monthly.

Digital Basic Service
Subscribers: 2,100.
Programming (via satellite): BBC America; Bloomberg Television; Bravo; Discovery Digital Networks; DMX Music; Fox Movie Channel; G4; Golf Channel; GSN; Halogen Network; Independent Film Channel; Outdoor Channel; Speed; Trinity Broadcasting Network; Versus; WE tv.
Fee: $8.70 monthly.

Pay Service 1
Pay Units: N.A.
Programming (via satellite): Cinemax; HBO.
Fee: $10.00 monthly (each).

Digital Pay Service 1
Pay Units: N.A.
Programming (via satellite): Cinemax (multiplexed); Encore (multiplexed); Flix; HBO (multiplexed); Showtime (multiplexed); Starz (multiplexed); The Movie Channel (multiplexed).
Fee: $10.00 monthly (Cinemax, HBO, Flix/Showtime/TMC, or Starz/Encore).

Video-On-Demand: No

Pay-Per-View
Addressable homes: 2,100.
iN DEMAND (delivered digitally); Playboy TV (delivered digitally); Fresh (delivered digitally).

Internet Service
Operational: Yes.
Broadband Service: Northland Express.
Fee: $42.99 monthly.

Telephone Service
Digital: Operational

Miles of Plant: 434.0 (coaxial); 18.0 (fiber optic). Additional miles planned: 32.0 (coaxial).
Plant Manager: Alan Boggs. Regional Manager: Bill Staley. Marketing Manager: Melinda Harbin. Office Manager: Sharon Martin. Technical Manager: Travis Blakely.
Ownership: Northland Communications Corp. (MSO).

SPARTANBURG—Charter Communications, 2 Digital Place, Simpsonville, SC 29681. Phone: 864-254-7260. Fax: 864-254-7345. Web Site: http://www.charter.com. Also serves Columbus, Landran, Lynn, Saluda & Tryon, NC; Abbeville, Abbeville County (portions), Anderson, Anderson County (portions), Blacksburg, Blue Ridge, Buffalo, Campobello, Central Pacolet, Cherokee County (unincorporated areas), Chesnee, Chester County (unincorporated areas), Clinton, Cowpens, Donalds, Due West, Duncan, Easley, Ebenezer, Enoree, Fairfield, Fountain Inn, Gaffney, Gray Court, Greenville County, Greer, Hornea Path, Inman, Iva, Joanna, Jonesville, Keowee Key, Landrum, Laurens, Laurens County (portions), Lockhart, Lyman, Marietta, Mauldin, Oconee County (unincorporated areas), Owings, Pacolet, Pacolet Mills, Pelzer, Pickens, Pickens County (portions), Pickett Post, Salem, Simpsonville, Spartanburg County, Starr, Travelers Rest, Union, Union County (portions), Wellford, West Pelzer, Williamston & Woodruff, SC. ICA: SC0003.
TV Market Ranking: 46 (Abbeville, Abbeville County (portions), Anderson, Anderson County (portions), Blacksburg, Blue Ridge, Buffalo, Campobello, Central Pacolet, Cherokee County (unincorporated areas), Chesnee, Chester County (unincorporated areas) (portions), Clinton, Columbus, Cowpens, Donalds, Due West, Duncan, Easley, Ebenezer, Enoree, Fairfield, Fountain Inn, Gaffney, Gray Court, Greenville County, Greer, Hornea Path, Inman, Iva, Jonesville, Keowee Key, Landran, Landrum, Laurens, Laurens County (portions) (portions), Lockhart, Lyman, Lynn, Marietta, Mauldin, Oconee County (unincorporated areas) (portions), Owings, Pacolet, Pacolet Mills, Pelzer, Pickens, Pickens County (portions), Pickett Post, Salem, Saluda, Simpsonville, SPARTANBURG, SPARTANBURG, Spartanburg County, Starr, Travelers Rest, Tryon, Union, Union County (portions) (portions), Wellford, West Pelzer, Williamston, Woodruff); Below 100 (Chester County (unincorporated areas) (portions), Oconee County (unincorporated areas) (portions), Union County (portions) (portions)); Outside TV Markets (Joanna, Laurens County (portions) (portions), Oconee County (unincorporated areas) (portions), Union County (portions) (portions)). Franchise award date: March 1, 1968. Franchise expiration date: N.A. Began: March 23, 1972.
Channel capacity: 116 (operating 2-way). Channels available but not in use: N.A.

Basic Service
Subscribers: 204,133.
Programming (received off-air): WGGS-TV (IND) Greenville; WHNS (FOX) Greenville; WLOS (ABC) Asheville; WMYA-TV (MNT) Anderson; WNTV (PBS) Greenville; WSPA-TV (CBS) Spartanburg; WUNF-TV (PBS) Asheville; WYCW (CW) Asheville; WYFF (NBC) Greenville.
Programming (via satellite): BET Networks; C-SPAN; C-SPAN 2; INSP; ION Television; QVC; Telemundo; The Weather Channel; TV Guide Network; Univision Studios; WGN America.
Fee: $49.95 installation.

Expanded Basic Service 1
Subscribers: 55,982.
Programming (via satellite): A&E Networks; ABC Family Channel; AmericanLife TV Network; Animal Planet; Bravo; Cartoon Network; CNBC; CNN; Comcast/Charter Sports Southeast (CSS); Comedy Central; Country Music TV; Discovery Channel; Disney Channel; DIY Network; E! Entertainment Television; ESPN; ESPN 2; Food Network; Fox News Channel; Fox Sports South; FX; G4; Golf Channel; GSN; Hallmark Channel; Headline News; HGTV; History Channel; Lifetime; MSNBC; MTV; MTV2; National Geographic Channel; Nickelodeon; Oxygen; SoapNet; Speed; Spike TV; SportSouth; Syfy; TBS Superstation; The Learning Channel; Toon Disney; Travel Channel; truTV; Turner Classic Movies; Turner Network TV; TV Land; USA Network; Versus; VH1; WE tv.
Fee: $31.36 installation; $44.50 monthly.

Digital Basic Service
Subscribers: N.A.
Programming (via satellite): BBC America; Bio; Bloomberg Television; Boomerang; Canales N; CNN International; Cooking Channel; Discovery Fit & Health; ESPN; ESPN Classic Sports; ESPNews; Eternal Word TV Network; Fox College Sports Atlantic; Fox College Sports Central; Fox College Sports Pacific; Fox Soccer; Fuel TV; Fuse; GalaVision; GAS; Great American Country; Halogen Network; HD Theater; HDNet; HDNet Movies; History Channel International; Independent Film Channel; Lifetime Movie Network; Lifetime Real Women; MTV Networks Digital Suite; Music Choice; NFL Network; Nick Jr.; Nick Too; NickToons TV; Sundance Channel; TV One; Weatherscan.

Digital Pay Service 1
Pay Units: N.A.
Programming (via satellite): Cinemax (multiplexed); Encore (multiplexed); Flix; HBO (multiplexed); HBO HD; Playboy TV; Showtime (multiplexed); Showtime HD; Starz (multiplexed); The Movie Channel (multiplexed).
Fee: $15.95 monthly.

Video-On-Demand: Yes

Pay-Per-View
iN DEMAND (delivered digitally); NASCAR In Car (delivered digitally); Playboy TV (delivered digitally); Fresh (delivered digitally); Shorteez (delivered digitally); NHL Center Ice (delivered digitally); MLB Extra Innings (delivered digitally).

Internet Service
Operational: Yes.
Broadband Service: Charter Pipeline.
Fee: $29.99 monthly.

Telephone Service
Digital: Operational

Miles of Plant: 8,182.0 (coaxial); 1,029.0 (fiber optic).
Vice President & General Manager: Anthony Pope. Operations Manager: Pat Hayes. Marketing Director: Brooke Sinclair.
Ownership: Charter Communications Inc. (MSO).

SPARTANBURG—Charter Communications. Now served by GREENVILLE/SPARTANBURG, SC [SC0003]. ICA: SC0004.

SPRINGFIELD—Formerly served by Almega Cable. No longer in operation. ICA: SC0163.

ST. GEORGE—Almega Cable, 4020 W Airport Freeway, Ste 549, Bedford, TX 76021. Phones: 817-685-9588; 877-725-6342. Fax: 817-685-6488. Web Site: http://almegacable.com. Also serves Dorchester County (unincorporated areas) & Reevesville. ICA: SC0078.
TV Market Ranking: Below 100 (Dorchester County (unincorporated areas) (portions)); Outside TV Markets (Dorchester County (unincorporated areas) (portions), Reevesville, ST. GEORGE). Franchise award date: January 1, 1981. Franchise expiration date: N.A. Began: August 8, 1983.
Channel capacity: 65 (not 2-way capable). Channels available but not in use: N.A.

Basic Service
Subscribers: 706.
Programming (received off-air): WCBD-TV (CW, NBC) Charleston; WCIV (ABC) Charleston; WCSC-TV (CBS) Charleston; WIS (NBC) Columbia; WITV (PBS) Charleston; WLTX (CBS) Columbia; WMMP (MNT) Charleston; WTAT-TV (FOX) Charleston.
Programming (via satellite): A&E Networks; ABC Family Channel; AMC; Animal Planet; BET Networks; Cartoon Network; CNBC; CNN; Discovery Channel; Disney Channel; E! Entertainment Television; ESPN; ESPN 2; FX; Great American Country; Headline News; HGTV; History Channel; Lifetime; MSNBC; National Geographic Channel; Nickelodeon; Speed; Spike TV; TBS Superstation; The Learning Channel; The Weather Channel; Travel Channel; truTV; Turner Classic Movies; Turner Network TV; USA Network; WE tv; WGN America.
Fee: $29.95 installation; $31.95 monthly.

Pay Service 1
Pay Units: N.A.
Programming (via satellite): Cinemax; HBO; Showtime; The Movie Channel.
Fee: $9.00 monthly (each).
Video-On-Demand: No
Internet Service
Operational: No.
Telephone Service
None
Miles of Plant: 69.0 (coaxial); None (fiber optic).
General Manager: Thomas Kurien.
Ownership: Almega Cable (MSO).

ST. STEPHEN—Formerly served by Pine Tree Cablevision. No longer in operation. ICA: SC0141.

SUMMERTON—Almega Cable, 4019 W Airport Freeway, Ste 548, Bedford, TX 76021. Phones: 817-685-9588; 877-725-6342. Fax: 817-685-6488. Web Site: http://almegacable.com. Also serves Davis Station, Goat Island Resort, Manning, Potato Creek & Taw Caw. ICA: SC0077.
TV Market Ranking: Below 100 (Davis Station, Goat Island Resort, Manning, Potato Creek, SUMMERTON, Taw Caw). Franchise award date: November 1, 1988. Franchise expiration date: November 1, 2008. Began: March 1, 1989.
Channel capacity: 62 (not 2-way capable). Channels available but not in use: N.A.
Basic Service
Subscribers: 952.
Programming (received off-air): WCBD-TV (CW, NBC) Charleston; WCIV (ABC) Charleston; WCSC-TV (CBS) Charleston; WIS (NBC) Columbia; WITV (PBS) Charleston; WLTX (CBS) Columbia; WTAT-TV (FOX) Charleston.
Programming (via satellite): A&E Networks; ABC Family Channel; CNBC; CNN; Country Music TV; C-SPAN; Discovery Channel; ESPN; ESPN 2; Golf Channel; Headline News; History Channel; Lifetime; MTV; Nickelodeon; Spike TV; Syfy; TBS Superstation; The Learning Channel; The Weather Channel; Travel Channel; Turner Classic Movies; Turner Network TV; USA Network; VH1; WGN America.
Fee: $34.95 installation; $19.95 monthly; $3.00 converter.
Pay Service 1
Pay Units: 42.
Programming (via satellite): Cinemax.
Fee: $10.00 installation; $10.95 monthly.
Pay Service 2
Pay Units: 42.
Programming (via satellite): HBO.
Fee: $10.00 installation; $10.95 monthly.
Pay Service 3
Pay Units: 42.
Programming (via satellite): Showtime.
Fee: $10.00 installation; $10.95 monthly.
Pay Service 4
Pay Units: 40.
Programming (via satellite): The Movie Channel.
Fee: $10.00 installation; $10.95 monthly.
Video-On-Demand: No
Internet Service
Operational: No.
Telephone Service
None
Miles of Plant: 83.0 (coaxial); None (fiber optic).
General Manager: Thomas Kurien. Regional Service Manager: Clarence Sumpter.
Ownership: Almega Cable (MSO).

SUMMERVILLE—Time Warner Cable. Now served by MYRTLE BEACH, SC [SC0007]. ICA: SC0012.

SURFSIDE BEACH—Time Warner Cable. Now served by MYRTLE BEACH, SC [SC0007]. ICA: SC0006.

SWANSEA—Formerly served by Pine Tree Cablevision. No longer in operation. ICA: SC0097.

THE SUMMIT—Formerly served by Adelphia Communications. No longer in operation. ICA: SC0142.

TRAVELERS REST—Charter Communications. Now served by GREENVILLE/SPARTANBURG, SC [SC0003]. ICA: SC0143.

TURBEVILLE—FTC Vision. Formerly [SC0085]. This cable system has converted to IPTV, 1101 E Main St, Kingstree, SC 29556. Phones: 888-218-5050; 843-382-1387. Web Site: http://www.ftcvision.com. ICA: SC5026.
Channel capacity: N.A. Channels available but not in use: N.A.
Internet Service
Operational: Yes.
Telephone Service
Digital: Operational
Chief Executive Officer: Brad Erwin.

TURBEVILLE—FTC Vision. This cable system has converted to IPTV. See Turbeville, SC [SC5029] & Olanta, SC [SC5027]. ICA: SC0085.

UNION—Charter Communications. Now served by GREENVILLE/SPARTANBURG, SC [SC0003]. ICA: SC0033.

WAGENER—Formerly served by Pine Tree Cablevision. No longer in operation. ICA: SC0102.

WALTERBORO—Comcast Cable, 4400 Belle Oaks Dr, North Charleston, SC 29405. Phone: 843-747-1403. Fax: 843-266-3272. E-mail: bill_watson@cable.comcast.com. Web Site: http://www.comcast.com. Also serves Colleton County. ICA: SC0145.
TV Market Ranking: Below 100 (Colleton County (portions)); Outside TV Markets (Colleton County (portions), WALTERBORO). Franchise award date: N.A. Franchise expiration date: N.A. Began: N.A.
Channel capacity: N.A. Channels available but not in use: N.A.
Basic Service
Subscribers: 4,300.
Programming (received off-air): WCBD-TV (CW, NBC) Charleston; WCIV (ABC) Charleston; WCSC-TV (CBS) Charleston; WIS (NBC) Columbia; WITV (PBS) Charleston; WJWJ-TV (PBS) Beaufort; WMMP (MNT) Charleston; WTAT-TV (FOX) Charleston.
Programming (via satellite): CW+; Fox Sports South; TBS Superstation; Turner Network TV.
Fee: $61.25 installation; $9.25 monthly.
Expanded Basic Service 1
Subscribers: N.A.
Programming (via satellite): A&E Networks; ABC Family Channel; AMC; Animal Planet; BET Networks; Cartoon Network; CNN; Comcast/Charter Sports Southeast (CSS); Comedy Central; Country Music TV; C-SPAN; Discovery Channel; Discovery Health Channel; Disney Channel; E! Entertainment Television; ESPN; ESPN 2; Food Network; Fox News Channel; FX; Golf Channel; Hallmark Channel; Headline News; HGTV; History Channel; INSP; Lifetime; MTV; Nickelodeon; QVC; Speed; Spike TV; Syfy; The Learning Channel; The Weather Channel; truTV; TV Land; USA Network; Versus.
Fee: $32.00 monthly.
Digital Basic Service
Subscribers: N.A.
Programming (via satellite): BBC America; Discovery Digital Networks; Encore (multiplexed); ESPNews; Flix; GAS; MTV Networks Digital Suite; Music Choice; Nick Jr.; Nick Too; SoapNet; Sundance Channel; Toon Disney.
Fee: $14.95 monthly.
Digital Pay Service 1
Pay Units: N.A.
Programming (via satellite): Cinemax (multiplexed); HBO (multiplexed); Showtime (multiplexed); The Movie Channel (multiplexed).
Fee: $11.85 monthly (each).
Video-On-Demand: No
Pay-Per-View
iN DEMAND; Playboy TV (delivered digitally); Fresh (delivered digitally); iN DEMAND (delivered digitally); Shorteez (delivered digitally); Pleasure (delivered digitally).
Internet Service
Operational: Yes.
Broadband Service: Comcast High Speed Internet.
Fee: $42.95 monthly.
Telephone Service
Digital: Operational
General Manager: Bill Watson. Technical Operations Director: Anthony Douglas. Marketing Director: Laura Scarborough. Chief Technician: Bob Bradshaw. Marketing Manager: Audrey Jones.
Ownership: Comcast Cable Communications Inc. (MSO).

WEST PELZER—Charter Communications. Now served by GREENVILLE/SPARTANBURG, SC [SC0003]. ICA: SC0009.

WHITMIRE—Charter Communications, 2 Digital Place, Simpsonville, SC 29681. Phone: 864-254-7260. Fax: 864-254-7345. Web Site: http://www.charter.com. Also serves Newberry County (unincorporated areas) & Union County (unincorporated areas). ICA: SC0065.
TV Market Ranking: 100,46 (Newberry County (unincorporated areas) (portions)); 46 (Union County (unincorporated areas) (portions)); Below 100 (Union County (unincorporated areas) (portions)); Outside TV Markets (WHITMIRE, Newberry County (unincorporated areas) (portions), Union County (unincorporated areas) (portions)). Franchise award date: April 14, 1980. Franchise expiration date: N.A. Began: February 1, 1982.
Channel capacity: N.A. Channels available but not in use: N.A.
Basic Service
Subscribers: 725.
Programming (received off-air): WBTV (CBS) Charlotte; WCCB (FOX) Charlotte; WGGS-TV (IND) Greenville; WIS (NBC) Columbia; WLOS (ABC) Asheville; WLTX (CBS) Columbia; WMYA-TV (MNT) Anderson; WOLO-TV (ABC) Columbia; WRLK-TV (PBS) Columbia; WSPA-TV (CBS) Spartanburg; WYCW (CW) Asheville; WYFF (NBC) Greenville.
Programming (via satellite): BET Networks; C-SPAN; C-SPAN 2; INSP; ION Television; QVC; Telemundo; The Weather Channel; TV Guide Network; Univision Studios; WGN America.
Fee: $49.95 installation; $3.50 converter.
Expanded Basic Service 1
Subscribers: 689.
Programming (via satellite): A&E Networks; ABC Family Channel; AMC; Animal Planet; Bravo; Cartoon Network; CNBC; CNN; Comcast/Charter Sports Southeast (CSS); Comedy Central; Country Music TV; Discovery Channel; Disney Channel; DIY Network; E! Entertainment Television; ESPN; ESPN 2; Food Network; Fox News Channel; Fox Sports South; FX; G4; Golf Channel; GSN; Hallmark Channel; Headline News; HGTV; History Channel; Lifetime; MSNBC; MTV; MTV2; National Geographic Channel; Nickelodeon; Oxygen; SoapNet; Speed; Spike TV; SportSouth; Syfy; TBS Superstation; The Learning Channel; Toon Disney; Travel Channel; truTV; Turner Classic Movies; Turner Network TV; TV Land; USA Network; Versus; VH1; WE tv.
Fee: $44.50 monthly.
Digital Basic Service
Subscribers: N.A.
Programming (via satellite): BBC America; Bio; Bloomberg Television; Boomerang; Canales N; CNN International; Cooking Channel; Discovery Fit & Health; ESPN; ESPN Classic Sports; ESPNews; Eternal Word TV Network; Fox College Sports Atlantic; Fox College Sports Central; Fox College Sports Pacific; Fox Movie Channel; Fox Soccer; Fuel TV; Fuse; GalaVision; GAS; Great American Country; Halogen Network; HD Theater; HDNet; HDNet Movies; History Channel International; Independent Film Channel; Lifetime Movie Network; Lifetime Real Women; MTV Networks Digital Suite; Music Choice; NFL Network; Nick Jr.; Nick Too; NickToons TV; Sundance Channel; TV One; Weatherscan.
Digital Pay Service 1
Pay Units: 83.
Programming (via satellite): HBO (multiplexed); HBO HD.
Fee: $13.95 monthly.
Digital Pay Service 2
Pay Units: 84.
Programming (via satellite): Showtime (multiplexed); Showtime HD.
Fee: $11.95 monthly.

Read what the Telecom elite read...
Communications Daily
Warren Communications News
FREE 30-day trial–call 800-771-9202 or visit www.warren-news.com

Digital Pay Service 3
Pay Units: N.A.
Programming (via satellite): Cinemax (multiplexed); Encore (multiplexed); Flix; Playboy TV; Starz (multiplexed); The Movie Channel (multiplexed).
Video-On-Demand: Yes

Pay-Per-View
iN DEMAND (delivered digitally); Playboy TV (delivered digitally); Fresh (delivered digitally); Shorteez (delivered digitally); NASCAR In Car (delivered digitally); ESPN (delivered digitally); NHL Center Ice (delivered digitally); MLB Extra Innings (delivered digitally).

Internet Service
Operational: Yes.
Broadband Service: Charter Pipeline.
Fee: $29.99 monthly; $3.95 modem lease.

Telephone Service
Digital: Operational
Fee: $29.99 monthly
Miles of Plant: 19.0 (coaxial); None (fiber optic).

Vice President & General Manager: Anthony Pope. Marketing Director: Brooke Sinclair. Operations Manager: Pat Hayes.
Ownership: Charter Communications Inc. (MSO).

WILD DUNES—US Cable of Coastal Texas. Now served by CHARLESTON, SC [SC0001]. ICA: SC0064.

WILLIAMSTON—Charter Communications. Now served by GREENVILLE/SPARTANBURG, SC [SC0003]. ICA: SC0062.

WINNSBORO—TruVista Communications, 112 York St, PO Box 160, Chester, SC 29706. Phones: 803-385-2191; 803-635-6459. Fax: 803-581-2226. Web Site: http://www.truvista.net. Also serves Fairfield County (portions) & Ridgeway. ICA: SC0048.
TV Market Ranking: 100 (Fairfield County (portions), Ridgeway, WINNSBORO). Franchise award date: N.A. Franchise expiration date: N.A. Began: October 15, 1980.
Channel capacity: N.A. Channels available but not in use: N.A.

Basic Service
Subscribers: N.A. Included in Chester
Programming (received off-air): WACH (FOX) Columbia; WIS (NBC) Columbia; WLTX (CBS) Columbia; WOLO-TV (ABC) Columbia; WRLK-TV (PBS) Columbia.
Programming (via satellite): C-SPAN 2; QVC; Trinity Broadcasting Network; TV Guide Network.
Fee: $45.00 installation; $23.90 monthly.

Digital Basic Service
Subscribers: N.A.
Programming (via satellite): A&E HD; BBC America; Bio; Bloomberg Television; Boomerang; CBS Sports Network; Church Channel; cloo; CMT Pure Country; CNN en Espanol; CNN International; Cooking Channel; Discovery Channel HD; Discovery en Espanol; Discovery Health Channel; Discovery Kids Channel; ESPN 2 HD; ESPN HD; ESPN U; ESPNews; Fox Deportes; Fox Movie Channel; FSN Digital Atlantic; FSN Digital Central; FSN Digital Pacific; Fuel TV; Fuse; Hallmark Movie Channel; HD Theater; HDNet; HDNet Movies; History Channel International; ID Investigation Discovery; Independent Film Channel; INSP; ION Television; Lifetime Movie Network; Lifetime Movie Network HD; Military Channel; MSNBC; MTV Hits; MTV Jams; MTV2; Music Choice; Nick Jr.; Nick Too; Ovation; PBS HD; Planet Green; Science; Speed HD; Sundance Channel; Syfy HD; TBS in HD; TeenNick; TLC HD; Tr3s; Turner Network TV HD; Universal HD; USA Network HD; Versus; VH1 Classic; VH1 Soul.

Digital Pay Service 1
Pay Units: N.A.
Programming (via satellite): Cinemax (multiplexed); Cinemax HD; Encore (multiplexed); Flix; HBO (multiplexed); HBO HD; Showtime (multiplexed); Showtime HD; Starz (multiplexed); Starz HDTV; The Movie Channel (multiplexed).
Video-On-Demand: No

Pay-Per-View
iN DEMAND (delivered digitally); ESPN Gameplan (delivered digitally); Special events (delivered digitally); Ten Xtsy (delivered digitally); Club Jenna (delivered digitally); Spice: Xcess (delivered digitally); Playboy en Espanol (delivered digitally); Playboy TV (delivered digitally); Fresh (delivered digitally); Shorteez (delivered digitally).

Internet Service
Operational: Yes.
Broadband Service: In-house.

Telephone Service
Digital: Operational
Miles of Plant: 48.0 (coaxial); None (fiber optic).
President & Chief Executive Officer: Brian Singleton. Vice President, Sales & Marketing: Allison Johnson. Marketing Manager: Bob Wilkinson. Video Service Manager: Tony Helms.
Ownership: TruVista Communications (MSO).

SOUTH DAKOTA

Total Systems: 119
Total Communities Served: 240
Franchises Not Yet Operating: 0
Applications Pending: 0
Communities with Applications: 0
Number of Basic Subscribers: 210,749
Number of Expanded Basic Subscribers: 650
Number of Pay Units: 34,046

Top 100 Markets Represented: Sioux Falls-Mitchell (85).

**For a list of cable communities in this section, see the Cable Community Index located in the back of Cable Volume 2.
For explanation of terms used in cable system listings, see p. D-11.**

ABERDEEN—Formerly served by ITC. No longer in operation. ICA: SD5061.

ABERDEEN TWP.—Midcontinent Communications, 24 First Ave NE, PO Box 1560, Aberdeen, SD 57402-1560. Phones: 800-888-1300; 605-229-1775. Fax: 605-229-0572. Web Site: http://www.midcocomm.com. Also serves Bath, Bowdle, Bristol, Brown County, Doland, Frederick, Ipswich, Java, Mina, Redfield, Roscoe, Roslyn, Selby, Warner, Waubay & Webster. ICA: SD0003.

TV Market Ranking: Below 100 (ABERDEEN TWP., Bath, Bristol, Brown County (portions), Frederick, Ipswich, Mina, Roslyn, Warner, Waubay, Webster); Outside TV Markets (Bowdle, Brown County (portions), Doland, Java, Redfield, Roscoe, Selby). Franchise award date: August 16, 1968. Franchise expiration date: N.A. Began: July 1, 1970.

Channel capacity: 69 (operating 2-way). Channels available but not in use: N.A.

Basic Service

Subscribers: 12,177.

Programming (received off-air): KABY-TV (ABC) Aberdeen; KCPO-LP Sioux Falls; KDLO-TV (CBS, MNT) Florence; KDLT-TV (NBC) Sioux Falls; KDSD-TV (PBS) Aberdeen; KTTM (FOX) Huron; KWSD (CW) Sioux Falls; 5 FMs.

Programming (via satellite): A&E Networks; ABC Family Channel; AMC; Animal Planet; BET Networks; Bravo; Cartoon Network; CNBC; CNN; Comedy Central; Country Music TV; C-SPAN; C-SPAN 2; Discovery Channel; Discovery Fit & Health; Discovery Health Channel; Disney Channel; E! Entertainment Television; ESPN; ESPN 2; ESPN Classic Sports; ESPNews; Eternal Word TV Network; Food Network; Fox Movie Channel; Fox News Channel; Fox Sports Net North; FX; G4; Headline News; HGTV; History Channel; INSP; Lifetime; MSNBC; MTV; Nickelodeon; Outdoor Channel; QVC; Speed; Spike TV; Syfy; TBS Superstation; The Learning Channel; The Weather Channel; Travel Channel; truTV; Turner Classic Movies; Turner Network TV; TV Guide Network; TV Land; USA Network; Versus; VH1; WE tv; WGN America.

Fee: $50.00 installation; $25.00 monthly.

Digital Basic Service

Subscribers: 2,454.

Programming (via satellite): BBC America; Bio; Bloomberg Television; Discovery Digital Networks; DMX Music; ESPNews; Fox Sports World; Fuse; GAS; Golf Channel; GSN; History Channel; Independent Film Channel; Lifetime Movie Network; Nick Jr.; Style Network; Sundance Channel; Toon Disney; VH1 Classic; VH1 Country; VH1 Soul.

Digital Pay Service 1

Pay Units: 4,261.

Programming (via satellite): Cinemax (multiplexed); Encore (multiplexed); HBO (multiplexed); Showtime (multiplexed); Starz (multiplexed); The Movie Channel (multiplexed).

Fee: $11.00 monthly (each).

Video-On-Demand: No

Pay-Per-View

Addressable homes: 2,454.

Hot Choice (delivered digitally); iN DEMAND; Sports PPV (delivered digitally).

Internet Service

Operational: Yes. Began: June 1, 1998.

Subscribers: 3,892.

Broadband Service: MidcoNet.

Fee: $35.00 installation; $19.95 monthly; $10.00 modem lease.

Telephone Service

Digital: Operational

Fee: $18.00 monthly

Miles of Plant: 433.0 (coaxial); 42.0 (fiber optic).

Manager: Clay Stevens. Marketing Director: Mark Powell. Customer Service Manager: Chris VanDover.

Ownership: Midcontinent Media Inc. (MSO).; Comcast Cable Communications Inc. (MSO).

ALEXANDRIA—TrioTel Communications Inc., 330 S Nebraska St, PO Box 630, Salem, SD 57058-0630. Phone: 605-425-2238. Fax: 605-425-2712. E-mail: customerservice@triotel.net. Web Site: http://www.triotel.net. Also serves Canova, Emery & Spencer. ICA: SD0097.

TV Market Ranking: 85 (ALEXANDRIA, Canova, Emery, Spencer). Franchise award date: N.A. Franchise expiration date: N.A. Began: November 1, 1983.

Channel capacity: 40 (operating 2-way). Channels available but not in use: N.A.

Basic Service

Subscribers: 480.

Programming (received off-air): KAUN-LP Sioux Falls; KCPO-LP Sioux Falls; KDLT-TV (NBC) Sioux Falls; KELO-TV (CBS, MNT) Sioux Falls; KSFY-TV (ABC) Sioux Falls; KTTM (FOX) Huron; KTTW (FOX) Sioux Falls; KUSD-TV (PBS) Vermillion.

Programming (via satellite): A&E Networks; ABC Family Channel; CNN; Country Music TV; Discovery Channel; Disney Channel; ESPN; ESPN 2; Eternal Word TV Network; Headline News; HGTV; History Channel; Lifetime; MTV; Nickelodeon; Outdoor Channel; QVC; Spike TV; TBS Superstation; The Weather Channel; Trinity Broadcasting Network; Turner Classic Movies; Turner Network TV; TV Land; USA Network; VH1; WGN America.

Fee: $20.00 installation; $23.95 monthly.

Digital Basic Service

Subscribers: 422.

Programming (via satellite): CW+; DMX Music; Eternal Word TV Network; LWS Local Weather Station; Paramount Network (UPN); QVC; Trinity Broadcasting Network; WGN America.

Fee: $20.95 monthly.

Digital Expanded Basic Service

Subscribers: N.A.

Programming (via satellite): A&E Networks; AMC; Animal Planet; Bloomberg Television; Bravo; Cartoon Network; CNBC; CNN; Comedy Central; Country Music TV; C-SPAN; Discovery Channel; Discovery Health Channel; Disney Channel; DIY Network; E! Entertainment Television; ESPN; ESPN 2; ESPN Classic Sports; ESPNews; Food Network; Fox Movie Channel; Fox News Channel; Fox Sports Net; FX; Golf Channel; Great American Country; GSN; Hallmark Channel; Headline News; HGTV; History Channel; Lifetime; Lifetime Real Women; MSNBC; MTV; MTV Hits; MTV2; National Geographic Channel; Nick Jr.; Nickelodeon; NickToons TV; Outdoor Channel; Oxygen; RFD-TV; SoapNet; Speed; Syfy; TBS Superstation; TeenNick; The Learning Channel; The Weather Channel; Toon Disney; Travel Channel; truTV; Turner Classic Movies; Turner Network TV; TV Land; USA Network; Versus; VH1; VH1 Classic; WE tv.

Fee: $22.95 monthly.

Pay Service 1

Pay Units: N.A.

Programming (via satellite): HBO.

Fee: $10.95 monthly.

Digital Pay Service 1

Pay Units: N.A.

Programming (via satellite): Cinemax (multiplexed); Encore (multiplexed); HBO (multiplexed); Playboy TV; Showtime (multiplexed); Starz (multiplexed); The Movie Channel.

Fee: $10.95 monthly (Playboy, Starz/Encore, Cinemax, or Showtime/TMC), $11.95 monthly (HBO).

Video-On-Demand: No

Pay-Per-View

iN DEMAND (delivered digitally); Spice (delivered digitally); Playboy TV (delivered digitally).

Internet Service

Operational: No, Both DSL & dial-up.

Telephone Service

None

Miles of Plant: 17.0 (coaxial); None (fiber optic).

General Manager & Chief Executive Officer: Bryan K. Roth. Chief Technician: Tim Wenande. Customer Service Manager: Heather Kranz.

Ownership: McCook Cooperative Telephone Co.

ALPENA (town)—Santel Communications. Formerly served by Mount Vernon, SD [SD0188]. This cable system has converted to IPTV, 308 S Dumont Ave, PO Box 67, Woonsocket, SD 57385-0067. Phones: 888-978-7777; 605-796-4411. Fax: 605-796-4419. E-mail: info@santel.net. Web Site: http://www.santel.net. ICA: SD5014.

TV Market Ranking: Below 100 (ALPENA, ALPENA (TOWN)).

Channel capacity: N.A. Channels available but not in use: N.A.

Basic Service

Subscribers: N.A.

Fee: $33.95 monthly.

Expanded Basic Service 1

Subscribers: N.A.

Fee: $43.95 monthly.

Limited Basic Service

Subscribers: N.A.

Fee: $21.95 monthly.

Pay Service 1

Pay Units: N.A.

Fee: $10.95 monthly (Cinemax, Encore/Starz, HBO, or Showtime).

Internet Service

Operational: Yes.

Fee: $25.00 installation; $24.95 monthly; $10.00 modem lease.

Telephone Service

Analog: Operational

Fee: $14.50 monthly

ARMOUR—Golden West Telecommunications, 415 Crown St, PO Box 411, Wall, SD 57790-0411. Phone: 605-279-2161. Fax: 605-279-2727. E-mail: info@goldenwest.com. Web Site: http://www.goldenwest.com. ICA: SD0149.

TV Market Ranking: 85 (ARMOUR). Franchise award date: January 1, 1981. Franchise expiration date: N.A. Began: March 1, 1982.

Channel capacity: 135 (not 2-way capable). Channels available but not in use: N.A.

Basic Service

Subscribers: 250.

Programming (received off-air): KDLV-TV (NBC) Mitchell; KELO-TV (CBS, MNT) Sioux Falls; KSFY-TV (ABC) Sioux Falls; KTSD-TV (PBS) Pierre.

Programming (via satellite): ABC Family Channel; CNN; Country Music TV; Discovery Channel; ESPN; Headline News; Spike TV; TBS Superstation; Turner Network TV; USA Network; WGN America.

Fee: $25.00 installation; $33.95 monthly.

Digital Basic Service

Subscribers: N.A.

Programming (via satellite): AmericanLife TV Network; Bio; Bloomberg Television; Bravo; Discovery Digital Networks; DMX Music; ESPN 2; ESPN Classic Sports; ESPNews; Fox Movie Channel; Fox Sports World; FX; G4; Golf Channel; GSN; HGTV; History Channel; History Channel Interna-

tional; Independent Film Channel; INSP; Lifetime Movie Network; MuchMusic Network; National Geographic Channel; Outdoor Channel; Speed; Style Network; Syfy; Toon Disney; Trinity Broadcasting Network; Turner Classic Movies; Versus; WE tv.
Fee: $10.00 installation; $14.95 monthly.

Pay Service 1
Pay Units: 17.
Programming (via satellite): HBO.
Fee: $11.95 monthly.

Pay Service 2
Pay Units: N.A.
Programming (via satellite): Cinemax.
Fee: $11.95 monthly.

Pay Service 3
Pay Units: N.A.
Programming (via satellite): Showtime.
Fee: $10.95 monthly.

Digital Pay Service 1
Pay Units: N.A.
Programming (via satellite): Cinemax (multiplexed); Encore (multiplexed); HBO (multiplexed); Showtime (multiplexed); Starz (multiplexed); The Movie Channel (multiplexed).
Fee: $11.95 monthly (Cinemax), $12.95 monthly (HBO), $13.95 monthly (Starz/Encore or Showtime/TMC).

Video-On-Demand: No

Pay-Per-View
Viewer's Choice (delivered digitally); Hot Choice (delivered digitally); Playboy TV (delivered digitally); Fresh (delivered digitally); ESPN Now (delivered digitally); ESPN (delivered digitally); Sports PPV (delivered digitally).

Internet Service
Operational: No, Both DSL & dial-up.

Telephone Service
None

Miles of Plant: 11.0 (coaxial); None (fiber optic).
General Manager: George Strandell. Marketing Director: Greg Oleson. Chief Technician: Randy Shepard. Cable Television Manager: Rick Reed. Customer Service Manager: Jody Bielmaier.
Ownership: Golden West Cablevision (MSO).

ARTESIAN—Santel Communications. Formerly served by Mount Vernon, SD [SD0188]. This cable system has converted to IPTV, 308 S Dumont Ave, PO Box 67, Woonsocket, SD 57385-0067. Phones: 888-978-7777; 605-796-4411. Fax: 605-796-4419. E-mail: info@santel.net. Web Site: http://www.santel.net. ICA: SD5015.
TV Market Ranking: 85 (ARTESIAN).
Channel capacity: N.A. Channels available but not in use: N.A.

Basic Service
Subscribers: N.A.
Fee: $33.95 monthly.

Expanded Basic Service 1
Subscribers: N.A.
Fee: $43.95 monthly.

Limited Basic Service
Subscribers: N.A.
Fee: $21.95 monthly.

Pay Service 1
Pay Units: N.A.
Fee: $10.95 monthly (Cinemax, Encore/Starz, Playboy, or Showtime).

Internet Service
Operational: Yes.
Fee: $25.00 installation; $24.95 monthly.

Telephone Service
Analog: Operational
Fee: $14.50 monthly

ASHTON—Midcontinent Communications, PO Box 5010, Sioux Falls, SD 57117. Phones: 800-456-0564; 605-229-1775. Fax: 605-229-0478. Web Site: http://www.midcocomm.com. ICA: SD0150.
TV Market Ranking: Below 100 (ASHTON). Franchise award date: N.A. Franchise expiration date: N.A. Began: N.A.
Channel capacity: 22 (2-way capable). Channels available but not in use: N.A.

Basic Service
Subscribers: 22.
Programming (received off-air): KABY-TV (ABC) Aberdeen; KDLT-TV (NBC) Sioux Falls; KDSD-TV (PBS) Aberdeen; KELO-TV (CBS, MNT) Sioux Falls; KTTM (FOX) Huron.
Programming (via satellite): A&E Networks; ABC Family Channel; AMC; CNN; Discovery Channel; Disney Channel; ESPN; ESPN 2; History Channel; Nickelodeon; Spike TV; TBS Superstation; Turner Network TV; USA Network; VH1; WGN America.
Fee: $31.95 monthly.

Pay Service 1
Pay Units: N.A.
Programming (via satellite): HBO.
Fee: $11.95 monthly.

Video-On-Demand: No

Internet Service
Operational: No.

Telephone Service
None

Miles of Plant: 2.0 (coaxial); None (fiber optic).
Manager: Doug Bierschbach. Chief Technician: Paul Schmidt.
Ownership: Midcontinent Media Inc. (MSO).

ASTORIA—ITC. Formerly served by Clear Lake, SD [SD0047]. This cable system has converted to IPTV, 312 Fourth St W, Clear Lake, SD 57226. Phones: 800-417-8667; 605-874-2181. Fax: 605-874-2014. E-mail: info@itctel.com. Web Site: http://www.itc-web.com. ICA: SD5037.
Channel capacity: N.A. Channels available but not in use: N.A.

Basic Service
Subscribers: N.A.
Fee: $35.50 monthly.

Expanded Basic Service 1
Subscribers: N.A.
Fee: $35.50 monthly.

Limited Basic Service
Subscribers: N.A.
Fee: $25.50 monthly.

Pay Service 1
Pay Units: N.A.
Fee: $10.95 monthly (Cinemax or Starz!), $11.95 monthly (Showtime), $13.95 monthly (HBO).

Internet Service
Operational: Yes.
Fee: $39.95 monthly.

Telephone Service
Digital: Operational

General Manager: Jerry Heiberger.

ASTORIA—Satellite Cable Services Inc. Now served by CLEAR LAKE, SD [SD0047]. ICA: SD0151.

AURORA—ITC. Formerly served by Clear Lake, SD [SD0047]. This cable system has converted to IPTV, 312 Fourth St W, Clear Lake, SD 57226. Phones: 800-417-8667; 605-874-2181. Fax: 605-874-2014. E-mail: info@itctel.com. Web Site: http://www.itc-web.com. ICA: SD5062.
Channel capacity: N.A. Channels available but not in use: N.A.

Basic Service
Subscribers: N.A.
Fee: $35.50 monthly.

Expanded Basic Service 1
Subscribers: N.A.
Fee: $46.95 monthly.

Limited Basic Service
Subscribers: N.A.
Fee: $25.50 monthly.

Pay Service 1
Pay Units: N.A.
Fee: $10.95 monthly (Cinemax or Starz!), $11.95 monthly (Showtime), $13.95 monthly (HBO).

Internet Service
Operational: Yes.
Fee: $39.95 monthly.

Telephone Service
Digital: Operational

General Manager: Jerry Heiberger.

AVON—Golden West Telecommunications, 415 Crown St, PO Box 411, Wall, SD 57790-0411. Phone: 605-279-2161. Fax: 605-279-2727. E-mail: info@goldenwest.com. Web Site: http://www.goldenwest.com. ICA: SD0079.
TV Market Ranking: Outside TV Markets (AVON). Franchise award date: N.A. Franchise expiration date: N.A. Began: April 1, 1982.
Channel capacity: 135 (not 2-way capable). Channels available but not in use: N.A.

Basic Service
Subscribers: 177.
Programming (received off-air): KCAU-TV (ABC) Sioux City; KDLV-TV (NBC) Mitchell; KELO-TV (CBS, MNT) Sioux Falls; KSFY-TV (ABC) Sioux Falls; KUSD-TV (PBS) Vermillion.
Programming (via satellite): TBS Superstation; WGN America.
Fee: $25.00 installation; $33.95 monthly.

Digital Basic Service
Subscribers: N.A.
Programming (via satellite): AmericanLife TV Network; Bio; Bloomberg Television; Bravo; Discovery Fit & Health; Discovery Kids Channel; DMX Music; ESPN 2; ESPN Classic Sports; ESPNews; Fox Movie Channel; Fox Sports World; G4; Golf Channel; GSN; Halogen Network; HGTV; History Channel; History Channel International; Independent Film Channel; Lifetime Movie Network; MuchMusic Network; National Geographic Channel; Outdoor Channel; Speed; Style Network; Syfy; Toon Disney; Trinity Broadcasting Network; Turner Classic Movies; Versus; WE tv.
Fee: $10.00 installation; $14.95 monthly.

Pay Service 1
Pay Units: 11.
Programming (via satellite): HBO.
Fee: $11.95 monthly.

Pay Service 2
Pay Units: N.A.
Programming (via satellite): Cinemax.
Fee: $11.95 monthly.

Pay Service 3
Pay Units: N.A.
Programming (via satellite): Showtime.
Fee: $10.95 monthly.

Pay Service 4
Pay Units: N.A.
Programming (via satellite): The Movie Channel.
Fee: $9.95 monthly.

Digital Pay Service 1
Pay Units: N.A.
Programming (via satellite): Cinemax (multiplexed); Encore (multiplexed); HBO (multiplexed); Showtime (multiplexed); Starz (multiplexed); The Movie Channel (multiplexed).
Fee: $11.95 monthly (Cinemax), $12.95 monthly (HBO), $13.95 monthly (Starz/Encore or Showtime/TMC).

Video-On-Demand: No

Pay-Per-View
Sports PPV (delivered digitally); ESPN Extra (delivered digitally); ESPN Now (delivered digitally); Fresh (delivered digitally); Playboy TV (delivered digitally); Hot Choice (delivered digitally).

Internet Service
Operational: No, Both DSL & dial-up.

Telephone Service
None

Miles of Plant: 10.0 (coaxial); None (fiber optic).
General Manager: George Strandell. Chief Technician: Randy Shepard. Marketing Director: Greg Oleson. Cable Television Manager: Rick Reed. Customer Service Manager: Jody Bielmaier.
Ownership: Golden West Cablevision (MSO).

BERESFORD—Beresford Cablevision Inc., 101 N 3rd St, Beresford, SD 57004-1741. Phone: 605-763-2500. Fax: 605-763-7112. E-mail: phone@bmtc.net. Web Site: http://www.bmtc.net. ICA: SD0032.
TV Market Ranking: 85 (BERESFORD). Franchise award date: N.A. Franchise expiration date: N.A. Began: January 1, 1983.
Channel capacity: 60 (operating 2-way). Channels available but not in use: N.A.

Basic Service
Subscribers: 764.
Programming (received off-air): KCAU-TV (ABC) Sioux City; KDLT-TV (NBC) Sioux Falls; KELO-TV (CBS, MNT) Sioux Falls; KMEG (CBS) Sioux City; KPTH (FOX, MNT) Sioux City; KSFY-TV (ABC) Sioux Falls; KTIV (CW, NBC) Sioux City; KTTW (FOX) Sioux Falls; KUSD-TV (PBS) Vermillion; KWSD (CW) Sioux Falls.
Fee: $25.00 installation; $14.79 monthly; $1.00 converter.

Expanded Basic Service 1
Subscribers: 650.
Programming (via satellite): A&E Networks; ABC Family Channel; AMC; Animal Planet; Boomerang; Bravo; Cartoon Network; CNN; Comedy Central; Country Music TV; C-SPAN; Discovery Channel; Disney Channel; DIY Network; ESPN; ESPN 2; ESPN Classic Sports; Food Network; Fox News Channel; Fox Sports Net; FX; HGTV; History Channel; Lifetime; MTV; National Geographic Channel; Nickelodeon; Outdoor Channel; Speed; Spike TV; Syfy; TBS Superstation; The Learning Channel; The Weather Channel; Turner Classic Movies; Turner Network TV; TV Land; USA Network; VH1; WGN America.
Fee: $15.85 monthly.

Digital Basic Service
Subscribers: N.A.
Programming (via satellite): AmericanLife TV Network; BBC America; Bio; Bloomberg Television; Bravo; CMT Pure Country; Discovery Fit & Health; Discovery Health Channel; Discovery Home Channel; Discovery Kids Channel; Discovery Times Channel; DMX Music; ESPN 2; ESPN Classic Sports; ESPNews; Fox College Sports Atlantic; Fox College Sports Central; Fox College Sports Pacific; Fox Movie Channel; Fox Soccer; Fuse; Golf Channel; Great American Country; GSN; Halogen Network; History Channel International; Independent Film Channel; Military Channel; MTV Jams; MTV2; Nick Jr.; NickToons TV; Outdoor Channel;

Ovation; Science; Speed; Style Network; Sundance Channel; TeenNick; Toon Disney; truTV; Versus; VH1 Classic; VH1 Soul; WE tv.
Fee: $34.00 monthly.
Pay Service 1
Pay Units: 131.
Programming (via satellite): Showtime.
Fee: $25.00 installation; $12.92 monthly.
Pay Service 2
Pay Units: 190.
Programming (via satellite): HBO.
Fee: $25.00 installation; $12.92 monthly.
Digital Pay Service 1
Pay Units: N.A.
Programming (via satellite): Cinemax (multiplexed); Encore; Flix; HBO (multiplexed); Showtime (multiplexed); Starz (multiplexed); The Movie Channel (multiplexed).
Fee: $8.50 monthly (Starz), $11.00 monthly (Cinemax), $13.50 monthly (HBO or Flix/Showtime/TMC).
Video-On-Demand: No
Internet Service
Operational: No, DSL.
Telephone Service
None
Miles of Plant: 47.0 (coaxial); None (fiber optic).
Manager: Todd Hansen. Marketing Director & Lead Technologist: Dean Jacobson. Cable Technician: Ted Lyle.
Ownership: Beresford Cablevision Inc.

BISON—West River Cable Television, 801 Coleman Ave, PO Box 39, Bison, SD 57620. Phones: 605-244-5236; 888-411-5651. Fax: 605-244-7288. E-mail: westriver@sdplains.com. Web Site: http://www.westrivercatv.com. Also serves Buffalo, Lemmon, McIntosh & Newell. ICA: SD0103.
TV Market Ranking: Below 100 (Newell); Outside TV Markets (BISON, Buffalo, Lemmon, McIntosh). Franchise award date: May 12, 1982. Franchise expiration date: N.A. Began: December 1, 1982.
Channel capacity: 78 (not 2-way capable). Channels available but not in use: N.A.
Basic Service
Subscribers: 696.
Programming (received off-air): KEVN-TV (FOX) Rapid City; KOTA-TV (ABC) Rapid City; KPSD-TV (PBS) Eagle Butte.
Programming (via microwave): KCNC-TV (CBS) Denver; KFYR-TV (NBC) Bismarck.
Programming (via satellite): A&E Networks; ABC Family Channel; AMC; Animal Planet; Cartoon Network; CNBC; CNN; Comedy Central; Country Music TV; C-SPAN; C-SPAN 2; Discovery Channel; Discovery Health Channel; Disney Channel; ESPN; ESPN 2; Eternal Word TV Network; Food Network; FX; Great American Country; Hallmark Channel; Hallmark Movie Channel; Headline News; HGTV; History Channel; INSP; Lifetime; Lifetime Movie Network; Lifetime Real Women; MTV; MTV2; National Geographic Channel; Nick Jr.; Nickelodeon; Outdoor Channel; QVC; Spike TV; Syfy; TBS Superstation; The Learning Channel; The Weather Channel; Travel Channel; truTV; Turner Classic Movies; Turner Network TV; TV Guide Network; TV Land; USA Network; Versus; VH1; WE tv; WGN America.
Fee: $35.00 installation; $37.95 monthly.
Video-On-Demand: No
Internet Service
Operational: No.
Telephone Service
None
Miles of Plant: 28.0 (coaxial); None (fiber optic).
Manager: Jerry Reisenauer. Assistant Manager: Colgan Huber. Telecommunications Manager: Colle Nash.
Ownership: West River Cooperative Telephone Co.

BOULDER CANYON—Midcontinent Communications, PO Box 5010, Sioux Falls, SD 57117. Phones: 605-229-1775; 800-888-1300; 605-342-1870. Fax: 605-229-0478. Web Site: http://www.midcocomm.com. ICA: SD0132.
TV Market Ranking: Below 100 (BOULDER CANYON). Franchise award date: N.A. Franchise expiration date: N.A. Began: September 1, 1983.
Channel capacity: N.A. Channels available but not in use: N.A.
Basic Service
Subscribers: 84.
Programming (received off-air): KBHE-TV (PBS) Rapid City; KCLO-TV (CBS) Rapid City; KCPL-LP Rapid City; KEVN-TV (FOX) Rapid City; KHSD-TV (ABC) Lead; KKRA-LP (ION) Rapid City; KNBN (NBC) Rapid City; KOTA-TV (ABC) Rapid City.
Programming (via satellite): A&E Networks; ABC Family Channel; AMC; Animal Planet; BET Networks; Bravo; Cartoon Network; CNBC; CNN; Comedy Central; Country Music TV; C-SPAN; C-SPAN 2; CW+; Discovery Channel; Discovery Fit & Health; Disney Channel; E! Entertainment Television; ESPN; ESPN 2; Eternal Word TV Network; Food Network; Fox News Channel; Fox Sports Net North; FX; Golf Channel; Great American Country; GSN; Hallmark Channel; Headline News; HGTV; History Channel; INSP; Lifetime; MSNBC; MTV; Nickelodeon; Outdoor Channel; Oxygen; QVC; Root Sports Rocky Mountain; Speed; Spike TV; Syfy; TBS Superstation; The Learning Channel; The Weather Channel; Toon Disney; Travel Channel; Trinity Broadcasting Network; truTV; Turner Classic Movies; Turner Network TV; TV Guide Network; TV Land; USA Network; Versus; VH1; WE tv; WGN America.
Fee: $35.00 installation; $35.05 monthly.
Digital Basic Service
Subscribers: N.A.
Programming (via satellite): 3 Angels Broadcasting Network; A&E HD; ABC Family HD; AmericanLife TV Network; Animal Planet HD; BBC America; Bio; Bloomberg Television; Boomerang; BTN; Canal Sur; CBS Sports Network; Cine Latino; Cine Mexicano; CMT Pure Country; CNN en Espanol; CNN HD; Cooking Channel; C-SPAN 3; Current; Discovery Channel HD; Discovery en Espanol; Discovery Health Channel; Discovery Kids Channel; Disney Channel HD; DIY Network; ESPN 2 HD; ESPN Classic Sports; ESPN Deportes; ESPN HD; ESPNews; EWTN en Espanol; Food Network HD; Fox Business Channel; Fox College Sports Atlantic; Fox College Sports Central; Fox College Sports Pacific; Fox Deportes; Fox Soccer; FSN HD; Fuse; Golf Channel; GolTV; Great American Country; GSN; Halogen Network; HD Theater; HDNet; HDNet Movies; HGTV HD; History Channel en Espanol; History Channel HD; History Channel International; ID Investigation Discovery; Independent Film Channel; ION Life; JCTV; Lifetime Movie Network; Military Channel; MTV Hits; MTV Jams; MTV2; mun2 television; Music Choice; National Geographic Channel; National Geographic Channel HD Network; NFL Network; NHL Network; Nick Jr.; Nick Too; NickToons TV; Palladia; PBS Kids Sprout; Pentagon Channel; Planet Green; Qubo; ReelzChannel; RFD-TV; Science; SoapNet; Style Network; Sundance Channel; Syfy HD; TBS in HD; TeenNick; Telemundo; Tennis Channel; TLC HD; Toon Disney; Toon Disney en Espanol; Tr3s; Trinity Broadcasting Network; Turner Network TV HD; TV One; TVE Internacional; TVG Network; Universal HD; USA Network HD; VeneMovies; Versus HD; VH1 Classic; VH1 Soul.
Digital Pay Service 1
Pay Units: N.A.
Programming (via satellite): Cinemax (multiplexed); Cinemax HD; Encore (multiplexed); Flix; HBO (multiplexed); HBO HD; Showtime (multiplexed); Showtime HD; Starz (multiplexed); Starz HDTV; The Movie Channel (multiplexed); The Movie Channel HD.
Video-On-Demand: No
Internet Service
Operational: No.
Telephone Service
None
Miles of Plant: 7.0 (coaxial); None (fiber optic).
Manager: Gary Steever. Chief Technician: Dave Gorsuch.
Ownership: Midcontinent Media Inc. (MSO).

BRADLEY—ITC. Formerly served by Clear Lake, SD [SD0047]. This cable system has converted to IPTV, 312 Fourth St W, Clear Lake, SD 57226. Phones: 800-417-8667; 605-874-2181. Fax: 605-874-2014. E-mail: info@itctel.com. Web Site: http://www.itc-web.com. ICA: SD5038.
Channel capacity: N.A. Channels available but not in use: N.A.
Basic Service
Subscribers: N.A.
Fee: $35.50 monthly.
Expanded Basic Service 1
Subscribers: N.A.
Fee: $46.95 monthly.
Limited Basic Service
Subscribers: N.A.
Fee: $25.50 monthly.
Pay Service 1
Pay Units: N.A.
Fee: $10.95 monthly (Cinemax or Starz!), $11.95 monthly (Showtime), $13.95 monthly (HBO).
Internet Service
Operational: Yes.
Fee: $39.95 monthly.
Telephone Service
Digital: Operational
General Manager: Jerry Heiberger.

BRANDT—ITC. Formerly served by Clear Lake, SD [SD0047]. This cable system has converted to IPTV, 312 Fourth St W, Clear Lake, SD 57226. Phones: 800-417-8667; 605-874-2181. Fax: 605-874-2014. E-mail: info@itctel.com. Web Site: http://www.itc-web.com. ICA: SD5039.
Channel capacity: N.A. Channels available but not in use: N.A.
Basic Service
Subscribers: N.A.
Fee: $35.50 monthly.
Expanded Basic Service 1
Subscribers: N.A.
Fee: $46.95 monthly.
Limited Basic Service
Subscribers: N.A.
Fee: $25.50 monthly.
Pay Service 1
Pay Units: N.A.
Fee: $10.95 monthly (Cinemax or Starz!), $11.95 monthly (Showtime), $13.95 monthly (HBO).
Internet Service
Operational: Yes.
Fee: $39.95 monthly.
Telephone Service
Digital: Operational
General Manager: Jerry Heiberger.

BRITTON—Venture Communications Cooperative, 218 Commercial Ave. SE, PO Box 157, Highmore, SD 57345-0157. Phones: 800-824-7282; 605-852-2224. Fax: 605-852-2404. E-mail: venture@venturecomm.net. Web Site: http://www.venturecomm.net. Also serves Eden, Langford & Pierpont. ICA: SD0041.
TV Market Ranking: Below 100 (Langford, Pierpont); Outside TV Markets (BRITTON, Eden). Franchise award date: N.A. Franchise expiration date: N.A. Began: May 1, 1979.
Channel capacity: N.A. Channels available but not in use: N.A.
Digital Basic Service
Subscribers: N.A. Included in Highmore
Programming (via satellite): C-SPAN; CW+; ESPN; Eternal Word TV Network; ION Television; Local Cable Weather; MyNetworkTV Inc.; QVC; The Weather Channel; Trinity Broadcasting Network; WGN America.
Fee: $19.95 monthly.
Digital Expanded Basic Service
Subscribers: N.A.
Programming (via satellite): A&E Networks; AMC; Animal Planet; BBC America; Bloomberg Television; Bravo; Cartoon Network; CNBC; CNN; Comedy Central; Country Music TV; C-SPAN 2; Discovery Channel; Discovery Health Channel; Discovery Kids Channel; Disney Channel; DIY Network; DMX Music; E! Entertainment Television; ESPN 2; ESPN Classic Sports; ESPNews; Food Network; Fox Movie Channel; Fox News Channel; Fox Sports Net North; FX; G4; Golf Channel; Great American Country; GSN; Hallmark Channel; Hallmark Movie Channel; Headline News; HGTV; History Channel; ID Investigation Discovery; Lifetime; Lifetime Movie Network; Lifetime Real Women; Military Channel; MSNBC; MTV; MTV Hits; MTV2; National Geographic Channel; NFL Network; Nick Jr.; Nickelodeon; NickToons TV; Outdoor Channel; Oxygen; Planet Green; RFD-TV; Science; SoapNet; Speed; Spike TV; Syfy; TBS Superstation; TeenNick; The Learning Channel; Toon Disney; Travel Channel; truTV; Turner Classic Movies; Turner Network TV; TV Land; USA Network; Versus; VH1; VH1 Classic; WE tv.
Fee: $18.00 monthly.
Digital Pay Service 1
Pay Units: N.A.
Programming (via satellite): Cinemax (multiplexed); Encore (multiplexed); HBO (multiplexed); Showtime (multiplexed); Starz (multiplexed); The Movie Channel.
Video-On-Demand: No
Pay-Per-View
Movies (delivered digitally); Playboy TV (delivered digitally); Fresh (delivered digitally).
Internet Service
Operational: No.
Telephone Service
None
General Manager: Randy Houdek. Assistant Manager: Randy Olson. Chief Technician: Brad Ryan. Member Services Manager: Rod Kusser.
Ownership: Venture Communications Cooperative (MSO).

BROOKINGS—Mediacom, 1504 2nd St SE, PO Box 110, Waseca, MN 56093. Phone: 507-835-2356. Fax: 507-835-4567. Web Site: http://www.mediacomcable.com. Also serves Arlington, Aurora, Bruce, Castlewood, Colman, De Smet, Egan, Elkton, Estelline, Flandreau, Hayti, Lake Norden, Lake Preston, Volga & White. ICA: SD0005.

TV Market Ranking: 85 (Colman, Egan); Below 100 (De Smet, Estelline, Hayti, Lake Norden); Outside TV Markets (Arlington, Aurora, BROOKINGS, Bruce, Elkton, Flandreau, Lake Preston, Volga, White). Franchise award date: June 1, 1989. Franchise expiration date: N.A. Began: July 1, 1970.

Channel capacity: 60 (operating 2-way). Channels available but not in use: N.A.

Basic Service

Subscribers: 3,035.

Programming (received off-air): KCPO-LP Sioux Falls; KDLT-TV (NBC) Sioux Falls; KELO-TV (CBS, MNT) Sioux Falls; KESD-TV (PBS) Brookings; KSFY-TV (ABC) Sioux Falls; KTTW (FOX) Sioux Falls; allband FM.

Programming (via satellite): C-SPAN; C-SPAN 2; ION Television; QVC; TV Guide Network; WGN America.

Fee: $44.30 installation; $26.28 monthly.

Expanded Basic Service 1

Subscribers: N.A.

Programming (via satellite): A&E Networks; ABC Family Channel; AMC; Animal Planet; Bravo; Cartoon Network; CNBC; CNN; Comedy Central; Discovery Channel; Disney Channel; E! Entertainment Television; ESPN; ESPN 2; Eternal Word TV Network; Food Network; Fox News Channel; Fox Sports Net North; FX; GalaVision; Great American Country; Hallmark Channel; Headline News; HGTV; History Channel; INSP; Lifetime; MSNBC; MTV; Nickelodeon; RFD-TV; Speed; Spike TV; Syfy; TBS Superstation; The Learning Channel; The Weather Channel; Travel Channel; Trinity Broadcasting Network; truTV; Turner Network TV; TV Land; USA Network; VH1; WE tv.

Digital Basic Service

Subscribers: N.A.

Programming (via satellite): AmericanLife TV Network; BBC America; Bio; Bloomberg Television; Canales N; Discovery Fit & Health; DMX Music; ESPN; ESPN 2; ESPNews; Fox Movie Channel; Fox Soccer; Fuse; G4; GAS; Golf Channel; GSN; Halogen Network; HD Theater; HDNet; HDNet Movies; History Channel International; Independent Film Channel; INHD (multiplexed); Lifetime Movie Network; Lime; MTV Networks Digital Suite; National Geographic Channel; Nick Jr.; NickToons TV; Outdoor Channel; Style Network; Turner Classic Movies; Universal HD.

Digital Pay Service 1

Pay Units: 906.

Programming (via satellite): Cinemax (multiplexed); Encore (multiplexed); Flix (multiplexed); HBO (multiplexed); HBO HD; Showtime (multiplexed); Showtime HD; Starz (multiplexed); Starz HDTV; Sundance Channel (multiplexed); The Movie Channel (multiplexed); The Movie Channel HD.

Fee: $6.75 monthly (Starz), $10.95 monthly (Cinemax, HBO or Showtime).

Video-On-Demand: No

Pay-Per-View

Mediacom PPV (delivered digitally); ESPN (delivered digitally); Fresh (delivered digitally); Shorteez (delivered digitally); Playboy TV (delivered digitally); Pleasure (delivered digitally).

Internet Service

Operational: Yes.

Broadband Service: Mediacom High Speed Internet.

Fee: $29.95 monthly; $10.00 modem lease.

Telephone Service

Digital: Operational

Miles of Plant: 644.0 (coaxial); 5.0 (fiber optic).

Vice President: Bill Jenson. Engineering Manager: Kraig Kaiser. Sales & Marketing Director: Lori Huberty.

Ownership: Mediacom LLC (MSO).

BROOKINGS (rural)—ITC. Formerly served by Clear Lake, SD [SD0047]. This cable system has converted to IPTV, 312 Fourth St W, Clear Lake, SD 57226. Phones: 800-417-8667; 605-874-2181. Fax: 605-874-2014. E-mail: info@itctel.com. Web Site: http://www.itc-web.com. ICA: SD5041.

Channel capacity: N.A. Channels available but not in use: N.A.

Basic Service

Subscribers: N.A.

Fee: $35.50 monthly.

Expanded Basic Service 1

Subscribers: N.A.

Fee: $46.95 monthly.

Limited Basic Service

Subscribers: N.A.

Fee: $25.50 monthly.

Pay Service 1

Pay Units: N.A.

Fee: $10.95 monthly (Cinemax or Starz!), $11.95 monthly (Showtime), $13.95 monthly (HBO).

Internet Service

Operational: Yes.

Fee: $39.95 monthly.

Telephone Service

Digital: Operational

General Manager: Jerry Heiberger.

BRUCE—Mediacom. Now served by BROOKINGS, SD [SD0005]. ICA: SD0153.

BRYANT—ITC. Formerly served by Clear Lake, SD [SD0047]. This cable system has converted to IPTV, 312 Fourth St W, Clear Lake, SD 57226. Phones: 800-417-8667; 605-874-2181. Fax: 605-874-2014. E-mail: info@itc-web.com. Web Site: http://www.itc-web.com. ICA: SD5049.

Channel capacity: N.A. Channels available but not in use: N.A.

Basic Service

Subscribers: N.A.

Fee: $35.50 monthly.

Expanded Basic Service 1

Subscribers: N.A.

Fee: $46.95 monthly.

Limited Basic Service

Subscribers: N.A.

Fee: $25.50 monthly.

Pay Service 1

Pay Units: N.A.

Fee: $10.95 monthly (Cinemax or Starz!), $11.95 monthly (Showtime), $13.95 (HBO).

Internet Service

Operational: Yes.

Fee: $39.95 monthly.

Telephone Service

Digital: Operational

General Manager: Jerry Heiberger.

BRYANT—Satellite Cable Services Inc. Now served by CLEAR LAKE, SD [SD0047]. ICA: SD0100.

BUFFALO—West River Cable Television. No longer in operation. ICA: SD0106.

BURKE—Golden West Telecommunications, 415 Crown St, PO Box 411, Wall, SD 57790-0411. Phone: 605-279-2161. Fax: 605-279-2727. E-mail: info@goldenwest.com. Web Site: http://www.goldenwest.com. ICA: SD0062.

TV Market Ranking: Outside TV Markets (BURKE). Franchise award date: N.A. Franchise expiration date: N.A. Began: September 1, 1980.

Channel capacity: 135 (not 2-way capable). Channels available but not in use: N.A.

Basic Service

Subscribers: 234.

Programming (received off-air): KDLV-TV (NBC) Mitchell; KMNE-TV (PBS) Bassett; KPLO-TV (CBS, MNT) Reliance; KPRY-TV (ABC) Pierre; KTSD-TV (PBS) Pierre.

Programming (via satellite): TBS Superstation; WGN America.

Fee: $25.00 installation; $33.95 monthly.

Digital Basic Service

Subscribers: 5.

Programming (via satellite): AmericanLife TV Network; Bio; Bloomberg Television; Bravo; DMX Music; ESPN 2; ESPN Classic Sports; ESPNews; Fox Movie Channel; Fox Sports World; Fuse; G4; Golf Channel; GSN; Halogen Network; HGTV; History Channel; History Channel International; Independent Film Channel; Lifetime Movie Network; National Geographic Channel; Outdoor Channel; Speed; Style Network; Syfy; Toon Disney; Trinity Broadcasting Network; Turner Classic Movies; Versus; WE tv.

Fee: $10.00 installation; $14.95 monthly.

Pay Service 1

Pay Units: 14.

Programming (via satellite): HBO.

Fee: $11.95 monthly.

Pay Service 2

Pay Units: 9.

Programming (via satellite): Cinemax.

Fee: $11.95 monthly.

Pay Service 3

Pay Units: N.A.

Programming (via satellite): Showtime; The Movie Channel.

Fee: $10.95 monthly.

Digital Pay Service 1

Pay Units: N.A.

Programming (via satellite): Cinemax (multiplexed); Encore (multiplexed); HBO (multiplexed); Showtime (multiplexed); Starz (multiplexed); The Movie Channel (multiplexed).

Fee: $10.95 monthly (Starz), $11.95 monthly (Cinemax, Showtime, or TMC), $12.95 monthly (HBO), $13.95 monthly (Encore).

Video-On-Demand: No

Pay-Per-View

Sports PPV (delivered digitally); ESPN Extra (delivered digitally); ESPN Now (delivered digitally); Fresh (delivered digitally); Playboy TV (delivered digitally); Hot Choice (delivered digitally).

Internet Service

Operational: No, Both DSL & dial-up.

Internet Service

Operational: No, Both DSL & dial-up.

Telephone Service

None

Miles of Plant: 26.0 (coaxial); None (fiber optic).

General Manager: George Strandell. Chief Technician: Randy Shepard. Marketing Director: Greg Oleson. Cable Television Manager: Rick Reed. Customer Service Manager: Jody Bielmaier.

Ownership: Golden West Cablevision (MSO).

CARTHAGE—Alliance Communications. Formerly [SD0244]. This cable system has converted to IPTV, 612 Third St, PO Box 349, Garretson, SD 57030. Phones: 800-701-4980; 605-594-3400. Fax: 605-594-6776. E-mail: email@alliancecom.net. Web Site: http://www.alliancecom.net. ICA: SD5079.

Channel capacity: N.A. Channels available but not in use: N.A.

Basic Service

Subscribers: N.A.

Fee: $29.95 monthly.

Expanded Basic Service 1

Subscribers: N.A.

Fee: $13.00 monthly.

Expanded Basic Service 2

Subscribers: N.A.

Fee: $8.00 monthly.

Pay Service 1

Pay Units: N.A.

Fee: $9.95 monthly (Cinemax or Starz/Encore), $10.95 monthly (Showtime) or $13.95 monthly (HBO).

Internet Service

Operational: Yes.

Fee: $14.95 monthly.

Telephone Service

Digital: Operational

Fee: $12.70 monthly

Manager: Don Snyder.

CARTHAGE—Alliance Communications. This cable system has converted to IPTV. See Carthage, SD [SD5079]. ICA: SD0244.

CASTLEWOOD—ITC. Formerly served by Clear Lake, SD [SD0047]. This cable system has converted to IPTV, 312 Fourth St W, Clear Lake, SD 57226. Phones: 800-417-8667; 605-874-2181. Fax: 605-874-2014. E-mail: info@itctel.com. Web Site: http://www.itc-web.com. ICA: SD5063.

Channel capacity: N.A. Channels available but not in use: N.A.

Basic Service

Subscribers: N.A.

Fee: $35.50 monthly.

Expanded Basic Service 1

Subscribers: N.A.

Fee: $46.95 monthly.

Limited Basic Service

Subscribers: N.A.

Fee: $25.50 monthly.

Pay Service 1

Pay Units: N.A.

Fee: $10.95 monthly (Cinemax or Starz!), $11.95 monthly (Showtime), $13.95 monthly (HBO).

Internet Service

Operational: Yes.

Fee: $39.95 monthly.

Telephone Service

Digital: Operational

General Manager: Jerry Heiberger.

CASTLEWOOD—Mediacom. Now served by BROOKINGS, SD [SD0005]. ICA: SD0098.

CAVOUR—Midcontinent Communications, PO Box 5010, Sioux Falls, SD 57117. Phones: 800-456-0564; 605-229-1775. Fax: 605-229-0478. Web Site: http://www.midcocomm.com. ICA: SD0155.

TV Market Ranking: Below 100 (CAVOUR). Franchise award date: N.A. Franchise expiration date: N.A. Began: N.A.

Channel capacity: 23 (not 2-way capable). Channels available but not in use: N.A.

Basic Service
Subscribers: 21.
Programming (received off-air): KABY-TV (ABC) Aberdeen; KDLO-TV (CBS, MNT) Florence; KDLT-TV (NBC) Sioux Falls; KESD-TV (PBS) Brookings; KTTM (FOX) Huron.
Programming (via satellite): A&E Networks; ABC Family Channel; AMC; CNN; Discovery Channel; Disney Channel; ESPN; ESPN 2; History Channel; Lifetime; Nickelodeon; Spike TV; TBS Superstation; Turner Network TV; USA Network; VH1; WGN America.
Fee: $31.95 monthly.
Pay Service 1
Pay Units: N.A.
Programming (via satellite): HBO.
Fee: $11.95 monthly.
Internet Service
Operational: No.
Telephone Service
None
Miles of Plant: 2.0 (coaxial); None (fiber optic).
Manager: Doug Bierschbach. Chief Technician: Paul Schmidt.
Ownership: Midcontinent Media Inc. (MSO).

CHERRY CREEK—Formerly served by Cheyenne River Sioux Tribe Telephone Authority. No longer in operation. ICA: SD0157.

CHESTER—Satellite Cable Services Inc. Now served by CLEAR LAKE, SD [SD0047]. ICA: SD0158.

CHESTER (rural)—ITC. Formerly served by Clear Lake, SD [SD0047]. This cable system has converted to IPTV, 312 Fourth St W, Clear Lake, SD 57226. Phones: 800-417-8667; 605-874-2181. Fax: 605-874-2014. E-mail: info@itc-web.com. Web Site: http://www.itc-web.com. ICA: SD5050.
Channel capacity: N.A. Channels available but not in use: N.A.
Internet Service
Operational: Yes.
Fee: $39.95 monthly.
Telephone Service
Digital: Operational
General Manager: Jerry Heiberger.

CLARK—ITC. Formerly served by Clear Lake, SD [SD0047]. This cable system has converted to IPTV, 312 Fourth St W, Clear Lake, SD 57226. Phones: 605-874-2181; 800-417-8667. Fax: 605-874-2014. E-mail: info@itc-web.com. Web Site: http://www.itc-web.com. ICA: SD5051.
Channel capacity: N.A. Channels available but not in use: N.A.
Basic Service
Subscribers: N.A.
Fee: $35.50 monthly.
Expanded Basic Service 1
Subscribers: N.A.
Fee: $46.95 monthly.
Limited Basic Service
Subscribers: N.A.
Fee: $25.50 monthly.
Pay Service 1
Pay Units: N.A.
Fee: $10.95 monthly (Cinemaz or Starz!), $11.95 monthly (Showtime), $13.95 monthly (HBO).
Internet Service
Operational: Yes.
Fee: $39.95 monthly.
Telephone Service
Digital: Operational
General Manager: Jerry Heiberger.

CLARK TWP.—Satellite Cable Services Inc. Now served by CLEAR LAKE, SD [SD0047]. ICA: SD0160.

CLEAR LAKE—Formerly served by HD Electric Cooperative. No longer in operation. ICA: SD0227.

CLEAR LAKE—ITC. Formerly [SD0047]. This cable system has converted to IPTV, 312 Fourth St W, Clear Lake, SD 57226. Phones: 800-417-8667; 605-874-2181. Fax: 605-874-2014. E-mail: info@itctel.com. Web Site: http://www.itc-web.com. ICA: SD5042.
Channel capacity: N.A. Channels available but not in use: N.A.
Basic Service
Subscribers: N.A.
Fee: $35.50 monthly.
Expanded Basic Service 1
Subscribers: N.A.
Fee: $46.95 monthly.
Limited Basic Service
Subscribers: N.A.
Fee: $25.50 monthly.
Pay Service 1
Pay Units: N.A.
Fee: $10.95 monthly (Cinemax or Starz!), $11.95 monthly (Showtime), $13.95 monthly (HBO).
Internet Service
Operational: Yes.
Fee: $39.95 monthly.
Telephone Service
Digital: Operational
General Manager: Jerry Heiberger.

CLEAR LAKE—ITC. This cable system has converted to IPTV. See Clear Lake, SD [SD5042]. ICA: SD0047.

COLMAN—Knology, 5100 S Broadband Ln, Sioux Falls, SD 57108-2207. Phone: 605-965-9393. Fax: 605-965-7867. Web Site: http://www.knology.com. Also serves Flandreau & Madison. ICA: SD0249. **Note:** This system is an overbuild.
TV Market Ranking: 85 (COLMAN, Flandreau, Madison).
Channel capacity: N.A. Channels available but not in use: N.A.
Basic Service
Subscribers: N.A. Included in Viborg
Programming (received off-air): KAUN-LP Sioux Falls; KCPO-LP Sioux Falls; KDLT-TV (NBC) Sioux Falls; KELO-TV (CBS, MNT) Sioux Falls; KSFY-TV (ABC) Sioux Falls; KTTW (FOX) Sioux Falls; KUSD-TV (PBS) Vermillion; KWSD (CW) Sioux Falls.
Programming (via satellite): A&E Networks; ABC Family Channel; AMC; Animal Planet; Bravo; Cartoon Network; CNBC; CNN; Comedy Central; Country Music TV; C-SPAN; Discovery Channel; Disney Channel; E! Entertainment Television; ESPN; ESPN 2; ESPN Classic Sports; Food Network; Fox News Channel; Fox Sports Net North; FX; G4; Golf Channel; Hallmark Channel; Headline News; HGTV; History Channel; Lifetime; Lifetime Movie Network; MSNBC; MTV; MyNetworkTV Inc.; National Geographic Channel; NFL Network; Nickelodeon; QVC; Speed; Spike TV; Syfy; TBS Superstation; The Learning Channel; The Weather Channel; Toon Disney; Travel Channel; truTV; Turner Classic Movies; Turner Network TV; TV Guide Network; TV Land; USA Network; VH1; WGN America.
Fee: $25.00 installation; $26.95 monthly.
Digital Basic Service
Subscribers: N.A.
Programming (via satellite): Bandamax; BBC America; Bio; Bloomberg Television; Boomerang; cloo; cloo on demand; CMT Pure Country; Cooking Channel; De Pelicula; De Pelicula Clasico; Discovery en Espanol; Discovery Fit & Health; Discovery Health Channel; Discovery Kids Channel; DIY Network; Encore Family; ESPN 2 HD; ESPN Deportes; ESPN Deportes On Demand; ESPN HD; ESPN On Demand; ESPN U; ESPN U On Demand; ESPNews; Eternal Word TV Network; Flix; Fox College Sports Atlantic; Fox College Sports Central; Fox College Sports Pacific; Fox Deportes; Fox Movie Channel; Fox Reality Channel; Fox Soccer; Fuse; G4; GMC; Golf Channel; GSN; HD Theater; HDNet; HDNet Movies; History Channel International; ID Investigation Discovery; Independent Film Channel; INSP; Lifetime Real Women; Military Channel; MTV Hits; MTV Jams; MTV2; Music Choice; National Geographic Channel; National Geographic Channel HD Network; National Geographic Channel On Demand; NFL Network HD; Nick Jr.; NickToons TV; Outdoor Channel; Outdoor Channel 2 HD; Outdoor Channel On Demand; Planet Green; QVC HD; RFD-TV; Ritmoson Latino; Science; SoapNet; Speed On Demand; Style Network; Sundance Channel; TBS in HD; TeenNick; Telehit; Turner Network TV HD; TV Guide SPOT; Universal HD; Versus; Versus HD; Versus On Demand; VH1 Classic; VH1 Soul; WE tv.
Pay Service 1
Pay Units: N.A.
Programming (via satellite): HBO (multiplexed); Showtime (multiplexed).
Fee: $10.00 installation; $8.85 monthly (Cinemax or Encore/Starz), $9.95 monthly (HBO or Showtime/TMC).
Digital Pay Service 1
Pay Units: N.A.
Programming (via satellite): Cinemax (multiplexed); Cinemax HD; Cinemax On Demand; Encore (multiplexed); HBO (multiplexed); HBO HD; HBO On Demand; Showtime (multiplexed); Showtime HD; Showtime On Demand; Starz (multiplexed); Starz HDTV; Starz On Demand; The Movie Channel (multiplexed); The Movie Channel On Demand.
Video-On-Demand: Yes
Pay-Per-View
iN DEMAND.
Internet Service
Operational: Yes.
Broadband Service: Knology.Net.
Telephone Service
Analog: Not Operational
Digital: Operational
General Manager: Scott Schroeder. Technical Operations Manager: Daryl Elcock. Marketing Manager: Scott Determan.
Ownership: Knology Inc. (MSO).

COLMAN—Mediacom. Now served by BROOKINGS, SD [SD0005]. ICA: SD0093.

CONDE—Satellite Cable Services Inc. Now served by GROTON, SD [SD0030]. ICA: SD0163.

CORSICA—Golden West Telecommunications, 415 Crown St, PO Box 411, Wall, SD 57790-0411. Phone: 605-279-2161. Fax: 605-279-2727. E-mail: info@goldenwest.com. Web Site: http://www.goldenwest.com. ICA: SD0094.
TV Market Ranking: 85 (CORSICA). Franchise award date: January 1, 1983. Franchise expiration date: N.A. Began: July 1, 1983.
Channel capacity: N.A. Channels available but not in use: N.A.
Basic Service
Subscribers: N.A.
Programming (received off-air): KDLT-TV (NBC) Sioux Falls; KPLO-TV (CBS, MNT) Reliance; KPRY-TV (ABC) Pierre; KTSD-TV (PBS) Pierre; KTTM (FOX) Huron.
Programming (via satellite): A&E Networks; ABC Family Channel; AMC; Animal Planet; Cartoon Network; CNBC; CNN; Comedy Central; Country Music TV; C-SPAN; C-SPAN 2; Discovery Channel; Discovery Health Channel; Disney Channel; DIY Network; E! Entertainment Television; ESPN; ESPN 2; Eternal Word TV Network; Fox News Channel; Great American Country; Hallmark Channel; Headline News; HGTV; History Channel; INSP; ION Television; Lifetime; MTV; National Geographic Channel; Nickelodeon; Outdoor Channel; QVC; Spike TV; Syfy; TBS Superstation; The Learning Channel; The Weather Channel; Travel Channel; Turner Network TV; TV Land; USA Network; VH1; WGN America.
Fee: $25.00 installation; $32.95 monthly.
Pay Service 1
Pay Units: 27.
Programming (via satellite): Cinemax; HBO (multiplexed).
Fee: $8.75 monthly (Cinemax), $11.95 monthly (HBO).
Video-On-Demand: No
Internet Service
Operational: No, Both DSL & dial-up.
Telephone Service
None
Miles of Plant: 4.0 (coaxial); None (fiber optic).
General Manager: George Strandell. Chief Technician: Randy Shepard. Marketing Director: Greg Oleson. Cable Television Manager: Rick Reed. Customer Service Manager: Jody Bielmaier.
Ownership: Golden West Cablevision (MSO).

CUSTER—Golden West Telecommunications, 415 Crown St, PO Box 411, Wall, SD 57790-0411. Phone: 605-279-2161. Fax: 605-279-2727. E-mail: info@goldenwest.com. Web Site: http://www.goldenwest.com. Also serves Buffalo Gap, Custer County (unincorporated areas), Edgemont, Fall River County, Hill City, Hot Springs & Oelrichs. ICA: SD0034.
TV Market Ranking: Below 100 (CUSTER, Custer County (unincorporated areas) (portions), Hill City); Outside TV Markets (Buffalo Gap, Custer County (unincorporated areas) (portions), Edgemont, Fall River County, Hot Springs, Oelrichs). Franchise

award date: N.A. Franchise expiration date: N.A. Began: September 1, 1980.
Channel capacity: N.A. Channels available but not in use: N.A.

Basic Service
Subscribers: 3,028.
Programming (received off-air): KBHE-TV (PBS) Rapid City; KCLO-TV (CBS) Rapid City; KEVN-TV (FOX) Rapid City; KKRA-LP (ION) Rapid City; KNBN (NBC) Rapid City; KOTA-TV (ABC) Rapid City; KWBH-LP Rapid City; allband FM.
Programming (via satellite): A&E Networks; ABC Family Channel; AMC; Animal Planet; Cartoon Network; CNBC; CNN; Comedy Central; Country Music TV; C-SPAN; Discovery Channel; Disney Channel; ESPN; ESPN 2; Eternal Word TV Network; Fox News Channel; FX; Headline News; HGTV; History Channel; KWGN-TV (CW) Denver; Lifetime; MTV; Nickelodeon; Outdoor Channel; QVC; Root Sports Rocky Mountain; Speed; Spike TV; Syfy; TBS Superstation; The Learning Channel; The Weather Channel; Trinity Broadcasting Network; Turner Classic Movies; Turner Network TV; TV Guide Network; TV Land; USA Network; VH1; WE tv.
Fee: $25.00 installation; $39.95 monthly.

Digital Basic Service
Subscribers: N.A.
Programming (via satellite): BBC America; Country Music TV; Current; Discovery Health Channel; Discovery Home Channel; Discovery Kids Channel; Discovery Times Channel; Fox Soccer; Fuse; History Channel International; Lifetime Movie Network; MTV Hits; MTV2; NFL Network; Nick Jr.; NickToons TV; Pentagon Channel; Science; Style Network; Sundance Channel; VH1 Classic; VH1 Soul.
Fee: $10.00 installation; $12.95 monthly.

Digital Pay Service 1
Pay Units: N.A.
Programming (via satellite): Cinemax (multiplexed); Encore (multiplexed); HBO (multiplexed); Showtime (multiplexed); Starz (multiplexed); The Movie Channel (multiplexed).
Fee: $12.00 monthly (HBO, Cinemax, Showtime/TMC or Starz/Encore).

Video-On-Demand: No

Internet Service
Operational: Yes.
Broadband Service: In-house.
Fee: $19.95 monthly.

Telephone Service
None

Miles of Plant: 85.0 (coaxial); None (fiber optic).
General Manager: George Strandell. Cable Television Manager: Rick Reed. Chief Technician: Randy Shepard. Marketing Director: Greg Oleson. Customer Service Manager: Jody Bielmaier.
Ownership: Golden West Cablevision (MSO).

DAKOTA DUNES—Long Lines, 501 4th St, Sergeant Bluff, IA 51054-8509. Phones: 712-884-2203; 712-271-4000. Fax: 712-271-2727. Web Site: http://www.longlines.com. ICA: SD0253. **Note:** This system is an overbuild.
TV Market Ranking: Below 100 (DAKOTA DUNES).
Channel capacity: N.A. Channels available but not in use: N.A.

Basic Service
Subscribers: 150.
Programming (received off-air): KCAU-TV (ABC) Sioux City; KELO-TV (CBS, MNT) Sioux Falls; KETV (ABC) Omaha; KMEG (CBS) Sioux City; KPTH (FOX, MNT) Sioux City; KSFY-TV (ABC) Sioux Falls; KSIN-TV (PBS) Sioux City; KTIV (CW, NBC) Sioux City; KUSD-TV (PBS) Vermillion.
Programming (via satellite): A&E Networks; ABC Family Channel; AMC; AmericanLife TV Network; Animal Planet; BTN; Cartoon Network; CNBC; CNN; Comedy Central; Country Music TV; C-SPAN; C-SPAN 2; CW+; Discovery Channel; Disney Channel; E! Entertainment Television; ESPN; ESPN 2; ESPN Classic Sports; Eternal Word TV Network; Food Network; Fox News Channel; Fox Sports Net North; FX; Golf Channel; Hallmark Channel; Headline News; HGTV; History Channel; INSP; Lifetime; Lifetime Movie Network; MSNBC; MTV; Nickelodeon; QVC; Speed; Spike TV; Syfy; TBS Superstation; The Learning Channel; The Weather Channel; Travel Channel; Trinity Broadcasting Network; truTV; Turner Classic Movies; Turner Network TV; TuTv; TV Guide Network; TV Land; USA Network; VH1; WGN America.
Fee: $41.99 monthly.

Digital Basic Service
Subscribers: N.A.
Programming (via satellite): BBC America; Bio; Cooking Channel; Discovery Fit & Health; Discovery Health Channel; Discovery Kids Channel; DIY Network; DMX Music; ESPN U; ESPNews; Fox College Sports Atlantic; Fox College Sports Central; Fox College Sports Pacific; Fox Movie Channel; Fox Soccer; G4; Great American Country; GSN; Halogen Network; History Channel International; ID Investigation Discovery; Independent Film Channel; Lifetime Real Women; Military Channel; MTV Hits; MTV Jams; MTV2; Nick Jr.; NickToons TV; Outdoor Channel; Planet Green; RFD-TV; Science; SoapNet; TeenNick; Toon Disney; Versus; VH1 Classic; VH1 Country; VH1 Soul; WE tv.
Fee: $9.99 monthly.

Digital Expanded Basic Service
Subscribers: N.A.
Programming (received off-air): KCAU-TV (ABC) Sioux City; KMEG (CBS) Sioux City; KPTH (FOX, MNT) Sioux City; KSIN-TV (PBS) Sioux City; KTIV (CW, NBC) Sioux City.
Programming (via satellite): BTN HD; Discovery Channel HD; ESPN 2 HD; ESPN HD; HDNet; HDNet Movies; Outdoor Channel 2 HD.
Fee: $9.95 monthly.

Digital Expanded Basic Service 2
Subscribers: N.A.
Programming (via satellite): Bandamax; De Pelicula; De Pelicula Clasico; Discovery en Espanol; ESPN Deportes; Fox Deportes; Ritmoson Latino; Telehit.
Fee: $2.95 monthly.

Pay Service 1
Pay Units: 31.
Programming (via satellite): HBO (multiplexed).
Fee: $14.95 monthly.

Pay Service 2
Pay Units: 10.
Programming (via satellite): Flix; Showtime (multiplexed); The Movie Channel.
Fee: $14.45 monthly.

Digital Pay Service 1
Pay Units: N.A.
Programming (via satellite): Cinemax (multiplexed); Cinemax HD; Encore (multiplexed); Flix; HBO (multiplexed); HBO HD; Showtime (multiplexed); Starz (multiplexed); Starz HDTV; The Movie Channel (multiplexed).
Fee: $11.95 monthly (Cinemax), $13.95 monthly (Starz/Encore), $14.45 monthly (Flix/Showtime/TMC), $14.95 monthly (HBO).

Video-On-Demand: Yes

Pay-Per-View
ESPN (delivered digitally); iN DEMAND (delivered digitally); Pleasure (delivered digitally).

Internet Service
Operational: Yes, Both DSL & dial-up.
Broadband Service: Long Lines Internet.
Fee: $39.95 monthly.

System Engineer: Tony Seubert. Marketing Manager: Pat McElroy. Office Manager: Denise Moberg.
Ownership: Long Lines (MSO).

DELL RAPIDS—Golden West Telecommunications, 415 Crown St, PO Box 411, Wall, SD 57790-0411. Phone: 605-279-2161. Fax: 605-279-2727. E-mail: info@goldenwest.com. Web Site: http://www.goldenwest.com. Also serves Minnehaha County. ICA: SD0028.
TV Market Ranking: 85 (DELL RAPIDS, Minnehaha County). Franchise award date: August 1, 1982. Franchise expiration date: N.A. Began: August 1, 1982.
Channel capacity: N.A. Channels available but not in use: N.A.

Basic Service
Subscribers: N.A.
Programming (received off-air): KDLT-TV (NBC) Sioux Falls; KPLO-TV (CBS, MNT) Reliance; KPRY-TV (ABC) Pierre; KTTM (FOX) Huron; KUSD-TV (PBS) Vermillion.
Programming (via satellite): A&E Networks; ABC Family Channel; AMC; Animal Planet; Cartoon Network; CNBC; CNN; Comedy Central; Country Music TV; C-SPAN; C-SPAN 2; Discovery Channel; Discovery Health Channel; Disney Channel; DIY Network; E! Entertainment Television; ESPN; ESPN 2; Eternal Word TV Network; Fox News Channel; Great American Country; Hallmark Channel; Headline News; HGTV; History Channel; INSP; ION Television; Lifetime; MTV; National Geographic Channel; Nickelodeon; Outdoor Channel; QVC; Spike TV; Syfy; TBS Superstation; The Learning Channel; The Weather Channel; Travel Channel; Turner Network TV; TV Land; USA Network; VH1; WGN America.
Fee: $25.00 installation; $33.95 monthly.

Pay Service 1
Pay Units: N.A.
Programming (via satellite): Encore; HBO; Showtime.
Fee: $2.30 monthly (Encore), $11.95 monthly (HBO or Showtime).

Video-On-Demand: No

Internet Service
Operational: No, Both DSL & dial-up.

Telephone Service
None

Miles of Plant: 29.0 (coaxial); None (fiber optic).
General Manager: George Strandell. Chief Technician: Randy Shepard. Marketing Director: Greg Oleson. Cable Television Manager: Rick Reed. Customer Service Manager: Jody Bielmaier.
Ownership: Golden West Cablevision (MSO).

DELMONT—Midstate Communications. Now served by PLATTE, SD [SD0049]. ICA: SD0141.

DUPREE—Cheyenne River Sioux Tribe Telephone Authority. Formerly served by Eagle Butte, SD [SD0164]. This cable system has converted to IPTV, PO Box 810, Eagle Butte, SD 57625. Phone: 605-964-2600. Fax: 605-964-1000. E-mail: info@crstta.com. Web Site: http://www.crstta.com. ICA: SD5047.
Channel capacity: N.A. Channels available but not in use: N.A.

Internet Service
Operational: Yes.

General Manager: J. D. Williams.

EAGLE BUTTE—Cheyenne River Sioux Tribe Telephone Authority. Formerly [SD0164]. This cable system has converted to IPTV, PO Box 810, Eagle Butte, SD 57625. Phone: 605-964-2600. Fax: 605-964-1000. E-mail: info@crstta.com. Web Site: http://www.crstta.com. ICA: SD5048.
Channel capacity: N.A. Channels available but not in use: N.A.

Internet Service
Operational: Yes.

General Manager: J. D. Williams.

EAGLE BUTTE—Cheyenne River Sioux Tribe Telephone. This cable system has converted to IPTV. See Eagle Butte, CA [SD5048]. ICA: SD0164.

EDEN—Venture Communications Cooperative. Now served by BRITTON, SD [SD0041]. ICA: SD0165.

EDGEMONT—Golden West Cablevision. Now served by WALL, SD [SD0068]. ICA: SD0043.

ELKTON (rural)—ITC. Formerly served by Clear Lake, SD [SD0047]. This cable system has converted to IPTV, 312 Fourth St W, Clear Lake, SD 57226. Phones: 800-417-8667; 605-874-2181. Fax: 605-874-2014. E-mail: info@itctel.com. Web Site: http://www.itc-web.com. ICA: SD5043.
Channel capacity: N.A. Channels available but not in use: N.A.

Basic Service
Subscribers: N.A.
Fee: $35.50 monthly.

Expanded Basic Service 1
Subscribers: N.A.
Fee: $46.95 monthly.

Limited Basic Service
Subscribers: N.A.
Fee: $25.50 monthly.

Pay Service 1
Pay Units: N.A.
Fee: $10.95 monthly (Cinemax or Starz!), $11.95 monthly (Showtime), $13.95 monthly (HBO).

Internet Service
Operational: Yes.
Fee: $39.95 monthly.

Telephone Service
Digital: Operational

General Manager: Jerry Heiberger.

EMERY—Emery Cable Vision Inc. Now served by ALEXANDRIA, SD [SD0097]. ICA: SD0107.

ESTELLINE—ITC. Formerly served by Clear Lake, SD [SD0047]. This cable system has converted to IPTV, 312 Fourth St W, Clear Lake, SD 57226. Phones: 800-417-8667; 605-874-2181. Fax: 605-874-2014. E-mail: info@itctel.com. Web Site: http://www.itc-web.com. ICA: SD5065.
Channel capacity: N.A. Channels available but not in use: N.A.

Basic Service
Subscribers: N.A.
Fee: $35.50 monthly.

Expanded Basic Service 1
Subscribers: N.A.
Fee: $46.95 monthly.
Limited Basic Service
Subscribers: N.A.
Fee: $25.50 monthly.
Pay Service 1
Pay Units: N.A.
Fee: $10.95 monthly (Cinemax or Starz!), $11.95 monthly (Showtime), $13.95 monthly (HBO).
Internet Service
Operational: Yes.
Fee: $39.95 monthly.
Telephone Service
Digital: Operational
General Manager: Jerry Heiberger.

ESTELLINE—Mediacom. Now served by BROOKINGS, SD [SD0005]. ICA: SD0076.

ETHAN—Santel Communications. Formerly served by Mount Vernon, SD [SD0188]. This cable system has converted to IPTV, 308 S Dumont Ave, PO Box 67, Woonsocket, SD 57385-0067. Phones: 888-978-7777; 605-796-4411. Fax: 605-796-4419. E-mail: info@santel.net. Web Site: http://www.santel.net. ICA: SD5016.
TV Market Ranking: 85 (ETHAN).
Channel capacity: N.A. Channels available but not in use: N.A.
Basic Service
Subscribers: N.A.
Fee: $33.95 monthly.
Expanded Basic Service 1
Subscribers: N.A.
Fee: $43.95 monthly.
Limited Basic Service
Subscribers: N.A.
Fee: $21.95 monthly.
Pay Service 1
Pay Units: N.A.
Fee: $10.95 monthly (Cinemax, Encore/ Starz, HBO, or Showtime).
Internet Service
Operational: Yes.
Fee: $25.00 installation; $24.95 monthly; $10.00 modem lease.
Telephone Service
Analog: Operational
Fee: $14.50 monthly

ETHAN—Santel Communications. Now served by MOUNT VERNON, SD [SD0188]. ICA: SD0167.

EUREKA—Valley Cable. Now served by HERREID, SD [SD0091]. ICA: SD0040.

EUREKA—Valley Telecommunications Coop. Assn. Formerly served by Herreid, SD [SD0091]. This cable system has converted to IPTV, PO Box 7, Herreid, SD 57632-0007. Phone: 605-437-2615. Fax: 605-437-2615. E-mail: valley@valleytel.net. Web Site: http://www.valleytelco.coop. ICA: SD5030.
Channel capacity: N.A. Channels available but not in use: N.A.
Basic Service
Subscribers: N.A.
Fee: $33.00 monthly.
Expanded Basic Service 1
Subscribers: N.A.
Fee: $42.00 monthly.
Internet Service
Operational: Yes.

FAIRFAX—Golden West Telecommunications, 415 Crown St, PO Box 411, Wall, SD 57790-0411. Phone: 605-279-2161. Fax: 605-279-2727. E-mail: info@goldenwest.com. Web Site: http://www.goldenwest.com. Also serves Bonesteel. ICA: SD0169.
TV Market Ranking: Outside TV Markets (Bonesteel, FAIRFAX). Franchise award date: N.A. Franchise expiration date: N.A. Began: April 1, 1987.
Channel capacity: 36 (not 2-way capable). Channels available but not in use: N.A.
Basic Service
Subscribers: 95.
Programming (received off-air): KARE (NBC) Minneapolis; KDLT-TV (NBC) Sioux Falls; KEVN-TV (FOX) Rapid City; KMNE-TV (PBS) Bassett; KPLO-TV (CBS, MNT) Reliance; KPRY-TV (ABC) Pierre.
Programming (via satellite): A&E Networks; ABC Family Channel; American Movie Classics; Animal Planet; Cartoon Network; CNBC; CNN; Comedy Central; Country Music TV; C-SPAN; C-SPAN 2; CW+; Discovery Channel; Disney Channel; ESPN; ESPN 2; ESPN Classic Sports; Eternal Word TV Network; Food Network; Fox News Channel; FX; Great American Country; Hallmark Channel; Headline News; HGTV; History Channel; INSP; ION Television; Lifetime Movie Network; MTV; NFL Network; Nickelodeon; QVC; RFD-TV; Spike TV; TBS Superstation; The Learning Channel; The Weather Channel; Trinity Broadcasting Network; Turner Classic Movies; Turner Network TV; TV Guide Network; TV Land; USA Network; VH1; WGN America.
Fee: $35.00 installation; $33.95 monthly.
Digital Basic Service
Subscribers: N.A.
Programming (via satellite): AmericanLife TV Network; Bio; Bloomberg Television; Bravo; Discovery Fit & Health; Discovery Kids Channel; DMX Music; ESPN 2; ESPN Classic Sports; ESPNews; Fox Movie Channel; Fuse; G4; Golf Channel; GSN; Halogen Network; HGTV; History Channel; ID Investigation Discovery; Independent Film Channel; Lifetime Movie Network; Military Channel; MTV2; National Geographic Channel; Nick Jr.; NickToons TV; Outdoor Channel; Planet Green; Science; Speed; Style Network; Syfy; TeenNick; Toon Disney; Trinity Broadcasting Network; Turner Classic Movies; Versus; VH1 Classic; VH1 Country; WE tv.
Fee: $14.95 monthly.
Pay Service 1
Pay Units: 17.
Programming (via satellite): HBO.
Fee: $11.95 monthly.
Pay Service 2
Pay Units: 5.
Programming (via satellite): Cinemax; Showtime; The Movie Channel.
Fee: $9.95 monthly (TMC), $10.95 monthly (Showtime), $11.95 (Cinemax).
Digital Pay Service 1
Pay Units: N.A.
Programming (via satellite): Cinemax (multiplexed); Encore (multiplexed); Flix; HBO (multiplexed); Showtime (multiplexed); Starz (multiplexed); The Movie Channel (multiplexed).
Fee: $11.95 monthly (Cinemax, Showtime or TMC), $12.95 monthly (HBO), $13.95 monthly (Starz/Encore).
Video-On-Demand: No
Internet Service
Operational: No, Both DSL & dial-up.
Telephone Service
None
General Manager: George Strandell. Chief Technician: Randy Shepard. Marketing Director: Greg Oleson. Cable Television Manager: Rick Reed. Customer Service Manager: Jody Bielmaier.
Ownership: Golden West Cablevision (MSO).

FAITH—West River Cable Television, 801 Coleman Ave, PO Box 39, Bison, SD 57620. Phones: 888-411-5651; 605-244-5236. Fax: 605-244-7288. E-mail: westriver@sdplains.com. Web Site: http://www.westrivercatv.com. ICA: SD0102.
TV Market Ranking: Outside TV Markets (FAITH). Franchise award date: April 1, 1986. Franchise expiration date: N.A. Began: March 1, 1983.
Channel capacity: 25 (not 2-way capable). Channels available but not in use: N.A.
Basic Service
Subscribers: 69.
Programming (received off-air): KCLO-TV (CBS) Rapid City; KEVN-TV (FOX) Rapid City; KOTA-TV (ABC) Rapid City; KPSD-TV (PBS) Eagle Butte.
Programming (via satellite): A&E Networks; ABC Family Channel; AMC; Animal Planet; CNN; Country Music TV; C-SPAN; Discovery Channel; Disney Channel; ESPN; ESPN 2; HGTV; KARE (NBC) Minneapolis; Lifetime; Nickelodeon; Spike TV; TBS Superstation; The Learning Channel; The Weather Channel; Turner Network TV; USA Network; WGN America.
Fee: $50.00 installation; $32.95 monthly.
Pay Service 1
Pay Units: 9.
Programming (via satellite): HBO.
Fee: $10.00 monthly.
Internet Service
Operational: No.
Telephone Service
None
Miles of Plant: 4.0 (coaxial); None (fiber optic).
General Manager: Jerry Reisonauer. Assistant Manager: Colgan Huber. Telecommunications Manager: Colle Nash.
Ownership: West River Cooperative Telephone Co. (MSO).

FAULKTON—Western Telephone Company, 111 N 9th Ave, PO Box 128, Faulkton, SD 57438. Phones: 605-852-2224; 605-598-6217. Fax: 605-598-4100. Web Site: http://www.westtelco.com. Also serves Cresbard. ICA: SD0170.
TV Market Ranking: Below 100 (Cresbard); Outside TV Markets (FAULKTON). Franchise award date: N.A. Franchise expiration date: N.A. Began: February 1, 1981.
Channel capacity: N.A. Channels available but not in use: N.A.
Basic Service
Subscribers: 300.
Programming (received off-air): KABY-TV (ABC) Aberdeen; KDLO-TV (CBS, MNT) Florence; KDLT-TV (NBC) Sioux Falls; KQSD-TV (PBS) Lowry; KTTM (FOX) Huron.
Programming (via satellite): A&E Networks; ABC Family Channel; AMC; Animal Planet; Cartoon Network; CNN; Comedy Central; Country Music TV; C-SPAN; C-SPAN 2; Discovery Channel; Disney Channel; E! Entertainment Television; ESPN; ESPN 2; Eternal Word TV Network; Food Network; Fox News Channel; Fox Sports Net; FX; Golf Channel; Hallmark Channel; Headline News; HGTV; History Channel; Lifetime; MTV; Nickelodeon; Speed; Spike TV; Syfy; TBS Superstation; The Learning Channel; The Weather Channel; Travel Channel; Trinity Broadcasting Network; truTV; Turner Classic Movies; Turner Network TV; TV Land; USA Network; Versus; VH1; WGN America.
Fee: $29.95 installation; $29.95 monthly.
Pay Service 1
Pay Units: 170.
Programming (via satellite): Cinemax; Encore; HBO; Showtime; The Movie Channel.
Fee: $10.00 installation; $9.95 monthly.
Video-On-Demand: No
Internet Service
Operational: No.
Telephone Service
None
Miles of Plant: 14.0 (coaxial); None (fiber optic).
General Manager: Randy Houdek. Assistant Manager: Randy Olson. Chief Technician: Brad Ryan. Member Services Manager: Rod Kusser.
Ownership: Venture Communications Cooperative (MSO).

FLORENCE—ITC. Formerly served by Clear Lake, SD [SD0047]. This cable system has converted to IPTV, 312 Fourth St W, Clear Lake, SD 57226. Phones: 800-417-8667; 605-874-2181. Fax: 605-874-2014. E-mail: info@itc-web.com. Web Site: http://www.itc-web.com. ICA: SD5052.
Channel capacity: N.A. Channels available but not in use: N.A.
Basic Service
Subscribers: N.A.
Fee: $35.50 monthly.
Expanded Basic Service 1
Subscribers: N.A.
Fee: $46.95 monthly.
Limited Basic Service
Subscribers: N.A.
Fee: $25.50 monthly.
Pay Service 1
Pay Units: N.A.
Fee: $10.95 monthly (Cinemax or Starz!), $11.95 monthly (Showtime), $13.95 monthly (HBO).
Internet Service
Operational: Yes.
Fee: $39.95 monthly.
Telephone Service
Digital: Operational
General Manager: Jerry Heiberger.

FLORENCE—Satellite Cable Services Inc. Now served by CLEAR LAKE, SD [SD0047]. ICA: SD0171.

FORT PIERRE—Midcontinent Communications, PO Box 5010, Sioux Falls, SD 57117. Phones: 800-888-1300 (Customer service); 605-223-9036 (Local office). Fax: 605-229-0478. Web Site: http://www.midcocomm.com. Also serves Pierre. ICA: SD0172.

TV Market Ranking: Below 100 (FORT PIERRE, Pierre). Franchise award date: June 17, 1985. Franchise expiration date: N.A. Began: N.A.
Channel capacity: 62 (operating 2-way). Channels available but not in use: N.A.
Basic Service
Subscribers: 5,339.
Programming (received off-air): KDLT-TV (NBC) Sioux Falls; KPLO-TV (CBS, MNT) Reliance; KPRY-TV (ABC) Pierre; KTSD-TV (PBS) Pierre; KTTW (FOX) Sioux Falls; 5 FMs.
Programming (via satellite): A&E Networks; ABC Family Channel; AMC; Animal Planet; Cartoon Network; CNBC; CNN; Comedy Central; Country Music TV; C-SPAN; C-SPAN 2; Discovery Channel; Discovery Fit & Health; Disney Channel; ESPN; ESPN 2; ESPN Classic Sports; ESPNews; Eternal Word TV Network; Food Network; Fox News Channel; Fox Sports Net North; FX; G4; Hallmark Channel; Headline News; HGTV; History Channel; INSP; ION Television; Lifetime; MSNBC; MTV; Nickelodeon; Outdoor Channel; QVC; Speed; Spike TV; Syfy; TBS Superstation; The Learning Channel; The Weather Channel; Travel Channel; truTV; Turner Classic Movies; Turner Network TV; TV Guide Network; TV Land; USA Network; Versus; VH1; WE tv; WGN America.
Fee: $25.00 installation; $38.95 monthly.
Digital Basic Service
Subscribers: 650.
Programming (via satellite): BBC America; Bio; Bloomberg Television; DMX Music; ESPN; Fox Soccer; Fuse; GAS; Golf Channel; GSN; HD Theater; HDNet; HDNet Movies; History Channel International; Independent Film Channel; Lifetime Movie Network; MTV Networks Digital Suite; Nick Jr.; NickToons TV; Style Network; Sundance Channel; Toon Disney.
Fee: $9.00 monthly.
Digital Pay Service 1
Pay Units: N.A.
Programming (via satellite): Cinemax (multiplexed); Encore (multiplexed); HBO (multiplexed); Showtime (multiplexed); Showtime HD; Starz (multiplexed); Starz HDTV (multiplexed); The Movie Channel (multiplexed).
Video-On-Demand: No
Pay-Per-View
Hot Choice (delivered digitally); iN DEMAND (delivered digitally); Sports PPV (delivered digitally).
Internet Service
Operational: Yes.
Subscribers: 1,686.
Broadband Service: MidcoNet.
Fee: $35.00 installation; $19.95 monthly; $10.00 modem lease; $39.00 modem purchase.
Telephone Service
Digital: Operational
Fee: $18.00 monthly
Miles of Plant: 77.0 (coaxial); 3.0 (fiber optic).
Manager: Lonnie Schumacher. Marketing Director: Fred Jamieson. Customer Service Manager: Kathy Fuhrmann.
Ownership: Comcast Cable Communications Inc. (MSO).; Midcontinent Media Inc. (MSO).

FRANKFORT—James Valley Telecommunications. Now served by GROTON, SD [SD0030]. ICA: SD0173.

FREEMAN—Mediacom, 750 22nd Ave S, Brookings, SD 57006-2822. Phones: 507-835-2356 (Waseca office); 605-692-5508 (Customer service). Fax: 605-692-6496. Web Site: http://www.mediacomcable.com. Also serves Bridgewater, Canistota, Marion, Menno, Olivet, Parkston, Salem & Scotland. ICA: SD0038.
TV Market Ranking: 85 (Bridgewater, Canistota, Marion, Parkston, Salem); Outside TV Markets (FREEMAN, Menno, Olivet, Scotland). Franchise award date: N.A. Franchise expiration date: N.A. Began: December 9, 1981.
Channel capacity: 150 (operating 2-way). Channels available but not in use: N.A.
Basic Service
Subscribers: 2,455.
Programming (received off-air): KDLT-TV (NBC) Sioux Falls; KELO-TV (CBS, MNT) Sioux Falls; KSFY-TV (ABC) Sioux Falls; KTTW (FOX) Sioux Falls; KUSD-TV (PBS) Vermillion; KWSD (CW) Sioux Falls.
Programming (via satellite): ABC Family Channel; CNN; C-SPAN; ION Television; QVC; TV Guide Network; WGN America.
Fee: $24.95 installation; $27.38 monthly.
Expanded Basic Service 1
Subscribers: N.A.
Programming (via satellite): A&E Networks; AMC; Animal Planet; Bravo; Cartoon Network; CNBC; Comedy Central; Country Music TV; C-SPAN 2; Discovery Channel; Discovery Fit & Health; Disney Channel; E! Entertainment Television; ESPN; ESPN 2; Food Network; Fox News Channel; FX; Hallmark Channel; Headline News; HGTV; History Channel; INSP; Lifetime; MSNBC; MTV; Nickelodeon; RFD-TV; SoapNet; Speed; Spike TV; Syfy; TBN Enlace USA; TBS Superstation; The Learning Channel; The Weather Channel; Toon Disney; Travel Channel; truTV; Turner Classic Movies; Turner Network TV; TV Land; Univision Studios; USA Network; VH1; WE tv.
Digital Basic Service
Subscribers: N.A.
Programming (received off-air): KSFY-TV (ABC) Sioux Falls.
Programming (via satellite): AmericanLife TV Network; BBC America; Bio; Bloomberg News Radio; Discovery Health Channel; Discovery Home Channel; Discovery Kids Channel; Discovery Times Channel; DMX Music; ESPNews; Fox Movie Channel; Fox Soccer; Fuse; G4; GAS; Golf Channel; GSN; History Channel International; Independent Film Channel; INSP; Lifetime Movie Network; Lime; MTV Hits; MTV2; National Geographic Channel; Nick Jr.; NickToons TV; Outdoor Channel; Science Television; Style Network; VH1 Classic.
Digital Pay Service 1
Pay Units: N.A.
Programming (via satellite): Canales N; Cinemax (multiplexed); Encore (multiplexed); HBO (multiplexed); Showtime (multiplexed); Starz (multiplexed); The Movie Channel (multiplexed).
Video-On-Demand: No
Pay-Per-View
ESPN; Fresh (delivered digitally); Shorteez (delivered digitally); Playboy TV (delivered digitally); Pleasure (delivered digitally).
Internet Service
Operational: Yes.
Broadband Service: Mediacom High Speed Internet.
Fee: $29.95 monthly; $10.00 modem lease.
Telephone Service
Analog: Not Operational
Digital: Operational
Miles of Plant: 9.0 (coaxial); None (fiber optic). Additional miles planned: 1.0 (coaxial).
Vice President: Bill Jensen. Manager: Ron Albritton.
Ownership: Mediacom LLC (MSO).

GARRETSON—Alliance Communications, 612 3rd St, PO Box 349, Garretson, SD 57030-0349. Phones: 800-701-4980; 605-582-6311; 605-594-3411. Fax: 605-594-6776. E-mail: email@alliancecom.net. Web Site: http://www.alliancecom.net. Also serves Brandon & Corson. ICA: SD0016.
TV Market Ranking: 85 (Brandon, Corson, GARRETSON). Franchise award date: N.A. Franchise expiration date: N.A. Began: December 10, 1981.
Channel capacity: 41 (not 2-way capable). Channels available but not in use: N.A.
Basic Service
Subscribers: 453.
Programming (received off-air): KCPO-LP Sioux Falls; KDLT-TV (NBC) Sioux Falls; KELO-TV (CBS, MNT) Sioux Falls; KSFY-TV (ABC) Sioux Falls; KTTW (FOX) Sioux Falls; KUSD-TV (PBS) Vermillion.
Programming (via satellite): A&E Networks; ABC Family Channel; AMC; Animal Planet; Bloomberg Television; Bravo; BTN; Cartoon Network; CNN; Comedy Central; Country Music TV; C-SPAN; Discovery Channel; Disney Channel; ESPN; ESPN 2; ESPN Classic Sports; Eternal Word TV Network; Food Network; Fox News Channel; Fox Sports Net; FX; Golf Channel; Great American Country; Hallmark Channel; Headline News; HGTV; History Channel; ION Television; Lifetime; LWS Local Weather Station; MTV; MyNetworkTV Inc.; National Geographic Channel; NFL Network; Nickelodeon; Outdoor Channel; QVC; Speed; Spike TV; Syfy; TBS Superstation; The Learning Channel; The Weather Channel; Travel Channel; truTV; Turner Classic Movies; Turner Network TV; TV Land; USA Network; VH1; WGN America.
Fee: $30.00 installation; $29.95 monthly.
Video-On-Demand: No
Internet Service
Operational: No.
Telephone Service
None
Miles of Plant: 75.0 (coaxial); None (fiber optic).
Manager: Don Snyders. Chief Technician: Bob Stietvater. Marketing Director: Amy Ahlers. Customer Service Manager: Chris Frerk.
Ownership: Alliance Communications.

GARY—ITC. Formerly served by Clear Lake, SD [SD0047]. This cable system has converted to IPTV, 312 Fourth St W, Clear Lake, SD 57226. Phones: 800-417-8667; 605-874-2181. Fax: 605-874-2014. E-mail: info@itc-web.com. Web Site: http://www.itc-web.com. ICA: SD5053.
Channel capacity: N.A. Channels available but not in use: N.A.
Basic Service
Subscribers: N.A.
Fee: $35.50 monthly.
Expanded Basic Service 1
Subscribers: N.A.
Fee: $46.95 monthly.
Limited Basic Service
Subscribers: N.A.
Fee: $25.50 monthly.
Pay Service 1
Pay Units: N.A.
Fee: $10.95 monthly (Cinemax or Starz!), $11.95 monthly (Showtime), $13.95 monthly (HBO).
Internet Service
Operational: Yes.
Fee: $39.95 monthly.
Telephone Service
Digital: Operational
General Manager: Jerry Heiberger.

GARY—Satellite Cable Services Inc. Now served by CLEAR LAKE, SD [SD0047]. ICA: SD0174.

GAYVILLE—Midcontinent Communications, PO Box 5010, Sioux Falls, SD 57117. Phone: 605-223-9036. Web Site: http://www.midcocomm.com. Also serves Vermillion & Yankton. ICA: SD0009.
TV Market Ranking: Below 100 (Vermillion); Outside TV Markets (GAYVILLE, Yankton). Franchise award date: N.A. Franchise expiration date: N.A. Began: April 1, 1980.
Channel capacity: 36 (operating 2-way). Channels available but not in use: N.A.
Basic Service
Subscribers: 5,264.
Programming (received off-air): KAUN-LP Sioux Falls; KCAU-TV (ABC) Sioux City; KDLT-TV (NBC) Sioux Falls; KELO-TV (CBS, MNT) Sioux Falls; KSFY-TV (ABC) Sioux Falls; KSIN-TV (PBS) Sioux City; KTIV (CW, NBC) Sioux City; KTTW (FOX) Sioux Falls; KUSD-TV (PBS) Vermillion; KXNE-TV (PBS) Norfolk.
Programming (via satellite): A&E Networks; ABC Family Channel; American Movie Classics; Animal Planet; Bravo; Cartoon Network; CNBC; CNN; Comedy Central; Country Music TV; C-SPAN; Discovery Channel; Disney Channel; E! Entertainment Television; ESPN; ESPN 2; Eternal Word TV Network; Food Network; Fox News Channel; Fox Sports Net North; FX; Hallmark Channel; Headline News; HGTV; History Channel; Home Shopping Network; INSP; Lifetime; MSNBC; MTV; Nickelodeon; QVC; SoapNet; Speed; Spike TV; Syfy; TBS Superstation; The Learning Channel; The Weather Channel; This TV; Travel Channel; Trinity Broadcasting Network; truTV; Turner Classic Movies; Turner Network TV; TV Guide Network; TV Land; Univision; USA Network; VH1; WE tv; WGN America.
Fee: $24.95 monthly.
Digital Basic Service
Subscribers: N.A.
Programming (via satellite): A&E HD; ABC Family HD; AMC HD; AmericanLife TV Network; Animal Planet HD; BBC America; Bio; Bloomberg News Radio; Boomerang; BTN; BTN HD; Canal Sur; CBS Sports Network; Centric; Cine Latino; Cine Mexicano; cloo; CMT Pure Country; CNN en Espanol; CNN HD; Cooking Channel; C-SPAN 2; C-SPAN 3; Current; Discovery Channel HD; Discovery en Espanol; Discovery Fit & Health; Discovery Health Channel; Disney Channel HD; Disney XD; Disney XD en Espanol; DIY Network; ESPN 2 HD; ESPN Classic Sports; ESPN Deportes; ESPN HD; ESPN U; ESPNews; EWTN en Espanol; Food Network HD; Fox College Sports Atlantic; Fox College Sports Central; Fox College Sports Pacific; Fox Movie Channel; Fox News HD; Fox Soccer; FSN HD; Fuse; FX HD; G4; GameHD; Golf Channel; Golf Channel HD; GolTV; GSN; Halogen Network; HD Theater; HGTV HD; History Channel en Espanol; History Channel HD; History Channel International; ID Investigation Discovery; Independent Film Channel; ION Life; Lifetime Movie Network; Military Channel; MLB Network; MLB Network HD; MTV Jams; mun2 television; Music Choice; National Geographic Channel; National Geographic Channel HD Network; NFL Network; NFL Network HD; NFL RedZone; NHL Network; Nick Jr.; Nick

Too; NickToons TV; Outdoor Channel; Palladia; PBS Kids Sprout; Pentagon Channel; Planet Green; Qubo; ReelzChannel; RFD-TV; Science; Science HD; SoapNet; Speed HD; Spike TV HD; Style Network; Syfy HD; TBS in HD; TeenNick; Telemundo; Tennis Channel; The Hub; The Sportsman Channel; The Weather Channel HD; TLC HD; Tr3s; Turner Network TV HD; TV One; TVE Internacional; TVG Network; Universal HD; Universal Sports; USA Network HD; VeneMovies; Versus; Versus HD; WE tv.
Fee: $24.95 monthly.

Digital Pay Service 1
Pay Units: 3,372.
Programming (via satellite): Cinemax (multiplexed); Cinemax HD; Encore (multiplexed); Flix (multiplexed); HBO (multiplexed); HBO HD; Showtime (multiplexed); Showtime HD; Starz (multiplexed); Starz HDTV; Sundance Channel (multiplexed); The Movie Channel (multiplexed); The Movie Channel HD.

Video-On-Demand: No

Pay-Per-View
ESPN (delivered digitally); Fresh (delivered digitally); Shorteez (delivered digitally); Playboy TV (delivered digitally); Pleasure (delivered digitally); Mediacom PPV (delivered digitally).

Internet Service
Operational: Yes.
Broadband Service: MidcoNet.
Fee: $35.00 installation; $19.95 monthly.

Telephone Service
Digital: Operational
Fee: $18.00 monthly

Miles of Plant: 91.0 (coaxial); None (fiber optic).
Ownership: Midcontinent Media Inc. (MSO).

GEDDES—Midstate Communications. Now served by PLATTE, SD [SD0049]. ICA: SD0175.

GETTYSBURG—Venture Communications Cooperative, 218 Commercial Ave. SE, PO Box 157, Highmore, SD 57345-0157. Phones: 800-824-7282; 605-852-2224. Fax: 605-852-2404. E-mail: venture@venturecomm.net. Web Site: http://www.venturecomm.net. Also serves Hoven. ICA: SD0036.
TV Market Ranking: Outside TV Markets (GETTYSBURG, Hoven). Franchise award date: January 6, 1992. Franchise expiration date: January 6, 2007. Began: February 1, 1980.
Channel capacity: N.A. Channels available but not in use: N.A.

Digital Basic Service
Subscribers: N.A. Included in Highmore
Programming (received off-air): KUSD-TV (PBS) Vermillion.
Programming (via satellite): CW+; Eternal Word TV Network; ION Television; QVC; The Weather Channel; Trinity Broadcasting Network; Weatherscan; WGN America.
Fee: $19.95 monthly.

Digital Expanded Basic Service
Subscribers: N.A.
Programming (via satellite): A&E Networks; ABC Family Channel; AMC; Animal Planet; BBC America; Bloomberg Television; Bravo; Cartoon Network; CNBC; CNN; Comedy Central; Country Music TV; C-SPAN; C-SPAN 2; Discovery Channel; Discovery Health Channel; Discovery Kids Channel; Disney Channel; DIY Network; DMX Music; E! Entertainment Television; ESPN; ESPN 2; ESPN Classic Sports; ESPNews; Food Network; Fox Movie Channel; Fox News Channel; Fox Sports Net North; FX; G4; GAS; Golf Channel; Great American Country; GSN; Hallmark Channel; Hallmark Movie Channel; Headline News; HGTV; History Channel; ID Investigation Discovery; Lifetime; Lifetime Movie Network; Lifetime Real Women; Military Channel; MSNBC; MTV; MTV Hits; MTV2; National Geographic Channel; NFL Network; Nick Jr.; Nickelodeon; NickToons TV; Outdoor Channel; Oxygen; Planet Green; RFD-TV; Science; SoapNet; Speed; Spike TV; Syfy; TBS Superstation; The Learning Channel; Toon Disney; Travel Channel; truTV; Turner Classic Movies; Turner Network TV; TV Land; USA Network; Versus; VH1; VH1 Classic; WE tv.
Fee: $18.00 monthly.

Digital Pay Service 1
Pay Units: N.A.
Programming (via satellite): Cinemax (multiplexed); Encore (multiplexed); HBO (multiplexed); Showtime (multiplexed); Starz (multiplexed); The Movie Channel.

Video-On-Demand: No

Pay-Per-View
Movies (delivered digitally); Playboy TV (delivered digitally); Shorteez (delivered digitally).

Internet Service
Operational: No.

Telephone Service
None

General Manager: Randy Houdek. Assistant Manager: Randy Olson. Chief Technician: Brad Ryan. Member Services Manager: Rod Kusser.
Ownership: Venture Communications Cooperative (MSO).

GLENHAM—Valley Cable. Now served by HERREID, SD [SD0091]. ICA: SD0143.

GLENHAM—Valley Telecommunications Coop. Assn. Formerly served by Herreid, SD [SD0091]. This cable system has converted to IPTV, PO Box 7, Herreid, SD 57632-0007. Phone: 605-437-2615. Fax: 605-437-2615. E-mail: valley@valleytel.net. Web Site: http://www.valleytelco.coop. ICA: SD5031.
Channel capacity: N.A. Channels available but not in use: N.A.

Basic Service
Subscribers: N.A.
Fee: $33.00 monthly.

Expanded Basic Service 1
Subscribers: N.A.
Fee: $42.00 monthly.

Internet Service
Operational: Yes.

GOODWIN—ITC. Formerly served by Clear Lake, SD [SD0047]. This cable system has converted to IPTV, 312 Fourth St W, Clear Lake, SD 57226. Phones: 800-417-8667; 605-874-2181. Fax: 605-874-2014. E-mail: info@itc-web.com. Web Site: http://www.itc-web.com. ICA: SD5054.
Channel capacity: N.A. Channels available but not in use: N.A.

Basic Service
Subscribers: N.A.
Fee: $35.50 monthly.

Expanded Basic Service 1
Subscribers: N.A.
Fee: $46.95 monthly.

Limited Basic Service
Subscribers: N.A.
Fee: $25.50 monthly.

Pay Service 1
Pay Units: N.A.
Fee: $10.95 monthly (Cinemax or Starz!), $11.95 monthly (Showtime), $13.95 monthly (HBO).

Internet Service
Operational: Yes.
Fee: $39.95 monthly.

Telephone Service
Digital: Operational

General Manager: Jerry Heiberger.

GREGORY—Golden West Telecommunications, 415 Crown St, PO Box 411, Wall, SD 57790-0411. Phone: 605-279-2161. Fax: 605-279-2727. E-mail: info@goldenwest.com. Web Site: http://www.goldenwest.com. ICA: SD0042.
TV Market Ranking: Outside TV Markets (GREGORY). Franchise award date: N.A. Franchise expiration date: N.A. Began: January 1, 1980.
Channel capacity: 135 (not 2-way capable). Channels available but not in use: N.A.

Basic Service
Subscribers: 489.
Programming (received off-air): KDLV-TV (NBC) Mitchell; KMNE-TV (PBS) Bassett; KPLO-TV (CBS, MNT) Reliance; KSFY-TV (ABC) Sioux Falls; KTSD-TV (PBS) Pierre.
Programming (via satellite): A&E Networks; ABC Family Channel; CNN; Discovery Channel; Disney Channel; ESPN; Nickelodeon; TBS Superstation; Turner Network TV; USA Network; WGN America.
Fee: $25.00 installation; $33.95 monthly.

Digital Basic Service
Subscribers: 9.
Programming (via satellite): AmericanLife TV Network; Bio; Bloomberg Television; Bravo; Discovery Fit & Health; DMX Music; ESPN 2; ESPN Classic Sports; ESPNews; Fox Movie Channel; Fox Sports World; Fuse; G4; Golf Channel; GSN; Halogen Network; HGTV; History Channel; History Channel International; Independent Film Channel; Lifetime Movie Network; National Geographic Channel; Outdoor Channel; Speed; Style Network; Syfy; Toon Disney; Trinity Broadcasting Network; Turner Classic Movies; Versus; WE tv.
Fee: $10.00 installation; $14.95 monthly.

Pay Service 1
Pay Units: 24.
Programming (via satellite): HBO.
Fee: $11.95 monthly.

Pay Service 2
Pay Units: 10.
Programming (via satellite): Cinemax.
Fee: $11.95 monthly.

Pay Service 3
Pay Units: N.A.
Programming (via satellite): Showtime; The Movie Channel.
Fee: $9.95 monthly (TMC), $10.95 monthly (Showtime).

Digital Pay Service 1
Pay Units: N.A.
Programming (via satellite): Cinemax (multiplexed); Encore (multiplexed); HBO (multiplexed); Showtime (multiplexed); Starz (multiplexed); The Movie Channel (multiplexed).
Fee: $11.95 monthly (Cinemax, Showtime or TMC), $12.95 monthly (HBO), $13.95 monthly (Starz/Encore).

Video-On-Demand: No

Pay-Per-View
Sports PPV (delivered digitally); ESPN Extra (delivered digitally); ESPN Now (delivered digitally); Fresh (delivered digitally); Playboy TV (delivered digitally); Hot Choice (delivered digitally).

Internet Service
Operational: No, Both DSL & dial-up.

Telephone Service
None

Miles of Plant: 26.0 (coaxial); None (fiber optic).
General Manager: George Strandell. Chief Technician: Randy Shepard. Marketing Director: Greg Oleson. Cable Television Manager: Rick Reed. Customer Service Manager: Jody Bielmaier.
Ownership: Golden West Cablevision (MSO).

GROTON—James Valley Telecommunications. Formerly [SD0030]. This cable system has converted to IPTV, 235 E First Ave, PO Box 260, Groton, SD 57445. Phones: 800-556-6525; 605-397-2323. Fax: 605-397-2350. E-mail: jvinfo@jamesvalley.com. Web Site: http://www.jamesvalley.com. ICA: SD5005.
TV Market Ranking: Below 100 (GROTON). Franchise award date: N.A. Franchise expiration date: N.A. Began: N.A.
Channel capacity: N.A. Channels available but not in use: N.A.

Internet Service
Operational: Yes.

Telephone Service
Digital: Operational

Chief Executive Officer: James Groft. Marketing Director: Kristi Larsen. Network Operations Manager: Russ Claussen. Plant Operations & Sales Manager: Rick Stugelmayer.

GROTON—James Valley Telecommunications. This cable system has converted to IPTV. See Groton, SD [SD5005]. ICA: SD0030.

HART RANCH—Midcontinent Communications, 1624 Concourse Ct, Rapid City, SD 57703. Phones: 605-342-1870; 605-343-0595. Fax: 605-338-9166. Web Site: http://www.midcocomm.com. ICA: SD0251.
TV Market Ranking: Below 100 (HART RANCH).
Channel capacity: N.A. Channels available but not in use: N.A.

Basic Service
Subscribers: 73.
Programming (received off-air): KBHE-TV (PBS) Rapid City; KCLO-TV (CBS) Rapid City; KCPM (MNT) Grand Forks; KEVN-TV (FOX) Rapid City; KKRA-LP (ION) Rapid City; KNBN (NBC) Rapid City; KOTA-TV (ABC) Rapid City; KWBH-LP Rapid City.
Programming (via satellite): A&E Networks; ABC Family Channel; AMC; Animal Planet; BET Networks; Bloomberg Television; Bravo; Cartoon Network; CNBC; CNN; Comedy Central; Country Music TV;

C-SPAN; C-SPAN 2; Discovery Channel; Discovery Fit & Health; Disney Channel; E! Entertainment Television; Encore; ESPN; ESPN 2; ESPN Classic Sports; ESPNews; Eternal Word TV Network; Food Network; Fox News Channel; Fox Sports Net North; FX; G4; Golf Channel; Great American Country; GSN; Hallmark Channel; Headline News; HGTV; History Channel; INSP; Lifetime; MSNBC; MTV; Nickelodeon; Outdoor Channel; Ovation; Oxygen; QVC; Root Sports Rocky Mountain; Speed; Spike TV; Syfy; TBS Superstation; The Learning Channel; The Weather Channel; Toon Disney; Travel Channel; Trinity Broadcasting Network; truTV; Turner Classic Movies; Turner Network TV; TV Guide Network; TV Land; USA Network; Versus; VH1; WE tv; WGN America.

Digital Basic Service
Subscribers: N.A.
Programming (via satellite): BBC America; Bio; Canales N; DMX Music; ESPN; Fuse; GAS; HD Theater; HDNet; HDNet Movies; History Channel International; Independent Film Channel; Lifetime Movie Network; MTV Networks Digital Suite; Nick Jr.; NickToons TV; Style Network; Sundance Channel.

Digital Pay Service 1
Pay Units: N.A.
Programming (via satellite): Cinemax (multiplexed); Encore (multiplexed); Flix; HBO (multiplexed); Showtime (multiplexed); Showtime; Starz (multiplexed); Starz HDTV (multiplexed); The Movie Channel.

Video-On-Demand: Yes

Pay-Per-View
iN DEMAND (delivered digitally); Hot Choice (delivered digitally); Playboy TV (delivered digitally); Sports PPV (delivered digitally).

Internet Service
Operational: Yes.
Broadband Service: MidcoNet.
Fee: $35.00 installation; $19.95 monthly.

Telephone Service
Digital: Operational
Fee: $18.00 monthly
Manager: Jerry Steever.
Ownership: Midcontinent Media Inc. (MSO).

HARTFORD—Golden West Telecommunications, 415 Crown St, PO Box 411, Wall, SD 57790-0411. Phone: 605-279-2161. Fax: 605-279-2727. E-mail: info@goldenwest.com. Web Site: http://www.goldenwest.com. Also serves Minnehaha County (southern portion). ICA: SD0057.
TV Market Ranking: 85 (HARTFORD, Minnehaha County (southern portion)). Franchise award date: January 1, 1983. Franchise expiration date: January 1, 2012. Began: December 1, 1983.
Channel capacity: N.A. Channels available but not in use: N.A.

Basic Service
Subscribers: 672.
Programming (received off-air): KCPO-LP Sioux Falls; KDLT-TV (NBC) Sioux Falls; KELO-TV (CBS, MNT) Sioux Falls; KSFY-TV (ABC) Sioux Falls; KTTW (FOX) Sioux Falls; KUSD-TV (PBS) Vermillion; KWSD (CW) Sioux Falls.
Programming (via satellite): A&E Networks; ABC Family Channel; AMC; Animal Planet; Bloomberg Television; Bravo; Cartoon Network; CNN; Comedy Central; Country Music TV; C-SPAN; Discovery Channel; Disney Channel; ESPN; ESPN 2; ESPN Classic Sports; Eternal Word TV Network; Food Network; Fox News Channel; Fox Sports Net North; FX; Golf Channel; Great American Country; Hallmark Channel; HGTV; History Channel; ION Television; Lifetime; MTV; NFL Network; Nickelodeon; Outdoor Channel; QVC; Speed; Spike TV; Syfy; TBS Superstation; The Learning Channel; The Weather Channel; Travel Channel; truTV; Turner Classic Movies; Turner Network TV; TV Guide Network; TV Land; USA Network; VH1; WGN America.
Fee: $25.00 installation; $31.95 monthly.

Pay Service 1
Pay Units: 280.
Programming (via satellite): Cinemax; Encore (multiplexed); Flix; HBO (multiplexed); Showtime (multiplexed); Starz (multiplexed); The Movie Channel (multiplexed).
Fee: $10.95 monthly (HBO or Cinemax), $12.95 monthly (Showtime/TMC or Starz/Encore).

Internet Service
Operational: No, Both DSL & dial-up.

Telephone Service
None
Miles of Plant: 25.0 (coaxial); 5.0 (fiber optic).
General Manager: George Strandell. Chief Technician: Randy Shepard. Marketing Director: Greg Oleson. Cable Television Manager: Rick Reed. Customer Service Manager: Jody Bielmaier.
Ownership: Golden West Cablevision (MSO).

HAYTI—ITC. Formerly served by Clear Lake, SD [SD0047]. This cable system has converted to IPTV, 312 Fourth St W, Clear Lake, SD 57226. Phones: 800-417-8667; 605-874-2181. Fax: 605-874-2014. E-mail: info@itctel.com. Web Site: http://www.itc-web.com. ICA: SD5067.
Channel capacity: N.A. Channels available but not in use: N.A.

Basic Service
Subscribers: N.A.
Fee: $35.50 monthly.

Expanded Basic Service 1
Subscribers: N.A.
Fee: $46.95 monthly.

Limited Basic Service
Subscribers: N.A.
Fee: $25.50 monthly.

Pay Service 1
Pay Units: N.A.
Fee: $10.95 monthly (Cinemax or Starz!), $11.95 monthly (Showtime), $13.95 monthly (HBO).

Internet Service
Operational: Yes.
Fee: $39.95 monthly.

Telephone Service
Digital: Operational
General Manager: Jerry Heiberger.

HAYTI—Mediacom. Now served by BROOKINGS, SD [SD0005]. ICA: SD0120.

HENRY—ITC. Formerly served by Clear Lake, SD [SD0047]. This cable system has converted to IPTV, 312 Fourth St W, Clear Lake, SD 57226. Phones: 800-417-8667; 605-874-2181. Fax: 605-874-2014. E-mail: info@itc-web.com. Web Site: http://www.itc-web.com. ICA: SD5055.
Channel capacity: N.A. Channels available but not in use: N.A.

Basic Service
Subscribers: N.A.
Fee: $35.50 monthly.

Expanded Basic Service 1
Subscribers: N.A.
Fee: $46.95 monthly.

Limited Basic Service
Subscribers: N.A.
Fee: $25.50 monthly.

Pay Service 1
Pay Units: N.A.
Fee: $10.95 monthly (Cinemax or Starz!), $11.95 monthly (Showtime), $13.95 monthly (HBO).

Internet Service
Operational: Yes.
Fee: $39.95 monthly.

Telephone Service
Digital: Operational
General Manager: Jerry Heiberger.

HENRY—Satellite Cable Services Inc. Now served by CLEAR LAKE, SD [SD0047]. ICA: SD0176.

HERREID—Valley Telecommunications Coop. Assn. Formerly [SD0091]. This cable system has converted to IPTV, PO Box 7, Herreid, SD 57632-0007. Phone: 605-437-2615. Fax: 605-437-2615. E-mail: valley@valleytel.net. Web Site: http://www.valleytelco.coop. ICA: SD5032.
Channel capacity: N.A. Channels available but not in use: N.A.

Basic Service
Subscribers: N.A.
Fee: $33.00 monthly.

Expanded Basic Service 1
Subscribers: N.A.
Fee: $42.00 monthly.

Internet Service
Operational: Yes.

HERREID—Valley Telecommunications Coop. Assn. This cable system has converted to IPTV. See Herreid, SD [SD5032]. ICA: SD0091.

HIGHMORE—Venture Communications Cooperative, 218 Commercial Ave. SE, PO Box 157, Highmore, SD 57345-0157. Phone: 605-852-2224. Fax: 605-852-2404. E-mail: venture@venturecomm.net. Web Site: http://www.venturecomm.net. Also serves Blunt, Harrold, Onaka, Ree Heights, Seneca & Tolstoy. ICA: SD0060.
TV Market Ranking: Below 100 (Blunt, Harrold); Outside TV Markets (HIGHMORE, Onaka, Ree Heights, Seneca, Tolstoy). Franchise award date: N.A. Franchise expiration date: N.A. Began: May 1, 1982.
Channel capacity: N.A. Channels available but not in use: N.A.

Basic Service
Subscribers: 320.
Programming (received off-air): KDLT-TV (NBC) Sioux Falls; KPLO-TV (CBS, MNT) Reliance; KPRY-TV (ABC) Pierre; KTTW (FOX) Sioux Falls; KUSD-TV (PBS) Vermillion; KWSD (CW) Sioux Falls.
Programming (via satellite): A&E Networks; ABC Family Channel; AMC; Animal Planet; Cartoon Network; Catholic Television Network; CNBC; CNN; Comedy Central; Country Music TV; C-SPAN; Discovery Channel; Disney Channel; ESPN; ESPN 2; Food Network; Fox News Channel; FX; Great American Country; Hallmark Channel; Headline News; HGTV; History Channel; ION Television; Lifetime; MTV; MyNetworkTV Inc.; Nickelodeon; QVC; Spike TV; Syfy; TBS Superstation; The Learning Channel; The Weather Channel; Travel Channel; Trinity Broadcasting Network; truTV; Turner Network TV; TV Land; USA Network; VH1; WGN America.
Fee: $20.00 installation; $29.95 monthly.

Digital Basic Service
Subscribers: 60 Includes Britton, Gettysburg, Onida, Rosholt, Sisseton, Wessington, & Wessington Springs.
Programming (via satellite): AmericanLife TV Network; BBC America; Bio; Bloomberg Television; Discovery Fit & Health; DMX Music; ESPN 2; ESPN Classic Sports; ESPNews; Fox Movie Channel; Fox Sports World; Fuse; G4; Golf Channel; GSN; Halogen Network; HGTV; History Channel; History Channel International; Independent Film Channel; Lifetime Movie Network; Lime; National Geographic Channel; Outdoor Channel; Speed; Style Network; Toon Disney; Trinity Broadcasting Network; Turner Classic Movies; Versus; WE tv.
Fee: $17.00 monthly.

Pay Service 1
Pay Units: 48.
Programming (via satellite): Showtime.
Fee: $15.00 installation; $10.95 monthly.

Digital Pay Service 1
Pay Units: N.A.
Programming (via satellite): Cinemax (multiplexed); Encore (multiplexed); Flix; HBO (multiplexed); Showtime (multiplexed); Starz (multiplexed); The Movie Channel (multiplexed).

Video-On-Demand: No

Pay-Per-View
Playboy TV (delivered digitally); Fresh (delivered digitally); Movies (delivered digitally); sports (delivered digitally); ESPN Now (delivered digitally).

Internet Service
Operational: No.

Telephone Service
None
Miles of Plant: 5.0 (coaxial); None (fiber optic).
General Manager: Randy Houdek. Assistant Manager: Randy Olson. Chief Technician: Brad Ryan. Member Services Manager: Rod Kusser.
Ownership: Venture Communications Cooperative (MSO).

HILL CITY—Golden West Cablevision. Now served by CUSTER, SD [SD0034]. ICA: SD0088.

HOSMER—Valley Cable & Satellite Communications, Inc. Now served by HERREID, SD [SD0091]. ICA: SD0117.

HOSMER—Valley Telecommunications Coop. Assn. Formerly served by Herreid, SD [SD0091]. This cable system has converted to IPTV, PO Box 7, Herreid, SD 57632-0007. Phone: 605-437-2615. Fax: 605-437-2615. E-mail: valley@valleytel.net. Web Site: http://www.valleytelco.coop. ICA: SD5033.
Channel capacity: N.A. Channels available but not in use: N.A.

Basic Service
Subscribers: N.A.
Fee: $33.00 monthly.

Expanded Basic Service 1
Subscribers: N.A.
Fee: $42.00 monthly.

Internet Service
Operational: Yes.

HOT SPRINGS—Golden West Telecommunications. Now served by CUSTER, SD [SD0034]. ICA: SD0018.

HOVEN—Venture Communications Cooperative. Now served by GETTYSBURG, SD [SD0036]. ICA: SD0082.

HOWARD—Alliance Communications. Formerly [SD0052]. This cable system has converted to IPTV, 612 Third St, PO Box 349, Garretson, SD 57030. Phones: 800-701-4980; 605-594-3400. Fax: 605-594-6776. E-mail: email@alliancecom.net. Web Site: http://www.alliancecom.net. ICA: SD5082.
Channel capacity: N.A. Channels available but not in use: N.A.
Basic Service
Subscribers: N.A.
Fee: $29.95 monthly.
Expanded Basic Service 1
Subscribers: N.A.
Fee: $13.00 monthly.
Expanded Basic Service 2
Subscribers: N.A.
Fee: $8.00 monthly.
Pay Service 1
Pay Units: N.A.
Fee: $9.95 monthly (Cinemax or Starz/Encore), $10.95 monthly (Showtime) or $13.95 monthly (HBO).
Internet Service
Operational: Yes.
Fee: $14.95 monthly.
Telephone Service
Digital: Operational
Fee: $12.70 monthly
Manager: Don Snyder.

HOWARD—Alliance Communications. This cable system has converted to IPTV. See Howard, SD [SD5082]. ICA: SD0052.

HUDSON—Alliance Communications. This cable system has converted to IPTV. See Hudson, SD [SD5083]. ICA: SD0254.

HUDSON—Sioux Valley Wireless. Now served by HUDSON, SD [SD0254]. ICA: SD0142.

HURON—Midcontinent Communications, PO Box 5010, Sioux Falls, SD 57117. Phone: 605-352-4302. Fax: 605-352-2413. Web Site: http://www.midcocomm.com. Also serves Beadle County, Miller, St. Lawrence & Wolsey. ICA: SD0006.
TV Market Ranking: Below 100 (HURON, Wolsey); Outside TV Markets (Beadle County, Miller, St. Lawrence). Franchise award date: December 1, 1984. Franchise expiration date: August 22, 2012. Began: December 1, 1968.
Channel capacity: 69 (operating 2-way). Channels available but not in use: N.A.
Basic Service
Subscribers: 5,157.
Programming (received off-air): KABY-TV (ABC) Aberdeen; KCPO-LP Sioux Falls; KDLO-TV (CBS, MNT) Florence; KDLT-TV (NBC) Sioux Falls; KELO-TV (CBS, MNT) Sioux Falls; KESD-TV (PBS) Brookings; KTTM (FOX) Huron; KTTW (FOX) Sioux Falls; KWSD (CW) Sioux Falls; 5 FMs.
Programming (via satellite): A&E Networks; ABC Family Channel; AMC; Animal Planet; BET Networks; Bravo; Cartoon Network; CNBC; CNN; Comedy Central; Country Music TV; C-SPAN; C-SPAN 2; Discovery Channel; Discovery Fit & Health; Discovery Health Channel; Disney Channel; E! Entertainment Television; ESPN; ESPN 2; ESPN Classic Sports; ESPNews; Eternal Word TV Network; Food Network; Fox Movie Channel; Fox News Channel; Fox Sports Net North; FX; G4; Hallmark Channel; Headline News; HGTV; History Channel; INSP; ION Television; Lifetime; MSNBC; MTV; Nickelodeon; Outdoor Channel; QVC; Speed; Spike TV; Syfy; TBS Superstation; The Learning Channel; The Weather Channel; Travel Channel; Trinity Broadcasting Network; truTV; Turner Classic Movies; Turner Network TV; TV Guide Network; TV Land; USA Network; Versus; VH1; WE tv; WGN America.
Fee: $50.00 installation; $25.00 monthly.
Digital Basic Service
Subscribers: 404.
Programming (received off-air): KELO-TV (CBS, MNT) Sioux Falls.
Programming (via satellite): BBC America; Bio; Bloomberg Television; DMX Music; ESPN; Fox Soccer; Fuse; Golf Channel; GSN; HD Theater; HDNet; HDNet Movies; History Channel International; Independent Film Channel; Lifetime Movie Network; MTV Networks Digital Suite; Nick Jr.; NickToons TV; Style Network; Sundance Channel; TeenNick; Toon Disney.
Digital Pay Service 1
Pay Units: N.A.
Programming (via satellite): Cinemax (multiplexed); Cinemax HD; Encore (multiplexed); HBO (multiplexed); HBO HD; Showtime (multiplexed); Showtime HD; Starz (multiplexed); Starz HDTV; The Movie Channel (multiplexed).
Video-On-Demand: No
Pay-Per-View
iN DEMAND (delivered digitally); NFL Network (delivered digitally); ESPN Sports PPV (delivered digitally); NBA TV (delivered digitally); MLS Direct Kick (delivered digitally); NHL Center Ice (delivered digitally); MLB Extra Innings (delivered digitally).
Internet Service
Operational: Yes. Began: June 1, 1998.
Subscribers: 1,556.
Broadband Service: MidcoNet.
Fee: $35.00 installation; $19.95 monthly.
Telephone Service
Digital: Operational
Fee: $18.00 monthly
Miles of Plant: 114.0 (coaxial); None (fiber optic).
Manager: Lonnie Schumacher. Marketing Director: Fred Jamieson. Customer Service Manager: Kathy Fuhrmann.
Ownership: Midcontinent Media Inc. (MSO).; Comcast Cable Communications Inc. (MSO).

IROQUOIS—Midcontinent Communications, PO Box 5010, Sioux Falls, SD 57117. Phones: 800-456-0564; 605-229-1775. Fax: 605-229-0478. Web Site: http://www.midcocomm.com. ICA: SD0128.
TV Market Ranking: Below 100 (IROQUOIS). Franchise award date: N.A. Franchise expiration date: N.A. Began: December 1, 1984.
Channel capacity: 26 (2-way capable). Channels available but not in use: N.A.
Basic Service
Subscribers: 61.
Programming (received off-air): KABY-TV (ABC) Aberdeen; KDLO-TV (CBS, MNT) Florence; KDLT-TV (NBC) Sioux Falls; KESD-TV (PBS) Brookings; KTTM (FOX) Huron.
Programming (via satellite): A&E Networks; ABC Family Channel; AMC; CNN; C-SPAN; Discovery Channel; Disney Channel; ESPN; ESPN 2; History Channel; Lifetime; Nickelodeon; Spike TV; Syfy; TBS Superstation; The Weather Channel; Turner Network TV; USA Network; VH1; WGN America.
Fee: $24.95 installation; $26.32 monthly.
Pay Service 1
Pay Units: 55.
Programming (via satellite): HBO.
Fee: $11.95 monthly.
Video-On-Demand: No
Internet Service
Operational: No.
Telephone Service
None
Miles of Plant: 5.0 (coaxial); None (fiber optic).
Manager: Doug Bierschbach. Chief Technician: Paul Schmidt.
Ownership: Midcontinent Media Inc. (MSO).

JEFFERSON—Jefferson Satellite Telecommunications Inc. Now served by SALIX, IA [IA0510]. ICA: SD0179.

KENNEBEC—Kennebec Telephone Co. Inc., 220 S Main St, PO Box 158, Kennebec, SD 57544-0158. Phone: 605-869-2220. Fax: 605-869-2221. E-mail: knbctel@kennebectelephone.com. Web Site: http://www.kennebectelephone.com. Also serves Presho. ICA: SD0130.
TV Market Ranking: Below 100 (KENNEBEC, Presho). Franchise award date: April 1, 1980. Franchise expiration date: N.A. Began: November 1, 1982.
Channel capacity: 78 (not 2-way capable). Channels available but not in use: N.A.
Basic Service
Subscribers: 247.
Programming (received off-air): KDLT-TV (NBC) Sioux Falls; KEVN-TV (FOX) Rapid City; KPLO-TV (CBS, MNT) Reliance; KPRY-TV (ABC) Pierre; KTSD-TV (PBS) Pierre.
Programming (via satellite): A&E Networks; ABC Family Channel; AMC; Animal Planet; Cartoon Network; CNBC; CNN; Comedy Central; Country Music TV; C-SPAN; C-SPAN 2; CW+; Discovery Channel; Disney Channel; ESPN; ESPN 2; ESPNews; Eternal Word TV Network; Food Network; Fox News Channel; FX; Great American Country; Hallmark Channel; Headline News; HGTV; History Channel; INSP; ION Television; KARE (NBC) Minneapolis; Lifetime; Local Cable Weather; MTV; Nickelodeon; QVC; RFD-TV; Spike TV; TBS Superstation; The Learning Channel; The Weather Channel; Trinity Broadcasting Network; Turner Classic Movies; Turner Network TV; TV Land; USA Network; VH1; WGN America.
Fee: $15.00 installation; $28.95 monthly.
Pay Service 1
Pay Units: 69.
Programming (via satellite): Cinemax; HBO; Showtime; The Movie Channel.
Fee: $8.95 monthly (Showtime or TMC), $10.95 monthly (HBO).
Video-On-Demand: No
Internet Service
Operational: No, DSL & dial-up.
Telephone Service
None
Miles of Plant: 17.0 (coaxial); None (fiber optic).
General Manager: Rod Bowar. Plant Manager: Matt Collins. Chief Technician: Ken Walling. Marketing Manager: Jason Thiry.
Ownership: Kennebec Telephone Co. Inc.

KIMBALL—Midstate Communications. Now served by WHITE LAKE, SD [SD0026]. ICA: SD0077.

LAKE ANDES—Satellite Cable Services Inc. Now served by TRIPP, SD [SD0087]. ICA: SD0072.

LAKE BENTON—ITC. Formerly served by Clear Lake, SD [SD0047]. This cable system has converted to IPTV, 312 Fourth St W, Clear Lake, SD 57226. Phones: 800-417-8667; 605-874-2181. Fax: 605-874-2014. E-mail: info@itctel.com. Web Site: http://www.itc-web.com. ICA: SD5068.
Channel capacity: N.A. Channels available but not in use: N.A.
Basic Service
Subscribers: N.A.
Fee: $35.50 monthly.
Expanded Basic Service 1
Subscribers: N.A.
Fee: $46.95 monthly.
Limited Basic Service
Subscribers: N.A.
Fee: $25.50 monthly.
Pay Service 1
Pay Units: N.A.
Fee: $10.95 monthly (Cinemax or Starz!), $11.95 monthly (Showtime), $13.95 monthly (HBO).
Internet Service
Operational: Yes.
Fee: $39.95 monthly.
Telephone Service
Digital: Operational
General Manager: Jerry Heiberger.

LAKE NORDEN—ITC. Formerly served by Clear Lake, SD [SD0047]. This cable system has converted to IPTV, 312 Fourth St W, Clear Lake, SD 57226. Phones: 800-417-8667; 605-874-2181. Fax: 605-874-2014. E-mail: info@itctel.com. Web Site: http://www.itc-web.com. ICA: SD5069.
Channel capacity: N.A. Channels available but not in use: N.A.
Basic Service
Subscribers: N.A.
Fee: $35.50 monthly.
Expanded Basic Service 1
Subscribers: N.A.
Fee: $46.95 monthly.
Limited Basic Service
Subscribers: N.A.
Fee: $25.50 monthly.
Pay Service 1
Pay Units: N.A.
Fee: $10.95 monthly (Cinemax or Starz!), $11.95 monthly (Showtime), $13.95 monthly (HBO).
Internet Service
Operational: Yes.
Fee: $39.95 monthly.
Telephone Service
Digital: Operational
General Manager: Jerry Heiberger.

LAKE NORDEN—Mediacom. Now served by BROOKINGS, SD [SD0005]. ICA: SD0114.

LANGFORD—Venture Communications Cooperative. Now served by BRITTON, SD [SD0041]. ICA: SD0095.

LEMMON—West River Cable TV. Now served by BISON, SD [SD0103]. ICA: SD0033.

LEOLA—Valley Cable & Satellite Communications Inc. Now served by HERREID, SD [SD0091]. ICA: SD0065.

LEOLA—Valley Telecommunications Coop. Assn. Formerly served by Herreid, SD [SD0091]. This cable system has converted to IPTV, PO Box 7, Herreid, SD 57632-0007. Phone: 605-437-2615. Fax: 605-437-2615. E-mail: valley@valleytel.net. Web Site: http://www.valleytelco.coop. ICA: SD5034.
Channel capacity: N.A. Channels available but not in use: N.A.
Basic Service
Subscribers: N.A.
Fee: $33.00 monthly.

Expanded Basic Service 1
Subscribers: N.A.
Fee: $42.00 monthly.
Internet Service
Operational: Yes.

LETCHER—Santel Communications. Formerly served by Mount Vernon, SD [SD0188]. This cable system has converted to IPTV, 308 S Dumont Ave, PO Box 67, Woonsocket, SD 57385-0067. Phones: 888-978-7777; 605-796-4411. Fax: 605-796-4419. E-mail: info@santel.net. Web Site: http://www.santel.net. ICA: SD5017.
TV Market Ranking: 85 (LETCHER).
Channel capacity: N.A. Channels available but not in use: N.A.
Basic Service
Subscribers: N.A.
Fee: $33.95 monthly.
Expanded Basic Service 1
Subscribers: N.A.
Fee: $43.95 monthly.
Limited Basic Service
Subscribers: N.A.
Fee: $21.95 monthly.
Pay Service 1
Pay Units: N.A.
Fee: $10.95 monthly (Cinemax, Encore/Starz, HBO, or Showtime).
Internet Service
Operational: Yes.
Fee: $25.00 installation; $24.95 monthly; $10.00 modem lease.
Telephone Service
Analog: Operational
Fee: $14.50 monthly

LOWER BRULE—Golden West Telecommunications, 415 Crown St, PO Box 411, Wall, SD 57790-0411. Phone: 605-279-2161. Fax: 605-279-2727. E-mail: info@goldenwest.com. Web Site: http://www.goldenwest.com. ICA: SD0247.
TV Market Ranking: Below 100 (LOWER BRULE). Franchise award date: N.A. Franchise expiration date: N.A. Began: N.A.
Channel capacity: N.A. Channels available but not in use: N.A.
Basic Service
Subscribers: 140.
Programming (received off-air): KDLT-TV (NBC) Sioux Falls; KPLO-TV (CBS, MNT) Reliance; KSFY-TV (ABC) Sioux Falls; KTSD-TV (PBS) Pierre.
Programming (via satellite): A&E Networks; ABC Family Channel; Cartoon Network; CNN; Discovery Channel; Disney Channel; ESPN; ESPN 2; Headline News; HGTV; History Channel; ION Television; QVC; Spike TV; TBS Superstation; The Weather Channel; Turner Network TV; TV Land; USA Network; WGN America.
Fee: $25.00 installation; $33.95 monthly.
Digital Basic Service
Subscribers: N.A.
Programming (via satellite): Bloomberg Television; Bravo; Discovery Fit & Health; Discovery Home Channel; Discovery Kids Channel; Discovery Times Channel; ESPN 2; ESPN Classic Sports; ESPNews; Fox Movie Channel; Fuse; G4; Golf Channel; GSN; HGTV; Lifetime Movie Network; MTV2; National Geographic Channel; Nick Jr.; NickToons TV; Outdoor Channel; Speed; Style Network; Syfy; Toon Disney; Trinity Broadcasting Network; Turner Classic Movies; VH1 Classic; WE tv.
Fee: $10.00 installation; $14.95 monthly.
Pay Service 1
Pay Units: N.A.

Digital Pay Service 1
Pay Units: N.A.
Programming (via satellite): Cinemax (multiplexed); Encore (multiplexed); HBO (multiplexed); Showtime (multiplexed); The Movie Channel (multiplexed).
Video-On-Demand: No
Internet Service
Operational: No, Both DSL & dial-up.
Telephone Service
None
Manager: George Strandell. Chief Technician: Randy Shepard. Marketing Director: Greg Oleson. Cable Television Manager: Rick Reed. Customer Service Manager: Jody Bielmaier.
Ownership: Golden West Cablevision (MSO).

McINTOSH—West River Cable Television. Now served by BISON, SD [SD0103]. ICA: SD0138.

MCLAUGHLIN—West River Cable Television, 801 Coleman Ave, PO Box 39, Bison, SD 57620. Phones: 888-411-5651; 605-244-5236. Fax: 605-244-7288. E-mail: westriver@sdplains.com. Web Site: http://www.westrivercatv.com. ICA: SD0185.
TV Market Ranking: Outside TV Markets (MCLAUGHLIN). Franchise award date: April 5, 1989. Franchise expiration date: N.A. Began: December 1, 1981.
Channel capacity: 41 (not 2-way capable). Channels available but not in use: N.A.
Basic Service
Subscribers: 170.
Programming (received off-air): KBMY (ABC) Bismarck; KFYR-TV (NBC) Bismarck; KNDX (FOX) Bismarck; KPLO-TV (CBS, MNT) Reliance; KQSD-TV (PBS) Lowry; KXMB-TV (CBS) Bismarck.
Programming (via satellite): A&E Networks; ABC Family Channel; AMC; Animal Planet; Cartoon Network; CNBC; CNN; Country Music TV; C-SPAN; Discovery Channel; Disney Channel; ESPN; ESPN 2; Eternal Word TV Network; FX; Headline News; HGTV; History Channel; Lifetime; Nickelodeon; Outdoor Channel; QVC; Spike TV; TBS Superstation; The Learning Channel; The Weather Channel; Turner Network TV; TV Land; USA Network; VH1; WE tv; WGN America.
Fee: $50.00 installation; $32.95 monthly.
Pay Service 1
Pay Units: 51.
Programming (via satellite): HBO; Showtime; The Movie Channel.
Fee: $20.00 installation; $10.00 monthly (Showtime or TMC), $10.95 monthly (HBO).
Video-On-Demand: No
Internet Service
Operational: No.
Telephone Service
None
Miles of Plant: 7.0 (coaxial); None (fiber optic).
General Manager: Jerry Reisenauer. Assistant Manager: Colgan Huber.
Ownership: West River Cooperative Telephone Co. (MSO).

MELLETTE—Satellite Cable Services Inc. Now served by GROTON, SD [SD0030]. ICA: SD0086.

MISSION TWP.—Golden West Telecommunications, 415 Crown St, PO Box 411, Wall, SD 57790. Phone: 605-279-2161. Fax: 605-279-2727. Web Site: http://www.goldenwest.com. ICA: SD0048.
TV Market Ranking: Outside TV Markets (MISSION TWP.). Franchise award date: January 1, 1983. Franchise expiration date: N.A. Began: January 1, 1984.
Channel capacity: 36 (2-way capable). Channels available but not in use: N.A.
Basic Service
Subscribers: 421.
Programming (received off-air): KDVR (FOX) Denver; KPLO-TV (CBS, MNT) Reliance; KPRY-TV (ABC) Pierre; KTSD-TV (PBS) Pierre; KUSA (NBC) Denver.
Programming (via satellite): A&E Networks; ABC Family Channel; Animal Planet; Cartoon Network; CNBC; CNN; Comedy Central; Country Music TV; C-SPAN; Discovery Channel; Disney Channel; ESPN; ESPN 2; Headline News; History Channel; KWGN-TV (CW) Denver; Lifetime; MTV; Nickelodeon; QVC; Spike TV; Syfy; The Learning Channel; The Weather Channel; Turner Classic Movies; Turner Network TV; USA Network; VH1; WGN-TV (CW, IND) Chicago; WPCH-TV (IND) Atlanta.
Fee: $39.95 installation; $33.45 monthly.
Pay Service 1
Pay Units: 109.
Programming (via satellite): The Movie Channel.
Fee: $9.95 monthly.
Pay Service 2
Pay Units: 166.
Programming (via satellite): HBO.
Fee: $10.95 monthly.
Video-On-Demand: No
Internet Service
Operational: No.
Telephone Service
None
Miles of Plant: 17.0 (coaxial); None (fiber optic).
Ownership: Golden West Cablevision (MSO).

MITCHELL—Midcontinent Communications, PO Box 5010, Sioux Falls, SD 57117. Phones: 800-888-1300; 605-229-1775. Fax: 605-996-6821. Web Site: http://www.midcocomm.com. ICA: SD0007.
TV Market Ranking: 85 (MITCHELL). Franchise award date: N.A. Franchise expiration date: N.A. Began: January 1, 1952.
Channel capacity: 67 (operating 2-way). Channels available but not in use: N.A.
Basic Service
Subscribers: 5,047.
Programming (received off-air): KCPO-LP Sioux Falls; KDLT-TV (NBC) Sioux Falls; KELO-TV (CBS, MNT) Sioux Falls; KESD-TV (PBS) Brookings; KSFY-TV (ABC) Sioux Falls; KTTM (FOX) Huron; KWSD (CW) Sioux Falls.
Programming (via satellite): A&E Networks; ABC Family Channel; AMC; Animal Planet; BET Networks; Bravo; Cartoon Network; CNBC; CNN; Comedy Central; Country Music TV; C-SPAN; C-SPAN 2; Discovery Channel; Discovery Health Channel; Disney Channel; E! Entertainment Television; ESPN; ESPN 2; ESPN Classic Sports; ESPNews; Eternal Word TV Network; Food Network; Fox News Channel; Fox Sports Net; FX; G4; Headline News; HGTV; History Channel; INSP; Lifetime; MSNBC; MTV; Nickelodeon; Outdoor Channel; QVC; Speed; Spike TV; Syfy; TBS Superstation; The Learning Channel; The Weather Channel; Travel Channel; truTV; Turner Classic Movies; Turner Network TV; TV Guide Network; TV Land; USA Network; Versus; VH1; WE tv; WGN America.
Fee: $30.00 installation; $21.00 monthly.

Digital Basic Service
Subscribers: 469.
Programming (via satellite): BBC America; Bio; Bloomberg Television; Discovery Digital Networks; DMX Music; ESPNews; Fox Sports World; GAS; Golf Channel; GSN; History Channel; Independent Film Channel; Lifetime Movie Network; MTV Networks Digital Suite; Nick Jr.; Style Network; Sundance Channel; Toon Disney.
Digital Pay Service 1
Pay Units: N.A.
Programming (via satellite): Cinemax; Encore; HBO (multiplexed); Showtime; Starz; The Movie Channel.
Video-On-Demand: No
Pay-Per-View
iN DEMAND (delivered digitally); Sports PPV (delivered digitally).
Internet Service
Operational: Yes.
Subscribers: 1,678.
Broadband Service: MidcoNet.
Fee: $35.00 installation; $19.95 monthly; $10.00 modem lease.
Telephone Service
Digital: Operational
Fee: $18.00 monthly
Miles of Plant: 81.0 (coaxial); 14.0 (fiber optic). Additional miles planned: 10.0 (coaxial).
Manager & Chief Technician: George Bosak. Marketing Director: Mark Powell.
Ownership: Midcontinent Media Inc. (MSO).; Comcast Cable Communications Inc. (MSO).

MOBRIDGE—Midcontinent Communications, PO Box 5010, Sioux Falls, SD 57117. Phones: 800-456-0564; 605-229-1775. Fax: 605-229-0478. Web Site: http://www.midcocomm.com. Also serves Walworth County. ICA: SD0186.
TV Market Ranking: Outside TV Markets (MOBRIDGE, Walworth County). Franchise award date: November 1, 1976. Franchise expiration date: N.A. Began: November 29, 1979.
Channel capacity: 67 (not 2-way capable). Channels available but not in use: N.A.
Basic Service
Subscribers: 1,302.
Programming (received off-air): KABY-TV (ABC) Aberdeen; KAUN-LP Sioux Falls; KDLO-TV (CBS, MNT) Florence; KDLT-TV (NBC) Sioux Falls; KDSD-TV (PBS) Aberdeen; KELO-TV (CBS, MNT) Sioux Falls; KFYR-TV (NBC) Bismarck; KTTM (FOX) Huron; KTTW (FOX) Sioux Falls; KUSD-TV (PBS) Vermillion; KXMB-TV (CBS) Bismarck; 1 FM.
Programming (via satellite): A&E Networks; ABC Family Channel; AMC; Animal Planet; BET Networks; Bravo; Cartoon Network; CNBC; CNN; Comedy Central; Country Music TV; C-SPAN; C-SPAN 2; CW+; Discovery Channel; Discovery Fit & Health; Discovery Health Channel; Disney Channel; E! Entertainment Television; ESPN; ESPN 2; Eternal Word TV Network; Food Network; Fox Movie Channel; Fox News Channel; Fox Sports Net North; FX; G4; Great American Country; Hallmark Channel; Headline News; HGTV; History Channel; INSP; Lifetime; MSNBC; MTV; MyNetworkTV Inc.; Nickelodeon; Outdoor Channel; QVC; Speed; Spike TV; Syfy; TBS Superstation; The Learning Channel; The Weather Channel; Travel Channel; truTV; Turner Classic Movies; Turner Network TV;

TV Guide Network; TV Land; USA Network; Versus; VH1; WE tv; WGN America.
Fee: $15.00 installation; $21.95 monthly; $15.00 additional installation.
Digital Basic Service
Subscribers: N.A.
Programming (via satellite): 3 Angels Broadcasting Network; A&E HD; ABC Family HD; AmericanLife TV Network; Animal Planet HD; BBC America; Bio; Bloomberg Television; Boomerang; BTN; Canal Sur; CBS Sports Network; Cine Latino; Cine Mexicano; CMT Pure Country; CNN en Espanol; CNN HD; Cooking Channel; C-SPAN 3; Current; Discovery Channel HD; Discovery en Espanol; Discovery Fit & Health; Discovery Health Channel; Discovery Kids Channel; Disney Channel HD; DIY Network; ESPN 2 HD; ESPN Classic Sports; ESPN Deportes; ESPN HD; ESPNews; EWTN en Espanol; Food Network HD; Fox Business Channel; Fox College Sports Atlantic; Fox College Sports Central; Fox College Sports Pacific; Fox Deportes; Fox Movie Channel; Fox Soccer; FSN HD; Fuse; G4; Golf Channel; GolTV; Great American Country; GSN; Halogen Network; HD Theater; HDNet; HDNet Movies; HGTV HD; History Channel en Espanol; History Channel HD; History Channel International; ID Investigation Discovery; Independent Film Channel; ION Life; JCTV; Lifetime Movie Network; Military Channel; MTV Hits; MTV Jams; MTV2; mun2 television; Music Choice; National Geographic Channel; National Geographic Channel HD Network; NFL Network; NHL Network; Nick Jr.; Nick Too; NickToons TV; Outdoor Channel; Palladia; PBS Kids Sprout; Pentagon Channel; Planet Green; Qubo; ReelzChannel; RFD-TV; Science; SoapNet; Style Network; Sundance Channel; Syfy HD; TBS in HD; TeenNick; Telemundo; Tennis Channel; TLC HD; Toon Disney; Toon Disney en Espanol; Tr3s; Trinity Broadcasting Network; Turner Classic Movies; Turner Network TV HD; TV One; TVE Internacional; TVG Network; Universal HD; USA Network HD; Versus; Versus HD; VH1 Classic; VH1 Soul; WE tv.
Digital Pay Service 1
Pay Units: N.A.
Programming (via satellite): Cinemax (multiplexed); Cinemax HD; Encore (multiplexed); Flix; HBO (multiplexed); HBO HD; HBO Latino; Showtime (multiplexed); Showtime HD; Starz (multiplexed); Starz HDTV; The Movie Channel (multiplexed); The Movie Channel HD.
Video-On-Demand: No
Pay-Per-View
iN DEMAND (delivered digitally); MLS Direct Kick (delivered digitally); NBA League Pass (delivered digitally); NHL Center Ice (delivered digitally); MLB Extra Innings (delivered digitally).
Internet Service
Operational: Yes.
Fee: $35.00 installation; $19.95 monthly.
Telephone Service
Digital: Operational
Fee: $18.00 monthly
Miles of Plant: 28.0 (coaxial); None (fiber optic).
Manager: Dale Hodgkins. Marketing Director: Dianna Aman. Chief Technician: Gary Reimer.
Ownership: Midcontinent Media Inc. (MSO).; Comcast Cable Communications Inc. (MSO).

MONROE—Formerly served by Sioux Valley Wireless. No longer in operation. ICA: SD0187.

MONTROSE—Golden West Telecommunications, 415 Crown St, PO Box 411, Wall, SD 57790-0411. Phone: 605-279-2161. Fax: 605-279-2727. E-mail: info@goldenwest.com. Web Site: http://www.goldenwest.com. ICA: SD0224.
TV Market Ranking: 85 (MONTROSE). Franchise award date: N.A. Franchise expiration date: N.A. Began: N.A.
Channel capacity: N.A. Channels available but not in use: N.A.
Basic Service
Subscribers: 123.
Programming (received off-air): KDLT-TV (NBC) Sioux Falls; KELO-TV (CBS, MNT) Sioux Falls; KSFY-TV (ABC) Sioux Falls; KTTW (FOX) Sioux Falls; KUSD-TV (PBS) Vermillion.
Programming (via satellite): ABC Family Channel; CNN; Discovery Channel; Disney Channel; ESPN; Nickelodeon; Spike TV; TBS Superstation; The Weather Channel; Turner Network TV; WGN America.
Fee: $25.00 installation; $33.95 monthly.
Pay Service 1
Pay Units: N.A.
Programming (via satellite): Cinemax (multiplexed); Encore (multiplexed); HBO (multiplexed); Showtime (multiplexed); Starz (multiplexed).
Fee: $10.95 monthly (HBO or Cinemax), $12.95 (Starz/Encore or Showtime).
Video-On-Demand: No
Internet Service
Operational: No, Both DSL & dial-up.
Telephone Service
None
Miles of Plant: 3.0 (coaxial); None (fiber optic).
Chief Executive Officer & General Manager: Denny Law.
Ownership: Golden West Cablevision (MSO).

MOUND CITY—Valley Telecommunications Coop. Assn. Formerly served by Herreid, SD [SD0091]. This cable system has converted to IPTV, PO Box 7, Herreid, SD 57632-0007. Phone: 605-437-2615. Fax: 605-437-2615. E-mail: valley@valleytel.net. Web Site: http://www.valleytelco.coop. ICA: SD5035.
Channel capacity: N.A. Channels available but not in use: N.A.
Basic Service
Subscribers: N.A.
Fee: $33.00 monthly.
Expanded Basic Service 1
Subscribers: N.A.
Fee: $42.00 monthly.
Internet Service
Operational: Yes.

MOUNT VERNON—Santel Communications. Formerly served by Mount Vernon, SD [SD0188]. This cable system has converted to IPTV, 308 S Dumont Ave, PO Box 67, Woonsocket, SD 57385-0067. Phones: 888-978-7777; 605-796-4411. Fax: 605-796-4419. E-mail: info@santel.net. Web Site: http://www.santel.net. ICA: SD5013.
TV Market Ranking: 85 (MOUNT VERNON). Franchise award date: N.A. Franchise expiration date: N.A. Began: N.A.
Channel capacity: N.A. Channels available but not in use: N.A.
Basic Service
Subscribers: N.A.
Fee: $33.95 monthly.
Expanded Basic Service 1
Subscribers: N.A.
Fee: $43.95 monthly.
Limited Basic Service
Subscribers: N.A.
Fee: $21.95 monthly.
Pay Service 1
Pay Units: N.A.
Fee: $10.95 monthly (Cinemax, Encore/Starz, HBO, or Showtime).
Video-On-Demand: No
Internet Service
Operational: Yes.
Fee: $25.00 installation; $24.95 monthly; $10.00 modem lease.
Telephone Service
Digital: Operational
Fee: $14.50 (local); $0-$4 monthly

MOUNT VERNON—Santel Communications. This cable system has converted to IPTV. See Mount Vernon, SD [SD5013]. ICA: SD0188.

NEW EFFINGTON—RCTV, 205 Main St, PO Box 196, New Effington, SD 57255-0196. Phones: 800-256-6854; 605-637-5211. Fax: 605-637-5302. E-mail: rctv@tnics.com. Web Site: http://www.tnics.com. Also serves Veblen. ICA: SD0189.
TV Market Ranking: Outside TV Markets (NEW EFFINGTON, Veblen). Franchise award date: N.A. Franchise expiration date: N.A. Began: N.A.
Channel capacity: 36 (not 2-way capable). Channels available but not in use: N.A.
Digital Basic Service
Subscribers: 1,041.
Programming (via satellite): A&E Networks; ABC Family Channel; AMC; Animal Planet; Bravo; Cartoon Network; CNN; CNN en Espanol; Comedy Central; C-SPAN; C-SPAN 2; Discovery Channel; DIY Network; DMX Music; E! Entertainment Television; ESPN; ESPN 2; ESPN Classic Sports; ESPNews; Food Network; Fox News Channel; Fox Sports Net North; FX; Great American Country; Hallmark Channel; Headline News; HGTV; History Channel; Lifetime; Lifetime Movie Network; MTV; National Geographic Channel; Nick Jr.; Nickelodeon; Oxygen; RFD-TV; SoapNet; Sorpresa; Spike TV; Syfy; TBS Superstation; TeenNick; The Learning Channel; The Weather Channel; Toon Disney; truTV; Turner Classic Movies; Turner Network TV; TV Land; USA Network; VH1; WGN America.
Fee: $29.95 installation; $17.95 monthly.
Digital Expanded Basic Service
Subscribers: N.A.
Programming (via satellite): Bloomberg Television; CNBC; Eternal Word TV Network; Fox Movie Channel; GSN; MSNBC; Outdoor Channel; Speed.
Digital Pay Service 1
Pay Units: N.A.
Programming (via satellite): Encore (multiplexed); HBO (multiplexed); Starz (multiplexed).
Video-On-Demand: No
Internet Service
Operational: No, DSL.
Telephone Service
None
Miles of Plant: 2.0 (coaxial); None (fiber optic).
General Manager: Scott Bostrom. Operations Manager: Colin Bronson. Sales Consultant & Programming Specialist: Sara Broz. Customer Service Manager: Wanda Heesch.
Ownership: RC Technologies Corp. (MSO).

NEWELL—West River Cable Television. No longer in operation. ICA: SD0078.

NUNDA (rural)—ITC. Formerly served by Clear Lake, SD [SD0047]. This cable system has converted to IPTV, 312 Fourth St W, Clear Lake, SD 57226. Phones: 800-417-8667; 605-874-2181. Fax: 605-874-2014. E-mail: info@itc-web.com. Web Site: http://www.itc-web.com. ICA: SD5056.
Channel capacity: N.A. Channels available but not in use: N.A.
Basic Service
Subscribers: N.A.
Fee: $35.50 monthly.
Expanded Basic Service 1
Subscribers: N.A.
Fee: $46.95 monthly.
Limited Basic Service
Subscribers: N.A.
Fee: $25.50 monthly.
Pay Service 1
Pay Units: N.A.
Fee: $10.95 monthly (Cinemax or Starz!), $11.95 monthly (Showtime), $13.95 monthly (HBO).
Internet Service
Operational: Yes.
Fee: $39.95 monthly.
Telephone Service
Digital: Operational
: Jerry Heiberger.

OACOMA—Midstate Communications. Now served by WHITE LAKE, SD [SD0026]. ICA: SD0135.

OELRICHS—Golden West Cablevision. Now served by WALL, SD [SD0068]. ICA: SD0190.

OLDHAM—Alliance Communications. Formerly [SD0191]. This cable system has converted to IPTV., 612 Third St, PO Box 349, Garretson, SD 57030. Phones: 800-701-4980; 605-594-3400. Fax: 605-594-6776. E-mail: email@alliancecom.net. Web Site: http://www.alliancecom.net. ICA: SD5010.
Channel capacity: N.A. Channels available but not in use: N.A.
Basic Service
Subscribers: N.A.
Fee: $29.95 monthly.
Expanded Basic Service 1
Subscribers: N.A.
Fee: $13.00 monthly.
Expanded Basic Service 2
Subscribers: N.A.
Fee: $8.00 monthly.
Pay Service 1
Pay Units: N.A.
Fee: $9.95 monthly (Cinemax or Starz/Encore), $10.95 monthly (Showtime) or $13.95 monthly (HBO).
Internet Service
Operational: Yes.
Fee: $14.95 monthly.
Telephone Service
Digital: Operational
Fee: $12.70 monthly
Manager: Don Snyder.

OLDHAM—Alliance Communications. This cable system has converted to IPTV. See Oldham, SD [SD5010]. ICA: SD0191.

ONIDA—Venture Communications Cooperative, 218 Commercial Ave. SE, PO Box 157, Highmore, SD 57345-0157. Phones: 800-824-7282; 605-852-2224. Fax: 605-852-2404. E-mail: venture@venturecomm.net. Web Site: http://www.venturecomm.net. ICA: SD0092.

TV Market Ranking: Below 100 (ONIDA). Franchise award date: N.A. Franchise expiration date: N.A. Began: May 1, 1982.
Channel capacity: N.A. Channels available but not in use: N.A.
Digital Basic Service
Subscribers: N.A. Included in Highmore
Programming (via satellite): CW+; Eternal Word TV Network; ION Television; MyNetworkTV Inc.; QVC; The Weather Channel; Trinity Broadcasting Network; WGN America.
Fee: $19.95 monthly.
Digital Expanded Basic Service
Subscribers: N.A.
Programming (via satellite): A&E Networks; ABC Family Channel; AMC; Animal Planet; BBC America; Bloomberg Television; Bravo; Cartoon Network; CNBC; CNN; Comedy Central; Country Music TV; C-SPAN 2; Discovery Channel; Discovery Health Channel; Discovery Kids Channel; Disney Channel; DIY Network; E! Entertainment Television; ESPN; ESPN 2; ESPN Classic Sports; ESPNews; Food Network; Fox Movie Channel; Fox News Channel; Fox Sports Net North; FX; G4; Golf Channel; Great American Country; GSN; Hallmark Channel; Hallmark Movie Channel; Headline News; HGTV; History Channel; ID Investigation Discovery; Lifetime; Lifetime Movie Network; Lifetime Real Women; Military Channel; MSNBC; MTV; MTV Hits; MTV2; Music Choice; National Geographic Channel; NFL Network; Nick Jr.; Nickelodeon; NickToons TV; Outdoor Channel; Oxygen; Planet Green; RFD-TV; Science; SoapNet; Speed; Spike TV; Syfy; TBS Superstation; TeenNick; The Learning Channel; Toon Disney; Travel Channel; truTV; Turner Classic Movies; Turner Network TV; TV Land; USA Network; Versus; VH1; VH1 Classic; WE tv.
Fee: $18.00 monthly.
Digital Pay Service 1
Pay Units: N.A.
Programming (via satellite): Cinemax (multiplexed); Encore (multiplexed); HBO (multiplexed); Showtime (multiplexed); Starz (multiplexed); The Movie Channel.
Video-On-Demand: No
Pay-Per-View
Movies (delivered digitally); Playboy TV (delivered digitally); Fresh (delivered digitally).
Internet Service
Operational: No.
Telephone Service
None
General Manager: Randy Houdek. Assistant Manager: Randy Olson. Chief Technician: Brad Ryan. Member Services Manager: Rod Kusser.
Ownership: Venture Communications Cooperative.

PARKSTON—Santel Communications. Formerly served by Mount Vernon, SD [SD0188]. This cable system has converted to IPTV, 308 S Dumont Ave, PO Box 67, Woonsocket, SD 57385-0067. Phones: 888-978-7777; 605-796-4411. Fax: 605-796-4419. E-mail: info@santel.net. Web Site: http://www.santel.net. ICA: SD5018.
TV Market Ranking: 85 (PARKSTON).
Channel capacity: N.A. Channels available but not in use: N.A.
Basic Service
Subscribers: N.A.
Fee: $33.95 monthly.
Expanded Basic Service 1
Subscribers: N.A.
Fee: $43.95 monthly.
Limited Basic Service
Subscribers: N.A.
Fee: $21.95 monthly.
Pay Service 1
Pay Units: N.A.
Fee: $10.95 monthly (Cinemax, Encore/Starz, HBO, or Showtime).
Internet Service
Operational: Yes.
Fee: $25.00 installation; $24.95 monthly; $10.00 modem lease.
Telephone Service
Analog: Operational
Fee: $14.50 monthly

PICKSTOWN—Satellite Cable Services Inc. Now served by TRIPP, SD [SD0087]. ICA: SD0193.

PIERPONT—Venture Communications Cooperative. Now served by BRITTON, SD [SD0041]. ICA: SD0194.

PINE RIDGE—Golden West Telecommunications, Billy Mills Hall, PO Box 420, Pine Ridge, SD 57770. Phone: 605-867-1166. Web Site: http://www.goldenwest.com. ICA: SD0037.
TV Market Ranking: Outside TV Markets (PINE RIDGE). Franchise award date: N.A. Franchise expiration date: N.A. Began: N.A.
Channel capacity: 52 (2-way capable). Channels available but not in use: N.A.
Basic Service
Subscribers: 500.
Programming (received off-air): KBHE-TV (PBS) Rapid City; KELO-TV (CBS, MNT) Sioux Falls; KEVN-TV (FOX) Rapid City; KNBN (NBC) Rapid City; KOTA-TV (ABC) Rapid City.
Programming (via satellite): A&E Networks; ABC Family Channel; Animal Planet; Cartoon Network; CNN; Discovery Channel; ESPN; ESPN 2; ESPNews; FX; Great American Country; Headline News; History Channel; Lifetime; MTV; Nickelodeon; QVC; Spike TV; Sundance Channel; Syfy; TBS Superstation; The Learning Channel; Trinity Broadcasting Network; Turner Network TV; TV Land; USA Network; VH1; WGN America.
Fee: $20.00 installation; $25.00 monthly.
Pay Service 1
Pay Units: 290.
Programming (via satellite): Cinemax; HBO; Showtime (multiplexed); The Movie Channel.
Fee: $10.00 monthly.
Video-On-Demand: No
Internet Service
Operational: Yes.
Telephone Service
None
Miles of Plant: 8.0 (coaxial); None (fiber optic).
General Manager: George Strandell.
Ownership: Golden West Cablevision (MSO).

PLANKINTON—Golden West Telecommunications, 415 Crown St, PO Box 411, Wall, SD 57790-0411. Phone: 605-279-2161. Fax: 605-279-2727. E-mail: info@goldenwest.com. Web Site: http://www.goldenwest.com. ICA: SD0248.
TV Market Ranking: 85 (PLANKINTON). Franchise award date: N.A. Franchise expiration date: N.A. Began: N.A.
Channel capacity: N.A. Channels available but not in use: N.A.
Basic Service
Subscribers: 250.
Programming (received off-air): KDLT-TV (NBC) Sioux Falls; KPLO-TV (CBS, MNT) Reliance; KPRY-TV (ABC) Pierre; KTSD-TV (PBS) Pierre; KTTM (FOX) Huron.
Programming (via satellite): A&E Networks; ABC Family Channel; AMC; Animal Planet; Cartoon Network; CNBC; CNN; Comedy Central; Country Music TV; C-SPAN; C-SPAN 2; Discovery Channel; Discovery Health Channel; Disney Channel; DIY Network; E! Entertainment Television; ESPN; ESPN 2; Eternal Word TV Network; Fox News Channel; Great American Country; Hallmark Channel; Headline News; HGTV; History Channel; INSP; ION Television; Lifetime; MTV; National Geographic Channel; Nickelodeon; Outdoor Channel; QVC; Spike TV; Syfy; TBS Superstation; The Learning Channel; The Weather Channel; Travel Channel; Turner Network TV; TV Land; USA Network; VH1; WGN America.
Fee: $25.00 installation; $32.95 monthly.
Pay Service 1
Pay Units: N.A.
Programming (via satellite): Cinemax; HBO.
Fee: $8.75 monthly (Cinemax), $11.95 monthly (HBO).
Video-On-Demand: No
Internet Service
Operational: No, Both DSL & dial-up.
Telephone Service
None
General Manager: George Strandell. Chief Technician: Randy Shepard. Marketing Director: Greg Oleson. Cable Television Manager: Rick Reed. Customer Service Manager: Jody Bielmaier.
Ownership: Golden West Cablevision (MSO).

PLATTE—Midstate Communications, 120 E First St, PO Box 48, Kimball, SD 57355-0048. Phone: 605-778-6221. Fax: 605-778-8080. Web Site: http://www.midstatesd.net. Also serves Delmont & Geddes. ICA: SD0049.
TV Market Ranking: 85 (Delmont); Outside TV Markets (Geddes, PLATTE). Franchise award date: N.A. Franchise expiration date: N.A. Began: January 1, 1981.
Channel capacity: N.A. Channels available but not in use: N.A.
Basic Service
Subscribers: N.A. Included in White Lake
Programming (received off-air): KAUN-LP Sioux Falls; KDLT-TV (NBC) Sioux Falls; KELO-TV (CBS, MNT) Sioux Falls; KSFY-TV (ABC) Sioux Falls; KTTM (FOX) Huron; KUSD-TV (PBS) Vermillion.
Programming (via satellite): A&E Networks; ABC Family Channel; AMC; Animal Planet; Cartoon Network; CNBC; CNN; Comedy Central; Country Music TV; C-SPAN; C-SPAN 2; Disney Channel; E! Entertainment Television; ESPN; Eternal Word TV Network; Food Network; Fox News Channel; Fox Sports Net North; FX; Great American Country; Hallmark Channel; Headline News; INSP; Lifetime; MSNBC; MTV; Nickelodeon; QVC; RFD-TV; Spike TV; TBS Superstation; The Learning Channel; The Weather Channel; Travel Channel; truTV; Turner Network TV; TV Land; USA Network; VH1; WGN America.
Fee: $57.00 installation; $30.95 monthly.
Pay Service 1
Pay Units: N.A.
Programming (via satellite): Cinemax; HBO; Showtime; The Movie Channel.
Fee: $11.95 monthly (each).
Video-On-Demand: No
Pay-Per-View
Sports PPV (delivered digitally); ESPN Extra (delivered digitally); ESPN Now (delivered digitally); Fresh (delivered digitally); Playboy TV (delivered digitally); Hot Choice (delivered digitally).
Internet Service
Operational: No, DSL.
Telephone Service
None
Miles of Plant: 10.0 (coaxial); None (fiber optic).
General Manager: Mark Benton. Plant Manager: Fay Jandreau. Marketing Manager: Chad Mutziger. Office Manager: Peg Reinesch.
Ownership: Midstate Communications (MSO).

POLLOCK—Valley Cable & Satellite Communications Inc. Now served by HERREID, SD [SD0091]. ICA: SD0195.

POLLOCK—Valley Telecommunications Coop. Assn. Formerly served by Herreid, SD [SD0091]. This cable system has converted to IPTV, PO Box 7, Herreid, SD 57632-0007. Phone: 605-437-2615. Fax: 605-437-2615. E-mail: valley@valleytel.net. Web Site: http://www.valleytelco.coop. ICA: SD5036.
Channel capacity: N.A. Channels available but not in use: N.A.
Basic Service
Subscribers: N.A.
Fee: $33.00 monthly.
Expanded Basic Service 1
Subscribers: N.A.
Fee: $42.00 monthly.
Internet Service
Operational: Yes.

PRAIRIE ACRES ESTATES—Comcast Cable. Now served by RAPID CITY, SD [SD0002]. ICA: SD0222.

PRAIRIEWOOD VILLAGE—Midcontinent Communications, PO Box 5010, Sioux Falls, SD 57117. Phones: 800-456-0564; 605-229-1775. Fax: 605-229-0478. Web Site: http://www.midcocomm.com. ICA: SD0196.
TV Market Ranking: Below 100 (PRAIRIEWOOD VILLAGE). Franchise award date: N.A. Franchise expiration date: N.A. Began: N.A.
Channel capacity: 29 (2-way capable). Channels available but not in use: N.A.
Basic Service
Subscribers: 49.
Programming (received off-air): KABY-TV (ABC) Aberdeen; KCPO-LP Sioux Falls; KDLO-TV (CBS, MNT) Florence; KDLT-TV (NBC) Sioux Falls; KDSD-TV (PBS) Aberdeen; KTTM (FOX) Huron; KWSD (CW) Sioux Falls.
Programming (via satellite): ABC Family Channel; CNN; Discovery Channel; ESPN; Eternal Word TV Network; QVC; TBS Superstation; The Weather Channel; TV Guide Network; WGN America.
Fee: $27.95 monthly.
Expanded Basic Service 1
Subscribers: N.A.
Programming (via satellite): A&E Networks; AMC; Animal Planet; BET Networks; Bravo; Cartoon Network; CNBC; Comedy Central; Country Music TV; C-SPAN; C-SPAN 2; Discovery Fit & Health; Discovery Health Channel; Disney Channel; E! Entertainment Television; ESPN 2; ESPN Classic Sports; Food Network; Fox Movie Channel; Fox News Channel; Fox Sports Net North; FX; Hallmark Channel; Headline News; HGTV; History Channel; INSP; Lifetime; MSNBC; MTV; Nickelodeon; Outdoor Channel; Speed; Spike TV; Syfy; The Learning Channel; Travel Channel; Turner Classic Movies; Turner Network TV; TV Land; USA Network; Versus; VH1; WE tv.

Digital Basic Service
Subscribers: N.A.
Programming (via satellite): AmericanLife TV Network; BBC America; Bio; Bloomberg Television; Boomerang; Canales N; Cooking Channel; C-SPAN 3; Current; Discovery Fit & Health; Discovery Health Channel; Discovery Home Channel; Discovery Kids Channel; Discovery Times Channel; DIY Network; DMX Music; ESPN Classic Sports; ESPNews; Fox College Sports Atlantic; Fox College Sports Central; Fox College Sports Pacific; Fox Movie Channel; Fox Soccer; G4; GAS; Golf Channel; GolTV; GSN; Halogen Network; History Channel International; Independent Film Channel; Lifetime Movie Network; MTV Networks Digital Suite; National Geographic Channel; NFL Network; Nick Jr.; Nick Too; NickToons TV; Outdoor Channel; Science Television; Style Network; Sundance Channel; Tennis Channel; Toon Disney; Trinity Broadcasting Network; Turner Classic Movies; TV One; TVG Network; Versus; WE tv.

Digital Pay Service 1
Pay Units: N.A.
Programming (via satellite): Cinemax (multiplexed); Encore (multiplexed); Flix; HBO (multiplexed); Showtime (multiplexed); Starz; The Movie Channel (multiplexed).
Fee: $11.95 monthly.

Video-On-Demand: No

Internet Service
Operational: No.

Telephone Service
None

Miles of Plant: 3.0 (coaxial); None (fiber optic).
Manager: Doug Bierschbach. Chief Technician: Paul Schmidt.
Ownership: Midcontinent Media Inc. (MSO).

RAPID CITY—Formerly served by USA Digital TV. No longer in operation. ICA: SD0233.

RAPID CITY—Knology, 809 Deadwood Ave, Rapid City, SD 57702. Phones: 877-243-4237; 605-716-3333. Fax: 605-342-1693. Web Site: http://www.knology.com. Also serves Lawrence County (portions), Meade County (portions) & Pennington County (portions). ICA: SD0252. **Note:** This system is an overbuild.
TV Market Ranking: Below 100 (Lawrence County (portions), Meade County (portions), Pennington County (portions), RAPID CITY).
Channel capacity: N.A. Channels available but not in use: N.A.

Basic Service
Subscribers: N.A. Included in Viborg
Programming (received off-air): KBHE-TV (PBS) Rapid City; KCLO-TV (CBS) Rapid City; KCPO-LP Sioux Falls; KEVN-TV (FOX) Rapid City; KKRA-LP (ION) Rapid City; KNBN (NBC) Rapid City; KOTA-TV (ABC) Rapid City; KWBH-LP Rapid City.
Programming (via satellite): A&E Networks; ABC Family Channel; AMC; AmericanLife TV Network; Animal Planet; BET Networks; Bravo; Cartoon Network; CNBC; CNN; Comedy Central; Country Music TV; C-SPAN; C-SPAN 2; Discovery Channel; Discovery Fit & Health; Disney Channel; DIY Network; E! Entertainment Television; ESPN; ESPN 2; ESPN Classic Sports; ESPNews; Eternal Word TV Network; Food Network; Fox News Channel; Fox Sports Net; Fox Sports World; FX; Golf Channel; Great American Country; GSN; Hallmark Channel; Headline News; HGTV; History Channel; INSP; Lifetime; MarketConnect Network; MoviePlex; MSNBC; MTV; National Geographic Channel; Nickelodeon; Outdoor Channel; Ovation; QVC; SoapNet; Speed; Spike TV; Style Network; Syfy; TBS Superstation; The Learning Channel; The Weather Channel; Toon Disney; Travel Channel; Trinity Broadcasting Network; truTV; Turner Classic Movies; Turner Network TV; TV Guide Network; TV Land; USA Network; Versus; VH1; WE tv; WGN America.
Fee: $25.00 installation; $29.95 monthly.

Digital Basic Service
Subscribers: 17,000.
Programming (via satellite): BBC America; Bio; Cinemax; Cooking Channel; Discovery Channel; Discovery Health Channel; Discovery Home Channel; Discovery Kids Channel; Discovery Times Channel; DIY Network; DMX Music; ESPN; Fuse; G4; GAS; HBO; HDNet; HDNet Movies; History Channel International; Independent Film Channel; Lifetime Movie Network; Military Channel; MTV Networks Digital Suite; Nick Jr.; Nick Too; Science; Showtime; The Movie Channel.
Fee: $6.95 converter.

Digital Pay Service 1
Pay Units: N.A.
Programming (via satellite): Cinemax (multiplexed); Encore (multiplexed); Flix; HBO (multiplexed); Showtime; Starz (multiplexed); Sundance Channel; The Movie Channel (multiplexed).

Video-On-Demand: Yes

Pay-Per-View
Sports PPV (delivered digitally).

Internet Service
Operational: Yes.
Broadband Service: Knology.Net.
Fee: $29.95 installation; $39.95 monthly.

Telephone Service
Analog: Not Operational
Digital: Operational

Miles of Plant: 840.0 (coaxial); 245.0 (fiber optic).
General Manager: Steve Schirber. Technical Operations Manager: Gary Hansen. Marketing Manager: Sherri Cribbs.
Ownership: Knology Inc. (MSO).

RAPID CITY—Midcontinent Communications, 1624 Concourse Ct, Rapid City, SD 57703. Phone: 605-343-0595. Fax: 605-388-9166. Web Site: http://www.midcocomm.com. Also serves Black Hawk, Box Elder, Countryside Mobile Home Park, Ellsworth AFB, Meade County (portions), Pennington County (portions), Piedmont, Prairie Acres Estates & Rimrock. ICA: SD0002.
TV Market Ranking: Below 100 (Black Hawk, Box Elder, Countryside Mobile Home Park, Ellsworth AFB, Meade County (portions), Pennington County (portions), Piedmont, Prairie Acres Estates, RAPID CITY, Rimrock); Outside TV Markets (Meade County (portions)). Franchise award date: N.A. Franchise expiration date: N.A. Began: October 6, 1958.
Channel capacity: N.A. Channels available but not in use: N.A.

Basic Service
Subscribers: 14,289.
Programming (received off-air): KBHE-TV (PBS) Rapid City; KCLO-TV (CBS) Rapid City; KCPL-LP Rapid City; KEVN-TV (FOX) Rapid City; KKRA-LP (ION) Rapid City; KOTA-TV (ABC) Rapid City.
Programming (via satellite): A&E Networks; ABC Family Channel; AMC; Animal Planet; BET Networks; Bloomberg Television; Bravo; Cartoon Network; CNBC; CNN; Comedy Central; Country Music TV; C-SPAN; C-SPAN 2; CW+; Discovery Channel; Disney Channel; E! Entertainment Television; ESPN; ESPN 2; ESPN Classic Sports; ESPNews; Eternal Word TV Network; Food Network; Fox News Channel; Fox Sports Net North; FX; G4; Golf Channel; Great American Country; GSN; Hallmark Channel; Headline News; HGTV; History Channel; INSP; KNBC (NBC) Los Angeles; Lifetime; MSNBC; MTV; Nickelodeon; Outdoor Channel; Oxygen; QVC; Root Sports Rocky Mountain; Speed; Spike TV; Syfy; TBS Superstation; The Learning Channel; The Weather Channel; Toon Disney; Travel Channel; Trinity Broadcasting Network; truTV; Turner Classic Movies; Turner Network TV; TV Guide Network; TV Land; USA Network; Versus; VH1; WE tv; WGN America.
Fee: $43.50 installation; $24.95 monthly; $3.25 converter; $21.75 additional installation.

Digital Basic Service
Subscribers: 4,541.
Programming (via satellite): 3 Angels Broadcasting Network; A&E HD; ABC Family HD; AmericanLife TV Network; Animal Planet HD; BBC America; Bio; Bloomberg Television; Boomerang; BTN; Canal Sur; CBS Sports Network; Cine Latino; Cine Mexicano; CMT Pure Country; CNN en Espanol; CNN HD; Cooking Channel; C-SPAN 3; Current; Discovery Channel HD; Discovery en Espanol; Discovery Health Channel; Discovery Kids Channel; Disney Channel HD; DIY Network; ESPN 2 HD; ESPN Deportes; ESPN HD; EWTN en Espanol; Food Network HD; Fox Business Channel; Fox College Sports Atlantic; Fox College Sports Central; Fox College Sports Pacific; Fox Deportes; Fox Sports World; FSN HD; Fuse; Golf Channel; GolTV; Great American Country; Halogen Network; HD Theater; HDNet; HDNet Movies; HGTV HD; History Channel en Espanol; History Channel HD; History Channel International; ID Investigation Discovery; Independent Film Channel; ION Life; JCTV; Lifetime Movie Network; Military Channel; MTV Hits; MTV Jams; MTV2; mun2 television; Music Choice; National Geographic Channel; National Geographic Channel HD Network; NFL Network; NHL Network; Nick Jr.; Nick Too; NickToons TV; Palladia; PBS Kids Sprout; Pentagon Channel; Planet Green; Qubo; ReelzChannel; RFD-TV; Science; SoapNet; Style Network; Sundance Channel; Syfy HD; TBS in HD; TeenNick; Telemundo; Tennis Channel; TLC HD; Toon Disney; Tr3s; Trinity Broadcasting Network; Turner Network TV HD; TV One; TVE Internacional; TVG Network; Universal HD; USA Network HD; VeneMovies; Versus HD; VH1 Classic; VH1 Soul.
Fee: $13.50 monthly.

Digital Pay Service 1
Pay Units: N.A.
Programming (via satellite): Cinemax (multiplexed); Cinemax HD; Encore (multiplexed); HBO (multiplexed); HBO HD; HBO Latino; Showtime (multiplexed); Showtime HD; Starz (multiplexed); Starz HDTV; The Movie Channel (multiplexed); The Movie Channel HD.

Video-On-Demand: Yes

Pay-Per-View
Addressable homes: 4,541.
iN DEMAND (delivered digitally); Hot Choice (delivered digitally); Playboy TV (delivered digitally).

Internet Service
Operational: Yes.
Subscribers: 6,667.
Broadband Service: MidcoNet.
Fee: $35.00 installation; $18.00 monthly.

Telephone Service
Digital: Operational
Fee: $18.00 monthly

Miles of Plant: 491.0 (coaxial); None (fiber optic).
Manager: Jerry Steever. Chief Technician: Dave Gorsuch.
Ownership: Midcontinent Media Inc. (MSO).

RAYMOND—ITC. Formerly served by Clear Lake, SD [SD0047]. This cable system has converted to IPTV, 312 Fourth St W, Clear Lake, SD 57226. Phones: 800-417-8667; 605-874-2181. Fax: 605-874-2014. E-mail: info@itc-web.com. Web Site: http://www.itc-web.com. ICA: SD5057.
Channel capacity: N.A. Channels available but not in use: N.A.

Basic Service
Subscribers: N.A.
Fee: $35.50 monthly.

Expanded Basic Service 1
Subscribers: N.A.
Fee: $46.95 monthly.

Limited Basic Service
Subscribers: N.A.
Fee: $25.50 monthly.

Pay Service 1
Pay Units: N.A.
Fee: $10.95 monthly (Cinemax or Starz!), $11.95 monthly (Showtime), $13.95 monthly (HBO).

Internet Service
Operational: Yes.
Fee: $39.95 monthly.

Telephone Service
Digital: Operational

General Manager: Jerry Heiberger.

RAYMOND—Satellite Cable Services Inc. Now served by CLEAR LAKE, SD [SD0047]. ICA: SD0199.

REDFIELD—Spink Electric. No longer in operation. ICA: SD0234.

RELIANCE—Golden West Telecommunications, 415 Crown St, PO Box 411, Wall, SD 57790-0411. Phone: 605-279-2161. Fax: 605-279-2727. E-mail: info@goldenwest.com. Web Site: http://www.goldenwest.com. ICA: SD0200.
TV Market Ranking: Below 100 (RELIANCE). Franchise award date: N.A. Franchise expiration date: N.A. Began: July 1, 1990.
Channel capacity: N.A. Channels available but not in use: N.A.

Basic Service
Subscribers: 33.
Programming (received off-air): KARE (NBC) Minneapolis; KDLT-TV (NBC) Sioux Falls; KPLO-TV (CBS, MNT) Reliance; KPRY-TV (ABC) Pierre; KTSD-TV (PBS) Pierre; KTTW (FOX) Sioux Falls.
Programming (via satellite): A&E Networks; ABC Family Channel; AMC; Animal Planet; Cartoon Network; CNBC; CNN; Comedy Central; Country Music TV; Discovery Channel; Disney Channel; ESPN; Food Network; Fox News Channel; FX; Hallmark Channel; Headline News; History Channel International; Lifetime; MTV; Nickelodeon; QVC; Spike TV; TBS Superstation; The Weather Channel; TLC; Trinity Broadcasting Network; Turner Network TV; TV Land; USA Network; VH1; WGN America.
Fee: $25.00 installation; $33.95 monthly.

Digital Basic Service
Subscribers: N.A.
Programming (via satellite): Bloomberg Television; Bravo; Discovery Fit & Health; Discovery Kids Channel; Discovery Times Channel; ESPN Classic Sports; Fox Movie Channel; Fuse; G4; Golf Channel; GSN; HGTV; Lifetime Movie Network (multiplexed); National Geographic Channel; Nick Jr.; Speed; Style Network; Syfy; Toon Disney; Turner Classic Movies; WE tv.
Fee: $10.00 installation; $14.95 monthly.
Pay Service 1
Pay Units: N.A.
Programming (via satellite): Cinemax; HBO; Showtime; The Movie Channel.
Digital Pay Service 1
Pay Units: N.A.
Programming (via satellite): HBO (multiplexed); Showtime (multiplexed).
Video-On-Demand: No
Internet Service
Operational: No, Both DSL & dial-up.
Telephone Service
None
General Manager: George Strandell. Chief Technician: Randy Shepard. Marketing Director: Greg Oleson. Cable Television Manager: Rick Reed. Customer Service Manager: Jody Bielmaier.
Ownership: Golden West Cablevision (MSO).

RIMROCK—Midcontinent Communications. Now served by RAPID CITY, SD [SD0002]. ICA: SD0221.

ROSEBUD—Golden West Telecommunications, 415 Crown St, PO Box 411, Wall, SD 57790. Phone: 605-279-2161. Fax: 605-279-2727. Web Site: http://www.goldenwest.com. ICA: SD0203.
TV Market Ranking: Outside TV Markets (ROSEBUD). Franchise award date: April 1, 1987. Franchise expiration date: N.A. Began: January 1, 1988.
Channel capacity: 36 (2-way capable). Channels available but not in use: N.A.
Basic Service
Subscribers: 243.
Programming (received off-air): KDVR (FOX) Denver; KPLO-TV (CBS, MNT) Reliance; KPRY-TV (ABC) Pierre; KTSD-TV (PBS) Pierre; KUSA (NBC) Denver; KWGN-TV (CW) Denver.
Programming (via satellite): A&E Networks; ABC Family Channel; Animal Planet; Cartoon Network; CNBC; CNN; Comedy Central; Country Music TV; C-SPAN; Discovery Channel; Disney Channel; ESPN; ESPN 2; Headline News; History Channel; Lifetime; MTV; Nickelodeon; QVC; Spike TV; Syfy; The Learning Channel; The Weather Channel; Turner Classic Movies; Turner Network TV; USA Network; VH1; WGN-TV (CW, IND) Chicago; WPCH-TV (IND) Atlanta.
Fee: $37.50 installation; $33.45 monthly.
Pay Service 1
Pay Units: 74.
Programming (via satellite): The Movie Channel.
Fee: $9.95 monthly.
Pay Service 2
Pay Units: 108.
Programming (via satellite): HBO.
Fee: $10.95 monthly.
Video-On-Demand: No
Internet Service
Operational: No.
Telephone Service
None
Miles of Plant: 16.0 (coaxial); None (fiber optic).
Ownership: Golden West Cablevision (MSO).

ROSHOLT—Venture Communications Cooperative, 218 Commercial Ave. SE, PO Box 157, Highmore, SD 57345-0157. Phone: 605-852-2224. Fax: 605-852-2404. E-mail: venture@venturecomm.net. Web Site: http://www.venturecomm.net. ICA: SD0115.
TV Market Ranking: Outside TV Markets (ROSHOLT). Franchise award date: N.A. Franchise expiration date: N.A. Began: December 1, 1979.
Channel capacity: N.A. Channels available but not in use: N.A.
Digital Basic Service
Subscribers: N.A. Included in Highmore
Programming (via satellite): C-SPAN; CW+; Eternal Word TV Network; ION Television; MyNetworkTV Inc.; QVC; The Weather Channel; Trinity Broadcasting Network; Weatherscan; WGN America.
Fee: $19.95 monthly.
Digital Expanded Basic Service
Subscribers: N.A.
Programming (via satellite): A&E Networks; ABC Family Channel; AMC; Animal Planet; BBC America; Bloomberg Television; Bravo; Cartoon Network; CNBC; CNN; Comedy Central; Country Music TV; C-SPAN 2; Discovery Channel; Discovery Health Channel; Discovery Kids Channel; Disney Channel; DIY Network; DMX Music; E! Entertainment Television; ESPN; ESPN 2; ESPN Classic Sports; ESPNews; Food Network; Fox Movie Channel; Fox News Channel; Fox Sports Net North; FX; G4; Golf Channel; Great American Country; GSN; Hallmark Channel; Hallmark Movie Channel; Headline News; HGTV; History Channel; ID Investigation Discovery; Lifetime; Lifetime Movie Network; Lifetime Real Women; Military Channel; MSNBC; MTV; MTV Hits; MTV2; National Geographic Channel; NFL Network; Nick Jr.; Nickelodeon; NickToons TV; Outdoor Channel; Oxygen; Planet Green; RFD-TV; Science; SoapNet; Speed; Spike TV; Syfy; TBS Superstation; TeenNick; The Learning Channel; Toon Disney; Travel Channel; truTV; Turner Classic Movies; Turner Network TV; TV Land; USA Network; Versus; VH1; VH1 Classic; WE tv.
Fee: $18.00 monthly.
Digital Pay Service 1
Pay Units: N.A.
Programming (via satellite): Cinemax (multiplexed); Encore (multiplexed); HBO (multiplexed); Showtime (multiplexed); Starz (multiplexed); The Movie Channel.
Video-On-Demand: No
Pay-Per-View
Movies (delivered digitally); Playboy TV (delivered digitally); Fresh (delivered digitally).
Internet Service
Operational: No.
Telephone Service
None
General Manager: Randy Houdek. Assistant Manager: Randy Olson. Chief Technician: Brad Ryan. Member Services Manager: Rod Kusser.
Ownership: Venture Communications Cooperative (MSO).

SHERMAN—Alliance Communications. Formerly served by Garretson, SD [SD0016]. This cable system has converted to IPTV, 612 Third St, PO Box 349, Garretson, SD 57030. Phones: 800-701-4980; 605-594-3400. Fax: 605-594-6776. E-mail: email@alliancecom.net. Web Site: http://www.alliancecom.net. ICA: SD5087.
Channel capacity: N.A. Channels available but not in use: N.A.
Basic Service
Subscribers: N.A.
Fee: $29.95 monthly.
Expanded Basic Service 1
Subscribers: N.A.
Fee: $13.00 monthly.
Expanded Basic Service 2
Subscribers: N.A.
Fee: $8.00 monthly.
Pay Service 1
Pay Units: N.A.
Fee: $9.95 monthly (Cinemax or Starz/Encore), $10.95 monthly (Showtime) or $13.95 monthly (HBO).
Internet Service
Operational: Yes.
Fee: $14.95 monthly.
Manager: Don Snyder.

SINAI (rural)—ITC. Formerly served by Clear Lake, SD [SD0047]. This cable system has converted to IPTV, 312 Fourth St W, Clear Lake, SD 57226. Phones: 800-417-8667; 605-874-2181. Fax: 605-874-2014. E-mail: info@itc-web.com. Web Site: http://www.itc-web.com. ICA: SD5058.
Channel capacity: N.A. Channels available but not in use: N.A.
Basic Service
Subscribers: N.A.
Fee: $35.50 monthly.
Expanded Basic Service 1
Subscribers: N.A.
Fee: $46.95 monthly.
Limited Basic Service
Subscribers: N.A.
Fee: $25.50 monthly.
Pay Service 1
Pay Units: N.A.
Fee: $10.95 monthly (Cinemax or Starz!), $11.95 monthly (Showtime), $13.95 monthly (HBO).
Internet Service
Operational: Yes.
Fee: $39.95 monthly.
Telephone Service
Digital: Operational
General Manager: Jerry Heiberger.

SIOUX FALLS—Midcontinent Communications, PO Box 5010, Sioux Falls, SD 57117. Phones: 605-339-3339 (Local office); 800-888-1300; 605-229-1775. Fax: 605-229-0572. Web Site: http://www.midcocomm.com. Also serves Baltic, Canton, Colton, Crooks, Humboldt, Madison & Renner. ICA: SD0001.
TV Market Ranking: 85 (Baltic, Canton, Colton, Crooks, Humboldt, Renner, SIOUX FALLS); Outside TV Markets (Madison). Franchise award date: May 30, 1969. Franchise expiration date: N.A. Began: December 29, 1969.
Channel capacity: N.A. Channels available but not in use: N.A.
Basic Service
Subscribers: 41,053.
Programming (received off-air): KAUN-LP Sioux Falls; KCPO-LP Sioux Falls; KDLT-TV (NBC) Sioux Falls; KELO-TV (CBS, MNT) Sioux Falls; KSFY-TV (ABC) Sioux Falls; KSMN (PBS) Worthington; KTTW (FOX) Sioux Falls; KUSD-TV (PBS) Vermillion; KWSD (CW) Sioux Falls.
Programming (via satellite): A&E Networks; ABC Family Channel; AMC; Animal Planet; BET Networks; Bravo; Cartoon Network; Celebrity Shopping Network; CNBC; CNN; Comedy Central; Country Music TV; C-SPAN; C-SPAN 2; Discovery Channel; Discovery Fit & Health; Discovery Health Channel; Disney Channel; E! Entertainment Television; ESPN; ESPN 2; Eternal Word TV Network; Food Network; Fox News Channel; Fox Sports Net North; FX; G4; Hallmark Channel; Headline News; HGTV; History Channel; INSP; Lifetime; MSNBC; MTV; MyNetworkTV Inc.; Nickelodeon; Outdoor Channel; QVC; Speed; Spike TV; Syfy; TBS Superstation; The Learning Channel; The Weather Channel; Travel Channel; truTV; Turner Classic Movies; Turner Network TV; TV Guide Network; TV Land; Univision Studios; USA Network; Versus; VH1; WE tv; WGN America.
Fee: $25.00 installation; $23.92 monthly; $2.00 converter.
Digital Basic Service
Subscribers: 10,090.
Programming (via satellite): 3 Angels Broadcasting Network; AmericanLife TV Network; BBC America; Bio; Bloomberg Television; Boomerang; CBS Sports Network; Cine Mexicano; CMT Pure Country; CNN en Espanol; Cooking Channel; C-SPAN 3; Current; Discovery en Espanol; Discovery Fit & Health; Discovery Health Channel; Discovery Home Channel; Discovery Kids Channel; Discovery Times Channel; DIY Network; ESPN 2 HD; ESPN Classic Sports; ESPN Deportes; ESPN HD; ESPNews; Fox Business Channel; Fox College Sports Atlantic; Fox College Sports Central; Fox College Sports Pacific; Fox Deportes; Fox Soccer; Fuse; G4; GAS; Golf Channel; GolTV; Great American Country; GSN; Halogen Network; HD Theater; HDNet; HDNet Movies; History Channel en Espanol; History Channel International; Independent Film Channel; JCTV; Lifetime Movie Network; Military Channel; MTV Hits; MTV Jams; MTV2; mun2 television; Music Choice; National Geographic Channel; National Geographic Channel HD Network; NHL Network; Nick Jr.; Nick Too; NickToons TV; Outdoor Channel; Palladia; PBS Kids Sprout; Science; SoapNet; Style Network; Sundance Channel; Telemundo; Tennis Channel; Toon Disney; Tr3s; Trinity Broadcasting Network; Turner Classic Movies; Turner Network TV HD; TV One; TVE Internacional; TVG Network; Universal HD; Versus HD; VH1 Classic; VH1 Soul; WE tv.
Digital Pay Service 1
Pay Units: 17,696.
Programming (via satellite): Cinemax (multiplexed); Cinemax HD; Encore (multiplexed); HBO (multiplexed); HBO HD; Showtime (multiplexed); Starz (multiplexed); Starz HDTV; The Movie Channel (multiplexed); The Movie Channel HD.
Fee: $25.00 installation; $11.35 monthly (each).
Video-On-Demand: No
Pay-Per-View
iN DEMAND (delivered digitally); MLS Direct Kick (delivered digitally); NBA League Pass (delivered digitally); Hot Choice (delivered digitally).
Internet Service
Operational: Yes. Began: June 1, 1998.
Subscribers: 15,618.
Broadband Service: MidcoNet.
Fee: $35.00 installation; $19.95 monthly; $10.00 modem lease.
Telephone Service
Digital: Operational
Fee: $18.00 monthly
Miles of Plant: 717.0 (coaxial); 98.0 (fiber optic).

Manager: Todd Curtis. Marketing Director: Trish McCann. Engineering Director: Tom Heier. Chief Technician: Dana Storm. Program Director: Wynne Haakenstad. Installation Manager: Mike Drummond.
Ownership: Midcontinent Media Inc. (MSO).; Comcast Cable Communications Inc. (MSO).

SISSETON—Venture Communications Cooperative, 218 Commercial Ave. SE, PO Box 157, Highmore, SD 57345-0157. Phones: 800-824-7282; 605-852-2224. Fax: 605-852-2404. E-mail: venture@venturecomm.net. Web Site: http://www.venturecomm.net. ICA: SD0023.
TV Market Ranking: Outside TV Markets (SISSETON). Franchise award date: N.A. Franchise expiration date: N.A. Began: February 1, 1977.
Channel capacity: N.A. Channels available but not in use: N.A.
Digital Basic Service
Subscribers: N.A. Included in Highmore
Programming (via satellite): C-SPAN; CW+; Eternal Word TV Network; ION Television; LWS Local Weather Station; MyNetworkTV Inc.; QVC; The Weather Channel; Trinity Broadcasting Network; WGN America.
Digital Expanded Basic Service
Subscribers: N.A.
Programming (via satellite): A&E Networks; ABC Family Channel; AMC; Animal Planet; BBC America; Bloomberg Television; Bravo; Cartoon Network; CNBC; CNN; Comedy Central; Country Music TV; Court TV; C-SPAN 2; Discovery Channel; Discovery Health Channel; Discovery Kids Channel; Disney Channel; DIY Network; DMX Music; E! Entertainment Television; ESPN; ESPN 2; ESPN Classic Sports; ESPNews; Food Network; Fox Movie Channel; Fox News Channel; Fox Sports Net North; FX; G4; Golf Channel; Great American Country; GSN; Hallmark Channel; Hallmark Movie Channel; Headline News; HGTV; History Channel; ID Investigation Discovery; Lifetime; Lifetime Movie Network; Lifetime Real Women; Military Channel; MSNBC; MTV Hits; MTV2; National Geographic Channel; NFL Network; Nick Jr.; Nickelodeon; NickToons TV; Outdoor Channel; Oxygen; Planet Green; RFD-TV; Science; SoapNet; Speed; Spike TV; Syfy; TBS Superstation; TeenNick; The Learning Channel; Toon Disney; Travel Channel; Turner Classic Movies; Turner Network TV; TV Land; USA Network; Versus; VH1; VH1 Classic; WE tv.
Digital Pay Service 1
Pay Units: 284.
Programming (via satellite): Cinemax (multiplexed); Encore (multiplexed); HBO (multiplexed); Showtime (multiplexed); Starz (multiplexed); The Movie Channel.
Fee: $10.00 monthly (HBO, TMC, or Starz/Encore).
Video-On-Demand: No
Pay-Per-View
Addressable homes: 94.
iN DEMAND (delivered digitally); Playboy TV (delivered digitally); Fresh (delivered digitally).
Internet Service
Operational: No.
Telephone Service
None
Miles of Plant: 17.0 (coaxial); None (fiber optic).
General Manager: Randy Houdek. Assistant Manager: Randy Olson. Chief Technician: Brad Ryan. Member Services Manager: Rod Kusser.
Ownership: Venture Communications Cooperative (MSO).

SPEARFISH—Midcontinent Communications, PO Box 5010, Sioux Falls, SD 57117. Phones: 800-888-1300; 605-229-1775. Fax: 605-229-0478. Web Site: http://www.midcocomm.com. Also serves Belle Fourche, Central City, Deadwood, Lawrence County (northern portion), Lead, Meade County (western portion) & Sturgis. ICA: SD0010.
TV Market Ranking: Below 100 (Belle Fourche, Central City, Deadwood, Lawrence County (northern portion), Lead, Meade County (western portion), SPEARFISH, Sturgis). Franchise award date: N.A. Franchise expiration date: N.A. Began: June 1, 1969.
Channel capacity: N.A. Channels available but not in use: N.A.
Basic Service
Subscribers: 3,173.
Programming (received off-air): KBHE-TV (PBS) Rapid City; KCLO-TV (CBS) Rapid City; KCPL-LP Rapid City; KEVN-TV (FOX) Rapid City; KHSD-TV (ABC) Lead; KKRA-LP (ION) Rapid City; KNBN (NBC) Rapid City; KWBH-LP Rapid City; allband FM.
Programming (via satellite): A&E Networks; ABC Family Channel; AMC; Animal Planet; BET Networks; Bravo; Cartoon Network; CNBC; CNN; Comedy Central; Country Music TV; C-SPAN; C-SPAN 2; Discovery Channel; Discovery Fit & Health; Disney Channel; Disney XD; E! Entertainment Television; ESPN; ESPN 2; Eternal Word TV Network; Food Network; Fox News Channel; Fox Sports Net North; FX; Golf Channel; Great American Country; GSN; Hallmark Channel; Headline News; HGTV; History Channel; Home Shopping Network; INSP; Lifetime; MSNBC; MTV; Nickelodeon; Outdoor Channel; Oxygen; QVC; Root Sports Rocky Mountain; Speed; Spike TV; Syfy; TBS Superstation; The Learning Channel; The Weather Channel; Travel Channel; Trinity Broadcasting Network; truTV; Turner Classic Movies; Turner Network TV; TV Guide Network; TV Land; USA Network; Versus; VH1; WE tv; WGN America.
Fee: $40.00 installation; $24.28 monthly; $10.00 additional installation.
Digital Basic Service
Subscribers: 536.
Programming (via satellite): 3 Angels Broadcasting Network; A&E HD; ABC Family HD; AMC HD; AmericanLife TV Network; Animal Planet HD; BBC America; Bio; Bloomberg Television; Boomerang; BTN; BTN HD; Canal Sur; CBS Sports Network; Centric; Cine Latino; Cine Mexicano; cloo; CMT Pure Country; CNN en Espanol; CNN HD; Cooking Channel; C-SPAN 3; Current; Discovery Channel HD; Discovery en Espanol; Discovery Fit & Health; Discovery Health Channel; Disney Channel HD; Disney XD; Disney XD en Espanol; DIY Network; ESPN 2 HD; ESPN Classic Sports; ESPN Deportes; ESPN HD; ESPN U; ESPNews; EWTN en Espanol; Food Network HD; Fox Business Channel; Fox College Sports Atlantic; Fox College Sports Central; Fox College Sports Pacific; Fox Deportes; Fox Movie Channel; Fox News HD; FSN HD; Fuse; FX HD; G4; Golf Channel; Golf Channel HD; GolTV; Great American Country; GSN; Halogen Network; HD Theater; HGTV HD; History Channel en Espanol; History Channel HD; History Channel International; ID Investigation Discovery; Independent Film Channel; ION Life; JCTV; Lifetime Movie Network; Military Channel; MLB Network; MLB Network HD; MTV Hits; MTV Jams; MTV2; mun2 television; Music Choice; National Geographic Channel; National Geographic Channel HD Network; NFL Network; NFL Network HD; NFL RedZone; NHL Network; Nick Jr.; Nick Too; NickToons TV; Outdoor Channel; Palladia; PBS Kids Sprout; Pentagon Channel; Planet Green; Qubo; ReelzChannel; RFD-TV; Russian Television Network; Science; Science HD; SoapNet; Speed HD; Spike TV HD; Style Network; Sundance Channel; Syfy HD; TBS in HD; TeenNick; Telemundo; Tennis Channel; The Hub; The Weather Channel HD; TLC HD; Tr3s; Trinity Broadcasting Network; Turner Classic Movies; Turner Network TV HD; TV One; TVE Internacional; TVG Network; Universal HD; USA Network HD; VeneMovies; Versus; Versus HD; VH1 Classic; WE tv.
Digital Pay Service 1
Pay Units: N.A.
Programming (via satellite): Cinemax (multiplexed); Cinemax HD; Encore (multiplexed); Flix; HBO (multiplexed); HBO HD; HBO Latino; Showtime (multiplexed); Showtime HD; Starz (multiplexed); Starz HDTV; The Movie Channel (multiplexed); The Movie Channel HD.
Video-On-Demand: No
Pay-Per-View
Addressable homes: 536.
iN DEMAND (delivered digitally); Sports PPV (delivered digitally).
Internet Service
Operational: Yes. Began: January 1, 1996.
Subscribers: 905.
Broadband Service: MidcoNet.
Fee: $35.00 installation; $19.95 monthly; $10.00 modem lease; $149.00 modem purchase.
Telephone Service
Digital: Operational
Fee: $18.00 monthly
Miles of Plant: 181.0 (coaxial); None (fiber optic).
Manager: Gerry Steevers. Chief Technician: Gary Reimer. Marketing Director: Dianna Aman.
Ownership: Midcontinent Media Inc. (MSO).; Comcast Cable Communications Inc. (MSO).

SPRINGFIELD—Golden West Telecommunications, 415 Crown St, PO Box 411, Wall, SD 57790-0411. Phone: 605-279-2161. Fax: 605-279-2727. E-mail: info@goldenwest.com. Web Site: http://www.goldenwest.com. ICA: SD0070.
TV Market Ranking: Outside TV Markets (SPRINGFIELD). Franchise award date: April 9, 1985. Franchise expiration date: July 1, 2013. Began: October 1, 1985.
Channel capacity: N.A. Channels available but not in use: N.A.
Basic Service
Subscribers: 250.
Programming (received off-air): KDLT-TV (NBC) Sioux Falls; KELO-TV (CBS, MNT) Sioux Falls; KSFY-TV (ABC) Sioux Falls; KUSD-TV (PBS) Vermillion.
Programming (via satellite): A&E Networks; ABC Family Channel; CNN; C-SPAN; Discovery Channel; Disney Channel; ESPN; ESPN 2; Eternal Word TV Network; HGTV; History Channel; INSP; Lifetime; Nickelodeon; TBS Superstation; The Learning Channel; The Weather Channel; Turner Network TV; USA Network; WGN America.
Fee: $25.00 installation; $31.95 monthly.
Pay Service 1
Pay Units: 9.
Programming (via satellite): Cinemax.
Fee: $11.95 monthly.
Pay Service 2
Pay Units: 12.
Programming (via satellite): HBO.
Fee: $11.95 monthly.
Pay Service 3
Pay Units: N.A.
Programming (via satellite): The Movie Channel.
Fee: $9.95 monthly.
Video-On-Demand: No
Internet Service
Operational: No, Both DSL & dial-up.
Telephone Service
None
Miles of Plant: 7.0 (coaxial); None (fiber optic).
General Manager: George Strandell. Chief Engineer: Randy Shepard. Marketing Director: Greg Oleson. Cable Television Manager: Rick Reed. Customer Service Manager: Jody Bielmaier.
Ownership: Golden West Cablevision (MSO).

ST. FRANCIS—Golden West Telecommunications, 415 Crown St, PO Box 411, Wall, SD 57790. Phone: 605-279-2161. Fax: 605-279-2727. Web Site: http://www.goldenwest.com. ICA: SD0050.
TV Market Ranking: Outside TV Markets (ST. FRANCIS). Franchise award date: July 1, 1989. Franchise expiration date: N.A. Began: September 1, 1989.
Channel capacity: 36 (2-way capable). Channels available but not in use: N.A.
Basic Service
Subscribers: 153.
Programming (received off-air): KPLO-TV (CBS, MNT) Reliance; KPRY-TV (ABC) Pierre; KTSD-TV (PBS) Pierre.
Programming (via satellite): A&E Networks; ABC Family Channel; Animal Planet; Cartoon Network; CNBC; CNN; Comedy Central; Country Music TV; C-SPAN; Discovery Channel; Disney Channel; ESPN; ESPN 2; Headline News; History Channel; KDVR (FOX) Denver; KUSA (NBC) Denver; KWGN-TV (CW) Denver; Lifetime; MTV; Nickelodeon; QVC; Spike TV; Syfy; The Learning Channel; The Weather Channel; Turner Classic Movies; Turner Network TV; USA Network; VH1; WGN-TV (CW, IND) Chicago; WPCH-TV (IND) Atlanta.
Fee: $39.95 installation; $33.45 monthly.
Pay Service 1
Pay Units: 63.
Programming (via satellite): The Movie Channel.
Fee: $9.95 monthly.
Pay Service 2
Pay Units: 86.
Programming (via satellite): HBO.
Fee: $10.95 monthly.
Video-On-Demand: No
Internet Service
Operational: No.
Telephone Service
None
Miles of Plant: 11.0 (coaxial); None (fiber optic).
Ownership: Golden West Cablevision (MSO).

SUMMIT (town)—Satellite Cable Services Inc. Now served by WILMOT, SD [SD0089]. ICA: SD0207.

TABOR—Satellite Cable Services Inc. Now served by TRIPP, SD [SD0087]. ICA: SD0208.

TAKINI—Formerly served by Cheyenne River Sioux Tribe Telephone Authority. No longer in operation. ICA: SD0209.

TIMBER LAKE—West River Cable Television, 801 Coleman Ave, PO Box 39, Bison, SD 57620. Phone: 605-244-5213. Fax: 605-244-7288. Web Site: http://www.westrivercatv.com. ICA: SD0085.

TV Market Ranking: Outside TV Markets (TIMBER LAKE). Franchise award date: January 16, 1986. Franchise expiration date: January 16, 2011. Began: November 1, 1982.

Channel capacity: 41 (not 2-way capable). Channels available but not in use: N.A.

Basic Service

Subscribers: 72.

Programming (received off-air): KNBN (NBC) Rapid City; KPLO-TV (CBS, MNT) Reliance; KPRY-TV (ABC) Pierre; KPSD-TV (PBS) Eagle Butte; KTTM (FOX) Huron; KXMB-TV (CBS) Bismarck; allband FM.

Programming (via satellite): A&E Networks; ABC Family Channel; AMC; Animal Planet; Cartoon Network; CNBC; CNN; Country Music TV; C-SPAN; Discovery Channel; Disney Channel; ESPN; ESPN 2; Fox Sports Net North; Headline News; HGTV; History Channel; INSP; Lifetime; Nickelodeon; QVC; Spike TV; TBS Superstation; The Learning Channel; The Weather Channel; Turner Network TV; TV Land; USA Network; VH1; WGN America.

Fee: $50.00 installation; $31.50 monthly.

Pay Service 1

Pay Units: 7.

Programming (via satellite): HBO.

Fee: $20.00 installation; $10.00 monthly.

Pay Service 2

Pay Units: N.A.

Programming (via satellite): Showtime.

Fee: $20.00 installation; $10.00 monthly.

Pay Service 3

Pay Units: N.A.

Programming (via satellite): The Movie Channel.

Fee: $20.00 installation.

Internet Service

Operational: No.

Telephone Service

None

Miles of Plant: 4.0 (coaxial); None (fiber optic).

Manager: Jerry Reisenauer. Chief Technician: Colle Nash.

Ownership: West River Cooperative Telephone Co. (MSO).

TORONTO—ITC. Formerly served by Clear Lake, SD [SD0047]. This cable system has converted to IPTV, 312 Fourth St W, Clear Lake, SD 57226. Phones: 800-417-8667; 605-874-2181. Fax: 605-874-2014. E-mail: info@itctel.com. Web Site: http://www.itc-web.com. ICA: SD5044.

Channel capacity: N.A. Channels available but not in use: N.A.

Basic Service

Subscribers: N.A.

Fee: $35.50 monthly.

Expanded Basic Service 1

Subscribers: N.A.

Fee: $46.95 monthly.

Limited Basic Service

Subscribers: N.A.

Fee: $25.50 monthly.

Pay Service 1

Pay Units: N.A.

Fee: $10.95 monthly (Cinemax or Starz!), $11.95 monthly (Showtime), $13.95 monthly (HBO).

Internet Service

Operational: Yes.

Fee: $39.95 monthly.

Telephone Service

Digital: Operational

General Manager: Jerry Heiberger.

TORONTO—Satellite Cable Services Inc. Now served by CLEAR LAKE, SD [SD0047]. ICA: SD0210.

TRENT—Golden West Telecommunications, 415 Crown St, PO Box 411, Wall, SD 57790-0411. Phone: 605-279-2161. Fax: 605-279-2727. E-mail: info@goldenwest.com. Web Site: http://www.goldenwest.com. ICA: SD0211.

TV Market Ranking: 85 (TRENT). Franchise award date: N.A. Franchise expiration date: N.A. Began: N.A.

Channel capacity: N.A. Channels available but not in use: N.A.

Basic Service

Subscribers: 20.

Programming (received off-air): KCPO-LP Sioux Falls; KDLT-TV (NBC) Sioux Falls; KELO-TV (CBS, MNT) Sioux Falls; KSFY-TV (ABC) Sioux Falls; KTTW (FOX) Sioux Falls; KUSD-TV (PBS) Vermillion.

Programming (via satellite): A&E Networks; ABC Family Channel; AMC; Animal Planet; Bloomberg Television; Bravo; Cartoon Network; CNN; Comedy Central; Country Music TV; C-SPAN; CW+; Discovery Channel; Disney Channel; ESPN; ESPN 2; ESPN Classic Sports; Eternal Word TV Network; Food Network; Fox News Channel; Fox Sports Net North; FX; Golf Channel; Great American Country; Hallmark Channel; Headline News; HGTV; History Channel; ION Television; Lifetime Movie Network; MTV; NFL Network; Nickelodeon; Outdoor Channel; QVC; Speed; Spike TV; Syfy; TBS Superstation; The Learning Channel; The Weather Channel; Travel Channel; truTV; Turner Classic Movies; Turner Network TV; TV Guide Network; TV Land; USA Network; VH1; WGN America.

Fee: $25.00 installation; $33.95 monthly.

Pay Service 1

Pay Units: N.A.

Programming (via satellite): Encore; HBO; Showtime.

Fee: $2.30 monthly (Encore), $11.95 monthly (HBO or Showtime).

Video-On-Demand: No

Internet Service

Operational: No, Both DSL & dial-up.

Telephone Service

None

Miles of Plant: 2.0 (coaxial); None (fiber optic).

General Manager: George Strandell. Chief Technician: Randy Shepard. Marketing Director: Greg Oleson. Cable Television Manager: Rick Reed. Customer Service Manager: Jody Bielmaier.

Ownership: Golden West Cablevision (MSO).

TRIPP—Fort Randall Cable, 1605 Laurel St, PO Box 608, Tyndall, SD 57066. Phones: 888-283-7667; 605-589-3366. E-mail: sharon@hcinet.net. Also serves Lake Andes, Pickstown, Tabor, Tyndall & Wagner. ICA: SD0087.

TV Market Ranking: Outside TV Markets (Lake Andes, Pickstown, Tabor, TRIPP, Tyndall, Wagner). Franchise award date: N.A. Franchise expiration date: N.A. Began: September 1, 1983.

Channel capacity: 135 (operating 2-way). Channels available but not in use: N.A.

Basic Service

Subscribers: 997.

Programming (received off-air): KDLV-TV (NBC) Mitchell; KELO-TV (CBS, MNT) Sioux Falls; KSFY-TV (ABC) Sioux Falls; KUSD-TV (PBS) Vermillion.

Programming (via satellite): ABC Family Channel; CNN; ESPN; TBS Superstation; USA Network; WGN America.

Fee: $29.95 installation; $28.95 monthly.

Digital Basic Service

Subscribers: N.A.

Programming (via satellite): AmericanLife TV Network; Bio; Bloomberg Television; Bravo; Discovery Fit & Health; DMX Music; ESPN 2; ESPN Classic Sports; ESPNews; Fox Movie Channel; Fox Sports World; Fuse; G4; Golf Channel; GSN; Halogen Network; HGTV; History Channel; History Channel International; Independent Film Channel; Lifetime Movie Network; National Geographic Channel; Outdoor Channel; Speed; Style Network; Syfy; Toon Disney; Trinity Broadcasting Network; Turner Classic Movies; Versus; WE tv.

Fee: $10.95 monthly.

Pay Service 1

Pay Units: 128.

Programming (via satellite): HBO.

Fee: $9.95 installation; $11.95 monthly.

Pay Service 2

Pay Units: 12.

Programming (via satellite): Cinemax.

Fee: $11.95 monthly.

Pay Service 3

Pay Units: 8.

Programming (via satellite): Showtime.

Fee: $9.45 installation; $11.95 monthly.

Digital Pay Service 1

Pay Units: N.A.

Programming (via satellite): Cinemax (multiplexed); Encore (multiplexed); HBO (multiplexed); Showtime (multiplexed); Starz (multiplexed); The Movie Channel (multiplexed).

Fee: $11.95 monthly (HBO, Cinemex, Starz/Encore or Showtime/TMC).

Video-On-Demand: No

Pay-Per-View

Sports PPV (delivered digitally); ESPN Extra (delivered digitally); ESPN Now (delivered digitally); Fresh (delivered digitally); Playboy TV (delivered digitally); Hot Choice (delivered digitally).

Internet Service

Operational: Yes.

Fee: $39.99 monthly.

Telephone Service

None

Manager: Bruce Hamson. Office Manager: Deb Wagner.

Ownership: Hanson Communications Inc. (MSO).

TRIPP—Santel Communications. Formerly served by Mount Vernon, SD [SD0188]. This cable system has converted to IPTV, 308 S Dumont Ave, PO Box 67, Woodsocket, SD 57365-0067. Phones: 888-978-7777; 605-796-4411. Fax: 605-796-4419. E-mail: info@santel.net. Web Site: http://www.santel.net. ICA: SD5019.

TV Market Ranking: 85 (TRIPP).

Channel capacity: N.A. Channels available but not in use: N.A.

Basic Service

Subscribers: N.A.

Fee: $33.95 monthly.

Expanded Basic Service 1

Subscribers: N.A.

Fee: $43.95 monthly.

Limited Basic Service

Subscribers: N.A.

Fee: $21.95 monthly.

Pay Service 1

Pay Units: N.A.

Fee: $10.95 monthly (Cinemaz, Encore/Starz, HBO, or Showtime).

Internet Service

Operational: Yes.

Fee: $25.00 installation; $24.95 monthly; $10.00 modem lease.

Telephone Service

Analog: Operational

Fee: $14.50 monthly

TYNDALL—Satellite Cable Services Inc. Now served by TRIPP, SD [SD0087]. ICA: SD0045.

VALLEY SPRINGS—Alliance Communications. Formerly [SD0084]. This cable system has converted to IPTV, 612 Third St, PO Box 349, Garretson, SD 57030. Phones: 800-701-4980; 605-594-3400. Fax: 605-594-6776. E-mail: email@alliancecom.net. Web Site: http://www.alliancecom.net. ICA: SD5089.

Channel capacity: N.A. Channels available but not in use: N.A.

Basic Service

Subscribers: N.A.

Fee: $29.95 monthly.

Expanded Basic Service 1

Subscribers: N.A.

Fee: $13.00 monthly.

Expanded Basic Service 2

Subscribers: N.A.

Fee: $8.00 monthly.

Pay Service 1

Pay Units: N.A.

Fee: $9.95 monthly (Cinemax or Starz/Encore), $10.95 monthly (Showtime) or $13.95 monthly (HBO).

Internet Service

Operational: Yes.

Fee: $14.95 monthly.

Telephone Service

Digital: Operational

Fee: $11.30 monthly

Manager: Don Snyder.

VALLEY SPRINGS—Alliance Communications. This cable system has converted to IPTV. See Valley Springs, SD [SD5089]. ICA: SD0084.

VERMILLION—Mediacom. Now served by GAYVILLE (formerly Yankton), SD [SD0009]. ICA: SD0012.

VIBORG—Knology, 5100 S Broadband Ln, Sioux Falls, SD 57108-2207. Phones: 706-645-3000 (Corporate office); 605-766-7793. Fax: 605-965-7867. Web Site: http://www.knology.com. Also serves Sioux City (northern portion), IA; Alcester, Canton (portions), Centerville, Chancellor, Elk Point, Gayville, Harrisburg, Hurley, Irene, Lennox, Parker, Tea, Wakonda, Worthing & Yankton, SD. ICA: SD0071. **Note:** This system is an overbuild.

TV Market Ranking: 85 (Canton (portions), Centerville, Chancellor, Harrisburg, Hurley, Lennox, Parker, Tea, VIBORG, Worthing); Below 100 (Elk Point, Gayville, Sioux City (northern portion)); Outside TV Markets (Alcester, Irene, Wakonda, Yankton). Franchise award date: February 7, 1983. Franchise expiration date: February 4, 2013. Began: July 1, 1983.

Channel capacity: N.A. Channels available but not in use: N.A.

Basic Service
Subscribers: 46,000 Includes Coleman, Rapid City, Watertown, Storm Lake IA, Ellsworth MN, & Marshall MN.
Programming (received off-air): KCAU-TV (ABC) Sioux City; KDLT-TV (NBC) Sioux Falls; KELO-TV (CBS, MNT) Sioux Falls; KSFY-TV (ABC) Sioux Falls; KSIN-TV (PBS) Sioux City; KTIV (CW, NBC) Sioux City; KTTW (FOX) Sioux Falls; KUSD-TV (PBS) Vermillion; KXNE-TV (PBS) Norfolk.
Programming (via satellite): A&E Networks; ABC Family Channel; AMC; Animal Planet; Bravo; Cartoon Network; CNBC; CNN; Comedy Central; Country Music TV; C-SPAN; Discovery Channel; Disney Channel; E! Entertainment Television; ESPN; ESPN 2; Eternal Word TV Network; Food Network; Fox Movie Channel; Fox News Channel; Fox Sports Net North; FX; Golf Channel; Headline News; HGTV; History Channel; INSP; ION Television; Lifetime; Lifetime Movie Network; MSNBC; MTV; Nickelodeon; Outdoor Channel; QVC; Speed; Spike TV; Syfy; TBS Superstation; The Learning Channel; The Weather Channel; Toon Disney; Travel Channel; truTV; Turner Classic Movies; Turner Network TV; TV Guide Network; TV Land; USA Network; VH1; WGN America.
Fee: $25.00 installation; $26.95 monthly.

Digital Basic Service
Subscribers: N.A.
Programming (via satellite): BBC America; Bio; Bloomberg Television; Cooking Channel; Discovery Fit & Health; DIY Network; Encore Family; ESPN; ESPNews; Flix; Fox College Sports Atlantic; Fox College Sports Central; Fox College Sports Pacific; Fox Soccer; Fuse; G4; GSN; Hallmark Channel; HD Theater; HDNet; HDNet Movies; History Channel International; Independent Film Channel; Lifetime Real Women; Lime; MTV Networks Digital Suite; Music Choice; National Geographic Channel; Nick Jr.; NickToons TV; SoapNet; Style Network; Sundance Channel; TeenNick; WE tv.

Pay Service 1
Pay Units: 931.
Programming (via satellite): HBO.
Fee: $10.00 installation; $9.85 monthly.

Pay Service 2
Pay Units: 923.
Programming (via satellite): Showtime.
Fee: $10.00 installation; $9.85 monthly.

Digital Pay Service 1
Pay Units: N.A.
Programming (via satellite): Canales N; Cinemax (multiplexed); Cinemax HD; Encore (multiplexed); HBO (multiplexed); HBO HD; Showtime (multiplexed); Showtime HD; Starz (multiplexed); The Movie Channel (multiplexed).

Video-On-Demand: Yes

Pay-Per-View
iN DEMAND (delivered digitally); Hot Choice (delivered digitally).

Internet Service
Operational: Yes.
Subscribers: 36,441.
Broadband Service: Knology.Net.
Fee: $29.95 installation; $39.95 monthly.

Telephone Service
Analog: Not Operational
Digital: Operational

General Manager: Scott Schroeder. Technical Operations Manager: Daryl Elcock. Marketing Manager: Scott Determan.
Ownership: Knology Inc. (MSO).

WAGNER—Satellite Cable Services Inc. Now served by TRIPP, SD [SD0087]. ICA: SD0039.

WALL—Golden West Telecommunications, 415 Crown St, PO Box 411, Wall, SD 57790-0411. Phone: 605-279-2161. Fax: 605-279-2727. E-mail: info@goldenwest.com. Web Site: http://www.goldenwest.com. Also serves Allen, Draper, Evergreen Housing, Horse Creek Housing, Kadoka, Kyle, Lake Waggoner, Manderson-White Horse Creek, Martin, Midland, Murdo, New Underwood, Philip, Porcupine, Tuthill, Vetal, Wanblee & White River. ICA: SD0068.
TV Market Ranking: Below 100 (Evergreen Housing, New Underwood); Outside TV Markets (Allen, Draper, Horse Creek Housing, Kadoka, Kyle, Lake Waggoner, Manderson-White Horse Creek, Martin, Midland, Murdo, Philip, Porcupine, Tuthill, Vetal, WALL, Wanblee, White River). Franchise award date: October 15, 1982. Franchise expiration date: N.A. Began: October 15, 1982.
Channel capacity: N.A. Channels available but not in use: N.A.

Basic Service
Subscribers: 2,300.
Programming (received off-air): KBHE-TV (PBS) Rapid City; KCLO-TV (CBS) Rapid City; KEVN-TV (FOX) Rapid City; KKRA-LP (ION) Rapid City; KNBN (NBC) Rapid City; KOTA-TV (ABC) Rapid City.
Programming (via satellite): A&E Networks; ABC Family Channel; AMC; Animal Planet; Cartoon Network; CNBC; CNN; Country Music TV; C-SPAN; C-SPAN 2; CW+; Discovery Channel; Disney Channel; ESPN; ESPN 2; ESPN Classic Sports; Eternal Word TV Network; Food Network; Fox News Channel; FX; Hallmark Channel; Headline News; HGTV; History Channel; INSP; Lifetime; MTV; National Geographic Channel; NFL Network; Nickelodeon; Outdoor Channel; QVC; Spike TV; TBS Superstation; The Learning Channel; The Weather Channel; Turner Classic Movies; Turner Network TV; TV Guide Network; TV Land; USA Network; VH1; WGN America.
Fee: $25.00 installation; $33.95 monthly.

Digital Basic Service
Subscribers: N.A.
Programming (via satellite): A&E Networks; AmericanLife TV Network; BBC America; Black Family Channel; Bloomberg Television; Current; Discovery Digital Networks; DMX Music; ESPN; ESPN Classic Sports; Fox Movie Channel; Fuse; G4; GAS; Golf Channel; GSN; Halogen Network; HGTV; History Channel; History Channel International; Independent Film Channel; Lifetime Movie Network; Lime; MTV Networks Digital Suite; National Geographic Channel; Nick Jr.; NickToons TV; Ovation; ShopNBC; Speed; Style Network; The Word Network; Toon Disney; Trinity Broadcasting Network; Versus; WE tv.
Fee: $14.95 monthly.

Pay Service 1
Pay Units: 1,870.
Programming (via satellite): HBO; Showtime; The Movie Channel.
Fee: $9.95 monthly (TMC), $10.95 monthly (Showtime), $11.95 monthly (HBO).

Digital Pay Service 1
Pay Units: N.A.
Programming (via satellite): Cinemax (multiplexed); Encore (multiplexed); Flix; HBO (multiplexed); Showtime (multiplexed); Starz (multiplexed); The Movie Channel (multiplexed).
Fee: $6.95 monthly (Encore), $11.95 monthly (Cinemax, Showtime, or TMC), $12.95 monthly (HBO), $13.95 monthly (Starz/Encore).

Video-On-Demand: No

Pay-Per-View
iN DEMAND (delivered digitally); Hot Choice (delivered digitally); Playboy TV (delivered digitally); Fresh (delivered digitally); Shorteez (delivered digitally).

Internet Service
Operational: No, Both DSL & dial-up.

Telephone Service
None

Miles of Plant: 175.0 (coaxial); None (fiber optic).
General Manager: George Strandell. Cable Television Manager: Rick Reed. Chief Technician: Randy Shepard. Marketing Director: Greg Oleson. Customer Service Manager: Jody Bielmaier.
Ownership: Golden West Cablevision (MSO).

WATERTOWN—Knology, 5100 S Broadband Ln, Sioux Falls, SD 57108-2207. Phone: 605-965-9393. Fax: 605-965-7867. Web Site: http://www.knology.com. ICA: SD0250.
Note: This system is an overbuild.
TV Market Ranking: Below 100 (WATERTOWN).
Channel capacity: N.A. Channels available but not in use: N.A.

Basic Service
Subscribers: 916.
Programming (received off-air): KABY-TV (ABC) Aberdeen; KAUN-LP Sioux Falls; KCPO-LP Sioux Falls; KDLO-TV (CBS, MNT) Florence; KDLT-TV (NBC) Sioux Falls; KTTW (FOX) Sioux Falls; KUSD-TV (PBS) Vermillion; KWSD (CW) Sioux Falls.
Programming (via satellite): A&E Networks; ABC Family Channel; AMC; Animal Planet; Bravo; Cartoon Network; CNBC; CNN; Comedy Central; Country Music TV; C-SPAN; Discovery Channel; Disney Channel; E! Entertainment Television; ESPN; ESPN 2; ESPN Classic Sports; Eternal Word TV Network; Food Network; Fox News Channel; Fox Sports Net North; FX; G4; Golf Channel; Hallmark Channel; Headline News; HGTV; History Channel; INSP; Lifetime; Lifetime Movie Network; MSNBC; MTV; MyNetworkTV Inc.; National Geographic Channel; NFL Network; Nickelodeon; QVC; Speed; Spike TV; Syfy; TBS Superstation; The Learning Channel; The Weather Channel; Toon Disney; Travel Channel; truTV; Turner Classic Movies; Turner Network TV; TV Guide Network; TV Land; USA Network; VH1; WGN America.
Fee: $25.00 installation; $26.95 monthly.

Digital Basic Service
Subscribers: N.A.
Programming (via satellite): Bandamax; BBC America; Bio; Bloomberg Television; Boomerang; cloo; cloo on demand; CMT Pure Country; Cooking Channel; De Pelicula; De Pelicula Clasico; Discovery Channel HD; Discovery en Espanol; Discovery Fit & Health; Discovery Health Channel; Discovery Home Channel; Discovery Kids Channel; DIY Network; ESPN 2 HD; ESPN Deportes; ESPN Deportes On Demand; ESPN HD; ESPN On Demand; ESPN U; ESPN U On Demand; ESPNews; Flix; Fox College Sports Atlantic; Fox College Sports Central; Fox College Sports Pacific; Fox Deportes; Fox Movie Channel; Fox Reality Channel; Fox Soccer; Fuse; G4; GMC; GSN; HDNet; HDNet Movies; History Channel International; ID Investigation Discovery; Independent Film Channel; Lifetime Real Women; Military Channel; MTV Hits; MTV Jams; MTV2; Music Choice; National Geographic Channel; National Geographic Channel On Demand; NFL Network HD; Nick Jr.; NickToons TV; Outdoor Channel; Outdoor Channel 2 HD; Outdoor Channel On Demand; RFD-TV; Ritmoson Latino; Science; SoapNet; Speed On Demand; Style Network; Sundance Channel; TeenNick; Telehit; Turner Network TV HD; TV Guide SPOT; Universal HD; Versus; Versus On Demand; VH1 Classic; VH1 Soul; WAM! America's Kidz Network; WE tv.

Pay Service 1
Pay Units: N.A.
Programming (via satellite): HBO; Showtime.
Fee: $10.00 installation; $9.85 monthly (each).

Digital Pay Service 1
Pay Units: N.A.
Programming (via satellite): Cinemax (multiplexed); Cinemax HD; Cinemax On Demand; Encore (multiplexed); HBO (multiplexed); HBO HD; HBO On Demand; Showtime (multiplexed); Showtime HD; Showtime On Demand; Starz (multiplexed); Starz HDTV; Starz On Demand; The Movie Channel (multiplexed); The Movie Channel On Demand.

Video-On-Demand: Yes

Pay-Per-View
iN DEMAND (delivered digitally); Special events (delivered digitally); Hot Choice (delivered digitally).

Internet Service
Operational: Yes.
Broadband Service: Knology.Net.

Telephone Service
Analog: Not Operational
Digital: Operational

General Manager: Scott Schroeder. Technical Operations Manager: Daryl Elcock. Marketing Manager: Scott Determan.
Ownership: Knology Inc. (MSO).

WATERTOWN—Midcontinent Communications, 222 9th Ave SE, Watertown, SD 57201. Phones: 605-882-9140 (Local office); 800-888-1300; 605-229-1775. Fax: 605-229-0478. Web Site: http://www.midcocomm.com. Also serves Big Stone City, Big Stone Twp., Ortonville & Ortonville Twp., MN; Codington County (portions), Grant County & Milbank, SD. ICA: SD0004.
TV Market Ranking: Below 100 (Codington County (portions), Grant County, WATERTOWN); Outside TV Markets (Big Stone City, Big Stone Twp., Milbank, Ortonville, Ortonville Twp.). Franchise award date: N.A. Franchise expiration date: N.A. Began: June 29, 1973.
Channel capacity: 68 (operating 2-way). Channels available but not in use: N.A.

Basic Service
Subscribers: 8,250.
Programming (received off-air): KABY-TV (ABC) Aberdeen; KCPO-LP Sioux Falls; KDLO-TV (CBS, MNT) Florence; KDLT-TV (NBC) Sioux Falls; KESD-TV (PBS) Brookings; KTTW (FOX) Sioux Falls; KWSD (CW) Sioux Falls; allband FM.
Programming (via satellite): A&E Networks; ABC Family Channel; AMC; Animal Planet; Bravo; Cartoon Network; CNBC; CNN; Comedy Central; Country Music TV; C-SPAN; C-SPAN 2; Discovery Channel; Discovery Health Channel; Disney Channel; E! Entertainment Television; Encore; ESPN; ESPN 2; ESPN Classic Sports; ESPNews; Eternal Word TV Network; Food Network; Fox News Channel; Fox Sports Net; FX; G4; Great American Country; Hall-

mark Channel; Headline News; HGTV; History Channel; INSP; Lifetime; MSNBC; MTV; Nickelodeon; Outdoor Channel; QVC; Speed; Spike TV; Starz; Syfy; TBS Superstation; The Learning Channel; The Weather Channel; Travel Channel; truTV; Turner Classic Movies; Turner Network TV; TV Guide Network; TV Land; USA Network; Versus; VH1; WE tv; WGN America.
Fee: $29.95 installation; $9.82 monthly; $.43 converter; $15.00 additional installation.

Digital Basic Service
Subscribers: 1,502.
Programming (via satellite): BBC America; Bio; Bloomberg Television; Discovery Digital Networks; DMX Music; ESPNOL; Fox Sports World; GAS; Golf Channel; GSN; History Channel; Independent Film Channel; Lifetime Movie Network; MTV2; Nick Jr.; Style Network; Sundance Channel; Toon Disney.

Pay Service 1
Pay Units: 729.
Programming (via satellite): Cinemax; HBO.
Fee: $15.00 installation; $9.95 monthly (each).

Digital Pay Service 1
Pay Units: 445.
Programming (via satellite): Cinemax (multiplexed); Encore (multiplexed); HBO (multiplexed); Showtime (multiplexed); Starz (multiplexed); The Movie Channel (multiplexed).

Video-On-Demand: No

Pay-Per-View
Addressable homes: 1,502.
iN DEMAND (delivered digitally); Hot Choice (delivered digitally); Fresh (delivered digitally).

Internet Service
Operational: Yes. Began: January 1, 1996.
Subscribers: 3,111.
Broadband Service: MidcoNet.
Fee: $35.00 installation; $19.95 monthly; $10.00 modem lease; $149.00 modem purchase.

Telephone Service
Digital: Operational
Fee: $18.00 monthly

Miles of Plant: 384.0 (coaxial); None (fiber optic).
Manager: Paul Foust. Chief Technician: Bob Spilde.
Ownership: Midcontinent Media Inc. (MSO).; Comcast Cable Communications Inc. (MSO).

WAUBAY—ITC. Formerly served by Clear Lake, SD [SD0047]. This cable system has converted to IPTV, 312 Fourth St W, Clear Lake, SD 57226. Phones: 800-417-8667; 605-874-2181. Fax: 605-874-2014. E-mail: info@itctel.com. Web Site: http://www.itc-web.com. ICA: SD5071.
Channel capacity: N.A. Channels available but not in use: N.A.

Basic Service
Subscribers: N.A.
Fee: $35.50 monthly.

Expanded Basic Service 1
Subscribers: N.A.
Fee: $46.95 monthly.

Limited Basic Service
Subscribers: N.A.
Fee: $25.50 monthly.

Pay Service 1
Pay Units: N.A.
Fee: $10.95 monthly (Cinemax or Starz!), $11.95 monthly (Showtime), $13.95 monthly (HBO).

Internet Service
Operational: Yes.
Fee: $39.95 monthly.

Telephone Service
Digital: Operational
General Manager: Jerry Heiberger.

WEBSTER—ITC. Formerly served by Clear Lake, SD [SD0047]. This cable system has converted to IPTV, 312 Fourth St W, Clear Lake, SD 57226. Phones: 800-417-8667; 605-874-2181. Fax: 605-874-2014. E-mail: info@itctel.com. Web Site: http://www.itc-web.com. ICA: SD5045.
Channel capacity: N.A. Channels available but not in use: N.A.

Basic Service
Subscribers: N.A.
Fee: $35.50 monthly.

Expanded Basic Service 1
Subscribers: N.A.
Fee: $46.95 monthly.

Limited Basic Service
Subscribers: N.A.
Fee: $25.50 monthly.

Pay Service 1
Pay Units: N.A.
Fee: $10.95 monthly (Cinemax or Starz!), $11.95 monthly (Showtime), $13.95 monthly (HBO).

Internet Service
Operational: Yes.
Fee: $39.95 monthly.

Telephone Service
Digital: Operational
General Manager: Jerry Heiberger.

WENTWORTH—Satellite Cable Services Inc. Now served by CLEAR LAKE, SD [SD0047]. ICA: SD0215.

WENTWORTH (rural)—ITC. Formerly served by Clear Lake, SD [SD0047]. This cable system has converted to IPTV, 312 Fourth St W, Clear Lake, SD 57226. Phones: 800-417-8667; 605-874-2181. Fax: 605-874-2014. E-mail: info@itc-web.com. Web Site: http://www.itc-web.com. ICA: SD5059.
Channel capacity: N.A. Channels available but not in use: N.A.

Basic Service
Subscribers: N.A.
Fee: $35.50 monthly.

Expanded Basic Service 1
Subscribers: N.A.
Fee: $46.95 monthly.

Limited Basic Service
Subscribers: N.A.
Fee: $25.50 monthly.

Pay Service 1
Pay Units: N.A.
Fee: $10.95 monthly (Cinemax or Starz!), $11.95 monthly (Showtime), $13.95 monthly (HBO).

Internet Service
Operational: Yes.
Fee: $39.95 monthly.

Telephone Service
Digital: Operational
General Manager: Jerry Heiberger.

WESSINGTON—Venture Communications Cooperative, 218 Commercial Ave. SE, PO Box 157, Highmore, SD 57345-0157. Phones: 800-847-7431; 605-852-2224. Fax: 605-852-2404. E-mail: venture@venturecomm.net. Web Site: http://www.venturecomm.net. Also serves Hitchcock & Tulare. ICA: SD0109.
TV Market Ranking: Below 100 (Hitchcock, Tulare, WESSINGTON). Franchise award date: N.A. Franchise expiration date: N.A. Began: September 1, 1985.
Channel capacity: N.A. Channels available but not in use: N.A.

Digital Basic Service
Subscribers: N.A. Included in Highmore
Programming (via satellite): A&E Networks; ABC Family Channel; AMC; Animal Planet; Cartoon Network; CNBC; CNN; Comedy Network; Country Music TV; C-SPAN; CW+; Discovery Channel; Disney Channel; ESPN; ESPN 2; Eternal Word TV Network; Food Network; Fox News Channel; FX; Great American Country; Hallmark Channel; Headline News; HGTV; History Channel; Lifetime; MTV; MyNetworkTV Inc.; Nickelodeon; QVC; Spike TV; Syfy; TBS Superstation; The Learning Channel; The Weather Channel; Travel Channel; Trinity Broadcasting Network; truTV; Turner Network TV; TV Land; USA Network; VH1; WGN America.
Fee: $46.95 monthly.

Digital Pay Service 1
Pay Units: N.A.
Programming (via satellite): Cinemax (multiplexed); Encore (multiplexed); HBO (multiplexed); Showtime (multiplexed); Starz (multiplexed); The Movie Channel.

Video-On-Demand: No

Pay-Per-View
Fresh (delivered digitally); Playboy TV (delivered digitally); Sports PPV (delivered digitally); ESPN Now (delivered digitally); Movies (delivered digitally).

Internet Service
Operational: No.

Telephone Service
None

Miles of Plant: 4.0 (coaxial); None (fiber optic).
General Manager: Randy Houdek. Assistant Manager: Randy Olson. Chief Technician: Brad Ryan. Member Services Manager: Rod Kusser.
Ownership: Venture Communications Cooperative (MSO).

WESSINGTON SPRINGS—Venture Communications Cooperative, 218 Commercial Ave. SE, PO Box 157, Highmore, SD 57345-0157. Phone: 605-852-2224. Fax: 605-852-2404. E-mail: venture@venturecomm.net. Web Site: http://www.venturecomm.net. ICA: SD0051.
TV Market Ranking: Below 100 (WESSINGTON SPRINGS). Franchise award date: N.A. Franchise expiration date: N.A. Began: December 15, 1980.
Channel capacity: N.A. Channels available but not in use: N.A.

Digital Basic Service
Subscribers: N.A. Included in Highmore
Programming (via satellite): C-SPAN; C-SPAN 2; CW+; Eternal Word TV Network; ION Television; Local Cable Weather; MyNetworkTV Inc.; QVC; Trinity Broadcasting Network; WGN America.
Fee: $19.95 monthly.

Digital Expanded Basic Service
Subscribers: N.A.
Programming (via satellite): A&E Networks; ABC Family Channel; AMC; Animal Planet; BBC America; Bloomberg Television; Bravo; Cartoon Network; CNBC; CNN; Comedy Central; Country Music TV; Discovery Channel; Discovery Health Channel; Discovery Kids Channel; Disney Channel; DIY Network; DMX Music; E! Entertainment Television; ESPN; ESPN 2; ESPN Classic Sports; ESPNews; Food Network; Fox Movie Channel; Fox News Channel; Fox Sports Net North; FX; G4; Golf Channel; Great American Country; GSN; Hallmark Channel; Headline News; HGTV; History Channel; ID Investigation Discovery; Lifetime; Lifetime Movie Network; Lifetime Real Women; Military Channel; MSNBC; MTV; MTV Hits; MTV2; National Geographic Channel; NFL Network; Nick Jr.; Nickelodeon; NickToons TV; Outdoor Channel; Oxygen; Planet Green; RFD-TV; Science; SoapNet; Speed; Spike TV; Syfy; TBS Superstation; TeenNick; The Learning Channel; Toon Disney; Travel Channel; truTV; Turner Classic Movies; Turner Network TV; TV Land; USA Network; Versus; VH1; VH1 Classic; WE tv.
Fee: $18.00 monthly.

Digital Pay Service 1
Pay Units: N.A.
Programming (via satellite): Cinemax (multiplexed); Encore (multiplexed); HBO (multiplexed); Showtime (multiplexed); Starz (multiplexed); The Movie Channel.

Video-On-Demand: No

Pay-Per-View
Movies (delivered digitally); Playboy TV (delivered digitally); Fresh (delivered digitally).

Internet Service
Operational: No.

Telephone Service
None

General Manager: Randy Houdek. Assistant Manager: Randy Olson. Chief Technician: Brad Ryan. Member Services Manager: Rod Kusser.
Ownership: Venture Communications Cooperative (MSO).

WEST WHITLOCK—Formerly served by Western Telephone Company. No longer in operation. ICA: SD0216.

WHITE—ITC. Formerly served by Clear Lake, SD [SD0047]. This cable system has converted to IPTV, 312 Fourth St W, Clear Lake, SD 57226. Phones: 800-417-8667; 605-874-2181. Fax: 605-874-2014. E-mail: info@itctel.com. Web Site: http://www.itc-web.com. ICA: SD5046.
Channel capacity: N.A. Channels available but not in use: N.A.

Basic Service
Subscribers: N.A.
Fee: $35.50 monthly.

Expanded Basic Service 1
Subscribers: N.A.
Fee: $46.95 monthly.

Limited Basic Service
Subscribers: N.A.
Fee: $25.50 monthly.

Pay Service 1
Pay Units: N.A.
Fee: $10.95 monthly (Cinemax or Starz!), $11.95 monthly (Showtime), $13.95 monthly (HBO).

Internet Service
Operational: Yes.
Fee: $39.95 monthly.

Telephone Service
Digital: Operational
General Manager: Jerry Heiberger.

WHITE—Mediacom. Now served by BROOKINGS, SD [SD0005]. ICA: SD0105.

WHITE LAKE—Midstate Communications, 120 E First St, PO Box 48, Kimball, SD 57355-0048. Phone: 605-778-6221. Fax: 605-778-8080. E-mail: midstate@midstatesd.net. Web Site: http://www.midstatesd.net. Also serves Chamberlain, Kimball, Oacoma, Pukwana & Stickney. ICA: SD0026.

TV Market Ranking: 85 (Stickney, WHITE LAKE); Below 100 (Chamberlain, Kimball, Oacoma, Pukwana). Franchise award date: December 7, 1988. Franchise expiration date: N.A. Began: N.A.

Channel capacity: 150 (operating 2-way). Channels available but not in use: N.A.

Basic Service

Subscribers: 2,500 Includes Platte.

Programming (received off-air): KCSD-TV (PBS) Sioux Falls; KDLT-TV (NBC) Sioux Falls; KPLO-TV (CBS, MNT) Reliance; KPRY-TV (ABC) Pierre; KTTW (FOX) Sioux Falls.

Programming (via satellite): A&E Networks; ABC Family Channel; CNBC; CNN; Comedy Central; Country Music TV; CW+; Discovery Channel; Disney Channel; E! Entertainment Television; ESPN; ESPN 2; Eternal Word TV Network; Fox News Channel; Fox Sports Net North; FX; Hallmark Channel; Headline News; History Channel; INSP; ION Television; Lifetime; Local Cable Weather; MTV; National Geographic Channel; NFL Network; Nickelodeon; QVC; RFD-TV; Spike TV; TBS Superstation; The Learning Channel; The Weather Channel; Travel Channel; Trinity Broadcasting Network; Turner Network TV; TV Land; USA Network; VH1; WGN America.

Fee: $57.00 installation; $30.95 monthly.

Digital Basic Service

Subscribers: N.A.

Programming (via satellite): A&E Networks; ABC Family Channel; AMC; Animal Planet; Bio; Bravo; Cartoon Network; CNBC; CNN; Comedy Central; Country Music TV; Crime & Investigation Network; C-SPAN; C-SPAN 2; CW+; Discovery Channel; Discovery Health Channel; Disney Channel; DIY Network; E! Entertainment Television; ESPN; ESPN 2; ESPN Classic Sports; ESPNews; Eternal Word TV Network; FamilyNet; Food Network; Fox College Sports Atlantic; Fox College Sports Central; Fox College Sports Pacific; Fox Movie Channel; Fox News Channel; Fox Sports Net North; FX; Golf Channel; Great American Country; GSN; Hallmark Channel; Headline News; HGTV; History Channel; History Channel International; INSP; ION Television; Lifetime; Military Channel; MSNBC; MTV; MTV2; NFL Network; Nick Jr.; Nickelodeon; NickToons TV; Outdoor Channel; QVC; RFD-TV; SoapNet; Speed; Spike TV; Syfy; TBS Superstation; TeenNick; The Learning Channel; The Weather Channel; Toon Disney; Travel Channel; Trinity Broadcasting Network; truTV; Turner Classic Movies; Turner Network TV; TV Land; USA Network; Versus; VH1; VH1 Classic; WE tv; WGN America.

Fee: $45.00 monthly.

Digital Pay Service 1

Pay Units: N.A.

Programming (via satellite): Cinemax (multiplexed); Encore (multiplexed); Flix; HBO (multiplexed); Showtime (multiplexed); Starz (multiplexed); The Movie Channel (multiplexed).

Fee: $8.45 monthly (Cinemax or Starz/Encore), $13.95 monthly (HBO or Showtime/TMC/Flix).

Video-On-Demand: No

Internet Service

Operational: No, DSL.

Telephone Service

None

General Manager: Mark Benton. Plant Manager: Fay Jandreau. Marketing Manager: Chad Mutziger. Office Manager: Peg Reinesch.

Ownership: Midstate Communications.

WHITEWOOD—Midcontinent Communications, 1624 Concourse Ct, Rapid City, SD 57703. Phones: 800-888-1300; 605-343-0595. Fax: 605-338-9166. Web Site: http://www.midcocomm.com. ICA: SD0219.

TV Market Ranking: Below 100 (WHITEWOOD). Franchise award date: N.A. Franchise expiration date: N.A. Began: April 1, 1983.

Channel capacity: 41 (not 2-way capable). Channels available but not in use: N.A.

Basic Service

Subscribers: 9.

Programming (received off-air): KBHE-TV (PBS) Rapid City; KCLO-TV (CBS) Rapid City; KCPL-LP Rapid City; KEVN-TV (FOX) Rapid City; KHSD-TV (ABC) Lead; KKRA-LP (ION) Rapid City; KNBN (NBC) Rapid City.

Programming (via satellite): A&E Networks; ABC Family Channel; AMC; Animal Planet; BET Networks; Bravo; Cartoon Network; CNBC; CNN; Comedy Central; Country Music TV; C-SPAN; C-SPAN 2; CW+; Discovery Channel; Discovery Fit & Health; Disney Channel; Disney XD; E! Entertainment Television; ESPN; ESPN 2; Eternal Word TV Network; Food Network; Fox News Channel; Fox Sports Net North; FX; Golf Channel; Great American Country; GSN; Hallmark Channel; Headline News; HGTV; History Channel; Home Shopping Network; INSP; Lifetime; MSNBC; MTV; Nickelodeon; Outdoor Channel; Oxygen; QVC; Root Sports Rocky Mountain; Speed; Spike TV; Syfy; TBS Superstation; The Learning Channel; The Weather Channel; Travel Channel; Trinity Broadcasting Network; truTV; Turner Classic Movies; Turner Network TV; TV Guide Network; TV Land; USA Network; Versus; VH1; WE tv; WGN America.

Fee: $24.95 monthly.

Digital Basic Service

Subscribers: N.A.

Programming (via satellite): 3 Angels Broadcasting Network; A&E HD; ABC Family HD; AmericanLife TV Network; Animal Planet HD; BBC America; Bio; Bloomberg Television; Boomerang; BTN; BTN HD; Canal Sur; CBS Sports Network; Centric; Cine Latino; Cine Mexicano; cloo; CMT Pure Country; CNN en Espanol; CNN HD; Cooking Channel; C-SPAN 2; C-SPAN 3; Current; Discovery Channel HD; Discovery en Espanol; Discovery Fit & Health; Discovery Health Channel; Disney Channel HD; Disney XD; Disney XD en Espanol; DIY Network; ESPN 2 HD; ESPN Classic Sports; ESPN Deportes; ESPN HD; ESPN U; ESPNews; EWTN en Espanol; Food Network HD; Fox Business Channel; Fox College Sports Atlantic; Fox College Sports Central; Fox College Sports Pacific; Fox Deportes; Fox Movie Channel; Fox News HD; Fox Soccer; FSN HD; Fuse; FX HD; G4; Golf Channel; Golf Channel HD; GolTV; Great American Country; GSN; Halogen Network; HD Theater; HGTV HD; History Channel en Espanol; History Channel HD; History Channel International; ID Investigation Discovery; Independent Film Channel; ION Life; JCTV; Lifetime Movie Network; Military Channel; MLB Network; MLB Network HD; MTV Hits; MTV Jams; MTV2; mun2 television; Music Choice; National Geographic Channel; National Geographic Channel HD Network; NFL Network; NFL Network HD; NFL RedZone; NHL Network; Nick Jr.; Nick Too; NickToons TV; Outdoor Channel; Palladia; PBS Kids Sprout; Pentagon Channel; Planet Green; Qubo; ReelzChannel; RFD-TV; Science; Science HD; SoapNet; Speed HD; Spike TV HD; Style Network; Sundance Channel; Syfy HD; TBS in HD; TeenNick; Telemundo; Tennis Channel; The Hub; The Weather Channel HD; TLC HD; Tr3s; Trinity Broadcasting Network; Turner Classic Movies; Turner Network TV HD; TV One; TVE Internacional; TVG Network; Universal HD; USA Network HD; VeneMovies; Versus; Versus HD; WE tv.

Digital Pay Service 1

Pay Units: N.A.

Programming (via satellite): Cinemax (multiplexed); Cinemax HD; Encore (multiplexed); Flix; HBO (multiplexed); HBO HD; Showtime (multiplexed); Showtime HD; Starz (multiplexed); Starz HDTV; The Movie Channel (multiplexed); The Movie Channel HD.

Video-On-Demand: Yes

Pay-Per-View

iN DEMAND (delivered digitally); NBA TV (delivered digitally); MLS Direct Kick (delivered digitally); MLB Extra Innings (delivered digitally); NHL Center Ice (delivered digitally); Hot Choice (delivered digitally); Playboy TV (delivered digitally).

Internet Service

Operational: Yes.

Broadband Service: MidcoNet.

Fee: $35.00 installation; $19.95 monthly.

Telephone Service

Digital: Operational

Fee: $18.00 monthly

Miles of Plant: 6.0 (coaxial); None (fiber optic).

Manager: Jerry Steever. Chief Technician: Dave Gorsuch.

Ownership: Midcontinent Media Inc. (MSO).

WILLOW LAKE—ITC. Formerly served by Clear Lake, SD [SD0047]. This cable system has converted to IPTV, 312 Fourth St W, Clear Lake, SD 57226. Phones: 800-417-8667; 605-874-2181. Fax: 605-874-2014. E-mail: info@itc-web.com. Web Site: http://www.itc-web.com. ICA: SD5060.

Channel capacity: N.A. Channels available but not in use: N.A.

Basic Service

Subscribers: N.A.

Fee: $35.50 monthly.

Expanded Basic Service 1

Subscribers: N.A.

Fee: $46.95 monthly.

Limited Basic Service

Subscribers: N.A.

Fee: $25.50 monthly.

Pay Service 1

Pay Units: N.A.

Fee: $10.95 monthly (Cinemax or Starz!), $11.95 monthly (Showtime), $13.95 monthly (HBO).

Internet Service

Operational: Yes.

Fee: $39.95 monthly.

Telephone Service

Digital: Operational

General Manager: Jerry Heiberger.

WILLOW LAKE—Satellite Cable Services Inc. Now served by CLEAR LAKE, SD [SD0047]. ICA: SD0112.

WILMOT—Formerly served by RCTV. No longer in operation. ICA: SD0089.

WINNER—Golden West Telecommunications, 415 Crown St, PO Box 411, Wall, SD 57790-0411. Phone: 605-279-2161. Fax: 605-279-2727. E-mail: info@goldenwest.com. Web Site: http://www.goldenwest.com. Also serves Colome. ICA: SD0021.

TV Market Ranking: Outside TV Markets (Colome, WINNER). Franchise award date: October 19, 1987. Franchise expiration date: October 19, 2011. Began: November 1, 1968.

Channel capacity: N.A. Channels available but not in use: N.A.

Basic Service

Subscribers: 1,164.

Programming (received off-air): KDLT-TV (NBC) Sioux Falls; KPLO-TV (CBS, MNT) Reliance; KPRY-TV (ABC) Pierre; KTSD-TV (PBS) Pierre; KTTM (FOX) Huron; allband FM.

Programming (via satellite): A&E Networks; ABC Family Channel; AMC; Animal Planet; Cartoon Network; CNBC; CNN; Comedy Central; Country Music TV; C-SPAN; C-SPAN 2; CW+; Discovery Channel; Disney Channel; ESPN; ESPN 2; Eternal Word TV Network; Food Network; Fox News Channel; Fox Sports Net North; FX; Hallmark Channel; Headline News; HGTV; History Channel; INSP; KWGN-TV (CW) Denver; Lifetime; MTV; Nickelodeon; Outdoor Channel; QVC; Speed; Spike TV; Syfy; TBS Superstation; The Learning Channel; The Weather Channel; Trinity Broadcasting Network; truTV; Turner Classic Movies; Turner Network TV; TV Guide Network; TV Land; USA Network; Versus; VH1; WE tv; WGN America.

Fee: $25.00 installation; $36.95 monthly.

Pay Service 1

Pay Units: 77.

Programming (via satellite): Cinemax.

Fee: $10.00 monthly.

Pay Service 2

Pay Units: 181.

Programming (via satellite): HBO.

Fee: $10.00 monthly.

Pay Service 3

Pay Units: 121.

Programming (via satellite): Showtime; The Movie Channel.

Fee: $10.00 monthly.

Video-On-Demand: No

Internet Service

Operational: Yes.

Fee: $22.95-$49.95 monthly.

Telephone Service

None

Miles of Plant: 22.0 (coaxial); None (fiber optic).

General Manager: George Strandell. Chief Technician: Randy Shepard. Marketing Director: Greg Oleson. Cable Television Manager: Rick Reed. Customer Service Manager: Jody Bielmaier.

Ownership: Golden West Cablevision (MSO).

WOLSEY—Santel Communications. Formerly served by Mount Vernon, SD [SD0188]. This cable system has converted to IPTV, 308 S Dumont Ave, PO Box 67, Woonsocket, SD 57385-0067. Phones: 888-978-7777; 605-796-4411. Fax: 605-796-4419. E-mail: info@santel.net. Web Site: http://www.santel.net. ICA: SD5021.

TV Market Ranking: Below 100 (WOLSEY).

Channel capacity: N.A. Channels available but not in use: N.A.

Basic Service

Subscribers: N.A.

Fee: $33.95 monthly.

Expanded Basic Service 1

Subscribers: N.A.

Fee: $43.95 monthly.

Limited Basic Service
Subscribers: N.A.
Fee: $21.95 monthly.
Pay Service 1
Pay Units: N.A.
Fee: $10.95 monthly (Cinemax, Encore/ Starz, HBO, or Showtime).
Internet Service
Operational: Yes.
Fee: $25.00 installation; $24.95 monthly; $10.00 modem lease.
Telephone Service
Analog: Operational
Fee: $16.50 monthly

WOONSOCKET—Santel Communications. Formerly served by Mount Vernon, SD [SD0188]. This cable system has converted to IPTV, 308 S Dumont Ave, PO Box 67, Woonsocket, SD 57385-0067. Phones: 888-978-7777; 605-796-4411. Fax: 605-796-4419. E-mail: info@santel.net. Web Site: http://www.santel.net. ICA: SD5020.
TV Market Ranking: 85 (WOONSOCKET).
Channel capacity: N.A. Channels available but not in use: N.A.
Basic Service
Subscribers: N.A.
Fee: $33.95 monthly.
Expanded Basic Service 1
Subscribers: N.A.
Fee: $43.95 monthly.
Limited Basic Service
Subscribers: N.A.
Fee: $21.95 monthly.
Pay Service 1
Pay Units: N.A.
Fee: $10.95 monthly (Cinemax, Encore/ Starz, HBO, or Showtime).
Internet Service
Operational: Yes.
Fee: $25.00 installation; $24.95 monthly; $10.00 modem lease.
Telephone Service
Analog: Operational
Fee: $14.50 monthly

WOONSOCKET—Santel Communications. This cable system has converted to IPTV. See Mount Vernon, SD [SD5013]. ICA: SD0096.

YALE—Midcontinent Communications, PO Box 5010, Sioux Falls, SD 57117. Phones: 800-456-0564; 605-229-1775. Fax: 605-229-0478. Web Site: http://www.midcocomm.com. ICA: SD0220.
TV Market Ranking: Below 100 (YALE). Franchise award date: N.A. Franchise expiration date: N.A. Began: N.A.
Channel capacity: 23 (2-way capable). Channels available but not in use: N.A.
Basic Service
Subscribers: 30.
Programming (received off-air): KABY-TV (ABC) Aberdeen; KDLV-TV (NBC) Mitchell; KELO-TV (CBS, MNT) Sioux Falls; KESD-TV (PBS) Brookings; KTTM (FOX) Huron.
Programming (via satellite): A&E Networks; AMC; CNN; Discovery Channel; Disney Channel; ESPN; ESPN 2; History Channel; Lifetime; Nickelodeon; Spike TV; TBS Superstation; Turner Network TV; USA Network; VH1; WGN America.
Fee: $26.32 monthly.
Pay Service 1
Pay Units: N.A.
Programming (via satellite): HBO.
Fee: $11.95 monthly.
Internet Service
Operational: No.
Telephone Service
None
Miles of Plant: 2.0 (coaxial); None (fiber optic).
Manager: Doug Bierschbach. Chief Technician: Paul Schmidt.
Ownership: Midcontinent Media Inc. (MSO).

TENNESSEE

Total Systems: **103**
Total Communities Served: **551**
Franchises Not Yet Operating: **0**
Applications Pending: **0**
Communities with Applications: **0**
Number of Basic Subscribers: **1,723,046**
Number of Expanded Basic Subscribers: **613,229**
Number of Pay Units: **353,522**

Top 100 Markets Represented: Memphis (26); Greenville-Spartanburg-Anderson, SC-Asheville, NC (46); Knoxville (71); Chattanooga (78); Huntsville-Decatur, AL (96).

For a list of cable communities in this section, see the Cable Community Index located in the back of Cable Volume 2.
For explanation of terms used in cable system listings, see p. D-11.

ALCOA—Charter Communications, 1774 Henry G Lane St, Maryville, TN 37801. Phone: 865-984-1400. Fax: 865-983-0382. Web Site: http://www.charter.com. Also serves Blount County (portions), Louisville, Maryville & Seymour. ICA: TN0151.

TV Market Ranking: 71 (ALCOA, Blount County (portions), Louisville, Maryville, Seymour). Franchise award date: January 1, 1979. Franchise expiration date: March 10, 2016. Began: January 1, 1979.

Channel capacity: N.A. Channels available but not in use: N.A.

Basic Service
Subscribers: 28,500.
Programming (received off-air): WATE-TV (ABC) Knoxville; WBIR-TV (NBC) Knoxville; WBXX-TV (CW) Crossville; WKOP-TV (PBS) Knoxville; WPXK-TV (ION) Jellico; WTNZ (FOX) Knoxville; WVLR (IND) Tazewell; WVLT-TV (CBS, MNT) Knoxville.
Programming (via satellite): Eternal Word TV Network; WGN America.
Fee: $29.99 installation.

Expanded Basic Service 1
Subscribers: 24,000.
Programming (via satellite): A&E Networks; ABC Family Channel; AMC; Animal Planet; BET Networks; Bravo; Cartoon Network; CNBC; CNN; Comcast/Charter Sports Southeast (CSS); Comedy Central; Country Music TV; C-SPAN; C-SPAN 2; Discovery Channel; Disney Channel; E! Entertainment Television; ESPN; ESPN 2; Food Network; Fox News Channel; Fox Sports South; FX; G4; Golf Channel; GSN; Hallmark Channel; Headline News; HGTV; History Channel; INSP; Lifetime; MSNBC; MTV; National Geographic Channel; Nickelodeon; Oxygen; QVC; SoapNet; Speed; Spike TV; SportSouth; Style Network; Syfy; TBS Superstation; Telemundo; The Learning Channel; The Weather Channel; Toon Disney; Travel Channel; Trinity Broadcasting Network; truTV; Turner Classic Movies; Turner Network TV; TV Guide Network; TV Land; USA Network; Versus; VH1; WE tv.
Fee: $50.99 monthly.

Digital Basic Service
Subscribers: N.A.
Programming (via satellite): BBC America; Bio; Bloomberg Television; CNN International; Cooking Channel; DIY Network; ESPN Classic Sports; ESPN HD; ESPNews; Fox College Sports Atlantic; Fox College Sports Central; Fox College Sports Pacific; Fox Movie Channel; Fox Sports World; Fuel TV; GAS; Great American Country; HD Theater; HDNet; HDNet Movies; History Channel International; Independent Film Channel; Jewelry Television; Lifetime Movie Network; Lifetime Real Women; MTV Networks Digital Suite; Music Choice; NFL Network; Nick Jr.; Nick Too; NickToons TV; Sundance Channel; TV Guide Interactive Inc.

Digital Pay Service 1
Pay Units: N.A.
Programming (via satellite): Cinemax (multiplexed); Encore (multiplexed); Flix; HBO (multiplexed); HBO HD; Showtime (multiplexed); Showtime HD; Starz (multiplexed); The Movie Channel (multiplexed).

Video-On-Demand: Yes

Pay-Per-View
Addressable homes: 3,400.
Special events.

Internet Service
Operational: Yes. Began: April 1, 1999.
Broadband Service: Charter Pipeline.
Fee: $29.99 monthly; $9.95 modem lease; $200.00 modem purchase.

Telephone Service
Digital: Operational
Fee: $29.99 monthly

Miles of Plant: 1,900.0 (coaxial); 243.0 (fiber optic).

Technical Operations Director: Grant Evans. Chief Technician: Mark Haley. Marketing Director: Pat Hollenbeck. Marketing Manager: Angie Lee. Government Relations Director: Nick Pavlis.

Ownership: Charter Communications Inc. (MSO).

ALTAMONT—Charter Communications. Now served by MONTEAGLE, TN [TN0016]. ICA: TN0126.

ASHLAND CITY—Comcast Cable, 660 Mainstream Dr, PO Box 280570, Nashville, TN 37228-0570. Phone: 615-244-7462. Fax: 615-255-6528. Web Site: http://www.comcast.com. Also serves Cheatham County. ICA: TN0052.

TV Market Ranking: 30 (ASHLAND CITY, Cheatham County). Franchise award date: January 1, 1981. Franchise expiration date: N.A. Began: June 1, 1981.

Channel capacity: 36 (not 2-way capable). Channels available but not in use: N.A.

Basic Service
Subscribers: 1,659.
Programming (received off-air): WKRN-TV (ABC) Nashville; WNPT (PBS) Nashville; WSMV-TV (NBC, TMO) Nashville; WTVF (CBS) Nashville; WUXP-TV (MNT) Nashville; WZTV (FOX) Nashville.
Programming (via satellite): ABC Family Channel; AMC; CNN; Country Music TV; Disney Channel; ESPN; Headline News; Lifetime; MTV; Nickelodeon; QVC; TBS Superstation; The Weather Channel; Turner Network TV; USA Network; WGN America.
Fee: $23.65 monthly.

Pay Service 1
Pay Units: 138.
Programming (via satellite): HBO; Showtime; The Movie Channel.
Fee: $10.00 monthly (each).

Video-On-Demand: No

Internet Service
Operational: Yes.
Fee: $42.95-$99.95 monthly.

Telephone Service
None

Miles of plant (coax & fiber combined) included in Nashville

Area Vice President & General Manager: John Gauder. Marketing Director: Martine Mahoney. Marketing Manager: Will Jefferson. Technical Operations Manager: Joe Pell.

Ownership: Comcast Cable Communications Inc. (MSO).

ATHENS—Comcast Cable, 2030 Polymer Dr, PO Box 182249, Chattanooga, TN 37421. Phone: 423-855-3900. Fax: 423-892-5893. Web Site: http://www.comcast.com. Also serves Benton, Delano, Englewood, Etowah, McMinn County (portions), Ocoee, Oldfort, Polk County (portions) & Riceville. ICA: TN0024.

TV Market Ranking: 78 (Benton, McMinn County (portions), Ocoee, Oldfort, Polk County (portions)); Below 100 (ATHENS, Delano, Englewood, Etowah, Riceville, McMinn County (portions), Polk County (portions)). Franchise award date: N.A. Franchise expiration date: N.A. Began: March 1, 1967.

Channel capacity: N.A. Channels available but not in use: N.A.

Basic Service
Subscribers: N.A. Included in Chattanooga
Programming (received off-air): WATE-TV (ABC) Knoxville; WBIR-TV (NBC) Knoxville; WDEF-TV (CBS) Chattanooga; WDSI-TV (FOX, MNT) Chattanooga; WELF-TV (TBN) Dalton; WFLI-TV (CW) Cleveland; WKOP-TV (PBS) Knoxville; WRCB (NBC) Chattanooga; WTCI (PBS) Chattanooga; WTVC (ABC) Chattanooga; WVLT-TV (CBS, MNT) Knoxville; allband FM.
Programming (via satellite): A&E Networks; ABC Family Channel; AMC; Animal Planet; BET Networks; Cartoon Network; CNN; Comcast/Charter Sports Southeast (CSS); Country Music TV; C-SPAN; C-SPAN 2; Discovery Channel; Discovery Health Channel; E! Entertainment Television; ESPN; ESPN 2; Food Network; Fox News Channel; Fox Sports Net; FX; Golf Channel; Hallmark Channel; Headline News; HGTV; History Channel; Home Shopping Network 2; ION Television; Lifetime; MTV; Nickelodeon; QVC; Speed; Spike TV; SportSouth; Syfy; TBS Superstation; The Learning Channel; The Weather Channel; truTV; Turner Network TV; TV Land; USA Network; Versus; VH1; WGN America.
Fee: $53.99 installation; $45.99 monthly.

Digital Basic Service
Subscribers: N.A.
Programming (via satellite): BBC America; C-SPAN 3; Discovery Digital Networks; Disney Channel; DMX Music; Encore Action; ESPNews; Flix; G4; GAS; MTV Networks Digital Suite; National Geographic Channel; Nick Jr.; Nick Too; SoapNet; Sundance Channel; Toon Disney; WAM! America's Kidz Network.
Fee: $14.95 monthly.

Digital Pay Service 1
Pay Units: 1,549.
Programming (via satellite): Cinemax (multiplexed); HBO (multiplexed); Showtime (multiplexed); Starz (multiplexed); The Movie Channel (multiplexed).
Fee: $12.00 monthly (each).

Video-On-Demand: Yes

Pay-Per-View
iN DEMAND (delivered digitally); Hot Choice (delivered digitally); Playboy TV (delivered digitally); Fresh (delivered digitally); Shorteez (delivered digitally); Pleasure (delivered digitally).

Internet Service
Operational: Yes.
Broadband Service: Comcast High Speed Internet.
Fee: $42.95 monthly.

Telephone Service
Digital: Operational

Miles of plant (coax & fiber) included in Chattanooga

Vice President & General Manager: Valerie Gillespie. Technical Operations Director: Tom Bailey. Marketing Director: Mike Kehrer.

Ownership: Comcast Cable Communications Inc. (MSO).

BENTON—Comcast Cablevision of the South. Now served by ATHENS, TN [TN0024]. ICA: TN0127.

BLEDSOE COUNTY (central portions)—Bledsoe Telephone Coop. Formerly served by Pikeville, TN [TN0158]. This cable system has converted to IPTV, 338 Cumberland Ave, PO Box 609, Pikeville, TN 37367-0609. Phone: 423-447-2121. E-mail: bledsoe@bledsoe.net. Web Site: http://www.bledsoe.net. ICA: TN5013.

TV Market Ranking: 78 (BLEDSOE COUNTY (CENTRAL PORTIONS) (portions)); Below 100 (BLEDSOE COUNTY (CENTRAL PORTIONS) (portions)).

Channel capacity: N.A. Channels available but not in use: N.A.

Internet Service
Operational: Yes.
Fee: $19.95 installation; $19.95 monthly.

Telephone Service
Digital: Operational
Fee: $12.95 monthly
General Manager: Greg Anderson.

BOLIVAR—NewWave Communications, 48 S Washington, Brownsville, TN 38012. Phones: 888-863-9928; 731-772-7296. Fax: 731-772-0197. E-mail: info@newwavecom.com. Web Site: http://www.newwavecom.com. Also serves Hardeman County (portions). ICA: TN0051.
TV Market Ranking: Below 100 (BOLIVAR, Hardeman County (portions)). Franchise award date: April 8, 1980. Franchise expiration date: N.A. Began: August 1, 1981.
Channel capacity: N.A. Channels available but not in use: N.A.
Basic Service
Subscribers: 909.
Programming (received off-air): WBBJ-TV (ABC) Jackson; WHBQ-TV (FOX) Memphis; WKNO (PBS) Memphis; WLJT-DT (PBS) Lexington; WLMT (CW) Memphis; WMC-TV (NBC) Memphis; WPTY-TV (ABC) Memphis; WPXX-TV (ION, MNT) Memphis; WREG-TV (CBS) Memphis.
Programming (via satellite): C-SPAN; C-SPAN 2; INSP; QVC; ShopNBC; Trinity Broadcasting Network; WGN America.
Fee: $29.95 installation; $15.95 monthly.
Expanded Basic Service 1
Subscribers: 810.
Programming (via satellite): A&E Networks; ABC Family Channel; AMC; Animal Planet; BET Networks; Bravo; Cartoon Network; CNBC; CNN; Comedy Central; Country Music TV; Discovery Channel; Disney Channel; E! Entertainment Television; ESPN; ESPN 2; ESPN Classic Sports; Food Network; Fox News Channel; Fox Sports South; FX; Golf Channel; Hallmark Channel; Headline News; HGTV; History Channel; Lifetime; MSNBC; MTV; Nickelodeon; Outdoor Channel; SoapNet; Speed; Spike TV; Syfy; TBS Superstation; The Learning Channel; The Weather Channel; Travel Channel; truTV; Turner Network TV; TV Land; USA Network; VH1.
Fee: $42.95 monthly.
Digital Basic Service
Subscribers: 110.
Programming (via satellite): BBC America; Bio; Black Family Channel; Bloomberg Television; cloo; Discovery Digital Networks; DMX Music; ESPNews; Fox Movie Channel; G4; GAS; Great American Country; Halogen Network; History Channel International; Independent Film Channel; Lifetime Movie Network; MTV Networks Digital Suite; Nick Jr.; NickToons TV; Style Network; The Word Network; Toon Disney; Turner Classic Movies; Versus.
Digital Pay Service 1
Pay Units: 264.
Programming (via satellite): Cinemax (multiplexed); Encore (multiplexed); Flix; HBO (multiplexed); Showtime (multiplexed); Starz (multiplexed); The Movie Channel (multiplexed).
Video-On-Demand: No
Pay-Per-View
iN DEMAND (delivered digitally); Hot Choice (delivered digitally); Playboy TV (delivered digitally); Fresh (delivered digitally); Shorteez (delivered digitally).
Internet Service
Operational: Yes.
Subscribers: 362.
Broadband Service: SpeedNet.
Fee: $40.00 installation; $31.99 monthly.
Telephone Service
Digital: Operational
Subscribers: 215.
Fee: $34.99 monthly
Miles of Plant: 72.0 (coaxial); None (fiber optic).
General Manager: Dennis Zeigler. Technical Operations Manager: Charles Elrod.
Ownership: NewWave Communications LLC (MSO).

BRADFORD—NewWave Communications. Now served by DYER, TN [TN0057]. ICA: TN0178.

BRISTOL—Charter Communications. Now served by KINGSPORT, TN [TN0007]. ICA: TN0198.

BROWNSVILLE—NewWave Communications, 48 S Washington, Brownsville, TN 38012. Phones: 888-863-9928; 731-772-7296. Fax: 731-772-0197. E-mail: info@newwavecom.com. Web Site: http://www.newwavecom.com. Also serves Gates, Halls, Haywood County (portions), Henning, Lauderdale County (unincorporated areas) & Ripley. ICA: TN0054.
TV Market Ranking: Below 100 (BROWNSVILLE, Haywood County (portions)); Outside TV Markets (Gates, Halls, Henning, Lauderdale County (unincorporated areas), Ripley). Franchise award date: N.A. Franchise expiration date: N.A. Began: March 1, 1981.
Channel capacity: N.A. Channels available but not in use: N.A.
Basic Service
Subscribers: 3,630.
Programming (received off-air): WBBJ-TV (ABC) Jackson; WDYR-CD Dyersburg; WHBQ-TV (FOX) Memphis; WKNO (PBS) Memphis; WLMT (CW) Memphis; WMC-TV (NBC) Memphis; WPTY-TV (ABC) Memphis; WPXX-TV (ION, MNT) Memphis; WREG-TV (CBS) Memphis.
Programming (via satellite): C-SPAN; C-SPAN 2; INSP; QVC; ShopNBC; Trinity Broadcasting Network; WGN America.
Fee: $29.95 monthly.
Expanded Basic Service 1
Subscribers: 3,368.
Programming (via satellite): A&E Networks; ABC Family Channel; AMC; Animal Planet; BET Networks; Bravo; Cartoon Network; CNBC; CNN; Comedy Central; Country Music TV; Discovery Channel; Disney Channel; E! Entertainment Television; ESPN; ESPN 2; ESPN Classic Sports; Food Network; Fox News Channel; Fox Sports South; FX; Golf Channel; GSN; Hallmark Channel; Headline News; HGTV; History Channel; Lifetime; MSNBC; MTV; Nickelodeon; Outdoor Channel; SoapNet; Speed; Spike TV; Syfy; TBS Superstation; The Learning Channel; The Weather Channel; Travel Channel; truTV; Turner Network TV; TV Land; USA Network; VH1.
Fee: $54.99 monthly.
Digital Basic Service
Subscribers: 745.
Programming (via satellite): BBC America; Bio; Black Family Channel; Bloomberg Television; cloo; Discovery Digital Networks; DMX Music; ESPNews; Fox Movie Channel; G4; GAS; Great American Country; Halogen Network; History Channel International; Independent Film Channel; Lifetime Movie Network; MTV Networks Digital Suite; Nick Jr.; NickToons TV; Style Network; The Word Network; Toon Disney; Turner Classic Movies; Versus.
Digital Pay Service 1
Pay Units: 1,411.
Programming (via satellite): Cinemax (multiplexed); Encore (multiplexed); Flix; HBO (multiplexed); Showtime (multiplexed); Starz (multiplexed); The Movie Channel (multiplexed).
Video-On-Demand: No
Pay-Per-View
Hot Choice (delivered digitally); Playboy TV (delivered digitally); Fresh (delivered digitally); Shorteez (delivered digitally); iN DEMAND (delivered digitally).
Internet Service
Operational: Yes.
Subscribers: 1,455.
Broadband Service: SpeedNet.
Fee: $40.00 installation; $31.99 monthly.
Telephone Service
Digital: Operational
Subscribers: 971.
Fee: $34.99 monthly
Miles of Plant: 264.0 (coaxial); None (fiber optic).
General Manager: Dennis Zeigler. Technical Operations Manager: Charles Elrod.
Ownership: NewWave Communications LLC (MSO).

BYRDSTOWN—Celina Cable, 17525 Highland Dr, McKenzie, TN 38201. Phone: 731-352-2980. Fax: 731-352-3533. Also serves Pickett County. ICA: TN0109.
TV Market Ranking: Below 100 (Pickett County (portions)); Outside TV Markets (BYRDSTOWN, Pickett County (portions)). Franchise award date: N.A. Franchise expiration date: January 1, 2007. Began: January 1, 1968.
Channel capacity: 36 (not 2-way capable). Channels available but not in use: N.A.
Basic Service
Subscribers: 322.
Programming (received off-air): WBKO (ABC, CW) Bowling Green; WCTE (PBS) Cookeville; WKRN-TV (ABC) Nashville; WNPT (PBS) Nashville; WSMV-TV (NBC, TMO) Nashville; WTVF (CBS) Nashville; WZTV (FOX) Nashville.
Programming (via satellite): A&E Networks; ABC Family Channel; CNBC; CNN; Country Music TV; C-SPAN; C-SPAN 2; Discovery Channel; Disney Channel; ESPN; Headline News; HGTV; Lifetime; Nickelodeon; Outdoor Channel; QVC; Spike TV; TBS Superstation; The Weather Channel; Turner Network TV; USA Network; WGN America.
Fee: $32.95 installation; $35.00 monthly.
Pay Service 1
Pay Units: 10.
Programming (via satellite): Cinemax.
Fee: $10.95 monthly.
Pay Service 2
Pay Units: N.A.
Programming (via satellite): Encore; Starz.
Fee: $8.95 monthly.
Pay Service 3
Pay Units: 17.
Programming (via satellite): HBO.
Fee: $12.95 monthly.
Internet Service
Operational: Yes.
Telephone Service
None
Miles of Plant: 25.0 (coaxial); None (fiber optic).
General Manager: Gary Blount.
Ownership: Celina Cable Communications (MSO).

CALHOUN—Charter Communications. Now served by CLEVELAND, TN [TN0013]. ICA: TN0129.

CARTHAGE—Comcast Cable. Now served by NASHVILLE, TN [TN0002]. ICA: TN0131.

CARTWRIGHT—Bledsoe Telephone Coop. Formerly served by Dunlap, TN [TN0040]. This cable system has converted to IPTV, 338 Cumberland Ave, PO Box 609, Pikeville, TN 37367-0609. Phone: 423-447-2121. E-mail: bledsoe@bledsoe.net. Web Site: http://www.bledsoe.net. ICA: TN5014.
TV Market Ranking: 78 (CARTWRIGHT).
Channel capacity: N.A. Channels available but not in use: N.A.
Internet Service
Operational: Yes.
Fee: $19.95 installation; $19.95 monthly.
Telephone Service
Digital: Operational
Fee: $12.95 monthly
General Manager: Greg Anderson.

CELINA—Celina Cable, 17525 Highland Dr, McKenzie, TN 38201. Phone: 731-352-2980. Fax: 731-352-3533. Also serves Clay County (unincorporated areas). ICA: TN0096.
TV Market Ranking: Below 100 (CELINA); Outside TV Markets (Clay County (unincorporated areas)). Franchise award date: N.A. Franchise expiration date: N.A. Began: July 1, 1988.
Channel capacity: 36 (not 2-way capable). Channels available but not in use: N.A.
Basic Service
Subscribers: N.A.
Programming (received off-air): WBKO (ABC, CW) Bowling Green; WCTE (PBS) Cookeville; WKRN-TV (ABC) Nashville; WNPX-TV (ION) Cookeville; WSMV-TV (NBC, TMO) Nashville; WTVF (CBS) Nashville; WZTV (FOX) Nashville.
Programming (via satellite): A&E Networks; ABC Family Channel; Comedy Central; C-SPAN; Lifetime; Nickelodeon; QVC.
Fee: $30.25 installation; $17.25 monthly.
Expanded Basic Service 1
Subscribers: N.A.
Programming (received off-air): WNAB (CW) Nashville.
Programming (via satellite): AMC; Animal Planet; Boomerang; Cartoon Network; CNBC; CNN; Country Music TV; Discovery Channel; Disney Channel; ESPN; ESPN 2; Fox News Channel; FX; G4; Headline News; HGTV; History Channel; MTV; Outdoor Channel; Syfy; TBS Superstation; The Learning Channel; The Weather Channel; Travel Channel; Trinity Broadcasting Network; Turner Network TV; TV Land; USA Network; VH1; WGN America.
Fee: $33.75 monthly.
Pay Service 1
Pay Units: N.A.
Programming (via satellite): Cinemax; HBO; The Movie Channel.
Fee: $11.18 monthly (each).
Video-On-Demand: No
Internet Service
Operational: Yes.
Telephone Service
None
Miles of Plant: 35.0 (coaxial); None (fiber optic).
General Manager: Gary Blount.
Ownership: Celina Cable Communications (MSO).

CENTERVILLE—Charter Communications, 1774 Henry G Lane St, Maryville, TN 37801. Phone: 865-984-1400. Fax: 865-983-0383. Web Site: http://www.charter.com. ICA: TN0204.

TV Market Ranking: Outside TV Markets (CENTERVILLE).
Channel capacity: N.A. Channels available but not in use: N.A.

Basic Service
Subscribers: N.A.
Programming (received off-air): WHTN (IND) Murfreesboro; WKRN-TV (ABC) Nashville; WNPT (PBS) Nashville; WNPX-TV (ION) Cookeville; WSMV-TV (NBC, TMO) Nashville; WTVF (CBS) Nashville; WUXP-TV (MNT) Nashville; WZTV (FOX) Nashville.
Programming (via satellite): Comcast/Charter Sports Southeast (CSS); C-SPAN; C-SPAN 2; Eternal Word TV Network; INSP; QVC; Trinity Broadcasting Network; TV Guide Network; WGN America; WNAB (CW) Nashville.

Expanded Basic Service 1
Subscribers: N.A.
Programming (via satellite): A&E Networks; ABC Family Channel; AMC; Animal Planet; BET Networks; Bravo; Cartoon Network; CNBC; CNN; Comedy Central; Country Music TV; Discovery Channel; Discovery Fit & Health; Disney Channel; E! Entertainment Television; ESPN; ESPN 2; Food Network; Fox News Channel; Fox Sports South; FX; G4; GalaVision; Golf Channel; GSN; Hallmark Channel; Headline News; HGTV; History Channel; Lifetime; MSNBC; MTV; National Geographic Channel; Nickelodeon; Oxygen; SoapNet; Speed; Spike TV; SportSouth; Syfy; TBS Superstation; Telemundo; The Learning Channel; The Weather Channel; Toon Disney; Travel Channel; truTV; Turner Classic Movies; Turner Network TV; TV Land; Univision Studios; USA Network; Versus; VH1; WE tv.

Digital Basic Service
Subscribers: N.A.
Programming (via satellite): BBC America; Bio; Bloomberg News Radio; Boomerang; CNN International; Discovery Health Channel; Discovery Home Channel; Discovery Kids Channel; Discovery Times Channel; DIY Network; DMX Music; ESPN Classic Sports; ESPNews; Fox College Sports Atlantic; Fox College Sports Pacific; Fox Soccer; Fuel TV; GAS; Great American Country; History Channel International; Independent Film Channel; Lifetime Movie Network; Lifetime Real Women; MTV Networks Digital Suite; NFL Network; Nick Jr.; Nick Too; NickToons TV; Outdoor Channel; Science; Sundance Channel.

Pay Service 1
Pay Units: N.A.
Programming (via satellite): Encore (multiplexed); Flix; Showtime (multiplexed); The Movie Channel (multiplexed).

Digital Pay Service 1
Pay Units: N.A.
Programming (via satellite): Cinemax (multiplexed); HBO (multiplexed); Starz (multiplexed).

Video-On-Demand: No

Pay-Per-View
Playboy TV (delivered digitally); Fresh (delivered digitally); Shorteez (delivered digitally).

Internet Service
Operational: No.

Telephone Service
None

Operations Manager: Sean Hendrix. Marketing Director: Pat Hollenbeck. Sales & Marketing Manager: Jo Ann Placke.
Ownership: Charter Communications Inc. (MSO).

CHAPEL HILL—Small Town Cable, PO Box 99, College Grove, TN 37046. Phones: 615-368-2115; 931-484-7994. Fax: 615-368-2295. Also serves Bedford County (unincorporated areas), Cornersville, Eagleville, Unionville & Williamson County (unincorporated areas). ICA: TN0089.
TV Market Ranking: 30 (Eagleville); Below 100 (Bedford County (unincorporated areas), CHAPEL HILL, Unionville, Williamson County (unincorporated areas)); Outside TV Markets (Cornersville). Franchise award date: April 11, 1985. Franchise expiration date: N.A. Began: April 1, 1985.
Channel capacity: N.A. Channels available but not in use: N.A.

Basic Service
Subscribers: 2,200.
Programming (received off-air): WHTN (IND) Murfreesboro; WKRN-TV (ABC) Nashville; WNPT (PBS) Nashville; WSMV-TV (NBC, TMO) Nashville; WTVF (CBS) Nashville; WUXP-TV (MNT) Nashville; WZTV (FOX) Nashville.
Programming (via satellite): TBS Superstation; WGN America.
Fee: $40.00 installation; $10.95 monthly.

Expanded Basic Service 1
Subscribers: 806.
Programming (via satellite): ABC Family Channel; AMC; Cartoon Network; CNN; Country Music TV; Discovery Channel; Disney Channel; ESPN; ESPN 2; History Channel; Lifetime; MTV; Nickelodeon; Spike TV; The Weather Channel; Turner Network TV; USA Network.
Fee: $39.10 monthly.

Digital Basic Service
Subscribers: 500.

Pay Service 1
Pay Units: N.A.
Programming (via satellite): Cinemax; Showtime.
Fee: $10.95 monthly (Cinemax), $12.95 monthly (Showtime).

Pay Service 2
Pay Units: 230.
Programming (via satellite): HBO.
Fee: $12.95 monthly.

Video-On-Demand: No

Internet Service
Operational: Yes.
Subscribers: 500.

Telephone Service
None

Miles of Plant: 240.0 (coaxial); 80.0 (fiber optic). Miles of plant include Lynnville, Minor Hill, Rogersville, & Summertown
General Manager: Vince King. Chief Technician: Brian Langham.
Ownership: Small Town Cable Corp. (MSO).

CHATTANOOGA—Comcast Cable, 2030 Polymer Dr, Chattanooga, TN 37421. Phone: 423-855-3900. Fax: 423-892-5893. Web Site: http://www.comcast.com. Also serves Dade County (unincorporated areas) & Lookout Mountain, GA; Collegedale, East Ridge, Hamilton County, Lakesite, Lookout Mountain, Marion County (unincorporated areas), Red Bank, Ridgeside, Sequatchie County (unincorporated areas), Signal Mountain, Soddy Daisy & Walden, TN. ICA: TN0003.
TV Market Ranking: 78 (CHATTANOOGA, Collegedale, Dade County (unincorporated areas), East Ridge, Hamilton County, Lakesite, Lookout Mountain (GA), Lookout Mountain (TN), Marion County (unincorporated areas), Red Bank, Ridgeside, Sequatchie County (unincorporated areas) (portions), Signal Mountain, Soddy Daisy, Walden); Outside TV Markets (Sequatchie County (unincorporated areas) (portions)). Franchise award date: October 6, 1970. Franchise expiration date: N.A. Began: May 25, 1977.
Channel capacity: N.A. Channels available but not in use: N.A.

Basic Service
Subscribers: 127,835 Includes Athens, La Fayette & Rossville, GA; Vonore, TN.
Programming (received off-air): WDEF-TV (CBS) Chattanooga; WDSI-TV (FOX, MNT) Chattanooga; WELF-TV (TBN) Dalton; WFLI-TV (CW) Cleveland; WRCB (NBC) Chattanooga; WTCI (PBS) Chattanooga; WTVC (ABC) Chattanooga.
Programming (via microwave): WNGH-TV (PBS) Chatsworth.
Programming (via satellite): A&E Networks; ABC Family Channel; AMC; Animal Planet; BET Networks; Bravo; Cartoon Network; CNBC; CNN; Comcast/Charter Sports Southeast (CSS); Comedy Central; Country Music TV; C-SPAN; C-SPAN 2; Discovery Channel; Discovery Health Channel; E! Entertainment Television; ESPN; ESPN 2; Food Network; Fox News Channel; Fox Sports Net; FX; Golf Channel; GSN; Hallmark Channel; Headline News; HGTV; History Channel; ION Television; Lifetime; MSNBC; MTV; Nickelodeon; QVC; Shop at Home; Speed; Spike TV; SportSouth; Style Network; Syfy; TBS Superstation; The Learning Channel; The Weather Channel; truTV; Turner Classic Movies; Turner Network TV; TV Guide Network; TV Land; USA Network; Versus; VH1; WGN America.
Fee: $53.99 installation; $49.99 monthly; $3.52 converter.

Digital Basic Service
Subscribers: 10,489.
Programming (via satellite): BBC America; Canales N; C-SPAN 3; Discovery Digital Networks; Disney Channel; DMX Music; Encore Action; ESPNews; Flix; G4; GAS; MTV Networks Digital Suite; National Geographic Channel; Nick Jr.; Nick Too; SoapNet; Sundance Channel; Toon Disney; WAM! America's Kidz Network; Weatherscan.
Fee: $14.95 monthly.

Digital Pay Service 1
Pay Units: 4,405.
Programming (via satellite): Cinemax (multiplexed).
Fee: $20.00 installation; $12.00 monthly.

Digital Pay Service 2
Pay Units: 4,175.
Programming (via satellite): Starz (multiplexed).
Fee: $20.00 installation; $12.00 monthly.

Digital Pay Service 3
Pay Units: 20,248.
Programming (via satellite): HBO (multiplexed).
Fee: $20.00 installation; $12.00 monthly.

Digital Pay Service 4
Pay Units: 8,708.
Programming (via satellite): Showtime (multiplexed).
Fee: $20.00 installation; $12.00 monthly.

Digital Pay Service 5
Pay Units: 2,540.
Programming (via satellite): The Movie Channel (multiplexed).
Fee: $12.00 monthly.

Video-On-Demand: Yes

Pay-Per-View
Addressable homes: 10,489.
iN DEMAND (delivered digitally); Hot Choice (delivered digitally); Sports PPV (delivered digitally); Playboy TV (delivered digitally); Fresh (delivered digitally); Shorteez (delivered digitally); Pleasure (delivered digitally); ESPN Gameplan (delivered digitally); ESPN Full Court (delivered digitally).

Internet Service
Operational: Yes.
Subscribers: 2,507.
Broadband Service: Comcast High Speed Internet.
Fee: $42.95 monthly; $7.00 modem lease.

Telephone Service
Digital: Operational

Miles of Plant: 4,537.0 (coaxial); 724.0 (fiber optic). Miles of plant (coax) include Athens, La Fayette & Rossville GA; Vonore, TN
Regional Vice President: Kirk Dale. Vice President & General Manager: Valerie Gillespie. Technical Operations Director: Tom Bailey. Marketing Director: Mike Kehrer.
Ownership: Comcast Cable Communications Inc. (MSO).

CLARKSVILLE—Charter Communications, 1774 Henry G Lane St, Maryville, TN 37801. Phone: 865-984-1400. Fax: 865-983-0383. Web Site: http://www.charter.com. Also serves Ashland City, Coopertown, Cunningham, Montgomery County, Pleasant View & Southside. ICA: TN0009.
TV Market Ranking: 30 (Ashland City, Coopertown, Cunningham, Pleasant View, Southside); Outside TV Markets (CLARKSVILLE, Montgomery County). Franchise award date: January 1, 1978. Franchise expiration date: N.A. Began: October 2, 1978.
Channel capacity: 34 (operating 2-way). Channels available but not in use: N.A.

Basic Service
Subscribers: 26,855.
Programming (received off-air): WCKV-LP (IND) Clarksville; WKAG-CA Hopkinsville; WKRN-TV (ABC) Nashville; WNAB (CW) Nashville; WNPT (PBS) Nashville; WPGD-TV (TBN) Hendersonville; WSMV-TV (NBC, TMO) Nashville; WTVF (CBS) Nashville; WUXP-TV (MNT) Nashville; WZTV (FOX) Nashville; allband FM.
Programming (via satellite): C-SPAN; C-SPAN 2; INSP; QVC; Shop at Home; TV Guide Network; Univision Studios; WGN America.
Fee: $39.95 installation.

Expanded Basic Service 1
Subscribers: 21,400.
Programming (via satellite): A&E Networks; ABC Family Channel; AMC; Animal Planet; BET Networks; Bravo; Cartoon Network; CNBC; CNN; Comcast/Charter Sports Southeast (CSS); Comedy Central; Country Music TV; Discovery Channel; Disney Channel; E! Entertainment Televi-

sion; ESPN; ESPN 2; Food Network; Fox News Channel; Fox Sports South; FX; G4; Golf Channel; Hallmark Channel; Headline News; HGTV; History Channel; Lifetime; MSNBC; MTV; National Geographic Channel; Nickelodeon; Oxygen; SoapNet; Speed; Spike TV; SportSouth; Style Network; Syfy; TBS Superstation; The Learning Channel; The Weather Channel; Toon Disney; Travel Channel; truTV; Turner Classic Movies; Turner Network TV; TV Land; USA Network; Versus; VH1.
Fee: $45.00 monthly.

Digital Basic Service
Subscribers: N.A.
Programming (via satellite): BBC America; Bio; Bloomberg Television; CNN en Espanol; CNN International; DIY Network; ESPN; ESPN Classic Sports; ESPNews; Fox College Sports Atlantic; Fox College Sports Central; Fox College Sports Pacific; Fox Movie Channel; Fox Soccer; Fuel TV; Fuse; GAS; Great American Country; GSN; HD Theater; History Channel International; Independent Film Channel; International Television (ITV); Lifetime Movie Network; Lifetime Real Women; MTV Networks Digital Suite; Music Choice; NFL Network; Nick Jr.; Nick Too; NickToons TV; Sundance Channel; TV Guide Interactive Inc.; WE tv.

Digital Pay Service 1
Pay Units: N.A.
Programming (via satellite): Cinemax (multiplexed); Encore; Flix; HBO (multiplexed); HBO HD; Showtime (multiplexed); Showtime HD; Starz; The Movie Channel (multiplexed).

Video-On-Demand: Yes

Pay-Per-View
iN DEMAND (delivered digitally); NASCAR In Car (delivered digitally); NHL Center Ice (delivered digitally); MLB Extra Innings (delivered digitally); Playboy TV (delivered digitally); Fresh (delivered digitally); Shorteez (delivered digitally).

Internet Service
Operational: Yes. Began: January 1, 2001.
Broadband Service: Charter Pipeline.
Fee: $29.99 monthly; $9.95 modem lease.

Telephone Service
Digital: Operational

Miles of Plant: 57.0 (coaxial); None (fiber optic). Additional miles planned: 50.0 (coaxial).
Operations Manager: Tony Fox. Technical Operations Director: Ron Janson. Marketing Director: Pat Hollenbeck. Marketing Manager: Wiley Bird.
Ownership: Charter Communications Inc. (MSO).

CLARKSVILLE—Formerly served by Virginia Communications Inc. No longer in operation. ICA: TN0182.

CLEVELAND—Charter Communications, 1235 King St SE, Cleveland, TN 37323. Phones: 423-478-1934; 865-984-1400 (Maryville office). Fax: 423-476-1621. Web Site: http://www.charter.com. Also serves Bradley County, Calhoun, Charleston, Dayton, Decatur, Graysville, McDonald & McMinn County. ICA: TN0013.
TV Market Ranking: 78 (Bradley County, Calhoun, Charleston, CLEVELAND, Dayton, Graysville, McDonald, McMinn County); Below 100 (Decatur). Franchise award date: N.A. Franchise expiration date: N.A. Began: October 1, 1976.
Channel capacity: N.A. Channels available but not in use: N.A.

Basic Service
Subscribers: 17,149.
Programming (received off-air): WDEF-TV (CBS) Chattanooga; WDSI-TV (FOX, MNT) Chattanooga; WELF-TV (TBN) Dalton; WFLI-TV (CW) Cleveland; WNGH-TV (PBS) Chatsworth; WRCB (NBC) Chattanooga; WTCI (PBS) Chattanooga; WTNB-CA Cleveland; WTVC (ABC) Chattanooga; 14 FMs.
Programming (via satellite): C-SPAN; C-SPAN 2; Eternal Word TV Network; INSP; ION Television; QVC; Shop at Home; Univision Studios; WGN America.
Fee: $29.99 installation.

Expanded Basic Service 1
Subscribers: 11,314.
Programming (via satellite): A&E Networks; ABC Family Channel; AMC; Animal Planet; BET Networks; Bravo; Cartoon Network; CNBC; CNN; Comcast/Charter Sports Southeast (CSS); Comedy Central; Country Music TV; Discovery Channel; Disney Channel; E! Entertainment Television; ESPN; Food Network; Fox News Channel; Fox Sports South; FX; G4; GalaVision; Golf Channel; GSN; Hallmark Channel; Headline News; HGTV; History Channel; Lifetime; MSNBC; MTV; National Geographic Channel; Nickelodeon; Oxygen; SoapNet; Speed; Spike TV; SportSouth; Syfy; TBS Superstation; Telemundo; The Learning Channel; The Weather Channel; Toon Disney; Travel Channel; truTV; Turner Classic Movies; Turner Network TV; TV Guide Network; TV Land; USA Network; Versus; VH1; WE tv.
Fee: $50.99 monthly.

Digital Basic Service
Subscribers: N.A.
Programming (via satellite): BBC America; Bio; Canales N; Discovery Digital Networks; DIY Network; ESPN Classic Sports; ESPNews; Fox College Sports Atlantic; Fox College Sports Central; Fox College Sports Pacific; Fox Movie Channel; Fox Soccer; Fuel TV; GAS; Great American Country; History Channel International; Independent Film Channel; Jewelry Television; Lifetime Movie Network; Lifetime Real Women; MTV2; Music Choice; NFL Network; Nick Jr.; Nick Too; NickToons TV; Sundance Channel; TV Guide Interactive Inc.; VH1 Classic.

Digital Pay Service 1
Pay Units: 3,019.
Programming (via satellite): Encore (multiplexed); Flix; HBO (multiplexed); Showtime (multiplexed); Starz (multiplexed); The Movie Channel (multiplexed).
Fee: $15.00 installation; $10.95 monthly (each).

Video-On-Demand: Yes

Pay-Per-View
Addressable homes: 13,900.
iN DEMAND (delivered digitally); Playboy TV (delivered digitally); Fresh (delivered digitally); Shorteez (delivered digitally); NASCAR In Car (delivered digitally); NHL Center Ice (delivered digitally); MLB Extra Innings (delivered digitally).

Internet Service
Operational: Yes.
Broadband Service: Charter Pipeline.
Fee: $29.99 monthly.

Telephone Service
Digital: Operational
Fee: $29.99 monthly

Miles of Plant: 500.0 (coaxial); None (fiber optic).
Operations Manager: Mike Burns. Technical Operations Director: Grant Evans. Technical Operations Manager: David Ogle. Marketing Director: Pat Hollenbeck. Office Manager: Connie Wilson.
Ownership: Charter Communications Inc. (MSO).

CLIFTON—Charter Communications, 1774 Henry G Lane St, Maryville, TN 37801. Phone: 865-984-1400. Fax: 865-983-0383. Web Site: http://www.charter.com. ICA: TN0120.
TV Market Ranking: Outside TV Markets (CLIFTON). Franchise award date: N.A. Franchise expiration date: N.A. Began: N.A.
Channel capacity: 42 (not 2-way capable). Channels available but not in use: N.A.

Basic Service
Subscribers: 267.
Programming (received off-air): WBBJ-TV (ABC) Jackson; WHDF (CW) Florence; WJKT (FOX) Jackson; WKRN-TV (ABC) Nashville; WLJT-DT (PBS) Lexington; WSMV-TV (NBC, TMO) Nashville; WTVF (CBS) Nashville.

Expanded Basic Service 1
Subscribers: 231.
Programming (via satellite): A&E Networks; AMC; Animal Planet; CNN; Country Music TV; C-SPAN; Discovery Channel; Disney Channel; ESPN; ESPN 2; Hallmark Channel; Headline News; History Channel; Lifetime; Spike TV; TBS Superstation; The Weather Channel; Travel Channel; truTV; Turner Network TV; USA Network.
Fee: $45.00 monthly.

Video-On-Demand: No

Internet Service
Operational: No.

Telephone Service
None

Miles of Plant: 15.0 (coaxial); None (fiber optic).
Operations Manager: Tony Fox. Technical Operations Manager: Ron Janson. Marketing Director: Pat Hollenbeck. Marketing Manager: Wiley Bird.
Ownership: Charter Communications Inc. (MSO).

COBBLY NOB—Comcast Cable. Now served by WALDEN CREEK, TN [TN0031]. ICA: TN0193.

COLUMBIA—Charter Communications, 1774 Henry G Lane St, Maryville, TN 37801. Phone: 865-984-1400. Fax: 865-983-0383. Web Site: http://www.charter.com. Also serves College Grove, Giles County (portions), Hohenwald, Lewis County (portions), Maury County (portions), Mount Pleasant, Pulaski, Spring Hill, Thompson's Station & Williamson County (portions). ICA: TN0017.
TV Market Ranking: 30 (Maury County (portions), Spring Hill, Thompson's Station, Williamson County (portions)); 96 (College Grove, Giles County (portions), Pulaski); Below 100 (Maury County (portions)); Outside TV Markets (COLUMBIA, Hohenwald, Lewis County (portions), Mount Pleasant, Maury County (portions)). Franchise award date: N.A. Franchise expiration date: N.A. Began: October 15, 1967.
Channel capacity: N.A. Channels available but not in use: N.A.

Basic Service
Subscribers: 34,645.
Programming (received off-air): WHTN (IND) Murfreesboro; WKRN-TV (ABC) Nashville; WNPT (PBS) Nashville; WNPX-TV (ION) Cookeville; WSMV-TV (NBC, TMO) Nashville; WTVF (CBS) Nashville; WUXP-TV (MNT) Nashville; WZTV (FOX) Nashville.
Programming (via satellite): Comcast/Charter Sports Southeast (CSS); C-SPAN; C-SPAN 2; Eternal Word TV Network; INSP; QVC; Trinity Broadcasting Network; TV Guide Network; WGN America; WNAB (CW) Nashville.
Fee: $34.32 installation.

Expanded Basic Service 1
Subscribers: N.A.
Programming (via satellite): A&E Networks; ABC Family Channel; AMC; Animal Planet; BET Networks; Bravo!; Cartoon Network; CNBC; CNN; Comedy Central; Country Music TV; Discovery Channel; Discovery Fit & Health; Disney Channel; E! Entertainment Television; ESPN; ESPN 2; Food Network; Fox News Channel; Fox Sports South; FX; G4; GalaVision; Golf Channel; GSN; Hallmark Channel; Headline News; HGTV; History Channel; Lifetime; MSNBC; MTV; National Geographic Channel; Nickelodeon; Oxygen; SoapNet; Speed; Spike TV; SportSouth; Syfy; TBS Superstation; Telemundo; The Learning Channel; The Weather Channel; Toon Disney; Travel Channel; truTV; Turner Classic Movies; Turner Network TV; TV Land; Univision Studios; USA Network; Versus; VH1; WE tv.
Fee: $45.00 monthly.

Digital Basic Service
Subscribers: N.A.
Programming (via satellite): BBC America; Bio; Bloomberg News Radio; Boomerang; CNN International; Discovery Health Channel; Discovery Home Channel; Discovery Kids Channel; Discovery Times Channel; DIY Network; DMX Music; ESPN Classic Sports; ESPNews; Fox College Sports Atlantic; Fox College Sports Central; Fox College Sports Pacific; Fox Soccer; Fuel TV; GAS; Great American Country; History Channel International; Independent Film Channel; Lifetime Movie Network; Lifetime Real Women; MTV Networks Digital Suite; NFL Network; Nick Jr.; Nick Too; NickToons TV; Outdoor Channel; Science Television; Sundance Channel.

Digital Pay Service 1
Pay Units: N.A.
Programming (via satellite): Cinemax (multiplexed); HBO (multiplexed); Starz (multiplexed).

Video-On-Demand: Yes

Pay-Per-View
Playboy TV (delivered digitally); Fresh (delivered digitally); Shorteez (delivered digitally).

Internet Service
Operational: Yes.
Broadband Service: Charter Pipeline.
Fee: $29.99 monthly.

Telephone Service
Digital: Operational
Fee: $29.99 monthly

Miles of Plant: 1,592.0 (coaxial); 100.0 (fiber optic). Additional miles planned: 7.0 (coaxial).
Operations Manager: Sean Hendrix. Marketing Director: Pat Hollenbeck. Sales & Marketing Manager: Jo Ann Placke.
Ownership: Charter Communications Inc. (MSO).

COLUMBIA—CPWS Broadband, 201 Pickens Lane, PO Box 379, Columbia, TN 38401. Phone: 931-388-4833. Fax: 931-388-5287. E-mail: johnna.watson@cpws.com. Web Site: http://www.cpws.com. ICA: TN0191. **Note:** This system is an overbuild.

TV Market Ranking: Outside TV Markets (COLUMBIA).

Channel capacity: N.A. Channels available but not in use: N.A.

Basic Service

Subscribers: 5,566.

Programming (received off-air): WHTN (IND) Murfreesboro; WKRN-TV (ABC) Nashville; WNAB (CW) Nashville; WNPT (PBS) Nashville; WSMV-TV (NBC, TMO) Nashville; WTVF (CBS) Nashville; WUXP-TV (MNT) Nashville; WZTV (FOX) Nashville.

Programming (via satellite): America One Television; INSP; QVC; TBS Superstation; The Weather Channel; Trinity Broadcasting Network; TV Guide Network; WGN America.

Fee: $21.00 monthly.

Expanded Basic Service 1

Subscribers: 4,852.

Programming (via satellite): A&E Networks; ABC Family Channel; AMC; Animal Planet; BET Networks; Bravo; Cartoon Network; CNBC; CNN; Comcast/Charter Sports Southeast (CSS); Comedy Central; Country Music TV; C-SPAN; C-SPAN 2; Discovery Channel; Disney Channel; E! Entertainment Television; ESPN; ESPN 2; ESPN Classic Sports; Eternal Word TV Network; Food Network; Fox News Channel; Fox Sports South; FX; G4; Golf Channel; Great American Country; GSN; Hallmark Channel; Headline News; HGTV; History Channel; ION Television; Lifetime; MSNBC; MTV; National Geographic Channel; Nickelodeon; Outdoor Channel; Oxygen; RFD-TV; SoapNet; Speed; Spike TV; SportSouth; Syfy; The Learning Channel; Toon Disney; Travel Channel; truTV; Turner Classic Movies; Turner Network TV; TV Land; Univision Studios; USA Network; Versus; VH1; WE tv; World Harvest Television.

Fee: $34.00 monthly.

Digital Basic Service

Subscribers: 570.

Programming (via satellite): 3 Angels Broadcasting Network; AmericanLife TV Network; BBC America; Bio; Bloomberg Television; Boomerang; CMT Pure Country; CNN International; Cooking Channel; Discovery Health Channel; Discovery Home Channel; Discovery Kids Channel; DIY Network; ESPNews; FamilyNet; Fox College Sports Atlantic; Fox College Sports Central; Fox College Sports Pacific; Fox Movie Channel; Fox Soccer; Fuse; History Channel International; ID Investigation Discovery; Independent Film Channel; JCTV; Lifetime Movie Network; Military Channel; MTV Jams; MTV2; Music Choice; Nick Jr.; NickToons TV; Science; Style Network; TeenNick; VH1 Classic; VH1 Soul; WAM! America's Kidz Network.

Fee: $4.00 monthly.

Digital Expanded Basic Service

Subscribers: N.A.

Programming (received off-air): WKRN-TV (ABC) Nashville; WSMV-TV (NBC, TMO) Nashville; WTVF (CBS) Nashville; WZTV (FOX) Nashville.

Programming (via satellite): A&E HD; Animal Planet HD; Cine Mexicano; CNN en Espanol; Discovery Channel HD; Discovery en Espanol; Discovery Familia; ESPN Deportes; ESPN HD; EWTN en Espanol; Food Network HD; Fox Deportes; HD Theater; HGTV HD; History Channel HD; La Familia Network; Latele Novela Network; mun2 television; Outdoor Channel 2 HD; Science HD; Sorpresa; TBN Enlace USA; TLC HD; Toon Disney en Espanol; Tr3s; Turner Network TV HD; TV Chile; TV Colombia; Universal HD; Video Rola.

Fee: $6.25 monthly (Canales), $12.95 monthly (HD Pak).

Pay Service 1

Pay Units: N.A.

Programming (via satellite): HBO (multiplexed).

Fee: $12.80 monthly.

Digital Pay Service 1

Pay Units: N.A.

Programming (via satellite): Cinemax (multiplexed); Cinemax HD; Encore (multiplexed); Flix; HBO (multiplexed); HBO HD; Showtime (multiplexed); Showtime HD; Starz (multiplexed); Starz HDTV; Sundance Channel; The Movie Channel (multiplexed); The Movie Channel HD.

Fee: $13.75 monthly (Cinemax), $15.85 monthly (Starz/Encore), $16.75 monthly (HBO), $17.76 monthly (Showtime/TMC).

Video-On-Demand: No

Pay-Per-View

sports (delivered digitally); iN DEMAND (delivered digitally).

Internet Service

Operational: Yes.

Broadband Service: XpressNet.

Fee: $29.95 monthly.

Telephone Service

None

General Manager: John Cobb. Chief Technician: Marty Helms. Marketing Director: Johnna Watson. Broadband Manager: Glenn Jerrigan.

Ownership: Columbia Power & Water Systems.

COOKEVILLE—Charter Communications, 1774 Henry G Lane St, Maryville, TN 37801. Phone: 865-984-1400. Fax: 865-983-0383. Web Site: http://www.charter.com. Also serves Algood, Baxter, Doyle, Monterey, Putnam County (portions), Sparta & White County (portions). ICA: TN0020.

TV Market Ranking: Below 100 (Algood, Baxter, COOKEVILLE, Doyle, Monterey, Putnam County (portions), Sparta, White County (portions)). Franchise award date: N.A. Franchise expiration date: N.A. Began: January 1, 1968.

Channel capacity: N.A. Channels available but not in use: N.A.

Basic Service

Subscribers: 19,380.

Programming (received off-air): WCTE (PBS) Cookeville; WKRN-TV (ABC) Nashville; WNAB (CW) Nashville; WNPT (PBS) Nashville; WNPX-TV (ION) Cookeville; WSMV-TV (NBC, TMO) Nashville; WTVF (CBS) Nashville; WUXP-TV (MNT) Nashville; WZTV (FOX) Nashville.

Programming (via satellite): ABC Family Channel; Comcast/Charter Sports Southeast (CSS); C-SPAN; C-SPAN 2; Eternal Word TV Network; INSP; QVC; Trinity Broadcasting Network; TV Guide Network; WGN America.

Expanded Basic Service 1

Subscribers: 11,700.

Programming (via satellite): A&E Networks; AMC; Animal Planet; BET Networks; Bravo; Cartoon Network; CNBC; CNN; Comedy Central; Country Music TV; Discovery Channel; Discovery Fit & Health; Disney Channel; E! Entertainment Television; ESPN; ESPN 2; Food Network; Fox News Channel; Fox Sports South; FX; G4; GalaVision; Golf Channel; GSN; Hallmark Channel; Headline News; HGTV; History Channel; Lifetime; MSNBC; MTV; National Geographic Channel; Nickelodeon; Oxygen; SoapNet; Speed; Spike TV; SportSouth; Syfy; TBS Superstation; Telemundo; The Learning Channel; The Weather Channel; Toon Disney; Travel Channel; truTV; Turner Classic Movies; Turner Network TV; TV Land; Univision Studios; USA Network; Versus; VH1; WE tv.

Fee: $45.00 monthly.

Digital Basic Service

Subscribers: N.A.

Programming (via satellite): BBC America; Bio; Bloomberg Television; Boomerang; CNN International; Discovery Digital Networks; DIY Network; DMX Music; ESPN Classic Sports; ESPNews; Fox College Sports Atlantic; Fox College Sports Central; Fox College Sports Pacific; Fox Movie Channel; Fox Soccer; Fuel TV; GAS; Great American Country; History Channel International; Independent Film Channel; Lifetime Movie Network; Lifetime Real Women; MTV Networks Digital Suite; NFL Network; Nick Jr.; Nick Too; NickToons TV; Outdoor Channel; Science Television; Style Network; Sundance Channel.

Digital Pay Service 1

Pay Units: N.A.

Programming (via satellite): Cinemax; HBO; Starz (multiplexed).

Video-On-Demand: No

Pay-Per-View

Playboy TV (delivered digitally); Fresh (delivered digitally); Shorteez (delivered digitally).

Internet Service

Operational: Yes.

Broadband Service: Charter Pipeline.

Fee: $29.99 monthly; $5.00 modem lease.

Telephone Service

Digital: Operational

Fee: $29.99 monthly

Miles of Plant: 585.0 (coaxial); None (fiber optic).

Operations Director: Sean Hendrix. Marketing Director: Pat Hollenbeck. Sales & Marketing Manager: Jo Ann Placke.

Ownership: Charter Communications Inc. (MSO).

CORNERSVILLE—Small Town Cable. Now served by CHAPEL HILL, TN [TN0089]. ICA: TN0133.

COUNCE—Pickwick Cablevision, 1845 Old SR 57, Counce, TN 38326. Phone: 731-689-5722. Fax: 731-689-3632. Web Site: http://www.pickwickcable.net. Also serves Hardin County (portions) & Pickwick Dam. ICA: TN0100.

TV Market Ranking: Below 100 (Hardin County (portions), Pickwick Dam); Outside TV Markets (COUNCE, Hardin County (portions)). Franchise award date: N.A. Franchise expiration date: N.A. Began: July 1, 1978.

Channel capacity: 52 (operating 2-way). Channels available but not in use: N.A.

Basic Service

Subscribers: 876.

Programming (received off-air): WBBJ-TV (ABC) Jackson; WHBQ-TV (FOX) Memphis; WJKT (FOX) Jackson; WKNO (PBS) Memphis; WMC-TV (NBC) Memphis; WREG-TV (CBS) Memphis.

Programming (via satellite): A&E Networks; ABC Family Channel; Cartoon Network; CNBC; CNN; Comcast/Charter Sports Southeast (CSS); Country Music TV; C-SPAN; Discovery Channel; ESPN; ESPN 2; Food Network; Fox News Channel; Fox Sports South; FX; Hallmark Channel; Headline News; HGTV; History Channel; Lifetime; National Geographic Channel; Nickelodeon; QVC; Spike TV; TBS Superstation; The Weather Channel; Turner Classic Movies; Turner Network TV; TV Land; USA Network; WGN America.

Fee: $25.00 installation; $34.95 monthly.

Digital Basic Service

Subscribers: N.A.

Programming (via satellite): BBC America; Bio; Bloomberg Television; Bravo; cloo; CMT Pure Country; Current; Discovery Digital Networks; DMX Music; Fox Movie Channel; Fuse; G4; GAS; GMC; Great American Country; GSN; Halogen Network; History Channel International; Independent Film Channel; Lifetime Movie Network; MTV Networks Digital Suite; National Geographic Channel; Nick Jr.; NickToons TV; Ovation; SoapNet; Style Network; Sundance Channel; The Word Network; WE tv.

Fee: $14.65 monthly.

Digital Expanded Basic Service

Subscribers: N.A.

Programming (via satellite): ESPN Classic Sports; ESPNews; Fox College Sports Atlantic; Fox College Sports Central; Fox College Sports Pacific; Fox Soccer; Golf Channel; Outdoor Channel; Speed; Versus.

Fee: $11.80 monthly.

Digital Expanded Basic Service 2

Subscribers: N.A.

Programming (via satellite): ESPN Classic Sports; ESPNews; Fox College Sports Atlantic; Fox College Sports Central; Fox College Sports Pacific; Fox Soccer; Golf Channel; Outdoor Channel; Speed; Versus.

Fee: $7.30 monthly.

Pay Service 1

Pay Units: N.A.

Programming (via satellite): Cinemax; HBO.

Fee: $15.00 installation; $8.60 monthly (Cinemax), $11.20 monthly (HBO).

Digital Pay Service 1

Pay Units: N.A.

Programming (via satellite): Cinemax (multiplexed); Encore (multiplexed); HBO (multiplexed); Showtime (multiplexed); Starz (multiplexed); The Movie Channel (multiplexed).

Fee: $9.00 monthly (Cinemax or TMC), $11.25 monthly (HBO), $13.50 monthly (Showtime).

Video-On-Demand: No

Internet Service

Operational: Yes.

Broadband Service: In-house.

Fee: $29.95-$59.95 monthly.

Telephone Service

None

Miles of Plant: 60.0 (coaxial); None (fiber optic).

Manager: Robert Campbell Sr.

Ownership: Pickwick Cablevision.

COVINGTON—Comcast Cable, 17370 Hwy 64, Somerville, TN 38068. Phones: 423-855-3900; 901-259-1442. Web Site: http://www.comcast.com. Also serves Brighton, Burlison, Garland, Gilt Edge & Tipton County. ICA: TN0066.

TV Market Ranking: 26 (Brighton, Burlison, COVINGTON, Gilt Edge, Tipton County (portions)); Outside TV Markets (Garland, Tipton County (portions)). Franchise award date: N.A. Franchise expiration date: N.A. Began: January 1, 1981.

Channel capacity: 36 (not 2-way capable). Channels available but not in use: N.A.

Basic Service
Subscribers: 2,065.
Programming (received off-air): WBBJ-TV (ABC) Jackson; WHBQ-TV (FOX) Memphis; WKNO (PBS) Memphis; WLMT (CW) Memphis; WMC-TV (NBC) Memphis; WPTY-TV (ABC) Memphis; WPXX-TV (ION, MNT) Memphis; WREG-TV (CBS) Memphis.
Programming (via satellite): ABC Family Channel; Headline News; Lifetime; QVC; TBS Superstation; The Weather Channel; WGN America.
Fee: $40.00 installation; $13.95 monthly.
Expanded Basic Service 1
Subscribers: 2,063.
Programming (via satellite): A&E Networks; AMC; Animal Planet; BET Networks; Cartoon Network; CNBC; CNN; Comedy Central; Country Music TV; C-SPAN; Discovery Channel; Disney Channel; E! Entertainment Television; ESPN; ESPN 2; ESPN Classic Sports; ESPNews; FamilyNet; Food Network; Fox News Channel; Fox Sports South; FX; Golf Channel; Great American Country; HGTV; History Channel; INSP; MSNBC; MTV; Nickelodeon; Outdoor Channel; Spike TV; The Learning Channel; Toon Disney; Travel Channel; Trinity Broadcasting Network; truTV; Turner Classic Movies; Turner Network TV; TV Land; USA Network; Versus; VH1.
Fee: $31.00 monthly.
Digital Basic Service
Subscribers: N.A.
Programming (via satellite): Bio; Boomerang; DIY Network; Fox Movie Channel; FSN Digital Atlantic; FSN Digital Central; FSN Digital Pacific; Fuse; G4; GAS; History Channel International; Lifetime Movie Network; MTV Networks Digital Suite; Music Choice; Nick Jr.; NickToons TV; Speed; Syfy.
Fee: $8.00 monthly.
Pay Service 1
Pay Units: N.A.
Programming (via satellite): HBO (multiplexed).
Fee: $15.25 monthly.
Digital Pay Service 1
Pay Units: N.A.
Programming (via satellite): Cinemax (multiplexed); Encore (multiplexed); Flix; HBO (multiplexed); Showtime (multiplexed); Starz (multiplexed); Sundance Channel; The Movie Channel (multiplexed).
Fee: $8.50 monthly (Encore), $13.95 monthly (Cinemax or Showtime/TMC/Flix/Sundance), $15.25 monthly (HBO), $16.35 monthly (Starz/Encore).
Video-On-Demand: No
Pay-Per-View
Playboy TV (delivered digitally); iN DEMAND (delivered digitally).
Internet Service
Operational: Yes.
Fee: $45.00 installation; $42.95 monthly.
Telephone Service
Digital: Operational
Miles of Plant: 180.0 (coaxial); None (fiber optic).
Manager: Harold Howard. Technical Operations Manager: Teri Dawson.
Ownership: Comcast Cable Communications Inc. (MSO).

CROSSVILLE—Charter Communications, 1774 Henry G Lane St, Maryville, TN 37801. Phone: 865-984-1400. Fax: 865-983-0383. Web Site: http://www.charter.com. Also serves Cumberland County & Lake Tansi. ICA: TN0134.
TV Market Ranking: Below 100 (CROSSVILLE, Cumberland County, Lake Tansi). Franchise award date: N.A. Franchise expiration date: N.A. Began: July 21, 1979.
Channel capacity: N.A. Channels available but not in use: N.A.
Basic Service
Subscribers: 5,992.
Programming (received off-air): WATE-TV (ABC) Knoxville; WBIR-TV (NBC) Knoxville; WBXX-TV (CW) Crossville; WCTE (PBS) Cookeville; WNPX-TV (ION) Cookeville; WSMV-TV (NBC, TMO) Nashville; WTNZ (FOX) Knoxville; WVLT-TV (CBS, MNT) Knoxville.
Programming (via satellite): Comcast/Charter Sports Southeast (CSS); C-SPAN; C-SPAN 2; Eternal Word TV Network; INSP; QVC; Trinity Broadcasting Network; TV Guide Network; WGN America.
Expanded Basic Service 1
Subscribers: N.A.
Programming (via satellite): A&E Networks; ABC Family Channel; AMC; Animal Planet; BET Networks; Bravo; Cartoon Network; CNBC; CNN; Comedy Central; Country Music TV; Discovery Channel; Discovery Fit & Health; Disney Channel; E! Entertainment Television; ESPN; ESPN 2; Food Network; Fox News Channel; Fox Sports South; FX; G4; GalaVision; Golf Channel; GSN; Hallmark Channel; Headline News; HGTV; History Channel; Lifetime; MSNBC; MTV; National Geographic Channel; Nickelodeon; Oxygen; SoapNet; Speed; Spike TV; SportSouth; Syfy; TBS Superstation; Telemundo; The Learning Channel; The Weather Channel; Toon Disney; Travel Channel; truTV; Turner Classic Movies; Turner Network TV; TV Land; Univision Studios; USA Network; Versus; VH1; WE tv.
Fee: $45.00 monthly.
Digital Basic Service
Subscribers: N.A.
Programming (via satellite): BBC America; Bio; Bloomberg Television; Boomerang; CNN International; Discovery Digital Networks; DIY Network; ESPN Classic Sports; ESPNews; Fox College Sports Atlantic; Fox College Sports Central; Fox College Sports Pacific; Fox Movie Channel; Fox Soccer; Fuel TV; Fuse; GAS; Great American Country; History Channel International; Independent Film Channel; Lifetime Movie Network; Lifetime Real Women; MTV Networks Digital Suite; NFL Network; Nick Jr.; Nick Too; NickToons TV; Outdoor Channel; Science Television; Style Network; Sundance Channel.
Digital Pay Service 1
Pay Units: N.A.
Programming (via satellite): Cinemax; HBO; Starz (multiplexed).
Video-On-Demand: No
Pay-Per-View
Playboy TV (delivered digitally); Fresh (delivered digitally); Shorteez (delivered digitally).
Internet Service
Operational: Yes.
Broadband Service: Charter Pipeline.
Fee: $29.99 monthly.
Telephone Service
None
Operations Manager: Sean Hendrix. Marketing Director: Pat Hollenbeck. Sales & Marketing Manager: Jo Ann Placke.
Ownership: Charter Communications Inc. (MSO).

CUMBERLAND COUNTY—Spirit Broadband, PO Box 249, College Grove, TN 37046. Phone: 615-368-2115. Fax: 615-368-2295. Web Site: http://www.spiritbb.com. Also serves Crab Orchard, Crossville & Pleasant Hill. ICA: TN0159.
TV Market Ranking: Below 100 (Crab Orchard, Crossville, CUMBERLAND COUNTY, Pleasant Hill). Franchise award date: N.A. Franchise expiration date: N.A. Began: July 1, 1988.
Channel capacity: N.A. Channels available but not in use: N.A.
Basic Service
Subscribers: 1,500.
Programming (received off-air): WATE-TV (ABC) Knoxville; WBIR-TV (NBC) Knoxville; WCTE (PBS) Cookeville; WTNZ (FOX) Knoxville; WTVF (CBS) Nashville.
Programming (via satellite): A&E Networks; AMC; Animal Planet; Cartoon Network; CNBC; CNN; Comedy Central; C-SPAN; C-SPAN 2; Discovery Channel; Disney Channel; ESPN; ESPN 2; ESPN Classic Sports; ESPNews; FamilyNet; Fox News Channel; Fox Sports South; Fox Sports World; FX; Golf Channel; Headline News; HGTV; History Channel; Lifetime; Lifetime Movie Network; MSNBC; MTV; MTV2; National Geographic Channel; Nick Jr.; Nickelodeon; NickToons TV; QVC; Speed; Spike TV; Syfy; TBS Superstation; The Learning Channel; The Weather Channel; Toon Disney; Travel Channel; Turner Network TV; TV Land; USA Network; Versus; VH1; WGN America.
Fee: $40.00 installation; $25.80 monthly.
Digital Basic Service
Subscribers: 80.
Fee: $29.00 monthly.
Pay Service 1
Pay Units: 35.
Programming (via satellite): Cinemax; HBO.
Fee: $12.00 monthly (each).
Video-On-Demand: Yes
Internet Service
Operational: Yes.
Subscribers: 320.
Fee: $32.95-$42.95 monthly.
Telephone Service
Digital: Operational
Fee: $29.95 monthly
Miles of Plant: 287.0 (coaxial); 120.0 (fiber optic).
President & General Manager: Vince King. Chief Technician: Brian Langham.
Ownership: Spirit Broadband.

DANDRIDGE—Haywood Cablevision, PO Box 778, Waynesville, NC 28786. Phone: 678-682-9726. Fax: 678-682-9727. Web Site: http://www.cbvnol.com. ICA: TN0201.
TV Market Ranking: 71 (DANDRIDGE).
Channel capacity: N.A. Channels available but not in use: N.A.
Basic Service
Subscribers: 106.
Programming (received off-air): WATE-TV (ABC) Knoxville; WBIR-TV (NBC) Knoxville; WBXX-TV (CW) Crossville; WETP-TV (PBS) Sneedville; WKOP-TV (PBS) Knoxville; WMAK (IND) Knoxville; WPXK-TV (ION) Jellico; WTNZ (FOX) Knoxville; WVLT-TV (CBS, MNT) Knoxville.
Programming (via satellite): C-SPAN; C-SPAN 2; Eternal Word TV Network; INSP; QVC; ShopNBC; Trinity Broadcasting Network.
Fee: $31.95 monthly.
Expanded Basic Service 1
Subscribers: N.A.
Programming (via satellite): A&E Networks; ABC Family Channel; AMC; CNN; Country Music TV; Discovery Channel; Disney Channel; DIY Network; ESPN; ESPN 2; ESPN Classic Sports; Fox News Channel; FX; Headline News; HGTV; History Channel; Lifetime; MTV; Nickelodeon; Spike TV; TBS Superstation; The Learning Channel; The Weather Channel; Toon Disney; Travel Channel; Turner Network TV; TV Land; USA Network; VH1.
Digital Basic Service
Subscribers: N.A.
Programming (via satellite): AmericanLife TV Network; Bio; Bloomberg Television; Discovery Fit & Health; ESPN Classic Sports; ESPNews; Fox College Sports Atlantic; Fox College Sports Central; Fox College Sports Pacific; Fox Movie Channel; G4; GAS; Golf Channel; Great American Country; GSN; Halogen Network; Independent Film Channel; Lime; MTV Networks Digital Suite; Music Choice; National Geographic Channel; Nick Jr.; NickToons TV; Outdoor Channel; Ovation; Speed; Sundance Channel; Toon Disney; Turner Classic Movies; Versus; WE tv.
Digital Pay Service 1
Pay Units: N.A.
Programming (via satellite): Cinemax (multiplexed); Encore (multiplexed); HBO (multiplexed); Showtime (multiplexed); The Movie Channel (multiplexed).
Video-On-Demand: No
Internet Service
Operational: Yes.
Broadband Service: In-house.
Fee: $43.95 monthly.
Telephone Service
None
Manager & Chief Technician: Joseph Stark.
Ownership: Carolina Mountain Cablevision Inc. (MSO).

DAYTON—Charter Communications. Now served by CLEVELAND, TN [TN0013]. ICA: TN0064.

DECATUR—Charter Communications. Now served by CLEVELAND, TN [TN0013]. ICA: TN0117.

DOVER—Mediacom. Now served by PEMBROKE, KY [KY0101]. ICA: TN0092.

DRESDEN—Dresden Cable Inc., 106 W Maple St, Dresden, TN 38225-1141. Phone: 731-364-5259. ICA: TN0102.
TV Market Ranking: Outside TV Markets (DRESDEN). Franchise award date: N.A. Franchise expiration date: N.A. Began: April 1, 1981.
Channel capacity: 17 (not 2-way capable). Channels available but not in use: N.A.
Basic Service
Subscribers: N.A.
Programming (received off-air): KBSI (FOX) Cape Girardeau; KFVS-TV (CBS, CW) Cape Girardeau; WBBJ-TV (ABC) Jackson; WHBQ-TV (FOX) Memphis; WKRN-TV (ABC) Nashville; WLJT-DT (PBS) Lexington; WPSD-TV (NBC) Paducah; WSMV-TV (NBC, TMO) Nashville; WTVF (CBS) Nashville.
Programming (via satellite): QVC; TBS Superstation; WGN America.
Fee: $25.00 installation; $15.40 monthly.
Expanded Basic Service 1
Subscribers: N.A.
Programming (via satellite): A&E Networks; AMC; Animal Planet; Christian Television Network; CNN; Country Music TV; C-SPAN; ESPN; Fox News Channel; Lifetime; MTV; Nickelodeon; Spike TV; The Weather Channel; Trinity Broadcasting Network; Turner Network TV; VH1.
Fee: $25.00 installation; $30.95 monthly.

Pay Service 1
Pay Units: 190.
Programming (via satellite): HBO; The Movie Channel.
Fee: $14.00 monthly (each).
Video-On-Demand: No
Internet Service
Operational: No.
Telephone Service
None
Miles of Plant: 12.0 (coaxial); None (fiber optic).
Manager: Kathleen Walden. Chief Technician: Richard Hutcherson.
Ownership: Dresden Cable Inc.

DUNLAP—Bledsoe Telephone Coop. Formerly [TN0040]. This cable system has converted to IPTV, 338 Cumberland Ave, PO Box 609, Pikeville, TN 37367-0609. Phone: 423-447-2121. E-mail: bledsoe@bledsoe.net. Web Site: http://www.bledsoe.net. ICA: TN5004.
TV Market Ranking: 78 (DUNLAP). Franchise award date: N.A. Franchise expiration date: N.A. Began: N.A.
Channel capacity: N.A. Channels available but not in use: N.A.
Video-On-Demand: No
Internet Service
Operational: Yes.
Fee: $19.95 installation; $19.95 monthly.
Telephone Service
Digital: Operational
Fee: $12.95 monthly
General Manager: Greg Anderson.

DUNLAP—Bledsoe Telephone Coop. This cable system has converted to IPTV. See Dunlap, TN [TN5004]. ICA: TN0040.

DYER—NewWave Communications, 2229 N Main St, Dyer, TN 38330. Phones: 731-692-3741; 888-863-9928. Fax: 731.692.3408. E-mail: info@newwavecom.com. Web Site: http://www.newwavecom.com. Also serves Bradford, Gibson County, Kenton, Obion County & Rutherford. ICA: TN0057.
TV Market Ranking: Below 100 (Bradford, DYER, Gibson County (portions)); Outside TV Markets (Gibson County (portions), Kenton, Obion County, Rutherford). Franchise award date: N.A. Franchise expiration date: N.A. Began: March 19, 1974.
Channel capacity: N.A. Channels available but not in use: N.A.
Basic Service
Subscribers: 1,409.
Programming (received off-air): KFVS-TV (CBS, CW) Cape Girardeau; WBBJ-TV (ABC) Jackson; WDYR-CD Dyersburg; WHBQ-TV (FOX) Memphis; WJKT (FOX) Jackson; WKNO (PBS) Memphis; WLJT-DT (PBS) Lexington; WMC-TV (NBC) Memphis; WPSD-TV (NBC) Paducah; WPTY-TV (ABC) Memphis; WREG-TV (CBS) Memphis.
Programming (via satellite): C-SPAN; C-SPAN 2; INSP; QVC; ShopNBC; Trinity Broadcasting Network; WGN America.
Fee: $29.95 monthly.
Expanded Basic Service 1
Subscribers: 1,276.
Programming (via satellite): A&E Networks; ABC Family Channel; AMC; Animal Planet; BET Networks; Bravo; Cartoon Network; CNBC; CNN; Comedy Central; Country Music TV; Discovery Channel; Disney Channel; E! Entertainment Television; ESPN; ESPN 2; ESPN Classic Sports; Food Network; Fox News Channel; Fox Sports South; FX; Golf Channel; GSN; Hallmark Channel; Headline News; HGTV; History Channel; Lifetime; MTV; Nickelodeon; Outdoor Channel; SoapNet; Speed; Spike TV; Syfy; TBS Superstation; The Learning Channel; The Weather Channel; Travel Channel; truTV; Turner Network TV; TV Land; USA Network; VH1.
Fee: $54.99 monthly.
Digital Basic Service
Subscribers: 232.
Programming (via satellite): BBC America; Bio; Black Family Channel; Bloomberg Television; cloo; Discovery Fit & Health; DMX Music; ESPNews; Fox Movie Channel; G4; GAS; Great American Country; Halogen Network; History Channel International; Independent Film Channel; Lifetime Movie Network; MTV Networks Digital Suite; Nick Jr.; NickToons TV; Style Network; The Word Network; Toon Disney; Turner Classic Movies; Versus.
Digital Pay Service 1
Pay Units: 376.
Programming (via satellite): Cinemax (multiplexed); Encore (multiplexed); Flix; HBO (multiplexed); Showtime (multiplexed); Starz (multiplexed); The Movie Channel.
Video-On-Demand: No
Pay-Per-View
Hot Choice (delivered digitally); Playboy TV (delivered digitally); Fresh (delivered digitally); Shorteez (delivered digitally); iN DEMAND (delivered digitally).
Internet Service
Operational: Yes.
Subscribers: 670.
Broadband Service: SpeedNet.
Fee: $40.00 installation; $31.99 monthly.
Telephone Service
Digital: Operational
Subscribers: 360.
Fee: $34.99 monthly
Miles of Plant: 93.0 (coaxial); None (fiber optic).
General Manager: Dennis Zeigler. Technical Operations Manager: Charles Elrod.
Ownership: NewWave Communications LLC (MSO).

DYERSBURG—Cable One, 416 W Court St, PO Box 888, Dyersburg, TN 38025-0888. Phone: 731-285-4174. Fax: 731-287-8040. Web Site: http://www.cableone.net. Also serves Dyer County, Finley, Friendship, Lenox, Roellen & Tigrett. ICA: TN0025.
TV Market Ranking: Below 100 (Dyer County (portions), DYERSBURG, Friendship, Tigrett); Outside TV Markets (Dyer County (portions), DYERSBURG, Finley, Lenox, Roellen). Franchise award date: May 24, 1966. Franchise expiration date: N.A. Began: April 1, 1967.
Channel capacity: 61 (operating 2-way). Channels available but not in use: N.A.
Basic Service
Subscribers: 7,624.
Programming (received off-air): KFVS-TV (CBS, CW) Cape Girardeau; WBBJ-TV (ABC) Jackson; WHBQ-TV (FOX) Memphis; WKNO (PBS) Memphis; WLJT-DT (PBS) Lexington; WLMT (CW) Memphis; WMC-TV (NBC) Memphis; WPSD-TV (NBC) Paducah; WPTY-TV (ABC) Memphis; WREG-TV (CBS) Memphis.
Programming (via satellite): A&E Networks; ABC Family Channel; AMC; Animal Planet; BET Networks; Cartoon Network; CNBC; CNN; Country Music TV; C-SPAN; C-SPAN 2; Discovery Channel; Disney Channel; ESPN; ESPN 2; Fox News Channel; Fox Sports South; FX; Headline News; HGTV; History Channel; ION Television; Lifetime; MSNBC; MTV; Nickelodeon; QVC; Spike TV; Syfy; TBS Superstation; The Learning Channel; The Weather Channel; Travel Channel; Trinity Broadcasting Network; Turner Classic Movies; Turner Network TV; TV Guide Network; TV Land; USA Network; VH1; WGN America.
Fee: $75.00 installation; $46.00 monthly.
Digital Basic Service
Subscribers: 3,000.
Programming (via satellite): 3 Angels Broadcasting Network; Bio; Boomerang; BYU Television; Canales N; Discovery Digital Networks; DMX Music; ESPN Classic Sports; ESPNews; FamilyNet; Fox College Sports Atlantic; Fox College Sports Central; Fox College Sports Pacific; Fox Movie Channel; Fox Soccer; Fuel TV; G4; Golf Channel; Great American Country; Hallmark Channel; History Channel International; INSP; National Geographic Channel; SoapNet; Speed; Toon Disney; Trinity Broadcasting Network; truTV; Turner Network TV HD; TVG Network; Universal HD.
Fee: $46.00 monthly.
Digital Pay Service 1
Pay Units: N.A.
Programming (via satellite): Cinemax (multiplexed); Encore (multiplexed); Flix (multiplexed); HBO (multiplexed); Showtime (multiplexed); Showtime HD; Starz (multiplexed); Sundance Channel (multiplexed); The Movie Channel (multiplexed); The Movie Channel HD.
Fee: $15.00 monthly.
Video-On-Demand: No
Pay-Per-View
Addressable homes: 3,092.
Movies (delivered digitally); Pleasure (delivered digitally); Ten Clips (delivered digitally); Ten Blox (delivered digitally); Ten Blue (delivered digitally).
Internet Service
Operational: Yes. Began: June 1, 2001.
Subscribers: 2,300.
Broadband Service: CableONE.net.
Fee: $75.00 installation; $43.00 monthly.
Telephone Service
Digital: Operational
Fee: $39.95 monthly
Miles of Plant: 280.0 (coaxial); 62.0 (fiber optic).
Manager: Jim Duck. Chief Technician: George Downs.
Ownership: Cable ONE Inc. (MSO).

EAGLEVILLE—Small Town Cable. Now served by CHAPEL HILL, TN [TN0089]. ICA: TN0136.

ELIZABETHTON—Charter Communications. Now served by KINGSPORT, TN [TN0007]. ICA: TN0199.

FAIRFIELD GLADE—Comcast Cable, 5720 Asheville Hwy, Knoxville, TN 37924-2701. Phone: 865-971-1544. Fax: 865-862-5092. Web Site: http://www.comcast.com. Also serves Crossville (unincorporated areas). ICA: TN0081.
TV Market Ranking: Below 100 (Crossville (unincorporated areas), FAIRFIELD GLADE). Franchise award date: April 20, 1981. Franchise expiration date: N.A. Began: December 1, 1981.
Channel capacity: 55 (not 2-way capable). Channels available but not in use: N.A.
Basic Service
Subscribers: 3,079.
Programming (received off-air): WATE-TV (ABC) Knoxville; WBIR-TV (NBC) Knoxville; WBXX-TV (CW) Crossville; WCTE (PBS) Cookeville; WKOP-TV (PBS) Knoxville; WTNZ (FOX) Knoxville; WVLT-TV (CBS, MNT) Knoxville; allband FM.
Programming (via satellite): A&E Networks; ABC Family Channel; AMC; Cartoon Network; CNBC; CNN; Comcast/Charter Sports Southeast (CSS); Comedy Central; C-SPAN; C-SPAN 2; Discovery Channel; Discovery Health Channel; E! Entertainment Television; ESPN; ESPN 2; Food Network; Fox News Channel; Fox Sports South; FX; Golf Channel; Great American Country; GSN; Hallmark Channel; Headline News; HGTV; History Channel; INSP; ION Television; Lifetime; Nickelodeon; QVC; Speed; Spike TV; SportSouth; Syfy; TBS Superstation; The Learning Channel; The Weather Channel; Travel Channel; Turner Classic Movies; Turner Network TV; TV Guide Network; TV Land; USA Network; Versus; VH1; WGN America.
Fee: $56.50 installation; $40.99 monthly.
Digital Basic Service
Subscribers: N.A.
Programming (via satellite): CMT Pure Country; Encore; Flix; GAS; MTV Networks Digital Suite; Music Choice; Nick Jr.; Nick Too.
Fee: $14.95 monthly.
Digital Pay Service 1
Pay Units: N.A.
Programming (via satellite): Cinemax (multiplexed); HBO (multiplexed); Showtime (multiplexed); Starz (multiplexed); The Movie Channel (multiplexed).
Fee: $9.95 monthly (Starz), $11.95 monthly (HBO, Showtime/TMC, or Cinemax).
Video-On-Demand: Planned
Pay-Per-View
iN DEMAND (delivered digitally); Hot Choice (delivered digitally).
Internet Service
Operational: Yes.
Telephone Service
Digital: Operational
Miles of Plant: 79.0 (coaxial); None (fiber optic).
Vice President & General Manager: Kirk Dale. Technical Operations Director: Charlie Goodreau. Engineering Manager: Hank Swindle. Marketing Director: Kristopher Workman. Government & Community Affairs Director: Russell Byrd.
Ownership: Comcast Cable Communications Inc. (MSO).

FAYETTEVILLE—Charter Communications, 1774 Henry G Lane St, Maryville, TN 37801. Phone: 865-984-1400. Fax: 865-983-0383. Web Site: http://www.charter.com. Also serves Lincoln County (portions). ICA: TN0185.
TV Market Ranking: 96 (FAYETTEVILLE, Lincoln County (portions)). Franchise award date: January 1, 1989. Franchise expiration date: January 1, 2009. Began: March 1, 1992.
Channel capacity: N.A. Channels available but not in use: N.A.
Basic Service
Subscribers: 2,688.
Programming (received off-air): WAAY-TV (ABC) Huntsville; WAFF (NBC) Huntsville; WHDF (CW) Florence; WHNT-TV (CBS) Huntsville; WKRN-TV (ABC) Nashville; WNAB (CW) Nashville; WNPT (PBS) Nashville; WSMV-TV (NBC, TMO) Nashville; WTVF (CBS) Nashville; WZDX (FOX, MNT) Huntsville; WZTV (FOX) Nashville.
Programming (via satellite): Comcast/Charter Sports Southeast (CSS); C-SPAN; C-

SPAN 2; INSP; Trinity Broadcasting Network; TV Guide Network; Univision Studios; WGN America.

Expanded Basic Service 1

Subscribers: 495.

Programming (via satellite): A&E Networks; ABC Family Channel; AMC; Animal Planet; BET Networks; Bravo; Cartoon Network; CNBC; CNN; Comedy Central; Country Music TV; Discovery Channel; Discovery Fit & Health; Disney Channel; E! Entertainment Television; ESPN; ESPN 2; Food Network; Fox News Channel; Fox Sports South; FX; G4; GalaVision; Golf Channel; GSN; Hallmark Channel; Headline News; HGTV; History Channel; Lifetime; MSNBC; MTV; National Geographic Channel; Nickelodeon; Outdoor Channel; Oxygen; SoapNet; Speed; Spike TV; SportSouth; Syfy; TBS Superstation; Telemundo; The Learning Channel; The Weather Channel; Toon Disney; Travel Channel; truTV; Turner Classic Movies; Turner Network TV; TV Land; USA Network; Versus; VH1; WE tv.

Fee: $45.00 monthly.

Digital Basic Service

Subscribers: N.A.

Programming (via satellite): BBC America; Bio; Bloomberg News Radio; Boomerang; CNN International; Discovery Digital Networks; DIY Network; ESPN Classic Sports; ESPNews; Fox College Sports Atlantic; Fox College Sports Central; Fox College Sports Pacific; Fox Movie Channel; Fox Soccer; Fuel TV; GAS; Great American Country; History Channel International; Independent Film Channel; Lifetime Movie Network; Lifetime Real Women; MTV Networks Digital Suite; Music Choice; NFL Network; Nick Jr.; Nick Too; Style Network; Sundance Channel.

Digital Pay Service 1

Pay Units: N.A.

Programming (via satellite): Cinemax (multiplexed); HBO (multiplexed); Starz (multiplexed).

Video-On-Demand: No

Pay-Per-View

Special events; Playboy TV (delivered digitally); Fresh (delivered digitally); Shorteez (delivered digitally).

Internet Service

Operational: Yes.

Broadband Service: Charter Pipeline.

Fee: $29.99 monthly.

Telephone Service

None

Miles of Plant: 54.0 (coaxial); None (fiber optic).

Operations Manager: Sean Hendrix. Marketing Director: Pat Hollenbeck. Sales & Marketing Manager: Jo Ann Placke.

Ownership: Charter Communications Inc. (MSO).

FAYETTEVILLE—Fayette Public Utilities, 408 W College St, PO Box 120, Fayetteville, TN 37334-0120. Phones: 800-379-2534; 931-433-1522. Fax: 931-433-0646. E-mail: customerservice@fpu-tn.com. Web Site: http://www.fpu-tn.com. ICA: TN0192.

Note: This system is an overbuild.

TV Market Ranking: 96 (FAYETTEVILLE). Franchise award date: N.A. Franchise expiration date: N.A. Began: March 21, 2001.

Channel capacity: 72 (operating 2-way). Channels available but not in use: N.A.

Basic Service

Subscribers: 2,300.

Programming (received off-air): WAAY-TV (ABC) Huntsville; WAFF (NBC) Huntsville; WHDF (CW) Florence; WHNT-TV (CBS) Huntsville; WKRN-TV (ABC) Nashville; WNPT (PBS) Nashville; WSMV-TV (NBC, TMO) Nashville; WTVF (CBS) Nashville; WZDX (FOX, MNT) Huntsville.

Programming (via satellite): C-SPAN; C-SPAN 2; ESPNews; Food Network; QVC; TBS Superstation; The Weather Channel; WGN America.

Fee: $21.36 monthly.

Expanded Basic Service 1

Subscribers: N.A.

Programming (via satellite): A&E Networks; ABC Family Channel; AMC; Animal Planet; BET Networks; Bravo; Cartoon Network; CNBC; CNN; Comedy Central; Country Music TV; Discovery Channel; Disney Channel; E! Entertainment Television; ESPN; ESPN 2; ESPN Classic Sports; Fox News Channel; Fox Sports South; FX; Golf Channel; Great American Country; GSN; Hallmark Channel; Headline News; HGTV; History Channel; ION Television; Lifetime; MSNBC; MTV; National Geographic Channel; Nickelodeon; Outdoor Channel; Speed; Spike TV; SportSouth; Syfy; The Learning Channel; Toon Disney; Travel Channel; Trinity Broadcasting Network; Turner Classic Movies; Turner Network TV; TV Land; USA Network; VH1; WE tv.

Fee: $41.00 monthly.

Digital Basic Service

Subscribers: N.A.

Programming (via satellite): BBC America; Bio; Discovery Digital Networks; DIY Network; DMX Music; Fuse; G4; History Channel International; Independent Film Channel; Lifetime Movie Network.

Fee: $14.45 monthly.

Pay Service 1

Pay Units: N.A.

Programming (via satellite): HBO (multiplexed).

Fee: $10.95 monthly.

Digital Pay Service 1

Pay Units: N.A.

Programming (via satellite): Cinemax (multiplexed); Encore (multiplexed); Flix; HBO (multiplexed); Showtime (multiplexed); Starz (multiplexed); Sundance Channel; The Movie Channel (multiplexed).

Fee: $8.95 monthly (Cinemax), $9.95 monthly (Starz/Encore), $12.95 monthly (HBO), $12.95 monthly (Flix/Showtime/Sundance/TMC).

Video-On-Demand: Planned

Pay-Per-View

Hot Choice (delivered digitally); iN DEMAND (delivered digitally).

Internet Service

Operational: Yes.

Broadband Service: In-house.

Fee: $39.45-$71.28 monthly; $10.00 modem lease.

Telephone Service

Digital: Operational

Miles of Plant: 30.0 (coaxial); None (fiber optic).

Chief Executive Officer & General Manager: Britt Dye.

Ownership: Fayetteville Public Utilities.

FLINTVILLE—Charter Communications, 1774 Henry G Lane St, Maryville, TN 37801. Phone: 865-984-1400. Fax: 865-983-0383. Web Site: http://www.charter.com. ICA: TN0189.

TV Market Ranking: 96 (FLINTVILLE). Franchise award date: N.A. Franchise expiration date: N.A. Began: N.A.

Channel capacity: N.A. Channels available but not in use: N.A.

Basic Service

Subscribers: 288.

Programming (received off-air): WAAY-TV (ABC) Huntsville; WAFF (NBC) Huntsville; WHDF (CW) Florence; WHNT-TV (CBS) Huntsville; WKRN-TV (ABC) Nashville; WNAB (CW) Nashville; WNPT (PBS) Nashville; WSMV-TV (NBC, TMO) Nashville; WTVF (CBS) Nashville; WZDX (FOX, MNT) Huntsville; WZTV (FOX) Nashville.

Programming (via satellite): QVC.

Expanded Basic Service 1

Subscribers: N.A.

Programming (via satellite): A&E Networks; ABC Family Channel; AMC; Animal Planet; Bravo; Cartoon Network; CNBC; CNN; Comcast/Charter Sports Southeast (CSS); Comedy Central; Country Music TV; C-SPAN; C-SPAN 2; Discovery Channel; Disney Channel; E! Entertainment Television; ESPN; ESPN 2; Food Network; Fox News Channel; Fox Sports South; FX; G4; Golf Channel; GSN; Hallmark Channel; Headline News; HGTV; History Channel; Lifetime; MSNBC; MTV; National Geographic Channel; Nickelodeon; Oxygen; SoapNet; Speed; Spike TV; Syfy; TBS Superstation; The Learning Channel; The Weather Channel; Toon Disney; Travel Channel; Trinity Broadcasting Network; truTV; Turner Classic Movies; Turner Network TV; TV Land; USA Network; Versus; VH1; WE tv; WGN America.

Fee: $45.00 monthly.

Digital Basic Service

Subscribers: N.A.

Programming (via satellite): BBC America; Bio; Bloomberg Television; Boomerang; CNN International; Discovery Digital Networks; DIY Network; ESPN Classic Sports; ESPNews; Fox College Sports Atlantic; Fox College Sports Central; Fox College Sports Pacific; Fox Movie Channel; Fox Soccer; Fuel TV; GAS; Great American Country; History Channel International; Independent Film Channel; Lifetime Movie Network; Lifetime Real Women; MTV Networks Digital Suite; Music Choice; NFL Network; Nick Jr.; Nick Too; NickToons TV; Outdoor Channel; Science Television; Style Network; Sundance Channel.

Digital Pay Service 1

Pay Units: N.A.

Programming (via satellite): Cinemax (multiplexed); HBO (multiplexed); Starz (multiplexed).

Video-On-Demand: No

Pay-Per-View

Playboy TV (delivered digitally); Fresh (delivered digitally); Shorteez (delivered digitally).

Internet Service

Operational: No.

Telephone Service

None

Operations Director: Sean Hendrix. Marketing Director: Pat Hollenbeck. Sales & Marketing Manager: Jo Ann Placke.

Ownership: Charter Communications Inc. (MSO).

FRIENDSVILLE—Comcast Cable, 241 W Summer St, Greeneville, TN 37743. Phones: 423-282-1370 (Gray office); 423-639-6342. Fax: 423-639-0145. Web Site: http://www.comcast.com. Also serves Greenback & Loudon County (portions). ICA: TN0062.

TV Market Ranking: 71 (FRIENDSVILLE, Greenback, Loudon County (portions)); Below 100 (Loudon County (portions)). Franchise award date: December 23, 1983. Franchise expiration date: N.A. Began: N.A.

Channel capacity: N.A. Channels available but not in use: N.A.

Basic Service

Subscribers: N.A. Included in Greeneville

Programming (received off-air): WATE-TV (ABC) Knoxville; WBIR-TV (NBC) Knoxville; WBXX-TV (CW) Crossville; WKOP-TV (PBS) Knoxville; WTNZ (FOX) Knoxville; WVLT-TV (CBS, MNT) Knoxville.

Programming (via satellite): CNN; ION Television; QVC; TBS Superstation; WGN America.

Fee: $40.00 installation; $18.95 monthly; $2.00 converter.

Expanded Basic Service 1

Subscribers: N.A.

Programming (received off-air): WVLR (IND) Tazewell.

Programming (via satellite): 3 Angels Broadcasting Network; A&E Networks; ABC Family Channel; AMC; Animal Planet; BET Networks; Bravo; Cartoon Network; CNBC; Comedy Central; Country Music TV; C-SPAN; C-SPAN 2; Discovery Channel; Disney Channel; E! Entertainment Television; ESPN; ESPN 2; Food Network; Fox News Channel; Fox Sports South; FX; GalaVision; Hallmark Channel; Headline News; HGTV; History Channel; INSP; Lifetime; MSNBC; MTV; Nickelodeon; Oxygen; Product Information Network; ShopNBC; Speed; Spike TV; SportSouth; Syfy; The Learning Channel; The Weather Channel; Toon Disney; Travel Channel; Trinity Broadcasting Network; truTV; Turner Network TV; TV Guide Network; TV Land; USA Network; VH1.

Fee: $27.05 monthly.

Digital Basic Service

Subscribers: N.A.

Programming (via satellite): AmericanLife TV Network; BBC America; Black Family Channel; Bloomberg Television; Canales N; Discovery Fit & Health; DIY Network; Fox Movie Channel; Fox Sports World; Fuse; G4; GAS; Great American Country; GSN; Halogen Network; Lifetime Movie Network; MTV Networks Digital Suite; National Geographic Channel; Nick Jr.; Nick Too; NickToons TV; SoapNet; The Word Network; Turner Classic Movies; WE tv.

Fee: $15.95 monthly.

Digital Expanded Basic Service

Subscribers: N.A.

Programming (via satellite): Bio; ESPN Classic Sports; ESPNews; FSN Digital Atlantic; FSN Digital Central; FSN Digital Pacific; Golf Channel; History Channel International; Independent Film Channel; Music Choice; Outdoor Channel; Sundance Channel; Versus.

Digital Pay Service 1

Pay Units: N.A.

Programming (via satellite): Cinemax (multiplexed); Encore (multiplexed); Flix; HBO (multiplexed); Showtime (multiplexed); Starz (multiplexed); The Movie Channel (multiplexed).

Fee: $15.95 monthly (each).

Video-On-Demand: No

Pay-Per-View

iN DEMAND (delivered digitally); Fresh (delivered digitally).

Internet Service

Operational: Yes.

Broadband Service: Comcast High Speed Internet.

Fee: $42.95 monthly.

Telephone Service

None

Miles of plant included in Greeneville

Vice President & General Manager: Dave Sanders. Operations Manager: Larry Matthews. Technical Operations Director: Tim Castor. Chief Technician: Gary Shoemaker. Marketing Manager: Sandra Munsey. Business Manager: Rhonda Humbert.

Ownership: Comcast Cable Communications Inc. (MSO).

GATLINBURG—Charter Communications, 1774 Henry G Lane St, Maryville, TN 37801. Phone: 865-984-1400. Fax: 865-983-0382. Web Site: http://www.charter.com. Also serves Pigeon Forge & Sevierville. ICA: TN0140.

TV Market Ranking: 71 (GATLINBURG, Pigeon Forge, Sevierville). Franchise award date: February 1, 1973. Franchise expiration date: N.A. Began: March 1, 1973.

Channel capacity: N.A. Channels available but not in use: N.A.

Basic Service

Subscribers: 10,700.

Programming (received off-air): WATE-TV (ABC) Knoxville; WBIR-TV (NBC) Knoxville; WBXX-TV (CW) Crossville; WKOP-TV (PBS) Knoxville; WLVT-TV (PBS) Allentown; WPXK-TV (ION) Jellico; WTNZ (FOX) Knoxville; WVLR (IND) Tazewell; WVLT-TV (CBS, MNT) Knoxville.

Programming (via satellite): QVC.

Fee: $29.99 installation.

Expanded Basic Service 1

Subscribers: 6,822.

Programming (via satellite): A&E Networks; ABC Family Channel; AMC; Animal Planet; BET Networks; Bravo; Cartoon Network; CNBC; CNN; Comcast/Charter Sports Southeast (CSS); Comedy Central; Country Music TV; C-SPAN; C-SPAN 2; Discovery Channel; Disney Channel; E! Entertainment Television; ESPN; ESPN 2; Food Network; Fox News Channel; Fox Sports South; FX; G4; Golf Channel; GSN; Hallmark Channel; Headline News; HGTV; History Channel; INSP; Lifetime; MSNBC; MTV; National Geographic Channel; Nickelodeon; Oxygen; SoapNet; Speed; Spike TV; SportSouth; Style Network; Syfy; TBS Superstation; Telemundo; The Learning Channel; The Weather Channel; Toon Disney; Travel Channel; Trinity Broadcasting Network; truTV; Turner Classic Movies; Turner Network TV; TV Guide Network; TV Land; USA Network; Versus; VH1; WE tv; WGN America.

Fee: $50.99 monthly.

Digital Basic Service

Subscribers: N.A.

Programming (via satellite): BBC America; Bio; Bloomberg Television; CNN International; Cooking Channel; DIY Network; ESPN Classic Sports; ESPN HD; Fox College Sports Atlantic; Fox College Sports Central; Fox College Sports Pacific; Fox Movie Channel; Fox Sports World; Fuel TV; GAS; Great American Country; HD Theater; HDNet; HDNet Movies; History Channel International; Independent Film Channel; Jewelry Television; Lifetime Movie Network; Lifetime Real Women; MTV Networks Digital Suite; Music Choice; NFL Network; Nick Jr.; Nick Too; NickToons TV; Sundance Channel; TV Guide Interactive Inc.

Digital Pay Service 1

Pay Units: N.A.

Programming (via satellite): Cinemax (multiplexed); Encore (multiplexed); Flix; HBO (multiplexed); HBO HD; Showtime (multiplexed); Starz (multiplexed); The Movie Channel (multiplexed).

Video-On-Demand: Yes

Pay-Per-View

Special events.

Internet Service

Operational: Yes.

Broadband Service: Charter Pipeline.

Fee: $29.99 monthly.

Telephone Service

Digital: Operational

Fee: $29.99 monthly

Technical Operations Director: Grant Evans. Chief Technician: Mark Haley. Marketing Director: Pat Hollenbeck. Marketing Manager: Angie Lee. Government Relations Director: Nick Pavlis.

Ownership: Charter Communications Inc. (MSO).

GRAY—Comcast Cable, 1794 Old Gray Station Rd, Gray, TN 37615-3869. Phone: 423-282-1370. Fax: 423-283-4855. Web Site: http://www.comcast.com. Also serves Braemar, Carter County, Erwin, Fall Branch, Hampton, Harmony, Johnson City (southwestern portion), Jonesborough, Mountain City, Unicoi County, Valley Forge & Washington County. ICA: TN0142.

TV Market Ranking: 46 (Unicoi County (portions)); Below 100 (Braemar, Carter County, Erwin, Fall Branch, GRAY, Hampton, Harmony, Johnson City (southwestern portion), Jonesborough, Mountain City, Valley Forge, Washington County, Unicoi County (portions)). Franchise award date: N.A. Franchise expiration date: N.A. Began: October 1, 1954.

Channel capacity: 75 (operating 2-way). Channels available but not in use: N.A.

Basic Service

Subscribers: 53,032 Includes Bluefield WV & Glade Spring VA.

Programming (received off-air): WAPK-CA (MNT) Kingsport; WCYB-TV (CW, NBC) Bristol; WEMT (FOX) Greeneville; WJHL-TV (CBS) Johnson City; WKPT-TV (ABC) Kingsport; WLFG (IND) Grundy.

Programming (via satellite): A&E Networks; ABC Family Channel; AMC; AmericanLife TV Network; Animal Planet; BET Networks; CNBC; CNN; Comcast/Charter Sports Southeast (CSS); Comedy Central; Country Music TV; C-SPAN; C-SPAN 2; Discovery Channel; Disney Channel; E! Entertainment Television; ESPN; ESPN 2; Food Network; Fox Sports Net; Golf Channel; GSN; Headline News; HGTV; History Channel; ION Television; Lifetime; MSNBC; MTV; MTV2; Nickelodeon; QVC; Sneak Prevue; Speed; Spike TV; Style Network; Syfy; TBS Superstation; The Learning Channel; The Weather Channel; Trinity Broadcasting Network; Turner Network TV; TV Guide Network; TV Land; USA Network; Versus; VH1; WGN America.

Fee: $58.61 installation; $10.95 monthly.

Digital Basic Service

Subscribers: 7,080.

Programming (via satellite): BBC America; Discovery Digital Networks; DMX Music; Encore Action; Flix; GAS; MTV Networks Digital Suite; Nick Jr.; Nick Too; Sundance Channel; WAM! America's Kidz Network; Weatherscan.

Fee: $14.95 monthly.

Digital Pay Service 1

Pay Units: N.A.

Programming (via satellite): Cinemax (multiplexed); HBO (multiplexed); Showtime (multiplexed); The Movie Channel (multiplexed).

Fee: $12.95 monthly (Starz/Encore), $13.95 monthly (Cinemax), $14.50 monthly (HBO or Showtime/TMC).

Video-On-Demand: Yes

Pay-Per-View

Addressable homes: 7,080.

iN DEMAND; Playboy TV; iN DEMAND (delivered digitally).

Internet Service

Operational: Yes.

Broadband Service: Comcast High Speed Internet.

Fee: $42.95 monthly.

Telephone Service

None

Miles of Plant: 1,171.0 (coaxial); None (fiber optic).

Vice President & General Manager: Dave Sanders. Technical Operations Director: Tim Castor. Marketing Manager: Sandra Munsey.

Ownership: Comcast Cable Communications Inc. (MSO).

GREENEVILLE—Comcast Cable, 241 W Summer St, Greeneville, TN 37743. Phones: 423-282-1370; 423-639-6342. Fax: 423-639-0145. Web Site: http://www.comcast.com. Also serves Afton, Baileyton, Bulls Gap, Chuckey, Greene County, Hamblen County, Hawkins County, Midway, Mosheim, Rheatown, Russellville, Tusculum & Whitesburg. ICA: TN0022.

TV Market Ranking: 46 (Greene County (portions)); Below 100 (Afton, Baileyton, Bulls Gap, Chuckey, GREENEVILLE, Hamblen County, Hawkins County, Midway, Mosheim, Rheatown, Russellville, Tusculum, Whitesburg, Greene County (portions)). Franchise award date: November 25, 1985. Franchise expiration date: N.A. Began: N.A.

Channel capacity: N.A. Channels available but not in use: N.A.

Basic Service

Subscribers: 52,181 Includes Friendsville, Whitesburg KY, Galax VA, Marion VA, Norton VA, & Pulaski VA.

Programming (received off-air): WAPK-CA (MNT) Kingsport; WATE-TV (ABC) Knoxville; WBIR-TV (NBC) Knoxville; WCYB-TV (CW, NBC) Bristol; WEMT (FOX) Greeneville; WETP-TV (PBS) Sneedville; WJHL-TV (CBS) Johnson City; WKPT-TV (ABC) Kingsport; WLFG (IND) Grundy; WLOS (ABC) Asheville.

Programming (via satellite): QVC; WGN America.

Fee: $45.00 installation; $18.95 monthly.

Expanded Basic Service 1

Subscribers: 16,721.

Programming (via satellite): 3 Angels Broadcasting Network; A&E Networks; ABC Family Channel; AMC; Animal Planet; BET Networks; Bravo; Cartoon Network; CNBC; CNN; Comedy Central; Country Music TV; C-SPAN; C-SPAN 2; Discovery Channel; Disney Channel; E! Entertainment Television; ESPN; ESPN 2; Food Network; Fox News Channel; Fox Sports South; FX; GalaVision; Hallmark Channel; Headline News; HGTV; History Channel; INSP; ION Television; Lifetime; MSNBC; MTV; Nickelodeon; Oxygen; Product Information Network; ShopNBC; Spike TV; Syfy; TBS Superstation; The Learning Channel; The Weather Channel; Travel Channel; Trinity Broadcasting Network; truTV; Turner Classic Movies; Turner Network TV; Turner South; TV Guide Network; TV Land; USA Network; VH1.

Fee: $27.05 monthly.

Digital Basic Service

Subscribers: 1,896.

Programming (via satellite): AmericanLife TV Network; BBC America; Black Family Channel; Bloomberg Television; Canales N; Country Music TV; Discovery Digital Networks; DIY Network; ESPN Classic Sports; ESPN HD; ESPN U; ESPNews; Fox Movie Channel; Fox Soccer; Fuse; G4; Great American Country; GSN; Halogen Network; HDNet; HDNet Movies; INHD; INHD2; Lifetime Movie Network; LOGO; MTV Networks Digital Suite; Music Choice; NickToons TV; SoapNet; Speed; Style Network; The Word Network; Toon Disney; TVG Network; WE tv.

Fee: $9.95 monthly.

Digital Expanded Basic Service

Subscribers: N.A.

Programming (via satellite): Bio; Flix; Fox Reality Channel; FSN Digital Atlantic; FSN Digital Central; FSN Digital Pacific; GAS; Golf Channel; History Channel International; Independent Film Channel; National Geographic Channel; Nick Jr.; Nick Too; Outdoor Channel; Sundance Channel; Versus.

Digital Pay Service 1

Pay Units: 524.

Programming (via satellite): Cinemax (multiplexed); Cinemax HD; Encore (multiplexed); Flix; HBO (multiplexed); HBO HD; Showtime (multiplexed); Showtime HD; Starz (multiplexed); Starz HDTV; The Movie Channel (multiplexed).

Fee: $15.95 monthly (each).

Video-On-Demand: No

Pay-Per-View

Addressable homes: 1,896.

iN DEMAND (delivered digitally); Playboy TV (delivered digitally).

Internet Service

Operational: Yes.

Broadband Service: Comcast High Speed Internet.

Fee: $42.95 monthly.

Telephone Service

None

Miles of Plant: 3,133.0 (coaxial); None (fiber optic). Miles of plant include Friendsville, Whitesburg KY, Galax VA, Marion VA, Norton VA, & Pulaski VA

Vice President & General Manager: Dave Sanders. Operations Manager: Larry Matthews. Technical Operations Director: Tim Castor. Chief Technician: Gary Shoemaker. Marketing Manager: Sandra Munsey. Business Manager: Rhonda Humbert.

Ownership: Comcast Cable Communications Inc. (MSO).

GRIMSLEY—Comcast Cable, 5720 Asheville Hwy, Knoxville, TN 37924-2701. Phone: 865-971-1544. Fax: 865-862-5092. Web Site: http://www.comcast.com. Also serves Clarkrange. ICA: TN0197.

TV Market Ranking: Below 100 (Clarkrange, GRIMSLEY).

Channel capacity: N.A. Channels available but not in use: N.A.

Basic Service

Subscribers: N.A.

Programming (received off-air): WATE-TV (ABC) Knoxville; WBIR-TV (NBC) Knoxville; WBXX-TV (CW) Crossville; WCTE (PBS) Cookeville; WETP-TV (PBS) Sneedville; WTNZ (FOX) Knoxville; WVLT-TV (CBS, MNT) Knoxville.

Programming (via satellite): CNBC; Comcast/Charter Sports Southeast (CSS); Fox News Channel; Outdoor Channel; QVC; TV Land; WGN America.

Fee: $56.50 installation; $39.95 monthly.

Expanded Basic Service 1

Subscribers: N.A.

Programming (via satellite): A&E Networks; ABC Family Channel; AMC; CNN; Country Music TV; C-SPAN; Discovery Channel; Disney Channel; ESPN; ESPN 2; Fox Sports South; FX; Headline News; HGTV; Lifetime; MTV; Nickelodeon; Spike TV; Syfy; TBS Superstation; The Weather Channel; Trinity Broadcasting Network; Turner Network TV; USA Network; VH1.

Digital Basic Service

Subscribers: N.A.

Programming (via satellite): BBC America; CMT Pure Country; Discovery Digital Networks; Encore (multiplexed); GAS; MTV Networks Digital Suite; Music Choice; Nick Jr.; Nick Too.

Fee: $14.95 monthly.

Digital Pay Service 1

Pay Units: N.A.

Programming (via satellite): Cinemax (multiplexed); HBO (multiplexed); Showtime (multiplexed); Starz; The Movie Channel.

Fee: $13.99 monthly (each).

Pay-Per-View

Hot Choice (delivered digitally); iN DEMAND (delivered digitally).

Internet Service

Operational: Yes.

Telephone Service

None

Vice President & General Manager: Kirk Dale. Government & Community Affairs Director: Russell Byrd. Marketing Director: Kristopher Workman. Technical Operations Director: Charlie Goodreau. Engineering Manager: Hank Swindle.

Ownership: Comcast Cable Communications Inc. (MSO).

HARRIMAN—Comcast Cable, 5720 Asheville Hwy, Knoxville, TN 37924-2701. Phone: 865-971-1544. Fax: 865-862-5092. Web Site: http://www.comcast.com. Also serves Anderson County (portions), Kingston, Roane County & Rockwood. ICA: TN0021.

TV Market Ranking: 71 (Anderson County (portions), HARRIMAN, Kingston, Roane County (portions)); Below 100 (Rockwood, Roane County (portions)). Franchise award date: N.A. Franchise expiration date: N.A. Began: January 1, 1966.

Channel capacity: N.A. Channels available but not in use: N.A.

Basic Service

Subscribers: 39,105.

Programming (received off-air): WATE-TV (ABC) Knoxville; WBIR-TV (NBC) Knoxville; WBXX-TV (CW) Crossville; WETP-TV (PBS) Sneedville; WKOP-TV (PBS) Knoxville; WMAK (IND) Knoxville; WPXK-TV (ION) Jellico; WTNZ (FOX) Knoxville; WVLR (IND) Tazewell; WVLT-TV (CBS, MNT) Knoxville; allband FM.

Programming (via satellite): C-SPAN; QVC; TBS Superstation; WGN America.

Fee: $56.50 installation; $13.75 monthly.

Expanded Basic Service 1

Subscribers: N.A.

Programming (via satellite): 10 News 2; A&E Networks; ABC Family Channel; AMC; Animal Planet; BET Networks; Bravo; Cartoon Network; CNBC; CNN; Comcast/Charter Sports Southeast (CSS); Comedy Central; Discovery Channel; Discovery Health Channel; Disney Channel; DIY Network; E! Entertainment Television; ESPN; ESPN 2; Food Network; Fox News Channel; Fox Sports South; FX; G4; Golf Channel; Great American Country; GSN; Hallmark Channel; Headline News; HGTV; History Channel; Lifetime; MTV; Nickelodeon; Speed; Spike TV; SportSouth; Style Network; Syfy; The Learning Channel; The Weather Channel; Travel Channel; Trinity Broadcasting Network; truTV; Turner Classic Movies; Turner Network TV; TV Guide Network; TV Land; USA Network; Versus; VH1.

Fee: $36.24 monthly.

Digital Basic Service

Subscribers: N.A.

Programming (via satellite): A&E HD; BBC America; Bio; CMT Pure Country; Cooking Channel; Country Music TV; C-SPAN 2; C-SPAN 3; Current; Encore (multiplexed); ESPN 2 HD; ESPN Classic Sports; ESPN HD; ESPNews; Eternal Word TV Network; Exercise TV; Flix; Fox College Sports Atlantic; Fox College Sports Central; Fox College Sports Pacific; Fox Reality Channel; Fox Soccer; GAS; GolTV; Halogen Network; HD Theater; History Channel International; INSP; Jewelry Television; Lifetime Movie Network; MoviePlex; MSNBC; MTV Networks Digital Suite; Music Choice; National Geographic Channel; National Geographic Channel HD Network; NBA TV; NFL Network; Nick Jr.; Nick Too; NickToons TV; Palladia; PBS Kids Sprout; ShopNBC; SoapNet; Sundance Channel; The Word Network; Toon Disney; Turner Network TV HD; TV One; Universal HD; Versus HD; Weatherscan.

Fee: $14.95 monthly.

Digital Pay Service 1

Pay Units: 1,156.

Programming (via satellite): Cinemax (multiplexed); Cinemax HD; HBO (multiplexed); HBO HD; HBO On Demand; Showtime (multiplexed); Showtime HD; Starz (multiplexed); Starz HDTV; The Movie Channel (multiplexed).

Fee: $10.00 installation; $13.99 monthly (each).

Video-On-Demand: Yes

Pay-Per-View

iN DEMAND (delivered digitally); Playboy TV (delivered digitally); Fresh (delivered digitally); Shorteez (delivered digitally); Pleasure (delivered digitally); Hot Choice (delivered digitally); Sports PPV (delivered digitally).

Internet Service

Operational: Yes.

Broadband Service: Comcast High Speed Internet.

Fee: $42.95 monthly.

Telephone Service

Digital: Operational

Miles of Plant: 221.0 (coaxial); None (fiber optic).

Vice President & General Manager: Kirk Dale. Technical Operations Director: Charlie Goodreau. Engineering Manager: Hank Swindle. Marketing Director: Kristopher Workman. Government & Community Affairs Director: Russell Byrd.

Ownership: Comcast Cable Communications Inc. (MSO).

HARTSVILLE—Comcast Cable. Now served by NASHVILLE, TN [TN0002]. ICA: TN0099.

HENDERSON—Charter Communications. Now served by JACKSON, TN [TN0008]. ICA: TN0074.

HENRY—Peoples CATV Inc., 4587 W Main St, PO Box 310, Erin, TN 37061-0310. Phone: 931-289-4221. Fax: 931-289-4220. Web Site: http://www.peoplescatv.com. ICA: TN0144.

TV Market Ranking: Outside TV Markets (HENRY). Franchise award date: April 12, 1983. Franchise expiration date: N.A. Began: January 1, 1985.

Channel capacity: 55 (not 2-way capable). Channels available but not in use: N.A.

Basic Service

Subscribers: 85.

Programming (received off-air): WBBJ-TV (ABC) Jackson; WLJT-DT (PBS) Lexington; WPSD-TV (NBC) Paducah; WSMV-TV (NBC, TMO) Nashville.

Programming (via satellite): CNN; ESPN; TBS Superstation; Turner Network TV; USA Network; WGN America.

Fee: $25.00 installation; $31.95 monthly.

Pay Service 1

Pay Units: 15.

Programming (via satellite): Cinemax.

Fee: $8.00 monthly.

Pay Service 2

Pay Units: 8.

Programming (via satellite): HBO.

Fee: $10.50 monthly.

Video-On-Demand: No

Internet Service

Operational: No.

Telephone Service

None

Miles of Plant: 11.0 (coaxial); None (fiber optic).

Manager: James H. Coakley. Marketing Director: Fay Lair. Chief Technician: Steve Hall. Program Director: Irene Wilbanks.

Ownership: Telephone Electronics Corp. (MSO).

HOHENWALD—Charter Communications. Now served by COLUMBIA, TN [TN0017]. ICA: TN0055.

HUMBOLDT—Infostructure Cable, 314 N 22nd Ave, Humboldt, TN 38343. Phone: 731-784-5000. Fax: 731-784-7474. E-mail: support@click1.net. Web Site: http://www.click1.net. Also serves Medina. ICA: TN0046.

TV Market Ranking: Below 100 (HUMBOLDT, Medina). Franchise award date: N.A. Franchise expiration date: N.A. Began: January 1, 1970.

Channel capacity: 116 (operating 2-way). Channels available but not in use: N.A.

Basic Service

Subscribers: 4,400.

Programming (received off-air): WBBJ-TV (ABC) Jackson; WDYR-CD Dyersburg; WHBQ-TV (FOX) Memphis; WJKT (FOX) Jackson; WKNO (PBS) Memphis; WLFT-CA (IND) Baton Rouge; WLJT-DT (PBS) Lexington; WLMT (CW) Memphis; WMC-TV (NBC) Memphis; WPTY-TV (ABC) Memphis; WPXX-TV (ION, MNT) Memphis; WREG-TV (CBS) Memphis.

Programming (via satellite): C-SPAN; C-SPAN 2; Gospel Music TV; QVC; TV Guide Network; WGN America.

Fee: $25.00 installation; $18.95 monthly; $1.25 converter; $12.50 additional installation.

Expanded Basic Service 1

Subscribers: 3,913.

Programming (via satellite): A&E Networks; ABC Family Channel; AMC; Animal Planet; BET Networks; Bravo; Cartoon Network; CNBC; CNN; Comcast/Charter Sports Southeast (CSS); Comedy Central; Country Music TV; Discovery Channel; Disney Channel; DIY Network; E! Entertainment Television; ESPN; ESPN 2; ESPN Classic Sports; Eternal Word TV Network; Food Network; Fox News Channel; Fox Sports Net Midwest; Fox Sports South; FX; Great American Country; Hallmark Channel; Headline News; HGTV; History Channel; INSP; Lifetime; MSNBC; MTV; National Geographic Channel; Nickelodeon; Oxygen; RFD-TV; SoapNet; Speed; Spike TV; SportSouth; Syfy; TBS Superstation; The Learning Channel; The Weather Channel; Travel Channel; Trinity Broadcasting Network; truTV; Turner Classic Movies; Turner Network TV; TV Land; USA Network; Versus; VH1; Weatherscan.

Fee: $37.00 monthly.

Digital Basic Service

Subscribers: 836.

Programming (via satellite): A&E HD; AmericanLife TV Network; BBC America; Bio; Bloomberg Television; CMT Pure Country; College Sports Television; Discovery Health Channel; Discovery Kids Channel; DMX Music; Encore; ESPN 2 HD; ESPN HD; ESPN U; ESPNews; Fox Business Channel; Fox College Sports Atlantic; Fox College Sports Central; Fox College Sports Pacific; Fox Movie Channel; Fuse; G4; Golf Channel; GSN; HD Theater; History Channel International; ID Investigation Discovery; JCTV; Lifetime Movie Network; Military Channel; MTV Hits; MTV Jams; MTV2; National Geographic Channel HD Network; Nick Jr.; NickToons TV; Outdoor Channel; Planet Green; Science; Style Network; TeenNick; Toon Disney; VH1 Classic; VH1 Soul; WAM! America's Kidz Network; WE tv.

Fee: $13.00 monthly.

Digital Pay Service 1

Pay Units: N.A.

Programming (via satellite): Cinemax (multiplexed); Flix; HBO (multiplexed); Showtime (multiplexed); Starz (multiplexed); Starz HDTV (multiplexed); Sundance Channel; The Movie Channel (multiplexed).

Fee: $14.00 monthly (Cinemax, HBO, Showtime/TMC/Flix or Starz/Encore).

Video-On-Demand: Yes

Pay-Per-View

Fresh (delivered digitally); Spice: Xcess (delivered digitally); Playboy TV (delivered digitally); Hot Choice (delivered digitally); iN DEMAND (delivered digitally).

Internet Service

Operational: Yes.

Subscribers: 1,400.

Fee: $29.95-$49.95 monthly.

Telephone Service

None

Miles of Plant: 105.0 (coaxial); None (fiber optic).

General Manager: Mark Love. Office Manager: Brandy Kemp.

Ownership: Warmath Communications Inc.

HUNTLAND—Mediacom, 123 Ware Dr NE, Huntsville, AL 35811-1061. Phones: 850-934-7700 (Gulf Breeze regional office); 256-852-7427. Fax: 256-851-7708. Web Site: http://www.mediacomcable.com. ICA: TN0116.

TV Market Ranking: 96 (HUNTLAND). Franchise award date: April 26, 1982. Franchise expiration date: N.A. Began: January 1, 1984.

Channel capacity: 36 (not 2-way capable). Channels available but not in use: N.A.

Basic Service

Subscribers: 326.

Programming (received off-air): WAAY-TV (ABC) Huntsville; WAFF (NBC) Huntsville; WHIQ (PBS) Huntsville; WHNT-TV (CBS) Huntsville; WKRN-TV (ABC) Nashville; WSMV-TV (NBC, TMO) Nashville; WZDX (FOX, MNT) Huntsville.

Fee: $5.11 monthly; $1.00 converter.

Expanded Basic Service 1

Subscribers: N.A.

Programming (via satellite): ABC Family Channel; AMC; CNN; Discovery Channel; ESPN; Lifetime; MTV; Nickelodeon; QVC;

Spike TV; TBS Superstation; Turner Network TV; USA Network; WGN America.
Fee: $15.68 monthly.

Pay Service 1
Pay Units: 68.
Programming (via satellite): Cinemax.
Fee: $9.95 monthly.

Pay Service 2
Pay Units: 73.
Programming (via satellite): HBO.
Fee: $9.95 monthly.

Pay Service 3
Pay Units: 65.
Programming (via satellite): Showtime.
Fee: $9.95 monthly.

Pay Service 4
Pay Units: 68.
Programming (via satellite): Flix.
Fee: $2.95 monthly.

Video-On-Demand: No

Internet Service
Operational: No.

Telephone Service
None

Miles of plant (coax) included in Huntsville, AL

Vice President: David Servies. General Manager: Tommy Hill. Technical Operations Supervisor: Mark Darwin. Sales & Marketing Manager: Joey Nagem. Customer Service Supervisor: Sandy Acklin.

Ownership: Mediacom LLC (MSO).

HUNTSVILLE—Comcast Cable, 5720 Asheville Hwy, Knoxville, TN 37924-2701. Phone: 865-971-1544. Fax: 865-862-5092. Web Site: http://www.comcast.com. Also serves Oneida, Scott County & Winfield. ICA: TN0195.

TV Market Ranking: Below 100 (HUNTSVILLE, Oneida, Scott County, Winfield).

Channel capacity: N.A. Channels available but not in use: N.A.

Basic Service
Subscribers: N.A.
Programming (received off-air): WATE-TV (ABC) Knoxville; WBIR-TV (NBC) Knoxville; WBXX-TV (CW) Crossville; WCTE (PBS) Cookeville; WETP-TV (PBS) Sneedville; WTNZ (FOX) Knoxville; WVLT-TV (CBS, MNT) Knoxville.
Programming (via satellite): CNBC; Comcast/Charter Sports Southeast (CSS); Outdoor Channel; WGN America.
Fee: $26.50 installation; $13.75 monthly.

Expanded Basic Service 1
Subscribers: N.A.
Programming (via satellite): A&E Networks; ABC Family Channel; AMC; Cartoon Network; CNN; Comedy Central; Country Music TV; C-SPAN; C-SPAN 2; Discovery Channel; Disney Channel; ESPN; ESPN 2; Fox News Channel; Fox Sports South; FX; Headline News; HGTV; History Channel; Lifetime; MTV; Nickelodeon; QVC; Spike TV; Syfy; TBS Superstation; The Weather Channel; Trinity Broadcasting Network; Turner Classic Movies; Turner Network TV; TV Land; USA Network; VH1.
Fee: $36.24 monthly.

Digital Basic Service
Subscribers: N.A.
Programming (via satellite): BBC America; CMT Pure Country; Discovery Digital Networks; Encore; GAS; MTV Networks Digital Suite; Music Choice; Nick Jr.; Nick Too.
Fee: $14.95 monthly.

Digital Pay Service 1
Pay Units: N.A.
Programming (via satellite): Cinemax (multiplexed); HBO (multiplexed); Showtime (multiplexed); Starz; The Movie Channel.
Fee: $13.99 monthly (each).

Video-On-Demand: No

Pay-Per-View
iN DEMAND (delivered digitally); Hot Choice (delivered digitally).

Internet Service
Operational: Yes.

Telephone Service
None

Vice President & General Manager: Kirk Dale. Technical Operations Director: Charlie Goodreau. Engineering Manager: Hank Swindle. Marketing Director: Kristopher Workman. Government & Community Affairs Director: Russell Byrd.

Ownership: Comcast Cable Communications Inc. (MSO).

JACKSON—Charter Communications, 1774 Henry G Lane St, Maryville, TN 37801. Phones: 865-984-1400 (Maryville office); 731-424-3290 (Local office). Fax: 865-983-0383. Web Site: http://www.charter.com. Also serves Alamo, Bells, Chester County (portions), Crockett County (portions), Gadsden, Henderson, Madison County (portions) & Maury City. ICA: TN0008.

TV Market Ranking: Below 100 (Alamo, Bells, Chester County (portions), Crockett County (portions), Gadsden, Henderson, JACKSON, Madison County (portions), Maury City).

Channel capacity: N.A. Channels available but not in use: N.A.

Basic Service
Subscribers: 27,454.
Programming (received off-air): WBBJ-TV (ABC) Jackson; WHBQ-TV (FOX) Memphis; WJKT (FOX) Jackson; WKNO (PBS) Memphis; WLJT-DT (PBS) Lexington; WMC-TV (NBC) Memphis; WPXX-TV (ION, MNT) Memphis; WREG-TV (CBS) Memphis; WSMV-TV (NBC, TMO) Nashville; WTVF (CBS) Nashville.
Programming (via satellite): WGN America.

Expanded Basic Service 1
Subscribers: N.A.
Programming (via satellite): A&E Networks; ABC Family Channel; AMC; Animal Planet; BET Networks; Bravo; Cartoon Network; CNBC; CNN; Comcast/Charter Sports Southeast (CSS); Comedy Central; Country Music TV; C-SPAN; C-SPAN 2; Discovery Channel; Disney Channel; E! Entertainment Television; ESPN; ESPN 2; Food Network; Fox News Channel; Fox Sports South; FX; G4; Golf Channel; GSN; Hallmark Channel; Headline News; HGTV; History Channel; INSP; Lifetime; MSNBC; MTV; National Geographic Channel; Nickelodeon; Oxygen; QVC; SoapNet; Speed; Spike TV; SportSouth; Style Network; Syfy; TBS Superstation; The Learning Channel; The Weather Channel; Toon Disney; Travel Channel; Trinity Broadcasting Network; truTV; Turner Classic Movies; Turner Network TV; TV Guide Network; TV Land; USA Network; VH1; WE tv.
Fee: $45.00 monthly.

Digital Basic Service
Subscribers: N.A.
Programming (via satellite): BBC America; Bio; Bloomberg Television; Boomerang; CNN en Espanol; DIY Network; ESPN; ESPN Classic Sports; ESPNews; Fox College Sports Atlantic; Fox College Sports Central; Fox College Sports Pacific; Fox Movie Channel; Fox Soccer; Fuel TV; Fuse; GAS; Great American Country; HD Theater; HDNet; HDNet Movies; History Channel International; Independent Film Channel; Lifetime Movie Network; Lifetime Real Women; MTV Networks Digital Suite; Music Choice; NFL Network; Nick Jr.; Nick Too; NickToons TV; Outdoor Channel; Sundance Channel; TV Guide Interactive Inc.

Digital Pay Service 1
Pay Units: N.A.
Programming (via satellite): Cinemax (multiplexed); Encore (multiplexed); HBO (multiplexed); HBO HD; Showtime (multiplexed); Showtime HD; Starz (multiplexed); The Movie Channel (multiplexed).

Video-On-Demand: Yes

Pay-Per-View
iN DEMAND (delivered digitally); NASCAR In Car (delivered digitally); NHL Center Ice (delivered digitally); MLB Extra Innings (delivered digitally); Playboy TV (delivered digitally); Fresh (delivered digitally); Shorteez (delivered digitally).

Internet Service
Operational: Yes.
Broadband Service: Charter Pipeline.
Fee: $29.99 monthly.

Telephone Service
Digital: Operational
Fee: $29.99 monthly

Miles of Plant: 620.0 (coaxial); None (fiber optic).

Operations Manager: Tony Fox. Technical Operations Director: Ron Janson. Marketing Director: Pat Hollenbeck. Marketing Manager: Wiley Bird.

Ownership: Charter Communications Inc. (MSO).

JAMESTOWN—Comcast Cable, 5720 Asheville Hwy, Knoxville, TN 37924-2701. Phone: 865-971-1544. Fax: 865-862-5092. Web Site: http://www.comcast.com. Also serves Allardt & Fentress County. ICA: TN0196.

TV Market Ranking: Below 100 (Allardt, Fentress County, JAMESTOWN).

Channel capacity: N.A. Channels available but not in use: N.A.

Basic Service
Subscribers: N.A.
Programming (received off-air): WATE-TV (ABC) Knoxville; WBIR-TV (NBC) Knoxville; WBXX-TV (CW) Crossville; WCTE (PBS) Cookeville; WETP-TV (PBS) Sneedville; WSMV-TV (NBC, TMO) Nashville; WTNZ (FOX) Knoxville; WTVF (CBS) Nashville; WVLT-TV (CBS, MNT) Knoxville.
Programming (via satellite): A&E Networks; ABC Family Channel; AMC; Cartoon Network; CNBC; CNN; Comcast/Charter Sports Southeast (CSS); Comedy Central; Country Music TV; C-SPAN; C-SPAN 2; Discovery Channel; Disney Channel; ESPN; ESPN 2; Fox News Channel; Fox Sports South; FX; Headline News; HGTV; History Channel; Lifetime; MTV; Nickelodeon; Outdoor Channel; QVC; Spike TV; Syfy; TBS Superstation; The Weather Channel; Trinity Broadcasting Network; Turner Classic Movies; Turner Network TV; TV Land; USA Network; VH1; WGN America.
Fee: $56.50 installation; $39.95 monthly.

Digital Basic Service
Subscribers: N.A.
Programming (via satellite): BBC America; CMT Pure Country; Discovery Digital Networks; Encore (multiplexed); GAS; MTV Networks Digital Suite; Music Choice; Nick Jr.; Nick Too.
Fee: $14.95 monthly.

Digital Pay Service 1
Pay Units: N.A.
Programming (via satellite): Cinemax (multiplexed); HBO (multiplexed); Showtime (multiplexed); Starz; The Movie Channel.
Fee: $13.99 monthly (each).

Video-On-Demand: No

Pay-Per-View
iN DEMAND (delivered digitally); Hot Choice (delivered digitally).

Internet Service
Operational: Yes.

Telephone Service
None

Vice President & General Manager: Kirk Dale. Technical Operations Director: Charlie Goodreau. Engineering Manager: Hank Swindle. Marketing Director: Kristopher Workman. Government & Community Affairs Director: Russell Byrd.

Ownership: Comcast Cable Communications Inc. (MSO).

JASPER—Charter Communications, 1235 King St SE, Cleveland, TN 37323. Phones: 865-984-1400 (Maryville office); 423-478-1934. Fax: 423-476-1621. Web Site: http://www.charter.com. Also serves Kimball, Marion County, New Hope, Powells Crossroads, Sequatchie, South Pittsburg, Whiteside & Whitwell. ICA: TN0070.

TV Market Ranking: 78 (JASPER, Kimball, Marion County, New Hope, Powells Crossroads, Sequatchie, South Pittsburg, Whiteside, Whitwell). Franchise award date: March 1, 1983. Franchise expiration date: N.A. Began: July 1, 1983.

Channel capacity: N.A. Channels available but not in use: N.A.

Basic Service
Subscribers: 9,790.
Programming (received off-air): WAAY-TV (ABC) Huntsville; WDEF-TV (CBS) Chattanooga; WDSI-TV (FOX, MNT) Chattanooga; WELF-TV (TBN) Dalton; WLFI-TV (CBS) Lafayette; WNGH-TV (PBS) Chatsworth; WRCB (NBC) Chattanooga; WTCI (PBS) Chattanooga; WTVC (ABC) Chattanooga; WXIA-TV (NBC) Atlanta.
Programming (via satellite): C-SPAN; C-SPAN 2; INSP; ION Television; QVC; Shop at Home; WGN America.
Fee: $25.00 installation; $9.05 monthly.

Expanded Basic Service 1
Subscribers: 390.
Programming (via satellite): A&E Networks; ABC Family Channel; AMC; Animal Planet; BET Networks; Bravo; Cartoon Network; CNBC; CNN; Comcast/Charter Sports Southeast (CSS); Comedy Central; Country Music TV; Discovery Channel; E! Entertainment Television; ESPN; ESPN 2; Food Network; Fox News Channel; Fox Sports South; FX; G4; Golf Channel;

GSN; Hallmark Channel; Headline News; HGTV; History Channel; Lifetime; MSNBC; MTV; National Geographic Channel; Nickelodeon; Oxygen; SoapNet; Speed; Spike TV; SportSouth; Syfy; TBS Superstation; The Learning Channel; The Weather Channel; Toon Disney; Travel Channel; truTV; Turner Classic Movies; Turner Network TV; TV Guide Network; TV Land; USA Network; Versus; VH1; WE tv.
Fee: $3.50 monthly.

Digital Basic Service
Subscribers: N.A.
Programming (via satellite): BBC America; Bio; Canales N; Discovery Fit & Health; DIY Network; ESPN Classic Sports; ESPNews; Fox College Sports Atlantic; Fox College Sports Central; Fox College Sports Pacific; Fox Movie Channel; Fox Soccer; Fuel TV; GAS; Great American Country; History Channel International; Independent Film Channel; Jewelry Television; Lifetime Movie Network; Lifetime Real Women; MTV2; Music Choice; NFL Network; Nick Jr.; Nick Too; NickToons TV; Style Network; Sundance Channel; TV Guide Interactive Inc.; VH1 Classic.

Digital Pay Service 1
Pay Units: N.A.
Programming (via satellite): Cinemax (multiplexed); Encore (multiplexed); HBO (multiplexed); Showtime (multiplexed); Starz (multiplexed); The Movie Channel (multiplexed).

Video-On-Demand: Yes

Internet Service
Operational: Yes.
Broadband Service: Charter Pipeline.
Fee: $29.99 monthly.

Telephone Service
Digital: Operational

Miles of Plant: 62.0 (coaxial); None (fiber optic). Additional miles planned: 12.0 (coaxial).

Operations Manager: Mike Burns. Technical Operations Manager: David Ogle. Marketing Director: Pat Hollenbeck.

Ownership: Charter Communications Inc. (MSO).

JELLICO—Access Cable Television Inc., 302 Enterprise Dr, Somerset, KY 42501. Phone: 606-677-2444. Fax: 606-677-2443. E-mail: cable@accesshsd.net. Also serves Emlyn & Whitley County (southern portion), KY; Newcomb & Oswego, TN. ICA: TN0056.

TV Market Ranking: Below 100 (Emlyn, JELLICO, Newcomb, Oswego, Whitley County (southern portion)). Franchise award date: N.A. Franchise expiration date: N.A. Began: April 1, 1979.

Channel capacity: N.A. Channels available but not in use: N.A.

Basic Service
Subscribers: 816.
Programming (received off-air): WAGV (IND) Harlan; WATE-TV (ABC) Knoxville; WBXX-TV (CW) Crossville; WETP-TV (PBS) Sneedville; WKSO-TV (PBS) Somerset; WKYT-TV (CBS, CW) Lexington; WLEX-TV (NBC) Lexington; WTNZ (FOX) Knoxville; WVLT-TV (CBS, MNT) Knoxville; WYMT-TV (CBS, CW) Hazard.
Programming (via satellite): AMC; CNN; Country Music TV; Discovery Channel; E! Entertainment Television; ESPN; Headline News; ION Television; MTV; Nickelodeon; QVC; Syfy; The Learning Channel; Trinity Broadcasting Network; VH1; WGN America.
Fee: $25.00 installation; $18.95 monthly; $3.00 converter; $15.00 additional installation.

Expanded Basic Service 1
Subscribers: 590.
Programming (via satellite): A&E Networks; ABC Family Channel; Cartoon Network; Disney Channel; ESPN 2; Fox News Channel; FX; Hallmark Channel; HGTV; History Channel; Lifetime; Outdoor Channel; Spike TV; TBS Superstation; The Weather Channel; Turner Network TV; TV Land; USA Network.
Fee: $10.80 monthly.

Pay Service 1
Pay Units: 35.
Programming (via satellite): Cinemax.
Fee: $11.95 monthly.

Pay Service 2
Pay Units: 43.
Programming (via satellite): HBO.
Fee: $11.95 monthly.

Video-On-Demand: No

Internet Service
Operational: Yes.

Telephone Service
Digital: Operational
Fee: $24.95 monthly

Miles of Plant: 90.0 (coaxial); None (fiber optic).

President & Manager: Roy Baker.

Ownership: Access Cable Television Inc. (MSO).

JOHNSON CITY—Charter Communications. Now served by KINGSPORT, TN [TN0007]. ICA: TN0010.

KINGSPORT—Charter Communications, 105 Jack White Dr, Kingsport, TN 37664. Phone: 423-247-7631. Fax: 423-247-1807. Web Site: http://www.charter.com. Also serves Blountville, Bluff City, Bristol, Carter County (portions), Church Hill, Colonial Heights, Elizabethton, Hawkins County, Johnson City, Lynn Garden, Mount Carmel, Sullivan County & Wautauga, TN; Bristol, Holston Valley, Scott County (portions) & Washington County (portions), VA. ICA: TN0007.

TV Market Ranking: Below 100 (Blountville, Bluff City, Bristol, Carter County (portions), Church Hill, Colonial Heights, Elizabethton, Hawkins County, Holston Valley, Johnson City, KINGSPORT, Lynn Garden, Mount Carmel, Scott County (portions), Sullivan County, Washington County (portions), Wautauga). Franchise award date: May 17, 1966. Franchise expiration date: January 20, 2007. Began: December 1, 1980.

Channel capacity: N.A. Channels available but not in use: N.A.

Basic Service
Subscribers: 91,042.
Programming (received off-air): WAPK-CA (MNT) Kingsport; WCYB-TV (CW, NBC) Bristol; WEMT (FOX) Greeneville; WETP-TV (PBS) Sneedville; WJHL-TV (CBS) Johnson City; WKPT-TV (ABC) Kingsport; WLFG (IND) Grundy; WSBN-TV (PBS) Norton; 16 FMs.
Programming (via satellite): Comcast/Charter Sports Southeast (CSS); C-SPAN; C-SPAN 2; INSP; ION Television; QVC; Shop at Home; The Weather Channel; TV Guide Network; WGN America.
Fee: $39.95 installation; $13.95 monthly.

Expanded Basic Service 1
Subscribers: 31,100.
Programming (received off-air): WBIR-TV (NBC) Knoxville.
Programming (via satellite): A&E Networks; ABC Family Channel; AMC; Animal Planet; BET Networks; Bravo; Cartoon Network; CNBC; CNN; Comedy Central; Country Music TV; Discovery Channel; Discovery Fit & Health; Disney Channel; E! Entertainment Television; ESPN; ESPN 2; Food Network; Fox News Channel; Fox Sports South; FX; G4; Golf Channel; GSN; Hallmark Channel; Headline News; HGTV; History Channel; Lifetime; MSNBC; MTV; National Geographic Channel; Nickelodeon; Oxygen; SoapNet; Speed; Spike TV; SportSouth; Style Network; Syfy; TBS Superstation; The Learning Channel; Toon Disney; Travel Channel; Trinity Broadcasting Network; truTV; Turner Classic Movies; Turner Network TV; TV Land; USA Network; Versus; VH1; WE tv.
Fee: $45.00 monthly.

Digital Basic Service
Subscribers: N.A.
Programming (via satellite): BBC America; Bio; Boomerang; CNN en Espanol; CNN International; DIY Network; ESPN; ESPN Classic Sports; ESPNews; Fox College Sports Atlantic; Fox College Sports Central; Fox College Sports Pacific; Fox Movie Channel; Fox Sports World; Fuel TV; GAS; Great American Country; HD Theater; HDNet; HDNet Movies; History Channel International; Independent Film Channel; Jewelry Television; Lifetime Movie Network; Lifetime Real Women; MTV Networks Digital Suite; Music Choice; NFL Network; Nick Jr.; Nick Too; NickToons TV; Outdoor Channel; Sundance Channel; TV Guide Interactive Inc.

Digital Pay Service 1
Pay Units: N.A.
Programming (via satellite): Cinemax (multiplexed); Encore (multiplexed); Flix; HBO (multiplexed); HBO HD; Showtime (multiplexed); Showtime HD; Starz (multiplexed); The Movie Channel (multiplexed).

Video-On-Demand: Yes

Pay-Per-View
Pleasure (delivered digitally); Playboy TV (delivered digitally); Fresh (delivered digitally); Shorteez (delivered digitally); iN DEMAND (delivered digitally); NASCAR In Car (delivered digitally); NHL Center Ice (delivered digitally); MLB Extra Innings (delivered digitally).

Internet Service
Operational: Yes.
Broadband Service: Charter Pipeline.
Fee: $29.99 monthly; $10.00 modem lease; $199.00 modem purchase.

Telephone Service
Digital: Operational
Subscribers: 10,000.
Fee: $29.99 monthly

Operations Manager: Tony Falin. Technical Operations Manager: Bruce Cocke. Marketing Director: Pat Hollenbeck. Sales & Marketing Manager: Kevin Kick.

Ownership: Charter Communications Inc. (MSO).

KNOXVILLE—Comcast Cable, 5720 Asheville Hwy, Knoxville, TN 37924-2701. Phone: 865-971-1544. Fax: 865-862-5092. Web Site: http://www.comcast.com. Also serves Blaine, Blount County (portions), Knox County, Luttrell, Maynardville, Powell, Rockford & Union County (portions). ICA: TN0004.

TV Market Ranking: 71 (Blaine, Blount County (portions), Knox County, KNOXVILLE, Luttrell, Maynardville, Powell, Rockford, Union County (portions)). Franchise award date: June 17, 1973. Franchise expiration date: N.A. Began: March 1, 1975.

Channel capacity: N.A. Channels available but not in use: N.A.

Basic Service
Subscribers: 107,334.
Programming (received off-air): WATE-TV (ABC) Knoxville; WBIR-TV (NBC) Knoxville; WBXX-TV (CW) Crossville; WKOP-TV (PBS) Knoxville; WPXK-TV (ION) Jellico; WTNZ (FOX) Knoxville; WVLR (IND) Tazewell; WVLT-TV (CBS, MNT) Knoxville; 2 FMs.
Programming (via satellite): QVC; WGN America.
Fee: $56.50 installation; $11.75 monthly.

Expanded Basic Service 1
Subscribers: 105,333.
Programming (via satellite): A&E Networks; ABC Family Channel; AMC; Animal Planet; BET Networks; Bravo; Cartoon Network; CNBC; CNN; Comcast/Charter Sports Southeast (CSS); Comedy Central; Country Music TV; C-SPAN; C-SPAN 2; Discovery Channel; Discovery Health Channel; Disney Channel; DIY Network; E! Entertainment Television; ESPN; ESPN 2; ESPN Classic Sports; Food Network; Fox News Channel; Fox Sports Net; FX; Golf Channel; Great American Country; GSN; Hallmark Channel; Headline News; HGTV; History Channel; Home Shopping Network 2; INSP; Lifetime; MSNBC; MTV; Nickelodeon; Shop at Home; Speed; Spike TV; Style Network; Syfy; TBS Superstation; The Learning Channel; The Weather Channel; Trinity Broadcasting Network; truTV; Turner Classic Movies; Turner Network TV; TV Guide Network; TV Land; USA Network; Versus; VH1; WBIR-TV (NBC) Knoxville.
Fee: $38.24 monthly.

Digital Basic Service
Subscribers: 16,245.
Programming (via satellite): BBC America; Bio; Cooking Channel; C-SPAN 3; Discovery Digital Networks; DMX Music; Encore Action; ESPNews; Flix; G4; GAS; History Channel International; MTV Networks Digital Suite; National Geographic Channel; Nick Jr.; Nick Too; SoapNet; Sundance Channel; Toon Disney; WAM! America's Kidz Network; Weatherscan.
Fee: $14.95 monthly.

Digital Pay Service 1
Pay Units: 10,000.
Programming (via satellite): Cinemax (multiplexed); HBO (multiplexed); Showtime (multiplexed); Starz (multiplexed); The Movie Channel (multiplexed).
Fee: $13.99 monthly (each).

Video-On-Demand: Yes

Pay-Per-View
Addressable homes: 26,245.
iN DEMAND (delivered digitally); Playboy TV (delivered digitally); Fresh (delivered digitally); Shorteez (delivered digitally); Pleasure (delivered digitally); ESPN Now (delivered digitally); Sports PPV (delivered digitally).

Internet Service
Operational: Yes. Began: January 1, 2001.
Broadband Service: Comcast High Speed Internet.
Fee: $42.95 monthly; $7.00 modem lease.

Telephone Service
Digital: Operational
Fee: $44.95 monthly

Miles of Plant: 2,625.0 (coaxial); 1,090.0 (fiber optic).

Vice President & General Manager: Kirk Dale. Technical Operations Director: Charlie Goodreau. Engineering Manager: Hank Swindle. Marketing Director: Kristopher Workman. Government & Community Affairs Director: Russell Byrd.

Ownership: Comcast Cable Communications Inc. (MSO).

KNOXVILLE—Formerly served by Tennessee Wireless Inc. No longer in operation. ICA: TN0180.

KNOXVILLE—Knology, 10115 Sherrill Blvd, Knoxville, TN 37932. Phones: 706-645-8553 (Corporate office); 865-357-1000 (Customer service). Fax: 865-357-1059. Web Site: http://www.knology.com. ICA: TN0208. **Note:** This system is an overbuild.

TV Market Ranking: 71 (KNOXVILLE).

Channel capacity: N.A. Channels available but not in use: N.A.

Basic Service

Subscribers: N.A.

Programming (received off-air): WATE-TV (ABC) Knoxville; WBIR-TV (NBC) Knoxville; WBXX-TV (CW) Crossville; WKOP-TV (PBS) Knoxville; WMAK (IND) Knoxville; WTNZ (FOX) Knoxville; WVLR (IND) Tazewell; WVLT-TV (CBS, MNT) Knoxville.

Programming (via satellite): MyNetworkTV Inc.; QVC.

Expanded Basic Service 1

Subscribers: N.A.

Programming (via satellite): A&E Networks; ABC Family Channel; American Movie Classics; Animal Planet; BET Networks; Bravo; Cartoon Network; CNBC; CNN; Comcast/Charter Sports Southeast (CSS); Comedy Central; Country Music TV; C-SPAN; C-SPAN 2; Discovery Channel; Discovery Health Channel; Disney Channel; E! Entertainment Television; ESPN; ESPN 2; Food Network; Fox News Channel; Fox Sports South; FX; G4; GMC; Golf Channel; Great American Country; Hallmark Channel; Headline News; HGTV; History Channel; ION Television; Lifetime; Lifetime Movie Network; MSNBC; MTV; Nickelodeon; Outdoor Channel; Oxygen; ShopNBC; Speed; Spike TV; SportSouth; Syfy; TBS Superstation; The Learning Channel; The Weather Channel; Toon Disney; Travel Channel; Trinity Broadcasting Network; truTV; Turner Classic Movies; Turner Network TV; TV Guide Network; TV Land; Univision Studios; USA Network; VH1; WGN America.

Digital Basic Service

Subscribers: N.A. Included in Valley AL

Programming (via satellite): Animal Planet HD; BBC America; Bio; Bloomberg Television; Church Channel; CMT Pure Country; Cooking Channel; C-SPAN 3; Discovery Fit & Health; Discovery Kids Channel; DIY Network; DMX Music; ESPN 2 HD; ESPN HD; ESPN U; Eternal Word TV Network; Fox Movie Channel; Fuse; Golf Channel; Hallmark Movie Channel; Halogen Network; HD Theater; HDNet; HDNet Movies; History Channel International; ID Investigation Discovery; Independent Film Channel; INSP; JCTV; Jewelry Television; Lifetime Real Women; Military Channel; MTV Hits; MTV Jams; MTV2; mtvU; NFL Network; Nick Jr.; Nick Too; NickToons TV; Planet Green; QVC HD; Science; Science HD; SoapNet; Style Network; TBS in HD; TeenNick; The Learning Channel; Tr3s; Turner Network TV HD; Universal HD; Versus; Versus HD; VH1 Classic; VH1 Soul; WE tv; Weatherscan.

Digital Pay Service 1

Pay Units: N.A.

Programming (via satellite): Cinemax (multiplexed); Cinemax HD; Discovery Channel HD; Encore (multiplexed); Flix; HBO (multiplexed); HBO HD; Showtime (multiplexed); Showtime HD; Starz (multiplexed); Starz HDTV; Sundance Channel; The Movie Channel (multiplexed).

Video-On-Demand: Yes

Pay-Per-View

iN DEMAND (delivered digitally); ESPN (delivered digitally); Fresh (delivered digitally); Playboy TV (delivered digitally); Shorteez (delivered digitally); Hot Choice (delivered digitally); Spice: Xcess (delivered digitally); Club Jenna (delivered digitally).

Internet Service

Operational: Yes.

Fee: $54.95 monthly.

Telephone Service

Digital: Operational

Fee: $19.80 monthly

General Manager: Jason Clabo. Marketing Manager: Jim Zink. Technical Operations Manager: Randy Zelenak.

Ownership: Knology Inc. (MSO).

KODAK—Comcast Cable, 5720 Asheville Hwy, Knoxville, TN 37924-2701. Phone: 865-971-1544. Fax: 865-862-5092. Web Site: http://www.comcast.com. ICA: TN0194.

TV Market Ranking: 71 (KODAK).

Channel capacity: N.A. Channels available but not in use: N.A.

Basic Service

Subscribers: N.A.

Programming (received off-air): WATE-TV (ABC) Knoxville; WBIR-TV (NBC) Knoxville; WBXX-TV (CW) Crossville; WETP-TV (PBS) Sneedville; WKOP-TV (PBS) Knoxville; WMAK (IND) Knoxville; WPXK-TV (ION) Jellico; WTNZ (FOX) Knoxville; WVLR (IND) Tazewell; WVLT-TV (CBS, MNT) Knoxville.

Programming (via satellite): C-SPAN 2; QVC; WGN America.

Fee: $56.50 installation; $13.75 monthly.

Expanded Basic Service 1

Subscribers: N.A.

Programming (via satellite): A&E Networks; ABC Family Channel; AMC; Animal Planet; BET Networks; Bravo; Cartoon Network; CNBC; CNN; Comcast/Charter Sports Southeast (CSS); Comedy Central; Country Music TV; C-SPAN; Discovery Channel; Discovery Health Channel; Disney Channel; DIY Network; E! Entertainment Television; ESPN; ESPN 2; ESPN Classic Sports; Food Network; Fox News Channel; Fox Sports South; FX; G4; Golf Channel; Great American Country; GSN; Hallmark Channel; Headline News; HGTV; History Channel; INSP; Lifetime; MSNBC; MTV; Nickelodeon; Speed; Spike TV; Style Network; Syfy; TBS Superstation; The Learning Channel; The Weather Channel; Travel Channel; Trinity Broadcasting Network; truTV; Turner Classic Movies; Turner Network TV; Turner South; TV Guide Network; TV Land; USA Network; Versus; VH1.

Fee: $36.24 monthly.

Digital Basic Service

Subscribers: N.A.

Programming (via satellite): BBC America; Bio; CMT Pure Country; Cooking Channel; C-SPAN 3; Current; Disney Channel; Encore (multiplexed); ESPN 2 HD; ESPN HD; ESPNews; Eternal Word TV Network; Flix; Fox College Sports Atlantic; Fox College Sports Central; Fox College Sports Pacific; Fox Reality Channel; Fox Soccer; GAS; GolTV; Halogen Network; HD Theater; History Channel International; INHD; Jewelry Television; Lifetime Movie Network; MoviePlex; MTV Networks Digital Suite; Music Choice; National Geographic Channel; NFL Network; Nick Jr.; Nick Too; NickToons TV; Palladia; PBS Kids Sprout; ShopNBC; SoapNet; Sundance Channel; The Word Network; Toon Disney; Turner Network TV HD; TV One; Versus HD; Weatherscan.

Fee: $14.95 monthly.

Digital Pay Service 1

Pay Units: N.A.

Programming (via satellite): Cinemax (multiplexed); Cinemax HD; HBO (multiplexed); HBO HD; Showtime (multiplexed); Showtime HD; Starz (multiplexed); Starz HDTV; The Movie Channel.

Fee: $13.99 monthly (each).

Video-On-Demand: Yes

Pay-Per-View

Movies (delivered digitally); NBA League Pass (delivered digitally); iN DEMAND (delivered digitally); Playboy TV (delivered digitally); Hot Choice (delivered digitally); Special events (delivered digitally).

Internet Service

Operational: Yes.

Broadband Service: Comcast High Speed Internet.

Fee: $42.95 installation.

Telephone Service

Digital: Operational

Fee: $44.95 monthly

Vice President & General Manager: Kirk Dale. Technical Operations Director: Charlie Goodreau. Engineering Manager: Hank Swindle. Marketing Director: Kristopher Workman. Government & Community Affairs Director: Russell Byrd.

Ownership: Comcast Cable Communications Inc. (MSO).

LA FOLLETTE—Comcast Cable, 5720 Asheville Hwy, Knoxville, TN 37924-2701. Phone: 865-971-1544. Fax: 865-862-5092. Web Site: http://www.comcast.com. Also serves Campbell County, Caryville, Jacksboro & Lake City. ICA: TN0035.

TV Market Ranking: 71 (Campbell County (portions), Caryville, Jacksboro, LA FOLLETTE, Lake City); Below 100 (Campbell County (portions)). Franchise award date: May 11, 1965. Franchise expiration date: N.A. Began: September 20, 1966.

Channel capacity: 67 (operating 2-way). Channels available but not in use: N.A.

Basic Service

Subscribers: 9,400.

Programming (received off-air): WATE-TV (ABC) Knoxville; WBIR-TV (NBC) Knoxville; WBXX-TV (CW) Crossville; WETP-TV (PBS) Sneedville; WMAK (IND) Knoxville; WPXK-TV (ION) Jellico; WTNZ (FOX) Knoxville; WVLR (IND) Tazewell; WVLT-TV (CBS, MNT) Knoxville; allband FM.

Programming (via satellite): C-SPAN; QVC; WGN America.

Fee: $56.50 installation; $13.75 monthly.

Expanded Basic Service 1

Subscribers: N.A.

Programming (via satellite): 10 News 2; A&E Networks; ABC Family Channel; AMC; Animal Planet; BET Networks; Bravo; Cartoon Network; CNBC; CNN; Comcast/Charter Sports Southeast (CSS); Comedy Central; Discovery Channel; Discovery Health Channel; Disney Channel; DIY Network; E! Entertainment Television; ESPN; ESPN 2; Food Network; Fox News Channel; Fox Sports South; FX; Golf Channel; Great American Country; Hallmark Channel; Headline News; HGTV; History Channel; Lifetime; MTV; Nickelodeon; Speed; Spike TV; Style Network; Syfy; TBS Superstation; The Learning Channel; The Weather Channel; Trinity Broadcasting Network; truTV; Turner Classic Movies; Turner Network TV; TV Guide Network; TV Land; USA Network; Versus; VH1.

Fee: $36.24 monthly.

Digital Basic Service

Subscribers: N.A.

Programming (via satellite): BBC America; Bio; CMT Pure Country; Country Music TV; C-SPAN 2; C-SPAN 3; Discovery Digital Networks; DMX Music; Encore (multiplexed); ESPN Classic Sports; ESPNews; Flix; GAS; GSN; History Channel International; Jewelry Television; MSNBC; MTV Networks Digital Suite; National Geographic Channel; Nick Jr.; Nick Too; NickToons TV; PBS Kids Sprout; SoapNet; Sundance Channel; Toon Disney; Weatherscan.

Fee: $14.95 monthly.

Digital Pay Service 1

Pay Units: 166.

Programming (via satellite): Cinemax (multiplexed); HBO (multiplexed); HBO On Demand; Showtime (multiplexed); Starz (multiplexed); The Movie Channel (multiplexed).

Fee: $13.99 monthly (each).

Video-On-Demand: Yes

Pay-Per-View

iN DEMAND (delivered digitally); Hot Choice (delivered digitally); Playboy TV (delivered digitally); Fresh (delivered digitally); Shorteez (delivered digitally); Pleasure (delivered digitally).

Internet Service

Operational: Yes.

Broadband Service: Comcast High Speed Internet.

Fee: $42.95 monthly.

Telephone Service

Digital: Operational

Miles of Plant: 280.0 (coaxial); 48.0 (fiber optic).

Area Vice President & General Manager: Kirk Dale. Technical Operations Director: Charlie Goodreau. Engineering Manager: Hank Swindle. Marketing Director: Kristopher Workman. Government & Community Affairs Director: Russell Byrd.

Ownership: Comcast Cable Communications Inc. (MSO).

LAFAYETTE—Comcast Cable. Now served by SCOTTSVILLE, KY [KY0073]. ICA: TN0085.

LAUREL BLOOMERY—Charter Communications. Now served by MOUNTAIN CITY, TN [TN0067]. ICA: TN0146.

LAWRENCEBURG—Charter Communications, 1774 Henry G Lane St, Maryville, TN 37801. Phone: 865-984-1400. Fax: 865-983-0383. Web Site: http://www.charter.com. Also serves Lawrence County (portions). ICA: TN0147.

TV Market Ranking: Below 100 (Lawrence County (portions), LAWRENCEBURG); Outside TV Markets (Lawrence County (portions)). Franchise award date: N.A. Franchise expiration date: N.A. Began: N.A.

Channel capacity: N.A. Channels available but not in use: N.A.

Basic Service

Subscribers: 4,640.

Programming (received off-air): WAAY-TV (ABC) Huntsville; WAFF (NBC) Huntsville; WHNT-TV (CBS) Huntsville; WKRN-TV (ABC) Nashville; WNAB (CW) Nashville; WNPT (PBS) Nashville; WSMV-TV (NBC, TMO) Nashville; WTVF (CBS) Nashville; WUXP-TV (MNT) Nashville; WZTV (FOX) Nashville.

Programming (via satellite): Comcast/Charter Sports Southeast (CSS); C-SPAN; C-SPAN 2; Eternal Word TV Network; INSP; Trinity Broadcasting Network; TV Guide Network; WGN America.

Expanded Basic Service 1

Subscribers: N.A.

Programming (via satellite): A&E Networks; ABC Family Channel; AMC; Animal Planet; BET Networks; Bravo; Cartoon Network; CNBC; CNN; Comedy Central; Country Music TV; Discovery Channel; Discovery Fit & Health; Disney Channel; E! Entertainment Television; ESPN; ESPN 2; Food Network; Fox News Channel; Fox Sports South; FX; G4; GalaVision; Golf Channel; GSN; Hallmark Channel; Headline News; HGTV; History Channel; Lifetime; MSNBC; MTV; National Geographic Channel; Nickelodeon; Oxygen; SoapNet; Speed; Spike TV; SportSouth; Syfy; TBS Superstation; Telemundo; The Learning Channel; The Weather Channel; Toon Disney; Travel Channel; truTV; Turner Classic Movies; Turner Network TV; TV Land; Univision Studios; USA Network; Versus; VH1; WE tv.

Fee: $45.00 monthly.

Digital Basic Service

Subscribers: N.A.

Programming (via satellite): BBC America; Bio; Bloomberg Television; Boomerang; CNN International; Discovery Digital Networks; DIY Network; ESPN Classic Sports; ESPNews; Fox College Sports Atlantic; Fox College Sports Central; Fox College Sports Pacific; Fox Movie Channel; Fox Soccer; Fuel TV; GAS; Great American Country; History Channel International; Independent Film Channel; Lifetime Movie Network; Lifetime Real Women; MTV Networks Digital Suite; Music Choice; NFL Network; Nick Jr.; Nick Too; NickToons TV; Outdoor Channel; Science Television; Style Network; Sundance Channel.

Digital Pay Service 1

Pay Units: N.A.

Programming (via satellite): Cinemax (multiplexed); HBO (multiplexed); Starz (multiplexed).

Video-On-Demand: Yes

Pay-Per-View

Playboy TV (delivered digitally); Fresh (delivered digitally); Shorteez (delivered digitally).

Internet Service

Operational: Yes.

Broadband Service: Charter Pipeline.

Fee: $29.99 monthly.

Telephone Service

Digital: Operational

Fee: $29.99 monthly

Operations Manager: Sean Hendrix. Marketing Director: Pat Hollenbeck. Sales & Marketing Manager: Jo Ann Placke.

Ownership: Charter Communications Inc. (MSO).

LEBANON—Charter Communications, 1774 Henry G Lane St, Maryville, TN 37801. Phone: 865-984-1400. Fax: 865-983-0383. Web Site: http://www.charter.com. Also serves Alexandria, Dowelltown, Gordonsville, Liberty, Smith County (unincorporated areas), Watertown & Wilson County (portions). ICA: TN0029.

TV Market Ranking: 30 (LEBANON, Wilson County (portions)); Below 100 (Alexandria, Dowelltown, Gordonsville, Liberty, Smith County (unincorporated areas), Watertown, Wilson County (portions)). Franchise award date: N.A. Franchise expiration date: N.A. Began: April 6, 1981.

Channel capacity: N.A. Channels available but not in use: N.A.

Basic Service

Subscribers: 10,315.

Programming (received off-air): WHTN (IND) Murfreesboro; WJFB (IND) Lebanon; WKRN-TV (ABC) Nashville; WNAB (CW) Nashville; WNPT (PBS) Nashville; WNPX-TV (ION) Cookeville; WPGD-TV (TBN) Hendersonville; WSMV-TV (NBC, TMO) Nashville; WTVF (CBS) Nashville; WUXP-TV (MNT) Nashville; WZTV (FOX) Nashville; allband FM.

Programming (via satellite): Comcast/Charter Sports Southeast (CSS); C-SPAN; C-SPAN 2; INSP; QVC; Trinity Broadcasting Network; TV Guide Network; WGN America.

Expanded Basic Service 1

Subscribers: N.A.

Programming (via satellite): A&E Networks; ABC Family Channel; AMC; Animal Planet; BET Networks; Bravo; Cartoon Network; CNBC; CNN; Comedy Central; Country Music TV; Discovery Channel; Discovery Fit & Health; Disney Channel; E! Entertainment Television; ESPN; ESPN 2; Food Network; Fox News Channel; Fox Sports South; FX; G4; GalaVision; Golf Channel; GSN; Hallmark Channel; Headline News; HGTV; History Channel; Lifetime; MSNBC; MTV; National Geographic Channel; Nickelodeon; Oxygen; SoapNet; Speed; Spike TV; SportSouth; Syfy; TBS Superstation; Telemundo; The Learning Channel; The Weather Channel; Toon Disney; Travel Channel; truTV; Turner Classic Movies; Turner Network TV; TV Land; Univision Studios; USA Network; Versus; VH1; WE tv.

Fee: $45.00 monthly.

Digital Basic Service

Subscribers: N.A.

Programming (via satellite): BBC America; Bio; Bloomberg Television; Boomerang; CNN International; Discovery Digital Networks; DIY Network; ESPN Classic Sports; ESPNews; Fox College Sports Atlantic; Fox College Sports Central; Fox College Sports Pacific; Fox Movie Channel; Fox Soccer; Fuel TV; GAS; Great American Country; History Channel International; Independent Film Channel; Lifetime Movie Network; Lifetime Real Women; MTV Networks Digital Suite; Music Choice; NFL Network; Nick Jr.; Nick Too; NickToons TV; Outdoor Channel; Science Television; Style Network; Sundance Channel.

Digital Pay Service 1

Pay Units: N.A.

Programming (via satellite): Cinemax; HBO (multiplexed); Starz.

Video-On-Demand: No

Pay-Per-View

Playboy TV (delivered digitally); Fresh (delivered digitally); Shorteez (delivered digitally).

Internet Service

Operational: Yes.

Broadband Service: Charter Pipeline.

Fee: $29.99 monthly.

Telephone Service

None

Miles of Plant: 158.0 (coaxial); None (fiber optic).

Operations Manager: Sean Hendrix. Marketing Director: Patt Hollenbeck. Sales & Marketing Manager: Jo Ann Placke.

Ownership: Charter Communications Inc. (MSO).

LEWISBURG—Charter Communications, 1774 Henry G Lane St, Maryville, TN 37801. Phone: 865-984-1400. Fax: 865-983-0383. Web Site: http://www.charter.com. Also serves Bedford County (portions), Belfast & Marshall County (portions). ICA: TN0049.

TV Market Ranking: Below 100 (Bedford County (portions), Belfast, Marshall County (portions)); Outside TV Markets (LEWISBURG, Marshall County (portions)). Franchise award date: December 6, 1967. Franchise expiration date: December 31, 2007. Began: April 1, 1974.

Channel capacity: N.A. Channels available but not in use: N.A.

Basic Service

Subscribers: 3,846.

Programming (received off-air): WAAY-TV (ABC) Huntsville; WAFF (NBC) Huntsville; WHNT-TV (CBS) Huntsville; WKRN-TV (ABC) Nashville; WNAB (CW) Nashville; WNPT (PBS) Nashville; WNPX-TV (ION) Cookeville; WSMV-TV (NBC, TMO) Nashville; WTVF (CBS) Nashville; WUXP-TV (MNT) Nashville; WZTV (FOX) Nashville; 14 FMs.

Programming (via satellite): Comcast/Charter Sports Southeast (CSS); C-SPAN; QVC; Trinity Broadcasting Network; TV Guide Network; USA Network; WGN America.

Expanded Basic Service 1

Subscribers: 3,023.

Programming (via satellite): A&E Networks; ABC Family Channel; AMC; Animal Planet; BET Networks; Cartoon Network; CNBC; CNN; Comedy Central; Country Music TV; Discovery Channel; Disney Channel; E! Entertainment Television; ESPN; ESPN 2; Fox News Channel; Fox Sports South; FX; Headline News; HGTV; History Channel; Lifetime; MTV; Nickelodeon; Spike TV; SportSouth; Syfy; TBS Superstation; The Learning Channel; The Weather Channel; Turner Network TV; TV Land; Versus; VH1.

Fee: $45.00 monthly.

Digital Basic Service

Subscribers: N.A.

Programming (via satellite): BBC America; Bio; Discovery Digital Networks; DMX Music; ESPN Classic Sports; ESPNews; Fox Soccer; Golf Channel; GSN; History Channel International; Independent Film Channel; Lifetime Movie Network; MTV Networks Digital Suite; Nick Jr.; Science Television; Speed; Toon Disney; Turner Classic Movies; WE tv.

Digital Pay Service 1

Pay Units: N.A.

Programming (via satellite): Cinemax (multiplexed); Encore (multiplexed); Flix; HBO (multiplexed); Showtime (multiplexed); Starz (multiplexed); The Movie Channel (multiplexed).

Video-On-Demand: Yes

Pay-Per-View

Playboy TV.

Internet Service

Operational: Yes.

Broadband Service: Charter Pipeline.

Fee: $29.99 monthly.

Telephone Service

Digital: Operational

Miles of Plant: 230.0 (coaxial); 40.0 (fiber optic).

Operations Manager: Sean Hendrix. Marketing Director: Pat Hollenbeck. Sales & Marketing Manager: Jo Ann Placke.

Ownership: Charter Communications Inc. (MSO).

LEXINGTON—Charter Communications, 1774 Henry G Lane St, Maryville, TN 37801. Phone: 865-984-1400. Fax: 865-983-0383. Web Site: http://www.charter.com. Also serves Decatur County, Decaturville, Henderson County & Parsons. ICA: TN0047.

TV Market Ranking: Below 100 (Decatur County (portions), Henderson County, LEXINGTON); Outside TV Markets (Decatur County (portions), Decaturville, Parsons). Franchise award date: October 10, 1964. Franchise expiration date: October 10, 2014. Began: January 1, 1965.

Channel capacity: N.A. Channels available but not in use: N.A.

Basic Service

Subscribers: 4,760.

Programming (received off-air): WBBJ-TV (ABC) Jackson; WHBQ-TV (FOX) Memphis; WJKT (FOX) Jackson; WLJT-DT (PBS) Lexington; WMC-TV (NBC) Memphis; WREG-TV (CBS) Memphis; WSMV-TV (NBC, TMO) Nashville; WTVF (CBS) Nashville.

Programming (via satellite): CW+; ION Television; WGN America.

Fee: $11.11 monthly.

Expanded Basic Service 1

Subscribers: 3,131.

Programming (via satellite): A&E Networks; ABC Family Channel; AMC; Animal Planet; BET Networks; Bravo; Cartoon Network; CNBC; CNN; Comedy Central; Country Music TV; C-SPAN; C-SPAN 2; Discovery Channel; Disney Channel; E! Entertainment Television; ESPN; ESPN 2; Food Network; Fox News Channel; Fox Sports South; FX; G4; Golf Channel; GSN; Hallmark Channel; Headline News; HGTV; History Channel; INSP; Lifetime; MSNBC; MTV; MTV2; National Geographic Channel; Nickelodeon; Oxygen; QVC; SoapNet; Speed; Spike TV; SportSouth; Syfy; TBS Superstation; The Learning Channel; The Weather Channel; Toon Disney; Travel Channel; Trinity Broadcasting Network; truTV; Turner Classic Movies; Turner Network TV; TV Land; USA Network; VH1.

Fee: $45.00 monthly.

Digital Basic Service

Subscribers: N.A.

Programming (via satellite): BBC America; Bio; Bloomberg Television; Boomerang; CNN en Espanol; Discovery Digital Networks; DIY Network; ESPN Classic Sports; ESPNews; Fox Movie Channel; Fox Soccer; FSN Digital Atlantic; FSN Digital Central; FSN Digital Pacific; Fuel TV; Fuse; GAS; Great American Country; History Channel International; Independent Film Channel; Lifetime Movie Network; Lifetime Real Women; MTV Networks Digital Suite; Music Choice; NFL Network; Nick Jr.; Nick Too; NickToons TV; Outdoor Channel; Science Television; Sundance Channel.

Digital Pay Service 1
Pay Units: N.A.
Programming (via satellite): Cinemax (multiplexed); Encore (multiplexed); Flix (multiplexed); HBO (multiplexed); Showtime (multiplexed); Starz (multiplexed); The Movie Channel (multiplexed).
Video-On-Demand: Yes
Pay-Per-View
Playboy TV (delivered digitally); Fresh (delivered digitally); Shorteez (delivered digitally); Sports PPV (delivered digitally); iN DEMAND (delivered digitally).
Internet Service
Operational: Yes.
Broadband Service: Charter Pipeline.
Fee: $29.99 monthly.
Telephone Service
Digital: Operational
Fee: $29.99 monthly
Miles of Plant: 214.0 (coaxial); None (fiber optic).
Manager: Ron Janson. Operations Manager: Tony Fox. Marketing Director: Pat Hollenbeck. Marketing Manager: Wiley Bird.
Ownership: Charter Communications Inc. (MSO).

LINDEN—Two Rivers Media, PO Box 555, Linden, TN 37096-0555. Phone: 931-589-2696. Fax: 931-589-2696. ICA: TN0098.
TV Market Ranking: Outside TV Markets (LINDEN). Franchise award date: N.A. Franchise expiration date: N.A. Began: June 16, 1981.
Channel capacity: N.A. Channels available but not in use: N.A.
Basic Service
Subscribers: N.A.
Programming (received off-air): WBBJ-TV (ABC) Jackson; WKRN-TV (ABC) Nashville; WNPT (PBS) Nashville; WSMV-TV (NBC, TMO) Nashville; WTVF (CBS) Nashville; WZTV (FOX) Nashville; allband FM.
Programming (via satellite): ESPN; Spike TV; TBS Superstation; Turner Network TV; WGN America.
Fee: $20.00 installation; $13.00 monthly.
Pay Service 1
Pay Units: N.A.
Programming (via satellite): HBO.
Fee: $9.00 monthly.
Internet Service
Operational: No.
Telephone Service
None
Additional miles planned: 21.0 (coaxial).
Manager: Dorothy Patterson. Chief Technician: Bert Patterson.
Ownership: Two Rivers Media (MSO).

LIVINGSTON—Comcast Cable, 2919 Ring Rd, Elizabethtown, KY 42701. Phone: 270-765-2731. Fax: 270-737-2731. Web Site: http://www.comcast.com. ICA: TN0078.
TV Market Ranking: Below 100 (LIVINGSTON). Franchise award date: November 4, 1963. Franchise expiration date: N.A. Began: May 1, 1966.
Channel capacity: N.A. Channels available but not in use: N.A.
Basic Service
Subscribers: N.A.
Programming (received off-air): WCTE (PBS) Cookeville; WKRN-TV (ABC) Nashville; WNPT (PBS) Nashville; WSMV-TV (NBC, TMO) Nashville; WTVF (CBS) Nashville; WZTV (FOX) Nashville; 1 FM.
Programming (via satellite): ABC Family Channel; AmericanLife TV Network; CNN; Country Music TV; Discovery Channel; Disney Channel; ESPN; Headline News; Lifetime; MTV; Nickelodeon; Spike TV; TBS Superstation; The Weather Channel; Turner Network TV; USA Network; WGN America.
Fee: $54.99 installation; $34.99 monthly.
Digital Basic Service
Subscribers: N.A.
Programming (via satellite): BBC America; Bio; CMT Pure Country; C-SPAN 3; Current; Discovery Digital Networks; Encore (multiplexed); ESPNews; Flix; GAS; History Channel International; Lifetime Movie Network; MoviePlex; MTV Networks Digital Suite; Music Choice; National Geographic Channel; NFL Network; Nick Jr.; Nick Too; NickToons TV; PBS Kids Sprout; SoapNet; Sundance Channel; Toon Disney; TV One.
Fee: $14.95 monthly.
Digital Pay Service 1
Pay Units: N.A.
Programming (via satellite): Cinemax (multiplexed); HBO (multiplexed); Showtime (multiplexed); Starz (multiplexed); The Movie Channel (multiplexed).
Fee: $13.05 monthly (each).
Video-On-Demand: No
Pay-Per-View
iN DEMAND (delivered digitally); Hot Choice (delivered digitally).
Internet Service
Operational: Yes. Began: May 4, 2004.
Broadband Service: Comcast High Speed Internet.
Fee: $42.95 monthly.
Telephone Service
None
Miles of Plant: 45.0 (coaxial); None (fiber optic).
General Manager: Tim Hagan. Technical Operations Director: Bob Tarp. Marketing Director: Laurie Nicholson.
Ownership: Comcast Cable Communications Inc. (MSO).

LOBELVILLE—Two Rivers Media, PO Box 555, Linden, TN 37096-0555. Phone: 931-589-2696. Fax: 931-589-2696. ICA: TN0149.
TV Market Ranking: Outside TV Markets (LOBELVILLE). Franchise award date: N.A. Franchise expiration date: N.A. Began: N.A.
Channel capacity: 12 (not 2-way capable). Channels available but not in use: N.A.
Basic Service
Subscribers: N.A.
Programming (received off-air): WBBJ-TV (ABC) Jackson; WKRN-TV (ABC) Nashville; WNPT (PBS) Nashville; WSMV-TV (NBC, TMO) Nashville; WTVF (CBS) Nashville; WZTV (FOX) Nashville.
Programming (via satellite): ESPN; Spike TV; TBS Superstation; Turner Network TV; WGN America.
Fee: $13.00 monthly.
Pay Service 1
Pay Units: N.A.
Programming (via satellite): HBO.
Fee: $9.00 monthly.
Internet Service
Operational: No.
Telephone Service
None
Manager: Dorothy Patterson. Chief Technician: Bert Patterson.
Ownership: Two Rivers Media (MSO).

LORETTO—Charter Communications, 1774 Henry G Lane St, Maryville, TN 37801. Phone: 731-984-9500. Fax: 865-983-0383. Web Site: http://www.charter.com. Also serves Lauderdale County (portions), AL; Iron City, Lawrence County (portions), St. Joseph & Westpoint, TN. ICA: TN0068.

TV Market Ranking: 96 (Lawrence County (portions)); Below 100 (Iron City, Lauderdale County (portions), LORETTO, St. Joseph, Westpoint, Lawrence County (portions)); Outside TV Markets (Lawrence County (portions)). Franchise award date: N.A. Franchise expiration date: August 1, 2006. Began: November 1, 1970.
Channel capacity: 61 (not 2-way capable). Channels available but not in use: N.A.
Basic Service
Subscribers: 2,447.
Programming (received off-air): WAAY-TV (ABC) Huntsville; WAFF (NBC) Huntsville; WHDF (CW) Florence; WHNT-TV (CBS) Huntsville; WKRN-TV (ABC) Nashville; WNPT (PBS) Nashville; WSMV-TV (NBC, TMO) Nashville; WTVF (CBS) Nashville; WZDX (FOX, MNT) Huntsville; allband FM.
Programming (via satellite): QVC; WGN America.
Expanded Basic Service 1
Subscribers: 1,939.
Programming (via satellite): A&E Networks; ABC Family Channel; AMC; Animal Planet; Bravo; Cartoon Network; CNBC; CNN; Comcast/Charter Sports Southeast (CSS); Comedy Central; Country Music TV; C-SPAN; Discovery Channel; Disney Channel; E! Entertainment Television; ESPN; ESPN 2; Food Network; Fox News Channel; Fox Sports South; FX; G4; Golf Channel; GSN; Hallmark Channel; Headline News; HGTV; History Channel; INSP; Lifetime; MTV; Nickelodeon; Oxygen; Speed; Spike TV; Syfy; TBS Superstation; The Learning Channel; The Weather Channel; Trinity Broadcasting Network; truTV; Turner Classic Movies; Turner Network TV; TV Land; USA Network; VH1; WE tv.
Fee: $45.00 monthly.
Digital Basic Service
Subscribers: N.A.
Programming (via satellite): BBC America; Bio; Bloomberg Television; Discovery Fit & Health; ESPN Deportes; Fox Deportes; Fox Movie Channel; Fox Soccer; Fuel TV; Fuse; GAS; History Channel International; Independent Film Channel; Lifetime Movie Network; Lifetime Real Women; MTV Networks Digital Suite; Music Choice; Nick Jr.; Nick Too; NickToons TV; Sundance Channel; Toon Disney; TV Guide Interactive Inc.; Versus.
Digital Pay Service 1
Pay Units: N.A.
Programming (via satellite): Cinemax (multiplexed); Encore (multiplexed); Flix; HBO (multiplexed); LOGO; Showtime (multiplexed); Starz (multiplexed); The Movie Channel (multiplexed).
Video-On-Demand: Yes
Pay-Per-View
Playboy TV (delivered digitally); Shorteez (delivered digitally); Fresh (delivered digitally); iN DEMAND (delivered digitally).
Internet Service
Operational: Yes.
Broadband Service: Charter Pipeline.
Fee: $29.99 monthly.
Telephone Service
Digital: Operational
Miles of Plant: 95.0 (coaxial); 25.0 (fiber optic).
Operations Manager: Sean Hendrix. Marketing Director: Pat Hollenbeck. Sales & Marketing Manager: Jo Ann Placke.
Ownership: Charter Communications Inc. (MSO).

LOUDON—Charter Communications, 1774 Henry G Lane St, Maryville, TN 37801. Phone: 865-984-1400. Fax: 865-983-0382. Web Site: http://www.charter.com. Also serves Concord, Farragut, Knox County, Lenoir City, Loudon County & Philadelphia. ICA: TN0148.
TV Market Ranking: 71 (Concord, Farragut, Knox County, Lenoir City, LOUDON, Loudon County (portions), Philadelphia); Below 100 (Loudon County (portions)). Franchise award date: N.A. Franchise expiration date: November 1, 2007. Began: August 1, 1977.
Channel capacity: N.A. Channels available but not in use: N.A.
Basic Service
Subscribers: 19,722.
Programming (received off-air): WATE-TV (ABC) Knoxville; WBIR-TV (NBC) Knoxville; WBXX-TV (CW) Crossville; WKOP-TV (PBS) Knoxville; WPXK-TV (ION) Jellico; WTNZ (FOX) Knoxville; WVLR (IND) Tazewell; WVLT-TV (CBS, MNT) Knoxville; allband FM.
Programming (via satellite): WGN America.
Fee: $29.99 installation.
Expanded Basic Service 1
Subscribers: 18,642.
Programming (via satellite): A&E Networks; ABC Family Channel; AMC; Animal Planet; BET Networks; Bravo; Cartoon Network; CNBC; CNN; Comcast/Charter Sports Southeast (CSS); Comedy Central; Country Music TV; C-SPAN; C-SPAN 2; Discovery Channel; Disney Channel; E! Entertainment Television; ESPN; ESPN 2; Food Network; Fox News Channel; Fox Sports South; FX; G4; Golf Channel; GSN; Hallmark Channel; Headline News; HGTV; History Channel; INSP; Lifetime; MSNBC; MTV; National Geographic Channel; Nickelodeon; Oxygen; QVC; SoapNet; Speed; Spike TV; SportSouth; Style Network; Syfy; TBS Superstation; Telemundo; The Learning Channel; The Weather Channel; Toon Disney; Travel Channel; Trinity Broadcasting Network; truTV; Turner Classic Movies; Turner Network TV; TV Guide Network; TV Land; USA Network; Versus; VH1; WE tv.
Fee: $50.99 monthly.
Digital Basic Service
Subscribers: N.A.
Programming (via satellite): BBC America; Bio; Bloomberg Television; CNN International; Cooking Channel; DIY Network; ESPN Classic Sports; ESPN HD; Fox College Sports Atlantic; Fox College Sports Central; Fox College Sports Pacific; Fox Movie Channel; Fox Sports World; Fuel TV; GAS; Great American Country; HD Theater; HDNet; HDNet Movies; History Chan-

nel International; Independent Film Channel; Jewelry Television; Lifetime Movie Network; Lifetime Real Women; MTV Networks Digital Suite; Music Choice; NFL Network; Nick Jr.; Nick Too; NickToons TV; Sundance Channel; TV Guide Interactive Inc.

Digital Pay Service 1
Pay Units: N.A.
Programming (via satellite): Cinemax (multiplexed); Encore (multiplexed); Flix; HBO (multiplexed); HBO HD; Showtime (multiplexed); Showtime HD; Starz (multiplexed); The Movie Channel (multiplexed).

Video-On-Demand: Yes

Pay-Per-View
Special events.

Internet Service
Operational: Yes.
Broadband Service: Charter Pipeline.
Fee: $29.99 monthly.

Telephone Service
Digital: Operational
Fee: $29.99 monthly

Technical Operations Director: Grant Evans. Marketing Director: Pat Hollenbeck. Marketing Manager: Angie Lee. Government Relations Director: Nick Pavlis.

Ownership: Charter Communications Inc. (MSO).

LYNCHBURG—Comcast Cable, 660 Mainstream Dr, PO Box 280570, Nashville, TN 37228-0570. Phones: 615-244-5900; 615-244-7462. Fax: 615-255-6528. Web Site: http://www.comcast.com. Also serves Cowan, Decherd, Estill Springs, Franklin County, Moore County (portions) & Winchester. ICA: TN0119.

TV Market Ranking: 96 (Franklin County (portions), Moore County (portions)); Below 100 (Moore County (portions)); Outside TV Markets (Cowan, Decherd, Estill Springs, LYNCHBURG, Winchester, Franklin County (portions), Moore County (portions)). Franchise award date: May 3, 1976. Franchise expiration date: N.A. Began: September 1, 1976.

Channel capacity: N.A. Channels available but not in use: N.A.

Basic Service
Subscribers: 217.
Programming (received off-air): WAAY-TV (ABC) Huntsville; WAFF (NBC) Huntsville; WDEF-TV (CBS) Chattanooga; WHNT-TV (CBS) Huntsville; WHTN (IND) Murfreesboro; WKRN-TV (ABC) Nashville; WNAB (CW) Nashville; WNPT (PBS) Nashville; WSMV-TV (NBC, TMO) Nashville; WTVF (CBS) Nashville; WZDX (FOX, MNT) Huntsville; WZTV (FOX) Nashville.
Programming (via satellite): ABC Family Channel; QVC.
Fee: $29.30 installation; $15.95 monthly.

Expanded Basic Service 1
Subscribers: 130.
Programming (via satellite): A&E Networks; AMC; Animal Planet; BET Networks; Cartoon Network; CNBC; CNN; Comcast/Charter Sports Southeast (CSS); Comedy Central; Country Music TV; C-SPAN; C-SPAN 2; Discovery Channel; Discovery Health Channel; Disney Channel; E! Entertainment Television; ESPN; ESPN 2; Food Network; Fox News Channel; Fox Sports Net; FX; Golf Channel; Great American Country; GSN; Hallmark Channel; Headline News; HGTV; History Channel; Home Shopping Network 2; INSP; Lifetime; MTV; Nickelodeon; Oxygen; Spike TV; Syfy; TBS Superstation; The Learning Channel; The Weather Channel; truTV; Turner Network TV; TV Guide Network; TV Land; Univision Studios; USA Network; Versus; VH1; WGN America.
Fee: $35.24 monthly.

Digital Basic Service
Subscribers: 88.
Programming (via satellite): BBC America; C-SPAN 3; Discovery Digital Networks; DMX Music; Encore Action; ESPNews; Flix; GAS; MTV Networks Digital Suite; Nick Jr.; Nick Too; SoapNet; Sundance Channel; Toon Disney; WAM! America's Kidz Network.

Pay Service 1
Pay Units: 48.
Programming (via satellite): Cinemax; HBO; Showtime.

Digital Pay Service 1
Pay Units: N.A.
Programming (via satellite): Cinemax (multiplexed); HBO (multiplexed); Showtime (multiplexed); Starz (multiplexed); The Movie Channel (multiplexed).

Video-On-Demand: No

Pay-Per-View
Addressable homes: 88.
iN DEMAND (delivered digitally); Playboy TV (delivered digitally); Fresh (delivered digitally); Shorteez (delivered digitally); Hot Choice (delivered digitally); Pleasure (delivered digitally).

Internet Service
Operational: Yes.
Subscribers: 42.
Broadband Service: Comcast High Speed Internet.
Fee: $42.95 monthly.

Telephone Service
Digital: Operational

Miles of plant (coax & fiber combined) included in Nashville

Area Vice President & General Manager: John Gauder. Technical Operations Director: Joe Pell. Marketing Director: Martine Mahoney. Marketing Manager: Will Jefferson.

Ownership: Comcast Cable Communications Inc. (MSO).

LYNNVILLE—Formerly served by Small Town Cable. No longer in operation. ICA: TN0123.

MADISONVILLE—Charter Communications, 1774 Henry G Lane St, Maryville, TN 37801. Phone: 865-984-1400. Fax: 865-983-0382. Web Site: http://www.charter.com. Also serves Monroe County & Sweetwater. ICA: TN0176.

TV Market Ranking: Below 100 (Monroe County (portions)); Outside TV Markets (MADISONVILLE, Monroe County (portions), Sweetwater). Franchise award date: N.A. Franchise expiration date: N.A. Began: N.A.

Channel capacity: N.A. Channels available but not in use: N.A.

Basic Service
Subscribers: 3,978.
Programming (received off-air): WATE-TV (ABC) Knoxville; WBIR-TV (NBC) Knoxville; WBXX-TV (CW) Crossville; WKOP-TV (PBS) Knoxville; WPXK-TV (ION) Jellico; WTNZ (FOX) Knoxville; WTVC (ABC) Chattanooga; WVLR (IND) Tazewell; WVLT-TV (CBS, MNT) Knoxville.
Programming (via satellite): WGN America.
Fee: $29.99 installation.

Expanded Basic Service 1
Subscribers: 3,758.
Programming (via satellite): A&E Networks; ABC Family Channel; AMC; Animal Planet; BET Networks; Bravo; Cartoon Network; CNBC; CNN; Comcast/Charter Sports Southeast (CSS); Comedy Central; Country Music TV; C-SPAN; C-SPAN 2; Discovery Channel; Disney Channel; E! Entertainment Television; ESPN; ESPN 2; Food Network; Fox News Channel; Fox Sports South; FX; G4; Golf Channel; GSN; Hallmark Channel; Headline News; HGTV; History Channel; INSP; Lifetime; MSNBC; MTV; National Geographic Channel; Nickelodeon; Oxygen; QVC; SoapNet; Speed; Spike TV; SportSouth; Style Network; Syfy; TBS Superstation; Telemundo; The Learning Channel; The Weather Channel; Toon Disney; Travel Channel; Trinity Broadcasting Network; truTV; Turner Classic Movies; Turner Network TV; TV Guide Network; TV Land; USA Network; Versus; VH1; WE tv.
Fee: $50.99 monthly.

Digital Basic Service
Subscribers: N.A.
Programming (via satellite): BBC America; Bio; Bloomberg Television; CNN International; Cooking Channel; DIY Network; ESPN Classic Sports; ESPN HD; Fox College Sports Atlantic; Fox College Sports Central; Fox College Sports Pacific; Fox Movie Channel; Fox Sports World; Fuel TV; GAS; Great American Country; HD Theater; HDNet; HDNet Movies; History Channel International; Independent Film Channel; Jewelry Television; Lifetime Movie Network; Lifetime Real Women; MTV Networks Digital Suite; Music Choice; NFL Network; Nick Jr.; Nick Too; NickToons TV; Sundance Channel.

Digital Pay Service 1
Pay Units: N.A.
Programming (via satellite): Cinemax (multiplexed); Encore (multiplexed); Flix; HBO (multiplexed); HBO HD; Showtime (multiplexed); Showtime HD; Starz (multiplexed); The Movie Channel (multiplexed).

Video-On-Demand: Yes

Internet Service
Operational: Yes.
Broadband Service: Charter Pipeline.
Fee: $29.99 monthly.

Telephone Service
Digital: Operational
Fee: $29.99 monthly

Technical Operations Director: Grant Evans. Marketing Director: Pat Hollenbeck. Marketing Manager: Angie Lee. Government Relations Director: Nick Pavlis.

Ownership: Charter Communications Inc. (MSO).

MARTIN—Charter Communications, 1774 Henry G Lane St, Maryville, TN 37801. Phone: 865-984-1400. Fax: 865-983-0383. Web Site: http://www.charter.com. Also serves Greenfield, Obion, Obion County (unincorporated areas), Rives, Sharon, Troy, Union City & Woodland Mills. ICA: TN0205.

TV Market Ranking: Outside TV Markets (Greenfield, MARTIN, Obion, Obion County (unincorporated areas), Rives, Sharon, Troy, Union City, Woodland Mills).

Channel capacity: N.A. Channels available but not in use: N.A.

Basic Service
Subscribers: N.A.
Programming (received off-air): KBSI (FOX) Cape Girardeau; KFVS-TV (CBS, CW) Cape Girardeau; WBBJ-TV (ABC) Jackson; WJKT (FOX) Jackson; WLJT-DT (PBS) Lexington; WMC-TV (NBC) Memphis; WPSD-TV (NBC) Paducah; WPTY-TV (ABC) Memphis; WTVF (CBS) Nashville.
Programming (via satellite): WGN America.

Digital Basic Service
Subscribers: N.A.
Programming (via satellite): A&E HD; AmericanLife TV Network; BBC America; Bio; Bloomberg Television; Boomerang; CMT Pure Country; CNN en Espanol; Cooking Channel; DIY Network; ESPN 2 HD; ESPN Classic Sports; ESPN HD; ESPN U; ESPNews; Fox Business Channel; Fox College Sports Atlantic; Fox College Sports Central; Fox College Sports Pacific; Fox Movie Channel; Fox Soccer; Fuel TV; Fuse; GMC; Great American Country; HD Theater; HDNet; HDNet Movies; History Channel HD; History Channel International; Independent Film Channel; Jewelry Television; Lifetime Movie Network; Lifetime Real Women; LOGO; MTV Networks Digital Suite; Music Choice; Nick Jr.; Nickelodeon; NickToons TV; Outdoor Channel; Palladia; PBS Kids Channel; Sundance Channel; TeenNick; Tennis Channel; Toon Disney; Turner Network TV HD; Universal HD; Versus HD; WE tv.

Digital Pay Service 1
Pay Units: N.A.
Programming (via satellite): Cinemax (multiplexed); Cinemax HD; Encore (multiplexed); Flix; HBO (multiplexed); HBO HD; Showtime (multiplexed); Showtime HD; Starz (multiplexed); Starz HDTV; The Movie Channel (multiplexed); The Movie Channel HD.

Video-On-Demand: No

Pay-Per-View
iN DEMAND (delivered digitally); Ten Clips (delivered digitally); Ten Blue (delivered digitally); Ten Blox (delivered digitally).

Internet Service
Operational: Yes.
Broadband Service: Charter Pipeline.
Fee: $29.99 monthly.

Telephone Service
Digital: Operational
Fee: $29.99 monthly

Operations Manager: Tony Fox. Technical Operations Manager: Ron Janson. Marketing Director: Pat Hollenbeck. Marketing Manager: Wiley Bird.

Ownership: Charter Communications Inc. (MSO).

MAYNARDVILLE—Comcast Cablevision of the South. Now served by KNOXVILLE, TN [TN0004]. ICA: TN0077.

MCEWEN—Charter Communications, 1774 Henry G Lane St, Maryville, TN 37801. Phone: 865-984-1400. Fax: 865-983-0383. Web Site: http://www.charter.com. ICA: TN0107.

TV Market Ranking: Outside TV Markets (MCEWEN). Franchise award date: February 10, 1983. Franchise expiration date: N.A. Began: December 1, 1984.

Channel capacity: N.A. Channels available but not in use: N.A.

Basic Service
Subscribers: 452.
Programming (received off-air): WHTN (IND) Murfreesboro; WKRN-TV (ABC) Nashville; WNAB (CW) Nashville; WNPT (PBS) Nashville; WSMV-TV (NBC, TMO) Nashville; WTVF (CBS) Nashville; WZTV (FOX) Nashville.
Programming (via satellite): C-SPAN; INSP; QVC; WGN America.

Expanded Basic Service 1
Subscribers: 446.
Programming (via satellite): A&E Networks; ABC Family Channel; AMC; Bravo; Cartoon Network; CNBC; CNN; Comedy Central; Country Music TV; Discovery Channel; Disney Channel; E! Entertainment Television; ESPN; ESPN 2; Fox News Channel; Fox Sports South; FX; G4; Golf Chan-

nel; Headline News; HGTV; History Channel; Lifetime; MTV; Nickelodeon; Oxygen; Speed; Spike TV; Syfy; TBS Superstation; The Learning Channel; The Weather Channel; Turner Classic Movies; Turner Network TV; TV Land; USA Network; VH1.
Fee: $45.00 monthly.

Digital Basic Service
Subscribers: N.A.
Programming (via satellite): BBC America; Bio; Bloomberg Television; Discovery Fit & Health; ESPN Classic Sports; ESPNews; Fox Movie Channel; Fox Soccer; Fuse; GAS; GSN; History Channel International; Independent Film Channel; Lifetime Movie Network; Lifetime Real Women; MTV Networks Digital Suite; Music Choice; Nick Jr.; Nick Too; NickToons TV; Style Network; Sundance Channel; Toon Disney; TV Guide Interactive Inc.; WE tv.

Digital Pay Service 1
Pay Units: N.A.
Programming (via satellite): Cinemax (multiplexed); Encore; Flix; HBO (multiplexed); Showtime (multiplexed); Starz (multiplexed); The Movie Channel (multiplexed).

Video-On-Demand: No

Pay-Per-View
iN DEMAND (delivered digitally); Playboy TV (delivered digitally); Fresh (delivered digitally).

Internet Service
Operational: No.

Telephone Service
None

Miles of Plant: 31.0 (coaxial); None (fiber optic).

Operations Manager: Tony Fox. Technical Operations Manager: Ron Janson. Marketing Director: Pat Hollenbeck. Marketing Manager: Wiley Bird.

Ownership: Charter Communications Inc. (MSO).

MCKENZIE—Charter Communications, 1774 Henry G Lane St, Maryville, TN 37801. Phone: 865-984-1400. Fax: 865-983-0383. Web Site: http://www.charter.com. Also serves Atwood, Bruceton, Buchanan, Clarksburg, Gibson, Gibson County, Gleason, Hollow Rock, Huntingdon, McLemoresville, Milan, Springville, Trezevant & Trimble. ICA: TN0063.

TV Market Ranking: Below 100 (Atwood, Clarksburg, Gibson, Gibson County (portions), Huntingdon, McLemoresville, Milan, Trezevant); Outside TV Markets (Bruceton, Buchanan, Gibson County (portions), Gleason, Hollow Rock, MCKENZIE, Springville, Trimble). Franchise award date: November 24, 1964. Franchise expiration date: December 5, 2006. Began: October 1, 1965.

Channel capacity: N.A. Channels available but not in use: N.A.

Basic Service
Subscribers: 30,099.
Programming (received off-air): WBBJ-TV (ABC) Jackson; WHBQ-TV (FOX) Memphis; WJKT (FOX) Jackson; WLJT-DT (PBS) Lexington; WMC-TV (NBC) Memphis; WPSD-TV (NBC) Paducah; WREG-TV (CBS) Memphis; WSMV-TV (NBC, TMO) Nashville; WTVF (CBS) Nashville; 1 FM.
Programming (via satellite): TV Guide Network; WGN America.

Expanded Basic Service 1
Subscribers: 17,766.
Programming (via satellite): A&E Networks; ABC Family Channel; AMC; Animal Planet; BET Networks; Bravo; Cartoon Network; CNBC; CNN; Comcast/Charter Sports Southeast (CSS); Comedy Central; Country Music TV; C-SPAN; C-SPAN 2; Discovery Channel; Disney Channel; E! Entertainment Television; ESPN; ESPN 2; Food Network; Fox News Channel; Fox Sports South; FX; G4; Golf Channel; GSN; Hallmark Channel; Headline News; HGTV; History Channel; INSP; Lifetime; MSNBC; MTV; National Geographic Channel; Nickelodeon; Oxygen; QVC; SoapNet; Speed; Spike TV; SportSouth; Syfy; TBS Superstation; The Learning Channel; The Weather Channel; Toon Disney; Travel Channel; Trinity Broadcasting Network; truTV; Turner Classic Movies; Turner Network TV; TV Land; USA Network; VH1; WE tv.
Fee: $45.00 monthly.

Digital Basic Service
Subscribers: N.A.
Programming (via satellite): BBC America; Bio; Bloomberg Television; Boomerang; CNN en Espanol; Discovery Digital Networks; DIY Network; ESPN Classic Sports; ESPNews; Fox Movie Channel; Fox Sports World; FSN Digital Atlantic; FSN Digital Central; FSN Digital Pacific; Fuel TV; Fuse; GAS; Great American Country; History Channel International; Independent Film Channel; Lifetime Movie Network; Lifetime Real Women; MTV Networks Digital Suite; Music Choice; NFL Network; Nick Jr.; Nick Too; NickToons TV; Outdoor Channel; Sundance Channel; TV Guide Interactive Inc.

Digital Pay Service 1
Pay Units: 11,073.
Programming (via satellite): Cinemax (multiplexed); Encore (multiplexed); Flix; HBO (multiplexed); Showtime (multiplexed); Starz (multiplexed); The Movie Channel (multiplexed).
Fee: $14.95 installation; $11.95 monthly (each).

Video-On-Demand: Yes

Pay-Per-View
Playboy TV (delivered digitally); Fresh (delivered digitally); Shorteez (delivered digitally); iN DEMAND (delivered digitally); NASCAR In Car (delivered digitally); NHL Center Ice (delivered digitally); MLB Extra Innings (delivered digitally); ESPN Now (delivered digitally).

Internet Service
Operational: Yes.
Broadband Service: Charter Pipeline.
Fee: $29.99 monthly.

Telephone Service
Digital: Operational
Fee: $29.99 monthly

Miles of Plant: 782.0 (coaxial); 18.0 (fiber optic).

Operations Manager: Tony Fox. Technical Operations Manager: Ron Janson. Marketing Director: Pat Hollenbeck. Marketing Manager: Wiley Bird.

Ownership: Charter Communications Inc. (MSO).

MEMPHIS—Comcast Cable, 6555 Quince Rd, Ste 400, Memphis, TN 38119-8225. Phone: 901-365-1770. Fax: 901-369-4515. Web Site: http://www.comcast.com. Also serves Crittenden County (eastern portion), Marion, Sunset & West Memphis, AR; Alcorn County (unincorporated areas), Brownfield, Byhalia, Coldwater, Como, Crenshaw, DeSoto County (unincorported areas), Harmontown, Hernando, Horn Lake, Marshall County (unincorporated areas), Olive Branch, Robinsonville, Sardis, Senatobia, Sledge, Southaven, Tate County (unincorporated ares), Tippah County (unincorporated areas), Tunica, Tunica County (unincorporated areas), Walls & Walnut, MS; Arlington, Bartlett, Braden, Collierville, Fayette County (unincorporated areas), Gallaway, Germantown, Grand Junction, Hardeman County (unincorporated areas), Haywood County (unincorporated areas), La Grange, Lakeland, Mason, Middleton, Moscow, Oakland, Piperton, Rossville, Saulsbury, Shelby County (unincorporated areas), Somerville, Stanton, Tipton County (southeastern portion), Whiteville & Williston, TN. ICA: TN0001.

TV Market Ranking: 26 (Arlington, Bartlett, Braden, Byhalia, Coldwater, Collierville, Crittenden County (eastern portion), DeSoto County (unincorported areas), Fayette County (unincorporated areas), Gallaway, Germantown, Hernando, Horn Lake, Lakeland, Marion, Marshall County (unincorporated areas), Mason, MEMPHIS, Moscow, Oakland, Olive Branch, Piperton, Robinsonville, Rossville, Senatobia, Shelby County (unincorporated areas), Southaven, Sunset, Tate County (unincorporated ares), Tipton County (southeastern portion), Tunica County (unincorporated areas), Walls, West Memphis, Williston); Below 100 (Brownfield, Como, Grand Junction, Hardeman County (unincorporated areas), Harmontown, Haywood County (unincorporated areas), La Grange, Saulsbury, Somerville, Stanton, Tippah County (unincorporated areas), Walnut, Whiteville); Outside TV Markets (Alcorn County (unincorporated areas), Crenshaw, Middleton, Sardis, Sledge, Tunica). Franchise award date: N.A. Franchise expiration date: N.A. Began: February 1, 1976.

Channel capacity: N.A. Channels available but not in use: N.A.

Basic Service
Subscribers: 210,000 Includes Earle, AR.
Programming (received off-air): WBUY-TV (TBN) Holly Springs; WHBQ-TV (FOX) Memphis; WKNO (PBS) Memphis; WLMT (CW) Memphis; WMC-TV (NBC) Memphis; WPTY-TV (ABC) Memphis; WPXX-TV (ION, MNT) Memphis; WREG-TV (CBS) Memphis.
Programming (via satellite): C-SPAN; C-SPAN 2; Eternal Word TV Network; QVC; Sneak Prevue.
Fee: $13.25 monthly.

Expanded Basic Service 1
Subscribers: N.A.
Programming (via satellite): A&E Networks; ABC Family Channel; AMC; Animal Planet; BET Networks; Cartoon Network; CNBC; CNN; Comedy Central; Discovery Channel; Disney Channel; E! Entertainment Television; Encore; ESPN; Food Network; Fox Movie Channel; Fox Sports South; FX; Hallmark Channel; Headline News; Lifetime; MSNBC; MTV; MTV2; Nickelodeon; Product Information Network; ShopNBC; Spike TV; SportSouth; TBS Superstation; The Learning Channel; The Weather Channel; Travel Channel; truTV; Turner Network TV; TV Land; USA Network; VH1; WGN America.
Fee: $44.69 monthly.

Digital Basic Service
Subscribers: 105,000.
Programming (via satellite): BBC America; Discovery Digital Networks; ESPN Classic Sports; Fox Sports World; G4; Golf Channel; GSN; History Channel; Lifetime Movie Network; MuchMusic Network; mun2 television; Music Choice; Nick Jr.; Outdoor Channel; Speed; Style Network; Sundance Channel; Toon Disney.
Fee: $15.76 monthly.

Digital Pay Service 1
Pay Units: N.A.
Programming (via satellite): Cinemax (multiplexed); HBO (multiplexed); Showtime (multiplexed); Starz (multiplexed); The Movie Channel (multiplexed).
Fee: $10.00 monthly (each).

Video-On-Demand: Yes

Pay-Per-View
Addressable homes: 105,000.
iN DEMAND; Playboy TV; Pleasure; Spice.

Internet Service
Operational: Yes. Began: October 1, 1997.
Subscribers: 71,000.
Broadband Service: Comcast High Speed Internet.
Fee: $42.95 monthly.

Telephone Service
Digital: Operational

Miles of Plant: 6,538.0 (coaxial); None (fiber optic). Miles of plant (coax & fiber combined) includes Earle, AR

Vice President & General Manager: Terry Kennedy. Technical Operations Director: Jim Davies. Plant Manager: Keith Bell. Marketing & Sales Director: Linda Brashear. Government Affairs Director: Otha Brandon.

Ownership: Comcast Cable Communications Inc. (MSO).

MILLINGTON—Millington CATV Inc., 5115 Easley St, PO Box 399, Millington, TN 38053-0399. Phone: 901-872-3600. Fax: 901-872-6703. E-mail: customerservice@xipline.com. Web Site: http://www.millingtoncable.com. Also serves Atoka, Drummonds, Munford & Northaven. ICA: TN0027.

TV Market Ranking: 26 (Atoka, Drummonds, MILLINGTON, Munford, Northaven). Franchise award date: June 1, 1982. Franchise expiration date: January 1, 2008. Began: May 1, 1982.

Channel capacity: 57 (operating 2-way). Channels available but not in use: N.A.

Basic Service
Subscribers: N.A.
Programming (received off-air): WBUY-TV (TBN) Holly Springs; WHBQ-TV (FOX) Memphis; WKNO (PBS) Memphis; WLMT (CW) Memphis; WMC-TV (NBC) Memphis; WPTY-TV (ABC) Memphis; WPXX-TV (ION, MNT) Memphis; WREG-TV (CBS) Memphis.
Programming (via satellite): A&E Networks; ABC Family Channel; AMC; Animal Planet; BET Networks; Cartoon Network; CNN; Comedy Central; Country Music TV; C-SPAN; Discovery Channel; Disney Channel; E! Entertainment Television; ESPN; ESPN 2; ESPN Classic Sports; Food Network; Fox News Channel; Fox Sports South; FX; Hallmark Channel; Headline News; HGTV; History Channel; Hot Choice; Lifetime; MTV; Nickelodeon; Out-

door Channel; Pentagon Channel; Speed; Spike TV; Syfy; TBS Superstation; The Learning Channel; The Weather Channel; Travel Channel; Turner Network TV; TV Guide Network; TV Land; USA Network; VH1; WGN America.
Fee: $34.52 monthly.

Digital Basic Service
Subscribers: N.A.
Programming (via satellite): A&E HD; Bio; Bloomberg Television; Boomerang; cloo; CMT Pure Country; Cooking Channel; Crime & Investigation Network; C-SPAN 3; Current; DIY Network; ESPN HD; Fuse; G4; GAS; GSN; HD Theater; HDNet; HDNet Movies; History Channel International; Military History Channel; MTV Networks Digital Suite; Music Choice; NASA TV; Nick Jr.; Nick Too; NickToons TV; RFD-TV; SoapNet; Toon Disney; Turner Classic Movies; Versus; WE tv.
Fee: $14.47 monthly.

Digital Expanded Basic Service
Subscribers: N.A.
Programming (via satellite): Canales N; ESPNews; Flix; Fox College Sports Atlantic; Fox College Sports Central; Fox College Sports Pacific; Fox Movie Channel; Fox Soccer; Fuel TV; Golf Channel; Independent Film Channel; Sundance Channel.
Fee: $2.99 monthly (sports, movies or Canales).

Pay Service 1
Pay Units: N.A.
Programming (via satellite): Cinemax; HBO.

Digital Pay Service 1
Pay Units: N.A.
Programming (via satellite): Cinemax (multiplexed); Cinemax HD; Encore (multiplexed); HBO (multiplexed); HBO HD; Showtime (multiplexed); Showtime HD; Starz (multiplexed); The Movie Channel (multiplexed); The Movie Channel HD.
Fee: $12.00 monthly (each).

Video-On-Demand: No

Pay-Per-View
iN DEMAND; iN DEMAND (delivered digitally); Ten Clips (delivered digitally); Ten Xtsy (delivered digitally); Ten Blue (delivered digitally); Ten Blox (delivered digitally).

Internet Service
Operational: Yes.
Fee: $44.95 monthly.

Telephone Service
None

Miles of Plant: 400.0 (coaxial); 17.0 (fiber optic).
President: Holly Starnes. Chief Technician: Gene Berry.
Ownership: Millington CATV Inc.

MINOR HILL—Small Town Cable, PO Box 99, College Grove, TN 37046. Phones: 931-484-7994; 615-368-2115. Fax: 615-368-2295. Also serves Giles County (unincorporated areas). ICA: TN0111.
TV Market Ranking: 96 (Giles County (unincorporated areas), MINOR HILL); Below 100 (Giles County (unincorporated areas) (portions)); Outside TV Markets (Giles County (unincorporated areas) (portions)). Franchise award date: N.A. Franchise expiration date: N.A. Began: N.A.
Channel capacity: N.A. Channels available but not in use: N.A.

Basic Service
Subscribers: N.A.
Programming (received off-air): WAAY-TV (ABC) Huntsville; WAFF (NBC) Huntsville; WHNT-TV (CBS) Huntsville; WKRN-TV (ABC) Nashville; WNPT (PBS) Nashville; WSMV-TV (NBC, TMO) Nashville; WTVF (CBS) Nashville; WZDX (FOX, MNT) Huntsville.
Programming (via satellite): Country Music TV; TBS Superstation; USA Network.
Fee: $40.00 installation; $10.95 monthly.

Expanded Basic Service 1
Subscribers: N.A.
Programming (via satellite): ABC Family Channel; AMC; Cartoon Network; CNN; Discovery Channel; Disney Channel; ESPN; ESPN 2; History Channel; MTV; Nickelodeon; Spike TV; The Weather Channel; Turner Network TV.
Fee: $13.00 monthly.

Digital Basic Service
Subscribers: N.A.

Pay Service 1
Pay Units: 61.
Programming (via satellite): Showtime.
Fee: $11.45 monthly.

Video-On-Demand: Yes

Internet Service
Operational: Yes.

Telephone Service
Analog: Not Operational
Digital: Operational

Miles of plant included in Chapel Hill
General Manager: Vince King. Chief Technician: Brian Langham.
Ownership: Small Town Cable Corp. (MSO).

MONTEAGLE—Charter Communications, 1774 Henry G Lane St, Maryville, TN 37801. Phone: 865-984-1400. Fax: 865-983-0383. Web Site: http://www.charter.com. Also serves Altamont, Beersheba Springs, Coalmont, Gruetli-Laager, Grundy County (portions), Palmer, Sewanee & Tracy City. ICA: TN0016.
TV Market Ranking: 78 (Gruetli-Laager, Grundy County (portions), Palmer, Tracy City); Outside TV Markets (Altamont, Beersheba Springs, Coalmont, MONTEAGLE, Sewanee, Grundy County (portions)). Franchise award date: N.A. Franchise expiration date: N.A. Began: July 1, 1968.
Channel capacity: 78 (operating 2-way). Channels available but not in use: N.A.

Basic Service
Subscribers: 8,339.
Programming (received off-air): WDEF-TV (CBS) Chattanooga; WDSI-TV (FOX, MNT) Chattanooga; WELF-TV (TBN) Dalton; WNAB (CW) Nashville; WRCB (NBC) Chattanooga; WTCI (PBS) Chattanooga; WTVC (ABC) Chattanooga; WTVF (CBS) Nashville; WUXP-TV (MNT) Nashville; WZTV (FOX) Nashville; allband FM.
Programming (via satellite): Comcast/Charter Sports Southeast (CSS); C-SPAN; C-SPAN 2; Eternal Word TV Network; INSP; QVC; The Learning Channel; Trinity Broadcasting Network; TV Guide Network; WGN America.
Fee: $29.95 installation; $11.95 monthly.

Expanded Basic Service 1
Subscribers: N.A.
Programming (via satellite): A&E Networks; ABC Family Channel; AMC; Animal Planet; BET Networks; Bravo; Cartoon Network; CNBC; CNN; Comedy Central; Country Music TV; Discovery Channel; Discovery Fit & Health; Disney Channel; E! Entertainment Television; ESPN; ESPN 2; Food Network; Fox News Channel; Fox Sports South; FX; G4; GalaVision; Golf Channel; GSN; Hallmark Channel; Headline News; HGTV; History Channel; Lifetime; MSNBC; MTV; National Geographic Channel; Nickelodeon; Oxygen; SoapNet; Speed; Spike TV; SportSouth; Syfy; TBS Superstation; Telemundo; The Weather Channel; Toon Disney; Travel Channel; truTV; Turner Classic Movies; Turner Network TV; TV Land; Univision Studios; USA Network; Versus; VH1; WE tv.
Fee: $45.00 monthly.

Digital Basic Service
Subscribers: N.A.
Programming (via satellite): BBC America; Bio; Bloomberg Television; Boomerang; CNN International; Discovery Digital Networks; DIY Network; DMX Music; ESPN Classic Sports; ESPNews; Fox College Sports Atlantic; Fox College Sports Central; Fox College Sports Pacific; Fox Movie Channel; Fox Soccer; Fuel TV; GAS; Great American Country; History Channel International; Independent Film Channel; Lifetime Movie Network; Lifetime Real Women; MTV Networks Digital Suite; NFL Network; Nick Jr.; Nick Too; NickToons TV; Outdoor Channel; Science Television; Style Network; Sundance Channel.

Digital Pay Service 1
Pay Units: N.A.
Programming (via satellite): Cinemax; HBO; Starz.

Video-On-Demand: Yes

Pay-Per-View
Playboy TV (delivered digitally); Fresh (delivered digitally); Shorteez (delivered digitally).

Internet Service
Operational: Yes.
Broadband Service: Charter Pipeline.
Fee: $29.99 monthly.

Telephone Service
Digital: Operational

Miles of Plant: 352.0 (coaxial); None (fiber optic).
Operations Manager: Sean Hendrix. Marketing Director: Pat Hollenbeck. Marketing Manager: Jo Ann Placke.
Ownership: Charter Communications Inc. (MSO).

MONTGOMERY COUNTY (portions)—Charter Communications. Now served by CLARKSVILLE, TN [TN0009]. ICA: TN0152.

MORRISTOWN—Charter Communications, 105 Jack White Dr, Kingsport, TN 37664. Phone: 423-247-7631. Fax: 423-247-1807. Web Site: http://www.charter.com. Also serves Baneberry, Bean Station, Cocke County, Dandridge, Grainger County (northeastern portion), Hamblen County, Jefferson City, Jefferson County, Mooresburg, New Market, Newport, Rutledge, Talbott & White Pine. ICA: TN0154.
TV Market Ranking: 71 (Dandridge, Hamblen County (portions), Jefferson City, Jefferson County (portions), New Market, Rutledge, Talbott); Below 100 (Baneberry, Bean Station, Cocke County, Grainger County (northeastern portion), Mooresburg, MORRISTOWN, Newport, White Pine, Hamblen County (portions), Jefferson County (portions)). Franchise award date: N.A. Franchise expiration date: N.A. Began: February 23, 1964.
Channel capacity: N.A. Channels available but not in use: N.A.

Basic Service
Subscribers: 28,500.
Programming (received off-air): WAGV (IND) Harlan; WATE-TV (ABC) Knoxville; WBIR-TV (NBC) Knoxville; WBXX-TV (CW) Crossville; WETP-TV (PBS) Sneedville; WMAK (IND) Knoxville; WPXK-TV (ION) Jellico; WTNZ (FOX) Knoxville; WVLR (IND) Tazewell; WVLT-TV (CBS, MNT) Knoxville; allband FM.
Programming (via satellite): C-SPAN; C-SPAN 2; INSP; QVC; The Weather Channel; TV Guide Network; Univision Studios; WBIR-TV (NBC) Knoxville; WGN America.

Expanded Basic Service 1
Subscribers: N.A.
Programming (via satellite): A&E Networks; ABC Family Channel; AMC; Animal Planet; BET Networks; Bravo; Cartoon Network; CNBC; CNN; Comcast/Charter Sports Southeast (CSS); Comedy Central; Country Music TV; Discovery Channel; Discovery Fit & Health; Disney Channel; E! Entertainment Television; ESPN; ESPN 2; Food Network; Fox News Channel; Fox Sports South; FX; G4; Golf Channel; GSN; Hallmark Channel; Headline News; HGTV; History Channel; Lifetime; MSNBC; MTV; National Geographic Channel; Nickelodeon; Oxygen; SoapNet; Speed; Spike TV; SportSouth; Style Network; Syfy; TBS Superstation; The Learning Channel; Toon Disney; Travel Channel; Trinity Broadcasting Network; truTV; Turner Classic Movies; Turner Network TV; TV Land; USA Network; Versus; VH1; WE tv.
Fee: $45.00 monthly.

Digital Basic Service
Subscribers: N.A.
Programming (via satellite): BBC America; Bio; Cooking Channel; Discovery Digital Networks; DIY Network; ESPN; ESPN Classic Sports; ESPNews; Fox College Sports Atlantic; Fox College Sports Central; Fox College Sports Pacific; Fox Movie Channel; Fox Sports World; Fuel TV; GAS; Great American Country; HDNet; HDNet Movies; History Channel International; Independent Film Channel; Jewelry Television; Lifetime Movie Network; Lifetime Real Women; MTV Networks Digital Suite; Music Choice; NFL Network; Nick Jr.; Nick Too; NickToons TV; Outdoor Channel; Sundance Channel.

Digital Pay Service 1
Pay Units: N.A.
Programming (via satellite): Cinemax (multiplexed); Encore (multiplexed); Flix (multiplexed); HBO (multiplexed); HBO HD; Showtime (multiplexed); Showtime HD; Starz (multiplexed); The Movie Channel (multiplexed).

Video-On-Demand: Yes

Pay-Per-View
Hot Choice; iN DEMAND; Fresh; Fresh (delivered digitally); Movies (delivered digitally); special events.

Internet Service
Operational: Yes.
Broadband Service: Charter Pipeline.
Fee: $29.99 monthly.

Telephone Service
Digital: Operational
Fee: $29.99 monthly

Miles of Plant: 471.0 (coaxial); None (fiber optic).
Operations Manager: Tony Falin. Marketing Director: Pat Hollenbeck. Sales & Marketing Manager: Kevin Kick.
Ownership: Charter Communications Inc. (MSO).

MOUNTAIN CITY—Charter Communications, 1121 Lenoir Rhyne Blvd SE, Hickory, NC 28602-5128. Phone: 828-322-2288. Fax: 828-322-5492. Web Site: http://www.charter.com. Also serves Johnson County & Laurel Bloomery. ICA: TN0067.
TV Market Ranking: Below 100 (Johnson County, Laurel Bloomery, MOUNTAIN CITY). Franchise award date: N.A. Fran-

chise expiration date: N.A. Began: July 1, 1963.

Channel capacity: N.A. Channels available but not in use: N.A.

Basic Service

Subscribers: 1,906.

Programming (received off-air): WCCB (FOX) Charlotte; WCYB-TV (CW, NBC) Bristol; WJHL-TV (CBS) Johnson City; WKPT-TV (ABC) Kingsport; WLFG (IND) Grundy; WUNE-TV (PBS) Linville.

Programming (via satellite): C-SPAN; INSP; QVC; Trinity Broadcasting Network.

Fee: $29.99 installation.

Expanded Basic Service 1

Subscribers: 1,656.

Programming (via satellite): A&E Networks; ABC Family Channel; AMC; Animal Planet; Bravo; Cartoon Network; CNBC; CNN; Comedy Central; Country Music TV; Discovery Channel; Disney Channel; E! Entertainment Television; ESPN; ESPN 2; Food Network; Fox News Channel; Fox Sports South; FX; G4; Golf Channel; Headline News; HGTV; History Channel; Lifetime; MSNBC; MTV; Nickelodeon; Outdoor Channel; Oxygen; Speed; Spike TV; Syfy; TBS Superstation; The Learning Channel; The Weather Channel; Toon Disney; Travel Channel; truTV; Turner Classic Movies; Turner Network TV; TV Land; USA Network; VH1; WE tv.

Fee: $47.99 monthly.

Digital Basic Service

Subscribers: N.A.

Programming (via satellite): BBC America; Bio; Bloomberg Television; Discovery Digital Networks; DIY Network; Fox Movie Channel; GAS; GSN; History Channel International; Independent Film Channel; Lifetime Movie Network; MTV Networks Digital Suite; Music Choice; National Geographic Channel; Nick Jr.; Nick Too; NickToons TV; Sundance Channel; TV Guide Interactive Inc.; Versus.

Fee: $43.08 monthly.

Digital Pay Service 1

Pay Units: 112.

Programming (via satellite): Cinemax (multiplexed).

Fee: $8.95 monthly.

Digital Pay Service 2

Pay Units: N.A.

Programming (via satellite): Encore; Flix; LOGO; Starz (multiplexed); The Movie Channel (multiplexed).

Fee: $8.95 monthly.

Digital Pay Service 3

Pay Units: 201.

Programming (via satellite): HBO (multiplexed).

Fee: $10.95 monthly.

Digital Pay Service 4

Pay Units: 157.

Programming (via satellite): Showtime (multiplexed).

Fee: $8.95 monthly.

Video-On-Demand: Yes

Pay-Per-View

iN DEMAND (delivered digitally); Playboy TV (delivered digitally); Fresh (delivered digitally); Shorteez (delivered digitally).

Internet Service

Operational: Yes.

Fee: $29.99 monthly.

Telephone Service

Digital: Operational

Miles of Plant: 53.0 (coaxial); None (fiber optic).

Vice President & General Manager: Anthony Pope. Operations Manager: Sam Scialabba. Marketing Director: Brooke Sinclair. Sales & Marketing Manager: Kren Sims.

Ownership: Charter Communications Inc. (MSO).

NASHVILLE—Comcast Cable, 660 Mainstream Dr, PO Box 280570, Nashville, TN 37228-0570. Phone: 615-244-7462. Fax: 615-255-6528. Web Site: http://www.comcast.com. Also serves Franklin & Simpson County, KY; Bellevue, Bon Aqua, Brentwood, Burns, Carthage, Cheatham County (portions), Coopertown, Cottontown, Cross Plains, Davidson County, Dickson, Dickson County, Elmwood, Fairview, Franklin, Gallatin, Goodlettsville, Greenbrier, Hartsville, Hendersonville, Hermitage, Humphreys County (portions), Joelton, Kingston Springs, La Vergne, Lyles, Macon County, Millersville, Mitchellville, Mount Juliet, Murfreesboro, New Deal, Nolensville, Old Hickory, Orlinda, Pegram, Portland, Robertson County (portions), Rutherford County, Smith County, Smyrna, South Carthage, Springfield, Sumner County (portions), Waverly, White Bluff, White House, Whites Creek & Williamson County (portions), TN. ICA: TN0002.

TV Market Ranking: 30 (Bellevue, Bon Aqua, Brentwood, Burns, Cheatham County (portions), Coopertown, Cottontown, Cross Plains, Davidson County, Dickson, Fairview, Franklin (Williamson County), Gallatin, Goodlettsville, Greenbrier, Hartsville, Hendersonville, Hermitage, Joelton, Kingston Springs, La Vergne, Lyles, Millersville, Mitchellville, Mount Juliet, Murfreesboro, NASHVILLE, New Deal, Nolensville, Old Hickory, Orlinda, Pegram, Portland, Robertson County (portions), Rutherford County, Simpson County (portions), Smyrna, Springfield, Sumner County (portions), White Bluff, White House, Whites Creek, Williamson County (portions)); Below 100 (Carthage, Elmwood, Franklin (Simpson County), Macon County, Smith County, South Carthage, Simpson County (portions)); Outside TV Markets (Franklin County, Humphreys County (portions), Waverly). Franchise award date: February 1, 1979. Franchise expiration date: May 4, 2010. Began: February 1, 1979.

Channel capacity: N.A. Channels available but not in use: N.A.

Basic Service

Subscribers: 330,216.

Programming (received off-air): WHTN (IND) Murfreesboro; WKRN-TV (ABC) Nashville; WNPT (PBS) Nashville; WPGD-TV (TBN) Hendersonville; WSMV-TV (NBC, TMO) Nashville; WTVF (CBS) Nashville; WUXP-TV (MNT) Nashville; WZTV (FOX) Nashville.

Programming (via satellite): Sneak Prevue; TBS Superstation; The Weather Channel; TV Guide Network; WGN America.

Fee: $33.02 installation; $8.69 monthly.

Expanded Basic Service 1

Subscribers: 290,400.

Programming (via satellite): A&E Networks; ABC Family Channel; AMC; BET Networks; Bravo; Cartoon Network; CNBC; CNN; Comedy Central; Country Music TV; C-SPAN; C-SPAN 2; Discovery Channel; Disney Channel; E! Entertainment Television; ESPN; Fox Movie Channel; Fox Sports South; FX; Hallmark Channel; Headline News; History Channel; Lifetime; MTV; Nickelodeon; QVC; ShopNBC; Spike TV; Syfy; The Learning Channel; truTV; Turner Network TV; TV Guide Network; USA Network; VH1.

Fee: $31.26 monthly.

Digital Basic Service

Subscribers: 128,489.

Programming (via satellite): BBC America; Bio; C-SPAN 3; Discovery Digital Networks; DMX Music; ESPN Classic Sports; Flix; Fox Sports World; GAS; Golf Channel; GSN; History Channel International; Independent Film Channel; INSP; Lifetime Movie Network; MTV Networks Digital Suite; MuchMusic Network; Nick Jr.; SoapNet; Speed; Sundance Channel; Toon Disney; Turner Classic Movies; Weatherscan.

Fee: $10.00 monthly.

Pay Service 1

Pay Units: 280,647.

Programming (via satellite): Cinemax; HBO; Showtime; The Movie Channel.

Fee: $8.00 monthly (each).

Digital Pay Service 1

Pay Units: N.A.

Programming (via satellite): Cinemax (multiplexed); Encore (multiplexed); HBO (multiplexed); Showtime (multiplexed); Starz (multiplexed); The Movie Channel (multiplexed).

Video-On-Demand: Yes

Pay-Per-View

Addressable homes: 128,589.

Hot Choice; Hot Choice (delivered digitally); iN DEMAND; iN DEMAND (delivered digitally); Playboy TV; Playboy TV (delivered digitally); Pleasure (delivered digitally); Fresh (delivered digitally); Shorteez (delivered digitally); Sports PPV (delivered digitally).

Internet Service

Operational: Yes.

Subscribers: 61,563.

Broadband Service: Comcast High Speed Internet.

Fee: $42.95 monthly; $15.00 modem lease; $240.00 modem purchase.

Telephone Service

Digital: Operational

Fee: $44.95 monthly

Miles of Plant: 11,000.0 (coaxial); None (fiber optic). Miles of plant (coax & fiber combined) include Fort Campbell KY, Ashland City, Lynchburg, Smithville, & Woodbury

Area Vice President & General Manager: John Gauder. Technical Operations Director: Joe Pell. Marketing Director: Martine Mahoney. Marketing Manager: Will Jefferson.

Ownership: Comcast Cable Communications Inc. (MSO).

NEW TAZEWELL—Communicomm Services, 3213 Hwy 25 E, Ste 1, PO Box 1526, New Tazewell, TN 37824-1526. Phone: 423-626-8817. Fax: 423-626-6304. Web Site: http://www.netcommander.com. Also serves Arthur, Cumberland Gap, Harrogate, Lone Mountain, Shawanee, Speedwell & Tazewell. ICA: TN0038.

TV Market Ranking: 71 (Lone Mountain); Below 100 (Arthur, Cumberland Gap, Harrogate, NEW TAZEWELL, Shawanee, Speedwell, Tazewell). Franchise award date: January 1, 1977. Franchise expiration date: January 1, 2018. Began: August 1, 1978.

Channel capacity: N.A. Channels available but not in use: N.A.

Basic Service

Subscribers: 5,700.

Programming (received off-air): WATE-TV (ABC) Knoxville; WBIR-TV (NBC) Knoxville; WBXX-TV (CW) Crossville; WETP-TV (PBS) Sneedville; WLFG (IND) Grundy; WMAK (IND) Knoxville; WPXK-TV (ION) Jellico; WTNZ (FOX) Knoxville; WVLR (IND) Tazewell; WVLT-TV (CBS, MNT) Knoxville; WYMT-TV (CBS, CW) Hazard.

Programming (via satellite): C-SPAN; Discovery Channel; QVC; TV Guide Network; WGN America.

Fee: $39.95 installation; $29.95 monthly.

Expanded Basic Service 1

Subscribers: N.A.

Programming (via satellite): A&E Networks; ABC Family Channel; AMC; Animal Planet; Boomerang; Bravo; Cartoon Network; CNBC; CNN; Comcast/Charter Sports Southeast (CSS); Comedy Central; Cooking Channel; Country Music TV; C-SPAN 2; Disney Channel; DIY Network; E! Entertainment Television; ESPN; ESPN 2; ESPN Classic Sports; ESPNews; Food Network; Fox Movie Channel; Fox News Channel; FX; G4; GMC; Great American Country; Hallmark Channel; Headline News; HGTV; History Channel; Lifetime; MSNBC; MTV; National Geographic Channel; Nick Jr.; Nickelodeon; Outdoor Channel; ShopNBC; Speed; Spike TV; SportSouth; Syfy; TBS Superstation; The Learning Channel; The Weather Channel; Travel Channel; Trinity Broadcasting Network; truTV; Turner Network TV; TV Land; USA Network; VH1; WE tv.

Fee: $19.96 monthly.

Digital Basic Service

Subscribers: 1,143.

Programming (via satellite): AmericanLife TV Network; BBC America; Bio; Bloomberg Television; Bravo; cloo; CMT Pure Country; Current; Daystar TV Network; Discovery Fit & Health; Discovery Health Channel; Discovery Home Channel; Discovery Kids Channel; Discovery Times Channel; DMX Music; Encore (multiplexed); ESPN 2; ESPN Classic Sports; ESPNews; Fox Movie Channel; Fox Soccer; Fuse; G4; GAS; Golf Channel; Great American Country; GSN; Halogen Network; HGTV; History Channel International; Independent Film Channel; Lifetime Movie Network; Military Channel; MTV Hits; MTV Jams; MTV2; National Geographic Channel; NickToons TV; Outdoor Channel; Ovation; RFD-TV; Science; SoapNet; Speed; Style Network; Syfy; The Word Network; Toon Disney; Trinity Broadcasting Network; Turner Classic Movies; TV One; Versus; VH1 Classic; VH1 Soul; WE tv.

Fee: $17.00 monthly.

Digital Pay Service 1

Pay Units: N.A.

Programming (via satellite): Cinemax (multiplexed); Flix; HBO (multiplexed); Showtime (multiplexed); Starz (multiplexed); The Movie Channel (multiplexed).

Fee: $13.95 monthly (each).

Video-On-Demand: No

Pay-Per-View
iN DEMAND (delivered digitally); ESPN (delivered digitally); Playboy TV (delivered digitally); Fresh (delivered digitally); Club Jenna (delivered digitally); Spice: Xcess (delivered digitally); Hot Choice (delivered digitally).
Internet Service
Operational: Yes.
Subscribers: 1,500.
Broadband Service: Net Commander.
Fee: $39.95 installation; $51.95 monthly.
Telephone Service
None
Miles of Plant: 200.0 (coaxial); None (fiber optic). Additional miles planned: 12.0 (coaxial).
General Manager & Chief Technician: Lloyd Walker. Customer Care Manager: Amy Cody.
Ownership: James Cable LLC (MSO).

NEWBERN—Charter Communications, 1774 Henry G Lane St, Maryville, TN 37801. Phone: 865-984-1400. Fax: 865-983-0383. Web Site: http://www.charter.com. ICA: TN0206.
TV Market Ranking: Outside TV Markets (NEWBERN).
Channel capacity: N.A. Channels available but not in use: N.A.
Basic Service
Subscribers: N.A.
Programming (received off-air): KFVS-TV (CBS, CW) Cape Girardeau; WBBJ-TV (ABC) Jackson; WHBQ-TV (FOX) Memphis; WJKT (FOX) Jackson; WLJT-DT (PBS) Lexington; WMC-TV (NBC) Memphis; WPSD-TV (NBC) Paducah; WPTY-TV (ABC) Memphis; WPXX-TV (ION, MNT) Memphis; WREG-TV (CBS) Memphis.
Programming (via satellite): WGN America.
Digital Basic Service
Subscribers: N.A.
Programming (via satellite): A&E HD; AmericanLife TV Network; BBC America; Bio; Bloomberg Television; Boomerang; CMT Pure Country; CNN en Espanol; Cooking Channel; DIY Network; ESPN 2 HD; ESPN Classic Sports; ESPN HD; ESPN U; ESPNews; Fox Business Channel; Fox College Sports Atlantic; Fox College Sports Central; Fox College Sports Pacific; Fox Movie Channel; Fox Soccer; Fuel TV; Fuse; GMC; Great American Country; HD Theater; HDNet; HDNet Movies; History Channel HD; History Channel International; Independent Film Channel; Jewelry Television; Lifetime Movie Network; Lifetime Real Women; LOGO; MTV Networks Digital Suite; Music Choice; Nick Jr.; Nick Too; NickToons TV; Outdoor Channel; Palladia; PBS KIDS/PBS KIDS GO!; Sundance Channel; TeenNick; Tennis Channel; Toon Disney; Turner Network TV HD; Universal HD; Versus HD; WE tv.
Digital Pay Service 1
Pay Units: N.A.
Programming (via satellite): Cinemax (multiplexed); Cinemax HD; Encore (multiplexed); Flix; HBO (multiplexed); HBO HD; Showtime (multiplexed); Showtime HD; Starz (multiplexed); Starz HDTV; The Movie Channel (multiplexed); The Movie Channel HD.
Video-On-Demand: No
Pay-Per-View
iN DEMAND (delivered digitally); Ten Clips (delivered digitally); Ten Blue (delivered digitally); Ten Blox (delivered digitally).
Internet Service
Operational: Yes.
Broadband Service: Charter Pipeline.
Fee: $29.99 monthly.
Telephone Service
None
Operations Manager: Tony Fox. Technical Operations Manager: Ron Jansen. Marketing Director: Pat Hollenbeck. Marketing Manager: Wiley Bird.
Ownership: Charter Communications Inc. (MSO).

NEWBERN—Charter Communications. Now served by NEWBERN, TN [TN0206]. ICA: TN0072.

NEWPORT—Haywood Cablevision, PO Box 778, Waynesville, NC 28786. Phone: 678-682-9726. Fax: 678-682-9727. Web Site: http://www.cbvnol.com. ICA: TN0203.
TV Market Ranking: 71 (NEWPORT).
Channel capacity: N.A. Channels available but not in use: N.A.
Basic Service
Subscribers: 238.
Programming (received off-air): WATE-TV (ABC) Knoxville; WBIR-TV (NBC) Knoxville; WEMT (FOX) Greeneville; WETP-TV (PBS) Sneedville; WVLT-TV (CBS, MNT) Knoxville.
Programming (via satellite): CNN; Country Music TV; Discovery Channel; Nickelodeon; Spike TV; The Weather Channel.
Fee: $29.91 monthly.
Expanded Basic Service 1
Subscribers: N.A.
Programming (via satellite): ABC Family Channel; Disney Channel; ESPN; ESPN 2; Fox News Channel; Headline News; HGTV; Lifetime; MTV; TBS Superstation; Trinity Broadcasting Network; Turner Classic Movies; Turner Network TV; USA Network; VH1.
Pay Service 1
Pay Units: N.A.
Programming (via satellite): HBO; Showtime.
Internet Service
Operational: Yes.
Fee: $43.95 monthly.
Telephone Service
None
Manager & Chief Technician: Joseph Stark.
Ownership: Carolina Mountain Cablevision Inc. (MSO).

NORRIS—Comcast Cable, 5720 Asheville Hwy, Knoxville, TN 37924-2701. Phone: 865-971-1544. Fax: 865-862-5092. Web Site: http://www.comcast.com. ICA: TN0156.
TV Market Ranking: 71 (NORRIS). Franchise award date: N.A. Franchise expiration date: N.A. Began: N.A.
Channel capacity: 67 (operating 2-way). Channels available but not in use: N.A.
Basic Service
Subscribers: N.A.
Programming (received off-air): WATE-TV (ABC) Knoxville; WBIR-TV (NBC) Knoxville; WBXX-TV (CW) Crossville; WETP-TV (PBS) Sneedville; WKOP-TV (PBS) Knoxville; WMAK (IND) Knoxville; WPXK-TV (ION) Jellico; WTNZ (FOX) Knoxville; WVLR (IND) Tazewell; WVLT-TV (CBS, MNT) Knoxville.
Programming (via satellite): C-SPAN; Discovery Health Channel; QVC; TBS Superstation; WGN America.
Fee: $56.50 installation; $13.75 monthly.
Expanded Basic Service 1
Subscribers: N.A.
Programming (via satellite): 10 News 2; A&E Networks; ABC Family Channel; AMC; BET Networks; Bravo; Cartoon Network; CNBC; CNN; Comcast/Charter Sports Southeast (CSS); Comedy Central; Discovery Channel; Disney Channel; DIY Network; E! Entertainment Television; ESPN; ESPN 2; Food Network; Fox Sports South; FX; Golf Channel; Great American Country; Hallmark Channel; Headline News; HGTV; History Channel; Lifetime; MTV; Nickelodeon; Speed; Spike TV; SportSouth; Style Network; Syfy; The Learning Channel; The Weather Channel; Travel Channel; Trinity Broadcasting Network; truTV; Turner Classic Movies; Turner Network TV; TV Guide Network; TV Land; USA Network; Versus; VH1.
Fee: $36.24 monthly.
Digital Basic Service
Subscribers: N.A.
Programming (via satellite): A&E HD; Animal Planet; BBC America; Bio; CMT Pure Country; Cooking Channel; Country Music TV; C-SPAN 2; C-SPAN 3; Current; Encore (multiplexed); ESPN 2 HD; ESPN Classic Sports; ESPN HD; ESPNews; Eternal Word TV Network; Exercise TV; Flix; Fox College Sports Atlantic; Fox College Sports Central; Fox College Sports Pacific; Fox News Channel; Fox Reality Channel; Fox Soccer; G4; GAS; GolTV; GSN; Halogen Network; HD Theater; History Channel International; INSP; Jewelry Television; Lifetime Movie Network; MoviePlex; MSNBC; MTV Networks Digital Suite; Music Choice; National Geographic Channel; National Geographic Channel HD Network; NBA TV; NFL Network; Nick Jr.; Nick Too; NickToons TV; Palladia; PBS Kids Sprout; ShopNBC; SoapNet; Sundance Channel; The Word Network; Toon Disney; Turner Network TV HD; TV One; Universal HD; Versus HD; Weatherscan.
Fee: $14.95 monthly.
Digital Pay Service 1
Pay Units: N.A.
Programming (via satellite): Cinemax (multiplexed); Cinemax HD; HBO (multiplexed); HBO HD; HBO On Demand; Showtime (multiplexed); Showtime HD; Starz (multiplexed); Starz HDTV; The Movie Channel (multiplexed).
Fee: $13.99 monthly (each).
Video-On-Demand: Yes
Pay-Per-View
Playboy TV (delivered digitally); Fresh (delivered digitally); Shorteez (delivered digitally); Pleasure (delivered digitally); ESPN Now (delivered digitally); ESPN (delivered digitally); iN DEMAND (delivered digitally).
Internet Service
Operational: Yes.
Broadband Service: Comcast High Speed Internet.
Fee: $42.95 monthly.
Telephone Service
Digital: Operational
Area Vice President & General Manager: Kirk Dale. Technical Operations Director: Charlie Goodreau. Engineering Manager: Hank Swindle. Marketing Director: Kristopher Workman. Government & Community Affairs: Russell Byrd.
Ownership: Comcast Cable Communications Inc. (MSO).

OAK RIDGE—Comcast Cable, 5720 Asheville Hwy, Knoxville, TN 37924-2701. Phone: 865-971-1544. Fax: 865-862-5092. Web Site: http://www.comcast.com. Also serves Anderson County (portions), Clinton, Oliver Springs & Roane County. ICA: TN0012.
TV Market Ranking: 71 (Anderson County (portions), Clinton, OAK RIDGE, Oliver Springs, Roane County (portions)); Below 100 (Roane County (portions)). Franchise award date: N.A. Franchise expiration date: N.A. Began: November 4, 1965.
Channel capacity: N.A. Channels available but not in use: N.A.
Basic Service
Subscribers: 19,547.
Programming (received off-air): WATE-TV (ABC) Knoxville; WBIR-TV (NBC) Knoxville; WBXX-TV (CW) Crossville; WETP-TV (PBS) Sneedville; WKOP-TV (PBS) Knoxville; WMAK (IND) Knoxville; WPXK-TV (ION) Jellico; WTNZ (FOX) Knoxville; WVLR (IND) Tazewell; WVLT-TV (CBS, MNT) Knoxville; allband FM.
Programming (via satellite): C-SPAN; QVC; TBS Superstation; WGN America.
Fee: $56.50 installation; $13.75 monthly.
Expanded Basic Service 1
Subscribers: N.A.
Programming (via satellite): 10 News 2; A&E Networks; ABC Family Channel; AMC; Animal Planet; BET Networks; Bravo; Cartoon Network; CNBC; CNN; Comcast/Charter Sports Southeast (CSS); Comedy Central; Discovery Channel; Discovery Health Channel; Disney Channel; DIY Network; E! Entertainment Television; ESPN; ESPN 2; Food Network; Fox News Channel; Fox Sports South; FX; G4; Golf Channel; Great American Country; Hallmark Channel; Headline News; HGTV; History Channel; Lifetime; MTV; Nickelodeon; Speed; Spike TV; SportSouth; Style Network; Syfy; The Learning Channel; The Weather Channel; Travel Channel; Trinity Broadcasting Network; truTV; Turner Classic Movies; Turner Network TV; TV Guide Network; TV Land; USA Network; Versus; VH1.
Fee: $36.24 monthly.
Digital Basic Service
Subscribers: N.A.
Programming (via satellite): A&E HD; BBC America; Bio; CMT Pure Country; Cooking Channel; Country Music TV; C-SPAN 2; C-SPAN 3; Current; Encore (multiplexed); ESPN 2 HD; ESPN Classic Sports; ESPN HD; ESPNews; Eternal Word TV Network; Exercise TV; Flix; Fox College Sports Atlantic; Fox College Sports Central; Fox College Sports Pacific; Fox Reality Channel; Fox Soccer; GAS; GolTV; GSN; Halogen Network; HD Theater; History Channel International; INSP; Jewelry Television; Lifetime Movie Network; MoviePlex; MSNBC; MTV Networks Digital Suite; Music Choice; National Geographic Channel; National Geographic Channel HD Network; NBA TV; NFL Network; Nick Jr.; Nick Too; NickToons TV; Palladia; PBS Kids Sprout; ShopNBC; SoapNet; Sundance Channel; The Word Network; Toon Disney; Turner Network TV HD; TV One; Universal HD; Versus HD; Weatherscan.
Fee: $14.95 monthly.
Digital Pay Service 1
Pay Units: N.A.
Programming (via satellite): Cinemax (multiplexed); Cinemax HD; HBO (multiplexed); HBO HD; HBO On Demand; Showtime (multiplexed); Showtime HD; Starz (multiplexed); Starz HDTV; The Movie Channel (multiplexed).
Fee: $13.99 monthly (each).
Video-On-Demand: Yes
Pay-Per-View
iN DEMAND (delivered digitally); Playboy TV (delivered digitally); Fresh (delivered digitally); Shorteez (delivered digitally); Pleasure (delivered digitally); ESPN Now (delivered digitally); Sports PPV (delivered digitally).

Internet Service
Operational: Yes.
Broadband Service: Comcast High Speed Internet.
Fee: $42.95 monthly.
Telephone Service
Digital: Operational
Miles of Plant: 526.0 (coaxial); None (fiber optic).
Area Vice President & General Manager: Kirk Dale. Technical Operations Director: Charlie Goodreau. Engineering Manager: Hank Swindle. Marketing Director: Kristopher Workman. Government & Community Affairs Director: Russell Byrd.
Ownership: Comcast Cable Communications Inc. (MSO).

OVERTON COUNTY (portions)—Overton County Cable, 17525 Highland Dr, McKenzie, TN 38201. Phones: 731-352-2980; 931-823-1114. Fax: 731-352-3533. ICA: TN0184.
TV Market Ranking: Below 100 (OVERTON COUNTY (PORTIONS)). Franchise award date: N.A. Franchise expiration date: N.A. Began: N.A.
Channel capacity: 40 (not 2-way capable). Channels available but not in use: N.A.
Basic Service
Subscribers: 2,000.
Programming (received off-air): WCTE (PBS) Cookeville; WKRN-TV (ABC) Nashville; WNAB (CW) Nashville; WSMV-TV (NBC, TMO) Nashville; WTVF (CBS) Nashville; WUXP-TV (MNT) Nashville; WZTV (FOX) Nashville.
Programming (via satellite): A&E Networks; ABC Family Channel; AMC; Animal Planet; Cartoon Network; CNBC; CNN; Country Music TV; C-SPAN; Discovery Channel; Disney Channel; ESPN; Fox Sports South; G4; HGTV; History Channel; Lifetime; MTV; Nickelodeon; Spike TV; SportSouth; Syfy; TBS Superstation; The Learning Channel; truTV; Turner Classic Movies; Turner Network TV; USA Network; VH1; WGN America.
Fee: $10.78 installation; $12.50 monthly.
Pay Service 1
Pay Units: 137.
Programming (via satellite): Cinemax.
Fee: $10.31 monthly.
Pay Service 2
Pay Units: 325.
Programming (via satellite): HBO.
Fee: $10.31 monthly.
Pay Service 3
Pay Units: 55.
Programming (via satellite): Showtime.
Fee: $10.31 monthly.
Video-On-Demand: No
Internet Service
Operational: Yes.
Telephone Service
None
Miles of Plant: 187.0 (coaxial); None (fiber optic).
General Manager: Gary Blount.
Ownership: Celina Cable Communications (MSO).

PARIS—Charter Communications, 1774 Henry G Lane St, Maryville, TN 37801. Phone: 865-984-1400. Fax: 865-983-0383. Web Site: http://www.charter.com. Also serves Camden & Henry County (unincorporated areas). ICA: TN0130.
TV Market Ranking: Outside TV Markets (Camden, Henry County (unincorporated areas), PARIS). Franchise award date: November 1, 1968. Franchise expiration date: November 1, 2008. Began: September 27, 1969.
Channel capacity: N.A. Channels available but not in use: N.A.
Basic Service
Subscribers: 1,831.
Programming (received off-air): WBBJ-TV (ABC) Jackson; WJKT (FOX) Jackson; WKMU (PBS) Murray; WKRN-TV (ABC) Nashville; WLJT-DT (PBS) Lexington; WNAB (CW) Nashville; WPSD-TV (NBC) Paducah; WSMV-TV (NBC, TMO) Nashville; WTVF (CBS) Nashville; WZTV (FOX) Nashville.
Programming (via satellite): WGN America.
Expanded Basic Service 1
Subscribers: N.A.
Programming (via satellite): A&E Networks; ABC Family Channel; AMC; Animal Planet; BET Networks; Bravo; Cartoon Network; CNBC; CNN; Comcast/Charter Sports Southeast (CSS); Comedy Central; Country Music TV; C-SPAN; C-SPAN 2; Discovery Channel; Disney Channel; E! Entertainment Television; ESPN; ESPN 2; Food Network; Fox News Channel; Fox Sports South; FX; G4; Golf Channel; GSN; Hallmark Channel; Headline News; HGTV; History Channel; INSP; Lifetime; MSNBC; MTV; MTV2; National Geographic Channel; Nickelodeon; Oxygen; QVC; SoapNet; Speed; Spike TV; SportSouth; Style Network; Syfy; TBS Superstation; The Learning Channel; The Weather Channel; Toon Disney; Travel Channel; Trinity Broadcasting Network; truTV; Turner Classic Movies; Turner Network TV; TV Land; USA Network; VH1; WE tv.
Fee: $45.00 monthly.
Digital Basic Service
Subscribers: N.A.
Programming (via satellite): BBC America; Bio; Bloomberg Television; Boomerang; CNN en Espanol; Discovery Digital Networks; DIY Network; ESPN Classic Sports; ESPNews; Fox College Sports Atlantic; Fox College Sports Central; Fox College Sports Pacific; Fox Movie Channel; Fox Soccer; Fuel TV; Fuse; GAS; Great American Country; History Channel International; Independent Film Channel; Lifetime Movie Network; Lifetime Real Women; MTV Networks Digital Suite; Music Choice; NFL Network; Nick Jr.; Nick Too; NickToons TV; Outdoor Channel; Science Television; Sundance Channel.
Pay Service 1
Pay Units: 210.
Programming (via satellite): Encore (multiplexed); Flix; Showtime; The Movie Channel.
Fee: $40.00 installation; $9.95 monthly (each).
Digital Pay Service 1
Pay Units: N.A.
Programming (via satellite): Cinemax; HBO; Starz (multiplexed).
Video-On-Demand: No
Pay-Per-View
Playboy TV (delivered digitally); Fresh (delivered digitally); Shorteez (delivered digitally).
Internet Service
Operational: Yes.
Broadband Service: Charter Pipeline.
Fee: $29.99 monthly.
Telephone Service
Digital: Operational
Fee: $29.99 monthly
Miles of Plant: 62.0 (coaxial); None (fiber optic). Additional miles planned: 10.0 (coaxial).
Operations Manager: Tony Fox. Technical Operations Manager: Ron Janson. Marketing Director: Pat Hollenbeck. Marketing Manager: Wiley Bird.
Ownership: Charter Communications Inc. (MSO).

PARSONS—Charter Communications. Now served by LEXINGTON, TN [TN0047]. ICA: TN0084.

PIKEVILLE—Bledsoe Telephone Coop. Formerly [TN0158]. This cable system has converted to IPTV, 338 Cumberland Ave, PO Box 609, Pikeville, TN 37367-0609. Phone: 423-447-2121. E-mail: bledsoe@bledsoe.net. Web Site: http://www.bledsoe.net. ICA: TN5005.
TV Market Ranking: Below 100 (PIKEVILLE). Franchise award date: N.A. Franchise expiration date: N.A. Began: N.A.
Channel capacity: N.A. Channels available but not in use: N.A.
Video-On-Demand: No
Internet Service
Operational: Yes.
Fee: $19.95 installation; $19.95 monthly.
Telephone Service
Digital: Operational
Fee: $12.95 monthly
General Manager: Greg Anderson.

PIKEVILLE—Bledsoe Telephone Coop. This cable system has converted to IPTV. See Pikeville, TN [TN5005]. ICA: TN0158.

PORTLAND—Comcast Cable. Now served by NASHVILLE, TN [TN0002]. ICA: TN0080.

PULASKI—Charter Communications. Now served by COLUMBIA, TN [TN0017]. ICA: TN0018.

RED BOILING SPRINGS—Celina Cable. Now served by SCOTTSVILLE, KY [KY0073]. ICA: TN0114.

RIPLEY—NewWave Communications. Now served by BROWNSVILLE, TN [TN0054]. ICA: TN0160.

ROGERSVILLE—Small Town Cable, PO Box 99, College Grove, TN 37046. Phones: 618-368-2115; 931-484-7994. Fax: 615-368-2295. Also serves Hawkins County (central portion) & Surgoinsville. ICA: TN0087.
TV Market Ranking: Below 100 (Hawkins County (central portion), ROGERSVILLE, Surgoinsville). Franchise award date: N.A. Franchise expiration date: N.A. Began: December 1, 1988.
Channel capacity: N.A. Channels available but not in use: N.A.
Basic Service
Subscribers: N.A. Included in Chapel Hill
Programming (received off-air): WBIR-TV (NBC) Knoxville; WCYB-TV (CW, NBC) Bristol; WETP-TV (PBS) Sneedville; WJHL-TV (CBS) Johnson City; WKPT-TV (ABC) Kingsport; WLOS (ABC) Asheville.
Programming (via satellite): A&E Networks; ABC Family Channel; CNN; Comedy Central; Country Music TV; Discovery Channel; Disney Channel; ESPN; Headline News; Lifetime; MTV; QVC; Spike TV; TBS Superstation; The Weather Channel; Turner Network TV; USA Network; WGN America.
Fee: $30.00 installation; $27.50 monthly.
Digital Basic Service
Subscribers: N.A. Included in Chapel Hill
Pay Service 1
Pay Units: N.A.
Programming (via satellite): HBO; Showtime.
Fee: $30.00 installation; $9.95 monthly (each).
Video-On-Demand: Yes
Internet Service
Operational: Yes.
Telephone Service
Analog: Not Operational
Digital: Operational
Miles of plant included in Chapel Hill
General Manager: Vince King. Chief Technician: Brian Langham.
Ownership: Small Town Cable Corp. (MSO).

ROGERSVILLE (portions)—Charter Communications, 105 Jack White Dr, Kingsport, TN 37664. Phone: 423-247-7631. Fax: 423-247-1807. Web Site: http://www.charter.com. ICA: TN0190.
TV Market Ranking: Below 100 (ROGERSVILLE). Franchise award date: N.A. Franchise expiration date: N.A. Began: N.A.
Channel capacity: N.A. Channels available but not in use: N.A.
Basic Service
Subscribers: 6,100.
Programming (received off-air): WAPK-CA (MNT) Kingsport; WATE-TV (ABC) Knoxville; WBIR-TV (NBC) Knoxville; WCYB-TV (CW, NBC) Bristol; WEMT (FOX) Greeneville; WETP-TV (PBS) Sneedville; WJHL-TV (CBS) Johnson City; WKPT-TV (ABC) Kingsport; WLFG (IND) Grundy; WVLT-TV (CBS, MNT) Knoxville.
Programming (via satellite): QVC; WGN America.
Expanded Basic Service 1
Subscribers: N.A.
Programming (via satellite): A&E Networks; ABC Family Channel; AMC; Animal Planet; BET Networks; Bravo; Cartoon Network; CNBC; CNN; Comedy Central; Country Music TV; C-SPAN; C-SPAN 2; Discovery Channel; Disney Channel; E! Entertainment Television; ESPN; ESPN 2; Food Network; Fox News Channel; Fox Sports South; FX; G4; Golf Channel; Headline News; HGTV; History Channel; INSP; ION Television; Lifetime; MSNBC; MTV; National Geographic Channel; Nickelodeon; Oxygen; SoapNet; Speed; Spike TV; SportSouth; Syfy; TBS Superstation; The Learning Channel; The Weather Channel; Toon Disney; Travel Channel; Trinity Broadcasting Network; truTV; Turner Classic Movies; Turner Network TV; TV Guide Network; TV Land; USA Network; Versus; VH1; WE tv.
Fee: $45.00 monthly.
Digital Basic Service
Subscribers: N.A.
Programming (via satellite): BBC America; Bio; Discovery Digital Networks; DIY Network; ESPN Classic Sports; Fox Sports World; GAS; Great American Country; GSN; History Channel International; Independent Film Channel; Lifetime Movie Network; MTV Networks Digital Suite; Music Choice; Nick Jr.; Sundance Channel.
Digital Pay Service 1
Pay Units: N.A.
Programming (via satellite): Cinemax (multiplexed); Encore (multiplexed); Flix; HBO (multiplexed); Showtime (multiplexed); Starz (multiplexed); The Movie Channel (multiplexed).
Video-On-Demand: Yes

Pay-Per-View
iN DEMAND (delivered digitally); Playboy TV (delivered digitally); Pleasure (delivered digitally); Fresh (delivered digitally); Shorteez (delivered digitally).
Internet Service
Operational: Yes.
Broadband Service: Charter Pipeline.
Fee: $29.99 monthly.
Telephone Service
Digital: Operational
Fee: $29.99 monthly
Miles of Plant: 210.0 (coaxial); 92.0 (fiber optic).
Vice President & General Manager: Fred Lutz. Sales & Marketing Manager: Betty Payne. Operations Manager: Tony Falin. Technical Supervisor: Bruce Cocke.
Ownership: Charter Communications Inc. (MSO).

SAVANNAH—Charter Communications, 1774 Henry G Lane St, Maryville, TN 37801. Phone: 865-984-1400. Fax: 865-983-0383. Web Site: http://www.charter.com. Also serves Crump, Hardin County, Milledgeville & Saltillo. ICA: TN0041.
TV Market Ranking: Below 100 (Hardin County (portions)); Outside TV Markets (Crump, Hardin County (portions), Milledgeville, Saltillo, SAVANNAH). Franchise award date: September 3, 1965. Franchise expiration date: N.A. Began: June 1, 1965.
Channel capacity: N.A. Channels available but not in use: N.A.
Basic Service
Subscribers: 5,320.
Programming (received off-air): WBBJ-TV (ABC) Jackson; WHBQ-TV (FOX) Memphis; WJKT (FOX) Jackson; WLJT-DT (PBS) Lexington; WMC-TV (NBC) Memphis; WREG-TV (CBS) Memphis; WSMV-TV (NBC, TMO) Nashville; WTVF (CBS) Nashville.
Programming (via satellite): C-SPAN; CW+; WGN America.
Expanded Basic Service 1
Subscribers: 4,632.
Programming (via satellite): A&E Networks; ABC Family Channel; AMC; Animal Planet; BET Networks; Bravo; Cartoon Network; CNBC; CNN; Comcast/Charter Sports Southeast (CSS); Comedy Central; Country Music TV; C-SPAN; C-SPAN 2; Discovery Channel; Disney Channel; E! Entertainment Television; ESPN; ESPN 2; Food Network; Fox News Channel; Fox Sports South; FX; G4; Golf Channel; GSN; Hallmark Channel; Headline News; HGTV; History Channel; INSP; Lifetime; Lifetime Real Women; MSNBC; MTV; MTV2; National Geographic Channel; Nickelodeon; Oxygen; QVC; SoapNet; Speed; Spike TV; SportSouth; Style Network; Syfy; TBS Superstation; The Learning Channel; The Weather Channel; Toon Disney; Travel Channel; Trinity Broadcasting Network; truTV; Turner Classic Movies; Turner Network TV; TV Land; USA Network; VH1; WE tv.
Fee: $45.00 monthly.
Digital Basic Service
Subscribers: N.A.
Programming (via satellite): BBC America; Bio; Bloomberg Television; Boomerang; CNN en Espanol; Discovery Digital Networks; DIY Network; ESPN Classic Sports; ESPNews; Fox College Sports Atlantic; Fox College Sports Central; Fox College Sports Pacific; Fox Movie Channel; Fox Soccer; Fuel TV; Fuse; GAS; Great American Country; History Channel International; Independent Film Channel; Lifetime Movie Network; MTV Networks Digital Suite; Music Choice; NFL Network; Nick Jr.; Nick Too; NickToons TV; Outdoor Channel; Science Television; Sundance Channel.
Digital Pay Service 1
Pay Units: N.A.
Programming (via satellite): Cinemax (multiplexed); HBO (multiplexed); Starz (multiplexed).
Video-On-Demand: Yes
Internet Service
Operational: Yes.
Broadband Service: Charter Pipeline.
Fee: $29.99 monthly.
Telephone Service
Digital: Operational
Fee: $29.99 monthly
Miles of Plant: 183.0 (coaxial); None (fiber optic). Additional miles planned: 30.0 (coaxial).
Operations Manager: Tony Fox. Technical Operations Manager: Ron Janson. Marketing Director: Pat Hollenbeck. Marketing Manager: Wiley Bird.
Ownership: Charter Communications Inc. (MSO).

SCOTTS HILL—Two Rivers Media, PO Box 555, Linden, TN 37096-0555. Phone: 931-589-2696. Fax: 931-589-2696. ICA: TN0166.
TV Market Ranking: Below 100 (SCOTTS HILL). Franchise award date: N.A. Franchise expiration date: N.A. Began: January 1, 1982.
Channel capacity: 12 (not 2-way capable). Channels available but not in use: N.A.
Basic Service
Subscribers: N.A.
Programming (received off-air): WBBJ-TV (ABC) Jackson; WKRN-TV (ABC) Nashville; WNPT (PBS) Nashville; WSMV-TV (NBC, TMO) Nashville; WTVF (CBS) Nashville; WZTV (FOX) Nashville.
Programming (via satellite): CNN; ESPN; Spike TV; TBS Superstation; Turner Network TV; WGN America.
Fee: $14.50 monthly.
Pay Service 1
Pay Units: N.A.
Programming (via satellite): HBO.
Fee: $9.00 monthly.
Internet Service
Operational: No.
Telephone Service
None
Manager: Dorothy Patterson. Chief Technician: Bert Patterson.
Ownership: Two Rivers Media (MSO).

SELMER—Charter Communications, 1774 Henry G Lane St, Maryville, TN 37801. Phone: 865-984-1400. Fax: 865-983-0383. Web Site: http://www.charter.com. Also serves Adamsville, Bethel Springs, McNairy & McNairy County (portions). ICA: TN0060.
TV Market Ranking: Below 100 (Bethel Springs, McNairy, McNairy County (portions), SELMER); Outside TV Markets (Adamsville, McNairy County (portions)). Franchise award date: June 1, 1965. Franchise expiration date: N.A. Began: June 1, 1965.
Channel capacity: N.A. Channels available but not in use: N.A.
Basic Service
Subscribers: 2,603.
Programming (received off-air): WBBJ-TV (ABC) Jackson; WHBQ-TV (FOX) Memphis; WJKT (FOX) Jackson; WKNO (PBS) Memphis; WLJT-DT (PBS) Lexington; WMC-TV (NBC) Memphis; WPXX-TV (ION, MNT) Memphis; WREG-TV (CBS) Memphis; WSMV-TV (NBC, TMO) Nashville; WTVF (CBS) Nashville; allband FM.
Programming (via satellite): WGN America.
Expanded Basic Service 1
Subscribers: N.A.
Programming (via satellite): A&E Networks; ABC Family Channel; AMC; Animal Planet; BET Networks; Bravo; Cartoon Network; CNBC; CNN; Comcast/Charter Sports Southeast (CSS); Comedy Central; Country Music TV; C-SPAN; C-SPAN 2; Discovery Channel; Disney Channel; E! Entertainment Television; ESPN; ESPN 2; Food Network; Fox News Channel; Fox Sports South; FX; G4; Golf Channel; GSN; Hallmark Channel; Headline News; HGTV; History Channel; INSP; Lifetime; MSNBC; MTV; MTV2; National Geographic Channel; Nickelodeon; Oxygen; QVC; SoapNet; Speed; Spike TV; SportSouth; Syfy; TBS Superstation; The Learning Channel; The Weather Channel; Toon Disney; Travel Channel; Trinity Broadcasting Network; truTV; Turner Classic Movies; Turner Network TV; TV Guide Network; TV Land; USA Network; VH1; WE tv.
Fee: $45.00 monthly.
Digital Basic Service
Subscribers: N.A.
Programming (via satellite): BBC America; Bio; Bloomberg Television; Boomerang; CNN en Espanol; DIY Network; ESPN; ESPN Classic Sports; ESPNews; Fox College Sports Atlantic; Fox College Sports Central; Fox College Sports Pacific; Fox Movie Channel; Fox Soccer; Fuel TV; Fuse; GAS; Great American Country; HD Theater; HDNet; HDNet Movies; History Channel International; Independent Film Channel; Lifetime Movie Network; Lifetime Real Women; MTV Networks Digital Suite; Music Choice; NFL Network; Nick Jr.; Nick Too; NickToons TV; Outdoor Channel; Science Television; Sundance Channel.
Digital Pay Service 1
Pay Units: N.A.
Programming (via satellite): Cinemax (multiplexed); HBO (multiplexed); Starz (multiplexed).
Video-On-Demand: Yes
Pay-Per-View
Playboy TV (delivered digitally); Fresh (delivered digitally); Shorteez (delivered digitally).
Internet Service
Operational: Yes.
Broadband Service: Charter Pipeline.
Fee: $29.99 monthly.
Telephone Service
Digital: Operational
Fee: $29.99 monthly
Miles of Plant: 110.0 (coaxial); None (fiber optic).
Operations Manager: Tony Fox. Technical Operations Manager: Ron Janson. Marketing Director: Pat Hollenbeck. Marketing Manager: Wiley Bird.
Ownership: Charter Communications Inc. (MSO).

SEQUATCHIE COUNTY (portions)—Bledsoe Telephone Coop. Formerly served by Dunlap, TN [TN0040]. This cable system has converted to IPTV, 338 Cumberland Ave, PO Box 609, Pikeville, TN 37367-0609. Phone: 423-447-2121. E-mail: bledsoe@bledsoe.net. Web Site: http://www.bledsoe.net. ICA: TN5015.
TV Market Ranking: 78 (SEQUATCHIE COUNTY (PORTIONS)).
Channel capacity: N.A. Channels available but not in use: N.A.
Internet Service
Operational: Yes.
Fee: $19.95 installation; $19.95 monthly.
Telephone Service
Digital: Operational
Fee: $12.95 monthly
General Manager: Greg Anderson.

SIMMERLY CREEK—Zito Media, 611 Vader Hill Rd, Coudersport, PA 16915. Phone: 814-260-9575. Web Site: http://www.zitomedia.com. Also serves Hampton & Roan Mountain. ICA: TN0105.
TV Market Ranking: Below 100 (Hampton, Roan Mountain, SIMMERLY CREEK). Franchise award date: N.A. Franchise expiration date: N.A. Began: June 1, 1990.
Channel capacity: N.A. Channels available but not in use: N.A.
Basic Service
Subscribers: 487.
Programming (received off-air): WCYB-TV (CW, NBC) Bristol; WEMT (FOX) Greeneville; WETP-TV (PBS) Sneedville; WJHL-TV (CBS) Johnson City; WKPT-TV (ABC) Kingsport.
Programming (via satellite): A&E Networks; ABC Family Channel; Animal Planet; CNN; Country Music TV; Discovery Channel; Disney Channel; ESPN; ESPN 2; HGTV; MTV; Nickelodeon; Spike TV; TBS Superstation; Trinity Broadcasting Network; Turner Classic Movies; Turner Network TV; USA Network; WGN America.
Fee: $29.95 installation; $19.95 monthly.
Pay Service 1
Pay Units: N.A.
Programming (via satellite): HBO.
Fee: $9.95 monthly.
Video-On-Demand: No
Pay-Per-View
iN DEMAND (delivered digitally); Hot Choice (delivered digitally); Playboy TV (delivered digitally); Fresh (delivered digitally); Shorteez (delivered digitally).
Internet Service
Operational: No.
Telephone Service
None
Miles of Plant: 32.0 (coaxial); None (fiber optic).
Public Relations Manager: Mark Laver.
Ownership: Zito Media (MSO).

SMITHVILLE—Comcast Cable, 660 Mainstream Dr, PO Box 280570, Nashville, TN 37228-0570. Phone: 615-244-7462. Fax: 615-255-6528. Web Site: http://www.comcast.com. Also serves DeKalb County. ICA: TN0076.
TV Market Ranking: Below 100 (DeKalb County, SMITHVILLE). Franchise award date: N.A. Franchise expiration date: N.A. Began: May 15, 1980.
Channel capacity: 56 (not 2-way capable). Channels available but not in use: N.A.
Basic Service
Subscribers: 2,557.
Programming (received off-air): WCTE (PBS) Cookeville; WKRN-TV (ABC) Nashville; WNAB (CW) Nashville; WNPT (PBS) Nashville; WNPX-TV (ION) Cookeville; WSMV-TV (NBC, TMO) Nashville; WTVF (CBS) Nashville; WUXP-TV (MNT) Nashville; WZTV (FOX) Nashville.
Fee: $29.30 installation; $15.95 monthly.
Expanded Basic Service 1
Subscribers: N.A.
Programming (via satellite): A&E Networks; ABC Family Channel; AMC; Animal Planet; Cartoon Network; CNBC; CNN; Comcast/Charter Sports Southeast (CSS); Comedy Central; Country Music TV; C-

SPAN; C-SPAN 2; Discovery Channel; Discovery Health Channel; Disney Channel; E! Entertainment Television; ESPN; ESPN 2; Food Network; Fox News Channel; Fox Sports Net; FX; Golf Channel; Great American Country; GSN; Headline News; HGTV; History Channel; Lifetime; MTV; Nickelodeon; QVC; Spike TV; TBS Superstation; The Learning Channel; The Weather Channel; truTV; Turner Network TV; TV Guide Network; TV Land; USA Network; Versus; VH1.
Fee: $60.00 installation; $35.24 monthly.

Digital Basic Service
Subscribers: 1,036.
Programming (via satellite): BBC America; C-SPAN 3; Discovery Digital Networks; DMX Music; Encore Action; ESPNews; Flix; GAS; MTV Networks Digital Suite; Nick Jr.; Nick Too; SoapNet; Sundance Channel; Toon Disney; WAM! America's Kidz Network.

Pay Service 1
Pay Units: N.A.
Programming (via satellite): HBO; Showtime.
Fee: $9.95 monthly (each).

Digital Pay Service 1
Pay Units: N.A.
Programming (via satellite): Cinemax (multiplexed); HBO (multiplexed); Showtime (multiplexed); Starz (multiplexed); The Movie Channel (multiplexed).

Video-On-Demand: No

Pay-Per-View
Addressable homes: 1,036.
iN DEMAND (delivered digitally); Playboy TV (delivered digitally); Fresh (delivered digitally); Shorteez (delivered digitally); Hot Choice (delivered digitally); Pleasure (delivered digitally).

Internet Service
Operational: Yes.
Broadband Service: Comcast High Speed Internet.
Fee: $42.95 monthly.

Telephone Service
Digital: Operational

Miles of plant (coax & fiber combined) included in Nashville

Area Vice President & General Manager: John Gauder. Technical Operations Director: Joe Pell. Marketing Director: Martine Mahoney. Marketing Manager: Will Jefferson.

Ownership: Comcast Cable Communications Inc. (MSO).

SNEEDVILLE—Zito Media, 611 Vader Hill Rd, Coudersport, PA 16915. Phone: 814-260-9575. Web Site: http://www.zitomedia.com. ICA: TN0113.

TV Market Ranking: Below 100 (SNEEDVILLE). Franchise award date: N.A. Franchise expiration date: N.A. Began: January 1, 1966.

Channel capacity: N.A. Channels available but not in use: N.A.

Basic Service
Subscribers: N.A.
Programming (received off-air): WATE-TV (ABC) Knoxville; WBIR-TV (NBC) Knoxville; WEMT (FOX) Greeneville; WETP-TV (PBS) Sneedville; WVLT-TV (CBS, MNT) Knoxville.
Programming (via satellite): C-SPAN; INSP; ION Television; QVC; Trinity Broadcasting Network; WGN America.
Fee: $29.95 installation; $19.95 monthly; $2.00 converter.

Expanded Basic Service 1
Subscribers: N.A.
Programming (via satellite): A&E Networks; ABC Family Channel; AMC; Bravo; Cartoon Network; CNBC; CNN; Comedy Central; Country Music TV; Discovery Channel; Disney Channel; E! Entertainment Television; ESPN; ESPN 2; Food Network; Fox News Channel; Fox Sports South; FX; Golf Channel; Hallmark Channel; Headline News; HGTV; History Channel; Lifetime; MSNBC; MTV; National Geographic Channel; Nickelodeon; Oxygen; Speed; Spike TV; SportSouth; Style Network; Syfy; TBS Superstation; The Learning Channel; The Weather Channel; Turner Classic Movies; Turner Network TV; TV Land; USA Network; VH1.

Digital Basic Service
Subscribers: N.A.
Programming (via satellite): BBC America; Bio; Bloomberg Television; Discovery Fit & Health; ESPN Classic Sports; ESPNews; Fox Movie Channel; Fox Sports World; Fuse; G4; GAS; GSN; History Channel International; Independent Film Channel; Lifetime Movie Network; MTV Networks Digital Suite; Music Choice; Nick Jr.; Nick Too; NickToons TV; SoapNet; Sundance Channel; Toon Disney; WE tv.

Digital Pay Service 1
Pay Units: N.A.
Programming (via satellite): Cinemax (multiplexed); Encore; Flix; HBO (multiplexed); Showtime (multiplexed); Starz (multiplexed); The Movie Channel (multiplexed).

Video-On-Demand: No

Pay-Per-View
Hot Choice; iN DEMAND; special events.

Internet Service
Operational: No.

Telephone Service
None

Miles of Plant: 26.0 (coaxial); None (fiber optic).

Public Relations Manager: Mark Laver.

Ownership: Zito Media (MSO).

SPRING CITY—Spring City Cable TV Inc., 140 Ellis St, PO Box 729, Spring City, TN 37381-0729. Phone: 423-365-7288. Fax: 423-365-4800. Also serves Rhea County. ICA: TN0086.

TV Market Ranking: 78 (Rhea County (portions)); Below 100 (SPRING CITY, Rhea County (portions)). Franchise award date: N.A. Franchise expiration date: N.A. Began: October 1, 1982.

Channel capacity: N.A. Channels available but not in use: N.A.

Basic Service
Subscribers: 1,350.
Programming (received off-air): WATE-TV (ABC) Knoxville; WBIR-TV (NBC) Knoxville; WBXX-TV (CW) Crossville; WDEF-TV (CBS) Chattanooga; WDSI-TV (FOX, MNT) Chattanooga; WELF-TV (TBN) Dalton; WFLI-TV (CW) Cleveland; WPXK-TV (ION) Jellico; WTCI (PBS) Chattanooga; WTNZ (FOX) Knoxville; WTVC (ABC) Chattanooga; WVLT-TV (CBS, MNT) Knoxville.
Programming (via satellite): TBS Superstation; WGN America.
Fee: $31.50 installation; $24.95 monthly.

Expanded Basic Service 1
Subscribers: N.A.
Programming (via satellite): A&E Networks; ABC Family Channel; Animal Planet; Cartoon Network; CBS Sports Network; CNBC; CNN; Comedy Central; Country Music TV; C-SPAN; C-SPAN 2; Discovery Channel; ESPN; ESPN 2; Food Network; Fox Movie Channel; Fox News Channel; Fox Sports South; FX; G4; Hallmark Channel; Headline News; HGTV; History Channel; Lifetime; MTV; Nickelodeon; Outdoor Channel; QVC; Speed; Spike TV; SportSouth; Syfy; The Learning Channel; The Weather Channel; Travel Channel; Turner Classic Movies; Turner Network TV; TV Land; USA Network; VH1.
Fee: $42.95 monthly.

Pay Service 1
Pay Units: 52.
Programming (via satellite): HBO.
Fee: $11.50 monthly.

Pay Service 2
Pay Units: 26.
Programming (via satellite): Cinemax.
Fee: $11.50 monthly.

Video-On-Demand: No

Internet Service
Operational: Yes.

Telephone Service
None

Miles of Plant: 32.0 (coaxial); None (fiber optic). Additional miles planned: 2.0 (coaxial).

Manager: Walter Hooper. Chief Technician: John Beasley.

Ownership: Spring City Cable TV Inc.

STONEY CREEK—Charter Communications, 105 Jack White Dr, Kingsport, TN 37664. Phone: 423-247-7631. Fax: 423-247-1807. Web Site: http://www.charter.com. ICA: TN0200.

TV Market Ranking: Below 100 (STONEY CREEK).

Channel capacity: N.A. Channels available but not in use: N.A.

Basic Service
Subscribers: N.A.
Programming (received off-air): WCYB-TV (CW, NBC) Bristol; WEMT (FOX) Greeneville; WETP-TV (PBS) Sneedville; WJHL-TV (CBS) Johnson City; WKPT-TV (ABC) Kingsport; WLFG (IND) Grundy.
Programming (via satellite): C-SPAN; QVC; Trinity Broadcasting Network.

Expanded Basic Service 1
Subscribers: N.A.
Programming (via satellite): A&E Networks; ABC Family Channel; AMC; Animal Planet; Bravo; Cartoon Network; CNBC; CNN; Comedy Central; Country Music TV; Discovery Channel; Disney Channel; E! Entertainment Television; ESPN; ESPN 2; Fox News Channel; FX; G4; Golf Channel; Headline News; HGTV; History Channel; MTV; Nickelodeon; Oxygen; SoapNet; Speed; Spike TV; Style Network; TBS Superstation; The Learning Channel; The Weather Channel; Turner Classic Movies; Turner Network TV; TV Land; USA Network; VH1.
Fee: $45.00 monthly.

Digital Basic Service
Subscribers: N.A.
Programming (via satellite): BBC America; Bio; Bloomberg Television; Discovery Fit & Health; Fox Movie Channel; Fox Sports World; Fuse; GAS; GSN; History Channel International; Independent Film Channel; Lifetime Movie Network; MTV Networks Digital Suite; Music Choice; Nick Jr.; Nick Too; NickToons TV; Sundance Channel; Toon Disney; TV Guide Interactive Inc.; WE tv.

Digital Pay Service 1
Pay Units: N.A.
Programming (via satellite): Cinemax (multiplexed); Encore; Flix; HBO (multiplexed); Showtime (multiplexed); Starz (multiplexed); The Movie Channel (multiplexed).

Video-On-Demand: No

Pay-Per-View
Playboy TV (delivered digitally); Fresh (delivered digitally); Shorteez (delivered digitally); iN DEMAND (delivered digitally).

Internet Service
Operational: Yes.
Fee: $19.99 monthly.

Telephone Service
Digital: Operational
Fee: $14.99 monthly

Miles of Plant: 62.0 (coaxial); 7.0 (fiber optic).

Operations Manager: Tony Falin. Technical Manager: Bruce Cocke. Sales & Marketing Manager: Kevin Kick.

Ownership: Charter Communications Inc. (MSO).

SUMMERTOWN—Small Town Cable, PO Box 99, College Grove, TN 37046. Phones: 615-368-2115; 931-484-7994. Fax: 615-368-2295. Also serves Ethridge & Lawrence County (unincorporated areas). ICA: TN0171.

TV Market Ranking: Outside TV Markets (Ethridge, Lawrence County (unincorporated areas), SUMMERTOWN). Franchise award date: July 18, 1988. Franchise expiration date: N.A. Began: N.A.

Channel capacity: N.A. Channels available but not in use: N.A.

Basic Service
Subscribers: N.A.
Programming (received off-air): WKRN-TV (ABC) Nashville; WNPT (PBS) Nashville; WSMV-TV (NBC, TMO) Nashville; WTVF (CBS) Nashville; WUXP-TV (MNT) Nashville; WZDX (FOX, MNT) Huntsville; WZTV (FOX) Nashville.
Programming (via satellite): C-SPAN; TBS Superstation.
Fee: $40.00 installation; $10.95 monthly.

Expanded Basic Service 1
Subscribers: N.A.
Programming (via satellite): ABC Family Channel; CNN; Discovery Channel; Disney Channel; ESPN; ESPN 2; History Channel; MTV; Nickelodeon; The Weather Channel; Turner Network TV; USA Network.
Fee: $13.00 monthly.

Digital Basic Service
Subscribers: N.A.

Pay Service 1
Pay Units: 35.
Programming (via satellite): Showtime.
Fee: $11.45 monthly.

Video-On-Demand: Yes

Internet Service
Operational: Yes.

Telephone Service
Analog: Not Operational
Digital: Operational

Miles of plant included in Chapel Hill

General Manager: Vince King. Chief Technician: Brian Langham.

Ownership: Small Town Cable Corp. (MSO).

TALBOTT—Haywood Cablevision, PO Box 778, Waynesville, NC 28786. Phone: 678-682-9726. Fax: 678-682-9727. Web Site: http://www.cbvnol.com. ICA: TN0202.

TV Market Ranking: Below 100 (TALBOTT).

Channel capacity: N.A. Channels available but not in use: N.A.

Basic Service
Subscribers: 132.
Programming (received off-air): WATE-TV (ABC) Knoxville; WBIR-TV (NBC) Knoxville; WEMT (FOX) Greeneville; WETP-TV (PBS) Sneedville; WJHL-TV (CBS) Johnson City; WKPT-TV (ABC) Kingsport; WVIR-TV (CW, NBC) Charlottesville; WVLT-TV (CBS, MNT) Knoxville.
Fee: $29.91 monthly.

Expanded Basic Service 1
Subscribers: N.A.
Programming (via satellite): ABC Family Channel; CNN; Country Music TV; Discovery Channel; Disney Channel; ESPN; ESPN 2; Fox News Channel; Headline News; HGTV; Lifetime; MTV; Nickelodeon; Spike TV; TBS Superstation; The Weather Channel; Trinity Broadcasting Network; Turner Classic Movies; Turner Network TV; USA Network; VH1.
Pay Service 1
Pay Units: N.A.
Programming (via satellite): HBO; Showtime.
Internet Service
Operational: Yes.
Fee: $43.95 monthly.
Telephone Service
None
Manager & Chief Technician: Joseph Stark.
Ownership: Carolina Mountain Cablevision Inc. (MSO).

TEN MILE—Charter Communications, 1235 King St SE, Cleveland, TN 37323. Phones: 865-984-1400 (Maryville office); 423-478-1934. Fax: 423-476-1621. Web Site: http://www.charter.com. Also serves Kingston & Midway. ICA: TN0073.
TV Market Ranking: 71 (Kingston); Below 100 (Midway, TEN MILE). Franchise award date: N.A. Franchise expiration date: N.A. Began: October 1, 1989.
Channel capacity: 40 (not 2-way capable). Channels available but not in use: N.A.
Basic Service
Subscribers: 1,339.
Programming (received off-air): WATE-TV (ABC) Knoxville; WBIR-TV (NBC) Knoxville; WBXX-TV (CW) Crossville; WDEF-TV (CBS) Chattanooga; WDSI-TV (FOX, MNT) Chattanooga; WFLI-TV (CW) Cleveland; WRCB (NBC) Chattanooga; WTCI (PBS) Chattanooga; WTVC (ABC) Chattanooga; WVLT-TV (CBS, MNT) Knoxville.
Programming (via satellite): QVC; WGN America.
Fee: $29.99 installation.
Expanded Basic Service 1
Subscribers: N.A.
Programming (via satellite): A&E Networks; ABC Family Channel; AMC; Bravo; Cartoon Network; CNBC; CNN; Comedy Central; Country Music TV; C-SPAN; Discovery Channel; Disney Channel; E! Entertainment Television; ESPN; ESPN 2; Fox News Channel; Fox Sports South; FX; G4; Golf Channel; Headline News; HGTV; History Channel; Lifetime; MTV; Nickelodeon; Oxygen; Speed; Spike TV; Syfy; TBS Superstation; The Learning Channel; The Weather Channel; Travel Channel; Trinity Broadcasting Network; Turner Network TV; TV Land; USA Network; VH1.
Fee: $50.99 monthly.
Digital Basic Service
Subscribers: N.A.
Programming (via satellite): BBC America; Bio; Bloomberg Television; Discovery Fit & Health; ESPN Classic Sports; Fox Soccer; GAS; History Channel International; Independent Film Channel; Lifetime Movie Network; MTV Networks Digital Suite; Music Choice; Nick Jr.; Nick Too; NickToons TV; Style Network; Sundance Channel; TV Guide Interactive Inc.; WE tv.
Digital Pay Service 1
Pay Units: N.A.
Programming (via satellite): Cinemax (multiplexed); Encore; Flix; HBO (multiplexed); Showtime (multiplexed); Starz (multiplexed); The Movie Channel (multiplexed).
Video-On-Demand: No
Internet Service
Operational: No.
Telephone Service
None
Miles of Plant: 100.0 (coaxial); None (fiber optic).
Operations Manager: Mike Burns. Technical Operations Director: Grant Evans. Technical Operations Manager: David Ogle. Marketing Director: Pat Hollenbeck. Office Manager: Connie Wilson.
Ownership: Charter Communications Inc. (MSO).

TENNESSEE RIDGE—Peoples CATV Inc., 4587 W Main St, PO Box 310, Erin, TN 37061-0310. Phone: 931-289-4221. Fax: 931-289-4220. Web Site: http://www.peoplescatv.com. Also serves Erin. ICA: TN0083.
TV Market Ranking: Outside TV Markets (Erin, TENNESSEE RIDGE). Franchise award date: March 1, 1983. Franchise expiration date: N.A. Began: March 1, 1984.
Channel capacity: 55 (2-way capable). Channels available but not in use: N.A.
Basic Service
Subscribers: 1,368.
Programming (received off-air): WKRN-TV (ABC) Nashville; WNAB (CW) Nashville; WNPT (PBS) Nashville; WSMV-TV (NBC, TMO) Nashville; WTVF (CBS) Nashville; WZTV (FOX) Nashville.
Programming (via satellite): C-SPAN; QVC; The Weather Channel; Trinity Broadcasting Network.
Fee: $25.00 installation; $9.95 monthly.
Expanded Basic Service 1
Subscribers: 1,114.
Programming (via satellite): A&E Networks; ABC Family Channel; Animal Planet; Cartoon Network; CNN; Comedy Central; Country Music TV; Discovery Channel; Disney Channel; E! Entertainment Television; ESPN; ESPN 2; Fox News Channel; Fox Sports South; FX; Golf Channel; Hallmark Channel; HGTV; History Channel; MTV; Nickelodeon; Oxygen; RFD-TV; Spike TV; Syfy; TBS Superstation; The Learning Channel; Travel Channel; Turner Classic Movies; Turner Network TV; TV Land; USA Network; VH1; WGN America.
Fee: $22.00 monthly.
Digital Basic Service
Subscribers: N.A.
Programming (via satellite): BBC America; Bio; Bravo; cloo; Discovery Digital Networks; DMX Music; ESPN Classic Sports; ESPNews; Fox Movie Channel; GAS; GSN; History Channel International; Independent Film Channel; Lime; MTV Networks Digital Suite; Nick Jr.; NickToons TV; Outdoor Channel; Speed; Style Network; Toon Disney; Versus; WE tv.
Fee: $19.95 monthly.
Pay Service 1
Pay Units: 139.
Programming (via satellite): Cinemax.
Fee: $25.00 installation; $11.95 monthly.
Pay Service 2
Pay Units: 151.
Programming (via satellite): HBO.
Fee: $11.95 monthly.
Digital Pay Service 1
Pay Units: N.A.
Programming (via satellite): Cinemax (multiplexed); Encore (multiplexed); HBO (multiplexed); Showtime (multiplexed); Starz (multiplexed); The Movie Channel (multiplexed).
Fee: $10.00 monthly (each).
Video-On-Demand: No
Internet Service
Operational: No.
Telephone Service
None
Miles of Plant: 108.0 (coaxial); None (fiber optic). Additional miles planned: 12.0 (coaxial).
Manager: James H. Coakley. Chief Technician: Steve Hall. Marketing Director: Fay Lair.
Ownership: Telephone Electronics Corp. (MSO).

TIPTONVILLE—NewWave Communications, 48 S Washington, Brownsville, TN 38012. Phones: 731-772-0197; 888-863-9928. Fax: 731-772-0197. Web Site: http://www.newwavecom.com. Also serves Hornbeak, Lake County, Ridgely, Samburg & Wynnburg. ICA: TN0059.
TV Market Ranking: Outside TV Markets (Hornbeak, Lake County, Ridgely, Samburg, TIPTONVILLE, Wynnburg). Franchise award date: February 9, 1978. Franchise expiration date: January 1, 2008. Began: July 1, 1979.
Channel capacity: N.A. Channels available but not in use: N.A.
Basic Service
Subscribers: 1,444.
Programming (received off-air): KBSI (FOX) Cape Girardeau; KFVS-TV (CBS, CW) Cape Girardeau; WBBJ-TV (ABC) Jackson; WDYR-CD Dyersburg; WHBQ-TV (FOX) Memphis; WKMU (PBS) Murray; WLJT-DT (PBS) Lexington; WMC-TV (NBC) Memphis; WPSD-TV (NBC) Paducah; WPTY-TV (ABC) Memphis.
Programming (via satellite): C-SPAN; INSP; Jewelry Television; QVC; ShopNBC; Trinity Broadcasting Network; WGN America.
Fee: $61.50 installation.
Expanded Basic Service 1
Subscribers: N.A.
Programming (via satellite): A&E Networks; ABC Family Channel; AMC; Animal Planet; BET Networks; Bravo; Cartoon Network; CNBC; CNN; Comedy Central; Country Music TV; C-SPAN 2; Discovery Channel; Disney Channel; E! Entertainment Television; ESPN; ESPN 2; ESPN Classic Sports; Food Network; Fox News Channel; Fox Sports South; FX; Golf Channel; Great American Country; GSN; Hallmark Channel; Headline News; HGTV; History Channel; Lifetime; MSNBC; MTV; National Geographic Channel; Nickelodeon; Outdoor Channel; Oxygen; SoapNet; Speed; Spike TV; Syfy; TBS Superstation; The Learning Channel; The Weather Channel; Travel Channel; truTV; Turner Classic Movies; Turner Network TV; TV Land; USA Network; Versus; VH1.
Fee: $34.95 monthly.
Digital Basic Service
Subscribers: N.A.
Programming (via satellite): A&E HD; BBC America; Bio; Bloomberg Television; Boomerang; cloo; CMT Pure Country; Discovery Fit & Health; Discovery Health Channel; Discovery Kids Channel; DIY Network; ESPN 2 HD; ESPN HD; ESPN U; ESPNews; Fox College Sports Atlantic; Fox College Sports Central; Fox College Sports Pacific; Fox Movie Channel; FSN HD; G4; GMC; HD Theater; HDNet; HDNet Movies; History Channel HD; History Channel International; HRTV; ID Investigation Discovery; Lifetime Movie Network; Lifetime Real Women; Military Channel; MTV Hits; MTV Jams; MTV2; Music Choice; Nick Jr.; NickToons TV; Palladia; Planet Green; Science; Style Network; TeenNick; The Weather Channel HD; Toon Disney; Turner Network TV HD; Versus HD; VH1 Classic; VH1 Soul.
Fee: $3.95 monthly.
Digital Pay Service 1
Pay Units: N.A.
Programming (via satellite): Cinemax (multiplexed); Cinemax HD; Encore (multiplexed); Flix; HBO (multiplexed); HBO HD; Showtime (multiplexed); Starz (multiplexed); Starz HDTV; The Movie Channel.
Video-On-Demand: No
Pay-Per-View
iN DEMAND (delivered digitally); ESPN Gameplan (delivered digitally); Ten Clips (delivered digitally); Ten Blue (delivered digitally); Ten Blox (delivered digitally).
Internet Service
Operational: Yes.
Fee: $40.00 installation; $31.99 monthly.
Telephone Service
Digital: Operational
Fee: $24.99 monthly
Miles of Plant: 52.0 (coaxial); None (fiber optic).
General Manager: Cameron Miller. Technical Operations Manager: Ralph Cales.
Ownership: NewWave Communications LLC (MSO).

TRENTON—Trenton TV Cable Co., 45 Howell Ln, PO Box 345, Trenton, TN 38382-0345. Phone: 731-855-2808. Fax: 731-855-9512. ICA: TN0071.
TV Market Ranking: Below 100 (TRENTON). Franchise award date: N.A. Franchise expiration date: N.A. Began: May 1, 1968.
Channel capacity: 60 (2-way capable). Channels available but not in use: N.A.
Basic Service
Subscribers: 1,374.
Programming (received off-air): KFVS-TV (CBS, CW) Cape Girardeau; WBBJ-TV (ABC) Jackson; WHBQ-TV (FOX) Memphis; WJKT (FOX) Jackson; WKNO (PBS) Memphis; WLJT-DT (PBS) Lexington; WMC-TV (NBC) Memphis; WPSD-TV (NBC) Paducah; WPTY-TV (ABC) Memphis; WREG-TV (CBS) Memphis.
Fee: $15.00 installation; $19.39 monthly.
Expanded Basic Service 1
Subscribers: 1,278.
Programming (via satellite): A&E Networks; ABC Family Channel; BET Networks; CNN; Country Music TV; C-SPAN; Discovery Channel; ESPN; ESPN 2; Fox Sports South; Headline News; HGTV; Lifetime; Spike TV; Syfy; TBS Superstation; The Weather Channel; Trinity Broadcasting Network; Turner Classic Movies; Turner Network TV; USA Network; VH1; WGN America.
Fee: $27.25 monthly.
Pay Service 1
Pay Units: N.A.
Programming (via satellite): Cinemax; HBO; Showtime; Starz.
Fee: $14.95 monthly (each).
Internet Service
Operational: Yes.
Subscribers: 287.
Broadband Service: In-house.
Fee: $25.95 monthly.
Telephone Service
None
Miles of Plant: 70.0 (coaxial); None (fiber optic).
Manager & Chief Technician: Stephen Nowell.
Ownership: Stephen Nowell.

TULLAHOMA—Charter Communications, 1774 Henry G Lane St, Maryville, TN 37801. Phone: 865-984-1400. Fax: 865-983-0383. Web Site: http://www.charter.com.

Also serves Bedford County (portions), Bell Buckle, Centertown, Coffee County (portions), Franklin County (portions), Manchester, McMinnville, Moore County (portions), Morrison, Shelbyville, Spencer, Van Buren County (portions), Viola, Warren County (portions) & Wartrace. ICA: TN0032.

TV Market Ranking: 96 (Franklin County (portions)); Below 100 (Bedford County (portions), Bell Buckle, Centertown, Coffee County (portions), Manchester, Moore County (portions), Morrison, Shelbyville, Spencer, TULLAHOMA, Van Buren County (portions), Warren County (portions), Wartrace); Outside TV Markets (Coffee County (portions), McMinnville, Moore County (portions), Viola, Franklin County (portions)). Franchise award date: N.A. Franchise expiration date: N.A. Began: May 1, 1969.

Channel capacity: N.A. Channels available but not in use: N.A.

Basic Service

Subscribers: 19,000.

Programming (received off-air): WHTN (IND) Murfreesboro; WKRN-TV (ABC) Nashville; WNAB (CW) Nashville; WNPT (PBS) Nashville; WNPX-TV (ION) Cookeville; WSMV-TV (NBC, TMO) Nashville; WTVF (CBS) Nashville; WUXP-TV (MNT) Nashville; WZTV (FOX) Nashville; 2 FMs.

Programming (via satellite): Comcast/Charter Sports Southeast (CSS); C-SPAN; C-SPAN 2; Eternal Word TV Network; INSP; QVC; Trinity Broadcasting Network; TV Guide Network; WGN America.

Expanded Basic Service 1

Subscribers: 16,600.

Programming (via satellite): A&E Networks; ABC Family Channel; AMC; Animal Planet; BET Networks; Bravo; Cartoon Network; CNBC; CNN; Comedy Central; Country Music TV; Discovery Channel; Discovery Fit & Health; Disney Channel; E! Entertainment Television; ESPN; ESPN 2; Food Network; Fox News Channel; Fox Sports South; FX; G4; GalaVision; Golf Channel; GSN; Hallmark Channel; Headline News; HGTV; History Channel; Lifetime; MSNBC; MTV; National Geographic Channel; Nickelodeon; Oxygen; SoapNet; Speed; Spike TV; SportSouth; Syfy; TBS Superstation; Telemundo; The Learning Channel; The Weather Channel; Toon Disney; Travel Channel; truTV; Turner Classic Movies; Turner Network TV; TV Land; Univision Studios; USA Network; VH1; WE tv.

Fee: $45.00 monthly.

Digital Basic Service

Subscribers: N.A.

Programming (via satellite): BBC America; Bio; Bloomberg Television; Boomerang; CNN International; Discovery Digital Networks; DIY Network; DMX Music; ESPN Classic Sports; ESPNews; Fox College Sports Atlantic; Fox College Sports Central; Fox College Sports Pacific; Fox Movie Channel; Fox Soccer; Fuel TV; GAS; Great American Country; History Channel International; Independent Film Channel; Lifetime Movie Network; Lifetime Real Women; MTV Networks Digital Suite; NFL Network; Nick Jr.; Nick Too; NickToons TV; Outdoor Channel; Science Television; Style Network; Sundance Channel; Versus.

Digital Pay Service 1

Pay Units: N.A.

Programming (via satellite): Cinemax (multiplexed); HBO (multiplexed); Starz (multiplexed).

Video-On-Demand: No

Pay-Per-View

Playboy TV (delivered digitally); Fresh (delivered digitally); Shorteez (delivered digitally).

Internet Service

Operational: Yes. Began: February 1, 2001.

Broadband Service: Charter Pipeline.

Fee: $29.99 monthly.

Telephone Service

Digital: Operational

Fee: $29.99 monthly

Miles of Plant: 583.0 (coaxial); None (fiber optic).

Operations Manager: Sean Hendrix. Marketing Director: Pat Hollenbeck. Sales & Marketing Manager: Jo Ann Placke.

Ownership: Charter Communications Inc. (MSO).

TURTLETOWN—Kudzu Cable TV Inc. Now served by BLUE RIDGE, GA [GA0075]. ICA: TN0065.

UNICOI—Shentel, 106 S Main St, Edinburg, VA 22824. Phones: 540-984-5224; 800-743-6835. Web Site: http://www.shentel.net. Also serves Erwin & Unicoi County (portions). ICA: TN0207.

TV Market Ranking: Below 100 (Erwin, UNICOI, Unicoi County (portions)).

Channel capacity: N.A. Channels available but not in use: N.A.

Basic Service

Subscribers: N.A.

Programming (received off-air): WCYB-TV (CW, NBC) Bristol; WJHL-TV (CBS) Johnson City; WKPT-TV (ABC) Kingsport.

Programming (via satellite): A&E Networks; ABC Family Channel; AMC; Animal Planet; Cartoon Network; CNBC; CNN; Comedy Central; Country Music TV; C-SPAN; C-SPAN 2; Discovery Channel; Disney Channel; E! Entertainment Television; ESPN; Fox News Channel; FX; G4; Headline News; HGTV; History Channel; INSP; MTV; Nickelodeon; Oxygen; QVC; SoapNet; Spike TV; Style Network; TBS Superstation; The Learning Channel; Trinity Broadcasting Network; Turner Network TV; TV Land; USA Network; VH1; WGN America.

Digital Basic Service

Subscribers: N.A.

Programming (via satellite): BBC America; Bio; Bloomberg Television; CMT Pure Country; Discovery Digital Networks; ESPN Classic Sports; Fox Movie Channel; Fox Soccer; Fuse; GSN; History Channel International; Independent Film Channel; Lifetime Movie Network; MTV Networks Digital Suite; Nick Jr.; Nick Too; NickToons TV; Sundance Channel; TeenNick; Toon Disney; WE tv.

Digital Pay Service 1

Pay Units: N.A.

Programming (via satellite): Cinemax (multiplexed); Encore; Flix; HBO (multiplexed); LOGO; Showtime (multiplexed); Starz (multiplexed); The Movie Channel (multiplexed).

Internet Service

Operational: No.

General Manager: Robert Harold. Chief Technician: Steve Adkins.

Ownership: Shenandoah Telecommunications Inc. (MSO).

UNION CITY—Formerly served by MetroVision. No longer in operation. ICA: TN0181.

VONORE—Comcast Cable, 2030 Polymer Dr, Chattanooga, TN 37421. Phone: 423-855-3900. Fax: 423-892-5893. Web Site: http://www.comcast.com. Also serves Niota & Tellico Plains. ICA: TN0115.

TV Market Ranking: 71 (VONORE); Below 100 (Niota, Tellico Plains). Franchise award date: N.A. Franchise expiration date: N.A. Began: June 1, 1982.

Channel capacity: N.A. Channels available but not in use: N.A.

Basic Service

Subscribers: N.A. Included in Chattanooga

Programming (received off-air): WATE-TV (ABC) Knoxville; WBIR-TV (NBC) Knoxville; WBXX-TV (CW) Crossville; WDEF-TV (CBS) Chattanooga; WDSI-TV (FOX, MNT) Chattanooga; WKOP-TV (PBS) Knoxville; WRCB (NBC) Chattanooga; WTCI (PBS) Chattanooga; WTNZ (FOX) Knoxville; WTVC (ABC) Chattanooga; WVLT-TV (CBS, MNT) Knoxville.

Programming (via satellite): ABC Family Channel; Animal Planet; Cartoon Network; CNN; Comedy Central; Country Music TV; C-SPAN; Discovery Channel; Disney Channel; ESPN; ESPN 2; Fox News Channel; Fox Sports South; Headline News; HGTV; History Channel; Lifetime; Nickelodeon; QVC; Speed; Spike TV; TBS Superstation; The Weather Channel; Trinity Broadcasting Network; Turner Classic Movies; Turner Network TV; TV Land; USA Network; VH1; WGN America.

Fee: $25.60 monthly.

Pay Service 1

Pay Units: 412.

Programming (via satellite): HBO.

Fee: $10.00 monthly.

Pay Service 2

Pay Units: 145.

Programming (via satellite): Cinemax.

Fee: $9.00 monthly.

Video-On-Demand: No

Internet Service

Operational: No.

Telephone Service

None

Miles of plant included in Chattanooga

Vice President & General Manager: Valerie Gillespie. Marketing Director: Mike Kehrer.

Ownership: Comcast Cable Communications Inc. (MSO).

WALDEN CREEK—Comcast Cable, 5720 Asheville Hwy, Knoxville, TN 37924-2701. Phone: 865-971-1544. Fax: 865-862-5092. Web Site: http://www.comcast.com. Also serves Blount County (portions), Cobbly Nob, Cosby, Pigeon Forge, Sevierville & Townsend. ICA: TN0031.

TV Market Ranking: 71 (Blount County (portions), Cobbly Nob, Pigeon Forge, Sevierville, Townsend, WALDEN CREEK); Below 100 (Cosby). Franchise award date: N.A. Franchise expiration date: N.A. Began: April 1, 1977.

Channel capacity: 63 (operating 2-way). Channels available but not in use: N.A.

Basic Service

Subscribers: N.A.

Programming (received off-air): WATE-TV (ABC) Knoxville; WBIR-TV (NBC) Knoxville; WBXX-TV (CW) Crossville; WETP-TV (PBS) Sneedville; WMAK (IND) Knoxville; WPXK-TV (ION) Jellico; WTNZ (FOX) Knoxville; WVLR (IND) Tazewell; WVLT-TV (CBS, MNT) Knoxville.

Programming (via satellite): C-SPAN 2; QVC; WGN America.

Fee: $56.50 installation; $13.75 monthly.

Expanded Basic Service 1

Subscribers: N.A.

Programming (via satellite): 10 News 2; A&E Networks; ABC Family Channel; AMC; Animal Planet; BET Networks; Bravo; Cartoon Network; CNBC; CNN; Comcast/Charter Sports Southeast (CSS); Comedy Central; Country Music TV; C-SPAN; Discovery Channel; Discovery Health Channel; Disney Channel; DIY Network; E! Entertainment Television; ESPN; ESPN 2; ESPN Classic Sports; Food Network; Fox News Channel; Fox Sports South; FX; G4; Golf Channel; Great American Country; GSN; Hallmark Channel; Headline News; HGTV; History Channel; INSP; Lifetime; MSNBC; MTV; Nickelodeon; Speed; Spike TV; Style Network; Syfy; TBS Superstation; The Learning Channel; The Weather Channel; Trinity Broadcasting Network; truTV; Turner Classic Movies; Turner Network TV; Turner South; TV Guide Network; TV Land; USA Network; Versus; VH1.

Fee: $36.24 monthly.

Digital Basic Service

Subscribers: N.A.

Programming (via satellite): BBC America; Bio; CMT Pure Country; Cooking Channel; C-SPAN 3; Discovery Digital Networks; Disney Channel; DMX Music; Encore; ESPNews; Flix (multiplexed); GAS; History Channel International; Lifetime Movie Network; Military History Channel; MoviePlex; MTV Networks Digital Suite; National Geographic Channel; Nick Jr.; Nick Too; NickToons TV; PBS Kids Sprout; SoapNet; Sundance Channel (multiplexed); Toon Disney; WAM! America's Kidz Network; Weatherscan.

Fee: $14.95 monthly.

Digital Pay Service 1

Pay Units: N.A.

Programming (via satellite): Cinemax (multiplexed); HBO (multiplexed); Showtime (multiplexed); Starz (multiplexed); The Movie Channel (multiplexed).

Fee: $13.99 monthly (each).

Video-On-Demand: Yes

Pay-Per-View

Playboy TV (delivered digitally); Fresh (delivered digitally); Shorteez (delivered digitally); Pleasure (delivered digitally); ESPN Now (delivered digitally); ESPN Extra (delivered digitally); iN DEMAND (delivered digitally).

Internet Service

Operational: Yes.

Broadband Service: Comcast High Speed Internet.

Fee: $42.95 monthly.

Telephone Service

Digital: Operational

Miles of Plant: 230.0 (coaxial); None (fiber optic).

Vice President & General Manager: Kirk Dale. Marketing Director: Kristopher Workman. Government & Community Affairs Director: Russell Byrd. Technical Operations Director: Charlie Goodreau. Engineering Manager: Hank Swindle.

Ownership: Comcast Cable Communications Inc. (MSO).

WARTBURG—Comcast Cable, 5720 Asheville Hwy, Knoxville, TN 37924-2701. Phone: 865-971-1544. Fax: 865-862-5092. Web Site: http://www.comcast.com. Also serves Burrville, Coalfield, Deer Lodge, Lancing, Morgan County, Oakdale, Petros & Sunbright. ICA: TN0019.

TV Market Ranking: 71 (Morgan County (portions), Oakdale, Petros); 96 (Coalfield); Below 100 (Burrville, Deer Lodge, Lancing, Sunbright, WARTBURG, Morgan County (portions)). Franchise award date: N.A.

Franchise expiration date: N.A. Began: June 1, 1982.
Channel capacity: N.A. Channels available but not in use: N.A.

Basic Service

Subscribers: 8,524.

Programming (received off-air): WATE-TV (ABC) Knoxville; WBIR-TV (NBC) Knoxville; WBXX-TV (CW) Crossville; WCTE (PBS) Cookeville; WETP-TV (PBS) Sneedville; WTNZ (FOX) Knoxville; WVLT-TV (CBS, MNT) Knoxville.

Programming (via satellite): CNBC; Comcast/Charter Sports Southeast (CSS); Fox News Channel; Outdoor Channel; QVC; TV Land; WGN America.

Fee: $56.50 installation; $12.50 monthly; $10.00 additional installation.

Expanded Basic Service 1

Subscribers: N.A.

Programming (via satellite): A&E Networks; ABC Family Channel; AMC; CNN; Country Music TV; C-SPAN; Discovery Channel; Disney Channel; ESPN; ESPN 2; Fox Sports South; FX; Headline News; HGTV; Lifetime; MTV; Nickelodeon; Spike TV; Syfy; TBS Superstation; The Weather Channel; Trinity Broadcasting Network; Turner Network TV; USA Network; VH1.

Fee: $28.45 monthly.

Digital Basic Service

Subscribers: N.A.

Programming (via satellite): BBC America; Country Music TV; Discovery Digital Networks; Encore (multiplexed); GAS; MTV Networks Digital Suite; Music Choice; Nick Jr.; Nick Too.

Fee: $14.95 monthly.

Digital Pay Service 1

Pay Units: N.A.

Programming (via satellite): Cinemax (multiplexed); HBO (multiplexed); Showtime (multiplexed); Starz; The Movie Channel.

Fee: $13.99 monthly (each).

Video-On-Demand: No

Pay-Per-View

iN DEMAND (delivered digitally); Hot Choice (delivered digitally).

Internet Service

Operational: No.

Telephone Service

None

Vice President & General Manager: Kirk Dale. Technical Operations Director: Charlie Goodreau. Engineering Manager: Hank Swindle. Government & Community Affairs Director: Russell Byrd.

Ownership: Comcast Cable Communications Inc. (MSO).

WAVERLY—Comcast Cable. Now served by NASHVILLE, TN [TN0002]. ICA: TN0075.

WAYNESBORO—Charter Communications, 1774 Henry G Lane St, Maryville, TN 37801. Phone: 865-984-1400. Fax: 865-983-0383. Web Site: http://www.charter.com. Also serves Collinwood & Wayne County (portions). ICA: TN0093.

TV Market Ranking: Below 100 (Collinwood, Wayne County (portions), WAYNESBORO); Outside TV Markets (Wayne County (portions)). Franchise award date: N.A. Franchise expiration date: N.A. Began: April 1, 1965.

Channel capacity: 42 (not 2-way capable). Channels available but not in use: N.A.

Basic Service

Subscribers: 1,707.

Programming (received off-air): WBBJ-TV (ABC) Jackson; WHDF (CW) Florence; WHNT-TV (CBS) Huntsville; WKRN-TV (ABC) Nashville; WNPT (PBS) Nashville; WSMV-TV (NBC, TMO) Nashville; WTVF (CBS) Nashville; WZTV (FOX) Nashville; allband FM.

Programming (via satellite): C-SPAN; QVC; The Learning Channel; WGN America.

Expanded Basic Service 1

Subscribers: 1,530.

Programming (via satellite): A&E Networks; ABC Family Channel; AMC; Animal Planet; BET Networks; CNBC; CNN; Country Music TV; Discovery Channel; Disney Channel; ESPN; ESPN 2; Fox News Channel; Fox Sports South; FX; Hallmark Channel; Headline News; HGTV; History Channel; Lifetime; MTV; Nickelodeon; Spike TV; TBS Superstation; The Weather Channel; Travel Channel; truTV; Turner Classic Movies; Turner Network TV; USA Network; VH1.

Fee: $45.00 monthly.

Digital Basic Service

Subscribers: N.A.

Programming (via satellite): Music Choice; TV Guide Interactive Inc.

Digital Pay Service 1

Pay Units: N.A.

Programming (via satellite): Cinemax (multiplexed); HBO (multiplexed).

Video-On-Demand: No

Internet Service

Operational: No.

Telephone Service

None

Miles of Plant: 77.0 (coaxial); 13.0 (fiber optic). Additional miles planned: 1.0 (coaxial).

Operations Manager: Tony Fox. Technical Operations Director: Ron Janson. Marketing Director: Pat Hollenbeck. Marketing Manager: Wiley Bird.

Ownership: Charter Communications Inc. (MSO).

WESTMORELAND—Comcast Cable. Now served by SCOTTSVILLE, KY [KY0073]. ICA: TN0104.

WESTPOINT—Charter Communications. Now served by LORETTO, TN [TN0068]. ICA: TN0124.

WHITE HOUSE—Comcast Cable. Now served by NASHVILLE, TN [TN0002]. ICA: TN0050.

WHITESBURG—Formerly served by Adelphia Communications. Now served GREENEVILLE, TN [TN0022]. ICA: TN0079.

WINCHESTER—Formerly served by Comcast Cable. No longer in operation. ICA: TN0045.

WOODBURY—Comcast Cable, 660 Mainstream Dr, PO Box 280570, Nashville, TN 37228-0570. Phones: 615-244-7462 (Administrative office); 615-244-5900 (Customer service). Fax: 615-255-6528. Web Site: http://www.comcast.com. Also serves Bradyville & Cannon County. ICA: TN0101.

TV Market Ranking: Below 100 (Bradyville, Cannon County, WOODBURY). Franchise award date: N.A. Franchise expiration date: N.A. Began: November 1, 1981.

Channel capacity: 39 (not 2-way capable). Channels available but not in use: N.A.

Basic Service

Subscribers: 940.

Programming (received off-air): WKRN-TV (ABC) Nashville; WNPT (PBS) Nashville; WSMV-TV (NBC, TMO) Nashville; WTVF (CBS) Nashville; WZTV (FOX) Nashville.

Fee: $45.10 installation; $12.40 monthly.

Expanded Basic Service 1

Subscribers: N.A.

Programming (via satellite): ABC Family Channel; CNBC; CNN; Discovery Channel; Disney Channel; ESPN; Headline News; Lifetime; MTV; Nickelodeon; Spike TV; TBS Superstation; Turner Network TV; USA Network; WGN America.

Fee: $14.91 monthly.

Pay Service 1

Pay Units: N.A.

Programming (via satellite): Cinemax; Encore; HBO; Showtime.

Fee: $1.50 monthly (Encore), $9.95 monthly (Cinemax, HBO or Showtime).

Internet Service

Operational: No.

Telephone Service

None

Miles of plant (coax & fiber combined) included in Nashville

Vice President & General Manager: John Gauder. Technical Operations Director: Joe Pell. Marketing Director: Martine Mahoney. Marketing Manager: Will Jefferson.

Ownership: Comcast Cable Communications Inc. (MSO).

TEXAS

Total Systems: 434
Total Communities Served: 1,392
Franchises Not Yet Operating: 0
Applications Pending: 0
Communities with Applications: 0
Number of Basic Subscribers: 4,884,775
Number of Expanded Basic Subscribers: 1,697,144
Number of Pay Units: 955,853

Top 100 Markets Represented: Dallas-Fort Worth (12); Houston (15); San Antonio (45); Texarkana, TX-Shreveport, LA (58); Beaumont-Port Arthur (88); Amarillo (95).

**For a list of cable communities in this section, see the Cable Community Index located in the back of Cable Volume 2.
For explanation of terms used in cable system listings, see p. D-11.**

ABERNATHY—Reach Broadband, 515 E Longview St, Arp, TX 75750. Phone: 800-687-1258. Web Site: http://www.reachbroadband.net. ICA: TX0388.
TV Market Ranking: Below 100 (ABERNATHY). Franchise award date: August 14, 1978. Franchise expiration date: N.A. Began: November 1, 1979.
Channel capacity: 61 (2-way capable). Channels available but not in use: N.A.
Basic Service
Subscribers: 318.
Programming (received off-air): KAMC (ABC) Lubbock; KBZO-LP (UNV) Lubbock; KCBD (NBC) Lubbock; KJTV-TV (FOX) Lubbock; KLBK-TV (CBS) Lubbock; KLCW-TV (CW) Wolfforth; KPTB-DT (IND) Lubbock; KRPV-DT (IND) Roswell; KTXT-TV (PBS) Lubbock; KXTQ-CA (TMO) Lubbock.
Programming (via satellite): A&E Networks; ABC Family Channel; AMC; CNN; Discovery Channel; Disney Channel; E! Entertainment Television; ESPN; ESPN 2; Fox News Channel; Fox Sports Southwest; FX; Great American Country; Headline News; HGTV; History Channel; INSP; Lifetime; MSNBC; MTV; National Geographic Channel; Nickelodeon; QVC; Spike TV; TBS Superstation; The Learning Channel; The Weather Channel; Turner Network TV; TV Land; USA Network; VH1.
Fee: $29.95 installation; $38.00 monthly.
Pay Service 1
Pay Units: 104.
Programming (via satellite): HBO.
Fee: $9.95 monthly.
Pay Service 2
Pay Units: 37.
Programming (via satellite): Showtime.
Fee: $9.95 monthly.
Video-On-Demand: No
Internet Service
Operational: No.
Telephone Service
None
Miles of Plant: 15.0 (coaxial); None (fiber optic).
Regional Manager: Ronnie Stafford. Office Manager: Jan Gibson.
Ownership: RB3 LLC (MSO).

ABILENE—Suddenlink Communications, 902 South Clack St, Abilene, TX 79606. Phones: 915-698-3585; 915-698-1510. Web Site: http://www.suddenlink.com. Also serves Dyess AFB, Taylor County (northern portion) & Tye. ICA: TX0019.
TV Market Ranking: Below 100 (ABILENE, Dyess AFB, Taylor County (northern portion), Tye). Franchise award date: January 1, 1964. Franchise expiration date: N.A. Began: April 1, 1965.
Channel capacity: N.A. Channels available but not in use: N.A.
Basic Service
Subscribers: 28,123.
Programming (received off-air): KIDZ-LP Abilene; KPCB-DT (IND) Snyder; KRBC-TV (NBC) Abilene; KTAB-TV (CBS) Abilene; KTES-LP (TMO) Abilene; KTXS-TV (ABC, CW, TMO) Sweetwater; KXVA (FOX) Abilene; allband FM.
Programming (via microwave): KERA-TV (PBS) Dallas.
Programming (via satellite): C-SPAN; C-SPAN 2; GalaVision; Product Information Network; QVC; The Weather Channel; TV Guide Network; Univision Studios.
Fee: $26.42 installation; $26.51 monthly.
Expanded Basic Service 1
Subscribers: 20,527.
Programming (via satellite): A&E Networks; ABC Family Channel; AMC; Animal Planet; BET Networks; Bravo; Cartoon Network; CNBC; CNN; Comedy Central; Country Music TV; CW+; Discovery Channel; Disney Channel; E! Entertainment Television; ESPN; ESPN 2; Food Network; Fox News Channel; Fox Sports Southwest; FX; Headline News; HGTV; History Channel; INSP; Lifetime; Lifetime Movie Network; MSNBC; MTV; MTV2; Nickelodeon; Oxygen; Speed; Spike TV; Syfy; TBS Superstation; The Learning Channel; Travel Channel; Turner Network TV; TV Land; USA Network; Versus; VH1.
Fee: $41.99 monthly.
Digital Basic Service
Subscribers: 7,596.
Programming (via satellite): A&E HD; Bandamax; BBC America; Bio; Bloomberg Television; Boomerang; CBS Sports Network; Cine Latino; Cine Mexicano; CMT Pure Country; CNN en Espanol; Cooking Channel; De Pelicula; De Pelicula Clasico; Discovery en Espanol; Discovery Health Channel; Discovery Home Channel; Discovery Kids Channel; DIY Network; Encore (multiplexed); ESPN 2 HD; ESPN Classic Sports; ESPN Deportes; ESPN HD; ESPN U; ESPNews; Eternal Word TV Network; EWTN en Espanol; Food Network HD; Fox College Sports Atlantic; Fox College Sports Central; Fox College Sports Pacific; Fox Deportes; Fox Soccer; FSN HD; Fuel TV; Fuse; G4; GalaVision; GMC; Golf Channel; Great American Country; GSN; Hallmark Channel; Halogen Network; HD Theater; HDNet; HDNet Movies; HGTV HD; History Channel en Espanol; History Channel International; ID Investigation Discovery; Independent Film Channel; Jewelry Television; Military Channel; MTV Hits; mtvU; mun2 television; Music Choice; National Geographic Channel; National Geographic Channel HD Network; Nick Jr.; NickToons en Espanol; NickToons TV; Nuvo TV; Outdoor Channel; Science; ShopNBC; SoapNet; Sorpresa; Sundance Channel; Sur Network; TeenNick; Telefutura; Telehit; Tennis Channel; Toon Disney; Toon Disney en Espanol; Tr3s; truTV; Turner Classic Movies; Turner Network TV HD; Universal HD; VH1 Classic; Video Rola; WE tv.
Fee: $14.95 monthly.
Pay Service 1
Pay Units: 2,671.
Programming (via satellite): Cinemax.
Fee: $2.00 installation; $11.38 monthly.
Pay Service 2
Pay Units: 9,368.
Programming (via satellite): Encore.
Fee: $8.81 installation; $1.75 monthly.
Pay Service 3
Pay Units: 3,986.
Programming (via satellite): HBO.
Fee: $2.00 installation; $11.38 monthly.
Pay Service 4
Pay Units: 1,273.
Programming (via satellite): Showtime.
Fee: $2.00 installation; $11.38 monthly.
Pay Service 5
Pay Units: 6,290.
Programming (via satellite): Starz.
Fee: $8.81 installation; $4.75 monthly.
Digital Pay Service 1
Pay Units: 7,596.
Programming (via satellite): Cinemax (multiplexed); Encore; HBO (multiplexed); HBO HD; HBO Latino; Showtime (multiplexed); Showtime HD; Starz (multiplexed); Starz HDTV; The Movie Channel (multiplexed).
Video-On-Demand: No
Pay-Per-View
iN DEMAND (delivered digitally); Playboy TV (delivered digitally); Fresh (delivered digitally); Shorteez (delivered digitally); Spice: Xcess (delivered digitally); Club Jenna (delivered digitally).
Internet Service
Operational: Yes. Began: December 1, 2000.
Subscribers: 9,664.
Broadband Service: Suddenlink High Speed Internet.
Fee: $49.95 installation; $24.95 monthly; $15.00 modem lease; $249.99 modem purchase.
Telephone Service
Digital: Operational
Fee: $48.95 monthly
Miles of Plant: 463.0 (coaxial); None (fiber optic).
Area Manager: Chris Christiansen. Regional Manager: Bill Flowers.
Ownership: Cequel Communications LLC (MSO).

ACE—Formerly served by Jones Broadcasting. No longer in operation. ICA: TX0995.

ACKERLY—Formerly served by National Cable Inc. No longer in operation. ICA: TX0681.

ADKINS—Formerly served by Almega Cable. No longer in operation. ICA: TX0346.

ADRIAN—Formerly served by Sunset Cablevision. No longer in operation. ICA: TX0706.

ALBA—Formerly served by Almega Cable. No longer in operation. ICA: TX0603.

ALBANY—Suddenlink Communications, 12444 Powerscourt Dr, Saint Louis, MO 63131-3660. Phones: 800-999-6845 (Customer service); 314-965-2020. Fax: 903-561-5485. Web Site: http://www.suddenlink.com. ICA: TX0337.
TV Market Ranking: Below 100 (ALBANY). Franchise award date: N.A. Franchise expiration date: N.A. Began: January 1, 1960.
Channel capacity: N.A. Channels available but not in use: N.A.
Basic Service
Subscribers: 765.
Programming (received off-air): KRBC-TV (NBC) Abilene; KTAB-TV (CBS) Abilene; KTXS-TV (ABC, CW, TMO) Sweetwater; 8 FMs.
Programming (via microwave): KERA-TV (PBS) Dallas; KTVT (CBS) Fort Worth; WFAA (ABC) Dallas.
Programming (via satellite): Discovery Channel; QVC; TBS Superstation; The Weather Channel; Trinity Broadcasting Network.
Fee: $39.95 installation; $19.95 monthly.
Expanded Basic Service 1
Subscribers: 650.
Programming (via satellite): ABC Family Channel; AMC; Animal Planet; Cartoon Network; CNBC; CNN; Disney Channel; ESPN; Fox News Channel; FX; Headline News; HGTV; Lifetime; MTV; Spike TV; The Learning Channel; Turner Network TV; USA Network.
Fee: $39.95 installation; $24.00 monthly.
Pay Service 1
Pay Units: N.A.
Programming (via satellite): Cinemax.
Fee: $10.95 monthly.
Pay Service 2
Pay Units: 128.
Programming (via satellite): HBO.
Fee: $13.65 monthly.
Pay Service 3
Pay Units: 236.
Programming (via satellite): Encore.
Fee: $1.75 monthly.
Pay Service 4
Pay Units: 156.
Programming (via satellite): Starz.
Fee: $6.75 monthly.
Video-On-Demand: No

Internet Service
Operational: Yes. Began: November 12, 2003.
Broadband Service: Suddenlink High Speed Internet.
Fee: $49.95 installation; $38.95 monthly.
Telephone Service
None
Miles of Plant: 26.0 (coaxial); None (fiber optic).
Regional Manager: Todd Cruthird. Plant Manager: Bobby Smith.
Ownership: Cequel Communications LLC (MSO).

ALGOA—Formerly served by Almega Cable. No longer in operation. ICA: TX0335.

ALICE—Time Warner Cable, 4060 S Padre Island Dr, Corpus Christi, TX 78411-4402. Phones: 972-899-7300 (Flower Mound office); 361-698-6259. Fax: 361-857-5038. Web Site: http://www.timewarnercable.com/Texas. Also serves Alice (unincorporated areas), Aqua Dulce, Ben Bolt, Benavides, Duval County (portions), Falfurrias, Premont & San Diego. ICA: TX0102.
TV Market Ranking: Outside TV Markets (ALICE, Alice (unincorporated areas), Aqua Dulce, Ben Bolt, Benavides, Duval County (portions), Falfurrias, Premont, San Diego). Franchise award date: N.A. Franchise expiration date: July 27, 2012. Began: March 1, 1971.
Channel capacity: N.A. Channels available but not in use: N.A.
Basic Service
Subscribers: N.A. Included in Corpus Christi
Programming (received off-air): KEDT (PBS) Corpus Christi; KIII (ABC) Corpus Christi; KORO (UNV) Corpus Christi; KRIS-TV (CW, NBC) Corpus Christi; KZTV (CBS) Corpus Christi.
Programming (via satellite): C-SPAN; Nickelodeon; WGN America.
Fee: $34.99 installation; $16.39 monthly.
Expanded Basic Service 1
Subscribers: 6,958.
Programming (via satellite): A&E Networks; ABC Family Channel; AMC; Animal Planet; BET Networks; Bravo; Cartoon Network; CNBC; CNN; Comedy Central; Country Music TV; C-SPAN; Discovery Channel; Discovery Health Channel; Disney Channel; E! Entertainment Television; ESPN; ESPN 2; ESPN Classic Sports; ESPNews; Eternal Word TV Network; Food Network; Fox News Channel; Fox Sports Southwest; FX; GalaVision; Golf Channel; Great American Country; Hallmark Channel; Headline News; HGTV; History Channel; Lifetime; Lifetime Movie Network; MSNBC; MTV; mun2 television; National Geographic Channel; Oxygen; QVC; Shop at Home; SoapNet; Speed; Spike TV; Syfy; TBS Superstation; The Learning Channel; The Weather Channel; Travel Channel; Trinity Broadcasting Network; truTV; Turner Classic Movies; Turner Network TV; TV Land; USA Network; Versus; VH1; WE tv.
Fee: $28.60 monthly.
Digital Basic Service
Subscribers: N.A.
Programming (via satellite): America's Store; BBC America; Bio; Bloomberg Television; Canales N; Cooking Channel; Discovery Kids Channel; DIY Network; DMX Music; FamilyNet; Fox College Sports Atlantic; Fox College Sports Central; Fox College Sports Pacific; Fox Movie Channel; Fox Sports World; Fuel TV; Fuse; G4; GAS; GSN; History Channel International; Independent Film Channel; Lifetime Real Women; MTV Networks Digital Suite; NBA TV; Nick Jr.; Nick Too; NickToons TV; Outdoor Channel; Ovation; Sundance Channel; Tennis Channel; Toon Disney; Trio.
Fee: $8.00 monthly.
Digital Pay Service 1
Pay Units: N.A.
Programming (via satellite): Cinemax (multiplexed); Encore; Flix; HBO; Showtime; Starz; The Movie Channel.
Fee: $12.95 monthly (each).
Video-On-Demand: Yes
Pay-Per-View
Hot Choice; Playboy TV; Fresh; Shorteez; Spice Hot.
Internet Service
Operational: Yes.
Broadband Service: Road Runner.
Fee: $49.99 installation; $44.95 monthly.
Telephone Service
Digital: Operational
Fee: $44.95 monthly
Miles of Plant: 203.0 (coaxial); None (fiber optic).
President: Connie Wharton. Vice President & General Manager: Mike McKee. Engineering Director: Charlotte Strong. Public Affairs Manager: Vicki Triplett.
Ownership: Time Warner Cable (MSO).; Advance/Newhouse Partnership (MSO).

ALLEN—Time Warner Cable. Now served by DALLAS, TX [TX0003]. ICA: TX0100.

ALLENDALE—Formerly served by Cebridge Connections. No longer in operation. ICA: TX0707.

ALPINE—US Cable of Coastal Texas LP, 108 S Lackey St, Alpine, TX 79830-5112. Phone: 432-837-3637. Fax: 432-837-2759. E-mail: dkoedyker@tx.uscable.com. Web Site: http://www.uscable.com. ICA: TX0875.
TV Market Ranking: Outside TV Markets (ALPINE). Franchise award date: July 5, 1985. Franchise expiration date: N.A. Began: July 1, 1985.
Channel capacity: 36 (not 2-way capable). Channels available but not in use: N.A.
Basic Service
Subscribers: 1,112.
Programming (received off-air): KASA-TV (FOX) Santa Fe; KMLM-DT (IND) Odessa; KOAT-TV (ABC) Albuquerque; KOSA-TV (CBS, MNT) Odessa; KPBT-TV (PBS) Odessa; KPEJ-TV (FOX) Odessa; KTLE-LP (TMO) Odessa; KUPB (UNV) Midland; KWES-TV (NBC) Odessa; allband FM.
Programming (via satellite): A&E Networks; ABC Family Channel; Animal Planet; Cartoon Network; CNBC; CNN; Comedy Central; Country Music TV; C-SPAN; Discovery Channel; Discovery Fit & Health; Disney Channel; E! Entertainment Television; ESPN; ESPN 2; Eternal Word TV Network; Fox News Channel; Fox Sports Southwest; FX; Great American Country; Hallmark Channel; Headline News; HGTV; History Channel; Lifetime; MTV; National Geographic Channel; Nickelodeon; Outdoor Channel; Oxygen; ShopNBC; Speed; Spike TV; Syfy; TBS Superstation; Telefutura; The Learning Channel; The Weather Channel; Trinity Broadcasting Network; Turner Classic Movies; Turner Network TV; TV Guide Network; TV Land; USA Network; VH1; WGN America.
Fee: $35.00 installation; $46.55 monthly; $.86 converter.
Digital Basic Service
Subscribers: N.A.
Programming (via satellite): BBC America; Bio; Bloomberg Television; Bravo; cloo; CMT Pure Country; Discovery Health Channel; Discovery Kids Channel; DMX Music; Encore (multiplexed); ESPN Classic Sports; ESPNews; Fox Movie Channel; Fox Soccer; Fuse; G4; Golf Channel; GSN; Halogen Network; History Channel International; ID Investigation Discovery; Independent Film Channel; Lifetime Movie Network; Military Channel; MTV2; Nick Jr.; Outdoor Channel; Planet Green; Science; Speed; Style Network; TeenNick; Toon Disney; Versus; VH1 Classic; WE tv.
Fee: $21.39 monthly.
Digital Expanded Basic Service
Subscribers: N.A.
Programming (via satellite): Cine Latino; Cine Mexicano; CNN en Espanol; Discovery en Espanol; ESPN Deportes; Fox Deportes; History Channel en Espanol; mun2 television; Tr3s; VeneMovies.
Fee: $4.95 monthly.
Pay Service 1
Pay Units: 30.
Programming (via satellite): Cinemax; HBO; Showtime.
Fee: $12.95 monthly (each).
Digital Pay Service 1
Pay Units: N.A.
Programming (via satellite): Cinemax (multiplexed); HBO (multiplexed); Showtime (multiplexed); Starz (multiplexed); The Movie Channel.
Fee: $8.95 monthly (Starz), $11.95 monthly (HBO, Cinemax, Showtime or TMC).
Video-On-Demand: No
Pay-Per-View
iN DEMAND (delivered digitally); Fresh (delivered digitally); Playboy TV (delivered digitally).
Internet Service
Operational: Yes.
Telephone Service
None
Miles of plant included in Seminole, TX
Manager: Daryl Koedyker. Chief Technician: Tim Davis. Marketing Director: Chandra Saldana.
Ownership: US Cable Corp. (MSO).; Comcast Cable Communications Inc. (MSO).

ALTO—Almega Cable, 4001 W Airport Freeway, Ste 530, Bedford, TX 76021. Phone: 817-685-9588. Fax: 817-685-6488. Web Site: http://www.almega.com. ICA: TX0435.
TV Market Ranking: Below 100 (ALTO). Franchise award date: N.A. Franchise expiration date: N.A. Began: June 1, 1983.
Channel capacity: 54 (not 2-way capable). Channels available but not in use: N.A.
Basic Service
Subscribers: 166.
Programming (received off-air): KETK-TV (NBC) Jacksonville; KFXK-TV (FOX) Longview; KRMA-TV (PBS) Denver; KTRE (ABC) Lufkin; KYTX (CBS, IND) Nacogdoches.
Programming (via satellite): A&E Networks; ABC Family Channel; AMC; Animal Planet; BET Networks; Cartoon Network; CNBC; CNN; C-SPAN; C-SPAN 2; Discovery Channel; Disney Channel; E! Entertainment Television; ESPN; ESPN 2; Food Network; Fox Sports Net; FX; Great American Country; Headline News; HGTV; History Channel; Lifetime; MTV; National Geographic Channel; Nickelodeon; Spike TV; Syfy; TBS Superstation; The Learning Channel; The Weather Channel; Trinity Broadcasting Network; Turner Classic Movies; Turner Network TV; Univision Studios; USA Network; VH1; WGN America.
Fee: $54.95 installation; $44.05 monthly.
Pay Service 1
Pay Units: 10.
Programming (via satellite): Cinemax.
Fee: $12.95 monthly.
Pay Service 2
Pay Units: 24.
Programming (via satellite): HBO.
Fee: $12.95 monthly.
Pay Service 3
Pay Units: 51.
Programming (via satellite): Showtime.
Fee: $12.95 monthly.
Pay Service 4
Pay Units: N.A.
Programming (via satellite): Flix.
Video-On-Demand: No
Internet Service
Operational: No.
Telephone Service
None
Miles of Plant: 14.0 (coaxial); None (fiber optic).
Ownership: Almega Cable (MSO).

ALTON—Time Warner Communications. Now served by PHARR, TX [TX0017]. ICA: TX0066.

ALUM CREEK—Time Warner Cable. No longer in operation. ICA: TX0615.

ALVARADO—Almega Cable, 4001 W Airport Frwy, Ste 530, Bedford, TX 76021. Phone: 817-685-9588. Fax: 817-685-6488. Web Site: http://www.almega.com. Also serves Grandview, Itasca, Keene, Maypearl & Venus. ICA: TX0270.
TV Market Ranking: 12 (ALVARADO, Grandview, Keene, Venus); Below 100 (Maypearl); Outside TV Markets (Itasca). Franchise award date: N.A. Franchise expiration date: N.A. Began: March 1, 1982.
Channel capacity: 52 (not 2-way capable). Channels available but not in use: N.A.
Basic Service
Subscribers: 1,316.
Programming (received off-air): KDAF (CW, IND) Dallas; KDFI (MNT) Dallas; KDFW-DT (FOX) Dallas; KDTN (ETV) Denton; KDTX-TV (TBN) Dallas; KERA-TV (PBS) Dallas; KFWD (IND) Fort Worth; KMPX (IND) Decatur; KPXD-TV (ION) Arlington; KSTR-DT (TEL) Irving; KTVT (CBS) Fort Worth; KTXA (IND) Fort Worth; KUVN-DT (UNV) Garland; KXAS-TV (NBC) Fort Worth; KXTX-TV (TMO) Dallas; WFAA (ABC) Dallas.
Programming (via satellite): Cartoon Network; C-SPAN; TBS Superstation; The Learning Channel; TV Guide Network; WGN America.
Fee: $54.95 installation; $20.95 monthly.
Expanded Basic Service 1
Subscribers: N.A.
Programming (via satellite): A&E Networks; ABC Family Channel; AMC; BET Networks; Bravo; CNN; Country Music TV; Discovery Channel; Disney Channel; E! Entertainment Television; ESPN; Fox Sports Southwest; Headline News; Lifetime; MTV; Nickelodeon; QVC; Spike TV; Syfy; The Weather Channel; Turner Network TV; TV Land; USA Network.
Fee: $23.10 monthly.
Pay Service 1
Pay Units: N.A.
Programming (via satellite): Cinemax; HBO; Showtime; The Movie Channel.

Fee: $12.95 monthly (each).
Video-On-Demand: No
Internet Service
Operational: No.
Telephone Service
None
Miles of Plant: 119.0 (coaxial); 3.0 (fiber optic).
Ownership: Almega Cable (MSO).

AMARILLO—Suddenlink Communications, 5800 W 45th Ave, Amarillo, TX 79109-5206. Phone: 806-358-4801. Fax: 806-354-7419. Web Site: http://www.suddenlink.com. Also serves Canyon, Lake Tanglewood & Rolling Hills. ICA: TX0014.
TV Market Ranking: 95 (AMARILLO, Canyon, Lake Tanglewood, Rolling Hills). Franchise award date: July 1, 1980. Franchise expiration date: N.A. Began: January 1, 1970.
Channel capacity: 78 (operating 2-way). Channels available but not in use: N.A.
Basic Service
Subscribers: 46,882.
Programming (received off-air): KACV-TV (PBS) Amarillo; KAMR-TV (NBC) Amarillo; KCIT (FOX) Amarillo; KCPN-LP Amarillo; KFDA-TV (CBS) Amarillo; KPTF-DT (IND) Farwell; KTMO-LP (TMO) Amarillo; KVII-TV (ABC, CW) Amarillo; 10 FMs.
Programming (via satellite): C-SPAN; CW+; Eternal Word TV Network; INSP; QVC; The Weather Channel; Trinity Broadcasting Network; TV Guide Network; Univision Studios; WGN America.
Fee: $35.00 installation; $9.22 monthly.
Expanded Basic Service 1
Subscribers: 31,077.
Programming (via satellite): A&E Networks; ABC Family Channel; AMC; Animal Planet; BET Networks; Bravo; Cartoon Network; CNBC; CNN; Comedy Central; Country Music TV; C-SPAN 2; Discovery Channel; Disney Channel; E! Entertainment Television; ESPN; ESPN 2; Food Network; Fox News Channel; Fox Sports Southwest; FX; GalaVision; Headline News; HGTV; History Channel; Lifetime; Lifetime Movie Network; MSNBC; MTV; MTV2; Nickelodeon; Speed; Spike TV; Syfy; TBS Superstation; The Learning Channel; Travel Channel; truTV; Turner Classic Movies; Turner Network TV; TV Land; USA Network; Versus; VH1.
Fee: $7.51 monthly.
Digital Basic Service
Subscribers: 15,805.
Programming (via satellite): A&E HD; Bandamax; BBC America; Bio; Bloomberg Television; Boomerang en Espanol; CBS Sports Network; Cine Latino; Cine Mexicano; CMT Pure Country; CNN en Espanol; Cooking Channel; De Pelicula; De Pelicula Clasico; Discovery en Espanol; Discovery Health Channel; Discovery Home Channel; Discovery Kids Channel; DIY Network; Encore (multiplexed); ESPN 2 HD; ESPN Classic Sports; ESPN Deportes; ESPN HD; ESPN U; ESPNews; EWTN en Espanol; Food Network HD; Fox College Sports Atlantic; Fox College Sports Central; Fox College Sports Pacific; Fox Deportes; Fox Soccer; FSN HD; Fuel TV; Fuse; G4; GalaVision; GMC; Golf Channel; Great American Country; GSN; Hallmark Channel; Halogen Network; HD Theater; HDNet; HDNet Movies; HGTV HD; History Channel en Espanol; History Channel International; ID Investigation Discovery; Independent Film Channel; Jewelry Television; Military Channel; MTV Hits; mtvU; mun2 television; National Geographic Channel; National Geographic Channel HD Network; Nick Jr.; NickToons en Espanol; NickToons TV; Nuvo TV; Outdoor Channel; Oxygen; Science; ShopNBC; SoapNet; Sorpresa; Sundance Channel; Sur Network; TeenNick; Telehit; Tennis Channel; Toon Disney; Toon Disney en Espanol; Tr3s; Turner Network TV HD; Universal HD; VH1 Classic; Video Rola; WE tv.
Pay Service 1
Pay Units: 5,645.
Programming (via satellite): Cinemax.
Fee: $10.95 monthly.
Pay Service 2
Pay Units: 309.
Programming (via satellite): Starz.
Pay Service 3
Pay Units: 7,596.
Programming (via satellite): Encore.
Pay Service 4
Pay Units: 6,609.
Programming (via satellite): HBO.
Fee: $12.95 monthly.
Pay Service 5
Pay Units: 5,277.
Programming (via satellite): Showtime.
Digital Pay Service 1
Pay Units: 14,477.
Programming (via satellite): Cinemax (multiplexed); HBO (multiplexed); HBO HD; HBO Latino; Showtime (multiplexed); Showtime HD; Starz (multiplexed); Starz HDTV; The Movie Channel (multiplexed).
Video-On-Demand: No
Pay-Per-View
iN DEMAND (delivered digitally); Playboy TV (delivered digitally); Fresh (delivered digitally); Shorteez (delivered digitally); Spice: Xcess (delivered digitally); Club Jenna (delivered digitally).
Internet Service
Operational: Yes.
Subscribers: 21,695.
Broadband Service: Suddenlink High Speed Internet.
Fee: $49.95 installation; $24.95 monthly.
Telephone Service
Digital: Operational
Fee: $48.95 monthly
Miles of Plant: 980.0 (coaxial); 100.0 (fiber optic). Additional miles planned: 15.0 (coaxial).
Vice President & Manager: Connie Wharton. Marketing Director: Alisa Mathies. Chief Technician: Charlie Johnson.
Ownership: Cequel Communications LLC (MSO).

ANAHUAC—Formerly served by Carrell Communications. No longer in operation. ICA: TX0376.

ANDERSON—Formerly served by National Cable Inc. No longer in operation. ICA: TX0666.

ANDREWS—Suddenlink Communications, 412 W Broadway St, Andrews, TX 79714-6222. Phones: 800-235-4233; 915-523-3081. Fax: 915-523-3325. Web Site: http://www.suddenlink.com. Also serves Andrews County. ICA: TX0141.
TV Market Ranking: Below 100 (ANDREWS, Andrews County (portions)); Outside TV Markets (Andrews County (portions)). Franchise award date: N.A. Franchise expiration date: N.A. Began: March 1, 1972.
Channel capacity: N.A. Channels available but not in use: N.A.
Basic Service
Subscribers: 3,313.
Programming (received off-air): KMID (ABC) Midland; KMLM-DT (IND) Odessa; KOSA-TV (CBS, MNT) Odessa; KPBT-TV (PBS) Odessa; KPEJ-TV (FOX) Odessa; KTLE-LP (TMO) Odessa; KUPB (UNV) Midland; KWES-TV (NBC) Odessa; KWWT (CW) Odessa.
Programming (via satellite): C-SPAN; MyNetworkTV Inc.; QVC; TBS Superstation; The Weather Channel; TV Guide Network; WGN America.
Fee: $38.00 installation; $6.22 monthly; $3.85 converter.
Expanded Basic Service 1
Subscribers: 2,339.
Programming (via satellite): A&E Networks; ABC Family Channel; AMC; Animal Planet; BET Networks; Bravo; Cartoon Network; CNBC; CNN; Comedy Central; Country Music TV; Discovery Channel; Disney Channel; E! Entertainment Television; ESPN; ESPN 2; Eternal Word TV Network; Food Network; Fox News Channel; Fox Sports Southwest; FX; Hallmark Channel; Headline News; HGTV; History Channel; Lifetime; Lifetime Movie Network; MSNBC; MTV; MTV2; mun2 television; Nickelodeon; Speed; Spike TV; Syfy; Telefutura; The Learning Channel; Travel Channel; Turner Classic Movies; Turner Network TV; TV Land; USA Network; Versus; VH1.
Fee: $38.00 installation; $24.93 monthly.
Digital Basic Service
Subscribers: N.A.
Programming (via satellite): A&E HD; Bandamax; BBC America; Bio; Bloomberg Television; Boomerang; Boomerang en Espanol; CBS Sports Network; Cine Latino; Cine Mexicano; CMT Pure Country; CNN en Espanol; Cooking Channel; De Pelicula; De Pelicula Clasico; Discovery en Espanol; Discovery Health Channel; Discovery Home Channel; Discovery Kids Channel; DIY Network; ESPN 2 HD; ESPN Classic Sports; ESPN Deportes; ESPN HD; ESPN U; ESPNews; EWTN en Espanol; Food Network HD; Fox College Sports Atlantic; Fox College Sports Central; Fox College Sports Pacific; Fox Deportes; Fox Soccer; FSN HD; Fuel TV; Fuse; G4; GalaVision; GMC; Golf Channel; Great American Country; GSN; Halogen Network; HD Theater; HDNet; HDNet Movies; HGTV HD; History Channel en Espanol; History Channel International; ID Investigation Discovery; Independent Film Channel; INSP; Jewelry Television; Military Channel; MTV Hits; mtvU; mun2 television; Music Choice; National Geographic Channel; National Geographic Channel HD Network; Nick Jr.; NickToons en Espanol; NickToons TV; Nuvo TV; Outdoor Channel; Oxygen; Science; ShopNBC; SoapNet; Sorpresa; Sundance Channel; Sur Network; TeenNick; Telefutura; Telehit; Tennis Channel; Toon Disney; Tr3s; Trinity Broadcasting Network; truTV; Turner Network TV HD; Universal HD; VH1 Classic; Video Rola; WE tv.
Pay Service 1
Pay Units: 285.
Programming (via satellite): Cinemax.
Fee: $9.95 monthly.
Pay Service 2
Pay Units: 344.
Programming (via satellite): HBO.
Fee: $13.00 monthly.
Pay Service 3
Pay Units: N.A.
Programming (via satellite): Starz.
Fee: $9.95 monthly.
Pay Service 4
Pay Units: 235.
Programming (via satellite): Showtime.
Fee: $9.95 monthly.
Digital Pay Service 1
Pay Units: N.A.
Programming (via satellite): Cinemax (multiplexed); Encore (multiplexed); HBO (multiplexed); HBO HD; HBO Latino; Showtime (multiplexed); Showtime HD; Starz (multiplexed); Starz HDTV; The Movie Channel (multiplexed).
Video-On-Demand: No
Pay-Per-View
iN DEMAND (delivered digitally); Playboy TV (delivered digitally); Fresh (delivered digitally); Shorteez (delivered digitally); Spice: Xcess (delivered digitally); Club Jenna (delivered digitally).
Internet Service
Operational: Yes. Began: January 1, 2003.
Broadband Service: Suddenlink High Speed Internet.
Fee: $45.95 installation; $29.95 monthly.
Telephone Service
Digital: Operational
Fee: $44.95 monthly
Miles of Plant: 95.0 (coaxial); None (fiber optic).
Manager: Archie Kountz. Marketing Director: Diane Bower. Chief Technician: Harold Vilas.
Ownership: Cequel Communications LLC (MSO).

ANGLETON—CMA Communications, 2514 N Velasco, Angleton, TX 77515-4720. Phone: 979-849-5728. Fax: 979-849-2955. Web Site: http://www.cmaaccess.com. Also serves Bailey's Prairie & Danbury. ICA: TX0091.
TV Market Ranking: Below 100 (ANGLETON, Bailey's Prairie, Danbury). Franchise award date: December 1, 1979. Franchise expiration date: N.A. Began: April 18, 1979.
Channel capacity: N.A. Channels available but not in use: N.A.
Basic Service
Subscribers: 3,320.
Programming (received off-air): KETH-TV (TBN) Houston; KFTH-DT (TEL) Alvin; KHOU (CBS) Houston; KIAH (CW) Houston; KLTJ (ETV) Galveston; KPRC-TV (NBC) Houston; KPXB-TV (ION) Conroe; KRIV (FOX) Houston; KTMD (TMO) Galveston; KTRK-TV (ABC) Houston; KTXH (MNT) Houston; KUBE-TV (IND) Baytown; KUHT (PBS) Houston; KXLN-DT (UNV) Rosenberg; KYAZ (IND) Katy; KZJL (IND) Houston.
Programming (via satellite): C-SPAN; QVC; TBS Superstation; WGN America.
Fee: $39.95 installation; $16.95 monthly; $12.95 additional installation.
Expanded Basic Service 1
Subscribers: N.A.
Programming (via satellite): A&E Networks; ABC Family Channel; AMC; Animal Planet; BET Networks; Bravo; Cartoon Network; CNBC; CNN; Country Music TV; Discovery Channel; ESPN; ESPN 2; ESPN Classic Sports; Food Network; Fox Deportes; Fox News Channel; Fox Sports Southwest; FX; Headline News; HGTV; History Channel; INSP; Lifetime; MSNBC; MTV; National Geographic Channel; Nickelodeon; SoapNet; Spike TV; Syfy; The Learning Channel; The Weather Channel; Travel Channel; truTV; Turner Classic Movies; Turner Network TV; TV Guide Network; TV Land; USA Network; VH1.
Fee: $29.50 monthly.
Digital Basic Service
Subscribers: N.A.
Programming (via satellite): BBC America; Bio; Bloomberg Television; DMX Mu-

sic; ESPN; ESPNews; Fox Movie Channel; Fox Soccer; G4; GAS; Golf Channel; GSN; HD Theater; History Channel International; Independent Film Channel; Lifetime Movie Network; MTV Networks Digital Suite; Nick Jr.; NickToons TV; Outdoor Channel; Speed; Universal HD; WE tv.
Fee: $12.95 monthly.

Pay Service 1
Pay Units: N.A.
Programming (via satellite): HBO.
Fee: $13.45 monthly.

Digital Pay Service 1
Pay Units: 364.
Programming (via satellite): Cinemax (multiplexed); Cinemax HD; Encore (multiplexed); Flix; HBO (multiplexed); HBO HD; Showtime (multiplexed); Showtime HD; Starz (multiplexed); The Movie Channel (multiplexed).
Fee: $12.95 monthly (Showtime, Cinemax, or Starz/Encore), $13.95 monthly (HBO).

Video-On-Demand: No

Pay-Per-View
iN DEMAND (delivered digitally); Playboy TV (delivered digitally); Fresh (delivered digitally); Shorteez (delivered digitally).

Internet Service
Operational: Yes.
Subscribers: 1,200.
Broadband Service: CMA.
Fee: $39.95 installation; $41.95 monthly; $2.95 modem lease; $39.95 modem purchase.

Telephone Service
Digital: Operational
Fee: $39.95 monthly

Miles of Plant: 165.0 (coaxial); None (fiber optic). Additional miles planned: 9.0 (coaxial).
General Manager: Jerry Smith. Marketing Director: Julie Ferguson.
Ownership: Cable Management Assoc. (MSO).

ANNA—Formerly served by Cebridge Connections. Now served by PILOT POINT, TX [TX0286]. ICA: TX0709.

ANSON—Suddenlink Communications, 12444 Powerscourt Dr, Saint Louis, MO 63131-3660. Phones: 800-999-6845 (Customer service); 314-315-9346; 314-965-2020. Fax: 903-561-5485. Web Site: http://www.suddenlink.com. Also serves Jones County (portions). ICA: TX0323.
TV Market Ranking: Below 100 (ANSON, Jones County (portions)). Franchise award date: July 1, 1962. Franchise expiration date: July 1, 2007. Began: August 1, 1968.
Channel capacity: N.A. Channels available but not in use: N.A.

Basic Service
Subscribers: 739.
Programming (received off-air): KRBC-TV (NBC) Abilene; KTAB-TV (CBS) Abilene; KTXS-TV (ABC, CW, TMO) Sweetwater; 4 FMs.
Programming (via satellite): BET Networks; C-SPAN; Lifetime; QVC; TBS Superstation; The Weather Channel.
Fee: $39.95 installation; $19.95 monthly.

Expanded Basic Service 1
Subscribers: 625.
Programming (via satellite): A&E Networks; ABC Family Channel; AMC; Animal Planet; Cartoon Network; CNN; Country Music TV; Discovery Channel; ESPN; Fox News Channel; Fox Sports Southwest; FX; HGTV; MTV; Nickelodeon; Spike TV; The Learning Channel; Turner Network TV; USA Network.
Fee: $39.95 installation; $23.00 monthly.

Pay Service 1
Pay Units: 72.
Programming (via satellite): Cinemax.
Fee: $12.50 monthly.

Pay Service 2
Pay Units: 170.
Programming (via satellite): Encore.
Fee: $1.71 monthly.

Pay Service 3
Pay Units: 84.
Programming (via satellite): HBO.
Fee: $13.00 monthly.

Pay Service 4
Pay Units: 111.
Programming (via satellite): Starz.
Fee: $6.75 monthly.

Video-On-Demand: No

Internet Service
Operational: Yes. Began: November 12, 2003.
Broadband Service: Suddenlink High Speed Internet.
Fee: $49.95 installation; $29.95 monthly.

Telephone Service
Digital: Operational
Fee: $44.95 monthly

Miles of Plant: 25.0 (coaxial); None (fiber optic).
Regional Manager: Todd Cruthird. Plant Manager: Bobby Smith.
Ownership: Cequel Communications LLC (MSO).

ANTON—Reach Broadband, 515 E Longview St, Arp, TX 75750. Phone: 800-687-1258. Web Site: http://www.reachbroadband.net. ICA: TX0506.
TV Market Ranking: Below 100 (ANTON). Franchise award date: July 21, 1982. Franchise expiration date: N.A. Began: October 15, 1982.
Channel capacity: 41 (not 2-way capable). Channels available but not in use: N.A.

Basic Service
Subscribers: 72.
Programming (received off-air): KAMC (ABC) Lubbock; KCBD (NBC) Lubbock; KJTV-TV (FOX) Lubbock; KLBK-TV (CBS) Lubbock; KRPV-DT (IND) Roswell; KTXT-TV (PBS) Lubbock; KXTQ-CA (TMO) Lubbock.
Programming (via satellite): ABC Family Channel; AMC; Cartoon Network; CNN; Discovery Channel; Disney Channel; ESPN; ESPN 2; Fox Sports Net; FX; Great American Country; Headline News; HGTV; History Channel; Lifetime; National Geographic Channel; Nickelodeon; Spike TV; Syfy; TBS Superstation; The Learning Channel; The Weather Channel; Trinity Broadcasting Network; Turner Network TV; Univision Studios; USA Network; VH1.
Fee: $29.95 installation; $38.00 monthly.

Pay Service 1
Pay Units: 21.
Programming (via satellite): Cinemax.
Fee: $9.95 monthly.

Pay Service 2
Pay Units: 28.
Programming (via satellite): HBO.
Fee: $9.95 monthly.

Video-On-Demand: No

Internet Service
Operational: No.

Telephone Service
None

Miles of Plant: 8.0 (coaxial); None (fiber optic).
Regional Manager: Ronnie Stafford. Office Manager: Jan Gibson.
Ownership: RB3 LLC (MSO).

AQUA VISTA—Formerly served by Cebridge Connections. No longer in operation. ICA: TX0912.

ARANSAS PASS—Cable One, 1045 S Commercial St, Aransas Pass, TX 78336-5305. Phone: 361-758-7621. Fax: 361-758-7096. E-mail: mschooley@cableone.net. Web Site: http://www.cableone.net. Also serves Aransas County, Gregory, Ingleside, Ingleside on the Bay, San Patricio County & Taft. ICA: TX0097.
TV Market Ranking: Below 100 (ARANSAS PASS, Arkansas County, City by the Sea, Gregory, Ingleside, Ingleside on the Bay, Palm Harbor, San Patricio County, Taft). Franchise award date: April 27, 1979. Franchise expiration date: April 1, 2009. Began: June 1, 1981.
Channel capacity: 62 (operating 2-way). Channels available but not in use: N.A.

Basic Service
Subscribers: 7,300.
Programming (received off-air): KEDT (PBS) Corpus Christi; KIII (ABC) Corpus Christi; KRIS-TV (CW, NBC) Corpus Christi; KTOV-LP Corpus Christi; KZTV (CBS) Corpus Christi.
Programming (via satellite): A&E Networks; ABC Family Channel; AMC; Animal Planet; BET Networks; Cartoon Network; CNBC; CNN; Comedy Central; Country Music TV; C-SPAN; C-SPAN 2; CW+; Discovery Channel; Disney Channel; ESPN; ESPN 2; Food Network; Fox Deportes; Fox News Channel; Fox Sports Southwest; FX; Headline News; HGTV; History Channel; ION Television; Lifetime; MSNBC; MTV; Nickelodeon; QVC; Syfy; TBS Superstation; Telemundo; The Learning Channel; The Weather Channel; Turner Classic Movies; TV Guide Network; TV Land; Univision Studios; USA Network; VH1.
Fee: $16.04 installation; $46.00 monthly; $1.68 converter; $12.50 additional installation.

Digital Basic Service
Subscribers: 2,912.
Programming (via satellite): DMX Music.
Fee: $4.95 installation; $11.15 monthly.

Digital Expanded Basic Service
Subscribers: 2,100.
Programming (received off-air): KEDT (PBS) Corpus Christi; KRIS-TV (CW, NBC) Corpus Christi; KZTV (CBS) Corpus Christi.
Programming (via satellite): 3 Angels Broadcasting Network; Bio; Boomerang; BYU Television; Canales N; Discovery Digital Networks; ESPN Classic Sports; ESPNews; FamilyNet; Fox College Sports Atlantic; Fox College Sports Central; Fox College Sports Pacific; Fox Movie Channel; Fox Soccer; Fuel TV; G4; Golf Channel; Great American Country; Hallmark Channel; History Channel International; INSP; National Geographic Channel; Outdoor Channel; SoapNet; Speed; Toon Disney; Trinity Broadcasting Network; truTV; Turner Network TV HD; Universal HD.
Fee: $4.00 monthly.

Digital Pay Service 1
Pay Units: N.A.
Programming (via satellite): Cinemax (multiplexed); Flix; HBO (multiplexed); Showtime (multiplexed); Showtime HD; The Movie Channel (multiplexed); The Movie Channel HD.
Fee: $20.00 installation; $15.00 monthly (each package).

Video-On-Demand: No

Pay-Per-View
Addressable homes: 2,799.
Pleasure (delivered digitally); Shorteez (delivered digitally); Shorteez (delivered digitally); ETC (delivered digitally); Playboy TV (delivered digitally); Playboy TV (delivered digitally); Fresh (delivered digitally); Fresh (delivered digitally).

Internet Service
Operational: Yes. Began: October 1, 2001.
Subscribers: 3,600.
Broadband Service: CableONE.net.
Fee: $75.00 installation; $43.00 monthly; $5.00 modem lease.

Telephone Service
Digital: Operational
Fee: $39.95 monthly

Miles of Plant: 160.0 (coaxial); 160.0 (fiber optic). Additional miles planned: 10.0 (coaxial).
Manager: David King. Chief Technician: Martin Schooley.
Ownership: Cable ONE Inc. (MSO).

ARCHER CITY—Time Warner Cable. Now served by WICHITA FALLS, TX [TX0026]. ICA: TX0710.

ARCOLA—Formerly served by Almega Cable. No longer in operation. ICA: TX0243.

ARGYLE—Formerly served by SouthTel Communications LP. No longer in operation. ICA: TX0533.

ARLINGTON—Time Warner Cable. Now served by DALLAS, TX [TX0003]. ICA: TX0011.

ARP—Zoom Media, PO Box 2126, Flint, TX 75762. Phone: 855-261-5304. Web Site: http://www.zoommediallc.com. Also serves New London, Overton, Troup & Turnertown. ICA: TX0374.
TV Market Ranking: Below 100 (ARP, New London, Overton, Troup, Turnertown). Franchise award date: N.A. Franchise expiration date: N.A. Began: February 1, 1981.
Channel capacity: 36 (not 2-way capable). Channels available but not in use: N.A.

Basic Service
Subscribers: 423.
Programming (received off-air): KCEB (CW) Longview; KETK-TV (NBC) Jacksonville; KFXK-TV (FOX) Longview; KLTS-TV (PBS) Shreveport; KLTV (ABC, TMO) Tyler; KYTX (CBS, IND) Nacogdoches.
Programming (via satellite): C-SPAN; Headline News; QVC; The Weather Channel; Trinity Broadcasting Network; Univision Studios.
Fee: $54.95 installation; $20.95 monthly.

Expanded Basic Service 1
Subscribers: 367.
Programming (via satellite): A&E Networks; ABC Family Channel; AMC; Animal Planet; BET Networks; Bio; Cartoon Network; CNBC; CNN; Discovery Channel; Disney Channel; E! Entertainment Television; ESPN; ESPN 2; Food Network; Fox News Channel; Fox Sports Southwest; FX; Great American Country; Lifetime; MSNBC; MTV; National Geographic Channel; Nickelodeon; Spike TV; TBS Superstation; The Learning Channel; Turner Classic Movies; Turner Network TV; USA Network.
Fee: $23.10 monthly.

Pay Service 1
Pay Units: 95.
Programming (via satellite): Cinemax.
Fee: $12.95 monthly.

Pay Service 2
Pay Units: 200.
Programming (via satellite): HBO.
Fee: $12.95 monthly.
Pay Service 3
Pay Units: 84.
Programming (via satellite): Showtime; The Movie Channel.
Fee: $12.95 monthly.
Video-On-Demand: No
Internet Service
Operational: No.
Telephone Service
None
Miles of Plant: 78.0 (coaxial); None (fiber optic).
Chief Executive Officer: Steve Houston.
Ownership: Zoom Media LLC (MSO).

ASHERTON—Time Warner Cable. Now served by CRYSTAL CITY, TX [TX0147]. ICA: TX0536.

ASPERMONT—Alliance Communications, 6125 Paluxy Dr, Tyler, TX 75703. Phones: 501-679-6619; 800-842-8160. Fax: 501-679-5694. Web Site: http://www.alliancecable.net. ICA: TX0461.
TV Market Ranking: Outside TV Markets (ASPERMONT). Franchise award date: July 1, 1980. Franchise expiration date: N.A. Began: March 15, 1981.
Channel capacity: N.A. Channels available but not in use: N.A.
Basic Service
Subscribers: 50.
Programming (received off-air): KIDZ-LP Abilene; KPCB-DT (IND) Snyder; KRBC-TV (NBC) Abilene; KRMA-TV (PBS) Denver; KTAB-TV (CBS) Abilene; KTXS-TV (ABC, CW, TMO) Sweetwater; KXVA (FOX) Abilene; allband FM.
Programming (via satellite): A&E Networks; ABC Family Channel; CNN; Country Music TV; Discovery Channel; ESPN; ESPN 2; HGTV; QVC; Spike TV; TBS Superstation; The Weather Channel; Turner Classic Movies; Turner Network TV; Univision Studios; USA Network; WGN America.
Fee: $29.95 installation; $38.00 monthly; $2.20 converter.
Pay Service 1
Pay Units: N.A.
Programming (via satellite): Cinemax; Encore Action (multiplexed); Flix; HBO; Showtime (multiplexed); The Movie Channel (multiplexed).
Fee: $20.00 installation; $10.50 monthly (each).
Video-On-Demand: No
Internet Service
Operational: No.
Telephone Service
None
Miles of Plant: 17.0 (coaxial); None (fiber optic).
Vice President & General Manager: John Brinker. Vice President, Programming: Julie Newman.
Ownership: Buford Media Group LLC (MSO).

ATASCOSA—Almega Cable, 4001 W Airport Freeway, Ste 530, Bedford, TX 76021. Phone: 817-685-9588. Fax: 817-685-6488. Web Site: http://www.almega.com. ICA: TX0309.
TV Market Ranking: 45 (ATASCOSA). Franchise award date: N.A. Franchise expiration date: N.A. Began: September 1, 1989.
Channel capacity: 54 (not 2-way capable). Channels available but not in use: N.A.
Basic Service
Subscribers: 182.
Programming (received off-air): KABB (FOX) San Antonio; KENS (CBS) San Antonio; KHCE-TV (TBN) San Antonio; KLRN (PBS) San Antonio; KMOL-LP Victoria; KMYS (CW) Kerrville; KSAT-TV (ABC) San Antonio; KVDA (TMO) San Antonio; KWEX-DT (UNV) San Antonio.
Programming (via satellite): A&E Networks; ABC Family Channel; AMC; Cartoon Network; CNN; Discovery Channel; Disney Channel; E! Entertainment Television; ESPN; ESPN 2; Eternal Word TV Network; Fox Sports Net; GalaVision; Great American Country; Headline News; HGTV; Lifetime; MTV; National Geographic Channel; Nickelodeon; SoapNet; Spike TV; TBS Superstation; The Learning Channel; The Weather Channel; Turner Network TV; USA Network.
Fee: $29.95 installation; $38.00 monthly.
Digital Basic Service
Subscribers: N.A.
Programming (via satellite): AmericanLife TV Network; Bloomberg Television; cloo; Discovery Health Channel; Discovery Kids Channel; DMX Music; ESPN 2; ESPN Classic Sports; ESPNews; Fox College Sports Atlantic; Fox College Sports Central; Fox College Sports Pacific; Fox Soccer; Fuse; G4; Golf Channel; GSN; Halogen Network; HGTV; History Channel; History Channel International; ID Investigation Discovery; Lifetime Movie Network; Military Channel; Outdoor Channel; Ovation; Planet Green; Science; ShopNBC; Speed; Style Network; Syfy; Trinity Broadcasting Network; Turner Classic Movies; Versus; WE tv.
Pay Service 1
Pay Units: 15.
Programming (via satellite): Cinemax.
Fee: $10.95 monthly.
Pay Service 2
Pay Units: 96.
Programming (via satellite): HBO.
Fee: $10.95 monthly.
Pay Service 3
Pay Units: 41.
Programming (via satellite): Showtime.
Fee: $5.95 monthly.
Digital Pay Service 1
Pay Units: N.A.
Programming (via satellite): Cinemax (multiplexed); Encore (multiplexed); Flix; HBO (multiplexed); Showtime (multiplexed); Starz (multiplexed); The Movie Channel (multiplexed).
Video-On-Demand: No
Pay-Per-View
iN DEMAND (delivered digitally); Playboy TV (delivered digitally); Shorteez (delivered digitally).
Internet Service
Operational: No.
Telephone Service
None
Miles of Plant: 61.0 (coaxial); None (fiber optic).
Ownership: Almega Cable (MSO).

ATHENS—Suddenlink Communications, 12444 Powerscourt Dr, Saint Louis, MO 63131-3660. Phones: 800-999-6845 (Customer service); 903-675-5917. Fax: 903-561-5485. Web Site: http://www.suddenlink.com. Also serves Henderson County. ICA: TX0711.
TV Market Ranking: Below 100 (ATHENS, Henderson County (portions)); Outside TV Markets (Henderson County (portions)). Franchise award date: N.A. Franchise expiration date: N.A. Began: October 15, 1968.
Channel capacity: N.A. Channels available but not in use: N.A.
Basic Service
Subscribers: N.A.
Programming (received off-air): KDAF (CW, IND) Dallas; KDFI (MNT) Dallas; KDFW-DT (FOX) Dallas; KERA-TV (PBS) Dallas; KETK-TV (NBC) Jacksonville; KHAS-TV (NBC) Hastings; KLTV (ABC, TMO) Tyler; KPXD-TV (ION) Arlington; KSTR-DT (TEL) Irving; KTVT (CBS) Fort Worth; KTXA (IND) Fort Worth; KUVN-DT (UNV) Garland; KXAS-TV (NBC) Fort Worth; KXTX-TV (TMO) Dallas; KYTX (CBS, IND) Nacogdoches; WFAA (ABC) Dallas; allband FM.
Programming (via satellite): C-SPAN; Jewelry Television; QVC; TBS Superstation; The Weather Channel; Trinity Broadcasting Network.
Fee: $38.00 installation; $14.78 monthly.
Expanded Basic Service 1
Subscribers: N.A.
Programming (via satellite): A&E Networks; ABC Family Channel; AMC; Animal Planet; BET Networks; Bravo; Cartoon Network; CNBC; CNN; Comedy Central; Country Music TV; Discovery Channel; Discovery Health Channel; Disney Channel; E! Entertainment Television; ESPN; ESPN 2; ESPN Classic Sports; Food Network; Fox News Channel; Fox Sports Southwest; FX; GalaVision; Great American Country; Headline News; HGTV; History Channel; Lifetime; Lifetime Movie Network; MSNBC; MTV; Nickelodeon; Outdoor Channel; Oxygen; Speed; Spike TV; Syfy; The Learning Channel; Toon Disney; Travel Channel; truTV; Turner Classic Movies; Turner Network TV; TV Guide Network; TV Land; USA Network; Versus; VH1; WE tv.
Fee: $14.17 monthly.
Digital Basic Service
Subscribers: N.A.
Programming (via satellite): A&E HD; Bandamax; BBC America; Bio; Bloomberg Television; Boomerang; CBS Sports Network; Cine Latino; Cine Mexicano; CMT Pure Country; CNN en Espanol; Cooking Channel; Cox Sports Television; De Pelicula; De Pelicula Clasico; Discovery en Espanol; Discovery Home Channel; Discovery Kids Channel; Discovery Times Channel; DIY Network; Encore (multiplexed); ESPN 2 HD; ESPN Deportes; ESPN HD; ESPN U; ESPNews; EWTN en Espanol; FamilyNet; Food Network HD; Fox Deportes; Fox Movie Channel; Fox Reality Channel; Fox Soccer; Fuel TV; Fuse; G4; GalaVision; GMC; Golf Channel; GSN; Hallmark Channel; Halogen Network; HD Theater; HDNet; HDNet Movies; HGTV HD; History Channel en Espanol; History Channel International; Independent Film Channel; Latele Novela Network; Military Channel; MTV Hits; MTV2; mun2 television; Music Choice; National Geographic Channel; National Geographic Channel HD Network; Nick Jr.; NickToons TV; Nuvo TV; Ritmoson Latino; Science; SoapNet; Sorpresa; Style Network; Sundance Channel; Sur Network; TBN Enlace USA; TeenNick; Telehit; Tennis Channel; Toon Disney en Espanol; Tr3s; Turner Network TV HD; TV Chile; TV One; Universal HD; VH1 Classic; VHUNO; Video Rola; Weatherscan.
Digital Pay Service 1
Pay Units: N.A.
Programming (via satellite): Cinemax (multiplexed); HBO (multiplexed); HBO HD; HBO Latino; Showtime (multiplexed); Showtime HD; Starz (multiplexed); Starz HDTV; The Movie Channel (multiplexed).
Fee: $26.95 monthly.
Video-On-Demand: No
Pay-Per-View
iN DEMAND (delivered digitally); Fresh (delivered digitally); Shorteez (delivered digitally); Playboy TV (delivered digitally); Playboy en Espanol (delivered digitally).
Internet Service
Operational: Yes.
Broadband Service: Suddenlink High Speed Internet.
Fee: $49.95 installation; $38.95 monthly.
Telephone Service
None
Miles of Plant: 92.0 (coaxial); None (fiber optic).
Manager: Nathan Geick. Chief Technician: Ronnie Babcock.
Ownership: Cequel Communications LLC (MSO).

ATLANTA—Cobridge Communications, 9450 Manchester Rd, Ste 200, St. Louis, MO 63119. Phones: 800-438-2427; 314-227-9500. Web Site: http://www.cobridge.net. Also serves Cass County (portions) & Queen City. ICA: TX0188.
TV Market Ranking: 58 (ATLANTA, Cass County (portions), Queen City); Below 100 (Cass County (portions)); Outside TV Markets (Cass County (portions)). Franchise award date: September 1, 1978. Franchise expiration date: N.A. Began: April 1, 1980.
Channel capacity: N.A. Channels available but not in use: N.A.
Basic Service
Subscribers: 482.
Programming (received off-air): KLTS-TV (PBS) Shreveport; KMSS-TV (FOX) Shreveport; KPXJ (CW) Minden; KSHV-TV (MNT) Shreveport; KSLA (CBS) Shreveport; KTAL-TV (NBC) Texarkana; KTBS-TV (ABC) Shreveport; allband FM.
Programming (via satellite): A&E Networks; ABC Family Channel; AMC; BET Networks; CNBC; CNN; Comedy Central; Country Music TV; Discovery Channel; ESPN; Fox Sports Southwest; Headline News; Lifetime; MTV; Nickelodeon; QVC; Spike TV; Trinity Broadcasting Network; Turner Network TV; TV Guide Network.
Fee: $53.00 installation; $29.82 monthly; $2.61 converter.
Expanded Basic Service 1
Subscribers: 1,213.
Programming (via satellite): Disney Channel; E! Entertainment Television; TBS Superstation; The Weather Channel; USA Network; WGN America.
Fee: $6.73 monthly.
Pay Service 1
Pay Units: 128.
Programming (via satellite): Cinemax.
Fee: $15.00 installation; $10.95 monthly.
Pay Service 2
Pay Units: 189.
Programming (via satellite): HBO.
Fee: $11.95 monthly.
Pay Service 3
Pay Units: 105.
Programming (via satellite): Showtime.
Fee: $10.95 monthly.
Pay Service 4
Pay Units: 67.
Programming (via satellite): The Movie Channel.
Fee: $10.95 monthly.
Video-On-Demand: No
Pay-Per-View
iN DEMAND.

Internet Service
Operational: No.
Telephone Service
None
Miles of Plant: 74.0 (coaxial); None (fiber optic).
Chief Executive Officer: Scott Widham. General Manager: Wayne Kelstrom.
Ownership: Cobridge Communications LLC (MSO).

AUSTIN—Grande Communications, 401 Carlson Circle, San Marcos, TX 78666. Phones: 512-878-4000 (Corporate office); 512-220-4600 (Customer service). Fax: 512-878-4010. E-mail: info@grandecom.com. Web Site: http://www.grandecom.com. Also serves San Marcos. ICA: TX0989. **Note:** This system is an overbuild.
TV Market Ranking: Below 100 (AUSTIN, San Marcos). Franchise award date: April 20, 2000. Franchise expiration date: N.A. Began: February 1, 2001.
Channel capacity: 75 (operating 2-way). Channels available but not in use: N.A.
Basic Service
Subscribers: N.A.
Programming (received off-air): KBVO-CD (TEL) Austin; KCWX (IND, MNT) Fredericksburg; KEYE-TV (CBS, TMO) Austin; KLRU (PBS) Austin; KNVA (CW) Austin; KTBC (FOX) Austin; KTFO-CD (TEL) Austin; KVUE (ABC) Austin; KXAN-TV (NBC) Austin.
Programming (via satellite): C-SPAN; C-SPAN 2; LWS Local Weather Station; QVC; TV Guide Network; WGN America.
Fee: $11.50 monthly.
Expanded Basic Service 1
Subscribers: N.A.
Programming (via satellite): A&E Networks; ABC Family Channel; AMC; Animal Planet; BET Networks; Bravo; Cartoon Network; CNBC; CNN; Comedy Central; Discovery Channel; Discovery Health Channel; Disney Channel; E! Entertainment Television; ESPN; ESPN 2; ESPN Classic Sports; Eternal Word TV Network; Food Network; Fox Deportes; Fox News Channel; Fox Sports Southwest; FX; G4; GalaVision; Golf Channel; Great American Country; GSN; Hallmark Channel; Headline News; HGTV; History Channel; Lifetime; MSNBC; MTV; mun2 television; Nickelodeon; Oxygen; SoapNet; Speed; Spike TV; Syfy; TBS Superstation; Telemundo; The Learning Channel; The Weather Channel; Toon Disney; Travel Channel; Trinity Broadcasting Network; truTV; Turner Network TV; TV Land; USA Network; VH1.
Fee: $32.00 monthly.
Digital Basic Service
Subscribers: N.A.
Programming (via satellite): BBC America; Bio; Bloomberg Television; Boomerang; Canales N; CBS Sports Network; Cooking Channel; DIY Network; ESPN; ESPNews; Fox College Sports Atlantic; Fox College Sports Central; Fox College Sports Pacific; Fox Movie Channel; Fox Soccer; Fuel TV; Fuse; GAS; GolTV; HD Theater; History Channel International; Independent Film Channel; INHD (multiplexed); Lifetime Movie Network; MTV Networks Digital Suite; Music Choice; National Geographic Channel; NBA TV; NFL Network; Nick Jr.; NickToons TV; Nuvo TV; Outdoor Channel; PBS Kids Channel; Style Network; Tennis Channel; The Word Network; Turner Classic Movies; Turner Network TV; TVG Network; Universal HD; Versus; WE tv.
Fee: $27.45 monthly.
Digital Pay Service 1
Pay Units: N.A.
Programming (via satellite): Cinemax (multiplexed); Cinemax HD; Encore (multiplexed); Flix (multiplexed); HBO (multiplexed); HBO HD; Showtime (multiplexed); Showtime HD; Starz (multiplexed); Starz HDTV; Sundance Channel (multiplexed); The Movie Channel (multiplexed).
Fee: $12.00 monthly (Cinemax, HBO, Showtime/Sundance/TMC/Flix, or Starz/Encore).
Video-On-Demand: No
Pay-Per-View
Movies (delivered digitally); special events (delivered digitally); sports (delivered digitally); Hot Choice (delivered digitally); Playboy TV (delivered digitally); Fresh (delivered digitally); Shorteez (delivered digitally).
Internet Service
Operational: Yes.
Broadband Service: Grande High Speed Internet.
Fee: $19.95 monthly.
Telephone Service
Digital: Operational
Fee: $9.00 monthly
Vice President & General Manager: Harris Bass. Manager: Randy Wink. Video Services Director: Diane Wigington.
Ownership: Grande Communications Networks Inc. (MSO).

AUSTIN—Time Warner Cable, 12012 N Mo Pac Expy, Austin, TX 78758-2904. Phone: 512-485-6100. Fax: 512-485-6105. Web Site: http://www.timewarnercable.com/centraltx. Also serves Bastrop, Bee Caves, Bertram, Briarcliff, Buda, Burnet, Cedar Park, Dripping Springs, Elgin, Fredericksburg, Gillespie County (portions), Granada Hills, Hays, Hays County (northeastern portion), Hutto, Jonestown, Kyle, Lago Vista, Lakeway, Leander, Liberty Hill, Lockhart, Luling, Manor, Marble Falls, Martindale, McDade, Mountain City, Point Venture, Rollingwood, Round Rock, San Leanna, San Marcos, Smithville, Spicewood, Sunset Valley, Taylor, The Hills, Thorndale, Thrall, Travis County, Volente, West Lake Hills, Wimberley & Woodcreek. ICA: TX0005. **Note:** This system is an overbuild.
TV Market Ranking: Below 100 (AUSTIN, Bastrop, Bee Caves, Bertram, Briarcliff, Buda, Burnet, Cedar Park, Dripping Springs, Elgin, Fredericksburg, Gillespie County (portions), Granada Hills, Hays, Hays County (northeastern portion), Hutto, Jonestown, Kyle, Lago Vista, Lakeway, Lakeway, Leander, Liberty Hill, Lockhart, Manor, Marble Falls, Martindale, McDade, Mountain City, Point Venture, Rollingwood, Round Rock, San Leanna, San Marcos, Spicewood, Sunset Valley, Taylor, The Hills, Thorndale, Thrall, Travis County, Volente, West Lake Hills, Wimberley, Woodcreek); Outside TV Markets (Luling, Smithville). Franchise award date: December 1, 1963. Franchise expiration date: August 12, 2011. Began: September 1, 1963.
Channel capacity: N.A. Channels available but not in use: N.A.
Basic Service
Subscribers: 330,000.
Programming (received off-air): KCWX (IND, MNT) Fredericksburg; KEYE-TV (CBS, TMO) Austin; KLRU (PBS) Austin; KNVA (CW) Austin; KTBC (FOX) Austin; KVUE (ABC) Austin; KXAN-TV (NBC) Austin; allband FM.
Programming (via satellite): C-SPAN; TV Guide Network; WGN America.
Fee: $50.51 installation; $19.95 monthly; $5.95 converter.
Expanded Basic Service 1
Subscribers: 194,000.
Programming (via satellite): A&E Networks; ABC Family Channel; AMC; Animal Planet; BET Networks; Bravo; Cartoon Network; CNBC; CNN; Comedy Central; Country Music TV; Discovery Channel; Disney Channel; E! Entertainment Television; ESPN; ESPN 2; Food Network; Fox News Channel; Fox Sports Southwest; FX; GalaVision; Golf Channel; Hallmark Channel; Headline News; HGTV; History Channel; ION Television; Lifetime; MSNBC; MTV; National Geographic Channel; Nickelodeon; Oxygen; QVC; SoapNet; Spike TV; Syfy; TBS Superstation; Telemundo; The Learning Channel; The Weather Channel; Travel Channel; truTV; Turner Classic Movies; Turner Network TV; TV Land; USA Network; VH1; WE tv.
Fee: $33.40 monthly.
Digital Basic Service
Subscribers: 77,685.
Programming (via satellite): A&E HD; A&E Networks; AMC; Animal Planet; BBC America; Bio; Bloomberg Television; Bravo; Celebrity Shopping Network; cloo; CNN; CNN HD; Comedy Central; Cooking Channel; Country Music TV; C-SPAN; C-SPAN 2; C-SPAN 3; Current; Discovery Channel; Discovery Fit & Health; Discovery Health Channel; Discovery Home Channel; Discovery Times Channel; DIY Network; E! Entertainment Television; ESPN; ESPN 2; ESPN 2 HD; ESPN Classic Sports; ESPN HD; ESPN U; ESPNews; Eternal Word TV Network; Food Network; Fox Business Channel; Fox News Channel; Fox Reality Channel; Fox Sports Southwest; Fuse; FX; G4; GemsTV; GMC; Great American Country; GSN; Halogen Network; HD Theater; Headline News; HGTV; History Channel; History Channel International; INSP; Jewelry Television; Lifetime; Lifetime Movie Network; Lifetime Real Women; LOGO; ME Television; Military Channel; MSNBC; MTV; MTV2; National Geographic Channel; News 8 Austin; Outdoor Channel; Ovation; Oxygen; Palladia; QVC; Science; Shop at Home; Shop Latino TV; ShopNBC; SoapNet; Spike TV; Style Network; Syfy; TBS in HD; TBS Superstation; Texas Cable News; The Learning Channel; The Weather Channel; The Word Network; Travel Channel; Trinity Broadcasting Network; truTV; Turner Classic Movies; Turner Network TV; Turner Network TV HD; TV Land; Universal HD; USA Network; VH1; VH1 Classic; WE tv.
Fee: $9.95 monthly.
Digital Expanded Basic Service
Subscribers: N.A.
Programming (via satellite): ABC Family Channel; Boomerang; Canal 24 Horas; Canal Sur; Cartoon Network; Cartoon Network Tambien en Espanol; CBS Sports Network; Cine Latino; CNN en Espanol; Discovery en Espanol; Discovery Kids Channel; Disney Channel; Docu TVE; Encore (multiplexed); ESPN Deportes; EWTN en Espanol; Fox College Sports Atlantic; Fox College Sports Central; Fox College Sports Pacific; Fox Deportes; Fox Movie Channel; Fox Soccer; Fuel TV; GalaVision; GAS; Golf Channel; Hallmark Channel; HTV Musica; Independent Film Channel; Infinito; ION Television; La Familia Network; mun2 television; NBA TV; Nick Jr.; Nick Too; Nickelodeon; NickToons TV; Nuvo TV; Puma TV; Shop Latino TV; Sorpresa; Speed; Sundance Channel; Telemundo; Tennis Channel; Toon Disney; Toon Disney en Espanol; Tr3s; TVE Internacional; Versus; Video Rola.
Digital Pay Service 1
Pay Units: 15,936.
Programming (via satellite): Cinemax (multiplexed); HBO (multiplexed); Showtime (multiplexed); Starz (multiplexed); The Movie Channel (multiplexed).
Fee: $12.95 monthly (HBO, Cinemax, Showtime/TMC or Starz), $16.95 monthly (Playboy).
Video-On-Demand: Yes
Pay-Per-View
ESPN Full Court (delivered digitally); ESPN Gameplan (delivered digitally); iN DEMAND (delivered digitally); NBA TV (delivered digitally); Playboy TV (delivered digitally).
Internet Service
Operational: Yes.
Subscribers: 91,628.
Broadband Service: Road Runner; EarthLink; AOL; Stick.net.
Fee: $99.95 installation; $44.95 monthly.
Telephone Service
Digital: Operational
Fee: $44.95 monthly
Miles of Plant: 2,788.0 (coaxial); 65.0 (fiber optic).
Division President: Katherine Brabson. Vice President, Marketing & Sales: Terri Weber Cumbie. Vice President, Public Affairs: Stacy Schmitt. Vice President, Engineering: Lew Suders. Vice President, Technical Operations: Ed Tagg. Vice President, Human Resources: Beth Bayes. Program Director: George Warmingham. Public Affairs Director: Roger Heaney.
Ownership: Time Warner Cable (MSO).; Advance/Newhouse Partnership (MSO).

AVINGER—Formerly served by Almega Cable. No longer in operation. ICA: TX0597.

AZTEC—Formerly served by Cebridge Connections. No longer in operation. ICA: TX0492.

BAIRD—Formerly served by Brownwood TV Cable Service Inc. No longer in operation. ICA: TX0212.

BALLINGER—Allegiance Communications, 707 W Saratoga St, Shawnee, OK 74804. Phones: 405-275-6923; 405-395-1131. Web Site: http://www.allegiance.tv. ICA: TX0964.
TV Market Ranking: Outside TV Markets (BALLINGER). Franchise award date: N.A. Franchise expiration date: N.A. Began: N.A.
Channel capacity: 36 (2-way capable). Channels available but not in use: N.A.
Basic Service
Subscribers: 2,135 Includes Miles & Winters.
Programming (received off-air): KERA-TV (PBS) Dallas; KLST (CBS) San Angelo; KPCB-DT (IND) Snyder; KRBC-TV (NBC) Abilene; KTAB-TV (CBS) Abilene; KTXA (IND) Fort Worth; KXVA (FOX) Abilene; WFAA (ABC) Dallas.
Programming (via satellite): CNN; C-SPAN; Headline News; INSP; QVC; Telefutura; Telemundo; The Weather Channel; Trinity Broadcasting Network; Univision Studios.
Fee: $38.00 installation; $21.95 monthly; $.25 converter.
Expanded Basic Service 1
Subscribers: 1,026.
Programming (via satellite): A&E Networks; ABC Family Channel; AMC; Cartoon Net-

work; CMT Pure Country; Discovery Channel; Disney Channel; ESPN; ESPN 2; Fox News Channel; Fox Sports Southwest; FX; Hallmark Channel; HGTV; Lifetime; MTV; NFL Network; Nickelodeon; Spike TV; TBS Superstation; The Learning Channel; Turner Network TV; TV Land; USA Network.
Fee: $38.00 installation; $24.50 monthly.

Digital Basic Service
Subscribers: N.A.
Programming (via satellite): AmericanLife TV Network; BBC America; Bio; Black Family Channel; Bloomberg Television; Bravo; Canal 52MX; Cine Latino; Cine Mexicano; cloo; CNN en Espanol; Current; Discovery en Espanol; Discovery Fit & Health; Discovery Health Channel; Discovery Home Channel; Discovery Kids Channel; Discovery Times Channel; DMX Music; Encore (multiplexed); ESPN 2; ESPN Classic Sports; ESPNews; Flix; Fox College Sports Atlantic; Fox College Sports Central; Fox College Sports Pacific; Fox Deportes; Fox Movie Channel; Fox Soccer; Fuse; G4; GAS; Golf Channel; Great American Country; GSN; Halogen Network; HGTV; History Channel; History Channel en Espanol; History Channel International; Independent Film Channel; Lifetime Movie Network; Military Channel; MTV Hits; MTV2; National Geographic Channel; Nick Jr.; NickToons TV; Outdoor Channel; Ovation; Science; ShopNBC; Speed; Style Network; Sundance Channel; Syfy; The Word Network; Toon Disney; Toon Disney en Espanol; Tr3s; Trinity Broadcasting Network; Turner Classic Movies; Versus; VH1 Classic; VH1 Country; VH1 Soul; WE tv.

Digital Pay Service 1
Pay Units: N.A.
Programming (via satellite): Cinemax (multiplexed); HBO (multiplexed); HBO Latino; Showtime (multiplexed); Starz (multiplexed); The Movie Channel (multiplexed).

Video-On-Demand: No

Pay-Per-View
iN DEMAND (delivered digitally); Hot Choice (delivered digitally); Playboy TV (delivered digitally); Fresh (delivered digitally); Shorteez (delivered digitally).

Internet Service
Operational: Yes.
Fee: $24.95 installation; $39.95 monthly.

Telephone Service
None

Miles of Plant: 33.0 (coaxial); None (fiber optic).
Chief Executive Officer: Bill Haggarty. Regional Vice President: Andrew Dearth. Vice President, Marketing: Tracy Bass.
Ownership: Allegiance Communications (MSO).

BALMORHEA—Balmorhea TV Cable, PO Box 1377, Alpine, TX 79831-1377. Phones: 800-446-5661; 432-837-2300. Fax: 432-837-5423. E-mail: mtnzone@sbcglobal.net. Web Site: http://www.mountainzonetv.net. ICA: TX0714.
TV Market Ranking: Outside TV Markets (BALMORHEA). Franchise award date: N.A. Franchise expiration date: January 1, 2010. Began: January 1, 1967.
Channel capacity: N.A. Channels available but not in use: N.A.

Basic Service
Subscribers: 125.
Programming (received off-air): KMID (ABC) Midland; KMLM-DT (IND) Odessa; KOSA-TV (CBS, MNT) Odessa; KPEJ-TV (FOX) Odessa; KWES-TV (NBC) Odessa; allband FM.
Programming (via microwave): KLRN (PBS) San Antonio.
Programming (via satellite): A&E Networks; ABC Family Channel; Animal Planet; Cartoon Network; CNN; C-SPAN; Discovery Channel; Disney Channel; ESPN; ESPN 2; Eternal Word TV Network; Food Network; Fox News Channel; GalaVision; Great American Country; HGTV; History Channel; Lifetime; MTV; NFL Network; Nickelodeon; TBS Superstation; Telefutura; Telemundo; The Learning Channel; The Weather Channel; Turner Classic Movies; Turner Network TV; TV Land; Univision Studios; USA Network; VH1; WGN America.
Fee: $25.00 installation; $42.00 monthly.

Pay Service 1
Pay Units: 34.
Programming (via satellite): HBO.
Fee: $10.00 installation; $10.00 monthly.

Pay Service 2
Pay Units: 20.
Programming (via satellite): Showtime.
Fee: $10.00 installation; $8.00 monthly.

Pay Service 3
Pay Units: 15.
Programming (via satellite): Cinemax.
Fee: $6.00 monthly.

Video-On-Demand: No

Internet Service
Operational: Yes.
Subscribers: 25.
Fee: $50.00 installation; $34.50 monthly.

Telephone Service
None

Miles of Plant: 5.0 (coaxial); None (fiber optic). Additional miles planned: 1.0 (coaxial).
Manager: Steve Neu. Office Manager: Lawrence Neu.
Ownership: Mountain Zone TV Systems (MSO).

BANDERA—Zoom Media, PO Box 2126, Flint, TX 75762. Phone: 855-261-5304. Web Site: http://www.zoommediallc.com. ICA: TX0445.
TV Market Ranking: Below 100 (BANDERA). Franchise award date: N.A. Franchise expiration date: December 31, 2006. Began: November 1, 1982.
Channel capacity: 48 (not 2-way capable). Channels available but not in use: N.A.

Basic Service
Subscribers: 371.
Programming (received off-air): KABB (FOX) San Antonio; KCWX (IND, MNT) Fredericksburg; KENS (CBS) San Antonio; KHCE-TV (TBN) San Antonio; KLRN (PBS) San Antonio; KMYS (CW) Kerrville; KPXL-TV (ION) Uvalde; KSAT-TV (ABC) San Antonio; KVDA (TMO) San Antonio; KWEX-DT (UNV) San Antonio; WOAI-TV (NBC) San Antonio.
Programming (via satellite): A&E Networks; AMC; Animal Planet; Cartoon Network; CNBC; CNN; Country Music TV; C-SPAN; C-SPAN 2; Discovery Channel; Disney Channel; E! Entertainment Television; ESPN; Fox News Channel; Fox Sports Southwest; FX; Headline News; HGTV; History Channel; Lifetime; MSNBC; Nickelodeon; QVC; ShopNBC; TBS Superstation; The Learning Channel; The Weather Channel; Trinity Broadcasting Network; truTV; Turner Network TV; USA Network; VH1.
Fee: $44.95 installation; $11.55 monthly.

Pay Service 1
Pay Units: N.A.
Programming (via satellite): Encore; HBO; Showtime; Starz; The Movie Channel.

Internet Service
Operational: Yes.
Fee: $20.99-$49.99 monthly.

Telephone Service
Digital: Operational
Fee: $49.95 monthly

Miles of plant included in San Antonio
Chief Executive Officer: Steve Houston.
Ownership: Zoom Media LLC (MSO).

BARSTOW—Formerly served by Almega Cable. No longer in operation. ICA: TX0616.

BARTLETT—Zoom Media, PO Box 2126, Flint, TX 75762. Phone: 855-261-5304. Web Site: http://www.zoommediallc.com. Also serves Granger. ICA: TX0287.
TV Market Ranking: Below 100 (BARTLETT, Granger). Franchise award date: September 28, 1994. Franchise expiration date: October 21, 2011. Began: May 1, 1982.
Channel capacity: 61 (not 2-way capable). Channels available but not in use: N.A.

Basic Service
Subscribers: 196.
Programming (received off-air): KCEN-TV (NBC, IND) Temple; KEYE-TV (CBS, TMO) Austin; KLRU (PBS) Austin; KNCT (PBS) Belton; KNVA (CW) Austin; KTBC (FOX) Austin; KVUE (ABC) Austin; KWTX-TV (CBS, CW) Waco; KXAN-TV (NBC) Austin; KXXV (ABC, TMO) Waco.
Programming (via satellite): A&E Networks; ABC Family Channel; AMC; Animal Planet; BET Networks; Cartoon Network; CNBC; CNN; Comedy Central; Country Music TV; C-SPAN; C-SPAN 2; Discovery Channel; E! Entertainment Television; ESPN; ESPN 2; Fox Sports Southwest; GalaVision; Headline News; HGTV; History Channel; ION Television; Lifetime; MSNBC; MTV; National Geographic Channel; Nick At Nite; Nickelodeon; QVC; Spike TV; TBS Superstation; The Learning Channel; The Weather Channel; Travel Channel; truTV; Turner Classic Movies; Turner Network TV; Univision Studios; USA Network; WGN America.
Fee: $50.51 installation; $37.82 monthly; $.69 converter.

Pay Service 1
Pay Units: N.A.
Programming (via satellite): Cinemax; HBO; Showtime.
Fee: $9.95 monthly (Cinemax or Showtime), $12.95 monthly (HBO).

Video-On-Demand: No

Internet Service
Operational: Yes.
Fee: $20.99-$49.99 monthly.

Telephone Service
Digital: Operational
Fee: $49.95 monthly

Miles of Plant: 52.0 (coaxial); None (fiber optic).
Chief Executive Officer: Steve Houston.
Ownership: Zoom Media LLC (MSO).

BATESVILLE—Formerly served by Almega Cable. No longer in operation. ICA: TX0886.

BAY CITY—Mid-Coast Cablevision, 505 N Mechanic St, PO Box 1269, El Campo, TX 77437. Phones: 866-532-3920; 979-543-6858. Also serves Markham, Matagorda, Matagorda County (unincorporated areas) & Van Vleck. ICA: TX0104.
TV Market Ranking: Outside TV Markets (BAY CITY, Markham, Matagorda, Matagorda County (unincorporated areas), Van Vleck). Franchise award date: N.A. Franchise expiration date: N.A. Began: February 1, 1972.
Channel capacity: 75 (2-way capable). Channels available but not in use: N.A.

Basic Service
Subscribers: 4,600.
Programming (received off-air): KAVU-TV (ABC) Victoria; KETH-TV (TBN) Houston; KFTH-DT (TEL) Alvin; KHOU (CBS) Houston; KIAH (CW) Houston; KLTJ (ETV) Galveston; KPRC-TV (NBC) Houston; KRIV (FOX) Houston; KTMD (TMO) Galveston; KTRK-TV (ABC) Houston; KTXH (MNT) Houston; KUBE-TV (IND) Baytown; KUHT (PBS) Houston; KXLN-DT (UNV) Rosenberg; KYAZ (IND) Katy; KZJL (IND) Houston.
Programming (via satellite): A&E Networks; BET Networks; Cartoon Network; CNBC; CNN; C-SPAN; Discovery Channel; ESPN; Food Network; Fox Deportes; Fox News Channel; Fox Sports Southwest; FX; Great American Country; Headline News; HGTV; SoapNet; TBS Superstation; The Learning Channel; The Weather Channel; Turner Network TV; TV Guide Network; USA Network.
Fee: $50.00 installation; $35.50 monthly; $2.00 converter.

Expanded Basic Service 1
Subscribers: 3,200.
Programming (via satellite): AMC; Animal Planet; Comedy Central; ESPN 2; Fox Movie Channel; History Channel; Lifetime; MTV; Nickelodeon; Spike TV; Syfy; Turner Classic Movies.
Fee: $15.00 installation; $45.45 monthly.

Digital Basic Service
Subscribers: N.A.
Programming (via satellite): BBC America; Bloomberg Television; Bravo; Discovery Fit & Health; DMX Music; Fox Movie Channel; G4; Golf Channel; GSN; Halogen Network; Independent Film Channel; Outdoor Channel; Speed; Syfy; Trinity Broadcasting Network; Versus; WE tv.
Fee: $47.99 monthly.

Pay Service 1
Pay Units: 210.
Programming (via satellite): Cinemax.
Fee: $15.00 installation; $9.95 monthly.

Pay Service 2
Pay Units: 1,380.
Programming (via satellite): HBO.
Fee: $15.00 installation; $10.50 monthly.

Digital Pay Service 1
Pay Units: N.A.
Programming (via satellite): Cinemax (multiplexed); Encore (multiplexed); HBO (multiplexed); Showtime (multiplexed); Starz (multiplexed); The Movie Channel (multiplexed).
Fee: $10.00 monthly (each).

Video-On-Demand: No

Pay-Per-View
Fresh (delivered digitally); Playboy TV (delivered digitally).

Internet Service
Operational: Yes.
Subscribers: 1,500.
Fee: $33.24-$53.24 monthly.

Telephone Service
None

Miles of Plant: 150.0 (coaxial); None (fiber optic).
Manager: Wayne Neal.
Ownership: Mid-Coast Cablevision (MSO).

BEACH CITY—Formerly served by Carrell Communications. No longer in operation. ICA: TX0373.

BEAUMONT—Time Warner Cable, 602 N Hwy 69, Nederland, TX 77627. Phones: 409-720-5500; 972-899-7300 (Flower

Mound office). Fax: 409-727-5050. Web Site: http://www.timewarnercable.com/Texas.

Also serves Bridge City, Groves, Hamshire, Kountze, Lumberton, Nederland, Orange, Pine Forest, Port Acres, Port Arthur, Port Neches, Sabine Pass, Silsbee, Vidor, West Orange & Winnie. ICA: TX0022.

TV Market Ranking: 88 (BEAUMONT, Bridge City, Groves, Hamshire, Kountze, Lumberton, Nederland, Orange, Pine Forest, Port Acres, Port Arthur, Port Neches, Sabine Pass, Silsbee, Vidor, West Orange, Winnie). Franchise award date: June 1, 1973. Franchise expiration date: April 1, 2009. Began: June 1, 1973.

Channel capacity: N.A. Channels available but not in use: N.A.

Basic Service

Subscribers: 90,000.

Programming (received off-air): KBMT (ABC) Beaumont; KBTV-TV (FOX) Port Arthur; KFDM (CBS, CW) Beaumont; KITU-TV (TBN) Beaumont; KUHT (PBS) Houston; 17 FMs.

Programming (via satellite): C-SPAN; C-SPAN 2; TV Guide Network; WGN America.

Fee: $50.51 installation; $17.19 monthly; $1.50 converter.

Expanded Basic Service 1

Subscribers: N.A.

Programming (via satellite): A&E Networks; ABC Family Channel; AMC; Animal Planet; BET Networks; Bravo; Cartoon Network; CNBC; CNN; Comedy Central; Country Music TV; Discovery Channel; Discovery Fit & Health; Discovery Health Channel; Disney Channel; E! Entertainment Television; ESPN; ESPN 2; Eternal Word TV Network; Food Network; Fox News Channel; Fox Sports Southwest; FX; GalaVision; Golf Channel; Great American Country; Hallmark Channel; Headline News; HGTV; History Channel; ION Television; Lifetime; Lifetime Movie Network; MoviePlex; MSNBC; MTV; National Geographic Channel; Nickelodeon; Oxygen; QVC; ShopNBC; SoapNet; Spike TV; Style Network; Syfy; TBS Superstation; Texas Cable News; The Learning Channel; The Weather Channel; Travel Channel; truTV; Turner Classic Movies; Turner Network TV; TV Land; Univision Studios; USA Network; Versus; VH1; WE tv.

Fee: $30.80 monthly.

Digital Basic Service

Subscribers: N.A.

Programming (via satellite): A&E Networks; ABC Family Channel; AMC; Animal Planet; BBC America; Bio; Bloomberg Television; Boomerang; Bravo; Cartoon Network; cloo; CNBC; CNN; Comedy Central; Cooking Channel; Country Music TV; C-SPAN; C-SPAN 2; C-SPAN 3; Current; Daystar TV Network; Discovery Channel; Discovery Fit & Health; Discovery Health Channel; Discovery Home Channel; Discovery Kids Channel; Discovery Times Channel; Disney Channel; DIY Network; E! Entertainment Television; ESPN; ESPN 2; ESPN 2 HD; ESPN Classic Sports; ESPN HD; ESPN U; ESPNews; Eternal Word TV Network; Exercise TV; FamilyNet; Food Network; Food Network On Demand; Fox Business Channel; Fox News Channel; Fox Reality Channel; Fox Soccer; Fox Sports Southwest; Fuse; FX; G4; GAS; Golf Channel; Great American Country; Hallmark Channel; HD Theater; HDNet; HDNet Movies; Headline News; HGTV; HGTV On Demand; History Channel; History Channel International; Howard TV; Independent Film Channel; ION Television; La Familia Network; Lifetime; Lifetime Movie Network; Lifetime Real Women; Military Channel; MoviePlex; MSNBC; MTV; MTV Hits; MTV2; Music Choice; National Geographic Channel; Nick Jr.; Nickelodeon; NickToons TV; Oxygen; QVC; Science; ShopNBC; SoapNet; Speed; Spike TV; Style Network; Syfy; TBS in HD; TBS Superstation; Texas Cable News; The Learning Channel; The Weather Channel; Toon Disney; Tr3s; Travel Channel; truTV; Turner Classic Movies; Turner Network TV; Turner Network TV HD; TV Guide Network; TV Guide SPOT; TV Land; Universal HD; USA Network; Versus; VH1; VH1 Classic; WE tv.

Fee: $5.00 monthly.

Digital Expanded Basic Service

Subscribers: N.A.

Programming (via satellite): Canal Sur; Cine Latino; CNN en Espanol; Discovery en Espanol; Encore (multiplexed); ESPN Deportes; Fox College Sports Atlantic; Fox College Sports Central; Fox College Sports Pacific; Fox Deportes; Fox Movie Channel; Fuel TV; GalaVision; HTV Musica; Infinito; La Familia Network; NBA TV; Puma TV; Speed; Sundance Channel; Telefutura; Tennis Channel; Toon Disney en Espanol; Tr3s; Univision Studios; Utilisima; VHUNO; Video Rola.

Digital Pay Service 1

Pay Units: N.A.

Programming (via satellite): Cinemax (multiplexed); Cinemax On Demand; HBO (multiplexed); HBO HD; HBO on Broadband; Showtime (multiplexed); Showtime HD; Showtime On Demand; Starz (multiplexed); The Movie Channel (multiplexed); The Movie Channel On Demand.

Fee: $12.95 monthly (each).

Video-On-Demand: Yes

Pay-Per-View

iN DEMAND (delivered digitally); Playboy TV (delivered digitally); NHL Center Ice (delivered digitally); Fresh (delivered digitally); Shorteez (delivered digitally); Hot Choice (delivered digitally); NBA League Pass (delivered digitally); ESPN Gameplan (delivered digitally); ESPN Full Court (delivered digitally); MLB Extra Innings (delivered digitally).

Internet Service

Operational: Yes. Began: July 1, 2001.

Broadband Service: Road Runner.

Fee: $49.99 installation; $44.95 monthly.

Telephone Service

Digital: Operational

Fee: $44.95 monthly

Miles of Plant: 2,500.0 (coaxial); None (fiber optic).

President: Connie Wharton. Vice President & General Manager: Roy Rudd. Engineering Director: Herscel Stracner. Public Affairs Manager: George Perrett.

Ownership: Time Warner Cable (MSO).; Advance/Newhouse Partnership (MSO).

BEAUMONT COLONY—Formerly served by Carrell Communications. No longer in operation. ICA: TX0564.

BEDFORD—Time Warner Cable. Now served by DALLAS, TX [TX0003]. ICA: TX0028.

BEDIAS—Formerly served by Almega Cable. No longer in operation. ICA: TX0669.

BEEVILLE—Time Warner Cable, 4060 S Padre Island Dr, Corpus Christi, TX 78411-4402. Phones: 972-899-7300 (Flower Mound office); 361-698-6259. Fax: 361-857-5038. Web Site: http://www.timewarnercable.com/Texas. Also serves Bee County & Skidmore. ICA: TX0113.

TV Market Ranking: Outside TV Markets (Bee County, BEEVILLE, Skidmore). Franchise award date: N.A. Franchise expiration date: N.A. Began: November 5, 1964.

Channel capacity: N.A. Channels available but not in use: N.A.

Basic Service

Subscribers: N.A. Included in Corpus Christi

Programming (received off-air): KEDT (PBS) Corpus Christi; KENS (CBS) San Antonio; KIII (ABC) Corpus Christi; KORO (UNV) Corpus Christi; KRIS-TV (CW, NBC) Corpus Christi; KSAT-TV (ABC) San Antonio; KZTV (CBS) Corpus Christi; allband FM.

Programming (via satellite): Cartoon Network; C-SPAN; Discovery Channel; Headline News; TBS Superstation; The Weather Channel.

Fee: $34.99 installation; $16.39 monthly.

Expanded Basic Service 1

Subscribers: N.A.

Programming (via satellite): ABC Family Channel; AMC; Animal Planet; CNBC; CNN; Disney Channel; ESPN; Fox News Channel; Fox Sports Southwest; FX; MTV; Nickelodeon; QVC; Spike TV; Turner Network TV; USA Network.

Fee: $28.60 monthly.

Digital Basic Service

Subscribers: N.A.

Programming (via satellite): BBC America; Bravo; Discovery Digital Networks; DMX Music; ESPN Classic Sports; Fox Sports World; Golf Channel; GSN; HGTV; History Channel; Independent Film Channel; Nick Jr.; Syfy; Turner Classic Movies; TV Land; Versus; WE tv.

Fee: $8.00 monthly.

Digital Pay Service 1

Pay Units: N.A.

Programming (via satellite): Encore (multiplexed); HBO (multiplexed); Showtime (multiplexed); Starz (multiplexed); The Movie Channel.

Fee: $12.95 monthly (each).

Video-On-Demand: Yes

Pay-Per-View

Hot Choice (delivered digitally); iN DEMAND (delivered digitally); Fresh (delivered digitally).

Internet Service

Operational: Yes.

Broadband Service: Road Runner.

Fee: $49.99 installation; $44.95 monthly.

Telephone Service

Digital: Operational

Fee: $44.95 monthly

Miles of Plant: 90.0 (coaxial); None (fiber optic).

President: Connie Wharton. Vice President & General Manager: Mike McKee. Engineering Director: Charlotte Strong. Public Affairs Manager: Vicki Triplett.

Ownership: Time Warner Cable (MSO).; Advance/Newhouse Partnership (MSO).

BELLEVUE—Formerly served by Cebridge Connections. No longer in operation. ICA: TX0716.

BELLVILLE—CMA Cablevision, 840 E Travis St, La Grange, TX 78945-2344. Phone: 979-968-6476. Fax: 979-968-5368. Web Site: http://www.cmaaccess.com. Also serves Sealy. ICA: TX0292.

TV Market Ranking: Below 100 (BELLVILLE, Sealy). Franchise award date: January 1, 1980. Franchise expiration date: N.A. Began: June 1, 1981.

Channel capacity: N.A. Channels available but not in use: N.A.

Basic Service

Subscribers: 1,025.

Programming (received off-air): KETH-TV (TBN) Houston; KFTH-DT (TEL) Alvin; KHOU (CBS) Houston; KIAH (CW) Houston; KLTJ (ETV) Galveston; KPRC-TV (NBC) Houston; KRIV (FOX) Houston; KTMD (TMO) Galveston; KTRK-TV (ABC) Houston; KTXH (MNT) Houston; KUHT (PBS) Houston; KXLN-DT (UNV) Rosenberg; KYAZ (IND) Katy; allband FM.

Programming (via satellite): C-SPAN.

Fee: $39.95 installation; $15.95 monthly; $12.95 additional installation.

Expanded Basic Service 1

Subscribers: 692.

Programming (via satellite): A&E Networks; ABC Family Channel; AMC; BET Networks; Cartoon Network; CNN; Country Music TV; Discovery Channel; ESPN; Fox News Channel; Fox Sports Southwest; History Channel; Lifetime; MTV; Nickelodeon; Spike TV; TBS Superstation; The Weather Channel; Turner Network TV; TV Land; USA Network.

Fee: $27.00 monthly.

Digital Basic Service

Subscribers: N.A.

Programming (via satellite): BBC America; Bio; Bloomberg Television; Bravo; Discovery Digital Networks; DMX Music; ESPN 2; ESPN Classic Sports; ESPNews; Fox Movie Channel; G4; GAS; Golf Channel; GSN; Halogen Network; HGTV; History Channel International; Independent Film Channel; Lifetime Movie Network; MTV Networks Digital Suite; National Geographic Channel; Nick Jr.; NickToons TV; Outdoor Channel; Speed; Syfy; Trinity Broadcasting Network; Turner Classic Movies; WE tv.

Fee: $13.95 monthly.

Pay Service 1

Pay Units: 136.

Programming (via satellite): Cinemax.

Fee: $14.95 installation; $10.95 monthly.

Pay Service 2

Pay Units: 102.

Programming (via satellite): Showtime.

Fee: $14.95 installation; $13.95 monthly.

Pay Service 3

Pay Units: 250.

Programming (via satellite): HBO.

Fee: $14.95 installation; $13.95 monthly.

Digital Pay Service 1

Pay Units: N.A.

Programming (via satellite): Cinemax (multiplexed); Encore (multiplexed); Flix; HBO (multiplexed); Showtime (multiplexed); Starz (multiplexed); Sundance Channel; The Movie Channel (multiplexed).

Fee: $10.95 monthly (Cinemax or Starz/Encore), $13.95 monthly (HBO or Showtime).

Video-On-Demand: No

Pay-Per-View

Hot Choice (delivered digitally); iN DEMAND (delivered digitally); Playboy TV (delivered digitally); Fresh (delivered digitally); Shorteez (delivered digitally).

Internet Service

Operational: Yes.

Subscribers: 150.

Broadband Service: CMA.

Fee: $39.95 installation; $36.95 monthly; $2.95 modem lease; $39.95 modem purchase.

Telephone Service

None

Miles of Plant: 130.0 (coaxial); None (fiber optic).

Manager: Jerry L. Smith. Plant Manager: Grady Daniels. Marketing Director: Julie Ferguson.
Ownership: Cable Management Assoc. (MSO).

BEN BOLT—National Cable Inc. Now served by ALICE, TX [TX0102]. ICA: TX0717.

BEN WHEELER—Zoom Media, PO Box 2126, Flint, TX 75762. Phone: 855-261-5304. Web Site: http://www.zoommediallc.com. Also serves Brownsboro, Edom, Henderson County (portions), Murchison, Van & Van Zandt County (portions). ICA: TX0487.
TV Market Ranking: Below 100 (BEN WHEELER, Brownsboro, Edom, Henderson County (portions), Murchison, Van, Van Zandt County (portions)). Franchise award date: January 1, 1989. Franchise expiration date: January 1, 2009. Began: July 11, 1989.
Channel capacity: N.A. Channels available but not in use: N.A.
Basic Service
Subscribers: 351.
Programming (received off-air): KDFI (MNT) Dallas; KDFW-DT (FOX) Dallas; KERA-TV (PBS) Dallas; KETK-TV (NBC) Jacksonville; KLTV (ABC, TMO) Tyler; KTVT (CBS) Fort Worth; KTXA (IND) Fort Worth; KXAS-TV (NBC) Fort Worth; KXTX-TV (TMO) Dallas; WFAA (ABC) Dallas.
Programming (via satellite): A&E Networks; ABC Family Channel; CNN; C-SPAN; Discovery Channel; Disney Channel; E! Entertainment Television; ESPN; ESPN 2; Fox News Channel; Fox Sports Net; FX; Great American Country; Headline News; HGTV; History Channel; ION Television; Lifetime; MSNBC; MTV; National Geographic Channel; Nickelodeon; Spike TV; TBS Superstation; The Weather Channel; Trinity Broadcasting Network; Turner Classic Movies; Turner Network TV; USA Network.
Fee: $54.95 installation; $44.05 monthly.
Expanded Basic Service 1
Subscribers: 293.
Digital Basic Service
Subscribers: N.A.
Programming (via satellite): BBC America; Bio; Bloomberg Television; cloo; Discovery Health Channel; Discovery Kids Channel; DMX Music; ESPN Classic Sports; ESPNews; Fox College Sports Atlantic; Fox College Sports Central; Fox College Sports Pacific; Fox Soccer; Fuse; G4; Golf Channel; GSN; HGTV; History Channel International; ID Investigation Discovery; Independent Film Channel; Military Channel; Planet Green; Science; ShopNBC; Style Network; Sundance Channel; Toon Disney; Trinity Broadcasting Network; Versus; WE tv.
Pay Service 1
Pay Units: 79.
Programming (via satellite): Cinemax.
Fee: $12.95 monthly.
Pay Service 2
Pay Units: 81.
Programming (via satellite): HBO.
Fee: $12.95 monthly.
Pay Service 3
Pay Units: 146.
Programming (via satellite): Showtime.
Fee: $12.95 monthly.
Digital Pay Service 1
Pay Units: N.A.
Programming (via satellite): Cinemax (multiplexed); Encore (multiplexed); Flix; HBO (multiplexed); Showtime (multiplexed); Starz (multiplexed); The Movie Channel (multiplexed).
Video-On-Demand: No
Pay-Per-View
iN DEMAND (delivered digitally); Playboy TV (delivered digitally).
Internet Service
Operational: No.
Telephone Service
None
Miles of Plant: 113.0 (coaxial); None (fiber optic).
Chief Executive Officer: Steve Houston.
Ownership: Zoom Media LLC (MSO).

BENAVIDES—Time Warner Cable. Now served by ALICE, TX [TX0102]. ICA: TX0477.

BENJAMIN—Formerly served by Jayroc Cablevision. No longer in operation. ICA: TX0718.

BENTSEN GROVE—Formerly served by CableDirect. No longer in operation. ICA: TX0235.

BEXAR COUNTY (portions)—GVTC Communications. Formerly served by Boerne (portions), TX [TX0315]. This cable system has converted to IPTV, 108 E Third St, Gridley, IL 61744. Phone: 309-747-2211. E-mail: info@gridcom.net. Web Site: http://www.gridtel.com. ICA: TX5471.
Channel capacity: N.A. Channels available but not in use: N.A.
Internet Service
Operational: Yes.

BIG LAKE—Suddenlink Communications, 12444 Powerscourt Dr, Saint Louis, MO 63131-3660. Phone: 314-965-2020. Web Site: http://www.suddenlink.com. ICA: TX0720.
TV Market Ranking: Outside TV Markets (BIG LAKE). Franchise award date: N.A. Franchise expiration date: N.A. Began: June 1, 1958.
Channel capacity: 22 (operating 2-way). Channels available but not in use: N.A.
Basic Service
Subscribers: 1,065.
Programming (received off-air): KLST (CBS) San Angelo; KMID (ABC) Midland; KMLM-DT (IND) Odessa; KOSA-TV (CBS, MNT) Odessa; KPEJ-TV (FOX) Odessa; KRMA-TV (PBS) Denver; KUPB (UNV) Midland; KWES-TV (NBC) Odessa; 12 FMs.
Programming (via satellite): GalaVision; QVC.
Fee: $20.00 installation; $18.00 monthly.
Expanded Basic Service 1
Subscribers: N.A.
Programming (via satellite): A&E Networks; ABC Family Channel; AMC; Animal Planet; Cartoon Network; CNBC; CNN; Comedy Central; C-SPAN; Discovery Channel; Disney Channel; E! Entertainment Television; ESPN; ESPN 2; Food Network; Fox News Channel; Fox Sports Southwest; FX; Great American Country; Hallmark Channel; Headline News; HGTV; History Channel; Lifetime; MSNBC; MTV; National Geographic Channel; Nickelodeon; Outdoor Channel; Shopping Channel; Spike TV; Syfy; TBS Superstation; The Learning Channel; The Weather Channel; Turner Classic Movies; Turner Network TV; TV Land; USA Network; VH1.
Fee: $19.95 monthly.

Digital Basic Service
Subscribers: N.A.
Programming (via satellite): BBC America; Bio; Bloomberg Television; cloo; Discovery Digital Networks; DMX Music; ESPN Classic Sports; ESPNews; Fox College Sports Atlantic; Fox College Sports Central; Fox College Sports Pacific; Fox Soccer; Fuse; G4; Golf Channel; GSN; History Channel International; Independent Film Channel; ShopNBC; Speed; Sundance Channel; Toon Disney; Trinity Broadcasting Network; Versus; WE tv.
Fee: $3.99 monthly.
Pay Service 1
Pay Units: 696.
Programming (via satellite): HBO.
Fee: $11.00 monthly.
Pay Service 2
Pay Units: N.A.
Programming (via satellite): Cinemax; Encore; Showtime.
Digital Pay Service 1
Pay Units: N.A.
Programming (via satellite): Cinemax (multiplexed); Encore (multiplexed); Flix; HBO (multiplexed); Showtime (multiplexed); Starz (multiplexed); The Movie Channel (multiplexed).
Pay-Per-View
iN DEMAND (delivered digitally); Playboy TV (delivered digitally); Fresh (delivered digitally); Shorteez (delivered digitally).
Internet Service
Operational: Yes. Began: January 28, 2004.
Broadband Service: Suddenlink High Speed Internet.
Fee: $49.95 installation; $38.95 monthly.
Telephone Service
None
Miles of Plant: 16.0 (coaxial); None (fiber optic).
Manager: Daniel Anderson. Chief Technician: Phil Pool.
Ownership: Cequel Communications LLC.

BIG SPRING—Suddenlink Communications, 2006 Birdwell Ln, Big Spring, TX 79702-6012. Phone: 915-267-3821. Fax: 915-264-0779. Web Site: http://www.suddenlink.com. Also serves Coahoma & Howard County. ICA: TX0063.
TV Market Ranking: Below 100 (BIG SPRING, Coahoma, Howard County). Franchise award date: January 1, 1961. Franchise expiration date: N.A. Began: September 1, 1961.
Channel capacity: N.A. Channels available but not in use: N.A.
Basic Service
Subscribers: 7,872.
Programming (received off-air): KERA-TV (PBS) Dallas; KMID (ABC) Midland; KMLM-DT (IND) Odessa; KOSA-TV (CBS, MNT) Odessa; KPEJ-TV (FOX) Odessa; KWAB-TV (NBC) Big Spring; WFAA (ABC) Dallas; all-band FM.
Programming (via satellite): ABC Family Channel; CNN; C-SPAN; C-SPAN 2; Headline News; TBS Superstation; The Learning Channel; The Weather Channel; TV Land.
Fee: $42.59 installation; $12.14 monthly.
Expanded Basic Service 1
Subscribers: 7,473.
Programming (via satellite): A&E Networks; AMC; BET Networks; CNBC; Discovery Channel; Disney Channel; ESPN; Fox Sports Southwest; Great American Country; HGTV; History Channel; Lifetime; Nickelodeon; Spike TV; Syfy; Turner Network TV; USA Network; VH1.
Fee: $11.12 monthly.
Digital Basic Service
Subscribers: N.A.
Programming (via satellite): Discovery Digital Networks; DMX Music; Encore Action; ESPN 2; ESPN Classic Sports; Speed; Versus; VH1 Classic; VH1 Country; WE tv.
Pay Service 1
Pay Units: 2,100.
Programming (via satellite): HBO; Showtime; The Movie Channel.
Fee: $35.00 installation; $9.88 monthly (each).
Digital Pay Service 1
Pay Units: N.A.
Programming (via satellite): Cinemax (multiplexed); HBO (multiplexed); Showtime (multiplexed); Starz (multiplexed); The Movie Channel (multiplexed).
Video-On-Demand: No
Pay-Per-View
iN DEMAND.
Internet Service
Operational: Yes.
Broadband Service: Suddenlink High Speed Internet.
Fee: $49.95 installation; $24.95 monthly.
Telephone Service
Digital: Operational
Fee: $48.95 monthly
Miles of Plant: 189.0 (coaxial); None (fiber optic).
Manager: Archie Kountz. Chief Technician: Vern Bloodworth.
Ownership: Cequel Communications LLC (MSO).

BIG WELLS—Formerly served by Almega Cable. No longer in operation. ICA: TX0887.

BIRCH CREEK—Reveille Broadband, PO Box 39, Lexington, TX 78947. Phone: 979-773-4700. Fax: 979-773-4733. E-mail: mariesullivan@reveillebroadband.com. Web Site: http://www.reveillebroadband.com. ICA: TX0885.
TV Market Ranking: Below 100 (BIRCH CREEK). Franchise award date: N.A. Franchise expiration date: N.A. Began: N.A.
Channel capacity: 36 (not 2-way capable). Channels available but not in use: N.A.
Basic Service
Subscribers: 77.
Programming (received off-air): KEYE-TV (CBS, TMO) Austin; KLRU (PBS) Austin; KNVA (CW) Austin; KTBC (FOX) Austin; KVUE (ABC) Austin; KXAN-TV (NBC) Austin.
Programming (via satellite): A&E Networks; ABC Family Channel; AMC; Animal Planet; BET Networks; Boomerang; Cartoon Network; CNN; Comedy Central; Country

Music TV; C-SPAN; C-SPAN 2; Discovery Channel; Disney Channel; E! Entertainment Television; ESPN; ESPN 2; Food Network; Fox News Channel; Fox Sports Southwest; FX; Great American Country; GSN; Hallmark Channel; Hallmark Movie Channel; Headline News; HGTV; History Channel; Lifetime; National Geographic Channel; Nick Jr.; Nickelodeon; QVC; Speed; Spike TV; Syfy; TBS Superstation; The Learning Channel; The Weather Channel; Travel Channel; Trinity Broadcasting Network; truTV; Turner Classic Movies; Turner Network TV; TV Land; Univision Studios; USA Network; VH1; WGN America.
Fee: $35.00 installation; $39.95 monthly.

Pay Service 1
Pay Units: N.A.
Programming (via satellite): HBO; The Movie Channel.
Fee: $10.95 monthly (each).

Internet Service
Operational: Yes.

Telephone Service
Analog: Not Operational
Digital: Operational

Miles of Plant: 13.0 (coaxial); None (fiber optic).
President: Jeff Sullivan. Chief Executive Officer: Marie Sullivan. Vice President: Cory Savage. Office Manager: Laura Tillery.
Ownership: Reveille Broadband (MSO).

BISHOP—Time Warner Cable. Now served by CORPUS CHRISTI, TX [TX0010]. ICA: TX0332.

BLACKWELL—CMA Cablevision, 1510 N 1st St, PO Box 549, Merkel, TX 79536-0549. Phones: 325-928-4750; 800-588-4750. Fax: 325-928-3452. Web Site: http://www.cmaaccess.com. ICA: TX0472.
TV Market Ranking: Below 100 (BLACKWELL). Franchise award date: N.A. Franchise expiration date: N.A. Began: December 1, 1987.
Channel capacity: N.A. Channels available but not in use: N.A.

Basic Service
Subscribers: 95.
Programming (received off-air): KLST (CBS) San Angelo; KPCB-DT (IND) Snyder; KRBC-TV (NBC) Abilene; KTAB-TV (CBS) Abilene; KTXS-TV (ABC, CW, TMO) Sweetwater; KXVA (FOX) Abilene.
Programming (via satellite): American Movie Classics; Animal Planet; CNN; Country Music TV; Discovery Channel; ESPN; History Channel; Lifetime; QVC; Spike TV; Syfy; TBS Superstation; The Learning Channel; The Weather Channel; Turner Classic Movies; Turner Network TV; USA Network; WGN America.
Fee: $39.95 installation; $33.45 monthly; $12.95 additional installation.

Pay Service 1
Pay Units: 51.
Programming (via satellite): HBO.
Fee: $14.95 installation; $13.95 monthly.

Internet Service
Operational: No.

Telephone Service
None

Miles of Plant: 18.0 (coaxial); None (fiber optic).
General Manager: Jerry Smith. Chief Technician: Joe Clark. Marketing Director: Julie Ferguson.
Ownership: Cable Management Assoc. (MSO).

BLANCO—Zoom Media, PO Box 2126, Flint, TX 75762. Phone: 855-261-5304. Web Site: http://www.zoommediallc.com. ICA: TX1022.
TV Market Ranking: Below 100 (BLANCO).
Channel capacity: N.A. Channels available but not in use: N.A.

Basic Service
Subscribers: 178.
Programming (received off-air): KABB (FOX) San Antonio; KBVO (MNT) Llano; KCWX (IND, MNT) Fredericksburg; KENS (CBS) San Antonio; KEYE-TV (CBS, TMO) Austin; KLRN (PBS) San Antonio; KNVA (CW) Austin; KSAT-TV (ABC) San Antonio; KTBC (FOX) Austin; KVUE (ABC) Austin; KXAN-TV (NBC) Austin.
Programming (via satellite): A&E Networks; ABC Family Channel; AMC; CNN; Comedy Central; Country Music TV; C-SPAN; C-SPAN 2; Discovery Channel; Disney Channel; E! Entertainment Television; ESPN; ESPN 2; Fox Sports World; Headline News; Lifetime; National Geographic Channel; Nickelodeon; Oxygen; Spike TV; TBS Superstation; The Learning Channel; The Weather Channel; Travel Channel; Trinity Broadcasting Network; truTV; Turner Network TV; USA Network; VH1; WGN America.

Pay Service 1
Pay Units: N.A.
Programming (via satellite): HBO.

Internet Service
Operational: Yes.
Fee: $20.99-$49.99 monthly.

Telephone Service
Digital: Operational
Fee: $49.95 monthly

Miles of plant included in San Antonio
Chief Executive Officer: Steve Houston.
Ownership: Zoom Media LLC (MSO).

BLANKET—Formerly served by National Cable Inc. No longer in operation. ICA: TX0643.

BLESSING—Bay City Cablevision, 505 N Mechanic St, PO Box 1269, El Campo, TX 77437-1269. Phones: 877-543-4850; 979-543-6858. Fax: 979-543-9501. Web Site: http://www.warpspeed1.net. Also serves Matagorda County (portions). ICA: TX0490.
TV Market Ranking: Outside TV Markets (BLESSING, Matagorda County (portions)). Franchise award date: November 1, 1982. Franchise expiration date: N.A. Began: August 24, 1983.
Channel capacity: 49 (operating 2-way). Channels available but not in use: N.A.

Basic Service
Subscribers: 210.
Programming (received off-air): KAVU-TV (ABC) Victoria; KHOU (CBS) Houston; KIAH (CW) Houston; KPRC-TV (NBC) Houston; KRIV (FOX) Houston; KTMD (TMO) Galveston; KTRK-TV (ABC) Houston; KTXH (MNT) Houston; KUBE-TV (IND) Baytown; KUHT (PBS) Houston; KXLN-DT (UNV) Rosenberg; KYAZ (IND) Katy; KZJL (IND) Houston; allband FM.
Programming (via satellite): A&E Networks; ABC Family Channel; AMC; BET Networks; Cartoon Network; CNBC; CNN; Country Music TV; C-SPAN; Discovery Channel; Discovery Fit & Health; ESPN; ESPN 2; ESPN Classic Sports; Food Network; Fox News Channel; Fox Sports Southwest; FX; Hallmark Channel; Headline News; HGTV; History Channel; Lifetime; MTV; Nickelodeon; Outdoor Channel; QVC; SoapNet; Spike TV; TBS Superstation; The Learning Channel; The Weather Channel; Trinity Broadcasting Network; truTV; Turner Network TV; TV Guide Network; TV Land; USA Network; VH1; WGN America.
Fee: $25.00 installation; $29.99 monthly; $15.00 additional installation.

Digital Basic Service
Subscribers: N.A.
Programming (via satellite): BBC America; Bloomberg Television; Canales N; Discovery Digital Networks; ESPNews; Fox Movie Channel; Fox Soccer; G4; Golf Channel; GSN; Independent Film Channel; Nick Jr.; NickToons TV; Speed; Turner Classic Movies; Versus; VH1 Classic (multiplexed); VH1 Country; WE tv.

Digital Pay Service 1
Pay Units: N.A.
Programming (via satellite): Cinemax; Encore (multiplexed); Flix; HBO (multiplexed); Showtime (multiplexed); The Movie Channel (multiplexed).

Video-On-Demand: No

Pay-Per-View
Playboy TV (delivered digitally).

Internet Service
Operational: Yes, Both DSL & dial-up.
Broadband Service: Warp Speed 1 Internet.
Fee: $17.05 installation; $34.99 monthly.

Telephone Service
None

Miles of Plant: 11.0 (coaxial); None (fiber optic). Additional miles planned: 1.0 (coaxial).
Manager: Wayne Neal. Chief Technician: Dickie Isaacs.
Ownership: Mid-Coast Cablevision (MSO).

BLOOMING GROVE—Formerly served by Almega Cable. No longer in operation. ICA: TX0424.

BLOOMINGTON—Almega Cable, 4001 W Airport Frwy, Ste 530, Bedford, TX 76021. Phone: 817-685-9588. Fax: 817-685-6488. Web Site: http://www.almega.com. ICA: TX0469.
TV Market Ranking: Below 100 (BLOOMINGTON). Franchise award date: N.A. Franchise expiration date: N.A. Began: March 1, 1976.
Channel capacity: 41 (2-way capable). Channels available but not in use: N.A.

Basic Service
Subscribers: 256.
Programming (received off-air): KAVU-TV (ABC) Victoria; KEDT (PBS) Corpus Christi; KENS (CBS) San Antonio; KMOL-LP Victoria; KSAT-TV (ABC) San Antonio; KUNU-LP Victoria; KVCT (FOX) Victoria; KXTS-LP Victoria; allband FM.
Programming (via satellite): A&E Networks; ABC Family Channel; Animal Planet; BET Networks; CNN; Discovery Channel; Disney Channel; ESPN; ESPN 2; Fox News Channel; Fox Sports Net; Headline News; HGTV; Lifetime; National Geographic Channel; Nickelodeon; SoapNet; Spike TV; Syfy; TBS Superstation; Telemundo; The Learning Channel; The Weather Channel; Turner Classic Movies; Turner Network TV; TV Land; USA Network; VH1.
Fee: $29.95 installation; $38.00 monthly.

Pay Service 1
Pay Units: 91.
Programming (via satellite): HBO.
Fee: $25.00 installation; $10.95 monthly.

Pay Service 2
Pay Units: 55.
Programming (via satellite): Showtime.
Fee: $9.95 monthly.

Video-On-Demand: No

Internet Service
Operational: No.

Telephone Service
None

Miles of Plant: 15.0 (coaxial); None (fiber optic).
Ownership: Almega Cable (MSO).

BOERNE (portions)—GVTV Communications. Formerly [TX0315]. This cable system has converted to IPTV, 108 E Third St, Gridley, TX 61744. Phone: 309-747-2211. E-mail: info@gridcom.net. Web Site: http://www.gridtel.com. Also serves BOERNE (portions). ICA: TX5465.
Channel capacity: N.A. Channels available but not in use: N.A.

Internet Service
Operational: Yes.

BOERNE (portions)—GVTV Communications. Formerly [TX0315]. This cable system has converted to IPTV. See Boerne (portions) [TX5465]. ICA: TX0315.

BOLING—Formerly served by Cebridge Connections. No longer in operation. ICA: TX0485.

BOOKER—Panhandle Telephone Coop. Inc., 2222 NW Hwy 64, Guymon, OK 73942. Phones: 580-338-2556; 800-562-2556. Fax: 580-338-8260. E-mail: support@ptsi.net. Web Site: http://www.ptsi.net. ICA: TX0456.
TV Market Ranking: Outside TV Markets (BOOKER). Franchise award date: N.A. Franchise expiration date: N.A. Began: September 1, 1955.
Channel capacity: N.A. Channels available but not in use: N.A.

Basic Service
Subscribers: N.A.
Programming (received off-air): KACV-TV (PBS) Amarillo; KAMR-TV (NBC) Amarillo; KCIT (FOX) Amarillo; KFDA-TV (CBS) Amarillo; KVII-TV (ABC, CW) Amarillo.
Programming (via satellite): CW Television Network; HBO; QVC; The Weather Channel; Trinity Broadcasting Network.
Fee: $18.99 monthly.

Expanded Basic Service 1
Subscribers: N.A.
Programming (via satellite): A&E Networks; ABC Family Channel; Animal Planet; CNN; Comedy Central; Discovery Channel; Disney Channel; E! Entertainment Television; ESPN; ESPN 2; Fox Deportes; Fox News Channel; Fox Sports Southwest; FX; Great American Country; GSN; Hallmark Channel; Headline News; History Channel; Lifetime; National Geographic Channel; Nickelodeon; Spike TV; TBS Superstation; Telemundo; TLC; TNT; TV Land; VH1.
Fee: $29.50 monthly.

Pay Service 1
Pay Units: 101.
Fee: $14.00 monthly.

Internet Service
Operational: Yes.
Broadband Service: In-house.
Fee: $39.99 installation.

Miles of Plant: 12.0 (coaxial); None (fiber optic).
President: Charles Russell.
Ownership: Panhandle Telephone Cooperative Inc. (MSO).

BORGER—Cable One, 201 E 10th St, Borger, TX 79007. Phone: 806-273-3744. Fax: 806-273-5258. Web Site: http://www.cableone.net. Also serves Dumas, Fritch, McLean, Pampa, Panhandle, Phillips, Stinnett, Sunray & White Deer. ICA: TX0068.

TV Market Ranking: 95 (Fritch, Panhandle); Below 100 (BORGER, Dumas, Phillips, Stinnett, Sunray, White Deer); Outside TV Markets (McLean, Pampa). Franchise award date: N.A. Franchise expiration date: N.A. Began: February 1, 1978.

Channel capacity: 54 (operating 2-way). Channels available but not in use: N.A.

Basic Service

Subscribers: 12,500.

Programming (received off-air): KACV-TV (PBS) Amarillo; KAMR-TV (NBC) Amarillo; KCIT (FOX) Amarillo; KEYU-LP Amarillo; KFDA-TV (CBS) Amarillo; KPTF-DT (IND) Farwell; KVII-TV (ABC, CW) Amarillo; 7 FMs.

Programming (via satellite): C-SPAN; C-SPAN 2; CW+; QVC; TBS Superstation; Telemundo; TV Guide Network; WGN America.

Fee: $46.00 monthly.

Expanded Basic Service 1

Subscribers: N.A.

Programming (via satellite): A&E Networks; ABC Family Channel; AMC; Animal Planet; BET Networks; Cartoon Network; CNBC; CNN; Discovery Channel; Disney Channel; ESPN; ESPN 2; Food Network; Fox Deportes; Fox News Channel; Fox Sports Southwest; FX; Headline News; HGTV; History Channel; Lifetime; MSNBC; MTV; Nickelodeon; Spike TV; Syfy; The Learning Channel; The Weather Channel; Trinity Broadcasting Network; Turner Classic Movies; Turner Network TV; TV Land; USA Network; VH1.

Fee: $46.00 monthly.

Digital Basic Service

Subscribers: 3,300.

Programming (via satellite): 3 Angels Broadcasting Network; Bio; Boomerang; BYU Television; Canales N; Discovery Digital Networks; DMX Music; ESPN Classic Sports; ESPNews; FamilyNet; Fox College Sports Atlantic; Fox College Sports Central; Fox College Sports Pacific; Fox Movie Channel; Fox Soccer; Fuel TV; G4; Golf Channel; Great American Country; Hallmark Channel; History Channel International; INSP; National Geographic Channel; Outdoor Channel; SoapNet; Speed; Toon Disney; Trinity Broadcasting Network; truTV; Turner Network TV HD; Universal HD.

Digital Pay Service 1

Pay Units: 363.

Programming (via satellite): Cinemax (multiplexed); Flix; HBO (multiplexed); Showtime (multiplexed); Showtime HD; Starz (multiplexed); Sundance Channel; The Movie Channel (multiplexed); The Movie Channel.

Fee: $15.00 installation; $15.00 monthly (each).

Video-On-Demand: No

Pay-Per-View

iN DEMAND (delivered digitally); Pleasure (delivered digitally); Ten Clips (delivered digitally); Ten Blox (delivered digitally); Ten Blue (delivered digitally).

Internet Service

Operational: Yes. Began: December 1, 2002.

Subscribers: 3,000.

Broadband Service: CableONE.net.

Fee: $75.00 installation; $43.00 monthly; $5.00 modem lease.

Telephone Service

Digital: Operational

Fee: $39.95 monthly

Miles of Plant: 339.0 (coaxial); None (fiber optic).

Manager: Terry Harris. Marketing Manager: Donna Litterell. Office Manager: Dawn Rowell. Chief Technician: Rodger Hooks.

Ownership: Cable ONE Inc. (MSO).

BOWIE—CommuniComm Services, 2804B S FM 51, PO Box 869, Decatur, TX 76234-0869. Phone: 940-627-8414. Fax: 940-627-8303. Web Site: http://www.netcommander.com. ICA: TX0191.

TV Market Ranking: Below 100 (BOWIE). Franchise award date: October 1, 1984. Franchise expiration date: N.A. Began: October 1, 1969.

Channel capacity: N.A. Channels available but not in use: N.A.

Basic Service

Subscribers: N.A. Included in Decatur

Programming (received off-air): KAUZ-TV (CBS, CW) Wichita Falls; KDAF (CW, IND) Dallas; KDFI (MNT) Dallas; KDFW-DT (FOX) Dallas; KDTN (ETV) Denton; KERA-TV (PBS) Dallas; KFDX-TV (NBC) Wichita Falls; KJTL (FOX) Wichita Falls; KMPX (IND) Decatur; KSWO-TV (ABC, TMO) Lawton; KTVT (CBS) Fort Worth; KXTX-TV (TMO) Dallas; 2 FMs.

Expanded Basic Service 1

Subscribers: 1,894.

Programming (received off-air): KPXD-TV (ION) Arlington.

Programming (via satellite): A&E Networks; ABC Family Channel; AMC; Animal Planet; BET Networks; Bravo; Cartoon Network; CNBC; CNN; Comedy Central; Country Music TV; C-SPAN; Discovery Channel; Disney Channel; ESPN; ESPN 2; Food Network; Fox News Channel; Fox Sports Southwest; FX; Headline News; HGTV; History Channel; Lifetime; MTV; Nick Jr.; Nickelodeon; QVC; Radar Channel; ShopNBC; Spike TV; Syfy; TBS Superstation; The Learning Channel; The Weather Channel; Travel Channel; Trinity Broadcasting Network; Turner Network TV; TV Guide Network; TV Land; USA Network; VH1; WE tv.

Fee: $43.95 monthly.

Digital Basic Service

Subscribers: N.A.

Programming (via satellite): BBC America; Bloomberg Television; Bravo; CMT Pure Country; Discovery Fit & Health; Discovery Health Channel; Discovery Home Channel; Discovery Kids Channel; DMX Music; ESPN 2; ESPN Classic Sports; ESPNews; Fox Soccer; G4; Golf Channel; GSN; Halogen Network; HGTV; History Channel; ID Investigation Discovery; Independent Film Channel; Military Channel; National Geographic Channel; Nick Jr.; NickToons TV; Outdoor Channel; Science; SoapNet; Speed; Syfy; Trinity Broadcasting Network; Turner Classic Movies; TV Land; Versus; VH1 Classic; WE tv.

Pay Service 1

Pay Units: N.A.

Programming (via satellite): Cinemax; Encore; HBO (multiplexed); Starz.

Digital Pay Service 1

Pay Units: N.A.

Programming (via satellite): Cinemax (multiplexed); Encore (multiplexed); Flix; HBO (multiplexed); Showtime (multiplexed); Starz (multiplexed); The Movie Channel (multiplexed).

Fee: $5.00 monthly (Encore), $11.00 monthly (Starz), $11.95 monthly (Cinemax), $13.95 monthly (HBO or Showtime/TMC/Flix).

Video-On-Demand: No

Pay-Per-View

iN DEMAND (delivered digitally); Playboy TV (delivered digitally); Fresh (delivered digitally); Club Jenna (delivered digitally).

Internet Service

Operational: Yes, Both DSL & dial-up.

Broadband Service: Net Commander.

Fee: $39.95 installation; $51.95 monthly.

Telephone Service

None

Miles of Plant: 42.0 (coaxial); None (fiber optic). Additional miles planned: 6.0 (coaxial).

Chief Technician: J. D. Sifford. Operations Manager: Wes Devall.

Ownership: James Cable LLC (MSO).

BOYD—Formerly served by SouthTel Communications LP. No longer in operation. ICA: TX0279.

BRACKETTVILLE—Almega Cable, 4001 W Airport Frwy, Ste 530, Bedford, TX 76021. Phone: 817-685-9588. Fax: 817-685-6488. Web Site: http://www.almega.com. Also serves Fort Clark Springs. ICA: TX0356.

TV Market Ranking: Below 100 (BRACKETTVILLE, Fort Clark Springs). Franchise award date: N.A. Franchise expiration date: N.A. Began: May 1, 1961.

Channel capacity: 60 (not 2-way capable). Channels available but not in use: N.A.

Basic Service

Subscribers: 132.

Programming (received off-air): KABB (FOX) San Antonio; KMOL-LP Victoria; 2 FMs.

Programming (via microwave): KENS (CBS) San Antonio; KLRN (PBS) San Antonio; KSAT-TV (ABC) San Antonio.

Programming (via satellite): QVC.

Fee: $29.95 installation; $19.95 monthly.

Expanded Basic Service 1

Subscribers: N.A.

Programming (via satellite): A&E Networks; ABC Family Channel; AMC; Animal Planet; Bravo; Cartoon Network; CNBC; CNN; Comedy Central; Country Music TV; Discovery Channel; Discovery Fit & Health; Disney Channel; E! Entertainment Television; ESPN; ESPN 2; Fox Deportes; Fox News Channel; Fox Sports Southwest; FX; G4; Headline News; HGTV; History Channel; Lifetime; MTV; Nickelodeon; Oxygen; Speed; Spike TV; Syfy; TBS Superstation; The Learning Channel; Travel Channel; Turner Classic Movies; Turner Network TV; TV Land; Univision Studios; USA Network; VH1.

Fee: $18.00 monthly.

Digital Basic Service

Subscribers: N.A.

Programming (via satellite): BBC America; Bio; Bloomberg Television; Discovery en Espanol; Discovery Health Channel; Discovery Kids Channel; DIY Network; ESPN Classic Sports; ESPNews; GSN; History Channel International; ID Investigation Discovery; Independent Film Channel; Lifetime Movie Network; Lifetime Real Women; Military Channel; MTV Jams; MTV2; Music Choice; Nick Jr.; Nick Too; NickToons TV; Planet Green; Science; SoapNet; Style Network; Sundance Channel; TeenNick; Toon Disney.

Digital Pay Service 1

Pay Units: N.A.

Programming (via satellite): Cinemax (multiplexed); Encore (multiplexed); Flix; HBO (multiplexed); Showtime (multiplexed); Starz (multiplexed); The Movie Channel (multiplexed).

Video-On-Demand: No

Pay-Per-View

iN DEMAND (delivered digitally).

Internet Service

Operational: No.

Telephone Service

None

Miles of Plant: 38.0 (coaxial); None (fiber optic).

Ownership: Almega Cable (MSO).

BRADY—Suddenlink Communications, 12444 Powerscourt Dr, Saint Louis, MO 63131-3660. Phone: 314-965-2020. Fax: 903-561-5485. Web Site: http://www.suddenlink.com. Also serves McCulloch County (portions). ICA: TX0180.

TV Market Ranking: Outside TV Markets (BRADY, McCulloch County (portions)). Franchise award date: N.A. Franchise expiration date: N.A. Began: September 1, 1965.

Channel capacity: 41 (operating 2-way). Channels available but not in use: N.A.

Basic Service

Subscribers: 1,768.

Programming (received off-air): KBVO (MNT) Llano; KIDY (FOX) San Angelo; KLST (CBS) San Angelo; KTXS-TV (ABC, CW, TMO) Sweetwater; 4 FMs.

Programming (via satellite): KRMA-TV (PBS) Denver; TV Guide Network.

Fee: $39.95 installation; $19.95 monthly.

Expanded Basic Service 1

Subscribers: N.A.

Programming (via satellite): A&E Networks; ABC Family Channel; AMC; Animal Planet; BET Networks; Bravo; Cartoon Network; CNBC; CNN; Comedy Central; C-SPAN; CW+; Discovery Channel; Disney Channel; E! Entertainment Television; ESPN; ESPN 2; ESPN Classic Sports; Eternal Word TV Network; Food Network; Fox News Channel; Fox Sports Southwest; FX; GalaVision; Golf Channel; Great American Country; Hallmark Channel; Headline News; HGTV; History Channel; INSP; Lifetime; MSNBC; MTV; National Geographic Channel; Nickelodeon; Outdoor Channel; QVC; Shop at Home; Shopping Channel; Speed; Spike TV; Syfy; TBS Superstation; Telemundo; The Learning Channel; The Weather Channel; Travel Channel; Trinity Broadcasting Network; Turner Classic Movies; Turner Network TV; TV Land; Univision Studios; USA Network; VH1.

Fee: $25.00 monthly.

Digital Basic Service

Subscribers: N.A.

Programming (via satellite): BBC America; Bio; Bloomberg Television; Canales N; cloo; Discovery Digital Networks; DMX Music;

ESPNews; Fox Movie Channel; Fox Soccer; Fuse; G4; GSN; History Channel International; Independent Film Channel; Sundance Channel; Toon Disney; Versus; WE tv.
Fee: $3.99 monthly.

Pay Service 1
Pay Units: 215.
Programming (via satellite): HBO.
Fee: $35.00 installation; $10.95 monthly.

Pay Service 2
Pay Units: 211.
Programming (via satellite): Showtime.
Fee: $9.95 monthly.

Pay Service 3
Pay Units: 199.
Programming (via satellite): The Movie Channel.
Fee: $7.95 monthly.

Digital Pay Service 1
Pay Units: N.A.
Programming (via satellite): Cinemax (multiplexed); Encore (multiplexed); HBO (multiplexed); Showtime (multiplexed); Starz (multiplexed); The Movie Channel (multiplexed).

Video-On-Demand: No

Pay-Per-View
iN DEMAND (delivered digitally); Playboy TV (delivered digitally); Fresh (delivered digitally); Shorteez (delivered digitally).

Internet Service
Operational: Yes. Began: June 23, 2002.
Broadband Service: Suddenlink High Speed Internet.
Fee: $45.95 installation; $29.95 monthly.

Telephone Service
Digital: Operational
Fee: $44.95 monthly

Miles of Plant: 46.0 (coaxial); None (fiber optic).
Regional Manager: Todd Cruthird. Chief Technician: Walt VanLue. Marketing Director: Beverly Gambell.
Ownership: Cequel Communications LLC (MSO).

BRAZORIA—Suddenlink Communications, 800 N Hwy 36, Brazoria, TX 77422. Phones: 800-999-6845 (Customer service); 314-965-2020. Fax: 281-385-9315. Web Site: http://www.suddenlink.com. Also serves Brazoria County & Jones Creek. ICA: TX0128.
TV Market Ranking: 15 (Brazoria County (portions)); Below 100 (BRAZORIA, Jones Creek, Brazoria County (portions)). Franchise award date: N.A. Franchise expiration date: N.A. Began: October 1, 1982.
Channel capacity: 40 (operating 2-way). Channels available but not in use: N.A.

Basic Service
Subscribers: 2,894.
Programming (received off-air): KETH-TV (TBN) Houston; KFTH-DT (TEL) Alvin; KHOU (CBS) Houston; KLTJ (ETV) Galveston; KPRC-TV (NBC) Houston; KRIV (FOX) Houston; KTMD (TMO) Galveston; KTRK-TV (ABC) Houston; KTXH (MNT) Houston; KUBE-TV (IND) Baytown; KUHT (PBS) Houston; KXLN-DT (UNV) Rosenberg; KYAZ (IND) Katy; KZJL (IND) Houston.
Programming (via satellite): INSP; QVC.
Fee: $15.00 installation; $19.95 monthly; $2.15 converter.

Expanded Basic Service 1
Subscribers: 2,783.
Programming (via satellite): A&E Networks; ABC Family Channel; AMC; BET Networks; Cartoon Network; CNBC; CNN; Discovery Channel; Disney Channel; E! Entertainment Television; ESPN; ESPN 2; Fox News Channel; Fox Sports Southwest; FX; Great American Country; Headline News; HGTV; History Channel; Lifetime; MTV; National Geographic Channel; Nickelodeon; Spike TV; TBS Superstation; The Learning Channel; The Weather Channel; Turner Network TV; USA Network; VH1.
Fee: $25.00 monthly.

Digital Basic Service
Subscribers: N.A.
Programming (via satellite): BBC America; Bio; Bloomberg Television; cloo; Discovery Digital Networks; DMX Music; ESPN Classic Sports; ESPNews; Fuse; G4; Golf Channel; GSN; History Channel International; Independent Film Channel; Outdoor Channel; Speed; Toon Disney; Turner Classic Movies; Versus; WE tv.

Pay Service 1
Pay Units: 230.
Programming (via satellite): Cinemax.
Fee: $10.95 monthly.

Pay Service 2
Pay Units: 623.
Programming (via satellite): HBO.
Fee: $10.95 monthly.

Pay Service 3
Pay Units: 488.
Programming (via satellite): Showtime; The Movie Channel.
Fee: $12.95 monthly.

Digital Pay Service 1
Pay Units: N.A.
Programming (via satellite): Cinemax (multiplexed); Encore (multiplexed); HBO (multiplexed); Showtime (multiplexed); Starz (multiplexed); The Movie Channel (multiplexed).

Video-On-Demand: No

Pay-Per-View
iN DEMAND (delivered digitally); Playboy TV (delivered digitally); Fresh (delivered digitally).

Internet Service
Operational: Yes. Began: October 23, 2003.
Broadband Service: Suddenlink High Speed Internet.
Fee: $45.95 installation; $29.95 monthly.

Telephone Service
Digital: Operational
Fee: $44.95 monthly

Miles of Plant: 154.0 (coaxial); None (fiber optic).
Manager: Mike Burns. Chief Technician: Mayla Zubeck.
Ownership: Cequel Communications LLC (MSO).

BRECKENRIDGE—Suddenlink Communications, 1207 W Walker St, Breckenridge, TX 76424. Phones: 877-423-2743 (Customer service); 314-965-2020. Fax: 903-561-5485. Web Site: http://www.suddenlink.com. ICA: TX0184.
TV Market Ranking: Outside TV Markets (BRECKENRIDGE). Franchise award date: N.A. Franchise expiration date: N.A. Began: January 1, 1952.
Channel capacity: 38 (operating 2-way). Channels available but not in use: N.A.

Basic Service
Subscribers: 2,544.
Programming (received off-air): KIDZ-LP Abilene; KPCB-DT (IND) Snyder; KRBC-TV (NBC) Abilene; KTAB-TV (CBS) Abilene; KTXS-TV (ABC, CW, TMO) Sweetwater; KXVA (FOX) Abilene; allband FM.
Programming (via microwave): KERA-TV (PBS) Dallas; KXTX-TV (TMO) Dallas; WFAA (ABC) Dallas.
Programming (via satellite): C-SPAN; QVC; Shopping Channel; The Weather Channel; Trinity Broadcasting Network; Univision Studios.
Fee: $39.95 installation; $19.95 monthly.

Expanded Basic Service 1
Subscribers: 2,103.
Programming (via satellite): A&E Networks; ABC Family Channel; AMC; Animal Planet; Cartoon Network; CNBC; CNN; Discovery Channel; Disney Channel; ESPN; ESPN 2; Food Network; Fox News Channel; Fox Sports Southwest; FX; Great American Country; Hallmark Channel; Headline News; HGTV; History Channel; INSP; Lifetime; MTV; National Geographic Channel; Nickelodeon; Outdoor Channel; Spike TV; Syfy; TBS Superstation; The Learning Channel; Travel Channel; Turner Network TV; TV Land; USA Network.
Fee: $39.95 installation; $25.00 monthly.

Digital Basic Service
Subscribers: N.A.
Programming (via satellite): BBC America; Bio; Bloomberg Television; Canales N; cloo; Discovery Digital Networks; DMX Music; ESPN Classic Sports; ESPNews; Fuse; G4; Golf Channel; GSN; History Channel International; Independent Film Channel; Speed; Toon Disney; Turner Classic Movies; Versus; WE tv.
Fee: $3.99 monthly.

Pay Service 1
Pay Units: 165.
Programming (via satellite): Cinemax.
Fee: $13.02 monthly.

Pay Service 2
Pay Units: 600.
Programming (via satellite): Encore.
Fee: $1.75 monthly.

Pay Service 3
Pay Units: 159.
Programming (via satellite): HBO.
Fee: $14.01 monthly.

Pay Service 4
Pay Units: 142.
Programming (via satellite): Showtime.
Fee: $14.01 monthly.

Pay Service 5
Pay Units: 351.
Programming (via satellite): Starz.
Fee: $6.75 monthly.

Digital Pay Service 1
Pay Units: N.A.
Programming (via satellite): Cinemax (multiplexed); Encore (multiplexed); HBO (multiplexed); Showtime (multiplexed); Starz (multiplexed); The Movie Channel (multiplexed).

Video-On-Demand: No

Pay-Per-View
iN DEMAND (delivered digitally); Playboy TV (delivered digitally); Fresh (delivered digitally).

Internet Service
Operational: Yes. Began: March 1, 2002.
Broadband Service: Suddenlink High Speed Internet.
Fee: $45.95 installation; $29.95 monthly.

Telephone Service
Digital: Operational
Fee: $44.95 monthly

Miles of Plant: 105.0 (coaxial); None (fiber optic).
Regional Manager: Todd Cruthird. Plant Manager: Bobby Smith.
Ownership: Cequel Communications LLC (MSO).

BREMOND—Zito Media, 611 Vader Hill Rd, Coudersport, PA 16915. Phone: 866-879-6235. E-mail: support@zitomedia.net. Web Site: http://www.zitomedia.com. ICA: TX0723.
TV Market Ranking: Outside TV Markets (BREMOND). Franchise award date: N.A. Franchise expiration date: N.A. Began: N.A.
Channel capacity: 41 (not 2-way capable). Channels available but not in use: N.A.

Basic Service
Subscribers: 105.
Programming (received off-air): KAKW-DT (UNV) Killeen; KCEN-TV (NBC, IND) Temple; KNCT (PBS) Belton; KWKT-TV (FOX, MNT) Waco; KWTX-TV (CBS, CW) Waco; KXXV (ABC, TMO) Waco.
Programming (via satellite): A&E Networks; ABC Family Channel; AMC; Animal Planet; BET Networks; Cartoon Network; CNN; C-SPAN; Discovery Channel; Disney Channel; ESPN; ESPN 2; Fox News Channel; Fuse; FX; Great American Country; Headline News; HGTV; INSP; Lifetime; Outdoor Channel; QVC; TBS Superstation; The Learning Channel; The Weather Channel; Turner Network TV; USA Network; WGN America.
Fee: $38.10 monthly.

Pay Service 1
Pay Units: N.A.
Programming (via satellite): Encore; HBO; Showtime.

Internet Service
Operational: No.

Telephone Service
None

Miles of Plant: 12.0 (coaxial); None (fiber optic).
President: James Rigas.
Ownership: Zito Media (MSO).

BRENHAM—Suddenlink Communications, 221 E Main St, Brenham, TX 77833. Phones: 800-999-6845 (Customer service); 314-965-2020. Web Site: http://www.suddenlink.com. Also serves Washington County (portions). ICA: TX0124.
TV Market Ranking: Below 100 (BRENHAM, Washington County (portions)). Franchise award date: September 1, 1964. Franchise expiration date: N.A. Began: September 1, 1971.
Channel capacity: N.A. Channels available but not in use: N.A.

Basic Service
Subscribers: 7,461.
Programming (received off-air): KAMU-TV (PBS) College Station; KBTX-TV (CBS, CW) Bryan; KHOU (CBS) Houston; KIAH (CW) Houston; KPRC-TV (NBC) Houston; KPXB-TV (ION) Conroe; KRIV (FOX) Houston; KTRK-TV (ABC) Houston; KTXH (MNT) Houston; KUHT (PBS) Houston; KVUE (ABC) Austin; KYAZ (IND) Katy; allband FM.
Programming (via satellite): A&E Networks; BET Networks; Cartoon Network; CNN; Discovery Channel; ESPN; Food Network; Fox Deportes; Fox News Channel; Fox Sports Southwest; FX; Headline News; HGTV; National Geographic Channel; QVC; TBS Superstation; Telemundo; The Learning Channel; The Weather Channel; Trinity Broadcasting Network; Turner Network TV; TV Guide Network; Univision Studios; USA Network.
Fee: $50.00 installation; $19.95 monthly.

Expanded Basic Service 1
Subscribers: N.A.
Programming (via satellite): Animal Planet; CNBC; Comedy Central; Country Music TV; C-SPAN; E! Entertainment Television; ESPN 2; Fox Movie Channel; Great American Country; Hallmark Channel; History Channel; Lifetime; MTV; Nickelodeon; Spike TV; Syfy; Turner Classic Movies; TV Land.
Fee: $50.00 installation; $23.00 monthly.

Digital Basic Service
Subscribers: N.A.
Programming (via satellite): AmericanLife TV Network; BBC America; Bloomberg Television; Bravo; Discovery Fit & Health; DMX Music; G4; Golf Channel; GSN; Halogen Network; Independent Film Channel; Outdoor Channel; Speed; TV Guide Interactive Inc.; Versus; WE tv.
Fee: $51.99 monthly.
Pay Service 1
Pay Units: 79.
Programming (via satellite): HBO.
Fee: $10.00 installation; $10.00 monthly.
Digital Pay Service 1
Pay Units: N.A.
Programming (via satellite): Cinemax; Encore (multiplexed); HBO (multiplexed); Showtime; Starz (multiplexed); The Movie Channel.
Video-On-Demand: No
Pay-Per-View
Sports PPV (delivered digitally); Playboy TV (delivered digitally); Fresh (delivered digitally).
Internet Service
Operational: Yes. Began: January 1, 2006.
Subscribers: 200.
Broadband Service: Suddenlink High Speed Internet.
Fee: $45.95 installation; $29.95 monthly.
Telephone Service
Digital: Operational
Fee: $44.95 monthly
Miles of Plant: 118.0 (coaxial); 17.0 (fiber optic). Additional miles planned: 2.0 (coaxial).
Manager: Ken Holle.
Ownership: Cequel Communications LLC (MSO).

BRIDGE CITY—Time Warner Cable. Now served by BEAUMONT, TX [TX0022]. ICA: TX0145.

BROOKELAND—Formerly served by Cebridge Connections. No longer in operation. ICA: TX0513.

BROOKSHIRE—Formerly served by Northland Cable Television. No longer in operation. ICA: TX0353.

BROWNFIELD—Reach Broadband, 515 E Longview St, Arp, TX 75750. Phone: 800-687-1258. Web Site: http://www.reachbroadband.net. Also serves Terry County. ICA: TX0151.
TV Market Ranking: Below 100 (BROWNFIELD, Terry County (portions)); Outside TV Markets (Terry County (portions)). Franchise award date: April 5, 1979. Franchise expiration date: N.A. Began: April 5, 1989.
Channel capacity: N.A. Channels available but not in use: N.A.
Basic Service
Subscribers: 2,378.
Programming (received off-air): KAMC (ABC) Lubbock; KCBD (NBC) Lubbock; KJTV-TV (FOX) Lubbock; KLBK-TV (CBS) Lubbock; KLCW-TV (CW) Wolfforth; KRPV-DT (IND) Roswell; KTXT-TV (PBS) Lubbock; KXTQ-CA (TMO) Lubbock.
Programming (via satellite): A&E Networks; ABC Family Channel; AMC; Animal Planet; BET Networks; Bravo; Cartoon Network; CNN; Comedy Central; Country Music TV; C-SPAN; Discovery Channel; Disney Channel; E! Entertainment Television; ESPN; ESPN 2; Food Network; Fox News Channel; Fox Sports Southwest; Headline News; HGTV; History Channel; ION Television; Lifetime; MTV; Nickelodeon; Outdoor Channel; RFD-TV; Speed; Spike TV; Syfy; TBS Superstation; The Learning Channel; The Weather Channel; Trinity Broadcasting Network; Turner Network TV; TV Guide Network; TV Land; Univision Studios; USA Network; WGN America.
Fee: $29.95 installation; $38.00 monthly; $1.60 converter.
Digital Basic Service
Subscribers: N.A.
Programming (via satellite): BBC America; Bio; Bloomberg Television; CMT Pure Country; Discovery en Espanol; Discovery Health Channel; Discovery Kids Channel; DIY Network; ESPN Classic Sports; ESPNews; GSN; History Channel International; ID Investigation Discovery; Military Channel; MTV Jams; MTV2; Music Choice; Nick Jr.; Planet Green; Science; SoapNet; Style Network; The New Encore; Toon Disney; Tr3s; VH1 Classic; VH1 Soul.
Pay Service 1
Pay Units: N.A.
Programming (via satellite): Encore.
Digital Pay Service 1
Pay Units: 225.
Programming (via satellite): Cinemax (multiplexed); Encore (multiplexed); Flix; HBO (multiplexed); Showtime (multiplexed); The Movie Channel (multiplexed).
Fee: $15.00 installation; $9.00 monthly.
Video-On-Demand: No
Pay-Per-View
iN DEMAND (delivered digitally); Hot Choice (delivered digitally).
Internet Service
Operational: No.
Telephone Service
None
Miles of Plant: 56.0 (coaxial); None (fiber optic).
Regional Manager: Ronnie Stafford. Office Manager: Jan Gibson.
Ownership: RB3 LLC (MSO).

BROWNSVILLE—Time Warner Communications. Now served by PHARR, TX [TX0017]. ICA: TX0726.

BROWNWOOD—Formerly served by Brownwood TV Cable Service Inc. No longer in operation. ICA: TX0059.

BRUNI—Windjammer Cable, 8500 W 110th St, Ste 600, Overland Park, KS 66210. Phone: 888-495-2881. Fax: 913-563-5454. Web Site: http://www.windjammercable.com. ICA: TX0680.
TV Market Ranking: Outside TV Markets (BRUNI). Franchise award date: N.A. Franchise expiration date: N.A. Began: N.A.
Channel capacity: N.A. Channels available but not in use: N.A.
Basic Service
Subscribers: 101.
Programming (received off-air): KGNS-TV (CW, NBC, TMO) Laredo; KLDO-TV (FOX, UNV) Laredo; KVTV (CBS) Laredo.
Programming (via satellite): A&E Networks; Animal Planet; Cartoon Network; CNN; Country Music TV; Discovery Channel; Disney Channel; ESPN; ESPN 2; Fox News Channel; Fox Sports Southwest; FX; GalaVision; KABB (FOX) San Antonio; Lifetime; MTV; Nickelodeon; Spike TV; TBS Superstation; Telefutura; Telemundo; The Learning Channel; The Weather Channel; Turner Classic Movies; Turner Network TV; USA Network; WABC-TV (ABC) New York.
Fee: $50.51 installation; $40.99 monthly.

Pay Service 1
Pay Units: 53.
Programming (via satellite): HBO; Showtime.
Fee: $12.95 monthly (each).
Pay Service 2
Pay Units: N.A.
Programming (via satellite): Encore.
Fee: $3.75 monthly.
Internet Service
Operational: No.
Telephone Service
None
Miles of Plant: 4.0 (coaxial); None (fiber optic).
General Manager: Timothy Evard. Operations Director: Belinda Graham. Engineering Director: Mike Earehart. Finance & Accounting Director: Cindy Johnson.
Ownership: Windjammer Communications LLC (MSO).

BRYAN—Suddenlink Communications, 4114 E 29th St, Bryan, TX 77802-4302. Phones: 888-822-5151; 979-846-2229. Fax: 979-268-0139. Web Site: http://www.suddenlink.com. Also serves Brazos County (unincorporated areas) & College Station. ICA: TX0020.
TV Market Ranking: Below 100 (Brazos County (unincorporated areas), BRYAN, College Station). Franchise award date: July 1, 1953. Franchise expiration date: N.A. Began: January 1, 1954.
Channel capacity: N.A. Channels available but not in use: N.A.
Basic Service
Subscribers: 51,162.
Programming (received off-air): KAGS-LD Bryan; KAMU-TV (PBS) College Station; KBTX-TV (CBS, CW) Bryan; KCEN-TV (NBC, IND) Temple; KRHD-CD (ABC) Bryan; KTRK-TV (ABC) Houston; KUHT (PBS) Houston; KXXV (ABC, TMO) Waco; KYLE-TV (FOX) Bryan; 21 FMs.
Programming (via satellite): C-SPAN; CW+; QVC; TBS Superstation; TV Guide Network; WGN America.
Fee: $35.00 installation; $22.16 monthly.
Expanded Basic Service 1
Subscribers: N.A.
Programming (via satellite): A&E Networks; ABC Family Channel; AMC; Animal Planet; BET Networks; Bravo; Cartoon Network; CNBC; CNN; Comedy Central; Country Music TV; C-SPAN 2; Discovery Channel; Disney Channel; E! Entertainment Television; ESPN; ESPN 2; Eternal Word TV Network; Food Network; Fox News Channel; Fox Sports Southwest; FX; GalaVision; Great American Country; Headline News; HGTV; History Channel; INSP; Jewelry Television; Lifetime; Lifetime Movie Network; MSNBC; MTV; MTV2; Nickelodeon; Outdoor Channel; Speed; Spike TV; Syfy; The Learning Channel; The Weather Channel; Travel Channel; Trinity Broadcasting Network; truTV; Turner Classic Movies; Turner Network TV; TV Land; USA Network; Versus; VH1.
Fee: $20.31 monthly.
Digital Basic Service
Subscribers: N.A.
Programming (via satellite): A&E HD; Bandamax; BBC America; Bio; Bloomberg Television; Boomerang; CBS Sports Network; Cine Latino; Cine Mexicano; CMT Pure Country; CNN en Espanol; Cooking Channel; Cox Sports Television; De Pelicula; De Pelicula Clasico; Discovery en Espanol; Discovery Health Channel; Discovery Home Channel; Discovery Kids Channel; DIY Network; Encore (multiplexed); ESPN 2 HD; ESPN Classic Sports; ESPN Deportes; ESPN HD; ESPN U; ESPNews; EWTN en Espanol; FamilyNet; Food Network HD; Fox Deportes; Fox Reality Channel; Fox Soccer; FSN HD; Fuel TV; Fuse; G4; GalaVision; GMC; Golf Channel; GSN; Hallmark Channel; Halogen Network; HD Theater; HDNet; HDNet Movies; HGTV HD; History Channel en Espanol; History Channel International; ID Investigation Discovery; Independent Film Channel; Latele Novela Network; Military Channel; MTV Hits; mtvU; mun2 television; Music Choice; National Geographic Channel; National Geographic Channel HD Network; Nick Jr.; NickToons en Espanol; NickToons TV; Nuvo TV; Oxygen; Palladia; Ritmoson Latino; Science; SoapNet; Sorpresa; Style Network; Sundance Channel; Sur Network; TBN Enlace USA; TeenNick; Telefutura; Telehit; Tennis Channel; Toon Disney; Toon Disney en Espanol; Tr3s; Turner Network TV HD; TV Chile; TV One; Universal HD; VH1 Classic; Video Rola; WE tv; Weatherscan.
Fee: $10.00 monthly.
Digital Pay Service 1
Pay Units: N.A.
Programming (via satellite): Cinemax (multiplexed); HBO (multiplexed); HBO HD; HBO Latino; Showtime (multiplexed); Showtime HD; Starz (multiplexed); Starz HDTV; The Movie Channel (multiplexed).
Fee: $21.95 monthly.
Video-On-Demand: No
Pay-Per-View
iN DEMAND (delivered digitally); Fresh (delivered digitally); Shorteez (delivered digitally); Playboy TV (delivered digitally); Club Jenna (delivered digitally); Hot Choice (delivered digitally); Spice: Xcess (delivered digitally); Playboy en Espanol (delivered digitally).
Internet Service
Operational: Yes.
Broadband Service: Suddenlink High Speed Internet.
Fee: $49.95 installation; $24.95 monthly.
Telephone Service
Digital: Operational
Fee: $48.95 monthly
Miles of Plant: 700.0 (coaxial); 50.0 (fiber optic).
Regional Vice President: Jim Ruel. Manager: Tom Way. Chief Technician: Mike Lavender. Customer Service Manager: Mike Kehere.
Ownership: Cequel Communications LLC (MSO).

BUCKHOLTS—Formerly served by National Cable Inc. No longer in operation. ICA: TX0903.

BUFFALO—Northland Cable Television, 515 W Tyler St, PO Box 112, Mexia, TX 76667-0112. Phones: 800-792-3087; 254-562-2872. Fax: 254-562-6454. E-mail: mexia@northlandcabletv.com. Web Site: http://www.northlandcabletv.com. ICA: TX0426.

TV Market Ranking: Outside TV Markets (BUFFALO). Franchise award date: June 2, 1975. Franchise expiration date: N.A. Began: December 1, 1975.

Channel capacity: 36 (not 2-way capable). Channels available but not in use: N.A.

Basic Service

Subscribers: N.A.

Programming (received off-air): KBTX-TV (CBS, CW) Bryan; KCEN-TV (NBC, IND) Temple; KERA-TV (PBS) Dallas; KTVT (CBS) Fort Worth; KWKT-TV (FOX, MNT) Waco; KWTX-TV (CBS, CW) Waco; KXAS-TV (NBC) Fort Worth; KXTX-TV (TMO) Dallas; KXXV (ABC, TMO) Waco; WFAA (ABC) Dallas.

Programming (via satellite): A&E Networks; AMC; BET Networks; Cartoon Network; CNN; Country Music TV; C-SPAN; Discovery Channel; ESPN; Fox News Channel; Fox Sports Southwest; Headline News; HGTV; Lifetime; QVC; Spike TV; TBS Superstation; The Weather Channel; Trinity Broadcasting Network; Turner Network TV; USA Network.

Fee: $49.95 installation; $31.99 monthly.

Pay Service 1

Pay Units: N.A.

Programming (via satellite): Cinemax; HBO; Showtime.

Fee: $11.00 monthly (HBO or Showtime).

Internet Service

Operational: No.

Telephone Service

None

Miles of Plant: 17.0 (coaxial); None (fiber optic).

Manager: Brent Richey. Chief Technician: Joe Lopez. Office Manager: Pamela Elliott.

Ownership: Northland Communications Corp. (MSO).

BUFFALO SPRINGS LAKE—Formerly served by Almega Cable. No longer in operation. ICA: TX0574.

BUNA—Formerly served by Cable Plus Inc. No longer in operation. ICA: TX0983.

BURKBURNETT—Suddenlink Communications, 12444 Powerscourt Dr, Saint Louis, MO 63131-3660. Phones: 877-423-2743 (Customer service); 314-315-9346; 314-965-2020. Web Site: http://www.suddenlink.com. Also serves Iowa Park. ICA: TX0154.

TV Market Ranking: Below 100 (BURKBURNETT, Iowa Park). Franchise award date: N.A. Franchise expiration date: N.A. Began: January 1, 1980.

Channel capacity: 37 (operating 2-way). Channels available but not in use: N.A.

Basic Service

Subscribers: 3,257.

Programming (received off-air): KAUZ-TV (CBS, CW) Wichita Falls; KFDX-TV (NBC) Wichita Falls; KJBO-LP (MNT) Wichita Falls; KJTL (FOX) Wichita Falls; KSWO-TV (ABC, TMO) Lawton; 2 FMs.

Programming (via satellite): INSP; QVC.

Programming (via translator): K44GS Wichita Falls.

Fee: $39.95 installation; $19.95 monthly.

Expanded Basic Service 1

Subscribers: 3,027.

Programming (via satellite): A&E Networks; ABC Family Channel; AMC; Animal Planet; Bravo; Cartoon Network; Celebrity Shopping Network; CNBC; CNN; Comedy Central; C-SPAN; Discovery Channel; Disney Channel; E! Entertainment Television; ESPN; ESPN 2; Food Network; Fox News Channel; Fox Sports Southwest; FX; GalaVision; Golf Channel; Great American Country; Hallmark Channel; Headline News; HGTV; History Channel; Lifetime; MSNBC; MTV; National Geographic Channel; Nickelodeon; Outdoor Channel; Speed; Spike TV; Syfy; TBS Superstation; The Learning Channel; The Weather Channel; Travel Channel; truTV; Turner Classic Movies; Turner Network TV; TV Guide Network; TV Land; Univision Studios; USA Network; VH1.

Fee: $39.95 installation; $25.00 monthly.

Digital Basic Service

Subscribers: N.A.

Programming (via satellite): BBC America; Bio; Bloomberg Television; cloo; Country Music TV; Discovery Digital Networks; DMX Music; ESPN Classic Sports; ESPNews; Fuse; G4; GAS; GSN; History Channel International; Independent Film Channel; Lifetime Movie Network; MTV Networks Digital Suite; Nick Jr.; NickToons TV; Style Network; Toon Disney; Trinity Broadcasting Network; Versus; WE tv.

Pay Service 1

Pay Units: 293.

Programming (via satellite): Cinemax.

Fee: $12.84 monthly.

Pay Service 2

Pay Units: 811.

Programming (via satellite): Encore.

Fee: $1.75 monthly.

Pay Service 3

Pay Units: 404.

Programming (via satellite): HBO.

Fee: $13.83 monthly.

Pay Service 4

Pay Units: 498.

Programming (via satellite): Starz.

Fee: $6.75 monthly.

Pay Service 5

Pay Units: N.A.

Programming (via satellite): Showtime.

Digital Pay Service 1

Pay Units: N.A.

Programming (via satellite): Cinemax (multiplexed); Encore (multiplexed); HBO (multiplexed); Showtime (multiplexed); Starz; The Movie Channel (multiplexed).

Video-On-Demand: No

Pay-Per-View

iN DEMAND (delivered digitally); Playboy TV (delivered digitally); Fresh (delivered digitally).

Internet Service

Operational: Yes. Began: April 1, 2002.

Broadband Service: Suddenlink High Speed Internet.

Fee: $45.95 installation; $29.95 monthly.

Telephone Service

Digital: Operational

Fee: $44.95 monthly

Miles of Plant: 102.0 (coaxial); None (fiber optic).

Regional Manager: Todd Cruthird. Area Manager: Larry Bryant. Plant Manager: Ron Johnson.

Ownership: Cequel Communications LLC (MSO).

BURLESON—Pathway. Formerly [TX0103]. This cable system has converted to IPTV, PO Box 1298, Joshua, TX 76058-1298. Phone: 817-484-2222. Fax: 817-447-0169. Web Site: http://www.usapathway.com. ICA: TX5530.

Channel capacity: N.A. Channels available but not in use: N.A.

Internet Service

Operational: Yes.

Telephone Service

Digital: Operational

BURLESON—Pathway. This cable system has converted to IPTV. See Burleson, TX [TX5530] & Joshua, TX [TX5531]. ICA: TX0103.

BURTON—Formerly served by Reveille Broadband. No longer in operation. ICA: TX0409.

BYERS—Formerly served by Byers-Petrolia Cable TV/North Texas Telephone Co. No longer in operation. ICA: TX0448.

CACTUS—Elk River TV Cable Co., 509 S Main St, PO Box 154, Troy, ID 83871. Phone: 208-369-4652. Web Site: http://www.elkrivertv.net. Also serves Etter. ICA: TX0730.

TV Market Ranking: Outside TV Markets (CACTUS, Etter). Franchise award date: N.A. Franchise expiration date: N.A. Began: N.A.

Channel capacity: 28 (not 2-way capable). Channels available but not in use: N.A.

Basic Service

Subscribers: N.A. Included in San Jon, NM

Programming (received off-air): KAMR-TV (NBC) Amarillo; KCIT (FOX) Amarillo; KFDA-TV (CBS) Amarillo; KVII-TV (ABC, CW) Amarillo.

Programming (via satellite): TBS Superstation; Turner Network TV.

Fee: $25.00 installation; $29.96 monthly.

Pay Service 1

Pay Units: N.A.

Programming (via satellite): Cinemax; Showtime.

Fee: $7.00 monthly (each).

Video-On-Demand: No

Internet Service

Operational: No.

Telephone Service

None

Manager: Dave & Leslie McGraw. Chief Technician: Justin McGraw.

Ownership: Elk River TV Cable Co. (MSO).

CADDO PEAK—North Texas Broadband, PO Box 676, Aubery, TX 76227. Phone: 940-365-2930. Web Site: http://northtxbroadband.com. Also serves Johnson County (portions) & Tarrant County (portions). ICA: TX0259.

TV Market Ranking: 12 (CADDO PEAK, Johnson County (portions), Tarrant County (portions)). Franchise award date: N.A. Franchise expiration date: N.A. Began: N.A.

Channel capacity: 36 (not 2-way capable). Channels available but not in use: N.A.

Basic Service

Subscribers: 55.

Programming (received off-air): KDAF (CW, IND) Dallas; KDFI (MNT) Dallas; KDFW-DT (FOX) Dallas; KERA-TV (PBS) Dallas; KTVT (CBS) Fort Worth; KTXA (IND) Fort Worth; KXAS-TV (NBC) Fort Worth; KXTX-TV (TMO) Dallas; WFAA (ABC) Dallas.

Programming (via satellite): A&E Networks; ABC Family Channel; AmericanLife TV Network; CNN; Country Music TV; Discovery Channel; Disney Channel; ESPN; Fox Sports Southwest; Headline News; Lifetime; Nickelodeon; Spike TV; TBS Superstation; Turner Network TV; USA Network; WGN America.

Fee: $40.00 installation; $39.95 monthly.

Pay Service 1

Pay Units: N.A.

Programming (via satellite): Cinemax; HBO; Showtime.

Video-On-Demand: No

Internet Service

Operational: Yes.

Fee: $50.00 installation; $24.95 monthly; $5.00 modem lease; $55.00 modem purchase.

Telephone Service

None

Miles of Plant: 69.0 (coaxial); None (fiber optic).

Manager: Curtis Davis.

Ownership: North Texas Broadband.

CALDWELL—Suddenlink Communications, 12444 Powerscourt Dr, Saint Louis, MO 63131-3660. Phone: 314-965-2020. Web Site: http://www.suddenlink.com. ICA: TX0206.

TV Market Ranking: Below 100 (CALDWELL). Franchise award date: October 13, 1970. Franchise expiration date: N.A. Began: October 1, 1971.

Channel capacity: N.A. Channels available but not in use: N.A.

Basic Service

Subscribers: 1,066.

Programming (received off-air): KAMU-TV (PBS) College Station; KBTX-TV (CBS, CW) Bryan; KCEN-TV (NBC, IND) Temple; KIAH (CW) Houston; KTBC (FOX) Austin; KTXH (MNT) Houston; KVUE (ABC) Austin; KWKT-TV (FOX, MNT) Waco; KXAN-TV (NBC) Austin; KYLE-TV (FOX) Bryan; allband FM.

Programming (via satellite): A&E Networks; ABC Family Channel; Cartoon Network; CNN; Country Music TV; Discovery Channel; Disney Channel; ESPN; Fox News Channel; Fox Sports Southwest; Headline News; HGTV; History Channel; Lifetime; Nickelodeon; QVC; Spike TV; TBS Superstation; The Learning Channel; The Weather Channel; Trinity Broadcasting Network; Turner Network TV; TV Land; USA Network; WGN America.

Fee: $39.95 installation; $19.95 monthly.

Pay Service 1

Pay Units: 170.

Programming (via satellite): HBO.

Fee: $10.95 monthly.

Pay Service 2

Pay Units: 122.

Programming (via satellite): Showtime.

Fee: $9.95 monthly.

Pay Service 3

Pay Units: 128.

Programming (via satellite): The Movie Channel.

Fee: $7.95 monthly.

Internet Service

Operational: Yes. Began: May 5, 2003.

Broadband Service: Suddenlink High Speed Internet.

Fee: $45.95 installation; $29.95 monthly.

Telephone Service

Digital: Operational

Fee: $44.95 monthly

Miles of Plant: 32.0 (coaxial); None (fiber optic).

Regional Manager: Todd Cruthird. Regional Marketing Manager: Beverly Gambell. Plant Manager: Carl Gillit.

Ownership: Cequel Communications LLC (MSO).

CALVERT—Zito Media, 611 Vader Hill Rd, Coudersport, PA 16915. Phone: 866-879-6235. E-mail: support@zitomedia.net. Web Site: http://www.zitomedia.com. ICA: TX0731.

TV Market Ranking: Below 100 (CALVERT). Franchise award date: N.A. Franchise expiration date: November 30, 2011. Began: N.A.

Channel capacity: 54 (not 2-way capable). Channels available but not in use: N.A.

Basic Service

Subscribers: 145.

Programming (received off-air): KBTX-TV (CBS, CW) Bryan; KCEN-TV (NBC, IND) Temple; KNCT (PBS) Belton; KWKT-TV (FOX, MNT) Waco; KWTX-TV (CBS, CW) Waco; KXXV (ABC, TMO) Waco.

Programming (via satellite): A&E Networks; ABC Family Channel; Animal Planet; BET Networks; Cartoon Network; CNN; C-SPAN; Discovery Channel; Disney Channel; ESPN; ESPN 2; Fox News Channel; Fuse; FX; Great American Country; Headline News; HGTV; History Channel; INSP; Lifetime; Outdoor Channel; QVC; TBS Superstation; The Learning Channel; The Weather Channel; Turner Classic Movies; Turner Network TV; USA Network; WGN America.

Fee: $38.25 monthly.

Pay Service 1

Pay Units: N.A.

Programming (via satellite): Encore; HBO; Showtime.

Internet Service

Operational: No.

Telephone Service

None

Miles of Plant: 9.0 (coaxial); None (fiber optic).

President: James Rigas.

Ownership: Zito Media (MSO).

CAMERON—Zito Media, 611 Vader Hill Rd, Coudersport, PA 16915. Phone: 866-879-6235. E-mail: support@zitomedia.net. Web Site: http://www.zitomedia.com. Also serves Milam County (portions). ICA: TX0160.

TV Market Ranking: Below 100 (CAMERON); Outside TV Markets (Milam County (portions)). Franchise award date: N.A. Franchise expiration date: N.A. Began: January 1, 1973.

Channel capacity: 61 (operating 2-way). Channels available but not in use: N.A.

Basic Service

Subscribers: 935.

Programming (received off-air): KCEN-TV (NBC, IND) Temple; KEYE-TV (CBS, TMO) Austin; KLRU (PBS) Austin; KNCT (PBS) Belton; KVUE (ABC) Austin; KWKT-TV (FOX, MNT) Waco; KWTX-TV (CBS, CW) Waco; KXXV (ABC, TMO) Waco; allband FM.

Programming (via satellite): A&E Networks; ABC Family Channel; AMC; Animal Planet; BET Networks; Cartoon Network; CNBC; CNN; Comedy Central; C-SPAN; Discovery Channel; Disney Channel; E! Entertainment Television; ESPN; Food Network; Fox News Channel; Fox Sports Southwest; Fuse; FX; Great American Country; Hallmark Channel; Headline News; HGTV; History Channel; INSP; Lifetime; QVC; Speed; TBS Superstation; The Learning Channel; The Weather Channel; Toon Disney; Travel Channel; Turner Classic Movies; Turner Network TV; USA Network; WGN America.

Fee: $30.00 installation; $41.60 monthly.

Digital Basic Service

Subscribers: 205.

Programming (via satellite): AmericanLife TV Network; BBC America; Bio; Bloomberg Television; Discovery Fit & Health; DMX Music; ESPN Classic Sports; ESPNews; Fox Sports World; FSN Digital Atlantic; FSN Digital Central; FSN Digital Pacific; G4; Golf Channel; GSN; History Channel International; National Geographic Channel; Outdoor Channel; Style Network; Syfy; WE tv.

Fee: $13.95 monthly.

Digital Expanded Basic Service

Subscribers: N.A.

Programming (via satellite): DMX Music; Encore; Fox Movie Channel; Lifetime Movie Network.

Fee: $13.95 monthly.

Pay Service 1

Pay Units: 1,026.

Programming (via satellite): HBO; Showtime.

Fee: $12.00 monthly (each).

Pay Service 2

Pay Units: N.A.

Programming (via satellite): Cinemax; The Movie Channel.

Digital Pay Service 1

Pay Units: N.A.

Programming (via satellite): Cinemax (multiplexed); Flix; HBO (multiplexed); Showtime (multiplexed); The Movie Channel (multiplexed).

Fee: $13.90 monthly.

Video-On-Demand: No

Pay-Per-View

Addressable homes: 191.

ESPN Now (delivered digitally); Hot Choice (delivered digitally); Movies (delivered digitally); Playboy TV (delivered digitally); Fresh (delivered digitally); Shorteez (delivered digitally); sports (delivered digitally); Urban Xtra (delivered digitally).

Internet Service

Operational: Yes.

Subscribers: 125.

Fee: $49.95 installation; $44.95 monthly.

Telephone Service

None

Miles of Plant: 41.0 (coaxial); None (fiber optic).

President: James Rigas.

Ownership: Zito Media (MSO).

CAMERON COUNTY (southern portion)—Formerly served by Ridgewood Cablevision. No longer in operation. ICA: TX1018.

CAMP WOODS—Formerly served by Cebridge Connections. No longer in operation. ICA: TX0559.

CAMPBELL—Formerly served by CableSouth Inc. No longer in operation. ICA: TX0581.

CANADIAN—Suddenlink Communications, 12444 Powerscourt Dr, Saint Louis, MO 63131-3660. Phones: 800-999-6845 (Customer service); 314-965-2020. Fax: 903-561-5485. Web Site: http://www.suddenlink.com. Also serves Hemphill County (portions). ICA: TX0334.

TV Market Ranking: Outside TV Markets (CANADIAN, Hemphill County (portions)). Franchise award date: N.A. Franchise expiration date: N.A. Began: September 1, 1958.

Channel capacity: N.A. Channels available but not in use: N.A.

Basic Service

Subscribers: 757.

Programming (received off-air): KCIT (FOX) Amarillo; KETA-TV (PBS) Oklahoma City.

Programming (via microwave): KAMR-TV (NBC) Amarillo; KFDA-TV (CBS) Amarillo; KVII-TV (ABC, CW) Amarillo.

Programming (via satellite): A&E Networks; ABC Family Channel; AMC; Animal Planet; CNN; Country Music TV; C-SPAN; Discovery Channel; Disney Channel; E! Entertainment Television; ESPN; Fox News Channel; Fox Sports Southwest; Headline News; History Channel; Lifetime; Nickelodeon; QVC; Spike TV; TBS Superstation; The Learning Channel; The Weather Channel; Trinity Broadcasting Network; Turner Network TV; TV Land; USA Network; WGN America.

Fee: $39.95 installation; $19.95 monthly.

Pay Service 1

Pay Units: 26.

Programming (via satellite): Cinemax.

Fee: $9.95 monthly.

Pay Service 2

Pay Units: 75.

Programming (via satellite): HBO.

Fee: $10.95 monthly.

Pay Service 3

Pay Units: 71.

Programming (via satellite): Showtime.

Fee: $9.95 monthly.

Pay Service 4

Pay Units: 111.

Programming (via satellite): The Movie Channel.

Fee: $7.95 monthly.

Video-On-Demand: No

Internet Service

Operational: Yes. Began: June 23, 2003.

Broadband Service: Suddenlink High Speed Internet.

Fee: $49.95 installation; $38.95 monthly.

Telephone Service

None

Miles of Plant: 23.0 (coaxial); None (fiber optic).

Marketing Director: Beverly Gambell. Chief Technician: Rick Rattan.

Ownership: Cequel Communications LLC (MSO).

CANTON—East Texas Cable Co., 24285 State Hwy 64, Canton, TX 75103-6187. Phone: 903-567-2260. Fax: 903-567-4048. E-mail: info@etcable.net. Web Site: http://www.etcable.net. ICA: TX0280.

TV Market Ranking: Outside TV Markets (CANTON). Franchise award date: N.A. Franchise expiration date: N.A. Began: July 1, 1983.

Channel capacity: 35 (operating 2-way). Channels available but not in use: N.A.

Basic Service

Subscribers: 1,425.

Programming (received off-air): KDAF (CW, IND) Dallas; KDFI (MNT) Dallas; KDFW-DT (FOX) Dallas; KDTX-TV (TBN) Dallas; KERA-TV (PBS) Dallas; KETK-TV (NBC) Jacksonville; KLTV (ABC, TMO) Tyler; KPDX (MNT) Vancouver; KSTR-DT (TEL) Irving; KTVT (CBS) Fort Worth; KTXA (IND) Fort Worth; KXAS-TV (NBC) Fort Worth; WFAA (ABC) Dallas.

Programming (via satellite): The Weather Channel; Univision Studios; WGN America.

Fee: $39.50 installation; $13.25 monthly.

Expanded Basic Service 1

Subscribers: N.A.

Programming (via satellite): A&E Networks; ABC Family Channel; AMC; Animal Planet; Bloomberg Television; Cartoon Network; CNBC; CNN; Country Music TV; C-SPAN; C-SPAN 2; Discovery Channel; Fox News Channel; Great American Country; Headline News; History Channel; Lifetime; MTV; National Geographic Channel; Speed; Spike TV; Syfy; TBS Superstation; The Learning Channel; Toon Disney; Travel Channel; Turner Classic Movies; TV Land; VH1; WE tv.

Fee: $25.00 monthly.

Expanded Basic Service 2

Subscribers: N.A.

Programming (via satellite): Disney Channel; ESPN; ESPN 2; Fox Sports Southwest; FX; HGTV; Nickelodeon; Turner Network TV; USA Network.

Fee: $9.50 monthly.

Digital Basic Service

Subscribers: N.A.

Programming (via satellite): AmericanLife TV Network; BBC America; Bio; Bloomberg Television; cloo; Current; Discovery Digital Networks; DMX Music; ESPN 2; ESPN Classic Sports; ESPNews; Fox Movie Channel; FSN Digital Atlantic; FSN Digital Central; FSN Digital Pacific; G4; GAS; Golf Channel; Great American Country; GSN; Halogen Network; HGTV; History Channel; History Channel International; MBC America; MTV Networks Digital Suite; National Geographic Channel; Nick Jr.; NickToons TV; Outdoor Channel; ShopNBC; Speed; Style Network; Syfy; The Word Network; Trinity Broadcasting Network; Turner Classic Movies; WE tv.

Fee: $20.00 monthly.

Pay Service 1

Pay Units: N.A.

Programming (via satellite): Cinemax; HBO; Showtime.

Fee: $8.95 monthly (Cinemax), $9.95 monthly (Showtime), $10.95 monthly (HBO).

Digital Pay Service 1

Pay Units: N.A.

Programming (via satellite): Cinemax (multiplexed); Encore (multiplexed); Flix; HBO (multiplexed); Showtime (multiplexed); Starz (multiplexed); Sundance Channel; The Movie Channel (multiplexed).

Fee: $7.95 monthly (Cinemax), $9.95 monthly (HBO), $10.95 monthly (Showtime/TMC or Starz/Encore).

Video-On-Demand: Yes

Pay-Per-View

iN DEMAND (delivered digitally); Hot Choice (delivered digitally); Playboy TV (delivered digitally); Fresh (delivered digitally); Shorteez (delivered digitally); ESPN Extra (delivered digitally); Sports PPV (delivered digitally).

Internet Service

Operational: Yes.

Subscribers: 720.

Broadband Service: In-house.

Fee: $25.95-$50.95 monthly; $70.00 modem purchase.

Telephone Service
Digital: Operational
Fee: $30.99 monthly
Miles of Plant: 54.0 (coaxial); None (fiber optic).
Manager & Chief Technician: Jim Roby. Office Manager: Stacey McGinnes.
Ownership: Jim Roby.

CANYON LAKE—GVTC Communications, 36101 FM 3159, New Braunfels, TX 78132-5900. Phone: 830-249-8181. Fax: 830-249-8107. E-mail: webhelp@gvtc.com. Web Site: http://www.gvtc.com. Also serves Comal County (portions). ICA: TX0199.
TV Market Ranking: 45 (CANYON LAKE, Comal County (portions)); Below 100 (Comal County (portions)); Outside TV Markets (Comal County (portions)). Franchise award date: N.A. Franchise expiration date: N.A. Began: January 1, 1983.
Channel capacity: 35 (not 2-way capable). Channels available but not in use: N.A.
Basic Service
Subscribers: 2,957.
Programming (received off-air): KABB (FOX) San Antonio; KCWX (IND, MNT) Fredericksburg; KENS (CBS) San Antonio; KHCE-TV (TBN) San Antonio; KLRN (PBS) San Antonio; KMYS (CW) Kerrville; KPXL-TV (ION) Uvalde; KSAT-TV (ABC) San Antonio; KVDA (TMO) San Antonio; KWEX-DT (UNV) San Antonio; WOAI-TV (NBC) San Antonio.
Programming (via satellite): A&E Networks; ABC Family Channel; AMC; CNBC; CNN; Country Music TV; C-SPAN; Discovery Channel; Disney Channel; ESPN; Fox News Channel; Fox Sports Southwest; Headline News; History Channel; Lifetime; MTV; Nickelodeon; QVC; Spike TV; TBS Superstation; The Learning Channel; The Weather Channel; Turner Network TV; USA Network; WGN America.
Fee: $25.00 installation; $61.95 monthly; $1.50 converter.
Digital Basic Service
Subscribers: 120.
Programming (via satellite): BBC America; Bio; Bravo; Discovery Digital Networks; DMX Music; Encore (multiplexed); ESPN 2; ESPN Classic Sports; Fox Sports World; GAS; Golf Channel; GSN; HGTV; History Channel International; Independent Film Channel; Lifetime Movie Network; National Geographic Channel; Nick Jr.; Speed; Syfy; Toon Disney; Turner Classic Movies; Versus; VH1 Classic; VH1 Country; WE tv.
Fee: $27.00 monthly.
Digital Pay Service 1
Pay Units: N.A.
Programming (via satellite): HBO (multiplexed); Showtime (multiplexed); Starz (multiplexed); The Movie Channel (multiplexed).
Fee: $14.95 monthly (each).
Video-On-Demand: No
Pay-Per-View
Addressable homes: 120.
iN DEMAND (delivered digitally).
Internet Service
Operational: Yes.
Fee: $19.95-$199.95 monthly.
Telephone Service
Digital: Operational
Miles of Plant: 90.0 (coaxial); None (fiber optic).
President & Chief Executive Officer: Ritchie Sorrells. Vice President, Sales & Marketing: Jeff Mnick.
Ownership: Guadalupe Valley Communications Systems LP (MSO).

CARLSBAD—Formerly served by Cebridge Connections. No longer in operation. ICA: TX0733.

CARMINE—Formerly served by Reveille Broadband. No longer in operation. ICA: TX0653.

CAROLINA COVE—Cablevision of Walker County, 1304 10th St, Huntsville, TX 77320. Phone: 936-291-2288. Fax: 936-291-0890. Web Site: http://www.walkercountycabletv.com. Also serves Walker County (portions). ICA: TX0568.
TV Market Ranking: Below 100 (CAROLINA COVE, Walker County (portions)). Franchise award date: N.A. Franchise expiration date: N.A. Began: February 1, 1985.
Channel capacity: 36 (not 2-way capable). Channels available but not in use: N.A.
Basic Service
Subscribers: 1,078.
Programming (received off-air): KBTX-TV (CBS, CW) Bryan; KHOU (CBS) Houston; KIAH (CW) Houston; KPRC-TV (NBC) Houston; KRIV (FOX) Houston; KTBU (IND) Conroe; KTRK-TV (ABC) Houston; KTXH (MNT) Houston; KUHT (PBS) Houston; KXLN-DT (UNV) Rosenberg.
Programming (via satellite): A&E Networks; ABC Family Channel; AMC; BET Networks; Bloomberg Television; CNBC; CNN; Country Music TV; Discovery Channel; Discovery Fit & Health; Disney Channel; ESPN; ESPN 2; Fox Sports Southwest; Headline News; History Channel; ION Television; Lifetime; Nickelodeon; Spike TV; Syfy; TBS Superstation; The Weather Channel; Trinity Broadcasting Network; Turner Classic Movies; Turner Network TV; USA Network; VH1.
Fee: $29.95 installation; $32.79 monthly.
Digital Basic Service
Subscribers: N.A.
Programming (via satellite): AmericanLife TV Network; BBC America; Bio; Discovery Digital Networks; DMX Music; ESPN 2; ESPN Classic Sports; ESPNews; Fox Movie Channel; Fox Sports World; Fuse; G4; GAS; Golf Channel; GSN; Halogen Network; HGTV; History Channel; History Channel International; Lifetime Movie Network; MTV Networks Digital Suite; National Geographic Channel; Nick Jr.; Outdoor Channel; Ovation; Speed; Style Network; Sundance Channel; Toon Disney; Trinity Broadcasting Network; Versus; WE tv.
Fee: $12.07 monthly.
Digital Pay Service 1
Pay Units: 18.
Programming (via satellite): Cinemax (multiplexed); Encore (multiplexed); HBO (multiplexed); Showtime (multiplexed); Starz (multiplexed); The Movie Channel (multiplexed).
Fee: $11.99 monthly (Showtime/TMC or Starz/Encore), $13.99 monthly (Cinemax/HBO).
Video-On-Demand: No
Pay-Per-View
iN DEMAND (delivered digitally); ESPN Now (delivered digitally); Sports PPV (delivered digitally).
Internet Service
Operational: No.
Telephone Service
None
Miles of Plant: 49.0 (coaxial); None (fiber optic).
General Manager: Caroline Walker. Chief Technician: Kenny Hanson.
Ownership: Cablevision of Walker County (MSO).

CARROLLTON—Charter Communications, 15100 Trinity Blvd, Ste 500, Fort Worth, TX 76155. Phones: 817-298-3600 (Fort Worth office); 940-898-0583 (Denton office). Web Site: http://www.charter.com. Also serves Addison. ICA: TX0734.
TV Market Ranking: 12 (Addison, CARROLLTON). Franchise award date: January 1, 1987. Franchise expiration date: N.A. Began: June 1, 1987.
Channel capacity: 55 (not 2-way capable). Channels available but not in use: N.A.
Basic Service
Subscribers: 1,803.
Programming (received off-air): KAZD (IND) Lake Dallas; KDAF (CW, IND) Dallas; KDFI (MNT) Dallas; KDFW-DT (FOX) Dallas; KDTN (ETV) Denton; KDTX-TV (TBN) Dallas; KERA-TV (PBS) Dallas; KFWD (IND) Fort Worth; KMPX (IND) Decatur; KPXD-TV (ION) Arlington; KSTR-DT (TEL) Irving; KTVT (CBS) Fort Worth; KTXA (IND) Fort Worth; KUVN-DT (UNV) Garland; KXAS-TV (NBC) Fort Worth; KXTX-TV (TMO) Dallas; WFAA (ABC) Dallas.
Programming (via satellite): C-SPAN; GalaVision; QVC; TBS Superstation.
Fee: $29.99 installation.
Expanded Basic Service 1
Subscribers: N.A.
Programming (via satellite): A&E Networks; ABC Family Channel; AMC; Animal Planet; BET Networks; Bravo; CNBC; CNN; Comedy Central; Country Music TV; Discovery Channel; Disney Channel; E! Entertainment Television; ESPN; ESPN 2; Fox News Channel; Fox Sports Southwest; Headline News; HGTV; History Channel; Lifetime; MTV; Nickelodeon; Spike TV; The Learning Channel; The Weather Channel; Toon Disney; Turner Network TV; TV Land; USA Network; VH1.
Fee: $48.99 monthly.
Digital Basic Service
Subscribers: N.A.
Programming (via satellite): BBC America; Bio; Bloomberg Television; Discovery Digital Networks; DIY Network; ESPN Classic Sports; G4; GAS; History Channel International; Lifetime Movie Network; MTV Networks Digital Suite; Music Choice; National Geographic Channel; Nick Jr.; SoapNet; Sundance Channel; WE tv.
Digital Expanded Basic Service
Subscribers: N.A.
Programming (via satellite): Fox Soccer; FSN Digital Atlantic; FSN Digital Central; FSN Digital Pacific; Fuel TV; NFL Network; Versus.
Digital Pay Service 1
Pay Units: N.A.
Programming (via satellite): Cinemax (multiplexed); Flix; HBO (multiplexed); Showtime (multiplexed); The Movie Channel (multiplexed).
Video-On-Demand: No
Pay-Per-View
Hot Choice (delivered digitally); Playboy TV (delivered digitally); Fresh (delivered digitally); Shorteez (delivered digitally); iN DEMAND (delivered digitally).
Internet Service
Operational: No.
Telephone Service
None
Miles of Plant: 181.0 (coaxial); 11.0 (fiber optic).
Marketing Director: Kathleen Griffin.
Ownership: Charter Communications Inc. (MSO).

CARTHAGE—Cobridge Communications, 9450 Manchester Rd, Ste 200, St. Louis, MO 63119. Phones: 800-438-2427; 314-227-9500. Web Site: http://www.cobridge.net. ICA: TX0193.
TV Market Ranking: Outside TV Markets (CARTHAGE). Franchise award date: January 1, 1972. Franchise expiration date: March 27, 2009. Began: April 1, 1973.
Channel capacity: 62 (not 2-way capable). Channels available but not in use: N.A.
Basic Service
Subscribers: 716.
Programming (received off-air): KETK-TV (NBC) Jacksonville; KLTS-TV (PBS) Shreveport; KMSS-TV (FOX) Shreveport; KPXJ (CW) Minden; KSHV-TV (MNT) Shreveport; KSLA (CBS) Shreveport; KTAL-TV (NBC) Texarkana; KTBS-TV (ABC) Shreveport; allband FM.
Programming (via satellite): A&E Networks; ABC Family Channel; Animal Planet; BET Networks; CNBC; C-SPAN; E! Entertainment Television; ESPN 2; FX; GalaVision; Lifetime; MTV; Nickelodeon; QVC; Syfy; TBS Superstation; The Learning Channel; The Weather Channel; Trinity Broadcasting Network; TV Land; WGN America.
Fee: $53.00 installation; $26.79 monthly; $2.61 converter.
Expanded Basic Service 1
Subscribers: N.A.
Programming (via satellite): AMC; Cartoon Network; CNN; Country Music TV; Discovery Channel; Discovery Fit & Health; Disney Channel; ESPN; Food Network; Fox Movie Channel; Fox News Channel; Fox Sports Southwest; Headline News; HGTV; History Channel; Spike TV; Turner Network TV; USA Network; Versus.
Fee: $17.63 monthly.
Pay Service 1
Pay Units: 195.
Programming (via satellite): Cinemax.
Fee: $25.00 installation; $11.95 monthly.
Pay Service 2
Pay Units: 294.
Programming (via satellite): HBO.
Fee: $25.00 installation; $11.95 monthly.
Pay Service 3
Pay Units: 170.
Programming (via satellite): Showtime.
Fee: $11.95 monthly.
Pay Service 4
Pay Units: 103.
Programming (via satellite): The Movie Channel.
Fee: $25.00 installation; $11.95 monthly.
Video-On-Demand: No
Pay-Per-View
Urban Xtra; iN DEMAND; Fresh.
Internet Service
Operational: No.
Telephone Service
None
Miles of Plant: 86.0 (coaxial); None (fiber optic).
Chief Executive Officer: Scott Widham. General Manager: Wayne Kelstrom.
Ownership: Cobridge Communications LLC (MSO).

CASTROVILLE—Charter Communications. Now served by HONDO, TX [TX0218]. ICA: TX0427.

CEDAR CREEK—Formerly served by Trust Cable. No longer in operation. ICA: TX0901.

CEDAR SPRINGS—Formerly served by Cebridge Connections. No longer in operation. ICA: TX0628.

CENTER—Suddenlink Communications, 12444 Powerscourt Dr, Saint Louis, MO 63131-3660. Phones: 877-423-2743 (Customer service); 314-965-2020; 314-315-9346. Fax: 903-561-5485. Web Site: http://www.suddenlink.com. Also serves San Augustine. ICA: TX0192.

TV Market Ranking: Below 100 (CENTER, San Augustine). Franchise award date: N.A. Franchise expiration date: N.A. Began: July 1, 1970.

Channel capacity: 105 (operating 2-way). Channels available but not in use: N.A.

Basic Service

Subscribers: 2,435.

Programming (received off-air): KLTS-TV (PBS) Shreveport; KMSS-TV (FOX) Shreveport; KPXJ (CW) Minden; KTAL-TV (NBC) Texarkana; KTBS-TV (ABC) Shreveport; KTRE (ABC) Lufkin; KYTX (CBS, IND) Nacogdoches; allband FM.

Programming (via satellite): C-SPAN; Trinity Broadcasting Network.

Fee: $39.95 installation; $19.95 monthly.

Expanded Basic Service 1

Subscribers: N.A.

Programming (via satellite): A&E Networks; ABC Family Channel; Animal Planet; BET Networks; Bravo; Cartoon Network; Celebrity Shopping Network; CNBC; CNN; Comedy Central; Discovery Channel; Disney Channel; E! Entertainment Television; ESPN; ESPN 2; Food Network; Fox News Channel; Fox Sports Southwest; FX; GalaVision; Golf Channel; Great American Country; Hallmark Channel; Headline News; HGTV; History Channel; Lifetime; MSNBC; MTV; National Geographic Channel; Nickelodeon; Outdoor Channel; QVC; Speed; Spike TV; Syfy; TBS Superstation; The Learning Channel; The Weather Channel; Travel Channel; Turner Classic Movies; Turner Network TV; TV Guide Network; TV Land; Univision Studios; USA Network; VH1.

Digital Basic Service

Subscribers: N.A.

Programming (via satellite): BBC America; Bio; Bloomberg Television; Canales N; cloo; Country Music TV; Discovery Digital Networks; DMX Music; ESPN Classic Sports; ESPNews; Fuse; G4; GAS; GSN; History Channel International; Independent Film Channel; Lifetime Movie Network; MTV Networks Digital Suite; Nick Jr.; NickToons TV; Style Network; Toon Disney; Versus; WE tv.

Pay Service 1

Pay Units: 593.

Programming (via satellite): HBO.

Fee: $10.00 monthly.

Pay Service 2

Pay Units: 326.

Programming (via satellite): Cinemax.

Fee: $10.00 monthly.

Pay Service 3

Pay Units: 149.

Programming (via satellite): The Movie Channel.

Fee: $10.00 monthly.

Pay Service 4

Pay Units: 240.

Programming (via satellite): Showtime.

Fee: $5.95 monthly.

Digital Pay Service 1

Pay Units: N.A.

Programming (via satellite): Cinemax (multiplexed); Encore (multiplexed); HBO (multiplexed); Showtime (multiplexed); Starz; The Movie Channel (multiplexed).

Video-On-Demand: No

Pay-Per-View

iN DEMAND (delivered digitally); Playboy TV (delivered digitally); Fresh (delivered digitally).

Internet Service

Operational: Yes. Began: May 12, 2003.

Broadband Service: Suddenlink High Speed Internet.

Fee: $45.95 installation; $29.95 monthly.

Telephone Service

Digital: Operational

Fee: $44.95 monthly

Miles of Plant: 65.0 (coaxial); None (fiber optic).

Area Manager: Marianne Bogy. Regional Manager: Todd Cruthird. Plant Manager: Henry Harris.

Ownership: Cequel Communications LLC (MSO).

CENTER POINT—Almega Cable, 4002 W Airport Frwy, Ste 531, Bedford, TX 76021. Phone: 817-685-9588. Fax: 817-685-6488. Web Site: http://www.almega.com. Also serves Woods. ICA: TX0913.

TV Market Ranking: Below 100 (CENTER POINT); Outside TV Markets (Woods). Franchise award date: N.A. Franchise expiration date: N.A. Began: N.A.

Channel capacity: 61 (2-way capable). Channels available but not in use: N.A.

Basic Service

Subscribers: 283.

Programming (received off-air): KABB (FOX) San Antonio; KCWX (IND, MNT) Fredericksburg; KENS (CBS) San Antonio; KMOL-LP Victoria; KMYS (CW) Kerrville; KSAT-TV (ABC) San Antonio; KVHC-LP Kerrville.

Programming (via satellite): A&E Networks; ABC Family Channel; Animal Planet; CNBC; CNN; Discovery Channel; Disney Channel; ESPN; ESPN 2; Fox News Channel; Fox Sports Southwest; FX; Great American Country; Headline News; HGTV; History Channel; ION Television; KRMA-TV (PBS) Denver; Lifetime; MSNBC; SoapNet; Spike TV; TBS Superstation; Telemundo; The Learning Channel; The Weather Channel; Trinity Broadcasting Network; Turner Classic Movies; Turner Network TV; TV Land; USA Network; VH1.

Fee: $29.95 installation; $38.00 monthly.

Pay Service 1

Pay Units: 24.

Programming (via satellite): Cinemax.

Fee: $9.95 monthly.

Pay Service 2

Pay Units: 87.

Programming (via satellite): HBO.

Fee: $10.95 monthly.

Pay Service 3

Pay Units: 41.

Programming (via satellite): Showtime.

Fee: $9.95 monthly.

Pay Service 4

Pay Units: 42.

Programming (via satellite): The Movie Channel.

Fee: $7.95 monthly.

Video-On-Demand: No

Internet Service

Operational: No.

Telephone Service

None

Miles of Plant: 18.0 (coaxial); None (fiber optic).

Ownership: Almega Cable (MSO).

CENTERVILLE—Formerly served by Almega Cable. No longer in operation. ICA: TX0463.

CENTRAL—Almega Cable, 4001 W Airport Frwy, Ste 530, Bedford, TX 76021. Phone: 817-685-9588. Fax: 817-685-6488. Web Site: http://www.almega.com. Also serves Angelina County (portions), Clawson & Redland. ICA: TX0339.

TV Market Ranking: Below 100 (Angelina County (portions), CENTRAL, Clawson, Redland). Franchise award date: N.A. Franchise expiration date: N.A. Began: N.A.

Channel capacity: 36 (not 2-way capable). Channels available but not in use: N.A.

Basic Service

Subscribers: 198.

Programming (received off-air): KETK-TV (NBC) Jacksonville; KSLA (CBS) Shreveport; KTRE (ABC) Lufkin.

Programming (via satellite): A&E Networks; ABC Family Channel; AMC; BET Networks; CNN; Country Music TV; Discovery Channel; Disney Channel; ESPN; Fox Sports Southwest; Headline News; Lifetime; Nickelodeon; Spike TV; TBS Superstation; The Weather Channel; Turner Network TV; USA Network; WGN America.

Fee: $54.95 installation; $44.05 monthly.

Pay Service 1

Pay Units: 38.

Programming (via satellite): Cinemax.

Fee: $12.95 monthly.

Pay Service 2

Pay Units: 37.

Programming (via satellite): HBO.

Fee: $12.95 monthly.

Pay Service 3

Pay Units: 126.

Programming (via satellite): Showtime.

Fee: $12.95 monthly.

Video-On-Demand: No

Internet Service

Operational: No.

Telephone Service

None

Miles of Plant: 79.0 (coaxial); None (fiber optic).

Ownership: Almega Cable (MSO).

CHANNING—Formerly served by Sunset Cablevision. No longer in operation. ICA: TX0737.

CHAPPELL HILL—Formerly served by Reveille Broadband. No longer in operation. ICA: TX0888.

CHARLOTTE—Zoom Media, PO Box 2126, Flint, TX 75762. Phone: 855-261-5304. Web Site: http://www.zoommediallc.com. Also serves Atascosa County. ICA: TX0508.

TV Market Ranking: 45 (Atascosa County (portions)); Outside TV Markets (CHARLOTTE, Atascosa County (portions)). Franchise award date: N.A. Franchise expiration date: July 1, 2011. Began: September 1, 1982.

Channel capacity: 56 (not 2-way capable). Channels available but not in use: N.A.

Basic Service

Subscribers: 43.

Programming (received off-air): KABB (FOX) San Antonio; KENS (CBS) San Antonio; KLRN (PBS) San Antonio; KMYS (CW) Kerrville; KPXL-TV (ION) Uvalde; KSAT-TV (ABC) San Antonio; KVDA (TMO) San Antonio; KWEX-DT (UNV) San Antonio; WOAI-TV (NBC) San Antonio.

Programming (via satellite): A&E Networks; ABC Family Channel; AMC; Animal Planet; Bravo; Cartoon Network; CNN; Comedy Central; C-SPAN; C-SPAN 2; E! Entertainment Television; ESPN; ESPN 2; Eternal Word TV Network; Food Network; Fox News Channel; Fox Sports Southwest; FX; GalaVision; Golf Channel; Great American Country; Hallmark Channel; Headline News; HGTV; History Channel; Lifetime; MSNBC; MTV; Nickelodeon; Oxygen; ShopNBC; Spike TV; Syfy; TBS Superstation; The Learning Channel; The Weather Channel; Travel Channel; Turner Classic Movies; Turner Network TV; TV Land; USA Network; WE tv.

Fee: $50.51 installation; $48.99 monthly.

Pay Service 1

Pay Units: N.A.

Programming (via satellite): Encore; HBO; Showtime; The Movie Channel.

Fee: $2.75 monthly (Encore), $10.45 monthly (TMC), $12.95 monthly (HBO or Showtime).

Internet Service

Operational: No.

Telephone Service

None

Miles of Plant: 10.0 (coaxial); None (fiber optic).

Chief Executive Officer: Steve Houston.

Ownership: Zoom Media LLC (MSO).

CHEEK—Formerly served by Cebridge Connections. No longer in operation. ICA: TX0576.

CHEROKEE COUNTY (northern portions)—Reach Broadband, 515 E Longview St, Arp, TX 75750. Phone: 800-687-1258. Web Site: http://www.reachbroadband.net. Also serves Smith County (southern portion). ICA: TX0988.

TV Market Ranking: Below 100 (CHEROKEE COUNTY (NORTHERN PORTIONS), Smith County (southern portion)). Franchise award date: N.A. Franchise expiration date: N.A. Began: N.A.

Channel capacity: 85 (not 2-way capable). Channels available but not in use: N.A.

Basic Service

Subscribers: 54.

Programming (received off-air): KETK-TV (NBC) Jacksonville; KFXK-TV (FOX) Longview; KLTV (ABC, TMO) Tyler; KTPN-LP Tyler; KYTX (CBS, IND) Nacogdoches.

Programming (via satellite): A&E Networks; Animal Planet; CNN; Comedy Central; C-SPAN; Discovery Channel; Disney Channel; ESPN; ESPN 2; Food Network; Fox News Channel; Fox Sports Southwest; Golf Channel; Great American Country; Headline News; HGTV; History Channel; KCNC-TV (CBS) Denver; Lifetime; MTV; Nickelodeon; Outdoor Channel; QVC; Spike TV; Syfy; TBS Superstation; The Learning Channel; The Weather Channel; Trinity Broadcasting Net-

work; truTV; Turner Classic Movies; Turner Network TV; TV Land; USA Network; VH1.
Fee: $54.95 installation; $44.05 monthly.
Pay Service 1
Pay Units: 148.
Programming (via satellite): Flix; Showtime; Sundance Channel; The Movie Channel.
Fee: $12.95 monthly.
Internet Service
Operational: No.
Telephone Service
None
Miles of Plant: 17.0 (coaxial); None (fiber optic).
Regional Manager: Ronnie Stafford. Office Manager: Jan Gibson.
Ownership: RB3 LLC (MSO).

CHESTER—Formerly served by Cebridge Connections. No longer in operation. ICA: TX0671.

CHILDRESS—Formerly served by Cebridge Connections. Now served by WELLINGTON, TX [TX0313]. ICA: TX0195.

CHILLICOTHE—Formerly served by Almega Cable. No longer in operation. ICA: TX0530.

CHILTON—Formerly served by Galaxy Cablevision. No longer in operation. ICA: TX0598.

CHINA—CMA Cablevision. Now served by SOUR LAKE, TX [TX0162]. ICA: TX0738.

CHRISTOVAL—Formerly served by Almega Cable. No longer in operation. ICA: TX0589.

CLARENDON—Suddenlink Communications, 12444 Powerscourt Dr, Saint Louis, MO 63131-3660. Phones: 800-999-6845; 314-965-2020. Fax: 903-561-5485. Web Site: http://www.suddenlink.com. ICA: TX0398.
TV Market Ranking: Outside TV Markets (CLARENDON). Franchise award date: N.A. Franchise expiration date: N.A. Began: June 15, 1962.
Channel capacity: N.A. Channels available but not in use: N.A.
Basic Service
Subscribers: 553.
Programming (received off-air): KACV-TV (PBS) Amarillo; KAMR-TV (NBC) Amarillo; KCIT (FOX) Amarillo; KFDA-TV (CBS) Amarillo; KVII-TV (ABC, CW) Amarillo; allband FM.
Programming (via satellite): ABC Family Channel; AMC; Animal Planet; CNN; Country Music TV; C-SPAN; Discovery Channel; Disney Channel; E! Entertainment Television; ESPN; Fox News Channel; Fox Sports Southwest; Headline News; HGTV; History Channel; Lifetime; Nickelodeon; QVC; Spike TV; Syfy; TBS Superstation; The Learning Channel; The Weather Channel; Turner Network TV; TV Land; USA Network; WGN America.
Fee: $39.95 installation; $19.95 monthly.
Pay Service 1
Pay Units: 59.
Programming (via satellite): HBO.
Fee: $20.00 installation; $10.95 monthly.
Pay Service 2
Pay Units: 26.
Programming (via satellite): Showtime.
Fee: $9.95 monthly.
Pay Service 3
Pay Units: 30.
Programming (via satellite): The Movie Channel.
Fee: $7.95 monthly.
Video-On-Demand: No
Internet Service
Operational: Yes. Began: June 11, 2004.
Broadband Service: Suddenlink High Speed Internet.
Fee: $49.95 installation; $38.95 monthly.
Telephone Service
None
Miles of Plant: 24.0 (coaxial); None (fiber optic).
Regional Manager: Todd Cruthird. Plant Manager: Rick Rattan. Regional Marketing Manager: Beverly Gambell.
Ownership: Cequel Communications LLC (MSO).

CLARKSVILLE—Suddenlink Communications, 12444 Powerscourt Dr, Saint Louis, MO 63131-3660. Phones: 877-423-2743 (Customer service); 314-965-2020. Fax: 903-561-5485. Web Site: http://www.suddenlink.com. Also serves Annona, Avery, Bagwell, Blossom, Bogata, Deport, Detroit, Lamar County (portions) & Talco. ICA: TX0200.
TV Market Ranking: Outside TV Markets (Annona, Avery, Bagwell, Blossom, Bogata, CLARKSVILLE, Deport, Detroit, Lamar County (portions), Talco). Franchise award date: N.A. Franchise expiration date: N.A. Began: March 1, 1963.
Channel capacity: 21 (operating 2-way). Channels available but not in use: N.A.
Basic Service
Subscribers: 3,454.
Programming (received off-air): KMSS-TV (FOX) Shreveport; KPXJ (CW) Minden; KTAL-TV (NBC) Texarkana; KTBS-TV (ABC) Shreveport; allband FM.
Programming (via microwave): KDFW-DT (FOX) Dallas; KERA-TV (PBS) Dallas; KTVT (CBS) Fort Worth; KXAS-TV (NBC) Fort Worth; WFAA (ABC) Dallas.
Programming (via satellite): QVC; The Weather Channel.
Fee: $39.95 installation; $19.95 monthly.
Expanded Basic Service 1
Subscribers: N.A.
Programming (via microwave): KDTX-TV (TBN) Dallas.
Programming (via satellite): A&E Networks; ABC Family Channel; AMC; Animal Planet; BET Networks; Cartoon Network; CNBC; CNN; Comedy Central; Discovery Channel; Disney Channel; E! Entertainment Television; ESPN; ESPN 2; Food Network; Fox News Channel; Fox Sports Southwest; FX; Great American Country; Headline News; HGTV; History Channel; Lifetime; MSNBC; MTV; National Geographic Channel; Nickelodeon; Outdoor Channel; Spike TV; Syfy; TBS Superstation; The Learning Channel; Travel Channel; Turner Classic Movies; Turner Network TV; TV Land; Univision Studios; USA Network; VH1.
Fee: $23.00 monthly.
Digital Basic Service
Subscribers: N.A.
Programming (via satellite): BBC America; Bio; Bloomberg Television; cloo; Discovery Digital Networks; DMX Music; ESPN Classic Sports; ESPNews; Fuse; G4; Golf Channel; GSN; History Channel International; Independent Film Channel; Speed; Style Network; Toon Disney; Trinity Broadcasting Network; Versus; WE tv.
Fee: $3.99 monthly.
Pay Service 1
Pay Units: 226.
Programming (via satellite): Cinemax.
Fee: $10.00 monthly.
Pay Service 2
Pay Units: 632.
Programming (via satellite): HBO.
Fee: $10.00 monthly.
Pay Service 3
Pay Units: 342.
Programming (via satellite): Showtime.
Fee: $5.95 monthly.
Pay Service 4
Pay Units: 182.
Programming (via satellite): The Movie Channel.
Fee: $10.00 monthly.
Digital Pay Service 1
Pay Units: N.A.
Programming (via satellite): Cinemax (multiplexed); Encore (multiplexed); HBO (multiplexed); Showtime (multiplexed); Starz; The Movie Channel (multiplexed).
Video-On-Demand: No
Pay-Per-View
iN DEMAND (delivered digitally); Playboy TV (delivered digitally); Fresh (delivered digitally).
Internet Service
Operational: Yes. Began: June 1, 2003.
Broadband Service: Suddenlink High Speed Internet.
Fee: $45.95 installation; $29.95 monthly.
Telephone Service
Digital: Operational
Fee: $44.95 monthly
Miles of Plant: 126.0 (coaxial); None (fiber optic).
Plant Manager: Sonny Myers. Regional Manager: Todd Cruthird. Area Manager: Marianne Bogy.
Ownership: Cequel Communications LLC (MSO).

CLAUDE—Formerly served by Almega Cable. No longer in operation. ICA: TX0516.

CLEBURNE—Charter Communications, 777 Harbor Lakes Dr, Granbury, TX 76048-2623. Phone: 817-279-9992. Web Site: http://www.charter.com. ICA: TX1003.
TV Market Ranking: 12 (CLEBURNE).
Channel capacity: N.A. Channels available but not in use: N.A.
Basic Service
Subscribers: N.A.
Programming (received off-air): KAZD (IND) Lake Dallas; KDAF (CW, IND) Dallas; KDFI (MNT) Dallas; KDFW-DT (FOX) Dallas; KDTN (ETV) Denton; KDTX-TV (TBN) Dallas; KERA-TV (PBS) Dallas; KFWD (IND) Fort Worth; KMPX (IND) Decatur; KPXD-TV (ION) Arlington; KSTR-DT (TEL) Irving; KTVT (CBS) Fort Worth; KTXA (IND) Fort Worth; KUVN-DT (UNV) Garland; KXAS-TV (NBC) Fort Worth; KXTX-TV (TMO) Dallas; WFAA (ABC) Dallas.
Programming (via satellite): A&E Networks; AMC; CNN; C-SPAN; C-SPAN 2; Discovery Channel; ESPN; ESPN 2; Eternal Word TV Network; Fox Sports Southwest; GalaVision; Headline News; HGTV; MTV; Nickelodeon; Product Information Network; QVC; ShopNBC; Texas Cable News; The Learning Channel; The Weather Channel; TV Land; VH1; WGN America.
Fee: $29.99 installation.
Expanded Basic Service 1
Subscribers: N.A.
Programming (via satellite): ABC Family Channel; Animal Planet; BET Networks; Bravo; Cartoon Network; CNBC; Comedy Central; Country Music TV; Disney Channel; E! Entertainment Television; Food Network; Fox Deportes; Fox News Channel; FX; G4; Golf Channel; GSN; Hallmark Channel; History Channel; Lifetime; MSNBC; mun2 television; National Geographic Channel; Oxygen; SoapNet; Speed; Spike TV; Style Network; Syfy; TBS Superstation; Toon Disney; Travel Channel; truTV; Turner Classic Movies; Turner Network TV; USA Network; Versus; WE tv.
Fee: $48.99 monthly.
Digital Basic Service
Subscribers: N.A.
Programming (via satellite): BBC America; Bio; Bloomberg Television; Canales N; Discovery Fit & Health; DIY Network; ESPN; ESPN Classic Sports; ESPNews; Fox College Sports Atlantic; Fox College Sports Central; Fox College Sports Pacific; Fox Movie Channel; Fox Soccer; Fuel TV; Fuse; GAS; Great American Country; Halogen Network; HD Theater; HDNet; HDNet Movies; History Channel International; Independent Film Channel; INSP; Lifetime Movie Network; MTV Networks Digital Suite; Music Choice; NFL Network; Nick Jr.; Nick Too; NickToons TV; Sundance Channel.
Digital Pay Service 1
Pay Units: N.A.
Programming (via satellite): Cinemax (multiplexed); Cinemax HD; Encore (multiplexed); Flix; HBO (multiplexed); HBO HD; Showtime (multiplexed); Showtime HD; Starz (multiplexed); The Movie Channel (multiplexed).
Video-On-Demand: Yes
Pay-Per-View
iN DEMAND (delivered digitally); TEN Clips (delivered digitally); Pleasure (delivered digitally); Fox Sports Net (delivered digitally).
Internet Service
Operational: Yes.
Broadband Service: Charter Pipeline.
Fee: $29.99 monthly.
Telephone Service
None
Miles of Plant: 14.0 (coaxial); 18.0 (fiber optic).
Vice President & General Manager: Wayne Cramp. Marketing Director: Kathleen Griffin. Technical Operations Director: John Linton. Chief Technician: Mike Carmack. Technical Supervisor: Sam Easley.
Ownership: Charter Communications Inc. (MSO).

CLEVELAND—CMA Cablevision, 630 W Barkley St, Sour Lake, TX 77659. Phones: 979-968-6476 (La Grange office); 409-287-3014. Fax: 979-968-5368. Web Site: http://www.cmaaccess.com. ICA: TX0170.
TV Market Ranking: Below 100 (CLEVELAND). Franchise award date: May 10, 1977. Franchise expiration date: May 10, 2007. Began: November 1, 1978.
Channel capacity: N.A. Channels available but not in use: N.A.
Basic Service
Subscribers: 1,120.
Programming (received off-air): KETH-TV (TBN) Houston; KFTH-DT (TEL) Alvin; KHOU (CBS) Houston; KIAH (CW) Houston; KLTJ (ETV) Galveston; KPRC-TV (NBC) Houston; KPXB-TV (ION) Conroe; KRIV (FOX) Houston; KTMD (TMO) Galveston; KTRK-TV (ABC) Houston; KTXH (MNT) Houston; KUHT (PBS) Houston; KXLN-DT (UNV) Rosenberg; KYAZ (IND) Katy.
Programming (via satellite): C-SPAN; QVC; WGN America.
Fee: $39.95 installation; $20.95 monthly; $12.95 additional installation.

Expanded Basic Service 1
Subscribers: N.A.
Programming (via satellite): A&E Networks; ABC Family Channel; AMC; Animal Planet; BET Networks; Bravo; Cartoon Network; CNBC; CNN; Comedy Central; Country Music TV; Discovery Channel; ESPN; ESPN 2; ESPN Classic Sports; Food Network; Fox News Channel; Fox Sports Southwest; FX; GalaVision; Headline News; History Channel; Lifetime; MTV; National Geographic Channel; Nickelodeon; Outdoor Channel; SoapNet; Spike TV; Syfy; TBS Superstation; The Learning Channel; The Weather Channel; truTV; Turner Network TV; TV Land; USA Network; VH1.
Fee: $25.50 monthly.

Digital Basic Service
Subscribers: N.A.
Programming (via satellite): BBC America; Bio; Discovery Digital Networks; DMX Music; Encore; ESPNews; Fox Sports World; GAS; Golf Channel; GSN; HGTV; History Channel International; Independent Film Channel; Lifetime Movie Network; MTV Networks Digital Suite; Nick Jr.; NickToons TV; Speed; Style Network; Turner Classic Movies; WE tv.
Fee: $13.95 monthly.

Pay Service 1
Pay Units: N.A.
Programming (via satellite): HBO.
Fee: $14.95 installation; $13.95 monthly.

Digital Pay Service 1
Pay Units: 156.
Programming (via satellite): Cinemax (multiplexed); Starz (multiplexed).
Fee: $10.95 monthly (Cinemax or Starz/Encore).

Digital Pay Service 2
Pay Units: 284.
Programming (via satellite): HBO (multiplexed).
Fee: $13.95 monthly.

Digital Pay Service 3
Pay Units: 183.
Programming (via satellite): Showtime (multiplexed).
Fee: $13.95 monthly.

Video-On-Demand: No

Pay-Per-View
iN DEMAND (delivered digitally); Playboy TV (delivered digitally).

Internet Service
Operational: Yes.
Broadband Service: CMA.
Fee: $39.95 installation; $41.95 monthly; $2.95 modem lease; $39.95 modem purchase.

Telephone Service
None

Miles of Plant: 84.0 (coaxial); None (fiber optic).
General Manager: Jerry L. Smith. Chief Technician: Dutch Bernsen. Marketing Director: Julie Ferguson.
Ownership: Cable Management Assoc. (MSO).

CLIFTON—Reach Broadband, 515 E Longview St, Arp, TX 75750. Phone: 800-687-1258. Web Site: http://www.reachbroadband.net. ICA: TX0288.
TV Market Ranking: Below 100 (CLIFTON). Franchise award date: N.A. Franchise expiration date: N.A. Began: February 1, 1982.
Channel capacity: N.A. Channels available but not in use: N.A.

Basic Service
Subscribers: 530.
Programming (received off-air): KCEN-TV (NBC, IND) Temple; KDAF (CW, IND) Dallas; KDFI (MNT) Dallas; KDFW-DT (FOX) Dallas; KERA-TV (PBS) Dallas; KSTR-DT (TEL) Irving; KTVT (CBS) Fort Worth; KWKT-TV (FOX, MNT) Waco; KWTX-TV (CBS, CW) Waco; KXAS-TV (NBC) Fort Worth; KXTX-TV (TMO) Dallas; KXXV (ABC, TMO) Waco; WFAA (ABC) Dallas.
Fee: $54.95 installation; $20.95 monthly.

Expanded Basic Service 1
Subscribers: N.A.
Programming (via satellite): A&E Networks; ABC Family Channel; AMC; Animal Planet; Cartoon Network; CNBC; CNN; Comedy Central; C-SPAN; Discovery Channel; Disney Channel; E! Entertainment Television; ESPN; ESPN 2; Food Network; Fox News Channel; Fox Sports Southwest; FX; Great American Country; Hallmark Channel; Headline News; HGTV; History Channel; INSP; Lifetime; MSNBC; MTV; Nickelodeon; Outdoor Channel; QVC; Speed; Spike TV; Syfy; TBS Superstation; The Learning Channel; The Weather Channel; Travel Channel; Turner Classic Movies; Turner Network TV; TV Land; USA Network; VH1.
Fee: $23.10 monthly.

Pay Service 1
Pay Units: 91.
Programming (via satellite): Cinemax.
Fee: $12.95 monthly.

Pay Service 2
Pay Units: 170.
Programming (via satellite): Encore.
Fee: $12.95 monthly.

Pay Service 3
Pay Units: 121.
Programming (via satellite): HBO.
Fee: $12.95 monthly.

Pay Service 4
Pay Units: 121.
Programming (via satellite): Starz.
Fee: $12.95 monthly.

Pay Service 5
Pay Units: N.A.
Programming (via satellite): Showtime.

Video-On-Demand: No

Internet Service
Operational: Yes.
Broadband Service: Rapid High Speed Internet.
Fee: $100.00 installation; $29.95 monthly.

Telephone Service
None

Miles of Plant: 24.0 (coaxial); None (fiber optic).
Regional Manager: Ronnie Stafford. Office Manager: Jan Gibson.
Ownership: RB3 LLC (MSO).

COLEMAN—Reach Broadband, 515 E Longview St, Arp, TX 75750. Phone: 800-687-1258. Web Site: http://www.reachbroadband.net. ICA: TX0178.
TV Market Ranking: Outside TV Markets (COLEMAN). Franchise award date: August 1, 1958. Franchise expiration date: N.A. Began: April 1, 1959.
Channel capacity: N.A. Channels available but not in use: N.A.

Basic Service
Subscribers: 1,910.
Programming (received off-air): KLST (CBS) San Angelo; KPCB-DT (IND) Snyder; KRBC-TV (NBC) Abilene; KRPV-DT (IND) Roswell; KTAB-TV (CBS) Abilene; KTXS-TV (ABC, CW, TMO) Sweetwater; KXVA (FOX) Abilene.
Programming (via microwave): KDFW-DT (FOX) Dallas; KERA-TV (PBS) Dallas; WFAA (ABC) Dallas.
Programming (via satellite): C-SPAN.
Fee: $29.95 installation; $19.95 monthly.

Expanded Basic Service 1
Subscribers: 1,780.
Programming (via satellite): A&E Networks; ABC Family Channel; AMC; Animal Planet; Bravo; Cartoon Network; CNBC; CNN; Comedy Central; Country Music TV; Disney Channel; E! Entertainment Television; ESPN; ESPN 2; Fox Movie Channel; Fox News Channel; Fox Sports Southwest; FX; G4; Golf Channel; Headline News; HGTV; History Channel; Lifetime; MTV; Nickelodeon; Outdoor Channel; Oxygen; SoapNet; Speed; Spike TV; Syfy; TBS Superstation; The Learning Channel; The Weather Channel; Turner Classic Movies; Turner Network TV; TV Land; Univision Studios; USA Network; VH1.
Fee: $18.00 monthly.

Digital Basic Service
Subscribers: N.A.
Programming (via satellite): BBC America; Bio; Bloomberg Television; CMT Pure Country; Discovery en Espanol; Discovery Fit & Health; Discovery Health Channel; Discovery Kids Channel; DIY Network; ESPN Classic Sports; GSN; History Channel International; ID Investigation Discovery; Independent Film Channel; Lifetime Movie Network; Music Choice; Nick Jr.; Nick Too; NickToons TV; Planet Green; Science; Style Network; Sundance Channel; TeenNick; Toon Disney; VH1 Classic; VH1 Soul; WE tv.

Digital Pay Service 1
Pay Units: 150.
Programming (via satellite): Cinemax (multiplexed); Encore (multiplexed); Flix; HBO (multiplexed); Showtime (multiplexed); Starz (multiplexed); The Movie Channel (multiplexed).
Fee: $20.00 installation; $9.95 monthly.

Video-On-Demand: No

Pay-Per-View
iN DEMAND (delivered digitally); Pleasure (delivered digitally); Ten Clips (delivered digitally).

Internet Service
Operational: No.

Telephone Service
None

Miles of Plant: 47.0 (coaxial); None (fiber optic).
Regional Manager: Ronnie Stafford. Office Manager: Jan Gibson.
Ownership: RB3 LLC (MSO).

COLETO CREEK—Formerly served by National Cable Inc. No longer in operation. ICA: TX0626.

COLMESNEIL—Formerly served by Carrell Communications. No longer in operation. ICA: TX0475.

COLORADO CITY—Cobridge Communications, 9450 Manchester Rd, Ste 200, St. Louis, MO 63119. Phones: 800-438-2427; 314-227-9500. Web Site: http://www.cobridge.net. Also serves Lake Colorado City & Mitchell County. ICA: TX0172.
TV Market Ranking: Below 100 (COLORADO CITY, Lake Colorado City, Mitchell County). Franchise award date: March 31, 1977. Franchise expiration date: March 31, 2007. Began: April 1, 1962.
Channel capacity: N.A. Channels available but not in use: N.A.

Basic Service
Subscribers: 688.
Programming (received off-air): KJTV-TV (FOX) Lubbock; KLCW-TV (CW) Wolfforth; KLST (CBS) San Angelo; KPCB-DT (IND) Snyder; KRBC-TV (NBC) Abilene; KRMA-TV (PBS) Denver; KTAB-TV (CBS) Abilene; KTXS-TV (ABC, CW, TMO) Sweetwater; KWAB-TV (NBC) Big Spring; 8 FMs.
Programming (via satellite): C-SPAN.
Fee: $27.90 installation; $9.26 monthly; $1.60 converter.

Expanded Basic Service 1
Subscribers: N.A.
Programming (via satellite): A&E Networks; ABC Family Channel; AMC; Bravo; Cartoon Network; CNBC; CNN; Comedy Central; Country Music TV; Discovery Channel; Disney Channel; E! Entertainment Television; ESPN; ESPN 2; Fox News Channel; Fox Sports Southwest; FX; G4; Headline News; HGTV; History Channel; Lifetime; MTV; Nickelodeon; Oxygen; SoapNet; Speed; Spike TV; Syfy; TBS Superstation; The Learning Channel; The Weather Channel; Turner Classic Movies; Turner Network TV; TV Land; Univision Studios; USA Network; Versus; VH1.
Fee: $20.00 installation; $14.69 monthly.

Digital Basic Service
Subscribers: N.A.
Programming (via satellite): BBC America; Bio; Bloomberg Television; Discovery Fit & Health; DIY Network; GAS; GSN; History Channel International; Independent Film Channel; Lifetime Movie Network; MTV Networks Digital Suite; Music Choice; Nick Jr.; Nick Too; NickToons TV; Science Television; Sundance Channel; Toon Disney; WE tv.

Pay Service 1
Pay Units: N.A.
Programming (via satellite): Encore (multiplexed); Flix; Showtime (multiplexed); The Movie Channel (multiplexed).

Digital Pay Service 1
Pay Units: 153.
Programming (via satellite): Cinemax (multiplexed); HBO (multiplexed); Starz (multiplexed).
Fee: $20.00 installation; $9.00 monthly.

Video-On-Demand: No

Pay-Per-View
iN DEMAND (delivered digitally); Pleasure (delivered digitally); ETC (delivered digitally).

Internet Service
Operational: No.

Telephone Service
None

Miles of Plant: 63.0 (coaxial); None (fiber optic).
Chief Executive Officer: Scott Widham. General Manager: Wayne Kelstrom.
Ownership: Cobridge Communications LLC (MSO).

COLUMBUS—Time Warner Cable, 900 Sidney Baker St, Kerrville, TX 78028-3353. Phones: 972-899-7300 (Flower Mound division office); 830-257-4709. Fax: 830-257-6776. Web Site: http://www.timewarnercable.com/Texas. Also serves Eagle Lake. ICA: TX0257.

TV Market Ranking: Below 100 (Eagle Lake); Outside TV Markets (COLUMBUS). Franchise award date: N.A. Franchise expiration date: N.A. Began: June 1, 1974.

Channel capacity: N.A. Channels available but not in use: N.A.

Basic Service

Subscribers: N.A. Included in Gonzales

Programming (received off-air): KETH-TV (TBN) Houston; KFTH-DT (TEL) Alvin; KHOU (CBS) Houston; KIAH (CW) Houston; KLTJ (ETV) Galveston; KPRC-TV (NBC) Houston; KPXB-TV (ION) Conroe; KRIV (FOX) Houston; KTMD (TMO) Galveston; KTRK-TV (ABC) Houston; KTXH (MNT) Houston; KUBE-TV (IND) Baytown; KUHT (PBS) Houston; KXLN-DT (UNV) Rosenberg; KYAZ (IND) Katy; KZJL (IND) Houston; 1 FM.

Programming (via satellite): ABC Family Channel; Cartoon Network; CNBC; CNN; C-SPAN; C-SPAN 2; Discovery Channel; TBS Superstation; The Weather Channel; Turner Network TV; WGN America.

Fee: $50.51 installation; $16.69 monthly.

Expanded Basic Service 1

Subscribers: N.A.

Programming (via satellite): A&E Networks; AMC; Animal Planet; BET Networks; Bravo; Country Music TV; Disney Channel; E! Entertainment Television; ESPN; ESPN 2; Food Network; Fox News Channel; Fox Sports Southwest; FX; Golf Channel; GSN; Hallmark Channel; Headline News; HGTV; History Channel; Lifetime; MoviePlex; MSNBC; MTV; mun2 television; National Geographic Channel; Nickelodeon; Oxygen; ShopNBC; SoapNet; Spike TV; Syfy; Texas Cable News; The Learning Channel; Travel Channel; truTV; Turner Classic Movies; TV Land; USA Network; VH1; WE tv.

Fee: $31.30 monthly.

Digital Basic Service

Subscribers: N.A.

Programming (via satellite): AmericanLife TV Network; America's Store; BBC America; Bloomberg Television; cloo; Cooking Channel; Current; Discovery Fit & Health; DIY Network; DMX Music; Encore (multiplexed); ESPN Classic Sports; ESPNews; Fox College Sports Atlantic; Fox College Sports Central; Fox College Sports Pacific; Fox Deportes; Fox Movie Channel; Fox Soccer; Fuse; G4; GAS; Great American Country; Independent Film Channel; Lifetime Movie Network; MTV Networks Digital Suite; NBA TV; Nick Jr.; NickToons TV; Outdoor Channel; Speed; Style Network; Sundance Channel (multiplexed); Tennis Channel; Toon Disney; Versus.

Fee: $5.00 monthly, $8.95 monthly (Value Tier, Sports Tier, or Movie Tier).

Digital Pay Service 1

Pay Units: N.A.

Programming (via satellite): Cinemax (multiplexed); HBO (multiplexed); Showtime (multiplexed); Starz (multiplexed); The Movie Channel.

Fee: $12.95 monthly (each).

Video-On-Demand: No

Internet Service

Operational: No.

Telephone Service

None

Miles of Plant: 65.0 (coaxial); None (fiber optic).

President: Connie Wharton. Vice President & General Manager: Mike McKee. Engineering Director: Charlotte Strong. Chief Technician: Bill Wilcox.

Ownership: Time Warner Cable (MSO).; Advance/Newhouse Partnership (MSO).

COMANCHE—Reach Broadband, 515 E Longview St, Arp, TX 75750. Phone: 800-687-1258. Web Site: http://www.reachbroadband.net. ICA: TX0227.

TV Market Ranking: Outside TV Markets (COMANCHE). Franchise award date: N.A. Franchise expiration date: N.A. Began: September 1, 1958.

Channel capacity: 57 (not 2-way capable). Channels available but not in use: N.A.

Basic Service

Subscribers: 348.

Programming (received off-air): KRBC-TV (NBC) Abilene; KTAB-TV (CBS) Abilene; allband FM.

Programming (via microwave): KDAF (CW, IND) Dallas; KDFW-DT (FOX) Dallas; KERA-TV (PBS) Dallas; KXAS-TV (NBC) Fort Worth; WFAA (ABC) Dallas.

Programming (via satellite): Disney Channel; QVC; The Learning Channel; Trinity Broadcasting Network.

Fee: $29.95 installation; $19.95 monthly; $3.51 converter.

Expanded Basic Service 1

Subscribers: N.A.

Programming (via satellite): A&E Networks; ABC Family Channel; AMC; Bravo; Cartoon Network; CNBC; CNN; Comedy Central; Country Music TV; Discovery Channel; E! Entertainment Television; ESPN; ESPN 2; Fox News Channel; FX; G4; GalaVision; Headline News; HGTV; History Channel; Lifetime; MTV; Nickelodeon; Oxygen; Speed; Spike TV; Syfy; TBS Superstation; The Weather Channel; Turner Classic Movies; Turner Network TV; TV Land; USA Network; VH1.

Fee: $18.00 monthly.

Digital Basic Service

Subscribers: N.A.

Programming (via satellite): BBC America; Bio; Bloomberg Television; CMT Pure Country; Discovery en Espanol; Discovery Fit & Health; Discovery Health Channel; Discovery Kids Channel; DIY Network; ESPN Classic Sports; GSN; History Channel International; ID Investigation Discovery; Lifetime Movie Network; Lifetime Real Women; Military Channel; MTV Hits; MTV2; Music Choice; Nick Jr.; Nick Too; NickToons TV; Planet Green; SoapNet; Style Network; Sundance Channel; TeenNick; Toon Disney; Tr3s; VH1 Classic; VH1 Soul.

Digital Pay Service 1

Pay Units: N.A.

Programming (via satellite): Cinemax (multiplexed); Encore; Flix; HBO (multiplexed); Showtime (multiplexed); Starz (multiplexed); The Movie Channel (multiplexed).

Video-On-Demand: No

Pay-Per-View

iN DEMAND (delivered digitally).

Internet Service

Operational: No.

Telephone Service

None

Miles of Plant: 50.0 (coaxial); None (fiber optic).

Regional Manager: Ronnie Stafford. Office Manager: Jan Gibson.

Ownership: RB3 LLC (MSO).

COMBINE—Formerly served by Charter Communications. No longer in operation. ICA: TX0917.

COMFORT—Comfort Cable Co., 523 8th St, PO Box 507, Comfort, TX 78013-0507. Phone: 830-995-2813. Fax: 830-995-2245. ICA: TX1015.

TV Market Ranking: Below 100 (COMFORT). Franchise award date: N.A. Franchise expiration date: N.A. Began: January 1, 1980.

Channel capacity: N.A. Channels available but not in use: N.A.

Basic Service

Subscribers: 119 Includes Lavernia.

Programming (received off-air): KABB (FOX) San Antonio; KCWX (IND, MNT) Fredericksburg; KENS (CBS) San Antonio; KLRN (PBS) San Antonio; KPXL-TV (ION) Uvalde; KSAT-TV (ABC) San Antonio; KVDA (TMO) San Antonio; KWEX-DT (UNV) San Antonio; WOAI-TV (NBC) San Antonio.

Programming (via satellite): A&E Networks; ABC Family Channel; AMC; CNN; Country Music TV; Discovery Channel; ESPN; ESPN 2; Fox News Channel; Fox Sports Southwest; GalaVision; Hallmark Channel; Headline News; HGTV; History Channel; Lifetime; Nickelodeon; QVC; RFD-TV; Spike TV; TBS Superstation; Telefutura; The Learning Channel; The Movie Channel; The Weather Channel; Turner Classic Movies; Turner Network TV; TV Land; USA Network; VH1; WGN America.

Pay Service 1

Pay Units: N.A.

Programming (via satellite): Showtime.

Internet Service

Operational: No.

Telephone Service

None

Miles of Plant: 23.0 (coaxial); None (fiber optic). Miles of plant include Lavernia

Manager & Chief Technician: David Petty.

Ownership: David Petty (MSO).

COMFORT—Formerly served by Cebridge Connections. No longer in operation. ICA: TX0400.

CONROE—Suddenlink Communications, 322 N Glenwood Blvd, Tyler, TX 75702. Phone: 903-595-4321. Web Site: http://www.suddenlink.com. Also serves Montgomery County, Panorama Village & Willis. ICA: TX0741.

TV Market Ranking: 15 (Montgomery County (portions)); Below 100 (CONROE, Panorama Village, Willis, Montgomery County (portions)). Franchise award date: N.A. Franchise expiration date: N.A. Began: September 1, 1969.

Channel capacity: N.A. Channels available but not in use: N.A.

Basic Service

Subscribers: 11,322.

Programming (received off-air): KETH-TV (TBN) Houston; KFTH-DT (TEL) Alvin; KHOU (CBS) Houston; KIAH (CW) Houston; KLTJ (ETV) Galveston; KPRC-TV (NBC) Houston; KPXB-TV (ION) Conroe; KRIV (FOX) Houston; KTBU (IND) Conroe; KTMD (TMO) Galveston; KTRK-TV (ABC) Houston; KTXH (MNT) Houston; KUBE-TV (IND) Baytown; KUHT (PBS) Houston; KXLN-DT (UNV) Rosenberg; KYAZ (IND) Katy; KZJL (IND) Houston; 1 FM.

Programming (via satellite): GalaVision; TBS Superstation; TV Guide Network.

Fee: $35.00 installation; $10.00 monthly.

Expanded Basic Service 1

Subscribers: N.A.

Programming (via satellite): A&E Networks; ABC Family Channel; AMC; Animal Planet; BET Networks; Bravo; Cartoon Network; CNBC; CNN; Comedy Central; Country Music TV; C-SPAN; C-SPAN 2; Discovery Channel; Disney Channel; E! Entertainment Television; ESPN; ESPN 2; Food Network; Fox News Channel; Fox Sports Southwest; FX; Great American Country; Headline News; HGTV; History Channel; Lifetime; MTV; Nickelodeon; Spike TV; Syfy; The Learning Channel; The Weather Channel; Travel Channel; truTV; Turner Network TV; USA Network; Versus; VH1.

Digital Basic Service

Subscribers: N.A.

Programming (via satellite): A&E HD; Bandamax; BBC America; Bio; Bloomberg Television; Cine Latino; Cine Mexicano; CMT Pure Country; CNN en Espanol; Cooking Channel; De Pelicula; De Pelicula Clasico; Discovery en Espanol; Discovery Health Channel; Discovery Home Channel; Discovery Kids Channel; Discovery Times Channel; DIY Network; Encore (multiplexed); ESPN 2 HD; ESPN Classic Sports; ESPN Deportes; ESPN HD; ESPN U; ESPNews; EWTN en Espanol; Food Network HD; Fox Deportes; Fox Soccer; Fuse; G4; Golf Channel; GSN; Hallmark Channel; Halogen Network; HD Theater; HDNet; HDNet Movies; HGTV HD; History Channel en Espanol; History Channel International; Independent Film Channel; Latele Novela Network; Lifetime Movie Network; Military Channel; MTV Hits; MTV2; mun2 television; Music Choice; National Geographic Channel; National Geographic Channel HD Network; Nick Jr.; NickToons TV; Outdoor Channel; Ritmoson Latino; Science; SoapNet; Sorpresa; Speed; Style Network; Sundance Channel; Sur Network; TBN Enlace USA; TeenNick; Telehit; Tennis Channel; Toon Disney; Toon Disney en Espanol; Tr3s; Turner Classic Movies; Turner Network TV HD; TV Chile; Universal HD; VH1 Classic; VHUNO; Video Rola.

Digital Pay Service 1

Pay Units: N.A.

Programming (via satellite): Cinemax (multiplexed); HBO (multiplexed); HBO HD; HBO Latino; Showtime (multiplexed); Showtime HD; Starz (multiplexed); Starz HDTV; The Movie Channel (multiplexed).

Video-On-Demand: Yes

Pay-Per-View

iN DEMAND (delivered digitally); Fresh (delivered digitally); Playboy TV (delivered digitally).

Internet Service

Operational: Yes.

Broadband Service: Suddenlink High Speed Internet.

Fee: $49.95 installation; $29.95 monthly.

Telephone Service

None

Miles of Plant: 169.0 (coaxial); None (fiber optic).

Manager: Nathan Geick.

Ownership: Cequel Communications LLC (MSO).

CONROE WEST—Suddenlink Communications, 12444 Powerscourt Dr, Saint Louis, MO 63131-3660. Phones: 800-999-6845; 314-965-2020. Fax: 903-561-5485. Web Site: http://www.suddenlink.com. Also serves Montgomery (unincorporated areas). ICA: TX0742.

TV Market Ranking: Below 100 (CONROE WEST, Montgomery (unincorporated areas)). Franchise award date: N.A. Franchise expiration date: N.A. Began: N.A.

Channel capacity: 36 (operating 2-way). Channels available but not in use: N.A.

Basic Service

Subscribers: 228.

Programming (received off-air): KETH-TV (TBN) Houston; KFTH-DT (TEL) Alvin; KHOU (CBS) Houston; KLTJ (ETV) Galveston; KPRC-TV (NBC) Houston; KPXB-TV (ION) Conroe; KRIV (FOX) Houston; KTBU (IND) Conroe; KTMD (TMO) Galveston; KTRK-TV (ABC) Houston; KTXH (MNT) Houston; KUBE-TV (IND) Baytown; KUHT (PBS) Houston; KXLN-DT (UNV) Rosenberg; KYAZ (IND) Katy; KZJL (IND) Houston.

Programming (via satellite): WGN America.

Fee: $19.05 monthly.

Expanded Basic Service 1

Subscribers: N.A.

Programming (via satellite): A&E Networks; ABC Family Channel; AMC; Animal Planet; BET Networks; Bravo; Cartoon Network; CNBC; CNN; Comedy Central; Country Music TV; C-SPAN; C-SPAN 2; Discovery Channel; Disney Channel; E! Entertainment Television; ESPN; ESPN 2; ESPN Classic Sports; Eternal Word TV Network; Food Network; Fox News Channel; Fox Soccer; Fox Sports Southwest; FX; Golf Channel; Hallmark Channel; Headline News; HGTV; History Channel; Lifetime; Lifetime Movie Network; MSNBC; MTV; Nickelodeon; Outdoor Channel; Oxygen; Shopping Channel; Speed; Spike TV; Syfy; TBS Superstation; The Learning Channel; The Weather Channel; Travel Channel; truTV; Turner Classic Movies; Turner Network TV; TV Guide Network; TV Land; USA Network; VH1; WE tv.

Fee: $23.90 monthly.

Digital Basic Service

Subscribers: N.A.

Programming (via satellite): BBC America; Bio; Bloomberg Television; cloo; C-SPAN 3; DIY Network; ESPN; ESPNews; Fox College Sports Atlantic; Fox College Sports Central; Fox College Sports Pacific; Fox Movie Channel; Fuel TV; Fuse; G4; GAS; GSN; HD Theater; HDNet; HDNet Movies; History Channel International; Independent Film Channel; Military History Channel; MTV Networks Digital Suite; Music Choice; National Geographic Channel; Nick Jr.; NickToons TV; SoapNet; Sundance Channel; Tennis Channel; Toon Disney; Versus; Weatherscan; WeatherVision.

Fee: $3.99 monthly.

Digital Pay Service 1

Pay Units: N.A.

Programming (via satellite): Cinemax (multiplexed); Encore (multiplexed); Flix; HBO (multiplexed); HBO HD; Showtime (multiplexed); Showtime HD; Starz (multiplexed); The Movie Channel (multiplexed).

Video-On-Demand: No

Pay-Per-View

iN DEMAND (delivered digitally); Playboy TV (delivered digitally).

Internet Service

Operational: Yes. Began: January 1, 2001.

Broadband Service: Suddenlink High Speed Internet.

Fee: $49.95 installation; $38.95 monthly.

Telephone Service

None

Miles of Plant: 30.0 (coaxial); None (fiber optic).

Regional Manager: Todd Cruthird. Plant Manager: Kyle Spell. Marketing Director: Beverly Gambell.

Ownership: Cequel Communications LLC (MSO).

COOLIDGE—Northland Cable Television, 515 W Tyler St, PO Box 112, Mexia, TX 76667-0112. Phones: 800-742-3087; 254-562-2872. Fax: 254-562-6454. Web Site: http://www.northlandcabletv.com. ICA: TX0569.

TV Market Ranking: Below 100 (COOLIDGE). Franchise award date: August 3, 1989. Franchise expiration date: N.A. Began: June 30, 1982.

Channel capacity: N.A. Channels available but not in use: N.A.

Basic Service

Subscribers: 190.

Programming (received off-air): KAKW-DT (UNV) Killeen; KCEN-TV (NBC, IND) Temple; KDAF (CW, IND) Dallas; KDFI (MNT) Dallas; KDFW-DT (FOX) Dallas; KERA-TV (PBS) Dallas; KTVT (CBS) Fort Worth; KTXA (IND) Fort Worth; KWKT-TV (FOX, MNT) Waco; KWTX-TV (CBS, CW) Waco; KXAS-TV (NBC) Fort Worth; KXTX-TV (TMO) Dallas; KXXV (ABC, TMO) Waco; WFAA (ABC) Dallas.

Programming (via satellite): BET Networks; Cartoon Network; CNN; Country Music TV; Discovery Channel; ESPN; Fox Sports Southwest; HGTV; Lifetime; TBS Superstation; Trinity Broadcasting Network; Turner Classic Movies; Turner Network TV.

Fee: $55.00 installation; $31.99 monthly.

Pay Service 1

Pay Units: 27.

Programming (via satellite): Cinemax.

Fee: $11.50 monthly.

Pay Service 2

Pay Units: 33.

Programming (via satellite): HBO.

Fee: $13.50 monthly.

Internet Service

Operational: No.

Telephone Service

None

Miles of Plant: 6.0 (coaxial); None (fiber optic).

Manager: Brent Richey. Chief Technician: Joe Lopez. Technician: Kelly Rogers. Office Manager: Pamela Elliott. Head Customer Service Representative: Elaine Norris.

Ownership: Northland Communications Corp. (MSO).

COOPER—Alliance Communications, 6125 Paluxy Dr, Tyler, TX 75703. Phones: 501-679-6619; 800-842-8160. Fax: 501-679-5694. Web Site: http://www.alliancecable.net. ICA: TX0099.

TV Market Ranking: Below 100 (COOPER). Franchise award date: N.A. Franchise expiration date: N.A. Began: April 1, 1963.

Channel capacity: N.A. Channels available but not in use: N.A.

Basic Service

Subscribers: 178.

Programming (received off-air): KDAF (CW, IND) Dallas; KDFI (MNT) Dallas; KDFW-DT (FOX) Dallas; KERA-TV (PBS) Dallas; KPXD-TV (ION) Arlington; KSTR-DT (TEL) Irving; KTAQ (IND) Greenville; KTVT (CBS) Fort Worth; KTXA (IND) Fort Worth; KUVN-DT (UNV) Garland; KXAS-TV (NBC) Fort Worth; KXTX-TV (TMO) Dallas; WFAA (ABC) Dallas; allband FM.

Programming (via satellite): C-SPAN; C-SPAN 2; QVC; Trinity Broadcasting Network; WGN America.

Fee: $45.10 installation; $7.02 monthly; $2.00 converter.

Expanded Basic Service 1

Subscribers: 111.

Programming (via satellite): A&E Networks; ABC Family Channel; AMC; Animal Planet; BET Networks; CNBC; CNN; Comedy Central; Country Music TV; Discovery Channel; Disney Channel; E! Entertainment Television; ESPN; ESPN 2; Food Network; Fox News Channel; Fox Sports Southwest; FX; Golf Channel; Hallmark Channel; Headline News; History Channel; Lifetime; MSNBC; MTV; Nickelodeon; Spike TV; TBS Superstation; Texas Cable News; The Learning Channel; The Weather Channel; truTV; Turner Classic Movies; Turner Network TV; TV Land; USA Network; Versus; VH1.

Fee: $13.51 installation; $28.25 monthly.

Digital Basic Service

Subscribers: 11.

Programming (via satellite): BBC America; Bio; Bravo; Cartoon Network; CMT Pure Country; Discovery Fit & Health; Discovery Health Channel; Discovery Home Channel; Discovery Kids Channel; Discovery Times Channel; Encore (multiplexed); ESPN Classic Sports; ESPNews; Fox Soccer; G4; GSN; Halogen Network; HGTV; History Channel International; Independent Film Channel; Lifetime Movie Network; Military Channel; MTV Jams; MTV2; Music Choice; National Geographic Channel; Nick Jr.; Nick Too; Outdoor Channel; Science; Speed; Style Network; Syfy; TeenNick; Toon Disney; Travel Channel; VH1 Classic; WE tv.

Digital Pay Service 1

Pay Units: N.A.

Programming (via satellite): Cinemax (multiplexed); HBO (multiplexed); Showtime (multiplexed); Starz (multiplexed); The Movie Channel (multiplexed).

Video-On-Demand: No

Pay-Per-View

iN DEMAND (delivered digitally); Playboy TV (delivered digitally); Fresh (delivered digitally); ESPN (delivered digitally).

Internet Service

Operational: Yes.

Broadband Service: In-house.

Telephone Service

Digital: Operational

Miles of Plant: 79.0 (coaxial); None (fiber optic).

Vice President & General Manager: John Brinker. Vice President, Programming: Julie Newman.

Ownership: Buford Media Group LLC (MSO).

CORPUS CHRISTI—Grande Communications, 401 Carlson Circle, San Marcos, TX 78666. Phones: 512-878-4000; 361-334-4600 (Customer service). Fax: 512-878-4010. Web Site: http://www.grandecom.com. ICA: TX0979. **Note:** This system is an overbuild.

TV Market Ranking: Below 100 (CORPUS CHRISTI). Franchise award date: November 10, 1999. Franchise expiration date: N.A. Began: July 1, 2000.

Channel capacity: N.A. Channels available but not in use: N.A.

Basic Service

Subscribers: N.A.

Programming (received off-air): KCBO-LP (IND) Corpus Christi; KCRP-CA (TEL) Corpus Christi; KDFW-DT (FOX) Dallas; KEDT (PBS) Corpus Christi; KIII (ABC) Corpus Christi; KORO (UNV) Corpus Christi; KRIS-TV (CW, NBC) Corpus Christi; KTMV-LP (IND) Corpus Christi; KTOV-LP Corpus Christi; KXPX-CA Corpus Christi; KZTV (CBS) Corpus Christi.

Programming (via satellite): Azteca America; C-SPAN 2; LWS Local Weather Station; QVC; Telemundo; TV Guide Network; WGN America.

Fee: $14.95 monthly.

Expanded Basic Service 1

Subscribers: N.A.

Programming (via satellite): A&E Networks; ABC Family Channel; AMC; Animal Planet; BET Networks; Bravo; Cartoon Network; CNBC; CNN; Comedy Central; Country Music TV; C-SPAN; Discovery Channel; Discovery Health Channel; Disney Channel; E! Entertainment Television; ESPN; ESPN 2; ESPN Classic Sports; Eternal Word TV Network; Food Network; Fox Deportes; Fox News Channel; Fox Sports Southwest; FX; G4; GalaVision; Golf Channel; Great American Country; GSN; Hallmark Channel; Headline News; HGTV; History Channel; Lifetime; MSNBC; MTV; mun2 television; National Geographic Channel; Nickelodeon; Oxygen; SoapNet; Speed; Spike TV; Syfy; TBS Superstation; The Learning Channel; The Weather Channel; Toon Disney; Travel Channel; Trinity Broadcasting Network; truTV; Turner Classic Movies; Turner Network TV; TV Land; USA Network; Versus; VH1.

Fee: $29.00 monthly.

Digital Basic Service

Subscribers: N.A.

Programming (via satellite): American-Life TV Network; BBC America; Bio; Boomerang; Canales N; CBS Sports Network; Colours; Cooking Channel; Discovery Fit & Health; DIY Network; ESPN; ESPNews; FamilyNet; Fox College Sports Atlantic; Fox College Sports Central; Fox College Sports Pacific; Fox Movie Channel; Fox Soccer; Fuel TV; Fuse; GAS; GolTV; HD Theater; History Channel International; INHD (multiplexed); Lifetime Movie Network; MTV Networks Digital Suite; Music Choice; NBA TV; NFL Network; Nick Jr.; Nick Too; NickToons TV; Nuvo TV; Radar Channel; Tennis Channel; Turner Network TV; TVG Network; Univision Studios.

Fee: $14.00 monthly.

Digital Pay Service 1

Pay Units: N.A.

Programming (via satellite): Cinemax (multiplexed); Cinemax HD; Encore (multiplexed); Flix (multiplexed); HBO (multiplexed); HBO HD; Showtime (multiplexed); Showtime HD; Starz (multiplexed); Sundance Channel (multiplexed); The Movie Channel (multiplexed).

Fee: $12.99 monthly (Cinemax, HBO, Starz/Encore or Showtime/FlixSundance/TMC).

Video-On-Demand: No

Pay-Per-View

Playboy TV (delivered digitally); Fresh (delivered digitally); ESPN Now (delivered digitally); Hot Choice (delivered digitally); iN DEMAND (delivered digitally); Pleasure (delivered digitally); Shorteez (delivered digitally); Sports PPV (delivered digitally).

Internet Service

Operational: Yes.

Broadband Service: Grande High Speed Internet.

Fee: $19.95 monthly.

Telephone Service

Digital: Operational

Fee: $9.00 monthly

General Manager: Dottie Lane. Video Services Director: Diane Wigington.

Ownership: Grande Communications Networks Inc. (MSO).

CORPUS CHRISTI—Time Warner Cable, 4060 S Padre Island Dr, Corpus Christi, TX 78411-4402. Phones: 972-899-7300 (Flower Mound office); 361-698-6259. Fax: 361-857-5038. Web Site: http://www.timewarnercable.com/Texas. Also serves Banquete, Bishop, Corpus Christi Naval Air Station, Driscoll, Nueces County, Odem, Robstown & San Patricio County. ICA: TX0010.

TV Market Ranking: Below 100 (Banquete, Bishop, CORPUS CHRISTI, Corpus Christi Naval Air Station, Driscoll, Nueces County, Odem, Robstown, San Patricio County). Franchise award date: N.A. Franchise expiration date: N.A. Began: February 1, 1972.

Channel capacity: N.A. Channels available but not in use: N.A.

Basic Service

Subscribers: 97,000 Includes Alice, Beeville, George West, Mathis, Orange Grove, Port O'Connor, & Seadrift.

Programming (received off-air): KDFW-DT (FOX) Dallas; KEDT (PBS) Corpus Christi; KIII (ABC) Corpus Christi; KORO (UNV) Corpus Christi; KRIS-TV (CW, NBC) Corpus Christi; KTMV-LP (IND) Corpus Christi; KTOV-LP Corpus Christi; KZTV (CBS) Corpus Christi; 14 FMs.

Programming (via satellite): Discovery Channel; Weatherscan; WGN America.

Fee: $34.99 installation; $16.39 monthly.

Expanded Basic Service 1

Subscribers: 46,921.

Programming (via satellite): A&E Networks; ABC Family Channel; AMC; Animal Planet; BET Networks; Bravo; Cartoon Network; CNBC; CNN; Comedy Central; Country Music TV; C-SPAN; C-SPAN 2; Disney Channel; E! Entertainment Television; ESPN; ESPN 2; ESPN Classic Sports; ESPNews; Eternal Word TV Network; Food Network; Fox News Channel; Fox Sports Southwest; FX; GalaVision; Golf Channel; Great American Country; Hallmark Channel; Headline News; HGTV; History Channel; Lifetime; Lifetime Movie Network; MSNBC; MTV; mun2 television; National Geographic Channel; Nickelodeon; Oxygen; QVC; Shop at Home; SoapNet; Speed; Spike TV; Syfy; TBS Superstation; Texas Cable News; The Learning Channel; The Weather Channel; Travel Channel; truTV; Turner Classic Movies; Turner Network TV; TV Land; USA Network; Versus; VH1; WE tv.

Fee: $28.60 monthly.

Digital Basic Service

Subscribers: N.A.

Programming (via satellite): AmericanLife TV Network; America's Store; BBC America; Bio; Bloomberg Television; Canales N; Cooking Channel; DIY Network; ESPN Full Court; ESPN HD; FamilyNet; Fox Soccer; Fuse; G4; GAS; GSN; HD Theater; HDNet; HDNet Movies; History Channel International; Independent Film Channel; INHD; Lifetime Real Women; MLB Extra Innings; MTV Networks Digital Suite; Music Choice; NASCAR In Car; NBA League Pass; NBA TV; NHL Center Ice; Nick Jr.; Nick Too; NickToons TV; Ovation; Toon Disney; Trinity Broadcasting Network; Trio; Turner Network TV HD.

Fee: $8.04 monthly.

Digital Expanded Basic Service

Subscribers: N.A.

Programming (via satellite): Fox College Sports Atlantic; Fox College Sports Central; Fox College Sports Pacific; Fuel TV; Outdoor Channel; Tennis Channel.

Fee: $8.95 monthly.

Digital Expanded Basic Service 2

Subscribers: N.A.

Programming (via satellite): Encore; Fox Movie Channel; Sundance Channel.

Fee: $8.95 monthly.

Digital Pay Service 1

Pay Units: N.A.

Programming (via satellite): Cinemax (multiplexed); Encore (multiplexed); Flix; HBO (multiplexed); HBO HD; Showtime (multiplexed); Showtime HD; Starz (multiplexed); The Movie Channel (multiplexed).

Fee: $12.95 monthly (each).

Video-On-Demand: Yes

Pay-Per-View

iN DEMAND; Hot Choice (delivered digitally); Fresh (delivered digitally); Shorteez (delivered digitally); Playboy TV (delivered digitally); Spice Live (delivered digitally).

Internet Service

Operational: Yes.

Broadband Service: Road Runner.

Fee: $44.99 installation; $44.95 monthly.

Telephone Service

Digital: Operational

Fee: $44.95 monthly

Miles of Plant: 1,149.0 (coaxial); None (fiber optic).

President: Connie Wharton. Vice President & General Manager: Mike McKee. Engineering Director: Charlotte Strong. Public Affairs Manager: Vicki Triplett.

Ownership: Time Warner Cable (MSO).; Advance/Newhouse Partnership (MSO).

CORRIGAN—Suddenlink Communications, 1415 S 1st St, Lufkin, TX 75901-4749. Phones: 800-584-5610; 936-639-1116. Fax: 936-634-6889. Web Site: http://www.suddenlink.com. Also serves Angelina County, Burke, Diboll, Fuller Springs, Lufkin & Polk County (portions). ICA: TX0051.

TV Market Ranking: Below 100 (Angelina County, Burke, CORRIGAN, Diboll, Fuller Springs, Lufkin, Polk County (portions)); Outside TV Markets (Polk County (portions)). Franchise award date: June 17, 1958. Franchise expiration date: N.A. Began: February 27, 1960.

Channel capacity: N.A. Channels available but not in use: N.A.

Basic Service

Subscribers: 12,733.

Programming (received off-air): KCEB (CW) Longview; KETK-LP (NBC) Lufkin; KFXK-TV (FOX) Longview; KFXL-LP Lufkin; KHOU (CBS) Houston; KIBN-LP Lufkin; KLUF-LP Lufkin; KPRC-TV (NBC) Houston; KTRE (ABC) Lufkin; KTRK-TV (ABC) Houston; KUHT (PBS) Houston; KXTX-TV (TMO) Dallas; KYTX (CBS, IND) Nacogdoches; 7 FMs.

Programming (via satellite): QVC; TBS Superstation; Univision Studios.

Fee: $38.00 installation; $29.78 monthly; $15.00 additional installation.

Expanded Basic Service 1

Subscribers: 1,126.

Programming (via satellite): A&E Networks; ABC Family Channel; Animal Planet; BET Networks; Bravo; Cartoon Network; CNBC; CNN; Comedy Central; Country Music TV; C-SPAN; C-SPAN 2; Discovery Channel; Discovery Health Channel; Disney Channel; E! Entertainment Television; ESPN; ESPN 2; Eternal Word TV Network; Food Network; Fox News Channel; Fox Sports Southwest; FX; Great American Country; Headline News; HGTV; History Channel; INSP; Jewelry Television; Lifetime; Lifetime Movie Network; MTV; MTV2; Nickelodeon; Spike TV; Syfy; The Learning Channel; The Weather Channel; Travel Channel; truTV; Turner Classic Movies; Turner Network TV; TV Guide Network; TV Land; USA Network; Versus; VH1.

Fee: $10.95 monthly.

Digital Basic Service

Subscribers: N.A.

Programming (via satellite): A&E HD; Bandamax; BBC America; Bio; Bloomberg Television; Boomerang; Boomerang en Espanol; CBS Sports Network; Cine Latino; Cine Mexicano; CMT Pure Country; CNN en Espanol; Cooking Channel; De Pelicula; De Pelicula Clasico; Discovery en Espanol; Discovery Home Channel; Discovery Kids Channel; DIY Network; Encore (multiplexed); ESPN Classic Sports; ESPN Deportes; ESPN HD; ESPN U; ESPNews; EWTN en Espanol; FamilyNet; Food Network HD; Fox Deportes; Fox Reality Channel; Fox Soccer; FSN HD; Fuel TV; Fuse; G4; GalaVision; Golf Channel; GSN; Hallmark Channel; Halogen Network; HD Theater; HDNet; HDNet Movies; HGTV HD; History Channel en Espanol; History Channel International; ID Investigation Discovery; Independent Film Channel; Latele Novela Network; Military Channel; MTV Hits; mun2 television; Music Choice; National Geographic Channel; National Geographic Channel HD Network; Nick Jr.; NickToons en Espanol; NickToons TV; Nuvo TV; Outdoor Channel; Ritmoson Latino; Science; SoapNet; Sorpresa; Speed; Style Network; Sundance Channel; Sur Network; TBN Enlace USA; TeenNick; Telefutura; Telehit; Tennis Channel; Toon Disney; Tr3s; Trinity Broadcasting Network; Turner Classic Movies; Turner Network TV HD; TV Chile; Universal HD; VH1 Classic; Video Rola; Weatherscan.

Digital Pay Service 1

Pay Units: N.A.

Programming (via satellite): Cinemax (multiplexed); HBO (multiplexed); HBO HD; HBO Latino; Showtime (multiplexed); Showtime HD; Starz (multiplexed); Starz HDTV; The Movie Channel (multiplexed).

Video-On-Demand: No

Pay-Per-View

iN DEMAND (delivered digitally); Fresh (delivered digitally); Shorteez (delivered digitally); Playboy TV (delivered digitally); Club Jenna (delivered digitally); Spice: Xcess (delivered digitally).

Internet Service

Operational: Yes.

Broadband Service: Suddenlink High Speed Internet.

Fee: $49.95 installation; $24.95 monthly.

Telephone Service

Digital: Operational

Fee: $48.95 monthly

Miles of Plant: 374.0 (coaxial); None (fiber optic).

Manager: Glenn Parker. Marketing Director: Mike Evans. Chief Technician: Jerry Teer.

Ownership: Cequel Communications LLC (MSO).

CORSICANA—Northland Cable Television, 1500 N Beaton St, PO Box 550, Corsicana, TX 75151. Phones: 800-872-3905; 903-872-3131. Fax: 903-872-6623. E-mail: corsicana@northlandcabletv.com. Web Site: http://www.northlandcabletv.com. ICA: TX0082.

TV Market Ranking: Outside TV Markets (CORSICANA). Franchise award date: N.A. Franchise expiration date: N.A. Began: May 1, 1971.

Channel capacity: 58 (operating 2-way). Channels available but not in use: N.A.

Basic Service

Subscribers: 5,700.

Programming (received off-air): KDAF (CW, IND) Dallas; KDFI (MNT) Dallas; KDFW-DT (FOX) Dallas; KDTN (ETV) Denton; KERA-TV (PBS) Dallas; KETK-TV (NBC) Jacksonville; KFWD (IND) Fort Worth; KSTR-DT (TEL) Irving; KTVT (CBS) Fort Worth; KTXA (IND) Fort Worth; KWTX-TV (CBS, CW) Waco; KXAS-TV (NBC) Fort Worth; KXTX-TV (TMO) Dallas; KXXV (ABC, TMO) Waco; WFAA (ABC) Dallas; 16 FMs.

Programming (via satellite): A&E Networks; Animal Planet; BET Networks; Cartoon Network; CNBC; CNN; C-SPAN; Discovery Channel; ESPN; ESPN 2; Fox News Channel; Fox Sports Southwest; GalaVision; Great American Country; Hallmark Channel; Headline News; HGTV; National Geographic Channel; QVC; Spike TV; Starz; TBS Superstation; The Learning Channel; The Weather Channel; Travel Channel; Trinity Broadcasting Network; Turner Network TV; TV Guide Network; Univision Studios; USA Network; WGN America.

Fee: $19.95 installation; $34.99 monthly.

Expanded Basic Service 1

Subscribers: N.A.

Programming (via satellite): ABC Family Channel; Comedy Central; E! Entertainment Television; Food Network; FX; Golf Channel; History Channel; Lifetime; MTV; Nickelodeon; Outdoor Channel; QVC; Syfy; Telemundo; Trinity Broadcasting Network; Turner Classic Movies; VH1.

Fee: $42.29 monthly.

Digital Basic Service

Subscribers: N.A.

Programming (via satellite): AmericanLife TV Network; BBC America; Bloomberg Television; Discovery Digital Networks; DMX Music; G4; Halogen Network; Speed.

Fee: $51.99 monthly.

Digital Expanded Basic Service

Subscribers: N.A.

Programming (via satellite): Bravo; Canales N; Discovery Fit & Health; GSN; Independent Film Channel; Versus; WE tv.

Pay Service 1

Pay Units: N.A.

Programming (via satellite): HBO.

Fee: $10.00 installation.

Digital Pay Service 1
Pay Units: N.A.
Programming (via satellite): Cinemax (multiplexed); Encore (multiplexed); Flix; HBO (multiplexed); Showtime (multiplexed); Starz (multiplexed); The Movie Channel (multiplexed).
Fee: $14.75 monthly (each).
Video-On-Demand: No
Internet Service
Operational: Yes.
Broadband Service: Northland Express.
Fee: $42.99 monthly.
Telephone Service
None
Miles of Plant: 130.0 (coaxial); None (fiber optic). Additional miles planned: 10.0 (coaxial).
Regional Manager: Richard Gammon. Plant Manager: Terry Granger. Chief Technician: Bobby Brady. Office Manager: Diane Ball.
Ownership: Northland Communications Corp.

COTULLA—Time Warner Cable. Now served by PEARSALL, TX [TX0196]. ICA: TX0266.

COUNTRY CLUB SHORES—Formerly served by CableSouth Inc. No longer in operation. ICA: TX0743.

COUNTRY HAVEN—Formerly served by Cebridge Connections. No longer in operation. ICA: TX0961.

CRANDALL—Formerly served by Almega Cable. No longer in operation. ICA: TX0554.

CRANE—Suddenlink Communications, 12444 Powerscourt Dr, Saint Louis, MO 63131-3660. Phone: 314-965-2020. Web Site: http://www.suddenlink.com. ICA: TX0228.
TV Market Ranking: Below 100 (CRANE). Franchise award date: April 30, 1987. Franchise expiration date: N.A. Began: April 1, 1978.
Channel capacity: N.A. Channels available but not in use: N.A.
Basic Service
Subscribers: 992.
Programming (received off-air): KMID (ABC) Midland; KMLM-DT (IND) Odessa; KOSA-TV (CBS, MNT) Odessa; KPBT-TV (PBS) Odessa; KPEJ-TV (FOX) Odessa; KWES-TV (NBC) Odessa; allband FM.
Programming (via satellite): A&E Networks; ABC Family Channel; AmericanLife TV Network; CNN; Country Music TV; C-SPAN; Discovery Channel; Disney Channel; ESPN; Fox Sports Southwest; GalaVision; Headline News; Lifetime; Nickelodeon; QVC; Spike TV; TBS Superstation; The Learning Channel; The Weather Channel; Turner Network TV; TV Land; USA Network; WGN America.
Fee: $39.95 installation; $19.95 monthly.
Pay Service 1
Pay Units: 211.
Programming (via satellite): HBO.
Fee: $10.95 monthly.
Pay Service 2
Pay Units: 93.
Programming (via satellite): Showtime.
Fee: $9.95 monthly.
Pay Service 3
Pay Units: 92.
Programming (via satellite): The Movie Channel.
Fee: $7.95 monthly.
Internet Service
Operational: Yes. Began: May 19, 2003.
Broadband Service: Suddenlink High Speed Internet.
Fee: $45.95 installation; $29.95 monthly.
Telephone Service
None
Miles of Plant: 28.0 (coaxial); None (fiber optic).
Regional Manager: Todd Cruthird. Plant Manager: Manuel Gonzales. Regional Marketing Manager: Beverly Gambell.
Ownership: Cequel Communications LLC (MSO).

CRANFILLS GAP—Formerly served by National Cable Inc. No longer in operation. ICA: TX0904.

CRAWFORD—Zito Media, 611 Vader Hill Rd, Coudersport, PA 16915. Phone: 866-879-6235. E-mail: support@zitomedia.net. Web Site: http://www.zitomedia.com. ICA: TX0584.
TV Market Ranking: Below 100 (CRAWFORD). Franchise award date: N.A. Franchise expiration date: N.A. Began: January 1, 1984.
Channel capacity: 54 (not 2-way capable). Channels available but not in use: N.A.
Basic Service
Subscribers: 57.
Programming (received off-air): KCEN-TV (NBC, IND) Temple; KNCT (PBS) Belton; KTVT (CBS) Fort Worth; KWKT-TV (FOX, MNT) Waco; KWTX-TV (CBS, CW) Waco; KXXV (ABC, TMO) Waco; WFAA (ABC) Dallas.
Programming (via satellite): A&E Networks; ABC Family Channel; AMC; Animal Planet; Cartoon Network; CNN; Discovery Channel; Disney Channel; ESPN; ESPN 2; Fox News Channel; Fuse; Great American Country; Headline News; HGTV; INSP; Lifetime; Outdoor Channel; QVC; TBS Superstation; The Learning Channel; Turner Network TV; USA Network; WGN America.
Fee: $30.00 installation; $36.50 monthly.
Pay Service 1
Pay Units: N.A.
Programming (via satellite): Cinemax; HBO; Showtime.
Fee: $12.00 monthly (each).
Internet Service
Operational: No.
Telephone Service
None
Miles of Plant: 8.0 (coaxial); None (fiber optic).
President: James Rigas.
Ownership: Zito Media (MSO).

CROCKETT—Northland Cable Television, 1202 E Houston Ave, PO Box 1228, Crockett, TX 75835. Phones: 800-615-1110; 936-544-2031. Fax: 936-544-9660. Web Site: http://www.northlandcabletv.com. ICA: TX0159.
TV Market Ranking: Outside TV Markets (CROCKETT). Franchise award date: N.A. Franchise expiration date: N.A. Began: August 1, 1963.
Channel capacity: 52 (2-way capable). Channels available but not in use: N.A.
Basic Service
Subscribers: 1,700.
Programming (received off-air): KBTX-TV (CBS, CW) Bryan; KETK-TV (NBC) Jacksonville; KFXL-LP Lufkin; KTRE (ABC) Lufkin; KYTX (CBS, IND) Nacogdoches; 5 FMs.
Programming (via microwave): KHOU (CBS) Houston; KIAH (CW) Houston; KRIV (FOX) Houston; KTRK-TV (ABC) Houston; KUHT (PBS) Houston.
Programming (via satellite): A&E Networks; BET Networks; Cartoon Network; CNBC; CNN; C-SPAN; Discovery Channel; ESPN; Fox News Channel; Fox Sports Southwest; Great American Country; Hallmark Channel; Headline News; HGTV; Outdoor Channel; QVC; TBS Superstation; Telemundo; The Learning Channel; The Weather Channel; Travel Channel; Trinity Broadcasting Network; Turner Network TV; TV Guide Network; Univision Studios; USA Network; WGN America.
Fee: $50.00 installation; $38.99 monthly.
Expanded Basic Service 1
Subscribers: 1,100.
Programming (via satellite): Animal Planet; E! Entertainment Television; ESPN 2; Food Network; Fox Movie Channel; History Channel; Lifetime; Nickelodeon; Spike TV; Syfy; Turner Classic Movies.
Fee: $49.99 monthly.
Digital Basic Service
Subscribers: 125.
Programming (via satellite): AmericanLife TV Network; Bloomberg Television; Bravo; Discovery Fit & Health; DMX Music; G4; Golf Channel; GSN; Halogen Network; Independent Film Channel; Speed; WE tv.
Fee: $54.99 monthly.
Pay Service 1
Pay Units: 200.
Programming (via satellite): HBO.
Fee: $14.00 monthly.
Digital Pay Service 1
Pay Units: 25.
Programming (via satellite): Cinemax (multiplexed).
Fee: $14.75 monthly.
Digital Pay Service 2
Pay Units: 30.
Programming (via satellite): Showtime (multiplexed); The Movie Channel (multiplexed).
Fee: $14.75 monthly.
Digital Pay Service 3
Pay Units: 100.
Programming (via satellite): Encore (multiplexed); Starz (multiplexed).
Fee: $14.75 monthly.
Digital Pay Service 4
Pay Units: N.A.
Programming (via satellite): HBO (multiplexed).
Fee: $14.75 monthly.
Video-On-Demand: No
Pay-Per-View
Sports PPV (delivered digitally); iN DEMAND (delivered digitally).
Internet Service
Operational: Yes.
Fee: $42.99 monthly.
Telephone Service
Analog: Not Operational
Digital: Planned
Miles of Plant: 69.0 (coaxial); None (fiber optic). Additional miles planned: 2.0 (coaxial).
Regional Manager: Brent Richey. Office Manager: Linda Richie. Chief Technician: John Guys.
Ownership: Northland Communications Corp. (MSO).

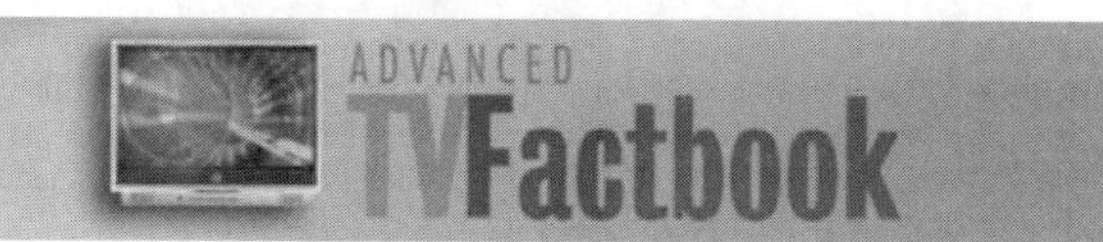

CROSBYTON—Reach Broadband, 515 E Longview St, Arp, TX 75750. Phone: 800-687-1258. Web Site: http://www.reachbroadband.net. ICA: TX0384.
TV Market Ranking: Below 100 (CROSBYTON). Franchise award date: October 1, 1978. Franchise expiration date: N.A. Began: October 1, 1978.
Channel capacity: 61 (not 2-way capable). Channels available but not in use: N.A.
Basic Service
Subscribers: 298.
Programming (received off-air): KAMC (ABC) Lubbock; KBZO-LP (UNV) Lubbock; KJTV-TV (FOX) Lubbock; KLBK-TV (CBS) Lubbock; KLCW-TV (CW) Wolfforth; KRPV-DT (IND) Roswell; KTXT-TV (PBS) Lubbock; allband FM.
Programming (via satellite): ABC Family Channel; AMC; Animal Planet; Cartoon Network; CNN; Discovery Channel; Disney Channel; E! Entertainment Television; ESPN; ESPN 2; Fox News Channel; Fox Sports Southwest; FX; Great American Country; Headline News; HGTV; History Channel; Lifetime; National Geographic Channel; Nickelodeon; QVC; Spike TV; TBS Superstation; The Learning Channel; The Weather Channel; Trinity Broadcasting Network; Turner Network TV; TV Land; USA Network; VH1.
Fee: $29.95 installation; $38.00 monthly.
Pay Service 1
Pay Units: 39.
Programming (via satellite): Cinemax.
Fee: $9.95 monthly.
Pay Service 2
Pay Units: 75.
Programming (via satellite): HBO.
Fee: $9.95 monthly.
Video-On-Demand: No
Internet Service
Operational: No.
Telephone Service
None
Miles of Plant: 12.0 (coaxial); None (fiber optic).
Regional Manager: Ronnie Stafford. Office Manager: Jan Gibson.
Ownership: RB3 LLC (MSO).

CROWELL—Alliance Communications, 6125 Paluxy Dr, Tyler, TX 75703. Phones: 501-679-6619; 800-842-8160. Fax: 501-679-5694. Web Site: http://www.alliancecable.net. ICA: TX0509.
TV Market Ranking: Outside TV Markets (CROWELL). Franchise award date: N.A. Franchise expiration date: N.A. Began: January 1, 1977.
Channel capacity: 61 (not 2-way capable). Channels available but not in use: N.A.
Basic Service
Subscribers: 64.
Programming (received off-air): KAUZ-TV (CBS, CW) Wichita Falls; KFDX-TV (NBC)

Wichita Falls; KJTL (FOX) Wichita Falls; KSWO-TV (ABC, TMO) Lawton; 1 FM.
Programming (via satellite): A&E Networks; ABC Family Channel; AMC; Animal Planet; Cartoon Network; CNN; Discovery Channel; Disney Channel; E! Entertainment Television; ESPN; ESPN 2; Fox Sports Southwest; FX; Great American Country; Headline News; History Channel; Lifetime; MSNBC; National Geographic Channel; Nickelodeon; QVC; Spike TV; Syfy; TBS Superstation; The Learning Channel; The Weather Channel; Trinity Broadcasting Network; Turner Network TV; TV Land; Univision Studios; USA Network; VH1.
Fee: $29.95 installation; $38.00 monthly.

Expanded Basic Service 1
Subscribers: 43.

Pay Service 1
Pay Units: N.A.
Programming (via satellite): Cinemax; HBO.

Video-On-Demand: No

Internet Service
Operational: No.

Telephone Service
None

Miles of Plant: 11.0 (coaxial); None (fiber optic).
Vice President & General Manager: John Brinker. Vice President, Programming: Julie Newman.
Ownership: Buford Media Group LLC (MSO).

CRYSTAL BEACH—Formerly served by Rapid Cable. No longer in operation. ICA: TX0132.

CRYSTAL CITY—Time Warner Cable, 1313 W Carlton Rd, Laredo, TX 78041. Phones: 972-899-7300 (Flower Mound office); 956-721-0607. Fax: 956-721-0612. Web Site: http://www.timewarnercable.com/Texas. Also serves Asherton, Carrizo Springs, Dimmit County & Zavala County. ICA: TX0147.
TV Market Ranking: Below 100 (Dimmit County (portions), Zavala County (portions)); Outside TV Markets (Asherton, Carrizo Springs, CRYSTAL CITY, Dimmit County (portions), Zavala County (portions)). Franchise award date: N.A. Franchise expiration date: N.A. Began: September 1, 1968.
Channel capacity: N.A. Channels available but not in use: N.A.

Basic Service
Subscribers: N.A. Included in Del Rio
Programming (received off-air): KGNS-TV (CW, NBC, TMO) Laredo; KPXL-TV (ION) Uvalde; allband FM.
Programming (via microwave): KENS (CBS) San Antonio; KLRN (PBS) San Antonio; KSAT-TV (ABC) San Antonio; KWEX-DT (UNV) San Antonio; WOAI-TV (NBC) San Antonio.
Programming (via satellite): AMC; Animal Planet; BET Networks; Bravo; Cartoon Network; CNN; Comedy Central; C-SPAN; C-SPAN 2; Discovery Channel; Discovery Health Channel; Disney Channel; E! Entertainment Television; ESPN; ESPN 2; ESPN Classic Sports; Eternal Word TV Network; Food Network; Fox Deportes; Fox News Channel; Fox Sports Southwest; FX; GalaVision; Golf Channel; Great American Country; Hallmark Channel; Headline News; HGTV; History Channel; KABB (FOX) San Antonio; Lifetime; MoviePlex; MSNBC; MTV; mun2 television; National Geographic Channel; Nickelodeon; Oxygen; QVC; ShopNBC; SoapNet; Spike TV; Style Network; Syfy; TBS Superstation; Telemundo; Texas Cable News; The Weather Channel; Travel Channel; Trinity Broadcasting Network; truTV; Turner Classic Movies; Turner Network TV; TV Guide Network; TV Land; USA Network; VH1; WE tv.
Fee: $33.74 installation; $40.99 monthly; $2.00 converter.

Digital Basic Service
Subscribers: N.A.
Programming (via satellite): BBC America; Bio; Bloomberg Television; Current; Discovery Digital Networks; Encore; ESPN Classic Sports; ESPNews; Fox College Sports Atlantic; Fox College Sports Central; Fox College Sports Pacific; Fox Movie Channel; Fox Soccer; Fuse; G4; GAS; GSN; History Channel International; Independent Film Channel; Lifetime Movie Network; MTV Networks Digital Suite; Music Choice; NBA TV; Nick Jr.; NickToons TV; Nuvo TV; Outdoor Channel; Speed; Sundance Channel (multiplexed); Tennis Channel; Toon Disney; Trio; Versus.
Fee: $7.00 monthy (value tier), $8.95 monthly (each additional tier).

Digital Pay Service 1
Pay Units: 173.
Programming (via satellite): Cinemax (multiplexed); HBO (multiplexed); Showtime (multiplexed); Starz (multiplexed); The Movie Channel.
Fee: $12.95 monthly (HBO, Showtime/TMC, Cinemax or Starz).

Video-On-Demand: No

Pay-Per-View
iN DEMAND (delivered digitally); Fresh (delivered digitally); Shorteez (delivered digitally); Playboy TV (delivered digitally); MLB Extra Innings (delivered digitally); NHL Center Ice (delivered digitally); NBA League Pass (delivered digitally); NASCAR In Car (delivered digitally).

Internet Service
Operational: Yes.

Telephone Service
Digital: Operational

Miles of Plant: 106.0 (coaxial); None (fiber optic).
President: Connie Wharton. Vice President & General Manager: Michael Carrosquiola. Operations Director: Marco Reyes. Technical Operations Manager: Eduardo Ruiz. Public Affairs Manager: Celinda Gonzalez.
Ownership: Time Warner Cable (MSO).; Advance/Newhouse Partnership (MSO).

CUERO—Time Warner Cable. Now served by GONZALES, TX [TX0209]. ICA: TX0202.

CUMBY—Formerly served by Cebridge Connections. No longer in operation. ICA: TX0567.

CUSHING—Almega Cable, 4001 W Airport Frwy, Ste 530, Bedford, TX 76021. Phone: 817-685-9588. Fax: 817-685-6488. Web Site: http://www.almega.com. ICA: TX0604.
TV Market Ranking: Below 100 (CUSHING). Franchise award date: N.A. Franchise expiration date: N.A. Began: February 1, 1984.
Channel capacity: 37 (not 2-way capable). Channels available but not in use: N.A.

Basic Service
Subscribers: 121.
Programming (received off-air): KLTV (ABC, TMO) Tyler; KSLA (CBS) Shreveport; KTAL-TV (NBC) Texarkana; KTBS-TV (ABC) Shreveport; KTRE (ABC) Lufkin.
Programming (via satellite): TBS Superstation; WGN America.
Fee: $54.95 installation; $44.05 monthly.

Pay Service 1
Pay Units: 15.
Programming (via satellite): Cinemax.
Fee: $12.95 monthly.

Pay Service 2
Pay Units: N.A.
Programming (via satellite): HBO.
Fee: $12.95 monthly.

Pay Service 3
Pay Units: 26.
Programming (via satellite): Showtime.
Fee: $12.95 monthly.

Video-On-Demand: No

Internet Service
Operational: No.

Telephone Service
None

Miles of Plant: 7.0 (coaxial); None (fiber optic).
Ownership: Almega Cable (MSO).

CUT AND SHOOT—Northland Cable Television, 22787 Antique Ln, PO Box 839, New Caney, TX 77357-0839. Phones: 800-689-2048; 281-689-2048. Fax: 281-689-7643. E-mail: newcaney@northlandcabletv.com. Web Site: http://www.northlandcabletv.com. Also serves Montgomery County (unincorporated ares). ICA: TX0746.
TV Market Ranking: Below 100 (CUT AND SHOOT, Montgomery County (unincorporated ares)). Franchise award date: N.A. Franchise expiration date: N.A. Began: July 1, 1987.
Channel capacity: 35 (not 2-way capable). Channels available but not in use: N.A.

Basic Service
Subscribers: 121.
Programming (received off-air): KHOU (CBS) Houston; KIAH (CW) Houston; KPRC-TV (NBC) Houston; KPXB-TV (ION) Conroe; KRIV (FOX) Houston; KTRK-TV (ABC) Houston; KTXH (MNT) Houston; KUHT (PBS) Houston; KYAZ (IND) Katy; KZJL (IND) Houston.
Programming (via satellite): A&E Networks; ABC Family Channel; Cartoon Network; CNN; C-SPAN; Discovery Channel; ESPN; ESPN 2; Headline News; History Channel; Lifetime; Nickelodeon; QVC; TBS Superstation; The Weather Channel; Trinity Broadcasting Network; Turner Classic Movies; Turner Network TV; USA Network; WGN America.
Fee: $55.00 installation; $37.88 monthly.

Pay Service 1
Pay Units: N.A.
Programming (via satellite): HBO; Showtime.
Fee: $13.50 monthly (each).

Internet Service
Operational: No.

Telephone Service
None

Miles of Plant: 30.0 (coaxial); None (fiber optic).
Manager: Richard Gammon. Marketing Director: Tammy Rogers. Chief Technician: Wade Caldwell.
Ownership: Northland Communications Corp. (MSO).

CYPRESS—Formerly served by Almega Cable. No longer in operation. ICA: TX0284.

DAINGERFIELD—Suddenlink Communications, 12444 Powerscourt Dr, Saint Louis, MO 63131-3660. Phone: 314-965-2020. Web Site: http://www.suddenlink.com. Also serves Cason, Hughes Springs, Lone Star & Morris County. ICA: TX0152.
TV Market Ranking: Below 100 (Hughes Springs, Lone Star, Morris County (portions)); Outside TV Markets (Cason, DAINGERFIELD, Morris County (portions)). Franchise award date: N.A. Franchise expiration date: N.A. Began: July 31, 1979.
Channel capacity: 62 (operating 2-way). Channels available but not in use: N.A.

Basic Service
Subscribers: 2,739.
Programming (received off-air): KLTS-TV (PBS) Shreveport; KLTV (ABC, TMO) Tyler; KMSS-TV (FOX) Shreveport; KSHV-TV (MNT) Shreveport; KSLA (CBS) Shreveport; KTAL-TV (NBC) Texarkana; KTBS-TV (ABC) Shreveport.
Programming (via satellite): QVC; The Weather Channel.
Fee: $19.95 installation; $12.00 monthly; $1.50 converter.

Expanded Basic Service 1
Subscribers: 2,592.
Programming (via satellite): A&E Networks; ABC Family Channel; AMC; Animal Planet; BET Networks; Cartoon Network; CNBC; CNN; Comedy Central; Discovery Channel; Disney Channel; E! Entertainment Television; ESPN; ESPN 2; Food Network; Fox News Channel; Fox Sports Southwest; FX; Great American Country; Hallmark Channel; Headline News; HGTV; History Channel; Lifetime; MSNBC; MTV; National Geographic Channel; Nickelodeon; Spike TV; Syfy; TBS Superstation; The Learning Channel; Trinity Broadcasting Network; truTV; Turner Classic Movies; Turner Network TV; TV Land; USA Network; VH1.
Fee: $25.00 monthly.

Digital Basic Service
Subscribers: N.A.
Programming (via satellite): BBC America; Bio; Bloomberg Television; cloo; Discovery Digital Networks; DMX Music; ESPN Classic Sports; ESPNews; Fuse; G4; Golf Channel; GSN; History Channel International; Independent Film Channel; Military History Channel; Outdoor Channel; Speed; Toon Disney; Versus; WE tv.
Fee: $3.99 monthly.

Pay Service 1
Pay Units: 252.
Programming (via satellite): Cinemax.
Fee: $7.95 monthly.

Pay Service 2
Pay Units: 448.
Programming (via satellite): HBO.
Fee: $10.95 monthly.

Pay Service 3
Pay Units: 401.
Programming (via satellite): Showtime; The Movie Channel.
Fee: $12.95 monthly (each).

Digital Pay Service 1
Pay Units: N.A.
Programming (via satellite): Cinemax (multiplexed); Encore (multiplexed); HBO (multiplexed); Showtime (multiplexed); Starz (multiplexed); The Movie Channel (multiplexed).

Pay-Per-View
iN DEMAND (delivered digitally); Fresh (delivered digitally); Playboy TV (delivered digitally).

Internet Service
Operational: Yes. Began: August 1, 2003.
Broadband Service: Suddenlink High Speed Internet.
Fee: $49.95 installation; $29.95 monthly.

Telephone Service
Digital: Operational
Fee: $44.95 monthly

Miles of Plant: 110.0 (coaxial); None (fiber optic).
Manager: Mike Burns.
Ownership: Cequel Communications LLC (MSO).

DALHART—Allegiance Communications, 707 W Saratoga St, Shawnee, OK 74804. Phones: 806-249-4820 (Customer service); 800-937-1397; 405-275-6923. Web Site: http://www.allegiance.tv. Also serves Dallam County & Hartley County. ICA: TX0182.
TV Market Ranking: Outside TV Markets (DALHART, Dallam County, Hartley County). Franchise award date: N.A. Franchise expiration date: N.A. Began: August 1, 1962.
Channel capacity: 46 (not 2-way capable). Channels available but not in use: N.A.
Basic Service
Subscribers: 2,372.
Programming (received off-air): KACV-TV (PBS) Amarillo; KAMR-TV (NBC) Amarillo; KCIT (FOX) Amarillo; KFDA-TV (CBS) Amarillo; KPTF-DT (IND) Farwell; KVII-TV (ABC, CW) Amarillo; 6 FMs.
Programming (via satellite): C-SPAN; C-SPAN 2; CW+; QVC; Telefutura; Telemundo; Texas Cable News; The Weather Channel; TV Guide Network; Univision Studios; WGN America.
Fee: $38.00 installation; $10.15 monthly.
Expanded Basic Service 1
Subscribers: N.A.
Programming (via satellite): A&E Networks; ABC Family Channel; AMC; Animal Planet; Bravo; CNBC; CNN; Comedy Central; Country Music TV; Discovery Channel; Disney Channel; ESPN; ESPN 2; Food Network; Fox Movie Channel; Fox News Channel; Fox Sports Southwest; FX; Hallmark Channel; Headline News; HGTV; INSP; Lifetime; MTV; NFL Network; Nickelodeon; RFD-TV; Spike TV; Syfy; TBS Superstation; The Learning Channel; Travel Channel; Turner Network TV; TV Land; USA Network; VH1.
Fee: $18.35 monthly.
Digital Basic Service
Subscribers: N.A.
Programming (via satellite): AmericanLife TV Network; BBC America; Bio; Bloomberg Television; Bravo; Cine Latino; Cine Mexicano; cloo; CMT Pure Country; CNN en Espanol; Current; Discovery en Espanol; Discovery Fit & Health; Discovery Health Channel; Discovery Home Channel; Discovery Kids Channel; DMX Music; Encore (multiplexed); ESPN 2; ESPN Classic Sports; ESPN Deportes; ESPNews; Flix; Fox College Sports Atlantic; Fox College Sports Central; Fox College Sports Pacific; Fox Deportes; Fox Movie Channel; Fox Soccer; Fuse; G4; GMC; Golf Channel; Great American Country; GSN; Halogen Network; HGTV; History Channel; History Channel en Espanol; History Channel International; ID Investigation Discovery; Independent Film Channel; Lifetime Movie Network; Military Channel; MTV Hits; MTV2; mun2 television; National Geographic Channel; Nick Jr.; NickToons TV; Outdoor Channel; Science; ShopNBC; Speed; Style Network; Sundance Channel; Syfy; TeenNick; The Word Network; Toon Disney; Tr3s; Trinity Broadcasting Network; Turner Classic Movies; VeneMovies; Versus; VH1 Classic; VH1 Soul; WE tv.
Pay Service 1
Pay Units: N.A.
Programming (via satellite): HBO.
Digital Pay Service 1
Pay Units: N.A.
Programming (via satellite): Cinemax (multiplexed); HBO (multiplexed); Showtime (multiplexed); Starz (multiplexed); The Movie Channel (multiplexed).
Video-On-Demand: No
Pay-Per-View
iN DEMAND (delivered digitally); Hot Choice (delivered digitally); Playboy TV (delivered digitally); Fresh (delivered digitally); Spice: Xcess (delivered digitally); Club Jenna (delivered digitally).
Internet Service
Operational: Yes.
Telephone Service
Digital: Operational
Miles of Plant: 60.0 (coaxial); None (fiber optic).
Chief Executive Officer: Bill Haggarty. Regional Vice President: Andrew Dearth. Vice President, Marketing: Tracy Bass.
Ownership: Allegiance Communications (MSO).

DALHART—XIT Communications. Formerly [TX1023]. This cable system has converted to IPTV, 1624 Tennessee Ave, Dalhart, TX 79022. Phones: 800-232-3312; 806-384-3311. Fax: 806-384-3311. E-mail: xitcom@xit.net. Web Site: http://www.xit.net. ICA: TX5049.
TV Market Ranking: Outside TV Markets (DALHART).
Channel capacity: N.A. Channels available but not in use: N.A.
Digital Basic Service
Subscribers: N.A.
Programming (via satellite): C-SPAN; C-SPAN 2; Eternal Word TV Network; INSP; ION Television; QVC; The Weather Channel; Trinity Broadcasting Network; WGN America; WPIX (CW, IND) New York.
Fee: $23.75 monthly.
Digital Expanded Basic Service
Subscribers: N.A.
Programming (via satellite): A&E Networks; ABC Family Channel; AMC; Animal Planet; BBC America; BET Networks; Cartoon Network; CNBC; CNN; Comedy Central; Cooking Channel; Country Music TV; Discovery Channel; Discovery en Espanol; Discovery Health Channel; Discovery Home Channel; Discovery Kids Channel; Disney Channel; DIY Network; E! Entertainment Television; Encore (multiplexed); ESPN; ESPN 2; ESPN Classic Sports; Food Network; Fox Deportes; Fox Movie Channel; Fox News Channel; Fox Sports Southwest; FX; G4; Golf Channel; Great American Country; GSN; Hallmark Channel; Headline News; HGTV; History Channel; ID Investigation Discovery; Lifetime; Lifetime Movie Network; Military Channel; MSNBC; MTV; NFL Network; Nick Jr.; Nickelodeon; Outdoor Channel; Oxygen; RFD-TV; Science; Speed; Spike TV; Syfy; TBS Superstation; The Learning Channel; Toon Disney; Travel Channel; Turner Classic Movies; Turner Network TV; TV Land; Univision Studios; USA Network; Versus; VH1; WE tv.
Fee: $27.82 monthly.
Digital Pay Service 1
Pay Units: N.A.
Programming (via satellite): Cinemax (multiplexed); Flix; HBO (multiplexed); Showtime (multiplexed); Starz (multiplexed); Sundance Channel; The Movie Channel (multiplexed).
Fee: $8.95 monthly (Cinemax or Starz), $13.95 monthly (Showtime, Flix, Sundance & TMC).
Internet Service
Operational: Yes.

Telephone Service
Digital: Operational
General Manager: Darrell Dennis.

DALHART—XIT Communications. This cable system has converted to IPTV. See Dalhart, TX [TX5049]. ICA: TX1023.

DALLAS—Time Warner Cable, 1565 Chenault St, Dallas, TX 75228. Phones: 214-328-2882 (Administrative office); 972-830-3800. Fax: 214-320-7484, 972-830-3921. Web Site: http://www.timewarnercable.com/dallas. Also serves Addison, Allen, Arlington, Bedford, Carrollton, Cedar Hill, Cockrell Hill, Colleyville, Coppell, Dallas County, Dalworthington Gardens, De Soto, Double Oak, Euless, Farmers Branch, Flower Mound, Frisco, Garland, Grand Prairie, Grapevine, Hebron, Highland Village, Hutchins, Irving, Lancaster, Las Colinas, Lewisville, McKinney, Mesquite, Murphy, Pantego, Parker, Plano, Princeton, Richardson, Rowlett, Sachse, St. Paul, Stonebridge Ranch, Sunnyvale, The Colony & Wylie. ICA: TX0003.
TV Market Ranking: 12 (Addison, Allen, Arlington, Bedford, Carrollton, Cedar Hill, Cockrell Hill, Colleyville, Coppell, DALLAS, Dallas County, Dalworthington Gardens, De Soto, Double Oak, Euless, Farmers Branch, Flower Mound, Frisco, Garland, Grand Prairie, Grapevine, Hebron, Highland Village, Hutchins, Irving, Lancaster, Las Colinas, Lewisville, McKinney, Mesquite, Murphy, Pantego, Parker, Plano, Princeton, Richardson, Rowlett, Rowlett, Sachse, St. Paul, Stonebridge Ranch, Sunnyvale, Wylie). Franchise award date: April 4, 1981. Franchise expiration date: N.A. Began: January 1, 1982.
Channel capacity: 100 (operating 2-way). Channels available but not in use: N.A.
Basic Service
Subscribers: 600,000 Includes Farmersville, Graham, Greenville, & Palestine.
Programming (received off-air): KAZD (IND) Lake Dallas; KDAF (CW, IND) Dallas; KDFI (MNT) Dallas; KDFW-DT (FOX) Dallas; KDTN (ETV) Denton; KDTX-TV (TBN) Dallas; KERA-TV (PBS) Dallas; KFWD (IND) Fort Worth; KMPX (IND) Decatur; KODF-LD Britton; KPXD-TV (ION) Arlington; KSTR-DT (TEL) Irving; KTAQ (IND) Greenville; KTVT (CBS) Fort Worth; KTXA (IND) Fort Worth; KUVN-DT (UNV) Garland; KXAS-TV (NBC) Fort Worth; KXTX-TV (TMO) Dallas; WFAA (ABC) Dallas; 22 FMs.
Programming (via satellite): C-SPAN 2; Discovery Channel; QVC; TBS Superstation; WGN America.
Fee: $47.47 installation; $11.35 monthly; $1.90 converter.
Expanded Basic Service 1
Subscribers: 134,702.
Programming (via satellite): A&E Networks; ABC Family Channel; Animal Planet; BET Networks; Cartoon Network; CNBC; CNN; Comedy Central; Country Music TV; C-SPAN; Disney Channel; E! Entertainment Television; ESPN; ESPN 2; ESPN Classic Sports; Eternal Word TV Network; Food Network; Fox News Channel; Fox Sports Southwest; FX; G4; GalaVision; Golf Channel; GSN; Headline News; HGTV; History Channel; Lifetime; MSNBC; MTV; MTV2; Nickelodeon; Oxygen; Spike TV; Style Network; Syfy; Texas Cable News; The Learning Channel; The Weather Channel; Travel Channel; truTV; Turner Classic Movies; Turner Network TV; TV One; USA Network; Versus; VH1.
Fee: $33.15 monthly.
Digital Basic Service
Subscribers: N.A.
Programming (via satellite): AMC; BBC America; Bio; Bloomberg Television; Boomerang; Bravo; Canales N; CNBC; CNN International; Cooking Channel; Country Music TV; C-SPAN 3; Current; DIY Network; ESPN Classic Sports; ESPNews; Eternal Word TV Network; FamilyNet; Fox College Sports Atlantic; Fox College Sports Central; Fox College Sports Pacific; Fox Movie Channel; Fox Soccer; Fuse; GAS; Great American Country; Hallmark Channel; Halogen Network; HD Theater; History Channel International; Independent Film Channel; INHD; INHD2; Lifetime Movie Network; Lifetime Real Women; Mnet; MSNBC; MTV Networks Digital Suite; Music Choice; National Geographic Channel; NBA TV; Nick Jr.; Nick Too; NickToons TV; Outdoor Channel; Speed; Sundance Channel; Tennis Channel; Toon Disney; Turner Network TV HD; TV Asia; TV Land; WE tv; Zee TV USA.
Fee: $9.95 monthly.
Digital Pay Service 1
Pay Units: N.A.
Programming (via satellite): Cinemax (multiplexed); Encore; Flix; HBO (multiplexed); Showtime (multiplexed); Showtime HD; Starz; Starz HDTV; The Movie Channel (multiplexed).
Fee: $16.99 monthly (each).
Video-On-Demand: Yes
Pay-Per-View
iN DEMAND; MLB Extra Innings (delivered digitally); Hot Choice (delivered digitally); Playboy TV (delivered digitally); Fresh (delivered digitally); Shorteez (delivered digitally); ESPN Full Court (delivered digitally); ESPN Gameplan (delivered digitally); NBA League Pass (delivered digitally); NHL Center Ice (delivered digitally).
Internet Service
Operational: Yes.
Broadband Service: Road Runner.
Fee: $29.95 installation; $42.95 monthly; $3.00 modem lease.
Telephone Service
Digital: Operational
Fee: $44.95 monthly
President & General Manager: Robert Moel. Vice President, Technical Operations: Michael McDonald. Vice President, Marketing: Robert Shurtleff. Vice President, Government & Public Affairs: Dick Kirby. Public Affairs Director: Gary Underwood.
Ownership: Time Warner Cable (MSO).

DALLAS (northwest suburbs)—Grande Communications, 7701 S Stemmons Rd, Ste 210, Corinth, TX 76210. Phones: 512-878-

4000 (San Marcos corporate office); 877-238-6891 (Customer service). Fax: 940-270-9600. Web Site: http://www.grandecom.com. Also serves Allen, Argyle, Arlington, Carrollton, Denton, Frisco, Lake Dallas, Lewisville, McKinney, Plano & Roanoke. ICA: TX1006.

Note: This system is an overbuild.

TV Market Ranking: 12 (Allen, Argyle, Arlington, Carrollton, DALLAS (NORTHWEST SUBURBS), Denton, Frisco, Lake Dallas, Lewisville, McKinney, Plano, Roanoke).

Channel capacity: N.A. Channels available but not in use: N.A.

Basic Service

Subscribers: N.A.

Programming (received off-air): KAZD (IND) Lake Dallas; KDAF (CW, IND) Dallas; KDFI (MNT) Dallas; KDFW-DT (FOX) Dallas; KDTN (ETV) Denton; KDTX-TV (TBN) Dallas; KERA-TV (PBS) Dallas; KFWD (IND) Fort Worth; KMPX (IND) Decatur; KSTR-DT (TEL) Irving; KTVT (CBS) Fort Worth; KTXA (IND) Fort Worth; KUVN-DT (UNV) Garland; KXAS-TV (NBC) Fort Worth; KXTX-TV (TMO) Dallas; WFAA (ABC) Dallas.

Programming (via satellite): C-SPAN.

Fee: $9.95 monthly.

Expanded Basic Service 1

Subscribers: N.A.

Programming (via satellite): A&E Networks; ABC Family Channel; AMC; Animal Planet; BET Networks; Bravo; Cartoon Network; CNBC; CNN; Comedy Central; Country Music TV; C-SPAN 2; Discovery Channel; Discovery Health Channel; Disney Channel; E! Entertainment Television; Encore; ESPN; ESPN 2; ESPN Classic Sports; Food Network; Fox News Channel; Fox Sports Net; FX; Golf Channel; Headline News; HGTV; History Channel; Lifetime; MSNBC; MTV; Nickelodeon; QVC; Spike TV; Syfy; TBS Superstation; The Learning Channel; The Weather Channel; Toon Disney; Travel Channel; truTV; Turner Classic Movies; Turner Network TV; TV Guide Network; TV Land; USA Network; VH1.

Fee: $28.95 monthly.

Digital Basic Service

Subscribers: N.A.

Programming (via satellite): BBC America; Bio; Bloomberg News Radio; Boomerang; CBS Sports Network; Cooking Channel; C-SPAN 3; Discovery Home Channel; Discovery Kids Channel; Discovery Times Channel; DIY Network; ESPNews; Fox Deportes; Fox Movie Channel; Fox Sports World; Fuel TV; Fuse; G4; GAS; History Channel International; Lifetime Movie Network; Military Channel; MTV Networks Digital Suite; National Geographic Channel; NBA TV; NFL Network; Nick Jr.; Nick Too; NickToons TV; Science Television; Speed; Style Network; Tennis Channel; Versus; WE tv.

Fee: $35.98 monthly.

Pay Service 1

Pay Units: N.A.

Programming (via satellite): Cinemax; HBO (multiplexed); Showtime; Starz; The Movie Channel.

Digital Pay Service 1

Pay Units: N.A.

Programming (via satellite): Cinemax (multiplexed); Encore (multiplexed); Flix; HBO (multiplexed); Showtime; Starz (multiplexed); Sundance Channel; The Movie Channel.

Video-On-Demand: No

Internet Service

Operational: Yes, Both DSL & dial-up.

Broadband Service: Grande High Speed Internet.

Fee: $19.95 monthly.

Telephone Service

Analog: Not Operational

Digital: Operational

Fee: $9.00 monthly

General Manager: J. Lyn Findley. Video Services Director: Diane Wigington.

Ownership: Grande Communications Networks Inc. (MSO).

DARROUZETT—Panhandle Telephone Coop. Inc., 2222 NW Hwy 64, Guymon, OK 73942. Phones: 580-338-2556; 800-562-2556. Fax: 580-338-8260. Web Site: http://www.ptci.net. ICA: TX0662.

TV Market Ranking: Outside TV Markets (DARROUZETT). Franchise award date: August 14, 1981. Franchise expiration date: N.A. Began: November 1, 1981.

Channel capacity: 36 (not 2-way capable). Channels available but not in use: N.A.

Basic Service

Subscribers: N.A.

Programming (received off-air): KACV-TV (PBS) Amarillo; KAMR-TV (NBC) Amarillo; KCIT (FOX) Amarillo; KFDA-TV (CBS) Amarillo; KVII-TV (ABC, CW) Amarillo.

Programming (via satellite): A&E Networks; ABC Family Channel; Cartoon Network; CNN; Discovery Channel; Disney Channel; ESPN; Hallmark Channel; HGTV; History Channel; INSP; Spike TV; Syfy; TBS Superstation; The Learning Channel; The Weather Channel; Turner Network TV; TV Land; USA Network.

Fee: $39.95 installation; $42.99 monthly.

Pay Service 1

Pay Units: 8.

Programming (via satellite): HBO.

Fee: $20.00 installation; $13.49 monthly.

Pay Service 2

Pay Units: 21.

Programming (via satellite): Showtime.

Fee: $13.95 monthly.

Internet Service

Operational: No.

Telephone Service

None

Miles of Plant: 4.0 (coaxial); None (fiber optic).

Plant Manager: Gary Burke.

Ownership: Panhandle Telephone Cooperative Inc. (MSO).

DE KALB—Allegiance Communications, 707 W Saratoga St, Shawnee, OK 74804. Phones: 405-395-1131; 405-275-6923. Web Site: http://www.allegiance.tv. Also serves Bowie County. ICA: TX0324.

TV Market Ranking: 58 (Bowie County (portions), DE KALB); Outside TV Markets (Bowie County (portions)). Franchise award date: N.A. Franchise expiration date: N.A. Began: March 1, 1980.

Channel capacity: N.A. Channels available but not in use: N.A.

Basic Service

Subscribers: 699.

Programming (received off-air): KLTS-TV (PBS) Shreveport; KMSS-TV (FOX) Shreveport; KPXJ (CW) Minden; KSHV-TV (MNT) Shreveport; KSLA (CBS) Shreveport; KTAL-TV (NBC) Texarkana; KTBS-TV (ABC) Shreveport.

Programming (via satellite): CNBC; CNN; C-SPAN; Discovery Channel; Headline News; QVC; Texas Cable News; The Weather Channel; Trinity Broadcasting Network; TV Guide Network; WGN America.

Fee: $34.13 installation; $10.65 monthly.

Expanded Basic Service 1

Subscribers: N.A.

Programming (via satellite): A&E Networks; ABC Family Channel; AMC; Animal Planet; BET Networks; Cartoon Network; Comedy Central; Country Music TV; Disney Channel; ESPN; ESPN 2; ESPN Classic Sports; Fox News Channel; Fox Sports Southwest; FX; Hallmark Channel; HGTV; History Channel; Lifetime; MoviePlex; MTV; NFL Network; Nickelodeon; Spike TV; Syfy; TBS Superstation; The Learning Channel; Turner Network TV; TV Land; USA Network; VH1.

Digital Basic Service

Subscribers: N.A.

Programming (via satellite): 3 Angels Broadcasting Network; A&E HD; AmericanLife TV Network; BBC America; Bio; Bloomberg Television; BYU Television; Church Channel; Cine Latino; Cine Mexicano; cloo; CMT Pure Country; CNN en Espanol; Colours; Daystar TV Network; Discovery en Espanol; Discovery Fit & Health; Discovery Health Channel; Discovery Kids Channel; DMX Music; Encore (multiplexed); ESPN Classic Sports; ESPN Deportes; ESPN HD; ESPNews; FamilyNet; Flix; Food Network HD; Fox College Sports Atlantic; Fox College Sports Central; Fox College Sports Pacific; Fox Deportes; Fox Movie Channel; Fox Soccer; Fuse; G4; GMC; Golden Eagle Broadcasting; Golf Channel; Great American Country; GSN; Halogen Network; HD Theater; HDNet; HDNet Movies; HGTV HD; History Channel; History Channel en Espanol; History Channel International; ID Investigation Discovery; Independent Film Channel; JCTV; La Familia Network; Latele Novela Network; Lifetime Movie Network; Military Channel; MTV Hits; MTV2; National Geographic Channel; National Geographic Channel HD Network; Nick Jr.; NickToons TV; Outdoor Channel; Outdoor Channel 2 HD; Planet Green; Science; ShopNBC; Speed; Style Network; Sundance Channel; Syfy; TBN Enlace USA; TeenNick; The Word Network; Toon Disney; Tr3s; Trinity Broadcasting Network; Turner Classic Movies; TV Chile; TV Colombia; Universal HD; Versus; VH1 Classic; WE tv; World Harvest Television.

Pay Service 1

Pay Units: 33.

Programming (via satellite): Encore; HBO; Showtime; Starz.

Fee: $11.95 monthly (HBO or Showtime).

Digital Pay Service 1

Pay Units: N.A.

Programming (via satellite): Cinemax (multiplexed); HBO (multiplexed); HBO HD; HBO Latino; Showtime (multiplexed); Showtime HD; Starz (multiplexed); Starz HDTV; The Movie Channel (multiplexed).

Pay-Per-View

iN DEMAND (delivered digitally); Hot Choice (delivered digitally); Playboy TV (delivered digitally); Fresh (delivered digitally); Spice: Xcess (delivered digitally); Club Jenna.

Internet Service

Operational: Yes.

Telephone Service

None

Miles of Plant: 21.0 (coaxial); None (fiber optic).

Chief Executive Officer: Bill Haggarty. Regional Vice President: Andrew Dearth. Vice President, Marketing: Tracy Bass.

Ownership: Allegiance Communications (MSO).

DE LEON—Reach Broadband, 515 E Longview St, Arp, TX 75750. Phone: 800-687-1258. Web Site: http://www.reachbroadband.net. ICA: TX0310.

TV Market Ranking: Outside TV Markets (DE LEON). Franchise award date: N.A. Franchise expiration date: N.A. Began: February 1, 1962.

Channel capacity: N.A. Channels available but not in use: N.A.

Basic Service

Subscribers: 496.

Programming (received off-air): KRBC-TV (NBC) Abilene; KTAB-TV (CBS) Abilene; all-band FM.

Programming (via microwave): KDFW-DT (FOX) Dallas; KERA-TV (PBS) Dallas; KTVT (CBS) Fort Worth; KXAS-TV (NBC) Fort Worth; WFAA (ABC) Dallas.

Programming (via satellite): C-SPAN; Discovery Channel; QVC; TBS Superstation; The Weather Channel.

Fee: $29.95 installation; $19.95 monthly.

Expanded Basic Service 1

Subscribers: N.A.

Programming (via satellite): ABC Family Channel; AMC; Animal Planet; Cartoon Network; CNBC; CNN; ESPN; Fox News Channel; Fox Sports Southwest; FX; Hallmark Channel; Headline News; HGTV; Lifetime; Spike TV; The Learning Channel; Turner Network TV; USA Network.

Fee: $20.00 monthly.

Pay Service 1

Pay Units: 75.

Programming (via satellite): Cinemax.

Fee: $12.90 monthly.

Pay Service 2

Pay Units: 260.

Programming (via satellite): Encore.

Fee: $1.75 monthly.

Pay Service 3

Pay Units: 87.

Programming (via satellite): HBO.

Fee: $12.90 monthly.

Pay Service 4

Pay Units: 139.

Programming (via satellite): Starz.

Fee: $6.75 monthly.

Video-On-Demand: No

Internet Service

Operational: Yes.

Broadband Service: Rapid High Speed Internet.

Fee: $100.00 installation; $29.95 monthly.

Telephone Service

None

Miles of Plant: 28.0 (coaxial); None (fiber optic).

Regional Manager: Ronnie Stafford. Office Manager: Jan Gibson.

Ownership: RB3 LLC (MSO).

DE SOTO—Time Warner Cable. Now served by DALLAS, TX [TX0003]. ICA: TX0053.

DECATUR—CommuniComm Services, 2804B S FM 51, PO Box 869, Decatur, TX 76234-0869. Phone: 940-627-8414. Fax: 940-627-8303. Web Site: http://www.netcommander.com. Also serves Alvord, Bridgeport, Chico, Lake Bridgeport & Runaway Bay. ICA: TX0168.

TV Market Ranking: Below 100 (Alvord, Bridgeport, Chico, DECATUR (VILLAGE), Lake Bridgeport, Runaway Bay). Franchise award date: September 1, 1979. Franchise expiration date: N.A. Began: June 1, 1980.

Channel capacity: N.A. Channels available but not in use: N.A.

Basic Service

Subscribers: 4,000 Includes Bowie, Jacksboro & Springtown.

Programming (received off-air): KAUZ-TV (CBS, CW) Wichita Falls; KDAF (CW, IND) Dallas; KDFI (MNT) Dallas; KDFW-DT (FOX) Dallas; KDTN (ETV) Denton; KERA-TV (PBS) Dallas; KSTR-DT (TEL) Irving; KTVT (CBS) Fort Worth; KTXA (IND) Fort Worth; KXAS-TV (NBC) Fort Worth; KXTX-TV (TMO) Dallas; WFAA (ABC) Dallas.

Expanded Basic Service 1

Subscribers: N.A.

Programming (received off-air): KMPX (IND) Decatur; KPXD-TV (ION) Arlington; KUVN-DT (UNV) Garland.

Programming (via satellite): A&E Networks; ABC Family Channel; AMC; Animal Planet; BET Networks; Bravo; Cartoon Network; CNBC; CNN; Comedy Central; Country Music TV; C-SPAN; Discovery Channel; Disney Channel; ESPN; ESPN 2; Food Network; Fox News Channel; Fox Sports Southwest; FX; Headline News; HGTV; History Channel; Lifetime; Local Cable Weather; MTV; Nick Jr.; Nickelodeon; QVC; ShopNBC; Spike TV; Syfy; TBS Superstation; The Learning Channel; The Weather Channel; Travel Channel; Trinity Broadcasting Network; Turner Network TV; TV Guide Network; TV Land; USA Network; VH1; WE tv.

Fee: $43.95 monthly.

Digital Basic Service

Subscribers: N.A.

Programming (via satellite): BBC America; Bloomberg Television; Bravo; CMT Pure Country; Discovery Fit & Health; Discovery Health Channel; Discovery Home Channel; Discovery Kids Channel; Discovery Times Channel; DMX Music; ESPN 2; ESPN Classic Sports; ESPNews; Fox Soccer; G4; Golf Channel; GSN; Halogen Network; HGTV; History Channel; Independent Film Channel; Military Channel; National Geographic Channel; Nick Jr.; NickToons TV; Outdoor Channel; Science; SoapNet; Speed; Syfy; Trinity Broadcasting Network; Turner Classic Movies; TV Land; Versus; VH1 Classic; WE tv.

Fee: $17.04 monthly.

Pay Service 1

Pay Units: N.A.

Programming (via satellite): Cinemax; Encore; HBO (multiplexed); Starz.

Digital Pay Service 1

Pay Units: N.A.

Programming (via satellite): Cinemax (multiplexed); Encore (multiplexed); Flix; HBO (multiplexed); Showtime (multiplexed); Starz (multiplexed); The Movie Channel (multiplexed).

Video-On-Demand: No

Pay-Per-View

iN DEMAND (delivered digitally); Playboy TV (delivered digitally); Spice (delivered digitally).

Internet Service

Operational: Yes.

Broadband Service: Net Commander.

Fee: $39.95 installation; $51.95 monthly.

Telephone Service

None

Miles of Plant: 77.0 (coaxial); None (fiber optic). Includes Bowie, Jacksboro & Springtown

Chief Technician: J. D. Sifford. Operations Manager: Wes Devall.

Ownership: James Cable LLC (MSO).

DEL RIO—Time Warner Cable, 1313 W Carlton Rd, Laredo, TX 78041. Phones: 956-721-0607; 972-899-7300 (Flower Mound office). Fax: 956-721-0612. Web Site: http://www.timewarnercable.com/Texas. Also serves Laughlin AFB. ICA: TX0056.

TV Market Ranking: Below 100 (DEL RIO, Laughlin AFB). Franchise award date: N.A. Franchise expiration date: N.A. Began: September 1, 1955.

Channel capacity: N.A. Channels available but not in use: N.A.

Basic Service

Subscribers: 35,000 Includes Crystal City, Eagle Pass, Encinal, Pearsall, Quemado & Uvalde.

Programming (received off-air): KABB (FOX) San Antonio; KENS (CBS) San Antonio; KLRN (PBS) San Antonio; KMYS (CW) Kerrville; KNIC-DT (TEL) Blanco; KPXL-TV (ION) Uvalde; KSAT-TV (ABC) San Antonio; KVDA (TMO) San Antonio; WOAI-TV (NBC) San Antonio; 3 FMs.

Programming (via microwave): KENS (CBS) San Antonio; KLRN (PBS) San Antonio; KSAT-TV (ABC) San Antonio; KWEX-DT (UNV) San Antonio; WOAI-TV (NBC) San Antonio.

Programming (via satellite): A&E Networks; ABC Family Channel; AMC; Animal Planet; Azteca America; BET Networks; Bravo; Cartoon Network; CNN; Comedy Central; Country Music TV; C-SPAN; C-SPAN 2; Discovery Channel; Discovery Health Channel; Disney Channel; E! Entertainment Television; ESPN; ESPN 2; Eternal Word TV Network; Food Network; Fox Deportes; Fox News Channel; Fox Sports Southwest; FX; GalaVision; Golf Channel; Great American Country; Hallmark Channel; Headline News; HGTV; History Channel; Lifetime; MoviePlex; MSNBC; MTV; National Geographic Channel; Nickelodeon; Oxygen; QVC; SoapNet; Spike TV; Style Network; Syfy; TBS Superstation; Telemundo; Texas Cable News; The Learning Channel; The Weather Channel; Travel Channel; Trinity Broadcasting Network; Turner Classic Movies; Turner Network TV; TV Guide Network; TV Land; USA Network; various Mexican stations; VH1; WE tv.

Fee: $50.51 installation; $45.99 monthly; $18.81 additional installation.

Digital Basic Service

Subscribers: N.A.

Programming (via satellite): A&E Networks; ABC Family Channel; AMC; Animal Planet; BBC America; BET Networks; Bio; Bloomberg Television; Boomerang; Bravo; Cartoon Network; cloo; CNN; Comedy Central; Country Music TV; C-SPAN; C-SPAN 2; C-SPAN 3; Discovery Channel; Discovery Fit & Health; Discovery Health Channel; Discovery Home Channel; Discovery Kids Channel; Discovery Times Channel; Disney Channel; DIY Network; E! Entertainment Television; ESPN; ESPN 2; ESPN 2 HD; ESPN Classic Sports; ESPN HD; ESPN U; ESPNews; Eternal Word TV Network; Food Network; Fox News Channel; Fox Reality Channel; Fuse; FX; G4; GalaVision; GAS; Golf Channel; Great American Country; GSN; Hallmark Channel; HD Theater; HDNet; HDNet Movies; Headline News; HGTV; History Channel; History Channel International; La Familia Network; Lifetime; Lifetime Movie Network; Military Channel; MoviePlex; MSNBC; MTV; MTV Hits; MTV2; mun2 television; Music Choice; National Geographic Channel; Nick Jr.; Nickelodeon; NickToons TV; Nuvo TV; Oxygen; QVC; Science Television; SoapNet; Speed; Spike TV; Style Network; Syfy; TBS Superstation; Texas Cable News; The Learning Channel; The Weather Channel; Toon Disney; Tr3s; Travel Channel; Trinity Broadcasting Network; Turner Classic Movies; Turner Network TV; Turner Network TV HD; TV Guide Network; TV Land; USA Network; Versus; VH1; VH1 Classic; VH1 Country; WE tv.

Fee: $4.99 monthly.

Digital Expanded Basic Service

Subscribers: N.A.

Programming (via satellite): Canal Sur; Cine Latino; CNN en Espanol; Discovery en Espanol; Encore (multiplexed); ESPN Deportes; Fox College Sports Atlantic; Fox College Sports Central; Fox College Sports Pacific; Fox Movie Channel; Fox Soccer; Fox Sports Southwest; Independent Film Channel; NBA TV; Puma TV; Sorpresa; Speed; Sundance Channel; Tennis Channel; Versus; VHUNO; Video Rola.

Digital Pay Service 1

Pay Units: 4,044.

Programming (via satellite): Cinemax (multiplexed); HBO (multiplexed); Showtime (multiplexed); Starz (multiplexed); The Movie Channel (multiplexed).

Fee: $12.95 monthly (each).

Video-On-Demand: No

Pay-Per-View

iN DEMAND (delivered digitally); Hot Choice (delivered digitally); Fresh (delivered digitally); Shorteez (delivered digitally); NBA League Pass (delivered digitally); MLB Extra Innings (delivered digitally); NHL Center Ice (delivered digitally).

Internet Service

Operational: Yes.

Broadband Service: Road Runner.

Fee: $49.99 installation; $44.95 monthly.

Telephone Service

Digital: Operational

Fee: $44.95 monthly

Miles of Plant: 190.0 (coaxial); None (fiber optic). Additional miles planned: 1.0 (coaxial).

President: Connie Wharton. Vice President & General Manager: Michael Carrosquiola. Technical Operations Manager: Eduardo Ruiz. Operations Director: Marco Reyes. Public Affairs Manager: Celinda Gonzalez.

Ownership: Time Warner Cable (MSO).; Advance/Newhouse Partnership (MSO).

DENTON—Charter Communications, 15100 Trinity Blvd, Ste 500, Fort Worth, TX 76155. Phones: 817-298-3600; 940-898-0583 (Denton). Web Site: http://www.charter.com. Also serves Corinth, Hickory Creek, Lake Dallas & Shady Shores. ICA: TX0040.

TV Market Ranking: 12 (Corinth, DENTON, Hickory Creek, Lake Dallas, Shady Shores). Franchise award date: January 20, 1979. Franchise expiration date: N.A. Began: November 1, 1979.

Channel capacity: N.A. Channels available but not in use: N.A.

Basic Service

Subscribers: 26,600.

Programming (received off-air): KDAF (CW, IND) Dallas; KDFI (MNT) Dallas; KDFW-DT (FOX) Dallas; KDLT-TV (NBC) Sioux Falls; KDTN (ETV) Denton; KDTX-TV (TBN) Dallas; KERA-TV (PBS) Dallas; KFTH-DT (TEL) Alvin; KFWD (IND) Fort Worth; KMPX (IND) Decatur; KPXD-TV (ION) Arlington; KTVT (CBS) Fort Worth; KTXA (IND) Fort Worth; KUVN-DT (UNV) Garland; KXAS-TV (NBC) Fort Worth; KXTX-TV (TMO) Dallas; WFAA (ABC) Dallas; 1 FM.

Programming (via satellite): C-SPAN; QVC.

Fee: $29.95 installation.

Expanded Basic Service 1

Subscribers: N.A.

Programming (via satellite): A&E Networks; ABC Family Channel; AMC; Animal Planet; BET Networks; Bravo; Cartoon Network; CNBC; CNN; Comedy Central; Country Music TV; Discovery Channel; Disney Channel; E! Entertainment Television; ESPN; ESPN 2; Food Network; Fox News Channel; Fox Sports Southwest; FX; G4; GalaVision; Hallmark Channel; Headline News; HGTV; History Channel; Lifetime; MSNBC; MTV; Nickelodeon; ShopNBC; Speed; Spike TV; Syfy; TBS Superstation; The Learning Channel; The Weather Channel; Travel Channel; Turner Classic Movies; Turner Network TV; TV Land; USA Network; Versus; VH1; Weatherscan.

Fee: $48.99 monthly.

Digital Basic Service

Subscribers: N.A.

Programming (via satellite): BBC America; Bio; Discovery Digital Networks; GAS; GSN; History Channel International; Independent Film Channel; Lifetime Movie Network; MTV Networks Digital Suite; Music Choice; National Geographic Channel; Nick Jr.; Nick Too; NickToons TV; Sundance Channel; Toon Disney; WE tv.

Digital Expanded Basic Service

Subscribers: N.A.

Programming (via satellite): Canales N; ESPNews; FSN Digital Atlantic; FSN Digital Central; FSN Digital Pacific; Fuel TV; Golf Channel; NFL Network.

Digital Pay Service 1

Pay Units: N.A.

Programming (via satellite): Cinemax (multiplexed); Encore (multiplexed); Flix; HBO (multiplexed); Showtime (multiplexed); Starz (multiplexed); The Movie Channel (multiplexed).

Video-On-Demand: No

Pay-Per-View

NASCAR In Car (delivered digitally); Playboy TV (delivered digitally); Fresh (delivered digitally); Shorteez (delivered digitally); iN DEMAND (delivered digitally).

Internet Service

Operational: Yes.

Broadband Service: Charter Pipeline.

Fee: $9.99 installation; $29.99 monthly.

Telephone Service

Digital: Operational

Fee: $29.95 monthly

Miles of Plant: 29,275.0 (coaxial); 516.0 (fiber optic).

Vice President & General Manager: Wayne Cramp. Marketing Director: Kathleen Griffin. Technical Operations Director: John Linton.

Ownership: Charter Communications Inc. (MSO).

DEVINE—Reach Broadband, 515 E Longview St, Arp, TX 75750. Phone: 800-687-1258. Web Site: http://www.reachbroadband.net. Also serves Lytle, Medina County (portions) & Natalia. ICA: TX0747.

TV Market Ranking: 45 (DEVINE, Lytle, Medina County (portions), Natalia); Below 100 (Medina County (portions)). Franchise award date: N.A. Franchise expiration date: N.A. Began: November 1, 1981.

Channel capacity: N.A. Channels available but not in use: N.A.

Basic Service

Subscribers: 663.

Programming (received off-air): KABB (FOX) San Antonio; KENS (CBS) San Antonio; KHCE-TV (TBN) San Antonio; KLRN (PBS) San Antonio; KMOL-LP Victoria; KMYS (CW) Kerrville; KPXL-TV (ION) Uvalde; KSAT-TV (ABC) San Antonio; KVDA (TMO) San Antonio; KWEX-DT (UNV) San Antonio.

Programming (via satellite): C-SPAN; ESPN; QVC.

Fee: $29.95 installation; $19.95 monthly.

Expanded Basic Service 1

Subscribers: N.A.

Programming (via satellite): A&E Networks; ABC Family Channel; AMC; Bravo; Cartoon Network; CNBC; CNN; Comedy Central; Country Music TV; Discovery Channel; Disney Channel; E! Entertainment Television; ESPN 2; Fox News Channel; Fox Sports Southwest; FX; G4; Headline News; HGTV; History Channel; Lifetime; MTV; Nickelodeon; Oxygen; Speed; Spike TV; Syfy; TBS Superstation; The Learning Channel; The Weather Channel; Travel Channel; Turner Classic Movies; Turner Network TV; TV Land; USA Network; VH1.

Fee: $20.00 monthly.

Digital Basic Service

Subscribers: N.A.

Programming (via satellite): BBC America; Bio; Bloomberg Television; Discovery Fit & Health; DIY Network; ESPN Classic Sports; ESPNews; GAS; GSN; History Channel International; Independent Film Channel; Lifetime Movie Network; MTV Networks Digital Suite; Music Choice; Nick Jr.; Nick Too; NickToons TV; SoapNet; Sundance Channel; Toon Disney; TV Guide Interactive Inc.; WE tv.

Digital Pay Service 1

Pay Units: 107.

Programming (via satellite): Cinemax (multiplexed).

Fee: $11.95 monthly.

Digital Pay Service 2

Pay Units: 131.

Programming (via satellite): HBO (multiplexed).

Fee: $11.95 monthly.

Digital Pay Service 3

Pay Units: 104.

Programming (via satellite): Showtime (multiplexed).

Fee: $11.95 monthly.

Digital Pay Service 4

Pay Units: 48.

Programming (via satellite): The Movie Channel (multiplexed).

Fee: $11.95 monthly.

Digital Pay Service 5

Pay Units: N.A.

Programming (via satellite): Encore (multiplexed); Flix; Starz (multiplexed).

Video-On-Demand: No

Pay-Per-View

iN DEMAND (delivered digitally).

Internet Service

Operational: No.

Telephone Service

None

Miles of Plant: 92.0 (coaxial); None (fiber optic).

Regional Manager: Ronnie Stafford. Office Manager: Jan Gibson.

Ownership: RB3 LLC (MSO).

DIANA—Almega Cable, 4001 W Airport Frwy, Ste 530, Bedford, TX 76021. Phone: 817-685-9588. Fax: 817-685-6488. Web Site: http://www.almega.com. Also serves Upshur County (portions). ICA: TX0566.

TV Market Ranking: Below 100 (DIANA, Upshur County (portions)). Franchise award date: January 1, 1989. Franchise expiration date: January 1, 2009. Began: June 26, 1989.

Channel capacity: 36 (not 2-way capable). Channels available but not in use: N.A.

Basic Service

Subscribers: 93.

Programming (received off-air): KERA-TV (PBS) Dallas; KETK-TV (NBC) Jacksonville; KFXK-TV (FOX) Longview; KLTV (ABC, TMO) Tyler; KSLA (CBS) Shreveport.

Programming (via satellite): ABC Family Channel; CNN; Country Music TV; Discovery Channel; ESPN; Lifetime; Nickelodeon; TBS Superstation; Turner Classic Movies; Turner Network TV; USA Network; WGN America.

Fee: $54.95 installation; $44.05 monthly.

Pay Service 1

Pay Units: 24.

Programming (via satellite): Cinemax.

Fee: $12.95 monthly.

Pay Service 2

Pay Units: 22.

Programming (via satellite): HBO.

Fee: $12.95 monthly.

Pay Service 3

Pay Units: 38.

Programming (via satellite): Showtime.

Fee: $12.95 monthly.

Video-On-Demand: No

Internet Service

Operational: No.

Telephone Service

None

Miles of Plant: 29.0 (coaxial); None (fiber optic).

Ownership: Almega Cable (MSO).

DICKENS—Formerly served by Almega Cable. No longer in operation. ICA: TX0748.

DILLEY—Time Warner Cable. Now served by PEARSALL, TX [TX0196]. ICA: TX0344.

DIME BOX—Formerly served by Reveille Broadband. No longer in operation. ICA: TX0601.

DIMMITT—Suddenlink Communications, 12444 Powerscourt Dr, Saint Louis, MO 63131-3660. Phones: 800-999-6845; 314-965-2020. Fax: 903-561-5485. Web Site: http://www.suddenlink.com. ICA: TX0255.

TV Market Ranking: Outside TV Markets (DIMMITT). Franchise award date: N.A. Franchise expiration date: N.A. Began: February 1, 1964.

Channel capacity: N.A. Channels available but not in use: N.A.

Basic Service

Subscribers: 1,154.

Programming (received off-air): KACV-TV (PBS) Amarillo; KAMR-TV (NBC) Amarillo; KCIT (FOX) Amarillo; KFDA-TV (CBS) Amarillo; KJTV-TV (FOX) Lubbock; KLBK-TV (CBS) Lubbock; KVII-TV (ABC, CW) Amarillo; allband FM.

Programming (via satellite): A&E Networks; ABC Family Channel; Animal Planet; CNN; Country Music TV; C-SPAN; Discovery Channel; Disney Channel; E! Entertainment Television; ESPN; Fox News Channel; Fox Sports Southwest; Headline News; History Channel; Nickelodeon; Spike TV; TBS Superstation; Telemundo; The Weather Channel; Turner Classic Movies; Turner Network TV; TV Land; USA Network; WGN America.

Fee: $39.95 installation; $19.95 monthly.

Pay Service 1

Pay Units: 162.

Programming (via satellite): HBO.

Fee: $15.00 installation; $10.95 monthly.

Pay Service 2

Pay Units: 98.

Programming (via satellite): Showtime.

Fee: $15.00 installation; $9.95 monthly.

Pay Service 3

Pay Units: 110.

Programming (via satellite): The Movie Channel.

Fee: $7.95 monthly.

Video-On-Demand: No

Internet Service

Operational: Yes. Began: June 19, 2003.

Broadband Service: Cebridge High Speed Cable Internet.

Fee: $49.95 installation; $25.95 monthly.

Telephone Service

None

Miles of Plant: 25.0 (coaxial); None (fiber optic).

Regional Manager: Todd Cruthird. Regional Marketing Manager: Beverly Gambell.

Ownership: Cequel Communications LLC (MSO).

DIXIE—Formerly served by Northland Communications Corp. No longer in operation. ICA: TX0911.

DRISCOLL—Time Warner Cable. Now served by CORPUS CHRISTI, TX [TX0010]. ICA: TX1007.

DUBLIN—Northland Cable Television, 975 N Lillian St, PO Box 70, Stephenville, TX 76401-0001. Phone: 254-968-4189. Fax: 254-968-8350. E-mail: brent_richey@northlandcabletv.com. Web Site: http://www.northlandcabletv.com. ICA: TX0749.

TV Market Ranking: Outside TV Markets (DUBLIN). Franchise award date: N.A. Franchise expiration date: N.A. Began: N.A.

Channel capacity: N.A. Channels available but not in use: N.A.

Basic Service

Subscribers: 584.

Programming (received off-air): KDAF (CW, IND) Dallas; KDFI (MNT) Dallas; KDFW-DT (FOX) Dallas; KERA-TV (PBS) Dallas; KPXD-TV (ION) Arlington; KSTR-DT (TEL) Irving; KTVT (CBS) Fort Worth; KTXA (IND) Fort Worth; KWTX-TV (CBS, CW) Waco; KXAS-TV (NBC) Fort Worth; KXTX-TV (TMO) Dallas; WFAA (ABC) Dallas.

Programming (via satellite): A&E Networks; Animal Planet; Cartoon Network; CNBC; CNN; Comedy Central; C-SPAN; Discovery Channel; Disney Channel; ESPN; ESPN 2; Food Network; Fox Movie Channel; Fox News Channel; FX; Golf Channel; Great American Country; Hallmark Channel; Headline News; HGTV; History Channel; Lifetime; MTV; Nickelodeon; Outdoor Channel; QVC; Spike TV; Syfy; TBS Superstation; The Learning Channel; The Weather Channel; Travel Channel; Trinity Broadcasting Network; Turner Classic Movies; Turner Network TV; TV Land; Univision Studios; USA Network; Versus; VH1.

Fee: $54.13 installation; $33.99 monthly.

Digital Basic Service

Subscribers: N.A.

Programming (via satellite): BBC America; Bloomberg Television; Bravo; Discovery Fit & Health; Discovery Health Channel; Discovery Kids Channel; DMX Music; ESPNews; Fox Soccer; G4; ID Investigation Discovery; Independent Film Channel; Military Channel; National Geographic Channel; Planet Green; Science; Speed; WE tv.

Digital Expanded Basic Service

Subscribers: N.A.

Programming (received off-air): KDFW-DT (FOX) Dallas; KERA-TV (PBS) Dallas; KXAS-TV (NBC) Fort Worth; WFAA (ABC) Dallas.

Programming (via satellite): ESPN HD; HD Theater; Turner Network TV HD; Universal HD.

Fee: $5.99 monthly.

Pay Service 1

Pay Units: 26.

Programming (via satellite): HBO.

Fee: $13.50 monthly.

Digital Pay Service 1

Pay Units: N.A.

Programming (via satellite): Cinemax (multiplexed); Encore (multiplexed); Flix; HBO (multiplexed); Showtime (multiplexed); Starz (multiplexed); The Movie Channel (multiplexed).

Fee: $14.75 monthly (HBO, Cinemax, Starz/Encore or Showtime/TMC/Flix).

Pay-Per-View

iN DEMAND (delivered digitally); Playboy TV (delivered digitally); Fresh (delivered digitally); Hot Choice (delivered digitally).

Internet Service

Operational: Yes.

Telephone Service

Digital: Operational

Miles of Plant: 35.0 (coaxial); None (fiber optic).

Regional Manager: Brent Richey. Office Manager: Linda Smith. Chief Technician: Greg Perry.

Ownership: Northland Communications Corp. (MSO).

DUNCANVILLE—Charter Communications, 15100 Trinity Blvd, Ste 500, Fort Worth, TX 76155. Phone: 817-298-3600. Web Site: http://www.charter.com. ICA: TX0080.

TV Market Ranking: 12 (DUNCANVILLE). Franchise award date: June 8, 1979. Franchise expiration date: N.A. Began: April 6, 1980.

Channel capacity: N.A. Channels available but not in use: N.A.

Basic Service

Subscribers: 4,371.

Programming (received off-air): KDAF (CW, IND) Dallas; KDFI (MNT) Dallas; KDFW-DT (FOX) Dallas; KDTN (ETV) Denton; KDTX-TV (TBN) Dallas; KERA-TV (PBS) Dallas; KFWD (IND) Fort Worth; KMPX (IND) Decatur; KPXD-TV (ION) Arlington; KSTR-DT (TEL) Irving; KTVT (CBS) Fort Worth; KTXA (IND) Fort Worth; KUVN-DT (UNV) Garland; KXAS-TV (NBC) Fort Worth; KXTX-TV (TMO) Dallas; WFAA (ABC) Dallas; 23 FMs.

Programming (via satellite): C-SPAN; INSP; WGN America.

Fee: $29.99 installation.

Expanded Basic Service 1
Subscribers: 4,290.
Programming (via satellite): A&E Networks; ABC Family Channel; AMC; Animal Planet; BET Networks; Bravo; Cartoon Network; CNBC; CNN; Comedy Central; Country Music TV; C-SPAN 2; Discovery Channel; Disney Channel; E! Entertainment Television; ESPN; ESPN 2; ESPN Classic Sports; Food Network; Fox News Channel; Fox Sports Southwest; FX; G4; GalaVision; Golf Channel; Great American Country; GSN; Hallmark Channel; Headline News; HGTV; History Channel; Lifetime; MSNBC; MTV; National Geographic Channel; Nickelodeon; Oxygen; QVC; SoapNet; Speed; Spike TV; Style Network; Syfy; TBS Superstation; Texas Cable News; The Learning Channel; The Weather Channel; Travel Channel; truTV; Turner Classic Movies; Turner Network TV; TV Land; USA Network; Versus; VH1; WE tv.
Fee: $48.99 monthly.

Digital Basic Service
Subscribers: N.A.
Programming (via satellite): BBC America; Bio; Bloomberg Television; Discovery Fit & Health; DIY Network; History Channel International; Independent Film Channel; Lifetime Movie Network; Music Choice; Sundance Channel; Toon Disney.

Digital Expanded Basic Service
Subscribers: N.A.
Programming (via satellite): Fox Deportes; FSN Digital Atlantic; FSN Digital Central; FSN Digital Pacific; Fuel TV; NFL Network.

Digital Pay Service 1
Pay Units: N.A.
Programming (via satellite): Cinemax (multiplexed); Encore (multiplexed); Flix; HBO (multiplexed); Showtime (multiplexed); Starz (multiplexed); The Movie Channel (multiplexed).

Video-On-Demand: No

Pay-Per-View
NASCAR In Car (delivered digitally); Hot Choice (delivered digitally); Fresh (delivered digitally); Shorteez (delivered digitally); iN DEMAND (delivered digitally).

Internet Service
Operational: Yes.
Broadband Service: Charter Pipeline.
Fee: $29.99 monthly.

Telephone Service
None

Miles of Plant: 114.0 (coaxial); 54.0 (fiber optic).
Vice President & General Manager: Wayne Cramp. Marketing Director: Kathleen Griffin. Technical Operations Director: John Linton.
Ownership: Charter Communications Inc. (MSO).

EAGLE LAKE—Time Warner Cable. Now served by COLUMBUS, TX [TX0257]. ICA: TX0278.

EAGLE PASS—Time Warner Cable, 1313 W Carlton Rd, Laredo, TX 78041. Phones: 972-899-7300 (Flower Mound office); 956-721-0607. Fax: 956-721-0612. Web Site: http://www.timewarnercable.com/Texas.
Also serves Maverick County. ICA: TX0067.
TV Market Ranking: Below 100 (EAGLE PASS, Maverick County). Franchise award date: N.A. Franchise expiration date: October 5, 2015. Began: September 1, 1959.
Channel capacity: N.A. Channels available but not in use: N.A.

Basic Service
Subscribers: N.A. Included in Del Rio
Programming (received off-air): KMYS (CW) Kerrville; KPXL-TV (ION) Uvalde; 4 FMs.
Programming (via microwave): KABB (FOX) San Antonio; KENS (CBS) San Antonio; KLRN (PBS) San Antonio; KSAT-TV (ABC) San Antonio; KWEX-DT (UNV) San Antonio; WOAI-TV (NBC) San Antonio.
Programming (via satellite): C-SPAN; C-SPAN 2; Disney Channel; QVC; various Mexican stations.
Fee: $50.51 installation; $18.49 monthly; $2.00 converter; $18.81 additional installation.

Expanded Basic Service 1
Subscribers: N.A.
Programming (via satellite): A&E Networks; AMC; Animal Planet; Bravo; Cartoon Network; CNN; Comedy Central; Discovery Channel; Discovery Health Channel; E! Entertainment Television; ESPN; ESPN 2; Eternal Word TV Network; Food Network; Fox Deportes; Fox News Channel; Fox Sports Southwest; FX; GalaVision; Golf Channel; Headline News; HGTV; History Channel; Lifetime; MSNBC; MTV; Nickelodeon; Oxygen; ShopNBC; SoapNet; Spike TV; Style Network; Syfy; TBS Superstation; Telemundo; Texas Cable News; The Learning Channel; The Weather Channel; Travel Channel; Turner Classic Movies; Turner Network TV; TV Land; USA Network; WE tv.
Fee: $27.50 monthly.

Digital Basic Service
Subscribers: N.A.
Programming (via satellite): BBC America; Bio; Bloomberg Television; Discovery Fit & Health; Discovery Home Channel; Discovery Kids Channel; ESPN Classic Sports; ESPNews; Fox Soccer; G4; GAS; GSN; History Channel International; INHD; Lifetime Movie Network; MTV Hits; MTV2; NBA TV; Nick Jr.; NickToons TV; Nuvo TV; Science Television; Toon Disney; Trio; Versus; VH1 Classic; VH1 Country.
Fee: $5.00 monthly.

Digital Expanded Basic Service
Subscribers: N.A.
Programming (via satellite): CNN en Espanol; DMX Music; Encore (multiplexed); Fox College Sports Atlantic; Fox College Sports Central; Fox College Sports Pacific; Fox Deportes; Fox Movie Channel; HTV Musica; Independent Film Channel; Infinito; La Familia Network; MTV Latin America; NBA TV; Puma TV; Speed; Sundance Channel; Tennis Channel; TVE Internacional; various Mexican stations; Versus; VHUNO; Video Rola.

Digital Pay Service 1
Pay Units: 478.
Programming (via satellite): Cinemax (multiplexed); HBO (multiplexed); Showtime (multiplexed); Starz (multiplexed); The Movie Channel (multiplexed).
Fee: $9.95 monthly (each).

Video-On-Demand: No

Pay-Per-View
Hot Choice (delivered digitally); Hot Choice (delivered digitally); iN DEMAND (delivered digitally); NASCAR In Car; adult (delivered digitally); adult (delivered digitally); adult (delivered digitally); adult (delivered digitally); director's cut- adult (delivered digitally); MLB Extra Innings (delivered digitally); NBA League Pass (delivered digitally).

Internet Service
Operational: Yes.
Broadband Service: Road Runner.
Fee: $49.99 installation; $44.95 monthly.

Telephone Service
Digital: Operational
Fee: $44.95 monthly

Miles of Plant: 159.0 (coaxial); None (fiber optic).
President: Connie Wharton. Vice President & General Manager: Michael Carrosquiola. Operations Director: Marco Reyes. Technical Operations Manager: Eduardo Ruiz. Public Affairs Manager: Celinda Gonzalez.
Ownership: Time Warner Cable (MSO).; Advance/Newhouse Partnership (MSO).

EAST GRAYSON COUNTY—TV Cable of Grayson County, 501 Hwy 120 N, Ste 6, PO Box 2084, Pottsboro, TX 75076. Phone: 903-786-7477. E-mail: tvcable@graysoncable.com. Web Site: http://www.graysoncable.com. Also serves Hendrix & Kemp, OK; Dennison, TX. ICA: TX1014.
TV Market Ranking: Below 100 (Dennison, EAST GRAYSON COUNTY, Hendrix, Kemp).
Channel capacity: N.A. Channels available but not in use: N.A.

Basic Service
Subscribers: N.A.
Programming (received off-air): KDAF (CW, IND) Dallas; KDFI (MNT) Dallas; KDFW-DT (FOX) Dallas; KERA-TV (PBS) Dallas; KTEN (ABC, CW, NBC) Ada; KTVT (CBS) Fort Worth; KXAS-TV (NBC) Fort Worth; KXII (CBS, FOX, MNT) Sherman; WFAA (ABC) Dallas.
Programming (via satellite): A&E Networks; ABC Family Channel; AMC; Animal Planet; Bloomberg Television; Boomerang; Cartoon Network; CNBC; CNN; Country Music TV; C-SPAN; C-SPAN 2; Discovery Channel; ESPN; ESPN 2; Fox Movie Channel; Fox News Channel; Fox Sports Southwest; FX; G4; Golf Channel; Great American Country; Headline News; HGTV; History Channel; Lifetime; MTV; National Geographic Channel; Nickelodeon; Outdoor Channel; QVC; Radar Channel; Speed; Spike TV; Syfy; TBS Superstation; The Learning Channel; The Weather Channel; Travel Channel; Trinity Broadcasting Network; truTV; Turner Network TV; TV Land; USA Network; VH1; WGN America.
Fee: $35.00 installation; $36.95 monthly; $20.00 additional installation.

Pay Service 1
Pay Units: N.A.
Programming (via satellite): HBO (multiplexed).

Video-On-Demand: No

Internet Service
Operational: Yes.
Broadband Service: Cable Rocket.
Fee: $35.00 installation; $24.99 monthly; $55.00 modem purchase.

Telephone Service
None

Manager: Chuck Davis.
Ownership: Chuck Davis (MSO).

EAST MOUNTAIN—Gilmer Cable, 111 E Marshall St, PO Box 1600, Gilmer, TX 75644. Phone: 903-843-5597. Fax: 903-843-2045. E-mail: cs@tatertv.com. Web Site: http://www.tatertv.com. Also serves Glenwood, Glenwood Acres & West Mountain. ICA: TX0750.
TV Market Ranking: Below 100 (EAST MOUNTAIN, Glenwood, Glenwood Acres, West Mountain). Franchise award date: November 14, 1988. Franchise expiration date: N.A. Began: November 1, 1990.
Channel capacity: N.A. Channels available but not in use: N.A.

Basic Service
Subscribers: 274.
Programming (via microwave): KDFW-DT (FOX) Dallas; KERA-TV (PBS) Dallas; KTVT (CBS) Fort Worth; KXAS-TV (NBC) Fort Worth.
Programming (via satellite): AMC; CNN; ESPN.
Fee: $32.95 installation; $14.30 monthly.

Expanded Basic Service 1
Subscribers: 212.
Programming (via satellite): A&E Networks; ABC Family Channel; Disney Channel; Fox Sports Southwest; MTV; Nickelodeon; USA Network.
Fee: $11.45 monthly.

Pay Service 1
Pay Units: 53.
Programming (via satellite): HBO.
Fee: $9.95 monthly.

Pay Service 2
Pay Units: 28.
Programming (via satellite): Showtime.
Fee: $7.95 monthly.

Video-On-Demand: No

Internet Service
Operational: Yes.
Fee: $29.95 installation; $34.95 monthly.

Telephone Service
None

Miles of Plant: 10.0 (coaxial); None (fiber optic).
President & General Manager: David P. Mooney. Plant Manager: Ken Beckwith. Marketing Director: Robbie Mooney.
Ownership: Gilmer Cable (MSO).

EASTLAND—Suddenlink Communications, 1504 N Main St, Monahans, TX 79756. Phones: 877-423-2743 (Customer service); 314-965-2020. Web Site: http://www.suddenlink.com. Also serves Cisco, Eastland County, Olden & Ranger. ICA: TX0131.
TV Market Ranking: Outside TV Markets (Cisco, EASTLAND, Eastland County, Olden, Ranger). Franchise award date: N.A. Franchise expiration date: N.A. Began: August 1, 1958.
Channel capacity: N.A. Channels available but not in use: N.A.

Basic Service
Subscribers: 3,290.
Programming (received off-air): KIDZ-LP Abilene; KPCB-DT (IND) Snyder; KRBC-TV (NBC) Abilene; KTAB-TV (CBS) Abilene; KTXS-TV (ABC, CW, TMO) Sweetwater; KXVA (FOX) Abilene; allband FM.

Programming (via microwave): KERA-TV (PBS) Dallas; WFAA (ABC) Dallas.
Programming (via satellite): C-SPAN; CW+; QVC; TV Guide Network; Univision Studios.
Fee: $39.95 installation; $19.95 monthly.

Expanded Basic Service 1
Subscribers: 2,761.
Programming (via satellite): A&E Networks; ABC Family Channel; AMC; Animal Planet; BET Networks; Bravo; Cartoon Network; Celebrity Shopping Network; CNBC; CNN; Comedy Central; Discovery Channel; Disney Channel; E! Entertainment Television; ESPN; ESPN 2; Food Network; Fox News Channel; Fox Sports Southwest; FX; GalaVision; Golf Channel; Great American Country; Hallmark Channel; Headline News; HGTV; History Channel; Jewelry Television; Lifetime; MSNBC; MTV; National Geographic Channel; Nickelodeon; Outdoor Channel; Speed; Spike TV; Syfy; TBS Superstation; The Learning Channel; The Weather Channel; Travel Channel; Turner Classic Movies; Turner Network TV; TV Land; USA Network; VH1.
Fee: $39.95 installation; $25.00 monthly.

Digital Basic Service
Subscribers: N.A.
Programming (via satellite): BBC America; Bio; Bloomberg Television; cloo; CMT Pure Country; Discovery Health Channel; Discovery Home Channel; Discovery Kids Channel; DMX Music; ESPN Classic Sports; ESPNews; Fuse; G4; GSN; History Channel International; ID Investigation Discovery; Independent Film Channel; Lifetime Movie Network; Military Channel; MTV2; Nick Jr.; NickToons TV; Science; Style Network; TeenNick; Toon Disney; Trinity Broadcasting Network; Versus; VH1 Classic; WE tv.
Fee: $3.99 monthly.

Pay Service 1
Pay Units: 223.
Programming (via satellite): Cinemax.
Fee: $12.90 monthly.

Pay Service 2
Pay Units: 911.
Programming (via satellite): Encore.
Fee: $1.75 monthly.

Pay Service 3
Pay Units: 426.
Programming (via satellite): HBO.
Fee: $12.90 monthly.

Pay Service 4
Pay Units: 171.
Programming (via satellite): Showtime.
Fee: $12.90 monthly.

Pay Service 5
Pay Units: 563.
Programming (via satellite): Starz.
Fee: $6.75 monthly.

Digital Pay Service 1
Pay Units: N.A.
Programming (via satellite): Cinemax (multiplexed); Encore (multiplexed); HBO (multiplexed); Showtime (multiplexed); Starz; The Movie Channel (multiplexed).

Video-On-Demand: No

Pay-Per-View
iN DEMAND (delivered digitally); Playboy TV (delivered digitally); Club Jenna (delivered digitally); Fresh (delivered digitally).

Internet Service
Operational: Yes. Began: March 2, 2002.
Broadband Service: Suddenlink High Speed Internet.
Fee: $45.95 installation; $29.95 monthly.

Telephone Service
Digital: Operational
Fee: $44.95 monthly

Miles of Plant: 124.0 (coaxial); None (fiber optic).
Regional Manager: Todd Cruthird.
Ownership: Cequel Communications LLC (MSO).

ECTOR—TV Cable of Grayson County, 501 Hwy 120 N, Ste 6, PO Box 2084, Pottsboro, TX 75076. Phone: 903-786-7477. E-mail: tvcable@graysoncable.com. Web Site: http://www.graysoncable.com. ICA: TX0585.
TV Market Ranking: Below 100 (ECTOR). Franchise award date: N.A. Franchise expiration date: N.A. Began: April 1, 1985.
Channel capacity: 54 (not 2-way capable). Channels available but not in use: N.A.

Basic Service
Subscribers: 57.
Programming (received off-air): KDFW-DT (FOX) Dallas; KERA-TV (PBS) Dallas; KPXD-TV (ION) Arlington; KTVT (CBS) Fort Worth; KXAS-TV (NBC) Fort Worth; KXII (CBS, FOX, MNT) Sherman; WFAA (ABC) Dallas.
Programming (via satellite): TBS Superstation.
Fee: $39.95 installation; $32.85 monthly.

Pay Service 1
Pay Units: 5.
Programming (via satellite): Cinemax.
Fee: $7.00 monthly.

Pay Service 2
Pay Units: N.A.
Programming (via satellite): HBO.
Fee: $12.00 monthly.

Pay Service 3
Pay Units: 20.
Programming (via satellite): Showtime.
Fee: $3.20 monthly.

Internet Service
Operational: Yes.
Fee: $35.00 installation; $49.95 monthly.

Telephone Service
None

Miles of Plant: 10.0 (coaxial); None (fiber optic).
Manager: Chuck Davis.
Ownership: Chuck Davis (MSO).

ECTOR COUNTY (portions)—Ridgewood Cablevision, 3700 S County Rd 1316, Odessa, TX 79765. Phone: 432-563-4330. Fax: 432-563-0104. E-mail: rwc@ridgewoodcable.com. Web Site: http://www.ridgewoodcable.com. ICA: TX1016.
TV Market Ranking: Below 100 (ECTOR COUNTY (PORTIONS)).
Channel capacity: N.A. Channels available but not in use: N.A.

Basic Service
Subscribers: 300 Includes Greenwood.
Programming (received off-air): KMID (ABC) Midland; KMLM-DT (IND) Odessa; KOSA-TV (CBS, MNT) Odessa; KPBT-TV (PBS) Odessa; KPEJ-TV (FOX) Odessa; KWES-TV (NBC) Odessa.
Programming (via satellite): A&E Networks; ABC Family Channel; AMC; Animal Planet; Cartoon Network; CNN; Country Music TV; C-SPAN; C-SPAN 2; Discovery Channel; Disney Channel; ESPN; ESPN 2; Food Network; Fox News Channel; Fox Sports Net; Hallmark Channel; Headline News; HGTV; History Channel; KUPB (UNV) Midland; Lifetime; MoviePlex; MTV; National Geographic Channel; Nickelodeon; QVC; Spike TV; Syfy; TBS Superstation; Telemundo; The Learning Channel; The Weather Channel; Toon Disney; Travel Channel; Turner Classic Movies; Turner Network TV; TV Land; USA Network; VH1; WGN America.
Fee: $37.95 monthly.

Pay Service 1
Pay Units: N.A.
Programming (via satellite): Cinemax (multiplexed); HBO (multiplexed); Showtime (multiplexed); The Movie Channel.
Fee: $6.95 monthly (Showtime & TMC), $7.95 montlhy (HBO & Cinemax).

Internet Service
Operational: No.

Manager & Chief Technician: Bob Randolph.
Ownership: Ridgewood Cable (MSO).

EDCOUCH—Time Warner Communications. Now served by PHARR, TX [TX0017]. ICA: TX0185.

EDEN—Reach Broadband, 515 E Longview St, Arp, TX 75750. Phone: 800-687-1258. Web Site: http://www.reachbroadband.net. Also serves Concho County (portions). ICA: TX0434.
TV Market Ranking: Below 100 (Concho County (portions)); Outside TV Markets (EDEN). Franchise award date: N.A. Franchise expiration date: N.A. Began: January 1, 1973.
Channel capacity: 41 (not 2-way capable). Channels available but not in use: N.A.

Basic Service
Subscribers: 245.
Programming (received off-air): KIDY (FOX) San Angelo; KLST (CBS) San Angelo; KRBC-TV (NBC) Abilene; KTXS-TV (ABC, CW, TMO) Sweetwater; 2 FMs.
Programming (via satellite): A&E Networks; ABC Family Channel; Animal Planet; Cartoon Network; CNN; Country Music TV; Discovery Channel; Disney Channel; ESPN; Fox News Channel; Fox Sports Southwest; Headline News; KRMA-TV (PBS) Denver; Lifetime; Nickelodeon; QVC; Spike TV; TBS Superstation; The Learning Channel; The Weather Channel; Trinity Broadcasting Network; Turner Classic Movies; Turner Network TV; TV Land; USA Network; WGN America.
Fee: $29.95 installation; $38.00 monthly.

Pay Service 1
Pay Units: 40.
Programming (via satellite): HBO.
Fee: $35.00 installation; $10.95 monthly.

Pay Service 2
Pay Units: 56.
Programming (via satellite): Showtime.
Fee: $9.95 monthly.

Pay Service 3
Pay Units: 48.
Programming (via satellite): The Movie Channel.
Fee: $7.95 monthly.

Video-On-Demand: No

Internet Service
Operational: No.

Telephone Service
None

Miles of Plant: 15.0 (coaxial); None (fiber optic).
Regional Manager: Ronnie Stafford. Office Manager: Jan Gibson.
Ownership: RB3 LLC (MSO).

EDNA—Mid-Coast Cablevision, 505 N Mechanic St, PO Box 1269, El Campo, TX 77437-1269. Phone: 979-543-6858. Fax: 979-543-9501. Web Site: http://www.warpspeed1.net. ICA: TX0207.
TV Market Ranking: Below 100 (EDNA). Franchise award date: N.A. Franchise expiration date: March 13, 2007. Began: January 1, 1959.
Channel capacity: 62 (operating 2-way). Channels available but not in use: N.A.

Basic Service
Subscribers: 1,897.
Programming (received off-air): KAVU-TV (ABC) Victoria; KHOU (CBS) Houston; KIAH (CW) Houston; KPRC-TV (NBC) Houston; KRIV (FOX) Houston; KTMD (TMO) Galveston; KTRK-TV (ABC) Houston; KTXH (MNT) Houston; KUBE-TV (IND) Baytown; KUHT (PBS) Houston; KXLN-DT (UNV) Rosenberg; KYAZ (IND) Katy; KZJL (IND) Houston; allband FM.
Programming (via satellite): A&E Networks; ABC Family Channel; AMC; BET Networks; Cartoon Network; CNBC; CNN; Country Music TV; C-SPAN; Discovery Channel; Discovery Fit & Health; ESPN; ESPN 2; ESPN Classic Sports; Food Network; Fox News Channel; Fox Sports Southwest; FX; Hallmark Channel; Headline News; HGTV; History Channel; Lifetime; MTV; Nickelodeon; Outdoor Channel; Paxson Communications Corp.; QVC; SoapNet; Spike TV; TBS Superstation; The Learning Channel; The Weather Channel; Trinity Broadcasting Network; truTV; Turner Network TV; TV Guide Network; TV Land; USA Network; VH1; WGN America.
Fee: $10.00 installation; $10.38 monthly.

Digital Basic Service
Subscribers: N.A.
Programming (via satellite): BBC America; Bloomberg Television; Canales N; Discovery Digital Networks; ESPNews; Fox Movie Channel; Fox Soccer; G4; Golf Channel; GSN; Independent Film Channel; Nick Jr.; NickToons TV; Speed; Turner Classic Movies; Versus; VH1 Classic; VH1 Country; WE tv.

Digital Pay Service 1
Pay Units: N.A.
Programming (via satellite): Cinemax (multiplexed); Encore (multiplexed); Flix; HBO (multiplexed); Showtime (multiplexed); The Movie Channel (multiplexed).

Video-On-Demand: No

Pay-Per-View
Addressable homes: 202.
Hot Choice; iN DEMAND.

Internet Service
Operational: Yes, Both DSL & dial-up.
Broadband Service: Warp Speed 1 Internet.
Fee: $17.05 installation; $34.99 monthly.

Telephone Service
None

Miles of Plant: 35.0 (coaxial); None (fiber optic). Additional miles planned: 5.0 (coaxial).
Manager: Wayne Neal.
Ownership: Mid-Coast Cablevision (MSO).

EGAN—North Texas Broadband, PO Box 676, Aubery, TX 76227. Phone: 940-365-2930. Web Site: http://www.northtxbroadband.com. Also serves Egan County (portions). ICA: TX0366.
TV Market Ranking: 12 (EGAN, Egan County (portions)); Outside TV Markets (Egan County (portions)). Franchise award date: N.A. Franchise expiration date: N.A. Began: N.A.
Channel capacity: 36 (not 2-way capable). Channels available but not in use: N.A.

Basic Service
Subscribers: 184.
Programming (received off-air): KDAF (CW, IND) Dallas; KDFI (MNT) Dallas; KDFW-DT (FOX) Dallas; KERA-TV (PBS) Dallas; KPXD-TV (ION) Arlington; KTVT (CBS) Fort Worth; KTXA (IND) Fort Worth; KXAS-TV (NBC) Fort Worth; KXTX-TV (TMO) Dallas; WFAA (ABC) Dallas.
Programming (via satellite): A&E Networks; ABC Family Channel; AMC; American-

Life TV Network; CNN; Country Music TV; Discovery Channel; Disney Channel; ESPN; Fox Sports Southwest; Lifetime; Nickelodeon; Spike TV; TBS Superstation; Trinity Broadcasting Network; Turner Network TV; USA Network; WGN America.
Fee: $39.95 installation; $31.50 monthly.

Pay Service 1
Pay Units: 11.
Programming (via satellite): Cinemax.
Fee: $10.95 monthly.

Pay Service 2
Pay Units: 21.
Programming (via satellite): HBO.
Fee: $10.95 monthly.

Pay Service 3
Pay Units: 34.
Programming (via satellite): Showtime.
Fee: $5.95 monthly.

Internet Service
Operational: Yes.

Telephone Service
None

Miles of Plant: 49.0 (coaxial); None (fiber optic).
Manager: Curtis Davis.
Ownership: North Texas Broadband (MSO).

EL CAMPO—Mid-Coast Cablevision, 505 N Mechanic St, PO Box 1269, El Campo, TX 77437-1269. Phones: 877-543-4850; 979-543-6858. Fax: 979-543-9501. Web Site: http://www.warpspeed1.net. ICA: TX0133.
TV Market Ranking: Outside TV Markets (EL CAMPO). Franchise award date: March 15, 1973. Franchise expiration date: August 25, 2017. Began: March 15, 1973.
Channel capacity: N.A. Channels available but not in use: N.A.

Basic Service
Subscribers: 3,548.
Programming (received off-air): KAVU-TV (ABC) Victoria; KETH-TV (TBN) Houston; KFTH-DT (TEL) Alvin; KHOU (CBS) Houston; KIAH (CW) Houston; KLTJ (ETV) Galveston; KPRC-TV (NBC) Houston; KRIV (FOX) Houston; KTBU (IND) Conroe; KTMD (TMO) Galveston; KTRK-TV (ABC) Houston; KTXH (MNT) Houston; KUBE-TV (IND) Baytown; KUHT (PBS) Houston; KXLN-DT (UNV) Rosenberg; KYAZ (IND) Katy; KZJL (IND) Houston; allband FM.
Programming (via satellite): ION Television; TV Guide Network; WGN America.
Fee: $25.00 installation; $10.38 monthly; $3.35 converter.

Expanded Basic Service 1
Subscribers: 3,422.
Programming (via satellite): A&E Networks; ABC Family Channel; AMC; BET Networks; Cartoon Network; CNBC; CNN; Country Music TV; C-SPAN; C-SPAN 2; Discovery Channel; Discovery Fit & Health; Disney Channel; ESPN; ESPN 2; ESPN Classic Sports; Eternal Word TV Network; Fox News Channel; Fox Sports Southwest; FX; Hallmark Channel; Headline News; HGTV; History Channel; INSP; Lifetime; MTV; Nickelodeon; Outdoor Channel; QVC; SoapNet; Speed; Spike TV; TBS Superstation; The Learning Channel; The Weather Channel; truTV; Turner Network TV; TV Land; USA Network; VH1.
Fee: $25.00 installation; $29.99 monthly.

Digital Basic Service
Subscribers: N.A.
Programming (via satellite): ABC News Now; BBC America; Bloomberg Television; Cine Latino; CMT Pure Country; CNN en Espanol; Discovery en Espanol; Discovery Health Channel; Discovery Kids Channel; ESPN 2 HD; ESPN U; ESPNews; Fox Deportes; Fox Movie Channel; Fox Reality Channel; Fox Soccer; Fuel TV; G4; Golf Channel; GSN; ID Investigation Discovery; Independent Film Channel; Military Channel; Nick Jr.; NickToons TV; PBS Kids Sprout; Science; Speed; Tr3s; Turner Classic Movies; TVE Internacional; Utilisima; Versus; VH1 Classic; WE tv.

Digital Pay Service 1
Pay Units: N.A.
Programming (via satellite): Cinemax (multiplexed); Encore (multiplexed); Flix; HBO (multiplexed); Showtime (multiplexed); Starz (multiplexed); The Movie Channel (multiplexed).

Video-On-Demand: No

Pay-Per-View
iN DEMAND (delivered digitally); Playboy TV (delivered digitally).

Internet Service
Operational: Yes, Both DSL & dial-up.
Broadband Service: Warp Speed 1 Internet.
Fee: $17.05 installation; $34.99 monthly.

Telephone Service
None

Miles of Plant: 87.0 (coaxial); 20.0 (fiber optic).
Manager: Wayne Neal. Chief Technician: Dickie Isaacs.
Ownership: Mid-Coast Cablevision (MSO).

EL PASO—Time Warner Cable, 7010 Airport Rd, El Paso, TX 79906. Phones: 972-899-7300 (Flower Mound division office); 915-772-1123. Fax: 915-772-4605. Web Site: http://www.timewarnercable.com/Texas. Also serves Anthony, Dona Ana County (portions), Santa Teresa & Sunland Park, NM; Anthony, Biggs Airfield, Canutillo, Clint, El Paso County, Fabens, Fort Bliss, Horizon City, Moon City, San Elizario, Socorro & Vinton, TX. ICA: TX0009.
TV Market Ranking: Below 100 (Anthony, Anthony, Biggs Airfield, Canutillo, Clint, Dona Ana County (portions), EL PASO, El Paso County, Fabens, Fort Bliss, Horizon City, Moon City, San Elizario, Santa Teresa, Socorro, Sunland Park, Vinton). Franchise award date: January 1, 1968. Franchise expiration date: March 1, 2007. Began: February 1, 1972.
Channel capacity: N.A. Channels available but not in use: N.A.

Basic Service
Subscribers: 120,000.
Programming (received off-air): KCOS (PBS) El Paso; KDBC-TV (CBS, MNT) El Paso; KFOX-TV (FOX) El Paso; KINT-TV (UNV) El Paso; KRWG-TV (PBS) Las Cruces; KSCE (ETV) El Paso; KTDO (TMO) Las Cruces; KTFN (TEL) El Paso; KTSM-TV (NBC) El Paso; KVIA-TV (ABC, CW) El Paso; 16 FMs.
Programming (via satellite): KTLA (CW) Los Angeles.
Fee: $50.51 installation; $9.70 monthly.

Expanded Basic Service 1
Subscribers: 115,000.
Programming (via satellite): A&E Networks; ABC Family Channel; AMC; Animal Planet; BET Networks; Bravo; Cartoon Network; CNBC; CNN; Comedy Central; Country Music TV; C-SPAN; C-SPAN 2; Discovery Channel; Discovery Health Channel; Disney Channel; E! Entertainment Television; ESPN; ESPN 2; ESPN Classic Sports; Eternal Word TV Network; Food Network; Fox Deportes; Fox News Channel; Fox Sports Southwest; FX; GalaVision; Golf Channel; Great American Country; Headline News; HGTV; History Channel; ION Television; Lifetime; Lifetime Movie Network; Metro Sports; MSNBC; MTV; National Geographic Channel; Nickelodeon; Oxygen; QVC; ShopNBC; SoapNet; Spike TV; Syfy; TBS Superstation; Texas Cable News; The Learning Channel; The Weather Channel; Travel Channel; truTV; Turner Classic Movies; Turner Network TV; TV Land; USA Network; VH1; WE tv.
Fee: $38.29 monthly.

Digital Basic Service
Subscribers: N.A.
Programming (via satellite): America's Store; BBC America; Bio; Boomerang; Canales N; cloo; Cooking Channel; Current; Discovery Fit & Health; DIY Network; ESPNews; Flix (multiplexed); Fox College Sports Atlantic; Fox College Sports Central; Fox College Sports Pacific; Fox Movie Channel; Fox Soccer; Fuel TV; G4; GAS; GSN; Hallmark Channel; History Channel International; Independent Film Channel; Lifetime Real Women; MTV Networks Digital Suite; mun2 television; NBA TV; Nick Jr.; NickToons TV; Outdoor Channel; Ovation; Science Television; Speed; Sundance Channel; Tennis Channel; Toon Disney; Versus.
Fee: $5.00 monthly, $8.94 monthly (Encore, Sports or Canales N tiers).

Digital Pay Service 1
Pay Units: N.A.
Programming (via satellite): Cinemax (multiplexed); Encore (multiplexed); HBO (multiplexed); Showtime (multiplexed); Starz (multiplexed); The Movie Channel (multiplexed).
Fee: $12.95 monthly (each).

Video-On-Demand: Yes

Pay-Per-View
iN DEMAND (delivered digitally); Hot Choice (delivered digitally); Playboy TV (delivered digitally); Fresh (delivered digitally); Shorteez (delivered digitally); NBA League Pass (delivered digitally); ESPN (delivered digitally); MLB Extra Innings (delivered digitally); NASCAR In Car (delivered digitally).

Internet Service
Operational: Yes. Began: September 1, 1997.
Subscribers: 5,500.
Broadband Service: Road Runner.
Fee: $49.99 installation; $44.95 monthly.

Telephone Service
Digital: Operational
Subscribers: 2,700.
Fee: $44.95 monthly

Miles of Plant: 2,562.0 (coaxial); 787.0 (fiber optic).
President: Connie Wharton. Vice President & General Manager: Michael G. Carrosquiola. Technical Operations Director: Ismael Molina. Public Affairs Director: Rene Hurtado.
Ownership: Time Warner Cable (MSO).; Advance/Newhouse Partnership (MSO).

ELDORADO—Reach Broadband, 515 E Longview St, Arp, TX 75750. Phone: 800-687-1258. Web Site: http://www.reachbroadband.net. Also serves Schleider County (portions). ICA: TX0342.
TV Market Ranking: Below 100 (Schleider County (portions)); Outside TV Markets (ELDORADO, Schleider County (portions)). Franchise award date: N.A. Franchise expiration date: N.A. Began: September 1, 1960.
Channel capacity: 41 (not 2-way capable). Channels available but not in use: N.A.

Basic Service
Subscribers: 314.
Programming (received off-air): KIDY (FOX) San Angelo; KLST (CBS) San Angelo; KSAN-TV (NBC) San Angelo; KTXS-TV (ABC, CW, TMO) Sweetwater; allband FM.
Programming (via satellite): A&E Networks; ABC Family Channel; Animal Planet; CNN; Country Music TV; C-SPAN; C-SPAN 2; Discovery Channel; Disney Channel; ESPN; Fox News Channel; Fox Sports Southwest; GalaVision; Headline News; KRMA-TV (PBS) Denver; Lifetime; Nickelodeon; QVC; Spike TV; TBS Superstation; The Learning Channel; The Weather Channel; Turner Classic Movies; Turner Network TV; TV Land; USA Network; WGN America.
Fee: $29.95 installation; $38.00 monthly.

Pay Service 1
Pay Units: 55.
Programming (via satellite): HBO.
Fee: $35.00 installation; $10.95 monthly.

Pay Service 2
Pay Units: 64.
Programming (via satellite): Showtime.
Fee: $9.95 monthly.

Pay Service 3
Pay Units: 56.
Programming (via satellite): The Movie Channel.
Fee: $7.95 monthly.

Video-On-Demand: No

Internet Service
Operational: No.

Telephone Service
None

Miles of Plant: 20.0 (coaxial); None (fiber optic).
Regional Manager: Ronnie Stafford. Office Manager: Jan Gibson.
Ownership: RB3 LLC (MSO).

ELECTRA—Suddenlink Communications, 12444 Powerscourt Dr, Saint Louis, MO 63131-3660. Phones: 800-999-6845; 314-965-2020. Fax: 903-561-5485. Web Site: http://www.suddenlink.com. ICA: TX0285.
TV Market Ranking: Below 100 (ELECTRA). Franchise award date: N.A. Franchise expiration date: N.A. Began: April 1, 1978.
Channel capacity: N.A. Channels available but not in use: N.A.

Basic Service
Subscribers: 507.
Programming (received off-air): KAUZ-TV (CBS, CW) Wichita Falls; KFDX-TV (NBC) Wichita Falls; KJTL (FOX) Wichita Falls; KSWO-TV (ABC, TMO) Lawton; allband FM.
Programming (via satellite): Discovery Channel; QVC; TBS Superstation; The Weather Channel; truTV.
Programming (via translator): KERA-TV (PBS) Dallas.
Fee: $39.95 installation; $19.95 monthly.

Expanded Basic Service 1
Subscribers: 483.
Programming (via satellite): ABC Family Channel; AMC; Animal Planet; Cartoon Network; CNBC; CNN; C-SPAN; ESPN; Fox News Channel; FX; Headline News; HGTV; Lifetime; MTV; Spike TV; The Learning Channel; Turner Network TV; USA Network.
Fee: $39.95 installation; $23.00 monthly.
Pay Service 1
Pay Units: 31.
Programming (via satellite): Cinemax.
Fee: $13.59 monthly.
Pay Service 2
Pay Units: 192.
Programming (via satellite): Encore.
Fee: $1.75 monthly.
Pay Service 3
Pay Units: 93.
Programming (via satellite): HBO.
Fee: $13.59 monthly.
Pay Service 4
Pay Units: 94.
Programming (via satellite): Starz.
Fee: $6.75 monthly.
Video-On-Demand: No
Internet Service
Operational: Yes. Began: November 12, 2003.
Broadband Service: Suddenlink High Speed Internet.
Fee: $49.95 installation; $43.95 monthly.
Telephone Service
None
Miles of Plant: 22.0 (coaxial); None (fiber optic).
Regional Manager: Todd Cruthird. Plant Manager: Ron Johnson.
Ownership: Cequel Communications LLC (MSO).

ELLINGER—Formerly served by National Cable Inc. No longer in operation. ICA: TX0751.

ELMO—Formerly served by Almega Cable. No longer in operation. ICA: TX0489.

EMORY—Formerly served by Alliance Communications. No longer in operation. ICA: TX0375.

ENCINAL—Windjammer Cable, 8500 W 110th St, Ste 600, Overland Park, KS 66210. Phone: 888-495-2881. Fax: 913-563-5454. Web Site: http://www.windjammercable.com. Also serves La Salle County (southern portion). ICA: TX0565.
TV Market Ranking: Outside TV Markets (ENCINAL, La Salle County (southern portion)). Franchise award date: N.A. Franchise expiration date: N.A. Began: July 1, 1983.
Channel capacity: N.A. Channels available but not in use: N.A.
Basic Service
Subscribers: N.A. Included in Del Rio
Programming (received off-air): KABB (FOX) San Antonio; KGNS-TV (CW, NBC, TMO) Laredo; KVTV (CBS) Laredo; WKRN-TV (ABC) Nashville.
Programming (via satellite): A&E Networks; ABC Family Channel; AMC; Animal Planet; Bravo; Cartoon Network; CNN; Comedy Central; C-SPAN; C-SPAN 2; Discovery Channel; E! Entertainment Television; Encore; ESPN; ESPN 2; Eternal Word TV Network; Food Network; Fox Deportes; Fox News Channel; Fox Sports Southwest; FX; GalaVision; Golf Channel; Great American Country; Hallmark Channel; Headline News; HGTV; History Channel; Lifetime; MSNBC; MTV; Nickelodeon; Oxygen; ShopNBC; Spike TV; Syfy; TBS Superstation; Telemundo; The Learning Channel; The Weather Channel; Travel Channel; Turner Classic Movies; Turner Network TV; TV Land; Univision Studios; USA Network; WABC-TV (ABC) New York; WE tv.
Fee: $50.51 installation; $40.99 monthly; $18.81 additional installation.
Pay Service 1
Pay Units: 62.
Programming (via satellite): Encore; HBO.
Fee: $2.75 monthly (Encore), 12.95 monthly (HBO).
Internet Service
Operational: No.
Telephone Service
None
Miles of Plant: 6.0 (coaxial); None (fiber optic).
General Manager: Timothy Evard. Operations Director: Belinda Graham. Engineering Director: Mike Earehart. Finance & Accounting Director: Cindy Johnson.
Ownership: Windjammer Communications LLC (MSO).

ENNIS—Charter Communications, 15100 Trinity Blvd, Ste 500, Fort Worth, TX 76155. Phones: 817-298-3600; 972-771-0202 (Waxahachie). Web Site: http://www.charter.com. Also serves Alma & Garrett. ICA: TX0123.
TV Market Ranking: 12 (ENNIS, Garrett); Outside TV Markets (Alma). Franchise award date: February 10, 1989. Franchise expiration date: N.A. Began: March 1, 1980.
Channel capacity: N.A. Channels available but not in use: N.A.
Basic Service
Subscribers: 2,015.
Programming (received off-air): KAZD (IND) Lake Dallas; KDAF (CW, IND) Dallas; KDFI (MNT) Dallas; KDFW-DT (FOX) Dallas; KDTN (ETV) Denton; KDTX-TV (TBN) Dallas; KERA-TV (PBS) Dallas; KFWD (IND) Fort Worth; KPXD-TV (ION) Arlington; KSTR-DT (TEL) Irving; KTVT (CBS) Fort Worth; KTXA (IND) Fort Worth; KUVN-DT (UNV) Garland; KXAS-TV (NBC) Fort Worth; KXTX-TV (TMO) Dallas; WFAA (ABC) Dallas.
Programming (via satellite): A&E Networks; ABC Family Channel; AMC; Animal Planet; BET Networks; Bravo; Cartoon Network; CNBC; CNN; Comedy Central; Country Music TV; C-SPAN; C-SPAN 2; Discovery Channel; Disney Channel; E! Entertainment Television; ESPN; ESPN 2; Eternal Word TV Network; Food Network; Fox News Channel; Fox Sports Southwest; Headline News; HGTV; History Channel; Lifetime; MTV; Nickelodeon; Outdoor Channel; Oxygen; Product Information Network; QVC; SoapNet; Spike TV; TBS Superstation; Texas Cable News; The Learning Channel; The Weather Channel; Toon Disney; Travel Channel; Turner Classic Movies; Turner Network TV; USA Network; VH1; WGN America.
Fee: $29.99 installation; $48.99 monthly; $1.65 converter.
Digital Basic Service
Subscribers: N.A.
Programming (via microwave): KDFW-DT (FOX) Dallas.
Programming (via satellite): BBC America; Bio; Bloomberg Television; Discovery Digital Networks; DIY Network; ESPN; Fox Movie Channel; Fuse; G4; GAS; Great American Country; HDNet; HDNet Movies; History Channel International; Independent Film Channel; KXAS-TV (NBC) Fort Worth; Lifetime Movie Network; MTV Networks Digital Suite; Music Choice; Nick Jr.; Nick Too; NickToons TV; Science Television; Style Network; Sundance Channel; TV Guide Interactive Inc.; WFAA (ABC) Dallas.
Digital Expanded Basic Service
Subscribers: N.A.
Programming (via satellite): Canales N; ESPN Classic Sports; ESPNews; Fox Soccer; FSN Digital Atlantic; FSN Digital Central; FSN Digital Pacific; Fuel TV; NFL Network.
Digital Pay Service 1
Pay Units: N.A.
Programming (via satellite): Cinemax (multiplexed); Encore (multiplexed); HBO (multiplexed); Showtime (multiplexed); Starz (multiplexed); The Movie Channel (multiplexed).
Video-On-Demand: No
Pay-Per-View
NASCAR In Car (delivered digitally); ETC (delivered digitally); Erotic Network (delivered digitally); Pleasure (delivered digitally); Playboy TV (delivered digitally); Fresh (delivered digitally); Shorteez (delivered digitally); iN DEMAND (delivered digitally).
Internet Service
Operational: Yes.
Broadband Service: Charter Pipeline.
Fee: $29.99 monthly.
Telephone Service
None
Miles of Plant: 39.0 (coaxial); 9.0 (fiber optic).
Vice President & General Manager: Wayne Cramp. Marketing Director: Kathleen Griffin. Technical Operations Director: John Linton. Technical Supervisor: Daryl Gross.
Ownership: Charter Communications Inc. (MSO).

EVANT—Formerly served by Almega Cable. No longer in operation. ICA: TX0631.

FAIR OAKS RANCH—GVTC Communications. Formerly served by Boerne (portions), TX [TX0315]. This cable system has converted to IPTV, 108 E Third St, Gridley, TX 61744. Fax: 309-783-3297. E-mail: info@gridcom.net. Web Site: http://www.gridtel.com. Also serves FAIR OAKS RANCH. ICA: TX5472.
Channel capacity: N.A. Channels available but not in use: N.A.
Internet Service
Operational: Yes.

FAIRFIELD—Northland Cable Television, 515 W Tyler St, PO Box 112, Mexia, TX 76667-0112. Phones: 800-792-3087; 254-562-2872. Fax: 254-562-6454. Web Site: http://www.northlandcabletv.com. Also serves Teague. ICA: TX0150.
TV Market Ranking: Outside TV Markets (FAIRFIELD, Teague). Franchise award date: February 1, 1965. Franchise expiration date: N.A. Began: November 1, 1968.
Channel capacity: 55 (not 2-way capable). Channels available but not in use: N.A.
Basic Service
Subscribers: 1,300.
Programming (received off-air): KCEN-TV (NBC, IND) Temple; KDAF (CW, IND) Dallas; KDFI (MNT) Dallas; KDFW-DT (FOX) Dallas; KERA-TV (PBS) Dallas; KFWD (IND) Fort Worth; KPXD-TV (ION) Arlington; KTVT (CBS) Fort Worth; KTXA (IND) Fort Worth; KWKT-TV (FOX, MNT) Waco; KWTX-TV (CBS, CW) Waco; KXAS-TV (NBC) Fort Worth; KXTX-TV (TMO) Dallas; KXXV (ABC, TMO) Waco; WFAA (ABC) Dallas; allband FM.
Programming (via satellite): A&E Networks; Animal Planet; BET Networks; Cartoon Network; CNBC; CNN; C-SPAN; Discovery Channel; ESPN; Food Network; Fox News Channel; Fox Sports Southwest; Great American Country; Hallmark Channel; Headline News; HGTV; History Channel; QVC; TBS Superstation; The Learning Channel; The Weather Channel; Trinity Broadcasting Network; Turner Network TV; TV Guide Network; Univision Studios; USA Network.
Fee: $55.00 installation; $38.99 monthly.
Expanded Basic Service 1
Subscribers: 830.
Programming (via satellite): Comedy Central; E! Entertainment Television; ESPN 2; Fox Movie Channel; Lifetime; MTV; Nickelodeon; Spike TV; Syfy; Turner Classic Movies.
Fee: $49.99 monthly.
Digital Basic Service
Subscribers: 140.
Programming (via satellite): AmericanLife TV Network; BBC America; Bloomberg Television; Bravo; Discovery Fit & Health; DMX Music; G4; Golf Channel; GSN; Halogen Network; Independent Film Channel; Outdoor Channel; Speed; Versus; WE tv.
Fee: $34.99 monthly.
Pay Service 1
Pay Units: 100.
Programming (via satellite): Encore; Starz.
Fee: $35.00 installation; $10.00 monthly.
Pay Service 2
Pay Units: 30.
Programming (via satellite): Showtime.
Fee: $35.00 installation; $10.00 monthly.
Pay Service 3
Pay Units: 200.
Programming (via satellite): HBO.
Fee: $35.00 installation; $14.00 monthly.
Digital Pay Service 1
Pay Units: 30.
Programming (via satellite): Cinemax (multiplexed); Encore (multiplexed); HBO (multiplexed); Showtime (multiplexed); Starz (multiplexed); The Movie Channel (multiplexed).
Fee: $14.75 monthly (HBO, Cinemax, Showtime/TMC or Starz/Encore).
Video-On-Demand: No
Pay-Per-View
Sports PPV (delivered digitally); iN DEMAND (delivered digitally).
Internet Service
Operational: Yes.
Fee: $42.99 monthly.
Telephone Service
None
Miles of Plant: 92.0 (coaxial); None (fiber optic).
Manager: Brent Richey. Chief Technician: Joe Lopez. Office Manager: Pamela Elliott.
Ownership: Northland Communications Corp. (MSO).

FALFURRIAS—Time Warner Cable. Now served by ALICE, TX [TX0102]. ICA: TX0269.

FANNETT—Almega Cable, 4001 W Airport Freeway, Ste 530, Bedford, TX 76021. Phone: 817-685-9588. Fax: 817-685-6488. Web Site: http://www.almega.com. Also serves Jefferson County (portions). ICA: TX0319.
TV Market Ranking: 88 (FANNETT, Jefferson County (portions)). Franchise award date:

N.A. Franchise expiration date: N.A. Began: September 1, 1989.
Channel capacity: 36 (not 2-way capable). Channels available but not in use: N.A.

Basic Service

Subscribers: 612.

Programming (received off-air): KBMT (ABC) Beaumont; KBTV-TV (FOX) Port Arthur; KFDM (CBS, CW) Beaumont; KITU-TV (TBN) Beaumont.

Programming (via satellite): A&E Networks; ABC Family Channel; CNN; Country Music TV; C-SPAN; Discovery Channel; Disney Channel; E! Entertainment Television; ESPN; Fox Sports Southwest; Hallmark Channel; Headline News; Lifetime; Nickelodeon; QVC; Spike TV; Syfy; TBS Superstation; The Weather Channel; Turner Network TV; USA Network; WGN America.

Fee: $54.95 installation; $44.05 monthly.

Pay Service 1

Pay Units: 64.

Programming (via satellite): Cinemax.

Fee: $12.95 monthly.

Pay Service 2

Pay Units: 81.

Programming (via satellite): HBO.

Fee: $12.95 monthly.

Pay Service 3

Pay Units: 127.

Programming (via satellite): Showtime.

Fee: $12.95 monthly.

Video-On-Demand: No

Internet Service

Operational: No.

Telephone Service

None

Miles of Plant: 81.0 (coaxial); None (fiber optic).

Ownership: Almega Cable (MSO).

FARMERSVILLE—Time Warner Cable, 1565 Chenault St, Dallas, TX 75228. Phones: 214-328-2882; 903-455-0012 (Greenville office). Fax: 214-320-7484. Web Site: http://www.timewarnercable.com. ICA: TX1000.

TV Market Ranking: 12 (FARMERSVILLE).

Channel capacity: N.A. Channels available but not in use: N.A.

Basic Service

Subscribers: N.A. Included in Dallas

Programming (received off-air): KAZD (IND) Lake Dallas; KDAF (CW, IND) Dallas; KDFI (MNT) Dallas; KDFW-DT (FOX) Dallas; KDTN (ETV) Denton; KDTX-TV (TBN) Dallas; KERA-TV (PBS) Dallas; KFWD (IND) Fort Worth; KMPX (IND) Decatur; KPXD-TV (ION) Arlington; KSTR-DT (TEL) Irving; KTAQ (IND) Greenville; KTVT (CBS) Fort Worth; KTXA (IND) Fort Worth; KUVN-DT (UNV) Garland; KXAS-TV (NBC) Fort Worth; KXTX-TV (TMO) Dallas; WFAA (ABC) Dallas.

Programming (via satellite): C-SPAN; C-SPAN 2; Discovery Channel; Eternal Word TV Network; QVC; WGN America.

Fee: $13.99 monthly.

Expanded Basic Service 1

Subscribers: N.A.

Programming (via satellite): A&E Networks; ABC Family Channel; AMC; Animal Planet; BET Networks; Cartoon Network; CNBC; CNN; Comedy Central; Country Music TV; Disney Channel; E! Entertainment Television; ESPN; ESPN 2; Food Network; Fox News Channel; Fox Sports Southwest; FX; GalaVision; Golf Channel; GSN; Hallmark Channel; Headline News; HGTV; History Channel; Lifetime; MSNBC; MTV; Nickelodeon; Oxygen; Spike TV; Syfy; TBS Superstation; Texas Cable News; The Learning Channel; The Weather Channel; Travel Channel; truTV; Turner Classic Movies; Turner Network TV; TV Land; TV One; USA Network; Versus; VH1.

Fee: $40.25 monthly.

Digital Basic Service

Subscribers: N.A.

Programming (via satellite): AMC; BBC America; Bravo; Cooking Channel; Discovery Health Channel; Discovery Kids Channel; DIY Network; Encore (multiplexed); ESPN Classic Sports; ESPNews; Fox Soccer; Hallmark Channel; Independent Film Channel; MTV Jams; Music Choice; Nick Jr.; Nick Too; Science; WE tv.

Digital Pay Service 1

Pay Units: N.A.

Programming (via satellite): Cinemax (multiplexed); HBO (multiplexed); Showtime (multiplexed); Starz (multiplexed); The Movie Channel (multiplexed).

Video-On-Demand: No

Pay-Per-View

iN DEMAND (delivered digitally); Playboy TV (delivered digitally); Fresh (delivered digitally).

Internet Service

Operational: Yes.

Broadband Service: Road Runner.

Telephone Service

None

President: Robert Moel. Vice President, Technical Operations: Michael McDonald. Vice President, Marketing: Robert Shurtleff. Vice President, Government & Public Affairs: Dick Kirby. Public Affairs Director: Gary Underwood. Office Manager: LaTonya Smiley-Rizby.

Ownership: Time Warner Cable (MSO).

FAYETTEVILLE—Grisham TV Cable Co., PO Box 65, Hallettsville, TX 77964-0065. Phone: 361-798-3611. ICA: TX0985.

TV Market Ranking: Outside TV Markets (FAYETTEVILLE). Franchise award date: N.A. Franchise expiration date: N.A. Began: N.A.

Channel capacity: 30 (not 2-way capable). Channels available but not in use: N.A.

Basic Service

Subscribers: 89.

Programming (received off-air): KCWX (IND, MNT) Fredericksburg; KEYE-TV (CBS, TMO) Austin; KHOU (CBS) Houston; KIAH (CW) Houston; KLRN (PBS) San Antonio; KPRC-TV (NBC) Houston; KRIV (FOX) Houston; KTBC (FOX) Austin; KTRK-TV (ABC) Houston; KTXH (MNT) Houston; KVUE (ABC) Austin; KXAN-TV (NBC) Austin.

Programming (via satellite): A&E Networks; CNN; Country Music TV; ESPN; History Channel; Spike TV; TBS Superstation; Turner Classic Movies; Turner Network TV; TV Land; WGN America.

Fee: $25.00 installation; $24.90 monthly.

Pay Service 1

Pay Units: 9.

Programming (via satellite): HBO.

Fee: $10.95 monthly.

Video-On-Demand: No

Internet Service

Operational: No.

Telephone Service

None

Miles of Plant: 2.0 (coaxial); None (fiber optic).

Manager: Clyde Grisham.

Ownership: Grisham TV Cable Co.

FENTRESS—Formerly served by National Cable Inc. No longer in operation. ICA: TX0611.

FLAT—Formerly served by National Cable Inc. No longer in operation. ICA: TX0699.

FLATONIA—Almega Cable, 4001 W Airport Freeway, Ste 530, Bedford, TX 76021. Phone: 817-685-9588. Fax: 817-685-6488. Web Site: http://www.almega.com. ICA: TX0755.

TV Market Ranking: Outside TV Markets (FLATONIA). Franchise award date: December 14, 1982. Franchise expiration date: N.A. Began: April 1, 1983.

Channel capacity: 36 (not 2-way capable). Channels available but not in use: N.A.

Basic Service

Subscribers: 163.

Programming (received off-air): KENS (CBS) San Antonio; KLRU (PBS) Austin; KRIV (FOX) Houston; KSAT-TV (ABC) San Antonio; KTBC (FOX) Austin; KTXH (MNT) Houston; KVUE (ABC) Austin; KXAN-TV (NBC) Austin; WOAI-TV (NBC) San Antonio.

Programming (via satellite): A&E Networks; ABC Family Channel; Cartoon Network; CNN; Country Music TV; Discovery Channel; Disney Channel; ESPN; Fox Sports Southwest; Headline News; Nickelodeon; Spike TV; TBS Superstation; The Learning Channel; The Weather Channel; Trinity Broadcasting Network; Turner Classic Movies; Turner Network TV; TV Land; USA Network; WGN America.

Fee: $29.95 installation; $38.00 monthly.

Pay Service 1

Pay Units: 92.

Programming (via satellite): HBO.

Fee: $10.00 installation; $10.95 monthly.

Pay Service 2

Pay Units: 25.

Programming (via satellite): Showtime.

Fee: $9.95 monthly.

Video-On-Demand: No

Internet Service

Operational: No.

Telephone Service

None

Miles of Plant: 6.0 (coaxial); None (fiber optic).

Ownership: Almega Cable (MSO).

FLORENCE—Windjammer Cable, 8500 W 110th St, Ste 600, Overland Park, KS 66210. Phone: 888-495-2881. Fax: 913-563-5454. Web Site: http://www.windjammercable.com. ICA: TX0539.

TV Market Ranking: Below 100 (FLORENCE). Franchise award date: September 6, 1994. Franchise expiration date: December 5, 2009. Began: July 1, 1983.

Channel capacity: 53 (not 2-way capable). Channels available but not in use: N.A.

Basic Service

Subscribers: N.A.

Programming (received off-air): KCEN-TV (NBC, IND) Temple; KEYE-TV (CBS, TMO) Austin; KLRU (PBS) Austin; KNCT (PBS) Belton; KNVA (CW) Austin; KTBC (FOX) Austin; KVUE (ABC) Austin; KWTX-TV (CBS, CW) Waco; KXAN-TV (NBC) Austin; KXXV (ABC, TMO) Waco.

Programming (via satellite): A&E Networks; ABC Family Channel; Animal Planet; Cartoon Network; CNBC; CNN; Comedy Central; Country Music TV; Discovery Channel; ESPN; ESPN 2; GalaVision; Headline News; HGTV; History Channel; ION Television; Lifetime; MSNBC; National Geographic Channel; Nick At Nite; Nickelodeon; Spike TV; TBS Superstation; The Learning Channel; The Weather Channel; Travel Channel; Turner Classic Movies; Turner Network TV; USA Network; WGN America.

Fee: $50.51 installation; $33.87 monthly; $.68 converter; $18.81 additional installation.

Pay Service 1

Pay Units: N.A.

Programming (via satellite): Cinemax; HBO; Showtime.

Fee: $9.95 monthly (Cinemax or Showtime), $12.95 monthly (HBO).

Internet Service

Operational: No.

Telephone Service

None

Miles of Plant: 8.0 (coaxial); None (fiber optic).

Ownership: Windjammer Communications LLC (MSO).

FLORESVILLE—Formerly served by Clear Vu Cable. No longer in operation. ICA: TX0236.

FLOWER MOUND—Time Warner Cable. Now served by DALLAS, TX [TX0003]. ICA: TX0107.

FLOYDADA—Suddenlink Communications, 119 E Kentucky St, Floydada, TX 79235-3426. Phone: 806-999-6845. Fax: 903-561-5485. Web Site: http://www.suddenlink.com. ICA: TX0237.

TV Market Ranking: Outside TV Markets (FLOYDADA). Franchise award date: N.A. Franchise expiration date: N.A. Began: January 1, 1979.

Channel capacity: 25 (not 2-way capable). Channels available but not in use: N.A.

Basic Service

Subscribers: 1,007.

Programming (received off-air): KAMC (ABC) Lubbock; KCBD (NBC) Lubbock; KJTV-TV (FOX) Lubbock; KLBK-TV (CBS) Lubbock; KPTB-DT (IND) Lubbock; KTXT-TV (PBS) Lubbock.

Programming (via satellite): C-SPAN; C-SPAN 2; Eternal Word TV Network; INSP; QVC; TBS Superstation; Telemundo; The Weather Channel; Trinity Broadcasting Network; TV Guide Network; Univision Studios; WGN America.

Fee: $35.00 installation; $10.00 monthly.

Expanded Basic Service 1

Subscribers: N.A.

Programming (via satellite): A&E Networks; ABC Family Channel; AMC; Animal Planet; BET Networks; CNBC; CNN; Comedy Central; Country Music TV; Discovery Channel; Disney Channel; E! Entertainment Television; ESPN; ESPN 2; Food Network; Fox News Channel; Fox Sports Southwest;

FX; GalaVision; Hallmark Channel; Headline News; HGTV; History Channel; ION Television; Lifetime; MSNBC; MTV; MTV2; mun2 television; Nickelodeon; Speed; Spike TV; Syfy; The Learning Channel; Travel Channel; truTV; Turner Network TV; TV Land; USA Network; VH1.
Fee: $43.65 monthly.

Digital Basic Service
Subscribers: N.A.
Programming (via satellite): AmericanLife TV Network; BBC America; Bio; Bloomberg Television; Bravo; Discovery Digital Networks; DMX Music; Encore; ESPN Classic Sports; ESPNews; Fox Movie Channel; Fox Sports World; Fuse; G4; Golf Channel; Great American Country; GSN; Halogen Network; History Channel International; Independent Film Channel; Lifetime Movie Network; MBC America; Outdoor Channel; ShopNBC; Sundance Channel; The Word Network; Toon Disney; Turner Classic Movies; Versus; WAM! America's Kidz Network.
Fee: $14.95 monthly.

Digital Pay Service 1
Pay Units: N.A.
Programming (via satellite): Cinemax (multiplexed); HBO (multiplexed); Showtime (multiplexed); Starz (multiplexed); The Movie Channel (multiplexed).

Video-On-Demand: No

Pay-Per-View
iN DEMAND (delivered digitally); ESPN (delivered digitally).

Internet Service
Operational: Yes.
Broadband Service: Suddenlink High Speed Internet.

Telephone Service
None

Miles of Plant: 21.0 (coaxial); None (fiber optic).
President: Connie Wharton. Manager: Pete Strom.
Ownership: Cequel Communications LLC (MSO).

FOLLETT—Panhandle Telephone Coop. Inc., 2222 NW Hwy 64, Guymon, OK 73942. Phones: 580-338-2556; 800-562-2556. Fax: 580-338-8260. Web Site: http://www.ptci.net. ICA: TX0610.
TV Market Ranking: Outside TV Markets (FOLLETT). Franchise award date: January 1, 1981. Franchise expiration date: N.A. Began: April 1, 1982.
Channel capacity: 36 (not 2-way capable). Channels available but not in use: N.A.

Basic Service
Subscribers: N.A.
Programming (received off-air): KAMR-TV (NBC) Amarillo; KCIT (FOX) Amarillo; KFDA-TV (CBS) Amarillo; KVII-TV (ABC, CW) Amarillo; KWET (PBS) Cheyenne.
Programming (via satellite): ABC Family Channel; Animal Planet; CNN; CW+; Discovery Channel; Disney Channel; ESPN; Fox Sports Southwest; Hallmark Channel; History Channel; Lifetime; National Geographic Channel; Nickelodeon; Spike TV; TBS Superstation; The Learning Channel; The Weather Channel; Trinity Broadcasting Network; Turner Network TV; TV Land; VH1.
Fee: $39.95 installation; $42.99 monthly.

Pay Service 1
Pay Units: 15.
Programming (via satellite): HBO.
Fee: $13.49 monthly.

Pay Service 2
Pay Units: 7.
Programming (via satellite): Showtime.
Fee: $13.95 monthly.

Internet Service
Operational: No.

Telephone Service
None

Miles of Plant: 7.0 (coaxial); None (fiber optic).
Plant Manager: Gary Burke.
Ownership: Panhandle Telephone Cooperative Inc. (MSO).

FORSAN—Formerly served by National Cable Inc. No longer in operation. ICA: TX0695.

FORT BEND COUNTY (portions)—Rapid Cable. Now served by ARCOLA, TX [TX0243]. ICA: TX1010.

FORT DAVIS—Fort Davis TV Cable, PO Box 1377, Alpine, TX 79831-1377. Phone: 432-837-2300. Fax: 432-837-5423. E-mail: mtnzone@sbcglobal.net. ICA: TX0531.
TV Market Ranking: Outside TV Markets (FORT DAVIS). Franchise award date: September 10, 1965. Franchise expiration date: N.A. Began: December 1, 1965.
Channel capacity: N.A. Channels available but not in use: N.A.

Basic Service
Subscribers: 290.
Programming (received off-air): KMID (ABC) Midland; KOSA-TV (CBS, MNT) Odessa; KWES-TV (NBC) Odessa; allband FM.
Programming (via satellite): A&E Networks; ABC Family Channel; CNN; Country Music TV; Discovery Channel; ESPN; GalaVision; KMGH-TV (ABC) Denver; KRMA-TV (PBS) Denver; Nickelodeon; Spike TV; TBS Superstation; The Learning Channel; The Weather Channel; Trinity Broadcasting Network; Turner Classic Movies; Turner Network TV; WGN America.
Fee: $35.00 installation; $42.00 monthly.

Pay Service 1
Pay Units: 97.
Programming (via satellite): Cinemax; HBO; Showtime.
Fee: $10.00 installation; $7.50 monthly.

Video-On-Demand: No

Internet Service
Operational: Yes. Began: April 1, 2006.
Fee: $50.00 installation; $25.50 monthly.

Telephone Service
None

Miles of Plant: 19.0 (coaxial); None (fiber optic).
Manager: Steve Neu. Office Manager: Lawrence Neu.
Ownership: Mountain Zone TV Systems (MSO).

FORT STOCKTON—US Cable of Coastal Texas LP, 611 W Ave A, Seminole, TX 79360. Phones: 432-758-9221; 800-996-8788. Fax: 432-758-3379. Web Site: http://www.uscable.com. ICA: TX1029.
TV Market Ranking: Outside TV Markets (FORT STOCKTON).
Channel capacity: N.A. Channels available but not in use: N.A.

Basic Service
Subscribers: 2,166.
Programming (received off-air): KMID (ABC) Midland; KMLM-DT (IND) Odessa; KOSA-TV (CBS, MNT) Odessa; KPBT-TV (PBS) Odessa; KPEJ-TV (FOX) Odessa; KTLE-LP (TMO) Odessa; KUPB (UNV) Midland; KWES-TV (NBC) Odessa; KWWT (CW) Odessa.
Programming (via satellite): ESPN Deportes; Eternal Word TV Network; Fox News Channel; Headline News; Home Shopping Network; Lifetime; ShopNBC; TBS Superstation; Telefutura; Trinity Broadcasting Network; TV Guide Network; WGN America.
Fee: $39.96 installation; $18.71 monthly.

Expanded Basic Service 1
Subscribers: N.A.
Programming (via satellite): A&E Networks; ABC Family Channel; American Movie Classics; Animal Planet; Cartoon Network; CNBC; CNN; Comedy Central; Country Music TV; C-SPAN; Discovery Channel; Discovery Fit & Health; Disney Channel; Fox Sports Net; FX; HGTV; History Channel; MoviePlex; MTV; Nick At Nite; Nickelodeon; Spike TV; Syfy; The Learning Channel; The Weather Channel; Turner Network TV; USA Network; VH1.
Fee: $29.83 monthly.

Digital Basic Service
Subscribers: N.A.
Programming (via satellite): BBC America; Bio; Bloomberg Television; Bravo; cloo; CMT Pure Country; Discovery Health Channel; Discovery Kids Channel; Disney XD; DMX Music; Encore (multiplexed); ESPNews; Fox Movie Channel; Fox Soccer; Fuse; G4; Golf Channel; GSN; Halogen Network; History Channel International; ID Investigation Discovery; Independent Film Channel; Lifetime Movie Network; Military Channel; MTV2; mun2 television; NFL Network; Nick Jr.; Planet Green; Science; Speed; Style Network; TeenNick; Turner Classic Movies; Versus; VH1 Classic; WE tv.
Fee: $23.39 monthly.

Digital Expanded Basic Service
Subscribers: N.A.
Programming (via satellite): ESPN Classic Sports; ESPNews; Fox Soccer; NFL Network; NFL RedZone; Outdoor Channel; Speed.
Fee: $3.95 monthly.

Digital Expanded Basic Service 2
Subscribers: N.A.
Programming (via satellite): Cine Latino; Cine Mexicano; CNN en Espanol; Discovery en Espanol; ESPN Deportes; History Channel en Espanol; mun2 television; Tr3s; VeneMovies.
Fee: $4.95 monthly.

Pay Service 1
Pay Units: N.A.
Programming (via satellite): Cinemax; HBO.
Fee: $13.95 monthly (each).

Digital Pay Service 1
Pay Units: N.A.
Programming (via satellite): Cinemax (multiplexed); HBO (multiplexed); Showtime (multiplexed); Starz (multiplexed); The Movie Channel (multiplexed).
Fee: $9.95 monthly (Starz), $12.95 monthly (HBO, Cinemax, Showtime or TMC).

Video-On-Demand: No

Pay-Per-View
Event Entertainment (delivered digitally); Movies (delivered digitally); Playboy TV (delivered digitally); Fresh (delivered digitally).

Internet Service
Operational: Yes.

Telephone Service
None

Regional Manager: Daryl Koedyker.
Ownership: US Cable Corp. (MSO).

FORT WORTH (northern portions)—Charter Communications, 15100 Trinity Blvd, Ste 500, Fort Worth, TX 76155. Phone: 817-298-3600. Web Site: http://www.charter.com. Also serves Aledo, Annetta, Annetta North, Annetta South, Benbrook, Blue Mound, Burleson, Crowley, Edgecliff Village, Everman, Forest Hill, Haltom City, Haslet, Hudson Oaks, Hurst, Keller, Kennedale, Lake Worth, Mansfield, Marshall Creek, North Richland Hills, Parker County (portions), Richland Hills, River Oaks, Roanoke, Saginaw, Sansom Park, Southlake, Trophy Club, Watauga, Westlake, Westover Hills, Westworth Village, White Settlement & Willow Park. ICA: TX0008.
TV Market Ranking: 12 (Aledo, Annetta, Annetta North, Annetta South, Benbrook, Blue Mound, Burleson, Crowley, Edgecliff Village, Everman, Forest Hill, FORT WORTH (NORTHERN PORTIONS), Haltom City, Haslet, Hudson Oaks, Hurst, Keller, Kennedale, Lake Worth, Mansfield, Marshall Creek, North Richland Hills, Parker County (portions), Richland Hills, River Oaks, Roanoke, Saginaw, Sansom Park, Southlake, Southlake, Trophy Club, Watauga, Westlake, Westover Hills, Westworth Village, White Settlement, Willow Park). Franchise award date: March 1, 1980. Franchise expiration date: N.A. Began: January 1, 1982.
Channel capacity: N.A. Channels available but not in use: N.A.

Basic Service
Subscribers: 122,914.
Programming (received off-air): KAZD (IND) Lake Dallas; KDAF (CW, IND) Dallas; KDFI (MNT) Dallas; KDFW-DT (FOX) Dallas; KDTN (ETV) Denton; KDTX-TV (TBN) Dallas; KERA-TV (PBS) Dallas; KFWD (IND) Fort Worth; KMPX (IND) Decatur; KPXD-TV (ION) Arlington; KSTR-DT (TEL) Irving; KTVT (CBS) Fort Worth; KTXA (IND) Fort Worth; KUVN-DT (UNV) Garland; KXAS-TV (NBC) Fort Worth; KXTX-TV (TMO) Dallas; WFAA (ABC) Dallas.
Programming (via satellite): C-SPAN; C-SPAN 2; Eternal Word TV Network; Product Information Network; QVC; ShopNBC; Texas Cable News; WGN America.
Fee: $30.00 installation.

Expanded Basic Service 1
Subscribers: N.A.
Programming (via satellite): A&E Networks; ABC Family Channel; AMC; AmericanLife TV Network; Animal Planet; BET Networks; Bravo; Cartoon Network; CNBC; CNN; Comedy Central; Country Music TV; Discovery Channel; Disney Channel; E! Entertainment Television; ESPN; ESPN 2; ESPN Classic Sports; Food Network; Fox Deportes; Fox News Channel; Fox Sports Southwest; FX; G4; GalaVision; Golf Channel; GSN; Hallmark Channel; Headline News; HGTV; History Channel; Lifetime; MSNBC; MTV; mun2 television; National Geographic Channel; Nickelodeon; Oxygen; Speed; Spike TV; Syfy; TBS Superstation; The Learning Channel; The Weather Channel; Toon Disney; Travel Channel; truTV; Turner Classic Movies; Turner Network TV; TV Land; USA Network; Versus; VH1; WE tv.
Fee: $48.99 monthly.

Digital Basic Service
Subscribers: 92,570.
Programming (via satellite): BBC America; Bio; Bloomberg Television; Discovery Digital Networks; DIY Network; Fox Movie Channel; Fox Sports World; Great American Country; History Channel International; Independent Film Channel; Lifetime Movie Network; Music Choice; SoapNet; Style Network; Sundance Channel; Weatherscan.

Digital Pay Service 1
Pay Units: 194,209.
Programming (via satellite): Cinemax (multiplexed); Encore (multiplexed); Flix; HBO (multiplexed); Showtime (multiplexed); Starz (multiplexed); The Movie Channel (multiplexed).
Fee: $7.95 monthly (Cinemax), $9.95 monthly (HBO, TMC, or Flix/Showtime).
Video-On-Demand: Yes
Pay-Per-View
Addressable homes: 92,570.
ETC (delivered digitally); iN DEMAND (delivered digitally); Pleasure (delivered digitally); sports (delivered digitally).
Internet Service
Operational: Yes.
Subscribers: 23,200.
Broadband Service: Charter Pipeline.
Fee: $29.99 monthly; $15.00 modem lease; $259.00 modem purchase.
Telephone Service
Digital: Operational
Fee: $29.99 monthly
Miles of Plant: 6,258.0 (coaxial); 90.0 (fiber optic).
Vice President & General Manager: Wayne Cramp. Technical Operations Director: John Linton. Marketing Director: Kathleen Griffin. Marketing Manager: Sherry Matlock.
Ownership: Charter Communications Inc. (MSO).

FRANKLIN—Zito Media, 611 Vader Hill Rd, Coudersport, PA 16915. Phone: 866-879-6235. E-mail: support@zitomedia.net. Web Site: http://www.zitomedia.com. ICA: TX0758.
TV Market Ranking: Below 100 (FRANKLIN). Franchise award date: N.A. Franchise expiration date: N.A. Began: N.A.
Channel capacity: 54 (not 2-way capable). Channels available but not in use: N.A.
Basic Service
Subscribers: 235.
Programming (received off-air): KBTX-TV (CBS, CW) Bryan; KCEN-TV (NBC, IND) Temple; KNCT (PBS) Belton; KWTX-TV (CBS, CW) Waco; KXXV (ABC, TMO) Waco.
Programming (via satellite): A&E Networks; ABC Family Channel; AMC; Animal Planet; BET Networks; Cartoon Network; CNN; C-SPAN; Discovery Channel; Disney Channel; E! Entertainment Television; ESPN; ESPN 2; Fox News Channel; Fox Sports Southwest; Fuse; FX; Great American Country; Hallmark Channel; Headline News; HGTV; History Channel; INSP; Lifetime; Outdoor Channel; QVC; TBS Superstation; The Learning Channel; The Weather Channel; Turner Network TV; USA Network; WGN America.
Fee: $39.50 monthly.
Pay Service 1
Pay Units: N.A.
Programming (via satellite): Encore; HBO; Showtime.
Internet Service
Operational: No.
Telephone Service
None
Miles of Plant: 11.0 (coaxial); None (fiber optic).
President: James Rigas.
Ownership: Zito Media (MSO).

FREDERICKSBURG—Time Warner Cable. Now served by AUSTIN, TX [TX0005]. ICA: TX0149.

FREER—Allegiance Communications, 6125 Paluxy Dr, Tyler, TX 75703. Phones: 501-679-6619; 800-842-8160. Fax: 501-679-5694. Web Site: http://www.alliancecable.net. Also serves Duval County (northern portion). ICA: TX0225.
TV Market Ranking: Outside TV Markets (Duval County (northern portion), FREER). Franchise award date: N.A. Franchise expiration date: N.A. Began: January 1, 1968.
Channel capacity: N.A. Channels available but not in use: N.A.
Basic Service
Subscribers: 245.
Programming (received off-air): KDFW-DT (FOX) Dallas; KEDT (PBS) Corpus Christi; KIII (ABC) Corpus Christi; KORO (UNV) Corpus Christi; KRIS-TV (CW, NBC) Corpus Christi; KUQI-DT (FOX) Corpus Christi; KZTV (CBS) Corpus Christi.
Programming (via satellite): A&E Networks; ABC Family Channel; AMC; Animal Planet; Bravo; Cartoon Network; CNBC; CNN; Comedy Central; Country Music TV; C-SPAN; CW+; Discovery Channel; Disney Channel; ESPN; ESPN 2; Eternal Word TV Network; Food Network; Fox News Channel; Fox Sports Southwest; FX; GalaVision; Hallmark Channel; Headline News; HGTV; History Channel; Lifetime; MSNBC; MTV; mun2 television; National Geographic Channel; Nickelodeon; Oxygen; QVC; SoapNet; Speed; Spike TV; Syfy; TBS Superstation; Telefutura; Telemundo; The Learning Channel; The Weather Channel; Travel Channel; Trinity Broadcasting Network; truTV; Turner Classic Movies; Turner Network TV; TV Land; USA Network; Versus; VH1; WE tv.
Fee: $34.99 installation; $52.99 monthly.
Pay Service 1
Pay Units: 79.
Programming (via satellite): Encore; HBO; Showtime; Starz; The Movie Channel.
Fee: $3.75 monthly (Encore), $12.95 monthly (Starz, TMC, Showtime or HBO).
Internet Service
Operational: No.
Telephone Service
None
Miles of Plant: 18.0 (coaxial); None (fiber optic).
Vice President & General Manager: John Brinker. Vice President, Programming: Julie Newman.
Ownership: Buford Media Group LLC (MSO).

FRIONA—Reach Broadband, 515 E Longview St, Arp, TX 75750. Phone: 800-687-1258. Web Site: http://www.reachbroadband.net. Also serves Bovina. ICA: TX0277.
TV Market Ranking: Below 100 (Bovina, FRIONA). Franchise award date: July 11, 1983. Franchise expiration date: N.A. Began: January 1, 1959.
Channel capacity: 41 (2-way capable). Channels available but not in use: N.A.
Basic Service
Subscribers: 298.
Programming (received off-air): KACV-TV (PBS) Amarillo; KAMR-TV (NBC) Amarillo; KCIT (FOX) Amarillo; KFDA-TV (CBS) Amarillo; KPTB-DT (IND) Lubbock; KVII-TV (ABC, CW) Amarillo; allband FM.
Programming (via satellite): A&E Networks; ABC Family Channel; AMC; American-Life TV Network; Animal Planet; Cartoon Network; CNN; Comedy Central; Country Music TV; C-SPAN; Discovery Channel; Disney Channel; E! Entertainment Television; ESPN; ESPN 2; Fox News Channel; Fox Sports Southwest; GalaVision; Headline News; HGTV; History Channel; Lifetime; Nickelodeon; QVC; Spike TV; Syfy; TBS Superstation; The Learning Channel; The Weather Channel; Travel Channel; Turner Network TV; TV Land; USA Network; VH1; WGN America.
Programming (via translator): KVDA (TMO) San Antonio.
Fee: $29.95 installation; $38.00 monthly.
Pay Service 1
Pay Units: 143.
Programming (via satellite): HBO.
Fee: $25.00 installation; $9.95 monthly.
Pay Service 2
Pay Units: 87.
Programming (via satellite): Showtime.
Fee: $9.95 monthly.
Pay Service 3
Pay Units: 82.
Programming (via satellite): The Movie Channel.
Fee: $9.95 monthly.
Video-On-Demand: No
Internet Service
Operational: No.
Telephone Service
None
Miles of Plant: 30.0 (coaxial); None (fiber optic).
Regional Manager: Ronnie Stafford. Office Manager: Jan Gibson.
Ownership: RB3 LLC (MSO).

FRUITVALE—Formerly served by Almega Cable. No longer in operation. ICA: TX0580.

GAINESVILLE—Suddenlink Communications, 12444 Powerscourt Dr, Saint Louis, MO 63131-3660. Phone: 314-965-2020. Web Site: http://www.suddenlink.com. Also serves Cooke County & Oak Ridge. ICA: TX0117.
TV Market Ranking: Below 100 (Cooke County (portions), GAINESVILLE); Outside TV Markets (Cooke County (portions), Oak Ridge). Franchise award date: N.A. Franchise expiration date: N.A. Began: March 2, 1967.
Channel capacity: N.A. Channels available but not in use: N.A.
Basic Service
Subscribers: 5,014.
Programming (received off-air): KDAF (CW, IND) Dallas; KDFW-DT (FOX) Dallas; KDTN (ETV) Denton; KERA-TV (PBS) Dallas; KMPX (IND) Decatur; KPXD-TV (ION) Arlington; KTVT (CBS) Fort Worth; KTXA (IND) Fort Worth; KUVN-DT (UNV) Garland; KXAS-TV (NBC) Fort Worth; KXII (CBS, FOX, MNT) Sherman; KXTX-TV (TMO) Dallas; WFAA (ABC) Dallas.
Programming (via satellite): Discovery Channel; Great American Country; QVC; TBS Superstation.
Fee: $38.97 installation; $9.40 monthly; $2.00 converter; $19.49 additional installation.
Expanded Basic Service 1
Subscribers: 4,608.
Programming (via satellite): A&E Networks; ABC Family Channel; AMC; BET Networks; CNBC; CNN; Country Music TV; C-SPAN; Disney Channel; ESPN; Fox News Channel; Fox Sports Southwest; FX; Headline News; Lifetime; MTV; Nickelodeon; Spike TV; The Weather Channel; Turner Network TV; USA Network.
Fee: $11.68 monthly.
Digital Basic Service
Subscribers: N.A.
Programming (via satellite): BBC America; Discovery Digital Networks; DMX Music; Encore; ESPN 2; ESPN Classic Sports; Fox Sports World; Golf Channel; GSN; HGTV; History Channel; MTV Networks Digital Suite; Speed; Syfy; Turner Classic Movies; TV Land; Versus; WE tv.
Pay Service 1
Pay Units: 139.
Programming (via satellite): Cinemax; Encore; HBO; Showtime.
Video-On-Demand: No
Pay-Per-View
Movies; special events.
Internet Service
Operational: Yes.
Broadband Service: Suddenlink High Speed Internet.
Fee: $45.95 installation; $29.95 monthly.
Telephone Service
Analog: Not Operational
Digital: Operational
Fee: $44.95 monthly
Miles of Plant: 121.0 (coaxial); None (fiber optic).
Ownership: Cequel Communications LLC (MSO).

GANADO—Mid-Coast Cablevision, 505 N Mechanic St, PO Box 1269, El Campo, TX 77437-1269. Phone: 979-543-6858. Fax: 979-543-9501. Web Site: http://www.warpspeed1.net. ICA: TX0428.
TV Market Ranking: Below 100 (GANADO). Franchise award date: N.A. Franchise expiration date: N.A. Began: January 1, 1961.
Channel capacity: N.A. Channels available but not in use: N.A.
Basic Service
Subscribers: 612.
Programming (received off-air): KAVU-TV (ABC) Victoria; KETH-TV (TBN) Houston; KFTH-DT (TEL) Alvin; KHOU (CBS) Houston; KIAH (CW) Houston; KLTJ (ETV) Galveston; KPRC-TV (NBC) Houston; KRIV (FOX) Houston; KTBU (IND) Conroe; KTMD (TMO) Galveston; KTRK-TV (ABC) Houston; KTXH (MNT) Houston; KUBE-TV (IND) Baytown; KUHT (PBS) Houston; KXLN-DT (UNV) Rosenberg; KYAZ (IND) Katy; KZJL (IND) Houston; allband FM.
Programming (via satellite): A&E Networks; ABC Family Channel; AMC; BET Networks; Cartoon Network; CNBC; CNN; Country Music TV; C-SPAN; C-SPAN 2; Discovery Channel; Discovery Fit & Health; Disney Channel; ESPN; ESPN 2; ESPN Classic Sports; Eternal Word TV Network; Fox News Channel; Fox Sports Southwest; FX; Hallmark Channel; Headline News; HGTV; History Channel; INSP; ION Television; Lifetime; MTV; Nickelodeon; Outdoor Channel; QVC; SoapNet; Speed; Spike TV; TBS Superstation; The Learning Channel; The Weather Channel; truTV; Turner Network

TV; TV Guide Network; TV Land; USA Network; WGN America.
Fee: $10.00 installation; $29.99 monthly.
Digital Basic Service
Subscribers: N.A.
Programming (via satellite): ABC News Now; BBC America; Bloomberg Television; Cine Latino; CMT Pure Country; Discovery en Espanol; Discovery Health Channel; Discovery Kids Channel; ESPN 2 HD; ESPN U; ESPNews; Fox Deportes; Fox Movie Channel; Fox Reality Channel; Fox Soccer; Fuel TV; G4; Golf Channel; GSN; ID Investigation Discovery; Independent Film Channel; Military Channel; Nick Jr.; NickToons TV; PBS Kids Sprout; Science; Speed; Tr3s; Turner Classic Movies; TVE Internacional; Utilisima; Versus; VH1 Classic; WE tv.
Digital Pay Service 1
Pay Units: N.A.
Programming (via satellite): Cinemax (multiplexed); Encore (multiplexed); Flix; HBO (multiplexed); Showtime (multiplexed); Starz (multiplexed); The Movie Channel (multiplexed).
Video-On-Demand: No
Pay-Per-View
iN DEMAND (delivered digitally); Playboy TV (delivered digitally).
Internet Service
Operational: Yes, Both DSL & dial-up.
Broadband Service: Warp Speed 1 Internet.
Fee: $17.05 installation; $34.99 monthly.
Telephone Service
None
Miles of Plant: 15.0 (coaxial); None (fiber optic).
Manager: Wayne Neal.
Ownership: Mid-Coast Cablevision (MSO).

GARDEN CITY—Formerly served by National Cable Inc. No longer in operation. ICA: TX0760.

GARDENDALE—Formerly served by Cebridge Connections. No longer in operation. ICA: TX0575.

GARLAND—Time Warner Cable. Now served by DALLAS, TX [TX0003]. ICA: TX0013.

GARRISON—Almega Cable, 4001 W Airport Frwy, Ste 530, Bedford, TX 76021. Phone: 817-685-9588. Fax: 817-685-6488. Web Site: http://www.almega.com. ICA: TX0528.
TV Market Ranking: Below 100 (GARRISON). Franchise award date: N.A. Franchise expiration date: N.A. Began: October 1, 1983.
Channel capacity: 54 (not 2-way capable). Channels available but not in use: N.A.
Basic Service
Subscribers: 109.
Programming (received off-air): KLTS-TV (PBS) Shreveport; KSLA (CBS) Shreveport; KTAL-TV (NBC) Texarkana; KTBS-TV (ABC) Shreveport; KTRE (ABC) Lufkin.
Programming (via satellite): TBS Superstation; WGN America.
Fee: $54.95 installation; $44.05 monthly.
Pay Service 1
Pay Units: 25.
Programming (via satellite): Cinemax.
Fee: $12.95 monthly.
Pay Service 2
Pay Units: 10.
Programming (via satellite): HBO.
Fee: $12.95 monthly.
Pay Service 3
Pay Units: 40.
Programming (via satellite): Showtime.
Fee: $12.95 monthly.
Video-On-Demand: No
Internet Service
Operational: No.
Telephone Service
None
Miles of Plant: 12.0 (coaxial); None (fiber optic).
Ownership: Almega Cable (MSO).

GARWOOD—Formerly served by National Cable Inc. No longer in operation. ICA: TX0573.

GARY—Formerly served by Almega Cable. No longer in operation. ICA: TX0399.

GATESVILLE—Suddenlink Communications, 2536 E Main St, Gatesville, TX 76528-2628. Phones: 888-822-5151 (Customer service); 254-865-5315. Fax: 254-865-8088. Web Site: http://www.suddenlink.com. Also serves Fort Gates. ICA: TX0167.
TV Market Ranking: Below 100 (Fort Gates, GATESVILLE). Franchise award date: N.A. Franchise expiration date: N.A. Began: January 1, 1952.
Channel capacity: N.A. Channels available but not in use: N.A.
Basic Service
Subscribers: N.A.
Programming (received off-air): KAKW-DT (UNV) Killeen; KCEN-TV (NBC, IND) Temple; KDYW (PBS) Waco; KNCT (PBS) Belton; KTBC (FOX) Austin; KWKT-TV (FOX, MNT) Waco; KWTX-TV (CBS, CW) Waco; KXXV (ABC, TMO) Waco; WFAA (ABC) Dallas; 4 FMs.
Programming (via satellite): CNBC; C-SPAN; Headline News; INSP; TBS Superstation; The Learning Channel; The Weather Channel; WGN America.
Fee: $10.00 installation; $9.00 monthly.
Expanded Basic Service 1
Subscribers: N.A.
Programming (via satellite): A&E Networks; ABC Family Channel; AMC; CNN; Discovery Channel; Disney Channel; ESPN; ESPN 2; Fox News Channel; Fox Sports Southwest; Great American Country; Independent Music Network; Lifetime; Nickelodeon; Spike TV; Turner Network TV; USA Network; VH1.
Digital Basic Service
Subscribers: N.A.
Programming (via satellite): BBC America; Bio; Bloomberg Television; Discovery Digital Networks; DMX Music; Encore; ESPN Classic Sports; ESPNews; Fox Soccer; Fuse; G4; Golf Channel; GSN; Halogen Network; HGTV; History Channel; History Channel International; Lifetime Movie Network; MBC America; Outdoor Channel; Speed; Sundance Channel; Syfy; The Word Network; Toon Disney; Trinity Broadcasting Network; Versus.
Digital Pay Service 1
Pay Units: 290.
Programming (via satellite): HBO (multiplexed); Showtime (multiplexed); Starz (multiplexed); The Movie Channel (multiplexed).
Fee: $10.00 monthly.
Digital Pay Service 2
Pay Units: N.A.
Programming (via satellite): Cinemax (multiplexed).
Video-On-Demand: No
Pay-Per-View
iN DEMAND (delivered digitally); Playboy TV (delivered digitally); Fresh (delivered digitally); Shorteez (delivered digitally).
Internet Service
Operational: No.
Telephone Service
Digital: Operational
Miles of Plant: 66.0 (coaxial); None (fiber optic).
Manager: Gail Ussery.
Ownership: Cequel Communications LLC (MSO).

GAUSE—Formerly served by National Cable Inc. No longer in operation. ICA: TX0660.

GEORGE WEST—Time Warner Cable, 4060 S Padre Island Dr, Corpus Christi, TX 78411-4402. Phones: 972-899-7300 (Flower Mound office); 361-698-6259. Fax: 361-857-5038. Web Site: http://www.timewarnercable.com/Texas. ICA: TX0343.
TV Market Ranking: Outside TV Markets (GEORGE WEST). Franchise award date: N.A. Franchise expiration date: December 31, 2019. Began: December 1, 1981.
Channel capacity: N.A. Channels available but not in use: N.A.
Basic Service
Subscribers: N.A. Included in Corpus Christi
Programming (received off-air): KDFW-DT (FOX) Dallas; KEDT (PBS) Corpus Christi; KIII (ABC) Corpus Christi; KORO (UNV) Corpus Christi; KRIS-TV (CW, NBC) Corpus Christi; KSAT-TV (ABC) San Antonio; KVDA (TMO) San Antonio; KZTV (CBS) Corpus Christi.
Programming (via satellite): Cartoon Network; QVC.
Fee: $34.99 installation; $16.39 monthly.
Expanded Basic Service 1
Subscribers: N.A.
Programming (via satellite): A&E Networks; ABC Family Channel; AMC; Animal Planet; Bravo; CNBC; CNN; Comedy Central; Country Music TV; C-SPAN; Discovery Channel; Disney Channel; E! Entertainment Television; ESPN; ESPN 2; Eternal Word TV Network; Food Network; Fox News Channel; Fox Sports Southwest; FX; GalaVision; Golf Channel; Great American Country; Headline News; HGTV; History Channel; Lifetime; MSNBC; MTV; National Geographic Channel; Nickelodeon; Oxygen; SoapNet; Speed; Spike TV; Syfy; TBS Superstation; The Learning Channel; The Weather Channel; Travel Channel; truTV; Turner Classic Movies; Turner Network TV; TV Land; USA Network; Versus; VH1.
Fee: $28.60 monthly.
Pay Service 1
Pay Units: 243.
Programming (via satellite): Encore; HBO; Showtime; Starz.
Fee: $3.75 monthly (Encore), $12.95 monthly (HBO, Starz or Showtime).
Internet Service
Operational: Yes.
Telephone Service
Digital: Operational
Miles of Plant: 21.0 (coaxial); None (fiber optic).
President: Connie Wharton. Vice President & General Manager: Mike McKee. Engineering Director: Charlotte Strong. Public Affairs Manager: Vicki Triplett.
Ownership: Time Warner Cable (MSO).; Advance/Newhouse Partnership (MSO).

GEORGETOWN—Suddenlink Communications, 111 N College St, Georgetown, TX 78626-4101. Phones: 512-930-3085; 512-869-1505. Fax: 512-869-2962. Web Site: http://www.suddenlink.com. ICA: TX0081.
TV Market Ranking: Below 100 (GEORGETOWN). Franchise award date: January 1, 1972. Franchise expiration date: N.A. Began: January 1, 1972.
Channel capacity: 80 (operating 2-way). Channels available but not in use: N.A.
Basic Service
Subscribers: 11,000.
Programming (received off-air): KAKW-DT (UNV) Killeen; KCEN-TV (NBC, IND) Temple; KEYE-TV (CBS, TMO) Austin; KLRU (PBS) Austin; KNVA (CW) Austin; KTBC (FOX) Austin; KVUE (ABC) Austin.
Programming (via satellite): C-SPAN; INSP; QVC; Telefutura; TV Guide Network; WGN America.
Fee: $35.00 installation; $5.99 monthly; $1.50 converter; $25.00 additional installation.
Expanded Basic Service 1
Subscribers: N.A.
Programming (via satellite): A&E Networks; ABC Family Channel; AMC; Animal Planet; BET Networks; Bravo; Cartoon Network; CNBC; CNN; Comedy Central; Country Music TV; C-SPAN 2; Discovery Channel; Disney Channel; E! Entertainment Television; ESPN; ESPN 2; Eternal Word TV Network; Food Network; Fox News Channel; Fox Sports Southwest; FX; GalaVision; Golf Channel; Great American Country; Headline News; HGTV; History Channel; Jewelry Television; Lifetime; Lifetime Movie Network; MSNBC; MTV; Nickelodeon; ShopNBC; Speed; Spike TV; Syfy; TBS Superstation; Telemundo; The Learning Channel; The Weather Channel; Travel Channel; Trinity Broadcasting Network; truTV; Turner Classic Movies; Turner Network TV; TV Land; USA Network; Versus; VH1.
Fee: $12.49 monthly.
Digital Basic Service
Subscribers: N.A.
Programming (via satellite): A&E HD; Bandamax; BBC America; Bio; Bloomberg Television; Boomerang; BYU Television; CBS Sports Network; Cine Latino; Cine Mexicano; CMT Pure Country; CNN en Espanol; Cooking Channel; Cox Sports Television; De Pelicula; De Pelicula Clasico; Discovery en Espanol; Discovery Health Channel; Discovery Home Channel; Discovery Kids Channel; Discovery Times Channel; DIY Network; Encore (multiplexed); ESPN 2 HD; ESPN Classic Sports; ESPN Deportes; ESPN HD; ESPN U; ESPNews; EWTN en Espanol; FamilyNet; Food Network HD; Fox Deportes; Fox Reality Channel; Fox Soccer; Fuel TV; Fuse; G4; GalaVision; GMC; GSN; Hallmark Channel; Halogen Network; HD Theater; HDNet; HDNet Movies; HGTV HD; History Channel en Espanol; History Channel International; Independent Film Channel; Latele Novela Network; Military Channel; MTV Hits; MTV2; mun2 television; Music Choice; National Geographic Channel; National Geographic Channel HD Network; Nick Jr.; NickToons TV; Nuvo TV; Outdoor Channel; Oxygen; Ritmoson Latino; Science; SoapNet; Sorpresa; Style Network; Sundance Channel; Sur Network; TBN Enlace USA; TeenNick; Telehit; Telemundo; Tennis Channel; Toon Disney; Toon Disney en Espanol; Tr3s; Turner Network TV HD; TV Chile; TV One; Universal HD; VH1 Classic; VHUNO; Video Rola; WE tv; Weatherscan.
Digital Pay Service 1
Pay Units: N.A.
Programming (via satellite): Cinemax (multiplexed); HBO (multiplexed); HBO HD; HBO Latino; Showtime (multiplexed); Showtime

HD; Starz (multiplexed); Starz HDTV; The Movie Channel (multiplexed).
Video-On-Demand: No
Pay-Per-View
iN DEMAND (delivered digitally); Fresh (delivered digitally); Shorteez (delivered digitally); Playboy TV (delivered digitally); Playboy en Espanol (delivered digitally); Playboy en Espanol (delivered digitally).
Internet Service
Operational: Yes.
Broadband Service: Suddenlink High Speed Internet.
Telephone Service
Digital: Operational
Miles of Plant: 228.0 (coaxial); 29.0 (fiber optic). Additional miles planned: 15.0 (coaxial).
Manager: Dale Hoffman. Chief Technician & Marketing Director: Wesley Houghteling.
Ownership: Cequel Communications LLC (MSO).

GILMER—Gilmer Cable, 111 E Marshall St, PO Box 1600, Gilmer, TX 75644. Phone: 903-843-5597. Fax: 903-843-2045. E-mail: cs@tatertv.com. Web Site: http://www.tatertv.com. ICA: TX0229.
TV Market Ranking: Below 100 (GILMER). Franchise award date: January 1, 1979. Franchise expiration date: October 27, 2007. Began: March 2, 1981.
Channel capacity: N.A. Channels available but not in use: N.A.
Basic Service
Subscribers: 1,510.
Programming (received off-air): KCEB (CW) Longview; KETK-TV (NBC) Jacksonville; KFXK-TV (FOX) Longview; KLTV (ABC, TMO) Tyler; KSLA (CBS) Shreveport; KTAL-TV (NBC) Texarkana; KTBS-TV (ABC) Shreveport; allband FM.
Programming (via microwave): KDFW-DT (FOX) Dallas; KERA-TV (PBS) Dallas; KYTX (CBS, IND) Nacogdoches.
Programming (via satellite): ESPN.
Fee: $32.95 installation; $14.30 monthly; $2.00 converter; $9.41 additional installation.
Expanded Basic Service 1
Subscribers: 390.
Programming (received off-air): KDAF (CW, IND) Dallas; KLTS-TV (PBS) Shreveport.
Programming (via microwave): KXAS-TV (NBC) Fort Worth.
Programming (via satellite): ABC Family Channel; Disney Channel; Fox Sports Southwest; MTV; Nickelodeon; USA Network; WGN America.
Fee: $6.90 monthly.
Expanded Basic Service 2
Subscribers: N.A.
Programming (via satellite): A&E Networks; AMC; Animal Planet; BET Networks; Bravo; Cartoon Network; CNN; Country Music TV; C-SPAN; C-SPAN 2; Discovery Channel; ESPN 2; Food Network; Fox News Channel; FX; Hallmark Channel; Hallmark Movie Channel; HGTV; History Channel; Lifetime; Spike TV; Syfy; TBS Superstation; The Learning Channel; The Weather Channel; Travel Channel; Trinity Broadcasting Network; Turner Classic Movies; Turner Network TV; TV Land; VH1.
Fee: $11.45 monthly.
Pay Service 1
Pay Units: 197.
Programming (via satellite): HBO.
Fee: $9.95 monthly.
Pay Service 2
Pay Units: 129.
Programming (via satellite): Showtime.
Fee: $7.95 monthly.
Video-On-Demand: No
Internet Service
Operational: Yes.
Fee: $29.95 installation; $34.95 monthly; $4.95 modem lease; $69.95 modem purchase.
Telephone Service
None
Miles of Plant: 37.0 (coaxial); None (fiber optic). Additional miles planned: 2.0 (coaxial).
President & General Manager: David P. Mooney. Plant Manager: Ken Beckwith. Marketing Director: Robbie Mooney.
Ownership: Gilmer Cable (MSO).

GLADEWATER—Suddenlink Communications, 507 NE Loop 485, Gladewater, TX 75647-2545. Phones: 903-845-4036; 903-595-4321. Fax: 903-845-4038. Web Site: http://www.suddenlink.com. Also serves Clarksville City, Liberty City, Union Grove, Warren City & White Oak. ICA: TX0558.
TV Market Ranking: Below 100 (Clarksville City, GLADEWATER, Liberty City, Union Grove, Warren City, White Oak). Franchise award date: N.A. Franchise expiration date: April 22, 2008. Began: March 1, 1974.
Channel capacity: 26 (operating 2-way). Channels available but not in use: N.A.
Basic Service
Subscribers: N.A.
Programming (received off-air): KCEB (CW) Longview; KERA-TV (PBS) Dallas; KETK-TV (NBC) Jacksonville; KFXK-TV (FOX) Longview; KLPN-LP (IND) Longview; KLTV (ABC, TMO) Tyler; KSLA (CBS) Shreveport; KXAS-TV (NBC) Fort Worth; KYTX (CBS, IND) Nacogdoches; WFAA (ABC) Dallas.
Programming (via satellite): Trinity Broadcasting Network.
Fee: $35.00 installation; $11.42 monthly.
Expanded Basic Service 1
Subscribers: N.A.
Programming (via satellite): A&E Networks; ABC Family Channel; AMC; Animal Planet; BET Networks; Bravo; Cartoon Network; CNBC; CNN; Comedy Central; C-SPAN; Discovery Channel; Disney Channel; E! Entertainment Television; ESPN; ESPN 2; Food Network; Fox News Channel; Fox Sports Southwest; FX; Great American Country; Headline News; HGTV; History Channel; Jewelry Television; Lifetime; MSNBC; MTV; National Geographic Channel; Nickelodeon; Outdoor Channel; Spike TV; Syfy; TBS Superstation; The Learning Channel; The Weather Channel; Travel Channel; Turner Classic Movies; Turner Network TV; TV Land; Univision Studios; USA Network; VH1.
Fee: $15.53 monthly.
Digital Basic Service
Subscribers: N.A.
Programming (via satellite): BBC America; Bloomberg Television; cloo; Discovery Digital Networks; DMX Music; ESPN Classic Sports; ESPNews; Fox College Sports Atlantic; Fox College Sports Central; Fox College Sports Pacific; Fox Soccer; Fuse; G4; Golf Channel; GSN; History Channel International; Independent Film Channel; ShopNBC; Speed; Style Network; Sundance Channel; Toon Disney; Versus; WE tv.
Pay Service 1
Pay Units: N.A.
Programming (via satellite): Cinemax; Flix; HBO; Showtime.

Digital Pay Service 1
Pay Units: N.A.
Programming (via satellite): Cinemax (multiplexed); Encore (multiplexed); Flix; HBO (multiplexed); Showtime (multiplexed); Starz (multiplexed); The Movie Channel (multiplexed).
Video-On-Demand: No
Pay-Per-View
iN DEMAND (delivered digitally); Playboy TV (delivered digitally); Fresh (delivered digitally); NBA TV (delivered digitally); ESPN Gameplan (delivered digitally); ESPN Now (delivered digitally).
Internet Service
Operational: Yes.
Broadband Service: Suddenlink High Speed Internet.
Fee: $49.95 installation; $38.95 monthly.
Telephone Service
None
Miles of Plant: 130.0 (coaxial); None (fiber optic).
Manager: Chris Downing. Chief Technician: Tim Moran.
Ownership: Cequel Communications LLC (MSO).

GLEN ROSE—Formerly served by Glen Rose CATV. No longer in operation. ICA: TX0362.

GODLEY—Formerly served by Almega Cable. No longer in operation. ICA: TX0562.

GOLDEN—Formerly served by Almega Cable. No longer in operation. ICA: TX0538.

GOLDSMITH—Formerly served by Cebridge Connections. No longer in operation. ICA: TX0670.

GOLDTHWAITE—Almega Cable, 4001 W Airport Freeway, Ste 530, Bedford, TX 76021. Phone: 817-685-9588. Fax: 817-685-6488. Web Site: http://www.almega.com. ICA: TX0761.
TV Market Ranking: Outside TV Markets (GOLDTHWAITE). Franchise award date: N.A. Franchise expiration date: N.A. Began: January 1, 1958.
Channel capacity: N.A. Channels available but not in use: N.A.
Basic Service
Subscribers: N.A.
Programming (received off-air): KBVO (MNT) Llano; KCEN-TV (NBC, IND) Temple; KNCT (PBS) Belton; KWKT-TV (FOX, MNT) Waco; KWTX-TV (CBS, CW) Waco; KXXV (ABC, TMO) Waco; allband FM.
Programming (via microwave): KDFW-DT (FOX) Dallas; KTVT (CBS) Fort Worth; WFAA (ABC) Dallas.
Programming (via satellite): A&E Networks; ABC Family Channel; AMC; Animal Planet; Cartoon Network; CNBC; CNN; Country Music TV; C-SPAN; Discovery Channel; Disney Channel; ESPN; ESPN 2; Fox Sports Southwest; GalaVision; HGTV; History Channel; Lifetime; Nickelodeon; Outdoor Channel; Oxygen; SoapNet; Spike TV; Syfy; TBS Superstation; The Learning Channel; The Weather Channel; Trinity Broadcasting Network; Turner Network TV; TV Land; Univision Studios; USA Network; VH1; WGN America.
Fee: $29.95 installation; $38.00 monthly.
Pay Service 1
Pay Units: 64.
Programming (via satellite): HBO.
Fee: $9.65 monthly.
Video-On-Demand: No
Pay-Per-View
iN DEMAND (delivered digitally); Hot Choice (delivered digitally); Playboy TV (delivered digitally); Fresh (delivered digitally); Shorteez (delivered digitally).
Internet Service
Operational: No.
Telephone Service
None
Miles of Plant: 26.0 (coaxial); None (fiber optic).
Ownership: Almega Cable (MSO).

GOLIAD—Reach Broadband, 515 E Longview St, Arp, TX 75750. Phone: 800-687-1258. Web Site: http://www.reachbroadband.net. ICA: TX0395.
TV Market Ranking: Below 100 (GOLIAD). Franchise award date: N.A. Franchise expiration date: N.A. Began: April 1, 1969.
Channel capacity: N.A. Channels available but not in use: N.A.
Basic Service
Subscribers: 643.
Programming (received off-air): KABB (FOX) San Antonio; KAVU-TV (ABC) Victoria; KENS (CBS) San Antonio; KLRN (PBS) San Antonio; KMOL-LP Victoria; KSAT-TV (ABC) San Antonio; KVCT (FOX) Victoria; KZTV (CBS) Corpus Christi; allband FM.
Programming (via satellite): ABC Family Channel; Bravo; Cartoon Network; CNN; Country Music TV; Discovery Fit & Health; E! Entertainment Television; ESPN; Headline News; Nickelodeon; Oxygen; QVC; Syfy; The Learning Channel; The Weather Channel; Travel Channel; Univision Studios; USA Network.
Fee: $29.95 installation; $19.95 monthly.
Expanded Basic Service 1
Subscribers: 606.
Programming (via satellite): A&E Networks; AMC; Animal Planet; CNBC; Discovery Channel; Disney Channel; Food Network; Fox News Channel; Fox Sports Southwest; FX; History Channel; Lifetime; MSNBC; MTV; Spike TV; TBS Superstation; Turner Network TV; TV Land; VH1.
Fee: $20.00 monthly.
Pay Service 1
Pay Units: 64.
Programming (via satellite): HBO.
Fee: $11.95 monthly.
Pay Service 2
Pay Units: 65.
Programming (via satellite): Showtime.
Fee: $11.95 monthly.
Pay Service 3
Pay Units: 33.
Programming (via satellite): The Movie Channel.

Fee: $11.95 monthly.
Video-On-Demand: No
Pay-Per-View
iN DEMAND (delivered digitally); Hot Choice (delivered digitally); Playboy TV (delivered digitally); Fresh (delivered digitally); Shorteez (delivered digitally).
Internet Service
Operational: No.
Telephone Service
None
Miles of Plant: 22.0 (coaxial); None (fiber optic).
Regional Manager: Ronnie Stafford. Office Manager: Jan Gibson.
Ownership: RB3 LLC (MSO).

GOLINDA—Formerly served by National Cable Inc. No longer in operation. ICA: TX0905.

GONZALES—Time Warner Cable, 900 Sidney Baker St, Kerrville, TX 78028-3353. Phones: 830-257-4709; 972-899-7300 (Flower Mound division office). Fax: 850-257-6776. Web Site: http://www.timewarnercable.com/Texas. Also serves Cuero, DeWitt County & Yoakum. ICA: TX0209.
TV Market Ranking: Below 100 (Cuero, DeWitt County (portions), Yoakum); Outside TV Markets (DeWitt County (portions), GONZALES). Franchise award date: N.A. Franchise expiration date: N.A. Began: November 15, 1973.
Channel capacity: N.A. Channels available but not in use: N.A.
Basic Service
Subscribers: 8,600 Includes Columbus.
Programming (received off-air): KABB (FOX) San Antonio; KAVU-TV (ABC) Victoria; KENS (CBS) San Antonio; KEYE-TV (CBS, TMO) Austin; KLRN (PBS) San Antonio; KMYS (CW) Kerrville; KSAT-TV (ABC) San Antonio; KTBC (FOX) Austin; KVDA (TMO) San Antonio; KWEX-DT (UNV) San Antonio; WOAI-TV (NBC) San Antonio; allband FM.
Programming (via satellite): C-SPAN.
Fee: $33.74 installation; $16.00 monthly; $16.69 converter.
Expanded Basic Service 1
Subscribers: 1,912.
Programming (via satellite): A&E Networks; ABC Family Channel; AMC; Animal Planet; BET Networks; Bravo!; Cartoon Network; CNBC; CNN; Comedy Central; Country Music TV; C-SPAN 2; Discovery Channel; Disney Channel; E! Entertainment Television; ESPN; ESPN 2; Eternal Word TV Network; Food Network; Fox News Channel; Fox Sports Southwest; FX; Golf Channel; Hallmark Channel; HD Theater; Headline News; HGTV; History Channel; Lifetime; MSNBC; MTV; mun2 television; National Geographic Channel; Nickelodeon; Oxygen; Paxson Communications Corp.; QVC; SoapNet; Spike TV; Syfy; TBS Superstation; Texas Cable News; The Learning Channel; The New Encore; The Weather Channel; Travel Channel; Trinity Broadcasting Network; truTV; Turner Classic Movies; Turner Network TV; Turner Network TV HD; TV Land; Univision Studios; USA Network; VH1; WE tv.
Fee: $31.30 monthly.
Digital Basic Service
Subscribers: N.A.
Programming (via satellite): AmericanLife TV Network; America's Store; BBC America; Bloomberg Television; Cooking Channel; Current; Discovery Digital Networks; DIY Network; DMX Music; Encore (multiplexed); ESPN Classic Sports; ESPN HD; ESPNews; Fox College Sports Atlantic; Fox College Sports Central; Fox College Sports Pacific; Fox Deportes; Fox Movie Channel; Fox Soccer; Fuse; G4; GAS; Great American Country; GSN; HDNet; HDNet Movies; Independent Film Channel; Lifetime Movie Network; MTV Networks Digital Suite; NBA TV; Nick Jr.; NickToons TV; Outdoor Channel; Speed; Sundance Channel; Tennis Channel; Toon Disney; Trio; Versus.
Fee: $5.00 monthly , $8.95 monthly (each tier).
Digital Pay Service 1
Pay Units: 94.
Programming (via satellite): Cinemax; HBO; Showtime; Starz; The Movie Channel.
Fee: $12.95 monthly (each).
Video-On-Demand: No
Pay-Per-View
iN DEMAND Previews (delivered digitally); MLB Extra Innings (delivered digitally); ESPN Full Court (delivered digitally); iN DEMAND (delivered digitally); Fresh (delivered digitally); Shorteez (delivered digitally); Hot Choice (delivered digitally); Playboy TV (delivered digitally); Spice Hot (delivered digitally); NASCAR In Car (delivered digitally); NBA League Pass (delivered digitally).
Internet Service
Operational: Yes.
Broadband Service: RoadRunner.
Fee: $44.95 monthly.
Telephone Service
Digital: Operational
Fee: $44.95 monthly
Miles of Plant: 185.0 (coaxial); None (fiber optic).
President: Connie Wharton. Vice President & General Manager: Mike McKee. Engineering Director: Charlotte Strong. Chief Technician: Bill Wilcox.
Ownership: Time Warner Cable (MSO).; Advance/Newhouse Partnership (MSO).

GOODRICH—Versalink Media, 511 Pan American Dr, Livingston, TX 77351. Phone: 877-689-6009. Web Site: http://www.versalinkus.com. Also serves Livingston. ICA: TX0174.
TV Market Ranking: Outside TV Markets (GOODRICH, Livingston). Franchise award date: N.A. Franchise expiration date: N.A. Began: N.A.
Channel capacity: 52 (not 2-way capable). Channels available but not in use: N.A.
Basic Service
Subscribers: 606.
Programming (received off-air): KBTX-TV (CBS, CW) Bryan; KCTL-LP Livingston; KETX-LP (IND) Livingston; KHOU (CBS) Houston; KIAH (CW) Houston; KPRC-TV (NBC) Houston; KPXB-TV (ION) Conroe; KRIV (FOX) Houston; KTRE (ABC) Lufkin; KTRK-TV (ABC) Houston; KTXH (MNT) Houston; KUHT (PBS) Houston.
Programming (via satellite): ABC Family Channel; CNN; TBS Superstation.
Fee: $54.95 installation; $20.95 monthly; $2.15 converter.
Expanded Basic Service 1
Subscribers: N.A.
Programming (via satellite): A&E Networks; AMC; BET Networks; CNBC; Country Music TV; Discovery Channel; Disney Channel; ESPN; Fox News Channel; Fox Sports Southwest; HGTV; History Channel; MTV; Nickelodeon; QVC; Spike TV; Syfy; The Weather Channel; Turner Network TV; USA Network; WGN America.
Fee: $23.10 monthly.
Pay Service 1
Pay Units: 87.
Programming (via satellite): Cinemax.
Fee: $12.95 monthly.
Pay Service 2
Pay Units: 164.
Programming (via satellite): HBO.
Fee: $12.95 monthly.
Pay Service 3
Pay Units: 191.
Programming (via satellite): Showtime; The Movie Channel.
Fee: $12.95 monthly.
Video-On-Demand: No
Internet Service
Operational: No.
Telephone Service
None
Miles of Plant: 135.0 (coaxial); None (fiber optic).
Ownership: VersaLink Media LLC (MSO).

GORDON—Formerly served by Mallard Cablevision. No longer in operation. ICA: TX0593.

GOREE—Formerly served by Jayroc Cablevision. No longer in operation. ICA: TX0762.

GORMAN—Reach Broadband, 515 E Longview St, Arp, TX 75750. Phone: 800-687-1258. Web Site: http://www.reachbroadband.net. ICA: TX0464.
TV Market Ranking: Outside TV Markets (GORMAN). Franchise award date: N.A. Franchise expiration date: N.A. Began: October 1, 1968.
Channel capacity: 35 (not 2-way capable). Channels available but not in use: N.A.
Basic Service
Subscribers: 267.
Programming (received off-air): KRBC-TV (NBC) Abilene; KTAB-TV (CBS) Abilene; KXTX-TV (TMO) Dallas; allband FM.
Programming (via microwave): KDFW-DT (FOX) Dallas; KERA-TV (PBS) Dallas; KTVT (CBS) Fort Worth; KXAS-TV (NBC) Fort Worth; WFAA (ABC) Dallas.
Programming (via satellite): Discovery Channel; FX; QVC; TBS Superstation; The Weather Channel.
Fee: $29.95 installation; $19.95 monthly.
Expanded Basic Service 1
Subscribers: N.A.
Programming (via satellite): ABC Family Channel; AMC; Animal Planet; Cartoon Network; CNBC; CNN; ESPN; Fox News Channel; Fox Sports Southwest; Headline News; HGTV; Spike TV; The Learning Channel; Turner Network TV; USA Network.
Fee: $18.00 monthly.
Pay Service 1
Pay Units: 56.
Programming (via satellite): Cinemax.
Fee: $12.90 monthly.
Pay Service 2
Pay Units: N.A.
Programming (via satellite): Encore; Showtime.
Pay Service 3
Pay Units: 64.
Programming (via satellite): HBO.
Fee: $12.90 monthly.
Pay Service 4
Pay Units: 159.
Programming (via satellite): Starz.
Fee: $6.75 monthly.
Video-On-Demand: No
Internet Service
Operational: No.
Telephone Service
None
Miles of Plant: 16.0 (coaxial); None (fiber optic).
Regional Manager: Ronnie Stafford. Office Manager: Jan Gibson.
Ownership: RB3 LLC (MSO).

GRAHAM—Windjammer Cable, 8500 W 110th St, Ste 600, Overland Park, KS 66210. Phones: 561-775-1208; 877-450-5558. Fax: 913-563-5454. Web Site: http://www.windjammercable.com. Also serves Young County. ICA: TX0142.
TV Market Ranking: Outside TV Markets (GRAHAM, Young County). Franchise award date: May 15, 1952. Franchise expiration date: N.A. Began: June 1, 1952.
Channel capacity: N.A. Channels available but not in use: N.A.
Basic Service
Subscribers: N.A. Included in Dallas
Programming (received off-air): KDTN (ETV) Denton; KMPX (IND) Decatur; KPXD-TV (ION) Arlington; KSTR-DT (TEL) Irving; KTAQ (IND) Greenville; WFAA (ABC) Dallas; 18 FMs.
Programming (via microwave): KAZD (IND) Lake Dallas; KDAF (CW, IND) Dallas; KDFI (MNT) Dallas; KDFW-DT (FOX) Dallas; KDTX-TV (TBN) Dallas; KERA-TV (PBS) Dallas; KFWD (IND) Fort Worth; KTVT (CBS) Fort Worth; KTXA (IND) Fort Worth; KXAS-TV (NBC) Fort Worth; KXTX-TV (TMO) Dallas; WFAA (ABC) Dallas.
Programming (via satellite): Azteca America; C-SPAN; C-SPAN 2; Discovery Channel; QVC; TBS Superstation; WGN America.
Fee: $39.95 installation; $19.70 monthly.
Expanded Basic Service 1
Subscribers: N.A.
Programming (via satellite): A&E Networks; ABC Family Channel; Animal Planet; BET Networks; Cartoon Network; CNBC; CNN; Comedy Central; Country Music TV; Disney Channel; E! Entertainment Television; ESPN; ESPN 2; ESPN Classic Sports; Eternal Word TV Network; Food Network; Fox News Channel; Fox Sports Southwest; FX; G4; GalaVision; Golf Channel; GSN; Headline News; HGTV; History Channel; Lifetime; MSNBC; MTV; MTV2; Nickelodeon; Oxygen; Shop at Home; Spike TV; Style Network; Syfy; Texas Cable News; The Learning Channel; The Weather Channel; Travel Channel; truTV; Turner Classic Movies; Turner Network TV; TV Guide Network; TV Land; TV One; Univision Studios; USA Network; Versus; VH1.
Digital Basic Service
Subscribers: N.A.
Programming (via satellite): AMC; BBC America; Bio; Bloomberg Television; Boomerang; Bravo; Canal Sur; Cartoon Network Tambien en Espanol; Cine Latino; CMT Pure Country; CNN en Espanol; CNN International; Cooking Channel; C-SPAN 3; Current; Discovery en Espanol; Discovery Fit & Health; Discovery Health Channel; Discovery Kids Channel; DIY Network; Encore (multiplexed); ESPN HD; ESPN U; ESPNews; EWTN en Espanol; FamilyNet; Fox College Sports Atlantic; Fox College Sports Central; Fox College Sports Pacific; Fox Deportes; Fox Movie Channel; Fox Soccer; Fuel TV; Fuse; GMC; Great American Country; Hallmark Channel; Halogen Network; HD Theater; HDNet; History Channel en Espanol; History Channel International; ID Investigation Discovery; Independent Film Channel; Infinito; La Familia Network; Lifetime Movie Network; Lifetime Real Women; Military Channel; Mnet; MTV Hits; MTV Jams; MTV2; mun2 television; Music Choice; National Geographic Channel; NBA TV; Nick Jr.; Nick Too; NickToons TV; Outdoor Channel; Planet Green; Science;

ShopNBC; Sorpresa; Speed; Sundance Channel; TBN Enlace USA; TeenNick; Tennis Channel; The Word Network; Toon Disney; Toon Disney en Espanol; Tr3s; Turner Network TV HD; TV Land; Universal HD; VH1 Classic; VH1 Soul; Video Rola; WE tv.

Digital Pay Service 1

Pay Units: N.A.

Programming (via satellite): Cinemax (multiplexed); Cinemax HD; Flix; HBO (multiplexed); HBO HD; Showtime (multiplexed); Showtime HD; Starz (multiplexed); Starz HDTV; The Movie Channel (multiplexed); TV Asia; Zee TV USA.

Video-On-Demand: No

Pay-Per-View

iN DEMAND (delivered digitally); Fresh (delivered digitally); Playboy TV (delivered digitally); Hot Choice (delivered digitally); Shorteez (delivered digitally); Playboy en Espanol (delivered digitally); ESPN (delivered digitally); NBA League Pass (delivered digitally); NHL Center Ice (delivered digitally); MLB Extra Innings (delivered digitally).

Internet Service

Operational: No.

Telephone Service

None

Miles of Plant: 62.0 (coaxial); None (fiber optic).

General Manager: Timothy Evard. Operations Director: Belinda Graham. Engineering Director: Mike Earehart. Finance & Accounting Director: Cindy Johnson.

Ownership: Windjammer Communications LLC (MSO).

GRANADA HILLS—Time Warner Cable. Now served by AUSTIN, TX [TX0005]. ICA: TX0763.

GRANBURY—Charter Communications, 777 Harbor Lakes Dr, Granbury, TX 76048-2623. Phone: 817-279-9992 (Granbury). Web Site: http://www.charter.com. Also serves Glen Rose, Hood County & Somervell County. ICA: TX0764.

TV Market Ranking: 12 (GRANBURY, Hood County (portions)); Outside TV Markets (Glen Rose, Somervell County, Hood County (portions)). Franchise award date: N.A. Franchise expiration date: N.A. Began: January 1, 1979.

Channel capacity: N.A. Channels available but not in use: N.A.

Basic Service

Subscribers: 13,000.

Programming (received off-air): KDAF (CW, IND) Dallas; KDFI (MNT) Dallas; KDFW-DT (FOX) Dallas; KDTN (ETV) Denton; KERA-TV (PBS) Dallas; KFWD (IND) Fort Worth; KMPX (IND) Decatur; KPXD-TV (ION) Arlington; KSTR-DT (TEL) Irving; KTVT (CBS) Fort Worth; KTXA (IND) Fort Worth; KXAS-TV (NBC) Fort Worth; KXTX-TV (TMO) Dallas; WFAA (ABC) Dallas.

Programming (via satellite): A&E Networks; ABC Family Channel; AMC; Animal Planet; Cartoon Network; CNBC; CNN; Comedy Central; Country Music TV; C-SPAN; Discovery Channel; Disney Channel; E! Entertainment Television; ESPN; ESPN 2; Fox News Channel; Fox Sports Southwest; Golf Channel; Headline News; HGTV; History Channel; Lifetime; MSNBC; MTV; Nickelodeon; Outdoor Channel; Spike TV; Syfy; TBS Superstation; The Learning Channel; The Weather Channel; Trinity Broadcasting Network; Turner Classic Movies; Turner Network TV; TV Land; USA Network; VH1; WGN America.

Fee: $29.95 installation.

Digital Basic Service

Subscribers: N.A.

Programming (via satellite): BBC America; Bio; Discovery Digital Networks; DMX Music; ESPN Classic Sports; GAS; GSN; History Channel International; Independent Film Channel; Lifetime Movie Network; MTV Networks Digital Suite; MuchMusic Network; Nick Jr.; Speed; Style Network; Toon Disney; Versus; WE tv.

Digital Pay Service 1

Pay Units: N.A.

Programming (via satellite): Cinemax (multiplexed); Encore (multiplexed); HBO (multiplexed); Showtime (multiplexed); Starz (multiplexed); The Movie Channel (multiplexed).

Fee: $20.00 installation; $9.95 monthly (each).

Video-On-Demand: Yes

Pay-Per-View

iN DEMAND (delivered digitally); Fresh (delivered digitally).

Internet Service

Operational: Yes.

Broadband Service: Charter Pipeline.

Fee: $29.99 monthly.

Telephone Service

None

Miles of Plant: 349.0 (coaxial); 123.0 (fiber optic).

Vice President & General Manager: Wayne Cramp. Marketing Director: Kathleen Griffin. Technical Operations Director: John Linton. Chief Technician: Mike Carmack. Technical Supervisor: Sam Easley.

Ownership: Charter Communications Inc. (MSO).

GRAND PRAIRIE—Time Warner Cable. Now served by DALLAS, TX [TX0003]. ICA: TX0030.

GRANDFALLS—Formerly served by Almega Cable. No longer in operation. ICA: TX0765.

GRAPE CREEK—CMA Cablevision, 1510 N 1st St, PO Box 549, Merkel, TX 79536-0549. Phones: 325-928-4750; 800-588-4750. Fax: 325-928-3452. Web Site: http://www.cmaaccess.com. ICA: TX0326.

TV Market Ranking: Below 100 (GRAPE CREEK). Franchise award date: October 1, 1980. Franchise expiration date: N.A. Began: July 1, 1982.

Channel capacity: N.A. Channels available but not in use: N.A.

Basic Service

Subscribers: 215.

Programming (received off-air): KIDY (FOX) San Angelo; KLST (CBS) San Angelo; KSAN-TV (NBC) San Angelo; KTXS-TV (ABC, CW, TMO) Sweetwater.

Programming (via satellite): A&E Networks; ABC Family Channel; AMC; Cartoon Network; CNN; Country Music TV; Disney Channel; ESPN; Lifetime; Spike TV; Syfy; TBS Superstation; The Learning Channel; The Weather Channel; Turner Network TV; TV Land; Univision Studios; USA Network; WGN America.

Fee: $39.95 installation; $25.95 monthly; $12.95 additional installation.

Pay Service 1

Pay Units: N.A.

Programming (via satellite): HBO.

Fee: $14.95 installation; $13.95 monthly.

Video-On-Demand: No

Internet Service

Operational: No.

Telephone Service

None

Miles of Plant: 45.0 (coaxial); None (fiber optic).

General Manager: Jerry Smith. Chief Technician: Joe Clark. Marketing Director: Julie Ferguson.

Ownership: Cable Management Assoc. (MSO).

GRAPELAND—Suddenlink Communications, 12444 Powerscourt Dr, Saint Louis, MO 63131-3660. Phones: 800-999-6845 (Customer service); 314-965-2020. Fax: 903-561-5485. Web Site: http://www.suddenlink.com. Also serves Latexo. ICA: TX0382.

TV Market Ranking: Outside TV Markets (GRAPELAND, Latexo). Franchise award date: N.A. Franchise expiration date: N.A. Began: April 1, 1974.

Channel capacity: N.A. Channels available but not in use: N.A.

Basic Service

Subscribers: 645.

Programming (received off-air): KFXK-TV (FOX) Longview; KLTV (ABC, TMO) Tyler; KTRE (ABC) Lufkin; KTVT (CBS) Fort Worth; allband FM.

Programming (via microwave): KXAS-TV (NBC) Fort Worth; WFAA (ABC) Dallas.

Programming (via satellite): CNN; Discovery Channel; ESPN; Nickelodeon; Spike TV; TBS Superstation; Turner Network TV; USA Network; WGN America.

Fee: $39.95 installation; $19.95 monthly.

Pay Service 1

Pay Units: 43.

Programming (via satellite): Showtime.

Fee: $11.00 monthly.

Pay Service 2

Pay Units: 11.

Programming (via satellite): Cinemax.

Fee: $10.95 monthly.

Pay Service 3

Pay Units: 26.

Programming (via satellite): HBO.

Fee: $10.95 monthly.

Video-On-Demand: No

Internet Service

Operational: Yes. Began: July 24, 2004.

Broadband Service: Suddenlink High Speed Internet.

Fee: $49.95 installation; $38.95 monthly.

Telephone Service

None

Miles of Plant: 35.0 (coaxial); None (fiber optic).

Regional Manager: Todd Cruthird. Plant Manager: David Burrell.

Ownership: Cequel Communications LLC (MSO).

GREENVILLE—GEUS, 2810 Wesley St, Greenville, TX 75401. Phone: 903-457-2800. Fax: 903-454-9249. E-mail: jtyler@geus.org. Web Site: http://www.geus.org. ICA: TX0998. **Note:** This system is an overbuild.

TV Market Ranking: Below 100 (GREENVILLE). Franchise award date: N.A. Franchise expiration date: N.A. Began: June 29, 2001.

Channel capacity: 78 (operating 2-way). Channels available but not in use: N.A.

Basic Service

Subscribers: 10,183.

Programming (received off-air): KDAF (CW, IND) Dallas; KDFI (MNT) Dallas; KDFW-DT (FOX) Dallas; KDTX-TV (TBN) Dallas; KERA-TV (PBS) Dallas; KPXD-TV (ION) Arlington; KSTR-DT (TEL) Irving; KTAQ (IND) Greenville; KTVT (CBS) Fort Worth; KTXA (IND) Fort Worth; KUVN-DT (UNV) Garland; KXAS-TV (NBC) Fort Worth; KXTX-TV (TMO) Dallas; WFAA (ABC) Dallas.

Programming (via satellite): Daystar TV Network; The Weather Channel; WGN America.

Fee: $28.50 installation; $12.95 monthly.

Expanded Basic Service 1

Subscribers: N.A.

Programming (via satellite): A&E Networks; ABC Family Channel; AMC; Animal Planet; BET Networks; Black Family Channel; Bravo; Cartoon Network; CNBC; CNN; Comedy Central; Country Music TV; C-SPAN; C-SPAN 2; Discovery Channel; Discovery Health Channel; Disney Channel; DIY Network; E! Entertainment Television; ESPN; ESPN 2; Eternal Word TV Network; FamilyNet; Food Network; Fox News Channel; Fox Sports Southwest; FX; GalaVision; Great American Country; Hallmark Channel; Headline News; HGTV; History Channel; Lifetime; MSNBC; MTV; National Geographic Channel; Nickelodeon; Oxygen; QVC; Spike TV; Syfy; TBS Superstation; The Learning Channel; Travel Channel; truTV; Turner Classic Movies; Turner Network TV; TV Land; USA Network; VH1.

Fee: $35.95 monthly.

Digital Basic Service

Subscribers: N.A.

Programming (via satellite): BBC America; Bio; Bloomberg Television; Discovery Fit & Health; DMX Music; ESPN; ESPN Classic Sports; ESPNews; Fox Movie Channel; Fox Soccer; FSN Digital Atlantic; FSN Digital Central; FSN Digital Pacific; Fuel TV; G4; GAS; Golf Channel; GSN; Halogen Network; HD Theater; HDNet; HDNet Movies; History Channel International; Independent Film Channel; Lifetime Movie Network; Lime; MTV Networks Digital Suite; NFL Network; Nick Jr.; NickToons TV; Outdoor Channel; SoapNet; Speed; Style Network; Toon Disney; Versus; WE tv.

Fee: $44.95 monthly.

Digital Pay Service 1

Pay Units: N.A.

Programming (via satellite): Canales N; Cinemax (multiplexed); Encore (multiplexed); Flix (multiplexed); Flix; HBO (multiplexed); Showtime (multiplexed); Starz (multiplexed); Sundance Channel (multiplexed); The Movie Channel (multiplexed).

Fee: $6.95 monthly (Canales n), $7.95 monthly (Cinemax), $10.95 monthly

(Starz & Encore), $12.95 monthly (HBO or Flix, Showtime, Sundance & TMC).
Video-On-Demand: Yes
Pay-Per-View
special events (delivered digitally); Movies (delivered digitally).
Internet Service
Operational: Yes.
Broadband Service: In-house.
Fee: $41.95 monthly.
Telephone Service
None
Miles of Plant: 250.0 (coaxial); None (fiber optic).
General Manager: David McCalla. Cable & Internet Manager: Jim Tyler. Engineering & Operations Manager: Mark Stapp. Marketing & Public Relations Supervisor: Cory Hogan. Customer Service Manager: Jimmy Dickey. Cable & Internet Customer Services Supervisor: Brenda Shelby.
Ownership: GEUS.

GREENVILLE—Time Warner Cable, 1565 Chenault St, Dallas, TX 75228. Phones: 214-328-2882; 903-455-0012 (Greenville office). Fax: 204-320-7484. Web Site: http://www.timewarnercable.com/dallas. ICA: TX0078.
TV Market Ranking: Below 100 (GREENVILLE). Franchise award date: November 1, 1966. Franchise expiration date: N.A. Began: June 1, 1967.
Channel capacity: N.A. Channels available but not in use: N.A.
Basic Service
Subscribers: N.A. Included in Dallas
Programming (received off-air): KDAF (CW, IND) Dallas; KDFI (MNT) Dallas; KDFW-DT (FOX) Dallas; KDTN (ETV) Denton; KDTX-TV (TBN) Dallas; KERA-TV (PBS) Dallas; KPXD-TV (ION) Arlington; KSTR-DT (TEL) Irving; KTAQ (IND) Greenville; KTVT (CBS) Fort Worth; KTXA (IND) Fort Worth; KUVN-DT (UNV) Garland; KXAS-TV (NBC) Fort Worth; KXTX-TV (TMO) Dallas; WFAA (ABC) Dallas.
Programming (via satellite): QVC; TV Guide Network; WGN America.
Fee: $13.99 monthly.
Expanded Basic Service 1
Subscribers: N.A.
Programming (via satellite): A&E Networks; ABC Family Channel; AMC; Animal Planet; BET Networks; Cartoon Network; CNBC; CNN; Comedy Central; Country Music TV; C-SPAN; C-SPAN 2; Discovery Channel; Disney Channel; E! Entertainment Television; ESPN; ESPN 2; Eternal Word TV Network; Food Network; Fox News Channel; Fox Sports Southwest; FX; GalaVision; Golf Channel; Great American Country; Hallmark Channel; Headline News; History Channel; Lifetime; MSNBC; MTV; mun2 television; Nickelodeon; Oxygen; Spike TV; TBS Superstation; Texas Cable News; The Learning Channel; The Weather Channel; Travel Channel; truTV; Turner Classic Movies; Turner Network TV; TV Land; USA Network; Versus; VH1.
Fee: $36.75 monthly.
Digital Basic Service
Subscribers: N.A.
Programming (via satellite): AmericanLife TV Network; BBC America; Bravo; CMT Pure Country; Discovery Fit & Health; Discovery Health Channel; Discovery Home Channel; Discovery Kids Channel; Discovery Times Channel; Encore (multiplexed); ESPN Classic Sports; ESPN HD; ESPNews; Fox Soccer; G4; GSN; HD Theater; HDNet; HGTV; Independent Film Channel; Lifetime Movie Network; Military Channel; MTV2; Music Choice; National Geographic Channel; Nick Jr.; Science; Style Network; Syfy; TeenNick; Trinity Broadcasting Network; Turner Network TV HD; Universal HD; VH1 Classic; WE tv.
Fee: $15.00 monthly.
Digital Expanded Basic Service
Subscribers: N.A.
Programming (via satellite): Bio; Bloomberg Television; Canal Sur; Cine Latino; CNN en Espanol; Discovery en Espanol; EWTN en Espanol; Fox Deportes; Fox Movie Channel; Fuse; Halogen Network; History Channel en Espanol; History Channel International; Infinito; MTV Jams; Nick Too; Outdoor Channel; Speed; TBN Enlace USA; Toon Disney; Toon Disney en Espanol; Tr3s; Video Rola.
Digital Pay Service 1
Pay Units: N.A.
Programming (via satellite): Cinemax (multiplexed); Cinemax HD; HBO (multiplexed); HBO HD; Showtime (multiplexed); Showtime HD; Starz (multiplexed); Starz HDTV; The Movie Channel.
Fee: $18.05 monthly (each).
Video-On-Demand: No
Pay-Per-View
iN DEMAND (delivered digitally); Fresh (delivered digitally); Playboy TV (delivered digitally); ESPN (delivered digitally).
Internet Service
Operational: Yes.
Broadband Service: Road Runner.
Telephone Service
Digital: Operational
Miles of Plant: 147.0 (coaxial); None (fiber optic).
President: Robert Moel. Vice President, Technical Operations: Michael McDonald. Vice President, Marketing: Robert Shurtleff. Vice President, Government & Public Affairs: Dick Kirby. Public Affairs Director: Gary Underwood. Office Manager: LaTonya Smiley-Rizby.
Ownership: Time Warner Cable (MSO).

GREENWOOD—Ridgewood Cablevision, 3700 S County Rd 1316, Odessa, TX 79765. Phone: 432-563-4330. Fax: 432-563-0104. E-mail: rwc@ridgewoodcable.com. Web Site: http://www.ridgewoodcable.com. ICA: TX1017.
TV Market Ranking: Below 100 (GREENWOOD).
Channel capacity: N.A. Channels available but not in use: N.A.
Basic Service
Subscribers: N.A. Included in Ector County (portions)
Programming (received off-air): KERA-TV (PBS) Dallas; KMLM-DT (IND) Odessa; KPEJ-TV (FOX) Odessa; KTVT (CBS) Fort Worth; KXAS-TV (NBC) Fort Worth; WFAA (ABC) Dallas.
Programming (via satellite): A&E Networks; ABC Family Channel; AMC; Animal Planet; Cartoon Network; CNN; Country Music TV; C-SPAN; C-SPAN 2; Discovery Channel; Disney Channel; ESPN; ESPN 2; Food Network; Fox News Channel; Fox Sports Southwest; Golf Channel; Headline News; HGTV; History Channel; Lifetime; MTV; National Geographic Channel; Nickelodeon; Outdoor Channel; QVC; Speed; Spike TV; Syfy; TBS Superstation; Telemundo; The Learning Channel; The Weather Channel; Toon Disney; Turner Classic Movies; Turner Network TV; TV Land; Univision Studios; USA Network; Versus; VH1; WGN America.
Fee: $37.95 monthly.
Pay Service 1
Pay Units: N.A.
Programming (via satellite): Cinemax (multiplexed); HBO (multiplexed); Showtime (multiplexed); The Movie Channel.
Fee: $6.95 monthly (Showtime & TMC), $7.95 monthly (HBO & Cinemax).
Internet Service
Operational: No.
Manager & Chief Technician: Bob Randolph.
Ownership: Ridgewood Cable (MSO).

GROOM—Formerly served by Almega Cable. No longer in operation. ICA: TX0458.

GROVETON—Formerly served by Almega Cable. No longer in operation. ICA: TX0486.

GRUVER—Elk River TV Cable Co., 509 S Main St, PO Box 154, Troy, ID 83871. Phone: 208-369-4652. Web Site: http://www.elkrivertv.net. ICA: TX0768.
TV Market Ranking: Outside TV Markets (GRUVER). Franchise award date: N.A. Franchise expiration date: N.A. Began: N.A.
Channel capacity: 12 (not 2-way capable). Channels available but not in use: N.A.
Basic Service
Subscribers: 175.
Programming (received off-air): KAMR-TV (NBC) Amarillo; KFDA-TV (CBS) Amarillo; KVII-TV (ABC, CW) Amarillo.
Programming (via satellite): CNN; Disney Channel; ESPN; Headline News; TBS Superstation; Turner Network TV; WGN America.
Fee: $25.00 installation; $31.70 monthly.
Pay Service 1
Pay Units: 16.
Programming (via satellite): HBO.
Fee: $12.00 monthly.
Video-On-Demand: No
Internet Service
Operational: No.
Telephone Service
None
Manager: Dave & Leslie McGraw. Chief Technician: Justin McGraw.
Ownership: Elk River TV Cable Co. (MSO).

GUN BARREL CITY—Northland Cable Television, 326 W Main St, PO Box 289, Gun Barrel City, TX 75147. Phones: 800-933-1046; 903-887-0240. Fax: 903-887-7395. E-mail: gunbarrel@northlandcabletv.com. Web Site: http://www.northlandcabletv.com. Also serves Enchanted Oaks, Mabank, Payne Springs, Seven Points (southern portion) & Tool. ICA: TX0084.
TV Market Ranking: Outside TV Markets (Enchanted Oaks, GUN BARREL CITY, Mabank, Payne Springs, Seven Points (southern portion), Tool). Franchise award date: April 9, 1980. Franchise expiration date: November 1, 2008. Began: September 1, 1981.
Channel capacity: 51 (not 2-way capable). Channels available but not in use: N.A.
Basic Service
Subscribers: 3,000.
Programming (received off-air): KDAF (CW, IND) Dallas; KDFI (MNT) Dallas; KDFW-DT (FOX) Dallas; KERA-TV (PBS) Dallas; KLTV (ABC, TMO) Tyler; KPXD-TV (ION) Arlington; KTVT (CBS) Fort Worth; KTXA (IND) Fort Worth; KXAS-TV (NBC) Fort Worth; KXTX-TV (TMO) Dallas; WFAA (ABC) Dallas.
Programming (via satellite): A&E Networks; ABC Family Channel; CNN; Discovery Channel; ESPN; ESPN 2; Great American Country; Headline News; HGTV; QVC; Spike TV; TBS Superstation; The Learning Channel; The Weather Channel; Trinity Broadcasting Network; Turner Network TV; TV Guide Network; WGN America.
Fee: $40.00 installation; $32.99 monthly.
Expanded Basic Service 1
Subscribers: N.A.
Programming (via satellite): AMC; Cartoon Network; Fox Movie Channel; Fox Sports Southwest; Lifetime; Nickelodeon; Turner Classic Movies; USA Network; VH1.
Fee: $41.29 monthly.
Digital Basic Service
Subscribers: N.A.
Programming (via satellite): BBC America; Discovery Digital Networks; Golf Channel; GSN; Halogen Network; Speed; WE tv.
Fee: $10.70 monthly.
Digital Expanded Basic Service
Subscribers: N.A.
Programming (via satellite): Bloomberg Television; Bravo; Discovery Fit & Health; DMX Music; G4; Independent Film Channel; Versus.
Pay Service 1
Pay Units: 700.
Programming (via satellite): HBO.
Fee: $11.95 monthly.
Digital Pay Service 1
Pay Units: N.A.
Programming (via satellite): Cinemax (multiplexed); Encore (multiplexed); Flix; HBO (multiplexed); Showtime (multiplexed); Starz (multiplexed); The Movie Channel (multiplexed).
Fee: $14.75 monthly (HBO, Cinemax, Showtime/TMC/Flix or Starz/Encore).
Video-On-Demand: No
Internet Service
Operational: Yes.
Fee: $42.99 monthly.
Telephone Service
Digital: Operational
Fee: $29.99 monthly
Miles of Plant: 149.0 (coaxial); 18.0 (fiber optic).
Regional Manager: Richard Gammon. Office Manager: Diane Ball. Chief Technician: Bobby Brady.
Ownership: Northland Communications Corp. (MSO).

GUSTINE—Formerly served by Cable Unlimited. No longer in operation. ICA: TX0605.

GUY—Formerly served by Cebridge Connections. No longer in operation. ICA: TX0439.

HALE CENTER—Reach Broadband, 515 E Longview St, Arp, TX 75750. Phone: 800-687-1258. Web Site: http://www.reachbroadband.net. ICA: TX0402.
TV Market Ranking: Below 100 (HALE CENTER). Franchise award date: August 7, 1978. Franchise expiration date: N.A. Began: August 1, 1981.
Channel capacity: 61 (2-way capable). Channels available but not in use: N.A.
Basic Service
Subscribers: 233.
Programming (received off-air): KAMC (ABC) Lubbock; KCBD (NBC) Lubbock; KJTV-TV (FOX) Lubbock; KLBK-TV (CBS) Lubbock; KTXT-TV (PBS) Lubbock; KVDA (TMO) San Antonio.
Programming (via satellite): A&E Networks; ABC Family Channel; AMC; AmericanLife TV Network; Cartoon Network; CNN; Country Music TV; Discovery Channel; Disney Channel; E! Entertainment Television; ESPN; Fox Sports Southwest; Headline

News; HGTV; History Channel; Lifetime; Nickelodeon; QVC; Spike TV; Syfy; TBS Superstation; The Learning Channel; The Weather Channel; Trinity Broadcasting Network; Turner Network TV; TV Land; USA Network; WGN America.
Fee: $29.95 installation; $38.00 monthly.

Pay Service 1
Pay Units: 68.
Programming (via satellite): HBO.
Fee: $10.95 monthly.

Pay Service 2
Pay Units: 38.
Programming (via satellite): Showtime.
Fee: $9.95 monthly.

Pay Service 3
Pay Units: 21.
Programming (via satellite): The Movie Channel.
Fee: $7.95 monthly.

Video-On-Demand: No

Internet Service
Operational: No.

Telephone Service
None

Miles of Plant: 14.0 (coaxial); None (fiber optic).
Regional Manager: Ronnie Stafford. Office Manager: Jan Gibson.
Ownership: RB3 LLC (MSO).

HAMILTON—Northland Cable Television, 975 N Lillian St, PO Box 70, Stephenville, TX 76401-0001. Phone: 254-968-4189. Fax: 254-968-8350. E-mail: brent_richey@northlandcabletv.com. Web Site: http://www.northlandcabletv.com. ICA: TX0267.
TV Market Ranking: Outside TV Markets (HAMILTON). Franchise award date: January 1, 1963. Franchise expiration date: April 1, 2007. Began: June 1, 1963.
Channel capacity: 47 (not 2-way capable). Channels available but not in use: N.A.

Basic Service
Subscribers: 762.
Programming (received off-air): KCEN-TV (NBC, IND) Temple; KDAF (CW, IND) Dallas; KDFW-DT (FOX) Dallas; KERA-TV (PBS) Dallas; KSTR-DT (TEL) Irving; KTVT (CBS) Fort Worth; KWTX-TV (CBS, CW) Waco; KXAS-TV (NBC) Fort Worth; KXXV (ABC, TMO) Waco; WFAA (ABC) Dallas; allband FM.
Programming (via satellite): C-SPAN; ESPN; Great American Country; Hallmark Channel; TBS Superstation; Telemundo; The Learning Channel; The Weather Channel; Travel Channel; Trinity Broadcasting Network; TV Guide Network; Univision Studios; WGN America.
Fee: $17.00 installation; $25.99 monthly; $1.00 converter.

Expanded Basic Service 1
Subscribers: N.A.
Programming (via satellite): A&E Networks; AMC; Cartoon Network; CNN; Discovery Channel; ESPN 2; Fox Sports Southwest; FX; Headline News; HGTV; Lifetime; Nickelodeon; QVC; Spike TV; Turner Classic Movies; Turner Network TV; USA Network.
Fee: $46.99 monthly.

Pay Service 1
Pay Units: 205.
Programming (via satellite): HBO.
Fee: $17.00 installation; $13.50 monthly.

Internet Service
Operational: No.

Telephone Service
None

Miles of Plant: 46.0 (coaxial); None (fiber optic).
Regional Manager: Brent Richey. Chief Engineer: Greg Perry. Office Manager: Linda Smith.
Ownership: Northland Communications Corp. (MSO).

HAMLIN—Suddenlink Communications, 12444 Powerscourt Dr, Saint Louis, MO 63131-3660. Phones: 800-999-6845 (Customer service); 314-965-2020. Web Site: http://www.suddenlink.com. Also serves Jones County (portions). ICA: TX0294.
TV Market Ranking: Below 100 (HAMLIN, Jones County (portions)). Franchise award date: June 16, 1966. Franchise expiration date: N.A. Began: August 1, 1968.
Channel capacity: N.A. Channels available but not in use: N.A.

Basic Service
Subscribers: 750.
Programming (received off-air): KRBC-TV (NBC) Abilene; KTAB-TV (CBS) Abilene; KTXS-TV (ABC, CW, TMO) Sweetwater; 4 FMs.
Programming (via satellite): BET Networks; C-SPAN; Lifetime; QVC; TBS Superstation; The Weather Channel.
Fee: $39.95 installation; $19.95 monthly.

Expanded Basic Service 1
Subscribers: 608.
Programming (via satellite): A&E Networks; ABC Family Channel; AMC; Animal Planet; Cartoon Network; CNN; Country Music TV; Discovery Channel; ESPN; Fox News Channel; Fox Sports Southwest; FX; HGTV; MTV; Nickelodeon; Spike TV; The Learning Channel; Turner Network TV; USA Network.
Fee: $39.95 installation; $23.00 monthly.

Pay Service 1
Pay Units: 83.
Programming (via satellite): Cinemax.
Fee: $12.50 monthly.

Pay Service 2
Pay Units: 186.
Programming (via satellite): Encore.
Fee: $1.71 monthly.

Pay Service 4
Pay Units: 99.
Programming (via satellite): HBO.
Fee: $13.00 monthly.

Pay Service 5
Pay Units: 113.
Programming (via satellite): Starz.
Fee: $6.75 monthly.

Video-On-Demand: No

Internet Service
Operational: Yes. Began: October 6, 2003.
Broadband Service: Suddenlink High Speed Internet.
Fee: $49.95 installation; $25.95 monthly.

Telephone Service
None

Miles of Plant: 22.0 (coaxial); None (fiber optic).
Regional Manager: Todd Cruthird. Plant Manager: Bobby Smith.
Ownership: Cequel Communications LLC (MSO).

HAPPY—Formerly served by Almega Cable. No longer in operation. ICA: TX0583.

HARBOR POINT—Formerly served by CableSouth Inc. No longer in operation. ICA: TX0769.

HARLINGEN—Time Warner Cable, 2921 S Expwy 83, PO Box 2327, Harlingen, TX 78551-2327. Phones: 972-899-7300 (Flower Mound division office); 956-425-7880. Fax: 956-412-0959. Web Site: http://www.timewarnercable.com/Texas. Also serves Alamo, Alton, Brownsville, Cameron County, Combes, Donna, Edcouch, Edinburg, Elsa, Escobares, Garceno, Garciasville, Hidalgo, Hidalgo County, Indian Lake, La Feria, La Grulla, La Joya, La Rosita, La Villa, Laguna Heights, Laguna Vista, Las Milpas, Lopezville, Los Barreras, Los Fresnos, Los Morenos, Los Saenz, Lyford, McAllen, Mercedes, Mission, Olmito, Palm Valley, Palmhurst, Palmview, Penitas, Pharr, Port Isabel, Primera, Rancho Viejo, Raymondville, Rio Del Sol, Rio Grande City, Rio Hondo, Roma, San Benito, San Juan (Hidalgo County), Santa Cruz, Santa Rosa, South Padre Island, Starr County, Sullivan City, Weslaco & Willacy County. ICA: TX0017.
TV Market Ranking: Below 100 (Alamo, Alton, Brownsville, Cameron County, Combes, Donna, Edcouch, Edinburg, Elsa, Escobares, Garceno, Garciasville, HARLINGEN, Hidalgo, Hidalgo County, Indian Lake, La Feria, La Grulla, La Joya, La Rosita, La Villa, Laguna Heights, Laguna Vista, Las Milpas, Lopezville, Los Barreras, Los Fresnos, Los Morenos, Los Saenz, Lyford, McAllen, Mercedes, Mission, Olmito, Palm Valley, Palmhurst, Palmview, Penitas, Pharr, Port Isabel, Primera, Rancho Viejo, Raymondville, Rio Del Sol, Rio Grande City, Rio Hondo, Roma, San Benito, San Juan (Hidalgo County), Santa Cruz, Santa Rosa, South Padre Island, Starr County, Sullivan City, Weslaco, Willacy County). Franchise award date: N.A. Franchise expiration date: N.A. Began: January 1, 1966.
Channel capacity: N.A. Channels available but not in use: N.A.

Basic Service
Subscribers: 109,000.
Programming (received off-air): KAZH-LP McAllen; KGBT-TV (CBS) Harlingen; KLUJ-TV (TBN) Harlingen; KMBH (PBS) Harlingen; KNVO (UNV) McAllen; KRGV-TV (ABC) Weslaco; KSFE-LP McAllen; KTLM (TMO) Rio Grande City; KVEO-TV (NBC) Brownsville; KVTF-CA (TEL) Brownsville.
Programming (via satellite): Bravo; C-SPAN; QVC; various Mexican stations.
Fee: $50.51 installation; $20.84 monthly.

Expanded Basic Service 1
Subscribers: N.A.
Programming (via satellite): A&E Networks; ABC Family Channel; AMC; Animal Planet; Cartoon Network; CNBC; CNN; Comedy Central; Country Music TV; C-SPAN 2; Discovery Channel; Disney Channel; E! Entertainment Television; ESPN; ESPN 2; Eternal Word TV Network; Food Network; Fox Deportes; Fox News Channel; Fox Soccer; Fox Sports Southwest; FX; GalaVision; Golf Channel; Great American Country; Hallmark Channel; Headline News; HGTV; History Channel; INSP; Jewelry Television; Lifetime; Lifetime Movie Network; MSNBC; MTV; mun2 television; National Geographic Channel; Nickelodeon; Oxygen; Shop at Home; Spike TV; Syfy; TBS Superstation; Texas Cable News; The Learning Channel; The Weather Channel; Travel Channel; truTV; Turner Classic Movies; Turner Network TV; TV Land; TVE Internacional; USA Network; VH1; WE tv.
Fee: $27.15 monthly.

Digital Basic Service
Subscribers: 32,561.
Programming (via satellite): A&E Networks; ABC Family Channel; AMC; Animal Planet; BBC America; BBC America On Demand; Bio; Bloomberg Television; Boomerang; Bravo; Cartoon Network; cloo; CNN; Comedy Central; Cooking Channel; Country Music TV; C-SPAN; C-SPAN 2; C-SPAN 3; Current; Daystar TV Network; Discovery Channel; Discovery Fit & Health; Discovery Health Channel; Discovery Home Channel; Discovery Kids Channel; Discovery Times Channel; Disney Channel; DIY Network; E! Entertainment Television; ESPN; ESPN 2; ESPN 2 HD; ESPN Classic Sports; ESPN HD; ESPN U; ESPNews; Eternal Word TV Network; Exercise TV; Food Network; Food Network On Demand; Fox Business Channel; Fox Deportes; Fox News Channel; Fox Reality Channel; Fox Soccer; Fox Sports Southwest; Fuse; FX; G4; GalaVision; GAS; Golf Channel; Great American Country; GSN; Hallmark Channel; HD Theater; HDNet; HDNet Movies; Headline News; HGTV; HGTV On Demand; History Channel; History Channel International; Howard TV; Independent Film Channel; INSP; Jewelry Television; Lifetime; Lifetime Movie Network; Lifetime Real Women; Military Channel; MSNBC; MTV; MTV Hits; MTV2; Music Choice; National Geographic Channel; National Geographic Channel On Demand; NBA TV; Nick Jr.; Nickelodeon; NickToons TV; Oxygen; Oxygen On Demand; QVC; Science; SoapNet; Speed On Demand; Spike TV; Style Network; Syfy; TBS Superstation; Telefutura; Texas Cable News; The Learning Channel; The Weather Channel; Toon Disney; Travel Channel; truTV; Turner Classic Movies; Turner Network TV; Turner Network TV HD; TV Guide SPOT; TV Land; Universal HD; USA Network; Versus; VH1; VH1 Classic; WE tv.
Fee: $5.00 monthly.

Digital Expanded Basic Service
Subscribers: N.A.
Programming (via satellite): Canal Sur; Cine Latino; CNN en Espanol; Discovery en Espanol; Encore; ESPN Deportes; EWTN en Espanol; Fox College Sports Atlantic; Fox College Sports Central; Fox College Sports Pacific; Fox Movie Channel; Fuel TV; HTV Musica; Infinito; La Familia Network; mun2 television; NBA TV; Puma TV; Sorpresa; Speed; Sundance Channel; Tennis Channel; Toon Disney en Espanol; Tr3s; Utilisima; VHUNO; Video Rola.

Digital Pay Service 1
Pay Units: 79,076.
Programming (via satellite): Cinemax (multiplexed); Cinemax On Demand; HBO (multiplexed); HBO HD; HBO on Broadband; Showtime (multiplexed); Showtime HD; Showtime On Demand; Starz (multiplexed); The Movie Channel (multiplexed); The Movie Channel On Demand.

Fee: $12.95 monthly (each).
Video-On-Demand: Yes
Pay-Per-View
Addressable homes: 32,561.
NBA League Pass (delivered digitally); NHL Center Ice (delivered digitally); ESPN Full Court (delivered digitally); ESPN Gameplan (delivered digitally); MLB Extra Innings (delivered digitally); Hot Choice (delivered digitally); iN DEMAND (delivered digitally); Playboy TV (delivered digitally); Fresh (delivered digitally); Shorteez (delivered digitally).
Internet Service
Operational: Yes. Began: November 30, 2001.
Subscribers: 19,769.
Broadband Service: Road Runner.
Fee: $49.99 installation; $44.95 monthly.
Telephone Service
Digital: Operational
Fee: $44.95 monthly
Miles of Plant: 2,289.0 (coaxial); None (fiber optic).
President: Gordon Harp. Vice President: Brad Wackley. Engineering Director: John Linton. Technical Operations Manager: Ana Rodriguez.
Ownership: Time Warner Cable (MSO).; Advance/Newhouse Partnership (MSO).

HARLINGEN—Time Warner Communications. Now served by PHARR, TX [TX0017]. ICA: TX0036.

HARPER—Formerly served by Cable Comm Ltd. No longer in operation. ICA: TX0622.

HARRIS COUNTY (northern portion)—Charter Communications. Now served by SPRING, TX [TX0044]. ICA: TX0213.

HART—Reach Broadband, 515 E Longview St, Arp, TX 75750. Phone: 800-687-1258. Web Site: http://www.reachbroadband.net. ICA: TX0534.
TV Market Ranking: Outside TV Markets (HART). Franchise award date: N.A. Franchise expiration date: N.A. Began: April 1, 1982.
Channel capacity: 36 (not 2-way capable). Channels available but not in use: N.A.
Basic Service
Subscribers: 128.
Programming (received off-air): KACV-TV (PBS) Amarillo; KAMC (ABC) Lubbock; KAMR-TV (NBC) Amarillo; KCBD (NBC) Lubbock; KCIT (FOX) Amarillo; KFDA-TV (CBS) Amarillo; KJTV-TV (FOX) Lubbock; KVII-TV (ABC, CW) Amarillo; allband FM.
Programming (via satellite): A&E Networks; ABC Family Channel; CNN; Country Music TV; Discovery Channel; Disney Channel; ESPN; History Channel; Nickelodeon; Spike TV; TBS Superstation; Telemundo; The Learning Channel; The Weather Channel; Trinity Broadcasting Network; Turner Network TV; TV Land; USA Network; WGN America.
Fee: $29.95 installation; $38.00 monthly.
Pay Service 1
Pay Units: 81.
Programming (via satellite): HBO.
Fee: $15.00 installation; $10.95 monthly.
Pay Service 2
Pay Units: 28.
Programming (via satellite): Showtime.
Fee: $15.00 installation; $9.95 monthly.
Video-On-Demand: No
Internet Service
Operational: No.
Telephone Service
None
Miles of Plant: 8.0 (coaxial); None (fiber optic).
Regional Manager: Ronnie Stafford. Office Manager: Jan Gibson.
Ownership: RB3 LLC (MSO).

HASKELL—Alliance Communications, 6125 Paluxy Dr, Tyler, TX 75703. Phones: 501-679-6619; 800-842-8160. Fax: 501-679-5694. Web Site: http://www.alliancecable.net. ICA: TX0321.
TV Market Ranking: Outside TV Markets (HASKELL). Franchise award date: N.A. Franchise expiration date: N.A. Began: January 1, 1962.
Channel capacity: 30 (not 2-way capable). Channels available but not in use: N.A.
Basic Service
Subscribers: 229.
Programming (received off-air): KIDZ-LP Abilene; KRBC-TV (NBC) Abilene; KRMA-TV (PBS) Denver; KTAB-TV (CBS) Abilene; KTXS-TV (ABC, CW, TMO) Sweetwater; KXVA (FOX) Abilene; 2 FMs.
Programming (via satellite): C-SPAN; QVC; Trinity Broadcasting Network.
Fee: $29.95 installation; $19.95 monthly.
Expanded Basic Service 1
Subscribers: 64.
Programming (via satellite): A&E Networks; ABC Family Channel; AMC; Animal Planet; Bravo; Cartoon Network; CNBC; CNN; Comedy Central; Country Music TV; Discovery Channel; Disney Channel; E! Entertainment Television; ESPN; ESPN 2; Fox Movie Channel; Fox News Channel; Fox Sports Southwest; FX; G4; Golf Channel; Headline News; HGTV; History Channel; Lifetime; MSNBC; MTV; Nickelodeon; Oxygen; SoapNet; Speed; Spike TV; Syfy; TBS Superstation; The Learning Channel; The Weather Channel; Travel Channel; Turner Classic Movies; Turner Network TV; TV Land; Univision Studios; USA Network; Versus; VH1.
Fee: $18.00 monthly.
Digital Basic Service
Subscribers: 48.
Programming (via satellite): BBC America; Bio; Bloomberg Television; Discovery Fit & Health; Discovery Health Channel; Discovery Home Channel; Discovery Kids Channel; Discovery Times Channel; DIY Network; ESPN Classic Sports; GAS; GSN; History Channel International; Independent Film Channel; Lifetime Movie Network; MTV Networks Digital Suite; Music Choice; Nick Jr.; Nick Too; NickToons TV; Science Television; Sundance Channel; Toon Disney; WE tv.
Fee: $12.95 monthly.
Pay Service 1
Pay Units: N.A.
Programming (via satellite): Cinemax; Encore; Flix; HBO; Showtime (multiplexed); The Movie Channel.
Fee: $35.00 installation; $3.95 monthly (Encore), $9.95 monthly (Cinemax, HBO or Showtime).
Digital Pay Service 1
Pay Units: N.A.
Programming (via satellite): Cinemax (multiplexed); HBO (multiplexed); Starz (multiplexed).
Video-On-Demand: No
Pay-Per-View
ETC (delivered digitally); Pleasure (delivered digitally).
Internet Service
Operational: No.
Telephone Service
None
Miles of Plant: 28.0 (coaxial); None (fiber optic).
Vice President & General Manager: John Brinker. Vice President, Programming: Julie Newman.
Ownership: Buford Media Group LLC (MSO).

HASSE—Formerly served by Cable Unlimited. No longer in operation. ICA: TX0550.

HAWKINS—Suddenlink Communications, 12444 Powerscourt Dr, Saint Louis, MO 63131-3660. Phones: 800-999-6845; 314-965-2020. Web Site: http://www.suddenlink.com. Also serves Big Sandy, Gladewater, Gregg County (portions), Smith County (portions), Winona & Wood County (portions). ICA: TX0289.
TV Market Ranking: Below 100 (Big Sandy, Gladewater, Gregg County (portions), HAWKINS, Smith County (portions), Winona, Wood County (portions)). Franchise award date: N.A. Franchise expiration date: April 1, 2007. Began: February 1, 1983.
Channel capacity: N.A. Channels available but not in use: N.A.
Basic Service
Subscribers: 1,170.
Programming (received off-air): KDFW-DT (FOX) Dallas; KERA-TV (PBS) Dallas; KFXK-TV (FOX) Longview; KLTV (ABC, TMO) Tyler; KTVT (CBS) Fort Worth; KXAS-TV (NBC) Fort Worth; WFAA (ABC) Dallas.
Programming (via satellite): ABC Family Channel; ESPN; TBS Superstation.
Fee: $39.95 installation; $19.95 monthly.
Pay Service 1
Pay Units: 61.
Programming (via satellite): Cinemax.
Fee: $7.00 monthly.
Pay Service 2
Pay Units: 109.
Programming (via satellite): Flix.
Fee: $1.95 monthly.
Pay Service 3
Pay Units: 87.
Programming (via satellite): HBO.
Fee: $12.00 monthly.
Pay Service 4
Pay Units: 140.
Programming (via satellite): Showtime.
Fee: $7.00 monthly.
Video-On-Demand: No
Internet Service
Operational: Yes. Began: August 1, 2003.
Broadband Service: Suddenlink High Speed Internet.
Fee: $49.95 installation; $25.95 monthly.
Telephone Service
Digital: Operational
Fee: $44.95 monthly
Miles of Plant: 89.0 (coaxial); None (fiber optic).
Plant Manager: Sonny Myers. Regional Manager: Todd Cruthird.
Ownership: Cequel Communications LLC (MSO).

HAWLEY—Formerly served by Jayroc Cablevision. No longer in operation. ICA: TX0974.

HEARNE—Suddenlink Communications, 4114 E 29th St, Bryan, TX 77802-4302. Phone: 888-822-5151. Fax: 979-268-0139. Web Site: http://www.suddenlink.com. ICA: TX0231.
TV Market Ranking: Below 100 (HEARNE). Franchise award date: November 1, 1968. Franchise expiration date: N.A. Began: November 1, 1968.
Channel capacity: 36 (2-way capable). Channels available but not in use: N.A.
Basic Service
Subscribers: 1,590.
Programming (received off-air): KAKW-DT (UNV) Killeen; KAMU-TV (PBS) College Station; KBTX-TV (CBS, CW) Bryan; KCEN-TV (NBC, IND) Temple; KXXV (ABC, TMO) Waco; KYLE-TV (FOX) Bryan; allband FM.
Programming (via satellite): A&E Networks; ABC Family Channel; AMC; AmericanLife TV Network; BET Networks; CNN; Country Music TV; C-SPAN; Discovery Channel; Disney Channel; ESPN; ESPN 2; Fox Sports Southwest; Great American Country; GSN; Headline News; HGTV; History Channel; ION Television; Lifetime; Nickelodeon; QVC; Spike TV; TBS Superstation; The Weather Channel; Trinity Broadcasting Network; Turner Network TV; TV Land; USA Network; WGN America.
Fee: $33.70 installation; $19.35 monthly; $12.50 additional installation.
Pay Service 1
Pay Units: 480.
Programming (via satellite): HBO.
Fee: $11.00 monthly.
Pay Service 2
Pay Units: 240.
Programming (via satellite): Cinemax.
Fee: $10.00 monthly.
Video-On-Demand: No
Internet Service
Operational: Yes.
Broadband Service: Suddenlink High Speed Internet.
Telephone Service
Digital: Operational
Miles of Plant: 30.0 (coaxial); None (fiber optic).
Manager: Randy Rodgers. Marketing Director: Jennie Kipp. Chief Technician: Jim Davis.
Ownership: Cequel Communications LLC (MSO).

HEBBRONVILLE—Alliance Communications, 6125 Paluxy Dr, Tyler, TX 75703. Phones: 800-842-8160; 501-679-6619. Fax: 501-679-5694. Web Site: http://www.alliancecable.net. ICA: TX0260.
TV Market Ranking: Outside TV Markets (HEBBRONVILLE). Franchise award date: N.A. Franchise expiration date: N.A. Began: January 1, 1968.
Channel capacity: N.A. Channels available but not in use: N.A.
Basic Service
Subscribers: 540.
Programming (received off-air): KDFW-DT (FOX) Dallas; KEDT (PBS) Corpus Christi; KIII (ABC) Corpus Christi; KRIS-TV (CW, NBC) Corpus Christi.
Programming (via microwave): KZTV (CBS) Corpus Christi.
Programming (via satellite): A&E Networks; ABC Family Channel; AMC; Animal Planet; Bravo; Cartoon Network; CNBC; CNN; Comedy Central; Country Music TV; C-SPAN; CW+; Discovery Channel; Disney Channel; ESPN; ESPN 2; Eternal Word TV Network; Fox News Channel; Fox Sports Southwest; FX; GalaVision; Hallmark Channel; Headline News; HGTV; History Channel; Lifetime; MSNBC; MTV; mun2 television; Nickelodeon; Oxygen; Spike TV; TBS Superstation; Telefutura; Telemundo; The Learning Channel; The Weather Channel; Travel Channel; Trinity Broadcasting Network; truTV; Turner Clas-

sic Movies; Turner Network TV; Univision Studios; USA Network; VH1; WE tv.
Fee: $50.51 installation; $48.99 monthly.

Digital Basic Service
Subscribers: 56.
Programming (via satellite): A&E Networks; ABC Family Channel; AMC; Animal Planet; BBC America; Bravo; Cartoon Network; CNBC; CNN; Comedy Central; Country Music TV; C-SPAN; C-SPAN 3; Discovery Fit & Health; Discovery Kids Channel; Disney Channel; DIY Network; ESPN; ESPN 2; ESPN Classic Sports; ESPN U; ESPNews; Eternal Word TV Network; Food Network; Fox Business Channel; Fox News Channel; Fox Reality Channel; Fox Soccer; Fox Sports Southwest; FX; GalaVision; Golf Channel; GSN; Hallmark Channel; Headline News; HGTV; History Channel; ID Investigation Discovery; Independent Film Channel; La Familia Network; Lifetime; Military Channel; MSNBC; MTV; mun2 television; Music Choice; National Geographic Channel; Nick Jr.; Nickelodeon; Oxygen; Planet Green; Science; Spike TV; Syfy; TBS Superstation; TeenNick; The Learning Channel; The Weather Channel; Toon Disney; Travel Channel; Trinity Broadcasting Network; truTV; Turner Classic Movies; Turner Network TV; TV Land; USA Network; Versus; VH1; VH1 Classic; WE tv.
Fee: $7.00 monthly.

Digital Expanded Basic Service
Subscribers: N.A.
Programming (via satellite): Encore (multiplexed).
Fee: $8.95 monthly.

Digital Pay Service 1
Pay Units: N.A.
Programming (via satellite): Cinemax (multiplexed); HBO (multiplexed); Showtime (multiplexed); Starz (multiplexed); The Movie Channel (multiplexed).
Fee: $12.95 monthly (each).

Video-On-Demand: No

Pay-Per-View
iN DEMAND (delivered digitally); Hot Choice (delivered digitally); Fresh (delivered digitally).

Internet Service
Operational: No.

Telephone Service
None

Miles of Plant: 35.0 (coaxial); None (fiber optic).
Vice President & General Manager: John Brinker. Vice President, Programming: Julie Newman.
Ownership: Buford Media Group LLC (MSO).

HEDLEY—Formerly served by Almega Cable. No longer in operation. ICA: TX0772.

HEIGHTS (unincorporated areas)—Almega Cable, 4001 W Airport Frwy, Ste 530, Bedford, TX 76021. Phone: 817-685-9588. Fax: 817-685-6488. Web Site: http://www.almega.com. Also serves Alvin (unincorporated areas) & Manvel (unincorporated areas). ICA: TX0143.
TV Market Ranking: 15 (Alvin (unincorporated areas), HEIGHTS (UNINCORPORATED AREAS), Manvel (unincorporated areas)). Franchise award date: N.A. Franchise expiration date: N.A. Began: N.A.
Channel capacity: 36 (not 2-way capable). Channels available but not in use: N.A.

Basic Service
Subscribers: 117.
Programming (received off-air): KETH-TV (TBN) Houston; KFTH-DT (TEL) Alvin; KHOU (CBS) Houston; KIAH (CW) Houston; KLTJ (ETV) Galveston; KPRC-TV (NBC) Houston; KRIV (FOX) Houston; KTMD (TMO) Galveston; KTRK-TV (ABC) Houston; KTXH (MNT) Houston; KUHT (PBS) Houston; KXLN-DT (UNV) Rosenberg; KYAZ (IND) Katy.
Programming (via satellite): A&E Networks; ABC Family Channel; AMC; CNN; Country Music TV; C-SPAN; Discovery Channel; Disney Channel; ESPN; Fox Sports Southwest; Headline News; Lifetime; Nickelodeon; Spike TV; TBS Superstation; The Weather Channel; Turner Network TV; USA Network; VH1; WGN America.
Fee: $54.95 installation; $44.05 monthly.

Pay Service 1
Pay Units: N.A.
Programming (via satellite): Cinemax; HBO; Showtime.
Fee: $12.95 monthly (each).

Video-On-Demand: No

Internet Service
Operational: No.

Telephone Service
None

Miles of Plant: 148.0 (coaxial); None (fiber optic).
Ownership: Almega Cable (MSO).

HEMPHILL—Almega Cable, 4003 W Airport Freeway, Ste 532, Bedford, TX 76021. Phone: 817-685-9588. Fax: 817-685-6488. Web Site: http://www.almega.com. Also serves Pineland. ICA: TX1019.
TV Market Ranking: Outside TV Markets (HEMPHILL, Pineland).
Channel capacity: N.A. Channels available but not in use: N.A.

Basic Service
Subscribers: 809.
Programming (received off-air): KALB-TV (CBS, NBC) Alexandria; KLAX-TV (ABC) Alexandria; KLPA-TV (PBS) Alexandria; KMSS-TV (FOX) Shreveport; KSHV-TV (MNT) Shreveport; KSLA (CBS) Shreveport; KTRE (ABC) Lufkin; KYTX (CBS, IND) Nacogdoches.
Programming (via satellite): QVC; The Weather Channel.
Fee: $54.95 installation; $20.95 monthly.

Expanded Basic Service 1
Subscribers: N.A.
Programming (via satellite): A&E Networks; ABC Family Channel; BET Networks; Cartoon Network; CNBC; CNN; C-SPAN; Discovery Channel; Disney Channel; E! Entertainment Television; ESPN; ESPN 2; Eternal Word TV Network; Fox News Channel; Fox Sports Southwest; FX; Great American Country; Headline News; HGTV; History Channel; Lifetime; MSNBC; MTV; National Geographic Channel; Nickelodeon; Outdoor Channel; Spike TV; TBS Superstation; The Learning Channel; Turner Classic Movies; Turner Network TV; TV Guide Network; USA Network.
Fee: $23.10 monthly.

Pay Service 1
Pay Units: N.A.
Programming (via satellite): HBO; Showtime.
Fee: $12.95 monthly (each).

Internet Service
Operational: No.

Telephone Service
None

Ownership: Almega Cable (MSO).

HEMPSTEAD—CMA Cablevision, 840 E Travis St, La Grange, TX 78945-2344. Phone: 979-968-6476. Fax: 979-968-5368.

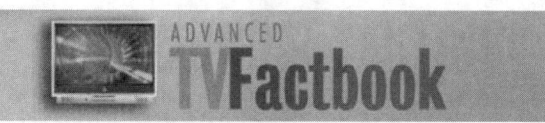

Web Site: http://www.cmaaccess.com. ICA: TX0305.
TV Market Ranking: Below 100 (HEMPSTEAD). Franchise award date: N.A. Franchise expiration date: June 23, 2009. Began: May 1, 1982.
Channel capacity: N.A. Channels available but not in use: N.A.

Basic Service
Subscribers: 275.
Programming (received off-air): KETH-TV (TBN) Houston; KFTH-DT (TEL) Alvin; KHOU (CBS) Houston; KIAH (CW) Houston; KLTJ (ETV) Galveston; KPRC-TV (NBC) Houston; KRIV (FOX) Houston; KTMD (TMO) Galveston; KTRK-TV (ABC) Houston; KTXH (MNT) Houston; KUHT (PBS) Houston; KXLN-DT (UNV) Rosenberg; KYAZ (IND) Katy; allband FM.
Programming (via satellite): C-SPAN.
Fee: $39.95 installation; $19.45 monthly; $12.95 additional installation.

Expanded Basic Service 1
Subscribers: N.A.
Programming (via satellite): A&E Networks; ABC Family Channel; AMC; BET Networks; Cartoon Network; CNN; Country Music TV; Discovery Channel; Disney Channel; ESPN; Fox News Channel; History Channel; Lifetime; MTV; Nickelodeon; Spike TV; TBS Superstation; The Weather Channel; Turner Network TV; TV Land; USA Network.
Fee: $21.50 monthly.

Digital Basic Service
Subscribers: N.A.
Programming (via satellite): BBC America; Bio; Bloomberg Television; Bravo; Discovery Digital Networks; DMX Music; ESPN 2; ESPN Classic Sports; ESPNews; Fox Movie Channel; Fuse; G4; Golf Channel; GSN; Halogen Network; HGTV; History Channel International; Independent Film Channel; Lifetime Movie Network; National Geographic Channel; Outdoor Channel; Speed; Sundance Channel; Syfy; Trinity Broadcasting Network; Turner Classic Movies; Versus; WE tv.
Fee: $16.95 monthly.

Pay Service 1
Pay Units: 8.
Programming (via satellite): Cinemax.
Fee: $14.95 installation; $10.95 monthly.

Pay Service 2
Pay Units: 10.
Programming (via satellite): Showtime.
Fee: $14.95 installation; $13.95 monthly.

Pay Service 3
Pay Units: 66.
Programming (via satellite): HBO.
Fee: $14.95 installation; $13.95 monthly.

Digital Pay Service 1
Pay Units: N.A.
Programming (via satellite): Cinemax (multiplexed); Encore (multiplexed); Flix; HBO (multiplexed); Showtime (multiplexed); Starz (multiplexed); The Movie Channel (multiplexed).
Fee: $10.95 monthly (Cinemax or Starz/Encore), $13.95 monthly (HBO or Showtime).

Video-On-Demand: No

Pay-Per-View
iN DEMAND (delivered digitally); Hot Choice (delivered digitally); Playboy TV (delivered digitally); Fresh (delivered digitally); Club Jenna (delivered digitally); Spice: Xcess (delivered digitally).

Internet Service
Operational: No.

Telephone Service
None

Miles of Plant: 31.0 (coaxial); None (fiber optic).
General Manager: Jerry L. Smith. Plant Manager: Grady Daniels. Marketing Director: Julie Ferguson.
Ownership: Cable Management Assoc. (MSO).

HENDERSON—Suddenlink Communications, 109 N High St, Henderson, TX 75652-3133. Phones: 888-722-5151 (Customer service); 903-657-3333. Fax: 903-657-7766. Web Site: http://www.suddenlink.com. Also serves Rusk County. ICA: TX0140.
TV Market Ranking: Below 100 (HENDERSON (PORTIONS), Rusk County). Franchise award date: January 1, 1968. Franchise expiration date: N.A. Began: September 5, 1968.
Channel capacity: N.A. Channels available but not in use: N.A.

Basic Service
Subscribers: N.A.
Programming (received off-air): KETK-TV (NBC) Jacksonville; KFXK-TV (FOX) Longview; KLPN-LP (IND) Longview; KLTV (ABC, TMO) Tyler; KYTX (CBS, IND) Nacogdoches; 6 FMs.
Programming (via microwave): KERA-TV (PBS) Dallas; KXTX-TV (TMO) Dallas.
Programming (via satellite): C-SPAN; QVC; TV Guide Network; Univision Studios; WGN America.
Fee: $35.00 installation; $9.51 monthly.

Expanded Basic Service 1
Subscribers: N.A.
Programming (via satellite): A&E Networks; ABC Family Channel; AMC; Animal Planet; BET Networks; Bravo; Cartoon Network; CNBC; CNN; Comedy Central; Country Music TV; C-SPAN 2; Discovery Channel; Disney Channel; E! Entertainment Television; ESPN; ESPN 2; Eternal Word TV Network; Food Network; Fox News Channel; Fox Sports Southwest; FX; GalaVision; Great American Country; Headline News; HGTV; History Channel; INSP; Jewelry Television; Lifetime; Lifetime Movie Network; MSNBC; MTV; Nickelodeon; Outdoor Channel; Speed; Spike TV; Syfy; TBS Superstation; The Learning Channel; The Weather Channel; Travel Channel; Trinity Broadcasting Network; truTV; Turner Classic Movies; Turner Network TV; TV Land; USA Network; Versus; VH1.
Fee: $18.99 monthly.

Digital Basic Service
Subscribers: N.A.
Programming (via satellite): A&E HD; Bandamax; BBC America; Bio; Bloomberg Television; Boomerang; CBS Sports Net-

work; Cine Latino; Cine Mexicano; CMT Pure Country; CNN en Espanol; Cooking Channel; Cox Sports Television; De Pelicula; De Pelicula Clasico; Discovery en Espanol; Discovery Health Channel; Discovery Home Channel; Discovery Kids Channel; Discovery Times Channel; DIY Network; Encore (multiplexed); ESPN 2 HD; ESPN Classic Sports; ESPN Deportes; ESPN HD; ESPN U; ESPNews; EWTN en Espanol; FamilyNet; Food Network HD; Fox Deportes; Fox Reality Channel; Fox Soccer; Fuel TV; Fuse; G4; GalaVision; GMC; Golf Channel; GSN; Hallmark Channel; Halogen Network; HD Theater; HDNet; HDNet Movies; HGTV HD; History Channel en Espanol; History Channel International; Independent Film Channel; Latele Novela Network; Military Channel; MTV Hits; MTV2; mun2 television; Music Choice; National Geographic Channel; National Geographic Channel HD Network; Nick Jr.; NickToons TV; Nuvo TV; Oxygen; Ritmoson Latino; Science; SoapNet; Sorpresa; Style Network; Sundance Channel; Sur Network; TBN Enlace USA; TeenNick; Telefutura; Telehit; Tennis Channel; Toon Disney; Toon Disney en Espanol; Tr3s; Turner Network TV HD; TV Chile; TV One; Universal HD; VH1 Classic; VHUNO; Video Rola; WE tv; Weatherscan.

Digital Pay Service 1
Pay Units: N.A.
Programming (via satellite): Cinemax (multiplexed); HBO (multiplexed); HBO HD; HBO Latino; Showtime (multiplexed); Showtime HD; Starz (multiplexed); Starz HDTV; The Movie Channel (multiplexed).

Video-On-Demand: No

Pay-Per-View
iN DEMAND (delivered digitally); Fresh (delivered digitally); Shorteez (delivered digitally); Playboy TV (delivered digitally); Playboy en Espanol (delivered digitally).

Internet Service
Operational: Yes.
Broadband Service: Suddenlink High Speed Internet.
Fee: $45.95 installation; $29.95 monthly.

Telephone Service
Digital: Operational
Fee: $44.95 monthly

Miles of Plant: 98.0 (coaxial); None (fiber optic). Additional miles planned: 2.0 (coaxial).
Manager: Ronnie Powell. Chief Technician: James McCain.
Ownership: Cequel Communications LLC (MSO).

HENRIETTA—Suddenlink Communications, 12444 Powerscourt Dr, Saint Louis, MO 63131-3660. Phones: 800-999-6845 (Customer service); 314-965-2020. Fax: 903-561-5485. Web Site: http://www.suddenlink.com. ICA: TX0314.
TV Market Ranking: Below 100 (HENRIETTA). Franchise award date: N.A. Franchise expiration date: N.A. Began: September 1, 1978.
Channel capacity: N.A. Channels available but not in use: N.A.

Basic Service
Subscribers: 700.
Programming (received off-air): KAUZ-TV (CBS, CW) Wichita Falls; KFDX-TV (NBC) Wichita Falls; KJTL (FOX) Wichita Falls; KSWO-TV (ABC, TMO) Lawton; allband FM.
Programming (via satellite): Discovery Channel; Hallmark Channel; QVC; TBS Superstation; The Weather Channel.
Programming (via translator): KERA-TV (PBS) Dallas.
Fee: $39.95 installation; $19.95 monthly.

Expanded Basic Service 1
Subscribers: 629.
Programming (via satellite): ABC Family Channel; AMC; Animal Planet; Cartoon Network; CNBC; CNN; C-SPAN; Disney Channel; ESPN; Fox News Channel; FX; Headline News; HGTV; Lifetime; MTV; Spike TV; The Learning Channel; truTV; Turner Network TV; USA Network.
Fee: $39.95 installation; $23.00 monthly.

Pay Service 1
Pay Units: 37.
Programming (via satellite): Cinemax.
Fee: $13.59 monthly.

Pay Service 2
Pay Units: 249.
Programming (via satellite): Encore.
Fee: $1.75 monthly.

Pay Service 3
Pay Units: 115.
Programming (via satellite): HBO.
Fee: $13.59 monthly.

Pay Service 4
Pay Units: 135.
Programming (via satellite): Starz.
Fee: $6.75 monthly.

Video-On-Demand: No

Internet Service
Operational: Yes. Began: May 1, 2003.
Broadband Service: Suddenlink High Speed Internet.
Fee: $49.95 installation; $25.95 monthly.

Telephone Service
None

Miles of Plant: 24.0 (coaxial); None (fiber optic).
Regional Manager: Todd Cruthird. Plant Manager: Ron Johnson.
Ownership: Cequel Communications LLC (MSO).

HEREFORD—XIT Communications, 12324 US Hwy 87, PO Box 1432, Dalhart, TX 79022. Phones: 806-364-1426; 806-384-3311 (Headquarters). Fax: 806-384-3340. E-mail: xitcom@xit.net. Web Site: http://www.xit.net. ICA: TX0125.
TV Market Ranking: 95 (Vega); Outside TV Markets (HEREFORD). Franchise award date: March 1, 1972. Franchise expiration date: April 22, 2012. Began: June 14, 1973.
Channel capacity: 55 (operating 2-way). Channels available but not in use: N.A.

Basic Service
Subscribers: 3,585.
Programming (received off-air): KACV-TV (PBS) Amarillo; KCIT (FOX) Amarillo; KFDA-TV (CBS) Amarillo; KPTF-DT (IND) Farwell; KVII-TV (ABC, CW) Amarillo; allband FM.
Programming (via satellite): A&E Networks; ABC Family Channel; AMC; Animal Planet; CNBC; CNN; Country Music TV; C-SPAN; C-SPAN 2; Discovery Channel; Disney Channel; ESPN; ESPN 2; Eternal Word TV Network; Food Network; Fox News Channel; Fox Sports Southwest; FX; GalaVision; Golf Channel; Hallmark Channel; Headline News; HGTV; History Channel; Lifetime; MSNBC; MTV; Nickelodeon; QVC; Spike TV; Syfy; TBS Superstation; Telemundo; The Learning Channel; The Weather Channel; Toon Disney; Travel Channel; Trinity Broadcasting Network; truTV; Turner Classic Movies; Turner Network TV; TV Land; USA Network; Versus; VH1; WGN America.
Fee: $18.39 installation; $37.25 monthly.

Pay Service 1
Pay Units: 135.
Programming (via satellite): Cinemax.
Fee: $10.05 monthly.

Pay Service 2
Pay Units: 313.
Programming (via satellite): HBO.
Fee: $11.60 monthly.

Pay Service 3
Pay Units: 100.
Programming (via satellite): Showtime.
Fee: $10.40 monthly.

Video-On-Demand: No

Internet Service
Operational: Yes.
Subscribers: 185.
Broadband Service: In-house.
Fee: $35.00 installation; $25.00 monthly.

Telephone Service
Digital: Planned

Miles of Plant: 68.0 (coaxial); 13.0 (fiber optic).
General Manager: Darrell Dennis. Area Manager & Chief Technician: Lloyd Ames.
Ownership: XIT Communications (MSO).

HICO—Northland Cable Television, 975 N Lillian St, PO Box 70, Stephenville, TX 76401-0001. Phone: 254-968-4189. Fax: 254-968-8350. E-mail: brent_richey@northlandcabletv.com. Web Site: http://www.northlandcabletv.com. ICA: TX0774.
TV Market Ranking: Outside TV Markets (HICO). Franchise award date: N.A. Franchise expiration date: N.A. Began: March 1, 1969.
Channel capacity: N.A. Channels available but not in use: N.A.

Basic Service
Subscribers: 262.
Programming (received off-air): KCEN-TV (NBC, IND) Temple; KDAF (CW, IND) Dallas; KDFI (MNT) Dallas; KDFW-DT (FOX) Dallas; KERA-TV (PBS) Dallas; KSTR-DT (TEL) Irving; KTVT (CBS) Fort Worth; KTXA (IND) Fort Worth; KWTX-TV (CBS, CW) Waco; KXAS-TV (NBC) Fort Worth; KXTX-TV (TMO) Dallas; KXXV (ABC, TMO) Waco; WFAA (ABC) Dallas; allband FM.
Programming (via satellite): ABC Family Channel; Cartoon Network; CityTV; Country Music TV; C-SPAN; ESPN; TBS Superstation; The Learning Channel; The Weather Channel; Trinity Broadcasting Network; Turner Classic Movies.
Fee: $21.65 installation; $32.98 monthly.

Pay Service 1
Pay Units: N.A.
Programming (via satellite): Showtime; The Movie Channel.

Internet Service
Operational: No.

Telephone Service
None

Miles of Plant: 15.0 (coaxial); None (fiber optic).
Chief Technician: Greg Perry. Office Manager: Linda Smith. Business Manager: David Castleberry.
Ownership: Northland Communications Corp. (MSO).

HIDALGO—Time Warner Communications. Now served by PHARR, TX [TX0017]. ICA: TX0244.

HIGGINS—Formerly served by Almega Cable. No longer in operation. ICA: TX0590.

HIGHLAND RANGE—Formerly served by Highland Cable. No longer in operation. ICA: TX0676.

HILLSBORO—Northland Cable Television, 303 Coke St, Hillsboro, TX 76645-2654. Phone: 254-582-9793. Fax: 254-582-8628. E-mail: hillsboro@northlandcabletv.com. Web Site: http://www.northlandcabletv.com. ICA: TX0175.
TV Market Ranking: Below 100 (HILLSBORO). Franchise award date: June 19, 1990. Franchise expiration date: N.A. Began: December 1, 1979.
Channel capacity: 52 (operating 2-way). Channels available but not in use: N.A.

Basic Service
Subscribers: 1,390.
Programming (received off-air): KCEN-TV (NBC, IND) Temple; KDAF (CW, IND) Dallas; KDFI (MNT) Dallas; KDFW-DT (FOX) Dallas; KDTN (ETV) Denton; KDTX-TV (TBN) Dallas; KERA-TV (PBS) Dallas; KFWD (IND) Fort Worth; KTVT (CBS) Fort Worth; KTXA (IND) Fort Worth; KWKT-TV (FOX, MNT) Waco; KWTX-TV (CBS, CW) Waco; KXAS-TV (NBC) Fort Worth; KXTX-TV (TMO) Dallas; KXXV (ABC, TMO) Waco; WFAA (ABC) Dallas.
Programming (via satellite): A&E Networks; Animal Planet; BET Networks; Cartoon Network; CNBC; CNN; C-SPAN; Discovery Channel; ESPN; ESPN 2; Food Network; Fox Movie Channel; Fox News Channel; Fox Sports Southwest; FX; Golf Channel; Great American Country; Headline News; HGTV; History Channel; Lifetime; MTV; National Geographic Channel; Nickelodeon; QVC; Spike TV; TBS Superstation; The Learning Channel; The Weather Channel; Turner Classic Movies; Turner Network TV; TV Land; Univision Studios; USA Network; WGN America.
Fee: $45.00 installation; $36.50 monthly.

Digital Basic Service
Subscribers: N.A.
Programming (via satellite): Discovery Health Channel; Discovery Kids Channel; DMX Music; ESPNews; Fox Soccer; Golf Channel; Lifetime Movie Network; Military Channel; Outdoor Channel; Science; Trinity Broadcasting Network; WE tv.
Fee: $44.99 monthly.

Pay Service 1
Pay Units: N.A.
Programming (via satellite): HBO.

Digital Pay Service 1
Pay Units: 280.
Programming (via satellite): Cinemax (multiplexed); Encore (multiplexed); Flix; HBO (multiplexed); Showtime (multiplexed); Starz (multiplexed); The Movie Channel (multiplexed).
Fee: $10.00 monthly (each).

Video-On-Demand: No

Pay-Per-View
iN DEMAND (delivered digitally); Playboy TV (delivered digitally); Fresh (delivered digitally).

Internet Service
Operational: Yes.
Broadband Service: Northland Express.
Fee: $39.99 monthly.

Telephone Service
None

Miles of Plant: 48.0 (coaxial); None (fiber optic).
Regional Manager: Mike Taylor. Marketing Director: Joanne Williams. Chief Technician: Bobby Brady.
Ownership: Northland Communications Corp. (MSO).

HOLIDAY LAKES—Formerly served by Cebridge Connections. No longer in operation. ICA: TX0514.

HOLLIDAY—Time Warner Cable. Now served by WICHITA FALLS, TX [TX0026]. ICA: TX0422.

HOMER—Almega Cable, 4001 W Airport Frwy, Ste 530, Bedford, TX 76021. Phone: 817-685-9588. Fax: 817-685-6488. E-mail: helpdesk@almegacable.com. Web Site: http://www.almega.com. Also serves Angelina County (portions), Bald Hill & Little Flock. ICA: TX0300.

TV Market Ranking: Below 100 (Angelina County (portions), Bald Hill, HOMER, Little Flock). Franchise award date: N.A. Franchise expiration date: N.A. Began: N.A.

Channel capacity: 36 (not 2-way capable). Channels available but not in use: N.A.

Basic Service

Subscribers: 214.

Programming (received off-air): KETK-TV (NBC) Jacksonville; KSLA (CBS) Shreveport; KTRE (ABC) Lufkin.

Programming (via satellite): ABC Family Channel; AMC; BET Networks; CNN; Country Music TV; Discovery Channel; ESPN; Fox Sports Southwest; Headline News; KMGH-TV (ABC) Denver; Lifetime; Nickelodeon; TBS Superstation; Turner Network TV; USA Network; WGN America; WXIA-TV (NBC) Atlanta.

Fee: $54.95 installation; $35.21 monthly.

Pay Service 1

Pay Units: 29.

Programming (via satellite): Cinemax.

Fee: $12.95 monthly.

Pay Service 2

Pay Units: 27.

Programming (via satellite): HBO.

Fee: $12.95 monthly.

Pay Service 3

Pay Units: 92.

Programming (via satellite): Showtime.

Fee: $12.95 monthly.

Video-On-Demand: No

Internet Service

Operational: No.

Telephone Service

None

Miles of Plant: 74.0 (coaxial); None (fiber optic).

Ownership: Almega Cable (MSO).

HONDO—Reach Broadband, 515 E Longview St, Arp, TX 75750. Phone: 800-687-1258. Web Site: http://www.reachbroadband.net. Also serves Castroville. ICA: TX0218.

TV Market Ranking: 45 (Castroville); Outside TV Markets (HONDO). Franchise award date: January 1, 1980. Franchise expiration date: N.A. Began: January 1, 1981.

Channel capacity: 30 (2-way capable). Channels available but not in use: N.A.

Basic Service

Subscribers: 1,213.

Programming (received off-air): KABB (FOX) San Antonio; KENS (CBS) San Antonio; KHCE-TV (TBN) San Antonio; KLRN (PBS) San Antonio; KMOL-LP Victoria; KMYS (CW) Kerrville; KPXL-TV (ION) Uvalde; KSAT-TV (ABC) San Antonio; KVDA (TMO) San Antonio; KWEX-DT (UNV) San Antonio.

Programming (via satellite): GalaVision; QVC.

Fee: $29.95 installation; $19.95 monthly; $1.71 converter.

Expanded Basic Service 1

Subscribers: 1,180.

Programming (via satellite): A&E Networks; ABC Family Channel; AMC; Animal Planet; Bravo; Cartoon Network; CNN; Comedy Central; Country Music TV; C-SPAN; Discovery Channel; Disney Channel; E! Entertainment Television; ESPN; ESPN 2; ESPN Classic Sports; Food Network; Fox Deportes; Fox News Channel; Fox Sports Southwest; Golf Channel; Headline News; HGTV; History Channel; Lifetime; MSNBC; MTV; Nickelodeon; Outdoor Channel; SoapNet; Speed; Spike TV; Syfy; TBS Superstation; The Learning Channel; The Weather Channel; Travel Channel; Turner Classic Movies; Turner Network TV; TV Land; USA Network; WGN America.

Fee: $18.00 monthly.

Digital Basic Service

Subscribers: N.A.

Programming (via satellite): BBC America; Bio; Bloomberg Television; CMT Pure Country; Discovery Digital Networks; DIY Network; History Channel International; Independent Film Channel; Lifetime Movie Network; Military History Channel; MTV Networks Digital Suite; Music Choice; Nick Jr.; Nick Too; Science; Style Network; TeenNick; Toon Disney.

Digital Pay Service 1

Pay Units: N.A.

Programming (via satellite): Cinemax (multiplexed); HBO (multiplexed); Showtime (multiplexed); The Movie Channel (multiplexed).

Video-On-Demand: No

Pay-Per-View

iN DEMAND (delivered digitally); Spice 2 (delivered digitally); Playboy TV (delivered digitally).

Internet Service

Operational: Yes.

Broadband Service: Rapid High Speed Internet.

Fee: $29.95 monthly.

Telephone Service

None

Miles of Plant: 31.0 (coaxial); None (fiber optic).

Regional Manager: Ronnie Stafford. Office Manager: Jan Gibson.

Ownership: RB3 LLC (MSO).

HONEY GROVE—Suddenlink Communications, 25 19th St SE, Paris, TX 75460-6101. Phones: 903-785-0086; 888-822-5151. Fax: 903-784-7099. Web Site: http://www.suddenlink.com. ICA: TX0776.

TV Market Ranking: Outside TV Markets (HONEY GROVE). Franchise award date: N.A. Franchise expiration date: N.A. Began: N.A.

Channel capacity: 25 (not 2-way capable). Channels available but not in use: N.A.

Basic Service

Subscribers: 655.

Programming (received off-air): KDAF (CW, IND) Dallas; KDFI (MNT) Dallas; KDFW-DT (FOX) Dallas; KERA-TV (PBS) Dallas; KTEN (ABC, CW, NBC) Ada; KTVT (CBS) Fort Worth; KTXA (IND) Fort Worth; KXAS-TV (NBC) Fort Worth; KXII (CBS, FOX, MNT) Sherman; KXTX-TV (TMO) Dallas; WFAA (ABC) Dallas.

Programming (via satellite): A&E Networks; ABC Family Channel; AMC; BET Networks; Cartoon Network; CNN; C-SPAN; Discovery Channel; Disney Channel; ESPN; Headline News; HGTV; Independent Music Network; INSP; Lifetime; Nickelodeon; Spike TV; TBS Superstation; The Learning Channel; The Weather Channel; Turner Network TV; USA Network; WGN America.

Fee: $35.00 installation; $20.69 monthly.

Digital Basic Service

Subscribers: N.A.

Programming (via satellite): BBC America; Bio; Bloomberg Television; Discovery Digital Networks; DMX Music; Encore; ESPNews; Fox Soccer; Fuse; G4; Golf Channel; GSN; Halogen Network; History Channel; History Channel International; Lifetime Movie Network; MBC America; Outdoor Channel; Speed; Sundance Channel; The Word Network; Toon Disney; Trinity Broadcasting Network; Urban American Television Network; Versus.

Digital Pay Service 1

Pay Units: N.A.

Programming (via satellite): Cinemax (multiplexed); HBO (multiplexed); Showtime (multiplexed); Starz (multiplexed); The Movie Channel (multiplexed).

Video-On-Demand: No

Pay-Per-View

iN DEMAND (delivered digitally); Playboy TV (delivered digitally); Fresh (delivered digitally); Shorteez (delivered digitally); ESPN Now (delivered digitally); ESPN Gameplan (delivered digitally); ActionMax (delivered digitally).

Internet Service

Operational: Yes.

Broadband Service: Suddenlink High Speed Internet.

Telephone Service

Digital: Operational

Manager: Tim Masters. Chief Technician: Bob Holmon.

Ownership: Cequel Communications LLC (MSO).

HOOKS—Allegiance Communications, 707 W Saratoga St, Shawnee, OK 74804. Phones: 405-395-1131; 405-275-6923. Web Site: http://www.allegiance.tv. Also serves Bowie County & Red River Army Depot. ICA: TX0272.

TV Market Ranking: 58 (Bowie County (portions), HOOKS, Red River Army Depot); Outside TV Markets (Bowie County (portions)). Franchise award date: N.A. Franchise expiration date: N.A. Began: February 1, 1980.

Channel capacity: 34 (not 2-way capable). Channels available but not in use: N.A.

Basic Service

Subscribers: 1,122.

Programming (received off-air): KLTS-TV (PBS) Shreveport; KMSS-TV (FOX) Shreveport; KPXJ (CW) Minden; KSHV-TV (MNT) Shreveport; KSLA (CBS) Shreveport; KTAL-TV (NBC) Texarkana; KTBS-TV (ABC) Shreveport.

Programming (via satellite): CNBC; CNN; C-SPAN; Headline News; QVC; Texas Cable News; The Weather Channel; Trinity Broadcasting Network; TV Guide Network; WGN America.

Fee: $34.02 installation; $10.05 monthly.

Expanded Basic Service 1

Subscribers: N.A.

Programming (via satellite): A&E Networks; ABC Family Channel; AMC; Animal Planet; BET Networks; Cartoon Network; CMT Pure Country; Comedy Central; Discovery Channel; Disney Channel; ESPN; ESPN 2; ESPN Classic Sports; Fox News Channel; Fox Sports Southwest; FX; Hallmark Channel; HGTV; History Channel; Lifetime; MoviePlex; MTV; NFL Network; Nickelodeon; Spike TV; Syfy; TBS Superstation; The Learning Channel; Turner Network TV; TV Land; USA Network; VH1.

Digital Basic Service

Subscribers: N.A.

Programming (via satellite): 3 Angels Broadcasting Network; BBC America; Bio; Black Family Channel; Bloomberg Television; B-Mania; Bravo; BYU Television; Church Channel; Cine Latino; Cine Mexicano; cloo; CNN en Espanol; Daystar TV Network; Discovery en Espanol; Discovery Fit & Health; Discovery Health Channel; Discovery Home Channel; Discovery Kids Channel; Discovery Times Channel; DMX Music; Encore (multiplexed); ESPN Classic Sports; ESPNews; FamilyNet; Flix; Fox College Sports Atlantic; Fox College Sports Central; Fox College Sports Pacific; Fox Deportes; Fox Movie Channel; Fox Soccer; Fuse; G4; GAS; Golden Eagle Broadcasting; Golf Channel; Gospel Music TV; Great American Country; GSN; History Channel; History Channel en Espanol; History Channel International; JCTV; La Familia Network; Latin Television (LTV); Lifetime Movie Network; Military Channel; MTV Hits; MTV2; National Geographic Channel; Nick Jr.; NickToons TV; Outdoor Channel; Puma TV; Science; ShopNBC; Speed; Style Network; Sundance Channel; Syfy; The Word Network; Toon Disney; Toon Disney en Espanol; Tr3s; Trinity Broadcasting Network; Turner Classic Movies; TV Chile; Versus; VH1 Classic; WE tv.

Pay Service 1

Pay Units: 82.

Programming (via satellite): Encore; HBO; Showtime; Starz.

Digital Pay Service 1

Pay Units: N.A.

Programming (via satellite): Cinemax (multiplexed); HBO (multiplexed); Showtime (multiplexed); Starz (multiplexed); The Movie Channel (multiplexed).

Pay-Per-View

iN DEMAND (delivered digitally); Hot Choice (delivered digitally); Playboy TV (delivered digitally); Fresh (delivered digitally); Shorteez (delivered digitally).

Internet Service

Operational: Yes.

Telephone Service

None

Miles of Plant: 36.0 (coaxial); None (fiber optic).

Chief Executive Officer: Bill Haggarty. Regional Vice President: Andrew Dearth. Vice President, Marketing: Tracy Bass.

Ownership: Allegiance Communications (MSO).

HOUSTON—Comcast Cable, 8590 W Tidwell Rd, Houston, TX 77040. Phone: 713-462-1900. Fax: 713-895-1239. Web Site: http://www.comcast.com. Also serves Alvin, Arbor Vineyard, Ashford Park, Autumn Run, Bacliff, Bammel Oaks, Barker's Landing, Barrett Station, Bayou Vista, Baytown, Bear Creek Farms, Bellaire, Bermuda Beach, Blue Bell, Brazoria County, Briar Creek, Briar Hills, Broken Bayou, Brook Hollow West, Brookside Village, Bunker Hill, Burger Estates, Chambers County (western portion), Channelview, Chimney Hill, Clear Lake Shores, Clute, Colonies, Concord Colony, Copperfield, Cornerstone Village North, Cottonwood, Crosby, Cypress Trails, Dayton, Deer Park, Deerfield Village, Dickinson, Easton Common Village, Ed-Lou, El Lago, Enclave at Pavillion, Fleetwood, Fleetwood Oaks, Forest Bend, Fort Bend County, Freeport, Frick Road Park, Friendswood, Galena Park, Galveston, Galveston County, Granada, Harris County, Hearthstone, Hearthstone Green, Heatherglen, Hedwig, Heritage Park, Highlands, Hillcrest Village, Hillshire, Hitchcock, Houston (eastern & western suburbs), Humble, Hunter Creek, Jacinto City, Jamaica Beach, Jamestown Colony, Jersey Village, Katy, Keegans Glen, Kemah, Klienbrook, La Marque, La Porte, Lake Jackson, Langham Colony, League City, Liberty, Magnolia, Maple Leaf Gardens, Memorial Thicket, Mills Walk, Mission Bend, Missouri City, Modot Village, Montgomery County, Morgans Point, Nassau Bay, Needville, North Cliffe Manor, North Pines Ranchetts, Northwest Green, Northwest Park, Oakland Village, Omega Bay, Paddock, Pasadena, Pearland, Pinedale, Piney Point, Pirate Beach, Pirate Cove, Reid Estates, Richmond, Richwood, Rolling Fork, Rosenberg, Santa Fe, Seabrook, Sepco Park, Settlers Village, Shenandoah (unincorporated areas), Shoreacres, Sommerall, South Creek, South Houston, Spring Valley, Spring Valley Creek, Stafford, Stone Creek, Stonehenge, Suffolk Chase, Sugar Land, Sundown, Tallowood, Taylor Lake Village, Texas City, The Meadows, The Woodlands, Thornhill Apartments, Tiki Island, Tomball, Turtle Lake, Waller County, Webster, Wedgewood, West Hollow, West Hollow Villa, West Trails, West University Place, White Oak Manor, Willow Point, Windfern, Windfern Manor, Windfern Meadow, Woodfern, Woodfern Manor, Woodgate & Yorkshire. ICA: TX0001.

TV Market Ranking: 15 (Alvin, Arbor Vineyard, Ashford Park, Autumn Run, Bacliff, Bammel Oaks, Barker's Landing, Barrett Station, Baytown, Bear Creek Farms, Bellaire, Blue Bell, Brazoria County (portions), Briar Creek, Briar Hills, Broken Bayou, Brook Hollow West, Brookside Village, Bunker Hill, Burger Estates, Chambers County (western portion), Channelview, Chimney Hill, Clear Lake Shores, Colonies, Concord Colony, Copperfield, Cornerstone Village North, Cottonwood, Crosby, Cypress Trails, Deer Park, Deerfield Village, Dickinson, Easton Common Village, Ed-Lou, El Lago, Enclave at Pavillion, Fleetwood, Fleetwood Oaks, Forest Bend, Fort Bend County (portions), Frick Road Park, Friendswood, Galena Park, Galveston (portions), Granada, Harris County, Hearthstone, Hearthstone Green, Heatherglen, Hedwig, Heritage Park, Highlands, Hillcrest Village, Hillshire, HOUSTON, Humble, Hunter Creek, Jacinto City, Jamestown Colony, Jersey Village, Katy, Keegans Glen, Kemah, Klienbrook, La Porte, Langham Colony, League City, Magnolia, Maple Leaf Gardens, Memorial Thicket, Mills Walk, Mission Bend, Missouri City, Modot Village, Montgomery County (portions), Morgans Point, Nassau Bay, North Cliffe Manor, North Pines Ranchetts, Northwest Green, Northwest Park, Oakland Village, Omega Bay, Paddock, Pasadena, Pearland, Pinedale, Piney Point, Reid Estates, Richmond, Rolling Fork, Rosenberg, Santa Fe, Seabrook, Sepco Park, Settlers Village, Shenandoah (unincorporated areas), Shoreacres, Sommerall, South Creek, South Houston, Spring Valley, Spring Valley Creek, Stafford, Stone Creek, Stonehenge, Suffolk Chase, Sugar Land, Sundown, Tallowood, Taylor Lake Village, The Meadows, The Woodlands, Thornhill Apartments, Tomball, Turtle Lake, Waller County, Webster, Wedgewood, West Hollow, West Hollow Villa, West Trails, West University Place, White Oak Manor, Willow Point, Windfern, Windfern Manor, Windfern Meadow, Woodfern, Woodfern Manor, Woodgate, Yorkshire); Below 100 (Bayou Vista, Bermuda Beach, Clute, Dayton, Freeport, Galveston, Hitchcock, Jamaica Beach, La Marque, Lake Jackson, Liberty, Needville, Pirate Beach, Pirate Cove, Richwood, Texas City, Tiki Island, Brazoria County (portions), Fort Bend County (portions), Galveston (portions), Montgomery County (portions)). Franchise award date: N.A. Franchise expiration date: N.A. Began: August 1, 1979.

Channel capacity: N.A. Channels available but not in use: N.A.

Basic Service

Subscribers: 790,000.

Programming (received off-air): KETH-TV (TBN) Houston; KFTH-DT (TEL) Alvin; KHOU (CBS) Houston; KIAH (CW) Houston; KLTJ (ETV) Galveston; KPRC-TV (NBC) Houston; KPXB-TV (ION) Conroe; KRIV (FOX) Houston; KTBU (IND) Conroe; KTMD (TMO) Galveston; KTRK-TV (ABC) Houston; KTXH (MNT) Houston; KUBE-TV (IND) Baytown; KUHT (PBS) Houston; KXLN-DT (UNV) Rosenberg; KYAZ (IND) Katy; KZJL (IND) Houston; 4 FMs.

Programming (via satellite): CNN International; ICTV; TV Guide Network; WGN America.

Fee: $42.95 installation; $16.42 monthly; $2.76 converter.

Expanded Basic Service 1

Subscribers: 526,208.

Programming (via satellite): A&E Networks; ABC Family Channel; AMC; Animal Planet; BET Networks; Bravo; Cartoon Network; CNBC; CNN; Comedy Central; C-SPAN; C-SPAN 2; Discovery Channel; Disney Channel; E! Entertainment Television; ESPN; ESPN 2; Food Network; Fox News Channel; Fox Sports Southwest; FX; GalaVision; Golf Channel; Hallmark Channel; Headline News; HGTV; History Channel; Lifetime; Lifetime Movie Network; MSNBC; MTV; mun2 television; National Geographic Channel; Nickelodeon; QVC; ShopNBC; Spike TV; Syfy; TBS Superstation; The Learning Channel; The Weather Channel; Travel Channel; truTV; Turner Classic Movies; Turner Network TV; USA Network; Versus; VH1; WE tv.

Fee: $25.39 installation; $28.79 monthly.

Digital Basic Service

Subscribers: 480,000.

Programming (via satellite): America's Store; BBC America; Black Family Channel; Bloomberg Television; CCTV-4; Country Music TV; C-SPAN 3; Discovery Fit & Health; ESPN Classic Sports; ESPNews; Eternal Word TV Network; Fox Sports World; Fuse; G4; Great American Country; Halogen Network; INSP; Lifetime Real Women; LWS Local Weather Station; MTV2; Music Choice; NASA TV; Nick Jr.; Oxygen; SoapNet; Style Network; Tennis Channel; Texas Cable News; Toon Disney; TV Land; VH1 Classic.

Fee: $3.00 monthly.

Digital Expanded Basic Service

Subscribers: N.A.

Programming (via satellite): Bio; Cooking Channel; Discovery Times Channel; DIY Network; FamilyNet; GSN; History Channel International; Ovation.

Fee: $5.00 monthly.

Digital Expanded Basic Service 2

Subscribers: N.A.

Programming (via satellite): FSN Digital Atlantic; FSN Digital Central; FSN Digital Pacific; Outdoor Channel; Speed.

Fee: $2.00 monthly.

Digital Pay Service 1

Pay Units: 79,857.

Programming (via satellite): Cinemax (multiplexed).

Fee: $4.95 installation; $10.00 monthly.

Digital Pay Service 2

Pay Units: 167,687.

Programming (via satellite): HBO (multiplexed).

Fee: $4.95 installation; $10.00 monthly.

Digital Pay Service 3

Pay Units: 31,971.

Programming (via satellite): The Movie Channel (multiplexed).

Fee: $4.95 installation; $10.00 monthly.

Digital Pay Service 4

Pay Units: 98,964.

Programming (via satellite): Showtime (multiplexed).

Fee: $10.00 monthly.

Digital Pay Service 5

Pay Units: N.A.

Programming (via satellite): ART America; Canales N; Chinese Television Network; Fox Movie Channel; Independent Film Channel; Korean Channel; RAI USA; Russian Television Network; Saigon Broadcasting Television Network; Starz (multiplexed); Sundance Channel; TV Asia; Zee TV USA; Zhong Tian Channel.

Fee: $4.95 installation; $3.00 monthly (Canales N or FMC, IFC, Sundance & Encore), $8.00 monthly (Starz!), $9.95 monthly (RAI or TV5), $11.95 monthly (CTN), $12.95 monthly ART or Korean), $14.95 monthly (RTN, SPN, TV Asia or Zee TV).

Video-On-Demand: Yes

Pay-Per-View

Addressable homes: 354,975.

Playboy TV; movies.

Internet Service

Operational: Yes. Began: October 1, 1999.

Subscribers: 430,000.

Broadband Service: Comcast High Speed Internet.

Fee: $99.99 installation; $44.95 monthly.

Telephone Service

Digital: Operational

Subscribers: 90,000.

Fee: $44.95 monthly

Miles of Plant: 21,500.0 (coaxial); None (fiber optic). Miles of plant (fiber) included in miles of plant (coax)

Vice President & General Manager: Tony Speller. Vice President, Operations: Keith Coogan. Vice President, Customer Care: Marie Grumbles. Vice President, Public Affairs: Ray Purser.

Ownership: Comcast Cable Communications Inc. (MSO).

HOUSTON—En-Touch Systems Inc., 11011 Richmond Ave, Ste 400, Houston, TX 77042. Phones: 832-590-5500; 281-225-1000 (Customer service). Fax: 832-225-0540. E-mail: marketing@entouch.net. Web Site: http://www.entouch.net. Also serves Blackhorse Ranch, Coles Crossing, Gleannlock Farms, Harris County (portions), Sienna Plantation, Stablegate, Summerwood & Westgate. ICA: TX0982. **Note:** This system is an overbuild.

TV Market Ranking: 15 (Blackhorse Ranch, Coles Crossing, Gleannock Farms, Harris County (portions), HOUSTON, Sienna Plantation, Stablegate, Summerwood, Westgate). Franchise award date: N.A. Franchise expiration date: N.A. Began: January 1, 1996.

Channel capacity: N.A. Channels available but not in use: N.A.

Basic Service

Subscribers: 10,000.

Programming (received off-air): KETH-TV (TBN) Houston; KFTH-DT (TEL) Alvin; KHOU (CBS) Houston; KIAH (CW) Houston; KLTJ (ETV) Galveston; KPRC-TV (NBC) Houston; KPXB-TV (ION) Conroe; KRIV (FOX) Houston; KTBU (IND) Conroe; KTMD (TMO) Galveston; KTRK-TV (ABC) Houston; KTXH (MNT) Houston; KUBE-TV (IND) Baytown; KUHT (PBS) Houston; KXLN-DT (UNV) Rosenberg; KYAZ (IND) Katy; KZJL (IND) Houston.

Programming (via satellite): ABC Family Channel; Animal Planet; BET Networks; Cartoon Network; CNBC; CNN; Country Music TV; Discovery Channel; Fox News Channel; Hallmark Channel; Headline News; Lifetime; MSNBC; MTV; Nickelodeon; QVC; SoapNet; TBS Superstation; The Learning Channel; The Weather Channel; Toon Disney; Travel Channel; Turner Network TV; TV Land; VH1.

Fee: $25.95 monthly.

Expanded Basic Service 1

Subscribers: N.A.

Programming (via satellite): A&E Networks; AMC; Bravo; Comedy Central; C-SPAN; C-SPAN 2; Discovery Fit & Health; Disney Channel; E! Entertainment Television; ESPN; ESPN 2; Food Network; Fox Sports Southwest; FX; HGTV; History Channel; Syfy; truTV; Turner Classic Movies; USA Network.

Fee: $24.00 monthly.

Digital Basic Service

Subscribers: 7,000.

Programming (via satellite): AmericanLife TV Network; BBC America; Bio; Bloomberg Television; DMX Music; ESPN Classic Sports; ESPN HD; Fuse; G4; Golf Channel; GSN; Halogen Network; HD Theater; HDNet; HDNet Movies; History Channel International; Lifetime Movie Network; Lime; MTV Networks Digital Suite; National Geographic Channel; Nick Jr.; NickToons TV; Outdoor Channel; TeenNick; Trio; Turner Network TV HD; WE tv.

Fee: $46.50 monthly.

Digital Expanded Basic Service

Subscribers: N.A.

Programming (via satellite): Canales N; Encore (multiplexed); ESPNews; Flix; Fox College Sports Atlantic; Fox College Sports Central; Fox College Sports Pacific; Fox Movie Channel; Fox Soccer; Independent Film Channel; Speed; Sundance Channel; Versus.

Fee: $3.50 monthly (sports tier), $4.50 monthly (movie tier or Americas tier).

Digital Pay Service 1

Pay Units: N.A.

Programming (via satellite): ART America; CCTV News; Chinese Television Network; Cinemax (multiplexed); HBO (multiplexed); HBO HD; MBC America; RAI International; Saigon Broadcasting Television Network; Showtime (multiplexed); Showtime HD; Starz (multiplexed); The Movie Channel (multiplexed); TV Asia; TV Japan; TV5 USA.

Fee: $7.95 monthly (Starz), $9.95 monthly (Cinemax), $15.95 (Showtime, TMC or HBO).

Video-On-Demand: Planned

Pay-Per-View

iN DEMAND (delivered digitally); Shorteez (delivered digitally); Playboy TV (delivered digitally); Hot Choice (delivered digitally); Fresh (delivered digitally); ESPN Gameplan (delivered digitally); NBA League Pass (delivered digitally); NHL Center Ice (delivered digitally); MLB Extra Innings (delivered digitally).

Internet Service

Operational: Yes.
Subscribers: 6,500.
Broadband Service: BroadbandNOW!.
Fee: $11.95 monthly; $14.95 modem lease.

Telephone Service

Digital: Operational
Fee: $48.50 monthly

Miles of Plant: 1,500.0 (coaxial); None (fiber optic).
President: Richard Gerstemeier. Operations Director: Wesley Pennix. Marketing Director: Tammy Kennedy. Marketing Manager: Arlene Thomas.
Ownership: En-Touch Systems Inc.

HOUSTON—Formerly served by Sprint Corp. No longer in operation. ICA: TX0893.

HOUSTON—Phonoscope Ltd., 6105 Westline Dr, Houston, TX 77036-3515. Phone: 713-272-4600. Fax: 713-271-4334. Web Site: http://www.phonoscope.com. Also serves Fort Bend County (portions), Richmond & Rosenberg. ICA: TX0777.

TV Market Ranking: 15 (Fort Bend County (portions) (portions), HOUSTON, Richmond, Rosenberg); Below 100 (Fort Bend County (portions) (portions)). Franchise award date: September 1, 1986. Franchise expiration date: N.A. Began: January 1, 1987.

Channel capacity: 110 (operating 2-way). Channels available but not in use: N.A.

Basic Service

Subscribers: 3,742.
Programming (received off-air): KETH-TV (TBN) Houston; KFTH-DT (TEL) Alvin; KHOU (CBS) Houston; KIAH (CW) Houston; KLTJ (ETV) Galveston; KPRC-TV (NBC) Houston; KPXB-TV (ION) Conroe; KRIV (FOX) Houston; KTBU (IND) Conroe; KTMD (TMO) Galveston; KTRK-TV (ABC) Houston; KTXH (MNT) Houston; KUBE-TV (IND) Baytown; KUHT (PBS) Houston; KXLN-DT (UNV) Rosenberg; KYAZ (IND) Katy; KZJL (IND) Houston.
Programming (via satellite): A&E Networks; ABC Family Channel; AMC; Animal Planet; BET Networks; Bloomberg Television; Cartoon Network; CCTV-4; CNBC; CNN; CNN International; Comedy Central; Country Music TV; C-SPAN; C-SPAN 2; C-SPAN 3; Current; Discovery Channel; Discovery Fit & Health; Disney Channel; E! Entertainment Television; ESPN; ESPN 2; ESPN Classic Sports; Food Network; Fox News Channel; Fox Sports Southwest; FX; Hallmark Channel; Headline News; HGTV; History Channel; Lifetime; MSNBC; MTV; NASA TV; Nickelodeon; Oxygen; QVC; Spike TV; Syfy; TBS Superstation; The Learning Channel; The Weather Channel; Travel Channel; truTV; Turner Classic Movies; Turner Network TV; TV Guide Network; TV Land; USA Network; VH1; WGN America.
Fee: $25.00 installation; $36.95 monthly.

Digital Basic Service

Subscribers: N.A.
Programming (via satellite): AmericanLife TV Network; BBC America; Bio; Black Family Channel; Canales N; CBS Sports Network; cloo; Colours; Cooking Channel; DIY Network; DMX Music; ESPNews; Eternal Word TV Network; Familyland Television Network; Flix; Food Network HD; Fox Movie Channel; Fox Soccer; FSN Digital Atlantic; FSN Digital Central; FSN Digital Pacific; Fuse; G4; GAS; Golf Channel; Great American Country; GSN; Halogen Network; HD Theater; Healthy Living Channel; HGTV HD; History Channel International; Independent Film Channel; INHD; INHD2; JCTV; Lifetime Movie Network; Lime; MTV Networks Digital Suite; National Geographic Channel; National Geographic Channel HD Network; NFL Network; Nick Jr.; NickToons TV; Outdoor Channel; Ovation; SoapNet; Soundtrack Channel; Speed; Style Network; Sundance Channel; Tennis Channel; The Word Network; Toon Disney; Trinity Broadcasting Network; Universal HD; Versus; WE tv; WealthTV.
Fee: $12.00 monthly.

Digital Pay Service 1

Pay Units: N.A.
Programming (via satellite): Cinemax (multiplexed); Encore (multiplexed); HBO (multiplexed); Showtime (multiplexed); Starz (multiplexed); The Movie Channel (multiplexed).
Fee: $9.95 monthly (Starz & Encore), $12.95 monthly (Showtime & TMC), $18.95 monthly (HBO & Cinemax).

Video-On-Demand: Planned

Pay-Per-View

iN DEMAND (delivered digitally); Fresh (delivered digitally); Shorteez (delivered digitally); Playboy TV (delivered digitally); Hustler TV (delivered digitally); Hot Choice (delivered digitally); ESPN (delivered digitally).

Internet Service

Operational: Yes.
Broadband Service: In-house.
Fee: $25.00 installation; $19.95 monthly.

Telephone Service

Digital: Operational
Fee: $29.95 monthly

President: Rhonda Druke. Marketing Manager: Tracy Garrett. Technical Operations Manager: Ron Cruz. Program Director: Otis Dyson.
Ownership: Phonoscope Ltd.

HOUSTON—TV Max, 10300 W Office Dr, Ste 200, Houston, TX 77042. Phones: 713-587-1238 (Customer service); 713-587-1200. Fax: 713-587-1212. Web Site: http://www.tvmax.com. ICA: TX1009.

TV Market Ranking: 15 (HOUSTON).
Channel capacity: N.A. Channels available but not in use: N.A.

Basic Service

Subscribers: N.A.
Programming (received off-air): KETH-TV (TBN) Houston; KFTH-DT (TEL) Alvin; KHOU (CBS) Houston; KIAH (CW) Houston; KLTJ (ETV) Galveston; KPRC-TV (NBC) Houston; KPXB-TV (ION) Conroe; KRIV (FOX) Houston; KTBU (IND) Conroe; KTMD (TMO) Galveston; KTRK-TV (ABC) Houston; KTXH (MNT) Houston; KUBE-TV (IND) Baytown; KUHT (PBS) Houston; KUVM-CD Dewalt; KXLN-DT (UNV) Rosenberg; KYAZ (IND) Katy; KZJL (IND) Houston.
Programming (via satellite): C-SPAN; Eternal Word TV Network; GalaVision; QVC; The Weather Channel; TV Guide Network; WGN America.
Fee: $25.00 installation; $13.99 monthly; $9.95 additional installation.

Expanded Basic Service 1

Subscribers: N.A.
Programming (via satellite): A&E Networks; ABC Family Channel; AMC; Animal Planet; BET Networks; Cartoon Network; CNBC; CNN; Comedy Central; Discovery Channel; Disney Channel; E! Entertainment Television; ESPN; ESPN 2; Food Network; Fox News Channel; Fox Sports Net; FX; Hallmark Channel; Headline News; HGTV; History Channel; Lifetime; MSNBC; MTV; Nickelodeon; Nuvo TV; SoapNet; Speed; Spike TV; Syfy; TBS Superstation; The Learning Channel; Travel Channel; truTV; Turner Network TV; TV Land; USA Network; VH1.
Fee: $33.99 monthly.

Digital Basic Service

Subscribers: N.A.
Programming (via satellite): ABC News Now; AmericanLife TV Network; AZ TV; BBC America; Bloomberg Television; Bravo; cloo; CMT Pure Country; Current; Daystar TV Network; Discovery Fit & Health; Discovery Health Channel; Discovery Home Channel; Discovery Kids Channel; DMX Music; ESPN Classic Sports; ESPN U; ESPNews; Fox Business Channel; Fox Reality Channel; Fox Soccer; Fuse; G4; GMC; Golf Channel; Great American Country; GSN; Halogen Network; ID Investigation Discovery; Independent Film Channel; Lifetime Movie Network; Military Channel; MTV Hits; MTV2; National Geographic Channel; Nick Jr.; NickToons TV; Outdoor Channel; Ovation; Science; ShopNBC; Style Network; Syfy; TeenNick; The Word Network; Toon Disney; Trinity Broadcasting Network; Turner Classic Movies; Versus; VH1 Classic; VH1 Soul; WE tv; WealthTV.
Fee: $46.99 monthly.

Digital Expanded Basic Service

Subscribers: N.A.
Programming (via satellite): Fox College Sports Atlantic; Fox College Sports Central; Fox College Sports Pacific.
Fee: $2.99 monthly.

Pay Service 1

Pay Units: N.A.
Programming (via satellite): HBO; Showtime.

Digital Pay Service 1

Pay Units: N.A.
Fee: $5.99 monthly (Canales N), $14.00 monthly (HBO, Showtime/TMC, Cinemax, or Starz).

Video-On-Demand: No

Pay-Per-View

Special events (delivered digitally); Movies (delivered digitally); Fresh (delivered digitally); Shorteez (delivered digitally); Playboy TV (delivered digitally); Club Jenna (delivered digitally); Hot Choice (delivered digitally).

Internet Service

Operational: Yes.
Broadband Service: In-house.
Fee: $30.00-$60.00 monthly.

Telephone Service

Digital: Operational
Fee: $35 monthly

Vice President, Operations: David Curtain. Office Manager: Sandra Harrison.
Ownership: TVMAX.

HOWARDWICK—Formerly served by Almega Cable. No longer in operation. ICA: TX0602.

HUBBARD—Almega Cable, 4001 W Airport Frwy, Ste 530, Bedford, TX 76021. Phone: 817-685-9588. Fax: 817-685-6488. E-mail: helpdesk@almegacable.com. Web Site: http://www.almega.com. Also serves Dawson. ICA: TX0393.

TV Market Ranking: Below 100 (HUBBARD); Outside TV Markets (Dawson). Franchise award date: N.A. Franchise expiration date: N.A. Began: July 1, 1983.
Channel capacity: 52 (not 2-way capable). Channels available but not in use: N.A.

Basic Service

Subscribers: 357.
Programming (received off-air): KDAF (CW, IND) Dallas; KDFI (MNT) Dallas; KDFW-DT (FOX) Dallas; KDTN (ETV) Denton; KDTX-TV (TBN) Dallas; KERA-TV (PBS) Dallas; KSTR-DT (TEL) Irving; KTVT (CBS) Fort Worth; KTXA (IND) Fort Worth; KUVN-DT (UNV) Garland; KWTX-TV (CBS, CW) Waco; KXAS-TV (NBC) Fort Worth; KXTX-TV (TMO) Dallas; WFAA (ABC) Dallas.
Programming (via satellite): C-SPAN; C-SPAN 2; WGN America.
Fee: $54.95 installation; $20.95 monthly.

Expanded Basic Service 1

Subscribers: N.A.
Programming (via satellite): ABC Family Channel; AMC; Animal Planet; CNBC; CNN; Country Music TV; Discovery Channel; Disney Channel; E! Entertainment Television; ESPN; ESPN 2; ESPNews; Fox Sports Southwest; Headline News; HGTV; History Channel; Lifetime; MTV; Nickelodeon; Spike TV; TBS Superstation; The Learning Channel; The Weather Channel; Toon Disney; Turner Network TV; TV Land; USA Network.
Fee: $23.10 monthly.

Pay Service 1

Pay Units: N.A.
Programming (via satellite): HBO; Showtime; The Movie Channel.
Fee: $12.95 monthly (each).

Video-On-Demand: No

Pay-Per-View

Hot Choice (delivered digitally); Playboy TV (delivered digitally); Fresh (delivered digitally); Shorteez (delivered digitally); iN DEMAND (delivered digitally).

Internet Service

Operational: No.

Telephone Service

None

Miles of Plant: 30.0 (coaxial); None (fiber optic).
Ownership: Almega Cable (MSO).

HUDSON—Suddenlink Communications, 1415 S 1st St, Lufkin, TX 75901-4749. Phone: 936-639-1116. Fax: 936-634-6889. Web Site: http://www.suddenlink.com. ICA: TX0357.

TV Market Ranking: Below 100 (HUDSON). Franchise award date: N.A. Franchise expiration date: N.A. Began: December 1, 1982.

Channel capacity: 59 (2-way capable). Channels available but not in use: N.A.

Basic Service

Subscribers: 814.

Programming (received off-air): KCEB (CW) Longview; KFXL-LP Lufkin; KHOU (CBS) Houston; KIBN-LP Lufkin; KLUF-LP Lufkin; KPRC-TV (NBC) Houston; KTRE (ABC) Lufkin; KTRK-TV (ABC) Houston; KUHT (PBS) Houston; KXTX-TV (TMO) Dallas; KYTX (CBS, IND) Nacogdoches.

Programming (via satellite): ION Television; QVC; TBS Superstation; Univision Studios.

Fee: $35.00 installation; $9.89 monthly.

Expanded Basic Service 1

Subscribers: N.A.

Programming (via satellite): A&E Networks; ABC Family Channel; BET Networks; Bravo; Cartoon Network; CNBC; CNN; Comedy Central; Country Music TV; C-SPAN; C-SPAN 2; Discovery Channel; Discovery Health Channel; Disney Channel; E! Entertainment Television; ESPN; ESPN 2; Eternal Word TV Network; Food Network; Fox News Channel; Fox Sports Southwest; FX; Great American Country; Headline News; HGTV; History Channel; INSP; Lifetime; MTV; MTV2; Nickelodeon; Spike TV; Syfy; The Learning Channel; The Weather Channel; Travel Channel; truTV; Turner Classic Movies; Turner Network TV; TV Guide Network; USA Network; Versus; VH1.

Fee: $39.18 monthly.

Digital Basic Service

Subscribers: N.A.

Programming (via satellite): BBC America; Bio; Bloomberg Television; Boomerang; Canales N; Cooking Channel; Discovery Fit & Health; DIY Network; Encore (multiplexed); ESPN; ESPN Classic Sports; ESPNews; FamilyNet; Fox Reality Channel; Fox Soccer; Fuel TV; Fuse; G4; GAS; Golf Channel; GSN; Hallmark Channel; Halogen Network; HD Theater; History Channel International; Independent Film Channel; INHD; Lifetime Movie Network; MTV Networks Digital Suite; Music Choice; National Geographic Channel; NBA TV; Nick Jr.; NickToons TV; Nuvo TV; Outdoor Channel; SoapNet; Speed; Style Network; Sundance Channel; Tennis Channel; Toon Disney; Trinity Broadcasting Network; Turner Classic Movies; Universal HD; Weatherscan.

Digital Pay Service 1

Pay Units: N.A.

Programming (via satellite): Cinemax (multiplexed); HBO (multiplexed); HBO HD; Showtime (multiplexed); Showtime HD; Starz (multiplexed); Starz HDTV; The Movie Channel (multiplexed).

Pay-Per-View

ESPN Gameplan (delivered digitally); NBA League Pass (delivered digitally); iN DEMAND (delivered digitally); MLS Direct Kick (delivered digitally); MLB Extra Innings (delivered digitally); NHL Center Ice (delivered digitally); Fresh (delivered digitally); Shorteez (delivered digitally); Playboy TV (delivered digitally); Hot Choice (delivered digitally).

Internet Service

Operational: No.

Telephone Service

None

Miles of Plant: 35.0 (coaxial); None (fiber optic).

Manager: Glenn Parker. Marketing Director: Mike Evans. Chief Technician: Jerry Teer.

Ownership: Cequel Communications LLC (MSO).

HULL—Formerly served by Carrell Communications. No longer in operation. ICA: TX0299.

HUNTINGTON—Formerly served by CommuniComm Services. No longer in operation. ICA: TX0417.

HUNTSVILLE—Suddenlink Communications, 1620 Normal Park D, Huntsville, TX 77340-4235. Phone: 888-822-5151. Fax: 409-295-5851. Web Site: http://www.suddenlink.com. Also serves Elkins Lake & Walker County. ICA: TX0094.

TV Market Ranking: Below 100 (Elkins Lake, HUNTSVILLE, Walker County (portions)); Outside TV Markets (Walker County (portions)). Franchise award date: N.A. Franchise expiration date: N.A. Began: August 9, 1962.

Channel capacity: N.A. Channels available but not in use: N.A.

Basic Service

Subscribers: 7,013.

Programming (received off-air): KBTX-TV (CBS, CW) Bryan; KFTH-DT (TEL) Alvin; KHOU (CBS) Houston; KHTX-LP (IND) Huntsville; KIAH (CW) Houston; KPRC-TV (NBC) Houston; KPXB-TV (ION) Conroe; KRIV (FOX) Houston; KTBU (IND) Conroe; KTMD (TMO) Galveston; KTRK-TV (ABC) Houston; KTXH (MNT) Houston; KUBE-TV (IND) Baytown; KUHT (PBS) Houston; KXLN-DT (UNV) Rosenberg; KYAZ (IND) Katy; allband FM.

Programming (via satellite): Eternal Word TV Network; Fox Sports Southwest; Jewelry Television; TBS Superstation; The Weather Channel.

Fee: $38.00 installation; $16.25 monthly; $2.25 converter.

Expanded Basic Service 1

Subscribers: N.A.

Programming (via satellite): A&E Networks; ABC Family Channel; AMC; Animal Planet; BET Networks; Bravo; Cartoon Network; CNBC; CNN; Comedy Central; Country Music TV; C-SPAN; C-SPAN 2; Discovery Channel; Discovery Health Channel; Disney Channel; E! Entertainment Television; ESPN; ESPN 2; Food Network; Fox News Channel; FX; GalaVision; Great American Country; Headline News; HGTV; History Channel; Lifetime; Lifetime Movie Network; MSNBC; MTV; Nickelodeon; Oxygen; QVC; Speed; Spike TV; The Learning Channel; Travel Channel; truTV; Turner Network TV; TV Land; USA Network; Versus; VH1.

Digital Basic Service

Subscribers: N.A.

Programming (via satellite): A&E HD; Bandamax; BBC America; Bio; Bloomberg Television; Boomerang en Espanol; CBS Sports Network; Cine Latino; Cine Mexicano; CMT Pure Country; CNN en Espanol; Cooking Channel; De Pelicula; De Pelicula Clasico; Discovery en Espanol; Discovery Home Channel; Discovery Kids Channel; DIY Network; Encore (multiplexed); ESPN 2 HD; ESPN Classic Sports; ESPN Deportes; ESPN HD; ESPN U; ESPNews; EWTN en Espanol; Food Network HD; Fox Deportes; Fox Reality Channel; Fox Soccer; FSN HD; Fuel TV; Fuse; G4; GalaVision; Golf Channel; GSN; Hallmark Channel; HD Theater; HDNet; HDNet Movies; HGTV HD; History Channel en Espanol; History Channel International; ID Investigation Discovery; Independent Film Channel; Latele Novela Network; Military Channel; MTV Hits; MTV2; mtvU; mun2 television; Music Choice; National Geographic Channel; National Geographic Channel HD Network; Nick Jr.; NickToons en Espanol; NickToons TV; Outdoor Channel; Palladia; Ritmoson Latino; Science; SoapNet; Sorpresa; Sundance Channel; Sur Network; Syfy; TBN Enlace USA; TeenNick; Telehit; Toon Disney; Toon Disney en Espanol; Tr3s; Turner Classic Movies; Turner Network TV HD; TV Chile; Universal HD; VH1 Classic; Video Rola.

Digital Pay Service 1

Pay Units: N.A.

Programming (via satellite): Cinemax (multiplexed); HBO (multiplexed); HBO HD; HBO Latino; Showtime (multiplexed); Showtime HD; Starz (multiplexed); Starz HDTV; The Movie Channel (multiplexed).

Video-On-Demand: No

Pay-Per-View

Playboy TV (delivered digitally); Fresh (delivered digitally); iN DEMAND (delivered digitally); NBA TV (delivered digitally); ESPN Gameplan (delivered digitally); ESPN Now (delivered digitally).

Internet Service

Operational: Yes.

Broadband Service: Suddenlink High Speed Internet.

Telephone Service

Digital: Operational

Miles of Plant: 183.0 (coaxial); None (fiber optic).

Manager: Johnnie D. Schmidt. Chief Technician: Mark Schmidt.

Ownership: Cequel Communications LLC (MSO).

IDALOU—Reach Broadband, 515 E Longview St, Arp, TX 75750. Phone: 800-687-1258. Web Site: http://www.reachbroadband.net. ICA: TX0406.

TV Market Ranking: Below 100 (IDALOU). Franchise award date: December 13, 1988. Franchise expiration date: N.A. Began: May 1, 1980.

Channel capacity: 61 (not 2-way capable). Channels available but not in use: N.A.

Basic Service

Subscribers: 195.

Programming (received off-air): KAMC (ABC) Lubbock; KCBD (NBC) Lubbock; KJTV-TV (FOX) Lubbock; KLBK-TV (CBS) Lubbock; KPTB-DT (IND) Lubbock; KTXT-TV (PBS) Lubbock.

Programming (via satellite): ABC Family Channel; AMC; Cartoon Network; CNN; Country Music TV; Discovery Channel; Disney Channel; E! Entertainment Television; ESPN; Fox News Channel; Fox Sports Southwest; Headline News; HGTV; History Channel; Lifetime; Nickelodeon; QVC; Spike TV; TBS Superstation; The Learning Channel; The Weather Channel; Travel Channel; Trinity Broadcasting Network; Turner Network TV; TV Land; USA Network; WGN America.

Programming (via translator): KVDA (TMO) San Antonio.

Fee: $29.95 installation; $38.00 monthly.

Pay Service 1

Pay Units: 40.

Programming (via satellite): Cinemax.

Fee: $9.95 monthly.

Pay Service 2

Pay Units: 79.

Programming (via satellite): HBO.

Fee: $9.95 monthly.

Video-On-Demand: No

Internet Service

Operational: No.

Telephone Service

None

Miles of Plant: 11.0 (coaxial); None (fiber optic).

Regional Manager: Ronnie Stafford. Office Manager: Jan Gibson.

Ownership: RB3 LLC (MSO).

IMPERIAL—Formerly served by Cebridge Connections. No longer in operation. ICA: TX0968.

INDIAN SPRINGS—Formerly served by Cebridge Connections. No longer in operation. ICA: TX0385.

INGRAM—Suddenlink Communications, 12444 Powerscourt Dr, Saint Louis, MO 63131-3660. Phone: 314-965-2020. Web Site: http://www.suddenlink.com. Also serves Hunt & Kerr County (portions). ICA: TX0232.

TV Market Ranking: Below 100 (Hunt, INGRAM, Kerr County (portions)). Franchise award date: N.A. Franchise expiration date: N.A. Began: November 1, 1966.

Channel capacity: 41 (operating 2-way). Channels available but not in use: N.A.

Basic Service

Subscribers: 1,946.

Programming (received off-air): KABB (FOX) San Antonio; KENS (CBS) San Antonio; KLRN (PBS) San Antonio; KMOL-LP Victoria; KMYS (CW) Kerrville; KPXL-TV (ION) Uvalde; KSAT-TV (ABC) San Antonio; KVHC-LP Kerrville; allband FM.

Fee: $39.95 installation; $18.95 monthly.

Expanded Basic Service 1

Subscribers: N.A.

Programming (via satellite): A&E Networks; ABC Family Channel; AMC; Animal Planet; Bravo; Cartoon Network; CNBC; CNN; Comedy Central; C-SPAN; Discovery Channel; Disney Channel; E! Entertainment Television; ESPN; ESPN 2; Food Network; Fox News Channel; Fox Sports Southwest; FX; GalaVision; Golf Channel; Great American Country; Hallmark Channel; Headline News; HGTV; History Channel; Lifetime; MSNBC; MTV; National Geographic Channel; Nickelodeon; Outdoor Channel; QVC; Shop at Home; Shopping Channel; Speed; Spike TV; Syfy; TBS Superstation; The Learning Channel; The Weather Channel; Travel Channel; Trinity Broadcasting Network; Turner Classic Movies; Turner Network TV; TV Land; Univision Studios; USA Network; VH1.

Fee: $26.00 monthly.

Digital Basic Service

Subscribers: N.A.

Programming (via satellite): BBC America; Bio; Bloomberg Television; cloo; Discovery Digital Networks; DMX Music; ESPN Classic Sports; ESPNews; Fox Soccer; Fuse; G4; GSN; History Channel International; Independent Film Channel; Military History Channel; Sundance Channel; Toon Disney; Versus; WE tv.

Fee: $3.99 monthly.

Pay Service 1

Pay Units: 74.

Programming (via satellite): Cinemax.

Fee: $9.95 monthly.

Pay Service 2
Pay Units: 206.
Programming (via satellite): HBO.
Fee: $10.95 monthly.
Pay Service 3
Pay Units: 150.
Programming (via satellite): Showtime.
Fee: $9.95 monthly.
Pay Service 4
Pay Units: 290.
Programming (via satellite): The Movie Channel.
Fee: $7.95 monthly.
Digital Pay Service 1
Pay Units: N.A.
Programming (via satellite): Cinemax (multiplexed); Encore (multiplexed); HBO (multiplexed); Showtime (multiplexed); Starz (multiplexed); The Movie Channel (multiplexed).
Pay-Per-View
iN DEMAND (delivered digitally); Playboy TV (delivered digitally); Fresh (delivered digitally); Shorteez (delivered digitally).
Internet Service
Operational: Yes. Began: July 1, 2002.
Broadband Service: Suddenlink High Speed Internet.
Fee: $45.95 installation; $29.95 monthly.
Telephone Service
Digital: Operational
Fee: $44.95 monthly
Miles of Plant: 112.0 (coaxial); None (fiber optic).
Regional Manager: Todd Cruthird. Plant Manager: Jimmy Welch. Regional Marketing Manager: Beverly Gambell.
Ownership: Cequel Communications LLC (MSO).

IOLA—Formerly served by National Cable Inc. No longer in operation. ICA: TX0677.

IOWA PARK—Formerly served by Cebridge Connections. Now served by BURKBURNETT, TX [TX0154]. ICA: TX0211.

IRAAN—US Cable of Coastal Texas LP, 611 W Ave A, Seminole, TX 79360. Phones: 432-758-9221; 800-996-8788. Fax: 432-758-3379. Web Site: http://www.uscable.com. ICA: TX1028.
TV Market Ranking: Outside TV Markets (IRAAN).
Channel capacity: N.A. Channels available but not in use: N.A.
Basic Service
Subscribers: 127.
Programming (received off-air): KMID (ABC) Midland; KMLM-DT (IND) Odessa; KOSA-TV (CBS, MNT) Odessa; KPBT-TV (PBS) Odessa; KPEJ-TV (FOX) Odessa; KTLE-LP (TMO) Odessa; KUPB (UNV) Midland; KWES-TV (NBC) Odessa; KWWT (CW) Odessa.
Programming (via satellite): A&E Networks; ABC Family Channel; C-SPAN; Hallmark Channel; Home Shopping Network; Lifetime; TBS Superstation; The Weather Channel; Trinity Broadcasting Network; WGN America.
Fee: $39.96 installation; $20.17 monthly.
Expanded Basic Service 1
Subscribers: N.A.
Programming (via satellite): American Movie Classics; Animal Planet; Cartoon Network; CNN; Country Music TV; Discovery Channel; Disney Channel; ESPN; ESPN 2; Fox News Channel; Fox Sports Net; History Channel; MoviePlex; MTV; National Geographic Channel; Nick At Nite; Nickelodeon; Spike TV; Syfy; Telefutura; The Learning Channel; Travel Channel; Turner Network TV; USA Network; VH1.
Fee: $28.35 monthly.
Digital Basic Service
Subscribers: N.A.
Programming (via satellite): BBC America; Bio; Bloomberg Television; Bravo; Centric; cloo; CMT Pure Country; Current; Discovery Fit & Health; Discovery Health Channel; Discovery Kids Channel; Disney XD; DMX Music; Encore (multiplexed); ESPN Classic Sports; ESPNews; Fox College Sports Atlantic; Fox College Sports Central; Fox College Sports Pacific; Fox Movie Channel; Fox Soccer; Fuse; G4; Golf Channel; Great American Country; GSN; Halogen Network; HGTV; History Channel International; ID Investigation Discovery; Independent Film Channel; Lifetime Movie Network; Military Channel; MTV Hits; MTV2; Nick Jr.; Outdoor Channel; Planet Green; Science; Speed; Style Network; TeenNick; The Word Network; Turner Classic Movies; Versus; VH1 Classic; VH1 Soul; WE tv.
Fee: $20.90 monthly.
Pay Service 1
Pay Units: N.A.
Programming (via satellite): HBO.
Fee: $13.95 monthly.
Digital Pay Service 1
Pay Units: N.A.
Programming (via satellite): Cinemax (multiplexed); HBO (multiplexed); Showtime (multiplexed); Starz (multiplexed); The Movie Channel (multiplexed).
Fee: $9.95 monthly (Starz), $12.95 monthly (HBO, Cinemax, Showtime or TMC).
Video-On-Demand: No
Pay-Per-View
Event Entertainment (delivered digitally); Movies (delivered digitally); Playboy TV (delivered digitally); Fresh (delivered digitally).
Internet Service
Operational: No.
Telephone Service
None
Regional Manager: Daryl Koedyker.
Ownership: US Cable Corp. (MSO).

IRVING—Time Warner Cable. Now served by DALLAS, TX [TX0003]. ICA: TX0016.

ITALY—Formerly served by Almega Cable. No longer in operation. ICA: TX1001.

JACKSBORO—CommuniComm Services, 2804B S FM 51, PO Box 869, Decatur, TX 76234-0869. Phone: 940-627-8414. Fax: 940-627-8303. Web Site: http://www.netcommander.com. Also serves Bryson, Graford & Possum Kingdom Lake. ICA: TX0781.
TV Market Ranking: Below 100 (JACKSBORO); Outside TV Markets (Bryson, Graford, Possum Kingdom Lake). Franchise award date: March 1, 1977. Franchise expiration date: March 1, 2007. Began: June 14, 1977.
Channel capacity: N.A. Channels available but not in use: N.A.
Basic Service
Subscribers: N.A. Included in Decatur
Programming (received off-air): KAUZ-TV (CBS, CW) Wichita Falls; KDAF (CW, IND) Dallas; KDFI (MNT) Dallas; KDFW-DT (FOX) Dallas; KERA-TV (PBS) Dallas; KFDX-TV (NBC) Wichita Falls; KJTL (FOX) Wichita Falls; KTVT (CBS) Fort Worth; KTXA (IND) Fort Worth; KXAS-TV (NBC) Fort Worth; KXTX-TV (TMO) Dallas; WFAA (ABC) Dallas; allband FM.

Expanded Basic Service 1
Subscribers: 2,763.
Programming (via satellite): A&E Networks; ABC Family Channel; AMC; Animal Planet; BET Networks; Bravo; Cartoon Network; CNBC; CNN; Comedy Central; Country Music TV; C-SPAN; Discovery Channel; Disney Channel; E! Entertainment Television; ESPN; ESPN 2; Eternal Word TV Network; Food Network; Fox News Channel; Fox Sports Southwest; FX; Headline News; HGTV; History Channel; Lifetime; MTV; Nick Jr.; Nickelodeon; QVC; Radar Channel; ShopNBC; Spike TV; Syfy; TBS Superstation; The Learning Channel; The Weather Channel; Travel Channel; Trinity Broadcasting Network; truTV; Turner Classic Movies; Turner Network TV; TV Guide Network; TV Land; Univision Studios; USA Network; VH1; WE tv.
Fee: $43.95 monthly.

Digital Basic Service
Subscribers: N.A.
Programming (via satellite): AmericanLife TV Network; BBC America; Bio; Bloomberg Television; Bravo; Church Channel; cloo; CMT Pure Country; Current; Discovery Fit & Health; Discovery Health Channel; Discovery Home Channel; Discovery Kids Channel; DMX Music; ESPN 2; ESPN Classic Sports; ESPNews; Fox Movie Channel; Fox Soccer; Fuse; G4; GMC; Golf Channel; Great American Country; GSN; Halogen Network; HGTV; History Channel; History Channel International; ID Investigation Discovery; Independent Film Channel; JCTV; Lifetime Movie Network; Military Channel; MTV Hits; MTV Jams; MTV2; National Geographic Channel; Nick Jr.; NickToons TV; Outdoor Channel; Ovation; Science; ShopNBC; SoapNet; Speed; Style Network; Sundance Channel; Syfy; TeenNick; The Word Network; Toon Disney; Trinity Broadcasting Network; Turner Classic Movies; Versus; VH1 Classic; VH1 Soul; WE tv.
Fee: $9.99 monthly.

Pay Service 1
Pay Units: N.A.
Programming (via satellite): Cinemax; Encore; HBO (multiplexed); Starz.
Fee: $20.00 installation.

Digital Pay Service 1
Pay Units: N.A.
Programming (via satellite): Cinemax (multiplexed); Encore (multiplexed); Flix; HBO (multiplexed); Showtime (multiplexed); Starz (multiplexed); The Movie Channel (multiplexed).
Fee: $20.00 installation; $5.00 monthly (Encore), $11.00 monthly (Starz), $11.95 monthly (Cinemax), $13.95 monthly (HBO or Showtime/TMC/Flix).
Video-On-Demand: No

Pay-Per-View
iN DEMAND (delivered digitally); Hot Choice (delivered digitally); Playboy TV (delivered digitally); Fresh (delivered digitally); Spice: Xcess (delivered digitally); Club Jenna (delivered digitally).

Internet Service
Operational: Yes.
Broadband Service: Net Commander.
Fee: $39.95 installation; $51.95 monthly.
Telephone Service
None
Miles of Plant: 33.0 (coaxial); None (fiber optic).
Chief Technician: J. D. Sifford. Operations Manager: Wes Devall.
Ownership: James Cable LLC (MSO).

JACKSONVILLE—Suddenlink Communications, 1009 S Jackson, Ste 365, Jacksonville, TX 75766-4966. Phone: 903-586-8122. Fax: 903-586-1752. Web Site: http://www.suddenlink.com. Also serves Cherokee County. ICA: TX0110.
TV Market Ranking: Below 100 (Cherokee County, JACKSONVILLE). Franchise award date: January 1, 1969. Franchise expiration date: N.A. Began: July 3, 1953.
Channel capacity: N.A. Channels available but not in use: N.A.
Basic Service
Subscribers: 4,220.
Programming (received off-air): KDFW-DT (FOX) Dallas; KERA-TV (PBS) Dallas; KETK-TV (NBC) Jacksonville; KFXK-TV (FOX) Longview; KLPN-LP (IND) Longview; KLTV (ABC, TMO) Tyler; KTVT (CBS) Fort Worth; KXAS-TV (NBC) Fort Worth; KXTX-TV (TMO) Dallas; WFAA (ABC) Dallas; 6 FMs.
Programming (via satellite): Comedy Central; Fox Sports Southwest; ION Television; Lifetime; QVC; TBS Superstation; truTV; TV Guide Network; VH1.
Fee: $49.95 installation; $10.00 monthly; $25.00 additional installation.
Expanded Basic Service 1
Subscribers: 4,038.
Programming (via satellite): A&E Networks; ABC Family Channel; Animal Planet; BET Networks; Cartoon Network; CNBC; CNN; C-SPAN; C-SPAN 2; Discovery Channel; ESPN; Food Network; Fox News Channel; Fox Sports Southwest; FX; GalaVision; Great American Country; Headline News; HGTV; INSP; MoviePlex; MSNBC; MTV; Nickelodeon; Spike TV; The Learning Channel; The Weather Channel; Turner Network TV; USA Network.
Fee: $19.25 monthly.
Digital Basic Service
Subscribers: N.A.
Programming (via satellite): Discovery Digital Networks; Encore; ESPN 2; ESPN Classic Sports; Fox Sports World; Golf Channel; GSN; History Channel; Speed; Syfy; Turner Classic Movies; TV Land; Versus; WE tv.
Pay Service 1
Pay Units: N.A.
Programming (via satellite): Cinemax; Encore; HBO; Showtime; Starz.
Fee: $1.75 monthly (Encore), $6.75 monthly (Starz), $9.00 monthly (Cinemax), $10.95 monthly (HBO).
Digital Pay Service 1
Pay Units: N.A.
Programming (via satellite): Cinemax (multiplexed); HBO (multiplexed); Showtime

(multiplexed); Starz (multiplexed); The Movie Channel (multiplexed).
Video-On-Demand: No
Pay-Per-View
iN DEMAND; iN DEMAND (delivered digitally).
Internet Service
Operational: Yes.
Broadband Service: Suddenlink High Speed Internet.
Fee: $45.95 installation; $29.95 monthly; $10.00 modem lease; $75.00 modem purchase.
Telephone Service
Digital: Operational
Fee: $44.95 monthly
Miles of Plant: 96.0 (coaxial); None (fiber optic).
Manager: Ronnie Powell. Chief Technician: Brad Casey.
Ownership: Cequel Communications LLC (MSO).

JARRELL—Suddenlink Communications, 111 N College St, Georgetown, TX 78626-4101. Phone: 512-930-3085. Fax: 512-869-2962. Web Site: http://www.suddenlink.com. ICA: TX0972.
TV Market Ranking: Below 100 (JARRELL). Franchise award date: N.A. Franchise expiration date: N.A. Began: N.A.
Channel capacity: N.A. Channels available but not in use: N.A.
Basic Service
Subscribers: 152.
Programming (received off-air): KCEN-TV (NBC, IND) Temple; KEYE-TV (CBS, TMO) Austin; KLRU (PBS) Austin; KNVA (CW) Austin; KTBC (FOX) Austin; KVUE (ABC) Austin; KWTX-TV (CBS, CW) Waco; KXXV (ABC, TMO) Waco.
Programming (via satellite): C-SPAN; QVC; TBS Superstation; TV Land; WGN America.
Fee: $12.49 monthly; $1.50 converter.
Expanded Basic Service 1
Subscribers: N.A.
Programming (via satellite): A&E Networks; ABC Family Channel; AMC; Animal Planet; CNBC; CNN; Country Music TV; Discovery Channel; Disney Channel; ESPN; Headline News; HGTV; History Channel; Lifetime; MTV; Nickelodeon; Spike TV; Syfy; The Learning Channel; The Weather Channel; Trinity Broadcasting Network; Turner Classic Movies; Turner Network TV; Univision Studios; USA Network; VH1.
Fee: $15.50 monthly.
Digital Basic Service
Subscribers: N.A.
Programming (via satellite): BBC America; Bio; Bloomberg Television; Discovery Health Channel; Discovery Home Channel; Discovery Kids Channel; Discovery Times Channel; DMX Music; Encore (multiplexed); ESPN Classic Sports; ESPNews; Fox Soccer; Fuse; G4; Golf Channel; GSN; Halogen Network; History Channel International; Lifetime Movie Network; Military Channel; Science; Speed; Sundance Channel; Toon Disney; Versus.
Pay Service 1
Pay Units: N.A.
Programming (via satellite): Cinemax (multiplexed); Encore; HBO; Showtime.
Fee: $8.99 monthly (Showtime), $9.99 monthly (Cinemax or Encore), $11.49 monthly (HBO).
Digital Pay Service 1
Pay Units: N.A.
Programming (via satellite): Cinemax (multiplexed); Encore; HBO (multiplexed); Showtime (multiplexed); Starz (multiplexed); The Movie Channel (multiplexed).
Video-On-Demand: No
Pay-Per-View
iN DEMAND (delivered digitally); Playboy TV (delivered digitally); Fresh (delivered digitally).
Internet Service
Operational: Yes.
Broadband Service: Suddenlink High Speed Internet.
Telephone Service
Digital: Operational
Manager: Dale E. Hoffman. Chief Technician & Marketing Director: Wesley Houghteling.
Ownership: Cequel Communications LLC (MSO).

JASPER—CMA Cablevision, 122 N Austin St, Jasper, TX 75951-4102. Phones: 979-968-6476 (La Grange office); 409-384-6862. Fax: 979-968-5368. Web Site: http://www.cmaaccess.com. ICA: TX0157.
TV Market Ranking: Outside TV Markets (JASPER). Franchise award date: November 14, 1977. Franchise expiration date: N.A. Began: August 1, 1967.
Channel capacity: N.A. Channels available but not in use: N.A.
Basic Service
Subscribers: 2,230.
Programming (received off-air): KBMT (ABC) Beaumont; KBTV-TV (FOX) Port Arthur; KFDM (CBS, CW) Beaumont; KVHP (FOX) Lake Charles; allband FM.
Programming (via microwave): KUHT (PBS) Houston.
Programming (via satellite): C-SPAN; ION Television; QVC; The Weather Channel; Trinity Broadcasting Network.
Fee: $39.95 installation; $17.95 monthly; $12.95 additional installation.
Expanded Basic Service 1
Subscribers: 2,125.
Programming (via satellite): A&E Networks; ABC Family Channel; AMC; Animal Planet; BET Networks; Cartoon Network; CNBC; CNN; Comedy Central; Country Music TV; Discovery Channel; ESPN; ESPN 2; Food Network; Fox News Channel; Fox Sports Southwest; FX; Hallmark Channel; Headline News; HGTV; History Channel; INSP; Lifetime; MTV; Nickelodeon; Outdoor Channel; Spike TV; Syfy; TBS Superstation; The Learning Channel; Travel Channel; Turner Classic Movies; Turner Network TV; TV Guide Network; TV Land; USA Network; VH1; WGN America.
Fee: $28.00 monthly.
Digital Basic Service
Subscribers: N.A.
Programming (via satellite): BBC America; Bio; Discovery Digital Networks; DMX Music; ESPN Classic Sports; ESPNews; Fox Sports World; GAS; Golf Channel; GSN; History Channel International; Independent Film Channel; Lifetime Movie Network; MTV Networks Digital Suite; MuchMusic Network; Speed; Versus; WE tv.
Fee: $13.95 monthly.
Digital Pay Service 1
Pay Units: 57.
Programming (via satellite): Cinemax (multiplexed).
Fee: $10.95 monthly.
Digital Pay Service 2
Pay Units: 95.
Programming (via satellite): HBO (multiplexed).
Fee: $13.95 monthly.
Digital Pay Service 3
Pay Units: 52.
Programming (via satellite): Showtime (multiplexed); The Movie Channel (multiplexed).
Fee: $13.95 monthly.
Digital Pay Service 4
Pay Units: 74.
Programming (via satellite): Encore (multiplexed); Starz (multiplexed).
Fee: $10.95 monthly (Starz & Encore).
Video-On-Demand: No
Pay-Per-View
iN DEMAND (delivered digitally); Club Jenna (delivered digitally); Playboy TV (delivered digitally).
Internet Service
Operational: Yes.
Broadband Service: CMA.
Fee: $39.95 installation; $41.95 monthly; $2.95 modem lease; $39.95 modem purchase.
Telephone Service
Digital: Operational
Fee: $39.95 monthly
Miles of Plant: 139.0 (coaxial); None (fiber optic). Additional miles planned: 20.0 (coaxial).
General Manager: Jerry L. Smith. Marketing Director: Julie Ferguson. Chief Technician: Bryce Beatty.
Ownership: Cable Management Assoc. (MSO).

JAYTON—Formerly served by Jayroc Cablevision. No longer in operation. ICA: TX0557.

JEWETT—Northland Cable Television, 515 W Tyler St, PO Box 112, Mexia, TX 76667-0112. Phones: 800-792-3087; 254-562-2872. Fax: 254-562-6454. E-mail: mexia@northlandcabletv.com. Web Site: http://www.northlandcabletv.com. ICA: TX0541.
TV Market Ranking: Outside TV Markets (JEWETT). Franchise award date: May 19, 1980. Franchise expiration date: N.A. Began: August 1, 1981.
Channel capacity: N.A. Channels available but not in use: N.A.
Basic Service
Subscribers: 237.
Programming (received off-air): KBTX-TV (CBS, CW) Bryan; KCEN-TV (NBC, IND) Temple; KDYW (PBS) Waco; KETK-TV (NBC) Jacksonville; KWKT-TV (FOX, MNT) Waco; KWTX-TV (CBS, CW) Waco; KXXV (ABC, TMO) Waco; WFAA (ABC) Dallas.
Programming (via satellite): A&E Networks; Cartoon Network; CNN; Country Music TV; Discovery Channel; ESPN; Fox Sports Southwest; Headline News; History Channel; Lifetime; QVC; TBS Superstation; Trinity Broadcasting Network; Turner Classic Movies; Turner Network TV; USA Network; WGN America.
Fee: $55.00 installation; $31.99 monthly.
Pay Service 1
Pay Units: N.A.
Programming (via satellite): Cinemax.
Pay Service 2
Pay Units: 57.
Programming (via satellite): HBO.
Fee: $10.00 monthly.
Internet Service
Operational: No.
Telephone Service
None
Miles of Plant: 28.0 (coaxial); None (fiber optic).
Manager: Brent Richey. Chief Technician: Joe Lopez. Office Manager: Pamela Elliott.
Ownership: Northland Communications Corp. (MSO).

JOHNSON CITY—Almega Cable, 4001 W Airport Frwy, Ste 530, Bedford, TX 76021. Phone: 817-685-9588. Fax: 817-685-6488. E-mail: helpdesk@almegacable.com. Web Site: http://www.almega.com. ICA: TX0560.
TV Market Ranking: Below 100 (JOHNSON CITY). Franchise award date: N.A. Franchise expiration date: N.A. Began: July 1, 1984.
Channel capacity: 37 (not 2-way capable). Channels available but not in use: N.A.
Basic Service
Subscribers: 120.
Programming (received off-air): KEYE-TV (CBS, TMO) Austin; KLRU (PBS) Austin; KNVA (CW) Austin; KTBC (FOX) Austin; KVUE (ABC) Austin; KXAN-TV (NBC) Austin.
Programming (via satellite): A&E Networks; ABC Family Channel; AMC; Animal Planet; CNBC; CNN; Country Music TV; C-SPAN; Discovery Channel; Disney Channel; ESPN; ESPN 2; Fox Sports Southwest; HGTV; History Channel; Lifetime; Nickelodeon; Spike TV; Syfy; TBS Superstation; The Learning Channel; The Weather Channel; Turner Network TV; TV Land; Univision Studios; USA Network; WGN America.
Fee: $29.95 installation; $38.00 monthly.
Pay Service 1
Pay Units: 30.
Programming (via satellite): HBO; The Movie Channel.
Video-On-Demand: No
Pay-Per-View
Hot Choice; Playboy TV; Fresh; Shorteez.
Internet Service
Operational: No.
Telephone Service
None
Miles of Plant: 8.0 (coaxial); None (fiber optic).
Ownership: Almega Cable (MSO).

JOSEPHINE—Formerly served by Almega Cable. No longer in operation. ICA: TX0784.

JOSHUA—Almega Cable, 4001 W Airport Freeway, Ste 530, Bedford, TX 76021. Phone: 817-685-9588. Fax: 817-685-6488. E-mail: helpdesk@almegacable.com. Web Site: http://www.almega.com. Also serves Burleson City & Johnson County (portions). ICA: TX0785.
TV Market Ranking: 12 (Burleson City, Johnson County (portions), JOSHUA). Franchise award date: N.A. Franchise expiration date: N.A. Began: February 1, 1984.
Channel capacity: N.A. Channels available but not in use: N.A.
Basic Service
Subscribers: 1,192.
Programming (received off-air): KDAF (CW, IND) Dallas; KDFI (MNT) Dallas; KDFW-DT (FOX) Dallas; KDTN (ETV) Denton; KERA-TV (PBS) Dallas; KFWD (IND) Fort Worth; KMPX (IND) Decatur; KSTR-DT (TEL) Irving; KTVT (CBS) Fort Worth; KTXA (IND) Fort Worth; KUVN-DT (UNV) Garland; KXAS-TV (NBC) Fort Worth; KXTX-TV (TMO) Dallas; WFAA (ABC) Dallas.
Programming (via satellite): A&E Networks; ABC Family Channel; Cartoon Network; CNBC; CNN; Comedy Central; Country Music TV; C-SPAN; Discovery Channel; Disney Channel; E! Entertainment Television; ESPN; ESPN 2; Fox Sports Southwest; FX; Hallmark Channel; Headline News; History Channel; Lifetime; MTV; Nickelodeon; Oxygen; SoapNet; Spike TV; TBS Superstation; The Learning Channel; The Weather Channel; Travel Channel; Trin-

ity Broadcasting Network; Turner Classic Movies; Turner Network TV; USA Network; WGN America.
Fee: $54.95 installation; $44.05 monthly.

Pay Service 1
Pay Units: N.A.
Programming (via satellite): Cinemax; HBO; Showtime.
Fee: $12.95 monthly (each).

Video-On-Demand: No

Internet Service
Operational: No.

Telephone Service
None

Miles of Plant: 85.0 (coaxial); 20.0 (fiber optic).
Ownership: Almega Cable (MSO).

JOSHUA—Pathway. Formerly served by Burleson, TX [TX0103]. This cable system has converted to IPTV, PO Box 1298, Joshua, TX 76058-1298. Phone: 817-484-2222. Fax: 817-447-0169. Web Site: http://www.usapathway.com. ICA: TX5531.
Channel capacity: N.A. Channels available but not in use: N.A.

Internet Service
Operational: Yes.

Telephone Service
Digital: Operational

JUNCTION—Suddenlink Communications, 12444 Powerscourt Dr, Saint Louis, MO 63131-3660. Phones: 800-999-6845 (Customer service); 314-965-2020. Fax: 903-561-5485. Web Site: http://www.suddenlink.com. Also serves Kimble County (portions). ICA: TX0320.
TV Market Ranking: Outside TV Markets (JUNCTION, Kimble County (portions)). Franchise award date: N.A. Franchise expiration date: N.A. Began: June 1, 1957.
Channel capacity: N.A. Channels available but not in use: N.A.

Basic Service
Subscribers: 832.
Programming (received off-air): KIDY (FOX) San Angelo; KLST (CBS) San Angelo; KTXS-TV (ABC, CW, TMO) Sweetwater; KXAN-TV (NBC) Austin; 4 FMs.
Programming (via microwave): KBVO (MNT) Llano; WFAA (ABC) Dallas.
Programming (via satellite): A&E Networks; ABC Family Channel; Animal Planet; CNN; Country Music TV; Discovery Channel; Disney Channel; ESPN; Fox News Channel; Fox Sports Southwest; Headline News; History Channel; KRMA-TV (PBS) Denver; Lifetime; Nickelodeon; QVC; Spike TV; TBS Superstation; Telemundo; The Learning Channel; The Weather Channel; Trinity Broadcasting Network; Turner Network TV; TV Land; USA Network; WGN America.
Fee: $39.95 installation; $18.95 monthly.

Pay Service 1
Pay Units: 91.
Programming (via satellite): HBO.
Fee: $10.00 installation; $10.95 monthly.

Pay Service 2
Pay Units: 130.
Programming (via satellite): Showtime.
Fee: $9.95 monthly.

Pay Service 3
Pay Units: 100.
Programming (via satellite): The Movie Channel.
Fee: $7.95 monthly.

Video-On-Demand: No

Internet Service
Operational: Yes. Began: January 26, 2004.
Broadband Service: Suddenlink High Speed Internet.
Fee: $49.95 installation; $25.95 monthly.

Telephone Service
Digital: Operational
Fee: $44.95 monthly

Miles of Plant: 27.0 (coaxial); None (fiber optic).
Regional Manager: Todd Cruthird. Plant Manager: Jimmy Welch. Regional Marketing Manager: Beverly Gambell.
Ownership: Cequel Communications LLC (MSO).

KATY (southern portion)—Formerly served by Cebridge Connections. No longer in operation. ICA: TX0786.

KAUFMAN—Northland Cable Television, 326 W Main St, PO Box 289, Gun Barrel City, TX 75147. Phones: 800-933-1046; 903-887-0240. Fax: 903-887-7395. E-mail: gunbarrel@northlandcabletv.com. Web Site: http://www.northlandcabletv.com. Also serves Oak Grove. ICA: TX0262.
TV Market Ranking: 12 (KAUFMAN, Oak Grove). Franchise award date: N.A. Franchise expiration date: N.A. Began: March 23, 1981.
Channel capacity: 52 (not 2-way capable). Channels available but not in use: N.A.

Basic Service
Subscribers: 1,000.
Programming (received off-air): KDAF (CW, IND) Dallas; KDFI (MNT) Dallas; KDFW-DT (FOX) Dallas; KDTX-TV (TBN) Dallas; KERA-TV (PBS) Dallas; KFWD (IND) Fort Worth; KMPX (IND) Decatur; KPXD-TV (ION) Arlington; KSTR-DT (TEL) Irving; KTVT (CBS) Fort Worth; KTXA (IND) Fort Worth; KUVN-DT (UNV) Garland; KXAS-TV (NBC) Fort Worth; KXTX-TV (TMO) Dallas; WFAA (ABC) Dallas.
Programming (via satellite): A&E Networks; Animal Planet; BET Networks; CNN; C-SPAN; Discovery Channel; ESPN; Fox News Channel; Fox Sports Southwest; GalaVision; Great American Country; Headline News; HGTV; QVC; Spike TV; TBS Superstation; The Weather Channel; Turner Network TV; TV Guide Network.
Fee: $40.00 installation; $32.99 monthly.

Expanded Basic Service 1
Subscribers: 358.
Programming (via satellite): AMC; Cartoon Network; CNBC; Comedy Central; ESPN 2; Fox Deportes; Fox Movie Channel; FX; Hallmark Channel; History Channel; Lifetime; MTV; Nickelodeon; Syfy; Turner Classic Movies; USA Network.
Fee: $41.29 monthly.

Digital Basic Service
Subscribers: N.A.
Programming (via satellite): AmericanLife TV Network; Bloomberg Television; Discovery Digital Networks; DMX Music; Encore; Golf Channel; GSN; Halogen Network; Outdoor Channel; Speed; Sundance Channel; Trinity Broadcasting Network; WE tv.
Fee: $10.70 monthly.

Pay Service 1
Pay Units: 84.
Programming (via satellite): Cinemax.
Fee: $11.00 monthly.

Pay Service 2
Pay Units: 241.
Programming (via satellite): Showtime.
Fee: $11.00 monthly.

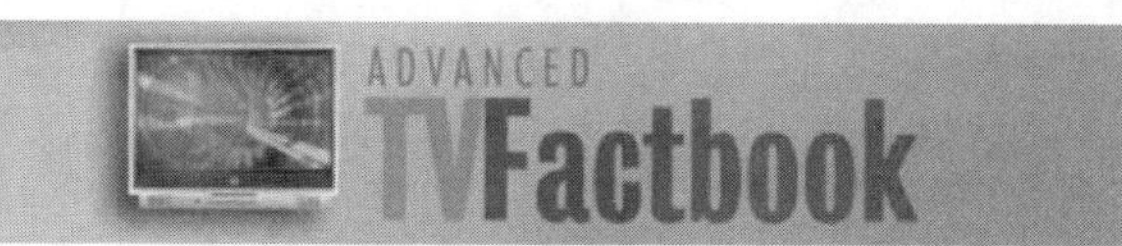

Pay Service 3
Pay Units: 90.
Programming (via satellite): HBO.
Fee: $13.50 monthly.

Digital Pay Service 1
Pay Units: N.A.
Programming (via satellite): Cinemax (multiplexed); Flix; HBO (multiplexed); Showtime (multiplexed); The Movie Channel (multiplexed).
Fee: $10.00 monthly (each).

Pay-Per-View
iN DEMAND (delivered digitally); Hot Choice (delivered digitally); Playboy TV (delivered digitally); Fresh (delivered digitally); ESPN Now (delivered digitally); Sports PPV (delivered digitally).

Internet Service
Operational: Yes.
Fee: $42.99 monthly.

Telephone Service
None

Miles of Plant: 61.0 (coaxial); None (fiber optic).
Regional Manager: Richard Gammon. Chief Technician: Bobby Brady. Office Manager: Diane Ball.
Ownership: Northland Communications Corp. (MSO).

KEMPNER—Formerly served by National Cable Inc. No longer in operation. ICA: TX0674.

KENDALL COUNTY (portions)—GVTV Communications. Formerly served by Boerne (portions), TX [TX0315]. This cable system has converted to IPTV, 108 E Third St, Gridley, TX 61744. Phone: 309-747-2211. E-mail: info@gridcom.net. Web Site: http://www.gridtel.com. ICA: TX5473.
Channel capacity: N.A. Channels available but not in use: N.A.

Internet Service
Operational: Yes.

KENEDY—Reach Broadband, 515 E Longview St, Arp, TX 75750. Phone: 800-687-1258. Web Site: http://www.reachbroadband.net. Also serves Karnes City. ICA: TX0281.
TV Market Ranking: Outside TV Markets (Karnes City, KENEDY). Franchise award date: N.A. Franchise expiration date: N.A. Began: July 1, 1977.
Channel capacity: 41 (2-way capable). Channels available but not in use: N.A.

Basic Service
Subscribers: 895.
Programming (received off-air): KABB (FOX) San Antonio; KENS (CBS) San Antonio; KLRN (PBS) San Antonio; KMYS (CW) Kerrville; KSAT-TV (ABC) San Antonio; KVDA (TMO) San Antonio; KWEX-DT (UNV) San Antonio; WOAI-TV (NBC) San Antonio; 1 FM.
Programming (via satellite): A&E Networks; ABC Family Channel; Animal Planet; CNN; Country Music TV; Discovery Channel; Disney Channel; ESPN; Eternal Word TV Network; Fox News Channel; Fox Sports Southwest; Headline News; Nickelodeon; QVC; Spike TV; TBS Superstation; The Learning Channel; The Weather Channel; Trinity Broadcasting Network; Turner Classic Movies; Turner Network TV; TV Land; USA Network; WGN America.
Fee: $29.95 installation; $38.00 monthly.

Pay Service 1
Pay Units: 171.
Programming (via satellite): HBO.
Fee: $25.00 installation; $10.95 monthly.

Pay Service 2
Pay Units: 178.
Programming (via satellite): Showtime.
Fee: $9.95 monthly.

Pay Service 3
Pay Units: 150.
Programming (via satellite): The Movie Channel.
Fee: $7.95 monthly.

Video-On-Demand: No

Internet Service
Operational: No.

Telephone Service
None

Miles of Plant: 65.0 (coaxial); None (fiber optic).
Regional Manager: Ronnie Stafford. Office Manager: Jan Gibson.
Ownership: RB3 LLC (MSO).

KENEFICK—Formerly served by Carrell Communications. No longer in operation. ICA: TX0438.

KERENS—Northland Cable Television, 1500 N Beaton St, PO Box 550, Corsicana, TX 75151. Phones: 800-872-3905; 903-872-3131. Fax: 903-872-6623. E-mail: corsicana@northlandcabletv.com. Web Site: http://www.northlandcabletv.com. ICA: TX0443.
TV Market Ranking: Outside TV Markets (KERENS). Franchise award date: June 3, 1980. Franchise expiration date: N.A. Began: N.A.
Channel capacity: 48 (not 2-way capable). Channels available but not in use: N.A.

Basic Service
Subscribers: N.A.
Programming (received off-air): KDAF (CW, IND) Dallas; KDFI (MNT) Dallas; KDFW-DT (FOX) Dallas; KERA-TV (PBS) Dallas; KETK-TV (NBC) Jacksonville; KSTR-DT (TEL) Irving; KTVT (CBS) Fort Worth; KTXA (IND) Fort Worth; KXAS-TV (NBC) Fort Worth; KXTX-TV (TMO) Dallas; WFAA (ABC) Dallas.
Programming (via satellite): A&E Networks; ABC Family Channel; Cartoon Network; CNN; C-SPAN; Discovery Channel; ESPN; Fox Sports Southwest; Great American Country; HGTV; Lifetime; Outdoor Channel; QVC; Spike TV; Syfy; TBS Superstation; Turner Classic Movies; Turner Network TV; USA Network; WGN America.
Fee: $40.00 installation; $36.99 monthly.

Pay Service 1
Pay Units: N.A.
Programming (via satellite): Cinemax; HBO.
Fee: $30.00 installation; $11.50 monthly (Cinemax), $13.50 monthly (HBO).

Internet Service
Operational: No.

Telephone Service
None
Chief Technician: Bobby Brady. Regional Manager: Mike Taylor. Office Manager: Diane Ball.
Ownership: Northland Communications Corp. (MSO).

KERMIT—Suddenlink Communications, 12444 Powerscourt Dr, Saint Louis, MO 63131-3660. Phone: 314-965-2020. Web Site: http://www.suddenlink.com. Also serves Winkler County (portions). ICA: TX0161.
TV Market Ranking: Below 100 (Winkler County (portions)); Outside TV Markets (KERMIT). Franchise award date: March 26, 1991. Franchise expiration date: N.A. Began: August 1, 1972.
Channel capacity: 70 (operating 2-way). Channels available but not in use: N.A.
Basic Service
Subscribers: 1,759.
Programming (received off-air): KMID (ABC) Midland; KMLM-DT (IND) Odessa; KOSA-TV (CBS, MNT) Odessa; KPEJ-TV (FOX) Odessa; KUPB (UNV) Midland; KWES-TV (NBC) Odessa.
Programming (via satellite): KMGH-TV (ABC) Denver; KRMA-TV (PBS) Denver; QVC.
Fee: $39.95 installation; $18.95 monthly.
Expanded Basic Service 1
Subscribers: N.A.
Programming (via satellite): A&E Networks; ABC Family Channel; AMC; Animal Planet; BET Networks; Bravo; Cartoon Network; CNBC; CNN; Comedy Central; C-SPAN; Discovery Channel; Disney Channel; E! Entertainment Television; ESPN; ESPN 2; Eternal Word TV Network; Food Network; Fox Deportes; Fox News Channel; Fox Sports Southwest; FX; GalaVision; Golf Channel; Great American Country; Hallmark Channel; Headline News; HGTV; History Channel; Lifetime; MSNBC; MTV; National Geographic Channel; Nickelodeon; Outdoor Channel; Shopping Channel; Spike TV; Syfy; TBS Superstation; Telemundo; The Learning Channel; The Weather Channel; Trinity Broadcasting Network; Turner Classic Movies; Turner Network TV; TV Guide Network; TV Land; USA Network; VH1.
Fee: $26.00 monthly.
Digital Basic Service
Subscribers: N.A.
Programming (via satellite): BBC America; Bio; Bloomberg Television; Canales N; cloo; Discovery Digital Networks; DMX Music; ESPN Classic Sports; ESPNews; Fox Soccer; Fuse; G4; GSN; History Channel International; Independent Film Channel; Military History Channel; Speed; Toon Disney; Versus; WE tv.
Fee: $3.99 monthly.
Pay Service 1
Pay Units: 83.
Programming (via satellite): Showtime.
Fee: $9.95 monthly.
Pay Service 2
Pay Units: 96.
Programming (via satellite): The Movie Channel.
Fee: $7.95 monthly.
Pay Service 3
Pay Units: 323.
Programming (via satellite): HBO.
Fee: $10.95 monthly.
Pay Service 4
Pay Units: N.A.
Programming (via satellite): Encore; Starz.
Fee: $6.95 monthly.
Digital Pay Service 1
Pay Units: N.A.
Programming (via satellite): Cinemax (multiplexed); Encore (multiplexed); HBO (multiplexed); Showtime (multiplexed); Starz (multiplexed); The Movie Channel (multiplexed).
Pay-Per-View
iN DEMAND (delivered digitally); Playboy TV (delivered digitally); Fresh (delivered digitally).
Internet Service
Operational: Yes. Began: June 23, 2002.
Broadband Service: Suddenlink High Speed Internet.
Fee: $45.95 installation; $29.95 monthly.
Telephone Service
Digital: Operational
Fee: $44.95 monthly
Miles of Plant: 33.0 (coaxial); None (fiber optic).
Regional Manager: Todd Cruthird. Area Manager: Chris Christiansen. Plant Manager: Manuel Gonzales. Regional Marketing Manager: Beverly Gambell.
Ownership: Cequel Communications LLC (MSO).

KERRVILLE—Time Warner Cable, 900 Sidney Baker St, Kerrville, TX 78028-3353. Phones: 972-899-7300 (Flower Mound division office); 830-257-4709. Fax: 830-257-6776. Web Site: http://www.timewarnercable.com/Texas. Also serves Kerr County. ICA: TX0061.
TV Market Ranking: Below 100 (Kerr County, KERRVILLE). Franchise award date: N.A. Franchise expiration date: N.A. Began: January 1, 1957.
Channel capacity: N.A. Channels available but not in use: N.A.
Basic Service
Subscribers: 11,000.
Programming (received off-air): KABB (FOX) San Antonio; KCWX (IND, MNT) Fredericksburg; KENS (CBS) San Antonio; KLRN (PBS) San Antonio; KMEX-DT (UNV) Los Angeles; KMYS (CW) Kerrville; KNIC-DT (TEL) Blanco; KPXL-TV (ION) Uvalde; KSAT-TV (ABC) San Antonio; KVDA (TMO) San Antonio; KVDF-CA (IND) San Antonio; WOAI-TV (NBC) San Antonio.
Programming (via satellite): TV Guide Network.
Fee: $50.51 installation; $16.99 monthly; $18.81 additional installation.
Expanded Basic Service 1
Subscribers: 9,780.
Programming (via satellite): A&E Networks; ABC Family Channel; AMC; Animal Planet; BET Networks; Bravo; Cartoon Network; CNBC; CNN; Comedy Central; Country Music TV; C-SPAN; C-SPAN 2; Discovery Channel; Discovery Health Channel; Disney Channel; E! Entertainment Television; ESPN; ESPN 2; Eternal Word TV Network; Food Network; Fox News Channel; Fox Sports Southwest; FX; GalaVision; Golf Channel; Great American Country; Hallmark Channel; Headline News; HGTV; History Channel; Lifetime; Lifetime Movie Network; MoviePlex; MSNBC; MTV; National Geographic Channel; Nickelodeon; Oxygen; QVC; ShopNBC; SoapNet; Spike TV; Style Network; Syfy; TBS Superstation; Texas Cable News; The Learning Channel; The Weather Channel; Travel Channel; Trinity Broadcasting Network; truTV; Turner Classic Movies; Turner Network TV; TV Land; USA Network; Versus; VH1; WE tv.
Fee: $31.00 monthly.
Digital Basic Service
Subscribers: N.A.
Programming (via satellite): A&E Networks; ABC Family Channel; AMC; AmericanLife TV Network; Animal Planet; BBC America; BET Networks; Bio; Bloomberg Television; Boomerang; Bravo; Cartoon Network; cloo; CNBC; CNN; Comedy Central; Cooking Channel; Country Music TV; C-SPAN; C-SPAN 2; C-SPAN 3; Daystar TV Network; Discovery Channel; Discovery Fit & Health; Discovery Health Channel; Discovery Home Channel; Discovery Kids Channel; Discovery Times Channel; Disney Channel; DIY Network; E! Entertainment Television; ESPN; ESPN 2; ESPN 2 HD; ESPN Classic Sports; ESPN HD; ESPN U; ESPNews; Eternal Word TV Network; Food Network; Fox Business Channel; Fox News Channel; Fox Reality Channel; Fox Sports Southwest; Fuse; FX; G4; GalaVision; GAS; Golf Channel; Great American Country; GSN; Hallmark Channel; HD Theater; HDNet; HDNet Movies; Headline News; HGTV; History Channel; History Channel International; La Familia Network; Lifetime; Lifetime Movie Network; Military Channel; MoviePlex; MSNBC; MTV; MTV Hits; MTV2; Music Choice; National Geographic Channel; NBA TV; Nick Jr.; Nickelodeon; NickToons TV; Outdoor Channel; Oxygen; QVC; Science Television; ShopNBC; SoapNet; Speed; Spike TV; Style Network; Syfy; TBS Superstation; Texas Cable News; The Learning Channel; The Weather Channel; Toon Disney; Travel Channel; Trinity Broadcasting Network; truTV; Turner Classic Movies; Turner Network TV; Turner Network TV HD; TV Land; Universal HD; USA Network; VH1; VH1 Classic; VH1 Country; WE tv.
Fee: $5.00 monthly.
Digital Expanded Basic Service
Subscribers: N.A.
Programming (via satellite): Encore (multiplexed); Fox College Sports Atlantic; Fox College Sports Central; Fox College Sports Pacific; Fox Deportes; Fox Movie Channel; Fox Soccer; Independent Film Channel; NBA TV; Sundance Channel; Tennis Channel; Versus.
Fee: $8.95 monthly (Sports Tier or Movie Tier).
Digital Pay Service 1
Pay Units: N.A.
Programming (via satellite): Cinemax (multiplexed); HBO (multiplexed); HBO HD; Showtime (multiplexed); Showtime HD; Starz (multiplexed); The Movie Channel (multiplexed).
Fee: $9.95 monthly (each).
Video-On-Demand: No
Pay-Per-View
iN DEMAND (delivered digitally); Hot Choice (delivered digitally); Shorteez (delivered digitally); Fresh (delivered digitally); Playboy TV (delivered digitally); ESPN Gameplan (delivered digitally); ESPN Full Court (delivered digitally); MLB Extra Innings (delivered digitally); NBA League Pass (delivered digitally); NHL Center Ice (delivered digitally).
Internet Service
Operational: Yes.
Broadband Service: RoadRunner.
Fee: $49.99 installation; $44.95 monthly.
Telephone Service
None
Miles of Plant: 233.0 (coaxial); 45.0 (fiber optic).
President: Connie Wharton. Vice President & General Manager: Mike McKee. Engineering Director: Charlotte Strong. Chief Technician: Jay Burton.
Ownership: Time Warner Cable (MSO).; Advance/Newhouse Partnership (MSO).

KILGORE—Almega Cable, 4001 W Airport Freeway, Ste 530, Bedford, TX 76021. Phone: 817-685-9588. Fax: 817-685-6488. E-mail: helpdesk@almegacable.com. Web Site: http://www.almega.com. Also serves Gregg County (portions). ICA: TX0505.
TV Market Ranking: Below 100 (Gregg County (portions), KILGORE). Franchise award date: N.A. Franchise expiration date: N.A. Began: N.A.
Channel capacity: 36 (not 2-way capable). Channels available but not in use: N.A.
Basic Service
Subscribers: 88.
Programming (received off-air): KETK-TV (NBC) Jacksonville; KLTS-TV (PBS) Shreveport; KLTV (ABC, TMO) Tyler; KSLA (CBS) Shreveport.
Programming (via satellite): ABC Family Channel; CNN; Country Music TV; Discovery Channel; ESPN; Spike TV; TBS Superstation; Turner Network TV; USA Network; WGN America.
Fee: $54.95 installation; $44.05 monthly.
Pay Service 1
Pay Units: 19.
Programming (via satellite): Cinemax.
Fee: $12.95 monthly.
Pay Service 2
Pay Units: 28.
Programming (via satellite): HBO.
Fee: $12.95 monthly.
Pay Service 3
Pay Units: 28.
Programming (via satellite): Showtime.
Fee: $12.95 monthly.
Video-On-Demand: No
Internet Service
Operational: No.
Telephone Service
None
Miles of Plant: 21.0 (coaxial); None (fiber optic).
Ownership: Almega Cable (MSO).

KILGORE—Kilgore Cable TV Co., 711 N High St, PO Box 4399, Longview, TX 75601. Phones: 800-903-0508; 903-758-9991 (Office); 903-983-7851 (Headend). Fax: 903-758-3083. E-mail: longviewcs@cablelynx.com. Web Site: http://www.longviewcabletv.com. ICA: TX0130.
TV Market Ranking: Below 100 (KILGORE). Franchise award date: March 8, 1977. Franchise expiration date: N.A. Began: February 9, 1978.
Channel capacity: 76 (operating 2-way). Channels available but not in use: N.A.
Basic Service
Subscribers: 4,000.
Programming (received off-air): KETK-TV (NBC) Jacksonville; KFXK-TV (FOX) Longview; KLPN-LP (IND) Longview; KLTV (ABC, TMO) Tyler; KSLA (CBS) Shreveport; KTAL-TV (NBC) Texarkana; KTBS-TV (ABC) Shreveport; KTXH (MNT) Houston; KYTX (CBS, IND) Nacogdoches; allband FM.
Programming (via microwave): KDFW-DT (FOX) Dallas; KERA-TV (PBS) Dallas; KXAS-TV (NBC) Fort Worth.
Programming (via satellite): A&E Networks; ABC Family Channel; AMC; Animal Planet; BET Networks; Cartoon Network; CNBC; CNN; Comedy Central; Country Music TV; C-SPAN; C-SPAN 2; Discovery Channel; Disney Channel; ESPN; ESPN 2;

Fox News Channel; Fox Sports Southwest; FX; GalaVision; Hallmark Channel; Headline News; HGTV; History Channel; ION Television; Lifetime; MTV; NASA TV; National Geographic Channel; Nickelodeon; ShopNBC; Spike TV; Syfy; TBS Superstation; Telemundo; The Learning Channel; The Weather Channel; Travel Channel; Trinity Broadcasting Network; Turner Classic Movies; Turner Network TV; TV Guide Network; TV Land; Univision Studios; USA Network; VH1.
Fee: $40.00 installation; $48.90 monthly.

Digital Basic Service
Subscribers: N.A.
Programming (via satellite): AmericanLife TV Network; BBC America; Bio; CMT Pure Country; Discovery Fit & Health; Discovery Health Channel; Discovery Kids Channel; DMX Music; ESPNews; Fox Soccer; FSN Digital Atlantic; FSN Digital Central; FSN Digital Pacific; G4; Golf Channel; Great American Country; GSN; Halogen Network; History Channel International; ID Investigation Discovery; Lifetime Movie Network; Military Channel; MTV Hits; MTV Jams; MTV2; National Geographic Channel; Nick Jr.; Nick Too; NickToons TV; Outdoor Channel; Planet Green; Science; SoapNet; Speed; Style Network; TeenNick; Toon Disney; Tr3s; VH1 Classic; VH1 Soul; WE tv.
Fee: $10.00 monthly.

Digital Expanded Basic Service
Subscribers: N.A.
Programming (received off-air): KETK-TV (NBC) Jacksonville; KFXK-TV (FOX) Longview; KLTS-TV (PBS) Shreveport; KLTV (ABC, TMO) Tyler; KTXH (MNT) Houston; KYTX (CBS, IND) Nacogdoches.
Programming (via satellite): Discovery Channel HD; ESPN HD; HDNet; HDNet Movies; Outdoor Channel 2 HD.
Fee: $5.00 monthly.

Digital Pay Service 1
Pay Units: N.A.
Programming (via satellite): Cinemax (multiplexed); Cinemax HD; Encore (multiplexed); HBO (multiplexed); HBO HD; Starz (multiplexed); Starz HDTV.
Fee: $12.95 monthly (HBO, Cinemax or Starz/Encore).

Video-On-Demand: No

Pay-Per-View
Sports PPV (delivered digitally); ESPN Gameplan (delivered digitally); iN DEMAND (delivered digitally).

Internet Service
Operational: Yes.
Broadband Service: Cablelynx.
Fee: $24.95-$44.95 monthly.

Telephone Service
Analog: Not Operational
Digital: Operational
Fee: $45.70 monthly

Miles of Plant: None (coaxial); 127.0 (fiber optic).
Vice President & Regional Manager: Don Deem. Manager: Brandi Turner. Plant Manager: George Doss. Business Manager: Cynthia Walters.
Ownership: WEHCO Video Inc. (MSO).

KILLEEN—Time Warner Cable, 12012 N Mo Pac Expy, Austin, TX 78758-2904. Phones: 512-485-6100; 254-776-2996 (Waco Office). Fax: 512-485-6105. Web Site: http://www.timewarnercable.com/Texas. Also serves Bell County, Belton, Copperas Cove, Coryell County (unincorporated areas), Fort Hood, Harker Heights, Holland, Kempner, Lampasas County (unincorporated areas), Nolanville & Temple. ICA: TX0023.
TV Market Ranking: Below 100 (Bell County, Belton, Copperas Cove, Coryell County (unincorporated areas), Fort Hood, Harker Heights, Holland, Kempner, KILLEEN, Lampasas County (unincorporated areas), Nolanville, Temple). Franchise award date: N.A. Franchise expiration date: N.A. Began: January 1, 1965.
Channel capacity: N.A. Channels available but not in use: N.A.

Basic Service
Subscribers: N.A. Included in Waco
Programming (received off-air): KAKW-DT (UNV) Killeen; KCEN-TV (NBC, IND) Temple; KEYE-TV (CBS, TMO) Austin; KNCT (PBS) Belton; KWKT-TV (FOX, MNT) Waco; KWTX-TV (CBS, CW) Waco; KXXV (ABC, TMO) Waco; allband FM.
Programming (via microwave): WFAA (ABC) Dallas.
Programming (via satellite): C-SPAN; C-SPAN 2; QVC; ShopNBC; TBS Superstation; TV Guide Network.
Fee: $43.95 installation; $14.95 monthly.

Expanded Basic Service 1
Subscribers: 23,944.
Programming (via satellite): A&E Networks; ABC Family Channel; AMC; Animal Planet; BET Networks; Bravo; Cartoon Network; CNBC; CNN; Comedy Central; Country Music TV; Discovery Channel; Disney Channel; E! Entertainment Television; ESPN; ESPN 2; ESPN Classic Sports; Eternal Word TV Network; Fox News Channel; Fox Sports Southwest; FX; Hallmark Channel; Headline News; HGTV; History Channel; ION Television; Lifetime; MSNBC; MTV; mun2 television; Nickelodeon; Shop at Home; Spike TV; Syfy; Telemundo; Texas Cable News; The Learning Channel; The Weather Channel; Travel Channel; Trinity Broadcasting Network; truTV; Turner Classic Movies; Turner Network TV; TV Land; USA Network; VH1.
Fee: $35.92 monthly.

Digital Basic Service
Subscribers: 23,000.
Programming (via satellite): BBC America; Bloomberg Television; Comedy Central; C-SPAN 3; Discovery Digital Networks; DMX Music; Encore; ESPN Classic Sports; Flix; Food Network; Fox Sports World; G4; Golf Channel; GSN; Lifetime Movie Network; MTV2; MuchMusic Network; Nick Jr.; Outdoor Channel; Ovation; Speed; Style Network; Syfy; Toon Disney; Turner Classic Movies.
Fee: $9.95 monthly.

Digital Pay Service 1
Pay Units: N.A.
Programming (via satellite): Cinemax (multiplexed); Fox Movie Channel; HBO (multiplexed); Showtime (multiplexed); Starz (multiplexed); The Movie Channel (multiplexed).
Fee: $12.95 monthly (Cinemax, HBO, Showtime, Starz, TMC, or FMC/Encore), $16.95 monthly (Playboy).

Video-On-Demand: Yes

Pay-Per-View
iN DEMAND (delivered digitally); Sports PPV (delivered digitally).

Internet Service
Operational: Yes. Began: April 1, 2000.
Subscribers: 11,000.
Broadband Service: Road Runner.
Fee: $79.00 installation; $44.95 monthly.

Telephone Service
Digital: Operational
Fee: $44.95 monthly

Miles of Plant: 1,466.0 (coaxial); None (fiber optic).
President: Katherine Brabson. Vice President, Engineering: Lew Suders. Vice President, Technical Operations: Ed Tagg. Vice President, Marketing & Sales: Terri Cumbie. Technical Operations Director: Deborah Brainard. Public Affairs Director: Roger Heaney.
Ownership: Time Warner Cable (MSO).; Advance/Newhouse Partnership (MSO).Day-to-Day operations are managed by Time Warner Cable.

KINGSVILLE—CMA Cablevision, 729 S 14th St, Kingsville, TX 78363. Phone: 361-595-5726. Fax: 361-355-4444. Web Site: http://www.cmaaccess.com. ICA: TX0926.
TV Market Ranking: Outside TV Markets (KINGSVILLE). Franchise award date: October 1, 1980. Franchise expiration date: N.A. Began: October 1, 1980.
Channel capacity: N.A. Channels available but not in use: N.A.

Basic Service
Subscribers: 4,115.
Programming (received off-air): K47DF Corpus Christi; KEDT (PBS) Corpus Christi; KIII (ABC) Corpus Christi; KORO (UNV) Corpus Christi; KRIS-TV (CW, NBC) Corpus Christi; KTOV-LP Corpus Christi; KZTV (CBS) Corpus Christi.
Programming (via satellite): C-SPAN; CW+; ESPN Classic Sports; Eternal Word TV Network; Food Network; Fox Deportes; Fox Sports South; GalaVision; National Geographic Channel; QVC; SoapNet; TBS Superstation; Telemundo; Trinity Broadcasting Network; TV Guide Network; TV Land; WGN America.
Fee: $39.95 installation; $15.95 monthly; $12.95 additional installation.

Expanded Basic Service 1
Subscribers: N.A.
Programming (via satellite): A&E Networks; ABC Family Channel; AMC; Animal Planet; BET Networks; Bravo!; Cartoon Network; CNN; Comedy Central; Country Music TV; Discovery Channel; E! Entertainment Television; ESPN; ESPN 2; Fox News Channel; FX; GSN; Headline News; HGTV; History Channel; Lifetime; Lifetime Movie Network; MTV; Nickelodeon; Spike TV; Syfy; The Learning Channel; The Weather Channel; Turner Network TV; USA Network; VH1.
Fee: $29.00 monthly.

Digital Basic Service
Subscribers: N.A.
Programming (via satellite): BBC America; Bio; Bloomberg Television; DMX Music; ESPNews; Fox Movie Channel; Fox Soccer; G4; GAS; Golf Channel; Halogen Network; HD Theater; History Channel International; Independent Film Channel; MTV Networks Digital Suite; Nick Jr.; NickToons TV; Outdoor Channel; Speed; Style Network; Trio; Turner Classic Movies; Universal HD; WE tv.
Fee: $13.95 monthly.

Pay Service 1
Pay Units: N.A.
Programming (via satellite): HBO.
Fee: $14.95 installation; $13.95 monthly.

Digital Pay Service 1
Pay Units: N.A.
Programming (via satellite): Cinemax (multiplexed); Encore (multiplexed); Flix; HBO (multiplexed); Showtime (multiplexed); Showtime HD; Starz (multiplexed); The Movie Channel (multiplexed).
Fee: $10.95 monthly (Cinemax or Starz/Encore), $13.95 monthly (HBO or Showtime).

Video-On-Demand: No

Pay-Per-View
iN DEMAND (delivered digitally); Playboy TV (delivered digitally); Fresh (delivered digitally).

Internet Service
Operational: Yes. Began: December 2, 2001.
Subscribers: 1,500.
Broadband Service: CMA.
Fee: $39.95 installation; $41.95 monthly; $2.95 modem lease; $39.95 modem purchase.

Telephone Service
Digital: Operational
Fee: $39.95 monthly

Miles of Plant: 114.0 (coaxial); 14.0 (fiber optic).
General Manager: Kenneth Herrington. Chief Technician: Dio Perez. Marketing Director: Julie Ferguson. Office Manager: Rosemary Garcia.
Ownership: Cable Management Assoc. (MSO).

KINGWOOD—Suddenlink Communications, 4103 W Lake Houston Pkwy, Kingwood, TX 77339. Phones: 800-999-6845; 314-965-2020; 281-360-7500. Web Site: http://www.suddenlink.com. Also serves Porter. ICA: TX0052.
TV Market Ranking: 15 (KINGWOOD, Porter). Franchise award date: January 1, 1972. Franchise expiration date: N.A. Began: September 1, 1974.
Channel capacity: 78 (operating 2-way). Channels available but not in use: N.A.

Basic Service
Subscribers: 15,611.
Programming (received off-air): KETH-TV (TBN) Houston; KFTH-DT (TEL) Alvin; KHOU (CBS) Houston; KIAH (CW) Houston; KLTJ (ETV) Galveston; KPRC-TV (NBC) Houston; KPXB-TV (ION) Conroe; KRIV (FOX) Houston; KTBU (IND) Conroe; KTMD (TMO) Galveston; KTRK-TV (ABC) Houston; KTXH (MNT) Houston; KUBE-TV (IND) Baytown; KUHT (PBS) Houston; KXLN-DT (UNV) Rosenberg; KYAZ (IND) Katy; KZJL (IND) Houston; 14 FMs.
Programming (via satellite): TV Guide Network; WGN America.
Fee: $52.65 installation; $18.95 monthly; $5.00 converter; $10.00 additional installation.

Expanded Basic Service 1
Subscribers: N.A.
Programming (via satellite): A&E Networks; ABC Family Channel; AMC; Animal Planet; BET Networks; Bravo; Cartoon Network; CNBC; CNN; Comedy Central; Country Music TV; C-SPAN; C-SPAN 2;

Discovery Channel; Disney Channel; E! Entertainment Television; ESPN; ESPN 2; Eternal Word TV Network; Food Network; Fox News Channel; Fox Sports Southwest; Fox Sports World; FX; Golf Channel; Hallmark Channel; Headline News; HGTV; History Channel; Lifetime; Lifetime Movie Network; MSNBC; MTV; Nickelodeon; Outdoor Channel; Oxygen; Speed; Spike TV; Syfy; TBS Superstation; The Learning Channel; The Weather Channel; Travel Channel; truTV; Turner Classic Movies; Turner Network TV; TV Land; USA Network; VH1.
Fee: $27.00 monthly.

Digital Basic Service
Subscribers: 6,500.
Programming (via satellite): BBC America; Bio; Bloomberg Television; C-SPAN 3; Discovery Digital Networks; DIY Network; DMX Music; ESPN Classic Sports; ESPNews; Fox Movie Channel; FSN Digital Atlantic; FSN Digital Central; FSN Digital Pacific; Fuse; G4; GAS; GSN; History Channel International; Independent Film Channel; MTV Networks Digital Suite; National Geographic Channel; Nick Jr.; NickToons TV; SoapNet; Style Network; Sundance Channel; Toon Disney; Versus; WE tv.
Fee: $3.99 monthly.

Digital Pay Service 1
Pay Units: 468.
Programming (via satellite): Cinemax (multiplexed); Encore (multiplexed); Flix; HBO (multiplexed); Showtime (multiplexed); Starz (multiplexed); The Movie Channel (multiplexed).
Fee: $8.95 monthly (Starz & Encore), $9.95 monthly (Cinemax), $11.95 monthly (Showtime & TMC), $12.95 monthly (HBO).

Video-On-Demand: No

Pay-Per-View
Addressable homes: 6,500.
iN DEMAND (delivered digitally); Playboy TV (delivered digitally); Fresh (delivered digitally).

Internet Service
Operational: Yes. Began: June 3, 2004.
Subscribers: 8,765.
Broadband Service: Suddenlink High Speed Internet.
Fee: $49.95 installation; $24.95 monthly.

Telephone Service
Digital: Operational
Fee: $48.95 monthly

Miles of Plant: 195.0 (coaxial); 34.0 (fiber optic).
Regional Manager: Todd Cruthird. Plant Manager: Kyle Spell. Marketing Director: Beverly Gambell.
Ownership: Cequel Communications LLC (MSO).

KIRBYVILLE—Formerly served by CommuniComm Services. No longer in operation. ICA: TX0345.

KNOX CITY—Alliance Communications, 6125 Paluxy Dr, Tyler, TX 75703. Phones: 800-842-8160; 501-679-6619. Fax: 501-679-5694. Web Site: http://www.alliancecable.net. Also serves O'Brien. ICA: TX0429.
TV Market Ranking: Outside TV Markets (KNOX CITY, O'Brien). Franchise award date: N.A. Franchise expiration date: January 1, 2007. Began: December 1, 1957.
Channel capacity: 41 (not 2-way capable). Channels available but not in use: N.A.

Basic Service
Subscribers: 123.
Programming (received off-air): KJTL (FOX) Wichita Falls; KRBC-TV (NBC) Abilene; KTAB-TV (CBS) Abilene; KTXS-TV (ABC, CW, TMO) Sweetwater; 1 FM.
Programming (via satellite): A&E Networks; ABC Family Channel; AMC; AmericanLife TV Network; Animal Planet; Cartoon Network; CNN; Country Music TV; C-SPAN; Discovery Channel; Disney Channel; E! Entertainment Television; ESPN; Fox News Channel; Fox Sports Southwest; Headline News; History Channel; Lifetime; Nickelodeon; QVC; Spike TV; TBS Superstation; The Learning Channel; The Weather Channel; Travel Channel; Trinity Broadcasting Network; Turner Network TV; TV Land; USA Network; WGN America.
Fee: $29.95 installation; $38.00 monthly.

Expanded Basic Service 1
Subscribers: 90.

Pay Service 1
Pay Units: 151.
Programming (via satellite): HBO.
Fee: $9.95 monthly.

Pay Service 2
Pay Units: 71.
Programming (via satellite): Showtime.
Fee: $9.95 monthly.

Video-On-Demand: No

Internet Service
Operational: No.

Telephone Service
None

Miles of Plant: 32.0 (coaxial); None (fiber optic).
Vice President & General Manager: John Brinker. Vice President, Programming: Julie Newman.
Ownership: Buford Media Group LLC (MSO).

KOUNTZE—Time Warner Cable. Now served by BEAUMONT, TX [TX0022]. ICA: TX0386.

KRESS—Formerly served by Almega Cable. No longer in operation. ICA: TX0588.

KRUM—Suddenlink Communications, 12444 Powerscourt Dr, Saint Louis, MO 63131-3660. Phones: 800-999-6845 (Customer service); 314-965-2020. Fax: 903-561-5485. Web Site: http://www.suddenlink.com. ICA: TX0517.
TV Market Ranking: Below 100 (KRUM). Franchise award date: N.A. Franchise expiration date: N.A. Began: August 1, 1984.
Channel capacity: 54 (operating 2-way). Channels available but not in use: N.A.

Basic Service
Subscribers: 297.
Programming (received off-air): KAZD (IND) Lake Dallas; KDFI (MNT) Dallas; KDFW-DT (FOX) Dallas; KDTN (ETV) Denton; KERA-TV (PBS) Dallas; KMPX (IND) Decatur; KPXD-TV (ION) Arlington; KSTR-DT (TEL) Irving; KTVT (CBS) Fort Worth; KTXA (IND) Fort Worth; KUVN-DT (UNV) Garland; KXAS-TV (NBC) Fort Worth; KXII (CBS, FOX, MNT) Sherman; KXTX-TV (TMO) Dallas; WFAA (ABC) Dallas.
Programming (via satellite): C-SPAN; GalaVision; QVC; TBS Superstation; Trinity Broadcasting Network; WGN America.
Fee: $39.95 installation; $19.95 monthly.

Expanded Basic Service 1
Subscribers: N.A.
Programming (via satellite): A&E Networks; ABC Family Channel; AMC; Animal Planet; BET Networks; Bravo; Cartoon Network; CNBC; CNN; Comedy Central; Discovery Channel; Disney Channel; E! Entertainment Television; ESPN; ESPN 2; Food Network; Fox News Channel; Fox Sports Southwest; FX; Golf Channel; Great American Country; Hallmark Channel; Headline News; HGTV; History Channel; Lifetime; MSNBC; MTV; National Geographic Channel; Nickelodeon; Outdoor Channel; Speed; Spike TV; Syfy; TBS Superstation; The Learning Channel; The Weather Channel; Travel Channel; truTV; Turner Classic Movies; Turner Network TV; TV Guide Network; TV Land; USA Network; VH1.
Fee: $24.95 monthly.

Digital Basic Service
Subscribers: N.A.
Programming (via satellite): BBC America; Bio; Bloomberg Television; Canales N; cloo; C-SPAN 3; ESPN; ESPN Classic Sports; ESPNews; Fox College Sports Atlantic; Fox College Sports Central; Fox College Sports Pacific; Fox Movie Channel; Fox Soccer; Fuel TV; Fuse; G4; GSN; HD Theater; HDNet; HDNet Movies; History Channel International; Independent Film Channel; Military History Channel; Music Choice; SoapNet; Sundance Channel; Toon Disney; Versus; WE tv.
Fee: $3.99 monthly.

Digital Pay Service 1
Pay Units: N.A.
Programming (via satellite): Cinemax (multiplexed); Encore (multiplexed); Flix; HBO (multiplexed); HBO HD; Showtime (multiplexed); Showtime HD; Starz (multiplexed); The Movie Channel (multiplexed).

Video-On-Demand: No

Pay-Per-View
iN DEMAND (delivered digitally); Playboy TV (delivered digitally).

Internet Service
Operational: Yes. Began: December 22, 2003.
Broadband Service: Suddenlink High Speed Internet.
Fee: $49.95 installation; $38.95 monthly.

Telephone Service
None

Miles of Plant: 10.0 (coaxial); None (fiber optic).
Regional Manager: Todd Cruthird. Area Manager: Rodney Fletcher. Plant Manager: Judy Cheney.
Ownership: Cequel Communications LLC (MSO).

LA GRANGE—CMA Cablevision, 840 E Travis St, La Grange, TX 78945-2344. Phone: 979-968-6476. Fax: 979-968-5368. Web Site: http://www.cmaaccess.com. Also serves Giddings, Hallettsville, Schulenburg & Weimar. ICA: TX0073.
TV Market Ranking: Outside TV Markets (Giddings, Hallettsville, LA GRANGE, Schulenburg, Weimar). Franchise award date: January 11, 1978. Franchise expiration date: N.A. Began: December 1, 1962.
Channel capacity: N.A. Channels available but not in use: N.A.

Basic Service
Subscribers: 4,100.
Programming (received off-air): KEYE-TV (CBS, TMO) Austin; KHOU (CBS) Houston; KLRU (PBS) Austin; KNVA (CW) Austin; KSAT-TV (ABC) San Antonio; KTBC (FOX) Austin; KTRK-TV (ABC) Houston; KTXH (MNT) Houston; KVUE (ABC) Austin; KXAN-TV (NBC) Austin; KXLN-DT (UNV) Rosenberg; KYAZ (IND) Katy; allband FM.
Programming (via satellite): A&E Networks; ABC Family Channel; AMC; BET Networks; Bravo!; Cartoon Network; CNBC; CNN; Country Music TV; C-SPAN; Discovery Channel; E! Entertainment Television; ESPN; ESPN 2; Fox News Channel; Fox Sports Southwest; GalaVision; Hallmark Channel; Headline News; HGTV; History Channel; Lifetime; MTV; Nickelodeon; QVC; SoapNet; Spike TV; Syfy; TBS Superstation; The Learning Channel; The Weather Channel; Trinity Broadcasting Network; Turner Network TV; TV Land; USA Network; VH1; WGN America.
Fee: $39.95 installation; $17.45 monthly; $1.31 converter; $12.95 additional installation.

Digital Basic Service
Subscribers: N.A.
Programming (via satellite): BBC America; Bio; Discovery Digital Networks; DMX Music; ESPN Classic Sports; ESPNews; Fox Sports World; GAS; Golf Channel; GSN; History Channel International; Independent Film Channel; Lifetime Movie Network; MTV Networks Digital Suite; National Geographic Channel; Nick Jr.; NickToons TV; Outdoor Channel; Speed; Turner Classic Movies; WE tv.
Fee: $13.45 monthly.

Pay Service 1
Pay Units: 543.
Programming (via satellite): Showtime.
Fee: $14.95 installation; $13.95 monthly.

Pay Service 2
Pay Units: 786.
Programming (via satellite): HBO.
Fee: $14.95 installation; $13.95 monthly.

Digital Pay Service 1
Pay Units: N.A.
Programming (via satellite): Cinemax (multiplexed); Encore (multiplexed); HBO (multiplexed); Showtime (multiplexed); Starz (multiplexed); The Movie Channel (multiplexed).
Fee: $10.95 monthly (Cinemax or Starz/Encore), $13.95 monthly (HBO or Showtime).

Video-On-Demand: No

Pay-Per-View
iN DEMAND (delivered digitally); Playboy TV (delivered digitally).

Internet Service
Operational: Yes.
Subscribers: 1,200.
Broadband Service: CMA.
Fee: $36.95 installation; $39.95 monthly; $2.95 modem lease; $39.95 modem purchase.

Telephone Service
None

Miles of Plant: 170.0 (coaxial); 56.0 (fiber optic).
General Manager: Jerry L. Smith. Plant Manager: Grady Daniels. Marketing Director: Julie Ferguson.
Ownership: Cable Management Assoc. (MSO).

LA GRULLA—Time Warner Cable. Now served by PHARR, TX [TX0017]. ICA: TX0788.

LA PRYOR—Formerly served by Almega Cable. No longer in operation. ICA: TX0789.

LAKE ARROWHEAD—Windjammer Cable, 8500 W 110th St, Ste 600, Overland Park, KY 66210. Phone: 888-495-2881. Fax: 913-563-5454. Web Site: http://www.windjammercable.com. ICA: TX0923.
TV Market Ranking: Below 100 (LAKE ARROWHEAD). Franchise award date: N.A. Franchise expiration date: N.A. Began: N.A.
Channel capacity: N.A. Channels available but not in use: N.A.

Basic Service
Subscribers: N.A. Included in Wichita Falls
Programming (received off-air): KAUZ-TV (CBS, CW) Wichita Falls; KENS (CBS) San Antonio; KERA-TV (PBS) Dallas; KFDX-TV (NBC) Wichita Falls; KJBO-LP (MNT) Wichita Falls; KJTL (FOX) Wichita Falls; KSWO-TV (ABC, TMO) Lawton.
Programming (via satellite): C-SPAN; FamilyNet; QVC; Trinity Broadcasting Network.
Fee: $50.41 installation; $15.89 monthly.

Expanded Basic Service 1
Subscribers: 207.
Programming (via satellite): A&E Networks; ABC Family Channel; AMC; Cartoon Network; CNBC; CNN; Discovery Channel; Disney Channel; E! Entertainment Television; ESPN; Fox Sports Southwest; Headline News; History Channel; Lifetime; MoviePlex; MTV; Nickelodeon; Spike TV; TBS Superstation; The Learning Channel; The Weather Channel; Travel Channel; truTV; Turner Network TV; USA Network; WGN America.
Fee: $32.10 monthly.

Pay Service 1
Pay Units: N.A.
Programming (via satellite): Cinemax; HBO; Showtime.
Fee: $12.95 monthly (each).

Internet Service
Operational: No.

Telephone Service
None

Miles of Plant: 27.0 (coaxial); None (fiber optic).
General Manager: Timothy Evard. Operations Director: Belinda Graham. Engineering Director: Mike Earehart. Finance & Accounting Director: Cindy Johnson.
Ownership: Windjammer Communications LLC (MSO).

LAKE BROWNWOOD—Formerly served by National Cable Inc. No longer in operation. ICA: TX0419.

LAKE BUCHANAN—Northland Cable Television, 1101 Mission Hill Dr, PO Box 366, Marble Falls, TX 78654-0366. Phone: 830-693-7500. Fax: 830-693-6056. E-mail: larson@nctv.com. Web Site: http://www.northlandcabletv.com. Also serves Inks Lake. ICA: TX0800.
TV Market Ranking: Below 100 (Inks Lake, LAKE BUCHANAN). Franchise award date: N.A. Franchise expiration date: N.A. Began: N.A.
Channel capacity: 65 (2-way capable). Channels available but not in use: N.A.

Basic Service
Subscribers: 900.
Programming (received off-air): KCWX (IND, MNT) Fredericksburg; KEYE-TV (CBS, TMO) Austin; KLRU (PBS) Austin; KNVA (CW) Austin; KTBC (FOX) Austin; KVUE (ABC) Austin; KXAN-TV (NBC) Austin.
Programming (via satellite): A&E Networks; ABC Family Channel; Cartoon Network; CNN; C-SPAN; Discovery Channel; ESPN; Fox News Channel; Fox Sports Southwest; Great American Country; Headline News; History Channel; Home & Garden Television; Lifetime; National Geographic Channel; QVC; Spike TV; Syfy; TBS Superstation; The Learning Channel; The Weather Channel; Trinity Broadcasting Network; Turner Classic Movies; Turner Network TV; TV Land; USA Network.
Fee: $50.00 installation; $38.99 monthly.

Pay Service 1
Pay Units: 84.
Programming (via satellite): HBO.
Fee: $13.50 monthly.

Pay Service 2
Pay Units: 47.
Programming (via satellite): Showtime.
Fee: $13.50 monthly.

Pay Service 3
Pay Units: N.A.
Programming (via satellite): Cinemax.

Internet Service
Operational: No.

Telephone Service
None

Miles of Plant: 6.0 (coaxial); None (fiber optic).
Marketing Director: Bonnie Moran. Regional Manager: Larson Lloyd. Plant Manager: Ron Gardner.
Ownership: Northland Communications Corp. (MSO).

LAKE CHEROKEE—Alliance Communications, 6125 Paluxy Dr, Tyler, TX 75703. Phones: 800-842-8160; 501-679-6619. Fax: 501-679-5694. Web Site: http://www.alliancecable.net. Also serves Beckville, Easton, Lakeport & Tatum. ICA: TX0795.
TV Market Ranking: Below 100 (Beckville, Easton, LAKE CHEROKEE, Lakeport, Tatum). Franchise award date: N.A. Franchise expiration date: N.A. Began: October 1, 1984.
Channel capacity: N.A. Channels available but not in use: N.A.

Basic Service
Subscribers: 745.
Programming (received off-air): KETK-TV (NBC) Jacksonville; KFXK-TV (FOX) Longview; KLTS-TV (PBS) Shreveport; KLTV (ABC, TMO) Tyler; KSLA (CBS) Shreveport; KTAL-TV (NBC) Texarkana; KTBS-TV (ABC) Shreveport; KYTX (CBS, IND) Nacogdoches.
Programming (via satellite): CW+; QVC; Univision Studios.
Fee: $54.95 installation; $20.95 monthly.

Expanded Basic Service 1
Subscribers: 678.
Programming (via satellite): A&E Networks; ABC Family Channel; AMC; Animal Planet; BET Networks; Bio; Cartoon Network; CNBC; CNN; Comedy Central; C-SPAN; Discovery Channel; Disney Channel; E! Entertainment Television; ESPN; ESPN 2; Food Network; Fox News Channel; Fox Sports Southwest; FX; Great American Country; Headline News; HGTV; History Channel; Lifetime; MSNBC; MTV; National Geographic Channel; Nickelodeon; Outdoor Channel; Spike TV; Syfy; TBS Superstation; The Learning Channel; The Weather Channel; Travel Channel; Trinity Broadcasting Network; Turner Classic Movies; Turner Network TV; TV Land; USA Network; VH1.
Fee: $23.10 monthly.

Pay Service 1
Pay Units: 181.
Programming (via satellite): Cinemax.
Fee: $12.95 monthly.

Pay Service 2
Pay Units: 341.
Programming (via satellite): HBO.
Fee: $12.95 monthly.

Pay Service 3
Pay Units: N.A.
Programming (via satellite): Flix.
Fee: $12.95 monthly.

Pay Service 4
Pay Units: 437.
Programming (via satellite): Showtime; The Movie Channel.

Fee: $12.95 monthly.

Video-On-Demand: No

Internet Service
Operational: Yes.
Fee: $100.00 installation; $29.95 monthly.

Telephone Service
None

Miles of Plant: 104.0 (coaxial); None (fiber optic).
Vice President & General Manager: John Brinker. Vice President, Programming: Julie Newman.
Ownership: Buford Media Group LLC (MSO).

LAKE GRAHAM—TGN Cable, Rte 2, PO Box 110, Olney, TX 76374. Phones: 800-687-7311; 940-873-4563. Fax: 940-873-4563. E-mail: bill@tgncable.net. Web Site: http://www.tgncable.com. ICA: TX1012.
TV Market Ranking: Outside TV Markets (LAKE GRAHAM).
Channel capacity: N.A. Channels available but not in use: N.A.

Basic Service
Subscribers: 155.
Programming (received off-air): KAUZ-TV (CBS, CW) Wichita Falls; KFDX-TV (NBC) Wichita Falls; KJTL (FOX) Wichita Falls; KSWO-TV (ABC, TMO) Lawton.
Programming (via satellite): ABC Family Channel; CNBC; CNN; C-SPAN; Discovery Channel; G4; Headline News; Paxson Communications Corp.; TBS Superstation; The Learning Channel; The Weather Channel; Toon Disney; Trinity Broadcasting Network; TV Land; WGN America.
Fee: $27.86 monthly.

Expanded Basic Service 1
Subscribers: N.A.
Programming (received off-air): KFDX-TV (NBC) Wichita Falls.
Programming (via satellite): A&E Networks; AMC; Animal Planet; Cartoon Network; Country Music TV; Disney Channel; ESPN; ESPN 2; Food Network; Fox News Channel; Fox Sports Southwest; FX; Hallmark Channel; HGTV; History Channel; Lifetime; MTV; Nickelodeon; Outdoor Channel; Shepherds Chapel Network; Speed; Syfy; Travel Channel; Turner Classic Movies; Turner Network TV; USA Network; VH1.
Fee: $16.91 monthly.

Digital Basic Service
Subscribers: N.A.
Programming (via satellite): BBC America; Bio; Bravo; cloo; Discovery Digital Networks; Fox College Sports Atlantic; Fox College Sports Central; Fox College Sports Pacific; Fox Movie Channel; Fox Sports World; Fuse; GAS; Golf Channel; Great American Country; GSN; Halogen Network; History Channel; History Channel International; Independent Film Channel; Lifetime Movie Network; MTV Networks Digital Suite; National Geographic Channel; Nick Jr.; NickToons TV; Ovation; ShopNBC; Style Network; Sundance Channel; Turner Classic Movies; Versus; WE tv.
Fee: $20.95 monthly.

Pay Service 1
Pay Units: N.A.
Programming (via satellite): Cinemax; HBO.
Fee: $13.47 monthly.

Digital Pay Service 1
Pay Units: N.A.
Programming (via satellite): Cinemax (multiplexed); Encore (multiplexed); Flix; HBO (multiplexed); Showtime (multiplexed); Starz (multiplexed); The Movie Channel (multiplexed).
Fee: $13.47 monthly (HBO/Cinemax), $7.01 monthly (Showtime/TMC or Starz/Encore).

Video-On-Demand: No

Internet Service
Operational: Yes.
Broadband Service: In-house.
Fee: $24.95 monthly; $5.00 modem lease; $59.95 modem purchase.

Telephone Service
None

Miles of Plant: 5.0 (coaxial); None (fiber optic).
Manager: Bill Tyler. Office Manager: Jan Tyler.
Ownership: Bill Tyler (MSO).

LAKE HILLS—Zoom Media, PO Box 2126, Flint, TX 75762. Phone: 855-261-5304. Web Site: http://www.zoommediallc.com. ICA: TX1021.
TV Market Ranking: 45 (LAKE HILLS).
Channel capacity: N.A. Channels available but not in use: N.A.

Basic Service
Subscribers: 58.
Programming (received off-air): KABB (FOX) San Antonio; KENS (CBS) San Antonio; KLRN (PBS) San Antonio; KMYS (CW) Kerrville; KPXL-TV (ION) Uvalde; KSAT-TV (ABC) San Antonio; KVDA (TMO) San Antonio; KWEX-DT (UNV) San Antonio.
Programming (via satellite): A&E Networks; ABC Family Channel; AMC; Animal Planet; Cartoon Network; CNBC; CNN; Comedy Central; C-SPAN; C-SPAN 2; Discovery Channel; Disney Channel; E! Entertainment Television; ESPN; ESPN 2; Fox News Channel; Fox Sports Southwest; FX; Headline News; HGTV; Lifetime; MTV; Nickelodeon; QVC; Spike TV; TBS Superstation; The Learning Channel; The Weather Channel; truTV; Turner Network TV; TV Land; USA Network; VH1.
Fee: $40.82 monthly.

Pay Service 1
Pay Units: N.A.
Programming (via satellite): Encore; HBO; Showtime; Starz.

Video-On-Demand: Yes

Internet Service
Operational: Yes.
Fee: $20.99-$49.99 monthly.

Telephone Service
Digital: Operational
Fee: $49.95 monthly

Chief Executive Officer: Steve Houston.
Ownership: Zoom Media LLC (MSO).

LAKE LIVINGSTON—Suddenlink Communications, 12444 Powerscourt Dr, Saint Louis, MO 63131-3660. Phones: 800-999-

6845 (Customer service); 888-707-1826; 314-965-2020. Fax: 903-561-5485. Web Site: http://www.suddenlink.com. Also serves Coldspring, Onalaska, Point Blank, Shepherd & Trinity. ICA: TX0851.

TV Market Ranking: Outside TV Markets (Coldspring, LAKE LIVINGSTON, Onalaska, Point Blank, Shepherd, Trinity). Franchise award date: N.A. Franchise expiration date: N.A. Began: January 31, 1972.

Channel capacity: 35 (operating 2-way). Channels available but not in use: N.A.

Basic Service

Subscribers: 7,200.

Programming (received off-air): KBTX-TV (CBS, CW) Bryan; KETK-TV (NBC) Jacksonville; KIAH (CW) Houston; KPRC-TV (NBC) Houston; KRIV (FOX) Houston; KTRE (ABC) Lufkin; KTRK-TV (ABC) Houston; KTXH (MNT) Houston; KUHT (PBS) Houston; KYTX (CBS, IND) Nacogdoches; 9 FMs.

Fee: $52.00 installation; $19.95 monthly.

Expanded Basic Service 1

Subscribers: N.A.

Programming (via satellite): A&E Networks; ABC Family Channel; AMC; Animal Planet; BET Networks; Cartoon Network; CNBC; CNN; Comedy Central; Discovery Channel; Disney Channel; E! Entertainment Television; ESPN; ESPN 2; Food Network; Fox News Channel; Fox Sports Southwest; FX; Great American Country; Headline News; HGTV; History Channel; Lifetime; MSNBC; MTV; National Geographic Channel; Nickelodeon; Outdoor Channel; Spike TV; Syfy; TBS Superstation; The Learning Channel; The Weather Channel; Trinity Broadcasting Network; Turner Classic Movies; Turner Network TV; USA Network.

Digital Basic Service

Subscribers: N.A.

Programming (via satellite): BBC America; Bio; Bloomberg Television; cloo; Discovery Digital Networks; DMX Music; ESPN Classic Sports; ESPNews; Fox College Sports Atlantic; Fox College Sports Central; Fox College Sports Pacific; Fox Soccer; Fuse; G4; Golf Channel; GSN; History Channel International; Independent Film Channel; ShopNBC; Speed; Style Network; Sundance Channel; Toon Disney; Versus; WE tv.

Pay Service 1

Pay Units: 250.

Programming (via satellite): Cinemax; HBO; Showtime.

Fee: $9.95 monthly (Cinemax or Showtime), $12.00 monthly (HBO).

Digital Pay Service 1

Pay Units: N.A.

Programming (via satellite): Cinemax (multiplexed); Encore (multiplexed); Flix; HBO (multiplexed); Showtime (multiplexed); Starz (multiplexed); The Movie Channel (multiplexed).

Video-On-Demand: No

Pay-Per-View

iN DEMAND (delivered digitally); Playboy TV (delivered digitally); Fresh (delivered digitally); Shorteez (delivered digitally).

Internet Service

Operational: Yes. Began: June 3, 2004.

Subscribers: 140.

Broadband Service: Suddenlink High Speed Internet.

Fee: $49.95 installation; $38.95 monthly.

Telephone Service

None

Miles of Plant: 200.0 (coaxial); 12.0 (fiber optic). Additional miles planned: 25.0 (coaxial); 31.0 (fiber optic).

Manager: Jim Cox. Marketing Manager: Beverly Gambell. Office Manager: Timmie Adams.

Ownership: Cequel Communications LLC (MSO).

LAKE PALESTINE EAST—Northland Cable Television, 10147 FM 346 West, PO Box 538, Flint, TX 75762-0538. Phones: 903-566-8757; 903-894-8200. Fax: 903-894-8204. E-mail: flint@northlandcabletv.com. Web Site: http://www.northlandcabletv.com. Also serves Big Eddy, Bullard, Emerald Bay, Flint (unincorporated areas), Gresham (unincorporated areas), Lake Tyler, New Chapel Hill, Noonday & Smith (unincorporated areas). ICA: TX0220.

TV Market Ranking: Below 100 (Big Eddy, Bullard, Emerald Bay, Flint (unincorporated areas), Gresham (unincorporated areas), LAKE PALESTINE EAST, Lake Tyler, New Chapel Hill, Noonday, Smith (unincorporated areas)). Franchise award date: November 17, 1982. Franchise expiration date: N.A. Began: April 1, 1983.

Channel capacity: 62 (operating 2-way). Channels available but not in use: N.A.

Basic Service

Subscribers: 4,900.

Programming (received off-air): KETK-TV (NBC) Jacksonville; KFXK-TV (FOX) Longview; KLTV (ABC, TMO) Tyler; KTPN-LP Tyler; KYTX (CBS, IND) Nacogdoches.

Programming (via microwave): KDFI (MNT) Dallas; KERA-TV (PBS) Dallas; WFAA (ABC) Dallas.

Programming (via satellite): Animal Planet; C-SPAN; CW+; QVC.

Fee: $49.95 installation; $19.95 additional installation.

Expanded Basic Service 1

Subscribers: 4,497.

Programming (via satellite): A&E Networks; BET Networks; Cartoon Network; CNBC; CNN; Comedy Central; Discovery Channel; E! Entertainment Television; ESPN; ESPN 2; Food Network; Fox Movie Channel; Fox News Channel; Fox Sports Southwest; FX; Golf Channel; Great American Country; Hallmark Channel; Headline News; HGTV; Lifetime; MTV; Nickelodeon; Spike TV; TBS Superstation; The Learning Channel; The Weather Channel; Travel Channel; Trinity Broadcasting Network; Turner Classic Movies; Turner Network TV; TV Land; USA Network.

Fee: $24.95 installation; $49.99 monthly; $10.00 additional installation.

Digital Basic Service

Subscribers: N.A.

Programming (via satellite): AmericanLife TV Network; BBC America; Bloomberg Television; Bravo; Discovery Health Channel; Discovery Home Channel; Discovery Kids Channel; Discovery Times Channel; DMX Music; ESPN HD; ESPNews; Fox Soccer; G4; Golf Channel; GSN; Halogen Network; HD Theater; History Channel; Independent Film Channel; Military Channel; National Geographic Channel; Outdoor Channel; Science; Speed; Syfy; Turner Network TV HD; Universal HD; Versus; WE tv.

Fee: $5.00 monthly.

Pay Service 1

Pay Units: N.A.

Programming (via satellite): HBO.

Fee: $13.50 monthly.

Digital Pay Service 1

Pay Units: 675.

Programming (via satellite): HBO (multiplexed).

Fee: $24.95 installation; $14.00 monthly; $10.00 additional installation.

Digital Pay Service 2

Pay Units: 340.

Programming (via satellite): Cinemax (multiplexed).

Fee: $24.95 installation; $14.00 monthly.

Digital Pay Service 3

Pay Units: 370.

Programming (via satellite): Flix; Showtime (multiplexed); The Movie Channel (multiplexed).

Fee: $24.95 installation; $14.00 monthly.

Digital Pay Service 4

Pay Units: 1,220.

Programming (via satellite): Encore (multiplexed); Starz (multiplexed).

Fee: $24.95 installation; $14.00 monthly.

Video-On-Demand: No

Pay-Per-View

iN DEMAND (delivered digitally); Playboy TV (delivered digitally); Fresh (delivered digitally); Hot Choice (delivered digitally).

Internet Service

Operational: Yes. Began: July 1, 2003.

Subscribers: 130.

Broadband Service: Northland Express.

Fee: $42.99 monthly; $2.99 modem lease; $90.00 modem purchase.

Telephone Service

Digital: Operational

Fee: $29.99 monthly

Miles of Plant: 450.0 (coaxial); 65.0 (fiber optic). Additional miles planned: 12.0 (fiber optic).

Manager: Mark Graves. Chief Technician: Tony Moffitt.

Ownership: Northland Communications Corp. (MSO).

LAKE PALESTINE WEST—Northland Cable Television, 10147 FM 346 West, PO Box 538, Flint, TX 75762-0538. Phones: 903-566-8757; 903-894-8200. Fax: 903-894-8204. E-mail: flint@northlandcabletv.com. Web Site: http://www.northlandcabletv.com. Also serves Anderson County (unincorporated areas), Berryville, Chandler, Frankston, Jackson's Landing (unincorporated aresas) & Red Ackers. ICA: TX0368.

TV Market Ranking: Below 100 (Anderson County (unincorporated areas), Berryville, Chandler, Frankston, Jackson's Landing (unincorporated aresas), LAKE PALESTINE WEST, Red Ackers). Franchise award date: June 7, 1982. Franchise expiration date: N.A. Began: June 1, 1983.

Channel capacity: 62 (operating 2-way). Channels available but not in use: N.A.

Basic Service

Subscribers: 2,426.

Programming (received off-air): KETK-TV (NBC) Jacksonville; KFXK-TV (FOX) Longview; KLTV (ABC, TMO) Tyler; KTPN-LP Tyler.

Programming (via microwave): KDFI (MNT) Dallas; KERA-TV (PBS) Dallas; KTVT (CBS) Fort Worth; WFAA (ABC) Dallas.

Programming (via satellite): A&E Networks; Animal Planet; Cartoon Network; CNN; C-SPAN; Discovery Channel; ESPN; Fox News Channel; Fox Sports Southwest; Great American Country; Hallmark Channel; Headline News; QVC; TBS Superstation; The Learning Channel; The Weather Channel; Travel Channel; Trinity Broadcasting Network; Turner Network TV; TV Guide Network; USA Network.

Fee: $49.95 installation; $34.70 monthly.

Expanded Basic Service 1

Subscribers: 1,742.

Programming (via satellite): CNBC; Comedy Central; E! Entertainment Television; ESPN 2; Food Network; Fox Movie Channel; FX; HGTV; Lifetime; MTV; Nickelodeon; Spike TV; Turner Classic Movies; TV Land.

Fee: $49.95 installation; $43.50 monthly.

Digital Basic Service

Subscribers: N.A.

Programming (via satellite): BBC America; Discovery Digital Networks; Golf Channel; GSN; Halogen Network; History Channel; Outdoor Channel; Speed; Syfy.

Fee: $51.99 monthly.

Digital Expanded Basic Service

Subscribers: N.A.

Programming (via satellite): AmericanLife TV Network; Bloomberg Television; Bravo; DMX Music; G4; Independent Film Channel; Versus; WE tv.

Pay Service 1

Pay Units: N.A.

Programming (via satellite): HBO.

Digital Pay Service 1

Pay Units: 315.

Programming (via satellite): Encore (multiplexed); Starz (multiplexed).

Fee: $49.95 installation; $9.95 monthly.

Digital Pay Service 2

Pay Units: 208.

Programming (via satellite): HBO (multiplexed).

Fee: $49.95 installation; $12.25 monthly.

Digital Pay Service 3

Pay Units: 83.

Programming (via satellite): Cinemax (multiplexed).

Fee: $49.95 installation; $9.95 monthly.

Digital Pay Service 4

Pay Units: 98.

Programming (via satellite): Showtime (multiplexed); The Movie Channel (multiplexed).

Fee: $49.95 installation; $11.95 monthly.

Video-On-Demand: No

Pay-Per-View

Addressable homes: 6,500.

iN DEMAND (delivered digitally).

Internet Service

Operational: Yes. Began: July 1, 2003.

Subscribers: 130.

Broadband Service: Northland Express.

Fee: $42.99 monthly.

Telephone Service

Digital: Operational

Fee: $29.99 monthly

Miles of Plant: 80.0 (coaxial); None (fiber optic).

Manager: Jim Wiggins. Chief Technician: Jim Bob Sanders. Billing Coordinator: Charlotte Griffen.

Ownership: Northland Communications Corp. (MSO).

LAMESA—Northland Cable Television, 1012 S 1st St, Lamesa, TX 79331-6147. Phone: 806-872-8561. Fax: 806-872-8825. E-mail: brent_richey@northlandcabletv.com. Web Site: http://www.northlandcabletv.com. Also serves Dawson County (unincorporated areas). ICA: TX0148.

TV Market Ranking: Below 100 (Dawson County (unincorporated areas) (portions)); Outside TV Markets (Dawson County (unincorporated areas) (portions), LAMESA). Franchise award date: January 1, 1966. Franchise expiration date: N.A. Began: April 1, 1966.

Channel capacity: 61 (operating 2-way). Channels available but not in use: N.A.

Basic Service

Subscribers: 2,758.

Programming (received off-air): KAMC (ABC) Lubbock; KCBD (NBC) Lubbock; KJTV-TV (FOX) Lubbock; KLBK-TV (CBS) Lubbock; KMID (ABC) Midland; KMLM-

DT (IND) Odessa; KPEJ-TV (FOX) Odessa; KPTB-DT (IND) Lubbock; KTXT-TV (PBS) Lubbock; KUPB (UNV) Midland; allband FM.

Programming (via satellite): A&E Networks; Animal Planet; Canales N; Cartoon Network; CNBC; CNN; Comedy Central; C-SPAN; Discovery Channel; ESPN; ESPN 2; Food Network; Fox Movie Channel; Fox News Channel; Fox Sports Southwest; FX; GalaVision; Great American Country; Hallmark Channel; Headline News; HGTV; History Channel; Lifetime; MTV; National Geographic Channel; Nickelodeon; QVC; SoapNet; Spike TV; Syfy; TBS Superstation; Telemundo; The Learning Channel; The Weather Channel; Travel Channel; Trinity Broadcasting Network; Turner Classic Movies; Turner Network TV; TV Guide Network; USA Network; VH1.

Fee: $50.00 installation; $33.99 monthly.

Digital Basic Service

Subscribers: N.A.

Programming (via satellite): BBC America; Discovery Digital Networks; Golf Channel; GSN; Halogen Network; Outdoor Channel; Speed.

Fee: $52.69 monthly.

Digital Expanded Basic Service

Subscribers: N.A.

Programming (via satellite): AmericanLife TV Network; Bloomberg Television; DMX Music; G4; Outdoor Channel; WE tv.

Digital Pay Service 1

Pay Units: 370.

Programming (via satellite): Cinemax (multiplexed); Encore (multiplexed); Flix; HBO (multiplexed); Showtime (multiplexed); Starz (multiplexed); The Movie Channel (multiplexed).

Video-On-Demand: No

Internet Service

Operational: Yes.

Broadband Service: Northland Express.

Fee: $42.99 monthly.

Telephone Service

None

Miles of Plant: 57.0 (coaxial); None (fiber optic). Additional miles planned: 3.0 (coaxial).

Regional Manager: Brent Richey. Manager & Chief Technician: Mickey Flanagan. Office Manager: Beverlee Kinnison.

Ownership: Northland Communications Corp. (MSO).

LAMPASAS—Suddenlink Communications, 403 E 3rd St, Lampasas, TX 76550. Phones: 512-556-8244; 314-965-2020. Web Site: http://www.suddenlink.com. Also serves Lampasas County. ICA: TX0183.

TV Market Ranking: Below 100 (LAMPASAS, Lampasas County (portions)); Outside TV Markets (Lampasas County (portions)). Franchise award date: March 29, 1962. Franchise expiration date: N.A. Began: January 1, 1964.

Channel capacity: 53 (operating 2-way). Channels available but not in use: N.A.

Basic Service

Subscribers: 2,309.

Programming (received off-air): KAKW-DT (UNV) Killeen; KCEN-TV (NBC, IND) Temple; KNCT (PBS) Belton; KNVA (CW) Austin; KTBC (FOX) Austin; KVUE (ABC) Austin; KWKT-TV (FOX, MNT) Waco; KWTX-TV (CBS, CW) Waco; KXXV (ABC, TMO) Waco.

Programming (via satellite): Shopping Channel; The Weather Channel; TV Guide Network.

Fee: $35.00 installation; $19.95 monthly; $1.02 converter; $15.37 additional installation.

Expanded Basic Service 1

Subscribers: N.A.

Programming (via satellite): A&E Networks; ABC Family Channel; AMC; Animal Planet; Cartoon Network; CNBC; CNN; Comedy Central; C-SPAN; C-SPAN 2; Discovery Channel; Disney Channel; E! Entertainment Television; ESPN; ESPN 2; Food Network; Fox News Channel; Fox Sports Southwest; FX; GalaVision; Great American Country; Headline News; HGTV; History Channel; INSP; Lifetime; MSNBC; MTV; National Geographic Channel; Nickelodeon; Outdoor Channel; QVC; Spike TV; Syfy; TBS Superstation; The Learning Channel; Turner Classic Movies; Turner Network TV; TV Land; USA Network.

Fee: $25.00 monthly.

Digital Basic Service

Subscribers: N.A.

Programming (via satellite): BBC America; Bio; cloo; Discovery Digital Networks; DMX Music; ESPN Classic Sports; ESPNews; Fox Soccer; Fuse; Golf Channel; GSN; History Channel International; Independent Film Channel; Speed; Toon Disney; Versus; WE tv.

Fee: $3.99 monthly.

Pay Service 1

Pay Units: 320.

Programming (via satellite): Cinemax.

Fee: $15.70 installation; $15.95 monthly.

Pay Service 2

Pay Units: 321.

Programming (via satellite): HBO.

Fee: $15.70 installation; $15.95 monthly.

Pay Service 3

Pay Units: 108.

Programming (via satellite): Showtime.

Fee: $15.70 installation; $12.95 monthly.

Pay Service 4

Pay Units: 108.

Programming (via satellite): The Movie Channel.

Fee: $15.70 installation; $12.95 monthly.

Digital Pay Service 1

Pay Units: N.A.

Programming (via satellite): Cinemax (multiplexed); Encore (multiplexed); HBO (multiplexed); Showtime (multiplexed); Starz (multiplexed); The Movie Channel (multiplexed).

Video-On-Demand: No

Pay-Per-View

iN DEMAND (delivered digitally); Playboy TV (delivered digitally).

Internet Service

Operational: Yes. Began: November 12, 2003.

Broadband Service: Suddenlink High Speed Internet.

Fee: $45.95 installation; $29.95 monthly; $9.95 modem lease.

Telephone Service

Digital: Operational

Fee: $44.95 monthly

Miles of Plant: 52.0 (coaxial); 3.0 (fiber optic).

Regional Manager: Todd Cruthird. Marketing Director: Beverly Gambell.

Ownership: Cequel Communications LLC (MSO).

LANEVILLE—Formerly served by Cebridge Connections. No longer in operation. ICA: TX0796.

LANSING—Zoom Media, PO Box 2126, Flint, TX 75762. Phone: 855-261-5304. Web Site: http://www.zoommediallc.com. Also serves Harrison County (portions). ICA: TX0336.

TV Market Ranking: Below 100 (Harrison County (portions), LANSING). Franchise award date: N.A. Franchise expiration date: N.A. Began: N.A.

Channel capacity: 36 (not 2-way capable). Channels available but not in use: N.A.

Basic Service

Subscribers: 121.

Programming (received off-air): KETK-TV (NBC) Jacksonville; KFXK-TV (FOX) Longview; KLTS-TV (PBS) Shreveport; KLTV (ABC, TMO) Tyler; KSLA (CBS) Shreveport.

Programming (via satellite): A&E Networks; ABC Family Channel; AmericanLife TV Network; CNN; Country Music TV; Discovery Channel; ESPN; Fox Sports Southwest; Spike TV; TBS Superstation; Turner Network TV; USA Network; WGN America.

Fee: $54.95 installation; $44.05 monthly.

Expanded Basic Service 1

Subscribers: 96.

Pay Service 1

Pay Units: 36.

Programming (via satellite): Cinemax.

Fee: $12.95 monthly.

Pay Service 2

Pay Units: 73.

Programming (via satellite): HBO.

Fee: $12.95 monthly.

Pay Service 3

Pay Units: 93.

Programming (via satellite): Showtime.

Fee: $12.95 monthly.

Video-On-Demand: No

Internet Service

Operational: No.

Telephone Service

None

Miles of Plant: 48.0 (coaxial); None (fiber optic).

Chief Executive Officer: Steve Houston.

Ownership: Zoom Media LLC (MSO).

LAREDO—Time Warner Cable, 1313 W Carlton Rd, Laredo, TX 78041. Phones: 956-721-0607; 972-899-7300 (Flower Mound division office). Fax: 956-721-0612. Web Site: http://www.timewarnercable.com/Texas. Also serves Rio Bravo & Webb County. ICA: TX0029.

TV Market Ranking: Below 100 (LAREDO, Rio Bravo, Webb County (portions)); Outside TV Markets (Webb County (portions)). Franchise award date: N.A. Franchise expiration date: N.A. Began: November 1, 1961.

Channel capacity: N.A. Channels available but not in use: N.A.

Basic Service

Subscribers: 32,000.

Programming (received off-air): KGNS-TV (CW, NBC, TMO) Laredo; KLDO-TV (FOX, UNV) Laredo; KVTV (CBS) Laredo; KXOF-CA (FOX) Laredo.

Programming (via microwave): KABB (FOX) San Antonio; KENS (CBS) San Antonio; KLRN (PBS) San Antonio; KSAT-TV (ABC) San Antonio.

Programming (via satellite): Azteca America; C-SPAN; C-SPAN 2; Eternal Word TV Network; QVC; ShopNBC; various Mexican stations (multiplexed); WGN America.

Fee: $50.51 installation; $11.24 monthly.

Expanded Basic Service 1

Subscribers: N.A.

Programming (via satellite): A&E Networks; ABC Family Channel; AMC; Animal Planet; Bravo; Cartoon Network; CNBC; CNN; Comedy Central; Country Music TV; Discovery Channel; Discovery Health Channel; Disney Channel; E! Entertainment Television; ESPN; ESPN 2; Food Network; Fox News Channel; Fox Sports Southwest; Fuse; FX; GalaVision; Golf Channel; Headline News; HGTV; History Channel; ION Television; Lifetime; Lifetime Movie Network; MSNBC; MTV; mun2 television; National Geographic Channel; Nickelodeon; Oxygen; ShopNBC; SoapNet; Spike TV; Style Network; Syfy; TBS Superstation; Telefutura; Telemundo; Texas Cable News; The Learning Channel; The Weather Channel; Tr3s; Travel Channel; truTV; Turner Network TV; TV Guide Network; TV Land; USA Network; VH1; WE tv.

Fee: $36.71 monthly.

Digital Basic Service

Subscribers: 13,869.

Programming (via satellite): A&E Networks; ABC Family Channel; AMC; Animal Planet; BBC America; Bio; Bloomberg Television; Boomerang; Bravo; Cartoon Network; cloo; CNBC; CNN; Comedy Central; Cooking Channel; Country Music TV; C-SPAN; C-SPAN 2; C-SPAN 3; Current; Daystar TV Network; Discovery Channel; Discovery Fit & Health; Discovery Health Channel; Discovery Home Channel; Discovery Kids Channel; Discovery Times Channel; Disney Channel; DIY Network; E! Entertainment Television; ESPN; ESPN 2; ESPN 2 HD; ESPN Classic Sports; ESPN HD; ESPN U; ESPNews; Eternal Word TV Network; Exercise TV; Food Network; Food Network On Demand; Fox Business Channel; Fox News Channel; Fox Reality Channel; Fox Sports Southwest; Fuse; FX; G4; Golf Channel; Great American Country; GSN; Hallmark Channel; HD Theater; HDNet; HDNet Movies; Headline News; HGTV; HGTV On Demand; History Channel; History Channel International; ION Television; La Familia Network; Lifetime; Lifetime Movie Network; Lifetime Real Women; Military Channel; MSNBC; MTV; MTV Hits; MTV2; Music Choice; National Geographic Channel; Nick Jr.; Nickelodeon; NickToons TV; Nuvo TV; Outdoor Channel; Ovation; Oxygen; QVC; Science; SoapNet; Speed; Spike TV; Style Network; Syfy; TBS Superstation; TeenNick; Texas Cable News; The Learning Channel; The Weather Channel; Toon Disney; Tr3s; Travel Channel; Trinity Broadcasting Network; truTV; Turner Classic Movies; Turner Network TV; Turner Network TV HD; TV Guide Network; TV Guide SPOT; Universal HD; USA Network; Versus; VH1; VH1 Classic; WE tv.

Fee: $5.04 monthly.

Digital Expanded Basic Service
Subscribers: N.A.
Programming (via satellite): Canal Sur; Cine Latino; CNN en Espanol; Discovery en Espanol; Encore; ESPN Deportes; EWTN en Espanol; Flix; Fox College Sports Atlantic; Fox College Sports Central; Fox College Sports Pacific; Fox Deportes; Fox Movie Channel; Fox Soccer; Fox Sports Southwest; Fuel TV; GalaVision; HTV Musica; Infinito; La Familia Network; mun2 television; NBA TV; Puma TV; Sorpresa; Sundance Channel; Tennis Channel; Toon Disney en Espanol; Tr3s; TVE Internacional; Utilisima; VHUNO; Video Rola.
Digital Pay Service 1
Pay Units: N.A.
Programming (via satellite): Cinemax (multiplexed); Cinemax On Demand; HBO (multiplexed); HBO HD; HBO on Broadband; Howard TV; Showtime (multiplexed); Showtime HD; Showtime On Demand; Starz (multiplexed); The Movie Channel (multiplexed); The Movie Channel On Demand.
Fee: $12.95 monthly (each).
Video-On-Demand: Yes
Pay-Per-View
Hot Choice (delivered digitally); NBA (delivered digitally); Game Plan (delivered digitally); ESPN Extra (delivered digitally); ESPN Now (delivered digitally); iN DEMAND (delivered digitally); Shorteez (delivered digitally); Fresh (delivered digitally); Variety; iN DEMAND (delivered digitally); Playboy TV (delivered digitally); Spice.
Internet Service
Operational: Yes. Began: April 1, 2001.
Subscribers: 9,074.
Broadband Service: Road Runner.
Fee: $49.99 installation; $44.95 monthly.
Telephone Service
Digital: Operational
Fee: $44.95 monthly
Miles of Plant: 634.0 (coaxial); 150.0 (fiber optic). Additional miles planned: 30.0 (coaxial); 2.0 (fiber optic).
President: Connie Wharton. Vice President & General Manager: Michael Carrosquiola. Operations Director: Marco Reyes. Technical Operations Manager: Eduardo Ruiz. Public Affairs Manager: Celinda Gonzalez.
Ownership: Time Warner Cable (MSO).; Advance/Newhouse Partnership (MSO).

LAS GALLINAS—Almega Cable, 4001 W Airport Frwy, Ste 530, Bedford, TX 76021. Phone: 817-685-9588. Fax: 817-685-6488. E-mail: helpdesk@almegacable.com. Web Site: http://www.almega.com. Also serves Bexar County (portions). ICA: TX0239.
TV Market Ranking: 45 (Bexar County (portions), LAS GALLINAS). Franchise award date: N.A. Franchise expiration date: N.A. Began: January 1, 1989.
Channel capacity: 54 (not 2-way capable). Channels available but not in use: N.A.
Basic Service
Subscribers: 246.
Programming (received off-air): KABB (FOX) San Antonio; KENS (CBS) San Antonio; KHCE-TV (TBN) San Antonio; KLRN (PBS) San Antonio; KMYS (CW) Kerrville; KSAT-TV (ABC) San Antonio; KVDA (TMO) San Antonio; KWEX-DT (UNV) San Antonio; WOAI-TV (NBC) San Antonio.
Programming (via satellite): CNN; Country Music TV; Discovery Channel; Disney Channel; ESPN; GalaVision; Headline News; MTV; Nickelodeon; Spike TV; TBS Superstation; Turner Network TV; USA Network.
Fee: $29.95 installation; $38.00 monthly.
Pay Service 1
Pay Units: 15.
Programming (via satellite): Cinemax.
Fee: $10.95 monthly.
Pay Service 2
Pay Units: 75.
Programming (via satellite): Showtime.
Fee: $10.95 monthly.
Pay Service 3
Pay Units: 40.
Programming (via satellite): HBO.
Fee: $10.95 monthly.
Video-On-Demand: No
Internet Service
Operational: No.
Telephone Service
None
Miles of Plant: 70.0 (coaxial); None (fiber optic).
Ownership: Almega Cable (MSO).

LAVERNIA—Comfort Cable Co., 523 8th St, PO Box 507, Comfort, TX 78013-0507. Phone: 830-995-2813. Fax: 830-995-2245. ICA: TX0441.
TV Market Ranking: 45 (LAVERNIA). Franchise award date: November 5, 1985. Franchise expiration date: N.A. Began: March 1, 1986.
Channel capacity: N.A. Channels available but not in use: N.A.
Basic Service
Subscribers: 119 Included in Comfort.
Programming (received off-air): KENS (CBS) San Antonio; KLRN (PBS) San Antonio; KSAT-TV (ABC) San Antonio; KWEX-DT (UNV) San Antonio; WOAI-TV (NBC) San Antonio.
Programming (via satellite): ABC Family Channel; ESPN; Headline News; Nickelodeon; TBS Superstation; The Movie Channel; Turner Network TV.
Fee: $21.95 monthly.
Video-On-Demand: No
Internet Service
Operational: No.
Telephone Service
None
Miles of plant included in Comfort
Manager & Chief Technician: David Petty.
Ownership: David Petty (MSO).

LEANDER—Suddenlink Communications, 409 Crystal Falls Pkwy, Leander, TX 78641. Phone: 512-930-3085. Fax: 512-869-2962. Web Site: http://www.suddenlink.com. ICA: TX0251.
TV Market Ranking: Below 100 (LEANDER). Franchise award date: January 1, 1980. Franchise expiration date: January 1, 2007. Began: December 1, 1981.
Channel capacity: 78 (operating 2-way). Channels available but not in use: N.A.
Basic Service
Subscribers: 3,000.
Programming (received off-air): KAKW-DT (UNV) Killeen; KCEN-TV (NBC, IND) Temple; KEYE-TV (CBS, TMO) Austin; KLRU (PBS) Austin; KNVA (CW) Austin; KTBC (FOX) Austin; KVUE (ABC) Austin.
Programming (via satellite): C-SPAN; INSP; QVC; Telefutura; TV Guide Network; WGN America.
Fee: $35.00 installation; $27.99 monthly; $1.50 converter.
Expanded Basic Service 1
Subscribers: N.A.
Programming (via satellite): A&E Networks; ABC Family Channel; AMC; Animal Planet; BET Networks; Bravo; Cartoon Network; CNBC; CNN; Comedy Central; Country Music TV; C-SPAN 2; Discovery Channel; Disney Channel; E! Entertainment Television; ESPN; ESPN 2; Eternal Word TV Network; Food Network; Fox News Channel; Fox Sports Southwest; FX; GalaVision; Golf Channel; Great American Country; Headline News; HGTV; History Channel; Jewelry Television; Lifetime; Lifetime Movie Network; MSNBC; MTV; Nickelodeon; ShopNBC; Speed; Spike TV; Syfy; TBS Superstation; Telemundo; The Learning Channel; The Weather Channel; Travel Channel; Trinity Broadcasting Network; truTV; Turner Classic Movies; Turner Network TV; TV Land; USA Network; Versus; VH1.
Fee: $15.50 monthly.
Digital Basic Service
Subscribers: N.A.
Programming (via satellite): A&E HD; Bandamax; BBC America; Bio; Bloomberg Television; Boomerang; BYU Television; Cine Latino; Cine Mexicano; CMT Pure Country; CNN en Espanol; Cooking Channel; Cox Sports Television; De Pelicula; De Pelicula Clasico; Discovery en Espanol; Discovery Health Channel; Discovery Home Channel; Discovery Kids Channel; Discovery Times Channel; DIY Network; Encore (multiplexed); ESPN 2 HD; ESPN Classic Sports; ESPN Deportes; ESPN HD; ESPN U; ESPNews; EWTN en Espanol; FamilyNet; Food Network HD; Fox Deportes; Fox Reality Channel; Fox Soccer; Fuel TV; Fuse; G4; GalaVision; GMC; GSN; Hallmark Channel; Halogen Network; HD Theater; HDNet; HDNet Movies; HGTV HD; History Channel en Espanol; History Channel International; Independent Film Channel; Latele Novela Network; Military Channel; MTV Hits; MTV2; mun2 television; Music Choice; National Geographic Channel; National Geographic Channel HD Network; Nick Jr.; NickToons TV; Nuvo TV; Outdoor Channel; Oxygen; Ritmoson Latino; Science; SoapNet; Sorpresa; Style Network; Sundance Channel; Sur Network; TBN Enlace USA; TeenNick; Telehit; Telemundo; Tennis Channel; Toon Disney; Toon Disney en Espanol; Tr3s; Turner Network TV HD; TV Chile; TV One; Universal HD; VH1 Classic; VHUNO; Video Rola; WE tv; Weatherscan.
Digital Pay Service 1
Pay Units: N.A.
Programming (via satellite): Cinemax (multiplexed); HBO (multiplexed); HBO HD; HBO Latino; Showtime (multiplexed); Showtime HD; Starz (multiplexed); Starz HDTV; The Movie Channel (multiplexed).
Video-On-Demand: No
Pay-Per-View
iN DEMAND (delivered digitally); Fresh (delivered digitally); Shorteez (delivered digitally); Playboy TV (delivered digitally); Playboy en Espanol (delivered digitally).
Internet Service
Operational: Yes.
Broadband Service: Suddenlink High Speed Internet.
Fee: $99.95 installation; $25.95 monthly; $10.00 modem lease.
Telephone Service
Digital: Operational
Fee: $44.95 monthly
Miles of Plant: 60.0 (coaxial); 9.0 (fiber optic).
Manager: Dale Hoffman. Chief Technician & Marketing Director: Wesley Houghteling.
Ownership: Cequel Communications LLC (MSO).

LEFORS—Formerly served by Almega Cable. No longer in operation. ICA: TX0563.

LEONA—Formerly served by Charter Communications. No longer in operation. ICA: TX0702.

LEONARD—Zoom Media, PO Box 2126, Flint, TX 75762. Phone: 855-261-5304. Web Site: http://www.zoommediallc.com. Also serves Celeste. ICA: TX0367.
TV Market Ranking: Below 100 (Celeste, LEONARD). Franchise award date: N.A. Franchise expiration date: N.A. Began: October 1, 1982.
Channel capacity: 54 (not 2-way capable). Channels available but not in use: N.A.
Basic Service
Subscribers: 65.
Programming (received off-air): KDAF (CW, IND) Dallas; KDFW-DT (FOX) Dallas; KERA-TV (PBS) Dallas; KTVT (CBS) Fort Worth; KXAS-TV (NBC) Fort Worth; KXTX-TV (TMO) Dallas; WFAA (ABC) Dallas; 13 FMs.
Programming (via satellite): Disney Channel; TBS Superstation; WGN America.
Fee: $54.95 installation; $44.05 monthly.
Pay Service 1
Pay Units: N.A.
Programming (via satellite): HBO; Showtime; The Movie Channel.
Video-On-Demand: No
Internet Service
Operational: No.
Telephone Service
None
Miles of Plant: 35.0 (coaxial); None (fiber optic).
Chief Executive Officer: Steve Houston.
Ownership: Zoom Media LLC (MSO).

LEVELLAND—Cobridge Communications, 9450 Manchester Rd, Ste 200, St. Louis, MO 63119. Phones: 314-227-9500; 800-438-2427. Web Site: http://www.cobridge.net. Also serves Hockley County, Littlefield & Morton. ICA: TX0112.
TV Market Ranking: Below 100 (Hockley County (portions), LEVELLAND, Littlefield); Outside TV Markets (Hockley County (portions), Morton). Franchise award date: January 1, 1966. Franchise expiration date: N.A. Began: January 1, 1966.
Channel capacity: 60 (not 2-way capable). Channels available but not in use: N.A.
Basic Service
Subscribers: 1,702.
Programming (received off-air): KAMC (ABC) Lubbock; KCBD (NBC) Lubbock; KJTV-TV (FOX) Lubbock; KLBK-TV (CBS) Lubbock; KPTB-DT (IND) Lubbock; KTXT-TV (PBS) Lubbock; KXTQ-CA (TMO) Lubbock.
Programming (via satellite): A&E Networks; ABC Family Channel; AMC; Animal Planet; BET Networks; Cartoon Network; CNN; Comedy Central; Country Music TV; C-SPAN; Discovery Channel; Disney Channel; E! Entertainment Television; ESPN; ESPN 2; Fox News Channel; Fox Sports Southwest; FX; G4; Headline News; HGTV; History Channel; ION Television; Lifetime; MTV; Nickelodeon; Oxygen; Spike TV; Syfy; TBS Superstation; The Learning Channel; The Weather Channel; Travel Channel; Turner Network TV; TV Guide Network; TV Land; Univision Studios; USA Network; VH1.
Fee: $28.00 installation; $38.51 monthly; $1.60 converter.
Digital Basic Service
Subscribers: N.A.
Programming (via satellite): BBC America; Bio; Bloomberg Television; Discovery Digital Networks; DIY Network; GAS; GSN;

History Channel International; Independent Film Channel; Lifetime Movie Network; MTV Networks Digital Suite; Music Choice; Nick Jr.; Nick Too; NickToons TV; Sundance Channel; TV Guide Interactive Inc.; WE tv.

Digital Pay Service 1
Pay Units: 518.
Programming (via satellite): Cinemax (multiplexed).
Fee: $20.00 installation; $9.00 monthly.

Digital Pay Service 2
Pay Units: 735.
Programming (via satellite): HBO (multiplexed).
Fee: $20.00 installation; $9.00 monthly.

Digital Pay Service 3
Pay Units: 507.
Programming (via satellite): Showtime (multiplexed).
Fee: $20.00 installation; $9.00 monthly.

Digital Pay Service 4
Pay Units: N.A.
Programming (via satellite): Encore (multiplexed); Flix; Starz (multiplexed); The Movie Channel (multiplexed).

Video-On-Demand: No

Pay-Per-View
iN DEMAND (delivered digitally); ETC (delivered digitally); Pleasure (delivered digitally).

Internet Service
Operational: No.

Telephone Service
None

Miles of Plant: 127.0 (coaxial); None (fiber optic).
Chief Executive Officer: Scott Widham. General Manager: Wayne Kelstrom.
Ownership: Cobridge Communications LLC (MSO).

LEXINGTON—Reveille Broadband, PO Box 39, Lexington, TX 78947. Phone: 979-773-4700. Fax: 979-773-4733. E-mail: mariesullivan@reveillebroadband.com. Web Site: http://www.reveillebroadband.com. ICA: TX0522.
TV Market Ranking: Outside TV Markets (LEXINGTON). Franchise award date: January 1, 1983. Franchise expiration date: N.A. Began: January 1, 1983.
Channel capacity: 32 (not 2-way capable). Channels available but not in use: N.A.

Basic Service
Subscribers: 299.
Programming (received off-air): KEYE-TV (CBS, TMO) Austin; KLRU (PBS) Austin; KNVA (CW) Austin; KTBC (FOX) Austin; KVUE (ABC) Austin; KXAN-TV (NBC) Austin.
Programming (via satellite): ABC Family Channel; AMC; Animal Planet; BET Networks; Boomerang; Cartoon Network; CNN; Comedy Central; Country Music TV; C-SPAN; C-SPAN 2; Discovery Channel; Disney Channel; E! Entertainment Television; ESPN; ESPN 2; Food Network; Fox News Channel; Fox Sports Southwest; FX; Great American Country; GSN; Hallmark Channel; Hallmark Movie Channel; Headline News; HGTV; History Channel; Lifetime; National Geographic Channel; Nick Jr.; Nickelodeon; QVC; Speed; Spike TV; Syfy; TBS Superstation; The Learning Channel; The Weather Channel; Travel Channel; Trinity Broadcasting Network; truTV; Turner Classic Movies; Turner Network TV; TV Land; Univision Studios; USA Network; VH1; WGN America.
Fee: $35.00 installation; $39.95 monthly.

Pay Service 1
Pay Units: 49.
Programming (via satellite): HBO; The Movie Channel.
Fee: $10.95 monthly.

Internet Service
Operational: Yes.
Fee: $50.00 installation; $39.95 monthly.

Telephone Service
Digital: Operational
Subscribers: 140.

Miles of Plant: 9.0 (coaxial); None (fiber optic). Additional miles planned: 2.0 (coaxial).
President: Jeff Sullivan. Chief Executive Officer: Marie Sullivan. Vice President: Cory Savage. Office Manager: Laura Tillery.
Ownership: Reveille Broadband (MSO).

LIBERTY—Time Warner Cable. Now served by HOUSTON, TX [TX0001]. ICA: TX0129.

LINDEN—Reach Broadband, 515 E Longview Dr, Arp, TX 75750. Phone: 800-687-1258. Web Site: http://www.reachbroadband.net. ICA: TX0381.
TV Market Ranking: 58 (LINDEN). Franchise award date: N.A. Franchise expiration date: N.A. Began: September 1, 1982.
Channel capacity: 42 (not 2-way capable). Channels available but not in use: N.A.

Basic Service
Subscribers: 241.
Programming (received off-air): KETK-TV (NBC) Jacksonville; KLTS-TV (PBS) Shreveport; KLTV (ABC, TMO) Tyler; KMSS-TV (FOX) Shreveport; KSHV-TV (MNT) Shreveport; KSLA (CBS) Shreveport; KTAL-TV (NBC) Texarkana; KTBS-TV (ABC) Shreveport.
Programming (via satellite): TBS Superstation; WGN America.
Fee: $54.95 installation; $20.95 monthly; $1.50 converter.

Expanded Basic Service 1
Subscribers: N.A.
Programming (via satellite): A&E Networks; ABC Family Channel; AMC; CNN; Country Music TV; Discovery Channel; Disney Channel; ESPN; Fox Sports Southwest; Lifetime; Nickelodeon; Spike TV; The Weather Channel; Trinity Broadcasting Network; Turner Network TV; TV Land; USA Network.
Fee: $23.10 monthly.

Pay Service 1
Pay Units: 105.
Programming (via satellite): HBO.
Fee: $12.95 monthly.

Pay Service 2
Pay Units: 90.
Programming (via satellite): Showtime; The Movie Channel.
Fee: $12.95 monthly (each).

Video-On-Demand: No

Internet Service
Operational: No.

Telephone Service
None

Miles of Plant: 19.0 (coaxial); None (fiber optic).
Regional Manager: Ronnie Stafford. Office Manager: Jan Gibson.
Ownership: RB3 LLC (MSO).

LIPAN—Formerly served by Almega Cable. No longer in operation. ICA: TX0987.

LITTLE RIVER-ACADEMY—Centrovision Inc., 8 E Barton Ave, PO Box 3157, Temple, TX 76505. Phone: 254-773-1163. Fax: 254-770-0778. E-mail: altonsheppard@centrovision.net. Web Site: http://www.centrovision.net/. ICA: TX0499.
TV Market Ranking: Below 100 (LITTLE RIVER-ACADEMY). Franchise award date: N.A. Franchise expiration date: N.A. Began: August 1, 1982.
Channel capacity: N.A. Channels available but not in use: N.A.

Basic Service
Subscribers: N.A.
Programming (received off-air): KCEN-TV (NBC, IND) Temple; KDYW (PBS) Waco; KEYE-TV (CBS, TMO) Austin; KNCT (PBS) Belton; KNVA (CW) Austin; KTBC (FOX) Austin; KWKT-TV (FOX, MNT) Waco; KWTX-TV (CBS, CW) Waco; KXAN-TV (NBC) Austin; KXXV (ABC, TMO) Waco; WFAA (ABC) Dallas.
Programming (via satellite): Univision Studios; WGN America.
Fee: $20.00 installation; $13.00 monthly.

Expanded Basic Service 1
Subscribers: N.A.
Programming (via satellite): A&E Networks; ABC Family Channel; AMC; Animal Planet; BET Networks; Cartoon Network; CNBC; CNN; Comedy Central; Country Music TV; C-SPAN; C-SPAN 2; Discovery Channel; Disney Channel; E! Entertainment Television; ESPN; ESPN 2; Food Network; Fox News Channel; Fox Sports Southwest; FX; Hallmark Channel; Headline News; HGTV; History Channel; ION Television; Lifetime; MSNBC; MTV; National Geographic Channel; Nickelodeon; QVC; SoapNet; Spike TV; Syfy; TBS Superstation; The Learning Channel; The Weather Channel; Travel Channel; Trinity Broadcasting Network; Turner Classic Movies; Turner Network TV; TV Land; USA Network; VH1 Classic.
Fee: $17.00 monthly.

Digital Basic Service
Subscribers: N.A.
Programming (via satellite): AmericanLife TV Network; BBC America; Bio; Bloomberg Television; Bravo; Daystar TV Network; Discovery Digital Networks; DMX Music; ESPN Classic Sports; ESPNews; Fox Movie Channel; Fox Sports World; FSN Digital Atlantic; FSN Digital Central; FSN Digital Pacific; G4; Golf Channel; Great American Country; GSN; Halogen Network; HGTV; History Channel; History Channel International; Independent Film Channel; International Television (ITV); Lifetime Movie Network; Lime; National Geographic Channel; Outdoor Channel; Ovation; ShopNBC; Speed; Style Network; Syfy; The Word Network; Toon Disney; Trinity Broadcasting Network; Turner Classic Movies; Versus; WE tv.
Fee: $15.00 installation; $49.00 monthly.

Digital Expanded Basic Service
Subscribers: N.A.
Programming (via satellite): GAS; MTV Networks Digital Suite; Nick Jr.; NickToons TV.

Pay Service 1
Pay Units: N.A.
Programming (via satellite): Showtime.
Fee: $11.00 monthly.

Digital Pay Service 1
Pay Units: N.A.
Programming (via satellite): Cinemax (multiplexed); Encore (multiplexed); HBO (multiplexed); Showtime (multiplexed); Starz (multiplexed).
Fee: $7.00 monthly (Cinemax), $11.00 monthly (HBO, Showtime, or Starz/Encore).

Video-On-Demand: No

Internet Service
Operational: Yes. Began: December 31, 2004.
Broadband Service: VVM Internet Services.
Fee: $20.00 installation; $40.00 monthly.

Telephone Service
Digital: Planned

Miles of Plant: 9.0 (coaxial); None (fiber optic).
Manager: Alton Sheppard. Chief Technician: Mike Wiggins.
Ownership: Centrovision Inc. (MSO).

LIVERPOOL—Almega Cable, 4001 W Airport Freeway, Ste 530, Bedford, TX 76021. Phone: 817-685-9588. Fax: 817-685-6488. E-mail: helpdesk@almegacable.com. Web Site: http://www.almega.com. ICA: TX0333.
TV Market Ranking: 15 (LIVERPOOL). Franchise award date: N.A. Franchise expiration date: N.A. Began: October 1, 1989.
Channel capacity: 62 (not 2-way capable). Channels available but not in use: N.A.

Basic Service
Subscribers: 189.
Programming (received off-air): KETH-TV (TBN) Houston; KFTH-DT (TEL) Alvin; KHOU (CBS) Houston; KIAH (CW) Houston; KLTJ (ETV) Galveston; KPRC-TV (NBC) Houston; KPXB-TV (ION) Conroe; KRIV (FOX) Houston; KTMD (TMO) Galveston; KTRK-TV (ABC) Houston; KTXH (MNT) Houston; KUBE-TV (IND) Baytown; KUHT (PBS) Houston; KYAZ (IND) Katy.
Programming (via satellite): A&E Networks; ABC Family Channel; AMC; CNN; Country Music TV; Discovery Channel; Disney Channel; ESPN; Fox Sports Southwest; Headline News; History Channel; Lifetime; MTV; Nickelodeon; QVC; Spike TV; Syfy; TBS Superstation; The Weather Channel; Turner Network TV; USA Network; VH1; WGN America.
Fee: $54.95 installation; $44.05 monthly.

Pay Service 1
Pay Units: 70.
Programming (via satellite): Cinemax.
Fee: $12.95 monthly.

Pay Service 2
Pay Units: 129.
Programming (via satellite): HBO.
Fee: $12.95 monthly.

Pay Service 3
Pay Units: 131.
Programming (via satellite): Showtime.
Fee: $12.95 monthly.

Video-On-Demand: No

Internet Service
Operational: No.

Telephone Service
None
Miles of Plant: 55.0 (coaxial); None (fiber optic).
Ownership: Almega Cable (MSO).

LIVINGSTON—Suddenlink Communications, 101 S Washington Ave, Livingston, TX 77351-3440. Phone: 936-327-4512. Web Site: http://www.suddenlink.com. Also serves Polk County (portions). ICA: TX0208.
TV Market Ranking: Outside TV Markets (LIVINGSTON, Polk County (portions)). Franchise award date: January 1, 1958. Franchise expiration date: N.A. Began: April 26, 1963.
Channel capacity: 36 (not 2-way capable). Channels available but not in use: N.A.
Basic Service
Subscribers: 1,892.
Programming (received off-air): KCTL-LP Livingston; KETX-LP (IND) Livingston; KPXB-TV (ION) Conroe; KTBU (IND) Conroe; KTRE (ABC) Lufkin; 15 FMs.
Programming (via microwave): KHOU (CBS) Houston; KIAH (CW) Houston; KPRC-TV (NBC) Houston; KRIV (FOX) Houston; KTRK-TV (ABC) Houston; KTXH (MNT) Houston; KUHT (PBS) Houston.
Programming (via satellite): BET Networks; CNN; C-SPAN; Discovery Channel; Disney Channel; ESPN; ESPN 2; Fox Sports Southwest; INSP; Lifetime; MTV; Nickelodeon; Spike TV; TBS Superstation; The Weather Channel; Turner Network TV; Univision Studios; USA Network; WGN America.
Fee: $37.95 installation; $17.80 monthly; $10.00 additional installation.
Pay Service 1
Pay Units: 147.
Programming (via satellite): Cinemax; HBO.
Fee: $9.95 monthly (Cinemax), $10.50 monthly (HBO).
Pay Service 2
Pay Units: 78.
Programming (via satellite): Showtime; The Movie Channel.
Fee: $7.95 monthly.
Video-On-Demand: No
Pay-Per-View
iN DEMAND.
Internet Service
Operational: Yes.
Broadband Service: Suddenlink High Speed Internet.
Fee: $45.95 installation; $29.95 monthly.
Telephone Service
None
Miles of Plant: 50.0 (coaxial); None (fiber optic).
Manager: Jerry Teer. Marketing Director: Wade Klein. Chief Technician: Jerry Teer.
Ownership: Cequel Communications LLC (MSO).

LLANO—Northland Cable Television, 1101 Mission Hill Dr, PO Box 366, Marble Falls, TX 78654-0366. Phone: 830-693-7500. Fax: 830-693-6056. E-mail: marblefalls@northlandcabletv.com. Web Site: http://www.northlandcabletv.com. ICA: TX0996.
TV Market Ranking: Below 100 (LLANO).
Channel capacity: 38 (not 2-way capable). Channels available but not in use: N.A.
Basic Service
Subscribers: N.A.
Programming (received off-air): KBVO (MNT) Llano; KCWX (IND, MNT) Fredericksburg; KEYE-TV (CBS, TMO) Austin; KLRU (PBS) Austin; KNVA (CW) Austin; KTBC (FOX) Austin; KVUE (ABC) Austin.
Programming (via satellite): A&E Networks; Animal Planet; Cartoon Network; CNN; C-SPAN; Discovery Channel; ESPN; Fox News Channel; Fox Sports Southwest; Great American Country; Hallmark Channel; Headline News; HGTV; History Channel; Lifetime; National Geographic Channel; QVC; Spike TV; Syfy; TBS Superstation; The Learning Channel; The Weather Channel; Trinity Broadcasting Network; Turner Classic Movies; Turner Network TV; TV Land; USA Network.
Fee: $38.99 monthly.
Pay Service 1
Pay Units: N.A.
Programming (via satellite): Cinemax; HBO.
Fee: $11.50 Cinemax (monthly) 13.50 monthly (HBO).
Internet Service
Operational: Yes.
Telephone Service
None
Regional Manager: Larson Lloyd. Plant Manager: Ron Gardner. Marketing Director: Gaye Tharett.
Ownership: Northland Communications Corp. (MSO).

LOCKHART—Time Warner Cable. Now served by AUSTIN, TX [TX0005]. ICA: TX0163.

LOCKNEY—Reach Broadband, 515 E Longview St, Arp, TX 75750. Phone: 800-687-1258. Web Site: http://www.reachbroadband.net. ICA: TX0414.
TV Market Ranking: Outside TV Markets (LOCKNEY). Franchise award date: December 10, 1980. Franchise expiration date: N.A. Began: May 15, 1981.
Channel capacity: 41 (2-way capable). Channels available but not in use: N.A.
Basic Service
Subscribers: 278.
Programming (received off-air): KAMC (ABC) Lubbock; KCBD (NBC) Lubbock; KJTV-TV (FOX) Lubbock; KLBK-TV (CBS) Lubbock; KTXT-TV (PBS) Lubbock; KVII-TV (ABC, CW) Amarillo.
Programming (via satellite): A&E Networks; ABC Family Channel; AMC; Cartoon Network; CNN; Country Music TV; Discovery Channel; Disney Channel; E! Entertainment Television; ESPN; Headline News; History Channel; Lifetime; Nickelodeon; QVC; Spike TV; Syfy; TBS Superstation; The Learning Channel; The Weather Channel; Turner Network TV; TV Land; USA Network; WGN America.
Fee: $29.95 installation; $38.00 monthly.
Pay Service 1
Pay Units: 35.
Programming (via satellite): Cinemax.
Fee: $9.95 monthly.
Pay Service 2
Pay Units: 86.
Programming (via satellite): HBO.
Fee: $9.95 monthly.
Video-On-Demand: No
Internet Service
Operational: No.
Telephone Service
None
Miles of Plant: 12.0 (coaxial); None (fiber optic).
Regional Manager: Ronnie Stafford. Office Manager: Jan Gibson.
Ownership: RB3 LLC (MSO).

LOLITA—Formerly served by Clearview Cable. No longer in operation. ICA: TX0637.

LOMETA—Almega Cable, 4001 W Airport Freeway, Ste 530, Bedford, TX 76021. Phone: 817-685-9588. Fax: 817-685-6488. E-mail: helpdesk@almegacable.com. Web Site: http://www.almega.com. ICA: TX0599.
TV Market Ranking: Outside TV Markets (LOMETA). Franchise award date: N.A. Franchise expiration date: N.A. Began: December 1, 1971.
Channel capacity: N.A. Channels available but not in use: N.A.
Basic Service
Subscribers: N.A.
Programming (received off-air): KCEN-TV (NBC, IND) Temple; KLST (CBS) San Angelo; KNCT (PBS) Belton; KTBC (FOX) Austin; KWKT-TV (FOX, MNT) Waco; KWTX-TV (CBS, CW) Waco; KXXV (ABC, TMO) Waco; allband FM.
Programming (via satellite): A&E Networks; ABC Family Channel; AMC; Animal Planet; Cartoon Network; CNN; Country Music TV; Discovery Channel; Disney Channel; ESPN; ESPN 2; Fox Sports Southwest; GalaVision; Headline News; HGTV; History Channel; Lifetime; Nickelodeon; Oxygen; Spike TV; Syfy; TBS Superstation; The Learning Channel; The Weather Channel; Turner Network TV; TV Land; Univision Studios; USA Network; WGN America.
Fee: $29.95 installation; $38.00 monthly.
Pay Service 1
Pay Units: 15.
Programming (via satellite): HBO.
Fee: $10.83 monthly.
Video-On-Demand: No
Pay-Per-View
iN DEMAND (delivered digitally); Hot Choice (delivered digitally); Playboy TV (delivered digitally); Fresh (delivered digitally); Shorteez (delivered digitally).
Internet Service
Operational: No.
Telephone Service
None
Miles of Plant: 7.0 (coaxial); None (fiber optic).
Ownership: Almega Cable (MSO).

LONGVIEW—Longview Cable Television, 711 N High St, PO Box 4399, Longview, TX 75601. Phones: 903-758-3052; 903-758-9991. Fax: 903-758-3083. E-mail: longviewcs@cablelynx.com. Web Site: http://www.longviewcabletv.com. ICA: TX0033.
TV Market Ranking: Below 100 (LONGVIEW). Franchise award date: June 1, 1965. Franchise expiration date: N.A. Began: August 1, 1972.
Channel capacity: 55 (operating 2-way). Channels available but not in use: N.A.
Basic Service
Subscribers: 24,930.
Programming (received off-air): KDFW-DT (FOX) Dallas; KERA-TV (PBS) Dallas; KETK-TV (NBC) Jacksonville; KFXK-TV (FOX) Longview; KLPN-LP (IND) Longview; KLTV (ABC, TMO) Tyler; KSLA (CBS) Shreveport; KTAL-TV (NBC) Texarkana; KTBS-TV (ABC) Shreveport; KXAS-TV (NBC) Fort Worth.
Programming (via satellite): A&E Networks; ABC Family Channel; AMC; Animal Planet; BET Networks; Cartoon Network; CNBC; CNN; Comedy Central; Country Music TV; C-SPAN; C-SPAN 2; Discovery Channel; Disney Channel; ESPN; ESPN 2; ESPN Classic Sports; Eternal Word TV Network; Food Network; Fox News Channel; Fox Sports Southwest; FX; GalaVision; Hallmark Channel; Headline News; HGTV; History Channel; ION Television; Lifetime; MTV; NASA TV; National Geographic Channel; Nickelodeon; QVC; ShopNBC; Spike TV; Syfy; TBS Superstation; Telemundo; The Learning Channel; The Weather Channel; Travel Channel; Trinity Broadcasting Network; Turner Classic Movies; Turner Network TV; TV Guide Network; TV Land; Univision Studios; USA Network; VH1.
Fee: $40.00 installation; $48.90 monthly; $3.65 converter; $20.95 additional installation.
Digital Basic Service
Subscribers: N.A.
Programming (via satellite): AmericanLife TV Network; BBC America; Bio; CMT Pure Country; Discovery Fit & Health; Discovery Health Channel; Discovery Kids Channel; DMX Music; ESPNews; Fox Soccer; FSN Digital Atlantic; FSN Digital Central; FSN Digital Pacific; G4; Golf Channel; Great American Country; GSN; Halogen Network; History Channel International; ID Investigation Discovery; Lifetime Movie Network; Military Channel; MTV Hits; MTV Jams; MTV2; National Geographic Channel; Nick Jr.; Nick Too; NickToons TV; Outdoor Channel; Planet Green; Science; SoapNet; Speed; Style Network; TeenNick; Toon Disney; Tr3s; VH1 Classic; VH1 Soul; WE tv.
Fee: $10.00 monthly.
Digital Expanded Basic Service
Subscribers: N.A.
Programming (received off-air): KETK-TV (NBC) Jacksonville; KFXK-TV (FOX) Longview; KLTS-TV (PBS) Shreveport; KLTV (ABC, TMO) Tyler; KYTX (CBS, IND) Nacogdoches.
Programming (via satellite): Discovery Channel HD; ESPN HD; HDNet; HDNet Movies; Outdoor Channel.
Fee: $5.00 monthly.
Digital Pay Service 1
Pay Units: N.A.
Programming (via satellite): Cinemax (multiplexed); Cinemax HD; Encore (multiplexed); HBO (multiplexed); HBO HD; Starz (multiplexed); Starz HDTV.
Fee: $12.95 monthly (Cinemax, HBO or Starz/Encore).
Video-On-Demand: No
Pay-Per-View
ESPN Gameplan (delivered digitally); Sports PPV (delivered digitally); iN DEMAND (delivered digitally).
Internet Service
Operational: Yes. Began: March 1, 2001.
Subscribers: 320.
Broadband Service: Cablelynx.
Fee: $24.95-$44.95 monthly; $10.00 modem lease.
Telephone Service
Digital: Operational
Fee: $45.70 monthly
Miles of Plant: 561.0 (coaxial); 32.0 (fiber optic). Additional miles planned: 50.0 (coaxial); 200.0 (fiber optic).
Vice President & Regional Manager: Don Deem. Vice President, Marketing & Programming: Lori Haight. Manager: Brandi Turner. Plant Manager: George Doss. Business Manager: Cynthia Walters.
Ownership: WEHCO Video Inc. (MSO).

LOOP—Formerly served by National Cable Inc. No longer in operation. ICA: TX0686.

LORAINE (town)—Formerly served by Almega Cable. No longer in operation. ICA: TX0529.

LORENA—Time Warner Cable. Now served by WACO, TX [TX0015]. ICA: TX0801.

LORENZO—Formerly served by Almega Cable. No longer in operation. ICA: TX0484.

LOS FRESNOS—Time Warner Communications. Now served by PHARR, TX [TX0017]. ICA: TX0264.

LOST PINES—Suddenlink Communications, 12444 Powerscourt Dr, Saint Louis, MO 63131-3660. Phones: 800-999-6845; 314-965-2020. Fax: 903-561-5485. Web Site: http://www.suddenlink.com. ICA: TX0950.

TV Market Ranking: Below 100 (LOST PINES). Franchise award date: N.A. Franchise expiration date: N.A. Began: N.A.

Channel capacity: N.A. Channels available but not in use: N.A.

Basic Service

Subscribers: 1,004.

Programming (received off-air): KEYE-TV (CBS, TMO) Austin; KLRU (PBS) Austin; KTBC (FOX) Austin; KVUE (ABC) Austin; KXAN-TV (NBC) Austin.

Programming (via satellite): A&E Networks; ABC Family Channel; BET Networks; CNN; Country Music TV; Discovery Channel; E! Entertainment Television; ESPN; Headline News; Lifetime; Nickelodeon; Spike TV; Syfy; TBS Superstation; The Weather Channel; Trinity Broadcasting Network; Turner Network TV; USA Network; WGN America.

Fee: $39.95 installation; $30.50 monthly.

Pay Service 1

Pay Units: 84.

Programming (via satellite): Cinemax.

Fee: $10.95 monthly.

Pay Service 2

Pay Units: 142.

Programming (via satellite): HBO.

Fee: $10.95 monthly.

Pay Service 3

Pay Units: 50.

Programming (via satellite): Showtime.

Fee: $10.95 monthly.

Video-On-Demand: No

Internet Service

Operational: Yes. Began: June 10, 2004.

Broadband Service: Suddenlink High Speed Internet.

Fee: $49.95 installation; $38.95 monthly.

Telephone Service

None

Miles of Plant: 86.0 (coaxial); None (fiber optic).

Regional Manager: Todd Cruthird. Plant Manager: Carl Gillit.

Ownership: Cequel Communications LLC (MSO).

LOTT—Zito Media, 611 Vader Hill Rd, Coudersport, PA 16915. Phone: 866-879-6235. E-mail: support@zitomedia.net. Web Site: http://www.zitomedia.com. ICA: TX0515.

TV Market Ranking: Below 100 (LOTT). Franchise award date: N.A. Franchise expiration date: June 27, 2007. Began: May 1, 1984.

Channel capacity: 54 (not 2-way capable). Channels available but not in use: N.A.

Basic Service

Subscribers: 66.

Programming (received off-air): KCEN-TV (NBC, IND) Temple; KNCT (PBS) Belton; KWKT-TV (FOX, MNT) Waco; KWTX-TV (CBS, CW) Waco; KXXV (ABC, TMO) Waco.

Programming (via satellite): A&E Networks; ABC Family Channel; Animal Planet; BET Networks; Cartoon Network; CNN; C-SPAN; Discovery Channel; Disney Channel; ESPN; ESPN 2; Fox News Channel; Fuse; GalaVision; Great American Country; Headline News; INSP; Lifetime; Outdoor Channel; TBS Superstation; The Learning Channel; The Weather Channel; Turner Classic Movies; Turner Network TV; USA Network; WGN America.

Fee: $30.00 installation; $36.50 monthly.

Pay Service 1

Pay Units: N.A.

Programming (via satellite): Cinemax; HBO; Showtime.

Fee: $9.00 monthly (each).

Internet Service

Operational: No.

Telephone Service

None

Miles of Plant: 9.0 (coaxial); None (fiber optic).

President: James Rigas.

Ownership: Zito Media (MSO).

LOUISE—Mid-Coast Cablevision, 505 N Mechanic St, PO Box 1269, El Campo, TX 77437-1269. Phones: 877-543-4850; 979-543-6858. Fax: 979-543-9501. Web Site: http://www.warpspeed1.net. ICA: TX0579.

TV Market Ranking: Outside TV Markets (LOUISE). Franchise award date: March 1, 1982. Franchise expiration date: N.A. Began: March 1, 1982.

Channel capacity: N.A. Channels available but not in use: N.A.

Basic Service

Subscribers: 239.

Programming (received off-air): KAVU-TV (ABC) Victoria; KETH-TV (TBN) Houston; KFTH-DT (TEL) Alvin; KHOU (CBS) Houston; KIAH (CW) Houston; KLTJ (ETV) Galveston; KPRC-TV (NBC) Houston; KRIV (FOX) Houston; KTBU (IND) Conroe; KTMD (TMO) Galveston; KTRK-TV (ABC) Houston; KTXH (MNT) Houston; KUBE-TV (IND) Baytown; KUHT (PBS) Houston; KXLN-DT (UNV) Rosenberg; KYAZ (IND) Katy; KZJL (IND) Houston.

Programming (via satellite): A&E Networks; ABC Family Channel; AMC; BET Networks; Cartoon Network; CNBC; CNN; Country Music TV; C-SPAN; C-SPAN 2; Discovery Channel; Discovery Fit & Health; Disney Channel; ESPN; ESPN 2; ESPN Classic Sports; Eternal Word TV Network; Fox News Channel; Fox Sports Southwest; FX; Hallmark Channel; Headline News; HGTV; History Channel; INSP; ION Television; Lifetime; MTV; Nickelodeon; Outdoor Channel; QVC; SoapNet; Speed; Spike TV; TBS Superstation; The Learning Channel; The Weather Channel; truTV; Turner Network TV; TV Guide Network; TV Land; USA Network; VH1; WGN America.

Fee: $25.00 installation; $29.99 monthly.

Digital Basic Service

Subscribers: N.A.

Programming (via satellite): ABC News Now; BBC America; Bloomberg Television; Cine Latino; CMT Pure Country; CNN en Espanol; Discovery en Espanol; Discovery Health Channel; Discovery Kids Channel; ESPN 2 HD; ESPN U; ESPNews; Fox Deportes; Fox Movie Channel; Fox Reality Channel; Fox Soccer; Fuel TV; G4; Golf Channel; GSN; ID Investigation Discovery; Independent Film Channel; Military Channel; Nick Jr.; NickToons TV; PBS Kids Sprout; Science; Speed; Tr3s; Turner Classic Movies; TVE Internacional; Utilisima; Versus; VH1 Classic; WE tv.

Digital Pay Service 1

Pay Units: N.A.

Programming (via satellite): Cinemax (multiplexed); Encore (multiplexed); Flix; HBO (multiplexed); Showtime (multiplexed); Starz (multiplexed); The Movie Channel (multiplexed).

Video-On-Demand: No

Pay-Per-View

iN DEMAND (delivered digitally); Playboy TV (delivered digitally).

Internet Service

Operational: Yes, Both DSL & dial-up.

Broadband Service: Warp Speed 1 Internet.

Fee: $17.05 installation; $34.99 monthly.

Telephone Service

None

Miles of Plant: 8.0 (coaxial); None (fiber optic).

Manager: Wayne Neal. Chief Technician: Dickie Isaacs.

Ownership: Mid-Coast Cablevision (MSO).

LOVELADY—Formerly served by Almega Cable. No longer in operation. ICA: TX0956.

LOWRY CROSSING—Suddenlink Communications, 12444 Powerscourt Dr, Saint Louis, MO 63131-3660. Phones: 800-999-6845; 314-965-2020. Fax: 903-561-5485. Web Site: http://www.suddenlink.com. Also serves New Hope. ICA: TX0256.

TV Market Ranking: 12 (LOWRY CROSSING, New Hope). Franchise award date: N.A. Franchise expiration date: N.A. Began: N.A.

Channel capacity: 54 (not 2-way capable). Channels available but not in use: N.A.

Basic Service

Subscribers: 793.

Programming (received off-air): KDAF (CW, IND) Dallas; KDFI (MNT) Dallas; KDFW-DT (FOX) Dallas; KDTN (ETV) Denton; KERA-TV (PBS) Dallas; KSTR-DT (TEL) Irving; KTVT (CBS) Fort Worth; KTXA (IND) Fort Worth; KXAS-TV (NBC) Fort Worth; KXTX-TV (TMO) Dallas; WFAA (ABC) Dallas.

Programming (via satellite): ABC Family Channel; CNN; Discovery Channel; Disney Channel; ESPN; Headline News; Lifetime; MTV; Nickelodeon; Spike TV; TBS Superstation; The Weather Channel; Turner Network TV; WGN America.

Fee: $39.95 installation; $41.95 monthly.

Pay Service 1

Pay Units: 133.

Programming (via satellite): HBO.

Fee: $12.00 monthly.

Pay Service 2

Pay Units: 82.

Programming (via satellite): The Movie Channel.

Fee: $9.00 monthly.

Pay Service 3

Pay Units: 268.

Programming (via satellite): Showtime.

Fee: $7.00 monthly.

Pay Service 4

Pay Units: 345.

Programming (via satellite): Flix.

Fee: $1.95 monthly.

Pay Service 5

Pay Units: 67.

Programming (via satellite): Cinemax.

Fee: $11.00 monthly.

Video-On-Demand: No

Internet Service

Operational: No.

Telephone Service

None

Miles of Plant: 86.0 (coaxial); None (fiber optic).

Area Manager: Rodney Fletcher. Regional Manager: Todd Cruthird.

Ownership: Cequel Communications LLC (MSO).

LUBBOCK—Reach Broadband, 515 E Longview St, Arp, TX 75750. Phone: 800-687-1258. Web Site: http://www.reachbroadband.net. Also serves Lubbock County (portions), Meadow, New Deal, Reese AFB, Ropesville, Shallowater, Smyer, West Lubbock & Wolfforth. ICA: TX0802.

TV Market Ranking: Below 100 (LUBBOCK, Lubbock County (portions), Meadow, New Deal, Reese AFB, Ropesville, Shallowater, Smyer, West Lubbock, Wolfforth). Franchise award date: N.A. Franchise expiration date: N.A. Began: N.A.

Channel capacity: 41 (not 2-way capable). Channels available but not in use: N.A.

Basic Service

Subscribers: 737.

Programming (received off-air): KAMC (ABC) Lubbock; KCBD (NBC) Lubbock; KJTV-TV (FOX) Lubbock; KLBK-TV (CBS) Lubbock; KTXT-TV (PBS) Lubbock.

Programming (via satellite): A&E Networks; ABC Family Channel; AMC; CNN; Country Music TV; Discovery Channel; ESPN; TBS Superstation; Turner Network TV; USA Network; WGN America.

Fee: $29.95 installation; $38.00 monthly.

Pay Service 1

Pay Units: 102.

Programming (via satellite): Cinemax.

Fee: $10.10 monthly.

Pay Service 2

Pay Units: 205.

Programming (via satellite): HBO.

Fee: $10.10 monthly.

Pay Service 3

Pay Units: 63.

Programming (via satellite): Showtime.

Fee: $10.10 monthly.

Video-On-Demand: No

Internet Service

Operational: No.

Telephone Service

None

Miles of Plant: 131.0 (coaxial); None (fiber optic).

Regional Manager: Ronnie Stafford. Office Manager: Jan Gibson.

Ownership: RB3 LLC (MSO).

LUBBOCK—Suddenlink Communications, 6710 Hartford Ave, Lubbock, TX 79401. Phones: 806-793-2222 (Customer service); 806-771-6001. Fax: 806-793-7818. Web Site: http://www.suddenlink.com. ICA: TX0012.

TV Market Ranking: Below 100 (LUBBOCK). Franchise award date: February 25, 1965. Franchise expiration date: N.A. Began: March 1, 1965.
Channel capacity: N.A. Channels available but not in use: N.A.

Basic Service
Subscribers: 51,262.
Programming (received off-air): KAMC (ABC) Lubbock; KBZO-LP (UNV) Lubbock; KCBD (NBC) Lubbock; KGLR-LP Lubbock; KJTV-TV (FOX) Lubbock; KLBK-TV (CBS) Lubbock; KLCW-TV (CW) Wolfforth; KPTB-DT (IND) Lubbock; KTXT-TV (PBS) Lubbock; KXTQ-CA (TMO) Lubbock; 10 FMs.
Programming (via satellite): C-SPAN; C-SPAN 2; Jewelry Television; QVC; Trinity Broadcasting Network; TV Guide Network; WGN America.
Fee: $42.04 installation; $27.64 monthly.

Expanded Basic Service 1
Subscribers: 30,096.
Programming (via satellite): A&E Networks; ABC Family Channel; AMC; Animal Planet; BET Networks; Bravo; Cartoon Network; CNBC; CNN; Comedy Central; Country Music TV; Discovery Channel; Disney Channel; E! Entertainment Television; ESPN; ESPN 2; Food Network; Fox News Channel; Fox Sports Southwest; FX; Hallmark Channel; Headline News; HGTV; History Channel; Lifetime; Lifetime Movie Network; MSNBC; MTV; MTV2; mun2 television; Nickelodeon; Speed; Spike TV; Syfy; TBS Superstation; Telefutura; The Learning Channel; The Weather Channel; Travel Channel; Turner Classic Movies; Turner Network TV; TV Land; USA Network; Versus; VH1.
Fee: $41.99 monthly.

Digital Basic Service
Subscribers: 21,166.
Programming (via satellite): A&E HD; Bandamax; BBC America; Bio; Bloomberg Television; Boomerang; Boomerang en Espanol; CBS Sports Network; Cine Latino; Cine Mexicano; CMT Pure Country; CNN en Espanol; Cooking Channel; De Pelicula; De Pelicula Clasico; Discovery en Espanol; Discovery Health Channel; Discovery Home Channel; Discovery Kids Channel; DIY Network; Encore (multiplexed); ESPN 2 HD; ESPN Classic Sports; ESPN Deportes; ESPN HD; ESPN U; ESPNews; Eternal Word TV Network; EWTN en Espanol; Food Network HD; Fox College Sports Atlantic; Fox College Sports Central; Fox College Sports Pacific; Fox Deportes; Fox Soccer; FSN HD; Fuel TV; Fuse; G4; GalaVision; GMC; Golf Channel; Great American Country; GSN; Halogen Network; HD Theater; HDNet; HDNet Movies; HGTV HD; History Channel en Espanol; History Channel International; ID Investigation Discovery; Independent Film Channel; INSP; Military Channel; MTV Hits; mtvU; mun2 television; Music Choice; National Geographic Channel; National Geographic Channel HD Network; Nick Jr.; NickToons en Espanol; NickToons TV; Nuvo TV; Outdoor Channel; Oxygen; Science; ShopNBC; SoapNet; Sorpresa; Sundance Channel; Sur Network; TeenNick; Telefutura; Telehit; Tennis Channel; Toon Disney; Toon Disney en Espanol; Tr3s; truTV; Turner Network TV HD; Universal HD; VH1 Classic; Video Rola; WE tv.
Fee: $14.95 monthly.

Pay Service 1
Pay Units: 44,927.
Programming (via satellite): Cinemax; HBO; Showtime; Starz.
Fee: $11.00 monthly (Cinemax, HBO, Starz or Showtime).

Digital Pay Service 1
Pay Units: 21,282.
Programming (via satellite): Cinemax (multiplexed); HBO (multiplexed); HBO HD; Showtime (multiplexed); Showtime HD; Starz (multiplexed); Starz HDTV; The Movie Channel (multiplexed).
Fee: $10.00 monthly (Cinemax, HBO, Starz or Showtime/TMC).

Video-On-Demand: No

Pay-Per-View
iN DEMAND (delivered digitally); Playboy TV (delivered digitally); Fresh (delivered digitally); Shorteez (delivered digitally); Spice: Xcess (delivered digitally); Club Jenna (delivered digitally).

Internet Service
Operational: Yes. Began: December 1, 2000.
Subscribers: 22,987.
Broadband Service: Suddenlink High Speed Internet.
Fee: $49.95 installation; $24.95 monthly; $15.00 modem lease; $249.00 modem purchase.

Telephone Service
Digital: Operational
Fee: $48.95 monthly

Miles of Plant: 668.0 (coaxial); 135.0 (fiber optic). Additional miles planned: 11.0 (coaxial).
Vice President & Manager: Connie Wharton. Marketing Director: Wayde Klein. Chief Technician: John Linton.
Ownership: Cequel Communications LLC (MSO).

LUBBOCK COUNTY (southeastern portion)—Formerly served by Almega Cable. No longer in operation. ICA: TX0348.

LUCAS—Suddenlink Communications, 12444 Powerscourt Dr, Saint Louis, MO 63131-3660. Phones: 800-999-6845 (Customer service); 314-965-2020. Fax: 903-561-5485. Web Site: http://www.suddenlink.com. Also serves Collin County (portions) & Fairview. ICA: TX0329.
TV Market Ranking: 12 (Collin County (portions), Fairview, LUCAS); Below 100 (Collin County (portions)). Franchise award date: N.A. Franchise expiration date: N.A. Began: January 1, 1983.
Channel capacity: 54 (not 2-way capable). Channels available but not in use: N.A.

Basic Service
Subscribers: 815.
Programming (received off-air): KDAF (CW, IND) Dallas; KDFW-DT (FOX) Dallas; KERA-TV (PBS) Dallas; KTVT (CBS) Fort Worth; KTXA (IND) Fort Worth; KXAS-TV (NBC) Fort Worth; KXTX-TV (TMO) Dallas; WFAA (ABC) Dallas.
Programming (via satellite): CNN; Disney Channel; ESPN; TBS Superstation; WGN America.
Fee: $39.95 installation; $41.95 monthly.

Pay Service 1
Pay Units: 130.
Programming (via satellite): HBO.
Fee: $12.00 monthly.

Pay Service 2
Pay Units: 68.
Programming (via satellite): The Movie Channel.
Fee: $9.00 monthly.

Pay Service 3
Pay Units: 172.
Programming (via satellite): Showtime.
Fee: $7.00 monthly.

Pay Service 4
Pay Units: 254.
Programming (via satellite): Flix.
Fee: $1.95 monthly.

Pay Service 5
Pay Units: 62.
Programming (via satellite): Cinemax.
Fee: $11.00 monthly.

Video-On-Demand: No

Internet Service
Operational: Yes.
Broadband Service: Suddenlink High Speed Internet.

Telephone Service
Digital: Operational

Miles of Plant: 83.0 (coaxial); None (fiber optic).
Regional Manager: Todd Cruthird. Plant Manager: Judy Cheney.
Ownership: Cequel Communications LLC (MSO).

LUEDERS—Formerly served by Jayroc Cablevision. No longer in operation. ICA: TX0803.

LULING—Time Warner Cable. Now served by AUSTIN, TX [TX0005]. ICA: TX0221.

LYONS—Reveille Broadband, PO Box 39, Lexington, TX 78947. Phone: 817-685-9588. Fax: 979-773-4733. E-mail: mariesullivan@reveillebroadband.com. Web Site: http://www.reveillebroadband.com. Also serves Burleson County (portions) & Somerville. ICA: TX0331.
TV Market Ranking: Below 100 (Burleson County (portions), LYONS, Somerville). Franchise award date: November 20, 1985. Franchise expiration date: N.A. Began: February 1, 1986.
Channel capacity: 50 (2-way capable). Channels available but not in use: None.

Basic Service
Subscribers: 297.
Programming (received off-air): KAMU-TV (PBS) College Station; KBTX-TV (CBS, CW) Bryan; KTBC (FOX) Austin; KVUE (ABC) Austin; KWKT-TV (FOX, MNT) Waco; KXAN-TV (NBC) Austin.
Programming (via microwave): KHOU (CBS) Houston; KTXH (MNT) Houston.
Programming (via satellite): A&E Networks; ABC Family Channel; AMC; BET Networks; Cartoon Network; CNN; Country Music TV; Discovery Channel; Disney Channel; ESPN; Fox Sports Southwest; HGTV; History Channel; MTV; Nickelodeon; QVC; Spike TV; TBS Superstation; The Learning Channel; The Weather Channel; Trinity Broadcasting Network; Turner Network TV; USA Network; WGN America.
Fee: $54.95 installation; $44.05 monthly.

Pay Service 1
Pay Units: 72.
Programming (via satellite): HBO.
Fee: $12.95 monthly.

Pay Service 2
Pay Units: 58.
Programming (via satellite): Showtime.
Fee: $12.95 monthly.

Pay Service 3
Pay Units: 63.
Programming (via satellite): The Movie Channel.
Fee: $12.95 monthly.

Video-On-Demand: No

Internet Service
Operational: Yes.

Telephone Service
None

Miles of Plant: 15.0 (coaxial); None (fiber optic).
President: Jeff Sullivan. Chief Executive Officer: Marie Sullivan. Vice President: Cory Savage. Office Manager: Laura Tillery.
Ownership: Reveille Broadband (MSO).

MADISONVILLE—Northland Cable Television, 1202 E Houston Ave, PO Box 1228, Crockett, TX 75835. Phones: 936-544-2031; 800-615-1110. Fax: 409-544-9660. Web Site: http://www.northlandcabletv.com. Also serves Madison County. ICA: TX0242.
TV Market Ranking: Below 100 (Madison County (portions), MADISONVILLE); Outside TV Markets (Madison County (portions)). Franchise award date: N.A. Franchise expiration date: N.A. Began: August 1, 1955.
Channel capacity: 52 (not 2-way capable). Channels available but not in use: N.A.

Basic Service
Subscribers: 900.
Programming (received off-air): KAMU-TV (PBS) College Station; KBTX-TV (CBS, CW) Bryan; KCEN-TV (NBC, IND) Temple; KETK-TV (NBC) Jacksonville; KHOU (CBS) Houston; KIAH (CW) Houston; KRHD-CD (ABC) Bryan; KRIV (FOX) Houston; KTRK-TV (ABC) Houston; KTXH (MNT) Houston; KYLE-TV (FOX) Bryan; allband FM.
Programming (via satellite): BET Networks; Cartoon Network; CNBC; C-SPAN; Discovery Channel; ESPN; Fox News Channel; Hallmark Channel; INSP; National Geographic Channel; QVC; TBS Superstation; Telemundo; The Learning Channel; The Weather Channel; Trinity Broadcasting Network; Turner Network TV; TV Guide Network; Univision Studios.
Fee: $38.99 monthly.

Expanded Basic Service 1
Subscribers: 775.
Programming (via satellite): A&E Networks; Animal Planet; CNN; ESPN 2; Food Network; Fox Movie Channel; Fox Sports Southwest; Headline News; HGTV; History Channel; Lifetime; Nickelodeon; Outdoor Channel; Spike TV; Syfy; Turner Classic Movies; Turner Network TV; USA Network.
Fee: $49.99 monthly.

Digital Basic Service
Subscribers: 80.
Programming (via satellite): AmericanLife TV Network; Discovery Digital Networks; DMX Music; G4; Golf Channel; GSN; Halogen Network; Speed.
Fee: $54.99 monthly.

Digital Expanded Basic Service
Subscribers: N.A.
Programming (via satellite): Bloomberg Television; Bravo; Discovery Fit & Health; Independent Film Channel; WE tv.

Pay Service 1
Pay Units: 100.
Programming (via satellite): HBO.
Fee: $14.00 monthly.

Pay Service 2
Pay Units: 45.
Programming (via satellite): Cinemax.

Pay Service 3
Pay Units: 45.
Programming (via satellite): Showtime.

Pay Service 4
Pay Units: 65.
Programming (via satellite): Encore; Starz.

Digital Pay Service 1
Pay Units: N.A.
Programming (via satellite): Cinemax (multiplexed); Encore (multiplexed); Flix; HBO

(multiplexed); Showtime (multiplexed); Starz (multiplexed); Sundance Channel.
Fee: $10.00 monthly (each).

Video-On-Demand: No

Internet Service
Operational: Yes.

Telephone Service
Digital: Operational

Miles of Plant: 49.0 (coaxial); None (fiber optic).

Manager: Brent Richey. Office Manager: Linda Richie. Chief Technician: John Guys.

Ownership: Northland Communications Corp. (MSO).

MAGNOLIA—Versalink Media, 511 Pan American Dr, Livingston, TX 77351. Phone: 877-689-6009. Web Site: http://www.versalinkus.com. Also serves Conroe (unincorporated areas) & Montgomery County (portions). ICA: TX0301.

TV Market Ranking: 15 (Conroe (unincorporated areas), Montgomery County (portions)); Below 100 (MAGNOLIA). Franchise award date: N.A. Franchise expiration date: N.A. Began: N.A.

Channel capacity: N.A. Channels available but not in use: N.A.

Basic Service
Subscribers: 248.
Programming (received off-air): KHOU (CBS) Houston; KIAH (CW) Houston; KPRC-TV (NBC) Houston; KRIV (FOX) Houston; KTRK-TV (ABC) Houston; KTXH (MNT) Houston; KUHT (PBS) Houston.
Programming (via satellite): A&E Networks; ABC Family Channel; CNN; Country Music TV; C-SPAN; Discovery Channel; Disney Channel; ESPN; Fox Sports Southwest; Headline News; INSP; Lifetime; Nickelodeon; QVC; Spike TV; TBS Superstation; The Weather Channel; Turner Network TV; USA Network.
Fee: $54.95 installation; $44.05 monthly.

Pay Service 1
Pay Units: 25.
Programming (via satellite): Cinemax.
Fee: $12.95 monthly.

Pay Service 2
Pay Units: 61.
Programming (via satellite): HBO.
Fee: $12.95 monthly.

Pay Service 3
Pay Units: 125.
Programming (via satellite): Showtime.
Fee: $12.95 monthly.

Video-On-Demand: No

Internet Service
Operational: No.

Telephone Service
None

Miles of Plant: 85.0 (coaxial); None (fiber optic).

Ownership: VersaLink Media LLC (MSO).

MALAKOFF—Northland Cable Television, 326 W Main St, PO Box 289, Gun Barrel City, TX 75147. Phones: 800-933-1046; 903-887-0240. Fax: 903-887-7395. E-mail: gunbarrel@northlandcabletv.com. Web Site: http://www.northlandcabletv.com. Also serves Caney City, Log Cabin, Star Harbor & Trinidad. ICA: TX0806.

TV Market Ranking: Outside TV Markets (Caney City, Log Cabin, MALKOFF, Star Harbor, Trinidad). Franchise award date: February 11, 1980. Franchise expiration date: N.A. Began: N.A.

Channel capacity: 51 (not 2-way capable). Channels available but not in use: N.A.

Basic Service
Subscribers: 950.
Programming (received off-air): KDAF (CW, IND) Dallas; KDFI (MNT) Dallas; KDFW-DT (FOX) Dallas; KERA-TV (PBS) Dallas; KETK-TV (NBC) Jacksonville; KLTV (ABC, TMO) Tyler; KPXD-TV (ION) Arlington; KSTR-DT (TEL) Irving; KTVT (CBS) Fort Worth; KTXA (IND) Fort Worth; KXAS-TV (NBC) Fort Worth; KXTX-TV (TMO) Dallas; WFAA (ABC) Dallas.
Programming (via satellite): A&E Networks; Cartoon Network; CNN; C-SPAN; Discovery Channel; ESPN; ESPN 2; Fox Sports Southwest; Great American Country; Headline News; HGTV; Lifetime; National Geographic Channel; QVC; Spike TV; TBS Superstation; The Weather Channel; Turner Classic Movies; Turner Network TV; USA Network; WGN America.
Fee: $40.00 installation; $30.99 monthly.

Digital Basic Service
Subscribers: N.A.
Programming (via satellite): American-Life TV Network; Bloomberg Television; Discovery Digital Networks; DMX Music; Fox Movie Channel; Golf Channel; GSN; Halogen Network; History Channel; Outdoor Channel; Speed; Trinity Broadcasting Network; WE tv.
Fee: $50.99 monthly.

Pay Service 1
Pay Units: 100.
Programming (via satellite): Cinemax.
Fee: $9.95 monthly.

Pay Service 2
Pay Units: 160.
Programming (via satellite): HBO.
Fee: $11.00 monthly.

Pay Service 3
Pay Units: 45.
Programming (via satellite): The Movie Channel.
Fee: $8.50 monthly.

Digital Pay Service 1
Pay Units: N.A.
Programming (via satellite): Cinemax (multiplexed); Encore (multiplexed); Flix; HBO (multiplexed); Showtime (multiplexed); Starz (multiplexed); Sundance Channel; The Movie Channel (multiplexed).
Fee: $10.00 monthly.

Internet Service
Operational: Yes.
Fee: $42.99 monthly.

Telephone Service
Digital: Operational
Fee: $29.99 monthly

Miles of Plant: 68.0 (coaxial); None (fiber optic).

Regional Manager: Richard Gammon. Chief Technician: Bobby Brady. Office Manager: Diane Ball.

Ownership: Northland Communications Corp. (MSO).

MANOR—Formerly served by Almega Cable. No longer in operation. ICA: TX0470.

MANVEL—Texas Mid-Gulf Cablevision, 1302 Wisteria St, Wharton, TX 77488. Phones: 979-532-8630; 866-532-3920. Fax: 979-532-8630. Web Site: http://www.warpspeed1.net. ICA: TX0986.

TV Market Ranking: 15 (MANVEL). Franchise award date: N.A. Franchise expiration date: N.A. Began: N.A.

Channel capacity: 62 (operating 2-way). Channels available but not in use: N.A.

Basic Service
Subscribers: N.A.
Programming (received off-air): KETH-TV (TBN) Houston; KFTH-DT (TEL) Alvin; KHOU (CBS) Houston; KIAH (CW) Houston; KLTJ (ETV) Galveston; KPRC-TV (NBC) Houston; KPXB-TV (ION) Conroe; KRIV (FOX) Houston; KTBU (IND) Conroe; KTMD (TMO) Galveston; KTRK-TV (ABC) Houston; KTXH (MNT) Houston; KUBE-TV (IND) Baytown; KUHT (PBS) Houston; KXLN-DT (UNV) Rosenberg; KYAZ (IND) Katy; KZJL (IND) Houston.
Programming (via satellite): C-SPAN 2; ESPN; TV Guide Network; WGN America.
Fee: $22.20 monthly.

Expanded Basic Service 1
Subscribers: N.A.
Programming (via satellite): A&E Networks; ABC Family Channel; AMC; Animal Planet; BET Networks; Bravo; Cartoon Network; CNN; Country Music TV; Discovery Channel; Disney Channel; E! Entertainment Television; ESPN 2; ESPN Classic Sports; Eternal Word TV Network; Food Network; Fox News Channel; FX; Halogen Network; Headline News; HGTV; History Channel; Lifetime; MSNBC; MTV; Nickelodeon; QVC; SoapNet; Speed; Spike TV; Syfy; TBS Superstation; The Learning Channel; The Weather Channel; Travel Channel; Turner Network TV; TV Land; USA Network; VH1.
Fee: $6.00 monthly.

Pay Service 1
Pay Units: N.A.
Fee: $12.95 monthly (each).

Video-On-Demand: No

Pay-Per-View
iN DEMAND (delivered digitally); Fresh (delivered digitally); Playboy TV (delivered digitally).

Internet Service
Operational: Yes, Both DSL & dial-up.
Broadband Service: Warp Speed 1 Internet.
Fee: $34.99 monthly.

Telephone Service
None

Chief Technician: Alan Boyd.

Ownership: Mid-Coast Cablevision (MSO).

MARATHON—Marathon TV Cable, PO Box 1377, Alpine, TX 79831-1377. Phone: 432-837-2300. Fax: 432-837-5423. E-mail: mtnzone@sbcglobal.net. ICA: TX0613.

TV Market Ranking: Outside TV Markets (MARATHON). Franchise award date: N.A. Franchise expiration date: N.A. Began: October 1, 1968.

Channel capacity: 36 (not 2-way capable). Channels available but not in use: N.A.

Basic Service
Subscribers: 140.
Programming (received off-air): KOSA-TV (CBS, MNT) Odessa; KPEJ-TV (FOX) Odessa; KWES-TV (NBC) Odessa; allband FM.
Programming (via satellite): A&E Networks; ABC Family Channel; CNN; Country Music TV; Discovery Channel; ESPN; GalaVision; KMGH-TV (ABC) Denver; KRMA-TV (PBS) Denver; Nickelodeon; Spike TV; TBS Superstation; The Learning Channel; The Weather Channel; Turner Classic Movies; Turner Network TV; WGN America.
Programming (via translator): KMID (ABC) Midland.
Fee: $25.00 installation; $38.00 monthly.

Pay Service 1
Pay Units: 48.
Programming (via satellite): HBO.
Fee: $10.00 installation.

Pay Service 2
Pay Units: 23.
Programming (via satellite): Showtime.
Fee: $10.00 installation.

Video-On-Demand: No

Internet Service
Operational: No.

Telephone Service
None

Miles of Plant: 8.0 (coaxial); None (fiber optic).

Manager: Steve Neu. Office Manager: Lawrence Neu.

Ownership: Mountain Zone TV Systems (MSO).

MARBLE FALLS—Northland Cable Television, 1101 Mission Hill Dr, PO Box 366, Marble Falls, TX 78654-0366. Phone: 830-693-7500. Fax: 830-693-6056. E-mail: marblefalls@northlandcabletv.com. Web Site: http://www.northlandcabletv.com. Also serves Burnet, Cottonwood Shores, Granite Shoals, Highland Haven, Horseshoe Bay, Kingsland, Lake L.B. Johnson, Meadowlakes & Sunrise Beach. ICA: TX0807.

TV Market Ranking: Below 100 (Burnet, Cottonwood Shores, Granite Shoals, Highland Haven, Horseshoe Bay, Kingsland, Lake L.B. Johnson, MARBLE FALLS, Meadowlakes, Sunrise Beach). Franchise award date: N.A. Franchise expiration date: N.A. Began: N.A.

Channel capacity: 65 (operating 2-way). Channels available but not in use: N.A.

Basic Service
Subscribers: 7,300.
Programming (received off-air): KBVO (MNT) Llano; KCWX (IND, MNT) Fredericksburg; KEYE-TV (CBS, TMO) Austin; KLRU (PBS) Austin; KNVA (CW) Austin; KTBC (FOX) Austin; KVUE (ABC) Austin.
Programming (via satellite): A&E Networks; AMC; Cartoon Network; CNBC; CNN; C-SPAN; Discovery Channel; ESPN; Food Network; Fox News Channel; Fox Sports Southwest; Great American Country; Hallmark Channel; Headline News; HGTV; History Channel; National Geographic Channel; QVC; TBS Superstation; Telemundo; The Learning Channel; The Weather Channel; Trinity Broadcasting Network; Turner Network TV; TV Guide Network; Univision Studios; USA Network.
Fee: $38.99 monthly.

Expanded Basic Service 1
Subscribers: 3,942.
Programming (via satellite): Animal Planet; Comedy Central; ESPN 2; Fox Movie Channel; FX; Lifetime; MTV; Nickelodeon; Outdoor Channel; Spike TV; Syfy; Turner Classic Movies; VH1.
Fee: $43.29 monthly.

Digital Basic Service
Subscribers: N.A.
Programming (via satellite): BBC America; Discovery Digital Networks; DMX Music; Golf Channel; GSN; Halogen Network; Outdoor Channel; Speed.
Fee: $51.99 monthly.

Digital Expanded Basic Service
Subscribers: N.A.
Programming (via satellite): Bloomberg Television; Bravo; Discovery Fit & Health; G4; Independent Film Channel; WE tv.

Pay Service 1
Pay Units: 1,250.
Programming (via satellite): Cinemax; HBO.
Fee: $11.95 monthly (Cinemax), $13.50 monthly (HBO).

Digital Pay Service 1
Pay Units: N.A.
Programming (via satellite): Cinemax (multiplexed); Encore (multiplexed); Flix; HBO (multiplexed); Showtime (multiplexed); Starz (multiplexed); The Movie Channel (multiplexed).

Video-On-Demand: No

Internet Service
Operational: Yes.
Broadband Service: Northland Express.
Fee: $42.99 monthly.

Telephone Service
Analog: Not Operational
Digital: Operational
Fee: $29.99 monthly

Miles of Plant: 213.0 (coaxial); 1.0 (fiber optic).
Regional Manager: Larson Lloyd. Marketing Director: Bonnie Moran. Plant Manager: Ron Gardner.
Ownership: Northland Communications Corp. (MSO).

MARFA—Marfa TV Cable Co. Inc., PO Box 1377, Alpine, TX 79831-1377. Phones: 800-446-5661; 432-837-2300. Fax: 432-837-5423. E-mail: mtnzone@sbcglobal.net. ICA: TX0360.
TV Market Ranking: Outside TV Markets (MARFA). Franchise award date: February 18, 1957. Franchise expiration date: N.A. Began: September 1, 1958.
Channel capacity: N.A. Channels available but not in use: N.A.

Basic Service
Subscribers: 682.
Programming (via satellite): A&E Networks; Animal Planet; Cartoon Network; CNN; Comedy Central; C-SPAN; Discovery Channel; Disney Channel; ESPN; ESPN 2; Eternal Word TV Network; Food Network; Fox News Channel; Fox Sports Southwest; GalaVision; Great American Country; Headline News; HGTV; History Channel; Lifetime; MTV; NFL Network; Nickelodeon; QVC; Syfy; TBS Superstation; Telefutura; Telemundo; The Learning Channel; The Weather Channel; Trinity Broadcasting Network; Turner Classic Movies; Turner Network TV; TV Land; Univision Studios; USA Network; VH1; WGN America.
Programming (via translator): KABB (FOX) San Antonio; KLRN (PBS) San Antonio; KMID (ABC) Midland; KMLM-DT (IND) Odessa; KOSA-TV (CBS, MNT) Odessa; KTSM-TV (NBC) El Paso; KVIA-TV (ABC, CW) El Paso; KWES-TV (NBC) Odessa.
Fee: $25.00 installation; $42.00 monthly.

Digital Basic Service
Subscribers: N.A.
Programming (via satellite): Bio; DMX Music; ESPN Classic Sports; History Channel International; Lifetime Movie Network; Style Network; Versus; WE tv.

Pay Service 1
Pay Units: 359.
Programming (via satellite): Cinemax; HBO; Showtime.

Digital Pay Service 1
Pay Units: N.A.
Programming (via satellite): Cinemax (multiplexed); Encore (multiplexed); HBO (multiplexed); Showtime (multiplexed); Starz (multiplexed).

Video-On-Demand: No

Internet Service
Operational: Yes. Began: June 1, 2005.
Fee: $50.00 installation; $25.50 monthly.

Telephone Service
None

Miles of Plant: 16.0 (coaxial); None (fiber optic).
Manager: Steve Neu. Office Manager: Lawrence Neu.
Ownership: Mountain Zone TV Systems (MSO).

MARLIN—Northland Cable Television, 515 W Tyler St, PO Box 112, Mexia, TX 76667-0112. Phones: 800-792-3087; 254-562-2872. Fax: 254-562-6454. E-mail: mexia@northlandcabletv.com. Web Site: http://www.northlandcabletv.com. ICA: TX0203.
TV Market Ranking: Below 100 (MARLIN). Franchise award date: January 1, 1964. Franchise expiration date: December 31, 2011. Began: March 1, 1965.
Channel capacity: 57 (not 2-way capable). Channels available but not in use: N.A.

Basic Service
Subscribers: 700.
Programming (received off-air): KCEN-TV (NBC, IND) Temple; KDYW (PBS) Waco; KERA-TV (PBS) Dallas; KTVT (CBS) Fort Worth; KTXA (IND) Fort Worth; KWKT-TV (FOX, MNT) Waco; KWTX-TV (CBS, CW) Waco; KXXV (ABC, TMO) Waco; WFAA (ABC) Dallas.
Programming (via satellite): INSP; QVC; Telemundo; Univision Studios.
Fee: $35.00 installation.

Expanded Basic Service 1
Subscribers: 600.
Programming (via satellite): A&E Networks; Animal Planet; BET Networks; Cartoon Network; CNBC; Comedy Central; C-SPAN; Discovery Channel; E! Entertainment Television; ESPN; ESPN 2; Food Network; Fox Movie Channel; Fox News Channel; Fox Sports Southwest; FX; Great American Country; Hallmark Channel; HGTV; History Channel; Lifetime; Nickelodeon; Outdoor Channel; Spike TV; Syfy; TBS Superstation; The Learning Channel; The Weather Channel; Turner Classic Movies; Turner Network TV; TV Land; USA Network.
Fee: $35.00 installation; $47.99 monthly.

Digital Basic Service
Subscribers: 20.
Programming (via satellite): Bravo; Discovery Fit & Health; Discovery Health Channel; Discovery Home Channel; Discovery Times Channel; DMX Music; ESPNews; Fox Soccer; G4; Golf Channel; Independent Film Channel; Lifetime Movie Network; Military Channel; RFD-TV; Science; ShopNBC; Speed; WE tv.
Fee: $8.00 monthly.

Pay Service 1
Pay Units: 40.
Programming (via satellite): HBO.
Fee: $11.50 monthly (Cinemax), $13.50 monthly (HBO).

Digital Pay Service 1
Pay Units: 35.
Programming (via satellite): Cinemax (multiplexed).
Fee: $14.00 monthly.

Digital Pay Service 2
Pay Units: 20.
Programming (via satellite): Encore (multiplexed); Starz (multiplexed).
Fee: $14.00 monthly.

Digital Pay Service 3
Pay Units: 15.
Programming (via satellite): Showtime (multiplexed); The Movie Channel (multiplexed).
Fee: $14.00 monthly.

Digital Pay Service 4
Pay Units: N.A.
Programming (via satellite): Flix; HBO (multiplexed).
Fee: $14.00 monthly.

Pay-Per-View
Sports PPV (delivered digitally); iN DEMAND (delivered digitally).

Internet Service
Operational: No.

Telephone Service
None

Miles of Plant: 41.0 (coaxial); None (fiber optic).
Manager: Brent Richey. Chief Technician: Joe Lopez. Office Manager: Pamela Elliott.
Ownership: Northland Communications Corp. (MSO).

MARSHALL—Cobridge Communications, 9450 Manchester Rd, Ste 200, St. Louis, MO 63119. Phones: 800-438-2427; 314-227-9500. Web Site: http://www.cobridge.net. Also serves Hallsville, Harrison County (portions), Jefferson & Marion County. ICA: TX0083.
TV Market Ranking: 58 (Harrison County (portions), Marion County, MARSHALL); Below 100 (Hallsville, Jefferson, Harrison County (portions), Marion County). Franchise award date: November 15, 1965. Franchise expiration date: N.A. Began: February 1, 1974.
Channel capacity: N.A. Channels available but not in use: N.A.

Basic Service
Subscribers: 3,929.
Programming (received off-air): KETK-TV (NBC) Jacksonville; KLTS-TV (PBS) Shreveport; KMSS-TV (FOX) Shreveport; KPXJ (CW) Minden; KSHV-TV (MNT) Shreveport; KSLA (CBS) Shreveport; KTAL-TV (NBC) Texarkana; KTBS-TV (ABC) Shreveport; allband FM.
Programming (via satellite): A&E Networks; ABC Family Channel; AMC; BET Networks; CNBC; Comedy Central; Country Music TV; C-SPAN; E! Entertainment Television; ESPN 2; Fox News Channel; FX; GalaVision; Headline News; INSP; Lifetime; MTV; Nickelodeon; QVC; Speed; Syfy; The Learning Channel; The Weather Channel; Trinity Broadcasting Network; TV Land.
Fee: $29.99 installation.

Digital Basic Service
Subscribers: N.A.
Programming (via satellite): BBC America; Bio; Discovery Digital Networks; DIY Network; ESPN Classic Sports; G4; GAS; History Channel International; Independent Film Channel; MTV Networks Digital Suite; Music Choice; Nick Jr.; Style Network; Toon Disney; TV Guide Interactive Inc.; WE tv.

Digital Pay Service 1
Pay Units: 776.
Programming (via satellite): Cinemax (multiplexed).
Fee: $25.00 installation; $11.95 monthly.

Digital Pay Service 2
Pay Units: 1,218.
Programming (via satellite): HBO (multiplexed).
Fee: $11.95 monthly.

Digital Pay Service 3
Pay Units: 266.
Programming (via satellite): Flix; The Movie Channel (multiplexed).
Fee: $11.95 monthly.

Digital Pay Service 4
Pay Units: 529.
Programming (via satellite): Showtime (multiplexed).
Fee: $11.95 monthly.

Video-On-Demand: No

Pay-Per-View
Hot Choice (delivered digitally); iN DEMAND (delivered digitally); Playboy TV (delivered digitally); Fresh (delivered digitally); Shorteez (delivered digitally).

Internet Service
Operational: Yes.
Broadband Service: Charter Pipeline.
Fee: $29.99 monthly.

Telephone Service
None

Miles of Plant: 274.0 (coaxial); None (fiber optic).
Chief Executive Officer: Scott Widham. General Manager: Wayne Kelstrom.
Ownership: Cobridge Communications LLC (MSO).

MART—Rapid Cable, 515 E Longview Dr, Arp, TX 75750. Phone: 903-859-6492. Fax: 903-859-3708. ICA: TX0359.
TV Market Ranking: Below 100 (MART). Franchise award date: N.A. Franchise expiration date: N.A. Began: January 1, 1983.
Channel capacity: N.A. Channels available but not in use: N.A.

Basic Service
Subscribers: 371.
Programming (received off-air): KCEN-TV (NBC, IND) Temple; KDFW-DT (FOX) Dallas; KERA-TV (PBS) Dallas; KTVT (CBS) Fort Worth; KWKT-TV (FOX, MNT) Waco; KWTX-TV (CBS, CW) Waco; KXAS-TV (NBC) Fort Worth; KXTX-TV (TMO) Dallas; KXXV (ABC, TMO) Waco; WFAA (ABC) Dallas.
Programming (via satellite): Discovery Channel; TBS Superstation; The Learning Channel.
Fee: $54.95 installation; $20.95 monthly.

Expanded Basic Service 1
Subscribers: N.A.
Programming (via satellite): ABC Family Channel; AMC; Animal Planet; Cartoon Network; CNBC; CNN; C-SPAN; Disney Channel; ESPN; Fox News Channel; FX; Headline News; HGTV; Lifetime; Nickelodeon; QVC; Spike TV; The Weather Channel; Turner Network TV; USA Network.
Fee: $23.10 monthly.

Pay Service 1
Pay Units: 108.
Programming (via satellite): Cinemax.
Fee: $12.95 monthly.

Pay Service 2
Pay Units: 173.
Programming (via satellite): Encore.
Fee: $12.95 monthly.

Pay Service 3
Pay Units: 133.
Programming (via satellite): HBO.
Fee: $12.95 monthly.

Pay Service 4
Pay Units: 122.
Programming (via satellite): Starz.
Fee: $6.75 monthly.
Video-On-Demand: No
Internet Service
Operational: Yes.
Broadband Service: Rapid High Speed Internet.
Fee: $100.00 installation; $29.95 monthly.
Telephone Service
None
Miles of Plant: 16.0 (coaxial); None (fiber optic).
Regional Manager: Mike Taylor. Chief Technician: Ronnie Stafford.
Ownership: RB3 LLC (MSO).

MASON—Reach Broadband, 515 E Longview St, Arp, TX 75750. Phone: 800-687-1258. Web Site: http://www.reachbroadband.net. Also serves Mason County (portions). ICA: TX0363.
TV Market Ranking: Below 100 (MASON, Mason County (portions)); Outside TV Markets (Mason County (portions)). Franchise award date: N.A. Franchise expiration date: N.A. Began: January 1, 1967.
Channel capacity: N.A. Channels available but not in use: N.A.
Basic Service
Subscribers: 455.
Programming (received off-air): KEYE-TV (CBS, TMO) Austin; KLRU (PBS) Austin; KLST (CBS) San Angelo; KTBC (FOX) Austin; KVUE (ABC) Austin; KXAN-TV (NBC) Austin; 8 FMs.
Programming (via satellite): A&E Networks; ABC Family Channel; CNN; Country Music TV; Discovery Channel; ESPN; Fox News Channel; Fox Sports Southwest; FX; HGTV; Spike TV; TBS Superstation; The Weather Channel; Trinity Broadcasting Network; Turner Network TV; TV Land; USA Network.
Fee: $29.95 installation; $38.00 monthly.
Pay Service 1
Pay Units: 64.
Programming (via satellite): HBO.
Fee: $10.63 monthly.
Pay Service 2
Pay Units: 30.
Programming (via satellite): Cinemax.
Fee: $10.95 monthly.
Pay Service 3
Pay Units: N.A.
Programming (via satellite): Encore; Starz.
Fee: $6.95 monthly.
Video-On-Demand: No
Internet Service
Operational: Yes.
Broadband Service: Rapid High Speed Internet.
Fee: $100.00 installation; $29.95 monthly.
Telephone Service
None
Miles of Plant: 24.0 (coaxial); None (fiber optic).
Regional Manager: Ronnie Stafford. Office Manager: Jan Gibson.
Ownership: RB3 LLC (MSO).

MATADOR (town)—Reach Broadband, 515 E Longview St, Arp, TX 75750. Phone: 800-687-1258. Web Site: http://www.reachbroadband.net. ICA: TX0500.
TV Market Ranking: Outside TV Markets (MATADOR (TOWN)). Franchise award date: N.A. Franchise expiration date: November 1, 2007. Began: November 1, 1957.
Channel capacity: 61 (not 2-way capable). Channels available but not in use: N.A.
Basic Service
Subscribers: 112.
Programming (received off-air): KAMC (ABC) Lubbock; KCBD (NBC) Lubbock; KJTV-TV (FOX) Lubbock; KLBK-TV (CBS) Lubbock.
Programming (via satellite): ABC Family Channel; AMC; AmericanLife TV Network; Animal Planet; Cartoon Network; CNN; Country Music TV; Discovery Channel; Disney Channel; E! Entertainment Television; ESPN; Fox Sports Southwest; Headline News; History Channel; KRMA-TV (PBS) Denver; Lifetime; QVC; Spike TV; TBS Superstation; The Learning Channel; The Weather Channel; Travel Channel; Trinity Broadcasting Network; Turner Network TV; TV Land; USA Network; WGN America.
Fee: $29.95 installation; $38.00 monthly.
Pay Service 1
Pay Units: 29.
Programming (via satellite): Cinemax.
Fee: $9.95 monthly.
Pay Service 2
Pay Units: 29.
Programming (via satellite): HBO.
Fee: $9.95 monthly.
Video-On-Demand: No
Internet Service
Operational: No.
Telephone Service
None
Miles of Plant: 11.0 (coaxial); None (fiber optic).
Regional Manager: Ronnie Stafford. Office Manager: Jan Gibson.
Ownership: RB3 LLC (MSO).

MATHIS—Time Warner Cable, 4060 S Padre Island Dr, Corpus Christi, TX 78411-4402. Phones: 972-899-7300 (Flower Mound office); 361-698-6259. Fax: 361-857-5038. Web Site: http://www.timewarnercable.com/Texas. Also serves Lake City, Refugio, Tynan & Woodsboro. ICA: TX0216.
TV Market Ranking: Outside TV Markets (Lake City, MATHIS, Refugio, Tynan, Woodsboro). Franchise award date: N.A. Franchise expiration date: October 20, 2010. Began: February 14, 1982.
Channel capacity: N.A. Channels available but not in use: N.A.
Basic Service
Subscribers: N.A. Included in Corpus Christi
Programming (received off-air): KDFW-DT (FOX) Dallas; KEDT (PBS) Corpus Christi; KIII (ABC) Corpus Christi; KORO (UNV) Corpus Christi; KRIS-TV (CW, NBC) Corpus Christi; KZTV (CBS) Corpus Christi.
Programming (via satellite): C-SPAN; Telemundo.
Fee: $34.99 installation; $16.39 monthly; $18.81 additional installation.
Expanded Basic Service 1
Subscribers: N.A.
Programming (via satellite): A&E Networks; ABC Family Channel; AMC; Animal Planet; BET Networks; Bravo; Cartoon Network; CNBC; CNN; Comedy Central; Country Music TV; Discovery Channel; Discovery Health Channel; Disney Channel; E! Entertainment Television; ESPN; ESPN 2; ESPN Classic Sports; ESPNews; Eternal Word TV Network; Food Network; Fox News Channel; Fox Sports Net; FX; GalaVision; Golf Channel; Great American Country; Hallmark Channel; Headline News; HGTV; History Channel; Lifetime; Lifetime Movie Network; MSNBC; MTV; mun2 television; National Geographic Channel; Nickelodeon; Oxygen; QVC; SoapNet; Speed; Spike TV; Syfy; TBS Superstation; Texas Cable News; The Learning Channel; The Weather Channel; Travel Channel; Trinity Broadcasting Network; truTV; Turner Classic Movies; Turner Network TV; TV Land; Versus; VH1; WE tv; Weatherscan.
Fee: $28.60 monthly.
Digital Basic Service
Subscribers: N.A.
Programming (via satellite): AmericanLife TV Network; America's Store; BBC America; Bio; Bloomberg Television; Canales N; Cooking Channel; Discovery Fit & Health; DIY Network; DMX Music; Encore Action; ESPN Now; FamilyNet; Fox Movie Channel; Fox Sports World; FSN Digital Atlantic; FSN Digital Central; FSN Digital Pacific; Fuel TV; Fuse; G4; GAS; GSN; History Channel International; Independent Film Channel; Lifetime Real Women; MTV2; NBA TV; Nick Jr.; Nick Too; NickToons TV; Outdoor Channel; Ovation; Sundance Channel; Tennis Channel; Toon Disney; VH1 Classic; VH1 Country.
Fee: $8.00 monthly.
Digital Pay Service 1
Pay Units: N.A.
Programming (via satellite): Cinemax (multiplexed); Flix (multiplexed); HBO (multiplexed); Showtime (multiplexed); Starz (multiplexed); The Movie Channel (multiplexed).
Fee: $12.95 monthly (each).
Video-On-Demand: Yes
Pay-Per-View
Sports PPV (delivered digitally); ESPN Gameplan (delivered digitally); iN DEMAND (delivered digitally); Events (delivered digitally); Movies (delivered digitally); Hot Choice (delivered digitally); Fresh (delivered digitally); Shorteez (delivered digitally); Playboy TV (delivered digitally).
Internet Service
Operational: Yes.
Broadband Service: Road Runner.
Fee: $49.99 installation; $44.95 monthly.
Telephone Service
Digital: Planned
Miles of Plant: 127.0 (coaxial); None (fiber optic).
President: Connie Wharton. Vice President & General Manager: Mike McKee. Engineering Director: Charlotte Strong. Public Affairs Manager: Vicki Triplett.
Ownership: Time Warner Cable (MSO).; Advance/Newhouse Partnership (MSO).

MAUD—Allegiance Communications, 707 W Saratoga St, Shawnee, OK 74804. Phones: 405-395-1131; 405-275-6923. Web Site: http://www.allegiance.tv. Also serves Bowie County. ICA: TX0482.
TV Market Ranking: 58 (Bowie County (portions), MAUD); Outside TV Markets (Bowie County (portions)). Franchise award date: N.A. Franchise expiration date: N.A. Began: August 1, 1981.
Channel capacity: 35 (not 2-way capable). Channels available but not in use: N.A.
Basic Service
Subscribers: 352.
Programming (received off-air): KLTS-TV (PBS) Shreveport; KMSS-TV (FOX) Shreveport; KSHV-TV (MNT) Shreveport; KSLA (CBS) Shreveport; KTAL-TV (NBC) Texarkana; KTBS-TV (ABC) Shreveport.
Programming (via satellite): Discovery Channel; QVC; TBS Superstation; The Weather Channel; WGN America.
Fee: $33.72 installation; $9.81 monthly.
Expanded Basic Service 1
Subscribers: 343.
Programming (via satellite): ABC Family Channel; AMC; Cartoon Network; CNBC; CNN; Disney Channel; ESPN; Fox News Channel; Fox Sports Southwest; FX; INSP; Lifetime; Nickelodeon; Spike TV; The Learning Channel; Turner Network TV; USA Network.
Fee: $11.10 monthly.
Digital Basic Service
Subscribers: N.A.
Programming (via satellite): BBC America; Black Family Channel; Bloomberg Television; Discovery Health Channel; Discovery Home Channel; Discovery Kids Channel; Discovery Times Channel; DMX Music; ESPNews; Fox Sports World; Fuse; G4; Golf Channel; GSN; Halogen Network; HGTV; Lifetime Movie Network; Outdoor Channel; Science; Speed; Sundance Channel; The Word Network; Toon Disney; Trinity Broadcasting Network; Versus.
Pay Service 1
Pay Units: 25.
Programming (via satellite): Encore; HBO; Showtime; Starz.
Digital Pay Service 1
Pay Units: N.A.
Programming (via satellite): Cinemax (multiplexed); Encore; HBO (multiplexed); Showtime (multiplexed); Starz (multiplexed); The Movie Channel (multiplexed).
Pay-Per-View
iN DEMAND (delivered digitally); Hot Choice (delivered digitally); Playboy TV (delivered digitally); Fresh (delivered digitally); Shorteez (delivered digitally).
Internet Service
Operational: Yes.
Telephone Service
None
Miles of Plant: 11.0 (coaxial); None (fiber optic).
Chief Executive Officer: Bill Haggarty. Regional Vice President: Andrew Dearth. Vice President, Marketing: Tracy Bass.
Ownership: Allegiance Communications (MSO).

MAURICEVILLE—Formerly served by Cebridge Connections. No longer in operation. ICA: TX0808.

MAY—Formerly served by Cable Unlimited. No longer in operation. ICA: TX0683.

McCAMEY—US Cable of Coastal Texas LP, 611 W Ave A, Seminole, TX 79360. Phones: 432-758-9221; 800-996-8788.

Fax: 432-758-3379. Web Site: http://www.uscable.com. ICA: TX1027.
TV Market Ranking: Outside TV Markets (McCAMEY).
Channel capacity: N.A. Channels available but not in use: N.A.

Basic Service
Subscribers: 320.
Programming (received off-air): KMID (ABC) Midland; KMLM-DT (IND) Odessa; KOSA-TV (CBS, MNT) Odessa; KPBT-TV (PBS) Odessa; KPEJ-TV (FOX) Odessa; KWES-TV (NBC) Odessa; KWWT (CW) Odessa.
Programming (via satellite): Animal Planet; C-SPAN; Fox News Channel; Home Shopping Network; KUPB (UNV) Midland; Lifetime; MSNBC; TBS Superstation; Telefutura; Trinity Broadcasting Network; Turner Network TV; WGN America.
Fee: $39.96 installation; $20.17 monthly.

Expanded Basic Service 1
Subscribers: N.A.
Programming (via satellite): A&E Networks; ABC Family Channel; American Movie Classics; Cartoon Network; CNN; Country Music TV; Discovery Channel; Discovery Fit & Health; Disney Channel; ESPN; ESPN 2; Fox Sports Net; FX; Hallmark Channel; History Channel; MoviePlex; MTV; National Geographic Channel; Nick At Nite; Nickelodeon; Spike TV; Syfy; The Learning Channel; USA Network; VH1.
Fee: $28.35 monthly.

Digital Basic Service
Subscribers: N.A.
Programming (via satellite): BBC America; Bio; Bloomberg Television; Bravo; Centric; cloo; CMT Pure Country; Current; Discovery Fit & Health; Discovery Health Channel; Discovery Kids Channel; Disney XD; DMX Music; Encore (multiplexed); ESPN Classic Sports; ESPNews; Fox College Sports Atlantic; Fox College Sports Central; Fox College Sports Pacific; Fox Movie Channel; Fox Soccer; Fuse; G4; Golf Channel; Great American Country; GSN; Halogen Network; HGTV; History Channel International; ID Investigation Discovery; Independent Film Channel; Lifetime Movie Network; Military Channel; MTV Hits; MTV2; Nick Jr.; Outdoor Channel; Planet Green; Science; Speed; Style Network; TeenNick; The Word Network; Turner Classic Movies; Versus; VH1 Classic; VH1 Soul; WE tv.
Fee: $20.90 monthly.

Pay Service 1
Pay Units: N.A.
Programming (via satellite): Cinemax; HBO.
Fee: $13.95 monthly (each).

Digital Pay Service 1
Pay Units: N.A.
Programming (via satellite): Cinemax (multiplexed); HBO (multiplexed); Showtime (multiplexed); Starz (multiplexed); The Movie Channel (multiplexed).
Fee: $9.95 monthly (Starz), $12.95 monthly (HBO, Cinemax, Showtime or TMC).

Video-On-Demand: No

Pay-Per-View
Event Entertainment (delivered digitally); Movies (delivered digitally); Playboy TV (delivered digitally); Fresh (delivered digitally).

Internet Service
Operational: Yes.

Telephone Service
None
Regional Manager: Daryl Koedyker.
Ownership: US Cable Corp. (MSO).

MEDINA—Formerly served by Medina Cable Ltd. No longer in operation. ICA: TX0684.

MEMPHIS—Reach Broadband, 515 E Longview St, Arp, TX 75750. Phone: 800-687-1258. Web Site: http://www.reachbroadband.net. Also serves Hall County (portions). ICA: TX0302.
TV Market Ranking: Outside TV Markets (Hall County (portions), MEMPHIS). Franchise award date: N.A. Franchise expiration date: N.A. Began: July 1, 1958.
Channel capacity: 29 (not 2-way capable). Channels available but not in use: N.A.

Basic Service
Subscribers: 542.
Programming (via microwave): KAMR-TV (NBC) Amarillo; KETA-TV (PBS) Oklahoma City; KFDA-TV (CBS) Amarillo; KVII-TV (ABC, CW) Amarillo.
Programming (via satellite): ABC Family Channel; Country Music TV; C-SPAN; Discovery Channel; Disney Channel; ESPN; INSP; Lifetime; MTV; Nickelodeon; Spike TV; TBS Superstation; The Weather Channel; Turner Classic Movies; Turner Network TV; USA Network; WGN America.
Fee: $29.99 installation; $38.00 monthly.

Pay Service 1
Pay Units: 45.
Programming (via satellite): Cinemax.
Fee: $20.00 installation; $11.65 monthly.

Pay Service 2
Pay Units: 71.
Programming (via satellite): HBO.
Fee: $11.65 monthly.

Internet Service
Operational: No.

Telephone Service
None
Miles of Plant: 23.0 (coaxial); None (fiber optic).
Regional Manager: Ronnie Stafford. Office Manager: Jan Gibson.
Ownership: RB3 LLC (MSO).

MENARD—Reach Broadband, 515 E Longview St, Arp, TX 75750. Phone: 800-687-1258. Web Site: http://www.reachbroadband.net. Also serves Menard County (portions). ICA: TX0392.
TV Market Ranking: Outside TV Markets (MENARD, Menard County (portions)). Franchise award date: N.A. Franchise expiration date: N.A. Began: November 1, 1958.
Channel capacity: 41 (not 2-way capable). Channels available but not in use: N.A.

Basic Service
Subscribers: 330.
Programming (received off-air): KIDY (FOX) San Angelo; KLST (CBS) San Angelo; KTXS-TV (ABC, CW, TMO) Sweetwater; 5 FMs.
Programming (via microwave): KDTX-TV (TBN) Dallas; KRBC-TV (NBC) Abilene.
Programming (via satellite): A&E Networks; ABC Family Channel; Animal Planet; CNN; Country Music TV; Discovery Channel; Disney Channel; ESPN; Fox News Channel; Fox Sports Southwest; Headline News; KRMA-TV (PBS) Denver; Lifetime; Nickelodeon; QVC; Spike TV; TBS Superstation; Telemundo; The Learning Channel; The Weather Channel; Trinity Broadcasting Network; Turner Classic Movies; Turner Network TV; TV Land; USA Network; WGN America.
Fee: $29.95 installation; $38.00 monthly.

Pay Service 1
Pay Units: 46.
Programming (via satellite): HBO.
Fee: $10.95 monthly.

Pay Service 2
Pay Units: 71.
Programming (via satellite): Showtime.
Fee: $9.95 monthly.

Pay Service 3
Pay Units: 62.
Programming (via satellite): The Movie Channel.
Fee: $7.95 monthly.

Video-On-Demand: No

Internet Service
Operational: No.

Telephone Service
None
Miles of Plant: 20.0 (coaxial); None (fiber optic).
Regional Manager: Ronnie Stafford. Office Manager: Jan Gibson.
Ownership: RB3 LLC (MSO).

MERIDIAN—Formerly served by Almega Cable. No longer in operation. ICA: TX0446.

MERKEL—CMA Cablevision, 1510 N 1st St, PO Box 549, Merkel, TX 79536-0549. Phones: 800-588-4750; 325-928-4750. Fax: 325-928-3452. Web Site: http://www.cmaaccess.com. ICA: TX0355.
TV Market Ranking: Below 100 (MERKEL). Franchise award date: September 20, 1971. Franchise expiration date: N.A. Began: July 1, 1972.
Channel capacity: N.A. Channels available but not in use: N.A.

Basic Service
Subscribers: 435.
Programming (received off-air): KRBC-TV (NBC) Abilene; KTAB-TV (CBS) Abilene; KTXS-TV (ABC, CW, TMO) Sweetwater; allband FM.
Programming (via satellite): A&E Networks; ABC Family Channel; CNN; Country Music TV; Discovery Channel; Disney Channel; ESPN; Lifetime; MTV; Nickelodeon; Spike TV; TBS Superstation; The Weather Channel; Turner Network TV; USA Network; WGN America.
Fee: $39.95 installation; $10.95 monthly; $9.95 additional installation.

Expanded Basic Service 1
Subscribers: N.A.
Programming (via satellite): AMC; Animal Planet; Cartoon Network; ESPN 2; Fox News Channel; Fox Sports Southwest; Headline News; HGTV; History Channel; INSP; QVC; Syfy; The Learning Channel; Turner Classic Movies; TV Land; VH1.
Fee: $24.00 monthly.

Pay Service 1
Pay Units: 169.
Programming (via satellite): HBO.
Fee: $9.95 installation; $11.95 monthly.

Video-On-Demand: No

Internet Service
Operational: Yes.
Subscribers: 50.
Broadband Service: CMA.
Fee: $39.95 installation; $40.95 monthly; $6.95 modem lease; $149.95 modem purchase.

Telephone Service
None
Miles of Plant: 18.0 (coaxial); None (fiber optic).
General Manager: Jerry Smith. Chief Technician: Joe Clark. Marketing Director: Julie Ferguson.
Ownership: Cable Management Assoc. (MSO).

MERTZON—Reach Broadband, 515 E Longview St, Arp, TX 75750. Phone: 800-687-1258. Web Site: http://www.reachbroadband.net. Also serves Irion County (portions) & Sherwood. ICA: TX0810.
TV Market Ranking: Below 100 (Irion County (portions), MERTZON, Sherwood). Franchise award date: N.A. Franchise expiration date: N.A. Began: June 1, 1981.
Channel capacity: 41 (not 2-way capable). Channels available but not in use: N.A.

Basic Service
Subscribers: 155.
Programming (received off-air): KIDY (FOX) San Angelo; KLST (CBS) San Angelo; KSAN-TV (NBC) San Angelo; KTXS-TV (ABC, CW, TMO) Sweetwater.
Programming (via satellite): A&E Networks; ABC Family Channel; AMC; Animal Planet; CNN; Country Music TV; Discovery Channel; Disney Channel; E! Entertainment Television; ESPN; Fox Sports Southwest; Headline News; Lifetime; QVC; Spike TV; Syfy; TBS Superstation; The Learning Channel; The Weather Channel; Travel Channel; Turner Network TV; TV Land; USA Network.
Fee: $29.95 installation; $38.00 monthly.

Pay Service 1
Pay Units: 67.
Programming (via satellite): HBO.
Fee: $9.95 monthly.

Pay Service 2
Pay Units: 31.
Programming (via satellite): Showtime.
Fee: $9.95 monthly.

Video-On-Demand: No

Internet Service
Operational: No.

Telephone Service
None
Miles of Plant: 20.0 (coaxial); None (fiber optic).
Regional Manager: Ronnie Stafford. Office Manager: Jan Gibson.
Ownership: RB3 LLC (MSO).

MEXIA—Northland Cable Television, 515 W Tyler St, PO Box 112, Mexia, TX 76667-0112. Phones: 800-792-3087; 254-562-2872. Fax: 254-562-6454. Web Site: http://www.northlandcabletv.com. Also serves Groesbeck, Lake Mexia, Shiloh & Tehuacana. ICA: TX0166.
TV Market Ranking: Outside TV Markets (Groesbeck, Lake Mexia, MEXIA, Shiloh, Tehuacana). Franchise award date: April 15, 1965. Franchise expiration date: December 14, 2008. Began: December 7, 1966.
Channel capacity: 54 (not 2-way capable). Channels available but not in use: N.A.

Basic Service
Subscribers: 2,900.
Programming (received off-air): KCEN-TV (NBC, IND) Temple; KDFI (MNT) Dallas; KDFW-DT (FOX) Dallas; KERA-TV (PBS) Dallas; KTVT (CBS) Fort Worth; KTXA (IND) Fort Worth; KWKT-TV (FOX, MNT) Waco; KWTX-TV (CBS, CW) Waco; KXAS-TV (NBC) Fort Worth; KXXV (ABC, TMO) Waco; WFAA (ABC) Dallas; allband FM.
Programming (via satellite): A&E Networks; Animal Planet; BET Networks; Cartoon Network; CNBC; CNN; C-SPAN; Discovery Channel; ESPN; Food Network; Fox Deportes; Fox News Channel; Fox Sports Southwest; Great American Country; Hallmark Channel; Headline News; HGTV; History Channel; National Geographic Channel; Outdoor Channel; QVC; TBS Superstation; Telemundo; The Learning Channel; The Weather Channel; Travel Channel; Trinity Broadcasting Network;

Turner Network TV; TV Guide Network; Univision Studios; USA Network.
Fee: $50.00 installation; $38.99 monthly.
Expanded Basic Service 1
Subscribers: 1,900.
Programming (via satellite): Comedy Central; E! Entertainment Television; ESPN 2; Fox Movie Channel; Lifetime; MTV; Nickelodeon; Spike TV; Syfy; Turner Classic Movies.
Fee: $49.99 monthly.
Digital Basic Service
Subscribers: 325.
Programming (via satellite): AmericanLife TV Network; BBC America; Bloomberg Television; Bravo; Discovery Fit & Health; DMX Music; G4; Golf Channel; GSN; Halogen Network; Independent Film Channel; Speed; Versus; WE tv.
Fee: $54.99 monthly.
Pay Service 1
Pay Units: 250.
Programming (via satellite): Encore; Starz.
Fee: $35.00 installation; $10.00 monthly.
Pay Service 2
Pay Units: 90.
Programming (via satellite): Showtime.
Fee: $35.00 installation; $10.00 monthly.
Pay Service 3
Pay Units: 300.
Programming (via satellite): HBO.
Fee: $35.00 installation; $14.00 monthly.
Digital Pay Service 1
Pay Units: 70.
Programming (via satellite): Cinemax (multiplexed); Encore (multiplexed); HBO (multiplexed); Showtime (multiplexed); Starz (multiplexed); Sundance Channel.
Fee: $10.00 monthly (each).
Video-On-Demand: No
Pay-Per-View
iN DEMAND (delivered digitally); Sports PPV (delivered digitally).
Internet Service
Operational: Yes.
Fee: $42.99 monthly.
Telephone Service
Analog: Not Operational
Digital: Operational
Fee: $29.99 monthly
Miles of Plant: 115.0 (coaxial); 19.0 (fiber optic).
Manager: Brent Richey. Chief Technician: Joe Lopez. Office Manager: Pamela Elliott.
Ownership: Northland Communications Corp. (MSO).

MIAMI—Elk River TV Cable Co., 509 S Main St, PO Box 154, Troy, ID 83871. Phone: 208-369-4652. E-mail: leslie@elkrivertv.net. Web Site: http://www.elkrivertv.net. ICA: TX0459.
TV Market Ranking: Outside TV Markets (MIAMI). Franchise award date: N.A. Franchise expiration date: N.A. Began: February 1, 1982.
Channel capacity: N.A. Channels available but not in use: N.A.
Basic Service
Subscribers: N.A. Included in San Jon, NM
Programming (received off-air): KAMR-TV (NBC) Amarillo; KFDA-TV (CBS) Amarillo; KVII-TV (ABC, CW) Amarillo; KWET (PBS) Cheyenne.
Programming (via satellite): C-SPAN; TBS Superstation; WGN America.
Fee: $35.00 installation; $9.00 monthly.
Pay Service 1
Pay Units: 162.
Programming (via satellite): The Movie Channel.
Fee: $11.00 monthly.
Video-On-Demand: No
Internet Service
Operational: No.
Telephone Service
None
Miles of Plant: 7.0 (coaxial); None (fiber optic).
Manager: Dave & Leslie McGraw. Chief Technician: Justin McGraw.
Ownership: Elk River TV Cable Co. (MSO).

MIDLAND—Suddenlink Communications, 2530 S Midkiss Rd, Midland, TX 79701. Phone: 432-694-7721. Web Site: http://www.suddenlink.com. Also serves Midland County (portions). ICA: TX0024.
TV Market Ranking: Below 100 (MIDLAND, Midland County (portions)). Franchise award date: N.A. Franchise expiration date: N.A. Began: October 19, 1968.
Channel capacity: 54 (operating 2-way). Channels available but not in use: N.A.
Basic Service
Subscribers: 26,753.
Programming (received off-air): KMID (ABC) Midland; KMLM-DT (IND) Odessa; KOSA-TV (CBS, MNT) Odessa; KPBT-TV (PBS) Odessa; KPEJ-TV (FOX) Odessa; KTLE-LP (TMO) Odessa; KUPB (UNV) Midland; KWES-TV (NBC) Odessa; 9 FMs.
Programming (via satellite): C-SPAN; C-SPAN 2; ION Television; QVC; TBS Superstation; The Weather Channel; TV Guide Network; WGN America.
Fee: $28.62 installation; $13.20 monthly.
Expanded Basic Service 1
Subscribers: 14,254.
Programming (via satellite): A&E Networks; ABC Family Channel; AMC; Animal Planet; BET Networks; Bravo; Cartoon Network; CNBC; CNN; Comedy Central; Country Music TV; Discovery Channel; Disney Channel; E! Entertainment Television; ESPN; ESPN 2; Eternal Word TV Network; Food Network; Fox News Channel; Fox Sports Southwest; FX; GSN; Hallmark Channel; Headline News; HGTV; History Channel; Lifetime; MoviePlex; MSNBC; MTV; MTV2; mun2 television; Nickelodeon; Spike TV; Syfy; The Learning Channel; Travel Channel; Turner Classic Movies; Turner Network TV; TV Land; USA Network; Versus; VH1.
Fee: $15.00 installation; $39.99 monthly.
Digital Basic Service
Subscribers: 12,499.
Programming (via satellite): BBC America; Bio; Bloomberg Television; Canales N; Cooking Channel; Discovery Channel; Discovery Digital Networks; DIY Network; Encore; ESPN; ESPN Classic Sports; ESPNews; Eternal Word TV Network; Fox Sports World; FSN Digital Atlantic; FSN Digital Central; FSN Digital Pacific; Fuel TV; Fuse; G4; GAS; GMC; Golf Channel; Great American Country; Halogen Network; History Channel International; iN DEMAND; Independent Film Channel; Lifetime Movie Network; MTV Networks Digital Suite; National Geographic Channel; NBA TV; Nick Jr.; NickToons TV; Nuvo TV; Outdoor Channel; Oxygen; ShopNBC; SoapNet; Sundance Channel; Tennis Channel; Toon Disney; Trinity Broadcasting Network; truTV; Universal HD; WAM! America's Kidz Network.
Fee: $14.95 monthly.
Pay Service 1
Pay Units: 16,872.
Programming (via satellite): Cinemax; HBO; Showtime; Starz.
Fee: $15.00 installation; $8.95 monthly (Cinemax), $9.95 monthly (Showtime), $10.95 monthly (TMC), $11.95 monthly (HBO).

Digital Pay Service 1
Pay Units: 14,563.
Programming (via satellite): Cinemax (multiplexed); Flix; HBO (multiplexed); HBO; Music Choice; Showtime (multiplexed); Showtime; Starz (multiplexed); Starz; The Movie Channel (multiplexed).
Fee: $10.00 monthly (each).
Video-On-Demand: No
Pay-Per-View
Addressable homes: 13,000.
iN DEMAND (delivered digitally); NBA TV (delivered digitally); Sports PPV (delivered digitally); Adult (delivered digitally).
Internet Service
Operational: Yes.
Broadband Service: Suddenlink High Speed Internet.
Fee: $49.95 installation; $24.95 monthly; $15.00 modem lease; $249.95 modem purchase.
Telephone Service
Digital: Operational
Fee: $48.95 monthly
Miles of Plant: 515.0 (coaxial); 18.0 (fiber optic). Additional miles planned: 294.0 (fiber optic).
Area Manager: Chris Christiansen. Regional Manager: Bill Flowers.
Ownership: Cequel Communications LLC (MSO).

MIDWAY—Formerly served by Almega Cable. No longer in operation. ICA: TX0675.

MILES—Allegiance Communications, 707 W Saratoga St, Shawnee, OK 74804. Phones: 405-395-1131; 405-275-6923. Web Site: http://www.allegiance.tv. ICA: TX0963.
TV Market Ranking: Below 100 (MILES). Franchise award date: N.A. Franchise expiration date: April 1, 2007. Began: N.A.
Channel capacity: 36 (not 2-way capable). Channels available but not in use: N.A.
Basic Service
Subscribers: N.A. Included with Ballinger
Programming (received off-air): KABC-TV (ABC) Los Angeles; KERA-TV (PBS) Dallas; KIDY (FOX) San Angelo; KLST (CBS) San Angelo; KPCB-DT (IND) Snyder; KTXA (IND) Fort Worth; WFAA (ABC) Dallas.
Programming (via satellite): TBS Superstation.
Fee: $38.00 installation; $13.50 monthly; $.25 converter.
Expanded Basic Service 1
Subscribers: N.A.
Programming (via satellite): A&E Networks; ABC Family Channel; AMC; Animal Planet; Cartoon Network; CMT Pure Country; CNN; Comedy Central; C-SPAN; Discovery Channel; ESPN; Fox News Channel; Fox Sports Southwest; Headline News; INSP; Lifetime; MTV; Nickelodeon; QVC; Spike TV; Syfy; Telefutura; The Learning Channel; The Weather Channel; Turner Network TV; Univision Studios; USA Network.
Fee: $38.00 installation; $24.50 monthly.
Pay-Per-View
iN DEMAND (delivered digitally); Hot Choice (delivered digitally); Playboy TV (delivered digitally); Fresh (delivered digitally); Shorteez (delivered digitally).
Internet Service
Operational: No.
Telephone Service
None
Miles of Plant: 9.0 (coaxial); None (fiber optic).
Chief Executive Officer: Bill Haggarty. Regional Vice President: Andrew Dearth. Vice President, Marketing: Tracy Bass.
Ownership: Allegiance Communications (MSO).

MILLSAP—Formerly served by Mallard Cablevision. No longer in operation. ICA: TX0523.

MINEOLA—Suddenlink Communications, 403 W Broad St, Mineola, TX 75773-2066. Phone: 903-569-2651. Fax: 903-569-2662. Web Site: http://www.suddenlink.com. Also serves Franklin County, Grand Saline, Lindale, Quitman, Smith County, Van Zandt County & Wood County. ICA: TX0812.
TV Market Ranking: Below 100 (Grand Saline, Lindale, MINEOLA, Quitman, Smith County (portions), Van Zandt County (portions), Wood County (portions)); Outside TV Markets (Franklin County, Smith County (portions), Van Zandt County (portions), Wood County (portions)). Franchise award date: N.A. Franchise expiration date: N.A. Began: January 1, 1963.
Channel capacity: 31 (operating 2-way). Channels available but not in use: N.A.
Basic Service
Subscribers: 5,800.
Programming (received off-air): KCEB (CW) Longview; KDFW-DT (FOX) Dallas; KERA-TV (PBS) Dallas; KETK-TV (NBC) Jacksonville; KFXK-TV (FOX) Longview; KLPN-LP (IND) Longview; KLTV (ABC, TMO) Tyler; KTXA (IND) Fort Worth; KXAS-TV (NBC) Fort Worth; KXTX-TV (TMO) Dallas; KYTX (CBS, IND) Nacogdoches; WFAA (ABC) Dallas; allband FM.
Programming (via satellite): C-SPAN; C-SPAN 2; QVC; TBS Superstation; The Weather Channel; TV Guide Network; WGN America.
Fee: $35.00 installation; $15.00 monthly.
Expanded Basic Service 1
Subscribers: 5,000.
Programming (via satellite): A&E Networks; ABC Family Channel; AMC; Animal Planet; BET Networks; Cartoon Network; CNBC; CNN; Comedy Central; Discovery Channel; Disney Channel; ESPN; ESPN 2; Food Network; Fox News Channel; Fox Sports Southwest; FX; Golf Channel; Great American Country; Headline News; HGTV; History Channel; INSP; Lifetime; MTV; Nickelodeon; Spike TV; Syfy; The Learning Channel; Trinity Broadcasting Network; Turner Classic Movies; Turner Network TV; TV Land; Univision Studios; USA Network; VH1.
Fee: $10.00 installation; $11.50 monthly.

Digital Basic Service
Subscribers: N.A.
Programming (via satellite): A&E HD; BBC America; Bio; Bloomberg Television; Boomerang; CBS Sports Network; CMT Pure Country; Cooking Channel; Discovery en Espanol; Discovery Health Channel; Discovery Home Channel; Discovery Kids Channel; Discovery Times Channel; DIY Network; Encore (multiplexed); ESPN Classic Sports; ESPN HD; ESPN U; ESPNews; FamilyNet; Food Network HD; Fox Soccer; Fuel TV; Fuse; G4; GMC; GSN; Hallmark Channel; Halogen Network; HD Theater; HDNet; HDNet Movies; HGTV HD; History Channel International; Lifetime Movie Network; Military Channel; MTV Hits; MTV2; Music Choice; National Geographic Channel; National Geographic Channel HD Network; Nick Jr.; NickToons TV; Outdoor Channel; Oxygen; Science; SoapNet; Speed; Style Network; Sundance Channel; TeenNick; Tennis Channel; Toon Disney; truTV; Turner Network TV HD; Universal HD; Versus; VH1 Classic; WE tv; Weatherscan.

Digital Pay Service 1
Pay Units: N.A.
Programming (via satellite): Cinemax (multiplexed); HBO (multiplexed); HBO HD; Showtime (multiplexed); Showtime HD; Starz (multiplexed); Starz HDTV; The Movie Channel.

Video-On-Demand: No

Pay-Per-View
iN DEMAND (delivered digitally); Playboy TV (delivered digitally); Fresh (delivered digitally).

Internet Service
Operational: Yes.
Broadband Service: Suddenlink High Speed Internet.
Fee: $49.95 installation; $38.95 monthly.

Telephone Service
None

Miles of Plant: 196.0 (coaxial); None (fiber optic).
Manager: Clyde Bowling. Chief Technician: Glen Lovette.
Ownership: Cequel Communications LLC (MSO).

MINERAL WELLS—Suddenlink Communications, 6501 Hwy 180 E, Mineral Wells, TX 76067. Phones: 940-325-9587 (Adminstrative office); 888-822-5151 (Customer service); 940-325-9586 (Administrative office); 940-328-1281. Web Site: http://www.suddenlink.com. Also serves Palo Pinto County (portions). ICA: TX0106.
TV Market Ranking: Below 100 (Palo Pinto County (portions)); Outside TV Markets (MINERAL WELLS, Palo Pinto County (portions)). Franchise award date: N.A. Franchise expiration date: N.A. Began: June 1, 1951.
Channel capacity: N.A. Channels available but not in use: N.A.

Basic Service
Subscribers: 4,569.
Programming (received off-air): KDAF (CW, IND) Dallas; KDFI (MNT) Dallas; KDFW-DT (FOX) Dallas; KDTN (ETV) Denton; KDTX-TV (TBN) Dallas; KERA-TV (PBS) Dallas; KHAS-TV (NBC) Hastings; KPXD-TV (ION) Arlington; KSTR-DT (TEL) Irving; KTVT (CBS) Fort Worth; KTXA (IND) Fort Worth; KUVN-DT (UNV) Garland; KXAS-TV (NBC) Fort Worth; KXTX-TV (TMO) Dallas; WFAA (ABC) Dallas; 13 FMs.
Programming (via satellite): C-SPAN; Jewelry Television; TBS Superstation; The Weather Channel; WGN America.
Fee: $38.24 installation; $9.85 monthly; $2.00 converter.

Expanded Basic Service 1
Subscribers: N.A.
Programming (via satellite): A&E Networks; ABC Family Channel; AMC; Animal Planet; BET Networks; Bravo; Cartoon Network; CNBC; CNN; Comedy Central; Country Music TV; C-SPAN 2; Discovery Channel; Discovery Health Channel; Disney Channel; E! Entertainment Television; ESPN; ESPN 2; ESPN Classic Sports; Eternal Word TV Network; Food Network; Fox News Channel; Fox Sports Southwest; FX; GalaVision; Great American Country; Headline News; HGTV; History Channel; INSP; Lifetime; Lifetime Movie Network; MSNBC; MTV; Nickelodeon; Outdoor Channel; Oxygen; QVC; Speed; Spike TV; The Learning Channel; Travel Channel; truTV; Turner Network TV; TV Guide Network; TV Land; USA Network; Versus; VH1.
Fee: $13.28 monthly.

Digital Basic Service
Subscribers: N.A.
Programming (via satellite): A&E HD; Bandamax; BBC America; Bio; Bloomberg Television; Boomerang en Espanol; CBS Sports Network; Cine Latino; Cine Mexicano; CMT Pure Country; CNN en Espanol; Cooking Channel; De Pelicula; De Pelicula Clasico; Discovery en Espanol; Discovery Home Channel; Discovery Kids Channel; DIY Network; Encore (multiplexed); ESPN 2 HD; ESPN Deportes; ESPN HD; ESPN U; ESPNews; EWTN en Espanol; Food Network HD; Fox Deportes; Fox Reality Channel; Fox Soccer; Fuel TV; Fuse; G4; GalaVision; Golf Channel; GSN; Hallmark Channel; HD Theater; HDNet; HDNet Movies; HGTV HD; History Channel en Espanol; History Channel HD; History Channel International; ID Investigation Discovery; Independent Film Channel; Latele Novela Network; Military Channel; MTV Hits; MTV2; mun2 television; Music Choice; National Geographic Channel; National Geographic Channel HD Network; Nick Jr.; NickToons en Espanol; NickToons TV; Ritmoson Latino; Science; SoapNet; Sorpresa; Sundance Channel; Sur Network; Syfy; TBN Enlace USA; TeenNick; Telehit; Toon Disney; Toon Disney en Espanol; Tr3s; Trinity Broadcasting Network; Turner Classic Movies; Turner Network TV HD; TV Chile; Universal HD; VH1 Classic; Video Rola; WE tv.

Pay Service 1
Pay Units: 421.
Programming (via satellite): Starz.
Fee: $10.00 installation; $10.95 monthly.

Digital Pay Service 1
Pay Units: N.A.
Programming (via satellite): Cinemax (multiplexed); HBO (multiplexed); HBO HD; Showtime (multiplexed); Showtime HD; Starz (multiplexed); Starz HDTV; The Movie Channel (multiplexed).

Video-On-Demand: No

Pay-Per-View
iN DEMAND (delivered digitally); Fresh (delivered digitally); Playboy TV (delivered digitally).

Internet Service
Operational: Yes.
Broadband Service: Suddenlink High Speed Internet.
Fee: $49.95 installation; $24.95 monthly.

Telephone Service
Digital: Operational
Fee: $48.95 monthly

Miles of Plant: 120.0 (coaxial); None (fiber optic).
Manager: Raymond Greenwood. Chief Technician: Scott Wilber.
Ownership: Cequel Communications LLC (MSO).

MONAHANS—Suddenlink Communications, 1504 N Main St, Monahans, TX 79756. Phones: 877-423-2743 (Customer service); 314-965-2020. Web Site: http://www.suddenlink.com. Also serves Thorntonville & Ward County. ICA: TX0134.
TV Market Ranking: Below 100 (Ward County (portions)); Outside TV Markets (MONAHANS, Thorntonville, Ward County (portions)). Franchise award date: July 24, 1990. Franchise expiration date: N.A. Began: December 1, 1972.
Channel capacity: N.A. Channels available but not in use: N.A.

Basic Service
Subscribers: 2,524.
Programming (received off-air): KMID (ABC) Midland; KMLM-DT (IND) Odessa; KOSA-TV (CBS, MNT) Odessa; KPBT-TV (PBS) Odessa; KPEJ-TV (FOX) Odessa; KTLE-LP (TMO) Odessa; KUPB (UNV) Midland; KWES-TV (NBC) Odessa; 6 FMs.
Fee: $35.00 installation; $19.95 monthly.

Expanded Basic Service 1
Subscribers: N.A.
Programming (via satellite): A&E Networks; ABC Family Channel; AMC; Animal Planet; BET Networks; Cartoon Network; CNBC; CNN; Comedy Central; C-SPAN; CW+; Discovery Channel; Disney Channel; E! Entertainment Television; ESPN; ESPN 2; Eternal Word TV Network; Food Network; Fox News Channel; Fox Sports Southwest; FX; GalaVision; Great American Country; Headline News; HGTV; History Channel; Lifetime; MSNBC; MTV; National Geographic Channel; Nickelodeon; QVC; Spike TV; Syfy; TBS Superstation; The Learning Channel; The Weather Channel; Travel Channel; Turner Classic Movies; Turner Network TV; TV Guide Network; TV Land; USA Network; VH1.
Fee: $24.00 monthly.

Digital Basic Service
Subscribers: N.A.
Programming (via satellite): BBC America; Bio; Canal 52MX; Cine Latino; Cine Mexicano; cloo; CMT Pure Country; CNN en Espanol; Discovery en Espanol; Discovery Health Channel; Discovery Home Channel; Discovery Kids Channel; DMX Music; ESPN Classic Sports; ESPN Deportes; ESPNews; Fox Deportes; Fox Soccer; Fuse; Golf Channel; GSN; History Channel en Espanol; History Channel International; ID Investigation Discovery; Independent Film Channel; Lifetime Movie Network; Military Channel; MTV2; Nick Jr.; Science; Speed; Style Network; TeenNick; Toon Disney; Tr3s; VeneMovies; Versus; VH1 Classic; WE tv.
Fee: $3.99 monthly.

Pay Service 1
Pay Units: 179.
Programming (via satellite): Cinemax.
Fee: $15.00 installation; $9.95 monthly.

Pay Service 2
Pay Units: 211.
Programming (via satellite): The Movie Channel.
Fee: $5.95 monthly.

Pay Service 3
Pay Units: 526.
Programming (via satellite): HBO.
Fee: $10.95 monthly.

Pay Service 4
Pay Units: 160.
Programming (via satellite): Showtime.
Fee: $9.95 monthly.

Digital Pay Service 1
Pay Units: N.A.
Programming (via satellite): Cinemax (multiplexed); Encore (multiplexed); HBO (multiplexed); Showtime (multiplexed); Starz; The Movie Channel (multiplexed).

Video-On-Demand: No

Pay-Per-View
iN DEMAND (delivered digitally); Playboy TV (delivered digitally); Club Jenna (delivered digitally).

Internet Service
Operational: Yes. Began: June 1, 2003.
Broadband Service: Suddenlink High Speed Internet.
Fee: $45.95 installation; $29.95 monthly.

Telephone Service
Digital: Operational
Fee: $44.95 monthly

Miles of Plant: 68.0 (coaxial); None (fiber optic).
Regional Manager: Todd Cruthird. Marketing Director: Beverly Gambell.
Ownership: Cequel Communications LLC (MSO).

MONT BELVIEU—Suddenlink Communications, 12444 Powerscourt Dr, Saint Louis, MO 63131-3660. Phones: 877-423-2743 (Customer service); 314-965-2020. Web Site: http://www.suddenlink.com. Also serves Chambers County (western portion), Harris County (southeastern portion), Liberty County (southeastern portion) & Old River-Winfree. ICA: TX0156.
TV Market Ranking: 15 (Harris County (southeastern portion), MONT BELVIEU, Old River-Winfree); 15,88 (Chambers County (western portion) (portions), Liberty County (southeastern portion) (portions)); Below 100 (Liberty County (southeastern portion) (portions)). Franchise award date: N.A. Franchise expiration date: N.A. Began: N.A.
Channel capacity: 62 (operating 2-way). Channels available but not in use: N.A.

Basic Service
Subscribers: 3,223.
Programming (received off-air): KETH-TV (TBN) Houston; KFTH-DT (TEL) Alvin; KHOU (CBS) Houston; KIAH (CW) Houston; KLTJ (ETV) Galveston; KPRC-TV (NBC) Houston; KRIV (FOX) Houston; KTBU (IND) Conroe; KTMD (TMO) Galveston; KTRK-TV (ABC) Houston; KTXH (MNT) Houston; KUBE-TV (IND) Baytown; KUHT (PBS) Houston; KXLN-DT (UNV) Rosenberg; KYAZ (IND) Katy; KZJL (IND) Houston.
Programming (via satellite): C-SPAN; Jewelry Television.
Fee: $19.95 monthly; $2.15 converter.

Expanded Basic Service 1
Subscribers: 3,141.
Programming (via satellite): A&E Networks; ABC Family Channel; Animal Planet; BET Networks; Cartoon Network; CNBC; CNN; Discovery Channel; Disney Channel; E! Entertainment Television; ESPN; ESPN 2; Fox News Channel; Fox Sports Southwest; FX; Great American Country; Headline News; HGTV; Lifetime; MTV; National Geographic Channel; Nickelodeon; QVC; Speed; Spike TV; Syfy; TBS Superstation; The Learning Channel; The Weather Channel; Turner Classic Movies; Turner Network TV; TV Land; USA Network; VH1.
Fee: $23.00 monthly.

Digital Basic Service

Subscribers: N.A.

Programming (via satellite): BBC America; Bio; Bloomberg Television; cloo; Discovery Health Channel; Discovery Kids Channel; DMX Music; Fuse; G4; GAS; History Channel; History Channel International; Independent Film Channel; Lifetime Movie Network; MTV2; Nick Jr.; NickToons TV; Science; Toon Disney; WE tv.

Fee: $3.99 monthly.

Digital Expanded Basic Service

Subscribers: N.A.

Programming (via satellite): ESPN Classic Sports; ESPNews; Golf Channel; GSN; Outdoor Channel; Versus.

Pay Service 1

Pay Units: 340.

Programming (via satellite): Cinemax.

Fee: $12.00 monthly.

Pay Service 2

Pay Units: 788.

Programming (via satellite): HBO.

Fee: $12.00 monthly.

Pay Service 3

Pay Units: 814.

Programming (via satellite): Showtime; The Movie Channel.

Fee: $12.95 monthly.

Digital Pay Service 1

Pay Units: N.A.

Programming (via satellite): Cinemax (multiplexed); Encore (multiplexed); HBO (multiplexed); Showtime (multiplexed); Starz; The Movie Channel (multiplexed).

Video-On-Demand: No

Pay-Per-View

iN DEMAND (delivered digitally); Playboy TV (delivered digitally); Fresh (delivered digitally).

Internet Service

Operational: Yes. Began: July 14, 2003.

Broadband Service: Suddenlink High Speed Internet.

Fee: $45.95 installation; $29.95 monthly.

Telephone Service

Digital: Operational

Fee: $44.95 monthly

Miles of Plant: 139.0 (coaxial); None (fiber optic).

Manager: Mike Burns. Chief Technician: Mayla Zubeck.

Ownership: Cequel Communications LLC (MSO).

MONTAGUE—Formerly served by Cebridge Connections. No longer in operation. ICA: TX0700.

MONTGOMERY COUNTY (unincorporated areas)—Versalink Media, 511 Pan American Dr, Livingston, TX 77351. Phone: 877-689-6009. Web Site: http://www.versalinkus.com. Also serves Hockley, Pinehurst & Tomball. ICA: TX0967.

TV Market Ranking: 15 (Hockley, MONTGOMERY COUNTY, Pinehurst, Tomball). Franchise award date: N.A. Franchise expiration date: N.A. Began: N.A.

Channel capacity: N.A. Channels available but not in use: N.A.

Basic Service

Subscribers: 947.

Programming (received off-air): KHOU (CBS) Houston; KIAH (CW) Houston; KPRC-TV (NBC) Houston; KPXB-TV (ION) Conroe; KRIV (FOX) Houston; KTRK-TV (ABC) Houston; KTXH (MNT) Houston; KUHT (PBS) Houston; KYAZ (IND) Katy.

Programming (via satellite): A&E Networks; ABC Family Channel; AMC; Animal Planet; Cartoon Network; CNBC; CNN; C-SPAN; Discovery Channel; Disney Channel; ESPN; ESPN 2; Fox Sports Southwest; Great American Country; Headline News; HGTV; History Channel; Lifetime; MSNBC; MTV; Nickelodeon; SoapNet; Spike TV; TBS Superstation; The Learning Channel; The Weather Channel; Trinity Broadcasting Network; Turner Network TV; USA Network; WGN America.

Fee: $54.95 installation; $44.05 monthly.

Pay Service 1

Pay Units: 156.

Programming (via satellite): Cinemax.

Fee: $12.95 monthly.

Pay Service 2

Pay Units: 260.

Programming (via satellite): HBO.

Fee: $12.95 monthly.

Pay Service 3

Pay Units: 412.

Programming (via satellite): Showtime.

Fee: $12.95 monthly.

Video-On-Demand: No

Internet Service

Operational: No.

Telephone Service

None

Miles of Plant: 224.0 (coaxial); None (fiber optic).

Ownership: VersaLink Media LLC (MSO).

MOODY—Centrovision Inc., 8 E Barton Ave, PO Box 3157, Temple, TX 76505. Phone: 254-773-1163. Fax: 254-770-0778. E-mail: altonsheppard@centrovision.net. Web Site: http://www.centrovision.net/. ICA: TX0501.

TV Market Ranking: Below 100 (MOODY). Franchise award date: N.A. Franchise expiration date: N.A. Began: April 1, 1981.

Channel capacity: N.A. Channels available but not in use: N.A.

Basic Service

Subscribers: N.A.

Programming (received off-air): KCEN-TV (NBC, IND) Temple; KDYW (PBS) Waco; KEYE-TV (CBS, TMO) Austin; KNCT (PBS) Belton; KNVA (CW) Austin; KTBC (FOX) Austin; KWKT-TV (FOX, MNT) Waco; KWTX-TV (CBS, CW) Waco; KXAN-TV (NBC) Austin; KXXV (ABC, TMO) Waco; WFAA (ABC) Dallas.

Programming (via satellite): Univision Studios; WGN America.

Fee: $20.00 installation; $13.00 monthly.

Expanded Basic Service 1

Subscribers: N.A.

Programming (via satellite): A&E Networks; ABC Family Channel; AMC; Animal Planet; BET Networks; Cartoon Network; CNBC; CNN; Comedy Central; Country Music TV; C-SPAN; C-SPAN 2; Discovery Channel; Disney Channel; E! Entertainment Television; ESPN; ESPN 2; Food Network; Fox News Channel; Fox Sports Southwest; FX; Hallmark Channel; Headline News; HGTV; History Channel; ION Television; Lifetime; MSNBC; MTV; National Geographic Channel; Nickelodeon; QVC; SoapNet; Spike TV; Syfy; TBS Superstation; The Learning Channel; The Weather Channel; Travel Channel; Trinity Broadcasting Network; Turner Classic Movies; Turner Network TV; TV Land; USA Network; VH1.

Fee: $17.00 monthly.

Digital Basic Service

Subscribers: N.A.

Programming (via satellite): AmericanLife TV Network; BBC America; Bio; Bloomberg Television; Bravo; Daystar TV Network; Discovery Digital Networks; DMX Music; ESPN Classic Sports; ESPNews; Fox Movie Channel; Fox Sports World; FSN Digital Atlantic; FSN Digital Central; FSN Digital Pacific; Fuse; G4; Golf Channel; Great American Country; GSN; Halogen Network; HGTV; History Channel; History Channel International; Independent Film Channel; International Television (ITV); Lifetime Movie Network; Lime; National Geographic Channel; Outdoor Channel; Ovation; ShopNBC; Speed; Style Network; Syfy; The Word Network; Toon Disney; Trinity Broadcasting Network; Turner Classic Movies; Versus; WE tv.

Fee: $15.00 installation; $49.00 monthly.

Pay Service 1

Pay Units: N.A.

Programming (via satellite): HBO; Showtime; The Movie Channel.

Fee: $11.00 monthly (HBO, Showtime or TMC), $13.50 monthly (Showtime & TMC), $19.50 monthly (HBO & TMC), $21.00 monthly (HBO & Showtime), $23.00 monthly (HBO, Showtime & TMC).

Digital Pay Service 1

Pay Units: N.A.

Programming (via satellite): Cinemax (multiplexed); Encore (multiplexed); HBO; Showtime (multiplexed); Starz (multiplexed).

Fee: $7.00 monthly (Cinemax), $11.00 monthly (HBO, Showtime, or Starz/Encore).

Video-On-Demand: No

Pay-Per-View

Hot Choice (delivered digitally); iN DEMAND (delivered digitally).

Internet Service

Operational: Yes. Began: December 31, 2004.

Broadband Service: VVM Internet Services.

Fee: $20.00 installation; $40.00 monthly.

Telephone Service

Digital: Planned

Miles of Plant: 10.0 (coaxial); None (fiber optic).

Manager: Alton Sheppard. Chief Technician: Mike Wiggins.

Ownership: Centrovision Inc. (MSO).

MORAN—Formerly served by Jayroc Cablevision. No longer in operation. ICA: TX0975.

MORGAN'S POINT RESORT—Centrovision Inc., 8 E Barton Ave, PO Box 3157, Temple, TX 76505. Phone: 254-773-1163. Fax: 254-770-0778. E-mail: altonsheppard@centrovision.net. Web Site: http://www.centrovision.net/. ICA: TX0814.

TV Market Ranking: Below 100 (MORGAN'S POINT RESORT). Franchise award date: N.A. Franchise expiration date: N.A. Began: N.A.

Channel capacity: N.A. Channels available but not in use: N.A.

Basic Service

Subscribers: N.A.

Programming (received off-air): KCEN-TV (NBC, IND) Temple; KDYW (PBS) Waco; KEYE-TV (CBS, TMO) Austin; KNCT (PBS) Belton; KNVA (CW) Austin; KTBC (FOX) Austin; KWKT-TV (FOX, MNT) Waco; KWTX-TV (CBS, CW) Waco; KXAN-TV (NBC) Austin; KXXV (ABC, TMO) Waco; WFAA (ABC) Dallas.

Programming (via satellite): Univision Studios; WGN America.

Fee: $20.00 installation; $13.00 monthly.

Expanded Basic Service 1

Subscribers: N.A.

Programming (via satellite): A&E Networks; ABC Family Channel; AMC; Animal Planet; BET Networks; Cartoon Network; CNBC; CNN; Comedy Central; Country Music TV; C-SPAN; C-SPAN 2; Discovery Channel; Disney Channel; E! Entertainment Television; ESPN; ESPN 2; Food Network; Fox News Channel; Fox Sports Southwest; FX; Hallmark Channel; Headline News; HGTV; History Channel; ION Television; Lifetime; MSNBC; MTV; National Geographic Channel; Nickelodeon; QVC; SoapNet; Spike TV; Syfy; TBS Superstation; The Learning Channel; The Weather Channel; Travel Channel; Trinity Broadcasting Network; Turner Classic Movies; Turner Network TV; TV Land; USA Network; VH1.

Fee: $17.00 monthly.

Digital Basic Service

Subscribers: N.A.

Programming (via satellite): AmericanLife TV Network; BBC America; Bio; Bloomberg Television; Bravo; Daystar TV Network; Discovery Digital Networks; DMX Music; ESPN Classic Sports; ESPNews; Fox Movie Channel; Fox Sports World; FSN Digital Atlantic; FSN Digital Central; FSN Digital Pacific; Fuse; G4; Golf Channel; Great American Country; GSN; Halogen Network; HGTV; History Channel; History Channel International; Independent Film Channel; International Television (ITV); Lifetime Movie Network; Lime; National Geographic Channel; Outdoor Channel; Ovation; ShopNBC; Speed; Style Network; Syfy; The Word Network; Toon Disney; Trinity Broadcasting Network; Turner Classic Movies; Versus; WE tv.

Fee: $15.00 installation; $49.00 monthly.

Pay Service 1

Pay Units: N.A.

Programming (via satellite): HBO; Showtime; The Movie Channel.

Fee: $11.00 monthly (HBO, Showtime or TMC), $13.50 monthly (Showtime & TMC), $19.50 monthly (HBO & TMC), $21.00 monthly (HBO & Showtime), $23.00 monthly (HBO, Showtime & TMC).

Digital Pay Service 1

Pay Units: N.A.

Programming (via satellite): Cinemax (multiplexed); Encore (multiplexed); HBO (multiplexed); Showtime (multiplexed); Starz (multiplexed).

Fee: $7.00 monthly (Cinemax), $11.00 monthly (HBO, Showtime, or Starz/Encore).

Video-On-Demand: No

Pay-Per-View

Hot Choice (delivered digitally); iN DEMAND (delivered digitally).

Internet Service
Operational: Yes. Began: December 31, 2004.
Broadband Service: VVM Internet Services.
Fee: $20.00 installation; $40.00 monthly.
Telephone Service
Digital: Planned
Miles of Plant: 10.0 (coaxial); None (fiber optic).
Manager: Alton Sheppard. Chief Technician: Mike Wiggins.
Ownership: Centrovision Inc. (MSO).

MOSS BLUFF—Formerly served by Carrell Communications. No longer in operation. ICA: TX0474.

MOULTON—Formerly served by National Cable Inc. No longer in operation. ICA: TX0497.

MOUND—Formerly served by National Cable Inc. No longer in operation. ICA: TX0701.

MOUNT ENTERPRISE—Formerly served by Cebridge Connections. No longer in operation. ICA: TX0973.

MOUNT PLEASANT—Suddenlink Communications, 1506 Shadywood Ln, Mount Pleasant, TX 75455-5630. Phone: 903-572-6107. Fax: 903-572-5669. Web Site: http://www.suddenlink.com. Also serves Titus County (portions). ICA: TX0089.
TV Market Ranking: Outside TV Markets (MOUNT PLEASANT, Titus County (portions)). Franchise award date: N.A. Franchise expiration date: N.A. Began: October 1, 1968.
Channel capacity: N.A. Channels available but not in use: N.A.
Basic Service
Subscribers: 3,929.
Programming (received off-air): KCEB (CW) Longview; KLTS-TV (PBS) Shreveport; KLTV (ABC, TMO) Tyler; KMSS-TV (FOX) Shreveport; KSHV-TV (MNT) Shreveport; KSLA (CBS) Shreveport; KTAL-TV (NBC) Texarkana; KTBS-TV (ABC) Shreveport; KYTX (CBS, IND) Nacogdoches; 9 FMs.
Programming (via microwave): KERA-TV (PBS) Dallas; KXAS-TV (NBC) Fort Worth; WFAA (ABC) Dallas.
Programming (via satellite): C-SPAN; Discovery Channel; QVC; TBS Superstation; The Weather Channel; WGN America.
Fee: $36.74 installation; $10.57 monthly; $2.00 converter; $18.37 additional installation.
Expanded Basic Service 1
Subscribers: 3,470.
Programming (via satellite): A&E Networks; ABC Family Channel; AMC; Animal Planet; BET Networks; Bravo; Cartoon Network; CNBC; CNN; Comedy Central; Country Music TV; C-SPAN 2; Disney Channel; E! Entertainment Television; ESPN; ESPN 2; Eternal Word TV Network; Food Network; Fox News Channel; Fox Sports Southwest; FX; GalaVision; Great American Country; Headline News; HGTV; History Channel; INSP; Jewelry Television; Lifetime; Lifetime Movie Network; MSNBC; MTV; Nickelodeon; Outdoor Channel; Speed; Spike TV; Telemundo; The Learning Channel; Travel Channel; Trinity Broadcasting Network; truTV; Turner Classic Movies; Turner Network TV; TV Land; Univision Studios; USA Network; Versus; VH1.
Fee: $11.15 monthly.
Digital Basic Service
Subscribers: N.A.
Programming (via satellite): A&E HD; Bandamax; BBC America; Bio; Bloomberg Television; Boomerang; Cine Latino; Cine Mexicano; CMT Pure Country; CNN en Espanol; Cooking Channel; Cox Sports Television; De Pelicula; De Pelicula Clasico; Discovery en Espanol; Discovery Health Channel; Discovery Home Channel; Discovery Kids Channel; Discovery Times Channel; DIY Network; Encore (multiplexed); ESPN 2 HD; ESPN Classic Sports; ESPN Deportes; ESPN HD; ESPN U; ESPNews; EWTN en Espanol; FamilyNet; Food Network HD; Fox Deportes; Fox Reality Channel; Fox Soccer; Fuel TV; Fuse; G4; GalaVision; GMC; Golf Channel; GSN; Hallmark Channel; Halogen Network; HD Theater; HDNet; HDNet Movies; HGTV HD; History Channel en Espanol; History Channel International; Independent Film Channel; Latele Novela Network; Military Channel; MTV Hits; MTV2; mun2 television; Music Choice; National Geographic Channel; National Geographic Channel HD Network; Nick Jr.; NickToons TV; Nuvo TV; Oxygen; Ritmoson Latino; Science; SoapNet; Sorpresa; Style Network; Sundance Channel; Sur Network; TBN Enlace USA; TeenNick; Telefutura; Telehit; Telemundo; Tennis Channel; Toon Disney; Toon Disney en Espanol; Tr3s; Turner Network TV HD; TV Chile; TV One; Universal HD; Univision Studios; VH1 Classic; VHUNO; Video Rola; WE tv; Weatherscan.
Digital Pay Service 1
Pay Units: N.A.
Programming (via satellite): Cinemax (multiplexed); HBO (multiplexed); HBO HD; Showtime (multiplexed); Showtime HD; Starz (multiplexed); Starz HDTV; The Movie Channel (multiplexed).
Video-On-Demand: No
Pay-Per-View
iN DEMAND (delivered digitally); Fresh (delivered digitally); Shorteez (delivered digitally); Playboy TV (delivered digitally); Playboy en Espanol (delivered digitally).
Internet Service
Operational: Yes.
Broadband Service: Suddenlink High Speed Internet.
Fee: $49.95 installation; $24.95 monthly.
Telephone Service
Digital: Operational
Fee: $48.95 monthly
Miles of Plant: 89.0 (coaxial); None (fiber optic).
Manager & Chief Technician: Ron Eubanks.
Ownership: Cequel Communications LLC (MSO).

MOUNT VERNON—Suddenlink Communications, 1506 Shadywood Ln, Mount Pleasant, TX 75455-5630. Phone: 903-572-6107. Fax: 903-572-5669. Web Site: http://www.suddenlink.com. Also serves Franklin County (portions). ICA: TX0311.
TV Market Ranking: Outside TV Markets (Franklin County (portions), MOUNT VERNON). Franchise award date: N.A. Franchise expiration date: N.A. Began: August 1, 1968.
Channel capacity: 35 (operating 2-way). Channels available but not in use: N.A.
Basic Service
Subscribers: 792.
Programming (received off-air): KCEB (CW) Longview; KETK-TV (NBC) Jacksonville; KFXK-TV (FOX) Longview; KLTV (ABC, TMO) Tyler; KSHV-TV (MNT) Shreveport; KSLA (CBS) Shreveport; KTBS-TV (ABC) Shreveport; KYTX (CBS, IND) Nacogdoches.
Programming (via microwave): KERA-TV (PBS) Dallas; KXAS-TV (NBC) Fort Worth; WFAA (ABC) Dallas.
Programming (via satellite): C-SPAN; Headline News; QVC; TBS Superstation; The Weather Channel; WGN America.
Fee: $36.78 installation; $10.23 monthly.
Expanded Basic Service 1
Subscribers: 691.
Programming (via satellite): A&E Networks; ABC Family Channel; AMC; Animal Planet; BET Networks; Bravo; Cartoon Network; CNBC; CNN; Comedy Central; Country Music TV; C-SPAN 2; Discovery Channel; Disney Channel; E! Entertainment Television; ESPN; ESPN 2; Eternal Word TV Network; Food Network; Fox News Channel; Fox Sports Southwest; FX; GalaVision; Great American Country; HGTV; History Channel; INSP; Jewelry Television; Lifetime; Lifetime Movie Network; MSNBC; MTV; Nickelodeon; Outdoor Channel; Speed; Spike TV; Syfy; Telemundo; The Learning Channel; Travel Channel; Trinity Broadcasting Network; truTV; Turner Classic Movies; Turner Network TV; TV Land; Univision Studios; USA Network; Versus; VH1.
Fee: $11.63 monthly.
Digital Basic Service
Subscribers: N.A.
Programming (via satellite): A&E HD; Bandamax; BBC America; Bio; Bloomberg Television; CBS Sports Network; Cine Latino; Cine Mexicano; CMT Pure Country; CNN en Espanol; Cooking Channel; Cox Sports Television; De Pelicula; De Pelicula Clasico; Discovery en Espanol; Discovery Health Channel; Discovery Home Channel; Discovery Kids Channel; Discovery Times Channel; DIY Network; Encore (multiplexed); ESPN 2 HD; ESPN Classic Sports; ESPN Deportes; ESPN HD; ESPN U; ESPNews; EWTN en Espanol; FamilyNet; Food Network HD; Fox Deportes; Fox Reality Channel; Fox Soccer; Fuel TV; Fuse; G4; GalaVision; GMC; Golf Channel; GSN; Hallmark Channel; Halogen Network; HD Theater; HDNet; HDNet Movies; HGTV HD; History Channel en Espanol; History Channel International; Independent Film Channel; Latele Novela Network; Military Channel; MTV Hits; MTV2; mun2 television; Music Choice; National Geographic Channel; National Geographic Channel HD Network; Nick Jr.; NickToons TV; Nuvo TV; Oxygen; Ritmoson Latino; Science; SoapNet; Sorpresa; Style Network; Sundance Channel; Sur Network; TBN Enlace USA; TeenNick; Telefutura; Telehit; Telemundo; Tennis Channel; Toon Disney; Toon Disney en Espanol; Tr3s; Turner Network TV HD; TV Chile; TV One; Universal HD; Univision Studios; VH1 Classic; VHUNO; Video Rola; WE tv; Weatherscan.
Digital Pay Service 1
Pay Units: N.A.
Programming (via satellite): Cinemax (multiplexed); HBO (multiplexed); HBO HD; HBO Latino; Showtime (multiplexed); Showtime HD; Starz (multiplexed); Starz HDTV; The Movie Channel (multiplexed).
Video-On-Demand: No
Pay-Per-View
iN DEMAND (delivered digitally); Fresh (delivered digitally); Shorteez (delivered digitally); Playboy TV (delivered digitally); Playboy en Espanol (delivered digitally).
Internet Service
Operational: Yes.
Broadband Service: Suddenlink High Speed Internet.
Fee: $49.95 installation; $29.95 monthly.
Telephone Service
None
Miles of Plant: 19.0 (coaxial); None (fiber optic).
Manager & Chief Technician: Ron Eubanks.
Ownership: Cequel Communications LLC (MSO).

MULESHOE—Reach Broadband, 515 E Longview St, Arp, TX 75750. Phone: 800-687-1258. Web Site: http://www.reachbroadband.net. Also serves Amherst, Earth & Sudan. ICA: TX0164.
TV Market Ranking: Below 100 (MULESHOE); Outside TV Markets (Amherst, Earth, Sudan). Franchise award date: January 1, 1959. Franchise expiration date: N.A. Began: February 1, 1959.
Channel capacity: N.A. Channels available but not in use: N.A.
Basic Service
Subscribers: 1,362.
Programming (received off-air): KAMC (ABC) Lubbock; KCBD (NBC) Lubbock; KENW (PBS) Portales; KJTV-TV (FOX) Lubbock; KLBK-TV (CBS) Lubbock; KPTB-DT (IND) Lubbock; KVII-TV (ABC, CW) Amarillo; allband FM.
Programming (via satellite): A&E Networks; ABC Family Channel; AMC; American-Life TV Network; Animal Planet; Cartoon Network; CNN; Comedy Central; Country Music TV; C-SPAN; Discovery Channel; Disney Channel; E! Entertainment Television; ESPN; Fox Sports Southwest; Headline News; History Channel; Lifetime; Nickelodeon; QVC; Spike TV; TBS Superstation; The Learning Channel; The Weather Channel; Trinity Broadcasting Network; Turner Network TV; TV Land; USA Network; WGN America.
Programming (via translator): KVDA (TMO) San Antonio.
Fee: $29.95 installation; $38.00 monthly.
Pay Service 1
Pay Units: 223.
Programming (via satellite): HBO.
Fee: $20.00 installation; $10.95 monthly.
Pay Service 2
Pay Units: 131.
Programming (via satellite): Showtime.
Fee: $9.95 monthly.
Pay Service 3
Pay Units: 126.
Programming (via satellite): The Movie Channel.
Fee: $7.95 monthly.
Video-On-Demand: No
Internet Service
Operational: No.
Telephone Service
None
Miles of Plant: 81.0 (coaxial); None (fiber optic).
Regional Manager: Ronnie Stafford. Office Manager: Jan Gibson.
Ownership: RB3 LLC (MSO).

MUNDAY—Alliance Communications, 6125 Paluxy Dr, Tyler, TX 75703. Phones: 800-842-8160; 501-679-6619. Fax: 501-679-5694. Web Site: http://www.alliancecable.net. ICA: TX0415.
TV Market Ranking: Outside TV Markets (MUNDAY). Franchise award date: N.A.

Franchise expiration date: N.A. Began: January 1, 1963.

Channel capacity: N.A. Channels available but not in use: N.A.

Basic Service

Subscribers: 150.

Programming (received off-air): KAUZ-TV (CBS, CW) Wichita Falls; KFDX-TV (NBC) Wichita Falls; KJTL (FOX) Wichita Falls; KRBC-TV (NBC) Abilene; KRMA-TV (PBS) Denver; KSWO-TV (ABC, TMO) Lawton; KTAB-TV (CBS) Abilene; KTXS-TV (ABC, CW, TMO) Sweetwater; allband FM.

Programming (via satellite): QVC; WGN America.

Fee: $29.99 installation; $19.95 monthly.

Expanded Basic Service 1

Subscribers: 107.

Programming (via satellite): ABC Family Channel; AMC; Animal Planet; CNN; Comedy Central; Country Music TV; C-SPAN; Discovery Channel; Disney Channel; E! Entertainment Television; ESPN; ESPN 2; Fox Sports Southwest; HGTV; History Channel; Lifetime; MSNBC; MTV; Nickelodeon; Oxygen; SoapNet; Spike TV; Syfy; TBS Superstation; The Learning Channel; The Weather Channel; Trinity Broadcasting Network; Turner Classic Movies; Turner Network TV; TV Land; Univision Studios; USA Network; VH1.

Fee: $18.00 monthly.

Pay Service 1

Pay Units: N.A.

Programming (via satellite): Cinemax; HBO; Showtime.

Fee: $30.00 installation; $9.95 monthly (each).

Video-On-Demand: No

Pay-Per-View

iN DEMAND (delivered digitally); Hot Choice (delivered digitally); Playboy TV (delivered digitally); Fresh (delivered digitally); Shorteez (delivered digitally).

Internet Service

Operational: No.

Telephone Service

None

Miles of Plant: 11.0 (coaxial); None (fiber optic).

Vice President & General Manager: John Brinker. Vice President, Programming: Julie Newman.

Ownership: Buford Media Group LLC (MSO).

MUSTANG RIDGE—Formerly served by Almega Cable. No longer in operation. ICA: TX0467.

MYRTLE SPRINGS—Formerly served by Cebridge Connections. No longer in operation. ICA: TX0625.

NACOGDOCHES—Suddenlink Communications, 409 N Fredonia St, Nacogdoches, TX 75961-5010. Phone: 888-822-5151. Web Site: http://www.suddenlink.com. Also serves Nacogdoches County. ICA: TX0065.

TV Market Ranking: Below 100 (NACOGDOCHES, Nacogdoches County). Franchise award date: N.A. Franchise expiration date: N.A. Began: September 1, 1960.

Channel capacity: N.A. Channels available but not in use: N.A.

Basic Service

Subscribers: 13,776.

Programming (received off-air): KFXK-TV (FOX) Longview; KPRC-TV (NBC) Houston; KSLA (CBS) Shreveport; KTRE (ABC) Lufkin; KYTX (CBS, IND) Nacogdoches; 6 FMs.

Programming (via microwave): KERA-TV (PBS) Dallas; KTVT (CBS) Fort Worth; KXTX-TV (TMO) Dallas.

Programming (via satellite): CNN; C-SPAN; ESPN; Fox Sports Southwest; Headline News; INSP; ION Television; TBS Superstation; The Learning Channel; The Weather Channel; Univision Studios.

Fee: $35.00 installation; $10.00 monthly.

Expanded Basic Service 1

Subscribers: N.A.

Programming (via satellite): A&E Networks; ABC Family Channel; AMC; Animal Planet; BET Networks; Bravo; Cartoon Network; CNBC; Comedy Central; Country Music TV; C-SPAN 2; Discovery Channel; Disney Channel; E! Entertainment Television; ESPN 2; Food Network; Fox News Channel; FX; G4; GalaVision; Great American Country; HGTV; History Channel; Lifetime; MSNBC; MTV; Nickelodeon; Outdoor Channel; Oxygen; Speed; Spike TV; Syfy; Travel Channel; Trinity Broadcasting Network; Turner Network TV; TV Guide Network; TV Land; USA Network; Versus; VH1; Video Rola; Weatherscan.

Digital Basic Service

Subscribers: N.A.

Programming (via satellite): BBC America; Bio; Bloomberg Television; Discovery Digital Networks; Encore Action; ESPN Classic Sports; ESPNews; Fox Sports World; Fuse; Golf Channel; GSN; Hallmark Channel; History Channel International; Independent Film Channel; Lifetime Movie Network; Music Choice; SoapNet; Sundance Channel; Toon Disney; Turner Classic Movies.

Pay Service 1

Pay Units: 1,050.

Programming (via satellite): Cinemax; HBO; Showtime; The Movie Channel.

Fee: $10.00 monthly (Showtime).

Digital Pay Service 1

Pay Units: N.A.

Programming (via satellite): Cinemax (multiplexed); Flix; HBO (multiplexed); Showtime (multiplexed); Starz (multiplexed); The Movie Channel (multiplexed).

Video-On-Demand: No

Pay-Per-View

iN DEMAND (delivered digitally); Playboy TV (delivered digitally); Hot Choice (delivered digitally); Fresh (delivered digitally); NBA TV (delivered digitally); ESPN Gameplan (delivered digitally); ESPN Now (delivered digitally).

Internet Service

Operational: Yes.

Broadband Service: Suddenlink High Speed Internet.

Fee: $49.95 installation; $24.95 monthly.

Telephone Service

Digital: Operational

Fee: $48.95 monthly

Miles of Plant: 202.0 (coaxial); None (fiber optic).

Manager: Brad Haile.

Ownership: Cequel Communications LLC (MSO).

NAPLES—Alliance Communications, 6125 Paluxy Dr, Tyler, TX 75703. Phones: 800-842-8160; 501-679-5694. Fax: 501-679-5694. Web Site: http://www.alliancecable.net. Also serves Omaha. ICA: TX0295.

TV Market Ranking: Outside TV Markets (NAPLES, Omaha). Franchise award date: N.A. Franchise expiration date: N.A. Began: N.A.

Channel capacity: 42 (not 2-way capable). Channels available but not in use: N.A.

Basic Service

Subscribers: 112.

Programming (received off-air): KMSS-TV (FOX) Shreveport; KSHV-TV (MNT) Shreveport; KSLA (CBS) Shreveport; KTAL-TV (NBC) Texarkana; KTBS-TV (ABC) Shreveport.

Programming (via microwave): KERA-TV (PBS) Dallas; WFAA (ABC) Dallas.

Programming (via satellite): TBS Superstation; WGN America.

Fee: $54.95 installation; $20.95 monthly.

Expanded Basic Service 1

Subscribers: N.A.

Programming (via satellite): A&E Networks; ABC Family Channel; BET Networks; CNN; Country Music TV; Discovery Channel; Disney Channel; ESPN; Fox Sports Southwest; Lifetime; MTV; Nickelodeon; Spike TV; Syfy; The Weather Channel; Trinity Broadcasting Network; Turner Network TV; TV Land; USA Network.

Fee: $23.10 monthly.

Pay Service 1

Pay Units: N.A.

Programming (via satellite): Cinemax; HBO.

Fee: $12.95 monthly.

Video-On-Demand: No

Internet Service

Operational: No.

Telephone Service

None

Miles of Plant: 33.0 (coaxial); None (fiber optic).

Vice President & Gneral Manager: John Brinker. Vice President, Programming: Julie Newman.

Ownership: Buford Media Group LLC (MSO).

NAVASOTA—Suddenlink Communications, 12444 Powerscourt Dr, Saint Louis, MO 63131-3660. Phones: 314-965-2020; 877-423-2743. Web Site: http://www.suddenlink.com. ICA: TX0210.

TV Market Ranking: Below 100 (NAVASOTA). Franchise award date: January 10, 1966. Franchise expiration date: N.A. Began: June 1, 1967.

Channel capacity: N.A. Channels available but not in use: N.A.

Basic Service

Subscribers: 1,774.

Programming (received off-air): KAMU-TV (PBS) College Station; KBTX-TV (CBS, CW) Bryan; KFTH-DT (TEL) Alvin; KHOU (CBS) Houston; KIAH (CW) Houston; KPRC-TV (NBC) Houston; KRIV (FOX) Houston; KTMD (TMO) Galveston; KTRK-TV (ABC) Houston; KTXH (MNT) Houston; KUHT (PBS) Houston; KYAZ (IND) Katy; allband FM.

Programming (via satellite): GalaVision.

Fee: $50.00 installation; $19.95 monthly; $20.00 additional installation.

Expanded Basic Service 1

Subscribers: 1,731.

Programming (via satellite): A&E Networks; Animal Planet; BET Networks; Cartoon Network; CNBC; CNN; Comedy Central; C-SPAN; Discovery Channel; ESPN; ESPN 2; Food Network; Fox Movie Channel; Fox News Channel; Fox Sports Southwest; FX; Great American Country; Hallmark Channel; Headline News; HGTV; History Channel; Lifetime; National Geographic Channel; Nickelodeon; Outdoor Channel; Spike TV; Syfy; TBS Superstation; The Learning Channel; The Weather Channel; Travel Channel; Trinity Broadcasting Network; Turner Classic Movies; Turner Network TV; TV Guide Network; Univision Studios; USA Network.

Fee: $50.00 installation; $23.00 monthly.

Pay Service 1

Pay Units: N.A.

Programming (via satellite): Cinemax; HBO.

Video-On-Demand: No

Internet Service

Operational: Yes.

Broadband Service: Suddenlink High Speed Internet.

Fee: $49.95 installation; $38.95 monthly.

Telephone Service

None

Miles of Plant: 39.0 (coaxial); None (fiber optic). Additional miles planned: 2.0 (coaxial).

Regional Manager: Todd Cruthird. Marketing Director: Beverly Gambell. Manager: Roberto Montalvo. Chief Technician: Jimmy Smith.

Ownership: Cequel Communications LLC (MSO).

NAZARETH—Elk River TV Cable Co., 509 S Main St, PO Box 154, Troy, ID 83871. Phone: 208-369-4652. E-mail: leslie@elkrivertv.net. Web Site: http://www.elkrivertv.net. ICA: TX0817.

TV Market Ranking: Outside TV Markets (NAZARETH). Franchise award date: N.A. Franchise expiration date: N.A. Began: N.A.

Channel capacity: N.A. Channels available but not in use: N.A.

Basic Service

Subscribers: N.A. Included in San Jon, NM

Programming (received off-air): KAMR-TV (NBC) Amarillo; KCIT (FOX) Amarillo; KFDA-TV (CBS) Amarillo; KVII-TV (ABC, CW) Amarillo.

Programming (via satellite): Turner Network TV.

Video-On-Demand: No

Internet Service

Operational: No.

Telephone Service

None

Manager: David & Leslie McGraw. Chief Technician: Justin McGraw.

Ownership: Elk River TV Cable Co. (MSO).

NEW BOSTON—Allegiance Communications, 707 W Saratoga St, Shawnee, OK 74804. Phones: 405-395-1131; 405-275-6923. Web Site: http://www.allegiance.tv. Also serves Bowie County (northern portion). ICA: TX0204.

TV Market Ranking: 58 (Bowie County (northern portion), NEW BOSTON). Franchise award date: N.A. Franchise expiration date: N.A. Began: January 1, 1979.

Channel capacity: 35 (operating 2-way). Channels available but not in use: N.A.

Basic Service
Subscribers: 1,796.
Programming (received off-air): KLTS-TV (PBS) Shreveport; KMSS-TV (FOX) Shreveport; KPXJ (CW) Minden; KSHV-TV (MNT) Shreveport; KSLA (CBS) Shreveport; KTAL-TV (NBC) Texarkana; KTBS-TV (ABC) Shreveport.
Programming (via satellite): CNBC; CNN; C-SPAN; Headline News; QVC; Texas Cable News; The Weather Channel; Trinity Broadcasting Network; TV Guide Network; WGN America.
Fee: $33.96 installation; $10.23 monthly.
Expanded Basic Service 1
Subscribers: 1,694.
Programming (via satellite): A&E Networks; ABC Family Channel; AMC; Animal Planet; BET Networks; Cartoon Network; CMT Pure Country; Comedy Central; Discovery Channel; Disney Channel; ESPN; ESPN 2; ESPN Classic Sports; Fox News Channel; Fox Sports Southwest; FX; Hallmark Channel; HGTV; History Channel; Lifetime; MoviePlex; MTV; NFL Network; Nickelodeon; Spike TV; Syfy; TBS Superstation; The Learning Channel; Turner Network TV; TV Land; USA Network; VH1.
Fee: $10.68 monthly.
Digital Basic Service
Subscribers: N.A.
Programming (via satellite): 3 Angels Broadcasting Network; A&E Networks; AmericanLife TV Network; BBC America; Black Family Channel; Bloomberg Television; B-Mania; Bravo; BYU Television; Church Channel; Cine Latino; Cine Mexicano; cloo; CMT Pure Country; CNN en Espanol; Daystar TV Network; Discovery en Espanol; Discovery Fit & Health; Discovery Health Channel; Discovery Kids Channel; DMX Music; Encore (multiplexed); ESPN Classic Sports; ESPNews; FamilyNet; Flix; Fox College Sports Atlantic; Fox College Sports Central; Fox College Sports Pacific; Fox Deportes; Fox Movie Channel; Fox Soccer; Fuse; G4; GAS; GMC; Golden Eagle Broadcasting; Golf Channel; Great American Country; GSN; Halogen Network; History Channel; History Channel en Espanol; History Channel International; ID Investigation Discovery; Independent Film Channel; JCTV; La Familia Network; Latin Television (LTV); Lifetime Movie Network; Military Channel; MTV Hits; MTV2; National Geographic Channel; Nick Jr.; NickToons TV; Outdoor Channel; Planet Green; Puma TV; Science; ShopNBC; Speed; Style Network; Sundance Channel; Syfy; The Word Network; Toon Disney; Toon Disney en Espanol; Tr3s; Trinity Broadcasting Network; Turner Classic Movies; TV Chile; Versus; VH1 Classic; WE tv.
Pay Service 1
Pay Units: 137.
Programming (via satellite): Encore; HBO; Showtime; Starz.
Fee: $11.95 monthly (each).
Digital Pay Service 1
Pay Units: N.A.
Programming (via satellite): Cinemax (multiplexed); HBO (multiplexed); Showtime (multiplexed); Starz (multiplexed); The Movie Channel (multiplexed).
Video-On-Demand: No
Pay-Per-View
iN DEMAND (delivered digitally); Hot Choice (delivered digitally); Playboy TV (delivered digitally); Fresh (delivered digitally); Shorteez (delivered digitally).
Internet Service
Operational: Yes.
Fee: $24.95 installation; $39.95 monthly.
Telephone Service
None
Miles of Plant: 34.0 (coaxial); None (fiber optic).
Chief Executive Officer: Bill Haggarty. Regional Vice President: Andrew Dearth. Vice President, Marketing: Tracy Bass.
Ownership: Allegiance Communications (MSO).

NEW CANEY—Northland Cable Television, 22787 Antique Ln, PO Box 839, New Caney, TX 77357-0839. Phones: 800-689-2048; 281-689-2048. Fax: 281-689-7643. E-mail: newcaney@northlandcabletv.com. Web Site: http://www.northlandcabletv.com. Also serves Grangerland, Harris County (northeastern portion), Huffman, Indian Shore, Lakewood, Patton Village, Porter Heights (unincorporated areas), Roman Forest, Splendora & Woodbranch Village. ICA: TX0105.
TV Market Ranking: 15 (Harris County (northeastern portion), Huffman, Indian Shore, Lakewood, NEW CANEY, Patton Village, Porter Heights (unincorporated areas), Roman Forest, Splendora, Woodbranch Village); Below 100 (Grangerland). Franchise award date: N.A. Franchise expiration date: N.A. Began: October 22, 1981.
Channel capacity: 62 (operating 2-way). Channels available but not in use: N.A.
Basic Service
Subscribers: 4,200.
Programming (received off-air): KFTH-DT (TEL) Alvin; KHOU (CBS) Houston; KIAH (CW) Houston; KPRC-TV (NBC) Houston; KPXB-TV (ION) Conroe; KRIV (FOX) Houston; KTBU (IND) Conroe; KTMD (TMO) Galveston; KTRK-TV (ABC) Houston; KTXH (MNT) Houston; KUHT (PBS) Houston; KXLN-DT (UNV) Rosenberg; KYAZ (IND) Katy; KZJL (IND) Houston; allband FM.
Programming (via satellite): C-SPAN; QVC.
Fee: $50.00 installation; $32.99 monthly; $20.00 additional installation.
Expanded Basic Service 1
Subscribers: 3,686.
Programming (via satellite): A&E Networks; Animal Planet; Cartoon Network; CNBC; CNN; Comedy Central; Discovery Channel; E! Entertainment Television; ESPN; ESPN 2; Food Network; Fox Movie Channel; Fox News Channel; Fox Sports Southwest; FX; Golf Channel; Great American Country; Hallmark Channel; Headline News; HGTV; History Channel; Lifetime; MTV; Nickelodeon; Spike TV; Syfy; TBS Superstation; The Learning Channel; The Weather Channel; Trinity Broadcasting Network; Turner Classic Movies; Turner Network TV; USA Network; VH1.
Fee: $55.00 installation; $44.25 monthly.
Digital Basic Service
Subscribers: N.A.
Programming (via satellite): BBC America; Bloomberg Television; Bravo; Discovery Fit & Health; Discovery Health Channel; Discovery Home Channel; Discovery Kids Channel; Discovery Times Channel; DMX Music; ESPN 2 HD; ESPN HD; ESPNews; Food Network HD; Fox Movie Channel; Fox Soccer; G4; Golf Channel; HD Theater; HDNet; HDNet Movies; HGTV HD; Independent Film Channel; Military Channel; National Geographic Channel; Outdoor Channel; Science; Speed; Turner Network TV HD; Universal HD; Versus; Versus HD; WE tv.
Fee: $55.00 installation; $52.99 monthly.
Pay Service 1
Pay Units: 566.
Programming (via satellite): Cinemax.
Fee: $35.00 installation; $13.50 monthly.
Pay Service 2
Pay Units: 730.
Programming (via satellite): HBO.
Fee: $35.00 installation; $13.50 monthly.
Digital Pay Service 1
Pay Units: N.A.
Programming (via satellite): Cinemax (multiplexed); Encore (multiplexed); Flix; HBO (multiplexed); Showtime (multiplexed); Starz (multiplexed); The Movie Channel (multiplexed).
Video-On-Demand: No
Pay-Per-View
Fresh (delivered digitally); Playboy TV (delivered digitally).
Internet Service
Operational: Yes.
Subscribers: 2,000.
Broadband Service: Northland Express.
Fee: $42.99 monthly.
Telephone Service
Analog: Not Operational
Digital: Operational
Fee: $29.99 monthly
Miles of Plant: 250.0 (coaxial); None (fiber optic). Additional miles planned: 20.0 (fiber optic).
Manager: Richard Gammon. Office Manager: Tammy Rogers. Chief Technician: Wade Caldwell.
Ownership: Northland Communications Corp. (MSO).

NEW SUMMERFIELD—Formerly served by Almega Cable. No longer in operation. ICA: TX0818.

NEW ULM—Formerly served by National Cable Inc. No longer in operation. ICA: TX0819.

NEW WAVERLY—Cablevision of Walker County, 1304 10th St, Huntsville, TX 77320-3804. Phone: 936-291-2288. Web Site: http://www.walkercountycabletv.com. ICA: TX0999.
TV Market Ranking: Below 100 (NEW WAVERLY).
Channel capacity: 36 (not 2-way capable). Channels available but not in use: N.A.
Basic Service
Subscribers: 160.
Programming (received off-air): KBTX-TV (CBS, CW) Bryan; KHOU (CBS) Houston; KIAH (CW) Houston; KPRC-TV (NBC) Houston; KRIV (FOX) Houston; KTBU (IND) Conroe; KTRK-TV (ABC) Houston; KTXH (MNT) Houston; KUHT (PBS) Houston; KXLN-DT (UNV) Rosenberg; KYAZ (IND) Katy.
Programming (via satellite): A&E Networks; AMC; BET Networks; C-SPAN; Discovery Channel; ESPN 2; Headline News; ION Television; Lifetime; MTV; Nickelodeon; SoapNet; Syfy; TBS Superstation; Trinity Broadcasting Network; VH1; WGN America.
Fee: $29.95 installation; $32.79 monthly.
Pay Service 1
Pay Units: N.A.
Programming (via satellite): Cinemax; HBO.
Fee: $13.99 monthly.
Video-On-Demand: No
Internet Service
Operational: No.
Telephone Service
None
General Manager: Caroline Walker. Chief Technician: Kenny Hanson.
Ownership: Cablevision of Walker County (MSO).

NEWCASTLE—TGN Cable, Rte 2, PO Box 110, Olney, TX 76374. Phones: 800-687-7311; 940-873-4563. Fax: 940-873-4563. Web Site: http://www.tgncable.com. ICA: TX1011.
TV Market Ranking: Outside TV Markets (NEWCASTLE (VILLAGE)).
Channel capacity: N.A. Channels available but not in use: N.A.
Basic Service
Subscribers: 155.
Programming (received off-air): KAUZ-TV (CBS, CW) Wichita Falls; KFDX-TV (NBC) Wichita Falls; KJTL (FOX) Wichita Falls; KSWO-TV (ABC, TMO) Lawton.
Programming (via satellite): ABC Family Channel; CNBC; CNN; C-SPAN; Discovery Channel; G4; Headline News; Paxson Communications Corp.; TBS Superstation; The Learning Channel; The Weather Channel; Toon Disney; Trinity Broadcasting Network; TV Land; WGN America.
Fee: $39.95 installation; $27.86 monthly.
Expanded Basic Service 1
Subscribers: N.A.
Programming (received off-air): KFDX-TV (NBC) Wichita Falls.
Programming (via satellite): A&E Networks; AMC; Animal Planet; Cartoon Network; Country Music TV; Disney Channel; ESPN; ESPN 2; Food Network; Fox News Channel; Fox Sports Southwest; FX; Hallmark Channel; HGTV; History Channel; Lifetime; MTV; Nickelodeon; Outdoor Channel; Shepherds Chapel Network; Speed; Spike TV; Syfy; Travel Channel; Turner Classic Movies; Turner Network TV; USA Network; VH1.
Fee: $16.91 monthly.
Digital Basic Service
Subscribers: N.A.
Programming (via satellite): BBC America; Bio; Bravo; cloo; Discovery Digital Networks; DMX Music; Fox College Sports Atlantic; Fox College Sports Central; Fox College Sports Pacific; Fox Movie Channel; Fox Sports World; Fuse; GAS; Golf Channel; Great American Country; GSN; Halogen Network; History Channel; History Channel International; Independent Film Channel; Lifetime Movie Network; MTV Networks Digital Suite; National Geographic Channel; Nick Jr.; NickToons TV; Ovation; ShopNBC; Style Network; Turner Classic Movies; Versus; WE tv.
Fee: $20.95 monthly.
Pay Service 1
Pay Units: N.A.
Programming (via satellite): Cinemax; HBO.
Fee: $13.47 monthly.
Digital Pay Service 1
Pay Units: N.A.
Programming (via satellite): Cinemax (multiplexed); Encore (multiplexed); HBO; Showtime (multiplexed); Starz (multiplexed); The Movie Channel (multiplexed).
Fee: $13.47 montlhly (HBO & Cinemax), $7.01 montlhly (Showtime/TMC or Starz/Encore).
Video-On-Demand: No
Internet Service
Operational: Yes.
Broadband Service: In-house.
Fee: $24.95 monthly; $5.00 modem lease; $59.95 modem purchase.
Telephone Service
None
Manager: Bill Tyler. Office Manager: Jan Tyler.
Ownership: Bill Tyler (MSO).

NIXON—Almega Cable, 4001 W Airport Freeway, Ste 530, Bedford, TX 76021. Phone: 817-685-9588. Fax: 817-685-6488. E-mail: helpdesk@almegacable.com. Web Site: http://www.almega.com. ICA: TX0431.

TV Market Ranking: Outside TV Markets (NIXON). Franchise award date: June 9, 1981. Franchise expiration date: N.A. Began: December 1, 1981.
Channel capacity: N.A. Channels available but not in use: N.A.

Basic Service
Subscribers: 184.
Programming (received off-air): KABB (FOX) San Antonio; KENS (CBS) San Antonio; KLRN (PBS) San Antonio; KMYS (CW) Kerrville; KSAT-TV (ABC) San Antonio; KVDA (TMO) San Antonio; KWEX-DT (UNV) San Antonio; WOAI-TV (NBC) San Antonio.
Programming (via satellite): A&E Networks; ABC Family Channel; Animal Planet; CNN; Country Music TV; Discovery Channel; Disney Channel; ESPN; Fox News Channel; Fox Sports Southwest; Headline News; Nickelodeon; Spike TV; TBS Superstation; The Learning Channel; The Weather Channel; Trinity Broadcasting Network; Turner Classic Movies; Turner Network TV; USA Network; WGN America.
Fee: $29.95 installation; $38.00 monthly.

Pay Service 1
Pay Units: 92.
Programming (via satellite): HBO.
Fee: $10.00 installation; $10.95 monthly.

Pay Service 2
Pay Units: 28.
Programming (via satellite): Showtime.
Fee: $9.95 monthly.

Video-On-Demand: No

Internet Service
Operational: No.

Telephone Service
None

Miles of Plant: 7.0 (coaxial); None (fiber optic).
Ownership: Almega Cable (MSO).

NOCONA—Suddenlink Communications, 12444 Powerscourt Dr, Saint Louis, MO 63131-3660. Phones: 800-999-6845; 314-965-2020. Fax: 903-561-5485. Web Site: http://www.suddenlink.com. ICA: TX0282.
TV Market Ranking: Outside TV Markets (NOCONA). Franchise award date: N.A. Franchise expiration date: N.A. Began: December 25, 1971.
Channel capacity: N.A. Channels available but not in use: N.A.

Basic Service
Subscribers: 1,170.
Programming (received off-air): KAUZ-TV (CBS, CW) Wichita Falls; KERA-TV (PBS) Dallas; KFDX-TV (NBC) Wichita Falls; KJTL (FOX) Wichita Falls; KSWO-TV (ABC, TMO) Lawton; KXAS-TV (NBC) Fort Worth; KXII (CBS, FOX, MNT) Sherman; WFAA (ABC) Dallas.
Programming (via satellite): C-SPAN; CW+.
Fee: $33.30 installation; $19.95 monthly.

Expanded Basic Service 1
Subscribers: N.A.
Programming (via satellite): A&E Networks; ABC Family Channel; AMC; Animal Planet; Bravo; Cartoon Network; Celebrity Shopping Network; CNBC; CNN; Comedy Central; Discovery Channel; Disney Channel; E! Entertainment Television; ESPN; ESPN 2; Food Network; Fox News Channel; Fox Sports Southwest; FX; Great American Country; Hallmark Channel; Headline News; HGTV; History Channel; INSP; Jewelry Television; Lifetime; MSNBC; MTV; National Geographic Channel; Nickelodeon; Outdoor Channel; Speed; Spike TV; Syfy; TBS Superstation; The Learning Channel; The Weather Channel; Travel Channel; Turner Classic Movies; Turner Network TV; TV Land; Univision Studios; USA Network; VH1.
Fee: $23.00 monthly.

Digital Basic Service
Subscribers: N.A.
Programming (via satellite): BBC America; Bio; Bloomberg Television; cloo; Discovery Health Channel; Discovery Home Channel; Discovery Kids Channel; DMX Music; ESPN Classic Sports; ESPNews; Fox College Sports Atlantic; Fox College Sports Central; Fox College Sports Pacific; Fox Soccer; Fuse; G4; Golf Channel; GSN; History Channel International; ID Investigation Discovery; Independent Film Channel; Military Channel; Science; ShopNBC; Style Network; Sundance Channel; Toon Disney; Trinity Broadcasting Network; Versus; WE tv.

Pay Service 1
Pay Units: 77.
Programming (via satellite): Encore; HBO; Showtime; Starz; The Movie Channel.

Digital Pay Service 1
Pay Units: N.A.
Programming (via satellite): Cinemax (multiplexed); Encore (multiplexed); Flix; HBO (multiplexed); Showtime (multiplexed); Starz (multiplexed); The Movie Channel (multiplexed).

Video-On-Demand: No

Pay-Per-View
iN DEMAND (delivered digitally); Playboy TV (delivered digitally); Club Jenna (delivered digitally); Fresh (delivered digitally); Spice: Xcess (delivered digitally).

Internet Service
Operational: Yes. Began: June 1, 2003.
Broadband Service: Suddenlink High Speed Internet.
Fee: $49.95 installation; $29.95 monthly.

Telephone Service
None

Miles of Plant: 25.0 (coaxial); None (fiber optic).
Regional Manager: Tod Cruthird. Chief Technician: Scott Wilber.
Ownership: Cequel Communications LLC (MSO).

NOME—Formerly served by Carrell Communications. No longer in operation. ICA: TX0644.

NORDHEIM—Formerly served by National Cable Inc. No longer in operation. ICA: TX0661.

NORMANGEE—Formerly served by Almega Cable. No longer in operation. ICA: TX0494.

NORTH SILSBEE—Formerly served by Carrell Communications. No longer in operation. ICA: TX0380.

NORTH ZULCH—Formerly served by Almega Cable. No longer in operation. ICA: TX0678.

NURSERY—Formerly served by National Cable Inc. No longer in operation. ICA: TX0555.

OAKWOOD—Formerly served by Charter Communications. No longer in operation. ICA: TX0526.

ODESSA—Cable One, 4701 E 52nd St, PO Box 14350, Odessa, TX 79768-4350. Phones: 877-692-2253; 432-363-7200. Fax: 432-363-2007. E-mail: jmorris@cableone.net. Web Site: http://www.cableone.net. Also serves Ector County & Mission Dorado. ICA: TX0025.

TV Market Ranking: Below 100 (Ector County, Mission Dorado, ODESSA). Franchise award date: November 10, 1970. Franchise expiration date: N.A. Began: December 10, 1968.
Channel capacity: 74 (operating 2-way). Channels available but not in use: N.A.

Basic Service
Subscribers: 22,418.
Programming (received off-air): KMID (ABC) Midland; KOSA-TV (CBS, MNT) Odessa; KPBT-TV (PBS) Odessa; KPEJ-TV (FOX) Odessa; KPTB-DT (IND) Lubbock; KTLE-LP (TMO) Odessa; KUPB (UNV) Midland; KWES-TV (NBC) Odessa; KWWT (CW) Odessa.
Programming (via satellite): GalaVision; LATV Networks; Telefutura.
Fee: $40.17 installation; $46.00 monthly.

Expanded Basic Service 1
Subscribers: N.A.
Programming (via satellite): A&E Networks; ABC Family Channel; AMC; Animal Planet; BET Networks; Bravo; Cartoon Network; CNBC; CNN; Comedy Central; Country Music TV; C-SPAN; C-SPAN 2; Discovery Channel; Disney Channel; E! Entertainment Television; ESPN; ESPN 2; ESPN Classic Sports; Eternal Word TV Network; Food Network; Fox News Channel; Fox Sports Southwest; FX; Golf Channel; Great American Country; Headline News; HGTV; History Channel; Lifetime; MSNBC; MTV; Nickelodeon; QVC; ShopNBC; Spike TV; Syfy; TBS Superstation; The Learning Channel; The Weather Channel; Travel Channel; Trinity Broadcasting Network; Turner Classic Movies; Turner Network TV; TV Guide Network; TV Land; USA Network; VH1.

Digital Basic Service
Subscribers: 12,000.
Programming (via satellite): 3 Angels Broadcasting Network; A&E HD; ABC Family HD; Bio; Boomerang; Boomerang en Espanol; BYU Television; Canales N; Cine Mexicano; CNN HD; Discovery Channel HD; Discovery Health Channel; Discovery Kids Channel; Disney Channel HD; ESPN 2 HD; ESPN Classic Sports; ESPN Deportes; ESPN HD; ESPN U; ESPNews; FamilyNet; Food Network HD; Fox College Sports Atlantic; Fox College Sports Central; Fox College Sports Pacific; Fox Deportes; Fox Movie Channel; Fox Soccer; Fuel TV; FX HD; Golf Channel; Great American Country; GSN; Hallmark Channel; HD Theater; HGTV HD; History Channel HD; History Channel International; INSP; La Familia Network; Latele Novela Network; Military Channel; mun2 television; Music Choice; National Geographic Channel; National Geographic Channel HD Network; Outdoor Channel; Science; SoapNet; Speed; TBS in HD; The Movie Channel HD; TLC HD; Toon Disney; Toon Disney en Espanol; Trinity Broadcasting Network; Turner Network TV HD; TVG Network; Universal HD; WE tv.
Fee: $12.95 monthly.

Pay Service 1
Pay Units: N.A.
Programming (via satellite): HBO.

Digital Pay Service 1
Pay Units: N.A.
Programming (via satellite): Cinemax (multiplexed); Encore (multiplexed); Flix; HBO (multiplexed); HBO HD; HBO Latino; Showtime (multiplexed); Showtime HD; Starz (multiplexed); Sundance Channel; The Movie Channel (multiplexed).
Fee: $10.00 installation; $15.00 monthly (each package).

Video-On-Demand: No

Pay-Per-View
Addressable homes: 9,196.
iN DEMAND (delivered digitally); special events (delivered digitally); ESPN (delivered digitally); Ten Clips (delivered digitally); Ten Blox (delivered digitally); Ten Blue (delivered digitally).

Internet Service
Operational: Yes. Began: September 19, 2002.
Subscribers: 6,000.
Broadband Service: CableONE.net.
Fee: $75.00 installation; $39.93 monthly; $5.00 modem lease.

Telephone Service
Digital: Operational
Fee: $39.95 monthly

Miles of Plant: 450.0 (coaxial); 16.0 (fiber optic). Additional miles planned: 2.0 (coaxial).
Manager: Terri Hale. Chief Technician: Jerry Morris. Marketing Director: Joni Holdridge.
Ownership: Cable ONE Inc. (MSO).

ODESSA—Grande Communications, 2401 IH-20, Odessa, TX 79766. Phones: 512-878-4000 (Administrative office); 432-272-4600 (Customer service). Fax: 432-272-3099. Web Site: http://www.grandecom.com. Also serves Midland. ICA: TX0984. **Note:** This system is an overbuild.
TV Market Ranking: Below 100 (Midland, ODESSA). Franchise award date: February 10, 2000. Franchise expiration date: N.A. Began: November 30, 2000.
Channel capacity: N.A. Channels available but not in use: N.A.

Basic Service
Subscribers: N.A.
Programming (received off-air): KMID (ABC) Midland; KMLM-DT (IND) Odessa; KOSA-TV (CBS, MNT) Odessa; KPBT-TV (PBS) Odessa; KPEJ-TV (FOX) Odessa; KTOV-LP Corpus Christi; KUPB (UNV) Midland; KWES-TV (NBC) Odessa.
Programming (via satellite): C-SPAN; C-SPAN 2; LWS Local Weather Station; QVC; Telefutura; Telemundo; TV Guide Network; WGN America.
Fee: $14.95 monthly.

Expanded Basic Service 1
Subscribers: N.A.
Programming (via satellite): A&E Networks; ABC Family Channel; AMC; Animal Planet; BET Networks; Bravo; Cartoon Network; CNBC; CNN; Comedy Central; Country Music TV; Discovery Channel; Discovery Health Channel; Disney Channel; E! Entertainment Television; ESPN; ESPN 2; ESPN

Classic Sports; Eternal Word TV Network; Food Network; Fox Deportes; Fox News Channel; Fox Sports Southwest; FX; G4; GalaVision; Golf Channel; Great American Country; GSN; Hallmark Channel; Headline News; HGTV; History Channel; Lifetime; MSNBC; MTV; mun2 television; National Geographic Channel; Nickelodeon; Oxygen; SoapNet; Special events; Speed; Spike TV; Syfy; TBS Superstation; The Learning Channel; The Weather Channel; Toon Disney; Travel Channel; Trinity Broadcasting Network; truTV; Turner Classic Movies; Turner Network TV; TV Land; USA Network; Versus; VH1.

Fee: $30.00 monthly.

Digital Basic Service

Subscribers: N.A.

Programming (via satellite): American-Life TV Network; BBC America; Bio; Boomerang; Canales N; CBS Sports Network; Cooking Channel; DIY Network; ESPN; ESPNews; FamilyNet; Fox College Sports Atlantic; Fox College Sports Central; Fox College Sports Pacific; Fox Movie Channel; Fox Soccer; Fuel TV; Fuse; GAS; Golf Channel; HD Theater; History Channel International; INHD; Lifetime Movie Network; MTV Networks Digital Suite; Music Choice; NBA TV; NFL Network; Nick Jr.; NickToons TV; Nuvo TV; Tennis Channel; Turner Network TV; TVG Network; Universal HD.

Fee: $24.00 monthly and $9.95 monthly HDTV tier.

Digital Pay Service 1

Pay Units: N.A.

Programming (via satellite): Cinemax (multiplexed); Cinemax; Encore (multiplexed); Flix (multiplexed); HBO (multiplexed); HBO; Showtime (multiplexed); Showtime; Starz (multiplexed); Starz HDTV; Sundance Channel (multiplexed); The Movie Channel (multiplexed).

Fee: $12.99 monthly (Cinemax, HBO, Starz/Encore, or Showtime/TMC/Flix/ Sundance).

Video-On-Demand: No

Pay-Per-View

Playboy TV (delivered digitally); Fresh (delivered digitally); Hot Choice (delivered digitally); iN DEMAND (delivered digitally); Pleasure (delivered digitally); Shorteez (delivered digitally); Sports PPV (delivered digitally).

Internet Service

Operational: Yes. Began: November 30, 2000.

Broadband Service: Grande High Speed Internet.

Fee: $19.95 monthly.

Telephone Service

Digital: Operational

Fee: $9.00 monthly

General Manager: Mark Machen. Video Services Director: Diane Wigington.

Ownership: Grande Communications Networks Inc. (MSO).

O'DONNELL—Reach Broadband, 515 E Longview St, Arp, TX 75750. Phone: 800-687-1258. Web Site: http://www.reachbroadband.net. ICA: TX0496.

TV Market Ranking: Outside TV Markets (O'DONNELL). Franchise award date: July 1, 1980. Franchise expiration date: N.A. Began: March 9, 1976.

Channel capacity: N.A. Channels available but not in use: N.A.

Basic Service

Subscribers: 259.

Programming (received off-air): KAMC (ABC) Lubbock; KCBD (NBC) Lubbock; KJTV-TV (FOX) Lubbock; KLBK-TV (CBS) Lubbock; KLCW-TV (CW) Wolfforth; KPTB-DT (IND) Lubbock; KTXT-TV (PBS) Lubbock; KXTQ-CA (TMO) Lubbock.

Programming (via satellite): A&E Networks; ABC Family Channel; Animal Planet; Cartoon Network; CNN; Comedy Central; Country Music TV; Discovery Channel; ESPN; ESPN 2; Fox Sports Southwest; HGTV; History Channel; Lifetime; Nickelodeon; QVC; Spike TV; TBS Superstation; The Learning Channel; The Weather Channel; Turner Classic Movies; Turner Network TV; TV Land; Univision Studios; USA Network; WGN America.

Fee: $29.95 installation; $38.00 monthly.

Pay Service 1

Pay Units: 94.

Programming (via satellite): HBO.

Fee: $20.00 installation; $10.50 monthly.

Pay Service 2

Pay Units: N.A.

Programming (via satellite): Cinemax.

Video-On-Demand: No

Internet Service

Operational: No.

Telephone Service

None

Miles of Plant: 9.0 (coaxial); None (fiber optic).

Regional Manager: Ronnie Stafford. Office Manager: Jan Gibson.

Ownership: RB3 LLC (MSO).

OILTON—Windjammer Cable, 8500 W 110th St, Ste 600, Overland Park, KS 66210. Phones: 877-450-5558; 561-775-1208. Fax: 913-563-5454. Web Site: http://www.windjammercable.com. Also serves Mirando City. ICA: TX0825.

TV Market Ranking: Below 100 (Mirando City, OILTON). Franchise award date: N.A. Franchise expiration date: N.A. Began: June 1, 1984.

Channel capacity: N.A. Channels available but not in use: N.A.

Basic Service

Subscribers: 150.

Programming (received off-air): KGNS-TV (CW, NBC, TMO) Laredo; KLDO-TV (FOX, UNV) Laredo; KVTV (CBS) Laredo.

Programming (via satellite): A&E Networks; Animal Planet; Cartoon Network; CNN; Country Music TV; Discovery Channel; Disney Channel; ESPN; ESPN 2; Fox News Channel; Fox Sports Southwest; FX; GalaVision; KABB (FOX) San Antonio; Lifetime; MTV; Nickelodeon; Spike TV; TBS Superstation; Telefutura; Telemundo; The Learning Channel; The Weather Channel; Turner Classic Movies; Turner Network TV; USA Network; WABC-TV (ABC) New York.

Fee: $50.51 installation; $40.99 monthly; $18.81 additional installation.

Pay Service 1

Pay Units: 79.

Programming (via satellite): HBO; Showtime.

Fee: $12.95 monthly (each).

Pay Service 2

Pay Units: N.A.

Programming (via satellite): Encore.

Fee: $3.75 monthly.

Internet Service

Operational: No.

Telephone Service

None

Miles of Plant: 9.0 (coaxial); None (fiber optic).

General Manager: Timothy Evard. Operations Director: Belinda Graham. Engineering Director: Mike Earhart. Finance & Accounting Director: Cindy Johnson.

Ownership: Windjammer Communications LLC (MSO).

OKLAHOMA—Suddenlink Communications, 12444 Powerscourt Dr, Saint Louis, MO 63131-3660. Phones: 800-999-6845 (Customer service); 314-965-2020. Fax: 903-561-5485. Web Site: http://www.suddenlink.com. Also serves Hardin County (portions), Lakewood & Montgomery County (portions). ICA: TX0308.

TV Market Ranking: 15 (Lakewood, Montgomery County (portions), OKLAHOMA); 88 (Hardin County (portions)). Franchise award date: N.A. Franchise expiration date: N.A. Began: N.A.

Channel capacity: 42 (not 2-way capable). Channels available but not in use: N.A.

Basic Service

Subscribers: 1,103.

Programming (received off-air): KHOU (CBS) Houston; KIAH (CW) Houston; KPRC-TV (NBC) Houston; KRIV (FOX) Houston; KTRK-TV (ABC) Houston; KTXH (MNT) Houston; KUHT (PBS) Houston.

Programming (via satellite): A&E Networks; ABC Family Channel; CNN; Country Music TV; C-SPAN; Discovery Channel; Disney Channel; ESPN; Fox Sports Southwest; Headline News; INSP; Lifetime; Nickelodeon; QVC; Spike TV; TBS Superstation; The Weather Channel; Turner Network TV; USA Network; VH1; WGN America.

Fee: $39.95 installation; $36.70 monthly.

Pay Service 1

Pay Units: 52.

Programming (via satellite): Cinemax.

Fee: $10.95 monthly.

Pay Service 2

Pay Units: 92.

Programming (via satellite): HBO.

Fee: $10.95 monthly.

Pay Service 3

Pay Units: 123.

Programming (via satellite): Showtime.

Fee: $10.95 monthly.

Video-On-Demand: No

Internet Service

Operational: Yes.

Broadband Service: Suddenlink High Speed Internet.

Telephone Service

None

Miles of Plant: 108.0 (coaxial); None (fiber optic).

Area Manager: Wanda Pyburn. Regional Manager: Todd Cruthird. Plant Manager: David Burrell.

Ownership: Cequel Communications LLC (MSO).

OLNEY—Suddenlink Communications, 12444 Powerscourt Dr, Saint Louis, MO 63131-3660. Phone: 314-965-2020. Web Site: http://www.suddenlink.com. Also serves Young County (portions). ICA: TX0215.

TV Market Ranking: Outside TV Markets (OLNEY, Young County (portions)). Franchise award date: N.A. Franchise expiration date: N.A. Began: October 1, 1971.

Channel capacity: N.A. Channels available but not in use: N.A.

Basic Service

Subscribers: 1,165.

Programming (received off-air): KAUZ-TV (CBS, CW) Wichita Falls; KFDX-TV (NBC) Wichita Falls; KJTL (FOX) Wichita Falls; KSWO-TV (ABC, TMO) Lawton; allband FM.

Programming (via satellite): C-SPAN; Discovery Channel; Hallmark Channel; QVC; TBS Superstation; The Learning Channel; The Weather Channel.

Programming (via translator): KERA-TV (PBS) Dallas; KTVT (CBS) Fort Worth; KXAS-TV (NBC) Fort Worth; WFAA (ABC) Dallas.

Fee: $39.95 installation; $19.95 monthly.

Expanded Basic Service 1

Subscribers: 932.

Programming (via satellite): ABC Family Channel; AMC; Animal Planet; Cartoon Network; CNBC; CNN; Disney Channel; ESPN; Fox News Channel; FX; Headline News; HGTV; Lifetime; MTV; Spike TV; truTV; Turner Network TV; USA Network.

Fee: $39.95 installation; $25.00 monthly.

Pay Service 1

Pay Units: 87.

Programming (via satellite): Cinemax.

Fee: $12.84 monthly.

Pay Service 2

Pay Units: 284.

Programming (via satellite): Encore.

Fee: $1.75 monthly.

Pay Service 3

Pay Units: 128.

Programming (via satellite): HBO.

Fee: $13.83 monthly.

Pay Service 4

Pay Units: 53.

Programming (via satellite): Showtime.

Fee: $13.83 monthly.

Pay Service 5

Pay Units: 198.

Programming (via satellite): Starz.

Fee: $6.75 monthly.

Internet Service

Operational: Yes. Began: June 5, 2003.

Broadband Service: Suddenlink High Speed Internet.

Fee: $49.95 installation; $25.95 monthly.

Telephone Service

None

Miles of Plant: 31.0 (coaxial); None (fiber optic).

Regional Manager: Todd Cruthird. Regional Marketing Manager: Beverly Gambell. Plant Manager: Ron Johnson.

Ownership: Cequel Communications LLC (MSO).

OLTON—Reach Broadband, 515 E Longview St, Arp, TX 75750. Phone: 800-687-1258. Web Site: http://www.reachbroadband.net. ICA: TX0387.

TV Market Ranking: Outside TV Markets (OLTON). Franchise award date: December 4, 1978. Franchise expiration date: N.A. Began: July 1, 1981.

Channel capacity: 41 (not 2-way capable). Channels available but not in use: N.A.

Basic Service

Subscribers: 288.

Programming (received off-air): KAMC (ABC) Lubbock; KCBD (NBC) Lubbock; KJTV-TV (FOX) Lubbock; KLBK-TV (CBS) Lubbock; KPTB-DT (IND) Lubbock; KTXT-TV (PBS) Lubbock.

Programming (via satellite): A&E Networks; ABC Family Channel; AMC; AmericanLife TV Network; Animal Planet; Cartoon Network; CNN; Country Music TV; Discovery Channel; Disney Channel; ESPN; Fox News Channel; Fox Sports Southwest; History Channel; Lifetime; Nickelodeon; QVC; Spike TV; Syfy; TBS Superstation; The Learning Channel; The Weather Channel; Trinity Broadcasting Network; Turner Network TV; TV Land; USA Network; WGN America.

Programming (via translator): KVDA (TMO) San Antonio.

Fee: $29.95 installation; $38.00 monthly.

Pay Service 1
Pay Units: 57.
Programming (via satellite): HBO.
Fee: $35.00 installation; $10.95 monthly.
Pay Service 2
Pay Units: 32.
Programming (via satellite): Showtime.
Fee: $9.95 monthly.
Pay Service 3
Pay Units: 33.
Programming (via satellite): The Movie Channel.
Fee: $7.95 monthly.
Video-On-Demand: No
Internet Service
Operational: No.
Telephone Service
None
Miles of Plant: 20.0 (coaxial); None (fiber optic).
Regional Manager: Ronnie Stafford. Office Manager: Jan Gibson.
Ownership: RB3 LLC (MSO).

ORANGE—Time Warner Cable. Now served by BEAUMONT, TX [TX0022]. ICA: TX0058.

ORANGE GROVE—Time Warner Cable, 4060 S Padre Island Dr, Corpus Christi, TX 78411-4402. Phones: 972-899-7300 (Flower Mound office); 361-698-6259. Fax: 361-857-5038. Web Site: http://www.timewarnercable.com/Texas. ICA: TX0510.
TV Market Ranking: Below 100 (ORANGE GROVE). Franchise award date: N.A. Franchise expiration date: February 19, 2014. Began: August 1, 1984.
Channel capacity: N.A. Channels available but not in use: N.A.
Basic Service
Subscribers: N.A. Included in Corpus Christi
Programming (received off-air): KEDT (PBS) Corpus Christi; KIII (ABC) Corpus Christi; KORO (UNV) Corpus Christi; KRIS-TV (CW, NBC) Corpus Christi; KZTV (CBS) Corpus Christi.
Programming (via satellite): C-SPAN; Telemundo; WGN America.
Fee: $34.99 installation; $16.39 monthly.
Expanded Basic Service 1
Subscribers: N.A.
Programming (received off-air): KCRP-CA (TEL) Corpus Christi.
Programming (via satellite): A&E Networks; ABC Family Channel; AMC; Animal Planet; BET Networks; Bravo; Cartoon Network; CNBC; CNN; Comedy Central; Country Music TV; C-SPAN 2; CW+; Discovery Channel; Discovery Health Channel; Disney Channel; E! Entertainment Television; ESPN; ESPN 2; ESPN Classic Sports; ESPNews; Eternal Word TV Network; Food Network; Fox News Channel; Fox Sports Southwest; FX; GalaVision; Golf Channel; Great American Country; Hallmark Channel; Headline News; HGTV; History Channel; Lifetime; Lifetime Movie Network; MSNBC; MTV; mun2 television; National Geographic Channel; Nickelodeon; Oxygen; QVC; ShopNBC; SoapNet; Speed; Spike TV; Syfy; TBS Superstation; Texas Cable News; The Learning Channel; The Weather Channel; Travel Channel; Trinity Broadcasting Network; truTV; Turner Classic Movies; Turner Network TV; TV Land; USA Network; Versus; VH1; WE tv.
Fee: $28.60 monthly.
Digital Basic Service
Subscribers: N.A.
Programming (via satellite): A&E Networks; ABC Family Channel; AMC; AmericanLife TV Network; Animal Planet; BBC America; BBC America On Demand; BET Networks; Bio; Bloomberg Television; Boomerang; Bravo; Canales N; Cartoon Network; cloo; CMT Pure Country; CNBC; CNN; Comedy Central; Cooking Channel; Country Music TV; C-SPAN; C-SPAN 2; C-SPAN 3; Current; CW+; Daystar TV Network; Disney Channel; DIY Network; E! Entertainment Television; Encore; ESPN; ESPN 2; ESPN Classic Sports; ESPN HD; ESPNews; Eternal Word TV Network; Exercise TV; FamilyNet; Flix; Food Network; Fox College Sports Atlantic; Fox College Sports Central; Fox College Sports Pacific; Fox Movie Channel; Fox News Channel; Fox Reality Channel; Fox Soccer; Fox Sports Southwest; Fuel TV; Fuse; FX; G4; GAS; Golf Channel; Great American Country; Great American Country On Demand; GSN; Hallmark Channel; HD Theater; HDNet; HDNet Movies; Headline News; HGTV; History Channel; History Channel International; Independent Film Channel; Lifetime; Lifetime Movie Network; Lifetime Real Women; LOGO; MSNBC; MTV Networks Digital Suite; Music Choice; National Geographic Channel; National Geographic Channel On Demand; NBA TV; Nick Jr.; Nick Too; Nickelodeon; NickToons TV; Outdoor Channel; Ovation; Oxygen; QVC; Radar Channel; SoapNet; Speed; Speed On Demand; Spike TV; Style Network; Sundance Channel; Syfy; TBS Superstation; Tennis Channel; Texas Cable News; The Learning Channel; The Weather Channel; Toon Disney; Travel Channel; Trinity Broadcasting Network; truTV; Turner Classic Movies; Turner Network TV; Turner Network TV HD; TV Land; Universal HD; USA Network; Versus; WE tv.
Fee: $8.04 monthly (value tier), $8.95 monthly (additional tiers).
Digital Pay Service 1
Pay Units: N.A.
Programming (via satellite): Cinemax (multiplexed); Cinemax On Demand; HBO (multiplexed); HBO HD; HBO On Demand; Showtime (multiplexed); Showtime HD; Showtime On Demand; Starz (multiplexed); The Movie Channel (multiplexed); The Movie Channel On Demand.
Fee: $12.95 monthly (each).
Video-On-Demand: Yes
Pay-Per-View
iN DEMAND (delivered digitally); Hot Choice (delivered digitally); NHL Center Ice (delivered digitally); Playboy TV (delivered digitally); Fresh (delivered digitally); Shorteez (delivered digitally); NBA League Pass (delivered digitally); ESPN Gameplan (delivered digitally); ESPN Full Court (delivered digitally); MLB Extra Innings (delivered digitally).
Internet Service
Operational: Yes.
Broadband Service: Road Runner.
Fee: $49.99 installation; $44.95 monthly.
Telephone Service
Digital: Planned
Miles of Plant: 7.0 (coaxial); None (fiber optic).
President: Connie Wharton. Vice President & General Manager: Mike McKee. Engineering Director: Charlotte Strong. Public Affairs Manager: Vicki Triplett.
Ownership: Time Warner Cable (MSO).; Advance/Newhouse Partnership (MSO).

ORE CITY—Reach Broadband, 515 E Longview St, Arp, TX 75750. Phones: 800-842-8160; 501-679-6619. E-mail: support@reachbroadband.net. Web Site: http://www.reachbroadband.net. Also serves Marion County (portions). ICA: TX0542.
TV Market Ranking: Below 100 (Marion County (portions), ORE CITY). Franchise award date: N.A. Franchise expiration date: N.A. Began: N.A.
Channel capacity: 62 (not 2-way capable). Channels available but not in use: N.A.
Basic Service
Subscribers: 161.
Programming (received off-air): KETK-TV (NBC) Jacksonville; KLTS-TV (PBS) Shreveport; KLTV (ABC, TMO) Tyler; KMSS-TV (FOX) Shreveport; KSHV-TV (MNT) Shreveport; KSLA (CBS) Shreveport; KTAL-TV (NBC) Texarkana; KTBS-TV (ABC) Shreveport.
Programming (via satellite): TBS Superstation; WGN America.
Fee: $54.95 installation; $20.95 monthly.
Expanded Basic Service 1
Subscribers: N.A.
Programming (via satellite): A&E Networks; ABC Family Channel; AMC; CNN; Country Music TV; Discovery Channel; Disney Channel; ESPN; Fox Sports Southwest; Lifetime; Nickelodeon; Spike TV; Syfy; The Weather Channel; Trinity Broadcasting Network; Turner Network TV; TV Land; USA Network.
Fee: $23.10 monthly.
Pay Service 1
Pay Units: 83.
Programming (via satellite): HBO.
Fee: $12.95 monthly.
Pay Service 2
Pay Units: 101.
Programming (via satellite): Showtime; The Movie Channel.
Fee: $12.95 monthly.
Video-On-Demand: No
Internet Service
Operational: No.
Telephone Service
None
Miles of Plant: 21.0 (coaxial); None (fiber optic).
Ownership: RB3 LLC (MSO).

OYSTER CREEK—Almega Cable, 4001 W Airport Frwy, Ste 530, Bedford, TX 76021. Phone: 817-685-9588. Fax: 817-685-6488. E-mail: helpdesk@almegacable.com. Web Site: http://www.almega.com. Also serves Brazoria County (portions) & Surfside Beach. ICA: TX0283.
TV Market Ranking: Below 100 (Brazoria County (portions), OYSTER CREEK, Surfside Beach). Franchise award date: N.A. Franchise expiration date: N.A. Began: N.A.
Channel capacity: 42 (not 2-way capable). Channels available but not in use: N.A.
Basic Service
Subscribers: 271.
Programming (received off-air): KETH-TV (TBN) Houston; KFTH-DT (TEL) Alvin; KHOU (CBS) Houston; KIAH (CW) Houston; KLTJ (ETV) Galveston; KPRC-TV (NBC) Houston; KRIV (FOX) Houston; KTMD (TMO) Galveston; KTRK-TV (ABC) Houston; KTXH (MNT) Houston; KUBE-TV (IND) Baytown; KUHT (PBS) Houston; KXLN-DT (UNV) Rosenberg.
Programming (via satellite): TBS Superstation; WGN America.
Fee: $54.95 installation; $20.95 monthly.
Expanded Basic Service 1
Subscribers: N.A.
Programming (via satellite): ABC Family Channel; CNN; Country Music TV; Discovery Channel; Disney Channel; ESPN; Fox Sports Southwest; Headline News; HGTV; History Channel; Lifetime; MTV; Nickelodeon; QVC; Spike TV; The Weather Channel; Turner Network TV; USA Network.
Fee: $23.10 monthly.
Pay Service 1
Pay Units: 188.
Programming (via satellite): HBO.
Fee: $12.95 monthly.
Pay Service 2
Pay Units: 163.
Programming (via satellite): Showtime; The Movie Channel.
Fee: $12.95 monthly.
Video-On-Demand: No
Internet Service
Operational: No.
Telephone Service
None
Miles of Plant: 35.0 (coaxial); None (fiber optic).
Ownership: Almega Cable (MSO).

OZONA—Circle Bar Cable TV Inc., 906 11th St, PO Box 777, Ozona, TX 76943. Phone: 325-392-3323. Fax: 325-392-5878. ICA: TX0252.
TV Market Ranking: Outside TV Markets (OZONA). Franchise award date: N.A. Franchise expiration date: January 1, 2014. Began: February 9, 1955.
Channel capacity: 37 (not 2-way capable). Channels available but not in use: N.A.
Basic Service
Subscribers: 778.
Programming (received off-air): KLST (CBS) San Angelo; KSAN-TV (NBC) San Angelo; 9 FMs.
Programming (via microwave): KMID (ABC) Midland; KPEJ-TV (FOX) Odessa.
Programming (via satellite): A&E Networks; ABC Family Channel; CNN; Discovery Channel; Disney Channel; ESPN; History Channel; KRMA-TV (PBS) Denver; Lifetime; Nickelodeon; Spike TV; TBS Superstation; Telemundo; The Learning Channel; The Weather Channel; Trinity Broadcasting Network; Turner Classic Movies; Turner Network TV; VH1; WGN America.
Fee: $30.00 installation; $30.23 monthly.
Pay Service 1
Pay Units: 121.
Programming (via satellite): HBO.
Fee: $10.00 installation; $10.00 monthly.
Video-On-Demand: No
Internet Service
Operational: No.
Telephone Service
None
Miles of Plant: 50.0 (coaxial); None (fiber optic).

Manager: Tony Shields.
Ownership: UNEV Communications Inc. (MSO).

PADUCAH (town)—Suddenlink Communications, 12444 Powerscourt Dr, Saint Louis, MO 63131-3660. Phones: 800-999-6845 (Customer service); 314-965-2020. Fax: 903-561-5485. Web Site: http://www.suddenlink.com. ICA: TX0405.
TV Market Ranking: Outside TV Markets (PADUCAH (TOWN)). Franchise award date: N.A. Franchise expiration date: N.A. Began: August 1, 1954.
Channel capacity: N.A. Channels available but not in use: N.A.

Basic Service
Subscribers: 552.
Programming (received off-air): KJTV-TV (FOX) Lubbock; allband FM.
Programming (via microwave): KACV-TV (PBS) Amarillo; KAMR-TV (NBC) Amarillo; KCIT (FOX) Amarillo; KFDA-TV (CBS) Amarillo; KTVT (CBS) Fort Worth; KVII-TV (ABC, CW) Amarillo.
Programming (via satellite): A&E Networks; ABC Family Channel; AMC; AmericanLife TV Network; Animal Planet; Cartoon Network; CNN; Country Music TV; Discovery Channel; Disney Channel; E! Entertainment Television; ESPN; Fox News Channel; Fox Sports Southwest; Headline News; History Channel; Lifetime; QVC; Spike TV; Syfy; TBS Superstation; The Learning Channel; The Weather Channel; Travel Channel; Trinity Broadcasting Network; Turner Network TV; TV Land; USA Network; WGN America.
Fee: $39.95 installation; $19.95 monthly.

Pay Service 1
Pay Units: 52.
Programming (via satellite): Cinemax.
Fee: $9.95 monthly.

Pay Service 2
Pay Units: 90.
Programming (via satellite): HBO.
Fee: $9.95 monthly.

Pay Service 3
Pay Units: 26.
Programming (via satellite): Showtime.
Fee: $9.95 monthly.

Video-On-Demand: No

Internet Service
Operational: Yes. Began: December 22, 2003.
Broadband Service: Suddenlink High Speed Internet.
Fee: $49.95 installation; $38.95 monthly.

Telephone Service
None
Miles of Plant: 16.0 (coaxial); None (fiber optic).
Regional Manager: Todd Cruthird. Regional Marketing Manager: Beverly Gambell. Plant Manager: Rick Rattan.
Ownership: Cequel Communications LLC (MSO).

PALACIOS—Bay City Cablevision, 1302 Wisteria St, Wharton, TX 77488. Phones: 979-532-8630; 866-532-3920. Fax: 979-532-8630. Web Site: http://www.warpspeed1.net. ICA: TX0223.
TV Market Ranking: Outside TV Markets (PALACIOS). Franchise award date: N.A. Franchise expiration date: N.A. Began: August 1, 1962.
Channel capacity: 62 (operating 2-way). Channels available but not in use: N.A.

Basic Service
Subscribers: 341.
Programming (received off-air): KAVU-TV (ABC) Victoria; KHOU (CBS) Houston; KIAH (CW) Houston; KPRC-TV (NBC) Houston; KRIV (FOX) Houston; KTMD (TMO) Galveston; KTRK-TV (ABC) Houston; KTXH (MNT) Houston; KUHT (PBS) Houston; KXLN-DT (UNV) Rosenberg; allband FM.
Programming (via satellite): ABC Family Channel; AMC; Bravo; CNBC; Comedy Central; Country Music TV; C-SPAN; Discovery Channel; Disney Channel; E! Entertainment Television; ESPN; ESPN 2; Food Network; Fox News Channel; Fox Sports Southwest; FX; GalaVision; Headline News; History Channel; Lifetime; Oxygen; QVC; SoapNet; Speed; Spike TV; Syfy; TBS Superstation; The Learning Channel; The Weather Channel; Travel Channel; Trinity Broadcasting Network; Turner Network TV; TV Land; USA Network; Versus; VH1; WGN America.
Fee: $15.00 installation; $21.10 monthly; $2.00 converter; $7.50 additional installation.

Digital Basic Service
Subscribers: 9.
Programming (via satellite): AmericanLife TV Network; BBC America; Bio; Bloomberg Television; CMT Pure Country; Current; Discovery Fit & Health; Discovery Health Channel; Discovery Kids Channel; Fox Movie Channel; Fuse; G4; Golf Channel; GSN; Halogen Network; HGTV; History Channel; ID Investigation Discovery; Independent Film Channel; Lifetime Movie Network; Military Channel; MTV2; Nick Jr.; Outdoor Channel; Planet Green; Science; Style Network; TeenNick; Toon Disney; Trinity Broadcasting Network; Turner Classic Movies; VH1 Classic; VH1 Soul; WE tv.

Pay Service 1
Pay Units: 50.
Programming (via satellite): Cinemax.
Fee: $9.95 monthly.

Pay Service 2
Pay Units: 96.
Programming (via satellite): HBO.
Fee: $10.00 monthly.

Pay Service 3
Pay Units: 10.
Programming (via satellite): The Movie Channel.
Fee: $9.95 monthly.

Pay Service 4
Pay Units: 17.
Programming (via satellite): Showtime.
Fee: $9.95 monthly.

Digital Pay Service 1
Pay Units: N.A.
Programming (via satellite): Cinemax (multiplexed); Encore (multiplexed); Flix; HBO (multiplexed); Showtime (multiplexed); Starz (multiplexed); The Movie Channel (multiplexed).

Video-On-Demand: No

Internet Service
Operational: Yes, Both DSL & dial-up.
Broadband Service: Warp Speed 1 Internet.
Fee: $17.05 installation; $34.99 monthly.

Telephone Service
None
Miles of Plant: 30.0 (coaxial); 9.0 (fiber optic).
General Manager: Wayne Neal. Chief Technician: Dickie Isaacs.
Ownership: Mid-Coast Cablevision (MSO).

PALESTINE—Windjammer Cable, 8500 W 110th St, Ste 600, Overland Park, KS 66. Phone: 888-495-2881. Fax: 913-563-5454. Web Site: http://www.windjammercable.com. Also serves Anderson County & Elkhart. ICA: TX0070.
TV Market Ranking: Below 100 (Anderson County (portions), Elkhart, PALESTINE); Outside TV Markets (Anderson County (portions)). Franchise award date: N.A. Franchise expiration date: N.A. Began: January 1, 1955.
Channel capacity: N.A. Channels available but not in use: N.A.

Basic Service
Subscribers: N.A. Included in Dallas
Programming (received off-air): KDTN (ETV) Denton; KETK-TV (NBC) Jacksonville; KFXK-TV (FOX) Longview; KTVT (CBS) Fort Worth; 18 FMs.
Programming (via microwave): KDFW-DT (FOX) Dallas; KERA-TV (PBS) Dallas; KXAS-TV (NBC) Fort Worth; KXTX-TV (TMO) Dallas; WFAA (ABC) Dallas.
Programming (via satellite): ABC Family Channel; BET Networks; CNN; C-SPAN; Lifetime; QVC; TBS Superstation; The Weather Channel; Trinity Broadcasting Network; WGN America.
Fee: $47.47 installation; $19.95 monthly; $15.00 additional installation.

Expanded Basic Service 1
Subscribers: 4,013.
Programming (via satellite): A&E Networks; AMC; Animal Planet; Cartoon Network; CNBC; Comedy Central; Country Music TV; Discovery Channel; Disney Channel; E! Entertainment Television; ESPN; ESPN 2; Eternal Word TV Network; Food Network; Fox News Channel; Golf Channel; Hallmark Channel; Headline News; HGTV; History Channel; INSP; MSNBC; MTV; Nickelodeon; Oxygen; Spike TV; Texas Cable News; The Learning Channel; Travel Channel; Turner Classic Movies; Turner Network TV; Univision Studios; USA Network; VH1.
Fee: $10.05 monthly.

Digital Basic Service
Subscribers: N.A.
Programming (via satellite): BBC America; Bio; Bloomberg Television; Bravo; Current; Discovery Fit & Health; Discovery Kids Channel; ESPN Classic Sports; ESPNews; Fox Movie Channel; Fox Soccer; Fuse; G4; GSN; Halogen Network; History Channel International; ID Investigation Discovery; Independent Film Channel; International Television (ITV); Lime; MTV Jams; MTV2; Music Choice; NBA TV; Nick Jr.; NickToons TV; Outdoor Channel; Ovation; Planet Green; Science; Speed; Sundance Channel; Syfy; TeenNick; Toon Disney; TV Land; Versus; WE tv.
Fee: $9.95 monthly.

Digital Pay Service 1
Pay Units: N.A.
Programming (via satellite): Cinemax (multiplexed); Encore (multiplexed); Flix; HBO (multiplexed); Showtime (multiplexed); Starz (multiplexed); The Movie Channel (multiplexed).
Fee: $16.99 monthly (Cinemax, Encore, Flix, HBO, Showtime, Starz, or TMC).

Video-On-Demand: No

Pay-Per-View
iN DEMAND (delivered digitally); Fresh (delivered digitally); Shorteez (delivered digitally); Playboy TV (delivered digitally); Barker (delivered digitally).

Internet Service
Operational: No.

Telephone Service
None
Miles of Plant: 187.0 (coaxial); None (fiber optic).
General Manager: Timothy Evard. Operations Director: Belinda Graham. Engineering Director: Mike Earehart. Finance & Accounting Director: Cindy Johnson.
Ownership: Windjammer Communications LLC (MSO).

PALO PINTO—Formerly served by Mallard Cablevision. No longer in operation. ICA: TX0639.

PARADISE—Formerly served by CableSouth Inc. No longer in operation. ICA: TX0679.

PARIS—Suddenlink Communications, 25 SE 19th St, Paris, TX 75460. Phone: 903-783-1715. Fax: 903-595-1929. Web Site: http://www.suddenlink.com. Also serves Lamar County (unincorporated areas), Reno (Lamar County) & Roxton. ICA: TX0060.
TV Market Ranking: Outside TV Markets (Lamar County (unincorporated areas), PARIS, Reno (Lamar County), Roxton). Franchise award date: June 11, 1984. Franchise expiration date: June 11, 2009. Began: April 1, 1956.
Channel capacity: 78 (operating 2-way). Channels available but not in use: N.A.

Basic Service
Subscribers: 9,349.
Programming (received off-air): KTEN (ABC, CW, NBC) Ada; KXII (CBS, FOX, MNT) Sherman; 14 FMs.
Programming (via microwave): KDFW-DT (FOX) Dallas; KERA-TV (PBS) Dallas; KTVT (CBS) Fort Worth; KXAS-TV (NBC) Fort Worth; WFAA (ABC) Dallas.
Programming (via satellite): C-SPAN; Trinity Broadcasting Network.
Fee: $38.00 installation; $10.51 monthly; $2.00 converter.

Expanded Basic Service 1
Subscribers: 9,042.
Programming (via satellite): A&E Networks; ABC Family Channel; AMC; Animal Planet; BET Networks; Cartoon Network; CNN; Comedy Central; C-SPAN 2; Discovery Channel; Disney Channel; E! Entertainment Television; ESPN; ESPN 2; Food Network; Fox News Channel; Fox Sports Southwest; FX; GalaVision; Great American Country; Headline News; HGTV; History Channel; Independent Music Network; Lifetime; MSNBC; MTV; Nickelodeon; Outdoor Channel; Spike TV; Syfy; The Learning Channel; The Weather Channel; Travel Channel; truTV; Turner Classic Movies; Turner Network TV; TV Land; USA Network; VH1.
Fee: $4.19 installation; $17.59 monthly.

Digital Basic Service
Subscribers: N.A.
Programming (via satellite): AmericanLife TV Network; BBC America; Bio; Bloomberg Television; Boomerang; Cooking Channel; Cox Sports Television; Discovery Fit & Health; DIY Network; Encore; ESPN Classic Sports; ESPNews; FamilyNet; Fox Movie Channel; Fox Soccer; Fuel TV; Fuse; G4; GMC; Golf Channel; GSN; Hallmark Channel; Halogen Network; History Channel International; Independent Film Channel; Lifetime Movie Network; Music Choice; National Geographic Channel; Oxygen; SoapNet; Speed; Sundance Channel; Tennis Channel; Toon Disney; TV One; Versus; WE tv.

Digital Pay Service 1
Pay Units: N.A.
Programming (via satellite): Cinemax (multiplexed); HBO (multiplexed); Showtime (multiplexed); Starz (multiplexed); The Movie Channel (multiplexed).

Video-On-Demand: Yes

Pay-Per-View
iN DEMAND (delivered digitally); Fresh (delivered digitally); Playboy TV (delivered digitally); Hot Choice (delivered digitally); Shorteez (delivered digitally).

Internet Service
Operational: No.

Telephone Service
None

Miles of Plant: 239.0 (coaxial); None (fiber optic). Additional miles planned: 5.0 (coaxial).

Manager: Tim Masters. Chief Technician: Bob Holmon.

Ownership: Cequel Communications LLC (MSO).

PARKWAY VILLAGE—Time Warner Cable. No longer in operation. ICA: TX0668.

PEARSALL—Time Warner Cable, 1313 W Carlton Rd, Laredo, TX 78041. Phones: 972-899-7300 (Flower Mound office); 956-721-0607. Fax: 956-721-0612. Web Site: http://www.timewarnercable.com/Texas.

Also serves Cotulla, Dilley, Frio County & La Salle County (portions). ICA: TX0196.

TV Market Ranking: 45 (Frio County (portions)); Outside TV Markets (Cotulla, Dilley, La Salle County (portions), PEARSALL, Frio County (portions)). Franchise award date: N.A. Franchise expiration date: N.A. Began: May 1, 1975.

Channel capacity: N.A. Channels available but not in use: N.A.

Basic Service
Subscribers: N.A. Included in Del Rio
Programming (received off-air): KABB (FOX) San Antonio; KENS (CBS) San Antonio; KLRN (PBS) San Antonio; KMYS (CW) Kerrville; KPXL-TV (ION) Uvalde; KSAT-TV (ABC) San Antonio; KVDA (TMO) San Antonio; KWEX-DT (UNV) San Antonio; WOAI-TV (NBC) San Antonio.
Programming (via satellite): A&E Networks; ABC Family Channel; AMC; Animal Planet; BET Networks; Bravo; Cartoon Network; CNBC; CNN; Comedy Central; Country Music TV; C-SPAN; C-SPAN 2; Discovery Channel; Discovery Health Channel; Disney Channel; E! Entertainment Television; ESPN; ESPN 2; Eternal Word TV Network; Food Network; Fox Deportes; Fox News Channel; Fox Sports Southwest; FX; GalaVision; Golf Channel; Great American Country; Hallmark Channel; Headline News; HGTV; History Channel; Lifetime; MoviePlex; MSNBC; MTV; mun2 television; National Geographic Channel; Nickelodeon; Outdoor Channel; Oxygen; QVC; ShopNBC; SoapNet; Spike TV; Style Network; Syfy; TBS Superstation; Texas Cable News; The Learning Channel; The Weather Channel; Travel Channel; Trinity Broadcasting Network; truTV; Turner Classic Movies; Turner Network TV; TV Guide Network; TV Land; USA Network; VH1; WE tv.
Fee: $33.74 installation; $40.99 monthly.

Digital Basic Service
Subscribers: N.A.
Programming (via satellite): BBC America; Bio; Bloomberg Television; Current; Discovery Fit & Health; Encore; ESPN Classic Sports; ESPNews; Fox College Sports Atlantic; Fox College Sports Central; Fox College Sports Pacific; Fox Movie Channel; Fox Soccer; Fuse; G4; GAS; GSN; History Channel International; Independent Film Channel; Lifetime Movie Network; MTV2; Music Choice; NBA TV; Nick Jr.; NickToons TV; Nuvo TV; Outdoor Channel; Speed; Sundance Channel (multiplexed); Tennis Channel; Toon Disney; Trio; Versus; VH1 Country.
Fee: $7.00 monthly (value tier), $8.95 monthly (each additional tier).

Digital Pay Service 1
Pay Units: N.A.
Programming (via satellite): Cinemax (multiplexed); HBO (multiplexed); Showtime (multiplexed); Starz (multiplexed); The Movie Channel (multiplexed).
Fee: $12.95 monthly (each).

Pay-Per-View
iN DEMAND (delivered digitally); Fresh (delivered digitally); Playboy TV (delivered digitally); Hot Choice (delivered digitally); NBA League Pass (delivered digitally); NASCAR In Car (delivered digitally); NHL Center Ice (delivered digitally); MLB Extra Innings (delivered digitally).

Internet Service
Operational: Yes.

Telephone Service
Digital: Operational

President: Connie Wharton. Vice President & General Manager: Michael Carrosquiola. Operations Director: Marcos Reyes. Technical Operations Manager: Eduardo Ruiz. Public Affairs Manager: Celinda Gonzalez.

Ownership: Time Warner Cable (MSO).; Advance/Newhouse Partnership (MSO).

PECOS—Suddenlink Communications, 12444 Powerscourt Dr, Saint Louis, MO 63131-3660. Phones: 800-999-6845; 314-965-2020. Web Site: http://www.suddenlink.com.

Also serves Reeves County (portions). ICA: TX0138.

TV Market Ranking: Outside TV Markets (PECOS, Reeves County (portions)). Franchise award date: July 12, 1979. Franchise expiration date: N.A. Began: March 17, 1955.

Channel capacity: 61 (operating 2-way). Channels available but not in use: N.A.

Basic Service
Subscribers: 2,980.
Programming (via microwave): KMID (ABC) Midland; KMLM-DT (IND) Odessa; KOSA-TV (CBS, MNT) Odessa; KPEJ-TV (FOX) Odessa; KWES-TV (NBC) Odessa.
Programming (via satellite): KMGH-TV (ABC) Denver; KRMA-TV (PBS) Denver; QVC; WGN America.
Fee: $35.00 installation; $18.95 monthly.

Expanded Basic Service 1
Subscribers: N.A.
Programming (via microwave): KUPB (UNV) Midland.
Programming (via satellite): A&E Networks; ABC Family Channel; AMC; Animal Planet; BET Networks; Bravo; Cartoon Network; CNBC; CNN; Comedy Central; C-SPAN; Discovery Channel; Disney Channel; E! Entertainment Television; ESPN; ESPN 2; Eternal Word TV Network; Food Network; Fox News Channel; Fox Sports Southwest; FX; GalaVision; Golf Channel; Great American Country; Hallmark Channel; Headline News; HGTV; History Channel; Lifetime; MSNBC; MTV; National Geographic Channel; Nickelodeon; Outdoor Channel; Shop at Home; Shopping Channel; Speed; Spike TV; Syfy; TBS Superstation; Telemundo; The Learning Channel; The Weather Channel; Travel Channel; Trinity Broadcasting Network; truTV; Turner Classic Movies; Turner Network TV; TV Guide Network; TV Land; USA Network; VH1.
Fee: $26.00 monthly.

Digital Basic Service
Subscribers: N.A.
Programming (via satellite): BBC America; Bio; Bloomberg Television; Canales N; cloo; Discovery Digital Networks; DMX Music; ESPN Classic Sports; ESPNews; Fox College Sports Atlantic; Fox College Sports Central; Fox College Sports Pacific; Fox Movie Channel; Fox Soccer; Fuse; G4; GSN; History Channel International; Independent Film Channel; Military History Channel; Sundance Channel; Toon Disney; Versus; WE tv.
Fee: $3.99 monthly.

Pay Service 1
Pay Units: 173.
Programming (via satellite): Cinemax.
Fee: $9.95 monthly.

Pay Service 2
Pay Units: 414.
Programming (via satellite): HBO.
Fee: $10.95 monthly.

Pay Service 3
Pay Units: 92.
Programming (via satellite): Showtime.
Fee: $9.95 monthly.

Pay Service 4
Pay Units: 189.
Programming (via satellite): The Movie Channel.
Fee: $5.95 monthly.

Digital Pay Service 1
Pay Units: N.A.
Programming (via satellite): Cinemax (multiplexed); Encore (multiplexed); HBO (multiplexed); Showtime (multiplexed); Starz (multiplexed); The Movie Channel (multiplexed).

Video-On-Demand: No

Pay-Per-View
iN DEMAND (delivered digitally); Playboy TV (delivered digitally); Fresh (delivered digitally); Shorteez (delivered digitally).

Internet Service
Operational: Yes. Began: March 1, 2002.
Broadband Service: Suddenlink High Speed Internet.
Fee: $45.95 installation; $29.95 monthly.

Telephone Service
Digital: Operational
Fee: $44.95 monthly

Miles of Plant: 64.0 (coaxial); None (fiber optic).

Regional Manager: Todd Cruthird. Marketing Director: Beverly Gambell.

Ownership: Cequel Communications LLC (MSO).

PELICAN BAY—Formerly served by SouthTel Communications LP. No longer in operation. ICA: TX0832.

PERRIN—Formerly served by Mallard Cablevision. No longer in operation. ICA: TX0640.

PERRYTON—Allegiance Communications, 707 W Saratoga St, Shawnee, OK 74804. Phones: 405-395-1131; 405-275-6923. Web Site: http://www.allegiance.tv. ICA: TX0165.

TV Market Ranking: Outside TV Markets (PERRYTON). Franchise award date: July 17, 1957. Franchise expiration date: N.A. Began: January 1, 1957.

Channel capacity: 42 (operating 2-way). Channels available but not in use: N.A.

Basic Service
Subscribers: 2,578.
Programming (received off-air): KACV-TV (PBS) Amarillo; KAMR-TV (NBC) Amarillo; KCIT (FOX) Amarillo; KFDA-TV (CBS) Amarillo; KPTF-DT (IND) Farwell; KVII-TV (ABC, CW) Amarillo.
Programming (via satellite): C-SPAN; C-SPAN 2; CW+; GalaVision; QVC; ShopNBC; Telefutura; Telemundo; Texas Cable News; The Weather Channel; TV Guide Network; Univision Studios; WGN America.
Fee: $38.00 installation; $21.95 monthly; $2.25 converter; $25.00 additional installation.

Expanded Basic Service 1
Subscribers: 2,193.
Programming (via satellite): A&E Networks; ABC Family Channel; AMC; Animal Planet; Bravo; Cartoon Network; CNBC; CNN; Comedy Central; Country Music TV; Discovery Channel; Disney Channel; ESPN; ESPN 2; Food Network; Fox News Channel; Fox Sports Southwest; FX; Hallmark Channel; Headline News; HGTV; History Channel; Lifetime; MoviePlex; MTV; NFL Network; Nickelodeon; Spike TV; TBS Superstation; The Learning Channel; Turner Network TV; TV Land; USA Network; VH1.
Fee: $15.77 monthly.

Digital Basic Service
Subscribers: N.A.
Programming (via satellite): AmericanLife TV Network; BBC America; Bio; Bloomberg Television; Bravo; Cine Latino; Cine Mexicano; cloo; CMT Pure Country; CNN en Espanol; Current; Discovery en Espanol; Discovery Fit & Health; Discovery Health Channel; Discovery Kids Channel; DMX Music; Encore (multiplexed); ESPN Classic Sports; ESPN Deportes; ESPNews; Flix; Fox College Sports Atlantic; Fox College Sports Central; Fox College Sports Pacific; Fox Deportes; Fox Movie Channel; Fox Soccer; Fuse; G4; GMC; Golf Channel; Great American Country; GSN; Halogen Network; HGTV; History Channel; History Channel en Espanol; History Channel International; ID Investigation Discovery; Independent Film Channel; Lifetime Movie Network; Military Channel; MTV Hits; MTV2; mun2 television; National Geographic Channel; Nick Jr.; NickToons TV; Outdoor Channel; Planet Green; Science; ShopNBC; Speed; Style Network; Sundance Channel; Syfy; TeenNick; The Word Network; Toon Disney; Tr3s; Trinity Broadcasting Network; Turner Classic Movies; VeneMovies; Versus; VH1 Classic; VH1 Soul; WE tv.

Pay Service 1
Pay Units: N.A.
Programming (via satellite): HBO.

Digital Pay Service 1
Pay Units: N.A.
Programming (via satellite): Cinemax (multiplexed); HBO (multiplexed); HBO Latino;

Showtime (multiplexed); Starz (multiplexed); The Movie Channel (multiplexed).
Video-On-Demand: No
Pay-Per-View
iN DEMAND (delivered digitally); Hot Choice (delivered digitally); Playboy TV (delivered digitally); Fresh (delivered digitally); Spice: Xcess (delivered digitally); Club Jenna (delivered digitally).
Internet Service
Operational: Yes.
Fee: $24.95 installation; $39.95 monthly.
Telephone Service
None
Miles of Plant: 43.0 (coaxial); None (fiber optic).
Chief Executive Officer: Bill Haggarty. Regional Vice President: Andrew Dearth. Vice President, Marketing: Tracy Bass.
Ownership: Allegiance Communications (MSO).

PETERSBURG—Formerly served by Almega Cable. No longer in operation. ICA: TX0483.

PETTUS—Formerly served by National Cable Inc. No longer in operation. ICA: TX0561.

PFLUGERVILLE—Suddenlink Communications, 322 N Glenwood Blvd, Tyler, TX 75702. Phones: 903-595-4321 (Tyler office); 512-930-3085; 800-999-6845 (Customer service). Fax: 512-869-2962. Web Site: http://www.suddenlink.com. ICA: TX0127.
TV Market Ranking: Below 100 (PFLUGERVILLE). Franchise award date: N.A. Franchise expiration date: January 17, 2015. Began: January 18, 1980.
Channel capacity: 78 (operating 2-way). Channels available but not in use: N.A.
Basic Service
Subscribers: 10,000.
Programming (received off-air): KEYE-TV (CBS, TMO) Austin; KLRU (PBS) Austin; KNVA (CW) Austin; KTBC (FOX) Austin; KVUE (ABC) Austin; KXAN-TV (NBC) Austin.
Programming (via satellite): C-SPAN; QVC; Trinity Broadcasting Network; TV Guide Network; WGN America.
Fee: $20.00 installation; $27.99 monthly; $1.50 converter.
Expanded Basic Service 1
Subscribers: 9,000.
Programming (via satellite): A&E Networks; ABC Family Channel; AMC; Animal Planet; BET Networks; Cartoon Network; CNBC; CNN; Comedy Central; Country Music TV; C-SPAN 2; Discovery Channel; Disney Channel; E! Entertainment Television; ESPN; ESPN 2; Food Network; Fox News Channel; Fox Sports Southwest; FX; Golf Channel; Headline News; HGTV; History Channel; Lifetime; MSNBC; MTV; Nickelodeon; Speed; Spike TV; Syfy; TBS Superstation; The Learning Channel; The Weather Channel; Travel Channel; truTV; Turner Classic Movies; Turner Network TV; TV Land; Univision Studios; USA Network; Versus; VH1.
Fee: $27.99 monthly.
Digital Basic Service
Subscribers: N.A.
Programming (via satellite): BBC America; Bio; Bloomberg Television; Cooking Channel; Discovery Digital Networks; DIY Network; Encore; ESPN Classic Sports; ESPNews; Fox Sports World; Fuse; G4; GSN; History Channel International; Lifetime Movie Network; Music Choice; Outdoor Channel; SoapNet; Sundance Channel; Toon Disney.
Pay Service 1
Pay Units: 581.
Programming (via satellite): Cinemax (multiplexed).
Fee: $9.99 monthly.
Pay Service 2
Pay Units: 350.
Programming (via satellite): Encore; Starz.
Fee: $9.99 monthly.
Pay Service 3
Pay Units: 1,523.
Programming (via satellite): HBO (multiplexed).
Fee: $11.99 monthly.
Pay Service 4
Pay Units: 1,172.
Programming (via satellite): Showtime.
Fee: $8.99 monthly.
Digital Pay Service 1
Pay Units: N.A.
Programming (via satellite): Cinemax (multiplexed); HBO (multiplexed); Showtime (multiplexed); Starz (multiplexed); The Movie Channel (multiplexed).
Video-On-Demand: No
Pay-Per-View
ESPN Gameplan (delivered digitally); ESPN Now (delivered digitally); Playboy TV (delivered digitally); Hot Choice (delivered digitally); Fresh (delivered digitally); iN DEMAND.
Internet Service
Operational: Yes.
Broadband Service: Suddenlink High Speed Internet.
Fee: $45.95 installation; $29.95 monthly.
Telephone Service
Digital: Operational
Fee: $44.95 monthly
Miles of Plant: 190.0 (coaxial); 18.0 (fiber optic). Additional miles planned: 20.0 (coaxial).
Manager: Dale Hoffman. Chief Technician & Marketing Director: Wesley Houghteling.
Ownership: Cequel Communications LLC (MSO).

PILOT POINT—Suddenlink Communications, 12444 Powerscourt Dr, Saint Louis, MO 63131-3660. Phones: 972-347-9779; 314-965-2020. Web Site: http://www.suddenlink.com. Also serves Anna, Aubrey, Celina, Gunter, Krugerville, Lakewood Village, Little Elm, Melissa, Oak Point, Prosper, Sanger & Tioga. ICA: TX0286.
TV Market Ranking: 12 (Lakewood Village, Little Elm, Oak Point, Prosper); Below 100 (Anna, Aubrey, Celina, Gunter, Krugerville, Melissa, PILOT POINT, Sanger, Tioga). Franchise award date: N.A. Franchise expiration date: N.A. Began: June 1, 1982.
Channel capacity: 54 (operating 2-way). Channels available but not in use: N.A.
Basic Service
Subscribers: 3,397.
Programming (received off-air): KAZD (IND) Lake Dallas; KDAF (CW, IND) Dallas; KDFI (MNT) Dallas; KDFW-DT (FOX) Dallas; KDTN (ETV) Denton; KERA-TV (PBS) Dallas; KMPX (IND) Decatur; KPXD-TV (ION) Arlington; KSTR-DT (TEL) Irving; KTVT (CBS) Fort Worth; KTXA (IND) Fort Worth; KUVN-DT (UNV) Garland; KXAS-TV (NBC) Fort Worth; KXII (CBS, FOX, MNT) Sherman; KXTX-TV (TMO) Dallas; WFAA (ABC) Dallas.
Programming (via satellite): C-SPAN; GalaVision; QVC; Trinity Broadcasting Network; WGN America.
Fee: $39.95 installation; $19.95 monthly.
Expanded Basic Service 1
Subscribers: N.A.
Programming (via satellite): A&E Networks; ABC Family Channel; AMC; Animal Planet; BET Networks; Bravo; Cartoon Network; CNBC; CNN; Comedy Central; Discovery Channel; Disney Channel; E! Entertainment Television; ESPN; ESPN 2; Food Network; Fox News Channel; Fox Sports Southwest; FX; Golf Channel; Great American Country; Hallmark Channel; Headline News; HGTV; History Channel; Lifetime; MSNBC; MTV; National Geographic Channel; Nickelodeon; Outdoor Channel; Speed; Spike TV; Syfy; TBS Superstation; The Learning Channel; The Weather Channel; Travel Channel; truTV; Turner Classic Movies; Turner Network TV; TV Guide Network; TV Land; USA Network; VH1.
Digital Basic Service
Subscribers: N.A.
Programming (via satellite): BBC America; Bio; Bloomberg Television; Canales N; cloo; C-SPAN 3; ESPN Classic Sports; ESPNews; Fox College Sports Atlantic; Fox College Sports Central; Fox College Sports Pacific; Fox Movie Channel; Fox Soccer; Fuel TV; Fuse; G4; GSN; HD Theater; HDNet; HDNet Movies; History Channel International; Independent Film Channel; Music Choice; SoapNet; Style Network; Sundance Channel; Toon Disney; Versus; WE tv.
Digital Pay Service 1
Pay Units: N.A.
Programming (via satellite): Cinemax (multiplexed); Encore (multiplexed); Flix; HBO (multiplexed); Showtime (multiplexed); Showtime HD; Starz (multiplexed); The Movie Channel (multiplexed).
Video-On-Demand: No
Pay-Per-View
iN DEMAND (delivered digitally); Playboy TV (delivered digitally).
Internet Service
Operational: Yes.
Broadband Service: Suddenlink High Speed Internet.
Fee: $49.95 installation; $25.95 monthly.
Telephone Service
Digital: Operational
Fee: $44.95 monthly
Miles of Plant: 158.0 (coaxial); None (fiber optic).
Regional Manager: Todd Cruthird.
Ownership: Cequel Communications LLC (MSO).

PITTSBURG—Suddenlink Communications, 1506 Shadywood Ln, Mount Pleasant, TX 75455-5630. Phone: 903-572-6107. Fax: 903-572-5669. Web Site: http://www.suddenlink.com. Also serves Camp County (portions). ICA: TX0219.
TV Market Ranking: Below 100 (Camp County (portions)); Outside TV Markets (Camp County (portions), PITTSBURG). Franchise award date: N.A. Franchise expiration date: N.A. Began: November 1, 1969.
Channel capacity: 36 (operating 2-way). Channels available but not in use: N.A.
Basic Service
Subscribers: 1,388.
Programming (received off-air): KETK-TV (NBC) Jacksonville; KFXK-TV (FOX) Longview; KLTV (ABC, TMO) Tyler; KSHV-TV (MNT) Shreveport; KSLA (CBS) Shreveport.
Programming (via microwave): KERA-TV (PBS) Dallas; KXAS-TV (NBC) Fort Worth; WFAA (ABC) Dallas.
Programming (via satellite): C-SPAN; Discovery Channel; Headline News; TBS Superstation; The Weather Channel.
Fee: $31.86 installation; $10.08 monthly.
Expanded Basic Service 1
Subscribers: 1,277.
Programming (via satellite): A&E Networks; ABC Family Channel; AMC; BET Networks; Cartoon Network; CNN; Discovery Health Channel; Disney Channel; ESPN; ESPN 2; Fox News Channel; Fox Sports Southwest; FX; GalaVision; ION Television; Lifetime; MoviePlex; MTV; Nickelodeon; QVC; Spike TV; The Learning Channel; Turner Network TV; Univision Studios; USA Network.
Fee: $10.97 monthly.
Digital Basic Service
Subscribers: N.A.
Programming (via satellite): BBC America; Bloomberg Television; Discovery Digital Networks; Encore; ESPN Classic Sports; ESPNews; Fox Sports World; Fuse; G4; Golf Channel; GSN; Lifetime Movie Network; Music Choice; Speed; Toon Disney; truTV.
Pay Service 1
Pay Units: 57.
Programming (via satellite): Cinemax; Encore; HBO; Showtime; Starz.
Fee: $25.00 installation; $11.00 monthly (Cinemax, HBO or Showtime).
Digital Pay Service 1
Pay Units: N.A.
Programming (via satellite): Cinemax (multiplexed); HBO (multiplexed); Showtime (multiplexed); Starz (multiplexed); The Movie Channel (multiplexed).
Video-On-Demand: No
Pay-Per-View
ESPN Extra (delivered digitally); ESPN Gameplan (delivered digitally); ESPN Now (delivered digitally); Fresh (delivered digitally); Hot Choice (delivered digitally); Barker (delivered digitally); iN DEMAND (delivered digitally).
Internet Service
Operational: Yes.
Broadband Service: Suddenlink High Speed Internet.
Fee: $49.95 installation; $25.95 monthly.
Telephone Service
None
Miles of Plant: 33.0 (coaxial); None (fiber optic).
Manager & Chief Technician: Ron Eubanks.
Ownership: Cequel Communications LLC (MSO).

PLACEDO—Formerly served by National Cable Inc. No longer in operation. ICA: TX0641.

PLAINS—Almega Cable, 4001 W Airport Frwy, Ste 530, Bedford, TX 76021. Phone: 817-685-9588. Fax: 817-685-6488. E-mail: helpdesk@almegacable.com. Web Site: http://www.almega.com. ICA: TX0457.
TV Market Ranking: Outside TV Markets (PLAINS). Franchise award date: September 1, 1988. Franchise expiration date: N.A. Began: July 1, 1979.
Channel capacity: 36 (not 2-way capable). Channels available but not in use: N.A.
Basic Service
Subscribers: 162.
Programming (received off-air): KAMC (ABC) Lubbock; KCBD (NBC) Lubbock; KENW (PBS) Portales; KJTV-TV (FOX) Lubbock; KLBK-TV (CBS) Lubbock.
Programming (via satellite): ABC Family Channel; ESPN; Spike TV; TBS Superstation.
Fee: $29.95 installation; $19.95 monthly.

Expanded Basic Service 1
Subscribers: N.A.
Programming (via satellite): Cartoon Network; CNN; Discovery Channel; Disney Channel; Fox Sports Southwest; Great American Country; Lifetime; National Geographic Channel; Nickelodeon; The Learning Channel; The Weather Channel; Trinity Broadcasting Network; Turner Classic Movies; Turner Network TV; TV Land; Univision Studios; USA Network; VH1.
Fee: $20.00 monthly.
Pay Service 1
Pay Units: 17.
Programming (via satellite): Showtime.
Fee: $9.95 monthly.
Pay Service 2
Pay Units: 43.
Programming (via satellite): HBO.
Fee: $11.95 monthly.
Video-On-Demand: No
Internet Service
Operational: No.
Telephone Service
None
Miles of Plant: 12.0 (coaxial); None (fiber optic).
Ownership: Almega Cable (MSO).

PLAINVIEW—Suddenlink Communications, 2301 W 5th St, PO Box 428, Plainview, TX 79073. Phone: 806-293-2551. Fax: 806-293-1152. Web Site: http://www.suddenlink.com. Also serves Hale County. ICA: TX0076.
TV Market Ranking: Below 100 (Hale County (portions)); Outside TV Markets (Hale County (portions), PLAINVIEW). Franchise award date: N.A. Franchise expiration date: N.A. Began: March 15, 1965.
Channel capacity: 116 (operating 2-way). Channels available but not in use: N.A.
Basic Service
Subscribers: 8,174.
Programming (received off-air): KAMC (ABC) Lubbock; KAMR-TV (NBC) Amarillo; KCBD (NBC) Lubbock; KJTV-TV (FOX) Lubbock; KLBK-TV (CBS) Lubbock; KPTB-DT (IND) Lubbock; KTXT-TV (PBS) Lubbock; KVII-TV (ABC, CW) Amarillo; allband FM.
Programming (via satellite): C-SPAN; Hallmark Channel; Telemundo; The Weather Channel; Trinity Broadcasting Network; TV Guide Network; WGN America.
Fee: $36.05 installation; $10.00 monthly.
Expanded Basic Service 1
Subscribers: N.A.
Programming (via satellite): A&E Networks; ABC Family Channel; AMC; Animal Planet; BET Networks; Cartoon Network; CNBC; CNN; Comedy Central; Discovery Channel; Disney Channel; E! Entertainment Television; ESPN; ESPN 2; Food Network; Fox News Channel; Fox Sports Southwest; FX; GalaVision; Great American Country; Headline News; HGTV; History Channel; ION Television; Lifetime; MSNBC; MTV; mun2 television; Nickelodeon; Outdoor Channel; Speed; Spike TV; Syfy; TBS Superstation; The Learning Channel; Travel Channel; Turner Classic Movies; Turner Network TV; TV Land; USA Network; Versus; VH1.
Digital Basic Service
Subscribers: N.A.
Programming (via satellite): BBC America; Bloomberg Television; Boomerang; Canales N; Discovery Digital Networks; Fox Sports World; G4; Golf Channel; GSN; Independent Film Channel; Lifetime Movie Network; MuchMusic Network; SoapNet; Sundance Channel; Toon Disney; truTV.
Pay Service 1
Pay Units: 2,500.
Programming (via satellite): Cinemax; Encore; HBO (multiplexed); Showtime; Starz; The Movie Channel.
Fee: $35.00 installation.
Digital Pay Service 1
Pay Units: N.A.
Programming (via satellite): Cinemax (multiplexed); Encore; HBO (multiplexed); Showtime (multiplexed); Starz (multiplexed); The Movie Channel (multiplexed).
Fee: $10.00 monthly (each).
Video-On-Demand: No
Pay-Per-View
iN DEMAND; iN DEMAND (delivered digitally); Sports PPV (delivered digitally).
Internet Service
Operational: Yes.
Broadband Service: Suddenlink High Speed Internet.
Fee: $49.95 installation; $24.95 monthly.
Telephone Service
Digital: Operational
Fee: $48.95 monthly
Miles of Plant: 123.0 (coaxial); 16.0 (fiber optic).
Manager: Pete Strom. Chief Technician: Roger Jones.
Ownership: Cequel Communications LLC (MSO).

PLANO—Time Warner Cable. Now served by DALLAS, TX [TX0003]. ICA: TX0833.

PLEAK—Almega Cable, 4001 W Airport Frwy, Ste 530, Bedford, TX 76021. Phone: 817-685-9588. Fax: 817-685-6488. E-mail: helpdesk@almegacable.com. Web Site: http://www.almega.com. Also serves Beasley, Fort Bend County (unincorporated areas), Hungerford & Kendleton. ICA: TX0265.
TV Market Ranking: Below 100 (Beasley, Fort Bend County (unincorporated areas), Hungerford, Kendleton); Outside TV Markets (PLEAK). Franchise award date: N.A. Franchise expiration date: N.A. Began: August 1, 1989.
Channel capacity: 52 (not 2-way capable). Channels available but not in use: N.A.
Basic Service
Subscribers: 112.
Programming (received off-air): KETH-TV (TBN) Houston; KHOU (CBS) Houston; KIAH (CW) Houston; KLTJ (ETV) Galveston; KPRC-TV (NBC) Houston; KRIV (FOX) Houston; KTMD (TMO) Galveston; KTRK-TV (ABC) Houston; KTXH (MNT) Houston; KUBE-TV (IND) Baytown; KUHT (PBS) Houston; KXLN-DT (UNV) Rosenberg; KYAZ (IND) Katy.
Programming (via satellite): A&E Networks; ABC Family Channel; AMC; BET Networks; CNN; Country Music TV; Discovery Channel; Disney Channel; ESPN; Fox Sports Southwest; Lifetime; MTV; Nickelodeon; QVC; Spike TV; TBS Superstation; The Weather Channel; Turner Network TV; USA Network; VH1; WGN America.
Fee: $54.95 installation; $44.05 monthly.
Pay Service 1
Pay Units: N.A.
Programming (via satellite): Cinemax; HBO; Showtime; The Movie Channel.
Fee: $12.95 monthly (each).
Video-On-Demand: No
Internet Service
Operational: No.
Telephone Service
None
Miles of Plant: 85.0 (coaxial); None (fiber optic).
Ownership: Almega Cable (MSO).

PLEASANT VALLEY—Formerly served by CableDirect. No longer in operation. ICA: TX0466.

PLEASANTON—Reach Broadband, 515 E Longview St, Arp, TX 75750. Phone: 800-687-1258. Web Site: http://www.reachbroadband.net. ICA: TX0194.
TV Market Ranking: 45 (PLEASANTON); Outside TV Markets (PLEASANTON). Franchise award date: October 2, 1979. Franchise expiration date: N.A. Began: October 31, 1980.
Channel capacity: N.A. Channels available but not in use: N.A.
Basic Service
Subscribers: 1,981.
Programming (received off-air): KABB (FOX) San Antonio; KENS (CBS) San Antonio; KLRN (PBS) San Antonio; KMOL-LP Victoria; KMYS (CW) Kerrville; KPXL-TV (ION) Uvalde; KSAT-TV (ABC) San Antonio; KVDA (TMO) San Antonio; KWEX-DT (UNV) San Antonio; 15 FMs.
Programming (via satellite): A&E Networks; ABC Family Channel; AMC; CNBC; Country Music TV; C-SPAN; ESPN; Fox Sports Southwest; GalaVision; Headline News; Lifetime; Nickelodeon; QVC; Spike TV; Syfy.
Fee: $29.95 installation; $19.95 monthly.
Expanded Basic Service 1
Subscribers: N.A.
Programming (via satellite): CNN; Discovery Channel; Disney Channel; E! Entertainment Television; MSNBC; MTV; TBS Superstation; Turner Network TV; USA Network; WGN America.
Fee: $18.00 monthly.
Pay Service 1
Pay Units: 61.
Programming (via satellite): Cinemax.
Fee: $11.95 monthly.
Pay Service 2
Pay Units: 225.
Programming (via satellite): HBO.
Fee: $11.95 monthly.
Pay Service 3
Pay Units: 114.
Programming (via satellite): The Movie Channel.
Fee: $11.95 monthly.
Pay Service 4
Pay Units: 219.
Programming (via satellite): Showtime.
Fee: $11.95 monthly.
Video-On-Demand: No
Internet Service
Operational: No.
Telephone Service
None
Miles of Plant: 56.0 (coaxial); None (fiber optic).
Regional Manager: Ronnie Stafford. Office Manager: Jan Gibson.
Ownership: RB3 LLC (MSO).

PLUM GROVE—Formerly served by Carrell Communications. No longer in operation. ICA: TX0437.

PONDER—Formerly served by SouthTel Communications LP. No longer in operation. ICA: TX0512.

PORT ARANSAS—Charter Communications. Now served by ROCKPORT, TX [TX0116]. ICA: TX0835.

PORT ARTHUR—Time Warner Cable. Now served by BEAUMONT, TX [TX0022]. ICA: TX0018.

PORT ISABEL—Time Warner Communications. Now served by PHARR, TX [TX0017]. ICA: TX0197.

PORT LAVACA—Cable One, 501 N Virginia St, Port Lavaca, TX 77979-3019. Phone: 361-552-9621. Fax: 361-552-7074. E-mail: dking@cableone.net. Web Site: http://www.cableone.net. Also serves Calhoun County & Point Comfort. ICA: TX0146.
TV Market Ranking: Below 100 (Calhoun County, Point Comfort, PORT LAVACA). Franchise award date: January 1, 1958. Franchise expiration date: N.A. Began: July 1, 1958.
Channel capacity: 78 (operating 2-way). Channels available but not in use: N.A.
Basic Service
Subscribers: 3,522.
Programming (received off-air): KAVU-TV (ABC) Victoria; KEDT (PBS) Corpus Christi; KVCT (FOX) Victoria; 12 FMs.
Programming (via microwave): KHOU (CBS) Houston; KHTV-LP Los Angeles; KPRC-TV (NBC) Houston; KTRK-TV (ABC) Houston.
Programming (via satellite): A&E Networks; ABC Family Channel; AMC; Animal Planet; BET Networks; Cartoon Network; CNBC; CNN; Comedy Central; Country Music TV; C-SPAN; C-SPAN 2; Discovery Channel; Disney Channel; ESPN; ESPN 2; Food Network; Fox Deportes; Fox News Channel; Fox Sports Southwest; FX; Headline News; HGTV; History Channel; Lifetime; MSNBC; MTV; Nickelodeon; Spike TV; Syfy; TBS Superstation; Telemundo; The Learning Channel; The Weather Channel; Turner Classic Movies; Turner Network TV; TV Guide Network; TV Land; USA Network; VH1.
Fee: $46.00 monthly; $10.00 additional installation.
Digital Basic Service
Subscribers: 1,036.
Programming (via satellite): Bio; Boomerang; Discovery Digital Networks; DMX Music; ESPN Classic Sports; ESPNews; History Channel International; National Geographic Channel; SoapNet; Speed; Toon Disney; truTV.
Digital Pay Service 1
Pay Units: N.A.
Programming (via satellite): Cinemax (multiplexed); Flix; HBO (multiplexed); Showtime (multiplexed); Sundance Channel; The Movie Channel (multiplexed).
Fee: $15.00 monthly (each).
Video-On-Demand: No
Pay-Per-View
Addressable homes: 1,036.
iN DEMAND (delivered digitally); Pleasure (delivered digitally); Ten Clips (delivered digitally); Ten Blox (delivered digitally); Ten Blue (delivered digitally); ESPN (delivered digitally).
Internet Service
Operational: Yes. Began: May 1, 2002.
Subscribers: 720.
Broadband Service: CableONE.net.
Fee: $75.00 installation; $43.00 monthly; $5.00 modem lease.
Telephone Service
Digital: Operational
Fee: $39.95 monthly

Miles of Plant: 82.0 (coaxial); None (fiber optic).
Manager: David King. Technical Operations Manager: Martin Schooley. Office Manager: Jamie Mosmeyer.
Ownership: Cable ONE Inc. (MSO).

PORT O'CONNOR—Time Warner Cable, 4060 S Padre Island Dr, Corpus Christi, TX 78411-4402. Phones: 972-899-7300 (Flower Mound office); 361-698-6259. Fax: 361-857-5038. Web Site: http://www.timewarnercable.com/Texas. ICA: TX0369.
TV Market Ranking: Outside TV Markets (PORT O'CONNOR). Franchise award date: N.A. Franchise expiration date: N.A. Began: December 1, 1972.
Channel capacity: N.A. Channels available but not in use: N.A.
Basic Service
Subscribers: N.A. Included in Corpus Christi
Programming (received off-air): KAVU-TV (ABC) Victoria; KHOU (CBS) Houston; KPRC-TV (NBC) Houston; KTRK-TV (ABC) Houston; KTXH (MNT) Houston; KUHT (PBS) Houston; KVCT (FOX) Victoria; allband FM.
Programming (via satellite): QVC; WGN America.
Fee: $34.99 installation; $16.39 monthly; $18.81 additional installation.
Expanded Basic Service 1
Subscribers: N.A.
Programming (via satellite): A&E Networks; AMC; Animal Planet; BET Networks; Bravo; Cartoon Network; CNBC; CNN; Comedy Central; Country Music TV; C-SPAN; C-SPAN 2; Discovery Channel; Disney Channel; E! Entertainment Television; ESPN; ESPN 2; Eternal Word TV Network; Food Network; Fox News Channel; Fox Sports Southwest; FX; GalaVision; Golf Channel; Headline News; HGTV; History Channel; Lifetime; Lifetime Movie Network; MTV; National Geographic Channel; Nickelodeon; Speed; Spike TV; TBS Superstation; The Learning Channel; The Weather Channel; Travel Channel; Trinity Broadcasting Network; truTV; Turner Classic Movies; Turner Network TV; USA Network; Versus; VH1.
Fee: $28.60 monthly.
Pay Service 1
Pay Units: 193.
Programming (via satellite): Encore; HBO; Showtime; Starz.
Fee: $3.75 monthly (Encore), $12.95 monthly (HBO, Showtime or Starz).
Internet Service
Operational: Yes.
Broadband Service: RoadRunner.
Telephone Service
Digital: Operational
Miles of Plant: 22.0 (coaxial); None (fiber optic).
President: Connie Wharton. Vice President & General Manager: Roy Rudd. Engineering Director: Charlotte Strong. Public Affairs Manager: Vicki Triplett.
Ownership: Time Warner Cable (MSO).; Advance/Newhouse Partnership (MSO).

PORTER—Suddenlink Communications, 12444 Powerscourt Dr, Saint Louis, MO 63131-3660. Phones: 800-999-6845 (Customer service); 314-965-2020. Fax: 903-561-5485. Web Site: http://www.suddenlink.com. Also serves Montgomery County (portions). ICA: TX0312.
TV Market Ranking: 15 (Montgomery County (portions), PORTER). Franchise award date: N.A. Franchise expiration date: N.A. Began: N.A.
Channel capacity: N.A. Channels available but not in use: N.A.
Basic Service
Subscribers: 630.
Programming (received off-air): KETH-TV (TBN) Houston; KFTH-DT (TEL) Alvin; KHOU (CBS) Houston; KIAH (CW) Houston; KLTJ (ETV) Galveston; KPRC-TV (NBC) Houston; KPXB-TV (ION) Conroe; KRIV (FOX) Houston; KTBU (IND) Conroe; KTMD (TMO) Galveston; KTRK-TV (ABC) Houston; KTXH (MNT) Houston; KUBE-TV (IND) Baytown; KUHT (PBS) Houston; KXLN-DT (UNV) Rosenberg; KYAZ (IND) Katy; KZJL (IND) Houston.
Programming (via satellite): WGN America.
Fee: $39.95 installation; $41.95 monthly.
Expanded Basic Service 1
Subscribers: N.A.
Programming (via satellite): A&E Networks; ABC Family Channel; AMC; Animal Planet; BET Networks; Bravo; Cartoon Network; CNBC; CNN; Comedy Central; Country Music TV; C-SPAN; C-SPAN 2; Discovery Channel; Disney Channel; E! Entertainment Television; ESPN; ESPN 2; ESPN Classic Sports; Eternal Word TV Network; Food Network; Fox News Channel; Fox Soccer; Fox Sports Southwest; FX; Golf Channel; Hallmark Channel; Headline News; HGTV; History Channel; Jewelry Television; Lifetime; Lifetime Movie Network; MSNBC; MTV; Nickelodeon; Outdoor Channel; Oxygen; Speed; Spike TV; Syfy; TBS Superstation; The Learning Channel; The Weather Channel; Travel Channel; truTV; Turner Classic Movies; Turner Network TV; TV Guide Network; TV Land; USA Network; VH1; WE tv.
Digital Basic Service
Subscribers: N.A.
Programming (via satellite): BBC America; Bio; Bloomberg Television; cloo; CMT Pure Country; C-SPAN 3; Discovery Health Channel; Discovery Home Channel; Discovery Kids Channel; DIY Network; ESPN 2 HD; ESPN HD; ESPN U; ESPNews; Food Network HD; Fox College Sports Atlantic; Fox College Sports Central; Fox College Sports Pacific; Fox Movie Channel; Fuel TV; Fuse; G4; GSN; HD Theater; HDNet; HDNet Movies; HGTV HD; History Channel International; ID Investigation Discovery; Independent Film Channel; Lifetime Real Women; LOGO; Military Channel; MTV Hits; MTV Jams; MTV2; Music Choice; National Geographic Channel; Nick Jr.; Nick Too; Nick-Toons TV; Science; SoapNet; Style Network; Sundance Channel; TeenNick; Tennis Channel; Toon Disney; Tr3s; Turner Network TV HD; Versus; VH1 Classic; VH1 Soul.
Digital Pay Service 1
Pay Units: N.A.
Programming (via satellite): Cinemax (multiplexed); Encore (multiplexed); Flix; HBO (multiplexed); HBO HD; Showtime (multiplexed); Showtime HD; Starz (multiplexed); The Movie Channel (multiplexed).
Video-On-Demand: No
Pay-Per-View
iN DEMAND (delivered digitally); Playboy TV (delivered digitally); Club Jenna (delivered digitally); Spice: Xcess (delivered digitally).
Internet Service
Operational: Yes.
Broadband Service: Suddenlink High Speed Internet.
Telephone Service
Digital: Operational
Miles of Plant: 54.0 (coaxial); None (fiber optic).
Regional Manager: Todd Cruthird.
Ownership: Cequel Communications LLC (MSO).

PORTLAND—Charter Communications. Now served by ROCKPORT, TX [TX0116]. ICA: TX0136.

POST—Suddenlink Communications, 12444 Powerscourt Dr, Saint Louis, MO 63131-3660. Phones: 800-999-6845; 314-965-2020. Fax: 903-561-5485. Web Site: http://www.suddenlink.com. ICA: TX0241.
TV Market Ranking: Outside TV Markets (POST). Franchise award date: August 3, 1964. Franchise expiration date: N.A. Began: November 10, 1968.
Channel capacity: N.A. Channels available but not in use: N.A.
Basic Service
Subscribers: 926.
Programming (received off-air): KAMC (ABC) Lubbock; KCBD (NBC) Lubbock; KJTV-TV (FOX) Lubbock; KLBK-TV (CBS) Lubbock; KPTB-DT (IND) Lubbock; KTXT-TV (PBS) Lubbock; allband FM.
Programming (via satellite): A&E Networks; ABC Family Channel; AMC; AmericanLife TV Network; Animal Planet; Cartoon Network; CNN; Country Music TV; Discovery Channel; Disney Channel; E! Entertainment Television; ESPN; Fox News Channel; Fox Sports Southwest; History Channel; Lifetime; Nickelodeon; QVC; Spike TV; Syfy; TBS Superstation; The Learning Channel; The Weather Channel; Turner Network TV; TV Land; USA Network; WGN America.
Programming (via translator): KVDA (TMO) San Antonio.
Fee: $39.95 installation; $19.95 monthly.
Pay Service 1
Pay Units: 79.
Programming (via satellite): Cinemax.
Fee: $9.95 monthly.
Pay Service 2
Pay Units: 62.
Programming (via satellite): Showtime.
Fee: $9.95 monthly.
Pay Service 3
Pay Units: 171.
Programming (via satellite): HBO.
Fee: $9.95 monthly.
Video-On-Demand: No
Internet Service
Operational: Yes. Began: November 12, 2003.
Broadband Service: Suddenlink High Speed Internet.
Fee: $45.95 installation; $29.95 monthly.
Telephone Service
Digital: Operational
Fee: $44.95 monthly
Miles of Plant: 23.0 (coaxial); None (fiber optic).
Regional Manager: Todd Cruthird. Regional Marketing Manager: Beverly Gambell.
Ownership: Cequel Communications LLC (MSO).

POTEET—Alliance Communications, 6125 Paluxy Dr, Tyler, TX 75703. Phones: 800-842-8160; 501-679-6619. Fax: 501-679-5694. Web Site: http://www.alliancecable.com. Also serves Atascosa County & Jourdanton. ICA: TX0238.
TV Market Ranking: 45 (Atascosa County (portions), Jourdanton, POTEET); Outside TV Markets (Atascosa County (portions)). Franchise award date: N.A. Franchise expiration date: December 31, 2006. Began: April 12, 1982.
Channel capacity: 63 (not 2-way capable). Channels available but not in use: N.A.
Basic Service
Subscribers: 295.
Programming (received off-air): KABB (FOX) San Antonio; KENS (CBS) San Antonio; KLRN (PBS) San Antonio; KMYS (CW) Kerrville; KPXL-TV (ION) Uvalde; KSAT-TV (ABC) San Antonio; KVDA (TMO) San Antonio; KWEX-DT (UNV) San Antonio; WOAI-TV (NBC) San Antonio.
Programming (via satellite): Turner Network TV.
Fee: $50.51 installation; $40.99 monthly; $18.81 additional installation.
Pay Service 1
Pay Units: N.A.
Programming (via satellite): Encore; HBO; Showtime; The Movie Channel.
Fee: $2.75 monthly (Encore), $12.95 monthly (HBO, TMC or Showtime).
Internet Service
Operational: No.
Telephone Service
None
Miles of Plant: 33.0 (coaxial); None (fiber optic).
Vice President & General Manager: John Brinker. Vice President, Programming: Julie Newman.
Ownership: Buford Media Group LLC (MSO).

POTOSI—Formerly served by Jayroc Cablevision. No longer in operation. ICA: TX0837.

POTTSBORO—TV Cable of Grayson County, 501 Hwy 120 N, Ste 6, PO Box 2084, Pottsboro, TX 75076. Phone: 903-786-7477. E-mail: tvcable@graysoncable.com. Web Site: http://www.graysoncable.com. ICA: TX0502.
TV Market Ranking: Below 100 (POTTSBORO). Franchise award date: N.A. Franchise expiration date: N.A. Began: June 1, 1983.
Channel capacity: 42 (not 2-way capable). Channels available but not in use: N.A.
Basic Service
Subscribers: 261.
Programming (received off-air): KDAF (CW, IND) Dallas; KDFI (MNT) Dallas; KERA-TV (PBS) Dallas; KTEN (ABC, CW, NBC) Ada; KTVT (CBS) Fort Worth; KTXA (IND) Fort Worth; KXAS-TV (NBC) Fort Worth; KXII (CBS, FOX, MNT) Sherman; KXTX-TV (TMO) Dallas; WFAA (ABC) Dallas.
Programming (via satellite): ABC Family Channel; CNN; Country Music TV; Discovery Channel; Disney Channel; ESPN; MTV; Nickelodeon; TBS Superstation; Turner Network TV; WGN America.
Fee: $35.00 installation; $17.95 monthly; $20.00 additional installation.
Pay Service 1
Pay Units: 6.
Programming (via satellite): HBO.
Fee: $11.95 monthly.
Pay Service 2
Pay Units: N.A.
Programming (via satellite): Encore; Starz.
Fee: $9.50 monthly.
Internet Service
Operational: No.
Telephone Service
None
Miles of Plant: 9.0 (coaxial); None (fiber optic).
Manager: Chuck Davis.
Ownership: Chuck Davis (MSO).

POWDERLY—Almega Cable, 4001 W Airport Frwy, Ste 530, Bedford, TX 76021. Phone: 817-685-9588. Fax: 817-685-6488. E-mail: helpdesk@almegacable.com. Web Site: http://www.almega.com. Also serves Lamar County (portions). ICA: TX0361.

TV Market Ranking: Outside TV Markets (Lamar County (portions), POWDERLY). Franchise award date: N.A. Franchise expiration date: N.A. Began: October 1, 1988.

Channel capacity: N.A. Channels available but not in use: N.A.

Basic Service

Subscribers: 198.

Programming (received off-air): KOED-TV (PBS) Tulsa; KTEN (ABC, CW, NBC) Ada; KXII (CBS, FOX, MNT) Sherman.

Programming (via satellite): A&E Networks; Cartoon Network; CNN; Country Music TV; Discovery Channel; Disney Channel; ESPN; Headline News; Spike TV; TBS Superstation; Trinity Broadcasting Network; Turner Classic Movies; Turner Network TV; USA Network; WGN America.

Fee: $54.95 installation; $44.05 monthly.

Pay Service 1

Pay Units: 11.

Programming (via satellite): Cinemax.

Fee: $12.95 monthly.

Pay Service 2

Pay Units: 57.

Programming (via satellite): HBO.

Fee: $12.95 monthly.

Pay Service 3

Pay Units: 44.

Programming (via satellite): Showtime.

Fee: $12.95 monthly.

Video-On-Demand: No

Internet Service

Operational: No.

Telephone Service

None

Miles of Plant: 58.0 (coaxial); None (fiber optic).

Ownership: Almega Cable (MSO).

PREMONT—Time Warner Cable. Now served by ALICE, TX [TX0102]. ICA: TX0352.

PRESIDIO—Presidio TV Cable, PO Box 1377, Alpine, TX 79831-1377. Phones: 800-446-5661; 432-837-2300. Fax: 432-837-5423. E-mail: mtnzone@sbcglobal.net. Web Site: http://www.mountainzonetv.net. ICA: TX0432.

TV Market Ranking: Outside TV Markets (PRESIDIO). Franchise award date: April 2, 1982. Franchise expiration date: April 2, 2007. Began: May 1, 1973.

Channel capacity: N.A. Channels available but not in use: N.A.

Basic Service

Subscribers: 430.

Programming (via satellite): A&E Networks; Animal Planet; Azteca America; Cartoon Network; CNN; Comedy Central; C-SPAN; Discovery Channel; Disney Channel; ESPN; ESPN 2; Eternal Word TV Network; Fox News Channel; Fox Sports Southwest; GalaVision; Great American Country; Headline News; HGTV; History Channel; KABB (FOX) San Antonio; KLRN (PBS) San Antonio; KMID (ABC) Midland; KMLM-DT (IND) Odessa; KOSA-TV (CBS, MNT) Odessa; KTSM-TV (NBC) El Paso; KVIA-TV (ABC, CW) El Paso; KWES-TV (NBC) Odessa; Lifetime; MTV; NFL Network; Nickelodeon; Syfy; TBS Superstation; Telefutura; Telemundo; The Learning Channel; The Weather Channel; Turner Classic Movies; Turner Network TV; TV Land; Univision Studios; USA Network; various Mexican stations; VH1; WGN America.

Fee: $25.00 installation; $42.00 monthly.

Pay Service 1

Pay Units: 98.

Programming (via satellite): Cinemax; HBO; Showtime.

Fee: $10.00 installation.

Video-On-Demand: No

Internet Service

Operational: Yes. Began: June 1, 2004.

Broadband Service: In-house.

Fee: $50.00 installation; $25.50 monthly.

Telephone Service

None

Miles of Plant: 25.0 (coaxial); None (fiber optic).

Manager: Steve Neu. Office Manager: Lawrence Neu.

Ownership: Mountain Zone TV Systems (MSO).

PRESTON PENINSULA—Allegiance Communications, 707 W Saratoga St, Shawnee, OK 74804. Phones: 405-275-6923; 405-395-1131. Web Site: http://www.allegiance.tv. ICA: TX0838.

TV Market Ranking: Below 100 (PRESTON PENINSULA). Franchise award date: January 17, 1989. Franchise expiration date: N.A. Began: August 1, 1983.

Channel capacity: N.A. Channels available but not in use: N.A.

Basic Service

Subscribers: N.A.

Programming (received off-air): KDAF (CW, IND) Dallas; KDFI (MNT) Dallas; KDFW-DT (FOX) Dallas; KERA-TV (PBS) Dallas; KTEN (ABC, CW, NBC) Ada; KTVT (CBS) Fort Worth; KTXA (IND) Fort Worth; KXAS-TV (NBC) Fort Worth; KXII (CBS, FOX, MNT) Sherman; KXTX-TV (TMO) Dallas; WFAA (ABC) Dallas.

Programming (via satellite): A&E Networks; ABC Family Channel; AMC; Animal Planet; Bravo; Cartoon Network; CNBC; CNN; Comedy Central; Country Music TV; C-SPAN; Discovery Channel; Disney Channel; E! Entertainment Television; ESPN; ESPN 2; Food Network; Fox News Channel; Fox Sports Southwest; FX; GSN; Hallmark Channel; Headline News; HGTV; History Channel; Lifetime; MSNBC; MTV; National Geographic Channel; Nickelodeon; Oxygen; QVC; SoapNet; Spike TV; Syfy; TBS Superstation; The Learning Channel; The Weather Channel; Travel Channel; Trinity Broadcasting Network; truTV; Turner Network TV; TV Land; USA Network; VH1.

Fee: $25.00 installation; $21.95 monthly.

Digital Basic Service

Subscribers: N.A.

Programming (via satellite): AmericanLife TV Network; BBC America; BET Networks; Bio; Bloomberg Television; Bravo; Discovery Fit & Health; DMX Music; Fox Movie Channel; Fuse; G4; GAS; Golf Channel; GSN; Halogen Network; HGTV; History Channel International; Independent Film Channel; Lifetime Movie Network; MTV Networks Digital Suite; Nick Jr.; Outdoor Channel; ShopNBC; Speed; Style Network; Toon Disney; Trinity Broadcasting Network; Turner Classic Movies; Versus; WE tv.

Pay Service 1

Pay Units: N.A.

Programming (via satellite): Cinemax; HBO; Showtime.

Fee: $9.00 monthly (each).

Digital Pay Service 1

Pay Units: N.A.

Programming (via satellite): Cinemax (multiplexed); Encore (multiplexed); Flix; HBO (multiplexed); Showtime (multiplexed); Starz (multiplexed); The Movie Channel (multiplexed).

Video-On-Demand: No

Pay-Per-View

Hot Choice (delivered digitally); Playboy TV (delivered digitally); Fresh (delivered digitally); Shorteez (delivered digitally); iN DEMAND (delivered digitally).

Internet Service

Operational: No.

Telephone Service

None

Miles of Plant: 90.0 (coaxial); 14.0 (fiber optic).

Chief Executive Officer: Bill Haggarty. Regional Vice President: Andrew Dearth. Vice President, Marketing: Tracy Bass.

Ownership: Allegiance Communications (MSO).

PRICE—Formerly served by Almega Cable. No longer in operation. ICA: TX0648.

PROGRESO—Formerly served by CableDirect. No longer in operation. ICA: TX0630.

QUANAH—Suddenlink Communications, 227 S Main, Quanah, TX 79252. Phones: 800-999-6845 (Customer service); 314-965-2020. Web Site: http://www.suddenlink.com. ICA: TX0839.

TV Market Ranking: Outside TV Markets (QUANAH). Franchise award date: N.A. Franchise expiration date: N.A. Began: April 1, 1963.

Channel capacity: N.A. Channels available but not in use: N.A.

Basic Service

Subscribers: 1,015.

Programming (received off-air): KAMR-TV (NBC) Amarillo; KAUZ-TV (CBS, CW) Wichita Falls; KFDA-TV (CBS) Amarillo; KFDX-TV (NBC) Wichita Falls; KJTL (FOX) Wichita Falls; KSWO-TV (ABC, TMO) Lawton; KWET (PBS) Cheyenne.

Programming (via satellite): A&E Networks; ABC Family Channel; AMC; AmericanLife TV Network; Animal Planet; CNN; Country Music TV; C-SPAN; Discovery Channel; Disney Channel; E! Entertainment Television; ESPN; Fox Sports Southwest; Hallmark Channel; Headline News; Lifetime; Nickelodeon; QVC; Spike TV; Syfy; TBS Superstation; The Learning Channel; The Weather Channel; Turner Network TV; TV Land; USA Network; WGN America.

Fee: $39.95 installation; $19.95 monthly.

Pay Service 1

Pay Units: 81.

Programming (via satellite): The Movie Channel.

Fee: $7.95 monthly.

Pay Service 2

Pay Units: 64.

Programming (via satellite): Showtime.

Fee: $9.95 monthly.

Pay Service 3

Pay Units: 113.

Programming (via satellite): HBO.

Fee: $10.95 monthly.

Video-On-Demand: No

Internet Service

Operational: Yes. Began: December 29, 2003.

Broadband Service: Suddenlink High Speed Internet.

Fee: $49.95 installation; $38.95 monthly.

Telephone Service

None

Miles of Plant: 33.0 (coaxial); None (fiber optic).

Regional Manager: Todd Cruthird. Plant Manager: Ron Johnson. Regional Marketing Manager: Beverly Gambell.

Ownership: Cequel Communications LLC (MSO).

QUEMADO—Time Warner Cable, 1313 W Carlton Rd, Laredo, TX 78041. Phones: 972-899-7300 (Flower Mound office); 956-721-0607. Fax: 956-721-0612. Web Site: http://www.timewarnercable.com/Texas. ICA: TX1008.

TV Market Ranking: Below 100 (QUEMADO).

Channel capacity: N.A. Channels available but not in use: N.A.

Basic Service

Subscribers: N.A. Included in Del Rio

Programming (received off-air): KENS (CBS) San Antonio; KLRN (PBS) San Antonio; KSAT-TV (ABC) San Antonio; KWEX-DT (UNV) San Antonio; WOAI-TV (NBC) San Antonio.

Programming (via satellite): A&E Networks; AMC; Animal Planet; Bravo; Cartoon Network; CNN; Discovery Channel; ESPN; ESPN 2; Food Network; Fox Sports Southwest; Golf Channel; Great American Country; Headline News; HGTV; History Channel; Lifetime; MSNBC; Nickelodeon; Oxygen; Spike TV; Syfy; TBS Superstation; The Learning Channel; The Weather Channel; Turner Network TV; TV Land; USA Network; various Mexican stations; WE tv.

Fee: $50.51 installation; $27.45 monthly; $18.81 additional installation.

Pay Service 1

Pay Units: N.A.

Programming (via satellite): HBO.

Fee: $12.90 monthly.

Internet Service

Operational: No.

Telephone Service

None

President: Connie Wharton. Vice President & General Manager: Michael Carrosquiola. Operations Director: Marco Reyes. Technical Operations Manager: Eduardo Ruiz. Public Affairs Manager: Celinda Gonzalez.

Ownership: Time Warner Cable (MSO).; Advance/Newhouse Partnership (MSO).

QUINLAN—Zoom Media, PO Box 2126, Flint, TX 75762. Phone: 855-261-5304. Web Site: http://www.zoommediallc.com. Also serves Caddo Mills, East Tawakoni, Hunt County (portions), Lone Oak, Rains County (portions) & West Tawakoni. ICA: TX0793.

TV Market Ranking: 12 (Hunt County (portions)); Below 100 (Caddo Mills, East Tawakoni, Lone Oak, QUINLAN, Rains County (portions), West Tawakoni, Hunt County (portions)). Franchise award date: N.A. Franchise expiration date: N.A. Began: October 1, 1982.

Channel capacity: 54 (not 2-way capable). Channels available but not in use: N.A.

Basic Service

Subscribers: 390.

Programming (received off-air): KDAF (CW, IND) Dallas; KDFI (MNT) Dallas; KDFW-DT (FOX) Dallas; KDTN (ETV) Denton; KDTX-TV (TBN) Dallas; KERA-TV (PBS) Dallas; KTAQ (IND) Greenville; KTVT (CBS) Fort Worth; KTXA (IND) Fort Worth; KXAS-TV (NBC) Fort Worth; KXTX-TV (TMO) Dallas; WFAA (ABC) Dallas.

Fee: $54.95 installation; $20.95 monthly.

Expanded Basic Service 1
Subscribers: 300.
Programming (received off-air): KPXD-TV (ION) Arlington; KSTR-DT (TEL) Irving; KUVN-DT (UNV) Garland.
Programming (via satellite): A&E Networks; ABC Family Channel; Cartoon Network; CNBC; CNN; Comedy Central; C-SPAN; Discovery Channel; Disney Channel; E! Entertainment Television; ESPN; ESPN 2; Fox News Channel; Fox Sports Southwest; FX; Great American Country; Headline News; HGTV; Lifetime; MTV; National Geographic Channel; Nickelodeon; Outdoor Channel; QVC; Speed; Spike TV; Syfy; TBS Superstation; The Learning Channel; The Weather Channel; Travel Channel; Turner Classic Movies; Turner Network TV; USA Network.
Fee: $23.10 monthly.
Digital Basic Service
Subscribers: 34.
Video-On-Demand: No
Internet Service
Operational: No.
Telephone Service
None
Miles of Plant: 201.0 (coaxial); None (fiber optic).
Chief Executive Officer: Steve Houston.
Ownership: Zoom Media LLC (MSO).

QUITAQUE—Formerly served by Almega Cable. No longer in operation. ICA: TX0840.

RALLS—Reach Broadband, 515 E Longview St, Arp, TX 75750. Phone: 800-687-1258. Web Site: http://www.reachbroadband.net. ICA: TX0377.
TV Market Ranking: Outside TV Markets (RALLS). Franchise award date: October 14, 1977. Franchise expiration date: N.A. Began: October 1, 1978.
Channel capacity: 61 (not 2-way capable). Channels available but not in use: N.A.
Basic Service
Subscribers: 236.
Programming (received off-air): KAMC (ABC) Lubbock; KCBD (NBC) Lubbock; KJTV-TV (FOX) Lubbock; KLBK-TV (CBS) Lubbock; KPTB-DT (IND) Lubbock; KTXT-TV (PBS) Lubbock.
Programming (via satellite): ABC Family Channel; AMC; CNN; Country Music TV; Discovery Channel; Disney Channel; E! Entertainment Television; ESPN; Fox Sports Southwest; History Channel; Lifetime; Nickelodeon; QVC; Spike TV; Syfy; TBS Superstation; The Learning Channel; The Weather Channel; Trinity Broadcasting Network; Turner Network TV; TV Land; USA Network; WGN America.
Programming (via translator): KVDA (TMO) San Antonio.
Fee: $29.95 installation; $38.00 monthly.
Pay Service 1
Pay Units: 28.
Programming (via satellite): Cinemax.
Fee: $9.95 monthly.
Pay Service 2
Pay Units: 63.
Programming (via satellite): HBO.
Fee: $9.95 monthly.
Video-On-Demand: No
Internet Service
Operational: No.
Telephone Service
None
Miles of Plant: 13.0 (coaxial); None (fiber optic).
Regional Manager: Ronnie Stafford. Office Manager: Jan Gibson.
Ownership: RB3 LLC (MSO).

RANKIN—US Cable of Coastal Texas LP, 611 W Ave A, Seminole, TX 79360. Phones: 432-758-9221; 800-996-8788. Fax: 432-758-3379. Web Site: http://www.uscable.com. ICA: TX1026.
TV Market Ranking: Outside TV Markets (RANKIN).
Channel capacity: N.A. Channels available but not in use: N.A.
Basic Service
Subscribers: 127.
Programming (received off-air): KMID (ABC) Midland; KMLM-DT (IND) Odessa; KOSA-TV (CBS, MNT) Odessa; KPBT-TV (PBS) Odessa; KPEJ-TV (FOX) Odessa; KUPB (UNV) Midland; KWES-TV (NBC) Odessa.
Programming (via satellite): Animal Planet; C-SPAN; Home Shopping Network; Lifetime; TBS Superstation; Trinity Broadcasting Network; WGN America.
Fee: $39.96 installation; $20.17 monthly.
Expanded Basic Service 1
Subscribers: N.A.
Programming (via satellite): A&E Networks; ABC Family Channel; American Movie Classics; Cartoon Network; CNN; Country Music TV; Discovery Channel; Discovery Fit & Health; Disney Channel; ESPN; ESPN 2; Food Network; Fox News Channel; Fox Sports Net; Hallmark Channel; HGTV; History Channel; MoviePlex; MTV; National Geographic Channel; Nick At Nite; Nickelodeon; Spike TV; Syfy; Telefutura; The Learning Channel; The Weather Channel; Turner Network TV; USA Network; VH1.
Fee: $28.35 monthly.
Digital Basic Service
Subscribers: N.A.
Programming (via satellite): BBC America; Bio; Bloomberg Television; Bravo; Centric; cloo; CMT Pure Country; Current; Discovery Health Channel; Discovery Kids Channel; Disney XD; DMX Music; Encore (multiplexed); ESPN Classic Sports; ESPNews; Fox College Sports Atlantic; Fox College Sports Central; Fox College Sports Pacific; Fox Movie Channel; Fox Soccer; Fuse; G4; Golf Channel; Great American Country; GSN; Halogen Network; HGTV; History Channel International; ID Investigation Discovery; Independent Film Channel; Lifetime Movie Network; Military Channel; MTV Hits; MTV2; Nick Jr.; Outdoor Channel; Planet Green; Science; Speed; Style Network; TeenNick; The Word Network; Turner Classic Movies; Versus; VH1 Classic; VH1 Soul; WE tv.
Fee: $20.90 monthly.
Pay Service 1
Pay Units: N.A.
Programming (via satellite): Cinemax; HBO.
Fee: $13.95 monthly (each).
Digital Pay Service 1
Pay Units: N.A.
Programming (via satellite): Cinemax (multiplexed); HBO (multiplexed); Showtime (multiplexed); Starz (multiplexed); The Movie Channel (multiplexed).
Fee: $9.95 monthly (Starz), $12.95 monthly (HBO, Cinemax, Showtime or TMC).
Video-On-Demand: No
Pay-Per-View
Event Entertainment (delivered digitally); Movies (delivered digitally); Playboy TV (delivered digitally); Fresh (delivered digitally).
Internet Service
Operational: Yes.
Telephone Service
None
Regional Manager: Daryl Koedyker.
Ownership: US Cable Corp. (MSO).

RAYMONDVILLE—Time Warner Communications. Now served by PHARR, TX [TX0017]. ICA: TX0173.

RAYWOOD—Formerly served by Cebridge Connections. No longer in operation. ICA: TX0340.

REALITOS—Formerly served by National Cable Inc. No longer in operation. ICA: TX0841.

REDWATER—Almega Cable, 4001 W Airport Frwy, Ste 530, Bedford, TX 76021. Phone: 817-685-9588. Fax: 817-685-6488. E-mail: helpdesk@almegacable.com. Web Site: http://www.almega.com. Also serves Bowie County (portions), Buchanan & Leary. ICA: TX0436.
TV Market Ranking: 58 (Bowie County (portions), Buchanan, Leary, REDWATER). Franchise award date: N.A. Franchise expiration date: N.A. Began: May 1, 1989.
Channel capacity: 54 (not 2-way capable). Channels available but not in use: N.A.
Basic Service
Subscribers: 489.
Programming (received off-air): KLTS-TV (PBS) Shreveport; KMSS-TV (FOX) Shreveport; KSHV-TV (MNT) Shreveport; KSLA (CBS) Shreveport; KTAL-TV (NBC) Texarkana; KTBS-TV (ABC) Shreveport.
Programming (via satellite): A&E Networks; CNN; Country Music TV; Discovery Channel; Disney Channel; ESPN; Headline News; History Channel; Lifetime; Nickelodeon; TBS Superstation; The Weather Channel; Trinity Broadcasting Network; Turner Network TV; USA Network; WGN America.
Fee: $54.95 installation; $44.05 monthly.
Pay Service 1
Pay Units: 184.
Programming (via satellite): HBO.
Fee: $12.95 monthly.
Pay Service 2
Pay Units: 17.
Programming (via satellite): Cinemax.
Fee: $12.95 monthly.
Pay Service 3
Pay Units: 67.
Programming (via satellite): Showtime.
Fee: $12.95 monthly.
Video-On-Demand: No
Internet Service
Operational: No.
Telephone Service
None
Miles of Plant: 93.0 (coaxial); None (fiber optic).
Ownership: Almega Cable (MSO).

REFUGIO—Time Warner Cable. Now served by MATHIS, TX [TX0216]. ICA: TX0214.

REKLAW—Formerly served by Almega Cable. No longer in operation. ICA: TX0698.

RENO (Parker County)—Formerly served by Almega County. No longer in operation. ICA: TX0261.

RICARDO—Formerly served by Riviera Cable TV. No longer in operation. ICA: TX0664.

RICHLAND SPRINGS—Formerly served by Almega Cable. No longer in operation. ICA: TX0632.

RIESEL—Formerly served by Cabletex Systems Inc. No longer in operation. ICA: TX0556.

RIO GRANDE CITY—Time Warner Communications. Now served by PHARR, TX [TX0017]. ICA: TX0181.

RIO VISTA—Formerly served by National Cable Inc. No longer in operation. ICA: TX0535.

RISING STAR—Formerly served by Brownwood TV Cable Service Inc. No longer in operation. ICA: TX0354.

RIVER OAKS (Tarrant County)—Charter Communications. Now served by FORT WORTH, TX [TX0008]. ICA: TX0884.

RIVERSIDE—Formerly served by Almega Cable. No longer in operation. ICA: TX0527.

RIVIERA—Formerly served by Riviera Cable TV. No longer in operation. ICA: TX0657.

ROARING SPRINGS (town)—Formerly served by Almega Cable. No longer in operation. ICA: TX0960.

ROBERT LEE—CMA Cablevision, 1510 N 1st St, PO Box 549, Merkel, TX 79536-0549. Phones: 800-588-4750; 325-928-4750. Fax: 325-928-3452. Web Site: http://www.cmaaccess.com. Also serves Bronte & Tom Green County (portions). ICA: TX0327.
TV Market Ranking: Below 100 (Bronte, ROBERT LEE, Tom Green County (portions)). Franchise award date: February 23, 1979. Franchise expiration date: N.A. Began: August 1, 1980.
Channel capacity: 40 (not 2-way capable). Channels available but not in use: N.A.
Basic Service
Subscribers: 385.
Programming (received off-air): KIDY (FOX) San Angelo; KLST (CBS) San Angelo; KSAN-TV (NBC) San Angelo; KTAB-TV (CBS) Abilene; KTXS-TV (ABC, CW, TMO) Sweetwater; allband FM.
Programming (via satellite): Animal Planet; ESPN 2; Fox News Channel; Fox Sports South; FX; Headline News; ION Television; Nickelodeon; QVC; TBS Superstation; The Weather Channel; Trinity Broadcasting Network; Turner Classic Movies; WGN America.
Fee: $39.95 installation; $19.95 monthly; $9.95 additional installation.
Expanded Basic Service 1
Subscribers: N.A.
Programming (via satellite): A&E Networks; ABC Family Channel; AMC; Cartoon Network; CNN; Country Music TV; Discovery Channel; ESPN; HGTV; History Channel; Lifetime; Spike TV; The Learning Channel; Turner Network TV; TV Land; USA Network.
Fee: $21.00 monthly.
Pay Service 1
Pay Units: 107.
Programming (via satellite): HBO.
Fee: $14.95 installation; $13.95 monthly.
Video-On-Demand: No
Internet Service
Operational: No.
Telephone Service
None
Miles of Plant: 41.0 (coaxial); None (fiber optic).

General Manager: Jerry Smith. Chief Technician: Joe Clark. Marketing Director: Julie Ferguson.
Ownership: Cable Management Assoc. (MSO).

ROBY—Formerly served by Almega Cable. No longer in operation. ICA: TX0844.

ROCHESTER—Formerly served by Jayroc Cablevision. No longer in operation. ICA: TX0845.

ROCKDALE—Suddenlink Communications, 12444 Powerscourt Dr, Saint Louis, MO 63131-3660. Phones: 877-423-2743 (Customer service); 314-965-2020. Web Site: http://www.suddenlink.com. ICA: TX0158.
TV Market Ranking: Outside TV Markets (ROCKDALE). Franchise award date: June 8, 1971. Franchise expiration date: N.A. Began: August 1, 1972.
Channel capacity: 58 (operating 2-way). Channels available but not in use: N.A.
Basic Service
Subscribers: 1,875.
Programming (received off-air): KCEN-TV (NBC, IND) Temple; KEYE-TV (CBS, TMO) Austin; KLRU (PBS) Austin; KTBC (FOX) Austin; KVUE (ABC) Austin; KWKT-TV (FOX, MNT) Waco; KWTX-TV (CBS, CW) Waco; KXAN-TV (NBC) Austin; allband FM.
Programming (via satellite): QVC; Univision Studios.
Fee: $35.00 installation; $19.95 monthly.
Expanded Basic Service 1
Subscribers: N.A.
Programming (via satellite): A&E Networks; ABC Family Channel; AMC; Animal Planet; BET Networks; Cartoon Network; CNBC; CNN; Comedy Central; C-SPAN; Discovery Channel; Disney Channel; E! Entertainment Television; ESPN; ESPN 2; Fox News Channel; Fox Sports Southwest; FX; Great American Country; Headline News; HGTV; History Channel; Lifetime; MSNBC; MTV; National Geographic Channel; Nickelodeon; Outdoor Channel; Shopping Channel; Spike TV; Syfy; TBS Superstation; The Learning Channel; The Weather Channel; Travel Channel; Trinity Broadcasting Network; Turner Classic Movies; Turner Network TV; TV Land; USA Network; VH1.
Fee: $24.00 monthly.
Digital Basic Service
Subscribers: N.A.
Programming (via satellite): BBC America; Bio; Canales N; cloo; Discovery Digital Networks; DMX Music; ESPN Classic Sports; ESPNews; Fox Soccer; Fuse; Golf Channel; GSN; History Channel International; Independent Film Channel; Military History Channel; Speed; Toon Disney; Versus; WE tv.
Fee: $3.99 monthly.
Pay Service 1
Pay Units: 218.
Programming (via satellite): The Movie Channel.
Fee: $5.95 monthly.
Pay Service 2
Pay Units: N.A.
Programming (via satellite): Cinemax.
Fee: $9.95 monthly.
Pay Service 3
Pay Units: 215.
Programming (via satellite): Showtime.
Fee: $9.95 monthly.
Pay Service 4
Pay Units: 212.
Programming (via satellite): HBO.
Fee: $9.95 monthly.
Digital Pay Service 1
Pay Units: N.A.
Programming (via satellite): Cinemax (multiplexed); Encore (multiplexed); HBO (multiplexed); Showtime (multiplexed); Starz (multiplexed); The Movie Channel (multiplexed).
Video-On-Demand: No
Pay-Per-View
iN DEMAND (delivered digitally); Playboy TV (delivered digitally).
Internet Service
Operational: Yes. Began: November 2, 2002.
Broadband Service: Suddenlink High Speed Internet.
Fee: $45.95 installation; $29.95 monthly.
Telephone Service
Digital: Operational
Fee: $44.95 monthly
Miles of Plant: 49.0 (coaxial); None (fiber optic).
Regional Manager: Todd Cruthird. Chief Technician: Walt VanLue. Marketing Director: Beverly Gambell.
Ownership: Cequel Communications LLC (MSO).

ROCKPORT—Cobridge Communications, 9450 Manchester Rd, Ste 200, St. Louis, MO 63119. Phones: 314-227-9500; 800-438-2427. Web Site: http://www.cobridge.net. Also serves Fulton, Holiday Beach, Port Aransas, Portland & Sinton. ICA: TX0116.
TV Market Ranking: Below 100 (Fulton, Port Aransas, Portland, ROCKPORT, Sinton); Outside TV Markets (Holiday Beach). Franchise award date: N.A. Franchise expiration date: N.A. Began: December 1, 1979.
Channel capacity: N.A. Channels available but not in use: N.A.
Basic Service
Subscribers: 9,301.
Programming (received off-air): KCBO-LP (IND) Corpus Christi; KEDT (PBS) Corpus Christi; KIII (ABC) Corpus Christi; KORO (UNV) Corpus Christi; KRIS-TV (CW, NBC) Corpus Christi; KTOV-LP Corpus Christi; KXPX-CA Corpus Christi; KZTV (CBS) Corpus Christi; 5 FMs.
Programming (via satellite): C-SPAN; GalaVision; QVC; The Weather Channel; Trinity Broadcasting Network; TV Guide Network; WGN America.
Fee: $25.00 installation; $17.94 monthly; $25.00 additional installation.
Expanded Basic Service 1
Subscribers: 6,700.
Programming (via satellite): A&E Networks; ABC Family Channel; AMC; Animal Planet; BET Networks; Cartoon Network; CNBC; CNN; Comedy Central; Country Music TV; Discovery Channel; Disney Channel; E! Entertainment Television; ESPN; ESPN 2; ESPN Classic Sports; Food Network; Fox Movie Channel; Fox News Channel; Fox Sports Southwest; FX; Headline News; HGTV; History Channel; Lifetime; MSNBC; MTV; Nickelodeon; Oxygen; SoapNet; Spike TV; Syfy; TBS Superstation; The Learning Channel; Toon Disney; Travel Channel; Turner Classic Movies; Turner Network TV; TV Land; USA Network; Versus; VH1; WE tv.
Fee: $4.57 monthly.
Digital Basic Service
Subscribers: N.A.
Programming (via satellite): BBC America; Bio; Bloomberg Television; Discovery Fit & Health; Discovery Health Channel; Discovery Home Channel; Discovery Kids Channel; Discovery Times Channel; DIY Network; Fox College Sports Atlantic; Fox College Sports Central; Fox College Sports Pacific; Fox Deportes; Fox Soccer; Fuel TV; G4; History Channel International; Independent Film Channel; Music Choice; Science Television; Sundance Channel; VHUNO.
Digital Pay Service 1
Pay Units: N.A.
Programming (via satellite): Cinemax (multiplexed); Encore (multiplexed); HBO (multiplexed); Starz (multiplexed).
Video-On-Demand: No
Pay-Per-View
Hot Choice (delivered digitally).
Internet Service
Operational: Yes. Began: January 1, 2003.
Broadband Service: Charter Pipeline.
Fee: $29.99 monthly; $10.00 modem lease.
Telephone Service
None
Miles of Plant: 404.0 (coaxial); None (fiber optic).
Chief Executive Officer: Scott Widham. General Manager: Wayne Kelstrom.
Ownership: Cobridge Communications LLC (MSO).

ROCKSPRINGS—Formerly served by Almega Cable. No longer in operation. ICA: TX0480.

ROCKWALL—Charter Communications, 15100 Trinity Blvd, Ste 500, Fort Worth, TX 76155. Phone: 817-298-3600. Web Site: http://www.charter.com. ICA: TX0155.
TV Market Ranking: 12 (ROCKWALL). Franchise award date: January 17, 1989. Franchise expiration date: N.A. Began: January 1, 1983.
Channel capacity: N.A. Channels available but not in use: N.A.
Basic Service
Subscribers: 2,595.
Programming (received off-air): KDAF (CW, IND) Dallas; KDFI (MNT) Dallas; KDFW-DT (FOX) Dallas; KDTN (ETV) Denton; KDTX-TV (TBN) Dallas; KERA-TV (PBS) Dallas; KMPX (IND) Decatur; KPXD-TV (ION) Arlington; KSTR-DT (TEL) Irving; KTAQ (IND) Greenville; KTVT (CBS) Fort Worth; KTXA (IND) Fort Worth; KUVN-DT (UNV) Garland; KXAS-TV (NBC) Fort Worth; KXTX-TV (TMO) Dallas; WFAA (ABC) Dallas.
Programming (via satellite): A&E Networks; ABC Family Channel; AMC; Animal Planet; BET Networks; Bravo; Cartoon Network; CNBC; CNN; Comedy Central; Country Music TV; C-SPAN; C-SPAN 2; Discovery Channel; Disney Channel; E! Entertainment Television; ESPN; ESPN 2; Food Network; Fox News Channel; Fox Sports Southwest; FX; G4; Golf Channel; GSN; Hallmark Channel; Headline News; HGTV; History Channel; INSP; Lifetime; MSNBC; MTV; National Geographic Channel; Nickelodeon; Oxygen; QVC; SoapNet; Speed; Spike TV; Syfy; TBS Superstation; The Learning Channel; The Weather Channel; Toon Disney; Travel Channel; truTV; Turner Network TV; TV Land; USA Network; VH1; WE tv.
Fee: $29.99 installation; $48.99 monthly.
Digital Basic Service
Subscribers: N.A.
Programming (via satellite): BBC America; Bio; Discovery Digital Networks; DMX Music; Fuse; GAS; History Channel International; Independent Film Channel; Lifetime Movie Network; MTV Networks Digital Suite; Nick Jr.; Style Network; Sundance Channel; Turner Classic Movies.
Digital Expanded Basic Service
Subscribers: N.A.
Programming (via satellite): ESPN Classic Sports; ESPNews; Fuel TV; NFL Network; Versus.
Digital Pay Service 1
Pay Units: N.A.
Programming (via satellite): Cinemax (multiplexed); Encore (multiplexed); HBO (multiplexed); Showtime (multiplexed); The Movie Channel (multiplexed).
Video-On-Demand: No
Pay-Per-View
Fresh (delivered digitally); ETC (delivered digitally); The Erotic Network (delivered digitally); iN DEMAND (delivered digitally).
Internet Service
Operational: Yes.
Broadband Service: Charter Pipeline.
Fee: $29.99 monthly.
Telephone Service
None
Miles of Plant: 110.0 (coaxial); 287.0 (fiber optic).
Vice President & General Manager: Wayne Cramp. Marketing Director: Kathleen Griffin. Technical Operations Director: John Linton.
Ownership: Charter Communications Inc. (MSO).

ROGERS—Centrovision Inc., 8 E Barton Ave, PO Box 3157, Temple, TX 76505. Phone: 254-773-1163. Fax: 254-770-0778. E-mail: altonsheppard@centrovision.net. Web Site: http://www.centrovision.net. ICA: TX0548.
TV Market Ranking: Below 100 (ROGERS). Franchise award date: N.A. Franchise expiration date: N.A. Began: June 1, 1983.
Channel capacity: N.A. Channels available but not in use: N.A.
Basic Service
Subscribers: N.A.
Programming (received off-air): KAKW-DT (UNV) Killeen; KBTX-TV (CBS, CW) Bryan; KCEN-TV (NBC, IND) Temple; KDYW (PBS) Waco; KNCT (PBS) Belton; KWKT-TV (FOX, MNT) Waco; KWTX-TV (CBS, CW) Waco; KXXV (ABC, TMO) Waco.
Programming (via satellite): Eternal Word TV Network; Local Cable Weather; QVC; Telemundo; Trinity Broadcasting Network; WGN America.
Fee: $20.00 installation; $12.00 monthly.
Expanded Basic Service 1
Subscribers: N.A.
Programming (received off-air): KEYE-TV (CBS, TMO) Austin; KNVA (CW) Austin; KTBC (FOX) Austin; KXAN-TV (NBC) Austin; WFAA (ABC) Dallas.
Programming (via satellite): A&E Networks; American Movie Classics; Animal Planet; BET Networks; Cartoon Network; CNBC; CNN; Comedy Central; Country Music TV; C-SPAN; C-SPAN 2; Discovery Channel; Disney Channel; DIY Network; E! Entertainment Television; ESPN; ESPN 2; Food Network; Fox News Channel; Fox Sports Net; FX; Golf Channel; Hallmark Channel; Headline News; HGTV; History Channel; ION Television; Lifetime; MSNBC; MTV; National Geographic Channel; Nickelodeon; RFD-TV; SoapNet; Speed; Spike TV; Syfy; TBS Superstation; The Learning Channel; The Weather Channel; Travel Channel; truTV; Turner Classic Movies; Turner Network TV; TV Land; USA Network; VH1.
Fee: $14.00 monthly.
Digital Basic Service
Subscribers: N.A.
Programming (via satellite): AmericanLife TV Network; BBC America; Bio; Bloomberg

Television; Bravo; cloo; CMT Pure Country; Current; Daystar TV Network; Discovery Fit & Health; ESPN Classic Sports; ESPNews; Fox College Sports Atlantic; Fox College Sports Central; Fox College Sports Pacific; Fox Movie Channel; Fox Soccer; G4; Great American Country; GSN; Halogen Network; History Channel International; Independent Film Channel; Lifetime Movie Network; Military History Channel; MTV Networks Digital Suite; Nick Jr.; NickToons TV; Outdoor Channel; Ovation; ShopNBC; Style Network; Sundance Channel; TeenNick; The Word Network; Toon Disney; Versus; WE tv.

Pay Service 1

Pay Units: N.A.

Programming (via satellite): HBO; Showtime; The Movie Channel.

Digital Pay Service 1

Pay Units: N.A.

Programming (via satellite): Cinemax (multiplexed); Encore (multiplexed); Flix; HBO (multiplexed); Showtime (multiplexed); Starz (multiplexed); The Movie Channel (multiplexed).

Video-On-Demand: No

Internet Service

Operational: Yes. Began: May 1, 2006.

Broadband Service: VVM Internet Services.

Fee: $20.00 installation; $40.00 monthly.

Telephone Service

Digital: Planned

Miles of Plant: 8.0 (coaxial); None (fiber optic).

Manager: Alton Sheppard. Chief Technician: Mike Wiggins.

Ownership: Centrovision Inc. (MSO).

ROMA—Time Warner Communications. Now served by PHARR, TX [TX0017]. ICA: TX0118.

ROSCOE—CMA Cablevision, 1510 N 1st St, PO Box 549, Merkel, TX 79536-0549. Phones: 800-588-4750; 325-928-4750. Fax: 325-928-3452. Web Site: http://www.cmaaccess.com. ICA: TX0471.

TV Market Ranking: Below 100 (ROSCOE). Franchise award date: November 20, 1968. Franchise expiration date: November 20, 2008. Began: August 1, 1971.

Channel capacity: N.A. Channels available but not in use: N.A.

Basic Service

Subscribers: 145.

Programming (received off-air): KPCB-DT (IND) Snyder; KRBC-TV (NBC) Abilene; KTAB-TV (CBS) Abilene; KTES-LP (TMO) Abilene; KTXS-TV (ABC, CW, TMO) Sweetwater; KXVA (FOX) Abilene; allband FM.

Programming (via satellite): ABC Family Channel; QVC; The Weather Channel; Univision Studios.

Fee: $39.95 installation; $16.95 monthly; $12.95 additional installation.

Expanded Basic Service 1

Subscribers: N.A.

Programming (via satellite): A&E Networks; AMC; Animal Planet; Cartoon Network; CNN; Country Music TV; Discovery Channel; ESPN; ESPN 2; Fox Sports Southwest; FX; HGTV; Lifetime; MTV; Nickelodeon; Spike TV; Syfy; TBS Superstation; The Learning Channel; Turner Classic Movies; Turner Network TV; TV Land; USA Network; VH1; WGN America.

Fee: $23.00 monthly.

Pay Service 1

Pay Units: 55.

Programming (via satellite): HBO.

Fee: $14.95 installation; $13.95 monthly.

Video-On-Demand: No

Internet Service

Operational: No.

Telephone Service

None

Miles of Plant: 13.0 (coaxial); None (fiber optic).

General Manager: Jerry Smith. Chief Technician: Joe Clark. Marketing Director: Julie Ferguson.

Ownership: Cable Management Assoc. (MSO).

ROSE CITY—Formerly served by Cebridge Connections. No longer in operation. ICA: TX0606.

ROSEBUD—DMS Cable TV, PO Box 268, Groesbeck, TX 76642-0268. Phone: 254-729-2221. ICA: TX0389.

TV Market Ranking: Below 100 (ROSEBUD). Franchise award date: N.A. Franchise expiration date: N.A. Began: January 1, 1966.

Channel capacity: 54 (operating 2-way). Channels available but not in use: N.A.

Basic Service

Subscribers: 344.

Programming (received off-air): KCEN-TV (NBC, IND) Temple; KLRU (PBS) Austin; KNCT (PBS) Belton; KWKT-TV (FOX, MNT) Waco; KWTX-TV (CBS, CW) Waco; KXXV (ABC, TMO) Waco; allband FM.

Programming (via satellite): A&E Networks; ABC Family Channel; AMC; BET Networks; Bloomberg Television; Cartoon Network; CNBC; CNN; Comedy Central; Country Music TV; Discovery Channel; Disney Channel; ESPN; ESPN 2; Food Network; Fox News Channel; GalaVision; Great American Country; Hallmark Channel; HGTV; History Channel; Lifetime; MTV; National Geographic Channel; Nickelodeon; Spike TV; Syfy; TBS Superstation; Telefutura; Telemundo; The Learning Channel; The Weather Channel; Trinity Broadcasting Network; Turner Classic Movies; Turner Network TV; TV Land; Univision Studios; USA Network; VH1; WGN America.

Fee: $25.00 installation; $22.00 monthly; $3.00 converter; $15.00 additional installation.

Digital Basic Service

Subscribers: 12.

Programming (via satellite): AmericanLife TV Network; BBC America; Bio; Bloomberg Television; Bravo; cloo; Current; Discovery Digital Networks; DMX Music; ESPN 2; ESPN Classic Sports; ESPNews; Fox Movie Channel; Fox Soccer; G4; GAS; Golf Channel; GSN; Halogen Network; HGTV; History Channel International; Independent Film Channel; Lifetime Movie Network; MTV Networks Digital Suite; National Geographic Channel; Nick Jr.; Outdoor Channel; Ovation; Speed; Style Network; Syfy; Toon Disney; Trinity Broadcasting Network; Turner Classic Movies; Versus; WE tv.

Fee: $23.99 monthly.

Digital Pay Service 1

Pay Units: 12.

Programming (via satellite): Cinemax (multiplexed); HBO (multiplexed).

Fee: $17.99 monthly.

Digital Pay Service 2

Pay Units: N.A.

Programming (via satellite): Encore (multiplexed); Showtime (multiplexed); Starz (multiplexed); The Movie Channel (multiplexed).

Fee: $17.99 monthly (Starz/Encore or Showtime/TMC).

Internet Service

Operational: No.

Telephone Service

None

Miles of Plant: 12.0 (coaxial); None (fiber optic).

Manager & Chief Technician: Danny Spurlock.

Ownership: Danny Spurlock.

ROTAN—Suddenlink Communications, 12444 Powerscourt Dr, Saint Louis, MO 63131-3660. Phones: 800-999-6845 (Customer service); 314-965-2020. Fax: 903-561-5485. Web Site: http://www.suddenlink.com. ICA: TX0365.

TV Market Ranking: Below 100 (ROTAN). Franchise award date: January 1, 1966. Franchise expiration date: January 1, 2009. Began: August 1, 1968.

Channel capacity: N.A. Channels available but not in use: N.A.

Basic Service

Subscribers: 555.

Programming (received off-air): KRBC-TV (NBC) Abilene; KTAB-TV (CBS) Abilene; KTXS-TV (ABC, CW, TMO) Sweetwater; 4 FMs.

Programming (via satellite): BET Networks; C-SPAN; Lifetime; QVC; TBS Superstation; The Weather Channel.

Fee: $39.95 installation; $19.95 monthly.

Expanded Basic Service 1

Subscribers: 437.

Programming (via satellite): A&E Networks; ABC Family Channel; AMC; Animal Planet; Cartoon Network; CNN; Country Music TV; Discovery Channel; ESPN; Fox News Channel; Fox Sports Southwest; FX; HGTV; MTV; Nickelodeon; Spike TV; The Learning Channel; Turner Network TV; USA Network.

Fee: $39.95 installation; $23.00 monthly.

Pay Service 1

Pay Units: 59.

Programming (via satellite): Cinemax.

Fee: $12.50 monthly.

Pay Service 2

Pay Units: 122.

Programming (via satellite): Encore.

Fee: $1.71 monthly.

Pay Service 3

Pay Units: 75.

Programming (via satellite): HBO.

Fee: $13.00 monthly.

Pay Service 4

Pay Units: 83.

Programming (via satellite): Starz.

Fee: $6.75 monthly.

Video-On-Demand: No

Internet Service

Operational: Yes. Began: November 12, 2003.

Broadband Service: Suddenlink High Speed Internet.

Fee: $49.95 installation; $38.95 monthly.

Telephone Service

None

Miles of Plant: 15.0 (coaxial); None (fiber optic).

Regional Manager: Todd Cruthird. Plant Manager: Bobby Smith.

Ownership: Cequel Communications LLC (MSO).

ROYSE CITY—Formerly served by Cebridge Connections. Now served by TERRELL, TX [TX0920]. ICA: TX0325.

RULE—Alliance Communications, 6125 Paluxy Dr, Tyler, TX 75703. Phones: 800-842-8160; 501-679-6619. Fax: 501-679-5694. Web Site: http://www.alliancecable.net. ICA: TX1005.

TV Market Ranking: Outside TV Markets (RULE).

Channel capacity: N.A. Channels available but not in use: N.A.

Basic Service

Subscribers: 48.

Programming (received off-air): KIDZ-LP Abilene; KRBC-TV (NBC) Abilene; KTAB-TV (CBS) Abilene; KTXS-TV (ABC, CW, TMO) Sweetwater; KXVA (FOX) Abilene.

Programming (via satellite): A&E Networks; ABC Family Channel; AMC; CNN; Comedy Central; Country Music TV; Discovery Channel; Disney Channel; E! Entertainment Television; ESPN; ESPN 2; History Channel; Lifetime; MSNBC; MTV; Nickelodeon; Oxygen; QVC; Spike TV; Syfy; TBS Superstation; The Learning Channel; The Weather Channel; Trinity Broadcasting Network; Turner Classic Movies; Turner Network TV; TV Land; Univision Studios; USA Network; VH1; WGN-TV (CW, IND) Chicago.

Fee: $29.95 installation; $38.00 monthly.

Pay Service 1

Pay Units: N.A.

Programming (via satellite): Cinemax; Encore (multiplexed); Flix; HBO; Showtime (multiplexed); The Movie Channel (multiplexed).

Video-On-Demand: No

Internet Service

Operational: No.

Telephone Service

None

Vice President & General Manager: John Brinker. Vice President, Programming: Julie Newman.

Ownership: Buford Media Group LLC (MSO).

RUNGE—Formerly served by Almega Cable. No longer in operation. ICA: TX0959.

RUSK—Suddenlink Communications, 12444 Powerscourt Dr, Saint Louis, MO 63131-3660. Phones: 800-999-6845; 314-965-2020. Fax: 903-561-5485. Web Site: http://www.suddenlink.com. Also serves Cherokee County (portions) & Dialville. ICA: TX0253.

TV Market Ranking: Below 100 (Cherokee County (portions), Dialville, RUSK). Franchise award date: N.A. Franchise expiration date: N.A. Began: January 1, 1963.

Channel capacity: N.A. Channels available but not in use: N.A.

Basic Service

Subscribers: 1,299.

Programming (received off-air): KETK-TV (NBC) Jacksonville; KFXK-TV (FOX) Longview; KLTV (ABC, TMO) Tyler; KSLA (CBS) Shreveport.

Programming (via microwave): KDFW-DT (FOX) Dallas; KERA-TV (PBS) Dallas; KTVT (CBS) Fort Worth; KXAS-TV (NBC) Fort Worth; WFAA (ABC) Dallas.

Programming (via satellite): A&E Networks; ABC Family Channel; CNN; Country Music TV; C-SPAN; Discovery Channel; ESPN; Fox Sports Southwest; Headline News; Lifetime; MTV; Nickelodeon; Spike TV; TBS Superstation; The Weather Channel; Turner Network TV.

Fee: $39.95 installation; $19.95 monthly.

Pay Service 1

Pay Units: 106.

Programming (via satellite): Cinemax.

Fee: $7.00 monthly.

Pay Service 2

Pay Units: 111.

Programming (via satellite): HBO.

Fee: $12.00 monthly.

Pay Service 3
Pay Units: 89.
Programming (via satellite): The Movie Channel.
Fee: $9.00 monthly.

Pay Service 4
Pay Units: 212.
Programming (via satellite): Showtime.
Fee: $7.00 monthly.

Pay Service 5
Pay Units: 247.
Programming (via satellite): Flix.
Fee: $1.95 monthly.

Video-On-Demand: No

Internet Service
Operational: Yes. Began: March 10, 2004.
Broadband Service: Suddenlink High Speed Internet.
Fee: $45.95 installation; $29.95 monthly.

Telephone Service
Digital: Operational
Fee: $44.95 monthly

Miles of Plant: 35.0 (coaxial); None (fiber optic).
Regional Manager: Todd Cruthird. Plant Manager: Henry Harris.
Ownership: Cequel Communications LLC (MSO).

SABINAL—Almega Cable, 4001 W Airport Frwy, Ste 530, Bedford, TX 76021. Phone: 817-685-9588. Fax: 817-685-6488. E-mail: helpdesk@almegacable.com. Web Site: http://www.almega.com. ICA: TX0442.
TV Market Ranking: Below 100 (SABINAL). Franchise award date: January 1, 1969. Franchise expiration date: N.A. Began: October 1, 1971.
Channel capacity: N.A. Channels available but not in use: N.A.

Basic Service
Subscribers: 232.
Programming (received off-air): KABB (FOX) San Antonio; KENS (CBS) San Antonio; KHCE-TV (TBN) San Antonio; KLRN (PBS) San Antonio; KMOL-LP Victoria; KMYS (CW) Kerrville; KPXL-TV (ION) Uvalde; KSAT-TV (ABC) San Antonio; KVDA (TMO) San Antonio; KWEX-DT (UNV) San Antonio.
Programming (via satellite): ABC Family Channel; AMC; Bravo; Cartoon Network; CNN; Country Music TV; C-SPAN; ESPN; Fox Sports Southwest; GalaVision; Headline News; QVC; Spike TV; The Learning Channel; Travel Channel; WGN America.
Fee: $29.95 installation; $19.95 monthly.

Expanded Basic Service 1
Subscribers: N.A.
Programming (via satellite): Discovery Channel; Nickelodeon; Syfy; TBS Superstation; Turner Network TV; USA Network.
Fee: $18.00 monthly.

Pay Service 1
Pay Units: 25.
Programming (via satellite): Cinemax.
Fee: $11.95 monthly.

Pay Service 2
Pay Units: 61.
Programming (via satellite): HBO.
Fee: $11.95 monthly.

Video-On-Demand: No

Internet Service
Operational: No.

Telephone Service
None

Miles of Plant: 13.0 (coaxial); None (fiber optic).
Ownership: Almega Cable (MSO).

SALADO—Centrovision Inc., 8 E Barton Ave, PO Box 3157, Temple, TX 76505. Phone: 254-773-1163. Fax: 254-770-0778. E-mail: altonsheppard@centrovision.net. Web Site: http://www.centrovision.net/. ICA: TX0504.
TV Market Ranking: Below 100 (SALADO). Franchise award date: N.A. Franchise expiration date: N.A. Began: February 1, 1982.
Channel capacity: N.A. Channels available but not in use: N.A.

Basic Service
Subscribers: N.A.
Programming (received off-air): KCEN-TV (NBC, IND) Temple; KDYW (PBS) Waco; KEYE-TV (CBS, TMO) Austin; KNCT (PBS) Belton; KNVA (CW) Austin; KTBC (FOX) Austin; KWKT-TV (FOX, MNT) Waco; KWTX-TV (CBS, CW) Waco; KXAN-TV (NBC) Austin; KXXV (ABC, TMO) Waco; WFAA (ABC) Dallas.
Programming (via satellite): Univision Studios; WGN America.
Fee: $20.00 installation; $12.00 monthly.

Expanded Basic Service 1
Subscribers: N.A.
Programming (via satellite): A&E Networks; ABC Family Channel; AMC; Animal Planet; BET Networks; Cartoon Network; CNBC; CNN; Comedy Central; Country Music TV; C-SPAN; C-SPAN 2; Discovery Channel; Disney Channel; E! Entertainment Television; ESPN; ESPN 2; Food Network; Fox News Channel; Fox Sports Southwest; FX; Hallmark Channel; Headline News; HGTV; History Channel; ION Television; Lifetime; MSNBC; MTV; National Geographic Channel; Nickelodeon; QVC; SoapNet; Spike TV; Syfy; TBS Superstation; The Learning Channel; The Weather Channel; Travel Channel; Trinity Broadcasting Network; Turner Classic Movies; Turner Network TV; TV Land; USA Network; VH1.
Fee: $18.00 monthly.

Digital Basic Service
Subscribers: N.A.
Programming (via satellite): AmericanLife TV Network; BBC America; Bio; Bloomberg Television; Bravo; Daystar TV Network; Discovery Digital Networks; DMX Music; ESPN Classic Sports; ESPNews; Fox Movie Channel; Fox Sports World; FSN Digital Atlantic; FSN Digital Central; FSN Digital Pacific; Fuse; G4; Golf Channel; Great American Country; GSN; Halogen Network; HGTV; History Channel; History Channel International; Independent Film Channel; International Television (ITV); Lifetime Movie Network; Lime; National Geographic Channel; Outdoor Channel; Ovation; ShopNBC; Speed; Style Network; Syfy; The Word Network; Toon Disney; Trinity Broadcasting Network; Turner Classic Movies; Versus; WE tv.
Fee: $15.00 installation; $49.00 monthly.

Pay Service 1
Pay Units: N.A.
Programming (via satellite): HBO; Showtime; The Movie Channel.
Fee: $11.00 monthly (HBO, Showtime or TMC), $13.50 monthly (Showtime & TMC), $19.50 monthly (HBO & TMC), $21.00 monthly (HBO & Showtime), $23.00 monthly (HBO, Showtime & TMC).

Digital Pay Service 1
Pay Units: N.A.
Programming (via satellite): Cinemax (multiplexed); Encore (multiplexed); HBO (multiplexed); Showtime (multiplexed); Starz (multiplexed).
Fee: $7.00 monthly (Cinemax), $11.00 monthly (HBO, Showtime or Starz & Encore).

Video-On-Demand: No

Pay-Per-View
Hot Choice (delivered digitally); iN DEMAND (delivered digitally).

Internet Service
Operational: Yes. Began: December 31, 2004.
Broadband Service: VVM Internet Services.
Fee: $20.00 installation; $40.00 monthly.

Telephone Service
Digital: Planned

Miles of Plant: 12.0 (coaxial); None (fiber optic).
Manager: Alton Sheppard. Chief Technician: Mike Wiggins.
Ownership: Centrovision Inc. (MSO).

SAN ANGELO—Suddenlink Communications, 4272 W Houston Harte Expy, San Angelo, TX 76901. Phone: 325-655-8911. Fax: 915-486-4182. Web Site: http://www.suddenlink.com. Also serves Goodfellow AFB & Harvest Acres. ICA: TX0021.
TV Market Ranking: Below 100 (Goodfellow AFB, Harvest Acres, SAN ANGELO). Franchise award date: October 1, 1957. Franchise expiration date: N.A. Began: October 1, 1958.
Channel capacity: N.A. Channels available but not in use: N.A.

Basic Service
Subscribers: 30,293.
Programming (received off-air): KANG-CA (TEL) San Angelo; KERA-TV (PBS) Dallas; KEUS-LP (UNV) San Angelo; KIDY (FOX) San Angelo; KLST (CBS) San Angelo; KSAN-TV (NBC) San Angelo; KTXE-LP San Angelo; WFAA (ABC) Dallas.
Programming (via satellite): C-SPAN; C-SPAN 2; CW+; INSP; QVC; TBS Superstation; Telemundo; Trinity Broadcasting Network; TV Guide Network.
Fee: $38.00 installation; $4.95 monthly; $3.36 converter.

Expanded Basic Service 1
Subscribers: 22,714.
Programming (via satellite): A&E Networks; ABC Family Channel; AMC; Animal Planet; BET Networks; Bravo; Cartoon Network; CNBC; CNN; Comedy Central; Country Music TV; Discovery Channel; Disney Channel; E! Entertainment Television; ESPN; ESPN 2; Food Network; Fox News Channel; Fox Sports Southwest; FX; GalaVision; Headline News; HGTV; History Channel; Lifetime; Lifetime Movie Network; MSNBC; MTV; MTV2; Nickelodeon; Speed; Spike TV; Syfy; The Learning Channel; The Weather Channel; Travel Channel; truTV; Turner Classic Movies; Turner Network TV; TV Land; USA Network; Versus; VH1.
Fee: $38.00 installation; $20.54 monthly.

Digital Basic Service
Subscribers: 7,579.
Programming (via satellite): A&E HD; Bandamax; BBC America; Bio; Bloomberg Television; Boomerang; Boomerang en Espanol; CBS Sports Network; Cine Latino; Cine Mexicano; CMT Pure Country; CNN en Espanol; Cooking Channel; De Pelicula; De Pelicula Clasico; Discovery en Espanol; Discovery Health Channel; Discovery Home Channel; Discovery Kids Channel; DIY Network; Encore (multiplexed); ESPN 2 HD; ESPN Classic Sports; ESPN Deportes; ESPN HD; ESPN U; ESPNews; Eternal Word TV Network; EWTN en Espanol; Food Network HD; Fox College Sports Atlantic; Fox College Sports Central; Fox College Sports Pacific; Fox Deportes; Fox Soccer; FSN HD; Fuel TV; Fuse; G4; GalaVision; GMC; Golf Channel; Great American Country; GSN; Hallmark Channel; Halogen Network; HD Theater; HDNet; HDNet Movies; HGTV HD; History Channel en Espanol; History Channel International; ID Investigation Discovery; Independent Film Channel; Jewelry Television; Military Channel; MTV Hits; mtvU; mun2 television; Music Choice; National Geographic Channel; National Geographic Channel HD Network; Nick Jr.; NickToons en Espanol; NickToons TV; Nuvo TV; Outdoor Channel; Oxygen; Science; ShopNBC; SoapNet; Sorpresa; Sundance Channel; Sur Network; TeenNick; Telehit; Tennis Channel; Toon Disney; Toon Disney en Espanol; Tr3s; Turner Network TV HD; Universal HD; VH1 Classic; Video Rola; WE tv.
Fee: $8.65 monthly.

Pay Service 1
Pay Units: 919.
Programming (via satellite): Cinemax.
Fee: $10.00 monthly.

Pay Service 2
Pay Units: 2,505.
Programming (via satellite): HBO (multiplexed).
Fee: $10.95 monthly.

Pay Service 3
Pay Units: 139.
Programming (via satellite): Encore; Showtime; Starz.
Fee: $3.97 monthly (Encore), $3.98 monthly (Starz), $6.75 monthly (Showtime).

Digital Pay Service 1
Pay Units: 6,544.
Programming (via satellite): Cinemax (multiplexed); HBO (multiplexed); HBO HD; HBO Latino; Showtime (multiplexed); Showtime HD; Starz (multiplexed); Starz HDTV; The Movie Channel (multiplexed).
Fee: $6.75 monthly (Showtime or TMC), $7.95 monthly (Starz), $12.95 monthly (HBO).

Video-On-Demand: No

Pay-Per-View
iN DEMAND (delivered digitally); Playgirl TV (delivered digitally); Fresh (delivered digitally); Shorteez (delivered digitally); Spice: Xcess (delivered digitally); Club Jenna (delivered digitally).

Internet Service
Operational: Yes. Began: October 1, 1999.
Subscribers: 12,015.
Broadband Service: Suddenlink High Speed Internet.
Fee: $49.95 installation; $24.95 monthly; $15.00 modem lease; $249.95 modem purchase.

Telephone Service
Digital: Operational
Fee: $48.95 monthly

Miles of Plant: 445.0 (coaxial); 30.0 (fiber optic).
Vice President & Manager: Connie Wharton. Technical Operations Manager: Robert E. Amo. Marketing Manager: Mike Johnson. Marketing Coordinator: Eric Wiemers. Customer Service Manager: Naomi Gonzales.
Ownership: Cequel Communications LLC (MSO).

SAN ANTONIO—Grande Communications, 6555 San Pedro Ave, San Antonio, TX 78216. Phones: 512-878-4000 (Corporate office); 210-320-4600 (Customer service). Fax: 210-320-4010. Web Site: http://www.grandecom.com. Also serves Alamo Heights, Balcones Heights, Castle Hills & Terrell

Hills. ICA: TX0990. **Note:** This system is an overbuild.

TV Market Ranking: 45 (Alamo Heights, Balcones Heights, Castle Hills, SAN ANTONIO, Terrell Hills). Franchise award date: May 18, 2000. Franchise expiration date: N.A. Began: February 1, 2001.

Channel capacity: 75 (operating 2-way). Channels available but not in use: N.A.

Basic Service

Subscribers: N.A.

Programming (received off-air): KABB (FOX) San Antonio; KCWX (IND, MNT) Fredericksburg; KENS (CBS) San Antonio; KHCE-TV (TBN) San Antonio; KLRN (PBS) San Antonio; KMYS (CW) Kerrville; KNIC-CA (TEL) San Antonio; KPXL-TV (ION) Uvalde; KSAT-TV (ABC) San Antonio; KVDA (TMO) San Antonio; KWEX-DT (UNV) San Antonio; WOAI-TV (NBC) San Antonio.

Programming (via satellite): Azteca America; C-SPAN; C-SPAN 2; LWS Local Weather Station; QVC; TV Guide Network; WGN America.

Fee: $14.95 monthly.

Expanded Basic Service 1

Subscribers: N.A.

Programming (via satellite): A&E Networks; ABC Family Channel; AMC; Animal Planet; BET Networks; Bravo; Cartoon Network; CNBC; CNN; Comedy Central; Country Music TV; Discovery Channel; Discovery Health Channel; Disney Channel; E! Entertainment Television; ESPN; ESPN 2; ESPN Classic Sports; Eternal Word TV Network; Food Network; Fox Deportes; Fox News Channel; Fox Sports Southwest; FX; G4; GalaVision; Golf Channel; Great American Country; GSN; Hallmark Channel; Headline News; HGTV; History Channel; INSP; Lifetime; MSNBC; MTV; mun2 television; Nickelodeon; Nuvo TV; Oxygen; SoapNet; Speed; Spike TV; Syfy; TBS Superstation; The Learning Channel; The Weather Channel; Toon Disney; Travel Channel; truTV; Turner Network TV; TV Land; USA Network; VH1.

Fee: $38.00 monthly.

Digital Basic Service

Subscribers: N.A.

Programming (received off-air): KENS (CBS) San Antonio.

Programming (via satellite): BBC America; Bio; Bloomberg Television; Boomerang; Canales N; CBS Sports Network; Cooking Channel; Discovery Kids Channel; DIY Network; ESPN; ESPNews; Fox College Sports Atlantic; Fox College Sports Central; Fox College Sports Pacific; Fox Movie Channel; Fox Soccer; Fuel TV; Fuse; GAS; GolTV; HD Theater; History Channel International; Independent Film Channel; INHD (multiplexed); Lifetime Movie Network; MTV Networks Digital Suite; Music Choice; National Geographic Channel; NBA TV; NFL Network; Nick Jr.; NickToons TV; Outdoor Channel; Style Network; Tennis Channel; The Word Network; Turner Classic Movies; Turner Network TV; TVG Network; Universal HD; Versus; WE tv.

Fee: $17.00 monthly; $5.00 converter.

Digital Pay Service 1

Pay Units: N.A.

Programming (via satellite): Cinemax (multiplexed); Cinemax HD; Encore (multiplexed); Flix (multiplexed); HBO (multiplexed); HBO HD; Showtime (multiplexed); Showtime HD; Starz (multiplexed); Starz HDTV; Sundance Channel (multiplexed); The Movie Channel (multiplexed).

Fee: $12.00 monthly (Cinemax, HBO, Showtime/Flix Sundance/TMC or Starz/Encore).

Video-On-Demand: No

Pay-Per-View

Sports PPV (delivered digitally); iN DEMAND (delivered digitally); Hot Choice (delivered digitally); Playboy TV (delivered digitally); Fresh (delivered digitally); Shorteez (delivered digitally).

Internet Service

Operational: Yes, Both DSL & dial-up.

Broadband Service: Grande High Speed Internet.

Fee: $19.95 monthly.

Telephone Service

Digital: Operational

Fee: $9.00 monthly

Vice President & General Manager: Carlos del Castillo. Video Services Director: Diane Wigington.

Ownership: Grande Communications Networks Inc. (MSO).

SAN ANTONIO—Time Warner Cable, 1900 Blue Crest Ln, San Antonio, TX 78247. Phone: 210-352-4600. Fax: 210-352-4278. Web Site: http://www.timewarnercable.com/SanAntonio. Also serves Alamo Heights, Balcones Heights, Bexar County, Brooks AFB, Bulverde, Castle Hills, China Grove, Cibolo, Comal County, Converse, Dominion, Elmendorf, Fort Sam Houston, Garden Ridge, Geronimo, Grey Forest, Guadalupe County, Helotes, Hill Country Village, Hollywood Park, Kelly AFB, Kirby, La Coste, Lackland AFB, Leon Valley, Live Oak, Marion, New Braunfels, Northcliff, Olmos Park, Randolph AFB, Schertz, Seguin, Selma, Shavano Park, Somerset, Terrell Hills, Universal City & Windcrest. ICA: TX0002.

TV Market Ranking: 45 (Alamo Heights, Balcones Heights, Bexar County, Brooks AFB, Bulverde, Castle Hills, China Grove, Cibolo, Comal County (portions), Converse, Dominion, Elmendorf, Fort Sam Houston, Garden Ridge, Geronimo, Grey Forest, Guadalupe County (portions), Helotes, Hill Country Village, Hollywood Park, Kelly AFB, Kirby, La Coste, Lackland AFB, Lakehills, Leon Valley, Live Oak, Marion, New Braunfels, Olmos Park, Randolph AFB, SAN ANTONIO, Schertz, Selma, Shavano Park, Somerset, Terrell Hills, Universal City, Windcrest); Below 100 (Blanco); Outside TV Markets (Seguin, Stockdale, Comal County (portions), Guadalupe County (portions)). Franchise award date: September 1, 1978. Franchise expiration date: N.A. Began: September 1, 1979.

Channel capacity: N.A. Channels available but not in use: N.A.

Basic Service

Subscribers: 364,991 Includes Stockdale.

Programming (received off-air): KABB (FOX) San Antonio; KCWX (IND, MNT) Fredericksburg; KENS (CBS) San Antonio; KHCE-TV (TBN) San Antonio; KLRN (PBS) San Antonio; KMYS (CW) Kerrville; KNIC-DT (TEL) Blanco; KPXL-TV (ION) Uvalde; KSAT-TV (ABC) San Antonio; KVDA (TMO) San Antonio; KWEX-DT (UNV) San Antonio; WOAI-TV (NBC) San Antonio; 28 FMs.

Programming (via satellite): Azteca America; GalaVision; Nickelodeon.

Fee: $44.83 installation; $12.75 monthly; $.17 converter.

Expanded Basic Service 1

Subscribers: 328,190.

Programming (via satellite): A&E Networks; ABC Family Channel; AMC; Animal Planet; BET Networks; Bravo; Cartoon Network; CNBC; CNN; Comedy Central; Country Music TV; C-SPAN; C-SPAN 2; Discovery Channel; Discovery Health Channel; Disney Channel; E! Entertainment Television; ESPN; ESPN 2; Food Network; Fox News Channel; Fox Sports Southwest; FX; Golf Channel; Hallmark Channel; Headline News; HGTV; History Channel; Lifetime; Lifetime Movie Network; MSNBC; MTV; mun2 television; National Geographic Channel; Oxygen; QVC; ShopNBC; Spike TV; Style Network; Syfy; The Learning Channel; The Weather Channel; Travel Channel; truTV; Turner Classic Movies; Turner Network TV; TV Guide Network; TV Land; USA Network; Versus; VH1; WE tv.

Fee: $36.10 monthly.

Expanded Basic Service 2

Subscribers: N.A.

Programming (via satellite): TBS Superstation; WGN America.

Fee: $2.50 monthly.

Digital Basic Service

Subscribers: 231,083.

Programming (via satellite): A&E HD; AmericanLife TV Network; BBC America; BBC America On Demand; Bio; Bloomberg Television; Boomerang; Canal Sur; Cartoon Network Tambien en Espanol; CBS Sports Network; Celebrity Shopping Network; Cine Latino; cloo; CNN en Espanol; CNN HD; CNN International; Cooking Channel; C-SPAN 3; Current; Discovery en Espanol; Discovery Fit & Health; Discovery Home Channel; Discovery Kids Channel; Discovery Times Channel; DIY Network; Encore (multiplexed); ESPN 2 HD; ESPN Classic Sports; ESPN Deportes; ESPN HD; ESPN U; ESPNews; EWTN en Espanol; Exercise TV; Flix; Food Network HD; Fox Business Channel; Fox College Sports Atlantic; Fox College Sports Central; Fox College Sports Pacific; Fox Deportes; Fox Movie Channel; Fox Reality Channel; Fox Soccer; Fuel TV; Fuse; G4; Great American Country; GSN; HD Theater; HDNet; HDNet Movies; HGTV HD; History Channel HD; History Channel International; HITN; Howard TV; HTV Musica; Independent Film Channel; Infinito; Jewelry Television; La Familia Network; Lifetime Movie Network HD; Lifetime Real Women; LOGO; Military Channel; MTV2; Music Choice; National Geographic Channel HD Network; National Geographic Channel On Demand; NBA TV; NHL Network; NHL Network HD; Nick Jr.; Nick Too; NickToons TV; Nuvo TV; Outdoor Channel; Ovation; Oxygen On Demand; Palladia; Science; Shop at Home; Shop Latino TV; SoapNet; Sorpresa; Speed; Speed On Demand; Sundance Channel; TBS in HD; TeenNick; Tennis Channel; Texas Cable News; Toon Disney; Toon Disney en Espanol; Tr3s; Turner Network TV HD; TV Guide SPOT; Universal HD; Versus HD; VH1 Classic; VHUNO; Video Rola; V-me TV.

Fee: $22.20 monthly; $3.07 converter.

Digital Pay Service 1

Pay Units: N.A.

Programming (via satellite): Cinemax HD; Cinemax On Demand; Deutsche Welle TV; Filipino Channel; HBO (multiplexed); HBO HD; HBO On Demand; Saigon Broadcasting Television Network; Showtime (multiplexed); Showtime HD; Showtime On Demand; Starz (multiplexed); Starz HDTV; The Movie Channel (multiplexed); The Movie Channel HD; The Movie Channel On Demand; TV Asia; TV Japan; Zee TV USA.

Fee: $9.00 monthly (Cinemax or TMC), $11.00 monthly (Starz), $11.95 monthly (Filipino Channel), $13.00 monthly (Showtime), $13.50 monthly (HBO), $14.95 monthly (SBTN), $ 24.95 monthly (Zee, TV Asia, Deutsche Weill, or TV Japan).

Video-On-Demand: Yes

Pay-Per-View

Playboy TV (delivered digitally); Playboy en Espanol (delivered digitally); NBA League Pass (delivered digitally); ESPN Gameplan (delivered digitally); MLB Extra Innings (delivered digitally); NHL Center Ice (delivered digitally); ESPN Full Court (delivered digitally); MLS Direct Kick (delivered digitally).

Internet Service

Operational: Yes. Began: May 1, 2000.

Subscribers: 237,800.

Broadband Service: Road Runner.

Fee: $39.95 installation; $39.95 monthly.

Telephone Service

Digital: Operational

Subscribers: 159,113.

Miles of Plant: 8,706.0 (coaxial); None (fiber optic). Miles of plant (coax & fiber combined) include Bandera, Blanco & Stockdale

President: John Owen. Vice President, Engineering: Norrie Bush. Vice President, Field Operations: Keith Coogan. Vice President, Marketing & New Product Development: Corky Roth. Vice President, Government & Public Affairs: Jon Gary Herrera. Public Affairs Manager: Melissa Sorola.

Ownership: Time Warner Cable (MSO).

SAN AUGUSTINE—Formerly served by Cebridge Connections. Now served by CENTER, TX [TX0192]. ICA: TX0317.

SAN CARLOS—Formerly served by CableDirect. No longer in operation. ICA: TX0624.

SAN LEON—Almega Cable, 4001 W Airport Frwy, Ste 530, Bedford, TX 76021. Phone: 817-685-9588. Fax: 817-685-6488. E-mail: helpdesk@almegacable.com. Web Site: http://www.almega.com. ICA: TX0240.

TV Market Ranking: 15 (SAN LEON). Franchise award date: N.A. Franchise expiration date: N.A. Began: December 10, 1987.

Channel capacity: 42 (not 2-way capable). Channels available but not in use: N.A.

Basic Service

Subscribers: 179.

Programming (received off-air): KETH-TV (TBN) Houston; KFTH-DT (TEL) Alvin; KHOU (CBS) Houston; KIAH (CW) Houston; KLTJ (ETV) Galveston; KPRC-TV (NBC) Houston; KPXB-TV (ION) Conroe; KRIV (FOX) Houston; KTMD (TMO) Galveston; KTRK-TV (ABC) Houston; KTXH (MNT) Houston; KUHT (PBS) Houston; KVVV-LP Houston; KXLN-DT (UNV) Rosenberg; KYAZ (IND) Katy.

Programming (via satellite): The Weather Channel.

Fee: $54.95 installation; $20.95 monthly.

Expanded Basic Service 1

Subscribers: N.A.

Programming (via satellite): A&E Networks; ABC Family Channel; Bio; CNBC; CNN; Discovery Channel; Disney Channel; ESPN; ESPN 2; Fox News Channel; Fox Sports Southwest; Headline News; HGTV; Lifetime; MTV; National Geographic Channel; Nickelodeon; QVC; Spike TV; Syfy; TBS Superstation; Turner Network TV; USA Network; VH1.

Fee: $23.10 monthly.

Pay Service 1

Pay Units: N.A.

Programming (via satellite): HBO; Showtime; The Movie Channel.

Fee: $12.95 monthly (each).
Video-On-Demand: No
Internet Service
Operational: No.
Telephone Service
None
Miles of Plant: 36.0 (coaxial); None (fiber optic).
Ownership: Almega Cable (MSO).

SAN MARCOS—Grande Communications. Now served by AUSTIN, TX [TX0989]. ICA: TX0991.

SAN MARCOS—Time Warner Cable. Now served by AUSTIN, TX [TX0005]. ICA: TX0849.

SAN PATRICIO COUNTY—Time Warner Cable. Now served by CORPUS CHRISTI, TX [TX0010]. ICA: TX0473.

SAN SABA—Suddenlink Communications, 12444 Powerscourt Dr, Saint Louis, MO 63131-3660. Phones: 800-999-6845; 314-965-2020. Web Site: http://www.suddenlink.com. ICA: TX0291.
TV Market Ranking: Below 100 (SAN SABA). Franchise award date: N.A. Franchise expiration date: N.A. Began: August 1, 1957.
Channel capacity: N.A. Channels available but not in use: N.A.
Basic Service
Subscribers: 782.
Programming (received off-air): KCEN-TV (NBC, IND) Temple; KNCT (PBS) Belton; KWKT-TV (FOX, MNT) Waco; KWTX-TV (CBS, CW) Waco; KXXV (ABC, TMO) Waco; 4 FMs.
Programming (via satellite): C-SPAN; Univision Studios.
Fee: $35.00 installation; $19.95 monthly.
Expanded Basic Service 1
Subscribers: N.A.
Programming (via satellite): A&E Networks; ABC Family Channel; AMC; Animal Planet; Cartoon Network; CNBC; CNN; Comedy Central; Discovery Channel; Disney Channel; E! Entertainment Television; ESPN; ESPN 2; Food Network; Fox News Channel; Fox Sports Southwest; FX; GalaVision; Great American Country; Hallmark Channel; Headline News; HGTV; History Channel; Jewelry Television; Lifetime; MSNBC; MTV; National Geographic Channel; Nickelodeon; Outdoor Channel; QVC; Spike TV; Syfy; TBS Superstation; The Learning Channel; The Weather Channel; Trinity Broadcasting Network; Turner Classic Movies; Turner Network TV; TV Land; USA Network; VH1.
Fee: $23.00 monthly.
Digital Basic Service
Subscribers: N.A.
Programming (via satellite): BBC America; Bio; Bloomberg Television; cloo; Discovery Health Channel; Discovery Home Channel; Discovery Kids Channel; DMX Music; ESPN Classic Sports; ESPNews; Fox College Sports Atlantic; Fox College Sports Central; Fox College Sports Pacific; Fox Soccer; Fuse; G4; Golf Channel; GSN; History Channel International; ID Investigation Discovery; Independent Film Channel; Military Channel; Science; ShopNBC; Speed; Style Network; Sundance Channel; Toon Disney; Versus; WE tv.
Pay Service 1
Pay Units: 94.
Programming (via satellite): The Movie Channel.
Fee: $5.95 monthly.
Pay Service 2
Pay Units: 99.
Programming (via satellite): Showtime.
Fee: $9.95 monthly.
Pay Service 3
Pay Units: 65.
Programming (via satellite): HBO.
Fee: $10.95 monthly.
Digital Pay Service 1
Pay Units: N.A.
Programming (via satellite): Cinemax (multiplexed); Encore (multiplexed); Flix; HBO (multiplexed); Showtime (multiplexed); Starz (multiplexed); The Movie Channel (multiplexed).
Video-On-Demand: No
Pay-Per-View
iN DEMAND (delivered digitally); Playboy TV (delivered digitally); Club Jenna (delivered digitally); Fresh (delivered digitally); Spice (delivered digitally).
Internet Service
Operational: Yes. Began: August 19, 2004.
Broadband Service: Suddenlink High Speed Internet.
Fee: $49.95 installation; $25.95 monthly.
Telephone Service
None
Miles of Plant: 36.0 (coaxial); None (fiber optic).
Marketing Director: Beverly Gambell.
Ownership: Cequel Communications LLC (MSO).

SAN YGNACIO—Time Warner Cable, 208 W Viggie St, Hebbronville, TX 78361-3048. Phones: 972-899-7300 (Flower Mound office); 361-527-3267. Fax: 361-527-3414. Web Site: http://www.timewarnercable.com/Texas. ICA: TX0647.
TV Market Ranking: Below 100 (SAN YGNACIO). Franchise award date: N.A. Franchise expiration date: N.A. Began: February 1, 1980.
Channel capacity: 31 (not 2-way capable). Channels available but not in use: N.A.
Basic Service
Subscribers: 140.
Programming (received off-air): KABB (FOX) San Antonio; KGNS-TV (CW, NBC, TMO) Laredo; KLDO-TV (FOX, UNV) Laredo; KVTV (CBS) Laredo.
Programming (via satellite): A&E Networks; Animal Planet; Cartoon Network; CNN; Discovery Channel; Disney Channel; ESPN; ESPN 2; FX; GalaVision; Lifetime; MoviePlex; MTV; Nickelodeon; Spike TV; TBS Superstation; Telefutura; Telemundo; The Learning Channel; The Weather Channel; Turner Classic Movies; Turner Network TV; USA Network; WABC-TV (ABC) New York.
Fee: $50.51 installation; $40.99 monthly.
Pay Service 1
Pay Units: N.A.
Programming (via satellite): HBO.
Fee: $12.95 monthly.
Video-On-Demand: No
Internet Service
Operational: No.
Telephone Service
None
Miles of Plant: 8.0 (coaxial); None (fiber optic).
President: Connie Wharton. Vice President & General Manager: Michael Carrosquiola. Chief Technician: Juve Morante. Office Manager: Nellie Garza.
Ownership: Time Warner Cable (MSO).; Advance/Newhouse Partnership (MSO).

SANDERSON—US Cable of Coastal Texas LP, 611 W Ave A, Seminole, TX 79360. Phone: 432-758-9221. Fax: 432-758-3379. Web Site: http://www.uscable.com. ICA: TX1025.
TV Market Ranking: Outside TV Markets (SANDERSON).
Channel capacity: N.A. Channels available but not in use: N.A.
Basic Service
Subscribers: 128.
Programming (received off-air): KMLM-DT (IND) Odessa; KOAT-TV (ABC) Albuquerque; KPBT-TV (PBS) Odessa; KPEJ-TV (FOX) Odessa; KRQE (CBS) Albuquerque; KTLE-LP (TMO) Odessa; KUPB (UNV) Midland; KWES-TV (NBC) Odessa; KWWT (CW) Odessa.
Programming (via satellite): ABC Family Channel; Animal Planet; Cartoon Network; CNN; Country Music TV; C-SPAN; Discovery Channel; Discovery Fit & Health; Disney Channel; E! Entertainment Television; ESPN; Food Network; Fox News Channel; Fox Sports Net; Hallmark Channel; Home Shopping Network; Lifetime; MTV; National Geographic Channel; Nick At Nite; Nickelodeon; Spike TV; Syfy; TBS Superstation; Texas Cable News; The Learning Channel; The Weather Channel; Trinity Broadcasting Network; Turner Classic Movies; Turner Network TV; USA Network; VH1; WGN America.
Fee: $39.96 installation; $44.60 monthly.
Digital Basic Service
Subscribers: N.A.
Programming (via satellite): BBC America; Bio; Bloomberg Television; Bravo; Centric; cloo; CMT Pure Country; Current; Discovery Health Channel; Discovery Kids Channel; Disney XD; DMX Music; Encore; ESPN Classic Sports; ESPNews; Fox College Sports Atlantic; Fox College Sports Central; Fox College Sports Pacific; Fox Movie Channel; Fox Soccer; Fuse; G4; Golf Channel; Great American Country; GSN; Halogen Network; HGTV; History Channel International; ID Investigation Discovery; Independent Film Channel; Lifetime Movie Network; Military Channel; MTV Hits; MTV2; Nick Jr.; Outdoor Channel; Planet Green; Science; Speed; Style Network; TeenNick; The Word Network; Turner Classic Movies; Versus; VH1 Classic; VH1 Soul; WE tv.
Fee: $20.90 monthly.
Pay Service 1
Pay Units: N.A.
Programming (via satellite): HBO; Showtime.
Fee: $13.95 monthly (each).
Digital Pay Service 1
Pay Units: N.A.
Programming (via satellite): Cinemax (multiplexed); HBO (multiplexed); Showtime (multiplexed); Starz (multiplexed); The Movie Channel (multiplexed).
Fee: $9.95 monthly (Starz), $12.95 monthly (HBO, Cinemax, Showtime or TMC).
Video-On-Demand: No
Pay-Per-View
Event Entertainment (delivered digitally); Movies (delivered digitally); Playboy TV (delivered digitally); Fresh (delivered digitally).
Internet Service
Operational: Yes.
Telephone Service
None
Regional Manager: Daryl Koedyker.
Ownership: US Cable Corp. (MSO).

SANDIA—Formerly served by National Cable Inc. No longer in operation. ICA: TX0667.

SANTA ANNA—Formerly served by Brownwood TV Cable Service Inc. No longer in operation. ICA: TX0425.

SANTA FE (unincorporated areas)—Formerly served by Almega Cable. No longer in operation. ICA: TX0411.

SARGENT—Formerly served by Almega Cable. No longer in operation. ICA: TX0248.

SEADRIFT—Time Warner Cable, 4060 S Padre Island Dr, Corpus Christi, TX 78411-4402. Phones: 972-899-7300 (Flower Mound office); 361-698-6259. Fax: 361-857-5038. Web Site: http://www.timewarnercable.com/Texas. ICA: TX0433.
TV Market Ranking: Below 100 (SEADRIFT). Franchise award date: N.A. Franchise expiration date: March 5, 2014. Began: December 1, 1981.
Channel capacity: N.A. Channels available but not in use: N.A.
Basic Service
Subscribers: N.A. Included in Corpus Christi
Programming (received off-air): KAVU-TV (ABC) Victoria; KEDT (PBS) Corpus Christi; KIII (ABC) Corpus Christi; KRIS-TV (CW, NBC) Corpus Christi; KVCT (FOX) Victoria; KZTV (CBS) Corpus Christi.
Programming (via satellite): QVC; WGN America.
Fee: $34.99 installation; $16.39 monthly; $18.81 additional installation.
Expanded Basic Service 1
Subscribers: N.A.
Programming (via satellite): A&E Networks; ABC Family Channel; Animal Planet; Cartoon Network; CNBC; CNN; Comedy Central; Discovery Channel; Disney Channel; E! Entertainment Television; ESPN; ESPN 2; Food Network; Fox News Channel; Fox Sports Southwest; FX; Headline News; HGTV; History Channel; Lifetime; MTV; National Geographic Channel; Nickelodeon; Speed; Spike TV; TBS Superstation; The Learning Channel; The Weather Channel; truTV; Turner Classic Movies; Turner Network TV; USA Network; Versus.
Fee: $28.60 monthly.
Pay Service 1
Pay Units: N.A.
Programming (via satellite): Encore; HBO; Showtime; Starz.
Fee: $3.75 monthly (Encore), $12.95 monthly (HBO, Starz or Showtime).
Internet Service
Operational: No.
Telephone Service
None
Miles of Plant: 9.0 (coaxial); None (fiber optic).
President: Connie Wharton. Vice President & General Manager: Mike McKee. Engineering Director: Charlotte Strong. Public Affairs Manager: Vicki Triplett.
Ownership: Time Warner Cable (MSO).; Advance/Newhouse Partnership (MSO).

SEALY—CMA Cablevision. Now served by BELLVILLE, TX [TX0292]. ICA: TX0994.

SEMINOLE—US Cable of Coastal Texas LP, 611 W Ave A, Seminole, TX 79360. Phones: 432-758-9221; 800-996-8788. Fax: 432-758-3379. E-mail: uscable@tx.uscable.com. Web Site: http://www.uscable.com. Also serves Denver City & Seagraves. ICA: TX0074.

TV Market Ranking: Below 100 (SEMINOLE); Outside TV Markets (Denver City, Seagraves). Franchise award date: N.A. Franchise expiration date: N.A. Began: July 1, 1953.

Channel capacity: 60 (operating 2-way). Channels available but not in use: N.A.

Basic Service

Subscribers: 2,714.

Programming (received off-air): KAMC (ABC) Lubbock; KBIM-TV (CBS) Roswell; KCBD (NBC) Lubbock; KJTV-TV (FOX) Lubbock; KMID (ABC) Midland; KMLM-DT (IND) Odessa; KOSA-TV (CBS, MNT) Odessa; KPEJ-TV (FOX) Odessa; KTXT-TV (PBS) Lubbock; KUPB (UNV) Midland; KUPT (MNT) Hobbs; KWES-TV (NBC) Odessa; KXTQ-CA (TMO) Lubbock; 1 FM.

Programming (via satellite): Fox News Channel; INSP; Lifetime; Turner Network TV; TV Guide Network; WGN America.

Fee: $35.28 installation; $20.42 monthly; $.90 converter.

Expanded Basic Service 1

Subscribers: N.A. Includes West Odessa, Carlsbad NM, Espanola NM, Hobbs NM, & Santa Clara Indian Reservation NM

Programming (via satellite): A&E Networks; ABC Family Channel; AMC; Animal Planet; Cartoon Network; CNBC; CNN; Country Music TV; C-SPAN; Discovery Channel; Discovery Fit & Health; Discovery Health Channel; Disney Channel; DIY Network; E! Entertainment Television; ESPN; ESPN 2; Food Network; Fox Sports Southwest; FX; Headline News; HGTV; History Channel; MoviePlex; MTV; National Geographic Channel; Nickelodeon; ShopNBC; Spike TV; Syfy; TBS Superstation; Telemundo; The Learning Channel; The Weather Channel; TV Land; USA Network; VH1.

Fee: $28.11 monthly.

Digital Basic Service

Subscribers: N.A.

Programming (via satellite): BBC America; Bio; Bloomberg Television; Bravo; DMX Music; Encore (multiplexed); ESPN Classic Sports; ESPNews; Fox College Sports Atlantic; Fox College Sports Central; Fox College Sports Pacific; Fox Movie Channel; Fox Soccer; Fuse; G4; GAS; Golf Channel; Great American Country; GSN; Halogen Network; History Channel International; Independent Film Channel; Lifetime Movie Network; MTV Networks Digital Suite; Nick Jr.; Outdoor Channel; Speed; Style Network; The Word Network; Toon Disney; Trinity Broadcasting Network; Trio; Turner Classic Movies; Versus; WE tv.

Fee: $20.90 monthly.

Pay Service 1

Pay Units: N.A.

Programming (via satellite): Cinemax; HBO.

Fee: $12.95 monthly (each).

Digital Pay Service 1

Pay Units: N.A.

Programming (via satellite): Cinemax (multiplexed); HBO (multiplexed); Showtime (multiplexed); Starz (multiplexed); The Movie Channel (multiplexed).

Fee: $8.95 monthly (Starz), $11.95 monthly (HBO, Cinemax, Showtime, or TMC).

Video-On-Demand: No

Pay-Per-View

Fresh (delivered digitally); Playboy TV (delivered digitally); iN DEMAND.

Internet Service

Operational: Yes.

Broadband Service: Warp Drive Online.

Fee: $27.95-$54.95 monthly.

Telephone Service

None

Miles of Plant: 1,292.0 (coaxial); None (fiber optic). Miles of plant include Alpine, West Odessa, Carlsbad NM, Chama NM, Dixon NM, Espanola NM, Jal NM, Hobbs NM, Penasco NM, & Santa Clara Indian Reservation NM

Regional Manager: Daryl Koedyker. Technical Operations Manager: Jess Webb. Office Manager: Kim Harris. Regional Administrative Assistant: Chandra Davis.

Ownership: US Cable Corp. (MSO).; Comcast Cable Communications Inc. (MSO).

SEVEN POINTS (northern portion)—Formerly served by Trust Cable. No longer in operation. ICA: TX0423.

SEYMOUR—Suddenlink Communications, 12444 Powerscourt Dr, Saint Louis, MO 63131-3660. Phones: 800-999-6845; 314-965-2020. Fax: 903-561-5485. Web Site: http://www.suddenlink.com. ICA: TX0254.

TV Market Ranking: Outside TV Markets (SEYMOUR). Franchise award date: N.A. Franchise expiration date: N.A. Began: February 1, 1977.

Channel capacity: N.A. Channels available but not in use: N.A.

Basic Service

Subscribers: 1,102.

Programming (received off-air): KAUZ-TV (CBS, CW) Wichita Falls; KFDX-TV (NBC) Wichita Falls; KJTL (FOX) Wichita Falls; KSWO-TV (ABC, TMO) Lawton; allband FM.

Programming (via satellite): C-SPAN; Discovery Channel; Hallmark Channel; Lifetime; QVC; TBS Superstation; The Learning Channel; The Weather Channel.

Fee: $39.95 installation; $19.95 monthly.

Expanded Basic Service 1

Subscribers: 874.

Programming (via satellite): ABC Family Channel; AMC; Animal Planet; Cartoon Network; CNN; Disney Channel; ESPN; Fox News Channel; FX; Headline News; HGTV; MTV; Nickelodeon; Spike TV; Turner Network TV; USA Network.

Fee: $39.95 installation; $25.00 monthly.

Pay Service 1

Pay Units: 47.

Programming (via satellite): Cinemax.

Fee: $12.84 monthly.

Pay Service 2

Pay Units: 332.

Programming (via satellite): Encore.

Fee: $1.75 monthly.

Pay Service 3

Pay Units: 140.

Programming (via satellite): HBO.

Fee: $13.83 monthly.

Pay Service 4

Pay Units: 188.

Programming (via satellite): Starz.

Fee: $6.75 monthly.

Video-On-Demand: No

Internet Service

Operational: Yes. Began: October 6, 2003.

Broadband Service: Suddenlink High Speed Internet.

Fee: $49.95 installation; $43.95 monthly.

Telephone Service

None

Miles of Plant: 29.0 (coaxial); None (fiber optic).

Regional Manager: Todd Cruthird. Plant Manager: Ron Johnson.

Ownership: Cequel Communications LLC (MSO).

SHAMROCK—Suddenlink Communications, 214 N Main St, Shamrock, TX 79079. Phones: 800-999-6845 (Customer service); 806-256-3944; 314-965-2020. Web Site: http://www.suddenlink.com. ICA: TX0318.

TV Market Ranking: Outside TV Markets (SHAMROCK). Franchise award date: N.A. Franchise expiration date: N.A. Began: August 1, 1957.

Channel capacity: N.A. Channels available but not in use: N.A.

Basic Service

Subscribers: 898.

Programming (received off-air): KWET (PBS) Cheyenne.

Programming (via microwave): KAMR-TV (NBC) Amarillo; KCIT (FOX) Amarillo; KETA-TV (PBS) Oklahoma City; KFDA-TV (CBS) Amarillo; KVII-TV (ABC, CW) Amarillo.

Programming (via satellite): ABC Family Channel; AMC; AmericanLife TV Network; Animal Planet; Cartoon Network; CNN; Country Music TV; Discovery Channel; Disney Channel; E! Entertainment Television; ESPN; Fox News Channel; Fox Sports Southwest; Headline News; HGTV; History Channel; INSP; Lifetime; Nickelodeon; QVC; Spike TV; Syfy; TBS Superstation; The Learning Channel; The Weather Channel; truTV; Turner Network TV; TV Land; USA Network; WGN America.

Fee: $35.00 installation; $19.95 monthly.

Pay Service 1

Pay Units: 45.

Programming (via satellite): The Movie Channel.

Fee: $5.95 monthly.

Pay Service 2

Pay Units: 41.

Programming (via satellite): Cinemax.

Fee: $9.95 monthly.

Pay Service 3

Pay Units: 46.

Programming (via satellite): Showtime.

Fee: $9.95 monthly.

Pay Service 4

Pay Units: 87.

Programming (via satellite): HBO.

Fee: $10.95 monthly.

Video-On-Demand: No

Internet Service

Operational: Yes. Began: February 11, 2004.

Broadband Service: Suddenlink High Speed Internet.

Fee: $49.95 installation; $25.95 monthly.

Telephone Service

Digital: Operational

Fee: $44.95 monthly

Miles of Plant: 25.0 (coaxial); None (fiber optic).

Marketing Director: Beverly Gambell. Chief Technician: Rick Rattan.

Ownership: Cequel Communications LLC (MSO).

SHEFFIELD—Formerly served by Ector Cable. No longer in operation. ICA: TX0691.

SHERIDAN—Formerly served by National Cable Inc. No longer in operation. ICA: TX0645.

SHERMAN—Cable One, 3720 Texoma Pkwy, PO Box 1223, Sherman, TX 75091-1223. Phone: 903-893-6548. Fax: 903-868-2754. E-mail: webmaster@cableone.net. Web Site: http://www.cableone.net. Also serves Bells, Bonham, Denison, Fannin County, Grayson County (northern portion), Howe, Knollwood, Savoy, Tom Bean, Van Alstyne & Whitewright. ICA: TX0042.

TV Market Ranking: Below 100 (Bells, Bonham, Denison, Fannin County, Grayson County (northern portion), Howe, Knollwood, Savoy, SHERMAN, Tom Bean, Van Alstyne, Whitewright). Franchise award date: March 7, 1966. Franchise expiration date: N.A. Began: August 1, 1957.

Channel capacity: 80 (operating 2-way). Channels available but not in use: N.A.

Basic Service

Subscribers: 23,400.

Programming (received off-air): KDAF (CW, IND) Dallas; KDFI (MNT) Dallas; KDFW-DT (FOX) Dallas; KDTX-TV (TBN) Dallas; KERA-TV (PBS) Dallas; KSTR-DT (TEL) Irving; KTAQ (IND) Greenville; KTEN (ABC, CW, NBC) Ada; KTVT (CBS) Fort Worth; KTXA (IND) Fort Worth; KUVN-DT (UNV) Garland; KXAS-TV (NBC) Fort Worth; KXII (CBS, FOX, MNT) Sherman; KXTX-TV (TMO) Dallas; WFAA (ABC) Dallas.

Programming (via satellite): Animal Planet; C-SPAN; C-SPAN 2; Daystar TV Network; Eternal Word TV Network; QVC; TV Guide Network.

Fee: $40.21 installation; $46.00 monthly; $.46 converter; $11.74 additional installation.

Expanded Basic Service 1

Subscribers: N.A.

Programming (via satellite): A&E Networks; ABC Family Channel; AMC; BET Networks; Bravo; Cartoon Network; CNBC; CNN; Comedy Central; Country Music TV; Discovery Channel; Disney Channel; ESPN; ESPN 2; Fox News Channel; Fox Sports Southwest; FX; Headline News; HGTV; History Channel; Lifetime; MSNBC; MTV; Nickelodeon; Spike TV; Syfy; TBS Superstation; The Learning Channel; The Weather Channel; Turner Classic Movies; Turner Network TV; TV Land; USA Network; VH1.

Fee: $46.00 monthly.

Digital Basic Service

Subscribers: 7,500.

Programming (via satellite): 3 Angels Broadcasting Network; Bio; Boomerang; BYU Television; Canales N; Discovery Digital Networks; DMX Music; ESPN Classic Sports; ESPNews; FamilyNet; Fox College Sports Atlantic; Fox College Sports Central; Fox College Sports Pacific; Fox HD; Fox Movie Channel; Fox Soccer; Fuel TV; G4; Golf Channel; Great American Country; Hallmark Channel; History Channel International; INSP; National Geographic Channel; Outdoor Channel; SoapNet; Speed; Toon Disney; Trinity Broadcasting Network; truTV; Turner Network TV HD; TVG Network; Universal HD.

Fee: $18.95 monthly.

Digital Pay Service 1

Pay Units: N.A.

Programming (via satellite): Cinemax (multiplexed); Encore (multiplexed); Flix; HBO (multiplexed); Showtime (multiplexed); Showtime HD; Starz (multiplexed); Sundance Channel; The Movie Channel (multiplexed); The Movie Channel HD.

Fee: $15.00 monthly (each).

Video-On-Demand: No

Pay-Per-View

iN DEMAND (delivered digitally); Pleasure (delivered digitally); Ten Clips (delivered digitally); Ten Blox (delivered digitally); Ten Blue (delivered digitally).

Internet Service

Operational: Yes. Began: October 1, 2001.

Subscribers: 7,500.

Broadband Service: CableONE.net.

Fee: $75.00 installation; $43.00 monthly; $5.00 modem lease.

Telephone Service
Digital: Operational
Fee: $39.95 monthly
Miles of Plant: 640.0 (coaxial); 65.0 (fiber optic).
Manager: Claude H. Edwards. Chief Technician: Rod Ralls. Program Director: Darla Hutcherson. Marketing Director: Donna Perry. Customer Service Manager: Donna Webb.
Ownership: Cable ONE Inc. (MSO).

SHERWOOD SHORES—TV Cable of Grayson County, 501 Hwy 120 N, Ste 6, PO Box 2084, Pottsboro, TX 75076. Phone: 903-786-7477. E-mail: tvcable@graysoncable.com. Web Site: http://www.graysoncable.com. Also serves Gordonville & Grayson County (portions). ICA: TX0413.
TV Market Ranking: Below 100 (Gordonville, Grayson County (portions), SHERWOOD SHORES). Franchise award date: N.A. Franchise expiration date: N.A. Began: N.A.
Channel capacity: 36 (not 2-way capable). Channels available but not in use: N.A.
Basic Service
Subscribers: 173.
Programming (received off-air): KDAF (CW, IND) Dallas; KDFI (MNT) Dallas; KERA-TV (PBS) Dallas; KTEN (ABC, CW, NBC) Ada; KTXA (IND) Fort Worth; KXAS-TV (NBC) Fort Worth; KXII (CBS, FOX, MNT) Sherman; KXTX-TV (TMO) Dallas; WFAA (ABC) Dallas.
Programming (via satellite): A&E Networks; ABC Family Channel; AMC; Animal Planet; CNN; C-SPAN; C-SPAN 2; Discovery Channel; Disney Channel; ESPN; ESPN 2; Fox Movie Channel; Fox News Channel; Fox Sports Southwest; FX; Golf Channel; Great American Country; Hallmark Channel; Headline News; HGTV; History Channel; Lifetime; MSNBC; MTV; National Geographic Channel; Nickelodeon; Outdoor Channel; QVC; Radar Channel; SoapNet; Speed; Spike TV; Syfy; TBS Superstation; The Learning Channel; The Weather Channel; Trinity Broadcasting Network; truTV; Turner Classic Movies; Turner Network TV; TV Land; USA Network; WGN America.
Fee: $39.95 installation; $32.17 monthly.
Pay Service 1
Pay Units: 5.
Programming (via satellite): HBO.
Fee: $12.00 monthly.
Pay Service 2
Pay Units: 25.
Programming (via satellite): Showtime.
Fee: $3.95 monthly.
Pay Service 3
Pay Units: 5.
Programming (via satellite): The Movie Channel.
Fee: $9.00 monthly.
Internet Service
Operational: No.
Telephone Service
None
Miles of Plant: 20.0 (coaxial); None (fiber optic).
Manager: Chuck Davis.
Ownership: Chuck Davis (MSO).

SHINER—Almega Cable, 4001 W Airport Frwy, Ste 530, Bedford, TX 76021. Phone: 817-685-9588. Fax: 817-685-6488. E-mail: helpdesk@almegacable.com. Web Site: http://www.almega.com. ICA: TX0383.
TV Market Ranking: Outside TV Markets (SHINER). Franchise award date: January 1, 1974. Franchise expiration date: N.A. Began: January 23, 1975.
Channel capacity: N.A. Channels available but not in use: N.A.
Basic Service
Subscribers: 737.
Programming (received off-air): KABB (FOX) San Antonio; KAVU-TV (ABC) Victoria; KENS (CBS) San Antonio; KLRN (PBS) San Antonio; KMOL-LP Victoria; KSAT-TV (ABC) San Antonio; KTBC (FOX) Austin; KVCT (FOX) Victoria; allband FM.
Programming (via satellite): A&E Networks; ABC Family Channel; AMC; Animal Planet; BET Networks; Bravo; Cartoon Network; CNBC; CNN; Comedy Central; Country Music TV; Discovery Channel; Disney Channel; E! Entertainment Television; ESPN; ESPN 2; Eternal Word TV Network; Fox News Channel; Fox Sports Southwest; FX; G4; Headline News; HGTV; History Channel; MTV; Nickelodeon; Oxygen; QVC; SoapNet; Speed; Spike TV; Syfy; TBS Superstation; The Learning Channel; Turner Network TV; TV Land; USA Network; VH1.
Fee: $29.95 installation; $19.95 monthly.
Digital Basic Service
Subscribers: N.A.
Programming (via satellite): BBC America; Bio; Bloomberg Television; Discovery Fit & Health; DIY Network; ESPN Classic Sports; ESPNews; GAS; GSN; History Channel International; Independent Film Channel; Lifetime Movie Network; MTV Networks Digital Suite; Music Choice; Nick Jr.; Nick Too; NickToons TV; Sundance Channel; Toon Disney; TV Guide Interactive Inc.; WE tv.
Digital Pay Service 1
Pay Units: 53.
Programming (via satellite): HBO (multiplexed).
Fee: $19.95 installation; $11.95 monthly.
Digital Pay Service 2
Pay Units: 51.
Programming (via satellite): Showtime (multiplexed).
Fee: $11.95 monthly.
Digital Pay Service 3
Pay Units: 20.
Programming (via satellite): The Movie Channel (multiplexed).
Fee: $11.95 monthly.
Digital Pay Service 4
Pay Units: N.A.
Programming (via satellite): Cinemax (multiplexed); Encore (multiplexed); Flix; Starz (multiplexed).
Video-On-Demand: No
Pay-Per-View
iN DEMAND (delivered digitally).
Internet Service
Operational: No.
Telephone Service
None
Miles of Plant: 30.0 (coaxial); None (fiber optic).
Ownership: Almega Cable (MSO).

SIERRA BLANCA—Formerly served by Sierra Cable TV. No longer in operation. ICA: TX0853.

SILSBEE—Time Warner Cable. Now served by BEAUMONT, TX [TX0022]. ICA: TX0079.

SILVERTON—Reach Broadband, 515 E Longview St, Arp, TX 75750. Phone: 800-687-1258. Web Site: http://www.reachbroadband.net. ICA: TX0525.
TV Market Ranking: Outside TV Markets (SILVERTON). Franchise award date: April 8, 1986. Franchise expiration date: N.A. Began: August 1, 1969.
Channel capacity: 41 (not 2-way capable). Channels available but not in use: N.A.
Basic Service
Subscribers: 94.
Programming (received off-air): KACV-TV (PBS) Amarillo; KAMR-TV (NBC) Amarillo; KCBD (NBC) Lubbock; KFDA-TV (CBS) Amarillo; KJTV-TV (FOX) Lubbock; KLBK-TV (CBS) Lubbock; KVII-TV (ABC, CW) Amarillo; 1 FM.
Programming (via satellite): ABC Family Channel; AMC; AmericanLife TV Network; CNN; Country Music TV; Discovery Channel; Disney Channel; ESPN; Fox News Channel; Fox Sports Southwest; Headline News; INSP; Lifetime; QVC; Spike TV; TBS Superstation; The Weather Channel; Travel Channel; Trinity Broadcasting Network; Turner Network TV; USA Network; WGN America.
Fee: $29.95 installation; $38.00 monthly.
Pay Service 1
Pay Units: 18.
Programming (via satellite): Cinemax.
Fee: $9.95 monthly.
Pay Service 2
Pay Units: 26.
Programming (via satellite): HBO.
Fee: $9.95 monthly.
Video-On-Demand: No
Internet Service
Operational: No.
Telephone Service
None
Miles of Plant: 8.0 (coaxial); None (fiber optic).
Regional Manager: Ronnie Stafford. Office Manager: Jan Gibson.
Ownership: RB3 LLC (MSO).

SINTON—Charter Communications. Now served by ROCKPORT, TX [TX0116]. ICA: TX0224.

SKELLYTOWN—Formerly served by Almega Cable. No longer in operation. ICA: TX0586.

SLATON—Cobridge Communications, 9450 Manchester Rd, Ste 200, St. Louis, MO 63119. Phones: 314-227-9500; 800-438-2427. Web Site: http://www.cobridge.net. ICA: TX0201.
TV Market Ranking: Below 100 (SLATON). Franchise award date: June 10, 1986. Franchise expiration date: N.A. Began: January 15, 1979.
Channel capacity: N.A. Channels available but not in use: N.A.
Basic Service
Subscribers: 342.
Programming (received off-air): KAMC (ABC) Lubbock; KCBD (NBC) Lubbock; KJTV-TV (FOX) Lubbock; KLBK-TV (CBS) Lubbock; KLCW-TV (CW) Wolfforth; KPTB-DT (IND) Lubbock; KTXT-TV (PBS) Lubbock; KXTQ-CA (TMO) Lubbock.
Programming (via satellite): A&E Networks; ABC Family Channel; AMC; Animal Planet; BET Networks; CNN; Country Music TV; C-SPAN; Discovery Channel; Disney Channel; ESPN; ESPN 2; Fox Sports Southwest; Headline News; HGTV; MTV; Nickelodeon; Outdoor Channel; Spike TV; TBS Superstation; The Weather Channel; Turner Network TV; Univision Studios; USA Network; WGN America.
Fee: $27.90 installation; $13.60 monthly; $1.55 converter.
Digital Basic Service
Subscribers: N.A.
Programming (via satellite): AmericanLife TV Network; BBC America; Bio; Bloomberg Television; Bravo; Discovery Fit & Health; DMX Music; ESPN Classic Sports; Fox Movie Channel; Fox Soccer; Fuse; G4; GAS; Golf Channel; GSN; Halogen Network; History Channel; History Channel International; Independent Film Channel; Lifetime Movie Network; MTV Networks Digital Suite; Nick Jr.; Speed; Syfy; Toon Disney; Trinity Broadcasting Network; Turner Classic Movies; Versus; WE tv.
Pay Service 1
Pay Units: 139.
Programming (via satellite): Cinemax.
Fee: $20.00 installation; $9.00 monthly.
Pay Service 2
Pay Units: 220.
Programming (via satellite): HBO.
Fee: $20.00 installation; $9.00 monthly.
Pay Service 3
Pay Units: 97.
Programming (via satellite): Showtime.
Fee: $20.00 installation; $9.00 monthly.
Digital Pay Service 1
Pay Units: N.A.
Programming (via satellite): Cinemax (multiplexed); Encore (multiplexed); Flix; HBO (multiplexed); Showtime (multiplexed); Starz (multiplexed); The Movie Channel (multiplexed).
Video-On-Demand: No
Pay-Per-View
iN DEMAND (delivered digitally); Hot Choice (delivered digitally); Playboy TV (delivered digitally); Fresh (delivered digitally); Shorteez (delivered digitally).
Internet Service
Operational: No.
Telephone Service
None
Miles of Plant: 38.0 (coaxial); None (fiber optic).
Chief Executive Officer: Scott Widham. General Manager: Wayne Kelstrom.
Ownership: Cobridge Communications LLC (MSO).

SMILEY—Formerly served by National Cable Inc. No longer in operation. ICA: TX0652.

SMITHVILLE—Reveille Broadband, PO Box 39, Lexington, TX 78947. Phone: 797-773-4700. Fax: 979-773-4733. E-mail: mariesullivan@reveillebroadband.com. Web Site: http://www.reveillebroadband.com. Also serves Lake Thunderbird Estates. ICA: TX0951.
TV Market Ranking: Below 100 (INDIAN LAKE, Lake Thunderbird Estates); Outside TV Markets (SMITHVILLE). Franchise award date: June 1, 2003. Franchise expiration date: N.A. Began: N.A.
Channel capacity: N.A. Channels available but not in use: N.A.
Basic Service
Subscribers: 138.
Programming (received off-air): KEYE-TV (CBS, TMO) Austin; KLRU (PBS) Austin; KNVA (CW) Austin; KTBC (FOX) Austin; KVUE (ABC) Austin; KXAN-TV (NBC) Austin.
Programming (via satellite): A&E Networks; ABC Family Channel; AMC; Animal Planet; BET Networks; Boomerang; Cartoon Network; CNN; Comedy Central; Country Music TV; Court TV; C-SPAN; C-SPAN 2; Discovery Channel; Disney Channel; E! Entertainment Television; ESPN; ESPN 2; Food Network; Fox News

Channel; Fox Sports Southwest; FX; Great American Country; GSN; Hallmark Channel; Hallmark Movie Channel; Headline News; HGTV; History Channel; Lifetime; National Geographic Channel; Nick Jr.; Nickelodeon; QVC; Speed; Spike TV; Syfy; TBS Superstation; The Learning Channel; The Weather Channel; Travel Channel; Trinity Broadcasting Network; Turner Classic Movies; Turner Network TV; TV Land; Univision Studios; USA Network; VH1; WGN America.
Fee: $35.00 installation; $39.95 monthly.

Pay Service 1
Pay Units: 20.
Programming (via satellite): HBO.
Fee: $10.95 monthly.

Pay Service 2
Pay Units: N.A.
Programming (via satellite): The Movie Channel.
Fee: $10.95 monthly.

Internet Service
Operational: Yes.

Telephone Service
Analog: Not Operational
Digital: Operational

Miles of Plant: 12.0 (coaxial); None (fiber optic).
President: Jeff Sullivan. Chief Executive Officer: Marie Sullivan. Vice President: Corey Savage. Office Manager: Laura Tillery.
Ownership: Reveille Broadband (MSO).

SNOOK—Formerly served by National Cable Inc. No longer in operation. ICA: TX0854.

SNYDER—Formerly served by Snyder Microwave Communications LC. No longer in operation. ICA: TX0897.

SNYDER—Suddenlink Communications, 2211 Avenue R, Snyder, TX 79549. Phones: 888-822-5151 (Customer service); 915-573-3536. Fax: 915-573-6360. Web Site: http://www.suddenlink.com. Also serves Hermleigh & Scurry County. ICA: TX0120.
TV Market Ranking: Below 100 (Hermleigh, Scurry County, SNYDER). Franchise award date: N.A. Franchise expiration date: N.A. Began: December 1, 1958.
Channel capacity: 30 (operating 2-way). Channels available but not in use: N.A.

Basic Service
Subscribers: 4,269.
Programming (received off-air): KCBD (NBC) Lubbock; KERA-TV (PBS) Dallas; KJTV-TV (FOX) Lubbock; KLBK-TV (CBS) Lubbock; KPCB-DT (IND) Snyder; KRBC-TV (NBC) Abilene; KTAB-TV (CBS) Abilene; KTES-LP (TMO) Abilene; KTXS-TV (ABC, CW, TMO) Sweetwater; KXVA (FOX) Abilene; WFAA (ABC) Dallas; allband FM.
Programming (via satellite): C-SPAN; C-SPAN 2; QVC; TV Guide Network; Univision Studios.
Fee: $10.00 installation; $7.03 monthly.

Expanded Basic Service 1
Subscribers: N.A.
Programming (via satellite): A&E Networks; ABC Family Channel; AMC; Animal Planet; BET Networks; Bravo; Cartoon Network; CNBC; CNN; Comedy Central; Country Music TV; CW+; Discovery Channel; Disney Channel; E! Entertainment Television; ESPN; ESPN 2; Food Network; Fox News Channel; Fox Sports Southwest; FX; Headline News; HGTV; History Channel; Lifetime; Lifetime Movie Network; MSNBC; MTV; MTV2; Nickelodeon; Oxygen; Speed; Spike TV; Syfy; TBS Superstation; The Learning Channel; The Weather Channel; Travel Channel; truTV; Turner Network TV; TV Land; USA Network; Versus; VH1.
Fee: $13.52 monthly.

Digital Basic Service
Subscribers: N.A.
Programming (via satellite): A&E HD; Bandamax; BBC America; Bio; Bloomberg Television; Boomerang; CBS Sports Network; Cine Latino; Cine Mexicano; CMT Pure Country; CNN en Espanol; Cooking Channel; De Pelicula; De Pelicula Clasico; Discovery en Espanol; Discovery Health Channel; Discovery Home Channel; Discovery Kids Channel; Discovery Times Channel; DIY Network; DMX Music; Encore (multiplexed); ESPN 2 HD; ESPN Classic Sports; ESPN Deportes; ESPN HD; ESPN U; ESPNews; Eternal Word TV Network; EWTN en Espanol; Food Network HD; Fox College Sports Atlantic; Fox College Sports Central; Fox College Sports Pacific; Fox Deportes; Fox Soccer; Fuel TV; Fuse; G4; GalaVision; GMC; Golf Channel; Great American Country; GSN; Hallmark Channel; Halogen Network; HD Theater; HDNet; HDNet Movies; HGTV HD; History Channel en Espanol; History Channel International; Independent Film Channel; Jewelry Television; Military Channel; MTV Hits; mun2 television; National Geographic Channel; National Geographic Channel HD Network; Nick Jr.; NickToons TV; Nuvo TV; Outdoor Channel; Science; ShopNBC; SoapNet; Sorpresa; Sundance Channel; Sur Network; TeenNick; Telefutura; Telehit; Tennis Channel; Toon Disney; Toon Disney en Espanol; Tr3s; Turner Classic Movies; Turner Network TV HD; Universal HD; VH1 Classic; VHUNO; Video Rola; WE tv.

Pay Service 1
Pay Units: 1,986.
Programming (via satellite): Cinemax; HBO; Showtime; Starz.
Fee: $40.00 installation; $10.50 monthly (each).

Digital Pay Service 1
Pay Units: N.A.
Programming (via satellite): Cinemax (multiplexed); Encore; HBO (multiplexed); HBO HD; HBO Latino; Showtime (multiplexed); Showtime HD; Starz (multiplexed); Starz HDTV; The Movie Channel.

Video-On-Demand: No

Pay-Per-View
iN DEMAND (delivered digitally); Fresh (delivered digitally); Shorteez (delivered digitally); Playboy TV (delivered digitally).

Internet Service
Operational: Yes.
Broadband Service: Suddenlink High Speed Internet.
Fee: $45.95 installation; $29.95 monthly.

Telephone Service
Digital: Operational
Fee: $44.95 monthly

Miles of Plant: 108.0 (coaxial); None (fiber optic).
Manager: Victor Means. Chief Technician: Peter Pena.
Ownership: Cequel Communications LLC (MSO).

SONORA—Suddenlink Communications, 12444 Powerscourt Dr, Saint Louis, MO 63131-3660. Phones: 877-423-2743 (Customer service); 314-965-2020. Web Site: http://www.suddenlink.com. ICA: TX0245.
TV Market Ranking: Outside TV Markets (SONORA). Franchise award date: N.A. Franchise expiration date: N.A. Began: April 1, 1955.
Channel capacity: N.A. Channels available but not in use: N.A.

Basic Service
Subscribers: 1,085.
Programming (received off-air): KIDY (FOX) San Angelo; KLST (CBS) San Angelo; KSAN-TV (NBC) San Angelo; KTXS-TV (ABC, CW, TMO) Sweetwater; 4 FMs.
Programming (via satellite): A&E Networks; ABC Family Channel; Animal Planet; CNN; Country Music TV; C-SPAN; Discovery Channel; Disney Channel; ESPN; Fox News Channel; Fox Sports Southwest; Headline News; History Channel; KRMA-TV (PBS) Denver; Lifetime; Nickelodeon; QVC; Spike TV; TBS Superstation; The Learning Channel; The Weather Channel; Trinity Broadcasting Network; Turner Classic Movies; Turner Network TV; TV Land; USA Network; WGN America.
Programming (via translator): KVDA (TMO) San Antonio.
Fee: $35.00 installation; $19.95 monthly.

Pay Service 1
Pay Units: 131.
Programming (via satellite): The Movie Channel.
Fee: $5.95 monthly.

Pay Service 2
Pay Units: 131.
Programming (via satellite): Showtime.
Fee: $9.95 monthly.

Pay Service 3
Pay Units: 167.
Programming (via satellite): HBO.
Fee: $10.95 monthly.

Video-On-Demand: No

Internet Service
Operational: Yes. Began: October 5, 2004.
Broadband Service: Suddenlink High Speed Internet.
Fee: $45.95 installation; $29.95 monthly.

Telephone Service
Digital: Operational
Fee: $44.95 monthly

Miles of Plant: 36.0 (coaxial); None (fiber optic).
Regional Manager: Todd Cruthird. Marketing Director: Beverly Gambell.
Ownership: Cequel Communications LLC (MSO).

SOUR LAKE—CMA Communications, 630 W Barkley St, Sour Lake, TX 77659. Phones: 979-968-6476 (La Grange office); 409-287-3014. Fax: 979-968-5368. Web Site: http://www.cmaaccess.com. Also serves Bevil Oaks, China & Jefferson County (portions). ICA: TX0162.
TV Market Ranking: 88 (Bevil Oaks, China, Jefferson County (portions), SOUR LAKE). Franchise award date: February 1, 1983. Franchise expiration date: N.A. Began: N.A.
Channel capacity: N.A. Channels available but not in use: N.A.

Basic Service
Subscribers: 2,240.
Programming (received off-air): KBMT (ABC) Beaumont; KBTV-TV (FOX) Port Arthur; KFDM (CBS, CW) Beaumont; KIAH (CW) Houston; KITU-TV (TBN) Beaumont; KRIV (FOX) Houston; KTRK-TV (ABC) Houston; KTXH (MNT) Houston; KUHT (PBS) Houston; KVHP (FOX) Lake Charles; KYAZ (IND) Katy.
Programming (via satellite): The Weather Channel.
Fee: $39.95 installation; $20.95 monthly; $12.95 additional installation.

Expanded Basic Service 1
Subscribers: N.A.
Programming (via satellite): A&E Networks; ABC Family Channel; AMC; Animal Planet; BET Networks; Bravo; CNBC; CNN; Comedy Central; Country Music TV; C-SPAN; Discovery Channel; ESPN; ESPN 2; Food Network; Fox News Channel; Fox Sports Net; FX; Hallmark Channel; Headline News; History Channel; Lifetime; MTV; Nickelodeon; Outdoor Channel; QVC; Spike TV; Syfy; TBS Superstation; The Learning Channel; Toon Disney; Travel Channel; truTV; Turner Network TV; TV Land; USA Network; VH1; WGN America.
Fee: $25.50 monthly.

Digital Basic Service
Subscribers: N.A.
Programming (via satellite): BBC America; Bio; Bloomberg Television; Discovery Digital Networks; ESPN Classic Sports; ESPNews; Fox Movie Channel; Fox Sports World; G4; GAS; Golf Channel; GSN; HGTV; History Channel International; Independent Film Channel; Lifetime Movie Network; National Geographic Channel; Nick Jr.; Speed; Style Network; Trinity Broadcasting Network; Turner Classic Movies; Versus; WE tv.
Fee: $13.95 monthly.

Digital Pay Service 1
Pay Units: N.A.
Programming (via satellite): DMX Music; Encore (multiplexed); HBO (multiplexed); Showtime (multiplexed); Starz; The Movie Channel (multiplexed).
Fee: $9.95 installation; $10.95 monthly (Cinemax or Starz/Encore), $13.95 monthly (HBO or Showtime).

Video-On-Demand: No

Pay-Per-View
iN DEMAND (delivered digitally); Club Jenna (delivered digitally); Fresh (delivered digitally); Playboy TV (delivered digitally).

Internet Service
Operational: Yes.
Broadband Service: CMA.
Fee: $39.95 installation; $41.95 monthly; $2.95 modem lease; $39.95 modem purchase.

Telephone Service
Digital: Operational
Fee: $39.95 monthly

Miles of Plant: 120.0 (coaxial); None (fiber optic).
General Manager: Jerry L. Smith. Chief Technician: Dutch Bernsen. Marketing Director: Jullie Ferguson.
Ownership: Cable Management Assoc. (MSO).

SOUTH SHORES—Formerly served by Cable Unlimited. No longer in operation. ICA: TX0966.

SOUTH SILSBEE—Formerly served by Cebridge Connections. No longer in operation. ICA: TX0614.

SPEARMAN—Panhandle Telephone Coop. Inc., 2222 NW Hwy 64, Guymon, OK 73942. Phones: 800-562-2556; 580-338-2556. Fax: 580-338-8260. E-mail: support@ptsi.net. Web Site: http://www.ptsi.net. ICA: TX0298.
TV Market Ranking: Outside TV Markets (SPEARMAN). Franchise award date: December 8, 1985. Franchise expiration date: N.A. Began: September 1, 1960.
Channel capacity: N.A. Channels available but not in use: N.A.

Basic Service
Subscribers: N.A.
Programming (received off-air): KACV-TV (PBS) Amarillo; KAMR-TV (NBC) Amarillo; KCIT (FOX) Amarillo; KETA-TV (PBS) Oklahoma City; KFDA-TV (CBS) Amarillo; KPTF-DT (IND) Farwell; KVII-TV (ABC, CW) Amarillo.
Programming (via satellite): QVC; Trinity Broadcasting Network.
Fee: $18.99 monthly.
Expanded Basic Service 1
Subscribers: N.A.
Programming (via satellite): A&E Networks; ABC Family Channel; American Movie Classics; Animal Planet; Cartoon Network; CNN; Comedy Central; CW Television Network; Discovery Channel; Disney Channel; E! Entertainment Television; ESPN; ESPN 2; Food Network; Fox News Channel; Fox Sports Southwest; FX; Great American Country; Headline News; History Channel; Home & Garden Television; Lifetime; MSNBC; MTV; National Geographic Channel; Nickelodeon; Outdoor Channel; Paramount Network (UPN); Speed; Spike TV; Syfy; TBS Superstation; Telemundo; The Weather Channel; TLC; TNT; Travel Channel; truTV; Turner Classic Movies; TV Land; Univision Studios; USA Network; VH1.
Fee: $33.00 monthly.
Pay Service 1
Pay Units: N.A.
Programming (via satellite): Cinemax; HBO; Showtime; The Movie Channel.
Fee: $13.49 monthly (Cinemax), $13.95 monthly (Showtime & TMC), $14.00 monthly (HBO).
Internet Service
Operational: Yes.
Fee: $44.99 monthly.
Telephone Service
Analog: Operational
Miles of Plant: 20.0 (coaxial); None (fiber optic).
President: Charles Russell.
Ownership: Panhandle Telephone Cooperative Inc.

SPICEWOOD BEACH—Formerly served by Charter Communications. No longer in operation. ICA: TX0633.

SPLENDORA—Almega Cable, 4001 W Airport Frwy, Ste 530, Bedford, TX 76021. Phone: 817-685-9588. Fax: 817-685-6488. E-mail: helpdesk@almegacable.com. Web Site: http://www.almega.com. Also serves Liberty County (portions) & Montgomery County (portions). ICA: TX0372.
TV Market Ranking: 15 (Montgomery County (portions), SPLENDORA); 88 (Liberty County (portions)). Franchise award date: N.A. Franchise expiration date: N.A. Began: N.A.
Channel capacity: 36 (not 2-way capable). Channels available but not in use: N.A.
Basic Service
Subscribers: 208.
Programming (received off-air): KHOU (CBS) Houston; KIAH (CW) Houston; KPRC-TV (NBC) Houston; KRIV (FOX) Houston; KTRK-TV (ABC) Houston; KTXH (MNT) Houston; KUHT (PBS) Houston.
Programming (via satellite): A&E Networks; ABC Family Channel; CNN; Country Music TV; C-SPAN; Discovery Channel; Disney Channel; ESPN; Fox Sports Southwest; Headline News; INSP; Lifetime; Nickelodeon; QVC; Spike TV; TBS Superstation; The Weather Channel; Turner Network TV; USA Network.
Fee: $54.95 installation; $44.05 monthly.
Pay Service 1
Pay Units: 51.
Programming (via satellite): Cinemax.
Fee: $12.95 monthly.
Pay Service 2
Pay Units: 69.
Programming (via satellite): HBO.
Fee: $12.95 monthly.
Pay Service 3
Pay Units: 149.
Programming (via satellite): Showtime.
Fee: $12.95 monthly.
Video-On-Demand: No
Internet Service
Operational: No.
Telephone Service
None
Miles of Plant: 108.0 (coaxial); None (fiber optic).
Ownership: Almega Cable (MSO).

SPRING—Charter Communications, 15100 Trinity Blvd, Ste 500, Fort Worth, TX 76155. Phone: 817-298-3600. Web Site: http://www.charter.com. Also serves Harris County (northern portion), Oak Ridge North, Rayford Forest, Shenandoah & Woodloch. ICA: TX0044.
TV Market Ranking: 15 (Harris County (northern portion), Oak Ridge North, Rayford Forest, Shenandoah, SPRING, Woodloch). Franchise award date: N.A. Franchise expiration date: N.A. Began: January 1, 1979.
Channel capacity: N.A. Channels available but not in use: N.A.
Basic Service
Subscribers: 13,657.
Programming (received off-air): KETH-TV (TBN) Houston; KFTH-DT (TEL) Alvin; KHOU (CBS) Houston; KIAH (CW) Houston; KLTJ (ETV) Galveston; KPRC-TV (NBC) Houston; KPXB-TV (ION) Conroe; KRIV (FOX) Houston; KTBU (IND) Conroe; KTMD (TMO) Galveston; KTRK-TV (ABC) Houston; KTXH (MNT) Houston; KUBE-TV (IND) Baytown; KUHT (PBS) Houston; KXLN-DT (UNV) Rosenberg; KYAZ (IND) Katy; KZJL (IND) Houston.
Programming (via satellite): ESPN; QVC; TBS Superstation; TV Guide Network; WGN America.
Fee: $28.00 installation; $13.25 monthly; $3.65 converter.
Expanded Basic Service 1
Subscribers: 13,257.
Programming (via satellite): A&E Networks; ABC Family Channel; AMC; Animal Planet; BET Networks; Bravo; Cartoon Network; CNBC; CNN; Comedy Central; C-SPAN; C-SPAN 2; Discovery Channel; Discovery Fit & Health; Disney Channel; E! Entertainment Television; ESPN 2; ESPN Classic Sports; Food Network; Fox News Channel; Fox Sports Southwest; FX; G4; GalaVision; Great American Country; GSN; Hallmark Channel; Headline News; HGTV; History Channel; Lifetime; MSNBC; MTV; National Geographic Channel; Nickelodeon; Oxygen; Product Information Network; SoapNet; Speed; Spike TV; Style Network; Syfy; The Learning Channel; The Weather Channel; Toon Disney; Travel Channel; truTV; Turner Network TV; TV Land; USA Network; Versus; VH1; WE tv.
Fee: $20.97 installation; $15.65 monthly.
Digital Basic Service
Subscribers: N.A.
Programming (via satellite): BBC America; Bio; Bloomberg Television; Discovery Health Channel; Discovery Home Channel; Discovery Kids Channel; Discovery Times Channel; DIY Network; ESPNews; Fox Movie Channel; Fox Soccer; Fuel TV; Golf Channel; History Channel International; Independent Film Channel; Lifetime Movie Network; Music Choice; Nick Jr.; Science Television; Sundance Channel; Turner Classic Movies; VHUNO.
Pay Service 1
Pay Units: 2,783.
Programming (via satellite): Encore (multiplexed); Flix; Showtime (multiplexed); The Movie Channel (multiplexed).
Fee: $8.00 monthly.
Digital Pay Service 1
Pay Units: N.A.
Programming (via satellite): Cinemax; HBO; Starz (multiplexed).
Video-On-Demand: No
Internet Service
Operational: Yes. Began: January 1, 2002.
Broadband Service: Charter Pipeline.
Fee: $29.99 monthly.
Telephone Service
None
Miles of Plant: 415.0 (coaxial); None (fiber optic).
Vice President & General Manager: Wayne Cramp. Technical Operations Director: John Linton. Technical Operations Manager: Robert Hurd. Marketing Director: Kathleen Griffin.
Ownership: Charter Communications Inc. (MSO).

SPRINGTOWN—CommuniComm Services, 2804B S FM 51, PO Box 869, Decatur, TX 76234-0869. Phone: 940-627-8414. Fax: 940-627-8303. Web Site: http://www.communicomm.com. ICA: TX0390.
TV Market Ranking: 12 (SPRINGTOWN). Franchise award date: September 1, 1983. Franchise expiration date: N.A. Began: September 1, 1983.
Channel capacity: N.A. Channels available but not in use: N.A.
Basic Service
Subscribers: N.A. Included in Decatur
Programming (received off-air): KDAF (CW, IND) Dallas; KDFI (MNT) Dallas; KDFW-DT (FOX) Dallas; KDTN (ETV) Denton; KDTX-TV (TBN) Dallas; KERA-TV (PBS) Dallas; KTVT (CBS) Fort Worth; KTXA (IND) Fort Worth; KXAS-TV (NBC) Fort Worth; KXTX-TV (TMO) Dallas; WFAA (ABC) Dallas.
Expanded Basic Service 1
Subscribers: N.A.
Programming (via satellite): A&E Networks; ABC Family Channel; AMC; CNBC; CNN; Country Music TV; C-SPAN; Discovery Channel; Disney Channel; ESPN; Fox Sports Southwest; Headline News; MTV; Nickelodeon; QVC; Spike TV; TBS Superstation; TeenNick; The Weather Channel; Turner Network TV; USA Network; WGN America.
Fee: $41.95 monthly.
Digital Basic Service
Subscribers: N.A.
Programming (via satellite): AmericanLife TV Network; BBC America; Bio; Bloomberg Television; Bravo; cloo; Discovery Fit & Health; Discovery Health Channel; Discovery Home Channel; Discovery Kids Channel; Discovery Times Channel; DMX Music; ESPN Classic Sports; ESPNews; Fox Soccer; Fuse; G4; Golf Channel; Great American Country; GSN; Halogen Network; HGTV; History Channel; History Channel International; Independent Film Channel; Lifetime Movie Network; Military Channel; MTV Hits; MTV2; National Geographic Channel; NickToons TV; Outdoor Channel; Science; Speed; Sundance Channel; Turner Classic Movies; Versus; WE tv.
Fee: $7.00 monthly.
Pay Service 1
Pay Units: N.A.
Programming (via satellite): Cinemax; HBO (multiplexed); Starz.
Digital Pay Service 1
Pay Units: N.A.
Programming (via satellite): Cinemax (multiplexed); Encore (multiplexed); Flix; HBO (multiplexed); Showtime (multiplexed); Starz (multiplexed); The Movie Channel (multiplexed).
Fee: $5.00 monthly (Encore), $11.00 monthly (Starz), $11.95 monthly (Cinemax), $13.95 monthly (HBO or Showtime/TMC/Flix).
Video-On-Demand: No
Pay-Per-View
iN DEMAND (delivered digitally); Hot Choice (delivered digitally); Playboy TV (delivered digitally); Spice (delivered digitally); Spice 2 (delivered digitally).
Internet Service
Operational: Yes.
Telephone Service
None
Miles of Plant: 44.0 (coaxial); None (fiber optic). Included in Decatur
Chief Technician: J. D. Sifford. Operations Manager: Wes Devall.
Ownership: James Cable LLC (MSO).

SPUR—Almega Cable, 4001 W Airport Freeway, Ste 530, Bedford, TX 76021. Phone: 817-685-9588. Fax: 817-685-6488. E-mail: helpdesk@almegacable.com. Web Site: http://www.almega.com. ICA: TX0358.
TV Market Ranking: Outside TV Markets (SPUR). Franchise award date: February 2, 1965. Franchise expiration date: N.A. Began: December 6, 1965.
Channel capacity: 41 (not 2-way capable). Channels available but not in use: N.A.
Basic Service
Subscribers: 140.
Programming (received off-air): KAMC (ABC) Lubbock; KCBD (NBC) Lubbock; KJTV-TV (FOX) Lubbock; KLBK-TV (CBS) Lubbock; KTXT-TV (PBS) Lubbock; 1 FM.
Programming (via satellite): ABC Family Channel; AMC; Animal Planet; Cartoon Network; CNN; Country Music TV; Discovery Channel; Disney Channel; E! Entertainment Television; ESPN; Fox News Channel; Fox Sports Southwest; Headline News; History Channel; Lifetime; Nickelodeon; QVC; Spike TV; Syfy; TBS Superstation; The Learning Channel; The Weather Channel; Trinity Broadcasting Network; Turner Network TV; TV Land; USA Network; WGN America.
Fee: $29.95 installation; $38.00 monthly.
Pay Service 1
Pay Units: 34.
Programming (via satellite): Cinemax.
Fee: $9.95 monthly.
Pay Service 2
Pay Units: 55.
Programming (via satellite): HBO.
Fee: $9.95 monthly.
Video-On-Demand: No
Internet Service
Operational: No.
Telephone Service
None
Miles of Plant: 14.0 (coaxial); None (fiber optic).
Ownership: Almega Cable (MSO).

SPURGER—Formerly served by Carrell Communications. No longer in operation. ICA: TX0882.

ST. FRANCIS VILLAGE—Formerly served by National Cable Inc. No longer in operation. ICA: TX0544.

ST. JO—Rapid Cable. Now served by VALLEY VIEW, TX [TX0792]. ICA: TX0571.

STAMFORD—Alliance Communications, 6125 Paluxy Dr, Tyler, TX 75703. Phones: 800-842-8160; 501-679-6619. Fax: 501-679-5694. Web Site: http://www.alliancecable.net. ICA: TX0247.
TV Market Ranking: Below 100 (STAMFORD). Franchise award date: N.A. Franchise expiration date: N.A. Began: April 1, 1961.
Channel capacity: N.A. Channels available but not in use: N.A.
Basic Service
Subscribers: 465.
Programming (received off-air): KIDZ-LP Abilene; KRBC-TV (NBC) Abilene; KRMA-TV (PBS) Denver; KTAB-TV (CBS) Abilene; KTXS-TV (ABC, CW, TMO) Sweetwater; KXVA (FOX) Abilene.
Programming (via satellite): C-SPAN; ESPN; ESPN 2; Fox Sports Southwest; MTV; QVC; TBS Superstation; Turner Network TV; WGN America.
Fee: $29.95 installation; $19.95 monthly.
Expanded Basic Service 1
Subscribers: 363.
Programming (received off-air): KDTX-TV (TBN) Dallas.
Programming (via satellite): A&E Networks; ABC Family Channel; AMC; Animal Planet; CNN; Comedy Central; Country Music TV; Discovery Channel; Disney Channel; E! Entertainment Television; Headline News; HGTV; History Channel; Lifetime; MSNBC; Nickelodeon; Oxygen; SoapNet; Spike TV; Syfy; The Learning Channel; The Weather Channel; Trinity Broadcasting Network; Turner Classic Movies; TV Land; Univision Studios; USA Network; Versus; VH1.
Fee: $18.00 monthly.
Digital Basic Service
Subscribers: 38.
Programming (via satellite): BBC America; Bio; Bloomberg Television; Discovery Digital Networks; DIY Network; ESPN Classic Sports; ESPNews; Flix; G4; History Channel International; Independent Film Channel; Music Choice; Style Network; Toon Disney.
Fee: $12.95 monthly.
Pay Service 1
Pay Units: N.A.
Programming (via satellite): Showtime.
Fee: $9.95 monthly.
Digital Pay Service 1
Pay Units: N.A.
Programming (via satellite): Cinemax (multiplexed); Encore (multiplexed); HBO (multiplexed); Showtime; The Movie Channel (multiplexed).
Video-On-Demand: No
Internet Service
Operational: No.
Telephone Service
None
Miles of Plant: 28.0 (coaxial); None (fiber optic).
Vice President & General Manager: John Brinker. Vice President, Programming: Julie Newman.
Ownership: Buford Media Group LLC (MSO).

STANTON—Formerly served by Almega Cable. No longer in operation. ICA: TX0350.

STEPHENVILLE—Northland Cable Television, 975 N Lillian St, PO Box 70, Stephenville, TX 76401-0001. Phone: 254-968-4189. Fax: 254-968-8350. Web Site: http://www.northlandcabletv.com. ICA: TX0098.
TV Market Ranking: Outside TV Markets (STEPHENVILLE). Franchise award date: N.A. Franchise expiration date: N.A. Began: July 15, 1967.
Channel capacity: 57 (not 2-way capable). Channels available but not in use: N.A.
Basic Service
Subscribers: 3,384.
Programming (received off-air): KDAF (CW, IND) Dallas; KDFI (MNT) Dallas; KDFW-DT (FOX) Dallas; KERA-TV (PBS) Dallas; KPXD-TV (ION) Arlington; KSTR-DT (TEL) Irving; KTVT (CBS) Fort Worth; KTXA (IND) Fort Worth; KWTX-TV (CBS, CW) Waco; KXAS-TV (NBC) Fort Worth; KXTX-TV (TMO) Dallas; WFAA (ABC) Dallas; allband FM.
Programming (via satellite): A&E Networks; Animal Planet; Cartoon Network; CNBC; CNN; Comedy Central; C-SPAN; Discovery Channel; Disney Channel; ESPN; ESPN 2; Food Network; Fox Movie Channel; Fox News Channel; Fox Sports Southwest; FX; Golf Channel; Great American Country; Hallmark Channel; Headline News; HGTV; History Channel; Lifetime; MTV; Nickelodeon; Outdoor Channel; QVC; Spike TV; Syfy; TBS Superstation; The Learning Channel; The Weather Channel; Travel Channel; Trinity Broadcasting Network; Turner Classic Movies; Turner Network TV; TV Land; Univision Studios; USA Network; Versus; VH1.
Fee: $45.99 monthly.
Digital Basic Service
Subscribers: N.A.
Programming (via satellite): BBC America; Bloomberg Television; Bravo; Discovery Fit & Health; Discovery Health Channel; Discovery Kids Channel; DMX Music; ESPNews; Fox Soccer; G4; ID Investigation Discovery; Independent Film Channel; Military Channel; National Geographic Channel; Planet Green; Science; Speed; WE tv.
Fee: $8.70 monthly.
Digital Expanded Basic Service
Subscribers: N.A.
Programming (via satellite): ESPN HD; HD Theater; Turner Network TV HD; Universal HD.
Fee: $5.99 monthly.
Pay Service 1
Pay Units: N.A.
Programming (via satellite): HBO.
Fee: $13.50 monthly.
Digital Pay Service 1
Pay Units: N.A.
Programming (via satellite): Cinemax (multiplexed); Encore (multiplexed); Flix; HBO (multiplexed); Showtime (multiplexed); Starz (multiplexed); The Movie Channel (multiplexed).
Fee: $14.75 monthly (Cinemax, HBO, Starz/Encore, or Showtime/TMC/Flix).
Video-On-Demand: No
Pay-Per-View
iN DEMAND (delivered digitally); Hot Choice (delivered digitally); Playboy TV (delivered digitally); Fresh (delivered digitally).
Internet Service
Operational: Yes.
Fee: $42.99 monthly.
Telephone Service
None
Miles of Plant: 96.0 (coaxial); None (fiber optic).
Manager: Melissa Gonzalez. Chief Technician: Bobby Smith.
Ownership: Northland Communications Corp. (MSO).

STERLING CITY—Reach Broadband, 515 E Longview St, Arp, TX 75750. Phone: 800-687-1258. Web Site: http://www.reachbroadband.net. ICA: TX0856.
TV Market Ranking: Outside TV Markets (STERLING CITY). Franchise award date: N.A. Franchise expiration date: N.A. Began: N.A.
Channel capacity: 22 (not 2-way capable). Channels available but not in use: N.A.
Basic Service
Subscribers: 166.
Programming (received off-air): KIDY (FOX) San Angelo; KLST (CBS) San Angelo; KSAN-TV (NBC) San Angelo; KTXS-TV (ABC, CW, TMO) Sweetwater.
Programming (via satellite): ABC Family Channel; AMC; Animal Planet; Cartoon Network; CNN; Country Music TV; Discovery Channel; Disney Channel; E! Entertainment Television; ESPN; Fox Sports Southwest; Headline News; Lifetime; QVC; Spike TV; Syfy; TBS Superstation; The Learning Channel; The Weather Channel; Trinity Broadcasting Network; Turner Network TV; TV Land; USA Network.
Fee: $29.99 installation; $38.00 monthly.
Pay Service 1
Pay Units: 19.
Programming (via satellite): Showtime.
Fee: $9.95 monthly.
Pay Service 2
Pay Units: 83.
Programming (via satellite): HBO.
Fee: $9.95 monthly.
Video-On-Demand: No
Internet Service
Operational: No.
Telephone Service
None
Miles of Plant: 200.0 (coaxial); None (fiber optic).
Regional Manager: Ronnie Stafford. Office Manager: Jan Gibson.
Ownership: RB3 LLC (MSO).

STOCKDALE—Windjammer Cable, 8500 W 110th St, Ste 600, Overland Park, KS 66210. Phone: 888-495-2881. Fax: 913-563-5454. Web Site: http://www.windjammercable.com. ICA: TX1020.
TV Market Ranking: Outside TV Markets (STOCKDALE).
Channel capacity: N.A. Channels available but not in use: N.A.
Basic Service
Subscribers: N.A. Included in San Antonio
Programming (received off-air): KABB (FOX) San Antonio; KENS (CBS) San Antonio; KLRN (PBS) San Antonio; KMYS (CW) Kerrville; KPXL-TV (ION) Uvalde; KSAT-TV (ABC) San Antonio; KVDA (TMO) San Antonio; KWEX-DT (UNV) San Antonio; WOAI-TV (NBC) San Antonio.
Programming (via satellite): A&E Networks; ABC Family Channel; AMC; Animal Planet; Cartoon Network; CNN; Comedy Central; Country Music TV; C-SPAN; C-SPAN 2; Discovery Channel; Disney Channel; ESPN; ESPN 2; Food Network; Fox News Channel; Fox Sports Southwest; FX; Headline News; HGTV; Lifetime; MTV; Nickelodeon; QVC; Spike TV; Syfy; TBS Superstation; The Learning Channel; The Movie Channel; The Weather Channel; Travel Channel; Turner Network TV; TV Land; USA Network.
Pay Service 1
Pay Units: N.A.
Programming (via satellite): Encore; HBO; Showtime; Starz (multiplexed).
Internet Service
Operational: No.
Telephone Service
None
Miles of plant included in San Antonio
General Manager: Timothy Evard. Operations Director: Belinda Graham. Engineering Director: Mike Earehart. Finance & Accounting Director: Cindy Johnson.
Ownership: Windjammer Communications LLC (MSO).

STONY POINT—Almega Cable, 4001 W Airport Frwy, Ste 530, Bedford, TX 76021. Phone: 817-685-9588. Fax: 817-685-6488. E-mail: helpdesk@almegacable.com. Web Site: http://www.almega.com. Also serves Garfield. ICA: TX0303.
TV Market Ranking: Below 100 (Garfield, STONY POINT). Franchise award date: July 3, 1986. Franchise expiration date: July 3, 2006. Began: May 1, 1988.
Channel capacity: 36 (not 2-way capable). Channels available but not in use: N.A.
Basic Service
Subscribers: N.A.
Programming (received off-air): KEYE-TV (CBS, TMO) Austin; KLRU (PBS) Austin; KTBC (FOX) Austin; KVUE (ABC) Austin; KXAN-TV (NBC) Austin.
Programming (via satellite): A&E Networks; ABC Family Channel; AMC; Animal Planet; BET Networks; Cartoon Network; CNN; Comedy Central; Country Music TV; C-SPAN; Discovery Channel; Disney Channel; ESPN; ESPN 2; Fox Sports Southwest; GalaVision; HGTV; History Channel; Lifetime; MTV; Nickelodeon; Speed; Spike TV; Syfy; TBS Superstation; The Learning Channel; The Weather Channel; Travel Channel; Turner Network TV; TV Land; Univision Studios; USA Network; WGN America.
Fee: $29.99 installation; $38.00 monthly.
Pay Service 1
Pay Units: 107.
Programming (via satellite): Cinemax; HBO.
Fee: $9.00 monthly (each).
Video-On-Demand: No
Pay-Per-View
iN DEMAND (delivered digitally); Hot Choice (delivered digitally); Playboy TV (delivered digitally); Fresh (delivered digitally); Shorteez (delivered digitally).
Internet Service
Operational: No.
Telephone Service
None
Miles of Plant: 32.0 (coaxial); None (fiber optic).
Ownership: Almega Cable (MSO).

STRATFORD—Almega Cable, 4001 W Airport Frwy, Ste 530, Bedford, TX 76021. Phone: 817-685-9588. Fax: 817-685-6488. E-mail: helpdesk@almegacable.com. Web Site: http://www.almega.com. ICA: TX0404.
TV Market Ranking: Outside TV Markets (STRATFORD). Franchise award date: N.A. Franchise expiration date: N.A. Began: April 1, 1963.
Channel capacity: N.A. Channels available but not in use: N.A.
Basic Service
Subscribers: 184.
Programming (received off-air): KAMR-TV (NBC) Amarillo; KCIT (FOX) Amarillo; KETA-

TV (PBS) Oklahoma City; KFDA-TV (CBS) Amarillo; KVII-TV (ABC, CW) Amarillo.
Programming (via satellite): A&E Networks; ABC Family Channel; AMC; Animal Planet; CNN; Country Music TV; C-SPAN; Discovery Channel; Disney Channel; ESPN; Fox News Channel; Hallmark Channel; Headline News; History Channel; Lifetime; Nickelodeon; QVC; Spike TV; Syfy; TBS Superstation; The Learning Channel; The Weather Channel; Turner Network TV; TV Land; USA Network; WGN America.
Fee: $29.95 installation; $38.00 monthly.

Pay Service 1
Pay Units: 51.
Programming (via satellite): The Movie Channel.
Fee: $5.95 monthly.

Pay Service 2
Pay Units: 55.
Programming (via satellite): Showtime.
Fee: $9.95 monthly.

Pay Service 3
Pay Units: 63.
Programming (via satellite): HBO.
Fee: $10.95 monthly.

Video-On-Demand: No

Internet Service
Operational: No.

Telephone Service
None

Miles of Plant: 19.0 (coaxial); None (fiber optic).
Ownership: Almega Cable (MSO).

STRAWN—Strawn TV Cable Inc., PO Box 48, Strawn, TX 76475-0048. Phone: 254-672-5296. ICA: TX0596.
TV Market Ranking: Outside TV Markets (STRAWN). Franchise award date: November 10, 1973. Franchise expiration date: N.A. Began: November 10, 1973.
Channel capacity: 28 (not 2-way capable). Channels available but not in use: N.A.

Basic Service
Subscribers: 70.
Programming (received off-air): KDAF (CW, IND) Dallas; KDFI (MNT) Dallas; KDFW-DT (FOX) Dallas; KERA-TV (PBS) Dallas; KRBC-TV (NBC) Abilene; KTVT (CBS) Fort Worth; KTXA (IND) Fort Worth; KTXS-TV (ABC, CW, TMO) Sweetwater; KXAS-TV (NBC) Fort Worth; KXTX-TV (TMO) Dallas; WFAA (ABC) Dallas; allband FM.
Programming (via satellite): Cartoon Network; CNN; Country Music TV; Discovery Channel; ESPN; Fox Sports Southwest; HGTV; History Channel; MTV; Nickelodeon; Spike TV; TBS Superstation; Telefutura; Telemundo; Turner Network TV; Univision Studios.
Fee: $20.00 installation; $22.50 monthly.

Pay Service 1
Pay Units: 21.
Programming (via satellite): Cinemax.
Fee: $10.00 monthly.

Pay Service 2
Pay Units: 22.
Programming (via satellite): HBO.
Fee: $10.00 monthly.

Video-On-Demand: No

Internet Service
Operational: No.

Telephone Service
None

Miles of Plant: 11.0 (coaxial); None (fiber optic).
Manager & Chief Technician: Buddy Talley. Marketing Director: Dorothy Talley.
Ownership: Albert A. & Dorothy Talley.

SULLIVAN CITY—Time Warner Communications. Now served by PHARR, TX [TX0017]. ICA: TX0328.

SULPHUR SPRINGS—Suddenlink Communications, 220 Linda Dr, Sulphur Springs, TX 75482-4355. Phone: 903-885-3757. Web Site: http://www.suddenlink.com. Also serves Hopkins County. ICA: TX0859.
TV Market Ranking: Below 100 (SULPHUR SPRINGS); Outside TV Markets (Hopkins County). Franchise award date: N.A. Franchise expiration date: N.A. Began: June 1, 1954.
Channel capacity: 42 (not 2-way capable). Channels available but not in use: N.A.

Basic Service
Subscribers: 5,956.
Programming (received off-air): KDFW-DT (FOX) Dallas; KERA-TV (PBS) Dallas; KETK-TV (NBC) Jacksonville; KLTV (ABC, TMO) Tyler; KTAQ (IND) Greenville; KTVT (CBS) Fort Worth; KXAS-TV (NBC) Fort Worth; KXTX-TV (TMO) Dallas; WFAA (ABC) Dallas; allband FM.
Programming (via satellite): C-SPAN; ESPN; Headline News; TBS Superstation; The Learning Channel; The Weather Channel; Trinity Broadcasting Network; TV Land.
Fee: $35.00 installation; $12.74 monthly.

Expanded Basic Service 1
Subscribers: N.A.
Programming (via satellite): ABC Family Channel; AMC; BET Networks; Cartoon Network; CNN; Discovery Channel; Disney Channel; Fox Sports Southwest; Great American Country; Lifetime; Nickelodeon; Spike TV; Syfy; Turner Network TV; USA Network; VH1.
Fee: $13.43 monthly.

A la Carte 1
Subscribers: N.A.
Programming (via satellite): TBS Superstation.
Fee: $.69 monthly.

Pay Service 1
Pay Units: 1,070.
Programming (via satellite): Cinemax; HBO; Showtime; Starz; The Movie Channel.
Fee: $21.95 monthly.

Video-On-Demand: No

Internet Service
Operational: Yes.
Broadband Service: Suddenlink High Speed Internet.

Telephone Service
Digital: Operational

Miles of Plant: 140.0 (coaxial); None (fiber optic).
Manager: Joe Suggs. Chief Technician: Tim Gaunder.
Ownership: Cequel Communications LLC (MSO).

SUNDOWN—Formerly served by Almega Cable. No longer in operation. ICA: TX0410.

SWEENY—Texas Mid-Gulf Cablevision, 1302 Wisteria St, Wharton, TX 77488. Phones: 979-532-8630; 866-532-3920. Fax: 979-532-8630. Web Site: http://www.warpspeed1.net. ICA: TX0246.
TV Market Ranking: Outside TV Markets (SWEENY). Franchise award date: N.A. Franchise expiration date: N.A. Began: May 1, 1980.
Channel capacity: N.A. Channels available but not in use: N.A.

Basic Service
Subscribers: 1,006.
Programming (received off-air): KHOU (CBS) Houston; KIAH (CW) Houston; KPRC-TV (NBC) Houston; KRIV (FOX) Houston; KTRK-TV (ABC) Houston; KTXH (MNT) Houston; KUHT (PBS) Houston; KXLN-DT (UNV) Rosenberg; allband FM.
Programming (via satellite): A&E Networks; ABC Family Channel; Bravo; CNN; Country Music TV; C-SPAN; E! Entertainment Television; ESPN; Fox Sports Southwest; Headline News; Lifetime; Nickelodeon; QVC; Syfy; Travel Channel; Turner Network TV.
Fee: $30.00 installation; $17.89 monthly.

Expanded Basic Service 1
Subscribers: 976.
Programming (via satellite): Discovery Channel; The Weather Channel; USA Network.
Fee: $2.26 monthly.

Expanded Basic Service 2
Subscribers: 966.
Programming (via satellite): Disney Channel; Spike TV; TBS Superstation.
Fee: $4.45 monthly.

Pay Service 1
Pay Units: 71.
Programming (via satellite): Cinemax.
Fee: $10.95 monthly.

Pay Service 2
Pay Units: 167.
Programming (via satellite): HBO.
Fee: $11.95 monthly.

Pay Service 3
Pay Units: 52.
Programming (via satellite): The Movie Channel.
Fee: $10.95 monthly.

Pay Service 4
Pay Units: 121.
Programming (via satellite): Showtime.
Fee: $10.95 monthly.

Video-On-Demand: No

Internet Service
Operational: Yes, Both DSL & dial-up.
Broadband Service: Warp Speed 1 Internet.
Fee: $17.05 installation; $34.99 monthly.

Telephone Service
None

Miles of Plant: 28.0 (coaxial); None (fiber optic).
Chief Technician: Alan Boyd.
Ownership: Mid-Coast Cablevision (MSO).

SWEETWATER—Suddenlink Communications, 1118 E Broadway St, PO Box 688, Sweetwater, TX 79556. Phone: 915-236-6375. Fax: 915-235-3164. Web Site: http://www.suddenlink.com. Also serves Nolan County (northern portion). ICA: TX0108.
TV Market Ranking: Below 100 (Nolan County (northern portion), SWEETWATER). Franchise award date: April 24, 1962. Franchise expiration date: April 21, 2010. Began: July 1, 1966.
Channel capacity: N.A. Channels available but not in use: N.A.

Basic Service
Subscribers: 3,836.
Programming (received off-air): KERA-TV (PBS) Dallas; KIDZ-LP Abilene; KPCB-DT (IND) Snyder; KRBC-TV (NBC) Abilene; KTAB-TV (CBS) Abilene; KTXS-TV (ABC, CW, TMO) Sweetwater; KXVA (FOX) Abilene; WFAA (ABC) Dallas.
Programming (via satellite): C-SPAN; C-SPAN 2; QVC; The Weather Channel; Trinity Broadcasting Network; TV Guide Network; Univision Studios.
Fee: $33.66 installation; $18.03 monthly; $3.00 converter; $16.83 additional installation.

Expanded Basic Service 1
Subscribers: N.A.
Programming (via satellite): A&E Networks; ABC Family Channel; AMC; Animal Planet; BET Networks; Bravo; Cartoon Network; CNBC; CNN; Comedy Central; Country Music TV; CW+; Discovery Channel; Disney Channel; E! Entertainment Television; ESPN; ESPN 2; Food Network; Fox News Channel; Fox Sports Southwest; FX; Headline News; HGTV; History Channel; INSP; Lifetime; Lifetime Movie Network; MSNBC; MTV; MTV2; Nickelodeon; Oxygen; Spike TV; Syfy; TBS Superstation; The Learning Channel; Travel Channel; Turner Network TV; TV Land; USA Network; Versus; VH1.
Fee: $12.59 monthly.

Digital Basic Service
Subscribers: N.A.
Programming (via satellite): A&E HD; Bandamax; BBC America; Bio; Bloomberg Television; Boomerang; Boomerang en Espanol; CBS Sports Network; Cine Latino; Cine Mexicano; CMT Pure Country; CNN en Espanol; Cooking Channel; De Pelicula; De Pelicula Clasico; Discovery en Espanol; Discovery Health Channel; Discovery Home Channel; Discovery Kids Channel; DIY Network; Encore (multiplexed); ESPN 2 HD; ESPN Classic Sports; ESPN Deportes; ESPN HD; ESPN U; ESPNews; Eternal Word TV Network; EWTN en Espanol; Food Network HD; Fox College Sports Atlantic; Fox College Sports Central; Fox College Sports Pacific; Fox Deportes; Fox Soccer; FSN HD; Fuel TV; Fuse; G4; GalaVision; GMC; Golf Channel; Great American Country; GSN; Hallmark Channel; Halogen Network; HD Theater; HDNet; HDNet Movies; HGTV HD; History Channel en Espanol; History Channel International; ID Investigation Discovery; Independent Film Channel; Jewelry Television; Military Channel; MTV Hits; mtvU; mun2 television; Music Choice; National Geographic Channel; National Geographic Channel HD Network; Nick Jr.; NickToons en Espanol; NickToons TV; Nuvo TV; Outdoor Channel; Science; ShopNBC; SoapNet; Sorpresa; Speed; Sundance Channel; Sur Network; TeenNick; Telefutura; Telehit; Tennis Channel; Toon Disney; Toon Disney en Espanol; Tr3s; truTV; Turner Classic Movies; Turner Network TV HD; Universal HD; VH1 Classic; Video Rola; WE tv.

Pay Service 1
Pay Units: 316.
Programming (via satellite): Cinemax; Encore; HBO; Showtime; Starz.
Fee: $10.00 installation; $1.75 monthly (Encore), $10.95 monthly (Cinemax, HBO or Showtime).

Digital Pay Service 1
Pay Units: N.A.
Programming (via satellite): Cinemax (multiplexed); Encore; HBO (multiplexed); HBO HD; HBO Latino; Showtime (multiplexed); Showtime HD; Starz (multiplexed); Starz HDTV; The Movie Channel.

Video-On-Demand: No

Pay-Per-View
iN DEMAND (delivered digitally); Playboy TV (delivered digitally); Fresh (delivered digitally); Shorteez (delivered digitally); Spice: Xcess (delivered digitally); Club Jenna (delivered digitally).

Internet Service
Operational: Yes.
Broadband Service: Suddenlink High Speed Internet.
Fee: $49.95 installation; $24.95 monthly.

Telephone Service
Digital: Operational
Fee: $48.95 monthly
Miles of Plant: 87.0 (coaxial); None (fiber optic).
Manager: Victor Means. Chief Technician: Bill Neely.
Ownership: Cequel Communications LLC (MSO).

TAHOKA—Reach Broadband, 515 E Longview St, Arp, TX 75750. Phone: 800-687-1258. Web Site: http://www.reachbroadband.net. ICA: TX0322.
TV Market Ranking: Below 100 (TAHOKA). Franchise award date: April 9, 1979. Franchise expiration date: N.A. Began: April 9, 1979.
Channel capacity: N.A. Channels available but not in use: N.A.
Basic Service
Subscribers: 604. Commercial subscribers: 2.
Programming (received off-air): KAMC (ABC) Lubbock; KCBD (NBC) Lubbock; KJTV-TV (FOX) Lubbock; KLBK-TV (CBS) Lubbock; KLCW-TV (CW) Wolfforth; KPTB-DT (IND) Lubbock; KTXT-TV (PBS) Lubbock; KXTQ-CA (TMO) Lubbock.
Programming (via satellite): A&E Networks; ABC Family Channel; Animal Planet; Cartoon Network; CNN; Country Music TV; Discovery Channel; Disney Channel; ESPN; ESPN 2; Fox Sports Southwest; HGTV; Lifetime; MTV; Nickelodeon; Outdoor Channel; QVC; Spike TV; TBS Superstation; The Learning Channel; The Weather Channel; Turner Classic Movies; Turner Network TV; TV Land; Univision Studios; USA Network; WGN America.
Fee: $29.95 installation; $38.00 monthly.
Pay Service 1
Pay Units: 160.
Programming (via satellite): HBO.
Fee: $20.00 installation; $11.50 monthly.
Pay Service 2
Pay Units: N.A.
Programming (via satellite): Cinemax.
Video-On-Demand: No
Internet Service
Operational: No.
Telephone Service
None
Miles of Plant: 19.0 (coaxial); None (fiber optic).
Regional Manager: Ronnie Stafford. Office Manager: Jan Gibson.
Ownership: RB3 LLC (MSO).

TARKINGTON PRAIRIE—Formerly served by Jones Broadcasting. No longer in operation. ICA: TX0997.

TEMPLE—Centrovision Inc., 8 E Barton Ave, PO Box 3157, Temple, TX 76505. Phone: 254-773-1163. Fax: 254-770-0778. E-mail: altonsheppard@centrovision.net. Web Site: http://www.centrovision.net. ICA: TX0861.
TV Market Ranking: Below 100 (TEMPLE). Franchise award date: N.A. Franchise expiration date: N.A. Began: N.A.
Channel capacity: N.A. Channels available but not in use: N.A.
Basic Service
Subscribers: 444.
Programming (received off-air): KAKW-DT (UNV) Killeen; KCEN-TV (NBC, IND) Temple; KDYW (PBS) Waco; KEYE-TV (CBS, TMO) Austin; KNCT (PBS) Belton; KNVA (CW) Austin; KTBC (FOX) Austin; KWKT-TV (FOX, MNT) Waco; KWTX-TV (CBS, CW) Waco; KXAN-TV (NBC) Austin; KXXV (ABC, TMO) Waco.
Programming (via satellite): A&E Networks; ABC Family Channel; AMC; AmericanLife TV Network; Animal Planet; BET Networks; Cartoon Network; CNBC; CNN; Comedy Central; Country Music TV; C-SPAN; C-SPAN 2; CW+; Discovery Channel; Disney Channel; DIY Network; E! Entertainment Television; ESPN; ESPN 2; Eternal Word TV Network; Food Network; Fox News Channel; Fox Sports Net; FX; Golf Channel; Hallmark Channel; Headline News; HGTV; History Channel; ION Television; Lifetime; Local Cable Weather; MSNBC; MTV; National Geographic Channel; Nickelodeon; QVC; RFD-TV; SoapNet; Speed; Spike TV; Syfy; TBS Superstation; Telemundo; The Learning Channel; The Weather Channel; Travel Channel; Trinity Broadcasting Network; truTV; Turner Classic Movies; Turner Network TV; TV Land; USA Network; VH1; WFAA (ABC) Dallas; WGN America.
Fee: $20.00 installation; $26.00 monthly.
Digital Basic Service
Subscribers: N.A.
Programming (via satellite): BBC America; Bio; Bloomberg Television; Bravo; cloo; CMT Pure Country; Current; Daystar TV Network; Discovery Fit & Health; Discovery Health Channel; Discovery Home Channel; Discovery Kids Channel; ESPN Classic Sports; ESPNews; Fox College Sports Atlantic; Fox College Sports Central; Fox College Sports Pacific; Fox Movie Channel; Fox Soccer; Fuse; G4; Golf Channel; Great American Country; GSN; Halogen Network; HGTV; History Channel; History Channel International; ID Investigation Discovery; Independent Film Channel; Lifetime Movie Network; Military Channel; MTV Hits; MTV2; Music Choice; National Geographic Channel; Nick Jr.; NickToons TV; Outdoor Channel; Ovation; Science; ShopNBC; Speed; Style Network; Syfy; TeenNick; The Word Network; Toon Disney; Trinity Broadcasting Network; Turner Classic Movies; Versus; VH1 Classic; VH1 Soul; WE tv.
Pay Service 1
Pay Units: N.A.
Programming (via satellite): HBO; Showtime; The Movie Channel.
Digital Pay Service 1
Pay Units: N.A.
Programming (via satellite): Cinemax (multiplexed); Encore (multiplexed); Flix; HBO (multiplexed); Showtime (multiplexed); Starz (multiplexed); Sundance Channel; The Movie Channel (multiplexed).
Video-On-Demand: No
Internet Service
Operational: Yes. Began: December 31, 2004.
Broadband Service: VVM Internet Services.
Fee: $20.00 installation; $40.00 monthly.
Telephone Service
Digital: Planned
Manager: Alton Sheppard. Chief Technician: Mike Wiggins.
Ownership: Centrovision Inc. (MSO).

TENAHA—Almega Cable, 4001 W Airport Frwy, Ste 530, Bedford, TX 76021. Phone: 817-685-9588. Fax: 817-685-6488. E-mail: helpdesk@almegacable.com. Web Site: http://www.almega.com. ICA: TX0507.
TV Market Ranking: Below 100 (TENAHA). Franchise award date: N.A. Franchise expiration date: N.A. Began: May 1, 1984.
Channel capacity: 54 (not 2-way capable). Channels available but not in use: N.A.
Basic Service
Subscribers: 87.
Programming (received off-air): KETK-TV (NBC) Jacksonville; KLTS-TV (PBS) Shreveport; KSLA (CBS) Shreveport; KTAL-TV (NBC) Texarkana; KTBS-TV (ABC) Shreveport; KTRE (ABC) Lufkin.
Programming (via satellite): ABC Family Channel; BET Networks; CNN; Discovery Channel; ESPN; Nickelodeon; TBS Superstation; Turner Network TV; USA Network; WGN America.
Fee: $54.95 installation; $44.05 monthly.
Pay Service 1
Pay Units: 22.
Programming (via satellite): Cinemax.
Fee: $12.95 monthly.
Pay Service 2
Pay Units: 11.
Programming (via satellite): HBO.
Fee: $12.95 monthly.
Pay Service 3
Pay Units: 28.
Programming (via satellite): Showtime.
Fee: $12.95 monthly.
Video-On-Demand: No
Internet Service
Operational: No.
Telephone Service
None
Miles of Plant: 14.0 (coaxial); None (fiber optic).
Ownership: Almega Cable (MSO).

TERRELL—Suddenlink Communications, 12444 Powerscourt Dr, Saint Louis, MO 63131-3660. Phones: 800-999-6845; 314-315-9346; 314-965-2020. Fax: 903-561-5485. Web Site: http://www.suddenlink.com. Also serves Balch Springs, Collin County (portions), Dallas County (portions), Fate, Forney, Happy Country Homes, Heath, Kaufman County, McClendon-Chisolm, Mobile City, Rockwall County (portions), Royse City & Seagoville. ICA: TX0920.
TV Market Ranking: 12 (Balch Springs, Collin County (portions), Dallas County (portions), Fate, Forney, Happy Country Homes, Heath, Kaufman County (portions), McClendon-Chisolm, Mobile City, Rockwall County (portions), Royse City, Seagoville, TERRELL); Outside TV Markets (Kaufman County (portions)). Franchise award date: N.A. Franchise expiration date: N.A. Began: N.A.
Channel capacity: 42 (operating 2-way). Channels available but not in use: N.A.
Basic Service
Subscribers: 9,693.
Programming (received off-air): KDAF (CW, IND) Dallas; KDFI (MNT) Dallas; KDFW-DT (FOX) Dallas; KDTN (ETV) Denton; KDTX-TV (TBN) Dallas; KERA-TV (PBS) Dallas; KFWD (IND) Fort Worth; KHAS-TV (NBC) Hastings; KMPX (IND) Decatur; KPXD-TV (ION) Arlington; KSTR-DT (TEL) Irving; KTAQ (IND) Greenville; KTVT (CBS) Fort Worth; KTXA (IND) Fort Worth; KUVN-DT (UNV) Garland; KXAS-TV (NBC) Fort Worth; KXTX-TV (TMO) Dallas; WFAA (ABC) Dallas.
Programming (via satellite): C-SPAN.
Fee: $39.95 installation; $19.95 monthly.
Expanded Basic Service 1
Subscribers: N.A.
Programming (via satellite): A&E Networks; ABC Family Channel; AMC; Animal Planet; BET Networks; Bravo; Cartoon Network; Celebrity Shopping Network; CNBC; CNN; Comedy Central; Discovery Channel; Disney Channel; E! Entertainment Television; ESPN; ESPN 2; ESPN Classic Sports; Food Network; Fox News Channel; Fox Sports Southwest; FX; GalaVision; Golf Channel; Great American Country; Hallmark Channel; Headline News; HGTV; History Channel; Lifetime; Lifetime Movie Network; MSNBC; MTV; National Geographic Channel; Nickelodeon; Outdoor Channel; Speed; Spike TV; Syfy; TBS Superstation; The Learning Channel; The Weather Channel; Travel Channel; truTV; Turner Classic Movies; Turner Network TV; TV Guide Network; TV Land; USA Network; VH1.
Digital Basic Service
Subscribers: N.A.
Programming (via satellite): BBC America; Bio; Bloomberg Television; Canales N; cloo; Country Music TV; C-SPAN 3; ESPNews; Fox College Sports Atlantic; Fox College Sports Central; Fox College Sports Pacific; Fox Movie Channel; Fox Soccer; Fuel TV; Fuse; G4; GAS; GSN; HD Theater; HDNet; HDNet Movies; History Channel International; Independent Film Channel; Lifetime Real Women; LOGO; MTV Networks Digital Suite; Music Choice; Nick Jr.; Nick Too; NickToons TV; SoapNet; Style Network; Sundance Channel; Toon Disney; Versus; WE tv.
Pay Service 1
Pay Units: 1,483.
Programming (via satellite): Cinemax.
Fee: $11.00 monthly.
Pay Service 2
Pay Units: 2,008.
Programming (via satellite): HBO.
Fee: $11.00 monthly.
Pay Service 3
Pay Units: 2,395.
Programming (via satellite): Showtime.
Fee: $11.00 monthly.
Pay Service 4
Pay Units: 1,223.
Programming (via satellite): The Movie Channel.
Fee: $10.95 monthly.
Digital Pay Service 1
Pay Units: N.A.
Programming (via satellite): Cinemax (multiplexed); Encore (multiplexed); Flix; HBO (multiplexed); Showtime (multiplexed); Showtime HD; Starz (multiplexed); The Movie Channel (multiplexed).
Video-On-Demand: No
Pay-Per-View
iN DEMAND (delivered digitally); Playboy TV (delivered digitally).
Internet Service
Operational: Yes. Began: August 1, 2002.
Broadband Service: Suddenlink High Speed Internet.
Fee: $49.95 installation; $38.95 monthly.
Telephone Service
None
Miles of Plant: 516.0 (coaxial); None (fiber optic).
Area Manager: Rodney Fletcher. Regional Manager: Todd Cruthird. Plant Manager: Steven Williams.
Ownership: Cequel Communications LLC (MSO).

TEXARKANA—Cable One, 401 Baylor St, Texarkana, TX 75501-3270. Phone: 903-838-2225. Fax: 903-792-3919. E-mail: jbutler@cableone.net. Web Site: http://www.cableone.net. Also serves Miller County & Texarkana, AR; Bowie County, Nash, Red Lick & Wake Village, TX. ICA: TX0031.
TV Market Ranking: 58 (Bowie County, Miller County, Nash, Red Lick, Texarkana, TEXARKANA, Wake Village). Franchise

award date: June 1, 1973. Franchise expiration date: N.A. Began: April 1, 1974.
Channel capacity: 78 (operating 2-way). Channels available but not in use: N.A.

Basic Service

Subscribers: 22,946.

Programming (received off-air): KETG (PBS) Arkadelphia; KLFI-LP Texarkana; KMSS-TV (FOX) Shreveport; KPXJ (CW) Minden; KSHV-TV (MNT) Shreveport; KSLA (CBS) Shreveport; KTAL-TV (NBC) Texarkana; KTBS-TV (ABC) Shreveport.

Programming (via microwave): KATV (ABC) Little Rock.

Programming (via satellite): A&E Networks; ABC Family Channel; AMC; Animal Planet; BET Networks; Bravo; Cartoon Network; CNBC; CNN; Comedy Central; Country Music TV; C-SPAN; C-SPAN 2; Discovery Channel; Disney Channel; ESPN; ESPN 2; Food Network; Fox News Channel; Fox Sports Southwest; FX; Headline News; HGTV; History Channel; ION Television; Lifetime; MSNBC; MTV; Nickelodeon; QVC; Spike TV; Syfy; TBS Superstation; Texas Cable News; The Learning Channel; The Weather Channel; Trinity Broadcasting Network; Turner Classic Movies; Turner Network TV; TV Guide Network; TV Land; USA Network; VH1; WGN America.

Fee: $46.00 monthly; $2.50 converter.

Digital Basic Service

Subscribers: 7,791.

Programming (via satellite): 24/7 News Channel; 3 Angels Broadcasting Network; Bio; Boomerang; BYU Television; Canales N; Discovery Digital Networks; DMX Music; ESPN Classic Sports; ESPNews; FamilyNet; Fox College Sports Atlantic; Fox College Sports Central; Fox College Sports Pacific; Fox Movie Channel; Fox Soccer; Fuel TV; G4; Golf Channel; Hallmark Channel; History Channel International; INSP; LWS Local Weather Station; National Geographic Channel; Outdoor Channel; SoapNet; Speed; Toon Disney; Trinity Broadcasting Network; truTV; Turner Network TV HD; TVG Network; Universal HD.

Fee: $9.95 installation; $46.00 monthly.

Digital Pay Service 1

Pay Units: N.A.

Programming (via satellite): Cinemax (multiplexed); Encore (multiplexed); Flix (multiplexed); HBO (multiplexed); Showtime (multiplexed); Showtime HD; Starz (multiplexed); Sundance Channel (multiplexed); The Movie Channel (multiplexed); The Movie Channel HD.

Fee: $9.95 installation; $15.00 monthly (each package).

Video-On-Demand: No

Pay-Per-View

Addressable homes: 7,791.

iN DEMAND (delivered digitally); Pleasure (delivered digitally); Ten Clips (delivered digitally); Ten Blox (delivered digitally); Ten Blue (delivered digitally).

Internet Service

Operational: Yes. Began: November 1, 2000.

Subscribers: 7,000.

Broadband Service: CableONE.net.

Fee: $75.00 installation; $43.00 monthly; $5.00 modem lease.

Telephone Service

Digital: Operational

Fee: $39.95 monthly

Miles of Plant: 510.0 (coaxial); 65.0 (fiber optic).

Manager: Jay Butler. Chief Technician: John Lanier. Marketing Director: Donna Chatman. Program Director: Jeannie Mitchell.

Ownership: Cable ONE Inc. (MSO).

TEXHOMA—Panhandle Telephone Coop. Inc., 2222 NW Hwy 64, Guymon, OK 73942. Phones: 580-338-2556; 800-562-2556. Fax: 580-338-8260. E-mail: support@ptsi.net. Web Site: http://www.ptsi.net. ICA: TX0476.

TV Market Ranking: Outside TV Markets (TEXHOMA).

Channel capacity: N.A. Channels available but not in use: N.A.

Basic Service

Subscribers: N.A.

Programming (received off-air): KACV-TV (PBS) Amarillo; KAMR-TV (NBC) Amarillo; KCIT (FOX) Amarillo; KETA-TV (PBS) Oklahoma City; KFDA-TV (CBS) Amarillo; KVII-TV (ABC, CW) Amarillo.

Programming (via satellite): QVC; The Weather Channel; Trinity Broadcasting Network; Univision Studios.

Fee: $18.99 monthly.

Expanded Basic Service 1

Subscribers: N.A.

Programming (via satellite): A&E Networks; ABC Family Channel; American Movie Classics; Animal Planet; BET Networks; Cartoon Network; CNN; C-SPAN; C-SPAN 2; Discovery Channel; Disney Channel; E! Entertainment Television; ESPN; ESPN 2; Food Network; Fox News Channel; Fox Sports Southwest; FX; GalaVision; Hallmark Channel; Headline News; Lifetime; MSNBC; MTV; Nickelodeon; Oxygen; Paramount Network (UPN); Spike TV; TBS Superstation; Telemundo; TLC; TNT; Travel Channel; truTV; USA Network; VH1; WGN America.

Fee: $25.00 monthly.

Internet Service

Operational: Yes.

President: Charles Russell.

Ownership: Panhandle Telephone Cooperative Inc. (MSO).

TEXLINE—Baja Broadband, 510 24th St, Alamogordo, NM 88310. Phone: 505-437-3101. Fax: 505-434-3439. Web Site: http://www.bajabroadband.com. ICA: TX0642.

TV Market Ranking: Outside TV Markets (TEXLINE). Franchise award date: N.A. Franchise expiration date: N.A. Began: August 1, 1977.

Channel capacity: N.A. Channels available but not in use: N.A.

Basic Service

Subscribers: 178.

Programming (received off-air): KAMR-TV (NBC) Amarillo; KCIT (FOX) Amarillo; KFDA-TV (CBS) Amarillo; KVII-TV (ABC, CW) Amarillo; KWGN-TV (CW) Denver.

Programming (via satellite): A&E Networks; ABC Family Channel; Animal Planet; CNN; Country Music TV; Discovery Channel; Disney Channel; E! Entertainment Television; ESPN; ESPN 2; HGTV; Lifetime; Nickelodeon; Oxygen; Spike TV; Syfy; TBS Superstation; The Learning Channel; The Weather Channel; Travel Channel; Trinity Broadcasting Network; Turner Classic Movies; Turner Network TV; TV Land; Univision Studios; USA Network; WGN America.

Fee: $54.95 installation; $35.99 monthly.

Pay Service 1

Pay Units: N.A.

Programming (via satellite): HBO; Showtime.

Video-On-Demand: No

Pay-Per-View

iN DEMAND (delivered digitally); Hot Choice (delivered digitally); Playboy TV (delivered digitally); Fresh (delivered digitally); Shorteez (delivered digitally).

Internet Service

Operational: No.

Telephone Service

None

Miles of Plant: 8.0 (coaxial); None (fiber optic).

Vice President & General Manager: Tom Jaskiewicz. Technical Operations Manager: Harold Vilas. Office Manager: Barbara Mick.

Ownership: Baja Broadband (MSO).

THORNTON—Formerly served by National Cable Inc. No longer in operation. ICA: TX0592.

THREE RIVERS—Reach Broadband, 515 E Longview St, Arp, TX 75750. Phone: 800-687-1258. Web Site: http://www.reachbroadband.net. ICA: TX0401.

TV Market Ranking: Outside TV Markets (THREE RIVERS). Franchise award date: January 1, 1978. Franchise expiration date: N.A. Began: October 1, 1978.

Channel capacity: N.A. Channels available but not in use: N.A.

Basic Service

Subscribers: 389.

Programming (received off-air): KABB (FOX) San Antonio; KEDT (PBS) Corpus Christi; KENS (CBS) San Antonio; KIII (ABC) Corpus Christi; KMOL-LP Victoria; KMYS (CW) Kerrville; KPXL-TV (ION) Uvalde; KRIS-TV (CW, NBC) Corpus Christi; KSAT-TV (ABC) San Antonio; KWEX-DT (UNV) San Antonio; KZTV (CBS) Corpus Christi; allband FM.

Programming (via satellite): ABC Family Channel; ESPN; Fox Sports Southwest; TBS Superstation; Turner Network TV.

Fee: $29.99 installation; $19.95 monthly; $10.00 additional installation.

Expanded Basic Service 1

Subscribers: N.A.

Programming (via satellite): CNN; Country Music TV; Discovery Channel; Disney Channel; Spike TV.

Fee: $20.00 monthly.

Pay Service 1

Pay Units: 27.

Programming (via satellite): Cinemax.

Fee: $11.95 monthly.

Pay Service 2

Pay Units: 70.

Programming (via satellite): HBO.

Fee: $11.95 monthly.

Pay Service 3

Pay Units: 84.

Programming (via satellite): Showtime.

Fee: $11.95 monthly.

Video-On-Demand: No

Pay-Per-View

iN DEMAND (delivered digitally); Hot Choice (delivered digitally); Playboy TV (delivered digitally); Fresh (delivered digitally); Shorteez (delivered digitally).

Internet Service

Operational: No.

Telephone Service

None

Miles of Plant: 15.0 (coaxial); None (fiber optic).

Regional Manager: Ronnie Stafford. Office Manager: Jan Gibson.

Ownership: RB3 LLC (MSO).

THROCKMORTON—TGN Cable, Rte 2, PO Box 110, Olney, TX 76374. Phones: 940-873-4563; 800-687-7311. Fax: 940-873-4563. E-mail: webmaster@tgncable.com. Web Site: http://www.tgncable.com. ICA: TX0511.

TV Market Ranking: Outside TV Markets (THROCKMORTON). Franchise award date: N.A. Franchise expiration date: N.A. Began: January 1, 1982.

Channel capacity: N.A. Channels available but not in use: N.A.

Basic Service

Subscribers: 330.

Programming (received off-air): KAUZ-TV (CBS, CW) Wichita Falls; KFDX-TV (NBC) Wichita Falls; KIDZ-LP Abilene; KJTL (FOX) Wichita Falls; KRBC-TV (NBC) Abilene; KSWO-TV (ABC, TMO) Lawton; 2 FMs.

Programming (via satellite): ABC Family Channel; CNBC; CNN; C-SPAN; Discovery Channel; Disney Channel; Paxson Communications Corp.; Spike TV; TBS Superstation; The Learning Channel; The Weather Channel; Trinity Broadcasting Network; TV Land; Univision Studios; WGN America.

Fee: $39.95 installation; $27.91 monthly.

Expanded Basic Service 1

Subscribers: N.A.

Programming (received off-air): KFDX-TV (NBC) Wichita Falls.

Programming (via satellite): A&E Networks; AMC; Animal Planet; Cartoon Network; Country Music TV; ESPN; ESPN 2; ESPN Classic Sports; Food Network; Fox News Channel; Fox Sports Southwest; FX; G4; Hallmark Channel; Headline News; HGTV; History Channel; Lifetime; MTV; Nickelodeon; Outdoor Channel; Speed; Syfy; Toon Disney; Travel Channel; Turner Network TV; USA Network; Versus; VH1.

Fee: $10.83 monthly.

Digital Basic Service

Subscribers: N.A.

Programming (via satellite): BBC America; Bio; Bravo; cloo; Discovery Digital Networks; DMX Music; Fox College Sports Atlantic; Fox College Sports Central; Fox College Sports Pacific; Fox Movie Channel; Fox Sports World; Fuse; GAS; Golf Channel; Great American Country; GSN; Halogen Network; History Channel; History Channel International; Independent Film Channel; Lifetime Real Women; MTV Networks Digital Suite; National Geographic Channel; Nick Jr.; NickToons TV; Ovation; ShopNBC; Style Network; Turner Classic Movies; Versus; WE tv.

Fee: $21.05 monthly.

Pay Service 1

Pay Units: N.A.

Programming (via satellite): Cinemax; HBO.

Fee: $13.55 monthly.

Digital Pay Service 1

Pay Units: N.A.

Programming (via satellite): Cinemax (multiplexed); Encore (multiplexed); Flix; HBO (multiplexed); Showtime (multiplexed); Starz; Sundance Channel; The Movie Channel (multiplexed).

Fee: $13.55 monthly (HBO/Cinemax), $7.01 monthly (Starz/Encore & Showtime/TMC).

Video-On-Demand: No

Internet Service

Operational: Yes.

Broadband Service: In-house.

Fee: $24.95 monthly; $5.00 modem lease; $59.95 modem purchase.

Telephone Service

None

Miles of Plant: 14.0 (coaxial); None (fiber optic).

Manager: Bill Tyler. Office Manager: Jan Tyler. Ownership: Bill Tyler (MSO).

THUNDERBIRD BAY—Formerly served by Cable Unlimited. No longer in operation. ICA: TX0408.

TILDEN—Formerly served by Almega Cable. No longer in operation. ICA: TX0663.

TIMPSON—Almega Cable, 4001 W Airport Frwy, Ste 530, Bedford, TX 76021. Phone: 817-685-9588. Fax: 817-685-6488. E-mail: helpdesk@almegacable.com. Web Site: http://www.almega.com. ICA: TX0572.

TV Market Ranking: Below 100 (TIMPSON). Franchise award date: N.A. Franchise expiration date: N.A. Began: January 1, 1985.

Channel capacity: 54 (not 2-way capable). Channels available but not in use: N.A.

Basic Service

Subscribers: 125.

Programming (received off-air): KLTS-TV (PBS) Shreveport; KSLA (CBS) Shreveport; KTAL-TV (NBC) Texarkana; KTBS-TV (ABC) Shreveport; KTRE (ABC) Lufkin.

Programming (via satellite): Animal Planet; BET Networks; CNN; Country Music TV; Discovery Channel; E! Entertainment Television; ESPN; Fox Sports Net; Headline News; Lifetime; Nickelodeon; Spike TV; TBS Superstation; The Weather Channel; Trinity Broadcasting Network; Turner Classic Movies; Turner Network TV; USA Network; Versus; WGN America.

Fee: $54.95 installation; $44.05 monthly.

Pay Service 1

Pay Units: 23.

Programming (via satellite): Cinemax.

Fee: $12.95 monthly.

Pay Service 2

Pay Units: 18.

Programming (via satellite): HBO.

Fee: $12.95 monthly.

Pay Service 3

Pay Units: 32.

Programming (via satellite): Showtime.

Fee: $12.95 monthly.

Video-On-Demand: No

Internet Service

Operational: No.

Telephone Service

None

Miles of Plant: 7.0 (coaxial); None (fiber optic).

Ownership: Almega Cable (MSO).

TOLAR—Formerly served by Charter Communications. No longer in operation. ICA: TX1002.

TOLEDO VILLAGE—Formerly served by Carrell Communications. No longer in operation. ICA: TX0864.

TRENT—Formerly served by Jayroc Cablevision. No longer in operation. ICA: TX0976.

TRINITY—Formerly served by Cebridge Connections. Now served by LAKE LIVINGSTON (formerly SHEPHERD), TX [TX0851]. ICA: TX0205.

TROY—Centrovision Inc., 8 E Barton Ave, PO Box 3157, Temple, TX 76505. Phone: 254-773-1163. Fax: 254-770-0778. E-mail: altonsheppard@centrovision.net. Web Site: http://www.centrovision.net/. ICA: TX0532.

TV Market Ranking: Below 100 (TROY). Franchise award date: N.A. Franchise expiration date: N.A. Began: October 1, 1981.

Channel capacity: N.A. Channels available but not in use: N.A.

Basic Service

Subscribers: N.A.

Programming (received off-air): KCEN-TV (NBC, IND) Temple; KDYW (PBS) Waco; KEYE-TV (CBS, TMO) Austin; KNCT (PBS) Belton; KNVA (CW) Austin; KTBC (FOX) Austin; KWKT-TV (FOX, MNT) Waco; KWTX-TV (CBS, CW) Waco; KXAN-TV (NBC) Austin; KXXV (ABC, TMO) Waco; WFAA (ABC) Dallas.

Programming (via satellite): Univision Studios; WGN America.

Fee: $20.00 installation; $12.00 monthly.

Expanded Basic Service 1

Subscribers: N.A.

Programming (via satellite): A&E Networks; ABC Family Channel; AMC; Animal Planet; BET Networks; Cartoon Network; CNBC; CNN; Comedy Central; Country Music TV; C-SPAN; C-SPAN 2; Discovery Channel; Disney Channel; E! Entertainment Television; ESPN; ESPN 2; Food Network; Fox News Channel; Fox Sports Southwest; FX; Hallmark Channel; Headline News; HGTV; History Channel; ION Television; Lifetime; MSNBC; MTV; National Geographic Channel; Nickelodeon; QVC; SoapNet; Spike TV; Syfy; TBS Superstation; The Learning Channel; The Weather Channel; Travel Channel; Trinity Broadcasting Network; Turner Classic Movies; Turner Network TV; TV Land; USA Network; VH1.

Fee: $18.00 monthly.

Digital Basic Service

Subscribers: N.A.

Programming (via satellite): AmericanLife TV Network; BBC America; Bio; Bloomberg Television; Bravo; Daystar TV Network; Discovery Digital Networks; DMX Music; ESPN Classic Sports; ESPNews; Fox Movie Channel; Fox Sports World; FSN Digital Atlantic; FSN Digital Central; FSN Digital Pacific; Fuse; G4; Golf Channel; Great American Country; GSN; Halogen Network; HGTV; History Channel; History Channel International; Independent Film Channel; Lifetime Movie Network; Lime; National Geographic Channel; Outdoor Channel; Ovation; ShopNBC; Speed; Style Network; Syfy; The Word Network; Toon Disney; Trinity Broadcasting Network; Turner Classic Movies; Versus; WE tv.

Fee: $15.00 installation; $49.00 monthly.

Pay Service 1

Pay Units: N.A.

Programming (via satellite): HBO; Showtime; The Movie Channel.

Fee: $11.00 monthly (HBO, Showtime or TMC), $13.50 monthly (Showtime & TMC), $19.50 monthly (HBO & TMC), $21.00 monthly (HBO & Showtime), $23.00 monthly (HBO, Showtime & TMC).

Digital Pay Service 1

Pay Units: N.A.

Programming (via satellite): Cinemax (multiplexed); Encore (multiplexed); HBO (multiplexed); Showtime (multiplexed); Starz (multiplexed).

Fee: $7.00 monthly (Cinemax), $11.00 monthly (HBO, Showtime or Starz & Encore).

Video-On-Demand: No

Internet Service

Operational: Yes. Began: December 31, 2004.

Broadband Service: VVM Internet Services.

Fee: $20.00 installation; $40.00 monthly.

Telephone Service

Digital: Planned

Miles of Plant: 8.0 (coaxial); None (fiber optic).

Manager: Alton Sheppard. Chief Technician: Mike Wiggins.

Ownership: Centrovision Inc. (MSO).

TULETA—Formerly served by National Cable Inc. No longer in operation. ICA: TX0907.

TULIA—Suddenlink Communications, 125 E Broadway Ave, Tulia, TX 79088. Phones: 806-995-4740; 314-965-2020. Web Site: http://www.suddenlink.com. ICA: TX0226.

TV Market Ranking: Outside TV Markets (TULIA). Franchise award date: June 17, 1980. Franchise expiration date: N.A. Began: January 10, 1965.

Channel capacity: N.A. Channels available but not in use: N.A.

Basic Service

Subscribers: 1,325.

Programming (received off-air): KACV-TV (PBS) Amarillo; KAMR-TV (NBC) Amarillo; KCIT (FOX) Amarillo; KFDA-TV (CBS) Amarillo; KLBK-TV (CBS) Lubbock; KVII-TV (ABC, CW) Amarillo; allband FM.

Programming (via satellite): A&E Networks; ABC Family Channel; AmericanLife TV Network; Animal Planet; CNN; Comedy Central; Country Music TV; Discovery Channel; Disney Channel; E! Entertainment Television; ESPN; ESPN 2; Fox News Channel; Fox Sports Southwest; Headline News; History Channel; INSP; Lifetime; Nickelodeon; QVC; Spike TV; Syfy; TBS Superstation; The Learning Channel; The Weather Channel; Trinity Broadcasting Network; Turner Classic Movies; Turner Network TV; TV Land; USA Network; WGN America.

Fee: $35.00 installation; $19.95 monthly.

Pay Service 1

Pay Units: 77.

Programming (via satellite): The Movie Channel.

Fee: $5.95 monthly.

Pay Service 2

Pay Units: 82.

Programming (via satellite): Showtime.

Fee: $9.95 monthly.

Pay Service 3

Pay Units: 169.

Programming (via satellite): HBO.

Fee: $10.95 monthly.

Video-On-Demand: No

Internet Service

Operational: Yes. Began: November 12, 2003.

Broadband Service: Suddenlink High Speed Internet.

Fee: $49.95 installation; $25.95 monthly.

Telephone Service

None

Miles of Plant: 30.0 (coaxial); None (fiber optic).

Marketing Director: Beverly Gambell. Chief Technician: Chris Christenson.

Ownership: Cequel Communications LLC (MSO).

TURKEY—Elk River TV Cable Co., 411 S Main St, PO Box 154, Troy, ID 83871. Phone: 208-369-4652. Fax: 207-835-5573. Web Site: http://www.elkrivertv.net. ICA: TX0900.

TV Market Ranking: Outside TV Markets (TURKEY). Franchise award date: N.A. Franchise expiration date: N.A. Began: August 1, 1991.

Channel capacity: 36 (not 2-way capable). Channels available but not in use: N.A.

Basic Service

Subscribers: N.A. Included in San Jon, NM

Programming (received off-air): KAMR-TV (NBC) Amarillo; KFDA-TV (CBS) Amarillo; KJTV-TV (FOX) Lubbock; KVII-TV (ABC, CW) Amarillo.

Programming (via satellite): ABC Family Channel; CNN; Discovery Channel; Disney Channel; ESPN; Spike TV; TBS Superstation; Turner Network TV; WGN America.

Fee: $25.00 installation; $19.79 monthly.

Pay Service 1

Pay Units: 70.

Programming (via satellite): Showtime; The Movie Channel.

Fee: $10.95 monthly (both).

Video-On-Demand: No

Internet Service

Operational: No.

Telephone Service

None

Miles of Plant: 5.0 (coaxial); None (fiber optic).

Manager: Dave & Leslie McGraw. Chief Technician: Justin McGraw.

Ownership: Elk River TV Cable Co. (MSO).

TUSCOLA—CMA Cablevision, 1510 N 1st St, PO Box 549, Merkel, TX 79536-0549. Phones: 800-588-4750; 325-928-4750. Fax: 325-928-3452. Web Site: http://www.cmaaccess.com. Also serves Buffalo Gap. ICA: TX0176.

TV Market Ranking: Below 100 (Buffalo Gap, TUSCOLA). Franchise award date: February 15, 1983. Franchise expiration date: February 15, 2008. Began: December 30, 1983.

Channel capacity: N.A. Channels available but not in use: N.A.

Basic Service

Subscribers: 110.

Programming (received off-air): KRBC-TV (NBC) Abilene; KTAB-TV (CBS) Abilene; KTXS-TV (ABC, CW, TMO) Sweetwater; KXVA (FOX) Abilene.

Programming (via satellite): Food Network; QVC; Syfy; TBS Superstation; The Weather Channel; Trinity Broadcasting Network; VH1; WGN America.

Fee: $39.95 installation; $14.90 monthly; $12.95 additional installation.

Expanded Basic Service 1

Subscribers: N.A.

Programming (via satellite): A&E Networks; ABC Family Channel; AMC; Animal Planet; CNN; Country Music TV; Discovery Channel; ESPN; ESPN 2; HGTV; Lifetime; MTV; Nickelodeon; Spike TV; The Learning Channel; Turner Network TV; TV Land; USA Network.

Fee: $23.55 monthly.

Pay Service 1

Pay Units: 60.

Programming (via satellite): HBO.

Fee: $14.95 installation; $13.95 monthly.

Video-On-Demand: No

Internet Service

Operational: No.

Telephone Service

None

Miles of Plant: 71.0 (coaxial); None (fiber optic).

General Manager: Jerry Smith. Chief Technician: Joe Clark. Marketing Director: Julie Ferguson.

Ownership: Cable Management Assoc. (MSO).

TYLER—Suddenlink Communications, 322 N Glenwood Blvd, Tyler, TX 75702. Phone: 903-595-4321. Fax: 903-593-6189. Web Site:

http://www.suddenlink.com. Also serves Smith County & Whitehouse. ICA: TX0027.

TV Market Ranking: Below 100 (Smith County, TYLER, Whitehouse). Franchise award date: January 1, 1970. Franchise expiration date: N.A. Began: March 1, 1951.

Channel capacity: N.A. Channels available but not in use: N.A.

Basic Service

Subscribers: 33,445.

Programming (received off-air): KCEB (CW) Longview; KDFW-DT (FOX) Dallas; KERA-TV (PBS) Dallas; KETK-TV (NBC) Jacksonville; KFXK-TV (FOX) Longview; KLPN-LP (IND) Longview; KLTV (ABC, TMO) Tyler; KXTX-TV (TMO) Dallas; KYTX (CBS, IND) Nacogdoches; WFAA (ABC) Dallas; 18 FMs.

Programming (via satellite): C-SPAN; Product Information Network; QVC; TBS Superstation; TV Guide Network; Univision Studios.

Fee: $38.00 installation; $10.75 monthly; $15.59 additional installation.

Expanded Basic Service 1

Subscribers: 28,200.

Programming (via satellite): A&E Networks; ABC Family Channel; AMC; Animal Planet; BET Networks; Bravo; Cartoon Network; CNBC; CNN; Comedy Central; Country Music TV; C-SPAN 2; Discovery Channel; Disney Channel; E! Entertainment Television; ESPN; ESPN 2; Eternal Word TV Network; Food Network; Fox News Channel; Fox Sports Southwest; FX; GalaVision; Great American Country; Headline News; HGTV; History Channel; INSP; Jewelry Television; Lifetime; Lifetime Movie Network; MSNBC; MTV; Nickelodeon; Outdoor Channel; ShopNBC; Speed; Spike TV; Syfy; The Learning Channel; The Weather Channel; Travel Channel; Trinity Broadcasting Network; truTV; Turner Classic Movies; Turner Network TV; TV Land; USA Network; Versus; VH1.

Fee: $14.26 monthly.

Digital Basic Service

Subscribers: N.A.

Programming (via satellite): A&E HD; Bandamax; BBC America; Bio; Bloomberg Television; Boomerang; CBS Sports Network; Cine Latino; Cine Mexicano; CMT Pure Country; CNN en Espanol; Cooking Channel; Cox Sports Television; De Pelicula; De Pelicula Clasico; Discovery en Espanol; Discovery Health Channel; Discovery Home Channel; Discovery Kids Channel; DIY Network; Encore (multiplexed); ESPN 2 HD; ESPN Classic Sports; ESPN Deportes; ESPN HD; ESPN U; ESPNews; EWTN en Espanol; FamilyNet; Food Network HD; Fox Deportes; Fox Reality Channel; Fox Soccer; FSN HD; Fuel TV; Fuse; G4; GalaVision; GMC; Golf Channel; GSN; Hallmark Channel; Halogen Network; HD Theater; HDNet; HDNet Movies; HGTV HD; History Channel en Espanol; History Channel International; ID Investigation Discovery; Independent Film Channel; Latele Novela Network; Military Channel; MTV Hits; MTV2; mun2 television; Music Choice; National Geographic Channel; National Geographic Channel HD Network; Nick Jr.; NickToons en Espanol; NickToons TV; Nuvo TV; Oxygen; Ritmoson Latino; Science; SoapNet; Sorpresa; Style Network; Sundance Channel; Sur Network; TBN Enlace USA; TeenNick; Telefutura; Telehit; Tennis Channel; Toon Disney; Toon Disney en Espanol; Tr3s; Turner Network TV HD; TV Chile; TV One; Universal HD; VH1 Classic; Video Rola; WE tv; Weatherscan.

Fee: $10.00 monthly.

Digital Pay Service 1

Pay Units: N.A.

Programming (via satellite): Cinemax (multiplexed); HBO (multiplexed); HBO HD; HBO Latino; Showtime (multiplexed); Showtime HD; Starz (multiplexed); Starz HDTV; The Movie Channel (multiplexed).

Fee: $6.75 monthly (Starz), $10.95 monthly (HBO), $11.50 monthly (Showtime or TMC).

Video-On-Demand: No

Pay-Per-View

iN DEMAND (delivered digitally); Fresh (delivered digitally); Shorteez (delivered digitally); Playboy TV (delivered digitally); Club Jenna (delivered digitally); Hot Choice (delivered digitally); Spice: Xcess (delivered digitally); Playboy en Espanol (delivered digitally).

Internet Service

Operational: Yes.

Broadband Service: Suddenlink High Speed Internet.

Fee: $49.95 installation; $24.95 monthly.

Telephone Service

Digital: Operational

Fee: $48.95 monthly

Miles of Plant: 652.0 (coaxial); None (fiber optic).

Manager: Vince Thomas.

Ownership: Cequel Communications LLC (MSO).

UNIVERSITY PARK—Charter Communications, 15100 Trinity Blvd, Ste 500, Fort Worth, TX 76155. Phone: 817-298-3600. Web Site: http://www.charter.com. Also serves Highland Park. ICA: TX0062.

TV Market Ranking: 12 (Highland Park, UNIVERSITY PARK). Franchise award date: April 1, 1979. Franchise expiration date: N.A. Began: January 1, 1980.

Channel capacity: N.A. Channels available but not in use: N.A.

Basic Service

Subscribers: 7,442.

Programming (received off-air): KAZD (IND) Lake Dallas; KDAF (CW, IND) Dallas; KDFI (MNT) Dallas; KDFW-DT (FOX) Dallas; KDTN (ETV) Denton; KDTX-TV (TBN) Dallas; KERA-TV (PBS) Dallas; KFWD (IND) Fort Worth; KMPX (IND) Decatur; KPXD-TV (ION) Arlington; KSTR-DT (TEL) Irving; KTVT (CBS) Fort Worth; KTXA (IND) Fort Worth; KUVN-DT (UNV) Garland; KXAS-TV (NBC) Fort Worth; KXTX-TV (TMO) Dallas; WFAA (ABC) Dallas; 23 FMs.

Programming (via satellite): C-SPAN; C-SPAN 2; INSP; QVC; WGN America.

Fee: $29.99 installation.

Expanded Basic Service 1

Subscribers: N.A.

Programming (via satellite): A&E Networks; ABC Family Channel; AMC; Animal Planet; Bravo; Cartoon Network; CNBC; CNN; Comedy Central; Country Music TV; Discovery Channel; Disney Channel; E! Entertainment Television; ESPN; ESPN 2; ESPN Classic Sports; Food Network; Fox News Channel; Fox Sports Southwest; FX; G4; Golf Channel; GSN; Hallmark Channel; Headline News; HGTV; History Channel; Lifetime; MSNBC; MTV; National Geographic Channel; Nickelodeon; Oxygen; SoapNet; Speed; Spike TV; Style Network; Syfy; TBS Superstation; Texas Cable News; The Learning Channel; The Weather Channel; Toon Disney; Travel Channel; truTV; Turner Classic Movies; Turner Network TV; TV Land; USA Network; Versus; VH1; WE tv.

Fee: $48.99 monthly.

Digital Basic Service

Subscribers: N.A.

Programming (via satellite): BBC America; Bio; Bloomberg Television; Discovery Digital Networks; DIY Network; GAS; History Channel International; Independent Film Channel; Lifetime Movie Network; MTV Networks Digital Suite; Music Choice; Nick Jr.; Nick Too; NickToons TV; Science Television; Sundance Channel.

Digital Expanded Basic Service

Subscribers: N.A.

Programming (via satellite): Fox Deportes; FSN Digital Atlantic; FSN Digital Central; FSN Digital Pacific; Fuel TV; NFL Network.

Digital Expanded Basic Service 2

Subscribers: N.A.

Programming (via microwave): KDFW-DT (FOX) Dallas.

Programming (via satellite): Discovery Channel; ESPN; HBO; HDNet; HDNet Movies; KXAS-TV (NBC) Fort Worth; Showtime; WFAA (ABC) Dallas.

Digital Pay Service 1

Pay Units: N.A.

Programming (via satellite): Cinemax (multiplexed); Encore; Flix (multiplexed); HBO (multiplexed); Showtime (multiplexed); Starz (multiplexed); The Movie Channel (multiplexed).

Video-On-Demand: No

Pay-Per-View

Hot Choice (delivered digitally); ETC (delivered digitally); The Erotic Network (delivered digitally); Pleasure (delivered digitally); iN DEMAND (delivered digitally); NASCAR In Car (delivered digitally); Fox Sports Net (delivered digitally).

Internet Service

Operational: Yes.

Broadband Service: Charter Pipeline.

Fee: $29.99 monthly.

Telephone Service

None

Miles of Plant: 82.0 (coaxial); 5.0 (fiber optic).

Vice President & General Manager: Wayne Cramp. Marketing Director: Kathleen Griffin. Technical Operations Director: John Linton.

Ownership: Charter Communications Inc. (MSO).

UVALDE—Time Warner Cable, 1313 W Carlton Rd, Laredo, TX 78041. Phones: 972-899-7300 (Flower Mound office); 956-721-0607. Fax: 956-721-0612. Web Site: http://www.timewarnercable.com/Texas. Also serves Knippa & Uvalde County (portions). ICA: TX0095.

TV Market Ranking: Below 100 (Knippa, UVALDE, Uvalde County (portions)). Franchise award date: N.A. Franchise expiration date: N.A. Began: June 25, 1955.

Channel capacity: N.A. Channels available but not in use: N.A.

Basic Service

Subscribers: N.A. Included in Del Rio

Programming (received off-air): KABB (FOX) San Antonio; KENS (CBS) San Antonio; KLRN (PBS) San Antonio; KMYS (CW) Kerrville; KNIC-CA (TEL) San Antonio; KPXL-TV (ION) Uvalde; KSAT-TV (ABC) San Antonio; KVDA (TMO) San Antonio; KWEX-DT (UNV) San Antonio; WOAI-TV (NBC) San Antonio; allband FM.

Programming (via satellite): Azteca America; C-SPAN 2; The Weather Channel; WGN America.

Fee: $50.51 installation; $14.54 monthly; $.92 converter.

Expanded Basic Service 1

Subscribers: 5,056.

Programming (via satellite): A&E Networks; ABC Family Channel; AMC; Animal Planet; BET Networks; Cartoon Network; CNBC; CNN; Comedy Central; Country Music TV; C-SPAN; Discovery Channel; Discovery Health Channel; Disney Channel; E! Entertainment Television; ESPN; ESPN 2; Eternal Word TV Network; Food Network; Fox News Channel; Fox Sports Southwest; FX; Golf Channel; Great American Country; Hallmark Channel; Headline News; HGTV; History Channel; Lifetime; MoviePlex; MSNBC; MTV; mun2 television; National Geographic Channel; Nickelodeon; Oxygen; QVC; ShopNBC; SoapNet; Spike TV; Style Network; Syfy; TBS Superstation; Texas Cable News; The Learning Channel; Travel Channel; Trinity Broadcasting Network; truTV; Turner Classic Movies; Turner Network TV; TV Guide Network; TV Land; USA Network; VH1; WE tv.

Fee: $33.45 monthly.

Digital Basic Service

Subscribers: N.A.

Programming (via satellite): A&E Networks; ABC Family Channel; AMC; Animal Planet; BBC America; BET Networks; Bio; Bloomberg Television; Boomerang; Bravo; Cartoon Network; cloo; CNBC; CNN; Comedy Central; Country Music TV; C-SPAN; C-SPAN 2; C-SPAN 3; Current; Discovery Channel; Discovery Fit & Health; Discovery Health Channel; Discovery Home Channel; Discovery Kids Channel; Discovery Times Channel; Disney Channel; DIY Network; E! Entertainment Television; ESPN 2; ESPN 2 HD; ESPN Classic Sports; ESPN HD; ESPN U; ESPNews; Eternal Word TV Network; Food Network; Fox Business Channel; Fox College Sports Atlantic; Fox College Sports Central; Fox College Sports Pacific; Fox Deportes; Fox News Channel; Fox Reality Channel; Fox Soccer; Fox Sports Southwest; Fuse; FX; G4; Golf Channel; Great American Country; GSN; Hallmark Channel; HD Theater; HDNet; HDNet Movies; Headline News; HGTV; History Channel; History Channel International; INHD; La Familia Network; Lifetime; Lifetime Movie Network; Military Channel; MoviePlex; MSNBC; MTV; MTV Hits; MTV2; mun2 television; Music Choice; National Geographic Channel; Nick Jr.; Nickelodeon; NickToons TV; Nuvo TV; Oxygen; QVC; Science; ShopNBC; SoapNet; Speed; Spike TV; Style Network; Syfy; TBS Superstation; TeenNick; Texas Cable News; The Learning Channel; The Weather Channel; Toon Disney; Tr3s; Travel Channel; Trinity Broadcasting Network; truTV; Turner Classic Movies; Turner Network TV; Turner Network TV HD; TV Guide Network; TV Land; USA Network; VH1; VH1 Classic; VH1 Country; WE tv.

Fee: $5.00 monthly.

Digital Expanded Basic Service

Subscribers: N.A.

Programming (via satellite): Boomerang; Canal Sur; Cine Latino; CNN en Espanol; Discovery en Espanol; Encore (multiplexed); ESPN Deportes; Fox Movie Channel; Independent Film Channel; NBA TV; Puma TV; Sorpresa; Speed; Sundance Channel; Tennis Channel; Tr3s; Versus; VHUNO; Video Rola.

Digital Pay Service 1

Pay Units: N.A.

Programming (via satellite): Cinemax (multiplexed); HBO (multiplexed); HBO HD; Showtime (multiplexed); Showtime HD; Starz (multiplexed); The Movie Channel.

Fee: $12.95 monthly (each).

Video-On-Demand: No

Pay-Per-View

iN DEMAND (delivered digitally); Fresh (delivered digitally); Playboy TV (delivered digitally); Hot Choice (delivered digitally); NBA League Pass (delivered digitally); MLS Direct Kick (delivered digitally); NHL Center Ice (delivered digitally); MLB Extra Innings (delivered digitally).

Internet Service

Operational: Yes.

Broadband Service: RoadRunner.

Fee: $49.99 installation; $44.95 monthly.

Telephone Service

Digital: Operational

Fee: $44.95 monthly

Miles of Plant: 104.0 (coaxial); None (fiber optic).

President: Connie Wharton. Vice President & General Manager: Michael Carrosquiola. Technical Operations Manager: Eduardo Ruiz. Operations Director: Marco Reyes. Public Affairs Manager: Celinda Gonzales.

Ownership: Time Warner Cable (MSO).; Advance/Newhouse Partnership (MSO).

VALENTINE—Valentine TV Cable, PO Box 1377, Alpine, TX 79831-1377. Phone: 432-837-2300. Fax: 432-837-5423. E-mail: mtnzone@sbcglobal.net. ICA: TX0692.

TV Market Ranking: Outside TV Markets (VALENTINE). Franchise award date: February 22, 1980. Franchise expiration date: January 1, 2016. Began: July 1, 1983.

Channel capacity: 36 (not 2-way capable). Channels available but not in use: N.A.

Basic Service

Subscribers: 32.

Programming (received off-air): KABB (FOX) San Antonio; KOSA-TV (CBS, MNT) Odessa; KSAT-TV (ABC) San Antonio; KWES-TV (NBC) Odessa; allband FM.

Programming (via satellite): A&E Networks; ABC Family Channel; Cartoon Network; CNN; Discovery Channel; ESPN; GalaVision; Great American Country; Nickelodeon; TBS Superstation; The Learning Channel; Turner Classic Movies; Turner Network TV; TV Land; Univision Studios; USA Network; WGN America.

Fee: $25.00 installation; $30.00 monthly.

Pay Service 1

Pay Units: 23.

Programming (via satellite): Cinemax; HBO.

Fee: $10.00 installation; $6.00 monthly.

Video-On-Demand: No

Internet Service

Operational: No.

Telephone Service

None

Miles of Plant: 3.0 (coaxial); None (fiber optic).

Manager: Steve Neu. Office Manager: Lawrence Neu.

Ownership: Mountain Zone TV Systems (MSO).

VALLEY MILLS—Reach Broadband, 515 E Longview Dr, Arp, TX 75750. Phone: 800-687-1258. Web Site: http://www.reachbroadband.net. ICA: TX0444.

TV Market Ranking: Below 100 (VALLEY MILLS). Franchise award date: July 15, 1989. Franchise expiration date: N.A. Began: December 28, 1983.

Channel capacity: 35 (not 2-way capable). Channels available but not in use: N.A.

Basic Service

Subscribers: 330.

Programming (received off-air): KCEN-TV (NBC, IND) Temple; KDFI (MNT) Dallas; KDYW (PBS) Waco; KERA-TV (PBS) Dallas; KSTR-DT (TEL) Irving; KTVT (CBS) Fort Worth; KUVN-DT (UNV) Garland; KWKT-TV (FOX, MNT) Waco; KWTX-TV (CBS, CW) Waco; KXAS-TV (NBC) Fort Worth; KXTX-TV (TMO) Dallas; KXXV (ABC, TMO) Waco; WFAA (ABC) Dallas.

Programming (via satellite): A&E Networks; ABC Family Channel; AMC; Animal Planet; Cartoon Network; CNN; Country Music TV; C-SPAN; Discovery Channel; Disney Channel; ESPN; ESPN 2; Fox Sports Southwest; Headline News; HGTV; History Channel; INSP; Lifetime; Nickelodeon; Speed; Spike TV; Syfy; TBS Superstation; The Learning Channel; The Weather Channel; Turner Network TV; TV Land; USA Network; VH1; WGN America.

Fee: $54.95 installation; $44.05 monthly.

Pay Service 1

Pay Units: 144.

Programming (via satellite): Cinemax; HBO.

Fee: $12.95 monthly (each).

Video-On-Demand: No

Internet Service

Operational: No.

Telephone Service

None

Miles of Plant: 9.0 (coaxial); None (fiber optic).

Regional Manager: Ronnie Stafford. Office Manager: Jan Gibson.

Ownership: RB3 LLC (MSO).

VALLEY VIEW—Nortex Communications, 205 N Walnut St, PO Box 587, Muenster, TX 76252-2780. Phone: 940-759-2251. Fax: 940-759-5557. E-mail: info@nortex.net. Web Site: http://www.nortex.com. Also serves Collinsville, Lake Kiowa, Lindsay, Muenster & St. Jo. ICA: TX0792.

TV Market Ranking: Below 100 (Collinsville, LAKE KIOWA, Muenster, St. Jo, Valley View); Outside TV Markets (Lindsay). Franchise award date: N.A. Franchise expiration date: N.A. Began: August 1, 1996.

Channel capacity: 62 (operating 2-way). Channels available but not in use: N.A.

Basic Service

Subscribers: 2,310.

Programming (received off-air): KDAF (CW, IND) Dallas; KDFI (MNT) Dallas; KFWD (IND) Fort Worth; KMPX (IND) Decatur; KTXA (IND) Fort Worth; KXTX-TV (TMO) Dallas.

Programming (via satellite): A&E Networks; ABC Family Channel; CNBC; CNN; Country Music TV; C-SPAN; Discovery Channel; Disney Channel; E! Entertainment Television; ESPN; ESPN 2; Eternal Word TV Network; Fox News Channel; Fox Sports Southwest; Golf Channel; Headline News; HGTV; History Channel; ION Television; Lifetime; MSNBC; Nickelodeon; QVC; ShopNBC; Spike TV; TBS Superstation; Telefutura; The Learning Channel; The Weather Channel; Travel Channel; Trinity Broadcasting Network; Turner Classic Movies; Turner Network TV; TV Land; USA Network; WGN America.

Fee: $40.00 installation; $38.95 monthly; $4.95 converter.

Digital Basic Service

Subscribers: N.A.

Programming (via satellite): Bio; Bloomberg Television; Discovery Fit & Health; DMX Music; ESPN Classic Sports; Fox Movie Channel; FSN Digital Atlantic; FSN Digital Central; FSN Digital Pacific; Fuse; G4; Great American Country; Halogen Network; History Channel International; Lifetime Movie Network; National Geographic Channel; Outdoor Channel; Speed; Style Network; Syfy; Toon Disney; Versus; WE tv.

Fee: $15.95 monthly; $4.95 converter.

Pay Service 1

Pay Units: N.A.

Programming (via satellite): Cinemax; HBO; Showtime.

Digital Pay Service 1

Pay Units: N.A.

Programming (via satellite): Cinemax (multiplexed); Encore (multiplexed); Flix; HBO (multiplexed); Showtime (multiplexed); Starz (multiplexed); The Movie Channel (multiplexed).

Fee: $10.00 monthly (each).

Video-On-Demand: No

Internet Service

Operational: Yes.

Fee: $29.95-$59.95 monthly.

Telephone Service

None

Miles of Plant: 111.0 (coaxial); 15.0 (fiber optic).

Chief Executive Officer: Alvin M. Fuhrman. Chief Operating Officer: Joey Anderson. Chief Financial Officer: Alan Rohmer. Marketing Manager: Carolyn McPherson. Network Engineer: Mack Isaacs.

Ownership: Nortex Communications (MSO).

VAN HORN—US Cable of Coastal Texas LP, 611 W Ave A, Seminole, TX 79360. Phones: 432-758-9221; 800-996-8788. Fax: 432-758-3379. Web Site: http://www.uscable.com. ICA: TX1024.

TV Market Ranking: Outside TV Markets (VAN HORN).

Channel capacity: N.A. Channels available but not in use: N.A.

Basic Service

Subscribers: 361.

Programming (received off-air): KDBC-TV (CBS, MNT) El Paso; KFOX-TV (FOX) El Paso; KPBT-TV (PBS) Odessa; KTSM-TV (NBC) El Paso; KVIA-TV (ABC, CW) El Paso; KWES-TV (NBC) Odessa.

Programming (via satellite): A&E Networks; ABC Family Channel; Animal Planet; Cartoon Network; CNN; Country Music TV; C-SPAN; Discovery Channel; Discovery Fit & Health; Disney Channel; ESPN; ESPN 2; Eternal Word TV Network; Fox Sports Net; FX; Hallmark Channel; Headline News; Home Shopping Network; Lifetime; MTV; National Geographic Channel; Nick At Nite; Nickelodeon; ShopNBC; Spike TV; Syfy; TBS Superstation; Telemundo; Texas Cable News; The Learning Channel; The Weather Channel; Trinity Broadcasting Network; Turner Classic Movies; Turner Network TV; Univision; USA Network; VH1; WGN America.

Fee: $39.96 installation; $45.93 monthly.

Digital Basic Service

Subscribers: N.A.

Programming (via satellite): BBC America; Bio; Bloomberg Television; Bravo; Centric; cloo; CMT Pure Country; Current; Discovery Health Channel; Discovery Kids Channel; Disney XD; DMX Music; Encore (multiplexed); ESPN Classic Sports; ESPNews; Fox Movie Channel; Fox Soccer; FSN Digital Atlantic; FSN Digital Central; FSN Digital Pacific; Fuse; G4; Golf Channel; Great American Country; GSN; Halogen Network; HGTV; History Channel International; ID Investigation Discovery; Independent Film Channel; Lifetime Movie Network; Military Channel; MTV Hits; MTV2; Nick Jr.; Outdoor Channel; Planet Green; Science; Speed; Style Network; TeenNick; The Word Network; Versus; VH1 Classic; VH1 Soul; WE tv.

Fee: $20.90 monthly.

Pay Service 1

Pay Units: N.A.

Programming (via satellite): HBO.

Fee: $13.95 monthly.

Digital Pay Service 1

Pay Units: N.A.

Programming (via satellite): Cinemax (multiplexed); HBO (multiplexed); Showtime (multiplexed); Starz (multiplexed); The Movie Channel (multiplexed).

Fee: $9.95 monthly (Starz), $12.95 monthly (HBO, Cinemax, Showtime or TMC).

Video-On-Demand: No

Pay-Per-View

Event Entertainment (delivered digitally); Playboy TV (delivered digitally); Fresh (delivered digitally); Movies (delivered digitally).

Internet Service

Operational: Yes.

Telephone Service

None

Regional Manager: Daryl Koedyker.

Ownership: US Cable Corp. (MSO).

VEGA—XIT Communications. Formerly served by Hereford, TX [TX0125]. This cable system has converted to IPTV, 1624 Tennessee Ave, Dalhart, TX 79022. Phones: 800-232-3312; 806-384-3311. E-mail: xitcom@xit.net. ICA: TX5081.

Channel capacity: N.A. Channels available but not in use: N.A.

Pay Service 1

Pay Units: N.A.

Fee: $8.95 monthly (Cinemax or Starz); $13.95 monthly (HBO or Showtime/TMC).

Internet Service

Operational: Yes.

Fee: $30.00 installation; $39.00 monthly.

Telephone Service

Digital: Operational

General Manager: Darrell Dennis.

VEGA—XIT Communications. Now served by HEREFORD, TX [TX0125]. ICA: TX0868.

VERNON—Suddenlink Communications, 2830 Wilbarger St, Vernon, TX 76384. Phones: 800-999-6845 (Customer service); 314-965-2020. Fax: 940-553-4551. Web Site: http://www.suddenlink.com. ICA: TX0119.

TV Market Ranking: Outside TV Markets (VERNON). Franchise award date: N.A. Franchise expiration date: N.A. Began: November 1, 1976.

Channel capacity: 37 (operating 2-way). Channels available but not in use: N.A.

Basic Service

Subscribers: 3,023.

Programming (received off-air): KAUZ-TV (CBS, CW) Wichita Falls; KFDX-TV (NBC) Wichita Falls; KJTL (FOX) Wichita Falls; KSWO-TV (ABC) Lawton; allband FM.

Programming (via satellite): C-SPAN; GalaVision; KRMA-TV (PBS) Denver; QVC; Shop at Home; The Weather Channel; TV Guide Network; Univision Studios.

Fee: $39.95 installation; $19.95 monthly.

Expanded Basic Service 1

Subscribers: 2,651.

Programming (via satellite): A&E Networks; ABC Family Channel; AMC; Animal

Planet; BET Networks; Bravo; Cartoon Network; CNBC; CNN; Comedy Central; Discovery Channel; Disney Channel; E! Entertainment Television; ESPN; ESPN 2; Eternal Word TV Network; Food Network; Fox News Channel; Fox Sports Southwest; FX; Golf Channel; Great American Country; Hallmark Channel; Headline News; HGTV; History Channel; Lifetime; MSNBC; MTV; National Geographic Channel; Nickelodeon; Outdoor Channel; Shopping Channel; Speed; Spike TV; Syfy; TBS Superstation; Telemundo; The Learning Channel; Travel Channel; truTV; Turner Classic Movies; Turner Network TV; TV Land; USA Network; VH1.
Fee: $39.95 installation; $24.00 monthly.

Digital Basic Service
Subscribers: N.A.
Programming (via satellite): BBC America; Bio; Bloomberg Television; cloo; Discovery Digital Networks; DMX Music; ESPN Classic Sports; ESPNews; Fox College Sports Atlantic; Fox College Sports Central; Fox College Sports Pacific; Fox Movie Channel; Fox Soccer; Fuse; G4; GSN; History Channel International; Independent Film Channel; Military History Channel; ShopNBC; Sundance Channel; Toon Disney; Trinity Broadcasting Network; Versus; WE tv.

Pay Service 1
Pay Units: 410.
Programming (via satellite): Cinemax.
Fee: $12.62 monthly.

Pay Service 2
Pay Units: 1,041.
Programming (via satellite): Encore.
Fee: $1.75 monthly.

Pay Service 3
Pay Units: 541.
Programming (via satellite): HBO.
Fee: $13.59 monthly.

Pay Service 4
Pay Units: 622.
Programming (via satellite): Starz.
Fee: $6.75 monthly.

Pay Service 5
Pay Units: N.A.
Programming (via satellite): Showtime.

Digital Pay Service 1
Pay Units: N.A.
Programming (via satellite): Cinemax (multiplexed); Encore (multiplexed); Flix; HBO (multiplexed); Showtime (multiplexed); Starz (multiplexed); The Movie Channel (multiplexed).

Video-On-Demand: No

Pay-Per-View
iN DEMAND (delivered digitally); Playboy TV (delivered digitally); Fresh (delivered digitally); Shorteez (delivered digitally).

Internet Service
Operational: Yes. Began: March 1, 2002.
Broadband Service: Suddenlink High Speed Internet.
Fee: $45.95 installation; $29.95 monthly.

Telephone Service
Digital: Operational
Fee: $44.95 monthly

Miles of Plant: 81.0 (coaxial); None (fiber optic).
Regional Manager: Todd Cruthird. Plant Manager: Ron Johnson.
Ownership: Cequel Communications LLC (MSO).

VICTORIA—Suddenlink Communications, 105 E Industrial Dr, Victoria, TX 77901-3344. Phone: 361-573-6301. Fax: 361-576-5295. Web Site: http://www.suddenlink.com. Also serves Victoria County (unincorporated areas). ICA: TX0043.
TV Market Ranking: Below 100 (VICTORIA, Victoria County (unincorporated areas)). Franchise award date: January 1, 1955. Franchise expiration date: N.A. Began: January 12, 1954.
Channel capacity: N.A. Channels available but not in use: N.A.

Basic Service
Subscribers: 19,460.
Programming (received off-air): KAVU-TV (ABC) Victoria; KMOL-LP Victoria; KTJA-CA (IND) Victoria; KVCT (FOX) Victoria; KVTX-LP (TMO) Victoria; KXTS-LP Victoria; 21 FMs.
Programming (via microwave): KENS (CBS) San Antonio; KLRN (PBS) San Antonio; KUHT (PBS) Houston; KUNU-LP Victoria.
Programming (via satellite): C-SPAN; C-SPAN 2; CW+; Eternal Word TV Network; INSP; QVC; The Weather Channel; Trinity Broadcasting Network; TV Guide Network; WGN America.
Fee: $35.00 installation; $11.32 monthly; $25.00 additional installation.

Expanded Basic Service 1
Subscribers: N.A.
Programming (via satellite): A&E Networks; ABC Family Channel; AMC; Animal Planet; BET Networks; Bravo; Cartoon Network; CNBC; CNN; Comedy Central; Country Music TV; Discovery Channel; Disney Channel; E! Entertainment Television; ESPN; ESPN 2; Food Network; Fox Deportes; Fox News Channel; Fox Sports Southwest; FX; GalaVision; Golf Channel; Great American Country; Headline News; HGTV; History Channel; Jewelry Television; Lifetime; Lifetime Movie Network; MSNBC; MTV; Nickelodeon; Outdoor Channel; Oxygen; Speed; Spike TV; Syfy; TBS Superstation; The Learning Channel; Travel Channel; truTV; Turner Classic Movies; Turner Network TV; TV Land; USA Network; Versus; VH1; WE tv; Weatherscan.
Fee: $20.63 monthly.

Digital Basic Service
Subscribers: N.A.
Programming (via satellite): A&E HD; Bandamax; BBC America; Bio; Bloomberg Television; Boomerang; Boomerang en Espanol; CBS Sports Network; Cine Latino; Cine Mexicano; CMT Pure Country; CNN en Espanol; Cooking Channel; De Pelicula; De Pelicula Clasico; Discovery en Espanol; Discovery Health Channel; Discovery Home Channel; Discovery Kids Channel; DIY Network; Encore (multiplexed); ESPN 2 HD; ESPN Classic Sports; ESPN Deportes; ESPN HD; ESPN U; ESPNews; EWTN en Espanol; Food Network HD; Fox Deportes; Fox Reality Channel; Fox Soccer; FSN HD; Fuel TV; Fuse; G4; GalaVision; GSN; Hallmark Channel; HD Theater; HDNet; HDNet Movies; HGTV HD; History Channel en Espanol; History Channel International; ID Investigation Discovery; Independent Film Channel; Latele Novela Network; Military Channel; MTV Hits; MTV Jams; MTV2; mun2 television; Music Choice; National Geographic Channel; National Geographic Channel HD Network; Nick Jr.; NickToons en Espanol; NickToons TV; Nuvo TV; Palladia; Ritmoson Latino; Science; SoapNet; Sorpresa; Style Network; Sundance Channel; Sur Network; TBN Enlace USA; TeenNick; Telefutura; Telehit; Tennis Channel; Toon Disney; Toon Disney en Espanol; Tr3s; Turner Network TV HD; TV Chile; Universal HD; VH1 Classic; VH1 Soul; Video Rola.
Fee: $8.65 monthly.

Digital Pay Service 1
Pay Units: N.A.
Programming (via satellite): Cinemax (multiplexed); HBO (multiplexed); HBO HD; HBO Latino; Showtime (multiplexed); Showtime HD; Starz (multiplexed); Starz HDTV; The Movie Channel (multiplexed).
Fee: $7.95 monthly (Starz & Encore), $10.00 monthly (Cinemax), $11.00 monthly (HBO).

Video-On-Demand: No

Pay-Per-View
iN DEMAND (delivered digitally); Fresh (delivered digitally); Shorteez (delivered digitally); Playboy TV (delivered digitally); Club Jenna (delivered digitally); Spice: Xcess (delivered digitally); Playboy en Espanol (delivered digitally).

Internet Service
Operational: Yes.
Broadband Service: Suddenlink High Speed Internet.
Fee: $49.95 installation; $24.95 monthly.

Telephone Service
Digital: Operational
Fee: $48.95 monthly

Miles of Plant: 350.0 (coaxial); None (fiber optic). Additional miles planned: 7.0 (coaxial).
Manager: Ray Griffith. Chief Technician: James Farrow.
Ownership: Cequel Communications LLC (MSO).

VIDOR—Time Warner Cable. Now served by BEAUMONT, TX [TX0022]. ICA: TX0093.

VIDOR (southern portion)—Formerly served by Cebridge Connections. No longer in operation. ICA: TX0551.

WACO—Grande Communications, 7200 Imperial Dr, Waco, TX 76712-6623. Phone: 254-235-4600. Fax: 254-235-2099. Web Site: http://www.grandecom.com. Also serves Hewitt & Woodway. ICA: TX0980. **Note:** This system is an overbuild.
TV Market Ranking: Below 100 (Hewitt, WACO, Woodway). Franchise award date: January 6, 1999. Franchise expiration date: N.A. Began: November 1, 1999.
Channel capacity: N.A. Channels available but not in use: N.A.

Basic Service
Subscribers: N.A.
Programming (received off-air): KAKW-DT (UNV) Killeen; KCEN-TV (NBC, IND) Temple; KDYW (PBS) Waco; KWKT-TV (FOX, MNT) Waco; KWTX-TV (CBS, CW) Waco; KXXV (ABC, TMO) Waco; WFAA (ABC) Dallas.
Programming (via satellite): C-SPAN; LWS Local Weather Station; QVC; Telemundo (multiplexed); Telemundo; WGN America.
Fee: $14.95 monthly.

Expanded Basic Service 1
Subscribers: N.A.
Programming (via satellite): A&E Networks; ABC Family Channel; AMC; Animal Planet; BET Networks; Bravo; Cartoon Network; CNBC; CNN; Comedy Central; Country Music TV; C-SPAN 2; Discovery Channel; Discovery Health Channel; Disney Channel; E! Entertainment Television; ESPN; ESPN 2; ESPN Classic Sports; Eternal Word TV Network; Food Network; Fox Deportes; Fox Movie Channel; Fox News Channel; Fox Sports Southwest; FX; G4; GalaVision; Golf Channel; Great American Country; GSN; Hallmark Channel; Headline News; HGTV; History Channel; Lifetime; Lifetime Movie Network; MSNBC; MTV; mun2 television; Nickelodeon; Oxygen; SoapNet; special events; Speed; Spike TV; Syfy; TBS Superstation; The Learning Channel; The Weather Channel; Toon Disney; Travel Channel; Trinity Broadcasting Network; truTV; Turner Classic Movies; Turner Network TV; TV Land; USA Network; Versus; VH1.
Fee: $28.00 monthly.

Digital Basic Service
Subscribers: N.A.
Programming (via satellite): American-Life TV Network; BBC America; Bio; Boomerang; Canales N; CBS Sports Network; Colours; Cooking Channel; Discovery Fit & Health; DIY Network; ESPN; ESPNews; FamilyNet; Fox College Sports Atlantic; Fox College Sports Central; Fox College Sports Pacific; Fox Soccer; Fuel TV; Fuse; GAS; GolTV; HD Theater; History Channel International; INHD; MTV Networks Digital Suite; Music Choice; National Geographic Channel; NBA TV; NFL Network; Nick Jr.; Nick Too; NickToons TV; Nuvo TV; Tennis Channel; Turner Network TV; TVG Network; Universal HD.
Fee: $16.00 monthly (basic), $4.00 monthly (Canales N), $9.95 monthly (HDTV Tier).

Digital Pay Service 1
Pay Units: N.A.
Programming (via satellite): Cinemax (multiplexed); Cinemax HD; Encore (multiplexed); Flix (multiplexed); HBO (multiplexed); HBO HD; Showtime (multiplexed); Showtime HD; Starz (multiplexed); Starz HDTV; Sundance Channel (multiplexed); The Movie Channel (multiplexed).
Fee: $9.99 monthly (Cinemax, HBO, Starz/Encore, or Showtime/TMC/Flix/Sundance).

Pay-Per-View
Playboy TV; Spice (delivered digitally); Shorteez (delivered digitally); Pleasure (delivered digitally); Hot Choice (delivered digitally); iN DEMAND (delivered digitally); Sports PPV (delivered digitally).

Internet Service
Operational: Yes. Began: January 1, 1999.
Broadband Service: Grande High Speed Internet.
Fee: $19.95 monthly.

Telephone Service
Digital: Operational
Fee: $9.00 monthly

General Manager: Matt Rohre.
Ownership: Grande Communications Networks Inc. (MSO).

WACO—Time Warner Cable, 12012 N Mo Pac Expy, Austin, TX 78758-2904. Phones: 254-776-2996 (Waco office); 512-485-6100. Fax: 512-485-6105. Web Site: http://www.timewarnercable.com/Texas. Also serves Bellmead, Beverly Hills, Bruceville-Eddy, China Spring, Elm Mott, Hewitt, Lacy-Lakeview, Lorena, McGregor, McLennan County (portions), Northcrest, Robinson & Woodway. ICA: TX0015.
TV Market Ranking: Below 100 (Bellmead, Beverly Hills, Bruceville-Eddy, China Spring, Elm Mott, Hewitt, Lacy-Lakeview, Lorena, McGregor, McLennan County (portions), Northcrest, Robinson, WACO, Woodway). Franchise award date: N.A. Franchise expiration date: N.A. Began: October 1, 1965.
Channel capacity: N.A. Channels available but not in use: N.A.

Basic Service
Subscribers: 115,000 Includes Killeen.
Programming (received off-air): KCEN-TV (NBC, IND) Temple; KDYW (PBS) Waco;

KNCT (PBS) Belton; KWKT-TV (FOX, MNT) Waco; KWTX-TV (CBS, CW) Waco; KXXV (ABC, TMO) Waco.
Programming (via satellite): C-SPAN; C-SPAN 2; Local Cable Weather; News 8 Austin; QVC; ShopNBC; TBS Superstation; Telemundo; TV Guide Network; Univision Studios.
Fee: $43.95 installation; $19.95 monthly.

Expanded Basic Service 1
Subscribers: N.A.
Programming (via satellite): A&E Networks; ABC Family Channel; AMC; Animal Planet; BET Networks; Bravo; Cartoon Network; CNBC; CNN; Comedy Central; Country Music TV; Discovery Channel; Discovery Health Channel; Disney Channel; E! Entertainment Television; ESPN; ESPN 2; Eternal Word TV Network; Food Network; Fox News Channel; Fox Sports Southwest; FX; GalaVision; Golf Channel; Hallmark Channel; Headline News; HGTV; History Channel; ION Television; Jewelry Television; Lifetime; Lifetime Movie Network; MSNBC; MTV; National Geographic Channel; Nickelodeon; Outdoor Channel; Oxygen; Shop at Home; Speed; Spike TV; Syfy; Telefutura; Texas Cable News; The Learning Channel; The Weather Channel; Travel Channel; Trinity Broadcasting Network; truTV; Turner Classic Movies; Turner Network TV; TV Land; USA Network; VH1; WE tv.
Fee: $22.79 monthly.

Digital Basic Service
Subscribers: N.A.
Programming (via satellite): A&E HD; BBC America; BBC America On Demand; Bio; Bloomberg Television; Boomerang; Canal Sur; Cartoon Network Tambien en Espanol; CBS Sports Network; Cine Latino; cloo; CNN en Espanol; CNN HD; Cooking Channel; C-SPAN 3; Current; Discovery en Espanol; Discovery Fit & Health; Discovery Home Channel; Discovery Kids Channel; Discovery Times Channel; DIY Network; Encore (multiplexed); ESPN 2 HD; ESPN Classic Sports; ESPN Deportes; ESPN HD; ESPN U; ESPNews; EWTN en Espanol; Exercise TV; Flix; Food Network HD; Fox Business Channel; Fox College Sports Atlantic; Fox College Sports Central; Fox College Sports Pacific; Fox Deportes; Fox Movie Channel; Fox Reality Channel; Fox Soccer; Fuel TV; Fuse; G4; GMC; Great American Country; GSN; Halogen Network; HD Theater; HDNet; HDNet Movies; HGTV HD; History Channel International; Howard TV; Independent Film Channel; INSP; La Familia Network; Lifetime Real Women; Military Channel; MTV2; Music Choice; National Geographic Channel On Demand; NBA TV; Nick Jr.; NickToons TV; Ovation; Oxygen On Demand; Science; SoapNet; Sorpresa; Speed On Demand; Style Network; TBS in HD; TeenNick; Tennis Channel; Toon Disney; Tr3s; Turner Network TV HD; TV Guide SPOT; Universal HD; Versus; VH1 Classic; Video Rola.
Fee: $20.00 installation; $9.95 monthly.

Digital Pay Service 1
Pay Units: N.A.
Programming (via satellite): Cinemax (multiplexed); Cinemax HD; HBO (multiplexed); HBO HD; Showtime (multiplexed); Showtime HD; Starz (multiplexed); Starz HDTV; The Movie Channel (multiplexed).
Fee: $12.95 monthly (each).
Video-On-Demand: Yes

Pay-Per-View
Addressable homes: 17,000.
Movies (delivered digitally); iN DEMAND (delivered digitally); Sports PPV (delivered digitally).

Internet Service
Operational: Yes.
Broadband Service: Road Runner.
Fee: $79.00 installation; $44.95 monthly.

Telephone Service
Digital: Operational
Fee: $44.95 monthly

Miles of Plant: 1,216.0 (coaxial); None (fiber optic).
President: Katherine Brabson. Vice President, Technical Operations: Ed Tagg. Vice President, Engineering: Lew Suders. Vice President, Marketing & Sales: Terri Cumbie. Vice President, Public Affairs: Stacy Schmitt. Technical Operations Director: Deborah Brainard. Public Affairs Director: Roger Heaney.
Ownership: Time Warner Cable (MSO).; Advance/Newhouse Partnership (MSO).

WAELDER—Formerly served by National Cable Inc. No longer in operation. ICA: TX0518.

WALDEN—Suddenlink Communications, 12444 Powerscourt Dr, Saint Louis, MO 63131-3660. Phones: 800-999-6845 (Customer service); 314-965-2020. Fax: 314-315-9496. Web Site: http://www.suddenlink.com. Also serves April Sound Subdivision, Lake Conroe East, Montgomery & Montgomery County. ICA: TX0869.
TV Market Ranking: 15 (Montgomery County (portions)); Below 100 (April Sound Subdivision, Lake Conroe East, Montgomery, WALDEN, Montgomery County (portions)). Franchise award date: N.A. Franchise expiration date: N.A. Began: September 1, 1984.
Channel capacity: 36 (operating 2-way). Channels available but not in use: N.A.

Basic Service
Subscribers: 7,400.
Programming (received off-air): KETH-TV (TBN) Houston; KFTH-DT (TEL) Alvin; KHOU (CBS) Houston; KIAH (CW) Houston; KLTJ (ETV) Galveston; KPRC-TV (NBC) Houston; KPXB-TV (ION) Conroe; KRIV (FOX) Houston; KTBU (IND) Conroe; KTMD (TMO) Galveston; KTRK-TV (ABC) Houston; KTXH (MNT) Houston; KUBE-TV (IND) Baytown; KUHT (PBS) Houston; KXLN-DT (UNV) Rosenberg; KYAZ (IND) Katy; KZJL (IND) Houston.
Programming (via satellite): WGN America.
Fee: $52.50 installation; $19.05 monthly.

Expanded Basic Service 1
Subscribers: N.A.
Programming (via satellite): A&E Networks; ABC Family Channel; AMC; Animal Planet; BET Networks; Bravo; Cartoon Network; CNBC; CNN; Comedy Central; Country Music TV; C-SPAN; C-SPAN 2; Discovery Channel; Disney Channel; E! Entertainment Television; ESPN; ESPN 2; ESPN Classic Sports; Eternal Word TV Network; Food Network; Fox News Channel; Fox Soccer; Fox Sports Southwest; FX; Golf Channel; Hallmark Channel; Headline News; HGTV; History Channel; Lifetime; Lifetime Movie Network; MSNBC; MTV; Nickelodeon; Outdoor Channel; Oxygen; Shopping Channel; Speed; Spike TV; Syfy; TBS Superstation; The Learning Channel; The Weather Channel; Travel Channel; truTV; Turner Classic Movies; Turner Network TV; TV Guide Network; TV Land; USA Network; VH1; WE tv.
Fee: $23.90 monthly.

Digital Basic Service
Subscribers: N.A.
Programming (via satellite): BBC America; Bio; Bloomberg Television; cloo; C-SPAN 3; DIY Network; ESPN; ESPNews; Fox College Sports Atlantic; Fox College Sports Central; Fox College Sports Pacific; Fox Movie Channel; Fuel TV; Fuse; G4; GAS; GSN; HD Theater; HDNet; HDNet Movies; History Channel International; Independent Film Channel; Military History Channel; MTV Networks Digital Suite; Music Choice; National Geographic Channel; Nick Jr.; NickToons TV; SoapNet; Sundance Channel; Tennis Channel; Toon Disney; Versus; Weatherscan; WeatherVision.
Fee: $3.99 monthly.

Digital Pay Service 1
Pay Units: N.A.
Programming (via satellite): Cinemax (multiplexed); Encore (multiplexed); Flix; HBO (multiplexed); HBO HD; Showtime (multiplexed); Showtime HD; Starz (multiplexed); The Movie Channel (multiplexed).
Video-On-Demand: No

Pay-Per-View
iN DEMAND (delivered digitally); Playboy TV (delivered digitally).

Internet Service
Operational: Yes. Began: January 1, 2001.
Subscribers: 529.
Broadband Service: Suddenlink High Speed Internet.
Fee: $49.95 installation; $29.95 monthly.

Telephone Service
Digital: Operational
Fee: $44.95 monthly

Regional Manager: Todd Cruthird. Plant Manager: Kyle Spell. Marketing Director: Beverly Gambell.
Ownership: Cequel Communications LLC (MSO).

WALLER—Suddenlink Communications, 12444 Powerscourt Dr, Saint Louis, MO 63131-3660. Phones: 800-999-6845 (Customer service); 314-965-2020. Fax: 903-561-5485. Web Site: http://www.suddenlink.com. Also serves Prairie View. ICA: TX0304.
TV Market Ranking: Below 100 (Prairie View, WALLER). Franchise award date: N.A. Franchise expiration date: N.A. Began: July 1, 1983.
Channel capacity: N.A. Channels available but not in use: N.A.

Basic Service
Subscribers: N.A.
Programming (received off-air): KHOU (CBS) Houston; KIAH (CW) Houston; KPRC-TV (NBC) Houston; KRIV (FOX) Houston; KTRK-TV (ABC) Houston; KTXH (MNT) Houston; KUHT (PBS) Houston; KYAZ (IND) Katy; KZJL (IND) Houston.
Programming (via satellite): A&E Networks; ABC Family Channel; AMC; Animal Planet; BET Networks; Cartoon Network; CNBC; CNN; Comedy Central; Country Music TV; C-SPAN; Discovery Channel; E! Entertainment Television; ESPN; ESPN 2; Fox News Channel; Hallmark Channel; Headline News; HGTV; History Channel; Lifetime; MTV; Nickelodeon; Syfy; TBS Superstation; The Learning Channel; The Weather Channel; Turner Classic Movies; Turner Network TV; TV Guide Network; USA Network; VH1.
Fee: $25.00 installation; $39.95 monthly.

Pay Service 1
Pay Units: N.A.
Programming (via satellite): Cinemax; HBO; Showtime.
Fee: $9.00 monthly (each).
Video-On-Demand: No

Internet Service
Operational: No.

Telephone Service
None

Miles of Plant: 44.0 (coaxial); None (fiber optic).
Regional Manager: Todd Cruthird.
Ownership: Cequel Communications LLC (MSO).

WALLIS—Formerly served by Rapid Cable. No longer in operation. ICA: TX0275.

WALNUT SPRINGS—Formerly served by National Cable Inc. No longer in operation. ICA: TX0871.

WATERWOOD—Cablevision of Walker County, 1304 10th St, Huntsville, TX 77320. Phone: 936-291-2288. Fax: 936-291-0890. Web Site: http://www.walkercountycabletv.com. Also serves San Jacinto County (portions). ICA: TX0872.
TV Market Ranking: Below 100 (San Jacinto County (portions), WATERWOOD); Outside TV Markets (San Jacinto County (portions)). Franchise award date: N.A. Franchise expiration date: N.A. Began: January 1, 1976.
Channel capacity: 52 (not 2-way capable). Channels available but not in use: N.A.

Basic Service
Subscribers: 450.
Programming (received off-air): KBTX-TV (CBS, CW) Bryan; KHOU (CBS) Houston; KPRC-TV (NBC) Houston; KPXB-TV (ION) Conroe; KRIV (FOX) Houston; KTBU (IND) Conroe; KTRK-TV (ABC) Houston; KTXH (MNT) Houston; KUHT (PBS) Houston.
Programming (via satellite): A&E Networks; ABC Family Channel; AMC; CNBC; CNN; Country Music TV; C-SPAN; Discovery Channel; ESPN; Food Network; Fox News Channel; Fox Sports Southwest; Golf Channel; Headline News; HGTV; History Channel; Lifetime; Nickelodeon; Spike TV; TBS Superstation; The Weather Channel; Turner Network TV; USA Network; VH1; WGN America.
Fee: $39.95 installation; $32.79 monthly.

Digital Basic Service
Subscribers: N.A.
Programming (via satellite): AmericanLife TV Network; BBC America; Bio; Bloomberg Television; Current; Discovery Fit & Health; Discovery Health Channel; Discovery Home Channel; Discovery Kids Channel; Discovery Travel & Living (Viajar y Vivir); DMX Music; ESPN 2; ESPN Classic Sports; ESPNews; Fox Movie Channel; Fox Sports World; Fuse; G4; GAS; Golf Channel; GSN; Halogen Network; HGTV; History Channel; History Channel International; Lifetime Movie Network; MTV Hits; MTV2; National Geographic Channel; Nick Jr.; Outdoor Channel; Ovation; Science Television; Speed; Style Network; Sundance Channel; Syfy; Toon Disney; Trinity Broadcasting Network; Trio; Turner Classic Movies; Versus; VH1 Classic; VH1 Country; VH1 Soul; WE tv.
Fee: $12.07 monthly.

Digital Pay Service 1
Pay Units: 81.
Programming (via satellite): Cinemax (multiplexed); HBO (multiplexed).
Fee: $13.99 monthly.

Digital Pay Service 2
Pay Units: 57.
Programming (via satellite): Showtime (multiplexed); The Movie Channel (multiplexed).
Fee: $11.99 monthly.
Digital Pay Service 3
Pay Units: N.A.
Programming (via satellite): Encore (multiplexed); Starz (multiplexed).
Fee: $11.99 monthly.
Video-On-Demand: No
Pay-Per-View
iN DEMAND (delivered digitally); ESPN Now (delivered digitally); Sports PPV (delivered digitally).
Internet Service
Operational: No.
Telephone Service
None
Miles of Plant: 26.0 (coaxial); None (fiber optic).
General Manager: Caroline Walker. Chief Technician: Kenny Hanson.
Ownership: Cablevision of Walker County (MSO).

WAXAHACHIE—Charter Communications, 5227 FM 813, Waxahachie, TX 75165-8919. Phone: 972-938-9288. Fax: 972-923-0039. Web Site: http://www.charter.com. Also serves Carlton, Ellis County, Ferris, Glenn Heights, Midlothian, Oak Leaf, Ovilla, Palmer, Pecan Hill, Red Oak, Rockett & Trumbull. ICA: TX0122.
TV Market Ranking: 12 (Ellis County, Ferris, Glenn Heights, Midlothian, Oak Leaf, Ovilla, Palmer, Pecan Hill, Red Oak, Rockett, Trumbull, WAXAHACHIE); Outside TV Markets (Carlton). Franchise award date: N.A. Franchise expiration date: N.A. Began: February 1, 1982.
Channel capacity: N.A. Channels available but not in use: N.A.
Basic Service
Subscribers: 5,072.
Programming (received off-air): KAZD (IND) Lake Dallas; KDAF (CW, IND) Dallas; KDFI (MNT) Dallas; KDFW-DT (FOX) Dallas; KDTN (ETV) Denton; KDTX-TV (TBN) Dallas; KERA-TV (PBS) Dallas; KFWD (IND) Fort Worth; KMPX (IND) Decatur; KPXD-TV (ION) Arlington; KSTR-DT (TEL) Irving; KTVT (CBS) Fort Worth; KTXA (IND) Fort Worth; KUVN-DT (UNV) Garland; KXAS-TV (NBC) Fort Worth; KXTX-TV (TMO) Dallas; WFAA (ABC) Dallas.
Programming (via satellite): Bravo; C-SPAN; C-SPAN 2; Eternal Word TV Network; History Channel; Product Information Network; QVC; Syfy; TBS Superstation; The Weather Channel; Turner Network TV; TV Land; USA Network; WGN America.
Fee: $29.99 installation.
Expanded Basic Service 1
Subscribers: N.A.
Programming (via satellite): A&E Networks; ABC Family Channel; AMC; BET Networks; CNN; Country Music TV; Discovery Channel; Disney Channel; E! Entertainment Television; ESPN; ESPN 2; Fox News Channel; Fox Sports Southwest; Headline News; Lifetime; MTV; Nickelodeon; Spike TV; Texas Cable News; The Learning Channel; Toon Disney.
Fee: $48.99 monthly.
Digital Basic Service
Subscribers: N.A.
Programming (via satellite): BBC America; Bio; Bloomberg Television; Discovery Digital Networks; DIY Network; ESPN Classic Sports; Fox Movie Channel; Fuse; G4; GAS; Great American Country; History Channel International; Independent Film Channel; Lifetime Movie Network; MTV Networks Digital Suite; Music Choice; Nick Jr.; Nick Too; NickToons TV; SoapNet; Style Network; Sundance Channel; WE tv.
Digital Expanded Basic Service
Subscribers: N.A.
Programming (via satellite): Canales N; ESPNews; Fox Soccer; FSN Digital Atlantic; FSN Digital Central; FSN Digital Pacific; Fuel TV; NFL Network.
Digital Pay Service 1
Pay Units: N.A.
Programming (via satellite): Cinemax (multiplexed); Encore (multiplexed); HBO (multiplexed); Showtime (multiplexed); Starz (multiplexed); The Movie Channel (multiplexed).
Video-On-Demand: No
Pay-Per-View
iN DEMAND (delivered digitally); ETC (delivered digitally); The Erotic Network (delivered digitally); Pleasure (delivered digitally); Playboy TV (delivered digitally); Fresh (delivered digitally); Shorteez (delivered digitally).
Internet Service
Operational: Yes.
Broadband Service: Charter Pipeline.
Fee: $29.99 monthly.
Telephone Service
None
Miles of Plant: 441.0 (coaxial); 103.0 (fiber optic).
Vice President & General Manager: Wayne Cramp. Marketing Director: Kathleen Griffin. Technical Operations Director: John Linton. Technical Supervisor: Daryl Gross.
Ownership: Charter Communications Inc. (MSO).

WEATHERFORD—Charter Communications, 777 Harbor Lakes Dr, Granbury, TX 76048-2623. Phone: 817-279-9992. Web Site: http://www.charter.com. ICA: TX1004.
TV Market Ranking: 12 (WEATHERFORD).
Channel capacity: N.A. Channels available but not in use: N.A.
Basic Service
Subscribers: N.A.
Programming (received off-air): KAZD (IND) Lake Dallas; KDAF (CW, IND) Dallas; KDFI (MNT) Dallas; KDFW-DT (FOX) Dallas; KDTN (ETV) Denton; KERA-TV (PBS) Dallas; KFWD (IND) Fort Worth; KMPX (IND) Decatur; KPXD-TV (ION) Arlington; KSTR-DT (TEL) Irving; KTVT (CBS) Fort Worth; KTXA (IND) Fort Worth; KUVN-DT (UNV) Garland; KXAS-TV (NBC) Fort Worth; KXTX-TV (TMO) Dallas; WFAA (ABC) Dallas.
Programming (via satellite): A&E Networks; AMC; CNN; C-SPAN; C-SPAN 2; Discovery Channel; ESPN; ESPN 2; Eternal Word TV Network; Fox Sports Southwest; GalaVision; Headline News; HGTV; MTV; Nickelodeon; Product Information Network; QVC; ShopNBC; Texas Cable News; The Learning Channel; The Weather Channel; TV Land; VH1; WGN America.
Fee: $29.99 installation.
Expanded Basic Service 1
Subscribers: N.A.
Programming (via satellite): ABC Family Channel; Animal Planet; BET Networks; Bravo; Cartoon Network; CNBC; Comedy Central; Country Music TV; Disney Channel; E! Entertainment Television; Food Network; Fox Deportes; Fox News Channel; FX; G4; Golf Channel; GSN; Hallmark Channel; History Channel; Lifetime; MSNBC; mun2 television; National Geographic Channel; Oxygen; SoapNet; Speed; Spike TV; Style Network; Syfy; TBS Superstation; Toon Disney; Travel Channel; truTV; Turner Classic Movies; Turner Network TV; USA Network; Versus; WE tv.
Fee: $48.99 monthly.
Digital Basic Service
Subscribers: N.A.
Programming (via satellite): BBC America; Bio; Bloomberg Television; Canales N; Discovery Fit & Health; DIY Network; ESPN; ESPN Classic Sports; ESPNews; Fox College Sports Atlantic; Fox College Sports Central; Fox College Sports Pacific; Fox Movie Channel; Fox Soccer; Fuel TV; Fuse; GAS; Great American Country; Halogen Network; HD Theater; HDNet; HDNet Movies; History Channel International; Independent Film Channel; INSP; Lifetime Movie Network; MTV Networks Digital Suite; Music Choice; NFL Network; Nick Jr.; Nick Too; NickToons TV; Sundance Channel.
Digital Pay Service 1
Pay Units: N.A.
Programming (via satellite): Cinemax; Encore (multiplexed); Flix; HBO (multiplexed); HBO HD; LOGO; Showtime (multiplexed); Showtime HD; Starz (multiplexed); The Movie Channel (multiplexed).
Video-On-Demand: Yes
Pay-Per-View
iN DEMAND (delivered digitally); Ten Clips (delivered digitally); Pleasure (delivered digitally); Fox Sports Net (delivered digitally).
Internet Service
Operational: Yes.
Broadband Service: Charter Pipeline.
Fee: $29.99 monthly.
Telephone Service
None
Miles of Plant: 101.0 (coaxial); None (fiber optic). Additional miles planned: 34.0 (fiber optic).
Vice President & General Manager: Wayne Cramp. Marketing Director: Kathleen Griffin. Technical Operations Director: John Linton. Chief Technician: Mike Carmack. Technical Supervisor: Sam Easley.
Ownership: Charter Communications Inc. (MSO).

WEINERT—Formerly served by Jayroc Cablevision. No longer in operation. ICA: TX0873.

WELCH—Formerly served by National Cable Inc. No longer in operation. ICA: TX0910.

WELLINGTON—Suddenlink Communications, 908 West Ave, Wellington, TX 79095. Phone: 314-965-2020. Web Site: http://www.suddenlink.com. Also serves Childress, Childress County & Collingsworth County. ICA: TX0313.
TV Market Ranking: Below 100 (Collingsworth County (portions)); Outside TV Markets (Childress, Childress County, Collingsworth County (portions), WELLINGTON). Franchise award date: May 2, 1955. Franchise expiration date: N.A. Began: May 1, 1955.
Channel capacity: N.A. Channels available but not in use: N.A.
Basic Service
Subscribers: 2,600.
Programming (via microwave): KAMR-TV (NBC) Amarillo; KCIT (FOX) Amarillo; KFDA-TV (CBS) Amarillo; KVII-TV (ABC, CW) Amarillo.
Programming (via satellite): ABC Family Channel; CNN; Country Music TV; C-SPAN; Discovery Channel; Disney Channel; ESPN; Hallmark Channel; Headline News; Lifetime; MTV; Nickelodeon; Spike TV; The Weather Channel; Turner Classic Movies; Turner Network TV; USA Network.
Fee: $20.00 installation; $19.95 monthly; $20.00 additional installation.
Pay Service 1
Pay Units: 521.
Programming (via satellite): Cinemax; HBO.
Fee: $20.00 installation; $12.00 monthly (each).
Video-On-Demand: No
Internet Service
Operational: Yes. Began: September 16, 2004.
Broadband Service: Suddenlink High Speed Internet.
Fee: $49.95 installation; $29.95 monthly.
Telephone Service
Digital: Operational
Fee: $49.95 monthly
Miles of Plant: 63.0 (coaxial); None (fiber optic).
Manager: Genarah Manuel. Chief Technician: Tim Cummings.
Ownership: Cequel Communications LLC (MSO).

WELLMAN—Formerly served by National Cable Inc. No longer in operation. ICA: TX0874.

WELLS—Formerly served by Cebridge Connections. No longer in operation. ICA: TX0546.

WESLACO—Time Warner Communications. Now served by PHARR, TX [TX0017]. ICA: TX0048.

WEST—Reach Broadband, 515 E Longview Dr, Arp, TX 75750. Phone: 800-687-1258. Web Site: http://www.reachbroadband.net. ICA: TX0371.
TV Market Ranking: Below 100 (WEST). Franchise award date: N.A. Franchise expiration date: N.A. Began: May 1, 1982.
Channel capacity: N.A. Channels available but not in use: N.A.
Basic Service
Subscribers: 468.
Programming (received off-air): KCEN-TV (NBC, IND) Temple; KDFW-DT (FOX) Dallas; KERA-TV (PBS) Dallas; KTVT (CBS) Fort Worth; KWKT-TV (FOX, MNT) Waco; KWTX-TV (CBS, CW) Waco; KXAS-TV (NBC) Fort Worth; KXTX-TV (TMO) Dallas; KXXV (ABC, TMO) Waco; WFAA (ABC) Dallas.
Programming (via satellite): Discovery Channel; TBS Superstation; The Learning Channel.
Fee: $54.95 installation; $20.95 monthly.
Expanded Basic Service 1
Subscribers: N.A.
Programming (via satellite): ABC Family Channel; AMC; Animal Planet; Cartoon Network; CNBC; CNN; C-SPAN; Disney Channel; ESPN; Fox News Channel; FX; Headline News; HGTV; Lifetime; Nickelodeon; QVC; Spike TV; The Weather Channel; Turner Network TV; USA Network.
Fee: $23.10 monthly.
Pay Service 1
Pay Units: 68.
Programming (via satellite): Cinemax.
Fee: $12.95 monthly.
Pay Service 2
Pay Units: 95.
Programming (via satellite): Encore.
Fee: $12.95 monthly.

Pay Service 3
Pay Units: 81.
Programming (via satellite): HBO.
Fee: $12.95 monthly.

Pay Service 4
Pay Units: 47.
Programming (via satellite): Starz.
Fee: $12.95 monthly.

Video-On-Demand: No

Internet Service
Operational: No.

Telephone Service
None

Miles of Plant: 19.0 (coaxial); None (fiber optic).

Regional Manager: Ronnie Stafford. Office Manager: Jan Gibson.

Ownership: RB3 LLC (MSO).

WEST COLUMBIA—Texas Mid-Gulf Cablevision, 1302 Wisteria St, Wharton, TX 77488. Phones: 979-543-6858; 866-532-3920. Fax: 979-532-8630. Web Site: http://www.warpspeed1.net. Also serves Columbia Lakes. ICA: TX0233.

TV Market Ranking: Below 100 (Columbia Lakes, WEST COLUMBIA). Franchise award date: N.A. Franchise expiration date: N.A. Began: January 1, 1973.

Channel capacity: N.A. Channels available but not in use: N.A.

Basic Service
Subscribers: 1,213.
Programming (received off-air): KHOU (CBS) Houston; KIAH (CW) Houston; KPRC-TV (NBC) Houston; KRIV (FOX) Houston; KTRK-TV (ABC) Houston; KTXH (MNT) Houston; KUHT (PBS) Houston; KXLN-DT (UNV) Rosenberg; allband FM.
Programming (via satellite): A&E Networks; Bravo; CNN; Country Music TV; C-SPAN; E! Entertainment Television; ESPN; Fox Sports Southwest; Headline News; INSP; Nickelodeon; QVC; Syfy; Travel Channel; Turner Network TV.
Fee: $30.00 installation; $17.79 monthly; $15.00 additional installation.

Expanded Basic Service 1
Subscribers: 1,179.
Programming (via satellite): Discovery Channel; Food Network; The Weather Channel; USA Network.
Fee: $1.88 monthly.

Expanded Basic Service 2
Subscribers: 1,153.
Programming (via satellite): Disney Channel; Spike TV; TBS Superstation.
Fee: $4.45 monthly.

Pay Service 1
Pay Units: 151.
Programming (via satellite): Cinemax.
Fee: $10.00 installation; $10.95 monthly.

Pay Service 2
Pay Units: 405.
Programming (via satellite): HBO.
Fee: $11.95 monthly.

Pay Service 3
Pay Units: 105.
Programming (via satellite): The Movie Channel.
Fee: $10.95 monthly.

Pay Service 4
Pay Units: 136.
Programming (via satellite): Showtime.
Fee: $10.95 monthly.

Video-On-Demand: No

Internet Service
Operational: Yes, Both DSL & dial-up.
Broadband Service: Warp Speed 1 Internet.
Fee: $17.05 installation; $34.99 monthly.

Telephone Service
None

Miles of Plant: 57.0 (coaxial); None (fiber optic).

Office Manager: Wayne Neal. Chief Technician: Alan Boyd.

Ownership: Mid-Coast Cablevision (MSO).

WEST GRAYSON COUNTY—TV Cable of Grayson County, 501 Hwy 120 N, Ste 6, PO Box 2084, Pottsboro, TX 75076. Phone: 903-786-7477. E-mail: tvcable@graysoncable.com. Web Site: http://www.graysoncable.com. Also serves Southmayd. ICA: TX1013.

TV Market Ranking: Below 100 (Southmayd, WEST GRAYSON COUNTY).

Channel capacity: N.A. Channels available but not in use: N.A.

Basic Service
Subscribers: N.A.
Programming (received off-air): KDAF (CW, IND) Dallas; KDFI (MNT) Dallas; KDFW-DT (FOX) Dallas; KERA-TV (PBS) Dallas; KSTR-DT (TEL) Irving; KTEN (ABC, CW, NBC) Ada; KTVT (CBS) Fort Worth; KTXA (IND) Fort Worth; KXAS-TV (NBC) Fort Worth; KXII (CBS, FOX, MNT) Sherman; WFAA (ABC) Dallas.
Programming (via satellite): A&E Networks; ABC Family Channel; AMC; AmericanLife TV Network; Animal Planet; Bloomberg Television; Boomerang; Cartoon Network; CNBC; CNN; C-SPAN; C-SPAN 2; Discovery Channel; Disney Channel; ESPN; ESPN 2; Fox Movie Channel; Fox News Channel; Fox Sports Southwest; FX; G4; Golf Channel; Great American Country; Hallmark Channel; Headline News; HGTV; History Channel; Lifetime; MSNBC; MTV; National Geographic Channel; Nickelodeon; Outdoor Channel; QVC; Radar Channel; SoapNet; Speed; Spike TV; Syfy; TBS Superstation; The Learning Channel; The Weather Channel; Travel Channel; Trinity Broadcasting Network; truTV; Turner Classic Movies; Turner Network TV; TV Land; USA Network; VH1; WGN America.
Fee: $35.00 installation; $17.95 monthly; $20.00 additional installation.

Pay Service 1
Pay Units: N.A.
Programming (via satellite): Encore; HBO (multiplexed); Showtime; Starz; The Movie Channel.

Video-On-Demand: No

Internet Service
Operational: Yes.
Broadband Service: Cable Rocket.
Fee: $35.00 installation; $24.99 monthly; $55.00 modem purchase.

Telephone Service
None

Manager: Chuck Davis.

Ownership: Chuck Davis (MSO).

WEST ODESSA—US Cable of Coastal Texas LP, 611 W Ave A, Seminole, TX 79360. Phones: 432-758-9221; 800-996-8788. Fax: 432-758-3379. E-mail: dkoedyker@tx.uscable.com. Web Site: http://www.uscable.com. Also serves Ector County. ICA: TX0969.

TV Market Ranking: Below 100 (Ector County, WEST ODESSA). Franchise award date: N.A. Franchise expiration date: N.A. Began: N.A.

Channel capacity: N.A. Channels available but not in use: N.A.

Basic Service
Subscribers: 1,122.
Programming (received off-air): KMID (ABC) Midland; KOSA-TV (CBS, MNT) Odessa; KPEJ-TV (FOX) Odessa; KRPV-DT (IND) Roswell; KUPB (UNV) Midland; KWES-TV (NBC) Odessa.
Programming (via satellite): Country Music TV; C-SPAN; Discovery Channel; Disney Channel; Fox News Channel; FX; Lifetime; Nickelodeon; Spike TV; TBS Superstation; Telemundo; The Weather Channel; Trinity Broadcasting Network; Turner Network TV; TV Guide Network; WGN America.
Fee: $39.96 installation; $26.18 monthly; $.90 converter.

Expanded Basic Service 1
Subscribers: N.A. Included in Seminole
Programming (via satellite): A&E Networks; ABC Family Channel; AMC; Animal Planet; Cartoon Network; CNN; Discovery Fit & Health; ESPN; ESPN 2; Fox Sports Southwest; Hallmark Channel; Headline News; HGTV; MoviePlex; MTV; Outdoor Channel; Syfy; The Learning Channel; USA Network; VH1.
Fee: $16.86 monthly.

Pay Service 1
Pay Units: N.A.
Programming (via satellite): HBO; Showtime.
Fee: $12.95 monthly (each).

Video-On-Demand: No

Pay-Per-View
Addressable homes: 224.
iN DEMAND (delivered digitally); Playboy TV (delivered digitally); Fresh (delivered digitally).

Internet Service
Operational: No.

Telephone Service
None

Miles of plant included in Seminole, TX

Manager: Daryl Koedyker. Marketing Director: Liz Lopez. Office Manager: Tammy Perez. Technical Operations Manager: Tim Davis.

Ownership: US Cable Corp. (MSO).; Comcast Cable Communications Inc. (MSO).

WESTBROOK—Formerly served by National Cable Inc. No longer in operation. ICA: TX0877.

WESTHOFF—Formerly served by National Cable Inc. No longer in operation. ICA: TX0909.

WHARTON—Texas Mid-Gulf Cablevision, 1302 Wisteria St, Wharton, TX 77488. Phones: 975-532-3920; 866-532-3920. Fax: 979-532-8630. Web Site: http://www.warpspeed1.net. ICA: TX0171.

TV Market Ranking: Below 100 (WHARTON). Franchise award date: N.A. Franchise expiration date: N.A. Began: November 1, 1973.

Channel capacity: N.A. Channels available but not in use: N.A.

Basic Service
Subscribers: 2,245.
Programming (received off-air): KETH-TV (TBN) Houston; KFTH-DT (TEL) Alvin; KHOU (CBS) Houston; KIAH (CW) Houston; KLTJ (ETV) Galveston; KPRC-TV (NBC) Houston; KRIV (FOX) Houston; KTBU (IND) Conroe; KTMD (TMO) Galveston; KTRK-TV (ABC) Houston; KTXH (MNT) Houston; KUBE-TV (IND) Baytown; KUHT (PBS) Houston; KXLN-DT (UNV) Rosenberg; KYAZ (IND) Katy; KZJL (IND) Houston; allband FM.
Programming (via satellite): A&E Networks; ABC Family Channel; AMC; Animal Planet; BET Networks; Bravo; Cartoon Network; CNN; Country Music TV; C-SPAN; C-SPAN 2; Discovery Channel; Disney Channel; E! Entertainment Television; ESPN; ESPN 2; ESPN Classic Sports; Eternal Word TV Network; Food Network; Fox News Channel; FX; Halogen Network; Headline News; HGTV; History Channel; ION Television; Lifetime; MSNBC; MTV; Nickelodeon; Oxygen; QVC; SoapNet; Speed; Spike TV; Syfy; TBS Superstation; The Learning Channel; The Weather Channel; Travel Channel; Turner Network TV; TV Guide Network; TV Land; USA Network; VH1; WGN America.
Fee: $30.00 installation; $18.34 monthly; $2.00 converter; $7.50 additional installation.

Digital Basic Service
Subscribers: N.A.
Programming (via satellite): BBC America; Bio; Bloomberg Television; Canal 52MX; Cine Latino; Cine Mexicano; CMT Pure Country; CNN en Espanol; Discovery en Espanol; Discovery Health Channel; Discovery Kids Channel; DIY Network; ESPN Deportes; ESPN HD; ESPNews; Fox Deportes; G4; Golf Channel; GSN; HD Theater; History Channel en Espanol; History Channel International; ID Investigation Discovery; Independent Film Channel; Military Channel; Nick Jr.; NickToons TV; Outdoor Channel 2 HD; Planet Green; RFD-TV; Science; Style Network; Toon Disney; Tr3s; Turner Classic Movies; VeneMovies; Versus; VH1 Classic; WE tv; WealthTV HD.

Digital Pay Service 1
Pay Units: N.A.
Programming (via satellite): Cinemax (multiplexed); Encore (multiplexed); Flix; HBO (multiplexed); HBO Latino; Showtime (multiplexed); Showtime HD; Starz (multiplexed); Starz HDTV; The Movie Channel (multiplexed); The Movie Channel HD.

Video-On-Demand: No

Pay-Per-View
iN DEMAND (delivered digitally); Fresh (delivered digitally); Playboy TV (delivered digitally).

Internet Service
Operational: Yes, Both DSL & dial-up. Began: January 1, 2002.
Broadband Service: Warp Speed 1 Internet.
Fee: $17.05 installation; $34.99 monthly.

Telephone Service
None

Miles of Plant: 77.0 (coaxial); None (fiber optic).

Manager: Tracy White. Chief Technician: Alan Boyd.

Ownership: Mid-Coast Cablevision (MSO).

WHEELER—Elk River TV Cable Co., 509 S Main St, PO Box 154, Troy, ID 83871. Phone: 208-369-4652. E-mail: leslie@elkrivertv.net. ICA: TX0460.

TV Market Ranking: Outside TV Markets (WHEELER). Franchise award date: N.A. Franchise expiration date: N.A. Began: March 1, 1958.

Channel capacity: 24 (not 2-way capable). Channels available but not in use: N.A.

Basic Service
Subscribers: 75.
Programming (received off-air): KCIT (FOX) Amarillo; KETA-TV (PBS) Oklahoma City.
Programming (via microwave): KAMR-TV (NBC) Amarillo; KFDA-TV (CBS) Amarillo; KVII-TV (ABC, CW) Amarillo.
Programming (via satellite): ABC Family Channel; AMC; CNN; Discovery Channel; Disney Channel; ESPN; Fox Sports Net; Headline News; Lifetime; Nickelodeon; QVC; Spike TV; TBS Superstation; Trinity Broadcasting Network; Turner Network

TV; Univision Studios; USA Network; WGN America.
Fee: $10.00 installation; $42.95 monthly.

Pay Service 1
Pay Units: 45.
Programming (via satellite): HBO.
Fee: $13.95 monthly.

Video-On-Demand: No

Internet Service
Operational: No.

Telephone Service
None

Miles of Plant: 11.0 (coaxial); None (fiber optic).
Managers: Dave McGraw.; Leslie McGraw. Chief Technician: Justin McGraw.
Ownership: Elk River TV Cable Co. (MSO).

WHITEFACE—Formerly served by Cebridge Connections. No longer in operation. ICA: TX0879.

WHITESBORO—Suddenlink Communications, 104 N Morris St, Gainesville, TX 76240-4242. Phone: 940-665-3241. Web Site: http://www.suddenlink.com. Also serves Sadler. ICA: TX0271.
TV Market Ranking: Below 100 (Sadler, WHITESBORO). Franchise award date: N.A. Franchise expiration date: N.A. Began: July 1, 1967.
Channel capacity: N.A. Channels available but not in use: N.A.

Basic Service
Subscribers: 1,121.
Programming (received off-air): KDAF (CW, IND) Dallas; KDFW-DT (FOX) Dallas; KDTN (ETV) Denton; KERA-TV (PBS) Dallas; KMPX (IND) Decatur; KTEN (ABC, CW, NBC) Ada; KTVT (CBS) Fort Worth; KTXA (IND) Fort Worth; KXAS-TV (NBC) Fort Worth; KXII (CBS, FOX, MNT) Sherman; KXTX-TV (TMO) Dallas; WFAA (ABC) Dallas.
Programming (via satellite): C-SPAN; Discovery Channel; QVC; TBS Superstation; The Weather Channel.
Fee: $39.60 installation; $10.08 monthly; $19.80 additional installation.

Expanded Basic Service 1
Subscribers: 1,024.
Programming (via satellite): ABC Family Channel; AMC; Animal Planet; Cartoon Network; CNBC; CNN; Disney Channel; ESPN; ESPN 2; Fox News Channel; Fox Sports Southwest; FX; Great American Country; Headline News; Lifetime; MoviePlex; Nickelodeon; Spike TV; The Learning Channel; truTV; Turner Network TV; USA Network; Versus.
Fee: $11.63 monthly.

Pay Service 1
Pay Units: 55.
Programming (via satellite): Encore; HBO; Showtime; Starz.
Fee: $7.50 installation; $10.95 monthly (HBO or Showtime).

Video-On-Demand: No

Internet Service
Operational: Yes.
Broadband Service: Suddenlink High Speed Internet.
Fee: $49.95 installation; $25.95 monthly.

Telephone Service
None

Miles of Plant: 27.0 (coaxial); None (fiber optic).
Manager: Ricky Allen. Chief Technician: Gary Hinkle.
Ownership: Cequel Communications LLC (MSO).

WHITNEY—Reach Broadband, 515 E Longview Dr, Arp, TX 75750. Phone: 800-687-1258. Web Site: http://www.reachbroadband.net. Also serves Lake Whitney. ICA: TX0403.
TV Market Ranking: Below 100 (Lake Whitney, WHITNEY). Franchise award date: N.A. Franchise expiration date: N.A. Began: October 1, 1982.
Channel capacity: 52 (not 2-way capable). Channels available but not in use: N.A.

Basic Service
Subscribers: 972.
Programming (received off-air): KDAF (CW, IND) Dallas; KDFI (MNT) Dallas; KDFW-DT (FOX) Dallas; KDTX-TV (TBN) Dallas; KDYW (PBS) Waco; KERA-TV (PBS) Dallas; KSTR-DT (TEL) Irving; KTVT (CBS) Fort Worth; KTXA (IND) Fort Worth; KUVN-DT (UNV) Garland; KWTX-TV (CBS, CW) Waco; KXAS-TV (NBC) Fort Worth; KXTX-TV (TMO) Dallas; WFAA (ABC) Dallas.
Programming (via satellite): A&E Networks; C-SPAN; WGN America.
Fee: $54.95 installation; $20.95 monthly.

Expanded Basic Service 1
Subscribers: N.A.
Programming (via satellite): ABC Family Channel; AMC; Animal Planet; CNN; Country Music TV; Discovery Channel; Disney Channel; E! Entertainment Television; ESPN; ESPN 2; ESPNews; Fox News Channel; Fox Sports Southwest; Headline News; HGTV; History Channel; Lifetime; MTV; National Geographic Channel; Nickelodeon; Spike TV; TBS Superstation; The Learning Channel; The Weather Channel; Toon Disney; Travel Channel; Turner Network TV; TV Land; USA Network.
Fee: $23.10 monthly.

Video-On-Demand: No

Pay-Per-View
Hot Choice (delivered digitally); Playboy TV (delivered digitally); Fresh (delivered digitally); Shorteez (delivered digitally); iN DEMAND (delivered digitally).

Internet Service
Operational: No.

Telephone Service
None

Miles of Plant: 62.0 (coaxial); None (fiber optic).
Regional Manager: Ronnie Stafford. Office Manager: Jan Gibson.
Ownership: RB3 LLC (MSO).

WICHITA FALLS—Time Warner Cable, 3225 Maurine St, Wichita Falls, TX 76306-6828. Phones: 940-855-4321; 972-899-7300 (Flower Mound office). Fax: 940-855-0465. Web Site: http://www.timewarnercable.com/Texas. Also serves Archer City, Holliday, Lakeside City, Sheppard AFB & Wichita County (unincorporated areas). ICA: TX0026.
TV Market Ranking: Below 100 (Archer City, Holliday, Lakeside City, Sheppard AFB, Wichita County (unincorporated areas), WICHITA FALLS). Franchise award date: N.A. Franchise expiration date: N.A. Began: November 1, 1979.
Channel capacity: N.A. Channels available but not in use: N.A.

Basic Service
Subscribers: 26,000 Includes Lake Arrowhead.
Programming (received off-air): KAUZ-TV (CBS, CW) Wichita Falls; KFDX-TV (NBC) Wichita Falls; KJBO-LP (MNT) Wichita Falls; KJTL (FOX) Wichita Falls; KSWO-TV (ABC, TMO) Lawton; 24 FMs.
Programming (via microwave): KERA-TV (PBS) Dallas.
Programming (via satellite): Christian Television Network; CW+; Radar Channel; WFTV (ABC) Orlando; WGN America.
Fee: $50.51 installation; $15.59 monthly.

Expanded Basic Service 1
Subscribers: N.A.
Programming (received off-air): KKTM-LP Altus.
Programming (via satellite): A&E Networks; ABC Family Channel; AMC; AmericanLife TV Network; Animal Planet; BET Networks; Bravo; Cartoon Network; CNBC; CNN; Comedy Central; Country Music TV; C-SPAN; C-SPAN 2; Discovery Channel; Discovery Health Channel; Disney Channel; E! Entertainment Television; ESPN; ESPN 2; Food Network; Fox Movie Channel; Fox News Channel; Fox Sports Southwest; FX; GalaVision; Golf Channel; Hallmark Channel; Headline News; HGTV; History Channel; ION Television; Lifetime; Lifetime Movie Network; MSNBC; MTV; National Geographic Channel; Nickelodeon; Oxygen; QVC; ShopNBC; Spike TV; Style Network; Sundance Channel; Syfy; TBS Superstation; Texas Cable News; The Learning Channel; The Weather Channel; Travel Channel; Trinity Broadcasting Network; truTV; Turner Network TV; TV Guide Network; TV Land; USA Network; VH1; WE tv.
Fee: $32.10 monthly.

Digital Basic Service
Subscribers: N.A.
Programming (via satellite): A&E Networks; ABC Family Channel; AMC; Animal Planet; BBC America; BBC America On Demand; BET Networks; Bloomberg Television; Boomerang; Bravo; Cartoon Network; cloo; CNBC; CNN; Comedy Central; Cooking Channel; Country Music TV; C-SPAN; C-SPAN 2; C-SPAN 3; Current; Daystar TV Network; Discovery Channel; Discovery Fit & Health; Discovery Health Channel; Discovery Home Channel; Discovery Kids Channel; Discovery Times Channel; Disney Channel; DIY Network; E! Entertainment Television; ESPN; ESPN 2; ESPN 2 HD; ESPN Classic Sports; ESPN HD; ESPN U; ESPNews; Eternal Word TV Network; EWTN en Espanol; Exercise TV; FamilyNet; Food Network; Food Network On Demand; Fox Business Channel; Fox Movie Channel; Fox News Channel; Fox Reality Channel; Fox Soccer; Fox Sports Southwest; Fuse; FX; G4; GalaVision; GAS; Golf Channel; Great American Country; Hallmark Channel; HD Theater; HDNet; HDNet Movies; Headline News; HGTV; HGTV On Demand; History Channel; Howard TV; Independent Film Channel; ION Television; La Familia Network; Lifetime; Lifetime Movie Network; Military Channel; MSNBC; MTV; MTV Hits; MTV2; Music Choice; National Geographic Channel; National Geographic Channel On Demand; NBA TV; Nick Jr.; Nickelodeon; NickToons TV; Ovation; Oxygen; Oxygen On Demand; QVC; Science; ShopNBC; SoapNet; Speed; Speed On Demand; Spike TV; Style Network; Syfy; TBS Superstation; Texas Cable News; The Learning Channel; The Weather Channel; Toon Disney; Travel Channel; Trinity Broadcasting Network; truTV; Turner Classic Movies; Turner Network TV; Turner Network TV HD; TV Guide Network; TV Land; Universal HD; USA Network; Versus; VH1; VH1 Classic; WE tv.
Fee: $5.00 monthly.

Digital Expanded Basic Service
Subscribers: N.A.
Programming (via satellite): Encore (multiplexed); Fox College Sports Atlantic; Fox College Sports Central; Fox College Sports Pacific; Fuel TV; Independent Film Channel; NBA TV; Speed; Tennis Channel.

Digital Pay Service 1
Pay Units: N.A.
Programming (via satellite): Cinemax (multiplexed); Cinemax On Demand; HBO (multiplexed); HBO HD; HBO on Broadband; Showtime (multiplexed); Showtime HD; Showtime On Demand; Starz (multiplexed); The Movie Channel (multiplexed); The Movie Channel On Demand.
Fee: $12.95 monthly (each).

Video-On-Demand: Yes

Pay-Per-View
iN DEMAND (delivered digitally); Fresh (delivered digitally); Shorteez (delivered digitally); Hot Choice (delivered digitally); NBA League Pass (delivered digitally); ESPN Gameplan (delivered digitally); ESPN Full Court (delivered digitally); MLB Extra Innings (delivered digitally); NHL Center Ice (delivered digitally).

Internet Service
Operational: Yes. Began: December 31, 2001.
Broadband Service: Road Runner.
Fee: $49.99 installation; $44.95 monthly.

Telephone Service
Digital: Operational
Fee: $44.95 monthly

Miles of Plant: 541.0 (coaxial); None (fiber optic). Miles of plant (coax & fiber combined) include Lake Arrowhead
President: Connie Wharton. Vice President & General Manager: Mike McKee. Public Affairs Manager: Vicki McCann.
Ownership: Time Warner Cable (MSO).; Advance/Newhouse Partnership (MSO).

WICKETT—Formerly served by Almega Cable. No longer in operation. ICA: TX0880.

WILDWOOD—Daybreak Communications, PO Box 899, Village Mills, TX 77663. Phone: 409-246-8750. ICA: TX0537.
TV Market Ranking: 88 (WILDWOOD). Franchise award date: N.A. Franchise expiration date: N.A. Began: N.A.
Channel capacity: 38 (not 2-way capable). Channels available but not in use: N.A.

Basic Service
Subscribers: 75.
Programming (received off-air): KBMT (ABC) Beaumont; KBTV-TV (FOX) Port Arthur; KFDM (CBS, CW) Beaumont; KITU-TV (TBN) Beaumont; KRMA-TV (PBS) Denver; KVHP (FOX) Lake Charles.
Programming (via satellite): A&E Networks; ABC Family Channel; CNBC; CNN; C-SPAN; Discovery Channel; Disney Channel; ESPN; ESPN 2; Fox Sports Southwest; FX; Golf Channel; Great American Country; HBO; Headline News; HGTV; History Channel; INSP; Lifetime; MSNBC; National Geographic Channel; Nickelodeon; Spike TV; TBS Superstation; The Weather Channel; Turner Classic Movies; Turner Network TV; USA Network.
Fee: $41.95 monthly.

Pay Service 1
Pay Units: 10.
Programming (via satellite): Cinemax.
Fee: $12.95 monthly.

Pay Service 2
Pay Units: 33.
Programming (via satellite): HBO.
Fee: $12.95 monthly.

Pay Service 3
Pay Units: 22.
Programming (via satellite): Showtime.
Fee: $12.95 monthly.

Internet Service
Operational: No.
Telephone Service
None
Miles of Plant: 21.0 (coaxial); None (fiber optic).
Ownership: Daybreak Communications.

WILLOW PARK—Mallard Cablevision. Now served by FORT WORTH, TX [TX0008]. ICA: TX0177.

WILLS POINT—Zoom Media, PO Box 2126, Flint, TX 75762. Phone: 855-261-5304. Web Site: http://www.zoommediallc.com. Also serves Edgewood. ICA: TX0338.
TV Market Ranking: Below 100 (Edgewood, WILLS POINT). Franchise award date: N.A. Franchise expiration date: N.A. Began: February 1, 1983.
Channel capacity: N.A. Channels available but not in use: N.A.
Basic Service
Subscribers: N.A.
Programming (received off-air): KDAF (CW, IND) Dallas; KDFI (MNT) Dallas; KDFW-DT (FOX) Dallas; KDTN (ETV) Denton; KDTX-TV (TBN) Dallas; KERA-TV (PBS) Dallas; KFWD (IND) Fort Worth; KLTV (ABC, TMO) Tyler; KSTR-DT (TEL) Irving; KTVT (CBS) Fort Worth; KTXA (IND) Fort Worth; KUVN-DT (UNV) Garland; KXAS-TV (NBC) Fort Worth; KXTX-TV (TMO) Dallas; WFAA (ABC) Dallas.
Programming (via satellite): A&E Networks; ABC Family Channel; AMC; Animal Planet; BET Networks; Bravo; Cartoon Network; CNBC; CNN; Comedy Central; Country Music TV; C-SPAN; Discovery Channel; Disney Channel; E! Entertainment Television; ESPN; ESPN 2; Food Network; Fox News Channel; Fox Sports Southwest; FX; Golf Channel; Hallmark Channel; Headline News; HGTV; History Channel; Lifetime; MTV; Nickelodeon; Oxygen; Speed; Spike TV; Syfy; TBS Superstation; The Learning Channel; The Weather Channel; Travel Channel; truTV; Turner Classic Movies; Turner Network TV; TV Land; USA Network; VH1.
Fee: $54.95 installation; $44.05 monthly.
Digital Basic Service
Subscribers: N.A.
Programming (via satellite): BBC America; Bio; Bloomberg Television; Discovery Fit & Health; DIY Network; Fox Movie Channel; G4; GAS; GSN; History Channel International; Independent Film Channel; Lifetime Movie Network; MTV Networks Digital Suite; Music Choice; Nick Jr.; Nick Too; NickToons TV; SoapNet; Style Network; Sundance Channel; Toon Disney; WE tv.
Digital Pay Service 1
Pay Units: N.A.
Programming (via satellite): Cinemax (multiplexed); Encore; Flix; HBO (multiplexed); Showtime (multiplexed); Starz (multiplexed); The Movie Channel (multiplexed).
Video-On-Demand: No
Pay-Per-View
Pleasure (delivered digitally); ETC (delivered digitally); The Erotic Network (delivered digitally); iN DEMAND (delivered digitally).
Internet Service
Operational: No.
Telephone Service
None
Miles of Plant: 47.0 (coaxial); None (fiber optic).
Chief Executive Officer: Steve Houston.
Ownership: Zoom Media LLC (MSO).

WILMER—Formerly served by Metro Cable. No longer in operation. ICA: TX0307.

WILSON—Formerly served by Charter Communications. No longer in operation. ICA: TX0650.

WINK—Almega Cable, 4001 W Airport Frwy, Ste 530, Bedford, TX 76021. Phone: 817-685-9588. Fax: 817-685-6488. E-mail: helpdesk@almegacable.com. Web Site: http://www.almega.com. ICA: TX0478.
TV Market Ranking: Outside TV Markets (WINK). Franchise award date: November 3, 1981. Franchise expiration date: N.A. Began: April 3, 1984.
Channel capacity: 52 (not 2-way capable). Channels available but not in use: N.A.
Basic Service
Subscribers: 220.
Programming (received off-air): KMLM-DT (IND) Odessa; KOSA-TV (CBS, MNT) Odessa; KPEJ-TV (FOX) Odessa; KWES-TV (NBC) Odessa.
Programming (via microwave): KMID (ABC) Midland.
Programming (via satellite): A&E Networks; ABC Family Channel; Animal Planet; Cartoon Network; CNN; Country Music TV; C-SPAN; Discovery Channel; Disney Channel; ESPN; Fox Sports Southwest; Headline News; History Channel; KRMA-TV (PBS) Denver; Lifetime; Nickelodeon; Spike TV; TBS Superstation; The Learning Channel; The Weather Channel; Turner Classic Movies; Turner Network TV; TV Land; USA Network; WGN America.
Fee: $29.99 installation; $38.00 monthly.
Pay Service 1
Pay Units: 55.
Programming (via satellite): Cinemax.
Fee: $10.95 monthly.
Pay Service 2
Pay Units: 65.
Programming (via satellite): HBO.
Fee: $11.95 monthly.
Video-On-Demand: No
Internet Service
Operational: No.
Telephone Service
None
Miles of Plant: 11.0 (coaxial); None (fiber optic).
Ownership: Almega Cable (MSO).

WINNIE—Time Warner Cable. Now served by BEAUMONT, TX [TX0022]. ICA: TX0258.

WINNSBORO—Suddenlink Communications, 816 W Coke Rd, Winnsboro, TX 75494-3010. Phone: 903-342-6080. Fax: 903-342-6080. Web Site: http://www.suddenlink.com. ICA: TX0978.
TV Market Ranking: Outside TV Markets (WINNSBORO). Franchise award date: N.A. Franchise expiration date: N.A. Began: N.A.
Channel capacity: 42 (not 2-way capable). Channels available but not in use: N.A.
Basic Service
Subscribers: N.A.
Programming (received off-air): KDFW-DT (FOX) Dallas; KERA-TV (PBS) Dallas; KETK-TV (NBC) Jacksonville; KFXK-TV (FOX) Longview; KLTV (ABC, TMO) Tyler; KSLA (CBS) Shreveport; KTVT (CBS) Fort Worth; KXAS-TV (NBC) Fort Worth; KXTX-TV (TMO) Dallas; WFAA (ABC) Dallas.
Programming (via satellite): Headline News; ION Television; TBS Superstation; The Weather Channel; Trinity Broadcasting Network; WGN America.
Fee: $14.05 monthly.
Expanded Basic Service 1
Subscribers: N.A.
Programming (via satellite): A&E Networks; ABC Family Channel; AMC; CNBC; CNN; Discovery Channel; ESPN; Fox Sports Southwest; Great American Country; Lifetime; Nickelodeon; Spike TV; Syfy; The Learning Channel; Turner Network TV; TV Land; USA Network.
Fee: $13.90 monthly.
Pay Service 1
Pay Units: N.A.
Programming (via satellite): HBO; Showtime; Starz; The Movie Channel.
Fee: $5.00 monthly (HBO), $6.00 monthly (Showtime & TMC), $7.95 monthly (Starz).
Video-On-Demand: No
Internet Service
Operational: Yes.
Broadband Service: Suddenlink High Speed Internet.
Telephone Service
Digital: Operational
Miles of Plant: 36.0 (coaxial); None (fiber optic).
Manager: Joe Suggs.
Ownership: Cequel Communications LLC (MSO).

WINTERS—Allegiance Communications, 707 W Saratoga St, Shawnee, OK 74804. Phones: 405-395-1131; 405-275-6923. Web Site: http://www.allegiance.tv. ICA: TX0965.
TV Market Ranking: Outside TV Markets (WINTERS). Franchise award date: N.A. Franchise expiration date: N.A. Began: N.A.
Channel capacity: N.A. Channels available but not in use: N.A.
Basic Service
Subscribers: N.A. Included in Ballinger
Programming (received off-air): KERA-TV (PBS) Dallas; KLST (CBS) San Angelo; KPCB-DT (IND) Snyder; KRBC-TV (NBC) Abilene; KTAB-TV (CBS) Abilene; KTXA (IND) Fort Worth; KTXS-TV (ABC, CW, TMO) Sweetwater; KXVA (FOX) Abilene; WFAA (ABC) Dallas.
Programming (via satellite): CNN; C-SPAN; Headline News; INSP; ION Television; QVC; Telefutura; Telemundo; The Weather Channel; Trinity Broadcasting Network; Univision Studios.
Fee: $38.00 installation; $10.90 monthly; $.25 converter.
Expanded Basic Service 1
Subscribers: 554.
Programming (via satellite): A&E Networks; ABC Family Channel; AMC; Animal Planet; CMT Pure Country; Discovery Channel; Disney Channel; ESPN; ESPN 2; Fox News Channel; Fox Sports Southwest; FX; Hallmark Channel; HGTV; Lifetime; MTV; NFL Network; Nickelodeon; Spike TV; TBS Superstation; The Learning Channel; Turner Network TV; USA Network.
Fee: $38.00 installation; $24.50 monthly.
Digital Basic Service
Subscribers: N.A.
Programming (via satellite): AmericanLife TV Network; BBC America; Bio; Bloomberg Television; Bravo; Canal 52MX; Cine Latino; Cine Mexicano; cloo; CMT Pure Country; CNN en Espanol; Current; Discovery en Espanol; Discovery Fit & Health; Discovery Health Channel; Discovery Kids Channel; DMX Music; Encore (multiplexed); ESPN 2; ESPN Classic Sports; ESPNews; Flix; Fox College Sports Atlantic; Fox College Sports Central; Fox College Sports Pacific; Fox Deportes; Fox Movie Channel; Fox Soccer; Fuse; G4; GAS; GMC; Golf Channel; Great American Country; GSN; Halogen Network; HGTV; History Channel; History Channel en Espanol; History Channel International; ID Investigation Discovery; Independent Film Channel; Lifetime Movie Network; Military Channel; MTV Hits; MTV2; National Geographic Channel; Nick Jr.; NickToons TV; Outdoor Channel; Ovation; Planet Green; Science; ShopNBC; Speed; Style Network; Sundance Channel; Syfy; The Word Network; Toon Disney; Toon Disney en Espanol; Tr3s; Trinity Broadcasting Network; Turner Classic Movies; Versus; VH1 Classic; VH1 Soul; WE tv.
Digital Pay Service 1
Pay Units: N.A.
Programming (via satellite): Cinemax (multiplexed); HBO (multiplexed); Showtime (multiplexed); Starz (multiplexed); The Movie Channel (multiplexed).
Pay-Per-View
iN DEMAND (delivered digitally); Playboy TV (delivered digitally); Fresh (delivered digitally); Shorteez (delivered digitally).
Internet Service
Operational: Yes.
Fee: $24.95 installation; $39.95 monthly.
Telephone Service
None
Miles of Plant: 19.0 (coaxial); None (fiber optic).
Chief Executive Officer: Bill Haggarty. Regional Vice President: Andrew Dearth. Vice President, Marketing: Tracy Bass.
Ownership: Allegiance Communications (MSO).

WODEN—Formerly served by Almega Cable. No longer in operation. ICA: TX0553.

WOLFE CITY—Zoom Media, PO Box 2126, Flint, TX 75762. Phone: 855-261-5304. Web Site: http://www.zoommediallc.com. Also serves Ladonia. ICA: TX0449.
TV Market Ranking: Below 100 (Ladonia, WOLFE CITY). Franchise award date: N.A. Franchise expiration date: N.A. Began: August 1, 1982.
Channel capacity: 52 (not 2-way capable). Channels available but not in use: N.A.
Basic Service
Subscribers: 84.
Programming (received off-air): KDFW-DT (FOX) Dallas; KERA-TV (PBS) Dallas; KTVT (CBS) Fort Worth; KXAS-TV (NBC) Fort Worth; KXTX-TV (TMO) Dallas; WFAA (ABC) Dallas.
Programming (via satellite): ABC Family Channel; CNN; Disney Channel; ESPN; Nickelodeon; TBS Superstation; The Weather Channel; Turner Classic Movies; USA Network; WGN America.
Fee: $54.95 installation; $33.28 monthly.
Pay Service 1
Pay Units: N.A.
Programming (via satellite): HBO; Showtime; The Movie Channel.
Fee: $12.95 monthly.
Video-On-Demand: No
Internet Service
Operational: No.
Telephone Service
None
Miles of Plant: 31.0 (coaxial); None (fiber optic).

Chief Executive Officer: Steve Houston.
Ownership: Zoom Media LLC (MSO).

WOODROW—Formerly served by Cebridge Connections. No longer in operation. ICA: TX0330.

WOODVILLE—CMA Cablevision, 122 N Austin St, Jasper, TX 75951-4102. Phones: 979-968-6476 (La Grange office); 409-384-6862. Fax: 979-968-5368. Web Site: http://www.cmaaccess.com. ICA: TX0981.
TV Market Ranking: Outside TV Markets (WOODVILLE). Franchise award date: N.A. Franchise expiration date: N.A. Began: N.A.
Channel capacity: N.A. Channels available but not in use: N.A.
Basic Service
Subscribers: 525.
Programming (received off-air): KBMT (ABC) Beaumont; KFDM (CBS, CW) Beaumont; KHOU (CBS) Houston; KIAH (CW) Houston; KRIV (FOX) Houston; KTRK-TV (ABC) Houston; KTXH (MNT) Houston; KUHT (PBS) Houston; KYTX (CBS, IND) Nacogdoches.
Programming (via satellite): Trinity Broadcasting Network.
Fee: $39.95 installation; $17.95 monthly; $12.95 additional installation.
Expanded Basic Service 1
Subscribers: 420.
Programming (via satellite): A&E Networks; ABC Family Channel; AMC; Animal Planet; BET Networks; CNN; Country Music TV; Discovery Channel; ESPN; Food Network; Fox News Channel; Fox Sports Southwest; FX; HGTV; History Channel; Lifetime; MTV; Nickelodeon; QVC; Spike TV; Syfy; TBS Superstation; The Learning Channel; The Weather Channel; Turner Network TV; TV Land; USA Network; VH1; WGN America.
Fee: $27.50 monthly.
Digital Basic Service
Subscribers: N.A.
Programming (via satellite): Bio; Discovery Digital Networks; DMX Music; ESPN Classic Sports; ESPNews; GAS; Golf Channel; GSN; History Channel; Lifetime Movie Network; MTV Networks Digital Suite; Nick Jr.; Speed; Versus.
Fee: $13.95 monthly.
Digital Pay Service 1
Pay Units: N.A.
Programming (via satellite): Cinemax (multiplexed); Encore (multiplexed); Flix; HBO (multiplexed); Showtime (multiplexed); Starz (multiplexed); The Movie Channel (multiplexed).
Fee: $10.95 monthly (Cinemax or Encore/Starz), $13.95 monthly (HBO or Showtime).
Video-On-Demand: No
Pay-Per-View
iN DEMAND (delivered digitally); Playboy TV (delivered digitally).
Internet Service
Operational: Yes.
Broadband Service: CMA.
Fee: $39.95 installation; $38.95 monthly; $2.95 modem lease; $39.95 modem purchase.
Telephone Service
None
Miles of Plant: 124.0 (coaxial); None (fiber optic).
General Manager: Jerry L. Smith. Chief Technician: Bryce Beatty. Marketing Director: Julie Ferguson.
Ownership: Cable Management Assoc. (MSO).

WORTHAM (town)—Northland Cable Television, 515 W Tyler St, PO Box 112, Mexia, TX 76667-0112. Phones: 800-792-3087; 254-562-2872. Fax: 254-562-6454. E-mail: brent_richey@northlandcabletv.com. Web Site: http://www.northlandcabletv.com. ICA: TX0549.
TV Market Ranking: Outside TV Markets (WORTHAM (TOWN)). Franchise award date: January 1, 1988. Franchise expiration date: N.A. Began: January 1, 1988.
Channel capacity: 53 (not 2-way capable). Channels available but not in use: N.A.
Basic Service
Subscribers: 225.
Programming (received off-air): KCEN-TV (NBC, IND) Temple; KDAF (CW, IND) Dallas; KDFI (MNT) Dallas; KDFW-DT (FOX) Dallas; KDTN (ETV) Denton; KERA-TV (PBS) Dallas; KFWD (IND) Fort Worth; KTVT (CBS) Fort Worth; KTXA (IND) Fort Worth; KWKT-TV (FOX, MNT) Waco; KWTX-TV (CBS, CW) Waco; KXAS-TV (NBC) Fort Worth; KXTX-TV (TMO) Dallas; KXXV (ABC, TMO) Waco; WFAA (ABC) Dallas.
Programming (via satellite): A&E Networks; Animal Planet; BET Networks; Bloomberg Television; Cartoon Network; CNN; C-SPAN; Discovery Channel; E! Entertainment Television; ESPN; ESPN 2; Food Network; Fox Movie Channel; Fox News Channel; Fox Sports Southwest; FX; Great American Country; Hallmark Channel; Headline News; HGTV; History Channel; Lifetime; Nickelodeon; Outdoor Channel; QVC; Spike TV; TBS Superstation; The Learning Channel; The Weather Channel; Trinity Broadcasting Network; Turner Classic Movies; Turner Network TV; TV Land; USA Network; Versus.
Fee: $55.00 installation; $31.99 monthly.
Pay Service 1
Pay Units: 7.
Programming (via satellite): HBO.
Fee: $14.75 monthly.
Internet Service
Operational: No.
Telephone Service
None
Miles of Plant: 16.0 (coaxial); None (fiber optic).
Regional Manager: Brent Richey. Chief Technician: Joe Lopez. Office Manager: Pamela Elliott.
Ownership: Northland Communications Corp. (MSO).

WYLIE—Time Warner Cable. Now served by DALLAS, TX [TX0003]. ICA: TX0109.

YOAKUM—Time Warner Cable. Now served by GONZALES, TX [TX0209]. ICA: TX0883.

YORKTOWN—Almega Cable, 4001 W Airport Frwy, Ste 530, Bedford, TX 76021. Phone: 817-685-9588. Fax: 817-685-6488. E-mail: helpdesk@almegacable.com. Web Site: http://www.almega.com. ICA: TX0349.
TV Market Ranking: Below 100 (YORKTOWN). Franchise award date: N.A. Franchise expiration date: N.A. Began: November 14, 1978.
Channel capacity: 41 (not 2-way capable). Channels available but not in use: N.A.
Basic Service
Subscribers: 427.
Programming (received off-air): KABB (FOX) San Antonio; KAVU-TV (ABC) Victoria; KENS (CBS) San Antonio; KLRN (PBS) San Antonio; KSAT-TV (ABC) San Antonio; KVCT (FOX) Victoria; KVDA (TMO) San Antonio; WOAI-TV (NBC) San Antonio; 1 FM.
Programming (via satellite): A&E Networks; ABC Family Channel; Animal Planet; CNN; Country Music TV; Discovery Channel; Disney Channel; ESPN; Fox News Channel; Fox Sports Southwest; Headline News; Nickelodeon; QVC; Spike TV; TBS Superstation; The Learning Channel; The Weather Channel; Trinity Broadcasting Network; Turner Classic Movies; Turner Network TV; TV Land; USA Network; WGN America.
Fee: $29.95 installation; $38.00 monthly.
Pay Service 1
Pay Units: 65.
Programming (via satellite): The Movie Channel.
Fee: $5.95 monthly.
Pay Service 2
Pay Units: 66.
Programming (via satellite): Showtime.
Fee: $9.95 monthly.
Pay Service 3
Pay Units: 70.
Programming (via satellite): HBO.
Fee: $10.95 monthly.
Video-On-Demand: No
Internet Service
Operational: No.
Telephone Service
None
Miles of Plant: 18.0 (coaxial); None (fiber optic).
Ownership: Almega Cable (MSO).

ZAPATA—Time Warner Cable, 208 W Viggie St, Hebbronville, TX 78361-3048. Phones: 972-899-7300 (Flower Mound office); 361-527-3267. Fax: 361-527-3414. Web Site: http://www.timewarnercable.com/Texas. ICA: TX0198.
TV Market Ranking: Outside TV Markets (ZAPATA). Franchise award date: N.A. Franchise expiration date: N.A. Began: September 1, 1973.
Channel capacity: N.A. Channels available but not in use: N.A.
Basic Service
Subscribers: 2,375.
Programming (received off-air): KGNS-TV (CW, NBC, TMO) Laredo; KLDO-TV (FOX, UNV) Laredo; allband FM.
Programming (via microwave): KIII (ABC) Corpus Christi; KZTV (CBS) Corpus Christi.
Programming (via satellite): A&E Networks; ABC Family Channel; AMC; Animal Planet; Bravo; Cartoon Network; CNBC; CNN; Comedy Central; Country Music TV; C-SPAN; Discovery Channel; Disney Channel; ESPN; ESPN 2; Eternal Word TV Network; Fox News Channel; Fox Sports Southwest; FX; GalaVision; Hallmark Channel; Headline News; HGTV; History Channel; KRMA-TV (PBS) Denver; Lifetime; MSNBC; MTV; mun2 television; Nickelodeon; Oxygen; Spike TV; TBS Superstation; Telemundo; The Learning Channel; The Weather Channel; Travel Channel; Trinity Broadcasting Network; truTV; Turner Classic Movies; Turner Network TV; USA Network; VH1; WE tv.
Fee: $50.51 installation; $40.99 monthly.
Digital Basic Service
Subscribers: N.A.
Programming (via satellite): BBC America; Discovery Digital Networks; Encore (multiplexed); ESPN Classic Sports; ESPNews; Fox Sports World; Golf Channel; GSN; Independent Film Channel; Music Choice; National Geographic Channel; Nick Jr.; Syfy; TV Land; Versus; VH1 Classic.
Digital Pay Service 1
Pay Units: N.A.
Programming (via satellite): Cinemax (multiplexed); HBO (multiplexed); Showtime (multiplexed); Starz (multiplexed); The Movie Channel (multiplexed).
Fee: $12.95 monthly (each).
Video-On-Demand: No
Pay-Per-View
iN DEMAND (delivered digitally); Hot Choice (delivered digitally).
Internet Service
Operational: Yes.
Broadband Service: RoadRunner.
Fee: $39.95 monthly.
Telephone Service
Digital: Operational
Fee: $44.99 monthly
Miles of Plant: 61.0 (coaxial); None (fiber optic).
President: Connie Wharton. Vice President & General Manager: Michael Carrosquiola. Chief Technician: Juve Morante. Office Manager: Nellie Garza.
Ownership: Time Warner Cable (MSO).; Advance/Newhouse Partnership (MSO).

ZAVALLA—Almega Cable, 4001 W Airport Frwy, Ste 530, Bedford, TX 76021. Phone: 817-685-9588. Fax: 817-685-6488. E-mail: helpdesk@almegacable.com. Web Site: http://www.almega.com. Also serves Angelina County (portions). ICA: TX0379.
TV Market Ranking: Below 100 (Angelina County (portions), ZAVALLA). Franchise award date: N.A. Franchise expiration date: N.A. Began: N.A.
Channel capacity: 36 (not 2-way capable). Channels available but not in use: N.A.
Basic Service
Subscribers: 166.
Programming (received off-air): KBTV-TV (FOX) Port Arthur; KFDM (CBS, CW) Beaumont; KTRE (ABC) Lufkin.
Programming (via satellite): A&E Networks; ABC Family Channel; CNN; Country Music TV; Discovery Channel; Disney Channel; ESPN; Headline News; Nickelodeon; TBS Superstation; Turner Network TV; USA Network; WBBM-TV (CBS) Chicago; WGN America; WXIA-TV (NBC) Atlanta.
Fee: $54.95 installation; $44.05 monthly.
Pay Service 1
Pay Units: 20.
Programming (via satellite): Cinemax.
Fee: $12.95 monthly.
Pay Service 2
Pay Units: 21.
Programming (via satellite): HBO.
Fee: $12.95 monthly.
Pay Service 3
Pay Units: 37.
Programming (via satellite): Showtime.
Fee: $12.95 monthly.
Video-On-Demand: No
Internet Service
Operational: No.
Telephone Service
None
Miles of Plant: 40.0 (coaxial); None (fiber optic).
Ownership: Almega Cable (MSO).

ZION HILL—Formerly served by National Cable Inc. No longer in operation. ICA: TX0766.

UTAH

Total Systems: 52
Total Communities Served: 210
Franchises Not Yet Operating: 0
Applications Pending: 0
Communities with Applications: 0
Number of Basic Subscribers: 324,867
Number of Expanded Basic Subscribers: 143,077
Number of Pay Units: 16,851

Top 100 Markets Represented: Salt Lake City (48).

**For a list of cable communities in this section, see the Cable Community Index located in the back of Cable Volume 2.
For explanation of terms used in cable system listings, see p. D-11.**

BEAVER—South Central Communications, 45 North 100 W, PO Box 555, Escalante, UT 84726-0555. Phone: 435-826-4211. Fax: 435-826-4900. Web Site: http://www.southcentralcommunications.com. ICA: UT0035.
TV Market Ranking: Outside TV Markets (BEAVER). Franchise award date: N.A. Franchise expiration date: December 31, 2006. Began: January 20, 1982.
Channel capacity: 45 (not 2-way capable). Channels available but not in use: N.A.
Basic Service
Subscribers: N.A. Included in Escalante
Programming (via satellite): A&E Networks; ABC Family Channel; AMC; Cartoon Network; CNN; Discovery Channel; Disney Channel; ESPN; ESPN 2; Fox News Channel; Fox Sports Net; Great American Country; Hallmark Channel; HGTV; INSP; Lifetime; MountainWest Sports Network; Nickelodeon; Outdoor Channel; Spike TV; TBS Superstation; Turner Classic Movies; Turner Network TV; USA Network; WGN America.
Programming (via translator): KBYU-TV (PBS) Provo; KJZZ-TV (MNT) Salt Lake City; KSL-TV (NBC) Salt Lake City; KSTU (FOX) Salt Lake City; KTVX (ABC) Salt Lake City; KUCW (CW) Ogden; KUED (PBS) Salt Lake City; KUTV (CBS) Salt Lake City.
Fee: $45.00 installation; $31.95 monthly.
Pay Service 1
Pay Units: 86.
Programming (via satellite): HBO.
Fee: $11.00 monthly.
Video-On-Demand: No
Internet Service
Operational: No.
Telephone Service
None
Miles of Plant: 16.0 (coaxial); None (fiber optic).
Manager & Chief Technician: Greg Barton.
Ownership: South Central Communications (MSO).

BLANDING—Emery Telcom, 445 E Hwy 29, PO Box 629, Orangeville, UT 84537. Phones: 877-895-2110; 435-748-2223. Web Site: http://www.emerytelcom.com. ICA: UT0032.
TV Market Ranking: Outside TV Markets (BLANDING). Franchise award date: N.A. Franchise expiration date: N.A. Began: November 1, 1981.
Channel capacity: 40 (operating 2-way). Channels available but not in use: N.A.
Basic Service
Subscribers: 369.
Programming (received off-air): KJZZ-TV (MNT) Salt Lake City; KPNZ (IND) Ogden; KUEN (ETV) Ogden; KUPX-TV (ION) Provo; KUWB-LD Bloomington.
Programming (via translator): KBYU-TV (PBS) Provo; KSL-TV (NBC) Salt Lake City; KSTU (FOX) Salt Lake City; KTVX (ABC) Salt Lake City; KUED (PBS) Salt Lake City; KUTV (CBS) Salt Lake City.
Fee: $29.95 installation; $10.70 monthly.
Expanded Basic Service 1
Subscribers: N.A.
Programming (via satellite): A&E Networks; ABC Family Channel; AMC; Animal Planet; Cartoon Network; CNBC; CNN; Comedy Central; Country Music TV; Discovery Channel; Disney Channel; ESPN; Fox News Channel; FX; Hallmark Channel; Lifetime; Nickelodeon; QVC; Root Sports Rocky Mountain; Spike TV; TBS Superstation; The Learning Channel; The Weather Channel; Turner Network TV; USA Network; WGN America.
Fee: $28.25 monthly.
Digital Basic Service
Subscribers: N.A.
Programming (via satellite): BBC America; Bio; Bravo; Discovery Digital Networks; DMX Music; ESPN 2; ESPN Classic Sports; ESPNews; Fox Sports World; FSN Digital Atlantic; FSN Digital Central; FSN Digital Pacific; Fuse; Golf Channel; Great American Country; GSN; HGTV; History Channel; History Channel International; Independent Film Channel; Lifetime Movie Network; MBC America; National Geographic Channel; ShopNBC; Speed; Style Network; Syfy; The Word Network; Toon Disney; Trio; Turner Classic Movies; Versus; WE tv.
Fee: $15.95 monthly.
Digital Pay Service 1
Pay Units: N.A.
Programming (via satellite): Cinemax (multiplexed); Encore (multiplexed); Flix; HBO (multiplexed); Showtime (multiplexed); Starz (multiplexed); The Movie Channel (multiplexed).
Fee: $12.95 monthly (each).
Video-On-Demand: No
Pay-Per-View
iN DEMAND (delivered digitally); Playboy TV (delivered digitally).
Internet Service
Operational: Yes.
Telephone Service
None
Miles of Plant: 11.0 (coaxial); None (fiber optic).
Manager: Greg Barton.
Ownership: Emery Telcom (MSO).

BRIAN HEAD—South Central Communications, 45 North 100 W, PO Box 555, Escalante, UT 84726-0555. Phone: 435-826-4211. Fax: 435-826-4900. Web Site: http://www.scwireless.com. ICA: UT0069.
TV Market Ranking: Below 100 (BRIAN HEAD). Franchise award date: N.A. Franchise expiration date: N.A. Began: January 1, 1981.
Channel capacity: 36 (not 2-way capable). Channels available but not in use: N.A.
Basic Service
Subscribers: N.A. Included in Escalante
Programming (via satellite): A&E Networks; ABC Family Channel; AMC; Animal Planet; CNN; Country Music TV; Discovery Channel; Disney Channel; ESPN; ESPN 2; Hallmark Channel; History Channel; Lifetime; MountainWest Sports Network; National Geographic Channel; Nickelodeon; Spike TV; TBS Superstation; The Learning Channel; The Weather Channel; Travel Channel; Turner Network TV; USA Network; VH1; WGN America.
Programming (via translator): KBYU-TV (PBS) Provo; KJZZ-TV (MNT) Salt Lake City; KSL-TV (NBC) Salt Lake City; KSTU (FOX) Salt Lake City; KTVX (ABC) Salt Lake City; KUED (PBS) Salt Lake City; KUTV (CBS) Salt Lake City.
Fee: $45.00 installation; $29.95 monthly.
Pay Service 1
Pay Units: 47.
Programming (via satellite): HBO.
Fee: $11.00 monthly.
Video-On-Demand: No
Internet Service
Operational: No.
Telephone Service
None
Miles of Plant: 5.0 (coaxial); None (fiber optic).
Manager & Chief Technician: Greg Barton.
Ownership: South Central Communications (MSO).

BRIGHAM CITY—Comcast Cable. Now served by OGDEN (formerly HOOPER), UT [UT0008]. ICA: UT0013.

CASTLE DALE—Emery Telcom, 445 E Hwy 29, PO Box 629, Orangeville, UT 84537. Phone: 435-748-2223. Web Site: http://www.emerytelcom.com. Also serves Emery County, Huntington & Orangeville. ICA: UT0017.
TV Market Ranking: Below 100 (Emery County); Outside TV Markets (CASTLE DALE, Huntington, Orangeville). Franchise award date: N.A. Franchise expiration date: N.A. Began: August 1, 1981.
Channel capacity: 40 (operating 2-way). Channels available but not in use: N.A.
Basic Service
Subscribers: 697.
Programming (received off-air): KJZZ-TV (MNT) Salt Lake City; KPNZ (IND) Ogden; KUEN (ETV) Ogden; KUPX-TV (ION) Provo; KUWB-LD Bloomington.
Programming (via translator): KBYU-TV (PBS) Provo; KSL-TV (NBC) Salt Lake City; KSTU (FOX) Salt Lake City; KTVX (ABC) Salt Lake City; KUED (PBS) Salt Lake City; KUTV (CBS) Salt Lake City.
Fee: $29.95 installation; $10.95 monthly; $1.50 converter; $40.00 additional installation.
Expanded Basic Service 1
Subscribers: N.A.
Programming (via satellite): A&E Networks; ABC Family Channel; AMC; Animal Planet; CNN; Comedy Central; Country Music TV; Discovery Channel; Disney Channel; ESPN; Fox News Channel; FX; Lifetime; Nickelodeon; QVC; Root Sports Rocky Mountain; Spike TV; TBS Superstation; The Learning Channel; The Weather Channel; Turner Network TV; USA Network; WGN America.
Fee: $25.00 monthly.
Digital Basic Service
Subscribers: N.A.
Programming (via satellite): BBC America; Bravo; Discovery Digital Networks; DMX Music; ESPN 2; ESPN Classic Sports; ESPNews; Fox Sports World; Golf Channel; GSN; HGTV; History Channel; Independent Film Channel; National Geographic Channel; Speed; Syfy; Turner Classic Movies; Versus; WE tv.
Fee: $16.95 monthly.
Digital Pay Service 1
Pay Units: N.A.
Programming (via satellite): Cinemax (multiplexed); Encore (multiplexed); HBO (multiplexed); Showtime (multiplexed); Starz (multiplexed); The Movie Channel (multiplexed).
Fee: $12.95 monthly (each).
Video-On-Demand: No
Pay-Per-View
iN DEMAND (delivered digitally); Playboy TV (delivered digitally).
Internet Service
Operational: No.
Telephone Service
None
Miles of Plant: 49.0 (coaxial); None (fiber optic).
Manager: Greg Barton.
Ownership: Emery Telcom (MSO).

CEDAR CITY—Bresnan Communications, 2502 Foresight Cir, Grand Junction, CO 81505. Phones: 877-273-7626; 435-586-8334 (Local office). Fax: 435-586-7675. Web Site: http://www.bresnan.com. ICA: UT0015.
TV Market Ranking: Below 100 (CEDAR CITY). Franchise award date: September 18, 1975. Franchise expiration date: N.A. Began: December 10, 1979.
Channel capacity: N.A. Channels available but not in use: N.A.
Basic Service
Subscribers: 2,850.
Programming (received off-air): KBYU-TV (PBS) Provo; KCNC-TV (CBS) Denver; KCSG (IND) Cedar City; KJZZ-TV (MNT) Salt Lake City; KSL-TV (NBC) Salt Lake City; KSTU (FOX) Salt Lake City; KTVX (ABC) Salt Lake City; KUCW (CW) Ogden; KUED (PBS) Salt Lake City; KUEN (ETV)

Ogden; KUTV (CBS) Salt Lake City; allband FM.
Programming (via satellite): C-SPAN; WGN America.
Programming (via translator): KSL-TV (NBC) Salt Lake City; KTVX (ABC) Salt Lake City; KUTV (CBS) Salt Lake City.
Fee: $44.95 installation; $48.99 monthly; $15.00 additional installation.

Expanded Basic Service 1
Subscribers: 2,301.
Programming (via satellite): A&E Networks; ABC Family Channel; Altitude Sports & Entertainment; AMC; Animal Planet; BYU Television; Cartoon Network; CNBC; CNN; Comedy Central; Country Music TV; C-SPAN 2; Discovery Channel; Disney Channel; E! Entertainment Television; ESPN; ESPN 2; Food Network; Fox News Channel; FX; Hallmark Channel; Headline News; HGTV; History Channel; INSP; Lifetime; MountainWest Sports Network; MSNBC; MTV; Nickelodeon; Oxygen; QVC; Root Sports Rocky Mountain; Spike TV; Syfy; TBS Superstation; The Learning Channel; The Weather Channel; Travel Channel; truTV; Turner Classic Movies; Turner Network TV; TV Guide Network; TV Land; USA Network; VH1.
Fee: $58.98 monthly.

Digital Basic Service
Subscribers: 388.
Programming (via satellite): A&E HD; Altitude Sports & Entertainment; American-Life TV Network; Bandamax; BBC America; Bio; Bloomberg Television; Bravo; CBS Sports Network; Cine Latino; Cine Mexicano; CMT Pure Country; CNN en Espanol; Cooking Channel; De Pelicula; De Pelicula Clasico; Discovery en Espanol; Discovery Fit & Health; Discovery Health Channel; Discovery Kids Channel; DIY Network; DMX Music; ESPN 2 HD; ESPN Classic Sports; ESPN Deportes; ESPN HD; ESPNews; Food Network HD; Fox College Sports Atlantic; Fox College Sports Central; Fox College Sports Pacific; Fox Deportes; Fox Movie Channel; Fox Reality Channel; Fox Soccer; Fuse; G4; GMC; Golf Channel; GolTV; GSN; Halogen Network; HD Theater; HDNet; HDNet Movies; HGTV HD; History Channel en Espanol; History Channel HD; History Channel International; ID Investigation Discovery; Independent Film Channel; Lifetime Movie Network; Lifetime Movie Network HD; Military Channel; MTV Hits; MTV Jams; MTV2; mun2 television; National Geographic Channel; National Geographic Channel HD Network; Nick Jr.; Nick Too; NickToons TV; Outdoor Channel; PBS Kids Sprout; Planet Green; RFD-TV; Science; SoapNet; Speed; Style Network; Syfy HD; TBS in HD; TeenNick; Telehit; Toon Disney; Tr3s; Trinity Broadcasting Network; Turner Network TV HD; Universal HD; USA Network HD; VeneMovies; Versus; Versus HD; VH1 Classic; VH1 Soul.
Fee: $72.95 monthly.

Digital Pay Service 1
Pay Units: N.A.
Programming (via satellite): Cinemax (multiplexed); Encore (multiplexed); Flix; HBO (multiplexed); HBO HD; Showtime (multiplexed); Showtime HD; Starz (multiplexed); Starz HDTV; The Movie Channel (multiplexed); The Movie Channel HD.
Fee: $1.75 monthly (Encore), $6.75 monthly (Starz), $13.15 monthly (HBO, Showtime or TMC).
Video-On-Demand: No

Pay-Per-View
Addressable homes: 388.
ESPN (delivered digitally); iN DEMAND (delivered digitally).
Internet Service
Operational: Yes.
Broadband Service: Bresnan OnLine.
Fee: $55.95 monthly.
Telephone Service
Digital: Operational
Fee: $49.99 monthly
Miles of Plant: 78.0 (coaxial); None (fiber optic). Additional miles planned: 3.0 (coaxial).
General Manager: Sean Hogue. Technical Operations Manager: Gary Young.
Ownership: Bresnan Communications Inc. (MSO). Sale pends to Cablevision Systems Corp.

CENTRAL—Central Telcom Services (CUTV). Now served by GUNNISON, UT [UT0037]. ICA: UT0070.

CLEVELAND—Emery Telcom, 445 E Hwy 29, PO Box 629, Orangeville, UT 84537. Phones: 435-564-3415; 435-748-2223 (Corporate office). Web Site: http://www.emerytelcom.com. Also serves Elmo. ICA: UT0055.
TV Market Ranking: Outside TV Markets (CLEVELAND, Elmo). Franchise award date: N.A. Franchise expiration date: N.A. Began: July 1, 1990.
Channel capacity: N.A. Channels available but not in use: N.A.
Basic Service
Subscribers: 133.
Programming (received off-air): KBYU-TV (PBS) Provo; KJZZ-TV (MNT) Salt Lake City; KSL-TV (NBC) Salt Lake City; KSTU (FOX) Salt Lake City; KTVX (ABC) Salt Lake City; KUED (PBS) Salt Lake City; KUTV (CBS) Salt Lake City.
Programming (via satellite): A&E Networks; ABC Family Channel; AMC; America's Store; Animal Planet; Cartoon Network; CNBC; CNN; Comedy Central; Country Music TV; C-SPAN; Discovery Channel; Disney Channel; ESPN; Fox News Channel; Fox Sports Net; Lifetime; Nickelodeon; Spike TV; Syfy; TBS Superstation; The Learning Channel; Travel Channel; Turner Network TV; USA Network; WGN America.
Fee: $49.95 installation; $26.45 monthly.
Pay Service 1
Pay Units: 37.
Programming (via satellite): Cinemax.
Fee: $10.95 monthly.
Pay Service 2
Pay Units: 40.
Programming (via satellite): HBO.
Fee: $10.95 monthly.
Video-On-Demand: No
Internet Service
Operational: Yes, Both DSL & dial-up.
Fee: $24.95 monthly.
Telephone Service
Analog: Operational
Digital: Not Operational
Miles of Plant: 12.0 (coaxial); None (fiber optic).
Manager: Greg Barton.
Ownership: Emery Telcom (MSO).

COALVILLE—Comcast Cable, 9602 S 300 W, Sandy, UT 84070. Phone: 801-401-2500. Fax: 801-401-3397. Web Site: http://www.comcast.com. Also serves Summit County (portions). ICA: UT0049.
TV Market Ranking: 48 (COALVILLE, Summit County (portions)). Franchise award date: N.A. Franchise expiration date: N.A. Began: January 1, 1984.
Channel capacity: N.A. Channels available but not in use: N.A.
Basic Service
Subscribers: N.A. Included in Salt Lake City
Programming (received off-air): KBYU-TV (PBS) Provo; KJZZ-TV (MNT) Salt Lake City; KSL-TV (NBC) Salt Lake City; KSTU (FOX) Salt Lake City; KTVX (ABC) Salt Lake City; KUED (PBS) Salt Lake City; KUTV (CBS) Salt Lake City.
Programming (via satellite): Discovery Channel; Hallmark Channel; Lifetime; TBS Superstation.
Fee: $43.99 installation; $8.68 monthly.
Expanded Basic Service 1
Subscribers: N.A.
Programming (via satellite): AMC; Animal Planet; Cartoon Network; CNBC; CNN; Country Music TV; Disney Channel; ESPN; Fox Sports Net; Spike TV; Turner Network TV; USA Network.
Fee: $43.60 monthly.
Pay Service 1
Pay Units: 65.
Programming (via satellite): Encore; HBO; Starz.
Fee: $6.99 monthly (Encore), $10.99 monthly (Starz), $14.99 monthly (HBO).
Internet Service
Operational: No.
Telephone Service
None
Miles of plant included in Salt Lake City
Area Vice President: Scott Tenney. Technical Operations Director: Mike Spaulding. Marketing Director: Dan Williams. Marketing Manager: Lisa Jenkins. Community & Government Affairs Director: Steve Proper.
Ownership: Comcast Cable Communications Inc. (MSO).

DELTA—Satview Broadband, 13495 S Hills Dr, PO Box 18143, Reno, NV 89511. Phone: 775-333-6626. Web Site: http://www.iwantone.tv. ICA: UT0024.
TV Market Ranking: Outside TV Markets (DELTA). Franchise award date: September 9, 1981. Franchise expiration date: N.A. Began: June 1, 1983.
Channel capacity: N.A. Channels available but not in use: N.A.
Basic Service
Subscribers: 90.
Programming (received off-air): KJZZ-TV (MNT) Salt Lake City; KUCW (CW) Ogden; KUEN (ETV) Ogden.
Programming (via satellite): TBS Superstation; WGN America.
Programming (via translator): KBYU-TV (PBS) Provo; KSL-TV (NBC) Salt Lake City; KSTU (FOX) Salt Lake City; KTVX (ABC) Salt Lake City; KUED (PBS) Salt Lake City; KUTV (CBS) Salt Lake City.
Fee: $44.95 installation; $48.99 monthly; $1.50 converter; $15.00 additional installation.
Expanded Basic Service 1
Subscribers: N.A.
Programming (via satellite): ABC Family Channel; AMC; Animal Planet; Cartoon Network; CNN; Comedy Central; Country Music TV; C-SPAN; C-SPAN 2; Discovery Channel; Disney Channel; ESPN; ESPN 2; Great American Country; Hallmark Channel; Headline News; History Channel; Lifetime; MountainWest Sports Network; MTV; Nickelodeon; QVC; Root Sports Rocky Mountain; Spike TV; Syfy; The Learning Channel; The Weather Channel; Travel Channel; Turner Network TV; TV Land; USA Network; VH1.
Fee: $58.98 monthly.
Digital Basic Service
Subscribers: N.A.
Programming (via satellite): BBC America; Bio; Bloomberg Television; Bravo; CMT Pure Country; Discovery Fit & Health; Discovery Health Channel; Discovery Kids Channel; DMX Music; ESPN Classic Sports; ESPNews; Fox Movie Channel; Fox Soccer; Fuse; G4; Golf Channel; GSN; Halogen Network; History Channel International; ID Investigation Discovery; Independent Film Channel; Lifetime Movie Network; Military Channel; MTV2; National Geographic Channel; Nick Jr.; NickToons TV; Outdoor Channel; Planet Green; Science; SoapNet; Speed; Style Network; TeenNick; Toon Disney; Trinity Broadcasting Network; Versus; VH1 Classic.
Fee: $72.95 monthly.
Digital Pay Service 1
Pay Units: N.A.
Programming (via satellite): Cinemax (multiplexed); Encore (multiplexed); HBO (multiplexed); Showtime (multiplexed); Starz (multiplexed); The Movie Channel (multiplexed).
Video-On-Demand: No
Internet Service
Operational: No.
Telephone Service
None
Miles of Plant: 25.0 (coaxial); None (fiber optic).
President: Tariq Ahmad.
Ownership: Satview Broadband Ltd. (MSO).

DUCHESNE—Strata Networks, 211 East 200 North, Roosevelt, UT 84066. Phone: 435-622-5007. Web Site: http://www.ubta-ubet.com. ICA: UT0052.
TV Market Ranking: Outside TV Markets (DUCHESNE). Franchise award date: N.A. Franchise expiration date: N.A. Began: October 1, 1981.
Channel capacity: 40 (operating 2-way). Channels available but not in use: N.A.
Basic Service
Subscribers: 145.
Programming (received off-air): KJZZ-TV (MNT) Salt Lake City; KPNZ (IND) Ogden; KUEN (ETV) Ogden; KUPX-TV (ION) Provo; KUWB-LD Bloomington.
Programming (via translator): KBYU-TV (PBS) Provo; KSL-TV (NBC) Salt Lake City; KSTU (FOX) Salt Lake City; KTVX (ABC) Salt Lake City; KUED (PBS) Salt Lake City; KUTV (CBS) Salt Lake City.
Fee: $29.95 installation; $10.70 monthly.
Expanded Basic Service 1
Subscribers: N.A.
Programming (via satellite): A&E Networks; ABC Family Channel; AMC; Animal Planet; Cartoon Network; CNBC; CNN; Comedy Central; Country Music TV; Discovery Channel; Disney Channel; ESPN; Fox News Channel; FX; Hallmark Channel; Lifetime; Nickelodeon; QVC; Root Sports Rocky Mountain; Spike TV; TBS Superstation; The Learning Channel; The Weather Channel; Turner Network TV; USA Network; WGN America.
Fee: $28.25 monthly.
Digital Basic Service
Subscribers: N.A.
Programming (via satellite): BBC America; Bio; Bravo; Discovery Digital Networks; DMX Music; ESPN 2; ESPN Classic Sports; ESPNews; Fox Sports World; FSN Digital

Atlantic; FSN Digital Central; FSN Digital Pacific; Fuse; Golf Channel; Great American Country; GSN; HGTV; History Channel; History Channel International; Independent Film Channel; Lifetime Movie Network; MBC America; National Geographic Channel; ShopNBC; Speed; Style Network; Syfy; The Word Network; Toon Disney; Trio; Turner Classic Movies; Versus; WE tv.
Fee: $15.95 monthly.

Digital Pay Service 1
Pay Units: N.A.
Programming (via satellite): Cinemax (multiplexed); Encore (multiplexed); Flix; HBO (multiplexed); Showtime (multiplexed); Starz (multiplexed); The Movie Channel (multiplexed).
Fee: $12.95 monthly (each).

Video-On-Demand: No

Pay-Per-View
iN DEMAND (delivered digitally); Playboy TV (delivered digitally).

Internet Service
Operational: No.

Telephone Service
None

Miles of Plant: 18.0 (coaxial); None (fiber optic).
Chief Executive Officer & General Manager: Bruce Todd. Chief Operating Officer: Jeff Goodrich. Marketing Manager: Tyler Rasmussen.
Ownership: Strata Networks (MSO).

DUGWAY—Central Telcom Services (CUTV), 35 S State St, PO Box 7, Fairview, UT 84629-0007. Phones: 877-427-2888; 435-831-4404. Fax: 435-427-3200. Web Site: http://www.centracom.com. ICA: UT0046.
TV Market Ranking: Outside TV Markets (DUGWAY). Franchise award date: N.A. Franchise expiration date: N.A. Began: October 15, 1980.
Channel capacity: N.A. Channels available but not in use: N.A.

Basic Service
Subscribers: 290.
Programming (received off-air): KBYU-TV (PBS) Provo; KJZZ-TV (MNT) Salt Lake City; KPNZ (IND) Ogden; KSL-TV (NBC) Salt Lake City; KSTU (FOX) Salt Lake City; KTVX (ABC) Salt Lake City; KUED (PBS) Salt Lake City; KUPX-TV (ION) Provo; KUTV (CBS) Salt Lake City.
Programming (via satellite): C-SPAN; Hallmark Channel; INSP; NASA TV; Pentagon Channel; QVC; The Weather Channel; WGN America.
Fee: $49.95 installation; $15.95 monthly.

Expanded Basic Service 1
Subscribers: 270.
Programming (via satellite): A&E Networks; ABC Family Channel; AMC; AmericanLife TV Network; Animal Planet; BET Networks; Cartoon Network; CNN; Comedy Central; Country Music TV; Discovery Channel; DIY Network; E! Entertainment Television; ESPN; ESPN 2; Food Network; Fox Movie Channel; Fox News Channel; Fox Sports Net; FX; G4; GSN; Headline News; HGTV; History Channel; Lifetime; MTV; Nickelodeon; Outdoor Channel; Oxygen; Spike TV; Syfy; TBS Superstation; The Learning Channel; truTV; Turner Classic Movies; Turner Network TV; TV Land; USA Network; VH1.
Fee: $18.00 monthly.

Pay Service 1
Pay Units: N.A.
Programming (via satellite): Cinemax; Encore; HBO (multiplexed); Showtime; Starz; The Movie Channel.

Video-On-Demand: No

Internet Service
Operational: Yes.
Subscribers: 275.
Broadband Service: In-house.
Fee: $19.95 installation; $35.95 monthly.

Telephone Service
None

Miles of Plant: 7.0 (coaxial); None (fiber optic).
General Manager: Eddie Lee. CATV Manager: George Lee. Chief Engineer: Kenny Roberts.
Ownership: CentraCom Interactive (MSO).

EAST CARBON—Emery Telcom, 445 E Hwy 29, PO Box 629, Orangeville, UT 84537. Phones: 435-613-9605; 435-748-2223. Web Site: http://www.emerytelcom.com. Also serves Columbia & Sunnyside. ICA: UT0050.
TV Market Ranking: Outside TV Markets (Columbia, EAST CARBON, Sunnyside). Franchise award date: N.A. Franchise expiration date: N.A. Began: November 1, 1980.
Channel capacity: 40 (operating 2-way). Channels available but not in use: N.A.

Basic Service
Subscribers: 427.
Programming (received off-air): KBYU-TV (PBS) Provo; KPNZ (IND) Ogden; KUEN (ETV) Ogden; KUPX-TV (ION) Provo; KUWB-LD Bloomington.
Programming (via translator): KJZZ-TV (MNT) Salt Lake City; KSL-TV (NBC) Salt Lake City; KSTU (FOX) Salt Lake City; KTVX (ABC) Salt Lake City; KUED (PBS) Salt Lake City; KUTV (CBS) Salt Lake City.
Fee: $29.95 installation; $10.70 monthly.

Expanded Basic Service 1
Subscribers: N.A.
Programming (via satellite): A&E Networks; ABC Family Channel; AMC; Animal Planet; Cartoon Network; CNBC; CNN; Comedy Central; Country Music TV; Discovery Channel; Disney Channel; ESPN; Fox News Channel; FX; Hallmark Channel; Lifetime; Nickelodeon; QVC; Root Sports Rocky Mountain; Spike TV; TBS Superstation; The Learning Channel; The Weather Channel; Turner Network TV; USA Network; WGN America.
Fee: $28.25 monthly.

Digital Basic Service
Subscribers: N.A.
Programming (via satellite): BBC America; Bio; Bravo; Discovery Digital Networks; DMX Music; ESPN 2; ESPN Classic Sports; ESPNews; Fox Sports World; FSN Digital Atlantic; FSN Digital Central; FSN Digital Pacific; Fuse; Golf Channel; Great American Country; GSN; HGTV; History Channel; History Channel International; Independent Film Channel; Lifetime Movie Network; MBC America; National Geographic Channel; ShopNBC; Speed; Style Network; Syfy; The Word Network; Toon Disney; Trio; Turner Classic Movies; Versus; WE tv.
Fee: $15.95 monthly.

Digital Pay Service 1
Pay Units: N.A.
Programming (via satellite): Cinemax (multiplexed); Encore (multiplexed); Flix; HBO (multiplexed); Showtime (multiplexed); Starz (multiplexed); The Movie Channel (multiplexed).
Fee: $12.95 monthly (each).

Video-On-Demand: No

Pay-Per-View
iN DEMAND (delivered digitally); Playboy TV (delivered digitally).

Internet Service
Operational: No.

Telephone Service
None

Miles of Plant: 9.0 (coaxial); None (fiber optic).
Manager: Greg Barton.
Ownership: Emery Telcom (MSO).

ENOCH—South Central Communications, 45 North 100 W, PO Box 555, Escalante, UT 84726-0555. Phone: 435-826-4211. Fax: 435-826-4900. Web Site: http://www.scwireless.com. ICA: UT0071.
TV Market Ranking: Below 100 (ENOCH). Franchise award date: March 1, 1988. Franchise expiration date: N.A. Began: September 15, 1988.
Channel capacity: N.A. Channels available but not in use: N.A.

Basic Service
Subscribers: N.A. Included in Escalante
Programming (received off-air): KCSG (IND) Cedar City.
Programming (via satellite): C-SPAN; C-SPAN 2; QVC; TV Guide Network.
Programming (via translator): KBYU-TV (PBS) Provo; KJZZ-TV (MNT) Salt Lake City; KSL-TV (NBC) Salt Lake City; KSTU (FOX) Salt Lake City; KTVX (ABC) Salt Lake City; KUCW (CW) Ogden; KUED (PBS) Salt Lake City; KUTV (CBS) Salt Lake City.
Fee: $45.00 installation; $10.95 monthly.

Expanded Basic Service 1
Subscribers: N.A.
Programming (via satellite): A&E Networks; ABC Family Channel; AMC; Animal Planet; Cartoon Network; CNBC; CNN; Comedy Central; Country Music TV; Discovery Channel; Disney Channel; E! Entertainment Television; ESPN; ESPN 2; Food Network; Fox News Channel; FX; Great American Country; Hallmark Channel; Headline News; HGTV; History Channel; INSP; Lifetime; MountainWest Sports Network; MSNBC; MTV; Nickelodeon; Outdoor Channel; Root Sports Rocky Mountain; Speed; Spike TV; Syfy; TBS Superstation; The Learning Channel; The Weather Channel; Travel Channel; Turner Classic Movies; Turner Network TV; TV Land; USA Network; Versus; VH1; WGN America.
Fee: $36.45 monthly.

Pay Service 1
Pay Units: 13.
Programming (via satellite): Cinemax.
Fee: $11.00 monthly.

Pay Service 2
Pay Units: 45.
Programming (via satellite): HBO.
Fee: $11.00 monthly.

Video-On-Demand: No

Pay-Per-View
iN DEMAND (delivered digitally); Playboy TV (delivered digitally); ESPN Extra (delivered digitally); ESPN Now (delivered digitally); Fresh (delivered digitally).

Internet Service
Operational: Yes, DSL.
Fee: $29.95 monthly.

Telephone Service
None

Miles of Plant: 74.0 (coaxial); None (fiber optic).
Manager & Chief Technician: Greg Barton.
Ownership: South Central Communications (MSO).

ENTERPRISE—South Central Communications, 45 North 100 W, PO Box 555, Escalante, UT 84726-0555. Phone: 435-826-4211. Fax: 435-826-4900. Web Site: http://www.scwireless.com. ICA: UT0056.
TV Market Ranking: Below 100 (ENTERPRISE). Franchise award date: November 13, 1986. Franchise expiration date: N.A. Began: September 21, 1987.
Channel capacity: 42 (not 2-way capable). Channels available but not in use: N.A.

Basic Service
Subscribers: N.A. Included in Escalante
Programming (received off-air): KUEN (ETV) Ogden.
Programming (via satellite): A&E Networks; ABC Family Channel; AMC; Animal Planet; CNN; Country Music TV; C-SPAN; Discovery Channel; Disney Channel; E! Entertainment Television; ESPN; ESPN 2; Headline News; HGTV; History Channel; KTLA (CW) Los Angeles; MountainWest Sports Network; Nickelodeon; Outdoor Channel; QVC; Root Sports Rocky Mountain; Spike TV; Syfy; TBS Superstation; The Learning Channel; The Weather Channel; Turner Classic Movies; Turner Network TV; TV Land; USA Network; VH1; WGN America.
Programming (via translator): KBYU-TV (PBS) Provo; KJZZ-TV (MNT) Salt Lake City; KSL-TV (NBC) Salt Lake City; KSTU (FOX) Salt Lake City; KTVX (ABC) Salt Lake City; KUCW (CW) Ogden; KUED (PBS) Salt Lake City; KUTV (CBS) Salt Lake City.
Fee: $45.00 installation; $30.95 monthly.

Pay Service 1
Pay Units: 19.
Programming (via satellite): HBO; Showtime.
Fee: $21.50 installation; $11.00 monthly (each).

Video-On-Demand: No

Internet Service
Operational: No.

Telephone Service
None

Miles of Plant: 8.0 (coaxial); None (fiber optic).
Manager & Chief Technician: Greg Barton.
Ownership: South Central Communications (MSO).

EPHRAIM—Central Telcom Services (CUTV). Now served by GUNNISON, UT [UT0037]. ICA: UT0022.

ESCALANTE—South Central Communications, 45 North 100 W, PO Box 555, Escalante, UT 84726-0555. Phones: 800-718-7288; 435-826-4211. Fax: 435-826-4900. Web Site: http://www.southcentralcommunications.com. ICA: UT0083.
TV Market Ranking: Outside TV Markets (ESCALANTE). Franchise award date: May 1, 1992. Franchise expiration date: May 1, 2007. Began: October 1, 1992.
Channel capacity: 46 (not 2-way capable). Channels available but not in use: N.A.

Basic Service
Subscribers: 2,000 Includes all South Central Communications systems.
Programming (received off-air): KBYU-TV (PBS) Provo; KJZZ-TV (MNT) Salt Lake City; KSL-TV (NBC) Salt Lake City; KSTU (FOX) Salt Lake City; KTVX (ABC) Salt Lake City; KUCW (CW) Ogden; KUED (PBS) Salt Lake City; KUTV (CBS) Salt Lake City.
Programming (via satellite): A&E Networks; ABC Family Channel; AMC; Animal Planet; Cartoon Network; CNN; Comedy Central; Country Music TV; Discovery Channel; Disney Channel; E! Entertainment Television; ESPN; ESPN 2; Fox News Channel; Hallmark Channel; HGTV; History Channel; Lifetime Movie Network; Nickelodeon; Outdoor Channel; QVC; Root Sports Rocky Moun-

tain; Spike TV; Syfy; TBS Superstation; The Learning Channel; Turner Classic Movies; Turner Network TV; TV Land; USA Network; VH1; WGN America.
Fee: $45.00 installation; $27.95 monthly.
Pay Service 1
Pay Units: 35.
Programming (via satellite): Cinemax.
Fee: $11.00 monthly.
Pay Service 2
Pay Units: 43.
Programming (via satellite): HBO.
Fee: $11.00 monthly.
Video-On-Demand: No
Internet Service
Operational: No.
Telephone Service
None
Miles of Plant: 13.0 (coaxial); None (fiber optic).
Manager & Chief Technician: Greg Barton. Marketing Director: James Harrison.
Ownership: South Central Communications (MSO).

EUREKA—Central Telcom Services (CUTV). Now served by GUNNISON, UT [UT0037]. ICA: UT0057.

FARMINGTON—Comcast Cable. Now served by OGDEN (formerly HOOPER), UT [UT0008]. ICA: UT0004.

FERRON—Emery Telcom, 445 E Hwy 29, PO Box 629, Orangeville, UT 84537. Phone: 435-748-2223. Web Site: http://www.emerytelcom.com. ICA: UT0054.
TV Market Ranking: Outside TV Markets (FERRON). Franchise award date: N.A. Franchise expiration date: N.A. Began: August 1, 1982.
Channel capacity: N.A. Channels available but not in use: N.A.
Basic Service
Subscribers: 90.
Programming (via satellite): A&E Networks; ABC Family Channel; AMC; Animal Planet; CNN; Country Music TV; C-SPAN; Discovery Channel; Disney Channel; ESPN; Fox Sports Net; Hallmark Channel; HGTV; Lifetime; Nickelodeon; QVC; Spike TV; TBS Superstation; The Learning Channel; The Weather Channel; Turner Network TV; USA Network; WGN America.
Programming (via translator): KBYU-TV (PBS) Provo; KSL-TV (NBC) Salt Lake City; KSTU (FOX) Salt Lake City; KTVX (ABC) Salt Lake City; KUED (PBS) Salt Lake City; KUTV (CBS) Salt Lake City.
Fee: $44.95 installation; $35.95 monthly.
Pay Service 1
Pay Units: 52.
Programming (via satellite): Cinemax.
Fee: $12.95 monthly.
Pay Service 2
Pay Units: 94.
Programming (via satellite): HBO.
Fee: $12.95 monthly.
Pay Service 3
Pay Units: 82.
Programming (via satellite): Starz.
Fee: $12.95 monthly.
Pay Service 4
Pay Units: 153.
Programming (via satellite): Encore.
Fee: $1.75 monthly.
Video-On-Demand: No
Internet Service
Operational: No.
Telephone Service
None
Miles of Plant: 15.0 (coaxial); None (fiber optic).
Manager: Greg Barton.
Ownership: Emery Telcom (MSO).

FIELDING—Comcast Cable. Now served by LOGAN, UT [UT0006]. ICA: UT0051.

FILLMORE—Satview Broadband, 45 North 100 W, PO Box 555, Escalante, UT 84726-0555. Phone: 435-826-4211. Fax: 435-826-4900. Web Site: http://www.iwantone.tv. ICA: UT0036.
TV Market Ranking: Outside TV Markets (FILLMORE). Franchise award date: N.A. Franchise expiration date: N.A. Began: March 1, 1985.
Channel capacity: 40 (operating 2-way). Channels available but not in use: N.A.
Basic Service
Subscribers: 346.
Programming (received off-air): KBYU-TV (PBS) Provo; KPNZ (IND) Ogden; KUCW (CW) Ogden; KUEN (ETV) Ogden; KUPX-TV (ION) Provo.
Programming (via translator): KJZZ-TV (MNT) Salt Lake City; KSL-TV (NBC) Salt Lake City; KSTU (FOX) Salt Lake City; KTVX (ABC) Salt Lake City; KUED (PBS) Salt Lake City; KUTV (CBS) Salt Lake City.
Fee: $49.95 installation; $10.95 monthly; $1.50 converter.
Expanded Basic Service 1
Subscribers: N.A.
Programming (via satellite): A&E Networks; ABC Family Channel; AMC; Animal Planet; CNN; Comedy Central; Country Music TV; Discovery Channel; Disney Channel; ESPN; Fox News Channel; FX; Lifetime; Nickelodeon; QVC; Root Sports Rocky Mountain; Spike TV; TBS Superstation; The Learning Channel; The Weather Channel; Turner Network TV; USA Network; WGN America.
Fee: $25.00 monthly.
Digital Basic Service
Subscribers: N.A.
Programming (via satellite): BBC America; Bio; Black Family Channel; Bravo; Discovery Digital Networks; DMX Music; ESPN 2; ESPN Classic Sports; ESPNews; Fox College Sports Atlantic; Fox College Sports Central; Fox College Sports Pacific; Fox Soccer; Fuse; Golf Channel; Great American Country; GSN; HGTV; History Channel; History Channel International; Independent Film Channel; Lifetime Movie Network; National Geographic Channel; ShopNBC; Speed; Style Network; The Word Network; Toon Disney; Trio; Turner Classic Movies; Versus; WE tv.
Fee: $15.95 monthly.
Digital Pay Service 1
Pay Units: N.A.
Programming (via satellite): Cinemax (multiplexed); Encore; Flix; HBO (multiplexed); Showtime (multiplexed); Starz (multiplexed); The Movie Channel (multiplexed).
Fee: $12.95 monthly (HBO, Cinemax, Showtime/TMC/Flix, or Starz/Encore).
Video-On-Demand: No
Pay-Per-View
iN DEMAND (delivered digitally); Playboy TV (delivered digitally).
Internet Service
Operational: Yes.
Fee: $29.95 monthly.
Telephone Service
None
Miles of Plant: 10.0 (coaxial); None (fiber optic).
Ownership: Satview Broadband Ltd. (MSO).

FRANCIS (town)—All West Communications. Formerly served by Kamas, UT [UT0053]. This cable system has converted to IPTV, 50 W 100 N, Kamas, UT 84036. Phones: 866-255-9378; 435-783-4361. Fax: 435-783-4928. E-mail: questions@allwest.net. Web Site: http://www.allwest.com. ICA: UT5030.
TV Market Ranking: Below 100 (FRANCIS (TOWN)).
Channel capacity: N.A. Channels available but not in use: N.A.
Internet Service
Operational: Yes.
Internet Service
Operational: Yes.

GLENWOOD—Central Telcom Services (CUTV), 35 S State St, PO Box 7, Fairview, UT 84629-0007. Phone: 435-427-3331. Fax: 435-427-3200. E-mail: g.lee@cut.net. Web Site: http://www.centracom.com. ICA: UT0084.
TV Market Ranking: Outside TV Markets (GLENWOOD). Franchise award date: N.A. Franchise expiration date: December 31, 2015. Began: January 1, 1988.
Channel capacity: 40 (not 2-way capable). Channels available but not in use: N.A.
Basic Service
Subscribers: 31.
Programming (received off-air): KBYU-TV (PBS) Provo; KJZZ-TV (MNT) Salt Lake City; KSL-TV (NBC) Salt Lake City; KSTU (FOX) Salt Lake City; KTVX (ABC) Salt Lake City; KUCW (CW) Ogden; KUED (PBS) Salt Lake City; KUEN (ETV) Ogden; KUTV (CBS) Salt Lake City.
Programming (via satellite): A&E Networks; ABC Family Channel; Animal Planet; CNN; Comedy Central; C-SPAN; Discovery Channel; Disney Channel; E! Entertainment Television; ESPN; HGTV; INSP; Lifetime; Nickelodeon; Outdoor Channel; QVC; Root Sports Rocky Mountain; Spike TV; TBS Superstation; The Learning Channel; Travel Channel; Turner Network TV; TV Land; USA Network; WGN America.
Fee: $49.95 installation; $29.95 monthly; $18.95 additional installation.
Pay Service 1
Pay Units: N.A.
Programming (via satellite): HBO.
Fee: $11.00 monthly.
Video-On-Demand: No
Internet Service
Operational: No, Both DSL & dial-up.
Telephone Service
None
Miles of Plant: 4.0 (coaxial); None (fiber optic).
General Manager: Eddie Cox. CATV Manager: George Lee. Chief Engineer: Kenny Roberts.
Ownership: CentraCom Interactive (MSO).

GOSHEN—Central Telcom Services (CUTV). Now served by GUNNISON, UT [UT0037]. ICA: UT0063.

GREEN RIVER—Emery Telcom, 445 E Hwy 29, PO Box 629, Orangeville, UT 84537. Phones: 435-564-3415; 435-748-2223. Web Site: http://www.emerytelcom.com. Also serves Emery County. ICA: UT0059.
TV Market Ranking: Outside TV Markets (Emery County, GREEN RIVER). Franchise award date: N.A. Franchise expiration date: N.A. Began: April 1, 1983.
Channel capacity: N.A. Channels available but not in use: N.A.
Basic Service
Subscribers: 238.
Programming (via satellite): ABC Family Channel; Bravo; CNN; Country Music TV; E! Entertainment Television; ESPN; Headline News; MTV; QVC; The Learning Channel; Turner Network TV; USA Network.
Programming (via translator): KBYU-TV (PBS) Provo; KSL-TV (NBC) Salt Lake City; KSTU (FOX) Salt Lake City; KTVX (ABC) Salt Lake City; KUED (PBS) Salt Lake City; KUTV (CBS) Salt Lake City.
Fee: $19.95 installation; $14.33 monthly.
Expanded Basic Service 1
Subscribers: 224.
Programming (via satellite): Discovery Channel; Disney Channel; Lifetime; Nickelodeon; Syfy.
Fee: $3.88 monthly.
Expanded Basic Service 2
Subscribers: 230.
Programming (via satellite): TBS Superstation; WGN America.
Fee: $2.15 monthly.
Pay Service 1
Pay Units: 34.
Programming (via satellite): Cinemax.
Fee: $10.50 monthly.
Pay Service 2
Pay Units: 64.
Programming (via satellite): HBO.
Fee: $10.50 monthly.
Internet Service
Operational: No, DSL.
Telephone Service
None
Miles of Plant: 12.0 (coaxial); None (fiber optic).
Manager: Greg Barker.
Ownership: Emery Telcom (MSO).

GUNNISON—Central Telcom Services (CUTV), 35 S State St, PO Box 7, Fairview, UT 84629-0007. Phone: 435-427-3331. Fax: 435-427-3200. Web Site: http://www.centracom.com. Also serves Annabella, Aurora, Austin, Centerfield, Central, Elsinore, Ephraim, Eureka, Fairview, Fountain Green, Goshen, Manti, Mayfield, Monroe, Moroni, Mount Pleasant, Redmond, Richfield, Salina, Sanpete County, Santaquin, Sevier County, Spring City & Utah County (portions). ICA: UT0037.
TV Market Ranking: Below 100 (Sanpete County, Utah County (portions), Eureka, Goshen, Santaquin); Outside TV Markets (Annabella, Aurora, Austin, Centerfield, Elsinore, Fairview, Fountain Green, GUNNISON, Manti, Monroe, Redmond, Sevier County, Spring City, Central, Ephraim, Mayfield, Moroni, Mount Pleasant, Richfield, Salina). Franchise award date: N.A. Franchise expiration date: N.A. Began: January 1, 1984.
Channel capacity: 72 (operating 2-way). Channels available but not in use: N.A.
Basic Service
Subscribers: 4,300.
Programming (received off-air): KJZZ-TV (MNT) Salt Lake City; KUEN (ETV) Ogden; KUPX-TV (ION) Provo.
Programming (via satellite): BYU Television.
Programming (via translator): KBYU-TV (PBS) Provo; KSL-TV (NBC) Salt Lake City; KSTU (FOX) Salt Lake City; KTVX (ABC) Salt Lake City; KUED (PBS) Salt Lake City; KUTV (CBS) Salt Lake City.
Fee: $49.95 installation; $10.70 monthly; $1.50 converter.
Expanded Basic Service 1
Subscribers: 3,300.
Programming (via satellite): A&E Networks; ABC Family Channel; AMC; Animal Planet;

Cartoon Network; CBS Sports Network; CNN; Comedy Central; Country Music TV; Discovery Channel; Disney Channel; ESPN; ESPN 2; Fox News Channel; Fox Sports Net; FX; Hallmark Channel; Lifetime; MTV; Nickelodeon; Outdoor Channel; QVC; Spike TV; TBS Superstation; The Learning Channel; The Mtn; The Weather Channel; Turner Network TV; TV Land; USA Network; VH1; WGN America.
Fee: $42.95 monthly.

Digital Basic Service
Subscribers: 850.
Programming (via satellite): BBC America; Bio; Bravo; cloo; Discovery Digital Networks; DMX Music; ESPN 2; ESPN Classic Sports; ESPNews; Fox Sports World; FSN Digital Atlantic; FSN Digital Central; FSN Digital Pacific; Fuse; GAS; Golf Channel; Great American Country; GSN; HGTV; History Channel; History Channel International; Independent Film Channel; Lifetime Movie Network; MBC America; MTV Networks Digital Suite; National Geographic Channel; Nick Jr.; ShopNBC; Speed; Style Network; Syfy; The Word Network; Toon Disney; Turner Classic Movies; Versus; WE tv.
Fee: $56.95 monthly.

Digital Pay Service 1
Pay Units: N.A.
Programming (via satellite): Cinemax (multiplexed); Encore (multiplexed); Flix; HBO (multiplexed); Showtime (multiplexed); Starz (multiplexed); The Movie Channel (multiplexed).
Fee: $11.95 monthly (Cinemax, Showtime/TMC, or Starz/Encore), $12.95 monthly (HBO).

Video-On-Demand: No

Pay-Per-View
Movies (delivered digitally); Special events (delivered digitally).

Internet Service
Operational: Yes.
Subscribers: 2,000.
Broadband Service: Precis Internet.
Fee: $39.95 monthly.

Telephone Service
Digital: Operational
Subscribers: 2.
Fee: $35.00 monthly
Miles of Plant: 350.0 (coaxial); 100.0 (fiber optic).
General Manager: Eddie Cox. CATV Manager: George Lee. Chief Engineer: Kenny Roberts.
Ownership: CentraCom Interactive (MSO).

HEBER CITY—Comcast Cable, 9602 S 300 W, Sandy, UT 84070. Phone: 801-401-2500. Fax: 801-401-3397. Web Site: http://www.comcast.com. Also serves Midway & Wasatch County. ICA: UT0018.
TV Market Ranking: 48 (HEBER CITY, Midway, Wasatch County (portions)); Below 100 (Wasatch County (portions)). Franchise award date: N.A. Franchise expiration date: N.A. Began: August 1, 1982.
Channel capacity: N.A. Channels available but not in use: N.A.

Basic Service
Subscribers: N.A. Included in Salt Lake City
Programming (received off-air): KBYU-TV (PBS) Provo; KJZZ-TV (MNT) Salt Lake City; KSL-TV (NBC) Salt Lake City; KSTU (FOX) Salt Lake City; KTVX (ABC) Salt Lake City; KUCW (CW) Ogden; KUED (PBS) Salt Lake City; KUTV (CBS) Salt Lake City.
Programming (via satellite): Discovery Channel; Hallmark Channel; QVC; TBS Superstation.
Fee: $43.99 installation; $12.67 monthly; $18.95 additional installation.

Expanded Basic Service 1
Subscribers: 1,451.
Programming (via satellite): ABC Family Channel; AMC; Animal Planet; Cartoon Network; CNBC; CNN; C-SPAN; Disney Channel; ESPN; Fox News Channel; Fox Sports Net; FX; Headline News; Lifetime; MoviePlex; MTV; Nickelodeon; Spike TV; The Learning Channel; The Weather Channel; Turner Network TV; USA Network.
Fee: $43.60 monthly.

Digital Basic Service
Subscribers: 336.
Programming (via satellite): American-Life TV Network; BBC America; Black Family Channel; Bravo; Discovery Digital Networks; DMX Music; ESPN 2; ESPN Classic Sports; ESPNews; Fox Sports World; FSN Digital Atlantic; FSN Digital Central; FSN Digital Pacific; G4; Golf Channel; Great American Country; GSN; HGTV; HTV Musica; Independent Film Channel; International Television (ITV); Music Choice; National Geographic Channel; Nick Jr.; ShopNBC; Style Network; Syfy; The Word Network; Trinity Broadcasting Network; Turner Classic Movies; TV Land; Versus; WE tv.
Fee: $14.95 monthly.

Digital Expanded Basic Service
Subscribers: N.A.
Programming (via satellite): Bio; Bloomberg Television; Discovery Fit & Health; Encore Action; Fox Movie Channel; Fuse; GAS; Halogen Network; History Channel International; Lifetime Movie Network; Lime; MTV Networks Digital Suite; NickToons TV; Outdoor Channel; Ovation; Speed; Sundance Channel; Toon Disney.
Fee: $5.00 monthly.

Pay Service 1
Pay Units: 104.
Programming (via satellite): Cinemax; HBO; Starz.
Fee: $10.99 monthly (Starz), $13.99 monthly (Cinemax), $14.99 monthly (HBO).

Pay Service 2
Pay Units: N.A.
Programming (via satellite): Encore.

Digital Pay Service 1
Pay Units: N.A.
Programming (via satellite): Canales N; Cinemax (multiplexed); Flix; HBO (multiplexed); Showtime (multiplexed); Starz (multiplexed); The Movie Channel (multiplexed).
Fee: $6.99 monthly (Canales N), $16.95 monthly (HBO, Cinemax, Starz, Showtime, or TMC).

Video-On-Demand: No

Pay-Per-View
Addressable homes: 336.
Sports PPV (delivered digitally); iN DEMAND (delivered digitally); Urban Xtra (delivered digitally); Fresh (delivered digitally); Shorteez (delivered digitally); Playboy TV (delivered digitally); ESPN Now (delivered digitally).

Internet Service
Operational: Yes.
Broadband Service: Comcast High Speed Internet.
Fee: $42.95 monthly.

Telephone Service
Digital: Operational
Miles of plant included in Salt Lake City
Area Vice President: Scott Tenney. Technical Operations Director: Mike Spaulding. Marketing Director: Dan Williams. Marketing Manager: Lisa Jenkins. Community & Government Affairs Director: Steve Proper.
Ownership: Comcast Cable Communications Inc. (MSO).

HUNTSVILLE—HLS Communications, 5500 West 10400 North, Ellwood, UT 84337. Phone: 435-257-5280. Also serves Eden. ICA: UT0064.
TV Market Ranking: 48 (Eden, HUNTSVILLE). Franchise award date: N.A. Franchise expiration date: N.A. Began: October 1, 1986.
Channel capacity: 42 (not 2-way capable). Channels available but not in use: N.A.

Basic Service
Subscribers: 39.
Programming (received off-air): KBYU-TV (PBS) Provo; KJZZ-TV (MNT) Salt Lake City; KSL-TV (NBC) Salt Lake City; KSTU (FOX) Salt Lake City; KTVX (ABC) Salt Lake City; KUCW (CW) Ogden; KUED (PBS) Salt Lake City; KUTV (CBS) Salt Lake City.
Programming (via satellite): A&E Networks; ABC Family Channel; AMC; Animal Planet; CNBC; CNN; Cooking Channel; C-SPAN; Discovery Channel; Disney Channel; DIY Network; ESPN; ESPN 2; G4; Great American Country; Headline News; HGTV; History Channel; Outdoor Channel; RFD-TV; ShopNBC; Spike TV; Syfy; TBS Superstation; The Learning Channel; Travel Channel; Turner Network TV; WGN America.
Fee: $25.00 installation; $26.95 monthly.

Pay Service 1
Pay Units: N.A.
Programming (via satellite): HBO.
Fee: $14.00 monthly.

Internet Service
Operational: No.

Telephone Service
None
Miles of Plant: 3.0 (coaxial); None (fiber optic).
Manager: Steve Haramoto. Chief Technician: Jeekenan Haramoto.
Ownership: Steven Haramoto.

HURRICANE—Charter Communications. Now served by ST. GEORGE, UT [UT0007]. ICA: UT0027.

KAMAS—All West Communications. Formerly [UT0053]. This cable system has converted to IPTV, 50 W 100 N, Kamas, UT 84036. Phones: 866-255-9378; 435-783-4361. Fax: 435-783-4928. E-mail: questions@allwest.net. Web Site: http://www.allwest.com. ICA: UT5013.
TV Market Ranking: Below 100 (KAMAS).
Channel capacity: N.A. Channels available but not in use: N.A.

Internet Service
Operational: Yes.

Telephone Service
Digital: Operational
Miles of Plant: None (coaxial); 130.0 (fiber optic).

KAMAS—All West Communications. This cable system has converted to IPTV. See Kamas, UT [UT5013]. ICA: UT0053.

KANAB—South Central Communications, 45 North 100 W, PO Box 555, Escalante, UT 84726-0555. Phone: 435-637-6813. Fax: 435-826-4900. Web Site: http://www.scwireless.com. Also serves Fredonia. ICA: UT0033.
TV Market Ranking: Outside TV Markets (Fredonia, KANAB). Franchise award date: N.A. Franchise expiration date: N.A. Began: February 1, 1982.
Channel capacity: 35 (operating 2-way). Channels available but not in use: N.A.

Basic Service
Subscribers: 341.
Programming (received off-air): KJZZ-TV (MNT) Salt Lake City; KPNZ (IND) Ogden; KUCW (CW) Ogden; KUEN (ETV) Ogden; KUPX-TV (ION) Provo.
Programming (via translator): KBYU-TV (PBS) Provo; KSL-TV (NBC) Salt Lake City; KSTU (FOX) Salt Lake City; KTVX (ABC) Salt Lake City; KUED (PBS) Salt Lake City; KUTV (CBS) Salt Lake City.
Fee: $49.95 installation; $10.95 monthly; $21.95 additional installation.

Expanded Basic Service 1
Subscribers: N.A.
Programming (via satellite): A&E Networks; ABC Family Channel; AMC; Animal Planet; CNN; Comedy Central; Country Music TV; Discovery Channel; Disney Channel; ESPN; Fox News Channel; FX; Lifetime; Nickelodeon; QVC; Root Sports Rocky Mountain; Spike TV; TBS Superstation; The Learning Channel; The Weather Channel; Turner Network TV; USA Network; WGN America.
Fee: $25.25 monthly.

Digital Basic Service
Subscribers: N.A.
Programming (via satellite): BBC America; Bio; Bravo; Discovery Digital Networks; DMX Music; ESPN 2; ESPN Classic Sports; ESPNews; Fox Soccer; FSN Digital Atlantic; FSN Digital Central; FSN Digital Pacific; Fuse; Golf Channel; Great American Country; GSN; HGTV; History Channel; History Channel International; Independent Film Channel; Lifetime Movie Network; MBC America; National Geographic Channel; ShopNBC; Speed; Style Network; The Word Network; Toon Disney; Trio; Turner Classic Movies; Versus; WE tv.
Fee: $15.95 monthly.

Digital Pay Service 1
Pay Units: N.A.
Programming (via satellite): Cinemax (multiplexed); Encore (multiplexed); Flix; HBO (multiplexed); Showtime (multiplexed); Starz (multiplexed); The Movie Channel (multiplexed).
Fee: $12.95 monthly (HBO, Cinemax, Showtime/TMC/Flix, or Starz/Encore).

Video-On-Demand: No

Pay-Per-View
iN DEMAND (delivered digitally); Playboy TV (delivered digitally).

Internet Service
Operational: Yes.
Fee: $29.95 monthly.

Telephone Service
None
Miles of Plant: 18.0 (coaxial); None (fiber optic).
Manager: Kerry Alvey.; Jeff Bushnell.
Ownership: South Central Communications (MSO).

KANARRAVILLE—South Central Communications, 45 North 100 W, PO Box 555, Escalante, UT 84726-0555. Phone: 435-826-4211. Fax: 435-826-4900. Web Site: http://www.scwireless.com. ICA: UT0067.
TV Market Ranking: Below 100 (KANARRAVILLE). Franchise award date: N.A. Franchise expiration date: N.A. Began: January 1, 1991.
Channel capacity: N.A. Channels available but not in use: N.A.

Basic Service
Subscribers: N.A. Included in Escalante
Programming (received off-air): KJZZ-TV (MNT) Salt Lake City.
Programming (via satellite): A&E Networks; ABC Family Channel; Cartoon Network; CNN; Comedy Central; C-SPAN; Discovery Channel; Disney Channel; E! Entertainment Television; ESPN; Mountain-West Sports Network; Nickelodeon; QVC; Root Sports Rocky Mountain; Spike TV; TBS Superstation; The Learning Channel; Turner Classic Movies; Turner Network TV; TV Land; WGN America.
Programming (via translator): KBYU-TV (PBS) Provo; KSL-TV (NBC) Salt Lake City; KSTU (FOX) Salt Lake City; KTVX (ABC) Salt Lake City; KUED (PBS) Salt Lake City; KUTV (CBS) Salt Lake City.
Fee: $45.00 installation; $31.95 monthly.
Pay Service 1
Pay Units: 6.
Programming (via satellite): Showtime.
Fee: $11.00 monthly.
Video-On-Demand: No
Internet Service
Operational: Yes, DSL.
Fee: $29.95 monthly.
Telephone Service
None
Miles of Plant: 6.0 (coaxial); None (fiber optic).
Manager & Chief Technician: Greg Barton.
Ownership: South Central Communications (MSO).

LINDON—Formerly served by Nuvont Communications. IPTV service no longer in operation. ICA: UT5028.

LINDON—UTOPIA, 2175 S Redwood Rd, West Valley City, UT 84119. Phones: 801-613-3800; 801-955-3790. Fax: 801-908-7225. Web Site: http://www.utopianet.org. Also serves Midvale, Murray, Orem, Payson & West Valley City. ICA: UT0092.
TV Market Ranking: 48 (LINDON, Midvale, Murray, Orem, West Valley City); Below 100 (Payson). Franchise award date: N.A. Franchise expiration date: N.A. Began: August 1, 2005.
Channel capacity: N.A. Channels available but not in use: N.A.
Basic Service
Subscribers: 2,000.
Programming (received off-air): KBYU-TV (PBS) Provo; KJZZ-TV (MNT) Salt Lake City; KPNZ (IND) Ogden; KSL-TV (NBC) Salt Lake City; KSTU (FOX) Salt Lake City; KTMW (IND) Salt Lake City; KTVX (ABC) Salt Lake City; KUED (PBS) Salt Lake City; KUPX-TV (ION) Provo; KUTH-DT (UNV) Provo; KUTV (CBS) Salt Lake City.
Programming (via satellite): BYU Television.
Digital Basic Service
Subscribers: 1,000.
Programming (via satellite): HD Theater; HDNet; HDNet Movies; Turner Network TV HD; Universal HD.
Fee: $19.00 monthly.
Digital Expanded Basic Service
Subscribers: N.A.
Programming (via satellite): A&E Networks; ABC Family Channel; AMC; Animal Planet; Bravo; Canales N; Cartoon Network; CNBC; CNN; Comedy Central; Country Music TV; C-SPAN; C-SPAN 2; C-SPAN 3; Discovery Channel; Discovery Fit & Health; Disney Channel; DIY Network; DMX Music; E! Entertainment Television; ESPN; ESPN 2; ESPN Classic Sports; Familyland Television Network; FamilyNet; Food Network; Fox Movie Channel; Fox News Channel; FX; GalaVision; Golf Channel; Great American Country; Hallmark Channel; Headline News; HGTV; History Channel; Lifetime; MSNBC; MTV; National Geographic Channel; Nickelodeon; Outdoor Channel; Ovation; Oxygen; Root Sports Rocky Mountain; SoapNet; Spike TV; Syfy; TBS Superstation; Telefutura; The Learning Channel; The Weather Channel; Travel Channel; truTV; Turner Network TV; TV Land; USA Network; Versus; VH1.
Digital Expanded Basic Service 2
Subscribers: N.A.
Programming (via satellite): AmericanLife TV Network; BBC America; Bio; Black Family Channel; Boomerang; Cooking Channel; C-SPAN 3; Current; Discovery Digital Networks; ESPNews; Fox College Sports Atlantic; Fox College Sports Central; Fox College Sports Pacific; Fox Soccer; Fuse; G4; GAS; GSN; Halogen Network; History Channel International; Independent Film Channel; Lifetime Movie Network; Lime; MTV Networks Digital Suite; Nick Jr.; NickToons TV; ShopNBC; Speed; Style Network; Toon Disney; Trinity Broadcasting Network; Trio; Turner Classic Movies; WE tv.
Digital Pay Service 1
Pay Units: N.A.
Programming (via satellite): Cinemax (multiplexed); Encore (multiplexed); Flix; HBO (multiplexed); Showtime (multiplexed); Showtime HD; Starz (multiplexed); Starz HDTV; Sundance Channel; The Movie Channel (multiplexed).
Video-On-Demand: Yes
Internet Service
Operational: Yes.
Telephone Service
Digital: Operational
Miles of Plant: None (coaxial); 360.0 (fiber optic). Additional miles planned: 1,132.0 (fiber optic).
Chief Operating Officer: Roger Black. Executive Director: Paul Morris. Executive Assistant: Cindy Patterson.
Ownership: UTOPIA (Utah Telecommunication Open Infrastructure Agency.

LOGAN—Comcast Cable, 9602 S 300 W, Sandy, UT 84070. Phone: 801-401-2500. Fax: 801-401-3397. Web Site: http://www.comcast.com. Also serves Bear River City, Cache County (portions), Clarkston, Corinne, Deweyville, Fielding, Garland, Honeyville, Hyde Park, Hyrum, Lewiston, Mendon, Millville, Newton, Nibley, North Logan, Paradise, Plymouth, Providence, Richmond, River Heights, Smithfield, Tremonton & Wellsville. ICA: UT0006.
TV Market Ranking: Below 100 (Bear River City, Cache County (portions), Corinne, Deweyville, Fielding, Garland, Honeyville, Hyrum, Lewiston, LOGAN, Mendon, Millville, Nibley, Paradise, Plymouth, Providence, Richmond, River Heights, Smithfield, Tremonton, Wellsville); Outside TV Markets (Cache County (portions), Clarkston, Hyde Park, Newton, North Logan). Franchise award date: December 22, 1970. Franchise expiration date: N.A. Began: January 7, 1971.
Channel capacity: 110 (operating 2-way). Channels available but not in use: N.A.
Basic Service
Subscribers: N.A. Included in Salt Lake City
Programming (received off-air): KBYU-TV (PBS) Provo; KCVB-CA (ION) Logan; KJZZ-TV (MNT) Salt Lake City; KPNZ (IND) Ogden; KSL-TV (NBC) Salt Lake City; KSTU (FOX) Salt Lake City; KTMW (IND) Salt Lake City; KTVX (ABC) Salt Lake City; KUCW (CW) Ogden; KUED (PBS) Salt Lake City; KUEN (ETV) Ogden; KUPX-TV (ION) Provo; KUTH-DT (UNV) Provo; KUTV (CBS) Salt Lake City; allband FM.
Programming (via satellite): C-SPAN; C-SPAN 2; TBS Superstation.
Fee: $43.99 installation; $8.68 monthly.
Expanded Basic Service 1
Subscribers: N.A.
Programming (via satellite): A&E Networks; ABC Family Channel; AMC; Animal Planet; BET Networks; BYU Television; Cartoon Network; CNBC; CNN; Comedy Central; Country Music TV; Discovery Channel; Disney Channel; E! Entertainment Television; ESPN; ESPN 2; Food Network; Fox News Channel; Fox Sports Net; GalaVision; Golf Channel; Great American Country; GSN; Hallmark Channel; Headline News; HGTV; History Channel; INSP; Lifetime; MSNBC; MTV; Nickelodeon; Oxygen; QVC; Spike TV; Style Network; Syfy; The Learning Channel; The Weather Channel; Travel Channel; Turner Network TV; TV Land; USA Network; Versus; VH1.
Fee: $43.60 monthly.
Digital Basic Service
Subscribers: 7,500.
Programming (via satellite): BBC America; Black Family Channel; Bravo; Cooking Channel; Discovery Digital Networks; DIY Network; DMX Music; Encore Action; ESPN Classic Sports; ESPNews; Fox Movie Channel; Fox Sports World; G4; Independent Film Channel; International Television (ITV); Music Choice; National Geographic Channel; NBA TV; Nick Jr.; ShopNBC; The Word Network; Trinity Broadcasting Network; Turner Classic Movies; WE tv.
Fee: $14.95 monthly.
Digital Expanded Basic Service
Subscribers: N.A.
Programming (via satellite): AmericanLife TV Network; Bio; Bloomberg Television; Discovery Fit & Health; FSN Digital Atlantic; FSN Digital Central; FSN Digital Pacific; Fuse; GAS; Halogen Network; History Channel International; Lifetime Movie Network; Lime; MTV Networks Digital Suite; NickToons TV; Outdoor Channel; Ovation; Speed; Sundance Channel; Toon Disney.
Fee: $5.00 monthly.
Digital Pay Service 1
Pay Units: 1,195.
Programming (via satellite): Cinemax (multiplexed).
Fee: $7.50 installation; $16.95 monthly.
Digital Pay Service 2
Pay Units: 1,069.
Programming (via satellite): Canales N.
Fee: $16.95 monthly.
Digital Pay Service 3
Pay Units: 536.
Programming (via satellite): Starz (multiplexed).
Fee: $16.95 monthly.
Digital Pay Service 4
Pay Units: 1,687.
Programming (via satellite): HBO (multiplexed).
Fee: $16.95 monthly.
Digital Pay Service 5
Pay Units: 1,290.
Programming (via satellite): Showtime (multiplexed).
Fee: $16.95 monthly.
Digital Pay Service 6
Pay Units: 578.
Programming (via satellite): Flix; The Movie Channel (multiplexed).
Fee: $16.95 monthly.
Video-On-Demand: Yes
Pay-Per-View
Addressable homes: 7,500.
iN DEMAND (delivered digitally); Urban Xtra (delivered digitally); Fresh (delivered digitally); Shorteez (delivered digitally); Playboy TV (delivered digitally); ESPN Now (delivered digitally); Sports PPV (delivered digitally); NBA League Pass (delivered digitally).
Internet Service
Operational: Yes. Began: March 1, 1999.
Subscribers: 2,050.
Broadband Service: Comcast High Speed Internet.
Fee: $42.95 monthly; $3.00 modem lease.
Telephone Service
Digital: Operational
Fee: $44.95 monthly
Miles of plant included in Salt Lake City
Area Vice President: Scott Tenney. Technical Operations Director: Mike Spaulding. Marketing Director: Dan Williams. Marketing Manager: Lisa Jenkins. Community & Government Affairs Director: Steve Proper.
Ownership: Comcast Cable Communications Inc. (MSO).

LYMAN—South Central Communications, 45 North 100 W, PO Box 555, Escalante, UT 84726-0555. Phones: 800-718-7288; 435-826-4211. Fax: 435-826-4900. Web Site: http://www.southcentralcommunications.com. Also serves Bicknell & Loa. ICA: UT0073.
TV Market Ranking: Outside TV Markets (Bicknell, Loa, LYMAN). Franchise award date: N.A. Franchise expiration date: N.A. Began: May 1, 1984.
Channel capacity: N.A. Channels available but not in use: N.A.
Basic Service
Subscribers: N.A. Included in Escalante
Programming (received off-air): KJZZ-TV (MNT) Salt Lake City; KUEN (ETV) Ogden.
Programming (via satellite): A&E Networks; ABC Family Channel; AMC; Animal Planet; Cartoon Network; CNBC; CNN; Country Music TV; CW+; Discovery Channel; Disney Channel; E! Entertainment Television; ESPN; ESPN 2; Fox News Channel; Headline News; History Channel; INSP; Lifetime; Nickelodeon; Outdoor Channel; QVC; RFD-TV; Root Sports Rocky Mountain; Spike TV; TBS Superstation; The Learning Channel; Travel Channel; Turner Network TV; TV Land; USA Network; WGN America.
Programming (via translator): KBYU-TV (PBS) Provo; KSL-TV (NBC) Salt Lake City; KSTU (FOX) Salt Lake City; KTVX (ABC)

Salt Lake City; KUED (PBS) Salt Lake City; KUTV (CBS) Salt Lake City.
Fee: $45.00 installation; $32.45 monthly; $18.95 additional installation.
Pay Service 1
Pay Units: 5.
Programming (via satellite): Cinemax.
Fee: $11.00 monthly.
Pay Service 2
Pay Units: 9.
Programming (via satellite): HBO.
Fee: $11.00 monthly.
Video-On-Demand: No
Internet Service
Operational: No.
Telephone Service
None
Miles of Plant: 24.0 (coaxial); None (fiber optic).
Manager & Chief Technician: Greg Barton.
Ownership: South Central Communications (MSO).

MANILA—Formerly served by Myvocom. No longer in operation. ICA: UT0058.

MARION—All West Communications. Formerly served by Kamas, UT [UT0053]. This cable system has converted to IPTV, 50 W 100 N, Kamas, UT 84036. Phone: 435-783-4361. Fax: 435-783-4928. E-mail: questions@allwest.net. Web Site: http://www.allwest.com. ICA: UT5033.
TV Market Ranking: 48 (MARION).
Channel capacity: N.A. Channels available but not in use: N.A.
Internet Service
Operational: Yes.

MAYFIELD—Central Telcom Services (CUTV). Now served by GUNNISON, UT [UT0037]. ICA: UT0088.

MIDVALE—Formerly served by Nuvont Communications. IPTV operations no longer in operation. ICA: UT5023.

MILFORD—South Central Communications, 45 North 100 W, PO Box 555, Escalante, UT 84726-0555. Phone: 435-826-4211. Fax: 435-826-4900. Web Site: http://www.scwireless.com. ICA: UT0074.
TV Market Ranking: Outside TV Markets (MILFORD). Franchise award date: N.A. Franchise expiration date: March 19, 2011. Began: March 1, 1983.
Channel capacity: 40 (operating 2-way). Channels available but not in use: N.A.
Basic Service
Subscribers: 253.
Programming (received off-air): KBYU-TV (PBS) Provo; KPNZ (IND) Ogden; KUCW (CW) Ogden; KUEN (ETV) Ogden; KUPX-TV (ION) Provo.
Programming (via translator): KJZZ-TV (MNT) Salt Lake City; KSL-TV (NBC) Salt Lake City; KSTU (FOX) Salt Lake City; KTVX (ABC) Salt Lake City; KUED (PBS) Salt Lake City; KUTV (CBS) Salt Lake City.
Fee: $49.95 installation; $10.95 monthly; $21.95 additional installation.
Expanded Basic Service 1
Subscribers: N.A.
Programming (via satellite): A&E Networks; ABC Family Channel; AMC; Animal Planet; CNN; Comedy Central; Country Music TV; Discovery Channel; Disney Channel; ESPN; Fox News Channel; FX; Lifetime; Nickelodeon; QVC; Root Sports Rocky Mountain; Spike TV; TBS Superstation; The Learning Channel; The Weather Channel; Turner Network TV; USA Network; WGN America.
Fee: $25.00 monthly.
Digital Basic Service
Subscribers: N.A.
Programming (via satellite): BBC America; Bio; Black Family Channel; Bravo; Discovery Digital Networks; DMX Music; ESPN 2; ESPN Classic Sports; ESPNews; Fox College Sports Atlantic; Fox College Sports Central; Fox College Sports Pacific; Fox Soccer; Fuse; Golf Channel; Great American Country; GSN; HGTV; History Channel; History Channel International; Independent Film Channel; Lifetime Movie Network; National Geographic Channel; ShopNBC; Speed; Style Network; The Word Network; Toon Disney; Trio; Turner Classic Movies; Versus; WE tv.
Fee: $15.95 monthly.
Digital Pay Service 1
Pay Units: N.A.
Programming (via satellite): Cinemax (multiplexed); Encore (multiplexed); Flix; HBO (multiplexed); Showtime (multiplexed); Starz (multiplexed); The Movie Channel (multiplexed).
Fee: $12.95 monthly (HBO, Cinemax, Showtime/TMC/Flix, or Starz/Encore).
Video-On-Demand: No
Pay-Per-View
iN DEMAND (delivered digitally); Playboy TV (delivered digitally).
Internet Service
Operational: Yes.
Fee: $29.95 monthly.
Telephone Service
None
Miles of Plant: 7.0 (coaxial); None (fiber optic).
Manager: Kerry Alvey.; Jeff Bushnell.
Ownership: South Central Communications (MSO).

MINERSVILLE—South Central Communications, 45 North 100 W, PO Box 555, Escalante, UT 84726-0555. Phone: 435-826-4211. Fax: 435-826-4900. Web Site: http://www.scwireless.com. ICA: UT0062.
TV Market Ranking: Outside TV Markets (MINERSVILLE). Franchise award date: N.A. Franchise expiration date: N.A. Began: July 10, 1991.
Channel capacity: 40 (operating 2-way). Channels available but not in use: N.A.
Basic Service
Subscribers: 124.
Programming (received off-air): KJZZ-TV (MNT) Salt Lake City; KPNZ (IND) Ogden; KUCW (CW) Ogden; KUEN (ETV) Ogden; KUPX-TV (ION) Provo.
Programming (via translator): KBYU-TV (PBS) Provo; KSL-TV (NBC) Salt Lake City; KSTU (FOX) Salt Lake City; KTVX (ABC) Salt Lake City; KUED (PBS) Salt Lake City; KUTV (CBS) Salt Lake City.
Fee: $49.95 installation; $10.95 monthly; $21.95 additional installation.
Expanded Basic Service 1
Subscribers: N.A.
Programming (via satellite): A&E Networks; ABC Family Channel; AMC; CNN; Comedy Central; Country Music TV; Discovery Channel; Disney Channel; ESPN; Fox News Channel; FX; Lifetime; Nickelodeon; QVC; Root Sports Rocky Mountain; Spike TV; TBS Superstation; The Learning Channel; The Weather Channel; Turner Network TV; USA Network; WGN America.
Fee: $25.00 monthly.
Digital Basic Service
Subscribers: N.A.
Programming (via satellite): Animal Planet; BBC America; Bio; Black Family Channel; Bravo; Discovery Digital Networks; DMX Music; ESPN 2; ESPN Classic Sports; ESPNews; Fox College Sports Atlantic; Fox College Sports Central; Fox College Sports Pacific; Fox Soccer; Fuse; Golf Channel; Great American Country; GSN; HGTV; History Channel; History Channel International; Independent Film Channel; Lifetime Movie Network; National Geographic Channel; ShopNBC; Speed; Style Network; The Word Network; Toon Disney; Trio; Turner Classic Movies; Versus; WE tv.
Fee: $15.95 monthly.
Digital Pay Service 1
Pay Units: N.A.
Programming (via satellite): Cinemax (multiplexed); Encore (multiplexed); Flix; HBO (multiplexed); Showtime (multiplexed); Starz (multiplexed); The Movie Channel (multiplexed).
Fee: $12.95 monthly (HBO, Cinemax, Showtime/TMC/Flix, or Starz/Encore).
Video-On-Demand: No
Pay-Per-View
iN DEMAND (delivered digitally); Playboy TV (delivered digitally).
Internet Service
Operational: Yes.
Fee: $29.95 monthly.
Telephone Service
None
Miles of Plant: 5.0 (coaxial); None (fiber optic).
Manager: Kerry Alvey.; Jeff Bushnell.
Ownership: South Central Communications (MSO).

MOAB—Emery Telcom, 445 E Hwy 29, PO Box 629, Orangeville, UT 84537. Phones: 800-924-7662; 435-637-6813. Web Site: http://www.emerytelcom.com. Also serves Grand County. ICA: UT0016.
TV Market Ranking: Below 100 (Grand County (portions)); Outside TV Markets (Grand County (portions), MOAB). Franchise award date: April 1, 1975. Franchise expiration date: N.A. Began: April 1, 1955.
Channel capacity: 40 (operating 2-way). Channels available but not in use: N.A.
Basic Service
Subscribers: 2,400.
Programming (received off-air): KBYU-TV (PBS) Provo; KJZZ-TV (MNT) Salt Lake City; KPNZ (IND) Ogden; KSTU (FOX) Salt Lake City; KUCW (CW) Ogden; KUEN (ETV) Ogden; KUPX-TV (ION) Provo; 7 FMs.
Programming (via microwave): KSL-TV (NBC) Salt Lake City; KTVX (ABC) Salt Lake City; KUED (PBS) Salt Lake City; KUTV (CBS) Salt Lake City.
Programming (via satellite): C-SPAN; QVC; TBS Superstation; The Weather Channel; WGN America.
Fee: $29.95 installation; $12.75 monthly; $1.50 converter.
Expanded Basic Service 1
Subscribers: 1,645.
Programming (via satellite): A&E Networks; ABC Family Channel; AMC; Animal Planet; Bravo; BYU Television; Cartoon Network; CNBC; CNN; Comedy Central; Country Music TV; C-SPAN 2; Discovery Channel; Disney Channel; E! Entertainment Television; ESPN; ESPN 2; Eternal Word TV Network; Food Network; Fox News Channel; FX; G4; GSN; Hallmark Channel; Headline News; HGTV; History Channel; Lifetime; MSNBC; MTV; National Geographic Channel; Nickelodeon; Outdoor Channel; Oxygen; Root Sports Rocky Mountain; SoapNet; Speed; Spike TV; Syfy; The Learning Channel; Travel Channel; truTV; Turner Network TV; TV Land; Univision Studios; USA Network; VH1.
Fee: $24.20 monthly.
Digital Basic Service
Subscribers: N.A.
Programming (via satellite): BBC America; Bio; Discovery Digital Networks; DMX Music; ESPN Classic Sports; ESPNews; Fox College Sports Atlantic; Fox College Sports Central; Fox College Sports Pacific; Fox Sports World; Fuse; GAS; Golf Channel; Great American Country; History Channel International; Independent Film Channel; Lifetime Movie Network; MTV2; Nick Jr.; Science Television; ShopNBC; The Word Network; Toon Disney; Turner Classic Movies; Versus; VH1 Classic; VH1 Country; WE tv.
Fee: $15.95 monthly.
Pay Service 1
Pay Units: 80.
Programming (via satellite): Cinemax (multiplexed).
Fee: $13.15 monthly.
Pay Service 2
Pay Units: 342.
Programming (via satellite): Encore (multiplexed); Starz (multiplexed).
Fee: $1.75 monthly (Encore), $6.75 monthly (Starz).
Pay Service 3
Pay Units: 217.
Programming (via satellite): HBO (multiplexed).
Fee: $13.15 monthly.
Pay Service 4
Pay Units: 96.
Programming (via satellite): Showtime; The Movie Channel.
Fee: $13.15 monthly.
Digital Pay Service 1
Pay Units: N.A.
Programming (via satellite): Cinemax (multiplexed); Encore (multiplexed); Flix; HBO (multiplexed); Showtime (multiplexed); Starz (multiplexed); The Movie Channel (multiplexed).
Fee: $12.95 monthly (each).
Video-On-Demand: No
Pay-Per-View
iN DEMAND (delivered digitally); Playboy TV (delivered digitally).
Internet Service
Operational: Yes.
Telephone Service
None
Miles of Plant: 85.0 (coaxial); None (fiber optic).
Manager: Greg Barton.
Ownership: Emery Telcom (MSO).

MONA—Central Telcom Services (CUTV), 35 S State St, PO Box 7, Fairview, UT 84629-0007. Phones: 800-427-8449; 435-427-3331. Fax: 435-427-3200. E-mail: g.lee@cut.net. Web Site: http://www.centracom.com. ICA: UT0065.
TV Market Ranking: Below 100 (MONA). Franchise award date: N.A. Franchise expiration date: September 26, 2018. Began: June 1, 1982.
Channel capacity: 40 (not 2-way capable). Channels available but not in use: N.A.
Basic Service
Subscribers: 17.
Programming (received off-air): KBYU-TV (PBS) Provo; KJZZ-TV (MNT) Salt Lake City; KSL-TV (NBC) Salt Lake City; KSTU (FOX)

Salt Lake City; KTVX (ABC) Salt Lake City; KUED (PBS) Salt Lake City; KUTV (CBS) Salt Lake City.
Programming (via satellite): A&E Networks; ABC Family Channel; Cartoon Network; CNN; Country Music TV; Discovery Channel; Disney Channel; ESPN; HGTV; Spike TV; TBS Superstation; Turner Classic Movies; Turner Network TV; USA Network; WGN America.
Fee: $49.95 installation; $29.45 monthly; $18.95 additional installation.

Pay Service 1
Pay Units: N.A.
Programming (via satellite): HBO.
Fee: $11.00 monthly.

Video-On-Demand: No

Internet Service
Operational: No, Both DSL & dial-up.

Telephone Service
Analog: Operational
Digital: Not Operational

Miles of Plant: 5.0 (coaxial); None (fiber optic).
General Manager: Eddie Cox. CATV Manager: George Lee. Chief Engineer: Kenny Rogers.
Ownership: CentraCom Interactive (MSO).

MONTICELLO—Emery Telcom, 445 E Hwy 29, PO Box 629, Orangeville, UT 84537. Phones: 877-895-2110; 435-748-2223. Web Site: http://www.emerytelcom.com. ICA: UT0044.
TV Market Ranking: Outside TV Markets (MONTICELLO). Franchise award date: N.A. Franchise expiration date: N.A. Began: August 20, 1980.
Channel capacity: 40 (operating 2-way). Channels available but not in use: N.A.

Basic Service
Subscribers: 304.
Programming (received off-air): KJZZ-TV (MNT) Salt Lake City; KPNZ (IND) Ogden; KUEN (ETV) Ogden; KUPX-TV (ION) Provo; KUWB-LD Bloomington.
Programming (via translator): KBYU-TV (PBS) Provo; KSL-TV (NBC) Salt Lake City; KSTU (FOX) Salt Lake City; KTVX (ABC) Salt Lake City; KUED (PBS) Salt Lake City; KUTV (CBS) Salt Lake City.
Fee: $29.95 installation; $10.70 monthly.

Expanded Basic Service 1
Subscribers: N.A.
Programming (via satellite): A&E Networks; ABC Family Channel; AMC; Animal Planet; Cartoon Network; CNBC; CNN; Comedy Central; Country Music TV; Discovery Channel; Disney Channel; ESPN; Fox News Channel; FX; Hallmark Channel; Lifetime; Nickelodeon; QVC; Root Sports Rocky Mountain; Spike TV; TBS Superstation; The Learning Channel; The Weather Channel; Turner Network TV; USA Network; WGN America.
Fee: $28.25 monthly.

Digital Basic Service
Subscribers: N.A.
Programming (via satellite): BBC America; Bio; Bravo; Discovery Digital Networks; DMX Music; ESPN 2; ESPN Classic Sports; ESPNews; Fox Sports World; FSN Digital Atlantic; FSN Digital Central; FSN Digital Pacific; Fuse; Golf Channel; Great American Country; GSN; HGTV; History Channel; History Channel International; Independent Film Channel; Lifetime Movie Network; MBC America; National Geographic Channel; ShopNBC; Speed; Style Network; Syfy; The Word Network; Toon Disney; Trio; Turner Classic Movies; Versus; WE tv.
Fee: $15.95 monthly.

Digital Pay Service 1
Pay Units: N.A.
Programming (via satellite): Cinemax (multiplexed); Encore (multiplexed); Flix; HBO; Showtime (multiplexed); Starz (multiplexed); The Movie Channel (multiplexed).
Fee: $12.95 monthly (each).

Video-On-Demand: No

Pay-Per-View
iN DEMAND (delivered digitally); Playboy TV (delivered digitally).

Internet Service
Operational: Yes.

Telephone Service
None

Miles of Plant: 9.0 (coaxial); None (fiber optic).
Manager: Greg Barton.
Ownership: Emery Telcom (MSO).

MORGAN CITY—Comcast Cable, 9602 S 300 W, Sandy, UT 84070. Phone: 801-401-2500. Fax: 801-401-3397. Web Site: http://www.comcast.com. Also serves Morgan County. ICA: UT0048.
TV Market Ranking: 48 (MORGAN CITY, Morgan County). Franchise award date: N.A. Franchise expiration date: N.A. Began: April 1, 1982.
Channel capacity: N.A. Channels available but not in use: N.A.

Basic Service
Subscribers: N.A. Included in Salt Lake City
Programming (received off-air): KBYU-TV (PBS) Provo; KJZZ-TV (MNT) Salt Lake City; KSL-TV (NBC) Salt Lake City; KSTU (FOX) Salt Lake City; KTVX (ABC) Salt Lake City; KUED (PBS) Salt Lake City; KUTV (CBS) Salt Lake City.
Programming (via satellite): A&E Networks; AMC; Animal Planet; Cartoon Network; CNBC; CNN; Country Music TV; Discovery Channel; Disney Channel; ESPN; Fox News Channel; Hallmark Channel; Headline News; Lifetime; MoviePlex; Nickelodeon; QVC; Root Sports Rocky Mountain; Spike TV; TBS Superstation; Turner Network TV; USA Network.
Fee: $43.99 installation; $50.60 monthly.

Digital Basic Service
Subscribers: N.A.
Programming (via satellite): BBC America; Bravo; CBS Sports Network; Country Music TV; Discovery Digital Networks; ESPN 2; ESPN Classic Sports; ESPNews; Fox Soccer; Fuse; G4; GAS; Golf Channel; GSN; HGTV; History Channel; Independent Film Channel; MTV Networks Digital Suite; National Geographic Channel; Nick Jr.; NickToons TV; PBS Kids Sprout; Style Network; Syfy; Trinity Broadcasting Network; Turner Classic Movies; TV Land; TV One; Versus; WE tv.
Fee: $14.95 monthly.

Digital Expanded Basic Service
Subscribers: N.A.
Programming (via satellite): Bio; Current; Discovery Digital Networks; Encore (multiplexed); Halogen Network; History Channel International; Lifetime Movie Network; MTV Networks Digital Suite; Sundance Channel; Toon Disney.

Digital Expanded Basic Service 2
Subscribers: N.A.
Programming (via satellite): Bloomberg Television; Fox Movie Channel; Lime; Outdoor Channel; Ovation; Speed.
Fee: $6.60 monthly.

Pay Service 1
Pay Units: 184.
Programming (via satellite): Cinemax; Encore; HBO; Starz.
Fee: $6.99 monthly (Encore), $10.99 monthly (Starz), $13.99 monthly (Cinemax), $14.99 monthly (HBO).

Digital Pay Service 1
Pay Units: N.A.
Programming (via satellite): Cinemax (multiplexed); HBO (multiplexed); Showtime (multiplexed); Starz (multiplexed); The Movie Channel (multiplexed).
Fee: $16.95 monthly (HBO, Cinemax, Showtime, TMC, or Starz).

Internet Service
Operational: No.

Telephone Service
None

Miles of plant included in Salt Lake City
Area Vice President: Scott Tenney. Technical Operations Director: Mike Spaulding. Marketing Director: Dan Williams. Marketing Manager: Lisa Jenkins. Community & Government Affairs Director: Steve Proper.
Ownership: Comcast Cable Communications Inc. (MSO).

MORONI—Central Telcom Services (CUTV). Now served by GUNNISON, UT [UT0037]. ICA: UT0042.

MOUNT PLEASANT—Central Telcom Services (CUTV). Now served by GUNNISON, UT [UT0037]. ICA: UT0023.

MURRAY—Formerly served by Nuvont Communications. IPTV service no longer in operation. ICA: UT5024.

NEPHI—Comcast Cable, 9602 S 300 W, Sandy, UT 84070. Phone: 801-401-2500. Fax: 801-401-3397. Web Site: http://www.comcast.com. ICA: UT0028.
TV Market Ranking: Outside TV Markets (NEPHI). Franchise award date: N.A. Franchise expiration date: N.A. Began: January 1, 1981.
Channel capacity: N.A. Channels available but not in use: N.A.

Basic Service
Subscribers: N.A. Included in Salt Lake City
Programming (received off-air): KBYU-TV (PBS) Provo; KJZZ-TV (MNT) Salt Lake City; KPNZ (IND) Ogden; KSL-TV (NBC) Salt Lake City; KSTU (FOX) Salt Lake City; KSVN-CA Ogden; KTMW (IND) Salt Lake City; KTVX (ABC) Salt Lake City; KUCW (CW) Ogden; KUED (PBS) Salt Lake City; KUEN (ETV) Ogden; KUPX-TV (ION) Provo; KUTH-DT (UNV) Provo; KUTV (CBS) Salt Lake City.
Programming (via satellite): BYU Television; C-SPAN; C-SPAN 2; Discovery Channel; FX; Lifetime; QVC; TBS Superstation.
Fee: $43.99 installation; $8.68 monthly; $18.95 additional installation.

Expanded Basic Service 1
Subscribers: 735.
Programming (via satellite): A&E Networks; ABC Family Channel; AMC; Animal Planet; BET Networks; Cartoon Network; CNBC; CNN; Comedy Central; Country Music TV; Disney Channel; E! Entertainment Television; ESPN; ESPN 2; Food Network; Fox News Channel; Fox Sports Net; GalaVision; Golf Channel; Great American Country; GSN; Hallmark Channel; Headline News; HGTV; History Channel; INSP; MSNBC; MTV; Nickelodeon; Oxygen; Spike TV; Style Network; Telemundo; The Learning Channel; The Weather Channel; Travel Channel; truTV; Turner Network TV; TV Land; USA Network; Versus; VH1.
Fee: $43.60 monthly.

Digital Basic Service
Subscribers: 194.
Programming (via satellite): BBC America; Black Family Channel; Bravo; Canales N; Cooking Channel; Discovery Digital Networks; DIY Network; DMX Music; ESPN; ESPN 2; ESPN Classic Sports; ESPNews; Fox Sports World; Independent Film Channel; INHD; International Television (ITV); Music Choice; National Geographic Channel; NBA TV; Nick Jr.; ShopNBC; Syfy; The Word Network; Trinity Broadcasting Network; Turner Classic Movies; TV Land; WE tv; Weatherscan.
Fee: $14.95 monthly.

Digital Expanded Basic Service
Subscribers: N.A.
Programming (via satellite): AmericanLife TV Network; Bio; Bloomberg Television; Discovery Fit & Health; Encore Action; Fox Movie Channel; FSN Digital Atlantic; FSN Digital Central; FSN Digital Pacific; Fuse; G4; GAS; Halogen Network; History Channel International; Lifetime Movie Network; Lime; MTV Networks Digital Suite; NickToons TV; Outdoor Channel; Ovation; Speed; Sundance Channel; Toon Disney.
Fee: $5.00 monthly.

Pay Service 1
Pay Units: 161.
Programming (via satellite): HBO; Showtime.
Fee: $13.99 monthly (Showtime), $14.99 monthly (HBO).

Digital Pay Service 1
Pay Units: N.A.
Programming (via satellite): Cinemax (multiplexed); Flix; HBO (multiplexed); Showtime (multiplexed); Starz (multiplexed); The Movie Channel (multiplexed).
Fee: $16.95 monthly (HBO, Cinemax, Starz, Showtime, or TMC).

Video-On-Demand: No

Pay-Per-View
Addressable homes: 194.
iN DEMAND (delivered digitally); Fresh (delivered digitally); Shorteez (delivered digitally); Playboy TV (delivered digitally); ESPN Now (delivered digitally); Sports PPV (delivered digitally); NBA League Pass (delivered digitally); Urban Xtra (delivered digitally).

Internet Service
Operational: Yes.
Broadband Service: Comcast High Speed Internet.
Fee: $42.95 monthly.

Telephone Service
None

Miles of plant included in Salt Lake City

MediaPrints
Map a Winning Business Strategy
Digital Cable and TV Coverage Maps.
Visit www.warren-news.com/mediaprints.htm

Area Vice President: Scott Tenney. Technical Operations Director: Mike Spaulding. Marketing Director: Dan Williams. Marketing Manager: Lisa Jenkins. Community & Government Affairs Director: Steve Proper.

Ownership: Comcast Cable Communications Inc. (MSO).

NEW HARMONY—Formerly served by South Central Communications. No longer in operation. ICA: UT0068.

OAKLEY—All West Communications. Formerly served by Kamas, UT [UT0053]. This cable system has converted to IPTV, 50 W 100 N, Kamas, UT 84036. Phones: 866-255-9378; 435-783-4361. Fax: 435-783-4928. E-mail: questions@allwest.net. Web Site: http://www.allwest.com. ICA: UT5034.

TV Market Ranking: 48 (OAKLEY).

Channel capacity: N.A. Channels available but not in use: N.A.

Internet Service

Operational: Yes.

OGDEN—Comcast Cable, 752 N Marshall Way, Layton, UT 84041. Phones: 801-444-4825 (Administrative office); 801-401-3400 (Sandy office); 801-444-4824 (Customer service). Web Site: http://www.comcast.com. Also serves Bountiful, Box Elder County (unincorporated areas), Brigham City, Centerville, Clearfield, Clinton, Davis County (portions), Farmington, Farr West, Fruit Heights, Harrisville, Hill AFB, Hooper, Kaysville, Layton, North Ogden, North Salt Lake, Perry, Plain City, Pleasant View, Riverdale, Roy, South Ogden, South Weber, Sunset, Syracuse, Uintah City, Washington Terrace, Weber County (portions), West Bountiful, West Haven, West Point, Willard & Woods Cross. ICA: UT0008.

TV Market Ranking: 48 (Bountiful, Centerville, Clearfield, Clearfield, Clinton, Clinton, Davis County (portions), Farmington, Fruit Heights, Harrisville, Hill AFB, Hooper, Kaysville, Layton, Layton, North Salt Lake, OGDEN, Riverdale, Roy, South Ogden, South Weber, South Weber, Sunset, Syracuse, Uintah City, Washington Terrace, Weber County (portions), Weber County (portions), West Bountiful, West Haven, West Point, Woods Cross); Below 100 (Box Elder County (unincorporated areas), Brigham City, Farr West, North Ogden, Perry, Plain City, Pleasant View, Willard, Weber County (portions)). Franchise award date: N.A. Franchise expiration date: N.A. Began: December 30, 1987.

Channel capacity: N.A. Channels available but not in use: N.A.

Basic Service

Subscribers: N.A. Included in Salt Lake City

Programming (received off-air): KBYU-TV (PBS) Provo; KJZZ-TV (MNT) Salt Lake City; KPNZ (IND) Ogden; KSL-TV (NBC) Salt Lake City; KSTU (FOX) Salt Lake City; KTMW (IND) Salt Lake City; KTVX (ABC) Salt Lake City; KUCW (CW) Ogden; KUED (PBS) Salt Lake City; KUEN (ETV) Ogden; KUPX-TV (ION) Provo; KUTV (CBS) Salt Lake City.

Programming (via satellite): Fox News Channel; Lifetime; QVC; TBS Superstation.

Fee: $40.95 installation; $11.28 monthly; $18.95 additional installation.

Expanded Basic Service 1

Subscribers: N.A.

Programming (via satellite): A&E Networks; ABC Family Channel; AMC; Animal Planet; CNBC; CNN; Country Music TV; C-SPAN; Discovery Channel; Disney Channel; ESPN; FX; Headline News; MTV; Nickelodeon; Root Sports Rocky Mountain; Spike TV; The Weather Channel; Turner Network TV; USA Network.

Fee: $40.95 monthly.

Digital Basic Service

Subscribers: 1,101.

Programming (via satellite): BBC America; Bravo; Discovery Digital Networks; DMX Music; ESPN 2; ESPN Classic Sports; ESPNews; Fox Sports World; Golf Channel; GSN; HGTV; Independent Film Channel; National Geographic Channel; Nick Jr.; Style Network; Syfy; The Word Network; Trinity Broadcasting Network; Turner Classic Movies; TV Land; Versus; WE tv.

Fee: $9.95 monthly.

Digital Expanded Basic Service

Subscribers: N.A.

Programming (via satellite): Bio; Bloomberg Television; Encore Action; Fox Movie Channel; Fuse; G4; GAS; Halogen Network; History Channel International; Lifetime Movie Network; Lime; MTV Networks Digital Suite; NickToons TV; Outdoor Channel; Speed; Sundance Channel; Toon Disney.

Fee: $5.00 monthly.

Pay Service 1

Pay Units: 1,055.

Programming (via satellite): HBO.

Fee: $15.25 installation; $14.99 monthly.

Digital Pay Service 1

Pay Units: 1,572.

Programming (via satellite): Cinemax (multiplexed); HBO (multiplexed); Showtime (multiplexed); Starz (multiplexed); The Movie Channel (multiplexed).

Fee: $11.09 monthly (each).

Pay-Per-View

Addressable homes: 1,101.

iN DEMAND (delivered digitally); Playboy TV (delivered digitally); Fresh (delivered digitally).

Internet Service

Operational: Yes.

Subscribers: 662.

Broadband Service: Comcast High Speed Internet.

Fee: $42.95 monthly; $3.00 modem lease.

Telephone Service

Analog: Operational

Miles of Plant: 252.0 (coaxial); None (fiber optic).

Area Vice President: Gary E. Waterfield. Manager: Mike Clarke.; Alan Hintze. Engineering Director: Craig Malang. Marketing Manager: Meagan Bunton.

Ownership: Comcast Cable Communications Inc. (MSO).

OREM—Formerly served by Nuvont Communications. IPTV service no longer in operation. ICA: UT5025.

PANGUITCH—South Central Communications, 45 North 100 W, PO Box 555, Escalante, UT 84726-0555. Phones: 800-718-7288; 435-826-4211. Fax: 435-826-4900. Web Site: http://www.southcentralcommunications.com. Also serves Bryce, Circleville & Tropic. ICA: UT0043.

TV Market Ranking: Outside TV Markets (Bryce, Circleville, PANGUITCH, Tropic). Franchise award date: N.A. Franchise expiration date: December 31, 2011. Began: February 22, 1982.

Channel capacity: 62 (not 2-way capable). Channels available but not in use: N.A.

Basic Service

Subscribers: N.A. Included in Escalante

Programming (via satellite): A&E Networks; ABC Family Channel; AMC; Animal Planet; Cartoon Network; CNN; Comedy Central; Country Music TV; Discovery Channel; Disney Channel; E! Entertainment Television; ESPN; ESPN 2; Fox News Channel; Hallmark Channel; HGTV; History Channel; Lifetime; MTV; Nickelodeon; Outdoor Channel; QVC; Root Sports Rocky Mountain; Spike TV; Syfy; TBS Superstation; The Learning Channel; Turner Classic Movies; Turner Network TV; TV Land; USA Network; VH1; WGN America.

Programming (via translator): KBYU-TV (PBS) Provo; KJZZ-TV (MNT) Salt Lake City; KSL-TV (NBC) Salt Lake City; KSTU (FOX) Salt Lake City; KTVX (ABC) Salt Lake City; KUCW (CW) Ogden; KUED (PBS) Salt Lake City; KUTV (CBS) Salt Lake City.

Fee: $45.00 installation; $28.95 monthly.

Pay Service 1

Pay Units: 30.

Programming (via satellite): Cinemax; HBO.

Fee: $11.00 monthly (each).

Video-On-Demand: No

Internet Service

Operational: No.

Telephone Service

None

Miles of Plant: 16.0 (coaxial); None (fiber optic).

Manager & Chief Technician: Greg Barton.

Ownership: South Central Communications (MSO).

PANGUITCH (portions)—South Central Communications. Now served by PANGUITCH, UT [UT0043]. ICA: UT0089.

PARAGONAH—South Central Communications. Now served by PAROWAN, UT [UT0034]. ICA: UT0085.

PARK CITY—Comcast Cable. Now served by SALT LAKE CITY, UT [UT0001]. ICA: UT0010.

PAROWAN—South Central Communications, 45 North 100 W, PO Box 555, Escalante, UT 84726-0555. Phone: 435-826-4211. Fax: 435-826-4900. Web Site: http://www.southcentralcommunications.com. Also serves Paragonah. ICA: UT0034.

TV Market Ranking: Below 100 (Paragonah, PAROWAN). Franchise award date: N.A. Franchise expiration date: N.A. Began: December 8, 1981.

Channel capacity: N.A. Channels available but not in use: N.A.

Basic Service

Subscribers: N.A. Included in Escalante

Programming (received off-air): KCSG (IND) Cedar City; KJZZ-TV (MNT) Salt Lake City; KUCW (CW) Ogden.

Programming (via satellite): A&E Networks; ABC Family Channel; AMC; Animal Planet; Cartoon Network; CNBC; CNN; Country Music TV; C-SPAN; Discovery Channel; Disney Channel; ESPN; ESPN 2; Food Network; Fox News Channel; FX; Great American Country; Hallmark Channel; Headline News; HGTV; History Channel; INSP; Lifetime; MSNBC; MTV; Nickelodeon; QVC; Root Sports Rocky Mountain; Speed; Spike TV; TBS Superstation; The Learning Channel; The Weather Channel; Travel Channel; Turner Classic Movies; Turner Network TV; TV Guide Network; TV Land; USA Network; Versus; VH1.

Programming (via translator): KBYU-TV (PBS) Provo; KSL-TV (NBC) Salt Lake City; KSTU (FOX) Salt Lake City; KTVX (ABC) Salt Lake City; KUED (PBS) Salt Lake City; KUTV (CBS) Salt Lake City.

Fee: $45.00 installation; $33.95 monthly.

Pay Service 1

Pay Units: 79.

Programming (via satellite): Cinemax; HBO.

Fee: $11.00 monthly (each).

Video-On-Demand: No

Internet Service

Operational: Yes, DSL. Began: April 1, 2006.

Subscribers: 99.

Fee: $39.99 monthly.

Telephone Service

None

Miles of Plant: 16.0 (coaxial); None (fiber optic).

Manager & Chief Technician: Greg Barton.

Ownership: South Central Communications (MSO).

PAYSON—Formerly served by Nuvont Communications. IPTV service no longer in operation. ICA: UT5026.

PEOA—All West Communications. Formerly served by Kamas, UT [UT0053]. This cable system has converted to IPTV, 50 W 100 N, Kamas, UT 84036. Phones: 866-255-9378; 435-783-4361. Fax: 435-783-4928. E-mail: questions@allwest.net. Web Site: http://www.allwest.com. ICA: UT5035.

TV Market Ranking: 48 (PEOA).

Channel capacity: N.A. Channels available but not in use: N.A.

Internet Service

Operational: Yes.

PRICE—Emery Telcom, 445 E Hwy 29, PO Box 629, Orangeville, UT 84537. Phones: 435-613-9605; 435-748-2223. Web Site: http://www.emerytelcom.com. Also serves Carbon County (portions), Helper, Kenilworth & Wellington. ICA: UT0011.

TV Market Ranking: Outside TV Markets (Carbon County (portions), Helper, Kenilworth, PRICE, Wellington). Franchise award date: N.A. Franchise expiration date: N.A. Began: July 1, 1979.

Channel capacity: N.A. Channels available but not in use: N.A.

Basic Service

Subscribers: 3,500.

Programming (received off-air): KJZZ-TV (MNT) Salt Lake City; KUEN (ETV) Ogden; 1 FM.

Programming (via satellite): A&E Networks; ABC Family Channel; AMC; Animal Planet; CNN; Country Music TV; C-SPAN; Discovery Channel; Disney Channel; ESPN; Fox News Channel; Fox Sports Net; FX; Headline News; Lifetime; MoviePlex; MTV; Nickelodeon; QVC; Spike TV; TBS Superstation; The Learning Channel; The Weather Channel; Turner Network TV; USA Network; WGN America.

Programming (via translator): KBYU-TV (PBS) Provo; KSL-TV (NBC) Salt Lake City; KSTU (FOX) Salt Lake City; KTVX (ABC) Salt Lake City; KUED (PBS) Salt Lake City; KUTV (CBS) Salt Lake City.

Fee: $44.95 installation; $10.95 monthly; $1.50 converter.

Digital Basic Service

Subscribers: 1,172.

Programming (via satellite): BBC America; Bravo; Discovery Digital Networks; ESPN 2; ESPN Classic Sports; Fox Sports World; Golf Channel; GSN; HGTV; History Channel; Independent Film Channel; Speed; Syfy; Turner Classic Movies; Versus; VH1 Classic; VH1 Country; WE tv.

Fee: $41.95 monthly.

Pay Service 1

Pay Units: 246.

Programming (via satellite): Cinemax (multiplexed).

Fee: $12.95 monthly.

Pay Service 2

Pay Units: 793.

Programming (via satellite): Encore; Starz (multiplexed); The Movie Channel.

Fee: $12.95 monthly.

Pay Service 3

Pay Units: 597.

Programming (via satellite): HBO (multiplexed).

Fee: $12.95 monthly.

Pay Service 4

Pay Units: 301.

Programming (via satellite): Showtime (multiplexed).

Fee: $12.95 monthly.

Video-On-Demand: No

Internet Service

Operational: No.

Telephone Service

None

Miles of Plant: 133.0 (coaxial); None (fiber optic).

Manager: Greg Barton.

Ownership: Emery Telcom (MSO).

PROVO—Comcast Cable, 9602 S 300 W, Sandy, UT 84070. Phone: 801-401-2500. Fax: 801-401-3397. Web Site: http://www.comcast.com. Also serves Elk Ridge, Payson, Salem, Spanish Fork, Spanish Fork City & Utah County (portions). ICA: UT0005.

TV Market Ranking: 48 (Utah County (portions)); Below 100 (Elk Ridge, Payson, PROVO, Salem, Spanish Fork, Spanish Fork City, Utah County (portions)). Franchise award date: N.A. Franchise expiration date: N.A. Began: November 1, 1975.

Channel capacity: N.A. Channels available but not in use: N.A.

Basic Service

Subscribers: N.A. Included in Salt Lake City

Programming (received off-air): KBYU-TV (PBS) Provo; KJZZ-TV (MNT) Salt Lake City; KPNZ (IND) Ogden; KSL-TV (NBC) Salt Lake City; KSTU (FOX) Salt Lake City; KTVX (ABC) Salt Lake City; KUCW (CW) Ogden; KUED (PBS) Salt Lake City; KUTV (CBS) Salt Lake City; allband FM.

Programming (via satellite): A&E Networks; Fox News Channel; QVC; TBS Superstation.

Fee: $43.99 installation; $12.87 monthly.

Expanded Basic Service 1

Subscribers: 27,124.

Programming (via satellite): ABC Family Channel; AMC; Animal Planet; Cartoon Network; CNBC; CNN; Country Music TV; Discovery Channel; Disney Channel; ESPN; Fox Sports Net; FX; Great American Country; Lifetime; Nickelodeon; Spike TV; Turner Network TV; USA Network.

Fee: $43.60 monthly.

Digital Basic Service

Subscribers: 5,817.

Programming (via satellite): BBC America; Bio; Bravo; Discovery Digital Networks; ESPN 2; ESPN Classic Sports; ESPNews; Fox Sports World; G4; Golf Channel; GSN; HGTV; History Channel; Independent Film Channel; INSP; MTV2; Music Choice; National Geographic Channel; Nick Jr.; Style Network; Syfy; Trinity Broadcasting Network; Turner Classic Movies; TV Land; Versus; WE tv.

Fee: $14.95 monthly.

Digital Expanded Basic Service

Subscribers: N.A.

Programming (via satellite): Bloomberg Television; Encore Action; Fox Movie Channel; Fuse; GAS; Halogen Network; History Channel International; Lifetime Movie Network; Lime; MTV Networks Digital Suite; NickToons TV; Outdoor Channel; Ovation; Speed; Sundance Channel; Toon Disney.

Fee: $5.00 monthly.

Pay Service 1

Pay Units: 1,070.

Programming (via satellite): HBO; Showtime.

Digital Pay Service 1

Pay Units: N.A.

Programming (via satellite): Cinemax (multiplexed); HBO (multiplexed); Showtime (multiplexed); Starz (multiplexed); The Movie Channel (multiplexed).

Fee: $16.95 monthly (HBO, Cinemax, Starz, Showtime, or TMC).

Video-On-Demand: Yes

Pay-Per-View

iN DEMAND (delivered digitally); Fresh (delivered digitally); Shorteez (delivered digitally); Playboy TV (delivered digitally).

Internet Service

Operational: Yes.

Subscribers: 3,496.

Broadband Service: Comcast High Speed Internet.

Fee: $42.95 monthly; $3.00 modem lease.

Telephone Service

Digital: Operational

Fee: $44.95 monthly

Miles of plant included in Salt Lake City

Area Vice President: Scott Tenney. Technical Operations Director: Mike Spaulding. Marketing Director: Dan Williams. Marketing Manager: Lisa Jenkins. Community & Government Affairs Director: Steve Proper.

Ownership: Comcast Cable Communications Inc. (MSO).

PROVO—Formerly served by Nuvont Communications. IPTV service no longer in operation. ICA: UT5027.

PROVO—Formerly served by Provo Cable. No longer in operation. ICA: UT0086.

RANDOLPH—All West Communications. Formerly [UT0066]. This cable system has converted to IPTV, 50 W 100 N, Kamas, UT 84036. Phones: 866-255-9378; 435-783-4361. Fax: 435-783-4928. E-mail: questions@allwest.net. Web Site: http://www.allwest.net. ICA: UT5015.

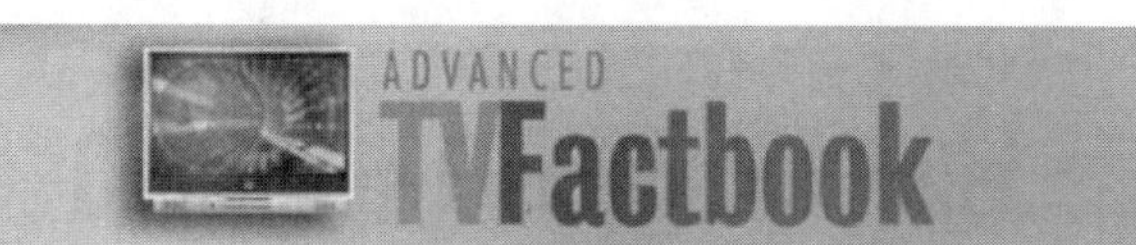

TV Market Ranking: Below 100 (RANDOLPH). Franchise award date: N.A. Franchise expiration date: N.A. Began: N.A.

Channel capacity: N.A. Channels available but not in use: N.A.

Internet Service

Operational: Yes, Both DSL & dial-up.

Telephone Service

Digital: Operational

RANDOLPH TWP.—All West Communications. This cable system has converted to IPTV. See Randolph, UT [UT5015]. ICA: UT0066.

RICHFIELD—Central Telcom Services (CUTV). Now served by GUNNISON, UT [UT0037]. ICA: UT0020.

RICHMOND—Comcast Cable. Now served by LOGAN, UT [UT0006]. ICA: UT0021.

RIVERDALE—Comcast Cable. Now served by OGDEN (formerly HOOPER), UT [UT0008]. ICA: UT0075.

ROCKVILLE—Baja Broadband, 111 W 700 S, Saint George, UT 84770-3550. Phone: 435-628-3681. Fax: 435-674-4225. Web Site: http://www.bajabroadband.com. Also serves Springdale. ICA: UT0077.

TV Market Ranking: Below 100 (ROCKVILLE, Springdale). Franchise award date: N.A. Franchise expiration date: N.A. Began: N.A.

Channel capacity: 54 (not 2-way capable). Channels available but not in use: N.A.

Basic Service

Subscribers: 130.

Programming (via satellite): A&E Networks; AMC; Animal Planet; CNBC; CNN; Country Music TV; Discovery Channel; Disney Channel; ESPN; Headline News; Lifetime; Nickelodeon; QVC; Speed; Spike TV; Syfy; TBS Superstation; The Learning Channel; Travel Channel; Turner Network TV; USA Network; VH1; WGN America.

Programming (via translator): KBYU-TV (PBS) Provo; KSL-TV (NBC) Salt Lake City; KSTU (FOX) Salt Lake City; KTVX (ABC) Salt Lake City; KUCW (CW) Ogden; KUED (PBS) Salt Lake City; KUTV (CBS) Salt Lake City.

Fee: $53.00 installation; $22.99 monthly.

Pay Service 1

Pay Units: 23.

Programming (via satellite): HBO.

Fee: $8.00 monthly.

Pay Service 2

Pay Units: 20.

Programming (via satellite): Showtime.

Fee: $8.00 monthly.

Video-On-Demand: No

Internet Service

Operational: No.

Telephone Service

None

Miles of Plant: 20.0 (coaxial); None (fiber optic).

Technical Operations Manager: Ed Farnum. Office Manager: Missy Snow.

Ownership: Baja Broadband (MSO).

ROOSEVELT—Strata Networks, 211 East 200 North, Roosevelt, UT 84066. Phone: 435-622-5007. Web Site: https://www.stratanetworks.com. ICA: UT0030.

TV Market Ranking: Outside TV Markets (ROOSEVELT). Franchise award date: N.A. Franchise expiration date: N.A. Began: August 1, 1981.

Channel capacity: 40 (not 2-way capable). Channels available but not in use: N.A.

Basic Service

Subscribers: 632.

Programming (received off-air): KJZZ-TV (MNT) Salt Lake City; KPNZ (IND) Ogden; KSL-TV (NBC) Salt Lake City; KUEN (ETV) Ogden; KUPX-TV (ION) Provo; KUWB-LD Bloomington.

Programming (via translator): KBYU-TV (PBS) Provo; KSL-TV (NBC) Salt Lake City; KSTU (FOX) Salt Lake City; KTVX (ABC) Salt Lake City; KUED (PBS) Salt Lake City; KUTV (CBS) Salt Lake City.

Fee: $29.95 installation; $10.70 monthly.

Expanded Basic Service 1

Subscribers: N.A.

Programming (via satellite): A&E Networks; ABC Family Channel; AMC; Animal Planet; Cartoon Network; CNBC; CNN; Comedy Central; Country Music TV; Discovery Channel; Disney Channel; ESPN; Fox News Channel; FX; Hallmark Channel; Lifetime; Nickelodeon; QVC; Root Sports Rocky Mountain; Spike TV; TBS Superstation; The Learning Channel; The Weather Channel; Turner Network TV; USA Network; WGN America.

Fee: $28.25 monthly.

Digital Basic Service

Subscribers: N.A.

Programming (via satellite): BBC America; Bio; Bravo; Discovery Digital Networks; DMX Music; ESPN 2; ESPN Classic Sports; ESPNews; Fox Sports World; Fuse; Golf Channel; Great American Country; GSN; HGTV; History Channel; History Channel International; Independent Film Channel; Lifetime Movie Network; MBC America; National Geographic Channel; ShopNBC; Speed; Style Network; Syfy; The Word Network; Toon Disney; Trio; Turner Classic Movies; Versus; WE tv.

Fee: $15.95 monthly.

Digital Pay Service 1

Pay Units: N.A.

Programming (via satellite): Cinemax (multiplexed); Encore (multiplexed); Flix; HBO (multiplexed); Showtime (multiplexed); Starz (multiplexed); The Movie Channel (multiplexed).

Fee: $12.95 monthly (each).

Video-On-Demand: No

Pay-Per-View

iN DEMAND (delivered digitally); Playboy TV (delivered digitally).

Internet Service

Operational: No.

Telephone Service

None

Miles of Plant: 22.0 (coaxial); None (fiber optic).

Marketing Manager: Tyler Rasmussen. Chief Executive Officer & General Manager:

Bruce Todd. Chief Operating Officer: Jeff Goodrich.
Ownership: Strata Networks (MSO).

SALEM—Comcast Cable. Now served by PROVO, UT [UT0005]. ICA: UT0009.

SALINA—Central Telcom Services (CUTV). Now served by GUNNISON, UT [UT0037]. ICA: UT0029.

SALT LAKE CITY—Comcast Cable, 9602 S 300 W, Sandy, UT 84070. Phone: 801-401-2500. Fax: 801-401-3397. Web Site: http://www.comcast.com. Also serves Alpine, American Fork, Bluffdale, Draper, Grantsville, Herriman, Highland, Lehi, Lindon, Mapleton, Midvale, Murray, Orem, Park City, Pleasant Grove, Riverton, Salt Lake County, Sandy, South Jordan, South Salt Lake City, Springville, Summit County (portions), Taylorsville, Tooele, Tooele County, Utah County (unincorporated areas), West Jordan & West Valley City. ICA: UT0001.

TV Market Ranking: 48 (Alpine, American Fork, Bluffdale, Draper, Grantsville, Herriman, Highland, Lehi, Lindon, Midvale, Murray, Orem, Park City, Pleasant Grove, Riverton, SALT LAKE CITY, Salt Lake County, Sandy, South Jordan, South Salt Lake City, Summit County (portions), Taylorsville, Tooele, Tooele County (portions), Utah County (unincorporated areas) (portions), West Jordan, West Valley City); Below 100 (Mapleton, Springville, Tooele County (portions), Utah County (unincorporated areas) (portions)); Outside TV Markets (Summit County (portions)). Franchise award date: January 1, 1966. Franchise expiration date: N.A. Began: March 1, 1970.

Channel capacity: N.A. Channels available but not in use: N.A.

Basic Service

Subscribers: 249,700 Includes Coalville, Heber City, Logan, Morgan City, Nephi, & Provo.

Programming (received off-air): KBYU-TV (PBS) Provo; KJZZ-TV (MNT) Salt Lake City; KPNZ (IND) Ogden; KSL-TV (NBC) Salt Lake City; KSTU (FOX) Salt Lake City; KSVN-CA Ogden; KTMW (IND) Salt Lake City; KTVX (ABC) Salt Lake City; KUED (PBS) Salt Lake City; KUEN (ETV) Ogden; KUPX-TV (ION) Provo; KUTV (CBS) Salt Lake City.

Programming (via satellite): C-SPAN; C-SPAN 2; Discovery Channel; FX; Hallmark Channel; INSP; Lifetime; QVC; TBS Superstation; Telemundo; Travel Channel; TV Land.

Programming (via translator): KUCW (CW) Ogden.

Fee: $43.99 installation; $12.87 monthly; $1.90 converter; $18.95 additional installation.

Expanded Basic Service 1

Subscribers: 100,610.

Programming (via satellite): A&E Networks; ABC Family Channel; AMC; Animal Planet; BET Networks; Cartoon Network; CNBC; CNN; Comedy Central; Country Music TV; Disney Channel; E! Entertainment Television; ESPN; ESPN 2; Food Network; Fox News Channel; GalaVision; Great American Country; GSN; Headline News; History Channel; MSNBC; MTV; Nickelodeon; Oxygen; Root Sports Rocky Mountain; Spike TV; The Learning Channel; The Weather Channel; truTV; Turner Network TV; USA Network; Versus; VH1.

Fee: $31.13 installation; $40.95 monthly.

Digital Basic Service

Subscribers: 22,341.

Programming (via satellite): BBC America; Black Family Channel; Bravo; Discovery Digital Networks; DMX Music; ESPN 2; ESPN Classic Sports; ESPNews; Fox Sports World; G4; Golf Channel; GSN; HGTV; Independent Film Channel; National Geographic Channel; NBA TV; Nick Jr.; ShopNBC; Style Network; Syfy; The Word Network; Trinity Broadcasting Network; Turner Classic Movies; TV Land; Versus; WE tv.

Fee: $14.95 monthly.

Digital Expanded Basic Service

Subscribers: N.A.

Programming (via satellite): AmericanLife TV Network; Bio; Bloomberg Television; Encore Action; Fox Movie Channel; FSN Digital Atlantic; FSN Digital Central; FSN Digital Pacific; Fuse; GAS; Halogen Network; History Channel International; Lifetime Movie Network; Lime; MTV Networks Digital Suite; NickToons TV; Outdoor Channel; Ovation; Speed; Sundance Channel; Toon Disney.

Fee: $5.00 monthly.

Digital Pay Service 1

Pay Units: N.A.

Programming (via satellite): Cinemax (multiplexed); HBO (multiplexed); Showtime (multiplexed); Starz (multiplexed); The Movie Channel (multiplexed).

Fee: $16.95 monthly (each).

Video-On-Demand: Yes

Pay-Per-View

Addressable homes: 22,341.

iN DEMAND (delivered digitally); Playboy TV (delivered digitally); Fresh (delivered digitally); Shorteez (delivered digitally).

Internet Service

Operational: Yes.

Subscribers: 13,426.

Broadband Service: Comcast High Speed Internet.

Fee: $42.95 monthly; $3.00 modem lease.

Telephone Service

Digital: Operational

Fee: $44.95 monthly

Miles of Plant: 9,080.0 (coaxial); None (fiber optic). Miles of plant include Coalville, Heber City, Logan, Morgan City, Nephi, & Provo

Area Vice President: Scott Tenney. Technical Operations Director: Mike Spaulding. Chief Technician: Everett Preece. Marketing Director: Dan Williams. Marketing Manager: Lisa Jenkins. Community & Government Affairs Director: Steve Proper.

Ownership: Comcast Cable Communications Inc. (MSO).

SALT LAKE CITY—Formerly served by TechnoVision Inc. No longer in operation. ICA: UT0082.

SANDY—Comcast Cable. Now served by SALT LAKE CITY, UT [UT0001]. ICA: UT0002.

SANTAQUIN—Central Telcom Services (CUTV). Now served by GUNNISON, UT [UT0037]. ICA: UT0041.

SOUTH JORDAN—CenturyLink. Formerly [UT0091]. This cable system has converted to IPTV., 1801 California St, Denver, CO 80202. Phones: 800-899-7780; 303-992-1400. Fax: 303-896-8515. Web Site: http://www.qwest.com. ICA: UT5021.

TV Market Ranking: 48 (SOUTH JORDAN). Franchise award date: N.A. Franchise expiration date: N.A. Began: N.A.

Channel capacity: N.A. Channels available but not in use: N.A.

Internet Service

Operational: Yes.

Telephone Service

Digital: Operational

SOUTH JORDAN—Qwest Choice TV. This cable system has converted to IPTV. See Randolph, UT [UT5021]. ICA: UT0091.

SPANISH FORK—Spanish Fork Community Network, 65 S 630 W, Spanish Fork, UT 84660-2077. Phones: 801-798-2877 (Customer service); 801-804-4500. Fax: 801-798-5025. E-mail: john@spanishfork.org. Web Site: http://www.sfcn.org. ICA: UT0090. **Note:** This system is an overbuild.

TV Market Ranking: Below 100 (SPANISH FORK).

Channel capacity: 77 (operating 2-way). Channels available but not in use: N.A.

Basic Service

Subscribers: 7,500.

Programming (received off-air): KBYU-TV (PBS) Provo; KJZZ-TV (MNT) Salt Lake City; KPNZ (IND) Ogden; KSL-TV (NBC) Salt Lake City; KSTU (FOX) Salt Lake City; KTMW (IND) Salt Lake City; KTVX (ABC) Salt Lake City; KUCW (CW) Ogden; KUED (PBS) Salt Lake City; KUEN (ETV) Ogden; KUPX-TV (ION) Provo; KUTV (CBS) Salt Lake City.

Programming (via satellite): BYU Television; C-SPAN; TBS Superstation; The Weather Channel.

Programming (via translator): KTVX (ABC) Salt Lake City.

Fee: $9.89 monthly.

Expanded Basic Service 1

Subscribers: N.A.

Programming (via satellite): A&E Networks; ABC Family Channel; AMC; Animal Planet; Cartoon Network; CBS Sports Network; CNBC; CNN; Comedy Central; Country Music TV; C-SPAN 2; Discovery Channel; Discovery Fit & Health; Discovery Health Channel; Disney Channel; DIY Network; E! Entertainment Television; ESPN; ESPN 2; ESPN Classic Sports; ESPNews; Food Network; Fox Movie Channel; Fox News Channel; FX; G4; Golf Channel; Great American Country; Hallmark Channel; Headline News; HGTV; History Channel; INSP; Lifetime; LiveTV; MoviePlex; MSNBC; MTV; National Geographic Channel; Nickelodeon; Outdoor Channel; Ovation; PBS Kids Channel; QVC; Root Sports Rocky Mountain; Speed; Spike TV; Syfy; The Learning Channel; The Mtn; Toon Disney; Travel Channel; truTV; Turner Classic Movies; Turner Network TV; TV Land; USA Network; Versus; VH1.

Fee: $41.44 monthly.

Digital Basic Service

Subscribers: N.A.

Programming (via satellite): BBC America; Bio; cloo; Discovery Channel HD; Discovery Kids Channel; DMX Music; ESPN HD; GSN; HDNet; HDNet Movies; History Channel International; ID Investigation Discovery; Independent Film Channel; Military Channel; MTV2; Nick Jr.; Planet Green; Science; TeenNick; VH1 Classic; VH1 Country; VH1 Soul; WE tv.

Fee: $8.57 monthly.

Digital Pay Service 1

Pay Units: N.A.

Programming (via satellite): Cinemax (multiplexed); Encore (multiplexed); Flix; HBO (multiplexed); Showtime (multiplexed); Starz (multiplexed); Sundance Channel; The Movie Channel (multiplexed).

Fee: $11.00 monthly (Starz/Encore), $12.00 monthly (Flix, Showtime, Sundance & TMC), $16.00 monthly (Cinemax & HBO).

Video-On-Demand: No

Pay-Per-View

Movies (delivered digitally).

Internet Service

Operational: Yes.

Subscribers: 3,000.

Broadband Service: In-house.

Fee: $28.00 monthly.

Telephone Service

None

Miles of Plant: 55.0 (coaxial); None (fiber optic).

Manager: John Bowcut. Chief Technician: Dan Henderson.

Ownership: Spanish Fork Community Network.

ST. GEORGE—Baja Broadband, 111 W 700 S, Saint George, UT 84770-3550. Phones: 435-673-6650; 435-628-3681; 980-235-7600 (Corporate office). Fax: 435-674-4225. E-mail: customersupportut@bajabb.tv. Web Site: http://www.bajabroadband.com. Also serves Harrisburg Junction, Hurricane, Ivins, La Verkin, Leeds, Santa Clara, Toquerville & Washington. ICA: UT0007.

TV Market Ranking: Below 100 (Harrisburg Junction, Hurricane, Ivins, La Verkin, Leeds, Santa Clara, ST. GEORGE, Toquerville, Washington). Franchise award date: October 1, 1977. Franchise expiration date: N.A. Began: December 15, 1978.

Channel capacity: 78 (operating 2-way). Channels available but not in use: N.A.

Basic Service

Subscribers: 5,222.

Programming (received off-air): KCSG (IND) Cedar City; KJZZ-TV (MNT) Salt Lake City; KMYU (IND, MNT) St. George; KPNZ (IND) Ogden; KSTU (FOX) Salt Lake City; KUCW (CW) Ogden; KUTH-DT (UNV) Provo.

Programming (via satellite): BYU Television; Product Information Network; QVC; TV Guide Network; WGN America.

Programming (via translator): KBYU-TV (PBS) Provo; KSL-TV (NBC) Salt Lake City; KSNV-DT (NBC) Las Vegas; KTVX (ABC) Salt Lake City; KUED (PBS) Salt Lake City; KUTV (CBS) Salt Lake City.

Fee: $53.00 installation; $20.00 monthly.

Expanded Basic Service 1

Subscribers: 5,187.

Programming (via satellite): A&E Networks; ABC Family Channel; AMC; Animal Planet; Bravo; Cartoon Network; CNBC; CNN; Comedy Central; Country Music TV; C-SPAN; C-SPAN 2; Discovery Channel; Discovery Fit & Health; Disney Channel; E! Entertainment Television; ESPN; ESPN 2; ESPN Classic Sports; Eternal Word TV Network; Food Network; Fox Movie Channel; Fox News Channel; FX; G4; GalaVision; Golf Channel; GSN; Hallmark Channel; Headline News; HGTV; History Channel; INSP; Lifetime; Lifetime Movie Network; MSNBC; MTV; National Geographic Channel; Nickelodeon; Root Sports Rocky Mountain; SoapNet; Speed; Spike TV; Syfy; TBS Superstation; The Learning Channel; The Mtn; The Weather Channel; Toon Disney; Travel Channel; truTV; Turner Classic Movies; Turner Network TV; TV Land; USA Network; Versus; VH1; WE tv.

Fee: $26.70 monthly.

Digital Basic Service
Subscribers: N.A.
Programming (via satellite): BBC America; Bio; Bloomberg Television; CMT Pure Country; Discovery en Espanol; Discovery Health Channel; Discovery Kids Channel; DIY Network; Fox Business Channel; Fox Reality Channel; Fuel TV; History Channel International; ID Investigation Discovery; Independent Film Channel; Lifetime Real Women; Military Channel; MTV Hits; MTV Jams; MTV2; Music Choice; Nick Jr.; Nick Too; Planet Green; Science; Style Network; Sundance Channel; TeenNick; Tr3s; VH1 Classic; VH1 Soul; VHUNO.
Fee: $11.95 monthly.

Digital Expanded Basic Service
Subscribers: N.A.
Programming (via satellite): CBS Sports Network; ESPNews; Fox College Sports Atlantic; Fox College Sports Central; Fox College Sports Pacific; Fox Soccer; Fuel TV; MavTV; Outdoor Channel.

Digital Expanded Basic Service 2
Subscribers: N.A.
Programming (received off-air): KSL-TV (NBC) Salt Lake City; KSTU (FOX) Salt Lake City; KUED (PBS) Salt Lake City; KUTV (CBS) Salt Lake City.
Programming (via satellite): A&E HD; ESPN HD; Food Network HD; FSN HD; FX HD; Golf Channel HD; HGTV HD; History Channel HD; National Geographic Channel HD Network; Speed HD; TBS in HD; Turner Network TV HD; Versus HD.

Digital Expanded Basic Service 3
Subscribers: N.A.
Programming (via satellite): HDNet; HDNet Movies; Universal HD.

Digital Pay Service 1
Pay Units: 472.
Programming (via satellite): Cinemax (multiplexed); Cinemax HD.
Fee: $10.50 monthly.

Digital Pay Service 2
Pay Units: 813.
Programming (via satellite): HBO (multiplexed); HBO HD.
Fee: $10.50 monthly.

Digital Pay Service 3
Pay Units: 577.
Programming (via satellite): Flix; Showtime (multiplexed); Showtime HD; The Movie Channel (multiplexed); The Movie Channel HD.
Fee: $10.50 monthly.

Digital Pay Service 4
Pay Units: 376.
Programming (via satellite): Encore (multiplexed).
Fee: $10.50 monthly.

Digital Pay Service 5
Pay Units: 359.
Programming (via satellite): Starz (multiplexed); Starz HDTV.
Fee: $10.50 monthly.

Video-On-Demand: No

Pay-Per-View
iN DEMAND (delivered digitally); Playboy TV (delivered digitally); Fresh (delivered digitally); Spice: Xcess (delivered digitally).

Internet Service
Operational: Yes. Began: September 1, 2000.
Subscribers: 425.
Broadband Service: In-house.
Fee: $49.99 installation; $34.99 monthly; $5.00 modem lease; $69.95 modem purchase.

Telephone Service
Digital: Operational
Miles of Plant: 392.0 (coaxial); None (fiber optic).
Chief Executive Officer: William A. Schuler. Chief Operating Officer: Phillip Klein. Technical Operations Manager: Ed Farnum. Office Manager: Misty Snow.
Ownership: Baja Broadband (MSO).

TOOELE—Comcast Cable. Now served by SALT LAKE CITY, UT [UT0001]. ICA: UT0012.

VERNAL—Bresnan Communications. No longer in operation. ICA: UT0014.

WENDOVER—Precis Communications. Now served by WENDOVER, NV [NV0054]. ICA: UT0025.

WEST VALLEY CITY—Formerly served by Nuvont Communications. IPTV service no longer in operation. ICA: UT5029.

WINCHESTER—Formerly served by South Central Communications. No longer in operation. ICA: UT0087.

WOODLAND—All West Communications. Formerly served by Kamas, UT [UT0053]. This cable system has converted to IPTV, 50 W 100 N, Kamas, UT 84036. Phones: 866-255-9378; 435-783-4361. Fax: 435-783-4928. E-mail: questions@allwest.net. Web Site: http://www.allwest.com. ICA: UT5038.
TV Market Ranking: Below 100 (WOODLAND).
Channel capacity: N.A. Channels available but not in use: N.A.

Internet Service
Operational: Yes.

WOODRUFF (town)—All West Communications. Formerly served by Randolph, UT [UT0066]. This cable system has converted to IPTV, 50 W 100 N, Kamas, UT 84036. Phones: 866-255-9378; 435-783-4361. Fax: 435-783-4928. E-mail: questions@allwest.net. Web Site: http://www.allwest.net. ICA: UT5020.
Channel capacity: N.A. Channels available but not in use: N.A.

Internet Service
Operational: Yes, Both DSL & dial-up.

Telephone Service
Digital: Operational

VERMONT

Total Systems: **12**
Total Communities Served: **236**
Franchises Not Yet Operating: **0**
Applications Pending: **0**
Communities with Applications: **0**
Number of Basic Subscribers: **37,038**
Number of Expanded Basic Subscribers: **73,931**
Number of Pay Units: **1,180**

Top 100 Markets Represented: Albany-Schenectady-Troy, NY (34).

For a list of cable communities in this section, see the Cable Community Index located in the back of Cable Volume 2.
For explanation of terms used in cable system listings, see p. D-11.

BARRE—Charter Communications. Now served by DANVILLE (TOWN) (formerly St. Johnsbury), VT [VT0009]. ICA: VT0005.

BENNINGTON—Comcast Cable, 43 Comcast Way, South Burlington, VT 05403-6056. Phones: 802-447-7850 (Bennington office); 802-419-6631. Fax: 802-658-5488. Web Site: http://www.comcast.com. Also serves Arlington, Bondville, Dorset, East Arlington, Manchester, Manchester Center, North Bennington, Old Bennington, Peru, Pownal, Sandgate, Shaftsbury, South Dorset, Stratton, Stratton Mountain, Sunderland, West Arlington (portions), Winhall & Woodford. ICA: VT0004.

TV Market Ranking: 34 (BENNINGTON, North Bennington, Old Bennington, Pownal, Shaftsbury, Woodford); Below 100 (Arlington, Stratton, Stratton Mountain, West Arlington (portions)); Outside TV Markets (Bondville, Dorset, East Arlington, Manchester, Manchester Center, Peru, Sandgate, South Dorset, Sunderland, Winhall). Franchise award date: October 1, 1961. Franchise expiration date: N.A. Began: April 1, 1962.

Channel capacity: 114 (operating 2-way). Channels available but not in use: N.A.

Basic Service

Subscribers: N.A. Included in Manchester, NH

Programming (received off-air): WCAX-TV (CBS) Burlington; WETK (PBS) Burlington; WMHT (PBS) Schenectady; WNYA (MNT) Pittsfield; WNYT (NBC) Albany; WPIX (CW, IND) New York; WRGB (CBS) Schenectady; WTEN (ABC) Albany; WVBK-CA Manchester; WXXA-TV (FOX) Albany; WYPX-TV (ION) Amsterdam; allband FM.

Programming (via satellite): Product Information Network; QVC; The Comcast Network; TV Guide Network.

Fee: $39.95 installation; $14.20 monthly.

Expanded Basic Service 1

Subscribers: 11,314.

Programming (via satellite): A&E Networks; ABC Family Channel; AMC; Animal Planet; Bravo; Cartoon Network; CNBC; CNN; Comcast SportsNet New England; Comedy Central; Country Music TV; C-SPAN; C-SPAN 2; Discovery Channel; Disney Channel; E! Entertainment Television; ESPN; ESPN 2; Eternal Word TV Network; Food Network; Fox News Channel; FX; Hallmark Channel; Headline News; HGTV; History Channel; Lifetime; MSNBC; MTV; New England Sports Network; Nickelodeon; Oxygen; ShopNBC; Speed; Spike TV; Syfy; TBS Superstation; The Learning Channel; The Weather Channel; Travel Channel; truTV; Turner Network TV; TV Land; USA Network; VH1.

Fee: $37.05 monthly.

Digital Basic Service

Subscribers: N.A.

Programming (via satellite): BBC America; Bio; Black Family Channel; Bloomberg Television; Canales N; CBS Sports Network; Cooking Channel; Country Music TV; Current; DIY Network; Encore (multiplexed); ESPN 2 HD; ESPN Classic Sports; ESPN HD; ESPNews; Flix; Fox Movie Channel; Fox Reality Channel; Fox Soccer; FSN Digital Atlantic; FSN Digital Central; FSN Digital Pacific; Fuse; G4; GAS; Golf Channel; GSN; Halogen Network; HD Theater; HDNet; HDNet Movies; History Channel International; Independent Film Channel; INHD; Lifetime Movie Network; LOGO; MTV Networks Digital Suite; Music Choice; National Geographic Channel; NFL Network; Nick Jr.; Nick Too; NickToons TV; Outdoor Channel; SoapNet; Speed; Style Network; Sundance Channel; The Word Network; Toon Disney; Trinity Broadcasting Network; Turner Classic Movies; Turner Network TV HD; Versus; WE tv.

Fee: $11.95 monthly.

Digital Pay Service 1

Pay Units: 400.

Programming (via satellite): ART America; CCTV-4; Cinemax (multiplexed); Cinemax On Demand; Encore (multiplexed); Filipino Channel; Flix; Flix On Demand; HBO (multiplexed); HBO HD; HBO On Demand; RAI International; Russian Television Network; Showtime (multiplexed); Showtime HD; Showtime On Demand; Starz (multiplexed); Starz HDTV; Starz On Demand; The Movie Channel (multiplexed); The Movie Channel On Demand; TV Asia; TV Japan; TV5 USA.

Video-On-Demand: Yes

Pay-Per-View

Playboy TV (delivered digitally); Fresh (delivered digitally); Hot Choice (delivered digitally); ESPN Gameplan (delivered digitally); MLB Extra Innings (delivered digitally); NHL Center Ice (delivered digitally); iN DEMAND (delivered digitally).

Internet Service

Operational: Yes.

Subscribers: 668.

Broadband Service: Comcast High Speed Internet.

Fee: $42.95 monthly.

Telephone Service

Digital: Operational

Miles of Plant: 508.0 (coaxial); None (fiber optic).

Regional Vice President: Steve Hackley. Area Vice President: Dan Blakeman. Vice President, Technical Operations: Raymond Kowalinski. Vice President, Sales & Marketing: Mark Adamy. Public Relations Manager: Marc Goodman.

Ownership: Comcast Cable Communications Inc. (MSO).

BERLIN—Comcast Cable. Now served by BURLINGTON, VT [VT0001]. ICA: VT0061.

BLOOMFIELD TWP.—Formerly served by Adelphia Communications. No longer in operation. ICA: VT0038.

BRADFORD—Charter Communications. Now served by DANVILLE (TOWN) (formerly St. Johnsbury), VT [VT0009]. ICA: VT0021.

BRAINTREE—Formerly served by Adelphia Cable-Berlin. Now served by BURLINGTON, VT [VT0001]. ICA: VT0039.

BRATTLEBORO—Comcast Cable, 74 Black Mountain Rd, Brattleboro, VT 05301-9178. Phones: 888-658-1000; 802-257-7371 (Administrative office). Fax: 802-257-9285. Web Site: http://www.comcast.com. Also serves Athens, Bellows Falls, Cambridgeport, Grafton, Guilford Twp., North Westminster, Rockingham, Saxtons River, Vernon & Westminster Twp. ICA: VT0010.

TV Market Ranking: Below 100 (BRATTLEBORO, Guilford Twp., Rockingham); Outside TV Markets (Athens, Bellows Falls, Cambridgeport, Grafton, North Westminster, Saxtons River, Vernon, Westminster Twp.). Franchise award date: N.A. Franchise expiration date: N.A. Began: January 1, 1954.

Channel capacity: 70 (operating 2-way). Channels available but not in use: N.A.

Basic Service

Subscribers: 10,947.

Programming (received off-air): WBIN-TV (IND) Derry; WBZ-TV (CBS) Boston; WCDC-TV (ABC) Adams; WCVB-TV (ABC) Boston; WEKW-TV (PBS) Keene; WGBY-TV (PBS) Springfield; WHDH (NBC) Boston; WMUR-TV (ABC) Manchester; WNNE (NBC) Hartford; WSBK-TV (CBS, MNT) Boston; WVBK-CA Manchester; WVTA (PBS) Windsor; allband FM.

Programming (via microwave): WFXT (FOX) Boston.

Programming (via translator): WCAX-TV (CBS) Burlington.

Fee: $39.95 installation; $18.00 monthly; $4.50 converter; $19.95 additional installation.

Expanded Basic Service 1

Subscribers: 9,481.

Programming (via satellite): A&E Networks; ABC Family Channel; AMC; Animal Planet; Bravo; Cartoon Network; CNBC; CNN; Comedy Central; C-SPAN; C-SPAN 2; Discovery Channel; Disney Channel; E! Entertainment Television; ESPN; ESPN 2; Eternal Word TV Network; FX; Hallmark Channel; Headline News; HGTV; History Channel; Lifetime; MSNBC; MTV; New England Cable News; New England Sports Network; Nickelodeon; Oxygen; Product Information Network; QVC; ShopNBC; Spike TV; Syfy; TBS Superstation; The Learning Channel; The Weather Channel; Travel Channel; truTV; Turner Network TV; TV Guide Network; USA Network; VH1.

Fee: $34.50 monthly.

Digital Basic Service

Subscribers: 924.

Programming (via satellite): AmericanLife TV Network; BBC America; Bio; Black Family Channel; Bloomberg Television; Discovery Fit & Health; DIY Network; ESPN Classic Sports; ESPNews; Fox Sports World; Fuse; G4; Golf Channel; Great American Country; GSN; Halogen Network; History Channel International; Outdoor Channel; SoapNet; Speed; Toon Disney; Trinity Broadcasting Network; Versus; WE tv.

Fee: $15.94 monthly.

Digital Expanded Basic Service

Subscribers: N.A.

Programming (via satellite): Canales N; DMX Music; GAS; Independent Film Channel; MTV Networks Digital Suite; National Geographic Channel; Nick Jr.; Nick Too; NickToons TV; Style Network; The Word Network; Turner Classic Movies.

Digital Pay Service 1

Pay Units: 279.

Programming (via satellite): ART America; CCTV-4; Cinemax (multiplexed); Encore (multiplexed); Filipino Channel; Flix; HBO (multiplexed); RAI International; Showtime (multiplexed); Starz (multiplexed); Sundance Channel; The Movie Channel (multiplexed); TV Asia; TV Japan; TV5, La Television International; Zee TV USA.

Fee: $15.95 monthly.

Video-On-Demand: Yes

Pay-Per-View

Addressable homes: 924.

Hot Choice (delivered digitally); iN DEMAND (delivered digitally); Fresh (delivered digitally).

Internet Service

Operational: Yes. Began: January 1, 2001.

Broadband Service: Comcast High Speed Internet.

Fee: $99.00 installation; $42.95 monthly; $3.00 modem lease.

Telephone Service

Digital: Operational

Miles of Plant: 120.0 (coaxial); None (fiber optic).

Area Vice President: Dan Blakeman. Regional Vice President: Steve Hackley. Vice President, Sales & Marketing: Mark Adamy. Vice President, Technical Operations: Raymond Kowalinski. Public Relations Manager: Marc Goodman.

Ownership: Comcast Cable Communications Inc. (MSO).

BURLINGTON—Comcast Cable, 43 Comcast Way, South Burlington, VT 05403-6056. Phones: 802-419-6631; 802-419-6650. Fax: 802-658-5488. Web Site: http://www.

comcast.com. Also serves Andover (town), Canaan (town), Claremont, Cornish (town), Cornish Flat, Danbury (town), Enfield, Grantham, Hanover, Hill (town), Lebanon, Meriden, New London, Newport, Plainfield (town), Salisbury (town), Sunapee, West Lebanon & Wilmot (town), NH; Barton, Beebe Plain, Berlin, Bethel, Bomoseen, Braintree, Brandon, Bridgewater, Bristol, Cabot, Cabot Twp., Calais, Castleton, Cavendish, Charleston, Charlotte, Chester, Chester Depot (village), Chittenden, Clarendon Twp., Colchester, Coventry, Danby, Derby, Derby Center, Derby Line, Duxbury, East Hardwick, East Middlebury, East Montpelier, East Poultney, Essex, Essex Junction, Fair Haven, Ferrisburg, Forest Dale, Georgia, Glover, Hardwick, Hinesburg, Huntington, Hyde Park, Hydeville, Irasburg, Jericho, Johnson, Killington, Londonderry, Ludlow, Marshfield Twp., Mendon, Middlebury, Middlesex, Milton, Montpelier, Moretown, Morristown, Morrisville, Mount Tabor, Newport, Newport Center, North Troy, Orleans, Pawlet, Perkinsville, Pittsford, Pittsford (village), Plainfield Twp., Plymouth, Poultney, Proctor Twp., Proctorsville, Randolph, Reading, Richmond, Rochester, Rutland, Shelburne, Sherburne (town), South Burlington, South Londonderry, Springfield, St. Albans (city), St. George (town), Starksboro Twp., Swanton (village), Taftsville, Troy Twp., Tyson, Underhill (town), Vergennes, Wallingford Twp., Waterbury, West Pawlet, West Rutland Twp., Weston, Weybridge (portions), Williston, Windsor, Winooski, Woodbury, Woodstock & Worcester, VT. ICA: VT0001.

TV Market Ranking: Below 100 (Andover (town), Bethel, Braintree, Bridgewater, Bristol, BURLINGTON, Canaan (town), Cavendish, Chester, Chester Depot (village), Chittenden, Claremont, Clarendon Twp., Colchester, Cornish (town), Cornish Flat, Danbury (town), Duxbury, East Middlebury, Enfield, Essex, Essex Junction, Etna, Ferrisburg, Georgia, Grantham, Hanover, Hill (town), Hinesburg, Huntington, Hyde Park, Jericho, Johnson, Killington, Lebanon, Londonderry, Ludlow, Mendon, Meriden, Middlebury, Middlesex, Milton, Montpelier, Moretown, Morristown, Morrisville, New London, Newport, Perkinsville, Plainfield (town), Plymouth, Proctorsville, Randolph, Reading, Richmond, Rochester, Rutland, Salisbury (town), Shelburne, Sherburne (town), South Burlington, South Londonderry, Springfield, St. Albans (city), St. George (town), Starksboro Twp., Sunapee, Swanton (village), Swanton Twp., Taftsville, Underhill (town), Vergennes, Wallingford Twp., Waterbury, West Lebanon, Weston, Weybridge (portions), Williston, Wilmot (town), Windsor, Winooski, Woodstock); Outside TV Markets (Barton, Beebe Plain, Berlin, Bomoseen, Brandon, Cabot, Cabot Twp., Calais, Castleton, Charleston, Charlotte, Chester Depot (village), Coventry, Danby, Derby, Derby Center, Derby Line, East Hardwick, East Montpelier, East Poultney, Fair Haven, Forest Dale, Glover, Hardwick, Hydeville, Irasburg, Marshfield Twp., Mount Tabor, Newport, Newport Center, North Troy, Orleans, Pawlet, Pittsford, Pittsford (village), Plainfield Twp., Poultney, Proctor Twp., Troy Twp., Tyson, West Pawlet, West Rutland Twp., Woodbury, Worcester). Franchise award date: January 1, 1952. Franchise expiration date: N.A. Began: May 1, 1952.

Channel capacity: N.A. Channels available but not in use: N.A.

Basic Service

Subscribers: N.A. Included in Manchester, NH

Programming (received off-air): WCAX-TV (CBS) Burlington; WCFE-TV (PBS) Plattsburgh; WETK (PBS) Burlington; WFFF-TV (CW, FOX) Burlington; WGMU-CA (MNT) Burlington; WPTZ (NBC) Plattsburgh; WVNY (ABC) Burlington; WWBI-LP Plattsburgh; 26 FMs.

Programming (via satellite): Product Information Network; TBS Superstation; The Learning Channel; TV Guide Network; WPIX (CW, IND) New York.

Fee: $39.95 installation; $17.50 monthly; $45.00 additional installation.

Expanded Basic Service 1

Subscribers: 40,627.

Programming (via satellite): A&E Networks; ABC Family Channel; Animal Planet; Cartoon Network; CNBC; CNN; Comedy Central; Country Music TV; C-SPAN; C-SPAN 2; Discovery Channel; Disney Channel; E! Entertainment Television; ESPN; ESPN 2; Eternal Word TV Network; Food Network; Fox News Channel; FX; Hallmark Channel; Headline News; HGTV; History Channel; INSP; ION Television; Lifetime; MSNBC; New England Cable News; Nickelodeon; Oxygen; QVC; ShopNBC; Spike TV; Syfy; The Weather Channel; Travel Channel; truTV; Turner Network TV; TV Land; WSBK-TV (CBS, MNT) Boston.

Fee: $36.75 monthly.

Digital Basic Service

Subscribers: N.A.

Programming (via satellite): AmericanLife TV Network; BBC America; Bio; Black Family Channel; Bloomberg Television; Discovery Fit & Health; DIY Network; ESPN Classic Sports; ESPNews; Fox Movie Channel; Fox Sports World; Fuse; G4; GAS; Golf Channel; Great American Country; GSN; Halogen Network; History Channel International; Music Choice; Nick Jr.; NickToons TV; Outdoor Channel; SoapNet; Speed; The Word Network; Toon Disney; Trinity Broadcasting Network; Versus; WE tv.

Digital Expanded Basic Service

Subscribers: N.A.

Programming (via satellite): Canales N; Independent Film Channel; MTV Networks Digital Suite; National Geographic Channel; Style Network; Sundance Channel; Turner Classic Movies.

Digital Pay Service 1

Pay Units: N.A.

Programming (via satellite): ART America; CCTV-4; Cinemax (multiplexed); Encore (multiplexed); Filipino Channel; Flix; HBO (multiplexed); RAI International; Russian Television Network; Showtime (multiplexed); Starz (multiplexed); The Movie Channel (multiplexed); TV Asia; TV Japan; TV5, La Television International; Zee TV USA.

Fee: $11.50 monthly (each).

Video-On-Demand: Yes

Pay-Per-View

Urban Xtra (delivered digitally); Hot Choice (delivered digitally); Shorteez (delivered digitally); Fresh (delivered digitally); HITS (delivered digitally); Playboy TV (delivered digitally); iN DEMAND.

Internet Service

Operational: Yes. Began: August 1, 1999.

Broadband Service: Comcast High Speed Internet.

Fee: $42.95 monthly.

Telephone Service

Digital: Operational

Miles of Plant: 3,667.0 (coaxial); None (fiber optic).

Area Vice President: Dan Blakeman. Regional Vice President: Steve Hackley. Vice President, Technical Operations: Raymond Kowalinski. Vice President, Sales & Marketing: Mark Adamy. Public Relations Manager: Marc Goodman.

Ownership: Comcast Cable Communications Inc. (MSO).

CHARLESTON—Comcast Cable. Now served by BURLINGTON, VT [VT0001]. ICA: VT0043.

CHELSEA—Charter Communications. Now served by DANVILLE (TOWN) (formerly St. Johnsbury), VT [VT0009]. ICA: VT0027.

COVENTRY TWP.—Formerly served by Adelphia Communications. No longer in operation. ICA: VT0044.

DANVILLE (town)—Charter Communications, 95 Higgins St, Worcester, MA 1606. Phone: 508-853-1515. Fax: 508-854-5042. Web Site: http://www.charter.com. Also serves Bath, Haverhill, North Haverhill, Piermont, Pike & Woodsville, NH; Barnet, Barre, Bradford, Burke, Chelsea, Concord, East Barre, East Burke, East Ryegate, East St. Johnsbury, Graniteville, Groton, Kirby, Lyndon, Lyndon Center, Lyndon Corners, Lyndonville, Marshfield, McIndoe Falls, Newbury, North Danville, Orange (town), Passumpsic, Peacham, Plainfield, Ryegate, Sheffield, South Royalton, South Ryegate, St. Johnsbury, St. Johnsbury Center, Sutton, Washington (town), Waterford, Websterville, Wells River, West Burke, Wheelock & Williamstown, VT. ICA: VT0009.

TV Market Ranking: Below 100 (Bradford, Chelsea, East Barre, Graniteville, Haverhill, Newbury, North Haverhill, Orange (town), Piermont, Pike, South Royalton, Websterville, Williamstown); Outside TV Markets (Barnet, Barre, Bath, Burke, Concord, DANVILLE (TOWN), East Burke, East Ryegate, East St. Johnsbury, Groton, Kirby, Lyndon, Lyndon Center, Lyndon Corners, Lyndonville, Marshfield, McIndoe Falls, North Danville, Passumpsic, Peacham, Plainfield, Ryegate, Sheffield, South Ryegate, St. Johnsbury, St. Johnsbury Center, Sutton, Waterford, Wells River, West Burke, Wheelock, Woodsville). Franchise award date: January 1, 1954. Franchise expiration date: N.A. Began: March 1, 1954.

Channel capacity: N.A. Channels available but not in use: N.A.

Basic Service

Subscribers: 12,624.

Programming (received off-air): WCAX-TV (CBS) Burlington; WETK (PBS) Burlington; WFFF-TV (CW, FOX) Burlington; WGMU-CA (MNT) Burlington; WLED-TV (PBS) Littleton; WMUR-TV (ABC) Manchester; WNNE (NBC) Hartford; WPTZ (NBC) Plattsburgh; WVNY (ABC) Burlington; WVTB (PBS) St. Johnsbury; allband FM.

Programming (via satellite): C-SPAN; C-SPAN 2; Eternal Word TV Network; INSP; ION Television; Product Information Network; QVC; ShopNBC; Trinity Broadcasting Network; TV Guide Network.

Expanded Basic Service 1

Subscribers: 6,677.

Programming (via satellite): A&E Networks; ABC Family Channel; AMC; Animal Planet; Bravo; Cartoon Network; CNBC; CNN; Comcast SportsNet New England; Comedy Central; Country Music TV; Discovery Channel; Disney Channel; E! Entertainment Television; ESPN; ESPN 2; Food Network; Fox News Channel; FX; G4; Golf Channel; GSN; Hallmark Channel; Headline News; HGTV; History Channel; Lifetime; MSNBC; MTV; MTV2; National Geographic Channel; New England Cable News; New England Sports Network; Nickelodeon; Oxygen; SoapNet; Speed; Spike TV; Style Network; Syfy; TBS Superstation; The Learning Channel; The Weather Channel; Toon Disney; Travel Channel; truTV; Turner Classic Movies; Turner Network TV; TV Land; USA Network; Versus; VH1.

Fee: $55.00 monthly.

Digital Basic Service

Subscribers: N.A.

Programming (via satellite): BBC America; Bio; Bloomberg Television; CBS Sports Network; Discovery Fit & Health; DIY Network; ESPN Classic Sports; ESPNews; Fox College Sports Atlantic; Fox College Sports Central; Fox College Sports Pacific; Fox Soccer; Fuel TV; Fuse; GAS; History Channel International; Independent Film Channel; Jewelry Television; Lifetime Movie Network; MTV Networks Digital Suite; Music Choice; Nick Jr.; Nick Too; NickToons TV; Sundance Channel; WE tv.

Digital Pay Service 1

Pay Units: N.A.

Programming (via satellite): Cinemax (multiplexed); Encore (multiplexed); HBO (multiplexed); Showtime (multiplexed); Starz (multiplexed); The Movie Channel (multiplexed).

Video-On-Demand: No

Pay-Per-View

Shorteez (delivered digitally); Playboy en Espanol (delivered digitally); Playboy TV (delivered digitally); Fresh (delivered digitally); NHL Center Ice (delivered digitally); MLB Extra Innings (delivered digitally); iN DEMAND (delivered digitally); NASCAR In Car (delivered digitally).

Internet Service

Operational: Yes.

Broadband Service: Charter Pipeline.

Fee: $29.99 monthly; $5.00 modem lease.

Telephone Service

None

Miles of Plant: 368.0 (coaxial); 650.0 (fiber optic).

Vice President & General Manager: Greg Garabedian. Technical Operations Director: George Duffy. Technical Operations Manager: Rick Smith. Marketing Director: Dennis Jerome.

Ownership: Charter Communications Inc. (MSO).

DERBY—Comcast Cable. Now served by BURLINGTON, VT [VT0001]. ICA: VT0013.

EAST CORINTH—Formerly served by Olsen TV. No longer in operation. ICA: VT0030.

ENOSBURG FALLS—Comcast Cable, 271 Main St, PO Box 576, Enosburg Falls, VT 05450-0576. Phone: 800-266-2278. Web Site: http://www.comcast.com. Also serves Bakersfield, East Berkshire, East Fairfield, Enosburg, Montgomery & Richford. ICA: VT0024.

TV Market Ranking: Below 100 (Bakersfield, East Fairfield); Outside TV Markets (East Berkshire, Enosburg, ENOSBURG FALLS, Montgomery, Richford). Franchise award date: N.A. Franchise expiration date: N.A. Began: August 1, 1981.

Channel capacity: 71 (operating 2-way). Channels available but not in use: N.A.

Basic Service

Subscribers: 1,500.

Programming (received off-air): WCAX-TV (CBS) Burlington; WCFE-TV (PBS) Plattsburgh; WETK (PBS) Burlington; WFFF-TV (CW, FOX) Burlington; WPTZ (NBC) Plattsburgh; WVNY (ABC) Burlington.

Programming (via satellite): CNN; C-SPAN; Encore; Headline News; Outdoor Channel; Speed; Spike TV; TBS Superstation; The Weather Channel; Turner Classic Movies; USA Network; various Canadian stations.

Fee: $25.00 installation; $22.00 monthly.

Expanded Basic Service 1

Subscribers: 360.

Programming (via satellite): A&E Networks; ABC Family Channel; Bravo; Comedy Central; Country Music TV; Daystar TV Network; Discovery Channel; Disney Channel; ESPN; ESPN 2; ESPN Classic Sports; Eternal Word TV Network; Fox News Channel; HGTV; Lifetime; MTV; National Geographic Channel; Nickelodeon; QVC; Syfy; The Learning Channel; Turner Network TV; TV Land; various Canadian stations; VH1.

Fee: $10.60 monthly.

Digital Basic Service

Subscribers: 25.

Programming (via satellite): AmericanLife TV Network; BBC America; Bio; Blackbelt TV; Bloomberg Television; Bravo; Current; Daystar TV Network; Discovery Digital Networks; DMX Music; ESPN Classic Sports; ESPNews; Fox Movie Channel; Fox Sports World; FSN Digital Atlantic; FSN Digital Central; FSN Digital Pacific; Fuse; G4; GAS; Golf Channel; Great American Country; GSN; Halogen Network; HGTV; History Channel; History Channel International; Independent Film Channel; Lifetime Movie Network; Lime; MBC America; MTV Networks Digital Suite; National Geographic Channel; Nick Jr.; NickToons TV; Outdoor Channel; Ovation; Speed; Style Network; Syfy; The Word Network; Toon Disney; Trinity Broadcasting Network; Trio; Turner Classic Movies; TVG Network; Versus; WE tv.

Fee: $21.15 monthly.

Pay Service 1

Pay Units: 85.

Programming (via satellite): HBO.

Fee: $11.75 monthly.

Digital Pay Service 1

Pay Units: N.A.

Programming (via satellite): Cinemax (multiplexed); Encore (multiplexed); Flix; HBO (multiplexed); Showtime (multiplexed); Starz (multiplexed); Sundance Channel; The Movie Channel (multiplexed).

Video-On-Demand: No

Pay-Per-View

Movies (delivered digitally).

Internet Service

Operational: Yes.

Subscribers: 200.

Broadband Service: Comcast High Speed Internet.

Fee: $50.00 installation; $25.00 monthly.

Telephone Service

Digital: Operational

Miles of Plant: 39.0 (coaxial); 11.0 (fiber optic). Additional miles planned: 12.0 (coaxial); 15.0 (fiber optic).

Manager: Gary Fiske.

Ownership: Comcast Cable Communications Inc. (MSO).

IRASBURG TWP.—Formerly served by Adelphia Communications. No longer in operation. ICA: VT0054.

JACKSONVILLE—Formerly served by Area Telecable. No longer in operation. ICA: VT0088.

JAMAICA TWP.—Southern Vermont Cable Co. Now served by PUTNEY, VT [VT0067]. ICA: VT0055.

JEFFERSONVILLE—Jeffersonville Cable TV Corp., 172 Thomas Ln, PO Box 453, Stowe, VT 5672. Phone: 802-253-9282. Fax: 802-253-7812. E-mail: stoweaccess@stoweaccess.com. Web Site: http://www.stoweaccess.com. Also serves Cambridge, Cambridge Junction & Smugglers Notch. ICA: VT0056.

TV Market Ranking: Below 100 (Cambridge, Cambridge Junction, JEFFERSONVILLE, Smugglers Notch). Franchise award date: N.A. Franchise expiration date: N.A. Began: July 1, 1988.

Channel capacity: 126 (operating 2-way). Channels available but not in use: N.A.

Basic Service

Subscribers: 909.

Programming (received off-air): WCAX-TV (CBS) Burlington; WETK (PBS) Burlington; WPTZ (NBC) Plattsburgh; WVNY (ABC) Burlington.

Programming (via satellite): A&E Networks; ABC Family Channel; CNN; Comedy Central; C-SPAN; Discovery Channel; Disney Channel; ESPN; Headline News; History Channel; New England Sports Network; Spike TV; Syfy; TBS Superstation; The Learning Channel; The Weather Channel; Turner Network TV; USA Network.

Fee: $60.00 installation; $26.63 monthly.

Expanded Basic Service 1

Subscribers: N.A.

Programming (via satellite): AMC; Animal Planet; CNBC; Country Music TV; ESPN 2; Food Network; Fox News Channel; G4; Great American Country; Lifetime; MTV; Nickelodeon; TV Land; VH1.

Digital Basic Service

Subscribers: N.A.

Programming (via satellite): Bio; Bravo; Discovery Digital Networks; ESPN 2; ESPN Classic Sports; ESPNews; Fox Movie Channel; Fox Sports World; GAS; Golf Channel; GSN; HGTV; History Channel International; Independent Film Channel; MTV Networks Digital Suite; Music Choice; Nick Jr.; NickToons TV; Outdoor Channel; Speed; Toon Disney; Turner Classic Movies; Versus.

Fee: $25.00 installation; $20.00 monthly.

Pay Service 1

Pay Units: N.A.

Programming (via satellite): HBO.

Fee: $10.00 monthly.

Digital Pay Service 1

Pay Units: N.A.

Programming (via satellite): Cinemax; Encore (multiplexed); Flix; HBO (multiplexed); Showtime (multiplexed); Starz; The Movie Channel (multiplexed).

Fee: $14.28 monthly (Showtime & TMC), $14.95 monthly (Starz & Encore), $17.00 monthly (HBO & Cinemax).

Video-On-Demand: No

Internet Service

Operational: Yes.

Broadband Service: In-house.

Fee: $75.00 installation; $40.00 monthly; $20.00 modem lease; $110.00 modem purchase.

Telephone Service

Digital: Operational

Fee: $29.95 monthly

Miles of Plant: 26.0 (coaxial); 36.0 (fiber optic). Includes Stowe

Manager & Chief Technician: Rick Rothammer.

Ownership: Richard Landy (MSO).

MANCHESTER—Formerly served by Adelphia Communications. Now served BENNINGTON, VT [VT0004]. ICA: VT0008.

MOUNT ASCUTNEY—Formerly served by New England Wireless Inc. No longer in operation. ICA: VT0091.

NEWFANE—Comcast Cable. Now served by PUTNEY, VT [VT0067]. ICA: VT0023.

NORTHFIELD (village)—Trans-Video Inc., 56 Depot Sq, Unit 1, Northfield, VT 05663-6723. Phone: 802-485-3811. Fax: 802-485-8451. E-mail: goodrich@trans-video.net. Web Site: http://www.trans-video.net. Also serves Northfield (town) & Riverton. ICA: VT0018.

TV Market Ranking: Outside TV Markets (Northfield (town), NORTHFIELD (VILLAGE), Riverton). Franchise award date: N.A. Franchise expiration date: N.A. Began: December 21, 1951.

Channel capacity: 64 (operating 2-way). Channels available but not in use: N.A.

Basic Service

Subscribers: 1,450.

Programming (received off-air): WCAX-TV (CBS) Burlington; WETK (PBS) Burlington; WFFF-TV (CW, FOX) Burlington; WPTZ (NBC) Plattsburgh; WVNY (ABC) Burlington; allband FM.

Programming (via satellite): Animal Planet; Discovery Channel; HGTV; TBS Superstation; The Learning Channel; Travel Channel.

Fee: $20.00 installation; $20.50 monthly; $3.15 converter.

Expanded Basic Service 1

Subscribers: 1,100.

Programming (via satellite): A&E Networks; ABC Family Channel; AMC; Bravo; Cartoon Network; CNBC; CNN; Comcast SportsNet Mid-Atlantic; Comedy Central; Country Music TV; Discovery Health Channel; Disney Channel; E! Entertainment Television; ESPN; ESPN 2; ESPN Classic Sports; Food Network; Fox News Channel; FX; Hallmark Channel; History Channel; Lifetime; Lifetime Movie Network; MTV; National Geographic Channel; New England Sports Network; Nickelodeon; Outdoor Channel; Speed; Spike TV; Syfy; The Weather Channel; truTV; Turner Classic Movies; Turner Network TV; TV Guide Network; TV Land; USA Network; Versus; VH1; WE tv; WGN America; WPIX (CW, IND) New York; WSBK-TV (CBS, MNT) Boston.

Fee: $20.00 installation; $49.69 monthly.

Digital Basic Service

Subscribers: N.A.

Programming (via satellite): A&E HD; BBC America; Bio; Chiller; CMT Pure Country; Cooking Channel; C-SPAN; C-SPAN 2; Discovery Fit & Health; Discovery Kids Channel; DIY Network; DMX Music; ESPN 2 HD; ESPN HD; ESPN U; ESPNews; Food Network HD; Fox Movie Channel; Fox Reality Channel; Fox Soccer; Fuse; G4; Golf Channel; GSN; HD Theater; HGTV HD; History Channel HD; History Channel International; ID Investigation Discovery; Independent Film Channel; Military Channel; MSNBC; MTV Hits; MTV Jams; MTV2; National Geographic Channel HD Network; New England Sports Network; Nick Jr.; Oxygen; PBS Kids Sprout; Planet Green; RFD-TV; Science; Style Network; Sundance Channel; TeenNick; Toon Disney; Trinity Broadcasting Network; Universal HD; VH1 Classic; VH1 Soul.

Fee: $19.95 monthly.

Digital Pay Service 1

Pay Units: N.A.

Programming (via satellite): Cinemax (multiplexed); Encore; Flix; HBO (multiplexed); Showtime (multiplexed); Starz (multiplexed); Starz HDTV; The Movie Channel (multiplexed).

Fee: $12.95 monthly (each).

Video-On-Demand: No

Pay-Per-View

Addressable homes: 330.

iN DEMAND (delivered digitally); Fresh (delivered digitally); Playboy TV (delivered digitally).

Internet Service

Operational: Yes. Began: August 1, 2000.

Broadband Service: Trans-video.net.

Fee: $32.95-$44.95 monthly.

Telephone Service

Digital: Operational

Fee: $34.95 monthly

Miles of Plant: 40.0 (coaxial); 6.0 (fiber optic).

Manager: George L. Goodrich III. Office Manager: Jill Goodrich.

Ownership: Trans-Video Inc.

PUTNEY—Southern Vermont Cable Co., PO Box 166, Bondville, VT 05340-0166. Phone: 800-544-5931. Fax: 802-297-3714. E-mail: escialabba@svcable.net. Web Site: http://www.svcable.net. Also serves Dummerston, East Jamaica, East Putney, Jamaica Twp., Newfane, Rawsonville, South Newfane, West Dummerston & Williamsville. ICA: VT0067.

TV Market Ranking: Below 100 (Dummerston, East Jamaica, East Putney, Newfane, PUTNEY, South Newfane, West Dummerston, Williamsville); Outside TV Markets (Jamaica Twp., Rawsonville). Franchise award date: October 1, 1988. Franchise expiration date: N.A. Began: January 1, 1978.

Channel capacity: N.A. Channels available but not in use: N.A.

Basic Service

Subscribers: 1,452 Includes Townshend.

Programming (received off-air): WBIN-TV (IND) Derry; WBZ-TV (CBS) Boston; WCDC-TV (ABC) Adams; WCVB-TV (ABC) Boston; WEKW-TV (PBS) Keene; WFXT (FOX) Boston; WHDH (NBC) Boston; WMUR-TV (ABC) Manchester; WNNE (NBC) Hartford; WPIX (CW, IND) New York; WVTA (PBS) Windsor; allband FM.

Programming (via satellite): Boston Catholic Television; C-SPAN; ION Televi-

sion; QVC; TV Guide Network; WSBK-TV (CBS, MNT) Boston.
Programming (via translator): WCAX-TV (CBS) Burlington.
Fee: $30.00 installation; $16.95 monthly; $11.00 additional installation.

Expanded Basic Service 1
Subscribers: 1,151 Includes Townshend.
Programming (via satellite): A&E Networks; AMC; Animal Planet; BBC America; Bravo!; Cartoon Network; CNBC; CNN; Comcast SportsNet New England; Comedy Central; Country Music TV; C-SPAN 2; Discovery Channel; Disney Channel; E! Entertainment Television; ESPN; ESPN 2; Eternal Word TV Network; FamilyNet; Food Network; Fox News Channel; FX; Hallmark Channel; Headline News; HGTV; History Channel; KTLA (CW) Los Angeles; Lifetime; MSNBC; MTV; New England Cable News; Nickelodeon; Oxygen; ShopNBC; Speed; Spike TV; Syfy; TBS Superstation; The Learning Channel; The Weather Channel; Travel Channel; truTV; Turner Classic Movies; Turner Network TV; TV Land; USA Network; Versus; VH1; WGN America.
Fee: $17.00 monthly.

Pay Service 1
Pay Units: 226 Includes Townshend.
Programming (via satellite): HBO; Showtime; The Movie Channel.
Fee: $27.50 installation; $9.95 monthly (HBO), $10.95 monthly (Showtime & TMC).

Video-On-Demand: No

Internet Service
Operational: Yes.
Subscribers: 1,180.
Fee: $55.00 installation; $19.95 monthly.

Telephone Service
Digital: Operational
Fee: $34.95 monthly

Miles of Plant: 97.0 (coaxial); None (fiber optic). Miles of plant include Townshend
Manager & Chief Technician: Ernest Scialabba.
Ownership: Southern Vermont Cable Co. (MSO).

RICHMOND—Formerly served by Adelphia Communications. Now served by BURLINGTON, VT [VT0001]. ICA: VT0068.

ROCHESTER—Formerly served by Adelphia Communications. Now served by BURLINGTON, VT [VT0001]. ICA: VT0069.

RUTLAND—Comcast Cable. Now served by BURLINGTON, VT [VT0001]. ICA: VT0003.

RUTLAND—Formerly served by Satellite Signals of New England. No longer in operation. ICA: VT0086.

SPRINGFIELD—Comcast Cable. Now served by BURLINGTON, VT [VT0001]. ICA: VT0002.

STOWE—Stowe Cablevision, Inc., 172 Thomas Ln, PO Box 453, Stowe, VT 5672. Phone: 802-253-9282. Fax: 802-253-7812. E-mail: stoweaccess@stoweaccess.com. Web Site: http://www.stoweaccess.com. ICA: VT0074.
TV Market Ranking: Below 100 (STOWE). Franchise award date: N.A. Franchise expiration date: N.A. Began: January 1, 1985.
Channel capacity: 126 (operating 2-way). Channels available but not in use: N.A.

Basic Service
Subscribers: 1,025.
Programming (received off-air): WCAX-TV (CBS) Burlington; WETK (PBS) Burlington; WFFF-TV (CW, FOX) Burlington; WPTZ (NBC) Plattsburgh; WVNY (ABC) Burlington.
Programming (via satellite): A&E Networks; ABC Family Channel; AMC; Animal Planet; CNBC; CNN; Comedy Central; Country Music TV; C-SPAN; Discovery Channel; Disney Channel; ESPN; ESPN 2; Food Network; Fox News Channel; G4; Great American Country; Headline News; History Channel; Lifetime; MTV; New England Sports Network; Nickelodeon; Spike TV; Syfy; TBS Superstation; The Learning Channel; The Weather Channel; Turner Network TV; TV Land; USA Network; VH1.
Fee: $60.00 installation; $28.63 monthly.

Digital Basic Service
Subscribers: N.A.
Programming (via satellite): Bio; Bravo; Discovery Digital Networks; ESPN 2; ESPN Classic Sports; ESPNews; Fox Movie Channel; Fox Sports World; Fuse; GAS; Golf Channel; GSN; HGTV; History Channel International; Independent Film Channel; Lifetime Movie Network; MTV Networks Digital Suite; Nick Jr.; NickToons TV; Outdoor Channel; Speed; Style Network; Toon Disney; Turner Classic Movies; Versus; WE tv.
Fee: $25.00 installation; $20.00 monthly.

Pay Service 1
Pay Units: N.A.
Programming (via satellite): HBO.
Fee: $10.00 monthly.

Digital Pay Service 1
Pay Units: N.A.
Programming (via satellite): Cinemax (multiplexed); Encore; Flix; HBO (multiplexed); Showtime (multiplexed); Starz (multiplexed); The Movie Channel (multiplexed).
Fee: $14.28 monthly (Showtime, TMC, & Flix), $14.95 monthly (Starz & Encore), $17.00 monthly (HBO & Cinemax).

Video-On-Demand: No

Pay-Per-View
Playboy TV (delivered digitally).

Internet Service
Operational: Yes. Began: January 1, 2001.
Subscribers: 200.
Broadband Service: Green Mountain Access.
Fee: $75.00 installation; $40.00 monthly; $20.00 modem lease; $110.00 modem purchase.

Telephone Service
Digital: Operational
Fee: $29.95 monthly

Miles of Plant: 26.0 (coaxial); 36.0 (fiber optic).
Manager & Chief Technician: Rick Rothammer.
Ownership: Richard Landy (MSO).

TOWNSHEND—Southern Vermont Cable Co., PO Box 166, Bondville, VT 05340-0166. Phone: 800-544-5931. Fax: 802-297-3714. E-mail: escialabba@svcable.net. Web Site: http://www.svcable.net. Also serves West Townshend. ICA: VT0076.
TV Market Ranking: Outside TV Markets (TOWNSHEND, West Townshend). Franchise award date: N.A. Franchise expiration date: April 30, 2011. Began: N.A.
Channel capacity: N.A. Channels available but not in use: N.A.

Basic Service
Subscribers: N.A. Included in Putney
Programming (received off-air): WBIN-TV (IND) Derry; WBPX-TV (ION) Boston; WBZ-TV (CBS) Boston; WCAX-TV (CBS) Burlington; WCDC-TV (ABC) Adams; WCVB-TV (ABC) Boston; WEKW-TV (PBS) Keene; WFXT (FOX) Boston; WHDH (NBC) Boston; WMUR-TV (ABC) Manchester; WNNE (NBC) Hartford; WPIX (CW, IND) New York; WSBK-TV (CBS, MNT) Boston; WVTA (PBS) Windsor.
Programming (via satellite): Boston Catholic Television; C-SPAN; ION Television; QVC; TV Guide Network.
Fee: $30.00 installation; $16.95 monthly.

Expanded Basic Service 1
Subscribers: N.A. Included in Putney
Programming (via satellite): A&E Networks; AMC; Animal Planet; BBC America; Bravo; Cartoon Network; CNBC; CNN; Comcast SportsNet New England; Comedy Central; Country Music TV; C-SPAN 2; Discovery Channel; Disney Channel; E! Entertainment Television; ESPN; ESPN 2; Eternal Word TV Network; FamilyNet; Food Network; Fox News Channel; FX; Hallmark Channel; Headline News; HGTV; History Channel; Lifetime; MSNBC; MTV; New England Cable News; New England Sports Network; Nickelodeon; Oxygen; ShopNBC; Speed; Spike TV; Syfy; TBS Superstation; The Learning Channel; The Weather Channel; Travel Channel; truTV; Turner Classic Movies; Turner Network TV; TV Land; USA Network; Versus; VH1; WGN America.
Fee: $17.00 monthly.

Pay Service 1
Pay Units: N.A. Included in Putney
Programming (via satellite): HBO; Showtime; The Movie Channel.
Fee: $9.95 monthly (HBO), $10.95 monthly each (Showtime & TMC).

Video-On-Demand: No

Internet Service
Operational: Yes.
Fee: $55.00 installation; $19.95 monthly.

Telephone Service
Digital: Operational
Fee: $34.95 monthly

Miles of plant included in Putney
Manager & Chief Technician: Ernest Scialabba.
Ownership: Southern Vermont Cable Co. (MSO).

WAITSFIELD—Waitsfield Cable Co., 3898 Main St, PO Box 9, Waitsfield, VT 05673-0009. Phone: 802-496-5800. Fax: 802-496-7040. E-mail: ghaskin@wcvt.com. Web Site: http://www.waitsfieldcable.com. Also serves Fayston, Moretown, Warren & Washington County (portions). ICA: VT0014.
TV Market Ranking: Below 100 (Fayston, Moretown, WAITSFIELD, Warren, Washington County (portions)); Outside TV Markets (Washington County (portions)). Franchise award date: N.A. Franchise expiration date: N.A. Began: October 1, 1982.
Channel capacity: N.A. Channels available but not in use: N.A.

Digital Basic Service
Subscribers: 3,382.
Programming (via satellite): C-SPAN; C-SPAN 2; C-SPAN 3; HD Theater; various Canadian stations; WGN America.
Fee: $25.00 installation; $18.50 monthly.

Digital Expanded Basic Service
Subscribers: 3,221.
Programming (via satellite): A&E HD; A&E Networks; ABC Family Channel; ABC Family HD; AMC; Animal Planet; Cartoon Network; CNBC; CNN; CNN HD; Comedy Central; Country Music TV; Discovery Channel; Disney Channel; Disney Channel HD; E! Entertainment Television; ESPN; ESPN 2; ESPN 2 HD; ESPN HD; Food Network; Food Network HD; Fox News Channel; FX; Headline News; History Channel; History Channel HD; Lifetime; MSNBC; MTV; National Geographic Channel; National Geographic Channel HD Network; New England Sports Network; NFL Network; NFL Network HD; Nickelodeon; Oxygen; Spike TV; TBS in HD; TBS Superstation; The Learning Channel; The Weather Channel; Toon Disney; Travel Channel; Travel Channel HD; truTV; Turner Network TV; Turner Network TV HD; TV Land; USA Network; Versus; VH1.
Fee: $27.20 monthly.

Digital Expanded Basic Service 2
Subscribers: N.A.
Programming (via satellite): BBC America; Bio; Bio HD; Bloomberg Television; Bravo; cloo; CMT Pure Country; Discovery Fit & Health; Discovery Health Channel; Discovery Kids Channel; DIY Network; DMX Music; ESPN Classic Sports; ESPN U; ESPNews; Fox Soccer; Fuse; G4; Golf Channel; GSN; Hallmark Channel; Halogen Network; HGTV; HGTV HD; History Channel International; HRTV; ID Investigation Discovery; Independent Film Channel; Lifetime Movie Network; Military Channel; MTV Hits; MTV2; Nick Jr.; Outdoor Channel; Outdoor Channel 2 HD; Planet Green; Science; Speed; Style Network; Sundance Channel; Syfy; TeenNick; Tennis Channel; Trinity Broadcasting Network; Turner Classic Movies; Versus HD; VH1 Classic; VH1 Soul; WE tv.
Fee: $15.10 monthly.

Digital Pay Service 1
Pay Units: N.A.
Programming (via satellite): Cinemax (multiplexed); Cinemax HD; Encore (multiplexed); HBO (multiplexed); HBO HD; Showtime (multiplexed); Showtime HD; Starz (multiplexed); Starz HDTV; The Movie Channel (multiplexed).
Fee: $12.95 monthly (HBO, Cinemax, Showtime/TMC, or Starz/Encore).

Video-On-Demand: No

Pay-Per-View
iN DEMAND (delivered digitally); MLB Extra Innings; NBA League Pass (delivered digitally).

Internet Service
Operational: No.
Broadband Service: DSL service only.

Telephone Service
None

Miles of Plant: 205.0 (coaxial); None (fiber optic).

President & Chief Executive Officer: Gregg Haskin. Technical Supervisor: Don Whittman. Customer Service Manager: Patricia Labnon.
Ownership: Waitsfield-Fayston Telephone Co.

WEST DOVER—Duncan Cable TV (formerly Area Telecable). Now served by WILMINGTON, VT [VT0017]. ICA: VT0016.

WHITINGHAM—Formerly served by Area Telecable. No longer in operation. ICA: VT0087.

WILLIAMSTOWN (portions)—Formerly served by North Valley Cable Systems Inc. No longer in operation. ICA: VT0084.

WILMINGTON—Duncan Cable TV Service, 48 Sunny Knoll Dr, PO Box 685, Wilmington, VT 05363-0685. Phone: 802-464-2233. Fax: 802-464-3232. E-mail: dctv8@sover.net. Web Site: http://www.duncancable.com. Also serves Wardsboro Twp. & West Dover. ICA: VT0017.
TV Market Ranking: Below 100 (Wardsboro Twp., West Dover, WILMINGTON). Franchise award date: N.A. Franchise expiration date: N.A. Began: January 1, 1966.
Channel capacity: N.A. Channels available but not in use: N.A.

Basic Service
Subscribers: 2,800.
Programming (received off-air): WNNE (NBC) Hartford; WTEN (ABC) Albany; WVTA (PBS) Windsor; allband FM.
Programming (via microwave): WBZ-TV (CBS) Boston; WCVB-TV (ABC) Boston; WFXT (FOX) Boston; WGBH-TV (PBS) Boston; WHDH (NBC) Boston; WLVI-TV (CW) Cambridge.
Programming (via satellite): A&E Networks; AMC; CNBC; CNN; Discovery Channel; Disney Channel; ESPN; HGTV; Lifetime; Nickelodeon; QVC; Spike TV; Syfy; TBS Superstation; The Learning Channel; truTV; Turner Network TV; VH1; WSBK-TV (CBS, MNT) Boston.
Fee: $49.95 installation; $23.89 monthly.

Pay Service 1
Pay Units: 190.
Programming (via satellite): HBO.
Fee: $12.95 monthly.
Video-On-Demand: No

Internet Service
Operational: Yes, Dial-up. Began: April 1, 2002.
Subscribers: 250.
Broadband Service: Sovernet.
Fee: $39.95 monthly.

Telephone Service
None
Miles of Plant: 52.0 (coaxial); 12.0 (fiber optic). Additional miles planned: 3.0 (coaxial).
Manager: Clifford Duncan.
Ownership: Clifford Duncan.

VIRGINIA

Total Systems: **106**
Total Communities Served: **572**
Franchises Not Yet Operating: **0**
Applications Pending: **0**
Communities with Applications: **0**
Number of Basic Subscribers: **1,961,115**
Number of Expanded Basic Subscribers: **419,291**
Number of Pay Units: **390,833**

Top 100 Markets Represented: Norfolk-Newport News-Portsmouth-Hampton (44); Richmond-Petersburg (63); Roanoke-Lynchburg (70); Washington, DC (9).

For a list of cable communities in this section, see the Cable Community Index located in the back of Cable Volume 2.
For explanation of terms used in cable system listings, see p. D-11.

ACCOMAC—Charter Communications, 216 Moore Ave, Suffolk, VA 23434. Phone: 757-539-0713. Fax: 757-539-1057. Web Site: http://www.charter.com. Also serves Accomack County, Belle Haven, Bloxom, Cheriton, Eastville, Exmore, Hallwood, Keller, Melfa, Nassawodox, Northampton County, Onancock, Onley, Painter, Parksley, Saxis & Wachapreague. ICA: VA0158.

TV Market Ranking: 44 (Cheriton, Eastville, Northampton County (portions)); Below 100 (Accomack County (portions), Hallwood, Saxis, Northampton County (portions)); Outside TV Markets (ACCOMAC, Accomack County (portions), Belle Haven, Bloxom, Exmore, Keller, Melfa, Nassawodox, Onancock, Onley, Painter, Parksley, Wachapreague, Northampton County (portions)). Franchise award date: N.A. Franchise expiration date: N.A. Began: June 5, 1970.

Channel capacity: N.A. Channels available but not in use: N.A.

Basic Service

Subscribers: 5,203.

Programming (received off-air): WAVY-TV (NBC) Portsmouth; WBOC-TV (CBS, FOX) Salisbury; WGNT (CW) Portsmouth; WHRO-TV (PBS) Hampton-Norfolk; WMDT (ABC, CW) Salisbury; WPXV-TV (ION) Norfolk; WTKR (CBS) Norfolk; WTVZ-TV (MNT) Norfolk; WVBT (FOX) Virginia Beach; WVEC (ABC) Hampton; 14 FMs.

Programming (via satellite): BET Networks; Bravo; Comcast SportsNet Mid-Atlantic; E! Entertainment Television; ESPN; ESPN 2; Golf Channel; INSP; Lifetime; QVC; Speed; The Weather Channel; Turner Classic Movies.

Fee: $29.99 installation.

Expanded Basic Service 1

Subscribers: 4,648.

Programming (via satellite): A&E Networks; ABC Family Channel; AMC; Cartoon Network; CNBC; CNN; Comedy Central; Country Music TV; C-SPAN; Discovery Channel; Disney Channel; Fox News Channel; FX; G4; Headline News; HGTV; History Channel; MTV; Nickelodeon; Oxygen; Spike TV; Syfy; TBS Superstation; The Learning Channel; Turner Network TV; TV Land; USA Network; VH1; WE tv.

Fee: $47.99 monthly.

Digital Basic Service

Subscribers: N.A.

Programming (via satellite): BBC America; Bio; Bloomberg Television; Discovery Fit & Health; DIY Network; ESPN Classic Sports; ESPNews; Fox College Sports Atlantic; Fox College Sports Central; Fox College Sports Pacific; Fox Movie Channel; Fox Soccer; Fuse; GAS; GSN; History Channel International; Independent Film Channel; Lifetime Movie Network; Mid-Atlantic Sports Network; MTV Networks Digital Suite; Music Choice; National Geographic Channel; Nick Jr.; Nick Too; SoapNet; Style Network; Sundance Channel; Toon Disney; TV Guide Interactive Inc.

Digital Pay Service 1

Pay Units: N.A.

Programming (via satellite): Cinemax (multiplexed); Encore; Flix; HBO (multiplexed); Showtime (multiplexed); Starz (multiplexed); The Movie Channel (multiplexed).

Video-On-Demand: No

Pay-Per-View

iN DEMAND (delivered digitally); Playboy TV (delivered digitally); Fresh (delivered digitally); Shorteez (delivered digitally).

Internet Service

Operational: No.

Telephone Service

None

Miles of Plant: 288.0 (coaxial); None (fiber optic).

Vice President & General Manager: Anthony Pope. Marketing Director: Brooke Sinclair. Marketing Manager: LaRisa Scales. Operations Manager: Tom Ross.

Ownership: Charter Communications Inc. (MSO).

ALEXANDRIA—Comcast Cable, 508 S Van Dorn St, Alexandria, VA 22304-4612. Phone: 703-789-8100 (Manassas office). Fax: 703-567-4444. Web Site: http://www.comcast.com. ICA: VA0009.

TV Market Ranking: 9 (ALEXANDRIA). Franchise award date: July 26, 1979. Franchise expiration date: June 18, 2009. Began: November 6, 1980.

Channel capacity: N.A. Channels available but not in use: N.A.

Basic Service

Subscribers: 38,400.

Programming (received off-air): WDCA (MNT) Washington; WDCW (CW) Washington; WETA-TV (PBS) Washington; WFDC-DT (UNV) Arlington; WHUT-TV (PBS) Washington; WJLA-TV (ABC) Washington; WMDO-CA (TEL) Washington; WMPT (PBS) Annapolis; WPXW-TV (ION) Manassas; WRC-TV (NBC) Washington; WTTG (FOX) Washington; WUSA (CBS) Washington; allband FM.

Programming (via microwave): NewsChannel 8.

Programming (via satellite): ESPN 2; Home Shopping Network 2; QVC; TBS Superstation; TV Guide Network.

Fee: $26.74 installation; $14.95 monthly; $1.45 converter.

Expanded Basic Service 1

Subscribers: N.A.

Programming (via satellite): A&E Networks; ABC Family Channel; AMC; Animal Planet; BET Networks; Bravo; Cartoon Network; CNBC; CNN; Comcast SportsNet Mid-Atlantic; Comedy Central; Country Music TV; C-SPAN; C-SPAN 2; Discovery Channel; Discovery Health Channel; Disney Channel; E! Entertainment Television; ESPN; Food Network; Fox News Channel; FX; Golf Channel; Great American Country; GSN; Headline News; HGTV; History Channel; Lifetime; MSNBC; MTV; Nickelodeon; Product Information Network; ShopNBC; Sneak Prevue; Speed; Spike TV; Style Network; Syfy; The Learning Channel; The Weather Channel; truTV; Turner Classic Movies; Turner Network TV; TV Land; TV One; Versus; VH1.

Fee: $26.74 installation; $38.25 monthly.

Digital Basic Service

Subscribers: N.A.

Programming (via satellite): BBC America; Cooking Channel; C-SPAN 3; Discovery Digital Networks; DIY Network; DMX Music; ESPN Classic Sports; ESPNews; Fox Sports World; G4; GAS; GolTV; Mid-Atlantic Sports Network; MTV Networks Digital Suite; MTV2; National Geographic Channel; NBA TV; Nick Jr.; Nick Too; SoapNet; Toon Disney; WAM! America's Kidz Network; Weatherscan.

Fee: $18.45 monthly.

Pay Service 1

Pay Units: 8,088.

Programming (via satellite): Cinemax.

Fee: $13.95 monthly.

Pay Service 2

Pay Units: N.A.

Programming (via satellite): The Movie Channel.

Fee: $13.95 monthly.

Pay Service 3

Pay Units: 12,528.

Programming (via satellite): HBO.

Fee: $16.95 monthly.

Pay Service 4

Pay Units: 4,556.

Programming (via satellite): Showtime.

Fee: $13.95 monthly.

Digital Pay Service 1

Pay Units: N.A.

Programming (via satellite): Canales N; Cinemax (multiplexed); Encore (multiplexed); Flix (multiplexed); HBO (multiplexed); International Television (ITV); Showtime (multiplexed); Sundance Channel (multiplexed); The Movie Channel.

Video-On-Demand: Yes

Pay-Per-View

iN DEMAND; Fresh; Hot Choice (delivered digitally); Playboy TV (delivered digitally); iN DEMAND (delivered digitally); Pleasure (delivered digitally); ESPN (delivered digitally); NBA (delivered digitally).

Internet Service

Operational: Yes.

Broadband Service: Comcast High Speed Internet.

Fee: $42.95 monthly; $7.00 modem lease; $180.00 modem purchase.

Telephone Service

Digital: Operational

Miles of Plant: 274.0 (coaxial); None (fiber optic).

Vice President & General Manager: Christine Whitaker. Technical Operations Director: Scott Shelley. Technical Operations Manager: Kelvin Webb. Marketing Director: Shawn Houston. Marketing Manager: Lyn Harmon.

Ownership: Comcast Cable Communications Inc. (MSO).

ALTAVISTA—Formerly served by Adelphia Communications. Now served by DANVILLE, VA [VA0012]. ICA: VA0068.

AMELIA COUNTY (portions)—Comcast Cable, 2277 Academy Rd, PO Box 100, Powhatan, VA 23139-0100. Phones: 804-598-8725; 804-915-5400. Fax: 804-598-2988. Web Site: http://www.comcast.com. ICA: VA0084.

TV Market Ranking: 63 (AMELIA COUNTY (PORTIONS)); Outside TV Markets (AMELIA COUNTY (PORTIONS)). Franchise award date: December 12, 1988. Franchise expiration date: N.A. Began: February 1, 1989.

Channel capacity: N.A. Channels available but not in use: N.A.

Basic Service

Subscribers: N.A. Included in Richmond

Programming (received off-air): WCVE-TV (PBS) Richmond; WRIC-TV (ABC) Petersburg; WRLH-TV (FOX, MNT) Richmond; WTVR-TV (CBS) Richmond; WUPV (CW) Ashland; WWBT (NBC) Richmond.

Programming (via satellite): C-SPAN; QVC; TBS Superstation; Trinity Broadcasting Network; WGN America.

Fee: $40.00 installation; $14.95 monthly.

Expanded Basic Service 1

Subscribers: N.A.

Programming (via satellite): A&E Networks; ABC Family Channel; AMC; BET Networks; Cartoon Network; CNBC; CNN; Country Music TV; Discovery Channel; Disney Channel; ESPN; ESPN 2; Fox News Channel; FX; Headline News; HGTV; History Channel; Lifetime; MTV; Nickelodeon; Spike TV; Syfy; The Learning Channel; The Weather Channel; Turner Network TV; TV Land; USA Network.

Digital Basic Service

Subscribers: N.A. Included in Richmond

Programming (via satellite): American-Life TV Network; BBC America; Bio; Black Family Channel; Bloomberg Television; Discovery Fit & Health; DMX Music; ESPN Classic Sports; ESPNews; Fox Sports World; Fuse; G4; GAS; Golf Channel; Great American Country; GSN; Halogen Network; History Channel International; Independent Film Channel; Lifetime Movie Network; Mid-Atlantic Sports Network; MTV Networks Digital Suite; National Geographic

Channel; Nick Jr.; NickToons TV; Outdoor Channel; Speed; Style Network; Sundance Channel; The Word Network; Toon Disney; Turner Classic Movies; Versus; WE tv.

Digital Pay Service 1

Pay Units: N.A.

Programming (via satellite): Cinemax (multiplexed); Encore; Flix; HBO (multiplexed); Showtime (multiplexed); The Movie Channel (multiplexed).

Video-On-Demand: No

Pay-Per-View

Urban American Television Network (delivered digitally); Hot Choice (delivered digitally); Fresh (delivered digitally); Playboy TV (delivered digitally); Hits Movies & Events (delivered digitally).

Internet Service

Operational: No.

Telephone Service

None

Miles of Plant: 65.0 (coaxial); None (fiber optic).

Vice President & General Manager: Kirby Brooks. Technical Operations Director: Stephen Hill. Technical Supervisor: Bob King. Marketing Director: Erin Powell. Public Relations Manager: Monica Smith-Callahan. Office Manager: Joyce Johnson.

Ownership: Comcast Cable Communications Inc. (MSO).

AMHERST COUNTY (southern portion)—Comcast Cable, 400 Westfield Rd, Charlottesville, VA 22901. Phone: 434-951-3700. Fax: 434-951-3705. Web Site: http://www.comcast.com. Also serves Amherst. ICA: VA0039.

TV Market Ranking: 70 (AMHERST, AMHERST COUNTY (SOUTHERN PORTION)). Franchise award date: January 1, 1968. Franchise expiration date: N.A. Began: January 1, 1970.

Channel capacity: N.A. Channels available but not in use: N.A.

Basic Service

Subscribers: 4,623.

Programming (received off-air): WBRA-TV (PBS) Roanoke; WCVE-TV (PBS) Richmond; WDBJ (CBS, MNT) Roanoke; WSET-TV (ABC) Lynchburg; WSLS-TV (NBC) Roanoke; WTVR-TV (CBS) Richmond; WWBT (NBC) Richmond; WWCW (CW, FOX) Lynchburg; allband FM.

Programming (via satellite): QVC; TBS Superstation; WGN America.

Fee: $50.00 installation; $22.95 monthly; $2.50 converter; $25.00 additional installation.

Expanded Basic Service 1

Subscribers: 4,564.

Programming (via satellite): A&E Networks; ABC Family Channel; BET Networks; Cartoon Network; CNN; Comcast SportsNet Mid-Atlantic; C-SPAN; Discovery Channel; Disney Channel; ESPN; Headline News; Lifetime; MTV; Nickelodeon; Spike TV; The Weather Channel; Turner Network TV; USA Network.

Pay Service 1

Pay Units: 531.

Programming (via satellite): Cinemax.

Fee: $11.50 monthly.

Pay Service 2

Pay Units: 723.

Programming (via satellite): HBO.

Fee: $11.50 monthly.

Pay Service 3

Pay Units: 256.

Programming (via satellite): Showtime.

Fee: $11.50 monthly.

Pay Service 4

Pay Units: 125.

Programming (via satellite): The Movie Channel.

Fee: $11.50 monthly.

Video-On-Demand: Yes

Internet Service

Operational: Yes.

Broadband Service: Comcast High Speed Internet.

Fee: $42.95 monthly.

Telephone Service

Digital: Operational

Miles of Plant: 152.0 (coaxial); None (fiber optic).

Vice President & General Manager: Tony Fitzhugh. Technical Operations Director: Tom Jacobs. Technical Operations Manager: Make Buckner. Marketing Director: Steve Miles.

Ownership: Comcast Cable Communications Inc. (MSO).

APPOMATTOX—Jet Broadband. Now served by RUSTBURG (formerly Timberlake), VA [VA0128]. ICA: VA0088.

ARLINGTON—Comcast Cable, 508 S Van Dorn St, Alexandria, VA 22304-4612. Phones: 703-789-8100 (Manassas office); 703-567-4600. Fax: 703-567-4444. Web Site: http://www.comcast.com. Also serves Fort Myer Army Base. ICA: VA0005.

TV Market Ranking: 9 (ARLINGTON, Fort Myer Army Base). Franchise award date: March 3, 1973. Franchise expiration date: June 30, 2013. Began: July 18, 1978.

Channel capacity: N.A. Channels available but not in use: N.A.

Basic Service

Subscribers: 50,538.

Programming (received off-air): WDCA (MNT) Washington; WDCW (CW) Washington; WETA-TV (PBS) Washington; WFDC-DT (UNV) Arlington; WHUT-TV (PBS) Washington; WJLA-TV (ABC) Washington; WMDO-CA (TEL) Washington; WMPT (PBS) Annapolis; WPXW-TV (ION) Manassas; WRC-TV (NBC) Washington; WTTG (FOX) Washington; WUSA (CBS) Washington.

Programming (via microwave): NewsChannel 8.

Programming (via satellite): Animal Planet; C-SPAN; FX; TBS Superstation; The Learning Channel; TV Guide Network.

Fee: $23.96 installation; $13.99 monthly.

Expanded Basic Service 1

Subscribers: N.A.

Programming (via satellite): A&E Networks; ABC Family Channel; AMC; BET Networks; Bravo; Cartoon Network; CNBC; CNN; Comcast SportsNet Mid-Atlantic; Comedy Central; Country Music TV; C-SPAN 2; Discovery Channel; Discovery Health Channel; Disney Channel; E! Entertainment Television; ESPN; ESPN 2; Food Network; Fox News Channel; Golf Channel; Great American Country; GSN; Headline News; HGTV; History Channel; Home Shopping Network 2; Lifetime; MSNBC; MTV; Nickelodeon; Product Information Network; QVC; ShopNBC; Sneak Prevue; Speed; Spike TV; Style Network; Syfy; Telemundo; The Weather Channel; truTV; Turner Classic Movies; Turner Network TV; TV Land; TV One; USA Network; Versus; VH1.

Fee: $33.08 monthly.

Digital Basic Service

Subscribers: N.A.

Programming (via satellite): BBC America; Cooking Channel; C-SPAN 3; Discovery Digital Networks; DIY Network; DMX Music; ESPN Classic Sports; ESPNews; G4; GAS; GolTV; Mid-Atlantic Sports Network; MTV Networks Digital Suite; National Geographic Channel; NBA TV; Nick Jr.; Nick Too; SoapNet; Toon Disney; WAM! America's Kidz Network; Weatherscan.

Pay Service 1

Pay Units: 5,308.

Programming (via satellite): Cinemax.

Fee: $15.00 installation; $10.95 monthly.

Pay Service 2

Pay Units: 11,560.

Programming (via satellite): The Movie Channel.

Fee: $15.00 installation; $10.95 monthly.

Pay Service 3

Pay Units: 15,537.

Programming (via satellite): HBO.

Fee: $15.00 installation; $10.95 monthly.

Pay Service 4

Pay Units: 4,152.

Programming (via satellite): Showtime (multiplexed).

Fee: $15.00 installation; $10.95 monthly.

Digital Pay Service 1

Pay Units: N.A.

Programming (via satellite): Canales N; Cinemax (multiplexed); Encore (multiplexed); Flix (multiplexed); HBO (multiplexed); International Television (ITV); Showtime (multiplexed); Sundance Channel (multiplexed); The Movie Channel (multiplexed).

Fee: $10.49 monthly (each).

Video-On-Demand: Yes

Pay-Per-View

Addressable homes: 11,613.

Fresh (delivered digitally); iN DEMAND; iN DEMAND (delivered digitally); Playboy TV (delivered digitally); Pleasure (delivered digitally); Hot Choice (delivered digitally); ESPN (delivered digitally); NBA (delivered digitally).

Internet Service

Operational: Yes.

Broadband Service: Comcast High Speed Internet.

Fee: $42.95 monthly; $7.00 modem lease; $199.00 modem purchase.

Telephone Service

Analog: Not Operational

Digital: Operational

Fee: $44.95 monthly

Miles of Plant: 450.0 (coaxial); 5.0 (fiber optic). Additional miles planned: 5.0 (coaxial).

Vice President & General Manager: Christine Whitaker. Technical Operations Director: Scott Shelley. Technical Operations Manager: Kelvin Webb. Marketing Director: Shawn Houston. Marketing Manager: Lynn Harmon.

Ownership: Comcast Cable Communications Inc. (MSO).

AUSTINVILLE—Citizens Telephone Coop. Now served by FORT CHISWELL, VA [VA0066]. ICA: VA5301.

BARREN SPRINGS—Citizens Telephone Coop. Now served by FORT CHISWELL, VA [VA0066]. ICA: VA5302.

BASTIAN—Formerly served by Almega Cable. No longer in operation. ICA: VA0124.

BEDFORD—Charter Communications. Now served by REDWOOD (formerly Franklin County), VA [VA0033]. ICA: VA0048.

BELLE HAVEN—Charter Communications. Now served by ACCOMAC, VA [VA0158]. ICA: VA0046.

BEN HUR—Formerly served by Adelphia Communications. Now served by NORTON, VA [VA0157]. ICA: VA0123.

BISHOP—Bishop TV Club Inc. Now served by RICHLANDS, VA [VA0041]. ICA: VA0118.

BLACKSBURG—Comcast Cable, 1415 S Main St, Blacksburg, VA 24060-5556. Phones: 434-951-3700 (Charlottesville office); 540-961-0389. Fax: 540-552-2416. Web Site: http://www.comcast.com. Also serves Alleghany Springs, Christiansburg, Elliston, Lafayette, Montgomery County & Shawsville. ICA: VA0020.

TV Market Ranking: 70 (Alleghany Springs, BLACKSBURG, Christiansburg, Elliston, Lafayette, Montgomery County, Shawsville). Franchise award date: December 1, 1964. Franchise expiration date: December 1, 2009. Began: July 1, 1970.

Channel capacity: N.A. Channels available but not in use: N.A.

Basic Service

Subscribers: 10,156.

Programming (received off-air): WBRA-TV (PBS) Roanoke; WDBJ (CBS, MNT) Roanoke; WDRL-TV (IND) Danville; WFXR (CW, FOX) Roanoke; WPXR-TV (ION) Roanoke; WSET-TV (ABC) Lynchburg; WSLS-TV (NBC) Roanoke; WWCW (CW, FOX) Lynchburg; allband FM.

Programming (via satellite): C-SPAN; C-SPAN 2; CW+; Product Information Network; QVC; TV Guide Network; WGN America.

Fee: $43.00 installation; $21.00 monthly; $3.25 converter; $33.00 additional installation.

Expanded Basic Service 1

Subscribers: N.A.

Programming (via satellite): A&E Networks; ABC Family Channel; AMC; Animal Planet; BET Networks; Bravo; Cartoon Network; CNBC; CNN; Comcast SportsNet Mid-Atlantic; Comedy Central; Country Music TV; Discovery Channel; Disney Channel; E! Entertainment Television; ESPN; ESPN 2; Eternal Word TV Network; Food Network; Fox News Channel; FX; Hallmark Channel; Headline News; HGTV; History Channel; INSP; Lifetime; MSNBC; MTV; Nickelodeon; Oxygen; ShopNBC; Spike TV; Syfy; TBS Superstation; The Learning Channel; The Weather Channel; Travel Channel; truTV; Turner Classic Movies; Turner Network TV; TV Land; USA Network; VH1.

Fee: $33.70 monthly.

Digital Basic Service

Subscribers: 8,000.

Programming (via satellite): A&E HD; Animal Planet HD; BBC America; Bio; Bloomberg Television; Canal 52MX; Cine Latino; Cine Mexicano; CMT Pure Country; CNN en Espanol; CNN HD; College Sports Television; C-SPAN 2; C-SPAN 3; Current; Daystar TV Network; Discovery Channel HD; Discovery en Espanol; Discovery Fit & Health; Discovery Health Channel; Discovery Home Channel; Discovery Kids Channel; DIY Network; Encore (multiplexed); ESPN 2 HD; ESPN Classic Sports; ESPN Deportes; ESPN HD; ESPNews; EWTN en Espanol; Flix; Food Network HD; Fox Business Channel; Fox College Sports Atlantic; Fox College Sports Central; Fox College Sports Pacific; Fox Deportes; Fox Movie Channel; Fox Reality Channel; Fox Soccer; Fuel TV; Fuse; G4; GalaVision; GMC; Golf Channel; Great American Country; GSN; Halogen Network; HD Theater;

HGTV HD; History Channel en Espanol; History Channel HD; History Channel International; Howard TV; ID Investigation Discovery; Independent Film Channel; Jewelry Television; Lifetime Movie Network; LOGO; Military Channel; MTV Hits; MTV Jams; MTV2; Music Choice; MyNetworkTV Inc.; National Geographic Channel; National Geographic Channel HD Network; NBA TV; NFL Network; NHL Network; Nick Jr.; Nick Too; NickToons TV; Outdoor Channel; Palladia; PBS Kids Sprout; Science; SoapNet; Speed; Style Network; Sundance Channel; Syfy HD; TBS in HD; TeenNick; Telefutura; The Word Network; TLC HD; Toon Disney; Toon Disney en Espanol; Tr3s; Trinity Broadcasting Network; Turner Network TV HD; TV One; TVG Network; Universal HD; USA Network HD; VeneMovies; Versus; Versus HD; VH1 Classic; VH1 Soul; WE tv.

Digital Pay Service 1
Pay Units: N.A.
Programming (via satellite): Cinemax (multiplexed); Cinemax HD; Cinemax On Demand; HBO (multiplexed); HBO HD; HBO On Demand; Showtime (multiplexed); Showtime HD; Showtime On Demand; Starz (multiplexed); Starz HDTV; Starz On Demand; The Movie Channel (multiplexed); The Movie Channel On Demand.

Video-On-Demand: Yes

Pay-Per-View
Playboy TV (delivered digitally); iN DEMAND (delivered digitally); Spice: Xcess (delivered digitally).

Internet Service
Operational: Yes. Began: July 1, 2001.
Subscribers: 2,000.
Broadband Service: Comcast High Speed Internet.
Fee: $50.00 installation; $34.95 monthly.

Telephone Service
Digital: Operational

Miles of Plant: 624.0 (coaxial); 624.0 (fiber optic).

Vice President & General Manager: Troy Fitzhugh. Technical Operations Director: Tom Jacobs. Plant Manager: John Van Lew. Chief Technician: Carl Brown. Marketing Director: Steve Miles. Office Manager: Donna Lincoln.

Ownership: Comcast Cable Communications Inc. (MSO).

BLACKSTONE—Nesbe Cable TV. Now served by CREWE, VA [VA0099]. ICA: VA0081.

BOWLING GREEN—MetroCast, 233 Colonial Ave, Colonial Beach, VA 22443. Phone: 800-633-8578. Web Site: http://www.metrocastcommunications.com. Also serves Caroline County. ICA: VA0093.

TV Market Ranking: 63 (Caroline County (portions)); Below 100 (BOWLING GREEN, Caroline County (portions)). Franchise award date: February 3, 1972. Franchise expiration date: September 3, 2007. Began: January 1, 1973.

Channel capacity: N.A. Channels available but not in use: N.A.

Basic Service
Subscribers: 961.
Programming (received off-air): WCVE-TV (PBS) Richmond; WCVW (PBS) Richmond; WDCA (MNT) Washington; WRIC-TV (ABC) Petersburg; WRLH-TV (FOX, MNT) Richmond; WTVR-TV (CBS) Richmond; WUPV (CW) Ashland; WUSA (CBS) Washington; WWBT (NBC) Richmond; allband FM.
Programming (via satellite): INSP; QVC; WGN America.
Fee: $35.64 installation; $20.10 monthly; $.75 converter.

Expanded Basic Service 1
Subscribers: 917.
Programming (via satellite): A&E Networks; ABC Family Channel; AMC; Animal Planet; BET Networks; Bravo; Cartoon Network; CNBC; CNN; Comcast SportsNet Mid-Atlantic; Comedy Central; Country Music TV; Discovery Channel; Disney Channel; E! Entertainment Television; ESPN; ESPN 2; Food Network; Fox News Channel; FX; G4; Golf Channel; Headline News; HGTV; History Channel; Lifetime; MSNBC; MTV; Nickelodeon; Oxygen; Speed; Spike TV; Syfy; TBS Superstation; The Learning Channel; The Weather Channel; Travel Channel; truTV; Turner Classic Movies; Turner Network TV; TV Land; USA Network; VH1; WE tv.
Fee: $13.95 monthly.

Digital Basic Service
Subscribers: N.A.
Programming (via satellite): BBC America; Bio; Bloomberg Television; Discovery Fit & Health; DIY Network; ESPN Classic Sports; ESPNews; Fox College Sports Atlantic; Fox College Sports Central; Fox College Sports Pacific; Fox Movie Channel; Fox Soccer; Fuse; GAS; GSN; History Channel International; Independent Film Channel; MTV Networks Digital Suite; Music Choice; National Geographic Channel; Nick Jr.; Nick Too; NickToons TV; SoapNet; Sundance Channel; Toon Disney; TV Guide Interactive Inc.

Digital Pay Service 1
Pay Units: 32.
Programming (via satellite): Cinemax (multiplexed).
Fee: $11.50 monthly.

Digital Pay Service 2
Pay Units: 75.
Programming (via satellite): HBO (multiplexed).
Fee: $11.50 monthly.

Digital Pay Service 3
Pay Units: N.A.
Programming (via satellite): Encore (multiplexed); Flix; Showtime (multiplexed); Starz (multiplexed); The Movie Channel (multiplexed).

Video-On-Demand: No

Pay-Per-View
iN DEMAND (delivered digitally); Playboy TV (delivered digitally); Fresh (delivered digitally); Shorteez (delivered digitally).

Internet Service
Operational: No.

Telephone Service
None

Miles of Plant: 49.0 (coaxial); None (fiber optic).

General Manager: Danny L. Jobe.

Ownership: Harron Communications LP (MSO).

BRISTOL—Formerly [VA0190]. BVU OptiNet. This cable system has converted to IPTV, 15022 Lee Hwy, Bristol, VA 24202. Phones: 276-821-6100; 866-835-1288. Fax: 276-821-6218. E-mail: help@bvu-optinet.com. Web Site: http://www.bvu-optinet.com. ICA: VA5201.

TV Market Ranking: Below 100 (BRISTOL).

Channel capacity: N.A. Channels available but not in use: N.A.

Internet Service
Operational: Yes.

Telephone Service
Digital: Operational

BRISTOL (portions)—BVU OptiNet. This cable system has converted to IPTV. See Bristol (portions), VA [VA5201]. ICA: VA0190.

BROOKNEAL—Comcast Cable, 560 Patton St, Danville, VA 24541. Phones: 434-951-3700 (Charlottesville office); 434-797-4135. Fax: 434-836-0120. Web Site: http://www.comcast.com. ICA: VA0125.

TV Market Ranking: 70 (BROOKNEAL). Franchise award date: May 17, 1983. Franchise expiration date: N.A. Began: N.A.

Channel capacity: N.A. Channels available but not in use: N.A.

Basic Service
Subscribers: N.A. Included with Danville, VA.
Programming (received off-air): WBRA-TV (PBS) Roanoke; WDBJ (CBS, MNT) Roanoke; WFXR (CW, FOX) Roanoke; WSET-TV (ABC) Lynchburg; WSLS-TV (NBC) Roanoke.
Programming (via satellite): BET Networks; ION Television; QVC; WGN America.
Fee: $50.00 installation; $5.55 monthly; $1.80 converter; $10.00 additional installation.

Expanded Basic Service 1
Subscribers: N.A.
Programming (via satellite): A&E Networks; ABC Family Channel; AMC; Animal Planet; BET Networks; CNBC; CNN; Comcast SportsNet Mid-Atlantic; Comedy Central; Country Music TV; C-SPAN; Discovery Channel; Disney Channel; E! Entertainment Television; ESPN; ESPN 2; Food Network; Fox News Channel; FX; Hallmark Channel; Headline News; HGTV; History Channel; INSP; Lifetime; MSNBC; MTV; Nickelodeon; ShopNBC; Spike TV; Syfy; TBS Superstation; The Learning Channel; The Weather Channel; Travel Channel; truTV; Turner Network TV; TV Land; USA Network; VH1.
Fee: $16.05 monthly.

Pay Service 1
Pay Units: N.A.
Programming (via satellite): Cinemax; HBO; Showtime.
Fee: $10.00 monthly (Cinemax or HBO), $11.95 monthly (Showtime).

Video-On-Demand: No

Internet Service
Operational: No.

Telephone Service
None

Miles of Plant: 14.0 (coaxial); None (fiber optic).

Vice President & General Manager: Troy Fitzhugh. Technical Operations Manager: Mike Buckner. Office Manager: Kathy Thomas.

Ownership: Comcast Cable Communications Inc. (MSO).

BROSVILLE—Chatmoss Cablevision, 12349 Martinsville Hwy, Danville, VA 24541-0855. Phone: 434-685-1521. Fax: 434-685-1803. E-mail: cs@chatmosscable.com. Web Site: http://chatmosscable.com. Also serves Bachelor's Hall, Cascade, Dry Fork, Tunstall (Pittsylvania County), Vandola & Whitmell. ICA: VA0075.

TV Market Ranking: Below 100 (Bachelor's Hall, BROSVILLE, Cascade, Dry Fork, Tunstall (Pittsylvania County), Vandola, Whitmell). Franchise award date: February 6, 1989. Franchise expiration date: N.A. Began: July 1, 1989.

Channel capacity: N.A. Channels available but not in use: N.A.

Basic Service
Subscribers: 2,300.
Programming (received off-air): WBRA-TV (PBS) Roanoke; WDBJ (CBS, MNT) Roanoke; WDRL-TV (IND) Danville; WFMY-TV (CBS) Greensboro; WFXR (CW, FOX) Roanoke; WGHP (FOX, IND) High Point; WGSR-LD (IND) Reidsville; WPXR-TV (ION) Roanoke; WSET-TV (ABC) Lynchburg; WSLS-TV (NBC) Roanoke; WUNL-TV (PBS) Winston-Salem; WXII-TV (NBC) Winston-Salem; WXLV-TV (ABC) Winston-Salem; 24 FMs.
Programming (via satellite): A&E Networks; ABC Family Channel; AMC; AmericanLife TV Network; BET Networks; Cartoon Network; CNBC; CNN; Comcast SportsNet Mid-Atlantic; Comedy Central; Country Music TV; C-SPAN; Discovery Channel; Disney Channel; ESPN; ESPN 2; Headline News; Lifetime; MTV; Nickelodeon; QVC; Spike TV; Syfy; TBS Superstation; The Learning Channel; The Weather Channel; Trinity Broadcasting Network; Turner Network TV; USA Network; VH1; WGN America.
Fee: $21.00 monthly; $2.50 converter.

Pay Service 1
Pay Units: 161.
Programming (via satellite): Cinemax.
Fee: $8.95 monthly.

Pay Service 2
Pay Units: 122.
Programming (via satellite): Showtime.
Fee: $8.95 monthly.

Pay Service 3
Pay Units: 344.
Programming (via satellite): HBO.
Fee: $9.95 monthly.

Video-On-Demand: No

Internet Service
Operational: Yes. Began: January 1, 2001.
Subscribers: 700.
Broadband Service: Fightstar.
Fee: $49.95 installation; $34.95 monthly; $10.00 modem lease; $250.00 modem purchase.

Telephone Service
None

Miles of Plant: 130.0 (coaxial); 20.0 (fiber optic).

Manager: Charles F. Lewis. Customer Service Manager: Ida S. Lewis.

Ownership: John P. Shoemaker Jr.

BUCHANAN—Shentel, 60 Long Ridge Rd, Ste 404, Stamford, CT 6902. Phones: 540-984-5224; 800-743-6835. Web Site: http://www.shentel.net. ICA: VA0126.

TV Market Ranking: 70 (BUCHANAN). Franchise award date: N.A. Franchise expiration date: N.A. Began: N.A.

Channel capacity: 37 (not 2-way capable). Channels available but not in use: N.A.

Basic Service

Subscribers: 300.

Programming (received off-air): WBRA-TV (PBS) Roanoke; WDBJ (CBS, MNT) Roanoke; WFXR (CW, FOX) Roanoke; WPXR-TV (ION) Roanoke; WSET-TV (ABC) Lynchburg; WSLS-TV (NBC) Roanoke.

Programming (via satellite): A&E Networks; ABC Family Channel; AMC; CNN; Discovery Channel; Disney Channel; ESPN; ESPN 2; Great American Country; History Channel; Lifetime; Nickelodeon; Spike TV; TBS Superstation; The Learning Channel; The Weather Channel; Turner Network TV; USA Network; WGN America.

Fee: $49.95 installation; $39.95 monthly.

Pay Service 1

Pay Units: N.A.

Programming (via satellite): HBO; Showtime; The Movie Channel.

Fee: $13.95 monthly (each).

Video-On-Demand: No

Internet Service

Operational: No.

Telephone Service

None

Miles of Plant: 14.0 (coaxial); None (fiber optic).

President: Christopher French. Vice President, Customer Service: David Ferguson. Marketing Manager: Chris Ranson.

Ownership: Shenandoah Telecommunications Inc. (MSO).

BUENA VISTA—Formerly served by Adelphia Communications. Now served by LEXINGTON, VA [VA0147]. ICA: VA0127.

CALLAGHAN—Clearview TV Cable, HC 81 Box 247 AA, Lewisburg, WV 24901. Phone: 304-645-1397. Also serves Hot Springs & Johnson Creek. ICA: VA0120. **Note:** This system is an overbuild.

TV Market Ranking: Below 100 (CALLAGHAN, Johnson Creek); Outside TV Markets (Hot Springs). Franchise award date: N.A. Franchise expiration date: N.A. Began: July 1, 1974.

Channel capacity: 27 (not 2-way capable). Channels available but not in use: N.A.

Basic Service

Subscribers: 602.

Programming (received off-air): WDBJ (CBS, MNT) Roanoke; WSET-TV (ABC) Lynchburg; WSLS-TV (NBC) Roanoke; WSWP-TV (PBS) Grandview; WVVA (CW, NBC) Bluefield.

Programming (via satellite): CNN; Headline News; TBS Superstation; Turner Network TV.

Fee: $30.00 installation; $32.50 monthly.

Pay Service 1

Pay Units: 15.

Programming (via satellite): HBO.

Fee: $12.00 monthly.

Video-On-Demand: No

Internet Service

Operational: No.

Telephone Service

None

Miles of Plant: 5.0 (coaxial); None (fiber optic).

Manager & Chief Technician: Chip James.

Ownership: Clearview Cable TV Inc. (MSO).

CHARLES CITY COUNTY (portions)—Comcast Cable, 2277 Academy Rd, PO Box 100, Powhatan, VA 23139-0100. Phones: 804-598-8725; 804-915-5400. Fax: 804-598-2988. Web Site: http://www.comcast.com. ICA: VA0078.

TV Market Ranking: 63 (CHARLES CITY COUNTY (PORTIONS)). Franchise award date: November 28, 1988. Franchise expiration date: N.A. Began: November 1, 1989.

Channel capacity: N.A. Channels available but not in use: N.A.

Basic Service

Subscribers: N.A. Included in Richmond

Programming (received off-air): WAVY-TV (NBC) Portsmouth; WCVE-TV (PBS) Richmond; WRIC-TV (ABC) Petersburg; WRLH-TV (FOX, MNT) Richmond; WTKR (CBS) Norfolk; WTVR-TV (CBS) Richmond; WUPV (CW) Ashland; WVEC (ABC) Hampton; WWBT (NBC) Richmond.

Programming (via satellite): QVC.

Fee: $40.00 installation; $16.95 monthly; $2.00 converter.

Expanded Basic Service 1

Subscribers: N.A.

Programming (via satellite): A&E Networks; ABC Family Channel; AMC; BET Networks; Cartoon Network; CNBC; CNN; Country Music TV; C-SPAN; C-SPAN 2; Discovery Channel; Disney Channel; ESPN; ESPN 2; Fox News Channel; FX; Headline News; HGTV; History Channel; Lifetime; MSNBC; MTV; Nickelodeon; Spike TV; Syfy; TBS Superstation; The Learning Channel; The Weather Channel; Turner Network TV; TV Land; USA Network; VH1.

Digital Basic Service

Subscribers: N.A. Included in Richmond

Programming (via satellite): BBC America; Bio; Black Family Channel; Bloomberg Television; Concert TV; Discovery Fit & Health; DMX Music; ESPN Classic Sports; ESPNews; Fox Movie Channel; Fox Sports World; Fuse; G4; GAS; Golf Channel; Great American Country; GSN; Halogen Network; Independent Film Channel; Mid-Atlantic Sports Network; MTV Networks Digital Suite; National Geographic Channel; Nick Jr.; Outdoor Channel; Style Network; Sundance Channel; The Word Network; Toon Disney; Trinity Broadcasting Network; truTV; Turner Classic Movies; Versus; WE tv.

Digital Expanded Basic Service

Subscribers: N.A.

Programming (via satellite): Speed.

Digital Pay Service 1

Pay Units: N.A.

Programming (via satellite): Cinemax (multiplexed); Encore; HBO (multiplexed); Showtime (multiplexed); The Movie Channel (multiplexed).

Video-On-Demand: No

Pay-Per-View

Hits Movies & Events (delivered digitally); Fresh (delivered digitally); Playboy TV (delivered digitally).

Internet Service

Operational: No.

Telephone Service

None

Miles of Plant: 140.0 (coaxial); None (fiber optic).

Vice President & General Manager: Kirby Brooks. Technical Operations Director: Stephen Hill. Technical Supervisor: Bob King. Marketing Director: Erin Powell. Public Relations Manager: Monica Smith-Callahan. Office Manager: Joyce Johnson.

Ownership: Comcast Cable Communications Inc. (MSO).

CHARLOTTESVILLE—Comcast Cable, 400 Westfield Rd, Charlottesville, VA 22901. Phone: 434-951-3700. Fax: 434-951-3705. Web Site: http://www.comcast.com. Also serves Albemarle County, Crozet & Lake Monticello. ICA: VA0131.

TV Market Ranking: Below 100 (Albemarle County, CHARLOTTESVILLE, Crozet, Lake Monticello). Franchise award date: January 1, 1963. Franchise expiration date: N.A. Began: February 1, 1963.

Channel capacity: N.A. Channels available but not in use: N.A.

Basic Service

Subscribers: 33,802.

Programming (received off-air): WAHU-CD Charlottesville; WCAV (CBS) Charlottesville; WHTJ (PBS) Charlottesville; WRIC-TV (ABC) Petersburg; WTTG (FOX) Washington; WVAW-LD Charlottesville; WVIR-TV (CW, NBC) Charlottesville; WVPT (PBS) Staunton; WWBT (NBC) Richmond.

Programming (via satellite): C-SPAN; QVC; ShopNBC; Trinity Broadcasting Network.

Fee: $50.00 installation; $30.95 monthly; $15.00 additional installation.

Expanded Basic Service 1

Subscribers: N.A.

Programming (via satellite): A&E Networks; ABC Family Channel; AMC; Animal Planet; BET Networks; Bravo; Cartoon Network; CNBC; CNN; Comcast SportsNet Mid-Atlantic; Comedy Central; Country Music TV; C-SPAN 2; Discovery Channel; Disney Channel; E! Entertainment Television; ESPN; ESPN 2; Eternal Word TV Network; Food Network; Fox News Channel; FX; Golf Channel; Hallmark Channel; Headline News; HGTV; History Channel; Lifetime; MSNBC; MTV; Nickelodeon; Oxygen; Spike TV; Syfy; TBS Superstation; The Learning Channel; The Weather Channel; Travel Channel; truTV; Turner Classic Movies; Turner Network TV; TV Guide Network; TV Land; USA Network; VH1.

Fee: $15.00 installation; $6.50 monthly.

Digital Basic Service

Subscribers: N.A.

Programming (via satellite): AmericanLife TV Network; BBC America; Bio; Black Family Channel; Bloomberg Television; Canales N; CBS Sports Network; Current; DIY Network; ESPN 2 HD; ESPN Classic Sports; ESPN HD; ESPNews; Fox Movie Channel; Fox Soccer; Fuel TV; Fuse; G4; Great American Country; GSN; Halogen Network; HD Theater; History Channel International; Independent Film Channel; Lifetime Movie Network; Music Choice; NFL Network; Outdoor Channel; PBS Kids Sprout; SoapNet; Speed; Sundance Channel; Tennis Channel; The Word Network; Toon Disney; Trinity Broadcasting Network; Turner Network TV HD; Versus; WE tv.

Digital Pay Service 1

Pay Units: 1,220.

Programming (via satellite): ART America; CCTV-4; Cinemax (multiplexed); Encore (multiplexed); Filipino Channel; Flix; HBO (multiplexed); HBO HD; RAI USA; Russian Television Network; Showtime (multiplexed); Showtime HD; Starz (multiplexed); The Movie Channel (multiplexed); TV Asia; TV Japan; TV5, La Television International; Zee TV USA; Zhong Tian Channel.

Video-On-Demand: No

Pay-Per-View

iN DEMAND (delivered digitally); Playboy TV (delivered digitally); Fresh (delivered digitally).

Internet Service

Operational: Yes.

Broadband Service: Comcast High Speed Internet.

Fee: $42.95 monthly.

Telephone Service

Digital: Operational

Miles of Plant: 927.0 (coaxial); 140.0 (fiber optic).

Vice President & General Manager: Troy Fitzhugh. Technical Operations Director: Tom Jacobs. Marketing Director: Steve Miles. Marketing Coordinator: Cassie Cool.

Ownership: Comcast Cable Communications Inc. (MSO).

CHARLOTTESVILLE—Formerly served by NTELOS. No longer in operation. ICA: VA0163.

CHASE CITY—Formerly served by Adelphia Communications. Now served by SOUTH HILL, VA [VA0062]. ICA: VA0095.

CHESAPEAKE—Mediacom. Now served by CAMDEN/CURRITUCK (formerly Currituck County, southern portion), NC [NC0083]. ICA: VA0183.

CHESTERFIELD COUNTY—Comcast Cable. Now served by RICHMOND, VA [VA0004]. ICA: VA0132.

CHINCOTEAGUE ISLAND—Charter Communications, 216 Moore Ave, Suffolk, VA 23434. Phone: 757-539-0713. Fax: 757-539-1057. Web Site: http://www.charter.com. ICA: VA0065.

TV Market Ranking: Below 100 (CHINCOTEAGUE ISLAND). Franchise award date: March 1, 1964. Franchise expiration date: N.A. Began: March 15, 1965.

Channel capacity: N.A. Channels available but not in use: N.A.

Basic Service

Subscribers: 2,352.

Programming (received off-air): WAVY-TV (NBC) Portsmouth; WBOC-TV (CBS, FOX) Salisbury; WCPB (PBS) Salisbury; WMDT (ABC, CW) Salisbury; WTKR (CBS) Norfolk; WVEC (ABC) Hampton; allband FM.

Programming (via satellite): C-SPAN; C-SPAN 2; INSP; ION Television; LWS Local Weather Station; QVC; Trinity Broadcasting Network; TV Guide Network.

Fee: $29.99 installation.

Expanded Basic Service 1

Subscribers: 1,751.

Programming (via satellite): A&E Networks; ABC Family Channel; AMC; Animal Planet; Cartoon Network; CNBC; CNN; Comcast SportsNet Mid-Atlantic; Comedy Central; Country Music TV; Discovery Channel; Disney Channel; E! Entertainment Television; ESPN; ESPN 2; Fox News Channel; FX; Headline News; HGTV; History Channel; Lifetime; MSNBC; MTV; Nickelodeon; SoapNet; Speed; Spike TV; Syfy; TBS Superstation; The Learning Channel; The Weather Channel; Toon Disney; Travel Channel; Turner Network TV; TV Land; USA Network; VH1.

Fee: $47.99 monthly.

Digital Basic Service

Subscribers: N.A.

Programming (via satellite): BBC America; Bio; Bloomberg Television; Discovery Fit & Health; DIY Network; ESPN Classic Sports; ESPNews; Fox College Sports Atlantic; Fox College Sports Central; Fox College Sports Pacific; Fox Movie Channel; Fox Soccer; Fuse; GAS; GSN; History Channel International; Independent Film Channel; Lifetime Movie Network; Mid-Atlantic Sports Network; MTV Networks Digital Suite; Music Choice; National Geographic Channel; Nick Jr.; Nick Too; NickToons TV; Style Network; Sundance Channel.

Digital Pay Service 1

Pay Units: N.A.

Programming (via satellite): Cinemax (multiplexed); Encore; Flix; HBO (multiplexed); Showtime (multiplexed); Starz (multiplexed); The Movie Channel (multiplexed).

Video-On-Demand: No

Pay-Per-View

iN DEMAND (delivered digitally); Playboy TV (delivered digitally); Fresh (delivered digitally); Shorteez (delivered digitally).

Internet Service

Operational: Yes.

Fee: $19.99 monthly.

Telephone Service

None

Miles of Plant: 55.0 (coaxial); None (fiber optic).

Vice President & General Manager: Anthony Pope. Marketing Director: Brooke Sinclair. Marketing Manager: LaRisa Scales. Operations Manager: Tom Ross.

Ownership: Charter Communications Inc. (MSO).

CLARAVILLE—Formerly served by Adelphia Communications. No longer in operation. ICA: VA0051.

CLARKSVILLE—Shentel, 60 Long Ridge Rd, Ste 404, Stamford, CT 6902. Phones: 540-984-5224; 800-743-6835. Web Site: http://www.shentel.net. Also serves Mecklenburg County (portions). ICA: VA0101.

TV Market Ranking: Outside TV Markets (CLARKSVILLE, Mecklenburg County (portions)). Franchise award date: June 12, 1979. Franchise expiration date: N.A. Began: February 20, 1981.

Channel capacity: N.A. Channels available but not in use: N.A.

Basic Service

Subscribers: 683.

Programming (received off-air): WDBJ (CBS, MNT) Roanoke; WLFL (CW) Raleigh; WNCN (NBC) Goldsboro; WRAL-TV (CBS) Raleigh; WRAY-TV (IND) Wilson; WRAZ (FOX) Raleigh; WRDC (MNT) Durham; WRPX-TV (ION) Rocky Mount; WSET-TV (ABC) Lynchburg; WSLS-TV (NBC) Roanoke; WTVD (ABC) Durham; WUNP-TV (PBS) Roanoke Rapids; 21 FMs.

Programming (via satellite): WGN America.

Fee: $49.95 installation; $18.95 monthly; $.75 converter; $10.00 additional installation.

Expanded Basic Service 1

Subscribers: 642.

Programming (via satellite): A&E Networks; ABC Family Channel; AMC; Animal Planet; BET Networks; Bravo; Cartoon Network; CNBC; CNN; Comedy Central; Country Music TV; Discovery Channel; Disney Channel; E! Entertainment Television; ESPN; ESPN 2; Food Network; Fox News Channel; FX; G4; Golf Channel; Headline News; HGTV; History Channel; INSP; Lifetime; MSNBC; MTV; Nickelodeon; Oxygen; QVC; Speed; Spike TV; Syfy; TBS Superstation; The Learning Channel; The Weather Channel; Travel Channel; truTV; Turner Classic Movies; Turner Network TV; TV Land; USA Network; VH1; WE tv.

Fee: $21.00 monthly.

Digital Basic Service

Subscribers: N.A.

Programming (via satellite): BBC America; Bio; Bloomberg Television; CMT Pure Country; Discovery Fit & Health; Discovery Health Channel; Discovery Kids Channel; DIY Network; DMX Music; ESPN Classic Sports; ESPNews; Fox College Sports Atlantic; Fox College Sports Central; Fox College Sports Pacific; Fox Movie Channel; Fox Soccer; Fuse; GSN; History Channel International; ID Investigation Discovery; Independent Film Channel; Military Channel; MTV Hits; MTV Jams; MTV2; National Geographic Channel; Nick Jr.; Nick Too; NickToons TV; Science; SoapNet; Sundance Channel; TeenNick; Toon Disney; Tr3s; TV Guide Interactive Inc.; VH1 Classic; VH1 Soul.

Fee: $13.00 monthly; $6.95 converter.

Digital Pay Service 1

Pay Units: 263.

Programming (via satellite): HBO (multiplexed).

Fee: $20.00 installation; $12.95 monthly.

Digital Pay Service 2

Pay Units: N.A.

Programming (via satellite): Cinemax (multiplexed); Encore (multiplexed); Flix; Showtime (multiplexed); Starz (multiplexed); The Movie Channel (multiplexed).

Fee: $12.95 monthly (Cinemax, Starz/Encore or Showtime/TMC/Flix).

Video-On-Demand: No

Pay-Per-View

iN DEMAND (delivered digitally); Playboy TV (delivered digitally); Fresh (delivered digitally); Shorteez (delivered digitally).

Internet Service

Operational: No.

Telephone Service

None

Miles of Plant: 30.0 (coaxial); None (fiber optic).

President: Christopher French. Vice President, Customer Service: David Ferguson. Marketing Manager: Chris Ranson.

Ownership: Shenandoah Telecommunications Inc. (MSO).

CLINTWOOD—Formerly served by Adelphia Communications. Now served by NORTON, VA [VA0157]. ICA: VA0057.

COLONIAL BEACH—MetroCast, 233 Colonial Ave, Colonial Beach, VA 22443. Phone: 800-633-8578. E-mail: support@metrocastcablevision.com. Web Site: http://www.metrocastcommunications.com/. Also serves Westmoreland County (unincorporated areas) & Westmoreland Shores. ICA: VA0063.

TV Market Ranking: Outside TV Markets (COLONIAL BEACH, Westmoreland County (unincorporated areas), Westmoreland Shores). Franchise award date: April 13, 1980. Franchise expiration date: April 8, 2008. Began: November 1, 1980.

Channel capacity: 64 (operating 2-way). Channels available but not in use: N.A.

Basic Service

Subscribers: 1,661.

Programming (received off-air): WDCA (MNT) Washington; WETA-TV (PBS) Washington; WFDC-DT (UNV) Arlington; WJLA-TV (ABC) Washington; WNVT (ETV) Goldvein; WRC-TV (NBC) Washington; WTTG (FOX) Washington; WTVR-TV (CBS) Richmond; WUSA (CBS) Washington; allband FM.

Programming (via satellite): C-SPAN; INSP; QVC; WGN America.

Fee: $32.07 installation; $11.34 monthly; $.75 converter.

Expanded Basic Service 1

Subscribers: 1,618.

Programming (via satellite): A&E Networks; ABC Family Channel; AMC; Animal Planet; BET Networks; Bravo; Cartoon Network; CNBC; CNN; Comcast SportsNet Mid-Atlantic; Comedy Central; Country Music TV; Discovery Channel; Disney Channel; E! Entertainment Television; ESPN; ESPN 2; Food Network; Fox News Channel; FX; G4; Golf Channel; Headline News; HGTV; History Channel; Lifetime; MSNBC; MTV; Nickelodeon; Oxygen; Speed; Spike TV; Syfy; TBS Superstation; The Learning Channel; The Weather Channel; Travel Channel; truTV; Turner Classic Movies; Turner Network TV; TV Land; USA Network; VH1; WE tv.

Fee: $12.28 monthly.

Digital Basic Service

Subscribers: N.A.

Programming (via satellite): BBC America; Bio; Bloomberg Television; Discovery Fit & Health; Discovery Home Channel; DIY Network; ESPN Classic Sports; ESPNews; Fox College Sports Atlantic; Fox College Sports Central; Fox College Sports Pacific; Fox Movie Channel; Fox Soccer; Fuse; GAS; GSN; History Channel International; Independent Film Channel; MTV Networks Digital Suite; Music Choice; National Geographic Channel; Nick Jr.; Nick Too; NickToons TV; SoapNet; Sundance Channel; Toon Disney; TV Guide Interactive Inc.

Digital Pay Service 1

Pay Units: 130.

Programming (via satellite): Showtime (multiplexed).

Fee: $11.50 monthly.

Digital Pay Service 2

Pay Units: 498.

Programming (via satellite): HBO (multiplexed).

Fee: $11.50 monthly.

Digital Pay Service 3

Pay Units: 218.

Programming (via satellite): The Movie Channel (multiplexed).

Fee: $11.50 monthly.

Digital Pay Service 4

Pay Units: N.A.

Programming (via satellite): Cinemax (multiplexed); Encore (multiplexed); Flix; Starz (multiplexed).

Video-On-Demand: No

Pay-Per-View

iN DEMAND (delivered digitally); Playboy TV (delivered digitally); Fresh (delivered digitally); Shorteez (delivered digitally).

Internet Service

Operational: Yes.

Fee: $49.95 installation; $29.95 monthly.

Telephone Service

None

Miles of Plant: 41.0 (coaxial); None (fiber optic). Additional miles planned: 10.0 (coaxial).

General Manager: Danny L. Jobe.

Ownership: Harron Communications LP (MSO).

COVINGTON—Shentel, Shentel Ctr, 500 Shentel Way, Edinburg, VA 22824. Phones: 800-743-6835; 540-984-5224. E-mail: complaints@shentel.net. Web Site: http://shentel.net. Also serves Alleghany County, Clifton Forge & Iron Gate. ICA: VA0036.

TV Market Ranking: 70 (Alleghany County (portions), COVINGTON); Below 100 (Clifton Forge, Iron Gate); Outside TV Markets (Alleghany County (portions)). Franchise award date: July 10, 1962. Franchise expiration date: N.A. Began: December 19, 1963.

Channel capacity: 122 (operating 2-way). Channels available but not in use: N.A.

Basic Service

Subscribers: 5,800.

Programming (received off-air): WBRA-TV (PBS) Roanoke; WDBJ (CBS, MNT) Roanoke; WFXR (CW, FOX) Roanoke; WPXR-TV (ION) Roanoke; WSET-TV (ABC) Lynchburg; WSLS-TV (NBC) Roanoke; WWCW (CW, FOX) Lynchburg; 1 FM.

Programming (via satellite): A&E Networks; ABC Family Channel; AMC; Animal Planet; Cartoon Network; CNN; Comedy Central; Country Music TV; Discovery Channel; ESPN; ESPN 2; ESPN Classic Sports; Food Network; Fox News Channel; Fox Sports Net; Hallmark Channel; Headline News; HGTV; History Channel; INSP; Lifetime; MSNBC; MTV; National Geographic Channel; Nickelodeon; QVC; Spike TV; Syfy; TBS Superstation; The Learning Channel; The Weather Channel; Travel Channel; Turner Network TV; TV Land; USA Network; VH1; WGN America.

Fee: $29.95 installation; $38.00 monthly; $2.16 converter.

Digital Basic Service

Subscribers: N.A.

Programming (via satellite): BBC America; Bio; Bloomberg News Radio; Discovery Kids Channel; DMX Music; Encore; ESPNews; Fox Movie Channel; Fox Sports World; G4; GAS; Golf Channel; GSN; History Channel International; Lifetime Movie Network; MTV Networks Digital Suite; Nick Jr.; NickToons TV; Outdoor Channel; Ovation; Speed; Sundance Channel; Turner Classic Movies.

Fee: $12.95 monthly.

Digital Pay Service 1

Pay Units: N.A.

Programming (via satellite): Cinemax (multiplexed); HBO (multiplexed); Showtime.

Video-On-Demand: No

Pay-Per-View

Addressable homes: 1,278.

iN DEMAND; special events.

Internet Service

Operational: Yes.

Broadband Service: Rapid High Speed Internet.

Fee: $50.00 installation; $24.95 monthly.

Telephone Service
None
Miles of Plant: 160.0 (coaxial); 20.0 (fiber optic).
Vice President, Customer Service: David Ferguson. General Manager: Robert Harold. Chief Technician: Steve Adkins.
Ownership: Shenandoah Telecommunications Inc. (MSO).

CRAIGSVILLE—Formerly served by Adelphia Communications. Now served by STAUNTON, VA [VA0026]. ICA: VA0133.

CRAWFORD MANOR—Crawford Manor Cable TV, 2806 NE Side Hwy, Elkton, VA 22827. Phone: 540-337-8450. ICA: VA0119.
TV Market Ranking: Below 100 (CRAWFORD MANOR). Franchise award date: N.A. Franchise expiration date: N.A. Began: August 1, 1982.
Channel capacity: 21 (not 2-way capable). Channels available but not in use: N.A.
Basic Service
Subscribers: 129.
Programming (received off-air): WDCA (MNT) Washington; WHSV-TV (ABC, MNT) Harrisonburg; WJLA-TV (ABC) Washington; WTTG (FOX) Washington; WUSA (CBS) Washington; WVIR-TV (CW, NBC) Charlottesville; WVPT (PBS) Staunton; WWBT (NBC) Richmond.
Programming (via satellite): A&E Networks; ABC Family Channel; CNN; Disney Channel; ESPN; TBS Superstation; Turner Network TV; USA Network.
Fee: $30.00 installation; $14.95 monthly.
Pay Service 1
Pay Units: 21.
Programming (via satellite): Showtime.
Fee: $9.00 monthly.
Video-On-Demand: No
Internet Service
Operational: No.
Telephone Service
None
Miles of Plant: 5.0 (coaxial); None (fiber optic).
Vice President: Atville Lear.
Ownership: Crawford Manor Cable TV.

CREWE—Shentel, 60 Long Ridge Rd, Ste 404, Stamford, CT 6902. Phones: 540-984-5224; 800-743-6835. Web Site: http://www.shentel.net. Also serves Blackstone, Burkeville & Pamplin. ICA: VA0099.
TV Market Ranking: 63 (Blackstone); 70 (Pamplin); Outside TV Markets (Burkeville, CREWE). Franchise award date: March 8, 1982. Franchise expiration date: N.A. Began: March 1, 1983.
Channel capacity: N.A. Channels available but not in use: N.A.
Basic Service
Subscribers: 1,135.
Programming (received off-air): WBRA-TV (PBS) Roanoke; WDBJ (CBS, MNT) Roanoke; WDRL-TV (IND) Danville; WFXR (CW, FOX) Roanoke; WPXR-TV (ION) Roanoke; WSET-TV (ABC) Lynchburg; WSLS-TV (NBC) Roanoke; WWCW (CW, FOX) Lynchburg.
Programming (via satellite): WGN America.
Fee: $49.95 installation; $19.95 monthly.
Expanded Basic Service 1
Subscribers: 958.
Programming (via satellite): A&E Networks; ABC Family Channel; AMC; Animal Planet; BET Networks; Bravo; Cartoon Network; CNBC; CNN; Comcast SportsNet Mid-Atlantic; Comedy Central; Country Music TV; C-SPAN; Discovery Channel; Disney Channel; E! Entertainment Television; ESPN; ESPN 2; Food Network; Fox Movie Channel; Fox News Channel; FX; Golf Channel; Great American Country; Hallmark Channel; Headline News; HGTV; History Channel; Lifetime; MSNBC; MTV; National Geographic Channel; Nickelodeon; Outdoor Channel; QVC; Speed; Spike TV; Syfy; TBS Superstation; The Learning Channel; The Weather Channel; Toon Disney; Travel Channel; Trinity Broadcasting Network; truTV; Turner Classic Movies; Turner Network TV; TV Land; USA Network; VH1.
Fee: $22.00 monthly.
Digital Basic Service
Subscribers: N.A.
Programming (via satellite): BBC America; Bio; cloo; CMT Pure Country; Discovery Digital Networks; DIY Network; ESPN Classic Sports; ESPN Deportes; ESPN U; ESPNews; Fox Soccer; Fuse; G4; GAS; GSN; History Channel International; Independent Film Channel; Lifetime Movie Network; MTV Networks Digital Suite; Music Choice; Nick Jr.; NickToons TV; Nuvo TV; Oxygen; SoapNet; Telemundo; Versus.
Fee: $14.95 monthly.
Digital Pay Service 1
Pay Units: N.A.
Programming (via satellite): Cinemax (multiplexed); Encore (multiplexed); Flix; HBO (multiplexed); Showtime (multiplexed); Starz (multiplexed); The Movie Channel (multiplexed).
Fee: $11.95 monthly (Starz/Encore or Cinemax), $12.95 monthly (HBO or Showtime/TMC).
Video-On-Demand: Planned
Internet Service
Operational: Yes.
Broadband Service: JetBroadband.
Fee: $49.95 installation; $49.95 monthly; $5.00 modem lease.
Telephone Service
None
Miles of Plant: 22.0 (coaxial); None (fiber optic).
President: Christopher French. Vice President, Customer Service: David Ferguson. Marketing Manager: Chris Ranson.
Ownership: Shenandoah Telecommunications Inc. (MSO).

CROZET—Formerly served by Adelphia Communications. Now served by CHARLOTTESVILLE, VA [VA0131]. ICA: VA0097.

CULPEPER—Formerly served by Adelphia Communications. Now served by CULPEPER COUNTY, VA [VA0182]. ICA: VA0047.

CULPEPER COUNTY—Comcast Cable, 15367 Brandy Rd, Culpeper, VA 22701-2547. Phones: 434-951-3700 (Charlottesville office); 540-825-5070. Fax: 540-829-6678. Web Site: http://www.comcast.com. Also serves Culpeper. ICA: VA0182.
TV Market Ranking: Below 100 (Culpeper, CULPEPER COUNTY). Franchise award date: N.A. Franchise expiration date: N.A. Began: January 1, 1994.
Channel capacity: N.A. Channels available but not in use: N.A.
Basic Service
Subscribers: 10,331.
Programming (received off-air): WDCA (MNT) Washington; WDCW (CW) Washington; WETA-TV (PBS) Washington; WHTJ (PBS) Charlottesville; WJLA-TV (ABC) Washington; WPXW-TV (ION) Manassas; WRC-TV (NBC) Washington; WTTG (FOX) Washington; WTVR-TV (CBS) Richmond; WUSA (CBS) Washington; WVIR-TV (CW, NBC) Charlottesville; WVPT (PBS) Staunton.
Programming (via satellite): C-SPAN; C-SPAN 2; QVC; ShopNBC; TBS Superstation; TV Guide Network.
Fee: $12.50 monthly; $3.95 converter.
Expanded Basic Service 1
Subscribers: 5,997.
Programming (via satellite): A&E Networks; ABC Family Channel; AMC; Animal Planet; BET Networks; Cartoon Network; CNBC; CNN; Comcast SportsNet Mid-Atlantic; Comedy Central; Country Music TV; Discovery Channel; Disney Channel; E! Entertainment Television; ESPN; ESPN 2; Eternal Word TV Network; Food Network; Fox News Channel; FX; Great American Country; Hallmark Channel; Headline News; HGTV; History Channel; Lifetime; MSNBC; MTV; Nickelodeon; Spike TV; Syfy; The Learning Channel; The Weather Channel; Travel Channel; truTV; Turner Network TV; TV Land; USA Network; VH1.
Fee: $19.49 monthly.
Digital Basic Service
Subscribers: 3,361.
Programming (via satellite): AmericanLife TV Network; BBC America; Bio; Bloomberg Television; Canales N; Discovery Fit & Health; DIY Network; DMX Music; ESPN Classic Sports; ESPNews; Fox Sports World; Fuse; G4; Golf Channel; GSN; Halogen Network; History Channel International; Independent Film Channel; Lifetime Movie Network; Mid-Atlantic Sports Network; Music Choice; National Geographic Channel; Outdoor Channel; SoapNet; Speed; Style Network; Toon Disney; Trinity Broadcasting Network; Turner Classic Movies; Versus; WE tv.
Pay Service 1
Pay Units: 2,578.
Programming (via satellite): HBO.
Fee: $11.99 monthly.
Digital Pay Service 1
Pay Units: 2,617.
Programming (via satellite): Cinemax (multiplexed); Encore (multiplexed); Flix; HBO (multiplexed); Showtime (multiplexed); Starz (multiplexed); The Movie Channel (multiplexed).
Video-On-Demand: No
Pay-Per-View
Addressable homes: 2,326.
iN DEMAND (delivered digitally); Playboy TV (delivered digitally); Fresh (delivered digitally); Shorteez (delivered digitally); Hot Choice (delivered digitally); Urban Xtra (delivered digitally).
Internet Service
Operational: Yes.
Subscribers: 1,574.
Broadband Service: Comcast High Speed Internet.
Fee: $42.95 monthly.
Telephone Service
Digital: Operational
Miles of Plant: 306.0 (coaxial); 75.0 (fiber optic).
Vice President & General Manager: Troy Fitzhugh. Technical Operations Manager: Richard Burke. Chief Technician: Delmer Seal. Marketing Coordinator: Cassie Cool. Office Manager: Melissa Marks.
Ownership: Comcast Cable Communications Inc. (MSO).

DAMASCUS—Zito Media, 611 Vader Hill Rd, Coudersport, PA 16915. Phone: 814-260-9575. Web Site: http://www.zitomedia.com. ICA: VA0134.
TV Market Ranking: Below 100 (DAMASCUS).
Channel capacity: N.A. Channels available but not in use: N.A.
Basic Service
Subscribers: N.A.
Programming (received off-air): WCYB-TV (CW, NBC) Bristol; WEMT (FOX) Greeneville; WETP-TV (PBS) Sneedville; WJHL-TV (CBS) Johnson City; WKPT-TV (ABC) Kingsport; WSBN-TV (PBS) Norton.
Programming (via satellite): A&E Networks; ABC Family Channel; AMC; Animal Planet; Bravo; Cartoon Network; CNBC; CNN; Comedy Central; Country Music TV; C-SPAN; C-SPAN 2; Discovery Channel; Disney Channel; E! Entertainment Television; ESPN; ESPN 2; Food Network; Fox News Channel; FX; G4; Golf Channel; Headline News; HGTV; History Channel; INSP; Lifetime; MSNBC; MTV; Nickelodeon; Outdoor Channel; Oxygen; QVC; Speed; Spike TV; Syfy; TBS Superstation; The Learning Channel; The Weather Channel; Travel Channel; Trinity Broadcasting Network; truTV; Turner Classic Movies; Turner Network TV; TV Land; USA Network; VH1; WE tv.
Fee: $29.95 installation; $19.95 monthly.
Digital Basic Service
Subscribers: N.A.
Programming (via satellite): BBC America; Bio; Bloomberg Television; CMT Pure Country; Discovery Digital Networks; DIY Network; Fox Movie Channel; Fox Soccer; GSN; History Channel International; Independent Film Channel; Lifetime Movie Network; MTV Networks Digital Suite; National Geographic Channel; Nick Jr.; Nick Too; NickToons TV; Style Network; Sundance Channel; TeenNick.
Digital Pay Service 1
Pay Units: N.A.
Programming (via satellite): Cinemax (multiplexed); Encore; Flix; HBO (multiplexed); LOGO; Showtime (multiplexed); Starz (multiplexed); The Movie Channel (multiplexed).
Internet Service
Operational: No.
Telephone Service
None
Public Relations Manager: Mark Laver.
Ownership: Zito Media (MSO).

DANVILLE—Comcast Cable, 560 Patton St, Danville, VA 24541. Phones: 434-951-3700 (Charlottesville office); 434-797-4135. Fax: 434-836-0120. Web Site: http://www.comcast.com. Also serves Caswell County (portions) & Yanceyville, NC; Altavista, Chatham, Glenwood, Gretna, Hurt, Pittsylvania County, Ringgold & Westover Hills, VA. ICA: VA0012.
TV Market Ranking: 47,73 (Caswell County (portions)); 70 (Altavista, Gretna, Hurt, Pittsylvania County (portions)); Below 100 (Chatham, DANVILLE, Glenwood, Ringgold, Westover Hills, Yanceyville, Caswell County (portions), Pittsylvania County (portions)). Franchise award date: March 3, 1987. Franchise expiration date: N.A. Began: January 1, 1969.
Channel capacity: N.A. Channels available but not in use: N.A.
Basic Service
Subscribers: 26,328 Includes subscribers for Brookneal.
Programming (received off-air): WBRA-TV (PBS) Roanoke; WDBJ (CBS, MNT)

Roanoke; WDRL-TV (IND) Danville; WFMY-TV (CBS) Greensboro; WFXR (CW, FOX) Roanoke; WGSR-LD (IND) Reidsville; WPXR-TV (ION) Roanoke; WSET-TV (ABC) Lynchburg; WSLS-TV (NBC) Roanoke; WUNC-TV (PBS) Chapel Hill; WWCW (CW, FOX) Lynchburg; WXII-TV (NBC) Winston-Salem; allband FM.

Programming (via satellite): QVC; WGN America.

Fee: $50.00 installation; $7.90 monthly; $1.80 converter.

Expanded Basic Service 1

Subscribers: 24,900.

Programming (via satellite): A&E Networks; ABC Family Channel; AMC; Animal Planet; BET Networks; Bravo; Cartoon Network; CNBC; CNN; Comcast SportsNet Mid-Atlantic; Comedy Central; Country Music TV; C-SPAN; C-SPAN 2; Discovery Channel; Disney Channel; E! Entertainment Television; ESPN; ESPN 2; Eternal Word TV Network; Food Network; Fox News Channel; FX; Golf Channel; Hallmark Channel; Headline News; HGTV; History Channel; INSP; Lifetime; MSNBC; MTV; Nickelodeon; Oxygen; ShopNBC; Speed; Spike TV; Syfy; TBS Superstation; The Learning Channel; The Weather Channel; Travel Channel; truTV; Turner Classic Movies; Turner Network TV; TV Guide Network; TV Land; Univision Studios; USA Network; VH1.

Fee: $32.08 monthly.

Digital Basic Service

Subscribers: N.A.

Programming (via satellite): A&E HD; ABC Family HD; Animal Planet HD; BBC America; Bio; Bloomberg Television; Canal 52MX; CBS Sports Network; Cine Latino; Cine Mexicano; CMT Pure Country; CNN en Espanol; CNN HD; C-SPAN 2; C-SPAN 3; Current; Daystar TV Network; Discovery Channel HD; Discovery en Espanol; Discovery Fit & Health; Discovery Health Channel; Discovery Kids Channel; DIY Network; DMX Music; Encore (multiplexed); ESPN 2 HD; ESPN Classic Sports; ESPN Deportes; ESPN HD; ESPNews; EWTN en Espanol; Flix; Food Network HD; Fox Business Channel; Fox College Sports Atlantic; Fox College Sports Central; Fox College Sports Pacific; Fox Deportes; Fox Movie Channel; Fox Reality Channel; Fox Soccer; Fuel TV; Fuse; G4; GalaVision; GMC; Great American Country; GSN; Halogen Network; HD Theater; HGTV HD; History Channel en Espanol; History Channel HD; History Channel International; ID Investigation Discovery; Independent Film Channel; Jewelry Television; Lifetime Movie Network; LOGO; Military Channel; MoviePlex; MTV2; National Geographic Channel; National Geographic Channel HD Network; NBA TV; NFL Network; NHL Network; Nick Jr.; Nick Too; NickToons TV; Outdoor Channel; Palladia; PBS Kids Sprout; Planet Green; Science; Science HD; SoapNet; Style Network; Sundance Channel; Syfy HD; TBS in HD; TeenNick; Telefutura; Tennis Channel; The Comcast Network; The Word Network; TLC HD; Toon Disney; Toon Disney en Espanol; Tr3s; Trinity Broadcasting Network; Turner Network TV HD; TV One; TVG Network; Universal HD; USA Network HD; VeneMovies; Versus; Versus HD; VH1 Classic; VH1 Soul; WE tv.

Digital Pay Service 1

Pay Units: N.A.

Programming (via satellite): ART America; CCTV-4; Cinemax (multiplexed); Cinemax HD; Filipino Channel; HBO (multiplexed); HBO HD; RAI International; Showtime (multiplexed); Showtime HD; Starz (multiplexed); Starz HDTV; The Movie Channel (multiplexed); TV Asia; TV Japan; TV5, La Television International; Zee TV USA; Zhong Tian Channel.

Video-On-Demand: Yes

Pay-Per-View

iN DEMAND (delivered digitally); Playboy TV (delivered digitally).

Internet Service

Operational: Yes.

Broadband Service: Comcast High Speed Internet.

Fee: $42.95 monthly.

Telephone Service

None

Miles of Plant: 688.0 (coaxial); None (fiber optic).

Vice President & General Manager: Troy Fitzhugh. Technical Operations Manager: Mike Buckner. Office Manager: Kathy Thomas.

Ownership: Comcast Cable Communications Inc. (MSO).

DILLWYN—Comcast Cable, 2277 Academy Rd, PO Box 100, Powhatan, VA 23139-0100. Phones: 804-915-5400; 804-598-8725. Fax: 804-598-2988. Web Site: http://www.comcast.com. Also serves Buckingham County (portions). ICA: VA0076.

TV Market Ranking: 70 (Buckingham County (portions)); Below 100 (DILLWYN, Buckingham County (portions)); Outside TV Markets (Buckingham County (portions)). Franchise award date: December 12, 1988. Franchise expiration date: N.A. Began: March 22, 1990.

Channel capacity: N.A. Channels available but not in use: N.A.

Basic Service

Subscribers: N.A. Included in Richmond

Programming (received off-air): WCVE-TV (PBS) Richmond; WRIC-TV (ABC) Petersburg; WRLH-TV (FOX, MNT) Richmond; WSET-TV (ABC) Lynchburg; WTVR-TV (CBS) Richmond; WUPV (CW) Ashland; WVIR-TV (CW, NBC) Charlottesville; WWBT (NBC) Richmond.

Programming (via satellite): C-SPAN; QVC; Trinity Broadcasting Network.

Fee: $40.00 installation; $14.95 monthly; $2.00 converter.

Digital Basic Service

Subscribers: N.A. Included in Richmond

Programming (via satellite): BBC America; Bloomberg Television; Discovery Fit & Health; DMX Music; ESPN Classic Sports; ESPNews; G4; Golf Channel; GSN; Halogen Network; Mid-Atlantic Sports Network; Nick Jr.; NickToons TV; Outdoor Channel; Versus; WE tv.

Pay Service 1

Pay Units: 139.

Programming (via satellite): HBO.

Fee: $15.00 installation; $10.95 monthly.

Pay Service 2

Pay Units: 251.

Programming (via satellite): Showtime.

Fee: $15.00 installation; $10.95 monthly.

Pay Service 3

Pay Units: 231.

Programming (via satellite): The Movie Channel.

Digital Pay Service 1

Pay Units: N.A.

Programming (via satellite): Cinemax (multiplexed); Encore; HBO (multiplexed); Showtime (multiplexed); The Movie Channel (multiplexed).

Video-On-Demand: No

Pay-Per-View

Fresh (delivered digitally); Playboy TV (delivered digitally); Hits Movies & Events (delivered digitally).

Internet Service

Operational: No.

Telephone Service

None

Miles of Plant: 107.0 (coaxial); None (fiber optic).

Vice President & General Manager: Kirby Brooks. Technical Operations Director: Stephen Hill. Technical Supervisor: Bob King. Marketing Director: Erin Powel. Public Relations Manager: Monica Smith-Callahan. Office Manager: Joyce Johnson.

Ownership: Comcast Cable Communications Inc. (MSO).

DUFFIELD—Formerly served by Adelphia Communications. Now served by NORTON, VA [VA0157]. ICA: VA0092.

EDINBURG—Shentel, 106 S Main St, Edinburg, VA 22824. Phone: 540-984-5224. Fax: 540-984-3438. Web Site: http://www.shentel.net. Also serves Maurertown, Mount Jackson, New Market, Shenandoah County, Strasburg, Toms Brook & Woodstock. ICA: VA0136.

TV Market Ranking: Below 100 (EDINBURG, Mount Jackson, New Market, Shenandoah County (portions)); Outside TV Markets (Maurertown, Shenandoah County (portions), Strasburg, Toms Brook, Woodstock). Franchise award date: N.A. Franchise expiration date: N.A. Began: September 1, 1981.

Channel capacity: 73 (not 2-way capable). Channels available but not in use: N.A.

Basic Service

Subscribers: 8,173.

Programming (received off-air): WAZT-CA (IND) Woodstock; WDCA (MNT) Washington; WDCW (CW) Washington; WHSV-TV (ABC, MNT) Harrisonburg; WJLA-TV (ABC) Washington; WRC-TV (NBC) Washington; WTTG (FOX) Washington; WUSA (CBS) Washington; WVPT (PBS) Staunton; WWPX-TV (ION) Martinsburg.

Programming (via satellite): TV Guide Network.

Fee: $35.00 installation; $19.95 monthly.

Expanded Basic Service 1

Subscribers: 4,985.

Programming (via satellite): A&E Networks; ABC Family Channel; AMC; Animal Planet; BET Networks; Bloomberg Television; Boomerang; Bravo; Cartoon Network; Chiller; CNBC; CNN; Comcast SportsNet Mid-Atlantic; Comedy Central; Country Music TV; C-SPAN; C-SPAN 2; Discovery Channel; Discovery Health Channel; Disney Channel; E! Entertainment Television; ESPN; ESPN 2; ESPN Classic Sports; Eternal Word TV Network; FamilyNet; Food Network; Fox News Channel; FX; Great American Country; Hallmark Channel; Headline News; HGTV; History Channel; Lifetime; MSNBC; MTV; National Geographic Channel; Nickelodeon; Outdoor Channel; Oxygen; QVC; RFD-TV; ShopNBC; Spike TV; Syfy; TBS Superstation; The Learning Channel; The Weather Channel; Travel Channel; Trinity Broadcasting Network; truTV; Turner Classic Movies; Turner Network TV; TV Land; USA Network; VH1; WE tv; WGN America.

Fee: $26.00 monthly.

Digital Basic Service

Subscribers: 2,079.

Programming (via satellite): AmericanLife TV Network; BBC America; Bio; cloo; CMT Pure Country; Cooking Channel; Discovery Fit & Health; Discovery Kids Channel; DIY Network; DMX Music; ESPNews; Fox Business Channel; Fox Movie Channel; Fox Reality Channel; Fuel TV; G4; GSN; History Channel International; ID Investigation Discovery; Military Channel; MTV Hits; MTV Jams; MTV2; Nick Jr.; NickToons TV; Planet Green; Science; SoapNet; Style Network; TeenNick; Toon Disney; Versus; VH1 Classic; VH1 Soul.

Fee: $4.00 monthly.

Digital Expanded Basic Service

Subscribers: N.A.

Programming (via satellite): Cine Mexicano; CNN en Espanol; Discovery en Espanol; ESPN Deportes; EWTN en Espanol; Fox College Sports Atlantic; Fox College Sports Central; Fox College Sports Pacific; Fox Deportes; Fox Soccer; Golf Channel; History Channel en Espanol; mun2 television; Speed; Telemundo; Tennis Channel; Tr3s; VeneMovies.

Fee: $4.95 monthly (sports package), $5.00 monthly (Spanish package).

Digital Expanded Basic Service 2

Subscribers: N.A.

Programming (received off-air): WDCA (MNT) Washington; WDCW (CW) Washington; WHSV-TV (ABC, MNT) Harrisonburg; WJLA-TV (ABC) Washington; WRC-TV (NBC) Washington; WTTG (FOX) Washington; WUSA (CBS) Washington; WVPT (PBS) Staunton.

Programming (via satellite): A&E HD; Bravo HD; CNBC HD+; Discovery Channel HD; ESPN HD; Food Network HD; FX HD; HDNet; HDNet Movies; HGTV HD; History Channel HD; National Geographic Channel HD Network; NFL Network HD; Speed HD; Syfy HD; TBS in HD; Turner Network TV HD; Universal HD; USA Network HD.

Fee: $9.95 monthly.

Digital Pay Service 1

Pay Units: 2,102.

Programming (via satellite): Cinemax (multiplexed); Cinemax HD; Encore (multiplexed); Flix; HBO (multiplexed); HBO HD; Showtime (multiplexed); Showtime HD; Starz (multiplexed); Starz HDTV; The Movie Channel (multiplexed).

Fee: $6.95 monthly (Encore), $9.95 monthly (Cinemax or Showtime/TMC/Flix), $11.95 monthly (Starz/Encore), $12.95 monthly (HBO).

Video-On-Demand: No

Internet Service

Operational: No.

Telephone Service
None
Miles of Plant: 175.0 (coaxial); None (fiber optic).
Vice President, Customer Service: David Ferguson. Chief Technician: David Brock.
Ownership: Shenandoah Telecommunications Inc.

EMPORIA—Comcast Cable, 2033 E Whitehill Dr, Prince George, VA 23875-1249. Phones: 804-915-5400 (Richmond office); 804-957-5739. Fax: 804-957-5830. Web Site: http://www.comcast.com. Also serves Greensville County. ICA: VA0053.
TV Market Ranking: 63 (Greensville County (portions)); Outside TV Markets (EMPORIA, Greensville County (portions)). Franchise award date: N.A. Franchise expiration date: November 16, 2006. Began: June 1, 1968.
Channel capacity: N.A. Channels available but not in use: N.A.

Basic Service
Subscribers: N.A. Included in Richmond
Programming (received off-air): WAVY-TV (NBC) Portsmouth; WCVE-TV (PBS) Richmond; WGNT (CW) Portsmouth; WNVN-LP Roanoke Rapids; WRIC-TV (ABC) Petersburg; WRLH-TV (FOX, MNT) Richmond; WTKR (CBS) Norfolk; WTVR-TV (CBS) Richmond; WVEC (ABC) Hampton; WWBT (NBC) Richmond; allband FM.
Programming (via satellite): C-SPAN; QVC; TV Guide Network; WGN America.
Fee: $31.45 monthly; $33.00 additional installation.

Expanded Basic Service 1
Subscribers: N.A.
Programming (via satellite): A&E Networks; ABC Family Channel; AMC; Animal Planet; BET Networks; Bravo; Cartoon Network; CNBC; CNN; Comcast SportsNet Mid-Atlantic; Comedy Central; Country Music TV; C-SPAN 2; Discovery Channel; Disney Channel; E! Entertainment Television; ESPN; ESPN 2; Food Network; Fox News Channel; FX; GSN; Hallmark Channel; Headline News; HGTV; History Channel; ION Television; Lifetime; MSNBC; MTV; Nickelodeon; Oxygen; Product Information Network; ShopNBC; Spike TV; Syfy; The Learning Channel; The Weather Channel; Travel Channel; Trinity Broadcasting Network; truTV; Turner Network TV; TV Land; USA Network; VH1; WE tv.

Digital Basic Service
Subscribers: N.A. Included in Richmond
Programming (via satellite): BBC America; Bio; Bloomberg Television; Discovery Fit & Health; DIY Network; ESPN Classic Sports; ESPNews; Fuse; G4; Golf Channel; Halogen Network; History Channel International; Mid-Atlantic Sports Network; Outdoor Channel; SoapNet; Speed; Toon Disney; Versus.

Digital Expanded Basic Service
Subscribers: N.A.
Programming (via satellite): Fox Movie Channel; GAS; MTV Networks Digital Suite; Music Choice; National Geographic Channel; Nick Jr.; Nick Too; NickToons TV; Style Network.

Pay Service 1
Pay Units: 531.
Programming (via satellite): Cinemax.
Fee: $11.50 monthly.

Pay Service 2
Pay Units: 893.
Programming (via satellite): HBO.
Fee: $11.50 monthly.

Pay Service 3
Pay Units: 295.
Programming (via satellite): The Movie Channel.
Fee: $11.50 monthly.

Digital Pay Service 1
Pay Units: N.A.
Programming (via satellite): Cinemax (multiplexed); Encore (multiplexed); HBO (multiplexed); Showtime (multiplexed); Starz (multiplexed); The Movie Channel (multiplexed).

Video-On-Demand: No

Pay-Per-View
Fresh (delivered digitally); Playboy TV (delivered digitally).

Internet Service
Operational: Yes.
Subscribers: 53.
Broadband Service: Comcast High Speed Internet.
Fee: $42.95 monthly.

Telephone Service
None
Miles of Plant: 66.0 (coaxial); 24.0 (fiber optic).
Vice President & General Manager: Kirby Brooks. Technical Operations Director: Stephen Hill. Marketing Director: Erin Powel. Public Relations Manager: Monica Smith-Callahan. Office Manager: Joyce Johnson.
Ownership: Comcast Cable Communications Inc. (MSO).

EWING—Zito Media, 611 Vader Hill Rd, Coudersport, PA 16915. Phone: 814-260-9575. Web Site: http://www.zitomedia.com. Also serves Rose Hill. ICA: VA0137.
TV Market Ranking: Below 100 (EWING, Rose Hill). Franchise award date: May 6, 1976. Franchise expiration date: N.A. Began: March 1, 1976.
Channel capacity: 28 (not 2-way capable). Channels available but not in use: N.A.

Basic Service
Subscribers: 460.
Programming (received off-air): WBIR-TV (NBC) Knoxville; WBXX-TV (CW) Crossville; WCYB-TV (CW, NBC) Bristol; WEMT (FOX) Greeneville; WETP-TV (PBS) Sneedville; WJHL-TV (CBS) Johnson City; WKPT-TV (ABC) Kingsport; WLFG (IND) Grundy; WSBN-TV (PBS) Norton; WVLT-TV (CBS, MNT) Knoxville.
Programming (via satellite): QVC; WGN America.
Fee: $35.00 installation; $14.00 monthly; $2.20 converter.

Expanded Basic Service 1
Subscribers: 410.
Programming (via satellite): A&E Networks; ABC Family Channel; CNN; Country Music TV; Discovery Channel; Disney Channel; ESPN; ESPN 2; Lifetime; Nickelodeon; Spike TV; TBS Superstation; Trinity Broadcasting Network; Turner Network TV; USA Network.
Fee: $19.95 monthly.

Digital Basic Service
Subscribers: N.A.
Programming (via satellite): BBC America; Bio; cloo; Discovery Digital Networks; DMX Music; ESPN Classic Sports; ESPNews; Fox Soccer; Fuse; GAS; Golf Channel; GSN; History Channel International; Independent Film Channel; Lifetime Movie Network; National Geographic Channel; Nick Jr.; Speed; Style Network; Syfy; Toon Disney; Turner Classic Movies; Versus; WE tv.

Digital Pay Service 1
Pay Units: N.A.
Programming (via satellite): Cinemax (multiplexed); Encore (multiplexed); Flix; HBO (multiplexed); Showtime (multiplexed); Starz (multiplexed); The Movie Channel (multiplexed).

Video-On-Demand: No

Pay-Per-View
iN DEMAND (delivered digitally); Playboy TV (delivered digitally).

Internet Service
Operational: No.

Telephone Service
None
Miles of Plant: 47.0 (coaxial); None (fiber optic).
Public Relations Manager: Mark Laver.
Ownership: Zito Media (MSO).

FAIRFAX COUNTY—Cox Communications, 3080 Centerville Rd, Herndon, VA 20171. Phone: 703-378-8400. Web Site: http://www.cox.com/fairfax. Also serves Alexandria (portions), Annandale, Burke, Centreville, Chantilly, Clifton, Fairfax, Fairfax Station, Falls Church, Great Falls, Herndon, Lorton, McLean, Oakton, Springfield & Vienna. ICA: VA0001.
TV Market Ranking: 9 (Alexandria (portions), Annandale, Burke, Centreville, Chantilly, Clifton, Fairfax, FAIRFAX COUNTY, Fairfax Station, Falls Church, Great Falls, Herndon, Lorton, McLean, Oakton, Springfield, Vienna). Franchise award date: September 1, 1983. Franchise expiration date: March 3, 2012. Began: August 1, 1983.
Channel capacity: 120 (operating 2-way). Channels available but not in use: N.A.

Basic Service
Subscribers: 242,861 Includes Fredericksburg.
Programming (received off-air): WDCA (MNT) Washington; WDCW (CW) Washington; WETA-TV (PBS) Washington; WFDC-DT (UNV) Arlington; WHUT-TV (PBS) Washington; WJLA-TV (ABC) Washington; WMPT (PBS) Annapolis; WNVC (ETV) Fairfax; WNVT (ETV) Goldvein; WPXW-TV (ION) Manassas; WRC-TV (NBC) Washington; WTTG (FOX) Washington; WUSA (CBS) Washington; 29 FMs.
Programming (via microwave): NewsChannel 8.
Programming (via satellite): C-SPAN; C-SPAN 2; NASA TV; QVC; ShopNBC; TV Guide Network; WGN America.
Fee: $29.99 installation; $12.70 monthly; $1.95 converter; $19.99 additional installation.

Expanded Basic Service 1
Subscribers: 200,851.
Programming (via satellite): A&E Networks; ABC Family Channel; AMC; Animal Planet; BET Networks; Bravo; Cartoon Network; CNBC; CNN; Comcast SportsNet Mid-Atlantic; Comedy Central; Country Music TV; Discovery Channel; Discovery Health Channel; Disney Channel; E! Entertainment Television; ESPN; ESPN 2; Eternal Word TV Network; Food Network; Fox News Channel; FX; Headline News; HGTV; History Channel; Lifetime; Mid-Atlantic Sports Network; MSNBC; MTV; Nickelodeon; Oxygen; Speed; Spike TV; Syfy; TBS Superstation; Telemundo; The Learning Channel; The Weather Channel; Travel Channel; Trinity Broadcasting Network; truTV; Turner Classic Movies; Turner Network TV; TV Land; USA Network; VH1.
Fee: $27.70 monthly.

Digital Basic Service
Subscribers: 121,776.
Programming (via satellite): BBC America; Bio; Bloomberg Television; Canales N; Cooking Channel; Discovery Digital Networks; DIY Network; ESPN Classic Sports; ESPNews; Fox Sports World; G4; Golf Channel; GSN; Hallmark Channel; History Channel International; Independent Film Channel; Lifetime Movie Network; MuchMusic Network; Music Choice; Ovation; SoapNet; Sundance Channel; Toon Disney; Versus; WE tv.
Fee: $20.90 monthly.

Pay Service 1
Pay Units: 37,218.
Programming (via satellite): Cinemax; HBO; Showtime; The Movie Channel.
Fee: $12.99 monthly (Cinemax), $13.99 monthly (HBO, Showtime or TMC).

Digital Pay Service 1
Pay Units: N.A.
Programming (via satellite): ART America; Cinemax (multiplexed); Encore; Filipino Channel; HBO (multiplexed); Korean Channel; Showtime (multiplexed); Starz (multiplexed); The Movie Channel (multiplexed); TV Asia.
Fee: $11.95 monthly (Filipino), $12.95 monthly (ART or Korean), $13.99 monthly (Cinemax, HBO, Showtime/TMC, or Starz/Encore), $14.95 monthly (TV Asia).

Video-On-Demand: Yes

Pay-Per-View
Addressable homes: 220,000.
ESPN Extra (delivered digitally); iN DEMAND; iN DEMAND (delivered digitally); NBA League Pass (delivered digitally); Playboy TV (delivered digitally); Fresh (delivered digitally); Shorteez (delivered digitally).

Internet Service
Operational: Yes.
Subscribers: 10,764.
Broadband Service: Cox High Speed Internet.
Fee: $99.95 installation; $44.95 monthly; $15.00 modem lease.

Telephone Service
Digital: Operational
Fee: $27.86 monthly
Miles of Plant: 4,300.0 (coaxial); 8.0 (fiber optic).
Vice President & General Manager: Janet Branard. Vice President, Network Development: Daryl Ladd. Marketing Manager: Byron Whitaker. Public Affairs Director: Alex Horwitz.
Ownership: Cox Communications Inc. (MSO).

FALLS CHURCH—RCN Corp. Formerly [VA0194]. This cable system has converted to IPTV, 196 Van Buren St, Herndon, VA 20170. Phone: 703-434-8200. Web Site: http://www.rcn.com. ICA: VA5184.
TV Market Ranking: 9 (FALLS CHURCH).
Channel capacity: N.A. Channels available but not in use: N.A.

Basic Service
Subscribers: N.A.
Fee: $61.44 monthly.

Video-On-Demand: Yes

Internet Service
Operational: Yes.
Broadband Service: RCN.
Fee: $38.00 monthly.

Telephone Service
Digital: Operational
Fee: $45.00 monthly
Chairman: Steven J. Simmons. Chief Executive Officer: Jim Holanda.

FALLS CHURCH—RCN Corp. This cable system has converted to IPTV. See Falls Church, VA [VA5184]. ICA: VA0194.

FARMVILLE—Shentel, 60 Long Ridge Rd, Ste 404, Stamford, CT 6902. Phones: 540-984-5224; 800-743-6835. Web Site: http://www.shentel.net. Also serves Cumberland County (southwestern portion), Hampden Sydney & Prince Edward County (northwestern portion). ICA: VA0050.

TV Market Ranking: Outside TV Markets (Cumberland County (southwestern portion), FARMVILLE (portions), Hampden Sydney, Prince Edward County (northwestern portion)). Franchise award date: January 10, 1991. Franchise expiration date: N.A. Began: November 11, 1979.

Channel capacity: N.A. Channels available but not in use: N.A.

Basic Service

Subscribers: 2,075.

Programming (received off-air): WCVE-TV (PBS) Richmond; WCVW (PBS) Richmond; WRIC-TV (ABC) Petersburg; WRLH-TV (FOX, MNT) Richmond; WSET-TV (ABC) Lynchburg; WTVR-TV (CBS) Richmond; WUPV (CW) Ashland; WWBT (NBC) Richmond; allband FM.

Programming (via satellite): C-SPAN; INSP; QVC; WGN America.

Fee: $24.95 installation; $15.55 monthly; $.75 converter.

Expanded Basic Service 1

Subscribers: 1,897.

Programming (via satellite): A&E Networks; ABC Family Channel; AMC; Animal Planet; BET Networks; Bravo; Cartoon Network; CNBC; CNN; Comcast SportsNet Mid-Atlantic; Comedy Central; Country Music TV; Discovery Channel; Disney Channel; E! Entertainment Television; ESPN; ESPN 2; Food Network; Fox News Channel; FX; G4; Golf Channel; Headline News; HGTV; History Channel; ION Television; Lifetime; MSNBC; MTV; Nickelodeon; Oxygen; Speed; Spike TV; Syfy; TBS Superstation; The Learning Channel; The Weather Channel; Travel Channel; truTV; Turner Classic Movies; Turner Network TV; TV Land; USA Network; VH1; WE tv.

Fee: $14.95 monthly.

Digital Basic Service

Subscribers: N.A.

Programming (via satellite): BBC America; Bio; Bloomberg Television; Discovery Fit & Health; DIY Network; ESPN Classic Sports; ESPNews; Fox College Sports Atlantic; Fox College Sports Central; Fox College Sports Pacific; Fox Movie Channel; Fox Soccer; Fuse; GAS; GSN; History Channel International; Independent Film Channel; MTV Networks Digital Suite; Music Choice; National Geographic Channel; Nick Jr.; Nick Too; NickToons TV; SoapNet; Sundance Channel; Toon Disney; TV Guide Interactive Inc.

Digital Pay Service 1

Pay Units: 397.

Programming (via satellite): HBO (multiplexed).

Fee: $14.95 installation; $11.50 monthly.

Digital Pay Service 2

Pay Units: 90.

Programming (via satellite): Showtime (multiplexed).

Fee: $14.95 installation; $11.50 monthly.

Digital Pay Service 3

Pay Units: N.A.

Programming (via satellite): Cinemax (multiplexed); Encore (multiplexed); Flix; Starz (multiplexed); The Movie Channel (multiplexed).

Video-On-Demand: No

Pay-Per-View

iN DEMAND (delivered digitally); Playboy TV (delivered digitally); Fresh (delivered digitally); Shorteez (delivered digitally).

Internet Service

Operational: Yes.

Fee: $49.95 installation; $49.95 monthly.

Telephone Service

None

Miles of Plant: 73.0 (coaxial); None (fiber optic).

President: Christopher French. Vice President, Customer Service: David Ferguson. Marketing Manager: Chris Ranson.

Ownership: Shenandoah Telecommunications Inc. (MSO).

FLOYD—Citizens Telephone Coop., 220 Webbs Mill Rd, Floyd, VA 24091. Phones: 540-745-6711; 800-941-0426. Fax: 540-745-3791. E-mail: gregsapp@citizens.coop. Web Site: http://www.citizens.coop. Also serves Floyd County, Franklin County (portions), Montgomery County (portions) & Patrick County (portions). ICA: VA0104.

TV Market Ranking: 70 (FLOYD, Floyd County (portions), Franklin County (portions), Montgomery County (portions), Patrick County (portions)); Outside TV Markets (Floyd County (portions), Patrick County (portions)). Franchise award date: August 13, 1983. Franchise expiration date: December 31, 2010. Began: December 1, 1986.

Channel capacity: N.A. Channels available but not in use: N.A.

Basic Service

Subscribers: 1,759.

Programming (received off-air): WBRA-TV (PBS) Roanoke; WDBJ (CBS, MNT) Roanoke; WDRL-TV (IND) Danville; WFXR (CW, FOX) Roanoke; WPXR-TV (ION) Roanoke; WSET-TV (ABC) Lynchburg; WSLS-TV (NBC) Roanoke.

Programming (via satellite): C-SPAN; C-SPAN 2; Eternal Word TV Network; INSP; QVC; TBS Superstation; The Learning Channel; The Weather Channel; WGN America.

Fee: $99.00 installation; $13.95 monthly; $79.00 additional installation.

Expanded Basic Service 1

Subscribers: 1,400.

Programming (via satellite): A&E Networks; ABC Family Channel; Cartoon Network; CNBC; CNN; Comedy Central; Country Music TV; Discovery Channel; Disney Channel; E! Entertainment Television; ESPN; ESPN 2; ESPN U; Food Network; Fox News Channel; FX; Hallmark Channel; Headline News; HGTV; History Channel; Lifetime; MSNBC; MTV; Nickelodeon; RFD-TV; Spike TV; Syfy; truTV; Turner Classic Movies; Turner Network TV; TV Land; USA Network; VH1.

Fee: $34.95 monthly.

Digital Basic Service

Subscribers: 300.

Programming (via satellite): Animal Planet; BET Networks; Bloomberg Television; CNN en Espanol; Comcast SportsNet Mid-Atlantic; Current; Daystar TV Network; DMX Music; ESPN Classic Sports; ESPNews; FamilyNet; Lifetime Movie Network; MTV Networks Digital Suite; Nick At Nite; Travel Channel; Trinity Broadcasting Network.

Fee: $44.95 monthly.

Digital Expanded Basic Service

Subscribers: 290.

Programming (via satellite): AMC; AmericanLife TV Network; BBC America; Bio; Boomerang; Bravo; Church Channel; CNN International; Discovery Digital Networks; DIY Network; Encore (multiplexed); Flix; Fox College Sports Atlantic; Fox College Sports Central; Fox College Sports Pacific; Fox Movie Channel; Fox Soccer; Fuel TV; Fuse; G4; GAS; Golf Channel; GolTV; Gospel Music TV; Great American Country; GSN; History Channel International; Independent Film Channel; National Geographic Channel; Nick Jr.; Nick Too; NickToons TV; Outdoor Channel; Oxygen; SoapNet; Speed; Sundance Channel; Toon Disney; Univision Studios; Versus; WE tv.

Fee: $59.95 monthly.

Digital Pay Service 1

Pay Units: 16.

Programming (via satellite): Cinemax (multiplexed).

Fee: $12.95 monthly.

Digital Pay Service 2

Pay Units: 33.

Programming (via satellite): HBO (multiplexed).

Fee: $14.95 monthly.

Digital Pay Service 3

Pay Units: 10.

Programming (via satellite): Showtime (multiplexed).

Fee: $12.95 monthly.

Digital Pay Service 4

Pay Units: N.A.

Programming (via satellite): Starz (multiplexed); The Movie Channel (multiplexed).

Video-On-Demand: No

Internet Service

Operational: No.

Telephone Service

None

Miles of Plant: 86.0 (coaxial); 70.0 (fiber optic).

General Manager: Greg Sapp. Assistant General Manager: Dennis Reece. Network Manager: Danny Vaughn.

Ownership: Citizens Cablevision Inc. (VA) (MSO).

FORT A.P. HILL—GMP Communications LP. Now served by KING GEORGE, VA [VA0058]. ICA: VA0189.

FORT BELVOIR ARMY BASE—Comcast Cable, 11101 University Blvd, Manassas, VA 20110. Phone: 703-789-8100. Fax: 703-789-8280. Web Site: http://www.comcast.com. ICA: VA0055.

TV Market Ranking: 9 (FORT BELVOIR ARMY BASE). Franchise award date: December 1, 1980. Franchise expiration date: N.A. Began: June 1, 1981.

Channel capacity: 64 (2-way capable). Channels available but not in use: N.A.

Basic Service

Subscribers: 2,268.

Programming (received off-air): WDCA (MNT) Washington; WDCW (CW) Washington; WETA-TV (PBS) Washington; WFDC-DT (UNV) Arlington; WHUT-TV (PBS) Washington; WJLA-TV (ABC) Washington; WMPT (PBS) Annapolis; WNVC (ETV) Fairfax; WNVT (ETV) Goldvein; WPXW-TV (ION) Manassas; WRC-TV (NBC) Washington; WTTG (FOX) Washington; WUSA (CBS) Washington.

Programming (via microwave): NewsChannel 8.

Programming (via satellite): A&E Networks; ABC Family Channel; AMC; BET Networks; Cartoon Network; CNBC; CNN; Comcast SportsNet Mid-Atlantic; Comedy Central; C-SPAN; C-SPAN 2; Discovery Channel; Disney Channel; E! Entertainment Television; ESPN; ESPN 2; FMX Cable FM System; Fox Movie Channel; FX; Great American Country; Hallmark Channel; Headline News; HGTV; History Channel; Lifetime; Mid-Atlantic Sports Network; MTV; Nickelodeon; QVC; Spike TV; Syfy; TBS Superstation; The Learning Channel; The Weather Channel; Turner Classic Movies; Turner Network TV; TV Guide Network; USA Network; VH1; WGN America.

Fee: $29.95 installation; $52.50 monthly.

Pay Service 1

Pay Units: 235.

Programming (via satellite): HBO; Showtime.

Fee: $9.95 monthly (Showtime or HBO).

Video-On-Demand: No

Pay-Per-View

Addressable homes: 1,000.

Fresh; iN DEMAND (delivered digitally); Hot Choice (delivered digitally); Playboy TV (delivered digitally); Fresh (delivered digitally); Shorteez (delivered digitally); Pleasure (delivered digitally); Barker (delivered digitally).

Internet Service

Operational: Yes.

Telephone Service

None

Miles of Plant: 40.0 (coaxial); None (fiber optic).

Vice President & General Manager: Christine Whitaker. Technical Operations Director: Scott Shelly. Marketing Director: Shawn Houston.

Ownership: Comcast Cable Communications Inc. (MSO).

FORT CHISWELL—Citizens Telephone Coop., 220 Webbs Mill Rd, Floyd, VA 24091. Phones: 540-745-6711; 800-941-0426. Fax: 540-745-3791. E-mail: gregsapp@citizens.coop. Web Site: http://www.citizens.coop. Also serves Austinville, Barren Springs, Carroll County (portions), Ivanhoe, Max Meadows & Wytheville. ICA: VA0066.

TV Market Ranking: Below 100 (Austinville, Barren Springs, Carroll County (portions), FORT CHISWELL, Ivanhoe, Max Meadows, Wytheville); Outside TV Markets (Carroll County (portions)). Franchise award date: N.A. Franchise expiration date: N.A. Began: January 1, 1985.

Channel capacity: 35 (2-way capable). Channels available but not in use: N.A.

Basic Service

Subscribers: 1,381.

Programming (received off-air): WBRA-TV (PBS) Roanoke; WDBJ (CBS, MNT) Roanoke; WDRL-TV (IND) Danville; WFXR (CW, FOX) Roanoke; WKRN-TV (ABC)

Nashville; WPXR-TV (ION) Roanoke; WSET-TV (ABC) Lynchburg; WSLS-TV (NBC) Roanoke.

Programming (via satellite): C-SPAN; QVC; TBS Superstation; WGN America.

Fee: $45.86 installation; $13.95 monthly; $31.74 additional installation.

Expanded Basic Service 1

Subscribers: 1,224.

Programming (via satellite): A&E Networks; ABC Family Channel; Animal Planet; BET Networks; Bloomberg Television; Cartoon Network; CNBC; CNN; CNN en Espanol; Comcast SportsNet Mid-Atlantic; Comedy Central; Country Music TV; C-SPAN 2; Daystar TV Network; Discovery Channel; Disney Channel; E! Entertainment Television; ESPN; ESPN 2; ESPN U; Eternal Word TV Network; Food Network; Fox News Channel; FX; Hallmark Channel; Headline News; HGTV; History Channel; INSP; Lifetime; Lifetime Movie Network; MSNBC; MTV; Nick At Nite; Nickelodeon; RFD-TV; Science Television; Spike TV; Syfy; The Learning Channel; The Weather Channel; Travel Channel; Trinity Broadcasting Network; truTV; Turner Classic Movies; Turner Network TV; TV Land; USA Network; VH1.

Fee: $34.95 monthly.

Digital Basic Service

Subscribers: N.A.

Programming (via satellite): AMC; AmericanLife TV Network; BBC America; Bio; Boomerang; Bravo; Church Channel; Discovery Digital Networks; DIY Network; FamilyNet; Flix; Fox College Sports Atlantic; Fox College Sports Central; Fox College Sports Pacific; Fox Movie Channel; Fox Soccer; Fuel TV; Fuse; G4; GAS; Golf Channel; GolTV; Gospel Music TV; Great American Country; GSN; History Channel International; Independent Film Channel; Military History Channel; MTV Networks Digital Suite; National Geographic Channel; Nick Jr.; Nick Too; NickToons TV; Outdoor Channel; Oxygen; SoapNet; Speed; Sundance Channel; Toon Disney; Univision Studios; Versus; WE tv.

Fee: $44.95 monthly.

Digital Pay Service 1

Pay Units: N.A.

Programming (via satellite): Cinemax (multiplexed); Encore (multiplexed); HBO (multiplexed); Showtime (multiplexed); Starz (multiplexed); The Movie Channel (multiplexed).

Fee: $14.95 monthly.

Video-On-Demand: No

Internet Service

Operational: No.

Telephone Service

Digital: Operational

Miles of Plant: 141.0 (coaxial); None (fiber optic).

Manager: Greg Sapp. Marketing Director: Robert Weeks. Network Manager: Danny Vaughn.

Ownership: Citizens Cablevision Inc. (VA) (MSO).

FORT CHISWELL—Citizens Telephone Coop. Now served by FORT CHISWELLI, VA [VA0066]. ICA: VA5303.

FRANKLIN—Charter Communications. Now served by SUFFOLK, VA [VA0025]. ICA: VA0023.

FREDERICKSBURG—Cox Communications, 1310 Belman Rd, PO Box 117, Fredericksburg, VA 22404-0117. Phones: 540-373-6343; 540-429-5091 (Customer service). Fax: 540-371-2391. Web Site: http://www.cox.com/fredericksburg. Also serves Spotsylvania County & Stafford County (southern portion). ICA: VA0019.

Note: This system is an overbuild.

TV Market Ranking: Below 100 (FREDERICKSBURG, Spotsylvania County, Stafford County (southern portion)). Franchise award date: August 1, 1964. Franchise expiration date: N.A. Began: August 15, 1964.

Channel capacity: 80 (operating 2-way). Channels available but not in use: N.A.

Basic Service

Subscribers: N.A. Included with Fairfax County

Programming (received off-air): WCVE-TV (PBS) Richmond; WDCA (MNT) Washington; WDCW (CW) Washington; WETA-TV (PBS) Washington; WHUT-TV (PBS) Washington; WJLA-TV (ABC) Washington; WNVC (ETV) Fairfax; WPXW-TV (ION) Manassas; WRC-TV (NBC) Washington; WRIC-TV (ABC) Petersburg; WTTG (FOX) Washington; WTVR-TV (CBS) Richmond; WUSA (CBS) Washington; WWBT (NBC) Richmond; 24 FMs.

Programming (via satellite): C-SPAN; C-SPAN 2; Eternal Word TV Network; QVC; ShopNBC; TBS Superstation; TV Guide Network.

Fee: $29.99 installation; $17.99 monthly; $2.00 converter; $30.00 additional installation.

Expanded Basic Service 1

Subscribers: 14,309.

Programming (via satellite): A&E Networks; ABC Family Channel; AMC; Animal Planet; BET Networks; Bravo; Cartoon Network; CNBC; CNN; Comcast SportsNet Mid-Atlantic; Comedy Central; Country Music TV; Discovery Channel; Discovery Health Channel; Disney Channel; E! Entertainment Television; ESPN; ESPN 2; Food Network; Fox News Channel; FX; Headline News; HGTV; History Channel; Lifetime; MSNBC; MTV; Nickelodeon; Oxygen; Speed; Spike TV; Syfy; Telemundo; The Learning Channel; The Weather Channel; Travel Channel; Trinity Broadcasting Network; truTV; Turner Classic Movies; Turner Network TV; TV Land; USA Network; VH1.

Fee: $26.00 monthly.

Digital Basic Service

Subscribers: 9,804.

Programming (via satellite): BBC America; Bio; Bloomberg Television; Cooking Channel; Discovery Digital Networks; DIY Network; ESPN Classic Sports; ESPNews; Fox Movie Channel; Fox Sports World; Fuse; G4; Golf Channel; GSN; Hallmark Channel; History Channel International; Independent Film Channel; Lifetime Movie Network; Mid-Atlantic Sports Network; SoapNet; Sundance Channel; Toon Disney; Versus.

Fee: $14.95 monthly.

Pay Service 1

Pay Units: 1,291.

Programming (via satellite): Cinemax.

Fee: $3.50 installation; $10.45 monthly.

Pay Service 2

Pay Units: 764.

Programming (via satellite): Showtime.

Fee: $3.50 installation; $10.45 monthly.

Pay Service 3

Pay Units: 2,713.

Programming (via satellite): HBO.

Fee: $3.50 installation; $10.45 monthly.

Pay Service 4

Pay Units: 679.

Programming (via satellite): The Movie Channel.

Fee: $3.50 installation; $10.45 monthly.

Digital Pay Service 1

Pay Units: N.A.

Programming (via satellite): Canales N; Cinemax (multiplexed); DMX Music; Encore (multiplexed); HBO (multiplexed); Showtime (multiplexed); Starz (multiplexed); The Movie Channel (multiplexed).

Fee: $13.99 monthly (each).

Video-On-Demand: Yes

Pay-Per-View

Addressable homes: 9,804.

iN DEMAND; Shorteez (delivered digitally); iN DEMAND (delivered digitally); Hot Choice (delivered digitally); Playboy TV (delivered digitally); Fresh (delivered digitally).

Internet Service

Operational: Yes.

Broadband Service: Cox High Speed Internet.

Fee: $39.95 monthly.

Telephone Service

Digital: Operational

Miles of Plant: 304.0 (coaxial); 9.0 (fiber optic). Additional miles planned: 9.0 (coaxial).

Vice President & General Manager: Janet Branard. Vice President, Network Development: Daryl Ladd. Marketing Coordinator: Stacy Thomas. Public Affairs Director: Alex Horwitz.

Ownership: Cox Communications Inc. (MSO).

FRONT ROYAL—Comcast Cable, 195 Rainville Rd, Winchester, VA 22602. Phones: 434-951-3700 (Charlottesville office); 540-504-0900. Fax: 540-504-0972. Web Site: http://www.comcast.com. Also serves Bentonville, Castleton, Chester Gap, Huntly, Riverton, Warren County & Washington. ICA: VA0139.

TV Market Ranking: Below 100 (Huntly); Outside TV Markets (Bentonville, Castleton, Chester Gap, FRONT ROYAL, Riverton, Warren County, Washington). Franchise award date: N.A. Franchise expiration date: N.A. Began: February 19, 1964.

Channel capacity: N.A. Channels available but not in use: N.A.

Basic Service

Subscribers: 8,844.

Programming (received off-air): WDCA (MNT) Washington; WDCW (CW) Washington; WETA-TV (PBS) Washington; WFDC-DT (UNV) Arlington; WHAG-TV (NBC) Hagerstown; WHSV-TV (ABC, MNT) Harrisonburg; WJLA-TV (ABC) Washington; WJZ-TV (CBS) Baltimore; WRC-TV (NBC) Washington; WTTG (FOX) Washington; WTVR-TV (CBS) Richmond; WUSA (CBS) Washington; WVPT (PBS) Staunton; WWPX-TV (ION) Martinsburg.

Programming (via satellite): QVC; TV Guide Network.

Fee: $33.00 installation; $10.00 monthly.

Expanded Basic Service 1

Subscribers: N.A.

Programming (via satellite): A&E Networks; ABC Family Channel; AMC; Animal Planet; BET Networks; Bravo; Cartoon Network; CNBC; CNN; Comcast SportsNet Mid-Atlantic; Comedy Central; Country Music TV; C-SPAN; Discovery Channel; Disney Channel; E! Entertainment Television; ESPN; ESPN 2; Eternal Word TV Network; Food Network; Fox News Channel; FX; Hallmark Channel; Headline News; HGTV; History Channel; Lifetime; Mid-Atlantic Sports Network; MSNBC; MTV; Nickelodeon; Oxygen; Spike TV; Syfy; TBS Superstation; The Learning Channel; The Weather Channel; Travel Channel; truTV; Turner Network TV; TV Land; USA Network; VH1.

Fee: $25.00 installation; $12.45 monthly.

Digital Basic Service

Subscribers: N.A.

Programming (via satellite): A&E HD; ABC Family HD; Animal Planet HD; BBC America; Bio; Bloomberg Television; CBS Sports Network; Cine Latino; CMT Pure Country; CNN en Espanol; CNN HD; C-SPAN 2; Current; Discovery Channel HD; Discovery en Espanol; Discovery Fit & Health; Discovery Health Channel; Discovery Kids Channel; DIY Network; Encore; ESPN 2 HD; ESPN Classic Sports; ESPN Deportes; ESPN HD; ESPNews; Flix; Food Network HD; Fox Business Channel; Fox College Sports Atlantic; Fox College Sports Central; Fox College Sports Pacific; Fox Deportes; Fox Movie Channel; Fox Reality Channel; Fox Soccer; Fuel TV; Fuse; G4; GMC; Golf Channel; Great American Country; GSN; Halogen Network; HD Theater; HGTV HD; History Channel en Espanol; History Channel HD; History Channel International; ID Investigation Discovery; Independent Film Channel; Lifetime Movie Network; LOGO; Military Channel; MTV2; mun2 television; Music Choice; National Geographic Channel; National Geographic Channel HD Network; NFL Network; Nick Jr.; Nick Too; NickToons TV; Outdoor Channel; Palladia; PBS Kids Sprout; Planet Green; RTN; Science; Science HD; SoapNet; Speed; Style Network; Sundance Channel; Syfy HD; TBS in HD; TeenNick; Tennis Channel; The Comcast Network; The Word Network; TLC HD; Toon Disney; Toon Disney en Espanol; Tr3s; Trinity Broadcasting Network; Turner Classic Movies; Turner Network TV HD; TV One; TVG Network; Universal HD; USA Network HD; VeneMovies; Versus; Versus HD; VH1 Classic; VH1 Soul; WE tv.

Digital Pay Service 1

Pay Units: N.A.

Programming (via satellite): ART America; CCTV-4; Cinemax (multiplexed); Cinemax HD; Filipino Channel; HBO (multiplexed); HBO HD; RAI USA; Showtime (multiplexed); Showtime HD; Starz (multiplexed); Starz HDTV; The Movie Channel (multiplexed); TV Asia; TV Japan; TV5, La Television International; Zee TV USA; Zhong Tian Channel.

Video-On-Demand: Yes

Pay-Per-View

iN DEMAND (delivered digitally); Playboy TV (delivered digitally).

Internet Service

Operational: Yes.

Broadband Service: Comcast High Speed Internet.

Fee: $42.95 monthly.

Telephone Service

None

Miles of Plant: 1,023.0 (coaxial); None (fiber optic). Miles of plant (coax) includes Winchester

Vice President & General Manager: Troy Fitzhugh. Technical Operations Director: Tom Jacobs. Technical Operations Manager: Richard Burke. Marketing Director: Steve Miles.

Ownership: Comcast Cable Communications Inc. (MSO).

GALAX—Comcast Cable, 112 W Washington St, Galax, VA 24333. Phones: 423-282-1370 (Gray, TN office); 276-236-0879. Fax: 276-236-4714. Web Site: http://www.comcast.com. Also serves Carroll County (portions), Fries, Grayson County (portions), Hillsville, Independence, Oldtown & Woodlawn. ICA: VA0140.

TV Market Ranking: Outside TV Markets (Carroll County (portions), Fries, GALAX, Grayson County (portions), Hillsville,

Independence, Oldtown, Woodlawn). Franchise award date: N.A. Franchise expiration date: N.A. Began: November 1, 1966.

Channel capacity: N.A. Channels available but not in use: N.A.

Basic Service

Subscribers: N.A. Included in Greeneville TN

Programming (received off-air): WBRA-TV (PBS) Roanoke; WDBJ (CBS, MNT) Roanoke; WFMY-TV (CBS) Greensboro; WFXR (CW, FOX) Roanoke; WPXR-TV (ION) Roanoke; WSLS-TV (NBC) Roanoke; WXII-TV (NBC) Winston-Salem; WXLV-TV (ABC) Winston-Salem.

Programming (via satellite): C-SPAN; QVC.

Fee: $40.00 installation; $9.55 monthly; $2.52 converter; $25.00 additional installation.

Expanded Basic Service 1

Subscribers: N.A.

Programming (via satellite): A&E Networks; ABC Family Channel; AMC; Animal Planet; BET Networks; CNBC; CNN; Comcast SportsNet Mid-Atlantic; Comedy Central; Country Music TV; C-SPAN 2; Discovery Channel; Disney Channel; E! Entertainment Television; ESPN; ESPN 2; Food Network; Fox News Channel; FX; Hallmark Channel; Headline News; INSP; Lifetime; MSNBC; MTV; Nickelodeon; Oxygen; Product Information Network; ShopNBC; Spike TV; TBS Superstation; The Learning Channel; The Weather Channel; Travel Channel; truTV; Turner Network TV; TV Guide Network; TV Land; USA Network; VH1.

Digital Basic Service

Subscribers: 1,327.

Programming (via satellite): BBC America; Bloomberg Television; Bravo; Discovery Fit & Health; DMX Music; ESPN Classic Sports; ESPNews; Fox Movie Channel; Fox Sports World; G4; Golf Channel; GSN; Halogen Network; HGTV; History Channel; Independent Film Channel; Lifetime Movie Network; Music Choice; NickToons TV; Outdoor Channel; Syfy; Toon Disney; Trinity Broadcasting Network; Versus; WE tv.

Digital Pay Service 1

Pay Units: 471.

Programming (via satellite): Cinemax (multiplexed); Encore (multiplexed); HBO (multiplexed); Showtime (multiplexed); Starz (multiplexed); The Movie Channel (multiplexed).

Video-On-Demand: No

Pay-Per-View

Addressable homes: 1,500.

iN DEMAND (delivered digitally); Playboy TV (delivered digitally); Fresh (delivered digitally).

Internet Service

Operational: Yes.

Subscribers: 776.

Broadband Service: Comcast High Speed Internet.

Fee: $42.95 monthly.

Telephone Service

Analog: Not Operational

Digital: Operational

Miles of plant included in Greeneville, TN

Vice President & General Manager: Dave Sanders. Manager: Hilda Sexton. Technical Operations Director: Tim Castor. Plant Manager: Travis Coomes. Marketing Coordinator: Debbie Frost. Office Manager: Ann Rouse.

Ownership: Comcast Cable Communications Inc. (MSO).

GATE CITY—Scott Telecom & Electronics, 121 Woodland St, PO Box 489, Gate City, VA 24251-0489. Phones: 800-833-9823; 276-452-9119. Fax: 276-452-2447. E-mail: sctc@sctc.org. Web Site: http://www.sctc.org. Also serves Daniel Boone, Hiltons, Nickelsville, Weber City & Yuma. ICA: VA0054.

TV Market Ranking: Below 100 (Daniel Boone, GATE CITY, Hiltons, Nickelsville, Weber City, Yuma). Franchise award date: March 15, 1965. Franchise expiration date: N.A. Began: May 5, 1965.

Channel capacity: 66 (2-way capable). Channels available but not in use: N.A.

Basic Service

Subscribers: 3,200.

Programming (received off-air): WAPK-CA (MNT) Kingsport; WCYB-TV (CW, NBC) Bristol; WEMT (FOX) Greeneville; WETP-TV (PBS) Sneedville; WJHL-TV (CBS) Johnson City; WKPT-TV (ABC) Kingsport; WSBN-TV (PBS) Norton; allband FM.

Programming (via satellite): A&E Networks; ABC Family Channel; AMC; AmericanLife TV Network; Animal Planet; BET Networks; Cartoon Network; CNBC; CNN; Comcast SportsNet Mid-Atlantic; Country Music TV; C-SPAN; C-SPAN 2; CW+; Discovery Channel; Discovery Fit & Health; Discovery Health Channel; Discovery Home Channel; Disney Channel; DIY Network; E! Entertainment Television; ESPN; ESPN 2; ESPN Classic Sports; Familyland Television Network; Food Network; Fox Movie Channel; Fox News Channel; FX; Gospel Music TV; Great American Country; GSN; Hallmark Channel; Headline News; HGTV; History Channel; INSP; ION Television; Lifetime; Lifetime Movie Network; Lifetime Real Women; MoviePlex; MSNBC; MTV; National Geographic Channel; Nickelodeon; Outdoor Channel; QVC; RFD-TV; Science; Speed; Spike TV; Style Network; Syfy; TBS Superstation; The Learning Channel; The Weather Channel; Toon Disney; Travel Channel; Trinity Broadcasting Network; truTV; Turner Network TV; TV Land; USA Network; Versus; VH1; WE tv; WGN America.

Fee: $45.50 installation; $28.00 monthly.

Digital Basic Service

Subscribers: N.A.

Programming (via satellite): BBC America; Bio; Bloomberg Television; Boomerang; CNN International; Discovery Times Channel; ESPNews; FamilyNet; Fox College Sports Atlantic; Fox College Sports Central; Fox College Sports Pacific; Fuse; G4; GAS; Golf Channel; History Channel International; HRTV; Military Channel; MTV Networks Digital Suite; Music Choice; Nick Jr.; Nick Too; NickToons TV; Oxygen; SoapNet; Tennis Channel; Turner Classic Movies.

Digital Pay Service 1

Pay Units: N.A.

Programming (via satellite): Cinemax (multiplexed); Encore (multiplexed); Flix; HBO (multiplexed); Showtime (multiplexed); Starz (multiplexed); The Movie Channel (multiplexed).

Video-On-Demand: No

Internet Service

Operational: No, DSL.

Telephone Service

None

Miles of Plant: 130.0 (coaxial); None (fiber optic). Additional miles planned: 20.0 (coaxial).

Manager: William J. Franklin. Marketing Director: Greg Hood. Chief Technician: Terry Holt.

Ownership: Scott County Telephone Cooperative.

GLADE SPRING—Comcast Cable, 1794 Old Gray Station Rd, Gray, TN 37615-3869. Phone: 423-282-1370. Fax: 423-283-4855. Web Site: http://www.comcast.com. Also serves Abingdon, Chilhowie, Saltville, Seven Mile Ford, Smyth County, Sugar Grove & Washington County. ICA: VA0032.

TV Market Ranking: Below 100 (Abingdon, Chilhowie, GLADE SPRING, Saltville, Seven Mile Ford, Smyth County, Sugar Grove, Washington County). Franchise award date: May 17, 1979. Franchise expiration date: N.A. Began: January 1, 1980.

Channel capacity: N.A. Channels available but not in use: N.A.

Basic Service

Subscribers: N.A. Included in Gray, TN

Programming (received off-air): WAPK-CA (MNT) Kingsport; WCYB-TV (CW, NBC) Bristol; WDBJ (CBS, MNT) Roanoke; WEMT (FOX) Greeneville; WJHL-TV (CBS) Johnson City; WKPT-TV (ABC) Kingsport; WLFG (IND) Grundy; WMSY-TV (PBS) Marion.

Programming (via satellite): ESPN; QVC.

Fee: $58.61 installation; $14.75 monthly.

Expanded Basic Service 1

Subscribers: N.A.

Programming (via satellite): A&E Networks; ABC Family Channel; AMC; Animal Planet; BET Networks; Bravo; Cartoon Network; CNBC; CNN; Comcast/Charter Sports Southeast (CSS); Comedy Central; Country Music TV; C-SPAN; Discovery Channel; Discovery Health Channel; Disney Channel; E! Entertainment Television; ESPN 2; Food Network; Fox News Channel; FX; Golf Channel; Great American Country; GSN; Hallmark Channel; Halogen Network; Headline News; HGTV; History Channel; Lifetime; MSNBC; MTV; Nickelodeon; Outdoor Channel; Paxson Communications Corp.; Speed; Spike TV; Style Network; Syfy; The Learning Channel; The Weather Channel; Trinity Broadcasting Network; truTV; Turner Classic Movies; Turner Network TV; TV Guide Network; TV Land; USA Network; Versus; VH1.

Fee: $28.24 monthly.

Digital Basic Service

Subscribers: N.A.

Programming (via satellite): BBC America; Bio; C-SPAN 3; DMX Music; Encore (multiplexed); ESPN; ESPNews; Flix (multiplexed); G4; GAS; HD Theater; History Channel International; INHD (multiplexed); MTV Networks Digital Suite; National Geographic Channel; NFL Network; Nick Jr.; Nick Too; NickToons TV; SoapNet; Sundance Channel (multiplexed); Toon Disney; Turner Network TV HD; WAM! America's Kidz Network; Weatherscan.

Digital Pay Service 1

Pay Units: N.A.

Programming (via satellite): Cinemax (multiplexed); Cinemax HD; HBO (multiplexed); HBO HD; Showtime (multiplexed); Showtime HD; Starz (multiplexed); Starz HDTV; The Movie Channel (multiplexed).

Fee: $13.95 monthly (each).

Video-On-Demand: Yes

Pay-Per-View

iN DEMAND (delivered digitally); Hot Choice (delivered digitally); Playboy TV (delivered digitally); Fresh (delivered digitally); Shorteez (delivered digitally); Pleasure (delivered digitally).

Internet Service

Operational: Yes.

Broadband Service: Comcast High Speed Internet.

Fee: $42.95 monthly.

Telephone Service

Digital: Operational

Miles of Plant: 732.0 (coaxial); 41.0 (fiber optic).

Vice President & General Manager: Dave Sanders. Technical Operations Director: Tim Castor. Marketing Manager: Sandra Munsey.

Ownership: Comcast Cable Communications Inc. (MSO).

GLASGOW—Formerly served by Adelphia Communications. Now served by LEXINGTON, VA [VA0147]. ICA: VA0103.

GLOUCESTER COUNTY—Cox Communications. Now served by HAMPTON ROADS (formerly Virginia Beach), VA [VA0002]. ICA: VA0031.

GORDONSVILLE—Comcast Cable, 400 Westfield Rd, Charlottesville, VA 22901. Phone: 434-951-3700. Fax: 434-951-3705. Web Site: http://www.comcast.com. Also serves Orange County (portions). ICA: VA0102.

TV Market Ranking: Below 100 (GORDONSVILLE, Orange County (portions)). Franchise award date: November 6, 1980. Franchise expiration date: N.A. Began: March 1, 1982.

Channel capacity: N.A. Channels available but not in use: N.A.

Basic Service

Subscribers: 500.

Programming (received off-air): WAHU-CD Charlottesville; WCVE-TV (PBS) Richmond; WRIC-TV (ABC) Petersburg; WTVR-TV (CBS) Richmond; WVIR-TV (CW, NBC) Charlottesville; WWBT (NBC) Richmond.

Programming (via satellite): A&E Networks; ABC Family Channel; AMC; BET Networks; CNN; Country Music TV; Discovery Channel; Disney Channel; ESPN; ESPN 2; Fox News Channel; Headline News; Lifetime; MTV; Nickelodeon; QVC; Spike TV; Syfy; TBS Superstation; The Learning Channel; The Weather Channel; Trinity Broadcasting Network; USA Network; WGN America.

Fee: $40.00 installation; $17.95 monthly; $2.00 converter.

Pay Service 1

Pay Units: 80.

Programming (via satellite): HBO.

Fee: $15.00 installation; $10.95 monthly.

Pay Service 2
Pay Units: 93.
Programming (via satellite): Showtime.

Pay Service 3
Pay Units: 88.
Programming (via satellite): The Movie Channel.

Video-On-Demand: No

Internet Service
Operational: Yes.

Telephone Service
Digital: Operational

Miles of Plant: 20.0 (coaxial); None (fiber optic).

Vice President & General Manager: Troy Fitzhugh. Technical Operations Director: Tom Jacobs. Marketing Director: Steve Miles. Marketing Coordinator: Cassie Cool.

Ownership: Comcast Cable Communications Inc. (MSO).

GOSHEN—Comcast Cable, 2154 Sycamore Ave, Buena Vista, VA 24416-3126. Phones: 434-951-3700; 540-261-4558. Fax: 540-261-7616. Web Site: http://www.comcast.com. ICA: VA0165.

TV Market Ranking: Outside TV Markets (GOSHEN). Franchise award date: October 1, 1990. Franchise expiration date: N.A. Began: December 1, 1990.

Channel capacity: 36 (not 2-way capable). Channels available but not in use: N.A.

Basic Service
Subscribers: 150.
Programming (received off-air): WDBJ (CBS, MNT) Roanoke; WFXR (CW, FOX) Roanoke; WSET-TV (ABC) Lynchburg; WSLS-TV (NBC) Roanoke; WVPT (PBS) Staunton.
Programming (via satellite): ABC Family Channel; CNN; Country Music TV; Discovery Channel; ESPN; Nickelodeon; TBS Superstation; Turner Network TV; USA Network; VH1; WGN America.
Fee: $35.00 installation; $17.50 monthly.

Pay Service 1
Pay Units: 54.
Programming (via satellite): HBO; Showtime; The Movie Channel.
Fee: $10.95 monthly (HBO), $11.95 monthly (Showtime/TMC).

Video-On-Demand: No

Internet Service
Operational: Yes.

Telephone Service
None

Miles of Plant: 8.0 (coaxial); None (fiber optic).

Vice President & General Manager: Troy Fitzhugh. Technical Operations Director: Tom Jacobs. Chief Technician: Joe Clements. Plant Manager: John Van Lew. Marketing Director: Steve Miles.

Ownership: Comcast Cable Communications Inc. (MSO).

GRUNDY—Time Warner Cable, 1430 2nd St, Richlands, VA 24641-2455. Phone: 276-964-1150. Fax: 276-596-9046. Web Site: http://www.timewarnercable.com. Also serves Big Rock, Deskins, Harman, Hurley, Maxie, Stacy, Vansant & Wolford. ICA: VA0044.

TV Market Ranking: Below 100 (Big Rock, Deskins, GRUNDY, Harman, Hurley, Maxie, Stacy, Vansant, Wolford). Franchise award date: N.A. Franchise expiration date: N.A. Began: N.A.

Channel capacity: N.A. Channels available but not in use: N.A.

Basic Service
Subscribers: 3,398.
Programming (received off-air): WAPK-CA (MNT) Kingsport; WCYB-TV (CW, NBC) Bristol; WJDW-LP Tazewell; WJHL-TV (CBS) Johnson City; WKPT-TV (ABC) Kingsport; WLFG (IND) Grundy; WSBN-TV (PBS) Norton; WVVA (CW, NBC) Bluefield.
Programming (via satellite): QVC; TBS Superstation.
Fee: $39.95 installation; $16.88 monthly; $3.25 converter.

Expanded Basic Service 1
Subscribers: 3,244.
Programming (via satellite): A&E Networks; CNBC; CNN; Comcast SportsNet Mid-Atlantic; Country Music TV; Discovery Channel; Disney Channel; ESPN; Headline News; Lifetime; MTV; Nickelodeon; Spike TV; The Weather Channel; Turner Network TV; USA Network; VH1.
Fee: $20.53 monthly.

Digital Basic Service
Subscribers: 3,100.
Programming (via satellite): BBC America; Bloomberg Television; Bravo; Country Music TV; Discovery Digital Networks; ESPN 2; ESPN Classic Sports; ESPNews; Fox Movie Channel; Fox Soccer; G4; Golf Channel; GSN; Halogen Network; HGTV; History Channel; Independent Film Channel; Music Choice; National Geographic Channel; Nick Jr.; NickToons TV; Outdoor Channel; Speed; Syfy; Trinity Broadcasting Network; Turner Classic Movies; TV Land; Versus; VH1 Classic; WE tv.
Fee: $5.35 monthly.

Digital Pay Service 1
Pay Units: N.A.
Programming (via satellite): Cinemax (multiplexed); Encore (multiplexed); HBO (multiplexed); Showtime (multiplexed); Starz (multiplexed); The Movie Channel (multiplexed).
Fee: $15.95 monthly (each).

Video-On-Demand: Planned

Pay-Per-View
Playboy TV (delivered digitally); NASCAR In Car (delivered digitally); Movies & Events (delivered digitally).

Internet Service
Operational: Yes.
Broadband Service: Road Runner.
Fee: $49.95 monthly.

Telephone Service
Digital: Planned

Miles of Plant: 211.0 (coaxial); None (fiber optic).

General Manager: C. K. Allen. Marketing Manager: Mark Cole. Chief Technician: Danny Nelson.

Ownership: Time Warner Cable (MSO).

HAMPTON ROADS—Cox Communications, 1341 Crossways Blvd, Chesapeake, VA 23320. Phone: 757-224-4269. Fax: 757-671-1501. Web Site: http://www.cox.com/hamptonroads. Also serves Chesapeake, Eltham, Fort Eustis Army Base, Fort Monroe, Fort Story, Gloucester County, Grafton, Hampton, James City County, King & Queen County (portions), Lanexa, Langley AFB, Mattaponi, New Kent, New Kent County (portions), Newport News, Norfolk, Norfolk Naval Base/Southside Hampton Roads, Poquoson, Portsmouth, Providence Forge, Quinton, Shacklefords, U.S. Coast Guard 5th District, U.S. Coast Guard Support Center, Virginia Beach, West Point, Williamsburg, York County, Yorktown & Yorktown Naval Weapons Station. ICA: VA0002.

TV Market Ranking: 44 (Chesapeake, Fort Eustis Army Base, Fort Monroe, Fort Story, Gloucester County (portions), Grafton, Hampton, HAMPTON ROADS, James City County, Langley AFB, Newport News, Norfolk, Norfolk Naval Base/Southside Hampton Roads, Portsmouth, U.S. Coast Guard 5th District, U.S. Coast Guard Support Center, Virginia Beach, Williamsburg, York County, Yorktown, Yorktown Naval Weapons Station); 63 (Eltham, King & Queen County (portions), Lanexa, New Kent, New Kent County (portions), Providence Forge, Quinton, West Point (portions)); Below 100 (Poquoson); Outside TV Markets (Mattaponi, Shacklefords, Gloucester County (portions), West Point (portions)). Franchise award date: N.A. Franchise expiration date: N.A. Began: January 16, 1978.

Channel capacity: N.A. Channels available but not in use: N.A.

Basic Service
Subscribers: 400,000.
Programming (received off-air): WAVY-TV (NBC) Portsmouth; WGNT (CW) Portsmouth; WHRO-TV (PBS) Hampton-Norfolk; WPXV-TV (ION) Norfolk; WSKY-TV (IND) Manteo; WTKR (CBS) Norfolk; WTVZ-TV (MNT) Norfolk; WUNC-TV (PBS) Chapel Hill; WVBT (FOX) Virginia Beach; WVEC (ABC) Hampton.
Programming (via satellite): Animal Planet; C-SPAN; C-SPAN 2; MarketConnect Network; QVC; Shop at Home; TBS Superstation; TV Guide Network; Univision Studios; WGN America.
Fee: $40.00 installation; $18.00 monthly; $10.00 additional installation.

Expanded Basic Service 1
Subscribers: N.A.
Programming (via satellite): A&E Networks; ABC Family Channel; AMC; BET Networks; Bravo; Cartoon Network; CNBC; CNN; Comcast SportsNet Mid-Atlantic; Comedy Central; Country Music TV; Discovery Channel; Discovery Health Channel; Disney Channel; E! Entertainment Television; ESPN; ESPN 2; Food Network; Fox News Channel; FX; Headline News; HGTV; History Channel; International Television (ITV); Lifetime; MSNBC; MTV; Nickelodeon; Speed; Spike TV; Syfy; The Learning Channel; The Weather Channel; Travel Channel; truTV; Turner Network TV; TV Land; USA Network; Versus; VH1.
Fee: $41.99 monthly.

Digital Basic Service
Subscribers: N.A.
Programming (via satellite): BBC America; Bio; Black Family Channel; Bloomberg Television; Cooking Channel; Discovery Digital Networks; DIY Network; Encore; ESPN Classic Sports; ESPNews; Flix; Fox Sports World; G4; GAS; Golf Channel; GSN; Hallmark Channel; History Channel International; Independent Film Channel; Lifetime Movie Network; LWS Local Weather Station; Mid-Atlantic Sports Network; MTV Networks Digital Suite; Music Choice; National Geographic Channel; NBA TV; Nick Jr.; NickToons TV; Oxygen; SoapNet; Sundance Channel; Toon Disney; Turner Classic Movies.
Fee: $9.45 monthly.

Pay Service 1
Pay Units: 167,271.
Programming (via satellite): Cinemax (multiplexed); Encore; HBO (multiplexed); Showtime; Starz; The Movie Channel.
Fee: $15.00 installation; $12.00 monthly (each).

Digital Pay Service 1
Pay Units: N.A.
Programming (via satellite): Cinemax (multiplexed); Filipino Channel; HBO (multiplexed); Showtime (multiplexed); Starz (multiplexed); The Movie Channel (multiplexed).

Video-On-Demand: Yes

Pay-Per-View
Hot Choice; iN DEMAND; special events; ESPN Now (delivered digitally); Adult PPV (delivered digitally); Sports PPV (delivered digitally).

Internet Service
Operational: Yes.
Broadband Service: Cox High Speed Internet.
Fee: $99.95 installation; $24.95 monthly; $15.00 modem lease; $299.00 modem purchase.

Telephone Service
Digital: Operational
Fee: $14.99 monthly

Miles of Plant: 4,687.0 (coaxial); 278.0 (fiber optic).

Vice President & Regional Manager: Gary McCollum. Vice President, Public & Government Affairs: Thom Prevette. Public Affairs Manager: Pamela Marino.

Ownership: Cox Communications Inc. (MSO).

HARRISONBURG—Comcast Cable, 400 Westfield Rd, Charlottesville, VA 22901. Phone: 434-951-3700. Fax: 434-951-3705. Web Site: http://www.comcast.com. Also serves Bridgewater, Broadway, Dayton, Elkton, Lacey Spring, McGaheysville, Mount Clinton, Mount Crawford, Page County (portions), Rawley Springs, Rockingham, Rockingham County, Shenandoah & Timberville. ICA: VA0016.

TV Market Ranking: Below 100 (Bridgewater, Broadway, Dayton, Elkton, HARRISONBURG, Lacey Spring, McGaheysville, Mount Clinton, Mount Crawford, Page County (portions), Rawley Springs, Rockingham, Rockingham County, Shenandoah, Timberville); Outside TV Markets (Page County (portions)). Franchise award date: January 1, 1952. Franchise expiration date: N.A. Began: August 1, 1952.

Channel capacity: N.A. Channels available but not in use: N.A.

Basic Service
Subscribers: 17,051.
Programming (received off-air): WAZT-CA (IND) Woodstock; WHSV-TV (ABC, MNT) Harrisonburg; WRC-TV (NBC) Washington; WRIC-TV (ABC) Petersburg; WTTG (FOX) Washington; WTVR-TV (CBS) Richmond; WUSA (CBS) Washington; WVIR-TV (CW, NBC) Charlottesville; WVPT (PBS) Staunton; WWBT (NBC) Richmond; allband FM.
Programming (via satellite): QVC.
Fee: $45.43 installation; $10.48 monthly; $1.87 converter.

Expanded Basic Service 1
Subscribers: 15,903.
Programming (via satellite): A&E Networks; ABC Family Channel; AMC; Animal Planet; BET Networks; Bravo; Cartoon Network; CNBC; CNN; Comcast SportsNet Mid-Atlantic; Comedy Central; Country Music TV; C-SPAN; C-SPAN 2; Discovery Channel; Disney Channel; E! Entertainment Television; ESPN; ESPN 2; Food Network; Fox News Channel; FX; Hallmark Channel; Headline News; HGTV; History Channel; ION Television; Lifetime; MSNBC; MTV; Nickelodeon; Oxygen; Product Information Network; ShopNBC; Speed; Spike TV; Syfy; TBS Superstation; The Learn-

ing Channel; The Weather Channel; Travel Channel; truTV; Turner Classic Movies; Turner Network TV; TV Guide Network; TV Land; USA Network; VH1.
Fee: $37.80 installation; $19.95 monthly.

Digital Basic Service
Subscribers: N.A.
Programming (via satellite): AmericanLife TV Network; BBC America; Bio; Black Family Channel; Bloomberg Television; Canales N; CBS Sports Network; CMT Pure Country; Current; DIY Network; ESPN 2 HD; ESPN Classic Sports; ESPN HD; ESPNews; Eternal Word TV Network; Fox College Sports Atlantic; Fox College Sports Central; Fox College Sports Pacific; Fox Movie Channel; Fox Reality Channel; Fox Soccer; Fuel TV; Fuse; G4; GAS; Golf Channel; Great American Country; GSN; Halogen Network; HD Theater; History Channel International; Howard TV; Independent Film Channel; INHD; Lifetime Movie Network; LOGO; MTV Networks Digital Suite; Music Choice; NFL Network; Nick Jr.; Nick Too; NickToons TV; Outdoor Channel; Palladia; PBS Kids Sprout; SoapNet; Sundance Channel; Tennis Channel; The Word Network; Toon Disney; Trinity Broadcasting Network; Turner Network TV HD; TVG Network; Universal HD; Versus; WE tv.

Digital Pay Service 1
Pay Units: 213.
Programming (via satellite): ART America; CCTV-4; Cinemax (multiplexed); Cinemax HD; Cinemax On Demand; Encore (multiplexed); Filipino Channel; Flix; HBO (multiplexed); HBO HD; HBO On Demand; RAI International; Showtime (multiplexed); Showtime HD; Showtime On Demand; Starz (multiplexed); Starz HDTV; Starz On Demand; The Movie Channel (multiplexed); The Movie Channel On Demand; TV Asia; TV Japan; TV5, La Television International; Zhong Tian Channel.

Video-On-Demand: Yes

Pay-Per-View
iN DEMAND (delivered digitally); Playboy TV (delivered digitally); Fresh (delivered digitally); Sports PPV (delivered digitally).

Internet Service
Operational: Yes. Began: April 1, 2001.
Subscribers: 6.
Broadband Service: Comcast High Speed Internet.
Fee: $42.55 monthly; $39.95 modem lease.

Telephone Service
Digital: Operational

Miles of Plant: 655.0 (coaxial); 15.0 (fiber optic). Miles of plant include Luray
Vice President & General Manager: Troy Fitzhugh. Technical Operations Director: Tom Jacobs. Marketing Director: Steve Miles. Marketing Coordinator: Cassie Cool.
Ownership: Comcast Cable Communications Inc. (MSO).

HARRISONBURG—Formerly served by NTELOS. No longer in operation. ICA: VA0179.

HAYSI—Formerly served by K & V Cable TV Co. No longer in operation. ICA: VA0116.

HENRICO COUNTY—Comcast Cable. Now served by RICHMOND, VA [VA0004]. ICA: VA0003.

HOT SPRINGS—Comcast Cable, 2154 Sycamore Ave, Buena Vista, VA 24416-3126. Phones: 434-951-3700 (Charlottesville office); 540-261-4558. Fax: 540-261-7616. Web Site: http://www.comcast.com. Also serves Bacova, Bath County & Warm Springs. ICA: VA0096.
TV Market Ranking: Outside TV Markets (Bacova, Bath County (portions), HOT SPRINGS, Warm Springs). Franchise award date: N.A. Franchise expiration date: N.A. Began: April 23, 1969.
Channel capacity: 36 (not 2-way capable). Channels available but not in use: N.A.

Basic Service
Subscribers: 819.
Programming (received off-air): WBRA-TV (PBS) Roanoke; WDBJ (CBS, MNT) Roanoke; WFXR (CW, FOX) Roanoke; WPXR-TV (ION) Roanoke; WSET-TV (ABC) Lynchburg; WSLS-TV (NBC) Roanoke; WVVA (CW, NBC) Bluefield; allband FM.
Programming (via satellite): A&E Networks; ABC Family Channel; AMC; CNN; Comcast SportsNet Mid-Atlantic; C-SPAN; Discovery Channel; Disney Channel; ESPN; ESPN 2; Headline News; History Channel; Lifetime; Nickelodeon; QVC; Spike TV; TBS Superstation; The Learning Channel; The Weather Channel; Trinity Broadcasting Network; Turner Network TV; USA Network; WGN America.
Fee: $50.00 installation; $24.95 monthly; $10.00 additional installation.

Pay Service 1
Pay Units: 82.
Programming (via satellite): HBO.
Fee: $15.00 installation; $11.95 monthly.

Pay Service 2
Pay Units: 57.
Programming (via satellite): Flix; Showtime; The Movie Channel.
Fee: $11.95 monthly.

Video-On-Demand: No

Internet Service
Operational: No.

Telephone Service
None

Miles of Plant: 30.0 (coaxial); None (fiber optic).
Vice President & General Manager: Troy Fitzhugh. Technical Operations Director: Tom Jacobs. Plant Manager: John Van Lew. Chief Technician: Joe Clemsents. Marketing Director: Steve Miles.
Ownership: Comcast Cable Communications Inc. (MSO).

HURT—Formerly served by Adelphia Communications. Now served by DANVILLE, VA [VA0012]. ICA: VA0087.

INDEPENDENCE—Formerly served by Adelphia Communications. Now served by GALAX, VA [VA0140]. ICA: VA0142.

IVANHOE—Citizens Telephone Coop. Now served by FORT CHISWELL, VA [VA0066]. ICA: VA5305.

JAMES CITY COUNTY—Cox Communications. Now served by HAMPTON ROADS (formerly Virginia Beach), VA [VA0002]. ICA: VA0027.

JARRATT—CWA Cable, 662 Blackridge Rd, La Crosse, VA 23950-2928. Phones: 800-448-0490; 434-636-6000. Fax: 434-636-2223. ICA: VA0114.
TV Market Ranking: 63 (JARRATT). Franchise award date: November 1, 1989. Franchise expiration date: N.A. Began: July 1, 1990.
Channel capacity: 50 (not 2-way capable). Channels available but not in use: N.A.

Basic Service
Subscribers: 200.
Programming (received off-air): WRAL-TV (CBS) Raleigh; WRIC-TV (ABC) Petersburg; WTVR-TV (CBS) Richmond; WWBT (NBC) Richmond.
Programming (via satellite): ABC Family Channel; BET Networks; CNN; C-SPAN; Discovery Channel; ESPN; MTV; Nickelodeon; QVC; Spike TV; TBS Superstation; The Weather Channel; Turner Network TV; USA Network; WGN America.
Fee: $45.00 installation; $24.70 monthly.

Pay Service 1
Pay Units: 20.
Programming (via satellite): Cinemax.
Fee: $10.00 monthly.

Pay Service 2
Pay Units: 20.
Programming (via satellite): HBO.
Fee: $10.00 monthly.

Internet Service
Operational: No.

Telephone Service
None

Miles of Plant: 40.0 (coaxial); 24.0 (fiber optic).
Ownership: Cathy Ashworth (MSO).

JONESVILLE—CC & S Cable TV. Now served by NORTON, VA [VA0157]. ICA: VA0115.

KEEN MOUNTAIN—Time Warner Cable, 1430 2nd St, Richlands, VA 24641-2455. Phone: 276-964-1150. Fax: 276-963-9358. Web Site: http://www.timewarnercable.com. Also serves Mavisdale, Oakwood, Pilgrims Knob & Whitewood. ICA: VA0083.
TV Market Ranking: Below 100 (KEEN MOUNTAIN, Mavisdale, Oakwood, Pilgrims Knob, Whitewood). Franchise award date: N.A. Franchise expiration date: N.A. Began: N.A.
Channel capacity: N.A. Channels available but not in use: N.A.

Basic Service
Subscribers: 751.
Programming (received off-air): WAPK-CA (MNT) Kingsport; WCYB-TV (CW, NBC) Bristol; WJHL-TV (CBS) Johnson City; WKPT-TV (ABC) Kingsport; WLFG (IND) Grundy; WSBN-TV (PBS) Norton; WVVA (CW, NBC) Bluefield.
Programming (via satellite): QVC; TBS Superstation.
Fee: $16.88 monthly; $3.25 converter.

Expanded Basic Service 1
Subscribers: 711.
Programming (via satellite): A&E Networks; CNBC; CNN; Comcast SportsNet Mid-Atlantic; Country Music TV; Discovery Channel; Disney Channel; ESPN; Lifetime; MTV; Nickelodeon; Spike TV; The Weather Channel; Turner Network TV; USA Network; VH1.
Fee: $20.53 monthly.

Digital Basic Service
Subscribers: 691.
Programming (via satellite): BBC America; Bloomberg Television; Bravo; Country Music TV; Discovery Digital Networks; ESPN 2; ESPN Classic Sports; ESPNews; Fox Movie Channel; Fox Soccer; G4; Golf Channel; GSN; Halogen Network; HGTV; History Channel; Independent Film Channel; Music Choice; National Geographic Channel; Nick Jr.; NickToons TV; Outdoor Channel; Speed; Syfy; Trinity Broadcasting Network; Turner Classic Movies; TV Land; Versus; VH1 Classic; WE tv.
Fee: $5.35 monthly.

Digital Pay Service 1
Pay Units: N.A.
Programming (via satellite): Cinemax (multiplexed); Encore (multiplexed); HBO (multiplexed); Showtime (multiplexed); Starz (multiplexed); The Movie Channel (multiplexed).
Fee: $15.95 monthly (each).

Video-On-Demand: Planned

Pay-Per-View
Fresh (delivered digitally); Movies & Events (delivered digitally); Playboy TV (delivered digitally); NASCAR In Car (delivered digitally).

Internet Service
Operational: No.

Telephone Service
Digital: Planned

Miles of Plant: 64.0 (coaxial); None (fiber optic).
General Manager: C. K. Allen. Marketing Manager: Mark Cole. Chief Technician: Danny Nelson.
Ownership: Time Warner Cable (MSO).

KENBRIDGE—Shentel, 60 Long Ridge Rd, Ste 404, Stamford, CT 6902. Phones: 540-984-5224; 800-743-6835. Web Site: http://www.shentel.net. Also serves Lunenburg County (portions). ICA: VA0110.
TV Market Ranking: Outside TV Markets (KENBRIDGE, Lunenburg County (portions)). Franchise award date: October 15, 1991. Franchise expiration date: N.A. Began: December 1, 1980.
Channel capacity: N.A. Channels available but not in use: N.A.

Basic Service
Subscribers: 288.
Programming (received off-air): WCVE-TV (PBS) Richmond; WCVW (PBS) Richmond; WRIC-TV (ABC) Petersburg; WRLH-TV (FOX, MNT) Richmond; WTVR-TV (CBS) Richmond; WWBT (NBC) Richmond; allband FM.
Programming (via satellite): INSP; Lifetime; QVC; WGN America.
Fee: $49.95 installation; $20.95 monthly; $10.00 additional installation.

Expanded Basic Service 1
Subscribers: 265.
Programming (via satellite): A&E Networks; ABC Family Channel; AMC; Animal Planet; BET Networks; Cartoon Network; CNBC; CNN; Comedy Central; Country Music TV; Discovery Channel; Disney Channel; E! Entertainment Television; ESPN; ESPN 2; Headline News; HGTV; History Channel; MTV; Nickelodeon; Spike TV; Syfy; TBS Superstation; The Learning Channel; The Weather Channel; Travel Channel; truTV; Turner Network TV; TV Land; USA Network; VH1.
Fee: $19.00 monthly.

Pay Service 1
Pay Units: 55.
Programming (via satellite): HBO.
Fee: $12.95 monthly.
Pay Service 2
Pay Units: N.A.
Programming (via satellite): Showtime.
Fee: $12.95 monthly.
Video-On-Demand: No
Pay-Per-View
iN DEMAND (delivered digitally); Hot Choice (delivered digitally); Urban Xtra (delivered digitally); ESPN Now (delivered digitally); Sports PPV (delivered digitally); Playboy TV (delivered digitally); Fresh (delivered digitally); Shorteez (delivered digitally).
Internet Service
Operational: No.
Telephone Service
None
Miles of Plant: 10.0 (coaxial); None (fiber optic).
President: Christopher French. Vice President, Customer Service: David Ferguson. Marketing Manager: Chris Ranson.
Ownership: Shenandoah Telecommunications Inc. (MSO).

KEYSVILLE—Shentel, 60 Long Ridge Rd, Ste 404, Stamford, CT 6902. Phones: 540-984-5224; 800-743-6835. Web Site: http://www.shentel.net. Also serves Charlotte County (eastern portion), Charlotte Court House, Drakes Branch & Phenix. ICA: VA0143.
TV Market Ranking: 70 (Phenix); Outside TV Markets (Charlotte County (eastern portion), Charlotte Court House, Drakes Branch, KEYSVILLE). Franchise award date: March 1, 1982. Franchise expiration date: N.A. Began: October 1, 1985.
Channel capacity: N.A. Channels available but not in use: N.A.
Basic Service
Subscribers: 675.
Programming (received off-air): WCVE-TV (PBS) Richmond; WDBJ (CBS, MNT) Roanoke; WRLH-TV (FOX, MNT) Richmond; WSET-TV (ABC) Lynchburg; WSLS-TV (NBC) Roanoke; WWCW (CW, FOX) Lynchburg.
Programming (via satellite): C-SPAN; INSP; QVC; WGN America.
Fee: $24.95 installation; $18.09 monthly; $.75 converter.
Expanded Basic Service 1
Subscribers: 580.
Programming (via satellite): A&E Networks; ABC Family Channel; AMC; Animal Planet; BET Networks; Cartoon Network; CNBC; CNN; Country Music TV; Discovery Channel; E! Entertainment Television; ESPN; ESPN 2; Food Network; HGTV; History Channel; Lifetime; Nickelodeon; Spike TV; Syfy; TBS Superstation; The Learning Channel; The Weather Channel; Travel Channel; truTV; Turner Network TV; TV Land; USA Network; VH1.
Fee: $13.66 monthly.
Digital Basic Service
Subscribers: N.A.
Programming (via satellite): AmericanLife TV Network; BBC America; Bio; Bloomberg Television; Discovery Fit & Health; DMX Music; ESPN Classic Sports; Fox Movie Channel; Fuse; G4; GAS; Golf Channel; GSN; Halogen Network; History Channel International; Independent Film Channel; Lifetime Movie Network; MTV Networks Digital Suite; Nick Jr.; Outdoor Channel; Speed; Toon Disney; Trinity Broadcasting Network; Turner Classic Movies; Versus; WE tv.
Pay Service 1
Pay Units: 58.
Programming (via satellite): Cinemax.
Fee: $11.50 monthly.
Pay Service 2
Pay Units: 86.
Programming (via satellite): HBO.
Fee: $11.50 monthly.
Digital Pay Service 1
Pay Units: N.A.
Programming (via satellite): Cinemax (multiplexed); Encore (multiplexed); HBO (multiplexed); Showtime (multiplexed); Starz (multiplexed); The Movie Channel (multiplexed).
Video-On-Demand: No
Pay-Per-View
iN DEMAND (delivered digitally); Hot Choice (delivered digitally); Playboy TV (delivered digitally); Fresh (delivered digitally); Shorteez (delivered digitally).
Internet Service
Operational: No.
Telephone Service
None
Miles of Plant: 57.0 (coaxial); None (fiber optic).
President: Christopher French. Vice President, Customer Service: David Ferguson. Marketing Manager: Chris Ranson.
Ownership: Shenandoah Telecommunications Inc. (MSO).

KING GEORGE—MetroCast Communications, 11387 Ridge Rd, King George, VA 22485-4048. Phones: 540-775-0699; 540-775-5689. Fax: 540-775-5313. Web Site: http://www.metrocastcommunications.com. Also serves Caroline County (unincorporated areas), Dahlgren, Fort A.P. Hill & Port Royal. ICA: VA0058.
TV Market Ranking: 63 (Caroline County (unincorporated areas) (portions), Fort A.P. Hill); Below 100 (Dahlgren, Port Royal, Caroline County (unincorporated areas) (portions)); Outside TV Markets (KING GEORGE, Caroline County (unincorporated areas) (portions)). Franchise award date: March 6, 1986. Franchise expiration date: N.A. Began: December 8, 1987.
Channel capacity: 100 (operating 2-way). Channels available but not in use: N.A.
Basic Service
Subscribers: 2,297.
Programming (received off-air): WCVE-TV (PBS) Richmond; WDCA (MNT) Washington; WDCW (CW) Washington; WETA-TV (PBS) Washington; WFDC-DT (UNV) Arlington; WJLA-TV (ABC) Washington; WNVC (ETV) Fairfax; WNVT (ETV) Goldvein; WPXW-TV (ION) Manassas; WRC-TV (NBC) Washington; WTTG (FOX) Washington; WTVR-TV (CBS) Richmond; WUSA (CBS) Washington; WWBT (NBC) Richmond.
Programming (via satellite): C-SPAN; Eternal Word TV Network (multiplexed); QVC; TBS Superstation; Trinity Broadcasting Network.
Fee: $60.00 installation; $14.75 monthly.
Expanded Basic Service 1
Subscribers: 2,067.
Programming (via satellite): A&E Networks; ABC Family Channel; AMC; Animal Planet; BET Networks; Bloomberg Television; Cartoon Network; CNBC; CNN; Comcast SportsNet Mid-Atlantic; Comedy Central; Country Music TV; C-SPAN 2; Discovery Channel; Disney Channel; E! Entertainment Television; ESPN; ESPN 2; Food Network; Fox Movie Channel; Fox News Channel; FX; G4; Headline News; HGTV; History Channel; Lifetime; MSNBC; MTV; Nickelodeon; Outdoor Channel; Pentagon Channel; Speed; Spike TV; Syfy; The Learning Channel; The Weather Channel; Travel Channel; truTV; Turner Classic Movies; Turner Network TV; TV Land; USA Network; Versus; VH1; WE tv; WGN America.
Fee: $27.50 monthly.
Digital Basic Service
Subscribers: 338.
Programming (via satellite): BBC America; Discovery Digital Networks; DMX Music; GSN; Lifetime Movie Network; National Geographic Channel; Nick Jr.; VH1 Classic; VH1 Country.
Fee: $8.95 monthly.
Digital Expanded Basic Service
Subscribers: N.A.
Programming (via satellite): Bravo; Encore (multiplexed); ESPN Classic Sports; ESPNews; Fox Soccer; Golf Channel; Independent Film Channel; Starz (multiplexed); WE tv.
Fee: $8.95 monthly.
Digital Pay Service 1
Pay Units: 94.
Programming (via satellite): Cinemax (multiplexed); HBO (multiplexed); Showtime (multiplexed).
Fee: $12.95 monthly (Cinemax, HBO or Showtime).
Video-On-Demand: No
Pay-Per-View
iN DEMAND (delivered digitally).
Internet Service
Operational: Yes.
Fee: $29.95-$69.95 monthly.
Telephone Service
Digital: Operational
Fee: $44.95 monthly
Miles of Plant: 140.0 (coaxial); None (fiber optic). Additional miles planned: 20.0 (coaxial).
General Manager: Danny Jobe. Manager: Hans Welch. Programming Director: Linda Stuchell.
Ownership: Harron Communications LP (MSO).

KING WILLIAM (portions)—Comcast Cable, 11101 University Blvd, Manassas, VA 20110. Phone: 703-789-8100. Fax: 703-789-8280. Web Site: http://www.comcast.com. Also serves Aylett & Central Garage. ICA: VA0166.
TV Market Ranking: 63 (Aylett, Central Garage, KING WILLIAM (PORTIONS)). Franchise award date: January 1, 1988. Franchise expiration date: N.A. Began: January 1, 1988.
Channel capacity: 40 (not 2-way capable). Channels available but not in use: N.A.
Basic Service
Subscribers: 399.
Programming (received off-air): WCVE-TV (PBS) Richmond; WCVW (PBS) Richmond; WRIC-TV (ABC) Petersburg; WRLH-TV (FOX, MNT) Richmond; WTVR-TV (CBS) Richmond; WUPV (CW) Ashland; WWBT (NBC) Richmond.
Programming (via satellite): CNN; The Weather Channel.
Fee: $40.00 installation; $16.95 monthly.
Expanded Basic Service 1
Subscribers: N.A.
Programming (via satellite): A&E Networks; ABC Family Channel; AMC; Animal Planet; BET Networks; Cartoon Network; Comcast SportsNet Mid-Atlantic; Country Music TV; C-SPAN; Discovery Channel; Disney Channel; ESPN; ESPN 2; Headline News; Lifetime; Mid-Atlantic Sports Network; MTV; Nickelodeon; QVC; Spike TV; Syfy; TBS Superstation; The Learning Channel; truTV; Turner Classic Movies; Turner Network TV; USA Network; VH1.
Fee: $52.50 monthly.
Pay Service 1
Pay Units: 240.
Programming (via satellite): Flix; HBO; Showtime; The Movie Channel.
Fee: $4.95 monthly (Flix), $10.95 monthly (HBO, Showtime or TMC).
Pay-Per-View
iN DEMAND (delivered digitally); Hot Choice (delivered digitally); Playboy TV (delivered digitally); Fresh (delivered digitally); Shorteez (delivered digitally); Pleasure (delivered digitally); ESPN Now (delivered digitally); Sports PPV (delivered digitally); ESPN Extra (delivered digitally); NBA TV (delivered digitally).
Internet Service
Operational: Yes.
Telephone Service
Digital: Operational
Miles of Plant: 27.0 (coaxial); None (fiber optic).
Vice President & General Manager: Christine Whitaker. Technical Operations Director: Scott Shelly. Marketing Director: Shawn Houston.
Ownership: Comcast Cable Communications Inc. (MSO).

LACEY SPRING—Formerly served by Adelphia Communications. Now served by HARRISONBURG, VA [VA0016]. ICA: VA0144.

LAKE GASTON—CWA Cable, 662 Blackridge Rd, La Crosse, VA 23950-2928. Phones: 800-448-0490; 434-636-6000. Fax: 434-636-2223. Also serves Bracey, Brunswick County (portions) & Mecklenburg County (portions). ICA: VA0170.
TV Market Ranking: Outside TV Markets (Bracey, Brunswick County (portions), LAKE GASTON, Mecklenburg County (portions)). Franchise award date: N.A. Franchise expiration date: N.A. Began: July 30, 1993.
Channel capacity: 60 (not 2-way capable). Channels available but not in use: N.A.
Basic Service
Subscribers: 750.
Programming (received off-air): WLFL (CW) Raleigh; WRAL-TV (CBS) Raleigh; WRDC (MNT) Durham; WRIC-TV (ABC) Petersburg; WTVD (ABC) Durham; WUNP-TV (PBS) Roanoke Rapids.
Programming (via satellite): A&E Networks; ABC Family Channel; CNN; C-SPAN; C-SPAN 2; Discovery Channel; ESPN; MTV; Nickelodeon; QVC; Spike TV; TBS Superstation; The Weather Channel; Travel Channel; Turner Network TV; USA Network; WGN America.
Fee: $45.00 installation; $32.95 monthly.
Pay Service 1
Pay Units: 78.
Programming (via satellite): HBO.
Fee: $10.00 monthly.
Internet Service
Operational: No.
Telephone Service
None
Miles of Plant: 30.0 (coaxial); None (fiber optic).
Ownership: Cathy Ashworth (MSO).

LANCASTER COUNTY—MetroCast Communications, 126 Urbanna Rd, PO Box 1147, Saluda, VA 23149-1147. Phone: 800-633-8578. Fax: 804-758-1215. Web Site: http://www.metrocastcommunications.com. Also serves Irvington (town), Kilmarnock (town), Northumberland County (portions) & White Stone (town). ICA: VA0146.

TV Market Ranking: Outside TV Markets (Irvington (town), Kilmarnock (town), LANCASTER COUNTY, Northumberland County (portions), White Stone (town)). Franchise award date: January 1, 1982. Franchise expiration date: October 1, 2011. Began: June 1, 1982.

Channel capacity: 116 (operating 2-way). Channels available but not in use: N.A.

Basic Service

Subscribers: 1,785.

Programming (received off-air): WAVY-TV (NBC) Portsmouth; WCVE-TV (PBS) Richmond; WHRO-TV (PBS) Hampton-Norfolk; WRIC-TV (ABC) Petersburg; WRLH-TV (FOX, MNT) Richmond; WTKR (CBS) Norfolk; WTVR-TV (CBS) Richmond; WUPV (CW) Ashland; WVEC (ABC) Hampton; WWBT (NBC) Richmond.

Programming (via satellite): A&E Networks; ABC Family Channel; AMC; Animal Planet; BET Networks; Bravo; Cartoon Network; CNBC; CNN; Comcast SportsNet Mid-Atlantic; Comedy Central; Country Music TV; C-SPAN; C-SPAN 2; Discovery Channel; Discovery Health Channel; Disney Channel; ESPN; ESPN 2; ESPN Classic Sports; Food Network; Fox News Channel; FX; Golf Channel; Hallmark Channel; Headline News; HGTV; History Channel; INSP; Lifetime; Lifetime Movie Network; MSNBC; MTV; National Geographic Channel; Nickelodeon; Outdoor Channel; Oxygen; QVC; Spike TV; Syfy; TBS Superstation; The Learning Channel; The Weather Channel; Travel Channel; truTV; Turner Network TV; TV Guide Network; TV Land; USA Network; VH1.

Fee: $60.00 installation; $45.95 monthly; $28.00 additional installation.

Digital Basic Service

Subscribers: 100.

Programming (via satellite): AmericanLife TV Network; BBC America; Bio; Bloomberg Television; Country Music TV; Discovery Home Channel; Discovery Kids Channel; DMX Music; ESPN 2 HD; ESPN HD; ESPNews; Fox College Sports Atlantic; Fox College Sports Central; Fox College Sports Pacific; Fox Movie Channel; Fox Soccer; Fuse; G4; Great American Country; GSN; Halogen Network; HD Theater; HDNet; HDNet Movies; History Channel International; ID Investigation Discovery; Independent Film Channel; Military Channel; MTV2; Nick Jr.; NickToons TV; Science; ShopNBC; TeenNick; The Word Network; Toon Disney; Trinity Broadcasting Network; Versus; VH1 Classic; VH1 Country; WE tv.

Fee: $16.90 monthly.

Digital Pay Service 1

Pay Units: N.A.

Programming (via satellite): Cinemax (multiplexed); Encore (multiplexed); Flix; HBO (multiplexed); Showtime (multiplexed); Starz (multiplexed); The Movie Channel (multiplexed).

Fee: $12.95 monthly (Cinemax), $16.50 monthly (Starz/Encore or Showtime/TMC), $19.00 monthly (HBO).

Video-On-Demand: No

Pay-Per-View

iN DEMAND (delivered digitally); Playboy TV (delivered digitally).

Internet Service

Operational: Yes, DSL.

Subscribers: 175.

Broadband Service: In-house.

Fee: $99.95 installation; $29.95-$58.95 monthly; $2.95 modem lease; $99.00 modem purchase.

Telephone Service

Digital: Operational

Fee: $29.95 monthly

Miles of Plant: 150.0 (coaxial); 65.0 (fiber optic).

General Manager: Danny L. Jobe.

Ownership: Harron Communications LP (MSO).

LANGLEY AFB—Cox Communications. Now served by HAMPTON ROADS (formerly Virginia Beach), VA [VA0002]. ICA: VA0008.

LAWRENCEVILLE—Shentel, 60 Long Ridge Rd, Ste 404, Stamford, CT 6902. Phones: 540-984-5224; 800-743-6835. Web Site: http://www.shentel.net. Also serves Alberta & Brunswick County. ICA: VA0089.

TV Market Ranking: 63 (Brunswick County (portions)); Outside TV Markets (Alberta, LAWRENCEVILLE, Brunswick County (portions)). Franchise award date: June 14, 1978. Franchise expiration date: December 14, 2008. Began: June 1, 1980.

Channel capacity: N.A. Channels available but not in use: N.A.

Basic Service

Subscribers: 707.

Programming (received off-air): WCVE-TV (PBS) Richmond; WCVW (PBS) Richmond; WNVN-LP Roanoke Rapids; WRAL-TV (CBS) Raleigh; WRIC-TV (ABC) Petersburg; WRLH-TV (FOX, MNT) Richmond; WTVR-TV (CBS) Richmond; WWBT (NBC) Richmond; allband FM.

Programming (via satellite): C-SPAN; INSP; QVC.

Fee: $24.95 installation; $19.40 monthly; $.75 converter.

Expanded Basic Service 1

Subscribers: 628.

Programming (via satellite): A&E Networks; ABC Family Channel; AMC; Animal Planet; BET Networks; Bravo; Cartoon Network; CNBC; CNN; Comedy Central; Country Music TV; Discovery Channel; Disney Channel; E! Entertainment Television; ESPN; ESPN 2; Food Network; Fox Movie Channel; FX; G4; Golf Channel; Headline News; HGTV; History Channel; Lifetime; MSNBC; MTV; Nickelodeon; Oxygen; Speed; Spike TV; Syfy; TBS Superstation; The Learning Channel; The Weather Channel; Travel Channel; truTV; Turner Classic Movies; Turner Network TV; TV Land; USA Network; VH1; WE tv.

Fee: $12.85 monthly.

Digital Basic Service

Subscribers: N.A.

Programming (via satellite): BBC America; Bio; Bloomberg Television; Discovery Fit & Health; DIY Network; ESPN Classic Sports; ESPNews; Fox College Sports Atlantic; Fox College Sports Central; Fox College Sports Pacific; Fox Movie Channel; Fox Soccer; Fuse; GAS; GSN; History Channel International; Independent Film Channel; MTV Networks Digital Suite; Music Choice; National Geographic Channel; Nick Jr.; Nick Too; NickToons TV; SoapNet; Sundance Channel; Toon Disney; TV Guide Interactive Inc.

Digital Pay Service 1

Pay Units: 217.

Programming (via satellite): HBO (multiplexed).

Fee: $14.95 installation; $11.95 monthly.

Digital Pay Service 2

Pay Units: N.A.

Programming (via satellite): Cinemax (multiplexed); Encore (multiplexed); Flix; Showtime (multiplexed); Starz (multiplexed); The Movie Channel (multiplexed).

Video-On-Demand: No

Pay-Per-View

iN DEMAND (delivered digitally); Playboy TV (delivered digitally); Fresh (delivered digitally); Shorteez (delivered digitally).

Internet Service

Operational: No.

Telephone Service

None

Miles of Plant: 25.0 (coaxial); None (fiber optic). Additional miles planned: 3.0 (coaxial).

President: Christopher French. Vice President, Customer Service: David Ferguson. Marketing Manager: Chris Ranson.

Ownership: Shenandoah Telecommunications Inc. (MSO).

LEBANON—Shentel, 60 Long Ridge Rd, Ste 404, Stamford, CT 6902. Phones: 540-984-5224; 800-743-6835. Web Site: http://www.shentel.net. Also serves Castlewood, Dante, Honaker, Russell County, St. Paul, Swords Creek & Wise. ICA: VA0035.

TV Market Ranking: Below 100 (Castlewood, Dante, Honaker, LEBANON, Russell County, St. Paul, Swords Creek, Wise). Franchise award date: N.A. Franchise expiration date: N.A. Began: October 1, 1964.

Channel capacity: N.A. Channels available but not in use: N.A.

Basic Service

Subscribers: 5,500.

Programming (received off-air): WAPK-CA (MNT) Kingsport; WCYB-TV (CW, NBC) Bristol; WEMT (FOX) Greeneville; WETP-TV (PBS) Sneedville; WJHL-TV (CBS) Johnson City; WKPT-TV (ABC) Kingsport; WLFG (IND) Grundy; WSBN-TV (PBS) Norton; allband FM.

Programming (via satellite): C-SPAN; Paxson Communications Corp.; QVC; The Weather Channel; Trinity Broadcasting Network; WGN America.

Fee: $53.64 installation; $9.25 monthly.

Expanded Basic Service 1

Subscribers: N.A.

Programming (via satellite): A&E Networks; ABC Family Channel; Animal Planet; Cartoon Network; CNN; Comcast SportsNet Mid-Atlantic; Comedy Central; Country Music TV; Discovery Channel; Disney Channel; E! Entertainment Television; ESPN; ESPN 2; Fox News Channel; FX; Headline News; HGTV; History Channel; Lifetime; MTV; Nickelodeon; Oxygen; Speed; Spike TV; Syfy; TBS Superstation; The Learning Channel; Travel Channel; Turner Classic Movies; Turner Network TV; TV Land; USA Network; VH1; WE tv.

Fee: $13.70 monthly.

Digital Basic Service

Subscribers: N.A.

Programming (via satellite): BBC America; Bio; Bloomberg Television; Discovery Digital Networks; DIY Network; GAS; GSN; History Channel International; Independent Film Channel; Lifetime Movie Network; MTV Networks Digital Suite; Music Choice; Nick Jr.; Nick Too; SoapNet; Style Network; Sundance Channel; Toon Disney; TV Guide Interactive Inc.

Digital Pay Service 1

Pay Units: N.A.

Programming (via satellite): Cinemax (multiplexed); Flix; HBO (multiplexed); Showtime (multiplexed); The Movie Channel (multiplexed).

Video-On-Demand: No

Pay-Per-View

Hot Choice (delivered digitally); iN DEMAND (delivered digitally).

Internet Service

Operational: Yes.

Broadband Service: JetBroadband.

Fee: $49.95 installation; $29.95 monthly.

Telephone Service

None

Miles of Plant: 175.0 (coaxial); None (fiber optic). Additional miles planned: 2.0 (coaxial).

President: Christopher French. Vice President, Customer Service: David Ferguson. Marketing Manager: Chris Ranson.

Ownership: Shenandoah Telecommunications Inc. (MSO).

LEBANON (portions)—Almega Cable, 4024 W Airport Freeway, Ste 553, Bedford, TX 76021. Phones: 877-725-6342; 817-685-9588. Fax: 817-685-6488. Web Site: http://almegacable.com. Also serves Carbo, Castlewood, Cleveland, Clinchfield, Hansonville & Spring City. ICA: VA0185. **Note:** This system is an overbuild.

TV Market Ranking: Below 100 (Carbo, Castlewood, Cleveland, Clinchfield, Hansonville, LEBANON (PORTIONS), Spring City). Franchise award date: N.A. Franchise expiration date: N.A. Began: N.A.

Channel capacity: 42 (2-way capable). Channels available but not in use: N.A.

Basic Service

Subscribers: 990.

Programming (received off-air): WCYB-TV (CW, NBC) Bristol; WEMT (FOX) Greeneville; WJHL-TV (CBS) Johnson City; WKPT-TV (ABC) Kingsport; WLFG (IND) Grundy; WSBN-TV (PBS) Norton.

Programming (via satellite): ABC Family Channel; AMC; CNN; Comcast SportsNet Mid-Atlantic; C-SPAN; Discovery Channel; Disney Channel; E! Entertainment Television; ESPN; ESPN 2; Great American Country; Headline News; History Channel; Lifetime; MTV; Nickelodeon; QVC; Spike TV; TBS Superstation; The Learning Channel; The Weather Channel; Travel Channel; Trinity Broadcasting Network; Turner Network TV; USA Network; Versus; VH1; WGN America.

Fee: $19.95 monthly.

Pay Service 1

Pay Units: 46.

Programming (via satellite): The Movie Channel.

Fee: $12.95 monthly.

Pay Service 2
Pay Units: 154.
Programming (via satellite): HBO.
Fee: $12.95 monthly.
Pay Service 3
Pay Units: 101.
Programming (via satellite): Showtime.
Fee: $12.95 monthly.
Video-On-Demand: No
Internet Service
Operational: Yes.
Fee: $29.95 monthly.
Telephone Service
None
Miles of Plant: 99.0 (coaxial); None (fiber optic).
Vice President, Operations: James Bradley. Vice President, Sales: Mike DeRosa. Manager: Thomas Kurien. Regional Service Manager: Rich Beesmer.
Ownership: Almega Cable (MSO).

LEXINGTON—Comcast Cable, 2154 Sycamore Ave, Buena Vista, VA 24416-3126. Phones: 434-951-3700 (Charlottesville office); 540-261-4558. Fax: 540-261-7616. Web Site: http://www.comcast.com. Also serves Buena Vista, Glasgow & Rockbridge County. ICA: VA0147.
TV Market Ranking: 70 (Buena Vista, Glasgow, LEXINGTON, Rockbridge County (portions)); Outside TV Markets (Rockbridge County (portions)). Franchise award date: N.A. Franchise expiration date: N.A. Began: July 1, 1975.
Channel capacity: N.A. Channels available but not in use: N.A.
Basic Service
Subscribers: 6,860.
Programming (received off-air): WBRA-TV (PBS) Roanoke; WDBJ (CBS, MNT) Roanoke; WPXR-TV (ION) Roanoke; WSET-TV (ABC) Lynchburg; WSLS-TV (NBC) Roanoke; WVPT (PBS) Staunton; WWCW (CW, FOX) Lynchburg.
Programming (via satellite): CNBC; QVC; TV Guide Network.
Fee: $32.00 installation; $16.90 monthly; $25.00 additional installation.
Expanded Basic Service 1
Subscribers: 6,354.
Programming (via satellite): A&E Networks; ABC Family Channel; AMC; Animal Planet; BET Networks; Bravo; CNN; Comcast SportsNet Mid-Atlantic; Comedy Central; Concert TV; Country Music TV; C-SPAN; C-SPAN 2; CW+; Discovery Channel; Disney Channel; E! Entertainment Television; ESPN; ESPN 2; Food Network; Fox News Channel; FX; Hallmark Channel; Headline News; HGTV; History Channel; ION Television; Lifetime; MSNBC; MTV; Nickelodeon; Oxygen; Product Information Network; Spike TV; Syfy; TBS Superstation; The Learning Channel; The Weather Channel; Toon Disney; Travel Channel; truTV; Turner Classic Movies; Turner Network TV; TV Land; USA Network; VH1.
Fee: $39.95 monthly.
Digital Basic Service
Subscribers: 1,663.
Programming (via satellite): AmericanLife TV Network; ART America; BBC America; Bio; Bloomberg Television; Canales N; CCTV-4; Chinese Television Network; Discovery Digital Networks; DIY Network; ESPN Classic Sports; ESPNews; Filipino Channel; Fox Sports World; G4; Golf Channel; GSN; Halogen Network; History Channel International; MuchMusic Network; Music Choice; National Geographic Channel; Outdoor Channel; RAI International; SoapNet; Speed; Style Network; Toon Disney; Trinity Broadcasting Network; TV Asia; TV Japan; TV5 USA; Versus; WE tv.
Fee: $9.95 monthly.
Pay Service 1
Pay Units: 381.
Programming (via satellite): Cinemax; HBO; Showtime.
Fee: $25.00 installation; $11.00 monthly (each).
Digital Pay Service 1
Pay Units: 1,879.
Programming (via satellite): Cinemax (multiplexed); Encore (multiplexed); HBO (multiplexed); Showtime (multiplexed); Starz (multiplexed).
Fee: $16.50 monthly (each).
Video-On-Demand: Yes
Pay-Per-View
iN DEMAND (delivered digitally).
Internet Service
Operational: Yes. Began: August 1, 2001.
Broadband Service: Comcast High Speed Internet.
Telephone Service
Digital: Operational
Miles of Plant: 139.0 (coaxial); 15.0 (fiber optic).
Vice President & General Manager: Troy Fitzhugh. Technical Operations Director: Tom Jacobs. Chief Technician: Joe Clements. Plant Manager: John Van Lew. Marketing Director: Steve Miles. Office Manager: Trudy McNew.
Ownership: Comcast Cable Communications Inc. (MSO).

LOUDOUN COUNTY—Comcast Cable, 21730 Red Rum Dr, Ste 192, Ashburn, VA 20147. Phones: 571-223-1340; 703-789-8100 (Manassas office). Fax: 571-223-2296. Web Site: http://www.comcast.com. Also serves Hamilton, Leesburg, Lovettsville, Middleburg, Purcellville, Round Hill & Sterling. ICA: VA0021.
TV Market Ranking: 9 (Leesburg, LOUDOUN COUNTY (portions), Sterling); Below 100 (Hamilton, Lovettsville, Middleburg, Purcellville, Round Hill, LOUDOUN COUNTY (portions)). Franchise award date: May 16, 1983. Franchise expiration date: N.A. Began: March 1, 1984.
Channel capacity: N.A. Channels available but not in use: N.A.
Basic Service
Subscribers: 32,100.
Programming (received off-air): WDCA (MNT) Washington; WDCW (CW) Washington; WETA-TV (PBS) Washington; WFDC-DT (UNV) Arlington; WHUT-TV (PBS) Washington; WJLA-TV (ABC) Washington; WMDO-CA (TEL) Washington; WPXW-TV (ION) Manassas; WRC-TV (NBC) Washington; WTTG (FOX) Washington; WUSA (CBS) Washington; WWPB (PBS) Hagerstown; WZDC-CA (TMO) Washington; 25 FMs.
Programming (via satellite): C-SPAN; Eternal Word TV Network; NewsChannel 8; QVC; The Comcast Network; WGN America.
Fee: $29.95 installation; $33.26 monthly.
Expanded Basic Service 1
Subscribers: N.A.
Programming (via satellite): A&E Networks; ABC Family Channel; Animal Planet; BET Networks; Bravo; Cartoon Network; CNBC; CNN; Comcast SportsNet Mid-Atlantic; Comedy Central; Discovery Channel; Disney Channel; E! Entertainment Television; ESPN; ESPN 2; Food Network; Fox News Channel; FX; Golf Channel; Headline News; HGTV; History Channel; Lifetime; Mid-Atlantic Sports Network; MSNBC; MTV; Nickelodeon; Spike TV; Syfy; TBS Superstation; The Learning Channel; The Weather Channel; Travel Channel; Turner Network TV; TV Land; USA Network; Versus; VH1.
Digital Basic Service
Subscribers: 17,500.
Programming (via satellite): A&E HD; AMC; Animal Planet HD; BBC America; Bio; Bloomberg Television; Cartoon Network Tambien en Espanol; CBS Sports Network; Cine Latino; Cine Mexicano; CMT Pure Country; CNN en Espanol; CNN HD; Cooking Channel; Country Music TV; C-SPAN 2; C-SPAN 3; Current; Discovery Channel HD; Discovery en Espanol; Discovery Fit & Health; Discovery Health Channel; Discovery Kids Channel; DIY Network; DMX Music; Encore (multiplexed); ESPN 2 HD; ESPN Deportes; ESPN HD; ESPNews; Flix; Food Network HD; Fox Business Channel; Fox College Sports Atlantic; Fox College Sports Central; Fox College Sports Pacific; Fox Deportes; Fox Movie Channel; Fox Reality Channel; Fox Soccer; Fuel TV; Fuse; G4; GMC; GolTV; Great American Country; GSN; Hallmark Channel; Halogen Network; HD Theater; HGTV HD; History Channel; History Channel en Espanol; History Channel HD; History Channel International; ID Investigation Discovery; Independent Film Channel; INSP; Jewelry Television; Lifetime Movie Network; LOGO; MHz Networks; Military Channel; MoviePlex; MTV2; mun2 television; National Geographic Channel; National Geographic Channel HD Network; NBA TV; NFL Network; NHL Network; Nick Jr.; Nick Too; NickToons TV; Outdoor Channel; Oxygen; Palladia; PBS Kids Sprout; Planet Green; Science; ShopNBC; SoapNet; Speed; Style Network; Sundance Channel; Syfy HD; TeenNick; The Word Network; TLC HD; Toon Disney; Tr3s; Trinity Broadcasting Network; truTV; Turner Classic Movies; Turner Network TV HD; TV Guide Interactive Inc.; TV One; TVG Network; Universal HD; USA Network HD; VeneMovies; VH1 Classic; VH1 Soul; WE tv.
Digital Pay Service 1
Pay Units: N.A.
Programming (via satellite): Cinemax (multiplexed); Cinemax HD; Filipino Channel; HBO (multiplexed); HBO HD; Showtime (multiplexed); Showtime HD; Starz HDTV; The Movie Channel (multiplexed); TV Asia; Zee TV USA; Zhong Tian Channel.
Video-On-Demand: Yes
Pay-Per-View
iN DEMAND (delivered digitally); Playboy TV (delivered digitally); Spice: Xcess (delivered digitally).
Internet Service
Operational: Yes. Began: July 1, 1997.
Subscribers: 700.
Broadband Service: Comcast High Speed Internet.
Fee: $42.95 monthly; $7.00 modem lease.
Telephone Service
Digital: Operational
Miles of Plant: 565.0 (coaxial); 95.0 (fiber optic). Additional miles planned: 30.0 (coaxial).
Vice President & General Manager: Christine Whitaker. Technical Operations Director: Scott Shelly. Technical Operations Manager: Ray Ness. Plant Manager: Michael Bova. Corporate Public Affairs: Joshua Kodeck. Marketing Director: Lynn Herman. Regional Public Relations Manager: Jay Lennon. Office Manager: Terese Martin.
Ownership: Comcast Cable Communications Inc. (MSO).

LOUISA—Comcast Cable. Now served by RICHMOND, VA [VA0004]. ICA: VA0090.

LOVINGSTON/SHIPMAN—Nelson Cable, 400 Front St, PO Box 395, Lovingston, VA 22949-0395. Phones: 800-376-8165; 434-263-4805. Fax: 434-263-4821. E-mail: joeleemc@aol.com. Web Site: http://www.nelsoncable.com. Also serves Shipman. ICA: VA0192.
TV Market Ranking: 70 (LOVINGSTON, SHIPMAN).
Channel capacity: N.A. Channels available but not in use: N.A.
Basic Service
Subscribers: N.A.
Programming (received off-air): WCVE-TV (PBS) Richmond; WDBJ (CBS, MNT) Roanoke; WDRL-TV (IND) Danville; WRIC-TV (ABC) Petersburg; WRLH-TV (FOX, MNT) Richmond; WSET-TV (ABC) Lynchburg; WSLS-TV (NBC) Roanoke; WTVR-TV (CBS) Richmond; WVIR-TV (CW, NBC) Charlottesville.
Programming (via satellite): A&E Networks; ABC Family Channel; AMC; BET Networks; Cartoon Network; CNN; Country Music TV; Discovery Channel; Disney Channel; ESPN; ESPN 2; Nickelodeon; Spike TV; The Weather Channel; Trinity Broadcasting Network; Turner Network TV; WPCH-TV (IND) Atlanta.
Fee: $26.00 monthly.
Pay Service 1
Pay Units: N.A.
Programming (via satellite): Cinemax; HBO.
Fee: $7.00 monthly (Cinemax), $7.50 monthly (HBO).
Video-On-Demand: No
Internet Service
Operational: No.
Telephone Service
None
President: Joe Lee McClellan. Chief Technician: Terry Engelhardt.
Ownership: Nelson County Cablevision Corporation (MSO).

LURAY—Comcast Cable, 400 Westfield Rd, Charlottesville, VA 22901. Phone: 434-951-3700. Fax: 434-951-3705. Web Site: http://www.comcast.com. Also serves Mount Sidney, Page City, Stanley & Weyers Cave. ICA: VA0042.
TV Market Ranking: Below 100 (LURAY, Mount Sidney, Page City, Stanley, Weyers Cave). Franchise award date: N.A. Franchise expiration date: N.A. Began: October 15, 1965.
Channel capacity: N.A. Channels available but not in use: N.A.
Basic Service
Subscribers: 6,500.
Programming (received off-air): WAZT-CA (IND) Woodstock; WDCA (MNT) Washington; WDCW (CW) Washington; WETA-TV (PBS) Washington; WFDC-DT (UNV) Arlington; WHSV-TV (ABC, MNT) Harrisonburg; WJLA-TV (ABC) Washington; WJZ-TV (CBS) Baltimore; WRC-TV (NBC) Washington; WTTG (FOX) Washington; WTVR-TV (CBS) Richmond; WUSA (CBS) Washington; WVIR-TV (CW, NBC) Charlottesville; WVPT (PBS) Staunton; WWPX-TV (ION) Martinsburg.
Programming (via satellite): QVC; TV Guide Network.
Fee: $35.00 installation; $11.95 monthly; $2.00 converter.

Expanded Basic Service 1
Subscribers: 5,735.
Programming (via satellite): A&E Networks; ABC Family Channel; AMC; Animal Planet; BET Networks; Bravo; Cartoon Network; CNBC; CNN; Comcast SportsNet Mid-Atlantic; Comedy Central; Country Music TV; C-SPAN; C-SPAN 2; Discovery Channel; Disney Channel; E! Entertainment Television; ESPN; ESPN 2; Eternal Word TV Network; Food Network; Fox News Channel; FX; Hallmark Channel; Headline News; HGTV; History Channel; Lifetime; MSNBC; MTV; Nickelodeon; Oxygen; Spike TV; Syfy; TBS Superstation; The Learning Channel; The Weather Channel; Travel Channel; truTV; Turner Network TV; TV Land; USA Network; VH1.

Digital Basic Service
Subscribers: N.A.
Programming (via satellite): AmericanLife TV Network; BBC America; Bio; Black Family Channel; Bloomberg Television; Canales N; CBS Sports Network; CMT Pure Country; Current; DIY Network; ESPN 2 HD; ESPN Classic Sports; ESPN HD; ESPNews; Flix; Fox College Sports Atlantic; Fox College Sports Central; Fox College Sports Pacific; Fox Movie Channel; Fox Reality Channel; Fuel TV; Fuse; G4; GAS; Golf Channel; Great American Country; GSN; Halogen Network; HD Theater; History Channel International; Independent Film Channel; INHD; Lifetime Movie Network; LOGO; MTV Networks Digital Suite; Music Choice; National Geographic Channel; NFL Network; Nick Too; NickToons TV; Outdoor Channel; PBS Kids Sprout; SoapNet; Speed; Style Network; Sundance Channel; Tennis Channel; The Word Network; Toon Disney; Trinity Broadcasting Network; Turner Classic Movies; Turner Network TV HD; TVG Network; Versus; WE tv.

Digital Pay Service 1
Pay Units: N.A.
Programming (via satellite): Arabic Channel; CCTV-4; Cinemax (multiplexed); Cinemax HD; Encore (multiplexed); Filipino Channel; HBO (multiplexed); HBO HD; RAI International; Showtime (multiplexed); Showtime HD; Starz (multiplexed); Starz HDTV; The Movie Channel (multiplexed); TV Asia; TV Japan; TV5, La Television International; Zhong Tian Channel.

Video-On-Demand: No

Pay-Per-View
Urban American Television Network (delivered digitally); Hot Choice (delivered digitally); Shorteez (delivered digitally); Fresh (delivered digitally); Playboy TV (delivered digitally).

Internet Service
Operational: Yes.
Broadband Service: Comcast High Speed Internet.
Fee: $42.95 monthly.

Telephone Service
None

Miles of plant included in Harrisonburg

Vice President & General Manager: Troy Fitzhugh. Technical Operations Director: Tom Jacobs. Marketing Director: Steve Miles.

Ownership: Comcast Cable Communications Inc. (MSO).

LYNCHBURG—Comcast Cable, 400 Westfield Rd, Charlottesville, VA 22901. Phone: 434-951-3700. Fax: 434-951-3705. Web Site: http://www.comcast.com. Also serves Bedford County (portions) & Campbell County. ICA: VA0013.

TV Market Ranking: 70 (Bedford County (portions), Campbell County, LYNCHBURG). Franchise award date: January 1, 1972. Franchise expiration date: N.A. Began: June 1, 1977.

Channel capacity: N.A. Channels available but not in use: N.A.

Basic Service
Subscribers: 21,631.
Programming (received off-air): WBRA-TV (PBS) Roanoke; WDBJ (CBS, MNT) Roanoke; WDRL-TV (IND) Danville; WFXR (CW, FOX) Roanoke; WPXR-TV (ION) Roanoke; WSET-TV (ABC) Lynchburg; WSLS-TV (NBC) Roanoke; WTLU-CA Lynchburg; WVPT (PBS) Staunton; WWCW (CW, FOX) Lynchburg.
Programming (via satellite): C-SPAN 2; Hallmark Channel; Product Information Network; QVC; ShopNBC; TV Guide Network; WGN America.
Fee: $39.76 installation; $29.82 monthly.

Expanded Basic Service 1
Subscribers: N.A.
Programming (via satellite): A&E Networks; ABC Family Channel; AMC; Animal Planet; BET Networks; Bravo; Cartoon Network; CNBC; CNN; Comcast SportsNet Mid-Atlantic; Comedy Central; Country Music TV; C-SPAN; Discovery Channel; Disney Channel; E! Entertainment Television; ESPN; ESPN 2; Food Network; Fox News Channel; FX; Headline News; HGTV; History Channel; INSP; Lifetime; MSNBC; MTV; Nickelodeon; Spike TV; Syfy; TBS Superstation; The Learning Channel; The Weather Channel; Travel Channel; truTV; Turner Classic Movies; Turner Network TV; TV Land; USA Network; VH1.

Digital Basic Service
Subscribers: N.A.
Programming (via satellite): AmericanLife TV Network; BBC America; Black Family Channel; Bloomberg Television; Canales N; CMT Pure Country; Discovery Digital Networks; DIY Network; ESPN Classic Sports; ESPN U; ESPNews; Flix; Fox Movie Channel; Fox Soccer; Fuse; G4; GAS; Great American Country; GSN; Halogen Network; Lifetime Movie Network; LOGO; MTV Networks Digital Suite; Music Choice; National Geographic Channel; Nick Jr.; Nick Too; NickToons TV; SoapNet; Speed; Style Network; The Word Network; Toon Disney; Trinity Broadcasting Network; WE tv.

Digital Expanded Basic Service
Subscribers: N.A.
Programming (via satellite): Bio; CBS Sports Network; Fox College Sports Atlantic; Fox College Sports Central; Fox College Sports Pacific; Fuel TV; Golf Channel; History Channel International; Independent Film Channel; NFL Network; Outdoor Channel; Sundance Channel; Tennis Channel; Versus.

Digital Pay Service 1
Pay Units: N.A.
Programming (via satellite): ART America; CCTV-4; Cinemax (multiplexed); Encore (multiplexed); Filipino Channel; Flix; HBO (multiplexed); RAI International; Showtime (multiplexed); Starz (multiplexed); The Movie Channel (multiplexed); TV Asia; TV Japan; TV5, La Television International; Zhong Tian Channel.

Video-On-Demand: No

Pay-Per-View
Movies (delivered digitally); Special events (delivered digitally); Playboy TV (delivered digitally); Fresh (delivered digitally); ESPN (delivered digitally); NHL Center Ice (delivered digitally); MLB Extra Innings (delivered digitally).

Internet Service
Operational: Yes.
Broadband Service: Comcast High Speed Internet.
Fee: $42.95 monthly; $7.00 modem lease.

Telephone Service
Digital: Operational

Miles of Plant: 368.0 (coaxial); 355.0 (fiber optic).

Vice President & General Manager: Troy Fitzhugh. Technical Operations Director: Tom Jacobs. Technical Operations Manager: Mike Buckner. Marketing Director: Steve Miles.

Ownership: Comcast Cable Communications Inc. (MSO).

MADISON—Comcast Cable, 15367 Brandy Rd, Culpeper, VA 22701-2547. Phones: 434-951-3700 (Charlottesville office); 540-825-5070. Fax: 540-829-6678. Web Site: http://www.comcast.com. Also serves Madison County. ICA: VA0106.

TV Market Ranking: Below 100 (MADISON, Madison County). Franchise award date: January 1, 1989. Franchise expiration date: January 1, 2009. Began: September 1, 1989.

Channel capacity: 62 (not 2-way capable). Channels available but not in use: N.A.

Basic Service
Subscribers: 1,307.
Programming (received off-air): WDCA (MNT) Washington; WETA-TV (PBS) Washington; WHSV-TV (ABC, MNT) Harrisonburg; WRIC-TV (ABC) Petersburg; WRLH-TV (FOX, MNT) Richmond; WTTG (FOX) Washington; WTVR-TV (CBS) Richmond; WUSA (CBS) Washington; WVIR-TV (CW, NBC) Charlottesville; WVPT (PBS) Staunton; WWBT (NBC) Richmond.
Programming (via satellite): A&E Networks; C-SPAN; QVC; TBS Superstation; The Weather Channel; Trinity Broadcasting Network; TV Guide Network.
Fee: $49.95 installation; $15.22 monthly.

Expanded Basic Service 1
Subscribers: 1,200.
Programming (via satellite): ABC Family Channel; AMC; BET Networks; Cartoon Network; CNBC; CNN; Comcast SportsNet Mid-Atlantic; Discovery Channel; Disney Channel; ESPN; ESPN 2; FX; Headline News; History Channel; Lifetime; Mid-Atlantic Sports Network; MTV; Nickelodeon; Spike TV; Syfy; The Weather Channel; Turner Network TV; TV Land; USA Network; VH1.
Fee: $12.95 monthly.

Pay Service 1
Pay Units: N.A.
Programming (via satellite): HBO; Showtime.
Fee: $11.99 monthly (each).

Video-On-Demand: No

Pay-Per-View
Addressable homes: 49.
TVN Digital Cable Television (delivered digitally).

Internet Service
Operational: No.

Telephone Service
Digital: Operational

Miles of Plant: 120.0 (coaxial); 50.0 (fiber optic).

Vice President & General Manager: Troy Fitzhugh. Technical Operations Manager: Richard Burke. Chief Technician: Delmer Seal. Marketing Coordinator: Cassie Cool. Office Manager: Melissa Marks.

Ownership: Comcast Cable Communications Inc. (MSO).

MARION—Comcast Cable, 112 W Washington St, Galax, VA 24333. Phones: 423-282-1370 (Gray, TN office); 276-236-0879. Fax: 276-236-4714. Web Site: http://www.comcast.com. Also serves Atkins & Smyth County. ICA: VA0149.

TV Market Ranking: Below 100 (Atkins, MARION, Smyth County). Franchise award date: N.A. Franchise expiration date: N.A. Began: October 19, 1983.

Channel capacity: N.A. Channels available but not in use: N.A.

Basic Service
Subscribers: N.A. Included in Greeneville, TN
Programming (received off-air): WCYB-TV (CW, NBC) Bristol; WDBJ (CBS, MNT) Roanoke; WEMT (FOX) Greeneville; WJHL-TV (CBS) Johnson City; WKPT-TV (ABC) Kingsport; WLFG (IND) Grundy; WMSY-TV (PBS) Marion; WSLS-TV (NBC) Roanoke; WVVA (CW, NBC) Bluefield.
Programming (via satellite): QVC.
Fee: $50.00 installation; $18.46 monthly; $2.00 converter.

Expanded Basic Service 1
Subscribers: N.A.
Programming (via satellite): A&E Networks; ABC Family Channel; AMC; Animal Planet; BET Networks; Bravo; CNBC; CNN; Comcast SportsNet Mid-Atlantic; Comedy Central; Country Music TV; C-SPAN; C-SPAN 2; Discovery Channel; Disney Channel; E! Entertainment Television; ESPN; ESPN 2; Food Network; Fox News Channel; FX; Hallmark Channel; Headline News; HGTV; History Channel; Lifetime; MSNBC; MTV; Nickelodeon; Oxygen; Product Information Network; ShopNBC; Spike TV; Syfy; TBS Superstation; The Learning Channel; The Weather Channel; Travel Channel; truTV; Turner Network TV; TV Guide Network; TV Land; USA Network; VH1; WGN America.

Digital Basic Service
Subscribers: N.A.
Programming (via satellite): BBC America; Bloomberg Television; Discovery Fit & Health; ESPN Classic Sports; ESPNews; Fox Movie Channel; G4; Golf Channel; GSN; Halogen Network; Music Choice; Outdoor Channel; Trinity Broadcasting Network; Versus; WE tv.

Digital Expanded Basic Service
Subscribers: N.A.
Programming (via satellite): NickToons TV.

Digital Pay Service 1
Pay Units: N.A.
Programming (via satellite): Cinemax (multiplexed); Encore (multiplexed); HBO

(multiplexed); Showtime (multiplexed); Starz (multiplexed); The Movie Channel (multiplexed).

Video-On-Demand: No

Pay-Per-View

Fresh (delivered digitally); HITS (delivered digitally); Playboy TV (delivered digitally).

Internet Service

Operational: Yes.

Subscribers: 640.

Broadband Service: Comcast High Speed Internet.

Fee: $42.95 monthly.

Telephone Service

Digital: Operational

Miles of plant included in Greeneville, TN

Manager: Hilda Sexton. Technical Operations Director: Time Castor. Plant Manager: Travis Coomes. Marketing Coordinator: Debbie Frost. Office Manager: Ann Rouse.

Ownership: Comcast Cable Communications Inc. (MSO).

MARTINSVILLE—Comcast Cable, 400 Westfield Rd, Charlottesville, VA 22901. Phone: 434-951-3700. Fax: 434-951-3705. Web Site: http://www.comcast.com. Also serves Axton, Bassett, Collinsville, Fieldale, Henry County, Horse Pasture, Ridgeway, Stanleytown & Villa Heights. ICA: VA0150.

TV Market Ranking: 70 (Bassett, Henry County (portions), Ridgeway); Below 100 (Axton, Collinsville, Fieldale, Horse Pasture, MARTINSVILLE, Stanleytown, Villa Heights, Henry County (portions)). Franchise award date: January 1, 1966. Franchise expiration date: April 28, 2010. Began: March 22, 1966.

Channel capacity: N.A. Channels available but not in use: N.A.

Basic Service

Subscribers: 19,551.

Programming (received off-air): WBRA-TV (PBS) Roanoke; WDBJ (CBS, MNT) Roanoke; WDRL-TV (IND) Danville; WFMY-TV (CBS) Greensboro; WFXR (CW, FOX) Roanoke; WGSR-LD (IND) Reidsville; WPXR-TV (ION) Roanoke; WSET-TV (ABC) Lynchburg; WSLS-TV (NBC) Roanoke; WWCW (CW, FOX) Lynchburg; WXII-TV (NBC) Winston-Salem; 12 FMs.

Programming (via satellite): QVC; WGN America.

Fee: $33.00 installation; $35.31 monthly.

Expanded Basic Service 1

Subscribers: N.A.

Programming (via satellite): A&E Networks; ABC Family Channel; AMC; Animal Planet; BET Networks; Bravo; Cartoon Network; CNBC; CNN; Comcast SportsNet Mid-Atlantic; Comedy Central; Country Music TV; C-SPAN; C-SPAN 2; Discovery Channel; Disney Channel; E! Entertainment Television; ESPN; ESPN 2; Eternal Word TV Network; Food Network; Fox News Channel; FX; Hallmark Channel; Headline News; HGTV; History Channel; INSP; Lifetime; MSNBC; MTV; Nickelodeon; Oxygen; Product Information Network; ShopNBC; Speed; Spike TV; Syfy; TBS Superstation; The Learning Channel; The Weather Channel; Travel Channel; truTV; Turner Classic Movies; Turner Network TV; TV Guide Network; TV Land; Univision Studios; USA Network; VH1.

Digital Basic Service

Subscribers: N.A.

Programming (via satellite): A&E HD; ABC Family HD; Animal Planet HD; BBC America; Bio; Bloomberg Television; Canal 52MX; CBS Sports Network; Cine Latino; Cine Mexicano; CMT Pure Country; CNN en Espanol; CNN HD; C-SPAN 2; C-SPAN 3; Current; Daystar TV Network; Discovery Channel HD; Discovery en Espanol; Discovery Fit & Health; Discovery Health Channel; Discovery Kids Channel; DIY Network; Encore (multiplexed); ESPN 2 HD; ESPN Classic Sports; ESPN Deportes; ESPN HD; ESPNews; EWTN en Espanol; Flix; Food Network HD; Fox Business Channel; Fox College Sports Atlantic; Fox College Sports Central; Fox College Sports Pacific; Fox Deportes; Fox Movie Channel; Fox Reality Channel; Fox Soccer; Fuel TV; Fuse; G4; GalaVision; GMC; Golf Channel; Great American Country; GSN; Halogen Network; HDNet; HGTV HD; History Channel en Espanol; History Channel HD; History Channel International; ID Investigation Discovery; Independent Film Channel; Jewelry Television; Lifetime Movie Network; LOGO; Military Channel; MoviePlex; MTV2; Music Choice; MyNetworkTV Inc.; National Geographic Channel; National Geographic Channel HD Network; NBA TV; NFL Network; NHL Network; Nick Jr.; NickToons TV; Outdoor Channel; Palladia; PBS Kids Sprout; Planet Green; Science; Science HD; SoapNet; Style Network; Sundance Channel; Syfy HD; TBS in HD; TeenNick; Telefutura; Tennis Channel; The Comcast Network; The Word Network; TLC HD; Toon Disney; Toon Disney en Espanol; Tr3s; Trinity Broadcasting Network; Turner Network TV HD; TV One; TVG Network; Universal HD; USA Network HD; VeneMovies; Versus; Versus HD; VH1 Classic; VH1 Soul; WE tv.

Digital Pay Service 1

Pay Units: N.A.

Programming (via satellite): ART America; CCTV-4; Cinemax (multiplexed); Cinemax HD; Filipino Channel; HBO (multiplexed); HBO HD; RAI International; Showtime (multiplexed); Showtime HD; Starz (multiplexed); Starz HDTV; The Movie Channel (multiplexed); TV Asia; TV Japan; TV5, La Television International; Zee TV USA; Zhong Tian Channel.

Video-On-Demand: Yes

Pay-Per-View

iN DEMAND (delivered digitally); Playboy TV (delivered digitally).

Internet Service

Operational: Yes.

Broadband Service: Comcast High Speed Internet.

Fee: $42.95 monthly; $7.00 modem lease.

Telephone Service

Digital: Operational

Miles of Plant: 653.0 (coaxial); 18.0 (fiber optic).

Vice President & General Manager: Troy Fitzhugh. Technical Operations Director: Tom Jacobs. Technical Operations Manager: Mike Buckner. Marketing Director: Steve Miles.

Ownership: Comcast Cable Communications Inc. (MSO).

MATHEWS—Comcast Cable, 10514 Buckley Hall Rd, Mathews, VA 23109-2200. Phones: 804-915-5400; 804-725-3412. Fax: 804-725-5209. Web Site: http://www.comcast.com. Also serves Mathews County. ICA: VA0056.

TV Market Ranking: 44 (MATHEWS, Mathews County). Franchise award date: March 22, 1988. Franchise expiration date: N.A. Began: December 1, 1988.

Channel capacity: 42 (not 2-way capable). Channels available but not in use: N.A.

Basic Service

Subscribers: N.A. Included with Richmond

Programming (received off-air): WAVY-TV (NBC) Portsmouth; WGNT (CW) Portsmouth; WHRO-TV (PBS) Hampton-Norfolk; WTKR (CBS) Norfolk; WTVZ-TV (MNT) Norfolk; WVBT (FOX) Virginia Beach; WVEC (ABC) Hampton.

Programming (via satellite): C-SPAN; C-SPAN 2; INSP; LWS Local Weather Station; QVC; TBS Superstation.

Fee: $28.95 installation; $13.40 monthly.

Expanded Basic Service 1

Subscribers: 1,915.

Programming (via satellite): A&E Networks; ABC Family Channel; BET Networks; CNBC; CNN; Comcast SportsNet Mid-Atlantic; Country Music TV; Discovery Channel; Disney Channel; ESPN; ESPN 2; Fox News Channel; Headline News; History Channel; Lifetime; MTV; Nickelodeon; Spike TV; Syfy; The Weather Channel; Turner Network TV; USA Network; VH1.

Fee: $17.00 monthly.

Digital Basic Service

Subscribers: N.A. Included with Richmond

Programming (via satellite): BBC America; Bloomberg Television; Bravo; Discovery Fit & Health; ESPN Classic Sports; ESPNews; Fox Movie Channel; G4; Golf Channel; GSN; Halogen Network; HGTV; National Geographic Channel; Nick Jr.; NickToons TV; Outdoor Channel; Speed; Trinity Broadcasting Network; Turner Classic Movies; Versus; VH1 Classic; VH1 Country; WE tv.

Digital Pay Service 1

Pay Units: N.A.

Programming (via satellite): Cinemax (multiplexed); Encore; HBO (multiplexed); Showtime (multiplexed); The Movie Channel (multiplexed).

Fee: $15.99 monthly (Starz, Cinemax, Showtime or TMC), $17.99 monthly (HBO).

Video-On-Demand: No

Pay-Per-View

Hits Movies & Events (delivered digitally); Fresh (delivered digitally); Playboy TV (delivered digitally).

Internet Service

Operational: No.

Telephone Service

None

Miles of Plant: 158.0 (coaxial); None (fiber optic).

Technical Operations Director: Stephen Hill. Chief Technician: Art Harris. Marketing Director: Erin Powell. Public Relations Manager: Monica Smith-Callahan. Office Manager: Shirley Winters.

Ownership: Comcast Cable Communications Inc. (MSO).

MAX MEADOWS—See Fort Chiswell, VA [VA0066]. ICA: VA5304.

MCKENNEY—Formerly served by Adelphia Communications. Now served by PETERSBURG (unincorporated areas), VA [VA0186]. ICA: VA0086.

MIDDLESEX COUNTY—MetroCast Communications, 126 Urbanna Rd, PO Box 1147, Saluda, VA 23149-1147. Phone: 800-633-8578. Fax: 804-758-1215. Web Site: http://www.metrocastcommunications.com. Also serves Deltaville, Saluda, Urbanna & Water View. ICA: VA0085.

TV Market Ranking: 44 (MIDDLESEX COUNTY); Below 100 (Water View); Outside TV Markets (Saluda, Urbanna). Franchise award date: March 1, 1983. Franchise expiration date: February 1, 2008. Began: April 2, 1984.

Channel capacity: 116 (operating 2-way). Channels available but not in use: N.A.

Basic Service

Subscribers: 2,723.

Programming (received off-air): WAVY-TV (NBC) Portsmouth; WCVE-TV (PBS) Richmond; WHRO-TV (PBS) Hampton-Norfolk; WRIC-TV (ABC) Petersburg; WRLH-TV (FOX, MNT) Richmond; WTKR (CBS) Norfolk; WTVR-TV (CBS) Richmond; WUPV (CW) Ashland; WVEC (ABC) Hampton; WWBT (NBC) Richmond.

Programming (via satellite): A&E Networks; ABC Family Channel; AMC; Animal Planet; BET Networks; Bravo; Cartoon Network; CNBC; CNN; Comcast SportsNet Mid-Atlantic; Comedy Central; C-SPAN; C-SPAN 2; Discovery Channel; Discovery Fit & Health; Discovery Health Channel; Disney Channel; ESPN; ESPN 2; ESPN Classic Sports; Food Network; Fox News Channel; FX; Golf Channel; Hallmark Channel; Headline News; HGTV; History Channel; INSP; Lifetime; Lifetime Movie Network; MSNBC; MTV; National Geographic Channel; Nickelodeon; Outdoor Channel; Oxygen; QVC; Speed; Spike TV; Syfy; TBS Superstation; The Learning Channel; The Weather Channel; Travel Channel; truTV; Turner Network TV; TV Guide Network; TV Land; USA Network; VH1; WGN America.

Fee: $60.00 installation; $45.90 monthly; $28.00 additional installation.

Digital Basic Service

Subscribers: 275.

Programming (via satellite): AmericanLife TV Network; BBC America; Bio; Bloomberg Television; Country Music TV; ESPN 2 HD; ESPN HD; ESPNews; Fox College Sports Atlantic; Fox College Sports Central; Fox College Sports Pacific; Fox Movie Channel; Fox Soccer; Fuse; G4; GAS; Great American Country; GSN; Halogen Network; HD Theater; HDNet; HDNet Movies; History Channel International; Independent Film Channel; MTV Networks Digital Suite; Nick Jr.; NickToons TV; ShopNBC; Style Network; The Word Network; Toon Disney; Trinity Broadcasting Network; Versus; WE tv.

Fee: $16.90 monthly.

Digital Pay Service 1

Pay Units: N.A.

Programming (via satellite): Cinemax (multiplexed); DMX Music; Encore (multiplexed); Flix; HBO (multiplexed); Showtime (multiplexed); Starz (multiplexed); The Movie Channel (multiplexed).

Fee: $32.50 installation; $12.95 monthly (Cinemax), $16.50 monthly (Starz/Encore or Showtime/TMC), $19.00 monthly (HBO).

Video-On-Demand: No

Pay-Per-View

Addressable homes: 2,000.

Hot Choice; iN DEMAND.

Internet Service

Operational: Yes.

Subscribers: 650.

Broadband Service: In-house.

Fee: $99.95 installation; $29.95-$58.95 monthly; $2.00 modem lease; $99.00 modem purchase.

Telephone Service

Digital: Operational

Fee: $29.95 monthly

Miles of Plant: 224.0 (coaxial); 87.0 (fiber optic).

General Manager: Danny L. Jobe.

Ownership: Harron Communications LP (MSO).

MONTEREY—Formerly served by Highland Communications. No longer in operation. ICA: VA0113.

MOUNT CLINTON—Formerly served by Adelphia Communications. Now served by HARRISONBURG, VA [VA0016]. ICA: VA0153.

NEW CASTLE (town)—Citizens Telephone Coop., 220 Webbs Mill Rd, Floyd, VA 24091. Phones: 540-745-2111; 800-941-0426. Fax: 540-745-3791. Web Site: http://www.citizens.coop. Also serves Craig County (portions). ICA: VA0105.

TV Market Ranking: 70 (Craig County (portions), NEW CASTLE (TOWN)). Franchise award date: N.A. Franchise expiration date: N.A. Began: N.A.

Channel capacity: 52 (2-way capable). Channels available but not in use: N.A.

Basic Service

Subscribers: 311.

Programming (received off-air): WBRA-TV (PBS) Roanoke; WDBJ (CBS, MNT) Roanoke; WFXR (CW, FOX) Roanoke; WPXR-TV (ION) Roanoke; WSET-TV (ABC) Lynchburg; WSLS-TV (NBC) Roanoke.

Programming (via satellite): C-SPAN; QVC; TBS Superstation; WGN America.

Fee: $45.86 installation; $12.81 monthly; $31.74 additional installation.

Expanded Basic Service 1

Subscribers: 54.

Programming (via satellite): ABC Family Channel; CNN; Country Music TV; Discovery Channel; Disney Channel; ESPN; ESPN 2; MSNBC; MTV; Nickelodeon; Spike TV; Syfy; The Learning Channel; The Weather Channel; Turner Classic Movies; Turner Network TV; USA Network.

Fee: $29.73 monthly.

Pay Service 1

Pay Units: 13.

Programming (via satellite): Cinemax.

Fee: $9.95 monthly.

Pay Service 2

Pay Units: 41.

Programming (via satellite): HBO.

Fee: $11.95 monthly.

Pay Service 3

Pay Units: 12.

Programming (via satellite): Showtime.

Fee: $9.95 monthly.

Video-On-Demand: No

Internet Service

Operational: Yes, DSL.

Telephone Service

None

Miles of Plant: 24.0 (coaxial); None (fiber optic).

Manager: Greg Sapp. Network Manager: Danny Vaughn. Marketing Director: Robert Weeks. Executive Administrative Assistant: Amanda Souiers.

Ownership: Citizens Cablevision Inc. (VA) (MSO).

NEW KENT—Cox Communications. Now served by HAMPTON ROADS (formerly Virginia Beach), VA [VA0002]. ICA: VA0156.

NICKELSVILLE—Formerly served by Scott Telecom & Electronics. No longer in operation. ICA: VA0187.

NORTHUMBERLAND COUNTY—MetroCast Communications, 126 Urbanna Rd, PO Box 1147, Saluda, VA 23149-1147. Phone: 800-633-8578. Web Site: http://www.metrocastcommunications.com. Also serves Burgess, Callao, Edwardsville, Heathsville, Lewisetta, Lottsburg, Ophelia, Reedville, Walmsley & Wicomico Church. ICA: VA0195.

TV Market Ranking: Outside TV Markets (Burgess, Callao, Edwardsville, Heathsville, Lewisetta, Lottsburg, NORTHUMBERLAND COUNTY, Ophelia, Reedville, Walmsley, Wicomico Church).

Channel capacity: N.A. Channels available but not in use: N.A.

Basic Service

Subscribers: N.A. Included in Richmond

Programming (received off-air): WAVY-TV (NBC) Portsmouth; WCVE-TV (PBS) Richmond; WGNT (CW) Portsmouth; WHRO-TV (PBS) Hampton-Norfolk; WRIC-TV (ABC) Petersburg; WRLH-TV (FOX, MNT) Richmond; WTVR-TV (CBS) Richmond; WUPV (CW) Ashland; WUSA (CBS) Washington; WWBT (NBC) Richmond.

Programming (via satellite): BET Networks; C-SPAN; C-SPAN 2; TBS Superstation; The Weather Channel.

Fee: $14.65 monthly.

Expanded Basic Service 1

Subscribers: N.A.

Programming (via satellite): A&E Networks; ABC Family Channel; CNBC; CNN; Comcast SportsNet Mid-Atlantic; Country Music TV; Discovery Channel; Disney Channel; ESPN; ESPN 2; Fox News Channel; Headline News; HGTV; Lifetime; MSNBC; MTV; Nickelodeon; QVC; Spike TV; Turner Network TV; TV Land; USA Network; VH1.

Digital Basic Service

Subscribers: N.A. Included with Richmond

Programming (via satellite): BBC America; Bloomberg Television; Bravo; CMT Pure Country; Discovery Digital Networks; DMX Music; ESPN Classic Sports; ESPNews; Fox Movie Channel; Fox Soccer; G4; Golf Channel; GSN; Halogen Network; History Channel; Independent Film Channel; National Geographic Channel; Nick Jr.; NickToons TV; Outdoor Channel; Speed; Trinity Broadcasting Network; Turner Classic Movies; Versus; VH1 Classic; WE tv.

Digital Pay Service 1

Pay Units: N.A.

Programming (via satellite): Cinemax (multiplexed); Encore (multiplexed); HBO (multiplexed); Showtime (multiplexed); Starz (multiplexed); The Movie Channel (multiplexed).

Pay-Per-View

Movies (delivered digitally); Special events (delivered digitally); Playboy TV (delivered digitally).

Internet Service

Operational: Yes.

Fee: $21.95-$58.95 monthly.

Telephone Service

Digital: Operational

Fee: $44.95 monthly

Miles of Plant: 220.0 (coaxial); None (fiber optic).

General Manager: Danny L. Jobe.

Ownership: Harron Communications LP (MSO).

NORTON—Comcast Cable, 838 Park Ave NE, Norton, VA 24273-1010. Phones: 423-282-1370 (Gray, TN office); 276-679-4001. Fax: 276-679-3431. Web Site: http://www.comcast.com. Also serves Appalachia, Banner, Ben Hur, Big Stone Gap, Bold Camp, Bond Town, Clinchco, Clinchport (portions), Clintwood, Coeburn, Crab Orchard, Dickenson County, Duffield, Esserville, Indian Creek, Jasper (portions), Jonesville, Josephine, Keokee, Lee County, Maytown, Pennington Gap, Poor Valley, Riverview, Stephens, Wise & Wise County. ICA: VA0157.

TV Market Ranking: Below 100 (Appalachia, Banner, Ben Hur, Big Stone Gap, Bold Camp, Bond Town, Clinchco, Clinchport (portions), Clintwood, Coeburn, Crab Orchard, Dickenson County, Duffield, Esserville, Indian Creek, Jasper (portions), Jonesville, Josephine, Keokee, Lee County (portions), Maytown, NORTON, Pennington Gap, Poor Valley, Riverview, Stephens, Wise, Wise County (portions)); Outside TV Markets (Lee County (portions), Wise County (portions)). Franchise award date: N.A. Franchise expiration date: N.A. Began: January 1, 1958.

Channel capacity: 54 (operating 2-way). Channels available but not in use: N.A.

Basic Service

Subscribers: N.A. Included in Greeneville, TN

Programming (received off-air): WCYB-TV (CW, NBC) Bristol; WDBJ (CBS, MNT) Roanoke; WEMT (FOX) Greeneville; WETP-TV (PBS) Sneedville; WKPT-TV (ABC) Kingsport; WSBN-TV (PBS) Norton; WYMT-TV (CBS, CW) Hazard; allband FM.

Programming (via satellite): A&E Networks; ABC Family Channel; AMC; Animal Planet; BET Networks; Cartoon Network; CNBC; CNN; Comcast SportsNet Mid-Atlantic; Comedy Central; Country Music TV; C-SPAN; C-SPAN 2; Discovery Channel; Disney Channel; E! Entertainment Television; ESPN; ESPN 2; Fox News Channel; FX; Golf Channel; Hallmark Channel; Headline News; HGTV; History Channel; ION Television; Lifetime; MSNBC; MTV; Nickelodeon; QVC; Speed; Spike TV; Syfy; TBS Superstation; The Learning Channel; The Weather Channel; Travel Channel; Trinity Broadcasting Network; truTV; Turner Network TV; TV Guide Network; TV Land; USA Network; Versus; VH1; WGN America.

Fee: $30.00 installation; $15.95 monthly; $10.00 additional installation.

Digital Basic Service

Subscribers: N.A.

Programming (via satellite): BBC America; Bloomberg Television; Discovery Fit & Health; ESPN Classic Sports; ESPNews; Fox Movie Channel; Fox Sports World; G4; GSN; Halogen Network; Music Choice; Outdoor Channel; Toon Disney; WE tv.

Digital Expanded Basic Service

Subscribers: N.A.

Programming (via satellite): National Geographic Channel; Nick Jr.; NickToons TV; Style Network; VH1 Classic; VH1 Country.

Digital Pay Service 1

Pay Units: 630.

Programming (via satellite): Cinemax (multiplexed); Encore (multiplexed); Flix; HBO (multiplexed); Showtime (multiplexed); Starz (multiplexed); The Movie Channel (multiplexed).

Video-On-Demand: No

Pay-Per-View

Fresh (delivered digitally); Playboy TV (delivered digitally); HITS (delivered digitally).

Internet Service

Operational: Yes.

Broadband Service: Comcast High Speed Internet.

Fee: $42.95 monthly.

Telephone Service

Digital: Operational

Miles of plant included in Greeneville, TN

Operations Manager: Larry Matthews. Technical Operations Director: Tim Castor. Marketing Manager: Sandra Munsey. Office Manager: Pam Owens.

Ownership: Comcast Cable Communications Inc. (MSO).

ORANGE—Comcast Cable, 15367 Brandy Rd, Culpeper, VA 22701-2547. Phones: 434-951-3700 (Charlottesville office); 540-825-5070. Fax: 540-829-6678. Web Site: http://www.comcast.com. Also serves Orange County. ICA: VA0073.

TV Market Ranking: Below 100 (ORANGE, Orange County).

Channel capacity: N.A. Channels available but not in use: N.A.

Basic Service

Subscribers: 3,092.

Programming (received off-air): WDCA (MNT) Washington; WDCW (CW) Washington; WETA-TV (PBS) Washington; WJLA-TV (ABC) Washington; WNVT (ETV) Goldvein; WPXW-TV (ION) Manassas; WRC-TV (NBC) Washington; WTTG (FOX) Washington; WTVR-TV (CBS) Richmond; WUSA (CBS) Washington; WVIR-TV (CW, NBC) Charlottesville; WVPT (PBS) Staunton.

Programming (via satellite): C-SPAN; C-SPAN 2; QVC; ShopNBC; TBS Superstation; TV Guide Network.

Expanded Basic Service 1

Subscribers: 2,178.

Programming (via satellite): A&E Networks; ABC Family Channel; AMC; Animal Planet; BET Networks; Cartoon Network; CNBC; CNN; Comcast SportsNet Mid-Atlantic; Comedy Central; Country Music TV; Discovery Channel; Disney Channel; E! Entertainment Television; ESPN; ESPN 2; Eternal Word TV Network; Food Network; Fox News Channel; FX; Great American Country; Hallmark Channel; Headline News; HGTV; History Channel; Lifetime; MSNBC; MTV; Nickelodeon; Spike TV; Syfy; The Learning Channel; The Weather Channel; Travel Channel; truTV; Turner Network TV; TV Land; USA Network; VH1.

Digital Basic Service

Subscribers: 846.

Programming (via satellite): AmericanLife TV Network; BBC America; Bio; Bloomberg Television; Discovery Fit & Health; DIY Network; Fox Sports World; Fuse; G4; GSN; Halogen Network; Lifetime Movie Network; Mid-Atlantic Sports Network; National Geographic Channel; SoapNet; Speed; Style Network; Toon Disney; Trinity Broadcasting Network; Turner Classic Movies; WE tv.

Digital Expanded Basic Service

Subscribers: N.A.

Programming (via satellite): Canales N; DMX Music; ESPN Classic Sports; ESP-

News; Flix; Golf Channel; History Channel International; Independent Film Channel; Outdoor Channel; Versus.

Digital Pay Service 1

Pay Units: N.A.

Programming (via satellite): Cinemax (multiplexed); Encore (multiplexed); HBO (multiplexed); Showtime (multiplexed); The Movie Channel (multiplexed).

Video-On-Demand: No

Pay-Per-View

Playboy TV (delivered digitally); Fresh (delivered digitally); Shorteez (delivered digitally); Hot Choice (delivered digitally); HITS (Headend In The Sky).

Internet Service

Operational: Yes.

Broadband Service: Comcast High Speed Internet.

Fee: $42.95 monthly.

Telephone Service

Digital: Operational

Miles of Plant: 110.0 (coaxial); 75.0 (fiber optic).

Vice President & General Manager: Troy Fitzhugh. Technical Operations Manager: Richard Burke. Chief Technician: Delmer Seal. Marketing Coordinator: Cassie Cool. Office Manager: Melissa Marks.

Ownership: Comcast Cable Communications Inc. (MSO).

PALMYRA—Comcast Cable, 400 Westfield Rd, Charlottesville, VA 22901. Phone: 434-951-3700. Fax: 434-951-3705. Web Site: http://www.comcast.com. ICA: VA0191.

TV Market Ranking: Below 100 (PALMYRA).

Channel capacity: N.A. Channels available but not in use: N.A.

Basic Service

Subscribers: N.A.

Programming (received off-air): WCAV (CBS) Charlottesville; WDCA (MNT) Washington; WHSV-TV (ABC, MNT) Harrisonburg; WHTJ (PBS) Charlottesville; WRIC-TV (ABC) Petersburg; WTTG (FOX) Washington; WTVR-TV (CBS) Richmond; WUPV (CW) Ashland; WVIR-TV (CW, NBC) Charlottesville; WVPT (PBS) Staunton; WWBT (NBC) Richmond.

Programming (via satellite): C-SPAN; ION Television; QVC; ShopNBC; TV Guide Network.

Expanded Basic Service 1

Subscribers: N.A.

Programming (via satellite): A&E Networks; ABC Family Channel; AMC; Animal Planet; BET Networks; Bravo; Cartoon Network; CNBC; CNN; Comcast SportsNet Mid-Atlantic; Comedy Central; Country Music TV; C-SPAN 2; Discovery Channel; Disney Channel; E! Entertainment Television; ESPN; ESPN 2; Eternal Word TV Network; Food Network; Fox News Channel; FX; Golf Channel; Hallmark Channel; Headline News; HGTV; History Channel; Lifetime; MSNBC; MTV; Nickelodeon; Oxygen; Spike TV; Syfy; TBS Superstation; The Learning Channel; The Weather Channel; Travel Channel; Trinity Broadcasting Network; truTV; Turner Classic Movies; Turner Network TV; TV Land; USA Network; VH1.

Digital Basic Service

Subscribers: N.A.

Programming (via satellite): AmericanLife TV Network; BBC America; Bloomberg Television; Discovery Fit & Health; Discovery Health Channel; Discovery Home Channel; Discovery Kids Channel; Discovery Times Channel; DIY Network; Fox Sports World; Fuse; G4; GSN; INSP; Lifetime Movie Network; Military Channel; National Geographic Channel; Science; SoapNet; Speed; Toon Disney; Trinity Broadcasting Network; WE tv.

Digital Expanded Basic Service

Subscribers: N.A.

Programming (via satellite): Arabic Channel; Bio; CCTV-4; ESPN Classic Sports; ESPNews; Filipino Channel; Flix (multiplexed); History Channel; Independent Film Channel; International Television (ITV); Music Choice; Outdoor Channel; RAI International; Sundance Channel; TV Asia; TV Japan; TV5, La Television International; Versus; Zhong Tian Channel.

Pay Service 1

Pay Units: N.A.

Programming (via satellite): HBO; Showtime.

Digital Pay Service 1

Pay Units: N.A.

Programming (via satellite): Cinemax; Encore (multiplexed); HBO (multiplexed); Showtime (multiplexed).

Video-On-Demand: No

Pay-Per-View

HITS 1 (delivered digitally); Hot Choice; Playboy TV (delivered digitally); Fresh (delivered digitally); Shorteez (delivered digitally).

Internet Service

Operational: Yes.

Broadband Service: Comcast High Speed Internet.

Fee: $42.95 monthly.

Telephone Service

Digital: Operational

Miles of Plant: 151.0 (coaxial); None (fiber optic).

Vice President & General Manager: Troy Fitzhugh. Technical Operations Director: Tom Jacobs. Marketing Director: Steve Miles. Marketing Coordinator: Cassie Cool.

Ownership: Comcast Cable Communications Inc. (MSO).

PEARISBURG—Charter Communications. Now served by BECKLEY, WV [WV0005]. ICA: VA0043.

PENNINGTON GAP—Formerly served by Adelphia Communications. Now served by NORTON, VA [VA0157]. ICA: VA0091.

PETERSBURG—Comcast Cable, 2033 E Whitehill Dr, Prince George, VA 23875-1249. Phones: 804-915-5400 (Richmond office); 804-957-5739. Fax: 804-957-5830. Web Site: http://www.comcast.com. Also serves Colonial Heights, Fort Lee, Hopewell, Prince George & Prince George County (portions). ICA: VA0015.

TV Market Ranking: 63 (Colonial Heights, Fort Lee, Hopewell, PETERSBURG, Prince George, Prince George County (portions)); Outside TV Markets (Prince George County (portions)). Franchise award date: January 1, 1968. Franchise expiration date: N.A. Began: October 14, 1968.

Channel capacity: N.A. Channels available but not in use: N.A.

Basic Service

Subscribers: N.A. Included in Richmond

Programming (received off-air): WCVE-TV (PBS) Richmond; WCVW (PBS) Richmond; WMYV (MNT) Greensboro; WRIC-TV (ABC) Petersburg; WRLH-TV (FOX, MNT) Richmond; WTVR-TV (CBS) Richmond; WWBT (NBC) Richmond.

Programming (via satellite): ABC Family Channel; C-SPAN; E! Entertainment Television; INSP; QVC; TBS Superstation; TV Guide Network; WGN America.

Fee: $11.95 monthly.

Expanded Basic Service 1

Subscribers: N.A.

Programming (via satellite): A&E Networks; AMC; Animal Planet; BET Networks; Bravo; Cartoon Network; CNBC; CNN; Comcast SportsNet Mid-Atlantic; Comedy Central; Country Music TV; C-SPAN 2; Discovery Channel; Disney Channel; ESPN; ESPN 2; Food Network; Fox News Channel; FX; Great American Country; Headline News; HGTV; History Channel; ION Television; Lifetime; MSNBC; MTV; Nickelodeon; Spike TV; Syfy; The Learning Channel; The Weather Channel; Travel Channel; Trinity Broadcasting Network; truTV; Turner Classic Movies; Turner Network TV; TV Land; Univision Studios; USA Network; VH1.

Fee: $23.00 monthly.

Digital Basic Service

Subscribers: N.A. Included in Richmond

Programming (via satellite): AmericanLife TV Network; BBC America; Bio; Bloomberg Television; Discovery Fit & Health; DIY Network; DMX Music; ESPN Classic Sports; ESPNews; Fox Sports World; Fuse; G4; Golf Channel; GSN; Halogen Network; History Channel International; Mid-Atlantic Sports Network; Music Choice; National Geographic Channel; Nick Jr.; Outdoor Channel; SoapNet; Speed; Style Network; Toon Disney; Versus; WE tv.

Fee: $10.95 monthly.

Digital Pay Service 1

Pay Units: 971.

Programming (via satellite): Canales N; Cinemax (multiplexed); Encore (multiplexed); Flix; HBO (multiplexed); Showtime (multiplexed); Starz (multiplexed); The Movie Channel (multiplexed).

Fee: $6.00 monthly (Canales N), $15.95 monthly (HBO, Cinemax, Showtime/TMC or Starz).

Video-On-Demand: No

Pay-Per-View

iN DEMAND (delivered digitally); Playboy TV (delivered digitally); Hot Choice (delivered digitally); Sports PPV (delivered digitally); Special events.

Internet Service

Operational: Yes. Began: July 1, 2002.

Subscribers: 80.

Broadband Service: Comcast High Speed Internet.

Fee: $42.95 monthly.

Telephone Service

Digital: Operational

Miles of Plant: 300.0 (coaxial); None (fiber optic).

Technical Operations Director: Stephen Hill. Marketing Director: Erin Powell. Public Relations Manager: Monica Smith-Callahan. Office Manager: Joyce Johnson.

Ownership: Comcast Cable Communications Inc. (MSO).

PETERSBURG (unincorporated areas)—Comcast Cable, 2033 E Whitehill Dr, Prince George, VA 23875-1249. Phones: 804-957-5739; 804-915-5400 (Richmond office). Fax: 804-957-5830. Web Site: http://www.comcast.com. Also serves Dinwiddie & McKenney. ICA: VA0186.

TV Market Ranking: 63 (Dinwiddie, McKenney, PETERSBURG (UNINCORPORATED AREAS)). Franchise award date: N.A. Franchise expiration date: N.A. Began: N.A.

Channel capacity: 59 (operating 2-way). Channels available but not in use: N.A.

Basic Service

Subscribers: N.A. Included in Richmond

Programming (received off-air): WCVE-TV (PBS) Richmond; WCVW (PBS) Richmond; WRIC-TV (ABC) Petersburg; WRLH-TV (FOX, MNT) Richmond; WTVR-TV (CBS) Richmond; WUPV (CW) Ashland; WWBT (NBC) Richmond.

Programming (via satellite): ABC Family Channel; E! Entertainment Television; INSP; QVC; TV Guide Network; WGN America.

Expanded Basic Service 1

Subscribers: N.A.

Programming (via satellite): A&E Networks; AMC; Animal Planet; BET Networks; Bravo; Cartoon Network; CNBC; CNN; Comcast SportsNet Mid-Atlantic; Comedy Central; Country Music TV; C-SPAN; C-SPAN 2; Discovery Channel; Disney Channel; ESPN; ESPN 2; Food Network; Fox News Channel; FX; Great American Country; Headline News; HGTV; History Channel; ION Television; Lifetime; MSNBC; MTV; Nickelodeon; Spike TV; Syfy; TBS Superstation; The Learning Channel; The Weather Channel; Travel Channel; Trinity Broadcasting Network; truTV; Turner Classic Movies; Turner Network TV; TV Land; Univision Studios; USA Network; VH1.

Digital Basic Service

Subscribers: N.A. Included in Richmond

Programming (via satellite): AmericanLife TV Network; BBC America; Bio; Bloomberg Television; Discovery Fit & Health; DIY Network; ESPN Classic Sports; ESPNews; Fox Sports World; Fuse; G4; Golf Channel; GSN; Halogen Network; History Channel International; Mid-Atlantic Sports Network; Music Choice; Outdoor Channel; SoapNet; Speed; Toon Disney; Trinity Broadcasting Network; Versus; WE tv.

Digital Expanded Basic Service

Subscribers: N.A.

Programming (via satellite): National Geographic Channel; Nick Jr.; Style Network.

Pay Service 1

Pay Units: 501.

Programming (via satellite): Cinemax; HBO.

Digital Pay Service 1

Pay Units: 302.

Programming (via satellite): Cinemax (multiplexed); Encore (multiplexed); Flix; HBO (multiplexed); Showtime (multiplexed); Starz (multiplexed); The Movie Channel (multiplexed).

Video-On-Demand: No

Pay-Per-View

Hot Choice (delivered digitally); Fresh (delivered digitally); HITS (delivered digitally); Playboy TV (delivered digitally).

Internet Service

Operational: Yes.

Broadband Service: Comcast High Speed Internet.

Fee: $42.95 monthly.

Telephone Service

None

Miles of Plant: 160.0 (coaxial); None (fiber optic).

Technical Operations Director: Stephen Hill. Marketing Director: Erin Powell. Public Relations Director: Monica Smith-Callahan. Office Manager: Joyce Johnson.

Ownership: Comcast Cable Communications Inc. (MSO).

POQUOSON—Cox Communications. Now served by HAMPTON ROADS (formerly Virginia Beach), VA [VA0002]. ICA: VA0180.

POWHATAN—Comcast Cable, 2277 Academy Rd, PO Box 100, Powhatan, VA 23139-0100. Phones: 804-598-8725; 804-915-5400 (Richmond office). Fax: 804-598-2988. Web Site: http://www.comcast.com. Also serves Ballsville, Flat

Rock, Jefferson, Macon, Powhatan County & Provost. ICA: VA0100.

TV Market Ranking: 63 (Ballsville, Flat Rock, Jefferson, Macon, POWHATAN, Powhatan County, Provost). Franchise award date: N.A. Franchise expiration date: N.A. Began: June 11, 1990.

Channel capacity: N.A. Channels available but not in use: N.A.

Basic Service

Subscribers: N.A. Included in Richmond

Programming (received off-air): WCVE-TV (PBS) Richmond; WCVW (PBS) Richmond; WRIC-TV (ABC) Petersburg; WRLH-TV (FOX, MNT) Richmond; WTVR-TV (CBS) Richmond; WWBT (NBC) Richmond.

Programming (via satellite): C-SPAN; Fox News Channel; QVC; Trinity Broadcasting Network; WGN America.

Fee: $5.00 monthly.

Expanded Basic Service 1

Subscribers: N.A.

Programming (via satellite): A&E Networks; ABC Family Channel; Animal Planet; BET Networks; Cartoon Network; CNBC; CNN; Comcast SportsNet Mid-Atlantic; Comedy Central; Country Music TV; Discovery Channel; Discovery Fit & Health; Disney Channel; E! Entertainment Television; ESPN; ESPN 2; ESPN Classic Sports; ESPNews; Food Network; Fox Sports World; FX; GAS; Golf Channel; Headline News; HGTV; History Channel; INSP; Lifetime; Lifetime Movie Network; MSNBC; Nick Jr.; Nickelodeon; Outdoor Channel; Ovation; SoapNet; Spike TV; Style Network; Syfy; TBS Superstation; The Learning Channel; The Weather Channel; Toon Disney; Travel Channel; truTV; Turner Classic Movies; Turner Network TV; TV Land; USA Network; Versus; VH1.

Fee: $17.95 monthly.

Digital Basic Service

Subscribers: N.A. Included in Richmond

Programming (via satellite): AmericanLife TV Network; BBC America; Bio; Bloomberg Television; Bravo; Discovery Digital Networks; Fox Movie Channel; G4; GSN; History Channel International; Independent Film Channel; Mid-Atlantic Sports Network; WE tv.

Digital Expanded Basic Service

Subscribers: N.A.

Programming (via satellite): Fuse; MTV Networks Digital Suite; Music Choice.

Digital Pay Service 1

Pay Units: N.A.

Programming (via satellite): Cinemax (multiplexed); HBO (multiplexed); Showtime (multiplexed); Starz (multiplexed); Sundance Channel; The Movie Channel (multiplexed).

Video-On-Demand: No

Pay-Per-View

Urban American Television Network; Hot Choice (delivered digitally); Shorteez (delivered digitally); Fresh (delivered digitally); Playboy TV (delivered digitally).

Internet Service

Operational: Yes.

Subscribers: 569.

Broadband Service: Comcast High Speed Internet.

Fee: $42.95 monthly.

Telephone Service

Digital: Operational

Miles of Plant: 224.0 (coaxial); None (fiber optic).

Technical Operations Director: Stephen Hill. Technical Supervisor: Bob King. Marketing Director: Erin Powell. Public Relations Manager: Monica Smith-Callahan. Office Manager: Joyce Johnson.

Ownership: Comcast Cable Communications Inc. (MSO).

PRINCE GEORGE—Formerly served by Adelphia Communications. Now served by PETERSBURG, VA [VA0015]. ICA: VA0022.

PRINCE WILLIAM COUNTY—Comcast Cable, 11101 University Blvd, Manassas, VA 20110. Phone: 703-789-8100. Fax: 703-789-8280. Web Site: http://www.comcast.com. Also serves Bristow, Catharpin, Dale City, Dumfries, Gainesville, Haymarket, Lake Ridge, Manassas, Montclair, Nokesville, Occoquan, Quantico, River Oaks, Southridge, Triangle & Woodbridge. ICA: VA0148.

TV Market Ranking: 9 (Bristow, Catharpin, Dale City, Dumfries, Gainesville, Haymarket, Lake Ridge, Manassas, Montclair, Nokesville, Occoquan, PRINCE WILLIAM COUNTY, Quantico, River Oaks, Southridge, Triangle, Woodbridge). Franchise award date: N.A. Franchise expiration date: N.A. Began: January 7, 1986.

Channel capacity: N.A. Channels available but not in use: N.A.

Basic Service

Subscribers: 90,463.

Programming (received off-air): WDCA (MNT) Washington; WDCW (CW) Washington; WETA-TV (PBS) Washington; WFDC-DT (UNV) Arlington; WHUT-TV (PBS) Washington; WJLA-TV (ABC) Washington; WMDO-CA (TEL) Washington; WMPT (PBS) Annapolis; WPXW-TV (ION) Manassas; WRC-TV (NBC) Washington; WTTG (FOX) Washington; WUSA (CBS) Washington; WZDC-CA (TMO) Washington.

Programming (via satellite): C-SPAN; C-SPAN 2; Eternal Word TV Network; NewsChannel 8; QVC; The Comcast Network; WGN America.

Fee: $25.00 installation; $19.00 monthly.

Expanded Basic Service 1

Subscribers: N.A.

Programming (via satellite): A&E Networks; ABC Family Channel; Animal Planet; BET Networks; Bravo; Cartoon Network; CNBC; CNN; Comcast SportsNet Mid-Atlantic; Comedy Central; Discovery Channel; Disney Channel; E! Entertainment Television; ESPN; ESPN 2; Food Network; Fox News Channel; FX; Golf Channel; Headline News; HGTV; History Channel; Lifetime; Mid-Atlantic Sports Network; MSNBC; MTV; Nickelodeon; Speed; Spike TV; Style Network; Syfy; TBS Superstation; The Learning Channel; The Weather Channel; Travel Channel; truTV; Turner Classic Movies; Turner Network TV; TV Land; USA Network; Versus; VH1.

Fee: $34.70 monthly.

Digital Basic Service

Subscribers: N.A.

Programming (via satellite): AMC; BBC America; Bio; Canales N; CBS Sports Network; CMT Pure Country; Cooking Channel; Country Music TV; C-SPAN 3; Current; DIY Network; Encore (multiplexed); ESPN 2 HD; ESPN HD; ESPNews; Flix; Fox College Sports Atlantic; Fox College Sports Central; Fox College Sports Pacific; Fox Reality Channel; Fox Soccer; G4; GAS; GolTV; Great American Country; GSN; Hallmark Channel; HD Theater; History Channel International; Howard TV; HRTV; INHD; INSP; Jewelry Television; Lifetime Movie Network; LOGO; Mid-Atlantic Sports Network; MoviePlex; MTV Networks Digital Suite; Music Choice; National Geographic Channel; National Geographic Channel HD Network; NBA TV; NFL Network; Nick Jr.; Nick Too; NickToons TV; Palladia; PBS Kids Sprout; SoapNet; Sundance Channel; Tennis Channel; Toon Disney; Turner Network TV HD; TV Asia; TV Guide Network; TV One; TVG Network; Versus HD; Weatherscan; Zee TV USA.

Fee: $13.00 monthly.

Pay Service 1

Pay Units: 5,200.

Programming (via satellite): HBO.

Fee: $16.95 monthly.

Pay Service 2

Pay Units: 5,075.

Programming (via satellite): Showtime.

Fee: $13.95 monthly.

Digital Pay Service 1

Pay Units: N.A.

Programming (via satellite): Cinemax (multiplexed); Cinemax HD; Cinemax On Demand; HBO (multiplexed); HBO HD; HBO On Demand; Showtime (multiplexed); Showtime HD; Showtime On Demand; Starz (multiplexed); Starz HDTV; Starz On Demand; The Movie Channel (multiplexed); The Movie Channel On Demand.

Fee: $13.95 monthly (each).

Video-On-Demand: Yes

Pay-Per-View

iN DEMAND (delivered digitally); Playboy TV (delivered digitally); Spice Hot (delivered digitally); ESPN Gameplan (delivered digitally); NBA League Pass (delivered digitally); MLS Direct Kick (delivered digitally); NHL Center Ice (delivered digitally).

Internet Service

Operational: Yes.

Subscribers: 10,488.

Broadband Service: Comcast High Speed Internet.

Fee: $42.95 monthly; $7.00 modem lease.

Telephone Service

Digital: Operational

Miles of Plant: 490.0 (coaxial); None (fiber optic).

Vice President & General Manager: Christine Whitaker. Technical Operations Director: Scott Shelly. Marketing Director: Shawn Houston. Marketing Manager: Lyn Harmon. Community Affairs Director: Marie Schuler.

Ownership: Comcast Cable Communications Inc. (MSO).

PULASKI—Comcast Cable, 641 E Main St, Pulaski, VA 24301-5115. Phones: 276-236-0879 (Galax office); 540-980-2206. Fax: 540-980-6219. Web Site: http://www.comcast.com. Also serves Dublin & Pulaski County. ICA: VA0159.

TV Market Ranking: Below 100 (Dublin, PULASKI, Pulaski County (portions)); Outside TV Markets (Pulaski County (portions)). Franchise award date: N.A. Franchise expiration date: N.A. Began: December 15, 1965.

Channel capacity: N.A. Channels available but not in use: N.A.

Basic Service

Subscribers: N.A. Included in Greeneville, TN

Programming (received off-air): WBRA-TV (PBS) Roanoke; WDBJ (CBS, MNT) Roanoke; WDRL-TV (IND) Danville; WFXR (CW, FOX) Roanoke; WPXR-TV (ION) Roanoke; WSET-TV (ABC) Lynchburg; WSLS-TV (NBC) Roanoke.

Programming (via satellite): C-SPAN; C-SPAN 2; FX; INSP; Product Information Network; QVC; TV Guide Network; WGN America.

Fee: $50.00 installation; $29.95 monthly; $2.00 converter.

Expanded Basic Service 1

Subscribers: 6,059.

Programming (via satellite): A&E Networks; ABC Family Channel; AMC; AmericanLife TV Network; Animal Planet; BET Networks; Bravo; Cartoon Network; CNBC; CNN; Comcast SportsNet Mid-Atlantic; Comedy Central; Country Music TV; Discovery Channel; Disney Channel; E! Entertainment Television; ESPN; ESPN 2; Food Network; Fox News Channel; Hallmark Channel; Headline News; HGTV; History Channel; INSP; Lifetime; MSNBC; MTV; Nickelodeon; Oxygen; ShopNBC; Spike TV; Syfy; TBS Superstation; The Learning Channel; The Weather Channel; Travel Channel; truTV; Turner Classic Movies; Turner Network TV; TV Land; USA Network; VH1.

Digital Basic Service

Subscribers: N.A.

Programming (via satellite): BBC America; Bio; Bloomberg Television; Discovery Fit & Health; DIY Network; ESPNews; Fox Sports World; Fuse; G4; Golf Channel; GSN; Halogen Network; History Channel International; Music Choice; Outdoor Channel; SoapNet; Speed; Toon Disney; Trinity Broadcasting Network; Versus; WE tv.

Digital Expanded Basic Service

Subscribers: N.A.

Programming (via satellite): National Geographic Channel; Style Network.

Pay Service 1

Pay Units: N.A.

Programming (via satellite): Cinemax; HBO; Showtime; The Movie Channel.

Digital Pay Service 1

Pay Units: N.A.

Programming (via satellite): ART America; Canales N; CCTV-4; Cinemax; Encore (multiplexed); Filipino Channel; Flix; HBO (multiplexed); RAI USA; Showtime (multiplexed); Starz (multiplexed); The Movie Channel (multiplexed); TV Asia; TV Japan; TV5, La Television International; Zee TV USA; Zhong Tian Channel.

Video-On-Demand: Yes

Pay-Per-View

iN DEMAND; Fresh (delivered digitally); Playboy TV (delivered digitally); Movies (delivered digitally).

Internet Service

Operational: Yes.

Subscribers: 1,000.

Broadband Service: Comcast High Speed Internet.
Fee: $42.95 monthly.
Telephone Service
Digital: Operational
Miles of plant included in Greeneville, TN
Technical Operations Director: Tim Castor. Chief Technician: Eddie Handy. Marketing Coordinator: Debbie Frost. Office Manager: Ann Rouse.
Ownership: Comcast Cable Communications Inc. (MSO).

RADFORD—Shentel, 60 Long Ridge Rd, Ste 404, Stamford, CT 6902. Phones: 540-984-5224; 800-743-6835. Web Site: http://www.shentel.net. Also serves Christiansburg, Fairlawn, Montgomery County & Pulaski County (portions). ICA: VA0029.
TV Market Ranking: 70 (Christiansburg, Fairlawn, Montgomery County, Pulaski County (portions), RADFORD); Below 100 (Pulaski County (portions)); Outside TV Markets (Pulaski County (portions)). Franchise award date: N.A. Franchise expiration date: N.A. Began: January 1, 1970.
Channel capacity: N.A. Channels available but not in use: N.A.
Basic Service
Subscribers: 10,000.
Programming (received off-air): WBRA-TV (PBS) Roanoke; WDBJ (CBS, MNT) Roanoke; WDRL-TV (IND) Danville; WFXR (CW, FOX) Roanoke; WPXR-TV (ION) Roanoke; WSET-TV (ABC) Lynchburg; WSLS-TV (NBC) Roanoke; allband FM.
Programming (via satellite): C-SPAN; INSP; QVC; TBS Superstation; Trinity Broadcasting Network; TV Guide Network; WGN America.
Fee: $29.95 installation; $7.83 monthly; $1.12 converter.
Expanded Basic Service 1
Subscribers: 9,844.
Programming (via satellite): A&E Networks; ABC Family Channel; AMC; Animal Planet; BET Networks; Bravo; Cartoon Network; CNBC; CNN; Comcast SportsNet Mid-Atlantic; Comedy Central; Country Music TV; Discovery Channel; Disney Channel; ESPN; ESPN 2; Fox News Channel; FX; Headline News; HGTV; History Channel; Lifetime; MSNBC; MTV; Nickelodeon; Speed; Spike TV; Syfy; The Learning Channel; The Weather Channel; Travel Channel; Turner Classic Movies; Turner Network TV; TV Land; USA Network; VH1.
Fee: $29.95 installation; $20.66 monthly.
Digital Basic Service
Subscribers: 2,541.
Programming (via satellite): BBC America; Bio; Discovery Digital Networks; DIY Network; GAS; History Channel International; Lifetime Movie Network; MTV Networks Digital Suite; Music Choice; Nick Jr.; Nick Too; Sundance Channel.
Fee: $9.95 monthly.
Digital Pay Service 1
Pay Units: 717.
Programming (via satellite): Cinemax (multiplexed).
Digital Pay Service 2
Pay Units: 966.
Programming (via satellite): HBO (multiplexed).
Fee: $10.00 monthly.
Digital Pay Service 3
Pay Units: 589.
Programming (via satellite): The Movie Channel (multiplexed).
Fee: $5.95 monthly.
Digital Pay Service 4
Pay Units: 633.
Programming (via satellite): Flix; Showtime (multiplexed).
Fee: $7.00 monthly.
Video-On-Demand: No
Pay-Per-View
Addressable homes: 2,541.
Hot Choice (delivered digitally); iN DEMAND (delivered digitally); Fresh (delivered digitally).
Internet Service
Operational: Yes.
Subscribers: 300.
Broadband Service: JetBroadband.
Fee: $49.95 installation; $29.95 monthly.
Telephone Service
None
Miles of Plant: 300.0 (coaxial); 8.0 (fiber optic).
President: Christopher French. Vice President, Customer Service: David Ferguson. Marketing Manager: Chris Ranson.
Ownership: Shenandoah Telecommunications Inc. (MSO).

REDWOOD—Suddenlink Communications, 613 2nd St, Radford, VA 24141. Phones: 540-639-0021; 866-472-2200. Fax: 540-731-4289. Web Site: http://www.suddenlink.com. Also serves Bedford, Bedford County (southwestern portion), Boones Mill, Ferrum, Franklin County, Gladehill, Moneta, Penhook, Pittsylvania County (northwestern portion), Rocky Mount, Scruggs, Smith Mountain Lake, Union Hall & Wirtz. ICA: VA0033.
TV Market Ranking: 70 (Bedford, Bedford County, Boones Mill, Ferrum, Franklin County, Gladehill, Moneta, Penhook, Pittsylvania County (northwestern portion) (portions), REDWOOD, Rocky Mount, Scruggs, Smith Mountain Lake, Union Hall, Wirtz); Below 100 (Pittsylvania County (northwestern portion) (portions)); Outside TV Markets (Pittsylvania County (northwestern portion) (portions)). Franchise award date: January 1, 1987. Franchise expiration date: N.A. Began: November 1, 1988.
Channel capacity: N.A. Channels available but not in use: N.A.
Basic Service
Subscribers: 11,080.
Programming (received off-air): WBRA-TV (PBS) Roanoke; WDBJ (CBS, MNT) Roanoke; WDRL-TV (IND) Danville; WFXR (CW, FOX) Roanoke; WPXR-TV (ION) Roanoke; WSET-TV (ABC) Lynchburg; WSLS-TV (NBC) Roanoke.
Programming (via satellite): A&E Networks; ABC Family Channel; AMC; Animal Planet; BET Networks; Cartoon Network; CNBC; CNN; Comcast SportsNet Mid-Atlantic; Comedy Central; Country Music TV; C-SPAN; Discovery Channel; Disney Channel; E! Entertainment Television; ESPN; ESPN 2; Fox News Channel; FX; GSN; Headline News; HGTV; History Channel; Lifetime; MTV; Nickelodeon; QVC; Spike TV; Syfy; TBS Superstation; The Learning Channel; The Weather Channel; Travel Channel; Trinity Broadcasting Network; Turner Classic Movies; Turner Network TV; TV Guide Network; TV Land; USA Network; VH1; WGN America.
Fee: $20.00 installation; $26.90 monthly.
Digital Basic Service
Subscribers: N.A.
Programming (via satellite): DMX Music; Encore Action; ESPN Classic Sports; ESPNews; Golf Channel; Speed; Versus; WE tv.
Digital Pay Service 1
Pay Units: N.A.
Programming (via satellite): Cinemax (multiplexed); HBO (multiplexed).
Fee: $10.00 installation; $9.00 monthly (Cinemax), $9.50 monthly (HBO).
Video-On-Demand: No
Pay-Per-View
iN DEMAND (delivered digitally); Playboy TV (delivered digitally).
Internet Service
Operational: Yes.
Broadband Service: Suddenlink High Speed Internet.
Fee: $49.95 installation; $29.99 monthly.
Telephone Service
None
Miles of Plant: 537.0 (coaxial); 78.0 (fiber optic). Additional miles planned: 20.0 (coaxial).
Vice President, Operations: David Bach. General Manager: Jack Ozminkowski. Technical Operations Director: Bob Legg. Marketing Director: Stan Howell. Marketing Manager: Kenny Phillips. Office Manager: Kay Hauschildt.
Ownership: Cequel Communications LLC (MSO).

RESTON—Comcast Cable, 11101 University Blvd, Manassas, VA 20110. Phone: 703-789-8100. Fax: 703-789-8280. Web Site: http://www.comcast.com. ICA: VA0017.
TV Market Ranking: 9 (RESTON). Franchise award date: N.A. Franchise expiration date: N.A. Began: January 1, 1970.
Channel capacity: N.A. Channels available but not in use: N.A.
Basic Service
Subscribers: 18,817.
Programming (received off-air): WDCA (MNT) Washington; WDCW (CW) Washington; WETA-TV (PBS) Washington; WFDC-DT (UNV) Arlington; WHUT-TV (PBS) Washington; WJLA-TV (ABC) Washington; WMDO-CA (TEL) Washington; WMPT (PBS) Annapolis; WPXW-TV (ION) Manassas; WRC-TV (NBC) Washington; WTTG (FOX) Washington; WUSA (CBS) Washington; allband FM.
Programming (via microwave): NewsChannel 8.
Programming (via satellite): ABC Family Channel; C-SPAN; C-SPAN 2; QVC; Telemundo; USA Network; WGN America.
Fee: $40.32 installation; $12.82 monthly.
Expanded Basic Service 1
Subscribers: 3,403.
Programming (via satellite): A&E Networks; AMC; Animal Planet; BET Networks; Bravo; Cartoon Network; CNBC; CNN; Comcast SportsNet Mid-Atlantic; Comedy Central; Discovery Channel; Discovery Health Channel; Disney Channel; E! Entertainment Television; ESPN; ESPN 2; Food Network; Fox News Channel; FX; Golf Channel; Great American Country; GSN; Headline News; HGTV; History Channel; Lifetime; MSNBC; MTV; Music Choice; Nickelodeon; Product Information Network; Speed; Spike TV; Style Network; Syfy; TBS Superstation; The Learning Channel; The Weather Channel; Travel Channel; truTV; Turner Classic Movies; Turner Network TV; TV Guide Network; TV Land; TV One; Versus; VH1.
Fee: $15.00 installation; $11.49 monthly.
Digital Basic Service
Subscribers: N.A.
Programming (via satellite): AMC; BBC America; Bio; CBS Sports Network; Comcast/Charter Sports Southeast (CSS); Cooking Channel; Country Music TV; C-SPAN 3; DIY Network; Encore (multiplexed); ESPN; ESPNews; Flix (multiplexed); FSN Digital Atlantic; FSN Digital Central; FSN Digital Pacific; G4; GAS; GolTV; GSN; HD Theater; History Channel International; HRTV; INHD (multiplexed); Lifetime Movie Network; LOGO; Mid-Atlantic Sports Network; MoviePlex; MTV Networks Digital Suite; National Geographic Channel; NBA TV; NFL Network; Nick Jr.; Nick Too; NickToons TV; PBS Kids Sprout; SoapNet; Sundance Channel (multiplexed); Tennis Channel; Toon Disney; Turner Network TV HD; TV Guide Network; TVG Network; WAM! America's Kidz Network; Weatherscan.
Pay Service 1
Pay Units: 11,094.
Programming (via satellite): HBO; Showtime.
Fee: $25.00 installation; $11.50 monthly (each).
Digital Pay Service 1
Pay Units: N.A.
Programming (via satellite): Cinemax (multiplexed); Cinemax HD; HBO (multiplexed); HBO HD; Showtime (multiplexed); Showtime HD; Starz (multiplexed); Starz HDTV; The Movie Channel (multiplexed).
Video-On-Demand: Yes
Pay-Per-View
iN DEMAND; Fresh; Hot Choice (delivered digitally); Playboy TV (delivered digitally); iN DEMAND (delivered digitally); Fresh (delivered digitally); Shorteez (delivered digitally); Pleasure (delivered digitally); Barker (delivered digitally).
Internet Service
Operational: Yes.
Broadband Service: Comcast High Speed Internet.
Fee: $42.95 monthly; $7.00 modem lease.
Telephone Service
Digital: Operational
Fee: $44.95 monthly
Miles of Plant: 144.0 (coaxial); None (fiber optic).
Vice President & General Manager: Christine Whitaker. Technical Operations Director: Scott Shelly. Marketing Director: Shawn Houston.
Ownership: Comcast Cable Communications Inc. (MSO).

RICHLANDS—Time Warner Cable, 1430 2nd St, Richlands, VA 24641-2455. Phone: 276-964-1150. Fax: 276-596-9046. Web Site: http://www.timewarnercable.com. Also serves Bandy, Bishop, Cedar Bluff, Doran, Gratton, North Tazewell, Paint Lick, Pounding Mill, Raven, Red Ash, Royal City, Steelburg, Swords Creek, Tazewell, Tiptop & Wardell. ICA: VA0041.
TV Market Ranking: Below 100 (Bandy, Bishop, Cedar Bluff, Gratton, North Tazewell, Paint Lick, Pounding Mill, Raven, Red Ash, RICHLANDS, Royal City, Tazewell, Tiptop, Wardell); Outside TV Markets (Doran, Steelburg, Swords Creek). Franchise award date: N.A. Franchise expiration date: N.A. Began: January 1, 1952.
Channel capacity: N.A. Channels available but not in use: N.A.
Basic Service
Subscribers: 8,949.
Programming (received off-air): WCYB-TV (CW, NBC) Bristol; WDBJ (CBS, MNT) Roanoke; WKPT-TV (ABC) Kingsport; WLFG (IND) Grundy; WOAY-TV (ABC) Oak Hill; WSBN-TV (PBS) Norton; WVVA (CW, NBC) Bluefield; allband FM.

Programming (via satellite): Concert TV; QVC.
Fee: $49.95 installation; $19.95 monthly; $3.25 converter.

Expanded Basic Service 1
Subscribers: 4,394.
Programming (via satellite): A&E Networks; ABC Family Channel; AMC; Animal Planet; BET Networks; Bravo; Cartoon Network; CNBC; CNN; Comcast SportsNet Mid-Atlantic; Comedy Central; Country Music TV; C-SPAN; C-SPAN 2; Discovery Channel; Disney Channel; E! Entertainment Television; ESPN; Food Network; FX; Hallmark Channel; Headline News; Lifetime; MTV; Nickelodeon; Oxygen; ShopNBC; Spike TV; TBS Superstation; The Learning Channel; The Weather Channel; Travel Channel; truTV; Turner Network TV; USA Network; VH1.
Fee: $27.25 monthly.

Digital Basic Service
Subscribers: 4,312.
Programming (via satellite): BBC America; Bloomberg Television; Discovery Fit & Health; ESPN 2; ESPN Classic Sports; ESPNews; Fox Movie Channel; Fox Sports World; G4; Golf Channel; GSN; Halogen Network; HGTV; History Channel; Independent Film Channel; Lifetime Movie Network; Music Choice; National Geographic Channel; Nick Jr.; NickToons TV; Outdoor Channel; Speed; Syfy; Toon Disney; Trinity Broadcasting Network; Turner Classic Movies; TV Land; Versus; VH1 Classic; VH1 Country; WE tv.
Fee: $6.00 monthly (per tier).

Digital Pay Service 1
Pay Units: N.A.
Programming (via satellite): Cinemax (multiplexed); Encore; HBO (multiplexed); Showtime (multiplexed); The Movie Channel (multiplexed).
Fee: $12.00 monthly (each).

Video-On-Demand: No

Pay-Per-View
Movies & Events (delivered digitally); Sports PPV (delivered digitally); Urban American Television Network (delivered digitally); Hot Choice (delivered digitally); Shorteez (delivered digitally); Fresh (delivered digitally); Playboy TV (delivered digitally).

Internet Service
Operational: Yes.
Subscribers: 1,581.
Broadband Service: Road Runner.
Fee: $44.95 monthly.

Telephone Service
Digital: Planned

Miles of Plant: 437.0 (coaxial); None (fiber optic).

General Manager: C. K. Allen. Marketing Manager: Mark Cole. Chief Technician: Danny Nelson.

Ownership: Time Warner Cable (MSO).

RICHMOND—Comcast Cable, 5401 Staples Mill Rd, Richmond, VA 23228. Phones: 804-915-5400; 804-743-1171. Fax: 804-915-5424. Web Site: http://www.comcast.com. Also serves Ashland, Chesterfield County, Goochland, Goochland County, Hanover County (portions), Henrico County (portions), Louisa, Louisa County & Mineral. ICA: VA0004.

TV Market Ranking: 63 (Ashland, Chesterfield County, Goochland, Goochland County (portions), Hanover County (portions), Henrico County (portions), Louisa County (portions), RICHMOND); Below 100 (Louisa, Mineral, Goochland County (portions), Louisa County (portions)). Franchise award date: January 1, 1978. Franchise expiration date: N.A. Began: June 25, 1980.

Channel capacity: 78 (operating 2-way). Channels available but not in use: N.A.

Basic Service
Subscribers: 285,000 Includes Amelia Co., Charles City Co., Dillwyn, Emporia, Mathews, Northumberland Co., Petersburg, Powhatan, & Westmoreland Co..
Programming (received off-air): WCVE-TV (PBS) Richmond; WCVW (PBS) Richmond; WRIC-TV (ABC) Petersburg; WRLH-TV (FOX, MNT) Richmond; WTVR-TV (CBS) Richmond; WUPV (CW) Ashland; WWBT (NBC) Richmond; allband FM.
Programming (via satellite): C-SPAN; C-SPAN 2; QVC; The Comcast Network; TV Guide Network; WGN America.
Fee: $51.34 installation; $12.25 monthly.

Expanded Basic Service 1
Subscribers: N.A.
Programming (via satellite): A&E Networks; ABC Family Channel; AMC; Animal Planet; BET Networks; Bravo; Cartoon Network; CNBC; CNN; Comcast SportsNet Mid-Atlantic; Comedy Central; Country Music TV; Discovery Channel; Discovery Health Channel; Disney Channel; E! Entertainment Television; ESPN; ESPN 2; Food Network; Fox News Channel; FX; Golf Channel; Great American Country; GSN; Hallmark Channel; Headline News; HGTV; History Channel; ION Television; Lifetime; MSNBC; MTV; Nickelodeon; Oxygen; Speed; Spike TV; Style Network; TBS Superstation; The Learning Channel; The Weather Channel; Toon Disney; Travel Channel; truTV; Turner Classic Movies; Turner Network TV; TV Land; TV One; Univision Studios; USA Network; Versus; VH1.
Fee: $40.20 monthly.

Digital Basic Service
Subscribers: 133,000 Includes Amelia Co., Charles City Co., Dillwyn, Emporia, Mathews, Northumberland Co., Petersburg, Powhatan, & Westmoreland Co..
Programming (via satellite): BBC America; Bio; Black Family Channel; Bloomberg Television; Canales N; CBS Sports Network; CMT Pure Country; Cooking Channel; Country Music TV; Current; DIY Network; Encore (multiplexed); ESPN 2 HD; ESPN Classic Sports; ESPN HD; ESPNews; Eternal Word TV Network; EWTN HD; FamilyNet; Flix; Fox College Sports Atlantic; Fox College Sports Central; Fox College Sports Pacific; Fox Movie Channel; Fox Reality Channel; Fox Soccer; Fuse; G4; GAS; GMC; GolTV; Great American Country; GSN; Halogen Network; HD Theater; History Channel International; Independent Film Channel; INHD; INSP; Lifetime Movie Network; LOGO; Mid-Atlantic Sports Network; MoviePlex; MTV Networks Digital Suite; Music Choice; MyNetworkTV Inc.; National Geographic Channel; NBA TV; NFL Network; Nick Jr.; Nick Too; NickToons TV; Outdoor Channel; Ovation; Palladia; PBS Kids Sprout; ShopNBC; SoapNet; Sundance Channel; Syfy; Tennis Channel; The Word Network; Trinity Broadcasting Network; Turner Network TV HD; TVG Network; Universal HD; Versus HD; WE tv; Weatherscan.
Fee: $16.15 monthly.

Pay Service 1
Pay Units: 38,830.
Programming (via satellite): HBO.
Fee: $15.00 installation; $9.95 monthly.

Digital Pay Service 1
Pay Units: N.A.
Programming (via satellite): BabyFirstTV; Cinemax (multiplexed); Cinemax HD; HBO (multiplexed); HBO HD; Playboy TV; Showtime (multiplexed); Showtime HD; Starz (multiplexed); Starz HDTV; The Movie Channel (multiplexed).
Fee: $17.35 monthly (each).

Video-On-Demand: Yes

Pay-Per-View
Addressable homes: 25,887.
iN DEMAND (delivered digitally); iN DEMAND; ESPN Gameplan (delivered digitally); Fresh (delivered digitally); Playboy TV (delivered digitally); NBA League Pass (delivered digitally); MLS Direct Kick (delivered digitally); NHL Center Ice (delivered digitally).

Internet Service
Operational: Yes.
Subscribers: 133,000.
Broadband Service: Comcast High Speed Internet.
Fee: $49.00 installation; $42.95 monthly; $249.00 modem purchase.

Telephone Service
Digital: Operational

Miles of Plant: 731.0 (coaxial); None (fiber optic).

Technical Operations Director: Stephen Hill. Marketing Director: Erin Powell. Marketing Coordinator: Dana Hughes. Public Relations Manager: Monica Smith-Callahan.

Ownership: Comcast Cable Communications Inc. (MSO).

RICHMOND—Formerly served by NTELOS. No longer in operation. ICA: VA0181.

RIVER OAKS—Comcast Cable. Now served by PRINCE WILLIAM COUNTY (formerly Manassas), VA [VA0148]. ICA: VA0178.

ROANOKE—Cox Communications, 5400 Fallowater Ln, Roanoke, VA 24036. Phones: 540-776-3848 (Customer service); 540-776-3845. Fax: 540-776-3849. Web Site: http://www.cox.com/roanoke. Also serves Roanoke County & Vinton. ICA: VA0007.

TV Market Ranking: 70 (ROANOKE, Roanoke County, Vinton). Franchise award date: January 20, 1975. Franchise expiration date: N.A. Began: November 18, 1976.

Channel capacity: N.A. Channels available but not in use: N.A.

Basic Service
Subscribers: 56,557.
Programming (received off-air): WBRA-TV (PBS) Roanoke; WDBJ (CBS, MNT) Roanoke; WDRL-TV (IND) Danville; WFXR (CW, FOX) Roanoke; WPXR-TV (ION) Roanoke; WSET-TV (ABC) Lynchburg; WSLS-TV (NBC) Roanoke; 8 FMs.
Programming (via satellite): C-SPAN; C-SPAN 2; QVC; TBS Superstation; WGN America.
Fee: $38.95 installation; $10.25 monthly; $1.15 converter; $16.71 additional installation.

Expanded Basic Service 1
Subscribers: N.A.
Programming (via satellite): A&E Networks; ABC Family Channel; AMC; Animal Planet; BET Networks; Bravo; Cartoon Network; CNBC; CNN; Comcast SportsNet Mid-Atlantic; Comedy Central; Country Music TV; Discovery Channel; Discovery Health Channel; Disney Channel; E! Entertainment Television; ESPN; ESPN 2; Food Network; Fox News Channel; FX; Hallmark Channel; Headline News; HGTV; History Channel; INSP; Lifetime; MSNBC; MTV; Nickelodeon; Oxygen; Product Information Network; Shop at Home; ShopNBC; Sneak Prevue; Speed; Spike TV; Syfy; The Learning Channel; The Weather Channel; Travel Channel; Trinity Broadcasting Network; truTV; Turner Network TV; TV Land; USA Network; Versus; VH1.
Fee: $18.99 installation; $32.04 monthly.

Digital Basic Service
Subscribers: 9,319.
Programming (via satellite): BBC America; Bio; Black Family Channel; Bloomberg Television; Discovery Digital Networks; ESPN Classic Sports; ESPNews; Eternal Word TV Network; Fox Sports World; G4; Golf Channel; Great American Country; GSN; Halogen Network; History Channel International; Independent Film Channel; Lifetime Movie Network; Mid-Atlantic Sports Network; MuchMusic Network; Music Choice; SoapNet; Sundance Channel; The Word Network; Toon Disney; Turner Classic Movies; Univision Studios.
Fee: $7.95 monthly.

Pay Service 1
Pay Units: 5,233.
Programming (via satellite): Cinemax (multiplexed).
Fee: $10.95 monthly.

Pay Service 2
Pay Units: 16,568.
Programming (via satellite): HBO (multiplexed).
Fee: $10.95 monthly.

Pay Service 3
Pay Units: 4,953.
Programming (via satellite): Showtime (multiplexed).
Fee: $10.95 monthly.

Pay Service 4
Pay Units: 3,517.
Programming (via satellite): Encore; Starz.
Fee: $10.95 monthly.

Pay Service 5
Pay Units: N.A.
Programming (via satellite): The Movie Channel.
Fee: $10.95 monthly.

Digital Pay Service 1
Pay Units: 1,541.
Programming (via satellite): Cinemax (multiplexed); Encore (multiplexed); Flix; HBO (multiplexed); Showtime (multiplexed); Starz (multiplexed); Sundance Channel; The Movie Channel (multiplexed).
Fee: $11.95 monthly (Cinemax, HBO, Flix/Showtime/Sundance/TMC, or Starz/Encore).

Video-On-Demand: Yes

Pay-Per-View
Addressable homes: 26,115.
TVN Entertainment; ESPN Now (delivered digitally); iN DEMAND (delivered digitally); Playboy TV (delivered digitally); Fresh (delivered digitally); sports (delivered digitally).
Internet Service
Operational: Yes.
Subscribers: 735.
Broadband Service: Cox High Speed Internet.
Fee: $49.95 installation; $39.95 monthly; $10.00 modem lease; $39.95 modem purchase.
Telephone Service
Digital: Operational
Fee: $12.20 monthly
Miles of Plant: 1,136.0 (coaxial); 231.0 (fiber optic).
General Manager: Marilyn Burrows. Technical Operations Director: Rick Neilson. Marketing Director: Jodi Muller-Stotser. Public Relations Director: Mike Pedelty.
Ownership: Cox Communications Inc. (MSO).

ROANOKE—Formerly served by NTELOS. No longer in operation. ICA: VA0173.

ROCKINGHAM—Formerly served by Adelphia Communications. Now served by HARRISONBURG, VA [VA0016]. ICA: VA0151.

ROSEDALE—Cable Plus, 5162 Redbud Hwy, PO Box 1030, Honaker, VA 24260-1030. Phones: 866-670-4828; 276-873-4828. Fax: 276-873-4882. E-mail: officestaff@cableplus.tv. Web Site: http://www.cableplus.tv. Also serves Belfast Mills & Breaks Interstate Park. ICA: VA0161.
TV Market Ranking: Below 100 (Belfast Mills, Breaks Interstate Park, ROSEDALE). Franchise award date: N.A. Franchise expiration date: N.A. Began: June 1, 1977.
Channel capacity: 28 (not 2-way capable). Channels available but not in use: N.A.
Basic Service
Subscribers: N.A.
Programming (received off-air): WAPK-CA (MNT) Kingsport; WCYB-TV (CW, NBC) Bristol; WEMT (FOX) Greeneville; WJDW-LP Tazewell; WJHL-TV (CBS) Johnson City; WKPT-TV (ABC) Kingsport; WSBN-TV (PBS) Norton; WVVA (CW, NBC) Bluefield.
Programming (via satellite): A&E Networks; ABC Family Channel; Animal Planet; Bravo; Cartoon Network; CNBC; CNN; Comcast/Charter Sports Southeast (CSS); Comedy Central; Country Music TV; C-SPAN; Discovery Channel; Disney Channel; E! Entertainment Television; ESPN; ESPN 2; ESPN Classic Sports; Food Network; Fox News Channel; FX; GMC; Golf Channel; Hallmark Channel; Headline News; HGTV; History Channel; ION Television; Lifetime; MSNBC; MTV; National Geographic Channel; NFL Network; Nickelodeon; Outdoor Channel; Oxygen; QVC; RFD-TV; Speed; Spike TV; Syfy; TBS Superstation; The Learning Channel; The Weather Channel; Toon Disney; Travel Channel; Trinity Broadcasting Network; Turner Classic Movies; Turner Network TV; TV Land; USA Network; VH1; WE tv; WGN America.
Pay Service 1
Pay Units: N.A.
Programming (via satellite): Cinemax; Encore; HBO; Showtime; The Movie Channel.
Video-On-Demand: No
Internet Service
Operational: Yes.
Fee: $29.95 monthly.
Telephone Service
None
Miles of Plant: 3.0 (coaxial); None (fiber optic).
Manager: Jody Eaton.
Ownership: Cable Plus.

RUCKERSVILLE—Comcast Cable, 400 Westfield Rd, Charlottesville, VA 22901. Phone: 434-951-3700. Fax: 434-951-3705. Web Site: http://www.comcast.com. Also serves Barboursville, Greene County & Stanardsville. ICA: VA0067.
TV Market Ranking: Below 100 (Barboursville, Greene County, RUCKERSVILLE, Stanardsville).
Channel capacity: N.A. Channels available but not in use: N.A.
Basic Service
Subscribers: 3,387.
Programming (received off-air): WAHU-CD Charlottesville; WAHU-LD Charlottesville; WCAV (CBS) Charlottesville; WHTJ (PBS) Charlottesville; WRIC-TV (ABC) Petersburg; WTTG (FOX) Washington; WTVR-TV (CBS) Richmond; WVAW-LD Charlottesville; WVIR-TV (CW, NBC) Charlottesville; WVPT (PBS) Staunton; WWBT (NBC) Richmond.
Programming (via satellite): C-SPAN; QVC; ShopNBC; The Comcast Network; Trinity Broadcasting Network; Weatherscan; WeatherVision.
Expanded Basic Service 1
Subscribers: N.A.
Programming (via satellite): A&E Networks; ABC Family Channel; AMC; Animal Planet; BET Networks; Bravo; Cartoon Network; CNBC; CNN; Comcast SportsNet Mid-Atlantic; Comedy Central; Country Music TV; C-SPAN 2; Discovery Channel; Disney Channel; E! Entertainment Television; ESPN; ESPN 2; Eternal Word TV Network; Food Network; Fox News Channel; FX; Golf Channel; Hallmark Channel; Headline News; HGTV; History Channel; Lifetime; MSNBC; MTV; Nickelodeon; Oxygen; Spike TV; Syfy; TBS Superstation; The Learning Channel; The Weather Channel; Travel Channel; truTV; Turner Classic Movies; Turner Network TV; TV Guide Network; TV Land; USA Network; Versus; VH1.
Digital Basic Service
Subscribers: N.A.
Programming (via satellite): A&E HD; Animal Planet HD; AZ TV; BBC America; Bio; Bloomberg Television; Canales N; CNN HD; College Sports Television; Comcast SportsNet Mid-Atlantic; Current; Discovery Channel HD; Discovery Fit & Health; DIY Network; ESPN 2 HD; ESPN Classic Sports; ESPN HD; ESPNews; Flix; Food Network HD; Fox Movie Channel; Fox Soccer; Fuel TV; Fuse; G4; GMC; Great American Country; GSN; Halogen Network; HD Theater; HGTV HD; History Channel HD; Independent Film Channel; Lifetime Movie Network; Military Channel; Music Choice; National Geographic Channel; National Geographic Channel HD Network; NFL Network; Outdoor Channel; Palladia; PBS Kids Sprout; SoapNet; Speed; Style Network; Sundance Channel; Syfy HD; TBS in HD; Tennis Channel; The Learning Channel; The Word Network; Toon Disney; Tr3s; Turner Network TV HD; Universal HD; USA Network HD; Versus HD; WE tv.
Digital Pay Service 1
Pay Units: N.A.
Programming (via satellite): Cinemax (multiplexed); Cinemax HD; Encore (multiplexed); HBO (multiplexed); HBO HD; Showtime (multiplexed); Showtime HD; Starz (multiplexed); Starz HDTV; The Movie Channel (multiplexed).
Video-On-Demand: No
Pay-Per-View
iN DEMAND (delivered digitally); Playboy TV (delivered digitally); Spice: Xcess (delivered digitally).
Internet Service
Operational: Yes.
Broadband Service: Comcast High Speed Internet.
Fee: $42.95 monthly.
Telephone Service
Digital: Operational
Vice President & General Manager: Troy Fitzhugh. Technical Operations Director: Tom Jacobs. Marketing Director: Steve Miles.
Ownership: Comcast Cable Communications Inc. (MSO).

RURAL RETREAT—Rural Retreat Cable TV Inc., 228 Sage Rd, Rural Retreat, VA 24368-5996. Phone: 276-686-5242. Fax: 276-686-5242. ICA: VA0109.
TV Market Ranking: Below 100 (RURAL RETREAT). Franchise award date: N.A. Franchise expiration date: N.A. Began: January 1, 1976.
Channel capacity: 38 (not 2-way capable). Channels available but not in use: N.A.
Basic Service
Subscribers: 600.
Programming (received off-air): WBRA-TV (PBS) Roanoke; WCYB-TV (CW, NBC) Bristol; WDBJ (CBS, MNT) Roanoke; WFXR (CW, FOX) Roanoke; WJHL-TV (CBS) Johnson City; WKPT-TV (ABC) Kingsport; WLFG (IND) Grundy; WPXR-TV (ION) Roanoke; WSLS-TV (NBC) Roanoke; WVVA (CW, NBC) Bluefield.
Programming (via satellite): Country Music TV; CW+; QVC; TBS Superstation; The Weather Channel.
Fee: $10.00 installation; $15.45 monthly.
Expanded Basic Service 1
Subscribers: N.A.
Programming (via satellite): A&E Networks; ABC Family Channel; Cartoon Network; CNN; Discovery Channel; ESPN; ESPN 2; FX; HGTV; Lifetime; MTV; NASA TV; Outdoor Channel; Spike TV; The Learning Channel; Turner Classic Movies; Turner Network TV; TV Land; USA Network; WGN America.
Pay Service 1
Pay Units: 200.
Programming (via satellite): HBO.
Fee: $10.00 monthly.
Internet Service
Operational: No.
Telephone Service
None
Miles of Plant: 25.0 (coaxial); None (fiber optic).
Manager: James P. Sage.
Ownership: James P. Sage.

RUSTBURG—Shentel, 60 Long Ridge Rd, Ste 404, Stamford, CT 6902. Phones: 540-984-5224; 800-743-6835. Web Site: http://www.shentel.net. Also serves Alta Vista, Appomattox, Appomattox County (portions), Bedford County (northern portion), Clarion, Concord, Evington, Forest, Goode & Timberlake. ICA: VA0128.
TV Market Ranking: 70 (Alta Vista, Appomattox, Appomattox County (portions), Bedford County (northern portion), Clarion, Concord, Evington, Forest, Goode, RUSTBURG, Timberlake). Franchise award date: N.A. Franchise expiration date: N.A. Began: December 1, 1984.
Channel capacity: N.A. Channels available but not in use: N.A.
Basic Service
Subscribers: 9,619.
Programming (received off-air): WBRA-TV (PBS) Roanoke; WDBJ (CBS, MNT) Roanoke; WDRL-TV (IND) Danville; WFXR (CW, FOX) Roanoke; WPXR-TV (ION) Roanoke; WSET-TV (ABC) Lynchburg; WSLS-TV (NBC) Roanoke; WWCW (CW, FOX) Lynchburg.
Programming (via satellite): WGN America.
Fee: $49.95 installation; $19.95 monthly.
Expanded Basic Service 1
Subscribers: N.A.
Programming (via satellite): A&E Networks; ABC Family Channel; AMC; Animal Planet; BET Networks; Bravo; Cartoon Network; CNBC; CNN; Comcast SportsNet Mid-Atlantic; Comedy Central; Country Music TV; C-SPAN; Discovery Channel; Disney Channel; E! Entertainment Television; ESPN; ESPN 2; Food Network; Fox Movie Channel; Fox News Channel; FX; Golf Channel; Great American Country; Hallmark Channel; Headline News; HGTV; History Channel; Lifetime; MSNBC; MTV; National Geographic Channel; Nickelodeon; Outdoor Channel; QVC; Speed; Spike TV; Syfy; TBS Superstation; The Learning Channel; The Weather Channel; Toon Disney; Travel Channel; Trinity Broadcasting Network; truTV; Turner Classic Movies; Turner Network TV; TV Land; USA Network; VH1.
Fee: $14.00 monthly.
Digital Basic Service
Subscribers: 1,925.
Programming (via satellite): BBC America; Bio; cloo; CMT Pure Country; Discovery Digital Networks; DIY Network; DMX Music; ESPN Classic Sports; ESPN U; ESPNews; Fox Soccer; Fuse; G4; GAS; GSN; History Channel International; Independent Film Channel; Lifetime Movie Network; Nick Jr.; NickToons TV; Oxygen; SoapNet; Versus.
Fee: $14.95 monthly.
Digital Pay Service 1
Pay Units: N.A.
Programming (via satellite): Cinemax (multiplexed); Encore (multiplexed); Flix; HBO (multiplexed); Showtime (multiplexed); Starz (multiplexed); The Movie Channel (multiplexed).
Fee: $11.95 monthly (Cinemax or Starz/Encore), $12.95 monthly (HBO or Showtime/TMC).
Video-On-Demand: Planned
Pay-Per-View
iN DEMAND (delivered digitally); Hot Choice (delivered digitally); Ten Blue (delivered digitally); Ten Blox (delivered digitally); Ten Clips (delivered digitally).
Internet Service
Operational: Yes.
Broadband Service: JetBroadband.
Fee: $49.95 installation; $29.95 monthly; $5.00 modem lease.
Telephone Service
Digital: Planned
Miles of Plant: 672.0 (coaxial); 60.0 (fiber optic).
President: Christopher French. Vice President, Customer Service: David Ferguson. Marketing Manager: Chris Ranson.
Ownership: Shenandoah Telecommunications Inc. (MSO).

RUTHER GLEN—Comcast Cable, 11101 University Blvd, Manassas, VA 20110. Phone: 703-789-8100. Fax: 703-789-8280. Web Site: http://www.comcast.com. Also serves Ladysmith & Woodford. ICA: VA0130.

TV Market Ranking: 63 (Ladysmith, RUTHER GLEN); Below 100 (Woodford). Franchise award date: N.A. Franchise expiration date: N.A. Began: October 1, 1989.

Channel capacity: 61 (2-way capable). Channels available but not in use: N.A.

Basic Service

Subscribers: 1,779.

Programming (received off-air): WCVE-TV (PBS) Richmond; WCVW (PBS) Richmond; WRIC-TV (ABC) Petersburg; WRLH-TV (FOX, MNT) Richmond; WTVR-TV (CBS) Richmond; WUPV (CW) Ashland; WWBT (NBC) Richmond.

Programming (via satellite): QVC; The Learning Channel.

Fee: $60.00 installation; $40.35 monthly.

Expanded Basic Service 1

Subscribers: N.A.

Programming (via satellite): A&E Networks; ABC Family Channel; AMC; Animal Planet; BET Networks; Cartoon Network; CNN; Comcast SportsNet Mid-Atlantic; Comedy Central; Country Music TV; C-SPAN; Discovery Channel; Disney Channel; ESPN; ESPN 2; HGTV; History Channel; Lifetime; Mid-Atlantic Sports Network; MTV; Nickelodeon; Spike TV; Syfy; TBS Superstation; The Weather Channel; truTV; Turner Classic Movies; Turner Network TV; TV Land; USA Network; VH1.

Fee: $12.15 monthly.

Pay Service 1

Pay Units: 1,068.

Programming (via satellite): Cinemax; Flix; HBO; Showtime; The Movie Channel.

Fee: $13.95 monthly (Cinemax, Showtime or TMC), $14.95 monthly (HBO).

Video-On-Demand: No

Pay-Per-View

Addressable homes: 712.

iN DEMAND; Hot Choice (delivered digitally); NBA TV (delivered digitally); Playboy TV (delivered digitally); Fresh (delivered digitally); Shorteez (delivered digitally); iN DEMAND (delivered digitally); Pleasure (delivered digitally); ESPN Now (delivered digitally); Sports PPV (delivered digitally); ESPN Extra (delivered digitally).

Internet Service

Operational: Yes.

Telephone Service

Digital: Operational

Vice President & General Manager: Christine Whitaker. Technical Operations Director: Scott Shelley. Marketing Director: Shawn Houston.

Ownership: Comcast Cable Communications Inc. (MSO).

SALEM—Comcast Cable, 21 S Bruffey St, Salem, VA 24153-4728. Phones: 434-951-3700 (Charlottesville office); 540-378-1160. Fax: 540-389-4338. Web Site: http://www.comcast.com. Also serves Roanoke County. ICA: VA0024.

TV Market Ranking: 70 (Roanoke County, SALEM). Franchise award date: January 1, 1969. Franchise expiration date: N.A. Began: July 1, 1970.

Channel capacity: N.A. Channels available but not in use: N.A.

Basic Service

Subscribers: 12,200.

Programming (received off-air): WBRA-TV (PBS) Roanoke; WDBJ (CBS, MNT) Roanoke; WDRL-TV (IND) Danville; WFXR (CW, FOX) Roanoke; WPXR-TV (ION) Roanoke; WSET-TV (ABC) Lynchburg; WSLS-TV (NBC) Roanoke; WWCW (CW, FOX) Lynchburg; 3 FMs.

Programming (via satellite): C-SPAN; C-SPAN 2; CW+; Product Information Network; QVC; TV Guide Network; WGN America.

Fee: $22.55 installation; $17.50 monthly.

Expanded Basic Service 1

Subscribers: 11,930.

Programming (via satellite): A&E Networks; ABC Family Channel; AMC; Animal Planet; BET Networks; Bravo; Cartoon Network; CNBC; CNN; Comcast SportsNet Mid-Atlantic; Comedy Central; Country Music TV; Discovery Channel; Disney Channel; E! Entertainment Television; ESPN; ESPN 2; Food Network; Fox News Channel; FX; Hallmark Channel; Headline News; HGTV; History Channel; Lifetime; MSNBC; MTV; Nickelodeon; Spike TV; Syfy; TBS Superstation; The Learning Channel; The Weather Channel; Travel Channel; Turner Network TV; TV Land; USA Network; VH1.

Fee: $22.75 installation; $37.20 monthly.

Digital Basic Service

Subscribers: 2,000.

Programming (received off-air): WBRA-TV (PBS) Roanoke.

Programming (via satellite): BBC America; Bio; Bloomberg Television; Canal 52MX; Cine Latino; CMT Pure Country; CNN en Espanol; College Sports Television; Current; Discovery en Espanol; Discovery Fit & Health; Discovery Health Channel; Discovery Home Channel; Discovery Kids Channel; DIY Network; Encore (multiplexed); ESPN 2 HD; ESPN Classic Sports; ESPN Deportes; ESPN HD; ESPNews; Eternal Word TV Network; Flix; Fox College Sports Atlantic; Fox College Sports Central; Fox College Sports Pacific; Fox Deportes; Fox Movie Channel; Fox Soccer; Fuel TV; Fuse; G4; GMC; Golf Channel; Great American Country; GSN; Halogen Network; HD Theater; History Channel en Espanol; History Channel International; ID Investigation Discovery; Independent Film Channel; Lifetime Movie Network; LOGO; Military Channel; MTV Hits; MTV Jams; MTV2; Music Choice; National Geographic Channel; NFL Network; NFL Network HD; Nick Jr.; Nick Too; NickToons TV; Outdoor Channel; Palladia; PBS Kids Sprout; Science; SoapNet; Speed; Style Network; Sundance Channel; TeenNick; Tennis Channel; The Word Network; Toon Disney; Toon Disney en Espanol; Tr3s; Trinity Broadcasting Network; Turner Classic Movies; Turner Network TV HD; TV One; Universal HD; VeneMovies; Versus; VH1 Classic; VH1 Soul; WAM! America's Kidz Network; WE tv.

Fee: $20.95 monthly.

Digital Pay Service 1

Pay Units: N.A.

Programming (via satellite): Cinemax (multiplexed); Cinemax HD; HBO (multiplexed); HBO HD; Showtime (multiplexed); Showtime HD; Starz (multiplexed); Starz HDTV; The Movie Channel (multiplexed).

Video-On-Demand: No

Pay-Per-View

iN DEMAND (delivered digitally); Playboy TV (delivered digitally); Spice: Xcess (delivered digitally).

Internet Service

Operational: Yes.

Broadband Service: Comcast High Speed Internet.

Fee: $42.95 monthly.

Telephone Service

Digital: Operational

Miles of Plant: 287.0 (coaxial); 40.0 (fiber optic). Additional miles planned: 15.0 (coaxial).

Vice President & General Manager: Troy Fitzhugh. Technical Operations Director: Tom Jacobs. Chief Technician: Rick Sturgill. Plant Manager: John Van Lew. Marketing Director: Steve Miles. Office Manager: Trudy McNew.

Ownership: Comcast Cable Communications Inc. (MSO).

SANDY RIDGE—Scott Telecom & Electronics, PO Box 489, Gate City, VA 24251-0489. Phone: 276-452-9119. Fax: 276-452-2447. E-mail: sctc@sctc.org. Web Site: http://www.sctc.org. ICA: VA0188.

TV Market Ranking: Below 100 (SANDY RIDGE). Franchise award date: N.A. Franchise expiration date: N.A. Began: N.A.

Channel capacity: 36 (not 2-way capable). Channels available but not in use: N.A.

Basic Service

Subscribers: 245.

Programming (received off-air): WCYB-TV (CW, NBC) Bristol; WEMT (FOX) Greeneville; WJHL-TV (CBS) Johnson City; WLFG (IND) Grundy; WSBN-TV (PBS) Norton.

Programming (via satellite): ABC Family Channel; Animal Planet; CNN; Country Music TV; Discovery Channel; Disney Channel; ESPN; Headline News; Spike TV; Syfy; TBS Superstation; Trinity Broadcasting Network; Turner Network TV; USA Network; WGN America.

Fee: $45.50 installation; $19.95 monthly.

Pay Service 1

Pay Units: N.A.

Programming (via satellite): The Movie Channel.

Fee: $12.00 monthly.

Video-On-Demand: No

Internet Service

Operational: No.

Telephone Service

None

Miles of Plant: 18.0 (coaxial); None (fiber optic).

Manager: William J. Franklin. Marketing Director: Greg Hood. Chief Technician: Terry Holt.

Ownership: Scott County Telephone Cooperative (MSO).

SCOTTSVILLE—Nelson Cable, 400 Front St, PO Box 395, Lovingston, VA 22949-0395. Phones: 800-376-8165; 434-263-4805. Fax: 804-263-4821. E-mail: joeleemc@aol.com. Web Site: http://www.nelsoncable.com. Also serves Albemarle County (portions), Buckingham County (portions) & Fluvanna County (portions). ICA: VA0111.

TV Market Ranking: 63 (Fluvanna County (portions)); 70 (Albemarle County (portions), Buckingham County (portions)); Below 100 (SCOTTSVILLE, Albemarle County (portions), Buckingham County (portions)); Outside TV Markets (Fluvanna County (portions), Buckingham County (portions)). Franchise award date: N.A. Franchise expiration date: N.A. Began: July 1, 1990.

Channel capacity: N.A. Channels available but not in use: N.A.

Basic Service

Subscribers: 104.

Programming (received off-air): WCVE-TV (PBS) Richmond; WRIC-TV (ABC) Petersburg; WRLH-TV (FOX, MNT) Richmond; WTVR-TV (CBS) Richmond; WVIR-TV (CW, NBC) Charlottesville; WWBT (NBC) Richmond.

Programming (via satellite): CNN; Discovery Channel; Disney Channel; ESPN; Hallmark Channel; Nickelodeon; Spike TV; TBS Superstation; Turner Network TV.

Fee: $26.00 monthly.

Pay Service 1

Pay Units: N.A.

Programming (via satellite): Cinemax; HBO.

Video-On-Demand: No

Internet Service

Operational: Yes.

Telephone Service

None

Miles of Plant: 10.0 (coaxial); None (fiber optic).

President: Joe Lee McClellan. Chief Technician: Terry Engelhardt.

Ownership: Nelson County Cablevision Corporation (MSO).

SHENANDOAH—Formerly served by Adelphia Communications. Now served by HARRISONBURG, VA [VA0016]. ICA: VA0060.

SOUTH BOSTON—Comcast Cable, 1711 Seymour Dr, PO Box 710, South Boston, VA 24592-0710. Phones: 434-951-3700; 434-575-5455. Fax: 434-575-5760. Web Site: http://www.timewarnercable.com. Also serves Halifax & Halifax County. ICA: VA0040.

TV Market Ranking: 70 (Halifax County (portions)); Below 100 (Halifax, SOUTH BOSTON, Halifax County (portions)); Outside TV Markets (Halifax County (portions)). Franchise award date: July 12, 1968. Franchise expiration date: February 3, 2007. Began: September 1, 1976.

Channel capacity: N.A. Channels available but not in use: N.A.

Basic Service

Subscribers: 4,148.

Programming (received off-air): WBRA-TV (PBS) Roanoke; WDBJ (CBS, MNT) Roanoke; WFXR (CW, FOX) Roanoke; WMYV (MNT) Greensboro; WPXR-TV (ION) Roanoke; WRAL-TV (CBS) Raleigh; WSET-TV (ABC) Lynchburg; WSLS-TV (NBC) Roanoke; WTVD (ABC) Durham; WUNP-TV (PBS) Roanoke Rapids.

Programming (via satellite): Concert TV; C-SPAN; QVC; TBS Superstation; WGN America.

Fee: $45.00 installation; $31.00 monthly; $3.25 converter.

Expanded Basic Service 1
Subscribers: N.A.
Programming (via satellite): A&E Networks; ABC Family Channel; AMC; Animal Planet; BET Networks; Bravo; Cartoon Network; CNBC; CNN; Comcast SportsNet Mid-Atlantic; Comedy Central; Country Music TV; Discovery Channel; Disney Channel; E! Entertainment Television; ESPN 2; Food Network; Fox News Channel; FX; Hallmark Channel; Headline News; HGTV; History Channel; INSP; MSNBC; Oxygen; Product Information Network; QVC; ShopNBC; Spike TV; Syfy; The Learning Channel; The Weather Channel; Travel Channel; truTV; Turner Network TV; TV Land.
Expanded Basic Service 2
Subscribers: N.A.
Programming (via satellite): ESPN; Lifetime; MTV; Nickelodeon; USA Network; VH1.
Digital Basic Service
Subscribers: 1,411.
Programming (via satellite): BBC America; Bio; Bloomberg Television; Discovery Fit & Health; DIY Network; ESPN Classic Sports; ESPNews; Fuse; G4; Golf Channel; GSN; Halogen Network; History Channel International; Outdoor Channel; SoapNet; Speed; Toon Disney; Trinity Broadcasting Network; Versus; WE tv.
Digital Expanded Basic Service
Subscribers: N.A.
Programming (via satellite): Fox Movie Channel; GAS; MTV Networks Digital Suite; Music Choice; National Geographic Channel; Nick Jr.; Nick Too; NickToons TV; Style Network.
Digital Pay Service 1
Pay Units: N.A.
Programming (via satellite): Cinemax (multiplexed); Encore (multiplexed); HBO (multiplexed); Showtime (multiplexed); Starz (multiplexed); The Movie Channel (multiplexed).
Video-On-Demand: No
Pay-Per-View
Fresh (delivered digitally); Playboy TV (delivered digitally).
Internet Service
Operational: Yes.
Subscribers: 614.
Broadband Service: Road Runner.
Fee: $42.95 monthly.
Telephone Service
Digital: Operational
Miles of Plant: 198.0 (coaxial); None (fiber optic).
Vice President & General Manager: Troy Fitzhugh. Marketing Director: Steve Miles. Technical Operations Manager: Mike Buckner. Technical Supervisor: Frank Berry. Office Manager: Kathy Thomas.
Ownership: Comcast Cable Communications Inc. (MSO).

SOUTH HILL—Comcast Cable, 1711 Seymour Dr, PO Box 710, South Boston, VA 24592-0710. Phones: 434-951-3700 (Charlottesville office); 434-575-5455. Fax: 434-575-5760. Web Site: http://www.comcast.com. Also serves Boydton, Chase City, La Crosse, Lunenburg County (portions), Mecklenburg County & Victoria. ICA: VA0062.
TV Market Ranking: Outside TV Markets (Boydton, Chase City, La Crosse, Lunenburg County (portions), Mecklenburg County, SOUTH HILL, Victoria). Franchise award date: July 1, 1968. Franchise expiration date: N.A. Began: March 1, 1977.
Channel capacity: N.A. Channels available but not in use: N.A.
Basic Service
Subscribers: 2,894.
Programming (received off-air): WCVE-TV (PBS) Richmond; WLFL (CW) Raleigh; WNCN (NBC) Goldsboro; WNVN-LP Roanoke Rapids; WRAL-TV (CBS) Raleigh; WRAY-TV (IND) Wilson; WRAZ (FOX) Raleigh; WRDC (MNT) Durham; WRIC-TV (ABC) Petersburg; WRLH-TV (FOX, MNT) Richmond; WRPX-TV (ION) Rocky Mount; WTVD (ABC) Durham; WTVR-TV (CBS) Richmond; WUNP-TV (PBS) Roanoke Rapids; WWBT (NBC) Richmond; allband FM.
Programming (via satellite): C-SPAN; C-SPAN 2; QVC; WGN America.
Fee: $45.00 installation; $28.50 monthly; $3.25 converter; $33.00 additional installation.
Expanded Basic Service 1
Subscribers: N.A.
Programming (via satellite): A&E Networks; ABC Family Channel; AMC; Animal Planet; BET Networks; Bravo; Cartoon Network; CNBC; CNN; Comedy Central; Country Music TV; Discovery Channel; Disney Channel; E! Entertainment Television; ESPN; ESPN 2; Food Network; Fox News Channel; FX; Headline News; HGTV; History Channel; Lifetime; MSNBC; MTV; Nickelodeon; Oxygen; Product Information Network; ShopNBC; Spike TV; Syfy; TBS Superstation; The Weather Channel; Travel Channel; truTV; Turner Network TV; TV Land; USA Network; VH1.
Digital Basic Service
Subscribers: 634.
Programming (via satellite): BBC America; Bio; Bloomberg Television; Discovery Fit & Health; DIY Network; ESPN Classic Sports; ESPNews; Fuse; G4; Golf Channel; GSN; Halogen Network; History Channel; Outdoor Channel; SoapNet; Speed; Toon Disney; Trinity Broadcasting Network; Versus; WE tv.
Digital Expanded Basic Service
Subscribers: N.A.
Programming (via satellite): Fox Movie Channel; GAS; MTV Networks Digital Suite; Music Choice; National Geographic Channel; Nick Jr.; Nick Too; NickToons TV; Style Network; The Learning Channel.
Digital Pay Service 1
Pay Units: N.A.
Programming (via satellite): Cinemax (multiplexed); Encore (multiplexed); HBO (multiplexed); Showtime (multiplexed); Starz (multiplexed); The Movie Channel (multiplexed).
Video-On-Demand: No
Pay-Per-View
Fresh (delivered digitally); Playboy TV (delivered digitally).
Internet Service
Operational: Yes.
Subscribers: 80.
Broadband Service: Comcast High Speed Internet.
Fee: $42.95 monthly.
Telephone Service
None
Miles of Plant: 140.0 (coaxial); None (fiber optic).
Vice President & General Manager: Troy Fitzhugh. Technical Supervisor: Frank Berry. Technical Operations Manager: Mike Buckner. Office Manager: Kathy Thomas.
Ownership: Comcast Cable Communications Inc. (MSO).

SPEEDWELL—R&S Communications LLC, PO Box 261, Castlewood, VA 24224. Phone: 800-801-4078. Web Site: http://randscommunications.com. Also serves Crockett & Rural Retreat (portions). ICA: VA0176. **Note:** This system is an overbuild.
TV Market Ranking: Below 100 (Crockett, Rural Retreat (portions), SPEEDWELL). Franchise award date: December 12, 1989. Franchise expiration date: N.A. Began: N.A.
Channel capacity: 45 (not 2-way capable). Channels available but not in use: N.A.
Basic Service
Subscribers: 11.
Programming (received off-air): WCYB-TV (CW, NBC) Bristol; WDBJ (CBS, MNT) Roanoke; WFXR (CW, FOX) Roanoke; WJHL-TV (CBS) Johnson City; WKPT-TV (ABC) Kingsport; WMSY-TV (PBS) Marion; WSLS-TV (NBC) Roanoke; WVVA (CW, NBC) Bluefield.
Programming (via satellite): ABC Family Channel; CNN; Country Music TV; C-SPAN; Discovery Channel; Disney Channel; E! Entertainment Television; ESPN; ESPN 2; Headline News; History Channel; Nickelodeon; Outdoor Channel; QVC; Spike TV; TBS Superstation; The Learning Channel; The Weather Channel; Travel Channel; Trinity Broadcasting Network; Turner Classic Movies; Turner Network TV; USA Network; WGN America.
Fee: $40.00 installation; $31.95 monthly; $1.95 converter.
Pay Service 1
Pay Units: N.A.
Programming (via satellite): HBO.
Fee: $12.95 monthly.
Pay Service 2
Pay Units: N.A.
Programming (via satellite): Showtime; The Movie Channel.
Fee: $12.95 monthly (each).
Video-On-Demand: No
Internet Service
Operational: Yes.
Fee: $29.95 monthly.
Telephone Service
None
Miles of Plant: 60.0 (coaxial); None (fiber optic).
Vice President, Operations: James Bradley. Vice President, Sales: Mike DeRosa. President & General Manager: Richard Beesmer. Regional Service Manager: Rich Beesmer.
Ownership: R&S Communications LLC.

SPOTSYLVANIA—Comcast Cable, 11101 University Blvd, Manassas, VA 20110. Phone: 703-789-8100. Fax: 703-789-8280. Web Site: http://www.comcast.com. Also serves Garrisonville, Lake of the Woods, Orange County (eastern portion), Spotsylvania County (northern portion) & Stafford County (northern portion). ICA: VA0018.
TV Market Ranking: 9 (Stafford County (northern portion) (portions)); Below 100 (Garrisonville, Lake of the Woods, Orange County (eastern portion), SPOTSYLVANIA, Spotsylvania County (northern portion) (portions), Stafford County (northern portion) (portions)); Outside TV Markets (Spotsylvania County (northern portion) (portions)). Franchise award date: N.A. Franchise expiration date: N.A. Began: May 1, 1982.
Channel capacity: N.A. Channels available but not in use: N.A.
Basic Service
Subscribers: 50,232 Includes Warrenton.
Programming (received off-air): WCVE-TV (PBS) Richmond; WDCA (MNT) Washington; WDCW (CW) Washington; WETA-TV (PBS) Washington; WHUT-TV (PBS) Washington; WJLA-TV (ABC) Washington; WNVC (ETV) Fairfax; WNVT (ETV) Goldvein; WPXW-TV (ION) Manassas; WRC-TV (NBC) Washington; WRIC-TV (ABC) Petersburg; WTTG (FOX) Washington; WTVR-TV (CBS) Richmond; WUSA (CBS) Washington; WWBT (NBC) Richmond.
Programming (via satellite): C-SPAN; C-SPAN 2; Fox News Channel; MSNBC; QVC; ShopNBC; TV Guide Network.
Fee: $47.54 installation; $10.17 monthly.
Expanded Basic Service 1
Subscribers: N.A.
Programming (via satellite): A&E Networks; ABC Family Channel; AMC; Animal Planet; BET Networks; Bravo; Cartoon Network; CNBC; CNN; Comcast SportsNet Mid-Atlantic; Comedy Central; Country Music TV; Discovery Channel; Disney Channel; E! Entertainment Television; ESPN; ESPN 2; Eternal Word TV Network; Food Network; FX; GSN; Hallmark Channel; Headline News; HGTV; History Channel; INSP; Lifetime; MTV; Nickelodeon; Oxygen; Product Information Network; Speed; Spike TV; Syfy; TBS Superstation; The Learning Channel; The Weather Channel; Travel Channel; Trinity Broadcasting Network; truTV; Turner Classic Movies; Turner Network TV; TV Land; Univision Studios; USA Network; VH1.
Fee: $11.78 monthly.
Digital Basic Service
Subscribers: N.A.
Programming (via satellite): AmericanLife TV Network; BBC America; Bio; Black Family Channel; Bloomberg Television; Discovery Fit & Health; DIY Network; ESPN Classic Sports; ESPNews; Fox Sports World; Fuse; G4; Golf Channel; Great American Country; Halogen Network; History Channel International; Mid-Atlantic Sports Network; Music Choice; Outdoor Channel; The Word Network; Toon Disney; Versus; WE tv.
Digital Expanded Basic Service
Subscribers: N.A.
Programming (via satellite): Fox Movie Channel; FSN Digital Atlantic; FSN Digital Central; FSN Digital Pacific; GAS; Independent Film Channel; Lifetime Movie Network; MTV Networks Digital Suite; National Geographic Channel; Nick Jr.; Nick Too; NickToons TV; SoapNet; Style Network; Sundance Channel.
Pay Service 1
Pay Units: N.A.
Programming (via satellite): Cinemax; HBO; Showtime; The Movie Channel.
Digital Pay Service 1
Pay Units: N.A.
Programming (via satellite): ART America; Canales N; CCTV-4; Cinemax (multiplexed); Encore (multiplexed); Filipino Channel; Flix; HBO (multiplexed); RAI USA; Russian Television Network; Showtime (multiplexed); Starz (multiplexed); The Movie Channel (multiplexed); TV Asia; TV Japan; TV5, La Television International; Zee TV USA; Zhong Tian Channel.
Video-On-Demand: Yes
Pay-Per-View
Urban Xtra (delivered digitally); Hot Choice (delivered digitally); Shorteez (delivered digitally); Fresh (delivered digitally); Playboy TV (delivered digitally).
Internet Service
Operational: Yes.
Broadband Service: Comcast High Speed Internet.
Fee: $42.95 monthly; $7.00 modem lease.
Telephone Service
Digital: Operational
Miles of Plant: 1,200.0 (coaxial); None (fiber optic).

Vice President & General Manager: Christine Whitaker. Technical Operations Director: Scott Shelly. Marketing Director: Shawn Houston.
Ownership: Comcast Cable Communications Inc. (MSO).

STAUNTON—Comcast Cable, 400 Westfield Rd, Charlottesville, VA 22901. Phones: 434-951-3700 (Charlottesville office); 888-683-1000. Fax: 434-951-3705. Web Site: http://www.comcast.com. Also serves Augusta, Augusta County (portions), Augusta Springs, Churchville, Craigsville, Crimora, Fishersville, Greenville, Grottoes, Harriston, Mint Spring, New Hope, Steeles Tavern, Stuarts Draft, Verona & Waynesboro. ICA: VA0026.
TV Market Ranking: Below 100 (Augusta, Augusta County (portions), Churchville, Crimora, Fishersville, Greenville, Grottoes, Harriston, Mint Spring, New Hope, STAUNTON, Stuarts Draft, Verona, Waynesboro); Outside TV Markets (Augusta County (portions), Augusta Springs, Craigsville, Steeles Tavern). Franchise award date: January 1, 1952. Franchise expiration date: N.A. Began: January 1, 1952.
Channel capacity: N.A. Channels available but not in use: N.A.
Basic Service
Subscribers: 25,412.
Programming (received off-air): WHSV-TV (ABC, MNT) Harrisonburg; WTTG (FOX) Washington; WUSA (CBS) Washington; WVIR-TV (CW, NBC) Charlottesville; WVPT (PBS) Staunton; allband FM.
Programming (via satellite): C-SPAN; CW+; Golf Channel; INSP; QVC; ShopNBC; TBS Superstation; The Comcast Network; Versus.
Fee: $33.00 installation; $10.00 monthly.
Expanded Basic Service 1
Subscribers: 23,723.
Programming (via satellite): A&E Networks; ABC Family Channel; AMC; Animal Planet; BET Networks; Bravo; Cartoon Network; CNBC; CNN; Comcast SportsNet Mid-Atlantic; Comedy Central; Country Music TV; Discovery Channel; Disney Channel; E! Entertainment Television; ESPN; ESPN 2; Food Network; Fox News Channel; FX; Hallmark Channel; Headline News; HGTV; History Channel; ION Television; Lifetime; MSNBC; MTV; Nickelodeon; Oxygen; Product Information Network; Speed; Spike TV; Syfy; The Learning Channel; The Weather Channel; Travel Channel; truTV; Turner Classic Movies; Turner Network TV; TV Land; USA Network; VH1.
Fee: $33.00 installation; $13.40 monthly.
Digital Basic Service
Subscribers: N.A.
Programming (via satellite): AmericanLife TV Network; BBC America; Bio; Bloomberg Television; Canal 52MX; CBS Sports Network; Cine Latino; CMT Pure Country; CNN en Espanol; C-SPAN 2; Discovery en Espanol; Discovery Fit & Health; Discovery Health Channel; Discovery Home Channel; Discovery Kids Channel; Discovery Times Channel; DIY Network; ESPN 2 HD; ESPN Classic Sports; ESPN Deportes; ESPN HD; ESPN U; ESPNews; Eternal Word TV Network; Fox College Sports Atlantic; Fox College Sports Central; Fox College Sports Pacific; Fox Deportes; Fox Movie Channel; Fox Sports World; Fuel TV; Fuse; G4; GMC; Golf Channel; Great American Country; GSN; Halogen Network; HD Theater; History Channel en Espanol; History Channel International; Independent Film Channel; Lifetime Movie Network; LOGO; Military Channel; MTV Hits; MTV Jams; MTV2; Music Choice; National Geographic Channel; NFL Network; Nick Jr.; Nick Too; NickToons TV; Outdoor Channel; Palladia; PBS Kids Sprout; Science; SoapNet; Style Network; Sundance Channel; TeenNick; Tennis Channel; The Word Network; Toon Disney; Toon Disney en Espanol; Tr3s; Trinity Broadcasting Network; TV One; TVG Network; Universal HD; VeneMovies; Versus; VH1 Classic; VH1 Soul; WE tv.
Digital Pay Service 1
Pay Units: N.A.
Programming (via satellite): ART America; CCTV-4; Cinemax (multiplexed); Cinemax HD; Encore (multiplexed); Filipino Channel; Flix; HBO (multiplexed); HBO HD; RAI USA; Showtime (multiplexed); Showtime HD; Starz (multiplexed); Starz HDTV; The Movie Channel (multiplexed); TV Asia; TV Japan; TV5, La Television International.
Video-On-Demand: Yes
Pay-Per-View
Urban Xtra (delivered digitally); Hot Choice (delivered digitally); Shorteez (delivered digitally); Fresh (delivered digitally); Playboy TV (delivered digitally); HITS (delivered digitally).
Internet Service
Operational: Yes.
Broadband Service: Comcast High Speed Internet.
Fee: $42.95 monthly.
Telephone Service
Digital: Operational
Miles of Plant: 817.0 (coaxial); None (fiber optic).
Vice President & General Manager: Troy Fitzhugh. Technical Operations Director: Tom Jacobs. Marketing Director: Steve Miles. Marketing Coordinator: Cassie Cool.
Ownership: Comcast Cable Communications Inc. (MSO).

STUART—Comcast Cable, 400 Westfield Rd, Charlottesville, VA 22901. Phone: 434-951-3700. Fax: 434-951-3705. Web Site: http://www.comcast.com. Also serves Patrick Springs. ICA: VA0069.
TV Market Ranking: Outside TV Markets (Patrick Springs, STUART). Franchise award date: April 16, 1983. Franchise expiration date: N.A. Began: April 16, 1983.
Channel capacity: 42 (not 2-way capable). Channels available but not in use: N.A.
Basic Service
Subscribers: 1,030.
Programming (received off-air): WBRA-TV (PBS) Roanoke; WCWG (CW) Lexington; WDBJ (CBS, MNT) Roanoke; WFMY-TV (CBS) Greensboro; WGHP (FOX, IND) High Point; WGPX-TV (ION) Burlington; WLXI (IND) Greensboro; WSLS-TV (NBC) Roanoke; WXII-TV (NBC) Winston-Salem; WXLV-TV (ABC) Winston-Salem.
Programming (via satellite): QVC; WGN America.
Fee: $47.50 installation; $9.00 monthly; $1.86 converter; $10.00 additional installation.
Expanded Basic Service 1
Subscribers: N.A.
Programming (via satellite): A&E Networks; ABC Family Channel; CNN; Comcast SportsNet Mid-Atlantic; Comedy Central; Country Music TV; C-SPAN; Discovery Channel; Disney Channel; ESPN; ESPN 2; Fox News Channel; FX; Headline News; INSP; Lifetime; Nickelodeon; Spike TV; Syfy; TBS Superstation; The Learning Channel; The Weather Channel; Turner Network TV; USA Network; VH1.
Fee: $15.18 monthly.
Digital Basic Service
Subscribers: N.A.
Programming (via satellite): Bravo; Encore (multiplexed); ESPN Classic Sports; HGTV; History Channel; Versus; WE tv.
Digital Pay Service 1
Pay Units: N.A.
Programming (via satellite): Cinemax (multiplexed); HBO (multiplexed); Showtime (multiplexed); Starz (multiplexed); The Movie Channel (multiplexed).
Video-On-Demand: No
Pay-Per-View
Hits Movies & Events (delivered digitally).
Telephone Service
None
Miles of Plant: 83.0 (coaxial); None (fiber optic).
Vice President & General Manager: Troy Fitzhugh. Technical Operations Director: Tom Jacobs. Technical Operations Manager: Mike Buckner. Marketing Director: Steve Miles. Marketing Manager: Donna Crisco.
Ownership: Comcast Cable Communications Inc. (MSO).

SUFFOLK—Charter Communications, 216 Moore Ave, Suffolk, VA 23434. Phone: 757-539-0713. Fax: 757-539-1057. Web Site: http://www.charter.com. Also serves Boykins, Branchville, Carrollton, Courtland, Franklin, Isle of Wight County, Ivor, Newsoms, Rushmere, Smithfield, Southampton County, Sussex County, Wakefield, Waverly & Windsor. ICA: VA0025.
TV Market Ranking: 44 (Carrollton, Franklin, Isle of Wight County, Ivor, Rushmere, Smithfield, Southampton County (portions), SUFFOLK, Sussex County (portions), Wakefield, Waverly, Windsor); Outside TV Markets (Boykins, Branchville, Courtland, Newsoms, Southampton County (portions), Sussex County (portions)). Franchise award date: February 1, 1984. Franchise expiration date: February 1, 2009. Began: October 24, 1984.
Channel capacity: N.A. Channels available but not in use: N.A.
Basic Service
Subscribers: 7,084.
Programming (received off-air): WAVY-TV (NBC) Portsmouth; WGNT (CW) Portsmouth; WHRO-TV (PBS) Hampton-Norfolk; WPXV-TV (ION) Norfolk; WSKY-TV (IND) Manteo; WTKR (CBS) Norfolk; WTVZ-TV (MNT) Norfolk; WVBT (FOX) Virginia Beach; WVEC (ABC) Hampton.
Programming (via satellite): C-SPAN; C-SPAN 2; INSP; LWS Local Weather Station; QVC; Trinity Broadcasting Network; WGN America.
Fee: $29.99 installation.
Expanded Basic Service 1
Subscribers: 6,354.
Programming (via satellite): A&E Networks; ABC Family Channel; AMC; Animal Planet; BET Networks; Bravo; Cartoon Network; CNBC; CNN; Comcast SportsNet Mid-Atlantic; Comedy Central; Country Music TV; Discovery Channel; Disney Channel; E! Entertainment Television; ESPN; ESPN 2; Food Network; Fox News Channel; FX; G4; Golf Channel; GSN; Hallmark Channel; Headline News; HGTV; History Channel; Lifetime; MSNBC; MTV; MTV2; National Geographic Channel; Nickelodeon; Oxygen; Shop at Home; ShopNBC; SoapNet; Speed; Spike TV; Style Network; Syfy; TBS Superstation; The Learning Channel; The Weather Channel; Toon Disney; Travel Channel; truTV; Turner Classic Movies; Turner Network TV; TV Guide Network; TV Land; USA Network; Versus; VH1; WE tv.
Fee: $47.99 monthly.
Digital Basic Service
Subscribers: N.A.
Programming (via satellite): BBC America; Bio; Bloomberg Television; Boomerang; Canales N; CNN en Espanol; CNN International; Discovery Fit & Health; DIY Network; ESPN; ESPN Classic Sports; ESPNews; Fox College Sports Atlantic; Fox College Sports Central; Fox College Sports Pacific; Fox Deportes; Fox Movie Channel; Fox Soccer; Fuel TV; GAS; Great American Country; HDNet; HDNet Movies; History Channel International; Independent Film Channel; Lifetime Movie Network; Mid-Atlantic Sports Network; MTV Networks Digital Suite; Music Choice; NFL Network; Nick Jr.; Nick Too; NickToons TV; Outdoor Channel; Sundance Channel; TV Guide Interactive Inc.
Digital Pay Service 1
Pay Units: N.A.
Programming (via satellite): Cinemax (multiplexed); Cinemax HD; Encore (multiplexed); HBO (multiplexed); HBO HD; Showtime (multiplexed); Showtime HD; Starz (multiplexed); Starz HDTV; The Movie Channel (multiplexed).
Video-On-Demand: Yes
Pay-Per-View
iN DEMAND (delivered digitally); NASCAR In Car (delivered digitally); Playboy TV (delivered digitally); Fresh (delivered digitally); Shorteez (delivered digitally).
Internet Service
Operational: Yes. Began: September 1, 2001.
Broadband Service: Charter Pipeline.
Fee: $29.99 monthly.
Telephone Service
None
Miles of Plant: 444.0 (coaxial); None (fiber optic).
Vice President & General Manager: Anthony Pope. Marketing Director: Brooke Sinclair. Sales & Marketing Manager: LaRisa Scales. Operations Manager: Tom Ross.
Ownership: Charter Communications Inc. (MSO).

TANGIER ISLAND—Charter Communications, 216 Moore Ave, Suffolk, VA 23434. Phone: 757-539-0713. Fax: 757-539-1057. Web Site: http://www.charter.com. ICA: VA0117.
TV Market Ranking: Outside TV Markets (TANGIER ISLAND). Franchise award

date: N.A. Franchise expiration date: N.A. Began: June 1, 1973.
Channel capacity: 12 (not 2-way capable). Channels available but not in use: N.A.

Basic Service
Subscribers: 127.
Programming (received off-air): WAVY-TV (NBC) Portsmouth; WBOC-TV (CBS, FOX) Salisbury; WCPB (PBS) Salisbury; WGNT (CW) Portsmouth; WHRO-TV (PBS) Hampton-Norfolk; WTKR (CBS) Norfolk; WTVZ-TV (MNT) Norfolk; WVEC (ABC) Hampton.
Programming (via satellite): CNN; Disney Channel; ESPN; Mid-Atlantic Sports Network; TBS Superstation.
Fee: $19.50 installation; $17.41 monthly.

Pay Service 1
Pay Units: 8.
Programming (via satellite): HBO.
Fee: $11.95 monthly.
Video-On-Demand: No

Internet Service
Operational: No.

Telephone Service
None
Miles of Plant: 3.0 (coaxial); None (fiber optic).
Vice President & General Manager: Anthony Pope. Marketing Director: Brooke Sinclair. Marketing Manager: LaRisa Scales. Operations Manager: Tom Ross.
Ownership: Charter Communications Inc. (MSO).

TAPPAHANNOCK—MetroCast, 233 Colonial Ave, Colonial Beach, VA 22443. Phone: 800-633-8578. Web Site: http://www.metrocastcommunications.com. Also serves Essex County (portions). ICA: VA0080.
TV Market Ranking: 63 (Essex County (portions)); Below 100 (TAPPAHANNOCK, Essex County (portions)); Outside TV Markets (Essex County (portions)). Franchise award date: February 1, 1972. Franchise expiration date: N.A. Began: March 1, 1972.
Channel capacity: N.A. Channels available but not in use: N.A.

Basic Service
Subscribers: 1,074.
Programming (received off-air): WCVE-TV (PBS) Richmond; WCVW (PBS) Richmond; WRIC-TV (ABC) Petersburg; WRLH-TV (FOX, MNT) Richmond; WTVR-TV (CBS) Richmond; WUPV (CW) Ashland; WWBT (NBC) Richmond; allband FM.
Programming (via satellite): C-SPAN; INSP; ION Television; QVC; WGN America.
Fee: $54.98 installation; $19.92 monthly; $.75 converter.

Expanded Basic Service 1
Subscribers: 976.
Programming (via satellite): A&E Networks; ABC Family Channel; AMC; Animal Planet; BET Networks; Bravo; Cartoon Network; CNBC; CNN; Comcast SportsNet Mid-Atlantic; Comedy Central; Country Music TV; Discovery Channel; Disney Channel; E! Entertainment Television; ESPN; ESPN 2; Food Network; Fox News Channel; FX; G4; Golf Channel; Headline News; HGTV; History Channel; Lifetime; MSNBC; MTV; Nickelodeon; Oxygen; Speed; Spike TV; Syfy; TBS Superstation; The Learning Channel; The Weather Channel; Travel Channel; truTV; Turner Classic Movies; Turner Network TV; TV Land; USA Network; VH1; WE tv.
Fee: $13.95 monthly.

Digital Basic Service
Subscribers: N.A.
Programming (via satellite): BBC America; Bio; Bloomberg Television; Discovery Fit & Health; DIY Network; ESPN Classic Sports; ESPNews; Fox College Sports Atlantic; Fox College Sports Central; Fox College Sports Pacific; Fox Movie Channel; Fox Soccer; Fuse; GAS; GSN; History Channel International; Independent Film Channel; MTV Networks Digital Suite; Music Choice; National Geographic Channel; Nick Jr.; Nick Too; NickToons TV; SoapNet; Sundance Channel; Toon Disney; TV Guide Interactive Inc.

Digital Pay Service 1
Pay Units: 43.
Programming (via satellite): Cinemax (multiplexed).
Fee: $11.50 monthly.

Digital Pay Service 2
Pay Units: 94.
Programming (via satellite): Encore (multiplexed); HBO (multiplexed).
Fee: $11.50 monthly.

Digital Pay Service 3
Pay Units: N.A.
Programming (via satellite): Flix; Showtime (multiplexed); Starz (multiplexed); The Movie Channel (multiplexed).
Video-On-Demand: No

Pay-Per-View
iN DEMAND (delivered digitally); Playboy TV (delivered digitally); Fresh (delivered digitally); Shorteez (delivered digitally).

Internet Service
Operational: Yes.
Fee: $29.95-$69.95 monthly.

Telephone Service
Digital: Operational
Fee: $44.95 monthly
Miles of Plant: 28.0 (coaxial); None (fiber optic). Additional miles planned: 2.0 (coaxial).
General Manager: Danny L. Jobe.
Ownership: Harron Communications LP (MSO).

TAZEWELL—Formerly served by Adelphia Communications. Now served by RICHLANDS, VA [VA0041]. ICA: VA0045.

TROUTVILLE—Comcast Cable, 21 S Bruffey St, Salem, VA 24153-4728. Phones: 434-951-3700 (Charlottesville office); 540-378-1160. Web Site: http://www.comcast.com. Also serves Bedford, Bedford County (portions), Blue Ridge, Botetourt County, Chamblissburg, Cloverdale, Daleville, Fincastle, Goodview, Huddleston, Moneta, Montvale, Nace, Stewartsville & Thaxton. ICA: VA0037.
TV Market Ranking: 70 (Bedford, Blue Ridge, Chamblissburg, Cloverdale, Daleville, Fincastle, Goodview, Huddleston, Moneta, Montvale, Nace, Stewartsville, Thaxton, TROUTVILLE); Below 100 (Bedford County (portions), Botetourt County). Franchise award date: April 30, 1982. Franchise expiration date: August 17, 2020. Began: November 1, 1983.
Channel capacity: N.A. Channels available but not in use: N.A.

Basic Service
Subscribers: 7,800.
Programming (received off-air): WBRA-TV (PBS) Roanoke; WDBJ (CBS, MNT) Roanoke; WDRL-TV (IND) Danville; WFXR (CW, FOX) Roanoke; WPXR-TV (ION) Roanoke; WSET-TV (ABC) Lynchburg; WSLS-TV (NBC) Roanoke.
Programming (via satellite): C-SPAN; C-SPAN 2; CW+; Product Information Network; QVC; TBS Superstation; TV Guide Network; WGN America.
Fee: $43.00 installation; $12.29 monthly; $.90 converter.

Expanded Basic Service 1
Subscribers: 7,421.
Programming (via satellite): A&E Networks; ABC Family Channel; AMC; Animal Planet; BET Networks; Bravo; Cartoon Network; CNBC; CNN; Comcast SportsNet Mid-Atlantic; Comedy Central; Country Music TV; Discovery Channel; Disney Channel; E! Entertainment Television; ESPN; ESPN 2; Eternal Word TV Network; Food Network; Fox News Channel; FX; Hallmark Channel; Headline News; HGTV; History Channel; INSP; Lifetime; MSNBC; MTV; Nickelodeon; Oxygen; ShopNBC; Spike TV; Syfy; The Learning Channel; The Weather Channel; Travel Channel; truTV; Turner Classic Movies; Turner Network TV; TV Land; USA Network; VH1.

Digital Basic Service
Subscribers: 3,000.
Programming (via satellite): AmericanLife TV Network; BBC America; Black Family Channel; Bloomberg Television; Canales N; Discovery Fit & Health; DIY Network; ESPN; ESPN 2; ESPN Classic Sports; ESPN U; ESPNews; Fox Movie Channel; Fox Soccer; Fuse; G4; GAS; Great American Country; GSN; Halogen Network; HD Theater; HDNet; HDNet Movies; INHD (multiplexed); Lifetime Movie Network; LOGO; MTV Networks Digital Suite; Music Choice; National Geographic Channel; NFL Network; Nick Jr.; Nick Too; NickToons TV; SoapNet; Speed; Style Network; The Word Network; Toon Disney; Trinity Broadcasting Network; TVG Network; WE tv.
Fee: $9.95 monthly.

Digital Expanded Basic Service
Subscribers: N.A.
Programming (via satellite): Bio; CBS Sports Network; Flix; Fox Reality Channel; FSN Digital Atlantic; FSN Digital Central; FSN Digital Pacific; Fuel TV; Golf Channel; History Channel International; Independent Film Channel; NFL Network; Outdoor Channel; Sundance Channel; Tennis Channel; Versus.

Digital Pay Service 1
Pay Units: N.A.
Programming (via satellite): Arabic Channel; CCTV-4; Cinemax (multiplexed); Cinemax HD; Encore (multiplexed); Filipino Channel; Flix; HBO (multiplexed); HBO HD; RAI International; Showtime (multiplexed); Showtime HD; Starz (multiplexed); Starz HDTV; The Movie Channel (multiplexed); TV Asia; TV Japan; TV5, La Television International; Zhong Tian Channel.
Video-On-Demand: Yes

Pay-Per-View
Movies (delivered digitally); Special events (delivered digitally); ESPN (delivered digitally); Playboy TV (delivered digitally); Fresh (delivered digitally); Shorteez (delivered digitally); Hot Choice (delivered digitally).

Internet Service
Operational: Yes.
Broadband Service: Comcast High Speed Internet.
Fee: $42.95 monthly.

Telephone Service
Digital: Operational
Miles of Plant: 525.0 (coaxial); None (fiber optic).
Vice President & General Manager: Troy Fitzhugh. Technical Operations Director: Tom Jacobs. Plant Manager: John Van Lew. Marketing Director: Steve Miles. Marketing Manager: Donna Crisco. Office Manager: Trudy McNew.
Ownership: Comcast Cable Communications Inc. (MSO).

VICTORIA—Formerly served by Adelphia Communications. Now served by SOUTH HILL, VA [VA0062]. ICA: VA0098.

WARRENTON—Comcast Cable, 11101 University Blvd, Manassas, VA 20110. Phone: 703-789-8100. Fax: 703-789-8280. Web Site: http://www.comcast.com. Also serves Bealeton, Catlett, Marshall & Remington. ICA: VA0034.
TV Market Ranking: Below 100 (Bealeton, Catlett, Marshall, Remington, WARRENTON). Franchise award date: December 1, 1986. Franchise expiration date: N.A. Began: December 1, 1986.
Channel capacity: N.A. Channels available but not in use: N.A.

Basic Service
Subscribers: N.A. Included in Spotsylvania
Programming (received off-air): WDCA (MNT) Washington; WDCW (CW) Washington; WETA-TV (PBS) Washington; WFDC-DT (UNV) Arlington; WJLA-TV (ABC) Washington; WMDO-CA (TEL) Washington; WPXW-TV (ION) Manassas; WRC-TV (NBC) Washington; WTTG (FOX) Washington; WUSA (CBS) Washington.
Programming (via satellite): C-SPAN; QVC; The Comcast Network.
Fee: $45.00 installation; $9.09 monthly.

Expanded Basic Service 1
Subscribers: 6,800.
Programming (received off-air): WZDC-CA (TMO) Washington.
Programming (via satellite): A&E Networks; ABC Family Channel; AMC; Animal Planet; BET Networks; Bravo; Cartoon Network; CNBC; CNN; Comcast SportsNet Mid-Atlantic; Comedy Central; Discovery Channel; Disney Channel; E! Entertainment Television; ESPN; ESPN 2; Eternal Word TV Network; Food Network; Fox News Channel; FX; Golf Channel; HGTV; History Channel; Lifetime; Mid-Atlantic Sports Network; MSNBC; MTV; Nickelodeon; Speed; Spike TV; Syfy; TBS Superstation; The Learning Channel; The Weather Channel; Travel Channel; Turner Classic Movies; Turner Network TV; USA Network; Versus; VH1; WGN America.
Fee: $13.34 monthly.

Digital Basic Service
Subscribers: N.A.
Programming (via satellite): A&E HD; Animal Planet HD; BBC America; Bio; Bloomberg Television; Cartoon Network Tambien en Espanol; CBS Sports Network; Cine Latino; Cine Mexicano; CMT Pure Country; CNN en Espanol; CNN HD; Cooking Channel; Country Music TV; C-SPAN 2; C-SPAN 3; Current; Discovery Channel HD; Discovery en Espanol; Discovery Fit & Health; Discovery Health Channel; DIY Network; Encore (multiplexed); ESPN 2 HD; ESPN Classic Sports; ESPN Deportes; ESPN HD; ESPNews; Flix; Food Network HD; Fox College Sports Atlantic; Fox College Sports Central; Fox College Sports Pacific; Fox Deportes; Fox Movie Channel; Fox Reality Channel; Fox Soccer; Fuel TV; Fuse; G4; GolTV; Gospel Music TV; Great American Country; GSN; Halogen Network; HD Theater; HGTV HD; History Channel en Espanol; History Channel HD; History Channel International; ID Investigation Discovery; Independent Film Channel; Jewelry Television; Lifetime Movie Net-

work; LOGO; MHz Worldview; Military Channel; MoviePlex; MTV2; mun2 television; Music Choice; National Geographic Channel; National Geographic Channel HD Network; NBA TV; NFL Network; Nick Jr.; Nick Too; NickToons TV; Outdoor Channel; Oxygen; Palladia; PBS Kids Sprout; Planet Green; Science; Science HD; ShopNBC; SoapNet; Style Network; Sundance Channel; TeenNick; Tennis Channel; The Word Network; TLC HD; Toon Disney; Tr3s; Trinity Broadcasting Network; truTV; Turner Network TV HD; TV Guide Interactive Inc.; TV One; TVG Network; Universal HD; USA Network HD; VeneMovies; Versus HD; VH1 Classic; VH1 Soul; WE tv.

Digital Pay Service 1
Pay Units: N.A.
Programming (via satellite): CCTV-4; Cinemax (multiplexed); Cinemax HD; Filipino Channel; HBO (multiplexed); HBO HD; RAI International; Showtime; Showtime HD; Starz (multiplexed); Starz HDTV; The Movie Channel (multiplexed); TV Asia; TV5 USA; Zee TV USA.

Video-On-Demand: No

Pay-Per-View
Hits Movies & Events (delivered digitally); Playboy TV (delivered digitally); Spice: Xcess (delivered digitally); NHL Center Ice (delivered digitally).

Internet Service
Operational: Yes.
Broadband Service: Comcast High Speed Internet.
Fee: $42.95 monthly.

Telephone Service
Digital: Operational

Miles of Plant: 330.0 (coaxial); None (fiber optic).
Vice President & General Manager: Christine Whitaker. Technical Operations Director: Scott Shelly. Marketing Director: Shawn Houston.
Ownership: Comcast Cable Communications Inc. (MSO).

WARSAW—MetroCast, 233 Colonial Ave, Colonial Beach, VA 22443. Phone: 800-633-8578. Web Site: http://www.metrocastcommunications.com. ICA: VA0094.
TV Market Ranking: Outside TV Markets (WARSAW). Franchise award date: April 1, 1984. Franchise expiration date: April 1, 2007. Began: February 13, 1986.
Channel capacity: N.A. Channels available but not in use: N.A.

Basic Service
Subscribers: 909.
Programming (received off-air): WCVE-TV (PBS) Richmond; WRIC-TV (ABC) Petersburg; WRLH-TV (FOX, MNT) Richmond; WTVR-TV (CBS) Richmond; WUPV (CW) Ashland; WWBT (NBC) Richmond.
Programming (via satellite): C-SPAN; C-SPAN 2; INSP; ION Television; QVC; WGN America.
Fee: $59.56 installation; $19.01 monthly; $.75 converter.

Expanded Basic Service 1
Subscribers: 837.
Programming (via satellite): A&E Networks; ABC Family Channel; AMC; Animal Planet; BET Networks; Bravo; Cartoon Network; CNBC; CNN; Comcast SportsNet Mid-Atlantic; Comedy Central; Country Music TV; Discovery Channel; Disney Channel; E! Entertainment Television; ESPN; ESPN 2; Food Network; Fox News Channel; FX; G4; Golf Channel; Headline News; HGTV; History Channel; Lifetime; MSNBC; MTV; Nickelodeon; Oxygen; Speed; Spike TV; Syfy; TBS Superstation; The Learning Channel; The Weather Channel; Travel Channel; truTV; Turner Classic Movies; Turner Network TV; TV Land; USA Network; VH1; WE tv.
Fee: $13.95 monthly.

Digital Basic Service
Subscribers: N.A.
Programming (via satellite): BBC America; Bio; Bloomberg Television; Discovery Fit & Health; DIY Network; ESPN Classic Sports; ESPNews; Fox College Sports Atlantic; Fox College Sports Central; Fox College Sports Pacific; Fox Movie Channel; Fox Soccer; Fuse; GAS; GSN; History Channel International; Independent Film Channel; MTV Networks Digital Suite; Music Choice; National Geographic Channel; Nick Jr.; Nick Too; NickToons TV; SoapNet; Sundance Channel; Toon Disney; TV Guide Interactive Inc.

Digital Pay Service 1
Pay Units: 50.
Programming (via satellite): Cinemax (multiplexed).
Fee: $11.50 monthly.

Digital Pay Service 2
Pay Units: 83.
Programming (via satellite): HBO (multiplexed).
Fee: $11.50 monthly.

Digital Pay Service 3
Pay Units: N.A.
Programming (via satellite): Encore (multiplexed); Flix; Showtime (multiplexed); Starz (multiplexed); The Movie Channel (multiplexed).

Video-On-Demand: No

Pay-Per-View
iN DEMAND (delivered digitally); Playboy TV (delivered digitally); Fresh (delivered digitally); Shorteez (delivered digitally).

Internet Service
Operational: Yes.
Fee: $29.95-$69.95 monthly.

Telephone Service
None

Miles of Plant: 46.0 (coaxial); None (fiber optic).
General Manager: Danny L. Jobe.
Ownership: Harron Communications LP (MSO).

WASHINGTON COUNTY (portions)—Formerly served by BRISTOL (portions), VA [VA0190]. BVU OptiNet. This cable system has converted to IPTV, 15022 Lee Hwy, Bristol, VA 24202. Phones: 276-821-6100; 866-835-1288. Fax: 276-821-6218. E-mail: help@bvu-optinet.com. Web Site: http://www.bvu-optinet.com. ICA: VA5204.
TV Market Ranking: Below 100 (WASHINGTON COUNTY (PORTIONS)).
Channel capacity: N.A. Channels available but not in use: N.A.

Internet Service
Operational: Yes.

Telephone Service
Digital: Operational

WESTMORELAND COUNTY—Comcast Cable, 410 Northumberland Hwy, Callao, VA 22422. Phones: 804-915-5400 (Richmond office); 804-725-3412. Fax: 804-725-5209. Web Site: http://www.comcast.com. Also serves Montross & Westmoreland. ICA: VA0049.
TV Market Ranking: Below 100 (Westmoreland, WESTMORELAND COUNTY (portions)); Outside TV Markets (Montross, WESTMORELAND COUNTY (portions)). Franchise award date: April 21, 1988. Franchise expiration date: N.A. Began: December 1, 1988.
Channel capacity: 42 (not 2-way capable). Channels available but not in use: N.A.

Basic Service
Subscribers: N.A. Included in Richmond
Programming (received off-air): WCVE-TV (PBS) Richmond; WETA-TV (PBS) Washington; WJLA-TV (ABC) Washington; WRC-TV (NBC) Washington; WRIC-TV (ABC) Petersburg; WRLH-TV (FOX, MNT) Richmond; WTTG (FOX) Washington; WTVR-TV (CBS) Richmond; WUSA (CBS) Washington; WWBT (NBC) Richmond.
Programming (via satellite): C-SPAN; C-SPAN 2; TBS Superstation.
Fee: $28.95 installation; $14.95 monthly.

Expanded Basic Service 1
Subscribers: 1,491.
Programming (via satellite): A&E Networks; ABC Family Channel; BET Networks; CNBC; CNN; Comcast SportsNet Mid-Atlantic; Country Music TV; Discovery Channel; Disney Channel; ESPN; Fox News Channel; Headline News; Lifetime; MTV; Nickelodeon; QVC; Spike TV; The Weather Channel; Turner Network TV; USA Network; VH1.

Digital Basic Service
Subscribers: N.A. Included in Richmond
Programming (via satellite): BBC America; Bloomberg Television; Bravo; Discovery Fit & Health; ESPN 2; ESPN Classic Sports; ESPNews; Fox Movie Channel; Fox Sports World; G4; Golf Channel; GSN; Halogen Network; HGTV; History Channel; Independent Film Channel; National Geographic Channel; Nick Jr.; NickToons TV; Outdoor Channel; Speed; Trinity Broadcasting Network; Turner Classic Movies; Versus; VH1 Classic; VH1 Country; WE tv.

Digital Expanded Basic Service
Subscribers: N.A.
Programming (via satellite): Music Choice.

Digital Pay Service 1
Pay Units: N.A.
Programming (via satellite): Cinemax (multiplexed); Encore; HBO (multiplexed); Showtime (multiplexed); The Movie Channel (multiplexed).

Video-On-Demand: No

Pay-Per-View
Hits Movies & Events (delivered digitally); Fresh (delivered digitally); Playboy TV (delivered digitally).

Internet Service
Operational: No.

Telephone Service
None

Miles of Plant: 190.0 (coaxial); None (fiber optic).
Chief Technician: Art Harris. Office Manager: Shirley Winters.
Ownership: Comcast Cable Communications Inc. (MSO).

WILLIAMSBURG—Cox Communications. Now served by HAMPTON ROADS (formerly Virginia Beach), VA [VA0002]. ICA: VA0177.

WINCHESTER—Comcast Cable, 195 Rainville Rd, Winchester, VA 22602. Phones: 434-951-3700 (Charlottesville office); 540-504-0900. Fax: 540-504-0972. Web Site: http://www.comcast.com. Also serves Berryville, Boyce, Clarke County, Frederick County & Stephens City. ICA: VA0014.
TV Market Ranking: Below 100 (Berryville, Boyce, Clarke County, Frederick County, Stephens City, WINCHESTER). Franchise award date: N.A. Franchise expiration date: January 1, 2010. Began: January 15, 1966.
Channel capacity: N.A. Channels available but not in use: N.A.

Basic Service
Subscribers: 22,808.
Programming (received off-air): WAZT-CA (IND) Woodstock; WDCA (MNT) Washington; WDCW (CW) Washington; WETA-TV (PBS) Washington; WFDC-DT (UNV) Arlington; WHAG-TV (NBC) Hagerstown; WHSV-TV (ABC, MNT) Harrisonburg; WJAL (IND) Hagerstown; WJLA-TV (ABC) Washington; WJZ-TV (CBS) Baltimore; WRC-TV (NBC) Washington; WTTG (FOX) Washington; WUSA (CBS) Washington; WWPX-TV (ION) Martinsburg; allband FM.
Programming (via microwave): WBAL-TV (NBC) Baltimore; WRC-TV (NBC) Washington; WTTG (FOX) Washington.
Programming (via satellite): ESPN; QVC; TV Guide Network.
Programming (via translator): WVPT (PBS) Staunton.
Fee: $44.00 installation; $11.50 monthly; $1.05 converter.

Expanded Basic Service 1
Subscribers: 22,200.
Programming (via satellite): A&E Networks; ABC Family Channel; AMC; Animal Planet; BET Networks; Bravo; Cartoon Network; CNBC; CNN; Comcast SportsNet Mid-Atlantic; Comedy Central; Country Music TV; C-SPAN; C-SPAN 2; Discovery Channel; Disney Channel; E! Entertainment Television; ESPN 2; Eternal Word TV Network; Food Network; Fox News Channel; FX; Hallmark Channel; Headline News; HGTV; History Channel; Lifetime; MSNBC; MTV; Nickelodeon; Oxygen; Spike TV; Syfy; TBS Superstation; The Learning Channel; The Weather Channel; Travel Channel; truTV; Turner Network TV; TV Land; USA Network; VH1.
Fee: $44.00 installation; $21.31 monthly.

Digital Basic Service
Subscribers: N.A.
Programming (via satellite): A&E HD; ABC Family HD; Animal Planet HD; BBC America; Bio; Bloomberg Television; CBS Sports Network; Cine Latino; CMT Pure Country; CNN en Espanol; CNN HD; C-SPAN 2; Current; Discovery Channel HD; Discovery en Espanol; Discovery Fit & Health; Discovery Health Channel; Disney Channel HD; DIY Network; Encore (multiplexed); ESPN 2 HD (multiplexed); ESPN Classic Sports; ESPN Deportes; ESPN HD; ESPNews; Flix; Food Network HD; Fox Business Channel; Fox College Sports Atlantic; Fox College Sports Central; Fox College Sports Pacific;

Fox Deportes; Fox Movie Channel; Fox Reality Channel; Fox Soccer; Fuel TV; Fuse; G4; GMC; Golf Channel; Great American Country; GSN; Halogen Network; HD Theater; HGTV HD; History Channel en Espanol; History Channel HD; History Channel International; ID Investigation Discovery; Independent Film Channel; Lifetime Movie Network; LOGO; Military Channel; MTV2; mun2 television; National Geographic Channel; National Geographic Channel HD Network; NFL Network; Nick Jr.; Nick Too; NickToons TV; Outdoor Channel; Palladia; PBS Kids Sprout; Planet Green; Science; Science HD; SoapNet; Speed; Style Network; Sundance Channel; Syfy HD; TBS in HD; TeenNick; The Comcast Network; The Word Network; TLC HD; Toon Disney; Toon Disney en Espanol; Tr3s; Trinity Broadcasting Network; Turner Classic Movies; Turner Network TV HD; TV One; TVG Network; Universal HD; USA Network HD; VeneMovies; Versus; VH1 Classic; VH1 Soul; WE tv.

Digital Pay Service 1

Pay Units: N.A.

Programming (via satellite): ART America; CCTV-4; Cinemax (multiplexed); Cinemax HD; Filipino Channel; HBO (multiplexed); HBO HD; RAI International; Showtime; Showtime HD; Starz HDTV; The Movie Channel (multiplexed); TV Asia; TV Japan; TV5, La Television International; Zee TV USA; Zhong Tian Channel.

Video-On-Demand: Yes

Pay-Per-View

iN DEMAND (delivered digitally); Playboy TV (delivered digitally).

Internet Service

Operational: Yes.

Broadband Service: Comcast High Speed Internet.

Fee: $42.95 monthly; $7.00 modem lease.

Telephone Service

Digital: Operational

Miles of plant included with Front Royal

Vice President & General Manager: Troy Fitzhugh. Technical Operations Director: Tom Jacobs. Technical Operations Manager: Richard Burke. Marketing Director: Steve Miles.

Ownership: Comcast Cable Communications Inc. (MSO).

WINTERGREEN—Nelson Cable, 400 Front St, PO Box 395, Lovingston, VA 22949-0395. Phones: 800-376-8165; 434-263-4805. Fax: 434-263-4821. E-mail: joeleemc@aol.com. Web Site: http://www.nelsoncable.com. Also serves Augusta County (portions), Nelson County (portions) & Rockfish. ICA: VA0112.

TV Market Ranking: 70 (Nelson County (portions), WINTERGREEN); Below 100 (Augusta County (portions), Rockfish, Nelson County (portions)); Outside TV Markets (Augusta County (portions)). Franchise award date: N.A. Franchise expiration date: N.A. Began: October 1, 1967.

Channel capacity: 42 (not 2-way capable). Channels available but not in use: N.A.

Basic Service

Subscribers: 296.

Programming (received off-air): WCVE-TV (PBS) Richmond; WDBJ (CBS, MNT) Roanoke; WRIC-TV (ABC) Petersburg; WSET-TV (ABC) Lynchburg; WSLS-TV (NBC) Roanoke; WTVR-TV (CBS) Richmond; WWBT (NBC) Richmond; WWCW (CW, FOX) Lynchburg; allband FM.

Programming (via satellite): CNN; Disney Channel; ESPN; Hallmark Channel; TBS Superstation.

Fee: $35.00 installation; $26.00 monthly.

Pay Service 1

Pay Units: 154.

Programming (via satellite): Cinemax; HBO; Playboy TV; Showtime.

Fee: $10.00 monthly (each).

Video-On-Demand: No

Internet Service

Operational: Yes.

Fee: $44.00 monthly.

Telephone Service

None

Miles of Plant: 42.0 (coaxial); None (fiber optic).

President: Joe Lee McClellan. Chief Technician: Terry Engelhardt.

Ownership: Nelson County Cablevision Corporation (MSO).

WYTHE COUNTY—Citizens Telephone Coop. Now served byy FORT CHISWELL, VA [VA0066]. ICA: VA5306.

WYTHEVILLE—Shentel, 60 Long Ridge Rd, Ste 404, Stamford, CT 6902. Phones: 800-743-6835; 540-984-5224. Web Site: http://www.shentel.net. Also serves Wythe County. ICA: VA0061.

TV Market Ranking: Below 100 (Wythe County, WYTHEVILLE). Franchise award date: N.A. Franchise expiration date: February 12, 2022. Began: December 1, 1969.

Channel capacity: 42 (not 2-way capable). Channels available but not in use: N.A.

Basic Service

Subscribers: 2,145.

Programming (received off-air): WBRA-TV (PBS) Roanoke; WDBJ (CBS, MNT) Roanoke; WKPT-TV (ABC) Kingsport; WSET-TV (ABC) Lynchburg; WSLS-TV (NBC) Roanoke; WVVA (CW, NBC) Bluefield; WWCW (CW, FOX) Lynchburg; allband FM.

Programming (via satellite): ABC Family Channel; Cartoon Network; Country Music TV; C-SPAN; C-SPAN 2; Discovery Channel; INSP; MSNBC; QVC; TBS Superstation; The Weather Channel; Travel Channel; Trinity Broadcasting Network.

Fee: $49.95 installation; $15.01 monthly; $21.95 additional installation.

Expanded Basic Service 1

Subscribers: 1,664.

Programming (via satellite): A&E Networks; AMC; Animal Planet; CNN; Comedy Central; Disney Channel; E! Entertainment Television; ESPN; ESPN 2; Fox News Channel; FX; Headline News; HGTV; Lifetime; MTV; Nickelodeon; Spike TV; Syfy; The Learning Channel; Turner Network TV; TV Land; USA Network.

Fee: $26.20 monthly.

Digital Basic Service

Subscribers: 383.

Programming (via satellite): BBC America; Bravo; Discovery Digital Networks; DMX Music; GSN; History Channel; Independent Film Channel; National Geographic Channel; Nick Jr.; Turner Classic Movies; VH1 Classic; VH1 Country; WE tv.

Fee: $4.00 monthly.

Digital Expanded Basic Service

Subscribers: N.A.

Programming (via satellite): ESPN Classic Sports; ESPNews; Fox Soccer; Golf Channel; Speed; Versus.

Fee: $4.00 monthly.

Digital Expanded Basic Service 2

Subscribers: N.A.

Programming (via satellite): Encore (multiplexed); Showtime (multiplexed); The Movie Channel (multiplexed).

Fee: $9.00 monthly.

Digital Pay Service 1

Pay Units: 363.

Programming (via satellite): Cinemax (multiplexed); HBO (multiplexed); Starz (multiplexed).

Fee: $12.95 installation; $13.00 monthly (each).

Video-On-Demand: No

Pay-Per-View

iN DEMAND (delivered digitally).

Internet Service

Operational: No.

Telephone Service

None

Miles of Plant: 125.0 (coaxial); None (fiber optic).

President: Christopher French. Vice President, Customer Service: David Ferguson. Marketing Manager: Chris Ranson.

Ownership: Shenandoah Telecommunications Inc. (MSO).

YORKTOWN—Cox Communications. Now served by HAMPTON ROADS (formerly Virginia Beach), VA [VA0002]. ICA: VA0162.

WASHINGTON

Total Systems: **103**
Total Communities Served: **463**
Franchises Not Yet Operating: **0**
Applications Pending: **0**
Communities with Applications: **0**
Number of Basic Subscribers: **1,746,219**
Number of Expanded Basic Subscribers: **552,753**
Number of Pay Units: **216,507**

Top 100 Markets Represented: Seattle-Tacoma (20).

For a list of cable communities in this section, see the Cable Community Index located in the back of Cable Volume 2.
For explanation of terms used in cable system listings, see p. D-11.

ABERDEEN—Comcast Cable. Now served by TACOMA, WA [WA0003]. ICA: WA0019.

ALMIRA—Formerly served by Almega Cable. No longer in operation. ICA: WA0143.

ANDERSON ISLAND—Millennium Digital Media/Broadstripe, 3633 136th Pl SE, Ste 107, Bellevue, WA 98006-1451. Phones: 800-829-2225; 425-747-4600. Fax: 425-644-4621. E-mail: contact_nw@mdm.net. Web Site: http://www.broadstripe.com. Also serves Herron Island & Key Peninsula. ICA: WA0157.

TV Market Ranking: 20 (ANDERSON ISLAND, Herron Island, Key Peninsula). Franchise award date: January 1, 1989. Franchise expiration date: N.A. Began: September 1, 1989.

Channel capacity: 54 (not 2-way capable). Channels available but not in use: N.A.

Basic Service

Subscribers: 850.

Programming (received off-air): KBTC-TV (PBS) Tacoma; KCPQ (FOX) Tacoma; KCTS-TV (PBS) Seattle; KING-TV (NBC) Seattle; KIRO-TV (CBS, IND) Seattle; KOMO-TV (ABC) Seattle; KONG (IND) Everett; KSTW (CW) Tacoma; KTBW-TV (TBN) Tacoma; KUNS-TV (UNV) Bellevue; KZJO (MNT) Seattle.

Programming (via satellite): A&E Networks; ABC Family Channel; AMC; CNBC; CNN; C-SPAN; Discovery Channel; Disney Channel; ESPN; Headline News; Lifetime; MTV; Nickelodeon; Northwest Cable News; QVC; Spike TV; Syfy; TBS Superstation; Turner Network TV; USA Network; VH1.

Fee: $29.95 installation; $39.99 monthly; $2.00 converter.

Digital Basic Service

Subscribers: N.A.

Programming (via satellite): A&E Networks; BBC America; Bravo; Discovery Digital Networks; DMX Music; ESPN 2; ESPNews; Fox Sports World; Golf Channel; GSN; HGTV; History Channel; History Channel International; Independent Film Channel; Lifetime Movie Network; National Geographic Channel; Speed; Style Network; Versus.

Fee: $15.40 monthly.

Digital Pay Service 1

Pay Units: N.A.

Programming (via satellite): Cinemax (multiplexed); Encore (multiplexed); HBO (multiplexed); Showtime (multiplexed); Starz (multiplexed); The Movie Channel (multiplexed).

Fee: $10.00 monthly (each).

Video-On-Demand: No

Pay-Per-View

Playboy TV (delivered digitally); iN DEMAND (delivered digitally).

Internet Service

Operational: Yes.

Fee: $39.95 installation; $37.95 monthly.

Telephone Service

Digital: Operational

Fee: $39.99 monthly

Miles of Plant: 18.0 (coaxial); None (fiber optic).

President & Chief Executive Officer: Bill Shreffler. Vice President & General Manager: Dave Walker. Vice President, Programming: Frank Scotello. Engineering Director: Dave Jacobs. Customer Service Manager: Steve Orona.

Ownership: Broadstripe (MSO).

ARLINGTON—Comcast Cable. Now served by SEATTLE, WA [WA0001]. ICA: WA0021.

AUBURN—Comcast Cable, 4020 Auburn Way N, Auburn, WA 98002. Phone: 253-288-7450. Fax: 253-288-7500. Web Site: http://www.comcast.com. Also serves Algona, Black Diamond, Burien, Covington, Des Moines, Enumclaw, Fall City, Federal Way, Issaquah, Kent, Maple Valley, Newcastle, Normandy Park, Pacific, Preston, Renton, Seatac, Snoqualmie & Tukwila. ICA: WA0211.

TV Market Ranking: 20 (Algona, AUBURN, Black Diamond, Burien, Covington, Des Moines, Enumclaw, Fall City, Federal Way, Issaquah, Kent, Maple Valley, Newcastle, Normandy Park, Pacific, Preston, Renton, Seatac, Snoqualmie, Tukwila, Tukwila).

Channel capacity: N.A. Channels available but not in use: N.A.

Basic Service

Subscribers: N.A. Included in Seattle

Programming (received off-air): KBCB (IND) Bellingham; KBTC-TV (PBS) Tacoma; KCPQ (FOX) Tacoma; KCTS-TV (PBS) Seattle; KFFV (IND) Seattle; KING-TV (NBC) Seattle; KIRO-TV (CBS, IND) Seattle; KOMO-TV (ABC) Seattle; KONG (IND) Everett; KSTW (CW) Tacoma; KTBW-TV (TBN) Tacoma; KUNS-TV (UNV) Bellevue; KWDK (ETV) Tacoma; KWPX-TV (ION) Bellevue; KZJO (MNT) Seattle.

Programming (via satellite): C-SPAN; C-SPAN 2; Discovery Channel; Hallmark Channel; Northwest Cable News; QVC; The Weather Channel; TVW; Univision Studios; various Canadian stations.

Fee: $43.99 installation; $12.55 monthly.

Expanded Basic Service 1

Subscribers: N.A.

Programming (via satellite): A&E Networks; ABC Family Channel; AMC; Animal Planet; BET Networks; Bravo; Cartoon Network; CNBC; CNN; Comedy Central; Country Music TV; Disney Channel; E! Entertainment Television; ESPN; ESPN 2; Food Network; Fox News Channel; FX; Golf Channel; Headline News; HGTV; History Channel; Lifetime; MSNBC; MTV; MTV2; Nickelodeon; Oxygen; Speed; Spike TV; Syfy; TBS Superstation; The Learning Channel; Travel Channel; truTV; Turner Network TV; USA Network; Versus; VH1.

Fee: $36.70 monthly.

Digital Basic Service

Subscribers: N.A.

Programming (via satellite): Arabic Channel; BBC America; Bio; Bloomberg Television; BYU Television; CBS Sports Network; CCTV-4; CMT Pure Country; Cooking Channel; Current; DIY Network; DMX Music (multiplexed); Encore (multiplexed); ESPN 2 HD; ESPN Classic Sports; ESPN HD; ESPNews; Eternal Word TV Network; Filipino Channel; Flix; Fox College Sports Atlantic; Fox College Sports Central; Fox College Sports Pacific; Fox Movie Channel; Fox Reality Channel; Fox Soccer; Fuse; G4; GAS; GMC; Great American Country; GSN; Halogen Network; HD Theater; History Channel International; Independent Film Channel; Jewelry Television; Lifetime Movie Network; LOGO (multiplexed); MoviePlex; MTV Networks Digital Suite; National Geographic Channel; NBA TV; NFL Network; Nick Jr.; Nick Too; NickToons TV; Outdoor Channel; Palladia; RAI International; Russian Television Network; Saigon Broadcasting Television Network; Style Network; Sundance Channel; The Word Network; Toon Disney; Turner Classic Movies; Turner Network TV HD; TV Asia; TV Japan; TV Land; TV One; TV5, La Television International; TVG Network; Universal HD; WE tv; Weatherscan; Zee TV USA; Zhong Tian Channel.

Fee: $11.99 monthly.

Digital Pay Service 1

Pay Units: N.A.

Programming (via satellite): Canales N; Cinemax (multiplexed); Cinemax HD; Flix; HBO (multiplexed); HBO HD; Showtime (multiplexed); Showtime HD; Starz (multiplexed); Starz HDTV; The Movie Channel.

Fee: $15.00 monthly (each).

Video-On-Demand: Yes

Pay-Per-View

ESPN (delivered digitally); NBA League Pass (delivered digitally); NHL Center Ice (delivered digitally); iN DEMAND (delivered digitally); Playboy TV (delivered digitally).

Internet Service

Operational: Yes.

Broadband Service: Comcast High Speed Internet.

Fee: $42.95 monthly.

Telephone Service

Digital: Operational

Fee: $44.95 monthly

Area Vice President: Ken Rhoades. Vice President, Engineering: Steve Taber. Vice President, Sales & Marketing: Tom Pierce. Public Relations Director: Steve Kipp.

Ownership: Comcast Cable Communications Inc. (MSO).

BAINBRIDGE ISLAND—Comcast Cable. Now served by TACOMA, WA [WA0003]. ICA: WA0024.

BAYVIEW—Wave Broadband. Now served by CAMANO ISLAND, WA [WA0046]. ICA: WA0149.

BELLEVUE—Comcast Cable. Now served by SEATTLE, WA [WA0001]. ICA: WA0212.

BELLINGHAM—Comcast Cable, 19909 120th Ave NE, Ste 200, Bothell, WA 98021. Phone: 425-398-6000. Fax: 425-398-6236. Web Site: http://www.comcast.com. Also serves Anacortes, Blaine, Deming, Everson, Ferndale, Glen Mobile Home Park, Island County (portions), Lummi Indian Reservation, Lynden, Maple Falls, Nooksack, Samish Lake, Skagit County (portions) & Whatcom County. ICA: WA0011.

TV Market Ranking: Below 100 (Anacortes, BELLINGHAM, Blaine, Deming, Everson, Ferndale, Glen Mobile Home Park, Island County (portions), Lummi Indian Reservation, Lynden, Maple Falls, Nooksack, Samish Lake, Skagit County (portions), Whatcom County (portions)); Outside TV Markets (Whatcom County (portions)). Franchise award date: N.A. Franchise expiration date: N.A. Began: February 1, 1949.

Channel capacity: N.A. Channels available but not in use: N.A.

Basic Service

Subscribers: N.A. Included in Seattle

Programming (received off-air): KBCB (IND) Bellingham; KCPQ (FOX) Tacoma; KCTS-TV (PBS) Seattle; KFFV (IND) Seattle; KING-TV (NBC) Seattle; KIRO-TV (CBS, IND) Seattle; KOMO-TV (ABC) Seattle; KONG (IND) Everett; KSTW (CW) Tacoma; KVOS-TV (IND) Bellingham; KWDK (ETV) Tacoma; KWPX-TV (ION) Bellevue; KZJO (MNT) Seattle; 20 FMs.

Programming (via satellite): C-SPAN; C-SPAN 2; Discovery Channel; Hallmark Channel; Northwest Cable News; QVC; The Comcast Network; Trinity Broadcasting Network; Univision Studios.

Fee: $43.99 installation; $12.55 monthly; $40.00 additional installation.

Expanded Basic Service 1

Subscribers: 31,009.

Programming (via satellite): A&E Networks; ABC Family Channel; AMC; Animal Planet; BET Networks; Bravo; Cartoon Network; CNBC; CNN; Comedy Central; Country Music TV; Disney Channel; E! Entertainment Television; ESPN; ESPN 2; Food Network; Fox News Channel; FX; Headline News; History Channel; Jewelry Television; Lifetime; MSNBC; MTV; MTV2; Nickelodeon; Oxygen; Product Information Network; Spike TV; TBS Superstation; The Learning Channel; The Weather Channel; Travel Channel;

truTV; Turner Network TV; TV Guide Network; USA Network; VH1.
Fee: $36.70 monthly.

Digital Basic Service
Subscribers: 11,449.
Programming (via satellite): American-Life TV Network; BBC America; Bio; Black Family Channel; Bloomberg Television; Discovery Digital Networks; DMX Music; ESPNews; Fox Movie Channel; Fox Sports World; FSN Digital Atlantic; FSN Digital Central; FSN Digital Pacific; Fuse; G4; GAS; Golf Channel; Great American Country; GSN; Halogen Network; HGTV; History Channel International; Independent Film Channel; Lifetime Movie Network; Lime; MTV Networks Digital Suite; National Geographic Channel; Nick Jr.; NickToons TV; Outdoor Channel; Ovation; Speed; Style Network; Sundance Channel; Syfy; The Word Network; Toon Disney; Turner Classic Movies; TV Land; Versus; WE tv; Weatherscan.
Fee: $11.99 monthly.

Digital Pay Service 1
Pay Units: 3,363.
Programming (via satellite): ART America; Canales N; CCTV-4; Cinemax (multiplexed); Encore (multiplexed); Filipino Channel; Flix; HBO (multiplexed); Korean Channel; RAI USA; Russian Television Network; Showtime (multiplexed); Starz (multiplexed); The Movie Channel (multiplexed); TV Asia; TV Japan; TV5 USA.
Fee: $15.00 monthly (each).

Video-On-Demand: Yes

Pay-Per-View
Addressable homes: 8,947.
Barker (delivered digitally); ESPN Now (delivered digitally); Hot Choice (delivered digitally); iN DEMAND (delivered digitally); Playboy TV (delivered digitally); Fresh (delivered digitally); Shorteez (delivered digitally); sports (delivered digitally).

Internet Service
Operational: Yes.
Subscribers: 14,373.
Broadband Service: Comcast High Speed Internet.
Fee: $42.95 monthly.

Telephone Service
Digital: Operational
Fee: $44.95 monthly

Miles of Plant: 1,188.0 (coaxial); None (fiber optic).

Area Vice President: John Dietrich. Vice President, Engineering: Steve Taber. Vice President, Sales & Marketing: Tom Pierce. General Manager: Brett Fontes. Public Relations Director: Steve Kipp.

Ownership: Comcast Cable Communications Inc. (MSO).

BELLINGHAM—Millennium Digital Media/Broadstripe, 3633 136th Pl SE, Ste 107, Bellevue, WA 98006-1451. Phones: 800-829-2225; 425-747-4600. Fax: 425-462-2092. E-mail: blam@mdm.net. Web Site: http://www.broadstripe.com. Also serves Whatcom County (portions). ICA: WA0080.

TV Market Ranking: Below 100 (BELLINGHAM, Whatcom County (portions)). Franchise award date: January 1, 1992. Franchise expiration date: January 1, 2017. Began: October 1, 1992.

Channel capacity: N.A. Channels available but not in use: N.A.

Basic Service
Subscribers: 1,081.
Programming (received off-air): KCPQ (FOX) Tacoma; KCTS-TV (PBS) Seattle; KING-TV (NBC) Seattle; KIRO-TV (CBS, IND) Seattle; KOMO-TV (ABC) Seattle; KSTW (CW) Tacoma; KVOS-TV (IND) Bellingham.
Programming (via satellite): A&E Networks; ABC Family Channel; AMC; CNN; C-SPAN; Discovery Channel; Disney Channel; ESPN; Headline News; History Channel; Lifetime; MTV; Nickelodeon; QVC; Spike TV; Syfy; TBS Superstation; The Learning Channel; Turner Network TV; TV Guide Network; USA Network; VH1; WGN America.
Fee: $30.00 installation; $40.39 monthly; $3.00 converter.

Pay Service 1
Pay Units: 135.
Programming (via satellite): HBO.
Fee: $8.95 monthly.

Pay Service 2
Pay Units: 79.
Programming (via satellite): Showtime.
Fee: $10.00 installation; $8.00 monthly.

Video-On-Demand: No

Internet Service
Operational: Yes.
Fee: $49.95 installation; $37.95 monthly.

Telephone Service
Digital: Operational
Fee: $39.99 monthly

Miles of Plant: 99.0 (coaxial); 10.0 (fiber optic).

President & Chief Executive Officer: Bill Shreffler. Engineering Director: Dane Jacobs. Customer Service Manager: Steve Orona.

Ownership: Broadstripe (MSO).

BIG LAKE—Wave Broadband. Now served by CAMANO ISLAND, WA [WA0046]. ICA: WA0085.

BREMERTON—Comcast Cable. No longer in operation. ICA: WA0017.

BREWSTER—Millennium Digital Media/Broadstripe, 3633 136th Pl SE, Ste 107, Bellevue, WA 98006-1451. Phones: 800-829-2225; 425-747-4600. Fax: 425-644-4621. Web Site: http://www.broadstripe.com. Also serves Bridgeport, Bridgeport Bar & Pateros. ICA: WA0060.

TV Market Ranking: Outside TV Markets (BREWSTER, Bridgeport, Bridgeport Bar, Pateros). Franchise award date: N.A. Franchise expiration date: N.A. Began: October 1, 1982.

Channel capacity: 35 (operating 2-way). Channels available but not in use: N.A.

Basic Service
Subscribers: 1,117.
Programming (received off-air): KAYU-TV (FOX) Spokane; KCTS-TV (PBS) Seattle; KHQ-TV (NBC) Spokane; KING-TV (NBC) Seattle; KIRO-TV (CBS, IND) Seattle; KOMO-TV (ABC) Seattle; KREM (CBS) Spokane; KXLY-TV (ABC, MNT) Spokane.
Programming (via satellite): A&E Networks; ABC Family Channel; AMC; CNN; Country Music TV; Discovery Channel; Disney Channel; ESPN; Fox News Channel; G4; Headline News; Lifetime; National Geographic Channel; Nickelodeon; Northwest Cable News; QVC; Spike TV; Syfy; TBS Superstation; Telemundo; The Learning Channel; Turner Network TV; TVW; Univision Studios; USA Network; WGN America.
Fee: $29.95 installation; $41.99 monthly.

Digital Basic Service
Subscribers: N.A.
Programming (via satellite): A&E Networks; BBC America; Bravo; Canales N; Discovery Digital Networks; DMX Music; ESPN 2; ESPNews; Fox Sports World; Golf Channel; GSN; HGTV; History Channel; History Channel International; Independent Film Channel; Lifetime Movie Network; Speed; Style Network; Versus.
Fee: $13.40 monthly.

Digital Pay Service 1
Pay Units: N.A.
Programming (via satellite): Cinemax (multiplexed); Encore (multiplexed); HBO (multiplexed); Showtime (multiplexed); Starz (multiplexed); The Movie Channel (multiplexed).
Fee: $10.00 monthly (each).

Video-On-Demand: No

Pay-Per-View
Playboy TV (delivered digitally); iN DEMAND (delivered digitally).

Internet Service
Operational: Yes.
Broadband Service: Millennium Cable-Speed.

Telephone Service
None

Miles of Plant: 47.0 (coaxial); None (fiber optic).

President & Chief Executive Officer: Bill Shreffler. Vice President & General Manager: Dave Walker. Vice President, Programming: Frank Scotello. Engineering Director: Dave Jacobs. Customer Service Manager: Steve Orona.

Ownership: Broadstripe (MSO).

BRIDGEHAVEN—Millennium Digital Media/Broadstripe, 3633 136th Pl SE, Ste 107, Bellevue, WA 98006-1451. Phones: 800-829-2225; 425-747-4600. Fax: 425-644-4621. E-mail: contact_nw@broadstripe.com. Web Site: http://www.broadstripe.com. Also serves Hood Canal. ICA: WA0199.

TV Market Ranking: 20 (BRIDGEHAVEN, Hood Canal). Franchise award date: N.A. Franchise expiration date: N.A. Began: N.A.

Channel capacity: N.A. Channels available but not in use: N.A.

Basic Service
Subscribers: 84.
Programming (received off-air): KCPQ (FOX) Tacoma; KCTS-TV (PBS) Seattle; KING-TV (NBC) Seattle; KIRO-TV (CBS, IND) Seattle; KOMO-TV (ABC) Seattle; KONG (IND) Everett; KSTW (CW) Tacoma; KTBW-TV (TBN) Tacoma; KUNS-TV (UNV) Bellevue; KVOS-TV (IND) Bellingham; KWPX-TV (ION) Bellevue; KZJO (MNT) Seattle; various Canadian stations.
Programming (via satellite): A&E Networks; ABC Family Channel; AMC; Cartoon Network; CNBC; CNN; C-SPAN; Discovery Channel; Disney Channel; ESPN; Fox News Channel; G4; Headline News; History Channel; Lifetime; Nickelodeon; Northwest Cable News; QVC; Spike TV; TBS Superstation; The Learning Channel; Turner Network TV; TVW; USA Network.
Fee: $29.95 installation; $37.99 monthly.

Digital Basic Service
Subscribers: N.A.
Programming (via satellite): DMX Music; Encore; Starz.
Fee: $13.40 monthly.

Digital Pay Service 1
Pay Units: N.A.
Programming (via satellite): HBO (multiplexed); Showtime (multiplexed).
Fee: $13.45 monthly (Showtime), $14.95 monthly (HBO).

Video-On-Demand: No

Pay-Per-View
Playboy TV (delivered digitally); Fresh (delivered digitally).

Internet Service
Operational: Yes.
Broadband Service: Millennium Cable-Speed.

Telephone Service
None

Miles of Plant: 73.0 (coaxial); None (fiber optic).

President & Chief Executive Officer: Bill Shreffler. Vice President & General Manager: Dave Walker. Vice President, Programming: Frank Scotello. Engineering Director: Dave Jacobs. Customer Service Manager: Steve Orona.

Ownership: Broadstripe (MSO).

BURIEN—Comcast Cable. Now served by AUBURN, WA [WA0211]. ICA: WA0210.

BURLINGTON—Comcast Cable. Now served by SEATTLE, WA [WA0001]. ICA: WA0018.

CAMANO ISLAND—Wave Broadband, 115 S Maple St, PO Box 1630, La Conner, WA 98257-1630. Phones: 866-928-3123 (Customer service); 804-648-5253; 800-442-8617; 360-466-3317. Fax: 360-466-3560. Web Site: http://www.wavebroadband.com. Also serves Arlington (northwestern portion), Bayview, Big Lake, Bryant, Clear Lake, Conway, Indian Beach, La Conner, Lake Goodwin, Lakewood, Lost Lake, Madrona Beach, Seven Lakes, Shelter Bay, Snohomish County (northwestern portion), Stanwood, Swinomish Indian Reservation, Utsalady & Whatcom County (southern portion). ICA: WA0046.

TV Market Ranking: 20 (CAMANO ISLAND (portions)); Below 100 (Arlington (northwestern portion), Bayview, Big Lake, Bryant, Clear Lake, Conway, Indian Beach, La Conner, Lake Goodwin, Lakewood, Lost Lake, Madrona Beach, Seven Lakes, Shelter Bay, Skagit County (unincorporated areas), Snohomish County (northwestern portion) (portions), Stanwood, Swinomish Indian Reservation, Utsalady, Whatcom County (southern portion), CAMANO ISLAND (portions)); Outside TV Markets (Snohomish County (northwestern portion) (portions)). Franchise award date: January 1, 1968. Franchise expiration date: N.A. Began: June 1, 1980.

Channel capacity: 50 (not 2-way capable). Channels available but not in use: N.A.

Basic Service
Subscribers: 3,915.
Programming (received off-air): KCPQ (FOX) Tacoma; KCTS-TV (PBS) Seattle; KFFV (IND) Seattle; KING-TV (NBC) Seattle; KIRO-TV (CBS, IND) Seattle; KOMO-TV (ABC) Seattle; KONG (IND) Everett; KSTW (CW) Tacoma; KUNS-TV (UNV) Bellevue; KVOS-TV (IND) Bellingham; KWPX-TV (ION) Bellevue; KZJO (MNT) Seattle; allband FM.
Programming (via satellite): C-SPAN; Jewelry Television; QVC; ShopNBC; Trinity Broadcasting Network; TV Guide Network; TVW; various Canadian stations.
Fee: $23.95 monthly.

Expanded Basic Service 1
Subscribers: 3,551.
Programming (via satellite): A&E Networks; ABC Family Channel; AMC; Animal Planet; BET Networks; Bravo; Cartoon Network; CNBC; CNN; Comedy Central; Country Music TV; Discovery Channel; Discovery Fit & Health; Disney Channel; E! Entertainment Television; ESPN; ESPN 2; Food Network; Fox Movie Channel; Fox News Channel; Fox Sports Net; FX; Great American Coun-

try; Hallmark Channel; Headline News; HGTV; History Channel; INSP; Lifetime; MSNBC; MTV; National Geographic Channel; Nickelodeon; Northwest Cable News; Outdoor Channel; Oxygen; Spike TV; Syfy; TBS Superstation; The Learning Channel; The Weather Channel; Travel Channel; Turner Classic Movies; Turner Network TV; TV Land; USA Network; VH1.
Fee: $50.00 installation; $23.55 monthly.

Digital Basic Service
Subscribers: N.A.
Programming (via satellite): BBC America; Bio; BYU Television; cloo; CMT Pure Country; Current; Discovery en Espanol; Discovery Health Channel; Discovery Kids Channel; Disney XD; DMX Music; Eternal Word TV Network; Fox Business Channel; History Channel International; Military Channel; MTV Hits; MTV Jams; MTV2; Nick Jr.; NickToons TV; PBS Kids Sprout; Planet Green; Science; SoapNet; TeenNick; Tr3s; VH1 Classic; VH1 Soul.
Fee: $10.00 monthly.

Digital Expanded Basic Service
Subscribers: N.A.
Programming (via satellite): American-Life TV Network; Bloomberg Television; Boomerang; Bravo; Cooking Channel; DIY Network; Fuse; G4; GSN; Hallmark Movie Channel; Halogen Network; Independent Film Channel; Lifetime Movie Network; Lifetime Real Women; Ovation; Style Network; truTV; WE tv.

Digital Expanded Basic Service 2
Subscribers: N.A.
Programming (received off-air): KCPQ (FOX) Tacoma; KCTS-TV (PBS) Seattle; KING-TV (NBC) Seattle; KIRO-TV (CBS, IND) Seattle; KOMO-TV (ABC) Seattle; KONG (IND) Everett; KSTW (CW) Tacoma.
Programming (via satellite): A&E HD; Animal Planet HD; Discovery Channel HD; Disney Channel HD; ESPN 2 HD; ESPN HD; Food Network HD; FSN HD; HD Theater; HDNet; HDNet Movies; HGTV HD; History Channel HD; MGM HD; National Geographic Channel HD Network; NFL Network HD; Science HD; TBS in HD; TLC HD; Travel Channel HD; Turner Network TV HD; Universal HD.

Digital Expanded Basic Service 3
Subscribers: N.A.
Programming (via satellite): CBS Sports Network; ESPN Classic Sports; ESPN U; ESPNews; Fox Soccer; FSN Digital Atlantic; FSN Digital Central; FSN Digital Pacific; Golf Channel; NFL Network; Speed; Tennis Channel; Versus.

Digital Pay Service 1
Pay Units: N.A.
Programming (via satellite): Cinemax (multiplexed); Cinemax HD; Encore (multiplexed); Flix; HBO (multiplexed); HBO HD; MoviePlex; Showtime (multiplexed); Showtime HD; Starz (multiplexed); Starz HDTV; The Movie Channel (multiplexed); The Movie Channel HD.
Fee: $12.00 monthly (Showtime/TMC/Flix), $15.00 monthly (HBO, Cinemax or Starz/Encore).

Video-On-Demand: Yes

Pay-Per-View
Sports PPV (delivered digitally); Movies (delivered digitally).

Internet Service
Operational: Yes.
Broadband Service: In-house.
Fee: $24.95-$74.95 monthly.

Telephone Service
Digital: Operational
Fee: $39.95 monthly

Miles of Plant: 134.0 (coaxial); None (fiber optic).
Manager: Jon Ulrich. Regional Office Manager: Bede Wells. Chief Technician: Ed Knipper. Marketing: Sue Campbell.
Ownership: WaveDivision Holdings LLC (MSO).

CARSON—Millennium Digital Media/Broadstripe, 3633 136th Pl SE, Ste 107, Bellevue, WA 98006-1451. Phones: 800-829-2225; 425-747-4600. Fax: 425-644-4621. E-mail: contact_nw@broadstripe.com. Web Site: http://www.broadstripe.com. Also serves Skamania & Stevenson. ICA: WA0061.
TV Market Ranking: 29 (Skamania); Outside TV Markets (CARSON, Stevenson). Franchise award date: N.A. Franchise expiration date: N.A. Began: January 1, 1953.
Channel capacity: 22 (operating 2-way). Channels available but not in use: N.A.

Basic Service
Subscribers: N.A.
Programming (received off-air): KATU (ABC) Portland; KGW (NBC) Portland; KOIN (CBS) Portland; KOPB-TV (PBS) Portland; KPDX (MNT) Vancouver; KPTV (FOX) Portland; allband FM.
Programming (via satellite): A&E Networks; ABC Family Channel; AMC; Animal Planet; CNN; C-SPAN; Discovery Channel; Disney Channel; ESPN; Fox News Channel; G4; Headline News; HGTV; History Channel; Lifetime; National Geographic Channel; Nickelodeon; Northwest Cable News; QVC; Spike TV; Syfy; TBS Superstation; The Learning Channel; The Weather Channel; Travel Channel; Turner Network TV; TV Land; USA Network; WGN America.
Fee: $29.95 installation; $42.99 monthly.

Digital Basic Service
Subscribers: N.A.
Programming (via satellite): A&E Networks; BBC America; Bravo; Discovery Digital Networks; DMX Music; ESPN 2; ESPNews; Fox Sports World; Golf Channel; GSN; History Channel International; Independent Film Channel; Lifetime Movie Network; Speed; Style Network; Versus.
Fee: $18.35 monthly.

Digital Pay Service 1
Pay Units: N.A.
Programming (via satellite): Cinemax (multiplexed); Encore (multiplexed); HBO (multiplexed); Showtime (multiplexed); Starz (multiplexed); The Movie Channel (multiplexed).
Fee: $6.00 monthly (each).

Video-On-Demand: No

Pay-Per-View
Playboy TV (delivered digitally); iN DEMAND (delivered digitally).

Internet Service
Operational: Yes.
Broadband Service: Millennium Cable-Speed.
Fee: $49.95 installation; $37.95 monthly.

Telephone Service
Digital: Operational
Fee: $39.99 monthly

Miles of Plant: 49.0 (coaxial); None (fiber optic).
President & Chief Executive Officer: Bill Shreffler. Vice President, Programming: Frank Scotello. Engineering Director: Dave Jacobs. Customer Service Manager: Steve Orona.
Ownership: Broadstripe (MSO).

CENTRALIA-CHEHALIS—Comcast Cable. Now served by TACOMA, WA [WA0003]. ICA: WA0022.

CHATTAROY—Formerly served by Almega Cable. No longer in operation. ICA: WA0181.

CHELAN—Millennium Digital Media/Broadstripe, 3633 136th Pl SE, Ste 107, Bellevue, WA 98006-1451. Phones: 800-829-2225; 425-747-4600. Fax: 425-644-4621. E-mail: contact_nw@broadstripe.com. Web Site: http://www.broadstripe.com. Also serves Chelan Falls, Manson & Upper South Shore. ICA: WA0058.
TV Market Ranking: Below 100 (Upper South Shore); Outside TV Markets (CHELAN, Chelan Falls, Manson). Franchise award date: N.A. Franchise expiration date: N.A. Began: May 1, 1954.
Channel capacity: 36 (operating 2-way). Channels available but not in use: N.A.

Basic Service
Subscribers: N.A.
Programming (received off-air): KCPQ (FOX) Tacoma; KHQ-TV (NBC) Spokane; KING-TV (NBC) Seattle; KIRO-TV (CBS, IND) Seattle; KOMO-TV (ABC) Seattle; KREM (CBS) Spokane; KSPS-TV (PBS) Spokane; KSTW (CW) Tacoma; KXLY-TV (ABC, MNT) Spokane; KZJO (MNT) Seattle; 8 FMs.
Programming (via satellite): A&E Networks; ABC Family Channel; AMC; CNBC; CNN; Comedy Central; C-SPAN; Discovery Channel; Disney Channel; ESPN; Fox News Channel; G4; Headline News; History Channel; Lifetime; National Geographic Channel; Nickelodeon; Northwest Cable News; QVC; Spike TV; TBS Superstation; The Learning Channel; Trinity Broadcasting Network; Turner Network TV; TVW; Univision Studios; USA Network.
Fee: $29.95 installation; $41.99 monthly.

Digital Basic Service
Subscribers: N.A.
Programming (via satellite): A&E Networks; BBC America; Bravo; Canales N; Discovery Digital Networks; DMX Music; Encore; ESPN 2; ESPNews; Fox Sports World; Golf Channel; GSN; HGTV; History Channel International; Independent Film Channel; Lifetime Movie Network; Speed; Style Network; Versus.
Fee: $13.40 monthly.

Digital Pay Service 1
Pay Units: N.A.
Programming (via satellite): Cinemax (multiplexed); HBO (multiplexed); Showtime (multiplexed).
Fee: $9.50 monthly (each).

Video-On-Demand: No

Pay-Per-View
iN DEMAND (delivered digitally); Playboy TV (delivered digitally).

Internet Service
Operational: Yes.
Broadband Service: Millennium Cable-Speed.
Fee: $49.95 installation; $24.95 monthly.

Telephone Service
Digital: Operational
Fee: $39.99 monthly

Miles of Plant: 82.0 (coaxial); None (fiber optic).
President & Chief Executive Officer: Bill Shreffler. Vice President & General Manager: Dave Walker. Vice President, Programming: Frank Scotello. Engineering Director: Dave Jacobs. Customer Service Manager: Steve Orona.
Ownership: Broadstripe (MSO).

CHENEY—Formerly served by Wave Broadband. No longer in operation. ICA: WA0045.

CHINOOK—Chinook Progressive Club TV, PO Box 15, Chinook, WA 98614-0015. Phone: 360-244-5660. ICA: WA0146.
TV Market Ranking: Outside TV Markets (CHINOOK). Franchise award date: N.A. Franchise expiration date: January 1, 2010. Began: January 1, 1961.
Channel capacity: 12 (not 2-way capable). Channels available but not in use: N.A.

Basic Service
Subscribers: 280.
Programming (received off-air): KATU (ABC) Portland; KGW (NBC) Portland; KOIN (CBS) Portland; KOPB-TV (PBS) Portland; KPTV (FOX) Portland.
Programming (via satellite): A&E Networks; ABC Family Channel; CNN; C-SPAN; Discovery Channel; ESPN; FX; QVC; Spike TV; TBS Superstation; The Learning Channel; The Weather Channel; Travel Channel; Trinity Broadcasting Network; Turner Network TV; USA Network.
Fee: $20.00 installation; $20.00 monthly; $15.00 additional installation.

Internet Service
Operational: No.

Telephone Service
None

Miles of Plant: 7.0 (coaxial); None (fiber optic).
Manager: Trophy W. Hughes. Chief Technician: Gary White.
Ownership: Chinook Progressive Club TV Inc.

CHINOOK PASS—Formerly served by Almega Cable. No longer in operation. ICA: WA0109.

CLALLAM BAY—Formerly served by Wave Broadband. No longer in operation. ICA: WA0095.

CLE ELUM—R & R Cable, 103 S Second St, PO Box 610, Roslyn, WA 98941. Phones: 509-649-2211; 509-649-2212. E-mail: cable@inlandnet.com. Web Site: http://www.rrcable.com. Also serves Kittitas County (northern portion) & South Cle Elum. ICA: WA0068.
TV Market Ranking: Below 100 (Kittitas County (northern portion) (portions)); Outside TV Markets (CLE ELUM, Kittitas County (northern portion) (portions), South Cle Elum). Franchise award date: N.A. Franchise expiration date: N.A. Began: December 1, 1954.
Channel capacity: N.A. Channels available but not in use: N.A.

Basic Service
Subscribers: N.A.
Programming (received off-air): KAPP (ABC, MNT) Yakima; KCYU-LD Yakima; KIMA-TV (CBS) Yakima; KNDO (NBC) Yakima; KYVE (PBS) Yakima; allband FM.
Programming (via microwave): KCPQ (FOX) Tacoma; KING-TV (NBC) Seattle; KIRO-TV (CBS, IND) Seattle; KOMO-TV (ABC) Seattle.
Programming (via satellite): A&E Networks; ABC Family Channel; AMC; Animal Planet; Bravo; Cartoon Network; CNN; Comedy Central; Country Music TV; C-SPAN; Discovery Channel; Discovery Fit & Health; E! Entertainment Television; ESPN; ESPN 2; ESPN Classic Sports; Food Network; Fox News Channel; FX; Hallmark Channel; Lifetime; Lifetime Movie Network; MSNBC; MTV; National Geographic Channel; Nickelodeon; NickToons TV; Northwest Cable News; Outdoor Channel; QVC; Spike TV; Syfy; TBS Superstation; The Learning Channel; The Weather Channel; Travel Channel; Trinity Broadcasting Network;

truTV; Turner Network TV; TV Guide Network; TV Land; TVW; USA Network; VH1; WGN America; WSBK-TV (CBS, MNT) Boston.
Fee: $32.95 monthly.

Digital Basic Service
Subscribers: N.A.
Programming (via satellite): BBC America; Bio; Bloomberg Television; cloo; Discovery Digital Networks; DMX Music; ESPNews; Fox College Sports Atlantic; Fox College Sports Central; Fox College Sports Pacific; Fox Movie Channel; Fox Soccer; Fuse; G4; GAS; Golf Channel; Great American Country; GSN; HGTV; History Channel; History Channel International; Independent Film Channel; MTV Networks Digital Suite; Nick Jr.; Speed; Style Network; Turner Classic Movies; Versus; WE tv.
Fee: $7.00 monthly.

Digital Pay Service 1
Pay Units: N.A.
Programming (via satellite): Cinemax (multiplexed); Encore (multiplexed); HBO (multiplexed); Showtime (multiplexed); Starz (multiplexed); The Movie Channel (multiplexed).
Fee: $7.00 monthly (Cinemax), $10.00 monthly (Starz & Encore), $12.00 monthly (Showtime & TMC), $13.00 monthly (HBO).

Video-On-Demand: No

Pay-Per-View
iN DEMAND (delivered digitally); Playboy TV (delivered digitally); Fresh (delivered digitally).

Internet Service
Operational: No.

Telephone Service
None

Miles of Plant: 23.0 (coaxial); None (fiber optic).
Manager: Doug Weiss. Chief Technician: Steven Vlahovich.
Ownership: Inland Telephone Co. (MSO).

COLFAX—Colfax Highline Cable Co., 300 North Mill St, Ste 2, PO Box 187, Colfax, WA 99111-0187. Phone: 509-397-2211. Fax: 509-397-3951. E-mail: service@stjohncable.com. Web Site: http://www.stjohncable.com. Also serves Steptoe. ICA: WA0075.
TV Market Ranking: Below 100 (COLFAX, Steptoe). Franchise award date: N.A. Franchise expiration date: N.A. Began: December 1, 1953.
Channel capacity: 42 (operating 2-way). Channels available but not in use: N.A.

Basic Service
Subscribers: 1,122.
Programming (received off-air): KAYU-TV (FOX) Spokane; KHQ-TV (NBC) Spokane; KLEW-TV (CBS) Lewiston; KREM (CBS) Spokane; KSKN (CW) Spokane; KSPS-TV (PBS) Spokane; KUID-TV (PBS) Moscow; KWSU-TV (PBS) Pullman; KXLY-TV (ABC, MNT) Spokane; allband FM.
Programming (via satellite): A&E Networks; ABC Family Channel; AMC; CNBC; CNN; Country Music TV; C-SPAN; C-SPAN 2; Discovery Channel; Disney Channel; E! Entertainment Television; ESPN; ESPN 2; ESPN Classic Sports; Eternal Word TV Network; Food Network; Fox News Channel; Headline News; HGTV; History Channel; ION Television; Lifetime; MTV; National Geographic Channel; Nickelodeon; Northwest Cable News; Outdoor Channel; Spike TV; Syfy; TBS Superstation; The Learning Channel; Toon Disney; Travel Channel; Turner Classic Movies; Turner Network TV; USA Network; VH1; WGN America.
Fee: $34.45 monthly.

Digital Basic Service
Subscribers: N.A.
Programming (via satellite): BBC America; Bio; Bravo; Discovery Digital Networks; DMX Music; ESPN 2; ESPN Classic Sports; Fox Sports World; Fuse; Golf Channel; GSN; History Channel International; Independent Film Channel; Lifetime Movie Network; National Geographic Channel; Speed; Style Network; Versus; WE tv.
Fee: $15.50 monthly.

Digital Pay Service 1
Pay Units: N.A.
Programming (via satellite): Cinemax (multiplexed); Encore (multiplexed); HBO (multiplexed); Showtime (multiplexed); Starz (multiplexed); The Movie Channel (multiplexed).
Fee: $8.00 monthly (Cinemax), $9.50 monthly (Starz/Encore), $10 monthly (Showtime/TMC), $12.00 monthly (HBO).

Video-On-Demand: No

Pay-Per-View
iN DEMAND (delivered digitally); Playboy TV (delivered digitally).

Internet Service
Operational: Yes.
Broadband Service: St. John Cable.
Fee: $25.00 installation; $34.95-$45.00 monthly.

Telephone Service
Analog: Operational
Digital: Not Operational

Miles of Plant: 25.0 (coaxial); None (fiber optic).
Manager & Chief Technician: Greg Morasch.
Ownership: Colfax Highline Cable Co.

COLVILLE—Charter Communications, 521 NE 136th Ave, Vancouver, WA 98684. Phone: 360-828-6600. Fax: 360-828-6795. Web Site: http://www.charter.com. Also serves Kettle Falls. ICA: WA0038.
TV Market Ranking: Outside TV Markets (COLVILLE, Kettle Falls). Franchise award date: April 20, 1954. Franchise expiration date: N.A. Began: August 1, 1953.
Channel capacity: 40 (not 2-way capable). Channels available but not in use: N.A.

Basic Service
Subscribers: 2,000.
Programming (received off-air): KAYU-TV (FOX) Spokane; KHQ-TV (NBC) Spokane; KQUP (IND) Pullman; KREM (CBS) Spokane; KSKN (CW) Spokane; KSPS-TV (PBS) Spokane; KXLY-TV (ABC, MNT) Spokane; allband FM.
Programming (via satellite): C-SPAN; INSP; QVC; TBS Superstation; The Weather Channel; Trinity Broadcasting Network; TVW; WGN America.
Fee: $29.95 installation.

Expanded Basic Service 1
Subscribers: N.A.
Programming (via satellite): A&E Networks; ABC Family Channel; AMC; Animal Planet; Cartoon Network; CNBC; CNN; Comedy Central; Country Music TV; Discovery Channel; Disney Channel; E! Entertainment Television; ESPN; ESPN 2; Food Network; Fox News Channel; FX; Hallmark Channel; Headline News; HGTV; History Channel; Lifetime; MSNBC; MTV; National Geographic Channel; Nickelodeon; Northwest Cable News; SoapNet; Spike TV; Syfy; The Learning Channel; Travel Channel; Turner Network TV; TV Land; USA Network; VH1; WE tv.
Fee: $42.99 monthly.

Digital Basic Service
Subscribers: N.A.
Programming (via satellite): BBC America; Bio; Bloomberg Television; Bravo; Discovery Digital Networks; DMX Music; Encore (multiplexed); ESPN Classic Sports; ESPNews; Fox Movie Channel; Fox Soccer; Fuse; G4; GAS; Golf Channel; GSN; History Channel International; Independent Film Channel; International Television (ITV); Lifetime Movie Network; MTV Networks Digital Suite; Nick Jr.; Outdoor Channel; Speed; Sundance Channel; Toon Disney; Turner Classic Movies; TV Guide Interactive Inc.; Versus.

Digital Pay Service 1
Pay Units: 328.
Programming (via satellite): HBO (multiplexed).
Fee: $25.95 installation; $11.95 monthly.

Digital Pay Service 2
Pay Units: 148.
Programming (via satellite): The Movie Channel (multiplexed).
Fee: $25.95 installation; $10.95 monthly.

Digital Pay Service 3
Pay Units: 251.
Programming (via satellite): Showtime (multiplexed).
Fee: $25.95 installation; $10.95 monthly.

Digital Pay Service 4
Pay Units: N.A.
Programming (via satellite): Cinemax (multiplexed); Starz (multiplexed).

Video-On-Demand: No

Pay-Per-View
iN DEMAND (delivered digitally); Playboy TV (delivered digitally); Fresh (delivered digitally); Shorteez (delivered digitally).

Internet Service
Operational: No.

Telephone Service
None

Miles of Plant: 71.0 (coaxial); None (fiber optic).
Vice President: Frank Antonovich. General Manager: Linda Kimberly. Technical Operations Director: Brian Lindholme. Marketing Director: Diane Long.
Ownership: Charter Communications Inc. (MSO).

CONCRETE—Millennium Digital Media/Broadstripe, 3633 136th Pl SE, Ste 107, Bellevue, WA 98006-1451. Phones: 800-829-2225; 425-747-4600. Fax: 425-644-4621. E-mail: contact_nw@broadstripe.com. Web Site: http://www.broadstripe.com. Also serves Hamilton & Lyman. ICA: WA0069.
TV Market Ranking: Below 100 (Hamilton, Lyman); Outside TV Markets (CONCRETE). Franchise award date: N.A. Franchise expiration date: N.A. Began: January 1, 1966.
Channel capacity: 35 (operating 2-way). Channels available but not in use: N.A.

Basic Service
Subscribers: 1,260.
Programming (received off-air): KCPQ (FOX) Tacoma; KCTS-TV (PBS) Seattle; KING-TV (NBC) Seattle; KIRO-TV (CBS, IND) Seattle; KOMO-TV (ABC) Seattle; KVOS-TV (IND) Bellingham; 1 FM.
Programming (via satellite): A&E Networks; ABC Family Channel; AMC; Bravo; Cartoon Network; CNN; Country Music TV; C-SPAN; Discovery Channel; Disney Channel; E! Entertainment Television; ESPN; Fox News Channel; FX; G4; Headline News; History Channel; Lifetime; National Geographic Channel; Northwest Cable News; QVC; Spike TV; Syfy; TBS Superstation; The Learning Channel; Turner Network TV; TV Land; USA Network; WGN America.
Fee: $29.95 installation; $41.99 monthly.

Digital Basic Service
Subscribers: N.A.
Programming (via satellite): A&E Networks; BBC America; Discovery Digital Networks; DMX Music; Encore; ESPN 2; ESPNews; Fox Sports World; Golf Channel; GSN; HGTV; History Channel International; Independent Film Channel; Lifetime Movie Network; Speed; Style Network; Versus.
Fee: $13.40 monthly.

Digital Pay Service 1
Pay Units: N.A.
Programming (via satellite): Cinemax (multiplexed); HBO (multiplexed); Showtime (multiplexed); The Movie Channel (multiplexed).
Fee: $10.00 monthly (each).

Video-On-Demand: No

Pay-Per-View
Playboy TV (delivered digitally); iN DEMAND (delivered digitally).

Internet Service
Operational: Yes.
Fee: $49.95 installation; $39.95 monthly.

Telephone Service
Digital: Operational
Fee: $39.99 monthly

Miles of Plant: 72.0 (coaxial); None (fiber optic).
President & Chief Executive Officer: Bill Shreffler. Vice President, Programming: Frank Scotello. Manager: Steve Orona. Engineering Director: Dave Jacobs.
Ownership: Broadstripe (MSO).

CONNELL—Northstar Broadband, PO Box 2576, Post Falls, ID 83877. Phones: 800-572-0902; 208-262-9394. Fax: 208-262-9314. E-mail: j.webb@northstarbroadband.net. Web Site: http://www.northstarbroadband.net. ICA: WA0090.
TV Market Ranking: Below 100 (CONNELL). Franchise award date: September 13, 1988. Franchise expiration date: N.A. Began: December 23, 1955.
Channel capacity: 64 (2-way capable). Channels available but not in use: N.A.

Basic Service
Subscribers: 251.
Programming (received off-air): KEPR-TV (CBS) Pasco; KHQ-TV (NBC) Spokane; KNDU (NBC) Richland; KSPS-TV (PBS) Spokane; KVEW (ABC, MNT) Kennewick; 7 FMs.
Programming (via satellite): A&E Networks; ABC Family Channel; AmericanLife TV Network; Animal Planet; Cartoon Network; Concert TV; Country Music TV; C-SPAN; Discovery Channel; Discovery

Health Channel; Eternal Word TV Network; Food Network; Fox News Channel; Hallmark Channel; HGTV; History Channel; ION Television; MSNBC; Nickelodeon; QVC; ShopNBC; TBS Superstation; Telefutura; The Learning Channel; Travel Channel; Trinity Broadcasting Network; TV Guide Network; TV Land; Versus; WGN America.
Fee: $20.00 installation; $22.27 monthly.

Expanded Basic Service 1
Subscribers: N.A.
Programming (via satellite): AMC; Bravo; CNBC; CNN; Comedy Central; Disney Channel; E! Entertainment Television; ESPN; ESPN 2; ESPN Classic Sports; FX; GalaVision; Headline News; Lifetime; MTV; National Geographic Channel; Northwest Cable News; Speed; Spike TV; Syfy; Toon Disney; truTV; Turner Classic Movies; Turner Network TV; Univision Studios; USA Network; VH1.
Fee: $12.31 monthly.

Pay Service 1
Pay Units: 98.
Programming (via satellite): Cinemax.
Fee: $5.00 installation; $5.25 monthly.

Pay Service 2
Pay Units: 118.
Programming (via satellite): HBO.
Fee: $5.00 installation; $9.60 monthly.

Pay Service 3
Pay Units: N.A.
Programming (via satellite): Showtime.
Fee: $5.00 installation; $8.65 monthly.

Video-On-Demand: No

Internet Service
Operational: No.

Telephone Service
None

Miles of Plant: 9.0 (coaxial); None (fiber optic).
Office Manager: Jennifer Webb. Operations Manager: Greg Lundwall.
Ownership: Northstar Broadband LLC (MSO).

COULEE CITY—Formerly served by Almega Cable. No longer in operation. ICA: WA0105.

COULEE DAM—Country Cable, 605 Tulip Ave, Coulee Dam, WA 99116. Phone: 509-633-2283. Fax: 208-772-8576. Also serves Lone Pine. ICA: WA0092.
TV Market Ranking: Outside TV Markets (COULEE DAM, Lone Pine). Franchise award date: September 1, 1954. Franchise expiration date: N.A. Began: September 1, 1954.
Channel capacity: 48 (2-way capable). Channels available but not in use: N.A.

Basic Service
Subscribers: 375.
Programming (received off-air): KAYU-TV (FOX) Spokane; KHQ-TV (NBC) Spokane; KREM (CBS) Spokane; KSPS-TV (PBS) Spokane; KXLY-TV (ABC, MNT) Spokane; allband FM.
Programming (via satellite): CNN; Discovery Channel; ESPN; Spike TV; TBS Superstation; Turner Network TV.
Fee: $25.00 installation; $16.50 monthly.

Pay Service 1
Pay Units: 80.
Programming (via satellite): HBO.
Fee: $9.95 monthly.

Pay Service 2
Pay Units: 40.
Programming (via satellite): Starz.
Fee: $6.25 monthly.

Video-On-Demand: No

Internet Service
Operational: Yes.
Subscribers: 150.
Fee: $25.00 installation; $34.00 monthly.

Telephone Service
Digital: Operational

Miles of Plant: 8.0 (coaxial); None (fiber optic).
Manager & Chief Technician: Jon Cooke.
Ownership: Country Cable (ID) (MSO).

COUPEVILLE—Comcast Cable. Now served by SEATTLE, WA [WA0001]. ICA: WA0071.

CRESTON—Millennium Digital Media/Broadstripe, 3633 136th Pl SE, Ste 107, Bellevue, WA 98006-1451. Phones: 800-829-2225; 425-747-4600. Fax: 425-462-2092. E-mail: contact_nw@broadstripe.com. Web Site: http://www.broadstripe.com. ICA: WA0150.
TV Market Ranking: Outside TV Markets (CRESTON). Franchise award date: October 6, 1989. Franchise expiration date: N.A. Began: May 1, 1989.
Channel capacity: 40 (not 2-way capable). Channels available but not in use: N.A.

Basic Service
Subscribers: 48.
Programming (received off-air): KAYU-TV (FOX) Spokane; KHQ-TV (NBC) Spokane; KREM (CBS) Spokane; KSPS-TV (PBS) Spokane; KXLY-TV (ABC, MNT) Spokane.
Programming (via satellite): A&E Networks; ABC Family Channel; AmericanLife TV Network; Animal Planet; CNN; Comedy Central; Country Music TV; C-SPAN; Discovery Channel; Disney Channel; ESPN; ESPN 2; Headline News; HGTV; History Channel; INSP; Lifetime; QVC; Spike TV; Syfy; TBS Superstation; The Learning Channel; The Weather Channel; Trinity Broadcasting Network; truTV; Turner Network TV; USA Network.
Fee: $29.95 installation; $34.99 monthly; $3.25 converter.

Digital Basic Service
Subscribers: N.A.
Programming (via satellite): A&E Networks; BBC America; Bloomberg Television; Bravo; Discovery Digital Networks; DMX Music; Fox Movie Channel; Fox Sports World; Fuse; G4; Golf Channel; GSN; Halogen Network; History Channel International; Independent Film Channel; Lifetime Movie Network; Outdoor Channel; Ovation; Speed; Style Network; Trinity Broadcasting Network; Turner Classic Movies; Versus; WE tv.
Fee: $20.40 monthly.

Digital Pay Service 1
Pay Units: N.A.
Programming (via satellite): Cinemax (multiplexed); Encore (multiplexed); HBO (multiplexed); Showtime (multiplexed); Starz (multiplexed); The Movie Channel (multiplexed).
Fee: $11.95 monthly (Showtime/TMC or Cinemax), $12.95 monthly (HBO).

Video-On-Demand: No

Internet Service
Operational: No.

Telephone Service
None

Miles of Plant: 6.0 (coaxial); None (fiber optic).
President & Chief Executive Officer: Bill Shreffler. Vice President, Programming: Frank Scotello. Engineering Director: Dave Jacobs. Customer Service Manager: Steven Orona.
Ownership: Broadstripe (MSO).

DARRINGTON—Millennium Digital Media/Broadstripe, 3633 136th Pl SE, Ste 107, Bellevue, WA 98006-1451. Phones: 800-829-2225; 425-747-4600. Fax: 425-644-4621. E-mail: contact_nw@broadstripe.com. Web Site: http://www.broadstripe.com. ICA: WA0078.
TV Market Ranking: Below 100 (DARRINGTON). Franchise award date: N.A. Franchise expiration date: N.A. Began: January 1, 1960.
Channel capacity: 21 (not 2-way capable). Channels available but not in use: N.A.

Basic Service
Subscribers: 664.
Programming (received off-air): KCPQ (FOX) Tacoma; KCTS-TV (PBS) Seattle; KING-TV (NBC) Seattle; KIRO-TV (CBS, IND) Seattle; KOMO-TV (ABC) Seattle; allband FM.
Programming (via satellite): A&E Networks; ABC Family Channel; AMC; Animal Planet; Cartoon Network; CNN; Comedy Central; Country Music TV; C-SPAN; Discovery Channel; Disney Channel; E! Entertainment Television; ESPN; ESPN 2; Fox News Channel; G4; Headline News; HGTV; History Channel; Northwest Cable News; QVC; Spike TV; Syfy; TBS Superstation; The Learning Channel; Turner Classic Movies; Turner Network TV; TV Guide Network; TV Land; USA Network.
Fee: $29.95 installation; $41.99 monthly.

Digital Basic Service
Subscribers: N.A.
Programming (via satellite): BBC America; Bio; Bravo; Discovery Digital Networks; DMX Music; GSN; History Channel International; Independent Film Channel; National Geographic Channel; Style Network.
Fee: $13.40 monthly.

Digital Expanded Basic Service
Subscribers: N.A.
Programming (via satellite): ESPNews; Fox Sports World; Golf Channel; Speed; Versus.
Fee: $5.00 monthly.

Digital Pay Service 1
Pay Units: N.A.
Programming (via satellite): Cinemax (multiplexed); Encore (multiplexed); HBO (multiplexed); Showtime (multiplexed); Starz (multiplexed); The Movie Channel (multiplexed).
Fee: $10.00 monthly (each).

Video-On-Demand: No

Pay-Per-View
Playboy PPV (delivered digitally); iN DEMAND (delivered digitally).

Internet Service
Operational: No.

Telephone Service
None

Miles of Plant: 29.0 (coaxial); None (fiber optic).
President & Chief Executive Officer: Bill Shreffler. Vice President & General Manager: Dave Walker. Vice President, Programming: Frank Scotello. Engineering Director: Dave Jacobs. Customer Service Manager: Steve Orona.
Ownership: Broadstripe (MSO).

DAVENPORT—Northstar Communications, PO Box 2576, Post Falls, ID 83877. Phones: 800-572-0902; 208-262-9394. Fax: 208-262-9314. E-mail: j.webb@northstarbroadband.net. Web Site: http://www.northstarbroadband.net. ICA: WA0089.
TV Market Ranking: Outside TV Markets (DAVENPORT).
Channel capacity: N.A. Channels available but not in use: N.A.

Basic Service
Subscribers: N.A.
Programming (received off-air): KAYU-TV (FOX) Spokane; KGPX-TV (ION) Spokane; KHQ-TV (NBC) Spokane; KREM (CBS) Spokane; KSKN (CW) Spokane; KSPS-TV (PBS) Spokane; KXLY-TV (ABC, MNT) Spokane.
Programming (via satellite): 3 Angels Broadcasting Network; A&E Networks; ABC Family Channel; American Movie Classics; Animal Planet; Cartoon Network; CNBC; CNN; C-SPAN; C-SPAN 2; Discovery Channel; Discovery Health Channel; Disney Channel; E! Entertainment Television; ESPN; ESPN 2; Fox News Channel; Fox Sports Net West; FX; Great American Country; HGTV; History Channel; Lifetime; MTV; Nickelodeon; Northwest Cable News; QVC; Spike TV; Syfy; TBS Superstation; The Learning Channel; The Weather Channel; Turner Network TV; USA Network; Versus; VH1.
Fee: $60.00 installation; $46.07 monthly.

Pay Service 1
Pay Units: N.A.
Programming (via satellite): HBO.
Fee: $13.60 monthly.

Telephone Service
None

Office Manager: Jennifer Webb. Operations Manager: Greg Lundwall.
Ownership: Northstar Broadband LLC (MSO).

DAYTON—Touchet Valley TV Inc., 107 S First St, PO Box 148, Dayton, WA 99328-0148. Phone: 509-382-2132. E-mail: tvcable@daytonwa.net. Web Site: http://www.touchetvalleytv.com. ICA: WA0070.
TV Market Ranking: Below 100 (DAYTON). Franchise award date: N.A. Franchise expiration date: N.A. Began: September 1, 1953.
Channel capacity: N.A. Channels available but not in use: N.A.

Basic Service
Subscribers: N.A.
Programming (received off-air): KHQ-TV (NBC) Spokane; KREM (CBS) Spokane; KSKN (CW) Spokane; KSPS-TV (PBS) Spokane; KVEW (ABC, MNT) Kennewick; allband FM.
Programming (via satellite): A&E Networks; ABC Family Channel; CNN; Country Music TV; Discovery Channel; ESPN; Fox News Channel; ION Television; Lifetime; Nickelodeon; Northwest Cable News; Outdoor Channel; QVC; Spike TV; Syfy; TBS Superstation; The Weather Channel; Turner Network TV; TV Land; Univision Studios; USA Network; VH1; WGN America.
Fee: $15.00 installation; $37.00 monthly.

Pay Service 1
Pay Units: N.A.
Programming (via satellite): HBO; Showtime.
Fee: $8.00 monthly (Showtime), $10.00 monthly (HBO).
Video-On-Demand: No
Internet Service
Operational: Yes.
Broadband Service: In-house.
Fee: $39.95 monthly.
Telephone Service
None
Miles of Plant: 25.0 (coaxial); None (fiber optic).
Manager: David Klingenstein. Chief Technician: Bob Truesdale.
Ownership: Ron Klingenstein.

DEER PARK—Northstar Broadband, PO Box 2576, Post Falls, ID 83877. Phones: 800-572-0902; 208-262-9394. Fax: 208-262-9314. E-mail: j.webb@northstarbroadband.net. Web Site: http://www.northstarbroadband.net. ICA: WA0081.
TV Market Ranking: 76 (DEER PARK).
Channel capacity: N.A. Channels available but not in use: N.A.
Basic Service
Subscribers: N.A.
Programming (received off-air): KAYU-TV (FOX) Spokane; KGPX-TV (ION) Spokane; KHQ-TV (NBC) Spokane; KQUP-LP Coeur d'Alene; KREM (CBS) Spokane; KSKN (CW) Spokane; KSPS-TV (PBS) Spokane; KXLY-TV (ABC, MNT) Spokane.
Programming (via satellite): 3 Angels Broadcasting Network; A&E Networks; ABC Family Channel; AmericanLife TV Network; Animal Planet; Cartoon Network; C-SPAN; C-SPAN 2; Discovery Channel; Disney Channel; Disney XD; ESPN; ESPN 2; ESPN Classic Sports; Eternal Word TV Network; Food Network; Fox News Channel; Fox Sports Net West; Great American Country; Hallmark Channel; Hallmark Movie Channel; HGTV; History Channel; National Geographic Channel; Nickelodeon; QVC; ShopNBC; TBS Superstation; The Learning Channel; The Weather Channel; Travel Channel; Trinity Broadcasting Network; TV Land; TVW; WGN America.
Fee: $60.00 installation; $40.06 monthly.
Expanded Basic Service 1
Subscribers: N.A.
Programming (via satellite): American Movie Classics; CNBC; CNN; Comedy Central; E! Entertainment Television; Fox Movie Channel; FX; Golf Channel; Lifetime; MTV; Northwest Cable News; Outdoor Channel; Speed; Spike TV; Syfy; Turner Classic Movies; Turner Network TV; USA Network; Versus; VH1.
Fee: $24.36 monthly.
Pay Service 1
Pay Units: N.A.
Programming (via satellite): Cinemax; HBO.
Fee: $12.15 monthly (Cinemax), $14.37 monthly (HBO).
Telephone Service
None
Office Manager: Jennifer Webb. Operations Manager: Greg Lundwall.
Ownership: Northstar Broadband LLC (MSO).

DIAMOND LAKE—Northstar Broadband, PO Box 2576, Post Falls, ID 83877. Phones: 800-572-0902; 208-262-9394. Fax: 208-262-9314. E-mail: j.webb@northstarbroadband.net. Web Site: http://www.northstarbroadband.net. ICA: WA0096.
TV Market Ranking: Outside TV Markets (DIAMOND LAKE).
Channel capacity: N.A. Channels available but not in use: N.A.
Basic Service
Subscribers: N.A.
Programming (received off-air): KAYU-TV (FOX) Spokane; KGPX-TV (ION) Spokane; KHQ-TV (NBC) Spokane; KREM (CBS) Spokane; KSKN (CW) Spokane; KSPS-TV (PBS) Spokane; KXLY-TV (ABC, MNT) Spokane.
Programming (via satellite): 3 Angels Broadcasting Network; A&E Networks; ABC Family Channel; CNN; C-SPAN; Discovery Channel; Disney Channel; ESPN; ESPN 2; Fox Sports Net West; Great American Country; Headline News; HGTV; History Channel; Home Shopping Network; Lifetime; MTV; Nickelodeon; Northwest Cable News; Spike TV; Superstation WGN; Syfy; TBS Superstation; The Learning Channel; The Weather Channel; Turner Classic Movies; Turner Network TV; USA Network; VH1.
Fee: $60.00 installation; $36.50 monthly.
Pay Service 1
Pay Units: N.A.
Programming (via satellite): HBO; Showtime; The Movie Channel.
Fee: $8.50 monthly (TMC), $11.50 monthly (Showtime), $12.95 monthly (HBO).
Telephone Service
None
Office Manager: Jennifer Webb. Operations Manager: Greg Lundwall.
Ownership: Northstar Broadband LLC (MSO).

DUVALL—Broadstripe, 604 Oakesdale Ave SW, Ste 101, Renton, WA 98057. Phones: 800-829-2225; 425-747-4600. Fax: 425-644-4621. E-mail: contact_nw@broadstripe.com. Web Site: http://www.broadstripe.com. Also serves Ames Lake, Carnation, Issaquah (southeastern portion), Redmond, Sahalee, Snoqualmie Valley & Woodinville. ICA: WA0043. **Note:** This system is an overbuild.
TV Market Ranking: 20 (Ames Lake, Carnation, DUVALL, Issaquah (southeastern portion), Redmond, Sahalee, Snoqualmie Valley, Woodinville). Franchise award date: January 1, 1981. Franchise expiration date: N.A. Began: January 1, 1982.
Channel capacity: 35 (operating 2-way). Channels available but not in use: N.A.
Basic Service
Subscribers: 2,130.
Programming (received off-air): KCPQ (FOX) Tacoma; KCTS-TV (PBS) Seattle; KFFV (IND) Seattle; KING-TV (NBC) Seattle; KIRO-TV (CBS, IND) Seattle; KOMO-TV (ABC) Seattle; KONG (IND) Everett; KSTW (CW) Tacoma; KTBW-TV (TBN) Tacoma; KUNS-TV (UNV) Bellevue; KWDK (ETV) Tacoma; KWPX-TV (ION) Bellevue; KZJO (MNT) Seattle.
Programming (via satellite): CCTV-4; C-SPAN; Eternal Word TV Network; QVC; ShopNBC; TV Guide Network; TVW; various Canadian stations.
Fee: $29.95 installation; $19.95 monthly.
Expanded Basic Service 1
Subscribers: N.A.
Programming (via satellite): A&E Networks; ABC Family Channel; AMC; Animal Planet; BET Networks; Bravo; Cartoon Network; Classic Arts Showcase; CNBC; CNN; Comedy Central; Cooking Channel; Country Music TV; Discovery Channel; Discovery Health Channel; Disney Channel; E! Entertainment Television; ESPN; ESPN 2; ESPN Classic Sports; Food Network; Fox News Channel; FX; G4; Golf Channel; GSN; Headline News; HGTV; History Channel; Independent Film Channel; Lifetime; MSNBC; MTV; National Geographic Channel; Nickelodeon; Northwest Cable News; Spike TV; Syfy; TBS Superstation; Telemundo; The Learning Channel; The Weather Channel; Travel Channel; truTV; Turner Classic Movies; Turner Network TV; TV Land; USA Network; VH1; WE tv.
Fee: $30.00 monthly.
Digital Basic Service
Subscribers: N.A.
Programming (via satellite): BBC America; CMT Pure Country; Discovery en Espanol; Discovery Home Channel; Discovery Kids Channel; Discovery Times Channel; DIY Network; Encore (multiplexed); ESPN HD; Food Network HD; Hallmark Channel; HD Theater; HDNet; HDNet Movies; HGTV HD; Military Channel; MTV Hits; MTV Jams; MTV2; Music Choice; Nick Jr.; Nick Too; NickToons TV; Science; Starz (multiplexed); Style Network; TeenNick; Tr3s; VH1 Classic; VH1 Soul.
Fee: $11.44 monthly.
Digital Expanded Basic Service
Subscribers: N.A.
Programming (via satellite): ESPNews; Fox College Sports Atlantic; Fox College Sports Central; Fox College Sports Pacific; Fox Soccer; Speed; Versus.
Fee: $5.99 monthly.
Digital Pay Service 1
Pay Units: N.A.
Programming (via satellite): Cinemax (multiplexed); Flix; HBO (multiplexed); Showtime (multiplexed); Sundance Channel; The Movie Channel (multiplexed); Zee TV USA.
Fee: $5.50 monthly (HBO, Cinemax or Showtime/TMC), $14.95 monthly (Zee TV).
Video-On-Demand: No
Pay-Per-View
Movies (delivered digitally); Special events (delivered digitally).
Internet Service
Operational: Yes.
Subscribers: 1,800.
Broadband Service: Millennium Cable-Speed.
Fee: $49.95 installation; $37.95 monthly.
Telephone Service
Digital: Operational
Fee: $39.99 monthly
Miles of Plant: 174.0 (coaxial); None (fiber optic).
President & Chief Executive Officer: Bill Shreffler. Vice President & General Manager: Dave Walker. Vice President, Programming: Frank Scotello. Engineering Director: Dave Jacobs. Customer Service Manager: Steve Orona.
Ownership: Broadstripe (MSO).

EASTON—Millennium Digital Media/Broadstripe, 3633 136th Pl SE, Ste 107, Bellevue, WA 98006-1451. Phones: 800-829-2225; 425-747-4600. Fax: 425-462-2092. E-mail: contact_nw@broadstripe.com. Web Site: http://www.broadstripe.com. Also serves Kittitas County (portions). ICA: WA0203.
TV Market Ranking: Outside TV Markets (EASTON, Kittitas County (portions)). Franchise award date: April 18, 1989. Franchise expiration date: April 18, 2014. Began: N.A.
Channel capacity: 56 (operating 2-way). Channels available but not in use: N.A.
Basic Service
Subscribers: 386.
Programming (received off-air): KCPQ (FOX) Tacoma; KCTS-TV (PBS) Seattle; KING-TV (NBC) Seattle; KIRO-TV (CBS, IND) Seattle; KOMO-TV (ABC) Seattle.
Programming (via satellite): A&E Networks; ABC Family Channel; AMC; AmericanLife TV Network; Animal Planet; Cartoon Network; CNBC; CNN; Country Music TV; Discovery Channel; Disney Channel; ESPN; ESPN 2; Fox Sports Net North; G4; Golf Channel; Headline News; History Channel; Lifetime; MSNBC; MTV; Nickelodeon; Northwest Cable News; QVC; Spike TV; TBS Superstation; The Learning Channel; The Weather Channel; Trinity Broadcasting Network; Turner Network TV; USA Network; VH1; WGN America.
Fee: $35.00 installation; $40.99 monthly.
Digital Basic Service
Subscribers: N.A.
Programming (via satellite): BBC America; Bio; Bloomberg Television; Bravo; Discovery Fit & Health; Discovery Health Channel; Discovery Kids Channel; DMX Music; Fox Movie Channel; GSN; Halogen Network; HGTV; History Channel International; ID Investigation Discovery; Independent Film Channel; Lifetime Movie Network; National Geographic Channel; Planet Green; Science; Style Network; Syfy; Trinity Broadcasting Network.
Fee: $14.40 monthly.
Digital Expanded Basic Service
Subscribers: N.A.
Programming (via satellite): ESPNews; Fox Soccer; Speed; Versus.
Fee: $5.00 monthly.
Digital Pay Service 1
Pay Units: N.A.
Programming (via satellite): Cinemax (multiplexed); Encore (multiplexed); HBO (multiplexed); Showtime (multiplexed); The Movie Channel (multiplexed).
Fee: $10.00 monthly (HBO, Cinemax, Starz/Encore or Showtime/TMC).
Video-On-Demand: No
Pay-Per-View
Club Jenna (delivered digitally); iN DEMAND (delivered digitally); Playboy TV (delivered digitally); Fresh (delivered digitally).
Internet Service
Operational: Yes.
Broadband Service: Millennium Cable-Speed.
Fee: $49.95 installation; $39.95 monthly.
Telephone Service
Digital: Operational
Fee: $39.99 monthly
Miles of Plant: 16.0 (coaxial); None (fiber optic).

President & Chief Executive Officer: Bill Shreffler. Vice President & General Manager: Dave Walker. Vice President, Programming: Frank Scotello. Engineering Director: Dave Jacobs. Customer Service Manager: Steven Orona.
Ownership: Broadstripe (MSO).

EATONVILLE—Rainier Cable, 104 Washington Ave N, PO Box 639, Eatonville, WA 98328-0639. Phones: 800-332-5725; 360-832-6161. Fax: 360-832-8817. E-mail: customerservice@rainierconnect.com. Web Site: http://www.rainierconnect.com. Also serves Centralia, Chehalis, Fife, Graham, Lakewood, Puyallup, Spanaway, Tacoma & University Place. ICA: WA0209.
Note: This system is an overbuild.
TV Market Ranking: 20 (EATONVILLE, Fife, Graham, Lakewood, Puyallup, Spanaway, Tacoma, University Place); Outside TV Markets (Centralia, Chehalis). Franchise award date: N.A. Franchise expiration date: N.A. Began: N.A.
Channel capacity: N.A. Channels available but not in use: N.A.
Basic Service
Subscribers: 2,300.
Programming (received off-air): KBTC-TV (PBS) Tacoma; KCPQ (FOX) Tacoma; KCTS-TV (PBS) Seattle; KING-TV (NBC) Seattle; KIRO-TV (CBS, IND) Seattle; KOMO-TV (ABC) Seattle; KONG (IND) Everett; KSTW (CW) Tacoma; KUNS-TV (UNV) Bellevue; KZJO (MNT) Seattle.
Programming (via satellite): A&E Networks; ABC Family Channel; AMC; Animal Planet; BET Networks; Boomerang; Bravo; BYU Television; Cartoon Network; CNBC; CNN; Comedy Central; Country Music TV; C-SPAN; C-SPAN 2; Daystar TV Network; Discovery Channel; Disney Channel; DIY Network; E! Entertainment Television; ESPN; ESPN 2; ESPN Classic Sports; Food Network; Fox News Channel; FX; Golf Channel; Hallmark Channel; Headline News; HGTV; History Channel; ION Television; Lifetime; MSNBC; MTV; National Geographic Channel; NFL Network; Nickelodeon; Northwest Cable News; Oxygen; QVC; Speed; Spike TV; Syfy; TBS Superstation; The Learning Channel; The Weather Channel; Travel Channel; Trinity Broadcasting Network; truTV; Turner Classic Movies; Turner Network TV; TV Guide Network; TV Land; TVW; USA Network; Versus; VH1; WE tv; WealthTV; WGN America.
Fee: $15.95 monthly.
Digital Basic Service
Subscribers: N.A.
Programming (via satellite): BBC America; Bio; Bloomberg Television; CBS Sports Network; Cine Latino; cloo; CMT Pure Country; CNN en Espanol; Discovery Channel HD; Discovery en Espanol; Discovery Home Channel; Discovery Kids Channel; Discovery Times Channel; DMX Music; Encore (multiplexed); ESPN HD; ESPNews; Food Network HD; Fox College Sports Atlantic; Fox College Sports Central; Fox College Sports Pacific; Fox Deportes; Fox Movie Channel; Fox Reality Channel; Fox Soccer; G4; GSN; Halogen Network; HDNet; HDNet Movies; HGTV HD; History Channel International; Independent Film Channel; Military Channel; MTV Hits; MTV2; National Geographic Channel HD Network; Nick Jr.; NickToons TV; Outdoor Channel; PBS Kids Sprout; Science; SoapNet; Style Network; Sundance Channel; TeenNick; Toon Disney; Toon Disney en Espanol; Tr3s; TVE Internacional; TVG Network; VeneMovies; VH1 Classic; VH1 Soul; WealthTV HD.
Fee: $19.00 monthly.
Digital Pay Service 1
Pay Units: N.A.
Programming (via satellite): Cinemax (multiplexed); Cinemax HD; Cinemax Selecciones; Filipino Channel; Flix; HBO (multiplexed); HBO en Espanol; HBO HD; Showtime (multiplexed); Showtime HD; Starz (multiplexed); Starz HDTV; The Movie Channel (multiplexed).
Fee: $9.99 monthly (Starz), $10.99 monthly (Showtime, TMC & Flix), $11.99 monthly (Cinemax), $12.99 monthly (HBO).
Video-On-Demand: No
Pay-Per-View
iN DEMAND (delivered digitally).
Internet Service
Operational: Yes, DSL.
Subscribers: 9,000.
Broadband Service: Rainer Connect.
Fee: $99.95 installation; $19.95-$55.95 monthly; $10.00 modem lease.
Telephone Service
Digital: Operational
Fee: $19.99 monthly
Miles of Plant: 100.0 (coaxial); None (fiber optic).
President: Brian Haynes. Vice President, Operations & Technology: Albert Weigand. Vice President, Sales & Marketing: Mike Villanueva. Marketing Manager: Debbie Reding.
Ownership: The Rainier Group (MSO).

Echo Lake/Snohomish—Millennium Digital Media/Broadstripe, 3633 136th Pl SE, Ste 107, Bellevue, WA 98006-1451. Phone: 800-829-2225. E-mail: contact_nw@broadstripe.com. Web Site: http://www.broadstripe.com. Also serves Snohomish County (southwestern portions). ICA: WA0205.
TV Market Ranking: 20 (ECHO LAKE/SNOHOMISH, Snohomish County (southwestern portions)). Franchise award date: August 22, 1990. Franchise expiration date: August 19, 2011. Began: November 18, 1987.
Channel capacity: 72 (operating 2-way). Channels available but not in use: N.A.
Basic Service
Subscribers: 1,409.
Programming (received off-air): KCPQ (FOX) Tacoma; KCTS-TV (PBS) Seattle; KING-TV (NBC) Seattle; KIRO-TV (CBS, IND) Seattle; KOMO-TV (ABC) Seattle; KONG (IND) Everett; KSTW (CW) Tacoma; KTBW-TV (TBN) Tacoma; KVOS-TV (IND) Bellingham; KWPX-TV (ION) Bellevue; KZJO (MNT) Seattle.
Programming (via satellite): A&E Networks; ABC Family Channel; AMC; AmericanLife TV Network; Animal Planet; Cartoon Network; CNBC; CNN; Comedy Central; Country Music TV; C-SPAN; Discovery Channel; Disney Channel; ESPN; ESPN 2; Fox Movie Channel; Fox News Channel; FX; G4; HGTV; History Channel; Lifetime; MTV; National Geographic Channel; Nickelodeon; Northwest Cable News; Outdoor Channel; QVC; Spike TV; Syfy; TBS Superstation; The Learning Channel; The Weather Channel; Turner Network TV; TV Land; USA Network; VH1.
Fee: $40.00 installation; $26.95 monthly.
Digital Basic Service
Subscribers: N.A.
Programming (via satellite): BBC America; Bio; Bravo; CMT Pure Country; Discovery Health Channel; Discovery Kids Channel; DMX Music; Golf Channel; GSN; Halogen Network; History Channel International; ID Investigation Discovery; Independent Film Channel; Lifetime Movie Network; Military Channel; MTV Hits; MTV2; Nick Jr.; NickToons TV; Planet Green; Science; ShopNBC; Style Network; TeenNick; Toon Disney; Trio; Turner Classic Movies; VH1 Classic; VH1 Soul; WE tv.
Pay Service 1
Pay Units: 60.
Programming (via satellite): Cinemax.
Fee: $11.95 monthly.
Pay Service 2
Pay Units: 133.
Programming (via satellite): Showtime.
Fee: $9.95 monthly.
Pay Service 3
Pay Units: 121.
Programming (via satellite): HBO.
Fee: $11.00 monthly.
Pay Service 4
Pay Units: 45.
Programming (via satellite): The Movie Channel.
Fee: $11.00 monthly.
Digital Pay Service 1
Pay Units: N.A.
Programming (via satellite): Cinemax (multiplexed); Encore (multiplexed); Flix; HBO (multiplexed); Showtime (multiplexed); Starz (multiplexed); The Movie Channel (multiplexed).
Video-On-Demand: No
Pay-Per-View
Movies (delivered digitally); Special events (delivered digitally).
Internet Service
Operational: Yes.
Fee: $49.95 installation; $37.95 monthly.
Telephone Service
Digital: Operational
Fee: $39.99 monthly
Miles of Plant: 1,012.0 (coaxial); 15.0 (fiber optic).
President & Chief Executive Officer: Bill Shreffler. Vice President & General Manager: Dave Walker. Vice President, Programming: Frank Scotello. Engineering Director: Dave Jacobs. Customer Service Manager: Steve Orona.
Ownership: Broadstripe (MSO).

EDMONDS—Comcast Cable. Now served by SEATTLE, WA [WA0001]. ICA: WA0012.

ELLENSBURG—Charter Communications, 1105 E. University Way, Ellensburg, WA 98926-0674. Phones: 509-783-0132 (Kennewick office); 509-925-9210. Fax: 509-962-2034. Web Site: http://www.charter.com. Also serves Kittitas. ICA: WA0023.
TV Market Ranking: Below 100 (ELLENSBURG, Kittitas). Franchise award date: N.A. Franchise expiration date: N.A. Began: August 1, 1954.
Channel capacity: N.A. Channels available but not in use: N.A.
Basic Service
Subscribers: 7,683.
Programming (received off-air): KAPP (ABC, MNT) Yakima; KCYU-LD Yakima; KIMA-TV (CBS) Yakima; KING-TV (NBC) Seattle; KIRO-TV (CBS, IND) Seattle; KNDO (NBC) Yakima; KOMO-TV (ABC) Seattle; KSTW (CW) Tacoma; KYVE (PBS) Yakima; 3 FMs.
Programming (via satellite): C-SPAN; C-SPAN 2; INSP; QVC; Travel Channel; Trinity Broadcasting Network; TV Guide Network; TVW; Univision Studios.
Fee: $29.99 installation.
Expanded Basic Service 1
Subscribers: 7,073.
Programming (via satellite): A&E Networks; ABC Family Channel; AMC; Animal Planet; BET Networks; Bravo; Cartoon Network; CNBC; CNN; Comedy Central; Country Music TV; Discovery Channel; Discovery Fit & Health; Disney Channel; E! Entertainment Television; ESPN; ESPN 2; Food Network; Fox News Channel; FX; G4; GalaVision; Golf Channel; GSN; Hallmark Channel; Headline News; HGTV; History Channel; Lifetime; MSNBC; MTV; MTV2; National Geographic Channel; Nickelodeon; Northwest Cable News; Oxygen; SoapNet; Speed; Spike TV; Style Network; Syfy; TBS Superstation; The Learning Channel; The Weather Channel; Toon Disney; truTV; Turner Classic Movies; Turner Network TV; TV Land; USA Network; Versus; VH1; WE tv.
Fee: $50.99 monthly.
Digital Basic Service
Subscribers: N.A.
Programming (via satellite): BBC America; Bio; Bloomberg Television; Discovery Digital Networks; DIY Network; ESPN Classic Sports; ESPNews; Fox College Sports Atlantic; Fox College Sports Central; Fox College Sports Pacific; Fox Movie Channel; Fox Soccer; Fuel TV; Fuse; GAS; History Channel International; Independent Film Channel; International Television (ITV); Lifetime Movie Network; Lifetime Real Women; Music Choice; NFL Network; Nick Jr.; Nick Too; NickToons TV; Outdoor Channel; TV Guide Interactive Inc.
Digital Pay Service 1
Pay Units: N.A.
Programming (via satellite): Cinemax (multiplexed); Encore (multiplexed); Flix; HBO (multiplexed); Showtime (multiplexed); Starz (multiplexed); The Movie Channel (multiplexed).
Video-On-Demand: No
Pay-Per-View
iN DEMAND (delivered digitally); NASCAR In Car (delivered digitally); en Espanol (delivered digitally); Playboy TV (delivered digitally); Fresh (delivered digitally); Shorteez (delivered digitally).
Internet Service
Operational: Yes. Began: June 1, 2002.
Broadband Service: Charter Pipeline.
Fee: $29.99 monthly.
Telephone Service
None
Miles of plant included in Kennewick

General Manager: Randy Lee. Technical Operations Manager: Jeff Hopkins. Chief Technician: Ron Graaff. Marketing Director: Diane Long. Program Director: Lloyd Swain.
Ownership: Charter Communications Inc. (MSO).

ENTIAT—Millennium Digital Media/Broadstripe, 3633 136th Pl SE, Ste 107, Bellevue, WA 98006-1451. Phones: 800-829-2225; 425-747-4600. Fax: 425-644-4621. E-mail: contact_nw@broadstripe.com. Web Site: http://www.broadstripe.com. ICA: WA0116.
TV Market Ranking: Outside TV Markets (ENTIAT). Franchise award date: N.A. Franchise expiration date: N.A. Began: February 1, 1983.
Channel capacity: 35 (operating 2-way). Channels available but not in use: N.A.
Basic Service
Subscribers: 137.
Programming (received off-air): KAYU-TV (FOX) Spokane; KHQ-TV (NBC) Spokane; KING-TV (NBC) Seattle; KIRO-TV (CBS, IND) Seattle; KOMO-TV (ABC) Seattle; KREM (CBS) Spokane; KSPS-TV (PBS) Spokane; KXLY-TV (ABC, MNT) Spokane.
Programming (via satellite): A&E Networks; ABC Family Channel; AMC; Cartoon Network; CNN; Country Music TV; Discovery Channel; Disney Channel; E! Entertainment Television; ESPN; Fox News Channel; Fox Sports Net; G4; Headline News; History Channel; Northwest Cable News; QVC; TBS Superstation; The Learning Channel; Turner Network TV; TV Guide Network; TVW; USA Network; WGN America.
Fee: $29.95 installation; $40.99 monthly; $20.00 additional installation.
Digital Basic Service
Subscribers: N.A.
Programming (via satellite): BBC America; Bio; Bravo; Discovery Digital Networks; DMX Music; GSN; HGTV; History Channel International; Independent Film Channel; National Geographic Channel; Style Network; Syfy.
Fee: $14.40 monthly.
Digital Expanded Basic Service
Subscribers: N.A.
Programming (via satellite): ESPN 2; ESPNews; Fox Sports World; Golf Channel; Speed; Versus.
Fee: $5.00 monthly.
Digital Pay Service 1
Pay Units: N.A.
Programming (via satellite): Cinemax (multiplexed); Encore (multiplexed); HBO (multiplexed); Showtime (multiplexed); Starz (multiplexed); The Movie Channel (multiplexed).
Fee: $10.00 monthly (each).
Video-On-Demand: No
Pay-Per-View
iN DEMAND (delivered digitally); Playboy TV (delivered digitally).
Internet Service
Operational: Yes.
Fee: $49.95 installation; $24.95 monthly.
Telephone Service
Digital: Operational
Fee: $39.99 monthly
Miles of Plant: 12.0 (coaxial); None (fiber optic).
President & Chief Executive Officer: Bill Shreffler. Vice President, Programming: Frank Scotello. Engineering Director: Dave Jacobs. Customer Service Manager: Steve Orona.
Ownership: Broadstripe (MSO).

EPHRATA—Northland Cable Television, 317 S Ash St, PO Box T, Moses Lake, WA 98837. Phone: 509-765-6151. Fax: 509-765-5132. E-mail: moseslake@northlandcabletv.com. Web Site: http://www.northlandcabletv.com. Also serves Grant County & Soap Lake. ICA: WA0039.
TV Market Ranking: Below 100 (Grant County (portions)); Outside TV Markets (EPHRATA, Grant County (portions), Soap Lake). Franchise award date: N.A. Franchise expiration date: N.A. Began: January 1, 1953.
Channel capacity: 63 (operating 2-way). Channels available but not in use: N.A.
Basic Service
Subscribers: 2,000.
Programming (received off-air): KAYU-TV (FOX) Spokane; KHQ-TV (NBC) Spokane; KREM (CBS) Spokane; KSKN (CW) Spokane; KSPS-TV (PBS) Spokane; KSTW (CW) Tacoma; KXLY-TV (ABC, MNT) Spokane; 14 FMs.
Programming (via microwave): KING-TV (NBC) Seattle; KIRO-TV (CBS, IND) Seattle; KOMO-TV (ABC) Seattle.
Programming (via satellite): A&E Networks; Animal Planet; CNBC; CNN; C-SPAN; Discovery Channel; ESPN; ESPN 2; Food Network; Fox News Channel; FX; Hallmark Channel; Headline News; History Channel; INSP; Lifetime; National Geographic Channel; Nickelodeon; Northwest Cable News; QVC; TBS Superstation; The Learning Channel; The Weather Channel; Turner Network TV; TV Guide Network; USA Network.
Fee: $45.00 installation; $31.49 monthly; $2.20 converter; $10.00 additional installation.
Expanded Basic Service 1
Subscribers: N.A.
Programming (via satellite): Cartoon Network; Fox Movie Channel; Great American Country; HGTV; Outdoor Channel; Spike TV; Syfy; Turner Classic Movies; VH1.
Fee: $5.00 monthly.
Digital Basic Service
Subscribers: N.A.
Programming (via satellite): BBC America; Bloomberg Television; Discovery Digital Networks; DMX Music; G4; GSN; Halogen Network; Speed; Trinity Broadcasting Network; Versus; WE tv.
Fee: $14.50 monthly.
Pay Service 1
Pay Units: N.A.
Programming (via satellite): HBO; Showtime.
Fee: $9.25 monthly (Showtime), $12.30 monthly (HBO).
Digital Pay Service 1
Pay Units: N.A.
Programming (via satellite): Cinemax (multiplexed); Encore (multiplexed); Flix; HBO (multiplexed); Showtime (multiplexed); Starz (multiplexed); The Movie Channel (multiplexed).
Fee: $14.75 monthly (HBO, Cinemax, Showtime/TMC/Flix or Starz/Encore).
Video-On-Demand: No
Pay-Per-View
Fresh (delivered digitally); Playboy TV (delivered digitally).
Internet Service
Operational: Yes. Began: December 1, 2002.
Subscribers: 12.
Broadband Service: Northland Express.
Fee: $42.95 monthly.
Telephone Service
None
Miles of Plant: 58.0 (coaxial); None (fiber optic).
Manager: Jon Ulrich. Chief Technician: Kim Svetich.
Ownership: Northland Communications Corp. (MSO).

EVERETT—Comcast Cable. Now served by SEATTLE, WA [WA0001]. ICA: WA0213.

FAIRCHILD AFB—Cable Montana. Now served by SPOKANE, WA [WA0004]. ICA: WA0153.

FAIRFIELD—Elk River TV Cable Co., 509 S Main St, PO Box 154, Troy, ID 83871. Phone: 208-369-4652. E-mail: leslie@elkrivertv.net. Web Site: http://www.elkrivertv.net. Also serves Rockford. ICA: WA0129.
TV Market Ranking: 76 (FAIRFIELD, Rockford). Franchise award date: N.A. Franchise expiration date: N.A. Began: January 12, 1983.
Channel capacity: N.A. Channels available but not in use: N.A.
Basic Service
Subscribers: 104.
Programming (received off-air): KAYU-TV (FOX) Spokane; KGPX-TV (ION) Spokane; KHQ-TV (NBC) Spokane; KREM (CBS) Spokane; KSKN (CW) Spokane; KSPS-TV (PBS) Spokane; KWSU-TV (PBS) Pullman; KXLY-TV (ABC, MNT) Spokane.
Programming (via satellite): A&E Networks; ABC Family Channel; Cartoon Network; CNN; Comedy Central; Discovery Channel; Disney Channel; Encore; ESPN; ESPN 2; HGTV; History Channel; Lifetime; MTV; National Geographic Channel; Nickelodeon; Northwest Cable News; Spike TV; Syfy; TBS Superstation; Turner Classic Movies; Turner Network TV; USA Network; WGN America.
Fee: $35.00 installation; $34.75 monthly.
Pay Service 1
Pay Units: 11.
Programming (via satellite): HBO (multiplexed).
Fee: $20.95 monthly.
Video-On-Demand: No
Internet Service
Operational: Yes.
Subscribers: 75.
Broadband Service: Elk River Cable.
Fee: $39.00 monthly.
Telephone Service
None
Miles of Plant: 5.0 (coaxial); None (fiber optic).
Managers: Dave McGraw.; Leslie McGraw. Chief Technician: Justin McGraw.
Ownership: Elk River TV Cable Co. (MSO).

FORKS—Millennium Digital Media/Broadstripe, 3633 136th Pl SE, Ste 107, Bellevue, WA 98006-1451. Phones: 800-829-2225; 425-747-4600. Fax: 425-644-4621. E-mail: contact_nw@broadstripe.com. Web Site: http://www.broadstripe.com. Also serves Beaver, Clallam County (southeastern portion) & Lake Creek. ICA: WA0048.
TV Market Ranking: Outside TV Markets (Beaver, Clallam County (southeastern portion), FORKS, Lake Creek). Franchise award date: N.A. Franchise expiration date: May 23, 2008. Began: December 30, 1965.
Channel capacity: 21 (not 2-way capable). Channels available but not in use: N.A.
Basic Service
Subscribers: 1,750.
Programming (received off-air): KCPQ (FOX) Tacoma; KCTS-TV (PBS) Seattle; KING-TV (NBC) Seattle; KIRO-TV (CBS, IND) Seattle; KOMO-TV (ABC) Seattle; KSTW (CW) Tacoma; KVOS-TV (IND) Bellingham; KZJO (MNT) Seattle; allband FM.
Programming (via satellite): A&E Networks; ABC Family Channel; AMC; Cartoon Network; CNN; Discovery Channel; Disney Channel; ESPN; Fox News Channel; History Channel; Northwest Cable News; QVC; Spike TV; TBS Superstation; Telemundo; The Learning Channel; Turner Classic Movies; Turner Network TV; TV Guide Network; USA Network; WGN America.
Fee: $29.95 installation; $41.99 monthly.
Digital Basic Service
Subscribers: N.A.
Programming (via satellite): BBC America; Bio; Bravo; Discovery Digital Networks; GSN; HGTV; History Channel International; Independent Film Channel; National Geographic Channel; Style Network; Syfy.
Fee: $13.40 monthly.
Digital Expanded Basic Service
Subscribers: N.A.
Programming (via satellite): ESPN 2; ESPNews; Fox Sports World; Golf Channel; Speed; Versus.
Fee: $5.00 monthly.
Digital Pay Service 1
Pay Units: N.A.
Programming (via satellite): Cinemax (multiplexed); Encore (multiplexed); HBO (multiplexed); Showtime (multiplexed); Starz (multiplexed); The Movie Channel (multiplexed).
Fee: $10.00 monthly (each).
Video-On-Demand: No
Pay-Per-View
iN DEMAND (delivered digitally); Playboy TV (delivered digitally).
Internet Service
Operational: No.
Telephone Service
None
Miles of Plant: 63.0 (coaxial); None (fiber optic).
President & Chief Executive Officer: Bill Shreffler. Vice President, Programming: Frank Scotello. Engineering Director: Dave Jacobs. Customer Service Manager: Steve Orona.
Ownership: Broadstripe (MSO).

FREELAND—Comcast Cable. Now served by SEATTLE, WA [WA0001]. ICA: WA0053.

FRIDAY HARBOR—Windjammer Cable, 8500 W 110th St, Ste 600, Overland Park, KS 66210. Phone: 888-495-2881. Fax: 913-563-5454. Web Site: http://www.windjammercable.com. Also serves San Juan County (portions). ICA: WA0084.
TV Market Ranking: Below 100 (FRIDAY HARBOR, San Juan County (portions)). Franchise award date: N.A. Franchise expiration date: N.A. Began: December 15, 1974.
Channel capacity: N.A. Channels available but not in use: N.A.
Basic Service
Subscribers: N.A.
Programming (received off-air): KCPQ (FOX) Tacoma; KCTS-TV (PBS) Seattle; KING-TV (NBC) Seattle; KIRO-TV (CBS, IND) Seattle; KOMO-TV (ABC) Seattle; KSTW (CW) Tacoma; KVOS-TV (IND) Bellingham; KWPX-TV (ION) Bellevue; KZJO (MNT) Seattle; allband FM.
Programming (via satellite): C-SPAN; QVC; TBS Superstation; Trinity Broadcasting Network; various Canadian stations.
Fee: $35.80 installation; $26.99 monthly; $23.00 additional installation.

Expanded Basic Service 1
Subscribers: N.A.
Programming (via satellite): A&E Networks; ABC Family Channel; Cartoon Network; CNBC; CNN; Comedy Central; Country Music TV; Discovery Channel; Disney Channel; E! Entertainment Television; ESPN; ESPN 2; Food Network; Fox News Channel; FX; Hallmark Channel; Headline News; HGTV; History Channel; Lifetime; MTV; Nickelodeon; Northwest Cable News; Spike TV; Syfy; The Learning Channel; The Weather Channel; truTV; Turner Classic Movies; Turner Network TV; TV Land; USA Network; VH1.
Fee: $35.72 monthly.
Digital Basic Service
Subscribers: 200.
Programming (via satellite): BBC America; Bio; Bloomberg Television; Bravo; CMT Pure Country; Discovery Health Channel; Discovery Kids Channel; ESPN Classic Sports; ESPNews; Fox Soccer; Fuse; G4; Golf Channel; GSN; Halogen Network; History Channel; History Channel International; Independent Film Channel; Military Channel; MTV Hits; MTV2; Music Choice; National Geographic Channel; Nick Jr.; Outdoor Channel; Planet Green; Science; Style Network; Sundance Channel; TeenNick; Versus; VH1 Classic; WE tv.
Fee: $11.99 monthly.
Digital Pay Service 1
Pay Units: 150.
Programming (via satellite): Cinemax (multiplexed); Encore (multiplexed); HBO (multiplexed); Showtime (multiplexed); Starz (multiplexed); The Movie Channel (multiplexed).
Fee: $15.95 monthly (each).
Video-On-Demand: No
Pay-Per-View
iN DEMAND (delivered digitally).
Internet Service
Operational: Yes.
Fee: $24.95 installation; $19.95-$44.95 monthly.
Telephone Service
None
Miles of plant included in Coeur d'Alene ID
General Manager: Timothy Evard. Operations Director: Belinda Graham. Engineering Director: Mike Earehart. Finance & Accounting Director: Cindy Johnson.
Ownership: Windjammer Communications LLC (MSO).

GARFIELD—Elk River TV Cable Co., 509 S Main St, PO Box 154, Troy, ID 83871. Phone: 208-369-4652. E-mail: leslie@elkrivertv.net. Web Site: http://www.elkrivertv.net. ICA: WA0117.
TV Market Ranking: Below 100 (GARFIELD). Franchise award date: N.A. Franchise expiration date: N.A. Began: January 16, 1984.
Channel capacity: N.A. Channels available but not in use: N.A.
Basic Service
Subscribers: 78.
Programming (received off-air): KAYU-TV (FOX) Spokane; KHQ-TV (NBC) Spokane; KREM (CBS) Spokane; KSKN (CW) Spokane; KSPS-TV (PBS) Spokane; KXLY-TV (ABC, MNT) Spokane.
Programming (via satellite): A&E Networks; ABC Family Channel; Cartoon Network; CNN; Comedy Central; Country Music TV; C-SPAN; Discovery Channel; Disney Channel; Encore; ESPN; ESPN 2; Fox Sports Net North; History Channel; ION Television; Lifetime; Nickelodeon; Northwest Cable News; Spike TV; Syfy; TBS Superstation; The Learning Channel; Turner Classic Movies; Turner Network TV; USA Network; WGN America.
Fee: $31.65 monthly.
Pay Service 1
Pay Units: 14.
Programming (via satellite): HBO.
Fee: $10.00 installation; $10.00 monthly.
Video-On-Demand: No
Internet Service
Operational: Yes.
Broadband Service: Elk River Cable.
Fee: $39.00 monthly.
Telephone Service
None
Miles of Plant: 5.0 (coaxial); None (fiber optic).
Managers: Dave McGraw.; Leslie McGraw. Chief Technician: Justin McGraw.
Ownership: Elk River TV Cable Co. (MSO).

GOLDENDALE—J & N Cable, 614 S Columbus Ave, Goldendale, WA 98620-9006. Phone: 509-773-5359. Fax: 509-773-7900. Web Site: http://www.jncable.com. ICA: WA0063.
TV Market Ranking: Outside TV Markets (GOLDENDALE). Franchise award date: N.A. Franchise expiration date: N.A. Began: July 1, 1960.
Channel capacity: 61 (not 2-way capable). Channels available but not in use: N.A.
Basic Service
Subscribers: 200.
Programming (received off-air): KATU (ABC) Portland; KGW (NBC) Portland; KING-TV (NBC) Seattle; KOIN (CBS) Portland; KOMO-TV (ABC) Seattle; KOPB-TV (PBS) Portland; KPDX (MNT) Vancouver; KPTV (FOX) Portland; allband FM.
Programming (via satellite): A&E Networks; ABC Family Channel; Animal Planet; CNBC; CNN; Comedy Central; C-SPAN; Discovery Channel; Disney Channel; E! Entertainment Television; ESPN; ESPN 2; Fox Movie Channel; Fox News Channel; FX; Headline News; HGTV; History Channel; Lifetime; MSNBC; MTV; Nickelodeon; Northwest Cable News; QVC; Spike TV; Style Network; TBS Superstation; The Learning Channel; The Weather Channel; Toon Disney; Trinity Broadcasting Network; Turner Classic Movies; Turner Network TV; TV Guide Network; TVW; USA Network; VH1; WGN America.
Fee: $35.00 installation; $17.95 monthly.
Video-On-Demand: No
Internet Service
Operational: No.
Telephone Service
None
Miles of Plant: 21.0 (coaxial); None (fiber optic).
General Manager: John Kusky.
Ownership: J & N Cable Systems Inc. (MSO).

GRAND COULEE—Charter Communications, 521 NE 136th Ave, Vancouver, WA 98684. Phone: 360-828-6600. Fax: 360-828-6795. Web Site: http://www.charter.com. Also serves Electric City, Elmer City & Grant County. ICA: WA0154.
TV Market Ranking: Outside TV Markets (Electric City, Elmer City, GRAND COULEE, Grant County). Franchise award date: N.A. Franchise expiration date: N.A. Began: August 1, 1980.
Channel capacity: 39 (not 2-way capable). Channels available but not in use: N.A.
Basic Service
Subscribers: 800.
Programming (via microwave): KAYU-TV (FOX) Spokane; KGPX-TV (ION) Spokane; KHQ-TV (NBC) Spokane; KREM (CBS) Spokane; KSKN (CW) Spokane; KSPS-TV (PBS) Spokane; KXLY-TV (ABC, MNT) Spokane.
Programming (via satellite): Discovery Channel; Hallmark Channel; Northwest Cable News; QVC; TBS Superstation; The Weather Channel; TV Guide Network; TVW.
Fee: $29.95 installation.
Expanded Basic Service 1
Subscribers: 678.
Programming (via satellite): A&E Networks; ABC Family Channel; AMC; Animal Planet; Cartoon Network; CNN; Disney Channel; E! Entertainment Television; ESPN; ESPN 2; Fox News Channel; FX; HGTV; Lifetime; MSNBC; MTV; Nickelodeon; Spike TV; The Learning Channel; Travel Channel; Turner Network TV; USA Network.
Fee: $42.99 monthly.
Digital Basic Service
Subscribers: N.A.
Programming (via satellite): AmericanLife TV Network; BBC America; Bio; Bloomberg Television; Bravo; Discovery Fit & Health; DMX Music; ESPN Classic Sports; ESPNews; Fox Movie Channel; Fuse; G4; GAS; Golf Channel; GSN; Halogen Network; History Channel; History Channel International; Independent Film Channel; Lifetime Movie Network; MTV Networks Digital Suite; Nick Jr.; Outdoor Channel; ShopNBC; Speed; Syfy; Toon Disney; Trinity Broadcasting Network; Turner Classic Movies; Versus; WE tv.
Pay Service 1
Pay Units: 73.
Programming (via satellite): Encore; HBO.
Fee: $13.15 monthly (HBO).
Pay Service 2
Pay Units: N.A.
Programming (via satellite): Cinemax; Showtime; Starz.
Digital Pay Service 1
Pay Units: N.A.
Programming (via satellite): Cinemax (multiplexed); Encore (multiplexed); Flix; HBO (multiplexed); Showtime (multiplexed); Starz (multiplexed); The Movie Channel (multiplexed).
Video-On-Demand: No
Pay-Per-View
iN DEMAND (delivered digitally); Hot Choice (delivered digitally); Playboy TV (delivered digitally); Fresh (delivered digitally); Shorteez (delivered digitally).
Internet Service
Operational: No.
Telephone Service
None
Miles of Plant: 39.0 (coaxial); 1.0 (fiber optic).
Vice President: Frank Antonovich. General Manager: Linda Kimberly. Technical Operations Director: Brian Lindholme. Marketing Director: Diane Long.
Ownership: Charter Communications Inc. (MSO).

GRANDVIEW—Charter Communications. Now served by YAKIMA, WA [WA0009]. ICA: WA0047.

GREENBANK—Millennium Digital Media/ Broadstripe, 3633 136th Pl SE, Ste 107, Bellevue, WA 98006-1451. Phone: 800-829-2225. E-mail: contact_nw@broadstripe.com. Web Site: http://www.broadstripe.com. ICA: WA0189.
TV Market Ranking: 20 (GREENBANK). Franchise award date: N.A. Franchise expiration date: N.A. Began: June 2, 1993.
Channel capacity: 24 (not 2-way capable). Channels available but not in use: N.A.
Basic Service
Subscribers: N.A.
Programming (received off-air): KCPQ (FOX) Tacoma; KCTS-TV (PBS) Seattle; KING-TV (NBC) Seattle; KIRO-TV (CBS, IND) Seattle; KOMO-TV (ABC) Seattle; KONG (IND) Everett; KSTW (CW) Tacoma; KTBW-TV (TBN) Tacoma; KUNS-TV (UNV) Bellevue; KVOS-TV (IND) Bellingham; KWPX-TV (ION) Bellevue; KZJO (MNT) Seattle.
Programming (via satellite): A&E Networks; ABC Family Channel; AMC; Cartoon Network; CNBC; CNN; Comedy Central; C-SPAN; Discovery Channel; Disney Channel; ESPN; ESPN 2; Fox News Channel; Fox Sports Net; G4; Headline News; HGTV; History Channel; Lifetime; Nickelodeon; Northwest Cable News; QVC; Spike TV; Syfy; TBS Superstation; The Learning Channel; Turner Network TV; USA Network; various Canadian stations.
Fee: $55.00 installation; $19.50 monthly.
Digital Basic Service
Subscribers: N.A.
Programming (via satellite): BBC America; Bio; Bravo; Discovery Digital Networks; DMX Music; Encore (multiplexed); GSN; HGTV; History Channel International; Independent Film Channel; Lifetime Movie Network; National Geographic Channel; Starz (multiplexed); Style Network.
Digital Expanded Basic Service
Subscribers: N.A.
Programming (via satellite): ESPNews; Fox Soccer; Golf Channel; Speed; Versus.
Digital Pay Service 1
Pay Units: N.A.
Programming (via satellite): Cinemax (multiplexed); HBO (multiplexed); Showtime (multiplexed); The Movie Channel (multiplexed).
Pay-Per-View
Movies (delivered digitally); Special events (delivered digitally); Adult PPV (delivered digitally).
Internet Service
Operational: Yes.
Fee: $49.95 installation; $37.95 monthly.
Telephone Service
Digital: Operational
Fee: $39.99 monthly
Miles of Plant: 4.0 (coaxial); None (fiber optic).
Vice President & General Manager: Dave Walker. Engineering Director: Dave Jacobs. Sales Manager: Rob Gouldsby. Customer Service Manager: Steve Orona.
Ownership: Broadstripe (MSO).

GUEMES ISLAND—Index Cable TV Inc., 12117 Bollenbaugh Hill Rd, Monroe, WA 98272-8663. Phone: 866-794-4283. Fax: 360-863-1306. Also serves Skagit County (portions). ICA: WA0207.

TV Market Ranking: Below 100 (GUEMES ISLAND); Outside TV Markets (Skagit County (portions)). Franchise award date: N.A. Franchise expiration date: N.A. Began: August 8, 1994.

Channel capacity: 36 (not 2-way capable). Channels available but not in use: N.A.

Basic Service

Subscribers: 177.

Programming (received off-air): KCPQ (FOX) Tacoma; KCTS-TV (PBS) Seattle; KING-TV (NBC) Seattle; KIRO-TV (CBS, IND) Seattle; KOMO-TV (ABC) Seattle; KONG (IND) Everett; KSTW (CW) Tacoma; KVOS-TV (IND) Bellingham; KZJO (MNT) Seattle.

Programming (via satellite): A&E Networks; ABC Family Channel; AMC; Animal Planet; BET Networks; Bloomberg Television; Bravo; CNBC; CNN; Comedy Central; C-SPAN; Discovery Channel; E! Entertainment Television; ESPN; ESPN 2; Food Network; Fox Movie Channel; Fox News Channel; Fox Soccer; FX; G4; Great American Country; Hallmark Channel; Headline News; HGTV; History Channel; ION Television; Lifetime; MSNBC; National Geographic Channel; Nickelodeon; Northwest Cable News; Outdoor Channel; QVC; Speed; Spike TV; TBS Superstation; The Learning Channel; The Weather Channel; Trinity Broadcasting Network; truTV; Turner Network TV; USA Network; various Canadian stations; WGN America.

Fee: $39.95 installation; $23.00 monthly.

Pay Service 1

Pay Units: 23.

Programming (via satellite): HBO.

Fee: $9.95 monthly.

Video-On-Demand: No

Internet Service

Operational: No.

Telephone Service

None

Miles of Plant: 13.0 (coaxial); None (fiber optic).

Owner: Ed Varhaug. Manager & Chief Technician: Matt Varhaug.

Ownership: Index Cable TV Inc.

HARRINGTON—Elk River TV Cable Co., 509 S Main St, PO Box 154, Troy, ID 83871. Phone: 208-369-4652. E-mail: leslie@elkrivertv.net. Web Site: http://www.elkrivertv.net. ICA: WA0120.

TV Market Ranking: Outside TV Markets (HARRINGTON). Franchise award date: N.A. Franchise expiration date: N.A. Began: May 31, 1983.

Channel capacity: N.A. Channels available but not in use: N.A.

Basic Service

Subscribers: 76.

Programming (received off-air): KAYU-TV (FOX) Spokane; KHQ-TV (NBC) Spokane; KREM (CBS) Spokane; KSKN (CW) Spokane; KSPS-TV (PBS) Spokane; KXLY-TV (ABC, MNT) Spokane.

Programming (via satellite): A&E Networks; ABC Family Channel; Cartoon Network; CNBC; CNN; Comedy Central; Country Music TV; C-SPAN; Discovery Channel; Disney Channel; ESPN; ESPN 2; Fox Sports Net; HGTV; History Channel; ION Television; Lifetime; Nickelodeon; Northwest Cable News; QVC; Spike TV; Syfy; TBS Superstation; The Learning Channel; Trinity Broadcasting Network; Turner Classic Movies; Turner Network TV; USA Network; Versus; VH1; WGN America.

Fee: $31.65 monthly.

Pay Service 1

Pay Units: 73.

Programming (via satellite): Cinemax; HBO.

Fee: $10.00 monthly (each).

Video-On-Demand: No

Internet Service

Operational: No.

Telephone Service

None

Miles of Plant: 5.0 (coaxial); None (fiber optic).

Managers: Dave McGraw.; Leslie McGraw. Chief Technician: Justin McGraw.

Ownership: Elk River TV Cable Co. (MSO).

INDEX—Iron Goat Networks LLC, PO Box 1232, Sultan, WA 98294. Phone: 360-799-0552. E-mail: info@irongoat.net. Web Site: http://www.irongoat.net. Also serves Snohomish County. ICA: WA0193.

TV Market Ranking: Below 100 (INDEX); Outside TV Markets (Snohomish County). Franchise award date: July 6, 1988. Franchise expiration date: N.A. Began: January 1, 1989.

Channel capacity: 72 (not 2-way capable). Channels available but not in use: N.A.

Basic Service

Subscribers: 75.

Programming (received off-air): KCPQ (FOX) Tacoma; KCTS-TV (PBS) Seattle; KING-TV (NBC) Seattle; KIRO-TV (CBS, IND) Seattle; KOMO-TV (ABC) Seattle.

Programming (via satellite): A&E Networks; ABC Family Channel; American Movie Classics; Animal Planet; Cartoon Network; CNN; Comedy Central; Country Music TV; C-SPAN; Discovery Channel; Disney Channel; E! Entertainment Television; ESPN; ESPN 2; Fox News Channel; Fox Sports Net West; Headline News; HGTV; History Channel; Northwest Cable News; QVC; Spike TV; Syfy; TBS Superstation; The Learning Channel; Turner Network TV; TV Land; USA Network.

Fee: $39.95 installation; $56.54 monthly; $4.00 converter.

Digital Basic Service

Subscribers: N.A.

Programming (via satellite): BBC America; Bio; Bloomberg Television; Bravo; Discovery Fit & Health; Discovery Health Channel; Discovery Kids Channel; DMX Music; ESPNews; Fox Movie Channel; Fox Soccer; GSN; Halogen Network; History Channel International; ID Investigation Discovery; Military Channel; National Geographic Channel; Outdoor Channel; Planet Green; Science; Speed; Style Network; Trinity Broadcasting Network; Versus.

Fee: $15.99 monthly; $6.95 converter.

Pay Service 1

Pay Units: 10.

Programming (via satellite): HBO.

Fee: $9.95 monthly.

Digital Pay Service 1

Pay Units: N.A.

Programming (via satellite): Cinemax (multiplexed); Encore (multiplexed); HBO (multiplexed); Showtime (multiplexed); Starz (multiplexed); The Movie Channel (multiplexed).

Fee: $14.99 monthly (Cinemax, Starz/ Encore or Showtime/TMC), $16.99 monthly (HBO).

Video-On-Demand: No

Pay-Per-View

Playboy TV (delivered digitally); Fresh (delivered digitally); Club Jenna (delivered digitally).

Internet Service

Operational: No.

Telephone Service

None

Miles of Plant: 10.0 (coaxial); None (fiber optic).

Vice President, Operations: Ryan Spott.

Ownership: Iron Goat Networks LLC.

IONE—Northstar Broadband, PO Box 2576, Post Falls, ID 83877. Phones: 800-572-0902; 208-262-9394. Fax: 208-262-9314. E-mail: j.webb@northstarbroadband.net. Web Site: http://www.northstarbroadband.net. ICA: WA0155.

TV Market Ranking: Outside TV Markets (IONE). Franchise award date: September 13, 1988. Franchise expiration date: N.A. Began: December 1, 1978.

Channel capacity: 62 (2-way capable). Channels available but not in use: N.A.

Basic Service

Subscribers: 222.

Programming (received off-air): KAYU-TV (FOX) Spokane; KHQ-TV (NBC) Spokane; KREM (CBS) Spokane; KSPS-TV (PBS) Spokane; KXLY-TV (ABC, MNT) Spokane.

Programming (via satellite): A&E Networks; ABC Family Channel; AmericanLife TV Network; Animal Planet; Cartoon Network; Country Music TV; C-SPAN; C-SPAN 2; Discovery Channel; Discovery Health Channel; Eternal Word TV Network; Food Network; Fox News Channel; Hallmark Channel; HGTV; History Channel; ION Television; Nickelodeon; Ovation; QVC; ShopNBC; TBS Superstation; The Learning Channel; Travel Channel; Trinity Broadcasting Network; truTV; TV Guide Network; TV Land; Versus; WGN America.

Fee: $20.00 installation; $29.10 monthly; $1.00 converter.

Expanded Basic Service 1

Subscribers: N.A.

Programming (via satellite): AMC; Bravo; CNBC; CNN; Comedy Central; Disney Channel; E! Entertainment Television; ESPN; ESPN 2; ESPN Classic Sports; Fox Movie Channel; FX; Headline News; Lifetime; MoviePlex; MSNBC; MTV; Northwest Cable News; Outdoor Channel; Speed; Spike TV; Syfy; Toon Disney; Turner Classic Movies; Turner Network TV; USA Network; VH1.

Fee: $16.02 monthly.

Pay Service 1

Pay Units: 57.

Programming (via satellite): HBO.

Fee: $5.00 installation; $9.60 monthly.

Pay Service 2

Pay Units: N.A.

Programming (via satellite): Cinemax; Showtime.

Fee: $5.00 installation; $5.25 monthly (Cinemax), $8.65 monthly (Showtime).

Video-On-Demand: No

Internet Service

Operational: No.

Telephone Service

None

Miles of Plant: 49.0 (coaxial); None (fiber optic).

Office Manager: Jennifer Webb. Operations Manager: Greg Lundwall.

Ownership: Northstar Broadband LLC (MSO).

KAHLOTUS—Formerly served by Community Cable Service. No longer in operation. ICA: WA0140.

KALA POINT—Millennium Digital Media/Broadstripe, 3633 136th Pl SE, Ste 107, Bellevue, WA 98006-1451. Phones: 800-829-2225; 425-747-4600. Fax: 425-644-4621. E-mail: contact_nw@broadstripe.com. Web Site: http://www.broadstripe.com. ICA: WA0156.

TV Market Ranking: 20 (KALA POINT). Franchise award date: N.A. Franchise expiration date: N.A. Began: July 1, 1991.

Channel capacity: 36 (operating 2-way). Channels available but not in use: N.A.

Basic Service

Subscribers: 223.

Programming (received off-air): KCPQ (FOX) Tacoma; KCTS-TV (PBS) Seattle; KFFV (IND) Seattle; KING-TV (NBC) Seattle; KIRO-TV (CBS, IND) Seattle; KOMO-TV (ABC) Seattle; KONG (IND) Everett; KSTW (CW) Tacoma; KTBW-TV (TBN) Tacoma; KUNS-TV (UNV) Bellevue; KVOS-TV (IND) Bellingham; KWDK (ETV) Tacoma; KWPX-TV (ION) Bellevue; KZJO (MNT) Seattle.

Programming (via satellite): QVC; ShopNBC; TV Guide Network; TVW; various Canadian stations.

Fee: $45.39 monthly; $29.95 converter.

Expanded Basic Service 1

Subscribers: N.A.

Programming (via satellite): A&E Networks; ABC Family Channel; AMC; Animal Planet; Cartoon Network; CNBC; CNN; Comedy Central; Country Music TV; C-SPAN; Discovery Channel; Disney Channel; ESPN; ESPN 2; ESPN Classic Sports; Food Network; Fox News Channel; FX; G4; Hallmark Channel; Headline News; HGTV; History Channel; Independent Film Channel; Lifetime; MTV; National Geographic Channel; Nickelodeon; Northwest Cable News; Spike TV; Syfy; TBS Superstation; The Learning Channel; Travel Channel; Turner Classic Movies; Turner Network TV; TV Land; USA Network.

Fee: $38.04 monthly.

Digital Basic Service

Subscribers: N.A.

Programming (via satellite): CMT Pure Country; Discovery Digital Networks; DIY Network; Encore (multiplexed); ESPN HD; Food Network HD; GAS; HDNet; HDNet Movies; HGTV HD; MTV; Music Choice; Nick Jr.; NickToons TV; Starz (multiplexed); Style Network; Turner Classic Movies.

Fee: $13.40 monthly.

Digital Expanded Basic Service

Subscribers: N.A.

Programming (via satellite): BBC America; ESPNews; Fox College Sports Atlantic; Fox College Sports Central; Fox College Sports Pacific; Fox Soccer; Golf Channel; Speed; Style Network; Versus.

Digital Pay Service 1

Pay Units: N.A.

Programming (via satellite): Cinemax (multiplexed); Flix; HBO (multiplexed); Showtime (multiplexed); Sundance Channel; The Movie Channel (multiplexed).

Fee: $5.50 monthly (each).

Video-On-Demand: No

Pay-Per-View

Movies (delivered digitally); Special events (delivered digitally).

Internet Service

Operational: Yes.

Broadband Service: Millennium Cable-Speed.

Fee: $49.95 installation; $37.95 monthly.

Telephone Service

Digital: Operational

Fee: $39.99 monthly

President & Chief Executive Officer: Bill Shreffler. Vice President, Programming: Frank Scotello. Engineering Director: Dave Ja-

cobs. Customer Service Manager: Steve Orona.
Ownership: Broadstripe (MSO).

KENNEWICK—Charter Communications, 639 N Kellogg St, Kennewick, WA 99336. Phones: 509-222-2500; 509-783-0132. Fax: 509-735-3795. Web Site: http://www.charter.com. Also serves Benton County, Franklin County, Pasco, Richland & Walla Walla County. ICA: WA0008.
TV Market Ranking: Below 100 (Benton County, Franklin County (portions), KENNEWICK, Pasco, Richland, Walla Walla County); Outside TV Markets (Franklin County (portions)). Franchise award date: January 1, 1951. Franchise expiration date: N.A. Began: January 1, 1952.
Channel capacity: N.A. Channels available but not in use: N.A.
Basic Service
Subscribers: 36,000.
Programming (received off-air): KEPR-TV (CBS) Pasco; KFFX-TV (FOX, IND) Pendleton; KNDU (NBC) Richland; KRLB-LD Richland; KTNW (PBS) Richland; KVEW (ABC, MNT) Kennewick; KVVK-CD (UNV) Kennewick, etc. 9 FMs.
Programming (via microwave): KCTS-TV (PBS) Seattle; KIRO-TV (CBS, IND) Seattle.
Programming (via satellite): C-SPAN; C-SPAN 2; GalaVision; ION Television; QVC; Telemundo; TV Guide Network; TVW; WGN America.
Fee: $29.99 installation.
Expanded Basic Service 1
Subscribers: N.A.
Programming (via satellite): A&E Networks; ABC Family Channel; AMC; Animal Planet; BET Networks; Bravo; Cartoon Network; CNBC; CNN; Comedy Central; Country Music TV; Discovery Channel; Disney Channel; DIY Network; E! Entertainment Television; ESPN; ESPN 2; Food Network; Fox News Channel; Fox Soccer; FX; G4; Golf Channel; GSN; Hallmark Channel; Headline News; HGTV; History Channel; Lifetime; MSNBC; MTV; MTV2; National Geographic Channel; Nickelodeon; Northwest Cable News; Outdoor Channel; Oxygen; SoapNet; Speed; Spike TV; Syfy; TBS Superstation; The Learning Channel; The Weather Channel; Toon Disney; Travel Channel; truTV; Turner Classic Movies; Turner Network TV; TV Land; USA Network; Versus; VH1; WE tv.
Fee: $50.99 monthly.
Digital Basic Service
Subscribers: N.A.
Programming (via satellite): 3 Angels Broadcasting Network; BBC America; Bio; Bloomberg Television; Boomerang; BYU Television; Canales N; CNN International; Discovery Fit & Health; ESPN; ESPN Classic Sports; ESPNews; Fox College Sports Atlantic; Fox College Sports Central; Fox College Sports Pacific; Fox Movie Channel; Fuel TV; Fuse; GAS; Great American Country; HD Theater; HDNet; HDNet Movies; History Channel International; Independent Film Channel; INSP; International Television (ITV); Lifetime Movie Network; Lifetime Real Women; MTV Networks Digital Suite; Music Choice; NFL Network; Nick Jr.; Nick Too; NickToons TV; Style Network; Sundance Channel.
Digital Pay Service 1
Pay Units: N.A.
Programming (via satellite): Cinemax (multiplexed); Cinemax HD; Encore (multiplexed); Flix; HBO (multiplexed); HBO HD; Showtime (multiplexed); Showtime HD; Starz (multiplexed); Starz HDTV; The Movie Channel (multiplexed).
Video-On-Demand: Yes
Pay-Per-View
iN DEMAND (delivered digitally).
Internet Service
Operational: Yes. Began: December 1, 2002.
Subscribers: 5,669.
Broadband Service: Charter Pipeline.
Fee: $29.99 monthly.
Telephone Service
Digital: Operational
Miles of Plant: 1,500.0 (coaxial); None (fiber optic). Miles of plant (fiber & coax combined) includes Ellensburg, Yakima, Burns OR, La Grande OR, & Pendleton OR
Vice President: Frank Antonovich. General Manager: Randy Lee. Technical Operations Manager: Jeff Hopkins. Marketing Director: Diane Long. Program Director: Lloyd Swain.
Ownership: Charter Communications Inc. (MSO).

LA CONNER—Wave Broadband. Now served by CAMANO ISLAND, WA [WA0046]. ICA: WA0158.

LAKE BAY—Millennium Digital Media/Broadstripe, 3633 136th Pl SE, Ste 107, Bellevue, WA 98006-1451. Phones: 800-829-2225; 425-747-4600. Fax: 425-644-4621. E-mail: contact_nw@broadstripe.com. Web Site: http://www.broadstripe.com. ICA: WA0201.
TV Market Ranking: 12 (LAKE BAY). Franchise award date: N.A. Franchise expiration date: N.A. Began: N.A.
Channel capacity: N.A. Channels available but not in use: N.A.
Basic Service
Subscribers: N.A.
Programming (received off-air): KBTC-TV (PBS) Tacoma; KCPQ (FOX) Tacoma; KCTS-TV (PBS) Seattle; KING-TV (NBC) Seattle; KIRO-TV (CBS, IND) Seattle; KOMO-TV (ABC) Seattle; KONG (IND) Everett; KSTW (CW) Tacoma; KTBW-TV (TBN) Tacoma; KZJO (MNT) Seattle.
Programming (via satellite): A&E Networks; ABC Family Channel; AMC; Animal Planet; Cartoon Network; CNBC; CNN; Comedy Central; C-SPAN; Discovery Channel; Disney Channel; ESPN; ESPN 2; Food Network; Fox News Channel; Fox Sports Net North; Hallmark Channel; Headline News; HGTV; History Channel; Lifetime; MTV; Nickelodeon; Northwest Cable News; QVC; Spike TV; Syfy; TBS Superstation; The Learning Channel; The Weather Channel; Travel Channel; Turner Network TV; USA Network; VH1.
Fee: $49.95 installation; $41.99 monthly.
Digital Basic Service
Subscribers: N.A.
Programming (via satellite): BBC America; Bio; Bloomberg Television; Bravo; CMT Pure Country; Daystar TV Network; Discovery Fit & Health; Discovery Health Channel; Discovery Kids Channel; DMX Music; Fox Movie Channel; Great American Country; GSN; Halogen Network; History Channel; History Channel International; ID Investigation Discovery; Independent Film Channel; Lifetime Movie Network; Military Channel; MTV Hits; MTV2; National Geographic Channel; Nick Jr.; NickToons TV; Planet Green; Science; ShopNBC; Style Network; TeenNick; The Word Network; VH1 Classic; VH1 Soul.
Fee: $13.40 monthly.

Digital Expanded Basic Service
Subscribers: N.A.
Programming (via satellite): ESPNews; Fox College Sports Atlantic; Fox College Sports Central; Fox College Sports Pacific; Fox Soccer; Golf Channel; Outdoor Channel; Speed; Versus.
Fee: $5.00 monthly.
Pay Service 1
Pay Units: N.A.
Programming (via satellite): Cinemax; HBO; Showtime.
Digital Pay Service 1
Pay Units: N.A.
Programming (via satellite): Cinemax (multiplexed); Encore (multiplexed); Flix; HBO (multiplexed); Showtime (multiplexed); Starz (multiplexed); Sundance Channel; The Movie Channel (multiplexed).
Fee: $10.00 monthly (each).
Video-On-Demand: No
Pay-Per-View
iN DEMAND (delivered digitally); Playboy TV (delivered digitally); Fresh (delivered digitally); Club Jenna (delivered digitally).
Internet Service
Operational: Yes.
Broadband Service: Millennium Cable-Speed.
Fee: $49.95 installation; $37.95 monthly.
Telephone Service
Digital: Operational
Fee: $39.99 monthly
Miles of Plant: 51.0 (coaxial); None (fiber optic).
President & Chief Executive Officer: Bill Shreffler. Vice President & General Manager: Dave Walker. Vice President, Programming: Frank Scotello. Engineering Director: Dave Jacobs. Customer Service Manager: Steve Orona.
Ownership: Broadstripe (MSO).

LAKE GOODWIN—Wave Broadband. Now served by CAMANO ISLAND, WA [WA0046]. ICA: WA0159.

LIBERTY LAKE—Northstar Broadband, PO Box 2576, Post Falls, ID 83877. Phones: 800-572-0902; 208-262-9394. Fax: 208-262-9314. E-mail: j.webb@northstarbroadband.net. Web Site: http://www.northstarbroadband.net. ICA: WA0123.
TV Market Ranking: 76 (LIBERTY LAKE). Franchise award date: N.A. Franchise expiration date: N.A. Began: N.A.
Channel capacity: 62 (operating 2-way). Channels available but not in use: N.A.
Basic Service
Subscribers: 1,482.
Programming (received off-air): KAYU-TV (FOX) Spokane; KHQ-TV (NBC) Spokane; KQUP-LP Coeur d'Alene; KREM (CBS) Spokane; KSKN (CW) Spokane; KSPS-TV (PBS) Spokane; KXLY-TV (ABC, MNT) Spokane.
Programming (via satellite): A&E Networks; ABC Family Channel; AmericanLife TV Network; Animal Planet; BYU Television; Cartoon Network; Country Music TV; C-SPAN; Discovery Channel; Discovery Health Channel; DIY Network; ESPN; ESPN 2; ESPN Classic Sports; Eternal Word TV Network; Food Network; Fox News Channel; Hallmark Channel; Hallmark Movie Channel; HGTV; History Channel; ION Television; National Geographic Channel; Nickelodeon; Ovation; QVC; ShopNBC; TBS Superstation; The Learning Channel; The Weather Channel; Travel Channel; Trinity Broadcasting Network; truTV; TV Guide Network; TV Land; WGN America.
Fee: $20.00 installation; $29.14 monthly.
Expanded Basic Service 1
Subscribers: N.A.
Programming (via satellite): AMC; Bloomberg Television; Bravo; CNBC; CNN; Comedy Central; C-SPAN 2; Disney Channel; E! Entertainment Television; Fox Movie Channel; FX; Golf Channel; Headline News; Lifetime; MoviePlex; MSNBC; MTV; Northwest Cable News; Outdoor Channel; Oxygen; Speed; Spike TV; Syfy; Toon Disney; Turner Classic Movies; Turner Network TV; TVW; USA Network; Versus; VH1.
Fee: $5.00 installation; $15.16 monthly.
Digital Basic Service
Subscribers: N.A.
Programming (via satellite): AmericanLife TV Network; BBC America; Bio; Bloomberg Television; Bravo; CMT Pure Country; Current; Discovery Digital Networks; DMX Music; ESPNews; Fox College Sports Atlantic; Fox College Sports Central; Fox College Sports Pacific; Fox Movie Channel; Fox Soccer; Fuse; G4; GAS; Golf Channel; Great American Country; GSN; Halogen Network; HGTV; History Channel; History Channel International; Independent Film Channel; Lifetime Movie Network; Lime; MTV Networks Digital Suite; National Geographic Channel; Nick Jr.; NickToons TV; Outdoor Channel; Ovation; ShopNBC; Speed; Style Network; Syfy; Toon Disney; Trinity Broadcasting Network; Turner Classic Movies; Turner Network TV HD; Versus; Versus HD; WE tv.
Fee: $5.00 installation; $7.48 monthly.
Pay Service 1
Pay Units: 152.
Programming (via satellite): Cinemax.
Fee: $5.00 installation; $4.95 monthly.
Pay Service 2
Pay Units: 89.
Programming (via satellite): Starz.
Fee: $5.00 installation; $4.95 monthly.
Pay Service 3
Pay Units: 225.
Programming (via satellite): HBO.
Fee: $5.00 installation; $9.60 monthly.
Pay Service 4
Pay Units: N.A.
Programming (via satellite): Showtime.
Fee: $5.00 installation; $9.60 monthly.
Digital Pay Service 1
Pay Units: N.A.
Programming (via satellite): Cinemax (multiplexed); Encore (multiplexed); Flix; HBO; Showtime (multiplexed); Starz (multiplexed); Sundance Channel; The Movie Channel (multiplexed).
Fee: $4.95 monthly (Cinemax), $6.90 monthly (Starz/Encore), $8.30 monthly

(Showtime/TMC/Sundance/Flix, $9.60 monthly (HBO).
Video-On-Demand: No
Internet Service
Operational: Yes, DSL.
Broadband Service: CCS Cable Internet.
Fee: $29.95 installation; $19.25 monthly.
Telephone Service
None
Office Manager: Jennifer Webb. Operations Manager: Greg Lundwall.
Ownership: Northstar Broadband LLC (MSO).

LIND—Northstar Broadband, PO Box 2576, Post Falls, ID 83877. Phones: 800-572-0902; 208-262-9394. Fax: 208-262-9314. E-mail: j.webb@northstarbroadband.net. Web Site: http://www.northstarbroadband.net. ICA: WA0115.
TV Market Ranking: Outside TV Markets (LIND). Franchise award date: N.A. Franchise expiration date: N.A. Began: December 1, 1953.
Channel capacity: 62 (2-way capable). Channels available but not in use: N.A.
Basic Service
Subscribers: 94.
Programming (received off-air): KAYU-TV (FOX) Spokane; KEPR-TV (CBS) Pasco; KHQ-TV (NBC) Spokane; KREM (CBS) Spokane; KSKN (CW) Spokane; KSPS-TV (PBS) Spokane; KWSU-TV (PBS) Pullman; KXLY-TV (ABC, MNT) Spokane; 8 FMs.
Programming (via satellite): A&E Networks; ABC Family Channel; AmericanLife TV Network; Animal Planet; Cartoon Network; Country Music TV; C-SPAN; C-SPAN 2; Discovery Channel; Discovery Health Channel; Eternal Word TV Network; Food Network; Fox News Channel; Hallmark Channel; HGTV; History Channel; ION Television; Nickelodeon; Ovation; QVC; ShopNBC; TBS Superstation; The Learning Channel; Travel Channel; Trinity Broadcasting Network; truTV; TV Land; WGN America.
Fee: $20.00 installation; $28.49 monthly; $35.00 converter.
Expanded Basic Service 1
Subscribers: N.A.
Programming (via satellite): AMC; Bravo; CNBC; CNN; Comedy Central; Disney Channel; E! Entertainment Television; ESPN; ESPN 2; ESPN Classic Sports; Fox Movie Channel; FX; Headline News; Lifetime; MoviePlex; MSNBC; MTV; Northwest Cable News; Outdoor Channel; Speed; Spike TV; Syfy; Toon Disney; Turner Classic Movies; Turner Network TV; USA Network; VH1.
Fee: $16.12 monthly.
Pay Service 1
Pay Units: 47.
Programming (via satellite): Cinemax.
Fee: $5.00 installation; $5.25 monthly.
Pay Service 2
Pay Units: 40.
Programming (via satellite): HBO.
Fee: $5.00 installation; $9.60 monthly.
Pay Service 3
Pay Units: 58.
Programming (via satellite): Showtime.
Fee: $5.00 installation; $8.65 monthly.
Video-On-Demand: No
Internet Service
Operational: No.
Telephone Service
None
Miles of Plant: 5.0 (coaxial); None (fiber optic). Additional miles planned: 1.0 (coaxial).
Office Manager: Jennifer Webb. Operations Manager: Greg Lundwall.
Ownership: Northstar Broadband LLC (MSO).

LONGVIEW—Comcast Cable, 9605 SW Nimbus Ave, Beaverton, OR 97008-7198. Phone: 503-605-6000. Fax: 503-605-6226. Web Site: http://www.comcast.com. Also serves Carrolls, Castle Rock, Cowlitz County, Kalama, Kelso, Rose Valley, Silver Lake, Toutle & Woodland. ICA: WA0013.
TV Market Ranking: 29 (Cowlitz County (portions), Kalama, Woodland); Below 100 (Carrolls, Rose Valley, Cowlitz County (portions)); Outside TV Markets (Castle Rock, Kelso, LONGVIEW, Silver Lake, Toutle, Rose Valley, Cowlitz County (portions)). Franchise award date: N.A. Franchise expiration date: N.A. Began: August 1, 1965.
Channel capacity: N.A. Channels available but not in use: N.A.
Basic Service
Subscribers: N.A. Included in Beaverton, OR
Programming (received off-air): KATU (ABC) Portland; KCTS-TV (PBS) Seattle; KGW (NBC) Portland; KOIN (CBS) Portland; KOMO-TV (ABC) Seattle; KOPB-TV (PBS) Portland; KPDX (MNT) Vancouver; KPTV (FOX) Portland; KRCW-TV (CW) Salem; KSTW (CW) Tacoma; 19 FMs.
Programming (via satellite): A&E Networks; Bravo; Cartoon Network; CNBC; CNN; Comedy Central; Country Music TV; C-SPAN; C-SPAN 2; Discovery Channel; Disney Channel; E! Entertainment Television; ESPN; ESPN 2; FX; Hallmark Channel; Headline News; History Channel; INSP; Lifetime; MSNBC; MTV; Nickelodeon; Northwest Cable News; Oxygen; QVC; Spike TV; Syfy; The Learning Channel; The Weather Channel; Travel Channel; truTV; TV Land; Univision Studios; USA Network; VH1.
Fee: $44.99 installation; $15.50 monthly; $2.00 converter.
Expanded Basic Service 1
Subscribers: N.A.
Programming (via satellite): AMC; Animal Planet; Food Network; Fox News Channel; HGTV; TBS Superstation; Turner Network TV.
Fee: $36.39 monthly.
Digital Basic Service
Subscribers: N.A.
Programming (via satellite): AmericanLife TV Network; Arabic Channel; BBC America; Black Family Channel; Bloomberg Television; Canales N; CCTV-4; Discovery Digital Networks; DMX Music; ESPNews; Filipino Channel; Fox Movie Channel; Fuse; G4; GAS; Golf Channel; Great American Country; GSN; Halogen Network; Lifetime Movie Network; MTV Networks Digital Suite; National Geographic Channel; Nick Jr.; Nick Too; NickToons TV; Nuvo TV; RAI International; Russian Television Network; SoapNet; Speed; Style Network; The Word Network; Toon Disney; Trinity Broadcasting Network; Turner Classic Movies; TV Asia; TV Japan; TV5, La Television International; WE tv; Zee TV USA; Zhong Tian Channel.
Fee: $10.95 monthly.
Digital Expanded Basic Service
Subscribers: N.A.
Programming (via satellite): Bio; DIY Network; ESPN Classic Sports; Flix; FSN Digital Atlantic; FSN Digital Central; FSN Digital Pacific; History Channel International; Independent Film Channel; Outdoor Channel; Versus.
Digital Pay Service 1
Pay Units: N.A.
Programming (via satellite): Cinemax (multiplexed); Encore; Flix; HBO (multiplexed); Showtime (multiplexed); The Movie Channel (multiplexed).
Fee: $18.15 monthly (each).
Video-On-Demand: Yes
Pay-Per-View
Addressable homes: 4,100.
Sports PPV (delivered digitally); Urban American Television Network (delivered digitally); Fresh (delivered digitally); Hot Choice (delivered digitally); Playboy TV (delivered digitally); iN DEMAND (delivered digitally).
Internet Service
Operational: Yes.
Broadband Service: Comcast High Speed Internet.
Fee: $42.95 monthly.
Telephone Service
Digital: Operational
Miles of plant included in Beaverton, OR
Senior Vice President: Curt Henninger. Vice President, Technical Operations: Mike Mason. Vice President, Marketing: Lars Lofas. Sales Director: Mike Williams. Marketing Director: Brad Nosler. Public Relations Director: Theressa Davis.
Ownership: Comcast Cable Communications Inc. (MSO).

LOOMIS—Formerly served by JKA Cable Systems. No longer in operation. ICA: WA0202.

LOON LAKE—Charter Communications. Now served by WENATCHEE, WA [WA0015]. ICA: WA0161.

LUMMI INDIAN RESERVATION—San Juan Cable & Construction, 2568 Mackenzie Rd, Bellingham, WA 98226-9204. Phone: 360-758-7879. ICA: WA0162.
TV Market Ranking: Below 100 (LUMMI INDIAN RESERVATION). Franchise award date: N.A. Franchise expiration date: N.A. Began: N.A.
Channel capacity: 39 (not 2-way capable). Channels available but not in use: N.A.
Basic Service
Subscribers: 450.
Programming (received off-air): KCPQ (FOX) Tacoma; KCTS-TV (PBS) Seattle; KING-TV (NBC) Seattle; KIRO-TV (CBS, IND) Seattle; KOMO-TV (ABC) Seattle; KSTW (CW) Tacoma; KVOS-TV (IND) Bellingham.
Fee: $24.95 monthly.
Pay Service 1
Pay Units: 120.
Programming (via satellite): HBO; Showtime.
Fee: $7.00 monthly (each).
Miles of Plant: 20.0 (coaxial); None (fiber optic).
Manager: Roy Budde. Chief Technician: Ben Waldren. Marketing Director: Shaun Morgon. Program Director: Richard Warbus.
Ownership: San Juan Cable & Construction.

LYLE—J & N Cable, 614 S Columbus Ave, Goldendale, WA 98620-9006. Phone: 509-773-5359. Fax: 509-773-7090. E-mail: john@jncable.com. Web Site: http://www.jncable.com. ICA: WA0163.
TV Market Ranking: Outside TV Markets (LYLE). Franchise award date: N.A. Franchise expiration date: N.A. Began: January 1, 1955.
Channel capacity: 22 (not 2-way capable). Channels available but not in use: N.A.
Basic Service
Subscribers: 70.
Programming (received off-air): KATU (ABC) Portland; KGW (NBC) Portland; KOIN (CBS) Portland; KOPB-TV (PBS) Portland; KPDX (MNT) Vancouver; KPTV (FOX) Portland; allband FM.
Programming (via satellite): AMC; CNN; Discovery Channel; Disney Channel; ESPN; ESPN 2; Northwest Cable News; TBS Superstation.
Fee: $25.00 installation; $19.00 monthly.
Video-On-Demand: No
Internet Service
Operational: No.
Telephone Service
None
Miles of Plant: 5.0 (coaxial); None (fiber optic).
Manager: John Kusky. Marketing Director: Nancy Kusky.
Ownership: J & N Cable Systems Inc. (MSO).

MALAGA—Formerly served by Almega Cable. No longer in operation. ICA: WA0164.

MANSFIELD—Millennium Digital Media/Broadstripe, 3633 136th Pl SE, Ste 107, Bellevue, WA 98006-1451. Phones: 800-829-2225 (Customer service); 425-747-4600. Fax: 425-644-4621. E-mail: contact_nw@broadstripe.com. Web Site: http://www.broadstripe.com. ICA: WA0136.
TV Market Ranking: Outside TV Markets (MANSFIELD). Franchise award date: N.A. Franchise expiration date: N.A. Began: January 1, 1982.
Channel capacity: 36 (2-way capable). Channels available but not in use: N.A.
Basic Service
Subscribers: 45.
Programming (received off-air): KAYU-TV (FOX) Spokane; KHQ-TV (NBC) Spokane; KREM (CBS) Spokane; KSPS-TV (PBS) Spokane; KXLY-TV (ABC, MNT) Spokane; KYVE (PBS) Yakima.
Programming (via satellite): A&E Networks; ABC Family Channel; AMC; AmericanLife TV Network; CNN; C-SPAN; Discovery Channel; Disney Channel; ESPN; Fox Sports Net; History Channel; Lifetime; Nickelodeon; QVC; Spike TV; Syfy; TBS Superstation; The Learning Channel; Turner Network TV; TV Land; TVW; USA Network; WGN America.
Fee: $29.95 installation; $34.99 monthly.
Digital Basic Service
Subscribers: N.A.
Programming (via satellite): BBC America; Bio; Bravo; Discovery Digital Networks; DMX Music; GSN; HGTV; History Channel International; National Geographic Channel; Style Network.
Fee: $20.40 monthly; $2.00 converter.
Digital Expanded Basic Service
Subscribers: N.A.
Programming (via satellite): ESPN 2; ESPNews; Fox Sports World; Golf Channel; Independent Film Channel; Speed; Versus.
Fee: $5.00 monthly.
Digital Pay Service 1
Pay Units: 9.
Programming (via satellite): Cinemax (multiplexed); Encore; HBO (multiplexed); Showtime (multiplexed); The Movie Channel (multiplexed).
Fee: $10.00 monthly (each).
Video-On-Demand: No
Pay-Per-View
Playboy TV (delivered digitally); iN DEMAND (delivered digitally).
Internet Service
Operational: No.

Telephone Service
None
Miles of Plant: 6.0 (coaxial); None (fiber optic).
President & Chief Executive Officer: Bill Shreffler. Vice President, Programming: Frank Scotello. Engineering Director: Dave Jacobs. Customer Service Manager: Steve Orona.
Ownership: Broadstripe (MSO).

MANSON—Millennium Digital Media. Now served by CHELAN, WA [WA0058]. ICA: WA0165.

MARBLEMOUNT—Millennium Digital Media/Broadstripe, 3633 136th Pl SE, Ste 107, Bellevue, WA 98006-1451. Phones: 800-829-2225; 425-747-4600. Fax: 425-644-4621. E-mail: contact_nw@broadstripe.com. Web Site: http://www.broadstripe.com. ICA: WA0194.
TV Market Ranking: Outside TV Markets (MARBLEMOUNT). Franchise award date: N.A. Franchise expiration date: N.A. Began: N.A.
Channel capacity: 36 (not 2-way capable). Channels available but not in use: N.A.
Basic Service
Subscribers: 74.
Programming (received off-air): KCPQ (FOX) Tacoma; KCTS-TV (PBS) Seattle; KING-TV (NBC) Seattle; KIRO-TV (CBS, IND) Seattle; KOMO-TV (ABC) Seattle.
Programming (via satellite): A&E Networks; ABC Family Channel; CNN; Comedy Central; Country Music TV; C-SPAN; Discovery Channel; ESPN; ShopNBC; Spike TV; Syfy; TBS Superstation; Trinity Broadcasting Network; Turner Network TV; USA Network; WGN America.
Fee: $29.95 installation; $33.99 monthly.
Pay Service 1
Pay Units: N.A.
Programming (via satellite): HBO.
Video-On-Demand: No
Pay-Per-View
iN DEMAND (delivered digitally); Hot Choice (delivered digitally); ESPN Now (delivered digitally); Fresh (delivered digitally); Playboy TV (delivered digitally); Shorteez (delivered digitally); Sports PPV (delivered digitally).
Internet Service
Operational: No.
Telephone Service
None
Miles of Plant: 8.0 (coaxial); None (fiber optic).
President & Chief Executive Officer: Bill Shreffler. Vice President & General Manager: Dave Walker. Vice President, Programming: Frank Scotello. Engineering Director: Dave Jacobs. Customer Service Manager: Steve Orona.
Ownership: Broadstripe (MSO).

MATTAWA—Formerly served by Almega Cable. No longer in operation. ICA: WA0098.

MAXWELTON—Comcast Cable. Now served by SEATTLE, WA [WA0001]. ICA: WA0141.

McCHORD AIR FORCE BASE—Comcast Cable. Now served by TACOMA, WA [WA0003]. ICA: WA0050.

MEDICAL LAKE—Formerly served by Wave Broadband. No longer in operation. ICA: WA0066.

METALINE FALLS—Northstar Broadband, PO Box 2576, Post Falls, ID 83877. Phones: 800-572-0902; 208-262-9394. Fax: 208-262-9314. E-mail: j.webb@northstarbroadband.net. Web Site: http://www.northstarbroadband.net. Also serves Metaline. ICA: WA0113.
TV Market Ranking: Outside TV Markets (Metaline, METALINE FALLS). Franchise award date: N.A. Franchise expiration date: N.A. Began: July 1, 1958.
Channel capacity: 35 (2-way capable). Channels available but not in use: N.A.
Basic Service
Subscribers: 213.
Programming (received off-air): KAYU-TV (FOX) Spokane; KHQ-TV (NBC) Spokane; KREM (CBS) Spokane; KSPS-TV (PBS) Spokane; KXLY-TV (ABC, MNT) Spokane; allband FM.
Programming (via satellite): A&E Networks; ABC Family Channel; AmericanLife TV Network; Animal Planet; Cartoon Network; Country Music TV; C-SPAN; C-SPAN 2; Discovery Channel; Discovery Health Channel; Eternal Word TV Network; Food Network; Fox News Channel; Hallmark Channel; HGTV; History Channel; ION Television; Nickelodeon; Ovation; QVC; ShopNBC; Showtime; TBS Superstation; The Learning Channel; Travel Channel; Trinity Broadcasting Network; truTV; TV Land; Versus; WGN America.
Fee: $20.00 installation; $29.10 monthly; $1.00 converter.
Expanded Basic Service 1
Subscribers: N.A.
Programming (via satellite): AMC; Bravo; CNBC; CNN; Comedy Central; Disney Channel; E! Entertainment Television; ESPN; ESPN 2; ESPN Classic Sports; Fox Movie Channel; Fox Sports Net; FX; Headline News; Lifetime; MoviePlex; MSNBC; MTV; Northwest Cable News; Outdoor Channel; Speed; Spike TV; Syfy; Toon Disney; Turner Classic Movies; Turner Network TV; USA Network; VH1.
Fee: $16.02 monthly.
Pay Service 1
Pay Units: 55.
Programming (via satellite): Cinemax.
Fee: $5.00 installation; $5.25 monthly.
Pay Service 2
Pay Units: 58.
Programming (via satellite): HBO.
Fee: $5.00 installation; $9.60 monthly.
Pay Service 3
Pay Units: N.A.
Programming (via satellite): Showtime.
Fee: $5.00 installation; $8.65 monthly.
Video-On-Demand: No
Internet Service
Operational: No.
Telephone Service
None
Miles of Plant: 8.0 (coaxial); None (fiber optic).
Office Manager: Jennifer Webb. Operations Manager: Greg Lundwall.
Ownership: Northstar Broadband LLC (MSO).

MINERAL—Comcast Cable, 410 Valley Ave NW, Ste 9, Puyallup, WA 98371. Phones: 425-398-6000 (Bothell office); 253-864-4200. Fax: 253-864-4352. Web Site: http://www.comcast.com. ICA: WA0132.
TV Market Ranking: Outside TV Markets (MINERAL). Franchise award date: N.A. Franchise expiration date: March 1, 2032. Began: June 1, 1984.
Channel capacity: 35 (not 2-way capable). Channels available but not in use: N.A.
Basic Service
Subscribers: 131.
Programming (received off-air): KCPQ (FOX) Tacoma; KCTS-TV (PBS) Seattle; KING-TV (NBC) Seattle; KIRO-TV (CBS, IND) Seattle; KOMO-TV (ABC) Seattle; KSTW (CW) Tacoma; allband FM.
Programming (via satellite): ABC Family Channel; AMC; Animal Planet; CNN; Discovery Channel; ESPN; Fox News Channel; Spike TV; Turner Network TV; USA Network.
Fee: $43.99 installation; $25.99 monthly.
Pay Service 1
Pay Units: N.A.
Programming (via satellite): Encore; HBO; Showtime; Starz.
Fee: $15.99 installation; $15.99 monthly (HBO, Showtime, or Starz/Encore).
Video-On-Demand: No
Internet Service
Operational: Yes.
Telephone Service
None
Miles of Plant: 9.0 (coaxial); None (fiber optic).
Area Vice President: Anne McMullan. Vice President, Sales & Marketing: Tom Pierce. Vice President, Engineering: Steve Tabor. Public Relations Director: Steve Kipp.
Ownership: Comcast Cable Communications Inc. (MSO).

MONTESANO—Comcast Cable. Now served by TACOMA, WA [WA0003]. ICA: WA0032.

MORTON—Broadstripe, 3633 136th Pl SE, Ste 107, Bellevue, WA 98006. Phone: 800-829-2225. Web Site: http://www.broadstripe.com. Also serves Lewis County. ICA: WA0082.
TV Market Ranking: Outside TV Markets (Lewis County, MORTON). Franchise award date: January 1, 1968. Franchise expiration date: April 1, 2016. Began: January 1, 1950.
Channel capacity: 52 (not 2-way capable). Channels available but not in use: N.A.
Basic Service
Subscribers: 473.
Programming (received off-air): KCPQ (FOX) Tacoma; KCTS-TV (PBS) Seattle; KING-TV (NBC) Seattle; KIRO-TV (CBS, IND) Seattle; KOMO-TV (ABC) Seattle; KONG (IND) Everett; KSTW (CW) Tacoma; allband FM.
Programming (via satellite): ABC Family Channel; CNN; Country Music TV; Discovery Channel; Headline News; HGTV; Nickelodeon; Northwest Cable News; Spike TV; TBS Superstation; WGN America.
Fee: $25.00 installation; $24.70 monthly; $15.00 additional installation.
Expanded Basic Service 1
Subscribers: 449.
Programming (via satellite): A&E Networks; Animal Planet; Comedy Central; Disney Channel; E! Entertainment Television; ESPN; ESPN 2; Fox News Channel; History Channel; National Geographic Channel; Outdoor Channel; Syfy; The Learning Channel; Turner Classic Movies; Turner Network TV; USA Network.
Fee: $10.00 installation; $13.00 monthly.
Digital Basic Service
Subscribers: N.A.
Programming (via satellite): AmericanLife TV Network; BBC America; Bio; Bloomberg Television; cloo; Discovery Fit & Health; DMX Music; Encore (multiplexed); ESPN 2; ESPN Classic Sports; ESPNews; Fox Movie Channel; Fox Soccer; FSN Digital Atlantic; FSN Digital Central; FSN Digital Pacific; Fuse; G4; Golf Channel; Great American Country; GSN; Halogen Network; HGTV; History Channel; History Channel International; Independent Film Channel; Lime; National Geographic Channel; Outdoor Channel; ShopNBC; Speed; Style Network; Syfy; Toon Disney; Trinity Broadcasting Network; Versus; WE tv.
Pay Service 1
Pay Units: 81.
Programming (via satellite): HBO.
Fee: $20.00 installation; $10.95 monthly.
Digital Pay Service 1
Pay Units: N.A.
Programming (via satellite): Cinemax (multiplexed); HBO (multiplexed); Showtime (multiplexed); Starz (multiplexed); The Movie Channel (multiplexed).
Video-On-Demand: No
Pay-Per-View
iN DEMAND (delivered digitally); Playboy TV (delivered digitally); Fresh (delivered digitally).
Internet Service
Operational: No.
Telephone Service
None
Miles of Plant: 30.0 (coaxial); None (fiber optic).
Customer Service Manager: Steve Orona.
Ownership: Broadstripe (MSO).

MOSES LAKE—Northland Cable Television, 317 S Ash St, PO Box T, Moses Lake, WA 98837. Phone: 509-765-6151. Fax: 509-765-5132. E-mail: moseslake@northlandcabletv.com. Web Site: http://www.northlandcabletv.com. Also serves Grant County. ICA: WA0167.
TV Market Ranking: Below 100 (Grant County (portions)); Outside TV Markets (Grant County (portions), MOSES LAKE). Franchise award date: N.A. Franchise expiration date: N.A. Began: January 1, 1954.
Channel capacity: 63 (operating 2-way). Channels available but not in use: N.A.
Basic Service
Subscribers: 5,829.
Programming (received off-air): KAYU-TV (FOX) Spokane; KHQ-TV (NBC) Spokane; KING-TV (NBC) Seattle; KIRO-TV (CBS, IND) Seattle; KOMO-TV (ABC) Seattle; KREM (CBS) Spokane; KSKN (CW) Spokane; KSPS-TV (PBS) Spokane; KSTW (CW) Tacoma; KXLY-TV (ABC, MNT) Spokane; 2 FMs.
Programming (via satellite): A&E Networks; Animal Planet; Cartoon Network; CNBC; CNN; C-SPAN; Discovery Channel; ESPN; Food Network; Fox Deportes; Fox News Channel; Great American Country; Hallmark Channel; Headline News; HGTV; INSP; Lifetime; National Geographic Channel; Northwest Cable News; QVC; TBS Superstation; Telemundo; The Learning Channel; The Weather Channel; Turner Network TV; TV Guide Network; Univision Studios; USA Network.
Fee: $45.00 installation.
Expanded Basic Service 1
Subscribers: N.A.
Programming (via satellite): Comedy Central; ESPN 2; Fox Movie Channel; FX; Golf Channel; History Channel; MTV; Nickelodeon; Spike TV; Syfy; Turner Classic Movies.
Fee: $10.00 monthly.
Digital Basic Service
Subscribers: 1,300.
Programming (via satellite): BBC America; Bloomberg Television; Bravo; Discovery Fit & Health; DMX Music; G4; GSN; Halogen Network; Independent Film Channel; Out-

door Channel; Speed; Trinity Broadcasting Network; Versus; WE tv.
Fee: $10.50 monthly.

Pay Service 1
Pay Units: N.A.
Programming (via satellite): Cinemax; HBO.

Digital Pay Service 1
Pay Units: N.A.
Programming (via satellite): Cinemax (multiplexed); Encore (multiplexed); HBO (multiplexed); Showtime (multiplexed); Starz (multiplexed); The Movie Channel (multiplexed).
Fee: $10.00 monthly (Cinemax, HBO or Showtime & TMC).

Video-On-Demand: No

Pay-Per-View
Fresh (delivered digitally); Playboy TV (delivered digitally).

Internet Service
Operational: Yes. Began: December 1, 2002.
Subscribers: 1,000.
Broadband Service: Northland Express.
Fee: $20.00 installation; $42.99 monthly.

Telephone Service
Analog: Not Operational
Digital: Operational
Fee: $29.99 monthly

Miles of Plant: 170.0 (coaxial); None (fiber optic).
Manager: Jon Ulrich. Chief Technician: Kim Svetich.
Ownership: Northland Communications Corp. (MSO).

MOSSYROCK—Comcast Cable, 410 Valley Ave NW, Ste 9, Puyallup, WA 98371. Phones: 425-398-6000 (Bothell office); 253-864-4200. Fax: 253-864-4352. Web Site: http://www.comcast.com. Also serves Lewis County & Mayfield Lake. ICA: WA0091.
TV Market Ranking: Outside TV Markets (Lewis County, Mayfield Lake, MOSSYROCK). Franchise award date: N.A. Franchise expiration date: March 1, 2032. Began: January 1, 1981.
Channel capacity: N.A. Channels available but not in use: N.A.

Basic Service
Subscribers: 469.
Programming (received off-air): KCPQ (FOX) Tacoma; KCTS-TV (PBS) Seattle; KING-TV (NBC) Seattle; KIRO-TV (CBS, IND) Seattle; KOMO-TV (ABC) Seattle; KSTW (CW) Tacoma; allband FM.
Programming (via satellite): A&E Networks; ABC Family Channel; AMC; Animal Planet; BET Networks; Cartoon Network; CNBC; CNN; Comedy Central; Country Music TV; Discovery Channel; Disney Channel; E! Entertainment Television; ESPN; Food Network; Fox News Channel; Hallmark Channel; Headline News; Lifetime; MoviePlex; MSNBC; MTV; Nickelodeon; Northwest Cable News; QVC; Spike TV; TBS Superstation; The Learning Channel; Travel Channel; truTV; Turner Network TV; Univision Studios; USA Network; VH1.
Fee: $23.99 installation; $17.46 monthly.

Digital Basic Service
Subscribers: N.A.
Programming (via satellite): BBC America; Black Family Channel; Bravo; Canales N; Discovery Health Channel; Discovery Kids Channel; DMX Music; ESPN 2; ESPN Classic Sports; ESPNews; Fox Soccer; Fuse; G4; GAS; Golf Channel; Great American Country; GSN; HGTV; History Channel; Independent Film Channel; MTV Networks Digital Suite; National Geographic Channel; Nick Jr.; NickToons TV; Nuvo TV; PBS Kids Sprout; Science; SoapNet; Style Network; Syfy; The Word Network; Trinity Broadcasting Network; Turner Classic Movies; TV Land; Versus; WE tv.

Digital Expanded Basic Service
Subscribers: N.A.
Programming (via satellite): Bio; CMT Pure Country; Discovery Fit & Health; Discovery Home Channel; Discovery Times Channel; Encore (multiplexed); Halogen Network; History Channel International; Lifetime Movie Network; Military History Channel; MTV Hits; Sundance Channel; Toon Disney.

Digital Pay Service 1
Pay Units: N.A.
Programming (via satellite): Cinemax (multiplexed); HBO (multiplexed); Showtime (multiplexed); Starz (multiplexed); The Movie Channel (multiplexed).

Video-On-Demand: No

Pay-Per-View
Movies (delivered digitally); Special events (delivered digitally); Fresh (delivered digitally); Club Jenna (delivered digitally); Shorteez (delivered digitally); Playboy TV (delivered digitally); Hot Choice (delivered digitally).

Internet Service
Operational: Yes.

Telephone Service
None

Miles of Plant: 30.0 (coaxial); None (fiber optic).
Area Vice President: Anne McMullen. Vice President, Sales & Marketing: Tom Pierce. Vice President, Engineering: Steve Tabor. Public Relations Director: Steve Kipp.
Ownership: Comcast Cable Communications Inc. (MSO).

NACHES—J & N Cable, 614 S Columbus Ave, Goldendale, WA 98620-9006. Phone: 509-773-5359. Fax: 509-773-7090. Web Site: http://www.jncable.com. Also serves Cowiche, Gleed, Tieton & Yakima County (unincorporated areas). ICA: WA0059.
TV Market Ranking: Below 100 (Cowiche, Gleed, NACHES, Tieton, Yakima County (unincorporated areas)). Franchise award date: N.A. Franchise expiration date: N.A. Began: January 1, 1984.
Channel capacity: 61 (not 2-way capable). Channels available but not in use: N.A.

Basic Service
Subscribers: 100.
Programming (received off-air): KAPP (ABC, MNT) Yakima; KCYU-LD Yakima; KIMA-TV (CBS) Yakima; KNDO (NBC) Yakima; KYVE (PBS) Yakima.
Programming (via satellite): A&E Networks; ABC Family Channel; Animal Planet; CNBC; CNN; C-SPAN; Discovery Channel; Disney Channel; E! Entertainment Television; ESPN; Fox Movie Channel; FX; Headline News; History Channel; Lifetime; MTV; Nickelodeon; QVC; Spike TV; Style Network; TBS Superstation; Toon Disney; Trinity Broadcasting Network; Turner Network TV; USA Network; VH1; WGN America.
Fee: $35.00 installation; $27.75 monthly.

Pay Service 1
Pay Units: N.A.
Programming (via satellite): HBO; Starz.

Video-On-Demand: No

Pay-Per-View
Pay-Per-View Channels (delivered digitally).

Internet Service
Operational: No.

Telephone Service
None

Miles of Plant: 72.0 (coaxial); None (fiber optic).
General Manager: John Kusky.
Ownership: J & N Cable Systems Inc. (MSO).

NAPAVINE—Millennium Digital Media/Broadstripe, 3633 136th Pl SE, Ste 107, Bellevue, WA 98006-1451. Phones: 800-829-2225; 425-747-4600. Fax: 425-644-4621. Web Site: http://www.broadstripe.com. ICA: WA0106.
TV Market Ranking: Outside TV Markets (NAPAVINE). Franchise award date: N.A. Franchise expiration date: January 1, 2008. Began: July 1, 1983.
Channel capacity: 35 (operating 2-way). Channels available but not in use: N.A.

Basic Service
Subscribers: 387.
Programming (received off-air): KCKA (PBS) Centralia; KCPQ (FOX) Tacoma; KCTS-TV (PBS) Seattle; KING-TV (NBC) Seattle; KIRO-TV (CBS, IND) Seattle; KOMO-TV (ABC) Seattle; KSTW (CW) Tacoma; KZJO (MNT) Seattle.
Programming (via satellite): A&E Networks; ABC Family Channel; AMC; Animal Planet; Cartoon Network; CNN; Discovery Channel; Disney Channel; E! Entertainment Television; ESPN; Fox News Channel; FX; Headline News; HGTV; History Channel; Nickelodeon; Northwest Cable News; QVC; Spike TV; Syfy; TBS Superstation; The Learning Channel; The Weather Channel; Turner Network TV; TV Land; TVW; USA Network; WGN America.
Fee: $29.95 installation; $41.99 monthly.

Digital Basic Service
Subscribers: N.A.
Programming (via satellite): BBC America; Bio; Bravo; Discovery Digital Networks; DMX Music; Encore (multiplexed); GSN; History Channel International; Independent Film Channel; National Geographic Channel; Style Network; Turner Classic Movies.
Fee: $9.40 monthly.

Digital Expanded Basic Service
Subscribers: N.A.
Programming (via satellite): ESPN 2; ESPNews; Fox Sports World; Golf Channel; Speed; Versus.
Fee: $5.00 monthly.

Pay Service 1
Pay Units: 58.
Programming (via satellite): HBO; Showtime.
Fee: $14.95 monthly (each).

Digital Pay Service 1
Pay Units: N.A.
Programming (via satellite): Cinemax (multiplexed); HBO (multiplexed); Showtime (multiplexed); The Movie Channel (multiplexed).
Fee: $10.00 monthly (each).

Video-On-Demand: No

Pay-Per-View
iN DEMAND (delivered digitally); Playboy TV (delivered digitally).

Internet Service
Operational: Yes.
Broadband Service: Millennium CableSpeed.
Fee: $49.95 installation; $37.95 monthly.

Telephone Service
Digital: Operational
Fee: $39.99 monthly

Miles of Plant: 129.0 (coaxial); None (fiber optic).
President & Chief Executive Officer: Bill Shreffler. Vice President, Programming: Frank Scotello. Engineering Director: Dave Jacobs. Customer Service Manager: Steve Orona.
Ownership: Broadstripe (MSO).

NESPELEM—Formerly served by Country Cable. No longer in operation. ICA: WA0170.

NEWPORT—Concept Cable, 412 S Union Ave, PO Box 810, Newport, WA 99156-0810. Phone: 208-437-4544. Fax: 208-437-2740. E-mail: staff@conceptcable.com. Web Site: http://www.conceptcable.com. Also serves Bonner County (unincorporated areas), Clark Fork, Oldtown & Priest River, ID; Pend Oreille County, WA. ICA: WA0195.
TV Market Ranking: Outside TV Markets (Bonner County (unincorporated areas), Clark Fork, NEWPORT, Oldtown, Pend Oreille County, Priest River). Franchise award date: August 1, 1993. Franchise expiration date: N.A. Began: January 1, 1994.
Channel capacity: N.A. Channels available but not in use: N.A.

Basic Service
Subscribers: 1,672.
Programming (received off-air): KAYU-TV (FOX) Spokane; KCDT (PBS) Coeur d'Alene; KHQ-TV (NBC) Spokane; KQUP (IND) Pullman; KREM (CBS) Spokane; KSKN (CW) Spokane; KSPS-TV (PBS) Spokane; KXLY-TV (ABC, MNT) Spokane.
Programming (via satellite): C-SPAN; Hallmark Channel; ION Television; Northwest Cable News; Trinity Broadcasting Network; Turner Classic Movies; TV Guide Network; WGN America.
Fee: $18.45 monthly; $.40 converter.

Expanded Basic Service 1
Subscribers: 965.
Programming (via satellite): A&E Networks; ABC Family Channel; AMC; American-Life TV Network; Animal Planet; Cartoon Network; CNBC; CNN; Comedy Central; Country Music TV; Discovery Channel; Discovery Health Channel; Disney Channel; DIY Network; E! Entertainment Television; ESPN; ESPN 2; Food Network; Fox Movie Channel; Fox News Channel; FX; G4; GSN; Headline News; HGTV; History Channel; Lifetime; MTV; National Geographic Channel; Nickelodeon; Outdoor Channel; Oxygen; SoapNet; Speed; Spike TV; Syfy; TBS Superstation; The Learning Channel; The Weather Channel; Toon Disney; Travel Channel; truTV; Turner Network TV; TV Land; USA Network; VH1.
Fee: $40.95 monthly.

Digital Basic Service
Subscribers: N.A.
Programming (via satellite): Bio; Bloomberg Television; Bravo; CMT Pure Country; Discovery Health Channel; Discovery Home Channel; Discovery Kids Channel; Discovery Times Channel; ESPN Classic Sports; ESPNews; Fox Soccer; Fuse; Golf Channel; Halogen Network; History Channel International; Independent Film Channel; Lifetime Movie Network; Military Channel; MTV2; Music Choice; National Geographic Channel; Nick Jr.; NickToons TV; Science; Style Network; Trio; Versus; VH1 Classic; WE tv.

Digital Pay Service 1
Pay Units: N.A.
Programming (via satellite): Cinemax (multiplexed); Encore (multiplexed); Flix; HBO (multiplexed); Showtime (multiplexed); Starz (multiplexed); The Movie Channel.
Fee: $9.95 monthly (Cinemax), $11.95 monthly (HBO, Starz/Encore or Showtime/TMC/Flix).

Video-On-Demand: No

Pay-Per-View
iN DEMAND (delivered digitally); Playboy TV (delivered digitally); Spice (delivered digitally).
Internet Service
Operational: Yes.
Fee: $19.95 installation; $24.95 monthly.
Telephone Service
None
Miles of Plant: 71.0 (coaxial); 10.0 (fiber optic).
Manager & Chief Technician: Keith Antcliff. Program & Marketing Director: Doris Dale.
Ownership: Keith Antcliff.

NORTH BONNEVILLE—North Bonneville Community Cable TV System, PO Box 7, North Bonneville, WA 98639-0007. Phone: 509-427-8182. Fax: 509-427-7214. ICA: WA0131.
TV Market Ranking: 29 (NORTH BONNEVILLE). Franchise award date: N.A. Franchise expiration date: N.A. Began: April 1, 1982.
Channel capacity: 35 (not 2-way capable). Channels available but not in use: N.A.
Basic Service
Subscribers: 158.
Programming (received off-air): KATU (ABC) Portland; KGW (NBC) Portland; KOIN (CBS) Portland; KOPB-TV (PBS) Portland; KPTV (FOX) Portland; allband FM.
Programming (via satellite): A&E Networks; ABC Family Channel; CNN; Discovery Channel; Disney Channel; ESPN; ESPN 2; FSN Digital Pacific; Great American Country; Hallmark Channel; Hallmark Movie Channel; HGTV; History Channel; MSNBC; Nickelodeon; Northwest Cable News; Spike TV; Syfy; TBS Superstation; The Learning Channel; Turner Classic Movies; Turner Network TV; WGN America.
Fee: $35.00 installation; $29.00 monthly.
Pay Service 1
Pay Units: 19.
Programming (via satellite): HBO.
Fee: $11.00 monthly.
Video-On-Demand: No
Pay-Per-View
Special events.
Internet Service
Operational: No. Began: January 1, 2004.
Telephone Service
None
Miles of Plant: 12.0 (coaxial); None (fiber optic).
Manager: Tom Payton. Chief Technician: Ray Hays.
Ownership: North Bonneville Community Cable TV System.

NORTHPORT—Formerly served by Almega Cable. No longer in operation. ICA: WA0172.

OAKESDALE—Elk River TV Cable Co., 509 S Main St, PO Box 154, Troy, ID 83871. Phone: 208-369-4652. E-mail: leslie@elkrivertv.net. Web Site: http://www.elkrivertv.net. ICA: WA0125.
TV Market Ranking: Below 100 (OAKESDALE). Franchise award date: N.A. Franchise expiration date: N.A. Began: December 1, 1983.
Channel capacity: N.A. Channels available but not in use: N.A.
Basic Service
Subscribers: 60.
Programming (received off-air): KAYU-TV (FOX) Spokane; KHQ-TV (NBC) Spokane; KREM (CBS) Spokane; KSKN (CW) Spokane; KSPS-TV (PBS) Spokane; KWSU-TV (PBS) Pullman; KXLY-TV (ABC, MNT) Spokane.
Programming (via satellite): A&E Networks; ABC Family Channel; CNN; Country Music TV; C-SPAN; Discovery Channel; Disney Channel; Encore; ESPN; ESPN 2; Fox Sports Net; History Channel; ION Television; Lifetime; Nickelodeon; Northwest Cable News; Outdoor Channel; Spike TV; Syfy; TBS Superstation; The Learning Channel; The Weather Channel; Turner Classic Movies; Turner Network TV; USA Network; VH1; WGN America.
Fee: $31.65 monthly.
Pay Service 1
Pay Units: 8.
Programming (via satellite): HBO.
Fee: $10.00 monthly.
Video-On-Demand: No
Internet Service
Operational: No.
Telephone Service
None
Miles of Plant: 6.0 (coaxial); None (fiber optic).
Managers: Dave McGraw.; Leslie McGraw. Chief Technician: Justin McGraw.
Ownership: Elk River TV Cable Co. (MSO).

OCEAN SHORES—Coast Communications Co. Inc., 349 Damon Rd NE, Ocean Shores, WA 98569-9226. Phone: 360-289-2252. Fax: 360-289-2750. E-mail: sales@coastaccess.com. Web Site: http://www.coastcommunications.com. Also serves Copalis Beach, Copalis Crossing, Grays Harbor County, Hogan's Corner, Ocean City & Pacific Beach. ICA: WA0042.
TV Market Ranking: Outside TV Markets (Copalis Beach, Copalis Crossing, Grays Harbor County, Hogan's Corner, Ocean City, OCEAN SHORES, Pacific Beach). Franchise award date: August 17, 1967. Franchise expiration date: N.A. Began: February 1, 1968.
Channel capacity: 60 (operating 2-way). Channels available but not in use: N.A.
Basic Service
Subscribers: 2,311.
Programming (via microwave): KCPQ (FOX) Tacoma; KCTS-TV (PBS) Seattle; KING-TV (NBC) Seattle; KIRO-TV (CBS, IND) Seattle; KOMO-TV (ABC) Seattle; KONG (IND) Everett; KSTW (CW) Tacoma; KZJO (MNT) Seattle.
Programming (via satellite): C-SPAN; C-SPAN 2; Food Network; ION Television; Northwest Cable News; Ovation; QVC; TBS Superstation; Travel Channel; Trinity Broadcasting Network; TVW.
Fee: $45.00 installation; $27.95 monthly; $2.95 converter; $10.00 additional installation.
Expanded Basic Service 1
Subscribers: N.A.
Programming (via satellite): A&E Networks; ABC Family Channel; Animal Planet; Bloomberg Television; Bravo; Cartoon Network; CNBC; CNN; Comedy Central; Discovery Channel; DIY Network; ESPN; ESPN 2; ESPN Classic Sports; Fox News Channel; Fox Sports Net; G4; Great American Country; Headline News; HGTV; History Channel; Lifetime; MuchMusic Network; National Geographic Channel; Syfy; The Learning Channel; The Weather Channel; truTV; Turner Classic Movies; Turner Network TV; TV Guide Network; TV Land; USA Network.
Fee: $22.00 monthly.
Digital Basic Service
Subscribers: N.A.
Programming (via satellite): BBC America; Bio; ESPN; ESPN 2; ESPN Classic Sports; ESPNews; Fox Sports World; FSN Digital Atlantic; FSN Digital Central; GAS; Golf Channel; HD Theater; History Channel International; MTV; Nick Jr.; Nick Too; Nickelodeon; Speed; Versus.
Fee: $11.00 monthly.
Digital Pay Service 1
Pay Units: N.A.
Programming (via satellite): Cinemax (multiplexed); DMX Music; Encore (multiplexed); HBO; Showtime (multiplexed); Starz (multiplexed); The Movie Channel (multiplexed).
Fee: $11.49 monthly (HBO, Cinemax/Starz, or Showtime/TMC).
Video-On-Demand: No
Pay-Per-View
iN DEMAND (delivered digitally).
Internet Service
Operational: Yes.
Broadband Service: Coast Access.
Fee: $42.95 monthly; $9.95 modem lease.
Telephone Service
Analog: Not Operational
Digital: Operational
Miles of Plant: 80.0 (coaxial); None (fiber optic).
Vice President & General Manager: Ronald Thomasson.
Ownership: Edward Hewson (MSO).

ODESSA (town)—Northstar Broadband, PO Box 2576, Post Falls, ID 83877. Phones: 800-572-0902; 208-262-9394. Fax: 208-262-9314. E-mail: j.webb@northstarbroadband.net. Web Site: http://www.northstarbroadband.net. ICA: WA0173.
TV Market Ranking: Outside TV Markets (ODESSA (TOWN)). Franchise award date: N.A. Franchise expiration date: N.A. Began: N.A.
Channel capacity: 62 (2-way capable). Channels available but not in use: N.A.
Basic Service
Subscribers: 179.
Programming (received off-air): KAYU-TV (FOX) Spokane; KHQ-TV (NBC) Spokane; KREM (CBS) Spokane; KSKN (CW) Spokane; KSPS-TV (PBS) Spokane; KXLY-TV (ABC, MNT) Spokane.
Programming (via satellite): A&E Networks; ABC Family Channel; AmericanLife TV Network; Animal Planet; Cartoon Network; Country Music TV; C-SPAN; C-SPAN 2; Discovery Channel; Discovery Health Channel; Eternal Word TV Network; Food Network; Fox News Channel; Hallmark Channel; HGTV; History Channel; ION Television; National Geographic Channel; Nickelodeon; Ovation; QVC; ShopNBC; TBS Superstation; The Learning Channel; Travel Channel; Trinity Broadcasting Network; truTV; TV Guide Network; TV Land; WGN America.
Fee: $20.00 installation; $28.99 monthly; $1.00 converter.
Expanded Basic Service 1
Subscribers: N.A.
Programming (via satellite): AMC; Bravo; CNBC; CNN; Comedy Central; Disney Channel; E! Entertainment Television; ESPN; ESPN 2; ESPN Classic Sports; Fox Movie Channel; FX; Golf Channel; Headline News; Lifetime; MoviePlex; MSNBC; MTV; Northwest Cable News; Speed; Spike TV; Syfy; Toon Disney; Turner Classic Movies; Turner Network TV; USA Network; Versus; VH1.
Fee: $16.60 monthly.
Pay Service 1
Pay Units: 74.
Programming (via satellite): Cinemax.
Fee: $5.00 installation; $5.25 monthly.
Pay Service 2
Pay Units: 83.
Programming (via satellite): HBO.
Fee: $5.00 installation; $9.60 monthly.
Pay Service 3
Pay Units: N.A.
Programming (via satellite): Showtime.
Fee: $5.00 installation; $8.65 monthly.
Video-On-Demand: No
Internet Service
Operational: No.
Telephone Service
None
Office Manager: Jennifer Webb. Operations Manager: Greg Lundwall.
Ownership: Northstar Broadband LLC (MSO).

OKANOGAN—Charter Communications. Now served by WENATCHEE, WA [WA0015]. ICA: WA0044.

OLYMPIA—Comcast Cable. Now served by TACOMA, WA [WA0003]. ICA: WA0007.

ORCAS ISLAND—Almega Cable, 4025 W Airport Frwy, Ste 554, Bedford, TX 76021. Phone: 817-685-9588. Fax: 817-685-6488. Web Site: http://almegacable.com. ICA: WA0083.
TV Market Ranking: Below 100 (ORCAS ISLAND). Franchise award date: N.A. Franchise expiration date: N.A. Began: August 15, 1989.
Channel capacity: 61 (not 2-way capable). Channels available but not in use: N.A.
Basic Service
Subscribers: 283.
Programming (received off-air): KBCB (IND) Bellingham; KCPQ (FOX) Tacoma; KCTS-TV (PBS) Seattle; KING-TV (NBC) Seattle; KIRO-TV (CBS, IND) Seattle; KOMO-TV (ABC) Seattle; KONG (IND) Everett; KSTW (CW) Tacoma; KVOS-TV (IND) Bellingham; KZJO (MNT) Seattle.
Programming (via satellite): A&E Networks; ABC Family Channel; AMC; Animal Planet; CNBC; CNN; C-SPAN; Discovery Channel; Disney Channel; ESPN; ESPN 2; Fox News Channel; Fox Sports Net; HGTV; History Channel; MTV; Nickelodeon; Northwest Cable News; Spike TV; Syfy; TBS Superstation; The Learning Channel; The Weather Channel; Turner Network TV; USA Network; Versus; VH1.
Fee: $29.95 installation; $19.95 monthly.
Pay Service 1
Pay Units: N.A.
Programming (via satellite): Cinemax; HBO.
Video-On-Demand: No
Internet Service
Operational: No.
Telephone Service
None
Miles of Plant: 53.0 (coaxial); None (fiber optic).
Ownership: Almega Cable (MSO).

OROVILLE—Charter Communications. Now served by WENATCHEE, WA [WA0015]. ICA: WA0073.

OTHELLO—Northland Cable Television, 317 S Ash St, PO Box T, Moses Lake, WA 98837. Phone: 509-765-6151. Fax: 509-765-5132. E-mail: moseslake@northlandcabletv.com. Web Site: http://www.northlandcabletv.com. Also serves Adams County. ICA: WA0049.
TV Market Ranking: Outside TV Markets (Adams County, OTHELLO). Franchise

award date: N.A. Franchise expiration date: N.A. Began: November 22, 1965.

Channel capacity: 63 (operating 2-way). Channels available but not in use: N.A.

Basic Service

Subscribers: 1,472.

Programming (received off-air): KAYU-TV (FOX) Spokane; KEPR-TV (CBS) Pasco; KHQ-TV (NBC) Spokane; KNDU (NBC) Richland; KREM (CBS) Spokane; KSKN (CW) Spokane; KSPS-TV (PBS) Spokane; KSTW (CW) Tacoma; KVEW (ABC, MNT) Kennewick; KXLY-TV (ABC, MNT) Spokane; 1 FM.

Programming (via microwave): KING-TV (NBC) Seattle; KIRO-TV (CBS, IND) Seattle.

Programming (via satellite): A&E Networks; Cartoon Network; CNN; Discovery Channel; ESPN; Fox Deportes; Fox News Channel; FX; GalaVision; Hallmark Channel; Headline News; HGTV; INSP; Lifetime; National Geographic Channel; Northwest Cable News; QVC; TBS Superstation; Telemundo; The Learning Channel; The Weather Channel; Turner Network TV; TV Guide Network; Univision Studios; USA Network.

Fee: $45.00 installation; $31.49 monthly; $2.20 converter.

Expanded Basic Service 1

Subscribers: N.A.

Programming (via satellite): Animal Planet; Canal Sur; Cine Mexicano; Comedy Central; C-SPAN; ESPN 2; Food Network; Fox Movie Channel; Golf Channel; History Channel; Latin Television (LTV); MTV; Nickelodeon; Spike TV; Syfy; Turner Classic Movies.

Fee: $10.00 monthly.

Digital Basic Service

Subscribers: N.A.

Programming (via satellite): BBC America; Bloomberg Television; Discovery Health Channel; Discovery Kids Channel; DMX Music; G4; GSN; Lifetime Movie Network; Military Channel; Outdoor Channel; Planet Green; Science; Speed; Trinity Broadcasting Network; Versus; WE tv.

Fee: $10.50 monthly.

Pay Service 1

Pay Units: N.A.

Programming (via satellite): HBO.

Digital Pay Service 1

Pay Units: N.A.

Programming (via satellite): Cinemax (multiplexed); Encore (multiplexed); Flix; HBO (multiplexed); Showtime (multiplexed); Starz (multiplexed); The Movie Channel (multiplexed).

Fee: $14.75 monthly (HBO, Cinemax, Showtime/TMC/Flix, or Starz/Encore).

Video-On-Demand: No

Pay-Per-View

iN DEMAND (delivered digitally); Playboy TV (delivered digitally); Fresh (delivered digitally).

Internet Service

Operational: Yes. Began: December 1, 2002.

Subscribers: 20.

Broadband Service: Northland Express.

Fee: $42.99 monthly.

Telephone Service

Digital: Operational

Fee: $29.99 monthly

Miles of Plant: 35.0 (coaxial); None (fiber optic).

Manager: Jon Ulrich. Chief Technician: Kim Svetich.

Ownership: Northland Communications Corp. (MSO).

PACKWOOD—Millennium Digital Media/Broadstripe, 3633 136th Pl SE, Ste 107, Bellevue, WA 98006-1451. Phones: 800-829-2225; 425-747-4600. Fax: 425-644-4621. E-mail: contact_nw@broadstripe.com. Web Site: http://www.broadstripe.com. Also serves Randle (portions) & Silver Brook. ICA: WA0074.

TV Market Ranking: Outside TV Markets (PACKWOOD, Randle (portions), Silver Brook). Franchise award date: N.A. Franchise expiration date: April 1, 2032. Began: December 1, 1983.

Channel capacity: 35 (operating 2-way). Channels available but not in use: N.A.

Basic Service

Subscribers: 619.

Programming (received off-air): KCPQ (FOX) Tacoma; KCTS-TV (PBS) Seattle; KING-TV (NBC) Seattle; KIRO-TV (CBS, IND) Seattle; KOMO-TV (ABC) Seattle.

Programming (via satellite): A&E Networks; ABC Family Channel; AMC; Animal Planet; CNN; Discovery Channel; Disney Channel; E! Entertainment Television; ESPN; Fox News Channel; G4; Great American Country; Headline News; HGTV; History Channel; Lifetime; National Geographic Channel; Nickelodeon; Northwest Cable News; QVC; Spike TV; Syfy; TBS Superstation; The Learning Channel; Turner Network TV; TV Guide Network; USA Network; WGN America.

Fee: $29.95 installation; $42.99 monthly.

Digital Basic Service

Subscribers: N.A.

Programming (via satellite): BBC America; Bio; Bravo; Discovery Digital Networks; DMX Music; Encore (multiplexed); GSN; History Channel International; Independent Film Channel; Lifetime Movie Network; Style Network.

Fee: $8.40 monthly.

Digital Expanded Basic Service

Subscribers: N.A.

Programming (via satellite): ESPN 2; ESPNews; Fox Sports World; Golf Channel; Speed; Versus.

Fee: $5.00 monthly.

Digital Pay Service 1

Pay Units: N.A.

Programming (via satellite): Cinemax (multiplexed); HBO (multiplexed); Showtime (multiplexed); The Movie Channel (multiplexed).

Fee: $10.00 monthly (each).

Video-On-Demand: No

Pay-Per-View

iN DEMAND (delivered digitally); Playboy TV (delivered digitally).

Internet Service

Operational: Yes.

Fee: $49.95 installation; $39.95 monthly.

Telephone Service

None

Miles of Plant: 32.0 (coaxial); None (fiber optic).

President & Chief Executive Officer: Bill Shreffler. Vice President & General Manager: Dave Walker. Vice President, Programming: Frank Scotello. Engineering Director: Dave Jacobs. Customer Service Manager: Steve Orona.

Ownership: Broadstripe (MSO).

PE ELL—Millennium Digital Media/Broadstripe, 3633 136th Pl SE, Ste 107, Bellevue, WA 98006-1451. Phones: 800-829-2225; 425-747-4600. Fax: 425-644-4600. E-mail: contact_nw@broadstripe.com. Web Site: http://www.broadstripe.com. Also serves Doty & Dryad. ICA: WA0103.

TV Market Ranking: Outside TV Markets (Doty, Dryad, PE ELL). Franchise award date: N.A. Franchise expiration date: January 1, 2007. Began: October 1, 1983.

Channel capacity: 35 (not 2-way capable). Channels available but not in use: N.A.

Basic Service

Subscribers: 322.

Programming (received off-air): KCKA (PBS) Centralia; KCPQ (FOX) Tacoma; KCTS-TV (PBS) Seattle; KING-TV (NBC) Seattle; KIRO-TV (CBS, IND) Seattle; KOMO-TV (ABC) Seattle; KSTW (CW) Tacoma; KZJO (MNT) Seattle.

Programming (via satellite): A&E Networks; ABC Family Channel; AMC; Animal Planet; Cartoon Network; CNN; Discovery Channel; Disney Channel; ESPN; Fox News Channel; G4; Headline News; HGTV; History Channel; Nickelodeon; Northwest Cable News; QVC; Spike TV; Syfy; TBS Superstation; The Learning Channel; Turner Network TV; TVW; USA Network; WGN America.

Fee: $29.95 installation; $40.99 monthly.

Digital Basic Service

Subscribers: N.A.

Programming (via satellite): BBC America; Bio; Bravo; Discovery Digital Networks; DMX Music; ESPN 2; ESPNews; Fox Sports World; Golf Channel; GSN; History Channel International; National Geographic Channel; Science Television; Speed; Versus.

Fee: $14.40 monthly.

Pay Service 1

Pay Units: 98.

Programming (via satellite): HBO; Showtime.

Fee: $14.95 monthly (each).

Digital Pay Service 1

Pay Units: N.A.

Programming (via satellite): Cinemax (multiplexed); Encore (multiplexed); HBO (multiplexed); Independent Film Channel; Showtime (multiplexed); Starz (multiplexed); The Movie Channel (multiplexed).

Fee: $10.00 monthly (each).

Video-On-Demand: No

Pay-Per-View

Playboy TV (delivered digitally); iN DEMAND (delivered digitally).

Internet Service

Operational: No.

Telephone Service

None

Miles of Plant: 18.0 (coaxial); None (fiber optic).

President & Chief Executive Officer: Bill Shreffler. Vice President, Programming: Frank Scotello. Engineering Director: Dave Jacobs. Customer Service Manager: Steve Orona.

Ownership: Broadstripe (MSO).

POINT ROBERTS—Delta Cable Vision, PO Box 869, Point Roberts, WA 98281-0869. Phones: 360-945-0456; 604-946-7676. Fax: 604-946-5627. E-mail: admin@deltacable.com. Web Site: http://www.deltacablevision.com. ICA: WA0076.

TV Market Ranking: Below 100 (POINT ROBERTS). Franchise award date: January 1, 1973. Franchise expiration date: January 1, 2018. Began: June 1, 1973.

Channel capacity: N.A. Channels available but not in use: N.A.

Basic Service

Subscribers: 650.

Programming (received off-air): KBCB (IND) Bellingham; KCPQ (FOX) Tacoma; KCTS-TV (PBS) Seattle; KING-TV (NBC) Seattle; KIRO-TV (CBS, IND) Seattle; KOMO-TV (ABC) Seattle; KSTW (CW) Tacoma; KVOS-TV (IND) Bellingham; allband FM.

Programming (via satellite): A&E Networks; ABC Family Channel; CNN; C-SPAN; Discovery Channel; Disney Channel; E! Entertainment Television; ESPN; ESPN Classic Sports; History Channel; Knowledge Network; Northwest Cable News; Spike TV; TBS Superstation; The Learning Channel; Turner Classic Movies; Turner Network TV; USA Network; WGN America.

Fee: $18.00 installation; $21.00 monthly; $5.00 converter.

Expanded Basic Service 1

Subscribers: N.A.

Programming (via satellite): Animal Planet; Bravo; Cartoon Network; Cooking Channel; DIY Network; Food Network; Fox Sports World; Golf Channel; Hallmark Channel; Headline News; HGTV; Speed; Syfy; truTV; Versus.

Fee: $9.95 monthly.

Pay Service 1

Pay Units: N.A.

Programming (via satellite): HBO.

Fee: $12.00 monthly.

Video-On-Demand: No

Internet Service

Operational: Yes.

Subscribers: 224.

Broadband Service: Delta Cable Communications.

Fee: $25.00 installation; $39.50 monthly.

Telephone Service

None

Miles of Plant: 30.0 (coaxial); 5.0 (fiber optic). Additional miles planned: 2.0 (coaxial); 2.0 (fiber optic).

President: John S. Thomas. General Manager: Larry Boule. Operations Manager: Craig Johnson. Engineering Manager: Gordie Duncan. Program Director: Adnan Hussain. Marketing Manager: Chris Rumbold. Customer Service Manager: Henri Wendel.

Ownership: Guiness Communications Inc.

POMEROY—Formerly served by Almega Cable. No longer in operation. ICA: WA0214.

PORT ANGELES—Wave Broadband, 725 E 1st St, Port Angeles, WA 98362-3604. Phones: 425-576-8200 (Administrative office); 866-928-3123 (Customer service); 800-244-7591; 360-452-8466. Fax: 805-643-1284. Web Site: http://www.wavebroadband.com. Also serves Clallam County (unincorporated areas) & Sequim. ICA: WA0020.

TV Market Ranking: Outside TV Markets (Clallam County (unincorporated areas), PORT ANGELES, Sequim). Franchise award date: May 1, 1960. Franchise expiration date: N.A. Began: May 1, 1960.

Channel capacity: 62 (not 2-way capable). Channels available but not in use: N.A.

Basic Service

Subscribers: 5,500.

Programming (received off-air): KBCB (IND) Bellingham; KCPQ (FOX) Tacoma; KCTS-TV (PBS) Seattle; KING-TV (NBC) Seattle; KIRO-TV (CBS, IND) Seattle; KOMO-TV (ABC) Seattle; KONG (IND) Everett; KSTW (CW) Tacoma; KVOS-TV (IND) Bellingham; KWPX-TV (ION) Bellevue; KZJO (MNT) Seattle; various Canadian stations.

Programming (via satellite): C-SPAN; QVC; TV Guide Network.

Fee: $50.00 installation; $22.95 monthly; $3.95 converter; $10.00 additional installation.

Expanded Basic Service 1
Subscribers: 4,878.
Programming (via satellite): A&E Networks; ABC Family Channel; AMC; Animal Planet; Bravo; Cartoon Network; CNBC; CNN; Comedy Central; Country Music TV; Discovery Channel; Disney Channel; E! Entertainment Television; ESPN; ESPN 2; Food Network; Fox Movie Channel; Fox News Channel; FX; Golf Channel; Great American Country; Hallmark Channel; Headline News; HGTV; History Channel; Lifetime; MSNBC; MTV; National Geographic Channel; Nickelodeon; Northwest Cable News; Oxygen; Spike TV; Syfy; TBS Superstation; The Learning Channel; The Weather Channel; Travel Channel; truTV; Turner Classic Movies; Turner Network TV; TV Land; USA Network; VH1.
Fee: $50.00 installation; $23.55 monthly.

Digital Basic Service
Subscribers: 570.
Programming (via satellite): BBC America; Bio; BYU Television; CMT Pure Country; C-SPAN 2; Discovery Fit & Health; Discovery Health Channel; Discovery Kids Channel; Disney XD; Eternal Word TV Network; Fox Business Channel; History Channel International; ID Investigation Discovery; Lifetime Real Women; Military Channel; MTV Hits; MTV2; Music Choice; Nick Jr.; NickToons TV; PBS Kids Sprout; Planet Green; Science; SoapNet; TeenNick; VH1 Classic; VH1 Soul.
Fee: $18.45 monthly.

Digital Expanded Basic Service
Subscribers: N.A.
Programming (received off-air): KCPQ (FOX) Tacoma; KCTS-TV (PBS) Seattle; KING-TV (NBC) Seattle; KIRO-TV (CBS, IND) Seattle; KOMO-TV (ABC) Seattle; KONG (IND) Everett; KSTW (CW) Tacoma.
Programming (via satellite): A&E HD; Animal Planet HD; Discovery Channel HD; Disney Channel HD; ESPN 2 HD; ESPN HD; Food Network HD; FSN HD; HD Theater; HDNet; HDNet Movies; HGTV HD; History Channel HD; MGM HD; National Geographic Channel HD Network; NFL Network HD; Science HD; TBS in HD; TLC HD; Travel Channel HD; Turner Network TV HD; Universal HD.

Digital Expanded Basic Service 2
Subscribers: N.A.
Programming (via satellite): Bloomberg Television; Boomerang; Bravo; Cooking Channel; DIY Network; Fuse; G4; GSN; Hallmark Movie Channel; Halogen Network; Independent Film Channel; Lifetime Movie Network; Style Network; Syfy; Trinity Broadcasting Network; WE tv.

Digital Expanded Basic Service 3
Subscribers: N.A.
Programming (via satellite): CBS Sports Network; ESPN Classic Sports; ESPN U; ESPNews; Fox Soccer; FSN Digital Atlantic; FSN Digital Central; FSN Digital Pacific; Golf Channel; NFL Network; Outdoor Channel; Speed; Tennis Channel; Versus.

Digital Pay Service 1
Pay Units: N.A.
Programming (via satellite): Cinemax (multiplexed); Cinemax HD; Encore (multiplexed); Flix; HBO (multiplexed); HBO HD; MoviePlex; Showtime (multiplexed); Showtime HD; Starz (multiplexed); Starz HDTV; The Movie Channel (multiplexed); The Movie Channel HD.
Fee: $12.00 monthly (Showtime/TMC/Flix), $15.00 monthly (HBO, Cinemax or Starz/Encore).

Video-On-Demand: Yes

Pay-Per-View
Movies (delivered digitally); Special events (delivered digitally); ESPN Gameplan (delivered digitally); NBA League Pass; Sports PPV (delivered digitally).

Internet Service
Operational: Yes.
Broadband Service: Wave Broadband.
Fee: $24.95-$74.95 monthly.

Telephone Service
Digital: Operational
Fee: $29.95-$49.95 monthly
Miles of Plant: 296.0 (coaxial); None (fiber optic). Additional miles planned: 5.0 (coaxial).
General Manager: Jon Ulrich.
Ownership: WaveDivision Holdings LLC (MSO).

PORT ORCHARD—Wave Broadband, 4519 SE Mile Hill Dr, Port Orchard, WA 98366. Phones: 425-576-8200; 800-244-7591. Web Site: http://www.wavebroadband.com. Also serves Allyn (portions), Bangor Submarine Base, Belfair, Holly, Jackson Park, Keyport, Keyport Naval Base, Kitsap Lake, Lake Symington, Lake Tahuya, Manchester, Mason County, North Shore, Olalla, Puget Sound Naval Shipyard, Seabeck, Silverdale, South Kitsap & Tahuya. ICA: WA0010.
TV Market Ranking: 20 (Allyn (portions), Bangor Submarine Base, Belfair, Holly, Jackson Park, Keyport, Keyport Naval Base, Kitsap Lake, Lake Symington, Lake Tahuya, Manchester, Mason County, North Shore, Olalla, PORT ORCHARD, Puget Sound Naval Shipyard, Seabeck, Silverdale, South Kitsap, Tahuya). Franchise award date: N.A. Franchise expiration date: N.A. Began: January 1, 1971.
Channel capacity: 42 (operating 2-way). Channels available but not in use: N.A.

Basic Service
Subscribers: 24,823.
Programming (received off-air): KBTC-TV (PBS) Tacoma; KCPQ (FOX) Tacoma; KCTS-TV (PBS) Seattle; KING-TV (NBC) Seattle; KIRO-TV (CBS, IND) Seattle; KOMO-TV (ABC) Seattle; KONG (IND) Everett; KSTW (CW) Tacoma; KTBW-TV (TBN) Tacoma; KUNS-TV (UNV) Bellevue; KWDK (ETV) Tacoma; KWPX-TV (ION) Bellevue; KZJO (MNT) Seattle; allband FM.
Programming (via satellite): C-SPAN; INSP; QVC; TV Guide Network; WGN America.
Fee: $45.00 installation; $23.95 monthly; $2.50 converter; $20.00 additional installation.

Expanded Basic Service 1
Subscribers: 20,000.
Programming (via satellite): A&E Networks; ABC Family Channel; AMC; Animal Planet; BET Networks; Bravo; Cartoon Network; CNBC; CNN; Comedy Central; Country Music TV; Discovery Channel; Discovery Fit & Health; Disney Channel; Disney XD; E! Entertainment Television; ESPN; ESPN 2; Food Network; Fox News Channel; FX; Golf Channel; Great American Country; Hallmark Channel; Headline News; HGTV; History Channel; Lifetime; MSNBC; MTV; National Geographic Channel; Nickelodeon; Northwest Cable News; Outdoor Channel; Oxygen; Speed; Spike TV; Syfy; TBS Superstation; The Learning Channel; The Weather Channel; Travel Channel; Turner Classic Movies; Turner Network TV; TV Land; USA Network; VH1.
Fee: $28.00 monthly.

Digital Basic Service
Subscribers: 12,900.
Programming (via satellite): BBC America; Bio; BYU Television; cloo; CMT Pure Country; Current; Discovery en Espanol; Discovery Health Channel; Discovery Kids Channel; Eternal Word TV Network; Fox Business Channel; History Channel International; ID Investigation Discovery; Military Channel; MTV Hits; MTV Jams; MTV2; Music Choice; Nick Jr.; NickToons TV; PBS Kids Sprout; Planet Green; Science; SoapNet; TeenNick; Tr3s; VH1 Classic; VH1 Soul.
Fee: $10.00 monthly.

Digital Expanded Basic Service
Subscribers: N.A.
Programming (via satellite): American-Life TV Network; Bloomberg Television; Boomerang; Cooking Channel; DIY Network; Fox Movie Channel; Fuse; G4; GSN; Hallmark Movie Channel; Halogen Network; Independent Film Channel; Lifetime Movie Network; Lifetime Real Women; Ovation; Style Network; truTV; WE tv.

Digital Expanded Basic Service 2
Subscribers: N.A.
Programming (via satellite): CBS Sports Network; ESPN Classic Sports; ESPN U; ESPNews; Fox Soccer; FSN Digital Atlantic; FSN Digital Central; FSN Digital Pacific; NFL Network; Tennis Channel; Versus.

Digital Expanded Basic Service 3
Subscribers: N.A.
Programming (received off-air): KCPQ (FOX) Tacoma; KCTS-TV (PBS) Seattle; KING-TV (NBC) Seattle; KIRO-TV (CBS, IND) Seattle; KOMO-TV (ABC) Seattle; KONG (IND) Everett; KSTW (CW) Tacoma.
Programming (via satellite): A&E HD; Disney Channel HD; ESPN 2 HD; ESPN HD; Food Network HD; FSN HD; HD Theater; HDNet; HDNet Movies; HGTV HD; History Channel HD; National Geographic Channel HD Network; NFL Network HD; Science HD; TBS in HD; Travel Channel HD; Turner Network TV HD; Universal HD.

Digital Pay Service 1
Pay Units: 2,153.
Programming (via satellite): Cinemax (multiplexed); Cinemax HD.
Fee: $20.00 installation; $10.95 monthly.

Digital Pay Service 2
Pay Units: 3,392.
Programming (via satellite): HBO (multiplexed); HBO HD.
Fee: $20.00 installation; $11.95 monthly.

Digital Pay Service 3
Pay Units: 3,173.
Programming (via satellite): Flix; Showtime (multiplexed); Showtime HD; Sundance Channel; The Movie Channel (multiplexed); The Movie Channel HD.
Fee: $20.00 installation; $10.95 monthly.

Digital Pay Service 4
Pay Units: N.A.
Programming (via satellite): Encore (multiplexed); Filipino Channel; here! TV; MoviePlex; Starz (multiplexed); Starz HDTV.

Video-On-Demand: Yes

Pay-Per-View
Addressable homes: 12,900.
Hot Choice (delivered digitally); iN DEMAND (delivered digitally); Fresh (delivered digitally); Shorteez (delivered digitally); Sports PPV (delivered digitally).

Internet Service
Operational: Yes. Began: December 1, 2000.
Subscribers: 11,000.
Broadband Service: Wave Broadband.
Fee: $150.00 installation; $24.95-$74.95 monthly.

Telephone Service
Digital: Operational
Fee: 29.95-$49.95 monthly
Miles of Plant: 1,105.0 (coaxial); None (fiber optic).
Manager: Jerry Rotondo. Chief Technician: Richard Rumrill. Marketing Director: Keith Tyrrell.
Ownership: WaveDivision Holdings LLC (MSO).

PORT TOWNSEND—Millennium Digital Media/Broadstripe, 3633 136th Pl SE, Ste 107, Bellevue, WA 98006-1451. Phones: 800-829-2225; 425-747-4600. Fax: 425-644-4621. Web Site: http://www.broadstripe.com. Also serves Brinnon, Port Hadlock, Port Ludlow & Quilcene. ICA: WA0027.
TV Market Ranking: 20 (Brinnon, Port Hadlock, Port Ludlow, Quilcene); Below 100 (PORT TOWNSEND). Franchise award date: January 1, 1977. Franchise expiration date: N.A. Began: December 28, 1977.
Channel capacity: 35 (operating 2-way). Channels available but not in use: N.A.

Basic Service
Subscribers: 3,800.
Programming (received off-air): KCPQ (FOX) Tacoma; KCTS-TV (PBS) Seattle; KFFV (IND) Seattle; KING-TV (NBC) Seattle; KIRO-TV (CBS, IND) Seattle; KOMO-TV (ABC) Seattle; KONG (IND) Everett; KSTW (CW) Tacoma; KTBW-TV (TBN) Tacoma; KUNS-TV (UNV) Bellevue; KVOS-TV (IND) Bellingham; KWDK (ETV) Tacoma; KWPX-TV (ION) Bellevue; KZJO (MNT) Seattle.
Programming (via satellite): QVC; ShopNBC; TV Guide Network; TVW; various Canadian stations.
Fee: $29.95 installation; $19.95 monthly.

Expanded Basic Service 1
Subscribers: N.A.
Programming (via satellite): A&E Networks; ABC Family Channel; AMC; Animal Planet; Cartoon Network; CNBC; CNN; Comedy Central; Country Music TV; C-SPAN; Discovery Channel; Disney Channel; ESPN; ESPN 2; ESPN Classic Sports; Food Network; Fox News Channel; FX; Hallmark Channel; Headline News; HGTV; History Channel; Independent Film Channel; Lifetime; MTV; National Geographic Channel; Nickelodeon; Northwest Cable News; Spike TV; Syfy; TBS Superstation; The Learning Channel; Travel Channel; Turner Classic Movies; Turner Network TV; TV Land; USA Network.
Fee: $27.08 monthly.

Digital Basic Service
Subscribers: N.A.
Programming (via satellite): CMT Pure Country; DIY Network; Encore (multiplexed); ESPN HD; Food Network HD; Fox

College Sports Central; Fox College Sports Pacific; GAS; HD Theater; HDNet; HDNet Movies; HGTV HD; MTV Networks Digital Suite; Music Choice; Nick Jr.; NickToons TV; Starz (multiplexed); Turner Classic Movies.
Fee: $13.40 monthly.
Digital Expanded Basic Service
Subscribers: N.A.
Programming (via satellite): BBC America; ESPNews; Fox College Sports Atlantic; Fox Sports World; G4; Golf Channel; Speed; Style Network; Versus.
Fee: $5.00 monthly (Arts & Entertainment or Sports).
Digital Pay Service 1
Pay Units: N.A.
Programming (via satellite): Cinemax (multiplexed); Flix; HBO (multiplexed); Showtime (multiplexed); Sundance Channel; The Movie Channel (multiplexed).
Fee: $5.50 monthly (each).
Video-On-Demand: No
Pay-Per-View
Movies (delivered digitally).
Internet Service
Operational: Yes.
Subscribers: 1,900.
Broadband Service: Millennium Cable-Speed.
Fee: $49.95 installation; $37.95 monthly.
Telephone Service
Digital: Operational
Fee: $39.99 monthly
Miles of Plant: 173.0 (coaxial); None (fiber optic).
President & Chief Executive Officer: Bill Shreffler. Vice President, Programming: Frank Scotello. Engineering Director: Dave Jacobs. Customer Service Manager: Steve Orona.
Ownership: Broadstripe (MSO).

PRESCOTT—Formerly served by Charter Communications. No longer in operation. ICA: WA0133.

QUINCY—J & N Cable, 614 S Columbus Ave, Goldendale, WA 98620-9006. Phone: 509-773-5359. Fax: 509-773-7090. Web Site: http://www.jncable.com. Also serves Crescent Bar & George. ICA: WA0057.
TV Market Ranking: Outside TV Markets (Crescent Bar, George, QUINCY). Franchise award date: N.A. Franchise expiration date: N.A. Began: August 1, 1978.
Channel capacity: 61 (not 2-way capable). Channels available but not in use: N.A.
Basic Service
Subscribers: 200.
Programming (received off-air): KAYU-TV (FOX) Spokane; KHQ-TV (NBC) Spokane; KING-TV (NBC) Seattle; KIRO-TV (CBS, IND) Seattle; KOMO-TV (ABC) Seattle; KREM (CBS) Spokane; KSPS-TV (PBS) Spokane; KSTW (CW) Tacoma; KXLY-TV (ABC, MNT) Spokane; 3 FMs.
Programming (via satellite): A&E Networks; ABC Family Channel; Animal Planet; Cartoon Network; CNN; Comedy Central; C-SPAN; Discovery Channel; Disney Channel; E! Entertainment Television; ESPN; ESPN 2; Fox Deportes; Fox News Channel; Fox Sports Net; FX; GalaVision; Headline News; HGTV; History Channel; Lifetime; MTV; Nickelodeon; Northwest Cable News; QVC; Spike TV; Syfy; TBS Superstation; Telemundo; Telenovelas; The Learning Channel; The Weather Channel; Toon Disney; Travel Channel; Turner Classic Movies; Turner Network TV; TV Guide Network; TV Land; TVW; USA Network; Versus; VH1; WGN America.
Fee: $39.95 installation; $29.52 monthly.
Digital Basic Service
Subscribers: N.A.
Programming (via satellite): Black Family Channel; Bravo; Discovery Digital Networks; DMX Music; GAS; Great American Country; GSN; History Channel International; MTV Networks Digital Suite; MuchMusic Network; National Geographic Channel; Nick Jr.; Science Television; Vision TV; WE tv.
Fee: $15.95 monthly.
Digital Expanded Basic Service
Subscribers: N.A.
Programming (via satellite): Canales N; Encore; ESPN Classic Sports; ESPNews; Fox Sports Net; Fox Sports World; Golf Channel; Independent Film Channel; Speed; Versus.
Fee: $15.95 monthly.
Pay Service 1
Pay Units: N.A.
Programming (via satellite): HBO.
Fee: $15.00 installation; $8.95 monthly (Cinemax), $10.95 monthly (HBO or Showtime).
Digital Pay Service 1
Pay Units: N.A.
Programming (via satellite): Cinemax (multiplexed); HBO (multiplexed); Showtime (multiplexed).
Fee: $10.00 monthly (Cinemax), $12.00 monthly (Showtime), $12.95 monthly (HBO).
Pay-Per-View
Playboy TV (delivered digitally); iN DEMAND (delivered digitally).
Internet Service
Operational: No.
Telephone Service
None
Miles of Plant: 43.0 (coaxial); 10.0 (fiber optic). Additional miles planned: 8.0 (coaxial).
General Manager: John Kusky.
Ownership: J & N Cable Systems Inc. (MSO).

RANDLE—Millennium Digital Media/Broadstripe, 3633 136th Pl SE, Ste 107, Bellevue, WA 98006-1451. Phones: 800-829-2225; 425-747-4600. Fax: 425-644-4621. E-mail: contact_nw@broadstripe.com. Web Site: http://www.broadstripe.com. Also serves Glenoma. ICA: WA0208.
TV Market Ranking: Outside TV Markets (Glenoma, RANDLE). Franchise award date: N.A. Franchise expiration date: N.A. Began: N.A.
Channel capacity: N.A. Channels available but not in use: N.A.
Basic Service
Subscribers: N.A.
Programming (received off-air): KCTS-TV (PBS) Seattle; KING-TV (NBC) Seattle; KIRO-TV (CBS, IND) Seattle; KOMO-TV (ABC) Seattle.
Programming (via satellite): A&E Networks; ABC Family Channel; AMC; CNN; Discovery Channel; Disney Channel; E! Entertainment Television; ESPN; Fox News Channel; Fox Sports Net; G4; Great American Country; Headline News; HGTV; History Channel; Lifetime; Nickelodeon; Northwest Cable News; QVC; Spike TV; Syfy; TBS Superstation; The Learning Channel; Trinity Broadcasting Network; Turner Classic Movies; Turner Network TV; TV Guide Network; USA Network; WGN America.
Fee: $29.95 installation; $41.99 monthly.
Digital Basic Service
Subscribers: N.A.
Programming (via satellite): BBC America; Bio; Bravo; Discovery Digital Networks; DMX Music; GSN; History Channel International; Independent Film Channel; Lifetime Movie Network; National Geographic Channel; Style Network.
Fee: $13.40 monthly.
Digital Expanded Basic Service
Subscribers: N.A.
Programming (via satellite): ESPN 2; ESPNews; Fox Sports World; Golf Channel; Speed; Versus.
Fee: $5.00 monthly.
Digital Pay Service 1
Pay Units: N.A.
Programming (via satellite): Cinemax (multiplexed); Encore (multiplexed); HBO (multiplexed); Showtime (multiplexed); Starz (multiplexed); The Movie Channel (multiplexed).
Fee: $10.00 monthly (each).
Video-On-Demand: No
Pay-Per-View
iN DEMAND (delivered digitally); Playboy TV (delivered digitally).
Internet Service
Operational: Yes.
Fee: $49.95 installation; $37.95 monthly.
Telephone Service
Digital: Operational
Fee: $39.99 monthly
Miles of Plant: 34.0 (coaxial); None (fiber optic).
President & Chief Executive Officer: Bill Shreffler. Vice President & General Manager: Dave Walker. Vice President, Programming: Frank Scotello. Engineering Director: Dave Jacobs. Customer Service Manager: Steve Orona.
Ownership: Broadstripe (MSO).

RAYMOND—Comcast Cable. Now served by TACOMA, WA [WA0003]. ICA: WA0040.

REARDAN—Elk River TV Cable Co., 509 S Main St, PO Box 154, Troy, ID 83871. Phone: 208-369-4652. E-mail: leslie@elkrivertv.net. Web Site: http://www.elkrivertv.net. ICA: WA0121.
TV Market Ranking: 76 (REARDAN). Franchise award date: N.A. Franchise expiration date: N.A. Began: May 31, 1983.
Channel capacity: N.A. Channels available but not in use: N.A.
Basic Service
Subscribers: 59.
Programming (received off-air): KAYU-TV (FOX) Spokane; KHQ-TV (NBC) Spokane; KREM (CBS) Spokane; KSKN (CW) Spokane; KSPS-TV (PBS) Spokane; KXLY-TV (ABC, MNT) Spokane.
Programming (via satellite): A&E Networks; ABC Family Channel; Cartoon Network; CNN; C-SPAN; Discovery Channel; Disney Channel; ESPN; ESPN 2; Fox Sports Net; Great American Country; HGTV; History Channel; ION Television; Lifetime; MTV; Nickelodeon; Northwest Cable News; Outdoor Channel; Spike TV; TBS Superstation; Turner Classic Movies; Turner Network TV; USA Network; Versus; WGN America.
Fee: $31.65 monthly.
Pay Service 1
Pay Units: 8.
Programming (via satellite): HBO.
Fee: $10.00 monthly.
Video-On-Demand: No
Internet Service
Operational: Yes.
Broadband Service: Elk River Cable.
Fee: $39.00 monthly.
Telephone Service
None
Miles of Plant: 5.0 (coaxial); None (fiber optic).
Managers: Dave McGraw.; Leslie McGraw. Chief Technician: Justin McGraw.
Ownership: Elk River TV Cable Co. (MSO).

REDMOND—Comcast Cable. Now served by SEATTLE, WA [WA0001]. ICA: WA0034.

REPUBLIC—Television Assn. of Republic, 147-18 N Clark St, PO Box 555, Republic, WA 99166-0555. Phone: 509-775-3822. Fax: 509-775-3822. E-mail: billing@rcabletv.com. Web Site: http://www.rcabletv.com. ICA: WA0177.
TV Market Ranking: Outside TV Markets (REPUBLIC). Franchise award date: December 1, 1953. Franchise expiration date: N.A. Began: December 1, 1953.
Channel capacity: N.A. Channels available but not in use: N.A.
Basic Service
Subscribers: 439.
Programming (received off-air): KAYU-TV (FOX) Spokane; KHQ-TV (NBC) Spokane; KREM (CBS) Spokane; KSPS-TV (PBS) Spokane; KXLY-TV (ABC, MNT) Spokane; various Canadian stations; allband FM.
Programming (via satellite): A&E Networks; ABC Family Channel; AMC; AmericanLife TV Network; Bravo; CNN; C-SPAN 2; Discovery Channel; Disney Channel; Encore; ESPN; ESPN 2; History Channel; Lifetime; Nickelodeon; Northwest Cable News; Syfy; TBS Superstation; The Learning Channel; Trinity Broadcasting Network; Turner Classic Movies; Turner Network TV; USA Network.
Fee: $40.00 installation; $25.00 monthly; $10.00 converter.
Expanded Basic Service 1
Subscribers: 220.
Programming (via satellite): Animal Planet; Cartoon Network; Country Music TV; C-SPAN; Discovery Health Channel; Food Network; Fox News Channel; Great American Country; HGTV; MTV; National Geographic Channel; Outdoor Channel; Speed; Spike TV; Travel Channel; TV Land; Versus; VH1; WGN America.
Fee: $6.50 monthly.
Pay Service 1
Pay Units: 79.
Programming (via satellite): HBO (multiplexed).
Fee: $10.50 monthly.
Internet Service
Operational: Yes. Began: October 1, 2000.
Subscribers: 300.
Broadband Service: In-house.
Fee: $60.00 installation; $30.50 monthly.
Telephone Service
None
Miles of Plant: 30.0 (coaxial); None (fiber optic).
Manager: Jerry Larson. Secretary-Treasurer: Sheila Wellaert.
Ownership: Television Assn. of Republic.

RITZVILLE—Northstar Broadband, PO Box 2576, Post Falls, ID 83877. Phones: 800-572-0902; 208-262-9394. Fax: 208-262-9314. E-mail: j.webb@northstarbroadband.net. Web Site: http://www.northstarbroadband.net. ICA: WA0178.
TV Market Ranking: Outside TV Markets (RITZVILLE). Franchise award date: N.A. Franchise expiration date: N.A. Began: June 1, 1981.
Channel capacity: N.A. Channels available but not in use: N.A.
Basic Service
Subscribers: 350.
Programming (received off-air): KAYU-TV (FOX) Spokane; KHQ-TV (NBC) Spokane;

KREM (CBS) Spokane; KSKN (CW) Spokane; KSPS-TV (PBS) Spokane; KWSU-TV (PBS) Pullman; KXLY-TV (ABC, MNT) Spokane.
Programming (via satellite): A&E Networks; ABC Family Channel; AmericanLife TV Network; Animal Planet; Cartoon Network; Country Music TV; C-SPAN; C-SPAN 2; Discovery Channel; Discovery Health Channel; Eternal Word TV Network; Food Network; Fox News Channel; Hallmark Channel; HGTV; History Channel; ION Television; MSNBC; National Geographic Channel; Nickelodeon; Ovation; QVC; ShopNBC; TBS Superstation; The Learning Channel; Travel Channel; Trinity Broadcasting Network; truTV; TV Guide Network; TV Land; Versus; WGN America.
Fee: $20.00 installation; $30.35 monthly.

Expanded Basic Service 1
Subscribers: N.A.
Programming (via satellite): AMC; Bravo; CNBC; CNN; Comedy Central; Disney Channel; E! Entertainment Television; ESPN; ESPN 2; ESPN Classic Sports; Fox Movie Channel; FX; Golf Channel; Headline News; Lifetime; MoviePlex; MTV; Northwest Cable News; Speed; Spike TV; Syfy; Toon Disney; Turner Classic Movies; Turner Network TV; USA Network; VH1.
Fee: $16.41 monthly.

Pay Service 1
Pay Units: 123.
Programming (via satellite): Cinemax (multiplexed).
Fee: $5.00 installation; $5.25 monthly.

Pay Service 2
Pay Units: 151.
Programming (via satellite): HBO (multiplexed).
Fee: $5.00 installation; $9.60 monthly.

Pay Service 3
Pay Units: N.A.
Programming (via satellite): Showtime.
Fee: $5.00 installation; $8.65 monthly.

Video-On-Demand: No

Internet Service
Operational: Yes, DSL.
Broadband Service: In-house.
Fee: $29.95 installation; $20.26 monthly.

Telephone Service
None

Office Manager: Jennifer Webb. Operations Manager: Greg Lundwall.
Ownership: Northstar Broadband LLC (MSO).

ROCHESTER—Comcast Cable. Now served by TACOMA, WA [WA0003]. ICA: WA0064.

ROSALIA—Elk River TV Cable Co., 509 S Main St, PO Box 154, Troy, ID 83871. Phone: 208-369-4652. E-mail: leslie@elkrivertv.net. Web Site: http://www.elkrivertv.net. ICA: WA0122.
TV Market Ranking: 76 (ROSALIA). Franchise award date: N.A. Franchise expiration date: N.A. Began: February 28, 1983.
Channel capacity: N.A. Channels available but not in use: N.A.

Basic Service
Subscribers: 92.
Programming (received off-air): KAYU-TV (FOX) Spokane; KHQ-TV (NBC) Spokane; KREM (CBS) Spokane; KSKN (CW) Spokane; KSPS-TV (PBS) Spokane; KXLY-TV (ABC, MNT) Spokane.
Programming (via satellite): A&E Networks; Cartoon Network; CNN; Country Music TV; Discovery Channel; Disney Channel; Encore; ESPN; ESPN 2; Fox News Channel; Fox Sports Net; HGTV; History Channel; Lifetime; MTV; Nickelodeon; Northwest Cable News; Outdoor Channel; Spike TV; TBS Superstation; The Learning Channel; The Weather Channel; Trinity Broadcasting Network; Turner Classic Movies; Turner Network TV; USA Network; WGN America.
Fee: $25.00 installation; $31.65 monthly.

Pay Service 1
Pay Units: 18.
Programming (via satellite): HBO.
Fee: $10.00 monthly.

Video-On-Demand: No

Internet Service
Operational: Yes.
Broadband Service: Elk River Cable.
Fee: $39.00 monthly.

Telephone Service
None

Miles of Plant: 6.0 (coaxial); None (fiber optic).
Managers: Dave McGraw.; Leslie McGraw.
Chief Technician: Justin McGraw.
Ownership: Elk River TV Cable Co. (MSO).

ROSLYN—R & R Cable, 103 S Second St, PO Box 610, Roslyn, WA 98941. Phones: 509-649-2211; 509-649-2212. Fax: 509-649-2555. E-mail: seth@inlandnet.com. Web Site: http://www.rrcable.com. Also serves Lake Cle Elum & Ronald. ICA: WA0179.
TV Market Ranking: Below 100 (Lake Cle Elum); Outside TV Markets (Ronald, ROSLYN). Franchise award date: N.A. Franchise expiration date: N.A. Began: February 1, 1955.
Channel capacity: 82 (operating 2-way). Channels available but not in use: None.

Basic Service
Subscribers: 850.
Programming (received off-air): KCPQ (FOX) Tacoma; KCYU-LD Yakima; KING-TV (NBC) Seattle; KIRO-TV (CBS, IND) Seattle; KOMO-TV (ABC) Seattle; allband FM.
Programming (via satellite): A&E Networks; ABC Family Channel; AMC; Animal Planet; Bravo; Cartoon Network; CNN; Comedy Central; Country Music TV; C-SPAN; Discovery Channel; Discovery Fit & Health; E! Entertainment Television; ESPN; ESPN 2; ESPN Classic Sports; Food Network; Fox News Channel; FX; Hallmark Channel; Lifetime; Lifetime Movie Network; MSNBC; MTV; National Geographic Channel; Nickelodeon; NickToons TV; Northwest Cable News; Outdoor Channel; QVC; Spike TV; Syfy; TBS Superstation; The Learning Channel; The Weather Channel; Travel Channel; Trinity Broadcasting Network; truTV; Turner Network TV; TV Guide Network; TV Land; TVW; USA Network; VH1; WGN America; WSBK-TV (CBS, MNT) Boston.
Programming (via translator): KAPP (ABC, MNT) Yakima; KIMA-TV (CBS) Yakima; KNDO (NBC) Yakima; KYVE (PBS) Yakima.
Fee: $19.95 installation; $32.95 monthly.

Digital Basic Service
Subscribers: N.A.
Programming (via satellite): BBC America; Bio; Bloomberg Television; cloo; Discovery Digital Networks; DMX Music; ESPNews; Fox College Sports Atlantic; Fox College Sports Central; Fox College Sports Pacific; Fox Movie Channel; Fox Soccer; Fuse; G4; GAS; Golf Channel; Great American Country; GSN; HGTV; History Channel; History Channel International; Independent Film Channel; MTV Networks Digital Suite; Nick Jr.; Speed; Style Network; Turner Classic Movies; Versus; WE tv.
Fee: $7.00 monthly.

Digital Pay Service 1
Pay Units: N.A.
Programming (via satellite): Cinemax (multiplexed); Encore (multiplexed); HBO (multiplexed); Showtime (multiplexed); Starz (multiplexed); The Movie Channel (multiplexed).
Fee: $7.00 monthly (Cinemax), $10.00 monthly (Starz & Encore), $12.00 monthly (Showtime & TMC), $13.00 monthly (HBO).

Video-On-Demand: No

Pay-Per-View
iN DEMAND (delivered digitally); Playboy TV (delivered digitally); Fresh (delivered digitally).

Internet Service
Operational: No, DSL.

Telephone Service
None

Miles of Plant: 112.0 (coaxial); 25.0 (fiber optic).
General Manager: Doug Weiss. Technical Operations Manager: Seth M. Digby.
Ownership: Inland Telephone Co.

ROYAL CITY—Formerly served by Almega Cable. No longer in operation. ICA: WA0118.

RUSTON—Comcast Cable. Now served by TACOMA, WA [WA0003]. ICA: WA0006.

RYDERWOOD—Comcast Cable, 410 Valley Ave NW, Ste 9, Puyallup, WA 98371. Phones: 425-398-6000 (Bothell office); 253-864-4352. Fax: 253-864-4352. Web Site: http://www.comcast.com. ICA: WA0127.
TV Market Ranking: Outside TV Markets (RYDERWOOD). Franchise award date: N.A. Franchise expiration date: N.A. Began: July 1, 1987.
Channel capacity: N.A. Channels available but not in use: N.A.

Basic Service
Subscribers: N.A. Included in Seattle
Programming (received off-air): KATU (ABC) Portland; KCKA (PBS) Centralia; KCPQ (FOX) Tacoma; KGW (NBC) Portland; KING-TV (NBC) Seattle; KIRO-TV (CBS, IND) Seattle; KOIN (CBS) Portland; KOPB-TV (PBS) Portland; KPTV (FOX) Portland; allband FM.
Programming (via satellite): ABC Family Channel; AMC; CNN; Discovery Channel; Disney Channel; E! Entertainment Television; ESPN; Fox News Channel; Fox Sports Net; TBS Superstation; Turner Network TV; USA Network.
Fee: $23.99 installation; $25.99 monthly.

Pay Service 1
Pay Units: N.A.
Programming (via satellite): Encore; HBO; Starz.

Video-On-Demand: No

Internet Service
Operational: Yes.

Telephone Service
None

Miles of Plant: 5.0 (coaxial); None (fiber optic).
Area Vice President: Anne McMullen. Vice President, Engineering: Steve Taber. Vice President, Sales & Marketing: Tom Pierce. Public Relations Director: Steve Kipp.
Ownership: Comcast Cable Communications Inc. (MSO).

SEATTLE—Comcast Cable, 19909 120th Ave NE, Ste 200, Bothell, WA 98021. Phone: 425-398-6000. Fax: 425-398-6236. E-mail: len_rozek@cable.comcast.com. Web Site: http://www.comcast.com. Also serves Arlington, Beaux Arts Village, Bellevue, Bothell, Brier, Burlington, Carnation, Cascade-Fairwood, Clinton, Clyde Hill, Coupeville, Des Moines, East Seattle, Edmonds, Everett, Freeland, Goldbar, Granite Falls, Inglewood-Finn Hill, Island County, Kenmore, King County, Kirkland, Lake Forest Park, Lake Stevens, Langley, Long Point, Lynwood, Madrona, Marysville, Maxwelton, Medina, Mercer Island, Mill Creek, Monroe, Mount Vernon, Mountlake Terrace, Mukiteo, Oak Harbor, Pine Lake, Redmond, Richmond Beach, Sedro Woolley, Shoreline, Skagit County, Snohomish, Snohomish County, Startup, Sultan, Whidbey Island, Whidbey Island Naval Air Station, Woodinville, Woodway & Yarrow Point. ICA: WA0001.
TV Market Ranking: 20 (Beaux Arts Village, Bellevue, Bothell, Brier, Carnation, Cascade-Fairwood, Clyde Hill, Des Moines, East Seattle, Edmonds, Everett, Goldbar, Inglewood-Finn Hill, Island County (portions), Kenmore, King County (portions), Kirkland, Lake Forest Park, Lake Stevens, Lynwood, Marysville, Maxwelton, Medina, Mercer Island, Mill Creek, Monroe, Mountlake Terrace, Mukiteo, Pine Lake, Redmond, Richmond Beach, SEATTLE, Shoreline, Snohomish, Snohomish County (portions), Startup, Sultan, Whidbey Island, Woodinville, Woodway, Yarrow Point); Below 100 (Arlington, Burlington, Clinton, Coupeville, Freeland, Granite Falls, Langley, Long Point, Madrona, Mount Vernon, Oak Harbor, Sedro Woolley, Skagit County (portions), Whidbey Island Naval Air Station, Island County (portions), King County (portions), Snohomish County (portions)); Outside TV Markets (Skagit County (portions), Island County (portions), King County (portions), Snohomish County (portions)). Franchise award date: N.A. Franchise expiration date: N.A. Began: March 1, 1952.
Channel capacity: N.A. Channels available but not in use: N.A.

Basic Service
Subscribers: 1,100,000 Includes Auburn, Bellingham, Ryderwood, Spokane, & Tacoma.
Programming (received off-air): KBCB (IND) Bellingham; KBTC-TV (PBS) Tacoma; KCPQ (FOX) Tacoma; KCTS-TV (PBS) Seattle; KFFV (IND) Seattle; KING-TV (NBC) Seattle; KIRO-TV (CBS, IND) Seattle; KOMO-TV (ABC) Seattle; KONG (IND) Everett; KSTW (CW) Tacoma; KTBW-TV (TBN) Tacoma; KUNS-TV (UNV) Bellevue; KWDK (ETV) Tacoma; KWPX-TV (ION) Bellevue; KZJO (MNT) Seattle; 28 FMs.
Programming (via satellite): C-SPAN; C-SPAN 2; Discovery Channel; Hallmark

Channel; Jewelry Television; Northwest Cable News; The Weather Channel; TV Guide Network; Univision Studios.
Fee: $43.99 installation; $12.55 monthly; $1.00 converter.

Expanded Basic Service 1
Subscribers: 318,109.
Programming (via satellite): A&E Networks; ABC Family Channel; AMC; Animal Planet; BET Networks; Bravo; Cartoon Network; CNBC; CNN; Comedy Central; Country Music TV; Disney Channel; E! Entertainment Television; ESPN; ESPN 2; Food Network; Fox News Channel; FX; Golf Channel; Headline News; HGTV; History Channel; International Television (ITV); Lifetime; MSNBC; MTV; MTV2; Nickelodeon; Oxygen; QVC; Speed; Spike TV; Syfy; TBS Superstation; The Learning Channel; Travel Channel; truTV; Turner Network TV; TVW; USA Network; Versus; VH1.
Fee: $36.70 monthly.

Digital Basic Service
Subscribers: 88,327.
Programming (via satellite): AmericanLife TV Network; BBC America; Bio; Bloomberg Television; BYU Television; Cooking Channel; Discovery Channel; Discovery Fit & Health; DIY Network; DMX Music; ESPN; ESPN Classic Sports; ESPNews; Eternal Word TV Network; Fox Movie Channel; Fox Sports World; FSN Digital Atlantic; FSN Digital Central; FSN Digital Pacific; Fuse; G4; Gaming Entertainment Television; GAS; Great American Country; GSN; Halogen Network; History Channel International; iN DEMAND; Independent Film Channel; Lifetime Movie Network; Lime; MBC America; MTV Networks Digital Suite; National Geographic Channel; NBA TV; NFL Network; Nick Jr.; Nick Too; NickToons TV; Outdoor Channel; Ovation; Style Network; Sundance Channel; The Word Network; Toon Disney; Turner Classic Movies; TV Land; WE tv; Weatherscan.
Fee: $11.99 monthly.

Digital Pay Service 1
Pay Units: 171,029.
Programming (via satellite): ART America; Canales N; CCTV-4; Cinemax (multiplexed); Encore (multiplexed); Filipino Channel; Flix; HBO (multiplexed); Korean Channel; RAI USA; Russian Television Network; Saigon Broadcasting Television Network; Showtime (multiplexed); Starz (multiplexed); The Movie Channel (multiplexed); TV Asia; TV Japan; TV5 USA; Zhong Tian Channel.
Fee: $39.95 installation; $15.00 monthly (each).

Video-On-Demand: Yes

Pay-Per-View
Addressable homes: 88,327.
ESPN Now (delivered digitally); Hot Choice (delivered digitally); MLB Extra Innings (delivered digitally); iN DEMAND (delivered digitally); Playboy TV (delivered digitally); Fresh (delivered digitally); Shorteez (delivered digitally); Urban Xtra (delivered digitally); NBA League Pass (delivered digitally); NHL Center Ice (delivered digitally).

Internet Service
Operational: Yes.
Subscribers: 35,000.
Broadband Service: Comcast High Speed Internet.
Fee: $99.95 installation; $42.95 monthly.

Telephone Service
Digital: Operational
Fee: $44.95 monthly

Miles of Plant: 8,609.0 (coaxial); None (fiber optic).
Area Senior Vice President: Len Rozek. Area Vice President: John Deitrech. Vice President, Engineering: Steve Tabor. Vice President, Marketing & Sales: Tom Pierce. Marketing Manager: Michelle Becker. Public Relations Director: Steve Kipp.
Ownership: Comcast Cable Communications Inc. (MSO).

SEATTLE—Formerly served by Sprint Corp. No longer in operation. ICA: WA0197.

SEATTLE (surrounding areas)—Wave Broadband, 4519 SE Mile Hill Dr, Port Orchard, WA 98366. Phones: 800-244-7591; 425-576-8200. Web Site: http://www.wavebroadband.com. ICA: WA0014. **Note:** This system is an overbuild.
TV Market Ranking: 20 (SEATTLE, SEATTLE (SURROUNDING AREAS)). Franchise award date: February 15, 1983. Franchise expiration date: N.A. Began: September 1, 1983.
Channel capacity: N.A. Channels available but not in use: N.A.

Basic Service
Subscribers: 11,896.
Programming (received off-air): KBTC-TV (PBS) Tacoma; KCPQ (FOX) Tacoma; KCTS-TV (PBS) Seattle; KFFV (IND) Seattle; KING-TV (NBC) Seattle; KIRO-TV (CBS, IND) Seattle; KOMO-TV (ABC) Seattle; KONG (IND) Everett; KSTW (CW) Tacoma; KTBW-TV (TBN) Tacoma; KUNS-TV (UNV) Bellevue; KWDK (ETV) Tacoma; KWPX-TV (ION) Bellevue; KZJO (MNT) Seattle; various Canadian stations.
Programming (via satellite): A&E Networks; ABC Family Channel; AMC; Animal Planet; BET Networks; Bravo; Cartoon Network; CNBC; CNN; Comedy Central; Cooking Channel; C-SPAN; Discovery Channel; Discovery Health Channel; Disney Channel; E! Entertainment Television; ESPN; ESPN 2; Food Network; Fox News Channel; FX; Headline News; HGTV; History Channel; Independent Film Channel; Lifetime; MSNBC; MTV; National Geographic Channel; Nickelodeon; Northwest Cable News; QVC; ShopNBC; Spike TV; Syfy; TBS Superstation; Telemundo; The Learning Channel; The Weather Channel; Travel Channel; Turner Network TV; TV Guide Network; TVW; Univision Studios; USA Network; VH1; WE tv.
Fee: $35.00 installation; $49.95 monthly.

Digital Basic Service
Subscribers: N.A.
Programming (via satellite): BBC America; Discovery Digital Networks; DIY Network; DMX Music; Encore (multiplexed); ESPNews; Fox Sports World; FSN Digital Atlantic; FSN Digital Central; FSN Digital Pacific; G4; GAS; Golf Channel; MTV Networks Digital Suite; Nick Jr.; Speed; Starz (multiplexed); Style Network; The Word Network; Versus.
Fee: $13.00 monthly.

Digital Pay Service 1
Pay Units: N.A.
Programming (via satellite): Cinemax (multiplexed); Encore (multiplexed); Flix; HBO (multiplexed); Showtime (multiplexed); Sundance Channel; The Movie Channel (multiplexed).
Fee: $5.50 monthly (each).

Video-On-Demand: Planned

Pay-Per-View
Addressable homes: 6,000.
iN DEMAND; Fresh; Movies; special events.

Internet Service
Operational: Yes.
Subscribers: 3,900.
Broadband Service: Millennium Cable-Speed.
Fee: $19.95 installation; $29.95 monthly; $7.50 modem lease.

Telephone Service
Analog: Not Operational
Digital: Operational
Fee: $39.99 monthly

Miles of Plant: 148.0 (coaxial); None (fiber optic).
Ownership: WaveDivision Holdings LLC (MSO).

SEQUIM—Wave Broadband. Now served by PORT ANGELES, WA [WA0020]. ICA: WA0029.

SHELTON—Comcast Cable. Now served by TACOMA, WA [WA0003]. ICA: WA0030.

SKAMOKAWA—Formerly served by Wright Cablevision. No longer in operation. ICA: WA0142.

SPANGLE—Formerly served by Elk River TV Cable Co. No longer in operation. ICA: WA0180.

SPOKANE—Comcast Cable, 19909 120th Ave NE, Ste 200, Bothell, WA 98021. Phone: 425-398-6000. Fax: 425-398-6236. Web Site: http://www.comcast.com. Also serves Airway Heights, Fairchild AFB, Millwood, Spokane County & Suncrest. ICA: WA0004.
TV Market Ranking: 76 (Airway Heights, Fairchild AFB, Millwood, SPOKANE, Spokane County, Suncrest). Franchise award date: December 23, 1974. Franchise expiration date: N.A. Began: September 30, 1976.
Channel capacity: N.A. Channels available but not in use: N.A.

Basic Service
Subscribers: N.A. Included in Seattle
Programming (received off-air): KAYU-TV (FOX) Spokane; KCDT (PBS) Coeur d'Alene; KHQ-TV (NBC) Spokane; KREM (CBS) Spokane; KSKN (CW) Spokane; KSPS-TV (PBS) Spokane; KXLY-TV (ABC, MNT) Spokane.
Programming (via satellite): C-SPAN; C-SPAN 2; Hallmark Channel; Northwest Cable News; Product Information Network; QVC; The Weather Channel; Trinity Broadcasting Network; TV Guide Network; TVW; WGN America.
Fee: $43.99 installation; $15.99 monthly.

Expanded Basic Service 1
Subscribers: 90,326.
Programming (via satellite): A&E Networks; ABC Family Channel; AMC; Animal Planet; BET Networks; Bravo; Cartoon Network; CNBC; CNN; Comedy Central; Country Music TV; Discovery Channel; E! Entertainment Television; ESPN; ESPN 2; Food Network; Fox Movie Channel; Fox News Channel; FX; Golf Channel; Headline News; HGTV; History Channel; Jewelry Television; Lifetime; MSNBC; MTV; Nickelodeon; Shop at Home; Speed; Spike TV; Syfy; TBS Superstation; The Learning Channel; Travel Channel; Turner Classic Movies; Turner Network TV; USA Network; Versus; VH1.
Fee: $30.50 monthly.

Digital Basic Service
Subscribers: 32,000.
Programming (via satellite): BBC America; Bio; Canales N; Discovery Digital Networks; DMX Music; Encore (multiplexed); ESPN Classic Sports; ESPNews; Fox Sports World; Fuse; G4; GAS; GSN; History Channel International; Independent Film Channel; Lifetime Movie Network; MTV Networks Digital Suite; National Geographic Channel; Nick Jr.; Ovation; Style Network; Sundance Channel; Toon Disney; TV Land; WE tv.
Fee: $11.99 monthly.

Digital Pay Service 1
Pay Units: 10,437.
Programming (via satellite): Cinemax (multiplexed); HBO (multiplexed); Showtime (multiplexed); Starz (multiplexed); The Movie Channel (multiplexed).
Fee: $3.00 installation; $15.00 monthly (each).

Video-On-Demand: Yes

Pay-Per-View
Addressable homes: 41,000.
iN DEMAND (delivered digitally); Shorteez (delivered digitally); Playboy TV (delivered digitally).

Internet Service
Operational: Yes.
Subscribers: 23,000.
Broadband Service: Comcast High Speed Internet.
Fee: $42.95 monthly.

Telephone Service
Digital: Operational
Fee: $44.95 monthly

Miles of Plant: 1,790.0 (coaxial); 422.0 (fiber optic).
Area Vice President: Ken Rhoades. Vice President, Engineering: Steve Tabor. Vice President, Sales & Marketing: Tom Pierce. General Manager: Kenneth Watts. Public Relations Director: Steve Kipp.
Ownership: Comcast Cable Communications Inc. (MSO).

SPOKANE—Formerly served by Video Wave Television. No longer in operation. ICA: WA0190.

SPRAGUE—Elk River TV Cable Co., 509 S Main St, PO Box 154, Troy, ID 83871. Phone: 208-369-4652. E-mail: leslie@elkrivertv.net. Web Site: http://www.elkrivertv.net. ICA: WA0130.
TV Market Ranking: Outside TV Markets (SPRAGUE). Franchise award date: N.A. Franchise expiration date: N.A. Began: June 9, 1983.
Channel capacity: N.A. Channels available but not in use: N.A.

Basic Service
Subscribers: 72.
Programming (received off-air): KAYU-TV (FOX) Spokane; KHQ-TV (NBC) Spokane; KREM (CBS) Spokane; KSKN (CW) Spokane; KSPS-TV (PBS) Spokane; KXLY-TV (ABC, MNT) Spokane.
Programming (via satellite): A&E Networks; ABC Family Channel; CNN; C-SPAN; Discovery Channel; Disney Channel; Encore; ESPN; ESPN 2; Fox Sports Net West; HGTV; History Channel; ION Television; Lifetime; Nickelodeon; Northwest Cable News; Outdoor Channel; Spike TV; Syfy; TBS Superstation; The Learning Channel; The Weather Channel; Turner Classic Movies; Turner Network TV; TV Land; USA Network; VH1; WGN America.
Fee: $38.37 monthly.

Pay Service 1
Pay Units: 11.
Programming (via satellite): HBO.
Fee: $10.95 monthly.

Video-On-Demand: No

Internet Service
Operational: No.

Telephone Service
None
Miles of Plant: 5.0 (coaxial); None (fiber optic).
Managers: Dave McGraw.; Leslie McGraw. Chief Technician: Justin McGraw.
Ownership: Elk River TV Cable Co. (MSO).

SPRINGDALE—Elk River TV Cable Co., 509 S Main St, PO Box 154, Troy, ID 83871. Phone: 208-369-4652. E-mail: leslie@elkrivertv.net. Web Site: http://www.elkrivertv.net. ICA: WA0182.
TV Market Ranking: 76 (SPRINGDALE). Franchise award date: August 1, 1988. Franchise expiration date: N.A. Began: July 1, 1989.
Channel capacity: N.A. Channels available but not in use: N.A.
Basic Service
Subscribers: 17.
Programming (received off-air): KAYU-TV (FOX) Spokane; KHQ-TV (NBC) Spokane; KREM (CBS) Spokane; KSPS-TV (PBS) Spokane; KXLY-TV (ABC, MNT) Spokane.
Programming (via satellite): A&E Networks; ABC Family Channel; Cartoon Network; CNN; Country Music TV; C-SPAN; Discovery Channel; Disney Channel; ESPN; Fox Sports Net; HGTV; History Channel; Lifetime; Nickelodeon; Northwest Cable News; Outdoor Channel; Spike TV; Syfy; TBS Superstation; The Learning Channel; The Weather Channel; Turner Classic Movies; Turner Network TV; USA Network; WGN America.
Fee: $31.65 monthly; $15.00 additional installation.
Pay Service 1
Pay Units: 5.
Programming (via satellite): HBO.
Fee: $10.00 monthly.
Video-On-Demand: No
Internet Service
Operational: No.
Telephone Service
None
Managers: Dave McGraw.; Leslie McGraw. Chief Technician: Justin McGraw.
Ownership: Elk River TV Cable Co. (MSO).

ST. JOHN—St. John Cable Co. Inc., 11 E Front St, St. John, WA 99171. Phone: 509-648-3322. Fax: 509-648-9900. E-mail: service@stjohncable.com. Web Site: http://www.stjohncable.com. Also serves Endicott & Lacrosse. ICA: WA0119.
TV Market Ranking: Below 100 (Endicott, Lacrosse, ST. JOHN). Franchise award date: N.A. Franchise expiration date: N.A. Began: January 1, 1983.
Channel capacity: 150 (operating 2-way). Channels available but not in use: N.A.
Basic Service
Subscribers: 400.
Programming (received off-air): KAYU-TV (FOX) Spokane; KGPX-TV (ION) Spokane; KHQ-TV (NBC) Spokane; KREM (CBS) Spokane; KSKN (CW) Spokane; KSPS-TV (PBS) Spokane; KUID-TV (PBS) Moscow; KWSU-TV (PBS) Pullman; KXLY-TV (ABC, MNT) Spokane.
Programming (via satellite): A&E Networks; ABC Family Channel; AMC; Cartoon Network; CNBC; CNN; Country Music TV; C-SPAN; C-SPAN 2; Discovery Channel; Disney Channel; E! Entertainment Television; ESPN; ESPN 2; ESPN Classic Sports; Food Network; Fox News Channel; Fox Sports Net; Headline News; HGTV; History Channel; Lifetime; MTV; National Geographic Channel; Nickelodeon; Outdoor Channel; Spike TV; Syfy; TBS Superstation; The Learning Channel; Travel Channel; Turner Classic Movies; Turner Network TV; USA Network; VH1; WGN America.
Fee: $10.00 installation; $30.00 monthly.
Digital Basic Service
Subscribers: N.A.
Programming (via satellite): BBC America; Bio; Bravo; Discovery Digital Networks; DMX Music; ESPN Classic Sports; ESPNews; Fox Sports World; Fuse; Golf Channel; GSN; History Channel International; Independent Film Channel; Lifetime Movie Network; National Geographic Channel; Speed; Style Network; Versus; WE tv.
Fee: $15.00 monthly.
Pay Service 1
Pay Units: N.A.
Programming (via satellite): Cinemax; HBO.
Fee: $11.00 monthly.
Digital Pay Service 1
Pay Units: N.A.
Programming (via satellite): Cinemax (multiplexed); Encore (multiplexed); HBO (multiplexed); Showtime (multiplexed); Starz (multiplexed); The Movie Channel (multiplexed).
Video-On-Demand: No
Pay-Per-View
iN DEMAND (delivered digitally); Playboy TV (delivered digitally).
Internet Service
Operational: Yes. Began: December 1, 2000.
Subscribers: 72.
Broadband Service: St. John Cable.
Fee: $30.00 monthly; $10.00 modem lease; $120.00 modem purchase.
Telephone Service
None
Manager: Greg Morasch. Chief Technician: Ole Olsen. Marketing Director: Donna Loomis.
Ownership: St. John Cable Co. Inc.

STARBUCK—Formerly served by Charter Communications. No longer in operation. ICA: WA0137.

SUDDEN VALLEY—Comcast Cable. No longer in operation. ICA: WA0067.

SUMAS—City of Sumas TV Cable System, PO Box 9, Sumas, WA 98295-0009. Phone: 360-988-5711. Fax: 360-988-8855. Web Site: http://www.cityofsumas.com. ICA: WA0099.
TV Market Ranking: Below 100 (SUMAS). Franchise award date: N.A. Franchise expiration date: N.A. Began: March 1, 1953.
Channel capacity: 43 (not 2-way capable). Channels available but not in use: N.A.
Basic Service
Subscribers: 360.
Programming (received off-air): KCPQ (FOX) Tacoma; KCTS-TV (PBS) Seattle; KING-TV (NBC) Seattle; KIRO-TV (CBS, IND) Seattle; KOMO-TV (ABC) Seattle; KONG (IND) Everett; KVOS-TV (IND) Bellingham; KZJO (MNT) Seattle; 1 FM.
Programming (via satellite): A&E Networks; CNN; C-SPAN; Discovery Channel; ESPN; FX; Hallmark Channel; HGTV; History Channel; Nickelodeon; Northwest Cable News; Outdoor Channel; QVC; Spike TV; TBS Superstation; The Learning Channel; Trinity Broadcasting Network; Turner Classic Movies; Turner Network TV; TV Land.
Fee: $25.00 installation; $22.50 monthly.
Pay Service 1
Pay Units: 99.
Programming (via satellite): Showtime.

Fee: $15.00 installation; $8.00 monthly.
Video-On-Demand: No
Internet Service
Operational: No.
Telephone Service
None
Miles of Plant: 13.0 (coaxial); None (fiber optic).
Manager: Rod Fadden. Chief Technician: Brian Swanson. Customer Service Manager: Shelly Neitch.
Ownership: City of Sumas TV Cable System.

SUNCREST—TV Max. Now served by SPOKANE, WA [WA0004]. ICA: WA0086.

SUNNYSIDE—Charter Communications. Now served by YAKIMA, WA [WA0009]. ICA: WA0033.

TACOMA—Click! Network, 3628 S 35th St, Tacoma, WA 98409-3115. Phone: 253-502-8900. E-mail: customercare@click-network.com. Web Site: http://www.clickcabletv.com. ICA: WA0206. **Note:** This system is an overbuild.
TV Market Ranking: 20 (TACOMA). Franchise award date: N.A. Franchise expiration date: N.A. Began: July 27, 1998.
Channel capacity: 76 (operating 2-way). Channels available but not in use: N.A.
Basic Service
Subscribers: 25,000.
Programming (received off-air): KBTC-TV (PBS) Tacoma; KCPQ (FOX) Tacoma; KCTS-TV (PBS) Seattle; KFFV (IND) Seattle; KING-TV (NBC) Seattle; KIRO-TV (CBS, IND) Seattle; KOMO-TV (ABC) Seattle; KONG (IND) Everett; KSTW (CW) Tacoma; KTBW-TV (TBN) Tacoma; KUNS-TV (UNV) Bellevue; KWDK (ETV) Tacoma; KWPX-TV (ION) Bellevue; KZJO (MNT) Seattle.
Programming (via satellite): C-SPAN; Northwest Cable News; QVC; TVW.
Fee: $42.50 installation; $12.45 monthly.
Expanded Basic Service 1
Subscribers: N.A.
Programming (via satellite): A&E Networks; ABC Family Channel; AMC; Animal Planet; BBC America; BET Networks; Bravo; Cartoon Network; CNBC; CNN; Comedy Central; Country Music TV; C-SPAN 2; Discovery Channel; Disney Channel; E! Entertainment Television; ESPN; ESPN 2; Food Network; Fox Movie Channel; Fox News Channel; FX; Golf Channel; Hallmark Channel; Headline News; HGTV; History Channel; Lifetime; MSNBC; MTV; National Geographic Channel; Nickelodeon; Oxygen; Speed; Spike TV; Syfy; TBS Superstation; The Learning Channel; The Weather Channel; Toon Disney; Travel Channel; truTV; Turner Classic Movies; Turner Network TV; TV Land; USA Network; various Canadian stations; Versus; VH1.
Fee: $37.50 monthly.
Digital Basic Service
Subscribers: N.A.
Programming (via satellite): AmericanLife TV Network; Bio; Bloomberg Television; BYU Television; CCTV-4; Cooking Channel; Discovery Digital Networks; DIY Network; Encore (multiplexed); ESPN Classic Sports; ESPNews; Eternal Word TV Network; Fox College Sports Atlantic; Fox College Sports Central; Fox College Sports Pacific; Fox Reality Channel; Fox Soccer; Fuse; G4; GAS; Great American Country; GSN; Halogen Network; History Channel International; Independent Film Channel; Lifetime Movie Network; Lifetime Real Women; MTV Networks Digital Suite; NFL Network; Nick Jr.; NickToons TV; Outdoor Channel; SoapNet; Style Network; The Word Network; WE tv.
Fee: $39.00 monthly.
Digital Expanded Basic Service
Subscribers: N.A.
Programming (via satellite): 3 Angels Broadcasting Network; Boomerang; CBS Sports Network; C-SPAN 3; Familyland Television Network; Fuel TV; GMC; Hallmark Channel; HRTV; PBS Kids Sprout; Tennis Channel.
Fee: $5.99 monthly.
Digital Pay Service 1
Pay Units: N.A.
Programming (via satellite): Cinemax (multiplexed); Flix; HBO (multiplexed); Playboy TV; Showtime (multiplexed); Starz (multiplexed); Sundance Channel; The Movie Channel (multiplexed).
Fee: $10.95 monthly (Cinemax), $11.25 monthly (Starz), $12.00 monthly (Playboy), $13.95 monthly (Flix, Showtime, Sundance, or TMC), $15.00 monthly (HBO).
Video-On-Demand: Yes
Pay-Per-View
Playboy TV; Fresh.
Internet Service
Operational: Yes. Began: December 1, 1999.
Subscribers: 5,500.
Broadband Service: Advanced Stream, HarborNet, Net-Venture.
Telephone Service
None
Miles of Plant: 670.0 (coaxial); None (fiber optic).
General Manager: Cyndi Wikstrom. Technical Operations Manager: Pat Bacon. Field Operations Manager: Rick Munson. Marketing & Business Operations Manager: Mitch Robinson. Network Services Manager: Terry Dillon. Government & Community Relations Manager: Diane R. Lachel.
Ownership: Tacoma Public Utilities.

TACOMA—Comcast Cable, 410 Valley Ave NW, Ste 9, Puyallup, WA 98371. Phones: 253-864-4200; 425-398-6000 (Bothell office). Fax: 253-864-4352. Web Site: http://www.comcast.com. Also serves Aberdeen, Bainbridge Island, Bonney Lake, Buckley, Carbonado, Central Park, Centralia-Chehalis, Cosmopolis, Du Pont, Eatonville, Edgewood, Elma, Fife, Fircrest, Fort Lewis, Fox Island, Gamblewood, Gig Harbor, Graham, Grayland, Grays Harbor, Grays Harbor County, Hansville, Hoquaim, Indianola (unincorporated areas), Kingston, Kitsap County, Lacey, Lake Holiday, Lakebay, Lakewood Center, Lewis County, Little Boston, Lofall, Mason County (southwestern portion), McChord AFB, McCleary, McKenna, Milton, Montesano, Oakville, Olympia, Orting, Pacific County, Poulsbo, Puyallup, Rainier, Raymond, Rochester, Roy, Ruston, Sandy Hook, Shelton, South Bend, South Prairie, Spanaway, Steilacoom, Summit, Sumner, Suquamish (unincorporated areas), Tenino, Thurston County, Tokeland, Tracyton, Turnwater, University Place, Vashon, Vashon Island, Westport, Wilkeson & Yelm. ICA: WA0003.

TV Market Ranking: 20 (Bainbridge Island, Bonney Lake, Buckley, Carbonado, Du Pont, Eatonville, Edgewood, Fife, Fircrest, Fort Lewis, Fox Island, Gamblewood, Gig Harbor, Graham, Hansville, Indianola (unincorporated areas), Kingston, Kitsap County, Lacey, Lake Holiday, Lakebay, Lakewood Center, Lewis County (portions), Little Boston, Lofall, Mason County (southwestern portion) (portions), McChord AFB, McKenna, Milton, Olympia, Orting, Poulsbo, Puyallup, Rainier, Roy, Ruston, Sandy Hook, Shelton, South Prairie, Spanaway, Steilacoom, Summit, Sumner, Suquamish (unincorporated areas), TACOMA, Tenino, Thurston County (portions), Tracyton, Turnwater, University Place, Vashon, Vashon Island, Wilkeson, Yelm); Outside TV Markets (Aberdeen, Central Park, Centralia-Chehalis, Cosmopolis, Elma, Grayland, Grays Harbor, Grays Harbor County, Hoquaim, McCleary, Montesano, Oakville, Pacific County, Raymond, Rochester, South Bend, Tokeland, Westport, Lewis County (portions), Mason County (southwestern portion) (portions), Thurston County (portions)). Franchise award date: N.A. Franchise expiration date: N.A. Began: January 1, 1967.

Channel capacity: N.A. Channels available but not in use: N.A.

Basic Service

Subscribers: N.A. Included in Seattle

Programming (received off-air): KBTC-TV (PBS) Tacoma; KCPQ (FOX) Tacoma; KCTS-TV (PBS) Seattle; KFFV (IND) Seattle; KING-TV (NBC) Seattle; KIRO-TV (CBS, IND) Seattle; KOMO-TV (ABC) Seattle; KONG (IND) Everett; KSTW (CW) Tacoma; KTBW-TV (TBN) Tacoma; KUNS-TV (UNV) Bellevue; KWDK (ETV) Tacoma; KWPX-TV (ION) Bellevue; KZJO (MNT) Seattle; 24 FMs.

Programming (via satellite): C-SPAN; C-SPAN 2; Discovery Channel; Hallmark Channel; Jewelry Television; Northwest Cable News; QVC; The Weather Channel; TV Guide Network; TVW; Univision Studios.

Fee: $43.99 installation; $12.30 monthly.

Expanded Basic Service 1

Subscribers: N.A.

Programming (via satellite): A&E Networks; ABC Family Channel; AMC; Animal Planet; BET Networks; Bravo; Cartoon Network; CNBC; CNN; Comedy Central; Country Music TV; Disney Channel; E! Entertainment Television; ESPN; ESPN 2; Food Network; Fox News Channel; FX; Headline News; History Channel; Lifetime; MSNBC; MTV; MTV2; Nickelodeon; Oxygen; Speed; Spike TV; Syfy; TBS Superstation; The Learning Channel; Travel Channel; truTV; Turner Network TV; USA Network; Versus; VH1.

Fee: $27.74 monthly.

Digital Basic Service

Subscribers: 39,874.

Programming (via satellite): AmericanLife TV Network; ART America; BBC America; Bio; Black Family Channel; Bloomberg Television; Canales N; CCTV-4; Discovery Digital Networks; DMX Music; ESPN Classic Sports; ESPNews; Filipino Channel; Fox Movie Channel; Fox Sports World; FSN Digital Atlantic; FSN Digital Central; FSN Digital Pacific; Fuse; G4; GAS; Golf Channel; Great American Country; GSN; Halogen Network; HGTV; History Channel International; Independent Film Channel; Korean Channel; Lifetime Movie Network; Lime; MTV Networks Digital Suite; National Geographic Channel; Nick Jr.; NickToons TV; Outdoor Channel; Ovation; RAI International; Russian Television Network; Saigon Broadcasting Television Network; Style Network; Sundance Channel; The Word Network; Toon Disney; Turner Classic Movies; TV Asia; TV Japan; TV Land; TV5 USA; WE tv; Weatherscan; Zee TV USA; Zhong Tian Channel.

Fee: $11.99 monthly.

Digital Pay Service 1

Pay Units: 12,000.

Programming (via satellite): Cinemax (multiplexed); Encore (multiplexed); Flix; HBO (multiplexed); Showtime (multiplexed); Starz (multiplexed); The Movie Channel (multiplexed).

Fee: $11.00 monthly (each).

Video-On-Demand: Yes

Pay-Per-View

Addressable homes: 39,874.

Barker (delivered digitally); Hot Choice (delivered digitally); Urban Xtra (delivered digitally); iN DEMAND (delivered digitally); Shorteez (delivered digitally); Playboy TV (delivered digitally); Fresh (delivered digitally); ESPN Now (delivered digitally); Sports PPV (delivered digitally).

Internet Service

Operational: Yes.

Subscribers: 18,884.

Broadband Service: Comcast High Speed Internet.

Fee: $42.95 monthly; $10.00 modem lease.

Telephone Service

Digital: Operational

Fee: $44.95 monthly

Miles of Plant: 3,401.0 (coaxial); None (fiber optic).

Area Vice President: Anne McMullen. Vice President, Engineering: Steve Taber. Vice President, Sales & Marketing: Tom Pierce. Marketing Manager: Jennifer Martinez. Public Relations Director: Steve Kipp.

Ownership: Comcast Cable Communications Inc. (MSO).

TEKOA—Northstar Broadband, PO Box 2576, Post Falls, ID 83877. Phones: 800-572-0902; 208-262-9394. Fax: 208-262-9314. E-mail: j.webb@northstarbroadband.net. Web Site: http://www.northstarbroadband.net. ICA: WA0114.

TV Market Ranking: 76 (TEKOA). Franchise award date: N.A. Franchise expiration date: N.A. Began: February 1, 1975.

Channel capacity: 62 (2-way capable). Channels available but not in use: N.A.

Basic Service

Subscribers: 101.

Programming (received off-air): KAYU-TV (FOX) Spokane; KHQ-TV (NBC) Spokane; KREM (CBS) Spokane; KSKN (CW) Spokane; KSPS-TV (PBS) Spokane; KWSU-TV (PBS) Pullman; KXLY-TV (ABC, MNT) Spokane; allband FM.

Programming (via satellite): A&E Networks; ABC Family Channel; AmericanLife TV Network; Animal Planet; Cartoon Network; Country Music TV; C-SPAN; C-SPAN 2; Discovery Channel; Discovery Health Channel; Eternal Word TV Network; Food Network; Fox News Channel; Hallmark Channel; HGTV; History Channel; ION Television; Nickelodeon; Ovation; QVC; ShopNBC; TBS Superstation; The Learning Channel; Travel Channel; Trinity Broadcasting Network; truTV; TV Land; TVW; WGN America.

Fee: $20.00 installation; $29.95 monthly.

Expanded Basic Service 1

Subscribers: N.A.

Programming (via satellite): AMC; Bravo; CNBC; CNN; Comedy Central; Disney Channel; E! Entertainment Television; ESPN; ESPN 2; ESPN Classic Sports; Fox Movie Channel; FX; Headline News; Lifetime; MoviePlex; MSNBC; MTV; Northwest Cable News; Outdoor Channel; Speed; Spike TV; Syfy; Toon Disney; Turner Classic Movies; Turner Network TV; USA Network; VH1.

Fee: $16.16 monthly.

Pay Service 1

Pay Units: 47.

Programming (via satellite): Cinemax.

Fee: $5.00 installation; $5.25 monthly.

Pay Service 2

Pay Units: 42.

Programming (via satellite): HBO.

Fee: $5.00 installation; $9.60 monthly.

Pay Service 3

Pay Units: 70.

Programming (via satellite): Showtime.

Fee: $5.00 installation; $8.65 monthly.

Video-On-Demand: No

Internet Service

Operational: No.

Telephone Service

None

Miles of Plant: 7.0 (coaxial); None (fiber optic).

Office Manager: Jennifer Webb. Operations Manager: Greg Lundwall.

Ownership: Northstar Broadband LLC (MSO).

THORP—Millennium Digital Media/Broadstripe, 3633 136th Pl SE, Ste 107, Bellevue, WA 98006-1451. Phones: 800-829-2225; 425-747-4600. Fax: 425-462-2092. E-mail: contact_nw@broadstripe.com. Web Site: http://www.broadstripe.com. ICA: WA0204.

TV Market Ranking: Below 100 (THORP). Franchise award date: October 6, 1989. Franchise expiration date: N.A. Began: N.A.

Channel capacity: 40 (not 2-way capable). Channels available but not in use: N.A.

Basic Service

Subscribers: 52.

Programming (received off-air): KAPP (ABC, MNT) Yakima; KAYU-TV (FOX) Spokane; KIMA-TV (CBS) Yakima; KNDO (NBC) Yakima; KYVE (PBS) Yakima.

Programming (via satellite): A&E Networks; ABC Family Channel; Animal Planet; CNN; Country Music TV; C-SPAN; Discovery Channel; Disney Channel; ESPN; ESPN 2; Fox News Channel; Headline News; HGTV; History Channel; Lifetime; Nickelodeon; Northwest Cable News; QVC; Spike TV; Syfy; TBS Superstation; The Learning Channel; The Weather Channel; Trinity Broadcasting Network; Turner Network TV; USA Network; WGN America.

Fee: $29.95 installation; $36.39 monthly.

Pay Service 1

Pay Units: 5.

Programming (via satellite): HBO.

Fee: $14.95 monthly.

Pay Service 2

Pay Units: N.A.

Programming (via satellite): Showtime.

Fee: $13.95 monthly.

Video-On-Demand: No

Internet Service

Operational: No.

Telephone Service

None

Miles of Plant: 6.0 (coaxial); None (fiber optic).

President & Chief Executive Officer: Bill Shreffler. Vice President & General Manager: Dave Walker. Vice President, Programming: Frank Scotello. Engineering Director: Dave Jacobs. Customer Service Manager: Steven Orona.

Ownership: Broadstripe (MSO).

TOLEDO—Formerly served by RGA Cable TV. No longer in operation. ICA: WA0107.

TULALIP INDIAN RESERVATION—Tulalip Tribes Broadband, 8825 34th Ave NE, Tulalip, WA 98271-7433. Phone: 360-716-3270. Fax: 360-716-3272. E-mail: cs@tulalipbroadband.net. Web Site: http://www.tulalipbroadband.com. ICA: WA0184.

TV Market Ranking: 20 (TULALIP INDIAN RESERVATION). Franchise award date: January 1, 1988. Franchise expiration date: N.A. Began: N.A.

Channel capacity: 71 (operating 2-way). Channels available but not in use: N.A.

Basic Service

Subscribers: 1,208.

Programming (received off-air): KCPQ (FOX) Tacoma; KCTS-TV (PBS) Seattle; KING-TV (NBC) Seattle; KIRO-TV (CBS, IND) Seattle; KOMO-TV (ABC) Seattle; KONG (IND) Everett; KSTW (CW) Tacoma; KTBW-TV (TBN) Tacoma; KVOS-TV (IND) Bellingham; KZJO (MNT) Seattle.

Programming (via satellite): A&E Networks; ABC Family Channel; AMC; Animal Planet; Bravo; Cartoon Network; CNN; Comedy Central; Country Music TV; C-SPAN; C-SPAN 2; Discovery Channel; Disney Channel; ESPN; ESPN 2; Food Network; History Channel; ION Television; Lifetime; MTV; National Geographic Channel; Nickelodeon; Northwest Cable News; Outdoor Channel; QVC; Spike TV; Syfy; TBS Superstation; The Learning Channel; Turner Classic Movies; Turner Network TV; TV Guide Network; TV Land; TVW; USA Network; VH1.

Fee: $78.00 installation; $33.00 monthly; $2.00 converter; $12.50 additional installation.

Digital Basic Service

Subscribers: 259.

Programming (via satellite): AZ TV; BBC America; Bio; Bloomberg Television; cloo; CMT Pure Country; Current; Discovery Fit & Health; Discovery Health Channel; Discovery Kids Channel; DMX Music; ESPN Classic Sports; ESPNews; Fox Movie Channel; Fox Soccer; G4; Golf Channel; GSN; Halogen Network; HGTV; History Channel International; ID Investigation Discovery; Independent Film Channel; Lifetime Movie Network; Military Channel; MTV2; Nick Jr.; Ovation; Planet Green; Science; Speed; Style Network; TeenNick; Toon Disney; Versus; VH1 Classic; VH1 Soul; WE tv.

Pay Service 1

Pay Units: N.A.

Programming (via satellite): HBO; Showtime.

Fee: $11.95 monthly (HBO), $10.95 monthly (Showtime).

Digital Pay Service 1

Pay Units: N.A.

Programming (via satellite): Cinemax (multiplexed); Encore (multiplexed); HBO (multiplexed); Showtime (multiplexed);

Starz (multiplexed); Sundance Channel; The Movie Channel (multiplexed).

Video-On-Demand: No

Pay-Per-View

iN DEMAND (delivered digitally); Playboy TV (delivered digitally); Fresh (delivered digitally); Spice (delivered digitally); Spice 2 (delivered digitally).

Internet Service

Operational: Yes.
Subscribers: 630.
Fee: $41.00 monthly.

Telephone Service

None

Miles of Plant: 100.0 (coaxial); None (fiber optic).

Manager: Richard A. Brown. Marketing Director & Customer Service Manager: Sharon Contraro. Chief Engineer: Rick Dechenne.

Ownership: The Tulalip Tribe Inc.

TWISP—Millennium Digital Media/Broadstripe, 3633 136th Pl SE, Ste 107, Bellevue, WA 98006-1451. Phones: 800-829-2225; 425-747-4600. Fax: 425-644-4621. E-mail: contact_nw@mdm.net. Web Site: http://www.broadstripe.com. Also serves Winthrop. ICA: WA0101.

TV Market Ranking: Outside TV Markets (TWISP, Winthrop). Franchise award date: N.A. Franchise expiration date: January 1, 2007. Began: March 1, 1983.

Channel capacity: 35 (operating 2-way). Channels available but not in use: N.A.

Basic Service

Subscribers: 144.

Programming (received off-air): KCTS-TV (PBS) Seattle; KING-TV (NBC) Seattle; KIRO-TV (CBS, IND) Seattle; KOMO-TV (ABC) Seattle.

Programming (via satellite): A&E Networks; ABC Family Channel; AMC; Animal Planet; CNN; Comedy Central; Country Music TV; Discovery Channel; Disney Channel; ESPN; Fox News Channel; G4; Headline News; HGTV; History Channel; Northwest Cable News; QVC; Spike TV; TBS Superstation; The Learning Channel; The Weather Channel; Turner Network TV; TV Guide Network; USA Network; WGN America.

Fee: $29.95 installation; $41.99 monthly.

Digital Basic Service

Subscribers: N.A.

Programming (via satellite): BBC America; Bio; Bravo; Discovery Digital Networks; DMX Music; ESPN 2; ESPNews; Fox Sports World; Golf Channel; GSN; History Channel International; National Geographic Channel; Science Television; Speed; Syfy; Versus.

Fee: $13.40 monthly.

Pay Service 1

Pay Units: 61.

Programming (via satellite): HBO; Showtime.

Fee: $11.95 monthly (Showtime), $12.95 monthly (HBO).

Digital Pay Service 1

Pay Units: N.A.

Programming (via satellite): Cinemax (multiplexed); Encore (multiplexed); HBO (multiplexed); Independent Film Channel; Showtime (multiplexed); Starz (multiplexed); The Movie Channel (multiplexed).

Fee: $10.00 monthly (each).

Video-On-Demand: No

Pay-Per-View

Playboy TV (delivered digitally); iN DEMAND (delivered digitally).

Internet Service

Operational: No.

Telephone Service

None

Miles of Plant: 23.0 (coaxial); None (fiber optic).

President & Chief Executive Officer: Bill Shreffler. Engineering Director: Dave Jacobs. Customer Service Manager: Steve Orona.

Ownership: Broadstripe (MSO).

UNION—Hood Canal Communications, 300 E Dalby Rd, PO Box 249, Union, WA 98592-9611. Phone: 360-898-2481. Fax: 360-898-2244. E-mail: support@hcc.net. Web Site: http://www.hctc.com. Also serves Agate, Colony Surf, Hoodsport, Lake Cushman, Lilliwaup Falls, Lower Hood Canal, Phillips Lake, Pickering, Shelton, Skokomish Valley & Timber Lakes. ICA: WA0052. **Note:** This system is an overbuild.

TV Market Ranking: 20 (Agate, Colony Surf, Hoodsport, Lilliwaup Falls, Lower Hood Canal, Phillips Lake, Pickering, Shelton, Skokomish Valley, Timber Lakes, UNION); Outside TV Markets (Lake Cushman). Franchise award date: N.A. Franchise expiration date: N.A. Began: N.A.

Channel capacity: 46 (operating 2-way). Channels available but not in use: N.A.

Basic Service

Subscribers: 2,400.

Programming (received off-air): KBTC-TV (PBS) Tacoma; KCPQ (FOX) Tacoma; KCTS-TV (PBS) Seattle; KING-TV (NBC) Seattle; KIRO-TV (CBS, IND) Seattle; KOMO-TV (ABC) Seattle; KONG (IND) Everett; KSTW (CW) Tacoma; KZJO (MNT) Seattle.

Programming (via satellite): A&E Networks; ABC Family Channel; AMC; Cartoon Network; CNBC; CNN; Comedy Central; C-SPAN; Discovery Channel; E! Entertainment Television; ESPN; Food Network; Fox News Channel; Headline News; History Channel; ION Television; Lifetime; MTV; Nickelodeon; Northwest Cable News; QVC; Spike TV; Syfy; TBS Superstation; The Learning Channel; Trinity Broadcasting Network; Turner Network TV; TV Guide Network; TV Land; TVW; USA Network; VH1.

Fee: $33.95 monthly; $4.00 converter.

Digital Basic Service

Subscribers: 400.

Programming (via satellite): AmericanLife TV Network; BBC America; Bio; Bloomberg Television; Discovery Digital Networks; ESPN 2; ESPN Classic Sports; ESPNews; Fox Movie Channel; Fox Sports World; G4; GAS; Golf Channel; GSN; Halogen Network; HGTV; History Channel International; MTV Networks Digital Suite; MuchMusic Network; Nick Jr.; Speed; Style Network; Turner Classic Movies; Versus; WE tv.

Fee: $10.00 monthly.

Digital Pay Service 1

Pay Units: 218.

Programming (via satellite): Cinemax (multiplexed).

Fee: $7.00 monthly.

Digital Pay Service 2

Pay Units: 363.

Programming (via satellite): HBO (multiplexed).

Fee: $13.00 monthly.

Digital Pay Service 3

Pay Units: N.A.

Programming (via satellite): Encore (multiplexed); Showtime (multiplexed); Starz (multiplexed); The Movie Channel (multiplexed).

Fee: $8.00 monthly (Starz & Encore), $10.00 monthly (Showtime & TMC).

Video-On-Demand: Yes

Pay-Per-View

Addressable homes: 400.

Playboy TV (delivered digitally); Hot Network (delivered digitally); Spice (delivered digitally).

Internet Service

Operational: Yes. Began: March 1, 2001.
Broadband Service: In-house.
Fee: $20.95 monthly.

Telephone Service

Digital: Operational
Subscribers: 15.
Fee: $22.00 monthly

Miles of Plant: 70.0 (coaxial); 100.0 (fiber optic).

President: Rick Buechel. Marketing Director: Kellie Nielsen. Chief Technician: David Collins. Program Director: Kelle Oblizalo.

Ownership: Hood Canal Communications.

VADER—Formerly served by Millennium Digital Media. No longer in operation. ICA: WA0126.

VANCOUVER—Comcast Cable, 9605 SW Nimbus Ave, Beaverton, OR 97008-7198. Phone: 503-605-6005. Fax: 503-605-6226. Web Site: http://www.comcast.com. Also serves Hayden Island, OR; Battle Ground, Camas, Clark County (unincorporated areas), Clark County (urban areas), La Center, Ridgefield & Washougal, WA. ICA: WA0005.

TV Market Ranking: 29 (Battle Ground, Camas, Clark County (unincorporated areas), Clark County (urban areas), Hayden Island, La Center, Ridgefield, VANCOUVER, Washougal). Franchise award date: November 26, 1981. Franchise expiration date: N.A. Began: October 1, 1982.

Channel capacity: 72 (operating 2-way). Channels available but not in use: N.A.

Basic Service

Subscribers: N.A. Included in Beaverton, OR

Programming (received off-air): KATU (ABC) Portland; KCTS-TV (PBS) Seattle; KGW (NBC) Portland; KNMT (TBN) Portland; KOIN (CBS) Portland; KOPB-TV (PBS) Portland; KPDX (MNT) Vancouver; KPTV (FOX) Portland; KPXG-TV (ION) Salem; KRCW-TV (CW) Salem.

Programming (via satellite): C-SPAN; C-SPAN 2; Discovery Channel; Hallmark Channel; QVC; ShopNBC; TV Guide Network; TVW; Univision Studios; WGN America.

Fee: $44.99 installation; $13.72 monthly; $1.60 converter.

Expanded Basic Service 1

Subscribers: 43,801.

Programming (via satellite): A&E Networks; ABC Family Channel; AMC; Animal Planet; BET Networks; Cartoon Network; CNBC; CNN; Comedy Central; Country Music TV; Disney Channel; E! Entertainment Television; ESPN; ESPN 2; Food Network; Fox News Channel; FX; Golf Channel; Headline News; HGTV; History Channel; International Television (ITV); Lifetime; MSNBC; MTV; Nickelodeon; Northwest Cable News; Oxygen; Spike TV; Syfy; TBS Superstation; The Learning Channel; The Weather Channel; Travel Channel; truTV; Turner Network TV; TV Land; USA Network; VH1.

Fee: $38.17 monthly.

Digital Basic Service

Subscribers: 18,680.

Programming (via satellite): American-Life TV Network; BBC America; Bio; Black Family Channel; Bloomberg Television; Bravo; Canales N; Discovery Fit & Health; DMX Music; Encore Action; ESPN Classic Sports; ESPNews; Eternal Word TV Network; Fox Movie Channel; Fox Sports World; FSN Digital Atlantic; FSN Digital Central; FSN Digital Pacific; Fuse; G4; GAS; Great American Country; GSN; Halogen Network; History Channel International; Independent Film Channel; Lifetime Movie Network; Lime; MTV Networks Digital Suite; National Geographic Channel; Nick Jr.; NickToons TV; Nuvo TV; Outdoor Channel; Ovation; Speed; Style Network; Sundance Channel; The Word Network; Toon Disney; Turner Classic Movies; Versus; WE tv; Weatherscan.

Fee: $10.95 monthly; $3.25 converter.

Digital Pay Service 1

Pay Units: 2,963.

Programming (via satellite): CCTV-4; Cinemax (multiplexed); Filipino Channel; Flix; HBO (multiplexed); Russian Television Network; Showtime (multiplexed); Starz (multiplexed); The Movie Channel (multiplexed).

Fee: $18.05 monthly (each).

Video-On-Demand: Yes

Pay-Per-View

Addressable homes: 18,680.

Fresh (delivered digitally); Sports PPV (delivered digitally); iN DEMAND (delivered digitally); Urban Xtra (delivered digitally); Shorteez (delivered digitally); Playboy TV (delivered digitally).

Internet Service

Operational: Yes.
Subscribers: 19,848.
Broadband Service: Comcast High Speed Internet.
Fee: $42.95 monthly; $3.00 modem lease.

Telephone Service

Digital: Operational
Fee: $44.95 monthly

Miles of plant included in Beaverton, OR

Senior Vice President: Curt Henninger. Vice President, Technical Operations: Mike Mason. Vice President, Marketing: Lars Lofas. Sales Director: Mike Williams. Marketing Director: Brad Nosler. Public Relations Director: Theressa Davis.

Ownership: Comcast Cable Communications Inc. (MSO).

WAITSBURG—Charter Communications. Now served by WALLA WALLA, WA [WA0016]. ICA: WA0088.

WALLA WALLA—Charter Communications, 639 N Kellogg St, Kennewick, WA 99336. Phones: 866-731-5420; 509-783-0132. Fax: 509-735-3795. Web Site: http://www.charter.com. Also serves Milton-Freewater & Umatilla County (unincorporated areas), OR; College Place, Dixie, Waitsburg & Walla Walla County (portions), WA. ICA: WA0016.

TV Market Ranking: Below 100 (College Place, Milton-Freewater, Umatilla County (unincorporated areas) (portions), Waitsburg, WALLA WALLA); Outside TV Markets (Dixie, Umatilla County (unincorporated areas) (portions), Walla Walla County (portions)). Franchise award date: N.A. Franchise expiration date: N.A. Began: October 1, 1953.

Channel capacity: N.A. Channels available but not in use: N.A.

Basic Service

Subscribers: 12,212.

Programming (received off-air): KEPR-TV (CBS) Pasco; KFFX-TV (FOX, IND) Pendleton; KNDU (NBC) Richland; KRLB-LD Richland; KTNW (PBS) Richland; KVEW (ABC, MNT) Kennewick.

Programming (via microwave): KCTS-TV (PBS) Seattle; KHQ-TV (NBC) Spokane; KIRO-TV (CBS, IND) Seattle; KREM (CBS) Spokane; KUNW-CA (UNV) Yakima.

Programming (via satellite): C-SPAN; C-SPAN 2; GalaVision; QVC; Telemundo; TV Guide Network; TVW; WGN America.

Fee: $37.44 installation; $9.85 monthly; $2.21 converter.

Expanded Basic Service 1

Subscribers: 9,100.

Programming (via satellite): A&E Networks; ABC Family Channel; AMC; Animal Planet; BET Networks; Bravo; Cartoon Network; CNBC; CNN; Comedy Central; Country Music TV; Discovery Channel; Disney Channel; DIY Network; E! Entertainment Television; ESPN; ESPN 2; Food Network; Fox News Channel; Fox Soccer; FX; G4; Golf Channel; GSN; Hallmark Channel; Headline News; HGTV; History Channel; Lifetime; MSNBC; MTV; National Geographic Channel; Nickelodeon; Northwest Cable News; Outdoor Channel; Oxygen; SoapNet; Speed; Spike TV; Syfy; TBS Superstation; The Learning Channel; The Weather Channel; Toon Disney; Travel Channel; truTV; Turner Classic Movies; Turner Network TV; TV Land; USA Network; Versus; WE tv.

Fee: $50.99 monthly.

Digital Basic Service

Subscribers: N.A.

Programming (via satellite): BBC America; Bio; Bloomberg Television; Boomerang; BYU Television; CNN en Espanol; CNN International; Discovery Fit & Health; ESPN Classic Sports; ESPNews; Fox College Sports Atlantic; Fox College Sports Central; Fox College Sports Pacific; Fox Deportes; Fox Movie Channel; Fuel TV; Fuse; Great American Country; HDNet; HDNet Movies; History Channel International; Independent Film Channel; INSP; International Television (ITV); Lifetime Movie Network; Lifetime Real Women; MTV Networks Digital Suite; Music Choice; NFL Network; Nick Jr.; Nick Too; NickToons TV; Science; Style Network; Sundance Channel; TeenNick.

Pay Service 1

Pay Units: 601.

Programming (via satellite): Encore (multiplexed); Flix; Showtime (multiplexed); The Movie Channel (multiplexed).

Fee: $1.75 monthly (Encore), $11.70 monthly (Cinemax), $14.00 monthly (HBO or Showtime).

Digital Pay Service 1

Pay Units: N.A.

Programming (via satellite): Cinemax; Cinemax HD; HBO (multiplexed); HBO HD; Showtime (multiplexed); Starz (multiplexed).

Video-On-Demand: Yes

Internet Service

Operational: Yes. Began: December 1, 2001.

Subscribers: 3,077.

Broadband Service: Charter Pipeline.

Fee: $29.99 monthly.

Telephone Service

Digital: Operational

Miles of Plant: 453.0 (coaxial); 24.0 (fiber optic).

General Manager: Randy Lee. Technical Operations Manager: Jeff Hopkins. Marketing Director: Diane Long. Program Director: Lloyd Swain.

Ownership: Charter Communications Inc. (MSO).

WARDEN—Northstar Broadband, PO Box 2576, Post Falls, ID 83877. Phones: 800-572-0902; 208-262-9394. Fax: 208-262-9314. E-mail: j.webb@northstarbroadband.net. Web Site: http://www.northstarbroadband.net. ICA: WA0185.

TV Market Ranking: Outside TV Markets (WARDEN). Franchise award date: N.A. Franchise expiration date: N.A. Began: N.A.

Channel capacity: N.A. Channels available but not in use: N.A.

Basic Service

Subscribers: 552.

Programming (received off-air): KAYU-TV (FOX) Spokane; KEPR-TV (CBS) Pasco; KHQ-TV (NBC) Spokane; KQUP (IND) Pullman; KREM (CBS) Spokane; KSKN (CW) Spokane; KSPS-TV (PBS) Spokane; KXLY-TV (ABC, MNT) Spokane.

Programming (via satellite): A&E Networks; ABC Family Channel; AmericanLife TV Network; Animal Planet; Cartoon Network; Country Music TV; C-SPAN; C-SPAN 2; Discovery Channel; Discovery Health Channel; Eternal Word TV Network; Food Network; Fox News Channel; GalaVision; Hallmark Channel; HGTV; History Channel; ION Television; National Geographic Channel; Nickelodeon; QVC; ShopNBC; TBS Superstation; Telefutura; The Learning Channel; Travel Channel; Trinity Broadcasting Network; truTV; TV Guide Network; TV Land; TVN Entertainment; Univision Studios; WGN America.

Fee: $20.00 installation; $29.97 monthly; $1.00 converter.

Expanded Basic Service 1

Subscribers: N.A.

Programming (via satellite): AMC; Bravo; CNBC; CNN; Comedy Central; Disney Channel; E! Entertainment Television; ESPN; ESPN 2; Fox Movie Channel; FX; Headline News; Lifetime; MoviePlex; MSNBC; MTV; Northwest Cable News; Speed; Spike TV; Syfy; Toon Disney; Turner Classic Movies; Turner Network TV; USA Network; Versus; VH1.

Fee: $5.00 installation; $15.15 monthly.

Pay Service 1

Pay Units: N.A.

Programming (via satellite): Showtime.

Fee: $5.00 installation; $8.65 monthly.

Pay Service 2

Pay Units: 92.

Programming (via satellite): HBO.

Fee: $5.00 installation; $9.60 monthly.

Pay Service 3

Pay Units: 125.

Programming (via satellite): Cinemax.

Fee: $5.00 installation; $5.25 monthly.

Video-On-Demand: No

Internet Service

Operational: Yes, DSL.

Broadband Service: In-house.

Fee: $26.95 installation; $20.26 monthly; $2.00 modem lease; $25.00 modem purchase.

Telephone Service

None

Office Manager: Jennifer Webb. Operations Manager: Greg Lundwall.

Ownership: Northstar Broadband LLC (MSO).

WASHTUCNA—Formerly served by Charter Communications. No longer in operation. ICA: WA0134.

WATERVILLE—Millennium Digital Media/Broadstripe, 3633 136th Pl SE, Ste 107, Bellevue, WA 98006-1451. Phones: 800-829-2225; 425-747-4600. Fax: 425-644-4621. E-mail: contact_nw@mdm.net. Web Site: http://www.broadstripe.com. ICA: WA0100.

TV Market Ranking: Below 100 (WATERVILLE). Franchise award date: N.A. Franchise expiration date: N.A. Began: January 1, 1953.

Channel capacity: N.A. Channels available but not in use: N.A.

Basic Service

Subscribers: 328.

Programming (received off-air): KAYU-TV (FOX) Spokane; KCTS-TV (PBS) Seattle; KHQ-TV (NBC) Spokane; KING-TV (NBC) Seattle; KIRO-TV (CBS, IND) Seattle; KOMO-TV (ABC) Seattle; KREM (CBS) Spokane; KSPS-TV (PBS) Spokane; KXLY-TV (ABC, MNT) Spokane; allband FM.

Programming (via satellite): A&E Networks; ABC Family Channel; AMC; Animal Planet; CNN; Discovery Channel; Disney Channel; E! Entertainment Television; ESPN; Fox News Channel; G4; Headline News; HGTV; History Channel; Nickelodeon; Northwest Cable News; QVC; Spike TV; Syfy; TBS Superstation; The Learning Channel; Turner Network TV; TVW; USA Network; WGN America.

Fee: $29.95 installation; $14.40 monthly.

Digital Basic Service

Subscribers: N.A.

Programming (via satellite): BBC America; Bio; Bravo; Discovery Digital Networks; DMX Music; ESPN 2; ESPNews; Fox Sports World; Golf Channel; GSN; History Channel International; National Geographic Channel; Science Television; Speed; Style Network; Versus.

Fee: $14.40 monthly.

Pay Service 1

Pay Units: N.A.

Programming (via satellite): HBO.

Fee: $14.95 monthly.

Digital Pay Service 1

Pay Units: N.A.

Programming (via satellite): Cinemax (multiplexed); Encore (multiplexed); HBO (multiplexed); Independent Film Channel; Showtime (multiplexed); Starz (multiplexed); The Movie Channel (multiplexed).

Fee: $10.00 monthly (each).

Video-On-Demand: No

Pay-Per-View

Playboy TV (delivered digitally); iN DEMAND (delivered digitally).

Internet Service

Operational: No.

Telephone Service

None

Miles of Plant: 15.0 (coaxial); None (fiber optic).

President & Chief Executive Officer: Bill Shreffler. Engineering Director: Dave Jacobs. Customer Service Manager: Steve Orona.

Ownership: Broadstripe (MSO).

WENATCHEE—Charter Communications, 521 NE 136th Ave, Vancouver, WA 98684. Phone: 360-828-6600. Fax: 360-828-6795. Web Site: http://www.charter.com. Also serves Cashmere, Chelan County, Chewelah, Deer Lake, Douglas County, East Wenatchee, Leavnworth, Loon Lake, Okanogan, Okanogan County (unincorporated areas), Omak, Oroville, Peshastin, Rock Island & Tonasket. ICA: WA0015.

TV Market Ranking: 76 (Deer Lake, LOON LAKE); Below 100 (Chelan County (portions), Douglas County (portions)); Outside TV Markets (Cashmere, Chelan County (portions), Chewelah, Douglas County (portions), East Wenatchee, Leavenworth, OKANOGAN, Okanogan County (unincorporated areas), Omak, OROVILLE, Peshastin, Rock Island, Tonasket, WENATCHEE). Franchise award date: January 1, 1953. Franchise expiration date: N.A. Began: August 1, 1953.

Channel capacity: N.A. Channels available but not in use: N.A.

Basic Service

Subscribers: 226,000.

Programming (received off-air): K36EW-D College Place; KWCC-LD Wenatchee; KWPX-TV (ION) Bellevue; 9 FMs.

Programming (via satellite): C-SPAN; C-SPAN 2; Eternal Word TV Network; Home Shopping Network; QVC; ShopNBC; The Weather Channel; Trinity Broadcasting Network.

Programming (via translator): KAYU-TV (FOX) Spokane; KCPQ (FOX) Tacoma; KCTS-TV (PBS) Seattle; KFFV (IND) Seattle; KHQ-TV (NBC) Spokane; KING-TV (NBC) Seattle; KIRO-TV (CBS, IND) Seattle; KOMO-TV (ABC) Seattle; KREM (CBS) Spokane; KSPS-TV (PBS) Spokane; KSTW (CW) Tacoma; KXLY-TV (ABC, MNT) Spokane; KZJO (MNT) Seattle.

Fee: $29.95 installation.

Expanded Basic Service 1

Subscribers: N.A.

Programming (via satellite): A&E Networks; ABC Family Channel; AMC; Animal Planet; BET Networks; Bravo; Cartoon Network; CNBC; CNN; Comedy Central; Country Music TV; Discovery Channel; Disney Channel; DIY Network; E! Entertainment Television; ESPN; ESPN 2; Flix; Food Network; Fox Deportes; Fox News Channel; FX; G4; Golf Channel; GSN; Hallmark Channel; Headline News; HGTV; History Channel; Lifetime; MSNBC; MTV; MTV2; National Geographic Channel; Nickelodeon; Northwest Cable News; Oxygen; Root Sports Northwest; SoapNet; Speed; Spike TV; Style Network; Syfy; TBS Superstation; Telemundo; The Learning Channel; Travel Channel; truTV; Turner Classic Movies; Turner Network TV; TV Land; TVW; USA Network; Versus; VH1.

Fee: $42.99 monthly.

Digital Basic Service

Subscribers: N.A.

Programming (via satellite): 3 Angels Broadcasting Network; A&E HD; AMC HD; AmericanLife TV Network; Animal Planet HD; Bandamax; BBC America; Bio; Bloomberg Television; Boomerang; Bravo HD; BYU Television; Canal 22 Mexico; Cartoon Network HD; CBS Sports Network; Centric; Church Channel; Cine Mexicano; CMT Pure Country; CNN en Espanol; CNN HD; CNN International; Comedy Central;

Comedy Central HD; Cooking Channel; Daystar TV Network; De Pelicula; De Pelicula Clasico; Discovery Channel HD; Discovery en Espanol; Discovery Fit & Health; Disney XD; ESPN 2 HD; ESPN Classic Sports; ESPN Deportes; ESPN HD; ESPN U; ESPNews; EWTN en Espanol; FamilyNet; Food Network HD; Fox Business Channel; Fox College Sports Atlantic; Fox College Sports Central; Fox College Sports Pacific; Fox Movie Channel; Fox News HD; Fox Soccer; Fuel TV; Fuse; FX HD; GalaVision; GMC; Golf Channel HD; GolTV; Great American Country; Hallmark Movie Channel HD; Halogen Network; HD Theater; HDNet; HDNet Movies; HGTV HD; History Channel en Espanol; History Channel HD; History Channel International; ID Investigation Discovery; Independent Film Channel; Infinito; INSP; JCTV; Jewelry Television; Latele Novela Network; Lifetime Movie Network; Lifetime Television HD; LOGO; MavTV; Military Channel; MLB Network HD; MTV Hits; MTV Jams; mtvU; mun2 television; Music Choice; National Geographic Channel HD Network; Nick Jr.; NickToons TV; Once TV Mexico; Outdoor Channel; Outdoor Channel 2 HD; OWN: Oprah Winfrey Network; Palladia; PBS Kids Sprout; Planet Green; ReelzChannel; RFD-TV; Science; Science HD; Smile of a Child; Smithsonian Channel HD; Sorpresa; Speed HD; Sundance Channel; Syfy HD; TBN Enlace USA; TBS in HD; TeenNick; Telefutura; Tennis Channel; The Hub; The Sportsman Channel; The Weather Channel HD; TLC HD; Tr3s; Trinity Broadcasting Network; Turner Network TV HD; TVG Network; Universal HD; USA Network HD; Utilisima; Versus HD; VH1 Classic; VH1 Soul; Video Rola; WE tv; World Fishing Network.

Digital Pay Service 1

Pay Units: 1,089.

Programming (via satellite): Cinemax (multiplexed); Cinemax HD; EPIX (multiplexed); HBO (multiplexed); HBO HD; Showtime (multiplexed); Showtime HD; Starz (multiplexed); Starz HDTV; The Movie Channel (multiplexed); The Movie Channel HD.

Fee: $13.15 monthly (Cinemax, HBO or Showtime).

Video-On-Demand: Yes

Pay-Per-View

iN DEMAND (delivered digitally); Ten Xtsy (delivered digitally); Playboy TV (delivered digitally); Fresh (delivered digitally); Spice: Xcess (delivered digitally).

Internet Service

Operational: Yes.

Broadband Service: Charter Pipeline.

Fee: $29.99 monthly.

Telephone Service

Digital: Operational

Fee: $29.99 monthly

Miles of Plant: 692.0 (coaxial); 142.0 (fiber optic).

Vice President: Frank Antonovich. General Manager: Linda Kimberly. Technical Operations Director: Brian Lindholme. Marketing Director: Diane Long.

Ownership: Charter Communications Inc. (MSO).

WEST RICHLAND—Charter Communications, 521 NE 136th Ave, Vancouver, WA 98684. Phone: 360-828-6600. Fax: 360-828-6795. Web Site: http://www.charter.com. Also serves Benton City & Benton County. ICA: WA0065.

TV Market Ranking: Below 100 (Benton City, Benton County, WEST RICHLAND). Franchise award date: N.A. Franchise expiration date: N.A. Began: January 1, 1982.

Channel capacity: 61 (operating 2-way). Channels available but not in use: N.A.

Basic Service

Subscribers: 500.

Programming (received off-air): KEPR-TV (CBS) Pasco; KFFX-TV (FOX, IND) Pendleton; KNDU (NBC) Richland; KTNW (PBS) Richland; KVEW (ABC, MNT) Kennewick.

Programming (via satellite): A&E Networks; ABC Family Channel; AMC; Animal Planet; CNBC; CNN; Comedy Central; C-SPAN; Discovery Channel; Disney Channel; E! Entertainment Television; ESPN; ESPN 2; Fox Movie Channel; Fox News Channel; FX; Great American Country; Hallmark Channel; Headline News; HGTV; History Channel; Lifetime; MSNBC; MTV; Nickelodeon; Northwest Cable News; QVC; Spike TV; Style Network; Syfy; TBS Superstation; The Learning Channel; The Weather Channel; Toon Disney; Trinity Broadcasting Network; Turner Classic Movies; Turner Network TV; TV Land; Univision Studios; USA Network; VH1; WGN America.

Fee: $35.00 installation; $35.99 monthly.

Digital Basic Service

Subscribers: N.A.

Programming (via satellite): BBC America; Bravo; Discovery Digital Networks; DMX Music; Encore; ESPN Classic Sports; ESPN Now; ESPNews; Golf Channel; GSN; Independent Film Channel; Nick Jr.; Speed; Versus; VH1 Classic; VH1 Country; WE tv.

Digital Pay Service 1

Pay Units: N.A.

Programming (via satellite): Cinemax (multiplexed); HBO (multiplexed); Showtime (multiplexed); The Movie Channel (multiplexed).

Video-On-Demand: No

Internet Service

Operational: Yes.

Broadband Service: Charter Pipeline.

Fee: $49.95 installation; $38.95 monthly.

Telephone Service

None

Miles of Plant: 25.0 (coaxial); None (fiber optic).

Manager: Linda Kimberly.

Ownership: Charter Communications Inc. (MSO).

WESTPORT—Comcast Cable. Now served by TACOMA, WA [WA0003]. ICA: WA0037.

WHIDBEY ISLAND—Millennium Digital Media/Broadstripe, 3633 136th Pl SE, Ste 107, Bellevue, WA 98006-1451. Phone: 800-829-2225. Web Site: http://www.broadstripe.com. ICA: WA0186.

TV Market Ranking: 20 (WHIDBEY ISLAND). Franchise award date: January 1, 1990. Franchise expiration date: N.A. Began: February 1, 1991.

Channel capacity: 40 (operating 2-way). Channels available but not in use: N.A.

Basic Service

Subscribers: 1,029.

Programming (received off-air): KCPQ (FOX) Tacoma; KCTS-TV (PBS) Seattle; KING-TV (NBC) Seattle; KIRO-TV (CBS, IND) Seattle; KOMO-TV (ABC) Seattle; KONG (IND) Everett; KSTW (CW) Tacoma; KTBW-TV (TBN) Tacoma; KVOS-TV (IND) Bellingham; KWPX-TV (ION) Bellevue; KZJO (MNT) Seattle.

Programming (via satellite): A&E Networks; ABC Family Channel; AMC; Cartoon Network; CNBC; CNN; Comedy Central; C-SPAN; Discovery Channel; Disney Channel; ESPN; ESPN 2; Fox News Channel; Headline News; HGTV; Lifetime; Nickelodeon; QVC; Spike TV; Syfy; The Learning Channel; Trinity Broadcasting Network; Turner Classic Movies; Turner Network TV; USA Network.

Fee: $29.95 installation; $41.99 monthly.

Digital Basic Service

Subscribers: N.A.

Programming (via satellite): AmericanLife TV Network; BBC America; Bloomberg Television; Bravo; Discovery Digital Networks; DMX Music; Fox Sports World; Fuse; G4; Golf Channel; GSN; Halogen Network; History Channel International; Outdoor Channel; Ovation; Speed; Style Network; Trinity Broadcasting Network; Versus; WE tv.

Fee: $13.40 monthly.

Digital Pay Service 1

Pay Units: N.A.

Programming (via satellite): Cinemax (multiplexed); Encore (multiplexed); Fox Movie Channel; HBO (multiplexed); Independent Film Channel; Showtime (multiplexed); Starz (multiplexed); The Movie Channel (multiplexed).

Fee: $7.50 monthly (each).

Video-On-Demand: No

Pay-Per-View

ESPN Now; Hot Choice; iN DEMAND; Playboy TV; Fresh; Shorteez; sports.

Internet Service

Operational: Yes.

Fee: $49.95 installation; $37.95 monthly.

Telephone Service

Digital: Operational

Fee: $49.99 monthly

Miles of Plant: 127.0 (coaxial); None (fiber optic).

Engineering Director: Dane Jacobs. Customer Service Manager: Steve Orona.

Ownership: Broadstripe (MSO).

WILBUR—Northstar Broadband, PO Box 2576, Post Falls, ID 83877. Phones: 800-572-0902; 208-262-9394. Fax: 208-262-9314. E-mail: j.webb@northstarbroadband.net. Web Site: http://www.northstarbroadband.net. ICA: WA0102.

TV Market Ranking: Outside TV Markets (WILBUR).

Channel capacity: N.A. Channels available but not in use: N.A.

Basic Service

Subscribers: N.A.

Programming (received off-air): KAYU-TV (FOX) Spokane; KGPX-TV (ION) Spokane; KHQ-TV (NBC) Spokane; KREM (CBS) Spokane; KSKN (CW) Spokane; KSPS-TV (PBS) Spokane; KXLY-TV (ABC, MNT) Spokane.

Programming (via satellite): 3 Angels Broadcasting Network; A&E Networks; ABC Family Channel; American Movie Classics; Animal Planet; Cartoon Network; CNBC; CNN; C-SPAN; C-SPAN 2; Discovery Channel; Discovery Health Channel; Disney Channel; E! Entertainment Television; ESPN; ESPN 2; Fox News Channel; Fox Sports Net West; FX; Great American Country; HGTV; History Channel; Lifetime; MTV; Nickelodeon; Northwest Cable News; QVC; Speed; Spike TV; Syfy; TBS Superstation; The Learning Channel; The Weather Channel; Turner Network TV; USA Network; Versus; VH1.

Fee: $60.00 installation; $40.77 monthly.

Pay Service 1

Pay Units: N.A.

Programming (via satellite): HBO.

Fee: $13.60 monthly.

Telephone Service

None

Office Manager: Jennifer Webb. Operations Manager: Greg Lundwall.

Ownership: Northstar Broadband LLC (MSO).

WILSON CREEK—Formerly served by Almega Cable. No longer in operation. ICA: WA0187.

WINLOCK—Comcast Cable, 410 Valley Ave NW, Ste 9, Puyallup, WA 98371. Phones: 425-398-6000 (Bothell office); 253-864-4200. Fax: 253-864-4352. Web Site: http://www.comcast.com. ICA: WA0094.

TV Market Ranking: Outside TV Markets (WINLOCK). Franchise award date: N.A. Franchise expiration date: N.A. Began: December 1, 1971.

Channel capacity: N.A. Channels available but not in use: N.A.

Basic Service

Subscribers: 397.

Programming (received off-air): KCKA (PBS) Centralia; KCPQ (FOX) Tacoma; KCTS-TV (PBS) Seattle; KGW (NBC) Portland; KING-TV (NBC) Seattle; KIRO-TV (CBS, IND) Seattle; KOIN (CBS) Portland; KOMO-TV (ABC) Seattle; KPTV (FOX) Portland; KSTW (CW) Tacoma; allband FM.

Programming (via satellite): A&E Networks; ABC Family Channel; AMC; Animal Planet; BET Networks; Cartoon Network; CNBC; CNN; Comedy Central; Country Music TV; Discovery Channel; Disney Channel; E! Entertainment Television; ESPN; Food Network; Fox News Channel; Hallmark Channel; Headline News; Lifetime; MSNBC; MTV; Nickelodeon; Northwest Cable News; QVC; Spike TV; TBS Superstation; The Learning Channel; Travel Channel; truTV; Turner Network TV; Univision Studios; USA Network; VH1.

Fee: $23.99 installation; $18.32 monthly.

Digital Basic Service

Subscribers: N.A.

Programming (via satellite): BBC America; Bio; Black Family Channel; Bravo; Canales N; Discovery Fit & Health; DMX Music; ESPN 2; ESPN Classic Sports; ESPNews; Fox Soccer; Fuse; G4; GAS; Golf Channel; Great American Country; GSN; Halogen Network; HGTV; History Channel; History Channel International; Independent Film Channel; Lifetime Movie Network; MoviePlex; MTV Networks Digital Suite; National Geographic Channel; Nick Jr.; NickToons TV; Nuvo TV; PBS Kids Sprout; Style Network; Sundance Channel; Syfy; The Word Network; Toon Disney; Trinity Broadcasting Network; Turner Classic Movies; TV Land; Versus; WE tv.

Digital Pay Service 1
Pay Units: N.A.
Programming (via satellite): Cinemax (multiplexed); Encore (multiplexed); HBO (multiplexed); Showtime (multiplexed); Starz (multiplexed); The Movie Channel (multiplexed).
Video-On-Demand: No
Pay-Per-View
Movies (delivered digitally); Special events (delivered digitally); Fresh (delivered digitally); Shorteez (delivered digitally); Playboy TV (delivered digitally).
Internet Service
Operational: No.
Telephone Service
Digital: Operational
Miles of Plant: 14.0 (coaxial); None (fiber optic).
Area Vice President: Anne McMullen. Vice President, Sales & Marketing: Tom Pierce. Vice President, Engineering: Steve Tabor. Public Relations Director: Steve Kipp.
Ownership: Comcast Cable Communications Inc. (MSO).

WISHRAM—Formerly served by J & N Cable. No longer in operation. ICA: WA0188.

YACOLT—J & N Cable, 614 S Columbus Ave, Goldendale, WA 98620-9006. Phone: 509-773-5359. Fax: 509-773-7090. E-mail: john@jncable.com. Web Site: http://www.jncable.com. ICA: WA0110.
TV Market Ranking: 29 (YACOLT). Franchise award date: November 1, 1988. Franchise expiration date: N.A. Began: July 1, 1989.
Channel capacity: 50 (not 2-way capable). Channels available but not in use: N.A.
Basic Service
Subscribers: 197.
Programming (received off-air): KATU (ABC) Portland; KGW (NBC) Portland; KOIN (CBS) Portland; KOPB-TV (PBS) Portland; KPDX (MNT) Vancouver; KPTV (FOX) Portland; KRCW-TV (CW) Salem.
Programming (via satellite): A&E Networks; ABC Family Channel; AMC; American-Life TV Network; Animal Planet; Cartoon Network; CNBC; CNN; Comedy Central; C-SPAN; Discovery Channel; Disney Channel; DIY Network; ESPN; ESPN 2; ESPNews; Eternal Word TV Network; FamilyNet; Food Network; Fox News Channel; Fox Sports Net; G4; Great American Country; Hallmark Channel; Headline News; HGTV; History Channel; Lifetime; MSNBC; Northwest Cable News; Outdoor Channel; QVC; ShopNBC; Speed; Style Network; Syfy; TBS Superstation; The Learning Channel; The Weather Channel; Travel Channel; Trinity Broadcasting Network; truTV; Turner Classic Movies; Turner Network TV; USA Network.
Fee: $39.95 installation; $15.95 monthly.
Pay Service 1
Pay Units: 30.
Programming (via satellite): The Movie Channel.
Fee: $10.95 monthly.
Pay Service 2
Pay Units: 30.
Programming (via satellite): Showtime (multiplexed).
Fee: $10.95 monthly.
Pay Service 3
Pay Units: 25.
Programming (via satellite): HBO (multiplexed).
Fee: $10.95 monthly.
Video-On-Demand: No
Internet Service
Operational: No.
Telephone Service
None
Miles of Plant: 4.0 (coaxial); None (fiber optic).
Manager: John Kusky. Marketing Manager: Nancy Kusky.
Ownership: J & N Cable Systems Inc. (MSO).

YAKIMA—Charter Communications, 1005 N 16th Ave, Yakima, WA 98902-1351. Phones: 589-783-0132 (Kennewick office); 509-575-8931. Fax: 509-735-3795. Web Site: http://www.charter.com. Also serves Grandview, Granger, Moxee City, Prosser, Sunnyside, Toppenish, Union Gap, Wapato, Yakima County, Yakima Indian Reservation & Zillah. ICA: WA0009.
TV Market Ranking: Below 100 (Grandview, Granger, Moxee City, Prosser, Sunnyside, Toppenish, Union Gap, Wapato, YAKIMA, Yakima County, Yakima Indian Reservation, Zillah). Franchise award date: January 1, 1963. Franchise expiration date: N.A. Began: November 1, 1979.
Channel capacity: N.A. Channels available but not in use: N.A.
Basic Service
Subscribers: 34,942.
Programming (received off-air): KAPP (ABC, MNT) Yakima; KCYU-LD Yakima; KIMA-TV (CBS) Yakima; KNDO (NBC) Yakima; KSTW (CW) Tacoma; KUNW-CA (UNV) Yakima; KYVE (PBS) Yakima.
Programming (via satellite): C-SPAN; C-SPAN 2; G4; QVC; Telemundo; Trinity Broadcasting Network; TV Guide Network; WGN-TV (CW, IND) Chicago.
Fee: $29.99 installation.
Expanded Basic Service 1
Subscribers: 22,594.
Programming (via satellite): A&E Networks; ABC Family Channel; AMC; Animal Planet; BET Networks; Bravo; Cartoon Network; CNBC; CNN; Comedy Central; Country Music TV; Discovery Channel; Disney Channel; DIY Network; E! Entertainment Television; ESPN; ESPN 2; Food Network; Fox News Channel; FX; GalaVision; Golf Channel; Hallmark Channel; Headline News; HGTV; History Channel; Lifetime; MSNBC; MTV; MTV2; National Geographic Channel; Nickelodeon; Northwest Cable News; Outdoor Channel; Oxygen; SoapNet; Speed; Spike TV; Style Network; Syfy; TBS Superstation; The Learning Channel; The Weather Channel; Toon Disney; Travel Channel; truTV; Turner Network TV; TV Land; USA Network; Versus; VH1; WE tv.
Fee: $50.99 monthly.
Digital Basic Service
Subscribers: N.A.
Programming (via satellite): BBC America; Bio; Bloomberg Television; Boomerang; BYU Television; CNN en Espanol; CNN International; ESPN; ESPN Classic Sports; ESPNews; Fox College Sports Atlantic; Fox College Sports Central; Fox College Sports Pacific; Fox Deportes; Fox Movie Channel; Fox Soccer; Fuel TV; Fuse; GAS; Great American Country; GSN; HDNet; HDNet Movies; History Channel International; Independent Film Channel; International Television (ITV); Lifetime Movie Network; Lifetime Real Women; MTV Networks Digital Suite; Music Choice; NFL Network; Nick Jr.; Nick Too; NickToons TV; Science Television; Sundance Channel; Turner Classic Movies.
Pay Service 1
Pay Units: 1,384.
Programming (via satellite): Encore (multiplexed); Flix; Showtime (multiplexed); The Movie Channel (multiplexed).
Fee: $15.00 installation; $12.05 monthly (each).
Digital Pay Service 1
Pay Units: N.A.
Programming (via satellite): Cinemax (multiplexed); HBO (multiplexed); Starz (multiplexed).
Video-On-Demand: Yes
Internet Service
Operational: Yes. Began: April 1, 2001.
Broadband Service: Charter Pipeline.
Fee: $29.99 monthly.
Telephone Service
Digital: Operational
Fee: $29.99 monthly
Miles of plant included in Kennewick
General Manager: Randy Lee. Technical Operations Manager: Jeff Hopkins. Marketing Director: Diane Long. Program Director: Lloyd Swain. Office Manager: Cathy Von Essen.
Ownership: Charter Communications Inc. (MSO).

YAKIMA—Formerly served by Wireless Broadcasting Systems of Yakima Inc. No longer in operation. ICA: WA0191.

WEST VIRGINIA

Total Systems: **130**
Total Communities Served: **1,020**
Franchises Not Yet Operating: **0**
Applications Pending: **0**
Communities with Applications: **0**
Number of Basic Subscribers: **488,580**
Number of Expanded Basic Subscribers: **212,227**
Number of Pay Units: **48,585**

Top 100 Markets Represented: Pittsburgh (10); Charleston-Huntington (36); Wheeling, WV-Steubenville, OH (90).

For a list of cable communities in this section, see the Cable Community Index located in the back of Cable Volume 2. For explanation of terms used in cable system listings, see p. D-11.

ALDERSON—Charter Communications. Now served by BECKLEY, WV [WV0005]. ICA: WV0091.

ALUM BRIDGE—Rapid Cable. Now served by WESTON, WV [WV0034]. ICA: WV0119.

ANSTED—Shentel, 106 S Main St, Edinburg, VA 22824. Phone: 540-984-5224. Web Site: http://www.shentel.net. Also serves Ames Heights, Lansing & Victor. ICA: WV0245.

TV Market Ranking: 36 (Ames Heights, ANSTED, Lansing, Victor). Franchise award date: N.A. Franchise expiration date: N.A. Began: N.A.

Channel capacity: N.A. Channels available but not in use: N.A.

Basic Service

Subscribers: 866.

Programming (received off-air): WCHS-TV (ABC) Charleston; WLFB (IND) Bluefield; WOAY-TV (ABC) Oak Hill; WSAZ-TV (MNT, NBC) Huntington; WSWP-TV (PBS) Grandview; WVAH-TV (FOX) Charleston; WVNS-TV (CBS) Lewisburg; WVVA (CW, NBC) Bluefield.

Programming (via satellite): A&E Networks; ABC Family Channel; Cartoon Network; CNN; Comedy Central; Country Music TV; C-SPAN; C-SPAN 2; Discovery Channel; ESPN; ESPN 2; Food Network; Fox News Channel; FX; Headline News; HGTV; History Channel; Lifetime; MSNBC; Nickelodeon; QVC; Spike TV; Syfy; The Learning Channel; The Weather Channel; Trinity Broadcasting Network; Turner Network TV; TV Land; USA Network; VH1.

Fee: $29.95 installation; $19.95 monthly; $1.50 converter.

Expanded Basic Service 1

Subscribers: N.A.

Programming (via satellite): AMC; Animal Planet; Disney Channel; TBS Superstation; WGN America.

Fee: $18.00 monthly.

Digital Basic Service

Subscribers: N.A.

Programming (via satellite): BBC America; Bio; Bloomberg Television; Bravo; Discovery Fit & Health; DMX Music; ESPN Classic Sports; Fox Movie Channel; Fox Soccer; Fuse; G4; GAS; Golf Channel; GSN; Halogen Network; History Channel International; Independent Film Channel; Lifetime Movie Network; MTV Networks Digital Suite; Nick Jr.; Outdoor Channel; Science Television; ShopNBC; Speed; Style Network; Toon Disney; Turner Classic Movies; Versus; WE tv.

Fee: $12.95 monthly.

Pay Service 1

Pay Units: N.A.

Programming (via satellite): HBO; Showtime; The Movie Channel.

Fee: $8.95 monthly (each).

Digital Pay Service 1

Pay Units: N.A.

Programming (via satellite): Cinemax (multiplexed); Encore (multiplexed); HBO (multiplexed); Showtime (multiplexed); Starz; The Movie Channel (multiplexed).

Video-On-Demand: No

Pay-Per-View

Hot Choice (delivered digitally); Playboy TV (delivered digitally); Fresh (delivered digitally); Shorteez (delivered digitally).

Internet Service

Operational: No.

Telephone Service

None

General Manager: Robert Harold. Chief Technician: Steve Adkins.

Ownership: Shenandoah Telecommunications Inc. (MSO).

ANTHONY CREEK—Windjammer Cable, 8500 W 110th St, Ste 600, Overland Park, KS 66210. Phone: 888-495-2881. Fax: 913-563-5454. Web Site: http://www.windjammercable.com. Also serves White Sulphur Springs. ICA: WV0254.

TV Market Ranking: Below 100 (ANTHONY CREEK, White Sulphur Springs). Franchise award date: N.A. Franchise expiration date: N.A. Began: N.A.

Channel capacity: N.A. Channels available but not in use: N.A.

Basic Service

Subscribers: 360.

Programming (received off-air): WFXR (CW, FOX) Roanoke; WOAY-TV (ABC) Oak Hill; WSWP-TV (PBS) Grandview; WVNS-TV (CBS) Lewisburg; WVVA (CW, NBC) Bluefield.

Programming (via satellite): A&E Networks; ABC Family Channel; AMC; CNN; Country Music TV; C-SPAN; Discovery Channel; Disney Channel; ESPN; ESPN 2; FX; Golf Channel; Lifetime; Nickelodeon; QVC; Spike TV; TBS Superstation; The Learning Channel; Trinity Broadcasting Network; Turner Network TV; USA Network; VH1; WGN America.

Fee: $39.95 installation; $27.52 monthly; $10.00 additional installation.

Digital Basic Service

Subscribers: N.A.

Programming (via satellite): BBC America; Bloomberg Television; Bravo; Discovery Digital Networks; ESPN Classic Sports; ESPNews; Fox Movie Channel; Fox Sports World; G4; GSN; Halogen Network; HGTV; History Channel; Independent Film Channel; MTV Networks Digital Suite; Music Choice; National Geographic Channel; Nick Jr.; NickToons TV; Outdoor Channel; Speed; Turner Classic Movies; Versus; WE tv.

Fee: $11.00 monthly.

Digital Pay Service 1

Pay Units: N.A.

Programming (via satellite): Cinemax (multiplexed); Encore (multiplexed); HBO (multiplexed); Showtime (multiplexed); Starz (multiplexed); The Movie Channel (multiplexed).

Fee: $15.95 monthly (each).

Video-On-Demand: No

Pay-Per-View

Hits Movies & Events (delivered digitally); Fresh (delivered digitally).

Internet Service

Operational: No.

Telephone Service

None

General Manager: Timothy Evard. Operations Director: Belinda Graham. Engineering Director: Mike Earehart. Finance & Accounting Director: Cindy Johnson.

Ownership: Windjammer Communications LLC (MSO).

APPLE GROVE—Windjammer Cable, 8500 W 110th St, Ste 600, Overland Park, KS 66210. Phone: 888-495-2881. Fax: 913-563-5454. Web Site: http://www.windjammercable.com. Also serves Cabell County (unincorporated areas), Glenwood, Green Bottom, Lesage & Mason City. ICA: WV0186.

TV Market Ranking: 36 (APPLE GROVE, Cabell County (unincorporated areas), Glenwood, Green Bottom, Lesage); Below 100 (Mason City). Franchise award date: N.A. Franchise expiration date: N.A. Began: January 1, 1988.

Channel capacity: 42 (not 2-way capable). Channels available but not in use: N.A.

Basic Service

Subscribers: 325.

Programming (received off-air): WCHS-TV (ABC) Charleston; WKAS (PBS) Ashland; WOWK-TV (CBS) Huntington; WPBY-TV (PBS) Huntington; WSAZ-TV (MNT, NBC) Huntington; WTSF (IND) Ashland; WVAH-TV (FOX) Charleston.

Programming (via satellite): C-SPAN; QVC; TBS Superstation; Trinity Broadcasting Network; WGN America.

Fee: $39.95 installation; $13.03 monthly; $2.00 converter.

Expanded Basic Service 1

Subscribers: 304.

Programming (via satellite): A&E Networks; ABC Family Channel; AMC; Bravo; CNN; Country Music TV; Discovery Channel; Disney Channel; E! Entertainment Television; ESPN; ESPN 2; Headline News; HGTV; History Channel; Lifetime; Nickelodeon; Spike TV; Syfy; The Weather Channel; Turner Network TV; TV Land; USA Network.

Fee: $26.61 monthly.

Digital Pay Service 1

Pay Units: N.A.

Programming (via satellite): Cinemax (multiplexed); Encore (multiplexed); HBO (multiplexed); Showtime (multiplexed); Starz (multiplexed); The Movie Channel (multiplexed).

Fee: $15.95 monthly (each).

Video-On-Demand: No

Internet Service

Operational: No.

Telephone Service

None

Miles of Plant: 30.0 (coaxial); None (fiber optic).

General Manager: Timothy Evard. Operations Director: Belinda Graham. Engineering Director: Mike Earehart. Finance & Accounting Director: Cindy Johnson.

Ownership: Windjammer Communications LLC (MSO).

ARNETTSVILLE—Formerly served by Adelphia Communications. No longer in operation. ICA: WV0046.

ASBURY—Windjammer Cable, 8500 W 110th St, Ste 600, Overland Park, KS 66210. Phone: 888-495-2881. Fax: 913-563-5454. Web Site: http://www.windjammercable.com. Also serves Alderson, Clintonville, Fort Spring, Lewisburg, Ronceverte & Rupert. ICA: WV0255.

TV Market Ranking: Below 100 (Alderson, ASBURY, Clintonville, Fort Spring, Lewisburg, Ronceverte, Rupert). Franchise award date: N.A. Franchise expiration date: N.A. Began: N.A.

Channel capacity: N.A. Channels available but not in use: N.A.

Basic Service

Subscribers: 441.

Programming (received off-air): WFXR (CW, FOX) Roanoke; WLFB (IND) Bluefield; WOAY-TV (ABC) Oak Hill; WSLS-TV (NBC) Roanoke; WSWP-TV (PBS) Grandview; WVNS-TV (CBS) Lewisburg; WVVA (CW, NBC) Bluefield.

Programming (via satellite): A&E Networks; ABC Family Channel; CNN; Country Music TV; C-SPAN; Discovery Channel; Disney Channel; ESPN; ESPN 2; Headline News; HGTV; INSP; Lifetime; Nickelodeon; Outdoor Channel; QVC; Spike TV; Syfy; TBS Superstation; The Learning Channel; The Weather Channel; Turner Classic Movies; Turner Network TV; TV Land; USA Network; VH1; WGN America.

Fee: $39.95 installation; $21.58 monthly.

Digital Basic Service

Subscribers: N.A.

Programming (via satellite): BBC America; Bloomberg Television; Bravo; Discovery Fit & Health; Discovery Health Channel; Discovery Kids Channel; ESPNews; Fox Movie Channel; Fox Soccer; G4; Golf Channel;

GSN; Halogen Network; History Channel; Independent Film Channel; Music Choice; Nick Jr.; NickToons TV; Science; Trinity Broadcasting Network; Versus; WE tv.

Pay Service 1

Pay Units: N.A.

Programming (via satellite): HBO.

Fee: $10.95 monthly.

Digital Pay Service 1

Pay Units: N.A.

Programming (via satellite): Cinemax (multiplexed); Encore (multiplexed); HBO (multiplexed); Showtime (multiplexed); Starz (multiplexed); The Movie Channel (multiplexed).

Video-On-Demand: No

Pay-Per-View

iN DEMAND (delivered digitally); Fresh (delivered digitally); Playboy TV (delivered digitally).

Internet Service

Operational: No.

Telephone Service

None

Miles of Plant: 25.0 (coaxial); None (fiber optic).

General Manager: Timothy Evard. Operations Director: Belinda Graham. Engineeering Director: Mike Earehart. Finance & Accounting Director: Cindy Johnson.

Ownership: Windjammer Communications LLC (MSO).

AUBURN—Formerly served by Cebridge Connections. No longer in operation. ICA: WV0161.

AUGUSTA—Comcast Cable, 15 Summit Park Dr, Pittsburgh, PA 15275. Phones: 412-747-6400; 304-788-2939 (Keyser office). Fax: 412-747-6401. Web Site: http://www.comcast.com. Also serves Hampshire County (portions) & Shanks. ICA: WV0117.

TV Market Ranking: Below 100 (AUGUSTA, Hampshire County (portions)); Outside TV Markets (Hampshire County (portions), Shanks). Franchise award date: N.A. Franchise expiration date: N.A. Began: N.A.

Channel capacity: N.A. Channels available but not in use: N.A.

Basic Service

Subscribers: N.A.

Programming (received off-air): WHAG-TV (NBC) Hagerstown; WJLA-TV (ABC) Washington; WTTG (FOX) Washington; WUSA (CBS) Washington; WWPX-TV (ION) Martinsburg; allband FM.

Programming (via satellite): ABC Family Channel; Discovery Channel; ESPN; Headline News; Spike TV; TBS Superstation; USA Network; WGN America.

Programming (via translator): WNPB-TV (PBS) Morgantown.

Fee: $39.95 installation; $16.85 monthly.

Pay Service 1

Pay Units: 37.

Programming (via satellite): Cinemax; HBO.

Fee: $10.95 monthly (each).

Video-On-Demand: No

Internet Service

Operational: Yes.

Telephone Service

None

Miles of Plant: 27.0 (coaxial); None (fiber optic).

Regional Vice President: Linda Hossinger. Vice President, Technical Operations: Randy Bender. Vice President, Marketing: Donna Corning. Vice President, Public Affairs: Jody Doherty. Chief Technician: Roy Blanchard. Office Manager: Nancy Nesselrodt.

Ownership: Comcast Cable Communications Inc. (MSO).

BALLARD—Windjammer Cable, 8500 W 110th St, Ste 600, Overland Park, KS 66210. Phone: 888-495-2881. Fax: 913-563-5454. Web Site: http://www.windjammercable.com. Also serves Monroe County (unincorporated areas). ICA: WV0113.

TV Market Ranking: Below 100 (BALLARD, Monroe County (unincorporated areas) (portions)); Outside TV Markets (Monroe County (unincorporated areas) (portions)). Franchise award date: N.A. Franchise expiration date: N.A. Began: February 1, 1988.

Channel capacity: 28 (not 2-way capable). Channels available but not in use: N.A.

Basic Service

Subscribers: 360.

Programming (received off-air): WLFB (IND) Bluefield; WOAY-TV (ABC) Oak Hill; WSWP-TV (PBS) Grandview; WVNS-TV (CBS) Lewisburg; WVVA (CW, NBC) Bluefield.

Programming (via satellite): A&E Networks; ABC Family Channel; AMC; CNN; Country Music TV; Discovery Channel; Disney Channel; ESPN; ESPN 2; Headline News; Lifetime; Nickelodeon; Spike TV; Syfy; TBS Superstation; The Weather Channel; Trinity Broadcasting Network; Turner Network TV; USA Network; WGN America.

Fee: $39.95 installation; $35.64 monthly.

Digital Basic Service

Subscribers: N.A.

Programming (via satellite): BBC America; Bloomberg Television; Bravo; Discovery Fit & Health; Discovery Health Channel; Discovery Kids Channel; ESPN Classic Sports; ESPNews; Fox Movie Channel; Fox Soccer; G4; Golf Channel; GSN; Halogen Network; HGTV; History Channel; Independent Film Channel; Music Choice; Nick Jr.; NickToons TV; Outdoor Channel; Science; Versus; WE tv.

Fee: $12.00 monthly.

Pay Service 1

Pay Units: 15.

Programming (via satellite): HBO.

Fee: $11.46 monthly.

Digital Pay Service 1

Pay Units: N.A.

Programming (via satellite): Cinemax (multiplexed); Encore (multiplexed); HBO (multiplexed); Showtime (multiplexed); Starz (multiplexed); The Movie Channel (multiplexed).

Fee: $16.95 monthly (each).

Video-On-Demand: No

Pay-Per-View

Hits Movies & Events (delivered digitally); Fresh (delivered digitally); Playboy TV (delivered digitally).

Internet Service

Operational: No.

Telephone Service

None

Miles of Plant: 32.0 (coaxial); None (fiber optic).

General Manager: Timothy Evard. Operations Director: Belinda Graham. Engineering Director: Mike Earehart. Finance & Accounting Director: Cindy Johnson.

Ownership: Windjammer Communications LLC (MSO).

BECKLEY—Suddenlink Communications, 115 Dye Dr, Beckley, WV 25801-2637. Phones: 304-252-6299; 304-757-8001 (Scott Depot office). Web Site: http://www.suddenlink.com. Also serves Giles County (portions), Glen Lyn, Narrows, Pearisburg, Pembroke & Rich Creek, VA; Alderson, Allen Junction, Amigo, Arnett, Athens, Charmco, Coal City, Corrinne, Crichton, Cunard, Dorothy, Eccles, Fairdale, Fairlea, Fayetteville, Flat Top, Glen White, Greenbrier County (portions), Helen, Hines, Hinton, Jumping Branch, Leslie, Lester, Lewisburg, Lochgelly, Mabscott, Matoaka, Mercer County, Midway, Monroe County, Mount Hope, Nimitz, Oak Hill, Pax, Peterstown, Pipestem, Princeton, Quinwood, Rainelle, Raleigh County (portions), Rhodell, Rupert, Shady Spring, Sophia, Stephenson, Summerlee, Summers County (unincorporated areas), White Sulphur Springs, Wyco & Wyoming County (portions), WV. ICA: WV0005.

TV Market Ranking: 36 (Fayetteville, Raleigh County (portions)); 70 (Giles County (portions)); Below 100 (Alderson, Allen Junction, Amigo, Amigo, Arnett, BECKLEY, Brooklyn, Charmco, Coal City, Corrinne, Crichton, Cunard, Dorothy, Eccles, Fairdale, Fairlea, Flat Top, Glen Lyn, Glen White, Greenbrier County (portions), Helen, Hines, Hinton, Jumping Branch, Leslie, Lester, Lewisburg, Lochgelly, Mabscott, Midway, Monroe County, Mount Hope, Narrows, Nimitz, Oak Hill, Pax, Pearisburg, Pembroke, Peterstown, Pipestem, Quinwood, Rainelle, Rhodell, Rich Creek, Rupert, Shady Spring, Sophia, Stephenson, Summerlee, Summers County (unincorporated areas), White Sulphur Springs, Wyco, Wyoming County (portions), Raleigh County (portions)); Outside TV Markets (Wyoming County (portions)). Franchise award date: N.A. Franchise expiration date: N.A. Began: October 1, 1964.

Channel capacity: 45 (operating 2-way). Channels available but not in use: N.A.

Basic Service

Subscribers: 41,294.

Programming (received off-air): WCHS-TV (ABC) Charleston; WLFB (IND) Bluefield; WOAY-TV (ABC) Oak Hill; WSAZ-TV (MNT, NBC) Huntington; WSWP-TV (PBS) Grandview; WVAH-TV (FOX) Charleston; WVNS-TV (CBS) Lewisburg; WVVA (CW, NBC) Bluefield; allband FM.

Programming (via satellite): C-SPAN; C-SPAN 2; INSP; ION Television; QVC; ShopNBC; Trinity Broadcasting Network; TV Guide Network.

Fee: $27.83 installation; $12.38 monthly.

Expanded Basic Service 1

Subscribers: 8,968.

Programming (via satellite): A&E Networks; ABC Family Channel; AMC; Animal Planet; BET Networks; Bravo; Cartoon Network; CNBC; CNN; Comedy Central; Country Music TV; Discovery Channel; Disney Channel; E! Entertainment Television; ESPN; ESPN 2; Food Network; Fox News Channel; FX; G4; Golf Channel; GSN; Hallmark Channel; Headline News; HGTV; History Channel; Lifetime; MSNBC; MTV; National Geographic Channel; Nickelodeon; Outdoor Channel; Oxygen; Root Sports Pittsburgh; SoapNet; Speed; Spike TV; Style Network; Syfy; TBS Superstation; The Learning Channel; The Weather Channel; Toon Disney; Travel Channel; truTV; Turner Classic Movies; Turner Network TV; TV Land; USA Network; Versus; VH1; WE tv.

Fee: $15.00 installation; $9.53 monthly.

Digital Basic Service

Subscribers: N.A.

Programming (via satellite): BBC America; Bio; Bloomberg Television; CBS Sports Network; DIY Network; ESPN; ESPN Classic Sports; ESPNews; Fox College Sports Atlantic; Fox College Sports Central; Fox College Sports Pacific; Fox Deportes; Fox Movie Channel; Fox Soccer; Fuel TV; Fuse; GAS; Great American Country; HD Theater; History Channel International; Independent Film Channel; Lifetime Movie Network; MTV Networks Digital Suite; Music Choice; NFL Network; Nick Jr.; Nick Too; NickToons TV; Sundance Channel; Turner Network TV HD; TVG Network.

Digital Pay Service 1

Pay Units: N.A.

Programming (via satellite): Cinemax (multiplexed); Cinemax HD; Encore (multiplexed); Flix; HBO (multiplexed); HBO HD; LOGO; Showtime (multiplexed); Showtime HD; Starz (multiplexed); Starz HDTV; The Movie Channel (multiplexed).

Video-On-Demand: Yes

Pay-Per-View

Playboy TV (delivered digitally); Fresh (delivered digitally); Shorteez (delivered digitally); iN DEMAND (delivered digitally); NASCAR In Car (delivered digitally); NHL Center Ice (delivered digitally); MLB Extra Innings (delivered digitally).

Internet Service

Operational: Yes.

Broadband Service: Suddenlink High Speed Internet.

Fee: $49.95 installation; $29.99 monthly.

Telephone Service

Digital: Operational

Miles of Plant: 1,012.0 (coaxial); None (fiber optic).

Vice President, Operations: David Bach. General Manager: Jack Ozminkowski. Technical Operations Director: Bob Legg. Technical Operations Manager: Ron Noor. Marketing Director: Stan Howell. Marketing Manager: Kenny Phillips. Office Manager: Susan Winston.

Ownership: Cequel Communications LLC (MSO).

BEECH BOTTOM—Blue Devil Cable TV Inc., 116 S 4th St, Toronto, OH 43964-1368. Phone: 800-931-9392. Fax: 740-537-2802. ICA: WV0114.

TV Market Ranking: 90 (BEECH BOTTOM). Franchise award date: N.A. Franchise expiration date: N.A. Began: January 1, 1952.

Channel capacity: 30 (not 2-way capable). Channels available but not in use: N.A.

Basic Service

Subscribers: 179.

Programming (received off-air): KDKA-TV (CBS) Pittsburgh; WNPB-TV (PBS) Morgantown; WPGH-TV (FOX) Pittsburgh; WPXI (IND, NBC) Pittsburgh; WQED (PBS) Pittsburgh; WTAE-TV (ABC) Pittsburgh; WTOV-TV (IND, NBC) Steubenville; WTRF-TV (CBS) Wheeling; allband FM.

Programming (via satellite): CNN; ESPN; TBS Superstation; USA Network.

Fee: $25.00 installation; $8.48 monthly.

Pay Service 1

Pay Units: 97.

Programming (via satellite): HBO.

Fee: $15.90 installation; $10.60 monthly.

Video-On-Demand: Planned

Internet Service

Operational: No.

Telephone Service

None

Miles of Plant: 10.0 (coaxial); None (fiber optic).

Manager: David Bates. Office Manager: Joanne Conner.

Ownership: Jefferson County Cable Inc. (MSO).

BEECH CREEK—Colane Cable TV Inc., PO Box 610, Omar, WV 25638. Phone: 304-946-2871. Fax: 304-946-4091. ICA: WV0272.

TV Market Ranking: Below 100 (BEECH CREEK).

Channel capacity: 44 (not 2-way capable). Channels available but not in use: N.A.

Basic Service

Subscribers: N.A. Included in Omar

Programming (received off-air): WCHS-TV (ABC) Charleston; WKPI-TV (PBS) Pikeville; WOWK-TV (CBS) Huntington; WPBY-TV (PBS) Huntington; WSAZ-TV (MNT, NBC) Huntington; WVVA (CW, NBC) Bluefield.

Programming (via satellite): QVC; TBS Superstation; Trinity Broadcasting Network; WGN America.

Fee: $20.00 installation; $22.50 monthly.

Expanded Basic Service 1

Subscribers: N.A.

Programming (via satellite): A&E Networks; ABC Family Channel; AMC; Animal Planet; Boomerang; Cartoon Network; CNN; Comedy Central; Country Music TV; Discovery Channel; ESPN; ESPN 2; FamilyNet; FX; Gospel Music TV; Hallmark Channel; Headline News; HGTV; History Channel; Lifetime; Nickelodeon; Outdoor Channel; Speed; Spike TV; Syfy; The Learning Channel; The Weather Channel; Turner Network TV; TV Land; USA Network; VH1.

Fee: $27.45 monthly.

Pay Service 1

Pay Units: N.A. Included in Omar

Programming (via satellite): HBO; Showtime; The Movie Channel.

Internet Service

Operational: Yes.

Telephone Service

None

General Manager: Gary Bowen. Office Manager: Rebecca Edwards.

Ownership: Colane Cable TV Inc. (MSO).

BELINGTON—Shentel, 106 S Main St, Edinburg, VA 22824. Phone: 540-984-5224. Web Site: http://www.shentel.net. Also serves Barbour County & Junior. ICA: WV0077.

TV Market Ranking: Below 100 (Barbour County, BELINGTON, Junior). Franchise award date: N.A. Franchise expiration date: N.A. Began: June 1, 1956.

Channel capacity: N.A. Channels available but not in use: N.A.

Basic Service

Subscribers: 1,006.

Programming (received off-air): WBOY-TV (NBC) Clarksburg; WDTV (CBS) Weston; WNPB-TV (PBS) Morgantown; WTAE-TV (ABC) Pittsburgh; WVFX (CW, FOX) Clarksburg; allband FM.

Programming (via satellite): C-SPAN; C-SPAN 2; QVC; TV Guide Interactive Inc.

Fee: $29.95 installation; $19.95 monthly.

Expanded Basic Service 1

Subscribers: N.A.

Programming (via satellite): A&E Networks; ABC Family Channel; AMC; Animal Planet; Cartoon Network; CNBC; CNN; Comedy Central; Country Music TV; Discovery Channel; Disney Channel; DMX Music; E! Entertainment Television; ESPN; ESPN 2; Fox News Channel; FX; G4; Headline News; HGTV; History Channel; INSP; Lifetime; MTV; Nickelodeon; Oxygen; Root Sports Pittsburgh; Speed; Spike TV; TBS Superstation; The Learning Channel; The Weather Channel; Travel Channel; Turner Network TV; TV Land; USA Network; VH1.

Fee: $18.00 monthly.

Video-On-Demand: No

Pay-Per-View

Fresh (delivered digitally); Shorteez (delivered digitally); Playboy TV (delivered digitally); iN DEMAND (delivered digitally).

Internet Service

Operational: No.

Telephone Service

None

Miles of Plant: 25.0 (coaxial); None (fiber optic).

General Manager: Robert Harold. Chief Technician: Steve Adkins.

Ownership: Shenandoah Telecommunications Inc. (MSO).

BENS CREEK—Charter Communications. Now served by OMAR, WV [WV0191]. ICA: WV0135.

BERGOO—Charter Communications. Now served by WEBSTER SPRINGS, WV [WV0080]. ICA: WV0163.

BETHANY—Comcast Cable, 300 Carliss St, Pittsburgh, PA 15220. Phones: 412-747-6400; 414-875-1100. Fax: 412-747-6111. Web Site: http://www.comcast.com. Also serves Brooke County (portions). ICA: WV0152.

TV Market Ranking: 10,90 (BETHANY, Brooke County (portions)). Franchise award date: March 1, 1991. Franchise expiration date: March 1, 2007. Began: March 1, 1991.

Channel capacity: 58 (2-way capable). Channels available but not in use: N.A.

Basic Service

Subscribers: 158.

Programming (received off-air): WINP-TV (IND, ION) Pittsburgh; WNPB-TV (PBS) Morgantown; WPGH-TV (FOX) Pittsburgh; WPMY (MNT) Pittsburgh; WQED (PBS) Pittsburgh; WTAE-TV (ABC) Pittsburgh; WTRF-TV (CBS) Wheeling.

Programming (via satellite): A&E Networks; ABC Family Channel; CNN; C-SPAN; Discovery Channel; ESPN; ESPN 2; Headline News; History Channel; MTV; Nickelodeon; QVC; Spike TV; Syfy; TBS Superstation; The Weather Channel; Turner Classic Movies; Turner Network TV; USA Network; WGN America.

Fee: $25.00 installation; $20.78 monthly.

Pay Service 1

Pay Units: 32.

Programming (via satellite): HBO.

Fee: $7.50 monthly.

Pay Service 2

Pay Units: 12.

Programming (via satellite): Cinemax.

Fee: $5.00 monthly.

Video-On-Demand: No

Internet Service

Operational: Yes.

Telephone Service

Digital: Operational

Miles of Plant: 6.0 (coaxial); None (fiber optic).

Regional Vice President: Doug Sansom.

Ownership: Comcast Cable Communications Inc. (MSO).

BEVERLY—Suddenlink Communications, 1513 Harrison Ave, Elkins, WV 26241. Phones: 314-965-2020; 304-472-4193. Fax: 304-472-0756. Web Site: http://www.suddenlink.com. Also serves East Dailey, Elkins, Huttonsville, Midland, Mill Creek, Montrose & Valley Bend. ICA: WV0015.

TV Market Ranking: Below 100 (BEVERLY, East Dailey, Elkins, Huttonsville, Midland, Mill Creek, Valley Bend); Outside TV Markets (Montrose). Franchise award date: December 14, 1979. Franchise expiration date: N.A. Began: December 1, 1979.

Channel capacity: 59 (operating 2-way). Channels available but not in use: N.A.

Basic Service

Subscribers: 6,803.

Programming (received off-air): KDKA-TV (CBS) Pittsburgh; WBOY-TV (NBC) Clarksburg; WCHS-TV (ABC) Charleston; WDTV (CBS) Weston; WNPB-TV (PBS) Morgantown; WTAE-TV (ABC) Pittsburgh; WTRF-TV (CBS) Wheeling; WVFX (CW, FOX) Clarksburg.

Programming (via satellite): Classic Arts Showcase; C-SPAN; Eternal Word TV Network; QVC; The Weather Channel; Trinity Broadcasting Network; TV Guide Network; WGN America.

Fee: $61.25 installation; $17.95 monthly; $2.27 converter.

Expanded Basic Service 1

Subscribers: 6,025.

Programming (via satellite): A&E Networks; ABC Family Channel; AMC; Animal Planet; BET Networks; Cartoon Network; CNBC; CNN; Comedy Central; C-SPAN 2; Discovery Channel; Disney Channel; E! Entertainment Television; ESPN; ESPN 2; ESPN Classic Sports; Food Network; Fox News Channel; FX; Great American Country; GSN; Hallmark Channel; Headline News; HGTV; History Channel; INSP; Lifetime; MSNBC; MTV; National Geographic Channel; Nickelodeon; Outdoor Channel; Root Sports Pittsburgh; SoapNet; Speed; Spike TV; Syfy; TBS Superstation; The Learning Channel; Travel Channel; Turner Network TV; TV Land; USA Network; VH1; WE tv.

Fee: $24.50 monthly.

Digital Basic Service

Subscribers: N.A.

Programming (via satellite): BBC America; Bio; Bloomberg Television; Discovery Digital Networks; DMX Music; ESPNews; Fox College Sports Atlantic; Fox College Sports Central; Fox College Sports Pacific; Fox Movie Channel; Fox Soccer; Fuse; G4; Golf Channel; History Channel International; Independent Film Channel; Lifetime Movie Network; ShopNBC; Style Network; Toon Disney; Turner Classic Movies; Versus.

Fee: $13.95 monthly.

Pay Service 1

Pay Units: 2,742.

Programming (via satellite): Cinemax; HBO; Showtime; The Movie Channel.

Fee: $17.50 installation; $7.95 monthly (Cinemax), $11.95 monthly (Showtime or HBO).

Digital Pay Service 1

Pay Units: N.A.

Programming (via satellite): Cinemax (multiplexed); Encore (multiplexed); HBO (multiplexed); Showtime (multiplexed); Starz (multiplexed); The Movie Channel (multiplexed).

Video-On-Demand: No

Pay-Per-View

iN DEMAND (delivered digitally); Playboy TV (delivered digitally); Fresh (delivered digitally).

Internet Service

Operational: Yes. Began: April 26, 2004.

Broadband Service: Suddenlink High Speed Internet.

Fee: $49.95 installation; $29.99 monthly.

Telephone Service

Digital: Operational

Fee: $49.99 monthly

Miles of Plant: 210.0 (coaxial); None (fiber optic).

Manager: Peter Brown.

Ownership: Cequel Communications LLC (MSO).

BIRCH RIVER—Windjammer Cable, 8500 W 110th St, Ste 600, Overland Park, KS 66210. Phones: 877-450-5558; 561-775-1208. Fax: 913-563-5454. Web Site: http://www.windjammercable.com. Also serves Clay County (unincorporated areas), Dille, Little Birch, Sutton & Widen. ICA: WV0090.

TV Market Ranking: 36 (Clay County (unincorporated areas) (portions)); Below 100 (Little Birch, Clay County (unincorporated areas) (portions)); Outside TV Markets (BIRCH RIVER, Dille, Sutton, Widen, Clay County (unincorporated areas) (portions)). Franchise award date: N.A. Franchise expiration date: N.A. Began: July 1, 1968.

Channel capacity: 28 (not 2-way capable). Channels available but not in use: N.A.

Basic Service

Subscribers: 527.

Programming (received off-air): WBOY-TV (NBC) Clarksburg; WCHS-TV (ABC) Charleston; WDTV (CBS) Weston; WOAY-TV (ABC) Oak Hill; WOWK-TV (CBS) Huntington; WSAZ-TV (MNT, NBC) Huntington; WSWP-TV (PBS) Grandview; WVAH-TV (FOX) Charleston.

Programming (via satellite): A&E Networks; ABC Family Channel; AMC; CNN; Discovery Channel; Disney Channel; ESPN; Great American Country; Spike TV; TBS Superstation; The Learning Channel; The Weather Channel; Trinity Broadcasting Network; Turner Network TV; USA Network; WGN America.

Fee: $39.95 installation; $36.27 monthly.

Digital Basic Service

Subscribers: N.A.

Programming (via satellite): BBC America; Bloomberg Television; Bravo; Discovery Fit & Health; Discovery Health Channel; Discovery Kids Channel; ESPN Classic Sports; ESPNews; Fox Movie Channel; Fox Soccer; G4; Golf Channel; GSN; Halogen Network; HGTV; History Channel; Independent Film Channel; Music Choice; Nick Jr.; NickToons TV; Outdoor Channel; Science; Syfy; Versus; WE tv.

Fee: $12.00 monthly.

Pay Service 1

Pay Units: 12.

Programming (via satellite): HBO.

Fee: $29.95 installation; $10.00 monthly.

Digital Pay Service 1

Pay Units: N.A.

Programming (via satellite): Cinemax (multiplexed); Encore (multiplexed); HBO (multiplexed); Showtime (multiplexed); Starz (multiplexed); The Movie Channel (multiplexed).

Fee: $16.95 monthly (each).

Video-On-Demand: No

Pay-Per-View

iN DEMAND (delivered digitally); Fresh (delivered digitally); Playboy TV (delivered digitally).

Internet Service

Operational: No.

Telephone Service

None

Miles of Plant: 39.0 (coaxial); None (fiber optic).

General Manager: Timothy Evard. Operations Director: Belinda Graham. Engineering Director: Mike Earehart. Finance & Accounting Director: Cindy Johnson.

Ownership: Windjammer Communications LLC (MSO).

BLUEFIELD—Comcast Cable, 1794 Old Gray Station Rd, Gray, TN 37615-3869. Phone: 423-282-1370. Fax: 423-283-4855. Web Site: http://www.comcast.com. Also serves Bland County (portions), Pocahontas, Rocky Gap & Tazewell County (portions), VA; Bluewell, Green Valley & Mercer County (portions), WV. ICA: WV0007.

TV Market Ranking: Below 100 (Bland County (portions), BLUEFIELD, Bluewell, Green Valley, Mercer County (portions), Pocahontas, Rocky Gap, Tazewell County (portions)). Franchise award date: February 26, 1954. Franchise expiration date: N.A. Began: January 1, 1956.

Channel capacity: N.A. Channels available but not in use: N.A.

Basic Service

Subscribers: N.A. Included in Gray, TN

Programming (received off-air): WBRA-TV (PBS) Roanoke; WDBJ (CBS, MNT) Roanoke; WLFB (IND) Bluefield; WOAY-TV (ABC) Oak Hill; WSWP-TV (PBS) Grandview; WVNS-TV (CBS) Lewisburg; WVVA (CW, NBC) Bluefield.

Programming (via satellite): C-SPAN; ION Television; QVC; TBS Superstation.

Fee: $59.95 installation; $14.75 monthly.

Expanded Basic Service 1

Subscribers: N.A.

Programming (via satellite): A&E Networks; ABC Family Channel; AMC; Animal Planet; BET Networks; Cartoon Network; CNBC; CNN; Comcast/Charter Sports Southeast (CSS); Comedy Central; Country Music TV; Discovery Channel; Discovery Health Channel; E! Entertainment Television; ESPN; ESPN 2; Food Network; Fox News Channel; FX; Golf Channel; Great American Country; GSN; Hallmark Channel; Halogen Network; Headline News; HGTV; History Channel; Lifetime; Lime; MTV; Nickelodeon; Root Sports Pittsburgh; Speed; Spike TV; Style Network; The Learning Channel; The Weather Channel; truTV; Turner Network TV; TV Guide Network; TV Land; USA Network; Versus; VH1.

Fee: $30.24 monthly.

Digital Basic Service

Subscribers: N.A.

Programming (via satellite): BBC America; Bio; Disney Channel; Encore (multiplexed); ESPN HD; ESPNews; Flix; G4; GAS; HD Theater; History Channel International; INHD; INHD2; MTV Networks Digital Suite; Music Choice; Nick Jr.; Nick Too; NickToons TV; SoapNet; Sundance Channel; Toon Disney; Turner Network TV HD; WAM! America's Kidz Network; Weatherscan.

Digital Pay Service 1

Pay Units: N.A.

Programming (via satellite): Cinemax (multiplexed); Cinemax HD; HBO (multiplexed); HBO HD; Showtime (multiplexed); Showtime HD; Starz (multiplexed); Starz HDTV; The Movie Channel (multiplexed).

Fee: $13.95 monthly (each).

Video-On-Demand: No

Pay-Per-View

iN DEMAND (delivered digitally); Hot Choice (delivered digitally); Playboy TV (delivered digitally); Fresh (delivered digitally).

Internet Service

Operational: Yes.

Broadband Service: Comcast High Speed Internet.

Fee: $42.95 monthly.

Telephone Service

None

Miles of Plant: 473.0 (coaxial); 33.0 (fiber optic).

Technical Operations Director: Tim Castor. Marketing Manager: Sandra Munsey.

Ownership: Comcast Cable Communications Inc. (MSO).

BOMONT—Vital Communications Group, PO Box 307, Behaven, NC 27810. Phone: 252-943-3800. Also serves Corton & Glen. ICA: WV0265.

TV Market Ranking: 36 (BOMONT, Corton, Glen).

Channel capacity: 43 (not 2-way capable). Channels available but not in use: N.A.

Basic Service

Subscribers: 176.

Programming (received off-air): WCHS-TV (ABC) Charleston; WLPX-TV (ION) Charleston; WOAY-TV (ABC) Oak Hill; WOWK-TV (CBS) Huntington; WPBY-TV (PBS) Huntington; WSAZ-TV (MNT, NBC) Huntington; WSWP-TV (PBS) Grandview; WVAH-TV (FOX) Charleston.

Programming (via satellite): A&E Networks; ABC Family Channel; Cartoon Network; CNN; Comedy Central; Country Music TV; C-SPAN; Discovery Channel; Disney Channel; ESPN; ESPN 2; FX; Headline News; HGTV; History Channel; INSP; Lifetime; MTV; Nickelodeon; Outdoor Channel; QVC; Root Sports Pittsburgh; Speed; Spike TV; Syfy; TBS Superstation; The Learning Channel; The Weather Channel; Trinity Broadcasting Network; Turner Classic Movies; Turner Network TV; TV Land; USA Network; VH1; WGN America.

Fee: $38.34 installation; $31.95 monthly.

Pay Service 1

Pay Units: 10.

Programming (via satellite): HBO.

Fee: $11.95 monthly.

Pay Service 2

Pay Units: 6.

Programming (via satellite): Cinemax.

Fee: $11.95 monthly.

Internet Service

Operational: No.

Miles of Plant: 20.0 (coaxial); None (fiber optic).

President: Jerry Stender.

Ownership: Vital Communications Group (MSO).

BOONE COUNTY (unincorporated areas)—Shentel, 106 S Main St, Edinburg, VA 22824. Phone: 540-984-5224. Web Site: http://www.shentel.net. ICA: WV0274.

TV Market Ranking: 36 (BOONE COUNTY (UNINCORPORATED AREAS) (portions)); Below 100 (BOONE COUNTY (UNINCORPORATED AREAS) (portions)).

Channel capacity: N.A. Channels available but not in use: N.A.

Basic Service

Subscribers: N.A.

Programming (received off-air): WCHS-TV (ABC) Charleston; WOAY-TV (ABC) Oak Hill; WOWK-TV (CBS) Huntington; WPBY-TV (PBS) Huntington; WSAZ-TV (MNT, NBC) Huntington; WVAH-TV (FOX) Charleston.

Programming (via satellite): A&E Networks; ABC Family Channel; AMC; Cartoon Network; CNN; Country Music TV; Discovery Channel; Disney Channel; ESPN; ESPN 2; FX; Headline News; History Channel; ION Television; Lifetime; MTV; Nickelodeon; QVC; Spike TV; Syfy; TBS Superstation; The Weather Channel; Trinity Broadcasting Network; Turner Network TV; USA Network; VH1; WGN America.

Pay Service 1

Pay Units: N.A.

Programming (via satellite): Cinemax; HBO; Showtime.

Internet Service

Operational: No.

Telephone Service

None

General Manager: Robert Harold. Chief Technician: Steve Adkins.

Ownership: Shenandoah Telecommunications Inc. (MSO).

BRANDYWINE—Formerly served by Brandywine Cablevision. No longer in operation. ICA: WV0168.

BROAD RUN—Rapid Cable. Now served by WESTON, WV [WV0034]. ICA: WV0155.

BROOKHAVEN—Formerly served by Adelphia Communications. No longer in operation. ICA: WV0170.

BRUNO—Colane Cable TV Inc., PO Box 610, Omar, WV 25638. Phone: 304-946-2871. Fax: 304-946-4091. ICA: WV0171.

TV Market Ranking: Below 100 (BRUNO). Franchise award date: October 1, 1991. Franchise expiration date: October 1, 2006. Began: N.A.

Channel capacity: N.A. Channels available but not in use: N.A.

Basic Service

Subscribers: N.A. Included in Omar

Programming (received off-air): WCHS-TV (ABC) Charleston; WOWK-TV (CBS) Huntington; WSAZ-TV (MNT, NBC) Huntington; WSWP-TV (PBS) Grandview; WVAH-TV (FOX) Charleston; WVVA (CW, NBC) Bluefield.

Programming (via satellite): ABC Family Channel; CNN; Country Music TV; ESPN; MTV; Nickelodeon; Spike TV; TBS Superstation; Turner Network TV; USA Network; WGN America.

Fee: $25.00 installation; $25.00 monthly.

Pay Service 1

Pay Units: N.A. Included in Omar

Programming (via satellite): HBO; Showtime; The Movie Channel.

Fee: $25.00 installation.

Video-On-Demand: No

Internet Service

Operational: Yes.

Telephone Service

None

Miles of plant included in Omar

General Manager: Gary Bowen. Office Manager: Rebecca Edwards.

Ownership: Colane Cable TV Inc. (MSO).

BUCKHANNON—Suddenlink Communications, 12444 Powerscourt Dr, Saint Louis, MO 63131-3660. Phones: 314-965-2020; 304-472-4193. Fax: 304-472-4193. Web Site: http://www.suddenlink.com. Also serves Adrian, French Creek, Harrison County (portions), Hodgesville, Kesling Mill, Lewis County (northern portion), Lorentz, Lost Creek, Rock Cave, Tennerton, Upshur County & WEST MILFORD. ICA: WV0024.

TV Market Ranking: Below 100 (Adrian, BUCKHANNON, French Creek, Harrison County (portions), Hodgesville, Kesling Mill, Lewis County (northern portion), Lorentz, Lost Creek, Rock Cave, Tennerton, Upshur County, West Milford). Franchise award date: February 15, 1987. Franchise expiration date: N.A. Began: November 1, 1966.

Channel capacity: 50 (operating 2-way). Channels available but not in use: N.A.

Basic Service

Subscribers: 5,094.

Programming (received off-air): KDKA-TV (CBS) Pittsburgh; WBOY-TV (NBC) Clarksburg; WCHS-TV (ABC) Charleston; WDTV (CBS) Weston; WNPB-TV (PBS) Morgantown; WTAE-TV (ABC) Pittsburgh; WTRF-TV (CBS) Wheeling; WVFX (CW, FOX) Clarksburg; allband FM.

Programming (via satellite): Classic Arts Showcase; C-SPAN; Eternal Word TV Network; QVC; The Weather Channel; Trinity Broadcasting Network; TV Guide Network; WGN America.

Fee: $61.25 installation; $17.95 monthly; $.65 converter.

Expanded Basic Service 1

Subscribers: 4,338.

Programming (via satellite): A&E Networks; ABC Family Channel; AMC; Animal Planet; BET Networks; Cartoon Network; Celebrity Shopping Network; CNBC; CNN; Comedy Central; C-SPAN 2; Discovery Channel; Disney Channel; E! Entertainment Television; ESPN; ESPN 2; ESPN Classic Sports; Food Network; Fox News Channel; FX; Great American Country; GSN; Hallmark Channel; Headline News; HGTV; History Channel; INSP; Lifetime; MSNBC; MTV; National Geographic Channel; Nickelodeon; Outdoor Channel; Root Sports Pittsburgh; SoapNet; Speed; Spike TV; Syfy; TBS Superstation; The Learning Channel; Travel Channel; Turner Network TV; TV Land; USA Network; VH1; WE tv.

Fee: $23.00 monthly.

Digital Basic Service

Subscribers: N.A.

Programming (via satellite): BBC America; Bio; Bloomberg Television; Country Music TV; Discovery Digital Networks; DMX Music; ESPNews; Fox College Sports Atlantic; Fox College Sports Central; Fox College Sports Pacific; Fox Movie Channel; Fox Soccer; Fuse; G4; GAS; Golf Channel; History Channel International; Independent Film Channel; Lifetime Movie Network; MTV Networks Digital Suite; Nick Jr.; NickToons TV; ShopNBC; Style Network; Toon Disney; Turner Classic Movies; Versus.

Fee: $13.95 monthly.

Pay Service 1

Pay Units: 398.

Programming (via satellite): Cinemax; HBO; Showtime; The Movie Channel.

Fee: $10.00 installation.

Digital Pay Service 1

Pay Units: N.A.

Programming (via satellite): Cinemax (multiplexed); Encore (multiplexed); HBO (multiplexed); Showtime (multiplexed); Starz (multiplexed); The Movie Channel (multiplexed).

Video-On-Demand: No

Pay-Per-View

iN DEMAND (delivered digitally); Playboy TV (delivered digitally); Fresh (delivered digitally).

Internet Service

Operational: Yes. Began: April 21, 2004.

Broadband Service: Suddenlink High Speed Internet.

Fee: $49.95 installation; $29.99 monthly.

Telephone Service

Analog: Not Operational

Digital: Operational

Fee: $49.99 monthly

Miles of Plant: 157.0 (coaxial); None (fiber optic).

Operations Director: Peter Brown.

Ownership: Cequel Communications LLC (MSO).

BUD—Formerly served by Bud-Alpoca TV Cable Club Inc. No longer in operation. ICA: WV0138.

BURNSVILLE—Charter Communications. Now served by WESTON, WV [WV0034]. ICA: WV0132.

CAIRO—Formerly served by Almega Cable. No longer in operation. ICA: WV0137.

CAMDEN ON GAULEY—Charter Communications. Now served by WEBSTER SPRINGS, WV [WV0080]. ICA: WV0230.

CAMERON—Zito Media, 611 Vader Hill Rd, Coudersport, PA 16915. Phone: 814-260-9575. Web Site: http://www.zitomedia.com. ICA: WV0085.

TV Market Ranking: 90 (CAMERON). Franchise award date: N.A. Franchise expiration date: N.A. Began: January 1, 1950.

Channel capacity: 39 (not 2-way capable). Channels available but not in use: N.A.

Basic Service

Subscribers: 422.

Programming (received off-air): KDKA-TV (CBS) Pittsburgh; WOUC-TV (PBS) Cambridge; WPGH-TV (FOX) Pittsburgh; WPXI (IND, NBC) Pittsburgh; WTAE-TV (ABC) Pittsburgh; WTOV-TV (IND, NBC) Steubenville; WTRF-TV (CBS) Wheeling; allband FM.

Programming (via satellite): C-SPAN; Trinity Broadcasting Network.

Fee: $29.95 installation; $19.95 monthly; $.73 converter.

Expanded Basic Service 1

Subscribers: N.A.

Programming (via satellite): A&E Networks; ABC Family Channel; AMC; CNN; Discovery Channel; Disney Channel; E! Entertainment Television; ESPN; ESPN 2; Fox News Channel; Great American Country; Headline News; HGTV; History Channel; Lifetime; MSNBC; MTV; National Geographic Channel; Nickelodeon; SoapNet; Spike TV; Syfy; TBS Superstation; The Weather Channel; Toon Disney; Turner Network TV; TV Land; USA Network; VH1.

Fee: $22.00 monthly.

Pay Service 1

Pay Units: 294.

Programming (via satellite): Cinemax; HBO; Showtime; The Movie Channel.

Fee: $17.50 installation; $7.95 monthly (Cinemax), $11.95 monthly (Showtime or TMC), $11.99 monthly (HBO).

Video-On-Demand: No

Pay-Per-View

iN DEMAND (delivered digitally); Playboy TV (delivered digitally); Fresh (delivered digitally).

Internet Service

Operational: No.

Telephone Service

None

Miles of Plant: 24.0 (coaxial); None (fiber optic).

Public Relations Manager: Mark Laver.

Ownership: Zito Media (MSO).

CANVAS—Econoco Inc., Rte 61, PO Box 147, Kincaid, WV 25119-0147. Phone: 304-469-2817. Fax: 304-469-2416. ICA: WV0172.

TV Market Ranking: Below 100 (CANVAS). Franchise award date: N.A. Franchise expiration date: N.A. Began: January 1, 1982.

Channel capacity: 36 (not 2-way capable). Channels available but not in use: N.A.

Basic Service

Subscribers: 153.

Programming (received off-air): WCHS-TV (ABC) Charleston; WDTV (CBS) Weston; WOAY-TV (ABC) Oak Hill; WOWK-TV (CBS) Huntington; WSAZ-TV (MNT, NBC) Huntington; WSWP-TV (PBS) Grandview; WVAH-TV (FOX) Charleston; WVVA (CW, NBC) Bluefield.

Programming (via satellite): A&E Networks; ABC Family Channel; CNN; Discovery Channel; ESPN; Fox Sports South; Lifetime; Spike TV; TBS Superstation; Turner Network TV; USA Network; WGN America.

Fee: $25.00 installation; $24.16 monthly.

Pay Service 1

Pay Units: N.A.

Fee: $15.00 installation; $10.00 monthly.

Video-On-Demand: No

Internet Service

Operational: No.

Telephone Service

None

Miles of Plant: 24.0 (coaxial); None (fiber optic).

Manager: Sheila Bills. Chief Technician: Eslie Bills.

Ownership: Econoco Inc. (MSO).

CAPON BRIDGE—Formerly served by Valley Cable Systems. No longer in operation. ICA: WV0123.

CASS—Milestone Communications LP, PO Box 7000, Monument, CO 80132-7000. Phone: 304-799-6229. ICA: WV0173.

TV Market Ranking: Outside TV Markets (CASS). Franchise award date: N.A. Franchise expiration date: May 15, 2015. Began: N.A.

Channel capacity: 39 (not 2-way capable). Channels available but not in use: N.A.

Basic Service

Subscribers: 30.

Programming (received off-air): WDBJ (CBS, MNT) Roanoke; WDTV (CBS) Weston; WSLS-TV (NBC) Roanoke.

Programming (via satellite): ABC Family Channel; CNN; Disney Channel; ESPN; Headline News; TBS Superstation; Trinity Broadcasting Network; Turner Network TV; USA Network; WGN America.

Fee: $50.00 installation; $22.95 monthly; $10.00 additional installation.

Internet Service

Operational: No.

Telephone Service

None

Miles of Plant: 3.0 (coaxial); None (fiber optic).

Owner: Barbara Mock.

Ownership: Milestone Communications LP (MSO).

CHAPEL—Windjammer Cable, 8500 W 110th St, Ste 600, Overland Park, KS 66210. Phone: 888-495-2881. Fax: 913-563-5454. Web Site: http://www.windjammercable.com. ICA: WV0260.

TV Market Ranking: Below 100 (CHAPEL).

Channel capacity: 12 (not 2-way capable). Channels available but not in use: N.A.

Basic Service

Subscribers: 24.

Programming (received off-air): WBOY-TV (NBC) Clarksburg; WCHS-TV (ABC) Charleston; WDTV (CBS) Weston; WOAY-TV (ABC) Oak Hill; WOWK-TV (CBS) Huntington; WSAZ-TV (MNT, NBC) Huntington; WSWP-TV (PBS) Grandview; WVAH-TV (FOX) Charleston.

Programming (via satellite): ABC Family Channel; ESPN; Lifetime; USA Network.

Fee: $39.95 installation; $20.61 monthly.

Video-On-Demand: No

Internet Service

Operational: No.

Telephone Service

None

Miles of Plant: 5.0 (coaxial); None (fiber optic).

General Manager: Timothy Evard. Operations Director: Belinda Graham. Engineering Director: Mike Earehart. Finance & Accounting Director: Cindy Johnson.

Ownership: Windjammer Communications LLC (MSO).

CHARLESTON—Suddenlink Communications, 3028 Michigan Ave, Shrewsbury, WV 25015-1936. Phones: 304-757-8001 (Scott Depot office); 304-343-3343. Fax: 304-357-6707. Web Site: http://www.suddenlink.com. Also serves Acme, Alkol, Alta, Arnett, Ashford, Beasley Hollow, Beech Glen, Belcher Road, Belle, Belva, Bentree, Bickmore, Big Chimney, Blakeley, Bloomingrose, Blue Creek, Blunt, Boomer, Boone County (portions), Branham Heights, Brownsville, Brush Creek, Cabin Creek, Camp Creek, Campbells Creek, Cane Fork, Carbon, Cedar Grove, Charlton Heights, Chelyan, Chesapeake, Cinco, Clay County (southern portion), Clendenin, Clover Drive, Coal Fork, Columbia, Comfort, Coonskin Drive, Coopertown, Costa, Crede, Cross Lanes, Crown Hill, Dameron, Davis Creek, Dawes, Decota, Deepwater, Diamond, Dixie, Dry Branch Drive, Drybranch, Dunbar, Dupont City, Dutch Road, East Bank, Edwight, Elk Forest, Elk Hills, Elk Two Mile, Elkridge, Elkview, Eskdale, Eunice, Falling Rock, Fallsview, Fola, Fosterville, Gallagher, Garrison, Gauley Bridge, Georges Creek, Giles, Glasgow, Glen Ferris, Handley, Hansford, Hernshaw, Holly, Holly Lawn, Hugheston, Hunter Road, Indore, Janie, Jodie, Julian, Kanawha County, Kanawha Falls, Kayford, Keith, Kimberly, Knowlwood, Laing, Laurel Fork, Leevale, Leewood, Lick Creek, Little Sandy, London, Longacre, Loudendale, MacDunn, Malden, Mammoth, Marmet, Masseyville, Meadowbrook, Miami, Millken, Montcoal, Montgomery, Montgomery Heights, Morris Drive, Morrisvale, Morrisville, Mount Carbon, Mulberry, Nabob, Nellis, Nitro, Noama, Ohley, Orgas, Packs Branch, Packsville, Paint Creek (portions), Paytona, Pettus, Pinch, Poca, Point Lick, Pond Gap, Port Amherst, Posey, Powellton, Pratt, Prenter, Prenter Road, Quarrier, Quincy, Racine, Rand, Rensford, Rich Creek, Ridgeview, Riverside, Robson, Rock Creek, Ronda, Route Six, Rumble, Ruthdale, Rutledge Road, Saxon, Seng Creek, Seth, Sharon, Shrewsbury, Smithers, Snow Hill, South Charleston, Spring Fork, Springfield, St. Albans, Stickney, Stover, Sundial, Swiss, Sylvester, Tad, Twentymile, Union Addition, Vaughan, West Belle, Wevaco, Whitesville, Winifrede, Witcher, Woodville & Youngs Bottom. ICA: WV0006.

TV Market Ranking: 36 (Acme, Alkol, Alta, Ashford, Beasley Hollow, Beech Glen, Belcher Road, Belle, Belva, Bentree, Bickmore, Big Chimney, Blakeley, Bloomingrose, Blue Creek, Blunt, Boomer, Boone County (portions), Branham Heights, Brownsville, Brush Creek, Cabin Creek, Camp Creek, Campbells Creek, Cane Fork, Carbon, Cedar Grove, CHARLESTON, Charlton Heights, Chelyan, Chesapeake, Cinco, Clay County (southern portion), Clendenin, Clover Drive, Coal Fork, Columbia, Comfort, Coonskin Drive, Coopertown, Costa, Crede, Cross Lanes, Crown Hill, Davis Creek, Dawes, Decota, Deepwater, Diamond, Dixie, Dry Branch Drive, Drybranch, Dunbar, Dupont City, Dutch Road, East Bank, Edwight, Elk Forest, Elk Hills, Elk Two Mile, Elkridge, Elkview, Eskdale, Eunice, Falling Rock, Fallsview, Fola, Fosterville, Gallagher, Garrison, Gauley Bridge, Georges Creek, Giles, Glasgow, Glen Ferris, Handley, Hansford, Hernshaw, Holly, Holly, Hugheston, Hunter Road, Indore, Janie, Jodie, Julian, Kanawha County, Kanawha Falls, Kayford, Keith, Kimberly, Knowlwood, Laing, Laurel Fork, Leevale, Leewood, Lick Creek, Little Sandy, London, Loudendale, MacDunn, Malden, Mammoth, Marmet, Meadowbrook, Miami, Millken, Montcoal, Montgomery, Montgomery Heights, Morris Drive, Morrisvale, Morrisville, Mount Carbon, Mulberry, Nabob, Nellis, Nitro, Noama, Ohley, Orgas, Packs Branch, Packsville, Paint Creek (portions), Paytona, Pettus, Pinch, Poca, Point Lick, Pond Gap, Port Amherst, Powellton, Pratt, Prenter, Prenter Road, Quarrier, Quincy, Racine, Rand, Rensford, Rich Creek, Ridgeview, Riverside, Robson, Rock Creek, Ronda, Route Six, Rumble, Ruthdale, Rutledge Road, Seng Creek, Seth, Sharon, Shrewsbury, Smithers, Snow Hill, South Charleston, Spring Fork, Springfield, St. Albans, Stickney, Sundial, Swiss, Sylvester, Tad, Twentymile, Union Addition, Vaughan, West Belle, Wevaco, Whitesville, Winifrede, Witcher, Woodville, Youngs Bottom); Below 100 (Arnett, Dameron, Masseyville, Posey, Saxon, Stover). Franchise award date: N.A. Franchise expiration date: N.A. Began: June 1, 1966.

Channel capacity: N.A. Channels available but not in use: N.A.

Basic Service

Subscribers: 71,261.

Programming (received off-air): WCHS-TV (ABC) Charleston; WLPX-TV (ION) Charleston; WOWK-TV (CBS) Huntington; WPBY-TV (PBS) Huntington; WQCW (CW) Portsmouth; WSAZ-TV (MNT, NBC) Huntington; WTSF (IND) Ashland; WVAH-TV (FOX) Charleston; WVPT (PBS) Staunton.

Programming (via satellite): C-SPAN; C-SPAN 2; Product Information Network; QVC; ShopNBC; TV Guide Network; WGN America.

Fee: $35.50 installation; $10.56 monthly; $.93 converter.

Expanded Basic Service 1

Subscribers: 71,000.

Programming (via satellite): A&E Networks; ABC Family Channel; AMC; AmericanLife TV Network; Animal Planet; BET Networks; Bravo; Cartoon Network; CNBC; CNN; Comedy Central; Country Music TV; Discovery Channel; Disney Channel; E! Entertainment Television; ESPN; ESPN 2; ESPN Classic Sports; Food Network; Fox News Channel; FX; G4; Golf Channel; Hallmark Channel; Headline News; HGTV;

History Channel; INSP; Lifetime; MSNBC; MTV; National Geographic Channel; Nickelodeon; Outdoor Channel; Oxygen; Root Sports Pittsburgh; SoapNet; Speed; Spike TV; Syfy; TBS Superstation; The Learning Channel; The Weather Channel; Toon Disney; Travel Channel; Trinity Broadcasting Network; truTV; Turner Classic Movies; Turner Network TV; TV Land; USA Network; Versus; VH1; WE tv.
Fee: $29.00 monthly.

Digital Basic Service
Subscribers: 6,551.
Programming (via satellite): BBC America; Bio; Bloomberg Television; Discovery Digital Networks; DIY Network; Fox Deportes; Fox Movie Channel; Fox Sports World; GAS; Great American Country; History Channel International; Independent Film Channel; Lifetime Movie Network; MTV Networks Digital Suite; Music Choice; Nick Jr.; Style Network; Sundance Channel.
Fee: $18.95 monthly.

Digital Pay Service 1
Pay Units: 9,553.
Programming (via satellite): Cinemax (multiplexed); Encore (multiplexed); HBO (multiplexed); Showtime (multiplexed); Starz (multiplexed); The Movie Channel (multiplexed).
Fee: $10.00 monthly (each).

Video-On-Demand: Yes

Pay-Per-View
Addressable homes: 6,551.
iN DEMAND (delivered digitally); Playboy TV (delivered digitally); Fresh (delivered digitally); Shorteez (delivered digitally); Sports PPV (delivered digitally).

Internet Service
Operational: Yes.
Broadband Service: Suddenlink High Speed Internet.
Fee: $49.95 installation; $29.99 monthly.

Telephone Service
Analog: Not Operational
Digital: Operational
Fee: $49.99 monthly

Miles of Plant: 1,021.0 (coaxial); 176.0 (fiber optic).
Vice President, Operations: David Bach. General Manager: Patrick Barclay. Technical Operations Director: Bob Legg. Marketing Director: Stan Howell. Marketing Manager: Kenny Phillips.
Ownership: Cequel Communications LLC (MSO).

CHATTAROY—Charter Communications. Now served by KERMIT, WV [WV0038]. ICA: WV0072.

CHESTER—Comcast Cable, 15 Summit Park Dr, Pittsburgh, PA 15275. Phone: 412-747-6400. Fax: 412-747-6401. Web Site: http://www.comcast.com. Also serves Hancock County (portions), Lawrenceville & Newell. ICA: WV0032.
TV Market Ranking: 10,90 (CHESTER, Hancock County (portions), Lawrenceville, Newell). Franchise award date: N.A. Franchise expiration date: N.A. Began: March 1, 1956.
Channel capacity: N.A. Channels available but not in use: N.A.

Expanded Basic Service 1
Subscribers: N.A.
Programming (via satellite): A&E Networks; ABC Family Channel; AMC; Animal Planet; BET Networks; Cartoon Network; CNBC; CNN; Comedy Central; Country Music TV; Discovery Channel; Disney Channel; E! Entertainment Television; ESPN; ESPN 2; Food Network; Fox News Channel; FX; G4; Golf Channel; GSN; Hallmark Channel; Headline News; HGTV; History Channel; Lifetime; MSNBC; MTV; Nickelodeon; Oxygen; Pittsburgh Cable News Channel; Root Sports Pittsburgh; Speed; Spike TV; Style Network; TBS Superstation; The Learning Channel; Travel Channel; truTV; Turner Classic Movies; Turner Network TV; TV Land; USA Network; Versus; VH1.
Fee: $36.49 monthly.

Digital Basic Service
Subscribers: 146.
Programming (via satellite): BBC America; Bio; Bloomberg Television; Bravo; CBS Sports Network; CMT Pure Country; Cooking Channel; C-SPAN 3; Current; Daystar TV Network; DIY Network; Encore; ESPN 2 HD; ESPN Classic Sports; ESPN HD; ESPNews; Flix; Fox College Sports Atlantic; Fox College Sports Central; Fox College Sports Pacific; Fox Movie Channel; Fox Reality Channel; Fox Soccer; Fuse; GAS; GMC; GolTV; Great American Country; Halogen Network; HD Theater; History Channel International; HRTV; Independent Film Channel; Jewelry Television; Lifetime Movie Network; LOGO; MoviePlex; MTV Networks Digital Suite; Music Choice; National Geographic Channel; National Geographic Channel HD Network; NBA TV; NFL Network; Nick Jr.; Nick Too; NickToons TV; Outdoor Channel; Palladia; PBS Kids Sprout; ShopNBC; SoapNet; Sundance Channel; Syfy; Tennis Channel; The Word Network; Toon Disney; Trinity Broadcasting Network; Turner Network TV HD; TV One; TVG Network; Universal HD; WE tv; Weatherscan.
Fee: $10.95 monthly.

Digital Pay Service 1
Pay Units: N.A.
Programming (via satellite): Cinemax (multiplexed); Cinemax HD; Flix; HBO (multiplexed); HBO HD; RAI International; Russian Television Network; Showtime (multiplexed); Showtime HD; Starz (multiplexed); Starz HDTV; The Movie Channel (multiplexed); TV Asia; Zee TV USA.

Video-On-Demand: Yes

Pay-Per-View
Addressable homes: 146.
iN DEMAND (delivered digitally); NASCAR In Car (delivered digitally); Sports PPV (delivered digitally); NBA TV (delivered digitally); MLB Extra Innings (delivered digitally); Fresh (delivered digitally); NHL Center Ice (delivered digitally); Playboy TV (delivered digitally); Hot Choice (delivered digitally).

Internet Service
Operational: Yes. Began: October 1, 2001.
Broadband Service: Comcast High Speed Internet.
Fee: $42.95 monthly.

Telephone Service
Digital: Operational
Fee: $44.95 monthly

Miles of Plant: 24.0 (coaxial); 5.0 (fiber optic).
Regional Vice President: Linda Hossinger. Vice President, Technical Operations: Jody Doherty. Vice President, Marketing: Donna Corning. Vice President, Public Affairs: Jody Doherty.
Ownership: Comcast Cable Communications Inc. (MSO).

CLARKSBURG—Country Cable, 224A Milford St, PO Box 1696, Clarksburg, WV 26302. Phone: 800-882-1206. Fax: 304-457-1691. Also serves Crooked Run, Isaacs Creek, Katy Lick & Sardis. ICA: WV0175.
TV Market Ranking: Below 100 (CLARKSBURG, Crooked Run, Isaacs Creek, Katy Lick, Sardis). Franchise award date: N.A. Franchise expiration date: N.A. Began: January 1, 1983.
Channel capacity: 24 (not 2-way capable). Channels available but not in use: N.A.

Basic Service
Subscribers: 200.
Programming (received off-air): WBOY-TV (NBC) Clarksburg; WDTV (CBS) Weston; WNPB-TV (PBS) Morgantown; WTAE-TV (ABC) Pittsburgh; WTRF-TV (CBS) Wheeling; WVFX (CW, FOX) Clarksburg.
Programming (via satellite): A&E Networks; ABC Family Channel; AMC; CNN; Discovery Channel; Disney Channel; ESPN; Headline News; Lifetime; Nickelodeon; Spike TV; TBS Superstation; The Weather Channel; Trinity Broadcasting Network; Turner Network TV; USA Network; WGN America.
Fee: $25.00 installation; $26.25 monthly.

Pay Service 1
Pay Units: 27.
Programming (via satellite): The Movie Channel.
Fee: $11.00 monthly.

Video-On-Demand: No

Internet Service
Operational: No.

Telephone Service
None

Miles of Plant: 25.0 (coaxial); None (fiber optic).
Manager: Jim Fink. Chief Technician: Duane Poling.
Ownership: Country Cable (WV) (MSO).

CLARKSBURG—Formerly served by Adelphia Communications. Now served by MORGANTOWN, WV [WV0198]. ICA: WV0174.

CLARKSBURG—Time Warner Cable, 507 Rosebud Plaza, Clarksburg, WV 26301-9380. Phone: 304-623-3933. Fax: 304-624-4805. Web Site: http://www.timewarnercable.com/clarksburg. Also serves Anmoore, Barrackville, Bridgeport, Fairmont, Harrison County (rural areas), Marion County (portions), Nutter Fort, Pleasant Valley, Stonewood & Taylor County (portions). ICA: WV0010.
TV Market Ranking: Below 100 (Anmoore, Barrackville, Bridgeport, CLARKSBURG, Fairmont, Harrison County (rural areas), Marion County (portions), Nutter Fort, Pleasant Valley, Stonewood, Taylor County (portions)). Franchise award date: N.A. Franchise expiration date: June 30, 2011. Began: July 1, 1953.
Channel capacity: N.A. Channels available but not in use: N.A.

Basic Service
Subscribers: 23,500.
Programming (received off-air): KDKA-TV (CBS) Pittsburgh; WBOY-TV (NBC) Clarksburg; WDTV (CBS) Weston; WNPB-TV (PBS) Morgantown; WTAE-TV (ABC) Pittsburgh; WVFX (CW, FOX) Clarksburg.
Programming (via satellite): ION Television; NASA TV; Product Information Network; QVC; Sneak Prevue; TV Guide Network.
Fee: $19.95 installation; $16.94 monthly; $.57 converter.

Expanded Basic Service 1
Subscribers: 22,020.
Programming (via satellite): A&E Networks; ABC Family Channel; AMC; AmericanLife TV Network; Animal Planet; BET Networks; Bravo; Cartoon Network; CNBC; CNN; Comedy Central; Country Music TV; C-SPAN; C-SPAN 2; Discovery Channel; Discovery Fit & Health; Discovery Health Channel; Disney Channel; E! Entertainment Television; ESPN; ESPN 2; ESPN Classic Sports; Eternal Word TV Network; Food Network; Fox News Channel; FX; Great American Country; Hallmark Channel; Headline News; HGTV; History Channel; INSP; Lifetime; MSNBC; MTV; Nickelodeon; Oxygen; Root Sports Pittsburgh; ShopNBC; Spike TV; TBS Superstation; The Learning Channel; The Weather Channel; Travel Channel; Trinity Broadcasting Network; truTV; Turner Network TV; TV Land; USA Network; VH1; WE tv.
Fee: $32.94 monthly.

Digital Basic Service
Subscribers: 9,431.
Programming (via satellite): BBC America; Bio; Bloomberg Television; Cooking Channel; Discovery Channel; DIY Network; Encore Action; ESPN; ESPNews; Flix; Fox Sports World; FSN Digital Atlantic; FSN Digital Central; FSN Digital Pacific; Fuel TV; Fuse; G4; GAS; Golf Channel; GSN; Halogen Network; HDNet; HDNet Movies; History Channel; iN DEMAND; Independent Film Channel; Lifetime Movie Network; MTV Networks Digital Suite; Music Choice; National Geographic Channel; NBA TV; Nick Jr.; NickToons TV; Outdoor Channel; Ovation; PBS Kids Channel; Speed; Syfy; Tennis Channel; Toon Disney; Turner Classic Movies; Turner Network TV; Versus.
Fee: $6.00 monthly (each tier).

Digital Pay Service 1
Pay Units: N.A.
Programming (via satellite): Cinemax (multiplexed); HBO (multiplexed); HBO HD; Showtime (multiplexed); Showtime HD; Starz (multiplexed); The Movie Channel (multiplexed).
Fee: $12.00 monthly (Cinemax, HBO, Showtime, Starz, or TMC).

Video-On-Demand: Yes

Pay-Per-View
iN DEMAND (delivered digitally); NASCAR In Car (delivered digitally); Fresh (delivered digitally); Shorteez (delivered digitally); Playboy TV (delivered digitally); Hot Choice (delivered digitally).

Internet Service
Operational: Yes.
Subscribers: 8,400.
Broadband Service: Road Runner.
Fee: $99.95 installation; $44.95 monthly.

Telephone Service
Analog: Not Operational
Digital: Operational
Subscribers: 2,700.
Fee: $44.95 monthly

Miles of Plant: 532.0 (coaxial); None (fiber optic). Additional miles planned: 3.0 (coaxial). Miles of plant (coax) include miles of plant (fiber)
General Manager: Lenny Hannigan. Chief Technician: Brian Lewis. Marketing Manager: Mari Patterson. Advertising Sales Manager: Brenda Jasper.
Ownership: Time Warner Cable (MSO).

CLAY (town)—Shentel, 106 S Main St, Edinburg, VA 22824. Phone: 540-984-5224. Web Site: http://www.shentel.net. ICA: WV0063.
TV Market Ranking: 36 (CLAY (TOWN)). Franchise award date: N.A. Franchise expiration date: N.A. Began: March 1, 1952.
Channel capacity: 36 (not 2-way capable). Channels available but not in use: N.A.

Basic Service
Subscribers: 104.
Programming (received off-air): WCHS-TV (ABC) Charleston; WDTV (CBS) Weston;

WLPX-TV (ION) Charleston; WOAY-TV (ABC) Oak Hill; WOWK-TV (CBS) Huntington; WSAZ-TV (MNT, NBC) Huntington; WSWP-TV (PBS) Grandview; WVAH-TV (FOX) Charleston; 5 FMs.
Programming (via satellite): QVC; WGN America.
Fee: $29.95 installation; $19.95 monthly.

Expanded Basic Service 1
Subscribers: N.A.
Programming (via satellite): A&E Networks; ABC Family Channel; AMC; Cartoon Network; CNN; Country Music TV; Discovery Channel; ESPN; ESPN 2; FX; Headline News; History Channel; Lifetime; MTV; Nickelodeon; Spike TV; Syfy; TBS Superstation; The Weather Channel; Turner Network TV; USA Network; VH1.
Fee: $20.00 monthly.

Pay Service 1
Pay Units: N.A.
Programming (via satellite): HBO.

Video-On-Demand: No

Internet Service
Operational: No.

Telephone Service
None

Miles of Plant: 34.0 (coaxial); None (fiber optic).
General Manager: Robert Harold. Chief Technician: Steve Adkins.
Ownership: Shenandoah Telecommunications Inc. (MSO).

COALTON—Country Cable, 224A Milford St, PO Box 1696, Clarksburg, WV 26302. Phone: 800-882-1206. Fax: 304-457-1691. ICA: WV0176.
TV Market Ranking: Below 100 (COALTON). Franchise award date: N.A. Franchise expiration date: January 1, 2010. Began: January 1, 1990.
Channel capacity: N.A. Channels available but not in use: N.A.

Basic Service
Subscribers: 69.
Programming (received off-air): WBOY-TV (NBC) Clarksburg; WDTV (CBS) Weston; WNPB-TV (PBS) Morgantown; WTAE-TV (ABC) Pittsburgh; WVFX (CW, FOX) Clarksburg.
Programming (via satellite): A&E Networks; ABC Family Channel; CNN; ESPN; Lifetime; Spike TV; TBS Superstation; Trinity Broadcasting Network; Turner Network TV; USA Network; WGN America.
Fee: $23.00 installation; $23.50 monthly.

Video-On-Demand: No

Internet Service
Operational: No.

Telephone Service
None

Miles of Plant: 2.0 (coaxial); None (fiber optic).
Manager: Jim Fink. Chief Technician: Duane Paling.
Ownership: Country Cable (WV) (MSO).

COLFAX—Formerly served by Adelphia Communications. Now served by MORGANTOWN, WV [WV0198]. ICA: WV0177.

COLLIERS—Jefferson County Cable Inc., 116 S 4th St, Toronto, OH 43964-1368. Phone: 740-537-2214. Fax: 740-537-2802. ICA: WV0146.
TV Market Ranking: 10,90 (COLLIERS). Franchise award date: N.A. Franchise expiration date: N.A. Began: February 1, 1972.
Channel capacity: 12 (not 2-way capable). Channels available but not in use: N.A.

Basic Service
Subscribers: 71.
Programming (received off-air): KDKA-TV (CBS) Pittsburgh; WINP-TV (IND, ION) Pittsburgh; WPGH-TV (FOX) Pittsburgh; WPXI (IND, NBC) Pittsburgh; WQED (PBS) Pittsburgh; WTOV-TV (IND, NBC) Steubenville; WTRF-TV (CBS) Wheeling.
Programming (via satellite): ESPN; TBS Superstation.
Programming (via translator): WNPB-TV (PBS) Morgantown.
Fee: $25.00 installation; $20.14 monthly.

Pay Service 1
Pay Units: 32.
Programming (via satellite): HBO.
Fee: $11.66 monthly.

Video-On-Demand: Planned

Internet Service
Operational: No.

Telephone Service
None

Miles of Plant: 4.0 (coaxial); None (fiber optic).
Manager: David Bates. Office Manager: Joanne Conner.
Ownership: Jefferson County Cable Inc. (MSO).

COTTAGEVILLE—Community Antenna Service, 1525 Dupont Rd, Parkersburg, WV 26101-9623. Phone: 304-420-2470. Fax: 304-420-2474. E-mail: info@cascable.com. Web Site: http://www.cascable.com. Also serves Evans, Evergreen Hill, Millwood, Ravenswood & Ripley. ICA: WV0062.
TV Market Ranking: 36 (COTTAGEVILLE, Evans, Evergreen Hill, Millwood, Ripley); Below 100 (Ravenswood). Franchise award date: N.A. Franchise expiration date: N.A. Began: November 1, 1981.
Channel capacity: N.A. Channels available but not in use: N.A.

Basic Service
Subscribers: 1,141.
Programming (received off-air): WCHS-TV (ABC) Charleston; WOUB-TV (PBS) Athens; WOWK-TV (CBS) Huntington; WPBY-TV (PBS) Huntington; WSAZ-TV (MNT, NBC) Huntington; WTAP-TV (FOX, MNT, NBC) Parkersburg; WVAH-TV (FOX) Charleston.
Programming (via satellite): A&E Networks; ABC Family Channel; Animal Planet; Cartoon Network; CNBC; CNN; Country Music TV; C-SPAN; C-SPAN 2; Discovery Channel; Discovery Health Channel; Disney Channel; ESPN; ESPN 2; ESPNews; Fox News Channel; FX; G4; Golf Channel; Great American Country; Hallmark Channel; Headline News; HGTV; History Channel; INSP; ION Television; Lifetime; MSNBC; National Geographic Channel; Nickelodeon; Outdoor Channel; QVC; Speed; Spike TV; Syfy; TBS Superstation; The Learning Channel; The Weather Channel; Travel Channel; Trinity Broadcasting Network; truTV; Turner Classic Movies; Turner Network TV; TV Guide Network; TV Land; USA Network; WGN America.
Fee: $45.00 installation; $51.85 monthly.

Pay Service 1
Pay Units: N.A.
Programming (via satellite): Cinemax; Encore; HBO; Starz.
Fee: $10.90 monthly (Starz & Encore), $10.95 monthly (Cinemax), $13.95 monthly (HBO).

Video-On-Demand: No

Internet Service
Operational: Yes.
Broadband Service: In-house.
Fee: $19.95 monthly.

Telephone Service
Analog: Not Operational
Digital: Operational
Fee: $29.95-$39.95 monthly

Miles of Plant: 59.0 (coaxial); None (fiber optic).
Manager: Arthur R. Cooper. Chief Technician: Steve Defibaugh. Marketing Director: Lisa Wilkinson.
Ownership: Arthur R. Cooper (MSO).

COWEN—Charter Communications. Now served by WEBSTER SPRINGS, WV [WV0080]. ICA: WV0096.

CRAIGSVILLE—Shentel, 106 S Main St, Edinburg, VA 22824. Phone: 540-984-5224. Web Site: http://www.shentel.net. Also serves Cottle. ICA: WV0071.
TV Market Ranking: Outside TV Markets (Cottle, CRAIGSVILLE). Franchise award date: N.A. Franchise expiration date: June 5, 2010. Began: November 1, 1973.
Channel capacity: 36 (not 2-way capable). Channels available but not in use: N.A.

Basic Service
Subscribers: N.A.
Programming (received off-air): WCHS-TV (ABC) Charleston; WDTV (CBS) Weston; WOAY-TV (ABC) Oak Hill; WOWK-TV (CBS) Huntington; WSAZ-TV (MNT, NBC) Huntington; WSWP-TV (PBS) Grandview; WVAH-TV (FOX) Charleston; allband FM.
Programming (via satellite): ABC Family Channel; C-SPAN; C-SPAN 2; CW+; INSP; ION Television; QVC; WGN America.
Fee: $29.95 installation; $19.95 monthly.

Expanded Basic Service 1
Subscribers: N.A.
Programming (via satellite): A&E Networks; AMC; Animal Planet; Cartoon Network; CNBC; CNN; Comedy Central; Country Music TV; Discovery Channel; Discovery Fit & Health; Disney Channel; E! Entertainment Television; ESPN; ESPN 2; ESPN Classic Sports; ESPNews; Eternal Word TV Network; Food Network; Fox News Channel; Fox Sports Net; FX; G4; Hallmark Channel; Headline News; HGTV; History Channel; Lifetime; MSNBC; MTV; National Geographic Channel; Nickelodeon; Outdoor Channel; Oxygen; SoapNet; Speed; Spike TV; Syfy; TBS Superstation; The Learning Channel; The Weather Channel; Travel Channel; truTV; Turner Network TV; TV Land; USA Network; VH1.
Fee: $18.00 monthly.

Digital Basic Service
Subscribers: N.A.
Programming (via satellite): BBC America; Bio; Bloomberg Television; Bravo; CMT Pure Country; Discovery Digital Networks; Fox College Sports Atlantic; Fox College Sports Central; Fox College Sports Pacific; Fox Movie Channel; Fox Soccer; Fuse; Golf Channel; GSN; History Channel International; Independent Film Channel; Lifetime Movie Network; MTV Networks Digital Suite; Nick Jr.; NickToons TV; Style Network; Sundance Channel; TeenNick; Toon Disney; Turner Classic Movies; Versus; WE tv.
Fee: $12.95 monthly.

Digital Pay Service 1
Pay Units: N.A.
Programming (via satellite): Cinemax (multiplexed); Encore (multiplexed); Flix; HBO (multiplexed); Showtime (multiplexed); Starz (multiplexed); The Movie Channel (multiplexed).

Video-On-Demand: No

Internet Service
Operational: No.

Telephone Service
None

General Manager: Robert Harold. Chief Technician: Steve Adkins.
Ownership: Shenandoah Telecommunications Inc. (MSO).

CRAWLEY CREEK ROAD—Colane Cable, PO Box 610, Omar, WV 25638. Phone: 304-946-2871. Also serves Chapmanville (portions). ICA: WV0236.
TV Market Ranking: 36 (Chapmanville (portions)); Below 100 (CRAWLEY CREEK ROAD). Franchise award date: N.A. Franchise expiration date: N.A. Began: N.A.
Channel capacity: 62 (not 2-way capable). Channels available but not in use: N.A.

Basic Service
Subscribers: 281.
Programming (received off-air): WCHS-TV (ABC) Charleston; WOWK-TV (CBS) Huntington; WPBY-TV (PBS) Huntington; WSAZ-TV (MNT, NBC) Huntington; WVAH-TV (FOX) Charleston.
Programming (via satellite): A&E Networks; ABC Family Channel; Cartoon Network; CNN; Comedy Central; Country Music TV; C-SPAN; Discovery Channel; ESPN; Headline News; Lifetime; MTV; Nickelodeon; QVC; Spike TV; Syfy; TBS Superstation; The Weather Channel; Trinity Broadcasting Network; Turner Network TV; USA Network; VH1; WGN America.
Fee: $38.85 installation; $33.30 monthly.

Pay Service 1
Pay Units: N.A.
Programming (via satellite): HBO.
Fee: $12.00 monthly.

Internet Service
Operational: No.

Telephone Service
None

Miles of Plant: 5.0 (coaxial); None (fiber optic).
General Manager: Gary Bowen. Office Manager: Rebecca Edwards.
Ownership: Colane Cable TV Inc. (MSO).

CROSSROADS—Formerly served by Crossroads TV Cable. No longer in operation. ICA: WV0235.

CURTIN—Charter Communications. Now served by WEBSTER SPRINGS, WV [WV0080]. ICA: WV0164.

DAWSON—Econoco Inc., Rte 61, PO Box 147, Kincaid, WV 25119-0147. Phone: 304-469-2817. Fax: 304-469-2416. ICA: WV0271.
TV Market Ranking: Below 100 (DAWSON). Franchise award date: N.A. Franchise expiration date: N.A. Began: June 1, 1996.
Channel capacity: 36 (not 2-way capable). Channels available but not in use: N.A.
Basic Service
Subscribers: 111.
Programming (received off-air): WCHS-TV (ABC) Charleston; WDTV (CBS) Weston; WOAY-TV (ABC) Oak Hill; WOWK-TV (CBS) Huntington; WSAZ-TV (MNT, NBC) Huntington; WSWP-TV (PBS) Grandview; WVAH-TV (FOX) Charleston; WVVA (CW, NBC) Bluefield.
Programming (via satellite): A&E Networks; ABC Family Channel; CNN; Discovery Channel; ESPN; Fox Sports South; Lifetime; Spike TV; TBS Superstation; Turner Network TV; USA Network; WGN America.
Fee: $25.00 installation; $25.99 monthly.
Pay Service 1
Pay Units: 6.
Programming (via satellite): Showtime.
Fee: $15.00 installation; $10.00 monthly.
Internet Service
Operational: No.
Telephone Service
None
Manager: Sheila Bills. Chief Technician: Elsie Bills.
Ownership: Econoco Inc. (MSO).

DELBARTON—Colane Cable TV Inc. Now served by OMAR, WV [WV0191]. ICA: WV0087.

DIANA—Country Cable, 224A Milford St, PO Box 1696, Clarksburg, WV 26302. Phone: 800-882-1206. Fax: 304-457-1691. Also serves Grassy Creek, Jumbo & Webster County (unincorporated areas). ICA: WV0127.
TV Market Ranking: Below 100 (DIANA, Grassy Creek, Jumbo, Webster County (unincorporated areas) (portions)); Outside TV Markets (Webster County (unincorporated areas) (portions)). Franchise award date: N.A. Franchise expiration date: N.A. Began: June 1, 1981.
Channel capacity: N.A. Channels available but not in use: N.A.
Basic Service
Subscribers: 120.
Programming (received off-air): WBOY-TV (NBC) Clarksburg; WCHS-TV (ABC) Charleston; WDTV (CBS) Weston; WOAY-TV (ABC) Oak Hill; WOWK-TV (CBS) Huntington; WSWP-TV (PBS) Grandview; WVAH-TV (FOX) Charleston.
Programming (via satellite): ABC Family Channel; CNN; ESPN; Syfy; TBS Superstation; Trinity Broadcasting Network; Turner Network TV; USA Network; WGN America.
Fee: $23.00 installation; $23.25 monthly.
Pay Service 1
Pay Units: 13.
Programming (via satellite): HBO.
Fee: $11.00 monthly.
Video-On-Demand: No
Internet Service
Operational: No.
Telephone Service
None
Miles of Plant: 15.0 (coaxial); None (fiber optic).
Manager: Jim Fink. Chief Technician: Duane Poling.
Ownership: Country Cable (WV) (MSO).

DINGESS—Shentel, 106 S Main St, Edinburg, VA 22824. Phone: 540-984-5224. Web Site: http://www.shentel.net. Also serves Breeden, Mingo County (unincorporated areas), Mount Gay, Mudfork & Verdunville. ICA: WV0079.
TV Market Ranking: Outside TV Markets (Breeden, DINGESS, Mingo County (unincorporated areas), Mount Gay, Mudfork, Verdunville). Franchise award date: September 18, 1985. Franchise expiration date: N.A. Began: N.A.
Channel capacity: N.A. Channels available but not in use: N.A.

Basic Service
Subscribers: 643.
Programming (received off-air): WCHS-TV (ABC) Charleston; WKPI-TV (PBS) Pikeville; WLPX-TV (ION) Charleston; WOWK-TV (CBS) Huntington; WPBY-TV (PBS) Huntington; WQCW (CW) Portsmouth; WSAZ-TV (MNT, NBC) Huntington; WTSF (IND) Ashland; WVAH-TV (FOX) Charleston.
Programming (via satellite): C-SPAN; TBS Superstation; Trinity Broadcasting Network; TV Guide Network; WGN America.
Fee: $29.95 installation; $19.95 monthly; $1.24 converter.

Expanded Basic Service 1
Subscribers: N.A.
Programming (via satellite): A&E Networks; ABC Family Channel; AMC; Animal Planet; Cartoon Network; CNBC; CNN; Comedy Central; Country Music TV; Discovery Channel; Disney Channel; E! Entertainment Television; ESPN; ESPN 2; Fox News Channel; FX; G4; Headline News; HGTV; History Channel; Lifetime; MTV; Nickelodeon; Oxygen; Speed; Spike TV; Syfy; The Learning Channel; The Weather Channel; Turner Classic Movies; Turner Network TV; TV Land; USA Network; VH1.
Fee: $18.00 monthly.

Digital Basic Service
Subscribers: N.A.
Programming (via satellite): BBC America; Bio; Bloomberg Television; Discovery Digital Networks; DMX Music; ESPN Classic Sports; ESPNews; Fox Movie Channel; Fox Soccer; Fuse; GAS; GSN; History Channel International; Independent Film Channel; Lifetime Movie Network; MTV Networks Digital Suite; Nick Jr.; Nick Too; NickToons TV; SoapNet; Style Network; Sundance Channel; Toon Disney; WE tv.
Fee: $12.95 monthly.

Digital Pay Service 1
Pay Units: N.A.
Programming (via satellite): Cinemax (multiplexed); Encore (multiplexed); Flix; HBO (multiplexed); Showtime (multiplexed); Starz (multiplexed); The Movie Channel (multiplexed).
Video-On-Demand: No

Pay-Per-View
iN DEMAND (delivered digitally); Fresh (delivered digitally); Shorteez (delivered digitally); Playboy TV (delivered digitally).

Internet Service
Operational: No.

Telephone Service
None
Miles of Plant: 43.0 (coaxial); None (fiber optic).
General Manager: Robert Harold. Chief Technician: Steve Adkins.
Ownership: Shenandoah Telecommunications Inc. (MSO).

DORCAS—C T & R Cable, 29 Water St, Petersburg, WV 26847-1544. Phone: 304-257-4891. Also serves Maysville. ICA: WV0224.
TV Market Ranking: Outside TV Markets (DORCAS, Maysville). Franchise award date: N.A. Franchise expiration date: N.A. Began: May 15, 1991.
Channel capacity: 23 (not 2-way capable). Channels available but not in use: N.A.
Basic Service
Subscribers: 325.
Programming (via satellite): ABC Family Channel; Cartoon Network; Discovery Channel; ESPN; ESPN 2; Fox News Channel; Spike TV; TBS Superstation; Turner Network TV; USA Network; WGN America.
Programming (via translator): WHSV-TV (ABC, MNT) Harrisonburg; WJAC-TV (NBC) Johnstown; WNPB-TV (PBS) Morgantown; WTTG (FOX) Washington; WUSA (CBS) Washington.
Fee: $25.00 installation; $20.00 monthly.
Pay Service 1
Pay Units: 44.
Programming (via satellite): Showtime.
Fee: $9.00 monthly.
Internet Service
Operational: No.
Telephone Service
None
Miles of Plant: 35.0 (coaxial); None (fiber optic).
Manager: Terry Hinkle. Chief Technician: Matt Alt.
Ownership: C T & R Cable LLC (MSO).

DOROTHY—Charter Communications. Now served by BECKLEY, WV [WV0005]. ICA: WV0246.

DRENNEN—Shentel, 106 S Main St, Edinburg, VA 22824. Phone: 540-984-5224. Web Site: http://www.shentel.net. Also serves Lockwood. ICA: WV0269.
TV Market Ranking: 36 (DRENNEN, Lockwood). Franchise award date: N.A. Franchise expiration date: April 13, 2013. Began: N.A.
Channel capacity: N.A. Channels available but not in use: N.A.
Basic Service
Subscribers: N.A.
Programming (received off-air): WCHS-TV (ABC) Charleston; WDTV (CBS) Weston; WOAY-TV (ABC) Oak Hill; WOWK-TV (CBS) Huntington; WSAZ-TV (MNT, NBC) Huntington; WSWP-TV (PBS) Grandview; WVAH-TV (FOX) Charleston; WVVA (CW, NBC) Bluefield.
Programming (via satellite): ABC Family Channel; CNN; Discovery Channel; ESPN; Spike TV; TBS Superstation; USA Network.
Pay Service 1
Pay Units: N.A.
Programming (via satellite): HBO.
Video-On-Demand: No
Pay-Per-View
Hot Choice (delivered digitally); Playboy TV (delivered digitally); Fresh (delivered digitally); Shorteez (delivered digitally); iN DEMAND (delivered digitally).
Internet Service
Operational: No.
Telephone Service
None
General Manager: Robert Harold. Chief Technician: Steve Adkins.
Ownership: Shenandoah Telecommunications Inc. (MSO).

DUNLOW—Formerly served by Almega Cable. No longer in operation. ICA: WV0179.

DURBIN—Milestone Communications LP, PO Box 7000, Monument, CO 80132-7000. Phone: 304-799-6229. Also serves Arborvale, Bartow, Frank, Green Bank & Pine Grove. ICA: WV0180.
TV Market Ranking: Outside TV Markets (Arborvale, Bartow, DURBIN, Frank, Green Bank, Pine Grove). Franchise award date: N.A. Franchise expiration date: May 15, 2015. Began: N.A.
Channel capacity: 62 (not 2-way capable). Channels available but not in use: N.A.
Basic Service
Subscribers: 307.
Programming (received off-air): WBOY-TV (NBC) Clarksburg; WDBJ (CBS, MNT) Roanoke; WDTV (CBS) Weston; WKRN-TV (ABC) Nashville; WSLS-TV (NBC) Roanoke; WVVA (CW, NBC) Bluefield.
Programming (via satellite): A&E Networks; ABC Family Channel; AMC; Animal Planet; CNN; Comedy Central; Country Music TV; C-SPAN; Discovery Channel; Disney Channel; E! Entertainment Television; ESPN; ESPN 2; Food Network; Fox News Channel; FX; Hallmark Channel; Headline News; HGTV; History Channel; Lifetime; MTV; Nickelodeon; Outdoor Channel; QVC; Root Sports Pittsburgh; Spike TV; Syfy; TBS Superstation; The Learning Channel; The Weather Channel; Travel Channel; Trinity Broadcasting Network; truTV; Turner Classic Movies; Turner Network TV; TV Land; USA Network; VH1; WE tv; WGN America.
Fee: $50.00 installation; $38.99 monthly; $20.00 additional installation.
Pay Service 1
Pay Units: 15.
Programming (via satellite): HBO.
Fee: $10.00 installation; $12.95 monthly.
Pay Service 2
Pay Units: 23.
Programming (via satellite): Showtime; The Movie Channel.
Fee: $10.00 installation; $12.95 monthly (each).
Internet Service
Operational: No.
Telephone Service
None
Miles of Plant: 32.0 (coaxial); 10.0 (fiber optic).
Owner: Barbara Mock.
Ownership: Milestone Communications LP (MSO).

EASTON—Formerly served by Adelphia Communications. No longer in operation. ICA: WV0181.

ELLAMORE—Windjammer Cable, 8500 W 110th St, Ste 600, Overland Park, KS 66210. Phone: 888-495-2881. Fax: 913-563-5454. Web Site: http://www.windjammercable.com. Also serves Belington, Buckhannon (portions), Coalton, Norton & Randolph County (unincorporated areas). ICA: WV0125.
TV Market Ranking: Below 100 (Belington, Buckhannon (portions), Coalton, ELLAMORE, Norton, Randolph County (unincorporated areas) (portions)); Outside TV Markets (Randolph County (unincorporated areas) (portions)). Franchise award date: N.A. Franchise expiration date: N.A. Began: N.A.
Channel capacity: 25 (not 2-way capable). Channels available but not in use: N.A.
Basic Service
Subscribers: 194.
Programming (received off-air): WBOY-TV (NBC) Clarksburg; WDTV (CBS) Weston; WNPB-TV (PBS) Morgantown; WTAE-TV

(ABC) Pittsburgh; WVFX (CW, FOX) Clarksburg.
Programming (via satellite): ABC Family Channel; AMC; CNN; C-SPAN; Discovery Channel; Disney Channel; ESPN; G4; Lifetime; Nickelodeon; QVC; Spike TV; TBS Superstation; The Weather Channel; Trinity Broadcasting Network; Turner Network TV; USA Network; WGN America; WXYZ-TV (ABC) Detroit.
Fee: $39.95 installation; $30.70 monthly.

Digital Basic Service
Subscribers: N.A.
Programming (via satellite): BBC America; Bloomberg Television; Bravo; Discovery Health Channel; Discovery Kids Channel; ESPN Classic Sports; ESPNews; Fox Movie Channel; Fox Soccer; Golf Channel; GSN; Halogen Network; HGTV; History Channel; Independent Film Channel; Music Choice; Nick Jr.; NickToons TV; Outdoor Channel; Science; Syfy; Versus; WE tv.
Fee: $11.00 monthly.

Pay Service 1
Pay Units: 15.
Programming (via satellite): HBO.
Fee: $11.46 monthly.

Digital Pay Service 1
Pay Units: N.A.
Programming (via satellite): Cinemax (multiplexed); Encore (multiplexed); HBO (multiplexed); Showtime (multiplexed); Starz (multiplexed); The Movie Channel (multiplexed).
Fee: $16.95 monthly (each).

Video-On-Demand: No

Pay-Per-View
Hits Movies & Events (delivered digitally); Fresh (delivered digitally).

Internet Service
Operational: No.

Telephone Service
None

Miles of Plant: 30.0 (coaxial); None (fiber optic).
General Manager: Timothy Evard. Operations Director: Belinda Graham. Engineering Director: Mike Earehart. Finance & Accounting Director: Cindy Johnson.
Ownership: Windjammer Communications LLC (MSO).

ELLENBORO—Charter Communications. Now served by WESTON, WV [WV0034]. ICA: WV0247.

FAIRMONT—Time Warner Cable. Now served by CLARKSBURG, WV [WV0010]. ICA: WV0014.

FLAT ROCK—Time Warner Cable, 225 Russell Rd, Ashland, KY 41101. Phone: 606-329-2201. Fax: 606-329-9579. Web Site: http://www.timewarnercable.com. Also serves Mason County (unincorporated areas). ICA: WV0108.
TV Market Ranking: 36 (FLAT ROCK, Mason County (unincorporated areas)). Franchise award date: N.A. Franchise expiration date: N.A. Began: N.A.
Channel capacity: N.A. Channels available but not in use: N.A.

Basic Service
Subscribers: 284.
Programming (received off-air): WCHS-TV (ABC) Charleston; WOWK-TV (CBS) Huntington; WPBY-TV (PBS) Huntington; WSAZ-TV (MNT, NBC) Huntington; WVAH-TV (FOX) Charleston.
Programming (via satellite): ABC Family Channel; CNN; Discovery Channel; Disney Channel; ESPN; FX; Headline News; Spike TV; TBS Superstation; Turner Network TV; USA Network; WGN America.
Fee: $39.95 installation; $27.74 monthly.

Digital Basic Service
Subscribers: N.A.
Programming (via satellite): BBC America; Bloomberg Television; Bravo; Discovery Digital Networks; ESPN Classic Sports; ESPNews; Fox Movie Channel; Fox Sports World; G4; Golf Channel; GSN; Halogen Network; HGTV; History Channel; Independent Film Channel; Music Choice; Nick Jr.; NickToons TV; Outdoor Channel; Syfy; Trinity Broadcasting Network; Versus; WE tv.
Fee: $11.00 monthly.

Pay Service 1
Pay Units: 75.
Programming (via satellite): HBO.
Fee: $10.00 monthly.

Digital Pay Service 1
Pay Units: N.A.
Programming (via satellite): Cinemax (multiplexed); Encore (multiplexed); HBO (multiplexed); Showtime (multiplexed); Starz (multiplexed); The Movie Channel (multiplexed).
Fee: $15.95 monthly (each).

Video-On-Demand: No

Pay-Per-View
HITS (Headend In The Sky) (delivered digitally); Fresh (delivered digitally).

Internet Service
Operational: No.

Telephone Service
None

Miles of Plant: 18.0 (coaxial); None (fiber optic).
General Manager: Russ Pomfrey. Technical Operations Manager: Mike Jones. Marketing Manager: Mark Cole. Technical Supervisor: Rod Frost. Business Manager: Tracy Tackett.
Ownership: Time Warner Cable (MSO).

FLEMINGTON—Suddenlink Communications, 12444 Powerscourt Dr, Saint Louis, MO 63131-3660. Phones: 314-965-2020; 304-472-4193. Web Site: http://www.suddenlink.com. Also serves Brownton, Galloway, Harrison County (portions), Rosemont & Simpson. ICA: WV0074.
TV Market Ranking: Below 100 (Brownton, FLEMINGTON, Galloway, Harrison County (portions), Rosemont, Simpson). Franchise award date: April 3, 1981. Franchise expiration date: N.A. Began: April 1, 1967.
Channel capacity: 29 (operating 2-way). Channels available but not in use: N.A.

Basic Service
Subscribers: 839.
Programming (received off-air): KDKA-TV (CBS) Pittsburgh; WBOY-TV (NBC) Clarksburg; WDTV (CBS) Weston; WNPB-TV (PBS) Morgantown; WTAE-TV (ABC) Pittsburgh; WTRF-TV (CBS) Wheeling; WVFX (CW, FOX) Clarksburg; allband FM.
Programming (via satellite): Eternal Word TV Network; QVC.
Fee: $61.25 installation; $17.95 monthly; $1.24 converter.

Expanded Basic Service 1
Subscribers: N.A.
Programming (via satellite): A&E Networks; ABC Family Channel; AMC; Animal Planet; Bravo; Cartoon Network; CNN; Comedy Central; C-SPAN; C-SPAN 2; Discovery Channel; Disney Channel; E! Entertainment Television; ESPN; ESPN 2; ESPN Classic Sports; Food Network; Fox News Channel; FX; G4; Great American Country; GSN; Hallmark Channel; Headline News; HGTV; History Channel; Lifetime; MSNBC; MTV; National Geographic Channel; Nickelodeon; Outdoor Channel; Root Sports Pittsburgh; SoapNet; Speed; Spike TV; Syfy; TBS Superstation; The Learning Channel; The Weather Channel; Trinity Broadcasting Network; truTV; Turner Network TV; TV Guide Network; TV Land; USA Network; VH1; WE tv.
Fee: $26.00 monthly.

Digital Basic Service
Subscribers: N.A.
Programming (via satellite): BBC America; Bio; Bloomberg Television; Discovery Digital Networks; DMX Music; ESPNews; Fox College Sports Atlantic; Fox College Sports Central; Fox College Sports Pacific; Fox Movie Channel; Fox Soccer; Fuse; Golf Channel; History Channel International; Independent Film Channel; Lifetime Movie Network; ShopNBC; Style Network; Toon Disney; Turner Classic Movies; Versus.
Fee: $13.95 monthly.

Pay Service 1
Pay Units: 146.
Programming (via satellite): Encore; HBO.
Fee: $17.50 installation; $11.99 monthly.

Pay Service 2
Pay Units: N.A.
Programming (via satellite): Cinemax; Showtime; The Movie Channel.
Fee: $7.95 monthly (Cinemax), $11.95 monthly (Showtime or TMC).

Digital Pay Service 1
Pay Units: N.A.
Programming (via satellite): Cinemax (multiplexed); Encore (multiplexed); HBO (multiplexed); Showtime (multiplexed); Starz (multiplexed); The Movie Channel (multiplexed).

Pay-Per-View
iN DEMAND (delivered digitally); Playboy TV (delivered digitally); Fresh (delivered digitally).

Internet Service
Operational: Yes. Began: November 1, 2004.
Broadband Service: Suddenlink High Speed Internet.
Fee: $49.95 installation; $29.99 monthly.

Telephone Service
Digital: Planned

Miles of Plant: 30.0 (coaxial); None (fiber optic). Additional miles planned: 5.0 (coaxial).
Operations Director: Peter Brown.
Ownership: Cequel Communications LLC (MSO).

FOLSOM—Jones TV Cable & Satellite Systems Inc., RR 1 Box 8, Folsom, WV 26348-9725. Phone: 304-334-6504. Also serves Wallace. ICA: WV0141.
TV Market Ranking: Below 100 (FOLSOM, Wallace). Franchise award date: N.A. Franchise expiration date: N.A. Began: April 1, 1985.
Channel capacity: 62 (not 2-way capable). Channels available but not in use: N.A.

Basic Service
Subscribers: 200.
Programming (received off-air): KDKA-TV (CBS) Pittsburgh; WBOY-TV (NBC) Clarksburg; WDTV (CBS) Weston; WNPB-TV (PBS) Morgantown; WTAE-TV (ABC) Pittsburgh; WTOV-TV (IND, NBC) Steubenville; WTRF-TV (CBS) Wheeling; WVFX (CW, FOX) Clarksburg.
Programming (via satellite): A&E Networks; ABC Family Channel; AmericanLife TV Network; CNN; Discovery Channel; Disney Channel; ESPN; ESPN 2; Headline News; History Channel; Spike TV; Syfy; TBS Superstation; The Learning Channel; Trinity Broadcasting Network; Turner Classic Movies; TV Land; USA Network; WGN America.

Pay Service 1
Pay Units: N.A.
Programming (via satellite): HBO.

Video-On-Demand: No

Internet Service
Operational: No.

Telephone Service
None

Miles of Plant: 9.0 (coaxial); None (fiber optic).
Manager & Chief Technician: Eugene Jones.
Ownership: Eugene Jones.

FRAME—Windjammer Cable, 8500 W 110th St, Ste 600, Overland Park, KS 66210. Phone: 888-495-2881. Fax: 913-563-5454. Web Site: http://www.windjammercable.com. Also serves Elkview & Sissonville (portions). ICA: WV0276.
TV Market Ranking: 36 (Elkview, FRAME, Sissonville).
Channel capacity: N.A. Channels available but not in use: N.A.

Basic Service
Subscribers: N.A.
Programming (received off-air): WCHS-TV (ABC) Charleston; WLPX-TV (ION) Charleston; WOWK-TV (CBS) Huntington; WPBY-TV (PBS) Huntington; WSAZ-TV (MNT, NBC) Huntington; WVAH-TV (FOX) Charleston.
Programming (via satellite): ABC Family Channel; BBC America; CNN; Discovery Channel; Discovery Health Channel; Discovery Kids Channel; Disney Channel; ESPN; ESPN 2; ESPN Classic Sports; ESPNews; Golf Channel; GSN; Halogen Network; Nickelodeon; QVC; Science; Spike TV; TBS Superstation; Trinity Broadcasting Network; Turner Network TV; USA Network; Versus; WGN America.
Fee: $39.95 installation; $34.47 monthly.

Digital Basic Service
Subscribers: N.A.
Programming (via satellite): BBC America; Bloomberg Television; Bravo; Discovery Fit & Health; Discovery Health Channel; Discovery Kids Channel; ESPN Classic Sports; ESPNews; Fox Movie Channel; G4; Golf Channel; GSN; Halogen Network; HGTV; History Channel; Independent Film Channel; Music Choice; Nick Jr.; NickToons TV; Outdoor Channel; Science; Syfy; Versus; WE tv.
Fee: $12.00 monthly.

Pay Service 1
Pay Units: N.A.
Programming (via satellite): HBO.

Digital Pay Service 1
Pay Units: N.A.
Programming (via satellite): Cinemax (multiplexed); Encore (multiplexed); HBO (multiplexed); Showtime (multiplexed); Starz (multiplexed); The Movie Channel (multiplexed).
Fee: $16.95 monthly (each).
Pay-Per-View
iN DEMAND (delivered digitally); Fresh (delivered digitally).
Internet Service
Operational: No.
Telephone Service
None
General Manager: Timothy Evard. Operations Director: Belinda Graham. Engineering Director: Mike Earehart. Finance & Accounting Director: Cindy Johnson.
Ownership: Windjammer Communications LLC (MSO).

FRAMETOWN—Windjammer Cable, 4400 PGA Blvd, Ste 902, Palm Beach Gardens, FL 33410. Phones: 877-450-5558; 561-775-1208. Fax: 561-775-7811. Web Site: http://www.windjammercable.com. Also serves Strange Creek. ICA: WV0252.
TV Market Ranking: Below 100 (FRAMETOWN); Outside TV Markets (Strange Creek). Franchise award date: N.A. Franchise expiration date: N.A. Began: N.A.
Channel capacity: N.A. Channels available but not in use: N.A.
Basic Service
Subscribers: 264.
Programming (received off-air): WBOY-TV (NBC) Clarksburg; WCHS-TV (ABC) Charleston; WDTV (CBS) Weston; WOAY-TV (ABC) Oak Hill; WOWK-TV (CBS) Huntington; WSAZ-TV (MNT, NBC) Huntington; WSWP-TV (PBS) Grandview; WVAH-TV (FOX) Charleston.
Programming (via satellite): ABC Family Channel; AMC; CNN; Country Music TV; Discovery Channel; Disney Channel; ESPN; Spike TV; TBS Superstation; The Learning Channel; The Weather Channel; Trinity Broadcasting Network; Turner Network TV; USA Network.
Fee: $39.95 installation; $34.89 monthly.
Digital Basic Service
Subscribers: N.A.
Programming (via satellite): BBC America; Bloomberg Television; Bravo; Discovery Fit & Health; Discovery Health Channel; Discovery Kids Channel; ESPN Classic Sports; ESPNews; Fox Movie Channel; Fox Soccer; G4; Golf Channel; GSN; Halogen Network; HGTV; History Channel; Independent Film Channel; Music Choice; Nick Jr.; NickToons TV; Outdoor Channel; Science; Syfy; Versus; WE tv.
Fee: $12.00 monthly.
Pay Service 1
Pay Units: N.A.
Programming (via satellite): HBO.
Fee: $10.00 monthly.
Digital Pay Service 1
Pay Units: N.A.
Programming (via satellite): Cinemax (multiplexed); Encore (multiplexed); HBO (multiplexed); Showtime (multiplexed); Starz (multiplexed); The Movie Channel (multiplexed).
Fee: $16.95 monthly (each).
Video-On-Demand: No
Pay-Per-View
Hits Movies & Events (delivered digitally); Fresh (delivered digitally); Playboy TV (delivered digitally).
Internet Service
Operational: No.
Telephone Service
None
Miles of Plant: 40.0 (coaxial); None (fiber optic).
General Manager: Timothy Evard. Operations Director: Belinda Graham. Engineering Director: Mike Earehart. Finance & Accounting Director: Cindy Johnson.
Ownership: Windjammer Communications LLC (MSO).

FRANKFORD—Clearview TV Cable, HC 81 Box 247 AA, Lewisburg, WV 24901. Phone: 304-645-1397. Also serves Anthony, Renick & Williamsburg. ICA: WV0098.
TV Market Ranking: Below 100 (Anthony, FRANKFORD, Renick, Williamsburg). Franchise award date: N.A. Franchise expiration date: N.A. Began: N.A.
Channel capacity: 27 (not 2-way capable). Channels available but not in use: N.A.
Basic Service
Subscribers: 515.
Programming (received off-air): WDBJ (CBS, MNT) Roanoke; WOAY-TV (ABC) Oak Hill; WSLS-TV (NBC) Roanoke; WSWP-TV (PBS) Grandview; WVVA (CW, NBC) Bluefield.
Programming (via satellite): ABC Family Channel; Discovery Channel; ESPN; Headline News; TBS Superstation; Turner Network TV; USA Network.
Fee: $33.30 installation; $34.10 monthly.
Pay Service 1
Pay Units: N.A.
Programming (via satellite): HBO.
Fee: $12.72 monthly.
Video-On-Demand: No
Internet Service
Operational: No.
Telephone Service
None
Miles of Plant: 45.0 (coaxial); None (fiber optic).
Manager: Chip James.
Ownership: Clearview Cable TV Inc. (MSO).

FRANKLIN—Shentel, 106 S Main St, Edinburg, VA 22824. Phone: 540-984-5224. Web Site: http://www.shentel.net. Also serves Pendleton County. ICA: WV0095.
TV Market Ranking: Below 100 (FRANKLIN, Pendleton County (portions)); Outside TV Markets (Pendleton County (portions)). Franchise award date: January 6, 1957. Franchise expiration date: N.A. Began: October 1, 1957.
Channel capacity: 29 (operating 2-way). Channels available but not in use: N.A.
Basic Service
Subscribers: 547.
Programming (received off-air): WDBJ (CBS, MNT) Roanoke; WDTV (CBS) Weston; WHSV-TV (ABC, MNT) Harrisonburg; WSLS-TV (NBC) Roanoke; allband FM.
Programming (via satellite): C-SPAN; QVC; The Weather Channel; Trinity Broadcasting Network; WGN America.
Fee: $29.95 installation; $19.95 monthly.
Expanded Basic Service 1
Subscribers: N.A.
Programming (via satellite): A&E Networks; ABC Family Channel; AMC; Animal Planet; Cartoon Network; CNBC; CNN; Comedy Central; C-SPAN 2; Discovery Channel; Disney Channel; ESPN; ESPN 2; ESPN Classic Sports; Food Network; Fox News Channel; FX; Great American Country; GSN; Hallmark Channel; HGTV; History Channel; Lifetime; National Geographic Channel; Nickelodeon; Outdoor Channel; Root Sports Pittsburgh; Spike TV; Syfy; TBS Superstation; The Learning Channel; Travel Channel; Turner Classic Movies; Turner Network TV; TV Land; USA Network.
Fee: $20.00 monthly.
Digital Basic Service
Subscribers: N.A.
Programming (via satellite): BBC America; Bio; Bloomberg Television; cloo; Discovery Digital Networks; DMX Music; ESPNews; Fox College Sports Atlantic; Fox College Sports Central; Fox College Sports Pacific; Fox Movie Channel; Fox Soccer; Fuse; G4; Golf Channel; History Channel International; Independent Film Channel; Lifetime Movie Network; ShopNBC; Speed; Style Network; Toon Disney; Versus; WE tv.
Pay Service 1
Pay Units: 150.
Programming (via satellite): HBO.
Fee: $11.99 monthly.
Pay Service 2
Pay Units: N.A.
Programming (via satellite): Cinemax.
Fee: $7.95 monthly.
Digital Pay Service 1
Pay Units: N.A.
Programming (via satellite): Cinemax (multiplexed); Encore (multiplexed); HBO (multiplexed); Showtime (multiplexed); Starz (multiplexed); The Movie Channel (multiplexed).
Video-On-Demand: No
Pay-Per-View
iN DEMAND (delivered digitally); Playboy TV (delivered digitally); Fresh (delivered digitally).
Internet Service
Operational: No.
Telephone Service
None
Miles of Plant: 30.0 (coaxial); None (fiber optic). Additional miles planned: 5.0 (coaxial).
General Manager: Robert Harold. Chief Technician: Steve Adkins.
Ownership: Shenandoah Telecommunications Inc. (MSO).

FRIENDLY—Windjammer Cable, 8500 W 110th St, Ste 600, Overland Park, KS 66210. Phone: 888-495-2881. Fax: 913-563-5454. Web Site: http://www.windjammercable.com. Also serves Sistersville. ICA: WV0133.
TV Market Ranking: Below 100 (FRIENDLY, Sistersville). Franchise award date: N.A. Franchise expiration date: N.A. Began: January 1, 1970.
Channel capacity: 22 (not 2-way capable). Channels available but not in use: N.A.
Basic Service
Subscribers: 118.
Programming (received off-air): WBOY-TV (NBC) Clarksburg; WDTV (CBS) Weston; WKRN-TV (ABC) Nashville; WNPB-TV (PBS) Morgantown; WTAP-TV (FOX, MNT, NBC) Parkersburg; WTOV-TV (IND, NBC) Steubenville; WTRF-TV (CBS) Wheeling; WVFX (CW, FOX) Clarksburg; allband FM.
Programming (via satellite): ABC Family Channel; WGN America.
Fee: $39.95 installation; $15.61 monthly; $.73 converter.
Expanded Basic Service 1
Subscribers: 94.
Programming (via satellite): AMC; CNN; Discovery Channel; ESPN; ESPN 2; HGTV; Spike TV; TBS Superstation; The Weather Channel; USA Network.
Fee: $12.08 monthly.
Pay Service 1
Pay Units: 24.
Programming (via satellite): HBO.
Fee: $29.95 installation; $11.99 monthly.
Digital Pay Service 1
Pay Units: N.A.
Programming (via satellite): Cinemax (multiplexed); Encore (multiplexed); HBO (multiplexed); Showtime (multiplexed); Starz; The Movie Channel.
Fee: $16.95 monthly (each).
Video-On-Demand: No
Internet Service
Operational: No.
Telephone Service
None
Miles of Plant: 6.0 (coaxial); None (fiber optic).
General Manager: Timothy Evard. Operations Director: Belinda Graham. Engineering Director: Mike Earehart. Finanace & Accounting Director: Cindy Johnson.
Ownership: Windjammer Communications LLC (MSO).

GANDEEVILLE—Econoco Inc., Rte 61, PO Box 147, Kincaid, WV 25119-0147. Phone: 304-469-2817. ICA: WV0183.
TV Market Ranking: 36 (GANDEEVILLE). Franchise award date: N.A. Franchise expiration date: N.A. Began: October 1, 1987.
Channel capacity: 36 (not 2-way capable). Channels available but not in use: N.A.
Basic Service
Subscribers: 125.
Programming (received off-air): WBOY-TV (NBC) Clarksburg; WCHS-TV (ABC) Charleston; WDTV (CBS) Weston; WOAY-TV (ABC) Oak Hill; WOWK-TV (CBS) Huntington; WSAZ-TV (MNT, NBC) Huntington; WSWP-TV (PBS) Grandview; WTAP-TV (FOX, MNT, NBC) Parkersburg; WVAH-TV (FOX) Charleston.
Programming (via satellite): A&E Networks; ABC Family Channel; Animal Planet; Cartoon Network; CNN; Country Music TV; Discovery Channel; ESPN; ESPN 2; Headline News; ION Television; Lifetime; QVC; Spike TV; Syfy; TBS Superstation; The Learning Channel; Travel Channel; Trinity Broadcasting Network; Turner Network TV; WGN America.
Fee: $25.00 installation; $25.99 monthly.
Pay Service 1
Pay Units: N.A.
Programming (via satellite): Showtime.
Fee: $15.00 installation; $10.00 monthly.
Video-On-Demand: No
Internet Service
Operational: No.
Telephone Service
None
Miles of Plant: 15.0 (coaxial); None (fiber optic).
Manager: Sheila Bills. Chief Technician: Eslie Bills.
Ownership: Econoco Inc. (MSO).

GASSAWAY—Shentel, 106 S Main St, Edinburg, VA 22824. Phone: 540-984-5224. Web Site: http://www.shentel.net. Also serves Braxton County, Flatwoods & Sutton. ICA: WV0061.
TV Market Ranking: Below 100 (Braxton County (portions), Flatwoods, GASSAWAY, Sutton); Outside TV Markets (Braxton County (portions)). Franchise award date: N.A. Franchise expiration date: N.A. Began: January 1, 1954.
Channel capacity: N.A. Channels available but not in use: N.A.

Basic Service
Subscribers: 2,000.
Programming (received off-air): WBOY-TV (NBC) Clarksburg; WCHS-TV (ABC) Charleston; WDTV (CBS) Weston; WLPX-TV (ION) Charleston; WNPB-TV (PBS) Morgantown; WOAY-TV (ABC) Oak Hill; WSAZ-TV (MNT, NBC) Huntington; WSWP-TV (PBS) Grandview; WVAH-TV (FOX) Charleston; allband FM.
Programming (via satellite): INSP; QVC; TV Guide Network.
Fee: $59.95 installation; $9.86 monthly.
Expanded Basic Service 1
Subscribers: 1,093.
Programming (via satellite): A&E Networks; ABC Family Channel; AMC; Animal Planet; Cartoon Network; CNBC; CNN; Comedy Central; Country Music TV; C-SPAN; Discovery Channel; Disney Channel; E! Entertainment Television; ESPN; ESPN 2; Fox News Channel; FX; G4; Golf Channel; Headline News; HGTV; History Channel; Lifetime; MTV; Nickelodeon; Oxygen; Root Sports Pittsburgh; Speed; Spike TV; Syfy; TBS Superstation; The Learning Channel; The Weather Channel; Travel Channel; Turner Classic Movies; Turner Network TV; TV Land; USA Network; VH1.
Fee: $9.93 monthly.
Digital Basic Service
Subscribers: N.A.
Programming (via satellite): BBC America; Bio; Bloomberg Television; Discovery Fit & Health; DMX Music; ESPN Classic Sports; ESPNews; Fox Movie Channel; Fuse; GAS; GSN; History Channel International; Independent Film Channel; Lifetime Movie Network; MTV Networks Digital Suite; Nick Jr.; Nick Too; NickToons TV; Science Television; SoapNet; Sundance Channel; Toon Disney; WE tv.
Digital Pay Service 1
Pay Units: N.A.
Programming (via satellite): Cinemax (multiplexed); Encore (multiplexed); Flix; HBO (multiplexed); Showtime (multiplexed); Starz (multiplexed); The Movie Channel (multiplexed).
Video-On-Demand: No
Pay-Per-View
Special events; iN DEMAND (delivered digitally); Fresh (delivered digitally); Shorteez (delivered digitally); Playboy TV (delivered digitally).
Internet Service
Operational: No.
Telephone Service
None
Miles of Plant: 45.0 (coaxial); None (fiber optic).
General Manager: David Hashimoto. Customer Service Manager: Angie Henline.
Ownership: Shenandoah Telecommunications Inc. (MSO).

GENOA—Lycom Communications, 305 E Pike St, Louisa, KY 41230. Phones: 606-638-3600; 800-489-0640; 606-638-0639. Fax: 606-638-4278. E-mail: info@lycomonline.com. Web Site: http://www.lycomonline.com. ICA: WV0214.
TV Market Ranking: Below 100 (GENOA). Franchise award date: N.A. Franchise expiration date: N.A. Began: June 1, 1977.
Channel capacity: N.A. Channels available but not in use: N.A.
Basic Service
Subscribers: 40.
Programming (received off-air): WCHS-TV (ABC) Charleston; WKAS (PBS) Ashland; WLPX-TV (ION) Charleston; WOWK-TV (CBS) Huntington; WPBY-TV (PBS) Huntington; WSAZ-TV (MNT, NBC) Huntington; WTSF (IND) Ashland; WVAH-TV (FOX) Charleston; WYMT-TV (CBS, CW) Hazard.
Programming (via satellite): A&E Networks; ABC Family Channel; AMC; Animal Planet; Cartoon Network; CNBC; CNN; Comedy Central; Country Music TV; C-SPAN; C-SPAN 2; CW+; Discovery Channel; Disney Channel; E! Entertainment Television; ESPN; ESPN 2; ESPN Classic Sports; Food Network; Fox News Channel; Fox Sports Net Ohio; FX; GMC; Great American Country; Hallmark Channel; Headline News; Healthy Living Channel; HGTV; History Channel; Lifetime; MTV; National Geographic Channel; Nickelodeon; QVC; RFD-TV; Speed; Spike TV; Syfy; TBS Superstation; The Learning Channel; The Weather Channel; Travel Channel; Trinity Broadcasting Network; truTV; Turner Classic Movies; Turner Network TV; TV Guide Network; TV Land; USA Network; VH1; WGN America.
Fee: $45.95 installation; $43.09 monthly.
Video-On-Demand: No
Internet Service
Operational: No.
Telephone Service
None
Managers: Steven Lycans.; Donna Lycans. Chief Technician: Aaron Lycans.
Ownership: Lycom Communications Inc. (MSO).

GILBERT—Colane Cable TV Inc. Now served by OMAR, WV [WV0191]. ICA: WV0075.

GILBOA—Shentel, 106 S Main St, Edinburg, VA 22824. Phone: 540-984-5224. Web Site: http://www.shentel.net. Also serves Poe. ICA: WV0268.
TV Market Ranking: 36 (GILBOA, Poe). Franchise award date: N.A. Franchise expiration date: April 13, 2013. Began: N.A.
Channel capacity: N.A. Channels available but not in use: N.A.
Basic Service
Subscribers: N.A.
Programming (received off-air): WCHS-TV (ABC) Charleston; WOAY-TV (ABC) Oak Hill; WOWK-TV (CBS) Huntington; WSAZ-TV (MNT, NBC) Huntington; WSWP-TV (PBS) Grandview; WVAH-TV (FOX) Charleston; WVVA (CW, NBC) Bluefield.
Programming (via satellite): A&E Networks; ABC Family Channel; CNN; Country Music TV; C-SPAN; Discovery Channel; ESPN; Headline News; Lifetime; QVC; Spike TV; TBS Superstation; USA Network; WGN America.
Pay Service 1
Pay Units: N.A.
Programming (via satellite): HBO.
Video-On-Demand: No
Pay-Per-View
iN DEMAND (delivered digitally); Hot Choice (delivered digitally); Playboy TV (delivered digitally); Fresh (delivered digitally); Shorteez (delivered digitally).
Internet Service
Operational: No.
Telephone Service
None
General Manager: Robert Harold. Chief Technician: Steve Adkins.
Ownership: Shenandoah Telecommunications Inc. (MSO).

GLEN DALE—Comcast Cable. Now served by WHEELING, WV [WV0004]. ICA: WV0223.

GLENHAYES—Formerly served by Lycom Communications. No longer in operation. ICA: WV0139.

GLENVILLE—Rapid Cable. Now served by WESTON, WV [WV0034]. ICA: WV0088.

GOLDTOWN—Econoco Inc., Rte 61, PO Box 147, Kincaid, WV 25119-0147. Phone: 304-469-2817. Also serves Kenna. ICA: WV0184.
TV Market Ranking: 36 (GOLDTOWN, Kenna). Franchise award date: N.A. Franchise expiration date: N.A. Began: June 1, 1989.
Channel capacity: 36 (not 2-way capable). Channels available but not in use: N.A.
Basic Service
Subscribers: 214.
Programming (received off-air): WCHS-TV (ABC) Charleston; WOAY-TV (ABC) Oak Hill; WOWK-TV (CBS) Huntington; WPBY-TV (PBS) Huntington; WSAZ-TV (MNT, NBC) Huntington; WVAH-TV (FOX) Charleston.
Programming (via satellite): A&E Networks; ABC Family Channel; Animal Planet; Cartoon Network; CNN; Country Music TV; Discovery Channel; ESPN; ESPN 2; Fox Sports South; FX; Headline News; HGTV; ION Television; Lifetime; QVC; Spike TV; Syfy; TBS Superstation; The Learning Channel; Travel Channel; Trinity Broadcasting Network; Turner Network TV; USA Network; WGN America.
Fee: $25.00 installation; $25.99 monthly.
Pay Service 1
Pay Units: N.A.
Programming (via satellite): Showtime.
Fee: $15.00 installation; $10.00 monthly.
Video-On-Demand: No
Internet Service
Operational: No.
Telephone Service
None
Miles of Plant: 25.0 (coaxial); None (fiber optic).
Manager: Sheila Bills. Chief Technician: Eslie Bills.
Ownership: Econoco Inc. (MSO).

GRAFTON—Comcast Cable. Now served by MORGANTOWN, WV [WV0198]. ICA: WV0028.

GRANT TOWN—Atlantic Broadband, 120 Southmont Blvd, Johnstown, PA 15905. Phones: 888-536-9600; 814-539-8971. Fax: 814-535-7749. E-mail: info@atlanticbb.com. Web Site: http://www.atlanticbb.com. Also serves Baxter & Fairview. ICA: WV0083.
TV Market Ranking: Below 100 (Baxter, Fairview, GRANT TOWN). Franchise award date: N.A. Franchise expiration date: N.A. Began: January 1, 1968.
Channel capacity: 21 (not 2-way capable). Channels available but not in use: N.A.
Basic Service
Subscribers: 925.
Programming (received off-air): KDKA-TV (CBS) Pittsburgh; WBOY-TV (NBC) Clarksburg; WDTV (CBS) Weston; WNPB-TV (PBS) Morgantown; WPGH-TV (FOX) Pittsburgh; WPXI (IND, NBC) Pittsburgh; WTAE-TV (ABC) Pittsburgh; WVFX (CW, FOX) Clarksburg; allband FM.
Programming (via satellite): C-SPAN; QVC.
Fee: $25.00 installation; $17.16 monthly.
Expanded Basic Service 1
Subscribers: N.A.
Programming (via satellite): A&E Networks; ABC Family Channel; AMC; Animal Planet; Cartoon Network; CNBC; CNN; Comedy Central; Country Music TV; Discovery Channel; Discovery Health Channel; Disney Channel; E! Entertainment Television; ESPN; ESPN 2; Food Network; Fox News Channel; FX; GSN; Hallmark Channel; Headline News; HGTV; History Channel; Lifetime; MSNBC; MTV; National Geographic Channel; Nickelodeon; Oxygen; Root Sports Pittsburgh; Spike TV; Syfy; TBS Superstation; The Learning Channel; The Weather Channel; Trinity Broadcasting Network; truTV; Turner Network TV; TV Guide; TV Land; USA Network; VH1.
Fee: $30.12 monthly.
Digital Basic Service
Subscribers: N.A.
Programming (via satellite): BBC America; Bio; Bloomberg Television; CMT Pure Country; Cooking Channel; Discovery Fit & Health; Discovery Kids Channel; DMX Music; Encore (multiplexed); ESPN Classic Sports; ESPNews; Fuse; G4; Golf Channel; Halogen Network; History Channel International; ID Investigation Discovery; Independent Film Channel; Lifetime Movie Network; Military Channel; MTV2; Nick Jr.; NickToons TV; Outdoor Channel; Planet Green; Science; SoapNet; Speed; Starz (multiplexed); Style Network; TeenNick; Toon Disney; Trinity Broadcasting Network; Turner Classic Movies; VH1 Classic.
Fee: $21.90 monthly.
Digital Pay Service 1
Pay Units: N.A.
Programming (via satellite): Cinemax (multiplexed); HBO (multiplexed); Showtime (multiplexed); The Movie Channel (multiplexed).
Fee: $15.95 monthly (HBO, Cinemax or Showtime & TMC).
Video-On-Demand: No
Pay-Per-View
iN DEMAND (delivered digitally); Hot Choice (delivered digitally); Playboy TV (delivered digitally); Fresh (delivered digitally); Shorteez (delivered digitally).
Internet Service
Operational: No.
Telephone Service
None
Miles of Plant: 35.0 (coaxial); None (fiber optic).
Vice President: David Dane. General Manager: Mike Papasergi. Technical Operations Director: Charles Sorchilla. Marketing & Customer Service Director: Dara Leslie. Marketing Manager: Natalie Kurchak.
Ownership: Atlantic Broadband (MSO).

GRANTSVILLE—Shentel, 106 S Main St, Edinburg, VA 22824. Phone: 540-984-5224. Web Site: http://www.shentel.net. Also serves Calhoun County & Mount Zion. ICA: WV0099.

TV Market Ranking: Below 100 (Calhoun County (portions), GRANTSVILLE); Outside TV Markets (Calhoun County (portions), Mount Zion). Franchise award date: N.A. Franchise expiration date: N.A. Began: January 1, 1971.
Channel capacity: N.A. Channels available but not in use: N.A.

Basic Service
Subscribers: 495.
Programming (received off-air): WBOY-TV (NBC) Clarksburg; WCHS-TV (ABC) Charleston; WDTV (CBS) Weston; WOWK-TV (CBS) Huntington; WSWP-TV (PBS) Grandview; WTAP-TV (FOX, MNT, NBC) Parkersburg; WVAH-TV (FOX) Charleston.
Programming (via satellite): QVC; Trinity Broadcasting Network; TV Guide Network; WGN America.
Fee: $29.95 installation; $19.95 monthly.

Expanded Basic Service 1
Subscribers: N.A.
Programming (via satellite): A&E Networks; ABC Family Channel; AMC; Animal Planet; Bravo!; Cartoon Network; CNBC; CNN; Comedy Central; Country Music TV; C-SPAN; Discovery Channel; Disney Channel; E! Entertainment Television; ESPN; ESPN 2; Fox News Channel; FX; G4; Golf Channel; Headline News; HGTV; History Channel; Lifetime; MSNBC; MTV; Nickelodeon; Oxygen; Root Sports Pittsburgh; Speed; Spike TV; Syfy; TBS Superstation; The Learning Channel; The Weather Channel; Turner Classic Movies; Turner Network TV; TV Land; USA Network; VH1.

Digital Basic Service
Subscribers: N.A.
Programming (via satellite): BBC America; Bio; Bloomberg Television; Discovery Fit & Health; DMX Music; ESPN Classic Sports; ESPNews; Fox Movie Channel; Fox Sports Net (multiplexed); Fuse; GAS; GSN; History Channel International; Independent Film Channel; Lifetime Movie Network; MTV Networks Digital Suite; Nick Jr.; Nick Too; NickToons TV; Science Television; SoapNet; Sundance Channel; Toon Disney; WE tv.

Digital Pay Service 1
Pay Units: N.A.
Programming (via satellite): Cinemax (multiplexed); Encore; Flix; HBO; Showtime (multiplexed); Starz (multiplexed); The Movie Channel.

Video-On-Demand: No

Pay-Per-View
iN DEMAND (delivered digitally); Pleasure (delivered digitally); Fresh (delivered digitally); Shorteez (delivered digitally); Playboy TV (delivered digitally).

Internet Service
Operational: No.

Telephone Service
None

Miles of Plant: 26.0 (coaxial); None (fiber optic).
General Manager: Robert Harold. Chief Technician: Steve Adkins.
Ownership: Shenandoah Telecommunications Inc. (MSO).

GRAYSVILLE—Windjammer Cable, 8500 W 110th St, Ste 600, Overland Park, KS 66210. Phone: 888-495-2881. Fax: 913-563-5454. Web Site: http://www.windjammercable.com. Also serves Marshall County (unincorporated areas). ICA: WV0185.
TV Market Ranking: 90 (GRAYSVILLE, Marshall County (unincorporated areas)). Franchise award date: N.A. Franchise expiration date: N.A. Began: January 1, 1987.
Channel capacity: 24 (not 2-way capable). Channels available but not in use: N.A.

Basic Service
Subscribers: 68.
Programming (received off-air): KDKA-TV (CBS) Pittsburgh; WNPB-TV (PBS) Morgantown; WOUC-TV (PBS) Cambridge; WPGH-TV (FOX) Pittsburgh; WPMY (MNT) Pittsburgh; WPXI (IND, NBC) Pittsburgh; WTAE-TV (ABC) Pittsburgh; WTOV-TV (IND, NBC) Steubenville; WTRF-TV (CBS) Wheeling.
Programming (via satellite): CNN; Discovery Channel; ESPN; Spike TV; TBS Superstation; USA Network.
Fee: $39.95 installation; $25.83 monthly; $.73 converter.

Pay Service 1
Pay Units: 16.
Programming (via satellite): HBO.
Fee: $16.95 monthly (each).

Video-On-Demand: No

Internet Service
Operational: No.

Telephone Service
None

Miles of Plant: 5.0 (coaxial); None (fiber optic).
General Manager: Timothy Evard. Operations Director: Belinda Graham. Engineering Director: Mike Earehart. Finance & Accounting Director: Cindy Johnson.
Ownership: Windjammer Communications LLC (MSO).

GREEN ACRES—Formerly served by Almega Cable. No longer in operation. ICA: WV0166.

HAMLIN—Armstrong Cable Services, 311 Main St, Hamlin, WV 25523-1413. Phone: 304-824-5114. Fax: 304-824-7711. E-mail: info@zoominternet.net. Web Site: http://cable.armstrongonewire.com. Also serves Pleasant View (Lincoln County) & West Hamlin. ICA: WV0047.
TV Market Ranking: 36 (HAMLIN, Pleasant View (Lincoln County), West Hamlin). Franchise award date: December 2, 1968. Franchise expiration date: N.A. Began: January 1, 1971.
Channel capacity: N.A. Channels available but not in use: N.A.

Digital Basic Service
Subscribers: 326.
Programming (via satellite): A&E Networks; ABC Family Channel; AMC; Animal Planet; Bravo; Cartoon Network; CNBC; CNN; Comedy Central; Country Music TV; C-SPAN; Discovery Channel; Disney Channel; E! Entertainment Television; ESPN; ESPN 2; ESPN Classic Sports; Eternal Word TV Network; Food Network; Fox News Channel; Fox Sports Net Ohio; FX; Headline News; HGTV; History Channel; INSP; Lifetime; MSNBC; MTV; Music Choice; Nickelodeon; NickToons TV; QVC; Root Sports Pittsburgh; ShopNBC; Spike TV; Syfy; TBS Superstation; The Learning Channel; The Weather Channel; Travel Channel; truTV; Turner Classic Movies; Turner Network TV; TV Guide Network; TV Land; USA Network; VH1.
Fee: $35.00 installation; $51.40 monthly.

Digital Expanded Basic Service
Subscribers: N.A.
Programming (via satellite): AmericanLife TV Network; BBC America; Bio; Bloomberg Television; Boomerang; Chiller; cloo; CMT Pure Country; Cooking Channel; Discovery Fit & Health; Discovery Health Channel; Discovery Kids Channel; DIY Network; ESPN Classic Sports; ESPNews; G4; Golf Channel; Great American Country; GSN; Hallmark Channel; Hallmark Movie Channel; History Channel International; HRTV; ID Investigation Discovery; Jewelry Television; Lifetime Movie Network; Military Channel; MTV Hits; MTV Jams; MTV2; mun2 television; National Geographic Channel; NFL Network; NHL Network; Nick Jr.; Nick Too; Outdoor Channel; Oxygen; PBS Kids Sprout; Pentagon Channel; Planet Green; RFD-TV; Science; SoapNet; Speed; TeenNick; Tennis Channel; Toon Disney; Tr3s; Versus; VH1 Classic; VH1 Soul; WE tv.
Fee: $12.00 monthly.

Digital Expanded Basic Service 2
Subscribers: N.A.
Programming (received off-air): WOWK-TV (CBS) Huntington; WSAZ-TV (MNT, NBC) Huntington.
Programming (via satellite): A&E HD; Animal Planet HD; Bravo HD; CNN HD; Discovery Channel HD; Disney Channel HD; ESPN 2 HD; ESPN HD; Food Network HD; Fox News HD; FX HD; Golf Channel HD; Hallmark Movie Channel HD; HD Theater; HDNet; HDNet Movies; HGTV HD; History Channel HD; MGM HD; National Geographic Channel HD Network; NFL Network HD; NHL Network HD; Outdoor Channel 2 HD; Palladia; PBS HD; QVC HD; Science HD; Syfy HD; TBS in HD; The Weather Channel HD; TLC HD; Turner Network TV HD; Universal HD; USA Network HD; Versus HD; WealthTV HD.
Fee: $9.00 monthly.

Digital Pay Service 1
Pay Units: N.A.
Programming (via satellite): Cinemax HD; Encore (multiplexed); Flix; HBO (multiplexed); HBO HD; RAI USA; Showtime (multiplexed); Showtime HD; Starz (multiplexed); Starz HDTV; The Movie Channel (multiplexed); TV5 USA.
Fee: $13.95 monthly (HBO, Cinemax, Showtime/TMC/Flix, or Starz/Encore).

Video-On-Demand: Yes

Pay-Per-View
ESPN Now (delivered digitally); Hot Choice (delivered digitally); iN DEMAND (delivered digitally); ESPN Sports, NHL/MLB (delivered digitally); ESPN Extra (delivered digitally).

Internet Service
Operational: Yes. Began: March 1, 2002.
Subscribers: 716.
Broadband Service: Armstrong Zoom.
Fee: $26.95-$39.95 monthly.

Telephone Service
Analog: Not Operational
Digital: Operational
Fee: $49.95 monthly

Miles of Plant: 70.0 (coaxial); None (fiber optic).
Vice President, Marketing: Jud D. Stewart. General Manager: Todd L. Barrett. Chief Technician: Russ Mutter.
Ownership: Armstrong Group of Companies (MSO).

HAMPDEN—Colane Cable TV Inc. Now served by OMAR, WV [WV0191]. ICA: WV0232.

HANOVER—Colane Cable TV Inc., PO Box 610, Omar, WV 25638. Phone: 304-946-2871. Fax: 304-946-4091. Also serves Wyoming County. ICA: WV0070.
TV Market Ranking: Below 100 (HANOVER, Wyoming County (portions)); Outside TV Markets (Wyoming County (portions)). Franchise award date: October 8, 1991. Franchise expiration date: October 8, 2006. Began: July 1, 1982.
Channel capacity: N.A. Channels available but not in use: N.A.

Basic Service
Subscribers: N.A. Included in Omar
Programming (received off-air): WCHS-TV (ABC) Charleston; WOAY-TV (ABC) Oak Hill; WOWK-TV (CBS) Huntington; WPBY-TV (PBS) Huntington; WSAZ-TV (MNT, NBC) Huntington; WSWP-TV (PBS) Grandview; WVAH-TV (FOX) Charleston; WVVA (CW, NBC) Bluefield.
Programming (via satellite): ABC Family Channel; CNN; Country Music TV; Discovery Channel; Disney Channel; ESPN; Headline News; Lifetime; Nickelodeon; Spike TV; TBS Superstation; Turner Network TV; USA Network; WGN America.
Fee: $48.18 installation; $25.00 monthly.

Pay Service 1
Pay Units: N.A. Included in Omar
Programming (via satellite): HBO; Showtime.
Fee: $25.00 installation.

Internet Service
Operational: No.

Telephone Service
None

Miles of plant included in Omar
General Manager: Gary Bowen. Office Manager: Rebecca Edwards.
Ownership: Colane Cable TV Inc. (MSO).

HARMAN—Formerly served by Harman Cable Corp. No longer in operation. ICA: WV0234.

HARRISVILLE—Rapid Cable. Now served by WESTON, WV [WV0034]. ICA: WV0102.

HARTS—Shentel, 106 S Main St, Edinburg, VA 22824. Phone: 540-984-5224. Web Site: http://www.shentel.net. Also serves Big Creek, Branchland, Chapmanville, Midkiff & Ranger. ICA: WV0270.
TV Market Ranking: 36 (Big Creek, Branchland, Chapmanville, HARTS, Midkiff, Ranger).
Channel capacity: N.A. Channels available but not in use: N.A.

Basic Service
Subscribers: N.A.
Programming (received off-air): WCHS-TV (ABC) Charleston; WKPI-TV (PBS) Pikeville; WLPX-TV (ION) Charleston; WOWK-TV (CBS) Huntington; WPBY-TV (PBS) Huntington; WQCW (CW) Portsmouth; WSAZ-TV (MNT, NBC) Huntington; WTSF (IND) Ashland; WVAH-TV (FOX) Charleston.
Programming (via satellite): C-SPAN; TBS Superstation; Trinity Broadcasting Network; TV Guide Network; WGN America.
Fee: $29.95 installation; $19.95 monthly.

Expanded Basic Service 1
Subscribers: N.A.
Programming (via satellite): A&E Networks; ABC Family Channel; AMC; Animal Planet; Cartoon Network; CNBC; CNN; Comedy Central; Country Music TV; Discovery Channel; Disney Channel; E! Entertainment Television; ESPN; ESPN 2; Fox News Channel; FX; G4; Headline News; HGTV; History Channel; Lifetime; MTV; Nickelodeon; Oxygen; Speed; Spike TV; Syfy; The Learning Channel; The Weather Channel; Turner Classic Movies; Turner Network TV; TV Land; USA Network; VH1.
Fee: $15.86 monthly.

Digital Basic Service
Subscribers: N.A.
Programming (via satellite): BBC America; Bio; Bloomberg Television; Discovery Digital Networks (multiplexed); DMX Music; ESPN Classic Sports; ESPNews; Fox Movie Channel; Fox Soccer; Fuse; GAS; GSN; History Channel International; Independent Film Channel; Lifetime Movie Network; MTV Networks Digital Suite; Nick Jr.; NickToons TV; SoapNet; Style Network; Sundance Channel; Toon Disney; WE tv.
Digital Pay Service 1
Pay Units: N.A.
Programming (via satellite): Cinemax (multiplexed); Encore (multiplexed); Flix; HBO (multiplexed); Showtime (multiplexed); Starz (multiplexed); The Movie Channel (multiplexed).
Pay-Per-View
iN DEMAND (delivered digitally); Fresh (delivered digitally); Shorteez (delivered digitally); Playboy TV (delivered digitally).
Internet Service
Operational: No.
Telephone Service
None
General Manager: Robert Harold. Chief Technician: Steve Adkins.
Ownership: Shenandoah Telecommunications Inc. (MSO).

HERNDON—Shentel, 99 Howard St, Welch, WV 24801. Phones: 540-984-5224; 800-743-6835. Web Site: http://www.shentel.net. Also serves Covel & Garwood. ICA: WV0273.
TV Market Ranking: Below 100 (Covel, Garwood, HERNDON).
Channel capacity: N.A. Channels available but not in use: N.A.
Basic Service
Subscribers: 73.
Programming (received off-air): WCHS-TV (ABC) Charleston; WOAY-TV (ABC) Oak Hill; WOWK-TV (CBS) Huntington; WSAZ-TV (MNT, NBC) Huntington; WSWP-TV (PBS) Grandview; WVAH-TV (FOX) Charleston; WVVA (CW, NBC) Bluefield.
Programming (via satellite): ABC Family Channel; CNN; Discovery Channel; ESPN; Great American Country; MTV; Nickelodeon; QVC; Spike TV; TBS Superstation; The Weather Channel; USA Network; WGN America.
Fee: $39.95 installation; $24.95 monthly.
Pay Service 1
Pay Units: N.A.
Programming (via satellite): HBO.
Fee: $11.95 monthly.
Internet Service
Operational: No.
Telephone Service
None
President: Christopher French. Vice President, Customer Service: David Ferguson. Marketing Manager: Chris Ranson.
Ownership: Shenandoah Telecommunications Inc. (MSO).

HEWETT—Colane Cable TV, PO Box 610, Omar, WV 25638. Phone: 304-946-2871. Fax: 304-946-4091. Also serves Jeffrey, Lake & Low Gap. ICA: WV0266.
TV Market Ranking: 36 (HEWETT, Jeffrey, Lake, Low Gap).
Channel capacity: 39 (not 2-way capable). Channels available but not in use: N.A.
Basic Service
Subscribers: 422.
Programming (received off-air): WCHS-TV (ABC) Charleston; WLPX-TV (ION) Charleston; WOAY-TV (ABC) Oak Hill; WOWK-TV (CBS) Huntington; WPBY-TV (PBS) Huntington; WSAZ-TV (MNT, NBC) Huntington; WSWP-TV (PBS) Grandview; WVAH-TV (FOX) Charleston; WVVA (CW, NBC) Bluefield.
Programming (via satellite): TBS Superstation; WGN America.
Fee: $38.34 installation; $22.50 monthly.
Expanded Basic Service 1
Subscribers: 462.
Programming (via satellite): A&E Networks; ABC Family Channel; Cartoon Network; CNN; Comedy Central; Country Music TV; C-SPAN; Discovery Channel; Disney Channel; ESPN; ESPN 2; FX; Headline News; INSP; Lifetime; MTV; Nickelodeon; QVC; Spike TV; Syfy; The Weather Channel; Trinity Broadcasting Network; truTV; Turner Classic Movies; Turner Network TV; TV Land; USA Network; VH1.
Fee: $17.45 monthly.
Pay Service 1
Pay Units: 27.
Programming (via satellite): HBO.
Fee: $11.95 monthly.
Pay Service 2
Pay Units: 15.
Programming (via satellite): Cinemax.
Fee: $11.95 monthly.
Internet Service
Operational: Yes.
Telephone Service
None
Miles of Plant: 26.0 (coaxial); None (fiber optic).
Manager: Gary Bowen. Office Manager: Rebecca Edwards.
Ownership: Colane Cable TV Inc. (MSO).

HINTON—Charter Communications. Now served by BECKLEY, WV [WV0005]. ICA: WV0059.

HUNTERSVILLE—Milestone Communications LP, PO Box 7000, Monument, CO 80132-7000. Phone: 304-799-6229. Also serves Minehaha Springs. ICA: WV0262.
TV Market Ranking: Below 100 (HUNTERSVILLE, Minehaha Springs). Franchise award date: N.A. Franchise expiration date: December 1, 2013. Began: N.A.
Channel capacity: 29 (not 2-way capable). Channels available but not in use: N.A.
Basic Service
Subscribers: 30.
Programming (received off-air): WDBJ (CBS, MNT) Roanoke; WSET-TV (ABC) Lynchburg; WSLS-TV (NBC) Roanoke; WVVA (CW, NBC) Bluefield.
Programming (via satellite): ABC Family Channel; CNN; ESPN; Spike TV; TBS Superstation; Trinity Broadcasting Network; Turner Network TV; WGN America.
Fee: $50.00 installation; $22.95 monthly.
Internet Service
Operational: No.
Telephone Service
None
Miles of Plant: 6.0 (coaxial); None (fiber optic).
Owner: Barbara Mock.
Ownership: Milestone Communications LP (MSO).

HUNTINGTON—Comcast Cable, 51 W 6th Ave, Huntington, WV 25701-1715. Phone: 304-522-0912. Fax: 304-523-5493. Web Site: http://www.comcast.com. Also serves Barboursville, East Pea Ridge, Guyan Estates, Lesage, Wayne County (northwestern portion) & West Pea Ridge. ICA: WV0002.

TV Market Ranking: 36 (Barboursville, East Pea Ridge, Guyan Estates, HUNTINGTON, Lesage, Wayne County (northwestern portion) (portions), West Pea Ridge); Below 100 (Wayne County (northwestern portion) (portions)). Franchise award date: N.A. Franchise expiration date: N.A. Began: N.A.
Channel capacity: N.A. Channels available but not in use: N.A.
Basic Service
Subscribers: 21,679.
Programming (received off-air): WCHS-TV (ABC) Charleston; WKAS (PBS) Ashland; WLPX-TV (ION) Charleston; WOWK-TV (CBS) Huntington; WPBY-TV (PBS) Huntington; WQCW (CW) Portsmouth; WSAZ-TV (MNT, NBC) Huntington; WTSF (IND) Ashland; WVAH-TV (FOX) Charleston; allband FM.
Programming (via satellite): ABC Family Channel; C-SPAN; C-SPAN 2; Eternal Word TV Network; Gospel Music TV; INSP; TBS Superstation; The Weather Channel; TV Guide Network; WGN America.
Fee: $50.00 installation; $1.38 converter.
Expanded Basic Service 1
Subscribers: N.A.
Programming (via satellite): A&E Networks; AMC; Animal Planet; BET Networks; Bio; Bravo; Cartoon Network; CNBC; CNN; Comedy Central; Country Music TV; Discovery Channel; Disney Channel; E! Entertainment Television; ESPN; ESPN 2; Food Network; Fox News Channel; Fox Sports Net Ohio; Golf Channel; Great American Country; Hallmark Channel; Headline News; HGTV; History Channel; Lifetime; MSNBC; MTV; National Geographic Channel; Nickelodeon; Outdoor Channel; Oxygen; Product Information Network; QVC; Root Sports Pittsburgh; ShopNBC; Speed; Spike TV; Syfy; The Learning Channel; Toon Disney; Travel Channel; truTV; Turner Network TV; TV Land; USA Network; VH1; WE tv.
Fee: $50.00 installation; $47.95 monthly.
Digital Basic Service
Subscribers: N.A.
Programming (via satellite): AmericanLife TV Network; BBC America; Bloomberg Television; Discovery Fit & Health; DIY Network; ESPN Classic Sports; ESPNews; Fox Movie Channel; Fox Sports World; Fuse; G4; GSN; History Channel International; Music Choice; SoapNet; Trinity Broadcasting Network; Turner Classic Movies; Versus.
Fee: $11.00 monthly.
Digital Expanded Basic Service
Subscribers: N.A.
Programming (via satellite): Nick Jr.; NickToons TV; Style Network; VH1 Classic; VH1 Country.
Digital Pay Service 1
Pay Units: 9,439.
Programming (via satellite): ART America; Canales N; CCTV-4; Cinemax (multiplexed); Encore (multiplexed); Filipino Channel; Flix; HBO (multiplexed); RAI USA; Showtime (multiplexed); Starz (multiplexed); Sundance Channel; The Movie Channel (multiplexed); TV Asia; TV Japan; TV5, La Television International; Zee TV USA; Zhong Tian Channel.
Fee: $15.95 monthly (each).
Video-On-Demand: Yes
Pay-Per-View
Urban Xtra (delivered digitally); Hot Choice (delivered digitally); Fresh (delivered digitally); Playboy TV (delivered digitally); HITS (delivered digitally).
Internet Service
Operational: Yes.
Broadband Service: Comcast High Speed Internet.
Fee: $42.95 monthly; $9.95 modem lease; $264.99 modem purchase.
Telephone Service
None
Miles of Plant: 341.0 (coaxial); None (fiber optic).
General Manager: Tim Hagan. Office Manager: Sandy Davis.
Ownership: Comcast Cable Communications Inc. (MSO).

HUTCHINSON—Formerly served by Adelphia Communications. Now served by MORGANTOWN, WV [WV0198]. ICA: WV0094.

IAEGER—Shentel, 99 Howard St, Welch, WV 24801. Phones: 540-984-5224; 800-743-6835. Web Site: http://www.shentel.net. Also serves Avondale, Beartown, Big Sandy, Bradshaw, Hensley, Jolo, McDowell County (portions), Raysal & Roderfield. ICA: WV0039.
TV Market Ranking: Below 100 (Avondale, Beartown, Big Sandy, Bradshaw, Hensley, IAEGER, Jolo, McDowell County (portions), Raysal, Roderfield). Franchise award date: N.A. Franchise expiration date: N.A. Began: March 1, 1953.
Channel capacity: 34 (not 2-way capable). Channels available but not in use: N.A.
Basic Service
Subscribers: 1,578.
Programming (received off-air): WCHS-TV (ABC) Charleston; WLFB (IND) Bluefield; WOAY-TV (ABC) Oak Hill; WSWP-TV (PBS) Grandview; WVNS-TV (CBS) Lewisburg; WVVA (CW, NBC) Bluefield.
Programming (via satellite): INSP; QVC; Trinity Broadcasting Network; WGN America.
Fee: $39.95 installation; $20.95 monthly; $2.20 converter; $10.00 additional installation.
Expanded Basic Service 1
Subscribers: N.A.
Programming (via satellite): A&E Networks; ABC Family Channel; CNBC; CNN; Country Music TV; Discovery Channel; Disney Channel; ESPN; ESPN 2; FX; Lifetime; MTV; Nickelodeon; Spike TV; Syfy; TBS Superstation; The Weather Channel; Turner Network TV; TV Land; USA Network.
Fee: $17.00 monthly.
Digital Basic Service
Subscribers: N.A.
Programming (via satellite): BBC America; Bio; Bloomberg Television; Discovery Health Channel; Discovery Kids Channel; DMX Music; ESPN Classic Sports; ESPNews; Fox Movie Channel; Fox Soc-

cer; Fuse; G4; Golf Channel; GSN; History Channel International; ID Investigation Discovery; Independent Film Channel; Lifetime Movie Network; Military Channel; National Geographic Channel; Nick Jr.; Outdoor Channel; Planet Green; Science; Speed; Style Network; TeenNick; Toon Disney; Turner Classic Movies; Versus; WE tv.
Fee: $14.00 monthly.

Pay Service 1
Pay Units: N.A.
Programming (via satellite): HBO; Showtime.

Digital Pay Service 1
Pay Units: N.A.
Programming (via satellite): Cinemax (multiplexed); Encore (multiplexed); Flix; HBO (multiplexed); Showtime (multiplexed); Starz (multiplexed); The Movie Channel (multiplexed).
Fee: $11.95 monthly (Cinemax or Starz/Encore), $12.95 monthly (HBO or Showtime/TMC/Flix).

Video-On-Demand: No

Pay-Per-View
iN DEMAND (delivered digitally); Playboy TV (delivered digitally); Fresh (delivered digitally).

Internet Service
Operational: No.

Telephone Service
None

Miles of Plant: 84.0 (coaxial); None (fiber optic).
President: Christopher French. Vice President, Customer Service: David Ferguson. General Manager: Anthony Barlage. Marketing Manager: Chris Ranson.
Ownership: Shenandoah Telecommunications Inc. (MSO).

INWOOD—Formerly served by Adelphia Communications. Now served by SHEPHERDSTOWN, WV [WV0016]. ICA: WV0021.

JENKINJONES—Formerly served by Obey's TV Cable. No longer in operation. ICA: WV0226.

KERMIT—Suddenlink Communications, County Rt 5, PO Box 1339, Mount Gay, WV 25637-1339. Phones: 304-752-4316; 304-757-8001. Fax: 304-752-5718. Web Site: http://www.suddenlink.com. Also serves Aflex, Beauty, Burnwell, Caney, Coldwater Creek, Davella, Debord, Elk Creek, Fairview, Goody, Hatfield, Hode, Huddy, Inez, Johnson County (portions), Leckieville, Lovely, McAndrews, Oppy, Paintsville, Pike County (unincorporated areas), Pilgrim, Pond Creek, Riverfront, Sharondale, Slater's Branch, South Williamson, Staton, Stone, Toler, Tomahawk, Turkey Creek, Warfield & Wolf Creek, KY; Blair, Boone County, Borderland, Chapmanville, Chattaroy, Crum, Cyclone, East Kermit, East Lovely, Grey Eagle, Lenore, Lobata, Logan, Logan County, Man, Marrowbone, Mitchell Heights, Myrtle, Naugatuck, Nolan, Ottawa, Rawl, Sharples-Clothier, Sprigg, Tripp, West Logan, Williamson, Wyoming County (portions) & Yolyn, WV. ICA: WV0038.
TV Market Ranking: 36 (Boone County (portions), Logan County (portions), Ottawa, Sharples-Clothier); Below 100 (Aflex, Borderland, Borderland, Burnwell, Chattaroy, Cyclone, Fairview, Goody, Huddy, Johnson County (portions), Leckieville, Lobata, Man, McAndrews, Pike County (unincorporated areas), Pond Creek, Rawl, Sharondale, Slater's Branch, South Williamson, Sprigg, Stone, Toler, Turkey Creek, Turkey Creek, Williamson, Wyoming County (portions), Boone County (portions), Logan County (portions)); Outside TV Markets (Beauty, Blair, Caney, Chapmanville, Coldwater Creek, Crum, Davella, Debord, East Kermit, East Lovely, Elk Creek, Grey Eagle, Hatfield, Hode, Inez, Johnson County (portions), KERMIT, Lenore, Lovely, Marrowbone, Mitchell Heights, Myrtle, Naugatuck, Nolan, Oppy, Paintsville, Pilgrim, Riverfront, Staton, Tomahawk, Tripp, Tripp, Warfield, West Logan, Wolf Creek, Wyoming County (portions), Yolyn, Logan County (portions)). Franchise award date: November 1, 1985. Franchise expiration date: N.A. Began: N.A.
Channel capacity: 37 (operating 2-way). Channels available but not in use: N.A.

Basic Service
Subscribers: 20,843.
Programming (received off-air): WCHS-TV (ABC) Charleston; WKPI-TV (PBS) Pikeville; WLPX-TV (ION) Charleston; WOWK-TV (CBS) Huntington; WPBY-TV (PBS) Huntington; WQCW (CW) Portsmouth; WSAZ-TV (MNT, NBC) Huntington; WTSF (IND) Ashland; WVAH-TV (FOX) Charleston; WYMT-TV (CBS, CW) Hazard.
Programming (via satellite): C-SPAN; C-SPAN 2; QVC; ShopNBC; WGN America.
Fee: $61.25 installation; $14.40 monthly; $1.24 converter.

Expanded Basic Service 1
Subscribers: 8,596.
Programming (via satellite): A&E Networks; ABC Family Channel; AMC; Animal Planet; BET Networks; Bravo; Cartoon Network; CNBC; CNN; Comedy Central; Country Music TV; Discovery Channel; Disney Channel; E! Entertainment Television; ESPN; ESPN 2; ESPN Classic Sports; Food Network; Fox News Channel; FX; G4; Golf Channel; GSN; Hallmark Channel; Headline News; HGTV; History Channel; INSP; Lifetime; MSNBC; MTV; National Geographic Channel; Nickelodeon; Outdoor Channel; Oxygen; Root Sports Pittsburgh; SoapNet; Speed; Spike TV; Style Network; Syfy; TBS Superstation; The Learning Channel; The Weather Channel; Toon Disney; Travel Channel; truTV; Turner Classic Movies; Turner Network TV; TV Land; USA Network; Versus; VH1; WE tv.
Fee: $17.10 monthly.

Digital Basic Service
Subscribers: N.A.
Programming (via satellite): BBC America; Bio; Bloomberg Television; DIY Network; ESPN; ESPNews; Fox College Sports Atlantic; Fox College Sports Central; Fox College Sports Pacific; Fox Deportes; Fox Movie Channel; Fox Soccer; Fuel TV; Fuse; GAS; Great American Country; HD Theater; History Channel International; Independent Film Channel; Lifetime Movie Network; MTV Networks Digital Suite; Music Choice; NFL Network; Nick Jr.; Nick Too; NickToons TV; Sundance Channel; TVG Network.

Digital Pay Service 1
Pay Units: N.A.
Programming (via satellite): Cinemax (multiplexed); Encore (multiplexed); HBO (multiplexed); Showtime (multiplexed); Starz (multiplexed); The Movie Channel (multiplexed).

Video-On-Demand: Yes

Pay-Per-View
Playboy TV (delivered digitally); Fresh (delivered digitally); Shorteez (delivered digitally); iN DEMAND (delivered digitally); NASCAR In Car (delivered digitally); NHL Center Ice (delivered digitally); MLB Extra Innings (delivered digitally).

Internet Service
Operational: Yes.
Broadband Service: Suddenlink High Speed Internet.
Fee: $49.95 installation; $29.99 monthly.

Telephone Service
Analog: Not Operational
Digital: Planned

Miles of Plant: 1,500.0 (coaxial); None (fiber optic).
Vice President, Operations: David Bach. General Manager: Jack Ozminkowski. Chief Technician: Joe Davis. Marketing Director: Stan Howell. Office Supervisor: Donna Vance.
Ownership: Cequel Communications LLC (MSO).

KEYSER—Comcast Cable, 15 Summit Park Dr, Pittsburgh, PA 15275. Phones: 412-747-6400; 304-788-2939 (Keyser office). Fax: 412-747-6401. Web Site: http://www.comcast.com. Also serves Allegany County (portions), Barton, Bloomington, Frostburg, Lonaconing, Luke, McCoole, Midland, Midlothian & Westernport, MD; Burlington, Mineral County, New Creek & Piedmont, WV. ICA: WV0020.
TV Market Ranking: Below 100 (Burlington); Outside TV Markets (Allegany County (portions), Barton, Bloomington, Frostburg, KEYSER, Lonaconing, Luke, McCoole, Midland, Midlothian, Mineral County, New Creek, Piedmont, Westernport). Franchise award date: October 1, 1965. Franchise expiration date: N.A. Began: April 1, 1952.
Channel capacity: 78 (operating 2-way). Channels available but not in use: N.A.

Basic Service
Subscribers: N.A.
Programming (received off-air): KDKA-TV (CBS) Pittsburgh; WJAC-TV (NBC) Johnstown; WJAL (IND) Hagerstown; WWPB (PBS) Hagerstown; allband FM.
Programming (via microwave): WDCA (MNT) Washington; WDCW (CW) Washington; WHAG-TV (NBC) Hagerstown; WJLA-TV (ABC) Washington; WJZ-TV (CBS) Baltimore; WTTG (FOX) Washington; WUSA (CBS) Washington.
Programming (via satellite): A&E Networks; ABC Family Channel; AMC; Animal Planet; BET Networks; Cartoon Network; CNBC; CNN; Comcast SportsNet Mid-Atlantic; Comedy Central; Country Music TV; C-SPAN; C-SPAN 2; Discovery Channel; Disney Channel; E! Entertainment Television; ESPN; ESPN 2; Eternal Word TV Network; Food Network; Fox News Channel; Fox Sports Net; FX; Halogen Network; Headline News; HGTV; History Channel; ION Television; Lifetime; MSNBC; MTV; Nickelodeon; Outdoor Channel; QVC; Spike TV; TBS Superstation; The Learning Channel; The Weather Channel; Travel Channel; Trinity Broadcasting Network; truTV; Turner Network TV; TV Land; USA Network; VH1; WGN America.
Programming (via translator): WNPB-TV (PBS) Morgantown.
Fee: $39.95 installation; $51.99 monthly.

Digital Basic Service
Subscribers: 955.
Programming (via satellite): BBC America; Bio; Bloomberg Television; Bravo; Country Music TV; Discovery Fit & Health; Discovery Health Channel; Discovery Kids Channel; ESPN Classic Sports; ESPNews; Fox College Sports Atlantic; Fox College Sports Central; Fox College Sports Pacific; Fox Movie Channel; Fox Soccer; Fuse; G4; GMC; Golf Channel; Great American Country; GSN; Halogen Network; History Channel; History Channel International; ID Investigation Discovery; Independent Film Channel; Lifetime Movie Network; Military Channel; MTV2; National Geographic Channel; Nick Jr.; NickToons TV; Planet Green; Science; Speed; Style Network; Syfy; TeenNick; The Word Network; Toon Disney; Turner Classic Movies; VH1 Classic; WE tv.
Fee: $10.95 monthly; $3.95 converter.

Digital Pay Service 1
Pay Units: N.A.
Programming (via satellite): Cinemax (multiplexed); Encore (multiplexed); HBO (multiplexed); Showtime (multiplexed); Starz (multiplexed); The Movie Channel (multiplexed).
Fee: $15.95 monthly (each).

Video-On-Demand: No

Pay-Per-View
iN DEMAND (delivered digitally); Playboy TV (delivered digitally); Club Jenna (delivered digitally); Fresh (delivered digitally).

Internet Service
Operational: Yes.
Broadband Service: Comcast High Speed Internet.
Fee: $42.95 monthly.

Telephone Service
None

Miles of Plant: 277.0 (coaxial); 71.0 (fiber optic). Additional miles planned: 2.0 (coaxial).
Regional Vice President: Linda Hossinger. Vice President, Technical Operations: Randy Bender. Vice President, Marketing: Donna Corning. Vice President, Public Affairs: Jody Doherty. Chief Technician: Roy Blanchard. Office Manager: Nancy Nesselrodt.
Ownership: Comcast Cable Communications Inc. (MSO).

KIMBALL—Comcast Cable. Now served by NORTHFORK, WV [WV0045]. ICA: WV0121.

KINGWOOD—Atlantic Broadband, 120 Southmont Blvd, Johnstown, PA 15905. Phones: 888-536-9600; 814-539-8971. Fax: 814-535-7749. E-mail: info@atlanticbb.com. Web Site: http://www.atlanticbb.com. Also serves Albright, Arthurdale, Bretz, Independence, Monongalia County (portions), Newburg, Preston County (portions), Reedsville & Terra Alta. ICA: WV0189.
TV Market Ranking: Below 100 (Arthurdale, Bretz, Independence, Monongalia County (portions), Newburg, Preston County (portions), Reedsville); Outside TV Markets (Albright, KINGWOOD, Monongalia County (portions), Preston County (portions), Terra Alta). Franchise award date: N.A. Franchise expiration date: N.A. Began: June 1, 1967.
Channel capacity: N.A. Channels available but not in use: N.A.

Basic Service
Subscribers: 3,104.
Programming (received off-air): KDKA-TV (CBS) Pittsburgh; WBOY-TV (NBC) Clarksburg; WDTV (CBS) Weston; WNPB-TV (PBS) Morgantown; WPGH-TV (FOX) Pittsburgh; WPMY (MNT) Pittsburgh; WPXI (IND, NBC) Pittsburgh; WTAE-TV (ABC) Pittsburgh; WVFX (CW, FOX) Clarksburg; WWCP-TV (FOX) Johnstown; allband FM.
Programming (via satellite): C-SPAN; C-SPAN 2; INSP; QVC; WGN America.
Fee: $25.00 installation; $19.38 monthly.

Expanded Basic Service 1
Subscribers: N.A.
Programming (via satellite): A&E Networks; ABC Family Channel; AMC; Animal Planet; Bravo; Cartoon Network; CNBC; CNN; Comedy Central; Country Music TV; Discovery Channel; Discovery Health Channel; Disney Channel; E! Entertainment Television; ESPN; ESPN 2; Food Network; Fox News Channel; FX; G4; Golf Channel; Hallmark Channel; Headline News; HGTV; History Channel; Lifetime; MSNBC; MTV; National Geographic Channel; Nickelodeon; Oxygen; Root Sports Pittsburgh; Speed; Spike TV; Style Network; Syfy; TBS Superstation; The Learning Channel; The Weather Channel; Travel Channel; truTV; Turner Network TV; TV Land; USA Network; VH1.
Fee: $34.61 monthly.

Digital Basic Service
Subscribers: N.A.
Programming (via satellite): A&E HD; BBC America; Bio; Bloomberg Television; Boomerang; CMT Pure Country; Discovery Kids Channel; DIY Network; Encore (multiplexed); ESPN Classic Sports; ESPN HD; ESPNews; Fuel TV; Great American Country; HD Theater; History Channel International; ID Investigation Discovery; Independent Film Channel; Lifetime Movie Network; Lifetime Real Women; Military Channel; MTV Hits; MTV Jams; MTV2; Music Choice; NFL Network; Nick Jr.; Nick Too; NickToons TV; Planet Green; Root Sports Pittsburgh; RTN; Science; SoapNet; Starz (multiplexed); Starz HDTV; Style Network; TeenNick; Toon Disney; Tr3s; Turner Network TV HD; VH1 Classic; VH1 Soul; WE tv; Weatherscan.
Fee: $18.95 monthly.

Digital Pay Service 1
Pay Units: N.A.
Programming (via satellite): Cinemax (multiplexed); Cinemax HD; Flix; HBO (multiplexed); HBO HD; Showtime (multiplexed); The Movie Channel (multiplexed).
Fee: $15.95 monthly (HBO, Cinemax or Showtime/Flix/TMC).

Video-On-Demand: No

Pay-Per-View
iN DEMAND (delivered digitally); Hot Choice (delivered digitally); Club Jenna (delivered digitally); Fresh (delivered digitally); Playboy TV (delivered digitally).

Internet Service
Operational: Yes.
Broadband Service: Atlantic Broadband High-Speed Internet.
Fee: $24.95-$57.95 monthly.

Telephone Service
Digital: Operational
Fee: $44.95 monthly

Miles of Plant: 94.0 (coaxial); None (fiber optic).
Vice President: David Dane. General Manager: Mike Papasergi. Technical Operations Director: Charles Sorchilla. Marketing & Customer Service Director: Dara Leslie. Marketing Manager: Natalie Kurchak.
Ownership: Atlantic Broadband (MSO).

LEFT HAND—Econoco Inc., Rte 61, PO Box 147, Kincaid, WV 25119-0147. Phone: 304-469-2817. Fax: 304-469-2416. Also serves Amma & Newton. ICA: WV0190.
TV Market Ranking: 36 (Amma, LEFT HAND, Newton). Franchise award date: N.A. Franchise expiration date: N.A. Began: October 1, 1989.
Channel capacity: 36 (not 2-way capable). Channels available but not in use: N.A.

Basic Service
Subscribers: 277.
Programming (received off-air): WCHS-TV (ABC) Charleston; WDTV (CBS) Weston; WOAY-TV (ABC) Oak Hill; WOWK-TV (CBS) Huntington; WSAZ-TV (MNT, NBC) Huntington; WSWP-TV (PBS) Grandview; WVAH-TV (FOX) Charleston.
Programming (via satellite): A&E Networks; ABC Family Channel; CNN; Country Music TV; ESPN; Fox Sports South; ION Television; QVC; Spike TV; TBS Superstation; Trinity Broadcasting Network; USA Network; WGN America.
Fee: $25.00 installation; $25.83 monthly.

Pay Service 1
Pay Units: N.A.
Programming (via satellite): Showtime.
Fee: $10.00 monthly.

Video-On-Demand: No

Internet Service
Operational: No.

Telephone Service
None

Miles of Plant: 58.0 (coaxial); None (fiber optic).
Manager: Sheila Bills. Chief Technician: Eslie Bills.
Ownership: Econoco Inc. (MSO).

LENORE—Charter Communications. Now served by KERMIT, WV [WV0038]. ICA: WV0050.

LEON—Vital Communications Group, PO Box 307, Belhaven, NC 27810. Phone: 252-943-3800. Also serves Arbuckle. ICA: WV0263.
TV Market Ranking: 26 (Arbuckle); 36 (LEON).
Channel capacity: 22 (not 2-way capable). Channels available but not in use: N.A.

Basic Service
Subscribers: 46.
Programming (received off-air): WCHS-TV (ABC) Charleston; WLPX-TV (ION) Charleston; WOUB-TV (PBS) Athens; WOWK-TV (CBS) Huntington; WPBY-TV (PBS) Huntington; WQCW (CW) Portsmouth; WSAZ-TV (MNT, NBC) Huntington; WVAH-TV (FOX) Charleston.
Programming (via satellite): ABC Family Channel; CNN; Discovery Channel; Disney Channel; ESPN; ESPN 2; Nickelodeon; QVC; Spike TV; TBS Superstation; Trinity Broadcasting Network; Turner Network TV; USA Network; WGN America.
Fee: $39.95 installation; $19.95 monthly; $28.69 additional installation.

Pay Service 1
Pay Units: N.A.
Programming (via satellite): HBO.
Fee: $15.00 installation; $11.95 monthly.

Internet Service
Operational: No.

Telephone Service
None

Miles of Plant: 7.0 (coaxial); None (fiber optic).
President: Jerry Stender.
Ownership: Vital Communications Group (MSO).

LEWISBURG—Charter Communications. Now served by BECKLEY, WV [WV0005]. ICA: WV0033.

LITTLE OTTER—Windjammer Cable, 8500 W 110th St, Ste 600, Overland Park, KS 66210. Phone: 888-495-2881. Fax: 913-563-5454. Web Site: http://www.windjammercable.com. ICA: WV0227.

TV Market Ranking: Below 100 (LITTLE OTTER). Franchise award date: N.A. Franchise expiration date: N.A. Began: February 15, 1979.
Channel capacity: N.A. Channels available but not in use: N.A.

Basic Service
Subscribers: 88.
Programming (received off-air): WBOY-TV (NBC) Clarksburg; WCHS-TV (ABC) Charleston; WDTV (CBS) Weston; WLPX-TV (ION) Charleston; WNPB-TV (PBS) Morgantown; WOAY-TV (ABC) Oak Hill; WQCW (CW) Portsmouth; WSAZ-TV (MNT, NBC) Huntington; WSWP-TV (PBS) Grandview; WVAH-TV (FOX) Charleston.
Programming (via satellite): A&E Networks; ABC Family Channel; AMC; Animal Planet; Cartoon Network; CNBC; CNN; Comedy Central; Country Music TV; C-SPAN; Discovery Channel; Disney Channel; E! Entertainment Television; ESPN; ESPN 2; Fox News Channel; FX; G4; Golf Channel; Halogen Network; Headline News; HGTV; History Channel; Lifetime; MTV; Nickelodeon; Oxygen; QVC; Root Sports Pittsburgh; Speed; Spike TV; TBS Superstation; The Learning Channel; The Weather Channel; Travel Channel; Turner Classic Movies; Turner Network TV; TV Land; USA Network; VH1.
Fee: $39.95 installation; $25.29 monthly.

Video-On-Demand: No

Internet Service
Operational: No.

Telephone Service
None

Miles of Plant: 3.0 (coaxial); None (fiber optic).
General Manager: Timothy Evard. Operations Director: Belinda Graham. Engineering Director: Mike Earehart. Finance & Accounting Director: Cindy Johnson.
Ownership: Windjammer Communications LLC (MSO).

LITTLETON—Zito Media, 611 Vader Hill Rd, Coudersport, PA 16915. Phone: 814-260-9575. E-mail: support@zitomedia.net. Web Site: http://www.zitomedia.com. Also serves Burton & Hundred. ICA: WV0106.
TV Market Ranking: 90 (Burton, Hundred, LITTLETON). Franchise award date: July 6, 1986. Franchise expiration date: N.A. Began: October 1, 1970.
Channel capacity: 35 (not 2-way capable). Channels available but not in use: N.A.

Basic Service
Subscribers: 227.
Programming (received off-air): KDKA-TV (CBS) Pittsburgh; WBOY-TV (NBC) Clarksburg; WDTV (CBS) Weston; WNPB-TV (PBS) Morgantown; WPGH-TV (FOX) Pittsburgh; WPMY (MNT) Pittsburgh; WPXI (IND, NBC) Pittsburgh; WQED (PBS) Pittsburgh; WTAE-TV (ABC) Pittsburgh; WTOV-TV (IND, NBC) Steubenville; WTRF-TV (CBS) Wheeling; allband FM.
Fee: $29.95 installation; $19.95 monthly; $1.24 converter.

Expanded Basic Service 1
Subscribers: N.A.
Programming (via satellite): ABC Family Channel; AMC; Animal Planet; CNN; Discovery Channel; Disney Channel; E! Entertainment Television; ESPN; ESPN 2; Great American Country; Lifetime; Nickelodeon; Spike TV; Syfy; TBS Superstation; The Weather Channel; Trinity Broadcasting Network; Turner Network TV; USA Network; WGN America.
Fee: $23.00 monthly.

Pay Service 1
Pay Units: 186.
Programming (via satellite): Cinemax; HBO; Showtime; The Movie Channel.
Fee: $10.00 installation; $7.95 monthly (Cinemax), $11.95 monthly (Showtime or TMC), $11.99 monthly (HBO).

Video-On-Demand: No

Internet Service
Operational: No.

Telephone Service
None

Miles of Plant: 17.0 (coaxial); None (fiber optic).
Public Relations Manager: Mark Laver.
Ownership: Zito Media (MSO).

LOGAN—Charter Communications. Now served by KERMIT, WV [WV0038]. ICA: WV0017.

LYBURN—Colane Cable TV, PO Box 610, Omar, WV 25638. Phone: 304-946-2871. Fax: 304-946-4091. Also serves Neibert. ICA: WV0237.
TV Market Ranking: Below 100 (LYBURN, Neibert). Franchise award date: N.A. Franchise expiration date: N.A. Began: N.A.
Channel capacity: 62 (not 2-way capable). Channels available but not in use: N.A.

Basic Service
Subscribers: 57.
Programming (received off-air): WCHS-TV (ABC) Charleston; WOWK-TV (CBS) Huntington; WPBY-TV (PBS) Huntington; WSAZ-TV (MNT, NBC) Huntington; WTSF (IND) Ashland; WVAH-TV (FOX) Charleston.
Programming (via satellite): ABC Family Channel; Country Music TV; ESPN; TBS Superstation; Turner Network TV; USA Network; WGN America.
Fee: $38.85 installation; $33.30 monthly.

Pay Service 1
Pay Units: N.A.
Programming (via satellite): HBO.
Fee: $12.00 monthly.

Internet Service
Operational: No.

Telephone Service
None

Miles of Plant: 5.0 (coaxial); None (fiber optic).
Manager: Gary Bowen. Office Manager: Rebecca Edwards.
Ownership: Colane Cable TV Inc. (MSO).

MADISON—Suddenlink Communications, 3028 Michigan Ave, Shrewsbury, WV 25015-1936. Phones: 304-757-8001 (Local office); 304-343-3343. Fax: 304-357-6707.

Web Site: http://www.suddenlink.com. Also serves Danville, Frontage Road, Quinland & Uneeda. ICA: WV0192.

TV Market Ranking: 36 (Danville, Frontage Road, MADISON, Quinland, Uneeda). Franchise award date: N.A. Franchise expiration date: N.A. Began: February 1, 1965.

Channel capacity: N.A. Channels available but not in use: N.A.

Basic Service

Subscribers: 1,764.

Programming (received off-air): WCHS-TV (ABC) Charleston; WLPX-TV (ION) Charleston; WOWK-TV (CBS) Huntington; WPBY-TV (PBS) Huntington; WQCW (CW) Portsmouth; WSAZ-TV (MNT, NBC) Huntington; WTSF (IND) Ashland; WVAH-TV (FOX) Charleston; WVPT (PBS) Staunton; allband FM.

Programming (via satellite): C-SPAN; C-SPAN 2; Product Information Network; QVC; ShopNBC; TV Guide Network; WGN America.

Fee: $25.00 installation.

Expanded Basic Service 1

Subscribers: N.A.

Programming (via satellite): A&E Networks; ABC Family Channel; AMC; Animal Planet; BET Networks; Bravo; Cartoon Network; CNBC; CNN; Comedy Central; Country Music TV; Discovery Channel; Disney Channel; E! Entertainment Television; ESPN; ESPN 2; ESPN Classic Sports; Food Network; Fox News Channel; FX; G4; Golf Channel; GSN; Hallmark Channel; Headline News; HGTV; History Channel; INSP; Lifetime; MSNBC; MTV; MTV2; National Geographic Channel; Nickelodeon; Outdoor Channel; Oxygen; Root Sports Pittsburgh; SoapNet; Speed; Spike TV; Style Network; Syfy; TBS Superstation; The Learning Channel; The Weather Channel; Toon Disney; Travel Channel; Trinity Broadcasting Network; truTV; Turner Classic Movies; Turner Network TV; TV Land; USA Network; Versus; VH1; WE tv.

Digital Basic Service

Subscribers: N.A.

Programming (via satellite): AmericanLife TV Network; BBC America; Bio; Bloomberg Television; Boomerang; CBS Sports Network; Discovery Fit & Health; DIY Network; ESPN; ESPNews; Fox College Sports Atlantic; Fox College Sports Central; Fox Deportes; Fox Movie Channel; Fox Soccer; Fuel TV; Fuse; GAS; GMC; Great American Country; Halogen Network; HD Theater; History Channel International; Independent Film Channel; Lifetime Movie Network; MTV Networks Digital Suite; Music Choice; Nick Jr.; Nick Too; NickToons TV; Sundance Channel; Turner Network TV HD; TVG Network.

Digital Pay Service 1

Pay Units: N.A.

Programming (via satellite): Cinemax (multiplexed); Cinemax HD; Encore; Flix; HBO (multiplexed); HBO HD; LOGO; Showtime (multiplexed); Showtime HD; Starz (multiplexed); Starz HDTV; The Movie Channel.

Video-On-Demand: Yes

Pay-Per-View

iN DEMAND (delivered digitally); NHL Center Ice (delivered digitally); MLB Extra Innings (delivered digitally); Playboy TV (delivered digitally); Fresh (delivered digitally); Shorteez (delivered digitally).

Internet Service

Operational: Yes.

Broadband Service: Suddenlink High Speed Internet.

Fee: $49.95 installation; $29.99 monthly.

Telephone Service

Digital: Planned

Miles of Plant: 30.0 (coaxial); None (fiber optic).

Vice President, Operations: David Bach. General Manager: Patrick Barclay. Technical Operations Director: Bob Legg. Marketing Director: Stan Howell. Marketing Manager: Kenny Phillips.

Ownership: Cequel Communications LLC (MSO).

MANNINGTON—Mannington TV Inc. Now served by MORGANTOWN, WV [WV0198]. ICA: WV0067.

MARLINGTON (town)—Shentel, 106 S Main St, Edinburg, VA 22824. Phone: 540-984-5224. Web Site: http://www.shentel.net. Also serves Buckeye, Campbelltown, Edray & Hillsboro. ICA: WV0193.

TV Market Ranking: Below 100 (Buckeye, Campbelltown, Hillsboro, MARLINGTON (TOWN)); Outside TV Markets (Edray). Franchise award date: N.A. Franchise expiration date: December 1, 2013. Began: May 15, 1954.

Channel capacity: N.A. Channels available but not in use: N.A.

Basic Service

Subscribers: 763.

Programming (received off-air): WDBJ (CBS, MNT) Roanoke; WDRL-TV (IND) Danville; WFXR (CW, FOX) Roanoke; WOAY-TV (ABC) Oak Hill; WSET-TV (ABC) Lynchburg; WSLS-TV (NBC) Roanoke; WSWP-TV (PBS) Grandview; WVNS-TV (CBS) Lewisburg; WVVA (CW, NBC) Bluefield; allband FM.

Programming (via satellite): A&E Networks; ABC Family Channel; AMC; Animal Planet; Bravo; Cartoon Network; CNN; Comedy Central; Country Music TV; C-SPAN; CW+; Discovery Channel; Disney Channel; E! Entertainment Television; ESPN; ESPN 2; ESPN Classic Sports; ESPNews; Fox News Channel; FX; G4; Hallmark Channel; Headline News; HGTV; History Channel; Lifetime; MSNBC; MTV; Nickelodeon; Outdoor Channel; QVC; Root Sports Pittsburgh; Speed; Spike TV; Syfy; TBS Superstation; The Learning Channel; The Weather Channel; Travel Channel; Trinity Broadcasting Network; truTV; Turner Classic Movies; Turner Network TV; TV Guide Network; TV Land; USA Network; VH1; WE tv; WGN America.

Fee: $29.95 installation; $37.99 monthly; $30.00 converter.

Digital Basic Service

Subscribers: N.A.

Programming (via satellite): BBC America; Bio; Bloomberg Television; CMT Pure Country; Discovery Fit & Health; Discovery Health Channel; Discovery Home Channel; Discovery Kids Channel; Fox College Sports Atlantic; Fox College Sports Central; Fox College Sports Pacific; Fox Movie Channel; Fuse; GSN; History Channel International; ID Investigation Discovery; Independent Film Channel; Lifetime Movie Network; Military Channel; MTV Hits; MTV Jams; MTV2; Nick Jr.; Nick Too; NickToons TV; Science; Style Network; Sundance Channel; TeenNick; Toon Disney; VH1 Classic; VH1 Soul; WE tv.

Digital Pay Service 1

Pay Units: N.A.

Programming (via satellite): Cinemax (multiplexed); Encore; Flix; HBO (multiplexed); Showtime (multiplexed); Starz (multiplexed); The Movie Channel (multiplexed).

Internet Service

Operational: No.

Telephone Service

None

Miles of Plant: 51.0 (coaxial); None (fiber optic).

Regional Manager: Tom Kenly. General Manager: Robert Harold. Chief Technician: Steve Adkins.

Ownership: Shenandoah Telecommunications Inc. (MSO).

MARTINSBURG—Formerly served by Adelphia Communications. Now served by SHEPHERDSTOWN, WV [WV0016]. ICA: WV0019.

MATEWAN—Formerly served by Charter Communications. No longer in operation. ICA: WV0073.

MAYSEL—Econoco Inc., Rte 61, PO Box 147, Kincaid, WV 25119-0147. Phone: 304-469-2817. Fax: 304-469-2416. Also serves Procious, Valley Fork & Wallback. ICA: WV0195.

TV Market Ranking: 36 (MAYSEL, Procious, Valley Fork, Wallback). Franchise award date: N.A. Franchise expiration date: N.A. Began: June 1, 1990.

Channel capacity: 36 (not 2-way capable). Channels available but not in use: N.A.

Basic Service

Subscribers: 329.

Programming (received off-air): WCHS-TV (ABC) Charleston; WOAY-TV (ABC) Oak Hill; WOWK-TV (CBS) Huntington; WPBY-TV (PBS) Huntington; WSAZ-TV (MNT, NBC) Huntington; WSWP-TV (PBS) Grandview; WVAH-TV (FOX) Charleston.

Programming (via satellite): ABC Family Channel; Animal Planet; Cartoon Network; CNN; Country Music TV; Discovery Channel; ESPN; ESPN 2; Fox Sports South; FX; Headline News; ION Television; Lifetime; Outdoor Channel; QVC; Spike TV; TBS Superstation; The Learning Channel; The Weather Channel; Travel Channel; Trinity Broadcasting Network; Turner Network TV; WGN America.

Fee: $25.00 installation; $25.46 monthly.

Pay Service 1

Pay Units: N.A.

Programming (via satellite): Showtime.

Fee: $10.00 installation; $10.00 monthly.

Video-On-Demand: No

Internet Service

Operational: No.

Telephone Service

None

Miles of Plant: 38.0 (coaxial); None (fiber optic).

Manager: Sheila Bills. Chief Technician: Eslie Bills.

Ownership: Econoco Inc. (MSO).

MEADOW BRIDGE—Vital Communications Group, PO Box 307, Behaven, NC 27810. Phone: 252-943-3800. Also serves Danese, Layland & Maplewood. ICA: WV0089.

TV Market Ranking: Below 100 (Danese, Layland, Maplewood, MEADOW BRIDGE). Franchise award date: February 23, 1981. Franchise expiration date: N.A. Began: November 1, 1981.

Channel capacity: 42 (not 2-way capable). Channels available but not in use: N.A.

Basic Service

Subscribers: 739.

Programming (received off-air): WCHS-TV (ABC) Charleston; WDBJ (CBS, MNT) Roanoke; WOAY-TV (ABC) Oak Hill; WSWP-TV (PBS) Grandview; WVAH-TV (FOX) Charleston; WVNS-TV (CBS) Lewisburg; WVVA (CW, NBC) Bluefield.

Programming (via satellite): ABC Family Channel; CNN; C-SPAN; Disney Channel; INSP; Lifetime; QVC; TBS Superstation; truTV; USA Network; WGN America.

Fee: $38.34 installation; $15.95 monthly; $1.26 converter; $15.47 additional installation.

Expanded Basic Service 1

Subscribers: 657.

Programming (via satellite): A&E Networks; Cartoon Network; Country Music TV; Discovery Channel; ESPN; ESPN 2; FX; Hallmark Channel; HGTV; MTV; Nickelodeon; Outdoor Channel; Root Sports Pittsburgh; Speed; Spike TV; Syfy; The Learning Channel; The Weather Channel; Turner Classic Movies; Turner Network TV; VH1.

Fee: $15.00 monthly.

Pay Service 1

Pay Units: 15.

Programming (via satellite): Cinemax.

Fee: $11.95 monthly.

Pay Service 2

Pay Units: 49.

Programming (via satellite): HBO.

Fee: $11.95 monthly.

Internet Service

Operational: No.

Telephone Service

None

Miles of Plant: 38.0 (coaxial); None (fiber optic).

President: Jerry Stender.

Ownership: Vital Communications Group (MSO).

MEADOWDALE—Formerly served by Adelphia Communications. No longer in operation. ICA: WV0109.

MIDDLEBOURNE—Richards TV Cable, PO Box 2, Jerusalem, OH 43747-0002. Phone: 740-926-1742. Fax: 740-926-1800. ICA: WV0105.

TV Market Ranking: Below 100 (MIDDLEBOURNE). Franchise award date: N.A. Franchise expiration date: N.A. Began: November 1, 1967.

Channel capacity: 32 (not 2-way capable). Channels available but not in use: N.A.

Basic Service

Subscribers: N.A. Included in Malaga Twp., OH

Programming (received off-air): WBOY-TV (NBC) Clarksburg; WDTV (CBS) Weston; WNPB-TV (PBS) Morgantown; WTAE-TV (ABC) Pittsburgh; WTAP-TV (FOX, MNT, NBC) Parkersburg; WTOV-TV (IND, NBC) Steubenville; WTRF-TV (CBS) Wheeling; allband FM.

Programming (via satellite): A&E Networks; ABC Family Channel; Animal Planet; Cartoon Network; CNN; Country Music TV; Discovery Channel; Disney Channel; ESPN; ESPN 2; Headline News; History Channel; Lifetime; Nickelodeon; QVC; Spike TV; TBS Superstation; The Learning Channel; The Weather Channel; Turner Classic Movies; Turner Network TV; TV Land; USA Network.

Fee: $10.30 installation; $25.00 monthly.

Pay Service 1

Pay Units: N.A.

Programming (via satellite): HBO.

Internet Service

Operational: No.

Telephone Service

None

Miles of plant included in Malaga Twp. OH

Manager: Paul E. Richards. Chief Technician: Mark Richards.

Ownership: Paul E. Richards (MSO).

MILTON—Suddenlink Communications, 4038 Teays Valley Rd, PO Box 1220, Scott Depot, WV 25560. Phone: 304-757-8001. Web Site: http://www.suddenlink.com. Also serves Barboursville, Cabell County, Culloden, Hurricane, Ona, Putnam County & Scott Depot. ICA: WV0012.

TV Market Ranking: 36 (Barboursville, Cabell County, Culloden, Hurricane, MILTON, Ona, Putnam County, Scott Depot). Franchise award date: December 1, 1975. Franchise expiration date: N.A. Began: March 1, 1976.

Channel capacity: N.A. Channels available but not in use: N.A.

Basic Service

Subscribers: 11,184.

Programming (received off-air): WCHS-TV (ABC) Charleston; WLPX-TV (ION) Charleston; WOWK-TV (CBS) Huntington; WPBY-TV (PBS) Huntington; WQCW (CW) Portsmouth; WSAZ-TV (MNT, NBC) Huntington; WTSF (IND) Ashland; WVAH-TV (FOX) Charleston; WVPT (PBS) Staunton.

Programming (via satellite): C-SPAN; C-SPAN 2; Product Information Network; QVC; ShopNBC; TV Guide Network; WGN America.

Fee: $61.25 installation; $14.40 monthly; $1.24 converter.

Expanded Basic Service 1

Subscribers: N.A.

Programming (via satellite): A&E Networks; ABC Family Channel; AMC; Animal Planet; BET Networks; Bravo; Cartoon Network; CNBC; CNN; Comedy Central; Country Music TV; Discovery Channel; Discovery Fit & Health; Disney Channel; E! Entertainment Television; ESPN; ESPN 2; ESPN Classic Sports; Food Network; Fox News Channel; FX; G4; Golf Channel; GSN; Hallmark Channel; Headline News; HGTV; History Channel; INSP; Lifetime; MSNBC; MTV; National Geographic Channel; Nickelodeon; Outdoor Channel; Oxygen; Root Sports Pittsburgh; SoapNet; Speed; Spike TV; Style Network; Syfy; TBS Superstation; The Learning Channel; The Weather Channel; Toon Disney; Travel Channel; Trinity Broadcasting Network; truTV; Turner Classic Movies; Turner Network TV; TV Land; USA Network; Versus; VH1; WE tv.

Fee: $17.32 monthly.

Digital Basic Service

Subscribers: N.A.

Programming (via satellite): BBC America; Bio; Bloomberg Television; DIY Network; ESPN; ESPNews; Fox College Sports Atlantic; Fox College Sports Central; Fox College Sports Pacific; Fox Deportes; Fox Movie Channel; Fox Sports World; Fuel TV; Fuse; GAS; Great American Country; HD Theater; History Channel International; Independent Film Channel; Lifetime Movie Network; MTV Networks Digital Suite; Music Choice; NFL Network; Nick Jr.; Nick Too; NickToons TV; Sundance Channel; TV Guide Interactive Inc.; TVG Network.

Digital Pay Service 1

Pay Units: N.A.

Programming (via satellite): Cinemax (multiplexed); Encore (multiplexed); Flix; HBO (multiplexed); Showtime (multiplexed); Starz (multiplexed); The Movie Channel (multiplexed).

Video-On-Demand: Yes

Pay-Per-View

iN DEMAND (delivered digitally); NASCAR In Car (delivered digitally); NHL Center Ice (delivered digitally); MLB Extra Innings (delivered digitally); Playboy TV (delivered digitally); Fresh (delivered digitally); Shorteez (delivered digitally).

Internet Service

Operational: Yes.

Broadband Service: Suddenlink High Speed Internet.

Fee: $49.95 installation; $29.99 monthly.

Telephone Service

None

Miles of Plant: 254.0 (coaxial); None (fiber optic).

Vice President, Operations: David Bach. General Manager: Patrick Barclay. Technical Operations Director: Bob Legg. Marketing Director: Stan Howell.

Ownership: Cequel Communications LLC (MSO).

MONONGAH—Formerly served by Adelphia Communications. Now served by MORGANTOWN, WV [WV0198]. ICA: WV0055.

MOOREFIELD—Atlantic Broadband, 120 Southmont Blvd, Johnstown, PA 15905. Phone: 814-539-8971. Fax: 814-535-7749. E-mail: info@atlanticbb.com. Web Site: http://www.atlanticbb.com. Also serves Durgon & Hardy County. ICA: WV0197.

TV Market Ranking: Below 100 (Hardy County (portions)); Outside TV Markets (Durgon, Hardy County (portions), MOOREFIELD). Franchise award date: N.A. Franchise expiration date: N.A. Began: July 1, 1969.

Channel capacity: N.A. Channels available but not in use: N.A.

Basic Service

Subscribers: 897.

Programming (received off-air): WHAG-TV (NBC) Hagerstown; WHSV-TV (ABC, MNT) Harrisonburg; WJAC-TV (NBC) Johnstown; WNPB-TV (PBS) Morgantown; WTTG (FOX) Washington; WUSA (CBS) Washington; WWCP-TV (FOX) Johnstown; WWPB (PBS) Hagerstown; WWPX-TV (ION) Martinsburg; allband FM.

Programming (via satellite): C-SPAN; QVC.

Fee: $29.95 installation; $16.95 monthly.

Expanded Basic Service 1

Subscribers: N.A.

Programming (via satellite): A&E Networks; ABC Family Channel; AMC; CNN; Comedy Central; Country Music TV; C-SPAN 2; Discovery Channel; Discovery Health Channel; Disney Channel; ESPN; ESPN 2; Fox News Channel; FX; Headline News; HGTV; History Channel; INSP; MTV; Nickelodeon; Spike TV; TBS Superstation; The Weather Channel; Turner Network TV; TV Land; USA Network; VH1.

Fee: $28.04 monthly.

Digital Basic Service

Subscribers: N.A.

Programming (via satellite): BBC America; Bio; Bloomberg Television; Cooking Channel; Discovery Fit & Health; Discovery Kids Channel; DMX Music; Encore (multiplexed); ESPN Classic Sports; ESPNews; Fuse; G4; Golf Channel; GSN; Halogen Network; History Channel International; Independent Film Channel; Lifetime Movie Network; MTV2; Nick Jr.; NickToons TV; Outdoor Channel; Science; Starz (multiplexed); Style Network; Toon Disney; Trinity Broadcasting Network; Turner Classic Movies.

Fee: $21.90 monthly.

Digital Pay Service 1

Pay Units: N.A.

Programming (via satellite): Cinemax (multiplexed); HBO (multiplexed); Showtime (multiplexed).

Fee: $15.95 monthly (each).

Video-On-Demand: No

Pay-Per-View

iN DEMAND (delivered digitally); Hot Choice (delivered digitally); Playboy TV (delivered digitally); Fresh (delivered digitally); Shorteez (delivered digitally).

Internet Service

Operational: No.

Telephone Service

None

Miles of Plant: 51.0 (coaxial); None (fiber optic).

Vice President: David Dane. General Manager: Dan Feiertag. Technical Operations Director: Charles Sorchilla. Marketing & Customer Service Director: Dara Leslie. Marketing Manager: Natalie Kuchak.

Ownership: Atlantic Broadband (MSO).

MORGANTOWN—Comcast Cable, 15 Summit Park Dr, Pittsburgh, PA 15275. Phones: 412-747-6400; 304-292-6188 (Morgantown office). Fax: 412-747-6401. Web Site: http://www.comcast.com. Also serves Bellview, Booth, Cassville, Clarksburg, Colfax, Core, Everettville, Fairmont, Grafton, Granville, Greentown, Hutchinson, Laurel Point, Maidsville, Mannington, Marion County, Monongah, Monongalia County (portions), Montana Mines, National, Osage, Pleasant Valley, Preston County (portions), Pursglove, Rachel, Rivesville, Rowlesburg, Star City, Taylor County (portions), Westover, Whitehall & Worthington. ICA: WV0198.

TV Market Ranking: 90 (Monongalia County (portions)); Below 100 (Bellview, Booth, Cassville, Clarksburg, Colfax, Core, Everettville, Fairmont, Grafton, Granville, Greentown, Hutchinson, Laurel Point, Maidsville, Marion County, Monongah, Montana Mines, MORGANTOWN, National, Osage, Pleasant Valley, Preston County (portions), Pursglove, Rachel, Rivesville, Star City, Taylor County (portions), Westover, Whitehall, Worthington, Monongalia County (portions)); Outside TV Markets (Preston County (portions), Rowlesburg, Monongalia County (portions)). Franchise award date: N.A. Franchise expiration date: N.A. Began: July 1, 1953.

Channel capacity: N.A. Channels available but not in use: N.A.

Basic Service

Subscribers: 35,240.

Programming (received off-air): KDKA-TV (CBS) Pittsburgh; WBOY-TV (NBC) Clarksburg; WDTV (CBS) Weston; WNPB-TV (PBS) Morgantown; WPCB-TV (IND) Greensburg; WPGH-TV (FOX) Pittsburgh; WPMY (MNT) Pittsburgh; WPXI (IND, NBC) Pittsburgh; WQED (PBS) Pittsburgh; WTAE-TV (ABC) Pittsburgh; WVFX (CW, FOX) Clarksburg; allband FM.

Programming (via satellite): A&E Networks; C-SPAN; C-SPAN 2; Eternal Word TV Network; Hallmark Channel; Headline News; Product Information Network; QVC; ShopNBC; Trinity Broadcasting Network; TV Guide Network; WGN America.

Fee: $39.95 installation; $13.85 monthly.

Expanded Basic Service 1

Subscribers: N.A.

Programming (via satellite): ABC Family Channel; AMC; Animal Planet; BET Networks; Bravo; Cartoon Network; CNBC; CNN; Comedy Central; Country Music TV; Discovery Channel; Disney Channel; E! Entertainment Television; ESPN; ESPN 2; Food Network; Fox News Channel; FX; HGTV; History Channel; INSP; ION Television; Lifetime; MSNBC; MTV; MTV2; Nick Jr.; Nickelodeon; Oxygen; Root Sports Pittsburgh; Speed; Spike TV; Style Network; Syfy; TBS Superstation; The Learning Channel; The Weather Channel; Travel Channel; truTV; Turner Network TV; TV Land; USA Network; VH1.

Fee: $28.00 monthly.

Digital Basic Service

Subscribers: 10,829.

Programming (via satellite): AmericanLife TV Network; BBC America; Black Family Channel; Bloomberg Television; Discovery Fit & Health; DIY Network; ESPN Classic Sports; ESPNews; Fox Movie Channel; Fox Sports World; Fuse; G4; Golf Channel; Great American Country; GSN; Halogen Network; History Channel International; Music Choice; Outdoor Channel; SoapNet; The Word Network; Toon Disney; Versus; WE tv.

Fee: $10.95 monthly.

Digital Expanded Basic Service

Subscribers: N.A.

Programming (via satellite): Bio; FSN Digital Atlantic; FSN Digital Central; FSN Digital Pacific; GAS; Independent Film Channel; MTV Networks Digital Suite; National Geographic Channel; Nick Too; NickToons TV.

Fee: $6.95 monthly.

Digital Pay Service 1

Pay Units: 8,721.

Programming (via satellite): ART America; Canales N; CCTV-4; Cinemax (multiplexed); Encore (multiplexed); Filipino Channel; Flix; HBO (multiplexed); RAI International; Russian Television Network; Showtime (multiplexed); Starz (multiplexed); The Movie Channel (multiplexed); TV Asia; TV Japan; TV5 USA; Zee TV USA; Zhong Tian Channel.

Fee: $15.95 monthly (each).

Video-On-Demand: No

Pay-Per-View

Addressable homes: 10,829.

Hot Choice (delivered digitally); Urban Xtra (delivered digitally); Playboy TV (delivered digitally); Fresh (delivered digitally); Shorteez (delivered digitally).

Internet Service

Operational: Yes.

Broadband Service: Comcast High Speed Internet.

Fee: $42.95 monthly.

Telephone Service

None

Miles of Plant: 562.0 (coaxial); None (fiber optic).

Regional Vice President: Linda Hossinger. Vice President, Technical Operations: Randy Bender. Vice President, Marketing: Donna Corning. Vice President, Public Affairs: Jody Doherty. Chief Technician: Ed

Hinkle. Customer Service Manager: Sheila Hall.
Ownership: Comcast Cable Communications Inc. (MSO).

MOUNDSVILLE—Comcast Cable. Now served by WHEELING, WV [WV0004]. ICA: WV0022.

MOUNT LOOKOUT—Econoco Inc., Rte 61, PO Box 147, Kincaid, WV 25119-0147. Phone: 304-469-2817. Fax: 304-469-2416. Also serves Mount Nebo & Nallen. ICA: WV0199.
TV Market Ranking: Below 100 (MOUNT LOOKOUT, Mount Nebo, Nallen). Franchise award date: N.A. Franchise expiration date: N.A. Began: January 1, 1984.
Channel capacity: 36 (not 2-way capable). Channels available but not in use: N.A.
Basic Service
Subscribers: 321.
Programming (received off-air): WCHS-TV (ABC) Charleston; WDTV (CBS) Weston; WOAY-TV (ABC) Oak Hill; WOWK-TV (CBS) Huntington; WSAZ-TV (MNT, NBC) Huntington; WSWP-TV (PBS) Grandview; WVAH-TV (FOX) Charleston.
Programming (via satellite): A&E Networks; ABC Family Channel; Cartoon Network; CNN; Country Music TV; Discovery Channel; ESPN; Fox Sports South; FX; ION Television; QVC; Spike TV; TBS Superstation; Trinity Broadcasting Network; Turner Network TV; USA Network; WGN America.
Fee: $25.00 installation; $24.16 monthly.
Video-On-Demand: No
Internet Service
Operational: No.
Telephone Service
None
Miles of Plant: 28.0 (coaxial); None (fiber optic).
Manager: Sheila Bills. Chief Technician: Eslie Bills.
Ownership: Econoco Inc. (MSO).

MOUNT STORM—Formerly served by Almega Cable. No longer in operation. ICA: WV0257.

MUD RIVER—Colane Cable TV, PO Box 130, Omar, WV 25638. Phone: 304-946-2871. Fax: 304-946-4091. ICA: WV0238.
TV Market Ranking: 36 (MUD RIVER). Franchise award date: N.A. Franchise expiration date: N.A. Began: N.A.
Channel capacity: 62 (not 2-way capable). Channels available but not in use: N.A.
Basic Service
Subscribers: 47.
Programming (received off-air): WCHS-TV (ABC) Charleston; WOWK-TV (CBS) Huntington; WPBY-TV (PBS) Huntington; WSAZ-TV (MNT, NBC) Huntington; WVAH-TV (FOX) Charleston.
Programming (via satellite): ABC Family Channel; ESPN; Turner Network TV; USA Network.
Fee: $38.85 installation; $33.30 monthly.
Pay Service 1
Pay Units: N.A.
Programming (via satellite): HBO.
Fee: $12.00 monthly.
Internet Service
Operational: No.
Telephone Service
None
Miles of Plant: 5.0 (coaxial); None (fiber optic).
Manager: Gary Bowen. Office Manager: Rebecca Edwards.
Ownership: Colane Cable TV Inc. (MSO).

MULLENS—Jet Broadband. Now served by PINEVILLE, WV [WV0204]. ICA: WV0086.

NEBO—Windjammer Cable, 8500 W 110th St, Ste 600, Overland Park, KS 66210. Phone: 888-495-2881. Fax: 913-563-5454. Web Site: http://www.windjammercable.com. Also serves Arnoldsburg, Chloe, Clay, Duck, Ivydale, Millstone & Orma. ICA: WV0253.
TV Market Ranking: 36 (Clay); Below 100 (Millstone, Orma); Outside TV Markets (Arnoldsburg, Chloe, Duck, Ivydale, NEBO). Franchise award date: N.A. Franchise expiration date: N.A. Began: N.A.
Channel capacity: N.A. Channels available but not in use: N.A.
Basic Service
Subscribers: 473.
Programming (received off-air): WCHS-TV (ABC) Charleston; WDTV (CBS) Weston; WOAY-TV (ABC) Oak Hill; WOWK-TV (CBS) Huntington; WSAZ-TV (MNT, NBC) Huntington; WSWP-TV (PBS) Grandview; WVAH-TV (FOX) Charleston.
Programming (via satellite): A&E Networks; ABC Family Channel; AMC; CNN; Country Music TV; Discovery Channel; Disney Channel; ESPN; Spike TV; TBS Superstation; The Learning Channel; The Weather Channel; Trinity Broadcasting Network; Turner Network TV; USA Network; WGN America.
Fee: $39.95 installation; $32.29 monthly.
Digital Basic Service
Subscribers: N.A.
Programming (via satellite): BBC America; Bloomberg Television; Bravo; Discovery Fit & Health; Discovery Health Channel; Discovery Kids Channel; ESPN Classic Sports; ESPNews; Fox Movie Channel; Fox Soccer; G4; Golf Channel; GSN; Halogen Network; HGTV; History Channel; Independent Film Channel; Music Choice; Nick Jr.; NickToons TV; Outdoor Channel; Science; Syfy; Versus; WE tv.
Fee: $11.00 monthly.
Pay Service 1
Pay Units: N.A.
Programming (via satellite): HBO.
Fee: $10.00 monthly.
Digital Pay Service 1
Pay Units: N.A.
Programming (via satellite): Cinemax (multiplexed); Encore (multiplexed); HBO (multiplexed); Showtime (multiplexed); Starz (multiplexed); The Movie Channel (multiplexed).
Fee: $15.95 monthly (each).
Video-On-Demand: No
Pay-Per-View
iN DEMAND (delivered digitally); Playboy TV (delivered digitally); Fresh (delivered digitally).
Internet Service
Operational: No.
Telephone Service
None
Miles of Plant: 60.0 (coaxial); None (fiber optic).
Ownership: Windjammer Communications LLC (MSO).

NETTIE—Windjammer Cable, 8500 W 110th St, Ste 600, Overland Park, KS 66210. Phone: 888-495-2881. Fax: 913-563-5454. Web Site: http://www.windjammercable.com. Also serves Calvin, Leivasy & Summersville (portions). ICA: WV0156.
TV Market Ranking: Below 100 (Calvin, Leivasy, NETTIE, Summersville (portions)). Franchise award date: N.A. Franchise expiration date: N.A. Began: April 1, 1981.
Channel capacity: 38 (not 2-way capable). Channels available but not in use: N.A.
Basic Service
Subscribers: 647.
Programming (received off-air): WCHS-TV (ABC) Charleston; WOAY-TV (ABC) Oak Hill; WOWK-TV (CBS) Huntington; WSAZ-TV (MNT, NBC) Huntington; WSWP-TV (PBS) Grandview; WVAH-TV (FOX) Charleston.
Programming (via satellite): A&E Networks; ABC Family Channel; AMC; Cartoon Network; CNN; Country Music TV; C-SPAN; Discovery Channel; Disney Channel; ESPN; ESPN 2; Fox News Channel; FX; Headline News; HGTV; History Channel; Lifetime; MTV; Nickelodeon; Outdoor Channel; QVC; Spike TV; TBS Superstation; The Learning Channel; The Weather Channel; Trinity Broadcasting Network; Turner Network TV; USA Network; VH1; WGN America.
Fee: $39.95 installation; $32.39 monthly; $.95 converter.
Digital Basic Service
Subscribers: N.A.
Programming (via satellite): Bravo; ESPN Classic Sports; Syfy; Versus; WE tv.
Fee: $11.00 monthly.
Pay Service 1
Pay Units: 69.
Programming (via satellite): HBO.
Fee: $10.95 monthly.
Digital Pay Service 1
Pay Units: N.A.
Programming (via satellite): Cinemax (multiplexed); Encore (multiplexed); HBO (multiplexed); Showtime (multiplexed); Starz (multiplexed); The Movie Channel (multiplexed).
Fee: $15.95 monthly (each).
Video-On-Demand: No
Pay-Per-View
iN DEMAND (delivered digitally); Club Jenna (delivered digitally).
Internet Service
Operational: No.
Telephone Service
None
Miles of Plant: 52.0 (coaxial); None (fiber optic).
General Manager: Timothy Evard. Operations Director: Belinda Graham. Engineering Director: Mike Earehart. Finance & Accounting Director: Cindy Johnson.
Ownership: Windjammer Communications LLC (MSO).

NEW CUMBERLAND—Comcast Cable, 15 Summit Park Dr, Pittsburgh, PA 15275. Phone: 412-747-6400. Fax: 412-747-6401. Web Site: http://www.comcast.com. Also serves Brooke County, Hancock County (portions), New Manchester & Weirton. ICA: WV0069.
TV Market Ranking: 10 (Brooke County, Weirton); 10,90 (Hancock County (portions), NEW CUMBERLAND, New Manchester). Franchise award date: N.A. Franchise expiration date: N.A. Began: June 1, 1970.
Channel capacity: N.A. Channels available but not in use: N.A.
Basic Service
Subscribers: N.A.
Programming (received off-air): KDKA-TV (CBS) Pittsburgh; WINP-TV (ION) Pittsburgh; WNEO (PBS) Alliance; WNPB-TV (PBS) Morgantown; WPCB-TV (IND) Greensburg; WPGH-TV (FOX) Pittsburgh; WPXI (IND, NBC) Pittsburgh; WQED (PBS) Pittsburgh; WTAE-TV (ABC) Pittsburgh; WTOV-TV (IND, NBC) Steubenville; WTRF-TV (CBS) Wheeling; allband FM.
Programming (via satellite): Hallmark Channel; QVC.
Fee: $14.00 monthly.
Expanded Basic Service 1
Subscribers: 9,993.
Programming (via satellite): A&E Networks; ABC Family Channel; AMC; Animal Planet; BET Networks; Cartoon Network; CNBC; CNN; Comedy Central; Country Music TV; C-SPAN; C-SPAN 2; Discovery Channel; Disney Channel; E! Entertainment Television; ESPN; ESPN 2; Eternal Word TV Network; Food Network; Fox News Channel; FX; Golf Channel; Headline News; HGTV; History Channel; ION Television; Lifetime; MSNBC; MTV; Nickelodeon; Oxygen; Pittsburgh Cable News Channel; Root Sports Pittsburgh; ShopNBC; Speed; Spike TV; TBS Superstation; The Learning Channel; The Weather Channel; Travel Channel; truTV; Turner Network TV; TV Guide Network; TV Land; USA Network; VH1.
Fee: $36.49 monthly.
Digital Basic Service
Subscribers: N.A.
Programming (via satellite): AmericanLife TV Network; BBC America; Bio; Black Family Channel; Bloomberg Television; Bravo; Discovery Digital Networks; DMX Music; ESPN Classic Sports; ESPNews; Fox Movie Channel; Fox Soccer; FSN Digital Atlantic; FSN Digital Central; FSN Digital Pacific; Fuse; G4; GAS; Great American Country; GSN; Halogen Network; History Channel International; Independent Film Channel; Lifetime Movie Network; Lime; MTV Networks Digital Suite; National Geographic Channel; Nick Jr.; NickToons TV; Outdoor Channel; Ovation; ShopNBC; Style Network; Sundance Channel; Syfy; The Word Network; Toon Disney; Trinity Broadcasting Network; Turner Classic Movies; Versus; WE tv; Weatherscan.
Fee: $10.95 monthly.
Digital Pay Service 1
Pay Units: N.A.
Programming (via satellite): Cinemax (multiplexed); Encore (multiplexed); Flix; HBO (multiplexed); Showtime (multiplexed); Starz (multiplexed); The Movie Channel (multiplexed).
Video-On-Demand: Yes
Pay-Per-View
ESPN Now (delivered digitally); Sports PPV (delivered digitally); NBA TV (delivered digitally); iN DEMAND (delivered digitally); Fresh (delivered digitally); Shorteez (delivered digitally); Playboy TV (delivered digitally); Hot Choice (delivered digitally).
Internet Service
Operational: Yes. Began: October 1, 2001.
Broadband Service: Comcast High Speed Internet.
Fee: $42.95 monthly.
Telephone Service
None
Miles of Plant: 136.0 (coaxial); 8.0 (fiber optic).
Regional Vice President: Linda Hossinger. Vice President, Technical Operations: Randy Bender. Vice President, Marketing: Donna Corning. Vice President, Public Affairs: Jody Doherty.
Ownership: Comcast Cable Communications Inc. (MSO).

NEW MARTINSVILLE—Charter Communications. Now served by PARKERSBURG, WV [WV0003]. ICA: WV0025.

NITRO—Charter Communications. Now served by CHARLESTON, (formerly Chelyan) WV [WV0006]. ICA: WV0009.

NORTHFORK—Shentel, Rt 16 Welch Pineville Rd, Welch, WV 24801. Phones: 540-984-5224; 800-743-6835. Web Site: http://www.shentel.net. Also serves Amonate, VA; Algoma, Asco, Canebrake, Capels, Caretta, Crumpler, Cucumber, Davy, Eckman, Elkhorn, Gilliam, Hartwell, Havaco, Hemphill, Kimball, Kyle, Landraff, Leckie, Maitland-Superior, Maybeury, Newhall, North Welch, Pageton, Powhatan, Skygusty, Squire, Switchback, Twin Branch, Vallscreek, Vivian, War, Welch & Worth, WV. ICA: WV0045.

TV Market Ranking: Below 100 (Algoma, Amonate, Asco, Canebrake, Capels, Caretta, Crumpler, Cucumber, Davy, Eckman, Elkhorn, Gary, Gilliam, Hartwell, Havaco, Hemphill, Kimball, Kyle, Landraff, Leckie, Maitland-Superior, Maybeury, Newhall, North Welch, NORTHFORK, Pageton, Powhatan, Skygusty, Squire, Switchback, Twin Branch, Vallscreek, Vivian, War, Welch, Worth). Franchise award date: N.A. Franchise expiration date: N.A. Began: December 1, 1951.

Channel capacity: 45 (operating 2-way). Channels available but not in use: N.A.

Basic Service

Subscribers: 1,171.

Programming (received off-air): WCHS-TV (ABC) Charleston; WLFB (IND) Bluefield; WOAY-TV (ABC) Oak Hill; WOWK-TV (CBS) Huntington; WSAZ-TV (MNT, NBC) Huntington; WSWP-TV (PBS) Grandview; WVNS-TV (CBS) Lewisburg; WVVA (CW, NBC) Bluefield; allband FM.

Programming (via satellite): QVC; TBS Superstation; Trinity Broadcasting Network; WGN America.

Fee: $39.95 installation; $20.95 monthly.

Expanded Basic Service 1

Subscribers: N.A.

Programming (via satellite): A&E Networks; ABC Family Channel; AMC; Animal Planet; BET Networks; Cartoon Network; CNBC; CNN; Country Music TV; C-SPAN; Discovery Channel; Disney Channel; ESPN; ESPN 2; Fox News Channel; FX; Headline News; HGTV; History Channel; Lifetime; MTV; Nickelodeon; Outdoor Channel; Root Sports Pittsburgh; Speed; Spike TV; Syfy; The Learning Channel; The Weather Channel; Trinity Broadcasting Network; Turner Classic Movies; Turner Network TV; TV Land; USA Network; VH1.

Fee: $20.00 monthly.

Digital Basic Service

Subscribers: 123.

Programming (via satellite): AmericanLife TV Network; BBC America; Bloomberg Television; Discovery Fit & Health; DMX Music; ESPN Classic Sports; ESPNews; Fox Soccer; G4; GAS; Golf Channel; GSN; MTV Networks Digital Suite; National Geographic Channel; Nick Jr.; NickToons TV; Style Network; Versus.

Fee: $14.00 monthly.

Pay Service 1

Pay Units: 350.

Programming (via satellite): HBO.

Fee: $11.95 monthly.

Pay Service 2

Pay Units: 350.

Programming (via satellite): Showtime.

Fee: $12.95 monthly.

Digital Pay Service 1

Pay Units: N.A.

Programming (via satellite): Cinemax (multiplexed); Encore (multiplexed); HBO (multiplexed); Showtime (multiplexed); Starz (multiplexed); The Movie Channel (multiplexed).

Fee: $11.95 monthly (Cinemax or Starz/Encore), $12.95 monthly (HBO or Showtime/TMC).

Video-On-Demand: No

Pay-Per-View

iN DEMAND (delivered digitally).

Internet Service

Operational: Yes. Began: November 1, 2004.

Broadband Service: JetBroadband.

Fee: $39.95 installation; $19.95 monthly.

Telephone Service

None

Miles of Plant: 65.0 (coaxial); 2.0 (fiber optic).

President: Christopher French. Vice President, Customer Service: David Ferguson. General Manager: Anthony Barlage. Marketing Manager: Chris Ranson.

Ownership: Shenandoah Telecommunications Inc. (MSO).

NORTON—Formerly served by Adelphia Communications. Now served by ELLAMORE, WV [WV0125]. ICA: WV0256.

OAK HILL—Charter Communications. Now served by BECKLEY, WV [WV0005]. ICA: WV0023.

OAKVALE—Shentel, 99 Howard St, Welch, WV 24801. Phones: 540-984-5224; 800-743-6835. Web Site: http://www.shentel.net. Also serves Elgood, Hardy, Ingleside, Kellysville, Mercer County & Willowton. ICA: WV0201.

TV Market Ranking: Below 100 (Elgood, Hardy, Ingleside, Kellysville, Mercer County, OAKVALE, Willowton). Franchise award date: N.A. Franchise expiration date: N.A. Began: N.A.

Channel capacity: 41 (not 2-way capable). Channels available but not in use: N.A.

Basic Service

Subscribers: 300.

Programming (received off-air): WBRA-TV (PBS) Roanoke; WDBJ (CBS, MNT) Roanoke; WFXR (CW, FOX) Roanoke; WOAY-TV (ABC) Oak Hill; WSLS-TV (NBC) Roanoke; WSWP-TV (PBS) Grandview; WVVA (CW, NBC) Bluefield.

Programming (via satellite): ABC Family Channel; Animal Planet; Cartoon Network; CNN; Discovery Channel; Disney Channel; ESPN; ESPN 2; FX; Golf Channel; Great American Country; Headline News; HGTV; INSP; Lime; MSNBC; Nickelodeon; Outdoor Channel; QVC; Root Sports Pittsburgh; Spike TV; Syfy; TBS Superstation; The Learning Channel; The Weather Channel; Travel Channel; Trinity Broadcasting Network; Turner Classic Movies; Turner Network TV; TV Land; USA Network; WGN America.

Fee: $39.95 installation; $36.50 monthly.

Pay Service 1

Pay Units: N.A.

Programming (via satellite): HBO; Showtime.

Fee: $10.95 monthly (Showtime), $11.95 monthly (HBO).

Video-On-Demand: Planned

Internet Service

Operational: No.

Telephone Service

None

President: Christopher French. Vice President, Customer Service: David Ferguson. General Manager: Anthony W. Barlage. Marketing Manager: Chris Ranson.

Ownership: Shenandoah Telecommunications Inc. (MSO).

OMAR—Colane Cable TV Inc., PO Box 610, Omar, WV 25638. Phone: 304-946-2871. Fax: 304-946-4091. Also serves Lawrence County (portions), Martin County (portions) & Pike County (portions), KY; Baisden, Barnabus, Bens Creek, Cow Creek, Delbarton, Gilbert, Hampden, Justice, Micco, Mingo County (portions), Ragland, Stirrat, Varney, Wayne County (portions) & Wharncliffe, WV. ICA: WV0191.

TV Market Ranking: Below 100 (Baisden, Barnabus, Cow Creek, Delbarton, Gilbert, Hampden, Justice, Micco, Mingo County (portions), OMAR, Ragland, Stirrat, Varney); Outside TV Markets (Bens Creek, Lawrence County (portions), Martin County (portions), Mingo County (portions), Pike County (portions), Wayne County (portions), Wharncliffe). Franchise award date: N.A. Franchise expiration date: N.A. Began: September 1, 1980.

Channel capacity: 46 (not 2-way capable). Channels available but not in use: N.A.

Basic Service

Subscribers: 3,000 Includes Beech Creek, Bruno, Hanover & Sarah Ann.

Programming (received off-air): WCHS-TV (ABC) Charleston; WLPX-TV (ION) Charleston; WOWK-TV (CBS) Huntington; WPBY-TV (PBS) Huntington; WQCW (CW) Portsmouth; WSAZ-TV (MNT, NBC) Huntington; WVAH-TV (FOX) Charleston; WVVA (CW, NBC) Bluefield.

Programming (via satellite): A&E Networks; ABC Family Channel; AMC; Boomerang; Cartoon Network; CNBC; CNN; Country Music TV; C-SPAN; Discovery Channel; Discovery Health Channel; ESPN; ESPN 2; ESPNews; Food Network; Fox News Channel; Fox Sports Net Ohio; FX; G4; Gaming Entertainment Television; GSN; Headline News; HGTV; History Channel; Lifetime; MTV; Nickelodeon; Outdoor Channel; QVC; Speed; Spike TV; Syfy; TBS Superstation; The Learning Channel; The Weather Channel; Trinity Broadcasting Network; Turner Classic Movies; Turner Network TV; TV Land; USA Network; VH1; WE tv; WGN America.

Fee: $20.00 installation; $25.00 monthly.

Pay Service 1

Pay Units: 600 Includes Beech Creek, Bruno, Hanover & Sarah Ann.

Programming (via satellite): HBO; Showtime; The Movie Channel.

Fee: $15.00 installation; $10.50 monthly (each).

Video-On-Demand: No

Internet Service

Operational: No.

Telephone Service

None

Miles of Plant: 102.0 (coaxial); None (fiber optic). Miles of plant includes Beech Creek, Bruno, Hanover & Sarah Ann

General Manager: Gary Bowen. Office Manager: Rebecca Edwards.

Ownership: Colane Cable TV Inc. (MSO).

PAGE—Shentel, 106 S Main St, Edinburg, VA 22824. Phone: 540-984-5224. Web Site: http://www.shentel.net. Also serves Ingram Branch, Johnson Branch, Kincaid, North Page & Wriston. ICA: WV0248.

TV Market Ranking: 36 (Ingram Branch, Johnson Branch, Kincaid, North Page, PAGE, Wriston). Franchise award date: N.A. Franchise expiration date: N.A. Began: N.A.

Channel capacity: N.A. Channels available but not in use: N.A.

Basic Service

Subscribers: 420.

Programming (received off-air): WCHS-TV (ABC) Charleston; WLFB (IND) Bluefield; WOAY-TV (ABC) Oak Hill; WOWK-TV (CBS) Huntington; WSAZ-TV (MNT, NBC) Huntington; WSWP-TV (PBS) Grandview; WVAH-TV (FOX) Charleston; WVNS-TV (CBS) Lewisburg; WVVA (CW, NBC) Bluefield.

Programming (via satellite): QVC.

Fee: $29.95 installation; $19.95 monthly; $1.50 converter.

Expanded Basic Service 1

Subscribers: N.A.

Programming (via satellite): A&E Networks; ABC Family Channel; AMC; Animal Planet; Bravo; Cartoon Network; CNBC; CNN; Comedy Central; Country Music TV; C-SPAN; Discovery Channel; Disney Channel; E! Entertainment Television; ESPN; ESPN 2; Food Network; Fox News Channel; FX; G4; Golf Channel; Headline News; HGTV; History Channel; Lifetime; MTV; Nickelodeon; Oxygen; Root Sports Pittsburgh; Speed; Spike TV; Syfy; TBS Superstation; The Learning Channel; The Weather Channel; Trinity Broadcasting Network; Turner Classic Movies; Turner Network TV; TV Land; USA Network; VH1; WGN America.

Fee: $18.00 monthly.

Digital Basic Service

Subscribers: N.A.

Programming (via satellite): BBC America; Bio; Bloomberg Television; Discovery Fit & Health; ESPN Classic Sports; ESPNews; Fox College Sports Atlantic; Fox College Sports Central; Fox College Sports Pacific; Fox Movie Channel; Fox Soccer; Fuse; GAS; GSN; History Channel International; Independent Film Channel; Lifetime Movie Network; MTV Networks Digital Suite; Music Choice; Nick Jr.; Nick Too; NickToons TV; Science Television; Style Network; Sundance Channel; Toon Disney; WE tv.

Fee: $12.95 monthly.

Pay Service 1

Pay Units: N.A.

Programming (via satellite): Flix; Showtime (multiplexed); The Movie Channel (multiplexed).

Fee: $8.95 monthly (each).

Digital Pay Service 1
Pay Units: N.A.
Programming (via satellite): Cinemax (multiplexed); HBO (multiplexed); Starz (multiplexed).
Video-On-Demand: No
Pay-Per-View
Playboy TV (delivered digitally); Fresh (delivered digitally); Shorteez (delivered digitally).
Internet Service
Operational: No.
Telephone Service
None
General Manager: Robert Harold. Chief Technician: Steve Adkins.
Ownership: Shenandoah Telecommunications Inc. (MSO).

PANTHER—Shentel, 99 Howard St, Welch, WV 24801. Phones: 540-984-5224; 800-743-6835. Web Site: http://www.shentel.net. Also serves Bull Creek, Isaban & Mohawk. ICA: WV0101.
TV Market Ranking: Below 100 (Bull Creek, Isaban, Mohawk, PANTHER). Franchise award date: N.A. Franchise expiration date: N.A. Began: January 1, 1973.
Channel capacity: 12 (not 2-way capable). Channels available but not in use: N.A.
Basic Service
Subscribers: 130.
Programming (received off-air): WOAY-TV (ABC) Oak Hill; WOWK-TV (CBS) Huntington; WSAZ-TV (MNT, NBC) Huntington; WVVA (CW, NBC) Bluefield.
Programming (via satellite): ABC Family Channel; CNN; Discovery Channel; ESPN; Spike TV; TBS Superstation; USA Network.
Fee: $39.95 installation; $23.25 monthly; $1.24 converter; $10.00 additional installation.
Video-On-Demand: No
Pay-Per-View
iN DEMAND (delivered digitally); Hot Choice (delivered digitally); Playboy TV (delivered digitally); Fresh (delivered digitally); Shorteez (delivered digitally).
Internet Service
Operational: No.
Telephone Service
None
Miles of Plant: 25.0 (coaxial); None (fiber optic).
President: Christopher French. Vice President, Customer Service: David Ferguson. General Manager: Anthony Barlage. Marketing Manager: Chris Ranson.
Ownership: Shenandoah Telecommunications Inc. (MSO).

PARKERSBURG—Suddenlink Communications, 1737 7th St, Parkersburg, WV 26101-5007. Phones: 304-757-8001 (Scott Depot office); 304-485-1700; 800-972-5757 (Customer service). Fax: 304-424-9656. Web Site: http://www.suddenlink.com. Also serves Addison Twp., Belpre, Cheshire, Cheshire Twp., Gallipolis, Marietta, Middleport, Pomeroy, Racine, Reno, Rutland, Springfield Twp., Syracuse & Washington County, OH; Belmont, Boaz, Bradley, Elizabeth, Gallipolis Ferry, Hartford, Henderson, Mason, Mineralwells, New Haven, New Martinsville, North Hills, Paden City, Pleasants County, Point Pleasant, Proctor, Ravenswood, Reno, Ripley, Sistersville, Spencer, St. Marys, Tyler County (portions), Vienna, Waverly, Wetzel County (portions), Williamstown & Wood County, WV. ICA: WV0003.
TV Market Ranking: 36 (Gallipolis, Gallipolis Ferry, Henderson, Point Pleasant, Ripley, Spencer); 90 (New Martinsville, Paden City, Proctor, Wetzel County (portions)); Below 100 (Belmont, Belpre, Boaz, Bradley, Elizabeth, Hartford, Marietta, Mason, Middleport, Mineralwells, New Haven, North Hills, PARKERSBURG, Pleasants County (portions), Pomeroy, Racine, Ravenswood, Reno, Reno, Rutland, St. Marys, Syracuse, Tyler County (portions), Vienna, Washington County, Waverly, Williamstown, Wood County); Outside TV Markets (Addison Twp., Cheshire, Cheshire Twp., Sistersville, Springfield Twp., Tyler County (portions)). Franchise award date: N.A. Franchise expiration date: N.A. Began: January 1, 1961.
Channel capacity: N.A. Channels available but not in use: N.A.
Basic Service
Subscribers: 50,032.
Programming (received off-air): WCHS-TV (ABC) Charleston; WOUB-TV (PBS) Athens; WOWK-TV (CBS) Huntington; WPBY-TV (PBS) Huntington; WSAZ-TV (MNT, NBC) Huntington; WTAP-TV (FOX, MNT, NBC) Parkersburg; WVAH-TV (FOX) Charleston; allband FM.
Programming (via microwave): WBNS-TV (CBS) Columbus; WSYX (ABC, MNT) Columbus.
Programming (via satellite): C-SPAN; C-SPAN 2; CW+; INSP; ION Television; QVC; ShopNBC; Trinity Broadcasting Network; WGN-TV (CW, IND) Chicago.
Fee: $59.95 installation; $10.42 monthly; $2.00 converter.
Expanded Basic Service 1
Subscribers: 24,059.
Programming (via satellite): A&E Networks; ABC Family Channel; AMC; Animal Planet; BET Networks; Bravo; Cartoon Network; CNBC; CNN; Comedy Central; Country Music TV; Discovery Channel; Disney Channel; E! Entertainment Television; ESPN; ESPN 2; Food Network; Fox News Channel; FX; G4; Golf Channel; GSN; Hallmark Channel; Headline News; HGTV; History Channel; Lifetime; MSNBC; MTV; National Geographic Channel; Nickelodeon; Ohio News Network; Outdoor Channel; Oxygen; Root Sports Pittsburgh; SoapNet; Speed; Spike TV; Style Network; Syfy; TBS Superstation; The Learning Channel; The Weather Channel; Toon Disney; Travel Channel; truTV; Turner Classic Movies; Turner Network TV; TV Guide Network; TV Land; USA Network; Versus; VH1; WE tv.
Fee: $13.56 monthly.
Digital Basic Service
Subscribers: N.A.
Programming (via satellite): BBC America; Bio; Bloomberg News Radio; Discovery Fit & Health; DIY Network; DMX Music; ESPN; ESPN Classic Sports; ESPNews; Fox College Sports Atlantic; Fox College Sports Central; Fox College Sports Pacific; Fox Deportes; Fox Movie Channel; Fox Soccer; Fuel TV; Fuse; GAS; Great American Country; HD Theater; History Channel International; Independent Film Channel; Lifetime Movie Network; MTV Networks Digital Suite; Music Choice; NFL Network; Nick Jr.; Nick Too; NickToons TV; Science Television; Sundance Channel; TVG Network.
Pay Service 1
Pay Units: 2,322.
Programming (via satellite): Encore (multiplexed); Flix; Showtime (multiplexed); The Movie Channel (multiplexed).
Digital Pay Service 1
Pay Units: N.A.
Programming (via satellite): Cinemax (multiplexed); HBO (multiplexed); HBO HD; Showtime; Starz (multiplexed).
Video-On-Demand: Yes
Pay-Per-View
Playboy TV (delivered digitally); Fresh (delivered digitally); Shorteez (delivered digitally).
Internet Service
Operational: Yes.
Broadband Service: Suddenlink High Speed Internet.
Fee: $49.95 installation; $29.99 monthly.
Telephone Service
Digital: Operational
Miles of Plant: 1,028.0 (coaxial); None (fiber optic).
Vice President, Operations: David Bach. General Manager: Patrick Barclay. Technical Operations Director: Bob Logg. Marketing Director: Stan Howell. Marketing Manager: Kenny Phillips.
Ownership: Cequel Communications LLC (MSO).

PARKERSBURG (southern portion)—Community Antenna Service, 1525 Dupont Rd, Parkersburg, WV 26101-9623. Phone: 304-420-2470. Fax: 304-420-2474. E-mail: info@cascable.com. Web Site: http://www.cascable.com. Also serves Belleville, Dallison, Davisville, Murphytown, Walker & Washington. ICA: WV0200. **Note:** This system is an overbuild.
TV Market Ranking: Below 100 (Belleville, Dallison, Davisville, Murphytown, PARKERSBURG (SOUTHERN PORTION), Walker, Washington). Franchise award date: N.A. Franchise expiration date: N.A. Began: June 1, 1981.
Channel capacity: 66 (not 2-way capable). Channels available but not in use: N.A.
Basic Service
Subscribers: 3,000.
Programming (received off-air): WCHS-TV (ABC) Charleston; WOUB-TV (PBS) Athens; WOWK-TV (CBS) Huntington; WPBY-TV (PBS) Huntington; WSAZ-TV (MNT, NBC) Huntington; WTAP-TV (FOX, MNT, NBC) Parkersburg; WVAH-TV (FOX) Charleston.
Programming (via satellite): A&E Networks; ABC Family Channel; AmericanLife TV Network; Animal Planet; Cartoon Network; CNBC; CNN; Country Music TV; C-SPAN; C-SPAN 2; CW+; Discovery Channel; Discovery Health Channel; Disney Channel; DIY Network; ESPN; ESPN 2; ESPNews; Food Network; Fox News Channel; Fox Sports Net Ohio; FX; G4; Golf Channel; Hallmark Channel; Headline News; HGTV; History Channel; INSP; ION Television; Lifetime; MSNBC; National Geographic Channel; Nickelodeon; Outdoor Channel; Ovation; Praise Television; QVC; Speed; Spike TV; Syfy; TBS Superstation; The Learning Channel; The Weather Channel; Travel Channel; Trinity Broadcasting Network; truTV; Turner Classic Movies; Turner Network TV; TV Guide Network; TV Land; USA Network; WGN America.
Fee: $45.00 installation; $37.95 monthly.
Digital Basic Service
Subscribers: N.A.
Programming (via satellite): Encore; Music Choice.
Fee: $15.80 monthly.
Pay Service 1
Pay Units: N.A.
Programming (via satellite): Cinemax; HBO; Showtime.
Fee: $10.95 monthly (Cinemax), $13.95 monthly (HBO or Showtime).
Digital Pay Service 1
Pay Units: N.A.
Programming (via satellite): Cinemax (multiplexed); Flix; HBO (multiplexed); Showtime (multiplexed); Sundance Channel; The Movie Channel (multiplexed).
Fee: $10.95 monthly (Cinemax), $13.95 monthly (HBO or Flix/Showtime/Sundance/TMC).
Video-On-Demand: No
Internet Service
Operational: Yes.
Broadband Service: In-house.
Fee: $19.95 monthly.
Telephone Service
Digital: Operational
Fee: 29.95-$39.95 monthly
Miles of Plant: 113.0 (coaxial); None (fiber optic).
Manager: Arthur R. Cooper. Program & Marketing Director: Lisa Wilkinson. Chief Technician: Steve Defibaugh.
Ownership: Arthur R. Cooper (MSO).

PAW PAW—Atlantic Broadband, 120 Southmont Blvd, Johnstown, PA 15905. Phones: 888-536-9600; 814-539-8971. Fax: 814-535-7749. E-mail: info@atlanticbb.com. Web Site: http://www.atlanticbb.com. ICA: WV0259.
TV Market Ranking: Outside TV Markets (PAW PAW).
Channel capacity: 38 (not 2-way capable). Channels available but not in use: N.A.
Basic Service
Subscribers: 105.
Programming (received off-air): WHAG-TV (NBC) Hagerstown; WJLA-TV (ABC) Washington; WNPB-TV (PBS) Morgantown; WTTG (FOX) Washington; WUSA (CBS) Washington.
Programming (via satellite): INSP; QVC.
Fee: $25.00 installation; $16.95 monthly.
Expanded Basic Service 1
Subscribers: N.A.
Programming (via satellite): A&E Networks; AMC; Animal Planet; Cartoon Network; CNN; Comedy Central; Country Music TV; Discovery Channel; Discovery Health Channel; Disney Channel; E! Entertainment Television; ESPN; Fox News Channel; FX; Hallmark Channel; History Channel; Lifetime; MSNBC; Nickelodeon; Spike TV; Syfy; TBS Superstation; The Learning Channel; The Weather Channel; truTV; Turner Network TV; TV Land; USA Network; VH1.
Fee: $23.04 monthly.
Digital Basic Service
Subscribers: N.A.
Programming (via satellite): BBC America; Bio; Bloomberg Television; CMT Pure Country; Cooking Channel; Discovery Fit & Health; Discovery Kids Channel; DMX Music; Encore (multiplexed); ESPN 2; ESPN Classic Sports; ESPNews; Fuse; G4; Golf Channel; GSN; Halogen Network; History Channel International; ID Investigation Discovery; Independent Film Channel; Lifetime Movie Network; Military Channel; MTV2; National Geographic Channel; Nick Jr.; NickToons TV; Outdoor Channel; Planet Green; Science; SoapNet; Speed; Starz (multiplexed); Style Network; Toon Disney; Trinity Broadcasting Network; Turner Classic Movies; VH1 Classic.
Fee: $21.90 monthly.

Digital Pay Service 1
Pay Units: N.A.
Programming (via satellite): Cinemax (multiplexed); HBO (multiplexed); Showtime; The Movie Channel (multiplexed).
Fee: $15.95 monthly (HBO, Cinemax, or Showtime/TMC).
Video-On-Demand: No
Pay-Per-View
iN DEMAND (delivered digitally).
Internet Service
Operational: No.
Telephone Service
None
Vice President: David Dane. General Manager: Mike Papasergi. Technical Operations Director: Charles Sorchilla. Marketing & Customer Service Director: Dara Leslie. Marketing Manager: Natalie Kurchak.
Ownership: Atlantic Broadband (MSO).

PAX—Charter Communications. Now served by BECKLEY, WV [WV0005]. ICA: WV0244.

PENNSBORO—Shentel, 106 S Main St, Edinburg, VA 22824. Phone: 540-984-5224. Web Site: http://www.shentel.net. ICA: WV0092.
TV Market Ranking: Below 100 (PENNSBORO). Franchise award date: December 11, 1965. Franchise expiration date: N.A. Began: November 1, 1966.
Channel capacity: 21 (operating 2-way). Channels available but not in use: N.A.
Basic Service
Subscribers: 378.
Programming (received off-air): WDTV (CBS) Weston; WNPB-TV (PBS) Morgantown; WOWK-TV (CBS) Huntington; WTAP-TV (FOX, MNT, NBC) Parkersburg; WTRF-TV (CBS) Wheeling; WVAH-TV (FOX) Charleston; WVFX (CW, FOX) Clarksburg.
Programming (via satellite): The Weather Channel; WABC-TV (ABC) New York; WGN America.
Fee: $29.95 installation; $19.95 monthly.
Expanded Basic Service 1
Subscribers: N.A.
Programming (via satellite): A&E Networks; ABC Family Channel; AMC; Animal Planet; Cartoon Network; CNN; C-SPAN; Discovery Channel; Disney Channel; E! Entertainment Television; ESPN; ESPN 2; ESPN Classic Sports; Fox News Channel; FX; Great American Country; GSN; Hallmark Channel; Headline News; HGTV; History Channel; Lifetime; MSNBC; MTV; Nickelodeon; Root Sports Pittsburgh; SoapNet; Speed; Spike TV; TBS Superstation; The Learning Channel; Turner Classic Movies; Turner Network TV; TV Land; USA Network; VH1; WE tv.
Fee: $18.00 monthly.
Digital Basic Service
Subscribers: N.A.
Programming (via satellite): BBC America; Bio; Bloomberg Television; cloo; Discovery Digital Networks; DMX Music; ESPNews; Fox College Sports Atlantic; Fox College Sports Central; Fox College Sports Pacific; Fox Movie Channel; Fox Soccer; Fuse; G4; Golf Channel; History Channel International; Independent Film Channel; Lifetime Movie Network; National Geographic Channel; Outdoor Channel; ShopNBC; Style Network; Toon Disney; Trinity Broadcasting Network; Versus.
Fee: $12.95 monthly.
Pay Service 1
Pay Units: N.A.
Programming (via satellite): Cinemax; HBO; Showtime; The Movie Channel.

Digital Pay Service 1
Pay Units: N.A.
Programming (via satellite): Cinemax (multiplexed); Encore (multiplexed); Flix; HBO (multiplexed); Showtime (multiplexed); Starz (multiplexed); The Movie Channel (multiplexed).
Video-On-Demand: No
Pay-Per-View
iN DEMAND (delivered digitally); Playboy TV (delivered digitally); Fresh (delivered digitally).
Internet Service
Operational: No.
Telephone Service
None
Miles of Plant: 23.0 (coaxial); None (fiber optic).
General Manager: Robert Harold. Chief Technician: Steve Adkins.
Ownership: Shenandoah Telecommunications Inc. (MSO).

PETERSBURG—Shentel, 106 S Main St, Edinburg, VA 22824. Phone: 540-984-5224. Web Site: http://www.shentel.net. Also serves Johnson Run, Meadow Ridge & North Fork. ICA: WV0064.
TV Market Ranking: Outside TV Markets (Johnson Run, Meadow Ridge, North Fork, PETERSBURG). Franchise award date: N.A. Franchise expiration date: N.A. Began: July 1, 1958.
Channel capacity: 38 (operating 2-way). Channels available but not in use: N.A.
Basic Service
Subscribers: 871.
Programming (received off-air): WHSV-TV (ABC, MNT) Harrisonburg; WJAC-TV (NBC) Johnstown; WNPB-TV (PBS) Morgantown; WTTG (FOX) Washington; WUSA (CBS) Washington; WWCP-TV (FOX) Johnstown; allband FM.
Programming (via satellite): C-SPAN; QVC; Trinity Broadcasting Network; WGN America.
Fee: $29.95 installation; $19.95 monthly; $1.24 converter.
Expanded Basic Service 1
Subscribers: N.A.
Programming (via satellite): A&E Networks; ABC Family Channel; AMC; CNN; Comedy Central; C-SPAN 2; Discovery Channel; Disney Channel; ESPN; ESPN 2; ESPN Classic Sports; Food Network; Fox News Channel; Great American Country; GSN; Headline News; Lifetime; MSNBC; MTV; Nickelodeon; Outdoor Channel; Root Sports Pittsburgh; SoapNet; Speed; Spike TV; Syfy; TBS Superstation; The Learning Channel; The Weather Channel; Toon Disney; Turner Network TV; TV Land; USA Network; VH1; WE tv.
Fee: $20.00 monthly.
Digital Basic Service
Subscribers: N.A.
Programming (via satellite): BBC America; Bio; Bloomberg Television; cloo; Discovery Digital Networks; ESPNews; Fox College Sports Atlantic; Fox College Sports Central; Fox College Sports Pacific; Fox Movie Channel; Fox Soccer; Fuse; G4; Golf Channel; HGTV; History Channel International; Independent Film Channel; Lifetime Movie Network; National Geographic Channel; ShopNBC; Style Network; Turner Classic Movies; Versus.
Fee: $12.95 monthly.

Digital cable and TV coverage maps.
Visit www.warren-news.com/mediaprints.htm
MediaPrints
Map a Winning Business Strategy

Pay Service 1
Pay Units: 774.
Programming (via satellite): Encore; HBO; Showtime.
Fee: $10.00 installation; $3.99 monthly (Encore), $11.95 monthly (Showtime), $11.99 monthly (HBO).
Pay Service 2
Pay Units: N.A.
Programming (via satellite): Cinemax; Starz; The Movie Channel.
Fee: $7.95 monthly (Cinemax), $11.95 monthly (TMC).
Digital Pay Service 1
Pay Units: N.A.
Programming (via satellite): Cinemax (multiplexed); Encore (multiplexed); Flix; HBO (multiplexed); Showtime (multiplexed); Starz (multiplexed); The Movie Channel (multiplexed).
Video-On-Demand: No
Pay-Per-View
iN DEMAND (delivered digitally); Playboy TV (delivered digitally); Fresh (delivered digitally).
Internet Service
Operational: No.
Telephone Service
None
Miles of Plant: 35.0 (coaxial); None (fiber optic).
General Manager: Robert Harold. Chief Technician: Steve Adkins.
Ownership: Shenandoah Telecommunications Inc. (MSO).

PETERSTOWN—Charter Communications. Now served by BECKLEY, WV [WV0005]. ICA: WV0251.

PHILIPPI—Philippi Communications System, PO Box 460, Philippi, WV 26416. Phone: 304-457-3700. Fax: 304-457-2703. Web Site: http://www.philippi.org/tv.htm. Also serves Barbour County (portions). ICA: WV0054.
TV Market Ranking: Below 100 (Barbour County (portions), PHILIPPI). Franchise award date: March 1, 1985. Franchise expiration date: N.A. Began: March 1, 1986.
Channel capacity: 46 (not 2-way capable). Channels available but not in use: N.A.
Basic Service
Subscribers: 1,270.
Programming (received off-air): KDKA-TV (CBS) Pittsburgh; WBOY-TV (NBC) Clarksburg; WDTV (CBS) Weston; WNPB-TV (PBS) Morgantown; WPXI (IND, NBC) Pittsburgh; WTAE-TV (ABC) Pittsburgh; WVFX (CW, FOX) Clarksburg.
Programming (via satellite): FX; Headline News; History Channel; Spike TV; TBS Superstation; The Weather Channel; Vision TV.
Fee: $50.00 installation; $16.84 monthly; $3.00 converter; $25.00 additional installation.
Expanded Basic Service 1
Subscribers: 1,100.
Programming (via satellite): A&E Networks; ABC Family Channel; AMC; Animal Planet; CNBC; CNN; Country Music TV; C-SPAN; Discovery Channel; Disney Channel; ESPN; ESPN 2; ESPNews; Lifetime; MTV; Nickelodeon; Outdoor Channel; Prime Sports Radio; Root Sports Pittsburgh; The Learning Channel; Turner Network TV; USA Network; VH1; WGN America.
Fee: $25.00 installation; $27.29 monthly.
Pay Service 1
Pay Units: 197.
Programming (via satellite): HBO.
Fee: $25.00 installation; $10.00 monthly.
Pay Service 2
Pay Units: 89.
Programming (via satellite): Showtime.
Fee: $25.00 installation; $10.00 monthly.
Pay Service 3
Pay Units: 49.
Programming (via satellite): Cinemax.
Fee: $25.00 installation; $9.00 monthly.
Video-On-Demand: No
Internet Service
Operational: Yes.
Fee: $39.95 monthly.
Telephone Service
None
Miles of Plant: 48.0 (coaxial); None (fiber optic).
Manager: Karen Weaver. Chief Technician: Carl Radcliff.
Ownership: City of Philippi.

PINE GROVE—Zito Media, 611 Vader Hill Rd, Coudersport, PA 16915. Phone: 814-260-9575. Web Site: http://www.zitomedia.com. Also serves Hastings, Jacksonburg, Reader & Wetzel County. ICA: WV0081.
TV Market Ranking: 90 (Wetzel County (portions)); Below 100 (Hastings, Jacksonburg, PINE GROVE, Reader, Wetzel County (portions)). Franchise award date: N.A. Franchise expiration date: N.A. Began: January 1, 1954.
Channel capacity: 29 (not 2-way capable). Channels available but not in use: N.A.
Basic Service
Subscribers: 468.
Programming (received off-air): KDKA-TV (CBS) Pittsburgh; WBOY-TV (NBC) Clarksburg; WDTV (CBS) Weston; WNPB-TV (PBS) Morgantown; WTAE-TV (ABC) Pittsburgh; WTOV-TV (IND, NBC) Steubenville; WTRF-TV (CBS) Wheeling; WVFX (CW, FOX) Clarksburg; allband FM.
Programming (via satellite): The Weather Channel; WABC-TV (ABC) New York; WGN America.
Fee: $29.95 installation; $19.95 monthly; $1.24 converter.
Expanded Basic Service 1
Subscribers: N.A.
Programming (via satellite): A&E Networks; ABC Family Channel; AMC; Animal Planet; Cartoon Network; CNN; C-SPAN; Discovery Channel; Disney Channel; E! Entertainment Television; ESPN; ESPN 2; Fox News Channel; FX; Great American Country; Hallmark Channel; HGTV; History Channel; Lifetime; Nickelodeon; Root Sports Pittsburgh; Spike TV; Syfy; TBS Superstation; The Learning Channel; Turner Network TV; TV Land; USA Network.
Fee: $22.00 monthly.

Digital Basic Service
Subscribers: N.A.
Programming (via satellite): BBC America; Bio; Bloomberg Television; cloo; Discovery Digital Networks; DMX Music; ESPN Classic Sports; ESPNews; Fox College Sports Atlantic; Fox College Sports Central; Fox College Sports Pacific; Fox Movie Channel; Fox Soccer; Fuse; G4; Golf Channel; GSN; History Channel International; Independent Film Channel; Lifetime Movie Network; National Geographic Channel; Outdoor Channel; ShopNBC; Speed; Style Network; Toon Disney; Trinity Broadcasting Network; Turner Classic Movies; Versus; WE tv.
Pay Service 1
Pay Units: 162.
Programming (via satellite): HBO.
Fee: $17.50 installation; $11.99 monthly.
Pay Service 2
Pay Units: N.A.
Programming (via satellite): Showtime.
Fee: $11.95 monthly.
Digital Pay Service 1
Pay Units: N.A.
Programming (via satellite): Cinemax (multiplexed); Encore (multiplexed); Flix; HBO (multiplexed); Showtime (multiplexed); Starz (multiplexed); The Movie Channel (multiplexed).
Video-On-Demand: No
Pay-Per-View
iN DEMAND (delivered digitally); Playboy TV (delivered digitally); Fresh (delivered digitally).
Internet Service
Operational: No.
Telephone Service
None
Miles of Plant: 32.0 (coaxial); None (fiber optic).
Public Relations Manager: Mark Laver.
Ownership: Zito Media (MSO).

PINEVILLE—Shentel, 60 Long Ridge Rd, Ste 404, Stamford, CT 6902. Phones: 540-984-5224; 800-743-6835. Web Site: http://www.shentel.net. Also serves Alpoca (portions), Brenton, Briar Creek, Bud (portions), Clear Fork, Corinne, Covel, Cyclone, Fanrock, Garwood, Glen Fork, Glen Rogers, Hotchkiss, Itmann, Jesse, Kopperstown, Maben, McGraws, Mullens, New Richmond, Oceana, Pierpoint, Ravencliff, Rock View, Sabine, Saulsville, Slab Fork & Wyoming County (portions). ICA: WV0204.
TV Market Ranking: Below 100 (Alpoca (portions), Brenton, Briar Creek, Bud (portions), Clear Fork, Corinne, Covel, Cyclone, Fanrock, Garwood, Glen Fork, Glen Rogers, Hotchkiss, Itmann, Jesse, Kopperstown, Maben, McGraws, Mullens, New Richmond, Oceana, Pierpoint, PINEVILLE, Ravencliff, Rock View, Sabine, Saulsville, Slab Fork, Wyoming County (portions)). Franchise award date: October 1, 1952. Franchise expiration date: N.A. Began: October 1, 1952.
Channel capacity: N.A. Channels available but not in use: N.A.
Basic Service
Subscribers: N.A.
Programming (received off-air): WCHS-TV (ABC) Charleston; WOAY-TV (ABC) Oak Hill; WSWP-TV (PBS) Grandview; WVNS-TV (CBS) Lewisburg; WVVA (CW, NBC) Bluefield; 12 FMs.
Programming (via satellite): INSP; QVC; TBS Superstation; Trinity Broadcasting Network.
Fee: $39.95 installation; $19.95 monthly; $10.00 additional installation.
Expanded Basic Service 1
Subscribers: N.A.
Programming (via satellite): A&E Networks; ABC Family Channel; AMC; Animal Planet; Cartoon Network; CNBC; CNN; C-SPAN; Discovery Channel; Disney Channel; ESPN; ESPN 2; Fox News Channel; FX; Golf Channel; Great American Country; Headline News; HGTV; History Channel; Lifetime; MSNBC; MTV; National Geographic Channel; Nickelodeon; Outdoor Channel; Root Sports Pittsburgh; Speed; Spike TV; Syfy; The Learning Channel; The Weather Channel; Toon Disney; Travel Channel; Turner Classic Movies; Turner Network TV; TV Land; USA Network; VH1.
Fee: $21.00 monthly.
Digital Basic Service
Subscribers: N.A.
Programming (via satellite): BBC America; Bio; cloo; CMT Pure Country; Discovery Fit & Health; Discovery Health Channel; Discovery Home Channel; Discovery Kids Channel; ESPN Classic Sports; ESPN U; ESPNews; Fox Soccer; Fuse; G4; GSN; History Channel International; ID Investigation Discovery; Independent Film Channel; Lifetime Movie Network; Military Channel; Music Choice; Nick Jr.; NickToons TV; Oxygen; Science; SoapNet; TeenNick; Versus.
Fee: $14.00 monthly.
Pay Service 1
Pay Units: 181.
Programming (via satellite): HBO; Showtime.
Fee: $10.90 monthly (Showtime), $11.95 monthly (HBO).
Digital Pay Service 1
Pay Units: N.A.
Programming (via satellite): Cinemax (multiplexed); Encore (multiplexed); Flix; HBO (multiplexed); Showtime (multiplexed); Starz (multiplexed); The Movie Channel (multiplexed).
Fee: $11.95 monthly (Cinemax or Starz/Encore), $12.95 monthly (HBO or Showtime/TMC).
Video-On-Demand: No
Pay-Per-View
iN DEMAND (delivered digitally); Hot Choice (delivered digitally); Ten Blue (delivered digitally); Ten Blox (delivered digitally); Ten Clips (delivered digitally).
Internet Service
Operational: Yes.
Broadband Service: JetBroadband.
Fee: $49.95 installation; $39.95 monthly; $5.00 modem lease.
Telephone Service
None
President: Christopher French. Vice President, Customer Service: David Ferguson. General Manager: Anthony W. Barlage. Marketing Manager: Chris Ranson.
Ownership: Shenandoah Telecommunications Inc. (MSO).

PIPESTEM—Charter Communications. Now served by BECKLEY, WV [WV0005]. ICA: WV0118.

PLINY—Bradley Communications, PO Box 41, Wharton, WV 25208-0041. Phones: 800-582-3546; 304-247-6231. Fax: 304-247-6255. Also serves Fraziers Bottom & Mason County (portions). ICA: WV0264.
TV Market Ranking: 36 (Fraziers Bottom, Mason County (portions), PLINY).
Channel capacity: 41 (not 2-way capable). Channels available but not in use: N.A.
Basic Service
Subscribers: 181.
Programming (received off-air): WCHS-TV (ABC) Charleston; WLPX-TV (ION) Charleston; WOUB-TV (PBS) Athens; WOWK-TV (CBS) Huntington; WPBY-TV (PBS) Huntington; WSAZ-TV (MNT, NBC) Huntington; WTSF (IND) Ashland; WVAH-TV (FOX) Charleston.
Programming (via satellite): TBS Superstation; WGN America.
Fee: $39.34 installation; $12.55 monthly.
Expanded Basic Service 1
Subscribers: 172.
Programming (via satellite): A&E Networks; ABC Family Channel; Cartoon Network; CNN; Comedy Central; Country Music TV; C-SPAN; Discovery Channel; Disney Channel; ESPN; ESPN 2; FX; Headline News; HGTV; INSP; Lifetime; MTV; Nickelodeon; Outdoor Channel; QVC; Root Sports Pittsburgh; Spike TV; Syfy; The Weather Channel; Trinity Broadcasting Network; truTV; Turner Classic Movies; Turner Network TV; TV Land; USA Network; VH1.
Fee: $5.40 monthly.
Pay Service 1
Pay Units: 12.
Programming (via satellite): HBO.
Fee: $11.95 monthly.
Pay Service 2
Pay Units: N.A.
Programming (via satellite): Cinemax.
Fee: $11.95 monthly.
Internet Service
Operational: No.
Telephone Service
None
Miles of Plant: 20.0 (coaxial); None (fiber optic).
Manager: Beth Jenkins. Chief Technician: Skip Brewer.

POINT PLEASANT—Charter Communications. Now served by PARKERSBURG, WV [WV0003]. ICA: WV0008.

PRICETOWN—Formerly served by Cebridge Connections. No longer in operation. ICA: WV0205.

PRICHARD—Windjammer Cable, 8500 W 110th St, Ste 600, Overland Park, KS 66210. Phone: 888-495-2881. Fax: 913-563-5454. Web Site: http://www.windjammercable.com. Also serves Boyd County (southern portion), Burnaugh & Cyrus, KY; Centerville & Wayne County (unincorporated areas), WV. ICA: KY0129.
TV Market Ranking: 36 (Boyd County (southern portion), Burnaugh, Centerville, Cyrus, PRICHARD, Wayne County (unincorporated areas)). Franchise award date: N.A. Franchise expiration date: N.A. Began: January 1, 1983.
Channel capacity: 32 (not 2-way capable). Channels available but not in use: N.A.
Basic Service
Subscribers: 1,125.
Programming (received off-air): WCHS-TV (ABC) Charleston; WKAS (PBS) Ashland; WOWK-TV (CBS) Huntington; WPBY-TV (PBS) Huntington; WQCW (CW) Portsmouth; WSAZ-TV (MNT, NBC) Huntington; WTSF (IND) Ashland; WVAH-TV (FOX) Charleston; WYMT-TV (CBS, CW) Hazard.
Programming (via satellite): QVC; WGN America.
Fee: $39.95 installation; $17.99 monthly.
Expanded Basic Service 1
Subscribers: N.A.
Programming (via satellite): A&E Networks; ABC Family Channel; AMC; CNBC; CNN; Country Music TV; Discovery Channel; Disney Channel; ESPN; ESPN 2; Headline News; Lifetime; Nickelodeon; Spike TV; TBS Superstation; The Learning Channel; The Weather Channel; Turner Network TV; USA Network.
Fee: $21.81 monthly.
Digital Basic Service
Subscribers: N.A.
Programming (via satellite): Bravo; ESPN Classic Sports; HGTV; History Channel; Syfy; Versus; WE tv.
Fee: $10.95 monthly.
Digital Pay Service 1
Pay Units: N.A.
Programming (via satellite): Cinemax (multiplexed); Encore (multiplexed); HBO (multiplexed); Showtime (multiplexed); Starz (multiplexed); The Movie Channel (multiplexed).
Fee: $16.95 monthly (each).
Video-On-Demand: No
Pay-Per-View
iN DEMAND (delivered digitally); Club Jenna (delivered digitally).
Internet Service
Operational: No.
Telephone Service
None
Miles of Plant: 93.0 (coaxial); None (fiber optic).
General Manager: Timothy Evard. Operations Director: Belinda Graham. Engineering Director: Mike Earehart. Finance & Accounting Director: Cindy Johnson.
Ownership: Windjammer Communications LLC (MSO).

PRINCETON—Charter Communications. Now served by BECKLEY, WV [WV0005]. ICA: WV0018.

PULLMAN—Formerly served by Cebridge Connections. No longer in operation. ICA: WV0159.

QUICK—Windjammer Cable, 8500 W 110th St, Ste 600, Overland Park, KS 66210. Phone: 888-495-2881. Fax: 913-563-5454. Web Site: http://www.windjammercable.com. ICA: WV0275.
TV Market Ranking: 36 (QUICK).
Channel capacity: N.A. Channels available but not in use: N.A.
Basic Service
Subscribers: N.A.
Programming (received off-air): WCHS-TV (ABC) Charleston; WLPX-TV (ION) Charleston; WOWK-TV (CBS) Huntington; WPBY-TV (PBS) Huntington; WSAZ-TV (MNT, NBC) Huntington; WVAH-TV (FOX) Charleston.
Programming (via satellite): ABC Family Channel; CNN; Discovery Channel; Disney Channel; ESPN; ESPN 2; Nickelodeon; QVC; Spike TV; TBS Superstation; Trinity Broadcasting Network; Turner Network TV; USA Network; WGN America.
Fee: $39.95 installation; $30.38 monthly.
Digital Basic Service
Subscribers: N.A.
Programming (via satellite): BBC America; Bloomberg Television; Bravo; Discovery Fit & Health; Discovery Health Channel; Discovery Kids Channel; ESPN Classic Sports; ESPNews; Fox Soccer; G4; Golf Channel; GSN; HGTV; History Channel; Independent Film Channel; INSP; NickToons TV; Nip-

pon Golden Network; Outdoor Channel; Science; Syfy; Versus; WE tv.
Fee: $11.00 monthly.

Pay Service 1
Pay Units: N.A.
Programming (via satellite): HBO.

Digital Pay Service 1
Pay Units: N.A.
Programming (via satellite): Cinemax (multiplexed); Encore (multiplexed); HBO (multiplexed); Showtime (multiplexed); Starz (multiplexed); The Movie Channel (multiplexed).
Fee: $15.95 monthly (each).

Pay-Per-View
iN DEMAND (delivered digitally); Playboy TV (delivered digitally); Club Jenna (delivered digitally); Fresh (delivered digitally).

Internet Service
Operational: No.

Telephone Service
None

Ownership: Windjammer Communications LLC (MSO).

RANSON—Comcast Cable, 302 N Mildred St, Ranson, WV 25438-1455. Phones: 434-951-3700 (Charlottesville office); 304-725-9185. Fax: 304-725-0930. Web Site: http://www.comcast.com. Also serves Keedysville & Sharpsburg, MD; Berkeley County (portions), Bolivar, Charles Town, Harpers Ferry, Hedgesville, Inwood, Jefferson County, Kearneysville, Martinsburg, Rippon, Shannondale, Shenandoah Junction (unincorporated areas), Sheperdstown & Summit Point, WV. ICA: WV0016.

TV Market Ranking: Below 100 (Berkeley County (portions), Bolivar, Charles Town, Harpers Ferry, Hedgesville, Inwood, Jefferson County, Kearneysville, Keedysville, Martinsburg, RANSON, Rippon, Shannondale, Sharpsburg, Shenandoah Junction (unincorporated areas), SHEPHERDSTOWN, Summit Point). Franchise award date: January 1, 1996. Franchise expiration date: N.A. Began: N.A.

Channel capacity: N.A. Channels available but not in use: N.A.

Basic Service
Subscribers: 31,452.
Programming (received off-air): WBAL-TV (NBC) Baltimore; WDCA (MNT) Washington; WDCW (CW) Washington; WETA-TV (PBS) Washington; WHAG-TV (NBC) Hagerstown; WJAL (IND) Hagerstown; WJLA-TV (ABC) Washington; WJZ-TV (CBS) Baltimore; WMAR-TV (ABC) Baltimore; WNPB-TV (PBS) Morgantown; WRC-TV (NBC) Washington; WTTG (FOX) Washington; WUSA (CBS) Washington; WWPB (PBS) Hagerstown; WWPX-TV (ION) Martinsburg.
Programming (via satellite): C-SPAN; C-SPAN 2; Eternal Word TV Network; NewsChannel 8; QVC; ShopNBC; Trinity Broadcasting Network; TV Guide Network.
Fee: $37.00 installation; $15.50 monthly; $1.99 converter.

Expanded Basic Service 1
Subscribers: 27,485.
Programming (via satellite): A&E Networks; ABC Family Channel; AMC; Animal Planet; BET Networks; Cartoon Network; CNBC; CNN; Comcast SportsNet Mid-Atlantic; Comedy Central; Country Music TV; Discovery Channel; Disney Channel; E! Entertainment Television; ESPN; ESPN 2; Food Network; FX; Headline News; HGTV; History Channel; Lifetime; MSNBC; MTV; Nickelodeon; Spike TV; Syfy; TBS Superstation; The Learning Channel; The Weather Channel; Turner Network TV; TV Land; USA Network; VH1.
Fee: $16.00 monthly.

Digital Basic Service
Subscribers: 5,901.
Programming (via satellite): BBC America; Bravo; Canales N; Discovery Digital Networks; DMX Music; ESPN Classic Sports; ESPNews; Fox Sports World; Golf Channel; GSN; National Geographic Channel; Nick Jr.; Speed; Versus; VH1 Classic; VH1 Country; WE tv.
Fee: $9.99 monthly.

Digital Pay Service 1
Pay Units: 7,817.
Programming (via satellite): Cinemax (multiplexed); Encore (multiplexed); HBO (multiplexed); Showtime (multiplexed); Starz (multiplexed); The Movie Channel (multiplexed).
Fee: $11.02 installation; $4.95 monthly (Encore); $10.95 monthly (Cinemax, HBO, Showtime or TMC).

Video-On-Demand: Yes

Pay-Per-View
Addressable homes: 5,901.
iN DEMAND (delivered digitally); Playboy TV (delivered digitally).

Internet Service
Operational: Yes.
Broadband Service: Comcast High Speed Internet.
Fee: $42.95 monthly.

Telephone Service
Digital: Operational

Miles of Plant: 4,113.0 (coaxial); 424.0 (fiber optic).

Vice President & General Manager: Troy Fitzhugh. Technical Operations Director: Tom Jacobs. Chief Technician: John W. Nichols. Marketing Director: Steve Miles. Office Manager: Penny Miller.

Ownership: Comcast Cable Communications Inc. (MSO).

RAVENCLIFF—Jet Broadband. Now served by PINEVILLE, WV [WV0204]. ICA: WV0093.

RED HOUSE—Comcast Cable, Rt. 34 North, PO Box 126, Red House, WV 25168-0126. Phone: 304-586-3701. Fax: 304-586-9410. Web Site: http://www.comcast.com. Also serves Bancroft, Buffalo, Eleanor, Elsinore, Hometown, Nitro (portions), Poca, Rock Branch, Scott Depot, St. Albans (portions) & Winfield. ICA: WV0027.

TV Market Ranking: 36 (Bancroft, Buffalo, Eleanor, Elsinore, Hometown, Nitro (portions), Poca, RED HOUSE, Rock Branch, Scott Depot, St. Albans (portions), Winfield). Franchise award date: N.A. Franchise expiration date: N.A. Began: February 15, 1977.

Channel capacity: N.A. Channels available but not in use: N.A.

Basic Service
Subscribers: 4,619.
Programming (received off-air): WCHS-TV (ABC) Charleston; WLPX-TV (ION) Charleston; WOWK-TV (CBS) Huntington; WPBY-TV (PBS) Huntington; WQCW (CW) Portsmouth; WSAZ-TV (MNT, NBC) Huntington; WVAH-TV (FOX) Charleston.
Programming (via satellite): ABC Family Channel; C-SPAN; C-SPAN 2; Eternal Word TV Network; Gospel Music TV; INSP; QVC; TBS Superstation; The Weather Channel; TV Guide Network; WGN America.
Fee: $54.99 installation.

Expanded Basic Service 1
Subscribers: N.A.
Programming (via satellite): AMC; Animal Planet; BET Networks; Bio; Bravo; Cartoon Network; CNBC; CNN; Comedy Central; Country Music TV; Discovery Channel; Disney Channel; E! Entertainment Television; ESPN; ESPN 2; Food Network; Fox News Channel; Fox Sports Net Ohio; FX; Golf Channel; Hallmark Channel; Headline News; HGTV; History Channel; Lifetime; MSNBC; MTV; National Geographic Channel; Nickelodeon; Outdoor Channel; Oxygen; Product Information Network; Root Sports Pittsburgh; ShopNBC; Speed; Spike TV; Syfy; The Learning Channel; Toon Disney; Travel Channel; truTV; Turner Network TV; TV Land; USA Network; VH1; WE tv.
Fee: $47.57 monthly.

Digital Basic Service
Subscribers: N.A.
Programming (via satellite): AmericanLife TV Network; BBC America; Bloomberg Television; Discovery Fit & Health; ESPN Classic Sports; ESPNews; Fox Movie Channel; Fox Sports World; G4; GSN; SoapNet; Trinity Broadcasting Network; Turner Classic Movies; Versus.
Fee: $11.95 monthly.

Digital Expanded Basic Service
Subscribers: N.A.
Programming (via satellite): A&E Networks; Canales N; Music Choice; Nick Jr.; NickToons TV; VH1 Classic; VH1 Country.

Digital Pay Service 1
Pay Units: N.A.
Programming (via satellite): ART America; CCTV-4; Cinemax (multiplexed); Encore (multiplexed); Filipino Channel; Flix; HBO (multiplexed); RAI International; Showtime (multiplexed); Starz (multiplexed); Sundance Channel; The Movie Channel (multiplexed); TV Asia; TV Japan; TV5, La Television International; Zee TV USA; Zhong Tian Channel.

Video-On-Demand: No

Pay-Per-View
Urban American Television Network (delivered digitally); Hot Choice (delivered digitally); Fresh (delivered digitally); Playboy TV (delivered digitally).

Internet Service
Operational: Yes.
Broadband Service: Comcast High Speed Internet.
Fee: $42.95 monthly.

Telephone Service
None

Miles of Plant: 145.0 (coaxial); None (fiber optic).

General Manager: Tim Hagan. Plant Manager: Rob Thacker.

Ownership: Comcast Cable Communications Inc. (MSO).

RICHWOOD—Shentel, 106 S Main St, Edinburg, VA 22824. Phone: 540-984-5224. Web Site: http://www.shentel.net. Also serves Fenwick, Holcomb & New Hope. ICA: WV0058.

TV Market Ranking: Below 100 (Fenwick, Holcomb, New Hope, RICHWOOD). Franchise award date: N.A. Franchise expiration date: July 7, 2010. Began: May 1, 1952.

Channel capacity: 37 (not 2-way capable). Channels available but not in use: N.A.

Basic Service
Subscribers: 1,372.
Programming (received off-air): WBOY-TV (NBC) Clarksburg; WCHS-TV (ABC) Charleston; WOAY-TV (ABC) Oak Hill; WOWK-TV (CBS) Huntington; WSAZ-TV (MNT, NBC) Huntington; WSWP-TV (PBS) Grandview; WVAH-TV (FOX) Charleston; allband FM.
Programming (via satellite): C-SPAN; QVC; WGN America.
Fee: $29.95 installation; $19.95 monthly; $1.24 converter.

Expanded Basic Service 1
Subscribers: N.A.
Programming (via satellite): A&E Networks; ABC Family Channel; AMC; Bravo; Cartoon Network; CNBC; CNN; Comedy Central; Country Music TV; Discovery Channel; Disney Channel; E! Entertainment Television; ESPN; ESPN 2; Fox News Channel; FX; G4; Golf Channel; Headline News; HGTV; History Channel; Lifetime; MTV; Nickelodeon; Oxygen; Speed; Spike TV; Syfy; TBS Superstation; The Learning Channel; The Weather Channel; Trinity Broadcasting Network; Turner Classic Movies; Turner Network TV; TV Land; USA Network; VH1.
Fee: $18.00 monthly.

Digital Basic Service
Subscribers: N.A.
Programming (via satellite): BBC America; Bio; Bloomberg Television; Discovery Fit & Health; ESPN Classic Sports; ESPNews; Fox College Sports Atlantic; Fox College Sports Central; Fox College Sports Pacific; Fox Movie Channel; Fox Sports World; Fuse; GAS; GSN; History Channel International; Independent Film Channel; Lifetime Movie Network; MTV Networks Digital Suite; Music Choice; Nick Jr.; Nick Too; NickToons TV; Style Network; Sundance Channel; Toon Disney; TV Guide Interactive Inc.; WE tv.
Fee: $12.95 monthly.

Digital Pay Service 1
Pay Units: N.A.
Programming (via satellite): Cinemax (multiplexed); Encore (multiplexed); Flix; HBO (multiplexed); Showtime (multiplexed); Starz (multiplexed); The Movie Channel (multiplexed).

Video-On-Demand: No

Internet Service
Operational: No.

Telephone Service
None

Miles of Plant: 32.0 (coaxial); None (fiber optic).

General Manager: Robert Harold. Chief Technician: Steve Adkins.

Ownership: Shenandoah Telecommunications Inc. (MSO).

RIG—C T & R Cable, 29 Water St, Petersburg, WV 26847-1544. Phone: 304-257-4891. ICA: WV0225.

TV Market Ranking: Outside TV Markets (RIG). Franchise award date: N.A. Franchise expiration date: N.A. Began: May 15, 1988.

Channel capacity: 23 (not 2-way capable). Channels available but not in use: N.A.

Basic Service
Subscribers: 100.
Programming (via satellite): ABC Family Channel; Cartoon Network; Discovery Channel; ESPN; ESPN 2; Fox News Channel; Spike TV; TBS Superstation; Turner Network TV; USA Network; WGN America.
Programming (via translator): WHSV-TV (ABC, MNT) Harrisonburg; WJAC-TV (NBC) Johnstown; WNPB-TV (PBS) Morgantown; WTTG (FOX) Washington; WUSA (CBS) Washington.
Fee: $25.00 installation; $20.00 monthly.
Pay Service 1
Pay Units: 23.
Programming (via satellite): Showtime.
Fee: $9.00 monthly.
Internet Service
Operational: No.
Telephone Service
None
Miles of Plant: 8.0 (coaxial); None (fiber optic).
Manager: Terry Hinkle. Chief Technician: Matt Alt.
Ownership: C T & R Cable LLC (MSO).

ROBSON—Charter Communications. Now served by CHARLESTON, WV (formerly Chelyan) [WV0006]. ICA: WV0153.

RONCEVERTE—Ronceverte TV Cable, PO Box 525, Ronceverte, WV 24970-0525. Phone: 304-645-4036. Fax: 304-645-1190. ICA: WV0208.
TV Market Ranking: Below 100 (RONCEVERTE). Franchise award date: February 1, 1991. Franchise expiration date: N.A. Began: N.A.
Channel capacity: 36 (not 2-way capable). Channels available but not in use: N.A.
Basic Service
Subscribers: 791.
Programming (received off-air): WDBJ (CBS, MNT) Roanoke; WOAY-TV (ABC) Oak Hill; WSLS-TV (NBC) Roanoke; WSWP-TV (PBS) Grandview; WVNS-TV (CBS) Lewisburg; WVVA (CW, NBC) Bluefield; allband FM.
Programming (via satellite): A&E Networks; ABC Family Channel; CNN; Country Music TV; Discovery Channel; ESPN; ESPN 2; Lifetime; Nickelodeon; Spike TV; Syfy; TBS Superstation; The Learning Channel; The Weather Channel; Trinity Broadcasting Network; Turner Classic Movies; Turner Network TV; USA Network; VH1; WGN America.
Fee: $27.75 installation; $35.00 monthly.
Pay Service 1
Pay Units: 90.
Programming (via satellite): HBO.
Fee: $14.00 monthly.
Video-On-Demand: No
Internet Service
Operational: No.
Telephone Service
None
Miles of Plant: 36.0 (coaxial); None (fiber optic).
Manager & Chief Technician: Gary W. Lemons.
Ownership: Ronceverte Television Corp.

RUPERT—Charter Communications. Now served by BECKLEY, WV [WV0009]. ICA: WV0209.

SALEM—Shentel, 500 Shentel Way, PO Box 459, Edinburg, VA 22824. Phone: 540-984-5224. Fax: 540-984-3438. Web Site: http://www.shentel.net. Also serves Bristol, Harrison County & Industrial. ICA: WV0066.
TV Market Ranking: Below 100 (Bristol, Harrison County, Industrial, SALEM). Franchise award date: N.A. Franchise expiration date: N.A. Began: July 20, 1962.
Channel capacity: 35 (operating 2-way). Channels available but not in use: N.A.
Basic Service
Subscribers: 998.
Programming (received off-air): WBOY-TV (NBC) Clarksburg; WDTV (CBS) Weston; WNPB-TV (PBS) Morgantown; WTRF-TV (CBS) Wheeling; WVFX (CW, FOX) Clarksburg; allband FM.
Programming (via satellite): C-SPAN; C-SPAN 2; QVC; WABC-TV (ABC) New York; WGN America.
Fee: $61.25 installation; $17.95 monthly; $1.24 converter.
Expanded Basic Service 1
Subscribers: 856.
Programming (via satellite): A&E Networks; ABC Family Channel; AMC; Animal Planet; Cartoon Network; CNBC; CNN; Comedy Central; Discovery Channel; Disney Channel; E! Entertainment Television; ESPN; ESPN 2; ESPN Classic Sports; Food Network; Fox News Channel; Great American Country; Headline News; HGTV; History Channel; ION Television; Lifetime; MSNBC; MTV; National Geographic Channel; Nickelodeon; Outdoor Channel; Root Sports Pittsburgh; SoapNet; Speed; Spike TV; Syfy; TBS Superstation; The Learning Channel; The Weather Channel; Toon Disney; Trinity Broadcasting Network; Turner Network TV; TV Land; USA Network; VH1; WE tv.
Fee: $25.00 monthly.
Digital Basic Service
Subscribers: N.A.
Programming (via satellite): BBC America; Bio; Bloomberg Television; cloo; Discovery Digital Networks; ESPNews; Fox College Sports Atlantic; Fox College Sports Central; Fox College Sports Pacific; Fox Movie Channel; Fox Soccer; Fuse; G4; Golf Channel; GSN; History Channel International; Independent Film Channel; Lifetime Movie Network; ShopNBC; Style Network; Turner Classic Movies; Versus.
Fee: $13.95 monthly.
Pay Service 1
Pay Units: 473.
Programming (via satellite): Cinemax; HBO.
Fee: $17.50 installation; $7.95 monthly (Cinemax), $11.99 monthly (HBO).
Pay Service 2
Pay Units: N.A.
Programming (via satellite): Showtime; The Movie Channel.
Digital Pay Service 1
Pay Units: N.A.
Programming (via satellite): Cinemax (multiplexed); Encore (multiplexed); Flix; HBO (multiplexed); Showtime (multiplexed); Starz (multiplexed); The Movie Channel (multiplexed).
Pay-Per-View
iN DEMAND (delivered digitally).
Internet Service
Operational: Yes. Began: December 31, 2005.
Broadband Service: Cebridge High Speed Cable Internet.
Fee: $49.95 installation; $29.99 monthly.
Telephone Service
Digital: Operational
Fee: $49.99 monthly
Miles of Plant: 25.0 (coaxial); None (fiber optic).
President: Christopher French. Vice President, Customer Service: David Ferguson.
Ownership: Shenandoah Telecommunications Inc. (MSO).

SALEM COLLEGE—Basco Electronics Inc., 420 W 2nd St, Weston, WV 26452-1702. Phone: 304-269-7530. Fax: 304-269-6581. ICA: WV0110.
TV Market Ranking: Below 100 (SALEM COLLEGE). Franchise award date: N.A. Franchise expiration date: N.A. Began: September 1, 1984.
Channel capacity: 25 (2-way capable). Channels available but not in use: N.A.
Basic Service
Subscribers: 140.
Programming (received off-air): WBOY-TV (NBC) Clarksburg; WDTV (CBS) Weston; WKRN-TV (ABC) Nashville; WNPB-TV (PBS) Morgantown; WVFX (CW, FOX) Clarksburg.
Programming (via satellite): ABC Family Channel; BET Networks; CNN; ESPN; MTV; TBS Superstation; The Learning Channel; Turner Network TV; TV Japan; USA Network; WE tv.
Fee: $6.30 monthly.
Video-On-Demand: No
Internet Service
Operational: No.
Telephone Service
None
Miles of Plant: 1.0 (coaxial); None (fiber optic).
Manager: Wilfred L. Sholes. Marketing Director: Sue Sholes. Chief Technician: Brian Queen.
Ownership: Basco Electronics Inc.

SALT ROCK—Windjammer Cable, 8500 W 110th St, Ste 600, Overland Park, KS 66210. Phone: 888-495-2881. Fax: 913-563-5454. Web Site: http://www.windjammercable.com. Also serves Cabell County (unincorporated areas). ICA: WV0084.
TV Market Ranking: 36 (Cabell County (unincorporated areas), SALT ROCK). Franchise award date: N.A. Franchise expiration date: N.A. Began: January 1, 1988.
Channel capacity: 32 (not 2-way capable). Channels available but not in use: N.A.
Basic Service
Subscribers: 780.
Programming (received off-air): WCHS-TV (ABC) Charleston; WOWK-TV (CBS) Huntington; WPBY-TV (PBS) Huntington; WSAZ-TV (MNT, NBC) Huntington; WVAH-TV (FOX) Charleston.
Programming (via satellite): ABC Family Channel; Headline News; TBS Superstation; Trinity Broadcasting Network; WGN America.
Fee: $39.95 installation; $12.66 monthly; $2.00 converter.
Expanded Basic Service 1
Subscribers: 678.
Programming (via satellite): A&E Networks; AMC; CNN; Country Music TV; Discovery Channel; Disney Channel; E! Entertainment Television; ESPN; Lifetime; MTV; Nickelodeon; Spike TV; Syfy; The Weather Channel; Turner Network TV; USA Network.
Fee: $22.91 monthly.
Digital Basic Service
Subscribers: N.A.
Programming (via satellite): BBC America; Bravo; Discovery Health Channel; Discovery Kids Channel; ESPN Classic Sports; ESPNews; Fox Soccer; Golf Channel; GSN; HGTV; History Channel; Independent Film Channel; Nick Jr.; Science; Versus; WE tv.
Fee: $10.95 monthly.
Digital Pay Service 1
Pay Units: N.A.
Programming (via satellite): Cinemax (multiplexed); Encore (multiplexed); HBO (multiplexed); Showtime (multiplexed); Starz (multiplexed); The Movie Channel (multiplexed).
Fee: $15.95 monthly (each).
Video-On-Demand: No
Pay-Per-View
HITS 1 (delivered digitally); HITS 2 (delivered digitally); HITS 3 (delivered digitally); HITS 4 (delivered digitally); HITS 5 (delivered digitally).
Internet Service
Operational: No.
Telephone Service
None
Miles of Plant: 41.0 (coaxial); None (fiber optic).
General Manager: Timothy Evard. Operations Director: Belinda Graham. Engineering Director: Mike Earehart. Finance & Accounting Director: Cindy Johnson.
Ownership: Windjammer Communications LLC (MSO).

SAND FORK—Rapid Cable. Now served by WESTON, WV [WV0034]. ICA: WV0147.

SANDYVILLE—Windjammer Cable, 8500 W 110th St, Ste 600, Overland Park, KS 66210. Phone: 888-495-2881. Fax: 913-563-5454. Web Site: http://www.windjammercable.com. Also serves Fairplain. ICA: WV0261.
TV Market Ranking: Below 100 (Fairplain, SANDYVILLE).
Channel capacity: N.A. Channels available but not in use: N.A.
Basic Service
Subscribers: N.A.
Programming (received off-air): WCHS-TV (ABC) Charleston; WOWK-TV (CBS) Huntington; WPBY-TV (PBS) Huntington; WSAZ-TV (MNT, NBC) Huntington; WVAH-TV (FOX) Charleston.
Programming (via satellite): A&E Networks; ABC Family Channel; Animal Planet; CNN; Discovery Channel; Disney Channel; ESPN; ESPN 2; Nickelodeon; QVC; Spike TV; TBS Superstation; Travel Channel; Trinity Broadcasting Network; Turner Network TV; USA Network; WGN America.
Fee: $39.95 installation; $33.20 monthly.
Pay Service 1
Pay Units: N.A.
Programming (via satellite): HBO.
Fee: $16.95 monthly.
Video-On-Demand: No
Internet Service
Operational: No.
Telephone Service
None
Miles of Plant: 12.0 (coaxial); None (fiber optic).
General Manager: Timothy Evard. Operations Director: Belinda Graham. Engineering Director: Mike Earehart. Finance & Accounting Director: Cindy Johnson.
Ownership: Windjammer Communications LLC (MSO).

SARAH ANN—Colane Cable TV Inc., PO Box 610, Omar, WV 25638. Phone: 304-946-2871. Fax: 304-946-4091. ICA: WV0148.
TV Market Ranking: Below 100 (SARAH ANN). Franchise award date: N.A. Franchise expiration date: N.A. Began: September 1, 1981.
Channel capacity: 57 (not 2-way capable). Channels available but not in use: N.A.

Basic Service
Subscribers: N.A. Included in Omar
Programming (received off-air): WCHS-TV (ABC) Charleston; WOWK-TV (CBS) Huntington; WPBY-TV (PBS) Huntington; WSAZ-TV (MNT, NBC) Huntington; WVAH-TV (FOX) Charleston; WVVA (CW, NBC) Bluefield.
Programming (via satellite): C-SPAN; ION Television; QVC; Trinity Broadcasting Network; WGN America.
Fee: $25.00 monthly.

Expanded Basic Service 1
Subscribers: N.A.
Programming (via satellite): A&E Networks; ABC Family Channel; AMC; Animal Planet; Boomerang; Cartoon Network; CNBC; CNN; Comedy Central; Country Music TV; Discovery Channel; Discovery Health Channel; ESPN; ESPN 2; ESPNews; Food Network; Fox News Channel; Fox Sports Net; FX; G4; Gospel Music TV; GSN; Hallmark Movie Channel; Headline News; HGTV; History Channel; Lifetime; MTV; Nickelodeon; Outdoor Channel; Speed; Spike TV; Syfy; TBS Superstation; The Learning Channel; The Weather Channel; Travel Channel; Turner Classic Movies; Turner Network TV; TV Land; USA Network; VH1; WE tv.
Fee: $29.95 monthly.

Pay Service 1
Pay Units: N.A. Included in Omar
Programming (via satellite): HBO; Showtime; The Movie Channel.

Internet Service
Operational: Yes.

Telephone Service
None

Miles of plant included in Omar
General Manager: Gary Bowen. Office Manager: Rebecca Edwards.
Ownership: Colane Cable TV Inc. (MSO).

SCARBRO—Shentel, 106 S Main St, Edinburg, VA 22824. Phone: 540-984-5224. Web Site: http://www.shentel.net. Also serves Dothan, Glen Jean, Harvey, Hilltop, Kingston, Mossy & Redstar. ICA: WV0031.
TV Market Ranking: 36 (Dothan, Kingston, Mossy); Below 100 (Glen Jean, Harvey, Hilltop, Redstar, SCARBRO). Franchise award date: N.A. Franchise expiration date: N.A. Began: January 1, 1952.
Channel capacity: 40 (not 2-way capable). Channels available but not in use: N.A.

Basic Service
Subscribers: 996.
Programming (received off-air): WCHS-TV (ABC) Charleston; WDRL-TV (IND) Danville; WLFB (IND) Bluefield; WOAY-TV (ABC) Oak Hill; WSWP-TV (PBS) Grandview; WVAH-TV (FOX) Charleston; WVNS-TV (CBS) Lewisburg; WVVA (CW, NBC) Bluefield.
Programming (via satellite): ABC Family Channel; Cartoon Network; CNN; Discovery Channel; ESPN; Headline News; Lifetime; QVC; Spike TV; The Weather Channel; Turner Network TV; USA Network; WGN America.
Fee: $29.95 installation; $19.95 monthly; $1.50 converter.

Expanded Basic Service 1
Subscribers: N.A.
Programming (via satellite): A&E Networks; AMC; Animal Planet; BET Networks; Bravo; CNBC; Comedy Central; Country Music TV; C-SPAN; Disney Channel; E! Entertainment Television; ESPN 2; Food Network; Fox News Channel; FX; G4; Golf Channel; HGTV; History Channel; MSNBC; MTV; National Geographic Channel; Nickelodeon; Oxygen; Root Sports Pittsburgh; Speed; Syfy; TBS Superstation; The Learning Channel; Travel Channel; Trinity Broadcasting Network; Turner Classic Movies; TV Land; VH1.
Fee: $18.00 monthly.

Digital Basic Service
Subscribers: N.A.
Programming (via satellite): BBC America; Bio; Bloomberg Television; Discovery Fit & Health; ESPN Classic Sports; ESPNews; Fox College Sports Atlantic; Fox College Sports Central; Fox College Sports Pacific; Fox Movie Channel; Fox Soccer; Fuse; GAS; GSN; History Channel International; Independent Film Channel; Lifetime Movie Network; MTV Networks Digital Suite; Music Choice; Nick Jr.; Nick Too; NickToons TV; Style Network; Sundance Channel; Toon Disney; TV Guide Interactive Inc.
Fee: $12.95 monthly.

Digital Pay Service 1
Pay Units: N.A.
Programming (via satellite): Cinemax (multiplexed); Encore; Flix; HBO (multiplexed); Showtime (multiplexed); Starz (multiplexed); The Movie Channel (multiplexed).

Video-On-Demand: No

Pay-Per-View
Fresh (delivered digitally); Shorteez (delivered digitally); Playboy TV (delivered digitally); iN DEMAND (delivered digitally).

Internet Service
Operational: No.

Telephone Service
None

Miles of Plant: 116.0 (coaxial); None (fiber optic).
General Manager: Robert Harold. Chief Technician: Steve Adkins.
Ownership: Shenandoah Telecommunications Inc. (MSO).

SHINNSTON—Suddenlink Communications, 12444 Powerscourt Dr, Saint Louis, MO 63131-3660. Phones: 314-965-2020; 304-472-4193. E-mail: gene.regan@suddenlink.com. Web Site: http://www.suddenlink.com. Also serves Enterprise, Farmington, Four States, Gypsy, Haywood, Hepzibah, Idamay, Lumberport, Marion County (portions), Spelter, Taylor County (eastern portion), Worthington & Wyatt. ICA: WV0029.
TV Market Ranking: Below 100 (Enterprise, Farmington, Four States, Gypsy, Haywood, Hepzibah, Idamay, Lumberport, Marion County (portions), SHINNSTON, Spelter, Taylor County (eastern portion), Worthington, Wyatt). Franchise award date: N.A. Franchise expiration date: N.A. Began: December 1, 1955.
Channel capacity: 36 (operating 2-way). Channels available but not in use: N.A.

Basic Service
Subscribers: 4,159.
Programming (received off-air): KDKA-TV (CBS) Pittsburgh; WBOY-TV (NBC) Clarksburg; WDTV (CBS) Weston; WNPB-TV (PBS) Morgantown; WTAE-TV (ABC) Pittsburgh; WTRF-TV (CBS) Wheeling; WVFX (CW, FOX) Clarksburg; allband FM.
Programming (via satellite): Eternal Word TV Network; QVC.
Fee: $61.25 installation; $17.95 monthly; $1.24 converter.

Expanded Basic Service 1
Subscribers: 3,939.
Programming (via satellite): A&E Networks; ABC Family Channel; AMC; Animal Planet; Bravo; Cartoon Network; CNN; Comedy Central; C-SPAN; C-SPAN 2; Discovery Channel; Disney Channel; E! Entertainment Television; ESPN; ESPN 2; ESPN Classic Sports; Food Network; Fox News Channel; FX; G4; Great American Country; GSN; Hallmark Channel; Headline News; HGTV; History Channel; Lifetime; MSNBC; MTV; National Geographic Channel; Nickelodeon; Outdoor Channel; Root Sports Pittsburgh; SoapNet; Speed; Spike TV; Syfy; TBS Superstation; The Learning Channel; The Weather Channel; Trinity Broadcasting Network; truTV; Turner Network TV; TV Guide Network; TV Land; USA Network; VH1; WE tv.
Fee: $26.00 monthly.

Digital Basic Service
Subscribers: N.A.
Programming (via satellite): BBC America; Bio; Bloomberg Television; Discovery Digital Networks; DMX Music; ESPNews; Fox College Sports Atlantic; Fox College Sports Central; Fox College Sports Pacific; Fox Movie Channel; Fox Soccer; Fuse; Golf Channel; History Channel International; Independent Film Channel; Lifetime Movie Network; ShopNBC; Style Network; Toon Disney; Turner Classic Movies; Versus.
Fee: $13.95 monthly.

Pay Service 1
Pay Units: 2,513.
Programming (via satellite): Cinemax; Encore; HBO; Showtime; The Movie Channel.
Fee: $17.50 installation; $3.99 monthly (Encore), $7.95 monthly (Cinemax), $11.95 monthly (Showtime & TMC), $11.99 monthly (HBO).

Digital Pay Service 1
Pay Units: N.A.
Programming (via satellite): Cinemax (multiplexed); Encore (multiplexed); HBO (multiplexed); Showtime (multiplexed); Starz (multiplexed); The Movie Channel (multiplexed).

Video-On-Demand: No

Pay-Per-View
iN DEMAND (delivered digitally); Playboy TV (delivered digitally); Fresh (delivered digitally).

Internet Service
Operational: Yes. Began: May 27, 2004.
Broadband Service: Suddenlink High Speed Internet.
Fee: $49.95 installation; $29.99 monthly.

Telephone Service
None

Miles of Plant: 153.0 (coaxial); None (fiber optic).
Operations Director: Peter Brown.
Ownership: Cequel Communications LLC (MSO).

SISSONVILLE—Suddenlink Communications, 68 5th St, Buckhannon, WV 26201. Phones: 314-965-2020 (Corporate office); 304-472-4193. Fax: 314-965-8500. Web Site: http://www.suddenlink.com. Also serves Pocatalico. ICA: WV0036.
TV Market Ranking: 36 (Pocatalico, SISSONVILLE). Franchise award date: N.A. Franchise expiration date: N.A. Began: January 1, 1982.
Channel capacity: 36 (operating 2-way). Channels available but not in use: N.A.

Basic Service
Subscribers: 3,594.
Programming (received off-air): WCHS-TV (ABC) Charleston; WLPX-TV (ION) Charleston; WOWK-TV (CBS) Huntington; WPBY-TV (PBS) Huntington; WQCW (CW) Portsmouth; WSAZ-TV (MNT, NBC) Huntington; WVAH-TV (FOX) Charleston.
Programming (via satellite): A&E Networks; ABC Family Channel; AMC; Animal Planet; Cartoon Network; Celebrity Shopping Network; CNN; Country Music TV; C-SPAN; Discovery Channel; Disney Channel; E! Entertainment Television; ESPN; ESPN 2; Fox News Channel; FX; Hallmark Channel; Headline News; HGTV; History Channel; Lifetime; MTV; Nickelodeon; Outdoor Channel; QVC; Root Sports Pittsburgh; Speed; Spike TV; Syfy; TBS Superstation; The Learning Channel; The Weather Channel; Trinity Broadcasting Network; Turner Network TV; TV Land; USA Network; VH1; WGN America.
Fee: $37.45 installation; $39.95 monthly.

Digital Basic Service
Subscribers: N.A.
Programming (via satellite): BBC America; Bio; Bloomberg Television; C-SPAN 3; Discovery Digital Networks; DIY Network; ESPN Classic Sports; ESPNews; Fox College Sports Atlantic; Fox College Sports Central; Fox College Sports Pacific; Fox Movie Channel; Fuse; G4; GSN; History Channel International; Independent Film Channel; Lifetime Movie Network; Music Choice; SoapNet; Style Network; Sundance Channel; Toon Disney; WE tv.

Pay Service 1
Pay Units: N.A.
Programming (via satellite): Cinemax; HBO; Showtime.

Digital Pay Service 1
Pay Units: N.A.
Programming (via satellite): Cinemax (multiplexed); Encore; Flix; HBO (multiplexed); Showtime (multiplexed); Starz (multiplexed); The Movie Channel (multiplexed).

Video-On-Demand: No

Pay-Per-View
iN DEMAND (delivered digitally); Playboy TV (delivered digitally).

Internet Service
Operational: Yes. Began: June 1, 2005.
Broadband Service: Suddenlink High Speed Internet.
Fee: $49.95 installation; $29.99 monthly.

Telephone Service
Digital: Operational
Fee: $49.99 monthly

Miles of Plant: 265.0 (coaxial); None (fiber optic).
Manager: Peter Brown. Chief Technician: Steve Adkins.
Ownership: Cequel Communications LLC (MSO).

SIX MILE—Colane Cable, PO Box 610, Omar, WV 25638. Phone: 304-946-2871. Also serves Greenview. ICA: WV0239.

TV Market Ranking: 36 (Greenview, SIX MILE). Franchise award date: N.A. Franchise expiration date: N.A. Began: N.A.

Channel capacity: 62 (not 2-way capable). Channels available but not in use: N.A.

Basic Service

Subscribers: 111.

Programming (received off-air): WCHS-TV (ABC) Charleston; WOWK-TV (CBS) Huntington; WPBY-TV (PBS) Huntington; WSAZ-TV (MNT, NBC) Huntington; WVAH-TV (FOX) Charleston.

Programming (via satellite): A&E Networks; ABC Family Channel; Cartoon Network; CNN; Comedy Central; Country Music TV; C-SPAN; Discovery Channel; ESPN; Headline News; Lifetime; MTV; Nickelodeon; QVC; Spike TV; Syfy; TBS Superstation; The Weather Channel; Trinity Broadcasting Network; Turner Network TV; USA Network; VH1; WGN America.

Fee: $38.85 installation; $33.30 monthly.

Pay Service 1

Pay Units: N.A.

Programming (via satellite): HBO.

Fee: $12.00 monthly.

Internet Service

Operational: No.

Telephone Service

None

Miles of Plant: 5.0 (coaxial); None (fiber optic).

General Manager: Gary Bowen. Office Manager: Rebecca Edwards.

Ownership: Colane Cable TV Inc. (MSO).

SMITHFIELD—Formerly served by Almega Cable. No longer in operation. ICA: WV0157.

SNOWSHOE—Windjammer Cable, 8500 W 110th St, Ste 600, Overland Park, KS 66210. Phone: 888-495-2881. Fax: 913-563-5454. Web Site: http://www.windjammercable.com. Also serves Silver Creek & Slatyfork. ICA: WV0212.

TV Market Ranking: Outside TV Markets (Silver Creek, Slatyfork, SNOWSHOE). Franchise award date: N.A. Franchise expiration date: N.A. Began: December 1, 1982.

Channel capacity: N.A. Channels available but not in use: N.A.

Basic Service

Subscribers: 901.

Programming (received off-air): WCHS-TV (ABC) Charleston; WDTV (CBS) Weston; WPBY-TV (PBS) Huntington; WSLS-TV (NBC) Roanoke; WVAH-TV (FOX) Charleston.

Programming (via satellite): A&E Networks; ABC Family Channel; AMC; Animal Planet; Cartoon Network; CNBC; CNN; Comedy Central; Discovery Channel; ESPN; ESPN 2; Fox News Channel; FX; Golf Channel; Headline News; HGTV; Lifetime; MTV; Nickelodeon; Spike TV; TBS Superstation; The Weather Channel; Travel Channel; Turner Network TV; TV Guide Network; USA Network; Versus; VH1; WGN America.

Fee: $29.95 installation; $32.68 monthly.

Digital Basic Service

Subscribers: N.A.

Programming (via satellite): BBC America; Bloomberg Television; Bravo; Discovery Health Channel; Discovery Kids Channel; ESPN Classic Sports; ESPNews; Fox Movie Channel; Fox Soccer; G4; GSN; Halogen Network; History Channel; Independent Film Channel; Music Choice; Nick Jr.; NickToons TV; Outdoor Channel; Science; Syfy; Trinity Broadcasting Network; WE tv.

Fee: $12.00 monthly.

Pay Service 1

Pay Units: 31.

Programming (via satellite): HBO.

Fee: $10.00 monthly.

Digital Pay Service 1

Pay Units: N.A.

Programming (via satellite): Cinemax (multiplexed); Encore (multiplexed); HBO (multiplexed); Showtime (multiplexed); Starz (multiplexed); The Movie Channel (multiplexed).

Fee: $16.95 monthly (each).

Video-On-Demand: No

Pay-Per-View

iN DEMAND (delivered digitally); Club Jenna (delivered digitally); Fresh (delivered digitally).

Internet Service

Operational: No.

Telephone Service

None

Miles of Plant: 17.0 (coaxial); None (fiber optic).

General Manager: Timothy Evard. Operations Director: Belinda Graham. Engineering Director: Mike Earehart. Finance & Accounting Director: Cindy Johnson.

Ownership: Windjammer Communications LLC (MSO).

SPENCER—Charter Communications. Now served by PARKERSBURG, WV [WV0003]. ICA: WV0053.

SPRINGFIELD—Comcast Cable, 15 Summit Park Dr, Pittsburgh, PA 15275. Phones: 412-747-6400; 304-788-2939 (Keyser office). Fax: 412-747-6401. Web Site: http://www.comcast.com. Also serves Green Spring. ICA: WV0258.

TV Market Ranking: Outside TV Markets (Green Spring, SPRINGFIELD). Franchise award date: N.A. Franchise expiration date: N.A. Began: N.A.

Channel capacity: 36 (not 2-way capable). Channels available but not in use: N.A.

Basic Service

Subscribers: N.A.

Programming (received off-air): WJAC-TV (NBC) Johnstown; WJAL (IND) Hagerstown; WJLA-TV (ABC) Washington; WNPB-TV (PBS) Morgantown; WTAJ-TV (CBS) Altoona; WTTG (FOX) Washington; WWPB (PBS) Hagerstown.

Programming (via satellite): A&E Networks; ABC Family Channel; CNN; C-SPAN; Discovery Channel; Disney Channel; ESPN; ESPN 2; History Channel; Spike TV; Syfy; TBS Superstation; Trinity Broadcasting Network; Turner Network TV; TV Land; USA Network; WGN America.

Fee: $19.95 monthly.

Pay Service 1

Pay Units: N.A.

Programming (via satellite): HBO.

Fee: $10.50 monthly.

Video-On-Demand: No

Internet Service

Operational: Yes.

Telephone Service

None

Miles of Plant: 23.0 (coaxial); None (fiber optic).

Regional Vice President: Linda Hossinger. Vice President, Technical Operations: Randy Bender. Vice President, Marketing: Donna Corning. Vice President, Public Affairs: Jody Doherty. Chief Technician: Roy Blanchard. Office Manager: Nancy Nesselrodt.

Ownership: Comcast Cable Communications Inc. (MSO).

ST. MARY'S—Charter Communications. Now served by PARKERSBURG, WV [WV0003]. ICA: WV0057.

SUMMERSVILLE—Shentel, Shentel Center, 500 Shentel Way, Edinburg, VA 22824. Phones: 800-743-6835; 540-984-5224. Web Site: http://www.shentel.com. Also serves Nicholas County. ICA: WV0213.

TV Market Ranking: 36 (Nicholas County (portions)); Below 100 (SUMMERSVILLE, Nicholas County (portions)); Outside TV Markets (Nicholas County (portions)). Franchise award date: N.A. Franchise expiration date: April 14, 2013. Began: August 1, 1960.

Channel capacity: N.A. Channels available but not in use: N.A.

Basic Service

Subscribers: 1,471.

Programming (received off-air): WCHS-TV (ABC) Charleston; WDTV (CBS) Weston; WLPX-TV (ION) Charleston; WOAY-TV (ABC) Oak Hill; WOWK-TV (CBS) Huntington; WSAZ-TV (MNT, NBC) Huntington; WSWP-TV (PBS) Grandview; WVAH-TV (FOX) Charleston; allband FM.

Programming (via satellite): ABC Family Channel; C-SPAN; C-SPAN 2; INSP; QVC; WGN America.

Fee: $29.95 installation; $19.95 monthly.

Expanded Basic Service 1

Subscribers: 1,348.

Programming (via satellite): A&E Networks; AMC; Animal Planet; Cartoon Network; CNBC; CNN; Comedy Central; Country Music TV; Discovery Channel; Discovery Fit & Health; Disney Channel; E! Entertainment Television; ESPN; ESPN 2; ESPN Classic Sports; ESPNews; Eternal Word TV Network; Food Network; Fox News Channel; FX; G4; Hallmark Channel; Headline News; HGTV; History Channel; Lifetime; MSNBC; MTV; National Geographic Channel; Nickelodeon; Outdoor Channel; Oxygen; Root Sports Pittsburgh; SoapNet; Speed; Spike TV; Syfy; TBS Superstation; The Learning Channel; The Weather Channel; Travel Channel; truTV; Turner Network TV; TV Land; USA Network; VH1.

Fee: $18.00 monthly.

Digital Basic Service

Subscribers: N.A.

Programming (via satellite): BBC America; Bio; Bloomberg Television; Bravo; CMT Pure Country; Discovery Digital Networks; DMX Music; Fox College Sports Atlantic; Fox College Sports Central; Fox College Sports Pacific; Fox Movie Channel; Fox Soccer; Fuse; Golf Channel; GSN; History Channel International; Independent Film Channel; Lifetime Movie Network; MTV Networks Digital Suite; Nick Jr.; NickToons TV; Style Network; Sundance Channel; TeenNick; Toon Disney; Turner Classic Movies; Versus; WE tv.

Fee: $12.95 monthly.

Digital Pay Service 1

Pay Units: N.A.

Programming (via satellite): Cinemax (multiplexed); Encore (multiplexed); Flix; HBO (multiplexed); Showtime (multiplexed); Starz (multiplexed); The Movie Channel (multiplexed).

Video-On-Demand: No

Internet Service

Operational: No.

Telephone Service

None

Miles of Plant: 32.0 (coaxial); None (fiber optic).

Vice President, Customer Service: David Ferguson. General Manager: Robert Harold. Chief Technician: Steve Adkins.

Ownership: Shenandoah Telecommunications Inc. (MSO).

TALCOTT—Windjammer Cable, 8500 W 110th St, Ste 600, Overland Park, KS 66210. Phone: 888-495-2881. Fax: 913-563-5454. Web Site: http://www.windjammercable.com. Also serves Hinton, Summers County (portions) & Summitview. ICA: WV0222.

TV Market Ranking: Below 100 (Hinton, Summers County (portions), Summitview, TALCOTT). Franchise award date: N.A. Franchise expiration date: N.A. Began: N.A.

Channel capacity: 36 (not 2-way capable). Channels available but not in use: N.A.

Basic Service

Subscribers: 427.

Programming (received off-air): WLFB (IND) Bluefield; WOAY-TV (ABC) Oak Hill; WSLS-TV (NBC) Roanoke; WSWP-TV (PBS) Grandview; WVVA (CW, NBC) Bluefield.

Programming (via satellite): A&E Networks; ABC Family Channel; AMC; Cartoon Network; CNN; Country Music TV; Discovery Channel; Disney Channel; ESPN; ESPN 2; Fox News Channel; Headline News; HGTV; History Channel; Lifetime; MTV; Nickelodeon; Outdoor Channel; QVC; Spike TV; TBS Superstation; The Learning Channel; The Weather Channel; Trinity Broadcasting Network; Turner Network TV; USA Network; VH1; WGN America.

Fee: $39.95 installation; $36.27 monthly.

Digital Basic Service

Subscribers: N.A.

Programming (via satellite): BBC America; Bloomberg Television; Bravo; Discovery Fit & Health; Discovery Health Channel; Discovery Kids Channel; ESPN Classic Sports; ESPNews; Fox Movie Channel; Fox Soccer; G4; Golf Channel; GSN; Halogen Network; Independent Film Channel; Music Choice; Nick Jr.; NickToons TV; Science; Syfy; Versus; WE tv.

Fee: $12.00 monthly.

Pay Service 1

Pay Units: 11.

Programming (via satellite): HBO.

Fee: $10.95 monthly.

Digital Pay Service 1

Pay Units: 11.

Programming (via satellite): Cinemax (multiplexed); Encore (multiplexed); HBO (multiplexed); Showtime (multiplexed); Starz (multiplexed); The Movie Channel (multiplexed).

Fee: $16.95 monthly (each).

Video-On-Demand: No

Pay-Per-View

iN DEMAND (delivered digitally); Playboy TV (delivered digitally); Club Jenna (delivered digitally); Fresh (delivered digitally).

Internet Service

Operational: No.

Telephone Service

None

Miles of Plant: 35.0 (coaxial); None (fiber optic).

General Manager: Timothy Evard. Operations Director: Belinda Graham. Engineering Director: Mike Earehart. Finance & Accounting Director: Cindy Johnson.

Ownership: Windjammer Communications LLC (MSO).

TANNER—Windjammer Cable, 8500 W 110th St, Ste 600, Overland Park, KS 66210. Phone: 888-495-2881. Fax: 913-563-5454. Web Site: http://www.windjammercable.com. ICA: WV0149.

TV Market Ranking: Below 100 (TANNER). Franchise award date: N.A. Franchise expiration date: N.A. Began: August 1, 1983.

Channel capacity: 35 (not 2-way capable). Channels available but not in use: N.A.

Basic Service

Subscribers: N.A.

Programming (received off-air): WBOY-TV (NBC) Clarksburg; WCHS-TV (ABC) Charleston; WDTV (CBS) Weston; WSAZ-TV (MNT, NBC) Huntington; WSWP-TV (PBS) Grandview; WVAH-TV (FOX) Charleston.

Programming (via satellite): ABC Family Channel; CNN; ESPN; Lifetime; Spike TV; TBS Superstation; Trinity Broadcasting Network; Turner Network TV; USA Network; WGN America.

Fee: $39.95 installation; $38.58 monthly.

Pay Service 1

Pay Units: N.A.

Programming (via satellite): HBO.

Fee: $15.95 monthly.

Video-On-Demand: No

Internet Service

Operational: No.

Telephone Service

None

Miles of Plant: 6.0 (coaxial); None (fiber optic).

General Manager: Timothy Evard. Operations Director: Belinda Graham. Engineering Director: Mike Earehart. Finance & Accounting Director: Cindy Johnson.

Ownership: Windjammer Communications LLC (MSO).

TUNNELTON—Community Antenna Service, 1525 Dupont Rd, Parkersburg, WV 26101-9623. Phone: 304-420-2470. Fax: 304-420-2472. E-mail: info@cascable.com. Web Site: http://www.cascable.com. Also serves Denver, Fellowsville & Kingwood. ICA: WV0112.

TV Market Ranking: Below 100 (Denver, Fellowsville, TUNNELTON); Outside TV Markets (Kingwood). Franchise award date: N.A. Franchise expiration date: N.A. Began: February 1, 1980.

Channel capacity: 36 (not 2-way capable). Channels available but not in use: N.A.

Basic Service

Subscribers: 624.

Programming (received off-air): KDKA-TV (CBS) Pittsburgh; WBOY-TV (NBC) Clarksburg; WDTV (CBS) Weston; WNPB-TV (PBS) Morgantown; WPGH-TV (FOX) Pittsburgh; WPXI (IND, NBC) Pittsburgh; WTAE-TV (ABC) Pittsburgh; WVFX (CW, FOX) Clarksburg.

Programming (via satellite): A&E Networks; ABC Family Channel; Animal Planet; Cartoon Network; CNBC; CNN; Country Music TV; C-SPAN; Discovery Channel; Discovery Health Channel; Disney Channel; ESPN; ESPN 2; ESPNews; Fox News Channel; FX; G4; Hallmark Channel; Headline News; INSP; Lifetime; MSNBC; National Geographic Channel; Nickelodeon; Outdoor Channel; Speed; Spike TV; Syfy; TBS Superstation; The Learning Channel; The Weather Channel; Trinity Broadcasting Network; truTV; Turner Classic Movies; Turner Network TV; TV Land; USA Network; WGN America.

Fee: $45.00 installation; $48.85 monthly.

Pay Service 1

Pay Units: N.A.

Programming (via satellite): Cinemax; HBO.

Fee: $10.95 monthly (Cinemax), $13.95 monthly (HBO).

Video-On-Demand: No

Internet Service

Operational: No.

Telephone Service

None

Miles of Plant: 37.0 (coaxial); None (fiber optic).

Manager: Arthur R. Cooper. Program & Marketing Director: Lisa Wilkinson. Chief Technician: Steve Defibaugh.

Ownership: Arthur R. Cooper (MSO).

TURTLE CREEK—Colane Cable, PO Box 610, Omar, WV 25638. Phone: 304-946-2871. Fax: 304-946-4191. ICA: WV0267.

TV Market Ranking: 36 (TURTLE CREEK).

Channel capacity: 39 (not 2-way capable). Channels available but not in use: N.A.

Basic Service

Subscribers: 241.

Programming (received off-air): WCHS-TV (ABC) Charleston; WLPX-TV (ION) Charleston; WOAY-TV (ABC) Oak Hill; WOWK-TV (CBS) Huntington; WPBY-TV (PBS) Huntington; WSAZ-TV (MNT, NBC) Huntington; WVAH-TV (FOX) Charleston.

Programming (via satellite): INSP; TBS Superstation; The Learning Channel; WGN America.

Fee: $38.34 installation; $13.65 monthly.

Expanded Basic Service 1

Subscribers: 225.

Programming (via satellite): A&E Networks; ABC Family Channel; Cartoon Network; CNN; Comedy Central; Country Music TV; C-SPAN; Discovery Channel; Disney Channel; ESPN; ESPN 2; FX; Headline News; HGTV; Lifetime; MTV; Nickelodeon; QVC; Spike TV; Syfy; The Weather Channel; Trinity Broadcasting Network; truTV; Turner Classic Movies; Turner Network TV; TV Land; USA Network; VH1.

Fee: $16.30 monthly.

Pay Service 1

Pay Units: 16.

Programming (via satellite): HBO.

Fee: $11.95 monthly.

Pay Service 2

Pay Units: N.A.

Programming (via satellite): Cinemax.

Fee: $11.95 monthly.

Internet Service

Operational: No.

Telephone Service

None

Miles of Plant: 13.0 (coaxial); None (fiber optic).

Manager: Beth Jenkins. Chief Technician: Skip Brewer.

Ownership: Colane Cable TV Inc. (MSO).

UNION—Vital Communications Group, PO Box 307, Behaven, NC 27810. Phone: 252-943-3800. ICA: WV0249.

TV Market Ranking: Below 100 (UNION). Franchise award date: January 1, 1985. Franchise expiration date: N.A. Began: January 1, 1986.

Channel capacity: N.A. Channels available but not in use: N.A.

Basic Service

Subscribers: 203.

Programming (received off-air): WBRA-TV (PBS) Roanoke; WDBJ (CBS, MNT) Roanoke; WLFB (IND) Bluefield; WOAY-TV (ABC) Oak Hill; WSET-TV (ABC) Lynchburg; WSLS-TV (NBC) Roanoke; WSWP-TV (PBS) Grandview; WVNS-TV (CBS) Lewisburg; WVVA (CW, NBC) Bluefield.

Programming (via satellite): ABC Family Channel; C-SPAN; C-SPAN 2; INSP; QVC; TBS Superstation; WGN America.

Fee: $40.00 installation; $14.95 monthly.

Expanded Basic Service 1

Subscribers: 177.

Programming (via satellite): A&E Networks; Animal Planet; Cartoon Network; CNBC; CNN; Comedy Central; Country Music TV; Discovery Channel; Disney Channel; ESPN; ESPN 2; ESPN Classic Sports; Fox News Channel; FX; Hallmark Channel; Headline News; HGTV; History Channel; Lifetime; MTV; Nickelodeon; Outdoor Channel; Root Sports Pittsburgh; Spike TV; Syfy; The Learning Channel; The Weather Channel; Turner Classic Movies; Turner Network TV; TV Land; USA Network; VH1.

Fee: $15.95 monthly.

Pay Service 1

Pay Units: 12.

Programming (via satellite): HBO.

Fee: $11.95 monthly.

Pay Service 2

Pay Units: N.A.

Programming (via satellite): Cinemax.

Fee: $11.95 monthly.

Internet Service

Operational: Yes.

Subscribers: 11.

Broadband Service: IBBS.

Fee: $39.95 monthly.

Telephone Service

None

Miles of Plant: 7.0 (coaxial); None (fiber optic).

President: Jerry Stender.

Ownership: Vital Communications Group (MSO).

UPPER TRACT—Formerly served by Cebridge Connections. No longer in operation. ICA: WV0136.

VAN—Colane Cable TV, PO Box 610, Omar, WV 25638. Phone: 304-946-2871. Fax: 304-946-4091. Also serves Bald Knob, Bandytown, Boone County (portions), Gordon, Twilight & Wharton. ICA: WV0167.

TV Market Ranking: 36 (Bald Knob, Bandytown, Boone County (portions), Gordon, Twilight, VAN, Wharton). Franchise award date: N.A. Franchise expiration date: N.A. Began: January 1, 1979.

Channel capacity: 42 (not 2-way capable). Channels available but not in use: N.A.

Basic Service

Subscribers: 460.

Programming (received off-air): WCHS-TV (ABC) Charleston; WLPX-TV (ION) Charleston; WOWK-TV (CBS) Huntington; WSAZ-TV (MNT, NBC) Huntington; WSWP-TV (PBS) Grandview; WVAH-TV (FOX) Charleston.

Programming (via satellite): ABC Family Channel; C-SPAN; Disney Channel; Headline News; INSP; Lifetime; QVC; TBS Superstation; Trinity Broadcasting Network; truTV; USA Network; WGN America.

Fee: $8.34 installation; $22.50 monthly; $1.26 converter; $15.47 additional installation.

Expanded Basic Service 1

Subscribers: 682.

Programming (via satellite): A&E Networks; Cartoon Network; CNN; Comedy Central; Country Music TV; Discovery Channel; ESPN; ESPN 2; FX; History Channel; MTV; Nickelodeon; Outdoor Channel; Root Sports Pittsburgh; Spike TV; Syfy; The Weather Channel; Turner Classic Movies; Turner Network TV; TV Land; VH1.

Fee: $29.95 monthly.

Pay Service 1

Pay Units: 56.

Programming (via satellite): HBO.

Fee: $11.95 monthly.

Pay Service 2

Pay Units: 17.

Programming (via satellite): Cinemax.

Fee: $11.95 monthly.

Internet Service

Operational: Yes.

Telephone Service

None

Miles of Plant: 54.0 (coaxial); None (fiber optic).

Manager: Gary Bowen. Office Manager: Rebecca Edwards.

Ownership: Colane Cable TV Inc.

VARNEY—Colane Cable TV Inc. Now served by OMAR, WV [WV0191]. ICA: WV0215.

WALKERSVILLE—Formerly served by Almega Cable. No longer in operation. ICA: WV0134.

WALTON—Formerly served by Windjammer Cable. No longer in operation. ICA: WV0277.

WAR—Suddenlink Communications. Now served by NORTHFORK, WV [WV0045]. ICA: WV0048.

WARDENSVILLE—Formerly served by Valley Cable Systems. No longer in operation. ICA: WV0124.

WARWOOD—Centre TV Cable, 510 Warwood Ave, Wheeling, WV 26003-6842. Phone: 304-277-2811. Also serves Beech Bottom, Power, RD No. 1 Trailer Courts, Short Creek & Windsor Heights. ICA: WV0043.

Note: This system is an overbuild.

TV Market Ranking: 10,90 (Beech Bottom, Power, RD No. 1 Trailer Courts, Short Creek, WARWOOD, Windsor Heights). Franchise award date: N.A. Franchise expiration date: N.A. Began: January 1, 1950.

Channel capacity: 45 (not 2-way capable). Channels available but not in use: N.A.

Basic Service

Subscribers: 1,478.

Programming (received off-air): WFMJ-TV (CW, NBC) Youngstown; WKBN-TV (CBS) Youngstown; WNPB-TV (PBS) Morgantown; WPGH-TV (FOX) Pittsburgh; WPMY (MNT) Pittsburgh; WQED (PBS) Pittsburgh; WTAE-TV (ABC) Pittsburgh; WTOV-TV (IND, NBC) Steubenville; WTRF-TV (CBS) Wheeling; WYTV (ABC, MNT) Youngstown; allband FM.

Programming (via satellite): A&E Networks; ABC Family Channel; Animal Planet; Cartoon Network; CNN; Comedy Central; Country Music TV; CW+; Discovery Channel; ESPN; ESPN 2; Eternal Word TV Network; Food Network; Fox News Channel; FX; Great American Country; Hallmark Channel; HGTV; History Channel; Lifetime; MTV; Nickelodeon; Outdoor Channel; QVC; Root Sports Pittsburgh; Speed; Spike TV; Syfy; TBS Superstation; The Learning Channel; The Weather Channel; Travel Channel; truTV; Turner Classic Movies; Turner Network TV; TV Guide Network; TV Land; USA Network; VH1; WGN America.

Fee: $26.00 monthly.

Pay Service 1

Pay Units: N.A.

Programming (via satellite): Encore; HBO (multiplexed).

Fee: $25.00 installation; $7.75 monthly (Encore), $12.00 monthly (HBO).

Video-On-Demand: No

Internet Service

Operational: No.

Telephone Service

None

Miles of Plant: 15.0 (coaxial); None (fiber optic).

Manager & Chief Technician: Kasmir Majewski.

Ownership: Kasmir Majewski (MSO).

WAYNE—Suddenlink Communications, 3028 Michigan Ave, Shrewsbury, WV 25015-1936. Phones: 304-757-8001 (Scott Depot office); 304-343-3343. Fax: 304-357-6707. Web Site: http://www.suddenlink.com. Also serves Atenville, Cove Gap, Crabtree, East Lynn, Ferrellsburg, Fort Gay, Hubball, Kitchen, Lavalette, Rockville & Sheridan. ICA: WV0035.

TV Market Ranking: 36 (Atenville, Cove Gap, Crabtree, East Lynn, Ferrellsburg, Fort Gay, Hubball, Kitchen, Lavalette, Rockville, Sheridan, WAYNE). Franchise award date: October 10, 1982. Franchise expiration date: October 10, 2032. Began: N.A.

Channel capacity: N.A. Channels available but not in use: N.A.

Basic Service

Subscribers: 2,984.

Programming (received off-air): WCHS-TV (ABC) Charleston; WLPX-TV (ION) Charleston; WOWK-TV (CBS) Huntington; WPBY-TV (PBS) Huntington; WQCW (CW) Portsmouth; WSAZ-TV (MNT, NBC) Huntington; WTSF (IND) Ashland; WVAH-TV (FOX) Charleston; WVPT (PBS) Staunton.

Programming (via satellite): C-SPAN; C-SPAN 2; Product Information Network; QVC; ShopNBC; TV Guide Network; WGN America.

Fee: $61.25 installation; $14.40 monthly; $1.24 converter.

Expanded Basic Service 1

Subscribers: N.A.

Programming (via satellite): A&E Networks; ABC Family Channel; AMC; Animal Planet; BET Networks; Bravo; Cartoon Network; CNBC; CNN; Comedy Central; Country Music TV; Discovery Channel; Disney Channel; E! Entertainment Television; ESPN; ESPN 2; ESPN Classic Sports; Food Network; Fox News Channel; FX; G4; Golf Channel; GSN; Hallmark Channel; Headline News; HGTV; History Channel; INSP; Lifetime; MSNBC; MTV; National Geographic Channel; Nickelodeon; Outdoor Channel; Oxygen; Root Sports Pittsburgh; SoapNet; Speed; Spike TV; Style Network; Syfy; TBS Superstation; The Learning Channel; The Weather Channel; Toon Disney; Travel Channel; Trinity Broadcasting Network; truTV; Turner Classic Movies; Turner Network TV; TV Land; USA Network; Versus; VH1; WE tv.

Fee: $15.02 monthly.

Digital Basic Service

Subscribers: N.A.

Programming (via satellite): BBC America; Bio; Bloomberg Television; DIY Network; ESPN; ESPNews; Fox College Sports Atlantic; Fox College Sports Central; Fox College Sports Pacific; Fox Deportes; Fox Movie Channel; Fox Sports World; Fuel TV; Fuse; GAS; Great American Country; HD Theater; History Channel International; Independent Film Channel; Lifetime Movie Network; MTV Networks Digital Suite; Music Choice; NFL Network; Nick Jr.; Nick Too; NickToons TV; Sundance Channel; TV Guide Interactive Inc.; TVG Network.

Digital Pay Service 1

Pay Units: N.A.

Programming (via satellite): Cinemax (multiplexed); Encore (multiplexed); Flix; HBO (multiplexed); Showtime (multiplexed); Starz (multiplexed); The Movie Channel (multiplexed).

Video-On-Demand: Yes

Internet Service

Operational: Yes.

Broadband Service: Suddenlink High Speed Internet.

Fee: $49.95 installation; $29.99 monthly.

Telephone Service

None

Miles of Plant: 153.0 (coaxial); None (fiber optic).

Vice President, Operations: David Bach. General Manager: Patrick Barclay. Technical Operations Director: Bob Legg. Marketing Director: Stan Howell. Marketing Manager: Kenny Phillips.

Ownership: Cequel Communications LLC (MSO).

WEBSTER SPRINGS—Shentel, 106 S Main St, Edinburg, VA 22824. Phone: 540-984-5224. Web Site: http://www.shentel.net. Also serves Bergoo, Camden (town), Camden on Gauley, Cowen, Curtin, Parcoal, Upperglade & Webster County (portions). ICA: WV0080.

TV Market Ranking: Below 100 (Camden (town), Webster County (portions)); Outside TV Markets (Bergoo, Camden on Gauley, Cowen, Curtin, Parcoal, Upperglade, Webster County (portions), WEBSTER SPRINGS). Franchise award date: N.A. Franchise expiration date: N.A. Began: January 1, 1953.

Channel capacity: N.A. Channels available but not in use: N.A.

Basic Service

Subscribers: 1,812.

Programming (received off-air): WBOY-TV (NBC) Clarksburg; WCHS-TV (ABC) Charleston; WDTV (CBS) Weston; WOAY-TV (ABC) Oak Hill; WSWP-TV (PBS) Grandview; allband FM.

Programming (via satellite): INSP; QVC; Trinity Broadcasting Network.

Fee: $29.95 installation; $19.95 monthly.

Expanded Basic Service 1

Subscribers: 894.

Programming (via satellite): A&E Networks; ABC Family Channel; AMC; Animal Planet; BET Networks; Bravo; Cartoon Network; CNBC; CNN; Comedy Central; Country Music TV; C-SPAN; Discovery Channel; Disney Channel; E! Entertainment Television; ESPN; ESPN 2; Food Network; Fox News Channel; FX; G4; Golf Channel; Headline News; HGTV; History Channel; Lifetime; MSNBC; MTV; National Geographic Channel; Nickelodeon; Outdoor Channel; Oxygen; Root Sports Pittsburgh; Speed; Spike TV; Syfy; TBS Superstation; The Learning Channel; The Weather Channel; Travel Channel; Turner Classic Movies; Turner Network TV; TV Land; USA Network; VH1.

Fee: $18.00 monthly.

Digital Basic Service

Subscribers: N.A.

Programming (via satellite): BBC America; Bio; Bloomberg Television; Discovery Fit & Health; ESPN Classic Sports; ESPNews; Fox College Sports Atlantic; Fox College Sports Central; Fox College Sports Pacific; Fox Movie Channel; Fox Sports World; Fuse; GAS; GSN; History Channel International; Independent Film Channel; Lifetime Movie Network; MTV Networks Digital Suite; Music Choice; Nick Jr.; Nick Too; NickToons TV; SoapNet; Sundance Channel; Toon Disney; TV Guide Interactive Inc.; WE tv.

Digital Pay Service 1

Pay Units: 79.

Programming (via satellite): Encore (multiplexed); HBO (multiplexed); Showtime (multiplexed).

Fee: $13.85 monthly.

Digital Pay Service 2

Pay Units: N.A.

Programming (via satellite): Cinemax (multiplexed); Flix; Starz (multiplexed); The Movie Channel (multiplexed).

Video-On-Demand: No

Pay-Per-View

iN DEMAND (delivered digitally); Fresh (delivered digitally); Shorteez (delivered digitally); Playboy TV (delivered digitally).

Internet Service

Operational: No.

Telephone Service

None

Miles of Plant: 25.0 (coaxial); None (fiber optic).

General Manager: Robert Harold. Chief Technician: Steve Adkins.

Ownership: Shenandoah Telecommunications Inc. (MSO).

WELCH—Jet Broadband. Now served by NORTHFORK, WV [WV0045]. ICA: WV0042.

WEST LIBERTY (town)—Comcast Cable. Now served by WHEELING, WV [WV0004]. ICA: WV0216.

WEST MILFORD—Formerly served by Cebridge Connections. Now served by BUCKHANNON, WV [WV0024]. ICA: WV0068.

WEST UNION—Shentel, 106 S Main St, Edinburg, VA 22824. Phone: 540-984-5224. Web Site: http://www.shentel.net. ICA: WV0104.

TV Market Ranking: Below 100 (WEST UNION). Franchise award date: N.A. Franchise expiration date: N.A. Began: January 1, 1966.

Channel capacity: 35 (not 2-way capable). Channels available but not in use: N.A.

Basic Service

Subscribers: 243.

Programming (received off-air): WBOY-TV (NBC) Clarksburg; WCHS-TV (ABC) Charleston; WDTV (CBS) Weston; WNPB-TV (PBS) Morgantown; WTAE-TV (ABC) Pittsburgh; WTAP-TV (FOX, MNT, NBC) Parkersburg; WTOV-TV (IND, NBC) Steubenville; WTRF-TV (CBS) Wheeling; WVFX (CW, FOX) Clarksburg; allband FM.

Programming (via satellite): E! Entertainment Television; History Channel; TBS Superstation; The Learning Channel; Trinity Broadcasting Network; TV Land; WGN America.

Fee: $29.95 installation; $19.95 monthly; $.73 converter.

Expanded Basic Service 1

Subscribers: N.A.

Programming (via satellite): ABC Family Channel; AMC; CNN; Discovery Channel; Disney Channel; ESPN; ESPN 2; Great American Country; Lifetime; Nickelodeon; Spike TV; Syfy; The Weather Channel; Turner Network TV; USA Network.

Fee: $18.00 monthly.

Pay Service 1

Pay Units: 22.

Programming (via satellite): HBO.

Fee: $17.50 installation; $11.99 monthly.

Pay Service 2

Pay Units: N.A.

Programming (via satellite): Cinemax.

Fee: $7.95 monthly.

Video-On-Demand: No

Internet Service

Operational: No.

Telephone Service

None

Miles of Plant: 10.0 (coaxial); None (fiber optic).

General Manager: Robert Harold. Chief Technician: Steve Adkins.

Ownership: Shenandoah Telecommunications Inc. (MSO).

WESTON—Shentel, Shentel Center, 500 Shentel Way, Edinburg, VA 22824. Phones: 304-517-1250; 800-409-1203. E-mail: complaints@shentel.net. Web Site: http://shentel.net. Also serves Alum Bridge, Broad Run, Burnsville, Camden, Ellenboro, Glenville, Harrisville, Jane Lew, Lewis County, Linn, Sand Fork, St. Marys & Troy. ICA: WV0034.

TV Market Ranking: Below 100 (Alum Bridge, Broad Run, Burnsville, Camden, Ellenboro, Glenville, Harrisville, Jane Lew, Lewis County, Linn, Sand Fork, St. Marys, Troy, WESTON). Franchise award date: N.A. Franchise expiration date: N.A. Began: January 1, 1954.

Channel capacity: N.A. Channels available but not in use: N.A.

Basic Service

Subscribers: 4,545.

Programming (received off-air): WBOY-TV (NBC) Clarksburg; WCHS-TV (ABC) Charleston; WDTV (CBS) Weston; WNPB-TV (PBS) Morgantown; WVFX (CW, FOX) Clarksburg; 20 FMs.

Programming (via microwave): WTAE-TV (ABC) Pittsburgh.

Programming (via satellite): C-SPAN; C-SPAN 2; INSP; QVC; Trinity Broadcasting Network; TV Guide Network.

Fee: $29.95 installation; $19.95 monthly; $2.00 converter.

Expanded Basic Service 1

Subscribers: N.A.

Programming (via satellite): A&E Networks; ABC Family Channel; AMC; Animal Planet; Cartoon Network; CNBC; CNN; Comedy Central; Country Music TV; Discovery Channel; Discovery Fit & Health; Disney Channel; E! Entertainment Television; ESPN; ESPN 2; Food Network; Fox News Channel; FX; G4; Headline News; HGTV; History Channel; Lifetime; MTV; Na-

tional Geographic Channel; Nickelodeon; Outdoor Channel; Oxygen; Root Sports Pittsburgh; SoapNet; Speed; Spike TV; Syfy; TBS Superstation; The Learning Channel; The Weather Channel; Toon Disney; Travel Channel; truTV; Turner Network TV; TV Land; USA Network.
Fee: $18.00 monthly.

Digital Basic Service
Subscribers: N.A.
Programming (via satellite): BBC America; Bravo!; Discovery Health Channel; Discovery Kids Channel; DMX Music; ESPN Classic Sports; ESPNews; Fox Soccer; Golf Channel; GSN; Independent Film Channel; Science Television; Turner Classic Movies; TV Guide Interactive Inc.; Versus; WE tv.
Fee: $12.95 monthly.

Digital Pay Service 1
Pay Units: N.A.
Programming (via satellite): Cinemax (multiplexed); Encore (multiplexed); HBO (multiplexed); Showtime (multiplexed); Starz (multiplexed); The Movie Channel (multiplexed).

Video-On-Demand: No

Pay-Per-View
iN DEMAND (delivered digitally); Playboy TV (delivered digitally).

Internet Service
Operational: Yes.
Fee: $50.00 installation; $39.95 monthly.

Telephone Service
None

Miles of Plant: 140.0 (coaxial); None (fiber optic).
Vice President, Customer Service: David Ferguson. General Manager: Robert Harold. Chief Technician: Steve Adkins.
Ownership: Shenandoah Telecommunications Inc. (MSO).

WESTOVER—Formerly served by Adelphia Communications. Now served by MORGANTOWN, WV [WV0198]. ICA: WV0056.

WHEELING—Comcast Cable, 15 Summit Park Dr, Pittsburgh, PA 15275. Phone: 412-747-6400. Fax: 412-747-6401. Web Site: http://www.comcast.com. Also serves Adena, Bannock, Barnesville, Bellaire, Belmont, Belmont County, Bethesda, Blaine, Bridgeport, Brilliant, Brookside, Colerain Twp., Connorsville, Cross Creek Twp. (Jefferson County), Dillonvale, Fairpoint, Flushing, Glen Robbins, Glencoe, Goshen Twp. (Belmont County), Hammondsville, Harrisville, Holloway, Irondale, Island Creek Twp. (Jefferson County), Key, Lafferty, Lansing Valley, Martins Ferry, Mead Twp., Mingo Junction, Mount Pleasant, Neffs, New Alexandria, Pease Twp. (Belmont County), Pultney Twp., Rayland, Richland Twp., Richmond, Saline Twp., Shadyside, Short Creek Twp., Smith Twp., Smithfield Twp. (Jefferson County), St. Clairsville, Steubenville, Tiltonsville, Warren Twp. (Belmont County), Wheeling Twp., Wintersville & Yorkville, OH; Benwood, Bethlehem, Brooke County (portions), Clearview, Follansbee, Glen Dale, Marshall County, McMechen, Moundsville, Mozart, Ohio County, Shawnee Hills, Triadelphia, Valley Grove, Wellsburg & West Liberty, WV. ICA: WV0004.

TV Market Ranking: 10 (Brilliant, Brooke County (portions), Follansbee, Mingo Junction, New Alexandria, Steubenville, Wellsburg); 90 (Adena, Bannock, Barnesville, Bellaire, Belmont, Belmont County, Benwood, Bethesda, Bethlehem, Blaine, Bridgeport, Brookside, Clearview, Colerain Twp., Connorsville, Cross Creek Twp. (Jefferson County), Dillonvale, Fairpoint, Flushing, Glen Robbins, Glencoe, Goshen Twp. (Belmont County), Hammondsville, Harrisville, Holloway, Irondale, Island Creek Twp. (Jefferson County), Key, Lafferty, Lansing Valley, Marshall County, Martins Ferry, McMechen, Mead Twp., Moundsville, Mount Pleasant, Mozart, Neffs, Ohio County, Pease Twp. (Belmont County), Pultney Twp., Rayland, Richland Twp., Richmond, Saline Twp., Shadyside, Shawnee Hills, Short Creek Twp., Smith Twp., Smithfield Twp. (Jefferson County), St. Clairsville, Tiltonsville, Triadelphia, Valley Grove, Warren Twp. (Belmont County), West Liberty, WHEELING, Wheeling Twp., Wintersville, Yorkville). Franchise award date: N.A. Franchise expiration date: N.A. Began: June 1, 1952.
Channel capacity: N.A. Channels available but not in use: N.A.

Basic Service
Subscribers: 63,249.
Programming (received off-air): CW+; KDKA-TV (CBS) Pittsburgh; WNPB-TV (PBS) Morgantown; WPGH-TV (FOX) Pittsburgh; WPXI (IND, NBC) Pittsburgh; WQED (PBS) Pittsburgh; WTAE-TV (ABC) Pittsburgh; WTOV-TV (IND, NBC) Steubenville; WTRF-TV (CBS) Wheeling; WYTV (ABC, MNT) Youngstown; 13 FMs.
Programming (via satellite): A&E Networks; ABC Family Channel; BET Networks; Cartoon Network; CNBC; CNN; C-SPAN; Discovery Channel; Hallmark Channel; Headline News; Lifetime; MTV; Nickelodeon; QVC; TBS Superstation; The Weather Channel; Turner Network TV.
Fee: $43.99 installation; $14.00 monthly; $4.00 converter.

Expanded Basic Service 1
Subscribers: 17,062.
Programming (via satellite): AMC; Animal Planet; Comedy Central; Country Music TV; C-SPAN 2; Disney Channel; E! Entertainment Television; ESPN; ESPN 2; Eternal Word TV Network; Food Network; Fox News Channel; FX; HGTV; History Channel; ION Television; MSNBC; Oxygen; Root Sports Pittsburgh; ShopNBC; Spike TV; The Learning Channel; Travel Channel; truTV; TV Land; USA Network; VH1.
Fee: $37.99 monthly.

Digital Basic Service
Subscribers: N.A.
Programming (via satellite): American-Life TV Network; BBC America; Bio; Black Family Channel; Bloomberg Television; Bravo; Discovery Digital Networks; DMX Music; ESPN Classic Sports; ESPNews; Fox Movie Channel; Fox Sports World; FSN Digital Atlantic; FSN Digital Central; FSN Digital Pacific; Fuse; G4; GAS; Golf Channel; Great American Country; GSN; Halogen Network; History Channel International; Independent Film Channel; Lifetime Movie Network; Lime; MTV Networks Digital Suite; National Geographic Channel; Nick Jr.; NickToons TV; Outdoor Channel; Ovation; ShopNBC; Speed; Style Network; Sundance Channel; Syfy; The Word Network; Toon Disney; Trinity Broadcasting Network; Turner Classic Movies; Versus; WE tv; Weatherscan.
Fee: $10.95 monthly.

Digital Pay Service 1
Pay Units: N.A.
Programming (via satellite): Cinemax (multiplexed); Encore (multiplexed); Flix; HBO (multiplexed); Showtime (multiplexed); Starz (multiplexed); The Movie Channel (multiplexed).

Video-On-Demand: Yes

Pay-Per-View
ESPN Now (delivered digitally); Sports PPV (delivered digitally); NBA TV (delivered digitally); iN DEMAND (delivered digitally); Urban Xtra (delivered digitally); Fresh (delivered digitally); Shorteez (delivered digitally); Playboy TV (delivered digitally); Hot Choice (delivered digitally).

Internet Service
Operational: Yes.
Broadband Service: Comcast High Speed Internet.
Fee: $42.95 monthly.

Telephone Service
Digital: Operational
Fee: $44.95 monthly

Miles of Plant: 1,162.0 (coaxial); None (fiber optic).
Regional Vice President: Linda Hossinger. Vice President, Technical Operations: Randy Bender. Vice President, Marketing: Donna Corning. Vice President, Public Affairs: Jody Doherty.
Ownership: Comcast Cable Communications Inc. (MSO).

WHITE SULPHUR SPRINGS—Charter Communications. Now served by BECKLEY, WV [WV0005]. ICA: WV0217.

WHITEHALL—Formerly served by Adelphia Communications. Now served by MORGANTOWN, WV [WV0198]. ICA: WV0040.

WILEYVILLE—Formerly served by Almega Cable. No longer in operation. ICA: WV0165.

WILLIAMSON—Charter Communications. Now served by KERMIT, WV [WV0038]. ICA: WV0030.

WORTHINGTON—Formerly served by Adelphia Communications. Now served by MORGANTOWN, WV [WV0198]. ICA: WV0151.

WYATT—Country Cable, 224A Milford St, PO Box 1696, Clarksburg, WV 26302. Phone: 800-882-1206. Fax: 304-457-1691. Also serves Mannington (northwestern portion), Peora, Pine Bluff & Shinnston (portions). ICA: WV0219.

TV Market Ranking: Below 100 (Mannington (northwestern portion), Peora, Pine Bluff, Shinnston (portions), WYATT). Franchise award date: N.A. Franchise expiration date: N.A. Began: October 1, 1983.
Channel capacity: 36 (not 2-way capable). Channels available but not in use: N.A.

Basic Service
Subscribers: 110.
Programming (received off-air): WBOY-TV (NBC) Clarksburg; WDTV (CBS) Weston; WNPB-TV (PBS) Morgantown; WTAE-TV (ABC) Pittsburgh; WTRF-TV (CBS) Wheeling; WVFX (CW, FOX) Clarksburg.
Programming (via satellite): A&E Networks; ABC Family Channel; CNN; ESPN; Headline News; Lifetime; Spike TV; Syfy; TBS Superstation; The Weather Channel; Trinity Broadcasting Network; Turner Network TV; USA Network; WGN America.
Fee: $23.00 installation; $25.50 monthly.

Pay Service 1
Pay Units: 13.
Programming (via satellite): The Movie Channel.
Fee: $11.00 monthly.

Video-On-Demand: No

Internet Service
Operational: No.

Telephone Service
None

Miles of Plant: 11.0 (coaxial); None (fiber optic).
Chief Technician: Duane Poling. Manager: Jim Fink.
Ownership: Country Cable (WV) (MSO).

WISCONSIN

Total Systems: **173**
Total Communities Served: **906**
Franchises Not Yet Operating: **0**
Applications Pending: **0**
Communities with Applications: **0**
Number of Basic Subscribers: **1,749,851**
Number of Expanded Basic Subscribers: **826,768**
Number of Pay Units: **173,656**

Top 100 Markets Represented: Minneapolis-St. Paul (13); Milwaukee (23); Green Bay (62); Duluth, MN-Superior, WI (89); Madison (93); Rockford-Freeport (97).

For a list of cable communities in this section, see the Cable Community Index located in the back of Cable Volume 2.
For explanation of terms used in cable system listings, see p. D-11.

ADAMS—Charter Communications, 165 Knights Way, Ste 100, Fond Du Lac, WI 54935-8061. Phone: 920-907-7720. Fax: 920-907-7723. Web Site: http://www.charter.com. Also serves Friendship & Preston. ICA: WI0099.
TV Market Ranking: Outside TV Markets (ADAMS, Friendship, Preston). Franchise award date: N.A. Franchise expiration date: N.A. Began: July 31, 1981.
Channel capacity: 35 (not 2-way capable). Channels available but not in use: N.A.
Basic Service
Subscribers: 591.
Programming (received off-air): WAOW (ABC, CW) Wausau; WEAU-TV (NBC) Eau Claire; WHA-TV (PBS) Madison; WISC-TV (CBS, MNT) Madison; WKOW (ABC) Madison; WMSN-TV (FOX) Madison; WMTV-TV (NBC) Madison; WSAW-TV (CBS, MNT) Wausau.
Programming (via satellite): C-SPAN; WGN America.
Fee: $29.99 installation.
Expanded Basic Service 1
Subscribers: N.A.
Programming (via satellite): A&E Networks; ABC Family Channel; AMC; Animal Planet; Bravo; CNN; C-SPAN 2; Discovery Channel; Disney Channel; ESPN; ESPN 2; HGTV; Lifetime; MSNBC; MTV; Nickelodeon; QVC; Spike TV; TBS Superstation; The Learning Channel; The Weather Channel; Turner Network TV; TV Land; USA Network.
Fee: $47.99 monthly.
Pay Service 1
Pay Units: 189.
Programming (via satellite): Cinemax.
Fee: $14.95 installation; $12.95 monthly.
Pay Service 2
Pay Units: 218.
Programming (via satellite): Showtime.
Fee: $14.95 installation; $12.95 monthly.
Pay Service 3
Pay Units: 246.
Programming (via satellite): HBO.
Fee: $14.95 installation; $12.95 monthly.
Video-On-Demand: No
Internet Service
Operational: No.
Telephone Service
None
Miles of Plant: 35.0 (coaxial); None (fiber optic).
Vice President & General Manager: Lisa Washa. Chief Technician: Jeff Gerner. Marketing Director: Traci Loonstra. Marketing Administrator: Rhonda Schelvan.
Ownership: Charter Communications Inc. (MSO).

ALBANY—Mediacom, 3033 Asbury Rd, Dubuque, IA 52001. Phone: 563-557-8025. Fax: 563-557-7413. Web Site: http://www.mediacomcable.com. ICA: WI0152.
TV Market Ranking: 97 (ALBANY).
Channel capacity: N.A. Channels available but not in use: N.A.
Basic Service
Subscribers: 50.
Programming (received off-air): WHA-TV (PBS) Madison; WIFR (CBS) Freeport; WISC-TV (CBS, MNT) Madison; WKOW (ABC) Madison; WMSN-TV (FOX) Madison; WMTV-TV (NBC) Madison; WQRF-TV (FOX) Rockford; WREX (CW, NBC) Rockford; WTVO (ABC, MNT) Rockford.
Programming (via satellite): A&E Networks; ABC Family Channel; AMC; Animal Planet; Bravo; Cartoon Network; CNBC; CNN; Comedy Central; Country Music TV; Discovery Channel; Discovery Fit & Health; ESPN; ESPN 2; Headline News; HGTV; History Channel; Lifetime; MTV; Nickelodeon; Oxygen; QVC; Speed; Spike TV; Syfy; TBS Superstation; The Learning Channel; The Weather Channel; Travel Channel; Trinity Broadcasting Network; truTV; Turner Network TV; TV Land; USA Network; VH1; WGN America.
Pay Service 1
Pay Units: N.A.
Programming (via satellite): HBO; Showtime.
Internet Service
Operational: No.
Telephone Service
None
Miles of plant included in Moline, IL
Regional Vice President: Cari Fenzel. Area Manager: Kathleen McMullen. Engineering Director: Mitch Carlson. Technical Operations Manager: Darren Dean. Marketing Director: Greg Evans.
Ownership: Mediacom LLC (MSO).

ALMA (town)—US Cable, 402 Red River Ave N, Unit 5, Cold Spring, MN 56320-1521. Phones: 320-685-7113; 800-783-2356. Fax: 320-685-2816. E-mail: help@mn.uscable.com. Web Site: http://www.uscable.com. Also serves Buffalo & Cochrane. ICA: WI0234.
TV Market Ranking: Below 100 (Buffalo, Cochrane); Outside TV Markets (ALMA (TOWN)). Franchise award date: N.A. Franchise expiration date: N.A. Began: January 1, 1960.
Channel capacity: N.A. Channels available but not in use: N.A.
Basic Service
Subscribers: N.A. Included in Cambridge
Programming (received off-air): KARE (NBC) Minneapolis; KSTC-TV (IND) Minneapolis; KSTP-TV (ABC) St. Paul; KTTC (CW, NBC) Rochester; WCCO-TV (CBS) Minneapolis; WEAU-TV (NBC) Eau Claire; WFTC (MNT) Minneapolis; WHLA-TV (PBS) La Crosse; WKBT-DT (CBS, MNT) La Crosse; WLAX (FOX) La Crosse; WUCW (CW) Minneapolis; WXOW (ABC, CW) La Crosse.
Programming (via satellite): Eternal Word TV Network; HGTV; QVC; Superstation WGN; The Weather Channel; Turner Classic Movies.
Fee: $22.99 monthly.
Expanded Basic Service 1
Subscribers: 825.
Programming (via satellite): A&E Networks; ABC Family Channel; Animal Planet; Bravo; Cartoon Network; CNBC; CNN; Comedy Central; Country Music TV; C-SPAN; C-SPAN 2; Discovery Channel; Disney Channel; E! Entertainment Television; ESPN; ESPN 2; Food Network; Fox News Channel; Fox Sports Net Wisconsin; FX; Great American Country; Hallmark Channel; Headline News; History Channel; Lifetime; MTV; National Geographic Channel; Nickelodeon; ShopNBC; SoapNet; Speed; Spike TV; Syfy; TBS Superstation; The Learning Channel; Travel Channel; truTV; Turner Network TV; TV Land; USA Network; VH1.
Fee: $25.08 monthly.
Digital Basic Service
Subscribers: N.A. Included in Cambridge
Programming (via satellite): BBC America; Bloomberg Television; cloo; Discovery Digital Networks; DMX Music; ESPN Classic Sports; ESPNews; Fox Soccer; Fuse; G4; Golf Channel; GSN; Independent Film Channel; Lifetime Movie Network; MTV2; Nick Jr.; Style Network; TeenNick; Toon Disney; Trinity Broadcasting Network; Versus; VH1 Classic; WE tv.
Fee: $12.90 monthly.
Digital Expanded Basic Service
Subscribers: N.A.
Programming (via satellite): Bio; CMT Pure Country; Discovery Fit & Health; Encore Action; Fox Movie Channel; Halogen Network; History Channel International; Military History Channel.
Fee: $2.95 monthly.
Digital Expanded Basic Service 2
Subscribers: N.A.
Programming (via satellite): NFL Network; Outdoor Channel.
Fee: $2.00 monthly.
Digital Pay Service 1
Pay Units: N.A. Included in Cambridge
Programming (via satellite): Cinemax (multiplexed); HBO (multiplexed); Showtime (multiplexed); Starz (multiplexed); The Movie Channel (multiplexed).
Fee: $6.95 monthly (Starz), $14.95 monthly (HBO, Cinemax, Showtime or TMC).
Video-On-Demand: No
Pay-Per-View
Fresh (delivered digitally); Playboy TV (delivered digitally); iN DEMAND (delivered digitally).
Internet Service
Operational: No.
Telephone Service
None
General Manager: Steve Johnson. Customer Service Director: Jackie Torborg.
Ownership: US Cable Corp. (MSO).

ALMOND—New Century Communications, 3588 Kennebec Dr, Eagan, MN 55122-1001. Phone: 651-688-2623. Fax: 651-688-2624. E-mail: info@ourcableia.com. ICA: WI0209.
TV Market Ranking: Outside TV Markets (ALMOND). Franchise award date: N.A. Franchise expiration date: N.A. Began: N.A.
Channel capacity: 40 (not 2-way capable). Channels available but not in use: N.A.
Basic Service
Subscribers: 31.
Programming (received off-air): WAOW (ABC, CW) Wausau; WEAU-TV (NBC) Eau Claire; WHRM-TV (PBS) Wausau; WLUK-TV (FOX) Green Bay; WSAW-TV (CBS, MNT) Wausau.
Programming (via satellite): A&E Networks; ABC Family Channel; AMC; Animal Planet; CNN; Comedy Central; Country Music TV; Discovery Channel; Disney Channel; ESPN; ESPN 2; History Channel; Lifetime; Nickelodeon; QVC; Showtime; Spike TV; TBS Superstation; The Learning Channel; The Weather Channel; Trinity Broadcasting Network; Turner Network TV; TV Land; USA Network; WGN America.
Fee: $30.00 installation; $32.95 monthly.
Pay Service 1
Pay Units: N.A.
Programming (via satellite): HBO.
Fee: $11.00 monthly.
Video-On-Demand: No
Internet Service
Operational: No.
Telephone Service
None
Miles of Plant: 4.0 (coaxial); None (fiber optic).
Manager & Chief Technician: Todd Anderson. Executive Vice President: Marty Walch.
Ownership: New Century Communications (MSO).

AMBERG—Packerland Broadband, 105 Kent St, PO Box 885, Iron Mountain, MI 49801. Phones: 800-236-8434; 906-774-6621. Fax: 906-776-2811. Web Site: http://www.packerlandbroadband.com. ICA: WI0326.
TV Market Ranking: Below 100 (AMBERG).
Channel capacity: 32 (not 2-way capable). Channels available but not in use: N.A.
Basic Service
Subscribers: 30.
Programming (received off-air): WACY-TV (MNT) Appleton; WBAY-TV (ABC, IND) Green Bay; WFRV-TV (CBS) Green Bay;

WGBA-TV (NBC) Green Bay; WLUC-TV (NBC) Marquette; WLUK-TV (FOX) Green Bay; WNMU (PBS) Marquette.
Programming (via satellite): A&E Networks; ABC Family Channel; CNBC; CNN; C-SPAN; Discovery Channel; ESPN; ESPN 2; Eternal Word TV Network; Fox Sports Net North; History Channel; Lifetime; MTV; Nickelodeon; QVC; Spike TV; TBS Superstation; The Learning Channel; The Weather Channel; Turner Classic Movies; Turner Network TV; USA Network; WGN America.
Fee: $42.95 monthly.

Pay Service 1
Pay Units: N.A.
Programming (via satellite): Cinemax; HBO.
Fee: $10.95 - $13.55 monthly (each).

Video-On-Demand: No

Internet Service
Operational: Yes.

Telephone Service
None

Miles of Plant: 5.0 (coaxial); None (fiber optic).
General Manager: Dan Plante. Technical Supervisor: Chad Kay.
Ownership: Cable Constructors Inc. (MSO).

AMERY—Northwest Community Communications, 120 Birch St W, Amery, WI 54001. Phone: 715-268-7101. Fax: 715-268-9194. E-mail: info@nwcomm.net. Web Site: http://www.nwcomm.net. Also serves Clayton (Polk County), Deer Park, Polk County (portions), Somerset & Turtle Lake. ICA: WI0080.
TV Market Ranking: 13 (Polk County (portions), Somerset); Outside TV Markets (AMERY, Clayton (Polk County), Deer Park, Turtle Lake, Polk County (portions)). Franchise award date: N.A. Franchise expiration date: N.A. Began: September 1, 1984.
Channel capacity: N.A. Channels available but not in use: N.A.

Basic Service
Subscribers: 3,000.
Programming (received off-air): KARE (NBC) Minneapolis; KMSP-TV (FOX) Minneapolis; KPXM-TV (ION) St. Cloud; KSTC-TV (IND) Minneapolis; KSTP-TV (ABC) St. Paul; KTCA-TV (PBS) St. Paul; KTCI-TV (PBS) St. Paul; WCCO-TV (CBS) Minneapolis; WEAU-TV (NBC) Eau Claire; WEUX (FOX) Chippewa Falls; WFTC (MNT) Minneapolis; WHWC-TV (PBS) Menomonie; WQOW (ABC, CW) Eau Claire; WUCW (CW) Minneapolis.
Programming (via satellite): A&E Networks; ABC Family Channel; AMC; Animal Planet; BTN; CNBC; CNN; Comedy Central; Country Music TV; C-SPAN; C-SPAN 2; Discovery Channel; Discovery Health Channel; Disney Channel; E! Entertainment Television; ESPN; ESPN 2; ESPN Classic Sports; Food Network; Fox News Channel; Fox Sports Net Minnesota; Fox Sports Net Wisconsin; FX; Golf Channel; Great American Country; Hallmark Channel; Hallmark Movie Channel; Headline News; HGTV; History Channel; Lifetime; MTV; National Geographic Channel; Nickelodeon; Outdoor Channel; Speed; Spike TV; Syfy; TBS Superstation; The Learning Channel; The Weather Channel; Travel Channel; Turner Classic Movies; Turner Network TV; TV Guide Network; TV Land; USA Network; VH1; WGN America.
Fee: $25.00 installation; $34.95 monthly.

Digital Basic Service
Subscribers: N.A.
Programming (via satellite): AmericanLife TV Network; BBC America; Bio; Bloomberg Television; cloo; CMT Pure Country; Discovery Fit & Health; Discovery Health Channel; Discovery Kids Channel; DMX Music; ESPN Classic Sports; ESPNews; Fox Movie Channel; Fox Soccer; FSN Digital Atlantic; FSN Digital Central; FSN Digital Pacific; Fuse; G4; GMC; Golf Channel; Halogen Network; History Channel International; ID Investigation Discovery; Independent Film Channel; Lifetime Movie Network; Military Channel; MTV Hits; MTV2; Nick Jr.; NickToons TV; Planet Green; Science; Style Network; TeenNick; Toon Disney; Trinity Broadcasting Network; Versus; VH1 Classic; VH1 Soul; WE tv.
Fee: $17.95 monthly.

Digital Expanded Basic Service
Subscribers: N.A.
Programming (received off-air): KARE (NBC) Minneapolis; KMSP-TV (FOX) Minneapolis; KSTP-TV (ABC) St. Paul; WCCO-TV (CBS) Minneapolis; WEAU-TV (NBC) Eau Claire; WFTC (MNT) Minneapolis; WQOW (ABC, CW) Eau Claire; WUCW (CW) Minneapolis.
Programming (via satellite): A&E HD; BTN HD; Discovery Channel HD; ESPN HD; HDNet; HDNet Movies; History Channel HD; National Geographic Channel HD Network; Outdoor Channel 2 HD; PBS HD; Universal HD.
Fee: $13.95 monthly.

Pay Service 1
Pay Units: 224.
Programming (via satellite): HBO (multiplexed).
Fee: $12.95 monthly.

Pay Service 2
Pay Units: 121.
Programming (via satellite): Showtime (multiplexed); The Movie Channel.
Fee: $10.95 monthly.

Pay Service 3
Pay Units: 54.
Programming (via satellite): Cinemax (multiplexed).
Fee: $10.95 monthly.

Digital Pay Service 1
Pay Units: N.A.
Programming (via satellite): Cinemax (multiplexed); Encore (multiplexed); Flix; HBO (multiplexed); Showtime (multiplexed); Starz (multiplexed); The Movie Channel.
Fee: $10.95 monthly (Cinemax, Starz/Encore or Showtime/TMC/Flix), $12.95 monthly (HBO).

Video-On-Demand: No

Internet Service
Operational: Yes.
Broadband Service: In-house.
Fee: $50.00 installation; $34.95 monthly.

Telephone Service
None

Miles of Plant: 39.0 (coaxial); None (fiber optic).
Manager: Michael Jensen.
Ownership: Northwest Community Communications (MSO).

AMHERST (village)—Amherst Telephone. This cable system has converted to IPTV. See Amherst (village), WI [WI5372]. ICA: WI0144.

ANGELICA—Northern Lakes Cable TV. Now served by KRAKOW, WI [WI0327]. ICA: WI0330.

ANTIGO—Charter Communications, 853 McIntosh St, Wausau, WI 54402. Phones: 715-845-4223; 715-842-3910. Fax: 715-848-0081. Web Site: http://www.charter.com. Also serves Rolling (town). ICA: WI0052.
TV Market Ranking: Below 100 (ANTIGO, Rolling (town)). Franchise award date: July 22, 1980. Franchise expiration date: N.A. Began: April 6, 1981.
Channel capacity: 78 (operating 2-way). Channels available but not in use: N.A.

Basic Service
Subscribers: 2,800.
Programming (received off-air): WAOW (ABC, CW) Wausau; WBAY-TV (ABC, IND) Green Bay; WFRV-TV (CBS) Green Bay; WFXS-DT (FOX) Wittenberg; WGBA-TV (NBC) Green Bay; WHRM-TV (PBS) Wausau; WJFW-TV (NBC) Rhinelander; WSAW-TV (CBS, MNT) Wausau.
Programming (via satellite): QVC; WGN America.
Fee: $29.99 installation.

Expanded Basic Service 1
Subscribers: N.A.
Programming (via satellite): A&E Networks; ABC Family Channel; AMC; Animal Planet; Bravo; Cartoon Network; CNBC; CNN; Comedy Central; Country Music TV; C-SPAN; C-SPAN 2; Discovery Channel; Disney Channel; E! Entertainment Television; ESPN; ESPN 2; ESPN Classic Sports; Eternal Word TV Network; Food Network; Fox News Channel; Fox Sports Net North; FX; G4; Golf Channel; Great American Country; GSN; Hallmark Channel; Headline News; HGTV; History Channel; INSP; Lifetime; MSNBC; MTV; National Geographic Channel; Nickelodeon; Oxygen; ShopNBC; SoapNet; Speed; Spike TV; Style Network; Syfy; TBS Superstation; The Learning Channel; The Weather Channel; Toon Disney; Travel Channel; truTV; Turner Classic Movies; Turner Network TV; TV Guide Network; TV Land; USA Network; Versus; VH1; WE tv.
Fee: $47.99 monthly.

Digital Basic Service
Subscribers: N.A.
Programming (via satellite): BBC America; Bio; Discovery Digital Networks; Fox College Sports Atlantic; Fox College Sports Central; Fox College Sports Pacific; Fox Soccer; Fuel TV; Fuse; GAS; History Channel International; Lifetime Movie Network; MTV Networks Digital Suite; Music Choice; NFL Network; Nick Jr.; Nick Too; NickToons TV; Sundance Channel; TV Guide Interactive Inc.

Digital Pay Service 1
Pay Units: N.A.
Programming (via satellite): Cinemax (multiplexed); Encore (multiplexed); Flix; HBO (multiplexed); Showtime (multiplexed); Starz (multiplexed); The Movie Channel (multiplexed).

Video-On-Demand: No

Pay-Per-View
iN DEMAND (delivered digitally); NASCAR In Car (delivered digitally); NHL Center Ice (delivered digitally); MLB Extra Innings (delivered digitally); Playboy TV (delivered digitally); Fresh (delivered digitally); Shorteez (delivered digitally).

Internet Service
Operational: Yes.
Broadband Service: Charter Pipeline.
Fee: $29.99 monthly.

Telephone Service
None

Miles of Plant: 55.0 (coaxial); None (fiber optic).
Vice President: Lisa Washa. Chief Technician: Bruce Wasleske. Marketing Director: Traci Loonstra.
Ownership: Charter Communications Inc. (MSO).

ARGYLE—Mediacom, 3033 Asbury Rd, Dubuque, IA 52001. Phones: 309-797-2580 (Regional office); 563-557-8025. Fax: 563-557-7413. Web Site: http://www.mediacomcable.com. ICA: WI0175.
TV Market Ranking: 93 (ARGYLE).
Channel capacity: N.A. Channels available but not in use: N.A.

Internet Service
Operational: No.

Telephone Service
None

Miles of plant included in Moline, IL
Regional Vice President: Cari Fenzel. Area Manager: Kathleen McMullen. Engineering Director: Mitch Carlson. Technical Operations Manager: Darren Dean. Marketing Director: Greg Evans.
Ownership: Mediacom LLC (MSO).

ARKANSAW—Chippewa Valley Cable Co. Inc., 318 3rd Ave W, PO Box 228, Durand, WI 54736. Phones: 715-946-3930; 715-672-4204. Fax: 715-672-4344. E-mail: cvc@nelson-tel.net. Web Site: http://www.nelson-tel.net. Also serves Durand, Eau Galle, Gilmanton, Mondovi & Plum City. ICA: WI0110.
TV Market Ranking: Below 100 (ARKANSAW, Durand, Eau Galle, Gilmanton, Mondovi); Outside TV Markets (Plum City). Franchise award date: January 1, 1968. Franchise expiration date: N.A. Began: September 1, 1968.
Channel capacity: 62 (operating 2-way). Channels available but not in use: N.A.

Basic Service
Subscribers: 2,230.
Programming (received off-air): KARE (NBC) Minneapolis; KSTC-TV (IND) Minneapolis; KSTP-TV (ABC) St. Paul; KTCA-TV (PBS) St. Paul; WCCO-TV (CBS) Minneapolis; WEAU-TV (NBC) Eau Claire; WEUX (FOX) Chippewa Falls; WFTC (MNT) Minneapolis; WKBT-DT (CBS, MNT) La Crosse; WQOW (ABC, CW) Eau Claire; WUCW (CW) Minneapolis; allband FM.
Programming (via satellite): A&E Networks; ABC Family Channel; AMC; Animal Planet; Cartoon Network; CNBC; CNN; Comedy Central; Country Music TV; C-SPAN; Discovery Channel; DIY Network; ESPN; ESPN 2; Eternal Word TV Network; Food Network; Fox News Channel; Fox Sports Net Wisconsin; FX; Golf Channel; Headline News; HGTV; History Channel; Lifetime; Lifetime Movie Network; MTV; National Geographic Channel; NFL Network; Nickelodeon; Outdoor Channel; QVC; Speed; Spike TV; Syfy; TBS Superstation; The Learning Channel; The Weather Channel; Turner Network TV; TV Guide Network; TV Land; USA Network; VH1; WGN America.
Fee: $45.00 installation; $31.90 monthly.

Digital Basic Service
Subscribers: 138.
Programming (via satellite): Animal Planet HD; Bio; Bloomberg Television; cloo; Discovery Channel HD; Discovery Health Channel; Discovery Kids Channel; DMX Music; ESPN HD; ESPNews; Fox Soccer; FSN HD; G4; Golf Channel; GSN; Hallmark Channel; HD Theater; HDNet; HDNet Movies; History Channel International; ID Investigation Discovery; Lifetime Movie Network; MTV2; mtvU; Nick Jr.; NickToons

TV; Outdoor Channel 2 HD; PBS HD; RFD-TV; Science; TeenNick; TLC HD; Turner Classic Movies; Versus; VH1 Classic; WE tv.
Fee: $8.95 monthly.
Digital Pay Service 1
Pay Units: 8.
Programming (via satellite): Cinemax (multiplexed); Cinemax HD; HBO HD; The Movie Channel (multiplexed).
Fee: $10.95 monthly.
Digital Pay Service 2
Pay Units: 16.
Programming (via satellite): Encore (multiplexed); Starz (multiplexed).
Fee: $12.95 monthly.
Digital Pay Service 3
Pay Units: 38.
Programming (via satellite): HBO (multiplexed).
Fee: $12.95 monthly.
Digital Pay Service 4
Pay Units: 15.
Programming (via satellite): Showtime (multiplexed).
Fee: $12.95 monthly.
Video-On-Demand: No
Pay-Per-View
iN DEMAND (delivered digitally); Club Jenna (delivered digitally).
Internet Service
Operational: No, DSL & dial-up.
Telephone Service
None
Miles of Plant: 51.0 (coaxial); 4.0 (fiber optic).
General Manager: Christy Berger. Office Manager: Laura Gullickson. Plant Supervisor: Dale Goss.
Ownership: Nelson Telephone Cooperative.

ASHLAND—Charter Communications, 1201 McCann Dr, Altoona, WI 54720-2561. Phone: 715-831-8940. Fax: 715-831-5862. Web Site: http://www.charter.com. Also serves Barksdale (town), Bayfield, Eileen (town), Red Cliff, Russell (town) & Washburn. ICA: WI0047.
TV Market Ranking: Outside TV Markets (ASHLAND, Barksdale (town), Bayfield, Eileen (town), Red Cliff, Russell (town), Washburn). Franchise award date: August 16, 1965. Franchise expiration date: N.A. Began: September 15, 1967.
Channel capacity: N.A. Channels available but not in use: N.A.
Basic Service
Subscribers: 4,300.
Programming (received off-air): KBJR-TV (MNT, NBC) Superior; KDLH (CBS, CW) Duluth; KQDS-TV (FOX) Duluth; WDIO-DT (ABC) Duluth; WDSE (PBS) Duluth; WLEF-TV (PBS) Park Falls.
Programming (via satellite): C-SPAN; Eternal Word TV Network; QVC; WGN America.
Fee: $50.00 installation.
Expanded Basic Service 1
Subscribers: N.A.
Programming (via satellite): A&E Networks; ABC Family Channel; AMC; Animal Planet; Bravo; Cartoon Network; CNBC; CNN; Comedy Central; Country Music TV; C-SPAN 2; Discovery Channel; Disney Channel; E! Entertainment Television; ESPN; ESPN 2; Food Network; Fox News Channel; Fox Sports Net North; FX; G4; GSN; Headline News; HGTV; History Channel; Lifetime; MSNBC; MTV; Nickelodeon; Oxygen; SoapNet; Speed; Spike TV; Syfy; TBS Superstation; The Learning Channel; The Weather Channel; Toon Disney; Travel Channel; truTV; Turner Classic Movies; Turner Network TV; TV Land; USA Network; Versus; VH1.
Fee: $47.99 monthly.
Digital Basic Service
Subscribers: N.A.
Programming (via satellite): BBC America; Bio; Bloomberg Television; Discovery Digital Networks; DIY Network; Fuse; GAS; History Channel International; Lifetime Movie Network; MTV Networks Digital Suite; Music Choice; Nick Jr.; Nick Too; Style Network; Sundance Channel; WE tv.
Fee: $7.00 monthly.
Digital Pay Service 1
Pay Units: 2,248.
Programming (via satellite): Cinemax (multiplexed); Flix; HBO (multiplexed); Showtime (multiplexed); The Movie Channel (multiplexed).
Fee: $10.00 monthly (Cinemax, HBO, Showtime, or Flix/TMC).
Video-On-Demand: No
Pay-Per-View
Shorteez (delivered digitally); Fresh (delivered digitally); Playboy TV (delivered digitally); iN DEMAND (delivered digitally); Hot Choice (delivered digitally).
Internet Service
Operational: Yes.
Broadband Service: Charter Pipeline.
Fee: $29.99 monthly.
Telephone Service
None
Miles of Plant: 98.0 (coaxial); None (fiber optic).
Vice President & General Manager: Lisa Washa. Operations Manager: Shirley Weibel. Engineering Director: Tim Normand. Marketing Director: Traci Loonstra. Sales & Marketing Manager: Chris Putzkey. Government Relations Manager: Mike Hill.
Ownership: Charter Communications Inc. (MSO).

AUBURNDALE—Packerland Broadband, 105 Kent St, PO Box 885, Iron Mountain, MI 49801. Phones: 800-236-8434; 906-774-6621. Fax: 906-776-2811. Web Site: http://www.packerlandbroadband.com. Also serves Hewitt & Marshfield (portions). ICA: WI0166.
TV Market Ranking: Below 100 (AUBURNDALE, Hewitt, Marshfield (portions)). Franchise award date: N.A. Franchise expiration date: N.A. Began: N.A.
Channel capacity: 40 (not 2-way capable). Channels available but not in use: N.A.
Basic Service
Subscribers: 61.
Programming (received off-air): WAOW (ABC, CW) Wausau; WEAU-TV (NBC) Eau Claire; WFXS-DT (FOX) Wittenberg; WHRM-TV (PBS) Wausau; WSAW-TV (CBS, MNT) Wausau.
Programming (via satellite): A&E Networks; ABC Family Channel; AMC; Animal Planet; CNBC; CNN; Country Music TV; Discovery Channel; Disney Channel; ESPN; ESPN 2; Fox Sports Net; History Channel; Lifetime; MTV; Nickelodeon; Spike TV; Syfy; TBS Superstation; The Learning Channel; The Weather Channel; Turner Network TV; TV Land; USA Network; VH1; WGN America.
Fee: $24.95 installation; $29.00 monthly; $1.50 converter.
Pay Service 1
Pay Units: 35.
Programming (via satellite): HBO.
Fee: $14.95 installation; $10.95 monthly.
Video-On-Demand: No
Internet Service
Operational: Yes.
Fee: $26.95 monthly.
Telephone Service
None
Miles of Plant: 22.0 (coaxial); None (fiber optic).
General Manager: Dan Plante. Technical Supervisor: Chad Kay.
Ownership: Cable Constructors Inc. (MSO).

AUGUSTA—Packerland Broadband, 105 Kent St, PO Box 885, Iron Mountain, MI 49801. Phones: 800-236-8434; 906-774-6621. Fax: 906-776-2811. Web Site: http://www.packerlandbroadband.com. ICA: WI0141.
TV Market Ranking: Below 100 (AUGUSTA). Franchise award date: March 1, 1976. Franchise expiration date: N.A. Began: September 1, 1978.
Channel capacity: N.A. Channels available but not in use: N.A.
Basic Service
Subscribers: 207.
Programming (received off-air): WEAU-TV (NBC) Eau Claire; WEUX (FOX) Chippewa Falls; WHWC-TV (PBS) Menomonie; WKBT-DT (CBS, MNT) La Crosse; WQOW (ABC, CW) Eau Claire.
Programming (via satellite): A&E Networks; ABC Family Channel; Animal Planet; CNN; Comedy Central; Country Music TV; Discovery Channel; Discovery Health Channel; ESPN; ESPN 2; Fox News Channel; FX; Great American Country; Hallmark Channel; Headline News; History Channel; Lifetime; MTV; Nickelodeon; QVC; Speed; Spike TV; Syfy; TBS Superstation; The Learning Channel; The Weather Channel; Travel Channel; Trinity Broadcasting Network; Turner Network TV; TV Land; USA Network; VH1; WGN America.
Fee: $35.00 installation; $32.43 monthly.
Pay Service 1
Pay Units: 70.
Programming (via satellite): Showtime.
Fee: $9.95 monthly.
Video-On-Demand: No
Internet Service
Operational: Yes.
Fee: $26.95 monthly.
Telephone Service
None
Miles of Plant: 12.0 (coaxial); None (fiber optic).
General Manager: Dan Plante. Technical Supervisor: Chad Kay.
Ownership: Cable Constructors Inc. (MSO).

AVOCA—Packerland Broadband, 105 Kent St, PO Box 885, Iron Mountain, MI 49801. Phones: 800-236-8434; 906-774-6621. Fax: 906-776-2811. Web Site: http://www.packerlandbroadband.com. ICA: WI0237.
TV Market Ranking: Outside TV Markets (AVOCA). Franchise award date: N.A. Franchise expiration date: N.A. Began: N.A.
Channel capacity: 36 (not 2-way capable). Channels available but not in use: N.A.
Basic Service
Subscribers: 34.
Programming (received off-air): WBUW (CW) Janesville; WHA-TV (PBS) Madison; WISC-TV (CBS, MNT) Madison; WKOW (ABC) Madison; WMSN-TV (FOX) Madison; WMTV-TV (NBC) Madison.
Programming (via satellite): QVC; TBS Superstation; WGN America.
Fee: $49.95 installation; $17.15 monthly.
Expanded Basic Service 1
Subscribers: N.A.
Programming (via satellite): A&E Networks; ABC Family Channel; Animal Planet; CNN; Country Music TV; Discovery Channel; Disney Channel; E! Entertainment Television; ESPN; ESPN 2; Headline News; History Channel; Lifetime; Nickelodeon; Spike TV; The Learning Channel; The Weather Channel; Turner Classic Movies; Turner Network TV; USA Network.
Fee: $21.10 monthly.
Pay Service 1
Pay Units: N.A.
Programming (via satellite): HBO.
Fee: $19.95 installation; $14.72 monthly.
Video-On-Demand: No
Internet Service
Operational: No.
Telephone Service
None
Miles of Plant: 4.0 (coaxial); None (fiber optic).
General Manager: Dan Plante. Technical Supervisor: Chad Kay.
Ownership: Cable Constructors Inc. (MSO).

BAGLEY (village)—Dairyland Cable Systems Inc., 2494 US Hwy 14 E, Richland Center, WI 53581-2983. Phones: 800-677-6383; 608-647-6383. Fax: 608-647-2093. ICA: WI0238.
TV Market Ranking: Below 100 (BAGLEY (VILLAGE)). Franchise award date: N.A. Franchise expiration date: N.A. Began: July 1, 1989.
Channel capacity: 13 (not 2-way capable). Channels available but not in use: N.A.
Basic Service
Subscribers: 108.
Programming (received off-air): KCRG-TV (ABC) Cedar Rapids; KRIN (PBS) Waterloo; KWWL (NBC) Waterloo; WISC-TV (CBS, MNT) Madison; WKBT-DT (CBS, MNT) La Crosse.
Programming (via satellite): CNN; Discovery Channel; ESPN; TBS Superstation; Turner Network TV; USA Network; WGN America.
Fee: $25.00 installation; $28.25 monthly.
Pay Service 1
Pay Units: 11.
Programming (via satellite): The Movie Channel.
Fee: $10.50 monthly.
Video-On-Demand: No
Internet Service
Operational: No.
Telephone Service
None
Manager: Jim Atkinson. Chief Technician: Rudy Marshall. Marketing Representative: Brian Sullivan.
Ownership: Dairyland Cable Systems Inc. (MSO).

BALDWIN (town)—Baldwin Telecom Inc. Formerly served by Baldwin (village), WI [WI0079]. This cable system has converted to IPTV, 930 Maple St, Baldwin, WI 54002. Phones: 877-684-3346; 715-684-3346. Fax: 715-684-4747. E-mail: info@baldwin-telecom.net. Web Site: http://www.baldwin-telecom.net. ICA: WI5201.
Channel capacity: N.A. Channels available but not in use: N.A.
Basic Service
Subscribers: N.A.
Fee: $46.50 monthly.
Expanded Basic Service 1
Subscribers: N.A.
Fee: $63.50 monthly.

Expanded Basic Service 2
Subscribers: N.A.
Fee: $6.95 monthly.
Pay Service 1
Pay Units: N.A.
Fee: $11.95 monthly (Cinemax, HBO, Showtime/TMC or Starz/Encore).
Internet Service
Operational: Yes.
Fee: $39.95 monthly.
Telephone Service
Digital: Operational
General Manager: Larry Knegendorf. Manager, Cable TV: Matt Knegendorf. Plant Manager: Duane Russett. Manager, Operations: Matt Sparks.

BALDWIN (village)—Baldwin Telecom Inc. Formerly served by Baldwin (village), WI [WI0079]. This cable system has converted to IPTV, 930 Maple St, Baldwin, WI 54002. Phones: 877-684-3346; 715-684-3346. Fax: 715-684-4747. E-mail: info@baldwin-telecom.net. Web Site: http://www.baldwin-telecom.net. ICA: WI5355.
Channel capacity: N.A. Channels available but not in use: N.A.
Basic Service
Subscribers: N.A.
Fee: $61.00 monthly.
Expanded Basic Service 1
Subscribers: N.A.
Fee: $6.95 monthly.
Pay Service 1
Pay Units: N.A.
Fee: $11.95 monthly.
Internet Service
Operational: Yes.
Fee: $39.95 monthly.
Telephone Service
Digital: Operational
General Manager: Larry Knegendorf. Cable TV Manager: Matt Knegendorf. Plant Manager: Duane Russett. Operations Manager: Matt Sparks.

BALDWIN (village)—Baldwin Telecom Inc. This cable system has converted to IPTV. See Baldwin (village), WI [WI5355]. ICA: WI0079.

BANCROFT—New Century Communications, 3588 Kennebec Dr, Eagan, MN 55122-1001. Phone: 651-688-2623. Fax: 651-688-2624. E-mail: info@ourcableia.com. ICA: WI0215.
TV Market Ranking: Outside TV Markets (BANCROFT). Franchise award date: N.A. Franchise expiration date: N.A. Began: N.A.
Channel capacity: 40 (not 2-way capable). Channels available but not in use: N.A.
Basic Service
Subscribers: 19.
Programming (received off-air): WAOW (ABC, CW) Wausau; WEAU-TV (NBC) Eau Claire; WFXS-DT (FOX) Wittenberg; WHRM-TV (PBS) Wausau; WSAW-TV (CBS, MNT) Wausau.
Programming (via satellite): A&E Networks; ABC Family Channel; AMC; CNN; Discovery Channel; ESPN; Lifetime; Nickelodeon; Showtime; Spike TV; TBS Superstation; The Learning Channel; Trinity Broadcasting Network; Turner Network TV; USA Network; WGN America.
Fee: $30.00 installation; $31.80 monthly.
Video-On-Demand: No
Internet Service
Operational: No.
Telephone Service
None
Miles of Plant: 4.0 (coaxial); None (fiber optic).
Executive Vice President: Marty Walch. Manager & Chief Technician: Todd Anderson.
Ownership: New Century Communications (MSO).

BAY CITY—US Cable, 402 Red River Ave N, Unit 5, Cold Spring, MN 56320-1521. Phones: 320-685-7113; 800-783-2356. Fax: 320-685-2816. E-mail: help@mn.uscable.com. Web Site: http://www.uscable.com. ICA: WI0239.
TV Market Ranking: Outside TV Markets (BAY CITY). Franchise award date: N.A. Franchise expiration date: N.A. Began: March 1, 1989.
Channel capacity: N.A. Channels available but not in use: N.A.
Basic Service
Subscribers: N.A. Included in Cambridge, MN
Programming (received off-air): KARE (NBC) Minneapolis; KMSP-TV (FOX) Minneapolis; KSTC-TV (IND) Minneapolis; KSTP-TV (ABC) St. Paul; KTCA-TV (PBS) St. Paul; KTCI-TV (PBS) St. Paul; WCCO-TV (CBS) Minneapolis; WEAU-TV (NBC) Eau Claire; WEUX (FOX) Chippewa Falls; WFTC (MNT) Minneapolis; WHMC (PBS) Conway; WKBT-DT (CBS, MNT) La Crosse; WUCW (CW) Minneapolis.
Programming (via satellite): A&E Networks; ABC Family Channel; Animal Planet; Cartoon Network; CNBC; CNN; Comedy Central; Country Music TV; C-SPAN; Discovery Channel; Disney Channel; ESPN; ESPN 2; Eternal Word TV Network; Food Network; Fox News Channel; Fox Sports Net North; FX; Hallmark Channel; Headline News; History Channel; Lifetime; MTV; Nickelodeon; QVC; Speed; Spike TV; TBS Superstation; The Learning Channel; The Weather Channel; Travel Channel; Turner Classic Movies; Turner Network TV; TV Land; USA Network; VH1; WGN America.
Fee: $47.58 monthly.
Digital Basic Service
Subscribers: N.A. Included in Cambridge, MN
Programming (via satellite): BBC America; Bio; Bloomberg Television; Bravo; cloo; CMT Pure Country; Discovery Fit & Health; DMX Music; Encore; ESPN Classic Sports; ESPNews; Fox Movie Channel; Fox Soccer; Fuse; G4; Golf Channel; GSN; Halogen Network; HGTV; History Channel International; Independent Film Channel; Lifetime Movie Network; Military History Channel; MTV Networks Digital Suite; Nick Jr.; Outdoor Channel; Style Network; Syfy; TeenNick; Toon Disney; Trinity Broadcasting Network; Versus; WE tv.
Fee: $12.90 monthly.
Digital Pay Service 1
Pay Units: N.A. Included in Cambridge, MN
Programming (via satellite): Cinemax (multiplexed); HBO (multiplexed); Showtime (multiplexed); Starz (multiplexed); The Movie Channel (multiplexed).
Fee: $6.95 monthly (Starz), $14.95 monthly (HBO, Cinemax, Showtime or TMC).
Video-On-Demand: No
Pay-Per-View
iN DEMAND (delivered digitally); Playboy TV; Club Jenna; Fresh (delivered digitally).
Internet Service
Operational: Yes.
Broadband Service: Warp Drive Online.
Fee: 24.95-$39.95 monthly.
Telephone Service
None
Miles of plant included in Cambridge, MN
General Manager: Steve Johnson. Customer Service Director: Jackie Torborg.
Ownership: US Cable Corp. (MSO).

BEAR CREEK—Charter Communications, 79 Main St, Clintonville, WI 54929. Phone: 888-438-2427. Web Site: http://www.charter.com. ICA: WI0240.
TV Market Ranking: Below 100 (BEAR CREEK). Franchise award date: N.A. Franchise expiration date: N.A. Began: May 1, 1990.
Channel capacity: N.A. Channels available but not in use: N.A.
Basic Service
Subscribers: 40.
Programming (received off-air): WAOW (ABC, CW) Wausau; WBAY-TV (ABC, IND) Green Bay; WFRV-TV (CBS) Green Bay; WGBA-TV (NBC) Green Bay; WLUK-TV (FOX) Green Bay; WPNE-TV (PBS) Green Bay; WSAW-TV (CBS, MNT) Wausau.
Programming (via satellite): A&E Networks; ABC Family Channel; CNBC; CNN; C-SPAN; Discovery Channel; Disney Channel; ESPN; ESPN 2; Eternal Word TV Network; Fox Sports Net Midwest; History Channel; ION Television; MTV; Nickelodeon; QVC; Spike TV; TBS Superstation; The Learning Channel; The Weather Channel; Turner Classic Movies; Turner Network TV; USA Network; WGN America.
Fee: $25.00 installation; $33.95 monthly.
Pay Service 1
Pay Units: N.A.
Programming (via satellite): Cinemax; HBO.
Fee: $11.50 monthly (each).
Video-On-Demand: Planned
Internet Service
Operational: Yes.
Fee: $19.99 monthly.
Telephone Service
Digital: Planned
Fee: $14.99 monthly
Miles of Plant: 6.0 (coaxial); None (fiber optic).
Vice President & General Manager: Lisa Washa.
Ownership: Charter Communications Inc. (MSO).

BELL CENTER—Richland-Grant Telephone Co-op. Formerly [WI0228]. This cable system has converted to IPTV, 202 N East St, PO Box 67, Blue River, WI 53518. Phone: 608-537-2461. Fax: 608-537-2222. E-mail: rgtc@mwt.net. Web Site: http://www.rgtelecom.com. ICA: WI5364.
Channel capacity: N.A. Channels available but not in use: N.A.
Internet Service
Operational: Yes.
President: Larry D. Jewell. Vice President: Keith D. Chamberlain. General Manager: Bradley Welp. Secretary-Treasurer: Byron D. Hillberry.

BELL CENTER—Richland-Grant Telephone Co-op. This cable system has converted to IPTV. See Bell Center, WI [WI5364]. ICA: WI0228.

BELLEVILLE—Charter Communications. Now served by MADISON, WI[WI0002]. ICA: WI0138.

BLACK RIVER FALLS—Charter Communications. Now served by ONALASKA, WI [WI0024]. ICA: WI0082.

BLANCHARDVILLE—Mediacom, 3033 Asbury Rd, Dubuque, IA 52001. Phones: 309-797-2580 (Regional office); 563-557-8025. Fax: 563-557-7413. Web Site: http://www.mediacomcable.com. ICA: WI0170.
TV Market Ranking: 93 (BLANCHARDVILLE).
Channel capacity: N.A. Channels available but not in use: N.A.
Basic Service
Subscribers: 32.
Programming (received off-air): WHA-TV (PBS) Madison; WISC-TV (CBS, MNT) Madison; WKOW (ABC) Madison; WMSN-TV (FOX) Madison; WMTV-TV (NBC) Madison.
Programming (via satellite): A&E Networks; ABC Family Channel; AMC; Animal Planet; Bravo; Cartoon Network; CNBC; CNN; Comedy Central; Country Music TV; C-SPAN; Discovery Channel; Discovery Fit & Health; Disney Channel; ESPN; ESPN 2; Food Network; Hallmark Channel; Headline News; HGTV; History Channel; INSP; Lifetime; MTV; Nickelodeon; Oxygen; QVC; Speed; Spike TV; Syfy; TBS Superstation; The Learning Channel; The Weather Channel; Travel Channel; Trinity Broadcasting Network; truTV; Turner Network TV; TV Land; USA Network; VH1; WGN America.
Pay Service 1
Pay Units: N.A.
Programming (via satellite): Cinemax; HBO; Showtime.
Internet Service
Operational: No.
Telephone Service
None
Miles of plant included in Moline, IL
Regional Vice President: Cari Fenzel. Area Manager: Kathleen McMullen. Engineering Director: Mitch Carlson. Technical Operations Manager: Darren Dean. Marketing Director: Greg Evans.
Ownership: Mediacom LLC (MSO).

BLOOMINGDALE—Formerly served by Midwest Cable Inc. No longer in operation. ICA: WI0232.

BLUE RIVER (village)—Dairyland Cable Systems Inc., 2494 US Hwy 14 E, Richland Center, WI 53581-2983. Phone: 608-647-6383. Fax: 608-647-2093. ICA: WI0242.
TV Market Ranking: Outside TV Markets (BLUE RIVER (VILLAGE)). Franchise award date: N.A. Franchise expiration date: N.A. Began: November 1, 1989.
Channel capacity: 16 (not 2-way capable). Channels available but not in use: N.A.
Basic Service
Subscribers: 77.
Programming (received off-air): WISC-TV (CBS, MNT) Madison; WKOW (ABC) Madison; WMSN-TV (FOX) Madison; WMTV-TV (NBC) Madison; WMVS (PBS) Milwaukee.
Programming (via satellite): CNN; Discovery Channel; ESPN; Nickelodeon; TBS Superstation; Turner Network TV; USA Network; VH1; WGN America.
Fee: $25.00 installation; $27.29 monthly.
Pay Service 1
Pay Units: 22.
Programming (via satellite): The Movie Channel.
Fee: $10.50 monthly.
Video-On-Demand: No
Internet Service
Operational: No.
Telephone Service
None
Manager: Jim Atkinson. Chief Technician: Randy Marshall. Marketing Representative: Brian Sullivan.
Ownership: Dairyland Cable Systems Inc. (MSO).

BLUFFVIEW MOBILE HOME PARK—HLM Cable Corp. Now served by MERRIMAC, WI [WI0154]. ICA: WI0212.

BOAZ—Village of Boaz, 25433 Jackson St, Muscoda, WI 53573. Phone: 608-536-3466. Fax: 608-536-3469. ICA: WI0229.
TV Market Ranking: Outside TV Markets (BOAZ). Franchise award date: N.A. Franchise expiration date: N.A. Began: N.A.
Channel capacity: 20 (not 2-way capable). Channels available but not in use: N.A.
Basic Service
Subscribers: 44.
Programming (received off-air): WHA-TV (PBS) Madison; WISC-TV (CBS, MNT) Madison; WKBT-DT (CBS, MNT) La Crosse; WKOW (ABC) Madison; WMSN-TV (FOX) Madison; WMTV-TV (NBC) Madison.
Programming (via satellite): CW+; Discovery Channel; ESPN; TBS Superstation; Turner Network TV; USA Network.
Fee: $13.00 monthly.
Internet Service
Operational: No.
Telephone Service
None
Miles of Plant: 3.0 (coaxial); None (fiber optic).
Village Clerk: Jean Welsh. Chief Technician: Dan Schwarz.
Ownership: Village of Boaz.

BONDUEL—Packerland Broadband, 105 Kent St, Iron Mountain, MI 49801. Phone: 800-236-8434. Web Site: http://www.packerlandbroadband.com. ICA: WI0163.
TV Market Ranking: 62 (BONDUEL). Franchise award date: May 1, 1981. Franchise expiration date: N.A. Began: February 1, 1983.
Channel capacity: 69 (not 2-way capable). Channels available but not in use: N.A.
Basic Service
Subscribers: 370.
Programming (received off-air): WACY-TV (MNT) Appleton; WBAY-TV (ABC, IND) Green Bay; WCWF (CW) Suring; WFRV-TV (CBS) Green Bay; WGBA-TV (NBC) Green Bay; WLUK-TV (FOX) Green Bay; WPNE-TV (PBS) Green Bay.
Programming (via satellite): A&E Networks; ABC Family Channel; AMC; Animal Planet; CNBC; CNN; Comedy Central; Country Music TV; C-SPAN; C-SPAN 2; Discovery Channel; Discovery Health Channel; Disney Channel; E! Entertainment Television; ESPN; ESPN 2; ESPNews; Eternal Word TV Network; Food Network; Fox News Channel; Fox Sports Net; FX; G4; Golf Channel; GSN; Hallmark Channel; Headline News; HGTV; History Channel; Lifetime; MSNBC; MTV; National Geographic Channel; Nickelodeon; Outdoor Channel; QVC; Speed; Spike TV; Syfy; TBS Superstation; The Learning Channel; The Weather Channel; Toon Disney; Travel Channel; truTV; Turner Classic Movies; Turner Network TV; TV Land; USA Network; Versus; VH1; WE tv; WGN America.
Fee: $31.95 monthly.
Pay Service 1
Pay Units: 86.
Programming (via satellite): Cinemax (multiplexed); HBO (multiplexed); Showtime (multiplexed).
Fee: $12.25 monthly.
Video-On-Demand: No
Internet Service
Operational: Yes.
Fee: $26.95-$44.95 monthly.
Telephone Service
None
Miles of Plant: 9.0 (coaxial); None (fiber optic).
General Manager: Joe Esbrook.
Ownership: Cable Constructors Inc.

BOULDER JUNCTION—Karban TV Systems Inc., 120 S Church St, PO Box 8, Bonduel, WI 54107-0008. Phones: 715-550-7613; 800-236-0233. Fax: 715-277-2339. E-mail: sales@ktvs.net. Web Site: http://www.ktvs.net. ICA: WI0243.
TV Market Ranking: Below 100 (BOULDER JUNCTION). Franchise award date: N.A. Franchise expiration date: N.A. Began: August 1, 1990.
Channel capacity: 77 (2-way capable). Channels available but not in use: N.A.
Basic Service
Subscribers: 161.
Programming (received off-air): WFXS-DT (FOX) Wittenberg; WJFW-TV (NBC) Rhinelander; WLEF-TV (PBS) Park Falls; WSAW-TV (CBS, MNT) Wausau; WYOW (ABC, CW) Eagle River.
Programming (via satellite): A&E Networks; ABC Family Channel; AMC; Animal Planet; CNBC; CNN; Comedy Central; Country Music TV; C-SPAN; CW+; Discovery Channel; Disney Channel; ESPN; ESPN 2; Eternal Word TV Network; Food Network; Fox News Channel; FX; Headline News; HGTV; History Channel; Lifetime; MSNBC; NFL Network; Nickelodeon; Outdoor Channel; QVC; Speed; Spike TV; Syfy; TBS Superstation; The Learning Channel; The Weather Channel; Travel Channel; Trinity Broadcasting Network; Turner Classic Movies; Turner Network TV; TV Land; USA Network; VH1; WGN America.
Fee: $75.00 installation; $40.00 monthly; $20.00 additional installation.
Pay Service 1
Pay Units: 15.
Programming (via satellite): Cinemax.
Fee: $10.00 monthly.
Pay Service 2
Pay Units: 25.
Programming (via satellite): HBO.
Fee: $10.00 monthly.
Video-On-Demand: No
Internet Service
Operational: No.
Telephone Service
None
Miles of Plant: 18.0 (coaxial); None (fiber optic).
Manager & Chief Technician: John Karban.
Ownership: Karban TV Systems Inc. (MSO).

BOYD/CADOTT—Charter Communications. Now served by EAU CLAIRE, WI [WI0011]. ICA: WI0131.

BRIGGSVILLE—New Century Communications, 3588 Kennebec Dr, Eagan, MN 55122-1001. Phone: 651-688-2623. Fax: 651-688-2624. E-mail: info@ourcableia.com. ICA: WI0216.
TV Market Ranking: Outside TV Markets (BRIGGSVILLE). Franchise award date: N.A. Franchise expiration date: N.A. Began: N.A.
Channel capacity: 40 (not 2-way capable). Channels available but not in use: N.A.
Basic Service
Subscribers: 31.
Programming (received off-air): WHA-TV (PBS) Madison; WISC-TV (CBS, MNT) Madison; WKOW (ABC) Madison; WMTV-TV (NBC) Madison.
Programming (via satellite): A&E Networks; ABC Family Channel; AMC; CNN; Discovery Channel; Disney Channel; ESPN; ESPN 2; History Channel; QVC; Showtime (multiplexed); Spike TV; TBS Superstation; The Learning Channel; Trinity Broadcasting Network; Turner Network TV; USA Network; WGN America.
Fee: $30.00 installation; $33.80 monthly.
Video-On-Demand: No
Internet Service
Operational: No.
Telephone Service
None
Miles of Plant: 4.0 (coaxial); None (fiber optic).
Executive Vice President: Marty Walch. Manager & Chief Technician: Todd Anderson.
Ownership: New Century Communications (MSO).

BROOKFIELD—Time Warner Cable. Now served by MILWAUKEE, WI [WI0001]. ICA: WI0028.

BURLINGTON—Time Warner Cable. Now served by MILWAUKEE, WI [WI0001]. ICA: WI0023.

BUTTERNUT—Packerland Broadband, 105 Kent St, PO Box 885, Iron Mountain, MI 49801. Phones: 800-236-8434; 906-774-6621. Fax: 906-776-2811. Web Site: http://www.packerlandbroadband.com. ICA: WI0214.
TV Market Ranking: Outside TV Markets (BUTTERNUT). Franchise award date: May 1, 1985. Franchise expiration date: N.A. Began: October 1, 1985.
Channel capacity: 50 (not 2-way capable). Channels available but not in use: N.A.
Basic Service
Subscribers: 117.
Programming (received off-air): WAOW (ABC, CW) Wausau; WFXS-DT (FOX) Wittenberg; WJFW-TV (NBC) Rhinelander; WLEF-TV (PBS) Park Falls; WSAW-TV (CBS, MNT) Wausau.
Programming (via satellite): A&E Networks; ABC Family Channel; CNN; Comedy Central; Discovery Channel; ESPN; ESPN 2; History Channel; MTV; Nickelodeon; Spike TV; Syfy; TBS Superstation; The Weather Channel; Turner Network TV; USA Network; VH1; WGN America.
Fee: $35.00 installation; $27.90 monthly.
Pay Service 1
Pay Units: 30.
Programming (via satellite): Flix; Showtime.
Fee: $9.95 monthly.
Video-On-Demand: No
Internet Service
Operational: Yes.
Fee: $34.95 monthly.
Telephone Service
Digital: Planned
Miles of Plant: 4.0 (coaxial); None (fiber optic).
General Manager: Dan Plante. Technical Supervisor: Chad Kay.
Ownership: Cable Constructors Inc. (MSO).

CASCO—CenturyTel, 212 Church Ave, Casco, WI 54205-9670. Phone: 888-835-2485. Fax: 920-837-2330. Web Site: http://www.centurytel.com. Also serves Casco (town), Casco (village), Forestville (village), Green Bay Twp., Luxemburg (town), Luxemburg (village), New Franken, Red River Twp. & Scott Twp. ICA: WI0115.
TV Market Ranking: 62 (CASCO, Casco (town), Casco (village), Forestville (village), Green Bay Twp., Luxemburg (town), Luxemburg (village), New Franken, Red River Twp., Scott Twp.). Franchise award date: February 1, 1983. Franchise expiration date: N.A. Began: February 1, 1983.
Channel capacity: 63 (not 2-way capable). Channels available but not in use: N.A.
Basic Service
Subscribers: 1,836.
Programming (received off-air): WACY-TV (MNT) Appleton; WBAY-TV (ABC, IND) Green Bay; WCWF (CW) Suring; WFRV-TV (CBS) Green Bay; WGBA-TV (NBC) Green Bay; WLUK-TV (FOX) Green Bay; WPNE-TV (PBS) Green Bay.
Programming (via satellite): A&E Networks; ABC Family Channel; AMC; Animal Planet; Cartoon Network; CNN; Comedy Central; Country Music TV; Discovery Channel; Disney Channel; ESPN; ESPN 2; Eternal Word TV Network; Food Network; Fox News Channel; Fox Sports Net North; FX; Hallmark Channel; HGTV; History Channel; Lifetime; MSNBC; MTV; Nickelodeon; QVC; Spike TV; Syfy; TBS Superstation; The Learning Channel; The Weather Channel; Travel Channel; Turner Classic Movies; Turner Network TV; TV Land; USA Network; VH1; WGN America.
Fee: $40.00 installation; $33.95 monthly.
Digital Basic Service
Subscribers: N.A.
Programming (via satellite): BBC America; Bio; Bloomberg News Radio; Bravo!; Discovery Fit & Health; Discovery Kids Channel; DMX Music; G4; GAS; GSN; History Channel International; International Television (ITV); MTV Networks Digital Suite; National Geographic Channel; Nick Jr.; NickToons TV; Ovation; Style Network; Toon Disney; Trinity Broadcasting Network; VH1 Classic; VH1 Country; WE tv.
Fee: $5.00 monthly; $4.95 converter.
Digital Expanded Basic Service
Subscribers: N.A.
Programming (via satellite): ESPN Classic Sports; ESPNews; Fox Movie Channel; Fox Sports World; Golf Channel; Independent Film Channel; Lifetime Movie Network; Outdoor Channel; Speed; Versus.
Fee: $3.00 monthly; $4.95 converter.
Digital Pay Service 1
Pay Units: N.A.
Programming (via satellite): Cinemax (multiplexed); HBO (multiplexed).
Fee: $15.95 monthly.
Pay-Per-View
iN DEMAND (delivered digitally).
Internet Service
Operational: No.
Telephone Service
None
Miles of Plant: 68.0 (coaxial); 5.0 (fiber optic).
Manager: Mary Gotstein. Chief Technician: Matt Gunderson.
Ownership: CenturyLink (MSO).

CASHTON—Mediacom, 4010 Alexandra Dr, Waterloo, IA 50702. Phone: 319-235-2197. Fax: 319-232-7841. Web Site: http://www.mediacomcable.com. Also serves Brookview Trailer Court, Gays Mills, Greenfield (La Crosse County), La Crosse, La Farge, Readstown, Shelby, Soldier's Grove, Viola, Viroqua & Westby. ICA: WI0068.
TV Market Ranking: Below 100 (Brookview Trailer Court, CASHTON, Greenfield (La Crosse County), La Crosse, La Farge, Shelby, Viola, VIROQUA, Westby); Outside TV Markets (Gays Mills, Readstown, Soldier's Grove). Franchise award date:

N.A. Franchise expiration date: N.A. Began: January 1, 1968.
Channel capacity: N.A. Channels available but not in use: N.A.

Basic Service
Subscribers: 4,310.
Programming (received off-air): WEAU-TV (NBC) Eau Claire; WHLA-TV (PBS) La Crosse; WKBT-DT (CBS, MNT) La Crosse; WLAX (FOX) La Crosse; WXOW (ABC, CW) La Crosse.
Programming (via satellite): C-SPAN; C-SPAN 2; Eternal Word TV Network; Paxson Communications Corp.; QVC; Trinity Broadcasting Network; TV Guide Network; WGN America.
Fee: $35.16 installation; $7.01 monthly; $1.58 converter.

Expanded Basic Service 1
Subscribers: 4,152.
Programming (via satellite): A&E Networks; ABC Family Channel; AMC; AmericanLife TV Network; Animal Planet; Bravo; Cartoon Network; CNBC; CNN; Comedy Central; Country Music TV; Discovery Channel; Disney Channel; E! Entertainment Television; ESPN; ESPN 2; Food Network; Fox Movie Channel; Fox News Channel; Fox Sports Net; FX; Hallmark Channel; Headline News; HGTV; History Channel; INSP; Lifetime; Lifetime Movie Network; MSNBC; MTV; Nickelodeon; RFD-TV; Speed; Spike TV; Syfy; TBS Superstation; The Learning Channel; The Weather Channel; Travel Channel; truTV; Turner Classic Movies; Turner Network TV; TV Land; USA Network; Versus; VH1.
Fee: $17.94 monthly.

Digital Basic Service
Subscribers: N.A.
Programming (via satellite): BBC America; Bio; Bloomberg Television; cloo; ESPN; ESPN 2; ESPNews; Fox Soccer; Fuse; G4; GAS; Golf Channel; GSN; Halogen Network; HD Theater; HDNet; HDNet Movies; History Channel International; Independent Film Channel; Lime; MTV Networks Digital Suite; Music Choice; National Geographic Channel; Nick Jr.; NickToons TV; Outdoor Channel; Style Network; TVG Network; Universal HD.

Digital Pay Service 1
Pay Units: N.A.
Programming (via satellite): Cinemax (multiplexed); Encore (multiplexed); Flix (multiplexed); HBO (multiplexed); HBO HD; Showtime (multiplexed); Showtime HD; Starz (multiplexed); Starz HDTV; Sundance Channel (multiplexed); The Movie Channel (multiplexed); The Movie Channel HD.

Video-On-Demand: No

Pay-Per-View
ESPN (delivered digitally); Fresh (delivered digitally); Shorteez (delivered digitally); Playboy TV (delivered digitally); Pleasure (delivered digitally); Ten Clips (delivered digitally).

Internet Service
Operational: Yes.
Broadband Service: Mediacom High Speed Internet.

Telephone Service
None

Miles of Plant: 108.0 (coaxial); None (fiber optic).
Regional Vice President: Doug Frank. General Manager: Doug Nix. Technical Operations Director: Greg Nank. Marketing Director: Steve Schuh. Marketing Coordinator: Joni Lindaur.
Ownership: Mediacom LLC (MSO).

CAZENOVIA—Community Antenna System Inc., 1010 Lake St, Hillsboro, WI 54634-9019. Phone: 608-489-2321. Fax: 608-489-2321. ICA: WI0222.
TV Market Ranking: Outside TV Markets (CAZENOVIA). Franchise award date: January 1, 1970. Franchise expiration date: N.A. Began: January 1, 1971.
Channel capacity: 39 (not 2-way capable). Channels available but not in use: N.A.

Basic Service
Subscribers: 135.
Programming (received off-air): WHA-TV (PBS) Madison; WISC-TV (CBS, MNT) Madison; WKBT-DT (CBS, MNT) La Crosse; WKOW (ABC) Madison; WMSN-TV (FOX) Madison; WMTV-TV (NBC) Madison.
Programming (via satellite): ABC Family Channel; ESPN; Spike TV; TBS Superstation; Turner Network TV; WGN America.
Fee: $25.00 installation; $28.00 monthly.

Pay Service 1
Pay Units: 35.
Programming (via satellite): Cinemax.
Fee: $6.95 monthly.

Internet Service
Operational: No.

Telephone Service
None

Miles of Plant: 2.0 (coaxial); None (fiber optic).
Manager: Randall Kubarski. Chief Technician: Gregory Kubarski.
Ownership: Community Antenna System Inc. (MSO).

CEDARBURG—Time Warner Cable. Now served by MILWAUKEE, WI [WI0001]. ICA: WI0031.

CHASEBURG—Mediacom. Now served by COON VALLEY, WI [WI0171]. ICA: WI0219.

CLINTONVILLE—Charter Communications, 853 McIntosh St, Wausau, WI 54402. Phones: 714-845-4223; 714-842-3910. Fax: 715-848-0081. Web Site: http://www.charter.com. Also serves Belle Plaine, Black Creek, Bovina, Caroline, Cloverleaf Lakes, Dayton (town), Embarrass, Farmington (town), Gresham, Hortonia (town), Hortonville, King, Larrabee (town), Lebanon (town), Liberty (town), Lind (town), Maple Creek (town), Marion, Matteson (town), Mukwa (town), New London, Richmond (town), Royalton (town), Shawano, Shioctin, Washington (town), Waukechon (town), Waupaca, Wescott (town) & Weyauwega. ICA: WI0073.
TV Market Ranking: 62 (Belle Plaine, Black Creek, Bovina, Embarrass, Maple Creek (town), Shawano, Shiocton, Washington (town), Waukechon (town)); Below 100 (Caroline, CLINTONVILLE, Gresham, Hortonia (town), Hortonville, King, Larrabee (town), Lebanon (town), Liberty (town), Lind (town), Marion, Matteson (town), Mukwa (town), New London, Richmond (town), Royalton (town), Waupaca, Wescott (town), Weyauwega); Outside TV Markets (Dayton (town), Farmington (town)). Franchise award date: N.A. Franchise expiration date: N.A. Began: December 1, 1980.
Channel capacity: N.A. Channels available but not in use: N.A.

Basic Service
Subscribers: 14,239.
Programming (received off-air): WACY-TV (MNT) Appleton; WBAY-TV (ABC, IND) Green Bay; WCWF (CW) Suring; WFRV-TV (CBS) Green Bay; WGBA-TV (NBC) Green

Access the most current data instantly.
FREE
TRIAL
@
ADVANCED
TVFactbook
www.warren-news.com/factbook.htm

Bay; WLUK-TV (FOX) Green Bay; WPNE-TV (PBS) Green Bay; WSAW-TV (CBS, MNT) Wausau.
Programming (via satellite): C-SPAN 2; QVC; WGN America.
Fee: $29.99 installation.

Expanded Basic Service 1
Subscribers: 13,304.
Programming (via satellite): A&E Networks; ABC Family Channel; AMC; Animal Planet; Bravo; Cartoon Network; CNBC; CNN; Comedy Central; Country Music TV; C-SPAN; Discovery Channel; Discovery Fit & Health; Disney Channel; E! Entertainment Television; ESPN; ESPN 2; ESPN Classic Sports; Eternal Word TV Network; Food Network; Fox News Channel; Fox Sports Net North; FX; G4; Golf Channel; Great American Country; GSN; Hallmark Channel; Headline News; HGTV; History Channel; INSP; ION Television; Lifetime; MSNBC; MTV; National Geographic Channel; Nickelodeon; Outdoor Channel; Oxygen; Product Information Network; ShopNBC; SoapNet; Speed; Spike TV; Style Network; Syfy; TBS Superstation; The Learning Channel; The Weather Channel; Toon Disney; Travel Channel; truTV; Turner Classic Movies; Turner Network TV; TV Guide Network; TV Land; USA Network; Versus; VH1; WE tv.
Fee: $47.99 monthly.

Digital Basic Service
Subscribers: N.A.
Programming (via satellite): BBC America; Bio; Discovery Digital Networks; DIY Network; ESPN; Fox College Sports Atlantic; Fox College Sports Central; Fox College Sports Pacific; Fox Soccer; Fuel TV; Fuse; GAS; HDNet; HDNet Movies; History Channel International; Lifetime Movie Network; MTV Networks Digital Suite; Music Choice; NFL Network; Nick Jr.; Nick Too; NickToons TV; Sundance Channel; TV Guide Interactive Inc.

Digital Pay Service 1
Pay Units: 6,436.
Programming (via satellite): Cinemax (multiplexed); Encore (multiplexed); Flix; HBO (multiplexed); HBO HD; Showtime (multiplexed); Showtime HD; Starz (multiplexed); The Movie Channel (multiplexed).
Fee: $10.00 monthly (Cinemax, HBO, Showtime, Flix/TMC, or Starz/Encore).

Video-On-Demand: Yes

Pay-Per-View
iN DEMAND (delivered digitally); Playboy TV (delivered digitally); Fresh (delivered digitally); Shorteez (delivered digitally); Sports PPV (delivered digitally).

Internet Service
Operational: Yes.
Broadband Service: Charter Pipeline.
Fee: $39.99 monthly.

Telephone Service
None

Miles of Plant: 441.0 (coaxial); 5.0 (fiber optic). Additional miles planned: 2.0 (coaxial).
Vice President: Lisa Washa. Chief Technician: Bruce Wasleske. Marketing Director: Traci Loonstra.
Ownership: Charter Communications Inc. (MSO).

COLEMAN—Packerland Broadband, 105 Kent St, PO Box 885, Iron Mountain, MI 49801. Phones: 800-236-8434; 906-774-6621. Fax: 906-776-2811. Web Site: http://www.packerlandbroadband.com. Also serves Pound. ICA: WI0173.
TV Market Ranking: Below 100 (COLEMAN, Pound). Franchise award date: February 1, 1982. Franchise expiration date: N.A. Began: December 31, 1982.
Channel capacity: N.A. Channels available but not in use: N.A.

Basic Service
Subscribers: 126.
Programming (received off-air): WACY-TV (MNT) Appleton; WBAY-TV (ABC, IND) Green Bay; WCWF (CW) Suring; WFRV-TV (CBS) Green Bay; WGBA-TV (NBC) Green Bay; WLUK-TV (FOX) Green Bay; WPNE-TV (PBS) Green Bay.
Programming (via satellite): C-SPAN; C-SPAN 2; QVC; WGN America.
Fee: $43.98 installation; $12.08 monthly.

Expanded Basic Service 1
Subscribers: 100.
Programming (via satellite): A&E Networks; ABC Family Channel; Animal Planet; Bravo; CNN; Country Music TV; Discovery Channel; Disney Channel; E! Entertainment Television; ESPN; Fox News Channel; Headline News; HGTV; History Channel; Lifetime; MSNBC; Nickelodeon; Speed; Spike TV; Syfy; TBS Superstation; The Learning Channel; The Weather Channel; Turner Network TV; TV Land; USA Network; VH1.
Fee: $28.37 monthly.

Pay Service 1
Pay Units: 48.
Programming (via satellite): Cinemax.
Fee: $14.72 monthly.

Pay Service 2
Pay Units: 50.
Programming (via satellite): HBO.
Fee: $14.72 monthly.

Video-On-Demand: No

Internet Service
Operational: Yes. Began: February 1, 2008.
Fee: $26.95 monthly.

Telephone Service
None

Miles of Plant: 14.0 (coaxial); None (fiber optic).
General Manager: Dan Plante. Technical Supervisor: Chad Kay.
Ownership: Cable Constructors Inc. (MSO).

COON VALLEY—Mediacom, 4010 Alexandra Dr, Waterloo, IA 50702. Phone: 319-235-2197. Fax: 319-232-7841. Web Site: http://www.mediacomcable.com. Also serves Chaseburg, Crawford County (portions), Ferryville & Stoddard. ICA: WI0171.
TV Market Ranking: Below 100 (Chaseburg, COON VALLEY, Crawford County, Ferryville, Stoddard). Franchise award date: May 7,

1968. Franchise expiration date: N.A. Began: February 1, 1969.
Channel capacity: N.A. Channels available but not in use: N.A.

Basic Service
Subscribers: 294.
Programming (received off-air): KWWL (NBC) Waterloo; WEAU-TV (NBC) Eau Claire; WHLA-TV (PBS) La Crosse; WKBT-DT (CBS, MNT) La Crosse; WLAX (FOX) La Crosse; WXOW (ABC, CW) La Crosse; allband FM.
Programming (via satellite): C-SPAN; C-SPAN 2; CW+; Eternal Word TV Network; ION Television; QVC; Trinity Broadcasting Network; WGN America.
Fee: $35.16 installation; $7.60 monthly; $1.58 converter.

Expanded Basic Service 1
Subscribers: 268.
Programming (via satellite): A&E Networks; ABC Family Channel; AMC; AmericanLife TV Network; Animal Planet; Bravo; Cartoon Network; CNBC; CNN; Comedy Central; Country Music TV; Discovery Channel; Disney Channel; E! Entertainment Television; ESPN; ESPN 2; Food Network; Fox Movie Channel; Fox News Channel; Fox Sports Net; FX; Hallmark Channel; Headline News; HGTV; History Channel; INSP; Lifetime; Lifetime Movie Network; MSNBC; MTV; Nickelodeon; RFD-TV; Speed; Spike TV; Syfy; TBS Superstation; The Learning Channel; The Weather Channel; Travel Channel; truTV; Turner Network TV; TV Land; USA Network; Versus; VH1.
Fee: $27.75 monthly.

Digital Basic Service
Subscribers: N.A.
Programming (via satellite): BBC America; Bio; Bloomberg Television; cloo; Discovery Channel HD; Discovery Fit & Health; Discovery Health Channel; Discovery Kids Channel; ESPN 2 HD; ESPN HD; ESPNews; Fox Soccer; Fuse; G4; Golf Channel; GSN; Halogen Network; HDNet; HDNet Movies; History Channel International; ID Investigation Discovery; Independent Film Channel; Military Channel; MTV Hits; MTV2; National Geographic Channel; NickToons TV; Outdoor Channel; Planet Green; Science; Style Network; Sundance Channel; TeenNick; Turner Classic Movies; TVG Network; Universal HD; VH1 Classic.

Digital Pay Service 1
Pay Units: N.A.
Programming (via satellite): Cinemax (multiplexed); Encore (multiplexed); Flix; HBO (multiplexed); HBO HD; Showtime (multiplexed); Showtime HD; Starz (multiplexed); Starz HDTV; Sundance Channel.

Video-On-Demand: No

Internet Service
Operational: Yes.
Broadband Service: Mediacom High Speed Internet.
Fee: $99.00 installation; $40.00 monthly.

Telephone Service
None

Miles of Plant: 8.0 (coaxial); None (fiber optic).
Regional Vice President: Doug Frank. General Manager: Doug Nlx. Technical Operations Director: Greg Nank. Marketing Director: Steve Schuh. Marketing Coordinator: Joni Lindauer.
Ownership: Mediacom LLC (MSO).

CRIVITZ—Howard Cable, 111 Pine St, PO Box 127, Peshtigo, WI 54157. Phone: 715-582-1141. Fax: 715-582-1142. E-mail: cableone@new.rr.com. Also serves Lake Noquebay. ICA: WI0321.
TV Market Ranking: Below 100 (CRIVITZ, Lake Noquebay). Franchise award date: January 1, 1986. Franchise expiration date: January 1, 2010. Began: January 1, 1985.
Channel capacity: 60 (not 2-way capable). Channels available but not in use: N.A.

Basic Service
Subscribers: 28.
Programming (received off-air): WACY-TV (MNT) Appleton; WBAY-TV (ABC, IND) Green Bay; WCWF (CW) Suring; WFRV-TV (CBS) Green Bay; WGBA-TV (NBC) Green Bay; WLUK-TV (FOX) Green Bay; WNMU (PBS) Marquette; WPNE-TV (PBS) Green Bay.
Programming (via satellite): ABC Family Channel; Eternal Word TV Network; HGTV; Lifetime; Nickelodeon; Spike TV; Turner Network TV; USA Network.
Fee: $19.95 monthly.

Expanded Basic Service 1
Subscribers: N.A.
Programming (via satellite): A&E Networks; AMC; Animal Planet; Bloomberg Television; Bravo; Classic Arts Showcase; CNN; Comedy Central; Country Music TV; Discovery Channel; Disney Channel; DIY Network; E! Entertainment Television; ESPN; ESPN 2; Food Network; Fox Movie Channel; Fox News Channel; FX; Great American Country; Hallmark Channel; Headline News; History Channel; MTV; National Geographic Channel; Outdoor Channel; QVC; Syfy; TBS Superstation; The Learning Channel; Toon Disney; Travel Channel; Trinity Broadcasting Network; truTV; Turner Classic Movies; TV Land; VH1; WGN America.
Fee: $10.00 monthly.

Pay Service 1
Pay Units: N.A.
Programming (via satellite): HBO.
Fee: $10.95 monthly.

Video-On-Demand: No

Internet Service
Operational: No.

Telephone Service
None

Miles of Plant: 6.0 (coaxial); None (fiber optic).
Manager & Chief Technician: Howard C. Lock.
Ownership: Howard Lock (MSO).

CUBA CITY—Mediacom, 3900 26th Ave, Moline, IL 61265. Phone: 309-797-2580. Fax: 309-797-2414. Web Site: http://www.mediacomcable.com. Also serves Belmont, Benton, Darlington, Hazel Green, Potosi, Shullsburg & Tennyson. ICA: WI0334.
Channel capacity: N.A. Channels available but not in use: N.A.

Basic Service
Subscribers: N.A.
Programming (received off-air): KFXA (FOX) Cedar Rapids; KWWL (NBC) Waterloo; WBUW (CW) Janesville; WHA-TV (PBS) Madison; WISC-TV (CBS, MNT) Madison; WKOW (ABC) Madison; WMSN-TV (FOX) Madison; WMTV-TV (NBC) Madison.
Programming (via satellite): C-SPAN; C-SPAN 2; Discovery Channel; QVC; WGN America.
Fee: $23.95 monthly.

Expanded Basic Service 1
Subscribers: N.A.
Programming (via satellite): A&E Networks; ABC Family Channel; AMC; Bravo; BTN; Cartoon Network; CNBC; CNN; Comedy Central; Country Music TV; Discovery Fit & Health; Disney Channel; E! Entertainment Television; ESPN; ESPN 2; Eternal Word TV Network; Food Network; Fox News Channel; Fox Sports Net; FX; Hallmark Channel; Headline News; HGTV; History Channel; INSP; Lifetime; MSNBC; MTV; Nickelodeon; SoapNet; Speed; Spike TV; Syfy; TBS Superstation; The Learning Channel; The Weather Channel; Travel Channel; Trinity Broadcasting Network; truTV; Turner Network TV; TV Land; USA Network; Versus; VH1; WE tv.
Fee: $34.00 monthly.

Digital Basic Service
Subscribers: N.A.
Programming (via satellite): ABC News Now; AmericanLife TV Network; BBC America; Bio; Bloomberg Television; Boomerang; CBS Sports Network; CCTV-4; Chiller; cloo; Discovery Health Channel; Discovery Kids Channel; ESPN U; ESPNews; Fox College Sports Atlantic; Fox College Sports Central; Fox College Sports Pacific; Fox Movie Channel; Fox Reality Channel; Fox Soccer; Fuel TV; Fuse; G4; Golf Channel; GolTV; GSN; History Channel International; ID Investigation Discovery; Independent Film Channel; ION Life; Lifetime Movie Network; Lifetime Real Women; Military Channel; MTV Hits; MTV2; Music Choice; National Geographic Channel; Nick Jr.; NickToons TV; Outdoor Channel; Planet Green; Qubo; ReelzChannel; Science; Style Network; Sundance Channel; TeenNick; Tennis Channel; TVG Network; VH1 Classic.
Fee: $22.95 monthly.

Digital Pay Service 1
Pay Units: N.A.
Programming (via satellite): Cinemax; Encore (multiplexed); Flix; HBO (multiplexed); HBO HD; Showtime (multiplexed); Showtime HD; Starz; Starz HDTV; Sundance Channel; The Movie Channel (multiplexed); The Movie Channel HD.
Fee: $9.00 monthly (Starz/Encore), $10.95 monthly (Cinemax or Showtime/TMC/Sundance/Flix), $4.95 monthly (HBO).

Video-On-Demand: No

Pay-Per-View
iN DEMAND (delivered digitally); Fresh (delivered digitally); Spice: Xcess (delivered digitally); Playboy TV (delivered digitally); Ten Clips (delivered digitally).

Internet Service
Operational: Yes.
Fee: $59.95 installation; $49.95 monthly.

Telephone Service
Digital: Operational

Miles of plant included in Moline, IL
Regional Vice President: Cari Fenzel. Area Manager: Kathleen McMullen. Technical Operations Manager: Darren Dean. Marketing Director: Greg Evans. Engineering Director: Mitch Carlson.
Ownership: Mediacom LLC (MSO).

DALLAS—Mosaic Media, 401 S First St, PO Box 664, Cameron, WI 54822. Phones: 800-924-3405; 715-458-5400. Fax: 715-458-5400. E-mail: chitel@mosaictelecom.net. Web Site: http://www.mosaictelecom.com/TV/index.html. Also serves Almena, Barron, Cameron, Hillsdale, Prairie Farm, Ridgeland & Sand Creek. ICA: WI0148. **Note:** This system is an overbuild.
TV Market Ranking: Below 100 (DALLAS, Hillsdale, Ridgeland, Sand Creek); Outside TV Markets (Almena, Barron, Cameron, Prairie Farm). Franchise award date: N.A. Franchise expiration date: N.A. Began: March 1, 1980.
Channel capacity: 35 (not 2-way capable). Channels available but not in use: N.A.

Basic Service
Subscribers: 1,747.
Programming (received off-air): KARE (NBC) Minneapolis; KMSP-TV (FOX) Minneapolis; KSTP-TV (ABC) St. Paul; KTCA-TV (PBS) St. Paul; WCCO-TV (CBS) Minneapolis; WEAU-TV (NBC) Eau Claire; WEUX (FOX) Chippewa Falls; WFTC (MNT) Minneapolis; WHWC-TV (PBS) Menomonie; WKBT-DT (CBS, MNT) La Crosse; WQOW (ABC, CW) Eau Claire; WUCW (CW) Minneapolis.
Fee: $14.95 monthly.

Expanded Basic Service 1
Subscribers: N.A.
Programming (via satellite): A&E Networks; ABC Family Channel; AMC; AmericanLife TV Network; Animal Planet; Bloomberg Television; CNBC; CNN; Comedy Central; Country Music TV; C-SPAN; C-SPAN 2; Discovery Channel; Discovery Fit & Health; Disney Channel; DIY Network; E! Entertainment Television; Encore Action; ESPN; ESPN 2; ESPNews; Flix; Fox News Channel; FX; Golf Channel; Headline News; HGTV; INSP; Lifetime; MTV; Nickelodeon; Outdoor Channel; QVC; Spike TV; Syfy; TBS Superstation; Telemundo; The Learning Channel; The Weather Channel; Trinity Broadcasting Network; truTV; Turner Network TV; TV Land; USA Network; Versus; VH1; WGN America.
Fee: $39.95 monthly.

Expanded Basic Service 2
Subscribers: N.A.
Programming (via satellite): Cartoon Network; Great American Country; GSN; Hallmark Channel; History Channel; Speed; Travel Channel; Turner Classic Movies; WE tv.
Fee: $5.95 monthly.

Pay Service 1
Pay Units: N.A.
Programming (via satellite): Cinemax (multiplexed); HBO (multiplexed); Showtime (multiplexed); The Movie Channel.
Fee: $11.95 monthly (Cinemax, Showtime or TMC), $9.00 monthly (HBO).

Video-On-Demand: Yes

Internet Service
Operational: No.

Telephone Service
None

Miles of Plant: 120.0 (coaxial); 50.0 (fiber optic).
Chief Executive Officer: Rick Vergin. Technical Operations Officer: Scott Hickock.
Ownership: Chibardun Cable TV Corporation.

DALTON—New Century Communications, 3588 Kennebec Dr, Eagan, MN 55122-1001. Phone: 651-688-2623. Fax: 651-688-2624. E-mail: info@ourcableia.com. ICA: WI0226.
TV Market Ranking: Outside TV Markets (DALTON). Franchise award date: N.A. Franchise expiration date: N.A. Began: N.A.
Channel capacity: 40 (not 2-way capable). Channels available but not in use: N.A.

Basic Service
Subscribers: 11.
Programming (received off-air): WHA-TV (PBS) Madison; WISC-TV (CBS, MNT) Madison; WKOW (ABC) Madison; WMTV-TV (NBC) Madison.
Programming (via satellite): A&E Networks; ABC Family Channel; AMC; CNN; Discovery Channel; Disney Channel; ESPN; Lifetime; Nickelodeon; QVC; Showtime; Spike TV; TBS Superstation; The Learning Channel; Trinity Broadcasting Network; Turner Network TV; USA Network; WGN America.
Fee: $30.00 installation; $33.80 monthly.

Video-On-Demand: No

Internet Service
Operational: No.
Telephone Service
None
Miles of Plant: 3.0 (coaxial); None (fiber optic).
Executive Vice President: Marty Walch. Manager & Chief Technician: Todd Anderson.
Ownership: New Century Communications (MSO).

DARIEN—Packerland Broadband, 105 Kent St, PO Box 885, Iron Mountain, MI 49801. Phones: 800-236-8434; 906-774-6621. Fax: 906-776-2811. Web Site: http://www.packerlandbroadband.com. ICA: WI0246.
TV Market Ranking: 97 (DARIEN). Franchise award date: N.A. Franchise expiration date: N.A. Began: December 1, 1988.
Channel capacity: N.A. Channels available but not in use: N.A.
Basic Service
Subscribers: 108.
Programming (received off-air): WBUW (CW) Janesville; WCGV-TV (MNT) Milwaukee; WDJT-TV (CBS) Milwaukee; WISC-TV (CBS, MNT) Madison; WISN-TV (ABC) Milwaukee; WITI (FOX, IND) Milwaukee; WKOW (ABC) Madison; WMTV-TV (NBC) Madison; WMVS (PBS) Milwaukee; WPXE-TV (ION) Kenosha; WTMJ-TV (NBC) Milwaukee; WVTV (CW) Milwaukee.
Programming (via satellite): A&E Networks; ABC Family Channel; AMC; CNN; Comedy Central; Discovery Channel; Disney Channel; ESPN; ESPN 2; History Channel; Lifetime; MTV; Nickelodeon; Spike TV; Syfy; TBS Superstation; The Learning Channel; The Weather Channel; Turner Network TV; USA Network; VH1; WGN America.
Fee: $24.95 installation; $29.00 monthly; $1.50 converter.
Pay Service 1
Pay Units: 26.
Programming (via satellite): HBO.
Fee: $10.95 monthly.
Internet Service
Operational: Yes.
Fee: $34.95 monthly.
Telephone Service
None
Miles of Plant: 9.0 (coaxial); None (fiber optic).
General Manager: Dan Plante. Technical Supervisor: Chad Kay.
Ownership: Cable Constructors Inc. (MSO).

DELAVAN—Charter Communications, 2701 Daniels St, Madison, WI 53718. Phone: 608-274-3822. Fax: 608-274-1436. Web Site: http://www.charter.com. ICA: WI0329.
TV Market Ranking: 97 (DELAVAN).
Channel capacity: N.A. Channels available but not in use: N.A.
Basic Service
Subscribers: N.A.
Programming (received off-air): WBUW (CW) Janesville; WCGV-TV (MNT) Milwaukee; WDJT-TV (CBS) Milwaukee; WISN-TV (ABC) Milwaukee; WITI (FOX, IND) Milwaukee; WMLW-CA (IND) Milwaukee; WMVS (PBS) Milwaukee; WMVT (PBS) Milwaukee; WPXE-TV (ION) Kenosha; WTMJ-TV (NBC) Milwaukee; WVTV (CW) Milwaukee.
Programming (via satellite): C-SPAN; C-SPAN 2; QVC; Shop at Home; TV Guide Network; Univision Studios; WGN America.
Expanded Basic Service 1
Subscribers: N.A.
Programming (via satellite): A&E Networks; ABC Family Channel; AMC; Animal Planet; BET Networks; Bravo; Cartoon Network; CNBC; CNN; Comedy Central; Country Music TV; Discovery Channel; Disney Channel; E! Entertainment Television; ESPN; ESPN 2; ESPN Classic Sports; Eternal Word TV Network; Food Network; Fox News Channel; Fox Sports Net North; FX; G4; Golf Channel; GSN; Hallmark Channel; Headline News; HGTV; History Channel; INSP; Lifetime; MSNBC; MTV; MTV2; National Geographic Channel; Nickelodeon; Oxygen; SoapNet; Speed; Spike TV; Style Network; Syfy; TBS Superstation; The Learning Channel; The Weather Channel; Toon Disney; Travel Channel; truTV; Turner Classic Movies; Turner Network TV; TV Land; USA Network; Versus; VH1; WE tv.
Digital Basic Service
Subscribers: N.A.
Programming (received off-air): WISN-TV (ABC) Milwaukee.
Programming (via satellite): BBC America; Bio; Canales N; CNN International; Discovery Digital Networks; DIY Network; ESPN; ESPNews; Fox College Sports Atlantic; Fox College Sports Central; Fox College Sports Pacific; Fox Movie Channel; Fox Soccer; Fuel TV; Fuse; GAS; HDNet; HDNet Movies; History Channel International; Independent Film Channel; Lifetime Movie Network; MTV Networks Digital Suite; Music Choice; NFL Network; Nick Jr.; Nick Too; NickToons TV; Sundance Channel; TV Guide Interactive Inc.
Digital Pay Service 1
Pay Units: N.A.
Programming (via satellite): Cinemax (multiplexed); Encore (multiplexed); Flix; HBO (multiplexed); HBO HD; Showtime (multiplexed); Showtime HD; Starz (multiplexed); The Movie Channel (multiplexed).
Video-On-Demand: Yes
Pay-Per-View
iN DEMAND (delivered digitally); NASCAR In Car (delivered digitally); NHL Center Ice (delivered digitally); MLB Extra Innings (delivered digitally); Playboy TV (delivered digitally); Spice Live (delivered digitally); Spice Platinum (delivered digitally); Hot Net Plus (delivered digitally); Spice Hot (delivered digitally).
Internet Service
Operational: Yes.
Broadband Service: Charter Pipeline.
Telephone Service
None
Vice President & General Manager: Lisa Washa. Technical Operations Director: Bruce Hummel. Marketing Director: Traci Loonstra. Government Relations Director: Tim Vowell.
Ownership: Charter Communications Inc. (MSO).

DOYLESTOWN—Formerly served by New Century Communications. No longer in operation. ICA: WI0223.

DRESSER—Charter Communications, 1201 McCann Dr, Altoona, WI 54720-2561. Phone: 715-831-8940. Fax: 715-831-5862. Web Site: http://www.charter.com. Also serves Laketown, Osceola & St. Croix Falls. ICA: WI0087.
TV Market Ranking: Outside TV Markets (DRESSER, Laketown, Osceola, St. Croix Falls). Franchise award date: January 1, 1982. Franchise expiration date: N.A. Began: January 1, 1982.
Channel capacity: N.A. Channels available but not in use: N.A.
Basic Service
Subscribers: 893.
Programming (received off-air): KARE (NBC) Minneapolis; KMSP-TV (FOX) Minneapolis; KPXM-TV (ION) St. Cloud; KSTC-TV (IND) Minneapolis; KSTP-TV (ABC) St. Paul; KTCA-TV (PBS) St. Paul; WCCO-TV (CBS) Minneapolis; WEAU-TV (NBC) Eau Claire; WHWC-TV (PBS) Menomonie; WUCW (CW) Minneapolis.
Programming (via satellite): QVC; WGN America.
Fee: $50.00 installation; $12.12 monthly.
Expanded Basic Service 1
Subscribers: 877.
Programming (via satellite): A&E Networks; ABC Family Channel; AMC; Animal Planet; Bravo; Cartoon Network; CNBC; CNN; Comedy Central; Country Music TV; C-SPAN; Discovery Channel; Disney Channel; E! Entertainment Television; ESPN; ESPN 2; ESPN Classic Sports; Food Network; Fox News Channel; Fox Sports Net North; FX; Headline News; HGTV; History Channel; Lifetime; MSNBC; MTV; Nickelodeon; Outdoor Channel; Oxygen; Spike TV; Syfy; TBS Superstation; The Learning Channel; The Weather Channel; Toon Disney; Travel Channel; truTV; Turner Network TV; TV Land; USA Network; VH1.
Fee: $31.95 monthly.
Digital Basic Service
Subscribers: N.A.
Programming (via satellite): BBC America; Bio; Bloomberg Television; Discovery Digital Networks; DIY Network; Fox College Sports Atlantic; Fox College Sports Central; Fox College Sports Pacific; Fox Soccer; Fuel TV; GAS; GSN; Hallmark Channel; History Channel International; Independent Film Channel; Lifetime Movie Network; MTV Networks Digital Suite; Music Choice; Nick Jr.; Nick Too; NickToons TV; Style Network; Sundance Channel; TV Guide Interactive Inc.; WE tv.
Digital Pay Service 1
Pay Units: N.A.
Programming (via satellite): Cinemax (multiplexed); Encore; Flix; HBO (multiplexed); Showtime (multiplexed); Starz (multiplexed); The Movie Channel.
Video-On-Demand: No
Pay-Per-View
iN DEMAND (delivered digitally); NASCAR In Car (delivered digitally); Playboy TV (delivered digitally); Fresh (delivered digitally); Shorteez (delivered digitally).
Internet Service
Operational: Yes.
Broadband Service: Charter Pipeline.
Fee: $29.99 monthly.
Telephone Service
None
Miles of Plant: 48.0 (coaxial); 7.0 (fiber optic).
Vice President & General Manager: Lisa Washa. Operations Manager: Shirley Weibel. Engineering Director: Tim Normand. Marketing Director: Traci Loonstra. Sales & Marketing Manager: Chris Putzkey. Government Relations Manager: Mike Hill.
Ownership: Charter Communications Inc. (MSO).

EAGLE RIVER—Charter Communications, 853 McIntosh St, Wausau, WI 54402. Phones: 715-845-4223; 715-842-3910. Fax: 715-848-0081. Web Site: http://www.charter.com. Also serves Lincoln & Washington. ICA: WI0103.
TV Market Ranking: Below 100 (EAGLE RIVER, Lincoln, Washington). Franchise award date: June 1, 1972. Franchise expiration date: N.A. Began: June 1, 1973.
Channel capacity: 54 (not 2-way capable). Channels available but not in use: N.A.
Basic Service
Subscribers: 731.
Programming (received off-air): WFXS-DT (FOX) Wittenberg; WJFW-TV (NBC) Rhinelander; WLEF-TV (PBS) Park Falls; WSAW-TV (CBS, MNT) Wausau; WYOW (ABC, CW) Eagle River.
Programming (via satellite): QVC; WGN America.
Fee: $29.99 installation.
Expanded Basic Service 1
Subscribers: N.A.
Programming (via satellite): A&E Networks; ABC Family Channel; AMC; Animal Planet; Bravo; Cartoon Network; CNBC; CNN; Comedy Central; Country Music TV; C-SPAN; C-SPAN 2; Discovery Channel; Disney Channel; E! Entertainment Television; ESPN; ESPN 2; Food Network; Fox News Channel; Fox Sports Net North; FX; G4; Golf Channel; Great American Country; GSN; Hallmark Channel; Headline News; HGTV; History Channel; INSP; Lifetime; MSNBC; MTV; National Geographic Channel; Nickelodeon; Oxygen; Speed; Spike TV; Syfy; TBS Superstation; The Learning Channel; The Weather Channel; Toon Disney; Travel Channel; truTV; Turner Classic Movies; Turner Network TV; TV Land; USA Network; Versus; VH1; WE tv.
Fee: $47.99 monthly.
Digital Basic Service
Subscribers: N.A.
Programming (via satellite): AmericanLife TV Network; BBC America; Bio; Bloomberg Television; Discovery Fit & Health; DMX Music; ESPN Classic Sports; ESPNews; Fox Movie Channel; Fox Soccer; Fuse; GAS; Halogen Network; History Channel International; Independent Film Channel; Lifetime Movie Network; MTV Networks Digital Suite; Nick Jr.; Outdoor Channel; ShopNBC; Style Network; Trinity Broadcasting Network.
Pay Service 1
Pay Units: 86.
Programming (via satellite): Cinemax.
Fee: $19.95 installation; $12.50 monthly.
Pay Service 2
Pay Units: 143.
Programming (via satellite): Showtime.
Fee: $19.95 installation; $12.50 monthly.
Pay Service 3
Pay Units: 110.
Programming (via satellite): HBO.
Fee: $19.95 installation; $12.95 monthly.
Digital Pay Service 1
Pay Units: N.A.
Programming (via satellite): Cinemax (multiplexed); Encore (multiplexed); Flix; HBO (multiplexed); Showtime (multiplexed); Starz (multiplexed); The Movie Channel (multiplexed); WAM! America's Kidz Network.
Video-On-Demand: No
Pay-Per-View
iN DEMAND (delivered digitally); ESPN Now (delivered digitally); ESPN (delivered digitally); Hot Choice (delivered digitally); Playboy TV (delivered digitally); Fresh (delivered digitally); Shorteez (delivered digitally).
Internet Service
Operational: Yes.
Fee: $19.99 monthly.
Telephone Service
Digital: Operational
Fee: $14.99 monthly
Miles of Plant: 28.0 (coaxial); None (fiber optic).

Vice President: Lisa Washa. Chief Technician: Bruce Wasleske. Marketing Director: Traci Loonstra.
Ownership: Charter Communications Inc. (MSO).

EAU CLAIRE—Charter Communications, 1201 McCann Dr, Altoona, WI 54720-2561. Phone: 715-831-8940. Fax: 715-831-5862. Web Site: http://www.charter.com. Also serves Altoona, Anson (town), Bloomer, Boyd, Brunswick Twp., Cadott, Chippewa Falls, Cornell, Eagle Point, Elk Mound (village), Hallie, Jim Falls, Lafayette, Lake Wissota, New Auburn, Stanley, Tilden, Union & Wheaton. ICA: WI0011.
TV Market Ranking: Below 100 (Altoona, Anson (town), Bloomer, Boyd, Brunswick Twp., Cadott, Chippewa Falls, Cornell, Eagle Point, EAU CLAIRE, Elk Mound (village), Hallie, Jim Falls, Lafayette, Lake Wissota, New Auburn, Stanley, Tilden, Union, Wheaton). Franchise award date: N.A. Franchise expiration date: N.A. Began: January 1, 1961.
Channel capacity: N.A. Channels available but not in use: N.A.

Basic Service
Subscribers: 39,386.
Programming (received off-air): KTCA-TV (PBS) St. Paul; WCCO-TV (CBS) Minneapolis; WEAU-TV (NBC) Eau Claire; WEUX (FOX) Chippewa Falls; WHWC-TV (PBS) Menomonie; WKBT-DT (CBS, MNT) La Crosse; WQOW (ABC, CW) Eau Claire.
Programming (via satellite): C-SPAN; TV Guide Network; WGN America.
Fee: $50.00 installation; $12.18 monthly.

Expanded Basic Service 1
Subscribers: N.A.
Programming (via satellite): A&E Networks; ABC Family Channel; AMC; Animal Planet; Cartoon Network; CNBC; CNN; Comedy Central; Country Music TV; C-SPAN 2; Discovery Channel; Disney Channel; E! Entertainment Television; ESPN; ESPN 2; Eternal Word TV Network; Food Network; Fox News Channel; Fox Sports Net North; FX; G4; Golf Channel; GSN; Headline News; HGTV; History Channel; Lifetime; MSNBC; MTV; National Geographic Channel; Nickelodeon; Outdoor Channel; Oxygen; QVC; SoapNet; Speed; Spike TV; Syfy; TBS Superstation; The Learning Channel; The Weather Channel; Toon Disney; Travel Channel; Trinity Broadcasting Network; truTV; Turner Network TV; TV Land; USA Network; Versus; VH1.
Fee: $47.99 monthly.

Digital Basic Service
Subscribers: 14,000.
Programming (via satellite): BBC America; Bio; Bravo; Discovery Digital Networks; DIY Network; Fuse; GAS; History Channel International; Lifetime Movie Network; MTV Networks Digital Suite; Music Choice; Nick Jr.; Nick Too; Sundance Channel.
Fee: $7.00 monthly.

Digital Pay Service 1
Pay Units: 8,652.
Programming (via satellite): Cinemax (multiplexed); Flix; HBO (multiplexed); Showtime (multiplexed).
Fee: $15.00 installation; $10.00 monthly (Cinemax, HBO, Showtime, Flix/TMC, or Starz/Encore).

Video-On-Demand: Yes

Pay-Per-View
Addressable homes: 14,000.
iN DEMAND (delivered digitally); Playboy TV (delivered digitally); Fresh (delivered digitally); Shorteez (delivered digitally).

Internet Service
Operational: Yes.
Broadband Service: Charter Pipeline.
Fee: $29.99 monthly; $4.95 modem lease.

Telephone Service
Digital: Operational
Fee: $29.99 monthly

Miles of Plant: 667.0 (coaxial); 110.0 (fiber optic).
Vice President & General Manager: Lisa Washa. Operations Manager: Shirley Weibel. Engineering Director: Tim Normand. Construction Manager: Pat Anderson. Marketing Director: Traci Loonstra. Sales & Marketing Manager: Chris Putzkey. Government Relations Manager: Mike Hill.
Ownership: Charter Communications Inc. (MSO).

ELCHO (town)—Packerland Broadband, 105 Kent St, PO Box 885, Iron Mountain, MI 49801. Phones: 800-236-8434; 906-774-6621. Fax: 906-776-2811. Web Site: http://www.packerlandbroadband.com. Also serves Oneida County (portions). ICA: WI0203.
TV Market Ranking: Below 100 (ELCHO (TOWN), Oneida County (portions)). Franchise award date: May 1, 1990. Franchise expiration date: N.A. Began: July 1, 1990.
Channel capacity: 54 (not 2-way capable). Channels available but not in use: N.A.

Basic Service
Subscribers: 630.
Programming (received off-air): WAOW (ABC, CW) Wausau; WFXS-DT (FOX) Wittenberg; WHRM-TV (PBS) Wausau; WJFW-TV (NBC) Rhinelander; WSAW-TV (CBS, MNT) Wausau.
Programming (via satellite): A&E Networks; ABC Family Channel; CNBC; CNN; Country Music TV; C-SPAN; Discovery Channel; ESPN; ESPN 2; Eternal Word TV Network; Food Network; Fox News Channel; Fox Sports Net; FX; Headline News; HGTV; History Channel; Lifetime; MSNBC; MTV; Nickelodeon; QVC; Speed; Spike TV; TBS Superstation; The Learning Channel; The Weather Channel; Turner Classic Movies; Turner Network TV; TV Land; USA Network; VH1; WGN America.
Fee: $25.00 installation; $31.60 monthly.

Pay Service 1
Pay Units: N.A.
Programming (via satellite): Cinemax; HBO.
Fee: $11.55 monthly (each).

Video-On-Demand: No

Internet Service
Operational: Yes.
Fee: $26.95 monthly.

Telephone Service
None

Miles of Plant: 85.0 (coaxial); None (fiber optic).
General Manager: Dan Plante. Technical Supervisor: Chad Kay.
Ownership: Cable Constructors Inc. (MSO).

ELLSWORTH—US Cable, 402 Red River Ave N, Unit 5, Cold Spring, MN 56320-1521. Phones: 320-685-7113; 800-783-2356. Fax: 320-685-2816. E-mail: help@mn.uscable.com. Web Site: http://www.uscable.com. ICA: WI0248.
TV Market Ranking: 13 (ELLSWORTH). Franchise award date: N.A. Franchise expiration date: N.A. Began: February 1, 1986.
Channel capacity: N.A. Channels available but not in use: N.A.

Basic Service
Subscribers: N.A. Included in Cambridge, MN
Programming (received off-air): KARE (NBC) Minneapolis; KMSP-TV (FOX) Minneapolis; KSTC-TV (IND) Minneapolis; KSTP-TV (ABC) St. Paul; KTCA-TV (PBS) St. Paul; WCCO-TV (CBS) Minneapolis; WEAU-TV (NBC) Eau Claire; WEUX (FOX) Chippewa Falls; WHMC (PBS) Conway; WKBT-DT (CBS, MNT) La Crosse.
Programming (via satellite): A&E Networks; ABC Family Channel; Animal Planet; CNBC; CNN; Comedy Central; Country Music TV; C-SPAN; Discovery Channel; Disney Channel; ESPN; ESPN 2; Food Network; Fox News Channel; Fox Sports Net; Headline News; History Channel; Lifetime; MTV; Nickelodeon; QVC; Spike TV; TBS Superstation; The Learning Channel; The Weather Channel; Travel Channel; Turner Classic Movies; Turner Network TV; TV Land; USA Network; WGN America.
Fee: $47.58 monthly.

Digital Basic Service
Subscribers: N.A. Included in Cambridge, MN
Programming (via satellite): BBC America; Bio; Bloomberg Television; Bravo; Discovery Digital Networks; DMX Music; Encore (multiplexed); ESPN Classic Sports; ESPNews; Fox Movie Channel; Fox Sports World; Fuse; G4; GAS; Golf Channel; GSN; Halogen Network; HGTV; History Channel International; Independent Film Channel; Lifetime Movie Network; MTV Networks Digital Suite; Nick Jr.; Outdoor Channel; Speed; Style Network; Syfy; Toon Disney; Trinity Broadcasting Network; Versus; WE tv.
Fee: $12.90 monthly.

Digital Pay Service 1
Pay Units: N.A. Included in Cambridge, MN
Programming (via satellite): Cinemax (multiplexed); HBO (multiplexed); Showtime (multiplexed); Starz (multiplexed); The Movie Channel (multiplexed).
Fee: $6.95 monthly (Starz), $14.95 monthly (HBO, Cinemax, Showtime or TMC).

Video-On-Demand: No

Pay-Per-View
Fresh (delivered digitally); Playboy TV (delivered digitally); iN DEMAND (delivered digitally).

Internet Service
Operational: Yes.
Broadband Service: Warp Drive Online.
Fee: $42.95 monthly.

Telephone Service
None

Miles of plant included in Cambridge, MN
General Manager: Steve Johnson. Customer Service Director: Jackie Torborg.
Ownership: US Cable Corp. (MSO).

ELMWOOD—Celect Communications, S131 McKay Ave, PO Box 189, Spring Valley, WI 54767. Phones: 800-285-7993; 715-788-6121. Fax: 715-778-5033. E-mail: celecthelp@celectcom.net. Web Site: http://www.celectcom.net. Also serves Bloomer, Bruce, Downsville, New Auburn & Spring Valley. ICA: WI0337.
TV Market Ranking: Below 100 (Bloomer, Downsville, New Auburn); Outside TV Markets (Bruce).
Channel capacity: 116 (not 2-way capable). Channels available but not in use: 2.

Basic Service
Subscribers: N.A.
Programming (received off-air): KARE (NBC) Minneapolis; KMSP-TV (FOX) Minneapolis; KSTC-TV (IND) Minneapolis; KSTP-TV (ABC) St. Paul; KTCA-TV (PBS) St. Paul; WCCO-TV (CBS) Minneapolis; WEAU-TV (NBC) Eau Claire; WEUX (FOX) Chippewa Falls; WFTC (MNT) Minneapolis; WHWC-TV (PBS) Menomonie; WKBT-DT (CBS, MNT) La Crosse; WQOW (ABC, CW) Eau Claire; WUCW (CW) Minneapolis.
Programming (via satellite): A&E Networks; ABC Family Channel; American Movie Classics; Animal Planet; Bravo; BTN; Cartoon Network; CNBC; CNN; Comedy Central; Country Music TV; C-SPAN; Discovery Channel; Disney Channel; DIY Network; E! Entertainment Television; ESPN; ESPN 2; ESPN Classic Sports; Eternal Word TV Network; Food Network; Fox News Channel; Fox Sports Net Minnesota; Fox Sports Net Wisconsin; FX; Golf Channel; Great American Country; GSN; Hallmark Channel; Headline News; HGTV; History Channel; Home Shopping Network; Lifetime; Lifetime Movie Network; MLB Network; MSNBC; MTV; National Geographic Channel; NFL Network; Nickelodeon; Outdoor Channel; QVC; RFD-TV; SoapNet; Speed; Spike TV; Syfy; TBS Superstation; The Learning Channel; The Sportsman Channel; The Weather Channel; Travel Channel; Trinity Broadcasting Network; truTV; Turner Classic Movies; Turner Network TV; TV Guide Network; TV Land; USA Network; Versus; VH1; WGN America.

Digital Basic Service
Subscribers: N.A.
Programming (via satellite): AmericanLife TV Network; BBC America; Bio; Bloomberg Television; Centric; Church Channel; cloo; CMT Pure Country; Cooking Channel; C-SPAN 2; Current; Discovery Health Channel; Disney XD; DMX Music; Fox Business Channel; Fox Movie Channel; Fuse; G4; GMC; Hallmark Movie Channel; Halogen Network; History Channel International; ID Investigation Discovery; Independent Film Channel; INSP; ION Television; JCTV; Jewelry Television; Military Channel; MTV Hits; MTV Jams; MTV2; Nick Jr.; NickToons TV; Oxygen; PBS Kids Sprout; Planet Green; Science; ShopNBC; Style Network; TeenNick; The Hub; The Word Network; VH1 Classic; VH1 Soul; WE tv.

Digital Expanded Basic Service
Subscribers: N.A.
Programming (received off-air): KARE (NBC) Minneapolis; KMSP-TV (FOX) Minneapolis; KSTP-TV (ABC) St. Paul; KTCA-TV (PBS) St. Paul; WCCO-TV (CBS) Minneapolis; WEAU-TV (NBC) Eau Claire; WEUX (FOX) Chippewa Falls; WFTC (MNT) Minneapolis; WHWC-TV (PBS) Menomonie; WKBT-DT (CBS, MNT) La Crosse; WQOW (ABC, CW) Eau Claire.
Programming (via satellite): A&E HD; Animal Planet HD; BTN HD; Discovery Channel HD; ESPN 2 HD; ESPN HD; Food Network HD; FSN Digital; HD Theater; HGTV HD; Lifetime Movie Network HD; Lifetime Television HD; MLB Network HD; National Geographic Channel HD Network; NFL Network HD; Science HD; Speed HD; TBS in HD; TLC HD; Turner Network TV HD; Universal HD.

Digital Pay Service 1
Pay Units: N.A.
Programming (via satellite): Cinemax (multiplexed); Cinemax HD; Encore (multiplexed); Flix; HBO (multiplexed); HBO HD; Showtime (multiplexed); Showtime HD; Starz (multiplexed); Starz HDTV (multiplexed); The Movie Channel.

Pay-Per-View
iN DEMAND (delivered digitally); Playboy TV (delivered digitally); Club Jenna (delivered digitally); Hot Choice (delivered digitally); Fresh (delivered digitally); Spice: Xcess (delivered digitally).

Internet Service
Operational: Yes.

Telephone Service
None

General Manager: Mike DeMarce.
Ownership: Celect Communications (MSO).

ELROY—Community Antenna System Inc., 1010 Lake St, Hillsboro, WI 54634-9019. Phone: 608-489-2321. Fax: 608-489-2321. ICA: WI0132.
TV Market Ranking: Outside TV Markets (ELROY). Franchise award date: January 1, 1963. Franchise expiration date: N.A. Began: October 1, 1963.
Channel capacity: 66 (operating 2-way). Channels available but not in use: N.A.

Basic Service
Subscribers: 590.
Programming (received off-air): WEAU-TV (NBC) Eau Claire; WHA-TV (PBS) Madison; WISC-TV (CBS, MNT) Madison; WKBT-DT (CBS, MNT) La Crosse; WKOW (ABC) Madison; WMSN-TV (FOX) Madison; WMTV-TV (NBC) Madison.
Programming (via satellite): ABC Family Channel; ESPN; Spike TV; TBS Superstation; Turner Network TV; WGN America.
Fee: $25.00 installation; $30.87 monthly.

Pay Service 1
Pay Units: 175.
Programming (via satellite): Cinemax.
Fee: $6.95 monthly.

Internet Service
Operational: Yes.
Broadband Service: In-house.
Fee: $27.99 monthly.

Telephone Service
None

Miles of Plant: 7.0 (coaxial); None (fiber optic).
Manager: Randall Kubarski. Chief Technician: Gregory Kubarski.
Ownership: Community Antenna System Inc. (MSO).

ENDEAVOR—New Century Communications, 3588 Kennebec Dr, Eagan, MN 55122-1001. Phone: 651-688-2623. Fax: 651-688-2624. E-mail: info@ourcableia.com. ICA: WI0218.
TV Market Ranking: Outside TV Markets (ENDEAVOR). Franchise award date: N.A. Franchise expiration date: N.A. Began: N.A.
Channel capacity: 40 (not 2-way capable). Channels available but not in use: N.A.

Basic Service
Subscribers: 9.
Programming (received off-air): WHA-TV (PBS) Madison; WISC-TV (CBS, MNT) Madison; WKOW (ABC) Madison; WMTV-TV (NBC) Madison.
Programming (via satellite): A&E Networks; ABC Family Channel; AMC; CNN; Discovery Channel; ESPN; ESPN 2; History Channel; Lifetime; Nickelodeon; QVC; Showtime (multiplexed); Spike TV; TBS Superstation; The Learning Channel; Trinity Broadcasting Network; Turner Network TV; USA Network; WGN America.
Fee: $30.00 installation; $32.75 monthly.

Video-On-Demand: No

Internet Service
Operational: No.

Telephone Service
None

Miles of Plant: 3.0 (coaxial); None (fiber optic).
Executive Vice President: Marty Walch. Manager & Chief Technician: Todd Anderson.
Ownership: New Century Communications (MSO).

FAIRWATER—Formerly served by CenturyTel. No longer in operation. ICA: WI0220.

FALL CREEK—Packerland Broadband, 105 Kent St, PO Box 885, Iron Mountain, MI 49801. Phones: 800-236-8434; 906-774-6621. Fax: 906-776-2811. Web Site: http://www.packerlandbroadband.com. ICA: WI0160.
TV Market Ranking: Below 100 (FALL CREEK). Franchise award date: January 1, 1973. Franchise expiration date: January 1, 2013. Began: December 1, 1975.
Channel capacity: 50 (not 2-way capable). Channels available but not in use: N.A.

Basic Service
Subscribers: 218.
Programming (received off-air): WEAU-TV (NBC) Eau Claire; WEUX (FOX) Chippewa Falls; WHWC-TV (PBS) Menomonie; WKBT-DT (CBS, MNT) La Crosse; WQOW (ABC, CW) Eau Claire.
Programming (via satellite): A&E Networks; ABC Family Channel; Animal Planet; CNN; Comedy Central; Country Music TV; Discovery Channel; Discovery Health Channel; ESPN; ESPN 2; Fox News Channel; Fox Sports Net Midwest; Great American Country; Hallmark Channel; Headline News; History Channel; Lifetime; MTV; Nickelodeon; QVC; Speed; Spike TV; Syfy; TBS Superstation; The Learning Channel; The Weather Channel; Trinity Broadcasting Network; truTV; Turner Network TV; TV Land; USA Network; VH1; WGN America.
Fee: $15.00 installation; $28.38 monthly.

Pay Service 1
Pay Units: 30.
Programming (via satellite): Flix; Showtime.
Fee: $9.95 monthly.

Video-On-Demand: No

Internet Service
Operational: Yes.
Fee: $26.95 monthly.

Telephone Service
None

Miles of Plant: 9.0 (coaxial); None (fiber optic).
General Manager: Dan Plante. Technical Supervisor: Chad Kay.
Ownership: Cable Constructors Inc. (MSO).

FENNIMORE—Mediacom, 4010 Alexandra Dr, Waterloo, IA 50702. Phone: 319-235-2197. Fax: 319-232-7841. Web Site: http://www.mediacomcable.com. Also serves Muscoda & Muscoda Twp. ICA: WI0335.
Channel capacity: N.A. Channels available but not in use: N.A.

Video-On-Demand: No

Internet Service
Operational: Yes.
Broadband Service: Mediacom High Speed Internet.

Telephone Service
None

Regional Vice President: Doug Frank. General Manager: Doug Nix. Technical Operations Director: Greg Nank. Marketing Director: Steve Schuh. Marketing Coordinator: Joni Lindauer.
Ownership: Mediacom LLC (MSO).

FIFIELD—Packerland Broadband, 105 Kent St, PO Box 885, Iron Mountain, MI 49801. Phones: 800-236-8434; 906-774-6621. Fax: 906-776-2811. Web Site: http://www.packerlandbroadband.com. ICA: WI0250.
TV Market Ranking: Outside TV Markets (FIFIELD). Franchise award date: January 1, 1991. Franchise expiration date: N.A. Began: N.A.
Channel capacity: 50 (not 2-way capable). Channels available but not in use: N.A.

Basic Service
Subscribers: 29.
Programming (received off-air): WAOW (ABC, CW) Wausau; WJFW-TV (NBC) Rhinelander; WLEF-TV (PBS) Park Falls; WSAW-TV (CBS, MNT) Wausau.
Programming (via satellite): A&E Networks; ABC Family Channel; Animal Planet; CNN; Comedy Central; Country Music TV; Discovery Channel; E! Entertainment Television; ESPN; ESPN 2; Hallmark Channel; Headline News; History Channel; MTV; Nickelodeon; QVC; Speed; Spike TV; Syfy; TBS Superstation; The Learning Channel; The Weather Channel; Trinity Broadcasting Network; Turner Network TV; TV Land; USA Network; VH1; WGN America.
Fee: $30.17 monthly.

Pay Service 1
Pay Units: N.A.
Programming (via satellite): Showtime.
Fee: $10.50 monthly.

Video-On-Demand: No

Internet Service
Operational: Yes.
Fee: $34.95 monthly.

Telephone Service
None

Miles of Plant: 4.0 (coaxial); None (fiber optic).
General Manager: Dan Plante. Technical Supervisor: Chad Kay.
Ownership: Cable Constructors Inc. (MSO).

FOND DU LAC—Charter Communications, 165 Knights Way, Ste 100, Fond Du Lac, WI 54935-8061. Phones: 715-831-8940 (Altoona office); 920-907-7720. Fax: 920-907-7723. Web Site: http://www.charter.com. Also serves Algoma, Aurora (town), Berlin, Black Wolf (town), Brandon, Brooklyn (town), Butte des Morts, Calumet (town), Campbellsport, Charlestown, Chilton, Eden (village), Eldorado (town), Empire (town), Friendship (town), Green Lake, Kiel, Lomira, Markesan, Mount Calvary, Nekimi (town), New Holstein, North Fond du Lac, Oakfield, Omro, Princeton, Ripon, Rosendale, Schleswig (town), St. Cloud, Taycheedah (town), Van Dyne & Winneconne (village). ICA: WI0018.
TV Market Ranking: 23 (Jackson, Jackson (Twp.), Polk (town), Richfield, West Bend, West Bend (town)); 62 (Algoma, Calumet (town), Charlestown, Chilton, Schleswig (town)); Below 100 (Aurora (town), Berlin, Black Wolf (town), Brandon, Brooklyn (town), Butte des Morts, Campbellsport, Eden (village), Eldorado (town), Empire (town), FOND DU LAC, Friendship (town), Green Lake, Kiel, Lomira, Markesan, Mount Calvary, Nekimi (town), New Holstein, North Fond du Lac, Oakfield, Omro, Princeton, Ripon, Rosendale, St. Cloud, Taycheedah (town), Van Dyne, Winneconne (village)). Franchise award date: N.A. Franchise expiration date: July 6, 2006. Began: November 1, 1979.
Channel capacity: N.A. Channels available but not in use: N.A.

Basic Service
Subscribers: 23,423.
Programming (received off-air): WACY-TV (MNT) Appleton; WBAY-TV (ABC, IND) Green Bay; WCGV-TV (MNT) Milwaukee; WCWF (CW) Suring; WDJT-TV (CBS) Milwaukee; WFRV-TV (CBS) Green Bay; WGBA-TV (NBC) Green Bay; WISN-TV (ABC) Milwaukee; WITI (FOX, IND) Milwaukee; WLUK-TV (FOX) Green Bay; WMVS (PBS) Milwaukee; WPNE-TV (PBS) Green Bay; WTMJ-TV (NBC) Milwaukee; WVTV (CW) Milwaukee.
Programming (via satellite): C-SPAN; C-SPAN 2; Product Information Network; QVC; ShopNBC; TV Guide Network; WGN America.
Fee: $29.99 installation.

Expanded Basic Service 1
Subscribers: 17,073.
Programming (via satellite): A&E Networks; ABC Family Channel; AMC; Animal Planet; Bravo; Cartoon Network; CNBC; CNN; Comedy Central; Country Music TV; Discovery Channel; Disney Channel; E! Entertainment Television; ESPN; ESPN 2; Eternal Word TV Network; Food Network; Fox News Channel; Fox Sports Net North; FX; G4; Golf Channel; GSN; Hallmark Channel; Headline News; HGTV; History Channel; Lifetime; MSNBC; MTV; National Geographic Channel; Nickelodeon; Oxygen; SoapNet; Speed; Spike TV; Syfy; TBS Superstation; The Learning Channel; The Weather Channel; Toon Disney; Travel Channel; truTV; Turner Classic Movies; Turner Network TV; TV Land; USA Network; Versus; VH1.
Fee: $47.99 monthly.

Digital Basic Service
Subscribers: 4,000.
Programming (via satellite): BBC America; Bio; Discovery Digital Networks; DIY Network; GAS; History Channel International; MTV Networks Digital Suite; MuchMusic Network; Music Choice; Nick Jr.; Nick Too; NickToons TV; Style Network; Sundance Channel; WE tv.
Fee: $7.00 monthly.

Digital Pay Service 1
Pay Units: 8,092.
Programming (via satellite): Cinemax (multiplexed); Encore (multiplexed); Flix; HBO (multiplexed); Showtime (multiplexed); Starz; The Movie Channel (multiplexed).
Fee: $10.00 monthly (Cinemax, HBO, Showtime, Flix/TMC, or Starz/Encore).

Video-On-Demand: Yes

Pay-Per-View
Addressable homes: 4,000.
Hot Choice (delivered digitally); Sports PPV (delivered digitally); Shorteez (delivered digitally); Fresh (delivered digitally); Playboy TV (delivered digitally); iN DEMAND (delivered digitally).

Internet Service
Operational: Yes.
Broadband Service: Charter Pipeline.
Fee: $29.99 monthly; $4.95 modem lease.

Telephone Service
Digital: Operational
Fee: $29.99 monthly

Miles of Plant: 575.0 (coaxial); 60.0 (fiber optic).
Vice President: Lisa Washa. Chief Technician: Jeff Gerner. Marketing Administrator: Traci Loonstra.; Rhonda Schelvan.
Ownership: Charter Communications Inc. (MSO).

FORT McCOY—Mediacom, 4010 Alexandra Dr, Waterloo, IA 50702. Phone: 319-235-2197. Fax: 319-232-7841. Web Site: http://www.mediacomcable.com. ICA: WI0312.

TV Market Ranking: Below 100 (FORT MCCOY). Franchise award date: March 24, 1995. Franchise expiration date: August 30, 2009. Began: February 1, 1996.

Channel capacity: N.A. Channels available but not in use: N.A.

Basic Service

Subscribers: 1,441.

Programming (received off-air): WEAU-TV (NBC) Eau Claire; WHLA-TV (PBS) La Crosse; WKBT-DT (CBS, MNT) La Crosse; WLAX (FOX) La Crosse; WXOW (ABC, CW) La Crosse.

Programming (via satellite): A&E Networks; ABC Family Channel; BET Networks; CNN; Comedy Central; Country Music TV; C-SPAN; C-SPAN 2; Discovery Channel; Disney Channel; E! Entertainment Television; ESPN; ESPN 2; Hallmark Channel; Headline News; History Channel; MTV; Pentagon Channel; RFD-TV; Spike TV; TBS Superstation; The Learning Channel; The Weather Channel; truTV; Turner Network TV; TV Guide Network; USA Network; Versus; VH1; WGN America.

Digital Basic Service

Subscribers: N.A.

Programming (via satellite): AmericanLife TV Network; BBC America; Bio; Bloomberg Television; cloo; Discovery Digital Networks; ESPNews; Fox Movie Channel; Fox Soccer; Fuse; G4; GAS; Golf Channel; GSN; Halogen Network; History Channel International; Independent Film Channel; Lifetime Movie Network; Lime; MTV Networks Digital Suite; Music Choice; National Geographic Channel; Nick Jr.; NickToons TV; Outdoor Channel; Style Network; Turner Classic Movies; TVG Network.

Digital Pay Service 1

Pay Units: N.A.

Programming (via satellite): Cinemax (multiplexed); Encore (multiplexed); Flix (multiplexed); HBO (multiplexed); Showtime (multiplexed); Starz (multiplexed); Sundance Channel (multiplexed); The Movie Channel (multiplexed).

Video-On-Demand: No

Pay-Per-View

ESPN (delivered digitally); Fresh (delivered digitally); Shorteez (delivered digitally); Playboy TV (delivered digitally); Pleasure (delivered digitally); Ten Clips (delivered digitally).

Internet Service

Operational: Yes.

Broadband Service: Mediacom High Speed Internet.

Telephone Service

None

Miles of Plant: 11.0 (coaxial); 12.0 (fiber optic).

Regional Vice President: Doug Frank. General Manager: Doug Nix. Technical Operations Director: Greg Nank. Marketing Director: Steve Schuh. Marketing Coordinator: Joni Lindauer.

Ownership: Mediacom LLC (MSO).

FOUNTAIN CITY—Charter Communications, 1201 McCann Dr, Altoona, WI 54720-2561. Phone: 715-831-8940. Fax: 715-831-5862. Web Site: http://www.charter.com. ICA: WI0178.

TV Market Ranking: Below 100 (FOUNTAIN CITY). Franchise award date: January 1, 1963. Franchise expiration date: N.A. Began: January 1, 1963.

Channel capacity: N.A. Channels available but not in use: N.A.

Basic Service

Subscribers: 293.

Programming (received off-air): KMSP-TV (FOX) Minneapolis; KSTP-TV (ABC) St. Paul; KTCA-TV (PBS) St. Paul; KTTC (CW, NBC) Rochester; WCCO-TV (CBS) Minneapolis; WEAU-TV (NBC) Eau Claire; WFTC (MNT) Minneapolis; WHLA-TV (PBS) La Crosse; WKBT-DT (CBS, MNT) La Crosse; WLAX (FOX) La Crosse; WXOW (ABC, CW) La Crosse.

Programming (via satellite): C-SPAN; C-SPAN 2; QVC; TV Guide Network; WGN America.

Fee: $50.00 installation; $12.00 monthly.

Expanded Basic Service 1

Subscribers: 217.

Programming (via satellite): A&E Networks; ABC Family Channel; AMC; Animal Planet; BET Networks; Bravo; Cartoon Network; CNBC; CNN; Comedy Central; Country Music TV; Discovery Channel; Disney Channel; E! Entertainment Television; ESPN; ESPN 2; Eternal Word TV Network; Food Network; Fox News Channel; Fox Sports Net North; FX; G4; Golf Channel; GSN; Hallmark Channel; Headline News; HGTV; History Channel; INSP; Lifetime; MSNBC; MTV; National Geographic Channel; Nickelodeon; Outdoor Channel; Oxygen; ShopNBC; SoapNet; Speed; Spike TV; Syfy; TBS Superstation; The Learning Channel; The Weather Channel; Toon Disney; Travel Channel; truTV; Turner Classic Movies; Turner Network TV; TV Land; USA Network; Versus; VH1; WE tv.

Fee: $31.95 monthly.

Digital Basic Service

Subscribers: 217.

Programming (via satellite): AmericanLife TV Network; BBC America; Bio; Bloomberg Television; Discovery Fit & Health; DMX Music; ESPNews; Fox Movie Channel; Fox Soccer; Fuse; GAS; Halogen Network; History Channel International; Independent Film Channel; Lifetime Movie Network; MTV Networks Digital Suite; Nick Jr.; Style Network; Trinity Broadcasting Network.

Fee: $6.05 monthly.

Digital Pay Service 1

Pay Units: N.A.

Programming (via satellite): Cinemax; Flix.

Fee: $19.25 installation; $13.95 monthly.

Digital Pay Service 2

Pay Units: N.A.

Programming (via satellite): HBO (multiplexed).

Fee: $19.25 installation; $13.95 monthly.

Digital Pay Service 3

Pay Units: N.A.

Programming (via satellite): Showtime (multiplexed).

Fee: $19.25 installation; $13.95 monthly.

Digital Pay Service 4

Pay Units: N.A.

Programming (via satellite): The Movie Channel (multiplexed).

Fee: $19.25 installation; $13.95 monthly.

Digital Pay Service 5

Pay Units: N.A.

Programming (via satellite): Encore (multiplexed); Starz (multiplexed).

Fee: $19.25 installation; $13.95 monthly.

Video-On-Demand: No

Pay-Per-View

iN DEMAND (delivered digitally); Hot Choice (delivered digitally); Playboy TV (delivered digitally); Fresh (delivered digitally); Shorteez (delivered digitally).

Internet Service

Operational: Yes.

Fee: $19.99 monthly.

Telephone Service

None

Miles of Plant: 6.0 (coaxial); None (fiber optic).

Vice President & General Manager: Lisa Washa. Operations Manager: Shirley Weibel. Engineering Director: Tim Normand. Marketing Director: Traci Loonstra. Government Relations Manager: Mike Hill.

Ownership: Charter Communications Inc. (MSO).

FREMONT—Mediacom, 4010 Alexandra Dr, Waterloo, IA 50702. Phone: 319-235-2197. Fax: 319-232-7841. Web Site: http://www.mediacomcable.com. ICA: WI0172.

TV Market Ranking: Below 100 (FREMONT). Franchise award date: N.A. Franchise expiration date: N.A. Began: March 1, 1985.

Channel capacity: N.A. Channels available but not in use: N.A.

Basic Service

Subscribers: 27.

Programming (received off-air): WACY-TV (MNT) Appleton; WBAY-TV (ABC, IND) Green Bay; WFRV-TV (CBS) Green Bay; WGBA-TV (NBC) Green Bay; WLUK-TV (FOX) Green Bay; WPNE-TV (PBS) Green Bay; WSAW-TV (CBS, MNT) Wausau.

Programming (via satellite): A&E Networks; ABC Family Channel; Animal Planet; CNN; Comedy Central; Country Music TV; Discovery Channel; ESPN; ESPN 2; FX; History Channel; Lifetime; Nickelodeon; QVC; Spike TV; Syfy; TBS Superstation; The Weather Channel; Turner Network TV; USA Network; VH1; WGN America.

Fee: $45.00 installation; $33.95 monthly.

Pay Service 1

Pay Units: 24.

Programming (via satellite): HBO; Showtime.

Fee: $11.99 monthly (each).

Video-On-Demand: No

Internet Service

Operational: No.

Telephone Service

None

Miles of Plant: 8.0 (coaxial); None (fiber optic).

Regional Vice President: Doug Frank. General Manager: Doug Nix. Technical Operations Director: Greg Nank. Marketing Director: Steve Schuh. Marketing Coordinator: Joni Lindauer.

Ownership: Mediacom LLC (MSO).

GENOA CITY—Charter Communications, 2701 Daniels St, Madison, WI 53718. Phone: 608-274-3822. Fax: 608-274-1436. Web Site: http://www.charter.com. Also serves Richmond, IL; Pell Lake & Twin Lakes, WI. ICA: WI0039.

TV Market Ranking: Below 100 (GENOA CITY, Pell Lake, Richmond, Twin Lakes). Franchise award date: N.A. Franchise expiration date: N.A. Began: June 1, 1982.

Channel capacity: N.A. Channels available but not in use: N.A.

Basic Service

Subscribers: 4,000.

Programming (received off-air): WBBM-TV (CBS) Chicago; WBUW (CW) Janesville; WCGV-TV (MNT) Milwaukee; WDJT-TV (CBS) Milwaukee; WFLD (FOX) Chicago; WISN-TV (ABC) Milwaukee; WITI (FOX, IND) Milwaukee; WLS-TV (ABC) Chicago; WMAQ-TV (NBC) Chicago; WMLW-CA (IND) Milwaukee; WMVS (PBS) Milwaukee; WMVT (PBS) Milwaukee; WPXE-TV (ION) Kenosha; WTMJ-TV (NBC) Milwaukee; WTTW (PBS) Chicago; WVTV (CW) Milwaukee; allband FM.

Programming (via satellite): C-SPAN; MTV2; QVC; TV Guide Network; Univision Studios; WGN-TV (CW, IND) Chicago.

Fee: $28.59 installation; $9.80 monthly; $2.47 converter; $14.30 additional installation.

Expanded Basic Service 1

Subscribers: 3,384.

Programming (via satellite): A&E Networks; ABC Family Channel; AMC; Animal Planet; BET Networks; Bravo; Cartoon Network; CNBC; CNN; Comedy Central; Country Music TV; C-SPAN 2; Discovery Channel; Disney Channel; E! Entertainment Television; ESPN; ESPN 2; ESPN Classic Sports; Eternal Word TV Network; Food Network; Fox News Channel; Fox Sports Net North; FX; G4; Golf Channel; GSN; Hallmark Channel; Headline News; HGTV; History Channel; INSP; Lifetime; MSNBC; MTV; National Geographic Channel; Nickelodeon; Oxygen; SoapNet; Speed; Spike TV; Syfy; TBS Superstation; The Learning Channel; The Weather Channel; Toon Disney; Travel Channel; truTV; Turner Classic Movies; Turner Network TV; TV Land; USA Network; Versus; VH1; WE tv.

Fee: $45.99 monthly.

Digital Basic Service

Subscribers: N.A.

Programming (via satellite): BBC America; Bio; Canales N; CNN International; Discovery Digital Networks; DIY Network; ESPN; ESPNews; Fox Movie Channel; Fox Soccer; FSN Digital Atlantic; FSN Digital Central; FSN Digital Pacific; Fuel TV; Fuse; GAS; HDNet; HDNet Movies; History Channel International; Independent Film Channel; Lifetime Movie Network; MTV Networks Digital Suite; Music Choice; NFL Network; Nick Jr.; Nick Too; NickToons TV; Sundance Channel; TV Guide Interactive Inc.

Digital Pay Service 1

Pay Units: 215.

Programming (via satellite): Cinemax (multiplexed); Encore (multiplexed); Flix; HBO (multiplexed); HBO HD; Showtime (multiplexed); Showtime HD; Starz (multiplexed); The Movie Channel (multiplexed).

Video-On-Demand: No

Pay-Per-View

iN DEMAND (delivered digitally); NASCAR In Car (delivered digitally); NHL Center Ice (delivered digitally); MLB Extra Innings (delivered digitally); Playboy TV (delivered digitally); Spice Live (delivered digitally); Spice Platinum (delivered digitally); Hot Net Plus (delivered digitally); Spice Hot (delivered digitally).

Internet Service

Operational: Yes. Began: January 1, 2002.

Broadband Service: Charter Pipeline.

Fee: $39.99 monthly.

Telephone Service

None

Miles of Plant: 134.0 (coaxial); None (fiber optic).

Vice President & General Manager: Lisa Washa. Engineering Director: Tim Sanderson. Technical Operations Director: Bruce Hummel. Marketing Director: Traci Loonstra. Government Relations Director: Tim Vowell.

Ownership: Charter Communications Inc. (MSO).

GILLETT—Packerland Broadband, 105 Kent St, PO Box 885, Iron Mountain, MI 49801. Phones: 800-236-8434; 906-774-6621. Fax:

906-776-2811. E-mail: inquires@plbb.us. Web Site: http://www.packerlandbroadband.com. Also serves Green Valley & Underhill. ICA: WI0181.

TV Market Ranking: 62 (GILLETT, Green Valley, Underhill). Franchise award date: April 1, 1981. Franchise expiration date: N.A. Began: December 31, 1982.

Channel capacity: N.A. Channels available but not in use: N.A.

Basic Service

Subscribers: 252.

Programming (received off-air): WACY-TV (MNT) Appleton; WBAY-TV (ABC, IND) Green Bay; WCWF (CW) Suring; WFRV-TV (CBS) Green Bay; WGBA-TV (NBC) Green Bay; WLUK-TV (FOX) Green Bay; WPNE-TV (PBS) Green Bay.

Programming (via satellite): C-SPAN; C-SPAN 2; QVC; WGN America.

Fee: $43.98 installation; $10.27 monthly.

Expanded Basic Service 1

Subscribers: 197.

Programming (via satellite): A&E Networks; ABC Family Channel; Animal Planet; Bravo; CNN; Country Music TV; Discovery Channel; Disney Channel; E! Entertainment Television; ESPN; Fox News Channel; Headline News; HGTV; History Channel; Lifetime; MSNBC; Nickelodeon; Speed; Spike TV; Syfy; TBS Superstation; The Learning Channel; The Weather Channel; Turner Network TV; TV Land; USA Network; VH1.

Fee: $24.50 monthly.

Pay Service 1

Pay Units: 71.

Programming (via satellite): Cinemax.

Fee: $14.72 monthly.

Pay Service 2

Pay Units: 76.

Programming (via satellite): HBO.

Fee: $14.72 monthly.

Video-On-Demand: No

Internet Service

Operational: Yes.

Broadband Service: In-house.

Fee: $39.95 installation; $34.95 monthly.

Telephone Service

None

Miles of Plant: 18.0 (coaxial); None (fiber optic).

General Manager: Dan Plante. Technical Supervisor: Chad Kay.

Ownership: Cable Constructors Inc. (MSO).

GILMAN—S & K TV Systems, 508 Miner Ave W, Ladysmith, WI 54848. Phones: 800-924-7880; 715-532-7321. Fax: 715-530-9583. E-mail: techsupport@skcable.com. Web Site: http://www.skcable.com. ICA: WI0333.

TV Market Ranking: Below 100 (GILMAN).

Channel capacity: 35 (not 2-way capable). Channels available but not in use: N.A.

Basic Service

Subscribers: 73.

Programming (received off-air): WAOW (ABC, CW) Wausau; WEAU-TV (NBC) Eau Claire; WEUX (FOX) Chippewa Falls; WHWC-TV (PBS) Menomonie; WSAW-TV (CBS, MNT) Wausau.

Programming (via satellite): A&E Networks; ABC Family Channel; AMC; Cartoon Network; CNN; C-SPAN; Discovery Channel; ESPN; ESPN 2; HGTV; History Channel; Lifetime; MSNBC; Nickelodeon; QVC; Spike TV; Syfy; TBS Superstation; The Weather Channel; Turner Classic Movies; Turner Network TV; TV Land; USA Network; VH1; WGN America.

Pay Service 1

Pay Units: N.A.

Programming (via satellite): HBO.

Internet Service

Operational: No.

Telephone Service

None

Manager: Randy Scott. Office Manager: Dave Scott.

Ownership: S & K TV Systems Inc. (MSO).

GLENWOOD CITY—Nextgen Communications, 234 E Oak St, PO Box 398, Glenwood City, WI 54013. Phones: 888-696-9146; 715-565-7742. Fax: 715-565-3001. E-mail: nextgen@nextgen-communications.net. Web Site: http://www.nextgen-communications.net. Also serves Boyceville & Downing. ICA: WI0251.

TV Market Ranking: Below 100 (Boyceville, Downing); Outside TV Markets (GLENWOOD CITY). Franchise award date: January 1, 1968. Franchise expiration date: N.A. Began: January 1, 1968.

Channel capacity: 78 (operating 2-way). Channels available but not in use: N.A.

Basic Service

Subscribers: 3,801.

Programming (received off-air): KARE (NBC) Minneapolis; KMSP-TV (FOX) Minneapolis; KSTC-TV (IND) Minneapolis; KSTP-TV (ABC) St. Paul; KTCA-TV (PBS) St. Paul; KUCW (CW) Ogden; WCCO-TV (CBS) Minneapolis; WEAU-TV (NBC) Eau Claire; WEUX (FOX) Chippewa Falls; WFTC (MNT) Minneapolis; WHWC-TV (PBS) Menomonie; WKBT-DT (CBS, MNT) La Crosse; WQOW (ABC, CW) Eau Claire.

Programming (via satellite): A&E Networks; ABC Family Channel; AMC; Animal Planet; Bravo; Cartoon Network; CNN; Comedy Central; Country Music TV; C-SPAN; C-SPAN 2; Discovery Channel; Disney Channel; E! Entertainment Television; ESPN; ESPN 2; ESPN Classic Sports; Food Network; Fox News Channel; Fox Sports Net; FX; Great American Country; GSN; Hallmark Channel; Headline News; HGTV; History Channel; ION Television; Lifetime; MSNBC; MTV; National Geographic Channel; Nickelodeon; Outdoor Channel; QVC; RFD-TV; SoapNet; Speed; Spike TV; Syfy; TBS Superstation; The Learning Channel; The Weather Channel; Travel Channel; Trinity Broadcasting Network; truTV; Turner Network TV; TV Land; USA Network; VH1; WGN America.

Fee: $29.95 monthly; $1.50 converter.

Digital Basic Service

Subscribers: 3,035.

Programming (via satellite): AmericanLife TV Network; BBC America; Bio; Bloomberg Television; Bravo; cloo; CMT Pure Country; Discovery Digital Networks; DMX Music; ESPN Classic Sports; ESPNews; Fox Movie Channel; Fuse; G4; GAS; Golf Channel; GSN; Halogen Network; History Channel International; Independent Film Channel; Lifetime Movie Network; MTV Networks Digital Suite; National Geographic Channel; Nick Jr.; Speed; Style Network; Trinity Broadcasting Network; Turner Classic Movies; Versus; WE tv.

Digital Pay Service 1

Pay Units: 324.

Programming (via satellite): Cinemax (multiplexed); Encore (multiplexed); Flix; HBO (multiplexed); Showtime (multiplexed); Starz (multiplexed); The Movie Channel.

Video-On-Demand: No

Pay-Per-View

Addressable homes: 1,298.

iN DEMAND (delivered digitally).

Internet Service

Operational: Yes.

Telephone Service

None

Miles of Plant: 78.0 (coaxial); 44.0 (fiber optic).

Ownership: Nextgen Communications (MSO).

GLIDDEN—Packerland Broadband, 105 Kent St, PO Box 885, Iron Mountain, MI 49801. Phones: 800-236-8434; 906-774-6621. Fax: 906-776-2811. Web Site: http://www.packerlandbroadband.com. ICA: WI0191.

TV Market Ranking: Outside TV Markets (GLIDDEN). Franchise award date: April 1, 1980. Franchise expiration date: N.A. Began: April 1, 1985.

Channel capacity: 30 (not 2-way capable). Channels available but not in use: N.A.

Basic Service

Subscribers: 96.

Programming (received off-air): KBJR-TV (MNT, NBC) Superior; KDLH (CBS, CW) Duluth; WDIO-DT (ABC) Duluth; WJFW-TV (NBC) Rhinelander; WLEF-TV (PBS) Park Falls; WSAW-TV (CBS, MNT) Wausau; WYOW (ABC, CW) Eagle River.

Programming (via satellite): A&E Networks; ABC Family Channel; Bloomberg Television; CNN; Discovery Channel; Disney Channel; ESPN; History Channel; MTV; Nickelodeon; Spike TV; Syfy; TBS Superstation; The Weather Channel; Turner Network TV; USA Network; VH1; WGN America.

Fee: $35.00 installation; $19.14 monthly.

Pay Service 1

Pay Units: 45.

Programming (via satellite): The Movie Channel.

Fee: $10.00 installation; $12.00 monthly.

Video-On-Demand: No

Internet Service

Operational: No.

Telephone Service

None

Miles of Plant: 6.0 (coaxial); None (fiber optic).

General Manager: Dan Plante. Technical Supervisor: Chad Kay.

Ownership: Cable Constructors Inc. (MSO).

GOODMAN—Packerland Broadband, 105 Kent St, PO Box 885, Iron Mountain, MI 49801. Phones: 800-236-8434; 906-774-6621. Fax: 906-776-2811. Web Site: http://www.packerlandbroadband.com. ICA: WI0206.

TV Market Ranking: Below 100 (GOODMAN). Franchise award date: N.A. Franchise expiration date: N.A. Began: September 1, 1988.

Channel capacity: 54 (not 2-way capable). Channels available but not in use: N.A.

Basic Service

Subscribers: 61.

Programming (received off-air): WAOW (ABC, CW) Wausau; WBAY-TV (ABC, IND) Green Bay; WFRV-TV (CBS) Green Bay; WGBA-TV (NBC) Green Bay; WJFW-TV (NBC) Rhinelander; WLUC-TV (NBC) Marquette; WLUK-TV (FOX) Green Bay; WPNE-TV (PBS) Green Bay.

Programming (via satellite): A&E Networks; ABC Family Channel; CNBC; CNN; Country Music TV; C-SPAN; Discovery Channel; ESPN; ESPN 2; Eternal Word TV Network; Fox News Channel; Fox Sports Net; History Channel; Lifetime; MTV; Nickelodeon; QVC; Spike TV; Syfy; TBS Superstation; The Weather Channel; Turner Classic Movies; Turner Network TV; TV Land; USA Network; VH1; WGN America.

Fee: $25.00 installation; $31.60 monthly.

Pay Service 1

Pay Units: N.A.

Programming (via satellite): Cinemax; HBO.

Fee: $11.55 monthly (each).

Video-On-Demand: No

Internet Service

Operational: Yes.

Fee: $26.95 monthly.

Telephone Service

None

Miles of Plant: 6.0 (coaxial); None (fiber optic).

General Manager: Dan Plante. Technical Supervisor: Chad Kay.

Ownership: Cable Constructors Inc. (MSO).

GRANTON—New Century Communications, 3588 Kennebec Dr, Eagan, MN 55122-1001. Phone: 651-688-2623. Fax: 651-688-2624. E-mail: info@ourcableia.com. ICA: WI0211.

TV Market Ranking: Outside TV Markets (GRANTON). Franchise award date: N.A. Franchise expiration date: N.A. Began: N.A.

Channel capacity: 40 (not 2-way capable). Channels available but not in use: N.A.

Basic Service

Subscribers: 21.

Programming (received off-air): WAOW (ABC, CW) Wausau; WEAU-TV (NBC) Eau Claire; WHRM-TV (PBS) Wausau; WLAX (FOX) La Crosse; WSAW-TV (CBS, MNT) Wausau.

Programming (via satellite): A&E Networks; ABC Family Channel; AMC; CNN; Discovery Channel; Disney Channel; ESPN; ESPN 2; History Channel; Lifetime; Nickelodeon; Showtime; Spike TV; TBS Superstation; The Learning Channel; Trinity Broadcasting Network; Turner Network TV; USA Network; WGN America.

Fee: $30.00 installation; $34.25 monthly.

Video-On-Demand: No

Internet Service

Operational: No.

Telephone Service

None

Miles of Plant: 4.0 (coaxial); None (fiber optic).

Executive Vice President: Marty Walch. Manager & Chief Technician: Todd Anderson.

Ownership: New Century Communications (MSO).

GRANTSBURG—Grantsburg Telcom, 139 W Madison Ave, PO Box 447, Grantsburg, WI 54840-0447. Phone: 715-463-5322. Fax: 715-463-5206. E-mail: office@grantsburgtelcom.com. Web Site: http://www.grantsburgtelcom.com. ICA: WI0252.

TV Market Ranking: Outside TV Markets (GRANTSBURG). Franchise award date: July 15, 1985. Franchise expiration date: N.A. Began: January 1, 1987.

Channel capacity: N.A. Channels available but not in use: N.A.

Basic Service

Subscribers: N.A.

Programming (received off-air): KARE (NBC) Minneapolis; KMSP-TV (FOX) Minneapolis; KPXM-TV (ION) St. Cloud; KSTC-TV (IND) Minneapolis; KSTP-TV (ABC) St. Paul; KTCA-TV (PBS) St. Paul; WCCO-TV (CBS) Minneapolis; WEAU-TV (NBC) Eau Claire; WEUX (FOX) Chippewa Falls; WFTC (MNT) Minneapolis; WHWC-TV (PBS) Menomonie; WQOW (ABC, CW) Eau Claire; WUCW (CW) Minneapolis.

Programming (via satellite): A&E Networks; ABC Family Channel; AMC; Animal Planet; Cartoon Network; CNBC; CNN; Comedy Central; Country Music TV; C-SPAN; C-SPAN 2; Discovery Channel; Disney Channel; DIY Network; E! Entertainment Television; ESPN; ESPN 2; ESPN Classic Sports; Eternal Word TV Network; Food Network; Fox News Channel; Fox Sports Net Minnesota; FX; Golf Channel; Hallmark Channel; Headline News; HGTV; History Channel; Lifetime; Lifetime Movie Network; Local Cable Weather; MTV; National Geographic Channel; Nickelodeon; Outdoor Channel; Oxygen; QVC; Speed; Spike TV; Syfy; TBS Superstation; The Learning Channel; The Weather Channel; Travel Channel; truTV; Turner Classic Movies; Turner Network TV; TV Guide Network; TV Land; USA Network; Versus; VH1; WGN America.

Fee: $24.95 installation; $38.95 monthly; $24.95 additional installation.

Digital Basic Service

Subscribers: N.A.

Programming (via satellite): AmericanLife TV Network; BBC America; Bio; cloo; CMT Pure Country; Discovery Fit & Health; Discovery Health Channel; Discovery Home Channel; Discovery Kids Channel; Discovery Times Channel; DMX Music; ESPN HD; ESPNews; Fox Movie Channel; GAS; Halogen Network; HDNet; HDNet Movies; History Channel International; Military Channel; MTV Hits; MTV2; Nick Jr.; NickToons TV; RFD-TV; Science; Toon Disney; Trinity Broadcasting Network; Universal HD; VH1 Classic; VH1 Soul; WE tv.

Fee: $49.95 installation; $21.00 monthly.

Pay Service 1

Pay Units: 14.

Programming (via satellite): Cinemax; HBO; Showtime.

Fee: $9.00 monthly (each).

Digital Pay Service 1

Pay Units: N.A.

Programming (via satellite): Cinemax (multiplexed); Encore (multiplexed); Flix; HBO (multiplexed); Showtime (multiplexed); Starz (multiplexed); The Movie Channel (multiplexed).

Fee: $11.95 monthly (each).

Video-On-Demand: No

Internet Service

Operational: Yes, Both DSL & dial-up.

Broadband Service: In-house.

Fee: $29.95 monthly.

Telephone Service

None

General Manager: Dana Olson.

Ownership: Farmers Independent Telephone Co.

GREEN BAY—Formerly served by Sprint Corp. No longer in operation. ICA: WI0305.

GREEN BAY—Time Warner Cable, 1001 W Kennedy Ave, PO Box 145, Kimberly, WI 54136-0145. Phones: 414-277-4032 (Milwaukee); 920-749-1400. Fax: 920-831-9372. Web Site: http://www.timewarnercable.com/wisconsin. Also serves Allouez, Appleton, Ashwaubenon, Bellevue, Buchanan (town), Center, Chase, Clayton (Winnebago County), Combined Locks, Dale, De Pere, Ellington, Freedom, Grand Chute (town), Greenville (town), Harrison (town), Hilbert (village), Hobart, Holland (town), Howard (village), Kaukauna, Kimberly, Lawrence (town), Ledgeview (town), Little Chute, Little Suamico, Medina, Menasha (town), Neenah (town), Oneida, Oshkosh, Pittsfield, Poy Sippi, Reedsville, Sherwood (village), St. Nazianz, Stockbridge, Suamico, Valders, Vandenbroek, Vinland (town), Winchester (town), Woodville (town) & Wrightstown. ICA: WI0006.

TV Market Ranking: 62 (Allouez, Appleton, Ashwaubenon, Bellevue, Buchanan (town), Center, Chase, Clayton (Winnebago County), Combined Locks, De Pere, Ellington, Freedom, Grand Chute (town), GREEN BAY, Greenville (town), Harrison (town), Hilbert (village), Hobart, Holland (town), Howard (village), Kaukauna, Kimberly, Lawrence (town), Ledgeview (town), Little Chute, Little Suamico, Medina, Menasha (town), Neenah (town), Oneida, Pittsfield, Reedsville, Sherwood (village), St. Nazianz, Stockbridge, Suamico, Valders, Vandenbroek, Woodville (town), Wrightstown); Below 100 (Dale, Oshkosh, Poy Sippi, Vinland (town), Winchester (town)). Franchise award date: January 1, 1980. Franchise expiration date: December 31, 2018. Began: July 1, 1973.

Channel capacity: 80 (operating 2-way). Channels available but not in use: N.A.

Basic Service

Subscribers: 153,000 Includes Marinette.

Programming (received off-air): WACY-TV (MNT) Appleton; WBAY-TV (ABC, IND) Green Bay; WCWF (CW) Suring; WFRV-TV (CBS) Green Bay; WGBA-TV (NBC) Green Bay; WLUK-TV (FOX) Green Bay; WPNE-TV (PBS) Green Bay; WVTV (CW) Milwaukee.

Programming (via satellite): C-SPAN; Eternal Word TV Network; WGN America.

Fee: $17.51 monthly.

Expanded Basic Service 1

Subscribers: 139,000 Includes Marinette.

Programming (via satellite): A&E Networks; ABC Family Channel; AMC; Animal Planet; Bravo; Cartoon Network; CNBC; CNN; Comedy Central; Country Music TV; C-SPAN 2; Discovery Channel; Discovery Health Channel; Disney Channel; E! Entertainment Television; ESPN; ESPN 2; ESPN Classic Sports; Food Network; Fox News Channel; Fox Sports Net; FX; Golf Channel; Hallmark Channel; Headline News; HGTV; History Channel; Lifetime; Lifetime Movie Network; MSNBC; MTV; National Geographic Channel; Nickelodeon; Oxygen; QVC; ShopNBC; Sneak Prevue; Spike TV; Syfy; TBS Superstation; The Learning Channel; The Weather Channel; Travel Channel; truTV; Turner Classic Movies; Turner Network TV; TV Guide Network; TV Land; Univision Studios; USA Network; Versus; VH1; WE tv.

Fee: $41.41 monthly.

Digital Basic Service

Subscribers: 79,000 Includes Marinette.

Programming (via satellite): America's Store; BBC America; Bio; Bloomberg Television; Cooking Channel; C-SPAN 3; Discovery Fit & Health; Discovery Home Channel; Discovery Kids Channel; Discovery Times Channel; DIY Network; ESPNews; Fox Sports World; FSN Digital Atlantic; FSN Digital Central; FSN Digital Pacific; Fuse; G4; GAS; Great American Country; GSN; History Channel International; Independent Film Channel; Lifetime Real Women; Military Channel; MTV2; NBA TV; Nick Jr.; Nick Too; Outdoor Channel; Ovation; Science; Speed; Style Network; Tennis Channel; Toon Disney; VH1 Classic; Weatherscan.

Fee: $53.49 monthly.

Digital Pay Service 1

Pay Units: N.A.

Programming (via satellite): Cinemax (multiplexed); Encore (multiplexed); HBO (multiplexed); Showtime (multiplexed); Starz (multiplexed); The Movie Channel (multiplexed).

Video-On-Demand: Yes

Pay-Per-View

iN DEMAND (delivered digitally); Playboy TV (delivered digitally); Movies (delivered digitally); Club Jenna (delivered digitally); ESPN (delivered digitally).

Internet Service

Operational: Yes. Began: August 1, 2000.

Subscribers: 82,000.

Broadband Service: Road Runner.

Fee: $44.95 installation; $39.99 monthly; $7.00 modem lease.

Telephone Service

Digital: Operational

Subscribers: 32,000.

Miles of Plant: 3,600.0 (coaxial); None (fiber optic). Miles of plant (coax & fiber combined) include Marinette

President: Jack Herbert. Vice President, Engineering: Randy Cicatello. Vice President, Marketing: Brenda Kinne. Vice President, Government & Public Affairs: Bev Greenburg. General Manager: Mike Fox. Public Affairs Manager: Bill Harken.

Ownership: Time Warner Cable (MSO).

GREENFIELD (Milwaukee County)—Time Warner Cable. Now served by MILWAUKEE, WI [WI0001]. ICA: WI0003.

GREENLEAF—Formerly served by CenturyTel. No longer in operation. ICA: WI0253.

GREENWOOD—Packerland Broadband, 105 Kent St, PO Box 885, Iron Mountain, MI 49801. Phones: 800-236-8434; 906-774-6621. Fax: 906-776-2811. Web Site: http://www.packerlandbroadband.com. ICA: WI0159.

TV Market Ranking: Outside TV Markets (GREENWOOD). Franchise award date: N.A. Franchise expiration date: N.A. Began: May 1, 1984.

Channel capacity: N.A. Channels available but not in use: N.A.

Basic Service

Subscribers: 178.

Programming (received off-air): WAOW (ABC, CW) Wausau; WEAU-TV (NBC) Eau Claire; WEUX (FOX) Chippewa Falls; WHRM-TV (PBS) Wausau; WKBT-DT (CBS, MNT) La Crosse; WSAW-TV (CBS, MNT) Wausau.

Programming (via satellite): A&E Networks; ABC Family Channel; Animal Planet; CNN; Comedy Central; Country Music TV; Discovery Channel; Discovery Health Channel; ESPN; ESPN 2; Fox News Channel; FX; Great American Country; Hallmark Channel; Headline News; History Channel; Lifetime; MTV; Nickelodeon; QVC; Speed; Spike TV; TBS Superstation; The Learning Channel; The Weather Channel; Travel Channel; Trinity Broadcasting Network; Turner Network TV; TV Land; USA Network; VH1; WGN America.

Fee: $25.00 installation; $33.95 monthly.

Pay Service 1

Pay Units: N.A.

Programming (via satellite): Flix; Showtime.

Fee: $9.95 monthly.

Video-On-Demand: No

Internet Service

Operational: No.

Telephone Service

None

Miles of Plant: 13.0 (coaxial); None (fiber optic).

General Manager: Dan Plante. Technical Supervisor: Chad Kay.

Ownership: Cable Constructors Inc. (MSO).

HAMMOND (village)—Baldwin Telecom Inc. Formerly served by Baldwin (village), WI [WI0079]. This cable system has converted to IPTV, 930 Maple St, Baldwin, WI 54002. Phones: 877-684-3346; 715-684-3346. Fax: 715-684-4747. E-mail: info@baldwin-telecom.net. Web Site: http://www.baldwin-telecom.net. ICA: WI5234.

Channel capacity: N.A. Channels available but not in use: N.A.

Basic Service

Subscribers: N.A.

Fee: $61.00 monthly.

Expanded Basic Service 1

Subscribers: N.A.

Fee: $6.95 monthly.

Pay Service 1

Pay Units: N.A.

Fee: $11.95 monthly (Cinemax, HBO, Showtime/TMC, or Starz/Encore).

Internet Service

Operational: Yes.

Fee: $39.90 monthly.

General Manager: Larry Knegendorf. Cable TV Manager: Matt Knegendorf. Plant Manager: Duane Russett. Operations Manager: Matt Sparks.

HAWKINS (village)—Packerland Broadband, 105 Kent St, PO Box 885, Iron Mountain, MI 49801. Phones: 800-236-8434; 906-774-6621. Fax: 906-776-2811. Web Site: http://www.packerlandbroadband.com. ICA: WI0254.

TV Market Ranking: Below 100 (HAWKINS (VILLAGE)). Franchise award date: N.A. Franchise expiration date: N.A. Began: N.A.

Channel capacity: 30 (not 2-way capable). Channels available but not in use: N.A.

Basic Service

Subscribers: 265.

Programming (received off-air): WAOW (ABC, CW) Wausau; WEAU-TV (NBC) Eau Claire; WEUX (FOX) Chippewa Falls; WLEF-TV (PBS) Park Falls; WSAW-TV (CBS, MNT) Wausau.

Programming (via satellite): A&E Networks; ABC Family Channel; Bloomberg Television; CNN; Comedy Central; Discovery Channel; Disney Channel; ESPN; ESPN 2; History Channel; MTV; Nickelodeon; Spike TV; Syfy; TBS Superstation; The Weather Channel; Turner Network TV; USA Network; VH1; WGN America.

Fee: $32.95 monthly.

Pay Service 1

Pay Units: N.A.

Programming (via satellite): Flix; Showtime.

Fee: $9.95 monthly.

Video-On-Demand: No

Internet Service

Operational: No.

Telephone Service
None
Miles of Plant: 4.0 (coaxial); None (fiber optic).
General Manager: Dan Plante. Technical Supervisor: Chad Kay.
Ownership: Cable Constructors Inc. (MSO).

HAYWARD—Charter Communications, 1201 McCann Dr, Altoona, WI 54720-2561. Phone: 715-831-8940. Fax: 715-831-5862. Web Site: http://www.charter.com. Also serves Bass Lake (town), Hayward (town), Sand Lake & Stone Lake. ICA: WI0085.
TV Market Ranking: Outside TV Markets (Bass Lake (town), HAYWARD, Hayward (town), Sand Lake, Stone Lake). Franchise award date: N.A. Franchise expiration date: N.A. Began: September 1, 1971.
Channel capacity: N.A. Channels available but not in use: N.A.
Basic Service
Subscribers: 1,245.
Programming (received off-air): KBJR-TV (MNT, NBC) Superior; KDLH (CBS, CW) Duluth; KMSP-TV (FOX) Minneapolis; KQDS-TV (FOX) Duluth; WDIO-DT (ABC) Duluth; WDSE (PBS) Duluth; WEAU-TV (NBC) Eau Claire; WEUX (FOX) Chippewa Falls; WLEF-TV (PBS) Park Falls; WQOW (ABC, CW) Eau Claire.
Programming (via satellite): Disney Channel; QVC; TV Guide Network; WGN America.
Fee: $50.00 installation; $12.00 monthly.
Expanded Basic Service 1
Subscribers: N.A.
Programming (via satellite): A&E Networks; ABC Family Channel; AMC; Animal Planet; Cartoon Network; CNBC; CNN; Comedy Central; Country Music TV; C-SPAN; Discovery Channel; E! Entertainment Television; ESPN; ESPN 2; ESPN Classic Sports; Eternal Word TV Network; Food Network; Fox News Channel; Fox Sports Net North; FX; G4; Golf Channel; GSN; Hallmark Channel; Headline News; HGTV; History Channel; Lifetime; MSNBC; MTV; Nickelodeon; Outdoor Channel; Oxygen; SoapNet; Speed; Spike TV; Syfy; TBS Superstation; The Learning Channel; The Weather Channel; Toon Disney; Travel Channel; Trinity Broadcasting Network; truTV; Turner Classic Movies; Turner Network TV; TV Land; USA Network; Versus; VH1.
Fee: $31.95 monthly.
Digital Basic Service
Subscribers: N.A.
Programming (via satellite): BBC America; Bio; Bloomberg Television; Boomerang; CNN en Espanol; CNN International; C-SPAN 3; Discovery Digital Networks; DIY Network; Encore; ESPN; ESPNews; Fox College Sports Atlantic; Fox College Sports Central; Fox College Sports Pacific; Fox Movie Channel; Fox Soccer; Fuel TV; Fuse; GAS; HDNet; HDNet Movies; History Channel International; Independent Film Channel; Lifetime Movie Network; MTV Networks Digital Suite; Music Choice; Nick Jr.; Nick Too; NickToons TV; Style Network; Sundance Channel; TV Guide Network.
Digital Pay Service 1
Pay Units: N.A.
Programming (via satellite): Cinemax (multiplexed); Encore (multiplexed); Flix; HBO (multiplexed); HBO HD; Showtime (multiplexed); Showtime HD; Starz (multiplexed); The Movie Channel (multiplexed).
Video-On-Demand: Yes
Pay-Per-View
iN DEMAND (delivered digitally); NASCAR In Car (delivered digitally); NHL Center Ice (delivered digitally); MLB Extra Innings (delivered digitally); Playboy TV (delivered digitally); Fresh (delivered digitally); Shorteez (delivered digitally).
Internet Service
Operational: Yes.
Broadband Service: Charter Pipeline.
Fee: $29.99 monthly.
Telephone Service
None
Miles of Plant: 53.0 (coaxial); None (fiber optic).
Vice President & General Manager: Lisa Washa. Operations Manager: Shirley Weibel. Engineering Director: Tim Normond. Marketing Director: Traci Loonstra. Sales & Marketing Manager: Chris Putzkey. Government Relations Manager: Mike Hill.
Ownership: Charter Communications Inc. (MSO).

HILLSBORO—Community Antenna System Inc., 1010 Lake St, Hillsboro, WI 54634-9019. Phone: 608-489-2321. ICA: WI0135.
TV Market Ranking: Outside TV Markets (HILLSBORO). Franchise award date: N.A. Franchise expiration date: N.A. Began: January 1, 1959.
Channel capacity: 66 (operating 2-way). Channels available but not in use: N.A.
Basic Service
Subscribers: 730.
Programming (received off-air): WEAU-TV (NBC) Eau Claire; WHA-TV (PBS) Madison; WISC-TV (CBS, MNT) Madison; WKBT-DT (CBS, MNT) La Crosse; WKOW (ABC) Madison; WMSN-TV (FOX) Madison; WMTV-TV (NBC) Madison.
Programming (via satellite): ABC Family Channel; ESPN; Spike TV; TBS Superstation; Turner Network TV; WGN America.
Fee: $25.00 installation; $30.87 monthly; $10.00 additional installation.
Pay Service 1
Pay Units: 98.
Programming (via satellite): Cinemax.
Fee: $6.95 monthly.
Internet Service
Operational: Yes.
Subscribers: 100.
Broadband Service: In-house.
Fee: $30.00 installation; $27.99 monthly.
Telephone Service
None
Miles of Plant: 5.0 (coaxial); None (fiber optic).
Manager: Randall Kubarski. Chief Technician: Gregory Kubarski.
Ownership: Community Antenna System Inc. (MSO).

HOLLANDALE—Packerland Broadband, 105 Kent St, PO Box 885, Iron Mountain, MI 49801. Phones: 800-236-8434; 906-774-6621. Fax: 906-776-2811. Web Site: http://www.packerlandbroadband.com. ICA: WI0278.
TV Market Ranking: 93 (HOLLANDALE). Franchise award date: N.A. Franchise expiration date: N.A. Began: June 1, 1989.
Channel capacity: N.A. Channels available but not in use: N.A.
Basic Service
Subscribers: 29.
Programming (received off-air): WBUW (CW) Janesville; WHA-TV (PBS) Madison; WISC-TV (CBS, MNT) Madison; WKOW (ABC) Madison; WMSN-TV (FOX) Madison; WMTV-TV (NBC) Madison.
Programming (via satellite): A&E Networks; QVC; TBS Superstation; WGN America.
Fee: $38.95 monthly.

Expanded Basic Service 1
Subscribers: 27.
Programming (via satellite): ABC Family Channel; CNN; Discovery Channel; Disney Channel; ESPN; ESPN 2; Fox Sports Net North; Headline News; Nickelodeon; Spike TV; The Learning Channel; The Weather Channel; Turner Classic Movies; Turner Network TV; TV Land; USA Network.
Fee: $21.10 monthly.
Pay Service 1
Pay Units: N.A.
Programming (via satellite): HBO.
Fee: $13.95 monthly.
Video-On-Demand: No
Internet Service
Operational: No.
Telephone Service
None
Miles of Plant: 2.0 (coaxial); None (fiber optic).
General Manager: Dan Plante. Technical Supervisor: Chad Kay.
Ownership: Cable Constructors Inc. (MSO).

HOWARDS GROVE—Time Warner Cable. Now served by RANDOM LAKE, WI [WI0059]. ICA: WI0097.

HUDSON (town)—Baldwin Telecom Inc. Formerly served by Baldwin (village), WI [WI0079]. This cable system has converted to IPTV, 930 Maple St, Baldwin, WI 54002. Phones: 877-684-3346; 715-684-3346. Fax: 715-684-4747. E-mail: info@baldwin-telecom.net. Web Site: http://www.baldwin-telecom.net. ICA: WI5044.
Channel capacity: N.A. Channels available but not in use: N.A.
Basic Service
Subscribers: N.A.
Fee: $61.00 monthly.
Expanded Basic Service 1
Subscribers: N.A.
Fee: $6.95 monthly.
Pay Service 1
Pay Units: N.A.
Fee: $11.95 monthly (Cinemax, HBO, Showtime/TMC, or Starz/Encore).
Internet Service
Operational: Yes.
Fee: $39.95 monthly.
General Manager: Larry Knegendorf. Cable TV Manager: Matt Knegendorf. Plant Manager: Duane Russett. Operations Manager: Matt Sparks.

HUDSON (town)—Baldwin Telecom Inc. Formerly served by Baldwin (village), WI [WI0126]. This cable system has converted to IPTV. See Hudson Twp., WI [WI5044]. ICA: WI0126.

HUSTISFORD—Charter Communications, 165 Knights Way, Ste 100, Fond Du Lac, WI 54935-8061. Phones: 888-843-2574; 920-907-7720. Fax: 920-907-7723. E-mail: rschelvan@chartercom.com. Web Site: http://www.charter.com. Also serves Beaver Dam, Burnett (town), Calamus, Chester, Clyman, Fox Lake, Horicon, Hubbard, Iron Ridge, Juneau, Lowell, Mayville, Neosho, Reeseville, Theresa, Waupun & Williamstown. ICA: WI0005.
TV Market Ranking: 93 (Calamus, Lowell, Reeseville); Below 100 (Beaver Dam, Burnett (town), Chester, Clyman, Fox Lake, Horicon, Hubbard, Iron Ridge, Juneau, Mayville, Neosho, Theresa, Waupun, Williamstown); Outside TV Markets (HUSTISFORD). Franchise award date: January 1, 1972. Franchise expiration date: N.A. Began: February 1, 1974.
Channel capacity: 80 (operating 2-way). Channels available but not in use: N.A.
Basic Service
Subscribers: 14,700.
Programming (received off-air): WCGV-TV (MNT) Milwaukee; WDJT-TV (CBS) Milwaukee; WHA-TV (PBS) Madison; WISC-TV (CBS, MNT) Madison; WISN-TV (ABC) Milwaukee; WITI (FOX, IND) Milwaukee; WMLW-CA (IND) Milwaukee; WMTV-TV (NBC) Madison; WMVS (PBS) Milwaukee; WMVT (PBS) Milwaukee; WPXE-TV (ION) Kenosha; WTMJ-TV (NBC) Milwaukee; WVTV (CW) Milwaukee.
Programming (via satellite): C-SPAN; C-SPAN 2; Product Information Network; QVC; ShopNBC; TV Guide Network; WGN America.
Fee: $45.00 installation; $13.19 monthly; $10.00 additional installation.
Expanded Basic Service 1
Subscribers: N.A.
Programming (via satellite): A&E Networks; ABC Family Channel; AMC; Animal Planet; Bravo; Cartoon Network; CNBC; CNN; Comedy Central; Country Music TV; Discovery Channel; Disney Channel; E! Entertainment Television; ESPN; ESPN 2; Eternal Word TV Network; Food Network; Fox News Channel; Fox Sports Net North; FX; G4; Golf Channel; GSN; Hallmark Channel; Headline News; HGTV; History Channel; Lifetime; MSNBC; MTV; National Geographic Channel; Nickelodeon; Oxygen; SoapNet; Speed; Spike TV; Syfy; TBS Superstation; The Learning Channel; The Weather Channel; Toon Disney; Travel Channel; truTV; Turner Classic Movies; Turner Network TV; TV Land; USA Network; Versus; VH1.
Fee: $29.76 monthly.
Digital Basic Service
Subscribers: N.A.
Programming (via satellite): BBC America; Bio; Discovery Digital Networks; DIY Network; ESPNews; GAS; History Channel International; MTV Networks Digital Suite; MuchMusic Network; Music Choice; Nick Jr.; Nick Too; Style Network; Sundance Channel; WE tv.
Fee: $7.00 monthly.
Digital Pay Service 1
Pay Units: N.A.
Programming (via satellite): Cinemax (multiplexed); Encore (multiplexed); Flix; HBO (multiplexed); Showtime (multiplexed); Starz (multiplexed); The Movie Channel (multiplexed).

Fee: $10.00 monthly (Cinemax, HBO, Showtime, Flix/TMC, or Starz/Encore).

Video-On-Demand: No

Pay-Per-View

Sports PPV (delivered digitally); Shorteez (delivered digitally); Fresh (delivered digitally); Playboy TV (delivered digitally); iN DEMAND (delivered digitally); Hot Choice (delivered digitally).

Internet Service

Operational: Yes. Began: July 1, 2001.

Broadband Service: Charter Pipeline.

Fee: $39.99 monthly; $4.95 modem lease.

Telephone Service

None

Miles of Plant: 300.0 (coaxial); None (fiber optic).

Vice President: Lisa Washa. Marketing Administrator: Rhonda Schelvan. Chief Technician: Jeff Gerner.

Ownership: Charter Communications Inc. (MSO).

INDEPENDENCE—Western Wisconsin Communications Cooperative, 23669 Washington St, Independence, WI 54747. Phones: 800-831-0610; 715-985-3004. Fax: 715-985-3261. E-mail: wwcc@triwest.net. Web Site: http://www2.tcc.coop. Also serves Alma Center, Arcadia, Blair, Eleva, Ettrick, Fairchild, Galesville, Hixton, Humbird, Lincoln Twp., Merillan, Northfield, Osseo, Pigeon, Pigeon Falls, Strum, Taylor, Trempealeau County & Whitehall. ICA: WI0032.

TV Market Ranking: Below 100 (Arcadia, Blair, Eleva, Ettrick, Fairchild, Galesville, INDEPENDENCE, Lincoln Twp., Osseo, Pigeon, Pigeon Falls, Strum, Taylor, Trempealeau County (portions), Whitehall); Outside TV Markets (Alma Center, Hixton, Humbird, Merillan, Northfield, Trempealeau County (portions)). Franchise award date: January 1, 1977. Franchise expiration date: June 1, 2007. Began: January 1, 1980.

Channel capacity: 78 (operating 2-way). Channels available but not in use: N.A.

Basic Service

Subscribers: 7,050.

Programming (received off-air): WEAU-TV (NBC) Eau Claire; WHLA-TV (PBS) La Crosse; WKBT-DT (CBS, MNT) La Crosse; WLAX (FOX) La Crosse; WXOW (ABC, CW) La Crosse; allband FM.

Programming (via satellite): A&E Networks; ABC Family Channel; Animal Planet; BTN; Cartoon Network; CNN; Comedy Central; Country Music TV; C-SPAN; CW+; Discovery Channel; Disney Channel; ESPN; ESPN 2; ESPN Classic Sports; Food Network; Fox News Channel; Fox Sports Net North; FX; Great American Country; Headline News; HGTV; History Channel; Lifetime; MSNBC; MTV; MyNetworkTV Inc.; NFL Network; Nickelodeon; Spike TV; Syfy; TBS Superstation; The Learning Channel; The Weather Channel; Travel Channel; Turner Classic Movies; Turner Network TV; TV Guide Network; TV Land; USA Network; VH1; Weatherscan; WGN America.

Fee: $25.00 installation; $56.14 monthly; $25.00 additional installation.

Digital Basic Service

Subscribers: 447.

Programming (via satellite): BBC America; BBC World News; Bio; Bloomberg Television; cloo; CMT Pure Country; Discovery Fit & Health; Discovery Kids Channel; DIY Network; DMX Music; ESPN U; ESPNews; Eternal Word TV Network; Fox Movie Channel; Fuse; G4; Golf Channel; GSN; Hallmark Channel; Halogen Network; History Channel International; ID Investigation Discovery; Lifetime Movie Network; Lifetime Real Women; Military Channel; MTV2; National Geographic Channel; Nick Jr.; NickToons TV; Outdoor Channel; PBS KIDS/PBS KIDS GO!; Planet Green; RFD-TV; Science; SoapNet; Speed; Style Network; TeenNick; Toon Disney; Trinity Broadcasting Network; Versus; VH1 Classic; WE tv.

Fee: $25.00 installation; $16.00 monthly.

Digital Expanded Basic Service

Subscribers: N.A.

Programming (received off-air): WEAU-TV (NBC) Eau Claire; WHLA-TV (PBS) La Crosse; WKBT-DT (CBS, MNT) La Crosse; WLAX (FOX) La Crosse; WXOW (ABC, CW) La Crosse.

Programming (via satellite): A&E HD; Animal Planet HD; BTN HD; Discovery Channel HD; ESPN 2 HD; ESPN HD; FSN HD; HD Theater; HDNet; HDNet Movies; History Channel HD; NFL Network HD; Outdoor Channel 2 HD; TBS in HD; Turner Network TV HD.

Fee: $10.00 monthly.

Digital Expanded Basic Service 2

Subscribers: N.A.

Programming (via satellite): Cine Latino; Cine Mexicano; CNN en Espanol; Discovery en Espanol; ESPN Deportes; Fox Deportes; History Channel en Espanol; mun2 television; Tr3s; VeneMovies.

Fee: $5.95 monthly.

Digital Pay Service 1

Pay Units: 216.

Programming (via satellite): Cinemax (multiplexed); Cinemax HD; HBO (multiplexed); HBO HD.

Fee: $19.99 monthly.

Digital Pay Service 2

Pay Units: 59.

Programming (via satellite): Encore (multiplexed); Starz (multiplexed).

Fee: $16.99 monthly.

Digital Pay Service 3

Pay Units: 29.

Programming (via satellite): Flix; Showtime (multiplexed); Sundance Channel; The Movie Channel (multiplexed).

Fee: $18.99 monthly.

Video-On-Demand: No

Pay-Per-View

Addressable homes: 447.

iN DEMAND (delivered digitally).

Internet Service

Operational: Yes.

Subscribers: 3,350.

Broadband Service: TriWest-Airstream.

Fee: $50.00 installation; $37.45-$53.45 monthly; $5.00 modem lease.

Telephone Service

None

Miles of Plant: 400.0 (coaxial); 125.0 (fiber optic).

Chief Executive Officer: Fred Weier. Chief Operating Officer: Cheryl Rue. Manager: Mark Schroeder. Chief Technician: Michael Flory.

Ownership: Tri-County Communications Cooperative Inc.

IOLA—Mediacom, 4010 Alexandra Dr, Waterloo, IA 50702. Phone: 319-235-2197. Fax: 319-232-7841. Web Site: http://www.mediacomcable.com. Also serves Scandinavia. ICA: WI0118.

TV Market Ranking: Outside TV Markets (IOLA, Scandinavia). Franchise award date: N.A. Franchise expiration date: December 22, 2013. Began: December 23, 1998.

Channel capacity: 42 (not 2-way capable). Channels available but not in use: N.A.

Basic Service

Subscribers: 465.

Programming (received off-air): WACY-TV (MNT) Appleton; WAOW (ABC, CW) Wausau; WBAY-TV (ABC, IND) Green Bay; WFRV-TV (CBS) Green Bay; WGBA-TV (NBC) Green Bay; WLUK-TV (FOX) Green Bay; WPNE-TV (PBS) Green Bay; WSAW-TV (CBS, MNT) Wausau.

Programming (via satellite): TBS Superstation; Trinity Broadcasting Network; WGN America.

Fee: $45.00 installation; $13.95 monthly.

Expanded Basic Service 1

Subscribers: 385.

Programming (via satellite): A&E Networks; ABC Family Channel; AMC; Animal Planet; CNN; Country Music TV; Discovery Channel; Disney Channel; ESPN; ESPN 2; HGTV; History Channel; Lifetime; MTV; Nickelodeon; Spike TV; Syfy; The Weather Channel; Travel Channel; Turner Network TV; TV Land; USA Network.

Fee: $22.00 monthly.

Pay Service 1

Pay Units: 91.

Programming (via satellite): Cinemax; HBO; Showtime.

Fee: $25.00 installation; $7.95 monthly (Cinemax), $11.99 monthly (HBO or Showtime).

Video-On-Demand: No

Internet Service

Operational: No.

Telephone Service

None

Miles of Plant: 18.0 (coaxial); None (fiber optic).

Regional Vice President: Doug Frank. General Manager: Doug Nix. Technical Operations Director: Greg Nank. Marketing Director: Steve Schuh. Marketing Coordinator: Joni Lindauer.

Ownership: Mediacom LLC (MSO).

IRONTON—Formerly served by Dairyland Cable Systems Inc. No longer in operation. ICA: WI0256.

JANESVILLE—Charter Communications, 2701 Daniels St, Madison, WI 53718. Phone: 608-274-3822. Fax: 608-274-1436. Web Site: http://www.charter.com. Also serves Harlem Twp., Rockton, Roscoe, Roscoe Twp. & South Beloit, IL; Afton, Albion, Aztalan, Beloit, Bradford, Brodhead, Center (town), Clarno, Clinton (village), Decatur, Edgerton, Evansville, Fort Atkinson, Fulton, Harmony, Jefferson, Johnson Creek, Koshkonong, Lake Mills, Milford, Milton (town), Monroe, New Glarus, Oconomowoc, Palmyra (village), Portland (town), Rock, Sullivan, Sumner, Turtle (town), Union, Waterloo, Watertown & Whitewater, WI. ICA: WI0007.

TV Market Ranking: 23 (Johnson Creek, Oconomowoc, Palmyra (village), Portland (town), Sullivan); 93 (Afton, Albion, Aztalan, Bradford, Brodhead, Clinton (village), Decatur, Edgerton, Evansville, Fort Atkinson, Jefferson, Koshkonong, Lake Mills, Milford, Milton (town), New Glarus, Sumner, Union, Waterloo, Watertown); 93,97 (Center (town), Clarno (town), Harmony, JANESVILLE, Monroe, Rock, Turtle (town)); 97 (Beloit, Fulton, Harlem Twp., Rockton, Roscoe, Roscoe Twp., South Beloit); Below 100 (Whitewater). Franchise award date: March 1, 1978. Franchise expiration date: N.A. Began: September 17, 1966.

Channel capacity: N.A. Channels available but not in use: N.A.

Basic Service

Subscribers: 81,300.

Programming (received off-air): WBUW (CW) Janesville; WHA-TV (PBS) Madison; WIFR (CBS) Freeport; WISC-TV (CBS, MNT) Madison; WKOW (ABC) Madison; WMSN-TV (FOX) Madison; WMTV-TV (NBC) Madison; WQRF-TV (FOX) Rockford; WREX (CW, NBC) Rockford; WTVO (ABC, MNT) Rockford; WVTV (CW) Milwaukee; 21 FMs.

Programming (via satellite): C-SPAN; C-SPAN 2; GRTV Network; QVC; TV Guide Network; WGN America.

Fee: $27.49 installation; $13.95 monthly; $1.10 converter.

Expanded Basic Service 1

Subscribers: 21,513.

Programming (via satellite): A&E Networks; ABC Family Channel; AMC; Animal Planet; BET Networks; Bravo; Cartoon Network; CNBC; CNN; Comedy Central; Country Music TV; Discovery Channel; Disney Channel; E! Entertainment Television; ESPN; ESPN 2; ESPN Classic Sports; Eternal Word TV Network; Food Network; Fox News Channel; Fox Sports Net North; FX; G4; Golf Channel; GSN; Hallmark Channel; Headline News; HGTV; History Channel; INSP; Lifetime; MSNBC; MTV; National Geographic Channel; Nickelodeon; Oxygen; SoapNet; Speed; Spike TV; Syfy; TBS Superstation; The Learning Channel; The Weather Channel; Toon Disney; Travel Channel; truTV; Turner Classic Movies; Turner Network TV; TV Land; USA Network; Versus; VH1; WE tv.

Fee: $28.40 monthly.

Digital Basic Service

Subscribers: N.A.

Programming (via satellite): BBC America; Bio; Discovery Digital Networks; DIY Network; ESPNews; History Channel International; MTV Networks Digital Suite; MuchMusic Network; Music Choice; Nick Jr.; Nick Too; Sundance Channel; TeenNick.

Fee: $12.95 monthly.

Digital Pay Service 1

Pay Units: 16,819.

Programming (via satellite): Cinemax (multiplexed); Encore (multiplexed); HBO (multiplexed); Showtime (multiplexed); Starz (multiplexed); The Movie Channel (multiplexed).

Fee: $12.95 monthly (Cinemax, HBO, TMC/Flix/Showtime, or Starz/Encore).

Video-On-Demand: Yes

Pay-Per-View

Shorteez (delivered digitally); Fresh (delivered digitally); Playboy TV (delivered digitally); iN DEMAND (delivered digitally).

Internet Service

Operational: Yes.

Broadband Service: Charter Pipeline.

Fee: $39.95 monthly.

Telephone Service

Digital: Operational

Fee: $39.95 monthly

Miles of Plant: 867.0 (coaxial); None (fiber optic).

Vice President & General Manager: Lisa Washa. Engineering Director: Tim Sanderson. Technical Operations Director: Bruce Hummel. Marketing Director: Traci Loonstra. Government Relations Director: Tim Vowell.

Ownership: Charter Communications Inc. (MSO).

JANESVILLE—Formerly served by Wireless Cable Systems Inc. No longer in operation. ICA: WI0307.

JUNCTION CITY—Packerland Broadband, 105 Kent St, PO Box 885, Iron Mountain, MI 49801. Phones: 800-236-8434; 906-774-6621. Fax: 906-776-2811. Web Site: http://www.packerlandbroadband.com. ICA: WI0257.

TV Market Ranking: Below 100 (JUNCTION CITY). Franchise award date: N.A. Franchise expiration date: N.A. Began: N.A.

Channel capacity: 40 (not 2-way capable). Channels available but not in use: N.A.

Basic Service

Subscribers: 53.

Programming (received off-air): WAOW (ABC, CW) Wausau; WEAU-TV (NBC) Eau Claire; WFXS-DT (FOX) Wittenberg; WHRM-TV (PBS) Wausau; WJFW-TV (NBC) Rhinelander; WSAW-TV (CBS, MNT) Wausau.

Programming (via satellite): A&E Networks; ABC Family Channel; AMC; Animal Planet; CNBC; CNN; Country Music TV; Discovery Channel; Disney Channel; ESPN; ESPN 2; Fox Sports Net; History Channel; Lifetime; MTV; Nickelodeon; Spike TV; Syfy; TBS Superstation; The Learning Channel; The Weather Channel; Turner Network TV; TV Land; USA Network; VH1; WGN America.

Fee: $24.95 installation; $33.95 monthly; $1.50 converter.

Pay Service 1

Pay Units: 13.

Programming (via satellite): HBO.

Fee: $10.95 monthly.

Video-On-Demand: No

Internet Service

Operational: No.

Telephone Service

None

Miles of Plant: 5.0 (coaxial); None (fiber optic).

General Manager: Dan Plante. Technical Supervisor: Chad Kay.

Ownership: Cable Constructors Inc. (MSO).

KELLNERSVILLE—New Century Communications, 3588 Kennebec Dr, Eagan, MN 55122-1001. Phone: 651-688-2623. Fax: 651-688-2624. E-mail: info@ourcableia.com. ICA: WI0258.

TV Market Ranking: 62 (KELLNERSVILLE). Franchise award date: N.A. Franchise expiration date: N.A. Began: August 1, 1990.

Channel capacity: 40 (not 2-way capable). Channels available but not in use: N.A.

Basic Service

Subscribers: 34.

Programming (received off-air): WACY-TV (MNT) Appleton; WBAY-TV (ABC, IND) Green Bay; WEAU-TV (NBC) Eau Claire; WFRV-TV (CBS) Green Bay; WLUK-TV (FOX) Green Bay; WPNE-TV (PBS) Green Bay.

Programming (via satellite): A&E Networks; ABC Family Channel; AMC; CNN; Discovery Channel; Disney Channel; ESPN; Lifetime; Nickelodeon; Showtime; Spike TV; TBS Superstation; The Learning Channel; Trinity Broadcasting Network; Turner Network TV; USA Network; WGN America.

Fee: $30.00 installation; $33.85 monthly.

Video-On-Demand: No

Internet Service

Operational: No.

Telephone Service

None

Miles of Plant: 2.0 (coaxial); None (fiber optic).

Executive Vice President: Marty Walch. Manager & Chief Technician: Todd Anderson.

Ownership: New Century Communications (MSO).

KENDALL—Community Antenna System Inc., 1010 Lake St, Hillsboro, WI 54634-9019. Phone: 608-489-2321. Fax: 608-489-2321. ICA: WI0201.

TV Market Ranking: Outside TV Markets (KENDALL). Franchise award date: January 1, 1961. Franchise expiration date: N.A. Began: January 1, 1963.

Channel capacity: 40 (not 2-way capable). Channels available but not in use: N.A.

Basic Service

Subscribers: 150.

Programming (received off-air): WEAU-TV (NBC) Eau Claire; WHA-TV (PBS) Madison; WISC-TV (CBS, MNT) Madison; WKBT-DT (CBS, MNT) La Crosse; WKOW (ABC) Madison; WMSN-TV (FOX) Madison; WMTV-TV (NBC) Madison.

Programming (via satellite): ABC Family Channel; ESPN; Spike TV; TBS Superstation; Turner Network TV; WGN America.

Fee: $27.05 installation; $28.05 monthly.

Pay Service 1

Pay Units: 34.

Programming (via satellite): Cinemax.

Fee: $6.95 monthly.

Internet Service

Operational: Yes.

Telephone Service

None

Miles of Plant: 4.0 (coaxial); None (fiber optic).

Manager: Randall Kubarski. Chief Technician: Gregory Kubarski.

Ownership: Community Antenna System Inc. (MSO).

KENOSHA—Time Warner Cable, 1320 N Dr Martin Luther King Dr, Milwaukee, WI 53212-4002. Phone: 414-277-4111. Fax: 414-277-8049. Web Site: http://www.timewarnercable.com. Also serves Bloomfield, Bristol, Caledonia, Elmwood Park, Geneva, Lake Geneva, Linn, Lyons, Mount Pleasant, North Bay, Paddock Lake, Pleasant Prairie, Racine, Randall, Randall (town), Raymond (town), Salem, Silver Lake, Somers, Spring Prairie, Sturtevant, Troy (town), Wheatfield, Wheatland & Wind Point. ICA: WI0009.

TV Market Ranking: 23 (Bristol, Caledonia, Elmwood Park, KENOSHA, Mount Pleasant, North Bay, Paddock Lake, Racine, Raymond (town), Salem, Somers, Sturtevant, Troy (town), Wheatfield, Wheatland, Wind Point); Below 100 (Bloomfield, Geneva, Lake Geneva, Linn, Lyons, Pleasant Prairie, Randall, Randall, Silver Lake, Spring Prairie). Franchise award date: July 5, 1983. Franchise expiration date: N.A. Began: June 1, 1984.

Channel capacity: N.A. Channels available but not in use: N.A.

Basic Service

Subscribers: N.A. Included in Milwaukee

Programming (received off-air): WBBM-TV (CBS) Chicago; WBME-TV (IND, TMO) Racine; WCGV-TV (MNT) Milwaukee; WDJT-TV (CBS) Milwaukee; WFLD (FOX) Chicago; WHA-TV (PBS) Madison; WISN-TV (ABC) Milwaukee; WITI (FOX, IND) Milwaukee; WLS-TV (ABC) Chicago; WMAQ-TV (NBC) Chicago; WMLW-CA (IND) Milwaukee; WMVS (PBS) Milwaukee; WMVT (PBS) Milwaukee; WPXE-TV (ION) Kenosha; WTMJ-TV (NBC) Milwaukee; WTTW (PBS) Chicago; WVCY-TV (IND) Milwaukee; WVTV (CW) Milwaukee; allband FM.

Programming (via satellite): ABC Family Channel; C-SPAN 2; Eternal Word TV Network; QVC; TBS Superstation; TV Guide Network; Univision Studios; WGN America.

Fee: $36.00 installation; $8.89 monthly; $.82 converter; $15.95 additional installation.

Expanded Basic Service 1

Subscribers: N.A. Included in Milwaukee

Programming (via satellite): A&E Networks; AMC; Animal Planet; BET Networks; Bravo!; Cartoon Network; CNBC; CNN; Comcast SportsNet California; Comedy Central; C-SPAN; Discovery Channel; Discovery Health Channel; Disney Channel; E! Entertainment Television; ESPN; ESPN 2; ESPN Classic Sports; Food Network; Fox News Channel; Fox Sports World; FX; Golf Channel; Great American Country; Hallmark Channel; Headline News; HGTV; History Channel; Jewelry Television; Lifetime; Lifetime Movie Network; MoviePlex; MSNBC; MTV; National Geographic Channel; Nickelodeon; Oxygen; Spike TV; Style Network; Syfy; Telemundo; The Learning Channel; The Weather Channel; Travel Channel; truTV; Turner Classic Movies; Turner Network TV; TV Land; USA Network; Versus; VH1; WE tv.

Fee: $17.15 monthly.

Digital Basic Service

Subscribers: N.A. Included in Milwaukee

Programming (via satellite): American-Life TV Network; America's Store; BBC America; Bio; Bloomberg Television; Boomerang; Canales N; CBS Sports Network; cloo; CNN International; Cooking Channel; Country Music TV; C-SPAN 3; Current; Discovery Fit & Health; Disney Channel; DIY Network; ESPN; ESPNews; Fox Sports Net; Fox Sports World; FSN Digital Atlantic; FSN Digital Central; FSN Digital Pacific; Fuel TV; G4; GAS; GSN; HD Theater; HDNet; HDNet Movies; History Channel; INHD (multiplexed); Lifetime Real Women; LWS Local Weather Station; MTV Networks Digital Suite; Music Choice; NBA TV; Nick Jr.; NickToons TV; Outdoor Channel; SoapNet; Speed; Tennis Channel; The Word Network; Toon Disney; Trinity Broadcasting Network; truTV; Turner Network TV HD.

Digital Pay Service 1

Pay Units: N.A.

Programming (via satellite): Cinemax (multiplexed); Encore (multiplexed); Flix; Fox Movie Channel; HBO (multiplexed); HBO HD; Independent Film Channel; RAI Internazional; Showtime (multiplexed); Showtime HD; Starz (multiplexed); Sundance Channel; The Movie Channel (multiplexed); TV Asia.

Video-On-Demand: Yes

Pay-Per-View

iN DEMAND (delivered digitally); Shorteez (delivered digitally); Sports PPV (delivered digitally); Playboy TV (delivered digitally); Ten Blox (delivered digitally); Ten Blue (delivered digitally); NBA League Pass (delivered digitally); MLS Direct Kick (delivered digitally); NHL Center Ice (delivered digitally); MLB Extra Innings (delivered digitally).

Internet Service

Operational: Yes.

Broadband Service: Road Runner.

Fee: $44.95 monthly.

Telephone Service

Digital: Operational

Fee: $44.95 monthly

Miles of plant included in Milwaukee

Division President: Jack Herbert. Vice President, Public Affairs: Bev Greenburg. Network Operations Director: Joseph Sherer. Marketing Director: Judith Gifford. Public Affairs Director: Celeste Flynn. Government Affairs Manager: Teresa Ferrante-Halbur.

Ownership: Time Warner Cable (MSO).

KINGSTON—New Century Communications, 3588 Kennebec Dr, Eagan, MN 55122-1001. Phone: 651-688-2623. Fax: 651-688-2624. E-mail: info@ourcableia.com. ICA: WI0213.

TV Market Ranking: Below 100 (KINGSTON). Franchise award date: N.A. Franchise expiration date: N.A. Began: N.A.

Channel capacity: 40 (not 2-way capable). Channels available but not in use: N.A.

Basic Service

Subscribers: 30.

Programming (received off-air): WHA-TV (PBS) Madison; WISC-TV (CBS, MNT) Madison; WKOW (ABC) Madison; WMTV-TV (NBC) Madison.

Programming (via satellite): A&E Networks; ABC Family Channel; AMC; CNN; Discovery Channel; Disney Channel; ESPN; Fox Sports Net; Lifetime; Nickelodeon; QVC; Showtime; Spike TV; TBS Superstation; The Learning Channel; Trinity Broadcasting Network; Turner Network TV; USA Network; WGN America.

Fee: $30.00 installation; $33.85 monthly.

Video-On-Demand: No

Internet Service

Operational: No.

Telephone Service

None

Miles of Plant: 3.0 (coaxial); None (fiber optic).

Executive Vice President: Marty Walch. Manager & Chief Technician: Todd Anderson.

Ownership: New Century Communications (MSO).

KNAPP (village)—Baldwin Telecom Inc. Formerly served by Baldwin (village), WI [WI0079]. This cable system has converted to IPTV, 930 Maple St, Baldwin, WI 54002. Phones: 877-684-3346; 715-684-3346. Fax: 715-684-4747. E-mail: info@baldwin-telecom.net. Web Site: http://www.baldwin-telecom.net. ICA: WI5247.

Channel capacity: N.A. Channels available but not in use: N.A.

Basic Service

Subscribers: N.A.

Fee: $61.00 monthly.

Expanded Basic Service 1

Subscribers: N.A.

Fee: $6.95 monthly.

Pay Service 1
Pay Units: N.A.
Fee: $11.95 monthly (Cinemax, HBO, Showtime/TMC, or Starz/Encore).
Internet Service
Operational: Yes.
Fee: $39.90 monthly.
General Manager: Larry Knegendorf. Cable TV Manager: Matt Knegendorf. Plant Manager: Duane Russett. Operations Manager: Matt Sparks.

KNAPP (village)—Baldwin Telecom Inc. No longer in operation. ICA: WI0259.

KNOWLES—Packerland Broadband, 105 Kent St, PO Box 885, Iron Mountain, MI 49801. Phones: 800-236-8434; 906-774-6621. Fax: 906-776-2811. Web Site: http://www.packerlandbroadband.com. Also serves Brownsville, Farmersville, Kekoskee, LeRoy & South Byron. ICA: WI0304.
TV Market Ranking: Below 100 (Brownsville, Farmersville, Kekoskee, KNOWLES, LeRoy, South Byron). Franchise award date: N.A. Franchise expiration date: N.A. Began: December 1, 1987.
Channel capacity: 40 (not 2-way capable). Channels available but not in use: N.A.
Basic Service
Subscribers: 181.
Programming (received off-air): WCGV-TV (MNT) Milwaukee; WFRV-TV (CBS) Green Bay; WISN-TV (ABC) Milwaukee; WITI (FOX, IND) Milwaukee; WLUK-TV (FOX) Green Bay; WMVS (PBS) Milwaukee; WTMJ-TV (NBC) Milwaukee; WVTV (CW) Milwaukee; WWRS-TV (TBN) Mayville.
Programming (via satellite): A&E Networks; ABC Family Channel; AMC; Animal Planet; CNN; Comedy Central; Country Music TV; Discovery Channel; Disney Channel; ESPN; ESPN 2; History Channel; Lifetime; MTV; Nickelodeon; Spike TV; Syfy; TBS Superstation; The Learning Channel; The Weather Channel; Turner Network TV; TV Land; USA Network; VH1; WGN America.
Fee: $24.95 installation; $41.95 monthly; $1.50 converter.
Pay Service 1
Pay Units: 23.
Programming (via satellite): HBO.
Fee: $14.95 installation; $13.95 monthly.
Video-On-Demand: No
Internet Service
Operational: Yes.
Fee: $26.95 monthly.
Telephone Service
None
Miles of Plant: 25.0 (coaxial); None (fiber optic).
General Manager: Dan Plante. Technical Supervisor: Chad Kay.
Ownership: Cable Constructors Inc.

KRAKOW—Packerland Broadband, 105 Kent St, PO Box 885, Iron Mountain, MI 49801. Phones: 800-236-8434; 906-774-6621. Fax: 906-776-2811. Web Site: http://www.packerlandbroadband.com. Also serves Angelica. ICA: WI0327.
TV Market Ranking: 62 (Angelica, KRAKOW).
Channel capacity: N.A. Channels available but not in use: N.A.
Basic Service
Subscribers: 55.
Programming (received off-air): WACY-TV (MNT) Appleton; WBAY-TV (ABC, IND) Green Bay; WFRV-TV (CBS) Green Bay; WGBA-TV (NBC) Green Bay; WLUK-TV (FOX) Green Bay; WPNE-TV (PBS) Green Bay.
Programming (via satellite): A&E Networks; ABC Family Channel; CNBC; CNN; C-SPAN; Discovery Channel; ESPN; ESPN 2; Eternal Word TV Network; Headline News; History Channel; ION Television; Lifetime; MTV; Nickelodeon; QVC; Spike TV; TBS Superstation; The Learning Channel; The Weather Channel; Turner Classic Movies; Turner Network TV; USA Network; WGN America.
Fee: $31.60 monthly.
Pay Service 1
Pay Units: N.A.
Programming (via satellite): HBO; Showtime.
Fee: $11.55 monthly (each).
Video-On-Demand: No
Internet Service
Operational: Yes.
Broadband Service: In-house.
Fee: $39.95 installation; $34.95 monthly.
Telephone Service
Digital: Operational
Miles of Plant: 6.0 (coaxial); None (fiber optic).
General Manager: Dan Plante. Technical Supervisor: Chad Kay.
Ownership: Cable Constructors Inc. (MSO).

LA CROSSE—Charter Communications. Now served by ONALASKA, WI [WI0024]. ICA: WI0017.

LA VALLE (village)—Packerland Broadband, 105 Kent St, PO Box 885, Iron Mountain, MI 49801. Phones: 800-236-8434; 906-774-6621. Fax: 906-776-2811. Web Site: http://www.packerlandbroadband.com. ICA: WI0260.
TV Market Ranking: Outside TV Markets (LA VALLE (VILLAGE)). Franchise award date: January 1, 1971. Franchise expiration date: N.A. Began: September 30, 1971.
Channel capacity: 40 (not 2-way capable). Channels available but not in use: N.A.
Basic Service
Subscribers: 162.
Programming (received off-air): WBUW (CW) Janesville; WHA-TV (PBS) Madison; WISC-TV (CBS, MNT) Madison; WKBT-DT (CBS, MNT) La Crosse; WKOW (ABC) Madison; WMSN-TV (FOX) Madison; WMTV-TV (NBC) Madison.
Programming (via satellite): QVC; WGN America.
Fee: $49.95 installation; $18.50 monthly; $19.95 additional installation.
Expanded Basic Service 1
Subscribers: 103.
Programming (received off-air): WBUW (CW) Janesville; WWRS-TV (TBN) Mayville.
Programming (via satellite): A&E Networks; ABC Family Channel; Animal Planet; CNN; Country Music TV; Discovery Channel; Disney Channel; E! Entertainment Television; ESPN; ESPN 2; Fox Sports Net North; Headline News; History Channel; MTV; Nickelodeon; Spike TV; TBS Superstation; The Learning Channel; The Weather Channel; Travel Channel; Turner Classic Movies; Turner Network TV; TV Land; USA Network.
Fee: $20.45 monthly.
Pay Service 1
Pay Units: 35.
Programming (via satellite): HBO.
Fee: $13.95 monthly.
Video-On-Demand: No
Internet Service
Operational: No.
Telephone Service
None
Miles of Plant: 35.0 (coaxial); None (fiber optic).
General Manager: Dan Plante. Technical Supervisor: Chad Kay.
Ownership: Cable Constructors Inc. (MSO).

LAC DU FLAMBEAU—Formerly served by Gauthier Cablevision. No longer in operation. ICA: WI0182.

LADYSMITH—Charter Communications, 1201 McCann Dr, Altoona, WI 54720-2561. Phone: 715-831-8940. Fax: 715-831-5862. Web Site: http://www.charter.com. Also serves Bruce, Flambeau, Grant & Tony (village). ICA: WI0081.
TV Market Ranking: Below 100 (Flambeau); Outside TV Markets (Bruce, Grant, LADYSMITH, Tony (village)). Franchise award date: N.A. Franchise expiration date: N.A. Began: June 1, 1967.
Channel capacity: N.A. Channels available but not in use: N.A.
Basic Service
Subscribers: 1,869.
Programming (received off-air): WCCO-TV (CBS) Minneapolis; WEAU-TV (NBC) Eau Claire; WEUX (FOX) Chippewa Falls; WHWC-TV (PBS) Menomonie; WQOW (ABC, CW) Eau Claire; WSAW-TV (CBS, MNT) Wausau.
Programming (via satellite): C-SPAN; C-SPAN 2; QVC; TV Guide Network; WGN America.
Fee: $50.00 installation; $12.00 monthly.
Expanded Basic Service 1
Subscribers: N.A.
Programming (via satellite): A&E Networks; ABC Family Channel; AMC; Animal Planet; Bravo; Cartoon Network; CNBC; CNN; Comedy Central; Country Music TV; Discovery Channel; Disney Channel; E! Entertainment Television; ESPN; ESPN 2; Food Network; Fox News Channel; Fox Sports Net North; FX; Headline News; HGTV; History Channel; Lifetime; MSNBC; MTV; Nickelodeon; Outdoor Channel; Oxygen; Spike TV; Syfy; TBS Superstation; The Learning Channel; The Weather Channel; Travel Channel; truTV; Turner Network TV; TV Land; USA Network; VH1.
Fee: $31.95 monthly.
Digital Basic Service
Subscribers: N.A.
Programming (via satellite): BBC America; Bio; Bloomberg Television; Discovery Fit & Health; DIY Network; Fox College Sports Atlantic; Fox College Sports Central; Fox College Sports Pacific; Fox Soccer; Fuel TV; GAS; GSN; Hallmark Channel; History Channel International; Independent Film Channel; Lifetime Movie Network; MTV Networks Digital Suite; Music Choice; Nick Jr.; Nick Too; NickToons TV; Style Network; Sundance Channel; TV Guide Interactive Inc.; WE tv.
Digital Pay Service 1
Pay Units: N.A.
Programming (via satellite): Cinemax (multiplexed); Encore (multiplexed); Flix; HBO (multiplexed); Showtime (multiplexed); Starz (multiplexed); The Movie Channel (multiplexed).
Video-On-Demand: No
Pay-Per-View
iN DEMAND (delivered digitally); NASCAR In Car (delivered digitally); Playboy TV (delivered digitally); Fresh (delivered digitally); Shorteez (delivered digitally).
Internet Service
Operational: Yes.
Broadband Service: Charter Pipeline.
Fee: $29.99 monthly.
Telephone Service
None
Miles of Plant: 26.0 (coaxial); None (fiber optic).
Vice President & General Manager: Lisa Washa. Operations Manager: Shirley Weibel. Engineering Director: Tim Normand. Marketing Director: Traci Loonstra. Sales & Marketing Manager: Chris Putzkey. Government Relations Manager: Mike Hill.
Ownership: Charter Communications Inc. (MSO).

LAKE HOLCOMBE—S & K TV Systems, 508 Miner Ave W, Ladysmith, WI 54848. Phones: 800-924-7880; 715-532-7321. Fax: 715-532-7583. E-mail: dave@skcable.com. Web Site: http://www.skcable.com. ICA: WI0147.
TV Market Ranking: Outside TV Markets (LAKE HOLCOMBE). Franchise award date: January 1, 1989. Franchise expiration date: N.A. Began: March 1, 1990.
Channel capacity: 40 (operating 2-way). Channels available but not in use: N.A.
Basic Service
Subscribers: 372.
Programming (received off-air): WEAU-TV (NBC) Eau Claire; WEUX (FOX) Chippewa Falls; WHWC-TV (PBS) Menomonie; WKBT-DT (CBS, MNT) La Crosse; WQOW (ABC, CW) Eau Claire.
Programming (via satellite): A&E Networks; ABC Family Channel; AMC; Animal Planet; CNN; Country Music TV; Discovery Channel; Disney Channel; ESPN; ESPN 2; Hallmark Channel; Headline News; HGTV; History Channel; Lifetime; MSNBC; Nickelodeon; Outdoor Channel; QVC; Spike TV; Syfy; TBS Superstation; The Weather Channel; Turner Classic Movies; Turner Network TV; TV Land; USA Network; WGN America.
Fee: $40.00 installation; $35.95 monthly; $25.00 additional installation.
Digital Basic Service
Subscribers: 27.
Programming (via satellite): Animal Planet; BBC America; Bio; Bloomberg Television; cloo; Discovery Fit & Health; DMX Music; ESPN 2; ESPN Classic Sports; ESPNews; Fox Movie Channel; Fox Sports World; Fuse; G4; GAS; Golf Channel; GSN; Halogen Network; HGTV; History Channel; History Channel International; Lifetime Movie Network; MTV Networks Digital Suite; Nick Jr.; NickToons TV; Outdoor Channel; Speed; Style Network; Syfy; The Learning Channel; Trinity Broadcasting Network; Turner Classic Movies; Versus; VH1.
Fee: $15.35 monthly.
Pay Service 1
Pay Units: 42.
Programming (via satellite): Cinemax.
Fee: $10.00 installation; $7.95 monthly.
Pay Service 2
Pay Units: 29.
Programming (via satellite): HBO.
Fee: $10.00 installation; $10.95 monthly.
Digital Pay Service 1
Pay Units: N.A.
Programming (via satellite): Cinemax (multiplexed); Encore (multiplexed); HBO (multiplexed); Showtime (multiplexed); Starz (multiplexed); The Movie Channel (multiplexed).
Video-On-Demand: No

Internet Service
Operational: Yes.
Fee: $30.00 installation; $24.95 monthly.
Telephone Service
None
Miles of Plant: 22.0 (coaxial); None (fiber optic).
Manager: Randy Scott. Office Manager: Dave Scott.
Ownership: S & K TV Systems Inc. (MSO).

LAKE NEBAGAMON—Charter Communications, 302 E Superior St, Duluth, MN 55802-2196. Phones: 507-289-8372 (Rochester administrative office); 218-529-8000. Fax: 507-285-6162. Web Site: http://www.charter.com. ICA: WI0133.
TV Market Ranking: 89 (LAKE NEBAGAMON). Franchise award date: August 1, 1989. Franchise expiration date: August 1, 2009. Began: June 1, 1990.
Channel capacity: 54 (not 2-way capable). Channels available but not in use: N.A.
Basic Service
Subscribers: 230.
Programming (received off-air): KBJR-TV (MNT, NBC) Superior; KDLH (CBS, CW) Duluth; WDIO-DT (ABC) Duluth; WDSE (PBS) Duluth.
Programming (via satellite): A&E Networks; ABC Family Channel; AMC; CNN; C-SPAN; Discovery Channel; ESPN; MTV; Nickelodeon; Spike TV; TBS Superstation; The Learning Channel; truTV; Turner Network TV; USA Network; WGN America.
Fee: $25.48 installation; $15.89 monthly.
Pay Service 1
Pay Units: 44.
Programming (via satellite): HBO.
Fee: $11.00 monthly.
Pay Service 2
Pay Units: 41.
Programming (via satellite): Showtime.
Fee: $11.00 monthly.
Video-On-Demand: No
Internet Service
Operational: No.
Telephone Service
None
Miles of Plant: 26.0 (coaxial); None (fiber optic).
Vice President & General Manager: John Crowley. Operations Manager: Tom Gorsuch. Marketing Director: Bill Haarstad.
Ownership: Charter Communications Inc. (MSO).

LANCASTER—Charter Communications, 2701 Daniels St, Madison, WI 53718. Phone: 608-274-3822. Fax: 608-274-1436. Web Site: http://www.charter.com. Also serves Bloomington, Cassville, Dickeyville & Patch Grove. ICA: WI0261.
TV Market Ranking: Below 100 (Bloomington, Cassville, Dickeyville, LANCASTER, Patch Grove). Franchise award date: January 1, 1980. Franchise expiration date: N.A. Began: June 1, 1967.
Channel capacity: 64 (not 2-way capable). Channels available but not in use: N.A.
Basic Service
Subscribers: 2,639.
Programming (received off-air): KCRG-TV (ABC) Cedar Rapids; KFXB-TV (IND) Dubuque; KGAN (CBS) Cedar Rapids; KRIN (PBS) Waterloo; KWWL (NBC) Waterloo; WHA-TV (PBS) Madison; WISC-TV (CBS, MNT) Madison; WKOW (ABC) Madison; WMSN-TV (FOX) Madison; WMTV-TV (NBC) Madison.
Programming (via satellite): A&E Networks; WGN America.
Fee: $49.95 installation; $16.26 monthly; $19.95 additional installation.
Expanded Basic Service 1
Subscribers: N.A.
Programming (via satellite): ABC Family Channel; Animal Planet; Cartoon Network; CNN; C-SPAN; Discovery Channel; Disney Channel; ESPN; ESPN 2; ESPNews; Eternal Word TV Network; Fox Sports Net North; FX; Great American Country; Headline News; HGTV; History Channel; Lifetime; Nickelodeon; Spike TV; Syfy; TBS Superstation; The Learning Channel; The Weather Channel; Turner Classic Movies; Turner Network TV; TV Land; USA Network; VH1.
Fee: $19.99 monthly.
Pay Service 1
Pay Units: 330.
Programming (via satellite): Cinemax; HBO.
Fee: $19.95 installation; $9.95 monthly (each).
Video-On-Demand: No
Pay-Per-View
Addressable homes: 62,819.
Hot Network (delivered digitally); Hot Zone (delivered digitally); iN DEMAND (delivered digitally); Playboy TV (delivered digitally); Spice (delivered digitally); Spice2 (delivered digitally).
Internet Service
Operational: No.
Telephone Service
None
Miles of Plant: 56.0 (coaxial); None (fiber optic).
Vice President & General Manager: Lisa Washa. Engineering Director: Tim Sanderson. Technical Operations Director: Bruce Hummel. Marketing Director: Traci Loonstra. Government Relations Director: Tim Vowell.
Ownership: Charter Communications Inc. (MSO).

LAND O'LAKES—Karban TV Systems Inc., 120 S Church St, PO Box 8, Bonduel, WI 54107-0008. Phones: 715-550-7613; 800-236-0233. Fax: 715-277-2339. E-mail: sales@ktvs.net. Web Site: http://www.ktvs.net. ICA: WI0262.
TV Market Ranking: Below 100 (LAND O'LAKES). Franchise award date: N.A. Franchise expiration date: N.A. Began: July 1, 1989.
Channel capacity: 77 (2-way capable). Channels available but not in use: N.A.
Basic Service
Subscribers: 80.
Programming (received off-air): WFXS-DT (FOX) Wittenberg; WJFW-TV (NBC) Rhinelander; WLEF-TV (PBS) Park Falls; WSAW-TV (CBS, MNT) Wausau; WYOW (ABC, CW) Eagle River.
Programming (via satellite): A&E Networks; ABC Family Channel; AMC; Animal Planet; CNBC; CNN; Comedy Central; Country Music TV; C-SPAN; CW+; Discovery Channel; Disney Channel; ESPN; ESPN 2; Eternal Word TV Network; Food Network; Fox News Channel; FX; Headline News; HGTV; History Channel; Lifetime; MSNBC; NFL Network; Nickelodeon; Outdoor Channel; QVC; Speed; Spike TV; Syfy; TBS Superstation; The Learning Channel; The Weather Channel; Travel Channel; Trinity Broadcasting Network; Turner Classic Movies; Turner Network TV; TV Land; USA Network; VH1; WGN America.
Fee: $75.00 installation; $40.00 monthly; $20.00 additional installation.

Pay Service 1
Pay Units: 12.
Programming (via satellite): Cinemax.
Fee: $10.00 monthly.
Pay Service 2
Pay Units: 19.
Programming (via satellite): HBO.
Fee: $10.00 monthly.
Video-On-Demand: No
Internet Service
Operational: No.
Telephone Service
None
Miles of Plant: 8.0 (coaxial); None (fiber optic).
Manager & Chief Technician: John Karban.
Ownership: Karban TV Systems Inc. (MSO).

LAONA—Packerland Broadband, 105 Kent St, PO Box 885, Iron Mountain, MI 49801. Phones: 800-236-8434; 906-774-6621. Fax: 906-776-2811. Web Site: http://www.packerlandbroadband.com. ICA: WI0143.
TV Market Ranking: Below 100 (LAONA). Franchise award date: N.A. Franchise expiration date: December 1, 2007. Began: June 1, 1989.
Channel capacity: 41 (not 2-way capable). Channels available but not in use: N.A.
Basic Service
Subscribers: 268.
Programming (received off-air): WACY-TV (MNT) Appleton; WAOW (ABC, CW) Wausau; WBAY-TV (ABC, IND) Green Bay; WFRV-TV (CBS) Green Bay; WGBA-TV (NBC) Green Bay; WJFW-TV (NBC) Rhinelander; WLUC-TV (NBC) Marquette; WLUK-TV (FOX) Green Bay; WNMU (PBS) Marquette; WSAW-TV (CBS, MNT) Wausau.
Programming (via satellite): A&E Networks; ABC Family Channel; CNBC; CNN; Country Music TV; C-SPAN; CW+; Discovery Channel; ESPN; ESPN 2; Eternal Word TV Network; Fox News Channel; Fox Sports Net North; FX; History Channel; Lifetime; MTV; Nickelodeon; QVC; Speed; Spike TV; TBS Superstation; The Learning Channel; The Weather Channel; Turner Classic Movies; Turner Network TV; TV Land; USA Network; VH1; WGN America.
Fee: $25.00 installation; $31.60 monthly.
Pay Service 1
Pay Units: N.A.
Programming (via satellite): Cinemax; HBO.
Fee: $11.55 monthly (each).
Video-On-Demand: No
Internet Service
Operational: Yes.
Fee: $26.95 monthly.
Telephone Service
None
Miles of Plant: 26.0 (coaxial); None (fiber optic).
General Manager: Dan Plante. Technical Supervisor: Chad Kay.
Ownership: Cable Constructors Inc. (MSO).

LENA—Packerland Broadband, 105 Kent St, PO Box 885, Iron Mountain, MI 49801. Phones: 800-236-8434; 906-774-6621. Fax: 906-776-2811. Web Site: http://www.packerlandbroadband.com. ICA: WI0204.
TV Market Ranking: 62 (LENA). Franchise award date: March 1, 1983. Franchise expiration date: N.A. Began: May 1, 1984.
Channel capacity: N.A. Channels available but not in use: N.A.
Basic Service
Subscribers: 88.
Programming (received off-air): WACY-TV (MNT) Appleton; WBAY-TV (ABC, IND) Green Bay; WCWF (CW) Suring; WFRV-TV (CBS) Green Bay; WGBA-TV (NBC) Green Bay; WLUK-TV (FOX) Green Bay; WPNE-TV (PBS) Green Bay.
Programming (via satellite): C-SPAN; C-SPAN 2; QVC; WGN America.
Fee: $56.73 installation; $12.08 monthly.
Expanded Basic Service 1
Subscribers: 73.
Programming (via satellite): A&E Networks; ABC Family Channel; Bravo; Cartoon Network; CNN; Country Music TV; Discovery Channel; Disney Channel; E! Entertainment Television; ESPN; ESPN 2; Fox News Channel; G4; Headline News; HGTV; History Channel; Lifetime; MSNBC; MTV; Nickelodeon; Spike TV; Syfy; TBS Superstation; The Learning Channel; Turner Network TV; TV Land; USA Network.
Fee: $24.79 monthly.
Pay Service 1
Pay Units: 31.
Programming (via satellite): Cinemax.
Fee: $14.72 monthly (each).
Pay Service 2
Pay Units: 42.
Programming (via satellite): HBO.
Fee: $12.95 monthly.
Video-On-Demand: No
Internet Service
Operational: Yes.
Broadband Service: In-house.
Fee: $39.95 installation; $34.95 monthly.
Telephone Service
None
Miles of Plant: 5.0 (coaxial); None (fiber optic).
General Manager: Dan Plante. Technical Supervisor: Chad Kay.
Ownership: Cable Constructors Inc. (MSO).

LOGANVILLE (village)—Dairyland Cable Systems Inc., 2494 US Hwy 14 E, Richland Center, WI 53581-2983. Phone: 608-647-6383. Fax: 608-647-2093. ICA: WI0263.
TV Market Ranking: Outside TV Markets (LOGANVILLE (VILLAGE)). Franchise award date: N.A. Franchise expiration date: N.A. Began: September 1, 1989.
Channel capacity: 13 (not 2-way capable). Channels available but not in use: N.A.
Basic Service
Subscribers: 76.
Programming (received off-air): WISC-TV (CBS, MNT) Madison; WKOW (ABC) Madison; WMSN-TV (FOX) Madison; WMTV-TV (NBC) Madison; WMVS (PBS) Milwaukee.
Programming (via satellite): CNN; ESPN; Nickelodeon; Spike TV; TBS Superstation;

Turner Network TV; USA Network; WGN America.
Fee: $25.00 installation; $27.31 monthly.

Pay Service 1
Pay Units: 27.
Programming (via satellite): HBO.
Fee: $10.50 monthly.

Video-On-Demand: No

Internet Service
Operational: No.

Telephone Service
None

Manager: Jim Atkinson. Chief Technician: Randy Mardall. Marketing Representative: Brian Sullivan.

Ownership: Dairyland Cable Systems Inc. (MSO).

MADISON—Charter Communications, 2701 Daniels St, Madison, WI 53718. Phone: 608-274-3822. Fax: 608-274-1436. Web Site: http://www.charter.com. Also serves Arlington, Belleville, Blooming Grove, Brooklyn, Burke, Cambridge, Christiana, Columbus, Cross Plains (village), De Forest, Deerfield, Dunkirk, Dunn, Elba (town), Exeter, Maple Bluff, Marshall, McFarland (village), Middleton, Monona, Morrisonville, Oakland (town), Oregon (village), Pleasant Springs (town), Shorewood Hills, Stoughton, Sun Prairie, Westport (town) & Windsor (town). ICA: WI0002.

TV Market Ranking: 93 (Arlington, Belleville, Blooming Grove, Brooklyn, Burke, Cambridge, Christiana, Columbus, Cross Plains (village), De Forest, Deerfield, Dunkirk, Dunn, Elba (town), Exeter, MADISON, Maple Bluff, Marshall, McFarland (village), Middleton, Monona, Morrisonville, Oakland (town), Oregon (village), Pleasant Springs (town), Shorewood Hills, Stoughton, Sun Prairie, Westport (town), Windsor (town)). Franchise award date: March 18, 1975. Franchise expiration date: N.A. Began: August 1, 1973.

Channel capacity: N.A. Channels available but not in use: N.A.

Basic Service
Subscribers: 83,607.
Programming (received off-air): WBUW (CW) Janesville; WHA-TV (PBS) Madison; WISC-TV (CBS, MNT) Madison; WKOW (ABC) Madison; WMSN-TV (FOX) Madison; WMTV-TV (NBC) Madison; 19 FMs.
Programming (via satellite): C-SPAN; C-SPAN 2; Headline News; Product Information Network; QVC; TV Guide Network; Univision Studios; WGN America.
Fee: $2.26 converter.

Expanded Basic Service 1
Subscribers: 75,313.
Programming (via satellite): A&E Networks; ABC Family Channel; AMC; Animal Planet; BET Networks; Bravo; Cartoon Network; CNBC; CNN; Comedy Central; Country Music TV; Discovery Channel; Disney Channel; E! Entertainment Television; ESPN; ESPN 2; ESPN Classic Sports; Eternal Word TV Network; Food Network; Fox News Channel; FX; G4; Golf Channel; GSN; Hallmark Channel; HGTV; History Channel; INSP; Lifetime; MSNBC; MTV; National Geographic Channel; Nickelodeon; Oxygen; SoapNet; Speed; Spike TV; Style Network; Syfy; TBS Superstation; The Learning Channel; The Weather Channel; Toon Disney; Travel Channel; truTV; Turner Classic Movies; Turner Network TV; TV Land; USA Network; Versus; VH1; WE tv.
Fee: $49.99 monthly.

Digital Basic Service
Subscribers: 62,819.
Programming (via satellite): BBC America; Bio; Canales N; Discovery Digital Networks; DIY Network; ESPNews; Fox Sports Net North; History Channel International; Independent Film Channel; Lifetime Movie Network; MTV Networks Digital Suite; Music Choice; Nick Jr.; Nick Too; ShopNBC; Sundance Channel; TeenNick.

Digital Pay Service 1
Pay Units: 62,355.
Programming (via satellite): Cinemax (multiplexed); Encore (multiplexed); Flix; HBO (multiplexed); Showtime (multiplexed); Starz (multiplexed); The Movie Channel (multiplexed).
Fee: $10.00 monthly (Cinemax, HBO, Showtime, Flix/TMC, or Starz/Encore).

Video-On-Demand: Yes

Pay-Per-View
Addressable homes: 62,819.
iN DEMAND (delivered digitally); Playboy TV (delivered digitally); Fresh (delivered digitally); Shorteez (delivered digitally).

Internet Service
Operational: Yes. Began: January 1, 2000.
Broadband Service: Charter Pipeline.
Fee: $49.95 installation; $39.99 monthly.

Telephone Service
Digital: Operational

Miles of Plant: 1,138.0 (coaxial); None (fiber optic).

Vice President & General Manager: Lisa Washa. Technical Operations Director: Bruce Hummel. Marketing Director: Traci Loonstra. Government Relations Director: Tim Vowell.

Ownership: Charter Communications Inc. (MSO).

MANAWA—Manawa Telecom Cable TV, 131 2nd St, PO Box 130, Manawa, WI 54949-0130. Phone: 920-596-2700. Fax: 920-596-3775. E-mail: manawa@wolfnet.net. Web Site: http://www.manawatelecomcable.com. Also serves Little Wolf & Royalton Twp. ICA: WI0127.

TV Market Ranking: Below 100 (Little Wolf, MANAWA, Royalton Twp.). Franchise award date: December 6, 1982. Franchise expiration date: December 1, 2012. Began: November 1, 1984.

Channel capacity: 58 (not 2-way capable). Channels available but not in use: N.A.

Basic Service
Subscribers: 499.
Programming (received off-air): WACY-TV (MNT) Appleton; WAOW (ABC, CW) Wausau; WBAY-TV (ABC, IND) Green Bay; WCWF (CW) Suring; WFRV-TV (CBS) Green Bay; WGBA-TV (NBC) Green Bay; WHRM-TV (PBS) Wausau; WLUK-TV (FOX) Green Bay; WPNE-TV (PBS) Green Bay; WSAW-TV (CBS, MNT) Wausau; allband FM.
Programming (via satellite): A&E Networks; ABC Family Channel; AMC; Animal Planet; Cartoon Network; CNBC; CNN; Comedy Central; Country Music TV; C-SPAN; Discovery Channel; Disney Channel; E! Entertainment Television; ESPN; ESPN 2; ESPN Classic Sports; Food Network; Fox News Channel; Fox Sports Net North; FX; G4; GSN; Hallmark Channel; Headline News; HGTV; History Channel; Lifetime; MTV; National Geographic Channel; Nickelodeon; Outdoor Channel; Oxygen; QVC; Speed; Spike TV; Syfy; TBS Superstation; The Learning Channel; The Weather Channel; Travel Channel; Trinity Broadcasting Network; truTV; Turner Classic Movies; Turner Network TV; TV Land; USA Network; VH1; WGN America.
Fee: $20.00 installation; $35.95 monthly; $2.00 converter; $10.00 additional installation.

Digital Basic Service
Subscribers: 164.
Programming (via satellite): A&E Networks; ABC Family Channel; AMC; Animal Planet; BTN; Cartoon Network; CNBC; CNN; Comedy Central; Country Music TV; C-SPAN; CW+; Discovery Channel; Discovery Health Channel; Discovery Kids Channel; Disney Channel; DMX Music; E! Entertainment Television; ESPN; ESPN 2; ESPN Classic Sports; ESPN U; ESPNews; Food Network; Fox News Channel; Fox Sports Net North; FX; G4; GSN; Hallmark Channel; Headline News; HGTV; History Channel; Lifetime; Lifetime Movie Network; MTV; National Geographic Channel; NFL Network; Nickelodeon; Outdoor Channel; Oxygen; QVC; Science; Speed; Spike TV; Syfy; TBS Superstation; The Learning Channel; The Weather Channel; Travel Channel; Trinity Broadcasting Network; truTV; Turner Classic Movies; Turner Network TV; TV Land; USA Network; VH1; WGN America.
Fee: $42.95 monthly.

Digital Expanded Basic Service
Subscribers: N.A.
Programming (via satellite): AmericanLife TV Network; BBC America; Bio; Bloomberg Television; Boomerang; Bravo; CNN International; C-SPAN 2; Discovery Fit & Health; Disney XD; DIY Network; Eternal Word TV Network; Fox Movie Channel; GMC; Golf Channel; History Channel International; ID Investigation Discovery; Lifetime Real Women; Military Channel; MSNBC; Ovation; Planet Green; RFD-TV; SoapNet; Style Network; Versus; WE tv.
Fee: $10.00 monthly.

Digital Expanded Basic Service 2
Subscribers: N.A.
Programming (via satellite): A&E HD; Discovery Channel HD; ESPN 2 HD; ESPN HD; History Channel HD; NFL Network HD; Turner Network TV HD.
Fee: $14.95 monthly.

Pay Service 1
Pay Units: 40.
Programming (via satellite): HBO.
Fee: $10.95 monthly.

Pay Service 2
Pay Units: 21.
Programming (via satellite): Showtime.
Fee: $10.95 monthly.

Digital Pay Service 1
Pay Units: N.A.
Programming (via satellite): Cinemax (multiplexed); Encore (multiplexed); Flix; HBO (multiplexed); Showtime (multiplexed); Starz (multiplexed); Sundance Channel; The Movie Channel (multiplexed).
Fee: $9.95 monthly (Cinemax), $11.95 monthly (HBO, Showtime/TMC/Sundance/Flix or Starz/Encore).

Video-On-Demand: No

Pay-Per-View
iN DEMAND (delivered digitally); Playboy TV (delivered digitally); Fresh (delivered digitally); Shorteez (delivered digitally).

Internet Service
Operational: No.

Telephone Service
None

Miles of Plant: 18.0 (coaxial); None (fiber optic).

Manager & Marketing Director: Brian J. Squires. Chief Technician: Thomas Squires.

Ownership: Manawa Telecom Inc.

MANITOWOC—Comcast Cable, 1614 Washington St, Manitowoc, WI 54220-5048. Phones: 920-682-7705; 920-682-6511. Fax: 920-682-9505. Web Site: http://www.comcast.com. Also serves Cato, Manitowoc (town), Manitowoc Rapids, Newton (town) & Whitelaw. ICA: WI0021.

TV Market Ranking: 62 (Cato, MANITOWOC, Manitowoc (town), Manitowoc Rapids, Whitelaw); Outside TV Markets (Newton (town)). Franchise award date: November 3, 1980. Franchise expiration date: N.A. Began: December 15, 1981.

Channel capacity: N.A. Channels available but not in use: N.A.

Basic Service
Subscribers: 9,368.
Programming (received off-air): WACY-TV (MNT) Appleton; WBAY-TV (ABC, IND) Green Bay; WCWF (CW) Suring; WFRV-TV (CBS) Green Bay; WGBA-TV (NBC) Green Bay; WLUK-TV (FOX) Green Bay; WPNE-TV (PBS) Green Bay; 22 FMs.
Programming (via satellite): C-SPAN; C-SPAN 2; Discovery Health Channel; Eternal Word TV Network; Headline News; MSNBC; Product Information Network; QVC; TBS Superstation; The Learning Channel; Trinity Broadcasting Network; TV Guide Network; WGN America.
Fee: $44.99 installation; $14.49 monthly; $13.99 additional installation.

Expanded Basic Service 1
Subscribers: N.A.
Programming (via satellite): A&E Networks; ABC Family Channel; AMC; Animal Planet; Cartoon Network; CNBC; CNN; Comedy Central; Discovery Channel; Disney Channel; E! Entertainment Television; ESPN; ESPN 2; Food Network; Fox News Channel; Fox Sports Net; FX; Golf Channel; Great American Country; GSN; Hallmark Channel; HGTV; History Channel; Lifetime; MTV; Nickelodeon; Speed; Spike TV; Style Network; Syfy; The Weather Channel; Travel Channel; truTV; Turner Classic Movies; Turner Network TV; TV Land; USA Network; Versus; VH1.
Fee: $6.00 installation; $34.00 monthly.

Digital Basic Service
Subscribers: 1,854.
Programming (via satellite): BBC America; Cooking Channel; Discovery Digital Networks; DIY Network; DMX Music; ESPNews; G4; GAS; MTV Networks Digital Suite; National Geographic Channel; NFL Network; Nick Jr.; Nick Too; NickToons TV; SoapNet; Toon Disney; WAM! America's Kidz Network.
Fee: $11.99 monthly.

Digital Pay Service 1
Pay Units: N.A.
Programming (via satellite): Cinemax (multiplexed); Encore (multiplexed); Flix; HBO (multiplexed); Showtime (multiplexed); Starz; Sundance Channel; The Movie Channel (multiplexed).

Video-On-Demand: No

Pay-Per-View
Addressable homes: 3,900.
Special events; iN DEMAND (delivered digitally); Hot Choice (delivered digitally); Playboy TV (delivered digitally); Fresh (delivered digitally); Shorteez (delivered digitally).

Internet Service
Operational: Yes.
Subscribers: 1,612.

Broadband Service: Comcast High Speed Internet.
Fee: $42.95 monthly.
Telephone Service
None
Miles of Plant: 219.0 (coaxial); 40.0 (fiber optic).
Office Manager: Ann Gadzinski. Chief Technician: Roberto Peronto. Operations Director: Jonathan Burns.
Ownership: Comcast Cable Communications Inc. (MSO).

MARINETTE—Time Warner Cable, 1001 W Kennedy Ave, PO Box 145, Kimberly, WI 54136-0145. Phones: 920-749-1400; 414-277-4032 (Milwaukee). Fax: 920-831-9372. Web Site: http://www.timewarnercable.com/wisconsin. Also serves Ingallston Twp. & Menominee Twp., MI; Menominee (town), Peshtigo & Porterfield, WI. ICA: WI0025.
TV Market Ranking: Below 100 (Peshtigo, Porterfield); Outside TV Markets (Ingallston Twp., MARINETTE, Menominee (town), Menominee Twp.). Franchise award date: August 9, 1966. Franchise expiration date: N.A. Began: March 1, 1970.
Channel capacity: 80 (operating 2-way). Channels available but not in use: N.A.
Basic Service
Subscribers: N.A. Included in Green Bay
Programming (received off-air): WACY-TV (MNT) Appleton; WBAY-TV (ABC, IND) Green Bay; WCWF (CW) Suring; WFRV-TV (CBS) Green Bay; WGBA-TV (NBC) Green Bay; WLUC-TV (NBC) Marquette; WLUK-TV (FOX) Green Bay; WNMU (PBS) Marquette; WPNE-TV (PBS) Green Bay; allband FM.
Programming (via satellite): C-SPAN; The Learning Channel; WGN America; WGN-TV (CW, IND) Chicago.
Fee: $37.62 installation; $10.47 monthly.
Expanded Basic Service 1
Subscribers: N.A. Included in Green Bay
Programming (via satellite): A&E Networks; ABC Family Channel; AMC; Animal Planet; Bravo; Cartoon Network; CNBC; CNN; Comedy Central; Country Music TV; C-SPAN 2; Discovery Channel; Discovery Health Channel; Disney Channel; E! Entertainment Television; ESPN; ESPN 2; ESPN Classic Sports; Eternal Word TV Network; Food Network; Fox News Channel; Fox Sports Net; FX; Golf Channel; Hallmark Channel; Headline News; HGTV; History Channel; Lifetime; Lifetime Movie Network; Michigan Government Television; MSNBC; MTV; National Geographic Channel; Nickelodeon; Oxygen; QVC; ShopNBC; Spike TV; Syfy; TBS Superstation; The Learning Channel; Travel Channel; truTV; Turner Classic Movies; Turner Network TV; TV Guide Network; TV Land; Univision Studios; USA Network; Versus; VH1; WE tv.
Fee: $30.55 monthly.
Digital Basic Service
Subscribers: N.A. Included in Green Bay
Programming (via satellite): America's Store; BBC America; Bio; Bloomberg Television; Cooking Channel; C-SPAN 3; Discovery Fit & Health; DIY Network; ESPN Classic Sports; ESPNews; Fox Sports World; FSN Digital Atlantic; FSN Digital Central; FSN Digital Pacific; Fuse; G4; GAS; Great American Country; GSN; History Channel International; Independent Film Channel; Lifetime Real Women; MTV2; NBA TV; Nick Jr.; Nick Too; Outdoor Channel; Ovation; Speed; Style Network; Tennis Channel; The Weather Channel; Toon Disney; VH1 Classic; Weatherscan.
Fee: $8.00 ala carte.
Digital Pay Service 1
Pay Units: 1,143.
Programming (via satellite): Cinemax (multiplexed); Encore (multiplexed); Fox Movie Channel; HBO (multiplexed); Independent Film Channel; Showtime (multiplexed); Starz (multiplexed); The Movie Channel (multiplexed).
Fee: $10.00 installation; $3.99 monthly (FMC, IFC & Encore), $10.00 monthly (Cinemax, HBO, Showtime, Starz or TMC).
Video-On-Demand: Yes
Pay-Per-View
iN DEMAND (delivered digitally); ESPN (delivered digitally); Playboy TV (delivered digitally); Club Jenna (delivered digitally); NBA League Pass (delivered digitally); NHL Center Ice (delivered digitally).
Internet Service
Operational: Yes, DSL.
Broadband Service: Road Runner, EarthLink, Internet.
Fee: $36.99 installation; $39.99 monthly.
Telephone Service
Digital: Operational
Fee: $39.95 monthly
Miles of plant included in Green Bay
President: Jack Herbert. Vice President, Engineering: Randy Cicatello. Vice President, Marketing: Brenda Kinne. Vice President, Government & Public Affairs: Bev Greenburg. General Manager: Mike Fox. Public Affairs Manager: Bill Harke.
Ownership: Time Warner Cable (MSO).

MARQUETTE—New Century Communications, 3588 Kennebec Dr, Eagan, MN 55122-1001. Phone: 651-688-2623. Fax: 651-688-2624. E-mail: info@ourcableia.com. ICA: WI0198.
TV Market Ranking: Below 100 (MARQUETTE). Franchise award date: N.A. Franchise expiration date: N.A. Began: N.A.
Channel capacity: 40 (not 2-way capable). Channels available but not in use: N.A.
Basic Service
Subscribers: 32.
Programming (received off-air): WHA-TV (PBS) Madison; WISC-TV (CBS, MNT) Madison; WKOW (ABC) Madison; WMTV-TV (NBC) Madison.
Programming (via satellite): A&E Networks; ABC Family Channel; AMC; CNN; Country Music TV; Discovery Channel; Disney Channel; ESPN; Lifetime; Nickelodeon; Showtime; Spike TV; TBS Superstation; The Learning Channel; Trinity Broadcasting Network; Turner Network TV; TV Land; USA Network; WGN America.
Fee: $30.00 installation; $33.80 monthly.
Video-On-Demand: No
Internet Service
Operational: No.
Telephone Service
None
Miles of Plant: 3.0 (coaxial); None (fiber optic).
Executive Vice President: Marty Walch. Manager & Chief Technician: Todd Anderson.
Ownership: New Century Communications (MSO).

MARSHFIELD—Charter Communications, 853 McIntosh St, Wausau, WI 54402. Phones: 715-845-4223; 715-842-3910. Fax: 715-848-0081. Web Site: http://www.charter.com. Also serves Cameron (town), Lincoln (town) & McMillan (town). ICA: WI0030.
TV Market Ranking: Below 100 (Cameron (town), MARSHFIELD, McMillan (town)); Outside TV Markets (Lincoln). Franchise award date: N.A. Franchise expiration date: N.A. Began: April 1, 1963.
Channel capacity: N.A. Channels available but not in use: N.A.
Basic Service
Subscribers: 6,400.
Programming (received off-air): WAOW (ABC, CW) Wausau; WEAU-TV (NBC) Eau Claire; WFXS-DT (FOX) Wittenberg; WHRM-TV (PBS) Wausau; WJFW-TV (NBC) Rhinelander; WKBT-DT (CBS, MNT) La Crosse; WSAW-TV (CBS, MNT) Wausau; 5 FMs.
Programming (via satellite): C-SPAN; C-SPAN 2; QVC; WGN America.
Fee: $29.95 installation; $1.50 converter.
Expanded Basic Service 1
Subscribers: 5,569.
Programming (via satellite): A&E Networks; ABC Family Channel; AMC; Animal Planet; Bravo; Cartoon Network; CNBC; CNN; Comedy Central; Country Music TV; Discovery Channel; Discovery Fit & Health; Disney Channel; E! Entertainment Television; ESPN; ESPN 2; ESPN Classic Sports; Eternal Word TV Network; Food Network; Fox News Channel; Fox Sports Net North; FX; G4; Golf Channel; Great American Country; GSN; Hallmark Channel; Headline News; HGTV; History Channel; INSP; ION Television; Lifetime; MSNBC; MTV; National Geographic Channel; Nickelodeon; Outdoor Channel; Oxygen; Product Information Network; ShopNBC; SoapNet; Speed; Spike TV; Style Network; Syfy; TBS Superstation; The Learning Channel; The Weather Channel; Toon Disney; Travel Channel; truTV; Turner Classic Movies; Turner Network TV; TV Guide Network; TV Land; USA Network; Versus; VH1; WE tv.
Fee: $47.99 monthly.
Digital Basic Service
Subscribers: N.A.
Programming (via satellite): BBC America; Bio; Discovery Digital Networks; DIY Network; ESPN; Fox College Sports Atlantic; Fox College Sports Central; Fox College Sports Pacific; Fox Soccer; Fuel TV; Fuse; GAS; HDNet; HDNet Movies; History Channel International; Lifetime Movie Network; MTV Networks Digital Suite; Music Choice; NFL Network; Nick Jr.; Nick Too; NickToons TV; Sundance Channel; TV Guide Interactive Inc.
Digital Pay Service 1
Pay Units: N.A.
Programming (via satellite): Cinemax (multiplexed); Encore (multiplexed); Flix; HBO (multiplexed); HBO HD; Showtime (multiplexed); Showtime HD; Starz (multiplexed); The Movie Channel (multiplexed).
Video-On-Demand: Yes
Pay-Per-View
iN DEMAND (delivered digitally); NASCAR In Car (delivered digitally); NHL Center Ice (delivered digitally); MLB Extra Innings (delivered digitally); Playboy TV (delivered digitally); Fresh (delivered digitally); Shorteez (delivered digitally).
Internet Service
Operational: Yes.
Broadband Service: Charter Pipeline.
Fee: $29.99 monthly; $3.95 modem lease.
Telephone Service
Digital: Operational
Fee: $29.99 monthly
Miles of Plant: 74.0 (coaxial); None (fiber optic). Additional miles planned: 8.0 (coaxial).
Vice President & General Manager: Lisa Washa. Chief Technician: Bruce Wasleske. Marketing Director: Traci Loonstra.
Ownership: Charter Communications Inc. (MSO).

MAUSTON—Mediacom, 4010 Alexandra Dr, Waterloo, IA 50702. Phone: 319-235-2197. Fax: 319-232-7841. Web Site: http://www.mediacomcable.com. Also serves Camp Douglas, Germantown, Hustler, Juneau County (unincorporated areas), Necedah & New Lisbon. ICA: WI0084.
TV Market Ranking: Outside TV Markets (Camp Douglas, Germantown, Hustler, Juneau County (unincorporated areas), MAUSTON, Necedah, New Lisbon). Franchise award date: N.A. Franchise expiration date: N.A. Began: April 1, 1977.
Channel capacity: N.A. Channels available but not in use: N.A.
Basic Service
Subscribers: 2,653.
Programming (received off-air): WEAU-TV (NBC) Eau Claire; WHLA-TV (PBS) La Crosse; WISC-TV (CBS, MNT) Madison; WKBT-DT (CBS, MNT) La Crosse; WKOW (ABC) Madison; WMSN-TV (FOX) Madison; WMTV-TV (NBC) Madison; allband FM.
Programming (via satellite): C-SPAN; C-SPAN 2; Eternal Word TV Network; Paxson Communications Corp.; QVC; Trinity Broadcasting Network; TV Guide Network; WGN America.
Fee: $35.16 installation; $9.59 monthly; $1.58 converter.
Expanded Basic Service 1
Subscribers: 2,542.
Programming (via satellite): A&E Networks; ABC Family Channel; AMC; AmericanLife TV Network; Animal Planet; Bravo; Cartoon Network; CNBC; CNN; Comedy Central; Country Music TV; Discovery Channel; Disney Channel; E! Entertainment Television; ESPN; ESPN 2; Food Network; Fox Movie Channel; Fox News Channel; Fox Sports Net; FX; Hallmark Channel; Headline News; HGTV; History Channel; INSP; Lifetime; MSNBC; MTV; Nickelodeon; RFD-TV; Speed; Spike TV; Syfy; TBS Superstation; The Learning Channel; The Weather Channel; Travel Channel; truTV; Turner Network TV; TV Land; USA Network; Versus; VH1.
Fee: $14.91 monthly.
Digital Basic Service
Subscribers: N.A.
Programming (via satellite): BBC America; Bio; Bloomberg Television; cloo; ESPN; ESPN 2; ESPNews; Fox Soccer; Fuse; G4; GAS; Golf Channel; GSN; Halogen Network; HD Theater; HDNet; HDNet Movies; History Channel International; Independent

Film Channel; Lifetime Movie Network; Lime; MTV; Music Choice; National Geographic Channel; Nick Jr.; NickToons TV; Outdoor Channel; Style Network; Turner Classic Movies; TVG Network; Universal HD.

Digital Pay Service 1

Pay Units: N.A.

Programming (via satellite): Cinemax (multiplexed); Encore (multiplexed); Flix (multiplexed); HBO (multiplexed); HBO HD; Showtime (multiplexed); Showtime HD; Starz (multiplexed); Starz HDTV; Sundance Channel (multiplexed); The Movie Channel (multiplexed); The Movie Channel HD.

Video-On-Demand: No

Pay-Per-View

ESPN (delivered digitally); Fresh (delivered digitally); Shorteez (delivered digitally); Playboy TV (delivered digitally); Pleasure (delivered digitally); Ten Clips (delivered digitally).

Internet Service

Operational: Yes.

Broadband Service: Mediacom High Speed Internet.

Fee: $99.00 installation; $40.00 monthly.

Telephone Service

None

Miles of Plant: 55.0 (coaxial); None (fiber optic).

Regional Vice President: Doug Frank. General Manager: Doug Nix. Technical Operations Director: Greg Nank. Marketing Director: Steve Schuh. Marketing Coordinator: Joni Lindauer.

Ownership: Mediacom LLC (MSO).

MAZOMANIE—Charter Communications, 2701 Daniels St, Madison, WI 53718. Phone: 608-274-3822. Fax: 608-274-1436. Web Site: http://www.charter.com. Also serves Arena (town), Arlington, Baraboo, Barneveld, Black Earth, Blue Mounds, Cobb, Columbia County, Dane, Dekorra (town), Dodgeville, Dunn (town), Edmund, Fitchburg, Gotham, Greenfield (town), Highland, Lake Delton, Linden, Livingston, Lodi, Lone Rock, Mineral Point, Monfort, Mount Horeb, North Freedom, Plain, Portage, Poynette, Prairie du Sac, Reedsburg, Richland Center, Ridgeway, Rock Springs, Roxbury, Sauk City, Sextonville, Spring Green, Springfield (town), Verona, Vienna (town), Waunakee, West Baraboo, West Point (town), Westport (town) & Wisconsin Dells. ICA: WI0116.

TV Market Ranking: 93 (Arena (town), Arlington, Baraboo, Barneveld, Black Earth, Blue Mounds, Columbia County, Dane, Dekorra (town), Dunn (town), Fitchburg, Lodi, MAZOMANIE, Mount Horeb, Plain, Portage, Poynette, Prairie du Sac, Ridgeway, Roxbury, Sauk City, Spring Green, Springfield (town), Verona, Verona (town), Vienna (town), Waunakee, West Baraboo, West Point (town), Westport (town)); Below 100 (Livingston, Monfort); Outside TV Markets (Cobb, Dodgeville, Edmund, Gotham, Greenfield (town), Highland, Lake Delton, Linden, Lone Rock, Mineral Point, North Freedom, Reedsburg, Richland Center, Rock Springs, Sextonville, Wisconsin Dells). Franchise award date: N.A. Franchise expiration date: N.A. Began: January 1, 1983.

Channel capacity: N.A. Channels available but not in use: N.A.

Basic Service

Subscribers: 32,823.

Programming (received off-air): WBUW (CW) Janesville; WHA-TV (PBS) Madison; WISC-TV (CBS, MNT) Madison; WKOW (ABC) Madison; WMSN-TV (FOX) Madison; WMTV-TV (NBC) Madison.

Programming (via satellite): C-SPAN; C-SPAN 2; GRTV Network; QVC; TV Guide Network; WGN America.

Fee: $13.95 monthly.

Expanded Basic Service 1

Subscribers: 28,743.

Programming (via satellite): A&E Networks; ABC Family Channel; AMC; Animal Planet; BET Networks; Bravo; Cartoon Network; CNBC; CNN; Comedy Central; Country Music TV; Discovery Channel; Disney Channel; E! Entertainment Television; ESPN; ESPN 2; ESPN Classic Sports; Eternal Word TV Network; Food Network; Fox News Channel; Fox Sports Net North; FX; G4; Golf Channel; GSN; Hallmark Channel; Headline News; HGTV; History Channel; INSP; Lifetime; MSNBC; MTV; National Geographic Channel; Nickelodeon; Oxygen; SoapNet; Speed; Spike TV; Syfy; TBS Superstation; The Learning Channel; The Weather Channel; Toon Disney; Travel Channel; truTV; Turner Classic Movies; Turner Network TV; TV Land; Univision Studios; USA Network; Versus; VH1; WE tv.

Fee: $28.40 monthly.

Digital Basic Service

Subscribers: 6,590.

Programming (via satellite): BBC America; Bio; Discovery Digital Networks; DIY Network; ESPNews; Fox Sports World; GAS; History Channel International; Independent Film Channel; Lifetime Movie Network; MTV Networks Digital Suite; Music Choice; Nick Jr.; Nick Too; Outdoor Channel; Sundance Channel.

Digital Pay Service 1

Pay Units: 8,531.

Programming (via satellite): Cinemax (multiplexed).

Fee: $12.95 monthly.

Digital Pay Service 2

Pay Units: 9,322.

Programming (via satellite): HBO (multiplexed).

Fee: $12.95 monthly.

Digital Pay Service 3

Pay Units: 9,521.

Programming (via satellite): Showtime (multiplexed).

Fee: $12.95 monthly.

Digital Pay Service 4

Pay Units: 6,531.

Programming (via satellite): Flix; The Movie Channel (multiplexed).

Fee: $12.95 monthly.

Digital Pay Service 5

Pay Units: 8,530.

Programming (via satellite): Encore (multiplexed); Starz (multiplexed).

Fee: $12.95 monthly.

Video-On-Demand: Yes

Pay-Per-View

Addressable homes: 6,590.

iN DEMAND (delivered digitally); Playboy TV (delivered digitally); Fresh (delivered digitally); Shorteez (delivered digitally).

Internet Service

Operational: Yes.

Broadband Service: Charter Pipeline.

Fee: $39.99 monthly.

Telephone Service

Digital: Operational

Miles of Plant: 699.0 (coaxial); None (fiber optic).

Vice President & General Manager: Lisa Washa. Engineering Director: Tim Sandersen. Technical Operations Director: Bruce Hummel. Marketing Director: Traci Loonstra.

Ownership: Charter Communications Inc. (MSO).

MEDFORD—Charter Communications, 853 McIntosh St, Wausau, WI 54402. Phones: 715-845-4223; 715-842-3910. Fax: 715-848-0081. Web Site: http://www.charter.com. ICA: WI0074.

TV Market Ranking: Outside TV Markets (MEDFORD). Franchise award date: July 7, 1981. Franchise expiration date: N.A. Began: July 1, 1982.

Channel capacity: N.A. Channels available but not in use: N.A.

Basic Service

Subscribers: 1,600.

Programming (received off-air): WAOW (ABC, CW) Wausau; WEAU-TV (NBC) Eau Claire; WFXS-DT (FOX) Wittenberg; WHRM-TV (PBS) Wausau; WJFW-TV (NBC) Rhinelander; WSAW-TV (CBS, MNT) Wausau.

Programming (via satellite): C-SPAN; C-SPAN 2; QVC; WGN America.

Fee: $29.95 installation.

Expanded Basic Service 1

Subscribers: N.A.

Programming (via satellite): A&E Networks; ABC Family Channel; AMC; Animal Planet; Bravo; Cartoon Network; CNBC; CNN; Comedy Central; Country Music TV; Discovery Channel; Discovery Fit & Health; Disney Channel; E! Entertainment Television; ESPN; ESPN 2; ESPN Classic Sports; Eternal Word TV Network; Food Network; Fox News Channel; Fox Sports Net North; FX; G4; Golf Channel; Great American Country; GSN; Hallmark Channel; Headline News; HGTV; History Channel; INSP; ION Television; Lifetime; MSNBC; MTV; National Geographic Channel; Nickelodeon; Outdoor Channel; Oxygen; Product Information Network; ShopNBC; SoapNet; Speed; Spike TV; Style Network; Syfy; TBS Superstation; The Learning Channel; The Weather Channel; Toon Disney; Travel Channel; truTV; Turner Classic Movies; Turner Network TV; TV Guide Network; TV Land; USA Network; Versus; VH1; WE tv.

Fee: $47.99 monthly.

Digital Basic Service

Subscribers: N.A.

Programming (via satellite): BBC America; Bio; Discovery Digital Networks; DIY Network; ESPN; Fox College Sports Atlantic; Fox College Sports Central; Fox College Sports Pacific; Fox Soccer; Fuel TV; Fuse; GAS; HDNet; HDNet Movies; History Channel International; Lifetime Movie Network; MTV Networks Digital Suite; Music Choice; NFL Network; Nick Jr.; Nick Too; NickToons TV; Sundance Channel; TV Guide Interactive Inc.

Digital Pay Service 1

Pay Units: N.A.

Programming (via satellite): Cinemax (multiplexed); Encore (multiplexed); Flix; HBO (multiplexed); HBO HD; Showtime (multiplexed); Showtime HD; Starz (multiplexed); The Movie Channel (multiplexed).

Video-On-Demand: Yes

Pay-Per-View

iN DEMAND (delivered digitally); NASCAR In Car (delivered digitally); NHL Center Ice (delivered digitally); MLB Extra Innings (delivered digitally); Playboy TV (delivered digitally); Fresh (delivered digitally); Shorteez (delivered digitally).

Internet Service

Operational: Yes.

Broadband Service: Charter Pipeline.

Fee: $39.99 monthly.

Telephone Service

None

Miles of Plant: 29.0 (coaxial); None (fiber optic).

Vice President & General Manager: Lisa Washa. Chief Technician: Bruce Wasleske. Marketing Director: Traci Loonstra.

Ownership: Charter Communications Inc. (MSO).

MELLEN—Packerland Broadband, 105 Kent St, PO Box 885, Iron Mountain, MI 49801. Phones: 800-236-8434; 906-774-6621. Fax: 906-776-2811. Web Site: http://www.packerlandbroadband.com. ICA: WI0165.

TV Market Ranking: Outside TV Markets (MELLEN). Franchise award date: March 1, 1978. Franchise expiration date: January 1, 2012. Began: March 1, 1979.

Channel capacity: 50 (not 2-way capable). Channels available but not in use: N.A.

Basic Service

Subscribers: 227.

Programming (received off-air): KBJR-TV (MNT, NBC) Superior; KDLH (CBS, CW) Duluth; WDIO-DT (ABC) Duluth; WJFW-TV (NBC) Rhinelander; WLEF-TV (PBS) Park Falls.

Programming (via satellite): A&E Networks; ABC Family Channel; CNN; Comedy Central; Discovery Channel; ESPN; History Channel; Lifetime; MTV; Nickelodeon; Spike TV; Syfy; TBS Superstation; The Learning Channel; The Weather Channel; Turner Network TV; TV Land; USA Network; VH1; WGN America.

Fee: $32.95 monthly.

Pay Service 1

Pay Units: 67.

Programming (via satellite): Flix; Showtime.

Fee: $9.95 monthly.

Video-On-Demand: No

Internet Service

Operational: No.

Telephone Service

None

Miles of Plant: 42.0 (coaxial); None (fiber optic).

General Manager: Dan Plante. Technical Supervisor: Chad Kay.

Ownership: Cable Constructors Inc. (MSO).

MELROSE—Charter Communications. Now served by ONALASKA, WI [WI0024]. ICA: WI0202.

MELVINA—Formerly served by Midwest Cable Inc. No longer in operation. ICA: WI0231.

MENOMONEE FALLS—Time Warner Cable. Now served by MILWAUKEE, WI [WI0001]. ICA: WI0027.

MENOMONIE—Charter Communications, 1201 McCann Dr, Altoona, WI 54720-2561. Phone: 715-831-8940. Fax: 715-831-5862. Web Site: http://www.charter.com. Also serves Colfax, Downsville, Menomonie (town), Red Cedar (town), Tainter (town) & Wheeler. ICA: WI0033.

TV Market Ranking: Below 100 (Colfax, Downsville, MENOMONEE, Menomonie (town), Red Cedar (town), Tainter (town), Wheeler). Franchise award date: August 31, 1992. Franchise expiration date: N.A. Began: May 1, 1962.

Channel capacity: N.A. Channels available but not in use: N.A.

Basic Service
Subscribers: 4,880.
Programming (received off-air): KARE (NBC) Minneapolis; KMSP-TV (FOX) Minneapolis; KSTP-TV (ABC) St. Paul; KTCA-TV (PBS) St. Paul; WCCO-TV (CBS) Minneapolis; WEAU-TV (NBC) Eau Claire; WEUX (FOX) Chippewa Falls; WHWC-TV (PBS) Menomonie; WKBT-DT (CBS, MNT) La Crosse; WQOW (ABC, CW) Eau Claire.
Programming (via satellite): C-SPAN; WGN America.
Fee: $50.00 installation; $12.00 monthly.

Expanded Basic Service 1
Subscribers: 4,271.
Programming (via satellite): A&E Networks; ABC Family Channel; AMC; Animal Planet; Bravo; Cartoon Network; CNBC; CNN; Comedy Central; Country Music TV; C-SPAN 2; Discovery Channel; Discovery Health Channel; Disney Channel; E! Entertainment Television; ESPN; ESPN 2; Eternal Word TV Network; Food Network; Fox News Channel; Fox Sports Net North; FX; G4; Golf Channel; GSN; Headline News; HGTV; History Channel; Lifetime; MSNBC; MTV; National Geographic Channel; Nickelodeon; Outdoor Channel; Oxygen; QVC; SoapNet; Speed; Spike TV; Syfy; TBS Superstation; The Learning Channel; The Weather Channel; Toon Disney; Travel Channel; Trinity Broadcasting Network; truTV; Turner Network TV; TV Land; USA Network; Versus; VH1.
Fee: $31.95 monthly.

Digital Basic Service
Subscribers: 490.
Programming (via satellite): BBC America; Bio; Discovery Digital Networks; DIY Network; Fuse; GAS; History Channel International; Lifetime Movie Network; MTV Networks Digital Suite; Music Choice; Nick Jr.; Nick Too; Sundance Channel.
Fee: $7.00 monthly.

Digital Pay Service 1
Pay Units: 2,449.
Programming (via satellite): Cinemax (multiplexed); Encore (multiplexed); Flix; HBO (multiplexed); Showtime (multiplexed); Starz (multiplexed); The Movie Channel (multiplexed).
Fee: $10.00 monthly (Cinemax, HBO, Showtime, Flix/TMC, or Starz/Encore).

Video-On-Demand: Yes

Pay-Per-View
Addressable homes: 490.
Sports PPV (delivered digitally); Shorteez (delivered digitally); Fresh (delivered digitally); Playboy TV (delivered digitally); iN DEMAND (delivered digitally).

Internet Service
Operational: Yes.
Broadband Service: Charter Pipeline.
Fee: $29.99 monthly; $4.95 modem lease.

Telephone Service
Digital: Operational
Fee: $29.99 monthly

Miles of Plant: 108.0 (coaxial); None (fiber optic).
Vice President & General Manager: Lisa Washa. Operations Manager: Shirley Weibel. Engineering Director: Tim Normand. Marketing Director: Traci Loonstra. Sales & Marketing Manager: Chris Putzkey. Government Relations Manager: Mike Hill.
Ownership: Charter Communications Inc. (MSO).

MEQUON—Time Warner Cable. Now served by MILWAUKEE, WI [WI0001]. ICA: WI0041.

MERCER—Karban TV Systems Inc., 120 S Church St, PO Box 8, Bonduel, WI 54107-0008. Phones: 715-550-7613; 800-236-0233. Fax: 715-277-2339. E-mail: sales@ktvs.net. Web Site: http://www.ktvs.net. ICA: WI0264.
TV Market Ranking: Outside TV Markets (MERCER). Franchise award date: N.A. Franchise expiration date: N.A. Began: March 1, 1988.
Channel capacity: 77 (not 2-way capable). Channels available but not in use: N.A.

Basic Service
Subscribers: 216.
Programming (received off-air): WFXS-DT (FOX) Wittenberg; WJFW-TV (NBC) Rhinelander; WLEF-TV (PBS) Park Falls; WSAW-TV (CBS, MNT) Wausau; WYOW (ABC, CW) Eagle River.
Programming (via satellite): A&E Networks; ABC Family Channel; AMC; Animal Planet; CNBC; CNN; Comedy Central; Country Music TV; C-SPAN; CW+; Discovery Channel; Disney Channel; ESPN; ESPN 2; Eternal Word TV Network; Food Network; Fox News Channel; FX; Headline News; HGTV; History Channel; Lifetime; MSNBC; NFL Network; Nickelodeon; Outdoor Channel; QVC; Speed; Spike TV; Syfy; TBS Superstation; The Learning Channel; The Weather Channel; Travel Channel; Trinity Broadcasting Network; Turner Classic Movies; Turner Network TV; TV Land; USA Network; VH1; WGN America.
Fee: $75.00 installation; $40.00 monthly; $20.00 additional installation.

Pay Service 1
Pay Units: 25.
Programming (via satellite): Cinemax.
Fee: $10.00 monthly.

Pay Service 2
Pay Units: 36.
Programming (via satellite): HBO.
Fee: $10.00 monthly.

Video-On-Demand: No

Internet Service
Operational: No.

Telephone Service
None

Miles of Plant: 16.0 (coaxial); None (fiber optic).
Manager & Chief Technician: John Karban.
Ownership: Karban TV Systems Inc. (MSO).

MERRILL—Charter Communications, 853 McIntosh St, Wausau, WI 54402. Phones: 715-842-3910; 715-845-4223. Fax: 715-848-0081. Web Site: http://www.charter.com. ICA: WI0054.
TV Market Ranking: Below 100 (MERRILL). Franchise award date: N.A. Franchise expiration date: N.A. Began: February 1, 1964.
Channel capacity: 78 (operating 2-way). Channels available but not in use: N.A.

Basic Service
Subscribers: 3,400.
Programming (received off-air): WAOW (ABC, CW) Wausau; WFXS-DT (FOX) Wittenberg; WHRM-TV (PBS) Wausau; WJFW-TV (NBC) Rhinelander; WSAW-TV (CBS, MNT) Wausau; 5 FMs.
Programming (via satellite): C-SPAN; C-SPAN 2; QVC; WGN America.
Fee: $29.99 installation.

Expanded Basic Service 1
Subscribers: 2,667.
Programming (via satellite): A&E Networks; ABC Family Channel; AMC; Animal Planet; Bravo; Cartoon Network; CNBC; CNN; Comedy Central; Country Music TV; Discovery Channel; Discovery Fit & Health; Disney Channel; E! Entertainment Television; ESPN; ESPN 2; ESPN Classic Sports; Eternal Word TV Network; Food Network; Fox News Channel; Fox Sports Net North; FX; G4; Golf Channel; Great American Country; GSN; Hallmark Channel; Headline News; HGTV; History Channel; INSP; ION Television; Lifetime; MSNBC; MTV; National Geographic Channel; Nickelodeon; Outdoor Channel; Oxygen; Product Information Network; ShopNBC; SoapNet; Speed; Spike TV; Style Network; Syfy; TBS Superstation; The Learning Channel; The Weather Channel; Toon Disney; Travel Channel; truTV; Turner Classic Movies; Turner Network TV; TV Guide Network; TV Land; USA Network; Versus; VH1; WE tv.
Fee: $47.99 monthly.

Digital Basic Service
Subscribers: N.A.
Programming (via satellite): BBC America; Bio; Discovery Digital Networks; DIY Network; ESPN; Fox College Sports Atlantic; Fox College Sports Central; Fox College Sports Pacific; Fox Soccer; Fuel TV; Fuse; HDNet; HDNet Movies; History Channel International; Lifetime Movie Network; MTV Networks Digital Suite; Music Choice; NFL Network; Nick Jr.; Nick Too; NickToons TV; Sundance Channel; TeenNick; TV Guide Interactive Inc.

Digital Pay Service 1
Pay Units: N.A.
Programming (via satellite): Cinemax (multiplexed); Encore (multiplexed); Flix; HBO (multiplexed); HBO HD; Showtime (multiplexed); Showtime HD; Starz (multiplexed); The Movie Channel.

Video-On-Demand: Yes

Pay-Per-View
iN DEMAND (delivered digitally); NASCAR In Car (delivered digitally); NHL Center Ice (delivered digitally); MLB Extra Innings (delivered digitally); Playboy TV (delivered digitally); Fresh (delivered digitally); Shorteez (delivered digitally).

Internet Service
Operational: Yes.
Broadband Service: Charter Pipeline.
Fee: $39.99 monthly.

Telephone Service
Digital: Operational
Fee: $29.99 monthly

Miles of Plant: 37.0 (coaxial); None (fiber optic). Additional miles planned: 9.0 (coaxial).
Vice President: Lisa Washa. Chief Technician: Bruce Wasleske. Marketing Director: Traci Loonstra.
Ownership: Charter Communications Inc. (MSO).

MERRIMAC—Merrimac Cable, 327 Palisade St, PO Box 40, Merrimac, WI 53561. Phone: 608-493-9470. Fax: 608-493-9902. E-mail: office@merr.com. Web Site: http://www.merr.com. Also serves Bluffview Mobile Home Park, Budnick Park, Caledonia (town), Merrimac (town) & Sumpter (town). ICA: WI0154.
TV Market Ranking: 93 (Caledonia (town), MERRIMAC, Merrimac (town)); Outside TV Markets (Bluffview Mobile Home Park, Budnick Park). Franchise award date: March 1, 1984. Franchise expiration date: N.A. Began: October 1, 1984.
Channel capacity: N.A. Channels available but not in use: N.A.

Basic Service
Subscribers: 549.
Programming (received off-air): WBUW (CW) Janesville; WCWF (CW) Suring; WHA-TV (PBS) Madison; WISC-TV (CBS, MNT) Madison; WKOW (ABC) Madison; WMSN-TV (FOX) Madison; WMTV-TV (NBC) Madison; 5 FMs.
Programming (via satellite): C-SPAN; C-SPAN 2; QVC; TV Guide Network; WGN America.
Fee: $25.00 installation; $19.95 monthly.

Expanded Basic Service 1
Subscribers: N.A.
Programming (via satellite): A&E Networks; ABC Family Channel; AMC; Animal Planet; Bravo; Cartoon Network; Classic Arts Showcase; CNBC; CNN; Comedy Central; Country Music TV; Discovery Channel; Disney Channel; DIY Network; E! Entertainment Television; ESPN; ESPN 2; ESPN Classic Sports; ESPN U; ESPNews; Eternal Word TV Network; Food Network; Fox News Channel; Fox Sports Net North; FX; Hallmark Channel; Headline News; HGTV; History Channel; INSP; Jewelry Television; Lifetime; MSNBC; MTV; NASA TV; National Geographic Channel; Nickelodeon; ShopNBC; Speed; Spike TV; Syfy; TBS Superstation; The Learning Channel; The Weather Channel; Travel Channel; Trinity Broadcasting Network; truTV; Turner Classic Movies; Turner Network TV; TV Land; USA Network; Versus; VH1; WE tv; WealthTV.
Fee: $20.00 monthly.

Digital Basic Service
Subscribers: 100.
Programming (via satellite): A&E HD; BBC America; Bio; Bloomberg Television; cloo; CMT Pure Country; Cooking Channel; Discovery Fit & Health; Discovery Health Channel; Discovery Kids Channel; DMX Music; ESPN 2 HD; ESPN HD; Food Network HD; Fox Business Channel; Fox Movie Channel; Fox Soccer; Fuse; G4; Golf Channel; GSN; HD Theater; HDNet; HDNet Movies; HGTV HD; History Channel International; ID Investigation Discovery; Independent Film Channel; Military Channel; MTV Hits; MTV2; National Geographic Channel HD Network; Nick Jr.; NickToons TV; Outdoor Channel; Planet Green; RFD-TV; Science; SoapNet; Style Network; Sundance Channel; TeenNick; Toon Disney; Universal HD; VH1 Classic; VH1 Soul.
Fee: $2.45 monthly (Sports), $2.95 monthly (Movies), $7.95 monthly (Family or HD Basic).

Digital Pay Service 1
Pay Units: N.A.
Programming (via satellite): Cinemax (multiplexed); Cinemax HD; Encore (multiplexed); Flix; HBO (multiplexed); HBO HD; Playboy TV; Showtime (multiplexed); Showtime HD; Starz (multiplexed); Starz HDTV; The Movie Channel (multiplexed).

Fee: $9.95 monthly (Playboy or Cinemax), $13.95 monthly (Showtime/TMC/Flix or Starz/Encore), $14.95 monthly (HBO).
Video-On-Demand: No

Pay-Per-View
Addressable homes: 14.
iN DEMAND (delivered digitally); Playboy TV (delivered digitally).

Internet Service
Operational: Yes, Dial-up.

Telephone Service
Analog: Not Operational
Digital: Operational
Fee: $14.99-$24.99 monthly
Miles of Plant: 35.0 (coaxial); 15.0 (fiber optic).
President: Bartlett Olson. Chief Financial Officer: Jean Buelow. Office Manager: Michelle Hopp.
Ownership: Merrimac Communications Ltd.

MIKANA—S & K TV Systems, 508 Miner Ave W, Ladysmith, WI 54848. Phones: 800-924-7880; 715-532-7321. Fax: 715-532-7583. E-mail: techsupport@skcable.com. Web Site: http://www.skcable.com. Also serves Birchwood & Edgewater. ICA: WI0265.
TV Market Ranking: Outside TV Markets (Birchwood, Edgewater, MIKANA). Franchise award date: January 1, 1989. Franchise expiration date: N.A. Began: November 1, 1989.
Channel capacity: 40 (not 2-way capable). Channels available but not in use: N.A.

Basic Service
Subscribers: 736.
Programming (received off-air): KQDS-TV (FOX) Duluth; WCCO-TV (CBS) Minneapolis; WEAU-TV (NBC) Eau Claire; WEUX (FOX) Chippewa Falls; WHWC-TV (PBS) Menomonie; WQOW (ABC, CW) Eau Claire.
Programming (via satellite): A&E Networks; ABC Family Channel; AMC; Animal Planet; CNN; Country Music TV; Discovery Channel; Disney Channel; ESPN; ESPN 2; Great American Country; Hallmark Channel; Headline News; HGTV; History Channel; Lifetime; MTV; Nickelodeon; Outdoor Channel; QVC; Spike TV; Syfy; TBS Superstation; The Learning Channel; The Weather Channel; Turner Classic Movies; Turner Network TV; TV Land; USA Network; VH1; WGN America.
Fee: $30.00 installation; $35.95 monthly.

Digital Basic Service
Subscribers: 48.
Programming (via satellite): BBC America; Bio; Bloomberg Television; CMT Pure Country; Discovery Fit & Health; Discovery Health Channel; Discovery Kids Channel; ESPN 2; ESPN Classic Sports; ESPNews; Fox Movie Channel; Fox Soccer; Fuse; G4; Golf Channel; GSN; Halogen Network; HGTV; History Channel; History Channel International; ID Investigation Discovery; Lifetime Movie Network; Military Channel; MTV2; Nick Jr.; NickToons TV; Outdoor Channel; Science; Speed; Style Network; Syfy; TeenNick; Trinity Broadcasting Network; Turner Classic Movies; Versus; VH1 Classic.
Fee: $15.35 monthly.

Pay Service 1
Pay Units: 21.
Programming (via satellite): Cinemax.
Fee: $7.95 monthly.

Pay Service 2
Pay Units: 12.
Programming (via satellite): HBO.
Fee: $10.95 monthly.

Digital Pay Service 1
Pay Units: N.A.
Programming (via satellite): Cinemax (multiplexed); Encore (multiplexed); HBO (multiplexed); Showtime (multiplexed); Starz (multiplexed); The Movie Channel (multiplexed).
Video-On-Demand: No

Internet Service
Operational: Yes.
Fee: $30.00 installation; $24.95 monthly.

Telephone Service
None
Miles of Plant: 12.0 (coaxial); None (fiber optic).
Manager: Randy Scott. Office Manager: Dave Scott.
Ownership: S & K TV Systems Inc. (MSO).

MILLADORE (town)—New Century Communications, 3588 Kennebec Dr, Eagan, MN 55122-1001. Phone: 651-688-2623. Fax: 651-688-2624. E-mail: info@ourcableia.com. ICA: WI0221.
TV Market Ranking: Below 100 (MILLADORE (TOWN)). Franchise award date: N.A. Franchise expiration date: N.A. Began: N.A.
Channel capacity: 40 (not 2-way capable). Channels available but not in use: N.A.

Basic Service
Subscribers: 14.
Programming (received off-air): WAOW (ABC, CW) Wausau; WEAU-TV (NBC) Eau Claire; WFXS-DT (FOX) Wittenberg; WHRM-TV (PBS) Wausau; WSAW-TV (CBS, MNT) Wausau.
Programming (via satellite): A&E Networks; ABC Family Channel; AMC; CNN; Discovery Channel; ESPN; Lifetime; Nickelodeon; Showtime; Spike TV; TBS Superstation; The Learning Channel; Trinity Broadcasting Network; Turner Network TV; TV Land; USA Network; WGN America.
Fee: $30.00 installation; $32.25 monthly.
Video-On-Demand: No

Internet Service
Operational: No.

Telephone Service
None
Miles of Plant: 3.0 (coaxial); None (fiber optic).
Executive Vice President: Marty Walch. Manager & Chief Technician: Todd Anderson.
Ownership: New Century Communications (MSO).

MILLTOWN—Lakeland Communications, 825 Innovation Ave, PO Box 40, Milltown, WI 54858. Phones: 715-825-2171; 715-472-2101. Fax: 715-825-4299. E-mail: shawnm@lakeland.ws. Web Site: http://www.lakeland.ws. Also serves Balsam Lake, Centuria, Cushing, Fox Creek, Frederic & Luck. ICA: WI0104.
TV Market Ranking: Outside TV Markets (Balsam Lake, Centuria, Fox Creek, Frederic, Luck, MILLTOWN). Franchise award date: July 15, 1985. Franchise expiration date: N.A. Began: December 1, 1985.
Channel capacity: 134 (operating 2-way). Channels available but not in use: N.A.

Basic Service
Subscribers: 1,090.
Programming (received off-air): KARE (NBC) Minneapolis; KMSP-TV (FOX) Minneapolis; KPXM-TV (ION) St. Cloud; KSTC-TV (IND) Minneapolis; KSTP-TV (ABC) St. Paul; KTCA-TV (PBS) St. Paul; WCCO-TV (CBS) Minneapolis; WEAU-TV (NBC) Eau Claire; WEUX (FOX) Chippewa Falls; WFTC (MNT) Minneapolis; WHWC-TV (PBS) Menomonie; WQOW (ABC, CW) Eau Claire; WUCW (CW) Minneapolis.
Programming (via satellite): A&E Networks; ABC Family Channel; AMC; Animal Planet; CNBC; CNN; Comedy Central; Country Music TV; C-SPAN; Discovery Channel; Disney Channel; DIY Network; E! Entertainment Television; ESPN; ESPN 2; ESPN Classic Sports; Eternal Word TV Network; Food Network; Fox News Channel; Fox Sports Net; Fox Sports Net Minnesota; Hallmark Channel; Headline News; HGTV; History Channel; Lifetime; Lifetime Movie Network; MTV; National Geographic Channel; Nickelodeon; Outdoor Channel; QVC; Spike TV; Syfy; TBS Superstation; The Learning Channel; The Weather Channel; Travel Channel; truTV; Turner Classic Movies; Turner Network TV; TV Guide Network; TV Land; USA Network; VH1; WGN America.
Fee: $39.50 installation; $27.95 monthly; $2.25 converter; $24.95 additional installation.

Pay Service 1
Pay Units: 300.
Programming (via satellite): Cinemax.
Fee: $9.00 monthly.

Pay Service 2
Pay Units: 157.
Programming (via satellite): Showtime.
Fee: $9.00 monthly.

Pay Service 3
Pay Units: 398.
Programming (via satellite): HBO.
Fee: $9.00 monthly.
Video-On-Demand: No

Internet Service
Operational: Yes, Both DSL & dial-up.

Telephone Service
None
Miles of Plant: 57.0 (coaxial); 18.0 (fiber optic).
President: John Klatt. Manager: Shawn McGinnity. Plant Manager: Darrell Otto. Office Manager: Sheri Thorsbakken.
Ownership: Lakeland Communications.

MILWAUKEE—Time Warner Cable, 1320 N Dr Martin Luther King Dr, Milwaukee, WI 53212-4002. Phones: 414-908-4877; 414-277-4032; 414-277-4111. Fax: 414-277-8049. Web Site: http://www.timewarnercable.com. Also serves Ashippun, Bayside, Big Bend, Brookfield, Brown Deer, Burlington, Butler (village), Cascade, Cedarburg, Chenequa, Cudahy, Delafield, Dousman, Dover (town), Eagle, East Troy, Elkhorn, Elm Grove (village), Fox Point, Franklin, Genesee (town), Germantown (village), Glendale, Grafton, Greendale, Greenfield, Hales Corners, Hartland (village), Ixonia, La Grange, Lafayette, Lannon, Lisbon, Lyons, Malibeka, Menomonee Falls, Mequon, Merton (town), Morton (town), Mukwonago, Muskego, Nashota (town), New Berlin, Newburg, North Prairie, Norway, Oak Creek, Oconomowoc (town), Oconomowoc Lake, Ottawa (town), Pewaukee, Port Washington, River Hills, Rochester, Saukville (village), Shorewood, South Milwaukee, St. Francis, Summit (town), Sussex, Theinsville (village), Union Grove, Vernon, Waldo, Waterford, Waukesha, Wauwatosa, West Allis, West Milwaukee (village), Whitefish Bay, Wind Lake & Yorkville. ICA: WI0001.
TV Market Ranking: 23 (Ashippun, Bayside, Big Bend, Brookfield, Brown Deer, Burlington, Butler (village), Cedarburg, Chenequa, Cudahy, Delafield, Dousman, Dover (town), Eagle, East Troy, Elm Grove (village), Fox Point, Franklin, Genesee (town), Germantown (village), Glendale, Grafton, Greendale, Greenfield, Hales Corners, Hartland (village), Ixonia, La Grange, Lafayette, Lannon, Lisbon, Lyons, Menomonee Falls, Mequon, Merton (town), MILWAUKEE, Morton (town), Mukwonago, Muskego, Nashota (town), New Berlin, Newburg, North Prairie, Norway, Oak Creek, Oconomowoc (town), Oconomowoc Lake, Ottawa (town), Pewaukee, Port Washington, River Hills, Rochester, Saukville (village), Shorewood, South Milwaukee, St. Francis, Summit (town), Sussex, Theinsville (village), Union Grove, Vernon, Waterford, Waukesha, Wauwatosa, West Allis, West Milwaukee (village), Whitefish Bay, Wind Lake, Yorkville); Below 100 (Cascade, Elkhorn, Malibeka, Waldo). Franchise award date: June 1, 1983. Franchise expiration date: N.A. Began: December 11, 1984.
Channel capacity: N.A. Channels available but not in use: N.A.

Basic Service
Subscribers: 543,595 Includes Kenosha & Random Lake.
Programming (received off-air): WBME-TV (IND, TMO) Racine; WCGV-TV (MNT) Milwaukee; WDJT-TV (CBS) Milwaukee; WISN-TV (ABC) Milwaukee; WITI (FOX, IND) Milwaukee; WMLW-CA (IND) Milwaukee; WMVS (PBS) Milwaukee; WMVT (PBS) Milwaukee; WPXE-TV (ION) Kenosha; WTMJ-TV (NBC) Milwaukee; WVCY-TV (IND) Milwaukee; WVTV (CW) Milwaukee; WWRS-TV (TBN) Mayville; 5 FMs.
Programming (via satellite): BET Networks; Cartoon Network; CNBC; C-SPAN 2; HGTV; History Channel; Jewelry Television; Lifetime; Lifetime Movie Network; MoviePlex; MSNBC; MTV; National Geographic Channel; Nickelodeon; Oxygen; Product Information Network; QVC; ShopNBC; Spike TV; Style Network; Syfy; TBS Superstation; Telemundo; The Learning Channel; The Weather Channel; TV Guide Network; Versus; VH1; WE tv; WGN America.
Fee: $41.00 installation; $10.20 monthly; $2.82 converter; $25.00 additional installation.

Expanded Basic Service 1
Subscribers: 399,000 Includes Kenosha & Random Lake.
Programming (via satellite): A&E Networks; ABC Family Channel; AMC; Animal Planet; Bravo; CNN; Comedy Central; Discovery Channel; Discovery Health Channel; Disney Channel; E! Entertainment Television; ESPN; ESPN 2; ESPN Classic Sports; Eternal Word TV Network; Food Network; Fox News Channel; Fox Sports World; FX; Golf Channel; Great American Country; Hallmark Channel; Headline News; Travel Channel; truTV; Turner Classic Movies; Turner Network TV; TV Land; Univision Studios; USA Network.
Fee: $19.54 monthly.

Digital Basic Service
Subscribers: 286,000 Includes Kenosha & Random Lake.
Programming (via satellite): America's Store; BBC America; Bio; Bloomberg Television; Boomerang; Canales N; CBS Sports Network; cloo; CNN International; Cooking Channel; Country Music TV; C-SPAN 3; Current; Discovery Fit & Health; Disney Channel; DIY Network; ESPN; ESPNews; Fox Sports Net; Fox Sports World; FSN Digital Atlantic; FSN Digital Central; FSN Digital Pacific; Fuel TV; Fuse; G4; GAS; GSN; HD Theater; HDNet; HDNet Movies; History Channel; INHD (multiplexed); Lifetime Real Women; LWS Local Weather Station; MTV Networks Digital Suite; Music Choice; NBA TV; Nick Jr.; NickToons TV;

Outdoor Channel; SoapNet; Speed; Tennis Channel; The Word Network; Toon Disney; truTV; Turner Network TV HD.
Fee: $3.95 monthly.

Digital Pay Service 1
Pay Units: N.A.
Programming (via satellite): Cinemax; Encore (multiplexed); Flix (multiplexed); Fox Movie Channel; HBO; HBO HD (multiplexed); Independent Film Channel; RAI International; Showtime; Showtime HD (multiplexed); Starz (multiplexed); Sundance Channel; The Movie Channel (multiplexed); TV Asia.

Video-On-Demand: Yes

Pay-Per-View
iN DEMAND (delivered digitally); Shorteez (delivered digitally); Sports PPV (delivered digitally); Playboy TV (delivered digitally); Ten Blox (delivered digitally); Ten Blue (delivered digitally); NBA League Pass (delivered digitally); MLS Direct Kick (delivered digitally); NHL Center Ice (delivered digitally); MLB Extra Innings (delivered digitally).

Internet Service
Operational: Yes.
Subscribers: 289,000.
Broadband Service: Road Runner.
Fee: $79.95 installation; $44.95 monthly.

Telephone Service
Digital: Operational
Subscribers: 125,000.
Fee: $44.95 monthly

Miles of Plant: 15,455.0 (coaxial); None (fiber optic). Miles of plant include Kenosha & Random Lake

President: Tom Adams. Vice President, Operations: Mike Fox. Vice President, Technical Operations: Ralph Newcomb. Vice President, Government Affairs: Celeste Flynn. Vice President, Communications: Marci Pelzer. Vice President, Sales & Marketing: Chuck Parshall.

Ownership: Time Warner Cable (MSO).

MINDORO—Charter Communications. Now served by ONALASKA, WI [WI0024]. ICA: WI0310.

MINOCQUA—Charter Communications, 853 McIntosh St, Wausau, WI 54402. Phones: 715-845-4223; 715-842-3910. Fax: 715-848-0081. Web Site: http://www.charter.com. Also serves Arbor Vitae & Woodruff. ICA: WI0071.

TV Market Ranking: Below 100 (Arbor Vitae, MINOCQUA, Woodruff). Franchise award date: January 1, 1972. Franchise expiration date: N.A. Began: June 1, 1973.

Channel capacity: N.A. Channels available but not in use: N.A.

Basic Service
Subscribers: 2,000.
Programming (received off-air): W02CF Minocqua; W31BA Minocqua; WFXS-DT (FOX) Wittenberg; WJFW-TV (NBC) Rhinelander; WLEF-TV (PBS) Park Falls; WSAW-TV (CBS, MNT) Wausau; WYOW (ABC, CW) Eagle River; allband FM.
Programming (via satellite): C-SPAN; QVC; WGN America.
Fee: $29.95 installation.

Expanded Basic Service 1
Subscribers: N.A.
Programming (via satellite): A&E Networks; ABC Family Channel; AMC; Animal Planet; Bravo; Cartoon Network; CNBC; CNN; Comedy Central; Country Music TV; C-SPAN 2; Discovery Channel; Disney Channel; E! Entertainment Television; ESPN; ESPN 2; ESPN Classic Sports; Eternal Word TV Network; Food Network; Fox News Channel; Fox Sports Net North; FX; G4; Golf Channel; Great American Country; Hallmark Channel; Headline News; HGTV; History Channel; INSP; Lifetime; MSNBC; MTV; National Geographic Channel; Nickelodeon; Outdoor Channel; Oxygen; ShopNBC; SoapNet; Speed; Spike TV; Syfy; TBS Superstation; The Learning Channel; The Weather Channel; Toon Disney; Travel Channel; truTV; Turner Classic Movies; Turner Network TV; TV Guide Network; TV Land; USA Network; Versus; VH1; WE tv.
Fee: $47.99 monthly.

Digital Basic Service
Subscribers: N.A.
Programming (via satellite): AmericanLife TV Network; BBC America; Bio; Bloomberg Television; Discovery Digital Networks; DMX Music; ESPNews; Fox Movie Channel; Fox Soccer; Fuse; GSN; Halogen Network; History Channel International; Independent Film Channel; Lifetime Movie Network; MTV Networks Digital Suite; Nick Jr.; ShopNBC; Style Network; Teen-Nick; Trinity Broadcasting Network; Turner Classic Movies.

Digital Pay Service 1
Pay Units: N.A.
Programming (via satellite): Cinemax (multiplexed); Encore (multiplexed); Flix; HBO (multiplexed); Showtime (multiplexed); Starz (multiplexed); The Movie Channel (multiplexed).

Video-On-Demand: No

Pay-Per-View
iN DEMAND (delivered digitally); ESPN Now (delivered digitally); ESPN (delivered digitally); Hot Choice (delivered digitally); Playboy TV (delivered digitally); Fresh (delivered digitally); Shorteez (delivered digitally).

Internet Service
Operational: Yes.
Broadband Service: Charter Pipeline.
Fee: $39.99 monthly.

Telephone Service
None

Miles of Plant: 80.0 (coaxial); None (fiber optic).

Vice President & General Manager: Lisa Washa. Chief Technician: Bruce Wasleske. Marketing Director: Traci Loonstra.

Ownership: Charter Communications Inc. (MSO).

MINONG—S & K TV Systems, 508 Miner Ave W, Ladysmith, WI 54848. Phones: 800-924-7880; 715-532-7321. Fax: 715-532-7583. E-mail: techsupport@skcable.com. Also serves Trego. ICA: WI0317.

TV Market Ranking: Outside TV Markets (MINONG, Trego). Franchise award date: August 4, 1987. Franchise expiration date: August 4, 2007. Began: N.A.

Channel capacity: 36 (not 2-way capable). Channels available but not in use: N.A.

Basic Service
Subscribers: 175.
Programming (received off-air): KBJR-TV (MNT, NBC) Superior; KDLH (CBS, CW) Duluth; KQDS-TV (FOX) Duluth; KSTP-TV (ABC) St. Paul; WDIO-DT (ABC) Duluth; WDSE (PBS) Duluth.
Programming (via satellite): A&E Networks; ABC Family Channel; AMC; AmericanLife TV Network; Animal Planet; CNN; Country Music TV; Discovery Channel; Disney Channel; ESPN; ESPN 2; Hallmark Channel; Headline News; HGTV; History Channel; Lifetime; MTV; Nickelodeon; Outdoor Channel; Spike TV; Syfy; TBS Superstation; The Learning Channel; The Weather Channel; Turner Classic Movies; Turner Network TV; TV Land; USA Network; VH1; WGN America.
Fee: $40.00 installation; $35.95 monthly; $25.00 additional installation.

Digital Basic Service
Subscribers: 17.
Programming (via satellite): BBC America; Bio; Bloomberg Television; Discovery Fit & Health; DMX Music; ESPN 2; ESPNews; Fox Movie Channel; Fox Sports World; Fuse; G4; GAS; Golf Channel; GSN; Halogen Network; HGTV; History Channel; History Channel International; Lifetime Movie Network; MTV Networks Digital Suite; Nick Jr.; NickToons TV; Outdoor Channel; Speed; Syfy; Toon Disney; Trinity Broadcasting Network; Turner Classic Movies; Versus.
Fee: $14.90 monthly.

Pay Service 1
Pay Units: 33.
Programming (via satellite): Cinemax.
Fee: $10.00 installation; $7.95 monthly.

Pay Service 2
Pay Units: 21.
Programming (via satellite): HBO.
Fee: $10.00 installation; $10.95 monthly.

Digital Pay Service 1
Pay Units: N.A.
Programming (via satellite): Cinemax (multiplexed); Encore (multiplexed); HBO (multiplexed); Showtime (multiplexed); Starz (multiplexed); The Movie Channel (multiplexed).

Video-On-Demand: No

Internet Service
Operational: No.

Telephone Service
None

Miles of Plant: 9.0 (coaxial); None (fiber optic).

Manager: Randy Scott. Office Manager: Dave Scott.

Ownership: S & K TV Systems Inc. (MSO).

MONTELLO—Charter Communications, 165 Knights Way, Ste 100, Fond Du Lac, WI 54935-8061. Phone: 920-907-7720. Fax: 920-907-7723. Web Site: http://www.charter.com. ICA: WI0122.

TV Market Ranking: Outside TV Markets (MONTELLO). Franchise award date: N.A. Franchise expiration date: N.A. Began: June 30, 1983.

Channel capacity: 35 (not 2-way capable). Channels available but not in use: N.A.

Basic Service
Subscribers: 567.
Programming (received off-air): WFRV-TV (CBS) Green Bay; WHA-TV (PBS) Madison; WISC-TV (CBS, MNT) Madison; WKOW (ABC) Madison; WLUK-TV (FOX) Green Bay; WMSN-TV (FOX) Madison; WMTV-TV (NBC) Madison; WVTV (CW) Milwaukee.
Programming (via satellite): QVC; WGN America.
Fee: $29.99 installation.

Expanded Basic Service 1
Subscribers: N.A.
Programming (via satellite): A&E Networks; ABC Family Channel; AMC; CNBC; CNN; Comedy Central; C-SPAN; Discovery Channel; Disney Channel; ESPN; ESPN 2; Eternal Word TV Network; Headline News; Lifetime; MSNBC; MTV; Nickelodeon; Spike TV; TBS Superstation; The Learning Channel; The Weather Channel; Turner Network TV; USA Network; VH1.
Fee: $47.99 monthly.

Pay Service 1
Pay Units: 92.
Programming (via satellite): Cinemax.
Fee: $14.95 installation; $12.95 monthly.

Pay Service 2
Pay Units: 147.
Programming (via satellite): Showtime.
Fee: $14.95 installation; $12.95 monthly.

Pay Service 3
Pay Units: 97.
Programming (via satellite): HBO.
Fee: $14.95 installation; $12.95 monthly.

Video-On-Demand: No

Internet Service
Operational: No.

Telephone Service
None

Miles of Plant: 16.0 (coaxial); None (fiber optic).

Vice President & General Manager: Lisa Washa. Chief Technician: Jeff Gerner. Marketing Director: Traci Loonstra. Marketing Administrator: Rhonda Schelvan.

Ownership: Charter Communications Inc. (MSO).

MONTICELLO—Mediacom, 3900 26th Ave, Moline, IL 61265. Phones: 309-797-2580 (Moline regional office); 563-557-8025. Fax: 309-797-2414. Web Site: http://www.mediacomcable.com. ICA: WI0153.

TV Market Ranking: 97 (MONTICELLO). Franchise award date: N.A. Franchise expiration date: June 22, 2013. Began: June 18, 1984.

Channel capacity: 42 (not 2-way capable). Channels available but not in use: N.A.

Basic Service
Subscribers: 275.
Programming (received off-air): WHA-TV (PBS) Madison; WIFR (CBS) Freeport; WISC-TV (CBS, MNT) Madison; WKOW (ABC) Madison; WMSN-TV (FOX) Madison; WMTV-TV (NBC) Madison; WQRF-TV (FOX) Rockford; WREX (CW, NBC) Rockford; WTVO (ABC, MNT) Rockford.
Programming (via satellite): A&E Networks; ABC Family Channel; AMC; Animal Planet; Cartoon Network; CNN; Country Music TV; Discovery Channel; ESPN; ESPN 2; Food Network; HGTV; Lifetime; MTV; Nickelodeon; Spike TV; Syfy; TBS Superstation; Travel Channel; Trinity Broadcasting Network; Turner Network TV; USA Network; VH1; WGN America.
Fee: $45.00 installation; $35.95 monthly.

Pay Service 1
Pay Units: 102.
Programming (via satellite): Cinemax; HBO.
Fee: $7.95 monthly (Cinemax), $11.99 monthly (HBO).

Video-On-Demand: No

Internet Service
Operational: No.

Telephone Service
None

Miles of plant (coax & fiber) included in Moline, IL

Regional Vice President: Cari Fenzel. Area Manager: Kathleen McMullen. Engineering Director: Mitch Carlson. Technical Operations Manager: Darren Dean. Marketing Director: Greg Evans.

Ownership: Mediacom LLC (MSO).

MUSKEGO—Time Warner Cable. Now served by MILWAUKEE, WI [WI0001]. ICA: WI0051.

NEW BERLIN—Time Warner Cable. Now served by MILWAUKEE, WI [WI0001]. ICA: WI0026.

NEW FRANKEN—CenturyLink. Now served by CASCO, WI [WI0115]. ICA: WI0269.

NEW RICHMOND—Northwest Community Communications, 120 Birch St W, Amery, WI 54001. Phone: 715-268-7011. Fax: 715-268-9194. Web Site: http://www.nwcomm.net. Also serves Richmond, Stanton, Star Prairie (town) & Star Prairie (village). ICA: WI0077.

TV Market Ranking: 13 (NEW RICHMOND, Richmond, Stanton, Star Prairie (town), Star Prairie (village)). Franchise award date: March 1, 1983. Franchise expiration date: N.A. Began: February 1, 1984.

Channel capacity: 55 (operating 2-way). Channels available but not in use: N.A.

Basic Service

Subscribers: 2,500.

Programming (received off-air): KARE (NBC) Minneapolis; KMSP-TV (FOX) Minneapolis; KSTP-TV (ABC) St. Paul; KTCA-TV (PBS) St. Paul; WCCO-TV (CBS) Minneapolis; WEAU-TV (NBC) Eau Claire; WFTC (MNT) Minneapolis; WHWC-TV (PBS) Menomonie; WKBT-DT (CBS, MNT) La Crosse; WQOW (ABC, CW) Eau Claire; WUCW (CW) Minneapolis.

Programming (via satellite): A&E Networks; ABC Family Channel; AMC; Animal Planet; Cartoon Network; CNN; Comedy Central; Country Music TV; Discovery Channel; ESPN; ESPN 2; ESPN Classic Sports; Food Network; Fox News Channel; Fox Sports Net; Hallmark Channel; Headline News; HGTV; History Channel; INSP; Lifetime; MSNBC; MTV; National Geographic Channel; Nickelodeon; QVC; Spike TV; Syfy; TBS Superstation; The Learning Channel; The Weather Channel; Travel Channel; Turner Network TV; TV Land; USA Network; VH1; WGN America.

Fee: $29.95 installation; $32.70 monthly.

Digital Basic Service

Subscribers: N.A.

Programming (via satellite): BBC America; Bio; Bloomberg Television; Discovery Kids Channel; DMX Music; ESPNews; Fox Movie Channel; Fox Sports World; G4; GAS; Golf Channel; GSN; History Channel International; Lifetime Movie Network; MTV Networks Digital Suite; Nick Jr.; NickToons TV; Outdoor Channel; Ovation; Speed; Sundance Channel; Turner Classic Movies.

Fee: $12.95 monthly.

Pay Service 1

Pay Units: 186.

Programming (via satellite): Cinemax; HBO; Showtime.

Fee: $10.25 monthly (Cinemax), $10.75 monthly (HBO or Showtime),.

Digital Pay Service 1

Pay Units: N.A.

Programming (via satellite): Cinemax (multiplexed); Encore (multiplexed); HBO (multiplexed); Showtime (multiplexed); Starz (multiplexed); The Movie Channel (multiplexed).

Fee: $12.50 monthly (HBO), $14.99 monthly (Showtime/TMC).

Video-On-Demand: No

Internet Service

Operational: Yes.

Fee: $29.95 installation; $39.95 monthly.

Telephone Service

None

Miles of Plant: 15.0 (coaxial); None (fiber optic).

Manager: Michael Jensen.

Ownership: Northwest Community Communications.

NEWBURG—Tiime Warner Cable. Now served by MILWAUKEE, WI [WI0001]. ICA: WI0270.

NIAGARA—Niagara Community TV Co-op, 1081 Main St, Apt 1, Niagara, WI 54151. Phone: 715-251-1526. Fax: 715-251-1527. Also serves Niagara (town). ICA: WI0271.

TV Market Ranking: Below 100 (NIAGARA, Niagara (town)). Franchise award date: N.A. Franchise expiration date: N.A. Began: August 1, 1954.

Channel capacity: 52 (not 2-way capable). Channels available but not in use: N.A.

Basic Service

Subscribers: 720.

Programming (received off-air): WACY-TV (MNT) Appleton; WBAY-TV (ABC, IND) Green Bay; WCWF (CW) Suring; WFRV-TV (CBS) Green Bay; WJFW-TV (NBC) Rhinelander; WLUC-TV (NBC) Marquette; WLUK-TV (FOX) Green Bay; WNMU (PBS) Marquette; WPNE-TV (PBS) Green Bay; allband FM.

Programming (via satellite): A&E Networks; ABC Family Channel; AMC; CNN; Country Music TV; C-SPAN; Discovery Channel; Discovery Fit & Health; Disney Channel; ESPN; Fox News Channel; FX; Hallmark Channel; Headline News; History Channel; Lifetime; Nickelodeon; Outdoor Channel; QVC; Shop at Home; SoapNet; Spike TV; TBS Superstation; The Learning Channel; The Weather Channel; Toon Disney; truTV; Turner Classic Movies; Turner Network TV; TV Land; USA Network; VH1; WGN America.

Fee: $100.00 installation; $23.42 monthly.

Digital Basic Service

Subscribers: 80.

Programming (via satellite): BBC America; Bio; Bloomberg Television; Bravo; Discovery Fit & Health; Discovery Kids Channel; DMX Music; ESPN 2; ESPN Classic Sports; ESPNews; Fuse; G4; GAS; Golf Channel; GSN; HGTV; History Channel International; Lifetime Movie Network; MTV2; Nick Jr.; NickToons TV; Speed; Style Network; VH1 Classic; VH1 Country.

Fee: $18.95 monthly.

Pay Service 1

Pay Units: 100.

Programming (via satellite): HBO; Showtime.

Fee: $9.00 monthly (Showtime), $10.95 monthly (HBO).

Digital Pay Service 1

Pay Units: N.A.

Programming (via satellite): Cinemax (multiplexed); Encore; HBO (multiplexed); Showtime (multiplexed); Starz (multiplexed); The Movie Channel (multiplexed).

Internet Service

Operational: No.

Telephone Service

None

Miles of Plant: 20.0 (coaxial); None (fiber optic).

Manager & Chief Technician: Gerald Kallenbach. Program & Marketing Director: Linda Weber.

Ownership: Niagara Community TV Co-op.

NICHOLS—Packerland Broadband, 105 Kent St, PO Box 885, Iron Mountain, MI 49801. Phones: 800-236-8434; 906-774-6621. Fax: 906-776-2811. Web Site: http://www.packerlandbroadband.com. ICA: WI0328.

TV Market Ranking: 62 (NICHOLS).

Channel capacity: 32 (not 2-way capable). Channels available but not in use: N.A.

Basic Service

Subscribers: 19.

Programming (received off-air): WACY-TV (MNT) Appleton; WAOW (ABC, CW) Wausau; WBAY-TV (ABC, IND) Green Bay; WFRV-TV (CBS) Green Bay; WGBA-TV (NBC) Green Bay; WLUK-TV (FOX) Green Bay; WPNE-TV (PBS) Green Bay; WSAW-TV (CBS, MNT) Wausau.

Programming (via satellite): A&E Networks; ABC Family Channel; CNBC; CNN; C-SPAN; Discovery Channel; ESPN; ESPN 2; Eternal Word TV Network; Fox News Channel; Fox Sports Net Midwest; History Channel; ION Television; MTV; Nickelodeon; QVC; Speed; Spike TV; TBS Superstation; The Learning Channel; The Weather Channel; Travel Channel; Turner Classic Movies; Turner Network TV; USA Network; WGN America.

Fee: $31.45 monthly.

Pay Service 1

Pay Units: N.A.

Programming (via satellite): Cinemax; HBO.

Fee: $11.50 monthly (each).

Video-On-Demand: No

Internet Service

Operational: No.

Telephone Service

None

Miles of Plant: 5.0 (coaxial); None (fiber optic).

General Manager: Dan Plante. Technical Supervisor: Chad Kay.

Ownership: Cable Constructors Inc. (MSO).

NORTH FREEDOM—Charter Communications. Now served by MAZOMANIE, WI [WI0116]. ICA: WI0325.

NORTH PRAIRIE—Time Warner Cable. Now served by MILWAUKEE, WI [WI0001]. ICA: WI0272.

NORWALK—Mediacom. Now served by ONTARIO, WI [WI0303]. ICA: WI0208.

OCONOMOWOC LAKE—Time Warner Cable. Now served by MILWAUKEE, WI [WI0001]. ICA: WI0273.

OCONTO—Charter Communications, 853 McIntosh St, Wausau, WI 54402. Phones: 715-845-4223; 715-842-3910. Fax: 715-848-0081. Web Site: http://www.charter.com. ICA: WI0075.

TV Market Ranking: 62 (OCONTO). Franchise award date: February 16, 1983. Franchise expiration date: N.A. Began: September 1, 1981.

Channel capacity: N.A. Channels available but not in use: N.A.

Basic Service

Subscribers: 1,339.

Programming (received off-air): WACY-TV (MNT) Appleton; WBAY-TV (ABC, IND) Green Bay; WCWF (CW) Suring; WFRV-TV (CBS) Green Bay; WGBA-TV (NBC) Green Bay; WLUK-TV (FOX) Green Bay; WPNE-TV (PBS) Green Bay; 1 FM.

Programming (via satellite): QVC; WGN America.

Fee: $29.99 installation.

Expanded Basic Service 1

Subscribers: 1,256.

Programming (via satellite): A&E Networks; ABC Family Channel; AMC; Animal Planet; Bravo; Cartoon Network; CNBC; CNN; Comedy Central; Country Music TV; C-SPAN; C-SPAN 2; Discovery Channel; Disney Channel; E! Entertainment Television; ESPN; ESPN 2; ESPN Classic Sports; Eternal Word TV Network; Food Network; Fox News Channel; Fox Sports Net North; FX; G4; Golf Channel; Great American Country; Hallmark Channel; Headline News; HGTV; History Channel; INSP; Lifetime; MSNBC; MTV; National Geographic Channel; Nickelodeon; Outdoor Channel; Oxygen; ShopNBC; SoapNet; Speed; Spike TV; Syfy; TBS Superstation; The Learning Channel; The Weather Channel; Toon Disney; Travel Channel; truTV; Turner Classic Movies; Turner Network TV; TV Guide Network; TV Land; USA Network; Versus; VH1; WE tv.

Fee: $47.99 monthly.

Digital Basic Service

Subscribers: N.A.

Programming (via satellite): AmericanLife TV Network; BBC America; Bio; Bloomberg Television; Discovery Fit & Health; DMX Music; ESPNews; Fox Movie Channel; Fox Soccer; Fuse; GAS; GSN; Halogen Network; History Channel International; Independent Film Channel; Lifetime Movie Network; MTV Networks Digital Suite; Nick Jr.; Style Network; Trinity Broadcasting Network.

Pay Service 1

Pay Units: 201.

Programming (via satellite): Cinemax.

Fee: $12.95 monthly.

Pay Service 2

Pay Units: 236.

Programming (via satellite): HBO.

Fee: $12.95 monthly.

Pay Service 3

Pay Units: 185.

Programming (via satellite): Showtime.

Fee: $12.95 monthly.

Digital Pay Service 1

Pay Units: N.A.

Programming (via satellite): Cinemax (multiplexed); Encore (multiplexed); HBO (multiplexed); Showtime (multiplexed); Starz (multiplexed); The Movie Channel (multiplexed).

Video-On-Demand: No

Pay-Per-View

iN DEMAND (delivered digitally); ESPN Now (delivered digitally); ESPN (delivered digitally); Hot Choice (delivered digitally); Playboy TV (delivered digitally); Fresh (delivered digitally); Shorteez (delivered digitally).

Internet Service

Operational: Yes.

Fee: $19.99 monthly.

Telephone Service

None

Miles of Plant: 38.0 (coaxial); None (fiber optic).

Vice President: Lisa Washa. Chief Technician: Bruce Wasleske. Marketing Director: Traci Loonstra.

Ownership: Charter Communications Inc. (MSO).

OCONTO FALLS—Oconto Falls Cable TV, 500 N Chestnut Ave, PO Box 70, Oconto Falls, WI 54154. Phone: 920-846-4507. Fax: 920-846-4516. Web Site: http://www.ci.ocontofalls.wi.us. ICA: WI0108.

TV Market Ranking: 62 (OCONTO FALLS). Franchise award date: N.A. Franchise expiration date: N.A. Began: December 20, 1981.

Channel capacity: 59 (operating 2-way). Channels available but not in use: N.A.

Basic Service

Subscribers: 996.

Programming (received off-air): WACY-TV (MNT) Appleton; WBAY-TV (ABC, IND) Green Bay; WFRV-TV (CBS) Green Bay; WGBA-TV (NBC) Green Bay; WLUK-TV

(FOX) Green Bay; WPNE-TV (PBS) Green Bay.
Programming (via satellite): C-SPAN; QVC; The Weather Channel.
Fee: $28.00 installation; $13.00 monthly; $15.00 additional installation.

Expanded Basic Service 1
Subscribers: 940.
Programming (via satellite): A&E Networks; ABC Family Channel; AMC; Animal Planet; Cartoon Network; CNBC; CNN; Comedy Central; C-SPAN 2; Discovery Channel; DIY Network; E! Entertainment Television; ESPN; ESPN 2; Food Network; Fox News Channel; Fox Sports Net North; GSN; Hallmark Channel; HGTV; History Channel; Lifetime; MTV; Nickelodeon; Outdoor Channel; Oxygen; SoapNet; Spike TV; Syfy; TBS Superstation; The Learning Channel; Travel Channel; truTV; Turner Classic Movies; Turner Network TV; TV Guide Network; TV Land; USA Network; VH1; WGN America.
Fee: $17.75 monthly.

Digital Basic Service
Subscribers: 45.
Programming (via satellite): BBC America; Bio; Bravo; Discovery Fit & Health; DMX Music; ESPNews; Fox College Sports Atlantic; Fox College Sports Central; Fox College Sports Pacific; Fox Movie Channel; Fuse; G4; GAS; Golf Channel; Great American Country; Halogen Network; History Channel International; Lifetime Movie Network; MTV Networks Digital Suite; Nick Jr.; NickToons TV; Speed; Trio; Versus.
Fee: $11.75 monthly.

Digital Pay Service 1
Pay Units: N.A.
Programming (via satellite): HBO (multiplexed); Showtime (multiplexed).
Fee: $11.75 monthly (each).

Video-On-Demand: No

Internet Service
Operational: No.

Telephone Service
None

Miles of Plant: 20.0 (coaxial); None (fiber optic).
Manager & Chief Technician: Chuck Grady.
Ownership: Oconto Falls Cable TV.

ONALASKA—Charter Communications, 1201 McCann Dr, Altoona, WI 54720-2561. Phone: 715-831-8940. Fax: 715-831-5862. Web Site: http://www.charter.com. Also serves La Crescent, MN; Adams, Angelo, Bangor, Barre, Black River Falls, Brockway, Campbell, Greenfield (town), Hamilton, Holland, Holmen, La Crosse, La Grange (town), Leon, Medary, Melrose, Mindoro, Oakdale, Rockland, Shelby, Sparta, Tomah, Warrens & West Salem, WI. ICA: WI0024.
TV Market Ranking: Below 100 (Adams, Angelo, Bangor, Barre, Campbell, Greenfield (town), Hamilton, Holland, Holmen, La Crescent, La Crosse, La Crosse, La Grange (town), Leon, Medary, Melrose, Mindoro, ONALASKA, Rockland, Shelby, Sparta, West Salem); Outside TV Markets (Black River Falls, Brockway, Oakdale, Tomah, Warrens). Franchise award date: October 1, 1973. Franchise expiration date: November 11, 2009. Began: November 1, 1974.
Channel capacity: N.A. Channels available but not in use: N.A.

Basic Service
Subscribers: 38,308.
Programming (received off-air): KIMT (CBS, MNT) Mason City; WEAU-TV (NBC) Eau Claire; WHLA-TV (PBS) La Crosse; WKBT-DT (CBS, MNT) La Crosse; WLAX (FOX) La Crosse; WXOW (ABC, CW) La Crosse.
Programming (via satellite): TV Guide Network; WGN America.
Fee: $50.00 installation; $12.00 monthly.

Expanded Basic Service 1
Subscribers: 31,094.
Programming (via satellite): A&E Networks; ABC Family Channel; AMC; Animal Planet; BET Networks; Bravo; Cartoon Network; CNBC; CNN; Comedy Central; Country Music TV; C-SPAN; Discovery Channel; Disney Channel; E! Entertainment Television; ESPN; ESPN 2; ESPN Classic Sports; Eternal Word TV Network; Fox News Channel; FX; Golf Channel; GSN; Hallmark Channel; Headline News; HGTV; History Channel; Lifetime; MSNBC; MTV; Nickelodeon; QVC; ShopNBC; SoapNet; Speed; Spike TV; Syfy; TBS Superstation; The Learning Channel; The Weather Channel; Toon Disney; Travel Channel; truTV; Turner Classic Movies; Turner Network TV; TV Land; USA Network; Versus; VH1; WE tv.
Fee: $31.95 monthly.

Digital Basic Service
Subscribers: 9,247.
Programming (via satellite): Bio; Discovery Digital Networks; DIY Network; History Channel International; Lifetime Movie Network; MTV Networks Digital Suite; MuchMusic Network; Nick Jr.; TeenNick.
Fee: $16.00 monthly; $8.95 converter.

Digital Pay Service 1
Pay Units: 2,140.
Programming (via satellite): HBO (multiplexed).
Fee: $13.95 monthly; $8.95 converter.

Digital Pay Service 2
Pay Units: 1,194.
Programming (via satellite): Cinemax (multiplexed).
Fee: $13.95 monthly; $8.95 converter.

Digital Pay Service 3
Pay Units: 967.
Programming (via satellite): Showtime (multiplexed).
Fee: $13.95 monthly; $8.95 converter.

Digital Pay Service 4
Pay Units: 939.
Programming (via satellite): The Movie Channel (multiplexed).
Fee: $13.95 monthly; $8.95 converter.

Video-On-Demand: Yes

Pay-Per-View
Addressable homes: 10,250.
iN DEMAND (delivered digitally).

Internet Service
Operational: Yes. Began: September 1, 1999.
Subscribers: 3,075.
Broadband Service: Charter Pipeline.
Fee: $29.99 monthly; $4.95 modem lease.

Telephone Service
Digital: Operational
Fee: $29.99 monthly

Miles of Plant: 741.0 (coaxial); 81.0 (fiber optic).
Vice President & General Manager: Lisa Washa. Operations Manager: Shirley Weibel. Engineering Director: Tim Normand. Marketing Director: Traci Loenstra. Sales & Marketing Manager: Chris Putzkey. Government Relations Director: Mike Hill.
Ownership: Charter Communications Inc. (MSO).

ONTARIO—Mediacom, 4010 Alexandra Dr, Waterloo, IA 50702. Phone: 319-235-2197. Fax: 319-232-7841. Web Site: http://www.mediacomcable.com. Also serves Norwalk & Wilton. ICA: WI0303.
TV Market Ranking: Below 100 (Norwalk, ONTARIO); Outside TV Markets (Wilton). Franchise award date: N.A. Franchise expiration date: February 9, 2009. Began: N.A.
Channel capacity: N.A. Channels available but not in use: N.A.

Basic Service
Subscribers: 515.
Programming (received off-air): WEAU-TV (NBC) Eau Claire; WHLA-TV (PBS) La Crosse; WKBT-DT (CBS, MNT) La Crosse; WKOW (ABC) Madison; WLAX (FOX) La Crosse; WMSN-TV (FOX) Madison; WMTV-TV (NBC) Madison; WXOW (ABC, CW) La Crosse.
Programming (via satellite): C-SPAN; C-SPAN 2; Eternal Word TV Network; Paxson Communications Corp.; QVC; Trinity Broadcasting Network; TV Guide Network; WGN America.
Fee: $35.16 installation; $9.03 monthly; $1.58 converter.

Expanded Basic Service 1
Subscribers: 162.
Programming (via satellite): A&E Networks; ABC Family Channel; AMC; AmericanLife TV Network; Animal Planet; Bravo; Cartoon Network; CNBC; CNN; Comedy Central; Country Music TV; Discovery Channel; Disney Channel; E! Entertainment Television; ESPN; ESPN 2; Food Network; Fox Movie Channel; Fox News Channel; Fox Sports Net; FX; Hallmark Channel; Headline News; HGTV; History Channel; INSP; Lifetime; MSNBC; MTV; Nickelodeon; RFD-TV; Speed; Spike TV; Syfy; TBS Superstation; The Learning Channel; The Weather Channel; Travel Channel; truTV; Turner Network TV; TV Land; USA Network; Versus; VH1.
Fee: $14.92 monthly.

Digital Basic Service
Subscribers: N.A.
Programming (via satellite): BBC America; Bio; Bloomberg Television; cloo; Discovery Digital Networks; ESPNews; Fox Soccer; Fuse; G4; GAS; Golf Channel; GSN; Halogen Network; History Channel International; Independent Film Channel; Lifetime Movie Network; Lime; MTV Networks Digital Suite; Music Choice; National Geographic Channel; Nick Jr.; NickToons TV; Outdoor Channel; Style Network; Turner Classic Movies; TVG Network.

Digital Pay Service 1
Pay Units: N.A.
Programming (via satellite): Cinemax (multiplexed); Encore (multiplexed); Flix (multiplexed); HBO (multiplexed); Showtime (multiplexed); Starz (multiplexed); Sundance Channel (multiplexed); The Movie Channel (multiplexed).

Video-On-Demand: No

Pay-Per-View
ESPN (delivered digitally); Fresh (delivered digitally); Shorteez (delivered digitally); Playboy TV (delivered digitally); Pleasure (delivered digitally); Ten Clips (delivered digitally).

Internet Service
Operational: Yes.
Broadband Service: Mediacom High Speed Internet.
Fee: $99.00 installation; $40.00 monthly.

Telephone Service
None

Miles of Plant: 12.0 (coaxial); None (fiber optic).
Regional Vice President: Doug Frank. General Manager: Doug Nix. Technical Operations Director: Greg Nank. Marketing Director: Steve Schuh. Marketing Coordinator: Joni Lindauer.
Ownership: Mediacom LLC (MSO).

ORFORDVILLE—Mediacom, 3900 26th Ave, Moline, IL 61265. Phones: 563-557-8025 (Dubuque office); 309-797-2580 (Moline regional office). Fax: 309-797-2414. Web Site: http://www.mediacomcable.com. Also serves Footville. ICA: WI0130.
TV Market Ranking: 93,97 (Footville, ORFORDVILLE). Franchise award date: September 26, 1983. Franchise expiration date: April 7, 2014. Began: October 24, 1984.
Channel capacity: N.A. Channels available but not in use: N.A.

Basic Service
Subscribers: 488.
Programming (received off-air): WHA-TV (PBS) Madison; WIFR (CBS) Freeport; WISC-TV (CBS, MNT) Madison; WKOW (ABC) Madison; WMSN-TV (FOX) Madison; WMTV-TV (NBC) Madison; WQRF-TV (FOX) Rockford; WREX (CW, NBC) Rockford; WTVO (ABC, MNT) Rockford.
Programming (via satellite): WGN America.
Fee: $45.00 installation; $13.95 monthly.

Expanded Basic Service 1
Subscribers: 441.
Programming (via satellite): A&E Networks; ABC Family Channel; AMC; Animal Planet; Cartoon Network; CNN; Comedy Central; Country Music TV; C-SPAN; Discovery Channel; Disney Channel; E! Entertainment Television; ESPN; ESPN 2; FX; History Channel; Lifetime; MTV; Nickelodeon; Spike TV; Syfy; TBS Superstation; The Weather Channel; Trinity Broadcasting Network; Turner Network TV; TV Land; USA Network.
Fee: $24.00 monthly.

Pay Service 1
Pay Units: 301.
Programming (via satellite): Cinemax; Encore; HBO; Showtime; Starz.
Fee: $5.99 monthly (Starz & Encore), $7.95 monthly (Cinemax), $11.99 monthly (HBO or Showtime).

Video-On-Demand: No

Internet Service
Operational: No.

Telephone Service
None

Miles of plant (coax & fiber) included in Moline, IL
Regional Vice President: Cari Fenzel. Area Manager: Kathleen McMullen. Engineering Director: Mitch Carlson. Technical Operations Manager: Darren Dean. Marketing Director: Greg Evans.
Ownership: Mediacom LLC (MSO).

OXFORD—New Century Communications, 3588 Kennebec Dr, Eagan, MN 55122-1001. Phone: 651-688-2623. Fax: 651-688-2624. E-mail: info@ourcableia.com. ICA: WI0314.
TV Market Ranking: Outside TV Markets (OXFORD). Franchise award date: N.A. Franchise expiration date: N.A. Began: N.A.
Channel capacity: N.A. Channels available but not in use: N.A.

Basic Service
Subscribers: 41.
Programming (received off-air): WHA-TV (PBS) Madison; WISC-TV (CBS, MNT) Madison; WKOW (ABC) Madison; WMTV-TV (NBC) Madison.
Programming (via satellite): A&E Networks; ABC Family Channel; AMC; Animal Planet; CNN; Comedy Central; Country Music TV; Discovery Channel; Disney Channel; ESPN; ESPN 2; Fox Sports Net; FX; History Channel; Lifetime; Showtime (multiplexed); Spike TV; TBS Superstation; The Learning Channel; The Weather Chan-

nel; Trinity Broadcasting Network; Turner Network TV; TV Land; USA Network; WGN America.
Fee: $30.00 installation; $32.95 monthly.

Pay Service 1
Pay Units: N.A.
Programming (via satellite): HBO.
Fee: $11.00 monthly.

Video-On-Demand: No

Internet Service
Operational: No.

Telephone Service
None

Executive Vice President: Marty Walch. Manager & Chief Technician: Todd Anderson.
Ownership: New Century Communications (MSO).

PACKWAUKEE—New Century Communications, 3588 Kennebec Dr, Eagan, MN 55122-1001. Phone: 651-688-2623. Fax: 651-688-2624. E-mail: info@ourcableia.com. ICA: WI0189.
TV Market Ranking: Outside TV Markets (PACKWAUKEE). Franchise award date: N.A. Franchise expiration date: N.A. Began: N.A.
Channel capacity: 40 (not 2-way capable). Channels available but not in use: N.A.

Basic Service
Subscribers: 21.
Programming (received off-air): WHA-TV (PBS) Madison; WISC-TV (CBS, MNT) Madison; WKOW (ABC) Madison; WMTV-TV (NBC) Madison.
Programming (via satellite): A&E Networks; ABC Family Channel; AMC; CNN; Country Music TV; Discovery Channel; Disney Channel; ESPN; ESPN 2; Fox Sports Net; History Channel; Lifetime; Showtime (multiplexed); Showtime; Spike TV; TBS Superstation; The Learning Channel; Trinity Broadcasting Network; Turner Network TV; TV Land; USA Network; WGN America.
Fee: $30.00 installation; $34.25 monthly.

Video-On-Demand: No

Internet Service
Operational: No.

Telephone Service
None

Miles of Plant: 10.0 (coaxial); None (fiber optic).
Executive Vice President: Marty Walch. Manager & Chief Technician: Todd Anderson.
Ownership: New Century Communications (MSO).

PARK FALLS—Charter Communications, 1201 McCann Dr, Altoona, WI 54720-2561. Phone: 715-831-8940. Fax: 715-831-5862. Web Site: http://www.charter.com. Also serves Eisenstein & Lake. ICA: WI0086.
TV Market Ranking: Outside TV Markets (Eisenstein, Lake, PARK FALLS). Franchise award date: N.A. Franchise expiration date: N.A. Began: May 10, 1966.
Channel capacity: N.A. Channels available but not in use: N.A.

Basic Service
Subscribers: 1,400.
Programming (received off-air): WAOW (ABC, CW) Wausau; WJFW-TV (NBC) Rhinelander; WLEF-TV (PBS) Park Falls; WSAW-TV (CBS, MNT) Wausau.
Programming (via satellite): C-SPAN; Eternal Word TV Network; QVC; ShopNBC; TV Guide Network; WGN America.
Fee: $50.00 installation; $12.00 monthly.

Expanded Basic Service 1
Subscribers: N.A.
Programming (via satellite): A&E Networks; ABC Family Channel; AMC; Animal Planet; Bravo; Cartoon Network; CNBC; CNN; Comedy Central; Country Music TV; C-SPAN 2; Discovery Channel; Disney Channel; E! Entertainment Television; ESPN; ESPN 2; Food Network; Fox News Channel; Fox Sports Net North; FX; G4; Golf Channel; GSN; Headline News; HGTV; History Channel; Lifetime; MSNBC; MTV; National Geographic Channel; Nickelodeon; Outdoor Channel; Oxygen; SoapNet; Speed; Spike TV; Syfy; TBS Superstation; The Learning Channel; The Weather Channel; Toon Disney; Travel Channel; Turner Classic Movies; Turner Network TV; TV Land; USA Network; Versus; VH1; WE tv.
Fee: $31.95 monthly.

Digital Basic Service
Subscribers: N.A.
Programming (via satellite): BBC America; Bio; Discovery Digital Networks; DIY Network; ESPN Classic Sports; ESPNews; Fox College Sports Atlantic; Fox College Sports Central; Fox College Sports Pacific; Fox Soccer; Fuel TV; Fuse; GAS; History Channel International; Lifetime Movie Network; MTV Networks Digital Suite; Music Choice; NFL Network; Nick Jr.; Nick Too; NickToons TV; TV Guide Network.

Digital Pay Service 1
Pay Units: N.A.
Programming (via satellite): Cinemax (multiplexed); Encore; Flix; HBO (multiplexed); Showtime (multiplexed); Starz (multiplexed); The Movie Channel (multiplexed).

Video-On-Demand: Planned

Pay-Per-View
iN DEMAND (delivered digitally); NASCAR In Car (delivered digitally); Playboy TV (delivered digitally); Fresh (delivered digitally); Shorteez (delivered digitally).

Internet Service
Operational: Yes.
Broadband Service: Charter Pipeline.
Fee: $29.99 monthly.

Telephone Service
Digital: Planned

Miles of Plant: 29.0 (coaxial); None (fiber optic).
Vice President & General Manager: Lisa Washa. Operations Manager: Shirley Weibel. Engineering Director: Tim Normand. Marketing Director: Traci Loonstra. Sales & Marketing Manager: Chris Putzkey. Government Relations Manager: Mike Hill.
Ownership: Charter Communications Inc. (MSO).

PEMBINE—Packerland Broadband, 105 Kent St, PO Box 885, Iron Mountain, MI 49801. Phones: 906-774-6621; 800-236-8434. Fax: 906-776-2811. Web Site: http://www.packerlandbroadband.com. Also serves Beecher. ICA: WI0331.
TV Market Ranking: Below 100 (Beecher, PEMBINE).
Channel capacity: N.A. Channels available but not in use: N.A.

Basic Service
Subscribers: 68.
Programming (received off-air): WACY-TV (MNT) Appleton; WBAY-TV (ABC, IND) Green Bay; WFRV-TV (CBS) Green Bay; WGBA-TV (NBC) Green Bay; WLUC-TV (NBC) Marquette; WLUK-TV (FOX) Green Bay; WNMU (PBS) Marquette.
Programming (via satellite): A&E Networks; ABC Family Channel; CNBC; CNN; C-SPAN; Discovery Channel; ESPN; ESPN 2; Eternal Word TV Network; Fox Sports Net; History Channel; Lifetime; MTV; Nickelodeon; QVC; Spike TV; TBS Superstation; The Learning Channel; The Weather Channel; Turner Classic Movies; Turner Network TV; USA Network; WGN America.
Fee: $31.60 monthly.

Pay Service 1
Pay Units: N.A.
Programming (via satellite): Cinemax; HBO.
Fee: $11.55 each.

Internet Service
Operational: Yes.
Fee: $26.95 monthly.

Telephone Service
None

Miles of Plant: 22.0 (coaxial); None (fiber optic).
General Manager: Dan Plante. Technical Supervisor: Chad Kay.
Ownership: Cable Constructors Inc. (MSO).

PEPIN—US Cable, 402 Red River Ave N, Unit 5, Cold Spring, MN 56320-1521. Phones: 320-685-7113; 800-642-5509. Fax: 320-685-2816. E-mail: help@mn.uscable.com. Web Site: http://www.uscable.com. Also serves Hager City & Nelson. ICA: WI0155.
TV Market Ranking: 13 (Hager City); Below 100 (PEPIN); Outside TV Markets (Nelson). Franchise award date: N.A. Franchise expiration date: N.A. Began: April 1, 1988.
Channel capacity: N.A. Channels available but not in use: N.A.

Basic Service
Subscribers: N.A. Included in Cambridge, MN
Programming (received off-air): KARE (NBC) Minneapolis; KSTC-TV (IND) Minneapolis; KSTP-TV (ABC) St. Paul; KTTC (CW, NBC) Rochester; WCCO-TV (CBS) Minneapolis; WEAU-TV (NBC) Eau Claire; WFTC (MNT) Minneapolis; WHLA-TV (PBS) La Crosse; WKBT-DT (CBS, MNT) La Crosse; WLAX (FOX) La Crosse; WUCW (CW) Minneapolis; WXOW (ABC, CW) La Crosse.
Programming (via satellite): Eternal Word TV Network; HGTV; QVC; The Weather Channel; Turner Classic Movies; WGN America.
Fee: $22.99 monthly.

Expanded Basic Service 1
Subscribers: N.A.
Programming (via satellite): A&E Networks; ABC Family Channel; Animal Planet; Bravo; BTN; Cartoon Network; CNBC; CNN; Comedy Central; Country Music TV; C-SPAN; Discovery Channel; Disney Channel; E! Entertainment Television; ESPN; ESPN 2; Food Network; Fox News Channel; Fox Sports Net Wisconsin; FX; Great American Country; Hallmark Channel; Headline News; History Channel; Lifetime; MTV; National Geographic Channel; Nickelodeon; ShopNBC; SoapNet; Speed; Spike TV; Syfy; TBS Superstation; The Learning Channel; Travel Channel; truTV; Turner Network TV; TV Land; USA Network; VH1.
Fee: $25.08 monthly.

Digital Basic Service
Subscribers: N.A. Included in Cambridge, MN
Programming (received off-air): KTCA-TV (PBS) St. Paul.
Programming (via satellite): BBC America; Bio; Bloomberg Television; cloo; CMT Pure Country; Discovery Fit & Health; Discovery Health Channel; Discovery Home Channel; Discovery Kids Channel; DMX Music; Encore (multiplexed); ESPN Classic Sports; ESPN HD; ESPNews; Fox Movie Channel; Fox Soccer; Fuse; G4; Golf Channel; GSN; Halogen Network; HD Theater; HDNet; HDNet Movies; History Channel International; ID Investigation Discovery; Independent Film Channel; Lifetime Movie Network; Military Channel; MTV2; National Geographic Channel HD Network; Nick Jr.; Science; Style Network; TeenNick; Toon Disney; Trinity Broadcasting Network; Universal HD; Versus; VH1 Classic; WE tv; WealthTV HD.
Fee: $12.90 monthly.

Digital Expanded Basic Service
Subscribers: N.A.
Programming (via satellite): NFL Network; Outdoor Channel.
Fee: $3.95 monthly.

Digital Pay Service 1
Pay Units: N.A. Included in Cambridge, MN
Programming (via satellite): Cinemax (multiplexed); HBO (multiplexed); Showtime (multiplexed); Starz (multiplexed); The Movie Channel (multiplexed).
Fee: $6.95 monthly (Starz), $14.95 monthly (HBO, Cinemax, Showtime or TMC).

Video-On-Demand: No

Pay-Per-View
iN DEMAND (delivered digitally); Playboy TV (delivered digitally); Fresh (delivered digitally); Club Jenna (delivered digitally).

Internet Service
Operational: No.

Telephone Service
None

Miles of plant included in Cambridge, MN
General Manager: Steve Johnson. Customer Service Director: Jackie Torborg.
Ownership: US Cable Corp. (MSO).

PHELPS—Upper Peninsula Communications, 397 N US Hwy 41, Carney, MI 49812-9757. Phone: 906-639-2194. Fax: 906-639-9936. E-mail: louied@alphacomm.net. ICA: WI0176.
TV Market Ranking: Outside TV Markets (PHELPS). Franchise award date: N.A. Franchise expiration date: N.A. Began: N.A.
Channel capacity: 40 (not 2-way capable). Channels available but not in use: N.A.

Basic Service
Subscribers: N.A.
Programming (received off-air): WAOW (ABC, CW) Wausau; WFXS-DT (FOX) Wittenberg; WJFW-TV (NBC) Rhinelander; WLEF-TV (PBS) Park Falls; WSAW-TV (CBS, MNT) Wausau; WYOW (ABC, CW) Eagle River.
Programming (via satellite): A&E Networks; ABC Family Channel; AMC; CNBC; CNN; Country Music TV; C-SPAN; Discovery Channel; Disney Channel; ESPN; ESPN 2; HGTV; History Channel; ION Television; Lifetime; Outdoor Channel; Spike TV; TBS Superstation; The Learning Channel; The Weather Channel; Trinity Broadcasting Network; Turner Network TV; TV Land; USA Network; WGN America.
Fee: $50.00 installation; $24.95 monthly.

Pay Service 1
Pay Units: N.A.
Programming (via satellite): Showtime.

Video-On-Demand: No

Internet Service
Operational: No.

Telephone Service
None

Miles of Plant: 16.0 (coaxial); None (fiber optic).
Manager & Chief Technician: Louis Dupont.
Ownership: Upper Peninsula Communications Inc. (MSO).

PHILLIPS—Price County Telephone Co. Formerly [WI5049]. This cable system has converted to IPTV, 105 N Avon Ave, PO Box 108, Phillips, WI 54555. Phone: 715-339-2151. Fax: 715-339-4512. ICA: WI5049.
TV Market Ranking: Outside TV Markets (PHILLIPS). Franchise award date: N.A. Franchise expiration date: N.A. Began: N.A.
Channel capacity: N.A. Channels available but not in use: N.A.
Video-On-Demand: No
Telephone Service
Digital: Operational

PHILLIPS—Price County Telephone Co. This cable system has converted to IPTV. See Phillips, WI [WI5049]. ICA: WI0119.

PITTSVILLE—Packerland Broadband, 105 Kent St, PO Box 885, Iron Mountain, MI 49801. Phones: 800-236-8434; 906-774-6621. Fax: 906-776-2811. Web Site: http://www.packerlandbroadband.com. ICA: WI0183.
TV Market Ranking: Outside TV Markets (PITTSVILLE). Franchise award date: January 1, 1987. Franchise expiration date: N.A. Began: January 1, 1988.
Channel capacity: 40 (not 2-way capable). Channels available but not in use: N.A.
Basic Service
Subscribers: 137.
Programming (received off-air): WAOW (ABC, CW) Wausau; WEAU-TV (NBC) Eau Claire; WFXS-DT (FOX) Wittenberg; WHRM-TV (PBS) Wausau; WSAW-TV (CBS, MNT) Wausau.
Programming (via satellite): A&E Networks; ABC Family Channel; AMC; Animal Planet; CNBC; CNN; Country Music TV; Discovery Channel; Disney Channel; ESPN; ESPN 2; Fox Sports Net; History Channel; Lifetime; MTV; Nickelodeon; Spike TV; Syfy; TBS Superstation; The Learning Channel; The Weather Channel; Turner Network TV; TV Land; USA Network; VH1; WGN America.
Fee: $24.95 installation; $29.00 monthly.
Pay Service 1
Pay Units: 24.
Programming (via satellite): HBO.
Fee: $10.95 monthly (HBO).
Video-On-Demand: No
Internet Service
Operational: Yes.
Fee: $26.95 monthly.
Telephone Service
None
Miles of Plant: 11.0 (coaxial); None (fiber optic).
General Manager: Dan Plante. Technical Supervisor: Chad Kay.
Ownership: Cable Constructors Inc. (MSO).

PLATTEVILLE—CenturyLink, 135 N Bonson St, Platteville, WI 53818-2504. Phone: 888-835-2485. Web Site: http://www.centurylink.com. Also serves Evergreen Trailer Court & Platteville Twp. (eastern portion). ICA: WI0056.
TV Market Ranking: Below 100 (Evergreen Trailer Court, PLATTEVILLE, Platteville Twp. (eastern portion)). Franchise award date: August 1, 1965. Franchise expiration date: N.A. Began: January 1, 1966.
Channel capacity: 48 (not 2-way capable). Channels available but not in use: N.A.
Basic Service
Subscribers: 2,984.
Programming (received off-air): KCRG-TV (ABC) Cedar Rapids; KFXB-TV (IND) Dubuque; KGAN (CBS) Cedar Rapids; KWWL (NBC) Waterloo; WBUW (CW) Janesville; WHA-TV (PBS) Madison; WISC-TV (CBS, MNT) Madison; WKOW (ABC) Madison; WMSN-TV (FOX) Madison; WMTV-TV (NBC) Madison.
Programming (via satellite): A&E Networks; ABC Family Channel; AMC; CNN; Comedy Central; Country Music TV; Discovery Channel; Disney Channel; ESPN; ESPN 2; Fox News Channel; Fox Sports Net North; HGTV; History Channel; Lifetime; MTV; Nickelodeon; QVC; Spike TV; TBS Superstation; The Learning Channel; The Weather Channel; Turner Classic Movies; Turner Network TV; TV Land; USA Network; VH1; WGN America.
Fee: $35.00 installation; $26.50 monthly.
Pay Service 1
Pay Units: N.A.
Programming (via satellite): Cinemax; Encore; HBO; Showtime.
Internet Service
Operational: No.
Telephone Service
None
Miles of Plant: 48.0 (coaxial); None (fiber optic).
Manager: Mary Gotstein. Chief Technician: Bob Jacob.
Ownership: CenturyLink (MSO).

PLATTEVILLE—Formerly served by Mediacom. No longer in operation. ICA: WI0320.

PLYMOUTH—Time Warner Cable. Now served by RANDOM LAKE, WI [WI0059]. ICA: WI0064.

PRAIRIE DU CHIEN—Mediacom, 4010 Alexandra Dr, Waterloo, IA 50702. Phone: 319-235-2197. Fax: 319-232-7841. Web Site: http://www.mediacomcable.com. Also serves Clayton, Clayton County, Elkader, Garnavillo, Guttenberg, Marquette, McGregor & Waukeon, IA; Boscobel, Bridgeport (town), Crawford County (unincorporated areas) & Grant County (unincorporated areas), WI. ICA: WI0066.
TV Market Ranking: Below 100 (Clayton County (portions), Crawford County (unincorporated areas) (portions), Grant County (unincorporated areas) (portions), Guttenberg); Outside TV Markets (Boscobel, Bridgeport (town), Clayton, Clayton County (portions), Crawford County (unincorporated areas) (portions), Elkader, Garnavillo, Grant County (unincorporated areas) (portions), Marquette, McGregor, PRAIRIE DU CHIEN, Waukon). Franchise award date: N.A. Franchise expiration date: N.A. Began: February 1, 1968.
Channel capacity: N.A. Channels available but not in use: N.A.
Basic Service
Subscribers: 9,809.
Programming (received off-air): KCRG-TV (ABC) Cedar Rapids; KFXB-TV (IND) Dubuque; KGAN (CBS) Cedar Rapids; KRIN (PBS) Waterloo; KWKB (CW, MNT) Iowa City; KWWL (NBC) Waterloo; WHLA-TV (PBS) La Crosse; WKBT-DT (CBS, MNT) La Crosse; WLAX (FOX) La Crosse; WMTV-TV (NBC) Madison; WXOW (ABC, CW) La Crosse; allband FM.
Fee: $8.00 monthly.
Expanded Basic Service 1
Subscribers: N.A.
Programming (via satellite): A&E Networks; ABC Family Channel; AMC; Animal Planet; Cartoon Network; CNBC; CNN; Country Music TV; C-SPAN; Discovery Channel; Disney Channel; ESPN; ESPN 2; Eternal Word TV Network; Fox Movie Channel; Fox Sports Net Midwest; Hallmark Channel; Headline News; HGTV; History Channel; ION Television; Lifetime; MSNBC; Nickelodeon; Spike TV; Syfy; TBS Superstation; The Learning Channel; The Weather Channel; Travel Channel; Trinity Broadcasting Network; truTV; Turner Classic Movies; Turner Network TV; TV Guide Network; TV Land; USA Network; VH1; WGN America.
Digital Basic Service
Subscribers: 1,746.
Programming (via satellite): AmericanLife TV Network; BBC America; Bio; Bloomberg Television; Discovery Digital Networks; DMX Music; Fox Sports World; Fuse; G4; Golf Channel; GSN; Halogen Network; History Channel International; Independent Film Channel; Lifetime Movie Network; Outdoor Channel; Style Network.
Digital Pay Service 1
Pay Units: 1,004.
Programming (via satellite): Cinemax (multiplexed); Encore (multiplexed); Flix; HBO (multiplexed); Showtime (multiplexed); Starz (multiplexed); Sundance Channel; The Movie Channel (multiplexed).
Fee: $20.00 installation; $10.00 monthly (Cinemax, HBO, Showtime, Flix, Sundance/TMC, or Starz/Encore).
Video-On-Demand: No
Pay-Per-View
Addressable homes: 1,746.
ESPN Now (delivered digitally); ETC (delivered digitally); Playboy TV (delivered digitally); Pleasure (delivered digitally); Fresh (delivered digitally); Shorteez (delivered digitally); TVN Entertainment (delivered digitally); sports (delivered digitally).
Internet Service
Operational: Yes.
Broadband Service: Mediacom High Speed Internet.
Telephone Service
None
Miles of Plant: 74.0 (coaxial); None (fiber optic).
Regional Vice President: Doug Frank. Manager: Doug Nix. Technical Operations Director: Greg Nank. Marketing Director: Steve Schuh. Marketing Coordinator: Joni Lindauer.
Ownership: Mediacom LLC (MSO).

PRENTICE—Packerland Broadband, 105 Kent St, PO Box 885, Iron Mountain, MI 49801. Phones: 800-236-8434; 906-774-6621. Fax: 906-776-2811. Web Site: http://www.packerlandbroadband.com. ICA: WI0200.
TV Market Ranking: Outside TV Markets (PRENTICE). Franchise award date: January 1, 1985. Franchise expiration date: N.A. Began: May 1, 1986.
Channel capacity: 50 (not 2-way capable). Channels available but not in use: N.A.
Basic Service
Subscribers: 104.
Programming (received off-air): WAOW (ABC, CW) Wausau; WEAU-TV (NBC) Eau Claire; WFXS-DT (FOX) Wittenberg; WJFW-TV (NBC) Rhinelander; WLEF-TV (PBS) Park Falls; WSAW-TV (CBS, MNT) Wausau.
Programming (via satellite): A&E Networks; ABC Family Channel; AMC; CNN; Comedy Central; Discovery Channel; Discovery Health Channel; ESPN; ESPN 2; History Channel; MTV; Nickelodeon; Spike TV; Syfy; TBS Superstation; The Learning Channel; The Weather Channel; Turner Network TV; TV Land; USA Network; VH1; WGN America.
Fee: $35.00 installation; $33.95 monthly.
Pay Service 1
Pay Units: 36.
Programming (via satellite): Flix; Showtime.
Fee: $9.95 monthly.
Video-On-Demand: No
Internet Service
Operational: No.
Telephone Service
None
Miles of Plant: 8.0 (coaxial); None (fiber optic).
General Manager: Dan Plante. Technical Supervisor: Chad Kay.
Ownership: Cable Constructors Inc. (MSO).

PULASKI—Nsight Teleservices. This cable system has converted to IPTV. See Pulaski, WI [WI5377]. ICA: WI0114.

PULASKI—Nsight. Formerly [WI0114]. This cable system has converted to IPTV, 450 Security Blvd, Green Bay, WI 54313. Phones: 800-826-5215; 920-617-7000. Fax: 920-826-5911. Web Site: http://www.nsight.com. ICA: WI5377.
Channel capacity: N.A. Channels available but not in use: N.A.
Basic Service
Subscribers: N.A.
Fee: $49.95 monthly.
Expanded Basic Service 1
Subscribers: N.A.
Fee: $59.95 monthly.
Expanded Basic Service 2
Subscribers: N.A.
Fee: $67.95 monthly.
Expanded Basic Service 3
Subscribers: N.A.
Fee: $9.95 monthly.
Pay Service 1
Pay Units: N.A.
Fee: $9.95 monthly (Cinemax), $13.95 monthly (Showtime/TMC or Starz/Encore) or $14.95 monthly (HBO).
Internet Service
Operational: Yes.
Fee: $28.95 monthly.
Telephone Service
Digital: Operational
Fee: ($49.95) installation; $24.95 monthly
President & Chief Executive Officer: Pat Riordan. Executive Vice President & Director, Corporate Development: Rob Riordan. Vice President, Corporate Technical Services & Chief Technical Officer: Jim Lienau.

RADISSON—S & K TV Systems, 508 Miner Ave W, Ladysmith, WI 54848. Phones: 800-924-7880; 715-532-7321. Fax: 715-530-9583. E-mail: techsupport@skcable.com. Web Site: http://www.skcable.com. Also serves Exeland & Winter. ICA: WI0336.
TV Market Ranking: Outside TV Markets (Exeland, RADISSON, Winter).
Channel capacity: 35 (not 2-way capable). Channels available but not in use: N.A.
Basic Service
Subscribers: 300.
Programming (received off-air): WCCO-TV (CBS) Minneapolis; WEAU-TV (NBC) Eau Claire; WEUX (FOX) Chippewa Falls; WHWC-TV (PBS) Menomonie; WQOW (ABC, CW) Eau Claire.
Programming (via satellite): A&E Networks; ABC Family Channel; AMC; AmericanLife TV Network; Animal Planet; CNN; Country Music TV; Discovery Channel; Disney Channel; Disney XD; ESPN; ESPN 2; Fox

News Channel; Great American Country; Hallmark Channel; Headline News; HGTV; History Channel; Lifetime; MTV; Nickelodeon; Outdoor Channel; QVC; Spike TV; Syfy; TBS Superstation; The Learning Channel; The Weather Channel; Turner Classic Movies; Turner Network TV; TV Land; USA Network; VH1; WGN America.
Fee: $40.00 installation; $37.45 monthly.

Digital Basic Service
Subscribers: N.A.
Programming (via satellite): BBC America; Bio; Bloomberg Television; cloo; CMT Pure Country; Discovery Fit & Health; Discovery Health Channel; Discovery Kids Channel; Disney XD; DMX Music; ESPN 2; ESPN Classic Sports; ESPNews; Fox Movie Channel; Fox Soccer; Fuse; G4; Golf Channel; GSN; HGTV; History Channel; History Channel International; ID Investigation Discovery; i-Lifetv; Lifetime Movie Network; Military Channel; MTV2; NickToons TV; Noggin; Outdoor Channel; Planet Green; Science; Speed; Style Network; Syfy; The N; Trinity Broadcasting Network; Turner Classic Movies; Versus; VH1 Classic.
Fee: $30.00 installation; $15.31 monthly.

Pay Service 1
Pay Units: N.A.
Programming (via satellite): Cinemax; HBO.
Fee: $7.95 monthly (Cinemax), $11.45 monthly (HBO).

Digital Pay Service 1
Pay Units: N.A.
Programming (via satellite): Cinemax (multiplexed); Encore; HBO (multiplexed); Showtime (multiplexed); Starz (multiplexed); The Movie Channel (multiplexed).
Fee: $9.95 monthly (Cinemax), $13.95 monthly (Showtime/TMC or Starz/Encore).

Internet Service
Operational: No.

Telephone Service
None

Manager: Randy Scott. Office Manager: Dave Scott.
Ownership: S & K TV Systems Inc. (MSO).

RANDOLPH—CenturyTel, 201 Stark St, PO Box 98, Randolph, WI 53956. Phones: 888-835-2485; 800-962-6104. Fax: 920-837-2330. Web Site: http://www.centurytel.com. Also serves Cambria, Courtland, Fall River, Fort Winnebago, Fountain Prairie, Fox Lake Twp., Lowville Twp., Marcellon, Otsego, Pacific Twp., Pardeeville, Rio & Wyocena Twp. ICA: WI0048.

TV Market Ranking: 93 (Cambria, Fall River, Fort Winnebago, Fountain Prairie, Fox Lake Twp., Lowville Twp., Marcellon, Otsego, Pacific Twp., Pardeeville, Rio, Wyocena Twp.); Below 100 (RANDOLPH); Outside TV Markets (Courtland). Franchise award date: N.A. Franchise expiration date: N.A. Began: October 1, 1982.

Channel capacity: 42 (not 2-way capable). Channels available but not in use: N.A.

Basic Service
Subscribers: 2,651.
Programming (received off-air): WBUW (CW) Janesville; WHA-TV (PBS) Madison; WISC-TV (CBS, MNT) Madison; WKOW (ABC) Madison; WMSN-TV (FOX) Madison; WMTV-TV (NBC) Madison; WMVS (PBS) Milwaukee.
Programming (via satellite): A&E Networks; ABC Family Channel; AMC; AmericanLife TV Network; CNN; Comedy Central; Country Music TV; C-SPAN; Discovery Channel; Disney Channel; ESPN; ESPN 2; Fox Sports Net North; Golf Channel; Halogen Network; HGTV; History Channel; Lifetime; Nickelodeon; Outdoor Channel; Spike TV; Syfy; TBS Superstation; The Learning Channel; The Weather Channel; Turner Network TV; TV Land; USA Network; WGN America.
Fee: $35.00 installation; $21.95 monthly.

Pay Service 1
Pay Units: N.A.
Programming (via satellite): Cinemax; HBO.
Fee: $9.95 monthly (each).

Video-On-Demand: No

Internet Service
Operational: Yes.
Fee: $29.95 monthly.

Telephone Service
Analog: Operational
Fee: $18.15 monthly

Miles of Plant: 104.0 (coaxial); 30.0 (fiber optic).
Manager: Mary Gotstein. Chief Technician: Tom Wolff.
Ownership: CenturyLink (MSO).

RANDOM LAKE—Time Warner Cable, 1320 N Dr Martin Luther King Dr, Milwaukee, WI 53212-4002. Phones: 414-277-4032; 414-277-4111. Fax: 414-277-8029. Web Site: http://www.timewarnercable.com. Also serves Adell, Belgium, Cedar Grove, Cleveland, Dacada Village, Elkhart Lake, Fredonia, Glenbeulah, Greenbush (town), Herman, Holland Twp., Howards Grove, Lima, Lyndon, Mosel, Oostburg, Plymouth, Rhine (town) & Sherman Twp. ICA: WI0059.

TV Market Ranking: 23 (Belgium, Dacada Village, Fredonia, Holland Twp., RANDOM LAKE); Below 100 (Adell, Cedar Grove, Elkhart Lake, Glenbeulah, Greenbush (town), Howards Grove, Lyndon, Mosel, Oostburg, Plymouth, Rhine (town), Sherman Twp.); Outside TV Markets (Cleveland, Herman, Lima). Franchise award date: N.A. Franchise expiration date: April 19, 2014. Began: December 1, 1984.

Channel capacity: N.A. Channels available but not in use: N.A.

Basic Service
Subscribers: N.A. Included in Milwaukee
Programming (received off-air): WBAY-TV (ABC, IND) Green Bay; WBME-TV (IND, TMO) Racine; WCGV-TV (MNT) Milwaukee; WDJT-TV (CBS) Milwaukee; WFRV-TV (CBS) Green Bay; WGBA-TV (NBC) Green Bay; WISN-TV (ABC) Milwaukee; WITI (FOX, IND) Milwaukee; WLUK-TV (FOX) Green Bay; WMVS (PBS) Milwaukee; WMVT (PBS) Milwaukee; WPNE-TV (PBS) Green Bay; WPXE-TV (ION) Kenosha; WTMJ-TV (NBC) Milwaukee; WVCY-TV (IND) Milwaukee; WVTV (CW) Milwaukee.
Programming (via satellite): ABC Family Channel; Discovery Channel; Eternal Word TV Network; TBS Superstation; TV One; Univision Studios; WGN America.
Fee: $75.00 installation; $10.39 monthly.

Expanded Basic Service 1
Subscribers: N.A. Included in Milwaukee
Programming (via satellite): A&E Networks; AMC; Animal Planet; BET Networks; Bravo; Cartoon Network; CNBC; CNN; Comedy Central; C-SPAN; Discovery Health Channel; Disney Channel; E! Entertainment Television; ESPN; ESPN 2; ESPN Classic Sports; Food Network; Fox News Channel; Fox Sports World; FX; Golf Channel; Great American Country; Hallmark Channel; Headline News; HGTV; History Channel; Jewelry Television; Lifetime; Lifetime Movie Network; MoviePlex; MSNBC; MTV; National Geographic Channel; Nickelodeon; Oxygen; QVC; Spike TV; Syfy; Telemundo; The Learning Channel; The Weather Channel; Travel Channel; Trinity Broadcasting Network; Turner Classic Movies; Turner Network TV; TV Guide Network; TV Land; USA Network; Versus; VH1; WE tv.

Digital Basic Service
Subscribers: N.A. Included in Milwaukee
Programming (via satellite): America's Store; BBC America; Bio; Bloomberg Television; Boomerang; Canales N; CBS Sports Network; CNN International; Cooking Channel; Country Music TV; C-SPAN 3; Discovery Home Channel; Discovery Kids Channel; Discovery Times Channel; Disney Channel; DIY Network; ESPNews; Fox Sports World; FSN Digital Atlantic; FSN Digital Central; FSN Digital Pacific; Fuel TV; G4; GAS; GSN; Healthy Living Channel; History Channel; Lifetime Real Women; Military Channel; MTV Networks Digital Suite; MuchMusic Network; Music Choice; NBA TV; Nick Jr.; NickToons TV; Outdoor Channel; Science; SoapNet; Speed; Tennis Channel; Toon Disney; Trio; truTV.

Digital Pay Service 1
Pay Units: N.A.
Programming (via satellite): Cinemax (multiplexed); Encore (multiplexed); Fox Movie Channel; HBO (multiplexed); Independent Film Channel; Showtime (multiplexed); Starz (multiplexed); Sundance Channel; The Movie Channel (multiplexed).

Video-On-Demand: Yes

Internet Service
Operational: Yes.
Broadband Service: Road Runner.
Fee: $44.95 monthly.

Telephone Service
Digital: Operational
Fee: $44.95 monthly

Miles of plant included in Milwaukee
President: Tom Adams. Vice President, Operations: Mike Fox. Vice President, Communications: Marci Pelzer. Vice President, Technical Operations: Ralph Newcomb. Vice President, Sales & Markets: Chuck Parshall.
Ownership: Time Warner Cable (MSO).

RHINELANDER—Charter Communications, 853 McIntosh St, Wausau, WI 54402. Phones: 715-845-4223; 715-842-3910. Fax: 715-848-0081. Web Site: http://www.charter.com. Also serves Argonne, Bradley (town), Cassian (town), Crandon, Crescent, Heafford Junction, Lincoln, Monico, Newbold, Nokomis, Pelican, Pine Lake, Stella, Tomahawk & Woodboro (town). ICA: WI0037.

TV Market Ranking: Below 100 (Argonne, Bradley (town), Cassian (town), Crandon, Crescent, Heafford Junction, Lincoln, Monico, Newbold, Nokomis, Pelican, Pine Lake, RHINELANDER, Stella, Tomahawk, Woodboro (town)). Franchise award date: N.A. Franchise expiration date: N.A. Began: February 1, 1954.

Channel capacity: N.A. Channels available but not in use: N.A.

Basic Service
Subscribers: 8,300.
Programming (received off-air): WFXS-DT (FOX) Wittenberg; WJFW-TV (NBC) Rhinelander; WLEF-TV (PBS) Park Falls; WSAW-TV (CBS, MNT) Wausau; WYOW (ABC, CW) Eagle River.
Programming (via satellite): QVC; WGN America.
Fee: $29.99 installation.

Expanded Basic Service 1
Subscribers: N.A.
Programming (via satellite): A&E Networks; ABC Family Channel; AMC; Animal Planet; Bravo; Cartoon Network; CNBC; CNN; Comedy Central; Country Music TV; C-SPAN; Discovery Channel; Disney Channel; E! Entertainment Television; ESPN; ESPN 2; Eternal Word TV Network; Food Network; Fox News Channel; Fox Sports Net North; FX; G4; Golf Channel; Great American Country; Hallmark Channel; Headline News; HGTV; History Channel; INSP; Lifetime; MSNBC; MTV; National Geographic Channel; Nickelodeon; Outdoor Channel; Oxygen; ShopNBC; SoapNet; Speed; Spike TV; Style Network; Syfy; TBS Superstation; The Learning Channel; The Weather Channel; Toon Disney; Travel Channel; truTV; Turner Classic Movies; Turner Network TV; TV Land; USA Network; Versus; VH1; WE tv.
Fee: $47.99 monthly.

Digital Basic Service
Subscribers: N.A.
Programming (via satellite): BBC America; Bio; Discovery Digital Networks; DIY Network; Fox College Sports Atlantic; Fox College Sports Central; Fox College Sports Pacific; Fox Soccer; Fuel TV; Fuse; GAS; History Channel International; Lifetime Movie Network; MTV Networks Digital Suite; Music Choice; NFL Network; Nick Jr.; Nick Too; NickToons TV; Sundance Channel; TV Guide Interactive Inc.

Digital Pay Service 1
Pay Units: N.A.
Programming (via satellite): Cinemax (multiplexed); Encore (multiplexed); Flix; HBO (multiplexed); Showtime (multiplexed); Starz (multiplexed); The Movie Channel (multiplexed).

Video-On-Demand: No

Pay-Per-View
iN DEMAND (delivered digitally); NASCAR In Car (delivered digitally); NHL Center Ice (delivered digitally); MLB Extra Innings (delivered digitally); Playboy TV (delivered digitally); Fresh (delivered digitally); Shorteez (delivered digitally).

Internet Service
Operational: Yes.
Broadband Service: Charter Pipeline.
Fee: $39.99 monthly.

Telephone Service
None

Miles of Plant: 300.0 (coaxial); 158.0 (fiber optic). Additional miles planned: 20.0 (coaxial); 14.0 (fiber optic).
Vice President: Lisa Washa. Chief Technician: Bruce Wasleske. Marketing Director: Traci Loonstra.
Ownership: Charter Communications Inc.

RIB LAKE—Formerly served by Citizens Communications. No longer in operation. ICA: WI0177.

RICE LAKE—Charter Communications, 1201 McCann Dr, Altoona, WI 54720-2561. Phone: 715-831-8940. Fax: 715-831-5862. Web Site: http://www.charter.com. Also serves Barron, Cameron, Chetek, Cumberland, Haugen & Prairie Lake (town). ICA: WI0055.

TV Market Ranking: Below 100 (Chetek, Prairie Lake (town)); Outside TV Markets (Barron, Cameron, Cumberland, Haugen, RICE LAKE). Franchise award date: January 1, 1951. Franchise expiration date: N.A. Began: October 1, 1957.

Channel capacity: 78 (operating 2-way). Channels available but not in use: N.A.

Basic Service
Subscribers: 6,400.
Programming (received off-air): KARE (NBC) Minneapolis; KMSP-TV (FOX)

Minneapolis; KSTP-TV (ABC) St. Paul; KTCA-TV (PBS) St. Paul; WCCO-TV (CBS) Minneapolis; WEAU-TV (NBC) Eau Claire; WEUX (FOX) Chippewa Falls; WFTC (MNT) Minneapolis; WHWC-TV (PBS) Menomonie; WKBT-DT (CBS, MNT) La Crosse; WQOW (ABC, CW) Eau Claire; WUCW (CW) Minneapolis; 8 FMs.
Programming (via satellite): Disney Channel; WGN America.
Fee: $50.00 installation; $12.00 monthly.

Expanded Basic Service 1
Subscribers: 5,800.
Programming (via satellite): A&E Networks; ABC Family Channel; AMC; Animal Planet; Bravo; Cartoon Network; CNBC; CNN; Comedy Central; Country Music TV; C-SPAN; C-SPAN 2; Discovery Channel; E! Entertainment Television; ESPN; ESPN 2; ESPN Classic Sports; Eternal Word TV Network; Food Network; Fox News Channel; Fox Sports Net North; FX; G4; Golf Channel; GSN; Hallmark Channel; Headline News; HGTV; History Channel; INSP; Lifetime; MSNBC; MTV; National Geographic Channel; Nickelodeon; Outdoor Channel; Oxygen; QVC; Speed; Spike TV; Syfy; TBS Superstation; The Learning Channel; The Weather Channel; Toon Disney; Travel Channel; Trinity Broadcasting Network; truTV; Turner Classic Movies; Turner Network TV; TV Guide Network; TV Land; USA Network; Versus; VH1; WE tv.
Fee: $31.95 monthly.

Digital Basic Service
Subscribers: N.A.
Programming (via satellite): BBC America; Bio; Discovery Digital Networks; DIY Network; GAS; History Channel International; Lifetime Movie Network; MTV Networks Digital Suite; MuchMusic Network; Music Choice; Nick Jr.; Nick Too; Sundance Channel.
Fee: $7.00 monthly.

Digital Pay Service 1
Pay Units: 2,060.
Programming (via satellite): Cinemax (multiplexed); Encore (multiplexed); Flix; HBO (multiplexed); Showtime (multiplexed); Starz (multiplexed); The Movie Channel (multiplexed).
Fee: $10.00 monthly (Cinemax, HBO, Showtime/Flix/TMC, or Starz/Encore).

Video-On-Demand: Planned

Pay-Per-View
Hot Choice (delivered digitally); iN DEMAND (delivered digitally); Playboy TV (delivered digitally); Fresh (delivered digitally); Shorteez (delivered digitally); Sports PPV (delivered digitally).

Internet Service
Operational: Yes.
Broadband Service: Charter Pipeline.
Fee: $29.99 monthly; $4.95 modem lease.

Telephone Service
Digital: Operational
Fee: $39.99 monthly

Miles of Plant: 63.0 (coaxial); None (fiber optic).
Vice President & General Manager: Lisa Washa. Operations Manager: Shirley Weibel. Engineering Director: Tim Normand. Marketing Director: Traci Loonstra. Sales & Marketing Manager: Chris Putzkey. Government Relations Manager: Mike Hill.
Ownership: Charter Communications Inc. (MSO).

RICHLAND CENTER—Richland Center Cable TV, 2358 Gatetree Ln SE, Grand Rapids, MI 49546. E-mail: richlandcentercabletv@mail.com. ICA: WI0277.
TV Market Ranking: Outside TV Markets (RICHLAND CENTER). Franchise award date: N.A. Franchise expiration date: N.A. Began: August 1, 1954.
Channel capacity: 76 (operating 2-way). Channels available but not in use: N.A.

Basic Service
Subscribers: 2,942.
Programming (received off-air): WHA-TV (PBS) Madison; WISC-TV (CBS, MNT) Madison; WKOW (ABC) Madison; WMSN-TV (FOX) Madison; WMTV-TV (NBC) Madison; 3 FMs.
Programming (via satellite): Bravo; C-SPAN; GRTV Network; ION Television; QVC; Spike TV; Turner Network TV; TV Guide Network.
Fee: $42.95 installation; $13.95 monthly.

Expanded Basic Service 1
Subscribers: 2,055.
Programming (via satellite): A&E Networks; ABC Family Channel; AMC; BET Networks; Bravo; Cartoon Network; CNBC; CNN; Comedy Central; Discovery Channel; Disney Channel; E! Entertainment Television; ESPN; ESPN Classic Sports; Eternal Word TV Network; Food Network; Fox News Channel; Fox Sports Net North; FX; G4; Golf Channel; GSN; Headline News; History Channel; INSP; Lifetime; MSNBC; National Geographic Channel; Nickelodeon; Oxygen; SoapNet; Syfy; TBS Superstation; The Learning Channel; The Weather Channel; Travel Channel; truTV; Turner Classic Movies; TV Land; Univision Studios; USA Network; WE tv.
Fee: $29.95 monthly.

Digital Basic Service
Subscribers: 2,109.
Programming (via satellite): Animal Planet; BBC America; Bio; Discovery Digital Networks; DIY Network; ESPN 2; ESPNews; Fox Sports World; GAS; HGTV; History Channel International; Independent Film Channel; Lifetime Movie Network; MTV Networks Digital Suite; Music Choice; Nick Jr.; Nick Too; Outdoor Channel; Speed; Sundance Channel; Toon Disney.

Digital Pay Service 1
Pay Units: 301.
Programming (via satellite): Cinemax (multiplexed).
Fee: $10.95 monthly.

Digital Pay Service 2
Pay Units: 242.
Programming (via satellite): HBO (multiplexed).
Fee: $10.95 monthly.

Digital Pay Service 3
Pay Units: 697.
Programming (via satellite): Encore (multiplexed); Starz (multiplexed).
Fee: $11.95 monthly.

Digital Pay Service 4
Pay Units: 310.
Programming (via satellite): Flix; Showtime (multiplexed); The Movie Channel (multiplexed).
Fee: $9.95 monthly (Showtime or Flix/TMC).

Video-On-Demand: No

Pay-Per-View
iN DEMAND (delivered digitally); Playboy TV (delivered digitally); Fresh (delivered digitally); Shorteez (delivered digitally).

Internet Service
Operational: Yes. Began: January 1, 2000.
Subscribers: 507.
Broadband Service: AOL for Broadband.
Fee: $49.95 installation; $32.95 monthly.

Telephone Service
None

Miles of Plant: 49.0 (coaxial); None (fiber optic).
Manager: Josh Perkins. Marketing Director: Sylvia Morrison. Customer Service Manager: Chris McElroy.
Ownership: CYS Inc.

ROBERTS (village)—Baldwin Telecom Inc. Formerly served by Baldwin (village), WI [WI0079]. This cable system has converted to IPTV, 930 Maple St, Baldwin, WI 54002. Phones: 877-684-3346; 715-684-3346. Fax: 715-684-4747. E-mail: info@baldwin-telecom.net. Web Site: http://www.baldwin-telecom.net. ICA: WI5274.
Channel capacity: N.A. Channels available but not in use: N.A.

Basic Service
Subscribers: N.A.
Fee: $61.00 monthly.

A la Carte 1
Subscribers: N.A.
Fee: $6.95 monthly.

Pay Service 1
Pay Units: N.A.
Fee: $11.95 Cinemax, Encore/Starz!, HBO or Showtime/The Movie Channel.

Internet Service
Operational: Yes.
Fee: $39.90 monthly.

General Manager: Larry Knegendorf. Cable TV Manager: Matt Knegendorf. Plant Manager: Duane Russett. Operations Manager: Matt Sparks.

ROME TWP.—Solarus, 440 E Grand Ave, PO Box 8045, Wisconsin Rapids, WI 54495. Phones: 800-421-9282; 715-421-8111. Fax: 715-421-6081. E-mail: support@solarus.net. Web Site: http://www.solarus.net. ICA: WI0279.
TV Market Ranking: Outside TV Markets (ROME TWP.). Franchise award date: N.A. Franchise expiration date: N.A. Began: January 1, 1984.
Channel capacity: N.A. Channels available but not in use: N.A.

Basic Service
Subscribers: 900.
Programming (received off-air): WAOW (ABC, CW) Wausau; WEAU-TV (NBC) Eau Claire; WFXS-DT (FOX) Wittenberg; WHRM-TV (PBS) Wausau; WSAW-TV (CBS, MNT) Wausau.
Programming (via satellite): Cartoon Network; CNN; Lifetime; Nickelodeon; TBS Superstation; Turner Classic Movies; USA Network; WGN America.
Fee: $25.00 installation; $28.95 monthly.

Pay Service 1
Pay Units: 127.
Programming (via satellite): HBO.
Fee: $10.00 monthly.

Pay Service 2
Pay Units: 80.
Programming (via satellite): Cinemax.
Fee: $8.00 monthly.

Video-On-Demand: No

Internet Service
Operational: Yes. Began: January 1, 2001.
Subscribers: 200.
Broadband Service: In-house.
Fee: $29.95 monthly; $6.95 modem lease.

Telephone Service
None

Miles of Plant: 50.0 (coaxial); None (fiber optic).
Chief Executive Officer & General Manager: Douglas Wenzlaff. Operations Director: Jamey Lysne. Sales & Marketing Director: Michael Meinel.
Ownership: Solarus.

ROSHOLT—New Century Communications, 3588 Kennebec Dr, Eagan, MN 55122-1001. Phone: 651-688-2623. Fax: 651-688-2624. E-mail: info@ourcableia.com. ICA: WI0280.
TV Market Ranking: Below 100 (ROSHOLT). Franchise award date: N.A. Franchise expiration date: N.A. Began: N.A.
Channel capacity: N.A. Channels available but not in use: N.A.

Basic Service
Subscribers: 91.
Programming (received off-air): WAOW (ABC, CW) Wausau; WGBA-TV (NBC) Green Bay; WHRM-TV (PBS) Wausau; WLUK-TV (FOX) Green Bay; WSAW-TV (CBS, MNT) Wausau.
Programming (via satellite): A&E Networks; ABC Family Channel; AMC; Animal Planet; Country Music TV; C-SPAN; C-SPAN 2; Discovery Channel; Disney Channel; ESPN; ESPN 2; Headline News; History Channel; Lifetime; MTV; Nickelodeon; QVC; Showtime; Spike TV; TBS Superstation; The Learning Channel; The Weather Channel; Trinity Broadcasting Network; Turner Network TV; TV Land; USA Network; VH1; WGN America.
Fee: $30.00 installation; $28.25 monthly.

Pay Service 1
Pay Units: N.A.
Programming (via satellite): HBO.
Fee: $11.00 monthly.

Video-On-Demand: No

Internet Service
Operational: Yes.
Broadband Service: IBBS.
Fee: $49.95 installation; $34.95 monthly.

Telephone Service
None

Miles of Plant: 6.0 (coaxial); None (fiber optic).
Executive Vice President: Marty Walch. Manager & Chief Technician: Todd Anderson.
Ownership: New Century Communications (MSO).

ROZELLVILLE—New Century Communications, 3588 Kennebec Dr, Eagan, MN 55122-1001. Phone: 651-688-2623. Fax: 651-688-2624. E-mail: info@ourcableia.com. ICA: WI0281.
TV Market Ranking: Below 100 (ROZELLVILLE). Franchise award date: N.A. Franchise expiration date: N.A. Began: N.A.
Channel capacity: 40 (not 2-way capable). Channels available but not in use: N.A.

Basic Service
Subscribers: 13.
Programming (received off-air): WAOW (ABC, CW) Wausau; WEAU-TV (NBC) Eau Claire; WFXS-DT (FOX) Wittenberg; WHRM-TV (PBS) Wausau; WSAW-TV (CBS, MNT) Wausau.
Programming (via satellite): A&E Networks; ABC Family Channel; AMC; CNN; Country Music TV; Discovery Channel; Disney Channel; ESPN; Lifetime; Nickelodeon; Showtime; Spike TV; TBS Superstation; The Learning Channel; Turner Network TV; USA Network; WGN America.
Fee: $30.00 installation; $33.85 monthly.

Video-On-Demand: No

Internet Service
Operational: No.

Telephone Service
None

Miles of Plant: 2.0 (coaxial); None (fiber optic).

Executive Vice President: Marty Walch. Manager & Chief Technician: Todd Anderson.
Ownership: New Century Communications (MSO).

RUDOLPH—Charter Communications, 3211 8th St S, wisconsin Rapids, WI 54494. Phone: 888-438-2427. Web Site: http://www.charter.com. ICA: WI0217.
TV Market Ranking: Below 100 (RUDOLPH). Franchise award date: N.A. Franchise expiration date: N.A. Began: N.A.
Channel capacity: 40 (not 2-way capable). Channels available but not in use: N.A.
Basic Service
Subscribers: 20.
Programming (received off-air): WAOW (ABC, CW) Wausau; WEAU-TV (NBC) Eau Claire; WFXS-DT (FOX) Wittenberg; WHRM-TV (PBS) Wausau; WJFW-TV (NBC) Rhinelander; WSAW-TV (CBS, MNT) Wausau.
Programming (via satellite): A&E Networks; ABC Family Channel; AMC; Animal Planet; CNBC; CNN; Country Music TV; Discovery Channel; Disney Channel; ESPN; ESPN 2; Fox Sports Net; History Channel; Lifetime; MTV; Nickelodeon; Spike TV; Syfy; TBS Superstation; The Learning Channel; The Weather Channel; Turner Network TV; TV Land; USA Network; VH1; WGN America.
Fee: $24.95 installation; $24.95 monthly; $1.50 converter.
Pay Service 1
Pay Units: N.A.
Programming (via satellite): HBO.
Fee: $10.95 monthly.
Video-On-Demand: Planned
Internet Service
Operational: No.
Telephone Service
Digital: Planned
Miles of Plant: 6.0 (coaxial); None (fiber optic).
Vice President & General Manager: Lisa Washa.
Ownership: Charter Communications Inc. (MSO).

SAXEVILLE—New Century Communications, 3588 Kennebec Dr, Eagan, MN 55122-1001. Phone: 651-688-2623. Fax: 651-688-2624. E-mail: info@ourcableia.com. ICA: WI0210.
TV Market Ranking: Below 100 (SAXEVILLE). Franchise award date: N.A. Franchise expiration date: N.A. Began: N.A.
Channel capacity: 40 (not 2-way capable). Channels available but not in use: N.A.
Basic Service
Subscribers: 17.
Programming (received off-air): WACY-TV (MNT) Appleton; WBAY-TV (ABC, IND) Green Bay; WFRV-TV (CBS) Green Bay; WGBA-TV (NBC) Green Bay; WLUK-TV (FOX) Green Bay; WPNE-TV (PBS) Green Bay.
Programming (via satellite): A&E Networks; ABC Family Channel; AMC; Discovery Channel; Disney Channel; ESPN; Headline News; Lifetime; Nickelodeon; Showtime; Spike TV; TBS Superstation; The Learning Channel; Trinity Broadcasting Network; Turner Network TV; USA Network; WGN America.
Fee: $30.00 installation; $33.85 monthly.
Video-On-Demand: No
Internet Service
Operational: No.
Telephone Service
None
Miles of Plant: 7.0 (coaxial); None (fiber optic).
Executive Vice President: Marty Walch. Manager & Chief Technician: Todd Anderson.
Ownership: New Century Communications (MSO).

SENECA (village)—Dairyland Cable Systems Inc., 2494 US Hwy 14 E, Richland Center, WI 53581-2983. Phone: 608-647-6383. Fax: 608-647-7394. Also serves Eastman (unincorporated areas), Lynxville (unincorporated areas) & Mount Sterling (unincorporated areas). ICA: WI0316.
TV Market Ranking: Outside TV Markets (Eastman (unincorporated areas), Lynxville (unincorporated areas), Mount Sterling (unincorporated areas), SENECA (VILLAGE)). Franchise award date: N.A. Franchise expiration date: N.A. Began: N.A.
Channel capacity: 36 (not 2-way capable). Channels available but not in use: N.A.
Basic Service
Subscribers: N.A.
Programming (received off-air): KWWL (NBC) Waterloo; WHLA-TV (PBS) La Crosse; WKBT-DT (CBS, MNT) La Crosse; WLAX (FOX) La Crosse; WMTV-TV (NBC) Madison; WQOW (ABC, CW) Eau Claire; WXOW (ABC, CW) La Crosse.
Programming (via satellite): A&E Networks; ABC Family Channel; American Movie Classics; Animal Planet; Bravo; CNN; Country Music TV; Discovery Channel; Disney Channel; ESPN; ESPN 2; Fox News Channel; HGTV; History Channel; Lifetime; Nickelodeon; Spike TV; TBS Superstation; The Learning Channel; Travel Channel; Turner Network TV; USA Network; WGN America.
Fee: $27.31 monthly.
Pay Service 1
Pay Units: 205.
Programming (via satellite): HBO.
Fee: $10.50 monthly.
Video-On-Demand: No
Internet Service
Operational: No.
Telephone Service
None
Miles of Plant: 17.0 (coaxial); None (fiber optic).
Manager: Jim Atkinson. Chief Technician: Randy Marshall. Marketing Representative: Brian Sullivan.
Ownership: Dairyland Cable Systems Inc.

SHARON—Charter Communications. Now served by HARVARD, IL [IL0073]. ICA: WI0140.

SHEBOYGAN—Charter Communications, 165 Knights Way, Ste 100, Fond Du Lac, WI 54935-8061. Phone: 920-907-7720. Fax: 920-907-7723. Web Site: http://www.charter.com. Also serves Kohler, Lima (town) & Sheboygan Falls. ICA: WI0014.
TV Market Ranking: Below 100 (Kohler, Sheboygan Falls); Outside TV Markets (Lima (town), SHEBOYGAN). Franchise award date: N.A. Franchise expiration date: N.A. Began: May 1, 1982.
Channel capacity: N.A. Channels available but not in use: N.A.
Basic Service
Subscribers: 21,600.
Programming (received off-air): WBAY-TV (ABC, IND) Green Bay; WCGV-TV (MNT) Milwaukee; WDJT-TV (CBS) Milwaukee; WFRV-TV (CBS) Green Bay; WGBA-TV (NBC) Green Bay; WISN-TV (ABC) Milwaukee; WITI (FOX, IND) Milwaukee; WLUK-TV (FOX) Green Bay; WMLW-CA (IND) Milwaukee; WMVS (PBS) Milwaukee; WMVT (PBS) Milwaukee; WPNE-TV (PBS) Green Bay; WPXE-TV (ION) Kenosha; WTMJ-TV (NBC) Milwaukee; WVTV (CW) Milwaukee.
Programming (via satellite): C-SPAN; C-SPAN 2; Product Information Network; QVC; ShopNBC; TV Guide Network; WGN America.
Fee: $29.99 installation.
Expanded Basic Service 1
Subscribers: 17,549.
Programming (via satellite): A&E Networks; ABC Family Channel; AMC; Animal Planet; Bravo; Cartoon Network; CNBC; CNN; Comedy Central; Country Music TV; Deutsche Welle TV; Discovery Channel; Disney Channel; E! Entertainment Television; ESPN; ESPN 2; ESPN Classic Sports; Eternal Word TV Network; Food Network; Fox News Channel; Fox Sports Net North; FX; G4; Golf Channel; GSN; Hallmark Channel; Headline News; HGTV; History Channel; Lifetime; MSNBC; MTV; National Geographic Channel; Nickelodeon; Oxygen; SoapNet; Speed; Spike TV; Style Network; Syfy; TBS Superstation; The Learning Channel; The Weather Channel; Toon Disney; Travel Channel; truTV; Turner Network TV; TV Land; Univision Studios; USA Network; Versus; VH1.
Fee: $47.99 monthly.
Digital Basic Service
Subscribers: N.A.
Programming (via satellite): BBC America; Bio; Discovery Digital Networks; DIY Network; Fox College Sports Atlantic; Fox College Sports Central; Fox College Sports Pacific; Fox Soccer; Fuel TV; Fuse; GAS; History Channel International; Lifetime Movie Network; MTV Networks Digital Suite; Music Choice; NFL Network; Nick Jr.; Nick Too; NickToons TV; Outdoor Channel; Sundance Channel; TV Guide Interactive Inc.; WE tv.
Digital Pay Service 1
Pay Units: N.A.
Programming (via satellite): Cinemax (multiplexed); Encore (multiplexed); Flix; HBO (multiplexed); Showtime (multiplexed); Starz (multiplexed); The Movie Channel (multiplexed).
Video-On-Demand: Yes
Pay-Per-View
Shorteez (delivered digitally); Shorteez (delivered digitally); Playboy TV (delivered digitally); iN DEMAND (delivered digitally); NASCAR In Car (delivered digitally); NHL Center Ice (delivered digitally); MLB Extra Innings (delivered digitally).
Internet Service
Operational: Yes.
Broadband Service: Charter Pipeline.
Fee: $29.99 monthly; $3.95 modem lease.
Telephone Service
Digital: Operational
Miles of Plant: 322.0 (coaxial); None (fiber optic).
Vice President: Lisa Washa. Chief Technician: Jeff Gerner. Marketing Director: Traci Loonstra. Marketing Administrator: Rhonda Schelvan.
Ownership: Charter Communications Inc. (MSO).

SIREN—Siren Communications, 7723 Main St, PO Box 506, Siren, WI 54872-0506. Phone: 715-349-2224. Fax: 715-349-2576. E-mail: sirentel@sirentel.net. Web Site: http://www.sirentel.com. Also serves Webster. ICA: WI0285.
TV Market Ranking: Outside TV Markets (SIREN, Webster). Franchise award date: July 1, 1986. Franchise expiration date: N.A. Began: June 1, 1987.
Channel capacity: N.A. Channels available but not in use: N.A.
Basic Service
Subscribers: 300.
Programming (received off-air): KARE (NBC) Minneapolis; KMSP-TV (FOX) Minneapolis; KPXM-TV (ION) St. Cloud; KSTP-TV (ABC) St. Paul; KTCA-TV (PBS) St. Paul; WCCO-TV (CBS) Minneapolis; WEAU-TV (NBC) Eau Claire; WEUX (FOX) Chippewa Falls; WFTC (MNT) Minneapolis; WHWC-TV (PBS) Menomonie; WQOW (ABC, CW) Eau Claire; WUCW (CW) Minneapolis.
Programming (via satellite): A&E Networks; ABC Family Channel; CNBC; CNN; C-SPAN; Discovery Channel; ESPN; ESPN 2; Fox Sports Net Midwest; Headline News; HGTV; History Channel; Lifetime; MTV; Nickelodeon; QVC; Spike TV; TBS Superstation; The Learning Channel; The Weather Channel; Turner Network TV; TV Land; USA Network; VH1; WGN America.
Fee: $39.50 installation; $36.00 monthly; $24.95 additional installation.
Pay Service 1
Pay Units: 51.
Programming (via satellite): Cinemax.
Fee: $9.00 monthly.
Pay Service 2
Pay Units: 19.
Programming (via satellite): Showtime.
Fee: $9.00 monthly.
Pay Service 3
Pay Units: 43.
Programming (via satellite): HBO.
Fee: $9.00 monthly.
Video-On-Demand: No
Internet Service
Operational: Yes.
Broadband Service: In-house.
Fee: $6.80 monthly.
Telephone Service
None
Miles of Plant: 22.0 (coaxial); None (fiber optic).
Manager: Sid Sherstad. Chief Technician: Kent Bassett.
Ownership: Siren Communications (MSO).

SISTER BAY—Charter Communications, 165 Knights Way, Ste 100, Fond Du Lac, WI 54935-8061. Phone: 920-907-7720. Fax: 920-907-7723. Web Site: http://www.charter.com. Also serves Baileys Harbor, Ephraim, Fish Creek, Gibraltar (town) & Liberty Grove (town). ICA: WI0309.
TV Market Ranking: Below 100 (Gibraltar (town), Liberty Grove (town)); Outside TV Markets (Baileys Harbor, Ephraim, Fish Creek, SISTER BAY). Franchise award date: N.A. Franchise expiration date: N.A. Began: N.A.
Channel capacity: N.A. Channels available but not in use: N.A.
Basic Service
Subscribers: 1,200.
Programming (received off-air): WACY-TV (MNT) Appleton; WBAY-TV (ABC, IND) Green Bay; WCWF (CW) Suring; WFRV-TV (CBS) Green Bay; WGBA-TV (NBC) Green Bay; WLUK-TV (FOX) Green Bay; WPNE-TV (PBS) Green Bay; WYTU-LP (TMO) Milwaukee.
Programming (via satellite): C-SPAN; C-SPAN 2; Product Information Network; QVC; ShopNBC; TV Guide Network; WGN America.
Fee: $29.99 installation; $2.29 converter.
Expanded Basic Service 1
Subscribers: 922.
Programming (via satellite): A&E Networks; ABC Family Channel; AMC; Animal Planet; Bravo; Cartoon Network; CNBC; CNN; Comedy Central; Country Music TV;

Discovery Channel; Disney Channel; E! Entertainment Television; ESPN; ESPN 2; ESPN Classic Sports; Eternal Word TV Network; Food Network; Fox News Channel; Fox Sports Net North; FX; G4; Golf Channel; GSN; Hallmark Channel; Headline News; HGTV; History Channel; Lifetime; MSNBC; MTV; National Geographic Channel; Nickelodeon; Oxygen; SoapNet; Speed; Spike TV; Style Network; Syfy; TBS Superstation; The Learning Channel; The Weather Channel; Toon Disney; Travel Channel; truTV; Turner Classic Movies; Turner Network TV; TV Land; USA Network; Versus; VH1.
Fee: $47.99 monthly.

Digital Basic Service
Subscribers: N.A.
Programming (via satellite): BBC America; Bio; Discovery Digital Networks; DIY Network; ESPN; Fox College Sports Atlantic; Fox College Sports Central; Fox College Sports Pacific; Fox Soccer; Fuel TV; Fuse; HDNet; HDNet Movies; History Channel International; Lifetime Movie Network; MTV Networks Digital Suite; Music Choice; NFL Network; Nick Jr.; Nick Too; NickToons TV; Outdoor Channel; Sundance Channel; TeenNick; TV Guide Interactive Inc.; WE tv.

Digital Pay Service 1
Pay Units: N.A.
Programming (via satellite): Cinemax (multiplexed); Encore (multiplexed); Flix; HBO (multiplexed); HBO HD; Showtime (multiplexed); Showtime HD; Starz (multiplexed); The Movie Channel (multiplexed).

Video-On-Demand: No

Pay-Per-View
iN DEMAND (delivered digitally); NASCAR In Car (delivered digitally); NHL Center Ice (delivered digitally); MLB Extra Innings (delivered digitally); Playboy TV (delivered digitally); Fresh (delivered digitally); Shorteez (delivered digitally).

Internet Service
Operational: Yes. Began: October 1, 2001.
Broadband Service: Charter Pipeline.
Fee: $29.99 monthly; $4.95 modem lease.

Telephone Service
Digital: Operational
Fee: $29.99 monthly

Miles of Plant: 44.0 (coaxial); None (fiber optic).

Vice President & General Manager: Lisa Washa. Chief Technician: Jeff Gerner. Marketing Director: Traci Loonstra. Marketing Administrator: Rhonda Schelvan.

Ownership: Charter Communications Inc. (MSO).

SOLON SPRINGS—Northwest Community Communications, 120 Birch St W, Amery, WI 54001. Phones: 715-268-6066; 715-268-7101. Fax: 715-268-9194. E-mail: info@nwcomm.net. Web Site: http://www.nwcomm.net. ICA: WI0286.

TV Market Ranking: 89 (SOLON SPRINGS). Franchise award date: N.A. Franchise expiration date: N.A. Began: January 1, 1989.

Channel capacity: 36 (not 2-way capable). Channels available but not in use: N.A.

Basic Service
Subscribers: 150.
Programming (received off-air): KARE (NBC) Minneapolis; KMSP-TV (FOX) Minneapolis; KPXM-TV (ION) St. Cloud; KSTP-TV (ABC) St. Paul; KTCA-TV (PBS) St. Paul; WCCO-TV (CBS) Minneapolis; WEAU-TV (NBC) Eau Claire; WEUX (FOX) Chippewa Falls; WFTC (MNT) Minneapolis; WHWC-TV (PBS) Menomonie; WQOW (ABC, CW) Eau Claire; WUCW (CW) Minneapolis.
Programming (via satellite): A&E Networks; ABC Family Channel; AMC; CNBC; CNN; C-SPAN; Discovery Channel; ESPN; ESPN 2; Fox Sports Net Midwest; Headline News; HGTV; History Channel; Lifetime; MTV; Nickelodeon; QVC; Spike TV; TBS Superstation; The Learning Channel; The Weather Channel; Turner Network TV; TV Land; USA Network; VH1; WGN America.
Fee: $39.50 installation; $27.95 monthly; $24.95 additional installation.

Pay Service 1
Pay Units: 47.
Programming (via satellite): Cinemax.
Fee: $9.00 monthly.

Pay Service 2
Pay Units: 15.
Programming (via satellite): Showtime.
Fee: $9.00 monthly.

Pay Service 3
Pay Units: 41.
Programming (via satellite): HBO.
Fee: $9.00 monthly.

Internet Service
Operational: No.

Telephone Service
None

Miles of Plant: 22.0 (coaxial); None (fiber optic).

Manager: Michael Jensen.

Ownership: Northwest Community Communications (MSO).

SOMERSET—Northwest Community Communications, 120 Birch St W, Amery, WI 54001. Phones: 715-247-3320; 715-268-7101. Fax: 715-268-9194. E-mail: info@nwcomm.net. Web Site: http://www.nwcomm.net. ICA: WI0146.

TV Market Ranking: 13 (SOMERSET). Franchise award date: N.A. Franchise expiration date: N.A. Began: November 1, 1988.

Channel capacity: N.A. Channels available but not in use: N.A.

Basic Service
Subscribers: 280.
Programming (received off-air): KARE (NBC) Minneapolis; KMSP-TV (FOX) Minneapolis; KPXM-TV (ION) St. Cloud; KSTC-TV (IND) Minneapolis; KSTP-TV (ABC) St. Paul; KTCA-TV (PBS) St. Paul; KTCI-TV (PBS) St. Paul; WCCO-TV (CBS) Minneapolis; WEAU-TV (NBC) Eau Claire; WEUX (FOX) Chippewa Falls; WFTC (MNT) Minneapolis; WHWC-TV (PBS) Menomonie; WQOW (ABC, CW) Eau Claire; WUCW (CW) Minneapolis.
Programming (via satellite): A&E Networks; ABC Family Channel; AMC; Animal Planet; BTN; CNBC; CNN; Comedy Central; Country Music TV; C-SPAN; C-SPAN 2; Discovery Channel; Discovery Health Channel; Disney Channel; E! Entertainment Television; ESPN; ESPN 2; ESPN Classic Sports; Food Network; Fox News Channel; Fox Sports Net Minnesota; Fox Sports Net Wisconsin; FX; Golf Channel; Great American Country; Hallmark Channel; Hallmark Movie Channel; Headline News; HGTV; History Channel; Lifetime; MTV; National Geographic Channel; Nickelodeon; Outdoor Channel; Speed; Spike TV; Syfy; TBS Superstation; The Learning Channel; The Weather Channel; Travel Channel; Turner Classic Movies; Turner Network TV; TV Guide Network; TV Land; USA Network; VH1; WGN America.
Fee: $25.00 installation; $34.95 monthly.

Digital Basic Service
Subscribers: N.A.
Programming (via satellite): AmericanLife TV Network; BBC America; Bio; Bloomberg Television; cloo; CMT Pure Country; Discovery Fit & Health; Discovery Health Channel; Discovery Kids Channel; DMX Music; ESPN Classic Sports; ESPNews; Fox Movie Channel; Fox Soccer; FSN Digital Atlantic; FSN Digital Central; FSN Digital Pacific; Fuse; G4; GMC; Halogen Network; History Channel International; ID Investigation Discovery; Independent Film Channel; Lifetime Movie Network; Military Channel; MTV Hits; MTV2; Nick Jr.; NickToons TV; Planet Green; Science; Style Network; TeenNick; Toon Disney; Trinity Broadcasting Network; Versus; VH1 Classic; VH1 Soul; WE tv.
Fee: $17.95 monthly.

Digital Expanded Basic Service
Subscribers: N.A.
Programming (received off-air): KARE (NBC) Minneapolis; KMSP-TV (FOX) Minneapolis; KSTP-TV (ABC) St. Paul; WCCO-TV (CBS) Minneapolis; WEAU-TV (NBC) Eau Claire; WFTC (MNT) Minneapolis; WQOW (ABC, CW) Eau Claire; WUCW (CW) Minneapolis.
Programming (via satellite): A&E HD; BTN HD; Discovery Channel HD; ESPN HD; HDNet; HDNet Movies; History Channel HD; National Geographic Channel HD Network; Outdoor Channel 2 HD; PBS HD; Universal HD.
Fee: $13.95 monthly.

Digital Pay Service 1
Pay Units: N.A.
Programming (via satellite): Cinemax (multiplexed); Encore (multiplexed); Flix; HBO (multiplexed); Showtime (multiplexed); Starz (multiplexed); The Movie Channel (multiplexed).
Fee: $10.95 monthly (Showtime/TMC/Flix, Cinemax or Starz/Encore), $12.95 monthly (HBO).

Video-On-Demand: No

Internet Service
Operational: No, Both DSL & dial-up.

Telephone Service
None

Manager: Victor Martinsen.

Ownership: Northwest Community Communications.

SPARTA—Charter Communications. Now served by ONALASKA, WI [WI0024]. ICA: WI0058.

SPENCER—Charter Communications, 853 McIntosh St, Wausau, WI 54402. Phones: 715-845-4223; 715-842-3910. Fax: 715-848-0081. Web Site: http://www.charter.com. Also serves Abbotsford, Athens, Colby, Dorchester, Edgar, Loyal, Neillsville, Owen, Stratford, Unity & Withee. ICA: WI0034.

TV Market Ranking: Below 100 (Abbotsford, Athens, Colby, Dorchester, Edgar, SPENCER (portions), Stratford, Unity); Outside TV Markets (Loyal, Neillsville, Owen, SPENCER (portions), Withee). Franchise award date: November 3, 1980. Franchise expiration date: N.A. Began: April 1, 1982.

Channel capacity: N.A. Channels available but not in use: N.A.

Basic Service
Subscribers: 4,300.
Programming (received off-air): WAOW (ABC, CW) Wausau; WEAU-TV (NBC) Eau Claire; WEUX (FOX) Chippewa Falls; WFXS-DT (FOX) Wittenberg; WHRM-TV (PBS) Wausau; WJFW-TV (NBC) Rhinelander; WQOW (ABC, CW) Eau Claire; WSAW-TV (CBS, MNT) Wausau.
Programming (via satellite): C-SPAN; QVC; WGN America.
Fee: $29.99 installation.

Expanded Basic Service 1
Subscribers: N.A.
Programming (via satellite): A&E Networks; ABC Family Channel; AMC; Animal Planet; Bravo; Cartoon Network; CNBC; CNN; Comedy Central; Country Music TV; C-SPAN 2; Discovery Channel; Discovery Fit & Health; Disney Channel; E! Entertainment Television; ESPN; ESPN 2; ESPN Classic Sports; Eternal Word TV Network; Food Network; Fox News Channel; Fox Sports Net North; FX; G4; Golf Channel; Great American Country; GSN; Hallmark Channel; Headline News; HGTV; History Channel; INSP; ION Television; Lifetime; MSNBC; MTV; National Geographic Channel; Nickelodeon; Outdoor Channel; Oxygen; Product Information Network; ShopNBC; SoapNet; Speed; Spike TV; Style Network; Syfy; TBS Superstation; The Learning Channel; The Weather Channel; Toon Disney; Travel Channel; truTV; Turner Classic Movies; Turner Network TV; TV Guide Network; TV Land; USA Network; Versus; VH1; WE tv.
Fee: $47.99 monthly.

Digital Basic Service
Subscribers: N.A.
Programming (via satellite): BBC America; Bio; Discovery Digital Networks; DIY Network; ESPN; Fox College Sports Atlantic; Fox College Sports Central; Fox College Sports Pacific; Fox Soccer; Fuel TV; Fuse; GAS; HDNet; HDNet Movies; History Channel International; Lifetime Movie Network; MTV Networks Digital Suite; Music Choice; NFL Network; Nick Jr.; Nick Too; NickToons TV; Sundance Channel; TV Guide Interactive Inc.

Digital Pay Service 1
Pay Units: N.A.
Programming (via satellite): Cinemax (multiplexed); Encore (multiplexed); Flix; HBO (multiplexed); HBO HD; Showtime (multiplexed); Showtime HD; Starz (multiplexed); The Movie Channel (multiplexed).

Video-On-Demand: No

Pay-Per-View
iN DEMAND (delivered digitally); NASCAR In Car (delivered digitally); NHL Center Ice (delivered digitally); MLB Extra Innings (delivered digitally); Playboy TV (delivered digitally); Fresh (delivered digitally); Shorteez (delivered digitally).

Internet Service
Operational: Yes.
Broadband Service: Charter Pipeline.
Fee: $29.99 monthly; $4.95 modem lease.

Telephone Service
None

Miles of Plant: 113.0 (coaxial); None (fiber optic).

Vice President: Lisa Washa. Chief Technician: Bruce Wasleske. Marketing Director: Traci Loonstra.

Ownership: Charter Communications Inc. (MSO).

SPOONER—Charter Communications, 1201 McCann Dr, Altoona, WI 54720-2561. Phone: 715-831-8940. Fax: 715-831-5862. Web Site: http://www.charter.com. Also serves Shell Lake. ICA: WI0096.

TV Market Ranking: Outside TV Markets (Shell Lake, SPOONER). Franchise award date: N.A. Franchise expiration date: March 20, 2013. Began: August 1, 1965.

Channel capacity: N.A. Channels available but not in use: N.A.

Basic Service
Subscribers: 1,520.
Programming (received off-air): KARE (NBC) Minneapolis; KBJR-TV (MNT, NBC)

Superior; KDLH (CBS, CW) Duluth; KQDS-TV (FOX) Duluth; KSTP-TV (ABC) St. Paul; KTCA-TV (PBS) St. Paul; WCCO-TV (CBS) Minneapolis; WDIO-DT (ABC) Duluth; WEAU-TV (NBC) Eau Claire; WEUX (FOX) Chippewa Falls; WFTC (MNT) Minneapolis; WHWC-TV (PBS) Menomonie; WQOW (ABC, CW) Eau Claire; WUCW (CW) Minneapolis; allband FM.
Programming (via satellite): C-SPAN; C-SPAN 2; QVC; ShopNBC; TV Guide Network; WGN America.
Fee: $50.00 installation; $12.00 monthly.

Expanded Basic Service 1
Subscribers: 1,400.
Programming (via satellite): A&E Networks; ABC Family Channel; AMC; Animal Planet; BET Networks; Bravo; Cartoon Network; CNBC; CNN; Comedy Central; Country Music TV; Discovery Channel; Discovery Fit & Health; Disney Channel; E! Entertainment Television; ESPN; ESPN 2; ESPN Classic Sports; Eternal Word TV Network; Food Network; Fox News Channel; Fox Sports Net North; FX; G4; Golf Channel; GSN; Hallmark Channel; Headline News; HGTV; History Channel; INSP; Lifetime; MSNBC; MTV; National Geographic Channel; Nickelodeon; Outdoor Channel; Oxygen; SoapNet; Speed; Spike TV; Style Network; Syfy; TBS Superstation; The Learning Channel; The Weather Channel; Toon Disney; Travel Channel; Trinity Broadcasting Network; truTV; Turner Classic Movies; Turner Network TV; TV Land; USA Network; Versus; VH1; WE tv.
Fee: $31.95 monthly.

Digital Basic Service
Subscribers: N.A.
Programming (via satellite): BBC America; Bio; Bloomberg Television; Boomerang; CNN en Espanol; CNN International; C-SPAN 3; Discovery Digital Networks; DIY Network; ESPN; ESPNews; Fox College Sports Atlantic; Fox College Sports Central; Fox College Sports Pacific; Fox Movie Channel; Fox Soccer; Fuel TV; Fuse; GAS; HDNet; HDNet Movies; History Channel International; Independent Film Channel; Lifetime Movie Network; MTV Networks Digital Suite; Music Choice; NFL Network; Nick Jr.; Nick Too; NickToons TV; Sundance Channel; TV Guide Interactive Inc.

Digital Pay Service 1
Pay Units: N.A.
Programming (via satellite): Cinemax (multiplexed); Encore; Flix; HBO (multiplexed); HBO HD; Showtime (multiplexed); Showtime HD; Starz (multiplexed); The Movie Channel (multiplexed).

Video-On-Demand: Yes

Pay-Per-View
iN DEMAND (delivered digitally); NHL Center Ice (delivered digitally); NASCAR In Car (delivered digitally); MLB Extra Innings (delivered digitally); Playboy TV (delivered digitally); Spice Live (delivered digitally); Spice Plaatinum (delivered digitally); Hot Net Plus (delivered digitally); Spice Hot (delivered digitally).

Internet Service
Operational: Yes.
Broadband Service: Charter Pipeline.
Fee: $29.99 monthly.

Telephone Service
Digital: Operational
Fee: $39.95 monthly

Miles of Plant: 20.0 (coaxial); None (fiber optic).
Vice President & General Manager: Lisa Washa. Operations Manager: Shirley Weibel. Engineering Director: Tim Normand. Marketing Director: Traci Loonstra. Sales & Marketing Manager: Chris Putzkey. Government Relations Manager: Mike Hill.
Ownership: Charter Communications Inc. (MSO).

ST. JOSEPH TWP.—Formerly served by Tele-Communications Cable Co. No longer in operation. ICA: WI0290.

STETSONVILLE—Charter Communications, 132 W State St, Medford, WI 54451. Phone: 888-438-2427. Web Site: http://www.charter.com. ICA: WI0291.
TV Market Ranking: Below 100 (STETSONVILLE). Franchise award date: January 1, 1988. Franchise expiration date: N.A. Began: October 1, 1988.
Channel capacity: 50 (not 2-way capable). Channels available but not in use: N.A.

Basic Service
Subscribers: 62.
Programming (received off-air): WAOW (ABC, CW) Wausau; WEAU-TV (NBC) Eau Claire; WFXS-DT (FOX) Wittenberg; WHRM-TV (PBS) Wausau; WJFW-TV (NBC) Rhinelander; WSAW-TV (CBS, MNT) Wausau.
Programming (via satellite): A&E Networks; ABC Family Channel; CNN; Comedy Central; Discovery Channel; ESPN; ESPN 2; MTV; Nickelodeon; Spike TV; Syfy; TBS Superstation; The Learning Channel; The Weather Channel; Turner Network TV; USA Network; VH1; WGN America.
Fee: $35.00 installation; $27.90 monthly.

Pay Service 1
Pay Units: N.A.
Programming (via satellite): Showtime.
Fee: $9.50 monthly.

Video-On-Demand: Planned

Internet Service
Operational: Yes.
Fee: $19.99 monthly.

Telephone Service
Digital: Planned
Fee: $14.99 monthly

Miles of Plant: 4.0 (coaxial); None (fiber optic).
Vice President & General Manager: Lisa Washa.
Ownership: Charter Communications Inc. (MSO).

STEUBEN—Formerly served by Steuben Community TV System. No longer in operation. ICA: WI0230.

STEVENS POINT—Charter Communications, 853 McIntosh St, Wausau, WI 54402. Phones: 715-845-4223; 715-842-3910. Fax: 715-848-0081. Web Site: http://www.charter.com. Also serves Hull, Linwood, Park Ridge (village), Plover, Plover (village), Stockton (town) & Whiting (village). ICA: WI0019.
TV Market Ranking: Below 100 (Hull, Linwood, Park Ridge (village), Plover, Plover (village), STEVENS POINT, Stockton (town), Whiting (village)). Franchise award date: October 1, 1977. Franchise expiration date: N.A. Began: February 25, 1985.
Channel capacity: N.A. Channels available but not in use: N.A.

Basic Service
Subscribers: 17,300.
Programming (received off-air): WAOW (ABC, CW) Wausau; WBAY-TV (ABC, IND) Green Bay; WEAU-TV (NBC) Eau Claire; WFRV-TV (CBS) Green Bay; WFXS-DT (FOX) Wittenberg; WHRM-TV (PBS) Wausau; WJFW-TV (NBC) Rhinelander; WSAW-TV (CBS, MNT) Wausau.
Programming (via satellite): C-SPAN; C-SPAN 2; QVC; WGN America.
Fee: $29.99 installation; $10.11 monthly.

Expanded Basic Service 1
Subscribers: 11,729.
Programming (via satellite): A&E Networks; ABC Family Channel; AMC; Animal Planet; Bravo; Cartoon Network; CNBC; CNN; Comedy Central; Country Music TV; Discovery Channel; Discovery Fit & Health; Disney Channel; E! Entertainment Television; ESPN; ESPN 2; ESPN Classic Sports; Eternal Word TV Network; Food Network; Fox News Channel; Fox Sports Net North; FX; G4; Golf Channel; Great American Country; GSN; Hallmark Channel; Headline News; HGTV; History Channel; INSP; ION Television; Lifetime; MSNBC; MTV; National Geographic Channel; Nickelodeon; Outdoor Channel; Oxygen; Product Information Network; ShopNBC; SoapNet; Speed; Spike TV; Style Network; Syfy; TBS Superstation; The Learning Channel; The Weather Channel; Toon Disney; Travel Channel; truTV; Turner Classic Movies; Turner Network TV; TV Guide Network; TV Land; USA Network; Versus; VH1; WE tv.
Fee: $33.84 monthly.

Digital Basic Service
Subscribers: N.A.
Programming (via satellite): BBC America; Bio; Discovery Digital Networks; DIY Network; ESPN; Fox College Sports Atlantic; Fox College Sports Central; Fox College Sports Pacific; Fox Soccer; Fuel TV; Fuse; GAS; HDNet; HDNet Movies; History Channel International; Lifetime Movie Network; MTV Networks Digital Suite; Music Choice; NFL Network; Nick Jr.; Nick Too; NickToons TV; Sundance Channel; TV Guide Interactive Inc.

Digital Pay Service 1
Pay Units: N.A.
Programming (via satellite): Cinemax (multiplexed); Encore (multiplexed); Flix; HBO (multiplexed); HBO HD; Showtime (multiplexed); Showtime HD; Starz (multiplexed); The Movie Channel (multiplexed).

Video-On-Demand: Yes

Pay-Per-View
iN DEMAND (delivered digitally); NASCAR In Car (delivered digitally); NHL Center Ice (delivered digitally); MLB Extra Innings (delivered digitally); Playboy TV (delivered digitally); Fresh (delivered digitally); Shorteez (delivered digitally).

Internet Service
Operational: Yes.
Broadband Service: Charter Pipeline.
Fee: $39.99 monthly; $3.95 modem lease.

Telephone Service
Digital: Operational
Fee: $29.99 monthly

Miles of Plant: 290.0 (coaxial); 43.0 (fiber optic).
Vice President: Lisa Washa. Chief Technician: Bruce Wasleske. Marketing Director: Traci Loonstra.
Ownership: Charter Communications Inc. (MSO).

STODDARD—Mediacom. Now served by COON VALLEY, WI [WI0171]. ICA: WI0161.

STURGEON BAY—Charter Communications, 165 Knights Way, Ste 100, Fond Du Lac, WI 54935-8061. Phone: 920-907-7720. Fax: 920-907-7723. Web Site: http://www.charter.com. Also serves Egg Harbor, Jacksonport, Nasawapi & Sevastapol. ICA: WI0043.
TV Market Ranking: Outside TV Markets (Egg Harbor, Jacksonport, Nasawapi, Sevastapol, STURGEON BAY). Franchise award date: March 2, 1982. Franchise expiration date: N.A. Began: December 31, 1982.
Channel capacity: N.A. Channels available but not in use: N.A.

Basic Service
Subscribers: 4,683.
Programming (received off-air): WACY-TV (MNT) Appleton; WBAY-TV (ABC, IND) Green Bay; WCWF (CW) Suring; WFRV-TV (CBS) Green Bay; WGBA-TV (NBC) Green Bay; WLUK-TV (FOX) Green Bay; WPNE-TV (PBS) Green Bay; WYTU-LP (TMO) Milwaukee; allband FM.
Programming (via satellite): C-SPAN 2; Product Information Network; QVC; ShopNBC; TV Guide Network; WGN America.
Fee: $29.99 installation.

Expanded Basic Service 1
Subscribers: 3,484.
Programming (via satellite): A&E Networks; ABC Family Channel; AMC; Animal Planet; Bravo; Cartoon Network; CNBC; CNN; Comedy Central; Country Music TV; C-SPAN; Discovery Channel; Disney Channel; E! Entertainment Television; ESPN; ESPN 2; ESPN Classic Sports; Eternal Word TV Network; Food Network; Fox News Channel; Fox Sports Net North; FX; G4; Golf Channel; GSN; Hallmark Channel; Headline News; HGTV; History Channel; Lifetime; MSNBC; MTV; National Geographic Channel; Nickelodeon; Oxygen; SoapNet; Speed; Spike TV; Style Network; Syfy; TBS Superstation; The Learning Channel; The Weather Channel; Toon Disney; Travel Channel; truTV; Turner Classic Movies; Turner Network TV; TV Land; USA Network; Versus; VH1.
Fee: $47.99 monthly.

Digital Basic Service
Subscribers: N.A.
Programming (via satellite): BBC America; Bio; Discovery Digital Networks; DIY Network; ESPN; Fox College Sports Atlantic; Fox College Sports Central; Fox College Sports Pacific; Fox Soccer; Fuel TV; Fuse; GAS; HDNet; HDNet Movies; History Channel International; Lifetime Movie Network; MTV Networks Digital Suite; Music Choice; NFL Network; Nick Jr.; Nick Too; NickToons TV; Outdoor Channel; Sundance Channel; TV Guide Interactive Inc.; WE tv.

Digital Pay Service 1
Pay Units: N.A.
Programming (via satellite): Cinemax (multiplexed); Encore (multiplexed); Flix; HBO (multiplexed); HBO HD; Showtime (multiplexed); Showtime HD; Starz (multiplexed); The Movie Channel (multiplexed).

Video-On-Demand: Yes

Pay-Per-View
iN DEMAND (delivered digitally); NASCAR In Car (delivered digitally); NHL Center Ice (delivered digitally); MLB Extra Innings (delivered digitally); Playboy TV (delivered digitally); Fresh (delivered digitally); Shorteez (delivered digitally).

Internet Service
Operational: Yes.
Broadband Service: Charter Pipeline.
Fee: $29.99 monthly.

Telephone Service
Digital: Operational
Fee: $29.99 monthly

Miles of Plant: 81.0 (coaxial); None (fiber optic).
Vice President: Lisa Washa. Chief Technician: Jeff Gerner. Marketing Director: Traci

Loonstra. Marketing Administrator: Rhonda Schelvan.
Ownership: Charter Communications Inc. (MSO).

SUGAR CREEK (town)—Mediacom, 3900 26th Ave, Moline, IL 61265. Phone: 309-797-2580. Fax: 309-797-2414. Web Site: http://www.mediacomcable.com. Also serves Elkhorn, La Grange Twp. & Lafayette Twp. ICA: WI0292.
TV Market Ranking: 23 (SUGAR CREEK (TOWN)); Below 100 (Elkhorn, La Grange Twp., Lafayette Twp.). Franchise award date: N.A. Franchise expiration date: N.A. Began: N.A.
Channel capacity: N.A. Channels available but not in use: N.A.
Basic Service
Subscribers: 324.
Programming (received off-air): WCGV-TV (MNT) Milwaukee; WDJT-TV (CBS) Milwaukee; WISN-TV (ABC) Milwaukee; WITI (FOX, IND) Milwaukee; WMVS (PBS) Milwaukee; WTMJ-TV (NBC) Milwaukee; WVTV (CW) Milwaukee.
Programming (via satellite): A&E Networks; ABC Family Channel; AMC; CNBC; CNN; Country Music TV; C-SPAN; Discovery Channel; Disney Channel; ESPN; ESPN 2; Headline News; Lifetime; MTV; Nickelodeon; QVC; Spike TV; TBS Superstation; The Learning Channel; The Weather Channel; Trinity Broadcasting Network; Turner Network TV; USA Network; VH1; WGN America.
Fee: $45.00 installation; $54.95 monthly.
Pay Service 1
Pay Units: 66.
Programming (via satellite): Showtime (multiplexed).
Fee: $9.95 monthly.
Video-On-Demand: No
Internet Service
Operational: No.
Telephone Service
None
Miles of plant included in Moline, IL
Regional Vice President: Cari Fenzel. Engineering Director: Mitch Carlson. Technical Operations Manager: Chris Toalson. Marketing Director: Greg Evans.
Ownership: Mediacom LLC (MSO).

THORP—CenturyTel, 405 N Washington St, Thorp, WI 54771-9538. Phone: 888-835-2485. Fax: 715-669-5501. Web Site: http://www.centurytel.com. ICA: WI0139.
TV Market Ranking: Below 100 (THORP). Franchise award date: June 23, 1981. Franchise expiration date: N.A. Began: October 1, 1982.
Channel capacity: 60 (not 2-way capable). Channels available but not in use: N.A.
Basic Service
Subscribers: 548.
Programming (received off-air): WAOW (ABC, CW) Wausau; WEAU-TV (NBC) Eau Claire; WEUX (FOX) Chippewa Falls; WHWC-TV (PBS) Menomonie; WKBT-DT (CBS, MNT) La Crosse; WQOW (ABC, CW) Eau Claire; WSAW-TV (CBS, MNT) Wausau.
Programming (via satellite): A&E Networks; ABC Family Channel; AMC; Animal Planet; Cartoon Network; CNN; Comedy Central; Country Music TV; Discovery Channel; Disney Channel; ESPN; ESPN 2; Food Network; Fox News Channel; FX; Hallmark Channel; HGTV; History Channel; Lifetime; MTV; Nickelodeon; QVC; Spike TV; Syfy; TBS Superstation; The Learning Channel; The Weather Channel; Travel Channel; Turner Classic Movies; Turner Network TV; TV Land; USA Network; VH1; WGN America.
Fee: $35.00 installation; $27.95 monthly.
Digital Basic Service
Subscribers: N.A.
Programming (via satellite): BBC America; Bio; Bloomberg Television; Bravo; Discovery Fit & Health; Discovery Kids Channel; DMX Music; ESPN Classic Sports; ESPNews; Fox Movie Channel; Fox Sports World; GAS; Golf Channel; GSN; Halogen Network; History Channel International; Independent Film Channel; International Television (ITV); Lifetime Movie Network; MTV Networks Digital Suite; National Geographic Channel; Nick Jr.; NickToons TV; Outdoor Channel; Ovation; Speed; Style Network; Toon Disney; Trinity Broadcasting Network; Versus; WE tv.
Fee: $12.95 monthly.
Pay Service 1
Pay Units: 68.
Programming (via satellite): Cinemax; HBO.
Fee: $15.95 monthly (each).
Pay Service 2
Pay Units: 48.
Programming (via satellite): Showtime; The Movie Channel.
Fee: $11.95 monthly.
Pay Service 3
Pay Units: N.A.
Programming (via satellite): Encore; Starz.
Fee: $10.95 monthly.
Digital Pay Service 1
Pay Units: N.A.
Programming (via satellite): Cinemax (multiplexed); Encore; HBO (multiplexed); Showtime (multiplexed); Starz; Sundance Channel (multiplexed); The Movie Channel (multiplexed).
Pay-Per-View
iN DEMAND (delivered digitally).
Internet Service
Operational: No.
Telephone Service
None
Miles of Plant: 14.0 (coaxial); None (fiber optic).
Manager: Mary Gotstein. Chief Technician: Dean Benzschawel.
Ownership: CenturyLink (MSO).

THREE LAKES—Karban TV Systems Inc., 120 S Church St, PO Box 8, Bonduel, WI 54107-0008. Phones: 715-493-7613; 800-236-0233. Fax: 715-277-2339. E-mail: sales@ktvs.net. Web Site: http://www.ktvs.net. ICA: WI0293.
TV Market Ranking: Below 100 (THREE LAKES). Franchise award date: N.A. Franchise expiration date: N.A. Began: January 1, 1986.
Channel capacity: 77 (2-way capable). Channels available but not in use: N.A.
Basic Service
Subscribers: 396.
Programming (received off-air): WFXS-DT (FOX) Wittenberg; WJFW-TV (NBC) Rhinelander; WLEF-TV (PBS) Park Falls; WSAW-TV (CBS, MNT) Wausau; WYOW (ABC, CW) Eagle River.
Programming (via satellite): A&E Networks; ABC Family Channel; AMC; Animal Planet; CNBC; CNN; Comedy Central; Country Music TV; C-SPAN; CW+; Discovery Channel; Disney Channel; ESPN; ESPN 2; Eternal Word TV Network; Food Network; Fox News Channel; FX; Headline News; HGTV; History Channel; Lifetime; MSNBC; NFL Network; Nickelodeon; Outdoor Channel; QVC; Speed; Spike TV; Syfy; TBS Superstation; The Learning Channel; The Weather Channel; Travel Channel; Trinity Broadcasting Network; Turner Classic Movies; Turner Network TV; TV Land; USA Network; VH1; WGN America.
Fee: $75.00 installation; $40.00 monthly; $20.00 additional installation.
Pay Service 1
Pay Units: 37.
Programming (via satellite): Cinemax.
Fee: $10.00 monthly.
Pay Service 2
Pay Units: 53.
Programming (via satellite): HBO.
Fee: $10.00 monthly.
Video-On-Demand: No
Internet Service
Operational: Yes.
Telephone Service
None
Miles of Plant: 60.0 (coaxial); 15.0 (fiber optic).
Manager & Chief Technician: John Karban.
Ownership: Karban TV Systems Inc. (MSO).

TIGERTON—Wittenberg Cable TV. Now served by WITTENBERG, WI [WI0158]. ICA: WI0169.

TOMAH—Charter Communications. Now served by ONALASKA, WI [WI0024]. ICA: WI0060.

TUSTIN—New Century Communications, 3588 Kennebec Dr, Eagan, MN 55122-1001. Phone: 651-688-2623. Fax: 651-688-2624. E-mail: info@ourcableia.com. Also serves Bloomfield (town). ICA: WI0225.
TV Market Ranking: Below 100 (Bloomfield (town), TUSTIN). Franchise award date: N.A. Franchise expiration date: N.A. Began: N.A.
Channel capacity: 40 (not 2-way capable). Channels available but not in use: N.A.
Basic Service
Subscribers: 20.
Programming (received off-air): WACY-TV (MNT) Appleton; WBAY-TV (ABC, IND) Green Bay; WFRV-TV (CBS) Green Bay; WGBA-TV (NBC) Green Bay; WLUK-TV (FOX) Green Bay; WPNE-TV (PBS) Green Bay.
Programming (via satellite): A&E Networks; ABC Family Channel; AMC; CNN; Discovery Channel; Disney Channel; ESPN; Lifetime; Nickelodeon; QVC; Showtime; Spike TV; TBS Superstation; The Learning Channel; Trinity Broadcasting Network; Turner Network TV; TV Land; USA Network; WGN America.
Fee: $30.00 installation; $33.85 monthly.
Video-On-Demand: No
Internet Service
Operational: No.
Telephone Service
None
Miles of Plant: 3.0 (coaxial); None (fiber optic).
Executive Vice President: Marty Walch. Manager & Chief Technician: Todd Anderson.
Ownership: New Century Communications (MSO).

TWO RIVERS—Charter Communications, 165 Knights Way, Ste 100, Fond Du Lac, WI 54935-8061. Phone: 920-907-7720. Fax: 920-907-7723. Web Site: http://www.charter.com. Also serves Algoma, Brillion, Carlton (town), Cooperstown (town), Denmark, Francis Creek, Gibson (town), Kewaunee, Kossuth (town), Maribel, Mishicot, Pierce, Potter & Rantoul (town). ICA: WI0035.
TV Market Ranking: 62 (Algoma, Brillion, Carlton (town), Cooperstown (town), Denmark, Francis Creek, Gibson (town), Kewaunee, Kossuth (town), Maribel, Mishicot, Pierce, Potter, Rantoul (town), TWO RIVERS). Franchise award date: July 8, 1980. Franchise expiration date: N.A. Began: September 23, 1981.
Channel capacity: 80 (operating 2-way). Channels available but not in use: N.A.
Basic Service
Subscribers: 6,908.
Programming (received off-air): WACY-TV (MNT) Appleton; WBAY-TV (ABC, IND) Green Bay; WCWF (CW) Suring; WFRV-TV (CBS) Green Bay; WGBA-TV (NBC) Green Bay; WLUK-TV (FOX) Green Bay; WPNE-TV (PBS) Green Bay; 18 FMs.
Programming (via satellite): C-SPAN; C-SPAN 2; Product Information Network; QVC; TV Guide Network; WGN America.
Fee: $29.99 installation.
Expanded Basic Service 1
Subscribers: N.A.
Programming (via satellite): A&E Networks; ABC Family Channel; AMC; Animal Planet; Bravo; Cartoon Network; CNBC; CNN; Comedy Central; Country Music TV; Discovery Channel; Disney Channel; E! Entertainment Television; ESPN; ESPN 2; Eternal Word TV Network; Food Network; Fox News Channel; Fox Sports Net North; FX; G4; Golf Channel; GSN; Hallmark Channel; Headline News; HGTV; History Channel; Lifetime; MSNBC; MTV; National Geographic Channel; Nickelodeon; Oxygen; SoapNet; Speed; Spike TV; Syfy; TBS Superstation; The Learning Channel; The Weather Channel; Toon Disney; Travel Channel; truTV; Turner Classic Movies; Turner Network TV; TV Land; USA Network; Versus; VH1.
Fee: $47.99 monthly.
Digital Basic Service
Subscribers: N.A.
Programming (via satellite): BBC America; Bio; Discovery Digital Networks; DIY Network; GAS; History Channel International; MTV Networks Digital Suite; MuchMusic Network; Music Choice; Nick Jr.; Nick Too; NickToons TV; Style Network; Sundance Channel; VH1; WE tv.
Fee: $7.00 monthly.
Digital Pay Service 1
Pay Units: 1,053.
Programming (via satellite): Cinemax (multiplexed).
Fee: $15.00 installation; $10.00 monthly.
Digital Pay Service 2
Pay Units: 1,382.
Programming (via satellite): HBO (multiplexed).
Fee: $15.00 installation; $10.00 monthly.
Digital Pay Service 3
Pay Units: 1,386.
Programming (via satellite): Flix; Showtime (multiplexed); The Movie Channel (multiplexed).
Fee: $15.00 installation; $10.00 monthly (Showtime or Flix/TMC).
Digital Pay Service 4
Pay Units: 1,328.
Programming (via satellite): Encore (multiplexed); Starz (multiplexed).
Fee: $10.00 monthly.
Video-On-Demand: No
Pay-Per-View
Sports PPV (delivered digitally); Shorteez (delivered digitally); Fresh (delivered digi-

tally); Playboy TV (delivered digitally); iN DEMAND (delivered digitally); Hot Choice (delivered digitally).

Internet Service

Operational: Yes.

Broadband Service: Charter Pipeline.

Fee: $29.99 monthly.

Telephone Service

None

Miles of Plant: 216.0 (coaxial); None (fiber optic).

Vice President: Lisa Washa. Chief Technician: Jeff Gerner. Marketing Director: Traci Loonstra. Marketing Administrator: Rhonda Schelvan.

Ownership: Charter Communications Inc. (MSO).

VESPER—Packerland Broadband, 105 Kent St, PO Box 885, Iron Mountain, MI 49801. Phones: 800-236-8434; 906-774-6621. Fax: 906-776-2811. Web Site: http://www.packerlandbroadband.com. Also serves Arpin (village). ICA: WI0295.

TV Market Ranking: Below 100 (Arpin (village), VESPER). Franchise award date: N.A. Franchise expiration date: N.A. Began: N.A.

Channel capacity: 40 (not 2-way capable). Channels available but not in use: N.A.

Basic Service

Subscribers: 128.

Programming (received off-air): WAOW (ABC, CW) Wausau; WEAU-TV (NBC) Eau Claire; WFXS-DT (FOX) Wittenberg; WHRM-TV (PBS) Wausau; WSAW-TV (CBS, MNT) Wausau.

Programming (via satellite): A&E Networks; ABC Family Channel; AMC; Animal Planet; CNBC; CNN; Country Music TV; Discovery Channel; Disney Channel; ESPN; ESPN 2; Fox Sports Net; History Channel; Lifetime; MTV; Nickelodeon; Spike TV; Syfy; TBS Superstation; The Learning Channel; The Weather Channel; Turner Network TV; TV Land; USA Network; VH1; WGN America.

Fee: $24.95 installation; $29.00 monthly; $1.50 converter.

Pay Service 1

Pay Units: 24.

Programming (via satellite): HBO.

Fee: $14.95 installation; $10.95 monthly.

Video-On-Demand: No

Internet Service

Operational: Yes.

Fee: $26.95 monthly.

Telephone Service

None

Miles of Plant: 18.0 (coaxial); None (fiber optic).

General Manager: Dan Plante. Technical Supervisor: Chad Kay.

Ownership: Cable Constructors Inc. (MSO).

WABENO—Packerland Broadband, 105 Kent St, PO Box 885, Iron Mountain, MI 49801. Phones: 906-774-6621; 800-236-8434. Fax: 906-776-2811. Web Site: http://www.packerlandbroadband.com. ICA: WI0332.

TV Market Ranking: Below 100 (WABENO).

Channel capacity: N.A. Channels available but not in use: N.A.

Basic Service

Subscribers: 123.

Programming (received off-air): WAOW (ABC, CW) Wausau; WFXS-DT (FOX) Wittenberg; WGBA-TV (NBC) Green Bay; WHRM-TV (PBS) Wausau; WJFW-TV (NBC) Rhinelander; WSAW-TV (CBS, MNT) Wausau.

Fee: $14.66 monthly.

Expanded Basic Service 1

Subscribers: 111.

Programming (via satellite): A&E Networks; ABC Family Channel; Animal Planet; CNN; Country Music TV; C-SPAN; Discovery Channel; Disney Channel; ESPN; ESPN 2; Eternal Word TV Network; Fox Sports Net North; G4; Headline News; HGTV; History Channel; Lifetime; MTV; Nickelodeon; Oxygen; Spike TV; Syfy; TBS Superstation; The Weather Channel; truTV; Turner Classic Movies; Turner Network TV; TV Land; USA Network; Versus; VH1; WGN America.

Fee: $21.15 monthly.

Pay Service 1

Pay Units: N.A.

Programming (via satellite): HBO (multiplexed); Showtime (multiplexed).

Fee: $14.72 monthly (HBO), $15.83 monthly (Showtime).

Internet Service

Operational: Yes.

Fee: $26.95 monthly.

Telephone Service

None

Miles of Plant: 23.0 (coaxial); None (fiber optic).

General Manager: Dan Plante. Technical Supervisor: Chad Kay.

Ownership: Cable Constructors Inc. (MSO).

WARRENS—Charter Communications. Now served by ONALASKA, WI [WI0024]. ICA: WI0319.

WAUSAU—Charter Communications, 853 McIntosh St, Wausau, WI 54402. Phones: 715-831-8940 (Altoona office); 715-845-4223; 715-842-3910. Fax: 715-848-0081. Web Site: http://www.charter.com. Also serves Aniwa (village), Bergen, Birnamwood, Bowler (village), Brokaw, Hatley (village), Kronenwetter, Maine, Marathon City, Mattoon (village), Mosinee, Rib Mountain, Ringle (town), Rothschild, Schofield, Stettin, Texas (town) & Weston. ICA: WI0012.

TV Market Ranking: Below 100 (Aniwa (village), Bergen, Birnamwood, Bowler (village), Brokaw, Hatley (village), Kronenwetter, Maine, Marathon City, Mattoon (village), Mosinee, Rib Mountain, Ringle (town), Rothschild, Schofield, Stettin, Texas (town), WAUSAU, Weston). Franchise award date: November 1, 1976. Franchise expiration date: April 14, 2008. Began: June 1, 1964.

Channel capacity: N.A. Channels available but not in use: N.A.

Basic Service

Subscribers: 24,100.

Programming (received off-air): WAOW (ABC, CW) Wausau; WFRV-TV (CBS) Green Bay; WFXS-DT (FOX) Wittenberg; WHRM-TV (PBS) Wausau; WJFW-TV (NBC) Rhinelander; WSAW-TV (CBS, MNT) Wausau.

Programming (via satellite): C-SPAN; C-SPAN 2; TBS Superstation; TV Guide Network; WGN America.

Fee: $29.99 installation.

Expanded Basic Service 1

Subscribers: 19,712.

Programming (via satellite): A&E Networks; ABC Family Channel; AMC; Animal Planet; Bravo; Cartoon Network; CNBC; CNN; Comedy Central; Country Music TV; Discovery Channel; Discovery Fit & Health; Disney Channel; E! Entertainment Television; ESPN; ESPN 2; ESPN Classic Sports; Eternal Word TV Network; Food Network; Fox News Channel; Fox Sports Net North; FX; G4; Golf Channel; Great American Country; GSN; Hallmark Channel; Headline News; HGTV; History Channel; INSP; ION Television; Lifetime; MSNBC; MTV; National Geographic Channel; Nickelodeon; Outdoor Channel; Oxygen; Product Information Network; QVC; ShopNBC; SoapNet; Speed; Spike TV; Style Network; Syfy; The Learning Channel; The Weather Channel; Toon Disney; Travel Channel; truTV; Turner Classic Movies; Turner Network TV; TV Guide Network; TV Land; USA Network; Versus; VH1; WE tv.

Fee: $47.99 monthly.

Digital Basic Service

Subscribers: N.A.

Programming (via satellite): BBC America; Bio; Discovery Digital Networks; DIY Network; DMX Music; Fox Soccer; Fuel TV; Fuse; History Channel International; Lifetime Movie Network; MTV Networks Digital Suite; NFL Network; Nick Jr.; Nick Too; NickToons TV; Science; Sundance Channel; TeenNick.

Digital Pay Service 1

Pay Units: N.A.

Programming (via satellite): Cinemax (multiplexed); Encore (multiplexed); Flix; HBO (multiplexed); Showtime (multiplexed); The Movie Channel (multiplexed).

Video-On-Demand: Yes

Pay-Per-View

Spice (delivered digitally); Spice2 (delivered digitally); Playboy TV; NHL Center Ice; iN DEMAND (delivered digitally).

Internet Service

Operational: Yes.

Broadband Service: Charter Pipeline.

Fee: $39.99 monthly; $3.95 modem lease.

Telephone Service

Digital: Operational

Fee: $29.99 monthly

Miles of Plant: 516.0 (coaxial); 77.0 (fiber optic).

Vice President: Lisa Washa. Chief Technician: Bruce Wasleske. Marketing Director: Traci Loonstra.

Ownership: Charter Communications Inc. (MSO).

WAUTOMA—Charter Communications, 165 Knights Way, Ste 100, Fond Du Lac, WI 54935-8061. Phone: 920-907-7720. Fax: 920-907-7723. Web Site: http://www.charter.com. Also serves Coloma, Dakota (town), Hancock, Lohrville, Marion (town), Neshkoro, Plainfield, Redgranite, Wautoma (town), Westfield & Wild Rose. ICA: WI0057.

TV Market Ranking: Outside TV Markets (Coloma, Dakota (town), Hancock, Lohrville, Marion (town), Neshkoro, Plainfield, Redgranite, WAUTOMA, Wautoma (town), Westfield, Wild Rose). Franchise award date: N.A. Franchise expiration date: N.A. Began: April 1, 1980.

Channel capacity: N.A. Channels available but not in use: N.A.

Basic Service

Subscribers: 3,100.

Programming (received off-air): WACY-TV (MNT) Appleton; WBAY-TV (ABC, IND) Green Bay; WFRV-TV (CBS) Green Bay; WGBA-TV (NBC) Green Bay; WISC-TV (CBS, MNT) Madison; WLUK-TV (FOX) Green Bay; WMTV-TV (NBC) Madison; WPNE-TV (PBS) Green Bay; WSAW-TV (CBS, MNT) Wausau.

Programming (via satellite): C-SPAN; WGN America.

Fee: $29.99 installation.

Expanded Basic Service 1

Subscribers: N.A.

Programming (via satellite): A&E Networks; ABC Family Channel; AMC; Animal Planet; Cartoon Network; CNBC; CNN; Comedy Central; Country Music TV; Discovery Channel; Disney Channel; E! Entertainment Television; ESPN; ESPN 2; Eternal Word TV Network; Fox News Channel; Fox Sports Net North; FX; G4; Headline News; HGTV; History Channel; Lifetime; MSNBC; MTV; Nickelodeon; Oxygen; QVC; Speed; Spike TV; Syfy; TBS Superstation; The Learning Channel; The Weather Channel; Toon Disney; truTV; Turner Network TV; TV Land; USA Network; VH1.

Fee: $47.99 monthly.

Digital Basic Service

Subscribers: N.A.

Programming (via satellite): BBC America; Bio; Bloomberg Television; Discovery Digital Networks; DIY Network; GSN; History Channel International; Independent Film Channel; MTV Networks Digital Suite; Music Choice; Nick Jr.; Nick Too; NickToons TV; Style Network; Sundance Channel; TeenNick; WE tv.

Digital Pay Service 1

Pay Units: N.A.

Programming (via satellite): Cinemax (multiplexed); Encore; Flix; HBO (multiplexed); Showtime (multiplexed); Starz (multiplexed); The Movie Channel (multiplexed).

Video-On-Demand: No

Pay-Per-View

iN DEMAND (delivered digitally); Playboy TV (delivered digitally); Fresh (delivered digitally).

Internet Service

Operational: Yes.

Fee: $19.99 monthly.

Telephone Service

Digital: Operational

Fee: $14.99 monthly

Miles of Plant: 110.0 (coaxial); None (fiber optic).

Vice President: Lisa Washa. Chief Technician: Jeff Gerner. Marketing Director: Traci Loonstra. Marketing Administrator: Rhonda Schelvan.

Ownership: Charter Communications Inc. (MSO).

WAUWATOSA—Time Warner Cable. Now served by MILWAUKEE, WI [WI0001]. ICA: WI0004.

WAUZEKA—Packerland Broadband, 105 Kent St, PO Box 885, Iron Mountain, MI 49801. Phones: 800-236-8434; 906-774-6621. Fax: 906-776-2811. Web Site: http://www.packerlandbroadband.com. ICA: WI0324.

TV Market Ranking: Outside TV Markets (WAUZEKA).

Channel capacity: N.A. Channels available but not in use: N.A.

Basic Service

Subscribers: 81.

Programming (received off-air): KWWL (NBC) Waterloo; WHA-TV (PBS) Madison; WKBT-DT (CBS, MNT) La Crosse; WKOW (ABC) Madison; WMSN-TV (FOX) Madison; WMTV-TV (NBC) Madison.

Programming (via satellite): CW+; TBS Superstation; WGN America.

Fee: $18.50 monthly.

Expanded Basic Service 1

Subscribers: 66.

Programming (via satellite): A&E Networks; ABC Family Channel; CNN; Country Music TV; Discovery Channel; Disney Channel; E! Entertainment Television; ESPN; ESPN 2; Fox Sports Net North; Headline News; History Channel; Nickelodeon; Spike TV; The Learning Channel; The Weather Channel;

Turner Classic Movies; Turner Network TV; USA Network.
Fee: $20.45 monthly.
Pay Service 1
Pay Units: N.A.
Programming (via satellite): HBO.
Fee: $13.95 monthly.
Video-On-Demand: No
Internet Service
Operational: No.
Telephone Service
None
Miles of Plant: 5.0 (coaxial); None (fiber optic).
General Manager: Dan Plante. Technical Supervisor: Chad Kay.
Ownership: Cable Constructors Inc. (MSO).

WEST BEND—Charter Communications, 165 Knights Way, Ste 100, Fond du Lac, WI 54935-8061. Phone: 920-907-7720. Fax: 920-907-7723. Web Site: http://www.charter.com. Also serves Addison (town), Allenton, Barton (town), Colgate, Farmington (town), Hartford, Hubertus, Jackson, Kewaskum, Polk, Richfield, Rubicon, Slinger & Trenton (town). ICA: WI0323.
TV Market Ranking: 23 (Addison (town), Allenton, Barton (town), Colgate, Farmington (town), Hartford, Hubertus, Jackson, Kewaskum, Polk, Richfield, Rubicon, Rubicon, Slinger, Trenton (town), WEST BEND).
Channel capacity: 80 (operating 2-way). Channels available but not in use: N.A.
Basic Service
Subscribers: 22,300.
Programming (received off-air): WCGV-TV (MNT) Milwaukee; WDJT-TV (CBS) Milwaukee; WISN-TV (ABC) Milwaukee; WITI (FOX, IND) Milwaukee; WMLW-CA (IND) Milwaukee; WMVS (PBS) Milwaukee; WMVT (PBS) Milwaukee; WPXE-TV (ION) Kenosha; WTMJ-TV (NBC) Milwaukee; WVCY-TV (IND) Milwaukee; WVTV (CW) Milwaukee.
Programming (via satellite): C-SPAN; C-SPAN 3; Product Information Network; QVC; ShopNBC; WGN America.
Fee: $29.99 installation.
Expanded Basic Service 1
Subscribers: N.A.
Programming (via satellite): A&E Networks; ABC Family Channel; AMC; Animal Planet; Bravo; Cartoon Network; CNBC; CNN; Comedy Central; Country Music TV; Discovery Channel; Disney Channel; E! Entertainment Television; ESPN; ESPN 2; Eternal Word TV Network; Food Network; Fox News Channel; Fox Sports Net North; FX; G4; Golf Channel; GSN; Hallmark Channel; Headline News; HGTV; History Channel; Lifetime; MSNBC; MTV; National Geographic Channel; Nickelodeon; Oxygen; SoapNet; Speed; Spike TV; Syfy; TBS Superstation; The Learning Channel; The Weather Channel; Toon Disney; Travel Channel; truTV; Turner Classic Movies; Turner Network TV; TV Land; USA Network; Versus; VH1.
Fee: $47.99 monthly.
Digital Basic Service
Subscribers: N.A.
Programming (via satellite): BBC America; Bio; Discovery Digital Networks; DIY Network; Fuse; History Channel International; MTV Networks Digital Suite; Music Choice; Nick Jr.; Nick Too; NickToons TV; Style Network; Sundance Channel; TeenNick; WE tv.
Fee: $7.00 monthly.
Digital Pay Service 1
Pay Units: N.A.
Programming (via satellite): Cinemax (multiplexed); Encore (multiplexed); Flix; HBO (multiplexed); Showtime (multiplexed); Starz (multiplexed); The Movie Channel (multiplexed).
Fee: $10.00 monthly (Cinemax, HBO, Showtime, Flix/TMC, or Starz/Encore).
Video-On-Demand: No
Pay-Per-View
Sports PPV (delivered digitally); Shorteez (delivered digitally); Fresh (delivered digitally); Playboy TV (delivered digitally); iN DEMAND (delivered digitally); Hot Choice (delivered digitally).
Internet Service
Operational: Yes.
Broadband Service: Charter Pipeline.
Fee: $29.99 monthly; $4.95 modem lease.
Telephone Service
None
Miles of Plant: 614.0 (coaxial); None (fiber optic).
Vice President: Linda Washa. Chief Technician: Jeff Gerner. Marketing Director: Traci Loonstra. Marketing Administrator: Rhonda Schelvan.
Ownership: Charter Communications Inc. (MSO).

WEYERHAEUSER—Formerly served by S & K TV Systems. No longer in operation. ICA: WI0297.

WHITE LAKE—Packerland Broadband, 105 Kent St, PO Box 885, Iron Mountain, MI 49801. Phones: 800-236-8434; 906-774-6621. Fax: 906-776-2811. Web Site: http://www.packerlandbroadband.com. ICA: WI0298.
TV Market Ranking: Below 100 (WHITE LAKE). Franchise award date: N.A. Franchise expiration date: N.A. Began: May 1, 1990.
Channel capacity: 32 (not 2-way capable). Channels available but not in use: N.A.
Basic Service
Subscribers: 70.
Programming (received off-air): WACY-TV (MNT) Appleton; WAOW (ABC, CW) Wausau; WBAY-TV (ABC, IND) Green Bay; WFRV-TV (CBS) Green Bay; WGBA-TV (NBC) Green Bay; WJFW-TV (NBC) Rhinelander; WLUK-TV (FOX) Green Bay; WPNE-TV (PBS) Green Bay; WSAW-TV (CBS, MNT) Wausau.
Programming (via satellite): A&E Networks; ABC Family Channel; CNBC; CNN; C-SPAN; Discovery Channel; Disney Channel; ESPN; ESPN 2; Fox Sports Net; History Channel; MTV; Nickelodeon; QVC; Spike TV; TBS Superstation; The Learning Channel; The Weather Channel; Turner Classic Movies; Turner Network TV; USA Network; WGN America.
Fee: $25.00 installation; $33.95 monthly.
Pay Service 1
Pay Units: N.A.
Programming (via satellite): HBO.
Fee: $10.95 monthly.
Pay Service 2
Pay Units: N.A.
Programming (via satellite): Cinemax.
Fee: $10.95 monthly.
Pay Service 3
Pay Units: N.A.
Programming (via satellite): Cinemax; HBO.
Fee: $17.95 monthly.
Video-On-Demand: No
Internet Service
Operational: No.
Telephone Service
None
Miles of Plant: 7.0 (coaxial); None (fiber optic).
General Manager: Dan Plante. Technical Supervisor: Chad Kay.
Ownership: Cable Constructors Inc. (MSO).

WHITEWATER—Charter Communications. Now served by JANESVILLE, WI [WI0007]. ICA: WI0045.

WILTON—Mediacom. Now served by ONTARIO, WI [WI0303]. ICA: WI0302.

WISCONSIN RAPIDS—Charter Communications, 853 McIntosh St, Wausau, WI 54402. Phones: 715-845-4223; 715-842-3910. Fax: 715-848-0081. Web Site: http://www.charter.com. Also serves Biron, Grand Rapids, Grant, Nekoosa, Port Edwards, Port Edwards (village), Rudolph (town), Saratoga & Seneca. ICA: WI0022.
TV Market Ranking: Below 100 (Rudolph (town), Saratoga); Outside TV Markets (Biron, Grand Rapids, Grant, Nekoosa, Port Edwards, Port Edwards (village), Seneca, WISCONSIN RAPIDS). Franchise award date: February 1, 1974. Franchise expiration date: N.A. Began: February 1, 1972.
Channel capacity: N.A. Channels available but not in use: N.A.
Basic Service
Subscribers: 13,000.
Programming (received off-air): WAOW (ABC, CW) Wausau; WEAU-TV (NBC) Eau Claire; WFRV-TV (CBS) Green Bay; WFXS-DT (FOX) Wittenberg; WHRM-TV (PBS) Wausau; WJFW-TV (NBC) Rhinelander; WSAW-TV (CBS, MNT) Wausau.
Programming (via satellite): WGN America.
Fee: $29.95 installation.
Expanded Basic Service 1
Subscribers: 10,308.
Programming (via satellite): A&E Networks; ABC Family Channel; AMC; Animal Planet; Bravo; Cartoon Network; CNBC; CNN; Comedy Central; Country Music TV; C-SPAN; C-SPAN 2; Discovery Channel; Discovery Fit & Health; Disney Channel; E! Entertainment Television; ESPN; ESPN 2; ESPN Classic Sports; Eternal Word TV Network; Food Network; Fox News Channel; Fox Sports Net North; FX; G4; Golf Channel; Great American Country; GSN; Hallmark Channel; Headline News; HGTV; History Channel; INSP; ION Television; Lifetime; MSNBC; MTV; National Geographic Channel; Nickelodeon; Outdoor Channel; Oxygen; Product Information Network; QVC; ShopNBC; SoapNet; Speed; Spike TV; Style Network; Syfy; TBS Superstation; The Learning Channel; The Weather Channel; Toon Disney; Travel Channel; truTV; Turner Classic Movies; Turner Network TV; TV Guide Network; TV Land; USA Network; Versus; VH1; WE tv.
Fee: $47.99 monthly.
Digital Basic Service
Subscribers: N.A.
Programming (via satellite): BBC America; Bio; Discovery Digital Networks; DIY Network; ESPN; Fox College Sports Atlantic; Fox College Sports Central; Fox College Sports Pacific; Fox Soccer; Fuel TV; Fuse; HDNet; HDNet Movies; History Channel International; Lifetime Movie Network; MTV Networks Digital Suite; Music Choice; NFL Network; Nick Jr.; Nick Too; NickToons TV; Sundance Channel; TeenNick; TV Guide Interactive Inc.
Digital Pay Service 1
Pay Units: N.A.
Programming (via satellite): Cinemax (multiplexed); Encore (multiplexed); Flix; HBO (multiplexed); HBO HD; Showtime (multiplexed); Showtime HD; Starz (multiplexed); The Movie Channel (multiplexed).
Video-On-Demand: Yes
Pay-Per-View
iN DEMAND (delivered digitally); NASCAR In Car (delivered digitally); NHL Center Ice (delivered digitally); MLB Extra Innings (delivered digitally); Playboy TV (delivered digitally); Fresh (delivered digitally); Shorteez (delivered digitally).
Internet Service
Operational: Yes.
Broadband Service: Charter Pipeline.
Fee: $29.99 monthly; $3.95 modem lease.
Telephone Service
Digital: Operational
Fee: $29.99 monthly
Miles of Plant: 351.0 (coaxial); 53.0 (fiber optic).
Vice President & General Manager: Lisa Washa. Chief Technician: Bruce Wasleske. Marketing Director: Traci Loonstra.
Ownership: Charter Communications Inc. (MSO).

WITTENBERG—Wittenberg Cable TV, 104 W Walker St, PO Box 160, Wittenberg, WI 54499-0160. Phones: 715-253-2111; 715-253-2828. Fax: 715-253-3497. E-mail: wittenbergtel@wittenbergnet.net. Web Site: http://www.wittenbergnet.net. Also serves Bevent, Eland, Elderdon, Galloway, Reid & Tigerton. ICA: WI0158.
TV Market Ranking: Below 100 (Bevent, Eland, ELDERDON, Galloway, Reid, WITTENBERG, Tigerton). Franchise award date: March 30, 1980. Franchise expiration date: N.A. Began: March 15, 1982.
Channel capacity: 36 (not 2-way capable). Channels available but not in use: N.A.
Basic Service
Subscribers: 800.
Programming (received off-air): WACY-TV (MNT) Appleton; WAOW (ABC, CW) Wausau; WBAY-TV (ABC, IND) Green Bay; WFRV-TV (CBS) Green Bay; WFXS-DT (FOX) Wittenberg; WGBA-TV (NBC) Green Bay; WHRM-TV (PBS) Wausau; WJFW-TV (NBC) Rhinelander; WLUK-TV (FOX) Green Bay; WSAW-TV (CBS, MNT) Wausau.
Programming (via satellite): A&E Networks; ABC Family Channel; AMC; Animal Planet; Bravo; CNN; Comedy Central; Country Music TV; C-SPAN; Discovery Channel; Disney Channel; ESPN; ESPN 2; ESPN Classic Sports; Fox News Channel; Fox Sports Net; FX; Hallmark Channel; HGTV; History Channel; Lifetime; MTV; Nickelodeon; Outdoor Channel; RFD-TV; Speed; Spike TV; Syfy; TBS Superstation; The Learning Channel; The Weather Channel; Travel Channel; Turner Classic Movies; Turner Network TV; TV Land; USA Network; VH1; WGN America.
Fee: $42.00 monthly; $15.00 additional installation.
Pay Service 1
Pay Units: 116.
Programming (via satellite): HBO.
Fee: $7.50 installation; $12.75 monthly.
Pay Service 2
Pay Units: 36.
Programming (via satellite): Showtime.
Fee: $12.75 monthly.
Video-On-Demand: No
Internet Service
Operational: No, DSL.
Telephone Service
None
Miles of Plant: 67.0 (coaxial); 19.0 (fiber optic). Additional miles planned: 16.0 (coaxial); 11.0 (fiber optic).

Manager & Chief Technician: Allen Mahnke.
Ownership: Wittenberg Telephone Co. (MSO).

WOLF RIVER—New Century Communications, 3588 Kennebec Dr, Eagan, MN 55122-1001. Phone: 651-688-2623. Fax: 651-688-2624. E-mail: info@ourcableia.com. ICA: WI0185.

TV Market Ranking: Below 100 (WOLF RIVER). Franchise award date: N.A. Franchise expiration date: N.A. Began: N.A.

Channel capacity: N.A. Channels available but not in use: N.A.

Basic Service

Subscribers: 35.

Programming (received off-air): WACY-TV (MNT) Appleton; WBAY-TV (ABC, IND) Green Bay; WCWF (CW) Suring; WFRV-TV (CBS) Green Bay; WGBA-TV (NBC) Green Bay; WLUK-TV (FOX) Green Bay; WPNE-TV (PBS) Green Bay.

Programming (via satellite): A&E Networks; ABC Family Channel; AMC; Animal Planet; CNN; Country Music TV; Discovery Channel; Disney Channel; ESPN; ESPN 2; Food Network; Fox Sports Net Wisconsin; FX; Golf Channel; HGTV; History Channel; Lifetime; MTV; Nickelodeon; Outdoor Channel; QVC; Speed; Spike TV; Syfy; TBS Superstation; The Learning Channel; The Weather Channel; Turner Network TV; TV Land; USA Network; VH1; WGN America.

Fee: $30.00 installation; $38.85 monthly.

Digital Basic Service

Subscribers: N.A.

Programming (via satellite): BBC America; Bio; Bloomberg Television; Bravo; cloo; CMT Pure Country; DMX Music; ESPN Classic Sports; ESPNews; Fox Movie Channel; Fox Soccer; Fuse; G4; GMC; GSN; Halogen Network; History Channel International; Independent Film Channel; Lifetime Movie Network; Military History Channel; MTV2; Nick Jr.; NickToons TV; Science; Style Network; TeenNick; Toon Disney; Trinity Broadcasting Network; Turner Classic Movies; Versus; VH1 Classic; WE tv.

Fee: $11.00 monthly.

Digital Pay Service 1

Pay Units: N.A.

Programming (via satellite): Cinemax (multiplexed); Encore (multiplexed); HBO (multiplexed); Showtime (multiplexed); Starz (multiplexed).

Fee: $9.95 monthly (Cinemax), $10.95 monthly (Starz & Encore), $12.95 monthly (Showtime), $13.95 monthly (HBO).

Video-On-Demand: No

Pay-Per-View

Playboy TV (delivered digitally); Spice (delivered digitally).

Internet Service

Operational: Yes.

Broadband Service: IBBS.

Fee: $49.95 installation; $34.95 monthly.

Telephone Service

None

Miles of Plant: 7.0 (coaxial); None (fiber optic).

Executive Vice President: Marty Walch. Manager & Chief Technician: Todd Anderson.

Ownership: New Century Communications (MSO).

WONEWOC—Packerland Broadband, 105 Kent St, PO Box 885, Iron Mountain, MI 49801. Phones: 800-236-8434; 906-774-6621. Fax: 906-776-2811. Web Site: http://www.packerlandbroadband.com. Also serves Union Center. ICA: WI0149.

TV Market Ranking: Outside TV Markets (Union Center, WONEWOC). Franchise award date: January 1, 1963. Franchise expiration date: N.A. Began: May 1, 1964.

Channel capacity: 42 (not 2-way capable). Channels available but not in use: N.A.

Basic Service

Subscribers: 171.

Programming (received off-air): WBUW (CW) Janesville; WEAU-TV (NBC) Eau Claire; WHA-TV (PBS) Madison; WISC-TV (CBS, MNT) Madison; WKBT-DT (CBS, MNT) La Crosse; WKOW (ABC) Madison; WMSN-TV (FOX) Madison; WMTV-TV (NBC) Madison.

Programming (via satellite): TBS Superstation; WGN America.

Fee: $18.50 monthly.

Expanded Basic Service 1

Subscribers: 136.

Programming (via satellite): A&E Networks; ABC Family Channel; CNN; Country Music TV; Discovery Channel; Disney Channel; E! Entertainment Television; ESPN; ESPN 2; Fox Sports Net North; Headline News; History Channel; Nickelodeon; Spike TV; The Learning Channel; The Weather Channel; Turner Classic Movies; Turner Network TV; TV Land; USA Network.

Fee: $20.45 monthly.

Pay Service 1

Pay Units: N.A.

Programming (via satellite): HBO.

Fee: $13.95 monthly.

Video-On-Demand: No

Internet Service

Operational: No.

Telephone Service

None

Miles of Plant: 9.0 (coaxial); None (fiber optic).

General Manager: Dan Plante. Technical Supervisor: Chad Kay.

Ownership: Cable Constructors Inc. (MSO).

WOODMAN—Formerly served by Woodman TV Cable System. No longer in operation. ICA: WI0300.

WOODVILLE (village)—Baldwin Telecom Inc. Formerly served by Baldwin (village), WI [WI0079]. This cable system has converted to IPTV, 930 Maple St, Baldwin, WI 54002. Phones: 877-684-3346; 715-684-3346. Fax: 715-684-4747. E-mail: info@baldwin-telecom.net. Web Site: http://www.baldwin-telecom.net. ICA: WI5293.

Channel capacity: N.A. Channels available but not in use: N.A.

Basic Service

Subscribers: N.A.

Fee: $61.00 monthly.

Expanded Basic Service 1

Subscribers: N.A.

Fee: $6.95 monthly.

Pay Service 1

Pay Units: N.A.

Fee: $11.95 monthly.

Internet Service

Operational: Yes.

Fee: $39.95 monthly.

Telephone Service

Digital: Operational

General Manager: Larry Knegendorf. Cable TV Manager: Matt Knegendorf. Plant Manager: Duane Russett. Operations Manager: Matt Sparks.

WYOMING

Total Systems: 53
Total Communities Served: 100
Franchises Not Yet Operating: 0
Applications Pending: 0
Communities with Applications: 0
Number of Basic Subscribers: 121,468
Number of Expanded Basic Subscribers: 79,761
Number of Pay Units: 17,689

Top 100 Markets Represented: N.A.

For a list of cable communities in this section, see the Cable Community Index located in the back of Cable Volume 2.
For explanation of terms used in cable system listings, see p. D-11.

AFTON (town)—Formerly served by KLiP Interactive. No longer in operation. ICA: WY0030.

BASIN—TCT West Inc. This cable system has converted to IPTV, 405 S 4th St, Basin, WY 82410. Phones: 800-354-2911; 307-568-3357. Fax: 307-568-2506. E-mail: support@tctwest.net. Web Site: http://www.tctwest.net. ICA: WY5003.
TV Market Ranking: Outside TV Markets (BASIN).
Channel capacity: N.A. Channels available but not in use: N.A.
Basic Service
Subscribers: 123.
Internet Service
Operational: Yes.
Telephone Service
Digital: Operational
Miles of Plant: None (coaxial); 500.0 (fiber optic). Miles of plant includes Basin, Burlington, Byron, Cowley, Emblem, Frannie, Greybull, Lovell, Manderson, Meeteetse, Otto, Shell, & Ten Sleep

BASIN—TCT West Inc. This cable system has converted to IPTV. See Basin, WY [WY5003]. ICA: WY0072.

BUFFALO—Bresnan Communications, 451 S Durbin St, Casper, WY 82601. Phones: 307-265-3136; 307-672-5841 (Sheridan office); 877-273-7626. Fax: 307-266-6821. Web Site: http://www.bresnan.com. Also serves Johnson County. ICA: WY0019.
TV Market Ranking: Below 100 (BUFFALO, Johnson County (portions)); Outside TV Markets (Johnson County (portions)). Franchise award date: March 7, 1995. Franchise expiration date: March 6, 2010. Began: April 1, 1964.
Channel capacity: N.A. Channels available but not in use: N.A.
Basic Service
Subscribers: 1,542.
Programming (received off-air): KCWC-DT (PBS) Lander; KSGW-TV (ABC) Sheridan; KTWO-TV (ABC) Casper; 5 FMs.
Programming (via satellite): C-SPAN; C-SPAN 2; Eternal Word TV Network; ION Television; KCNC-TV (CBS) Denver; KDVR (FOX) Denver; KMGH-TV (ABC) Denver; KRMA-TV (PBS) Denver; KTVD (MNT) Denver; KUSA (NBC) Denver; KWGN-TV (CW) Denver; Lifetime; QVC; TBS Superstation; TV Guide Network; WGN America.
Fee: $40.95 installation; $23.34 monthly; $13.95 additional installation.
Expanded Basic Service 1
Subscribers: 1,259.
Programming (via satellite): A&E Networks; ABC Family Channel; Altitude Sports & Entertainment; AMC; Animal Planet; Cartoon Network; CNBC; CNN; Comedy Central; Country Music TV; Discovery Channel; Disney Channel; E! Entertainment Television; ESPN; ESPN 2; Food Network; Fox News Channel; FX; Great American Country; Hallmark Channel; Headline News; HGTV; History Channel; INSP; MSNBC; MTV; Nickelodeon; Oxygen; Root Sports Rocky Mountain; Spike TV; Syfy; The Learning Channel; The Weather Channel; Travel Channel; truTV; Turner Classic Movies; Turner Network TV; TV Land; USA Network; VH1.
Fee: $36.40 monthly.

Digital Basic Service
Subscribers: 168.
Programming (via satellite): A&E HD; AmericanLife TV Network; BBC America; Bio; Bloomberg Television; Bravo; BYU Television; CBS Sports Network; CMT Pure Country; Cooking Channel; Discovery Fit & Health; Discovery Health Channel; Discovery Kids Channel; DIY Network; DMX Music; ESPN 2 HD; ESPN Classic Sports; ESPN HD; ESPNews; Fox College Sports Atlantic; Fox College Sports Central; Fox College Sports Pacific; Fox Movie Channel; Fox Reality Channel; Fox Soccer; FSN HD; Fuse; G4; GMC; Golf Channel; GSN; Halogen Network; HD Theater; HDNet; HDNet Movies; History Channel International; HRTV; ID Investigation Discovery; Independent Film Channel; ION Television; Lifetime Movie Network; Military Channel; MountainWest Sports Network; MTV Hits; MTV Jams; MTV2; National Geographic Channel; National Geographic Channel HD Network; NFL Network; NFL Network HD; Nick Jr.; Nick Too; NickToons TV; Outdoor Channel; PBS Kids Sprout; Planet Green; RFD-TV; Science; SoapNet; Speed; Style Network; TeenNick; Toon Disney; Tr3s; Trinity Broadcasting Network; Turner Network TV HD; Universal HD; Versus; Versus HD; VH1 Classic; VH1 Soul.
Fee: $64.24 monthly; $6.70 converter.

Pay Service 1
Pay Units: 227.
Programming (via satellite): HBO.
Fee: $14.95 installation; $12.70 monthly.

Digital Pay Service 1
Pay Units: 163.
Programming (via satellite): Cinemax (multiplexed); Encore (multiplexed); Flix; HBO (multiplexed); HBO HD; Showtime (multiplexed); Showtime HD; Starz (multiplexed); Starz HDTV; The Movie Channel (multiplexed).
Fee: $49.99 installation; $12.00 monthly (Starz/Encore), $16.15 monthly (Cinemax, HBO or Showtime/TMC).
Video-On-Demand: No

Pay-Per-View
iN DEMAND (delivered digitally).

Internet Service
Operational: Yes.
Broadband Service: Bresnan OnLine.
Fee: $29.95-$52.95 monthly; $3.99 modem lease.
Telephone Service
Digital: Operational
Fee: $46.99 monthly
Miles of Plant: 39.0 (coaxial); 7.0 (fiber optic).
General Manager: Clint Rodeman.
Ownership: Bresnan Communications Inc. (MSO). Sale pends to Cablevision Systems Corp.

BURLINGTON—Formerly served by Basin, WY [WY0072]. TCT West Inc. This cable system has converted to IPTV, 405 S 4th St, Basin, WY 82410. Phones: 800-354-2911; 307-568-3357. Fax: 307-568-2506. E-mail: support@tctwest.net. Web Site: http://www.tctwest.net. ICA: WY5004.
TV Market Ranking: Outside TV Markets (BURLINGTON).
Channel capacity: N.A. Channels available but not in use: N.A.
Internet Service
Operational: Yes.
Telephone Service
Digital: Operational

BURNS—B & C Cablevision Inc., 4683 US Hwy 6, Wiggins, CO 80654-8912. Phone: 970-483-7820. Fax: 970-483-7822. E-mail: bccable@rtebb.net. ICA: WY0070.
TV Market Ranking: Below 100 (BURNS). Franchise award date: August 18, 1994. Franchise expiration date: August 18, 2009. Began: May 1, 1995.
Channel capacity: 50 (not 2-way capable). Channels available but not in use: N.A.
Basic Service
Subscribers: 40.
Programming (received off-air): KDEV-LP (MNT) Cheyenne; KGWN-TV (CBS, CW) Cheyenne; KLWY (FOX) Cheyenne.
Programming (via satellite): A&E Networks; ABC Family Channel; CNN; Discovery Channel; Disney Channel; ESPN; Fox News Channel; HGTV; History Channel; ION Television; KDVR (FOX) Denver; KMGH-TV (ABC) Denver; KRMA-TV (PBS) Denver; KUSA (NBC) Denver; KWGN-TV (CW) Denver; Root Sports Rocky Mountain; Spike TV; TBS Superstation; The Weather Channel; Turner Classic Movies; Turner Network TV; USA Network; WGN America.
Fee: $30.00 installation; $26.00 monthly; $3.00 converter.
Pay Service 1
Pay Units: N.A.
Programming (via satellite): HBO.
Fee: $10.00 monthly.
Internet Service
Operational: No.
Telephone Service
None
Miles of Plant: 3.0 (coaxial); None (fiber optic).
Manager: Bill Rogers. Marketing Director: Carol Rogers. Chief Technician: Harv Humphrey. Office Manager: Teather Leitner.
Ownership: B & C Cablevision Inc. (MSO).

BYRON—Formerly served by Basin, WY [WY0072]. TCT West Inc. This cable system has converted to IPTV, 405 S 4th St, Basin, WY 82410. Phones: 800-354-2911; 307-568-3357. Fax: 307-568-2506. E-mail: support@tctwest.net. Web Site: http://www.tctwest.net. ICA: WY5019.
TV Market Ranking: Outside TV Markets (BYRON).
Channel capacity: N.A. Channels available but not in use: N.A.
Internet Service
Operational: Yes.
Telephone Service
Digital: Operational

BYRON—Formerly served by Byron Cable TV. No longer in operation. ICA: WY0071.

CASPER—Bresnan Communications, 451 S Durbin St, Casper, WY 82601. Phones: 307-265-3136; 307-265-3529; 877-273-7626. Fax: 307-266-6821. Web Site: http://www.bresnan.com. Also serves Bar Nunn, Evansville, Mills, Mountain View (Natrona County), Natrona County & Paradise Valley. ICA: WY0001.
TV Market Ranking: Below 100 (Bar Nunn, CASPER, Evansville, Mills, Mountain View (Natrona County), Natrona County (portions), Paradise Valley); Outside TV Markets (Natrona County (portions)). Franchise award date: N.A. Franchise expiration date: March 1, 2007. Began: December 24, 1953.
Channel capacity: N.A. Channels available but not in use: N.A.
Basic Service
Subscribers: 19,400.
Programming (received off-air): KCWC-DT (PBS) Lander; KCWY-DT (NBC) Casper; KFNB (FOX) Casper; KGWC-TV (CBS) Casper; KTWO-TV (ABC) Casper; 6 FMs.
Programming (via satellite): BYU Television; C-SPAN; Discovery Channel; KWGN-TV (CW) Denver; QVC; TBS Superstation; TV Guide Network; WGN America.
Fee: $33.39 installation; $23.34 monthly; $3.00 converter.
Expanded Basic Service 1
Subscribers: 15,600.
Programming (via satellite): A&E Networks; ABC Family Channel; Altitude Sports & Entertainment; AMC; Animal Planet; Cartoon Network; CNBC; CNN; Comedy Central; Country Music TV; C-

SPAN 2; Disney Channel; E! Entertainment Television; ESPN; ESPN 2; Eternal Word TV Network; Food Network; Fox News Channel; FX; Hallmark Channel; Headline News; HGTV; History Channel; ION Television; Lifetime; MSNBC; MTV; Nickelodeon; Oxygen; Root Sports Rocky Mountain; Spike TV; Syfy; The Learning Channel; The Weather Channel; Travel Channel; truTV; Turner Classic Movies; Turner Network TV; TV Land; USA Network; VH1.

Fee: $42.40 monthly.

Digital Basic Service

Subscribers: N.A.

Programming (via satellite): A&E HD; ABC Family HD; Altitude Sports & Entertainment; AmericanLife TV Network; Animal Planet HD; BBC America; Bio; Bloomberg Television; Bravo; CBS Sports Network; CMT Pure Country; CNN HD; Cooking Channel; C-SPAN 3; Discovery Channel HD; Discovery Fit & Health; Discovery Health Channel; Discovery Kids Channel; Disney Channel HD; DIY Network; DMX Music; ESPN 2 HD; ESPN Classic Sports; ESPN HD; ESPNews; Food Network HD; Fox Movie Channel; Fox Reality Channel; Fox Soccer; FSN HD; Fuse; G4; Golf Channel; Great American Country; GSN; Halogen Network; HD Theater; HDNet; HDNet Movies; HGTV HD; History Channel HD; History Channel International; HRTV; ID Investigation Discovery; Independent Film Channel; ION Life; Lifetime Movie Network; Lifetime Movie Network HD; Military Channel; MountainWest Sports Network; MTV Hits; MTV2; mun2 television; National Geographic Channel; National Geographic Channel HD Network; NFL Network HD; NHL Network; Nick Jr.; NickToons TV; Outdoor Channel; PBS Kids Sprout; Planet Green; Qubo; RFD-TV; Science; Science HD; ShopNBC; SoapNet; Speed; Style Network; Syfy HD; TBS in HD; TeenNick; The Weather Channel HD; TLC HD; Toon Disney; Tr3s; Trinity Broadcasting Network; Turner Network TV HD; Universal HD; USA Network HD; Versus; Versus HD; VH1 Classic; VH1 Soul.

Fee: $64.24 monthly; $6.70 converter.

Digital Pay Service 1

Pay Units: N.A.

Programming (via satellite): Cinemax (multiplexed); Cinemax HD; Encore (multiplexed); Flix; HBO (multiplexed); HBO HD; Showtime (multiplexed); Showtime HD; Starz (multiplexed); Starz HDTV; The Movie Channel (multiplexed); The Movie Channel HD.

Fee: $12.00 monthly (Starz/Encore), $16.15 monthly (Cinemax, HBO or Showtimw/TMC).

Video-On-Demand: Yes

Pay-Per-View

iN DEMAND (delivered digitally); ESPN (delivered digitally); Discovery en Espanol (delivered digitally); Fox Deportes (delivered digitally); mun2 television (delivered digitally); Cine Latino (delivered digitally); History Channel en Espanol (delivered digitally); Tr3s (delivered digitally); CNN en Espanol (delivered digitally); ESPN Deportes On Demand (delivered digitally); Cine Mexicano (delivered digitally); GolTV (delivered digitally); Bandamax (delivered digitally); De Pelicula (delivered digitally); De Pelicula Clasico (delivered digitally); Telehit (delivered digitally); Movies (delivered digitally); Sports PPV (delivered digitally); MLS Direct Kick (delivered digitally); HBO On Demand (delivered digitally); Showtime On Demand (delivered digitally); Starz On Demand (delivered digitally); WWE 24/7 (delivered digitally); Free Speech TV on Demand (delivered digitally); The SPOT on Demand (delivered digitally); MLB Extra Innings (delivered digitally); NHL Center Ice (delivered digitally); Fox College Sports Atlantic (delivered digitally); Fox College Sports Central (delivered digitally); Fox College Sports Pacific (delivered digitally); VeneMovies (delivered digitally).

Internet Service

Operational: Yes.

Subscribers: 1,400.

Broadband Service: Bresnan OnLine.

Fee: $49.99 installation; $29.95-$62.90 monthly; $3.99 modem lease.

Telephone Service

Analog: Not Operational

Digital: Operational

Fee: $46.99 monthly

Miles of Plant: 369.0 (coaxial); 21.0 (fiber optic).

General Manager: Clint Rodeman.

Ownership: Bresnan Communications Inc. (MSO). Sale pends to Cablevision Systems Corp.

CHEYENNE—Bresnan Communications, 506 W 17th St, Cheyenne, WY 82001. Phones: 307-632-8114; 877-273-7626. Fax: 307-637-5973. Web Site: http://www.bresnan.com. Also serves Fox Farm College, Laramie County, South Greeley & Warren AFB. ICA: WY0002.

TV Market Ranking: Below 100 (CHEYENNE, Fox Farm College, Laramie County (portions), South Greeley, Warren AFB); Outside TV Markets (Laramie County (portions)). Franchise award date: N.A. Franchise expiration date: N.A. Began: December 1, 1968.

Channel capacity: N.A. Channels available but not in use: N.A.

Basic Service

Subscribers: 23,379.

Programming (received off-air): KCWC-DT (PBS) Lander; KCWY-DT (NBC) Casper; KGWN-TV (CBS, CW) Cheyenne; KLWY (FOX) Cheyenne; KQCK (IND) Cheyenne; 18 FMs.

Programming (via microwave): KCNC-TV (CBS) Denver; KMGH-TV (ABC) Denver; KRMA-TV (PBS) Denver; KUSA (NBC) Denver.

Programming (via satellite): C-SPAN; C-SPAN 2; CW+; Eternal Word TV Network; Lifetime; Oxygen; QVC; TBS Superstation; Travel Channel; TV Guide Network; Univision Studios.

Fee: $60.00 installation; $23.34 monthly; $2.28 converter; $19.67 additional installation.

Expanded Basic Service 1

Subscribers: 20,277.

Programming (via satellite): A&E Networks; ABC Family Channel; Altitude Sports & Entertainment; AMC; Animal Planet; BET Networks; Cartoon Network; CNBC; CNN; Comedy Central; Country Music TV; Discovery Channel; Disney Channel; E! Entertainment Television; ESPN; ESPN 2; Food Network; Fox News Channel; FX; Great American Country; Hallmark Channel; Headline News; HGTV; History Channel; ION Television; MSNBC; MTV; Nickelodeon; Root Sports Rocky Mountain; Spike TV; Syfy; The Learning Channel; The Weather Channel; truTV; Turner Classic Movies; Turner Network TV; TV Land; USA Network; VH1.

Fee: $42.40 monthly.

Digital Basic Service

Subscribers: N.A.

Programming (received off-air): KLWY (FOX) Cheyenne.

Programming (via satellite): A&E HD; ABC Family HD; Altitude Sports & Entertainment; AmericanLife TV Network; Animal Planet HD; BBC America; Bio; Bloomberg Television; BlueHighways TV; Bravo; BYU Television; CBS Sports Network; CMT Pure Country; CNN HD; Cooking Channel; C-SPAN 3; Discovery Channel HD; Discovery Fit & Health; Discovery Health Channel; Discovery Kids Channel; Disney Channel HD; DIY Network; DMX Music; ESPN 2 HD; ESPN Classic Sports; ESPN HD; ESPNews; Food Network HD; Fox Movie Channel; Fox Reality Channel; Fox Soccer; FSN HD; Fuse; G4; GMC; Golf Channel; GSN; Halogen Network; HD Theater; HDNet; HDNet Movies; HGTV HD; History Channel; History Channel HD; History Channel International; HRTV; ID Investigation Discovery; Independent Film Channel; ION Television; Lifetime Movie Network; Lifetime Movie Network HD; Military Channel; MountainWest Sports Network; MTV Hits; MTV Jams; MTV2; mun2 television; National Geographic Channel; National Geographic Channel HD Network; Nick Jr.; Nick Too; NickToons TV; Outdoor Channel; Outdoor Channel 2 HD; PBS Kids Sprout; Planet Green; RFD-TV; Science; Science HD; SoapNet; Speed; Speed HD; Style Network; Syfy HD; TBS in HD; TeenNick; Telefutura; Tennis Channel; The Weather Channel HD; TLC HD; Toon Disney; Tr3s; Trinity Broadcasting Network; Turner Network TV HD; Universal HD; USA Network HD; Versus; VH1 Classic; VH1 Soul.

Fee: $64.20 monthly; $6.70 converter.

Pay Service 1

Pay Units: 1,973.

Programming (via satellite): HBO; Showtime; Starz.

Digital Pay Service 1

Pay Units: N.A.

Programming (via satellite): Cinemax (multiplexed); Encore (multiplexed); Flix; HBO (multiplexed); HBO HD; Showtime (multiplexed); Showtime HD; Starz (multiplexed); Starz HDTV; The Movie Channel (multiplexed); The Movie Channel HD; Versus HD.

Fee: $12.00 monthly (Starz/Encore), $16.15 monthly (Cinemax, HBO or Showtime/TMC).

Video-On-Demand: Yes

Pay-Per-View

iN DEMAND (delivered digitally); ESPN (delivered digitally); mun2 television (delivered digitally); Cine Latino (delivered digitally); History Channel en Espanol (delivered digitally); Tr3s (delivered digitally); CNN en Espanol (delivered digitally); ESPN Deportes (delivered digitally); Cine Mexicano (delivered digitally); GolTV (delivered digitally); Bandamax (delivered digitally); De Pelicula (delivered digitally); De Pelicula Clasico (delivered digitally); Telehit (delivered digitally); Univision Studios (delivered digitally); Movies (delivered digitally); sports (delivered digitally); NFL Network (delivered digitally); Cinemax On Demand (delivered digitally); HBO On Demand (delivered digitally); Showtime On Demand (delivered digitally); Starz On Demand (delivered digitally); WWE 24/7 (delivered digitally); Free Speech TV on Demand (delivered digitally); The SPOT On Demand (delivered digitally); careerSPOT On Demand (delivered digitally); homeSPOT On Demand (delivered digitally); Fox College Sports Atlantic (delivered digitally); NFL Network HD (delivered digitally); Fox College Sports Central (delivered digitally); Fox College Sports Pacific (delivered digitally); VeneMovies (delivered digitally); Discovery en Espanol (delivered digitally); Fox Deportes (delivered digitally).

Internet Service

Operational: Yes.

Subscribers: 3,430.

Broadband Service: Bresnan OnLine.

Fee: $49.99 installation; $29.95-$62.90 monthly; $3.99 modem lease.

Telephone Service

Analog: Not Operational

Digital: Operational

Fee: $46.99 monthly

Miles of Plant: 540.0 (coaxial); None (fiber optic).

Regional Vice President: Clint Rodeman. General Manager: Wes Frost. Technical Operations Manager: Mitch Winter.

Ownership: Bresnan Communications Inc. (MSO). Sale pends to Cablevision Systems Corp.

CODY—Bresnan Communications, 2432 Sheridan Ave, Cody, WY 82414-4004. Phone: 307-587-9459. Fax: 307-587-5912. Web Site: http://www.bresnan.com. Also serves Park County. ICA: WY0010.

TV Market Ranking: Outside TV Markets (CODY, Park County). Franchise award date: N.A. Franchise expiration date: N.A. Began: October 1, 1954.

Channel capacity: N.A. Channels available but not in use: N.A.

Basic Service

Subscribers: 3,100.

Programming (via microwave): KHMT (FOX) Hardin; KSVI (ABC) Billings; KTVQ (CBS, CW) Billings; KULR-TV (NBC) Billings.

Programming (via satellite): BYU Television; C-SPAN; C-SPAN 2; CW+; ION Television; KRMA-TV (PBS) Denver; Lifetime; QVC; TBS Superstation; TV Guide Network; WGN America.

Programming (via translator): KCWC-DT (PBS) Lander; KTWO-TV (ABC) Casper.

Fee: $25.00 installation; $23.40 monthly; $4.50 converter.

Expanded Basic Service 1

Subscribers: 2,640.

Programming (via satellite): A&E Networks; ABC Family Channel; Altitude Sports & Entertainment; AMC; Animal Planet; Bravo; Cartoon Network; CNBC; CNN; Comedy Central; Country Music TV; Discovery Channel; Disney Channel; E! Entertainment Television; ESPN; ESPN 2; Eternal Word TV Network; Food Network; Fox News Channel; FX; Great American Country; Hallmark Channel; Headline News; HGTV; History Channel; INSP; MSNBC; MTV; Nickelodeon; Oxygen; Root Sports Rocky Mountain; Spike TV; Syfy; The Learning Channel; The Weather Channel; Travel Channel; truTV; Turner Classic Movies; Turner Network TV; TV Land; USA Network; VH1.

Fee: $42.34 monthly.

Digital Basic Service

Subscribers: N.A.

Programming (via satellite): A&E HD; Altitude Sports & Entertainment; AmericanLife TV Network; Animal Planet HD; BBC America; Bio; Bloomberg Television; CBS Sports Network; CMT Pure Country; Cooking Channel; Discovery Channel HD; Discovery Fit & Health; Discovery Health Channel; Discovery Kids Channel; DIY Network; DMX Music; ESPN 2 HD; ESPN Classic Sports; ESPN HD; ESPNews; Fox Movie Channel; Fox Reality Channel; Fox Soccer; FSN HD; Fuse; G4; GMC; Golf Channel; GSN; Halogen Network; HD Theater; HD-

Net; HDNet Movies; History Channel International; HRTV; ID Investigation Discovery; Independent Film Channel; ION Television; Lifetime Movie Network; Military Channel; MountainWest Sports Network; MTV Hits; MTV Jams; MTV2; National Geographic Channel; National Geographic Channel HD Network; Nick Jr.; Nick Too; NickToons TV; Outdoor Channel; PBS Kids Sprout; Planet Green; RFD-TV; Science; Science HD; SoapNet; Speed; Style Network; TeenNick; TLC HD; Toon Disney; Tr3s; Trinity Broadcasting Network; Turner Network TV HD; Universal HD; Versus; Versus HD; VH1 Classic; VH1 Soul.
Fee: $64.24 monthly; $6.70 converter.

Pay Service 1
Pay Units: N.A.
Programming (via satellite): HBO.

Digital Pay Service 1
Pay Units: N.A.
Programming (via satellite): Cinemax (multiplexed); Encore (multiplexed); Flix; HBO (multiplexed); HBO HD; Showtime (multiplexed); Showtime HD; Starz (multiplexed); Starz HDTV; The Movie Channel (multiplexed).
Fee: $12.00 monthly (Starz/Encore), $16.15 monthly (Cinemax, HBO or Showtime/TMC).

Video-On-Demand: No

Pay-Per-View
ESPN (delivered digitally); iN DEMAND (delivered digitally).

Internet Service
Operational: Yes.
Broadband Service: Bresnan OnLine.
Fee: $49.99 installation; $29.95-$62.95 monthly; $3.99 modem lease.

Telephone Service
Analog: Not Operational
Digital: Operational
Fee: $46.99 monthly

Miles of Plant: 84.0 (coaxial); 15.0 (fiber optic).
Regional Vice President & General Manager: Clint Rodeman. Chief Technician: Dan Higgins.
Ownership: Bresnan Communications Inc. (MSO). Sale pends to Cablevision Systems Corp.

COKEVILLE—All West Communications. This cable system has converted to IPTV. See Cokeville (town), WY [WY5014]. ICA: WY0054.

COKEVILLE (town)—All West Communications. Formerly [WY0054]. This cable system has converted to IPTV, 50 West 100 North, Kamas, UT 84036. Phones: 866-255-9378; 435-783-4361. Fax: 435-783-4928. E-mail: bsupport@allwest.net. Web Site: http://www.allwest.com. ICA: WY5014.
TV Market Ranking: Outside TV Markets (COKEVILLE (TOWN)). Franchise award date: N.A. Franchise expiration date: N.A. Began: N.A.
Channel capacity: N.A. Channels available but not in use: N.A.

Internet Service
Operational: Yes.

Telephone Service
Digital: Operational

COWLEY—Formerly served by Basin, WY [WY0072]. TCT West Inc. This cable system has converted to IPTV, 405 S 4th St, Basin, WY 82410. Phones: 800-354-2911; 307-568-3357. Fax: 307-568-2506. E-mail: support@tctwest.net. Web Site: http://www.tctwest.net. ICA: WY5005.
TV Market Ranking: Outside TV Markets (COWLEY).
Channel capacity: N.A. Channels available but not in use: N.A.

Internet Service
Operational: Yes.

Telephone Service
Digital: Operational

COWLEY—Formerly served by Cowley Telecable Inc. No longer in operation. ICA: WY0043.

DOUGLAS—CommuniComm Services, 234 Wind River Dr, Douglas, WY 82633-2338. Phones: 800-759-8448 (local access only); 307-358-3861. Fax: 307-358-3849. Web Site: http://www.netcommander.com. ICA: WY0012.
TV Market Ranking: Outside TV Markets (DOUGLAS). Franchise award date: November 1, 1973. Franchise expiration date: N.A. Began: October 1, 1975.
Channel capacity: 75 (operating 2-way). Channels available but not in use: N.A.

Basic Service
Subscribers: 1,581.
Programming (received off-air): KCWY-DT (NBC) Casper; KFNB (FOX) Casper; KGWC-TV (CBS) Casper; KTWO-TV (ABC) Casper.
Programming (via microwave): KCNC-TV (CBS) Denver; KMGH-TV (ABC) Denver; KRMA-TV (PBS) Denver; KTVD (MNT) Denver; KUSA (NBC) Denver; KWGN-TV (CW) Denver.
Programming (via satellite): WGN America.
Fee: $39.95 installation; $29.95 monthly; $2.95 converter.

Expanded Basic Service 1
Subscribers: 1,556.
Programming (via satellite): A&E Networks; ABC Family Channel; AMC; Animal Planet; Bravo; Cartoon Network; CNBC; CNN; Comedy Central; Country Music TV; C-SPAN; C-SPAN 2; Discovery Channel; Discovery Health Channel; E! Entertainment Television; ESPN; ESPN 2; ESPNews; Food Network; Fox News Channel; FX; G4; Hallmark Channel; Headline News; HGTV; History Channel; Lifetime; MSNBC; MTV; Nick Jr.; Nickelodeon; Outdoor Channel; QVC; Root Sports Rocky Mountain; Spike TV; Syfy; TBS Superstation; The Learning Channel; The Weather Channel; Travel Channel; Trinity Broadcasting Network; truTV; Turner Network TV; TV Guide Network; TV Land; USA Network; VH1; WE tv.
Fee: $19.04 monthly.

Digital Basic Service
Subscribers: 540.
Programming (via satellite): AmericanLife TV Network; BBC America; Bio; Blackbelt TV; Bloomberg Television; Bravo; Current; Discovery Fit & Health; DMX Music; ESPN 2; ESPN Classic Sports; ESPNews; Fox Movie Channel; Fox Soccer; FSN Digital Atlantic; FSN Digital Central; FSN Digital Pacific; Fuse; G4; Golf Channel; Great American Country; GSN; Halogen Network; HGTV; History Channel; History Channel International; Independent Film Channel; International Television (ITV); Lifetime Movie Network; Lime; MBC America; MTV Networks Digital Suite; National Geographic Channel; Nick Jr.; NickToons TV; Outdoor Channel; Ovation; ShopNBC; Speed; Style Network; Sundance Channel; Syfy; TeenNick; The Word Network; Trinity Broadcasting Network; Trio; Turner Classic Movies; TV Land; Versus; WE tv.
Fee: $11.95 monthly.

Digital Pay Service 1
Pay Units: N.A.
Programming (via satellite): Cinemax (multiplexed); Encore (multiplexed); Flix; HBO (multiplexed); Showtime (multiplexed); Starz (multiplexed); The Movie Channel (multiplexed).
Fee: $11.95 monthly (Cinemax), $13.95 monthly (HBO, Starz/Encore, Showtime/Flix or TMC).

Video-On-Demand: No

Pay-Per-View
iN DEMAND (delivered digitally); Hot Choice (delivered digitally); Playboy TV (delivered digitally); Fresh (delivered digitally); Shorteez (delivered digitally).

Internet Service
Operational: Yes. Began: August 1, 1998.
Subscribers: 979.
Broadband Service: Net Commander.
Fee: $39.95 installation; $51.95 monthly.

Telephone Service
None

Miles of Plant: 32.0 (coaxial); None (fiber optic).
General Manager: Merritt Engleberetsen. Technical Operations Manager: Eric Garland. Marketing Director: Darby Edelman.
Ownership: James Cable LLC (MSO).

DUBOIS—Formerly served by KLiP Interactive. No longer in operation. ICA: WY0040.

EDGERTON—Formerly served by Tongue River Cable TV Inc. No longer in operation. ICA: WY0032.

EMBLEM—Formerly served by Basin, WY [WY0072]. TCT West Inc. This cable system has converted to IPTV, 405 S 4th St, Basin, WY 82410. Phones: 800-354-2911; 307-568-3357. Fax: 307-568-2506. E-mail: support@tctwest.net. Web Site: http://www.tctwest.net. ICA: WY5006.
TV Market Ranking: Outside TV Markets (EMBLEM).
Channel capacity: N.A. Channels available but not in use: N.A.

Telephone Service
Digital: Operational

ENCAMPMENT—CommuniComm Services, 234 Wind River Dr, Douglas, WY 82633-2338. Phone: 307-358-3861. Fax: 307-358-3849. Web Site: http://www.communicomm.com. Also serves Riverside. ICA: WY0073.
TV Market Ranking: Outside TV Markets (ENCAMPMENT, Riverside).
Channel capacity: N.A. Channels available but not in use: N.A.

Basic Service
Subscribers: 42.
Programming (via microwave): KTWO-TV (ABC) Casper.
Programming (via satellite): ABC Family Channel; Animal Planet; CNN; Country Music TV; Discovery Channel; ESPN; KCNC-TV (CBS) Denver; KDVR (FOX) Denver; KMGH-TV (ABC) Denver; KUSA (NBC) Denver; KWGN-TV (CW) Denver; Nick Jr.; Nickelodeon; QVC; Spike TV; Syfy; TBS Superstation; The Learning Channel; Travel Channel; Turner Network TV; VH1; WGN America.

Pay Service 1
Pay Units: N.A.
Programming (via satellite): Cinemax; HBO.

Internet Service
Operational: No.

Telephone Service
None

General Manager: Merritt Engleberetson.
Ownership: James Cable LLC (MSO).

EVANSTON (portions)—Windjammer Cable, 8500 W 110th St, Ste 600, Overland Park, KS 66210. Phone: 888-495-2881. Fax: 913-563-5454. Web Site: http://www.windjammercable.com. Also serves Uinta County (portions). ICA: WY0009.
TV Market Ranking: Outside TV Markets (EVANSTON (PORTIONS), Uinta County (portions)). Franchise award date: N.A. Franchise expiration date: N.A. Began: January 1, 1978.
Channel capacity: N.A. Channels available but not in use: N.A.

Basic Service
Subscribers: 1,406.
Programming (via microwave): KJZZ-TV (MNT) Salt Lake City; KSL-TV (NBC) Salt Lake City; KSTU (FOX) Salt Lake City; KTVX (ABC) Salt Lake City; KTWO-TV (ABC) Casper; KUCW (CW) Ogden; KUED (PBS) Salt Lake City; KUTH-DT (UNV) Provo; KUTV (CBS) Salt Lake City.
Programming (via satellite): A&E Networks; AMC; Animal Planet; BET Networks; Bravo; Cartoon Network; CNBC; CNN; Comedy Central; Country Music TV; C-SPAN; C-SPAN 2; Discovery Channel; Disney Channel; E! Entertainment Television; ESPN; ESPN 2; Fox News Channel; Fox Sports Net West; FX; Hallmark Channel; Headline News; HGTV; History Channel; Lifetime; MSNBC; MTV; National Geographic Channel; Nickelodeon; Oxygen; QVC; ShopNBC; Syfy; The Learning Channel; The Weather Channel; Toon Disney; Travel Channel; truTV; TV Land; Univision Studios; USA Network; VH1; WGN America.
Fee: $39.95 installation; $42.23 monthly.

Expanded Basic Service 1
Subscribers: 1,238.
Programming (via satellite): ABC Family Channel; Spike TV; TBS Superstation; Turner Network TV.
Fee: $8.75 monthly.

Digital Basic Service
Subscribers: 531.
Programming (via satellite): BBC America; Bloomberg Television; Discovery Digital Networks; ESPN Classic Sports; ESPNews; Fox Movie Channel; Fox Sports World; G4; GAS; Golf Channel; GSN; Halogen Network; MTV Networks Digital Suite; Music Choice; Nick Jr.; NickToons TV; Outdoor Channel; Trinity Broadcasting Network; Versus; WE tv.
Fee: $10.99 monthly.

Digital Pay Service 1
Pay Units: N.A.
Programming (via satellite): Cinemax (multiplexed); Encore (multiplexed); HBO (multiplexed); Showtime (multiplexed); Starz (multiplexed); The Movie Channel (multiplexed).
Fee: $15.95 monthly (each).

Video-On-Demand: Planned

Pay-Per-View
Fresh (delivered digitally); Playboy TV (delivered digitally).

Internet Service
Operational: Yes.
Subscribers: 463.
Broadband Service: In-house.
Fee: $99.95 installation; $44.95 monthly.

Telephone Service
Analog: Not Operational
Digital: Planned

Miles of Plant: 74.0 (coaxial); None (fiber optic).
Ownership: Windjammer Communications LLC (MSO).

FRANNIE—Formerly served by Basin, WY [WY0072]. TCT West Inc. This cable system has converted to IPTV, 405 S 4th St, Basin, WY 82410. Phones: 800-354-2911; 307-568-3357. Fax: 307-568-2506. E-mail: support@tctwest.net. Web Site: http://www.tctwest.net. ICA: WY5018.

TV Market Ranking: Outside TV Markets (FRANNIE).

Channel capacity: N.A. Channels available but not in use: N.A.

Internet Service

Operational: Yes.

Telephone Service

Digital: Operational

GILLETTE—Bresnan Communications, 410 W Boxelder Rd, Gillette, WY 82718-5315. Phones: 307-265-3136; 307-682-4303; 800-788-9457. Fax: 307-266-6821. Web Site: http://www.bresnan.com. Also serves Campbell County & Sleepy Hollow. ICA: WY0005.

TV Market Ranking: Outside TV Markets (Campbell County, GILLETTE, Sleepy Hollow). Franchise award date: August 1, 1992. Franchise expiration date: July 31, 2007. Began: April 1, 1964.

Channel capacity: 86 (operating 2-way). Channels available but not in use: N.A.

Basic Service

Subscribers: 7,900.

Programming (via microwave): KEVN-TV (FOX) Rapid City; KGWC-TV (CBS) Casper; KSGW-TV (ABC) Sheridan; KTWO-TV (ABC) Casper.

Programming (via satellite): ABC Family Channel; BYU Television; C-SPAN; C-SPAN 2; Fox News Channel; FX; ION Television; KCNC-TV (CBS) Denver; KDVR (FOX) Denver; KMGH-TV (ABC) Denver; KRMA-TV (PBS) Denver; KTVD (MNT) Denver; KUSA (NBC) Denver; KWGN-TV (CW) Denver; Lifetime; MSNBC; Nickelodeon; QVC; Spike TV; TBS Superstation; The Learning Channel; TV Guide Network; WGN America.

Programming (via translator): KCWC-DT (PBS) Lander.

Fee: $40.95 installation; $23.49 monthly; $1.65 converter; $13.95 additional installation.

Expanded Basic Service 1

Subscribers: 6,339.

Programming (via satellite): A&E Networks; Altitude Sports & Entertainment; AMC; Animal Planet; Cartoon Network; CNBC; CNN; Comedy Central; Country Music TV; Discovery Channel; Disney Channel; E! Entertainment Television; ESPN; ESPN 2; Food Network; Hallmark Channel; Headline News; HGTV; History Channel; MTV; Oxygen; Root Sports Rocky Mountain; Syfy; The Weather Channel; Travel Channel; truTV; Turner Classic Movies; Turner Network TV; TV Land; USA Network; VH1.

Fee: $41.95 monthly.

Digital Basic Service

Subscribers: 1,923.

Programming (via satellite): A&E HD; Altitude Sports & Entertainment; AmericanLife TV Network; BBC America; Bio; Bloomberg Television; Bravo; CBS Sports Network; CMT Pure Country; Cooking Channel; Discovery Fit & Health; Discovery Health Channel; Discovery Kids Channel; DIY Network; DMX Music; ESPN 2 HD; ESPN Classic Sports; ESPN HD; ESPNews; Eternal Word TV Network; Food Network HD; Fox Movie Channel; Fox Reality Channel; Fox Soccer; FSN HD; Fuse; G4; GMC; Golf Channel; Great American Country; GSN; Halogen Network; HD Theater; HDNet; HDNet Movies; HGTV HD; History Channel HD; History Channel International; HRTV; ID Investigation Discovery; Independent Film Channel; ION Life; ION Television; Lifetime Movie Network; Lifetime Movie Network HD; Military Channel; Mountain-West Sports Network; MTV Hits; MTV2; National Geographic Channel; National Geographic Channel HD Network; Nick Jr.; NickToons TV; Outdoor Channel; PBS Kids Sprout; Planet Green; Qubo; RFD-TV; Science; ShopNBC; SoapNet; Speed; Style Network; Syfy HD; TBS in HD; TeenNick; Toon Disney; Trinity Broadcasting Network; Turner Network TV HD; Universal HD; USA Network HD; Versus; Versus HD; VH1 Classic; VH1 Soul.

Fee: $64.74 monthly; $6.70 converter.

Pay Service 1

Pay Units: 1,868.

Programming (via satellite): HBO.

Fee: $11.93 monthly.

Digital Pay Service 1

Pay Units: 1,923.

Programming (via satellite): Cinemax (multiplexed); Encore (multiplexed); Flix; HBO (multiplexed); HBO HD; Showtime (multiplexed); Showtime HD; Starz (multiplexed); Starz HDTV (multiplexed); The Movie Channel (multiplexed); The Movie Channel HD.

Fee: $12.00 monthly (Starz/Encore), $16.15 monthly (Cinemax, HBO or Showtime/TMC).

Video-On-Demand: Yes

Pay-Per-View

iN DEMAND (delivered digitally); ESPN (delivered digitally); Home Theatre (delivered digitally); Cinemax On Demand (delivered digitally); HBO On Demand (delivered digitally); Showtime On Demand (delivered digitally); Starz On Demand (delivered digitally); Free Speech TV on Demand (delivered digitally); The SPOT On Demand (delivered digitally); careerOn Demand (delivered digitally); homeOn Demand (delivered digitally); NFL Network HD (delivered digitally); WWE 24/7 (delivered digitally); Movies (delivered digitally); sports (delivered digitally).

Internet Service

Operational: Yes.

Broadband Service: Bresnan OnLine.

Fee: $29.95-$62.90 monthly; $3.99 modem lease.

Telephone Service

Digital: Operational

Fee: $46.99 monthly

Miles of Plant: 285.0 (coaxial); 40.0 (fiber optic).

General Manager: Clint Rodeman. Chief Technician: Dan Higgins.

Ownership: Bresnan Communications Inc. (MSO). Sale pends to Cablevision Systems Corp.

GLENDO—Formerly served by CommuniComm Services. No longer in operation. ICA: WY0055.

GLENROCK—CommuniComm Services, 234 Wind River Dr, Douglas, WY 82633-2338. Phones: 307-358-3861; 800-759-8448 (Local only). Fax: 307-358-3849. Web Site: http://www.communicomm.com. Also serves Rolling Hills. ICA: WY0018.

TV Market Ranking: Below 100 (GLENROCK, Rolling Hills). Franchise award date: June 1, 1972. Franchise expiration date: N.A. Began: February 3, 1974.

Channel capacity: N.A. Channels available but not in use: N.A.

Basic Service

Subscribers: 643.

Programming (received off-air): KCWC-DT (PBS) Lander; KFNB (FOX) Casper; KGWC-TV (CBS) Casper; KTWO-TV (ABC) Casper.

Programming (via microwave): KCWY-DT (NBC) Casper.

Programming (via satellite): KUSA (NBC) Denver; KWGN-TV (CW) Denver; QVC; WGN America.

Fee: $39.95 installation; $29.95 monthly.

Expanded Basic Service 1

Subscribers: 639.

Programming (via satellite): A&E Networks; ABC Family Channel; AMC; Animal Planet; Bravo; Cartoon Network; CNBC; CNN; Comedy Central; Country Music TV; C-SPAN; C-SPAN 2; Discovery Channel; Discovery Health Channel; E! Entertainment Television; ESPN; ESPN 2; ESPN Classic Sports; ESPNews; Food Network; Fox News Channel; FX; Great American Country; Hallmark Channel; Headline News; HGTV; History Channel; Lifetime; MSNBC; MTV; Nick Jr.; Nickelodeon; Outdoor Channel; Root Sports Rocky Mountain; Spike TV; Syfy; TBS Superstation; The Learning Channel; The Weather Channel; Travel Channel; Trinity Broadcasting Network; truTV; Turner Classic Movies; Turner Network TV; TV Land; USA Network; VH1; WE tv.

Fee: $19.04 monthly.

Digital Basic Service

Subscribers: 206.

Programming (via satellite): AmericanLife TV Network; BBC America; Bio; Blackbelt TV; Bloomberg Television; Bravo; Current; Discovery Fit & Health; DMX Music; ESPN 2; ESPN Classic Sports; ESPNews; Fox Movie Channel; Fox Soccer; FSN Digital Atlantic; FSN Digital Central; FSN Digital Pacific; Fuse; G4; GAS; Golf Channel; Great American Country; GSN; Halogen Network; HGTV; History Channel; History Channel International; Independent Film Channel; International Television (ITV); Lifetime Movie Network; Lime; MBC America; MTV Networks Digital Suite; National Geographic Channel; Nick Jr.; NickToons TV; Outdoor Channel; Ovation; ShopNBC; Speed; Style Network; Sundance Channel; Syfy; The Word Network; Trinity Broadcasting Network; Trio; Turner Classic Movies; TV Land; Versus; WE tv.

Fee: $11.95 monthly.

Digital Pay Service 1

Pay Units: 131.

Programming (via satellite): HBO (multiplexed).

Fee: $13.95 monthly.

Digital Pay Service 2

Pay Units: 117.

Programming (via satellite): Cinemax (multiplexed).

Fee: $11.95 monthly.

Digital Pay Service 3

Pay Units: 135.

Programming (via satellite): Encore (multiplexed); Starz (multiplexed).

Fee: $13.95 monthly.

Digital Pay Service 4

Pay Units: 44.

Programming (via satellite): Flix; Showtime (multiplexed); The Movie Channel (multiplexed).

Fee: $13.95 monthly (Showtime/Flix or TMC).

Video-On-Demand: No

Pay-Per-View

iN DEMAND (delivered digitally); Hot Choice (delivered digitally); Playboy TV (delivered digitally); Fresh (delivered digitally); Shorteez (delivered digitally).

Internet Service

Operational: Yes.

Subscribers: 278.

Broadband Service: Net Commander.

Fee: $39.95 installation; $51.95 monthly.

Telephone Service

None

Miles of Plant: 28.0 (coaxial); None (fiber optic).

General Manager: Merritt Engleberetsen. Technical Operations Manager: Eric Garland. Marketing Director: Darby Edelman.

Ownership: James Cable LLC (MSO).

GREEN RIVER—Sweetwater Cable TV Co. Inc., 151 E Flaming Gorge Way, Green River, WY 82935-4322. Phones: 307-875-2506; 307-362-3773. Fax: 307-875-5834. E-mail: swtv@sweetwaterhsa.com. Web Site: http://www.sweetwaterhsa.com. Also serves James Town & Sweetwater County. ICA: WY0008.

TV Market Ranking: Below 100 (GREEN RIVER, James Town, Sweetwater County (portions)); Outside TV Markets (Sweetwater County (portions)). Franchise award date: January 1, 1956. Franchise expiration date: N.A. Began: October 1, 1958.

Channel capacity: 116 (operating 2-way). Channels available but not in use: N.A.

Basic Service

Subscribers: 3,500.

Programming (received off-air): KGWR-TV (CBS) Rock Springs; KTWO-TV (ABC) Casper; 12 FMs.

Programming (via microwave): KJZZ-TV (MNT) Salt Lake City; KSL-TV (NBC) Salt Lake City; KSTU (FOX) Salt Lake City; KTVX (ABC) Salt Lake City; KUCW (CW) Ogden; KUED (PBS) Salt Lake City; KUTV (CBS) Salt Lake City.

Programming (via satellite): BYU Television; Eternal Word TV Network; INSP; QVC; TBS Superstation; The Weather Channel; TV Guide Network; Univision Studios.

Fee: $30.00 installation; $17.00 monthly; $15.00 additional installation.

Expanded Basic Service 1

Subscribers: N.A.

Programming (via satellite): A&E Networks; ABC Family Channel; AMC; Animal Planet; Bravo; Cartoon Network; CBS Sports Network; CNBC; CNN; Comedy Central; Country Music TV; C-SPAN; C-SPAN 2; Discovery Channel; Disney Channel; E! Entertainment Television; ESPN; ESPN Classic Sports; Food Network; Fox News Channel; Fox Sports Net; FX; Hallmark Channel; Headline News; History Channel; Lifetime; MSNBC; MTV; National Geographic Channel; NFL Network; Nickelodeon; ShopNBC; Speed; Spike TV; Syfy; Telemundo; The Learning Channel; The Mtn; Travel Channel; truTV; Turner Network TV; TV Land; USA Network; VH1.

Fee: $34.90 monthly.

Digital Basic Service

Subscribers: 362.

Programming (via satellite): AmericanLife TV Network; AZ TV; BBC America; Bio; Bloomberg Television; Canal 52MX; Cine Latino; cloo; CMT Pure Country; CNBC World; CNN en Espanol; Discovery en Espanol; Discovery Fit & Health; Discovery Health Channel; Discovery Home Channel; Discovery Kids Channel; Discovery Times Channel; DMX Music; ESPN HD; ESPNews;

Fox Deportes; Fox Movie Channel; G4; GAS; Golf Channel; GSN; Halogen Network; HD Theater; HDNet; HDNet Movies; HGTV; History Channel en Espanol; History Channel International; Independent Film Channel; Military Channel; MTV Hits; MTV Latin America; MTV2; Nick Jr.; NickToons TV; Outdoor Channel; Science; Toon Disney en Espanol; Trinity Broadcasting Network; Turner Classic Movies; VeneMovies; Versus; VH1 Classic; VH1 Soul.
Fee: $19.00 monthly.

Pay Service 1
Pay Units: 975.
Programming (via satellite): HBO (multiplexed).
Fee: $12.50 installation; $9.95 monthly.

Digital Pay Service 1
Pay Units: 295.
Programming (via satellite): Cinemax (multiplexed); Encore (multiplexed); Flix; HBO (multiplexed); Showtime (multiplexed); Showtime HD; Starz (multiplexed); The Movie Channel (multiplexed).
Fee: $10.00 monthly (each).

Video-On-Demand: No

Pay-Per-View
Addressable homes: 1,020.
iN DEMAND (delivered digitally); ESPN (delivered digitally); Spice: Xcess (delivered digitally); Hot Choice (delivered digitally); Club Jenna (delivered digitally); Fresh (delivered digitally); Playboy TV (delivered digitally).

Internet Service
Operational: Yes. Began: November 8, 2001.
Subscribers: 782.
Broadband Service: ZCorum.
Fee: $49.00 installation; $22.90-$54.95 monthly; $99.95 modem purchase.

Telephone Service
Digital: Operational
Fee: $39.95 monthly

Miles of Plant: 56.0 (coaxial); 10.0 (fiber optic). Additional miles planned: 2.0 (coaxial).

Manager: Al Carollo Jr. Chief Technician: Lawrence Gessner. Program & Marketing Director & Customer Service Manager: John Carollo.

Ownership: Sweetwater Cable TV Co. Inc. (MSO).

GREYBULL—Bresnan Communications, 2432 Sheridan Ave, Cody, WY 82414-4004. Phone: 307-682-4303. Web Site: http://www.bresnan.com. Also serves Basin & Big Horn County. ICA: WY0022.

TV Market Ranking: Below 100 (Big Horn County (portions)); Outside TV Markets (Basin, Big Horn County (portions), GREYBULL). Franchise award date: N.A. Franchise expiration date: N.A. Began: March 1, 1956.

Channel capacity: N.A. Channels available but not in use: N.A.

Basic Service
Subscribers: 600.
Programming (via microwave): KCWC-DT (PBS) Lander; KHMT (FOX) Hardin; KTVQ (CBS, CW) Billings; KTWO-TV (ABC) Casper; KULR-TV (NBC) Billings.
Programming (via satellite): C-SPAN; C-SPAN 2; CW+; Hallmark Channel; KCNC-TV (CBS) Denver; KMGH-TV (ABC) Denver; KRMA-TV (PBS) Denver; QVC; TBS Superstation; TV Guide Network; WGN America.
Fee: $39.99 installation; $13.88 monthly; $9.99 additional installation.

Expanded Basic Service 1
Subscribers: 530.
Programming (via satellite): A&E Networks; ABC Family Channel; Altitude Sports & Entertainment; AMC; Animal Planet; BYU Television; Cartoon Network; CNBC; CNN; Comedy Central; Country Music TV; Discovery Channel; Disney Channel; E! Entertainment Television; ESPN; ESPN 2; Food Network; Fox News Channel; FX; Great American Country; Headline News; HGTV; History Channel; INSP; ION Television; Lifetime; MSNBC; MTV; Nickelodeon; Oxygen; Root Sports Rocky Mountain; Spike TV; Syfy; The Learning Channel; The Weather Channel; Travel Channel; truTV; Turner Classic Movies; Turner Network TV; TV Land; USA Network; VH1.
Fee: $24.68 monthly.

Digital Basic Service
Subscribers: N.A.
Programming (via satellite): A&E HD; ABC Family HD; AmericanLife TV Network; Animal Planet HD; BBC America; Bio; Bloomberg Television; Bravo; CBS Sports Network; CMT Pure Country; Discovery Channel HD; Discovery Fit & Health; Discovery Health Channel; Discovery Kids Channel; Disney Channel HD; DMX Music; ESPN Classic Sports; ESPN HD; ESPNews; Food Network HD; Fox Movie Channel; Fox Reality Channel; Fox Soccer; Fuse; G4; GMC; Golf Channel; GSN; Halogen Network; HD Theater; HGTV HD; History Channel HD; History Channel International; HRTV; ID Investigation Discovery; Independent Film Channel; ION Television; Lifetime Movie Network; Military Channel; MountainWest Sports Network; MTV Hits; MTV2; National Geographic Channel; National Geographic Channel HD Network; Nick Jr.; NickToons TV; Outdoor Channel; PBS Kids Sprout; Planet Green; RFD-TV; Science; Science HD; SoapNet; Speed; Style Network; Syfy HD; TeenNick; Toon Disney; Trinity Broadcasting Network; Universal HD; USA Network HD; Versus; VH1 Classic; VH1 Soul.
Fee: $52.99 monthly; $6.70 converter.

Pay Service 1
Pay Units: N.A.
Programming (via satellite): HBO.

Digital Pay Service 1
Pay Units: 195.
Programming (via satellite): Cinemax (multiplexed).
Fee: $12.95 installation; $16.15 monthly.

Digital Pay Service 2
Pay Units: 410.
Programming (via satellite): Starz (multiplexed); Starz HDTV.
Fee: $12.00 monthly.

Digital Pay Service 3
Pay Units: 264.
Programming (via satellite): HBO (multiplexed); HBO HD.
Fee: $16.16 monthly.

Digital Pay Service 4
Pay Units: 507.
Programming (via satellite): Encore (multiplexed).
Fee: $12.00 monthly.

Digital Pay Service 5
Pay Units: N.A.
Programming (via satellite): Showtime (multiplexed); The Movie Channel (multiplexed).
Fee: $16.15 monthly.

Video-On-Demand: No

Pay-Per-View
iN DEMAND (delivered digitally).

Internet Service
Operational: Yes.
Broadband Service: Bresnan OnLine.
Fee: $49.99 installation; $29.95-$62.90 monthly; $3.99 modem lease.

Telephone Service
Digital: Operational
Fee: $46.99 monthly

Miles of Plant: 25.0 (coaxial); 8.0 (fiber optic).

Regional Vice President & General Manager: Clint Rodeman. Chief Technician: Dan Higgins.

Ownership: Bresnan Communications Inc. (MSO). Sale pends to Cablevision Systems Corp.

GREYBULL—Formerly served by Basin, WY [WY0072]. TCT West Inc. This cable system has converted to IPTV, 405 S 4th St, Basin, WY 82410. Phones: 800-354-2911; 307-568-3357. Fax: 307-568-2506. E-mail: support@tctwest.net. Web Site: http://www.tctwest.net. ICA: WY5007.

TV Market Ranking: Outside TV Markets (GREYBULL).

Channel capacity: N.A. Channels available but not in use: N.A.

Internet Service
Operational: Yes.

Telephone Service
Digital: Operational

GUERNSEY—CAMS Cable, 55 S Wyoming St, Guernsey, WY 82214. Phone: 888-291-2415. E-mail: cam@camscable.com. Web Site: http://www.camscable.com. Also serves Fort Laramie & Hartville. ICA: WY0026.

TV Market Ranking: Outside TV Markets (Fort Laramie, GUERNSEY, Hartville). Franchise award date: N.A. Franchise expiration date: N.A. Began: March 16, 1978.

Channel capacity: 47 (operating 2-way). Channels available but not in use: N.A.

Basic Service
Subscribers: 153.
Programming (via microwave): KDUH-TV (ABC) Scottsbluff; KGWN-TV (CBS, CW) Cheyenne; KSTF (CBS, CW) Scottsbluff; KTNE-TV (PBS) Alliance; KTWO-TV (ABC) Casper.
Programming (via satellite): ABC Family Channel; Cartoon Network; CNN; ESPN; Headline News; KCNC-TV (CBS) Denver; KMGH-TV (ABC) Denver; KRMA-TV (PBS) Denver; KUSA (NBC) Denver; KWGN-TV (CW) Denver; Spike TV; TBS Superstation; Turner Classic Movies; Turner Network TV; USA Network.
Fee: $34.95 installation; $39.95 monthly.

Pay Service 1
Pay Units: 33.
Programming (via satellite): Encore; HBO; Starz.
Fee: $2.00 monthly (Encore), $11 monthly (Starz/Encore), $14 monthly (HBO).

Video-On-Demand: No

Internet Service
Operational: Yes.
Subscribers: 115.
Fee: $34.95 installation; $29.95 monthly.

Telephone Service
None

Miles of Plant: 16.0 (coaxial); None (fiber optic).

General Manager: Cameron Stone.

Ownership: CAMS Cable (MSO).

HULETT—Tongue River Communications, 620 Betty St, PO Box 759, Ranchester, WY 82839-0759. Phones: 800-953-9011; 307-655-9011. Fax: 307-655-9021. Web Site: http://tonguerivercomm.com. ICA: WY0044.

TV Market Ranking: Outside TV Markets (HULETT). Franchise award date: N.A. Franchise expiration date: N.A. Began: N.A.

Channel capacity: 42 (not 2-way capable). Channels available but not in use: N.A.

Basic Service
Subscribers: 120.
Programming (received off-air): KIVV-TV (FOX) Lead; KOTA-TV (ABC) Rapid City.
Programming (via satellite): A&E Networks; ABC Family Channel; AMC; Animal Planet; CNN; Country Music TV; C-SPAN; Discovery Channel; Disney Channel; E! Entertainment Television; ESPN; ESPN 2; Headline News; History Channel; KCNC-TV (CBS) Denver; KRMA-TV (PBS) Denver; KUSA (NBC) Denver; KWGN-TV (CW) Denver; Lifetime; MTV; Nickelodeon; Outdoor Channel; Spike TV; TBS Superstation; The Learning Channel; The Weather Channel; Trinity Broadcasting Network; Turner Network TV; USA Network; WGN America.
Fee: $40.00 installation; $39.00 monthly; $15.00 additional installation.

Pay Service 1
Pay Units: 10.
Programming (via satellite): Cinemax.
Fee: $10.00 installation; $10.00 monthly.

Pay Service 2
Pay Units: 19.
Programming (via satellite): HBO.
Fee: $10.00 installation; $12.00 monthly.

Pay Service 3
Pay Units: N.A.
Programming (via satellite): Encore.
Fee: $3.00 monthly.

Internet Service
Operational: No.

Telephone Service
None

Miles of Plant: 4.0 (coaxial); None (fiber optic).

General Manager: Rob Hium.

Ownership: Lynda & Robert Jacobson (MSO).

JACKSON (town)—Bresnan Communications, 3575 S Park Dr, PO Box 2650, Jackson, WY 83001. Phones: 307-265-3136; 877-273-7626; 307-733-6030. Fax: 307-266-6821. Web Site: http://www.bresnan.com. Also serves Rafter J Ranch, South Park, Teton County, Teton Village & Wilson. ICA: WY0007.

TV Market Ranking: Below 100 (JACKSON (TOWN), Rafter J Ranch, South Park, Teton County, Teton Village, Wilson). Franchise award date: N.A. Franchise expiration date: N.A. Began: December 1, 1954.

Channel capacity: N.A. Channels available but not in use: N.A.

Read what the Telecom elite read...
Communications Daily
Warren Communications News
FREE 30-day trial–call 800-771-9202 or visit www.warren-news.com

Basic Service
Subscribers: 6,500.
Programming (received off-air): KJWY (NBC) Jackson; 15 FMs.
Programming (via satellite): C-SPAN; C-SPAN 2; CW+; Lifetime; QVC; TBS Superstation; TV Guide Network; WGN America; WGN-TV (CW, IND) Chicago.
Programming (via translator): KCWC-DT (PBS) Lander; KFXP (FOX) Pocatello; KIDK (CBS, MNT) Idaho Falls; KIFI-TV (ABC, CW, TEL) Idaho Falls; KTWO-TV (ABC) Casper.
Fee: $39.99 installation; $23.34 monthly; $3.50 converter; $9.99 additional installation.

Expanded Basic Service 1
Subscribers: 4,500.
Programming (via satellite): A&E Networks; ABC Family Channel; Altitude Sports & Entertainment; AMC; Animal Planet; Bravo; Cartoon Network; CNBC; CNN; Comedy Central; Country Music TV; Discovery Channel; Disney Channel; E! Entertainment Television; ESPN; ESPN 2; Eternal Word TV Network; Food Network; Fox News Channel; FX; GSN; Hallmark Channel; Headline News; HGTV; History Channel; ION Television; MSNBC; MTV; Nickelodeon; Oxygen; Root Sports Rocky Mountain; Spike TV; Syfy; Tennis Channel; The Learning Channel; The Weather Channel; Travel Channel; truTV; Turner Classic Movies; Turner Network TV; TV Land; Univision Studios; USA Network; VH1.
Fee: $42.40 monthly.

Digital Basic Service
Subscribers: 1,940.
Programming (via satellite): A&E HD; ABC Family HD; Altitude Sports & Entertainment; American Movie Classics; AmericanLife TV Network; Animal Planet HD; BBC America; Bio; Bloomberg Television; Bravo HD; CBS Sports Network; CMT Pure Country; CNBC HD+; CNN HD; CNN International; Cooking Channel; C-SPAN 3; Discovery Channel HD; Discovery Fit & Health; Discovery Health Channel; Discovery Kids Channel; Disney Channel HD; DIY Network; DMX Music; ESPN 2 HD; ESPN Classic Sports; ESPN HD; ESPNews; Food Network HD; Fox Movie Channel; Fox Reality Channel; Fox Soccer; FSN HD; Fuse; G4; GMC; Golf Channel; Halogen Network; HD Theater; HDNet; HDNet Movies; HGTV HD; History Channel HD; History Channel International; HRTV; ID Investigation Discovery; Independent Film Channel; ION Life; Lifetime Movie Network; Lifetime Movie Network HD; Military Channel; MountainWest Sports Network; MTV Hits; MTV Jams; MTV2; mun2 television; National Geographic Channel; National Geographic Channel HD Network; Nick Jr.; Nick Too; NickToons TV; Outdoor Channel; Outdoor Channel 2 HD; Palladia; PBS Kids Sprout; Planet Green; Qubo; RFD-TV; Science; Science HD; SoapNet; Speed; Speed HD; Style Network; Syfy HD; TBS in HD; TeenNick; The Weather Channel HD; TLC HD; Toon Disney; Tr3s; Trinity Broadcasting Network; Turner Network TV HD; Universal HD; USA Network HD; Versus; Versus HD; VH1 Classic; VH1 Soul.
Fee: $12.95 installation; $64.24 monthly; $6.70 converter.

Pay Service 1
Pay Units: 458.
Programming (via satellite): Encore; HBO; Starz.
Fee: $6.99 monthly (Starz or Encore), $13.70 monthly (HBO).

Digital Pay Service 1
Pay Units: N.A.
Programming (via satellite): Cinemax (multiplexed); Cinemax HD; Encore (multiplexed); Flix; HBO (multiplexed); HBO HD; Showtime (multiplexed); Showtime HD; Starz (multiplexed); Starz HDTV; The Movie Channel (multiplexed); The Movie Channel HD.
Fee: $12.00 monthly (Starz/Encore), $16.15 monthly (Cinemax, HBO or Showtime/TMC).

Video-On-Demand: No

Pay-Per-View
iN DEMAND (delivered digitally); ESPN (delivered digitally); Discovery en Espanol (delivered digitally); Fox Deportes (delivered digitally); mun2 television (delivered digitally); Cine Latino (delivered digitally); History Channel en Espanol (delivered digitally); Tr3s (delivered digitally); CNN en Espanol (delivered digitally); ESPN Deportes (delivered digitally); Cine Mexicano (delivered digitally); MLB Extra Innings (delivered digitally); GolTV (delivered digitally); AYM Sports (delivered digitally); Bandamax (delivered digitally); De Pelicula (delivered digitally); De Pelicula Clasico (delivered digitally); Telehit (delivered digitally); NFL Network HD (delivered digitally); NHL Center Ice (delivered digitally); NFL Network (delivered digitally); Fox College Sports Atlantic (delivered digitally); Fox College Sports Central (delivered digitally); Fox College Sports Pacific (delivered digitally); NHL Network (delivered digitally); VeneMovies (delivered digitally).

Internet Service
Operational: Yes. Began: July 1, 2003.
Broadband Service: Bresnan OnLine.
Fee: $49.99 installation; $29.95-$62.90 monthly; $3.99 modem lease.

Telephone Service
Digital: Operational
Fee: $49.99 monthly

Miles of Plant: 174.0 (coaxial); None (fiber optic). Additional miles planned: 11.0 (coaxial).

General Manager: Clint Rodeman. Chief Technician: Dan Higgins.

Ownership: Bresnan Communications Inc. (MSO). Sale pends to Cablevision Systems Corp.

KEMMERER—Formerly served by KLiP Interactive. No longer in operation. ICA: WY0021.

LANDER—Bresnan Communications. Now served by RIVERTON, WY [WY0059]. ICA: WY0056.

LARAMIE—Bresnan Communications, 506 W 17th St, Cheyenne, WY 82001. Phone: 307-587-9459. Web Site: http://www.bresnan.com. Also serves Albany County. ICA: WY0003.

TV Market Ranking: Below 100 (Albany County (portions), LARAMIE); Outside TV Markets (Albany County (portions)). Franchise award date: N.A. Franchise expiration date: N.A. Began: March 1, 1954.

Channel capacity: N.A. Channels available but not in use: N.A.

Basic Service
Subscribers: 8,034.
Programming (received off-air): KFCT (FOX) Fort Collins; 4 FMs.
Programming (via microwave): KCWC-DT (PBS) Lander; KGWN-TV (CBS, CW) Cheyenne.
Programming (via satellite): C-SPAN; C-SPAN 2; ION Television; KCNC-TV (CBS) Denver; KMGH-TV (ABC) Denver; KRMA-TV (PBS) Denver; KTVD (MNT) Denver; KUSA (NBC) Denver; KWGN-TV (CW) Denver; Lifetime; QVC; TBS Superstation; TV Guide Network.
Programming (via translator): KCWY-DT (NBC) Casper; KTWO-TV (ABC) Casper.
Fee: $39.99 installation; $23.34 monthly; $3.00 converter; $9.99 additional installation.

Expanded Basic Service 1
Subscribers: 6,867.
Programming (via satellite): A&E Networks; ABC Family Channel; Altitude Sports & Entertainment; AMC; Animal Planet; Cartoon Network; CBS Sports Network; CNBC; CNN; Comedy Central; Country Music TV; Discovery Channel; Disney Channel; E! Entertainment Television; ESPN; ESPN 2; Eternal Word TV Network; Food Network; Fox News Channel; FX; Hallmark Channel; Headline News; HGTV; History Channel; MSNBC; MTV; Nickelodeon; Oxygen; Root Sports Rocky Mountain; Spike TV; Syfy; The Learning Channel; The Weather Channel; Travel Channel; truTV; Turner Classic Movies; Turner Network TV; TV Land; Univision Studios; USA Network; VH1.
Fee: $42.40 monthly.

Digital Basic Service
Subscribers: N.A.
Programming (via satellite): A&E HD; ABC Family HD; Altitude Sports & Entertainment; American Movie Classics; AmericanLife TV Network; Animal Planet HD; BBC America; Bio; Bloomberg Television; BlueHighways TV; Bravo; Bravo HD; BYU Television; CMT Pure Country; CNBC HD+; CNN HD; Cooking Channel; Discovery Channel HD; Discovery Fit & Health; Discovery Health Channel; Discovery Kids Channel; Disney Channel HD; DIY Network; DMX Music; ESPN 2 HD; ESPN Classic Sports; ESPN HD; ESPNews; Food Network HD; Fox Movie Channel; Fox Reality Channel; Fox Soccer; FSN HD; Fuse; G4; GMC; Golf Channel; GSN; Halogen Network; HD Theater; HDNet; HDNet Movies; HGTV HD; History Channel HD; History Channel International; HRTV; ID Investigation Discovery; Independent Film Channel; ION Life; ION Television; Lifetime Movie Network; Lifetime Movie Network HD; Military Channel; MountainWest Sports Network; MTV Hits; MTV Jams; MTV2; mun2 television; National Geographic Channel; National Geographic Channel HD Network; Nick Jr.; Nick Too; NickToons TV; Outdoor Channel; Outdoor Channel 2 HD; Palladia; PBS Kids Sprout; Planet Green; Qubo; RFD-TV; Science; Science HD; SoapNet; Speed; Speed HD; Style Network; Syfy HD; TBS in HD; TeenNick; The Weather Channel HD; TLC HD; Toon Disney; Tr3s; Trinity Broadcasting Network; Turner Network TV HD; Universal HD; USA Network HD; Versus; Versus HD; VH1 Classic; VH1 Soul.
Fee: $64.24 monthly; $6.70 converter.

Pay Service 1
Pay Units: 616.
Programming (via satellite): HBO.
Fee: $20.00 installation; $13.20 monthly.

Digital Pay Service 1
Pay Units: N.A.
Programming (via satellite): Cinemax (multiplexed); Cinemax HD; Encore (multiplexed); Flix; HBO (multiplexed); HBO HD; Showtime (multiplexed); Showtime HD; Starz (multiplexed); Starz HDTV; The Movie Channel (multiplexed); The Movie Channel HD.
Fee: $12.00 monthly (Starz/Encore), $16.15 monthly (Cinemax, HBO or Showtime/TMC).

Video-On-Demand: Yes

Pay-Per-View
iN DEMAND (delivered digitally); ESPN (delivered digitally); NHL Network (delivered digitally); VeneMovies (delivered digitally); Discovery en Espanol (delivered digitally); Fox Deportes (delivered digitally); mun2 television (delivered digitally); Cine Latino (delivered digitally); History Channel en Espanol (delivered digitally); Tr3s (delivered digitally); CNN en Espanol (delivered digitally); NBA League Pass (delivered digitally); ESPN Deportes (delivered digitally); Cine Mexicano (delivered digitally); GolTV (delivered digitally); Bandamax (delivered digitally); De Pelicula (delivered digitally); De Pelicula Clasico (delivered digitally); Telehit (delivered digitally); Univision Studios (delivered digitally); Movies (delivered digitally); MLS Direct Kick (delivered digitally); sports (delivered digitally); Home Theatre (delivered digitally); Cinemax On Demand (delivered digitally); HBO On Demand (delivered digitally); Showtime On Demand (delivered digitally); Starz On Demand (delivered digitally); WWE 24/7 (delivered digitally); MLB Extra Innings (delivered digitally); Free Speech TV on Demand (delivered digitally); The SPOT On Demand (delivered digitally); careerSPOT On Demand (delivered digitally); homeSPOT On Demand (delivered digitally); NHL Center Ice (delivered digitally); NFL Network (delivered digitally); Fox College Sports Atlantic (delivered digitally); Fox College Sports Central (delivered digitally); Fox College Sports Pacific (delivered digitally).

Internet Service
Operational: Yes. Began: October 1, 2002.
Broadband Service: Bresnan OnLine.
Fee: $49.99 installation; $29.95-$62.90 monthly; $3.99 modem lease.

Telephone Service
Digital: Operational
Fee: $46.99 monthly

Miles of Plant: 118.0 (coaxial); 29.0 (fiber optic).

Regional Vice President: Clint Rodeman. General Manager: Wes Frost. Technical Operations Manager: Mitch Winter.

Ownership: Bresnan Communications Inc. (MSO). Sale pends to Cablevision Systems Corp.

LOVELL—Formerly [WY0024]. TCT West Inc. This cable system has converted to IPTV, 405 S 4th St, Basin, WY 82410. Phones: 800-354-2911; 307-568-3357. Fax: 307-568-2506. E-mail: support@tctwest.

net. Web Site: http://www.tctwest.net. ICA: WY5009.
TV Market Ranking: Outside TV Markets (LOVELL).
Channel capacity: N.A. Channels available but not in use: N.A.
Internet Service
Operational: Yes.
Telephone Service
Digital: Operational

LOVELL—TCT West Inc. This cable system has converted to IPTV. See Lovell, WY [WY5009]. ICA: WY0024.

LUSK—CommuniComm Services, 234 Wind River Dr, Douglas, WY 82633-2338. Phones: 800-759-8448; 307-358-3861. Fax: 307-358-3849. Web Site: http://www.communicomm.com. ICA: WY0027.
TV Market Ranking: Outside TV Markets (LUSK). Franchise award date: November 1, 1978. Franchise expiration date: N.A. Began: May 1, 1980.
Channel capacity: N.A. Channels available but not in use: N.A.
Basic Service
Subscribers: 347.
Programming (via microwave): KCWY-DT (NBC) Casper; KDUH-TV (ABC) Scottsbluff; KTWO-TV (ABC) Casper.
Programming (via satellite): KCNC-TV (CBS) Denver; KDVR (FOX) Denver; KMGH-TV (ABC) Denver; KRMA-TV (PBS) Denver; KTVD (MNT) Denver; KUSA (NBC) Denver; KWGN-TV (CW) Denver; QVC; WGN America.
Fee: $39.95 installation; $29.95 monthly; $20.00 additional installation.
Expanded Basic Service 1
Subscribers: 342.
Programming (via satellite): A&E Networks; ABC Family Channel; AMC; Animal Planet; Bravo; Cartoon Network; CNBC; CNN; Comedy Central; Country Music TV; C-SPAN; C-SPAN 2; Discovery Channel; Discovery Health Channel; E! Entertainment Television; ESPN; ESPN 2; ESPNews; Food Network; Fox News Channel; FX; G4; Hallmark Channel; Headline News; HGTV; History Channel; Lifetime; MSNBC; MTV; Nick Jr.; Nickelodeon; Root Sports Rocky Mountain; Spike TV; Syfy; TBS Superstation; The Learning Channel; The Weather Channel; Travel Channel; truTV; Turner Network TV; TV Land; USA Network; VH1; WE tv.
Fee: $19.04 monthly.
Digital Basic Service
Subscribers: 91.
Programming (via satellite): AmericanLife TV Network; BBC America; Bio; Blackbelt TV; Bloomberg Television; Bravo; Current; Discovery Fit & Health; DMX Music; E! Entertainment Television; ESPN 2; ESPN Classic Sports; ESPNews; Fox Movie Channel; Fox Sports World; FSN Digital Atlantic; FSN Digital Central; FSN Digital Pacific; Fuse; G4; GAS; Golf Channel; Great American Country; GSN; Halogen Network; HGTV; History Channel; History Channel International; Independent Film Channel; International Television (ITV); Lifetime Movie Network; Lime; MBC America; MTV Networks Digital Suite; National Geographic Channel; Nick Jr.; NickToons TV; Outdoor Channel; Ovation; ShopNBC; Speed; Sundance Channel; Syfy; The Word Network; Trinity Broadcasting Network; Trio; Turner Classic Movies; TV Land; Versus; WE tv.
Fee: $11.95 monthly.
Digital Pay Service 1
Pay Units: 81.
Programming (via satellite): HBO (multiplexed).
Fee: $13.95 monthly.
Digital Pay Service 2
Pay Units: 71.
Programming (via satellite): Cinemax (multiplexed).
Fee: $11.95 monthly.
Digital Pay Service 3
Pay Units: 77.
Programming (via satellite): Encore (multiplexed); Starz (multiplexed).
Fee: $10.95 monthly.
Digital Pay Service 4
Pay Units: 20.
Programming (via satellite): Flix; Showtime (multiplexed); The Movie Channel (multiplexed).
Fee: $13.95 monthly (Showtime/Flix or TMC).
Video-On-Demand: No
Pay-Per-View
iN DEMAND (delivered digitally); Hot Choice (delivered digitally); Playboy TV (delivered digitally); Fresh (delivered digitally); Shorteez (delivered digitally).
Internet Service
Operational: Yes.
Subscribers: 190.
Broadband Service: Net Commander.
Fee: $39.95 installation; $51.95 monthly.
Telephone Service
None
Miles of Plant: 17.0 (coaxial); None (fiber optic).
General Manager: Merritt Engleberetsen. Technical Operations Manager: Eric Garland. Marketing Director: Darby Edelman.
Ownership: James Cable LLC (MSO).

MAMMOTH HOT SPRINGS—Formerly served by North Yellowstone Cable TV. No longer in operation. ICA: WY0048.

MANDERSON—Formerly served by Basin, WY [WY0072]. TCT West Inc. This cable system has converted to IPTV, 405 S 4th St, Basin, WY 82410. Phones: 800-354-2911; 307-568-3357. Fax: 307-568-2506. E-mail: support@tctwest.net. Web Site: http://www.tctwest.net. ICA: WY5010.
TV Market Ranking: Outside TV Markets (MANDERSON).
Channel capacity: N.A. Channels available but not in use: N.A.
Internet Service
Operational: Yes.
Telephone Service
Digital: Operational

MEDICINE BOW—Medicine Bow Cable, PO Box 127, Medicine Bow, WY 82329. Phone: 307-379-2594. E-mail: jsheehan@klipia.com. ICA: WY0045.
TV Market Ranking: Outside TV Markets (MEDICINE BOW). Franchise award date: N.A. Franchise expiration date: N.A. Began: February 3, 1981.
Channel capacity: 45 (not 2-way capable). Channels available but not in use: N.A.
Basic Service
Subscribers: 18.
Programming (received off-air): KGWC-TV (CBS) Casper; KTWO-TV (ABC) Casper.
Programming (via satellite): A&E Networks; ABC Family Channel; AMC; CNN; Discovery Channel; Disney Channel; ESPN; ESPN 2; Fox News Channel; FX; History Channel; KCNC-TV (CBS) Denver; KDVR (FOX) Denver; KMGH-TV (ABC) Denver; KRMA-TV (PBS) Denver; KUSA (NBC) Denver; Lifetime; Outdoor Channel; QVC; Spike TV; TBS Superstation; The Weather Channel; Turner Network TV; TV Land; USA Network; WGN America.
Fee: $29.95 installation; $31.75 monthly.
Pay Service 1
Pay Units: N.A.
Programming (via satellite): HBO; Showtime; The Movie Channel.
Fee: $10.00 installation; $10.95 monthly (each).
Internet Service
Operational: No.
Telephone Service
None
Miles of Plant: 3.0 (coaxial); None (fiber optic).
Chief Executive Officer: Joseph A. Sheehan. General Manager East: Mark Miller. General Manager West: Vance Johnson.
Ownership: Medicine Bow Cable (MSO).

MEETEETSE—Formerly served by Basin, WY [WY0072]. TCT West Inc. This cable system has converted to IPTV, 405 S 4th St, Basin, WY 82410. Phones: 800-354-2911; 307-568-3357. Fax: 307-568-2506. E-mail: support@tctwest.net. Web Site: http://www.tctwest.net. ICA: WY5011.
TV Market Ranking: Outside TV Markets (MEETEETSE).
Channel capacity: N.A. Channels available but not in use: N.A.
Internet Service
Operational: Yes.
Telephone Service
Digital: Operational

MEETEETSE—Formerly served by KLiP Interactive. No longer in operation. ICA: WY0047.
Channel capacity: 45 (not 2-way capable). Channels available but not in use: N.A.
Miles of Plant: 6.0 (coaxial); None (fiber optic).

MOORCROFT—Tongue River Communications, 620 Betty St, PO Box 759, Ranchester, WY 82839-0759. Phones: 800-953-9011; 307-665-9011. Fax: 307-655-9021. Web Site: http://www.tonguerivercomm.com. ICA: WY0033.
TV Market Ranking: Outside TV Markets (MOORCROFT). Franchise award date: January 9, 1995. Franchise expiration date: January 8, 2015. Began: January 1, 1979.
Channel capacity: 36 (not 2-way capable). Channels available but not in use: N.A.
Basic Service
Subscribers: 68.
Programming (via satellite): A&E Networks; ABC Family Channel; Altitude Sports & Entertainment; AMC; Animal Planet; Cartoon Network; CNBC; CNN; C-SPAN; C-SPAN 2; Discovery Channel; Disney Channel; E! Entertainment Television; ESPN; Headline News; KCNC-TV (CBS) Denver; KRMA-TV (PBS) Denver; KUSA (NBC) Denver; Lifetime; MTV; Nickelodeon; QVC; Spike TV; TBS Superstation; The Learning Channel; The Weather Channel; Travel Channel; truTV; Turner Network TV; USA Network.
Programming (via translator): KGWC-TV (CBS) Casper; KIVV-TV (FOX) Lead; KOTA-TV (ABC) Rapid City; KTWO-TV (ABC) Casper.
Fee: $40.95 installation; $28.49 monthly; $13.95 additional installation.
Pay Service 1
Pay Units: 55.
Programming (via satellite): HBO.
Fee: $14.95 installation; $13.65 monthly.
Pay Service 2
Pay Units: 102.
Programming (via satellite): Encore.
Fee: $14.95 installation; $1.75 monthly.
Internet Service
Operational: No.
Telephone Service
None
Miles of Plant: 9.0 (coaxial); None (fiber optic).
General Manager: Rob Hium.
Ownership: Lynda & Robert Jacobson (MSO).

MOUNTAIN VIEW (Uinta County)—Union Cable Co., 850 N Hwy 414, PO Box 160, Mountain View, WY 82939-0160. Phones: 888-926-2273; 307-782-6131. Fax: 307-787-7043. Web Site: http://www.unionwireless.com. ICA: WY0023.
TV Market Ranking: Outside TV Markets (MOUNTAIN VIEW (UINTA COUNTY)). Franchise award date: N.A. Franchise expiration date: N.A. Began: December 1, 1962.
Channel capacity: 27 (not 2-way capable). Channels available but not in use: N.A.
Basic Service
Subscribers: 29.
Programming (via microwave): KJZZ-TV (MNT) Salt Lake City; KSL-TV (NBC) Salt Lake City; KSTU (FOX) Salt Lake City; KTVX (ABC) Salt Lake City; KTWO-TV (ABC) Casper; KUED (PBS) Salt Lake City; KUTV (CBS) Salt Lake City.
Programming (via satellite): ABC Family Channel; CNN; Disney Channel; ESPN; Spike TV; TBS Superstation; The Weather Channel; Turner Network TV; WGN America.
Fee: $35.00 installation; $18.00 monthly.
Expanded Basic Service 1
Subscribers: N.A.
Programming (via satellite): A&E Networks; Country Music TV; Discovery Channel; ESPN 2; History Channel; Nickelodeon; VH1.
Fee: $8.00 monthly.
Pay Service 1
Pay Units: N.A.
Programming (via satellite): Encore; Fox Movie Channel; HBO; Starz.
Fee: $8.00 monthly.
Internet Service
Operational: No.
Telephone Service
None
Miles of Plant: 15.0 (coaxial); None (fiber optic).

Manager & Chief Technician: Chuck Fagnant. Marketing Director: Rob Elwood.
Ownership: Union Telephone Co.–Mountain View, WY (MSO).

NEWCASTLE—Bresnan Communications, 410 W Boxelder Rd, Gillette, WY 82718-5315. Phone: 307-265-3136. Fax: 307-266-6821. Web Site: http://www.bresnan.com. Also serves Weston County. ICA: WY0020.
TV Market Ranking: Below 100 (Weston County (portions)); Outside TV Markets (NEWCASTLE, Weston County (portions)). Franchise award date: May 19, 1994. Franchise expiration date: May 18, 2014. Began: November 1, 1976.
Channel capacity: N.A. Channels available but not in use: N.A.
Basic Service
Subscribers: 700.
Programming (received off-air): KEVN-TV (FOX) Rapid City; KOTA-TV (ABC) Rapid City.
Programming (via microwave): KGWC-TV (CBS) Casper; KTWO-TV (ABC) Casper.
Programming (via satellite): A&E Networks; ABC Family Channel; Altitude Sports & Entertainment; AMC; Animal Planet; Cartoon Network; CNBC; CNN; Comedy Central; C-SPAN; C-SPAN 2; CW+; Discovery Channel; Disney Channel; E! Entertainment Television; ESPN; ESPN 2; Food Network; Fox News Channel; FX; Hallmark Channel; Halogen Network; Headline News; HGTV; KCNC-TV (CBS) Denver; KRMA-TV (PBS) Denver; KUSA (NBC) Denver; Lifetime; MSNBC; MTV; Nickelodeon; QVC; Spike TV; Syfy; TBS Superstation; The Learning Channel; The Weather Channel; Travel Channel; Turner Classic Movies; Turner Network TV; TV Land; USA Network; VH1; WGN America.
Fee: $39.99 installation; $53.74 monthly; $9.99 additional installation.
Digital Basic Service
Subscribers: 400.
Programming (via satellite): BBC America; Bio; Bloomberg Television; CBS Sports Network; CMT Pure Country; Discovery Fit & Health; Discovery Health Channel; Discovery Kids Channel; DMX Music; ESPN Classic Sports; ESPNews; Fox Movie Channel; Fox Soccer; Fuse; G4; Golf Channel; GSN; History Channel; History Channel International; ID Investigation Discovery; Lifetime Movie Network; Military Channel; MountainWest Sports Network; MTV2; National Geographic Channel; Nick Jr.; NickToons TV; Outdoor Channel; Planet Green; Science; SoapNet; Speed; Style Network; TeenNick; Toon Disney; Trinity Broadcasting Network; Versus; VH1 Classic.
Fee: $61.24 monthly.
Digital Pay Service 1
Pay Units: 216.
Programming (via satellite): Cinemax (multiplexed); Encore (multiplexed); HBO (multiplexed); Showtime; Starz (multiplexed); The Movie Channel (multiplexed).
Fee: $12.00 monthly (Starz/Encore), $16.15 monthly (Cinemax, HBO or Showtime/TMC).
Video-On-Demand: No
Pay-Per-View
Addressable homes: 216.
iN DEMAND.
Internet Service
Operational: Yes.
Fee: $39.95 monthly.
Telephone Service
Digital: Operational
Fee: $49.99 monthly
Miles of Plant: 38.0 (coaxial); None (fiber optic).
General Manager: Clint Rodeman. Chief Technician: Dan Higgins.
Ownership: Bresnan Communications Inc. (MSO). Sale pends to Cablevision Systems Corp.

OSAGE—Formerly served by Tongue River Cable TV Inc. No longer in operation. ICA: WY0049.

OTTO—Formerly served by Basin, WY [WY0072]. TCT West Inc. This cable system has converted to IPTV, 405 S 4th St, Basin, WY 82410. Phones: 800-354-2911; 307-568-3357. Fax: 307-568-2506. E-mail: support@tctwest.net. Web Site: http://www.tctwest.net. ICA: WY5012.
TV Market Ranking: Outside TV Markets (OTTO).
Channel capacity: N.A. Channels available but not in use: N.A.
Internet Service
Operational: Yes.
Telephone Service
Digital: Operational

PINE BLUFFS—CAMS Cable, 210 Main St, Pine Bluffs, WY 82082. Phone: 888-291-2415. E-mail: cam@camscable.com. Web Site: http://www.camscable.com. ICA: WY0031.
TV Market Ranking: Outside TV Markets (PINE BLUFFS). Franchise award date: November 7, 1962. Franchise expiration date: N.A. Began: July 1, 1957.
Channel capacity: 47 (operating 2-way). Channels available but not in use: None.
Basic Service
Subscribers: 197.
Programming (via microwave): KDUH-TV (ABC) Scottsbluff; KGWN-TV (CBS, CW) Cheyenne; KSTF (CBS, CW) Scottsbluff; KTNE-TV (PBS) Alliance; KTWO-TV (ABC) Casper.
Programming (via satellite): ABC Family Channel; CNN; ESPN; KCNC-TV (CBS) Denver; KMGH-TV (ABC) Denver; KRMA-TV (PBS) Denver; KUSA (NBC) Denver; KWGN-TV (CW) Denver; TBS Superstation; Turner Network TV; USA Network.
Fee: $34.95 installation; $39.95 monthly.
Pay Service 1
Pay Units: 20.
Programming (via satellite): Encore; HBO; Starz.
Fee: $2.00 monthly (Encore), $11 monthly (Starz/Encore), $14 monthly (HBO).
Video-On-Demand: No
Internet Service
Operational: Yes.
Subscribers: 130.
Fee: $34.95 installation; $29.95 monthly.
Telephone Service
None
Miles of Plant: 8.0 (coaxial); None (fiber optic).
General Manager: Cameron Stone.
Ownership: CAMS Cable (MSO).

PINE HAVEN—Tongue River Communications, 620 Betty St, PO Box 759, Ranchester, WY 82839-0759. Phones: 800-953-9011; 307-655-9011. Fax: 307-655-9021. Web Site: http://tonguerivercomm.com. ICA: WY0052.
TV Market Ranking: Outside TV Markets (PINE HAVEN). Franchise award date: September 1, 1987. Franchise expiration date: N.A. Began: October 1, 1987.
Channel capacity: 42 (not 2-way capable). Channels available but not in use: N.A.
Basic Service
Subscribers: 63.
Programming (received off-air): KEVN-TV (FOX) Rapid City; KGWC-TV (CBS) Casper; KOTA-TV (ABC) Rapid City; KPSD-TV (PBS) Eagle Butte.
Programming (via satellite): A&E Networks; ABC Family Channel; AMC; CNN; Country Music TV; C-SPAN; Discovery Channel; Disney Channel; ESPN; Headline News; KCNC-TV (CBS) Denver; Lifetime; Nickelodeon; Spike TV; TBS Superstation; The Weather Channel; Turner Network TV; USA Network; WGN America; WWOR-TV (MNT) Secaucus.
Fee: $40.00 installation; $39.00 monthly; $3.00 converter; $15.00 additional installation.
Pay Service 1
Pay Units: 10.
Programming (via satellite): HBO.
Fee: $10.00 installation; $12.00 monthly.
Pay Service 2
Pay Units: 13.
Programming (via satellite): Cinemax.
Fee: $10.00 monthly.
Pay Service 3
Pay Units: 12.
Programming (via satellite): Encore.
Fee: $3.00 monthly.
Internet Service
Operational: No.
Telephone Service
None
Miles of Plant: 6.0 (coaxial); None (fiber optic).
General Manager: Rob Hium.
Ownership: Lynda & Robert Jacobson (MSO).

PINEDALE—Formerly served by KLiP Interactive. No longer in operation. ICA: WY0025.

POWELL—Bresnan Communications, 2432 Sheridan Ave, Cody, WY 82414-4004. Phone: 307-587-9459. Fax: 307-587-5912. Web Site: http://www.bresnan.com. ICA: WY0015.
TV Market Ranking: Outside TV Markets (POWELL). Franchise award date: N.A. Franchise expiration date: N.A. Began: December 1, 1965.
Channel capacity: N.A. Channels available but not in use: N.A.
Basic Service
Subscribers: 1,681.
Programming (via microwave): KTWO-TV (ABC) Casper.
Programming (via satellite): ABC Family Channel; BYU Television; CNBC; CNN; Comedy Central; Country Music TV; C-SPAN; C-SPAN 2; CW+; Eternal Word TV Network; KRMA-TV (PBS) Denver; Lifetime; MSNBC; MTV; Nickelodeon; QVC; TBS Superstation; The Weather Channel; TV Guide Network; VH1; WGN America.
Programming (via translator): KCWC-DT (PBS) Lander; KHMT (FOX) Hardin; KSVI (ABC) Billings; KTVQ (CBS, CW) Billings; KULR-TV (NBC) Billings.
Fee: $39.99 installation; $21.74 monthly.
Expanded Basic Service 1
Subscribers: 1,575.
Programming (via satellite): A&E Networks; Altitude Sports & Entertainment; AMC; Animal Planet; Bravo; Cartoon Network; Discovery Channel; Disney Channel; E! Entertainment Television; ESPN; ESPN 2; Food Network; Fox News Channel; FX; Great American Country; Hallmark Channel; Headline News; HGTV; History Channel; ION Television; Oxygen; Root Sports Rocky Mountain; Spike TV; Syfy; The Learning Channel; Travel Channel; truTV; Turner Classic Movies; Turner Network TV; TV Land; Univision Studios; USA Network.
Fee: $40.25 monthly.
Digital Basic Service
Subscribers: N.A.
Programming (via satellite): A&E HD; Altitude Sports & Entertainment; AmericanLife TV Network; Animal Planet HD; BBC America; Bio; Bloomberg Television; CBS Sports Network; CMT Pure Country; Cooking Channel; Discovery Channel HD; Discovery Fit & Health; Discovery Health Channel; DIY Network; DMX Music; ESPN 2 HD; ESPN Classic Sports; ESPN HD; ESPNews; Fox Movie Channel; Fox Reality Channel; Fox Soccer; FSN HD; Fuse; G4; GMC; Golf Channel; GSN; Halogen Network; HD Theater; HDNet; HDNet Movies; History Channel International; HRTV; ID Investigation Discovery; Independent Film Channel; Lifetime Movie Network; Military Channel; MTV Hits; MTV Jams; MTV2; National Geographic Channel; National Geographic Channel HD Network; Nick Jr.; Nick Too; NickToons TV; Outdoor Channel; PBS Kids Sprout; Planet Green; RFD-TV; Science; Science HD; SoapNet; Speed; Style Network; TeenNick; TLC HD; Toon Disney; Tr3s; Trinity Broadcasting Network; Turner Network TV HD; Universal HD; Versus; Versus HD; VH1 Classic; VH1 Soul.
Fee: $6.70 installation; $60.49 monthly.
Pay Service 1
Pay Units: 97.
Programming (via satellite): HBO.
Digital Pay Service 1
Pay Units: N.A.
Programming (via satellite): Cinemax (multiplexed); Encore (multiplexed); Flix; HBO (multiplexed); HBO HD; Showtime (multiplexed); Showtime HD; Starz (multiplexed); Starz HDTV; The Movie Channel (multiplexed).
Fee: $12.00 monthly (Starz/Encore), $16.15 monthly (Cinemax, HBO or Showtime/TMC).
Video-On-Demand: No
Pay-Per-View
iN DEMAND (delivered digitally); NBA League Pass (delivered digitally); MLS Direct Kick (delivered digitally); NFL Network; NFL Network HD (delivered digitally); Fox College Sports Atlantic (delivered digitally); Fox College Sports Central (delivered digitally); Fox College Sports Pacific (delivered digitally).
Internet Service
Operational: Yes. Began: July 20, 2002.
Broadband Service: Bresnan OnLine.
Fee: $49.99 installation; $29.95-$62.90 monthly; $3.50 modem lease.
Telephone Service
Analog: Not Operational
Digital: Operational
Fee: $46.99 monthly
Miles of Plant: 40.0 (coaxial); 7.0 (fiber optic).
Regional Vice President & General Manager: Clint Rodeman. Chief Technician: Dan Higgins.
Ownership: Bresnan Communications Inc. (MSO). Sale pends to Cablevision Systems Corp.

RANCHESTER—Tongue River Communications, 620 Betty St, PO Box 759, Ranchester, WY 82839-0759. Phones: 800-953-9011; 307-655-9011. Fax: 307-655-9021.

Web Site: http://tonguerivercomm.com. Also serves Dayton. ICA: WY0028.

TV Market Ranking: Below 100 (Dayton, RANCHESTER). Franchise award date: January 1, 1979. Franchise expiration date: N.A. Began: December 18, 1979.

Channel capacity: N.A. Channels available but not in use: N.A.

Basic Service

Subscribers: 350.

Programming (received off-air): KCWC-DT (PBS) Lander; KGWC-TV (CBS) Casper; KHMT (FOX) Hardin; KSGW-TV (ABC) Sheridan; KTVQ (CBS, CW) Billings; KTWO-TV (ABC) Casper.

Programming (via satellite): A&E Networks; ABC Family Channel; AMC; Animal Planet; Cartoon Network; CNBC; CNN; Country Music TV; C-SPAN; C-SPAN 2; Discovery Channel; Disney Channel; E! Entertainment Television; ESPN; ESPN 2; Headline News; HGTV; History Channel; KCNC-TV (CBS) Denver; KRMA-TV (PBS) Denver; KTLA (CW) Los Angeles; KUSA (NBC) Denver; KWGN-TV (CW) Denver; Lifetime; MSNBC; MTV; Nickelodeon; Outdoor Channel; Spike TV; Syfy; TBS Superstation; The Learning Channel; The Weather Channel; Travel Channel; Trinity Broadcasting Network; truTV; Turner Network TV; USA Network; VH1; WGN America; WPIX (CW, IND) New York.

Fee: $40.00 installation; $43.00 monthly; $15.00 additional installation.

Pay Service 1

Pay Units: N.A.

Programming (via satellite): Cinemax; Encore; HBO.

Fee: $10.00 installation; $12.00 monthly (HBO), $10.00 monthly (Cinemax), $3.00 monthly (Encore).

Video-On-Demand: No

Internet Service

Operational: Yes.

Subscribers: 200.

Broadband Service: In-house.

Fee: $45.00 monthly.

Telephone Service

Digital: Planned

Miles of Plant: 24.0 (coaxial); None (fiber optic).

General Manager: Rob Hium.

Ownership: Lynda & Robert Jacobson (MSO).

RAWLINS—Bresnan Communications, 451 S Durbin St, Casper, WY 82601. Phones: 307-265-3136; 877-273-7626; 307-324-2286 (Customer service). Fax: 307-266-6821. Web Site: http://www.bresnan.com. Also serves Sinclair. ICA: WY0011.

TV Market Ranking: Below 100 (RAWLINS, Sinclair). Franchise award date: N.A. Franchise expiration date: N.A. Began: September 1, 1955.

Channel capacity: N.A. Channels available but not in use: N.A.

Basic Service

Subscribers: 2,500.

Programming (received off-air): KFNR (FOX) Rawlins; 3 FMs.

Programming (via microwave): KCWC-DT (PBS) Lander; KCWY-DT (NBC) Casper; KTWO-TV (ABC) Casper.

Programming (via satellite): C-SPAN; Discovery Channel; ION Television; KCNC-TV (CBS) Denver; KDVR (FOX) Denver; KMGH-TV (ABC) Denver; KTVD (MNT) Denver; KWGN-TV (CW) Denver; TBS Superstation.

Fee: $39.99 installation; $23.74 monthly; $9.99 additional installation.

Expanded Basic Service 1

Subscribers: 2,025.

Programming (via satellite): A&E Networks; ABC Family Channel; Altitude Sports & Entertainment; AMC; Animal Planet; BYU Television; Cartoon Network; CNBC; CNN; Comedy Central; Country Music TV; C-SPAN 2; Disney Channel; E! Entertainment Television; ESPN; ESPN 2; Food Network; Fox News Channel; FX; Hallmark Channel; Headline News; HGTV; History Channel; INSP; Lifetime; MSNBC; MTV; Nickelodeon; Oxygen; QVC; Root Sports Rocky Mountain; Spike TV; Syfy; Telefutura; The Learning Channel; The Weather Channel; Travel Channel; truTV; Turner Classic Movies; Turner Network TV; TV Guide Network; TV Land; Univision Studios; USA Network; VH1.

Fee: $42.00 monthly.

Digital Basic Service

Subscribers: 1,500.

Programming (via satellite): A&E HD; ABC Family HD; Altitude Sports & Entertainment; AmericanLife TV Network; Animal Planet HD; BBC America; Bio; Bloomberg Television; Bravo; CBS Sports Network; CMT Pure Country; CNN HD; Cooking Channel; Discovery Channel HD; Discovery Fit & Health; Discovery Health Channel; Discovery Kids Channel; Disney Channel HD; DIY Network; DMX Music; ESPN 2 HD; ESPN Classic Sports; ESPN HD; ESPNews; Food Network HD; Fox Movie Channel; Fox Reality Channel; Fox Soccer; FSN HD; Fuse; G4; GMC; Golf Channel; GSN; Halogen Network; HD Theater; HDNet; HDNet Movies; HGTV HD; History Channel HD; History Channel International; HRTV; ID Investigation Discovery; Independent Film Channel; Lifetime Movie Network; Lifetime Movie Network HD; Military Channel; MountainWest Sports Network; MTV Hits; MTV Jams; MTV2; mun2 television; National Geographic Channel; National Geographic Channel HD Network; Nick Jr.; Nick Too; NickToons TV; Outdoor Channel; PBS Kids Sprout; Planet Green; RFD-TV; Science; Science HD; SoapNet; Speed; Style Network; Syfy HD; TBS in HD; TeenNick; The Weather Channel HD; TLC HD; Toon Disney; Tr3s; Trinity Broadcasting Network; Turner Network TV HD; Universal HD; USA Network HD; Versus; Versus HD; VH1 Classic; VH1 Soul.

Fee: $64.24 monthly; $6.70 converter.

Pay Service 1

Pay Units: 346.

Programming (via satellite): HBO.

Fee: $19.95 installation.

Digital Pay Service 1

Pay Units: N.A.

Programming (via satellite): Cinemax (multiplexed); Cinemax HD; Encore (multiplexed); HBO (multiplexed); HBO HD; Showtime (multiplexed); Showtime HD; Starz (multiplexed); Starz HDTV; The Movie Channel (multiplexed); The Movie Channel HD.

Fee: $12.00 monthly (Starz/Encore), $16.15 monthly (Cinemax, HBO or Showtime/TMC).

Video-On-Demand: No

Pay-Per-View

iN DEMAND (delivered digitally); NFL Network (delivered digitally); History Channel en Espanol (delivered digitally); Tr3s (delivered digitally); CNN en Espanol (delivered digitally); ESPN Deportes (delivered digitally); Cine Mexicano (delivered digitally); GolTV (delivered digitally); Bandamax (delivered digitally); De Pelicula (delivered digitally); De Pelicula Clasico (delivered digitally); Fox College Sports Atlantic (delivered digitally); Telehit (delivered digitally); Univision Studios (delivered digitally); Telefutura (delivered digitally); NFL Network HD (delivered digitally); Fox College Sports Central (delivered digitally); Fox College Sports Pacific (delivered digitally); VeneMovies (delivered digitally); Discovery en Espanol (delivered digitally); Fox Deportes (delivered digitally); mun2 television (delivered digitally); Cine Latino (delivered digitally).

Internet Service

Operational: Yes.

Broadband Service: Bresnan OnLine.

Fee: $49.99 installation; $29.95-$62.90 monthly; $3.99 modem lease.

Telephone Service

Digital: Operational

Fee: $46.99 monthly

Miles of Plant: 80.0 (coaxial); None (fiber optic).

General Manager: Clint Rodeman. Chief Technician: Dan Higgins.

Ownership: Bresnan Communications Inc. (MSO). Sale pends to Cablevision Systems Corp.

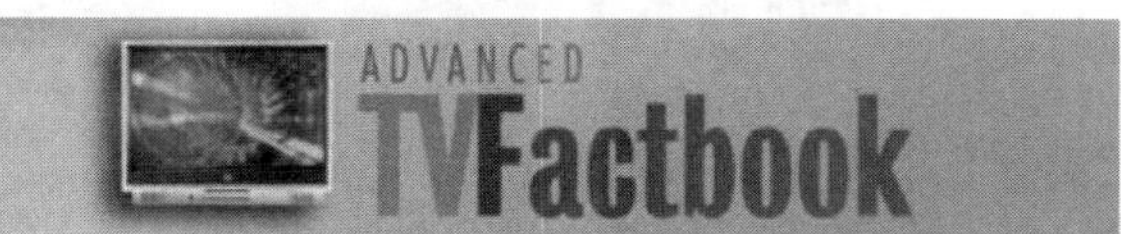

RIVERTON—Bresnan Communications, 451 S Durbin St, Casper, WY 82601. Phones: 307-265-3136; 877-273-7626; 307-856-3248. Fax: 307-266-6821. Web Site: http://www.bresnan.com. Also serves Fremont County & Lander. ICA: WY0059.

TV Market Ranking: Below 100 (Fremont County (portions), Lander, RIVERTON); Outside TV Markets (Fremont County (portions)). Franchise award date: January 1, 1958. Franchise expiration date: June 23, 2025. Began: June 1, 1958.

Channel capacity: N.A. Channels available but not in use: N.A.

Basic Service

Subscribers: 5,000.

Programming (received off-air): KCWC-DT (PBS) Lander; KFNE (FOX) Riverton; KGWL-TV (CBS) Lander.

Programming (via microwave): KCWY-DT (NBC) Casper; KTWO-TV (ABC) Casper.

Programming (via satellite): BYU Television; C-SPAN; C-SPAN 2; CW+; Discovery Channel; Eternal Word TV Network; INSP; ION Television; QVC; TBS Superstation; TV Guide Network.

Fee: $40.95 installation; $48.99 monthly.

Expanded Basic Service 1

Subscribers: 2,970.

Programming (via satellite): A&E Networks; ABC Family Channel; Altitude Sports & Entertainment; AMC; Animal Planet; Bravo; Cartoon Network; CNBC; CNN; Comedy Central; Country Music TV; Disney Channel; E! Entertainment Television; ESPN; ESPN 2; Food Network; Fox News Channel; FX; Hallmark Channel; Headline News; HGTV; History Channel; Lifetime; MSNBC; MTV; Nickelodeon; Outdoor Channel; Oxygen; Root Sports Rocky Mountain; Spike TV; Syfy; The Learning Channel; The Weather Channel; Travel Channel; truTV; Turner Classic Movies; Turner Network TV; TV Land; USA Network; VH1.

Fee: $42.40 monthly.

Digital Basic Service

Subscribers: 1,030.

Programming (via satellite): A&E HD; ABC Family HD; Altitude Sports & Entertainment; AmericanLife TV Network; Animal Planet HD; BBC America; Bio; Bloomberg Television; CBS Sports Network; CMT Pure Country; CNN HD; Cooking Channel; Discovery Channel HD; Discovery Fit & Health; Discovery Health Channel; Discovery Kids Channel; Disney Channel HD; DIY Network; DMX Music; ESPN 2 HD; ESPN Classic Sports; ESPN HD; ESPNews; Food Network HD; Fox Movie Channel; Fox Reality Channel; Fox Soccer; FSN HD; Fuse; G4; Golf Channel; Gospel Music TV; Great American Country; GSN; Halogen Network; HD Theater; HDNet; HDNet Movies; HGTV HD; History Channel HD; History Channel International; HRTV; ID Investigation Discovery; Independent Film Channel; ION Life; Lifetime Movie Network; Lifetime Movie Network HD; Military Channel; MountainWest Sports Network; MTV Hits; MTV Jams; MTV2; National Geographic Channel; National Geographic Channel HD Network; Nick Jr.; Nick Too; NickToons TV; PBS Kids Sprout; Planet Green; Qubo; RFD-TV; Science; Science HD; SoapNet; Speed; Style Network; Syfy HD; TBS in HD; TeenNick; The Weather Channel HD; TLC HD; Toon Disney; Tr3s; Trinity Broadcasting Network; Turner Network TV HD; Universal HD; USA Network HD; Versus; Versus HD; VH1 Classic; VH1 Soul.

Fee: $39.99 installation; $23.34 monthly; $9.99 additional installation.

Pay Service 1

Pay Units: 900.

Programming (via satellite): HBO.

Fee: $13.83 installation; $13.83 monthly.

Digital Pay Service 1

Pay Units: 630.

Programming (via satellite): Cinemax (multiplexed); Cinemax HD; Encore (multiplexed); Flix; HBO (multiplexed); HBO HD; Showtime (multiplexed); Showtime HD; Starz (multiplexed); Starz HDTV; The Movie Channel (multiplexed); The Movie Channel HD.

Fee: $12.00 monthly (Starz/Encore), $16.15 monthly (Cinemax, HBO or Showtime/TMC).

Video-On-Demand: No

Pay-Per-View

Addressable homes: 100.

iN DEMAND (delivered digitally); ESPN (delivered digitally); NHL Network (delivered digitally); NFL Network HD (delivered digitally); NBA League Pass (delivered digitally); MLS Direct Kick (delivered digitally); MLB Extra Innings (delivered digitally); NHL Center Ice (delivered digitally); NFL Network (delivered digitally); Fox College Sports Atlantic (delivered digitally); Fox College Sports Central (delivered digitally); Fox College Sports Pacific (delivered digitally).

Internet Service
Operational: Yes.
Broadband Service: Bresnan OnLine.
Fee: $49.99 installation; $29.95-$62.90 monthly; $3.99 modem lease.
Telephone Service
Digital: Operational
Fee: $49.99 monthly
Miles of Plant: 64.0 (coaxial); None (fiber optic).
Manager: Clint Rodeman. Chief Technician: Dan Higgins.
Ownership: Bresnan Communications Inc. (MSO). Sale pends to Cablevision Systems Corp.

ROCK SPRINGS—Sweetwater Cable TV Co. Inc., 602 Broadway St, Rock Springs, WY 82901-6348. Phone: 307-362-3773. Fax: 307-382-2781. E-mail: swtv@sweetwaterhsa.com. Web Site: http://www.sweetwaterhsa.com. Also serves North Rock Springs, Reliance & Sweetwater County (unincorporated areas). ICA: WY0004.
TV Market Ranking: Below 100 (North Rock Springs, Reliance, ROCK SPRINGS, Sweetwater County (unincorporated areas) (portions)); Outside TV Markets (Sweetwater County (unincorporated areas) (portions)). Franchise award date: January 1, 1954. Franchise expiration date: N.A. Began: December 1, 1956.
Channel capacity: 116 (operating 2-way). Channels available but not in use: N.A.
Basic Service
Subscribers: 7,100.
Programming (received off-air): KGWR-TV (CBS) Rock Springs; 12 FMs.
Programming (via microwave): KJZZ-TV (MNT) Salt Lake City; KSL-TV (NBC) Salt Lake City; KSTU (FOX) Salt Lake City; KTVX (ABC) Salt Lake City; KTWO-TV (ABC) Casper; KUCW (CW) Ogden; KUED (PBS) Salt Lake City; KUTV (CBS) Salt Lake City.
Programming (via satellite): BYU Television; Eternal Word TV Network; INSP; QVC; TBS Superstation; The Weather Channel; TV Guide Network; Univision Studios.
Fee: $30.00 installation; $17.00 monthly; $15.00 additional installation.
Expanded Basic Service 1
Subscribers: N.A.
Programming (via satellite): A&E Networks; ABC Family Channel; AMC; Animal Planet; Bravo; Cartoon Network; CBS Sports Network; CNBC; CNN; Comedy Central; Country Music TV; C-SPAN; C-SPAN 2; Discovery Channel; Disney Channel; E! Entertainment Television; ESPN; ESPN Classic Sports; Food Network; Fox News Channel; Fox Sports Net; FX; Hallmark Channel; Headline News; History Channel; Lifetime; MSNBC; MTV; National Geographic Channel; NFL Network; Nickelodeon; ShopNBC; Speed; Spike TV; Syfy; Telemundo; The Learning Channel; The Mtn; Travel Channel; truTV; Turner Network TV; TV Land; USA Network; VH1.
Fee: $20.90 monthly.
Digital Basic Service
Subscribers: 983.
Programming (via satellite): AmericanLife TV Network; AZ TV; BBC America; Bio; Bloomberg Television; Canal 52MX; Cine Latino; cloo; CMT Pure Country; CNBC World; CNN en Espanol; Discovery en Espanol; Discovery Fit & Health; Discovery Health Channel; Discovery Kids Channel; DMX Music; ESPN HD; ESPNews; Fox Deportes; Fox Movie Channel; G4; Golf Channel; GSN; Halogen Network; HD Theater; HDNet; HDNet Movies; HGTV; History Channel en Espanol; History Channel International; ID Investigation Discovery; Independent Film Channel; Military Channel; MTV Hits; MTV Latin America; MTV2; Nick Jr.; NickToons TV; Outdoor Channel; Planet Green; Science; TeenNick; Toon Disney en Espanol; Trinity Broadcasting Network; Turner Classic Movies; VeneMovies; Versus; VH1 Classic; VH1 Soul.
Fee: $16.00 monthly.
Pay Service 1
Pay Units: 2,236.
Programming (via satellite): HBO (multiplexed).
Fee: $12.50 installation; $9.95 monthly.
Digital Pay Service 1
Pay Units: N.A.
Programming (via satellite): Cinemax (multiplexed); Encore (multiplexed); HBO (multiplexed); Showtime (multiplexed); Showtime HD; Starz (multiplexed); The Movie Channel (multiplexed).
Fee: $10.00 monthly (each).
Video-On-Demand: No
Pay-Per-View
Addressable homes: 756.
ESPN (delivered digitally); Spice: Xcess (delivered digitally); Hot Choice (delivered digitally); iN DEMAND (delivered digitally); Club Jenna (delivered digitally); Playboy TV (delivered digitally); Fresh (delivered digitally).
Internet Service
Operational: Yes. Began: March 4, 2001.
Subscribers: 1,550.
Broadband Service: ZCorum.
Fee: $49.00 installation; $22.90-$54.95 monthly; $64.95 modem purchase.
Telephone Service
Digital: Operational
Miles of Plant: 110.0 (coaxial); 20.0 (fiber optic).
President: Al Carollo Jr. Vice President & Marketing Manager: John Carollo. Chief Technician: Lawrence Gessner. Office Manager: Mandy Krueth.
Ownership: Sweetwater Cable TV Co. Inc. (MSO).

SARATOGA—CommuniComm Services, 234 Wind River Dr, Douglas, WY 82633-2338. Phones: 307-358-3861; 800-759-8448 (Local access only). Fax: 307-358-3849. Web Site: http://www.communicomm.com. Also serves Carbon County (portions), Hanna & Old Baldy. ICA: WY0016.
TV Market Ranking: Below 100 (Carbon County (portions), Hanna, SARATOGA); Outside TV Markets (Carbon County (portions), Old Baldy). Franchise award date: N.A. Franchise expiration date: N.A. Began: November 1, 1979.
Channel capacity: N.A. Channels available but not in use: N.A.
Basic Service
Subscribers: 496.
Programming (via microwave): KCWY-DT (NBC) Casper; KTWO-TV (ABC) Casper.
Programming (via satellite): A&E Networks; ABC Family Channel; AMC; Animal Planet; Bravo; Cartoon Network; CNBC; CNN; Comedy Central; Country Music TV; C-SPAN; C-SPAN 2; Discovery Channel; Discovery Health Channel; Disney Channel; E! Entertainment Television; ESPN; ESPN 2; ESPN Classic Sports; ESPNews; Food Network; Fox News Channel; Fox Sports Net; FX; Great American Country; Hallmark Channel; Headline News; HGTV; History Channel; KCNC-TV (CBS) Denver; KDVR (FOX) Denver; KMGH-TV (ABC) Denver; KRMA-TV (PBS) Denver; KTVD (MNT) Denver; KUSA (NBC) Denver; KWGN-TV (CW) Denver; Lifetime; MSNBC; MTV; Nick Jr.; Nickelodeon; Outdoor Channel; QVC; Spike TV; Syfy; TBS Superstation; The Learning Channel; The Weather Channel; Travel Channel; Trinity Broadcasting Network; truTV; Turner Classic Movies; Turner Network TV; TV Land; USA Network; VH1; WE tv; WGN America.
Fee: $39.95 installation; $29.95 monthly; $2.95 converter.
Digital Basic Service
Subscribers: 142.
Programming (via satellite): AmericanLife TV Network; BBC America; Bio; Blackbelt TV; Bloomberg Television; Bravo; Current; DMX Music; ESPN 2; ESPN Classic Sports; ESPNews; Fox Movie Channel; Fox Soccer; FSN Digital Atlantic; FSN Digital Central; FSN Digital Pacific; Fuse; G4; Golf Channel; Great American Country; GSN; Halogen Network; HGTV; History Channel; History Channel International; Independent Film Channel; International Television (ITV); Lifetime Movie Network; Lime; MBC America; MTV Networks Digital Suite; National Geographic Channel; Nick Jr.; NickToons TV; Outdoor Channel; Ovation; ShopNBC; Speed; Style Network; Sundance Channel; Syfy; TeenNick; The Word Network; Trinity Broadcasting Network; Trio; Turner Classic Movies; TV Land; Versus; WE tv.
Fee: $9.95 monthly.
Digital Pay Service 1
Pay Units: 5.
Programming (via satellite): HBO (multiplexed).
Fee: $13.95 monthly.
Digital Pay Service 2
Pay Units: 6.
Programming (via satellite): Cinemax (multiplexed).
Fee: $13.95 monthly.
Digital Pay Service 3
Pay Units: N.A.
Programming (via satellite): Encore (multiplexed); Starz (multiplexed).
Fee: $13.95 monthly.
Digital Pay Service 4
Pay Units: 24.
Programming (via satellite): Flix; Showtime (multiplexed); The Movie Channel (multiplexed).
Fee: $13.95 monthly (Showtime/Flix or TMC).
Video-On-Demand: No
Pay-Per-View
Hot Choice (delivered digitally); Playboy TV (delivered digitally); Fresh (delivered digitally); Shorteez (delivered digitally); iN DEMAND (delivered digitally).
Internet Service
Operational: Yes.
Subscribers: 100.
Broadband Service: Net Commander.
Fee: $39.95 installation; $51.95 monthly.
Telephone Service
None
Miles of Plant: 30.0 (coaxial); None (fiber optic).
General Manager: Merritt Engleberetsen. Technical Operations Manager: Eric Garland. Marketing Director: Darby Edelman.
Ownership: James Cable LLC (MSO).

SHELL—Formerly served by Basin, WY [WY0072]. TCT West Inc. This cable system has converted to IPTV, 405 S 4th St, Basin, WY 82410. Phones: 800-354-2911; 307-568-3357. Fax: 307-568-2506. E-mail: support@tctwest.net. Web Site: http://www.tctwest.net. ICA: WY5013.
TV Market Ranking: Outside TV Markets (SHELL).
Channel capacity: N.A. Channels available but not in use: N.A.
Internet Service
Operational: Yes.
Telephone Service
Digital: Operational

SHERIDAN—Bresnan Communications, 451 S Durbin St, Casper, WY 82601. Phones: 307-265-3136; 877-273-7626; 307-672-5841 (Customer service). Fax: 307-266-6821. Web Site: http://www.bresnan.com. Also serves Sheridan County. ICA: WY0006.
TV Market Ranking: Below 100 (SHERIDAN, Sheridan County (portions)); Outside TV Markets (Sheridan County (portions)). Franchise award date: N.A. Franchise expiration date: N.A. Began: September 1, 1955.
Channel capacity: N.A. Channels available but not in use: N.A.
Basic Service
Subscribers: 5,841.
Programming (received off-air): KSGW-TV (ABC) Sheridan; KULR-TV (NBC) Billings.
Programming (via microwave): KCWC-DT (PBS) Lander; KTVQ (CBS, CW) Billings; KTWO-TV (ABC) Casper.
Programming (via satellite): Altitude Sports & Entertainment; C-SPAN; C-SPAN 2; CW+; ION Television; KDVR (FOX) Denver; KRMA-TV (PBS) Denver; Oxygen; QVC.
Fee: $39.99 installation; $8.09 monthly; $9.99 additional installation.
Expanded Basic Service 1
Subscribers: 5,628.
Programming (via satellite): A&E Networks; ABC Family Channel; AMC; Animal Planet; Cartoon Network; CNBC; CNN; Comedy Central; Country Music TV; Discovery Channel; Disney Channel; E! Entertainment Television; ESPN; ESPN 2; Eternal Word TV Network; Food Network; Fox News Channel; FX; Golf Channel; Hallmark Channel; Headline News; HGTV; History Channel; Lifetime; MSNBC; MTV; Nickelodeon; Root Sports Rocky Mountain; Spike TV; Syfy; TBS Superstation; The Learning Channel; The Weather Channel; Travel Channel; truTV; Turner Classic Movies; Turner Network TV; TV Guide Network; TV Land; USA Network; Versus; VH1.
Fee: $57.65 monthly.
Digital Basic Service
Subscribers: N.A.
Programming (via satellite): A&E HD; ABC Family HD; American Movie Classics; AmericanLife TV Network; Animal Planet HD; BBC America; Bio; Bloomberg Television; Bravo; Bravo HD; BYU Television; CBS Sports Network; CMT Pure Country; CNBC HD+; CNN HD; Cooking Channel; Discovery Channel HD; Discovery Fit & Health; Discovery Health Channel; Discovery Kids Channel; Disney Channel HD; DIY Network; DMX Music; ESPN 2 HD; ESPN Classic Sports; ESPN HD; ESPNews; Fox Movie Channel; Fox Reality Channel; Fox Soccer; Fuse; G4; GMC; Golf Channel; Great American Country; GSN; Halogen Network; HD Theater; HDNet; HDNet Movies; History Channel HD; History Channel International; HRTV; ID Investigation Discovery; Independent Film Channel; ION Life; Lifetime Movie Network; Military Channel; MountainWest Sports Network; MTV Hits; MTV Jams; MTV2; mun2 television; National Geographic Channel; National Geographic Channel HD Network; Nick Jr.; Nick Too; NickToons TV; Outdoor

Channel; Outdoor Channel 2 HD; Palladia; PBS Kids Sprout; Planet Green; Qubo; RFD-TV; Science; Science HD; SoapNet; Speed; Speed HD; Style Network; TeenNick; The Weather Channel HD; TLC HD; Toon Disney; Tr3s; Trinity Broadcasting Network; Turner Network TV HD; Universal HD; Versus HD; VH1 Classic; VH1 Soul.
Fee: $64.24 monthly.

Digital Pay Service 1
Pay Units: N.A.
Programming (via satellite): Cinemax (multiplexed); Cinemax HD; Encore (multiplexed); Flix; HBO (multiplexed); HBO HD; Showtime (multiplexed); Showtime HD; Starz (multiplexed); Starz HDTV; The Movie Channel (multiplexed).
Fee: $12.00 monthly (Starz/Encore), $16.15 monthly (Cinemax, HBO or Showtime/TMC).

Video-On-Demand: No

Pay-Per-View
iN DEMAND (delivered digitally); NBA League Pass (delivered digitally); VeneMovies (delivered digitally); Discovery en Espanol (delivered digitally); Fox Deportes (delivered digitally); mun2 television (delivered digitally); Cine Latino (delivered digitally); History Channel en Espanol (delivered digitally); Tr3s (delivered digitally); CNN en Espanol (delivered digitally); ESPN Deportes (delivered digitally); MLS Direct Kick (delivered digitally); Cine Mexicano (delivered digitally); NFL Network HD (delivered digitally); MLB Extra Innings (delivered digitally); NHL Center Ice (delivered digitally); NFL Network (delivered digitally); Fox College Sports Atlantic (delivered digitally); Fox College Sports Central (delivered digitally); Fox College Sports Pacific (delivered digitally); NHL Network (delivered digitally).

Internet Service
Operational: Yes.
Broadband Service: Bresnan OnLine.
Fee: $49.99 installation; $29.95-$62.90 monthly.

Telephone Service
Digital: Operational
Fee: $46.95 monthly

Miles of Plant: 120.0 (coaxial); 22.0 (fiber optic).
General Manager: Clint Rodeman. Chief Technician: Dan Higgins.
Ownership: Bresnan Communications Inc. (MSO). Sale pends to Cablevision Systems Corp.

SHERIDAN—Formerly served by Sprint Corp. No longer in operation. ICA: WY0068.

SHOSHONI—Formerly served by Winhill Corp. No longer in operation. ICA: WY0060.

STORY—Tongue River Communications, 620 Betty St, PO Box 759, Ranchester, WY 82839-0759. Phones: 800-953-9011; 307-655-9011. Fax: 307-655-9021. Web Site: http://tonguerivercomm.com. ICA: WY0034.
TV Market Ranking: Below 100 (STORY). Franchise award date: N.A. Franchise expiration date: N.A. Began: July 1, 1980.
Channel capacity: N.A. Channels available but not in use: N.A.

Basic Service
Subscribers: 300.
Programming (received off-air): KCWC-DT (PBS) Lander; KGWC-TV (CBS) Casper; KHMT (FOX) Hardin; KSGW-TV (ABC) Sheridan; KTVQ (CBS, CW) Billings; KTWO-TV (ABC) Casper.
Programming (via satellite): A&E Networks; ABC Family Channel; AMC; Animal Planet; Cartoon Network; CNBC; CNN; Country Music TV; C-SPAN; C-SPAN 2; Discovery Channel; Disney Channel; E! Entertainment Television; ESPN; ESPN 2; Headline News; HGTV; History Channel; KCNC-TV (CBS) Denver; KRMA-TV (PBS) Denver; KTLA (CW) Los Angeles; KUSA (NBC) Denver; KWGN-TV (CW) Denver; Lifetime; MSNBC; MTV; Nickelodeon; Outdoor Channel; Spike TV; Syfy; TBS Superstation; The Learning Channel; The Weather Channel; Travel Channel; Trinity Broadcasting Network; truTV; Turner Network TV; USA Network; VH1; WGN America; WPIX (CW, IND) New York.
Fee: $40.00 installation; $43.00 monthly; $15.00 additional installation.

Pay Service 1
Pay Units: 28.
Programming (via satellite): Cinemax.
Fee: $10.00 installation; $10.00 monthly.

Pay Service 2
Pay Units: 38.
Programming (via satellite): HBO.
Fee: $10.00 installation; $12.00 monthly.

Video-On-Demand: No

Internet Service
Operational: Yes.
Subscribers: 200.
Broadband Service: In-house.
Fee: $45.00 monthly.

Telephone Service
None

Miles of Plant: 13.0 (coaxial); None (fiber optic). Additional miles planned: 1.0 (coaxial).
General Manager: Rob Hium.
Ownership: Lynda & Robert Jacobson (MSO).

SUNDANCE—Tongue River Communications, 620 Betty St, PO Box 759, Ranchester, WY 82839-0759. Phones: 800-953-9011; 307-655-9011. Fax: 307-655-9021. Web Site: http://tonguerivercomm.com. ICA: WY0061.
TV Market Ranking: Below 100 (SUNDANCE). Franchise award date: N.A. Franchise expiration date: N.A. Began: November 1, 1980.
Channel capacity: N.A. Channels available but not in use: N.A.

Basic Service
Subscribers: 350.
Programming (received off-air): KCWC-DT (PBS) Lander; KGWC-TV (CBS) Casper; KIVV-TV (FOX) Lead; KOTA-TV (ABC) Rapid City; KPSD-TV (PBS) Eagle Butte; KTWO-TV (ABC) Casper.
Programming (via satellite): A&E Networks; ABC Family Channel; AMC; Animal Planet; Cartoon Network; CNBC; CNN; Country Music TV; C-SPAN; C-SPAN 2; Discovery Channel; Disney Channel; E! Entertainment Television; ESPN; ESPN 2; Headline News; HGTV; History Channel; KCNC-TV (CBS) Denver; KTLA (CW) Los Angeles; KUSA (NBC) Denver; KWGN-TV (CW) Denver; Lifetime; MSNBC; MTV; Nickelodeon; Outdoor Channel; Spike TV; Syfy; TBS Superstation; The Learning Channel; The Weather Channel; Travel Channel; Trinity Broadcasting Network; truTV; Turner Network TV; USA Network; VH1; WGN America; WPIX (CW, IND) New York.
Fee: $40.00 installation; $43.00 monthly; $15.00 additional installation.

Pay Service 1
Pay Units: 45.
Programming (via satellite): Cinemax.
Fee: $10.00 installation; $10.00 monthly.

Pay Service 2
Pay Units: 40.
Programming (via satellite): Encore.
Fee: $10.00 installation; $3.00 monthly.

Pay Service 3
Pay Units: 68.
Programming (via satellite): HBO.
Fee: $10.00 installation; $12.00 monthly.

Video-On-Demand: No

Internet Service
Operational: Yes.
Subscribers: 40.
Broadband Service: In-house.
Fee: $45.00 monthly.

Telephone Service
None

General Manager: Rob Hium.
Ownership: Lynda & Robert Jacobson (MSO).

TEN SLEEP—Formerly served by Basin, WY [WY0072]. TCT West Inc. This cable system has converted to IPTV, 405 S 4th St, Basin, WY 82410. Phones: 800-354-2911; 307-568-3357. Fax: 307-568-2506. E-mail: support@tctwest.net. Web Site: http://www.tctwest.net. ICA: WY5017.
TV Market Ranking: Outside TV Markets (TEN SLEEP).
Channel capacity: N.A. Channels available but not in use: N.A.

Internet Service
Operational: Yes.

Telephone Service
Digital: Operational

TEN SLEEP—TCT West. No longer in operation. ICA: WY0046.

THERMOPOLIS—Bresnan Communications, 451 S Durbin St, Casper, WY 82601. Phones: 307-265-3136; 307-856-3248 (Customer service). Fax: 307-266-6821. Web Site: http://www.bresnan.com. Also serves East Thermopolis & Hot Springs County. ICA: WY0062.
TV Market Ranking: Below 100 (Hot Springs County (portions)); Outside TV Markets (East Thermopolis, Hot Springs County (portions), THERMOPOLIS). Franchise award date: N.A. Franchise expiration date: October 6, 2010. Began: N.A.
Channel capacity: N.A. Channels available but not in use: N.A.

Basic Service
Subscribers: 1,200.
Programming (received off-air): KCWC-DT (PBS) Lander; KFNE (FOX) Riverton; KGWL-TV (CBS) Lander.
Programming (via microwave): KCWY-DT (NBC) Casper; KTWO-TV (ABC) Casper.
Programming (via satellite): ABC Family Channel; BYU Television; CNN; Comedy Central; C-SPAN; C-SPAN 2; CW+; Discovery Channel; Eternal Word TV Network; Headline News; INSP; ION Television; Lifetime; Nickelodeon; QVC; TBS Superstation; WGN America.
Fee: $39.99 installation; $32.34 monthly; $9.99 additional installation.

Expanded Basic Service 1
Subscribers: 1,030.
Programming (via satellite): A&E Networks; Altitude Sports & Entertainment; AMC; Animal Planet; Bravo; Cartoon Network; CNBC; Country Music TV; Disney Channel; E! Entertainment Television; ESPN; ESPN 2; Food Network; Fox News Channel; FX; Hallmark Channel; HGTV; History Channel; MSNBC; MTV; Oxygen; Root Sports Rocky Mountain; Spike TV; Syfy; The Learning Channel; The Weather Channel; Travel Channel; truTV; Turner Classic Movies; Turner Network TV; TV Guide Network; TV Land; USA Network; VH1.
Fee: $33.40 monthly.

Digital Basic Service
Subscribers: 360.
Programming (via satellite): A&E HD; AmericanLife TV Network; Animal Planet HD; BBC America; Bio; Bloomberg Television; CBS Sports Network; CMT Pure Country; Cooking Channel; Discovery Channel HD; Discovery Fit & Health; Discovery Health Channel; Discovery Kids Channel; DIY Network; DMX Music; ESPN Classic Sports; ESPN HD; ESPNews; Food Network HD; Fox Movie Channel; Fox Reality Channel; Fox Soccer; Fuse; G4; GMC; Golf Channel; Great American Country; GSN; Halogen Network; HD Theater; HGTV HD; History Channel HD; History Channel International; HRTV; ID Investigation Discovery; Independent Film Channel; ION Television; Lifetime Movie Network; Military Channel; MountainWest Sports Network; MTV Hits; MTV Jams; MTV2; National Geographic Channel; National Geographic Channel HD Network; Nick Jr.; Nick Too; NickToons TV; Outdoor Channel; PBS Kids Sprout; Planet Green; RFD-TV; Science; Science HD; SoapNet; Speed; Style Network; Syfy HD; TeenNick; Toon Disney; Tr3s; Trinity Broadcasting Network; Universal HD; USA Network HD; Versus; VH1 Classic; VH1 Soul.
Fee: $64.24 monthly.

Digital Pay Service 1
Pay Units: N.A.
Programming (via satellite): Cinemax (multiplexed); Encore (multiplexed); Flix; HBO (multiplexed); HBO HD; Showtime (multiplexed); Starz (multiplexed); Starz HDTV; The Movie Channel (multiplexed).
Fee: $12.00 monthly (Starz/Encore), $16.15 monthly (Cinemax, HBO or Showtime/TMC).

Video-On-Demand: No

Pay-Per-View
iN DEMAND (delivered digitally); NFL Network (delivered digitally); Fox College Sports Atlantic (delivered digitally); Fox College Sports Central (delivered digitally); Fox College Sports Pacific (delivered digitally).

Internet Service
Operational: Yes.
Broadband Service: Bresnan OnLine.
Fee: $49.99 installation; $29.95-$62.90 monthly; $3.99 modem lease.

Telephone Service
Digital: Operational
Fee: $49.99 monthly

Miles of Plant: 19.0 (coaxial); 8.0 (fiber optic).
General Manager: Clint Rodeman. Chief Technician: Dan Higgins.
Ownership: Bresnan Communications Inc. (MSO). Sale pends to Cablevision Systems Corp.

TORRINGTON—CommuniComm Services, 234 Wind River Dr, Douglas, WY 82633-2338. Phone: 307-358-3861. Fax: 307-385-3849. Web Site: http://www.communicomm.com. Also serves Goshen County (unincorporated areas) & Lingle. ICA: WY0014.
TV Market Ranking: Below 100 (Goshen County (unincorporated areas) (portions), TORRINGTON); Outside TV Markets (Goshen County (unincorporated areas) (portions), Lingle). Franchise award date: January 1, 1962. Franchise expiration date: N.A. Began: November 1, 1964.
Channel capacity: N.A. Channels available but not in use: N.A.

Basic Service
Subscribers: 2,053.
Programming (received off-air): KCWC-DT (PBS) Lander; KCWY-DT (NBC) Casper; KDUH-TV (ABC) Scottsbluff; KGWN-TV (CBS, CW) Cheyenne; KLWY (FOX) Cheyenne; KSTF (CBS, CW) Scottsbluff; KTNE-TV (PBS) Alliance.
Programming (via microwave): KCNC-TV (CBS) Denver; KMGH-TV (ABC) Denver; KTVD (MNT) Denver; KUSA (NBC) Denver; KWGN-TV (CW) Denver.
Programming (via satellite): QVC.
Fee: $39.95 installation; $29.95 monthly; $20.00 additional installation.

Expanded Basic Service 1
Subscribers: 1,995.
Programming (via satellite): A&E Networks; ABC Family Channel; AMC; Animal Planet; Bravo; Cartoon Network; CNBC; CNN; Comedy Central; Country Music TV; C-SPAN; C-SPAN 2; Discovery Channel; Discovery Health Channel; E! Entertainment Television; ESPN; ESPN 2; ESPNews; Food Network; Fox News Channel; FX; G4; Hallmark Channel; Headline News; HGTV; History Channel; Lifetime; MSNBC; MTV; Nick Jr.; Nickelodeon; Outdoor Channel; Root Sports Rocky Mountain; Spike TV; Syfy; TBS Superstation; The Learning Channel; The Weather Channel; Travel Channel; Trinity Broadcasting Network; truTV; Turner Network TV; TV Guide Network; TV Land; Univision Studios; USA Network; VH1; WE tv.
Fee: $19.04 monthly.

Digital Basic Service
Subscribers: 457.
Programming (via satellite): AmericanLife TV Network; BBC America; Bio; Blackbelt TV; Bloomberg Television; Bravo; Current; DMX Music; ESPN 2; ESPN Classic Sports; ESPNews; Fox Movie Channel; Fox Soccer; FSN Digital Atlantic; FSN Digital Central; FSN Digital Pacific; Fuse; G4; Golf Channel; Great American Country; GSN; Halogen Network; HGTV; History Channel; History Channel International; Independent Film Channel; International Television (ITV); Lifetime Movie Network; Lime; MBC America; MTV Networks Digital Suite; National Geographic Channel; Nick Jr.; NickToons TV; Outdoor Channel; Ovation; ShopNBC; Speed; Style Network; Sundance Channel; TeenNick; The Word Network; Trio; Turner Classic Movies; TV Land; Versus; WE tv.
Fee: $11.95 monthly.

Digital Pay Service 1
Pay Units: 437.
Programming (via satellite): HBO (multiplexed).
Fee: $13.95 monthly.

Digital Pay Service 2
Pay Units: 384.
Programming (via satellite): Cinemax (multiplexed).
Fee: $11.95 monthly.

Digital Pay Service 3
Pay Units: 417.
Programming (via satellite): Encore (multiplexed); Starz (multiplexed).
Fee: $13.95 monthly.

Digital Pay Service 4
Pay Units: 74.
Programming (via satellite): Flix; Showtime (multiplexed); The Movie Channel (multiplexed).
Fee: $13.95 monthly (Showtime/Flix or TMC).

Video-On-Demand: No

Pay-Per-View
iN DEMAND (delivered digitally); Hot Choice (delivered digitally); Playboy TV (delivered digitally); Fresh (delivered digitally); Shorteez (delivered digitally).

Internet Service
Operational: Yes.
Subscribers: 912.
Broadband Service: Net Commander.
Fee: $39.95 installation; $51.95 monthly.

Telephone Service
None
Miles of Plant: 67.0 (coaxial); None (fiber optic).
Manager: Merritt Engebretsen. Technical Operations Manager: Eric Garland. Marketing Director: Darby Edelman.
Ownership: James Cable LLC (MSO).

UPTON—Tongue River Communications, 620 Betty St, PO Box 759, Ranchester, WY 82839-0759. Phones: 800-953-9011; 307-665-9011. Fax: 307-655-9021. Web Site: http://www.tonguerivercomm.com. ICA: WY0036.
TV Market Ranking: Outside TV Markets (UPTON). Franchise award date: June 7, 1990. Franchise expiration date: June 6, 2015. Began: November 1, 1978.
Channel capacity: 36 (not 2-way capable). Channels available but not in use: N.A.

Basic Service
Subscribers: 227.
Programming (received off-air): KEVN-TV (FOX) Rapid City; KOTA-TV (ABC) Rapid City.
Programming (via satellite): A&E Networks; ABC Family Channel; Altitude Sports & Entertainment; AMC; Animal Planet; Cartoon Network; CNBC; CNN; C-SPAN; C-SPAN 2; CW+; Discovery Channel; Disney Channel; E! Entertainment Television; ESPN; Hallmark Channel; Headline News; ION Television; KCNC-TV (CBS) Denver; KRMA-TV (PBS) Denver; KUSA (NBC) Denver; Lifetime; MSNBC; MTV; Nickelodeon; QVC; Spike TV; TBS Superstation; The Learning Channel; The Weather Channel; truTV; Turner Network TV; USA Network.
Programming (via translator): KTWO-TV (ABC) Casper.
Fee: $40.95 installation; $28.49 monthly; $1.65 converter; $13.95 additional installation.

Pay Service 1
Pay Units: 67.
Programming (via satellite): HBO.
Fee: $13.05 monthly.

Pay Service 2
Pay Units: 107.
Programming (via satellite): Encore.
Fee: $1.75 monthly.

Internet Service
Operational: No.

Telephone Service
None
Miles of Plant: 14.0 (coaxial); None (fiber optic).
General Manager: Rob Hium.
Ownership: Lynda & Robert Jacobson (MSO).

WAMSUTTER—Formerly served by Sweetwater Cable TV Co. Inc. No longer in operation. ICA: WY0039.

WHEATLAND—CommuniComm Services, 234 Wind River Dr, Douglas, WY 82633-2338. Phone: 307-358-3861. Fax: 307-358-3849. Web Site: http://www.communicomm.com. Also serves Platte County (unincorporated areas). ICA: WY0017.
TV Market Ranking: Outside TV Markets (Platte County (unincorporated areas), WHEATLAND). Franchise award date: January 1, 1962. Franchise expiration date: N.A. Began: September 1, 1963.
Channel capacity: N.A. Channels available but not in use: N.A.

Basic Service
Subscribers: 1,868.
Programming (received off-air): KCWC-DT (PBS) Lander; KCWY-DT (NBC) Casper; KDUH-TV (ABC) Scottsbluff; KGWN-TV (CBS, CW) Cheyenne; KSTF (CBS, CW) Scottsbluff.
Programming (via satellite): KCNC-TV (CBS) Denver; KDVR (FOX) Denver; KMGH-TV (ABC) Denver; KTVD (MNT) Denver; KUSA (NBC) Denver.
Fee: $39.95 installation; $29.95 monthly.

Expanded Basic Service 1
Subscribers: 1,851.
Programming (via satellite): A&E Networks; ABC Family Channel; AMC; Animal Planet; Bravo; Cartoon Network; CNBC; CNN; Country Music TV; C-SPAN; C-SPAN 2; Discovery Channel; Discovery Health Channel; E! Entertainment Television; ESPN; ESPN 2; ESPNews; Food Network; Fox News Channel; FX; G4; Hallmark Channel; Headline News; HGTV; History Channel; KWGN-TV (CW) Denver; Lifetime; MSNBC; MTV; Nick Jr.; Nickelodeon; Outdoor Channel; QVC; Root Sports Rocky Mountain; Spike TV; Syfy; TBS Superstation; The Learning Channel; The Weather Channel; Travel Channel; Trinity Broadcasting Network; truTV; Turner Network TV; TV Guide Network; TV Land; Univision Studios; USA Network; VH1; WE tv; WGN America.
Fee: $19.04 monthly.

Digital Basic Service
Subscribers: 212.
Programming (via satellite): AmericanLife TV Network; BBC America; Bio; Blackbelt TV; Bloomberg Television; Bravo; Current; Discovery Fit & Health; DMX Music; E! Entertainment Television; ESPN 2; ESPN Classic Sports; ESPNews; Fox Movie Channel; Fox Soccer; FSN Digital Atlantic; FSN Digital Central; FSN Digital Pacific; Fuse; G4; Golf Channel; Great American Country; GSN; Halogen Network; HGTV; History Channel; History Channel International; Independent Film Channel; International Television (ITV); Lifetime Movie Network; Lime; MBC America; MTV Networks Digital Suite; National Geographic Channel; Nick Jr.; NickToons TV; Outdoor Channel; Ovation; ShopNBC; Speed; Sundance Channel; Syfy; TeenNick; The Word Network; Trinity Broadcasting Network; Trio; Turner Classic Movies; TV Land; Versus; WE tv.
Fee: $11.95 monthly.

Digital Pay Service 1
Pay Units: 174.
Programming (via satellite): HBO.
Fee: $13.95 monthly.

Digital Pay Service 2
Pay Units: 150.
Programming (via satellite): Cinemax (multiplexed).
Fee: $11.95 monthly.

Digital Pay Service 3
Pay Units: 177.
Programming (via satellite): Encore (multiplexed); Starz (multiplexed).
Fee: $13.95 monthly.

Digital Pay Service 4
Pay Units: 28.
Programming (via satellite): Flix; Showtime (multiplexed); The Movie Channel (multiplexed).
Fee: $13.95 monthly (Showtime/Flix or TMC).

Video-On-Demand: No

Internet Service
Operational: Yes. Began: August 1, 1998.
Subscribers: 434.
Broadband Service: Net Commander.
Fee: $39.95 installation; $51.95 monthly.

Telephone Service
None
Miles of Plant: 41.0 (coaxial); None (fiber optic).
General Manager: Merritt Engleberetsen. Technical Operations Manager: Eric Garland. Marketing Director: Darby Edelman.
Ownership: James Cable LLC (MSO).

WORLAND—Bresnan Communications, 714 Coburn Ave, Worland, WY 82401-3315. Phones: 877-273-7626; 307-347-3245. Fax: 307-347-8339. Web Site: http://www.bresnan.com. Also serves Washakie County. ICA: WY0013.
TV Market Ranking: Outside TV Markets (Washakie County, WORLAND). Franchise award date: N.A. Franchise expiration date: N.A. Began: May 1, 1954.
Channel capacity: N.A. Channels available but not in use: N.A.

Basic Service
Subscribers: 1,600.
Programming (received off-air): KCWC-DT (PBS) Lander; KCWY-DT (NBC) Casper; KFNE (FOX) Riverton; KGWL-TV (CBS) Lander; KTVQ (CBS, CW) Billings; 1 FM.
Programming (via microwave): KTWO-TV (ABC) Casper.
Programming (via satellite): BYU Television; C-SPAN 2; CW+; Discovery Channel; QVC; TBS Superstation; TV Guide Network; WGN America.
Fee: $39.99 installation; $23.34 monthly; $9.99 additional installation.

Expanded Basic Service 1
Subscribers: 900.
Programming (via satellite): A&E Networks; ABC Family Channel; Altitude Sports & Entertainment; AMC; Animal Planet; Bravo; Cartoon Network; CNBC; CNN; Comedy Central; Country Music TV; C-SPAN; Disney Channel; E! Entertainment Television; ESPN; ESPN 2; Eternal Word TV Network; Food Network; Fox News Channel; FX; Hallmark Channel; Headline News; HGTV; History Channel; ION Television; Lifetime; MSNBC; MTV; Nickelodeon; Oxygen; Root Sports Rocky Mountain; Spike TV; Syfy;

The Learning Channel; The Weather Channel; Travel Channel; truTV; Turner Classic Movies; Turner Network TV; TV Land; Univision Studios; USA Network; VH1.
Fee: $42.40 monthly.

Digital Basic Service
Subscribers: 500.
Programming (via satellite): A&E HD; ABC Family HD; AmericanLife TV Network; Animal Planet HD; BBC America; Bio; Bloomberg Television; CBS Sports Network; Cooking Channel; Country Music TV; Discovery Channel HD; Discovery Fit & Health; Discovery Health Channel; Discovery Kids Channel; Disney Channel HD; DIY Network; DMX Music; ESPN Classic Sports; ESPN HD; ESPNews; Food Network HD; Fox Movie Channel; Fox Reality Channel; Fox Soccer; Fuse; G4; GMC; Golf Channel; GSN; Halogen Network; HD Theater; HGTV HD; History Channel HD; History Channel International; HRTV; ID Investigation Discovery; Independent Film Channel; Lifetime Movie Network; Military Channel; MountainWest Sports Network; MTV Hits; MTV2; National Geographic Channel; National Geographic Channel HD Network; Nick Jr.; NickToons TV; Outdoor Channel; PBS Kids Sprout; Planet Green; RFD-TV; Science; Science HD; SoapNet; Speed; Style Network; Syfy HD; TeenNick; Toon Disney; Tr3s; Trinity Broadcasting Network; Universal HD; USA Network HD; Versus; VH1 Classic; VH1 Soul.
Fee: $64.24 monthly.

Pay Service 1
Pay Units: 171.
Programming (via satellite): HBO.
Fee: $14.19 monthly.

Digital Pay Service 1
Pay Units: N.A.
Programming (via satellite): Cinemax (multiplexed); Encore (multiplexed); Flix; HBO (multiplexed); HBO HD; Showtime (multiplexed); Starz (multiplexed); Starz HDTV; The Movie Channel (multiplexed).
Fee: $12.00 monthly (Starz/Encore), $16.15 monthly (Cinemax, HBO or Showtime/TMC).

Video-On-Demand: No

Pay-Per-View
iN DEMAND (delivered digitally); NFL Network (delivered digitally); History Channel en Espanol (delivered digitally); Tr3s (delivered digitally); CNN en Espanol (delivered digitally); ESPN Deportes (delivered digitally); Cine Mexicano (delivered digitally); Fox College Sports Atlantic (delivered digitally); Fox College Sports Central (delivered digitally); Fox College Sports Pacific (delivered digitally); VeneMovies (delivered digitally); Discovery en Espanol (delivered digitally); Fox Deportes (delivered digitally); mun2 television (delivered digitally); Cine Latino (delivered digitally).

Internet Service
Operational: Yes.
Broadband Service: Bresnan OnLine.
Fee: $49.99 installation; $29.95-$62.90 monthly.

Telephone Service
Digital: Operational
Fee: $46.99 monthly
Miles of Plant: 42.0 (coaxial); 6.0 (fiber optic).

Regional Vice President & General Manager: Clint Rodeman. Chief Technician: Dan Higgins.
Ownership: Bresnan Communications Inc. (MSO). Sale pends to Cablevision Systems Corp.

WRIGHT—Bresnan Communications, 451 S Durbin St, Casper, WY 82601. Phone: 307-682-4303. Web Site: http://www.bresnan.com. Also serves Reno Junction. ICA: WY0029.
TV Market Ranking: Outside TV Markets (Reno Junction, WRIGHT). Franchise award date: October 13, 1989. Franchise expiration date: October 12, 2009. Began: August 1, 1976.
Channel capacity: 36 (not 2-way capable). Channels available but not in use: N.A.

Basic Service
Subscribers: 72.
Programming (received off-air): KTWO-TV (ABC) Casper; 1 FM.
Programming (via satellite): A&E Networks; ABC Family Channel; AMC; Animal Planet; Cartoon Network; CNN; C-SPAN; C-SPAN 2; Discovery Channel; Disney Channel; E! Entertainment Television; ESPN; ESPN 2; Hallmark Channel; HGTV; History Channel; KCNC-TV (CBS) Denver; KDVR (FOX) Denver; KMGH-TV (ABC) Denver; KRMA-TV (PBS) Denver; KTVD (MNT) Denver; KUSA (NBC) Denver; KWGN-TV (CW) Denver; MoviePlex; MSNBC; Nickelodeon; Spike TV; TBS Superstation; The Learning Channel; The Weather Channel; truTV; Turner Network TV; USA Network.
Fee: $40.95 installation; $27.99 monthly.

Pay Service 1
Pay Units: N.A.
Programming (via satellite): Encore; HBO; Starz.
Fee: $14.95 installation; $12.65 monthly.

Internet Service
Operational: No.

Telephone Service
None
Miles of Plant: 10.0 (coaxial); None (fiber optic).
General Manager: Clint Rodeman. Chief Technician: Dan Higgins.
Ownership: Bresnan Communications Inc. (MSO). Sale pends to Cablevision Systems Corp.

WYODAK—Formerly served by Tongue River Cable TV Inc. No longer in operation. ICA: WY0035.

CUBA

Total Systems: 1
Total Communities Served: 1
Franchises Not Yet Operating: 0
Applications Pending: 0
Communities with Applications: 0
Number of Basic Subscribers: 976
Number of Expanded Basic Subscribers: 0
Number of Pay Units: 858

Top 100 Markets Represented: N.A.

**For a list of cable communities in this section, see the Cable Community Index located in the back of Cable Volume 2.
For explanation of terms used in cable system listings, see p. D-11.**

GUANTANAMO BAY—Phoenix Cable, 17 S Franklin Tpke, Ramsey, NJ 7446. Phone: 201-825-9090. Fax: 201-825-8794. ICA: CU0001.

TV Market Ranking: Outside TV Markets (GUANTANAMO BAY). Franchise award date: December 5, 1986. Franchise expiration date: December 5, 2010. Began: March 1, 1987.

Channel capacity: 35 (not 2-way capable). Channels available but not in use: N.A.

Basic Service

Subscribers: 976.

Programming (via satellite): A&E Networks; ABC Family Channel; BET Networks; Cartoon Network; CNN; Comedy Central; Country Music TV; C-SPAN; Discovery Channel; ESPN; ESPN 2; Headline News; History Channel; Lifetime; MTV; Nickelodeon; OpenTV; Spike TV; Syfy; TBS Superstation; Telemundo; The Learning Channel; Turner Classic Movies; Turner Network TV; TV Guide Network; TV Land; VH1; WGN America; WNBC (NBC) New York; WPIX (CW, IND) New York; WSEE-TV (CBS, CW) Erie.

Fee: $10.00 installation; $29.00 monthly; $1.68 converter.

Pay Service 1

Pay Units: 252.

Programming (via satellite): Cinemax.

Fee: $9.00 monthly.

Pay Service 2

Pay Units: 135.

Programming (via satellite): Showtime.

Fee: $9.00 monthly.

Pay Service 3

Pay Units: 384.

Programming (via satellite): HBO.

Fee: $9.00 monthly.

Pay Service 4

Pay Units: 87.

Programming (via satellite): The Movie Channel.

Fee: $9.00 monthly.

Video-On-Demand: No

Internet Service

Operational: Yes.

Telephone Service

None

Miles of Plant: 40.0 (coaxial); None (fiber optic).

Manager: Jim Feeney, Jr.

Ownership: Phoenix Cable Inc. (MSO).

GUAM

Total Systems: **1**
Total Communities Served: **20**
Franchises Not Yet Operating: **0**
Applications Pending: **0**
Communities with Applications: **0**
Number of Basic Subscribers: **48,646**
Number of Expanded Basic Subscribers: **0**
Number of Pay Units: **2,631**

Top 100 Markets Represented: N.A.

For a list of cable communities in this section, see the Cable Community Index located in the back of Cable Volume 2.
For explanation of terms used in cable system listings, see p. D-11.

AGANA—MCV Broadband, 600 Harmon Loop Rd, Dededo, GU 96929. Phone: 671-635-4628. Fax: 671-635-1500. Web Site: http://www.mcvguam.com. Also serves Agana Heights, Agat, Asan-Maina, Barrigada, Chalan Pago-Ordot, Dededo, Hagatna, Inarajan, Mangilao, Merizo, Mongmong-Toto-Maite, Piti, Santa Rita, Sinajana, Talofofo, Tamuning, Umatac, Yigo & Yona. ICA: GU0001.

TV Market Ranking: Below 100 (AGANA, Agana Heights, Agat, Asan-Maina, Barrigada, Chalan Pago-Ordot, Dededo, Hagatna, Inarajan, Mangilao, Merizo, Mongmong-Toto-Maite, Piti, Santa Rita, Sinajana, Talofofo, Tamuning, Umatac, Yigo, Yona). Franchise award date: N.A. Franchise expiration date: N.A. Began: October 1, 1970.

Channel capacity: N.A. Channels available but not in use: N.A.

Basic Service

Subscribers: 40,414.

Programming (received off-air): KGTF (PBS) Agana; KTGM (ABC) Tamuning; KUAM-TV (NBC) Hagatna; allband FM.

Programming (via satellite): A&E Networks; ABC Family Channel; AMC; Animal Planet; BET Networks; Cartoon Network; CNBC World; CNN; CNN International; Comedy Central; Country Music TV; Discovery Channel; Discovery Channel Australia; Disney Channel; E! Entertainment Television; ESPN; ESPN 2; ESPN Classic Sports; Eternal Word TV Network; Food Network; Fox News Channel; FX; G4; Golf Channel; Headline News; HGTV; History Channel; ION Television; Lifetime; MTV; Navy Office of Information (OI-03); Nickelodeon; Outdoor Channel; Pentagon Channel; SoapNet; Spike TV; Syfy; The Learning Channel; The Weather Channel; Turner Classic Movies; Turner Network TV; TV Guide Network; TV Land; USA Network; VH1; WE tv.

Fee: $38.20 installation; $49.99 monthly; $4.95 converter; $16.95 additional installation.

Digital Basic Service

Subscribers: 8,232.

Programming (via satellite): A&E HD; BBC America; BBC World News; Bio; Bravo; BYU Television; Discovery Health Channel; Discovery Kids Channel; DIY Network; ESPN 2 HD; ESPN HD; ESPNews; Fox College Sports Atlantic; Fox College Sports Central; Fox College Sports Pacific; Fox Movie Channel; Fox Soccer; Hallmark Channel; HD Theater; History Channel International; Hope Channel; ID Investigation Discovery; JCTV; Lifetime Movie Network; Military Channel; MSNBC; MTV Hits; MTV Jams; MTV2; Music Choice; NASA TV; National Geographic Channel; National Geographic Television; Nick Jr.; NickToons TV; Oxygen; Planet Green; Science; Speed; TeenNick; Toon Disney; Trinity Broadcasting Network; Universal HD; VH1 Classic.

Fee: $49.95 installation; $11.99 monthly.

Pay Service 1

Pay Units: 2,631.

Programming (via satellite): Filipino Channel; GMA Pinoy TV; Mix.

Digital Pay Service 1

Pay Units: N.A.

Programming (via satellite): Cinemax; Encore (multiplexed); Filipino Channel; Flix; GMA Life TV; HBO (multiplexed); MBC America; Mix; Showtime (multiplexed); Starz (multiplexed); The Movie Channel; YemenTV.

Video-On-Demand: Yes

Pay-Per-View

iN DEMAND (delivered digitally).

Internet Service

Operational: Yes.

Subscribers: 20,788.

Fee: $89.99 installation; $14.99-$79.99 monthly.

Telephone Service

Digital: Operational

Subscribers: 5,286.

Fee: $19.99 monthly

Miles of Plant: 709.0 (coaxial); 97.0 (fiber optic).

Vice President, Marketing: Thomas Higa. General Manager: John Cruikshank. Technical Operations Director: Wilis Cannon.

Ownership: Marianas Cablevision Inc. (MSO).

MARIANA ISLANDS

Total Systems: 1
Total Communities Served: 3
Franchises Not Yet Operating: 0
Applications Pending: 0
Communities with Applications: 0
Number of Basic Subscribers: 6,500
Number of Expanded Basic Subscribers: 0
Number of Pay Units: 440

Top 100 Markets Represented: N.A.

For a list of cable communities in this section, see the Cable Community Index located in the back of Cable Volume 2.
For explanation of terms used in cable system listings, see p. D-11.

SAIPAN—MCV Broadband, PO Box 501298, Saipan, MP 96950. Phone: 670-235-4628. Fax: 670-235-0965. Web Site: http://www.mcvcnmi.com. Also serves Rota & Tinian. ICA: MR0001.

TV Market Ranking: Below 100 (Rota, SAIPAN, Tinian). Franchise award date: N.A. Franchise expiration date: N.A. Began: June 1, 1976.

Channel capacity: N.A. Channels available but not in use: N.A.

Basic Service

Subscribers: 6,500.
Programming (received off-air): KGTF (PBS) Agana; KUAM-TV (NBC) Hagatna.
Programming (via satellite): ABC Family Channel; Chinese Television Network; CNBC World; CNN International; ESPN; Fox News Channel; Korean Channel; Nickelodeon; The Weather Channel; USA Network.
Fee: $37.84 installation; $30.95 monthly; $1.95 converter.

Expanded Basic Service 1

Subscribers: N.A.
Programming (received off-air): KFVE (MNT) Honolulu; KHNL (NBC) Honolulu; KHON-TV (CW, FOX) Honolulu.
Programming (via satellite): A&E Networks; AMC; Animal Planet; Cartoon Network; Comedy Central; Discovery Channel; ESPN 2; Eternal Word TV Network; Food Network; G4; Golf Channel; HGTV; History Channel; ION Television; Lifetime; MTV; SoapNet; Spike TV; Syfy; The Learning Channel; Turner Classic Movies; Turner Network TV; TV Land; VH1.
Fee: $13.55 monthly.

Pay Service 1

Pay Units: 440.
Programming (via satellite): Cinemax; HBO; Showtime; Starz; The Movie Channel.
Fee: $12.58 monthly (Cinemax, Starz or HBO), $15.74 monthly (Showtime/TMC/Sundance).

Pay Service 2

Pay Units: N.A.
Programming (via satellite): Filipino Channel; GMA Pinoy TV; TV Japan.
Fee: $10.48 monthly (Japanese or Filipino channels), $22.10 monthly (Korean channel).

Video-On-Demand: No

Internet Service

Operational: Yes.
Broadband Service: In-house.
Fee: $62.95 monthly.

Telephone Service

None

Miles of Plant: 90.0 (coaxial); 20.0 (fiber optic). Additional miles planned: 25.0 (coaxial).

System Manager: Mark Birmingham. Chief Technician: Bryan Pitt.

Ownership: Marianas Cablevision Inc. (MSO).

PUERTO RICO

Total Systems:	3	**Communities with Applications:**	0
Total Communities Served:	86	**Number of Basic Subscribers:**	339,550
Franchises Not Yet Operating:	0	**Number of Expanded Basic Subscribers:**	102,000
Applications Pending:	0	**Number of Pay Units:**	48,334

Top 100 Markets Represented: N.A.

For a list of cable communities in this section, see the Cable Community Index located in the back of Cable Volume 2.
For explanation of terms used in cable system listings, see p. D-11.

CEIBA NAVAL BASE—Formerly served by Americable International. No longer in operation. ICA: PR0011.

LEVITTOWN—OneLink Communications. Now served by SAN JUAN, PR [PR0001]. ICA: PR0009.

LUQUILLO—Liberty Cablevision of Puerto Rico, PO Box 719, Luquillo, PR 00773-0719. Phones: 787-355-3535; 787-657-3050. Fax: 787-889-4900. E-mail: info@libertypr.com. Web Site: http://www.libertypr.com. Also serves Aguas Buenas, Aibonito, Arecibo, Barceloneta, Barranquitas, Caguas, Camuy, Canovanas, Cayey, Ceiba, Ciales, Cidra, Comerio, Corozal, Dorado, Fajardo, Gurabo, Hatillo, Humacao, Juncos, Lares, Las Piedras, Loiza, Manati, Morovis, Naguabo, Naranjito, Orocovis, Rio Grande, San Lorenzo, San Sebastion, Utuado, Vega Alta, Vega Baja & Yabucoa. ICA: PR0003.

TV Market Ranking: Below 100 (Aguas Buenas, Aibonito, Arecibo, Barceloneta, Barranquitas, Caguas, Camuy, Canovanas, Cayey, Ceiba, Ciales, Cidra, Comerio, Corozal, Dorado, Fajardo, Gurabo, Hatillo, Humacao, Juncos, Lares, Las Piedras, Loiza, LUQUILLO, Manati, Morovis, Naguabo, Naranjito, Orocovis, Rio Grande, San Lorenzo, San Sebastion, Utuado, Vega Alta, Vega Baja, Yabucoa). Franchise award date: N.A. Franchise expiration date: September 25, 2011. Began: December 1, 1985.

Channel capacity: N.A. Channels available but not in use: N.A.

Digital Basic Service

Subscribers: 89,550.

Programming (received off-air): WCBS-TV (CBS) New York.

Programming (via satellite): CaribeVision Television Networks; GSN; QVC; ReelzChannel; Telemundo Puerto Rico; Televisa Networks; TuTv; Univision Studios; WABC-TV (ABC) New York; WGN America; WNBC (NBC) New York; WPIX (CW, IND) New York.

Fee: $42.99 monthly.

Digital Expanded Basic Service

Subscribers: N.A.

Programming (via satellite): A&E HD; A&E Networks; ABC Family Channel; Animal Planet; Animal Planet HD; Antena 3; Azteca America; Bio HD; Bravo; Bravo HD; Caracol TV; Cartoon Network; CNBC; CNN; Comedy Central; Discovery Channel; Discovery Channel HD; Disney Channel; Disney Channel HD; E! Entertainment Television; ESPN; ESPN 2; ESPN 2 HD; ESPN Deportes; ESPN HD; ESPNU HD; Food Network; FX; Golf Channel; GolTV; HD Theater; Headline News; HGTV; History Channel; History Channel HD; Latele Novela Network; Lifetime; MSNBC; MTV; mun2 television; Music Choice; National Geographic Channel HD Network; Nickelodeon; Planet Green HD; Science HD; SoapNet; Sorpresa; Spike TV; Syfy; Syfy HD; TBS Superstation; The Learning Channel; The Weather Channel; TLC HD; Travel Channel; Travel Channel HD; truTV; Turner Network TV; TV Land; Universal HD; USA Network; USA Network HD; VeneMovies; VH1; WGN America.

Fee: $42.99 monthly.

Digital Expanded Basic Service 2

Subscribers: N.A.

Programming (via satellite): BBC America; Bio; Bloomberg Television; Boomerang; Chiller; cloo; CNN en Espanol; CNN International; Discovery en Espanol; Discovery Fit & Health; Discovery Health Channel; Discovery Home Channel; Discovery Kids Channel; Discovery Times Channel; Discovery Travel & Living (Viajar y Vivir); Disney XD; DIY Network; ESPN Classic Sports; ESPN U; ESPNews; Eternal Word TV Network; Fox Deportes; Fuse; G4; GAS; History Channel International; ID Investigation Discovery; Independent Film Channel; Lifetime Movie Network; Lifetime Real Women; Military Channel; MTV2; National Geographic Channel; Nick Jr.; NickToons TV; Outdoor Channel; Planet Green; Radar Channel; Science; Speed; Style Network; Tennis Channel; Toon Disney; Tr3s; Turner Classic Movies; TVE Internacional; TVG Network; Versus; VH1 Classic; VH1 Country; VHUNO.

Fee: $14.99 monthly.

Digital Pay Service 1

Pay Units: 48,334.

Programming (via satellite): Cinemax (multiplexed); Cinemax HD; Encore (multiplexed); HBO (multiplexed); HBO HD; Showtime (multiplexed); Showtime HD; Starz (multiplexed); Starz HDTV; The Movie Channel (multiplexed); The Movie Channel HD.

Fee: $15.99 monthly (HBO, Cinemax, Showtime/TMC or Starz/Encore).

Video-On-Demand: Yes

Pay-Per-View

iN DEMAND (delivered digitally); Club Jenna (delivered digitally); Playboy TV (delivered digitally); Ten Blox (delivered digitally); Spice: Xcess (delivered digitally); MLB Extra Innings (delivered digitally).

Internet Service

Operational: Yes.

Subscribers: 2,000.

Broadband Service: In-house.

Telephone Service

Analog: Operational

Digital: Operational

Miles of Plant: 2,920.0 (coaxial); 492.0 (fiber optic).

Executive Director: Naji Khoury. Vice President, Technical Operations: Ivan Rosa. Vice President, Sales & Marketing: Gabriel Palerm. Marketing Manager: Dalila Roldan.

Ownership: Liberty Cablevision of Puerto Rico Ltd.

MERCEDITA—Centennial de Puerto Rico. Now served by MAYAGUEZ, PR [PR0008]. ICA: PR0005.

PONCE—Choice Cable, PO Box 204, Mercedita, PR 00715-0204. Phones: 787-651-9867; 877-717-0400. Fax: 787-651-9884. Web Site: http://www.choicecable.com. Also serves Adjuntas, Aguada, Aguadilla, Anasco, Arroyo, Caba Rojo, Coamo, Guanica, Guayama, Guayanilla, Hormigueros, Isabela, Jayuya, Juana Diaz, Lajas, Las Marias, Maricao, Maunabo, Mayaguez, Mercedita, Moca, Patillas, Penuelas, Playa de Ponce, Quebradillas, Rincon, Sabanna Grande, Salinas, San German, Santa Isabel, Tallaboa, Villalba & Yauco. ICA: PR0008.

TV Market Ranking: Below 100 (Adjuntas, Adjuntas, Aguada, Aguadilla, Anasco, Arroyo, Arroyo, Caba Rojo, Coamo, Coamo, Guanica, Guayama, Guayanilla, Guayanilla, Hormigueros, Isabela, Jayuya, Jayuya, Juana Diaz, Juana Diaz, Lajas, Las Marias, Maricao, Maunabo, Maunabo, Mayaguez, Moca, Patillas, Penuelas, Playa de Ponce, PONCE, Quebradillas, Rincon, Sabanna Grande, Salinas, San German, Santa Isabel, Tallaboa, Tallaboa, Villalba, Yauco). Franchise award date: June 1, 1984. Franchise expiration date: N.A. Began: June 16, 1986.

Channel capacity: N.A. Channels available but not in use: N.A.

Digital Basic Service

Subscribers: 110,000.

Programming (via satellite): A&E Networks; ABC Family Channel; AMC; Animal Planet; Bloomberg Television; Boomerang; Bravo; Cartoon Network; CNBC; CNN; CNN en Espanol; Comedy Central; C-SPAN; Discovery Channel; Discovery en Espanol; Discovery Health Channel; E! Entertainment Television; ESPN; ESPN 2; ESPN Classic Sports; Eternal Word TV Network; Fashion TV; Food Network; Fox Deportes; Fox News Channel; G4; Golf Channel; Headline News; HGTV; History Channel; HTV Musica; Lifetime; Lifetime Movie Network; MSNBC; MTV; Music Choice; National Geographic Channel; Nickelodeon; NickToons TV; Outdoor Channel; QVC; Sorpresa; Spike TV; Syfy; The Learning Channel; The Weather Channel; Travel Channel; Trinity Broadcasting Network; truTV; Turner Classic Movies; TV Land; USA Network; VH1; WE tv.

Digital Expanded Basic Service

Subscribers: N.A.

Programming (via satellite): BBC America; Bio; Discovery Home Channel; Discovery Kids Channel; Discovery Times Channel; Discovery Travel & Living (Viajar y Vivir); ESPN Deportes; ESPNews; Flix; Fox College Sports Central; Fox College Sports Pacific; Fox Movie Channel; Fox Soccer; GAS; History Channel International; Lifetime Real Women; Military Channel; MoviePlex; MTV Hits; MTV Jams; MTV2; Music Choice; Nick Jr.; Science; Versus; VH1 Classic; VHUNO.

Digital Pay Service 1

Pay Units: N.A.

Programming (via satellite): Cinemax (multiplexed); Encore (multiplexed); HBO (multiplexed); Showtime (multiplexed); Starz (multiplexed); The Movie Channel (multiplexed).

Video-On-Demand: Yes

Pay-Per-View

iN DEMAND (delivered digitally).

Internet Service

Operational: Yes.

Broadband Service: Choice OnLine.

Telephone Service

Digital: Operational

Miles of Plant: 3,363.0 (coaxial); 600.0 (fiber optic).

President & General Manager: Michael Carrosquil. Vice President, Technical Operations & Chief of Operations: Jim Olanda. Marketing Director: Tomas Montilla.

Ownership: HM Capital Partners LLC (MSO).

SAN JUAN—OneLink Communications, PO Box 192296, San Juan, PR 00919-2296. Phone: 787-766-0909. Fax: 787-250-6532. E-mail: servicio@onelinkpr.com. Web Site: http://www.onelinkpr.com. Also serves Bayamon, Carolina, Catano, Guaynabo, Levittown, Toa Alta, Toa Baja & Trujillo Alto. ICA: PR0001.

TV Market Ranking: Below 100 (Bayamon, Carolina, Catano, Guaynabo, Levittown, SAN JUAN, Toa Alta, Toa Baja, Trujillo Alto). Franchise award date: January 1, 1971. Franchise expiration date: N.A. Began: April 1, 1972.

Channel capacity: N.A. Channels available but not in use: N.A.

Basic Service

Subscribers: 140,000.

Programming (received off-air): WAPA-TV (IND) San Juan; WCCV-TV (IND) Arecibo; WDWL (IND) Bayamon; WECN (IND) Naranjito; WIDP (IND) Guayama; WIPR-TV (PBS) San Juan; WJPX (IND) San Juan; WKAQ-TV (TMO) San Juan; WLII-DT (UNV) Caguas; WMTJ (PBS) Fajardo; WORO-DT (IND) Fajardo; WPRU-LP (ABC) Aguadilla; WRFB (IND) Carolina; WSJP-LP (CW) Aguadilla; WSJU-TV (IND) San Juan; WSJX-LP (FOX) Aquadilla; WSTE-DT (IND) Ponce; WTCV (IND) San Juan; WUJA (ETV) Caguas; WVXF (IND) Charlotte Amalie.

Programming (via satellite): WNBC (NBC) New York.

Fee: $45.00 installation; $36.60 monthly.

Expanded Basic Service 1
Subscribers: 102,000.
Programming (via satellite): A&E Networks; ABC Family Channel; Animal Planet; BBC World News; Bravo; Cartoon Network; CNBC; CNN; CNN en Espanol; Comedy Central; C-SPAN 2; Discovery Channel; Discovery Kids en Espanol; Disney Channel; Docu TVE; E! Entertainment Television; ESPN; ESPN 2; ESPN Classic Sports; Eternal Word TV Network; Food Network; Fox Deportes; FX; Headline News; HGTV; History Channel; Lifetime; Lifetime Movie Network; MSNBC; MTV; MTV2; mun2 television; Nickelodeon; QVC; Spike TV; Syfy; TBS Superstation; The Learning Channel; The Weather Channel; Travel Channel; Turner Classic Movies; Turner Network TV; TV Guide Network; TV Land; TVE Internacional; USA Network; VH1; WGN America.
Fee: $13.40 monthly.

Digital Basic Service
Subscribers: N.A.
Programming (via satellite): Anime Network; Antena 3; BBC America; Bio; Bloomberg Television; Boomerang; cloo; CNN International; Cooking Channel; Discovery Fit & Health; Discovery Health Channel; Discovery Home Channel; Discovery Kids Channel; Discovery Times Channel; ESPN Deportes; ESPN HD; ESPNews; Fox Movie Channel; G4; GAS; Golf Channel; Halogen Network; HD Theater; HDNet; HDNet Movies; History Channel en Espanol; History Channel International; Independent Film Channel; Lifetime Real Women; LOGO; Military Channel; MTV Hits; Music Choice; National Geographic Channel; Nick Jr.; NickToons TV; Ovation; Oxygen; Science; SoapNet; Sorpresa; Speed; Style Network; Telefe International; Tennis Channel; Toon Disney en Espanol; Tr3s; Trinity Broadcasting Network; VeneMovies; VH1 Classic; VH1 Soul; VHUNO; WE tv; WealthTV; WealthTV HD.
Fee: $6.50 monthly.

Digital Pay Service 1
Pay Units: N.A.
Programming (via satellite): ART America; BabyFirstTV; CCTV-4; Cinemax (multiplexed); Cinemax HD; Cinemax On Demand; Encore (multiplexed); Filipino Channel; Flix; HBO (multiplexed); HBO HD; HBO On Demand; RAI International; Showtime (multiplexed); Showtime HD; Showtime On Demand; Starz (multiplexed); Starz HDTV; The Movie Channel (multiplexed); The Movie Channel On Demand; TV Asia; TV Japan; TV5, La Television International; Zhong Tian Channel.

Video-On-Demand: Yes

Pay-Per-View
Playboy TV (delivered digitally); Fresh (delivered digitally); Sports PPV (delivered digitally); Movies & Events (delivered digitally).

Internet Service
Operational: Yes.
Subscribers: 22,000.
Fee: $99.95 installation; $55.95 monthly.

Telephone Service
Digital: Operational

Miles of Plant: 1,620.0 (coaxial); 247.0 (fiber optic).

General Manager: William Chain. Technical Operations Director: Nestor Cardona. Marketing Manager: Juan Gonzalez. Video Products Manager: Sarah Padilla.

Ownership: OneLink Communications.

VIRGIN ISLANDS

Total Systems: **2**
Total Communities Served: **3**
Franchises Not Yet Operating: **0**
Applications Pending: **0**
Communities with Applications: **0**
Number of Basic Subscribers: **42,923**
Number of Expanded Basic Subscribers: **22,622**
Number of Pay Units: **16,845**

Top 100 Markets Represented: N.A.

For a list of cable communities in this section, see the Cable Community Index located in the back of Cable Volume 2.
For explanation of terms used in cable system listings, see p. D-11.

ST. CROIX—Innovative Cable TV St. Croix, 4006 Estate Diamond, Christiansted, VI 820. Phones: 866-240-2999; 340-712-5053. Fax: 340-772-5053. Web Site: http://www.innovativecable.com. ICA: VI0002.

TV Market Ranking: Below 100 (ST. CROIX). Franchise award date: January 1, 1981. Franchise expiration date: January 1, 2015. Began: April 1, 1981.

Channel capacity: 60 (not 2-way capable). Channels available but not in use: N.A.

Basic Service

Subscribers: 10,750.

Programming (received off-air): WCVI-TV (CW) Christiansted; WKAQ-TV (TMO) San Juan; WSVI (ABC) Christiansted; WTJX-TV (PBS) Charlotte Amalie; WVGN-LP (NBC) Charlotte Amalie; WVXF (IND) Charlotte Amalie; 17 FMs.

Programming (via satellite): ABC Family Channel; CNBC; Discovery Channel; Eternal Word TV Network; QVC; TBS Superstation; The Learning Channel; The Weather Channel; Trinity Broadcasting Network; TV Guide Network; WGN America.

Fee: $34.71 installation; $21.46 monthly.

Expanded Basic Service 1

Subscribers: 8,650.

Programming (via satellite): A&E Networks; Animal Planet; BET Networks; Bravo; CNN; C-SPAN; C-SPAN 2; Disney Channel; E! Entertainment Television; ESPN; ESPN 2; Headline News; History Channel; Lifetime; MTV; Nickelodeon; Syfy; TBS Superstation; Tempo; Travel Channel; truTV; Turner Classic Movies; Turner Network TV; USA Network; VH1.

Fee: $21.44 monthly.

Digital Basic Service

Subscribers: 7,319.

Programming (via satellite): 3 Angels Broadcasting Network; BBC America; Boomerang; Cartoon Network; Cine Latino; CNN en Espanol; Comedy Central; Discovery en Espanol; Discovery Health Channel; Discovery Home Channel; Discovery Kids Channel; Discovery Times Channel; DMX Music; ESPNews; Food Network; Fox Deportes; Fox Sports Net; GAS; HGTV; History Channel en Espanol; HRTV; Lifetime Movie Network; Lifetime Real Women; Military Channel; MTV Hits; MTV2; NBA TV; NFL Network; Nick Jr.; NickToons TV; Science; SoapNet; Spike TV; Tennis Channel; Toon Disney en Espanol; Tr3s; TV Land; VH1 Classic; VHUNO; WAPA America.

Digital Pay Service 1

Pay Units: 6,196.

Programming (via satellite): Cinemax (multiplexed); Flix; HBO (multiplexed); Showtime (multiplexed); The Movie Channel (multiplexed).

Fee: $40.00 installation.

Video-On-Demand: No

Pay-Per-View

Addressable homes: 12,950.

Hot Network; iN DEMAND.

Internet Service

Operational: No.

Telephone Service

None

Miles of Plant: 480.0 (coaxial); None (fiber optic).

President & General Manager: Jennifer Matarangas-King. Assistant General Manager: Graciela Rivera. Chief Technician: Douglas Pompey.

Ownership: Innovative Communications Corp.

ST. THOMAS—Innovative Cable TV St. Thomas-St. John, 4611 Tutu Park, Ste 300, St. Thomas, VI 802. Phones: 866-240-2999; 340-776-2150. Fax: 340-774-5029. Web Site: http://www.innovativecable.com. Also serves St. John. ICA: VI0001.

TV Market Ranking: Below 100 (St. John, ST. THOMAS). Franchise award date: October 21, 1985. Franchise expiration date: N.A. Began: January 1, 1966.

Channel capacity: 77 (operating 2-way). Channels available but not in use: N.A.

Basic Service

Subscribers: 15,138.

Programming (received off-air): WCVI-TV (CW) Christiansted; WEON-LP (FOX) Frederiksted; WKAQ-TV (TMO) San Juan; WSVI (ABC) Christiansted; WTJX-TV (PBS) Charlotte Amalie; WVGN-LP (NBC) Charlotte Amalie; WVXF (IND) Charlotte Amalie; 23 FMs.

Programming (via satellite): A&E Networks; ABC Family Channel; America's Store; Bravo; CNBC; Comedy Central; C-SPAN; C-SPAN 2; Discovery Channel; Eternal Word TV Network; QVC; The Learning Channel; The Weather Channel; Travel Channel; Trinity Broadcasting Network; TV Guide Network; TV2; WGN America.

Fee: $53.96 installation; $13.30 monthly; $3.05 converter.

Expanded Basic Service 1

Subscribers: 13,972.

Programming (via satellite): AMC; Animal Planet; BET Networks; Cartoon Network; CNN; Discovery Health Channel; Disney Channel; ESPN; ESPN 2; ESPN Classic Sports; Food Network; Headline News; History Channel; Lifetime; MTV; NFL Network; Nickelodeon; Spike TV; Syfy; TBS Superstation; Tempo; Tennis Channel; truTV; Turner Network TV; TV Land; USA Network; VH1; WE tv.

Fee: $2.00 installation; $33.25 monthly.

Digital Basic Service

Subscribers: 9,716.

Programming (via satellite): 3 Angels Broadcasting Network; BBC America; Canales N; Discovery Digital Networks; E! Entertainment Television; ESPN Deportes; ESPNews; GAS; Halogen Network; HRTV; INSP; Lifetime Movie Network; Lifetime Real Women; MTV Networks Digital Suite; NBA TV; Nick Jr.; NickToons TV; Oxygen; SoapNet; Toon Disney.

Fee: $29.26 monthly.

Digital Pay Service 1

Pay Units: 10,649.

Programming (via satellite): Cinemax (multiplexed); Encore (multiplexed); Flix; HBO (multiplexed); Showtime (multiplexed); Starz (multiplexed); Sundance Channel; The Movie Channel (multiplexed).

Fee: $7.35 monthly (Cinemax), $9.45 monthly (Starz/Encore), $10.50 monthly (Showtime/TMC), $14.18 monthly (HBO).

Video-On-Demand: No

Pay-Per-View

iN DEMAND (delivered digitally); Playboy TV (delivered digitally); Fresh (delivered digitally); Shorteez (delivered digitally).

Internet Service

Operational: No.

Telephone Service

None

Miles of Plant: 386.0 (coaxial); 5.0 (fiber optic). Additional miles planned: 7.0 (coaxial).

President & General Manager: Jennifer Matarangas-King. Assistant General Manager: Debra Thomas-Smith. Chief Technician: Bernard A. Ray.

Ownership: Innovative Communications Corp. (MSO).

Ownership of Cable Systems in the United States

Comprises all persons or companies which have interest in cable systems or franchises. Ownership of all systems is assumed to be 100% unless otherwise noted.

ACCESS CABLE TELEVISION INC.

5215 S. Hwy. 27
PO Box 4005
West Somerset, KY 42501
Phone: 606-676-0616
E-mail: royb@sharpehouseboat.com
Officer:
Roy Baker, President
Cable Systems (5):
KENTUCKY: CUMBERLAND; GREENSBURG; HUSTONVILLE; WHITLEY CITY.
TENNESSEE: JELLICO.

ADAMS CATV INC.

19 N Main St
Carbondale, PA 18407-2303
Phones: 570-282-6121; 888-222-0077
Fax: 570-282-3787
E-mail: frontdesk@echoes.net
Web site: http://www.adamscable.com
Officers:
Dorotha T. Adams, President
Douglas V.R. Adams, Vice President
Ownership: Dorotha T Adams.
Cable Systems (2):
PENNSYLVANIA: CARBONDALE; LOOMIS LAKE.

ADVANCE/NEWHOUSE PARTNERSHIP

5000 Campus Wood Dr.
East Syracuse, NY 13057-4250
Phone: 315-438-4100
Fax: 315-438-4643
E-mail: michael.mayer@mybrighthouse.com
Web site: http://www.brighthouse.com/corporate.aspx
Officers:
Steven A. Miron, President
Naomi M. Bergman, Executive Vice President, Strategy & Development
William A. Futera, Executive Vice President & Chief Financial Officer
Yixin J. Chen, Vice President, Advanced Technology
Kashif Haq, Vice President, Broadband Data Services
Mark A. Rinefierd, Vice President & Controller
Mark D. Wasserstrom, Vice President, Financial Planning
Ownership: Advance Publications, 61.24%; Newhouse Broadcasting Corp., 38.76%.
Represented (legal): Sabin, Bermant & Gould LLP.
Cable Systems (91):
CALIFORNIA: BARSTOW.
MASSACHUSETTS: ATHOL; PITTSFIELD.
NEBRASKA: AUBURN; COLUMBUS; FAIRBURY; FALLS CITY; FREMONT; LINCOLN; YORK.
NEW YORK: ALBANY; BATAVIA; BINGHAMTON; CHAMPLAIN; CORTLAND; ELMIRA/CORNING; GENEVA; HORNELL; ILION; ITHACA; JAMESTOWN; MASSENA; ONEONTA; OSWEGO; PORT HENRY (village); ROCHESTER; ROME; SYRACUSE; SYRACUSE (suburbs); WATERTOWN.
NORTH CAROLINA: ALBEMARLE; CARRBORO; CARY; CEDAR ISLAND; CHAPEL HILL; CHARLOTTE; DURHAM; ELIZABETHTOWN; FARMVILLE; FAYETTEVILLE; GASTONIA; GOLDSBORO; GREENSBORO; HENDERSON; JACKSONVILLE; KANNAPOLIS; LUMBERTON; MONROE; NEWPORT; PAMLICO COUNTY; RALEIGH; ROCKINGHAM; SALISBURY; SELMA/GARNER; SHELBY; SOUTHERN PINES; WADESBORO; WILMINGTON; WILSON.
PENNSYLVANIA: MONTROSE; SAYRE; ULYSSES.
SOUTH CAROLINA: COLUMBIA; MYRTLE BEACH.
TEXAS: ALICE; AUSTIN; BEAUMONT; BEEVILLE; COLUMBUS; CORPUS CHRISTI; CRYSTAL CITY; DEL RIO; EAGLE PASS; EL PASO; GEORGE WEST; GONZALES; HARLINGEN; KERRVILLE; KILLEEN; LAREDO; MATHIS; ORANGE GROVE; PEARSALL; PORT O'CONNOR; QUEMADO; SAN YGNACIO; SEADRIFT; UVALDE; WACO; WICHITA FALLS; ZAPATA.
Newspapers:
National: Sporting News
Cable Holdings:
Time Warner Entertainment Co. LP-Advance/Newhouse Partnership 33.3% interest; Manager of Bright House Networks LLC see listing
Other Holdings:
Magazine: Golf Digest

ADVENT CHRISTIAN VILLAGE INC.

PO Box 4345
Dowling Park, FL 32064
Phones: 386-658-5291; 800-647-3353
Fax: 386-658-5151
E-mail: acvillage@acvillage.net
Web site: http://www.acvillage.net
Officer:
Tim Goyette, Director, Operations
Cable Systems (1):
FLORIDA: ADVENT CHRISTIAN VILLAGE.

ALABAMA BROADBAND LLC

Ste 101
3447 Parkwood Rd SE
Bessemer, AL 35022
Phones: 205-426-3432; 877-840-5040
E-mail: contact@alabamabroadband.net
Web site: http://www.alabamabroadband.net/
Cable Systems (8):
ALABAMA: ADDISON (town); ASHVILLE; BLOUNT COUNTY; GOOD HOPE; HAYNEVILLE; LOWNDES COUNTY; MARGARET; SELBROOK.

ALGONA MUNICIPAL UTILITIES

104 W. Call St.
PO Box 10
Algona, IA 50511
Phone: 515-295-3584
Fax: 515-295-3364
E-mail: info@netamu.com
Web site: http://www.netamu.com
Cable Systems (1):
IOWA: ALGONA.

ALLEGHANY CABLEVISION INC.

105 N. Main St.
PO Box 429
Sparta, NC 28675
Phone: 336-372-5801
E-mail: alleghanycablevision@yahoo.com
Ownership: George L Sheets, President.
Cable Systems (1):
NORTH CAROLINA: SPARTA.

ALLEGIANCE COMMUNICATIONS

707 W Saratoga
Shawnee, OK 74804
Phones: 405-275-6923; 800-937-1397
Fax: 405-275-0276
E-mail: mendy.mcentire@allegiancecatv.com
Web site: http://allegiance.tv
Officers:
William Haggarty, Chief Executive Officer
Woody Wood, Vice President, Operations & Regional Manager

Branch Offices:
PERRYTON
217 S Ash St
Perryton, TX 79070
OTTAWA
118 W 15th St
Ottawa, KS 66067
NEW BOSTON
118 N West St
New Boston, TX 75570
MENA
509 Mena St
Mena, AR 71953
MEDICINE LODGE
108 N Main
Medicine Lodge, KS 67104
McGEHEE
501 E Ash St
McGehee, AR 71654
GUYMON
215 NW 5th St
Guymon, OK 73942
FORT RILEY
6422 Normandy Dr
Fort Riley, KS 66442
DALHART
1619 Tennessee Blvd
Dalhart, TX 79022
ATCHINSON
625 Commercial
Ste 1
Atchison, KS 66002
McALESTER
205 E Cherokee
McAlester, OK 74501
SHAWNEE
1819 Airport Drive
Shawnee, OK 74804
Phone: 405-395-1104
Fax: 405-788-4314
Cable Systems (134):
ARKANSAS: CORNING; DAISY; DE QUEEN; DIERKS; DUMAS; FAIRFIELD BAY; FULTON; LAKE VILLAGE; MCCASKILL; McCRORY; McGEHEE; MENA; MINERAL SPRINGS; MURFREESBORO.
KANSAS: ATCHISON; BEATTIE; BUHLER; CHETOPA; CONWAY SPRINGS; DOUGLASS; ELLINWOOD; FORT RILEY; FREDONIA; GREENLEAF; HARPER; HAVEN; HERINGTON; LINN; MEADE; MEDICINE LODGE; OTTAWA; OXFORD; PEABODY; SEDAN; SHARON; STAFFORD.
MISSOURI: BRAYMER; CAMDEN POINT; GOWER; HAMILTON; LATHROP; MAYSVILLE; PLATTSBURG; SELIGMAN.
OKLAHOMA: ADAIR; ALLEN (town); BEGGS; BOSWELL; BRAGGS; BRISTOW; CALVIN; CAMERON; CHANDLER; CLAYTON (town); COLCORD; CROMWELL; DELAWARE; DEPEW; DUSTIN; FORT GIBSON; GANS; GLENCOE; GOODWELL; GORE; GUYMON; HARTSHORNE; HASKELL; HOLDENVILLE; HOWE; HULBERT; INOLA; KANSAS; KELLYVILLE; KEOTA; KETCHUM; KONAWA; LANGSTON; LONGTOWN; LUTHER; MAUD; McALESTER; McCURTAIN; MORRIS; MORRISON; MOUNDS; NEWKIRK; OKAY; OKEMAH; OOLOGAH; PANAMA; PAWHUSKA; PORTER; PORUM; PORUM LANDING; QUINTON; RALSTON; RATTAN; SALINA; SAVANNA; SCHULTER; SHAWNEE; STIGLER; STILWELL; STRANG; STRATFORD; STROUD; STUART; TALIHINA; TRYON; TURPIN; TYRONE; VALLIANT; VERDIGRIS; VIAN; WELCH; WELEETKA; WELLSTON; WESTVILLE; WETUMKA; WILBURTON; WISTER; WRIGHT CITY; WYANDOTTE.
TEXAS: BALLINGER; DALHART; DE KALB; HOOKS; MAUD; MILES; NEW BOSTON; PERRYTON; PRESTON PENINSULA; WINTERS.

ALLEN'S TV CABLE SERVICE INC.

800 Victor II Blvd.
PO Box 2643
Morgan City, LA 70380
Phone: 985-384-8335
Fax: 504-384-5243
E-mail: info@atvci.net
Web site: http://www.atvci.net
Officers:
Gregory A. Price, President
Chris Price, Vice President
Angela P. Governale, Secretary-Treasurer
Ownership: Elizabeth Price; Gregory A Price, jointly.
Represented (legal): Cole, Raywid & Braverman LLP.
Cable Systems (2):
LOUISIANA: GRAND COTEAU; MORGAN CITY.

ALLIANCE COMMUNICATIONS NETWORK

290 S Broadview
Greenbrier, AR 72058
Phone: 800-842-8160
Web site: http://alliancecable.net

Cable Systems (3):
LOUISIANA: MELVILLE; WATERPROOF.
OKLAHOMA: CYRIL.

ALLIANCE COMMUNICATIONS
612 3rd St
PO Box 349
Garretson, SD 57030
Phone: 605-594-3411
E-mail: kvegas@alliancecom.net
Web site: http://www.alliancecom.net
Cable Systems (4):
IOWA: INWOOD; LARCHWOOD.
MINNESOTA: HILLS.
SOUTH DAKOTA: GARRETSON.

ALMEGA CABLE
Ste 530
4001 W Airport Fwy
Bedford, TX 76021
Phones: 817-685-9588; 877-725-6342
Fax: 817-685-6488
E-mail: kurien@almega.com
Web site: http://www.almega.com
Officers:
Thomas Kurien, President
James Bradley, Vice President, Operations
Mike DeRosa, Vice President, Sales
Steve Varghese, Regional Sales Manager

Branch Offices:
MIDDLETOWN
1385 Hwy 35
Middletown, NJ 07748
SHADY COVE
6655 Rogue River Dr
Shady Cove, OR 97539
MIDDLETOWN
4001 W Airport Frwy
Suite 530
Bedford, TX 76021
Phone: 817-685-9588
Fax: 817-685-6488
Ownership: Techcore.
Cable Systems (63):
ARKANSAS: ALTHEIMER; WILMAR.
CALIFORNIA: DORRIS; FALL RIVER MILLS; KLAMATH; TULELAKE; WILLOW CREEK.
OREGON: BUTTE FALLS; CHILOQUIN; ENTERPRISE; GLENDALE; MALIN; MERRILL; PROSPECT; SHADY COVE.
SOUTH CAROLINA: BOWMAN; HOLLY HILL; SANTEE; ST. GEORGE; SUMMERTON.
TEXAS: ALTO; ALVARADO; ATASCOSA; BLOOMINGTON; BRACKETTVILLE; CENTER POINT; CENTRAL; CUSHING; DIANA; FANNETT; FLATONIA; GARRISON; GOLDTHWAITE; HEIGHTS (unincorporated areas); HEMPHILL; HOMER; HUBBARD; JOHNSON CITY; JOSHUA; KILGORE; LAS GALLINAS; LIVERPOOL; LOMETA; NIXON; OYSTER CREEK; PLAINS; PLEAK; POWDERLY; REDWATER; SABINAL; SAN LEON; SHINER; SPLENDORA; SPUR; STONY POINT; STRATFORD; TENAHA; TIMPSON; WINK; YORKTOWN; ZAVALLA.
VIRGINIA: LEBANON (portions).
WASHINGTON: ORCAS ISLAND.

ALTATEC
223 Main St
Alta, IA 51002
Phone: 712-200-1122
Fax: 712-200-9600
E-mail: altatec@alta-tec.net
Web site: http://www.alta-tec.net
Cable Systems (1):
IOWA: ALTA.

ALTA VISTA MUNICIPAL CABLE
PO Box 115
Alta Vista, IA 50603
Phone: 614-364-2975
Fax: 614-364-2975
Ownership: City of Alta Vista.
Cable Systems (1):
IOWA: ALTA VISTA (town).

AMERICAN BROADBAND COMMUNICATIONS INC.
Ste 250
1348 Matthews Twp Pkwy
Matthews, NC 28105
Phone: 704-845-2263
Fax: 704-845-2299
E-mail: jduda@americanbb.com
Web site: http://www.americanbroadband.com
Officers:
Patrick L. Eudy, President & Chief Executive Officer
John P Duda, Executive Vice President & Chief Operating Officer
Cable Systems (10):
ILLINOIS: GRIDLEY.
MISSOURI: POMME DE TERRE.
NEBRASKA: BASSETT; BLAIR; ELSIE; LAUREL; LYONS; OAKLAND; TEKAMAH; WAYNE.

ANGOON CABLEVISION
PO Box 189
Angoon, AK 99820
Phone: 907-788-3653
Fax: 907-788-3821
Officer:
Alan Zuboff, Chief Operating Officer
Ownership: Community owned--Angoon, AK.
Cable Systems (1):
ALASKA: ANGOON.

KEITH ANTCLIFF
PO Box 157
Dugway, UT 84022
Phone: 801-831-4404
E-mail: staff@conceptcable.com
Web site: http://www.conceptcable.com
Cable Systems (1):
WASHINGTON: NEWPORT.

APPLIED COMMUNICATIONS TECHNOLOGY
524 Nebraska Ave
PO Box 300
Arapahoe, NE 68922
Phones: 308-962-7298; 866-222-7873
E-mail: atccable@atcjet.net
Web site: http://www.atcjet.net
Cable Systems (1):
NEBRASKA: ARAPAHOE.

ARGENT COMMUNICATIONS LLC
PO Box 278
Bristol, NH 03222
Phones: 603-922-7025; 877-295-1254
Fax: 206-202-1415
E-mail: service@argentcommunications.com
Web site: http://www.argentcommunications.com
Officer:
Andrew Bauer, Vice President, Business & Marketing
Cable Systems (7):
MAINE: RANGELEY (town).
NEW HAMPSHIRE: MILAN (town); NELSON (town); SPOFFORD; STODDARD; STRATFORD (town); TROY.

ARLINGTON TV COOPERATIVE INC.
PO Box 184
Arlington, OR 97812
Phone: 541-454-2707
Officers:
Judity Hughes, Vice President
Della Foster, Secretary-Treasurer
Ownership: Subscriber owned--Arlington, OR.
Cable Systems (1):
OREGON: ARLINGTON.

ARMSTRONG GROUP OF COMPANIES
One Armstrong Pl
Butler, PA 16001
Phone: 724-283-0925
Fax: 724-283-9655
Web site: http://cable.armstrongonewire.com
Officers:
Jay L. Sedwick, Chairman
Kirby J. Campbell, Vice Chairman
Dru A. Sedwick, President
William C Stewart, Corporate Officer
Bryan Cipoletti, Chief Financial Officer
David R Jamieson, General Counsel
Christopher King, Vice President, Financial Reporting
Mark S Miko, Chief Information Officer
Jeffrey A. Ross, President, Armstrong Utilities Inc. (Broadband)
Cable Systems (15):
MARYLAND: BEL AIR.
OHIO: ASHLAND; BOARDMAN; MEDINA; ORRVILLE; SOUTH POINT.
PENNSYLVANIA: BUTLER; CONNELLSVILLE; GROVE CITY; MEADVILLE; NEW WILMINGTON; NORTH CLARION; OXFORD; ZELIENOPLE.
WEST VIRGINIA: HAMLIN.

CATHY ASHWORTH
PO Box 1048
Littleton, NC 27850
Phone: 434-636-6000
Cable Systems (2):
VIRGINIA: JARRATT; LAKE GASTON.
Other Holdings:
Cable construction: CWA Enterprises

ATC
407 W. 11th St.
PO Box 2027
Alma, GA 31510
Phone: 912-632-8603
E-mail: kbrooks@atc.cc; info@atc.cc; sales@atc.cc
Web site: http://homepage.accessatc.net
Officer:
Greg Davis, President

Branch Offices:
BLACKSHEAR
3349 Hwy. 84 W
Ste 104
Blackshear, GA 31516
Phone: 912-449-5443
BAXLEY
371 W Parker St
Baxley, GA 31513
Phone: 912-705-5000
Ownership: Alma Telephone Co..
Cable Systems (4):
GEORGIA: ALMA; BAXLEY; BLACKSHEAR; PATTERSON.

ATKINS TELEPHONE CO.
85 Main Ave
PO Box 157
Atkins, IA 52206
Phone: 319-446-7331
Fax: 319-446-9100
E-mail: jtraut@atkinstelephone.com
Web site: http://www.atkinstelephone.com
Officer:
Jody Traut, Manager
Cable Systems (1):
IOWA: ATKINS.

ATLANTIC BROADBAND
Suite 405
One Batterymarch Park
Quincy, MA 02169
Phone: 617-786-8800
Fax: 617-786-8803
E-mail: info@atlanticbb.com
Web site: http://www.atlanticbb.com
Officers:
David J. Keefe, Chief Executive Officer
Edward T. Holleran Jr., President & Chief Operating Officer
Patrick Bratton, Chief Financial Officer
Christopher S. Daly, Chief Marketing Officer
Almis (Al) J. Kuolas, Chief Technology Officer
Donna Garofano, Senior Vice President, Government & Regulatory Affairs
Bartlett Leber, Senior Vice President & Legal Council
Matthew M. Murphy, Senior Vice President, Corporate Development
Thomas F Roundtree, Senior Vice President, Human Resources
Richard J. Shea, Senior Vice President & Chief Information Officer
Ownership: ABRY Partners LLC; Oak Hill Capital Partners LP; ABRY ownership:; Royce Yudkoff. Yudkoff is also principal of Nexstar Broadcasting Group Inc., see listing.
Cable Systems (29):
DELAWARE: MIDDLETOWN (town).
FLORIDA: MIAMI BEACH.
MARYLAND: CUMBERLAND; GRASONVILLE.
NEW YORK: LIMESTONE; SALAMANCA.
PENNSYLVANIA: ALTOONA; BRADFORD; CLEARFIELD; DERRY/DECATUR; GRAMPIAN; JOHNSTOWN; LIMESTONE; McALEVYS FORT; MIFFLINBURG; SHIPPENVILLE; SHIPPENVILLE; UNION TWP. (Huntingdon County); UNIONTOWN; WARREN; WOODBURY.
SOUTH CAROLINA: AIKEN; ALLENDALE; BAMBERG; BARNWELL.
WEST VIRGINIA: GRANT TOWN; KINGWOOD; MOOREFIELD; PAW PAW.

ATWOOD CABLE SYSTEMS INC.
423 State St.
Atwood, KS 67730
Phone: 785-626-3261
Fax: 785-626-9005
E-mail: cableinfo@atwoodtv.net
Web site: http://www.atwoodcable.com
Officers:
Harold Dunker, President
Robert J. Dunker, Vice President
Kerry L. Dunker, Vice President, Operations
Ownership: Harold Dunker.
Cable Systems (1):
KANSAS: ATWOOD.

AYRSHIRE COMMUNICATIONS
1405 Silver Lake Ave
PO Box 248
Ayrshire, IA 50515
Phone: 712-426-2815
Fax: 712-426-2008
Web site: http://www.ayrshireia.com
Officers:
John Higgins, President
William Myers, Vice President
Ownership: Ayrshire Farmers Mutual Telephone Co..

Cable Systems (3):
IOWA: AYRSHIRE; GILLETT GROVE; WHITTEMORE.

BAGLEY PUBLIC UTILITIES
18 Main Ave S
PO Box M
Bagley, MN 56621-1012
Phone: 218-694-2300
Fax: 218-694-6632
E-mail: vfletcher@bagleymn.us
Web site: http://www.bagleymn.us
Officers:
Mark Edevold, Chairman
Doug Lindgren, Secretary-Treasurer
Michael Jensen, General Manager
Ownership: Community owned--Bagley, MN.
Cable Systems (1):
MINNESOTA: BAGLEY.

BAILEY CABLE TV INC.
807 Church St
Port Gibson, MS 39150
Phones: 601-437-8300; 601-892-5249
Fax: 601-437-6860
E-mail: cs@baileycable.net
Web site: http://www.baileycable.net
Ownership: David A Bailey.
Cable Systems (6):
LOUISIANA: ANGOLA; ST. FRANCISVILLE.
MISSISSIPPI: CRYSTAL SPRINGS; MAGEE; MENDENHALL; PORT GIBSON.

LEON M. BAILEY JR.
115 N Main St
PO Box 368
Ripley, MS 38663
Phone: 662-837-4881
Fax: 662-837-9332
E-mail: leon@ripleycable.net
Web site: http://www.ripleycable.net
Cable Systems (1):
MISSISSIPPI: RIPLEY.

BAJA BROADBAND
Ste 100
1061 521 Corporate Center Dr
Fort Mill, SC 29707
Phone: 980-235-7600
Web site: http://www.bajabroadband.com
Officers:
William A. Schuler, Chief Executive Officer
Phillip Klein, Chief Operating Officer
Robert Calgi, Vice President, Marketing & Business Development
Sharon Levesque, Vice President, Finance
Kathleen Davis, Vice President, Regulatory Affairs
Ownership: Columbia Capital; M/C Venture Partners; Oak Investment Partners, investors.
Cable Systems (21):
COLORADO: BURLINGTON; CORTEZ; ESTES PARK; FORT CARSON; LAS ANIMAS; SPRINGFIELD.
NEVADA: BATTLE MOUNTAIN; CARLIN; ELKO; LOGANDALE; MESQUITE.
NEW MEXICO: ALAMOGORDO; CARRIZOZO; CLAYTON (town); HIGH ROLLS MOUNTAIN PARK; LOGAN; RUIDOSO; TRUTH OR CONSEQUENCES.
TEXAS: TEXLINE.
UTAH: ROCKVILLE; ST. GEORGE.

B & C CABLE
PO Box 548
Norwood, CO 81423
Phone: 970-327-4521
Fax: 970-327-4080
Officers:
Craig Greager, President
Mediatrica Greager, Vice President
Ownership: Craig Greager, 50%; Mediatrica Greager, 50%.
Cable Systems (1):
COLORADO: NORWOOD.

B & C CABLEVISION INC.
4683 Hwy. 6
Wiggins, CO 80654
Phone: 970-483-7820
Fax: 970-483-7822
Officers:
Carol Rogers, President
Bill Rogers, Secretary-Treasurer
Ownership: Bill Rogers; Carol Rogers, Principals.
Cable Systems (1):
WYOMING: BURNS.

B & L TECHNOLOGIES LLC
3329 270th St.
Lenox, IA 50851
Phone: 800-798-5488
Fax: 641-348-2240
Officer:
Robert Hintz, Chairman, President & Chief Operating Officer
Ownership: Greta Pierce; Robert Dean Pierce.
Cable Systems (21):
IOWA: ADAIR; AFTON; BLOCKTON; CINCINNATI; CLEARFIELD; DIAGONAL; FONTANELLE; GRAND RIVER; HUMESTON; MASSENA; MORAVIA; MOULTON; MYSTIC; VAN WERT.
MISSOURI: BURLINGTON JUNCTION; CONCEPTION JUNCTION; GRANT CITY; HOPKINS; PARNELL; RAVENWOOD; SHERIDAN.

BARBOURVILLE UTILITY COMMISSION
PO Box 1600
Barbourville, KY 40906
Phones: 606-546-4127; 606-545-9206
Fax: 606-546-4848
Web site: http://www.barbourville.com
Officers:
Randall Young, Superintendent
Wilhem Brewer, Assistant Superintendent
Ownership: Community owned--Barbourville, KY.
Cable Systems (1):
KENTUCKY: BARBOURVILLE.

CITY OF BARDSTOWN
220 N 5th St
Bardstown, KY 40004
Phone: 502-348-9711
Fax: 502-348-2433
Web site: http://www.bardstowncable.net
Officers:
Bill Sheckles, City Mayor
Mike Abell, Chief Financial Officer
Bobbie Blincoe, City Clerk
Ownership: Community owned--Bardstown, KY.
Cable Systems (1):
KENTUCKY: BARDSTOWN.

CITY OF BARNESVILLE
102 Front St N
PO Box 550
Barnesville, MN 56514
Phones: 218-354-2292; 800-354-2292
Web site: http://www.barnesvillemn.com
Ownership: Community owned--Barnesville, MN.
Cable Systems (1):
MINNESOTA: BARNESVILLE.

BASCO ELECTRONICS INC.
420 W 2nd St
Weston, WV 26452
Phone: 304-269-7530
Fax: 304-269-6581
E-mail: bascoelec@yahoo.com
Officers:
Wilfred L. Sholes, President
Virginia Sue Sholes, Secretary-Treasurer
Ownership: Virginia Sue Sholes; Wilfred L Sholes.
Represented (legal): Hogan Lovells.
Cable Systems (1):
WEST VIRGINIA: SALEM COLLEGE.

BASE CABLEVISION INC.
PO Box 553
Kennett, MO 63857
Phone: 573-717-1568
Officers:
Larry V. Jones, Acting President
John Scott, Secretary
Gerald Gamble, Treasurer
Cable Systems (1):
MISSOURI: HORNERSVILLE.

CITY OF BAXTER SPRINGS
1445 Military Ave
PO Box 577
Baxter Springs, KS 66713
Phone: 620-856-2114
Fax: 620-856-2460
Web site: http://baxtersprings.us
Ownership: Community owned--Baxter Springs, KS.
Cable Systems (1):
KANSAS: BAXTER SPRINGS.

BAYOU CABLE TV
378 Main St.
Marion, LA 71260
Phone: 318-292-4774
Fax: 318-292-4775
Officers:
Allen Booker, President & Chief Executive Officer
Cathy Booker, Vice President & Secretary-Treasurer
Ownership: Allen Booker; Cathy Booker.
Cable Systems (5):
ARKANSAS: HUTTIG; STRONG.
LOUISIANA: MARION; ROCKY BRANCH; STERLINGTON.

BEAMSPEED LLC
2481 E. Palo Verde St.
Yuma, AZ 85365
Phones: 928-726-0896; 928-317-6866
Fax: 928-726-8232
E-mail: support@beamspeed.net
Web site: http://www.beamspeed.net
Officer:
Phil Merrill, Manager
Cable Systems (1):
ARIZONA: WELLTON.

BEAVER CREEK COOPERATIVE TELEPHONE CO.
15223 SE Henrici Rd.
Oregon City, OR 97045
Phone: 503-632-3113
Fax: 503-632-4159
E-mail: info@bctonline.com
Web site: http://www.bctelco.com
Officers:
Tom Linstrom, President & Chief Executive Officer
Paul Hauer, Executive Vice President, Finance
Mark Beaudry, Vice President, Operations
Brandon Drake, Vice President Network Operations
Cable Systems (1):
OREGON: BEAVERCREEK.

BEAVER VALLEY CABLE INC.
36150 Rte 187
Rome, PA 18837
Phone: 570-247-2512
Fax: 570-247-2494
E-mail: bvc@cableracer.com
Web site: http://www.beavervalleycable.com
Cable Systems (1):
PENNSYLVANIA: ROME.

BEE LINE INC.
PO Box 431
Skowhegan, ME 04976
Phones: 207-474-2727; 800-439-4611
Fax: 207-474-0966
Web site: http://www.getbeeline.com
Officers:
Paul W. Hannigan, President
George C Allen, Vice President
Ownership: Paul W Hannigan, 5%.
Represented (legal): Garvey Schubert Barer.
Cable Systems (2):
MAINE: MADISON; MILLINOCKET.

BELHAVEN CABLE TV INC.
PO Box 8
235 Pamlico St
Belhaven, NC 27810-0008
Phone: 252-943-3736
Fax: 252-943-3738
Web site: http://www.belhavencabletv.com
Officers:
Guinn Leverett, Chairman & Chief Executive Officer
Ben Johnson, Chief Operating Officer
Corki Leverett, Secretary-Treasurer
Ownership: Corki Leverett.
Cable Systems (1):
NORTH CAROLINA: BELHAVEN.

BENKELMAN TELEPHONE CO.
607 Chief St
Benkelman, NE 69021
Phone: 308-423-2000
Fax: 308-423-2399
E-mail: bwtelcom@bwtelcom.net
Web site: http://www.bwtelcom.net
Cable Systems (3):
NEBRASKA: BENKELMAN; HAIGLER; WAUNETA.

BERESFORD CABLEVISION INC.
101 N 3rd St
Beresford, SD 57004
Phone: 605-763-2500
Fax: 605-763-7112
E-mail: phone@bmtc.net
Web site: http://www.bmtc.net
Officer:
Todd Hanson, Manager
Ownership: Community owned--Beresford, SD.
Cable Systems (1):
SOUTH DAKOTA: BERESFORD.

BERKELEY CABLE TV CO. INC.
579 Stoney Landing Rd.
PO Box 1194
Moncks Corner, SC 29461

Phones: 843-761-8188; 843-471-2200
Fax: 843-761-9120
Web site: http://www.homesc.com
Ownership: Robert L. Helmly, President. Helmly is also President & General Manager of Home Telephone Co. Inc., Moncks Corner, SC.
Cable Systems (1):
SOUTH CAROLINA: MONCKS CORNER.

BEULAH LAND COMMUNICATIONS INC.

8611 Central Ave
PO Box 188
Beulah, CO 81023
Phone: 719-485-3400
Fax: 719-485-3500
E-mail: pdtelco@pinedrivetel.com
Web site: http://www.pinedrivetel.com/
Ownership: Richard Sellers, Principal.
Cable Systems (1):
COLORADO: BEULAH.

BEVCOMM

191 2nd St SE
Wells, MN 56097
Phone: 507-553-3144
Fax: 507-553-6700
E-mail: info@bevcomm.net
Web site: http://www.bevcomm.net

Branch Office:
NEW PRAGUE
115 Main St W
New Prague, MN 56071
Phone: 952-758-2501
Fax: 952-758-4343
Cable Systems (5):
MINNESOTA: BLUE EARTH; BRICELYN; MINNESOTA LAKE; MORRISTOWN; VERMILLION.

BIG SKY COMMUNICATIONS INC.

124 Tailgate Ln
Hamilton, MT 59840
Phones: 406-363-0700; 800-859-2525
Fax: 406-363-0800
E-mail: sales@bigskycommunications.com
Web site: http://www.bigskycommunications.com
Cable Systems (1):
MONTANA: WHITEHALL.

BLAKELY CABLE TV INC.

65 Liberty St.
Blakely, GA 39823
Phone: 229-723-3555
Fax: 229-723-2000
Officer:
Charles Deloach Jr., President
Ownership: Charles Deloach Jr., 51%; Wayne R Foster, 49%.
Cable Systems (3):
GEORGIA: BLAKELY; LEARY; MORGAN.

BLOCK COMMUNICATIONS INC.

Ste 2100
405 Madison Ave
Toledo, OH 43604
Phones: 419-724-6212; 419-724-6035
Fax: 419-724-6167
E-mail: askus@cablesystem.com
Web site: http://www.blockcommunications.com
Officers:
Allan J. Block, Chairman
John R. Block, Vice Chairman
Gary J. Blair, President
David M. Beihoff, Vice President, Newspaper Operations
Jodi L. Miehls, Assistant Secretary
Ownership: Allan J Block, 25%; John R Block, 25%; William Block Marital Trusts, Karen D Johnese, Trustee, 25%; Family Trust No. 2, William Block Jr, Chairperson of Trustees, 25%. votes.
Represented (legal): Dow Lohnes PLLC.
Cable Systems (2):
OHIO: SANDUSKY; TOLEDO.
TV Stations:
Idaho: KTRV-TV Nampa.
Illinois: WAND Decatur.
Indiana: WMYO Salem.
Kentucky: WDRB Louisville.
Ohio: WLIO Lima.
LPTV Stations:
Illinois: W31BX-D Danville; W40CV-D Jacksonville.
Ohio: WFND-LP Findlay; WLMO-LP Lima; WLQP-LP Lima; WOHL-CD Lima.
Newspapers:
Ohio: Toledo Blade
Pennsylvania: Pittsburgh Post-Gazette
Other Holdings:
Construction: Metro Fiber & Cable Construction Co. (Toledo)
Outdoor advertising: Community Communications Services, advertising distribution company
Telephone service: Buckeye Telesystem Inc. (Toledo)

BLUE DEVIL CABLE TV INC.

116 S. 4th St.
Toronto, OH 43964-1368
Phones: 740-537-2214; 740-537-2030
Fax: 740-537-2802
Web site: http://bluedevilcabletv.com
Cable Systems (3):
PENNSYLVANIA: AVELLA; BURGETTSTOWN; CLAYSVILLE.

BLUE MOUNTAIN TV CABLE CO.

PO Box 267
Mount Vernon, OR 97865
Phone: 541-932-4613
Fax: 541-932-4613
Web site: http://www.bmtvcable.com
Ownership: Jack McKenna.
Cable Systems (4):
OREGON: DAYVILLE; MOUNT VERNON; PRAIRIE CITY; SENECA.

BLUE SKY CABLE LLC

412 W. Blackwell
Blackwell, OK 74631-2859
Phone: 580-363-5580
Web site: http://www.blueskycable.com
Cable Systems (2):
KANSAS: BENTLEY; MARQUETTE.

BOB BOALDIN

610 S Cosmos
Elkhart, KS 67950
Phone: 316-697-4466
E-mail: etc@elkhart.com
Web site: http://www.epictouch.com
Cable Systems (1):
KANSAS: ELKHART.

VILLAGE OF BOAZ

Rte 1
Muscoda, WI 53573
Phone: 608-536-3493
E-mail: villofboaz@mwt.net
Ownership: Local investors.
Cable Systems (1):
WISCONSIN: BOAZ.

BOONEVILLE CABLEVISION

PO Box 232
Combs, KY 41729
Phone: 606-439-2542
Fax: 606-436-4777
Cable Systems (1):
KENTUCKY: LEROSE.

DAN BOWLING

652 Owls Nest Rd.
PO Box 522
Hyden, KY 41749-0522
Phone: 606-672-3479
Cable Systems (1):
KENTUCKY: HYDEN.

BOYCOM CABLEVISION INC.

RR 10
PO Box 333
Poplar Bluff, MO 63901
Phones: 573-686-3218; 573-686-9101
Fax: 573-686-4722
E-mail: info@boycomonline.com
Web site: http://www.boycom.com
Officers:
Steven D. Boyers, Chairman, President. & Chief Executive & Operating Officer
Patricia Jo Boyers, Vice President, Secretary-Treasurer & Chief Financial Officer
Ownership: Steven D Boyers, 50%; Patricia Jo Boyers, 50%.
Cable Systems (19):
ARKANSAS: BIGGERS.
MISSOURI: ALTON; BIRCH TREE; BUTLER COUNTY; DONIPHAN; DUDLEY; ELLINGTON; ELLSINORE; EMINENCE; FISK; MARBLE HILL; MOUNTAIN VIEW; NAYLOR; PIEDMONT; PUXICO; QULIN; VAN BUREN; WAPPAPELLO; WINONA.

BRESNAN COMMUNICATIONS INC.

One Manhattanville Rd.
Purchase, NY 10577-2596
Phone: 914-641-3300
Fax: 914-641-3301
E-mail: mdambra@bresnan.com
Web site: http://www.bresnan.com
Officers:
Jeffrey S. DeMond, President & Chief Executive Officer
Steven M. Brookstein, Executive Vice President, Operations & Chief Operating Officer
Andrew C Kober, Executive Vice President & Chief Financial Officer
Patrick J Bresnan, Senior Vice President
Margot C Bright, Senior Vice President & Treasurer
Jackie Heitman, Senior Vice President, Marketing
Leonard Higgins, Senior Vice President, Advanced Services
Pragash Pillai, Senior Vice President, Engineering & Technology
Jeanne Rudell, Senior Vice President, Human Resources
Terry St. Marie, Senior Vice President, Operations
Shawn Beqay, Vice President, Public Affairs
Ownership: Bresnan Broadband Holdings LLC; BBHLLC ownership:; Providence Equity Partners Inc., lead investor; Comcast Corp., 30%; Quadrangle Corp. LLC; TD Capital Communications Partners; Bresnan Management, equity owners.
Cable Systems (71):
COLORADO: ALAMOSA; ANTONITO; BUENA VISTA; CANON CITY; COLORADO CITY; CRAIG; DEL NORTE; DELTA; DOLORES; DOVE CREEK; DURANGO; DURANGO WEST; FORT MORGAN; GRAND JUNCTION; LA JUNTA; LAMAR; LEADVILLE; MANASSA; MEEKER; MONTROSE; NUCLA; PAONIA; RANGELY; SALIDA; SAN LUIS; STERLING; VICTOR; WALDEN; WALSENBURG.
MONTANA: ALBERTON; ANACONDA; BILLINGS; BOULDER; BOZEMAN; BUTTE; CASCADE; CHINOOK; CUT BANK; DEER LODGE; DILLON; FORT BENTON; GLASGOW; GREAT FALLS; HAMILTON; HARLEM; HAVRE; HELENA; KALISPELL; LIVINGSTON; MALTA; MISSOULA; POLSON; STEVENSVILLE; TOWNSEND.
UTAH: CEDAR CITY.
WYOMING: BUFFALO; CASPER; CHEYENNE; CODY; GILLETTE; GREYBULL; JACKSON (town); LARAMIE; NEWCASTLE; POWELL; RAWLINS; RIVERTON; SHERIDAN; THERMOPOLIS; WORLAND; WRIGHT.

BRIGHTGREEN COMMUNICATIONS

PO Box 127
Gillespie, IL 62033
Phones: 217-839-1498; 217-839-3732
E-mail: support@brightgreencable.com
Web site: http://www.brightgreencable.com
Officer:
Phillip Claro, President
Cable Systems (3):
ILLINOIS: BRIGHTON; GREENFIELD; HARDIN.

BRIGHT HOUSE NETWORKS LLC

Ste 600
65 S Keller Rd
Orlando, FL 32801
Phone: 407-291-2500
E-mail: stephen.colafrancesco@mybrighthouse.com
Web site: http://www.brighthouse.com
Officers:
Steven Miron, Chairman & Chief Executive Officer
Nomi Bergman, President
Kevin Hyman, Executive Vice President, Cable Operations
Craig Cowden, Senior Vice President, Network Engineering & Operations
Dick Amell, Corporate Vice President, Video Engineering & Operations
Pam Hagan, Corporate Vice President, Human Resources
Stephen Colafrancesco, Vice President, Marketing
Kevin Hord, Vice President, Corporate Procurement & Materials Management
Jennifer Mooney, Vice President, Corporate Government & Public Affairs
Todd A Stewart, Vice President, Advertising Sales

Branch Office:
Central Florida
1670 E. Hwy. 50
Suite D
Clermont, FL 34711
Phone: 407-295-9119
Fax: 352-243-7592
Ownership: Advance/Newhouse Partnership, see listing, majority interest; Time Warner Cable Inc., see listing. Advance/Newhouse has 100% beneficial ownership of Bright House Networks assets listings.
Cable Systems (36):
ALABAMA: BIRMINGHAM; CLIO; EUFAULA; FLORALA; GENEVA; GREENVILLE; SAMSON; WETUMPKA.
CALIFORNIA: AVENAL; BAKERSFIELD; TEHACHAPI.
FLORIDA: AUBURNDALE; BLOUNTSTOWN; BRADENTON; CANTONMENT; CEDAR KEY; CENTURY; CHATTAHOOCHEE; CHIPLEY; DE FUNIAK SPRINGS; DELAND; HERNANDO

COUNTY; HILLSBOROUGH COUNTY (portions); HOMOSASSA; MELBOURNE; MIAMI (portions); ORLANDO; ORLANDO; PASCO COUNTY (central & eastern portions); PASCO COUNTY (western portion); PINELLAS COUNTY (portions); WELLINGTON; WILDWOOD.
INDIANA: INDIANAPOLIS (portions); MARION.
MICHIGAN: LIVONIA.

BRISTOL BAY TELEPHONE COOPERATIVE INC.

1 Main St
King Salmon, AK 99613
Phone: 907-246-3403
Fax: 907-246-1115
E-mail: bbtcmanager@bristolbay.com
Web site: http://www.bristolbay.com
Officer:
Todd Hoppe, General Manager
Ownership: Subscriber owned--Bristol Bay, AK.
Cable Systems (1):
ALASKA: KING SALMON.

BROADSTRIPE

Ste 1310
13455 Noel Rd
Dallas, TX 75420
Phone: 972-663-6971
Fax: 972-663-6973
E-mail: customerservicemd@broadstripe.com
Web site: http://www.broadstripe.com/
Officers:
Gustavo Prilick, Chief Executive Officer
Rudy Tober, Chief Operating Officer
Debra Wood, Chief Financial Officer
Eric Freesmeier, Chief People Officer
Tony Lent, Chief Commerical Officer
David Irons, Executive Vice President & General Manager, Northwest Operations
Terie Hannay, Senior Vice President, Customer Care
Gilbert Nichols, Senior Vice President, Operations
Frank Scotello, Senior Vice President, Programming & New Business Development
Tamara Shelman, Senior Vice President, Customer Care
Peter C. Smith, Senior Vice President, Programming & Product Development
Tim Valley, Senior Vice President, Finance
Mark Jordan, Vice President, Engineering & Technical Operations
Tom Martinson, Vice President, IT/ISP Services
Bruce E Beard, General Counsel

Branch Offices:
NORTHWEST REGION
10427 ML King Jr Way
Tukwila, WA 98178
Phone: 800-829-2225
CENTRAL REGION
2512 Lansing Rd
Charlotte, MI 48813
Phone: 800-444-6997
MID-ATLANTIC REGION
406 Headquarters Dr
Ste 201
Millersville, MD 21108
Phone: 877-882-7623
Ownership: Highland Capital Management, controlling investor; Broadstripe filed January 2, 2009 for Chapter 11 bankruptcy protection with the US Bankruptcy Court in Delaware.. It was announced August 24, 2011 that Broadstripe would sell its assets to Wave Broadband (WaveDivision Holdings LLC) & WideOpenWest LLC, see listings.
Cable Systems (35):
MARYLAND: MILLERSVILLE.
MICHIGAN: DIMONDALE; UNION CITY; VERMONTVILLE.
OREGON: DEPOE BAY; OTIS.
WASHINGTON: ANDERSON ISLAND; BELLINGHAM; BREWSTER; BRIDGEHAVEN; CARSON; CHELAN; CONCRETE; CRESTON; DARRINGTON; DUVALL; EASTON; Echo Lake/ Snohomish; ENTIAT; FORKS; GREENBANK; KALA POINT; LAKE BAY; MANSFIELD; MARBLEMOUNT; MORTON; NAPAVINE; PACKWOOD; PE ELL; PORT TOWNSEND; RANDLE; THORP; TWISP; WATERVILLE; WHIDBEY ISLAND.
Other Holdings:
Data service: US Net; Pacifier; OneNet Communications Inc.; Northwest Link; EZ.net; Europa Communications

BROCKWAY TV INC.

501 Main St
Brockway, PA 15824
Phone: 814-268-6565
Fax: 814-265-1300
E-mail: lwayne@brockwaytv.com
Web site: http://www.brockwaytv.com
Officers:
Laurie Wayne, Borough Manager
Lugene Inzana, Vice Chairman
Chris Bensen, Vice President
Ownership: Subscriber owned--Brockway, PA.
Represented (legal): Ferraro & Young.
Cable Systems (1):
PENNSYLVANIA: BROCKWAY.

BRYAN MUNICIPAL UTILITIES

841 E Edgerton St
Bryan, OH 43506
Phones: 419-633-3031; 419-633-6130
Fax: 419-636-8026
E-mail: bmuvideo@cityofbyran.com
Web site: http://www.cityofbryan.net
Officer:
Jim Funderburg, Superintendent
Cable Systems (1):
OHIO: BRYAN.

BUFORD MEDIA GROUP LLC

6125 Paluxy Drive
Tyler, TX 75703
Phone: 903-561-4411
Fax: 903-561-4031
E-mail: info@bufordmedia.com
Web site: http://www.bufordmedia.com
Officers:
Ben Hooks, Chief Executive Officer
Bennett Hooks, President
Cable Systems (47):
ALABAMA: UNIONTOWN.
ARKANSAS: DES ARC; GREENBRIER; JUNCTION CITY; LAKE VIEW; LEE COUNTY (southern portion); LEWISVILLE; LONOKE; MARSHALL; MAYFLOWER; PLUMERVILLE.
LOUISIANA: ARCADIA; BASILE; BERNICE; COLFAX; GIBSLAND; KENTWOOD; MERRYVILLE; MONTGOMERY; NATCHEZ; NEWELLTON; OLLA; PLAIN DEALING.
MISSISSIPPI: BASSFIELD; CROWDER; JONESTOWN; LEAKESVILLE; RICHTON; SHUBUTA; SUMRALL.
OKLAHOMA: ANTLERS; PRYOR; WALTERS; WAURIKA.
TEXAS: ASPERMONT; COOPER; CROWELL; FREER; HASKELL; HEBBRONVILLE; KNOX CITY; LAKE CHEROKEE; MUNDAY; NAPLES; POTEET; RULE; STAMFORD.
Other Holdings:
Manages Allegiance Communications, see listing

BULLDOG CABLE

455 Gees Mill Business Ct
Conyers, GA 30013
Phone: 800-388-6577
E-mail: info@bulldogcable.com
Web site: http://www.bulldogcable.com
Officer:
Joe Sheehan, Chief Executive Officer
Cable Systems (18):
GEORGIA: ABBEVILLE; BALDWIN COUNTY (northern portion); COLQUITT; DUDLEY; GORDON; MILAN; RENTZ; ROCHELLE; SEMINOLE COUNTY; SPARTA; WRENS.
MONTANA: BIG SKY; CULBERTSON; ENNIS; PLENTYWOOD; POPLAR; SCOBEY; WEST YELLOWSTONE.

CABLEAMERICA CORP.

4120 E Valley Auto Dr
Mesa, AZ 85206
Phones: 480-315-1820; 480-558-7300
Fax: 480-545-0656
Web site: http://www.cableamerica.com
Officers:
Alan C. Jackson, Vice President
Eric W. Jackson, Vice President
William H. Lewis, Vice President
Ownership: William G Jackson, 90%; Gloria J Jackson, 10%.
Represented (legal): Cole, Raywid & Braverman LLP.
Cable Systems (6):
MICHIGAN: EAGLE HARBOR TWP..
MISSOURI: LAKE SHERWOOD; MARYLAND HEIGHTS; PORTAGE DES SIOUX; REPUBLIC; WAYNESVILLE.
Other Holdings:
SMATV

CABLE COMMUNICATIONS OF WILLSBORO INC.

3669 Essex Rd., Ste. 1
PO Box 625
Willsboro, NY 12996
Phone: 518-963-4116
Fax: 518-963-7405
E-mail: adksr4us@yahoo.com
Officers:
Herb Longware, President
Shirley Longware, Chief Financial Officer
Ownership: Herb Longware; Eileen Longware.
Cable Systems (1):
NEW YORK: WILLSBORO (town).

CABLE CONSTRUCTORS INC.

105 Kent St
PO Box 885
Iron Mountain, MI 49801
Phones: 906-774-6621; 800-236-8434
Fax: 906-776-2811
E-mail: inquiries@plbb.us
Web site: http://www.packerlandbroadband.com
Cable Systems (37):
ILLINOIS: GEM SUBURBAN MOBILE HOME PARK; UNION.
MICHIGAN: MELLEN TWP.; STEPHENSON.
WISCONSIN: AMBERG; AUBURNDALE; AUGUSTA; AVOCA; BONDUEL; BUTTERNUT; COLEMAN; DARIEN; ELCHO (town); FALL CREEK; FIFIELD; GILLETT; GLIDDEN; GOODMAN; GREENWOOD; HAWKINS (village); HOLLANDALE; JUNCTION CITY; KNOWLES; KRAKOW; LA VALLE (village); LAONA; LENA; MELLEN; NICHOLS; PEMBINE; PITTSVILLE; PRENTICE; VESPER; WABENO; WAUZEKA; WHITE LAKE; WONEWOC.

CABLE COOPERATIVE INC.

27 E. College St.
Oberlin, OH 44074
Phone: 440-775-4001
Fax: 440-775-1635
E-mail: support@oberlin.net
Web site: http://www.oberlin.net
Officers:
Andrew Ruckman, Chairman
Ralph Potts, Chief Operating Officer
Dayton Livingston, Chief Financial Officer
Ownership: Subscriber-owned--Oberlin, OH.
Cable Systems (1):
OHIO: OBERLIN.

CABLE MANAGEMENT ASSOC.

Ste 2100
13355 Noel Rd
Dallas, TX 75240
Phone: 972-233-9616
Fax: 972-385-9601
E-mail: feedback@cmaaccess.com
Web site: http://cmaaccess.com
Officers:
Nathan A. Levine, Chairman & Chief Executive Officer
Douglas K. Bridges, Chief Operating Officer
Dave Beasley, Vice President, Marketing
Mark Reaves, Vice President, Operations
Ownership: Nathan A Levine.
Represented (legal): Dow Lohnes PLLC.
Cable Systems (37):
LOUISIANA: BELLE CHASSE; BLANCHARD; CALHOUN; COLUMBIA; DELHI; FARMERVILLE; HOMER; LAKE PROVIDENCE; LOGANSPORT; MANSFIELD; MONROE; SPRINGHILL; TALLULAH; WISNER.
MISSISSIPPI: ANGUILLA; ARCOLA; HOLLANDALE; LELAND; QUITMAN; WAYNESBORO.
NEVADA: LAUGHLIN; PAHRUMP.
TEXAS: ANGLETON; BELLVILLE; BLACKWELL; CLEVELAND; GRAPE CREEK; HEMPSTEAD; JASPER; KINGSVILLE; LA GRANGE; MERKEL; ROBERT LEE; ROSCOE; SOUR LAKE; TUSCOLA; WOODVILLE.
Other Holdings:
Service company: Credit Protection Assoc. Inc., collection agency for cable receivables.; 50% of Alpha Data Systems Inc., national computer company specializing in cellular telephone billing services and third party administration for insurance companies;

CABLE ONE INC.

3rd Fl
1314 N 3rd St
Phoenix, AZ 85004
Phone: 602-364-6000
Fax: 602-364-6011
Web site: http://www.cableone.net
Officers:
Thomas O. Might, President
Julia M. Laulis, Chief Operating Officer
Stephen A. Fox, Chief Technical Officer
Gerald W. McKenna, Chief Marketing Officer
T. Mitchell Bland, Vice President, Central Division
John D. Gosch, Vice President, West Division
Michael E. Bowker, Vice President, Advertising Sales
Aldo R. Casartelli, Vice President, Internet Services
Patrick A. Dolohanty, Vice President & Treasurer
Joe Felbab, Vice President, Marketing
James J. Hannan, Vice President, Engineering
Alan H. Silverman, Vice President & General Counsel
Janiece St. Cyr, Vice President, Human Resources

Ownership: The Washington Post Co. The Washington Post Co. has broadcast, newspaper, periodical, publishing & other interests, see listing for Post-Newsweek Stations Inc. in Commercial TV Station Ownership.

Represented (legal): Fleischman & Harding LLP.

Cable Systems (53):
ALABAMA: ANNISTON.
ARIZONA: BISBEE; CLIFTON; COTTONWOOD; GLOBE-MIAMI; PAGE; PRESCOTT; SAFFORD; SHOW LOW.
IDAHO: BOISE; CALDWELL; COUNCIL; IDAHO FALLS; LEWISTON; POCATELLO; TWIN FALLS.
IOWA: SIOUX CITY.
KANSAS: CHANUTE; EMPORIA; INDEPENDENCE; PARSONS.
MISSISSIPPI: BILOXI; BROOKHAVEN; CLARKSDALE; CLEVELAND; COLUMBUS; LONG BEACH; NATCHEZ; PASCAGOULA; WINONA.
MISSOURI: JOPLIN; KIRKSVILLE.
NEBRASKA: NORFOLK.
NEW MEXICO: RIO RANCHO; ROSWELL.
NORTH DAKOTA: FARGO.
OKLAHOMA: ADA; ALTUS; ARDMORE/LONE GROVE; BARTLESVILLE; DUNCAN; ELK CITY; HOBART; MIAMI; PONCA CITY; VINITA.
TENNESSEE: DYERSBURG.
TEXAS: ARANSAS PASS; BORGER; ODESSA; PORT LAVACA; SHERMAN; TEXARKANA.

CABLE OPTIONS INC.

PO Box 1404
Fairhope, AL 36533
Phone: 251-550-5796
E-mail: cabopt@yahoo.com
Officer:
J. Alex Bowab, Chief Operating Officer
Ownership: Alex Bowab; John Riley, Principals.
Cable Systems (1):
ALABAMA: BALDWIN COUNTY (portions).

CABLE PLUS

PO Box 1030
Honaker, VA 24260-1030
Phone: 276-873-4828
Fax: 276-873-6331
E-mail: officestaff@cableplus.tv
Web site: http://www.cableplus.tv
Cable Systems (1):
VIRGINIA: ROSEDALE.

CABLE SERVICES INC.

308 2nd St SW
PO Box 1995
Jamestown, ND 58402
Phones: 701-252-5281; 701-252-2225; 701-845-4383
E-mail: info@csicable.com
Web site: http://csicable.com
Officer:
Roy A. Sheppard, Chief Executive & Operating Officer
Cable Systems (4):
NORTH DAKOTA: JAMESTOWN; LISBON; OAKES; VALLEY CITY.

CABLE SOUTH MEDIA III LLC

301 W First Ave
Crossett, AR 71635
Phone: 870-305-1241
Cable Systems (7):
ARKANSAS: CROSSETT; FORDYCE.
LOUISIANA: FERRIDAY; JENA; JONESVILLE; WINNSBORO.
MISSISSIPPI: COLUMBIA.

CABLESTAR INC.

PO Box 145
Ragland, AL 35131-0145
Phone: 205-472-2141
Fax: 205-472-2145
E-mail: peggydickinson@ragland.net
Web site: http://www.ragland.net
Ownership: Bob Dickinson, Principal.
Cable Systems (1):
ALABAMA: RAGLAND.
Other Holdings:
Telephone

CABLE TV OF STANTON

100 Ivy St.
Stanton, NE 68779
Phones: 402-439-5000; 402-439-2264
Fax: 402-439-7777
E-mail: info@stanton.net
Web site: http://www.stanton.net/cabletv.html
Officer:
Leona Paden, Secretary
Ownership: Leona Paden, 55%; John Paden, 15%; Richard A Paden, 15%; Robert J Paden, 15%.
Cable Systems (1):
NEBRASKA: STANTON.

CABLEVISION OF WALKER COUNTY

1304 10th St.
Huntsville, TX 77320
Phone: 936-291-2288
Fax: 936-291-0890
Web site: http://www.walkercountycabletv.com
Cable Systems (3):
TEXAS: CAROLINA COVE; NEW WAVERLY; WATERWOOD.

CABLEVISION SYSTEMS CORP.

1111 Stewart Ave.
Bethpage, NY 11714
Phone: 516-803-2300
Fax: 516-803-2368
Web site: http://www.cablevision.com
Officers:
Charles F. Dolan, Chairman, Cablevision Systems Corp. & Executive Chairman, AMC Networks Inc.
Hank J. Ratner, Vice Chairman
James L. Dolan, President & Chief Executive Officer
Tom Rutledge, Chief Operating Officer
Gregg Seibert, Chief Financial Officer & Executive Vice President
John Bickham, President, Cable & Communications
Wilt Hildenbrand, Senior Advisor, Engineering & Technology
James Blackley, Executive Vice President, Corporate Engineering & Technology
David Ellen, Executive Vice President & General Counsel
Jonathan Hargis, Executive Vice President, Marketing & Advertising
Michael Huseby, Executive Vice President & Chief Financial Officer
Lisa Rosenblum, Executive Vice President, Government & Public Affairs
Gregg Seibert, Executive Vice President
John Trierwelier, Executive Vice President, Product Management
Todd Brecher, Senior Vice President, Associate General Counsel of Business Affairs
Chris Coffee, Senior Vice President, Field Operations
Tom Donohue, Senior Vice President, Technology, Local Media Group
Valerie Green, Senior Vice President, Marketing, Local Media Group
P Kevin Smith, Senior Vice President & Chief Security Officer
Ownership: Publicly held.; Charles F Dolan, majority stockholder; Harbinger Capital Management, 7.5%. Dolan's attempt to take company private was denied by stockholders October 24, 2007.
Represented (legal): DLA Piper International; Mintz Levin Cohn Ferris Glovsky & Popeo.
Cable Systems (29):
CONNECTICUT: BRIDGEPORT; LITCHFIELD; NORWALK.
NEW JERSEY: BAYONNE; BERGENFIELD; DOVER; ELIZABETH; HAMILTON TWP. (Mercer County); HOBOKEN; MONMOUTH COUNTY; NEWARK; OAKLAND; PATERSON; RARITAN.
NEW YORK: BRONX; BROOKLYN; DOVER PLAINS; MAMARONECK; OSSINING; PORT CHESTER; RAMAPO (town); RIVERHEAD; ROCKLAND; SUFFOLK COUNTY; WARWICK; WOODBURY; YONKERS; YORKTOWN.
PENNSYLVANIA: MATAMORAS.
Newspapers:
New York: 97% of Newsday (Long Island & New York City)
Other Holdings:
Madison Square Garden, Radio City Music Hall
Cable advertising representative: Rainbow Advertising Sales Corp.
Common Carrier: Optimum Lightpath
Data service: IO: Interactive Optimum digital television, Optimum Online high-speed Internet, Optimum Voice digital voice-over-cable & Optimum Lightpath integrated business communications services
Motion picture holdings: Clearview Cinemas
Professional sports team: New York Knicks, Rangers and WNBA Liberty
Program source: fuse; Much Music; Fox Sports Net New York, Fox Sports Net Chicago, 50% of Fox Sports Net New England, 60% of Fox Sports Net Bay Area; News 12 Bronx; News 12 Connecticut; News 12 Long Island; Rainbow Media Holdings LLC was spun off as AMC Networks Inc. June 30, 2011; News 12 Westchester; Wedding Central; New 12 New Jersey
Telecommunications company: Lightpath CLEC

CALIFORNIA-OREGON BROADCASTING INC.

125 S. Fir St.
PO Box 1489
Medford, OR 97501
Phones: 541-779-5555; 1-800-821-8108
Fax: 541-779-1151
E-mail: kobi@kobi5.com
Web site: http://localnewscomesfirst.com
Ownership: Patricia C Smullin, President.
Represented (legal): Wiley Rein LLP.
Cable Systems (3):
OREGON: LA PINE; MADRAS; PRINEVILLE.
TV Stations:
Oregon: KLSR-TV Eugene; KOTI Klamath Falls; KOBI Medford; KPIC Roseburg.
LPTV Stations:
California: K34KJ-D Crescent City, etc.; K13HU Fort Jones, etc.; K05ET-D Likely; K47DV-D South Yreka; K04HE Yreka, etc..
Oregon: K04ER Applegate Valley; K07JT-D Brookings; K07PP Camas Valley; K43DI Canyonville; K07KT Canyonville, etc.; K07PZ Cave Junction; K07PS Chemult; K06NS-D Chiloquin; K14MQ-D Coos Bay; K30BN-D Coos Bay; K36BX-D Coos Bay; K14GW-D Corvallis; KEVU-CD Eugene; K19GH-D Eugene, etc.; K26HO-D Glide; K25EN-D Gold Beach; K02FT Gold Hill; K50FW Grants Pass; K04EY Grants Pass, etc.; K13JR-D Jacksonville, etc.; K04ES Klamath Falls; K07NR-D Lakeview, etc.; K32DY Medford; K36IB-D Midland, etc.; K49JE-D Murphy, etc.; K13HM Myrtle Creek; K13JQ North Bend & Empire; K08AK-D Port Orford, etc.; K33FE Roseburg; K41JQ Roseburg; K11RM Silver Lake; K13MI Squaw Valley; K03EI Tolo, etc.; K11GH Tri-City, etc.; K07HS Williams; K32FI Yoncalla; K39CL Yoncalla.

JEWEL B. CALLAHAM REVOCABLE TRUST

PO Box 548
Broken Bow, OK 74728
Phone: 580-584-3340
Ownership: Esta Callaham; John B Callaham; Angela G Wisenhunt.
Cable Systems (1):
OKLAHOMA: BROKEN BOW.
LPTV Stations:
Oklahoma: K28DJ Broken Bow.
Other Holdings:
Telephone: Pine Telephone Co. Inc

CALNEVA BROADBAND LLC

322 Ash St
PO Box 1470
Westwood, CA 96137
Phones: 530-256-2028; 866-330-2028
Fax: 530-256-3123
Web site: http://blog.calneva.org
Cable Systems (4):
CALIFORNIA: FRAZIER PARK; LAKE ALMANOR; NEEDLES.
NEVADA: WINNEMUCCA.

TOWN OF CAMPBELLTON

PO Box 38
Campbellton, FL 32426
Phones: 850-263-4535; 850-263-8502
Cable Systems (1):
FLORIDA: CAMPBELLTON.

CAMS CABLE

8221 Dolly Madison Dr
Colorado Springs, CO 80902
Phone: 888-291-2415
E-mail: cam@camscable.com
Web site: http://www.camscable.com
Cable Systems (3):
COLORADO: LYONS (town).
WYOMING: GUERNSEY; PINE BLUFFS.

C & W CABLE INC.

7920 Hwy. 30W
Annville, KY 40402-9748
Phone: 606-364-5357
Officers:
Brett Williams, President & Chief Executive & Operating Officer
Viola Williams, Vice President, Secretary-Treasurer & Chief Financial Officer
Ownership: Don Williams; Judy C Williams.
Cable Systems (1):
KENTUCKY: ANNVILLE.

CARNEGIE CABLE

25 S. Colorado
PO Box 96
Carnegie, OK 73015
Phone: 580-654-1002
Fax: 580-654-2699
E-mail: jpowers@carnegiecable.com
Web site: http://www.carnegietelco.com
Officers:
Lyn Johnson, President & Chief Executive Officer
Gary Woodruff, Vice President & Chief Operating Officer
Leslie Powers, Secretary & Treasurer

Darrin Cornelison, Central Officer Manager
James Powers, Operations Manager
Travis Ridgeway, Outside Plant Manager
Ownership: H. S Scott, 97%; Troy Scott, 1%; Wade Scott, 1%; Suzanne Scott, 1%.
Cable Systems (1):
OKLAHOMA: CARNEGIE.

CARNESVILLE GUMLOG CABLE

1591 S Fairview Rd
Lavonia, GA 30553
Phone: 706-356-1714
E-mail: gumlogsales@gumlog.net
Web site: http://www.gumlog.net
Ownership: John Williamson.
Cable Systems (1):
GEORGIA: CARNESVILLE.

CAROLINA MOUNTAIN CABLEVISION INC.

4930 Jonathan Creek Rd.
PO Box 298
Waynesville, NC 28785
Phone: 828-926-2288
Fax: 828-926-2114
Web site: http://www.cbvnol.com
Officers:
John Dixson, President
Terry Sersland, Chief Technology Officer
Ownership: Stewart Corbett; Gerald Aldridge; Ed Stark, Principals.
Cable Systems (4):
NORTH CAROLINA: WAYNESVILLE.
TENNESSEE: DANDRIDGE; NEWPORT; TALBOTT.

CITY OF CASCADE LOCKS CABLE TV

PO Box 308
Cascade Locks, OR 97014
Phones: 541-374-8484; 541-374-8752
Web site: http://www.clbb.net
Officer:
Robert Willoughby, General Manager
Ownership: Municipally owned--Cascade Locks, OR.
Cable Systems (1):
OREGON: CASCADE LOCKS.

CASEY MUTUAL TELEPHONE CO.

108 E. Logan St.
Casey, IA 50048
Phone: 641-746-2222
Fax: 641-746-2221
E-mail: caseymutual@netins.net
Officer:
John Breining, Manager
Cable Systems (1):
IOWA: CASEY.

CASPIAN COMMUNITY TV CORP.

301 W Caspian Ave
Caspian, MI 49915
Phone: 906-265-4747
Officers:
Vic Shepich, President
Chalmers McGreaham, Vice President
Robert Watts, Secretary-Treasurer
Ownership: Subscriber owned--Caspian, MI.
Cable Systems (1):
MICHIGAN: CASPIAN.

CASS CABLE TV INC.

100 Rosebud Rd.
PO Box 200
Virginia, IL 62691
Phones: 217-452-7725; 800-252-1799
Fax: 217-452-7030
E-mail: solutions@casscomm.com
Web site: http://home.casscomm.com
Officers:
Gerald E. Gill, Chairman & President
Donald L. Bell, Vice President & Chief Executive Officer
Gerald S. Gill II, Vice President
Thomas D. Allen, Chief Financial Officer
Ownership: Gerald E. Gill. Gill owns Cass Telephone Co., Cass Long Distance, Cass Communications Management Inc. & has cellular telephone holdings.
Represented (legal): Cole, Raywid & Braverman LLP.
Cable Systems (2):
ILLINOIS: PITTSFIELD; VIRGINIA.

CATALINA CABLE TV CO.

222 Metropole Ave
PO Box 2143
Avalon, CA 90704
Phone: 310-510-0255
E-mail: catcable@catalinaisp.com
Web site: http://www.catalinaisp.com
Officer:
Ralph J. Morrow Jr., Chief Executive Officer
Ownership: Patricia L Morrow; Ralph J Morrow Jr..
Cable Systems (1):
CALIFORNIA: AVALON/CATALINA ISLAND.

CATV SERVICE INC.

115 Mill St
PO Box 198
Danville, PA 17821
Phone: 570-275-3101
Fax: 570-275-3888
E-mail: catvserv@ptd.net
Web site: http://catvservice.com
Officer:
Samuel Haulman, President & General Manager
Ownership: Margaret Walsonavich, Pres..
Represented (legal): Womble, Carlyle, Sandridge & Rice.
Cable Systems (1):
PENNSYLVANIA: DANVILLE.

CEDAR FALLS MUNICIPAL COMMUNICATIONS UTILITY

PO Box 769
Cedar Falls, IA 50613
Phone: 319-266-1761
E-mail: cfu@cfu.net
Web site: http://www.cfunet.net
Officers:
Pamela Taylor, Chairman
Richard Eades, Vice Chairman
Vilas L. Morris Jr., Secretary
Ownership: Municipally owned--Cedar Falls, IA.
Cable Systems (1):
IOWA: CEDAR FALLS.

CELECT COMMUNICATIONS

S131 McKay Ave
PO Box 189
Spring Valley, WI 54767
Phones: 715-778-6121; 800-285-7993
Fax: 715-778-5033
E-mail: celecthelp@celectcom.net
Web site: http://www.celectcom.net
Officers:
Randy Sailer, President
Max Downs, Vice President
Mike DeMarce, Chief Operating Officer
Jim Smart, Secretary
Dennis Bachman, Treasurer
Cable Systems (1):
WISCONSIN: ELMWOOD.

CELINA CABLE COMMUNICATIONS

538 Cedar St.
McKenzie, TN 38201
Phone: 731-352-2980
Fax: 731-352-3533
Officer:
Gary Blount, Owner
Cable Systems (3):
TENNESSEE: BYRDSTOWN; CELINA; OVERTON COUNTY (portions).

CENTER CABLE TV

PO Box 117
Greeley, NE 68842
Phone: 308-428-2915
E-mail: greeleycitizen@centercable.tv
Officer:
Martin Callahan, Owner
Ownership: Martin Callahan, 50%; Thomas Callahan, 50%.
Cable Systems (1):
NEBRASKA: GREELEY.

CENTER JUNCTION TELEPHONE CO.

513 Main St.
Center Junction, IA 52212
Phone: 563-487-2631
Fax: 563-487-3701
Officers:
Dennis Orris, President
Judy Paulsen, Secretary-Treasurer
Cable Systems (1):
IOWA: CENTER JUNCTION.

CENTRACOM INTERACTIVE

35 S. State St.
PO Box 7
Fairview, UT 84629
Phones: 435-427-3331; 800-427-8449
Fax: 435-427-3200
Web site: http://www.centracom.com
Ownership: Lynch Interactive Corp..
Cable Systems (9):
NEVADA: ELY; EUREKA; MCGILL; RUTH; WENDOVER.
UTAH: DUGWAY; GLENWOOD; GUNNISON; MONA.

CENTRAL VALLEY CABLE TV LLC

38951 S. Hwy. One
PO Box 429
Gualala, CA 95445
Phone: 559-298-1464
Fax: 707-884-4116
Ownership: Tom Gelardi, Chief Operating Officer.
Cable Systems (1):
CALIFORNIA: THE SEA RANCH.

CENTROVISION INC.

8 E. Barton Ave.
PO Box 3157
Temple, TX 76501
Phone: 254-773-1163
Web site: http://www.centrovision.net
Ownership: Alton Sheppard, Pres. & Principal.
Cable Systems (7):
TEXAS: LITTLE RIVER-ACADEMY; MOODY; MORGAN'S POINT RESORT; ROGERS; SALADO; TEMPLE; TROY.

CEQUEL COMMUNICATIONS LLC

12444 Powerscourt Dr.
St. Louis, MO 63131
Phones: 314-965-2020; 314-315-9346
Web site: http://www.suddenlink.com
Officers:
Jerald L. Kent, Chairman & Chief Executive Officer
Thomas P McMillin, Executive Vice President & Chief Operating Officer
Mary E Meduski, Executive Vice President & Chief Financial Officer
Wendy Knudsen, Executive Vice President & Secretary
Jerry Dow, Chief Marketing & Sales Officer
Terry M Cordova, Senior Vice President & Chief Technology Officer
James Fox, Senior Vice President & Chief Accounting Officer
Robert L Putnam, Senior Vice President & Chief Information Officer
Peter M Abel, Senior Vice President, Corporate Communications
John E Fuhler, Senior Vice President, Fiscal Operations
Gibbs Jones, Senior Vice President, Customer Experience
Ralph G Kelly, Senior Vice President, Treasurer
Patricia L McCaskill, Senior Vice President, Programming
Mary R Meier, Senior Vice President, Marketing
Craig L Rosenthal, Senior Vice President, General Counsel
Kevin A Stephens, Senior Vice President, Commerical & Advertising Operations
Douglas G Wiley, Senior Vice President, Human Resources
Heather L Wood, Senior Vice President, Corporate Development
Phil Ahlschlager, Senior Vice President, Operations-North Carolina Region, Suddenlink
Dave Bach, Senior Vice President, Operations-Atlantic Region, Suddenlink
Todd Cruthird, Senior Vice President, Operations-Texoma Region, Suddenlink
Dave Gilles, Senior Vice President, Operations-West Region, Suddenlink
Randy Goad, Senior Vice President, Operations-Mid South Region, Suddenlink
Pat O'Connor, Senior Vice President, Operations-Central Region, Suddenlink
Ownership: Oaktree Capital Management, majority owner; Cequel III LLC, minority owner. Note: All systems managed by Cequel III LLC.
Cable Systems (272):
ARIZONA: BULLHEAD CITY; FLAGSTAFF; KINGMAN; LAKE HAVASU CITY; PARKER; PAYSON (town); PINE; SEDONA.
ARKANSAS: ARKADELPHIA; ATKINS; BATESVILLE; BOONEVILLE; CABOT; CHARLESTON; CLARKSVILLE; COAL HILL; DANVILLE; DE WITT; DOVER; EL DORADO; GURDON; HARRELL; HAZEN; HEBER SPRINGS; HECTOR; HELENA; HOT SPRINGS VILLAGE; HUGHES; JONESBORO; LONDON; MAGNOLIA; MALVERN; MARVELL; MORRILTON; MOUNT IDA; MOUNTAIN HOME; NASHVILLE; NEWPORT; OZARK; PARIS; POCAHONTAS; RUSSELLVILLE; STUTTGART; WALDRON; WALNUT RIDGE; WHITEHALL.
CALIFORNIA: BISHOP; BLYTHE; EUREKA; FORESTHILL; FORT ORD; JUNE LAKE; LAKE OF THE PINES; MAMMOTH LAKES; SHAVER LAKE; TRUCKEE.
IDAHO: OROFINO; OSBURN; ST. MARIES; TWIN LAKES.
ILLINOIS: ARGENTA; BETHANY; BLUE MOUND; MOWEAQUA.
INDIANA: JASONVILLE; ODON; ROCKVILLE.
KANSAS: ANTHONY; FORT SCOTT; PAOLA.

KENTUCKY: ADAIRVILLE; FRAKES; GRAYSON; GREASY CREEK; PIKEVILLE; PRESTONSBURG; RUSSELLVILLE.
LOUISIANA: BASTROP; BOSSIER CITY; BOYCE; DE RIDDER; FORT POLK; IOWA; JONESBORO; LAKE CHARLES; LECOMPTE; LEESVILLE; MANY; MINDEN; MOREAUVILLE; NATCHITOCHES; NEW IBERIA; PINEVILLE; RUSTON; SIBLEY; ST. JOSEPH; SULPHUR; VILLE PLATTE; WINNFIELD.
MISSISSIPPI: GREENVILLE; GREENWOOD.
MISSOURI: BOONVILLE; BRANSON; BROOKFIELD; CARTHAGE; CLEVER; COLE COUNTY (portions); FAYETTE; GLASGOW; LAMAR; LEXINGTON; MARYVILLE; MONETT; NEOSHO; NIXA; ST. JOSEPH; TRENTON.
NEVADA: VERDI.
NEW MEXICO: CLOVIS.
NORTH CAROLINA: ENFIELD; GREENVILLE; PARMELE; SCOTLAND NECK; SIMPSON; WASHINGTON.
OHIO: BLOOMINGDALE; KNOXVILLE; NELSON TWP.; SENECAVILLE.
OKLAHOMA: ALVA; ANADARKO; BLACKWELL; CHICKASHA; CRESCENT; CUSHING; DRUMRIGHT; ENID; FAIRVIEW; FORT SILL; GROVE; HEALDTON; HEAVENER; HUGO; IDABEL; LINDSAY; MUSKOGEE; OKMULGEE; PAULS VALLEY; PERRY; POTEAU; PURCELL; SALLISAW; SEMINOLE; SPIRO; STILLWATER; WEATHERFORD; WOODWARD.
PENNSYLVANIA: CAMP HILL CORRECTIONAL INSTITUTE; DALLAS CORRECTIONAL INSTITUTE; RETREAT CORRECTIONAL INSTITUTION.
TEXAS: ABILENE; ALBANY; AMARILLO; ANDREWS; ANSON; ATHENS; BIG LAKE; BIG SPRING; BRADY; BRAZORIA; BRECKENRIDGE; BRENHAM; BRYAN; BURKBURNETT; CALDWELL; CANADIAN; CENTER; CLARENDON; CLARKSVILLE; CONROE; CONROE WEST; CORRIGAN; CRANE; DAINGERFIELD; DIMMITT; EASTLAND; ELECTRA; FLOYDADA; GAINESVILLE; GATESVILLE; GEORGETOWN; GLADEWATER; GRAPELAND; HAMLIN; HAWKINS; HEARNE; HENDERSON; HENRIETTA; HONEY GROVE; HUDSON; HUNTSVILLE; INGRAM; JACKSONVILLE; JARRELL; JUNCTION; KERMIT; KINGWOOD; KRUM; LAKE LIVINGSTON; LAMPASAS; LEANDER; LIVINGSTON; LOST PINES; LOWRY CROSSING; LUBBOCK; LUCAS; MIDLAND; MINEOLA; MINERAL WELLS; MONAHANS; MONT BELVIEU; MOUNT PLEASANT; MOUNT VERNON; NACOGDOCHES; NAVASOTA; NOCONA; OKLAHOMA; OLNEY; PADUCAH (town); PARIS; PECOS; PFLUGERVILLE; PILOT POINT; PITTSBURG; PLAINVIEW; PORTER; POST; QUANAH; ROCKDALE; ROTAN; RUSK; SAN ANGELO; SAN SABA; SEYMOUR; SHAMROCK; SNYDER; SONORA; SULPHUR SPRINGS; SWEETWATER; TERRELL; TULIA; TYLER; VERNON; VICTORIA; WALDEN; WALLER; WELLINGTON; WHITESBORO; WINNSBORO.
VIRGINIA: REDWOOD.
WEST VIRGINIA: BECKLEY; BEVERLY; BUCKHANNON; CHARLESTON; FLEMINGTON; KERMIT; MADISON; MILTON; PARKERSBURG; SHINNSTON; SISSONVILLE; WAYNE.

CHAMBERS COMMUNICATIONS CORP.

2295 Coburg Rd., Suite 200
PO Box 7009
Eugene, OR 97401
Phone: 541-485-5611
Fax: 541-342-2695
E-mail: info@chamberscable.com
Web site: http://www.chamberscable.com
Ownership: Carolyn S Chambers Estate, see also Soda Mountain Broadcasting Inc..
Represented (legal): Arnold, Gallagher, Saydack, Percell, Roberts & Potter PC.

Cable Systems (1):
OREGON: SUNRIVER.
TV Stations:
Oregon: KOHD Bend; KEZI Eugene; KDKF Klamath Falls; KDRV Medford.
LPTV Stations:
Oregon: K11GT College Hill, etc.; K27CL-D Coos Bay; K07JS North Bend; K07IA Oakland; K04OS-D Reedsport; K53CU Roseburg; K06IO Scottsburg; K11BX-D Sutherlin; K07IL Winston.
Other Holdings:
Multimedia: Chambers Production Group, Chambers Multimedia Connection Inc.

CHARTER COMMUNICATIONS INC.

Charter Plz
12405-12444 Powerscourt Dr.
St. Louis, MO 63131
Phone: 314-965-0555
Fax: 315-965-9745
Web site: http://www.charter.com
Officers:
Eric L Zinterhofer, Chairman
Michael Lovett, President & Chief Executive Officer
Steven E Apodaca, President, Operations
James M Heneghan, President, Charter Media
Chris Bowick, Interim Chief Technology Officer
Don Detampel, Executive Vice President, Technology & President, Commercial Services
Robert E Quicksilver, Executive Vice President & Chief Administrative Officer
Christopher Winfrey, Executive Vice President & Chief Financial Officer
John Birrer, Senior Vice President, Customer Experience
Rich DiGeronimo, Senior Vice President, Product & Strategy
Rick Dykhouse, Senior Vice President, General Counsel & Corporate Secretary
Kevin D Howard, Senior Vice President, Controller & Interim Chief Financial Officer
Jim McGann, Senior Vice President
Don Poulter, Senior Vice President, Commercial Operations
Lynne F. Ramsey, Senior Vice President, Human Resources
Jay A Rolls, Senior Vice President & Chief Technology Officer
Allan Sampson, Senior Vice President, Marketing
Allan Singer, Senior Vice President, Programming
Joseph R Stackhouse, Senior Vice President, Customer Operations

Branch Offices:

Charter Southern Wisconsin
2701 Daniels St.
Madison, WI 53718
Phone: 608-274-3822

Charter Tennessee
1774 Henry G. Lane St.
Maryville, TN 37801
Phone: 865- 273-2701

Charter New England
95 Higgins St.
Worchester, MA 01606
Phone: 508-853-1515

Charter Alabama
2100 Columbiana Rd.
Vestavia Hills, AL 35216
Phone: 205-824-5400

Charter Minnesota & Nebraska
3380 Northern Valley Place NE
Rochester, MN 55906

Charter South Carolina
2 Digital Place
4th Floor
Simpsonville, SC 29681
Phone: 800-955-7766

Charter Georgia
1925 Breckinridge Plaza
Suite 100
Duluth, GA 30096
Phone: 770-806-7060

Charter Los Angeles Metro
4781 Irwindale Ave.
Irwindale, CA 91706

Charter Central States
941 Charter Commons Dr.
St. Louis, MO 63017
Phone: 636-207-7044

Charter Northwest
521 NE 136th Ave.
Vancouver, WA 98684

Charter Nevada
9335 Prototype Way
Reno, NV 89521
Phone: 775-850-1200

Charter North Michigan
701 S. Airport Rd.
Traverse City, MI 49686
Phone: 231-947-5221

Charter East Michigan
7372 Davison Rd.
Davison, MI 48423
Phone: 810-652-1402

Charter West Michigan
1433 Fulton St.
Grand Haven, MI 49417
Phone: 616-647-6201

Charter Central California
270 Bridge St.
San Luis Obispo, CA 93401
Phone: 805-544-1962

Charter Louisiana
1304 Ridgefield Rd.
Thibodaux, LA 70301
Phone: 985-446-4941

Charter Fort Worth
4800 Blue Mound Rd.
Forth Worth, TX 76106
Phone: 817-509-6272

Charter Inland Empire
7337 Central Ave.
Riverside, CA 92504
Phone: 951-343-5100

Charter North Wisconsin
165 Knights Way
Fon du Lac, WI 54935
Phone: 920-907-7751

Ownership: Paul Allen, 2%. equity; 3% voting.
Cable Systems (447):
ALABAMA: ALBERTVILLE; ATHENS; BEULAH; BRIDGEPORT; CURRY; DECATUR; FAIRFIELD; GUNTERSVILLE; GURLEY; JASPER; LEEDS; MENTONE; MONTGOMERY; MOULTON; PIEDMONT; RUSSELLVILLE; SELMA; SHELBY LAKE; SOUTHSIDE; WESTOVER.
CALIFORNIA: ALHAMBRA; ALTURAS; ARCADIA; AZUSA; BIG BEAR LAKE; BORON; BOX CANYON; CALIFORNIA CITY; CALIFORNIA HOT SPRINGS; CERRITOS; CRESCENT CITY; FOREST FALLS; GILROY; GLENDALE; GREENFIELD; HESPERIA; JACK RANCH/POSEY; KING CITY; LAKE ARROWHEAD; LONG BEACH; LOS ALAMOS; MALIBU; MEYERS; MOJAVE; NORTH EDWARDS; NORTHSTAR; PHELAN; PORTERVILLE; RED BLUFF; REDDING; RIVERSIDE; SAN BERNARDINO; SAN LUIS OBISPO; SOLEDAD; SOUTH LAKE TAHOE; THOUSAND OAKS; TURLOCK; VENTURA; WATSONVILLE; WHITTIER.
CONNECTICUT: ASHFORD; NEWTOWN (borough); WINSTED.
GEORGIA: ATHENS; CARROLLTON; CEDARTOWN; CHATSWORTH; COLUMBUS; COVINGTON; DALTON; DOUGLAS; DUBLIN; DULUTH; GAINESVILLE; LAGRANGE; MANCHESTER; MILLEDGEVILLE; NEWNAN; PINE MOUNTAIN; RINGGOLD; ROCKMART; ROSWELL; SMYRNA; STOCKBRIDGE; SUMMERVILLE; THOMASTON; TRENTON; VILLA RICA; WAVERLY HALL; WEST POINT.
ILLINOIS: BELLEVILLE; BREESE; CAHOKIA; CARLYLE; EAST ST. LOUIS; FARMERSVILLE; GILLESPIE; HARVARD; MARYVILLE; NOKOMIS; OKAWVILLE; PANA; RAYMOND; ROXANA; SALEM; SCOTT AFB; SHELBYVILLE; VIRDEN; WATERLOO; WOODLAWN.
LOUISIANA: BOGALUSA; BOURG; BUNKIE; HAMMOND; MARKSVILLE; PINE PRAIRIE; SLIDELL; ST. LANDRY PARISH; THIBODAUX.
MARYLAND: CRISFIELD.
MASSACHUSETTS: BELCHERTOWN; CHARLTON; CHICOPEE; HINSDALE; LANESBORO; PEPPERELL; RUTLAND (town); UXBRIDGE; WALES; WEST STOCKBRIDGE; WESTPORT; WORCESTER.
MICHIGAN: ALLEGAN; ALLENDALE; ALMA; ALMONT; ALPENA; ARNOLD LAKE; AU GRES; BALDWIN (village); BAY CITY; BERLIN TWP. (St. Clair County); BIG PRAIRIE TWP.; BIG RAPIDS; BIG STAR LAKE; BILLINGS; BROOMFIELD VALLEY TRAILER PARK; BUTMAN TWP.; CADILLAC; CANADIAN LAKES; CHEBOYGAN; CHESANING; CHESTER TWP. (Ottawa County); CHIPPEWA TWP. (Isabella County); COLDWATER; COLEMAN; CUSTER; DAVISON; DELTON; DURAND; ELSIE; ESCANABA; EVART; FENTON; FRASER TWP.; FREDERIC TWP.; GRAND LAKE; GRANT; GRAYLING; GREENVILLE; HALE; HAMLIN TWP. (Mason County); HART; HESPERIA; HIGGINS LAKE; HIGHLAND PARK; HOPE TWP. (Midland County); HOUGHTON; HOUGHTON LAKE; HOWARD CITY; INDIAN RIVER; IONIA; IRON MOUNTAIN; IRONWOOD; KALAMAZOO; KINCHELOE; LAKE GEORGE; LAKEVIEW; LAPEER; LEVERING; LILLEY TWP.; LIVINGSTON COUNTY; LUDINGTON; MACKINAC ISLAND; MACKINAW CITY; MARQUETTE; MECOSTA; MIDDLEVILLE/CALEDONIA; MIDLAND; MIO; MONROE; MONTROSE; MOUNT PLEASANT; NEWBERRY; NORTH BRANCH TWP.; OMER; OSCODA; OWOSSO; OXFORD; PELLSTON; PENTWATER; REED CITY; REMUS; RIVERDALE; ROCKFORD; ROGERS CITY; ROSCOMMON; ROSE CITY; RUTLAND TWP.; SAGE TWP.; SAGINAW; SAULT STE. MARIE; SKIDWAY LAKE; ST. HELEN; ST. JOHNS; THETFORD TWP.; TRAVERSE CITY; VASSAR; WEIDMAN; WHITE CLOUD; WHITEHALL; WHITTEMORE.
MINNESOTA: ALBANY; ALBERT LEA; ALEXANDRIA; AUSTIN; BRAINERD; BUFFALO; COTTONWOOD; DULUTH; FARIBAULT; FERGUS FALLS; GLENWOOD; LITTLE FALLS; MANKATO; MARSHALL; MELROSE; MONTEVIDEO; OWATONNA; PARK RAPIDS; PEQUOT LAKES; RED WING; ROCHESTER; ROSEMOUNT; SAUK CENTRE; ST. CLOUD; TRACY; WADENA; WILLMAR; WINONA.
MISSISSIPPI: PICAYUNE.
MISSOURI: BARNHART; CAPE GIRARDEAU; CLINTON; COLUMBIA; FARMINGTON; FERGUSON; FULTON; IMPERIAL; LAKE ST. LOUIS; NEW MADRID; OLIVETTE; OSAGE BEACH; OVERLAND; PERRYVILLE; ST. CHARLES; ST. LOUIS; STE. GENEVIEVE; SULLIVAN; WARRENSBURG; WARRENTON.
MONTANA: SUN PRAIRIE.
NEBRASKA: ALLIANCE; BEATRICE; GRAND ISLAND; HASTINGS; JUNIATA; KEARNEY; KENESAW; KIMBALL; NORTH PLATTE; OGALLALA; SCOTTSBLUFF; SIDNEY; SPRINGFIELD.
NEVADA: CARSON CITY; CRYSTAL BAY; FALLON; FERNLEY; GARDNERVILLE; HAWTHORNE; RENO; SILVER SPRINGS.
NEW YORK: BERLIN (town); CHATHAM; PLATTSBURGH.
NORTH CAROLINA: ASHEVILLE; BOONE; BUIES CREEK; BURNSVILLE; GATES COUNTY; HICKORY; HOLLY RIDGE; KENLY; MANTEO; MARION; NORTH WILKESBORO; ROANOKE RAPIDS; ROXBORO; TROY; WAYNESVILLE.
OREGON: ASTORIA; BROOKINGS; BURNS; COOS BAY; COTTAGE GROVE; DALLAS; FLORENCE; GOLD BEACH; GRANTS PASS; KLAMATH FALLS; LA GRANDE; LAKEVIEW;

LINCOLN CITY; MEDFORD; PENDLETON; ROSEBURG; THE DALLES.
SOUTH CAROLINA: ANCHOR POINT; HARTWELL VILLAS; SPARTANBURG; WHITMIRE.
TENNESSEE: ALCOA; CENTERVILLE; CLARKSVILLE; CLEVELAND; CLIFTON; COLUMBIA; COOKEVILLE; CROSSVILLE; FAYETTEVILLE; FLINTVILLE; GATLINBURG; JACKSON; JASPER; KINGSPORT; LAWRENCEBURG; LEBANON; LEWISBURG; LEXINGTON; LORETTO; LOUDON; MADISONVILLE; MARTIN; MCEWEN; MCKENZIE; MONTEAGLE; MORRISTOWN; MOUNTAIN CITY; NEWBERN; PARIS; ROGERSVILLE (portions); SAVANNAH; SELMER; STONEY CREEK; TEN MILE; TULLAHOMA; WAYNESBORO.
TEXAS: CARROLLTON; CLEBURNE; DENTON; DUNCANVILLE; ENNIS; FORT WORTH (northern portions); GRANBURY; ROCKWALL; SPRING; UNIVERSITY PARK; WAXAHACHIE; WEATHERFORD.
VERMONT: DANVILLE (town).
VIRGINIA: ACCOMAC; CHINCOTEAGUE ISLAND; SUFFOLK; TANGIER ISLAND.
WASHINGTON: COLVILLE; ELLENSBURG; GRAND COULEE; KENNEWICK; WALLA WALLA; WENATCHEE; WEST RICHLAND; YAKIMA.
WISCONSIN: ADAMS; ANTIGO; ASHLAND; BEAR CREEK; CLINTONVILLE; DELAVAN; DRESSER; EAGLE RIVER; EAU CLAIRE; FOND DU LAC; FOUNTAIN CITY; GENOA CITY; HAYWARD; HUSTISFORD; JANESVILLE; LADYSMITH; LAKE NEBAGAMON; LANCASTER; MADISON; MARSHFIELD; MAZOMANIE; MEDFORD; MENOMONIE; MERRILL; MINOCQUA; MONTELLO; OCONTO; ONALASKA; PARK FALLS; RHINELANDER; RICE LAKE; RUDOLPH; SHEBOYGAN; SISTER BAY; SPENCER; SPOONER; STETSONVILLE; STEVENS POINT; STURGEON BAY; TWO RIVERS; WAUSAU; WAUTOMA; WEST BEND; WISCONSIN RAPIDS.

CHEROKEE CABLEVISION INC.
PO Box 487
Cherokee, NC 28719
Phone: 828-497-4861
Fax: 828-497-4983
Ownership: Ken Blankenship, Pres..
Cable Systems (1):
NORTH CAROLINA: CHEROKEE INDIAN RESERVATION.

CHIBARDUN CABLE TV CORPORATION
401 S 1st St
PO Box 664
Cameron, WI 54822
Phones: 715-458-5400; 800-924-3405
Fax: 715-458-2112
E-mail: chitel@mosaictelecom.net
Web site: http://www.mosaictelecom.com
Officers:
Rick S. Vergin, Chief Executive Officer
Scott J. Hickok, Vice President, Programming & Chief Operating Officer
Cable Systems (1):
WISCONSIN: DALLAS.

CHINOOK PROGRESSIVE CLUB TV INC.
PO Box 15
Chinook, WA 98614
Phone: 360-777-8412
Fax: 360-777-8255
Officers:
Terry Krager, President
Dale Hughes, Chief Executive Officer
Trophy W. Hughes, Chief Operating Officer
Rhoda Hughes, Secretary-Treasurer
Ownership: Subscriber owned--Chinook, WA.
Cable Systems (1):
WASHINGTON: CHINOOK.

CHRISTIAN ENTERPRISES
PO Box 300
Pioche, NV 89043
Phones: 775-962-5200; 775-962-5111
Officers:
John Christian, President
Paul Christian, Vice President
Cable Systems (2):
NEVADA: ALAMO; PANACA.

CIM TEL CABLE INC.
103-D Cimarron St
PO Box 266
Mannford, OK 74044
Phones: 918-865-3314; 800-722-2651
Fax: 918-865-3187
E-mail: staff@cimtel.net
Web site: http://www.cimtel.net
Officers:
V. David Miller II, President
H. Gene Baldwin, Chief Executive Officer
Dan Overland, Chief Financial Officer
Ownership: Cimarron Telephone; CT ownership: MBO Corp.
Cable Systems (1):
OKLAHOMA: MANNFORD.

CITIZENS CABLE TV
134 N. Bailey Ave.
PO Box 465
Leslie, GA 31764
Phones: 229-853-1600; 229-268-2288
Fax: 229-877-2211
Web site: http://www.citizenscatv.com
Cable Systems (4):
GEORGIA: LAKE BLACKSHEAR; SMITHVILLE; WARWICK; WILEY ACRES.

CITIZENS CABLEVISION INC.
26 S Main St
PO Box 217
Hammond, NY 13646
Phones: 315-324-6000; 315-324-5911
Fax: 315-324-6289
E-mail: citizens@cit-tele.com
Web site: http://www.cit-tele.com
Officer:
Don Ceresoli Jr., President
Ownership: Citizens Telephone Co..
Cable Systems (1):
NEW YORK: ALEXANDRIA BAY.

CITIZENS CABLEVISION INC. (VA)
220 Webbs Mill Rd
PO Box 196
Floyd, VA 24091-0137
Phones: 540-745-6711; 800-941-0426
Fax: 540-745-3791
E-mail: cable@citizens.coop
Web site: http://www.citizens.coop
Officers:
Greg Sapp, Manager
Lori Worrell, Sales & Marketing Manager
Ownership: Citizens Telephone Cooperative Inc..
Cable Systems (3):
VIRGINIA: FLOYD; FORT CHISWELL; NEW CASTLE (town).
Other Holdings:
Telephone.

CITIZENS TELEPHONE CO. (MISSOURI)
1905 Walnut St
PO Box 737
Higginsville, MO 64037
Phone: 800-321-4282
E-mail: customerservice@ctcis.net
Web site: http://www.ctcis.net
Officer:
Brian Cornelius, President
Ownership: Employee owned..
Cable Systems (1):
MISSOURI: ALMA.

CITIZENS TELEPHONE CORP.
426 N. Wayne St.
PO Box 330
Warren, IN 46792
Phone: 260-375-2115
Fax: 260-375-2244
E-mail: info@citznet.com
Web site: http://www.citznet.com/
Officers:
Gordon L. Laymon, President & Chief Executive Officer
Neil Laymon, Secretary-Treasurer
Ellen Laymon, Chief Financial Officer
Cable Systems (1):
INDIANA: WARREN.

CLARENDON TV ASSOCIATION
PO Box 315
Clarendon, PA 16313
Phone: 814-726-3972
Officer:
Marlene Kay, Secretary-Treasurer
Ownership: Subscriber owned--Clarendon, PA.
Cable Systems (1):
PENNSYLVANIA: CLARENDON.

CLEAR CREEK TELEPHONE & TELEVISION
18238 South Fischers Mill Rd
Oregon City, OR 97045
Phone: 503-631-2101
Fax: 503-631-2098
E-mail: info@clearcreek.coop
Web site: http://www.ccmtc.com
Officer:
Mitchell Moore, President
Cable Systems (1):
OREGON: OREGON CITY (unincorporated areas).

CLEARVIEW CABLE INC.
PO Box 7
28795 Commerce St
Gantt, AL 36038
Phone: 334-388-2716
Fax: 334-388-2718
E-mail: support@andycable.com
Web site: http://www.andycable.com
Officer:
Mike Russell, Owner & Manager
Ownership: Ivan Bishop; J. Mike Russell. Ivan Bishop is executive with TV Cable Co. of Andalusia, see listing.
Cable Systems (5):
ALABAMA: BEATRICE; CASTLEBERRY; CHANCELLOR; HEATH; McKENZIE.

CLEARVIEW CABLE TV INC.
Rte 4
Lewisburg, WV 24901
Phone: 304-445-7575
Ownership: Chip James; Shawn James.
Cable Systems (2):
VIRGINIA: CALLAGHAN.
WEST VIRGINIA: FRANKFORD.

CLEARVISION CABLE SYSTEMS INC.
1785 Rte. 40
Greenup, IL 62428
Phone: 217-923-5594
Fax: 217-923-5681
Cable Systems (15):
ILLINOIS: BEECHER CITY; BROCTON; COWDEN; EDGEWOOD; EFFINGHAM COUNTY; GRANTFORK (village); HUME (village); KINMUNDY; MONTROSE; MULBERRY GROVE; PATOKA; PIERRON; POCAHONTAS; SIDELL (village); ST. PETER.

CLIMAX TELEPHONE CO.
13800 E Michigan Ave
Galesburg, MI 49053
Phones: 269-746-4411; 800-627-5287
Fax: 269-746-9914
E-mail: info@ctstelecom.com
Web site: http://www.ctstelecom.com
Officers:
Jim Burnham, President & Chief Executive Officer
Bob Stewart, Vice President
Ownership: CTS Communications Corp..
Cable Systems (1):
MICHIGAN: CLIMAX TWP..

CLINTON CABLE INC.
PO Box 900
Clinton, AR 72031
Phone: 501-745-4040
Fax: 501-745-4663
E-mail: clintoncable@clintoncable.net
Web site: http://www.clintoncable.net
Officer:
John Hastings, Owner
Ownership: John Hastings.
Cable Systems (1):
ARKANSAS: CLINTON.

CND ACQUISITION CO. LLC
PO Box 880
Rossville, GA 30741
Phone: 706-866-0901
Fax: 706-866-0902
Ownership: William J Cooke; David P Daniel, jointly.
Cable Systems (1):
NORTH CAROLINA: MURPHY.

COAXIAL CABLE TV CORP.
105 Walker Dr
Edinboro, PA 16412
Phone: 814-734-1424
Fax: 814-734-8898
E-mail: info@coaxpa.com
Web site: http://www.coaxialcabletv.com
Officers:
Michael Mead, President
Edward M. Mead, Executive Vice President
Ownership: Mead Newspapers. Mead Newspapers owns Erie (PA) News, Times & Times News; Warren (PA) Times-Observer.
Represented (legal): The McDonald Group LLP.
Cable Systems (1):
PENNSYLVANIA: EDINBORO.

COAXIAL PROPERTIES INC.
Suite 805
4564 Telephone Rd
Ventura, CA 93003

Phone: 805-658-1579
E-mail: commserv@cablerocket.com
Web site: http://www.commservcable.com
Officer:
Phil Shockley, President
Cable Systems (1):
CALIFORNIA: POINT MUGU NAVAL AIR STATION.

COBRIDGE COMMUNICATIONS LLC

Ste 200
9450 Manchester Rd
Saint Louis, MO 63119
Phones: 314-227-9500; 800-438-2427
Fax: 312-372-3939
Web site: http://www.cobridge.net
Officers:
Mark Barber, Chief Operating Officer
Linda Kondrick, Chief Accounting Officer
Bruce Herman, Chief Financial Officer
Chad Rycenga, Chief Information Officer
Larry Schutz, Vice President, Technology

Branch Office:
Chicago Office
307 N Michigan Ave
Ste 1020
Chicago, IL 60601
Phone: 636-778-0646
Fax: 312-372-3939
Ownership:Cobridge is affiliated with The Gores Group, a Los Angeles-based private equity firm.
Cable Systems (35):
ALABAMA: BAILEYTON; CLANTON; COLUMBIANA; DOUBLE SPRINGS; ELGIN; HALEYVILLE; HEFLIN; HENAGAR; LAY LAKE; LEIGHTON; RAINSVILLE; THORSBY; TROY.
ARKANSAS: BEEBE; HARDY; MAUMELLE; McALMONT; SHANNON HILLS; VILONIA; WEST PULASKI.
GEORGIA: FORT GORDON; LAKE PARK.
LOUISIANA: POINTE COUPEE.
MISSOURI: EL DORADO SPRINGS; HARRISONVILLE; NEVADA; THAYER; WEST PLAINS.
TEXAS: ATLANTA; CARTHAGE; COLORADO CITY; LEVELLAND; MARSHALL; ROCKPORT; SLATON.

COLANE CABLE TV INC.

PO Box 610
Omar, WV 25638
Phone: 304-946-2871
E-mail: garyg.bowen@lightlynx.net
Ownership: William Stark.
Cable Systems (12):
WEST VIRGINIA: BEECH CREEK; BRUNO; CRAWLEY CREEK ROAD; HANOVER; HEWETT; LYBURN; MUD RIVER; OMAR; SARAH ANN; SIX MILE; TURTLE CREEK; VAN.

COLDWATER BOARD OF PUBLIC UTILITIES

1 Grand St
Coldwater, MI 49036
Phone: 517-279-9531
Fax: 517-278-2947
E-mail: jroyer@coldwater.org
Web site: http://www.coldwater.org/Content/documents/DigitalFlyer1-11.pdf
Officer:
David Sattler, Public Works
Cable Systems (1):
MICHIGAN: COLDWATER.

COLFAX HIGHLINE CABLE CO.

N. 301 Mill St.
Colfax, WA 99111
Phone: 509-397-2211
Fax: 509-397-2274
Ownership: St. John Cable Co. Inc., see listing, 50%; Ken Julian, 50%.
Cable Systems (1):
WASHINGTON: COLFAX.

CITY OF COLLINS

PO Box 400
City Hall
Collins, MS 39428
Phone: 601-765-4491
Fax: 601-765-0050
Web site: http://www.cityofcollins.com
Officers:
V. O. Smith, Mayor & Manager
April Kirkley, Cable Clerk
Ownership: Municipally owned--Collins, MS.
Cable Systems (1):
MISSISSIPPI: COLLINS.

COLLINSVILLE TV CABLE

332 Davis St.
Collinsville, AL 35961
Phone: 256-524-2267
Web site: http://www.collinsvillealabama.net/tv.htm
Ownership: Mary Ann Pendergrass, Principal.
Cable Systems (1):
ALABAMA: COLLINSVILLE.

COLTONTEL

PO Box 68
20983 S Hwy 211
Colton, OR 97017
Phone: 503-824-3211
Fax: 503-824-9944
Web site: http://www.coltontel.com/
Cable Systems (1):
OREGON: COLTON.

COLUMBIA POWER & WATER SYSTEMS

PO Box 379
201 Pickens Ln
Columbia, TN 38402-0379
Phone: 931-388-4833
Fax: 931-388-5287
E-mail: support@cpws.com
Web site: http://www.cpws.com
Cable Systems (1):
TENNESSEE: COLUMBIA.

COMCAST CABLE COMMUNICATIONS INC.

1701 JFK Blvd
Philadelphia, PA 19102
Phones: 215-286-1700; 215-981-7613
Fax: 215-981-8548
Web site: http://www.comcast.com
Officers:
Brian L. Roberts, Chairman & Chief Executive Officer, Comcast Corp.
Ralph J. Roberts, Chairman, Executive & Finance Committee, Comcast Corp.
Kyle McSlarrow, President, Comcast/NBCUniversal, Washington, DC
Neil Smit, President
Michael J. Angelakis, Chief Financial Officer, Comcast Corp.
Stephen B Burke, Executive Vice President
Kenneth Carrig, Executive Vice President, Human Resources
David L. Cohen, Executive Vice President, Comcast Corp.
Susan Adams, Senior Vice President, Engineering & Operations
Catherine Avgiris, Senior Vice President & General Manager, Communications & Data Services
C. Stephen Backstrom, Senior Vice President, Taxation
Amy L. Banse, Senior Vice President, Comcast Corp. & President, Comcast Interactive Media
Mark A. Coblitz, Senior Vice President, Strategic Planning, Comcast Corp.
Kristine Dankenbrink, Senior Vice President, Taxation
Mike DeCandido, Senior Vice President, Call Center Operations
Marlene S. Dooner, Senior Vice President, Investor Relations, Comcast Corp.
William E Dordelman, Senior Vice President & Treasurer
Doug Guthrie, Senior Vice President, Houston Region
Cynthia Hook, Senior Vice President & General Auditor, Comcast Corp.
Aljit Joy, Senior Vice President, Strategy & Communications Product Development
Grace Killelea, Senior Vice President, Talent
Melissa Maxfield, Senior Vice President, Congressional & Federal Government Affairs
Mary McLaughlin, Senior Vice President, Western New England
Robert S. Pick, Senior Vice President, Corporate Development, Comcast Corp.
Ron Phillips, Senior Vice President, Employee Engagement
D'Arcy F. Rudnay, Senior Vice President, Corporate Communciations, Comcast Corp.
Lawrence J. Salva, Senior Vice President, Chief Accounting Officer & Controller, Comcast Corp.
Robert S Victor, Senior Vice President, Strategic & Financial Planning
Tina Waters, Senior Vice President, Human Performance
Kathy Zachem, Senior Vice President, Regulatory & State Legislative Affairs
Ownership: Comcast Corp.. Comcast Corp. has interest in wired telecommunications including telephone services; wireless telecommunications including cellular, personal communications services and direct-to-home satellite television.; Publicly held. On December 3, 2009, it was announced that Comcast Corp. & GE would form a joint venture including the assets of NBC Universal & Comcast's cable networks. Comcast will have 51% interest, GE 49% interest. The FCC approved the deal January 18, 2011.
Represented (legal): LeBoeuf, Lamb, Greene & MacRae LLP; Dow Lohnes PLLC.
Cable Systems (676):
ALABAMA: ABBEVILLE; ATTALLA; CLAYTON (town); DAUPHIN ISLAND; DOTHAN; FLORENCE; GADSDEN; HUNTSVILLE; MOBILE; TUSCALOOSA.
ARIZONA: PIMA COUNTY.
ARKANSAS: EARLE; LITTLE ROCK.
CALIFORNIA: CHICO; CHOWCHILLA; COALINGA; CONCORD; FRANCISCAN MOBILE HOME PARK; FRESNO; GRASS VALLEY; HURON; LE GRAND; LODI; MERCED; MODESTO & OAKDALE; MONTEREY; NAPA/SONOMA; NEWMAN; OAKLAND; PLACERVILLE; PLANADA; RIVERDALE; SACRAMENTO; SAN ANDREAS; SAN FRANCISCO; SAN JOSE; SANTA CRUZ; SANTA MARIA; STOCKTON; TRACY; TWAIN HARTE; UKIAH; WILLIAMS; YUBA CITY.
COLORADO: ASPEN; AVON; COLORADO SPRINGS; CONIFER; CRIPPLE CREEK; DENVER; DENVER (suburbs); EATON; FORT COLLINS; GILCREST; GRANBY; GREELEY; JOHNSTOWN; KREMMLING; LAKEWOOD; LONGMONT; PARACHUTE; PUEBLO; RIFLE; SILVERTHORNE; STEAMBOAT SPRINGS; TABLE MOUNTAIN; TRINIDAD; WOODLAND PARK.
CONNECTICUT: BRANFORD; CLINTON; DANBURY; GROTON; HARTFORD; LAKEVILLE; MIDDLETOWN; NEW HAVEN; NORWICH; OLD LYME; PLAINVILLE (town); SEYMOUR; VERNON; WATERBURY.
DELAWARE: DOVER; REHOBOTH BEACH; WILMINGTON.
DISTRICT OF COLUMBIA: WASHINGTON.
FLORIDA: ARCADIA; ARCHER; BARTOW; BELLE GLADE; BIG CYPRESS SEMINOLE INDIAN RESERVATION; BOWLING GREEN; BRANDON (northern portion); BRIGHTON SEMINOLE RESERVE; BROWARD COUNTY (portions); CELEBRATION; CRESCENT CITY; DEBARY; DELRAY BEACH; ENGLEWOOD; HASTINGS; HILLIARD; IMMOKALEE SEMINOLE INDIAN RESERVATION; INVERNESS; JACKSONVILLE; JASPER; JENNINGS; KEY WEST; LAKE BUTLER; LAKE CITY; LAKE WALES; LEESBURG; MACCLENNY; MADISON; MARIANNA; MAYO; MIAMI; MIMS; MONTICELLO; MOORE HAVEN; NAPLES; OKEECHOBEE; ORANGE COUNTY (unincorporated areas); ORTONA; OSCEOLA COUNTY (eastern portion); OSCEOLA COUNTY (western portion); PALATKA; PALM BAY; PALM BEACH GARDENS; PANAMA CITY; PERRY; PORT CHARLOTTE; SARASOTA; SEBRING; SILVER SPRINGS SHORES; SPRING LAKE; ST. AUGUSTINE; STUART; TALLAHASSEE; TRENTON; VENICE; VERO BEACH; WALDO; WAUCHULA; WELAKA (town); WEST PALM BEACH; WILLISTON; YULEE.
GEORGIA: ADRIAN; ATLANTA (metro area); ATLANTA (northern portion); ATLANTA (perimeter north); ATLANTA (perimeter south); AUGUSTA; BRUNSWICK; CLAXTON; COLONELS ISLAND; DARIEN; ELBERTON; EULONIA; FAIRBURN; FOLKSTON; GLENNVILLE; GUYTON; HINESVILLE; HOMERVILLE; JEKYLL ISLAND; LA FAYETTE; LINCOLNTON; LOUISVILLE; METTER; MILLEN; MONTEZUMA; MOUNT VERNON; NAHUNTA; PEMBROKE; QUITMAN; ROSSVILLE; SAVANNAH; SOPERTON; ST. MARY'S; SYLVANIA; TALLAPOOSA; TWIN CITY; TYBEE ISLAND; WARRENTON; WASHINGTON; WAYNESVILLE; WOODBINE; WRIGHTSVILLE.
ILLINOIS: AMBOY; BLOOMINGTON; CANTON; CHICAGO; CHICAGO (southern suburbs); DIXON; DU QUOIN; FRANKLIN GROVE; FREEPORT; GALESBURG; KEWANEE; LADD; MACOMB; MONMOUTH; NEWMAN; OAK BROOK; OLNEY; ONARGA; PEKIN; PEORIA; PERU; PIPER CITY; PRINCETON; QUINCY; ROCKFORD; SCHAUMBURG; SPRINGFIELD; STERLING; URBANA.
INDIANA: ANDERSON; ATTICA; AVILLA; BATESVILLE; BEDFORD; BLOOMINGTON; BROOKVILLE (town); BROWNSTOWN; COLUMBUS; CONNERSVILLE; COVINGTON; CRAWFORDSVILLE; FLORA; FORT WAYNE; FRANKFORT; GREENCASTLE; GREENSBURG; GREENWOOD; HARTFORD CITY; HUNTINGTON; INDIANAPOLIS; KOKOMO; LA PORTE; LAFAYETTE; LAWRENCEBURG; LIBERTY (town); LINTON; LOGANSPORT; MARTINSVILLE; MICHIGAN CITY; MONROEVILLE (town); MONROVIA; MONTICELLO; MUNCIE; NOBLESVILLE; PERU; PORTLAND; RICHMOND; RUSHVILLE; SEYMOUR; SHELBYVILLE; SOUTH BEND; TELL CITY; THORNTOWN; VEEDERSBURG; WABASH; WINCHESTER.
KANSAS: OLATHE.
KENTUCKY: ELIZABETHTOWN; FORT CAMPBELL; GREENVILLE; HORSE CAVE; LEITCHFIELD; PADUCAH; WHITESBURG.
LOUISIANA: HOSSTON; HOUMA; LA PLACE; SHREVEPORT; WEST MONROE.
MAINE: BRUNSWICK (town).
MARYLAND: ANNE ARUNDEL COUNTY (portions); BALTIMORE; BALTIMORE COUNTY; CAMBRIDGE; CECILTON; CHARLES COUNTY; DEEP CREEK LAKE; ELKTON; FREDERICK; GRANTSVILLE; HANCOCK; HARFORD COUNTY; HOWARD COUNTY (portions); MONTGOMERY COUNTY (portions); OCEAN CITY; PRINCE FREDERICK; PRINCE GEORGE'S COUNTY (portions); SALISBURY; WESTMINSTER.
MASSACHUSETTS: BOSTON; SPRINGFIELD;

TAUNTON; WESTFORD.
MICHIGAN: ADDISON (village); ANN ARBOR; BATTLE CREEK; BENTON HARBOR; BROWN CITY; CAPAC; CASSOPOLIS; CHESTERFIELD TWP.; DECKERVILLE; DETROIT; EAST LANSING; FLINT; GRAND RAPIDS; HARTLAND; HILLSDALE; HOLLAND; HUDSON; JACKSON; LANSING; LAWTON; LEXINGTON; LOWELL; MUSKEGON; NILES; OSHTEMO TWP.; PIGEON; PLYMOUTH TWP.; PONTIAC; RICHLAND; ROYAL OAK; SANDUSKY; SAUGATUCK; SOUTH HAVEN; SOUTHFIELD; ST. JOSEPH TWP.; STERLING HEIGHTS; TAYLOR; THREE RIVERS; WALDRON VILLAGE; WALLED LAKE; WATERVLIET; WEST BLOOMFIELD TWP.; YALE.
MINNESOTA: BROWNS VALLEY; HALLOCK; MINNEAPOLIS; OSLO; PLAINVIEW; ROUND LAKE; SABIN; ST. PAUL; WABASHA.
MISSISSIPPI: BENTONIA; CANTON; HATTIESBURG; JACKSON; LAUREL; MERIDIAN; PAULDING; PEARL; PUCKETT; TUPELO.
MISSOURI: EDINA; HANNIBAL; INDEPENDENCE; JONESBURG; LOUISIANA; MADISON; MEXICO; MOBERLY; PERRY; WINFIELD.
MONTANA: BROADUS.
NEBRASKA: CODY.
NEW HAMPSHIRE: MANCHESTER.
NEW JERSEY: AVALON; BURLINGTON COUNTY; CARLSTADT BOROUGH; EAST WINDSOR; GLOUCESTER COUNTY; HILLSBOROUGH; JERSEY CITY; LAMBERTVILLE; LONG BEACH TWP.; LONG HILL TWP.; MAPLE SHADE; MONMOUTH COUNTY; OCEAN COUNTY; PLAINFIELD; PORT MURRAY; PRINCETON; TOMS RIVER; TRENTON; UNION; VINELAND; VOORHEES; WILDWOOD.
NEW MEXICO: ALBUQUERQUE; ANGEL FIRE; CARLSBAD; CHAMA; CIMARRON; DEMING; DIXON; ESPANOLA; FARMINGTON; GALLUP; GRANTS; HATCH; HOBBS; JAL; LAS CRUCES; LAS VEGAS; LOS ALAMOS; LOS LUNAS; LOVINGTON; PECOS; PENASCO; POJOAQUE; PORTALES; QUESTA; RATON; RED RIVER; SANTA CLARA INDIAN RESERVATION; SANTA FE; SILVER CITY; SOCORRO; SPRINGER; TAOS; THOREAU; TUCUMCARI.
NEW YORK: CARMEL.
NORTH DAKOTA: ARVILLA; BEACH; BEULAH; BOWMAN; CARRINGTON; CASSELTON; COOPERSTOWN; DEVILS LAKE; ESMOND; FOREST RIVER; GACKLE; GRAFTON; GRAND FORKS; HANKINSON; HARVEY; LA MOURE; LANGDON; LARIMORE; LEEDS; MANDAN; MANVEL; MCCLUSKY; MINNEWAUKAN; MINOT; MINTO; MOTT; ROLETTE; RUGBY; SOUTH HEART; WAHPETON; WILLISTON; WISHEK.
OHIO: CONVOY; EAST LIVERPOOL; FORT RECOVERY (village); NEW MIDDLETOWN; PAYNE.
OREGON: BEAVERTON; CORVALLIS; EUGENE; PORTLAND; SALEM.
PENNSYLVANIA: ADAMS TWP. (Cambria County); ARMAGH; AUBURN; BEAVER FALLS; BEAVER VALLEY; BEDFORD; BENSALEM TWP.; BETHEL PARK; BLAIRSVILLE; CENTRAL CITY BOROUGH; CLARION BOROUGH; COALPORT; COATESVILLE; CRESSON; DALLAS; DUNMORE; ELIZABETHTOWN; GETTYSBURG; GREENSBURG; HARRISBURG; HUNTINGDON; JAMISON; KANE; KENNETT SQUARE; KING OF PRUSSIA; KISKIMINETAS TWP.; LA PORTE BOROUGH; LANCASTER; LANSDALE; LEBANON; LEVITTOWN; LEWISTOWN; LOCK HAVEN; LOWER MERION TWP.; LYKENS; MARKLEYSBURG; MEYERSDALE; MONROEVILLE; NEWPORT; NEWTOWN; NORRISTOWN; OIL CITY; PHILADELPHIA (area 2); PHILADELPHIA (areas 1, 3 & 4); PHILIPSBURG BOROUGH; PITTSBURGH; POTTSTOWN; POTTSVILLE; PULASKI; PUNXSUTAWNEY; READING; REEDSVILLE; ROCHESTER; SCRANTON; SELLERSVILLE; SHIPPENSBURG; SMETHPORT; STATE COLLEGE; TARENTUM BOROUGH; TOWANDA; TRAPPE; WALLINGFORD; WAYNESBURG; WEST ALEXANDER; WILLIAMSPORT; WILLOW GROVE; YORK.
SOUTH CAROLINA: BEAUFORT USMC AIR STATION; CALHOUN FALLS; CHARLESTON; HAMPTON; LADY'S ISLAND; NEWBERRY; WALTERBORO.
SOUTH DAKOTA: ABERDEEN TWP.; FORT PIERRE; HURON; MITCHELL; MOBRIDGE; SIOUX FALLS; SPEARFISH; WATERTOWN.
TENNESSEE: ASHLAND CITY; ATHENS; CHATTANOOGA; COVINGTON; FAIRFIELD GLADE; FRIENDSVILLE; GRAY; GREENEVILLE; GRIMSLEY; HARRIMAN; HUNTSVILLE; JAMESTOWN; KNOXVILLE; KODAK; LA FOLLETTE; LIVINGSTON; LYNCHBURG; MEMPHIS; NASHVILLE; NORRIS; OAK RIDGE; SMITHVILLE; VONORE; WALDEN CREEK; WARTBURG; WOODBURY.
TEXAS: ALPINE; HOUSTON; SEMINOLE; WEST ODESSA.
UTAH: COALVILLE; HEBER CITY; LOGAN; MORGAN CITY; NEPHI; OGDEN; PROVO; SALT LAKE CITY.
VERMONT: BENNINGTON; BRATTLEBORO; BURLINGTON; ENOSBURG FALLS.
VIRGINIA: ALEXANDRIA; AMELIA COUNTY (portions); AMHERST COUNTY (southern portion); ARLINGTON; BLACKSBURG; BROOKNEAL; CHARLES CITY COUNTY (portions); CHARLOTTESVILLE; CULPEPER COUNTY; DANVILLE; DILLWYN; EMPORIA; FORT BELVOIR ARMY BASE; FRONT ROYAL; GALAX; GLADE SPRING; GORDONSVILLE; GOSHEN; HARRISONBURG; HOT SPRINGS; KING WILLIAM (portions); LEXINGTON; LOUDOUN COUNTY; LURAY; LYNCHBURG; MADISON; MARION; MARTINSVILLE; MATHEWS; NORTON; ORANGE; PALMYRA; PETERSBURG; PETERSBURG (unincorporated areas); POWHATAN; PRINCE WILLIAM COUNTY; PULASKI; RESTON; RICHMOND; RUCKERSVILLE; RUTHER GLEN; SALEM; SOUTH BOSTON; SOUTH HILL; SPOTSYLVANIA; STAUNTON; STUART; TROUTVILLE; WARRENTON; WESTMORELAND COUNTY; WINCHESTER.
WASHINGTON: AUBURN; BELLINGHAM; LONGVIEW; MINERAL; MOSSYROCK; RYDERWOOD; SEATTLE; SPOKANE; TACOMA; VANCOUVER; WINLOCK.
WEST VIRGINIA: AUGUSTA; BETHANY; BLUEFIELD; CHESTER; HUNTINGTON; KEYSER; MORGANTOWN; NEW CUMBERLAND; RANSON; RED HOUSE; SPRINGFIELD; WHEELING.
WISCONSIN: MANITOWOC.
Other Holdings:
Professional sports: Owns 66% of sports venture that includes Philadelphia Flyers (hockey team), Philadelphia 76ers (basketball team); CoreStates Center & CoreStates Spectrum (sports arenas); Phantoms of American Hockey League; Spectacor
Program source: 8.34% of MLB Network; 30% of Pittsburgh Cable News; 12.4% of Music Choice; 15.6% of NHL Network; 10% of Current Media LLC owner of Current TV

COM-LINK INC.

206 Hardaway Ave E
Union Springs, AL 36089
Phone: 334-738-2204
Fax: 334-738-5555
E-mail: jfischer@ustconline.net
Web site: http://www.comlinkinc.net
Officer:
John Fischer, Chief Executive Officer
Ownership: Ropir Industries; Mrs. R. M. Pirnie, Principals. Pirnie has telephone holdings.
Cable Systems (3):
ALABAMA: LAKE MARTIN RESORT; NOTASULGA; UNION SPRINGS.

COMMUNITY ANTENNA SYSTEM INC.

1010 Lake St
Hillsboro, WI 54634
Phone: 608-489-2321
Fax: 608-489-2321
Officers:
Bernice Kubarski, Chairman
Randall Kubarski, President
Gregory Kubarski, Vice President
Cable Systems (4):
WISCONSIN: CAZENOVIA; ELROY; HILLSBORO; KENDALL.

COMMUNITY CABLE CORP. OF PENNSYLVANIA

4145 Rte 549
Mansfield, PA 16933
Phones: 570-549-3805; 570-549-4788
Fax: 570-549-2500
E-mail: nptinfo@npacc.net
Web site: http://www.northpenntelephone.com
Officers:
Robert H. Wagner, President
Pete McClure, Vice President

Branch Office:
PRATTSBURGH
34 Main St
Prattsburgh, NY 14873
Phone: 607-522-3712
Ownership: North Penn Telephone Co..
Cable Systems (1):
PENNSYLVANIA: EAST SMITHFIELD.
Other Holdings:
Telephone

COMMUNITY CABLE TV CORP.

102 S Eastern St
PO Box 489
Sanborn, IA 51248
Phone: 712-930-5593
Fax: 712-930-5595
E-mail: tca@tcaexpress.net
Web site: http://www.tcaexpress.com
Officer:
D. J. Weber, Manager
Ownership: Community owned--Sanborn, IA.
Cable Systems (1):
IOWA: SANBORN.

COMMUNITY CABLEVISION CO.

PO Box 307
1550 W Rogers Blvd
Skiatook, OK 74070-0307
Phone: 918-396-3019
Fax: 918-896-2081
E-mail: dennis@communitycablevision.com
Web site: http://www.communitycablebroadband.com
Officer:
Dennis Soule, President
Ownership: Ann E Hamilton; Georgie G Hamilton.
Cable Systems (13):
OKLAHOMA: AVANT; BARNSDALL; COLLINSVILLE; COPAN; HOMINY; KAW CITY; OCHELATA; OILTON; RAMONA; SHIDLER; SKIATOOK; WYNONA; YALE.
Cable Holdings:
Community Cable & Broadband Inc.

COMMUNITY COMMUNICATIONS CO.

1920 Hwy 425 N
Monticello, AR 71655
Phones: 870-367-7300; 800-272-2191
Fax: 870-367-9770
Web site: http://www.ccc-cable.net
Ownership: Paul Gardner, Pres..
Cable Systems (26):
ARKANSAS: AMITY; ARKANSAS CITY; BISMARCK; CARPENTER DAM; CURTIS; EAST CAMDEN; EUDORA; FRIENDSHIP; GILLETT; GLENWOOD; GOULD; HOOKER/LADD; JONES MILL; MAGIC SPRINGS; MONTICELLO; NORMAN; PEARCY; REED; RISON; ROYAL; SALINE COUNTY (unincorporated areas); STAR CITY; WARREN; WATSON.
LOUISIANA: KILBOURNE.
MISSISSIPPI: ROSEDALE.

COMMUNITY NETWORK SERVICES

111 Victoria Pl
Thomasville, GA 31799
Phone: 229-227-7001
Fax: 229-227-3366
E-mail: answers@cns-internet.com
Web site: http://www.cns-internet.com
Officers:
Mark Furhman, General Manager
Sherri Nix, Marketing Coordinator
Cable Systems (5):
GEORGIA: BACONTON; CAIRO; CAMILLA; MOULTRIE; THOMASVILLE.

COMMUNITY TELECOM SERVICES

49 Hardwood Dr
PO Box 579
Monticello, KY 42633
Phones: 606-348-8416; 877-279-1323
Fax: 606-348-6397
E-mail: info@ctsmediagroup.com
Web site: http://www.ctsmediagroup.com
Officer:
Shane Stockton, General Manager
Cable Systems (1):
KENTUCKY: MONTICELLO.

COMMUNITY TV INC.

364 Riverview Dr.
Hazard, KY 41701
Phone: 606-436-4593
Officer:
Don Dresher, President
Ownership: Non-profit organization--Walkertown Station, KY.
Cable Systems (1):
KENTUCKY: WALKERTOWN.

COMPORIUM COMMUNICATIONS

330 E. Black St.
Rock Hill, SC 29730
Phone: 803-324-9011
Web site: http://www.comporium.com
Ownership: Comporium Group.
Cable Systems (3):
NORTH CAROLINA: BREVARD.
SOUTH CAROLINA: GILBERT; ROCK HILL.

COMPUTER DEVELOPMENT SERVICES/CDSINET LLC

122 N Lafayette
Marshall, MO 65340
Phone: 660-886-4045
E-mail: support@cdsinet.net
Web site: http://www.cdsinet.net
Ownership: James R. Kiser.

COMSERV LTD.

111 W 2nd St
PO Box 310
Schaller, IA 51053
Phone: 712-275-4215
Fax: 712-275-4121
Officer:
Steven Reimers, Chairman
Ownership: Schaller Telephone Co..

Cable Systems (1):
IOWA: SCHALLER.

COMSOUTH CORP.

99 Broad St
PO Box 1298
Hawkinsville, GA 31036
Phone: 478-783-4001
Fax: 478-892-3055
E-mail: sales@dsl.cstel.net
Web site: http://www.comsouth.net
Cable Systems (2):
GEORGIA: FORT VALLEY; PERRY.

COMSTAR CABLE TV INC.

8358 W Scott Rd
PO Box 975
Beatrice, NE 68310
Phone: 402-228-0683
Fax: 402-228-3766
Ownership: Tim Schwarz, Pres..
Cable Systems (5):
NEBRASKA: ALEXANDRIA; DAYKIN; FILLEY; PICKRELL; SWANTON.

COMSTOCK COMMUNITY TV INC.

PO Box 9
Virginia City, NV 89440
Phone: 775-847-0572
Officers:
Marilou Walling, President
Barbara Bowers, Secretary-Treasurer
Ownership: Non-profit organization--Virginia City, NV.
Cable Systems (1):
NEVADA: VIRGINIA CITY.

CONSOLIDATED CABLE INC.

PO Box 6147
6900 Van Dorn St
Lincoln, NE 68506
Phones: 402-489-2728; 800-742-7464
Fax: 402-489-9034
E-mail: support@nebnet.net
Web site: http://www.nebnet.net
Cable Systems (7):
NEBRASKA: BIG SPRINGS; CURTIS; DUNNING; FARNAM; HYANNIS; MAXWELL; WALLACE.

CONSOLIDATED TELECOM

507 S Main
PO Box 1408
Dickinson, ND 58602
Phone: 701-483-4000
Fax: 701-483-0001
Web site: http://www.ctctel.com
Cable Systems (1):
NORTH DAKOTA: DICKINSON.

CONWAY CORP.

1307 Prairie St.
PO Box 99
Conway, AR 72033
Phone: 501-450-6000
Fax: 501-450-6099
E-mail: comments@conwaycorp.net
Web site: http://www.conwaycorp.net
Officers:
Barbara Money, Chairman
Richard Arnold, Chief Executive Officer
Tommy Shackelford, Chief Operating Officer
Bret Carroll, Chief Financial Officer
Ownership: Community owned--Conway, AR.
Cable Systems (1):
ARKANSAS: CONWAY.

COON CREEK TELEPHONE & CABLEVISION

312 Locust St.
PO Box 150
Blairstown, IA 52209
Phone: 319-454-6234
Fax: 319-454-6480
Web site: http://www.cooncreektelephone.com
Cable Systems (1):
IOWA: BLAIRSTOWN.

COON RAPIDS MUNICIPAL CABLE SYSTEM

123 3rd Ave. S
PO Box 207
Coon Rapids, IA 50058
Phone: 712-999-2225
Fax: 712-999-5148
E-mail: crmu@crmu.net
Web site: http://www.crmu.net/index-4.html
Officers:
Brad Honold, General Manager
Kevin Dorpinghaus, Technician
Ownership: Community owned--Coon Rapids, IA.
Cable Systems (1):
IOWA: COON RAPIDS.

COON VALLEY CABLEVISION

516 Sherman St.
Menlo, IA 50164
Phone: 641-524-2111
Fax: 641-524-2112
Web site: http://www.coonvalleytelco.com
Officer:
Jim Nelson, General Manager
Cable Systems (1):
IOWA: MENLO.

ARTHUR R. COOPER

1525 Dupont Rd
Parkersburg, WV 26101
Phone: 304-420-2470
Fax: 304-420-2474
E-mail: info@cascable.com
Web site: http://www.cascable.com
Cable Systems (3):
WEST VIRGINIA: COTTAGEVILLE; PARKERSBURG (southern portion); TUNNELTON.

COOSA CABLE CO.

1701 Cogswell Ave.
Pell City, AL 35125
Phone: 205-884-4545
Fax: 205-884-4510
E-mail: coosacable@coosahs.net
Web site: http://www.coosahs.net
Officers:
Jeff Smith, President
Arthur M. Smith, Chief Executive Officer
Jacqueline I. Smith, Secretary-Treasurer
Ownership: Arthur M Smith, 53%. Arthur M. Smith is 50% owner of Trinity Cablevision Inc., see listing; Jeff Smith, 30%; N. L Smith, 15%; Jacqueline I Smith, 2%.
Cable Systems (1):
ALABAMA: PELL CITY.

COPPER MOUNTAIN CONSOLIDATED METROPOLITAN DISTRICT

PO Box 3002
Copper Mountain, CO 80443
Phone: 970-968-2537
Fax: 970-968-2932
Web site: http://www.coppermtnmetro.org/cable.html
Officers:
Thomas J. Malmgren, Chairman & Chief Executive Officer
Elizabeth Black, Chief Operating & Financial Officer
Ownership: Community owned--Copper Mountain, CO.
Cable Systems (1):
COLORADO: COPPER MOUNTAIN.

CORDES LAKES CABLEVISION

20269 Conestoga Dr.
Cordes Lakes, AZ 86333
Phone: 928-379-0348
Fax: 928-632-5258
Ownership: Dave Conchola.
Cable Systems (1):
ARIZONA: CORDES LAKES.

COUNCIL GROVE TELECOMMUNICATIONS

1410 Lilac Lake
Wamego, KS 66547
Phone: 785-456-2287
E-mail: councilgrovecs@cablerocket.com
Web site: http://www.councilgrove.cablerocket.com
Cable Systems (1):
KANSAS: COUNCIL GROVE.

COUNTRY CABLE (ID)

PO Box 997
Hayden, ID 83835
Phone: 208-762-8825
Fax: 208-772-8576
E-mail: cs@couleedam.net
Web site: http://www.couleedam.net
Officers:
Jon Cooke, President
Tim Devine, Secretary-Treasurer
Ownership: Jon Cooke, 50%; Tim Devine, 50%.
Cable Systems (2):
IDAHO: BONNERS FERRY.
WASHINGTON: COULEE DAM.

COUNTRY CABLE TV

196 S Main St
Pleasant Gap, PA 16823
Phone: 814-359-3161
Fax: 814-359-2145
Ownership: Lee Dorman.
Cable Systems (1):
PENNSYLVANIA: UNION TWP. (Centre County).

COUNTRY CABLEVISION LTD.

2003 25th St SE
PO Box 12038
Salem, OR 97309-0038
Phone: 503-588-8247
Fax: 503-588-0544
E-mail: management@countrycablevision.net
Web site: http://www.countrycablevision.net
Ownership: John P Johnson, Pres..
Cable Systems (2):
OREGON: GILCHRIST; MACLEAY.

COUNTRY CABLE (WV)

PO Box 1696
Clarksburg, WV 26302
Phone: 800-882-1206
Cable Systems (4):
WEST VIRGINIA: CLARKSBURG; COALTON; DIANA; WYATT.

COWLEY TELECABLE INC.

27 West 1st South
PO Box 687
Cowley, WY 82420
Phone: 307-548-7888
Officers:
Jerrie Townsend, President
Tim Townsend, Chief Executive Officer
Ownership: Jerri Townsend; Tim Townsend.
Cable Systems (2):
MONTANA: BELFRY; DRUMMOND.

CRAIG CABLE TV INC.

PO Box 131
Craig, AK 99921
Phone: 907-826-3470
Fax: 907-826-3469
E-mail: office@craigcabletv.com
Web site: http://www.craigcabletv.com
Cable Systems (1):
ALASKA: CRAIG.

CRAWFORD MANOR CABLE TV

2806 NE Side Hwy.
Elkton, VA 22827
Phone: 540-337-8450
Cable Systems (1):
VIRGINIA: CRAWFORD MANOR.

CROSSLAKE COMMUNICATIONS

35910 County Rd 66
PO Box 70
Crosslake, MN 56442
Phone: 218-692-2777
Fax: 218-692-2410
Web site: http://www.crosslake.net
Officer:
Paul Hoge, General Manager
Ownership: Community owned--Crosslake, MN.
Cable Systems (1):
MINNESOTA: CROSSLAKE.

CRYSTAL BROADBAND NETWORKS

PO Box 180336
Chicago, IL 60618
Phones: 630-206-0447; 877-319-0328
E-mail: info@crystalbn.com
Web site: http://crystalbn.com
Cable Systems (36):
ARKANSAS: ASH FLAT; HORSESHOE BEND.
ILLINOIS: BARRY; BLUFFS; GRIGGSVILLE; MAROA; PLEASANT HILL; WARRENSBURG; WAVERLY; WINCHESTER.
KENTUCKY: BEATTYVILLE; BREMEN; HAWESVILLE; LEWISPORT; STANTON.
MISSOURI: BOWLING GREEN; CALIFORNIA; ELSBERRY; HOLDEN; LAMPE; MISSIONARY; NOEL; POTOSI; SENECA; TIPTON; VANDALIA; VERSAILLES; VIBURNUM; WARSAW; WINDSOR.
NORTH CAROLINA: HALIFAX; HOLLISTER; NASH COUNTY; OAK CITY; PINETOPS; WHITAKERS.

CITY OF CRYSTAL FALLS

401 Superior Ave
Crystal Falls, MI 49920
Phone: 906-875-3212
Fax: 906-875-3767
E-mail: cfclerk@up.net
Web site: http://www.crystalfalls.org
Ownership: Community owned--Crystal Falls, MI.

Cable Systems (1):
MICHIGAN: CRYSTAL FALLS.

C T & R CABLE LLC
29 Water St.
Petersburg, WV 26847
Phone: 304-257-4891
Ownership: Matthew Alt, 50%; Terry Hinkle, 50%.
Cable Systems (2):
WEST VIRGINIA: DORCAS; RIG.

CUNNINGHAM COMMUNICATIONS
220 W Main St
Glen Elder, KS 67446
Phone: 800-287-8495
Fax: 785-527-3277
E-mail: brent@ctctelephony.tv
Web site: http://www.cunninghamtelephoneandcable.com

Branch Offices:
BELLEVILLE
1809 N St
Belleville, KS 66935
Phone: 785-527-2226
BELOIT
110 W Main St
Beloit, KS 67420
Phone: 785-534-1111
CONCORDIA
407 W 6th St
Concordia, KS 66901
Phone: 785-243-4068
Cable Systems (1):
KANSAS: CONCORDIA.

CYS INC.
2358 Gatetree Lane SE
Grand Rapids, MI 49546-7590

Cable Systems (1):
WISCONSIN: RICHLAND CENTER.
LPTV Stations:
Alabama: W08DC Birmingham.
California: K08LT Modesto.

DAIRYLAND CABLE SYSTEMS INC.
2494 Hwy 14 E
Richland Center, WI 53581
Phone: 608-647-6383
Fax: 608-647-2093
Officer:
Frannie Hasburgh, Manager
Ownership: Lonnie Freeman, Principal.
Cable Systems (4):
WISCONSIN: BAGLEY (village); BLUE RIVER (village); LOGANVILLE (village); SENECA (village).

DAK COMMUNICATIONS INC.
Suite A
26685 Madison Ave.
Mirrieta, CA 92562
Phones: 951-677-9593; 800-203-6469
Fax: 951-679-1819
Officers:
Edward W. Ellis, President
Jeanne Ellis, Vice President
Ownership: Edward W Ellis, 50%; Jeanne M Ellis, 50%.
Represented (legal): Edward John Nowakoski.
Cable Systems (1):
CALIFORNIA: RAINBOW.
Other Holdings:
SMATV: California: Glen Eden Sun Club, Inland Valley Medical Center, Park Place Mobile Home Park, Rainbow (San Diego County), Rancho Springs Medical Center, Stoneridge Mobile Home Park

DALE-MEDIA INC.
1121 SE 2nd St
PO Box 368
Snow Hill, NC 28580
Phone: 252-747-5682
Fax: 252-747-3061
Cable Systems (1):
NORTH CAROLINA: SNOW HILL.

D & P COMMUNICATIONS INC.
4200 Teal Rd.
PO Box 566
Petersburg, MI 49270
Phones: 734-279-1339; 800-311-7340
Fax: 734-279-2640
E-mail: help@cass.net
Web site: http://www.d-pcommunications.com

Branch Offices:
124 Tecumseh St.
Dundee, MI 48131
Phone: 800-311-7340
137 S. Lane St.
Blissfield, MI 49228
Phone: 800-311-7340
Cable Systems (1):
MICHIGAN: PETERSBURG.

DARIEN COMMUNICATIONS
PO Box 575
1011 North St
Darien, GA 31305
Phone: 912-437-4111
Fax: 912-437-7006
E-mail: dtcadmin@darientel.net
Web site: http://www.darientelephone.com
Officers:
Mary Lou Jackson Forsyth, President
Reginald V. Jackson, Vice President
Mary Alice Forsyth Thomas, Secretary-Treasurer
Cable Systems (1):
GEORGIA: DARIEN.

CHUCK DAVIS
501 Hwy 120 N, Ste 65
PO Box 2084
Pottsboro, TX 75076
Phone: 903-786-7477
E-mail: tvcable@graysoncable.com
Web site: http://www.graysoncable.com
Cable Systems (5):
TEXAS: EAST GRAYSON COUNTY; ECTOR; POTTSBORO; SHERWOOD SHORES; WEST GRAYSON COUNTY.

MICKEY DAVIS
314 W Main St
PO Box 237
Mountain View, OK 73062
Phone: 800-980-7912
Fax: 580-347-2179
Cable Systems (10):
OKLAHOMA: BINGER; CORN; DILL CITY; FORT COBB; GRACEMONT; GRANITE; MOUNTAIN VIEW; ROOSEVELT TWP.; SENTINEL; VERDEN.

DAYBREAK COMMUNICATIONS
PO Box 899
Village Mills, TX 77663-0899
Phone: 409-834-2190
Cable Systems (1):
TEXAS: WILDWOOD.

DEAN HILL CABLE
PO Box 128
Parkdale, AR 71661
Phone: 870-473-2802
Cable Systems (3):
ARKANSAS: MONTROSE; PORTLAND; WILMOT.

DONALD G. DEE
PO Box 38
Houlton, ME 04730
Phone: 207-532-4451
Cable Systems (1):
MAINE: MATTAWAMKEAG (town).

DEMOPOLIS CATV CO.
105 S Cedar Ave
PO Box 477
Demopolis, AL 36732
Phone: 334-289-0727
Fax: 334-289-2707
E-mail: lgoldman@demopoliscatv.com
Web site: http://www.demopoliscatv.com
Officers:
Lynn Goldman, President & Chief Executive Officer
Debbie Goldman, Vice President
Ownership: Lynn Goldman, 99.5%; Richard Manley, 0.5%.
Cable Systems (1):
ALABAMA: DEMOPOLIS.

DENISON COMMUNICATIONS INC.
Suite B
11919 Sunray Ave.
Baton Rouge, LA 70816
Phone: 504-291-9698
Cable Systems (4):
MISSISSIPPI: MCLAURIN; SANFORD; SEMINARY; SUNRISE.

DIODE CABLE CO. INC.
300 Commercial St
PO Box 236
Diller, NE 68342
Phone: 402-793-5330
Fax: 402-793-5139
E-mail: diodedonna@diodecom.net
Web site: http://www.diodecom.net
Ownership: Diller Telephone Co..
Cable Systems (2):
NEBRASKA: DILLER; HEBRON.
Other Holdings:
Telephone

DIRECT COMMUNICATIONS
150 S Main St
PO Box 270
Rockland, ID 83271
Phones: 208-548-2345; 866-675-1639
Fax: 208-548-9911
E-mail: support@directcom.com
Web site: http://www.directcom.com
Officers:
Leonard May, President
Garrin Bott, General Manager
Jeremy Smith, General Manager, Starwest (Internet & Television)
Kip Wilson, General Manager, Direct Communications, Cedar Valley
Cable Systems (7):
IDAHO: ABERDEEN; ARCO; ASHTON; CHALLIS; MALAD CITY; SODA SPRINGS; VICTOR.

DIVERSE COMMUNICATIONS INC.
246 N. Division St.
Woodhull, IL 61490
Phone: 309-334-2150
Fax: 309-334-2989
E-mail: woodhulltel@yahoo.com
Web site: http://www.woodhulltel.com
Officers:
Jerry Krueger, President
Roscoe Lowrey, Executive Vice President
Ownership: Woodhull Community Telephone Co..
Cable Systems (1):
ILLINOIS: ALPHA.

DIXON TELEPHONE CO.
608 Davenport St
PO Box 10
Dixon, IA 52745
Phone: 563-843-2901
Fax: 563-843-2481
E-mail: dixontel@netins.net
Officer:
Keith Steward, President
Cable Systems (1):
IOWA: DIXON.

CITY OF DOERUN
223 W. Broad Ave.
PO Box 37
Doerun, GA 31744
Phone: 229-782-5444
Fax: 229-782-5224
Ownership: Community owned--Doerun, GA.
Cable Systems (1):
GEORGIA: DOERUN.

KEN DOUVIA
730 Burlington
Grand Ridge, IL 61325
Phone: 815-249-5517
Represented (legal): Timothy J. Creedon III.
Cable Systems (1):
ILLINOIS: GRAND RIDGE.

DRESDEN CABLE INC.
106 W. Maple St.
Dresden, TN 38225
Phone: 731-364-5259
Ownership: Richard Hutcherson, Pres..
Cable Systems (1):
TENNESSEE: DRESDEN.

DUMONT TELEPHONE CO.
506 Pine St
PO Box 349
Dumont, IA 50625
Phones: 641-857-3211; 800-328-6543
Fax: 641-857-3300
E-mail: dumontel@netins.net
Web site: http://www.dumonttelephone.com
Ownership: Shareholder owned.
Cable Systems (2):
IOWA: DUMONT; GENEVA.

CLIFFORD DUNCAN
PO Box 685
Wilmington, VT 05363
Phone: 802-464-2233
Fax: 802-464-1289
E-mail: dctv8@sover.net
Web site: http://www.duncancable.com
Cable Systems (1):
VERMONT: WILMINGTON.

RAY S. DYER JR.
922 Main St
PO Box 157
Locke, NY 13092
Phone: 315-497-0444
Fax: 315-497-7653
E-mail: sbadman@scccinternet.com

Cable Systems (1):
NEW YORK: MORAVIA.

EAGLE CABLEVISION

101 Hill St.
Lodge Grass, MT 59050
Phone: 406-639-2570
Fax: 406-639-2570
Ownership: Cliff Schollmeyer, Principal.
Cable Systems (2):
MONTANA: LAME DEER; LODGE GRASS.

EAGLE CABLEVISION INC.

205 1st Ave NE
PO Box 39
Remer, MN 56672
Phones: 218-566-2302; 800-903-1987
Web site: http://www.jtc-companies.com
Officers:
Conrad Johnson, President
Ron Johnson, Vice President
Donna Gunderson, Secretary
Ownership: Conrad Johnson; Donna Johnson; Dwayne Johnson; Lowell Johnson; Ronald Johnson. Lowell & Ronald Johnson are execs. with the Johnson Telephone Co., Remer, MN.
Cable Systems (1):
MINNESOTA: REMER.

EAGLE COMMUNICATIONS INC. (KS)

2703 Hall St, Ste 15
PO Box 817
Hays, KS 67601
Phone: 785-625-4000
Fax: 785-625-8030
E-mail: support@eaglecom.net
Web site: http://www.eaglecom.net
Officers:
Robert E. Schmidt, Chairman
Gary Shorman, President & Chief Executive Officer
Ownership: Robert E Schmidt.
Represented (legal): Wiley Rein LLP.
Cable Systems (24):
COLORADO: WRAY.
KANSAS: ABILENE; CHAPMAN; CLAY CENTER; CUBA; ELLSWORTH; GOODLAND; HAYS; HOPE; HOXIE; LINCOLN; MARION; McDONALD; MILFORD; MINNEAPOLIS; OBERLIN; RILEY; RUSSELL; SOLOMON; ST. FRANCIS; WAKEENEY; WAKEFIELD; WHITE CITY; WOODBINE.
Radio Stations:
Kansas: KVGB-AM-FM Great Bend; KAYS (AM), KHAZ (FM), KJLS (FM) Hays; KKQY (FM) Hill City; KHOK (FM) Hoisington; KHUT (FM), KWBW (AM) Hutchinson; KBGL (FM) Larned; KFIX (FM) Plainville; KHMY (FM) Pratt; KINA (AM), KSKG (FM) Salina
Missouri: KSJQ (FM) Savannah; KFEQ (AM), KKJO-FM, KSFT (AM) St. Joseph
Nebraska: KAAQ (FM), KCOW (AM) Alliance; KQSK (FM) Chadron; KELN, KOOQ (AM) North Platte

EAGLES MERE & LA PORTE CABLEVISION INC.

513 Jordan Ave.
Montoursville, PA 17754
Phone: 570-368-3266
Fax: 570-368-8154
Web site: http://www.emlcable.com
Officers:
C. Dale Criswell, Chairman
Roxanne Y. Criswell, President
Timothy J. Criswell, Secretary-Treasurer
Ownership: C. Dale Criswell; Roxanne Y Criswell; Timothy J Criswell, jointly.
Cable Systems (1):
PENNSYLVANIA: LEWIS TWP..

EAGLE VALLEY COMMUNICATIONS

349 First St.
PO Box 180
Richland, OR 97870
Phones: 541-893-6116; 800-366-0795
Fax: 541-893-6903
Web site: http://www.eagletelephone.com
Ownership: Eagle Telephone System.
Cable Systems (1):
OREGON: RICHLAND.

EAST CLEVELAND CABLE TV LLC

1395 Hayden Ave.
East Cleveland, OH 44112
Phone: 216-851-2215
Fax: 216-851-0231
E-mail: jimmy@ecctv.tv
Web site: http://www.ecctv.tv
Ownership: Jerry Smart; Alan Thompson.
Cable Systems (1):
OHIO: EAST CLEVELAND.

EASTERN CABLE

PO Box 126
Corbin, KY 40701
Phone: 606-528-6400
Fax: 606-523-0427
E-mail: cablecsr@2geton.net
Web site: http://www.easterncable.net
Cable Systems (1):
KENTUCKY: GRAY.

EASTON UTILITIES COMMISSION

201 N Washington St
PO Box 1189
Easton, MD 21601
Phone: 410-822-6110
Fax: 410-822-0743
E-mail: info@eastonutilities.com
Web site: http://www.eastonutilities.com
Officer:
Hugh E. Grunden, President & Chief Executive Officer
Cable Systems (1):
MARYLAND: EASTON.

ECONOCO INC.

Rte 61
PO Box 147
Kincaid, WV 25119
Phone: 304-469-2817
Fax: 304-469-2416
Ownership: Sheila Bills, Principal.
Cable Systems (7):
WEST VIRGINIA: CANVAS; DAWSON; GANDEEVILLE; GOLDTOWN; LEFT HAND; MAYSEL; MOUNT LOOKOUT.

ELBERTON UTILITIES

230 N. MacIntosh St.
Elberton, GA 30635
Phones: 706-213-3100; 706-213-3278
Fax: 706-213-3279
E-mail: customerservice@cityofelberton.net
Web site: http://www.elberton.net
Officer:
Amy Bond, Director, Marketing
Ownership: City of Elberton.
Cable Systems (1):
GEORGIA: ELBERTON.

ELGIN TV ASSN. INC.

830 Adler
PO Box 246
Elgin, OR 97827
Phone: 541-437-4575
E-mail: cs@elgintv.com
Web site: http://elgin.elgintv.com
Officers:
Allen Williams, President
Harlan Scott, Vice President
Risa Hallgarth, Secretary-Treasurer
Ownership: Subscriber owned--Elgin, OR.
Cable Systems (1):
OREGON: ELGIN.

ELK RIVER TV CABLE CO.

PO Box 154
Troy, ID 83871
Phone: 877-874-4900
Fax: 208-835-5773
Web site: http://www.elkrivertv.net
Cable Systems (21):
IDAHO: BOVILL; DEARY; ELK RIVER; RIGGINS; TROY; WORLEY.
NEW MEXICO: SAN JON.
TEXAS: CACTUS; GRUVER; MIAMI; NAZARETH; TURKEY; WHEELER.
WASHINGTON: FAIRFIELD; GARFIELD; HARRINGTON; OAKESDALE; REARDAN; ROSALIA; SPRAGUE; SPRINGDALE.

ELLIJAY TELEPHONE CO.

PO Box 0
Ellijay, GA 30540
Phones: 706-276-2271; 800-660-6826
Fax: 706-276-9888
E-mail: info@ellijay.com
Web site: http://etcnow.com
Officers:
Albert E. Harrison, President
Marion Harrison, Secretary
Ownership: Albert E Harrison, 36.3%; Marion Harrison, 35.2%; John Harrison, 28.5%.
Cable Systems (2):
GEORGIA: BLUE RIDGE; ELLIJAY.

EMERY TELCOM

445 E Hwy 29
PO Box 629
Orangeville, UT 84537
Phone: 435-748-2223
Web site: http://www.emerytelcom.com
Officer:
Brock Johansen, Chief Executive Officer & General Manager
Cable Systems (9):
UTAH: BLANDING; CASTLE DALE; CLEVELAND; EAST CARBON; FERRON; GREEN RIVER; MOAB; MONTICELLO; PRICE.

ENVISION MEDIA INC.

300 N 5th Ave
Rome, GA 30165
Phones: 256-779-8700; 800-653-3511
Fax: 706-295-1286
E-mail: service@envisionalabama.com
Web site: http://www.envisionalabama.com
Cable Systems (2):
ALABAMA: CEDAR BLUFF; LEESBURG.

EVARTS TV INC.

113 Yocum St
PO Box 8
Evarts, KY 40828
Phone: 606-837-2505
Fax: 606-837-3738
Cable Systems (1):
KENTUCKY: EVARTS.

EVERTEK INC.

216 N Main
PO Box 270
Everly, IA 51338
Phones: 712-834-2255 (Billing); 800-242-0154
Web site: http://www.evertek.net
Officers:
Roxanne White, General Manager
Chris Dodd, Marketing & Sales
Jerry Weatherman, Internet Systems Supervisor
Ownership: United Farmer's Telephone Co..
Cable Systems (13):
IOWA: KINGSLEY; MOVILLE.

EYECOM INC.

Suite 100
201 E. 56th Ave.
Anchorage, AK 99518
Phone: 907-563-2003
Fax: 907-550-1675
Web site: http://www.telalaska.com
Officers:
Jack Rhyner, Chairman & President
David J. Goggins, Vice President, Plant
Ownership: TelAlaska Inc..
Represented (legal): Dorsey & Whitney.
Cable Systems (3):
ALASKA: GALENA; GIRDWOOD; UNALASKA.

FARMERS INDEPENDENT TELEPHONE CO.

139 W. Madison Ave.
Grantsburg, WI 54840
Phone: 715-463-5322
Fax: 715-463-5206
E-mail: dana@grantsburgtelcom.com
Web site: http://www.grantsburgtelcom.net
Officer:
Dana Olson, General Manager
Cable Systems (1):
WISCONSIN: GRANTSBURG.

FARMERS MUTUAL COOPERATIVE TELEPHONE CO.

PO Box 220
410 Broad St.
Stanton, IA 51573-0220
Phones: 712-829-2111; 800-469-2111
Fax: 712-829-2509
Web site: http://home.myfmtc.com
Officers:
Max Peterson, President
Clayton Johnson, Vice President
Wayne Sederburg, Secretary-Treasurer
Cable Systems (2):
IOWA: EARLING; STANTON.

FARMERS MUTUAL TELEPHONE CO.

608 E Congress
Nora Springs, IA 50458
Phone: 641-749-2531
Fax: 641-749-9578
E-mail: question@omnitel.biz
Web site: http://www.omnitel.biz
Officer:
Ron Laudner, Chief Executive Officer
Cable Systems (6):
IOWA: PLYMOUTH; RUDD.
MINNESOTA: HANLEY FALLS; LAKE LILLIAN; RAYMOND; WATSON.

FAYETTEVILLE PUBLIC UTILITIES

408 College St W
PO Box 120
Fayetteville, TN 37334
Phone: 931-433-1522
Fax: 931-433-0646
E-mail: customerservice@fpu-tn.com
Web site: http://www.fpu-tn.com

Officer:
Britt Dye, Chief Executive Officer
Cable Systems (1):
TENNESSEE: FAYETTEVILLE.

FENTON COOPERATIVE TELEPHONE CO.

300 2nd St
PO Box 77
Fenton, IA 50539
Phone: 515-889-2785
Fax: 515-889-2255
E-mail: fntn@netins.net
Cable Systems (1):
IOWA: FENTON.

THEODORE W. FILSON

Suite 19
215 W. Kellner Blvd.
Rensselaer, IN 47978
Phone: 219-866-7101
Fax: 219-866-5785

Branch Office:
110 E. Adams
Winamac, IN 46996
Phone: 219-946-3813
Cable Systems (3):
INDIANA: MOROCCO; RENSSELAER; WINAMAC.

FIRST CABLE OF MISSOURI INC.

605 Concannon
PO Box 1010
Moberly, MO 65270-0875
Phones: 660-263-6300; 800-892-7139
Fax: 660-263-3238
Officers:
Alan D. Steinbach, President
Jesse W. Wamsley, Vice President
Craig H. Plaster, Secretary-Treasurer
Ownership: Alan D Steinbach; Jesse W Wamsley; Craig H Plaster, each, 33.33%. Principals also own Mississippi Valley Communications Inc., regional CATV contracting firm.
Represented (legal): McDowell, Rice, Smith & Buchanan; Blackwell Sanders.
Cable Systems (1):
MISSOURI: CLARKSVILLE.

JAMES W. FITZPATRICK

PO Box 35
Whitesville, NY 14897
Phone: 607-356-3117
Cable Systems (1):
NEW YORK: WHITESVILLE.

FLINT CABLE TELEVISION INC.

PO Box 669
Reynolds, GA 31076
Phones: 478-847-3101; 888-593-7782
Fax: 478-847-2010
E-mail: customerservice@pstel.com
Web site: http://www.flintcatv.com
Officers:
Donald E. Bond, President & General Manager
E. Kelly Bond, Vice President
Cable Systems (7):
GEORGIA: BUENA VISTA; BUTLER; CRAWFORD COUNTY (portions); LIZELLA; REYNOLDS; ROBERTA; YATESVILLE.

FLORIDA CABLE INC.

SR 40
PO Box 498
Astor, FL 32102
Phones: 352-759-2788; 800-779-2788
Fax: 352-759-3577
E-mail: support@floridacable.com
Web site: http://www.floridacable.com
Officers:
Walter Tucker, President
Bob Samuel, Secretary-Treasurer
Ownership: Walter Tucker; Bob Samuel.
Cable Systems (26):
FLORIDA: ASTOR; BRADENTON; BRONSON (town); CHRISTMAS; CITRA; CLAY COUNTY; FANNING SPRINGS; FLORAHOME; FRUITLAND PARK; HAMPTON; HERNANDO COUNTY; HOLOPAW; KENANSVILLE; LAKE MARY JANE; LAWTEY; LIVE OAK; MARION COUNTY (southern portion); NORTH OLD TOWN; ORANGE SPRINGS; PAISLEY; PENNEY FARMS; PUTNAM COUNTY (eastern portion); PUTNAM COUNTY (western portion); SHARPES FERRY; SMITH LAKE SHORES MOBILE HOME PARK; ZELLWOOD.

FORSYTH CABLE

26 N Jackson St
PO Box 1447
Forsyth, GA 31029
Phone: 478-992-5096
Fax: 478-992-1002
E-mail: cablemgr@forsythcable.com
Web site: http://www.forsythcable.com
Cable Systems (1):
GEORGIA: FORSYTH.

FORT JENNINGS TELEPHONE CO.

PO Box 146
65 W 3rd St
Fort Jennings, OH 45844
Phone: 419-286-2181
Fax: 419-286-2193
E-mail: fjtc@bright.net
Web site: http://www.fjtelephone.com
Officer:
Mike Metvger, General Manager
Cable Systems (1):
OHIO: FORT JENNINGS.

FOSSIL COMMUNITY TV INC.

401 Main St
PO Box 209
Fossil, OR 97830-0209
Phone: 541-763-2698
Cable Systems (1):
OREGON: FOSSIL.

CITY OF FOSSTON CABLE TV

220 E First St
PO Box 607
Fosston, MN 56542
Phone: 218-435-1737
Fax: 218-435-1961
E-mail: chuck.lucken@fosston.com
Web site: http://www.fosston.com
Ownership: Community owned--Fosston, MN.
Cable Systems (1):
MINNESOTA: FOSSTON.

FRANKFORT PLANT BOARD

PO Box 308
Frankfort, KY 40602
Phones: 502-352-4372; 888-312-4372
Fax: 502-223-4449
Web site: http://fewpb.cc
Officers:
Joseph Smith, Chairman
Warner J. Caines, Chief Executive Officer
Ownership: Community owned--Frankfort, KY.
Cable Systems (1):
KENTUCKY: FRANKFORT.

FULL CIRCLE COMMUNICATIONS

PO Box 56
Rockey, OK 73661
Phone: 580-562-3521
Fax: 580-666-2252
Ownership: Craig Holman, Owner.
Cable Systems (3):
OKLAHOMA: ARAPAHO; BURNS FLAT; CANUTE.

GAINES WATROUS TV ASSOCIATION INC.

RD Box 30
Gaines, PA 16921
Phone: 814-435-6578
Fax: 814-435-8585
Officers:
Nancy Holleran, President
Amy Smith, Secretary-Treasurer
Melvin Lowrey, Chief Operating Officer
Ownership: Subscriber owned--Gaines, PA.
Cable Systems (1):
PENNSYLVANIA: GAINES.

GALI ESTATE

c/o Skyview TV Cable
PO Box 445
Broadus, MT 59317
Phone: 406-436-2820
Cable Systems (1):
MONTANA: BROADUS.

GAP CABLE TV INC.

1 Washington Rd.
Annville, PA 17003
Phone: 717-865-0511
E-mail: sales@gapbroadband.com
Web site: http://www.gapbroadband.com
Officers:
Carolyn A. Bryce, President
George Bryce, Chief Operating Officer
Ray Funck, Vice President
Ruth Ann Funck, Secretary
Ownership: Carolyn A Bryce.
Cable Systems (1):
PENNSYLVANIA: FORT INDIANTOWN GAP.

GENERAL COMMUNICATION INC.

PO Box 99016
Anchorage, AK 99509
Phones: 907-265-5600; 800-800-4800
Fax: 907-265-5676
Web site: http://www.gci.com
Officers:
Ronald A. Duncan, President & Chief Executive Officer
G. Wilson Hughes, Executive Vice President & General Manager
William C. Behnke, Senior Vice President, Strategic Initiatives
Gregory F. Chapados, Senior Vice President
Richard P. Dowling, Senior Vice President, Corporate Development
John M. Lowber, Senior Vice President & Chief Financial Officer
Megan Delany, Vice President, Federal Governmental Affairs & Counsel
Ownership: Publicly held.
Represented (legal): Hartig, Rhodes, Hoge & Lekisch PC.
Cable Systems (18):
ALASKA: ANCHORAGE; BARROW; BETHEL; CORDOVA; FAIRBANKS; HOMER; JUNEAU; KETCHIKAN; KODIAK; KOTZEBUE; NOME; PETERSBURG; SEWARD; SITKA; SOLDOTNA; VALDEZ; WASILLA; WRANGELL.

GEUS

2810 Wesley St
Greenville, TX 75401
Phone: 903-457-2800
Fax: 903-454-9249
Web site: http://www.geus.org
Cable Systems (1):
TEXAS: GREENVILLE.

GIANT COMMUNICATIONS

Suite C
418 W. 5th St.
Holton, KS 66436
Phones: 785-362-9331; 800-346-9084
Fax: 785-362-2144
Web site: http://portal.giantcomm.net
Officer:
Gene Morris, General Manager
Ownership: Lynch Multi-Media Corp.; Rainbow Communications & Electronics; Robert C Carson.
Cable Systems (8):
KANSAS: HOLTON; HOYT; MAYETTA; McLOUTH; NORTONVILLE; OZAWKIE; VALLEY FALLS; WINCHESTER.

GILMER CABLE

111 Marshall St
PO Box 1004
Gilmer, TX 75644
Phone: 903-843-5597
Fax: 903-843-2045
E-mail: dpmooney@tatertv.com
Web site: http://gilmer.tatertv.com/
Ownership: David P. Mooney.
Represented (legal): Cole, Raywid & Braverman LLP.
Cable Systems (4):
ARKANSAS: HOPE; HOT SPRINGS.
TEXAS: EAST MOUNTAIN; GILMER.

GLENWOOD TELECOMMUNICATIONS

510 W Gage St
PO Box 97
Blue Hill, NE 68930
Phones: 402-756-3130; 866-756-4746
Fax: 402-756-3134
E-mail: info@gtmc.net; info@shopglenwood.net
Web site: http://www.gtmc.net
Officers:
Phil Boyd, President
Ron Ostdiek, Secretary-Treasurer
Ownership: Glenwood Telephone Membership Corp..
Represented (legal): Dunmire, Fisher & Hastings.
Cable Systems (3):
NEBRASKA: BLUE HILL; GUIDE ROCK; SUPERIOR.
Other Holdings:
Telephone

GLIDE CABLEVISION

1918 One N Umpqua Hwy
PO Box 609
Glide, OR 97443
Phone: 541-496-0515
Fax: 541-496-0515
Ownership: Richard Arwood Sr.; Gean M Arwood, Principals.

Cable Systems (1):
OREGON: GLIDE.

GLW BROADBAND INC.

993 Commerce Dr.
PO Box 67
Grafton, OH 44044
Phone: 440-926-3230
Fax: 440-926-2889
Web site: http://www.glwb.net
Cable Systems (1):
OHIO: WELLINGTON.

GOLDEN VALLEY CABLE & COMMUNICATIONS INC.

Ste A
4206 W Hwy 68
Golden Valley, AZ 86413
Phone: 928-565-4190
E-mail: cs@goldenvalleycable.com
Web site: http://goldenvalleycable.com
Cable Systems (1):
ARIZONA: GOLDEN VALLEY.

GOLDEN WEST CABLEVISION

415 Crown St.
Box 411
Wall, SD 57790-0411
Phone: 605-279-2161
Fax: 605-279-2727
Web site: http://www.goldenwest.com
Officers:
Lee Briggs, President
George Strandell, Chief Executive Officer & General Manager
Robert Fronek, Secretary

Branch Office:
District Manager
Ownership: Golden West Telecommunications.
Represented (legal): Riter, Rogers, Wattier & Brown LLP.
Cable Systems (21):
SOUTH DAKOTA: ARMOUR; AVON; BURKE; CORSICA; CUSTER; DELL RAPIDS; FAIRFAX; GREGORY; HARTFORD; LOWER BRULE; MISSION TWP.; MONTROSE; PINE RIDGE; PLANKINTON; RELIANCE; ROSEBUD; SPRINGFIELD; ST. FRANCIS; TRENT; WALL; WINNER.
Other Holdings:
Cellular radio

GOLDFIELD COMMUNICATION SERVICES CORP.

536 N Main
PO Box 67
Goldfield, IA 50542
Phone: 515-825-3888
Fax: 515-825-3801
E-mail: gold@goldfieldaccess.net
Web site: http://www.goldfieldaccess.net
Officers:
Kenneth Axon, President
Troy Seaba, Secretary-Treasurer
Ownership: Goldfield Telephone Co..
Cable Systems (3):
IOWA: BADGER; GOLDFIELD; WOOLSTOCK.
Other Holdings:
Cellular telephone

GORGE NETWORKS INC.

616 Industrial Ave, Ste 401
PO Box 1107
Hood River, OR 97031
Phones: 541-436-1234; 888-508-2363
E-mail: sales@gorge.net
Web site: http://new.gorge.net

GOVERNMENT CAMP CABLE

PO Box 10
Government Camp, OR 97028
Phone: 503-272-3333
Fax: 503-272-3800
Ownership: Charlie Sperr.
Cable Systems (1):
OREGON: GOVERNMENT CAMP.

GOWRIE CABLEVISION INC.

1112 1/2 Beek St
PO Box 145
Gowrie, IA 50543
Phone: 515-352-5227
Ownership: Paul Johnson, Pres..
Cable Systems (3):
IOWA: CALHOUN COUNTY (portions); GOWRIE; PATON.

GRAND RIVER CABLEVISION

102 W 2nd St
PO Box 249
Leaf River, IL 61047
Phone: 815-738-2225
Fax: 815-738-6060
Web site: http://www.grcblvsn.com
Officers:
K. L. Barney, President
Eugene J. Barney, Vice President
Maxine L. Palmer, Secretary-Treasurer
Cable Systems (1):
ILLINOIS: LEAF RIVER.

GREAT AUK WIRELESS LLC

118 Main St
Brattleboro, VT 05301
Phone: 877-220-2873
Fax: 866-229-4956
E-mail: info@gaw.com
Web site: http://gaw.com
Officers:
H. Josh Garza, Chief Executive Officer
Gregg R. Noble, Chief Operating Officer
Nick Huanca, Chief Technology Officer
London Frost, Customer Service Manager

GREAT PLAINS COMMUNICATIONS INC.

1600 Great Plains Centre
PO Box 500
Blair, NE 68008
Phones: 402-426-9511; 888-343-8014
Fax: 402-426-6475
Web site: http://www.gpcom.com
Cable Systems (12):
NEBRASKA: ARNOLD; BANCROFT; BLOOMFIELD; CHADRON; CHAPMAN; ELGIN; GRANT; McCOOK; NORTH BEND; SUTHERLAND; TRENTON; WOLBACH.

GREENE COUNTY PARTNERS INC.

100 Redbud Rd
PO Box 200
Virginia, IL 62691
Phones: 217-452-7725; 800-252-1799
Fax: 217-452-7030
Web site: http://www.casscomm.com
Officers:
Gerald E. Gill, Chairman & President
Gerald S. Gill, Vice President
Cable Systems (3):
ILLINOIS: CARROLLTON; JERSEYVILLE; WILLIAMSVILLE.

R. M. GREENE INC.

2400 Sportsman Dr
Phenix City, AL 36868
Phone: 334-298-7000
Fax: 334-298-0833
Web site: http://www.ctvea.net/
Officers:
Roy M. Greene, Chairman
Lynne G. Frakes, President
Vicki Abbot, Chief Operating Officer
Cable Systems (1):
ALABAMA: PHENIX CITY.
LPTV Stations:
Alabama: W06BH Phenix City, etc..

GRISHAM TV CABLE CO.

PO Box 65
Hallettsville, TX 77964
Phone: 361-798-3611
Fax: 361-798-3611
Ownership: Shirley Grisham.
Cable Systems (1):
TEXAS: FAYETTEVILLE.

GRISWOLD CO-OP TELEPHONE CO.

607 Main St
PO Box 640
Griswold, IA 51535
Phone: 712-778-2121
E-mail: gctc@netins.net
Web site: http://www.griswoldtelco.com
Cable Systems (1):
IOWA: GRISWOLD.

GROVE CABLE CO.

115 Glenwood Rd.
Marquette, MI 49855
Phone: 906-249-1057
E-mail: helpdesk@cablemo.net
Ownership: Robert Grove.
Cable Systems (4):
MICHIGAN: GRAND MARAIS; REPUBLIC TWP.; SENEY TWP.; SHINGLETON.

GRUNDY CENTER MUNICIPAL LIGHT & POWER

706 6th St
PO Box 307
Grundy Center, IA 50638
Phone: 319-825-5207
E-mail: gcmuni@gcmuni.net
Web site: http://www.gcmuni.net
Cable Systems (1):
IOWA: GRUNDY CENTER.

GUADALUPE VALLEY COMMUNICATIONS SYSTEMS LP

36101 FM 3159
New Braunfels, TX 78132-1604
Phones: 830-885-4411; 800-367-4882
Fax: 830-885-2100
Web site: http://www.gvtc.com
Officers:
Ritchie Sorrells, President & Chief Executive Officer
Robert Hunt, Vice President, Regulatory Affairs & Business Operations
Jeff Mnick, Vice President, Sales & Marketing
Mark Gitter, Chief Financial Officer

Branch Office:
1221 S. Main St.
Boerne, TX 78006
Phone: 830-249-8181
Ownership: Community owned--Guadalupe Valley.
Cable Systems (1):
TEXAS: CANYON LAKE.
Other Holdings:
Telephone

GUINESS COMMUNICATIONS INC.

5381 48th Ave
Delta, BC V4K 1W7
Phones: 604-946-1144; 604-946-7676
Fax: 604-946-5627
E-mail: customerservice@deltacable.com
Web site: http://www.deltacablevision.com
Officers:
Larry Boule, General Manager
Monica Barrett, Finance Director
Cable Systems (1):
WASHINGTON: POINT ROBERTS.
Cable Holdings:
Canada: Delta, BC

HAEFELE TV INC.

PO Box 312
Spencer, NY 14883
Phones: 607-589-6235; 800-338-6330
E-mail: htv@htva.net
Web site: http://www.htva.net
Officer:
Denise Laue, Vice President
Ownership: Lee Haefele, Principal.
Cable Systems (3):
NEW YORK: ENFIELD; SMITHVILLE; SPENCER.

HAINES & SKAGWAY CABLE TV

715 Main St
PO Box 1229
Haines, AK 99827
Phones: 907-766-237 (Haines); 907-983-2205 (Skagway)
Fax: 907-766-2345
Web site: http://www.hainescable.tvheaven.com/
Ownership: Patty Campbell, Pres..
Cable Systems (2):
ALASKA: HAINES; SKAGWAY.

HAMILTON COUNTY/GORE MOUNTAIN CABLE TV INC.

PO Box 275
Wells, NY 12190
Phones: 518-924-2013; 800-562-1560
Fax: 518-381-4833
Web site: http://www.hcctelevision.com
Officers:
Paul F. Schonewolf, President & Chief Operating Officer
George M. Williams, Chief Financial Officer
Ownership: Paul F Schonewolf, 80.1%; George M Williams, 19.9%.
Represented (legal): Koerner & Olender PC.
Cable Systems (3):
NEW YORK: INDIAN LAKE (town); JOHNSBURG (town); WELLS.

HANCEL INC.

34 Read St
PO Box 608
Hancock, NY 13783-0608
Phones: 607-637-2568; 800-360-4664
Fax: 607-637-9999
E-mail: telco@hancock.net
Web site: http://www.hancockvideo.com
Officers:
Robert C. Wrighter Sr., Chairman, President & Chief Operating Officer
Lewis Martin, Chief Financial Officer
Ownership: Hancock Telephone Co..

Cable Systems (2):
NEW YORK: HANCOCK.
PENNSYLVANIA: LAKEWOOD.

H & B CABLE SERVICE INC.
108 N Main St
PO Box 108
Holyrood, KS 67450
Phones: 785-252-4000; 800-432-8296
Fax: 785-252-3229
E-mail: commentsquestions@hbcomm.net
Web site: http://www.hbcomm.net
Officers:
Robert Koch, President & General Manager
Don Nash, Vice President & Chief Financial Officer
Kathy Koch, Vice President
Del Jeane Nash, Secretary-Treasurer
Ownership: Betty Koch; Harold Koch.
Cable Systems (1):
KANSAS: HOLYROOD.

HANSON COMMUNICATIONS INC.
227 S Main St
Clara City, MN 56222
Phone: 320-847-2211
Fax: 320-847-2736
Officer:
Bruce Hanson, President
Cable Systems (9):
MINNESOTA: BELVIEW; CLEMENTS; COMFREY; ECHO; NICOLLET; WABASSO; WOOD LAKE.
NEBRASKA: ATKINSON.
SOUTH DAKOTA: TRIPP.

STEVEN HARAMOTO
500 West 10400 North
Elwood, UT 84337

Cable Systems (1):
UTAH: HUNTSVILLE.

HARLAN COMMUNITY TV INC.
124 S 1st St
PO Box 592
Harlan, KY 40831
Phone: 606-573-2945
E-mail: hctv@harlanonline.net
Web site: http://www.harlantv.com
Officers:
James Morgan, President
Mark Lawrence, Vice President
Jack Hale, Secretary-Treasurer
Ownership: Subscriber owned--Harlan, KY.
Represented (legal): Greene & Forester.
Cable Systems (1):
KENTUCKY: HARLAN.

HARLAN MUNICIPAL UTILITIES
PO Box 71
405 Chatburn Ave
Harlan, IA 51537
Phone: 712-755-5182
Fax: 712-755-2320
E-mail: hmu@harlannet.com
Web site: http://www.harlannet.com
Cable Systems (1):
IOWA: HARLAN.

HARRON COMMUNICATIONS LP
70 E. Lancaster Ave.
Frazer, PA 19355
Phone: 610-644-7500
Fax: 610-993-1100
E-mail: administration@harron.com
Web site: http://www.harron.com
Officers:
James J Bruder Jr., Chairman & Chief Executive Officer
Thomas M Marturano, President & Chief Operating Officer
Ryan F Pearson, Executive Vice President & General Counsel
Shawn P Flannery, Chief Financial Officer & Treasurer
Steve A Murdough, Vice President, Operations
Joshua S Barstow, Vice President, Advanced Services
Linda C Stuchell, Vice President, Programming & Marketing
Constance S Prince, Chief Administrative Officer
Cable Systems (44):
ALABAMA: RED BAY.
CONNECTICUT: NEW LONDON.
MAINE: SANFORD.
MARYLAND: ST. MARY'S COUNTY.
MISSISSIPPI: ABERDEEN; AMORY; ASHLAND; BALDWYN; BOONEVILLE; BRUCE; CALHOUN CITY; CARTHAGE; COFFEEVILLE; FOREST; HICKORY FLAT; HOLLY SPRINGS; IUKA; KOSCIUSKO; MABEN; NETTLETON; NEW ALBANY; OXFORD; PHILADELPHIA; PONTOTOC; POTTS CAMP; RALEIGH; STARKVILLE.
NEW HAMPSHIRE: BELMONT; ROCHESTER.
PENNSYLVANIA: BERWICK; POCONO; SCHUYLKILL TWP.; SPRUCE CREEK TWP.; SUGAR GROVE; THREE SPRINGS.
SOUTH CAROLINA: BENNETTSVILLE.
VIRGINIA: BOWLING GREEN; COLONIAL BEACH; KING GEORGE; LANCASTER COUNTY; MIDDLESEX COUNTY; NORTHUMBERLAND COUNTY; TAPPAHANNOCK; WARSAW.
LPTV Stations:
Pennsylvania: WYLN-LP Hazleton; W05BG Williamsport.
Other Holdings:
Boston Ventures communications equity firm

HART CABLE
196 N Forest Ave
PO Box 388
Hartwell, GA 30643
Phone: 706-856-2288
Fax: 706-376-2009
Web site: http://www.hartcom.net
Officer:
J. Lee Barton, President & Chief Executive Officer
Ownership: Lintel Inc..
Cable Systems (1):
GEORGIA: HARTWELL (unincorporated areas).

HART ELECTRIC INC.
102 S. Main St.
PO Box 282
Lostant, IL 61334
Phone: 815-368-3341
Fax: 815-368-3342
Web site: http://www.hihart.net
Cable Systems (3):
ILLINOIS: LEONORE; LOSTANT; MALDEN.

HARTINGTON TELEPHONE CO.
104 W Centre St
PO Box 157
Hartington, NE 68739
Phones: 402-254-3933; 402-254-3901
Fax: 402-254-2453
E-mail: htc@hartel.net
Web site: http://www.hartel.net
Cable Systems (1):
NEBRASKA: HARTINGTON.

JAMES DALE HASLETT
PO Box 386
Waldport, OR 97394
Phone: 541-563-4807
Fax: 541-563-7341
Cable Systems (1):
OREGON: WALDPORT.

HAVILAND TELEPHONE CO.
104 N. Main St.
PO Box 308
Haviland, KS 67059
Phones: 620-862-5211; 800-339-8052
E-mail: custserv@havilandtelco.com
Web site: http://www.havilandtelco.com
Officer:
Gene Morris, President
Cable Systems (1):
KANSAS: HAVILAND.

CITY OF HAWARDEN
1150 Central Ave.
Hawarden, IA 51023
Phone: 712-551-2565
Fax: 712-551-1117
Web site: http://www.cityofhawarden.com
Officer:
Gary Tucker, City Administrator
Cable Systems (1):
IOWA: HAWARDEN.

HAWKEYE TV CO.
115 W. Main St.
PO Box 250
Hawkeye, IA 52147
Phone: 563-427-3222
Fax: 563-427-7553
E-mail: hawkitel@netins.net
Officers:
William Strudthoff, President
Chuck Gray, Chief Executive & Financial Officer & Secretary-Treasuer
Michael Johnson, Chief Operating Officer
Ownership: Hawkeye Telephone Co..
Cable Systems (1):
IOWA: HAWKEYE.

JIM HAYS
251 Broadway
PO Box 186
Irvine, KY 40336
Phone: 606-723-4240
Fax: 606-723-4723
E-mail: jim@irvineonline.net
Web site: http://www.irvine-cable.net
Cable Systems (1):
KENTUCKY: IRVINE.

HAZARD TV CO. INC.
655 Main St.
Hazard, KY 41702
Phones: 606-436-2522; 606-436-3165
Fax: 606-436-3447
Officers:
William D. Gorman Sr., Chairman & Chief Executive Officer
William D. Gorman Jr., Chief Operating Officer
Ownership: William D Gorman Sr., 52%; D. A Davis Estate, 48%.
Cable Systems (1):
KENTUCKY: HAZARD.

H C CABLE HOLDINGS LLC
c/o NuLink
70B Sewell Rd
Newnan, GA 30263
Phone: 770-683-5516
E-mail: info@nulinkdigital.com
Officer:
John Brooks, Chairman & Chief Executive Officer
Ownership: Halyard Capital.
Cable Systems (1):
GEORGIA: NEWNAN.

HEARTLAND CABLE INC. (ILLINOIS)
167 W 5th
PO Box 7
Minonk, IL 61760
Phones: 309-432-2075; 800-448-4320
Fax: 309-432-2500
Officers:
Steve Allen, Chief Executive & Operating Officer
Marshall Smith, Vice President
Jessica Meister, Secretary
Jaime Ruestman, Secretary
Ownership: Steve Allen; Ken Nevius; Marshall Smith, Principals.
Cable Systems (7):
ILLINOIS: ARMINGTON (village); COMPTON; FLANAGAN; KENNEY; SIBLEY (village); SUBLETTE (village); TONICA.

HEART OF THE LAKES CABLE
9938 State Hwy. 55 NW
PO Box 340
Annandale, MN 55302
Phones: 320-274-5800; 800-288-7694
Fax: 320-274-7178
E-mail: sysop@lakedalelink.net
Officers:
John M. Bishop, Chief Executive Officer
Gene R. South Sr., Chief Operating Officer
Ownership: Lakedale Communications.
Cable Systems (1):
MINNESOTA: ANNANDALE.

STEVEN HECK
601 7th St
PO Box 517
Armstrong, IA 50514
Phone: 712-864-3431
Cable Systems (3):
IOWA: LAKOTA; RENWICK.
MINNESOTA: EMMONS.

HECTOR COMMUNICATIONS CORP.
211 S Main St
PO Box 428
Hector, MN 55342
Phones: 320-848-6611; 320-848-6231
Fax: 320-848-2323
E-mail: unisupport@newulmtel.net
Web site: http://www.hectorcom.com
Officers:
Curtis A. Sampson, Chairman & Chief Executive Officer
Steven H. Sjugren, President & Chief Operating Officer
Paul N. Hanson, Vice President & Secretary-Treasurer
Represented (legal): Lindquist & Vennum PLLP.
Cable Systems (32):
MINNESOTA: ADA; BIG FALLS; BIGFORK; BOVEY; DELAVAN; DEXTER; EASTON; FERTILE; FOUNTAIN; GARDEN CITY; GARY; GREEN ISLE; HAWLEY; HAYWARD; LEWISVILLE; MADISON LAKE; MAHNOMEN; MAPLEVIEW; NEW AUBURN; NEW MARKET; OSTRANDER; PELICAN LAKE; PELICAN RAPIDS; PINE ISLAND; PLATO; RACINE; RED ROCK; ROSE CREEK; ULEN; VERNON CENTER; WARSAW; WYKOFF.

HELIX COMMUNICATIONS
200 Concord St
PO Box 326
Helix, OR 97835

Phone: 541-457-2385
Fax: 541-457-2111
E-mail: info@helixcommunications.com
Web site: http://helixcommunications.com
Officers:
James A. Smith, President
Timothy J. Smith, Secretary-Treasurer
Ownership: James A Smith, 50%; Timothy J Smith, 50%.
Cable Systems (1):
OREGON: HELIX.

DICK HERLIHY
548 Wetherby Terr.
c/o Mid-Missouri Broadband & Cable
Ballwin, MO 63021
Phones: 636-484-2736; 636-552-0028
Cable Systems (1):
MISSOURI: LOOSE CREEK.

HERR CABLE CO.
RR 2
Paxinos, PA 17860
Phone: 570-435-2780
Ownership: Al Herr; Ralph Herr; Rita Herr; Barry Herr, jointly.
Cable Systems (1):
PENNSYLVANIA: ELDRED TWP..

EDWARD HEWSON
349 Damon Rd. NE
Ocean Shores, WA 98569
Phones: 360-289-2252; 360-289-5760
E-mail: sales@coastaccess.com
Web site: http://www.coastcommunications.com
Cable Systems (1):
WASHINGTON: OCEAN SHORES.

HILLTOP COMMUNICATIONS INC.
PO Box 352
Germantown, NY 12526
Phone: 518-537-7827
Fax: 518-537-6700
Officers:
Madeline Bohnsack, President
Bruce Bohnsack, Vice President & General Manager
A. Joel Bohnsack, Secretary-Treasurer
Ownership: Germantown Telephone Inc..
Cable Systems (1):
NEW YORK: GERMANTOWN.
Other Holdings:
Telephone

HINTON CATV CO.
Hinton, OK 73047
Phone: 405-542-3211
E-mail: hintoncatv@hintonet.net
Web site: http://www.hintonet.net
Officers:
Kenneth Doughty, President
Florene Doughty, Vice President
Kerry Allen, Secretary-Treasurer
Cable Systems (1):
OKLAHOMA: HINTON.

HM CAPITAL PARTNERS LLC
Ste 1600
200 Crescent Ct
Dallas, TX 75201
Phone: 214-740-7300
Fax: 214-720-7888
E-mail: jmuse@hmcapital.com
Web site: http://www.hmcapital.com
Officers:
John R. Muse, Chairman, President & Chief Executive Officer
Jack D. Furst, Chief Operating Officer & Partner
Cable Systems (1):
PUERTO RICO: PONCE.

HOLWAY TELEPHONE CO.
208 Ash St.
Maitland, MO 64466
Phone: 660-935-2211
Fax: 660-935-2213
Web site: http://www.abbmissouri.com/holway_default.asp
Cable Systems (1):
MISSOURI: MAITLAND.

HOOD CANAL COMMUNICATIONS
300 E Dalby Rd
Union, WA 98592-0249
Phone: 360-898-2481
Fax: 360-898-2244
E-mail: rbuechel@hctc.com
Web site: http://www.hcc.net
Officer:
Rick Buechel, President

Branch Office:
2218 Olympic Hwy. N
Shelton, WA 98584-2955
Phone: 360-462-4282
Fax: 360-898-2245
Cable Systems (1):
WASHINGTON: UNION.
Other Holdings:
Cellular radio

HORIZON CABLE TV INC.
PO Box 1240
520 Mesa Road
Point Reyes Station, CA 94956
Phones: 415-6639610; 888-883-9251
Fax: 415-382-0814
E-mail: horizon-info@horizoncable.com
Web site: http://www.horizoncable.com
Officer:
Kevin Daniel, President
Ownership: Ken Daniel, Principal.
Cable Systems (2):
CALIFORNIA: NOVATO; POINT REYES STATION.

HOT SPRINGS TELEPHONE CO.
216 Main St
PO Box 627
Hot Springs, MT 59845
Phone: 406-741-2751
Web site: http://www.hotsprgs.net/
Cable Systems (1):
MONTANA: HOT SPRINGS.

RUTH & RICK HOWARD
Rte 40
PO Box 229
Salyersville, KY 41465
Phone: 606-349-3317
Cable Systems (1):
KENTUCKY: SALYERSVILLE.

HTC CABLECOM
107 2nd Ave S
Hospers, IA 51238
Phone: 712-752-8100
E-mail: htc@hosperstel.com
Web site: http://www.hosperstel.com
Ownership: Hospers Telephone Exchange Inc..
Cable Systems (1):
IOWA: SHELDON.

HUBBARD CO-OP CABLE
306 E Maple St
Hubbard, IA 50122
Phone: 641-864-2216
Fax: 641-864-2666
E-mail: hubbard@netins.net
Web site: http://www.hubbardtelephone.com
Cable Systems (1):
IOWA: HUBBARD.

WALTER E HUSSMAN JR
2nd Floor
115 E Capitol Ave
Little Rock, AR 72201
Phone: 501-378-3400
Fax: 501-376-8594
E-mail: camdencabletvtech@cablelynx.com
Web site: http://www.wehco.com/
Cable Systems (1):
ARKANSAS: CAMDEN.
Cable Holdings:
WEHCO Video Inc., see listing

ICE CABLE HOLDINGS LLC
Suite 2501
New York, NY 10169
Phone: 212-414-0200 ext. 555
Fax: 212-414-0210
Officers:
Michele James, President
Gary Sugarman, Vice President

Branch Office:
40 County Rd. 600
Suite F
Pagosa Springs, CO 81147
Phone: 970-731-2211
Ownership: Chip James; Gary Sugarman, Managing Partners; Avalon Equity Fund, Investor.
Cable Systems (11):
COLORADO: BAYFIELD; BLACK HAWK; CREEDE; HOTCHKISS; LAKE CITY; NEDERLAND; OLATHE; PAGOSA SPRINGS; SAGUACHE; SILVERTON; SOUTH FORK.

IDAHO CITY CABLE TV
PO Box 70
Idaho City, ID 83631
Phone: 208-392-4290
Fax: 208-392-4505
Ownership: Don Campbell.
Cable Systems (1):
IDAHO: IDAHO CITY.

INDCO CABLE TV
2700 N St Louis
PO Box 3799
Batesville, AR 72503-3799
Phone: 870-793-4174
Fax: 870-793-7439
E-mail: indco@indco.net
Web site: http://www.indco.net
Officers:
J. D. Pierce, President
Boyce E. Barnett, Secretary-Treasurer
Ownership: J. D Pierce, 50%; Boyce E Barnett, 50%.
Cable Systems (25):
ARKANSAS: BLACK ROCK; BRADFORD; CALDWELL; CALICO ROCK; CAVE CITY; CUSHMAN; DIAMOND CITY; EVENING SHADE; GREENE COUNTY (unincorporated areas); GUION; GUM SPRINGS; MELBOURNE; MORO; MOUNT PLEASANT; MOUNTAIN VIEW; NEWARK; OIL TROUGH; PANGBURN; PLAINVIEW; PLEASANT PLAINS; RUSSELL; SIDNEY; TUMBLING SHOALS; TUPELO; YELLVILLE.

INDEPENDENCE LIGHT & POWER TELECOMMUNICATIONS
700 7th Ave. NE
Independence, IA 50644
Phone: 319-332-0100
Fax: 319-332-0101
Web site: http://www.indytel.com
Cable Systems (1):
IOWA: INDEPENDENCE.

INDEVIDEO CO. INC.
5901 E. McKellips Rd., Suite 109
PO Box 422
Mesa, AZ 85215
Phone: 800-234-8333
Fax: 480-656-8704
E-mail: indevideo2@juno.com
Cable Systems (4):
ARIZONA: GISELA; GRAND CANYON; TUBA CITY; TUSAYAN.

INDEX CABLE TV INC.
12117 Bollenbaugh Hill Rd
Monroe, WA 98272-8663
Phones: 866-794-4283; 360-853-2660
Fax: 360-863-1306
E-mail: indexcable@cablerocket.com
Web site: http://indexcatv.com/
Officer:
Ed Varhaug, General Manager
Cable Systems (1):
WASHINGTON: GUEMES ISLAND.

INLAND TELEPHONE CO.
103 S 2nd St
PO Box 171
Roslyn, WA 98941
Phone: 509-649-2212
Fax: 509-649-2555
E-mail: custserv@inlandnetworks.com
Web site: http://www.inlandnetworks.com
Officers:
Douglas W. Weis, President
Nathan R. Weis, Secretary-Treasurer

Branch Office:
PO Box 221
Uniontown, WA 99179
Phone: 509-229-3311
Ownership: Western Elite Inc. Services.
Cable Systems (2):
WASHINGTON: CLE ELUM; ROSLYN.

INNOVATIVE COMMUNICATIONS CORP.
4006 Estate Diamond
PO Box 7450
Christiansted, VI 00820
Phones: 340-779-9999; 866-240-3999
Fax: 340-778-6011
Web site: http://www.innovativevi.net
Cable Systems (2):
VIRGIN ISLANDS: ST. CROIX; ST. THOMAS.

INSIDE CONNECT CABLE LLC
4890 Knob Creek Rd
Brooks, KY 40109
Phone: 502-955-4882
Fax: 502-543-7553
E-mail: sales@insideconnect.net
Web site: http://www.insideconnect.net

Cable Systems (1):
KENTUCKY: SHEPHERDSVILLE.

INSIGHT COMMUNICATIONS CO.

810 7th Ave., 41st Fl
New York, NY 10019
Phone: 917-286-2300
Fax: 917-286-2301
Web site: http://www.myinsight.com
Officers:
Sidney R. Knafel, Chairman
Michael S. Willner, Vice Chairman & Chief Executive Officer
Dinni Jain, President & Chief Operating Officer
John Abbot, Executive Vice President & Chief Financial Officer
Hamid Heidary, Executive Vice President, Central Operations & Chief Technology Officer
Christopher Slattery, Executive Vice President, Operations
Keith Hal, Executive Vice President, Government Relations
Elliot Brecher, Senior Vice President & General Counsel
Sandra D Colony, Senior Vice President, Corporate Communications
Kevin Dowell, Senior Vice President, Insight Media
Pamela Euler Halling, Senior Vice President, Brand
Ishmel Goodrum, Senior Vice President, Network Operations Center
Gregg Graff, Senior Vice President, Field Operations
Melani Griffith, Senior Vice President, Programming & Video Services
John W Hutton, Senior Vice President, Operations
Rocco Laurenzano, Senior Vice President, Project Management
Bam Liem, Senior Vice President, Advanced Services Engineering
Daniel Mannino, Senior Vice President & Chief Accounting Officer
Paul Meltzer, Senior Vice President, Product Management
Jim Morgan, Senior Vice President, Human Resources
Scott Schneiderman, Senior Vice President, Operational Finance
Keely Bostock, Vice President, Programming & Video Services
Diane Quennoz, Vice President, Marketing
Ankur Sharma, Vice President, E-Commerce
Mitch Weinraub, Vice President, Product Development
Ownership: The Carlyle Group, 42%; Crestview Partners; MidOcean Partners, 42%. jointly; Management & Employees, 18%.
Represented (legal): Fleischman & Harding LLP.
Cable Systems (12):
ILLINOIS: ROCKFORD.
INDIANA: EVANSVILLE; JASPER.
KENTUCKY: BLOOMFIELD; BOWLING GREEN; COVINGTON; DAWSON SPRINGS; LEXINGTON; LOUISVILLE; PROVIDENCE; WARSAW.
OHIO: COLUMBUS.

INTER-COUNTY CABLE CO.

127 Jackson St.
PO Box 578
Brooklyn, IA 52211
Phone: 641-522-9211
Fax: 641-522-5001
Officer:
Tim Atkinson, General Manager
Ownership: Brooklyn Mutual Telephone Co..
Cable Systems (1):
IOWA: BROOKLYN.

INTER-MOUNTAIN CABLE INC.

PO Box 159
Harold, KY 41635
Phone: 606-478-9406
Fax: 606-478-1680
Web site: http://www.imctv.com
Officers:
Paul R. Gearheart, President
Paul D. Gearheart, Vice President
Elaine Gearheart, Secretary-Treasurer
Ownership: Elaine Gearhart, 50%; Paul R Gearhart, 50%.
Cable Systems (5):
KENTUCKY: FALLSBURG; HAROLD; JENKINS; LOWMANSVILLE; VARNEY.

INTERNET AMERICA INC.

PO Box 690753
Houston, TX 77269-0753
Phone: 800-232-4335
E-mail: president@airmail.net
Web site: http://www.internetamerica.com
Officer:
Ross McAlpine, President

INTERNET TEXOMA INC.

PO Box 2543
Sherman, TX 75091-2543
Phones: 903-813-4500; 800-697-0206
Fax: 903-868-8551
Web site: http://www.texoma.net

INTERSTATE COMMUNICATIONS

404 Howland St.
Emerson, IA 51533
Phone: 712-824-7231
Fax: 641-765-4204
E-mail: customerservice@interstatecom.com
Web site: http://www.interstatecom.com

Branch Office:
105 N. West St.
Truro, IA 50257
Phone: 641-765-4201
Cable Systems (6):
IOWA: ANDREW; CARSON; EMERSON; MURRAY; SUN VALLEY LAKE; TRURO.
Other Holdings:
Telephone: Southwest Telephone Exchange Inc., Emerson, IA (affiliated with independent telephone cos.); Interstate '35' Telephone Co., Truro, IA;

INVISIMAX

126 W Johnson Ave
Warren, MN 56762
Phones: 218-745-6030; 866-745-6030
Fax: 218-745-6040
Web site: http://www.invisimax.com
Officers:
Dave Giles, Chief Executive Officer
Phil Hebert, Vice President, Sales
Josh Benson, Sales Manager
Mark Wimpfheimer, Customer Service Manager
Rick Kroll, Operations Manager
Luke Lundin, Controller
Ownership: Dave Giles; Phil Hebert.

IRON GOAT NETWORKS LLC

PO Box 1232
Sultan, WA 98294
E-mail: info@irongoat.net
Web site: http://www.irongoat.net
Officer:
Ryan Spott, Vice President, Operations
Ownership: Caroline Spott.
Cable Systems (1):
WASHINGTON: INDEX.

IRON RIVER COOPERATIVE TV ANTENNA CORP.

316 N 2nd Ave
Iron River, MI 49935
Phone: 906-265-3810
Fax: 906-265-3020
E-mail: ircable@ironriver.tv
Web site: http://www.ironriver.tv
Officer:
Pete Nocerini, President
Ownership: Subscriber owned--Iron River, MI.
Cable Systems (1):
MICHIGAN: IRON RIVER.

ISP MANAGEMENT

409 Gratiot Ave
Alma, MI 48801
Phones: 989-466-6104; 877-466-6104
Web site: http://www.ispmgt.com
Officer:
Jimmy Blake, Information Contact
Ownership: Jeff Hall; Raedene Shunk.

IT WIFI.NET LLC

745 Jordan Lake Ave
Lake Odessa, MI 48849
Phones: 616-374-7787; 800-383-4784
E-mail: info@itwifi.net
Web site: http://ittechnique.com/itwifi.html
Ownership: Micah Sneed; Robin Sneed.

JACKSON MUNICIPAL TV SYSTEM

80 W Ashley St
Jackson, MN 56143
Phone: 507-847-3225
Fax: 507-847-5586
Ownership: Community owned--Jackson, MI.
Cable Systems (1):
MINNESOTA: JACKSON.

LYNDA & ROBERT JACOBSON

620 Betty St
PO Box 759
Ranchester, WY 82839
Phone: 307-655-9011
Fax: 307-655-9021
E-mail: tvcatv@tvcable.tv
Web site: http://tonguerivercomm.com
Officers:
Robert Jacobson, President
Lynda Lee Jacobson, Secretary-Treasurer
Cable Systems (7):
WYOMING: HULETT; MOORCROFT; PINE HAVEN; RANCHESTER; STORY; SUNDANCE; UPTON.

JADE COMMUNICATIONS LLC

129 Santa Fe Ave.
PO Box 1138
Alamosa, CO 81101
Phones: 719-589-5140; 719-379-3839
Fax: 719-379-5233
E-mail: jade@GoJade.Org
Web site: http://www.gojade.org
Cable Systems (1):
COLORADO: BLANCA.

JAMES CABLE LLC

Ste 310
901 Tower Dr
Troy, MI 48098
Phone: 800-392-2662
E-mail: al-support@communicomm.com
Web site: http://www.jamescable.com
Officers:
Kate Adams, Chief Executive Officer
Dan Shoemaker, Chief Financial Officer
Kevin Gardner, Vice President, Marketing
Scott Madison, Vice President, Technology
Represented (legal): Davis Wright Tremaine LLP.
Cable Systems (47):
ALABAMA: ASHLAND; DADEVILLE; GUIN; HACKLEBURG; HOLLIS CROSSROADS; LAFAYETTE; PHIL CAMPBELL; ROANOKE; SULLIGENT; WADLEY; WEDOWEE.
COLORADO: OTIS (town).
FLORIDA: ALACHUA; BRANFORD; CHIEFLAND; CROSS CITY; HAWTHORNE; HIGH SPRINGS; MICANOPY (town); ORANGE LAKE; STEINHATCHEE.
GEORGIA: CRAWFORD; EATONTON; GRAY; GREENSBORO.
LOUISIANA: KINDER; LAKE ARTHUR; VINTON (town); WESTLAKE.
OKLAHOMA: COALGATE; DURANT; SAND POINT; STRINGTOWN; TISHOMINGO; WAPANUCKA.
TENNESSEE: NEW TAZEWELL.
TEXAS: BOWIE; DECATUR; JACKSBORO; SPRINGTOWN.
WYOMING: DOUGLAS; ENCAMPMENT; GLENROCK; LUSK; SARATOGA; TORRINGTON; WHEATLAND.

J & N CABLE SYSTEMS INC.

614 S Columbus Ave
Goldendale, WA 98620-9006
Phone: 509-773-5359
Fax: 509-773-7090
E-mail: john@jncable.com
Web site: http://www.jncable.com
Officer:
John Kusky, President
Ownership: John Kusky; Nancy Kusky, 100% jointly.
Cable Systems (9):
OREGON: CONDON; MORO; RAINIER; WASCO.
WASHINGTON: GOLDENDALE; LYLE; NACHES; QUINCY; YACOLT.

J. B. CABLE

PO Box 268
Minersville, PA 17954
Phone: 570-544-5582
Ownership: John Dunleavy, 50%; Thomas O'Brien, 50%.
Cable Systems (1):
PENNSYLVANIA: PRIMROSE.

JB-NETS LLC

1158 Green Valley Dr
Bidwell, OH 45614-9478
Phones: 740-446-2975; 740-645-4947
Web site: http://www.jbnets.net
Ownership: Jacob Kline.

JEFFERSON COUNTY CABLE INC.

116 S. 4th
Toronto, OH 43964
Phones: 740-537-2214; 800-931-9392
Fax: 740-537-2802
Web site: http://www.voiceflight.biz
Officer:
Bob Loveridge, General Manager
Ownership: Marvin L Bates Sr., Principal.

Cable Systems (4):
OHIO: RUSH RUN; TORONTO.
WEST VIRGINIA: BEECH BOTTOM; COLLIERS.

JESUP FARMER'S MUTUAL TELEPHONE CO.

PO Box 249
Jesup, IA 50648-0249
Phone: 319-827-3434
E-mail: jesupfmt@jtt.net
Web site: http://www.jtt.net
Officers:
Gerald Bloes, President
Russell Rock, Chief Operating Officer
Ownership: Cooperative.
Cable Systems (1):
IOWA: JESUP.

JOHNSONBURG COMMUNITY TV CO. INC.

424 Center St
PO Box 248
Johnsonburg, PA 15845
Phone: 814-965-4888
Officers:
Archie Shuer, President
Harry Horne, Chief Operating Officer & Secretary
Sam Guaglianone, Chief Financial Officer
Ownership: Community owned--Johnsonburg, PA.
Cable Systems (1):
PENNSYLVANIA: JOHNSONBURG.

EUGENE JONES

Rte 1
PO Box 8
Folsum, WV 26348
Phone: 304-334-6504
Fax: 304-334-6504
Cable Systems (1):
WEST VIRGINIA: FOLSOM.

JORDAN NETWORKS INC.

PO Box 5093
Ellsworth, ME 04605
Phones: 207-667-7414; 866-856-7009
Web site: http://www.jordannetworks.com
Ownership: Charles Crawford; Danette Rogers; Dwight Rogers.

K2 COMMUNICATIONS

PO Box 232
Mead, CO 80542
Phone: 303-535-6323
E-mail: info@k2cable.com
Web site: http://www.k2cable.com
Cable Systems (1):
COLORADO: MEAD.

CITY OF KAHOKA

c/o Scott Groben
250 N. Morgan
Kahoka, MO 63445-1433
Phone: 660-727-3711
Fax: 660-727-3750
E-mail: cityofkahoka@kahoka.com
Officers:
Herb Butler, Mayor
Sandie Hopp, Cable Director
Ownership: Community owned--Kahoka, MO.
Cable Systems (1):
MISSOURI: KAHOKA.

KARBAN TV SYSTEMS INC.

73A St. Stevens St.
Rhinelander, WI 54501
Phone: 715-362-4550
E-mail: sales@ktvs.net
Web site: http://www.ktvs.net
Ownership: John Karban.
Cable Systems (4):
WISCONSIN: BOULDER JUNCTION; LAND O'LAKES; MERCER; THREE LAKES.

KELLIN COMMUNICATIONS

6203 Valley High
Larkspur, CO 80118
Phones: 303-349-9815; 719-785-7200
Web site: http://www.kellin.net
Officer:
Kelly Judy, Chief Technician

KENNEBEC TELEPHONE CO. INC.

220 S Main St
PO Box 158
Kennebec, SD 57544-0158
Phone: 605-869-2220
Fax: 605-869-2221
E-mail: knbctel@kennebectelphone.com
Web site: http://www.kennebectelephone.com
Officer:
Rod Bowar, President & Manager
Ownership: Kennebec Telephone, Inc..
Cable Systems (1):
SOUTH DAKOTA: KENNEBEC.

J. ROGER KENNEDY JR.

PO Box 2059
Reidsville, GA 30453
Phone: 912-557-6133
Fax: 912-557-6545
Cable Systems (2):
GEORGIA: COLLINS; REIDSVILLE.
Other Holdings:
Cable construction: Kennedy Network Services Inc.

KENTEC COMMUNICATIONS INC.

915 W. Main St.
Sterling, CO 80751
Phone: 970-522-8107
Fax: 970-521-9457
E-mail: support@kci.net
Web site: http://www.kci.net
Cable Systems (4):
COLORADO: MERINO.

KEYSTONE FARMERS COOPERATIVE TELEPHONE CO.

86 Main St.
Keystone, IA 52249
Phone: 319-442-3241
E-mail: keystone@netins.net
Web site: http://www.keystonecommunications.com
Officer:
DuWayne Schirm, President
Cable Systems (1):
IOWA: KEYSTONE.
Other Holdings:
Cellular radio

KEYSTONE WILCOX CABLE TV INC.

PO Box 431
DuBois, PA 15801-0431
Phone: 814-371-1550
Officers:
James A. Rickard Jr., President & Chief Operating Officer
Shirley A. McCoy, Secretary-Treasurer

Branch Office:
749 Treasure Lake
Dubois, PA 15801
Phone: 814-371-2939
Ownership: Shirley A McCoy, 50%; James Rickard Jr., 50%.
Cable Systems (1):
PENNSYLVANIA: WESTLINE.
Other Holdings:
SMATV

KIROCK CABLE

1483-F-70 Rd.
Delta, CO 81416
Phone: 970-249-4506
Fax: 970-240-8122
Cable Systems (1):
COLORADO: COLLBRAN (town).

RON KLINGENSTEIN

204 E Main St
PO Box 148
Dayton, WA 99328
Phone: 509-382-2132
E-mail: tvcable@daytonwa.net
Web site: http://www.touchetvalleytv.com
Cable Systems (1):
WASHINGTON: DAYTON.

KLM TELEPHONE CO.

PO Box 30
Rich Hill, MO 64779
Phone: 417-395-2121
Fax: 417-395-2120
E-mail: klminfo@abbmissouri.com
Web site: http://www.abbmissouri.com/KLM_default.asp
Cable Systems (3):
MISSOURI: MAITLAND; RICH HILL; SCHELL CITY.

KMHC INC.

107 Jefferson
PO Box 21
Kingston Mines, IL 61539
Phone: 309-389-5782
Ownership: Community owned--Kingston Mines, IL.
Cable Systems (1):
ILLINOIS: KINGSTON MINES.

KNOLOGY INC.

1241 O. G. Skinner Dr.
West Point, GA 31833
Phone: 706-634-2500
Fax: 706-645-1446
Web site: http://www.knology.com
Officers:
Rodger L Johnson, Chairman & Chief Executive Officer
M. Todd Holt, President
Robert Mills, Chief Financial Officer
John Treece, Chief Technology Officer
Bret T. McCants, Executive Vice President, Operations
Felix L. Boccucci Jr., Vice President, Regulatory Affairs
Weldon A. Feightner, Vice President, Regional Operations
Allan H. Goodson, Vice President, Regional Operations
Ronald K. Johnson, Vice President, Sales
Marcus R. Luke, Vice President, Chief Scientist
Anthony Palermo, Vice President, Marketing
Richard D. Perkins, Vice President, Information Technology & Billing
Andy M. Sivell, Vice President, Network Operations
Brad M. Vanacore, Vice President, Human Resources
Chad S. Wachter, Vice President, General Counsel & Corporate Secretary
Ownership: Privately held.
Cable Systems (21):
ALABAMA: ATHENS; DOTHAN; HUNTSVILLE; MONTGOMERY; VALLEY.
FLORIDA: PANAMA CITY BEACH; PINELLAS COUNTY (portions).
GEORGIA: AUGUSTA; COLUMBUS.
IOWA: STORM LAKE.
KANSAS: LAWRENCE.
MINNESOTA: ADRIAN; ELLSWORTH; JASPER; MARSHALL.
SOUTH CAROLINA: CHARLESTON.
SOUTH DAKOTA: COLMAN; RAPID CITY; VIBORG; WATERTOWN.
TENNESSEE: KNOXVILLE.

ARTHUR J. KRAUS

305 State St.
Manhattan, IL 60442
Phones: 815-357-6678; 815-478-4000
Web site: http://www.krausonline.com
Cable Systems (3):
ILLINOIS: GARDNER; MANHATTAN; SENECA.

KUHN COMMUNICATIONS

301 W Main St
PO Box 277
Walnut Bottom, PA 17266
Phone: 717-532-8857
E-mail: kuhncom1@kuhncom.net, tech@kuhncom.net
Web site: http://www.kuhncom.net
Ownership: Earl Kuhn.
Cable Systems (2):
PENNSYLVANIA: PERRY COUNTY; WALNUT BOTTOM.

LAKE COMMUNICATIONS

4849 S 190th Rd
Half Way, MO 65663
Phone: 877-242-3830
Officer:
Tony Gilbert, President & General Manager
Cable Systems (2):
MISSOURI: GRAVOIS MILLS; PORTER MILLS.

CITY OF LAKEFIELD PUBLIC UTILITIES

301 Main St.
PO Box 1023
Lakefield, MN 56150
Phone: 507-662-5457
Fax: 507-662-5990
Web site: http://www.lakefieldmn.com
Officers:
Mark Steffen, Chairman
Doug Anderson, Vice Chairman
Joni Hanson, Secretary
Jim Koep, City Superintendent
Cable Systems (1):
MINNESOTA: LAKEFIELD.

LAKELAND CABLE TV INC.

PO Box 118
Crowder, OK 74430
Phone: 918-334-6200
Officers:
Charles O. Smith, Chairman
Janet Brooks, Secretary
Ownership: Charles Smith; Betty Smith; Orlean Smith, Principals. Charles Smith is Pres. & Gen. Mgr. and Betty Smith is exec. of the Canadian Valley Telephone Co., Crowder, OK.
Cable Systems (1):
OKLAHOMA: CANADIAN.

LAKELAND COMMUNICATIONS

PO Box 40
Milltown, WI 54858

Phone: 715-472-2101
Fax: 715-472-2707
E-mail: info@lakeland.ws
Web site: http://www.lakeland.ws
Cable Systems (1):
WISCONSIN: MILLTOWN.

LAKEVIEW CABLE INC.
PO Box 460
Cache, OK 73527
Phone: 580-429-8800
Fax: 580-429-6599
Web site: http://www.lvcisp.com
Officer:
Bill Rowell, President
Cable Systems (9):
OKLAHOMA: BLAIR; CACHE; COMANCHE COUNTY (unincorporated area); GERONIMO; LAKE ELLSWORTH; LAKE LAWTONKA; MEDICINE PARK; MOUNTAIN PARK; TIPTON.

RICHARD LANDY
PO Box 453
Stowe, VT 05672
Phone: 802-253-9282
E-mail: stoweaccess@stoweaccess.com
Web site: http://www.stoweaccess.com/
Cable Systems (2):
VERMONT: JEFFERSONVILLE; STOWE.

LAUREL CABLE LP
PO Box 125
Berlin, PA 15530
Phones: 814-443-6250; 800-732-5604
Fax: 814-445-1876
Ownership: David Maust.
Cable Systems (1):
PENNSYLVANIA: NEW BALTIMORE.

LAURENS MUNICIPAL POWER & COMMUNICATIONS
272 N. 3rd St.
PO Box 148
Laurens, IA 50554
Phone: 712-841-4610
Fax: 712-841-4611
Web site: http://www.laurens-ia.com
Officer:
Chad Cleveland, General Manager
Cable Systems (1):
IOWA: LAURENS.

DON T. LEAP
PO Box 703
Hyndman, PA 15545
Phone: 814-842-3370
Cable Systems (1):
PENNSYLVANIA: LONDONDERRY TWP. (Bedford County).

CINCINNATI BELL EXTENDED TERRITORIES
125 S. Sycamore St.
Lebanon, OH 45036
Phone: 513-933-7201
Fax: 513-933-7208
Web site: http://www.cincinnatibell.com/main.asp
Officer:
Darrick Zucco, Director
Cable Systems (1):
OHIO: LEBANON.

LEHIGH SERVICES INC.
9090 Taylor Rd
PO Box 137
Lehigh, IA 50557
Phone: 515-359-2211
Fax: 515-359-2424
E-mail: info@lvcta.net
Web site: http://lvcta.net
Ownership: Lehigh Valley Cooperative Telephone Assn..
Cable Systems (1):
IOWA: LEHIGH.

LENOX MUNICIPAL CABLEVISION
PO Box 96
Lenox, IA 50851
Phone: 641-333-2550
Fax: 641-333-2582
Web site: http://lenoxia.com/CityofLenox/Utility/LenoxMunicipalCable.htm
Cable Systems (1):
IOWA: LENOX.

LEWISTON COMMUNICATIONS
3250 S Van Wagoner Ave
Fremont, MI 49412-8008
Phones: 231-924-8060; 800-443-0758
Fax: 231-924-4882
E-mail: help@lewistoncomm.com
Web site: http://portal.lewistoncomm.com
Cable Systems (3):
MICHIGAN: FREEPORT; LEWISTON; MEARS.

LIBERTY CABLEVISION OF PUERTO RICO LTD.
12300 Liberty Blvd.
Englewood, CO 80112
Phones: 303-220-6600; 877-772-1518
Fax: 303-220-6601
Web site: http://www.Lgi.com
Ownership: Liberty Global Inc.. John C. Malone, Chmn.; Michael T. Fries, Pres. & Chief Exec. Officer; LGI ownership:; Liberty Media International; United Global Communications, jointly.
Cable Systems (1):
PUERTO RICO: LUQUILLO.
Other Holdings:
Background music service: 56% of DMX
Broadcast holdings: 2% of Viacom Inc. (see listing); 39.56% of Telemundo Communications Group (see listing); 17% of The News Corp. Ltd. (see Fox Television Stations Inc.)
Cable Network: 21% of USA Networks Inc.; 100% of Starz Encore Group LLC; 100% of QVC Inc.; 90% of International Channel; 4% of Gemstar-TV Guide International Inc.; 10% of E! Entertainment Television; 50% of Discovery Communications; 50% of Court TV Production: 67% of MacNeil/Lehrer Productions

LINCOLN TELEPHONE CO.
111 Stemple Pass Rd
Lincoln, MT 59639
Phone: 406-362-4216
Fax: 406-362-4606
E-mail: ltc@linctel.net
Web site: http://www.linctel.net
Ownership: Stockholder owned.
Cable Systems (1):
MONTANA: LINCOLN.

LINCOLNVILLE COMMUNICATIONS INC.
PO Box 200
Lincolnville Center, ME 04850
Phone: 207-763-9900
Fax: 207-763-3028
E-mail: billing@tidewater.net
Web site: http://www.lintelco.net
Officers:
Jethro Pease, Chairman
Shirley Manning, President & Chief Executive Officer
Ronald McIntyre, Chief Financial Officer
Ownership: Lincolnville Telephone Co..
Cable Systems (1):
MAINE: LINCOLNVILLE.
Other Holdings:
Telephone

LIVERMORE CABLE
806 Okoboji Ave
PO Box 163
Milford, IA 51351
Phone: 712-338-4967
Ownership: Cliff Plagman, Principal. Plagman also has interest in Milford Cable TV, see listing.
Cable Systems (1):
IOWA: LIVERMORE.

MARY S. LOAR
PO Box 222
Soper, OK 74759
Phone: 580-345-2898
Cable Systems (1):
OKLAHOMA: SOPER.

HOWARD LOCK
111 Pine St
PO Box 127
Peshtigo, WI 54157
Phones: 715-582-1141; 800-472-0576
Fax: 715-582-1142
Represented (legal): Cinnamon Mueller.
Cable Systems (2):
MICHIGAN: STEPHENSON.
WISCONSIN: CRIVITZ.

LONE PINE TV INC.
310 Jackson St
PO Box 867
Lone Pine, CA 93545
Phone: 760-876-5461
Fax: 760-876-9101
Web site: http://lonepine.lonepinetv.com
Ownership: Bruce Branson, Chmn. & Pres..
Cable Systems (1):
CALIFORNIA: LONE PINE.

LONG LINES
501 4th St
Sergeant Bluff, IA 51054
Phone: 712-271-4000
Fax: 712-271-2727
E-mail: info@longlines.com
Web site: http://www.longlines.com
Officers:
Chuck Long, Chairman
Jon Winkel, Chief Executive Officer
Ownership: Publicly held..
Cable Systems (14):
IOWA: ANTHON; BLENCOE; DANBURY; LOGAN; MAPLETON; MISSOURI VALLEY; MOORHEAD; ONAWA; ORANGE CITY; SALIX; SOLDIER; UTE; WHITING.
SOUTH DAKOTA: DAKOTA DUNES.
Other Holdings:
Mapleton Communications Inc., see listing

DEL LOTT
102 S. Hayden St.
Belzoni, MS 39038
Phone: 662-247-1834
Fax: 662-247-3237
E-mail: office@belzonicable.com
Web site: http://www.belzonicable.com
Officers:
Del Lott, President
Genelle Lott, Secretary-Treasurer & Chief Financial Officer
Cable Systems (1):
MISSISSIPPI: BELZONI.

LOWELL COMMUNITY TV CORP.
Water St
PO Box 364
Lowell, OH 45744
Phone: 740-896-2626
Officers:
Ron Bauerbach, President & Manager
Debbie Cline, Secretary-Treasurer
Ownership: Subscriber owned--Lowell, OH.
Cable Systems (1):
OHIO: LOWELL.

LYCOM COMMUNICATIONS INC.
305 E. Pike St.
PO Box 1114
Louisa, KY 41230
Phone: 606-638-0639
Fax: 606-638-4278
E-mail: info@lycomonline.com
Web site: http://www.lycomonline.com
Ownership: Donna Lycans.
Cable Systems (3):
KENTUCKY: LAWRENCE COUNTY (southern portion); LOUISA.
WEST VIRGINIA: GENOA.

MADDOCK AREA DEVELOPMENT CORP.
PO Box 0368
Maddock, ND 58348
Phone: 701-438-2541
Web site: http://www.maddocknd.com/EconomicDevelopment/MaddockEDC/tabid/1787/Default.aspx
Officers:
Bruce Terpening, President
Larry Summers, Vice President
Beth Olson, Secretary
Rod Maddock, Treasurer
Cable Systems (1):
NORTH DAKOTA: MADDOCK.

MADISON COMMUNICATIONS CO.
21668 Double Arch Rd
Staunton, IL 62088-4374
Phone: 618-635-5000
E-mail: infomtc@madisontelco.com
Web site: http://www.gomadison.com
Officers:
Robert W. Schwartz, Chairman
Len J. Schwartz, Chief Operating Officer
Mary J. Westernold, Chief Financial Officer
Cable Systems (2):
ILLINOIS: SORENTO/NEW DOUGLAS; STAUNTON.

MADISON COMMUNICATIONS INC.
216 S. Marion St.
Athens, AL 35611-2504
Phone: 256-536-3724
Cable Systems (1):
ARKANSAS: HUNTSVILLE.

KASMIR MAJEWSKI
510 Warwood Ave
Wheeling, WV 26003
Phones: 304-277-2811; 740-795-5005

Branch Office:
Powhatan Cable
PO Box 67
140 First St
Powhatan Point, OH 54942
Phone: 740-795-5005

Cable Systems (3):
OHIO: BARTON; POWHATAN POINT.
WEST VIRGINIA: WARWOOD.

MANAWA TELECOM INC.
131 2nd St
PO Box 130
Manawa, WI 54949
Phone: 920-596-2700
Fax: 920-596-3775
Web site: http://www.wolfnet.net
Officers:
Thomas R. Squires, President
Robert E. Squires, Vice President
Brian J. Squires, Secretary-Treasurer
Ownership: Manawa Telecommunications Inc..
Cable Systems (1):
WISCONSIN: MANAWA.
Other Holdings:
Telephone

MANNING MUNICIPAL COMMUNICATION & TV SYSTEM UTILITY
719 3rd St
PO Box 386
Manning, IA 51455
Phone: 712-655-2660
Fax: 712-655-3304
E-mail: info@mmctsu.com
Web site: http://www.mmctsu.com
Ownership: Community owned--Manning, IA.
Cable Systems (1):
IOWA: MANNING.

MAPLETON COMMUNICATIONS INC.
513 Main
Mapleton, IA 51034
Phone: 712-271-400
Fax: 712-881-2726
Web site: http://www.mapletoncomm.net
Officer:
Thomas LeFebvre, Chairman
Ownership: City owned--Mapleton, IA, 50%; Long Lines, see listing,, 50%.
Cable Systems (1):
IOWA: MAPLETON.

MARCO ISLAND CABLE
926 Windward Dr.
PO Box 344
Marco Island, FL 34145
Phone: 239-642-4545
Fax: 239-394-4895
E-mail: marcocable@marcocable.com
Web site: http://marcocable.net
Ownership: William Gaston, Gen. Mgr..
Cable Systems (1):
FLORIDA: MARCO ISLAND.

MARGARETVILLE TELEPHONE CO.
50 Swart St
PO Box 260
Margaretville, NY 12455
Phones: 845-586-3311; 845-586-2288
Fax: 845-586-4050
E-mail: mtc@catskill.net
Web site: http://www.mtctelcom.com
Cable Systems (1):
NEW YORK: MARGARETVILLE.

MARIANAS CABLEVISION INC.
Chalan Kanea
PO Box 1298
Saipan, MP 96950
E-mail: mcv.service@saipan.com
Web site: http://www.mcvcnmi.com
Officers:
Peter Sinclair, President
Robert O'Connor, Vice President
Michael Saislan, Secretary-Treasurer
Chris Kurz, Chief Financial Officer
Ownership: UMDA.
Cable Systems (2):
GUAM: AGANA.
MARIANA ISLANDS: SAIPAN.

MARNE & ELK HORN TELEPHONE CO.
4242 Main St
PO Box 120
Elk Horn, IA 51531
Phone: 712-764-6141
Fax: 712-764-2773
E-mail: metc@metc.net
Web site: http://www.metc.net
Cable Systems (1):
IOWA: ELK HORN.

MARTELLE COOPERATIVE TELEPHONE ASSOCIATION
204 South St
PO Box 128
Martelle, IA 52305
Phone: 319-482-2381
Fax: 319-482-3018
E-mail: martelle@netins.net
Web site: http://www.martellecom.com
Officers:
John O. Miller, President
Richard Strother, Secretary-Treasurer
Ownership: Sandra Davis, Principal.
Cable Systems (1):
IOWA: MARTELLE.

MASSILLON CABLE TV INC.
814 Cable Crt NW
PO BOx 1000
Massillon, OH 44648-1000
Phone: 330-833-4134
Fax: 330-833-7522
Web site: http://www.massilloncabletv.com/index.php
Officers:
Richard W. Gessner, Chairman, Treasurer & Chief Financial Officer
Robert B. Gessner, President
David Hoffer, Chief Operating Officer
Susan R. Gessner, Secretary
Ownership: Richard W Gessner; Susan R Gessner, jointly, 54%; 100 stockholders, each with less than 5%.
Represented (legal): Womble, Carlyle, Sandridge & Rice.
Cable Systems (2):
OHIO: MASSILLON; WOOSTER.

MASTER VISION CABLE
25167 Weed Rd
Union City, PA 16438
Phones: 814-694-3682; 888-827-2259
Cable Systems (1):
PENNSYLVANIA: CANADOHTA LAKE.

WALTER MATKOVICH
PO Box 67
Powhatan, OH 43942
Phone: 614-795-5005
Cable Systems (2):
OHIO: BARTON; POWHATAN POINT.

EDWARD MATTOX
716 S. 3rd. St.
Parsons, KS 67357
Phone: 620-421-2322
Cable Systems (1):
KANSAS: ST. PAUL.

MCCOOK COOPERATIVE TELEPHONE CO.
330 S Nebraska St
PO Box 630
Salem, SD 57058
Phones: 605-425-2238; 605-239-4302
Fax: 605-425-2712
E-mail: customerservice@triotel.net
Web site: http://www.triotel.net
Cable Systems (1):
SOUTH DAKOTA: ALEXANDRIA.

MONTY MCCULLOUGH
PO Box 1115
Salem, AR 72576
Phone: 870-895-4993
Fax: 870-895-4905
Cable Systems (2):
ARKANSAS: SALEM; VIOLA.

MCNABB CABLE & SATELLITE INC.
308 W Main St
PO Box 218
McNabb, IL 61335
Phone: 815-882-2202
Fax: 815-882-2141
Web site: http://www.nabbnet.com
Officer:
Sally Walin, Secretary
Ownership: McNabb Telephone Co..
Cable Systems (1):
ILLINOIS: MCNABB.

MEDIACOM LLC
100 Crystal Run Rd.
Middletown, NY 10941
Phones: 845-695-2600; 845-695-2664
Fax: 845-695-2679
Web site: http://www.mediacomllc.com
Officers:
Rocco B. Commisso, Chairman & Chief Executive Officer
Mark E. Stephan, Executive Vice President & Chief Financial Officer
John G. Pascarelli, Executive Vice President, Operations
Charles J. Bartolotta, Senior Vice President, Customer Operations
Italia Commisso Weinand, Senior Vice President, Programming & Human Resources
Calvin G. Craib, Senior Vice President, Business Development
Dan Templin, Senior Vice President, Mediacom Business
Brian M. Walsh, Senior Vice President & Corporate Controller
Joseph E. Young, Senior Vice President, General Counsel & Secretary
Joseph Selvage, Group Vice President, IP Networks
Suzanne Sosiewicz-Leggio, Vice President, Financial Services
Ownership: Rocco B Commisso. On November 15, 2010 the board of directors' special committee accepted the offer of Rocco B Commisso to take Mediacom private. Mediacom became privately held March 4, 2011. Mediacom plans to relocate its headquarters to Blooming Grove, NY in the fall of 2012.
Represented (legal): Sonnenschein, Nath & Rosenthal.
Cable Systems (271):
ALABAMA: ARDMORE; BIG COVE; CAMDEN; CODEN; DAPHNE; FAIRHOPE; GREENSBORO; HUNTSVILLE; LINDEN; LIVINGSTON; MOBILE COUNTY; PERDIDO BEACH; ROBERTSDALE; THOMASVILLE.
ARIZONA: AJO; APACHE JUNCTION; NOGALES.
CALIFORNIA: CLEARLAKE OAKS; KERNVILLE; RIDGECREST; SUN CITY; VALLEY CENTER.
DELAWARE: DAGSBORO.
FLORIDA: GULF BREEZE; HAVANA (town); WEWAHITCHKA.
GEORGIA: ALBANY; AMERICUS; BAINBRIDGE; CAMILLA; COLUMBUS; CUTHBERT; EASTMAN; FITZGERALD; HAZLEHURST; MOULTRIE; PEARSON; THOMASVILLE; TIFTON; VALDOSTA.
ILLINOIS: ABINGDON; ALTAMONT; APOLLO ACRES; ARENZVILLE; ASTORIA; ATLANTA; BRIMFIELD; BURLINGTON (village); CALEDONIA; CARTHAGE; CHARLESTON; CHILLICOTHE; CLAY CITY; CLINTON; COFFEEN; CORTLAND (village); COULTERVILLE; DELAVAN; EFFINGHAM; ELMWOOD; FAIRBURY; FARMER CITY; GERMAN VALLEY; GIBSON CITY; GOOD HOPE; GREENUP; HEBRON (village); HERRICK; HEYWORTH; INDUSTRY; IPAVA; IRVING; JACKSONVILLE; KINCAID; KIRKLAND; LACON; LE ROY; LENA; LOUISVILLE; MAHOMET; MARION; MARTINSVILLE; MATTOON; MINERAL; MOLINE; MONTICELLO; MORRIS; MURPHYSBORO; NAUVOO; NEOGA; PEARL CITY (village); PONTIAC; POPLAR GROVE; RANTOUL; ROANOKE; ROBINSON; ROSEVILLE; SCALES MOUND; SHIPMAN; SPRING GROVE (village); STREATOR; SUGAR GROVE; SULLIVAN; TAMPICO; TOWER HILL; TUSCOLA; VERMONT; VICTORIA; WASHINGTON PARK; WATSEKA; WILSONVILLE; WYOMING; ZEIGLER.
INDIANA: ANGOLA; BLUFFTON; BUTLER; KENDALLVILLE; KENTLAND; KNOX; LAGRANGE; LIGONIER; NORTH MANCHESTER; NORTH WEBSTER; ROME CITY; ROSELAWN; SAN PIERRE; WALKERTON.
IOWA: AMES; ATLANTIC; BUFFALO CENTER; BURLINGTON; CEDAR RAPIDS; CENTERVILLE; CHARLES CITY; CLINTON; DECORAH; DES MOINES; DUBUQUE; FORT DODGE; GILMORE CITY; GLADBROOK; HAMPTON; INDEPENDENCE; IOWA FALLS; KEOKUK; LANSING; MASON CITY; MOUNT PLEASANT; NEW ALBIN; NEW HAMPTON; OSAGE; OSKALOOSA; OTTUMWA; SPENCER; SPIRIT LAKE; SWEA CITY; WATERLOO; WAVERLY.
KANSAS: ALTOONA; BALDWIN CITY; BURLINGTON; EUREKA; OSWEGO; THAYER; TORONTO.
KENTUCKY: BURKESVILLE; CADIZ; CALLOWAY COUNTY; CANEYVILLE; CASEY COUNTY (southwestern portion); HENDERSON (southern portion); LINCOLN COUNTY (eastern portion); MARION; MARSHALL COUNTY; MORGANTOWN; MUNFORDVILLE; NEBO; NORTONVILLE; PARK CITY; RUSSELL COUNTY (unincorporated areas); SUMMER SHADE; TOMPKINSVILLE; TRENTON; WHITESVILLE.
MICHIGAN: MARCELLUS; MATTAWAN; MENDON (village).
MINNESOTA: APPLETON; BROWNTON; CALEDONIA; CANNON FALLS; CHATFIELD; CHOKIO; CLARA CITY; CLOQUET; COOK; DODGE CENTER; ELKO; EVELETH; GRAND MARAIS; GRAND RAPIDS; HIBBING; HOWARD LAKE; IVANHOE; LAKE CITY; LAKE MINNETONKA; MONTGOMERY; MOOSE LAKE; MOUNTAIN LAKE; NORWOOD; OLIVIA; PIPESTONE; PRIOR LAKE; REDWOOD FALLS; SILVER BAY; WASECA; WORTHINGTON.
MISSISSIPPI: BEAUMONT; LUCEDALE; ST. ANDREWS; UNION; WAVELAND; WIGGINS.
MISSOURI: ALBANY; APPLETON CITY; BETHANY; BUTLER; CAMERON; CARL JUNCTION; CARROLLTON; CARUTHERSVILLE; CASSVILLE; COLUMBIA; EVERTON; EXCELSIOR SPRINGS; FORSYTH; GRANBY; HERMANN; JEFFERSON CITY; LOWRY CITY; MARCELINE; NORBORNE; OSCEOLA; RICHMOND; SALISBURY; SEYMOUR; SPRINGFIELD.
NORTH CAROLINA: CAMDEN/CURRITUCK; EDENTON; PLYMOUTH (town); RICH

SQUARE.
OHIO: HICKSVILLE.
SOUTH DAKOTA: BROOKINGS; FREEMAN.
TENNESSEE: HUNTLAND.
WISCONSIN: ALBANY; ARGYLE; BLANCHARDVILLE; CASHTON; COON VALLEY; CUBA CITY; FENNIMORE; FORT McCOY; FREMONT; IOLA; MAUSTON; MONTICELLO; ONTARIO; ORFORDVILLE; PRAIRIE DU CHIEN; SUGAR CREEK (town).

MEDIAPOLIS CABLEVISION CO.

652 Main St.
Mediapolis, IA 52637
Phones: 319-394-3456; 800-762-1527
Fax: 319-394-9155
E-mail: office@mepotelco.net
Web site: http://www.mtctech.net
Officer:
William Malcom, General Manager
Ownership: Mediapolis Telephone Co..
Cable Systems (1):
IOWA: MEDIAPOLIS.

MEDICINE BOW CABLE

PO Box 127
Medicine Bow, WY 82329
Phone: 307-379-2594
Ownership: Vernon Scott; Vickie Scott.
Cable Systems (1):
WYOMING: MEDICINE BOW.

MERRIMAC COMMUNICATIONS LTD.

327 Palisade St
Merrimac, WI 53561
Phones: 608-493-9470; 877-493-9470
Fax: 608-493-9902
E-mail: office@merr.com
Web site: http://www.merr.com
Officers:
Bartlett A. Olson, President & Chief Executive Officer
Charlotte A. Olson, Vice President & Secretary-Treasurer
Ownership: Bartlett Olson; Charlotte Olson, jointly.
Cable Systems (1):
WISCONSIN: MERRIMAC.

MI-CONNECTION

435 S Broad St
Mooresville, NC 28115
Phone: 704-662-3255
E-mail: manager@MI-Connection.com
Web site: http://www.mi-connection.com
Cable Systems (1):
NORTH CAROLINA: MOORESVILLE.

MID-COAST CABLEVISION

505 N. Mechanic St.
PO Box 1269
El Campo, TX 77437
Phone: 979-543-6858
Fax: 979-543-9501
E-mail: khermenitt@warpspeed1.net
Web site: http://www.warpspeed1.net
Officers:
William McDonald Jr., President
Wayne Neal, Area Manager
Ownership: McDonald Investment Group, Principal.
Represented (legal): Dow Lohnes PLLC.
Cable Systems (11):
TEXAS: BAY CITY; BLESSING; EDNA; EL CAMPO; GANADO; LOUISE; MANVEL; PALACIOS; SWEENY; WEST COLUMBIA; WHARTON.

MIDCONTINENT MEDIA INC.

Ste 700
3600 Minnesota Dr
Minneapolis, MN 55435
Phone: 952-844-2600
Fax: 952-844-2660
Web site: http://www.midcocomm.com
Officers:
Patrick McAdaragh, President & Chief Executive Officer
Steven E. Grosser, Senior Vice President, Finance
W. Tom Simmons, Senior Vice President, Public Policy
Dick Busch, Vice President, Information Technology
Ownership: Midcontinent Media; Midcontinent Media ownership:; N. L Bentson, 67.7%; Joseph H Floyd, 30.27%; Mark S Niblick, 2.03%.
Represented (legal): Leventhal, Senter & Lerman PLLC; Dow Lohnes PLLC.
Cable Systems (66):
MINNESOTA: ALTURA; BABBITT; BALATON; BEMIDJI; BROWNS VALLEY; CANBY; ELY; FAIRMONT; HALLOCK; INTERNATIONAL FALLS; LITTLEFORK; OSLO; SABIN; STOCKTON; TOWER.
NEBRASKA: CODY.
NORTH DAKOTA: ARVILLA; BEACH; BEULAH; BOWMAN; CARRINGTON; CASSELTON; COOPERSTOWN; DEVILS LAKE; ESMOND; FOREST RIVER; GACKLE; GRAFTON; GRAND FORKS; HANKINSON; HARVEY; LA MOURE; LANGDON; LARIMORE; LEEDS; MANDAN; MANVEL; MCCLUSKY; MINNEWAUKAN; MINOT; MINTO; MOTT; ROLETTE; RUGBY; SOUTH HEART; WAHPETON; WILLISTON; WISHEK.
SOUTH DAKOTA: ABERDEEN TWP.; ASHTON; BOULDER CANYON; CAVOUR; FORT PIERRE; GAYVILLE; HART RANCH; HURON; IROQUOIS; MITCHELL; MOBRIDGE; PRAIRIEWOOD VILLAGE; RAPID CITY; SIOUX FALLS; SPEARFISH; WATERTOWN; WHITEWOOD; YALE.
Other Holdings:
Regional Cable Channel: Midco Sports Network.

MID-HUDSON CABLEVISION INC.

200 Jefferson Heights
PO Box 399
Catskill, NY 12414
Phone: 518-943-6600
Fax: 518-943-6603
E-mail: info@mhcable.com; cable@mid-hudson.com
Web site: http://www.mid-hudson.com; http://www2.mhcable.com
Officers:
James M. Reynolds, Chief Executive Officer
Jeff Rose, Chief Financial Officer
Stuart W. Smith, Operations Manager
Cable Systems (2):
NEW YORK: CATSKILL; DURHAM.

MID-KANSAS CABLE SERVICES INC.

805 N Main St
McPherson, KS 67460-2839
Phones: 620-241-6955; 620-345-2831
Fax: 620-345-6106
Officers:
Carl Krehbiel, President
Kathryn Krehbiel, Secretary-Treasurer
Ownership: Carl C Krehbiel Trust, 50%; Kathryn Krehbiel Trust, 50%.
Cable Systems (2):
KANSAS: GOESSEL; MOUNDRIDGE.
Other Holdings:
Cellular radio
Telephone

MID-MISSOURI BROADBAND & CABLE LLC

PO Box 524
Linn, MO 65051
Phone: 573-417-4004
E-mail: customer@osagenet.com
Web site: http://midmobroadband.com
Cable Systems (2):
MISSOURI: CHAMOIS; LINN.

MID-STATE COMMUNITY TV INC.

1001 12th St.
Aurora, NE 68818
Phone: 402-694-5101
Fax: 402-694-2848
E-mail: midstate@midstatetv.com
Web site: http://www.midstatetv.com
Officers:
Phillip C. Nelson, President
Betty Van Luchene, Secretary
Ownership: Phillip C Nelson. Nelson is Pres. of the Hamilton Telephone Co., Aurora, NE.
Cable Systems (1):
NEBRASKA: AURORA.

MIDVALE TELEPHONE EXCHANGE INC.

2205 Keithly Creek Rd.
Midvale, ID 83645
Phone: 208-355-2211
Fax: 208-355-2222
E-mail: info@midvaletelephone.com
Web site: http://www.midvaletelephone.com
Officers:
Lane Williams, President & Chief Operating Officer
Mary Williams, Chief Financial Officer
Cable Systems (1):
IDAHO: MIDVALE.

MILAN INTERACTIVE COMMUNICATIONS

PO Box 240
312 S Main
Milan, MO 63556
Phone: 660-265-7174
Officers:
Rick Gardener, President & General Manager
Sara Gardener, Vice President
Cable Systems (3):
MISSOURI: CLARENCE; MILAN; RENICK.

MILESTONE COMMUNICATIONS LP

43 Herrn Lane
Castle Rock, CO 80108
Phone: 303-393-3557
Fax: 303-993-3559
Officer:
Michael W. Drake, President
Ownership: Milestone Media Management Inc., Gen. Partner; MMMI ownership:; Michael W. Drake, sole shareholder & Pres.; Michael W. Drake, Ltd. Partner; Randy Mock, Ltd. Partner.
Represented (legal): Cinnamon Mueller.
Cable Systems (3):
WEST VIRGINIA: CASS; DURBIN; HUNTERSVILLE.

MILFORD CABLE TV

806 Okoboji Ave
PO Box 163
Milford, IA 51351
Phones: 712-338-4967; 888-404-2525
Fax: 712-338-4719
E-mail: support@milfordcable.net
Web site: http://www.milfordcable.net
Officers:
Cliff Plagman, Chairman & President
Matt Plagman, Chief Operating Officer
Cable Systems (3):
IOWA: BLAIRSBURG; MILFORD; THOR.
Other Holdings:
Cliff Plagman is Principal of Livermore Cable, see listing

RAY V. MILLER GROUP

9449 State Hwy 197S
Burnsville, NC 28714
Phone: 828-682-4074
Fax: 828-682-6895
Web site: http://www.ccvn.com
Officers:
Ray V. Miller, Chairman
Randall Miller, President
Bryan Hyder, Secretary-Treasurer
Represented (legal): Cole, Raywid & Braverman LLP.
Cable Systems (1):
NORTH CAROLINA: BURNSVILLE.
Other Holdings:
Cable Network: Interest in The Outdoor Channel
Telecommunications company: Interest in World Multicast.Com Inc.

V. DAVID & BILLIE LYNN MILLER

PO Box 509
Warner, OK 74469
Phone: 918-463-2921
Fax: 918-463-2551
Represented (legal): Ronald Comingdeer.
Cable Systems (1):
OKLAHOMA: WARNER.

MILLHEIM TV TRANSMISSION CO.

PO Box 365
Millheim, PA 16854
Phone: 814-349-4837
Officers:
Earl Heckman, President
Harold Benfer, Secretary-Treasurer & Manager
Ownership: Subscriber owned--Millheim, PA.
Cable Systems (1):
PENNSYLVANIA: MILLHEIM.

MILLINGTON CATV INC.

5115 Easley
PO Box 399
Millington, TN 38053
Phone: 901-872-3600
Fax: 901-872-6703
E-mail: customerservice@xipline.com
Web site: http://www.millingtoncable.com
Officers:
Holly Starnes, President
Laura Howard, Secretary

Branch Office:
1464 Munford Ave.
Munford, TN 38058
Phone: 901-837-3600
Ownership: Holly Starnes, 25%; 3 others, each with 25%.
Represented (legal): J. Houston Gordon.
Cable Systems (1):
TENNESSEE: MILLINGTON.

MINBURN CABLEVISION INC.

416 Chestnut St
Po Box 206
Minburn, IA 50167-0206
Phone: 515-677-2100
Fax: 515-677-2007
E-mail: minburn@minburncomm.com

Web site: http://www.minburncom.com
Officers:
Greg Burket, President
William Wright, Vice President
Michele Blair, Secretary-Treasurer
Ownership: Minburn Telephone Co..
Cable Systems (1):
IOWA: MINBURN.

MINERVA VALLEY CABLEVISION INC.
104 N Pine
PO Box 176
Zearing, IA 50278
Phone: 641-487-7399
Fax: 641-487-7599
E-mail: minerva@netins.net
Web site: http://www.minervavalley.com
Cable Systems (1):
IOWA: ZEARING.

MLGC
301 Dewey St.
Enderlin, ND 58027
Phone: 701-437-3300
Fax: 701-437-3022
E-mail: mandl@mlgc.com
Web site: http://www.mlgc.com

Branch Office:
905 Lenham Ave.
Cooperstown, ND 58425
Phone: 701-797-3301
Fax: 701-797-2541
Cable Systems (4):
NORTH DAKOTA: ENDERLIN; FINLEY; KINDRED; NORTHWOOD.

MM & G ENTERPRISES LLC
1910 Mockingbird Ln
Paragould, AR 72450
Phones: 870-586-0216; 870-919-1454
Web site: http://www.fusion-media.tv
Cable Systems (1):
ARKANSAS: OAK GROVE HEIGHTS.

JAMES MOGG TV
PO Box 328
Cheyenne, OK 73628
Phone: 580-497-2182
Officers:
James M. Mogg, President
Lura Mae Mogg, Vice President
Ownership: James M Mogg, 50%; Lura Mae Mogg, 50%.
Cable Systems (1):
OKLAHOMA: CHEYENNE.

CITY OF MONROE, WATER, LIGHT & GAS COMMISSION
215 N. Broad St.
PO Box 725
Monroe, GA 30655
Phone: 770-267-3429
Fax: 770-267-3698
Web site: http://www.monroeutilities.net
Ownership: Community owned--Monroe, GA.
Represented (legal): Preston & Malcolm PC.
Cable Systems (1):
GEORGIA: MONROE.

MONTEZUMA MUTUAL TELEPHONE CO.
107 N 4th St
PO Box 10
Montezuma, IA 50171
Phone: 641-623-5654
Fax: 641-623-2199
Web site: http://www.netins.net/ricweb/telco/montztel.htm
Cable Systems (1):
IOWA: DEEP RIVER.

MOOSEHEAD ENTERPRISES INC.
3 Lakeview St
Greenville, ME 04441
Phone: 207-695-3337
Fax: 207-695-3571
Officers:
Scott Richardson, Chairman & Chief Executive Officer
Earl Richardson Jr., President & Chief Operating & Financial Officer
Ownership: Earl Richardson.
Cable Systems (6):
MAINE: BINGHAM; GREENVILLE; GUILFORD; JACKMAN; MONSON; ROCKWOOD.
Other Holdings:
SMATV

MOREHEAD STATE UNIVERSITY
Dept. of Telecommunications
110 Ginger Hall
Morehead, KY 40351
Phone: 606-783-9090
Web site: http://www.moreheadstate.edu
Cable Systems (1):
KENTUCKY: MOREHEAD STATE UNIVERSITY.

CITY OF MORGANTON
305 E Union St
Morganton, NC 28680-3448
Phone: 828-438-5353
E-mail: compasdept@ci.morganton.nc.us
Web site: http://www.compascable.net
Officer:
Randy Loop, General Manager
Ownership: Community owned--Morganton, NC..
Cable Systems (1):
NORTH CAROLINA: MORGANTON.

WAYNE E. MORGAN
85 Cordell Lane
Coos Bay, OR 97420
Phone: 503-267-4788
Cable Systems (1):
OREGON: GREEN ACRES.

MORRIS COMMUNICATIONS CO LLC
725 Broad St
Augusta, GA 30901
Phone: 800-622-6358
Web site: http://morriscomm.com/
Officers:
William S Morris III, Chairman & Chief Executive Officer
James C Currow, Executive Vice President, Newspapers
Craig S Mitchell, Senior Vice President, Finance & Secretary-Treasurer
Steve K Stone, Senior Vice President & Chief Financial Officer
Susan Morris Baker, Vice President
Terry K House Jr., Assistant Secretary & Tax Director
Ownership: Privately held..
Cable Systems (4):
NORTH CAROLINA: FRANKLIN/SYLVA; HENDERSONVILLE; NEBO; WEST JEFFERSON.
Newspapers:
Alaska: Juneau Empire, Peninsula Clarion (Kenai).
Arkansas: Log Cabin Democrat (Conway)
Florida: The Florida Times Union (Jacksonville), The St. Augustine Record.
Georgia: Athens Banner-Herald, The Augusta Chronicle, Savannah Morning News.
Kansas: The Topeka Capital-Journal.
Minnesota: Brainerd Dispatch.
Non-daily: Publishes 28 non-daily newspapers in Alaska, Florida, Georgia, Minnesota, South Carolina & Texas.
South Carolina: Bluffton Today.
Texas: Amarillo Globe-News, Lubbock Avalanche-Journal.
Radio Stations:
Alaska: KBRJ (FM), KEAG (FM), KFQD (AM), KHAR (AM), KMXS (FM) & KWHL (FM) Anchorage.
California: KCLB-FM & KNWZ (AM) Coachella, KKUU (FM) Indio, KNWQ (AM) Palm Springs, KFUT (AM) & KXPS (AM) Thousand Palms, KDGL (FM) & KNWH (AM) Yucca Valley.
Kansas: KABI (AM) & KSAJ-FM Abilene, KBLS (FM) North Fort Riley, KSAL (AM), KSAL-FM & KYEZ (FM) Salina, WIBW (AM) & WIBW-FM Topeka.
Texas: KGNC (AM) & KGNC-FM Amarillo.
Washington: KDUX-FM & KXRO (AM) Aberdeen, KWOK (AM) & KXXK (FM) Hoquiam, KWIQ (AM) & KWIQ-FM Moses Lake, KKRT (FM) & KKRV (FM) Wenatchee, KWLN (FN) Wilson Creek.
Other Holdings:
Magazine: Publishes 21 periodicals through Morris Magazines plus 41 magazines and shoppers through Morris Publishing Group.
Outdoor advertising: Fairway Outdoor Advertising.
Publishing holdings: Globe Pequot Press

MOULTRIE TELECOMMUNICATIONS INC.
111 State & Broadway
PO Box 350
Lovington, IL 61937
Phone: 217-873-5211
Fax: 217-873-4990
Web site: http://www.moultriemulticorp.com
Officer:
David A. Bowers, President & Chief Financial Officer
Represented (legal): John V. Freeman.
Cable Systems (1):
ILLINOIS: LOVINGTON.

MOUNTAIN ZONE TV SYSTEMS
PO Box 1377
Alpine, TX 79831-1377
Phones: 432-837-2300; 432-837-5423
E-mail: mtnzone@sbcglobal.net
Web site: http://www.mountainzonetv.net
Officer:
Steve Neu, Manager
Represented (legal): Cinnamon Mueller.
Cable Systems (6):
TEXAS: BALMORHEA; FORT DAVIS; MARATHON; MARFA; PRESIDIO; VALENTINE.

MULLAN CABLE TV INC.
202 N 2nd St
PO Box 615
Mullan, ID 83846
Phone: 208-744-1223
Fax: 208-556-5609
E-mail: cs@mctvusa.tv
Web site: http://www.mctvusa.tv
Ownership: James R. Dahl, Chmn. & Pres..
Cable Systems (1):
IDAHO: MULLAN.

MURRAY ELECTRIC SYSTEM
401 Olive St
PO Box 1095
Murray, KY 42071-1095
Phone: 270-753-5312
Fax: 270-753-6494
E-mail: murrayelectric@murray-ky.net
Web site: http://www2.murray-ky.net
Cable Systems (1):
KENTUCKY: MURRAY.

MUSCATINE POWER & WATER
3205 Cedar St
PO Box 899
Muscatine, IA 52761-0075
Phone: 563-262-2631
Fax: 563-262-3373
E-mail: onlinecs@mpw.org
Web site: http://www.mpw.org
Cable Systems (1):
IOWA: MUSCATINE.

MWR CABLE
599 Tomales Rd.
Petaluma, CA 94952-5000
Phone: 707-765-7343
Fax: 707-765-7329
Cable Systems (1):
CALIFORNIA: PETALUMA COAST GUARD STATION.

NALMAN ELECTRONICS
4440 26th St W
Bradenton, FL 34207
Phone: 941-758-5533
Fax: 941-756-5460
Cable Systems (1):
FLORIDA: SARALAKE ESTATES MOBILE HOME PARK.

NEBONET INC.
656 N Main #7
Nephi, UT 84648
Phones: 435-623-1435; 435-623-7010
Fax: 888-288-3015
E-mail: sales@nebonet.com
Web site: http://www.nebonet.com
Ownership: J C Mickelson.

NEBRASKA CENTRAL TELECOM INC.
PO Box 700
Gibbon, NE 68840
Phones: 308-468-6341; 888-873-6282
Fax: 308-468-9929
E-mail: customer-service@nctc.net
Web site: http://www.nctc.net
Cable Systems (12):
NEBRASKA: ANSLEY; ARCADIA; ASHTON; BOELUS; BURWELL; DANNEBROG; ELBA; MASON CITY; NORTH LOUP; SARGENT; SCOTIA; TAYLOR.

CITY OF NEGAUNEE CABLE TV
City Hall, Silver St
PO Box 70
Negaunee, MI 49866
Phones: 906-475-7400; 906-475-7700
Fax: 906-475-9994
E-mail: dpwcable@cityofnegaunee.com
Web site: http://www.cityofnegaunee.com/Cable.html
Ownership: Community owned--Negaunee, MI.

Cable Systems (1):
MICHIGAN: NEGAUNEE.

NELSON COUNTY CABLEVISION CORPORATION

400 Front St.
PO Box 395
Lovingston, VA 22949
Phones: 434-263-4805; 800-376-8165
Fax: 434-263-4821
E-mail: info@cyberwind.net
Web site: http://www.nelsoncable.com
Officers:
Joe Lee McClellan, Chairman & President
W. Burkes Fortune, Vice President & Treasurer
Ownership: Joe Lee McClellan.
Cable Systems (3):
VIRGINIA: LOVINGSTON/SHIPMAN; SCOTTSVILLE; WINTERGREEN.

NELSONVILLE TV CABLE INC.

One W. Columbus St.
Nelsonville, OH 45764
Phone: 740-753-2686
Fax: 740-753-3326
Web site: http://www.nelsonvilletv.com
Officers:
Eugene R. Edwards, President
Betty Edwards, Secretary-Treasurer
Ownership: Eugene R Edwards, 99.6%; Betty Edwards, 0.4%.
Cable Systems (1):
OHIO: NELSONVILLE.

NEMONT TELEPHONE COOP

61 Hwy 13 S
PO Box 600
Scobey, MT 59263
Phone: 800-636-6680
Fax: 406-783-5283
E-mail: nemont@nemont.coop
Web site: http://www.nemont.net
Cable Systems (1):
MONTANA: WOLF POINT.

NEPSK INC.

12 Brewer Rd.
PO Box 1149
Presque Isle, ME 04769
Phone: 207-764-4461
Fax: 207-764-5329
Web site: http://www.wagmtv.com
Officers:
Gordon Wark, President
Peter P. Kozloski, Chief Executive Officer
Catherine Donovan, Vice President & Chief Financial Officer
Carole M. Kozloski, Vice President

Branch Office:
72 Main
PO Box 610
Houlton, ME 04730
Phone: 207-532-2579
Fax: 207-532-4025
Ownership: Peter P Kozloski.
Cable Systems (8):
MAINE: DANFORTH; HOULTON; HOWLAND; ISLAND FALLS; MEDWAY; MONTICELLO (town); OAKFIELD; PATTEN.
TV Stations:
Maine: WAGM-TV Presque Isle.
LPTV Stations:
Maine: W11AA Madawaska.

NEW CENTURY COMMUNICATIONS

3588 Kennebec Dr
Eagan, MN 55122
Phone: 651-688-2623
Fax: 651-688-2624
Officers:
Robert Smith, President
Richard Anderson, Vice President
Ownership: Cable Systems Services.
Cable Systems (26):
IOWA: DELHI; HOPKINTON; LUXEMBURG; WORTHINGTON.
MINNESOTA: CANOSIA TWP.; KNIFE LAKE TWP.; KNIFE RIVER; LONG LAKE; ROUND LAKE TWP..
WISCONSIN: ALMOND; BANCROFT; BRIGGSVILLE; DALTON; ENDEAVOR; GRANTON; KELLNERSVILLE; KINGSTON; MARQUETTE; MILLADORE (town); OXFORD; PACKWAUKEE; ROSHOLT; ROZELLVILLE; SAXEVILLE; TUSTIN; WOLF RIVER.

NEW DAY BROADBAND

Ste D
9155 Deschutes Rd
Palo Cedro, CA 96073
Phone: 530-547-2226
Cable Systems (6):
ARIZONA: WILLIAMS.
CALIFORNIA: HAYFORK; LEWISTON; PALO CEDRO; TEHAMA; WEAVERVILLE.

NEW KNOXVILLE TELEPHONE & CABLE CO.

PO Box 219
301 W South St
New Knoxville, OH 45871
Phone: 419-753-5000
Fax: 419-753-2950
E-mail: info@nktelco.net
Web site: http://www.nktelco.net
Officers:
Preston Meyer, Chief Executive Officer
John H. Hoge, Secretary-Treasurer
Cable Systems (1):
OHIO: NEW KNOXVILLE.

TOM NEWMAN

PO Box 3
Waterfall, PA 16689
Phone: 814-685-3464
Cable Systems (1):
PENNSYLVANIA: WATERFALL.

NEW PARIS TELEPHONE CO.

19066 E. Market St.
PO Box 7
New Paris, IN 46553
Phone: 574-831-2225
E-mail: qualcabl@bnin.net
Web site: http://www.nptel.com
Officers:
Mark Grady, Vice President
Myrna Rapp, Chief Financial Officer
Cable Systems (1):
INDIANA: NEW PARIS.

NEW RIVER CABLEVISION INC.

11401 SW State Rte. 231-235
Brooker, FL 32622
Phone: 352-485-1362
Fax: 352-485-1352
Ownership: Cable Diversified Installations.
Cable Systems (1):
FLORIDA: BROOKER.

NEWWAVE COMMUNICATIONS LLC

4th Fl
One Montgomery Plz
Sikeston, MO 63801
Phones: 573-472-9500; 888-863-9928
Fax: 573-481-9809
E-mail: info@newwavecom.com
Web site: http://www.newwavecom.com
Officers:
James M. Gleason, President & Chief Executive Officer
Keith Davidson, Chief Financial Officer
Larry Eby, Senior Vice President, Operations
Cable Systems (57):
ARKANSAS: ASHDOWN; RECTOR.
ILLINOIS: ALBION; ANNA; CAIRO; CARLINVILLE; ENFIELD; EVANSVILLE; FAIRFIELD; GRAYVILLE; GREENVILLE; HILLSBORO; LITCHFIELD; MCLEANSBORO; MOUNT CARMEL; NEWTON; NORRIS CITY; RAMSEY; SESSER; SPARTA; TAMMS; TAYLORVILLE; VANDALIA; WAYNE CITY.
INDIANA: WADESVILLE.
KENTUCKY: BEAVER DAM; BULAN; CORBIN; FLAT LICK; FULTON; GARRARD; HOPKINSVILLE; LIBERTY; MADISONVILLE; MAYFIELD; MCKINNEY; MIDDLESBORO; MURRAY; PINEVILLE; SEBREE; SOMERSET; WILLIAMSBURG.
MISSOURI: CLARKTON; DEXTER; PARMA; PORTAGEVILLE; STEELE.
SOUTH CAROLINA: CHESTERFIELD (town); PAGELAND.
TENNESSEE: BOLIVAR; BROWNSVILLE; DYER; TIPTONVILLE.
Cable Holdings:
Avenue Broadband Communications Inc., see listing.

NEXHORIZON COMMUNICATIONS INC.

9737 Wadsworth Pkwy
PO Box 7208
Westminster, CO 80021
Phone: 303-404-9700
Fax: 303-404-9702
E-mail: info@nexhorizon.us
Web site: http://www.nexhorizon.us
Officers:
Calvin D. Smiley Sr., Chairman & Chief Executive Officer
Daniel M. Smith, Chief Operating Officer
John T. Conroy, Executive Vice President, Strategic Development
Jeff Vaglio, Vice President, Technical Operations
Ronald VanDzura, Controller
Cable Systems (12):
CALIFORNIA: CHULA VISTA.
COLORADO: CHEYENNE WELLS; EADS; FLAGLER COUNTY (portions); GRANADA; HOLLY; HUGO; LARIMER COUNTY; ORDWAY; STRATTON; WALSH; WELD COUNTY.

NEXTGEN COMMUNICATIONS

234 E Oak St
PO Box 398
Glenwood City, WI 54013
Phones: 715-565-7742; 888-696-9146
Fax: 715-565-3001
E-mail: nextgen@nextgen-communications.net
Web site: http://nextgen-communications.net
Cable Systems (1):
WISCONSIN: GLENWOOD CITY.

NIAGARA COMMUNITY TV CO-OP

1081 Main St, Ste 1
PO Box 256
Niagara, WI 54151
Phone: 715-251-1526
Fax: 715-251-1527
E-mail: linda@niagaracable.com
Web site: http://www.niagaracable.com
Officers:
Rick Steeno, President
Mark Zenko, Vice President
Debbie Kallenbach, Secretary
Bruce Nygard, Treasurer
Ownership: Subscriber owned--Niagara, WI..
Cable Systems (1):
WISCONSIN: NIAGARA.

NITTANY MEDIA INC.

18 W Juniata St
PO Box 111
Lewistown, PA 17044
Phone: 717-248-3733
Fax: 717-248-3732
Web site: http://www.nittanymedia.com
Ownership: Harry J Hain; Anna A Hain, Principals.
Cable Systems (2):
PENNSYLVANIA: LEWISTOWN; McCLURE.

NORTEX COMMUNICATIONS

Drawer 587
205 N Walnut St
Muenster, TX 76252
Phone: 940-759-2251
Fax: 940-759-5557
Web site: http://www.nortex.com
Officers:
Alvin M. Fuhrman, President
Joey Anderson, Vice President, Operations
Alan Rohmer, Vice President, Finance
Ownership: Alvin M Fuhrman, 50%; Ellen G Fuhrman, 50%. Fuhrmans are affiliated with the Nortex Communications Co., Muenster, TX.
Cable Systems (1):
TEXAS: VALLEY VIEW.

NORTH BONNEVILLE COMMUNITY CABLE TV SYSTEM

PO Box 7
North Bonneville, WA 98639
Phone: 509-427-8182
Fax: 509-427-7214
E-mail: info@northbonneville.net
Ownership: Community owned--North Bonneville, WA.
Represented (legal): Woodrich & Archer LLP.
Cable Systems (1):
WASHINGTON: NORTH BONNEVILLE.

NORTHEAST CABLE TV

PO Box 4177
Youngstown, OH 44515
Phone: 330-793-7434
Fax: 330-793-7434
Ownership: Albert F Pezzenti.
Cable Systems (5):
OHIO: BROOKFIELD TWP. (Trumbull County); HUBBARD TWP. (Trumbull County); WARREN TWP. (Trumbull County); WEATHERSFIELD TWP.; YOUNGSTOWN.

NORTHEAST IOWA TELEPHONE CO.

800 N Main
Monona, IA 52159
Phone: 563-539-2122
Fax: 563-539-2003
E-mail: neitel@neitel.com
Web site: http://www.neitel.com
Officers:
Keith Mohs, President
Arlyn Schroeder, Secretary-Treasurer

Cable Systems (1):
IOWA: MONONA.

NORTHEAST LOUISIANA TELEPHONE CO. INC.

Drawer 185
6402 Howell Ave
Collinston, LA 71229
Phone: 318-874-7011
Fax: 318-874-2041
E-mail: info@ne-tel.com
Web site: http://www.northeasttel.net
Officers:
Rector L. Hopgood, President
William A. Norsworthy, Vice President
Dorothy Anne George, Secretary
Mike George, Treasurer
Ownership: Rector L Hopgood, 50%; William A Norsworthy, 50%.
Cable Systems (1):
LOUISIANA: COLLINSTON.

NORTHLAND COMMUNICATIONS CORP.

Suite 700
101 Stewart St.
Seattle, WA 98101
Phone: 206-621-1351
Fax: 206-623-9015
Web site: http://www.northlandcabletv.com
Officers:
John S. Whetzell, Chairman & Chief Executive Officer
Gary S. Jones, President
Richard I. Clark, Executive Vice President
Richard J. Dyste, Senior Vice President & Technical Services
Rick J. McElwee, Vice President & Controller
H. Lee Johnson, Director & Vice President, Southeast Operations
Paul Milan, Vice President & Senior Counsel
John E. Iverson, Secretary
R. Gregory Ferrer, Treasurer

Branch Office:
32 E. Vine
Statesboro, GA 30458
Phone: 912-489-1065
Represented (legal): Cole, Raywid & Braverman LLP; Cairncross & Hempelman PS.
Cable Systems (52):
ALABAMA: ALICEVILLE; MILLPORT.
CALIFORNIA: COARSEGOLD; LUSHMEADOWS; MARIPOSA; MOUNT SHASTA; OAKHURST; YREKA.
GEORGIA: CLAYTON; ROYSTON; SANDERSVILLE; STATESBORO; SWAINSBORO; TOCCOA; VIDALIA.
IDAHO: SANDPOINT.
NORTH CAROLINA: FOREST CITY; HARRIS; HIGHLANDS.
SOUTH CAROLINA: FIVE POINTS; GREENWOOD; SENECA.
TEXAS: BUFFALO; COOLIDGE; CORSICANA; CROCKETT; CUT AND SHOOT; DUBLIN; FAIRFIELD; GUN BARREL CITY; HAMILTON; HICO; HILLSBORO; JEWETT; KAUFMAN; KERENS; LAKE BUCHANAN; LAKE PALESTINE EAST; LAKE PALESTINE WEST; LAMESA; LLANO; MADISONVILLE; MALAKOFF; MARBLE FALLS; MARLIN; MEXIA; NEW CANEY; STEPHENVILLE; WORTHAM (town).
WASHINGTON: EPHRATA; MOSES LAKE; OTHELLO.

NORTHSIDE TV CORP.

521 Vulcan St
Iron Mountain, MI 49801-2333
Phone: 906-774-1351
Fax: 906-774-1351
Web site: http://www.upnorthcable.com
Ownership: Subscriber owned--Iron Mountain.
Cable Systems (1):
MICHIGAN: IRON MOUNTAIN.

NORTHSTAR BROADBAND LLC

PO Box 2576
Post Falls, ID 83877
Phones: 208-262-9394; 800-572-0902
E-mail: j.webb@northstarbroadband.net
Web site: http://www.northstarbroadband.net/
Officers:
Greg Lundwall, General Operations
Jennifer Webb, Office Manager
Cable Systems (13):
WASHINGTON: CONNELL; DAVENPORT; DEER PARK; DIAMOND LAKE; IONE; LIBERTY LAKE; LIND; METALINE FALLS; ODESSA (town); RITZVILLE; TEKOA; WARDEN; WILBUR.

NORTHSTATE CABLEVISION CO.

180 NE 2nd St
PO Box 297
Dufur, OR 97021
Phone: 541-467-2409
Officers:
J. W. Damon, President
Barbara Damon, Vice President
Helen Saunders, Secretary-Treasurer
Cable Systems (1):
OREGON: DUFUR.
Other Holdings:
Telephone: Northstate Telephone Co., Dufur, OR.

NORTH TEXAS BROADBAND

PO Box 676
Aubery, TX 76227
Phones: 940-365-2030; 888-207-0204
E-mail: customerservice@northtxbroadband.com
Web site: http://northtxbroadband.com
Cable Systems (2):
TEXAS: CADDO PEAK; EGAN.

NORTHWEST COMMUNICATIONS INC.

844 Wood St
PO Box 186
Havelock, IA 50546
Phone: 712-776-2222
Fax: 712-776-4444
E-mail: nis@ncn.net
Web site: http://www.northwest.coop
Officers:
Thomas Eberle, President
Donald D. Miller, Executive Vice President
Donald Banwart, Secretary-Treasurer
Ownership: Northwest Telephone Cooperative.
Cable Systems (1):
IOWA: HAVELOCK.

NORTHWEST COMMUNITY COMMUNICATIONS

120 Birch St W
Amery, WI 54001
Phone: 715-268-7101
Fax: 715-268-9194
E-mail: info@nwcomm.net
Web site: http://www.nwcomm.net
Ownership: Amery Telcom.
Cable Systems (4):
WISCONSIN: AMERY; NEW RICHMOND; SOLON SPRINGS; SOMERSET.
Other Holdings:
Telephone

CITY OF NORWAY CATV

915 Main St.
Norway, MI 49870
Phone: 906-563-9961
Fax: 906-563-7502
E-mail: catv@norwaymi.com
Web site: http://www.norwaymi.com/?CATVinformation
Ownership: Community owned--Norway, MI.
Cable Systems (1):
MICHIGAN: NORWAY.

NOVA CABLEVISION INC.

PO Box 1412
Galesburg, IL 61402
Phone: 309-342-9681
Fax: 309-342-4408
Web site: http://www.novacablevision.com
Ownership: Robert G Fischer Jr., Chief Exec. & Operating Officer.
Cable Systems (10):
ILLINOIS: CAMERON; GLADSTONE; KEITHSBURG; KIRKWOOD; LAKE BRACKEN; LITTLE YORK; NEW BOSTON; RIO; TRIVOLI; WEE-MA-TUK HILLS.

RANDY NOVAKOVICH

215 North B St
Bridger, MT 59014
Phone: 406-662-3516
E-mail: randy@brmt.net
Cable Systems (1):
MONTANA: BRIDGER.

STEPHEN NOWELL

Hwy 45
PO Box 345
Trenton, TN 38382
Phone: 731-855-2808
Fax: 731-855-9512
Cable Systems (1):
TENNESSEE: TRENTON.

NUSHAGAK COOPERATIVE INC.

557 Kenny Wren Rd.
PO Box 350
Dillingham, AK 99576
Phone: 907-842-5251
Fax: 907-842-2799
E-mail: nushtel@nushtel.com
Web site: http://www.nushtel.com
Officers:
Nick Wahl, President
Frank Corbin, Chief Executive Officer
Pete Andrew, Vice President
Rae Belle S. Whitcomb, Secretary
Mary Ford, Treasurer
Jana Lamb, Executive Secretary
Nancy Favors, Customer Service Manager
Cable Systems (1):
ALASKA: DILLINGHAM.

NWS COMMUNICATIONS

79 Mainline Dr
Westfield, MA 01085-3313
Phone: 800-562-7081
Fax: 413-562-5415
E-mail: deleo@nwscorp.net
Web site: http://www.nwscorp.net
Officer:
Douglas J De Leo, Founder
Cable Systems (1):
CALIFORNIA: SAN DIEGO NAVAL BASE.

OCONTO FALLS CABLE TV

500 N Chestnut
PO Box 70
Oconto Falls, WI 54154
Phone: 920-846-4507
Fax: 920-846-4516
Officers:
Jim Kandoskee, President
John Dougherty, Chief Financial Officer
Ownership: Community owned--Oconto Falls, WI.
Cable Systems (1):
WISCONSIN: OCONTO FALLS.

OGDEN TELEPHONE CO.

113 SW 3rd St
PO Box 457
Ogden, IA 50212-0457
Phone: 515-275-2050
Fax: 515-275-2599
Web site: http://www.ogdentelephone.com
Cable Systems (1):
IOWA: OGDEN.

OLDTOWN COMMUNITY SYSTEMS INC.

PO Box 75
Oldtown, MD 21555
Phone: 301-478-5700
Fax: 301-478-5711
Officers:
David Bennett, President
Jacqueline Malcolm, Treasurer
Ownership: Non-profit cooperative--Oldtown, MD.
Cable Systems (1):
MARYLAND: OLDTOWN.

OLIN TELEPHONE & CABLEVISION CO.

318 S Jackson St
Olin, IA 52320
Phone: 319-484-2200
Fax: 319-484-2800
Web site: http://www.olintelephone.com
Officer:
Rodney Cozart, General Manager
Cable Systems (1):
IOWA: OLIN.

OMNI III CABLE TV INC.

224 S 4th St
PO Box 308
Jay, OK 74346
Phone: 918-253-4545
Fax: 918-253-3400
Web site: http://www.grand.net/nsomni.htm
Officers:
Teresa A. Aubrey, President
Rex Ray Brixey, Executive Vice President & Treasurer
Tim Etris, Vice President, Operations & Assistant Manager
Norma R. Holt, Vice President, Industry Relations
Sherri Stephens, Secretary
Ownership: Teresa Aubrey, 51%; Norma Holt, 49%. Aubrey & Holt are execs. with the Grand Telephone Co., Jay, OK.
Cable Systems (1):
OKLAHOMA: DISNEY.
Other Holdings:
Cellular radio

ONELINK COMMUNICATIONS

PO Box 192296
San Juan, PR 00919-2296
Phones: 787-766-0909; 787-622-1400
Fax: 787-250-6532
E-mail: servicio@onelinkpr.com
Web site: http://onelinkpr.com
Officers:
Bill Chain, General Manager

Jorge Hernandez, Vice President & Chief Financial Officer
Nestor Cardona, Chief Operating Officer
Jeffrey Engleman, Director, Customer Service
Francisco Marrero, Director, Information Technology (IT)
Vidia Arill, Director, Human Resources
Ownership: MidOcean Partners; Crestview Partners; MP ownership:; Tyler Zachem, Managing Dir.; CP ownership:; Jeffrey A. Marcus, Managing Dir..
Cable Systems (1):
PUERTO RICO: SAN JUAN.

ONEONTA TELEPHONE CO. INC.

PO Box 1500
Oneonta, AL 35121
Phone: 205-625-3591
Officers:
R. C. Corr, Chairman & Chief Executive Officer
Bryan Corr, President
Doris Corr, Vice President & Secretary-Treasurer
Cable Systems (1):
ALABAMA: ONEONTA.
Other Holdings:
Cellular radio

ONLINENW

340 Ford St
McMinnville, OR 97128
Phones: 503-883-9200; 866-876-4052
Web site: http://www.onlinenw.com

ONSLOW COOPERATIVE TELEPHONE ASSOCIATION

102 Anamosa Ave
PO Box 6
Onslow, IA 52321
Phone: 563-485-2833
Fax: 563-485-3891
Web site: http://www.yourclosestconnection.com/membership.asp?id=154
Officer:
Ron Fagan, Chairman
Cable Systems (1):
IOWA: ONSLOW.

OPP CABLEVISION

108 North Main St
Opp, AL 36467
Phone: 334-493-4571
Fax: 334-493-6666
E-mail: support@oppcatv.com
Web site: http://www.oppcatv.com
Ownership: Community owned--Opp, AL..
Cable Systems (1):
ALABAMA: OPP.

ORBITEL COMMUNICATIONS

Ste B-9
21116 N John Wayne Pkwy
Maricopa, AZ 85239
Phone: 877-274-5269
Web site: http://www.orbitelcom.com
Ownership: MGC Capital Corp..
Cable Systems (1):
ARIZONA: MARICOPA.

OTEC COMMUNICATION CO.

245 W 3rd St
PO Box 427
Ottoville, OH 45876-0427
Phone: 419-453-3324
Fax: 419-453-2468
E-mail: tomtc@bright.net
Web site: http://www.ottovillemutual.com
Officers:
Basil Alt, President
Ray Kaufman, Secretary-Treasurer
Ownership: Non-profit organization--Ottoville, OH.
Cable Systems (1):
OHIO: OTTOVILLE.

OUR CABLE

112 E Main St
PO Box 190
Breda, IA 51436
Phone: 877-873-8715
E-mail: info@ourcableia.com
Web site: http://ourcableia.com
Cable Systems (7):
IOWA: HAMBURG; MALVERN; OAKLAND; SIDNEY; TABOR; TREYNOR.
NEBRASKA: BEAVER LAKE.

PALMER MUTUAL TELEPHONE CO.

306 Main St
PO Box 155
Palmer, IA 50571
Phone: 712-359-2411
Fax: 712-359-2200
E-mail: palmerone@PalmerOne.com
Web site: http://www.palmerone.com
Officer:
Verne Metzger, President
Cable Systems (1):
IOWA: PALMER.

P & W TV CABLE SYSTEMS INC.

109 Depot Rd
Paintsville, KY 41240
Phone: 606-789-7603
Fax: 606-789-3391
Cable Systems (1):
KENTUCKY: TUTOR KEY.

PANORA COOPERATIVE CABLEVISION ASSN. INC.

114 E Main St
PO Box 217
Panora, IA 50216
Phone: 641-755-2200
Fax: 641-755-2425
E-mail: panora@netins.net
Web site: http://www.panoratelco.com
Officer:
Ron Reynolds, Chairman
Cable Systems (3):
IOWA: BAGLEY; JAMAICA; PANORA.
Other Holdings:
Cellular radio
Telephone

PARAGOULD LIGHT WATER & CABLE

1901 Jones Rd
PO Box 9
Paragould, AR 72450
Phone: 870-239-7700
Fax: 870-239-7727
E-mail: support@paragould.net
Web site: http://www.clwc.com
Cable Systems (1):
ARKANSAS: PARAGOULD.

PARK TV & ELECTRONICS INC.

205 E Fire Lane Dr
Cissna Park, IL 60924
Phones: 815-457-2659; 800-474-9488
Fax: 815-457-2735
Cable Systems (22):
ILLINOIS: ARMSTRONG; BIRDS; BISMARCK; BUCKLEY (village); CISSNA PARK (village); POTOMAC (village); RANKIN (village); WEST SALEM; WHITE HEATH.
INDIANA: BOSWELL; CLOVERDALE; DARLINGTON; JAMESTOWN; MONTEZUMA; NEW MARKET; NEWPORT; OXFORD; PERRYSVILLE; ROACHDALE; WAYNETOWN; WEST LEBANON; WORTHINGTON.

PARTNER COMMUNICATIONS COOPERATIVE

101 E Church St
PO Box 8
Gilman, IA 50106
Phones: 641-498-7701; 877-433-7701
Fax: 641-498-7308
E-mail: custsvc@partnercom.net
Web site: http://www.pcctel.net
Officers:
J. Harry Scurr Jr., President
Bill Hotger, Vice President
Daniel Carnahan, Secretary

Branch Offices:
128 W Main St
State Center, IA 50247
Phone: 641-483-7701
PO Box 100
316 Railroad St
Kellogg, IA 50135
Phone: 641-526-8585
Cable Systems (1):
IOWA: GILMAN.

PC TELCORP

240 S Interocean Ave
PO Box 387
Holyoke, CO 80734
Phone: 970-854-2201
Fax: 970-854-2668
E-mail: customerservice@pctelcom.coop
Web site: http://www.pctelcom.coop
Officers:
Vincent Kropp, General Manager
Pete Markle, Director of Operations
Lonnie Krueger, Lead Network/Broadband Technician
Cable Systems (4):
COLORADO: FLEMING; HOLYOKE; JULESBURG; SEDGWICK.

PENASCO VALLEY TELECOMMUNICATIONS

4011 W. Main St.
Artesia, NM 88210
Phone: 505-748-1241
Fax: 505-746-4142
E-mail: csr@pvt.com
Web site: http://www.pvt.com
Officers:
Bob L. Mayberry, President
Mike G. Casabonne, Vice President
Peggy L. Bell, Secretary
Elizabeth F. Mahill, Treasurer

Branch Offices:
1311 W. Main St.
Artersia, NM 88210
Phone: 505-746-9844
118824001 W. Pierce
Calrsbad, NM 88220
Phone: 505-628-0604
2400 N. Grimes
Hobbs, NM 88240
Phone: 505-392-9958
2682 Hwy. 82
Mayhill, NM 88339
Phone: 505-687-2600
110 W. College
Roswell, NM 88201
Phone: 505-627-9424
823 S. White Sands Blvd.
Alamogordo, NM 88310
Phone: 505-443-0411
Cable Systems (2):
NEW MEXICO: ARTESIA; ELEPHANT BUTTE.

PENCOR SERVICES INC.

656 Delaware Ave
Palmerton, PA 18071
Phones: 610-826-2552; 610-826-7311
Fax: 610-826-7626
E-mail: custserv@corp.ptd.net
Web site: http://www.pencorsuperstore.com
Officers:
Donald G. Reinhard, Chairman
Fred A. Reinhard, President
Richard Semmel, Vice President, Operations
Mark Masenheimer, Vice President & General Manager, Blue Ridge Communications
Jeff Gehman, Treasurer
Cable Systems (19):
PENNSYLVANIA: ARNOT; BEACH LAKE; BENTLEY CREEK; DUNCANNON; DUSHORE; EPHRATA; GALETON; GREENTOWN; HAWLEY; HEMLOCK FARMS DEVELOPMENT; HONESDALE; LEROY TWP.; MESHOPPEN; MILFORD; NEWBERRY TWP.; PALMERTON; STROUDSBURG; TROY; WELLSBORO.
Newspapers:
Pennsylvania: Lehighton Times News
Other Holdings:
Telephone: Palmerton Telephone Co.

PEREGRINE COMMUNICATIONS

Suite 16A
14818 W. 6th Ave.
Golden, CO 80401
Phones: 303-278-9660; 800-344-5404
Fax: 303-278-9685
E-mail: peregrine.info@perecom.com
Web site: http://www.perecom.com
Ownership: John Post, Pres. & Chief Exec. Officer.
Cable Systems (2):
NEBRASKA: PAXTON; STRATTON.

DAVID PETTY

523 8th St
Comfort, TX 78013
Phone: 830-995-2813
Fax: 830-995-2245
Cable Systems (2):
TEXAS: COMFORT; LAVERNIA.

PHOENIX CABLE INC.

17 S Franklin Tpk
Ramsey, NJ 07446
Phone: 201-825-9090
Fax: 201-825-8794
Officers:
James Feeney, President
Charles D. Himerlick, Assistant Vice President, Operations
Danielle Bean, Assistant Vice President
Represented (legal): Cole, Raywid & Braverman LLP.
Cable Systems (5):
CUBA: GUANTANAMO BAY.
NEW YORK: LONG LAKE; MINERVA (town); NEWCOMB; SUMMIT (town).

PHONOSCOPE LTD.

6105 Westline Dr
Houston, TX 77036
Phone: 713-272-4600
Fax: 713-271-4334
E-mail: trouble@phonoscope.com
Web site: http://www.phonoscope.com
Ownership: Partnership.

Cable Systems (1):
TEXAS: HOUSTON.
Other Holdings:
Data service: private data networks; Internet
Data Services: Private Fiber Networks; Digital Video Streaming; High Speed Internet; IP Telephony; Ethernet Circuits
Video production: Videoconferencing

PICKWICK CABLEVISION
1845 Old SR 57
PO Box 12
Pickwick Dam, TN 38365
Phone: 731-689-5722
Fax: 731-689-3632
Web site: http://www.pickwickcable.net
Ownership: Bob Campbell.
Cable Systems (1):
TENNESSEE: COUNCE.

PIEDMONT TELEPHONE MEMBERSHIP CORP.
191 Reeds Baptist Church Rd
Lexington, NC 27295
Phone: 336-787-5433
Fax: 336-787-5246
E-mail: ptmc@ptmc.net
Web site: http://www.ptmc.net/TV/index.htm
Ownership: Surry Telephone Membership Corp..
Represented (legal): Crisp, Page & Currin LLP.
Cable Systems (1):
NORTH CAROLINA: REEDS CROSS ROADS.

PINE RIVER CABLE
PO Box 96
McBain, MI 49657
Phone: 888-244-2288
Fax: 231-825--0191
Cable Systems (31):
MICHIGAN: AKRON/FAIRGROVE; ASHLEY; BARRYTON; BARTON CITY; BEAVER ISLAND; BOARDMAN TWP. (southern portion); BRETHREN; BRUTUS; CARSON CITY; FALMOUTH; FINE LAKE; GLENNIE (village); KALEVA (village); LE ROY (village); LUZERNE; MAPLE RAPIDS; MARION; MCBAIN; MESICK; MIKADO TWP.; MISSAUKEE COUNTY (unincorporated areas); NASHVILLE; PERRINTON; STERLING; UNIONVILLE; WELLSTON; WEST BRANCH; WOLF LAKE; WOODLAND (village).
OKLAHOMA: CATOOSA; TULSA COUNTY (western portion).

PINPOINT COMMUNICATIONS INC.
611 Patterson
PO Box 490
Cambridge, NE 69022
Phone: 308-697-3375
Fax: 308-697-3631
Web site: http://www.pnpt.com
Officers:
Alec Geist, Chief Executive Officer
J. Richard Shoemaker, President

Branch Office:
302 W. B St.
McCook, NE 69001
Phone: 308-345-3870
Ownership: PinPoint Holdings Inc..
Cable Systems (4):
NEBRASKA: BEAVER CITY; CAMBRIDGE; CULBERTSON; OXFORD.

PIONEER COMMUNICATIONS
120 W Kansas Ave
PO Box 707
Ulysses, KS 67880-2001
Phones: 620-356-3211; 800-308-7536
Fax: 620-356-3242
E-mail: marketing@pioncomm.net
Web site: http://www.pioncomm.net
Officers:
William Nicholas, President
Bill Boekhaus, Director
Leon Young, Director

Branch Offices:
JOHNSON CITY
110 Chestnut
Johnson City, KS 67855
SATANTA
211 S Sequoyah
Satanta, KS 67870
Phone: 620-649-2225
SYRACUSE
PO Box 1445
210 N Main
Syracuse, KS 67878
Phone: 620-384-7721
SCOTT CITY
411 Main St
Scott City, KS 67871
Phone: 620-872-2998
LAKIN
PO Box 724
201 N Main
Lakin, KS 67860
Phone: 260-355-7355
HUGOTON
PO Box 460
114 E 6th
Hugoton, KS 67951
Phone: 316-544-4392
Represented (legal): Lukas, Nace, Gutierrez & Sachs.
Cable Systems (1):
KANSAS: ULYSSES.

PITCAIRN COMMUNITY ANTENNA SYSTEM
582 6th St
Pitcairn, PA 15140
Phone: 412-372-6500
Fax: 412-373-1464
Web site: http://www.pitcairnborough.us
Officers:
Orelio Vecchio, President
Gary Parks, Secretary-Treasurer
Ownership: Community owned--Pitcairn, PA.
Cable Systems (1):
PENNSYLVANIA: PITCAIRN.

PLANTATION CABLEVISION INC.
865 Harmony Rd NE
PO Box 494
Eatonton, GA 31024
Phones: 706-485-7740; 800-652-3044
Fax: 706-485-2590
Web site: http://www.plantationcable.net
Officers:
James H. Hall, President
Joel H. Hall, Chief Operating Officer
John H. Hall, Vice President, Engineering
Cable Systems (1):
GEORGIA: GREENE COUNTY (unincorporated areas).

POLAR COMMUNICATIONS
110 4th St E
PO Box 270
River, ND 58270
Phones: 702-284-7221; 800-284-7222
Fax: 701-284-7205
Web site: http://www.polarcomm.com

Branch Office:
112 W Main St
Mayville, ND 58257
Phone: 701-788-7221
Fax: 701-284-9622
Ownership: David Drucker; Penny Drucker. Druckers also have interest in Cayo Hueso Networks LLC, Denver Digital Television LLC, Echonet Corp., GreenTV Corp. & Ketchikan TV LLC, see listings.
Cable Systems (2):
NORTH DAKOTA: LAKOTA; PEMBINA.

PONDEROSA CABLEVISION
47034 Rd 201
O'Neals, CA 93645
Phones: 559-868-6000; 800-682-1878
E-mail: cherylf@ponderosatel.com
Web site: http://www.goponderosa.com

Branch Office:
Service & Engineering Offices
47671 Rd 200
O'Neals, CA 93645
Phone: 559-868-6000
Cable Systems (1):
CALIFORNIA: NORTH FORK.

POPLAR BLUFF MUNICIPAL UTILITIES
3000 N. Westwood
Poplar Bluff, MO 63901
Phone: 573-686-8020
Fax: 573-686-8695
E-mail: dlpresley@pbutilities.com
Web site: http://www.mycitycable.com
Officer:
Dave Presley, Technical Manager
Cable Systems (1):
MISSOURI: POPLAR BLUFF.

PREMIER COMMUNICATIONS INC.
339 1st Ave. NE
Sioux Center, IA 51250
Phone: 712-722-3451
Fax: 712-722-1113
E-mail: dboone@mypremieronline.com
Web site: http://www.mypremieronline.com
Cable Systems (8):
IOWA: DICKENS; LE MARS; LITTLE ROCK; MELVIN; OCHEYEDAN; ORANGE CITY; ROCK RAPIDS; SIOUX CENTER.
Other Holdings:
Telephone

PRINCETOWN CABLE CO. INC.
878 Ennis Rd
Schenectady, NY 12306
Phones: 518-887-5500; 518-887-2815
Web site: http://www.princetowncable.com
Ownership: Barbara Price, Principal.
Cable Systems (1):
NEW YORK: PRINCETOWN (town).

CITY OF PROTIVIN
117 N. Main
PO Box 53
Protivin, IA 52163
Phone: 563-569-8401
Ownership: Community owned--Protivin, IA..
Cable Systems (1):
IOWA: PROTIVIN.

PROVINCIAL CABLE & DATA
Ste A
123 W Main St
Odessa, MO 64076
Phones: 816-633-1626; 866-284-3346
E-mail: mrunyan@provincial-cable.com
Cable Systems (8):
MISSOURI: ADRIAN; BUFFALO; COLE CAMP; LA MONTE; LINCOLN; SMITHTON; STOVER; STURGEON.

THE RAINIER GROUP
104 Washington Ave. N
Eatonville, WA 98328
Phone: 360-832-6161
Fax: 360-832-8817
Web site: http://www.rainierconnect.com
Ownership: Mashell Telecom.
Cable Systems (1):
WASHINGTON: EATONVILLE.

RAMCO BROADBAND SERVICES
Ste 320-119
726 Rt 202
Bridgewater, NJ 08807
Phone: 903-424-2015
E-mail: info@rmnj.net
Web site: http://www.rmnj.net
Officer:
Robert Motyka, President & General Manager
Cable Systems (1):
ALABAMA: CHEROKEE.

R&S COMMUNICATIONS LLC
PO Box 261
Castlewood, VA 24224
Phone: 800-801-4078
Web site: http://randscommunications.com
Officer:
Richard Beesmer, President & General Manager
Cable Systems (1):
VIRGINIA: SPEEDWELL.

RAPID COMMUNICATIONS LLC
19336 Goddard Ranch Ct
Suite 220
Morrison, CO 80465
Phone: 303-805-8085
Fax: 303-697-2217
Officers:
Tom Semptimphelter, President & Chief Executive Officer
Steve Rice, Vice President & Chief Technology Officer
Belinda Murphy, Vice President
Thomas Gelardi, Chief Operating Officer
Ownership: Alta Communications; Columbia Capital; Housatonic Partners.
Cable Systems (16):
ALABAMA: ALTOONA.
ARIZONA: GOLDEN SHORES.
ARKANSAS: FOUKE; HIGGINSON; LOCUST BAYOU; PLAINVIEW.
NEW MEXICO: FORT SUMNER; MELROSE; SANTA ROSA; TATUM.
OREGON: BOARDMAN; BROWNSVILLE; KNAPPA; MAPLETON; UMATILLA; WESTON.

RB3 LLC
515 E Longview St
Arp, TX 75780
Phone: 800-687-1258
Web site: http://www.reachbroadband.net
Ownership: TS Communications Inc.; TSCI ownership:; Tom Semptimphelter.
Cable Systems (47):
OKLAHOMA: ERICK; EUFAULA; FLETCHER; RUSH SPRINGS; VELMA.
TEXAS: ABERNATHY; ANTON; BROWNFIELD; CHEROKEE COUNTY (northern portions); CLIFTON; COLEMAN; COMANCHE; CROSBY-TON; DE LEON; DEVINE; EDEN; ELDORADO; FRIONA; GOLIAD; GORMAN; HALE CENTER; HART; HONDO; IDALOU; KENEDY; LINDEN; LOCKNEY; LUBBOCK; MART; MASON; MATADOR (town); MEMPHIS; MENARD; MERTZON; MULESHOE; O'DONNELL; OLTON; ORE CITY; PLEASANTON; RALLS; SILVER-

TON; STERLING CITY; TAHOKA; THREE RIVERS; VALLEY MILLS; WEST; WHITNEY.

RC TECHNOLOGIES CORP.
205 Main St
PO Box 196
New Effington, SD 57255
Phones: 605-637-5211; 800-256-6854
Fax: 605-637-5302
Web site: http://www.tnics.com
Officers:
Pamela Harrington, General Manager
Scott Bostrom, Operations Manager
Rachel Bartnick, Marketing & Sales Manager
Paul Gravdahl, Controller
Ownership: Roberts County Telephone Cooperative Assn..
Cable Systems (1):
SOUTH DAKOTA: NEW EFFINGTON.

READLYN TELEPHONE CO.
121 Main St
PO Box 159
Readlyn, IA 50668
Phones: 319-279-3375; 800-590-7747
Fax: 319-279-7575
E-mail: readlyn@netins.net
Web site: http://www.readlyntelco.com
Officer:
Burton Thies, President
Ownership: Cooperative -- Readlyn, IA.
Cable Systems (1):
IOWA: READLYN.

REALSTAR COMMUNICATIONS
Ste 525
1020 19th St NW
Washington, DC 20036
Phone: 202-379-3115
Web site: http://www.realstartv.com
Officers:
Antonn Muhammad, Chairman & President
Kelvin Smith, Chief Executive Officer
Varick Baiyina, Chief Communications Officer
Cable Systems (12):
ARIZONA: BLACK CANYON CITY; DUDLEYVILLE; ELOY; HEBER; KEARNY; MAMMOTH; ORACLE; SAN MANUEL; ST. JOHNS; SUPERIOR; YARNELL.
NEVADA: TONOPAH.

REBELTEC COMMUNICATIONS LLC
185 South 1st East St.
Cheyenne Wells, CO 80810
Phones: 719-767-8902; 866-879-7824
Fax: 719-767-8906
E-mail: tech@rebeltec.net
Web site: http://www.rebeltec.net
Cable Systems (1):
COLORADO: KIT CARSON.

RED RIVER CABLE TV
PO Box 674
Coushatta, LA 71019
Phone: 318-932-4991
Fax: 318-932-5123
Ownership: Jim Hardy, Principal.
Cable Systems (3):
LOUISIANA: CAMPTI; CLARENCE; COUSHATTA.

RED'S TV CABLE INC.
601 W Horne Ave
PO Box 202
Farmville, NC 27828
Phone: 252-753-3074
E-mail: cable@redcable.com
Ownership: Frank Styers.
Cable Systems (1):
NORTH CAROLINA: BATH.

RELIANCE CONNECTS
301 S Broadway
PO Box 1283
Estacada, OR 97023
Phone: 503-630-3545
Fax: 503-630-4464
E-mail: support@rconnects.com
Web site: http://www.relianceconnects.com
Officer:
Brenda Crosby, Manager
Ownership: Cascade Connects LLC.
Cable Systems (1):
OREGON: ESTACADA.

RESERVATION TELEPHONE COOPERATIVE
24 Main St N
Parshall, ND 58770
Phone: 701-862-3115
Fax: 701-862-3008
E-mail: rtc@restel.com
Web site: http://www.reservationtelephone.com
Cable Systems (5):
NORTH DAKOTA: GARRISON; KENMARE; MAX; PARSHALL; WATFORD CITY.

RESORTS CABLE TV
2190 S. Hwy. 27
Somerset, KY 42501
Phone: 606-679-3427
Cable Systems (1):
SOUTH CAROLINA: DAUFUSKIE ISLAND.

REVEILLE BROADBAND
614 Wheatley St
PO Box 39
Lexington, TX 78947
Phones: 979-773-4700; 866-489-4739
Fax: 979-773-4733
E-mail: mariesullivan@reveillebroadband.com
Web site: http://www.reveillebroadband.com
Officers:
Marie Sullivan, Chairman & Chief Executive Officer
Jeff Sullivan, President
Cable Systems (4):
TEXAS: BIRCH CREEK; LEXINGTON; LYONS; SMITHVILLE.
Cable Holdings:
Central Texas Cable Partners, Inc. DBa ReveilleBroadband

REYNOLDS CABLE TV INC.
PO Box 782
Swainsboro, GA 30401
Phone: 800-822-8650
E-mail: reynolds@reynoldscable.net
Web site: http://www.reynoldscable.net
Officer:
Terry Reynolds, Chairman, President & Chief Executive Officer
Ownership: Terry Reynolds, 51%; Randy Forehand, 44%; Bill McWhorter, 5%.
Represented (legal): Reddy, Begley & McCormick LLP.
Cable Systems (1):
GEORGIA: BOLINGBROKE.

RF CABLE LLC
19999 Hwy 61
Rolling Fork, MS 39159
Phone: 662-873-6983
Fax: 662-873-6090
Ownership: Mississippi Delta Wireless LLC; MDWLLC ownership:; George Martin; Johnny Sanders Sr..
Cable Systems (1):
MISSISSIPPI: ROLLING FORK.

PAUL E. RICHARDS
51684 Main St
PO Box D-2
Jerusalem, OH 43747
Phone: 740-926-1742
Fax: 740-926-1800
Cable Systems (3):
OHIO: MALAGA TWP.; NEW ATHENS.
WEST VIRGINIA: MIDDLEBOURNE.

RIDGEWOOD CABLE
3700 S County Rd 1316
Odessa, TX 79765
Phone: 432-563-4330
Fax: 432-563-0134
Web site: http://www.ridgewoodcable.com
Cable Systems (2):
TEXAS: ECTOR COUNTY (portions); GREENWOOD.

RINGSTED TELEPHONE CO.
PO Box 187
Ringsted, IA 50578
Phone: 712-866-8000
Fax: 712-866-0002
E-mail: tjohnson@ringtelco.com
Web site: http://www.ringstedtelephone.com
Officer:
Dale Johansen, Chairman & Chief Executive Officer
Represented (legal): Anderson, Pelzer & Hart.
Cable Systems (1):
IOWA: RINGSTED.
Other Holdings:
Cellular telephone
Telephone

RITTER COMMUNICATIONS
3300 One Place
Jonesboro, AR 72404
Phone: 870-934-3434
E-mail: pwaits@ritternet.com
Web site: http://www.callritter.com
Officers:
Paul Waits, President
Harold Kennel, Director, Cable Operations
Cable Systems (3):
ARKANSAS: LESLIE; MARKED TREE; WESTERN GROVE.

RIVIERA UTILITIES CABLE TV
413 E Laurel Ave
PO Box 2050
Foley, AL 36536
Phone: 251-943-5001
Fax: 251-943-5275
E-mail: mdugger@riviera-utilities.com
Web site: http://www.rivierautilities.com
Officers:
Michael M Dugger, Chief Executive Officer & General Manager
David A. Horton, Superintendent, Public Affairs, Marketing and Cable
Ownership: Community owned--Foley, AL.
Represented (legal): Bryan Cave LLP.
Cable Systems (1):
ALABAMA: FOLEY.

JIM ROBY
24285 S. Hwy. 64
Canton, TX 75103
Phone: 903-567-2260
Web site: http://www.etcable.net
Cable Systems (1):
TEXAS: CANTON.

ROCK PORT TELEPHONE CO.
107 Opp St
PO Box 147
Rock Port, MO 64482
Phones: 660-744-5314; 877-202-1764
Fax: 660-744-2120
E-mail: rptel@rpt.coop
Web site: http://www.rptel.net
Officers:
Robert L. Stanton, President
Keith Ottmann, Vice President
Stanley Griffin, Secretary
Dan LaHue, Treasurer
Cable Systems (1):
MISSOURI: ROCKPORT.

ROCKWELL COOPERATIVE TELEPHONE ASSOCIATION
111 N 4th St
PO Box 416
Rockwell, IA 50469-0416
Phone: 641-822-3211
Fax: 641-822-3550
Web site: http://www.rockwellcoop.com/index.php
Officers:
Robert Amosson, President
Tom Worley, Vice President
Robert Corporon, Secretary
David Severin, General Manager
Ruth Reimers, Billing & Collection Manager
Cable Systems (2):
IOWA: MESERVEY; THORNTON.

RONCEVERTE TELEVISION CORP.
PO Box 525
Ronceverte, WV 24970-0525
Phone: 304-647-5455
Officers:
Donald R. Honaker, President
Keith E. Morgan, Secretary-Treasurer
Ownership: Subscriber owned--Ronceverte, WV.
Cable Systems (1):
WEST VIRGINIA: RONCEVERTE.

ROOME TELECOMMUNICATIONS INC.
705 W 2nd St
PO Box 227
Halsey, OR 97348
Phones: 503-369-2211; 800-343-2211
Fax: 503-369-2233
E-mail: support@rtinet.com
Web site: http://www.rtinet.com
Officer:
Randal L. Roome, Chief Executive Officer
Cable Systems (1):
OREGON: HALSEY.
Other Holdings:
Telephone

ROYAL TELEPHONE CO.
PO Box 80
Royal, IA 51357
Phone: 712-933-2615
E-mail: info@royaltelco.com
Web site: http://www.royaltelco.com

Cable Systems (1):
IOWA: ROYAL.

RUNESTONE TELECOM ASSOCIATION

100 Runestone Dr
PO Box 336
Hoffman, MN 56339
Phone: 320-986-2013
Fax: 320-986-2050
E-mail: help@runestone.net
Web site: http://www.runestone.net/rta
Cable Systems (1):
MINNESOTA: BARRETT.

RURAL ROUTE VIDEO

360 Browning Ave
PO Box 640
Ignacio, CO 81137-0640
Phone: 970-563-9593
Fax: 970-563-9381
Officers:
Christopher L. May, President
Nancy Howley, Secretary
Cable Systems (2):
COLORADO: IGNACIO; SUNNYSIDE.

RURAL TELEPHONE CO.

892 W. Madison Ave.
Glenns Ferry, ID 83623
Phones: 208-366-2614; 888-366-7821
Fax: 208-366-2615
E-mail: mark.martell@ruraltel.org
Web site: http://www.rtci.net
Ownership: James R Martell.
Cable Systems (6):
IDAHO: GLENNS FERRY.
KANSAS: LENORA; MUNJOR; PHILLIPSBURG; PLAINVILLE; SMITH CENTER.

RURALWEST - WESTERN RURAL BROADBAND INC.

PO Box 52968
Bellevue, WA 98015-2968
Phone: 425-451-1470
Fax: 425-451-1471
E-mail: corporatestaff@ruralwest.com
Web site: http://www.ruralwest.com

Branch Offices:
Vandenberg Broadband
PO Box 6009
Vandenberg AFB, CA 93437
Phone: 805-734-5578
Fax: 805-734-0158
Peterson Broadband
301 Mitchell St.
Colorado Springs, CO 80916
Phone: 719-597-0873
Fax: 719-597-0164
Ownership: David Boland, 50%; Jim Hershey, 50%.
Cable Systems (2):
CALIFORNIA: VANDENBERG AFB.
COLORADO: PETERSON AFB.

RUSSELL MUNICIPAL CABLE TV

Town Hall, 65 Main St
PO Box 408
Russell, MA 01071
Phone: 413-862-4707
Fax: 413-862-3103
E-mail: information@russellma.net
Web site: http://www2.russellma.net
Officers:
Louis E. Garlo, Chief Executive Officer
Susan B. Maxwell, Chief Operating Officer
Ownership: Community owned--Russell, MA.
Cable Systems (1):
MASSACHUSETTS: RUSSELL.

SAC COUNTY MUTUAL TELEPHONE CO.

108 S Maple St
PO Box 582
Odebolt, IA 51458
Phone: 712-668-2200
Fax: 712-668-2100
E-mail: odetelco@netins.net
Web site: http://www.odebolt.net/sac_co__mutual_telco.html
Officer:
Dale Schaefer, Manager
Ownership: Publicly owned..
Cable Systems (2):
IOWA: ARTHUR; BATTLE CREEK.

JAMES P. SAGE

228 Sage Rd.
Rural Retreat, VA 24368
Phones: 276-686-5242; 276-686-5242
Cable Systems (1):
VIRGINIA: RURAL RETREAT.

ST. JOHN CABLE CO. INC.

PO Box 268
St. John, WA 99171
Phone: 509-648-3322
E-mail: service@stjohncable.com
Web site: http://www.stjohncable.com
Cable Systems (1):
WASHINGTON: ST. JOHN.
Other Holdings:
Cable: 50% interest in Colfax Highline Cable Co., see listing
Telephone

SALTILLO TV CABLE CORP.

PO Box 89
Saltillo, PA 17253
Phone: 814-448-9182
Fax: 814-448-9182
Officers:
Rodney Thomas, President
Marsha M. Dell, Secretary-Treasurer
Cable Systems (1):
PENNSYLVANIA: SALTILLO.

SAN BRUNO MUNICIPAL CABLE TV

398 El Camino Real
San Bruno, CA 94066
Phone: 650-616-3111
Fax: 650-871-5526
E-mail: info@sanbrunocable.com
Web site: http://www.sanbrunocable.com
Ownership: Municipally owned -- San Bruno, CA.
Cable Systems (1):
CALIFORNIA: SAN BRUNO.

SAN CARLOS APACHE TELECOMMUNICATIONS UTILITY INC.

10 Telecom Ln
PO Box 1000
Peridot, AZ 85542
Phone: 928-475-2433
Fax: 928-475-7047
Web site: http://www.scatui.net
Officer:
Richard Gomez, Chief Technology Officer
Ownership: Hal Williams, Court Trustee.
Cable Systems (3):
ARIZONA: BYLAS; GILA COUNTY; SAN CARLOS.

S & K TV SYSTEMS INC.

508 Miner Ave W
Ladysmith, WI 54848
Phones: 715-532-7321; 800-924-7880
Fax: 715-532-7583
E-mail: techsupport@skcable.com
Web site: http://www.skcable.com
Officer:
Randy Scott, Manager
Ownership: Randy Scott; Tom Krenz.
Cable Systems (5):
WISCONSIN: GILMAN; LAKE HOLCOMBE; MIKANA; MINONG; RADISSON.

S & T COMMUNICATIONS INC.

320 Kansas Ave
PO Box 99
Brewster, KS 67732
Phones: 785-694-2256; 800-432-8294
Web site: http://www.sttelcom.com
Officers:
Steve Richards, Chief Executive Officer
Gary Slough, Branches/Sales/Marketing Director
Fritz Doke, Systems Manager
Clint Felzien, CATV Manager
Shawna Kersenbrock, Marketing Manager
Tracey Purvis, Computer Services Manager
Dwayne Randolph, Outside Plant Manager
Carolyn Somers, Chief Financial Officer
Cable Systems (6):
KANSAS: BREWSTER; COLBY; DIGHTON; GOODLAND; HEALY; OAKLEY.

SAN JUAN CABLE & CONSTRUCTION

2568 MacKenzie Rd.
Bellingham, WA 98226-9204
Phone: 360-758-7879
Officers:
Fred J. Morgan, Chairman
Roy M. Budde, Chief Executive Officer
Edward Warner, Chief Operating Officer
Richard Warbus, Chief Financial Officer
Cable Systems (1):
WASHINGTON: LUMMI INDIAN RESERVATION.

SAN SIMEON COMMUNITY CABLE INC.

PO Box 84
San Simeon, CA 93452-0084
Phone: 805-927-5555
Web site: http://www.slocounty.ca.gov/Page9332.aspx
Cable Systems (1):
CALIFORNIA: SAN SIMEON ACRES.

SATELLITE OPERATIONS INC.

517 Petrie Ave.
St. Joseph, MI 49085-1927
Phones: 616-983-0206; 269-424-5737
E-mail: cs@sisterlakescable.com
Web site: http://www.sisterlakescable.com
Ownership: Tim Olmstead, 50%; Art Schmidt Jr., 50%.
Cable Systems (1):
MICHIGAN: KEELER TWP..

SAT STAR COMMUNICATIONS LLC

11449 Challenger Ave
Odessa, FL 33556
Phone: 800-445-1139
Fax: 813-249-2809
Web site: http://www.satstartech.com
Cable Systems (1):
FLORIDA: RIVER RANCH.

SATVIEW BROADBAND LTD.

Suite 5
137 Vassar St.
Reno, NV 89502
Phones: 775-333-6626; 800-225-0605
Fax: 775-333-0255
E-mail: taroil@yahoo.com
Web site: http://www.iwantone.tv
Officers:
James W. Charlton, Co-President
David Scott Charlton, Co-President
Ownership: James W Charlton, 50%; David Scott Charlton, 48%; HFU Inc., 2%.
Cable Systems (9):
CALIFORNIA: BRIDGEPORT; COLEVILLE; CROWLEY LAKE.
NEVADA: JACKPOT; TOPAZ LAKE; WELLINGTON; WELLS.
UTAH: DELTA; FILLMORE.

SAVAGE COMMUNICATIONS INC.

206 Power Ave N
PO Box 810
Hinckley, MN 55037-0810
Phones: 320-384-7442; 800-222-9809
Fax: 320-384-7446
Web site: http://www.scibroadband.com
Officers:
Ronald W. Savage, President
Mike Danielson, Vice President, Operations
Paula Savage, Secretary-Treasurer
Ownership: Ron Savage, Principal; Mike Danielson; Pat McCabe; Jerry Meier.
Cable Systems (9):
MINNESOTA: BARNUM; FLOODWOOD; HILL CITY; ISLE; MCGREGOR; PENGILLY; PILLAGER; SANDSTONE; VERNDALE.

SBC-TELE

PO Box 226
Kinsman, OH 44428
Phones: 330-876-0294; 330-876-0500
Fax: 330-876-0294
Ownership: Scott Bryer.
Cable Systems (2):
OHIO: MOUNT ORAB; VERNON.

SCHURZ COMMUNICATIONS INC.

1301 E Douglas Rd
Mishawaka, IN 46545
Phone: 574-247-7237
Fax: 574-247-7238
E-mail: info@schurz.com
Web site: http://www.schurz.com
Officers:
Franklin D. Schurz Jr., Chairman
Scott C Schurz, Vice Chairman
Todd F Schurz, President & Chief Executive Officer
Marcia K. Burdick, Senior Vice President, Electronic Division
Gary N Hoipkemier, Senior Vice President, Secretary & Treasurer & Chief Financial Officer
Charles V Pittman, Senior Vice President, Publishing
Sally J Brown, Vice President, Radio-Indiana
David C Ray, Vice President
Martin D Switalski, Vice President, Finance & Administration & Assistant Treasurer
Judy A Felty, Assistant Secretary

Ownership: Franklin D. Schurz Jr.; Mary Schurz; James M. Schurz; Scott C. Schurz, 75.2%. votes, Trustees; David C Ray, V.P., 15.2%. votes, 4.06% assets; Robin S Bruni, 9.6, votes, 4.37% assets%; Todd F Schurz, 7.36%. assets; Franklin D Schurz Jr, 7.14%. assets; Scott C Schurz, 3.76%. assets; Scott C Schurz Jr, 3.17%. assets.
Represented (legal): Wilmer Cutler Pickering Hale & Dorr LLP.
Cable Systems (3):
FLORIDA: CORAL SPRINGS; WESTON.
MARYLAND: HAGERSTOWN.
TV Stations:
Alaska: KTUU-TV Anchorage.
Georgia: WAGT Augusta.
Indiana: WSBT-TV South Bend.
Kansas: KBSD-DT Ensign; KBSL-DT Goodland; KBSH-DT Hays; KWCH-DT Hutchinson; KSCW-DT Wichita.
Missouri: KYTV Springfield.
Virginia: WDBJ Roanoke.
LPTV Stations:
Alaska: K04DS Kenai River; K10NC Kenai, etc.; K09JE Palmer.
Indiana: WBND-LD South Bend; WBND-LP South Bend.
Missouri: K17DL-D Branson; K15CZ Springfield.
Virginia: W04AG-D Garden City, etc..
Newspapers:
California: Adelante Valle (El Centro), Imperial Valley Press
Indiana: Times Mail (Bedford), Herald Times (Bloomington), Reporter Times (Martinsville), Mooresville-Decatur Times, Noblesville Daily Times, South Bend Tribune
Kentucky: The Advocate-Messenger (Danville), The Jessamine Journal (Nicholasville), The Interior Journal (Stanford), The Winchester Sun
Maryland: Herald-Mail (Hagerstown)
Michigan: Charlevoix Courier, Gaylord Herald Times, The Petoskey News-Review
Pennsylvania: Daily American (Somerset)
South Dakota: American News (Aberdeen)
Radio Stations:
Indiana: WASK (AM), WHKY (AM), WKDA (AM), WXXB (FM) Lafayette; WNSN (FM), WSBT (AM) South Bend
South Dakota: KFXS (FM), KKLS (AM), KKMK (FM), KOUT (FM), KRCS (FM) Rapid City; KBHB (AM) Sturgis

SCI CABLE INC.
6700 SW Topeka Blvd
Topeka, KS 66619
Phone: 785-862-1950
E-mail: scicable@sbcglobal.net
Officer:
Kirk A. Keberlein, President
Cable Systems (4):
KANSAS: GRANTVILLE; MERIDEN; PERRY; ST. GEORGE.

S CORPORATION
510 Rte 302 W
PO Box 586
West Van Lear, KY 41268
Phones: 606-789-3455; 888-789-3455
E-mail: info@bigsandybb.com
Web site: http://www.bigsandybb.com
Officer:
Paul D. Butcher, Vice President
Cable Systems (1):
KENTUCKY: VAN LEAR.

SCOTTSBORO ELECTRIC POWER BOARD
404 East Willow St
PO Box 550
Scottsboro, AL 35768
Phone: 256-574-2682
Fax: 256-574-5085
E-mail: feedback@scottsboropower.com
Web site: http://www.scottsboropower.com
Cable Systems (1):
ALABAMA: SCOTTSBORO.

SCRANTON TELEPHONE CO.
1200 Main St
PO Box 8
Scranton, IA 51462
Phone: 712-652-3355
Fax: 712-652-3777
E-mail: jingles@netins.net
Web site: http://www.netins.net/ricweb/telco/scrantel.htm
Cable Systems (1):
IOWA: SCRANTON.

SEMO COMMUNICATIONS INC.
107 Semo Ln
PO Box C
Sikeston, MO 63801
Phone: 573-471-6594
Fax: 573-471-6878
E-mail: semosupport@cablerocket.com
Web site: http://www.semocommunications.com
Officers:
Travis E. Garrett, Chairman
Tyrone Garrett, President
Shannon Garrett, Vice President & Secretary-Treasurer
Ownership: Tyrone Garrett, 50.1%; Shannon Garrett, 34.9%; Denise Antrobus, 15%.
Represented (legal): William Clayton Vandivort.
Cable Systems (1):
MISSOURI: MORLEY.
Other Holdings:
Cable Consulting

SERVICE ELECTRIC CABLE TV INC.
201 W Centre St
Mahanoy City, PA 17948
Phones: 570-773-2585; 570-874-1010
Fax: 570-773-0276
E-mail: corporateoffice@secv.com
Web site: http://www.secable.com
Officers:
John Walson Jr., President
Joe Macus, Vice President
Steve Salash, Marketing Director
Arlean Lilly, Regulatory Affairs Director
Ownership: Margaret Walson.
Represented (legal): Womble, Carlyle, Sandridge & Rice.
Cable Systems (8):
NEW JERSEY: HUNTERDON COUNTY; SPARTA.
PENNSYLVANIA: BIRDSBORO; HAZLETON; LEHIGH VALLEY; MAHANOY CITY; SUNBURY; WILKES-BARRE.
Other Holdings:
Common Carrier

SHADE GAP TV ASSN.
HC 83 Box 398
Shade Gap, PA 17255
Phone: 814-259-3673
Officers:
Richard Price, President
Mary McMullen, Secretary-Treasurer
Ownership: Community owned--Shade Gap.
Cable Systems (1):
PENNSYLVANIA: SHADE GAP.

SHELLSBURG CABLEVISION INC.
PO Box 390
Shellsburg, IA 53332
Phone: 319-436-2224
E-mail: frmutshe@fmtcs.com
Web site: http://www.usacomm.coop
Officers:
Roy M. Fish, President
Rex Miller, Vice President
Robert H. Smith, Secretary
Warren Richart, Treasurer
Ownership: Community owned--Shellsburg, IA.
Cable Systems (3):
IOWA: COGGON; RYAN; SHELLSBURG.
Other Holdings:
Telephone

SHENANDOAH TELECOMMUNICATIONS INC.
PO Box 459
Edinburg, VA 22824
Phone: 540-984-5224
E-mail: complaints@shentel.net
Web site: http://www.shentel.com
Officers:
Christopher E French, President
Earle A MacKenzie, Chief Operating Officer & Executive Vice President
Adele M Skolits, Chief Financial Officer & Vice President, Finance
David E Ferguson, Vice President, Customer Services
William L Pirtle, Vice President, Marketing & Sales
Cable Systems (46):
MARYLAND: OAKLAND.
OHIO: BERLIN TWP. (Mahoning County); COITSVILLE TWP..
TENNESSEE: UNICOI.
VIRGINIA: BUCHANAN; CLARKSVILLE; COVINGTON; CREWE; EDINBURG; FARMVILLE; KENBRIDGE; KEYSVILLE; LAWRENCEVILLE; LEBANON; RADFORD; RUSTBURG; WYTHEVILLE.
WEST VIRGINIA: ANSTED; BELINGTON; BOONE COUNTY (unincorporated areas); CLAY (town); CRAIGSVILLE; DINGESS; DRENNEN; FRANKLIN; GASSAWAY; GILBOA; GRANTSVILLE; HARTS; HERNDON; IAEGER; MARLINGTON (town); NORTHFORK; OAKVALE; PAGE; PANTHER; PENNSBORO; PETERSBURG; PINEVILLE; RICHWOOD; SALEM; SCARBRO; SUMMERSVILLE; WEBSTER SPRINGS; WEST UNION; WESTON.
Other Holdings:
Telephone: Shenandoah Telephone Co.

SHEN-HEIGHTS TV ASSN. INC.
38 N Main St
Shenandoah, PA 17976
Phone: 570-462-1911
Fax: 570-462-1948
Web site: http://www.shenhgts.net
Officers:
Martin F. Brophy, Chairman & Chief Executive Officer
Francis T. Brophy, Secretary-Treasurer
Ownership: Frank Brophy; Martin P Brophy; Tony Brophy.
Represented (legal): Williamson, Friedberg & Jones LLC.
Cable Systems (1):
PENNSYLVANIA: SHENANDOAH.

SHERMAN CABLEVISION
PO Box 38
Houlton, ME 04730
Phone: 207-532-3320
Ownership: Ronald Dee.
Cable Systems (1):
MAINE: SHERMAN.

JOHN P. SHOEMAKER JR.
PO Box 5064
Martinsville, VA 24115
Phone: 804-685-1521
Cable Systems (1):
VIRGINIA: BROSVILLE.

SHREWSBURY'S COMMUNITY CABLEVISION
100 Maple Ave.
Shrewsbury, MA 01545
Phone: 508-841-8500
Fax: 508-842-9419
E-mail: customerservice@ci.shrewsbury.ma.us
Web site: http://www.shrewsbury-ma.gov/selco
Officer:
Richard A. Corbi, Finance & Administration
Ownership: Community owned--Shrewsbury, MA.
Cable Systems (1):
MASSACHUSETTS: SHREWSBURY.

SIERRA DAWN ESTATES HOMEOWNERS ASSN.
950 S. Lyon
Hemet, CA 92343
Phones: 714-925-6026; 714-925-6502
Cable Systems (1):
CALIFORNIA: SIERRA DAWN ESTATES.

SIERRA NEVADA COMMUNICATIONS
PO Box 281
Sonora, CA 95373
Phone: 209-588-9601
E-mail: cust@gosnc.com
Web site: http://www.snccable.com
Cable Systems (3):
CALIFORNIA: GROVELAND; LONG BARN; PINECREST.

SIGNAL INC.
PO Box 435
West Bend, IA 50597
Phone: 515-887-4591
E-mail: msignal@ncn.net
Cable Systems (1):
IOWA: LU VERNE.

SIREN COMMUNICATIONS
7723 W Main St
PO Box 506
Siren, WI 54872-0506
Phone: 715-349-2224
Fax: 715-349-2576
Web site: http://www.sirentel.com
Ownership: Siren Telephone Co..
Cable Systems (1):
WISCONSIN: SIREN.

SITKA TV CABLE SYSTEM
964 Broadway Plaza
Paintsville, KY 41240
Phone: 606-789-3391
Cable Systems (1):
KENTUCKY: SITKA.

SIX MILE RUN TV ASSOCIATION
1171 Six Mile Run Rd.
Six Mile Run, PA 16679
Phone: 814-928-4897
Officers:
Richard W. White, President

Susan K. White, Secretary-Treasurer
Ownership: Community owned--Six Mile Run, PA.
Cable Systems (1):
PENNSYLVANIA: SIX MILE RUN.

SJOBERG'S CABLE TV INC.

315 N. Main
Thief River Falls, MN 56701
Phone: 218-681-3044
E-mail: office1@mncable.net
Web site: http://trf.mncable.net/
Officers:
Richard Sjoberg, President
Stan Sjoberg, Secretary-Treasurer
Ownership: Richard Sjoberg, 50%; Stan Sjoberg, 50%.
Represented (legal): Cole, Raywid & Braverman LLP.
Cable Systems (11):
MINNESOTA: BADGER; BAUDETTE; GREENBUSH; KARLSTAD; MIDDLE RIVER; NEWFOLDEN; RED LAKE FALLS; ROSEAU; THIEF RIVER FALLS; WARREN; WARROAD.

SKISAT

555 Valley St., Bldg. 51
Providence, RI 02908-5600
Phone: 401-272-2558
E-mail: tech@skisat.net
Web site: http://www.skisat.net
Ownership: Tom Corcoran, 50%; Philip R DeSano, 50%.
Cable Systems (1):
NEW HAMPSHIRE: WATERVILLE VALLEY.

SKY CABLEVISION LTD.

PO Box 65
Meridian, MS 39302
Phone: 601-485-6980
Fax: 601-483-0103
E-mail: helpdesk@24hoursupport.com
Web site: http://www.skycablevision.com
Ownership: Berry Ward.
Cable Systems (9):
ALABAMA: BELLAMY; BOLIGEE; CENTREVILLE; CHATOM; EUTAW; FORKLAND; MARION; PROVIDENCE; SWEET WATER.

SMALL TOWN CABLE CORP.

225 Highland Villa
Nashville, TN 37211
Phone: 877-368-2110
Officers:
Doc Collins, Vice President
T. Hasbrouck, Controller
Ownership: Vince King, Managing Partner.
Cable Systems (4):
TENNESSEE: CHAPEL HILL; MINOR HILL; ROGERSVILLE; SUMMERTOWN.

SOLARUS

440 E Grand Ave
PO Box 8045
Wisconsin Rapids, WI 54495-8045
Phones: 715-421-8111; 800-421-9282
Fax: 715-421-6081
E-mail: support@solarus.net
Web site: http://www.solarus.net
Officer:
Douglas Wenzlaff, Chief Executive Officer & General Manager
Ownership: Cooperative.
Cable Systems (1):
WISCONSIN: ROME TWP..

SOMERFIELD CABLE TV CO.

6511 National Pike
Addison, PA 15411
Phone: 814-395-3084
E-mail: sc-tv@sc-tv.net
Web site: http://www.sc-tv.net
Ownership: Michael J Diehl, Chmn. & Chief Exec. Officer.
Cable Systems (1):
PENNSYLVANIA: ADDISON TWP. (southern portion).

SOUTH ARKANSAS TELEPHONE CO. INC.

PO Box 778
Hampton, AR 71744
Phone: 870-798-2201
E-mail: help@sat-co.net
Web site: http://www.sat-co.net
Cable Systems (1):
ARKANSAS: HAMPTON.

SOUTH CENTRAL COMMUNICATIONS

45 North 100 West
PO Box 555
Escalante, UT 84726
Phone: 435-826-4211
Fax: 435-826-4900
Web site: http://www.scwireless.com
Cable Systems (12):
UTAH: BEAVER; BRIAN HEAD; ENOCH; ENTERPRISE; ESCALANTE; KANAB; KANARRAVILLE; LYMAN; MILFORD; MINERSVILLE; PANGUITCH; PAROWAN.

SOUTHEAST CABLE TV INC.

Suite 200
3902 Corporex Park Dr.
Tampa, FL 33619-1132
Phone: 813-630-5500
Officers:
James F. Cavanaugh, President
Bob Heide, Vice President

Branch Office:
PO Box 584
Boston, GA 31626-0584
Phone: 912-498-4191
Cable Systems (6):
FLORIDA: HOSFORD; KEATON BEACH.
GEORGIA: BOSTON; COOLIDGE; OCHLOCKNEE; PAVO.

SOUTHERN CABLEVISION INC.

112 First St NW
Grand Meadow, MN 55936-1200
Phone: 507-754-5117
Ownership: Martinsen Communication Inc..
Cable Systems (1):
MINNESOTA: GRAND MEADOW.

SOUTHERN KANSAS TELEPHONE CO.

128 N. Gorin
Clearwater, KS 67026
Phones: 620-584-2255; 888-758-8976
Fax: 620-584-2260
E-mail: customerservice@sktc.net
Web site: http://www.sktmainstreet.com
Officers:
Kendall S. Mikesell, President
Gregory L. Mikesell, Controller
Cable Systems (2):
KANSAS: CLEARWATER.
NEBRASKA: DALTON.

SOUTHERN PLAINS CABLE

PO Box 88
Sterling, OK 73567
Phone: 580-365-4235
Fax: 580-365-4126
E-mail: office@wichitaonline.net
Web site: http://southernplainscommunications.com
Cable Systems (5):
OKLAHOMA: ALEX; APACHE; CEMENT; GRANDFIELD; STERLING.

SOUTHERN VERMONT CABLE CO.

PO Box 166
Bondville, VT 05340-0166
Phone: 518-843-3037
E-mail: escialabba@svcable.net
Web site: http://www.svcable.net
Officers:
Herbert Scialabba, Chairman
Ernest Scialabba, President
Carol Scialabba, Secretary-Treasurer
Ownership: Ernest Scialabba; Herbert Scialabba.
Cable Systems (2):
VERMONT: PUTNEY; TOWNSHEND.

SOUTH HOLT CABLEVISION INC.

PO Box 227
Oregon, MO 64473
Phone: 816-446-3391
Ownership: Robert Williams, Chmn. & Chief Exec. Officer.
Cable Systems (1):
MISSOURI: OREGON.

SOUTH SHORE CABLE TV INC.

6301 Broad Branch Rd.
Chevy Chase, MD 20815

Cable Systems (2):
GEORGIA: LUTHERSVILLE.
MICHIGAN: MASON.

SPANISH FORK COMMUNITY NETWORK

65 South 630 West
Spanish Fork, UT 84660
Phones: 801-798-5000; 801-798-2877
E-mail: info@sfcn.org
Web site: http://www.sfcn.org
Ownership: City of Spanish Fork.
Cable Systems (1):
UTAH: SPANISH FORK.

SPENCER MUNICIPAL UTILITIES

712 N Grand Ave
PO Box 222
Spencer, IA 51301-0222
Phone: 712-262-3027
E-mail: jeffrey.rezabek@smunet.net
Web site: http://www.smunet.net
Cable Systems (1):
IOWA: SPENCER.

SPILLWAY CABLEVISION INC.

PO Box 337
Maringouin, LA 70757
Phone: 504-625-2311
Officers:
Craig Greene, President
Mark Greene, Secretary-Treasurer
Ownership: Craig Greene; Mark Greene, Principals.
Cable Systems (2):
LOUISIANA: KROTZ SPRINGS; MARINGOUIN.

SPIRIT BROADBAND

PO Box 249
College Grove, TN 37046
Phone: 615-368-2115
Fax: 615-368-2295
Web site: http://www.spiritbb.com/
Cable Systems (1):
TENNESSEE: CUMBERLAND COUNTY.

SPRING CITY CABLE TV INC.

PO Box 729
Spring City, TN 37381
Phone: 423-365-7288
Cable Systems (1):
TENNESSEE: SPRING CITY.

SPRINGFIELD CABLE TELEVISION

3529 E 3rd St
Springfield, FL 32401-6001
Phone: 850-872-7570
Fax: 850-747-5663
Web site: http://www.springfieldfl.org/296098.html
Officer:
Annette Williams, General Manager
Ownership:Formerly known as Springfield Cablevision.
Cable Systems (1):
FLORIDA: SPRINGFIELD.

SPRINGPORT TELEPHONE CO.

400 E Main St
PO Box 208
Springport, MI 49284
Phone: 517-857-3500
Web site: http://www3.springcom.com
Cable Systems (1):
MICHIGAN: SPRINGPORT TWP..

SPRINGVILLE COOPERATIVE TELEPHONE ASSN. INC.

207 Broadway
Springville, IA 52336
Phone: 319-854-6500
E-mail: springvl@netins.net
Web site: http://www.springvilletelephone.com
Cable Systems (1):
IOWA: SPRINGVILLE.

DANNY SPURLOCK

PO Box 268
Groesbeck, TX 76642
Phones: 254-729-2221; 800-822-0198
Cable Systems (1):
TEXAS: ROSEBUD.

SRT COMMUNICATIONS INC.

3615 N Broadway
PO Box 2027
Minot, ND 58702-2027
Phones: 701-858-1200; 800-737-9130
Fax: 701-858-1428
E-mail: email@srt.com
Web site: http://www.srt.com
Officers:
Ardel Rice, President
Steve Lysne, General Manager & Chief Executive Officer
John Reiser, Chief Operating Officer
Cassidy Kersten, Corporate Communications Director
Ownership: Subscriber owned--Minot, ND..
Represented (legal): Pringle & Herigstad PC.
Cable Systems (1):
NORTH DAKOTA: VELVA.
Other Holdings:
Telephone

STANDARD TOBACCO CO. INC.
626 Forest Ave
PO Box 100
Maysville, KY 41056
Phone: 606-564-5678
Officers:
James A. Finch, Chairman, President & Chief Executive Officer
Ivan Cracraft, Chief Operating & Financial Officer
Ronald Buerkley, Vice President, Cable
Karen Campbell, Secretary
Ownership: James A Finch Jr., 90%. Finch owns WFTM-AM-FM, Maysville, KY; Barbara Tucker, 10%.
Represented (legal): Royse, Zweigart, Kirk, Brammer & Caudill.
Cable Systems (2):
KENTUCKY: MAYSVILLE; MOUNT OLIVET.
Radio Stations:
Kentucky: WFTM (AM) Maysville

STANLEY CABLEVISION INC.
PO Box 400
Stanley, ND 58784
Phone: 701-628-3333
Ownership: Fred Beehler; Gordon Wilhelmi; James Wilhelmi; Mark Wilhelmi.
Cable Systems (1):
NORTH DAKOTA: STANLEY.

STARVISION INC.
3850 N US Hwy 421
PO Box 319
Clinton, NC 28329
Phone: 910-564-7888
Fax: 910-564-5410
E-mail: adsales@stmc.net
Web site: http://www.starvisions.tv
Officers:
Robert Hester, President
Lyman Horne, Chief Operating Officer
Robert Thornton, Secretary-Treasurer
Jeff Nethercutt, Chief Financial Officer

Branch Office:
ELIZABETHTOWN, NC
3112 Martin Luther King Dr.
Elizabethtown, NC 28337
Phone: 910-645-1111
Ownership: Star Telephone Membership Corp..
Represented (legal): Holland, Poole, Holland & Sanderson PA.
Cable Systems (1):
NORTH CAROLINA: CLINTON.

STARWEST INC.
PO Box 98
Atkins, IA 52206
Phones: 319-293-6336; 800-568-4992
Fax: 319-446-7858
Ownership: John Stookesberry, Principal.
Cable Systems (7):
IOWA: AINSWORTH; BRIGHTON; FARMINGTON; FREMONT; HEDRICK; KEOSAUQUA; RICHLAND.

STRATA NETWORKS
211 E 200 N
Roosevelt, UT 84066
Phone: 435-622-5007
E-mail: company@stratanetworks.com
Web site: http://www.stratanetworks.com
Officer:
Bruce Todd, Chief Executive Officer & General Manager
Ownership:Formerly UBTA-UBET Communications.
Cable Systems (2):
UTAH: DUCHESNE; ROOSEVELT.

STRATFORD MUTUAL TELEPHONE
1001 Tennyson St
PO BOx 438
Stratford, IA 50249
Phone: 515-838-2390
E-mail: info@globalccs.net
Web site: http://www.stratfordtelephone.com
Officers:
Gary W. Davis, Chief Executive Officer
Dave Prichard, Chief Operating Officer
Cable Systems (1):
IOWA: STRATFORD.

RICHARD STURTZ
PO Box 445
Broadus, MT 59317
Phone: 406-436-2820
Cable Systems (1):
MONTANA: BROADUS.

CITY OF SUMAS TV CABLE SYSTEM
433 Cherry St.
PO Box 9
Sumas, WA 98295
Phone: 360-988-5711
Fax: 360-988-8855
Web site: http://cityofsumas.homestead.com
Ownership: Community owned--Sumas, WA.
Cable Systems (1):
WASHINGTON: SUMAS.

SUMNER COMMUNICATIONS
117 W. Harvey
Wellington, KS 67152
Phone: 316-326-8989
Fax: 316-326-3290
E-mail: sumnertv@sutv.com
Web site: http://sutv.com/
Ownership: Jack Mitchell; Jeanne Mitchell.
Cable Systems (1):
KANSAS: WELLINGTON.

SUNRISE COMMUNICATIONS LLC
20938 Washington Ave
PO Box 733
Onaway, MI 49765
Phone: 989-733-8100
Fax: 989-733-8155
E-mail: info@src-mi.com
Web site: http://www.src-mi.com
Cable Systems (2):
MICHIGAN: PICKFORD TWP.; POSEN.

SUPERVISION CABLE TV
PO Box 872100
Wasilla, AK 99687-3809
Phone: 907-373-6007
Fax: 907-336-7195
Web site: http://www.yukontel.com
Ownership: Clifton Eller, Pres..
Cable Systems (2):
ALASKA: TANANA; WHITTIER.

SWAYZEE TELE BROADBAND
PO Box 70
Swayzee, IN 46986
Phone: 765-922-7928
Fax: 765-922-7966
E-mail: swayzee@swayzee.com
Web site: http://www.swayzee.com
Officer:
S. M. Samuels, President
Cable Systems (1):
INDIANA: SWAYZEE.
Other Holdings:
Telephone

SWEETWATER CABLE TV CO. INC.
602 Broadway
PO Box 8
Rock Springs, WY 82901
Phone: 307-362-3773
Web site: http://www2.sweetwaterhsa.com/index.html
Officers:
Albert M. Carollo Sr., Chairman
Albert M. Carollo Jr., President
John B. Carollo, Chief Operating Officer
James R. Carollo, Vice President
Leona Carollo, Secretary-Treasurer
Ownership: Albert M Carollo Jr., 25%; James R Carollo, 25%; John B Carollo, 25%; Albert M Carollo Sr., 25%. Carollo family owns Pilot Butte Transmission Co. (Common Carrier) & TV Translator station in WY.
Represented (legal): Cole, Raywid & Braverman LLP.
Cable Systems (2):
WYOMING: GREEN RIVER; ROCK SPRINGS.

TACOMA PUBLIC UTILITIES
3628 S. 35th St.
PO Box 11007
Tacoma, WA 98409
Phones: 253-502-8900; 800-752-6745
Fax: 253-502-8493
Web site: http://www.mytpu.org
Cable Systems (1):
WASHINGTON: TACOMA.

ALBERT A. & DOROTHY TALLEY
PO Box 48
Strawn, TX 76475-0048
Phone: 254-672-5296
Fax: 254-672-5296
Cable Systems (1):
TEXAS: STRAWN.

TALOGA CABLE TV
PO Box 218
Taloga, OK 73667
Phone: 405-328-5262
Ownership: Glenn Gore.
Cable Systems (1):
OKLAHOMA: TALOGA.

TELE-MEDIA CORP.
320 W College Ave
PO Box 5301
Pleasant Gap, PA 16823-5301
Phone: 814-359-3481
Fax: 814-359-5390
Web site: http://www.tele-media.com
Officers:
Robert E. Tudek, Chairman & Chief Executive Officer
Tony S. Swain, President
Richard W. Shore, Senior Vice President, Corporate Development
Allen C. Jacobson, Senior Vice President, Legal Affairs & Secretary
Frank R. Vicente, Senior Vice President, Operations & Assistant Secretary
Robert D. Stemler, Senior Vice President, Finance & Treasurer
Russell G. Bamburger, Senior Vice President & President, Tele-Media Constructors Co.
Charles J. Hilderbrand, Vice President & Director, Purchasing
Randall S. Lewis, Vice President & General Sales Manager
Thomas T. Wolanski, Vice President, Tax Affairs
Steven E. Koval, Vice President, Information Technology
Jonathan P. Young, Vice President, Legal Affairs
Dean Colbert III, Assistant Vice President & Assistant General Manager
Jean C. Brown, Administrative Vice President & Assistant Secretary
Elsie M. Tudek, Administrative Vice President & Assistant Secretary-Treasurer
Ownership: Robert E Tudek.
Represented (legal): Fleischman & Harding LLP.
Cable Systems (3):
NORTH CAROLINA: BALD HEAD ISLAND.
PENNSYLVANIA: SNOW SHOE; ZION.

TELEPHONE ELECTRONICS CORP.
4587 W Main St
Erin, TN 37061
Phone: 931-289-4221
Fax: 931-289-4220
E-mail: HumanResources@tec.com
Web site: http://www.tec.com/home.aspx
Officers:
Joseph D. Fail, Chairman & President
James H. Coakley Jr., Chief Operating Officer
Cable Systems (2):
TENNESSEE: HENRY; TENNESSEE RIDGE.

TELE-SERVICES LTD.
PO Box 250
Breda, IA 51436-0250
Phone: 712-382-1773
Ownership: Ott Boeckman, Principal.
Cable Systems (3):
IOWA: BREDA; FARRAGUT; WESTSIDE.
Other Holdings:
Telephone

TELEVISION ASSN. OF REPUBLIC
147 N Clark
PO Box 555
Republic, WA 99166
Phone: 509-775-3822
Web site: http://www.rcabletv.com
Officers:
Charles Sublett, Chairman & President
Sheila Welvaert, Secretary-Treasurer
Ownership: Subscriber owned - Republic, WA.
Cable Systems (1):
WASHINGTON: REPUBLIC.

TEL-STAR CABLEVISION INC.
1295 Lourdes Rd
Metamora, IL 61548-8416
Phones: 309-383-2677; 888-842-0258
Fax: 309-383-2657
Web site: http://www.telstar-online.net
Ownership: James L Perley, Chmn. & Chief Exec. Officer.
Cable Systems (2):
ILLINOIS: EDWARDS; WOODLAND HEIGHTS.

TEMPLETON TELEPHONE CO.
115 Main
PO Box 77
Templeton, IA 51463
Phone: 712-669-3311
Fax: 712-669-3312
E-mail: citytemp@netins.net
Officer:
Loretta Friedman, Chairman & President

Cable Systems (1):
IOWA: TEMPLETON.

TER TEL ENTERPRISES
PO Box 100
Terril, IA 51364
Phone: 712-853-6121
Fax: 712-853-6185
Cable Systems (4):
IOWA: TERRIL.
MINNESOTA: TRIMONT; TRUMAN; WELCOME.
Other Holdings:
Telephone

3 RIVERS TELEPHONE COOPERATIVE INC.
202 5th St S
Box 429
Fairfield, MT 59436
Phones: 406-467-2535; 800-796-4567
Fax: 406-467-3490
E-mail: 3rt@3rivers.net
Web site: http://www.3rivers.net/
Ownership: 3 Rivers Communications.
Cable Systems (3):
MONTANA: CHOTEAU; CONRAD; SHELBY.

TIP TOP COMMUNICATION
200 Center St.
Arcadia, IA 51480
Phone: 712-689-2238
Fax: 712-689-2600
Ownership: Arcadia Telephone Cooperative.
Cable Systems (3):
IOWA: DELOIT; DUNLAP; SCHLESWIG.

TITONKA TELEPHONE CO.
247 Main St N
PO Box 363
Titonka, IA 50480
Phones: 515-928-2120; 515-928-2859
Fax: 515-928-2897
E-mail: Titonka@TBCtel.com
Web site: http://www.tbctel.com
Officers:
Norman Cooper, President
Vicky Nelson, Secretary-Treasurer
Cable Systems (1):
IOWA: TITONKA.
Other Holdings:
Telephone: The Burt Telephone Co.

TRANS-VIDEO INC.
Village Common
Northfield, VT 05663
Phone: 802-485-3811
E-mail: info@trans-video.net
Web site: http://trans-video.net
Officers:
George L. Goodrich Jr., President
Robert H. Goodrich, Vice President
Ownership: George L Goodrich Jr., 50%; Robert H Goodrich, 50%.
Represented (legal): Young, Monte & Lyford Law Office.
Cable Systems (1):
VERMONT: NORTHFIELD (village).

TRI-COUNTY COMMUNICATIONS INC.
PO Box 460
Belhaven, NC 27810
Phone: 252-964-2100
Fax: 252-964-2211
Officer:
Dennis M. Wallace Jr., Chief Executive Officer
Ownership: Tri-County Telephone Membership Corp..
Represented (legal): Harvey W. Raynor III.
Cable Systems (1):
NORTH CAROLINA: BELHAVEN.

TRINITY CABLEVISION INC.
1701 Cogswell Ave.
Pell City, AL 35125
Phone: 205-884-4549
Ownership: Alton D Elliot, 50%; Arthur M Smith, 50%. Smith is principal of Coosa Cable Co., see listing.
Cable Systems (1):
ALABAMA: TRINITY.

TROY CABLEVISION
1006 S Brundidge St
PO Box 1228
Troy, AL 36081
Phone: 334-566-3310
Fax: 334-566-3304
E-mail: support@troycable.net
Web site: http://www.troycable.net
Ownership: Freeman Family.
Cable Systems (3):
ALABAMA: DALEVILLE; LUVERNE; TROY.

TRUST COMMUNICATIONS
PO Box 16512
Jackson, MS 39236
Phone: 888-536-2947
E-mail: steven@trustcable.com
Web site: http://www.trustcable.com
Cable Systems (2):
LOUISIANA: ETHEL.
MISSISSIPPI: CENTREVILLE.

TRUVISTA COMMUNICATIONS
112 York St
PO Box 160
Chester, SC 29706
Phone: 803-385-2191
Fax: 803-581-2223
E-mail: ajohnson@truvista.biz
Web site: http://www.truvista.net
Officers:
Brian Singleton, President & Chief Executive Officer
David Brunt, Vice President & Chief Financial Offficer
Allison Johnson, Vice President, Sales & Marketing
David Redys, Vice President, Network Services & Technology
Tom Harper, Director, Administration & Regulatory Affairs
Richard Johnson, Director, Business Operations
Tracy D Starnes, Director, Field Services
Patricia Joyner, Business Solutions Manager
Bob Wilkinson, Strategic Marketing Manager
Tony Helms, Manager, Switching & Video Services
Tony Miles, Manager, Purchasing & Property Services
Cheryl Wylie, Controller

Branch Offices:
501 Dearborn St.
Great Falls, SC 29055
Phone: 803-482-2191

295 S. Means St.
Ridgeway, SC 29180
Phone: 803-337-2291

736 US Hwy. 321 Business S
Winnsboro, SC 29180
Phone: 803-635-6459

2629 Broad St.
Camden, SC 29020
Phone: 803-432-3461
Cable Systems (3):
SOUTH CAROLINA: CAMDEN; CHESTER; WINNSBORO.

THE TULALIP TRIBE INC.
6326 33rd Ave. NE
Marysville, WA 98271
Phone: 360-651-3270
Fax: 360-651-3272
Officers:
Herman Williams, Jr., Chairman
Chris Henry, Chief Executive Officer
Represented (legal): Bell & Ingram PS.
Cable Systems (1):
WASHINGTON: TULALIP INDIAN RESERVATION.

ROBERT E. TURNER
Rte. 4
Windom, MN 56101
Phone: 507-831-4176
Cable Systems (3):
MINNESOTA: LAMBERTON; REVERE; WALNUT GROVE.

TV CABLE ASSOCIATES INC.
PO Box 101
Loganton, PA 17747
Phone: 717-725-2733
Officer:
William Sayers, President
Ownership: Community owned--Loganton, PA.
Cable Systems (1):
PENNSYLVANIA: LOGANTON.

TV CABLE CO. OF ANDALUSIA INC.
PO Box 34
Andalusia, AL 36420
Phone: 205-222-6464
E-mail: jmike@andycable.com
Web site: http://www.andycable.com
Officers:
Ivan Bishop, President
J. Dige Bishop, Vice President
Ownership: Ivan Bishop, 23.35%; Linda Whitman, 18.82%; Julia H Bishop Trust, 16.09%; John Anderson, 9.86%; Jane Anthony, 7.42%; William H Albritton, 6.97%; Ophelia Albritton, 5.34%; Ann L Albritton, 4.25%; Harold & Virginia Broughton, 2.53%; Drew Cowen, 2.26%; Tyler Cowen, 2.26%; J. Dige Bishop Trust, 0.9%. Ivan Bishop is part owner of Clearview Cable Inc., see listing.
Cable Systems (1):
ALABAMA: ANDALUSIA.

TVC INC.
3095 Sheridan Rd.
PO Box 369
Lennon, MI 48449
Phones: 810-621-3363; 888-204-1077
Fax: 810-621-9600
E-mail: customerserv@lentel.com
Web site: http://www.lentel.com
Cable Systems (1):
MICHIGAN: LENNON.

TVMAX
Suite 1000
1111 W. Mockingbird Lane
Dallas, TX 75247
Phones: 214-634-3800; 512-480-2234
Fax: 214-634-3850
Web site: http://www.tvmax.com
Officer:
Ron Dorchester, President
Ownership: Managed by Anchor Pacific Corp..
Cable Systems (1):
TEXAS: HOUSTON.

TV SERVICE INC.
Hwy 550
PO Box 1410
Hindman, KY 41822
Phone: 606-785-3450
E-mail: tvs@tvscable.com
Web site: http://www.tvscable.com
Officers:
Robert C. Thacker, President, Chief Operating & Financial Officer
Archie W. Everage, Vice President, Operations
Junell Thacker, Secretary-Treasurer
Ownership: Robert C Thacker. Thacker is part owner of Thacker-Grigsby Telephone Co., Hindman, KY.
Represented (legal): Slone & Bates.
Cable Systems (2):
KENTUCKY: HINDMAN; VANCLEVE.
Other Holdings:
Telephone

TWO RIVERS MEDIA
102 Hill St Y Rd
PO Box 555
Linden, TN 37096
Phone: 615-589-2696
Ownership: Bert Patterson; Mrs. Edwin Patterson, Principals.
Cable Systems (3):
TENNESSEE: LINDEN; LOBELVILLE; SCOTTS HILL.

TYKESON & ASSOCIATES
63090 Sherman Rd
Bend, OR 97701
Phone: 541-382-5551
Fax: 541-385-3271
Web site: http://www.bendbroadband.com
Officers:
Donald E. Tykeson, Chairman
William P. Morton, President & Chief Operating Officer
Amy C. Tykeson, Chief Executive Officer
David Jones, Vice President, Advertising Sales
Ann Lum, Secretary-Treasurer
Thomas H. Palmer, Chief Financial Officer
Daniel Heller, Director, Engineering Operations
Ownership: Donald E Tykeson.
Represented (legal): Wiley Rein LLP.
Cable Systems (1):
OREGON: BEND.

BILL TYLER
Rte 2
PO Box 110
Olney, TX 76374
Phones: 940-873-4563; 800-687-7311
Fax: 940-873-4563
E-mail: bill@tgncable.net
Web site: http://www.tgncable.com
Cable Systems (3):
TEXAS: LAKE GRAHAM; NEWCASTLE; THROCKMORTON.
Cable Holdings:
TGN Cable Systems located in Throckmorton, Newcastle and Lake Graham, Texas.

TYLERSVILLE COMMUNITY TV ASSOCIATION INC.
1133 Summer Mountain Rd.
Loganton, PA 17747
Phone: 570-725-3865
Officer:
Jim Breon, President
Ownership: Community owned--Tylersville, PA.

Cable Systems (1):
PENNSYLVANIA: TYLERSVILLE.

UNEV COMMUNICATIONS INC.
PO Box 1077
Lovelock, NV 89419
Phone: 702-273-2020
Ownership: Tom Mitchell.
Cable Systems (2):
NEVADA: LOVELOCK.
TEXAS: OZONA.

UNION TELEPHONE CO.--MOUNTAIN VIEW, WY
PO Box 160
Mountain View, WY 82939
Phones: 307-787-7043; 888-926-2273
E-mail: webmaster@unionwireless.com
Web site: http://www.unionwireless.com
Cable Systems (1):
WYOMING: MOUNTAIN VIEW (Uinta County).

CITY OF UNIONVILLE CABLE TV
1611 Grant St.
PO Box 255
Unionville, MO 63565
Phone: 660-947-3818
Fax: 660-947-7756
Officer:
Jerry Tilden, Chief Operating Officer
Cable Systems (1):
MISSOURI: UNIONVILLE.

UNITED COMMUNICATIONS ASSN. INC.
1107 McArtor Rd.
PO Box 117
Dodge City, KS 67801
Phone: 620-227-8645
Fax: 620-227-7032
E-mail: utasupport@unitedtelcom.net
Web site: http://www.unitedtelcom.net
Officers:
Laurence Vierthaler, President
Don Howell, Vice President
Sharon Batman, Secretary-Treasurer
Ownership: Subscriber owned--Dodge City, KS.
Cable Systems (2):
KANSAS: BUCKLIN; CIMARRON.

UNITED ENTERPRISES
PO Box 14375
Grand Forks, ND 58208-4375
Phone: 701-772-7191
Ownership: David A Ramage.
Cable Systems (2):
NEVADA: INDIAN SPRINGS; NELLIS AFB.

UNITED TELEPHONE MUTUAL AID CORP.
411 7th Ave
PO Box 729
Langdon, ND 58259
Phone: 701-256-5156
Fax: 701-256-5150
E-mail: customerservice@utma.com
Web site: http://www.utma.com
Officer:
Harold Estenson, President
Ownership: Community cooperative--Munich, ND.
Represented (legal): Scott Stewart.
Cable Systems (2):
NORTH DAKOTA: MUNICH; SOURIS.

UNITE WIRELESS OF WEATHERFORD LLC
111 W Church St
Weatherford, TX 76086
Phones: 817-550-9022; 866-859-0843
E-mail: support@unitewireless.com
Web site: http://www.unitewireless.com
Officers:
Phil Gilbert, President
Dan Gilbert, Vice President, Operations
Brad Shaw, Network Administrator
Kevin Grace, Web Solutions Director
Billy Ritchmond, Infrastructure Management

Branch Office:
7477 Airport Fwy
Fort Worth, TX 76118

UNIVERSAL CABLEVISION INC.
4440 26th St. W
Bradenton, FL 33507
Phone: 813-756-5460
Officers:
John L. Manny, Chairman, Chief Executive, Operating & Financial Officer
Bonnie J. Manny, Vice President
Ownership: Bonnie J Manny; John L Manny, Principals.
Cable Systems (1):
FLORIDA: BRADENTON (unincorporated areas).

UPPER PENINSULA COMMUNICATIONS INC.
PO Box 66
Carney, MI 49812
Phone: 906-639-2194
Officer:
L. G. Matthews, Secretary-Treasurer
Ownership: Louis DuPont; L. G Matthews (Mrs.), Principals.
Cable Systems (13):
MICHIGAN: ALPHA (village); AMASA; CHAMPION TWP.; DE TOUR (village); ENGADINE; GARDEN TWP.; GERMFASK; MARENISCO TWP.; MICHIGAMME; PORTAGE TWP.; POWERS; WOLVERINE (village).
WISCONSIN: PHELPS.

USA COMPANIES
Ste B
920 E 56th St
Kearney, NE 68847
Phones: 308-236-1510; 877-234-0102
E-mail: support@usacommunications.tv
Web site: http://www.cableusa.com
Officers:
Russell G. Hilliard, President, Chief Executive & Financial Officer
Stuart Gilbertson, Corporate Engineer

Branch Office:
PO Box 1448
Kearney, NE 68848-1448
Ownership: Russell G. Hilliard.
Represented (legal): Cole, Raywid & Braverman LLP.
Cable Systems (47):
CALIFORNIA: BOMBAY BEACH; BORREGO SPRINGS; CALIPATRIA; JULIAN; MECCA; OCOTILLO; SALTON CITY; SALTON SEA BEACH; THERMAL.
MONTANA: ABSAROKEE; BIG TIMBER; BILLINGS (western portion); COLSTRIP; FORSYTH; FROMBERG; HARDIN; JOLIET; LAUREL; RED LODGE.
NEBRASKA: AINSWORTH; ALBION; ALMA TWP.; BELLWOOD; CEDAR RAPIDS; CENTRAL CITY; DUNCAN; FULLERTON; GENEVA; GENOA; HUMPHREY; MEADOW GROVE; MONROE; NAPER; NEWMAN GROVE; O'NEILL; OSCEOLA; PALMER; PLATTE CENTER; POLK; RICHLAND; SCHUYLER; SHELBY; SILVER CREEK; SPALDING; ST. EDWARD; STROMSBURG; VALENTINE.

US CABLE CORP.
Montvale Plaza
28 W. Grand Ave.
Montvale, NJ 07645
Phone: 201-930-9000
Fax: 201-930-9232
E-mail: info@uscable.com
Web site: http://www.uscable.com
Officers:
Stephen E. Myers, Chairman
James D. Pearson, President & Chief Executive Officer
Michael C. Anderson, Executive Vice President
G. Joseph Appio, Vice President, Operations
Ownership: Stephen E Myers, 88%; Michael C Anderson, 10%; James D Pearson, 2%.
Represented (legal): Dow Lohnes PLLC.
Cable Systems (53):
COLORADO: CONIFER; CRIPPLE CREEK; EATON; GILCREST; JOHNSTOWN; TABLE MOUNTAIN; WOODLAND PARK.
MINNESOTA: ALDEN; BREWSTER; CAMBRIDGE; CEYLON; DUNNELL; GLENVILLE; GRANADA; HERON LAKE; MINNEOTA; NORTHROP; PLAINVIEW; ROUND LAKE; STORDEN; WABASHA; WANAMINGO.
MISSOURI: EDINA; HANNIBAL; JONESBURG; LOUISIANA; MADISON; MEXICO; MOBERLY; PERRY; WINFIELD.
NEW JERSEY: PARAMUS.
NEW MEXICO: CARLSBAD; CHAMA; DIXON; ESPANOLA; HOBBS; JAL; PENASCO; SANTA CLARA INDIAN RESERVATION.
TEXAS: ALPINE; FORT STOCKTON; IRAAN; McCAMEY; RANKIN; SANDERSON; SEMINOLE; VAN HORN; WEST ODESSA.
WISCONSIN: ALMA (town); BAY CITY; ELLSWORTH; PEPIN.
Other Holdings:
SMATV systems

UTE MOUNTAIN INDIAN TRIBE
PO Box 33
Towaoc, CO 81334
Phone: 303-565-9574
Cable Systems (1):
COLORADO: TOWAOC.

UTOPIA (UTAH TELECOMMUNICATION OPEN INFRASTRUCTURE AGENCY
2175 S Redwood Rd
West Valley City, UT 84119
Phones: 801-990-5450; 888-342-3748
Fax: 801-908-7225
E-mail: mstreet@orem.org
Web site: http://www.utopianet.org
Cable Systems (1):
UTAH: LINDON.

VALLEY CABLE SYSTEMS
PO Box 78
Doylesburg, PA 17219
Phone: 717-349-7717
Officer:
Barry Kepner, Chairman
Ownership: Barry L Kepner, 50%; Sandy Kepner, 50%.
Cable Systems (2):
PENNSYLVANIA: DOYLESBURG; METAL TWP..

VALLEY TV CO-OP INC.
PO Box 450
Parkdale, OR 97401
Phone: 503-352-6760
Cable Systems (2):
OREGON: ODELL; PARKDALE.

VALPARAISO COMMUNICATION SYSTEMS
465 Valparaiso Pkwy
PO Box 296
Valparaiso, FL 32580
Phone: 904-729-5404
E-mail: support@valp.net
Web site: http://www.valp.net
Officer:
Helen J. Bourgeois, Chief Financial Officer & City Clerk
Ownership: Community owned--Valparaiso, FL.
Cable Systems (1):
FLORIDA: VALPARAISO.

VAN HORNE TELEPHONE CO.
204 Main St.
Van Horne, IA 52346
Phone: 319-228-8791
Fax: 319-228-8784
E-mail: vanhorne@netins.net
Officers:
Ralph Petersen, President
Wayne Eichmeyer, Vice President
Patrice Smith, Secretary-Treasurer
Cable Systems (1):
IOWA: VAN HORNE.
Other Holdings:
Cellular radio: Navenroh Communications Inc.

VAXEO TECHNOLOGIES LLC
13632 E 460 RD
Claremore, OK 74017
Phone: 918-283-1715
E-mail: info@vaxeo.com
Web site: http://www.vaxeo.com

VERNONIA CATV INC.
536 S. First Ave.
Vernonia, OR 97064
Phones: 503-427-8327; 503-429-5103
Ownership: Bud Foster, Pres..
Cable Systems (1):
OREGON: VERNONIA.

VERSALINK MEDIA LLC
511 Pan American Dr
Livingston, TX 77351
Phone: 877-689-6009
Web site: http://www.versalinkus.com/media.html
Cable Systems (3):
TEXAS: GOODRICH; MAGNOLIA; MONTGOMERY COUNTY (unincorporated areas).

VIDEO INC.
PO Box 708
Bay Springs, MS 39422
Phone: 601-764-3143
Fax: 601-764-4900
Officers:
Joseph D. Fail, President & Chief Executive Officer
R. A. McFarland, Vice President
D. Wayne Skelton, Secretary-Treasurer

Robert J. Healea, Chief Financial Officer
Ownership: Telephone Electronics Corp.. Affiliated with the Bay Springs Telephone Co. Inc., Bay Springs, MS.
Cable Systems (1):
MISSISSIPPI: BAY SPRINGS.

VIDEO SERVICES LTD.
PO Box 123
Bode, IA 50519
Phone: 515-379-1558
E-mail: office@trvnet.net
Ownership: Mark Steil, Principal.
Cable Systems (1):
IOWA: BODE.

VISION COMMUNICATIONS LLC (LOUISIANA)
115 W 10th Blvd
Larose, LA 70373
Phones: 985-693-0123; 800-256-5665
E-mail: callaiscable@yahoo.com
Web site: http://www.myviscom.com
Ownership: James Callahan.
Represented (legal): Arter & Hadden LLP.
Cable Systems (1):
LOUISIANA: GOLDEN MEADOW.

VITAL COMMUNICATIONS GROUP
PO Box 307
Belhaven, NC 28710
Phone: 252-943-3800
Cable Systems (4):
WEST VIRGINIA: BOMONT; LEON; MEADOW BRIDGE; UNION.

VI-TEL INC.
223 Broadway
PO Box 789
Davenport, OK 74026-0789
Phone: 918-377-2347
Fax: 918-377-2506
E-mail: info@cotc.net
Web site: http://www.cotc.net
Officers:
Steven Guest, President
David Guest, Vice President
Ownership: Central Oklahoma Telephone Co..
Cable Systems (1):
OKLAHOMA: DAVENPORT.
Other Holdings:
Telephone

VOLCANO COMMUNICATIONS CO.
PO Box 1070
20000 Hwy 88
Pine Grove, CA 95665
Phone: 209-274-2660
E-mail: info@volcanotel.com
Web site: http://www.volcanocommunications.com
Ownership: Sharon Lundgren, Chmn. & Principal.
Represented (legal): Cooper, White & Cooper LLP.
Cable Systems (2):
CALIFORNIA: IONE; PINE GROVE.
Other Holdings:
Cellular radio: Volcano Cellular Inc.
Telephone: Volcano Telephone Co.

WABASH INDEPENDENT NETWORKS
113 Hagen Dr
PO Box 719
Flora, IL 62839
Phones: 618-665-9946; 877-878-2120
Fax: 618-665-3400
E-mail: winita@wabash.net
Web site: http://www.wabash.net
Cable Systems (6):
ILLINOIS: CISNE; FLORA; GEFF; LOUISVILLE; NOBLE; XENIA.

WADSWORTH COMMUNICATIONS
120 Maple St.
Wadsworth, OH 44281
Phone: 330-335-2888
E-mail: support@wadsnet.com
Web site: http://www.wadsnet.com
Ownership: City of Wadsworth.
Cable Systems (1):
OHIO: WADSWORTH.

WAINWRIGHT CABLE INC.
PO Box 614
Norman Park, GA 31771
Phone: 229-769-3785
Cable Systems (2):
GEORGIA: FUNSTON; NORMAN PARK.

WAITSFIELD-FAYSTON TELEPHONE CO.
Rte 100
PO Box 9
Waitsfield, VT 05673
Phone: 802-496-5800
E-mail: ghaskin@wcvt.com
Web site: http://www.waitsfieldcable.com
Officers:
Dana Haskin, Chairman
Gregg Haskin, President & Chief Executive Officer
Roger Nishi, Vice President, Industry
Cable Systems (1):
VERMONT: WAITSFIELD.

WARMATH COMMUNICATIONS INC.
314 N 22nd Ave
Humboldt, TN 38343
Phone: 731-784-5000
Fax: 731-784-7474
E-mail: mlove@click1.net
Web site: http://www.click1.net/
Officer:
John Warmath, President
Ownership: J. Frank Warmath Estate, 70.66%; John F Warmath, 14.67%; James C Warmath, 14.67%. John F. Warmath also has microwave holdings.
Cable Systems (1):
TENNESSEE: HUMBOLDT.
Newspapers:
Tennessee: The Courier-Chronicle
Radio Stations:
Tennessee: WIRJ (AM) Humboldt

W.A.T.C.H. TV
3225 W. Elm St.
Lima, OH 45805
Phones: 419-859-2144; 800-589-3837
Fax: 419-859-2150
E-mail: info@watchtv.net
Web site: http://www.watchtv.net
Officers:
William Jones, Chairman
Kimberly Stumpp, Vice President & General Manager
Represented (legal): Thompson Hine LLP.
Cable Systems (1):
OHIO: BENTON RIDGE.

WAVEDIVISION HOLDINGS LLC
Ste 500
401 Kirkland Park Pl
Kirkland, WA 98033
Phone: 425-576-8200
Fax: 425-576-8221
Web site: http://www.wavebroadband.com/
Officers:
Steven Weed, Chief Executive Officer
Steve Friedman, Chief Operating Officer
Angela Higham, Marketing Director
Ownership: Steven Weed, Founder.
Cable Systems (19):
CALIFORNIA: CARSON; CONCORD; CRESCENT MILLS; GARBERVILLE; PLACER COUNTY (southwestern portion); PORTOLA; RIO VISTA; SAN FRANCISCO (southern portion); WEST SACRAMENTO.
OREGON: LACOMBE; SANDY; SHERIDAN; SILVERTON; STAYTON; WOODBURN.
WASHINGTON: CAMANO ISLAND; PORT ANGELES; PORT ORCHARD; SEATTLE (surrounding areas).

WAVE WIRELESS LLC
PO Box 921
Parsons, KS 67357
Phone: 620-423-9283
E-mail: support@wavewls.com
Web site: http://www.wavewls.com/
Cable Systems (1):
KANSAS: ALTAMONT.

W. E. COMMUNICATIONS INC.
35 First Ave NE
PO Box 308
Harmony, MN 55939
Phone: 507-886-2525
Fax: 507-886-2500
E-mail: info@harmonytel.com
Web site: http://www.harmonytel.com
Officers:
Lorren Tingesdal, Chief Executive Officer
Craig Otterness, Chief Financial Officer
Cable Systems (1):
MINNESOTA: HARMONY.

WEHCO VIDEO INC.
PO Box 2221
Little Rock, AR 72203
Phone: 501-378-3529
Fax: 501-376-8594
Web site: http://www.wehcovideo.com
Officers:
Walter E. Hussman Jr., Chairman & Chief Executive Officer
J. P. Morbeck, Chief Operating Officer
Allen Berry, Chief Financial Officer
Ownership: Walter E Hussman Jr., see listing, Principal; Camden News Publishing Company.
Represented (legal): Covington & Burling.
Cable Systems (11):
ARKANSAS: BRINKLEY; CAMDEN; FORREST CITY; HOPE; HOT SPRINGS; PINE BLUFF; SEARCY.
MISSISSIPPI: VICKSBURG.
OKLAHOMA: TAHLEQUAH.
TEXAS: KILGORE; LONGVIEW.
Newspapers:
Arkansas: The Weekly Vista (Bella Vista); Benton County Daily Record; Camden News; El Dorado News-Times; White River Valley News (Elkins); Northwest Arkansas Democrat-Gazette, Northwest Arkansas Times, Noticias Libres No
Tennessee: Chattanooga Times Free Press, Noticias Libres Sureste de Tennessee (Chattanooga)
Texas: Texarkana Gazette
Other Holdings:
Common Carrier: 100% owned by United WEHCO Inc.

WEST ALABAMA TV CABLE CO. INC.
108 First St. SW
Fayette, AL 35555
Phone: 205-932-4100
E-mail: cable@watvc.com
Web site: http://www.watvc.com
Ownership: Stephen W Vaughan, Pres..
Cable Systems (3):
ALABAMA: FAYETTE; HAMILTON; WINFIELD.

CITY OF WESTBROOK
PO Box 308
Westbrook, MN 56183
Phone: 507-274-6712
Fax: 507-274-5569
Officer:
Dennis Jutting, Superintendent
Cable Systems (1):
MINNESOTA: WESTBROOK.

WESTERN BROADBAND LLC
Ste 108
9666 E Riggs Rd
Sun Lakes, AZ 85248
Phone: 480-895-8084
Fax: 480-895-8010
Web site: http://www.westernbroadband.net
Officer:
Tom Basinger, President & Chief Executive Officer
Ownership: Evergreen Pacific Partners.
Cable Systems (3):
ARIZONA: ROBSON RANCH; SADDLEBROOKE; SUN LAKES.

WESTERN CABLE OF OPPORTUNITY INC.
PO Box 913
Butte, MT 59703
Phone: 406-723-3362
Fax: 406-782-6541
Cable Systems (1):
MONTANA: OPPORTUNITY.

WESTERN IOWA TELEPHONE
202 Cedar St
PO Box 38
Lawton, IA 51030
Phones: 712-944-5711; 800-469-0811
Fax: 712-944-5722
E-mail: wiatel@wiatel.com
Web site: http://www.wiatel.com
Officers:
Phil Robinson, Operations Manager
Pam Clark, Marketing & Sales
Susan Kolker, Office Manager
Cable Systems (1):
IOWA: LAWTON.

WESTERN MONTANA COMMUNITY TELEPHONE
312 Main St SW
Ronan, MT 59864
Phone: 406-676-0798
Cable Systems (5):
MONTANA: PLAINS; SEELEY LAKE; ST. IGNATIUS; SUPERIOR; THOMPSON FALLS.

WESTFIELD COMMUNITY ANTENNA ASSN. INC.
121 Strang St.
Westfield, PA 16950
Phone: 814-367-5190
Fax: 814-367-5586
Officer:
Faun James, Office Manager
Ownership: Subscriber owned--Westfield, PA.

Cable Systems (1):
PENNSYLVANIA: WESTFIELD.

WEST IOWA TELEPHONE CO.
12 E 3rd St
PO Box 330
Remsen, IA 51050
Phone: 712-786-1181
Fax: 712-786-2400
E-mail: support@westelsystems.com; acctinfo@westelsystems.com
Web site: http://www.westelsystems.com
Cable Systems (3):
IOWA: ANITA; MARCUS.
NEBRASKA: HOOPER.

WESTPA.NET INC.
216 Pennsylvania Ave W
PO Box 703
Warren, PA 16365
Phones: 814-726-9462; 877-726-9462
Fax: 814-723-9585
E-mail: info@westpa.net
Web site: http://www.westpa.net
Cable Systems (2):
PENNSYLVANIA: SHEFFIELD; SHEFFIELD.

WETHERELL CABLE TV SYSTEM
407 W. Grace St.
Cleghorn, IA 51014
Phone: 712-436-2266
Ownership: Ronald Wetherell; Todd Wetherell.
Cable Systems (1):
IOWA: CLEGHORN.

WFL CABLE TELEVISION ASSOCIATES INC.
114 N. Rutherford St.
Wadesboro, NC 28170
Phone: 704-694-9409
Fax: 704-694-6803
Officers:
William F. Lee, President
H. P. Taylor Jr., Chief Operating Officer
Ownership: William F Lee, 50%; H. P Taylor Jr., 50%.
Cable Systems (1):
NORTH CAROLINA: MORVEN.

WHEAT STATE TELECABLE INC.
106 W 1st St
PO Box 320
Udall, KS 67146
Phone: 620-782-3347
Fax: 620-782-3302
E-mail: support@wheatstate.com
Web site: http://www.wheatstate.com
Officers:
Greg Reed, Chairman, President & Chief Executive Officer
Arturo Macias, Chief Operating Officer & Secretary-Treasurer
Ownership: Golden Wheat Inc.. Also owns Wheat State Telephone Co.
Represented (legal): James M. Caplinger Chartered.
Cable Systems (1):
KANSAS: UDALL.

TIMOTHY A. WHITNEY
PO Box 47
Keene Valley, NY 12943
Phone: 518-576-4510
Cable Systems (1):
NEW YORK: KEENE VALLEY.

WIDEOPENWEST LLC
900 W. Castleton Rd.
Castle Rock, CO 80104
Phones: 303-663-0771; 925-371-1011
Web site: http://www.wowway.com
Officers:
Colleen Abdoulah, Chairman & Chief Executive Officer
Steven Cochran, President & Chief Financial Officer
Cash Hagen, Chief Technical Officer
Cathy Kuo, Chief Marketing Officer
Mark Dineen, Senior Vice President & General Manager, Michigan
Kelvin Fee, Senior Vice President & General Manager, Illinois
Scott Neesley, Senior Vice President & General Manager, Ohio
Michael Furst, Senior Vice President, Customer Care
Janice Turner, Senior Vice President, Human Resources
Robert DiNardo, Vice President & General Manager, Evansville
Craig Martin, General Counsel
Kirk Zerkle, Vice President & General Manager, Cleveland
Janice Turner, Vice President, Human Resources
Craig Martin, General Counsel
Ownership: Avista Capital Partners.
Cable Systems (7):
ILLINOIS: CHICAGO (southern portion); NAPERVILLE.
INDIANA: EVANSVILLE; HAMMOND.
MICHIGAN: DETROIT.
OHIO: CLEVELAND; COLUMBUS.

WILCOP CABLE TV
PO Box 558
Brodhead, KY 40409
Phone: 606-758-8320
Ownership: Johnny Wilcop.
Cable Systems (1):
KENTUCKY: BRODHEAD.

ANDY WILLIAMS
PO Box 2598
Starkville, MS 39759
Phone: 662-324-5121
Cable Systems (6):
MISSISSIPPI: ARTESIA; CRAWFORD; EUPORA; MACON; OKTIBBEHA COUNTY; SCOOBA.

CITY OF WILLIAMSTOWN CABLE TV
400 N Main St
PO Box 147
Williamstown, KY 41097
Phone: 859-824-3633
Fax: 859-824-6320
E-mail: jhartinger@wtownky.org
Web site: http://www.wtownky.org
Officers:
Chuck Hudson, Chairman, Chief Executive & Operating Officer
Vivian Link, Chief Financial Officer
Ownership: Community owned--Williamstown, KY.
Cable Systems (1):
KENTUCKY: WILLIAMSTOWN.

WILSON COMMUNICATIONS
2504 Ave D
PO Box 190
Wilson, KS 67490-0190
Phones: 785-658-2111; 800-432-7607
Fax: 785-658-3344
Web site: http://www.wilsoncommunications.us
Officers:
Brian Boisvert, General Manager
Scott Grauer, Vice President, Marketing
Gary Everett, Controller
Ownership: Bob Grauer; Eva Grauer; Scott Grauer.
Cable Systems (1):
KANSAS: WILSON.

WINDBREAK CABLE
1140 10th St.
Gering, NE 69341
Phone: 308-436-4650
Fax: 308-436-4779
Web site: http://www.windbreak.com
Officer:
William D. Bauer, President & Chief Executive Officer
Ownership: WIlliam D. Bauer, Pres. & Chief Exec. Officer.
Cable Systems (3):
NEBRASKA: HARRISON; LYMAN; OSHKOSH.
Other Holdings:
Multimedia: InterTECH Interactive Technologies Inc.

WINDJAMMER COMMUNICATIONS LLC
Ste 902
4400 PGA Blvd
Palm Beach Gardens, FL 33410
Phones: 561-775-1208; 877-450-5558
Fax: 561-775-7811
Web site: http://www.windjammercable.com
Officers:
Timothy Evard, Executive Director
Belinda Graham, Operations Manager
Cindy Johnson, Director, Finance & Accounting
Stephen Flessner, Regulatory Compliance & Contract Administrator
Ownership: Communications Construction Services; MAST Capital Management LLC.
Cable Systems (81):
ALABAMA: CULLMAN; FORT PAYNE.
CALIFORNIA: BURNEY; SUSANVILLE.
GEORGIA: FORT BENNING.
IDAHO: MOUNTAIN HOME.
ILLINOIS: CAVE-IN-ROCK.
INDIANA: WILLIAMSBURG.
KANSAS: LIBERAL.
KENTUCKY: BROOKS; CAMPTON; CLOVERPORT; CORINTH; CROMWELL; DUNMOR; FRANKFORT/STONEWALL; FRENCHBURG; HARDINSBURG; IRVINGTON; ISLAND; JACKSON; LESLIE COUNTY (northern portion); MOUNT STERLING; MOZELLE; PLEASANT RIDGE; ROCHESTER; SLAUGHTERS; WELCHS CREEK.
MAINE: SEARSMONT; TEMPLE (town).
MISSOURI: CHILLICOTHE; KENNETT; MARSHALL.
MONTANA: LIBBY; TROY.
NEW MEXICO: LA MESA.
NORTH CAROLINA: FOUNTAIN; MID LAKES TRAILER PARK; OAK CITY; ROBBINS.
OHIO: AMSTERDAM; CROWN CITY; EDON; EUREKA; FREEPORT TWP.; HANNIBAL; NEWPORT; PEDRO; SALINEVILLE.
SOUTH CAROLINA: McCLELLANVILLE.
TEXAS: BRUNI; ENCINAL; FLORENCE; GRAHAM; LAKE ARROWHEAD; OILTON; PALESTINE; STOCKDALE.
WASHINGTON: FRIDAY HARBOR.
WEST VIRGINIA: ANTHONY CREEK; APPLE GROVE; ASBURY; BALLARD; BIRCH RIVER; CHAPEL; ELLAMORE; FRAME; FRAMETOWN; FRIENDLY; GRAYSVILLE; LITTLE OTTER; NEBO; NETTIE; PRICHARD; QUICK; SALT ROCK; SANDYVILLE; SNOWSHOE; TALCOTT; TANNER.
WYOMING: EVANSTON (portions).

WINDWAVE COMMUNICATIONS
162 N Main St
PO Box 815
Heppner, OR 97836
Phones: 541-676-9663; 800-862-8508
Fax: 541-676-9655
E-mail: windsales@windwave.org
Web site: http://www.windwave.org/corpinfo.htm
Officers:
Nate Arbogast, President
Don Russel, Vice President
Gary Neal, Secretary-Treasurer
Randall Kowalke, Director
Cable Systems (1):
OREGON: HEPPNER.

SCOTT WINGER
210 N Main St
Sweetser, IN 46937
Phone: 317-384-5444
E-mail: sweetser@comteck.com
Web site: http://ww2.comteck.com
Cable Systems (1):
INDIANA: SWEETSER.

WINNEBAGO COOPERATIVE TELEPHONE ASSN.
704 E. Main
Lake Mills, IA 50450
Phone: 641-592-6105
Fax: 641-592-6102
E-mail: wcta@wctatel.net
Web site: http://www.wctatel.net
Ownership: Subscriber owned--Lake Mills, IA.
Cable Systems (4):
IOWA: BUFFALO CENTER; FOREST CITY; LAKE MILLS; THOMPSON.

WIRE TELE-VIEW CORP.
603 E. Market St.
Pottsville, PA 17901
Phone: 570-622-4501
Fax: 570-622-8340
Web site: http://www.wtvaccess.com
Officers:
Deborah A. Stabinsky, President
J. Richard Kirn, Secretary
Mary Louise Schoffstall, Treasurer
Ownership: Mary Louise Schoffstall, 30.4%; Deborah A Stabinsky, 12.2%; J. Richard Kirn, 9.6%; remainder undisclosed.
Cable Systems (2):
PENNSYLVANIA: POTTSVILLE; TREMONT.

WITTENBERG TELEPHONE CO.
104 W Walker St
PO Box 160
Wittenberg, WI 54499
Phone: 715-253-2111
Fax: 715-253-3497
E-mail: wittenbergtel@wittenbergnet.net
Web site: http://www.wittenbergnet.net
Officers:
Sydney R. Peterson, President
Allen Mahnke, Vice President
Lucy Lopez, Secretary
Larry Winter, Treasurer
Cable Systems (1):
WISCONSIN: WITTENBERG.

BRYAN WIXTROM
45 Howell Ln
PO Box 345
Trenton, TN 38382

Phone: 731-855-2808
Fax: 731-855-9512
Cable Systems (6):
MINNESOTA: ALVARADO; ARGYLE; KENNEDY; LAKE BRONSON; LANCASTER; STEPHEN.

CITY OF WOODSFIELD, OH

221 S Main St
Woodsfield, OH 43793
Phone: 740-472-1865
Cable Systems (1):
OHIO: WOODSFIELD.

WOODSTOCK TELEPHONE CO.

PO Box C
Ruthton, MN 56170
Phones: 507-658-3830; 800-752-9397
Web site: http://www.woodstocktel.net
Officers:
Ken Knuth, Chief Executive & Financial Officer
Doug Folkerts, Chief Operating Officer
Cable Systems (5):
MINNESOTA: GOOD THUNDER; LISMORE; RUSHMORE; RUTHTON; WILMONT.

WORTH CABLE SERVICES

PO Box 1733
Darien, GA 31305
Phone: 912-437-3422
Fax: 912-437-2065
Ownership: Dennis B Wortham.
Cable Systems (3):
GEORGIA: HOBOKEN; SURRENCY; UVALDA.

WYANDOTTE MUNICIPAL SERVICES

3005 Biddle Ave.
Wyandotte, MI 48192
Phones: 313-282-7100; 313-324-7130
E-mail: jfrench@wyan.org
Web site: http://www.wyan.org
Ownership: Community owned--Wyandotte, MI.
Cable Systems (1):
MICHIGAN: WYANDOTTE.

YOUNGSVILLE TV CORP.

3 W Main St
Youngsville, PA 16371
Phone: 814-563-3336
E-mail: ytv@eaglezip.net
Web site: http://youngsvilletv.com
Officers:
Richard Hutley, President
Scott Barber Sr, General Manager
Ownership: Community owned--Youngsville, PA.
Cable Systems (1):
PENNSYLVANIA: YOUNGSVILLE.

ZAMPELLI TV

PO Box 830
Lewistown, PA 17044
Phone: 717-248-1544
Fax: 717-248-4465
Ownership: Frank P Zampelli, Principal.
Cable Systems (4):
PENNSYLVANIA: BELLEVILLE; LIVERPOOL; McVEYTOWN; MOUNT PLEASANT MILLS.

TOM ZELKA

PO Box 338
Hardin, MT 59034
Phone: 406-665-2103
Cable Systems (1):
MONTANA: CROW AGENCY.

ZITO MEDIA

611 Vader Hill Rd.
Coudersport, PA 16915
Phone: 814-260-9575
Web site: http://www.zitomedia.com
Officer:
James Rigas, Manager
Ownership: The Rigas Family.
Cable Systems (103):
ALABAMA: BOOTH; BUTLER; GROVE HILL.
ILLINOIS: ALEXANDER COUNTY (portions); BUNCOMBE; CARRIER MILLS; FREEMAN SPUR; GOLCONDA; JACKSON COUNTY; LAKE OF EGYPT; ROSICLARE; SALINE COUNTY (portions); WILLIAMSON COUNTY (portions).
KANSAS: ALMA; AMERICUS; BLUE RAPIDS; CLIFTON; ESKRIDGE; HARTFORD; MAPLE HILL; MELVERN; NEOSHO RAPIDS; OLPE; OVERBROOK; PAXICO; POMONA; RICHMOND; ROSSVILLE; STRONG CITY; WAVERLY; WILLIAMSBURG.
KENTUCKY: BLACK MOUNTAIN; GRAVES COUNTY; HAZEL; HICKMAN; KUTTAWA; WALLINS CREEK; WHITLEY COUNTY; WICKLIFFE.
MISSISSIPPI: LUMBERTON; MERIDIAN NAVAL AIR STATION; POPLARVILLE; TYLERTOWN.
NEBRASKA: BEAVER CROSSING; BRADSHAW; BRAINARD; BYRON; CERESCO; CHESTER; CLAY CENTER; DESHLER; GARLAND; GLENVILLE; GRAND ISLAND; GRESHAM; GRETNA; MALCOLM; NELSON; PERU; RAYMOND; STAPLEHURST (village); SYRACUSE; ULYSSES; VALPARAISO; WACO; WESTERN; WILBER.
NORTH CAROLINA: BRYSON CITY; CRESTON (southern portion); ROBBINSVILLE.
OHIO: CORNING; DENMARK TWP.; GALLIPOLIS; ROCK CREEK; THOMPSON TWP. (Geauga County); WARNER.
PENNSYLVANIA: BRAVE; CANTON; COGAN STATION; COUDERSPORT; HAZEN; JOHNSONBURG; OSWAYO; RALSTON; SABULA; SPARTANSBURG; ST. MARY'S; TREASURE LAKE; WEEDVILLE; WILCOX.
TENNESSEE: SIMMERLY CREEK; SNEEDVILLE.
TEXAS: BREMOND; CALVERT; CAMERON; CRAWFORD; FRANKLIN; LOTT.
VIRGINIA: DAMASCUS; EWING.
WEST VIRGINIA: CAMERON; LITTLETON; PINE GROVE.

ZOOM MEDIA LLC

PO Box 2126
Flint, TX 75762
Phone: 855-261-5304
Web site: http://www.zoommediallc.com
Cable Systems (47):
ALABAMA: ARLEY; CUBA; JASPER; NAUVOO; ORRVILLE; PENNINGTON; PINE HILL; THOMASTON.
ARKANSAS: BEARDEN; CLARENDON; ENGLAND; HAMBURG; PINEBERGEN; SHERIDAN; SMACKOVER; STEPHENS.
LOUISIANA: BENTON; CLAYTON (town); COTTON VALLEY; DRY PRONG; EFFIE; MARKSVILLE; SIMPSON; WALLACE RIDGE.
MISSISSIPPI: CHUNKY; CORINTH; DE KALB; LAKE; MACEDONIA; MONTICELLO; PONTOTOC; PRENTISS; STATE LINE; TAYLORSVILLE.
OKLAHOMA: CLAREMORE.
TEXAS: ARP; BANDERA; BARTLETT; BEN WHEELER; BLANCO; CHARLOTTE; LAKE HILLS; LANSING; LEONARD; QUINLAN; WILLS POINT; WOLFE CITY.

Pay TV & Satellite Services

Total Subscribers are included only when they are provided by companies. Listings in ***italics*** are planned services.

PAY TV & SATELLITE SERVICES CROSS REFERENCE LISTS

AUDIO ONLY

AP ALL NEWS RADIO
BLOOMBERG NEWS RADIO
CHRISTIANNET
CNN RADIO NOTICIAS
CNN RADIO
C-SPAN AUDIO NETWORKS
DMX CANADA
DMX MUSIC
ESPN DEPORTES RADIO
FMX CABLE FM SYSTEM
MUSIC CHOICE
PRIME SPORTS RADIO
SPORTING NEWS RADIO
TALKLINE COMMUNICATIONS RADIO NETWORK
WALN CABLE RADIO
WFMT RADIO NETWORKS
WTEM SPORTS RADIO
YESTERDAY USA

CANADIAN

ABORIGINAL PEOPLES TELEVISION NETWORK
ACCESS THE EDUCATION STATION
ASIAN TELEVISION NETWORK
ASIAN TELEVISION NETWORK INTERNATIONAL
BBC CANADA
BOOK TELEVISION
BRAVO!
CABLE PUBLIC AFFAIRS CHANNEL
CANADIAN LEARNING TELEVISION
CANAL D
CBC/RADIO-CANADA
CITYTV
COMEDY NETWORK
COSMOPOLITANTV
COUNTRY MUSIC TV CANADA
COURTTV CANADA
CP24
CTV NEWS 1
CTV NEWSNET
CTV TRAVEL
DIRECT TO YOU
DISCOVERY CHANNEL CANADA
DRIVE-IN CLASSICS
ENCORE AVENUE
EQUESTRIAN PLANET
FASHION TELEVISION
THE FIGHT NETWORK
HGTV CANADA
HISTORY TELEVISION
KNOWLEDGE NETWORK
LE CANAL VIE
LE RESEAU DES SPORTS
LEARNING & SKILLS TELEVISION OF ALBERTA
LIFE NETWORK
MESCAPE
METEOMEDIA
MOVIE CENTRAL EXPRESS
MOVIE CENTRAL HD
MOVIE CENTRAL
MPIX
MUCHLOUD
MUCHMORE RETRO
MUCHMOREMUSIC
MUCHMUSIC NETWORK
MUSIMAX & MUSIQUEPLUS
ODYSSEY TELEVISION NETWORK
OUTDOOR LIFE NETWORK (CANADA)
OUTTV
PRIDEVISION TV
PULSE 24
RCS TELEVISION
RESEAU DE L'INFORMATION
ROGERS SPORTSNET
SCORE
SEXTV:THE CHANNEL
SHOP TV CANADA
SHOPPING CHANNEL
SHOWCASE TELEVISION
SMART LIVING TELEVISION
SOCCER TELEVISION
SPACE - THE IMAGINATION STATION
SPORTS NETWORK
STAR!
SUPER CHANNEL
TALENTVISION
TELELATINO NETWORK
TELEQUEBEC
TELETOON
TMN-THE MOVIE NETWORK (1-4)
TORSTAR MEDIA GROUP TELEVISION (TORONTO STAR TV)
TREEHOUSE TV
TV5, LA TELEVISION INTERNATIONAL
VIEWER'S CHOICE CANADA
VISION TV
WEATHER NETWORK
WILD TV
YTV CANADA

INTERACTIVE SERVICES

MOVIELINK
STARSIGHT
SWRV
TV GUIDE INTERACTIVE INC.

LOCAL NEWS SERVICES

ARIZONA NEWS CHANNEL
BERKS COUNTY NEWS 5
CAPITAL NEWS 9
CENTRAL FLORIDA NEWS 13
CHICAGOLAND TELEVISION NEWS
CNWG-10
5 NEWS
NEW ENGLAND CABLE NEWS
NEW YORK 1 NEWS
NEWS 8 AUSTIN
NEWS 12 CONNECTICUT
NEWS 12 LONG ISLAND
NEWS 12 NEW JERSEY
NEWS 12 THE BRONX
NEWS 12 WESTCHESTER
NEWSCHANNEL 8
NEWSWATCH 15
NORTHWEST CABLE NEWS
OHIO NEWS NETWORK
PITTSBURGH CABLE NEWS CHANNEL
REGIONAL NEWS NETWORK
RHODE ISLAND NEWS CHANNEL
10 NEWS CHANNEL
WBIR-TV

ON LINE SERVICES

ADRENALINE NATION TV (ANTV)
AFRICAST TV ONLINE
AFRICAST TV
AMERICAN INDIAN TV
ANHUI SATELLITE TV
ANHUI TV
ASIA TRAVEL TV
ATV
BLACK FAMILY CHANNEL
BLINKX BROADBAND TV
CAPTIVATE NETWORK
CCTV-ENTERTAINMENT
CCTV NEWS
CCTV-OPERA
CHINESE ENTERTAINMENT TELEVISION (CETV)
CHONGQING TV INTERNATIONAL CHANNEL
CMT LOADED
CNET TV
DISCOVERY CHANNEL BEYOND
ELECTION CHANNEL
EPIX HD
EPIX 2 HD
EPIX
ESPN MOBILE TV
ESPN3.COM
ESPN360.COM
FANGORIA
FASTCOMPANY.TV
FOX SOCCER CHANNEL BROADBAND
GAMETAP
GEKTV
GOOD TV
GUANGDONG SOUTHERN TELEVISION (TVS)
HBO GO
HBO ON BROADBAND
HOLLYWOODPRESSTV.COM
HULU
HUNAN SATELLITE TV (HTV)
HWAZAN TV
IAVC
ICTV
IDEA CHANNEL
IN2TV
INTERNATIONAL FAMILY TELEVISION
INTERTAINER
JEWISH TELEVISION NETWORK/JTN PRODUCTIONS
JIA YU CHANNEL
JIANGSU INTERNATIONAL CHANNEL
JUMP TV
KARMALOOP TV
KIDCARE TELEVISION NETWORK
KIDSWB.COM
KUNLUN THEATER
KYLINTV
LEGISLATIVE COUNSEL BUREAU - BROADCAST AND PRODUCTION SERVICES
LIVEWIRE
MACAU ASIA SATELLITE TV (MASTV)
MACTV
MARTIAL ARTS CHANNEL
MASTV
MAX GO
MAXIMUM TV
MEDIAZONE
MUSIC PLUS TELEVISION NETWORK
MY DAMN CHANNEL
NATIVE AMERICAN TELEVISION
NTN BUZZTIME
OPEN STUDENT TELEVISION NETWORK (OSTN)
PETCARE TELEVISION NETWORK
PGA TV
PHOENIX INFO NEWS
PHOENIX NORTH AMERICA
PHOENIX PREMIUM CHANNELS
POKERTV NETWORK
POPCORNFLIX.COM
POWER LINK
PULSE
THE REAL ESTATE CHANNEL
SHENZHEN SATELLITE TV
SIVOO
SKY LINK TV
SKY LINK VOD THEATER
SPEED2
STARZ PLAY
STARZ TICKET
SUDDENLINK2GO
SUN-TV
TEXAS SENATE MEDIA
TINSELVISION
TITAN TV NETWORK
TRADING DAY
TRAVEL CHANNEL BEYOND
TV GUIDE BROADBAND
TV GUIDE ONLINE
29 HD NETWORK
UCTV
UTH TV
VOY TV
WB.COM
WHEELSTV
WOMAN TV
WORLDGATE SERVICE
XIAMEN TV
XTV
YANGTSE RIVER DRAMA
ZHEJIANG TV

OTHER

CRACKLE
XFINITY

PAY SERVICES

ART AMERICA
@MAX
CCTV-4
CCTV-E
CHINESE TELEVISION NETWORK
CINEMAX ON DEMAND
CINEMAX
CINEMAX HD
CTC MEDIA
CYRTV (CHINESE YELLOW RIVER TV)
ENCORE ACTION
ENCORE DRAMA
ENCORE LOVE
ENCORE MYSTERY
ENCORE WAM
ENCORE WESTERNS
ENCORE
ESPN FULL COURT
ESPN GAMEPLAN
EXXXOTICA
FITTV
5STARMAX
FLIX ON DEMAND
FLIX
FOX MOVIE CHANNEL
FOX SOCCER PLUS
FUJIAN STRAITS TV
HBO ASIA
HBO COMEDY
HBO FAMILY
HBO HUNGARY
HBO INTERNATIONAL
HBO LATINO
HBO ON DEMAND
HBO SIGNATURE
HBO 2
HBO ZONE
HBO
HOME BOX OFFICE
HOWARD TV ON DEMAND
I-LIFETV
INDEPENDENT FILM CHANNEL
JADE CHANNEL
MOREMAX
THE MOVIE CHANNEL
MOVIEPLEX
MULTIMAX
NEWS 10 NOW
NIPPON GOLDEN NETWORK
OPTIMUM ONLINE
OUTERMAX
PENTHOUSE HD
PENTHOUSE TV
PHOENIX TV
PILLSBURY CHANNEL
PLAYBOY EN ESPANOL
PLAYBOY HD
PLAYBOY TV
PLAYGIRL TV
PURSUIT CHANNEL
RAI INTERNATIONAL
RIO DE LA PLATA
SHORTSHD
SHOWTIME FAMILYZONE
SHOWTIME HD
SHOWTIME NEXT
SHOWTIME ON DEMAND
SHOWTIME SHOWCASE
SHOWTIME TOO
SHOWTIME WOMEN
SHOWTIME
SONY ENTERTAINMENT TELEVISION ASIA
STARZ CINEMA HD
STARZ CINEMA
STARZ COMEDY HD
STARZ COMEDY
STARZ EDGE HD
STARZ EDGE
STARZ HDTV
STARZ IN BLACK HD
STARZ IN BLACK
STARZ INDIEPLEX HD
STARZ INDIEPLEX
STARZ KIDS & FAMILY HD
STARZ KIDS & FAMILY
STARZ RETROPLEX HD
STARZ RETROPLEX
STARZ
SUNDANCE CHANNEL
THE JEWISH CHANNEL
THRILLERMAX
TV ASIA
TV JAPAN
TV POLONIA
VENEMOVIES
VUTOPIA
WMAX
ZILLIONTV

PAY-PER-VIEW

BET ACTION PAY-PER-VIEW
CLUB JENNA
EVENT ENTERTAINMENT
FRESH
GAMEHD
GONZOX
HOT CHOICE
HUSTLER TV
IN DEMAND
MLB EXTRA INNINGS
MLS DIRECT KICK
NBA LEAGUE PASS
NHL CENTER ICE
PLEASURE
SHORTEEZ
SPICE HD
SPICE HOT
SPICE LIVE
SPICE PLATINUM
SPICE 2
SPICE ULTIMATE
SPICE: XCESS
SPICE
SPORTS PPV
TEAMHD
TEN BLOX
TEN BLUE
TEN CLIPS
TEN MAX
TEN ON DEMAND
TEN XTSY
TIGERVISION
TRUE BLUE
VIDEO SEAT
WORLD CHAMPIONSHIP WRESTLING

PLANNED SERVICES

AMERICA CHANNEL
AMERICAN NATIONAL NETWORK
BLACK TELEVISION NEWS CHANNEL
BOUNCE TV
BOXTV: THE BOXING CHANNEL
BROADWAY TELEVISION NETWORK
CUBAPLAY TELEVISION
DISNEY JUNIOR
.2 NETWORK
ENCORE ESPANOL
HBCU NETWORK
LEGACY.TV
LONGHORN NETWORK
MOVE NETWORKS INC.
MUSL TV
PAC-12 NETWORK
PB&J
THE SYZYGY NETWORK
UNINOVELAS
UNIVISION DEPORTES
UNIVISION 24/7
U.S. MILITARY TV NETWORK
VELOCITY
WWE NETWORK

REGIONAL PROGRAMMING

ACTION 36 CABLE 6
ALTITUDE SPORTS & ENTERTAINMENT
ATLANTA INTERFAITH BROADCASTERS
BAY NEWS 9
BAY NEWS 9 ESPANOL
BEACHTV
BOSTON KIDS & FAMILY
BRAVESVISION
BRIGHT HOUSE SPORTS NETWORK
CABLE TV NETWORK OF NEW JERSEY
CALIFORNIA CHANNEL
CATCH 47
CATHOLIC TELEVISION NETWORK
CET - COMCAST ENTERTAINMENT TV
CHANNEL 4 SAN DIEGO
CN8
CN|2
COMCAST/CHARTER SPORTS SOUTHEAST (CSS)
COMCAST HOMETOWN NETWORK
COMCAST SPORTSNET CHICAGO
COMCAST SPORTS SOUTHWEST (CSS)
COMCAST SPORTSNET BAY AREA
COMCAST SPORTSNET CALIFORNIA
COMCAST SPORTSNET MID-ATLANTIC
COMCAST SPORTSNET NEW ENGLAND
COMCAST SPORTSNET NORTHWEST
COMCAST SPORTSNET PHILADELPHIA
FOX SPORTS SOUTH
COMCAST SPORTSNET WEST
THE COMCAST NETWORK
COUNTY TELEVISION NETWORK SAN DIEGO
COX SPORTS TELEVISION
CT-N
THE DENVER CHANNEL - KMGH
DISCOVERY CHANNEL ASIA
DISCOVERY EN ESPANOL
DOLPHINS TELEVISION NETWORK
ECOLOGY CABLE SERVICE
ECUMENICAL TV CHANNEL
ENGLISH ON DEMAND
FALCONSVISION
FIOS1
FLORIDA CHANNEL
FOX DEPORTES
FOX SPORTS NET ARIZONA
FOX SPORTS NET DETROIT
FOX SPORTS NET FLORIDA
FOX SPORTS NET HOUSTON
FOX SPORTS NET INDIANA
FOX SPORTS NET MID-ATLANTIC
FOX SPORTS NET MIDWEST
FOX SPORTS NET MINNESOTA
FOX SPORTS NET NEW YORK
FOX SPORTS NET NORTH
FOX SPORTS NET OHIO
FOX SPORTS NET PHILADELPHIA
FOX SPORTS NET PRIME TICKET
FOX SPORTS NET WEST 2
FOX SPORTS NET WEST
FOX SPORTS NET WISCONSIN
FOX SPORTS NET
FOX SPORTS SOUTHWEST
FOX SPORTS WORLD
GBH KIDS
GEORGIA PUBLIC BROADCASTING
GLOBAL VILLAGE NETWORK
GREEK CHANNEL
HELENA CIVIC TELEVISION (HCT)
ILLINOIS CHANNEL
INTERNATIONAL TELEVISION (ITV)
IOWA COMMUNICATIONS NETWORK
JTV
KANSAS NOW 22
KENTUCKY EDUCATIONAL TELEVISION (KET5)
KLRU-TOO
K-MTN TELEVISION
KOREA ONE: CHICAGOLAND KOREAN TV
LAS VEGAS ONE
LIBRARY LITERACY CHANNEL / GHTV
LIVE WELL NETWORK
LNC 5
LOCAL CABLE WEATHER
LOCAL NEWS ON CABLE
LWS LOCAL WEATHER STATION
LOTTERY CHANNEL
LOUISIANA LEGISLATIVE NETWORK
ME TELEVISION
METROCHANNELS
METRO SPORTS
MHZ NETWORKS
MHZ WORLDVIEW
MICHIGAN GOVERNMENT TELEVISION
MID-ATLANTIC SPORTS NETWORK
MIDCO SPORTS NETWORK
MINNESOTA HOUSE & SENATE TELEVISION
MKTV
MSG PLUS
MSG 3D
MSG VARSITY
MSG
THE MTN
MXENERGYTV
NATIONAL GREEK TELEVISION
NBC CHICAGO NONSTOP
NBC MIAMI NONSTOP
NBC NEW YORK NONSTOP
NBC PHILADELPHIA NONSTOP
NBC WASHINGTON NONSTOP
NEW ENGLAND SPORTS NETWORK
NEW YORK NETWORK
NEW YORK 1 NOTICIAS
NEW YORK RACING CHANNEL
NEW YORK STATE ASSEMBLY RADIO TELEVISION
NEWS CHANNEL 5+
NEWS CHANNEL 3 ANYTIME
NEWS NOW 53
NEWS ON ONE - WOWT
NEWS 12 BROOKLYN
NEWS 12 TRAFFIC & WEATHER
NEWS 14 CAROLINA
NIPPON GOLDEN NETWORK ON DEMAND
NIPPON GOLDEN NETWORK 3
NIPPON GOLDEN NETWORK 2
NJTV
OHIO CHANNEL
OLELO
OREGON PUBLIC AFFAIRS NETWORK
PENN NATIONAL RACING ALIVE
PENNSYLVANIA CABLE NETWORK
PHILADELPHIA PARK LIVE
PIKES PEAK COMMUNITY COLLEGE
PLAY & WIN CHANNEL
PORTUGUESE CHANNEL
PRAYER CHANNEL
R NEWS
RHODE ISLAND STATEWIDE INTERCONNECT
ROCHESTER'S CW
ROOT SPORTS NORTHWEST
ROOT SPORTS PITTSBURGH
ROOT SPORTS ROCKY MOUNTAIN
ROOT SPORTS UTAH
RTP-USA
SAN DIEGO NEWS CHANNEL 10 - KGTV
SINO TV
6 NEWS
SNN 6
SPORTSOUTH
SPORTSCHOICE
SPORTSTIME OHIO
SPORTSNET NEW YORK
SUNSPORTS TV
TAMPA BAY ON DEMAND
TELECARE
TELEMIAMI
TEMPO
10 NEWS 2
TEXAS CABLE NEWS
TEXAS HOUSE OF REPRESENTATIVES VIDEO/ AUDIO SERVICES

TIME WARNER CABLE SPORTS
TKMI LIVE BROADCASTING
TRAVEL WEATHER NOW
TROJAN VISION
TV2
TVW
24/7 NEWS CHANNEL
WASHINGTON KOREAN TV
WCTY CHANNEL 16
WGBH CREATE
WGBH HD
WGBH ON DEMAND
WGBH-TV
WGBH WORLD
WISCONSINEYE
WKYT-TV
WUCF TV
YES 3D
YNN-CENTRAL NEW YORK

RELIGIOUS GROUPS

ADVENTIST TELEVISION NETWORK
CORNERSTONE TELEVISION
DOMINION SKY ANGEL
GOD TV
NHK WORLD TV
SON BROADCASTING
TAIWAN MACROVIEW TV

SATELLITE PROGRAMMERS

A TASTE OF SPICE
A&E HD
A&E
AAPKA COLORS
AARP TV
ABC FAMILY CHANNEL
ABC FAMILY HD
ABC NEWS NOW
ABU DHABI SPORT
ACTIONMAX
ADULT SWIM
AFRICA CHANNEL HD
AFRICA CHANNEL
AFRICAN TV NETWORK (ATVN)
AL FORAT
AL-IRAQIYA
AL JAZEERA ENGLISH
AL KARMA TV
AL MAGHRIBIA
ALMAVISION
ALPHA MOM TV
ALTERNA'TV
AMC HD
AMC
AMERICA ONE TELEVISION
AMERICAN DESI
AMERICANLIFE TV NETWORK
AMERICAN LIFE TV ON DEMAND
AMERICAN MOVIE CLASSICS
AMERICAN NETWORK
AMERICAN NEWS NETWORK
AMERICANLIFE TV NETWORK HD
AMERICA'S STORE
AMRITA TV
ANA TELEVISION NETWORK
ANGEL ONE
ANGEL TWO
ANHUI TV INTERNATIONAL
ANIMAL PLANET HD
ANIMAL PLANET
ANIME NETWORK
ANNENBERG CHANNEL
ANTENA 3
ANTENNA SATELLITE TV/USA
ANTENNA TV
ARABIC CHANNEL
ARIANA AFGHANISTAN MEDIA
ARIANA TV
ARMENIAN PUBLIC CHANNEL
ARMENIAN RUSSIAN TELEVISION NETWORK (ARTN)
ASC FLIX
ASC XTRA
ASIANET NEWS
ASIANET PLUS
ASIANET USA
ASSYRIASAT
AUCTION TV
AUDIENCE NETWORK
AYM SPORTS
AZ TV
AZTECA AMERICA
B-MANIA
BABYFIRSTTV
BANDAMAX
BARKER
BBC AMERICA ON DEMAND
BBC AMERICA
BBC ARABIC
BBC HD
BBC WORLD NEWS
BEAUTY AND FASHION CHANNEL
BEAUTY TV
BEIJING TV
BEN TELEVISION
BET GOSPEL
BET J
BET NETWORKS
BETSOUNDZ
BETTER LIFE MEDIA
BIO HD
BIO
BLACK BROADCASTING NETWORK
BLACKBELT TV
BLOOMBERG TELEVISION HD
BLOOMBERG TELEVISION
BLUEHIGHWAYS TV
BN BOSNIA
BOLLYWOOD HITS ON DEMAND
BOLLYWOOD ON DEMAND
BOOK TV
BOOMERANG EN ESPANOL
BOOMERANG
BOSTEL
BOSTON CATHOLIC TELEVISION
BRAVO HD
BRAVO
BRIDGES TV
BTN HD
BTN
BUSINESSVISION
BYU TELEVISION
CABLE IN THE CLASSROOM
CANAL ALGERIE
CANAL DE LAS ESTRELLAS
CANAL 52MX
CANAL SUR MEXICO
CANAL SUR
CANAL 24 HORAS
CANALES N
CAPITAL OFF TRACK BETTING TELEVISION NETWORK
CARACOL TV
CAREER ENTERTAINMENT TELEVISION
CARIBEVISION TELEVISION NETWORKS
CARS.TV
CARTOON NETWORK HD
CARTOON NETWORK TAMBIEN EN ESPANOL
CARTOON NETWORK
CASA CLUB TV
CASINO & GAMING TELEVISION
CATALOG TV
CATHOLICTV
CB TELEVISION MICHOACAN
CBS SPORTS NETWORK HD
CBS SPORTS NETWORK
CCTV-9 (DOCUMENTARY CHANNEL)
CCTV-6
CELEBRITY SHOPPING NETWORK
CELTIC VISION
CENTRIC
CHANNEL ONE RUSSIA
CHANNEL ONE
CHERIETV
CHILLER
CHINA MOVIE CHANNEL
CHINESE COMMUNICATION CHANNEL
CHRISTIAN TELEVISION NETWORK
CHURCH CHANNEL
CI HD
CINE LATINO
CINE MEXICANO
CINEMA GOLDEN CHOICE
CINEMAX SELECCIONES
CLASSIC ARTS SHOWCASE
CMT HD
CMT PURE COUNTRY
CNBC HD+
CNBC
CNN EN ESPANOL
CNN ENHANCED TV
CNN HD
CNN INTERNATIONAL
CNN
COLLEGE & SCHOOL NETWORK
COLLEGE SPORTS TELEVISION
COLOURS
COMCAST SPORTSNET PLUS HD
COMEDY CENTRAL HD
COMEDY CENTRAL
COMEDY.TV
CONCERT TV
CONDISTA
COOKING CHANNEL
THECOOLTV
COUNTRY MUSIC TV
COUNTRY MUSIC TV (ASIA/PACIFIC RIM)
COUNTRY MUSIC TV (LATIN AMERICA)
THE COUNTRY NETWORK
COURT TV
CRIME & INVESTIGATION NETWORK
CRIME CHANNEL
CSN+ HD
CSN+
C-SPAN EXTRA
C-SPAN 2 HD
C-SPAN HD
C-SPAN S
C-SPAN 3 HD
C-SPAN 3
C-SPAN 2
C-SPAN
CTN: CAMBODIAN CHANNEL
CURRENT
CW11 NEW YORK
CW+
DALLAS COWBOYS CHANNEL
DATING ON DEMAND
DAYSTAR TV NETWORK
DE PELICULA CLASICO
DE PELICULA
DEEP DISH TV
DESTINY CHANNEL
DEUTSCHE WELLE TV
DIRECT SHOPPING NETWORK
DIRECTV CINEMA 3D
DISCOVERY CHANNEL AFRICA
DISCOVERY CHANNEL AUSTRALIA
DISCOVERY CHANNEL BRAZIL
DISCOVERY CHANNEL EUROPE
DISCOVERY CHANNEL GERMANY
DISCOVERY CHANNEL HD
DISCOVERY CHANNEL INDIA
DISCOVERY CHANNEL ITALY
DISCOVERY CHANNEL JAPAN
DISCOVERY CHANNEL MIDDLE EAST
DISCOVERY CHANNEL
DISCOVERY DIGITAL NETWORKS
DISCOVERY FAMILIA
DISCOVERY FIT & HEALTH
HD THEATER
DISCOVERY HEALTH CHANNEL
DISCOVERY HEALTH ON CALL
DISCOVERY HOME CHANNEL
DISCOVERY KIDS CHANNEL
DISCOVERY KIDS EN ESPANOL
DISCOVERY KIDS CHANNEL HD
DISCOVERY TIMES CHANNEL
DISCOVERY TRAVEL & LIVING (VIAJAR Y VIVIR)
DISNEY CHANNEL HD
DISNEY CHANNEL
DISNEY FAMILY MOVIES
DISNEY TRAVEL ON DEMAND
DISNEY XD EN ESPANOL
DISNEY XD HD
DISNEY XD
DIY NETWORK HD
DIY NETWORK
DMTV7
DOCU TVE
DOCUMENTARY CHANNEL
DODGERS ON DEMAND
DIY NETWORK ON DEMAND
DRAGONTV
DREAM TELEVISION NETWORK
DRIVERTV
DUBAI TV
E! ENTERTAINMENT TELEVISION HD
E! ENTERTAINMENT TELEVISION
EBRU TV
ECUAVISIA INTERNACIONAL
EMIRATES DUBAI TELEVISION
EMPLOYMENT & CAREER CHANNEL
ENCORE HD
ES.TV
ESPN AMERICA HD
ESPN AMERICA
ESPN CLASSIC HD
ESPN CLASSIC SPORTS
ESPN DEPORTES ON DEMAND
ESPN DEPORTES
ESPN EXTRA
ESPN NOW
ESPN ON DEMAND
ESPN/SPORTSTICKER
ESPN 3D
ESPN 2
ESPN U ON DEMAND
ESPN U
ESPN
ESPNEWS HD
ESPNEWS
ESPN HD
ESPNOL
ESPN PREMIER LEAGUE
ESPN 2 HD
ESPNU HD
ESTRELLA TV
ET-GLOBAL
ET-NEWS
ETERNAL WORD TV NETWORK
EUROCINEMA
EURONEWS
EWTN HD
EWTN
EWTN EN ESPANOL
EXERCISE TV
EXPO TV
FAITH TELEVISION NETWORK
FAMILY CHRISTIAN TELEVISION
FAMILYLAND TELEVISION NETWORK
FAMILYNET
FANZ-TV
FASHION NETWORK
FASHION TV
FEARNET
FESTIVAL DIRECT
FIGHT NOW TV
FILIPINO CHANNEL
FILIPINO ON DEMAND
FILM FESTIVAL CHANNEL
FINE LIVING NETWORK
FINE LIVING ON DEMAND
FOOD NETWORK HD
FOOD NETWORK ON DEMAND
FOOD NETWORK

FOX BUSINESS CHANNEL HD
FOX BUSINESS CHANNEL
FOX COLLEGE SPORTS ATLANTIC
FOX COLLEGE SPORTS CENTRAL
FOX COLLEGE SPORTS PACIFIC
FOX COLLEGE SPORTS
FOX ENHANCED TV
FOX HD
FOX NEWS CHANNEL
FOX NEWS HD
FOX REALITY CHANNEL
FOX SOCCER
FOX SPORTS NET CAROLINAS
FOX SPORTS NET KANSAS CITY
FOX SPORTS NET NORTHWEST
FOX SPORTS NET PITTSBURGH
FOX SPORTS NET ROCKY MOUNTAIN
FOX SPORTS NET TENNESSEE
FOX SPORTS NET UTAH
FRANCE 24
FREE SPEECH TV
FRIGHT CHANNEL
FSN HD
FTV HD
FUEL TV HD
FUEL TV
FUNIMATION CHANNEL
FUSE HD
FUSE ON DEMAND
FUSE
FX HD
FX PREVIEW CHANNEL
FX
G4
GALAVISION HD
GALAVISION
GALLERYPLAYER ON DEMAND
GAME SHOW NETWORK
GAMING ENTERTAINMENT TELEVISION
GAS STATION TV
GEM SHOPPING NETWORK
GEMSTV
GLOBECAST WORLDTV
GMA PINOY TV
GMA LIFE TV
GOLDEN EAGLE BROADCASTING
GOLF CHANNEL HD
GOLF CHANNEL
GOLTV
GOSCOUT HOMES
GOSPEL MUSIC CHANNEL HD
GOSPEL MUSIC CHANNEL
GOSPEL MUSIC TV
GRAN CINE
GREAT AMERICAN COUNTRY HD
GREAT AMERICAN COUNTRY
GRTV NETWORK
GSN HD
GSN
GUARDIAN TELEVISION NETWORK (GTN)
GUYTV
HALLMARK CHANNEL HD
HALLMARK CHANNEL
HALLMARK MOVIE CHANNEL HD
HALLMARK MOVIE CHANNEL
HALOGEN NETWORK
HAVOC TV
HAZARDOUS
HBO EN ESPANOL
HBO HD
HBO THE WORKS
HD ON DEMAND
HDNET MOVIES
HDNET
HEADLINE NEWS HD
HEADLINE NEWS
HEALTHINATION
HEALTHY LIVING CHANNEL
HERE! ON DEMAND
HERE! TV
HGTV HD
HGTV ON DEMAND
HGTV
HISTORY CHANNEL EN ESPANOL
HISTORY CHANNEL HD
HISTORY CHANNEL INTERNATIONAL
HISTORY CHANNEL
HITN
HITS EN ESPANOL
HITS (HEADEND IN THE SKY)
HLN
HOLLYWOOD.COM TV
HOME & GARDEN TELEVISION
HOME SHOPPING NETWORK EN ESPANOL
HOME SHOPPING NETWORK HD
HOME SHOPPING NETWORK 2
HOME THEATRE
HOME SHOPPING NETWORK
HOOKS AND BULLETS
HOPE CHANNEL
HORROR CHANNEL
HORROR NET
HORSETV CHANNEL
HOWARD TV
HRTV
HTV MUSICA
ID INVESTIGATION DISCOVERY HD
ID INVESTIGATION DISCOVERY
IDRIVETV
IFC FILMS ON DEMAND
IFC FREE
IFC HD
IFC IN THEATERS
I-HEALTH
IMETRO
IMPACT
INDEPENDENT MUSIC NETWORK
INFINITO
INHD2
INHD
INSP
INSPIRATION ON DEMAND
INTELLICAST
ION LIFE
ION TELEVISION HD
ION TELEVISION
I-SHOP
ITALIAN AMERICAN NETWORK
JCTV
JEWELRY TELEVISION
JEWISH LIFE TV
KARAOKE CHANNEL
KOREAN CHANNEL
KTLA LOS ANGELES
KTV - KIDS & TEENS TELEVISION
KUWAIT TV
KYLIN KIDS LEARNING CHINESE
LA FAMILIA NETWORK
LATELE NOVELA NETWORK
LATIN TELEVISION (LTV)
LATINO AMERICA TV
LATV NETWORKS
THE LEARNING CHANNEL
LMN ESPANOL ON DEMAND
LIFETIME MOVIE NETWORK HD
LIFETIME MOVIE NETWORK
LIFETIME ON DEMAND
LIFETIME REAL WOMEN
LIFETIME TELEVISION HD
LIFETIME
LIME
LIVETV
LIVE WELL HD NETWORK
LIVING FAITH TELEVISION
LMN HD
LOGO
MAC TV
MADISON SQUARE GARDEN NETWORK
MAG RACK
THE MAJESTIC
MALL TV
MARIAVISION
MARTHA STEWART ON DEMAND
MASMUSICA TEVE NETWORK
MAVTV
MBC AMERICA
MDTV: MEDICAL NEWS NOW
ME-TV
MEADOWS RACING NETWORK
MEDIASET ITALIA
MEGA TV
MEN7 NETWORK
MEZZO LIVE HD
MEXICANAL
MGM CHANNEL
MGM HD
MGM PLUS
MI CINE ON DEMAND
MI CINE
MILITARY CHANNEL
MILITARY HISTORY CHANNEL
MLB NETWORK
MLB NETWORK HD
MNET
MOJO MIX
MOMENTUM TV
MONSTER ON DEMAND
MOODY BROADCASTING NETWORK
MOUNTAINWEST SPORTS NETWORK
THE MOVIE CHANNEL HD
THE MOVIE CHANNEL ON DEMAND
MSNBC
MTC PERSIAN TELEVISION
MTV HITS
MTV JAMS
MTV LATIN AMERICA
MTV NETWORKS DIGITAL SUITE
MTV NETWORKS EUROPE
MTV NETWORKS HD
MTV2
MTV
MTVU
MULTIMEDIOS TELEVISION
MUN2 TELEVISION
MYDESTINATION.TV
MYNETWORKTV INC.
MYX TV
N3D ON DEMAND
N3D
NARRATIVE TELEVISION NETWORK
NASA TV HD
NASA TV
NASCAR HOTPASS
NASCAR IN CAR
NAT GEO WILD HD
NAT GEO WILD
NATIONAL GEOGRAPHIC CHANNEL
NATIONAL GEOGRAPHIC CHANNEL HD NETWORK
NATIONAL GEOGRAPHIC CHANNEL ON DEMAND
NATIONAL IRANIAN TELEVISION
NATIONAL JEWISH TV (NJT)
NATIONAL LAMPOON NETWORK
NBA TV HD
NBA TV
NDTV THE DOMINICAN CHANNEL
NEO CRICKET
NETLINK INTERNATIONAL
NETWORK ONE
THE NEW ENCORE
NEWS 12 INTERACTIVE
NEWSDAY TV
NEW TANG DYNASTY TV
NFL NETWORK HD
NFL NETWORK
NFL REDZONE
NHL NETWORK HD
NHL NETWORK
NICK AT NITE
NICK HD
NICK JR.
NICK TOO
NICKELODEON
NICKTOONS EN ESPANOL
NICKTOONS TV
NOGGIN
NTN24
NTV AMERICA
NTV HAYAT
NUVO TV HD
NUVO TV
OASIS TV
OLE TV
OLEC NETWORK
OLYMPUSAT HISPANIC PACK
101 NETWORK
ONSPOT DIGITAL NETWORK
OUTDOOR CHANNEL HD
OUTDOOR CHANNEL ON DEMAND
OUTDOOR CHANNEL 2 HD
OUTDOOR CHANNEL
OUTSIDE TELEVISION
OVATION
OWN: OPRAH WINFREY NETWORK
OXYGEN ON DEMAND
OXYGEN
PACVIA TV
PALLADIA
PANDAAMERICA SHOPPING NETWORK
PARENTS TV
PATRIOTS ON DEMAND
PAXSON COMMUNICATIONS CORP.
PBS HD
PBS KIDS CHANNEL
PBS KIDS/PBS KIDS GO!
PBS KIDS SPROUT
PBS WORLD
PEGASUSTV
PENTAGON CHANNEL
PEOPLE'S NETWORK
PETS.TV
PLANET GREEN HD
PLANET GREEN
PLAYERS NETWORK
PLAZA TV
PLUM TV
PRAISE TELEVISION
PRIMETIME 24
PRODUCT INFORMATION NETWORK
PROMOTER
PUBLIC INTEREST VIDEO NETWORK
PUMA TV
PUMPTOP TV
PUPPY CHANNEL
QATARTV
QUBO
QVC HD
QVC
RADAR CHANNEL
RAI USA
RANG-A-RANG TELEVISION
REACTV
REAL HIP-HOP NETWORK
REAL MADRID TV
RECIPE.TV
REELZCHANNEL
RESEARCH CHANNEL
RFD HD
RFD-TV
RGT
RITMOSON LATINO
RLTV
RSC ROMANIA
RSN RESORT TV
RT
RTN
RTN+
RTR PLANETA
RTV21
RTVI
RUSSIA TODAY
RUSSIAN TELEVISION NETWORK
SAFE TV
SAIGON BROADCASTING TELEVISION NETWORK
SALAAM TV
SAMANYOLU TV
SAUDITV
SCIENCE HD
SCIENCE TELEVISION
SCIENCE

SCI-FI CHANNEL
SCOLA
SELECT ON DEMAND
SEMINAR TV
THE SET3
THE SET2
THE SET (SOUTHERN ENTERTAINMENT TV)
SETANTA SPORTS USA
SHALOM TV
SHALOM USA AMERICA
SHANGHAI DRAGON TV
SHARJAHTV
SHEPHERDS CHAPEL NETWORK
SHOP AT HOME
SHOP LATINO TV
SHOPNBC
SHORT TV
SHOWCASE HD
SHOWTIME BEYOND
SHOWTIME EN ESPANOL
SHOWTIME EXTREME
SI TV
SIMAYE AZADI TV
SIX NEWS NOW
THE SKI CHANNEL
SLEUTH ON DEMAND
SLEUTH
SMILE OF A CHILD
SMITHSONIAN CHANNEL HD
SMITHSONIAN CHANNEL ON DEMAND
SMITHSONIAN CHANNEL
SNEAK PREVUE
SOAPNET
SOCIETY OF PORTUGUESE TELEVISION
SOL VIDEO ON DEMAND
SONY MOVIE CHANNEL
SORPRESA
SOUNDTRACK CHANNEL
SOUTHEASTERN CHANNEL
SPEED HD
SPEED ON DEMAND
SPEED
SPIKE TV HD
SPIKE TV
SPIRIT TELEVISION NETWORK
SPORTING CHANNEL
SPORTS GAMING PLAYERS NETWORK
SPORTSKOOL
THE SPORTSMAN CHANNEL HD
THE SPORTSMAN CHANNEL
SPORTS VIEW PLUS
SPORTSVUE
STAR CHINESE CHANNEL
STAR INDIA GOLD
STAR INDIA NEWS
STAR INDIA PLUS
STAR ONE
STARFISH TELEVISION NETWORK
START OVER
STARZ ON DEMAND
STUDENT FILM NETWORK
STUFF TV
STYLE NETWORK
SUDANTV
SUNDANCE CHANNEL HD
SUNDANCE SELECT
SUPERCANAL CARIBE
SUPERCHANNEL
SUPERSTATION WGN
SUR MEX
SUR NETWORK
SUR PERU
SYFY HD
SYFY
SYRIANTV
TALKLINE COMMUNICATIONS TV NETWORK
TAPESHTV
TAVSIR IRAN
TBN ENLACE USA
TBN HD
TBS IN HD
TBS SUPERSTATION
TEENNICK
TELE 5
TELE PADRE PIO
TELEFE INTERNATIONAL
TELEFORMULA
TELEFUTURA HD
TELEFUTURA
TELEHIT
TELEMICRO INTERNACIONAL
TELEMUNDO INTERNACIONAL
TELEMUNDO PUERTO RICO
TELEMUNDO
TELENOVELAS
TELEPACE
TELEVISA NETWORKS
TELEVISION KOREA 24
TENNIS CHANNEL HD
TENNIS CHANNEL
TETRIS TV
TEVE-DE-MENTE
THE HUB
THE N
THIS TV
3 ANGELS BROADCASTING NETWORK
3NET
TIME WARNER HITS
TL NOVELAS
TLC HD
TLC
TOTAL LIVING NETWORK
TMC XTRA
TNT
TOO MUCH FOR TV ON DEMAND
TOON DISNEY
TOP CHANNEL TV
TRAVEL CHANNEL HD
TRAVEL CHANNEL LATIN AMERICA
TRAVEL CHANNEL
TR3S
TRINITY BROADCASTING NETWORK
TRUTV HD
TRUTV
TUFF.TV
TURBO
TURNER CLASSIC MOVIES
TURNER CLASSIC MOVIES HD
TURNER NETWORK TV HD
TURNER NETWORK TV
TURNER SOUTH
TUTV
TV CHILE
TV COLOMBIA
TV GUIDE NETWORK ON DEMAND
TV GUIDE NETWORK
TV GUIDE SPOT
TV LAND HD
TV LAND
TV ONE HD
TV ONE
TV ORIENT
TV ROMANIA INTERNATIONAL
TVE INTERNACIONAL
TV5 USA
TVG NETWORK
TVK (CAMBODIAN)
TVK (KOREAN)
TVK2
TVN ENTERTAINMENT
TVU MUSIC TELEVISION
CANAL 22 MEXICO
2M MAROC
ULTIMATE SHOPPING NETWORK
UNICABLE
UNION ON DEMAND
UNIQUE BUSINESS NEWS
UNIQUE SATELLITE TV
UNIVERSAL HD
UNIVERSITY OF CALIFORNIA TV (UCTV)
UNIVISION HD
UNIVISION ON DEMAND
UNIVISION
URBAN AMERICAN TELEVISION NETWORK
USA NETWORK HD
USA NETWORK
UTILISIMA US
UTILISIMA
VEGAS CHANNEL
VEHIX TV ON DEMAND
VERIA TV
VERSUS HD
VERSUS ON DEMAND
VERSUS
VH1 HD
VH1 CLASSIC
VH1 COUNTRY
VH1 SOUL
VH1
VHUNO
VIDA VISION
VIDEO ROLA
VIJAY
VIVA TELEVISION NETWORK
V-ME KIDS
VOY
VSEN-TV
VUDU
W NETWORK
WAM! AMERICA'S KIDZ NETWORK
WAPA AMERICA
WE ON DEMAND
WE TV HD
WE TV
WEALTHTV
WEALTHTV HD
WEALTHTV 3D
THE WEATHER CHANNEL HD
THE WEATHER CHANNEL
WEATHERNATION
WEATHERSCAN
WEATHERVISION
WEBMD TELEVISION
WFN HD
WGN AMERICA HD
WGN AMERICA
WGN
WICKED ON DEMAND
WINE NETWORK
WIZEBUYS TV
WOMEN'S TELEVISION NETWORK
THE WORD NETWORK
WORLD CINEMA HD
WORLD FIGHT CHANNEL (WFC)
WORLD FISHING NETWORK
WORLD HARVEST TELEVISION
WORSHIP NETWORK
WPIX
WTBS
WWE 24/7
XFINITY 3D
XY.TV
YANKEES ENTERTAINMENT & SPORTS
YEMENTV
YES HD
ZEE CINEMA
ZEE GOLD
ZEE TV USA
ZHONG TIAN CHANNEL

SPANISH LANGUAGE PROGRAMMING

BARCA TV
CENTROAMERICA TV
LO MEJOR ON DEMAND
NAT GEO MUNDO
ONCE TV MEXICO
PASIONES
SEMILLITAS
TELEMUNDO NETWORK GROUP
TELEVISION DOMINICANA
UNIVISION STUDIOS
V-ME TV

TEXT SERVICES

NEWS PLUS

PAY TV & SATELLITE SERVICES COMPANIES

A TASTE OF SPICE — See Fresh.

A&E
235 E 45th St
New York, NY 10017
Phone: 212-210-1400
Fax: 212-692-9269
E-mail: michael.feeney@aetn.com
Web Site: http://www.aetv.com
Abbe Raven, President & Chief Executive Officer
Robert DeBitetto, President & General Manager, A&E
Whitney Goit, Senior Executive Vice President, AETN
Gerard Gruosso, Chief Financial Officer & Executive Vice President, AETN
Melvin Berning, Executive Vice President, Ad Sales, AETN
Jim Greiner, Executive Vice President, New Enterprises, Production & Internet Services
David McKillop, Executive Vice President, Programming
David Zagin, Executive Vice President, Distribution
Jim Agius, Senior Vice President, Ad Sales, A&E & Biography
David Desocio, Senior Vice President, Partnerships, AETN
Michael Feeney, Senior Vice President, Corporate Communications
Elaine Frontain Bryant, Senior Vice President, Nonfiction & Alternative Programming
Paul Jelinek, Senior Vice President, Digital Media
Nina Lederman, Senior Vice President, Series Programming
Tina Lopez, Senior Vice President, Original Movies
David Marans, Senior Vice President, Research & Insights
Melinda McLaughlin, Senior Vice President, Insights & Marketing Solutions
Thomas Moody, Senior Vice President, Programming Planning & Acquisitions
Dan Silverman, Senior Vice President, Publicity
Nancy Alpert, Vice President, Deputy General Counsel
Liz Dickler, Vice President, Drama Programming
Laura Fleury, Vice President, Non-Fiction & Alternative Programming
Mark Garner, Vice President, Affiliate Distribution & Business Development
Chris Lenge, Vice President, Sales Strategy
Alexandra MacDowell, Vice President, Production Management
Lily Neumeyer, Vice President, Nonfiction & Alternative Programming
Lori Peterzell, Vice President, Marketing, A&E
Maggie Reilly-Brooks, Vice President, Deputy General Counsel
Don Roberts, Vice President, Corporate Research & Consumer Insight
Risa Rosenthal, Vice President, Direct Response Advertising
Richard Shirley, Vice President, Distribution Business Development
Steve Stander, Vice President, Deputy General Counsel
Marcela Tabares, Vice President, Ad Sales Research

Molly Thompson, Vice President, A&E IndieFilms
Emory R Walton III, Vice President, Distribution Field Sales, West
Kate Winn, Vice President, Video Sales & Mktg, Consumer Products
Richard Shirley, Senior Director, Distribution & Business Development
Stephen Harris, Director, Nonfiction & Alternative Programming
Melissa Hudson, Director, Digital Mktg.
Gina Nocero, Director, Program Publicity, A&E
Kerri Tarmey, Director, Corporate Communications
Carrie Trimmer, Director, Licensing, Consumer Products

Sales Offices:
ATLANTA: One Buckhead Plaza, 3060 Peachtree Rd NW, Ste 875, Atlanta, GA 30305. Phone: 404-816-8880.

CHICAGO: 111 E Wacker Dr, Ste 2206, Chicago, IL 60601. Phone: 312-819-1486.

DETROIT: 201 W Beaver Rd, Ste 1010, Troy, MI 48084. Phone: 248-740-1300. Fax: 248-740-2686.

LOS ANGELES: 1925 Century Park E, Ste 1000, Los Angeles, CA 90067. Phone: 310-286-6060. Fax: 310-286-1240.
Type of service: Basic & video on demand.
Satellites: Galaxy I, transponder 12.
Operating hours/week: 168.
Uplink: Stamford, CT.
Programming: Original series, Biography, mysteries & special presentations.
Began: February 1, 1984.
Means of Support: Advertising, subscriber fees & program licensing fees.
Total subscribers: 100,100,000.
Distribution method: Available to cable systems.
Scrambled signal: Yes.
Ownership: Hearst Corp., NBCUniversal LLC & The Walt Disney Co.

A&E HD — See A&E.
Began: September 1, 2006.

AAPKA COLORS
Viacom 18 Media Pvt. Ltd.
30-H, Simran Center, 3rd Fl, Parsi Panchay Rd
Andheri (E), Mumbai 400069
India
Phones: 022-42325300; 022-42325369
Fax: 022-67652663
Web Site: http://www.aapkacolors.com
Haresh Chawla, Group Chief Executive Officer, Viacom 18 & Network 18
Rajesh Kamat, Group Chief Operating Officer, Viacom 18 & Chief Executive Officer, Aapka Colors
Bhavneet Singh, Managing Director & Executive Vice President, Emerging Networks, MTV Networks International
Chris Kuelling, Vice President, International Programing, DISH Network
Sonia Huria, Senior Manager, Communications

Branch Offices:
Delhi Branch Office: Viacom 18 Media Pvt. Ltd., Times Tower, 7th Fl, Sector- 28, Mg Rd, Opp. Gurgaon Central Mall, Gurgaon, Haryana 122002, India. Phone: 0124 4758800.
Programming: Offers scripted series, reality shows, game shows and blockbuster Bollywood films for the south Asian community.
Began: January 27, 2010, in the United States. Service launched July 21, 2008 in India.
Total subscribers: 40,000,000 (Figure is subscribers worldwide.).
Distribution method: Available to DISH Network subscribers.
Scrambled signal: Yes.
Ownership: Viacom Inc. & Network 18.

AARP TV
601 E St NW
Washington, DC 20049
Phone: 888-687-2277
Web Site: http://www.aarp.org/tv
Type of service: Basic.
Programming: Information & entertainment for viewers 50 plus.
Began: March 10, 2008.
Total subscribers: 29,000,000.
Distribution method: Available to cable systems & satellite providers.

ABC FAMILY CHANNEL
10960 Wilshire Blvd
23rd Fl
Los Angeles, CA 90024
Phone: 310-235-5100
Fax: 310-235-5102
E-mail: press@abcfamily.com
Web Site: http://www.abcfamily.go.com
Michael Riley, President
John Burns III, President, Distribution
Joel Andryc, Executive Vice President, Kids Programming & Development
Tom Cosgrove, Executive Vice President, ABC Family Channel
Eytan Keller, Executive Vice President, Reality Programming & Specials
Laura Nathanson, Executive Vice President, Sales
Janice Arouh, Senior Vice President, Affiliate Sales, ABC Family Channel
Brooke Bowman, Senior Vice President, Original Programming & Development
Tom Halleen, Senior Vice President, Primetime Programming & Development
Laura Kuhn, Senior Vice President, Strategic Sales Insights
Tracey Lawrence, Senior Vice President & General Manager, ABC Family Channel
Donna Mitroff, Senior Vice President, Educational Policies & Program Practices
Nicole Nichols, Senior Vice President, Corporate Communications & Publicity
Mark Rejtig, Senior Vice President, National Sales Manager
Todd Schoen, Senior Vice President, Affiliate Marketing & Local Advertising Sales
Patricia La Vigne, Senior Vice President, On-Air Promotion
Doug Yates, Senior Vice President, Marketing
Vicki Applegate, Vice President, Business & Legal Affairs
Wayne Baker, Vice President, Ad Sales
Elizabeth Boykewich, Vice President, Casting, Series & Movies
Jennifer Brawley, Vice President, Midwest Advertising Sales
Jeffrey Brechtelsbauer, Vice President, Information Technology
Tamara Brown, Vice President, Marketing
Felicia Brulato, Vice President, National Corporate Accounts
Brian Casentini, Vice President, Current Programming
Kim Christianson, Vice President, Programming & Development
Ovie Cowles, Vice President, Affiliate Ad Sales
Jennifer Dingwall, Vice President, Domestic Sales
Stephen R. Fisch, Vice President, Business & Legal Affairs
Eric Fisher, Vice President, Advertising Sales
Annie Fort, Vice President, Media Relations
Janice Forti, Vice President, Human Resources & Benefits
Ed Georger, Vice President, Advertising Sales
Jill Goldfarb, Vice President, Planning & Scheduling
Michael Hartounian, Vice President, Business & Legal Affairs
Terry Holmstrom, Vice President, Promotions
Fred Poston, Vice President, On-Air Promotion Operations
Nancy Redford, Vice President, Programming & Development
Jonathan Rosenthal, Vice President, Development
Marc Saputo, Vice President, Sales Development & Research
Matt Turner, Vice President, Ad Sales
Marlene Zakovich, Vice President, Corporate Communications & Publicity
Matthew Weiss, Regional Vice President, New York
Type of service: Basic.
Satellites: Galaxy V, transponder 11 (east coast); Satcom C-3, transponder 1 (west coast).
Operating hours/week: 168.
Programming: Family-oriented entertainment, including original series for kids.
Began: April 29, 1997, as The Family Channel; Relaunched as ABC Family Channel on August 15, 1998.
Means of Support: Advertising & system fees.
Total subscribers: 96,000,000.
Distribution method: Available to home dish audiences & cable systems.
Equipment: VideoCipher II.
Ownership: Disney-ABC Television Group.

ABC FAMILY HD — See ABC Family.

ABC NEWS NOW
7 W 66th St
New York, NY 10023
Web Site: http://abcnews.go.com/abcnews-now
Type of service: Digital & video on demand.
Operating hours/week: 168.
Programming: Breaking news, headlines & coverage of other ABC News shows.
Began: July 1, 2004.
Total subscribers: 34,000,000.
Distribution method: Available to cable, broadband & mobile providers.

ABORIGINAL PEOPLES TELEVISION NETWORK
339 Portage Ave
Winnipeg, MB R3B 2C3
Canada
Phones: 204-947-9331; 888-330-2786
Fax: 204-947-9307
E-mail: apowell@aptn.ca
Web Site: http://aptn.ca
Jean LaRose, Chief Executive Officer
Sky Bridges, Chief Operating Officer
Peter Strutt, Director of Programming
Wayne McKenzie, Director of Operations
Mike Peterkin, Director of Business Development, Strategic Planning
Vera Houle, Director of News & Current Affairs
Lea Todd, Director of Creative Services & Scheduling
Aimee Powell, Director of Sales

Branch Office:
YELLOWKNIFE: 5120 49th St, Box 3, Yellowknife, NT X1A 1P8. Phone: 867-873-2862. Fax: 867-873-3786.
Satellites: Anik E-1, transponder 10-A.
Operating hours/week: 168.
Operating areas: Portions of Newfoundland, The Northwest Territories, Quebec & Yukon Provinces.
Uplink: Iqaluit, Whitehorse & Yellowknife, NT.
Programming: Children's shows, accredited & general interest educational programming, cultural & current affairs shows, documentary features, phone-in shows, northern political coverage & special events.
Began: September 1, 1999.
Means of Support: Advertising & government contributions.
Total subscribers: 10,000,000.
Distribution method: Available to home dish audiences & cable systems.

ABU DHABI SPORT — See GlobeCast WorldTV.
PO Box 63
Abu Dhabi
United Arab Emirates
Phone: 971-2-4144000
Web Site: http://www.emi.ae
Type of service: Basic.
Operating hours/week: 168.
Programming: Live sports, news coverage, biographies, game shows & coverage of popular events throughout the Middle East.
Distribution method: Available on GlobeCast WorldTV satellite service.

ACCESS THE EDUCATION STATION
10212 Jasper Ave
Edmonton, AB T5J 5A3
Canada
Phone: 780-440-7777
Fax: 780-440-8899
E-mail: pam.hnytka@chumtv.com
Web Site: http://www.accesstv.ca
Tito Margiotta, Manager, Operations
Jill Bonenfant, Program Director
Richard Hiron, Managing, Sales & Marketing Director
Type of service: Basic.
Satellites: Anik E-1, transponder 20.
Operating hours/week: 168.
Operating areas: Provinces of Alberta, British Columbia, Manitoba, the Northwest Territories, Saskatchewan & the Yukon.
Uplink: Calgary, AB.
Programming: Offers educational, informational, documentaries & lifelong learning shows.
Began: January 1, 1975.
Means of Support: Advertising, sponsored air time sales.
Distribution method: Available to home dish audiences and cable systems.
Scrambled signal: Yes. Equipment: DVC MPEG2; DSR 4400.
Ownership: CHUM Ltd.

ACTION 36 CABLE 6
2102 Commerce Dr
San Jose, CA 95131
Phone: 408-953-3636
Fax: 408-953-3620
E-mail: general.manager@ktvu.com
Web Site: http://www.ktvu.com/kicu
Type of service: Basic.
Programming: News, entertainment & sports.

ACTIONMAX — See Cinemax.
Programming: Action movies, blockbusters, westerns, war movies & martial arts films.
Began: August 1, 1980.

ADRENALINE NATION TV (ANTV)
PO Box 3136
Holiday, FL 34692

Phone: 206-338-2365
Web Site: http://www.brandedentertainment.tv/antv
Keith Dressel, Chief Executive Officer
John Furlow, Chief of Operations
Charles Bednarek, Senior Director, Production
Mark Hughes, Marketing & Strategy
Jeff Greenfield, Branded Entertainment
Type of service: IPTV.
Programming: Independent music, entertainment & adrenaline sports.
Began: April 15, 2007.

ADULT SWIM
One Time Warner Center
New York, NY 10019
Phone: 212-275-6825
Fax: 212-275-7132
E-mail: advertisewithus@turner.com
Web Site: http://www.adultswim.com
John O'Hara, Executive Vice President & General Sales Manager
Patty Gillette, Senior Vice President, Brand Activation & Media Partnerships
Type of service: Basic & video on demand.
Operating hours/week: 37.
Programming: Adult targeted animated series.
Total subscribers: 95,800,000.
Distribution method: Available to cable & satellite providers.
Ownership: Time Warner.

ADVENTIST TELEVISION NETWORK — See Hope Channel.

ADVERTISING TELEVISION — No longer planned.

AFRICA CHANNEL
11135 Magnolia Blvd
Ste 110
North Hollywood, CA 91601
Phone: 818-655-9977
Fax: 818-655-9944
E-mail: info@theafricachannel.com
Web Site: http://www.theafricachannel.com
Jacob Arback, Co-Founder
Richard E Hammer, Co-Founder
James Makawa, Co-Founder
Elrick Williams, President & Chief Executive Officer
Shirley Neal, Executive Vice President, Programming & Production
Fred Paccone, Executive Vice President & Chief Financial Officer
Bob Reid, Executive Vice President & General Manager
Mark Walton, Executive Vice President, Ad Sales & Corporate Development
Cheryl Dorsey, Vice President, Affiliate Sales, Southern Region & West Coast
Irene Markantonis, Vice President, Production & Operations, S.A.
Darrell Smith, Vice President, Community Development & Marketing
Sherrice Smith, Vice President, Affiliate Sales, East Coast & Midwest Region
Marco Williams, Vice President, Affiliate Marketing
Operating hours/week: 168.
Programming: Africa-centric news magazines, biographies, current business analysis, cultural & historical programming, travel & lifestyle series, talk shows, soap operas & feature films.
Began: September 1, 2005.
Total subscribers: 15,100,000.
Scrambled signal: Yes.

AFRICA CHANNEL HD — See Africa Channel.
Began: August 1, 2010.

AFRICAN TV NETWORK (ATVN)
7376 Hickory Log Circle
Columbia, MD 21045
Phone: 443-498-8335
Web Site: http://www.africantvnetwork.com
Clement Afforo, Founder, President
Daniel Egbe, Chief Operating Officer
Dagnet Worjloh, Director, Affiliate Relations
Stephanie King, Director, Productions & Network Operations
Bob Reid, Executive Vice President, Network General Manager
Cheryl Dorsey, Vice President Affiliate Sales, Western Division
Sherrice Smith, Vice President Affiliate Sales, Eastern Division
Operating hours/week: 168.
Programming: Authentic African programs including news, sports & entertainment targeted to African & non-African audience.
Began: July 1, 2002.

AFRICAST TV
606 Post Rd E
Ste 638
Westport, CT 06880
Phone: 800-957-4406
E-mail: info@africast.com
Web Site: http://www.africast.tv
Type of service: IPTV.
Operating hours/week: 168.
Programming: Currently delivers African films to hotels through On Command. Movies, news & entertainment from African television services.
Scrambled signal: Yes.

AFRICAST TV ONLINE
606 Post Rd E
Ste 638
Westport, CT 06880
Phone: 800-957-4406
E-mail: info@africast.com
Web Site: http://www.africast.tv
John Sarpong, Chairman & Chief Executive Officer
Michael Day, Chief Financial Officer
George J. Stoulil, Chief Operating Officer
Alvin D. James, Vice President, Corporate Development
Joseph Lawson, Vice President, Marketing & Affiliate Sales
Antoinette Alexander Sarpong, Programming Director
Leonard Chaikind, Director
Type of service: Broadband.
Programming: Live & on demand programming from Africa. Includes movies, news, sports & entertainment from broadcasters in Ghana, Nigeria, Kenya, Malawi, Botswana & Zambia.
Began: N.A.

AL FORAT — See GlobeCast WorldTV.
E-mail: info@alforattv.net
Web Site: http://www.alforattv.net
Type of service: Basic.
Programming: Iraqi news.
Distribution method: Available on GlobeCast WorldTV satellite service.

AL-IRAQIYA — See GlobeCast WorldTV.
Web Site: http://www.iraqimedianet.net/tv

AL JAZEERA ENGLISH
1627 K St NW
Ste 1100
Washington, DC 20006-1710
Phones: 202-496-4500; 974-489-0222
Fax: 974-442-6265
Web Site: http://www.aljazeera.net/english
Nigel Parsons, Managing Director
Morgan Almeida, Creative Design Director
Steve Clark, News Director
Scott Ferguson, Non-News Programming Director
Type of service: Basic & broadband.
Operating hours/week: 168.
Programming: News features, analysis, documentaries, live debates, current affairs, business & sports.
Began: November 15, 2006, Reflects broadband launch.
Total subscribers: 110,000,000 (Reflects worldwide subscribers).
Distribution method: Available to cable & satellite systems & online.

AL KARMA TV
PO Box 3610
Seal Beach, CA 90740
Phone: 714-709-4300
Fax: 925-226-4034
E-mail: info@alkarmatv.com
Web Site: http://www.alkarmatv.com
Type of service: Basic, broadband.
Operating hours/week: 168.
Programming: Christian Arabic family programming.
Began: October 17, 2005.
Distribution method: Available to satellite providers & online.

AL MAGHRIBIA — See 2M Maroc.
Operating hours/week: 84.
Programming: Arabic, French & Amazigh language news & entertainment for Moroccans living abroad.
Distribution method: Available to satellite providers.
Scrambled signal: Yes.
Ownership: Joint venture between Radio Television Marocaine & 2M.

ALMAVISION
PO Box 26590
Santa Ana, CA 92799
Phones: 213-627-8711; 877-316-5159
Fax: 213-627-8712
E-mail: info@almavision.com
Web Site: http://www.almavision.com
Operating hours/week: 168.
Began: August 1, 2003.
Distribution method: Available to satellite programmers.

ALPHA MOM TV
1173A 2nd Ave
Ste 314
New York, NY 10021
Phone: 212-752-7400
Fax: 212-752-7411
E-mail: contact@alphamom.com
Web Site: http://www.alphamom.com
Isabel Kallman, Chief Executive Officer
Type of service: Broadband & video on demand.
Programming: How-to advice & information targeted to parents raising children; from infants to toddlers & older.
Began: May 1, 2005.
Total subscribers: 11,500,000.
Distribution method: Comcast On Demand, Cox On Demand.

ALTERNA'TV
Rodolfo Gaona 86, 2nd Floor
Col. Lomas de Sotelo
Mexico City, D.F. 11200
Mexico
Phone: 877-728-6391
E-mail: clemente.cabello@satmex.com.mx
Web Site: http://www.alternatv.com.mx
Branch Offices:
AFFILIATE SALES: Castalia Communications, 1532 Dunwoody Village Pkwy, Ste 203, Atlanta, GA 30338. Phone: 770-396-7850.
Type of service: Packaged channels & video on demand.
Programming: Comprised of several selected Spanish language channels originating in Latin America; arts, entertainment, news, music, sports, talk shows & family programming.
Means of Support: Subscribers.
Total subscribers: 6,000,000.
Distribution method: Available to cable systems & satellite providers.

ALTITUDE SPORTS & ENTERTAINMENT
1000 Chopper Cir
Denver, CO 80204
Phone: 303-405-6100
Fax: 303-925-2994
E-mail: salesandmarketing@altitude.tv
Web Site: http://www.altitudesports.com
Matt Hutchings, President & Chief Executive Officer
Tom Philand, Senior Vice President, Media & Sponsorship Sales
Shelly Harper, Senior Vice President, Programming & Production
Dave Zur, Senior Vice President, Operations
Phillip Mallios, Senior Vice President, Affiliate Sales & Marketing
Type of service: Digital basic & video on demand.
Operating hours/week: 168.
Operating areas: Western U.S.
Programming: Featuring regional high-school, college & professional sports, including basketball, soccer, hockey, baseball, lacrosse, boxing, cycling, outdoor & extreme sports. Official network of the Denver Nuggets, Colorado Avalanche, Colorado Mammoth & Colorado Rapids; broadcasting regular season & playoff games.
Began: September 2, 2004.
Distribution method: Available to cable & satellite providers.

AMC
200 Jericho Quadrangle
Jericho, NY 11753
Phone: 516-803-3000
Fax: 516-803-3003
E-mail: info@amctv.com
Web Site: http://www.amctv.com
Joshua Sapan, President & Chief Executive Officer, AMC Networks Inc.
Charlie Collier, Executive Vice President & General Manager
Scott Collins, Executive Vice President, Advertising Sales
Kim Martin, Executive Vice President, Distribution & Affiliate Marketing
Marnie Black, Senior Vice President, Public Relations
Sid Eshleman, Senior Vice President, Western Region
Jason Fisher, Senior Vice President, Production
Tom Halleen, Senior Vice President, Programming & Scheduling
Marc Krok, Senior Vice President, AMC TV Advertising Sales
Joel Stillerman, Senior Vice President, Original Programming, Production & Digital Content
Marci Wiseman, Senior Vice President, Business Affairs
Bob Bel Bruno, Vice President, Ad Sales
Joshua Berger, Vice President, Programming Operations

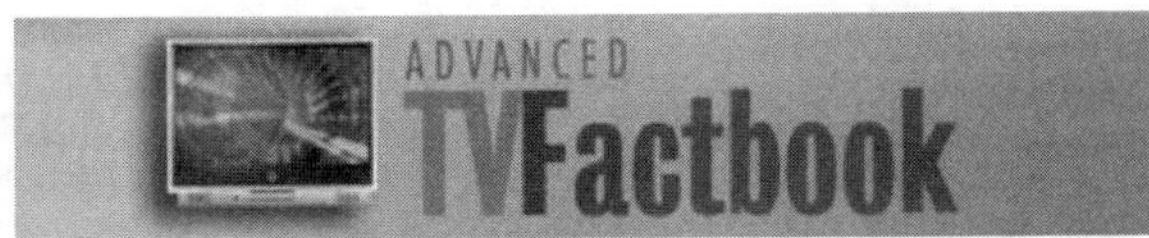

Ben Davis, Vice President, Scripted Programming
Olivia Dupuis, Vice President, Public Relations
Jeremy Elice, Vice President, Original Programming Series
Sean Fassett, Vice President, Research
Joe Glennon, Vice President, Central Region
Susan Goldberg, Vice President, Production
Melani Griffith, Vice President, Eastern Region
Allison Hoffman, Vice President, Creative & Brand Strategy
Nancy Kane Leidersdorff, Vice President, Media Planning
Joe Leonard, Vice President, Affiliate Marketing
Bob Marino, Vice President, Ad Sales
Nancy McKenna, Vice President, Production
David Sehring, Vice President, Programming Acquisition
Krista Sonne, Vice President, Scheduling & Program Planning
Vlad Wolynetz, Vice President

Regional Offices:
Atlanta, GA; Des Plaines, IL; Detroit, MI; Santa Monica, CA.
Type of service: Basic.
Satellites: Satcom C-4, transponder 1.
Operating hours/week: 168.
Uplink: Floral Park, NY.
Programming: Features classic motion pictures, series & original specials.
Began: October 1, 1984, AMC HD launched in 2008.
Means of Support: Subscriber fees.
Total subscribers: 94,000,000 (On Demand service has 20,000,000 subscribers).
Distribution method: Available to home dish audiences & cable systems.
Scrambled signal: Yes. Equipment: VideoCipher II.
Ownership: AMC Networks Inc. Formerly Rainbow Media Holdings LLC owned by Cablevision Systems Corp., it became a publicly held company under the new name June 30, 2011.

AMC HD — See AMC.

AMERICA CHANNEL
801 International Pkwy
5th Fl
Heathrow, FL 32746
Phone: 407-333-3031
E-mail: info@americachannel.us
Web Site: http://www.americachannel.us
Doron Gorshein, Chairman & Chief Executive Officer
Craig Haffner, Creative Advisor
Type of service: Plans digital basic.
Programming: Plans regional sports & lifestyle coverage & new non-fiction programming that tells the extraordinary stories of ordinary people in America. Will focus on how real Americans face challenges, overcome obstacles, work, play & explore this country.
Scheduled to begin: Unannounced.
Means of Support: Plans Ad Supported.
Distribution method: Plans cable, telco and DBS systems.
Ownership: Independent investors.

AMERICAN NATIONAL NETWORK
1601 Cloverfield Blvd
2nd Fl, South Tower
Santa Monica, CA 90404
Phone: 310-460-3527
Fax: 310-309-4702
E-mail: sacpatriot@sentinel-america.com
Web Site: http://www.sentinel-america.com
Michael W Leighton, Chairman, President & Chief Executive Officer
Michael R Ricci, Chief Operating Officer
John L Donovan, Director
William G Schneider, Director
Parker L Shelton, Director
Edwin Meese, III, Director Elect
Jhoon Rhee, Director Elect
Capt. William Schira, Director Elect
Operating hours/week: 168.
Programming: News & entertainment focused on patriotic & traditional American themes.
Scheduled to begin: Unannounced.
Ownership: Sentinel America Corp.

AMERICA ONE TELEVISION
6125 Airport Freeway
Ste 100
Haltom City, TX 76117
Phone: 817-546-1400
Fax: 682-647-0756
E-mail: jheibel@americaone.com
Web Site: http://www.americaone.com
Robb Hudspeth, Program Director
Josh Heibel, Affiliate / RSN Relations
Allen Miller, Operations Manager
Leann Bowden, Traffic Manager
Type of service: Basic.
Satellites: Galaxy 23, transponder 18.
Operating hours/week: 168.
Uplink: Southwest Micronet, Cedar Hill, TX.
Programming: Family-oriented entertainment, sports & movies.
Began: February 1, 1995.
Total subscribers: 20,000,000.
Distribution method: Available to LP, FP, Regional Sports Networks and cable systems.
Scrambled signal: Yes.
Ownership: USFR Media Group.

AMERICAN DESI
120 Wood Ave S
Ste 300
Iselin, NJ 08830
Phone: 732-623-2222
Web Site: http://www.americandesi.tv
Vimal Verma, Chairman & Chief Executive Officer
Divya Ohri, Senior Vice President, Programming
Kenneth F. Gelb, Senior Vice President, Sales
Type of service: Basic.
Programming: 24-hour English-language television network for South Asians in America.
Began: January 1, 2005.

AMERICAN INDIAN TV
245 E 19th St
Ste 11R
New York, NY 10003
Phone: 212-982-2152
E-mail: info@americanindiantv.com
Web Site: http://www.americanindiantv.com
Michael Starobin, Chief Executive Officer
Harold (Jerry) Ashton, Co-Founder & President
Joseph Franklyn McElroy, Co-Founder & Chief Technology Officer
Donna McElroy, Co-Founder & Vice President, Administration
Type of service: IPTV.
Operating hours/week: 168.
Programming: Features powwows, news, arts, crafts, original films by Native American filmakers & educational programs dedicated to preserving & protecting American Indian & Alaskan Native culture.
Began: March 1, 2007.

AMERICAN LEGAL NETWORK — No longer planned.

AMERICANLIFE TV NETWORK
650 Massachusetts Ave NW
Washington, DC 20001
Phones: 202-289-6633; 800-446-6388
Fax: 202-289-6632
Web Site: http://www.americanlifetv.com
Lawrence Meli, President & Chief Operating Officer
Richard Freedman, Senior Vice President, Affiliate Sales & Relations
Hiroshi Goto, Chief Financial Officer
Darlene Chapman-Holmes, Senior Vice President, Marketing
Mark Ringwald, Vice President, Programming
John Baghdassarian, Regional Vice President, Affiliate Sales West Coast
Linda Moffat, Regional Vice President, Affiliate Sales Northeast
Matt Coren, Marketing Director
Nancy Becker, Program Scheduling Manager
Type of service: Basic & video on demand.
Satellites: G-15, transponder 22; G-4R, transponder HITS 6; G-15, transponder HITS 14.
Operating hours/week: 168.
Uplink: Denver, CO.
Programming: Lifestyle, entertainment & information programming for the baby boomer generation.
Began: February 1, 1985, as Goodlife TV. Relaunched as AmericanLife TV Network on March 1, 2005.
Means of Support: System fees & advertising.
Total subscribers: 12,700,000.
Distribution method: Available to cable systems.
Scrambled signal: Yes.
Ownership: ComStar Media Fund LP.

AMERICAN LIFE TV ON DEMAND — See AmericanLife TV Network.
Began: September 3, 2007.

AMERICAN MOVIE CLASSICS — See AMC.

AMERICAN NETWORK — See Televisa Networks.
E-mail: americannetwork@televisanetworks.tv

AMERICAN NEWS NETWORK
7742 Spalding Dr
Ste 475
Norcross, GA 30092
Phone: 770-953-3232
Fax: 770-953-3211
E-mail: vannnews@yahoo.com
Vincent Castelli, Chief Executive Officer
Al Alvarez, President
Cida Bormann, Marketing & Affiliate Relations Director
Steve Marcum, Chief Engineer
Type of service: Basic.
Programming: National syndicated news & special edition services & programs.
Began: January 6, 2003.
Means of Support: Advertising & subscriptions.
Total subscribers: 85,793,000.

AMERICANLIFE TV NETWORK HD — See AmericanLife TV Network.

AMERICA'S STORE
One HSN Dr
St. Petersburg, FL 33729
Phone: 727-872-1000
Fax: 727-872-7130
E-mail: spanoc@hsn.net
Barry Diller, Chairman
James Held, President & Chief Executive Officer
Barry Augenbraun, Executive Vice President & General Counsel
Louise I. Cleary, Vice President, Corporate Communications
Ray Brown, Operating Vice President
Cynthia Spano, Manager, Broadcast Marketing
Type of service: Basic.
Satellites: Satcom C-3, transponder 10.
Operating hours/week: 168.
Programming: Electronic retailer.
Began: June 5, 1995, as Spree!.
Means of Support: Commissions on merchandise sold.
Total subscribers: 33,000,000.
Distribution method: Available to cable systems & home dish audiences.
Ownership: Home Shopping Network.

AMP TV — No longer planned.

AMRITA TV
Gandhi Nagar, Vazhuthacaud
Thiruvananthapuram-695014
India
Phones: 91-471-2321500; 91-471-2328901
Fax: 91-471-2328900
E-mail: info@amritatv.com
Web Site: http://www.amritatv.com
Sudhaka Jayaram, Director & Chief Executive Officer
Shyamaprasad, President, Programmes
Neelan, Chief Executive Officer
A. Sushil Kumar, Global Head, Marketing & Communications
G.P. Nair, Head, Engineering & IT
Radhakrishnan, Senior Vice President, Sales
Anil Kumar, General Manager, Programmes
Binoj, General Manager, Sales
Harikumar MG, General Manager, Human Resource & Administration

Branch Offices:
US OFFICE: PO Box 68, San Ramon, CA 94583. Phone: 925-967-0221.
Programming: Family entertainment, including dramas, musical performances, game shows, competitions & spiritual growth shows about the history of India.
Distribution method: Available to satellite providers.

ANA TELEVISION NETWORK
1510 H St NW
Ste 900
Washington, DC 20005-1008
Phone: 202-898-8222
Fax: 202-898-8088
E-mail: mbc-tv@allied-media.com
Omar Akrouk, President
Tukki Al Shabanah, Chief Executive Officer

Amanda Hartford, Operations
Angela Adams, Sales & Marketing Director
Abe El Masry, TV Programming & Production Director
Type of service: Pay.
Satellites: Galaxy VI, transponder 10.
Operating hours/week: 168.
Operating areas: Detroit, MI & Washington, DC.
Uplink: Staten Island, NY.
Programming: Arabic language news, entertainment, public affairs, sports, special interest & children's programs.
Began: December 1, 1991.
Means of Support: Advertising & subscriber fees.
Distribution method: Available to home dish audiences & cable systems.

ANGEL ONE — See Dominion Sky Angel.

ANGEL TWO — See Dominion Sky Angel.

ANHUI SATELLITE TV — See KyLinTV.

ANHUI TV — See KyLinTV.

ANHUI TV INTERNATIONAL — See KyLinTV.

Web Site: http://www.ahtv.cn
Type of service: Video on demand.
Programming: Offered as part of KyLinTV's great Wall Package, Anhui TV International is a variety channel offering overseas Chinese viewers programs in four categories.: Anhui Today, Anhui Flavor, Entertaining and Home Theatre.
Means of Support: Advertising & subscriber fees.
Distribution method: IPTV and cable systems.
Scrambled signal: Yes.

ANIMAL PLANET

One Discovery Pl
Silver Spring, MD 20910
Phone: 240-662-2000
Web Site: http://animal.discovery.com
Marjorie Kaplan, President & General Manager
Bill Goodwyn, President, Domestic Distribution & Enterprises
Lori McFarling, Chief Operating Officer
Carole Tomko, Executive Vice President, Production
Rick Holzman, Senior Vice President, Programming
Victoria Lowell, Senior Vice President, Marketing & Operations
Jason Carey, Vice President, Production
Marc Etkind, Vice President, Development
Andy Weissberg, Vice President, Program Planning & Scheduling
William Graff, Programming Director

Branch Office:
LOS ANGELES: 1801 Century Park E, Ste 1430, Los Angeles, CA 90067. Phone: 310-551-1611. Fax: 310-551-1684.
Type of service: Basic.
Satellites: Satcom C-3., transponder 22.; West Coast Feed: AMC-10, transponder 14.
Operating hours/week: 168.
Programming: Animal Planet is the worldÆs only entertainment brand that immerses viewers in the full range of life in the animal kingdom with rich, deep content on multiple platforms. APM offers animal lovers and pet owners access to a centralized online, television and mobile community for immersive, engaging, high-quality entertainment, information and enrichment. Programming highlights on Animal Planet include Whale Wars, River Monsters, Fatal Attractions, Monsters Inside Me, Pit Bulls and Parolees and Dogs 101.
Began: June 1, 1996.
Total subscribers: 97,000,000.
Distribution method: Available to cable systems.
Scrambled signal: Yes.
Ownership: Discovery Communications Inc.

ANIMAL PLANET HD — See Animal Planet.

ANIME NETWORK

10114 W Sam Houston Pkwy S
Houston, TX 77099
Phone: 713-341-7100
Fax: 713-587-0286
E-mail: info@theanimenetwork.com
Web Site: http://www.theanimenetwork.com
Mark Williams, General Manager & Chief Technology Officer
Kevin McFeeley, Vice President, Affiliate Sales & New Media
Stacey Dodson, Director, Programming & Operations
Emily Olman, National Advertising Manager
Type of service: Digital basic, video on demand & mobile.
Operating hours/week: 168.
Programming: Animation from Japan. Also featuring j-pop & j-rock music videos & Asian movies.
Began: November 1, 2002.
Total subscribers: 31,500,000.
Scrambled signal: Yes.
Ownership: A.D. Vision Inc.

ANNENBERG CHANNEL

c/o Harvard-Smithsonian Center for Astrophysics
60 Garden St, MS 82
Cambridge, MA 02138
Phone: 800-228-8030
Fax: 617-496-7670
E-mail: channel@learner.org
Web Site: http://www.learner.org
Pete Neal, General Manager
Larisa M. Kirgan, Operations Officer
Kathryn Koczot, Administrative Assistant
Michele McLeod, Senior Program Officer
Yolanda Odunsi, Manager, Interactive Services

Branch Office:
WASHINGTON: 401 9th St NW, Washington, DC 20004. Phone: 202-879-9654. Fax: 202-879-9696.
Type of service: Basic.
Satellites: GE-3, transponder 23.
Programming: Adult educational programs & professional development series for K-12 educators.
Began: January 1, 1998.
Means of Support: Funding.
Distribution method: Distributed by Ku-band DBS; available for nonexclusive rebroadcast without cost to non-commercial broadcasters, cable channels and/or schools, colleges/universities or educational agencies.
Equipment: DigiCipher II.
Ownership: Annenberg/CPB.

ANTENA 3

Avda. Isla Graciosa 13
28700 San Sebastian de los Reyes
Madrid
Spain
Web Site: http://www.antena3tv.es
Programming: General entertainment.
Began: September 1, 1996.
Total subscribers: 1,500,000 (Reflects U.S. subscribers).
Ownership: Antena 3 Television.

ANTENNA SATELLITE TV/USA

520 Thomas Blvd
Orange, NJ 07050
Phone: 201-673-6500
Fax: 201-674-8289
E-mail: satellite@antenna.gr
Web Site: http://www.antennasatellite.gr
Mike Kelly, Information Contact

Branch Offices:
Kifissias Ave 10-12, Marousi, Athens 151 25, Greece. Phone: 30-210-6886-490-2. Fax: 30-210-6893-750.
Type of service: Pay.
Satellites: Galaxy III, transponder 9.
Operating hours/week: 12.
Operating areas: New York, New Jersey.
Uplink: Orange, NJ.
Programming: Greek language programming.
Began: June 1, 1992.
Means of Support: Advertising & subscription fees.
Distribution method: Available to home dish audiences & cable systems.
Equipment: VideoCipher II Plus.

ANTENNA TV

2501 W Bradley Pl
Chicago, IL 60618-4718
Phone: 773-528-2311
E-mail: programming@antennatv.tv
Web Site: http://www.antennatv.tv
Sean Compton, President, Programming, Tribune Broadcasting
Steve Farber, Vice President & Director of Operations
Marc Archer, Vice President, Sales Development
Greg Chassman, Vice President, Sales
Bina Roy, Affiliates Manager

Branch Offices:
WorldLink: 6100 Wilshire Blvd, Ste 1400, Los Angeles, CA 90048. Phone: 323-866-5900.
Type of service: Digital multicast network airing on local TV stations.
Operating areas: Available throughout the U.S.
Programming: Digital multicast network airing on local TV stations throughout the U.S. that features classic TV series and movies.
Began: January 1, 2011.
Total subscribers: 50,000,000.
Distribution method: Service leases unused digital sub channel and then relies on cable systems to pick up the station and the distribute signal.
Scrambled signal: Yes.
Ownership: Tribune Broadcasting.

AP ALL NEWS CHANNEL — see AP Television News.

AP ALL NEWS RADIO

1100 13th St
Ste 700
Washington, DC 20005
Phone: 202-736-1100
Fax: 202-736-1199
Web Site: http://www.apbroadcast.com
James R. Williams, II, Vice President & Director, Broadcast Services
Greg Groce, Director, Business Operations & Development
Brad Kalbfeld, Managing Editor
Lee Perryman, Deputy Director, Broadcast Services & Director, Broadcast Technology
Roger Lockhart, Director, Marketing & Communications
Type of service: Audio.
Satellites: GE 3; Satcom C-5.
Operating hours/week: 168.
Programming: All news radio service.
Began: June 1, 1994.
Means of Support: Subscriber fees.
Ownership: Associated Press.

ARABIC CHANNEL

366 86th St
1st Fl
Brooklyn, NY 11209
Phone: 718-238-2450
Fax: 718-238-2465
E-mail: gmt@ethnicnet.com
Web Site: http://www.thearabicchannel.tv
Gamil Tawfik, President & Chief Executive Officer
Marguerite Moore, Vice President
Type of service: Basic, Pay, Digital & Satellite.
Satellites: Telstar 5.
Operating hours/week: 168.
Programming: Full-time family entertainment in the Arabic language (most programs subtitled in English).
Began: April 8, 1991.
Means of Support: Advertising & leased time programming.
Total subscribers: 1,300,000.
Scrambled signal: Yes.
Ownership: GMT Productions LP.

ARIANA AFGHANISTAN MEDIA

15375 Barranca Pkwy
Ste A-103
Irvine, CA 92618
Phone: 949-825-7400
Fax: 949-825-7474
E-mail: sales@aa-tv.com
Web Site: http://www.aa-tv.com
Nabil Miskinyar, President & Founder
Satellites: Telstar 5, transponder 8.
Operating hours/week: 168.
Programming: Cultural, religious, sporting, artistic & community-related shows.
Distribution method: Available to satellite providers.

ARIANA TV

Parker Plaza
400 Kelby St, 16th Fl
Fort Lee, NJ 07024
Phone: 201-302-0400
Fax: 201-301-0406
E-mail: feedback@arianatelevision.com
Web Site: http://www.arianatelevision.com
Operating hours/week: 168.
Programming: Afghani news & events in English, Pashto & Dari.
Distribution method: Available to satellite providers.

ARIZONA NEWS CHANNEL

c/o KTVK
5555 N 7th Ave
Phoenix, AZ 85010
Phone: 602-207-3333
Fax: 602-207-3397
E-mail: feedback@azfamily.com
Web Site: http://www.azfamily.com
Lawrence Nicholson, President & General Manager
Brad Remington, Executive News Director
Teri Lane, Marketing Director
Jim Cole, Engineering Director
Mark Demopoulos, Program & Research Director
Operating hours/week: 168.
Programming: 24-hour news service covering local issues.
Began: November 4, 1997.
Means of Support: Advertising & subscriber fees.

Total subscribers: 630,000.
Ownership: Belo Corp. & Cox Cable.

ARMENIAN PUBLIC CHANNEL
E-mail: support@armtv.com
Web Site: http://www.armtv.com
Operating hours/week: 168.
Programming: Armenian language movies, game shows, soap operas, family & children's shows, cultural documentaries sporting events & news reports.
Distribution method: Available to satellite providers.

ARMENIAN RUSSIAN TELEVISION NETWORK (ARTN)
4401 San Fernando Rd
Glendale, CA 91204
Phone: 818-553-3737
Fax: 818-552-3710
E-mail: info@artn.tv
Web Site: http://www.artn.tv
Robert Oglakhchyan, President & Chief Executive Officer
Type of service: Basic.
Operating hours/week: 168.
Programming: Armenian & Russian language shows including travel, food, children's & game shows, soap operas, cultural & entertainment shows featuring artists, politicians, lawyers & doctors.
Began: January 1, 1985.
Distribution method: Available to cable systems & satellite providers.

ART AMERICA
Arab Radio & Television
PO Box 51668
Knoxville, TN 37950
Phone: 423-539-8260
Fax: 423-470-4320
E-mail: artamerica1@aol.com
Web Site: http://www.art-tv.net; http://www.firstnettv.net
Hani Gharbieh, General Manager
Fadi Gharbieh, Sales & Marketing
Salvatore Vecchuzzio, Public Relations & Marketing
Type of service: Pay.
Satellites: EchoStar I.
Operating hours/week: 48.
Programming: Arabic programming including news, movies, music videos, cultural documentaries, children's shows, sports & live events.
Began: March 3, 1996.
Means of Support: Subscription fees.
Distribution method: Available to home dish audiences.
Ownership: Arab Radio & Television.

ASC FLIX — See GlobeCast WorldTV.
Web Site: http://www.asctvusa.com
Operating hours/week: 168.
Programming: Focused on all aspects of the Indian & Bollywood entertainment industry, including movies, behind-the-scenes, interviews, news, music videos & live performances.
Began: January 1, 2001, Formerly SBC-TV.
Distribution method: Available to cable & satellite providers.

ASC XTRA — See GlobeCast WorldTV.
Web Site: http://www.asctvusa.com
Operating hours/week: 168.
Programming: Hindi dramas, serials, thrillers, epics, news from India & the U.S. community, talk shows, debates on topical issues, game shows, fashion shows, youth & educational programming, comedies, devotional music, sports highlights featuring cricket matches from India, Pakistan, Bangladesh & Sri Lanka.
Distribution method: Available to cable & satellite providers.

ASIA TRAVEL TV — See KyLinTV.
Type of service: IPTV.
Programming: Travel shows.
Began: January 1, 2004.

ASIAN TELEVISION NETWORK
130 Pony Dr
Newmarket, ON L3Y 7B6
Canada
Phone: 905-836-6460
Fax: 905-853-5212
E-mail: atn@asiantelevision.com
Web Site: http://www.asiantelevision.com
Shan Chandrasekar, President
Satellites: AlphaStar.
Operating hours/week: 168.
Programming: South Asian movies, sports, news, music, dance, drama, variety, talk & game shows, children's programming & adult education in native languages & English. Available to U.S. customers via AlphaStar Digital Television.
Began: February 1, 1996 in Canada; November 28, 1996 in US.
Distribution method: Available to home dish audiences.

ASIAN TELEVISION NETWORK INTERNATIONAL
130 Pony Dr
Newmarket, ON L3Y 7B6
Phone: 905-836-6460
Fax: 905-853-5212
E-mail: atn@asiantelevision.com
Web Site: http://www.asiantelevision.com
Programming: Channels include ATN-Asian Sports Network, ATN-Cricket Channel I & ATN-Cricket Channel II.

ASIANET USA
9920 Rhode Island Ave
College Park, MD 20740-1460
Phones: 301-345-1139; 888-898-0020
Fax: 301-345-8160
E-mail: info@asianetusa.tv
Web Site: http://www.asianetusa.tv
Sathya Viswanath, President & Producer
Nandini Sikand, Assistant Producer
Type of service: Basic.
Satellites: SBS-6, transponder 13.
Operating hours/week: 168.
Programming: Malayalam news, serials, sports, movies, current affairs & family programming.
Began: September 1, 1993, relaunched in U.S. on May 1, 2003.
Means of Support: Advertising & subscription fees.
Total subscribers: 7,000.
Distribution method: Available to home dish audiences & cable systems.
Ownership: Deepak Viswanath, Principal.

ASIANET NEWS — See Asianet USA.
Web Site: http://www.asianetglobal.com

ASIANET PLUS — See Asianet USA.
Web Site: http://www.asianetplus.tv

ASSYRIASAT
PO Box 4116
Modesto, CA 95352
Phone: 209-538-4130
Fax: 209-538-2795
Web Site: http://www.betnahrain.org
Programming: Assyrian focused family programming, from news & general entertainment to cultural & educational shows.
Distribution method: Available to satellite providers.

@MAX — See Cinemax.
Programming: Offers contemporary movies.
Began: May 1, 2001.

ATLANTA INTERFAITH BROADCASTERS
1075 Spring St NW
Atlanta, GA 30309
Phone: 404-892-0454
Fax: 404-892-8687
E-mail: info@aibtv.com
Web Site: http://www.aibtv.com
Collie Burnett, Jr., President & Chief Executive Officer
Patsy E. Williams, Vice President, Operations
Angela H. Rice, Programming & Production Director
Dennis Mills, Chief Engineer
Sharon Phillip, Production
Deloris Keith, Programming & News Manager
Type of service: Regional.
Operating hours/week: 168.
Operating areas: Georgia.
Programming: Interfaith teaching, talk shows, worship & call-in shows.
Began: February 1, 1981.
Means of Support: Time sales, production fees & contributions.
Total subscribers: 850,000.

ATV — See KyLinTV.
25-37 Dai Shing Street
Tai Po Industrial Estate
N.T., Hong Kong
China
Phones: 852-2992-8888; 852-2992-9298
Fax: 852-2338-0438
E-mail: atv@atv.com.hk
Web Site: http://www.hkatv.com
Operating hours/week: 168.
Programming: Cantonese channel, providing a wide range of programming, including synchronization with the Hong Kong press reports and commentaries on current affairs, as well as variety shows and classic series. Offered by DISH Network & KyLinTV.
Distribution method: Available to available to home dish audiences and the internet.
Scrambled signal: Yes.
Asia TV Limited.

AUCTION HD — No longer planned.

AUCTION TV — See i-Shop.

AUDIENCE NETWORK
DirecTV
2230 E Imperial Hwy
El Segundo, CA 90245
Phone: 310-535-5000
Fax: 310-535-5225
Web Site: http://www.directv.com
Derek Chang, Executive Vice President, Content Strategy & Development
Operating hours/week: 168.
Programming: Offers premium quality entertainment channel for of extra charge. Popular series, movies, sports & entertainment are featured. Relaunched under present name June 1, 2011. Formerly known as the 101 Network.
Began: June 5, 2006.
Total subscribers: 19,400,000.
Distribution method: Available to DirecTV subscribers only.
Scrambled signal: Yes.

AYM SPORTS
Avenida Chapultepec 409
Col. Juarez, Del. Cuauhtemoc
D.F. 06600
Mexico
E-mail: contactoaym@aymcorp.com
Web Site: http://www.aymsports.com.mx
Programming: Coverage of Mexican sports.
Began: April 1, 2004.
Ownership: AYM Sports SA de CV.

AZ TV
AZ1011 M.Huseyn 1
Baku, Azerbaijan
Phone: 99-412-4923807
Fax: 99-412-4972020
E-mail: webmaster@aztv.az
Web Site: http://www.aztv.az
Type of service: Basic.
Satellites: Galaxy 25, transponder K21.
Operating hours/week: 168.
Programming: News, serials, sports & musical events from Azerbaijan.
Distribution method: Available to satellite providers.

AZTECA AMERICA
1139 Grand Central Ave
Glendale, CA 91201
Phone: 818-247-0400
Fax: 818-241-5483
E-mail: bturner@aztecaamerica.com
Web Site: http://www.corporate-aztecaamerica.com
Luis J. Echarte, Chairman
Martin K. Breidsprecher, Chief Executive Officer
Jorge Jaidar, General Manager
Alberto Santini Lara, Executive Vice President, Production, Programming & Marketing
John DeSimone, Vice President & General Manager, TV Spot Sales
Roberto Romagnoli, Vice President, Production & Entertainment
Rawdon Messenger, Director, New Media & Product Integration
Juan Pablo Alvarez, Affiliate Relations Manager
Bob Turner, Sales Manager
Karen Davis, Strategic Consultant
Operating hours/week: 168.
Programming: Spanish language broadcast network for the U.S. Hispanic market, featuring news, sports & entertainment.
Began: January 1, 2001, (U.S. launch).
Distribution method: Satellite.
Ownership: TV Azteca.

B-MANIA — See M-2 (Movie Mania) TV Network.

BABYFIRSTTV
10390 Santa Monica Blvd
3rd Fl
Los Angeles, CA 90025
Phone: 888-251-2229
Web Site: http://www.babyfirsttv.com
Guy Oranim, Chief Executive Officer
Sharon Rechter, Executive Vice President, Business Development & Marketing
Arik Kerman, Senior Vice President, Programming & Operations
Itamar Daube, Vice President, Creative
Arthur Pober, Chief Educational Advisor
Type of service: Basic & video on demand.
Satellites: Telstar, transponder 10.
Operating hours/week: 168.
Programming: Shows for babies & toddlers to age three.
Began: May 1, 2006.
Distribution method: Available to cable & satellite providers.

Scrambled signal: Yes.
Ownership: Regency Enterprises, Kardan NV & Bellco Capital.

BANDAMAX — See Televisa Networks.
E-mail: bandamax@televisanetworks.tv
Web Site: http://www.esmas.com/bandamax
Programming: Features music videos as well as live original programming, the latest celebrity news and exclusive concerts.
Began: May 1, 2003, U.S. launch.
Total subscribers: 150,000 (U.S. subscribers).
Scrambled signal: Yes.
Ownership: TuTv, joint venture between Univision & Televisa.

BARCA TV
Web Site: http://www.fcbarcelona.com

BARKER
1332 Enterprise Dr
Ste 200
West Chester, PA 19380
Fax: 215-692-6487
Tom Fannell, Vice President, Sales
Bill Higginbotham, Information Contact
Satellites: Satcom C-4, transponder 12.
Uplink: West Chester, PA.
Programming: Pay-per-view promotion channel.
Total subscribers: 10,000,000.
Distribution method: Available to cable systems.
Ownership: StarNet.

BAY NEWS 9
700 Carillon Pkwy
Ste 9
St. Petersburg, FL 33716
Phone: 727-329-2300
E-mail: comments@baynews9.com
Web Site: http://www.baynews9.com
Elliott Wiser, Corporate Vice President, Local Programming, Brighthouse
Rod Gramer, Vice President & General Manager
Mike Gautreau, News Director
Sylvia Setheras, General Sales Manager
Jason Bishop, Assistant News Director
Maggie Daniell, Business Affairs Director
Linda Granger, Marketing Director
Type of service: Basic.
Operating hours/week: 168.
Programming: 24-hour news channel covering the Tampa Bay area.
Began: September 24, 1997.
Means of Support: Advertising.
Total subscribers: 1,000,000.
Distribution method: Available to cable systems.
Ownership: Advance Newhouse.

BAY NEWS 9 ESPANOL — See Bay News 9.

BBC AMERICA
747 3rd Ave
6th Fl
New York, NY 10017
Phone: 212-705-9300
Fax: 212-705-9420
E-mail: amy.mulcair@bbc.co.uk
Web Site: http://www.bbcamerica.com
Herb Scannell, President
Perry Simon, General Manager
Andrew Bott, Chief Financial Officer
Ann Sarnoff, Chief Operating Officer
Luke Bradley-Jones, Executive Vice President, Development & Digital Media
Candace Carlisle, Executive Vice President, Co-Productions & TV Sales
Burton Cromer, Executive Vice President, Consumer Products
Michele Grant, Executive Vice President, News & Sport
Jo Petherbridge, Executive Vice President, Communications
Michael Ross, Executive Vice President, Business Affairs & Operations
Paul Telegdy, Executive Vice President, TV Sales, Content & Production
Nick Ascheim, Senior Vice President, Digital Media
Megan Branigan, Senior Vice President, Video Marketing & BBC Direct
Valerie Bruce, Senior Vice President, Business Affairs
Miranda Cresswell, Senior Vice President, Strategy & Operations, BBC.com
Richard De Croce, Senior Vice President, Programming
Mark Gail, Senior Vice President, Digital Sales
Linda Giambrone, Senior Vice President, Production
Ian Moffitt, Senior Vice President, Programming & Content Strategy
Susanna Pollack, Senior Vice President, TV Sales, Co-Productions & Children's
Mary Pratt-Henaghan, Senior Vice President, Operations & Administration
Aimee White, Senior Vice President, Sales & Operations, Consumer Products
Joy Chilcowicz, Vice President, US Ad Sales, BBC.com
Joe Czarkowski, Vice President, National Sales Manager
Charles Douglass, Vice President, Ad Sales, West Coast
Scott Gregory, Vice President, Scheduling
Greg Heanue, Vice President, Marketing
Brian Matthews, Vice President, Ad Sales, East Coast
Mike Neeves, Vice President, Program Scheduling
Mark Richardson, Vice President, Ad Sales, Midwest
Rachel Smith, Vice President, Original Programming
John Taite, Vice President, Multiplatform Programming
Type of service: Basic.
Satellites: Satcom C-3, transponder 22.
Operating hours/week: 168.
Programming: British programs & shows.
Began: March 29, 1998.
Means of Support: Advertising sold by Discovery Communications.
Total subscribers: 67,000,000.
Distribution method: Available to cable systems & satellite providers.
Ownership: British Broadcasting Corp.

BBC AMERICA ON DEMAND — See BBC America.
Type of service: Video on demand.

BBC ARABIC — See BBC World News
Web Site: http://www.bbcarabic.com
Type of service: Mobile, broadband & digital basic.
Operating hours/week: 84.
Programming: News headlines & summaries.
Began: March 11, 2008.
Distribution method: Online & satellite.
Scrambled signal: Yes.

BBC CANADA
121 Bloor St E
Ste 200
Toronto, ON M4W 3M5
Canada
Phones: 416-967-3249; 866-813-3222
Fax: 416-967-0044

E-mail: media@canwest.com
Web Site: http://www.bbccanada.com
Programming: British television, comedies, dramas & life & style series.
Ownership: Alliance Atlantis.

BBC HD — See BBC Worldwide Ltd.

BBC WORLD NEWS
BBC World Ltd.
Woodlands, 80 Wood Ln
London W12 0TT
UK
Phone: 44-0-20-8433-2000
Fax: 44-0-20-8749-0538
Web Site: http://www.bbcworld.com
Richard Sambrook, BBC World Service & Global News Director
Anne Barnard, Chief Operating Officer
Sian Kevill, Editorial Director
Jeff Hazell, Sales & Distribution Director
Jonathan Howlett, Airtime Sales Director
Jane Gorard, Marketing & Communications Director
Simone Pennie, Finance Director
Type of service: Digital.
Operating hours/week: 168.
Programming: Global news & events.
Began: April 30, 2006, (Reflects U.S. launch date).
Total subscribers: 274,000,000 (Includes 2,300,000 U.S. subscribers).
Distribution method: Available to cable operators.

BEACHTV
1250 Bellflower Blvd
Long Beach, CA 90840
Phone: 562-985-4352
Web Site: http://cslbtv.amp.csulb.edu
Type of service: Basic.
Programming: Campus, local, national & international news & entertainment.
Distribution method: Available to cable systems.

BEAUTY AND FASHION CHANNEL
4100 E Mississippi Ave
19th Fl
Glendale, CO 80246
Phone: 303-839-5303
Fax: 303-839-5335
Web Site: http://www.beautyfashiontv.com
Programming: Features news & trends in fashion & style.
Total subscribers: 32,000,000.
Distribution method: Available to cable systems & satellite providers.
Ownership: Turner Media Group.

BEAUTY TV
214 Main St
Ste 245
El Segundo, CA 90245
Phone: 310-281-6225
Fax: 310-356-4917
Web Site: http://beautytv.me
Type of service: Basic & IPTV.
Operating hours/week: 168.
Programming: Shows on beauty, fashion & health including beauty tips, trends, spas, news & product reviews.
Began: January 9, 2007.
Distribution method: Available to cable & satellite systems.

BEIJING TV
Jianguo Rd
Chaoyang District
Beijing, No. 98 100022
China
E-mail: btvsuggest@btv.com.cn
Web Site: http://www.btv.org
Programming: Chinese language television service comprised of 14 channels, covering the arts, life, science and sports.
Ownership: Government owned.

BEN TELEVISION
25 Ashley Rd
London N17 9LJ
UK
Phones: +44 0 208808 8800; +44 0 208801 3888
Web Site: http://www.bentelevision.com
Alistair Soyode, Chief Executive Officer
Satellites: F1.
Programming: Also known as Bright Entertainment Network, delivers Africa-centric content, including news & entertainment from African broadcasters.
Began: N.A.
Distribution method: Available to Sky Digital subscribers & online.

BERKS COUNTY NEWS 5
400 Riverfront Dr
Reading, PA 19602
Phone: 610-378-4660
Fax: 610-378-4697
Liz Sterner, Area Director of Communications
Bill Saunders, News Director
Operating areas: Berks County, PA.
Programming: Regional all news channel.
Began: September 5, 1995.
Total subscribers: 100,000.
Distribution method: Available to cable systems.
Ownership: AT&T Cable Services.

BET ACTION PAY-PER-VIEW — See TVN Entertainment.

BET GOSPEL — See BET Networks.

BET J — See Centric.
Replaced by Centric September 28, 2009.

BET NETWORKS
(Black Entertainment Television)
1 BET Plaza, 1235 W St, NW
Washington, DC 20018
Phone: 202-608-2000
Fax: 202-608-2589
E-mail: adsales@bet.net
Web Site: http://www.bet.com
Debra L. Lee, Chairman & Chief Executive Officer
Scott Mills, President & Chief Operating Officer
Louis Carr, President, Broadcast Media Sales
Stephen G. Hill, President, Programming
Loretha Jones, President, Programming

Michael Pickrum, Chief Financial Officer
James A. Ebron, Executive Vice President, Publishing Advertising Sales
Carl D. Folta, Executive Vice President, Corporate Communications
Sheila Crump Johnson, Executive Vice President, Corporate Affairs
Byron Marchant, Executive Vice President, Legal Affairs & Chief Financial Officer
Janet Rolle, Executive Vice President & Chief Marketing Officer
Darrell E. Walker, Executive Vice President & General Counsel
Barbara Zaneri, Executive Vice President, Programming, Strategy, Scheduling & Acquisitions
Lee Chaffin, Senior Vice President, Affiliate Sales & Marketing
Curtis Gadson, Senior Vice President, Network Operations & Entertainment Programming
Brett King, Senior Vice President, Scripted Programming
Robyn Lattaker-Johnson, Senior Vice President, Development Reality Programming
Jeanine Liburd, Senior Vice President, Communications & Public Affairs
Kelli Richardson, Senior Vice President, Corporate Marketing
Reggie Williams, Senior Vice President, Music Strategy & Operations
Carla Kelly, Vice President, Marketing, BET Interactive
Cindy Mahmaud, Vice President, Entertainment & Special Projects
Rayna Swann, Vice President, Corporate Marketing, BET Holdings Inc.
Leyla Turkkan, Vice President, Music Development, BET.com
Stacie Turner, Vice President, Marketing, BET.com
Kevin Morrison, Director, Development, Los Angeles
Shirley Salomon, Director, Production for Development
Navarrow Wright, Chief Technology Officer, BET.com

Office Locations:
Network Operations: 1900 W Place NE, Washington, DC 20018. Phone: 202-608-2000.

BET Productions: 2000 W Place NE, Washington, DC 20018. Phone: 202-608-2601.

Branch Offices:
BURBANK: 2801 W Olive Ave, Burbank, CA 91505. Phone: 818-566-9948. Fax: 818-566-1655.

CENTURY CITY: 1840 Century Park E, Ste 600, Los Angeles, CA 90067. Phone: 310-552-8400. Fax: 310-552-8444.

CHICAGO: 180 N Stetson Ct, Ste 4350, Chicago, IL 60601. Phone: 312-819-8600. Fax: 312-819-8684.

NEW YORK: 380 Madison Ave, 20th Floor, New York, NY 10017. Phone: 212-697-5500. Fax: 212-697-2050.
Type of service: Basic & video on demand.
Satellites: Galaxy V, transponder 20.
Operating hours/week: 168.
Programming: Sports, news, entertainment, specials, children's programming & gospel programming.
Began: January 25, 1980, in U.S.; October 1, 1998 in Canada.
Means of Support: Advertising.
Total subscribers: 87,000,000 (Also has 4,000,000 Canadian subscribers & 10,000,000 UK subscribers).
Distribution method: Available to cable & satellite systems.
Scrambled signal: Yes.
Ownership: Viacom Inc.

BETSOUNDZ
One BET Plaza
1900 W Place NE
Washington, DC 20018-1211
Phone: 202-608-2208
Fax: 202-608-2590
Debra Lee, Chairman & Chief Executive Officer
Curtis Symonds, Executive Vice President, Affiliate Sales
Gregory C. King, Senior Manager, Corp. Communications
Type of service: Basic.
Operating hours/week: 168.
Programming: Package of digital music networks including BET J, BET Inspirations, BET Soundz of R & B, BET World Music Beat & Rap and Hip Hop.
Began: May 5, 1998.
Distribution method: Available to cable systems.
Ownership: BET Holdings Inc.

BETTER LIFE MEDIA
200 Swisher Rd
Lake Dallas, TX 75065
Phone: 877-929-0439
Fax: 817-442-1390
E-mail: info@betterlifemedia.com
Web Site: http://www.betterlifemedia.com
Michael Burgess, President
Tom Weise, Executive Vice President, Business Development
Linda Domholt, Vice President, Talent Relations
Type of service: Video on demand.
Programming: Motivational & self-improvement programming available through select major hotels.
Scrambled signal: Yes.

BIO HD — See Bio.
Began: November 28, 2007.

BIO
235 E 45th St
New York, NY 10017
Phone: 212-210-1400
Fax: 212-692-9269
E-mail: michael.feeney@aetn.com
Web Site: http://www.biography.com
Robert DeBitetto, President & General Manager
David McKillop, Executive Vice President, Programming
Thomas Moody, Senior Vice President, Programming Planning & Acquisitions
Peter Olsen, Senior Vice President, Advertising Sales
Dan Silverman, Senior Vice President, Publicity
Guy Slatery, Senior Vice President, Marketing
John Haringer, Vice President, Marketing
Peter Tarshis, Vice President, Programming
Type of service: Digital & video on demand.
Satellites: Galaxy IX, transponder 23.
Programming: Focused on true stories & celebrity profiles. Includes talk shows & documentary-style programs.
Began: December 1, 1998, Formerly The Biography Channel, re-launched as Bio July 16, 2007.
Total subscribers: 47,000,000.
Distribution method: Available to cable systems.
Scrambled signal: Yes.
Ownership: Hearst Corp., NBCUniversal LLC & The Walt Disney Co.

BLACK BROADCASTING NETWORK
5315 B. FM 1960 W
Ste 333
Houston, TX 77069
Phone: 888-823-4256
Fax: 888-823-4256
E-mail: admin@blackbroadcasting.com
Web Site: http://blackbroadcasting.com
Ricky Anderson, Chairman & Chief Executive Officer
Yusef Muhammad, President & Chief Operating Officer
Operating hours/week: 168.
Programming: Offers popular entertainemtn and a variety of program genres to the urban 18-34 demographic. Programs feature African American and Latino artists, casts, comedians, producers, filmmakers and athletes.
Began: December 21, 2009.
Means of Support: Subscribers.
Distribution method: Available to cable systems and FiOS subscribers.

BLACK FAMILY CHANNEL
800 Forrest St NW
Atlanta, GA 30313
Phones: 404-350-2509; 404-748-8000
Fax: 404-350-0356
Web Site: http://www.blackfamilychannel.com
Rick Newberger, Chief Executive Officer
Robert Townsend, Chief Executive Officer & President, Production
Willie E. Gary, Chairman
Evander Holyfield, Co-Vice Chairman
Cecil G. Fielder, Co-Vice Chairman
Type of service: Broadband.
Uplink: Atlanta, GA.
Programming: Responsible programming targeting the African American family: sports, movies, information, news & entertainment. See also Gospel Music Channel.
Began: June 1, 1999, as cable channel; relaunched as broadband & merged cable operations with Gospel Music Channel on May 1, 2007.
Means of Support: Advertising & subscription fees.
Total subscribers: 16,000,000.
Distribution method: Online.
Ownership: Programming Acquisitions LLC.

BLACK TELEVISION NEWS CHANNEL
600 13th St NW
Ste 790
Washington, DC 20005
Phone: 202-207-2854
Fax: 202-207-2853
E-mail: fwatson@btnc.tv
Web Site: http://www.btnc.tv
Robert Brillante, Co-Manager
JC C Watts, Co-Manager
Frank Watson, General Manager
Type of service: Plans basic.
Operating hours/week: Plans 168.
Programming: The mission of Black Television News Channel (BTNC) an innovative, life-changing television network is to provide intelligent programming that is informative, educational, entertaining, inspiring, and empowering for its African American audience.
Scheduled to begin: Plans to launch November 2011.
Distribution method: Will be available to cable systems & satellite providers.
Scrambled signal: Yes.

BLACKBELT TV
1649 11th St
Santa Monica, CA 90404
Phone: 310-452-8899
Fax: 310-452-0736
E-mail: info@blackbelt.com
Web Site: http://www.blackbelt.com
Larry Kasanoff, Chairman
Lisa Kruglov, Senior Vice President, Sales
Operating hours/week: Plans 168.
Programming: Martial arts fights, movies, animations & tv shows.
Began: N.A.

BLINKX BROADBAND TV
1 Market Plaza
Spear Tower, 19th Floor
San Francisco, CA 94105
Phone: 415-848-2986
E-mail: feedback@blinkx.com

Branch Offices:
105 Piccadilly, London W1J 7NJ, UK. Phone: 44-0-20-8906-6857.
Type of service: Broadband.
Programming: Independent films & television shows integrated with internet search functionality.
Began: April 2, 2008.

BLOOMBERG NEWS RADIO
731 Lexington Ave
New York, NY 10022
Phones: 212-318-2390; 800-448-5678
Fax: 201-935-3307
Web Site: http://www.bloomberg.com
Neal Cortell, TV Distribution, U.S. & Canada
Jaime H. Cohen, News & Programming Director
Operating hours/week: 168.
Operating areas: New York, New Jersey & Connecticut.
Programming: Business, financial, national & local news.
Began: January 1, 1993.

BLOOMBERG TELEVISION
731 Lexington Ave
New York, NY 10022
Phone: 212-617-2201
Fax: 917-369-5086
Web Site: http://www.bloomberg.com/tv
Peter Grauer, Chairman, Bloomberg LP
Dan Doctoroff, Chief Executive Officer, Bloomberg LP
Andy Lack, Chief Executive Officer, Bloomberg Media Group
Andrew Morse, President, Bloomberg Television, US
Sid Amira, Affiliate Team Leader
Steve Males, Affiliate & Consumer Marketing
Tracy Bedell, Affiliate Sales, Northeast Region
William Loesel, Affiliate Sales, Western Region
Sandra Mosiello, Affiliate Sales, Southeast Region
Dave Noguerol, Affiliate Sales, Mid-Atlantic Region
Kevin Connolly, Cable & Satellite Distribution
Type of service: Basic.
Satellites: HITS; Satcom C-3, transponder 8; G11.
Operating hours/week: 168.
Programming: Financial news from 126 news bureaus. Providing local, regional & international news that moves markets through live interviews & coverage of major events.
Began: February 1, 1994.
Total subscribers: 48,000,000 (Includes full-time subscribers only; part-time

subscribers comprise an additional 86,000,000).
Distribution method: Available to home dish & cable systems.

BLOOMBERG TELEVISION HD — See Bloomberg Television.
Began: April 25, 2011.

BLUEHIGHWAYS TV
111 Shivel Dr
Hendersonville, TN 37075
Phones: 866-454-2488; 615-264-3292
Fax: 615-264-3308
E-mail: dhitchcock@bluehighwaystv.com
Web Site: http://www.bluehighwaystv.com
Stan Hitchcock, Chairman & Chief Executive Officer
Davida Shear, Senior Vice President, Affiliate Relations
Type of service: Basic digital, video on demand, broadband.
Satellites: AMC 10, transponder T-15.
Sales representative: Davida M. Shear.
Operating hours/week: 168.
Uplink: Atlanta, GA.
Programming: Americana programming featuring roots music, backroads travel, western & equesterian shows.
Began: July 1, 2004, reflects video on demand launch; linear channel launched March 11, 2007.
Total subscribers: 6,000,000 (reflects video on demand service).
Distribution method: Satellite, TVN, Broadband.
Scrambled signal: No.
Ownership: Network Creative Group.

BN BOSNIA — See GlobeCast WorldTV.
Web Site: http://www.bnsat.com
Operating hours/week: 168.
Programming: Bosnian news & political shows.
Began: January 1, 1998.
Distribution method: Available to satellite providers.

BOB: BRIEF ORIGINAL BROADCASTS — No longer planned.

BOLLYWOOD HITS ON DEMAND
4100 E Dry Creek Rd
Centennial, CO 80122
Phones: 303-712-5400; 303-712-5401
Web Site: http://www.mybhod.com
Type of service: Video on demand.
Programming: Bollywood movies & music videos.
Began: September 1, 2006.
Distribution method: Available to cable systems.
Ownership: International Networks & Eros.

BOLLYWOOD ON DEMAND
212 Media
72 Madison Ave, 5th Floor
New York, NY 10016
Phone: 212-710-3080
Fax: 646-349-4013
E-mail: info@212media.com
Web Site: http://www.bollywoodondemand.com
Vinodt Bhat, Partner, 212 Media
Joe Schramm, Partner, Schramm Sports & Entertainment
Anjali Jindal, Marketing & Creative Services
Type of service: Video on demand.
Programming: Bollywood hits & entertainment.
Began: August 1, 2004.
Distribution method: Available to cable systems.
Ownership: 212 Media & Schramm Sports & Entertainment.

BOOK TELEVISION
10212 Jasper Ave
Edmonton, AB T5J 5A3
Canada
Phone: 780-440-7777
Fax: 780-440-8899
E-mail: info@booktelevision.com
Web Site: http://www.booktelevision.com
Operating hours/week: 168.
Programming: Features books & writers.

BOOK TV
400 N Capitol St NW
Ste 650
Washington, DC 20001
Phone: 202-737-3220
Fax: 202-737-0508
E-mail: booktv@c-span.org
Web Site: http://www.booktv.org
Robin Scullin, Media Relations Manager
Connie Doebele, Senior Executive Producer
Type of service: Basic.
Operating hours/week: 48. 8a.m. Sat.- 8a.m. Mon.
Uplink: Washington, D.C.
Programming: Featuring works of non-fiction authors and classics that have impacted public policy, history, or culture; historical fiction/non-fiction books for children and young adults; tours of unique bookstores & libraries; live call-in forums. Available on C-SPAN 2.
Began: December 9, 1998.
Total subscribers: 85,000,000.
Distribution method: Available to cable systems.
Ownership: C-SPAN.

BOOMERANG
Turner Broadcasting System
1 CNN Center
Atlanta, GA 30303
Phone: 404-827-1700
Web Site: http://www.cartoonnetwork.com/boomerang
Mark Norman, Senior Vice President & General Manager
Tom Alexander, Vice President, Trade Marketing
Adina Pitt, Vice President, Content Acquisitions & Co-Productions
Stuart Snyder, President & Chief Operating Officer, Turner Animation, Young Adults & Kids Media
Rico Hill, Vice President, Programming & Acquisitions
Laurie Goldberg, Media Contact
Satellites: Galaxy I-R, transponder 15.
Operating hours/week: 168.
Programming: Classic cartoons. SAP where available.
Began: April 1, 2000.
Total subscribers: 18,000,000.
Ownership: Turner Broadcasting System Inc.

BOOMERANG EN ESPANOL — See Boomerang.
Web Site: http://www.boomerangla.com
Turner Network Television.

BOSTEL — See GlobeCast WorldTV.
E-mail: marketing@rtvbostel.com
Web Site: http://www.rtvbostel.com
Operating hours/week: 168.
Programming: Traditional music, sports, business, art & technology focused shows for Bosnian community in U.S.
Began: January 1, 2001.

BOSTON KIDS & FAMILY — See WGBH TV.

BOSTON CATHOLIC TELEVISION — See CatholicTV.

BOUNCE TV
323 A Edgewood Ave
Atlanta, GA 30312
Phone: 770-960-8733
Fax: 404-577-1786
E-mail: jweiss@bouncetv.com
Web Site: http://www.bouncetv.com
Rob Hardy, Chief Content Officer
Will Packer, Chief Strategy & Marketing Officer
Ryan Glover, Executive Vice President
Jonathan Katz, Executive Vice President
Jeffrey Wolf, Executive Vice President, Distribution
Jim Weiss, Information Contact
Type of service: Plans basic.
Operating areas: Plans nationwide.
Programming: Will offer a programming mix of theatrical motion pictures, live sporting events, documentaries, specials, inspirational faith-based programs off-net sales, original programming and more available 24/7. Target audience will be African Americans between the ages of 25-54.
Scheduled to begin: Plans to launch September 26, 2011.
Means of Support: Plans advertising.
Distribution method: Terrestrial service will be carried on stations digital sub channels. Has signed distribution deals with Raycom Media, LIN TV Corp. & Nexstar Broadcasting Group Inc.
Scrambled signal: Planned.
Ownership: Andrew Young, Andrew 'Bo' Young III, Martin Luther King III, Rob Hardy & Will Packer, Co-Founders.

BOX — No longer in operation; see MTV2.

BOXTV: THE BOXING CHANNEL
819 4th St
Secaucus, NJ 07094
Phone: 212-731-2151
Fax: 212-202-4265
E-mail: bricco@boxtv.org
Web Site: http://www.boxtv.org
Brian Ricco, President & Chief Executive Officer
Operating hours/week: Plans 168.
Operating areas: To be available nationwide.
Scheduled to begin: First quarter 2012. Has provided periodic service on PPV and Video on Demand since fall of 2007.

BRAVESVISION
2925 Courtyards Dr
Norcross, GA 30071
David Williams, General Manager, Channel Operations
Type of service: Digital.
Programming: Live Atlanta Braves home games in high-definition, pre/post game coverage, player interviews & classic games.
Began: September 21, 2004.
Total subscribers: 750,000.
Ownership: Comcast Corp.

BRAVO
30 Rockefeller Plz
8th Fl E
New York, NY 10112
E-mail: bravofeedback@bravotv.com
Web Site: http://www.bravotv.com
Joshua Sapan, Chief Executive Officer, Rainbow Media Holdings Inc.
Frances Berwick, President, Bravo Media
Holly Tang, Chief Financial Officer
Ed Carroll, Executive Vice President
Joseph A. Cantwell, Executive Vice President, Bravo New Media
Andrew Cohen, Executive Vice President, Original Programming & Development
Gregg Hill, Executive Vice President, Affiliate Sales & Marketing
Lisa Hsia, Executive Vice President, Bravo Digital Media
Steve Mandala, Executive Vice President, Cable Ad Sales, NBCU
Cameron Blanchard, Senior Vice President, Communications
Cynthia Burnell, Senior Vice President, General Manager, Bravo International
Tony Cardinale, Senior Vice President, Research & Strategic Insights
John Duff, Senior Vice President, Western Division/Local Ad Sales
Jennifer Geisser, Senior Vice President, Communications
Michael Haggerty, Senior Vice President, Research
Jerry Leo, Senior Vice President, Program Strategy & Acquisitions
Shari Levine, Senior Vice President, Production
Susan Malfa, Senior Vice President, Ad Sales
David O'Connell, Senior Vice President, Production & Operations
Ed Palluth, Senior Vice President, Eastern Division
Ellen Stone, Senior Vice President, Marketing
Christian Barcellos, Vice President, Production
Kim Becker, Vice President, Public Relations
Bill Bergmann, Vice President, Finance
Eric Cavanaugh, Vice President, Program Research
Jennifer DeGuzman, Vice President, Communications
Ryan Flynn, Vice President, Production
Kevin Granger, Vice President, Sales Strategy & National Accounts
Caroline Kaplan, Vice President, Film & Program Development
David Kaplan, Vice President, Ad Sales Research, Bravo Media
Eli Lehrer, Vice President, Development
Jenn Levy, Vice President, Development & Production
Christian McLaughlin, Vice President, Production
Ryan Pinette, Vice President, Production & Operations
Corey Silverman, Vice President, National Advertising Sales, Eastern Division
Lara Spotts, Vice President, East Coast Development
Jennifer Turner, Vice President, Licensing & Strategic Partnerships
Jim Urick, Vice President, Finance

Krissie Verbic, Vice President, National Accounts & Affiliate Marketing
Emily Yeomans, Communications Director

Regional Offices:
Chicago, IL; Westlake, TX; Santa Monica, CA; New York, NY.
Type of service: Basic.
Satellites: AMC 11, transponder 24; AMC 10, transponder 13; Satcom C4, transponder 7.
Operating hours/week: 168.
Programming: Feature films, performing arts series & specials from around the world.
Began: December 1, 1980.
Means of Support: Subscriber fees & advertising.
Total subscribers: 85,000,000.
Scrambled signal: Yes.
Ownership: NBCUniversal LLC.

BRAVO HD — See Bravo.

BRAVO!
299 Queen St W
Toronto, ON M5V 2Z5
Canada
Phone: 416-591-5757
Fax: 416-591-7482
E-mail: bravomail@bravo.ca
Web Site: http://www.bravo.ca
Paul Gratton, General Manager
Programming: Performing arts.
Began: January 1, 1995.
Ownership: CHUM International.

BRIDAL CHANNEL — No longer planned.

BRIDGES TV
227 Thorn Ave
Studio V
Orchard Park, NY 14127
Phone: 716-961-3142
Fax: 716-961-3142
E-mail: info@bridgestv.com
Web Site: http://www.bridgestv.com
Muzzammil Hassan, President & Chief Executive Officer
Joan Lence, Program Director
Ambereen Shaikh, Advertising Sales
Samina Salahuddin, Media Relations
Type of service: Digital basic & broadband.
Programming: Programming for American Muslims focusing on entertainment, family, news, children's shows, sports & religion.
Began: December 14, 2004.
Means of Support: Subscribers, advertising.
Total subscribers: 1,000,000.
Distribution method: Available via satellite & cable.

BRIGHT HOUSE SPORTS NETWORK
7901 66th St N
Pinellas Park, FL 33781
Phone: 727-329-2417
Fax: 727-329-2359
Web Site: http://www.brighthouse.com
Paul Kosuth, Station Manager
Glen Richard, Programming Manager
Mindy Smith, Accounting Mgr.
Mike Stanford, Marketing Manager
Lou Bruno, Engineering Manager
Chris Elias, Sports Director
Type of service: Digital.
Operating hours/week: 168.
Operating areas: Florida.
Programming: Regional sports network, inlcuding coverage of high school & college sports, fishing, auto racing, boxing, soccer & extreme sports.
Began: September 17, 2008.
Distribution method: Available to cable systems.
Ownership: Bright House Networks.

BROADWAY TELEVISION NETWORK
268 W 44th St
3rd Fl
New York, NY 10036
Phone: 212-471-6060
Fax: 212-471-6088
E-mail: bmb@broadwaytv.com
Web Site: http://www.broadwayonline.com
Kay Koplovitz, Chairman
Bruce Brandwen, Chief Executive Officer
Don Roy King, Creative Director
Jerry Zaks, Creative Director
Type of service: Digital basic, pay-per-view, video on demand.
Operating hours/week: Plans 168.
Programming: Plans programming from Broadway, off Broadway, off off Broadway, London's West End, regional & local theatre. Including musicals, plays, reality shows, travel/news/documentaries, major motion pictures & original talk shows.
Scheduled to begin: Unannounced.
Means of Support: Advertising.
Distribution method: Available to cable systems & home dish audiences.
Scrambled signal: Yes.
Ownership: The Shubert Organization; The Nederlander Organization; Jujamcyn Theatres & SFX Entertainment, investors.

BTN
600 W Chicago
Ste 875
Chicago, IL 60610
Phone: 312-665-0700
Fax: 312-665-0740
Web Site: http://bigtennetwork.com
Mark Silverman, President
Michael Calderon, Vice President, Digital & Interactive Media
Elizabeth Conlisk, Vice President, Communications & University Relations
Michael Fuller, Vice President, Programming
Erin Harvego, Vice President, Marketing
Mark Hulsey, Vice President, Production & Executive Producer
Roy Seinfeld, Vice President, Ad Sales
Mike Vest, Media Relations Manager
Type of service: Basic.
Operating hours/week: 168.
Operating areas: Available nationwide and across Canada.
Programming: Sports & other programming from 11-member Big Ten schools. Formerly known as Big Ten Network. Service was rebranded May 31, 2011.
Began: August 30, 2007.
Total subscribers: 80,000,000.
Distribution method: Available to cable systems & satellite providers.
Scrambled signal: Yes.
Ownership: Big Ten Conference 51%, Fox Cable Networks 49%.

BTN HD — See BTN.

BUSINESSVISION
930 N National Pkwy
Ste 505
Schaumburg, IL 60173
Phone: 800-424-0840
Fax: 800-517-8744
Von Polk, Chairman & Chief Executive Officer, WingsNet Inc.
Lloyd Singer, President & Chief Operating Officer
Stephen Reitmeister, Vice President, Marketing
Satellites: Echostar.
Programming: Training videos, live panel discussions & financial, legal & business news.
Began: April 1, 1996.
Distribution method: Available to home dish audiences & business sites.
Ownership: Video Publishing House Inc. & Broadcast International.

BYU TELEVISION
2000 Ironton Blvd
Provo, UT 84606
Phone: 866-662-9888
E-mail: byutv@byu.edu
Web Site: http://www.byutv.org
Type of service: Basic.
Operating hours/week: 168.
Operating areas: Utah, Arizona, Nevada, Montana, California, Washington & Wyoming.
Programming: Devotionals & forums, conference broadcasts, BYU sporting events, documentaries, musical performance. Aimed at alumni & friends of BYU & the LDS Church.
Means of Support: Viewer-supported.
Total subscribers: 39,000,000.
Distribution method: Available to cable & satellite providers & online.
Ownership: Brigham Young University & the Church of Jesus Christ of Latter-Day Saints.

CABLE PUBLIC AFFAIRS CHANNEL
PO Box 81099
Ottawa, ON K1P 1B1
Canada
Phone: 877-287-2722
Fax: 613-567-2749
Web Site: http://www.cpac.ca
Satellites: Anik F-1, transponder T5.
Operating hours/week: 168.
Programming: Coverage of Parliamentary proceedings & political events as well as specials & documentary reports.
Began: January 1, 1992, as Cable Parliamentary Channel; relaunched as Cable Public Affairs Channel in 1996.
Total subscribers: 22,000,000.

CABLE TV NETWORK OF NEW JERSEY
124 W State S
Trenton, NJ 08608
Phone: 609-392-3223
Fax: 609-392-8682
E-mail: ctnofnj124@aol.com
James A. DeBold, Executive Director
Cliff Potent, Vice President, Engineering
Albert Stender, Vice President, Counsel
Mary Murphy, Sales Coordinator & Administrative Assistant
Type of service: Basic.
Operating hours/week: 168.
Operating areas: New Jersey.
Programming: Offers Gavel to Gavel, coverage of New Jersey State Senate & Assembly when in session, plus additional programming.
Began: January 17, 1983.
Means of Support: Advertising (program & spot).
Total subscribers: 1,800,000.
Distribution method: Available to cable systems.

CABLE IN THE CLASSROOM
25 Massachusetts Ave NW
Ste 100
Washington, DC 20001
Phone: 202-222-2335
Fax: 202-222-2336
Web Site: http://www.ciconline.org
Helen Soule, Executive Director
Frank Gallagher, Education Director
Douglas Levin, Senior Director, Education Policy
Rachel Macias, Cable System Relations Director
Type of service: Basic.
Satellites: Various.
Operating hours/week: Varies.
Programming: Cable in the Classroom (CIC), the cable industry's education foundation, works to expand & enhance learning opportunities for children & youth. Created to help schools take advantage of educational cable programming & technology. An advocate for media literacy education & for the use of technology & media for learning, as well as a resource of educational cable content & services for policymakers, educators & industry leaders.
Began: January 1, 1989.
Means of Support: Public service initiative of local cable companies & cable networks.
Distribution method: Available to cable systems & schools.

CALIFORNIA CHANNEL
1121 L St
Ste 110
Sacramento, CA 95814
Phone: 916-444-9792
Fax: 916-444-9812
E-mail: contact_us@calchannel.com
Web Site: http://www.calchannel.com
John Hancock, President
Jim Gualtieri, Broadcast Operations Director
Type of service: Basic.
Satellites: Satcom C-4, transponder 5.
Operating hours/week: 32.5.
Operating areas: California.
Programming: Statewide non-profit public affairs network providing gavel-to-gavel coverage of state government proceedings.
Began: February 1, 1991.
Total subscribers: 5,000,000.
Distribution method: Available to cable & satellite systems.

CANADIAN LEARNING TELEVISION
10212 Jasper Ave
Edmonton, AB T5J 5A3
Canada
Phone: 780-440-7777
Fax: 780-440-8899
E-mail: pam.hnytka@chumtv.com
Web Site: http://www.clt.ca
Ross Mayot, Vice President, Learning Services

Branch Offices:
TORONTO: 299 Queen St W, Toronto, ON M5V 2Z5, Canada. Phone: 416-591-7400. Fax: 416-591-5117.
Satellites: Anik, transponder E2.
Operating hours/week: 168.
Programming: National educational television specialty service providing entertaining, informative & educational programs to adult viewers & lifelong learners in all parts of Canada.
Began: September 1, 1999.
Means of Support: Advertising & subscriber fees.
Ownership: CHUM Ltd.

CANAL ALGERIE — See GlobeCast WorldTV.
Programming: General entertainment in French & Arabic.

CANAL DE LAS ESTRELLAS — See Televisa Networks.
E-mail: estrellaslatinoamerica@televisanetworks.tv

CANAL 52MX
Blvd Puerto Aereo 486
Col Montezuma
Mexico City 15500
Mexico
Phone: 555-764-83-67
Fax: 555-764-83-53
E-mail: canal52@mvs.com
Web Site: http://www.canal52.com
Type of service: Digital.
Programming: Spanish language programming featuring original productions, sporting events, Mexican films & news.
Began: June 8, 2005.
Total subscribers: 5,000,000.
Distribution method: Cable.
Ownership: MVS Television.

CANAL SUR — See Sur Network.

CANAL SUR MEXICO
7311 NW 12th St
Ste 29
Miami, FL 33126-1924
Phones: 305-468-6602; 877-890-1787
Fax: 305-436-1953
Satellites: Galaxy 23, transponder 10C.
Programming: Offering Mexicans living in the U.S. a full schedule of news, events, and entertainment programming.
Began: January 1, 1992.
Means of Support: Advertising and subscriber fees.
Total subscribers: 2,000,000.
Distribution method: Available to home dish audiences and cable subscribers.
Scrambled signal: Yes.

CANAL 24 HORAS
Edifico Prado del Rey, despacho 2/162
28233 Pozuelo de Alarcon
Madrid
Spain
E-mail: rtve.dircom@rtve.es
Web Site: http://www.rtve.es
Programming: Spanish news & headlines from Madrid's TVE news network.
Total subscribers: 180,000.
Ownership: State owned.

CANAL D
2100 Ste. Catherine St W
Ste 700
Montreal, QC H3H 2T3
Canada
Phone: 514-939-3150
Fax: 514-939-3151
Web Site: http://www.canald.com
Pierre Roy, President & Chief Executive Officer
Judith Brosseau, Senior Vice President, Programming & Communications
Type of service: Basic.
Satellites: Anik E-2.
Programming: French language programming focusing on documentaries, biographies, cult series & classic movies.
Began: January 1, 1995.
Ownership: Astral Media Inc.

CANALES N — See HITS (Headend In The Sky).

CAPITAL NEWS 9
104 Watervliet Ave Extension
Albany, NY 12206
Phone: 518-459-9999
Fax: 518-641-7025
E-mail: albanynews@ynn.com
Web Site: http://capitalregion.ynn.com
Al Marlin, General Manager
Rich Hahn, Sales Manager
Scott Christiansen, Marketing Manager
Chris Brunner, News Director
Type of service: Basic.
Sales representative: Advertising.
Operating hours/week: 168.
Programming: Local news channel.
Began: October 11, 2002.
Total subscribers: 320,000.
Scrambled signal: Yes.
Ownership: Time Warner Inc.

CAPITAL OFF TRACK BETTING TELEVISION NETWORK
510 Smith St
Schenectady, NY 12305
Phone: 518-344-5204
E-mail: jimb@capitalotb.com
Web Site: http://www.capitalotb.com
Programming: Live horse races & information on racing & betting for the Capital region of Upstate NY.
Began: July 1, 1974.
Live Horse Racing and Horse Racing informational programming.

CAPTIVATE NETWORK
2 Executive Dr
3rd Fl, Ste 301
Chelmsford, MA 01824
Phone: 888-383-3737
Fax: 978-392-0312
E-mail: contactus@captivate.com
Web Site: http://www.captivate.com
Mike DiFranza, President & General Manager
Type of service: Broadband.
Operating areas: GA, MA, IL, TX, MO, CA, CO, CT, AZ, NY, TN, FL, MN, PA, WA, DC.
Programming: News & entertainment programming from cable, online & news organizations; targeted to professionals in major business centers.
Distribution method: Available wirelessly to elevator networks in professional office buildings.
Ownership: Gannett.

CARACOL TV
1441 Brickell Ave
Ste 1010
Miami, FL 33131
Phone: 305-960-2018
Fax: 305-960-2017
E-mail: loic@mediamundi.com.br
Web Site: http://www.caracoltvinternacional.com
Camilo Cano, International Vice President

Angelica Guerra, International Director
Jimena Mejia, International Sales Executive
Andres Uribe, Affiliate Sales
Roberto Prieto, Advertising Sales
Diana Visbal, Administration & Marketing Manager

Branch Offices:
BOGOTA: Calle 103 No. 50-45, Bogota, Colombia. Phone: 57-1-6-430-430.
Satellites: PanamSat 9 6C.
Programming: Colombian telenovelas, news broadcasts, variety magazines & entertainment shows, reality & travel programs.
Began: September 1, 2003.
Total subscribers: 1,500,000.
Ownership: Caracol Television Inc.

CAREER ENTERTAINMENT TELEVISION
10573 W Pico Blvd
Ste 168
Los Angeles, CA 90064-2348
Phone: 310-277-2388
Fax: 310-277-1037
E-mail: info@ce.tv
Web Site: http://www.ce.tv
Margaret A. Loesch, Advisory Board
Connie Johnson, Founder & President
Karen Barnes, Executive Vice President, Development & Programming
Jeffrey D. Torkelson, Senior Vice President, Communications
Samantha Brown, Senior Vice President, Affiliate Sales
Rick D'Andrea, Senior Vice President, Business Development
Amy Cox, Senior Vice President, Marketing
Darren E. Barker, Vice President, Finance
Hugh Cadden, Vice President, Programming & Development
Monica Deeter, Production Manager
Type of service: Digital basic & video on demand.
Programming: Entertainment & education-based programming devoted to work & the workplace.
Began: September 1, 2004.
Distribution method: Available to cable & satellite systems.

CARIBEVISION TELEVISION NETWORKS
1520 NW 79th Ave
Miami, FL 33126
E-mail: vgomez@caribevision.com
Web Site: http://www.caribevision.com
Operating hours/week: 168.
Operating areas: Florida, New York & Puerto Rico.
Programming: Spanish-language entertainment, sports, news, Caribbean cultural & lifestyle shows.
Began: September 11, 2007.
Total subscribers: 7,000,000.
Ownership: Pegaso TV & Barba Television.

CARS.TV
1925 Century Park E
Ste 1025
Los Angeles, CA 90067
Phone: 310-277-3500
E-mail: eric@es.tv
Web Site: http://www.es.tv/category/shows/carstv/
Byron Allen, Chairman & Chief Executive Officer
Darren Galatt, Vice President, Ad Sales
Type of service: Digital broadband.
Operating hours/week: 168.
Operating areas: Available nationwide.
Programming: Features shows geared towards the auto enthusiast.
Began: May 11, 2009.
Total subscribers: 1,900,000.
Distribution method: Available to Verizon FiOS and Frontier Communications subscribers.
Scrambled signal: No.
Ownership: Entertainment Studios.

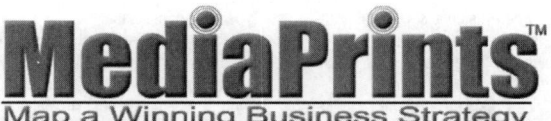

CARTOON NETWORK
1050 Techwood Dr NW
Atlanta, GA 30318-5264
Phones: 404-827-1717; 404-885-2263
Fax: 404-885-4594
E-mail: sgc2c@turner.com
Web Site: http://www.cartoonnetwork.com
Stuart Snyder, President & Chief Operating Officer, Turner Animation
David Levy, President, Turner Broadcasting Sales
Robert Sorcher, Chief Content Officer
Beth Goss, Executive Vice President, Ad Sales, Marketing & Enterprises
Timothy Hall, Executive Vice President
John O'Hara, Executive Vice President & General Sales Manager
Finn Arnesen, Senior Vice President, Original Series & Int'l Development
Paul Condolora, Senior Vice President, Digital, Animation, Young Adults & Kids Media Group
Peter Dougherty, Senior Vice President, Branding
Phyllis Ehrlich, Senior Vice President, Promotions Marketing
Josh Feldman, Senior Vice President, Ad Sales
Lisa Fernow, Senior Vice President, Global Marketing & Strategy
Patty Gillette, Senior Vice President, Brand Activation & Media Partnerships
Bob Higgins, Senior Vice President, Programming
Stacy Isenhower, Senior Vice President, Programming & Scheduling
Craig Steven McAnsh, Senior Vice President, Marketing
John J. O'Hara, Senior Vice President, Ad Sales
James Anderson, Vice President, Public Relations
William Blair, Vice President, Ad Sales, Promotions & Marketing
Pola Chagnon, Vice President & Executive Producer, Cartoon Network Online
Molly Chase, Vice President & Executive Producer, New Media
Keith Crofford, Vice President, Production
Brenda Guttman, Vice President, Creative Services
Russell Hicks, Vice President, Marketing
Sharon Lieblein, Vice President, Casting & Talent Development

Brian Miller, Vice President & General Manager, Cartoon Network Studios
Michael Ouweleen, Vice President & Creative Director
Adina Pitt, Vice President, Content Acquisitions & Co-Productions
Lisa Richardson, Vice President, Marketing
Phil Sharpe, Vice President, Technology, Cartoon Network Online
Robert Swartz, Vice President, Original Series
Michelle Allario, Consumer Marketing Director
Deena Boykin, Senior Director, Retail Development
Daria Cronin, Softlines Director
Lisa Wilson, Trade Marketing Director
Courtenay Purcell, Public Relations Director
Peter Yoder, Hardlines Director
Type of service: Basic, video on demand.
Satellites: Galaxy I/I-R, transponder 8.
Sales representative: Turner Broadcasting Sales Inc.
Operating hours/week: 168.
Programming: Cartoons from Hanna-Barbera, MGM, Warner Brothers & Paramount.
Began: October 1, 1992.
Means of Support: Advertising.
Total subscribers: 100,600,000.
Distribution method: Available to home dish audiences, cable systems & mobile video.
Ownership: Time Warner & Turner Broadcasting.

CARTOON NETWORK HD — See Cartoon Network.

CARTOON NETWORK TAMBIEN EN ESPANOL — See Cartoon Network.

CASA CLUB TV

MGM Networks Latin America, LLC
2800 Ponce de Leon Blvd, Ste 1320
Coral Gables, FL 33134
Phone: 305-445-4350
Fax: 305-445-2058
Web Site: http://www.casaclubtv.com
Gustavo Pupo-Mayo, President & Chief Executive Officer
Melvin Perez, Executive Vice President & Chief Financial Officer
Raoul DeSota, Senior Vice President, Business Development
Anjelica Cohn, Senior Vice President, Advertising Sales & New Business
Marcello Coltro, Vice President, Sales & Marketing
Ricardo Montagnana, Sales & Marketing Director
Sandra Austin, Finance Director
Patricia Schille Hubalek, Affiliate Sales
Programming: Spanish language home & lifestyle programming.
Began: June 1, 2003.
Ownership: MGM Worldwide, United Global Communications Inc.

CASINO & GAMING TELEVISION

1800 Century Park E
Ste 600
Los Angeles, CA 90067
Phone: 310-407-5115
Fax: 310-229-5799
E-mail: rac@cgtv.com
Web Site: http://www.cgtv.com
Nickolas J. Rhodes, President & Chief Executive Officer
William Keenan, Chief Financial Officer & Chief Operating Officer
Steven Cheskin, Executive Vice President, Programming & Production
Terry Debono, President, CGTV Canada
John Brosseau, Marketing Director, CGTV Canada
Type of service: Basic.
Programming: First & only 24-hour entertainment & information cable network devoted to the gaming industry & lifestyle. Focusing on casino games, recreation & tournaments.
Began: September 1, 2005, Launched in Canada.

CATALOG TV — See i-Shop.

CATALOGUE TV — No longer planned.

CATCH 47 — See Bay News 9.

CATHOLIC TELEVISION NETWORK

PO Box 301825
St. Thomas, VI 00803
Phone: 340-777-4828
Fax: 340-777-4828
Benny Gibbs, Director
Ronaldo A. Boschuite, Operations Director
Type of service: Basic.
Operating areas: U.S. Virgin Islands.
Programming: Mix of local religious programming with Trinity Bcstg. Network.
Distribution method: Available to cable systems.

CATHOLICTV

PO Box 9196
34 Chestnut St
Watertown, MA 02471
Phone: 617-923-0220
Fax: 617-965-6587
E-mail: bctv@catholictv.org
Web Site: http://www.catholictv.com
Father Robert Reed, Executive Director
Jay Fadden, General Manager
Bonnie Rodgers, Programming & Affiliate Relations
Kevin Nelson, Producer
Matthew Weber, Producer
Kate Andrews, Associate Producer
Type of service: Basic, Digital.
Operating hours/week: 168.
Programming: Connecting people of faith through relevant, inspiring & prayerful programming; educating, teaching the Wisdom of God in the Catholic Tradition, endeavoring to move people of all ages, cultures & attitudes toward the Fullness of Life.
Began: January 1, 1983, CatholicTV has been broadcasting since the 1950s (on cable since 1983).
Means of Support: Sponsorship.
Distribution method: Satellite, Fiber.
Scrambled signal: Yes.

CB TELEVISION MICHOACAN — See Alterna'TV.
Programming: General, locally focused entertainment shows covering economics, sports, tourism & news for Michoacanos in Mexico & abroad.

CBC/RADIO-CANADA

PO Box 3220
Station C
Ottawa, ON K1Y 1E4
Canada
Phones: 613-288-6033; 866-220-6045
Fax: 613-288-6045
E-mail: liaison@radio-canada.ca
Web Site: http://www.cbc.radio-canada.ca
Timothy Casgrain, Chairman
Hubert T. Lacroix, President & Chief Executive Officer
Sylvain Lafrance, Executive Vice President, French Services
Richard Stursberg, Executive Vice President, English Services
Johanne Charbonneau, Vice President & Chief Financial Officer
Raymond Carnovale, Vice President & Chief Technology Officer
William B. Chambers, Vice President, Communications
Reaches Canadians through its national TV and radio networks, specialty cable services, Internet, satellite and podcast services, full service websites, international services, and continuous music network.

CBS SPORTS NETWORK

85 10th Ave, 3rd Fl
New York, NY 10011
Phone: 212-342-8700
Fax: 212-342-8899
E-mail: lwade@cbs.com
Web Site: http://cstv.collegesports.com/mm/
Sean McManus, Chairman
David Berson, President
Ken Aagaard, Executive Vice President, Operations, Engineering & Production Services
Mike Aresco, Executive Vice President, Programming
Chris Bevilacqua, Executive Vice President
Bob Rose, Executive Vice President, Distribution
Marty Kaye, Senior Vice President, Finance
Patty Power, Senior Vice President, Operations
Harold Bryant, Vice President, Production
Type of service: Basic.
Programming: Live regular season & championship events across a broad spectrum of men's & women's sports including football, basketball, baseball, soccer, ice hockey & lacrosse.
Began: April 7, 2003, as College Sports Television; relaunched as CBS College Sports March 16, 2008. Rebranded as CBS Sports Network February 15, 2011.
Total subscribers: 95,000,000.
Distribution method: Available to cable systems & satellite providers.
Scrambled signal: Yes.
Ownership: CBS.

CBS SPORTS NETWORK HD — See CBS Sports Network.

CCTV-9 (DOCUMENTARY CHANNEL)

11B Fuming Rd
Beijing 100038
China
E-mail: documentary@cctv.com
Web Site: http://cctv.cntv.cn/documentary/
Operating hours/week: 168.
Operating areas: Available nationwide.
Programming: Offers Chinese-language documentaries focusing on nature, history, the humanities and society. Available as part of the 'Great Wall' package through KyLinTV.
Began: January 1, 2011, in China; available 2/15/2011 in North America, Europe and Singapore.
Scrambled signal: Yes.

CCTV-ENTERTAINMENT — See KyLinTV.

CCTV NEWS

11B Fuxing Rd
Media Center
Beijing 100038
China
E-mail: cctv-9@cctv.com
Web Site: http://www.cctv.com
Type of service: IPTV.
Programming: Chinese news available on KyLinTV.
Began: September 25, 2000.

CCTV-OPERA — See KyLinTV.

CCTV-4

11835 W Olympic Blvd
Ste 1150
Los Angeles, CA 90064
Phones: 626-912-3388; 310-268-2271
Fax: 310-477-4544
E-mail: cctv4mail@mail.cctv-4.com
Web Site: http://www.cctv-4.com
Fang Jiqing, Information Contact

Branch Office:
BEIJING: CCTV, 11 Fuxing Rd, Beijing 100859, China.
Type of service: Pay.
Satellites: Galaxy VII, transponder 24.
Operating hours/week: 168.
Programming: Offers news & documentaries in Mandarin, plus some English-language newscasts. Also available on International Premium Networks.
Began: April 1, 1998.
Distribution method: Available to cable & telco systems.
Ownership: China Central Television.

CCTV-6 — See KyLinTV.
Programming: Also known as China Movie Channel.

CCTV-E — See KyLinTV.
Programming: Broadcasts programming in Spanish, includes educational, entertainment, features and news shows.
Began: March 5, 2010, Date shown is when broadcasts began in China.

CELEBRITY SHOPPING NETWORK

c/o Revenue Frontier LLC
3250 Ocean Park Blvd, Ste 200
Santa Monica, CA 90405
Phone: 310-584-9200
E-mail: info@revenuefrontier.tv
Web Site: http://www.revenuefrontier.tv
Type of service: Basic.
Programming: Beauty, fashion, health & style products from celebrity models & actors.
Distribution method: Satellite.

CELTIC VISION

8 N Marketplace
Faneuil Hall
Boston, MA 02109
Phone: 617-973-6441
Fax: 617-973-6444
Web Site: http://www.celticvision.com
Lawrence Baker, Chairman & President
Roger P. Day, Chief Operating Officer
John-Philip Foley, Vice President & General Counsel
Daniel J. Leahy, Vice President, Development
James Tobin, Vice President, Advertising
Kathleen Held, Executive Producer
Steve Groh, Production Manager
Brendan Canning, Regional Manager

Network Operations:
BROOKLINE: 179 Amory St, Brookline, MA 02146. Phone: 617-566-4844.

Regional Offices:
NEW YORK:. Phone: 212-557-4887.

SAN FRANCISCO:. Phone: 415-452-3155.

Program Operations:
DUBLIN: 8 Crow St, Dublin 2, Ireland. Phone: 353-1-671-2101. Fax: 353-1-676-2344. Voice Mail: 353-1-700-3229.
Type of service: Basic.
Satellites: GE-3.
Operating hours/week: 168.

Operating areas: Massachusetts.
Programming: Entertainment, news & sports from Europe.
Began: March 17, 1995.
Means of Support: Advertising & subscription.
Distribution method: Available home dish audiences & cable systems.
Ownership: Celtic Vision Productions Ltd. (Dublin, Ireland).

CENTRAL FLORIDA NEWS 13
20 N Orange Ave
Ste 13
Orlando, FL 32801
Phone: 407-513-1300
Fax: 407-513-1310
E-mail: rsmythe@cfnews13.com
Web Site: http://www.cfnews13.com
Robin Smythe, Vice President & General Manager
Stephen Chavarie, News Programming Director
Rick Chattin, Finance Director
Deirdre Treacy, Marketing Director
Fletcher Christian, Operations Manager
Operating areas: Orlando-Daytona Beach-Melbourne, FL.
Programming: Regional 24-hour all local news channel.
Began: October 27, 1997.
Means of Support: Advertising & subscriber fees.
Total subscribers: 750,000.
Distribution method: Available to Bright House Networks customers only.
Scrambled signal: No.
Ownership: Bright House Networks.

CENTRIC
1235 W St NE
Washington, DC 20018
Phone: 202-608-2000
Fax: 202-269-9335
Web Site: http://www.centrictv.com/
Debra L. Lee, Chairman & Chief Executive Officer, BET Networks
Scott Mills, President & Chief Operating Officer, BET Networks
Reginald Hudlin, President, Entertainment
Paxton Baker, Executive Vice President & General Manager, Centric
Cybelle Brown, Vice President, Sales & Business Development, BET Digital Networks
Derek Lewis, Vice President, Production, BET Event Productions
Eileen Littlejohn, Vice President, Network Operations, BET Digital Networks
Gail Northern, Vice President, Programming, BET Digital Networks

Branch Offices:
New York: 1515 Broadway, New York, NY 10036. Phone: 212-846-5000.
Type of service: Digital.
Satellites: Galaxy 11, transponder 3.
Operating hours/week: 168.
Operating areas: Available nationwide.
Programming: Entertainment network featuring the artists, music, series, movies and reality programming reflecting the lifestyle and sophistication of today's African-American and multi-cultural adult.
Began: January 15, 1996, ; as BET On Jazz. Re-launched as BET J on March 1, 2006. Re-launched as Centric September 28, 2009.
Means of Support: Advertising.
Total subscribers: 32,000,000.
Distribution method: Available to cable & satellite providers.
Scrambled signal: Yes.
Ownership: BET Networks, a division of Viacom Inc.

CENTROAMERICA TV
7291 NW 74th St
c/o US Imagina LLC
Miami, FL 33166
Phone: 305-777-1900
Fax: 305-820-9046
E-mail: info@centroamericatv.tv
Web Site: http://www.centroamericatv.tv
Spanish language programming focusing on Central American communities.

CET - COMCAST ENTERTAINMENT TV
1601 Mile High Stadium Cir
Denver, CO 80204
Phone: 303-603-6332
E-mail: denver_cet@cable.comcast.com
Web Site: http://www.comcast.com/cet
Type of service: Digital & video on demand.
Operating hours/week: 168.
Operating areas: Colorado.
Programming: Documentaries, movies, high school sports, music & lifestyle shows related to Colorado communities.
Began: September 1, 2004.
Distribution method: Available to Comcast cable subscribers.
Ownership: Comcast.

CHANNEL 500 — No longer planned.

CHANNEL 4 SAN DIEGO
350 10th Ave
Ste 500
San Diego, CA 92101
Phone: 619-686-1900
Fax: 619-595-0168
Web Site: http://4sd.signonsandiego.com
Tom Ceterski, Executive Producer & Director
Dan Novak, Vice President, Programming
Nick Davis, Senior Producer
Tom Morgigno, Station Manager
Type of service: Basic.
Operating areas: San Diego, CA region.
Programming: Carries San Diego Padres major league baseball games, features and shows about baseball, the Padres ballclub, and the team's community activities, San Diego State U. football & basketball, local news magazine show & local biography show.
Began: March 1, 1997.
Total subscribers: 500,000.
Distribution method: Available to cable systems, distributed by fiber optic.
Scrambled signal: Yes.
Ownership: Cox Communications Inc.

CHANNEL ONE
151 W 26th St
11th Fl
New York, NY 10001
Phone: 800-251-4039
E-mail: feedback@channelone.com
Web Site: http://www.channelonenetwork.com
Kent Haehl, Chief Executive Officer
Beth Mayall, Senior Vice President, Creative Development
Angela Hunter, Senior Vice President & Executive Producer, Channel One News
Andy Cheatwood, Web Development Manager
James Gladden, Art Director
Stephanie L. Smith, Senior Editor

Branch Office:
LOS ANGELES: 6300 Wilshire Blvd, Ste 2150, Los Angeles, CA 90048.
Type of service: Basic.

Operating hours/week: 1.
Programming: Daily news reports targeted to middle & high school students.
Began: March 1, 1990.
Total subscribers: 7,000,000.
Ownership: Primedia Inc.

CHANNEL ONE RUSSIA
19 Akademika Korolyova St
Moscow 127427
Russian Federation
Phones: 7 495 617 55 78; 7 495 617 99 33
Fax: 7 495 617 51 14
E-mail: distribution@1tvrus.com
Web Site: http://eng.1tvrus.com
Nikolay Dubovoy, Director General
Type of service: Premium.
Operating areas: Available nationwide.
Programming: Offers digital thematic broadcasting in Russian. Currently provides five different channels of entertainment: Dom Kino (movies), Muzika Pervogo (music videos), Telecafe (food channel), TV Nanny (children's programming) & Vremya (biographies).
Means of Support: Subscriber fees and advertising.
Distribution method: Available to cable subscribers.

CHERIETV — See Playgirl TV.

CHICAGOLAND TELEVISION NEWS
2501 W Bradley Pl
Chicago, IL 60618-4718
Phone: 773-528-2311
E-mail: programming@cltv.com
Web Site: http://www.cltv.com
Marty Wilke, Vice President & General Manager
Steve Farber, Vice President, Operations
Ron Goldberg, Sales Director
Greg Caputo, News Director
Jennifer Lyons, Assistant News Director
Type of service: Regional.
Operating hours/week: 168.
Operating areas: Chicago, IL area; Rockford, IL; and South Bend, IN.
Programming: Chicago area news and informational programming.
Began: January 1, 1993.
Means of Support: Advertising & subscriber fees.
Total subscribers: 1,500,000.
Distribution method: Available to cable systems.
Scrambled signal: Yes.
Ownership: Tribune Co.

CHILLER
900 Sylvan Ave
1 CNBC Plz
Englewood Cliffs, NJ 07632
E-mail: feedback@chillertv.com
Web Site: http://www.chillertv.com
Dave Howe, President
Ted A'Zary, Senior Vice President, Research
Susan Lape, Vice President, Primary Research
Type of service: Basic, video on demand & broadband.
Satellites: AMC 11, transponder 24.
Programming: Horror & thriller series & films from NCB Universal's library.
Began: March 1, 2007.
Total subscribers: 33,000,000.
Distribution method: Available to cable systems & satellite providers.
Scrambled signal: Yes.
Ownership: NBCUniversal LLC.

CHINA MOVIE CHANNEL — See KyLinTV.
Programming: Also known as CCTV-6.
Scrambled signal: Yes.

CHINESE COMMUNICATION CHANNEL
4107 Sarilee Ave
Rosemead, CA 91770-1359
Yuan-Shiung Kuo, Chairman & Chief Executive Officer
Eddie C. L. Wang, President & General Manager
Raymond Wang, Executive Vice President

Branch Office:
ROSEMEAD: 500 W Montebello Blvd, Rosemead, CA 91770. Phone: 213-722-8889.
Type of service: Basic.
Satellites: Satcom K-2, transponder 8.
Operating hours/week: 168.
Programming: News, sports & in-house programs in Mandarin, Cantonese & Taiwanese.
Began: September 1, 1989.
Total subscribers: 750,000.
Ownership: North American Television.

CHINESE ENTERTAINMENT TELEVISION (CETV) — See KyLinTV.
Type of service: IPTV.
Programming: General entertainment from Hong Kong, Beijing, Guangzhou & Shenzhen.

CHINESE TELEVISION NETWORK
1995 Broadway
Ste 602
New York, NY 10023
Phone: 212-501-8088
Fax: 212-501-7533
Web Site: http://av.sina.com/ctn/index.html

Branch Offices:
London; Los Angeles; New York; Paris; San Francisco; Singapore; Taipei; Tokyo; Vancouver; Washington, DC.
Type of service: Pay.
Satellites: Galaxy IV, transponder 7.
Uplink: Hong Kong.
Programming: Offers news, informational & educational programming in Chinese.
Began: September 1, 1994.
Means of Support: Advertising & subscriber fees.
Distribution method: Available to home dish audiences & cable systems.

CHONGQING TV INTERNATIONAL CHANNEL — See KyLin TV.

CHRISTIANNET
7140 S Lewis Ave

One Technology Plaza
Tulsa, OK 74136-5422
Phones: 918-499-6800; 800-831-4641
Fax: 918-499-6868
Todd Ragsdale, Product Manager
Type of service: Audio.
Operating hours/week: 168.
Programming: Radio shows for conservative Christian listeners.
Began: September 1, 1995.
Means of Support: Subscriber fees.
Distribution method: Available to home dish audiences.

CHRISTIAN TELEVISION NETWORK
6922 142nd Ave
Largo, FL 33771
Phone: 727-535-5622
Fax: 727-531-2497
E-mail: comments@ctnonline.com
Web Site: http://www.ctnonline.com
Bob D'Andrea, President & Founder

Branch Offices:
PO Box 6922, Clearwater, FL 33758.
Type of service: Basic.
Operating hours/week: 168.
Programming: Inspirational & Christian programming.
Began: October 24, 1979.
Means of Support: Viewer supported.
Total subscribers: 15,000,000.
Distribution method: Available to cable & satellite systems.

CHURCH CHANNEL
2442 Michelle Dr
Tustin, CA 92780
Phones: 714-665-2110; 714-832-2950
Fax: 714-832-0645
E-mail: rhenke@tbn.org
Web Site: http://www.churchchannel.tv
Paul F. Crouch, President & Founder
Paul Crouch Jr., Chief of Staff
Rodney Henke, Vice President, Media
Bob Higley, Vice President, Cable & Satellite Relations
David Adcock, National Director, Affiliate Sales & Relations
Diane Adcock, Director, Southeast Cable Affiliates
Type of service: Digital.
Satellites: Galaxy 14, transponder 1.
Operating hours/week: 168.
Programming: Features prominent & favorite church leaders from across the nation, traditional, contemporary & cutting edge programs.
Began: January 1, 2002.
Total subscribers: 15,776,000.
Distribution method: Available to cable systems.
Ownership: Non-profit Corp.

CI HD — See Crime & Investigation Network.

CINE LATINO — See Condista.
Condista
10752 Coral Way
Miami, FL 33165
Phone: 305-554-1876
Web Site: http://www.cinelatino.com/usa
Programming: Contemporary Spanish-language films.
Began: January 1, 1999.
Total subscribers: 2,300,000 (Reflects U.S. subscribers).
Ownership: MVS Television.

CINE MEXICANO — See OlympuSat Hispanic Pack.
Web Site: http://www.cinemexicano.tv
Type of service: Basic & video on demand.
Programming: Mexican movies from the 1990's to today.
Began: November 1, 2004, reflects U.S. launch.
Total subscribers: 875,000,000.
Ownership: Cine Mexicano LLC.

CINEMA GOLDEN CHOICE — See Televisa Networks.
E-mail: goldenchoice@televisanetworks.tv

CINEMAX
Home Box Office
1100 Avenue of the Americas
New York, NY 10036
Phone: 212-512-1000
Fax: 212-512-1166
Web Site: http://www.cinemax.com
Olivia Smashum, Senior Vice President, Subscriber Marketing & Business Development

Branch Offices
ATLANTA: Lenox Bldg, 3399 Peachtree Rd NE, Atlanta, GA 30328. Phone: 404-239-6600. Fax: 404-261-4186. Sandra Mitchell, Senior Vice President & General Manager, Affiliate Operations; Pat Conner, Manager, Affiliate Public Relations.

CHICAGO: 6250 N River Rd, Ste 10-300, Rosemont, IL 60018. Phone: 847-318-5100. Fax: 847-825-1333. Jane Moyer, Senior Vice President & General Manager, Affiliate Operations; Cheryl Procter, Manager, Affiliate Public Relations.

DALLAS: 12750 Merit Dr, Ste 1105, Dallas, TX 75251. Phone: 972-450-1000. Fax: 972-387-5570. Michael Hopper, Manager, Affiliate Relations.

DENVER: The Quadrant, 5445 DTC Pkwy, Ste 700, Englewood, CO 80111, 303-220-2900. Fax: 303-220-9668. Jane Moyer, Senior Vice President & General Manager, Affiliate Operations.

LOS ANGELES: 2049 Century Park E, Ste 4100, Los Angeles, CA 90067. Phone: 310-201-9200. Fax: 310-201-9310. Janice Aull, Senior Vice President & General Manager, Affiliate Operations; David Castro, Manager, Affiliate Public Relations.

PHILADELPHIA: 401 City Ave, Ste 620, Bala Cynwyd, PA 19004. Phone: 610-668-6500. Fax: 610-668-9318. Steve Davidson, Senior Vice President & General Manager, Affiliate Operations.

SAN FRANCISCO: 353 Sacramento St, 20th Floor, San Francisco, CA 94111. Phone: 415-785-7700. Fax: 415-788-0183. Janice Aull, Senior Vice President & General Manager.
Type of service: Pay.
Satellites: Galaxy 1-R, transponder 23 (Cinemax ETW); Galaxy 1-R, transponder 19 (Cinemax east); Galaxy V, transponder 16 (Cinemax west).
Operating hours/week: 168.
Uplink: Hauppauge, NY.
Programming: 24-hour all movie service.
Began: August 1, 1980.
Means of Support: Subscriber fees.
Total subscribers: 40,000,000 (includes subscribers for HBO).
Equipment: General Instrument.
Ownership: AOL Time Warner.

CINEMAX ON DEMAND — See Cinemax.
Type of service: Video on demand.

CINEMAX SELECCIONES — See Cinemax.

CINEMAX HD — See Cinemax.

CITYTV
299 Queen St W
Toronto, ON M5V 2Z5
Canada
Phone: 416-591-5757
Fax: 416-591-8523
E-mail: interactivesiteadmin@citytv.com
Web Site: http://www.citytv.com
Allan Waters, Chairman, President & Director, CHUM Ltd.
Jay Switzer, President, Programming, CHUM Television
Ron Waters, Senior Vice President, CHUM Ltd.
Moses Znaimer, President & Executive Producer, Citytv
Stephen Tapp, Vice President & General Manager, Citytv
Marcia Martin, Vice President, Production
Stephen Hurlbut, Vice President, News Programming
Allan Schwebel, Vice President, Affiliate Sales & Marketing
Type of service: Basic.
Satellites: Anik E-2; Cancom.
Operating hours/week: 168.
Programming: Canadian superstation.
Began: September 28, 1972.
Means of Support: Advertising.
Total subscribers: 4,000,000.
Distribution method: Available to home dish audiences & cable systems.
Ownership: CHUM Ltd.

CLASSIC ARTS SHOWCASE
PO Box 828
Burbank, CA 91503
Phone: 323-878-0283
Fax: 323-878-0329
E-mail: casmail@sbcglobal.net
Web Site: http://www.classicartsshowcase.org
Jamie D. Rigler, President & Programming Director
Charlie Mount, General Manager
Peter Zeeman, Operations
Type of service: Basic.
Satellites: Galaxy 15, transponder 5.
Operating hours/week: 168.
Programming: All classic arts video featuring: animation, architectural art, ballet, chamber & choral music, dance, documentary, folk art, museum art, musical theatre, opera, orchestral, recital, solo instrumental & vocal & theatrical performance.
Began: May 3, 1994.
Means of Support: Underwritten by the Lloyd E. Rigler-Lawrence E. Deutsch Foundation.
Total subscribers: 48,000,000.
Distribution method: Available to home dish audiences & cable systems.
Ownership: Rigler-Deutsch Foundation, Lloyd E. Rigler & Lawrence Deutsch, founders.

CLUB JENNA
9242 Beverly Blvd
Beverly Hills, CA 90210
Phone: 310-246-4000
Fax: 310-246-4050
Type of service: Pay-per-view.
Programming: Adult entertainment. Formerly Hot Network.
Distribution method: Available to cable systems & satellite providers.

CMT HD — See Country Music TV.
Lisa Chader, Senior Vice President, Corporate Communications

CMT LOADED — See Country Music TV.
Type of service: Broadband.
Programming: Music, news, TV, movies & highlights from the CMT cable network.
Began: July 24, 2006.

CMT PURE COUNTRY — See Country Music TV.
Began: May 26, 2006, originally launched as VH1 Country.
Total subscribers: 17,000,000.

CN8 CREATIVE — See branch office listings for The Comcast Network.

CNBC HD+ — See listing for CNBC.
Began: October 1, 2007.

CNBC
900 Sylvan Ave
Englewood Cliffs, NJ 07632
Phone: 201-735-2622
Fax: 201-585-6244
E-mail: john.kelly@nbcuni.com
Web Site: http://www.cnbc.com
Mark Hoffman, President
Tom O'Brien, Chief Revenue Officer
Andrew Warren, Chief Financial Officer & Vice President
Bruno Cohen, Executive Vice President, Programming
Lilach Asofsky, Senior Vice President, Marketing & Research
John Kelley, Senior Vice President, CNBC Sales
Lou Tosto, Senior Vice President, Digital & Mobile Ad Sales
Joe Berini, Vice President, Cable Network Operations
Robert Foothorap, Vice President, Global Sales Leader
Brian Hunt, Vice President, Affiliate Advertising Sales & Promotion
George Jamison, Vice President, Media Relations & Corporate Communications
Andrea Kane, Vice President, Employee Relations
Mark Miller, Vice President, CNBC Advertising Sales
Stacey Nachtaler, Vice President, Advertising Sales Marketing
Bob Reichblum, Vice President, Current Prime Time Programming
Dan Renaldo, Vice President & Quality Leader
Ken Wilkey, Vice President, Engineering & Operations
Vic Bhagat, Information Technology Vice President
Paul Capelli, Public Relations Vice President
Thomas Clendenin, Marketing Vice President
Scott Drake, Information Technology Vice President
Vince Erardi, Finance Vice President
Thomas A. Quick, Human Resources Vice President
Steve Sherman, Research Vice President
Barry Stoddard, Research Vice President
Allen Wastler, Managing Editor
Marian Caracciolo, Director, Direct Response & Paid Programming
David Bitler, Communications Director
Barry Fitzsimmons, On-Air Promotion Director
John Henderson, Eastern Sales Director
Charles MacLachlan, Marketing Director
Jennifer Sobel, Finance Director
Barbara Stelzner, News Director, CNBC Europe
Howard Homonoff, General Counsel

Branch Offices:
BURBANK: 3000 W Alameda Ave., Suite C-288, Burbank, CA 91523. Phone: 818-840-3214. Fax: 818-840-4181.

CHICAGO: 454 City Front Plaza, Chicago, IL 60611. Phone: 312-836-5836.

TROY: 2855 Coolidge Hwy., Suite 201A, Troy, MI 48084. Phone: 313-643-9033.

WASHINGTON, DC: 1825 K St. NW, Suite 1003, Washington, DC 20006. Phone: 202-467-5400. Fax: 202-467-6267.
Type of service: Basic.
Satellites: Galaxy 5, transponder 13.
Operating hours/week: 168.
Programming: A division of NBC Universal Cable, this cable network provides financial news & information. On the weekends CNBC offers other programming such as The Wall Street Journal Report. International divisions include CNBC Asia, CNBC Europe & CNBC World & provides news & information online.
Began: April 17, 1989.
Means of Support: Advertising & license fees.
Total subscribers: 97,000,000.
Distribution method: Available to home dish audiences, cable systems & mobile video.
Scrambled signal: Yes. Equipment: VideoCipher.
Ownership: NBCUniversal LLC.

CN8 — See The Comcast Network.

CNET TV
235 2nd St
San Francisco, CA 94105
Phone: 415-344-2218
E-mail: sarah.cain@cnet.com
Web Site: http://www.cnet.com
Type of service: Broadband & video on demand.
Programming: 2500 hours of computer & technology related content, including user generated video, coverage of industry-related news & special events.
Began: N.A.
Distribution method: Available to cable & satellite providers.
Ownership: Partnership with Cox Communications, TiVo Inc. & TVN Networks.

CNN
(Cable Network News)
One CNN Center
Atlanta, GA 30303
Phone: 404-827-1700
E-mail: simone.santos@cnn.com
Web Site: http://www.cnn.com
Burt Reinhardt, Vice Chairman
Jim Walton, President
Ken Jautz, President, CNN U.S.
Eason Jordan, Chief News Executive, CNN News Group
Greg D'Alba, Executive Vice President & Chief Operating Officer
Jonathan Davies, Executive Vice President, International Ad Sales
Gail Evans, Executive Vice President
Bob Furnad, Executive Vice President, Programming
Jack Womack, Executive Vice President, CNN Newsource
David Bohrman, Senior Vice President & Chief Innovation Officer, CNN Worldwide
K C Estenson, Senior Vice President & General Manager, CNN International Digital
Robin Garfield, Senior Vice President, CNN Research
David Payne, Senior Vice President, Business Operations for Domestic Networks
Rolando Santos, Senior Vice President, International Relations
Scott T. Weller, Senior Vice President & National Sales Manager
Meredith Artley, Vice President, Managing Editor, CNN.com
Gordon Castle, Vice President, Research & Development
Gene Cooper, Vice President, Audience & Marketing Research, CNN News Group
Joseph Dugan, Vice President, Sales
Louis Gump, Vice President, Mobile
Andrew W. Gyves, Vice President, Sales
Judy Milestone, Vice President, CNN Network Booking
Clare O'Brien, Vice President, CNN Interactive Advertising Sales
Stephen L. Pollack, Vice President & Sales Manager, Western Region
Timothy E. Russell, Vice President, Sales
Anne Woodward, Vice President, Technical Operations
Mark Whitaker, Managing Editor, CNN Worldwide
Type of service: Basic & video on demand.
Satellites: Galaxy I, transponder 7.
Operating hours/week: 168.
Uplink: Atlanta, GA.
Programming: Coverage of major news stories & daily reports on business, finance, medicine, nutrition, sports, weather, fashion & entertainment.
Began: June 1, 1980.
Means of Support: System pays 24-33 cents per subscriber; advertising.
Total subscribers: 101,000,000.
Distribution method: Available to cable systems & mobile video.
Equipment: VideoCipher II.
Ownership: AOL Time Warner.

CNN EN ESPANOL
One CNN Center
12 S
Atlanta, GA 30303
Web Site: http://www.cnn.com/espanol
Tony Madox, Executive Vice President & Managing Director, CNN International
Cynthia Hudson, General Manager
Eduardo Suarez, Vice President, Programming

Branch Offices:
Latin America - Miami: Courvoisier Center II, 601 Brickell Jey Dr, Ste 403, Miami, FL 33131-4330. Phone: 305-603-2000. Fax: 305-603-2505.

Turner International - Argentina: Av. Eduardo Madero 1020, Piso 14, Buenos Aires C1106ACX, Argentina. Phone: 54-11-4312-9900. Fax: 54-11-4312-4581.

Turner International - Mexico: Blvd. Manuel Avila Camacho No. 1, Piso 8, Despacho 805, Col. Chapultepec, Polanco, Mexico DF 11009, Mexico. Phone: 52-55-5395-3066. Fax: 52-55-5395-3055.

Turner International - Brasil: Av. das Nacoes Unidas N, 12.901, 17 Andar CJ 1701 Chacara, Itaim, Sao Paulo 04578-000, Brasil. Phone: 55-11-5501-6700. Fax: 55-11-5507-7080.
Programming: News & analysis.
Began: January 1, 1997.
Total subscribers: 5,000,000.
Ownership: Turner Broadcasting System, Inc.

CNN ENHANCED TV — See CNN.

CNN HD — See CNN.
Began: September 1, 2007.

CNN INTERNATIONAL — See CNN.
Katherine Green, Senior Vice President, Programming
Peter Bale, Vice President & General Manager, CNN International Digital
Mike McCarthy, Vice President, Coverage & Feature Programming

CNN RADIO — See CNN.

CNN RADIO NOTICIAS — See CNN.

CN — 2|
4701 Commerce Crossing Dr
Louisville, KY 40229-2167
Phone: 502-357-4400
Web Site: http://mycn2.com
Caroline Imler, Director, Broadcast Operations
Type of service: Regional basic.
Operating areas: Indiana & Kentucky.
Programming: Offers 24-hour local news, weather and sports, plus political news and analysis.
Began: June 24, 2010.
Means of Support: Advertising.
Total subscribers: 600,000.
Distribution method: Available to Insight cable subscribers in the Louisville, KY region.
Scrambled signal: No.
Ownership: Insight Communications Co.

CNWG-10
PO Box 241
Rome, GA 30162
Phone: 706-235-4851
Fax: 706-232-1644
Ben Clearig, News & Programming Manager
Type of service: Basic.
Operating areas: Floyd & Gordon Counties, GA.
Programming: Local weeknight live newscast, other live local programming.
Began: April 1, 1992.
Distribution method: Fiber optic to cable systems.
Ownership: Comcast Cable Communications Inc.

COLLEGE & SCHOOL NETWORK
c/o North American Catholic Educational Programming Foundation
2419 Hartford Ave
Johnston, RI 02919-1719
Phone: 401-934-1100
Fax: 401-934-2240
E-mail: tchodelka@nacepf.net
Web Site: http://www.csn-ed.net
John Primeau, Director
Type of service: Basic.
Operating hours/week: 54.
Operating areas: Nationwide.
Programming: Offers distance learning, full semester educational courses to public, private & parochial schools & the general subscribing public.
Began: N.A.
Distribution method: Available to cable systems.
Ownership: North American Catholic Educational Programming Foundation.

COLLEGE SPORTS TELEVISION —
See CBS College Sports Network.

COLOURS
200 Quebec St
Bldg 600, Ste 209
Denver, CO 80230
Phone: 303-326-0088
Fax: 303-326-0087
E-mail: info@colourstv.org
Web Site: http://www.colourstv.org
Tracy Jenkins Winchester, President & Chief Executive Officer
Arthur O. Thomas, Executive Vice President
Programming: Multicultural & multi-ethnic programming offering movies, original series, short films, documentaries & sports.
Total subscribers: 14,000,000.
Ownership: Black Star Communications.

COMCAST/CHARTER SPORTS SOUTHEAST (CSS)
2925 Courtyards Dr
Norcross, GA 30071
Phone: 770-559-7800
E-mail: css@css-sports.com
Web Site: http://www.css-sports.com
Mark Fuhrman, Vice President & General Manager
Operating hours/week: 168.
Operating areas: AL, AR, FL, GA, KY, LA, MS, NC, SC, TN, TX, VA & WV.
Programming: Live sports, news & analysis geared toward the Southern sports fan.
Began: September 3, 1999.
Total subscribers: 6,000,000.
Scrambled signal: Yes.
Ownership: NBCUniversal Inc. (majority interest) & Charter Communications Inc.

COMCAST HOMETOWN NETWORK
3055 Comcast Pl
Livermore, CA 94551
Phone: 925-424-0100
E-mail: Comcast_hometown@cable.comcast.com
Web Site: http://www.comcasthometown.com
Jeff Giles, Director
Bryan Byrd, Director, Communications

Branch Offices:
Hayward Studio: 23525 Clawiter Rd, Hayward, CA 94545. Phone: 510-266-3200.

San Francisco Studio: 2741 16th St, San Francisco, CA 94103. Phone: 415-863-8500.

Stockton Studio: 6343 Tam O'Shantar Dr, Stockton, CA 95219. Phone: 209-473-4955.
Type of service: Regional cable service.
Operating hours/week: 168.
Operating areas: Northern & Central California.
Programming: Local programs that show local high school sports and local community life from South Valley to Yuba to the San Francisco Coast.
Began: March 2, 2007.
Total subscribers: 1,600,000.
Distribution method: Available to cable systems.

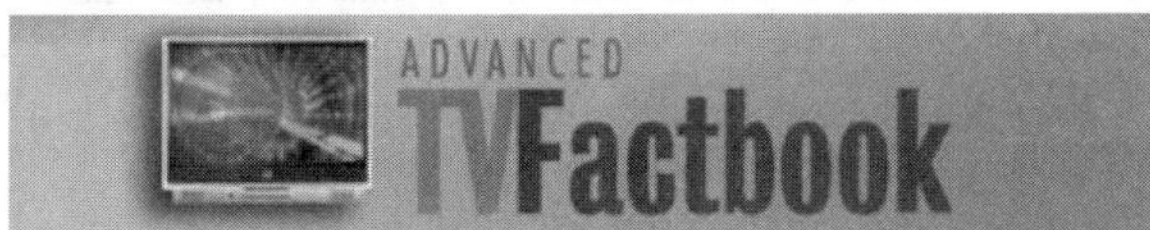

Scrambled signal: Yes.
Ownership: Comcast Corp.

COMCAST SPORTSNET CHICAGO

350 N Orleans St
Ste S1-100
Chicago, IL 60654
Phone: 312-222-6000
Fax: 312-527-4028
E-mail: jnuich@comcastsportsnet.com
Web Site: http://www.csnchicago.com
Jim Corno Sr., President & General Manager
Phil Bedella, Assistant General Manager & Vice President, Ad Sales
Jaclene Tetzlaff, Vice President, Marketing
Greg Bowman, Vice President, Programming
Joyce Brewer, Vice President, Finance & Human Resources
Wesley Albury, Senior Engineering Director
Jeff Nuich, Senior Communications Director
Brian Sanderlin, Senior Operations Director
Charles Schumacher, Senior News Director
Jim Corno Jr., Senior Executive Producer, Live Events
D. J. Maragos, Director, Affiliate Marketing
Type of service: Basic.
Operating hours/week: 168.
Programming: Regular, pre & post season games for the Blackhawks, Bulls, Cubs & White Sox.
Began: October 1, 2004.
Total subscribers: 4,800,000.
Distribution method: Available to cable systems & satellite providers.
Scrambled signal: Yes.
Ownership: NBCUniversal LLC; Bulls TV LLC; W Sports Media LLC; Sox TV LLC; Chicago Baseball Holdings LLC, 20% each.

COMCAST SPORTS SOUTHWEST (CSS)

2925 Courtyards Dr
Norcross, GA 30062
Phone: 770-559-7800
E-mail: css@css-sports.com
Web Site: http://www.comcastsportssouthwest.com
Mark Thurman, Vice President & General Manager
Type of service: Basic.
Operating areas: Texas (Houston area).
Programming: Local sports channel that provides comprehensive local college and high school sports coverage in the Houston, TX area.
Began: September 1, 2009, Service is managed through Comcast/Charter Sports Southeast.
Distribution method: Available to Comcast subscribers.
Ownership: NBCUniversal LLC.

COMCAST SPORTSNET BAY AREA

370 3rd St
Ste 200
San Francisco, CA 94107
Phone: 415-296-8900
Fax: 415-615-4793
E-mail: info@csnbayarea.com
Web Site: http://www.csnbayarea.com
Ted Griggs, Vice President & General Manager
John Feeley, Vice President, Sales & Syndication
Tom Pellack, Vice President, Marketing
Peter Schofield, Senior Director, Operations
Chris McDonald, Senior Director, Finance & Human Resources
David Koppett, Senior Executive Producer
Jen Franklin, Senior Director, Digital Media
Chris Olivere, News Director
Kyleen Bell, Programming Director
Jay Dela Cruz, Communications Director
Marisa Veroneau, Affiliate Marketing Manager
Type of service: Basic.
Satellites: GE-1, transponder 16.
Sales representative: Rasco.
Operating hours/week: 168.
Operating areas: California (northern portion) & Nevada (northern portion).
Programming: Regional sports service offering San Francisco Giants baseball, Golden State Warriors basketball, PAC 10 & Stanford U. sports, as well as original news sports programming – SportsNet Central and Chronicle Live. Formerly FSN Bay Area and SportChannel Pacific.
Began: April 4, 1990, on March 31, 2009, entity obtained present name.
Means of Support: Advertising & affiliate fees.
Total subscribers: 3,600,000.
Distribution method: Available to cable systems & satellite providers.
Scrambled signal: Yes.
Ownership: NBCUniversal LLC 60%, News Corp 40%.

COMCAST SPORTSNET CALIFORNIA

4450 E Commerce Ave
2nd Fl
Sacramento, CA 95834
Phones: 415-296-8900; 415-296-8900
Fax: 915-515-2770
E-mail: info@csncalifornia.com
Web Site: http://www.csncalifornia.com
Larry Eldridge, Vice President & General Manager
John Feeley, Vice President, Sales & Syndication
Tom Pellack, Vice President, Marketing
Peter Schofield, Senior Director, Operations
Chris McDonald, Senior Director, Finance & Human Resources
Jen Franklin, Senior Director, Digital Media
Richard Zinn, Executive Producer
Richard Leeson, Programming Director
Jay Dela Cruz, Communications Director
Marisa Veroneau, Affiliate Marketing Manager
Type of service: Basic.
Operating areas: California (northern portions), Nevada (portions) & Oregon (portions).
Programming: Regional sports service offering Oakland Athletics baseball, Sacramento Kings basketball, San Jose Sharks hockey, San Jose Earthquakes soccer, and PAC 10 & U. of California Berkeley sports. Formerly Comcast SportsNet West.
Began: November 2, 2004, Launched as Comcast SportsNet West. Renamed Comcast SportsNet California 2008.
Total subscribers: 50,000,000 (Reflects combined total of Comcast SportsNet channels).
Distribution method: Available to Comcast and Dish Network subscribers.
Scrambled signal: Yes.

COMCAST SPORTSNET MID-ATLANTIC

7700 Wisconsin Ave
Ste 200
Bethesda, MD 20814
Phone: 301-718-3200
Fax: 301-718-3300
E-mail: viewermail@csnwashington.com
Web Site: http://www.csnwashington.com; http://www.csnbaltimore.com
Rebecca Schulte, Senior Vice President & General Manager
Mark Lapidus, Vice President, Digital Manager
Marc LeSage, Vice President, Ad Sales
George Psillos, Vice President, Finance & Business Administration
Austin Krablin, Senior Director, Marketing & Creative Services
Brian H. Potter, Senior Director, Communications
Frank Crisafulli, News Director
Tom Pahnke, Operations Director
Lisa Pendleton, Programming Director
Lynne Cotton, Human Resources Specialist
Type of service: Regional basic.
Satellites: GE-3, transponder 6.
Operating hours/week: 168.
Operating areas: Delaware, District of Columbia, Maryland, North Carolina, Pennsylvania, Virginia & West Virginia.
Programming: The official sports network of the Washington Redskins, Baltimore Ravens, Washington Capitals, Washington Wizards, D.C. United, Atlantic Coast Conference and Colonial Athletic Association, delivers more than 500 live sporting events per year, along with Emmy Award-winning news, analysis and entertainment programming, to more than 4.7 million homes throughout the District of Columbia, Maryland and Virginia. Comcast SportsNet's digital portfolio, highlighted by CSNwashington.com and CSNbaltimore.com, is the region's leading source for online sports news and information.
Began: April 4, 1984, Launched as Home Team Sports, it assumed current name when acquired by Comcast April 4, 2001.
Means of Support: System fees & advertising.
Total subscribers: 4,700,000.
Distribution method: Available to Comcast, DirecTV & Dish Network subscribers.
Scrambled signal: Yes.
Ownership: NBCUniversal LLC.

COMCAST SPORTSNET NEW ENGLAND

42 3rd Ave
Burlington, MA 01803
Phone: 781-270-7200
Fax: 781-221-7408
E-mail: fans@comcastportsnet.com
Web Site: http://www.csnne.com
Bill Bridgen, General Manager & Executive Vice President
Len Mead, Vice President, Production & Programming
Gregg Sanders, Vice President, Business Development & Marketing
Type of service: Basic.
Satellites: GE-1, transponder 14.
Sales representative: Rasco.
Operating areas: Connecticut, Maine, Massachusetts, New Hampshire, Rhode Island & Vermont.
Programming: Regional sports service offering Boston Celtics basketball, New England Revolution soccer, CT Suns women's basketball. PAC 10, Big 12 and CAA football and basketball. America East and A-10 basketball, plus nightly sports news, SportsNet Central.
Began: November 6, 1981, 7 when Cablevision sold out to Comcast.
Means of Support: Advertising & subscriber fees.
Total subscribers: 4,000,000.
Distribution method: Available to home dish audiences & cable systems.
Scrambled signal: Yes.
Ownership: NBCUniversal LLC.

COMCAST SPORTSNET NORTHWEST

300 N Winning Way
Portland, OR 97227
Phone: 503-736-5140
Fax: 503-736-5135
Web Site: http://www.csnnw.com
David Manougian, General Manager
Casey Waage, Ad Sales Director
Ken Lotka, Programming Director
Satellites: Galaxy 14 (HD), transponder 4.
Operating areas: Alaska (portions), Idaho, Montana, Oregon & Washington.
Programming: Regional sports service providing NBA Portland Trail Blazers basketball and surrounding programming; NHL Vancouver Canucks hockey & other NHL; Emerald Downs horse racing; PAC-10 football & basketball; Big Sky football & basketball; Portland and Seattle sports radio; original outdoor programming: Outdoor GPS, Northwest Wild Country, WANTED, The Wild Life with Jeremy, Adrenaline Hunter, and more.
Began: September 1, 1989.
Total subscribers: 2,400,000.
Distribution method: Available to home dish audiences, cable systems, MMDS & SMATVs.
Scrambled signal: Yes.
Ownership: NBCUniversal LLC.

COMCAST SPORTSNET PHILADELPHIA

3601 S Broad St
Wells Fargo Center
Philadelphia, PA 19148-5290
Phone: 215-336-3500
Fax: 215-952-5756
E-mail: mquilter@comcastsportsnet.com
Web Site: http://www.csnphilly.com
Brian Monihan, Senior Vice President & General Manager
Joe Croce, Vice President, Advertising Sales
Cynthia Weiss, Vice President, Marketing
Todd Berman, Senior Director, Digital Media
John Braun, National Sales Manager
Bo Koelle, Advertising Sales Director
Maureen Quilter, Communications Director
Dan Rudley, Digital Sales Manager
Mike Garrity, Sponsorship Sales Manager
Type of service: Basic.
Operating hours/week: 168.
Programming: The leading regional sports network reaching over three million viewers in and around Philadelphia, Southern New Jersey and Delaware. Together with The Comcast Network, Comcast SportsNet Philadelphia provides local sports fans with the most sports coverage including more than 250 live game broadcasts of the NHL's Philadelphia Flyers, NBA's Philadelphia 76ers, MLB's Philadelphia Phillies, plus NCAA coverage, as well as Emmy Award-winning sports news and analysis.

Began: October 1, 1997.
Total subscribers: 50,000,000 (Reflects combined total of Comcast SportsNet channels).
Distribution method: Available to cable systems & Verizon FiOS.
Scrambled signal: Yes.
Ownership: NBCUniversal LLC.

COMCAST SPORTSNET PLUS HD — See Comcast SportsNet Plus.

FOX SPORTS SOUTH

1175 Peachtree St NE
Bldg 100, Ste 200
Atlanta, GA 30361
Phone: 404-230-7300
Fax: 404-230-7399
E-mail: FSSouth@foxsports.net
Web Site: http://www.foxsportssouth.com
Jeffrey Genthner, Vice President & General Manager
Type of service: Basic.
Satellites: Galaxy 11, transponder 4.
Operating hours/week: 168.
Operating areas: Alabama, Georgia, Kentucky & Mississippi.
Programming: Regional sports coverage, including Atlanta Hawks basketball games, Atlanta Braves & Baltimore Orioles baseball games, NASCAR, SEC & ACC events, access to more than 40 college football & 200 college basketball games.
Began: August 29, 1990.
Means of Support: Advertising & subscriber fees.
Total subscribers: 7,000,000.
Distribution method: Available to home dish audiences & cable systems.
Ownership: News Corp., Liberty Media & Scripps Howard.

COMCAST SPORTSNET WEST — See Comcast SportsNet California

THE COMCAST NETWORK

386 Washington St
Norwell, MA 02061
Phones: 781-659-1235; 877-862-9374
Fax: 781-659-9855
Web Site: http://http://csnphilly.com/pages/comcastnetwork
Melissa Kennedy, Vice President, Marketing Communications

Branch Offices:

TRENTON STUDIO: 940 Prospect St, Trenton, NJ 08618. Phone: 609-394-3860. Fax: 609-394-6983.

UNION STUDIO: 800 Rahway Ave, Union, NJ 07083. Phone: 732-602-7492. Fax: 908-851-8916.

NEW CASTLE STUDIO: 2215 N DuPont Hwy, New Castle, DE 19720. Phone: 302-661-4203. Fax: 302-661-4201.

PHILADELPHIA STUDIO: 1351 S Columbus Blvd, Philadelphia, PA 19147. Phone: 215-468-2222. Fax: 215-463-5922.

MOORESTOWN OFFICE (CN8 CREATIVE): 650 Centerton Rd, Moorestown, NJ 08057. Phone: 856-638-4000. Fax: 856-206-0727.

OAKS OFFICE: 200 Cresson Blvd, Oaks, PA 19456. Phone: 610-650-1000. Fax: 610-650-2909.

NEW ENGLAND AD SALES: 179 Amory St, Brookline, MA 02446. Phone: 617-264-5749. Fax: 617-731-6456.
Type of service: Regional basic & video on demand.
Sales representative: Eric Fortune.
Operating hours/week: 168.
Operating areas: Maine, Massachusetts, New Hampshire, Pennsylvania, Maryland, New Jersey, Connecticut, Delaware & Virginia.
Programming: New England and Mid-Atlantic regional programming featuring entertainment, sports, news and information & other locally produced programming.
Began: January 1, 2009, Launched in 1996 as CN8. Reorganized in late 2008 and relaunched as The Comcast Network in early 2009.
Total subscribers: 10,000,000.
Distribution method: Available to Comcast cable systems.
Scrambled signal: Yes.
Ownership: NBCUniversal LLC.

COMEDY CENTRAL

1775 Broadway
10th Fl
New York, NY 10019
Phone: 212-767-8600
Web Site: http://www.comedycentral.com
Doug Herzog, President, MTV Networks Entertainment Group
Michelle Ganeless, President
Kent Alterman, President, Original Programming & Development
David Bernath, Executive Vice President, Program Strategy & Multiplatform Programming
John Cucci, Executive Vice President & Chief Operating Officer
Tony Fox, Executive Vice President, Corporate Communications
Walter Levitt, Executive Vice President-Marketing
Jeff Lucas, Executive Vice President, Ad Sales
Melissa Bear, Senior Vice President, Business & Legal Affairs, East Coast
Val Boreland, Senior Vice President, Progeamming, Promotion & Multiplatform
Erik Flannigan, Senior Vice President, Digital Media
Mitch Fried, Senior Vice President, Promotions Marketing
Steve Grimes, Senior Vice President, Digital Media
Lisa Leingang, Senior Vice President, Original Programming & Development, East Coast
Bob Pederson, Senior Vice President & Creative Director
Chris Pergola, Senior Vice President, Finance
Elizabeth Porter, Senior Vice President, Specials & Talent
Peter Rafisi, Senior Vice President, Brand Marketing & Executive Creative Director
Bob Salazar, Senior Vice President, Creative Director, Brand Creative
Jim Sharp, Senior Vice President, Original Programming & Development, West Coast
Michael Tenzer, Senior Vice President, Legal Affairs, West Coast
Lou Wallach, Senior Vice President, Original Programming & Development, East Coast
Caleb Weinstein, Senior Vice President, Strategy & Business Development
Joella West, Senior Vice President, Business & Legal Affairs
Paul Beddoe-Stephens, Vice President, Digital Media
Kelleigh Dulany, Vice President, Public Responsibility
JoAnn Grigioni, Vice President, Talent
Scott Landsman, Vice President, Original Programming & Development

Sharon Light, Vice President, Ad Sales Research
Arian Sultan Rothman, Vice President, Business & Legal Affairs, East Coast
Type of service: Basic & video on demand.
Satellites: Galaxy I-R, transponder 1 (west coast); Satcom C-3, transponder 21 (east coast).
Operating hours/week: 168.
Programming: Original & syndicated comedy programming.
Began: April 1, 1991.
Means of Support: Advertising.
Total subscribers: 93,000,000.
Distribution method: Available to cable systems, satellite providers & mobile video.
Scrambled signal: Yes.
Ownership: Viacom Inc.

COMEDY CENTRAL HD — See Comedy Central.

COMEDY NETWORK

PO Box 1000
Station O
Toronto, ON M4A 2W3
Canada
Phone: 416-332-5300
Fax: 416-332-5301
E-mail: mail@thecomedynetwork.ca
Web Site: http://www.thecomedynetwork.ca
Susanne Boyce, Senior Vice President, Programming
Roman Melnyk, Vice President, Business Affairs
Ed Robinson, Vice President, Programming
Frank Abels, Director, Affiliate Relations & Marketing
Type of service: Basic.
Operating hours/week: 168.
Programming: 24-hour service featuring Canadian & international programs devoted exclusively to comedy sketches, standup comedy & ongoing comedy series.
Began: October 17, 1997.
Ownership: Shaw Communications.

COMEDY.TV

1925 Century Park E
Ste 1025
Los Angeles, CA 90067
Phone: 310-277-3500
E-mail: eric@es.tv
Web Site: http://www.comedy.tv
Byron Allen, Chairman & Chief Executive Officer
Darren Galatt, Vice President, Ad Sales
Type of service: Digital broadband.
Operating hours/week: 168.
Operating areas: Available nationwide.
Programming: Features live performances, talk & variety shows, sitcoms & movies.
Began: May 11, 2009.
Total subscribers: 1,900,000.
Distribution method: Available to Verizon FiOS and Frontier Communications sybscribers.
Scrambled signal: No.
Ownership: Entertainment Studios.

COMPUTER TELEVISION NETWORK — No longer planned.

CONCERT TV

730 Wellington
Montreal, Quebec H3C 1T4
CANADA
Phone: 514-664-1244
Fax: 514-664-1143
E-mail: info@concerttv.com
Web Site: http://www.concerttv.com/
Programming: View a selection of concerts On Demand for free and purchase full length concerts of some of your favorite musicians. We bring you some of the best talent in the world in every style of music including Black Eyed Peas, Norah Jones, Garth Brooks, Kanye West, Santana and The Rolling Stones.
Began: Launched in 2003 Concert TV is now available to viewers across the United States, where it reaches close to 30 million households and is so.
Total subscribers: 30,000,000.
Distribution method: Digital cable, satellite & IPTV.
Ownership: Stingray Digital Group Inc.

CONDISTA

2029 SW 105 Ct
Miami, FL 33165
Phone: 305-554-1876
Fax: 305-554-6776
E-mail: jorge@condista.com
Web Site: http://www.condista.com
Programming: Digital-ready, Spanish language programming.
Total subscribers: 12,000,000.
Scrambled signal: Yes.

CONSTRUCTION CABLE NETWORK — No longer planned.

COOKING CHANNEL

75 9th Ave
New York, NY 10011
Phone: 212-398-8836
Fax: 212-736-7716
Web Site: http://www.cookingchanneltv.com
Michael Smith, General Manager
Bruce Seidel, Senior Vice President, Programming & Production
Type of service: Digital basic.
Programming: Formerly Fine Living Network, now it's for food people, by food people. Experts offer indepth and detailed information including unconventional how-tos, global cuisine, wines and spirits, international travel and classic favorites.
Began: March 1, 2002, Originally launched as Fine Living Network, channel was relaunched as Cooking Channel May 31, 2010.
Total subscribers: 58,000,000.
Scrambled signal: Yes.
Ownership: Scripps Networks Interactive Inc.

THECOOLTV

PO Box 514
Lawrence, KS 66044
Phone: 888-342-8761
Fax: 773-439-8804
E-mail: info@coolmusicnetwork.com
Web Site: http://www.thecooltv.com
Joe Comparato, Chief Executive Officer

David Hampe, Chief Operating Officer
John (Digger) Pelaez, Senior Vice President, On Demand & Chief Marketing Officer
Bobby Tarantino, Senior Vice President, Artist & Label Relations
Type of service: Basic.
Operating hours/week: 168.
Programming: Multiplatform digital subchannel television network that connects audiences with their favorite music.
Began: March 2, 2009.
Means of Support: Advertising.
Distribution method: Available nationwide.
Scrambled signal: Yes.
Ownership: Cool Music Network LLC.

CORNERSTONE TELEVISION

1 Signal Dr
Wall, PA 15148-1499
Phone: 412-824-3930
Fax: 412-824-5442
E-mail: info@ctvn.org
Web Site: http://www.ctvn.org
Ron Hembree, President
Blake Richert, Vice President, Engineering
Tim Burgan, Vice President, Ministry
Satellites: AMC-4.
Operating hours/week: 168.
Programming: Offers multiple programs, including original in-house productions ministering salvation, encouragement & healing.
Began: April 15, 1979.
Total subscribers: 52,000,000.

COSMOPOLITAN CHANNEL — No longer planned.

COSMOPOLITANTV

Corus Specialty Television
64 Jefferson Ave, Unit 18
Toronto, ON M6K 3H4
Canada
Phone: 416-534-1191
E-mail: info@cosmotv.ca
Web Site: http://cosmotv.ca
Type of service: Digital basic.
Operating hours/week: 168.
Programming: Women's programming.
Began: February 14, 2008.
Total subscribers: 5,000,000.
Distribution method: Available to cable systems.
Ownership: Corus Entertainment & Hearst Publications.

COUNTRY MUSIC TV

(CMT)
2806 Opryland Dr
Nashville, TN 37214
Phones: 615-457-8500; 615-457-8501
Fax: 615-457-8520
E-mail: cmtviewerservices@country.com
Web Site: http://www.cmt.com
Ann Sarnoff, Chief Operating Officer
Brian Philips, President, New Media
Bob Kusbit, Head of Development
Richard Gay, Executive Vice President, Strategy & Operations
Jay Frank, Senior Vice President, Music Strategy
David Giles, Senior Vice President, Research
John Hamlin, Senior Vice President, Production & Development
Brad Johnson, Senior Vice President, Series Development
Dee McLaughlin, Senior Vice President, Brand Marketing
Suzanne Norman, Senior Vice President, Strategy & Business Operations
Rich Cornish, Vice President, Ad Sales Research
Stacey Killian Hagewood, Vice President, Creative Services
Claire McCabe, Vice President, Development-Nashville
Melanie Moreau, Vice President, Development-Los Angeles
Chris Parr, Vice President, Music Programming
Kaye Zusmann, Vice President, Programming & Production
Evan Kroft, Senior Director, Music Programming
Laurissa Ryan, Senior Director, Artist Development & Relations
Jim Babchak, Marketing Director
Jama Bowen, Communications Director
Andrew Whitney, Development Manager

Branch Office:
NEW YORK: 1515 Broadway, 25th Floor, New York, NY 10036.
Type of service: Basic & video on demand.
Satellites: Satcom C-4, transponder 24.
Operating hours/week: 168.
Programming: Country music videos, interviews & specials.
Began: March 6, 1983.
Means of Support: Advertising.
Total subscribers: 87,000,000.
Distribution method: Available to home dish audiences & cable systems.
Scrambled signal: Yes.
Ownership: Viacom Inc.

COUNTRY MUSIC TV (ASIA/PACIFIC RIM) — See Country Music TV.

COUNTRY MUSIC TV (LATIN AMERICA) — See Country Music TV.

COUNTRY MUSIC TV CANADA

64 Jefferson Ave
Unit 9
Toronto, ON M6K 3H4
Canada
Phone: 416-534-1191
Fax: 416-530-5206
Web Site: http://www.cmtcanada.com
Brian Bolli, Vice President, Sales & Marketing
John Willson, Creative Director
Satellites: Anik E-1, transponder 2-H.
Sales representative: TeleRep Inc.
Operating hours/week: 168.
Programming: Country music videos.
Began: December 31, 1994.
Means of Support: Advertising & subscriber fees.
Total subscribers: 8,000,000.
Ownership: Corus Entertainment.

THE COUNTRY NETWORK

40 Music Sq W
Nashville, TN 37212
Phone: 877-655-2351
E-mail: billjones@tcncountry.com
Web Site: http://www.afncountry.com
Tammy Genovese, President, TCN Nashville
Chris Butterick, President, TCN Broadcasting
Warren Hansen, Chief Operating Officer
Kim Bullard, Executive Vice President
Bill Jones, Programming Director
Type of service: Basic.
Operating hours/week: 168.
Operating areas: Available nationwide.
Programming: Television network dedicated exclusively to airing country music videos, all Country Music, all the time.
Began: June 15, 2010, Originally launched January 7, 2009 as the Artists & Fans Network. Became the American Music Video Network August 2009. Renamed The Country.
Total subscribers: 17,700,000 (Includes viewers of Sinclair Broadcast Group stations, which carries service on its digital subcha).
Distribution method: Available to cable systems and on Sinclair Broadcast Group stations.
Ownership: Founded by Chad Brock & Warren Hansen.

COUNTY TELEVISION NETWORK SAN DIEGO

1600 Pacific Hwy
Rm 208
San Diego, CA 92101-2481
Phone: 619-595-4600
Fax: 619-557-4027
E-mail: michael.russo@sdcounty.ca.gov
Web Site: http://www.ctn.org
Michael Workman, Director
Michael Russo, Program & Production Manager
Type of service: Basic.
Operating hours/week: 168.
Operating areas: San Diego, CA.
Programming: Government access programmer for San Diego County. Largest of its kind in the county.
Began: July 1, 1996.
Total subscribers: 725,000.
Ownership: San Diego County.

COURT TV — See truTV.

COURTTV CANADA

9 Channel Nine Ct
Scarborough, ON M1S 4B5
Canada
Phone: 416-332-5000
Web Site: http://www.courttvcanada.ca
Programming: Specialty television service featuring entertaining programs about police, forensic science, the law, the courts, rescue & emergency medicine.
Ownership: CTVglobemedia.

COX SPORTS TELEVISION

2121 Airline Dr
2nd Floor W
Metairie, LA 70001
Phone: 504-304-2740
Fax: 504-304-2243
E-mail: coxsportstv@cox.com
Web Site: http://www.coxsportstv.com
Amaliya Lenz, Administrative Asst.
Programming: CST is the exclusive regional sports network home of the New Orleans Hornets, New Orleans Saints, LSU Tigers & the New Orleans VooDoo. Showcases over 350 events each year.
Began: October 1, 2002.
Total subscribers: 2,000,000. Total systems served: 16.
Scrambled signal: Yes.

CP24

299 Queen St W
Toronto, ON M5V 2Z5
Phone: 416-591-5757
Fax: 416-593-6397
E-mail: news@pulse24.com
Web Site: http://www.pulse24.com
Operating hours/week: 168.
Programming: 24-hour Toronto news.
Began: January 1, 1998.
Ownership: Chum Television.

CRACKLE

10202 W Washington Blvd
Culver City, CA 90232
Web Site: http://www.crackle.com
Programming: Crackle is a multi-platform next-generation video entertainment network that distributes digital content including original short form series and full-length traditional programming from Sony Pictures' vast library of television series and feature films. Crackle is one of the fastest growing entertainment destinations on the Internet today, offering audiences quality programming in a variety of genres including comedy, action, sci-fi, horror, music and reality. Crackle reaches an impressive audience through its diverse online and mobile distribution.
Scrambled signal: Yes.
Ownership: Sony Pictures Entertainment Co.

CRIME & INVESTIGATION NETWORK — See Arts & Entertainment.

CRIME CHANNEL

78206 Varner Rd
Ste D131
Palm Desert, CA 92211
Phone: 760-360-6151
Fax: 760-360-3258
E-mail: crimechannel@dc.rr.com
Web Site: http://www.thecrimechannel.com
Arnold Frank, President
Gary Miller, Executive Vice President, Sales & Marketing
Sheldon Altfeld, Vice President, Network Operations
Dan Blackburn, Vice President, Production
Type of service: Basic.
Satellites: Satcom C-1, transponder 11.
Operating hours/week: 2.
Uplink: Network I.
Programming: Crime-related programs.
Began: July 4, 1993.
Means of Support: Advertising.
Total subscribers: 16,000,000.
Distribution method: Available to home dish audiences and cable systems.
Ownership: Arnold Frank.

CSN+ — See Comcast SportsNet Plus.

CSN+ HD — See Comcast SportsNet Plus.

C-SPAN

400 N Capitol St NW
Ste 650
Washington, DC 20001
Phone: 202-737-3220
Fax: 202-737-3323
E-mail: pkiley@c-span.org
Web Site: http://www.c-span.org
Brian P. Lamb, Chief Executive Officer
Susan Swain, Co-President
Robert Kennedy, Co-President
Terry Murphy, Vice President, Programming
Marty Dominguez, Vice President, Marketing
John Jackson, Vice President, Human Resources
Bruce D. Collins, Vice President & General Counsel
Kathy Murphy, Vice President, Programming Operations
Roxane Kerr, Vice President, Corporate Engineering
Peter Kiley, Vice President, Affiliate Relations
Type of service: Basic. C-SPAN3 Digital.
Satellites: AMC 11, transponder 7.
Operating hours/week: 168 for C-SPAN, C-SPAN 2 & C-SPAN 3.
Uplink: Fairfax County, VA.
Programming: Cable industry's cooperative for 24-hour public affairs programming including live coverage of U.S. House of Representatives, House & Senate hearings,

press conferences, conventions and other public events from around the nation.
Began: March 19, 1979.
Means of Support: For C-SPAN, system fee per month; for C-SPAN 2 & 3, free with C-SPAN.
Total subscribers: 100,000,000.
Distribution method: Available to home dish audiences and cable systems.
Ownership: Cable industry cooperative.

C-SPAN AUDIO NETWORKS — See C-SPAN.

C-SPAN EXTRA — See C-SPAN.

C-SPAN HD — See C-SPAN.
Began: June 28, 2010.

C-SPAN 2 HD — See C-SPAN.

C-SPAN S — See C-SPAN.

C-SPAN 3 — See C-SPAN.
Began: January 22, 2001.

C-SPAN 3 HD — See C-SPAN.
Began: June 28, 2010.

C-SPAN 2 — See C-SPAN.
Began: June 2, 1986.

CTC MEDIA
15A Pravda St
Moscow 125124
Russia
Phone: 7-495-785-6333
E-mail: info@ctcmedia.ru
Web Site: http://www.ctcmedia.ru
Anton Kudryashov, Chief Executive Officer
Vyacheslav Murugov, Chief Content Officer & General Director
Boris Podolsky, Chief Financial Officer
Ekaterina Osadchaya, Head of PR & Corporate Communications, Press Secretary
Angelika Larionova, PR & Corporate Communications Manager
Satellites: DISH Network.
Operating hours/week: 168.
Programming: Russian family entertainment channel.
Began: December 21, 2009.
Means of Support: Available to home dish audiences.
Distribution method: Available to home dish audiences.

CT-N
Capitol Place, 21 Oak St
Ste 605
Hartford, CT 06106
Phone: 860-246-1553
Fax: 860-246-1547
E-mail: paul.giguere@cga.ct.gov
Web Site: http://www.ctn.state.ct.us
Paul Giguere, Chief Executive Officer
Bill Mendoza, Director, Operations
Joseph Patriss, Assistant Director, Operations
Dominique Avery, Executive Producer
William A. Bevacqua, Marketing Director
Type of service: Basic, digital & video on demand.
Operating hours/week: 168.
Programming: Gavel to gavel coverage of all three branches of Connecticut state government & other statewide public policy events.
Began: January 1, 1999.
Distribution method: Available to cable systems.

CTN: CAMBODIAN CHANNEL
c/o Globecast World TV
7291 NW 74th St
Miami, FL 33166
Phone: 305-887-1600
Fax: 305-391-4424
Web Site: http://www.ctncambodia.com
Satellites: Galaxy 5.
Programming: News, culture, drama, entertainment & sports from Cambodia.
Began: March 8, 2003.

CTV NEWS 1
PO Box 9
Station O
Scarborough, ON M4A 2M9
Canada
Phones: 416-332-7400; 416-332-5000
Fax: 416-291-5337
E-mail: news@ctv.ca
Web Site: http://www.ctv.ca
Kirk Lapont, Senior Vice President, News
Dennis MacIntosh, Vice President, News
Tom Habersloh, Executive Producer
Programming: Continually updated headline news, business, sports, weather & entertainment every 15 minutes.
Ownership: CTV Inc.

CTV NEWSNET — See CTV News 1.

CTV TRAVEL
c/o CTV
9 Channel Nine Ct
Agincourt, ON M1S 4B5
Canada
Phone: 416-332-5000
Fax: 416-332-4571
E-mail: sharon@glassbox.tv
Web Site: http://www.ctvtravel.ca
Sharon Stevens, Director Of Programming, GlassBOX Television
Type of service: Digital.
Programming: Travel & lifestyle programming.
Distribution method: Available to cable & satellite providers.

CUBAPLAY TELEVISION
560 Village Blvd, Suite 250
c/o Olympusat Inc.
West Palm Beach, FL 33409
Phone: 561-684-5657
Fax: 561-684-9690
Web Site: http://www.olympusat.com
Tom Mohler, President, Olympusat
Albert Hammond, Director of Operations
Programming: Programming from all six of Cuba's broadcast stations. Genres will include sports, movies, documentaries, children's shows, telenovelas and comedy. Content will be free of any political affiliation or ideological influence.
Scheduled to begin: Unannounced.
Distribution method: Will be available to cable systems.
Scrambled signal: Yes.
Ownership: Olympusat Inc.

CURRENT
118 King St
San Francisco, CA 94107
Phone: 415-995-8200
Fax: 415-995-8201
E-mail: info@current.com
Web Site: http://www.current.com
Al Gore, Chairman
Joel Hyatt, Vice Chairman
Mark Rosenthal, Chief Executive Officer
Mark Goldman, Chief Operating Officer
Ofer Shaked, Chief Technology Officer
Paul Hollerbach, Chief Financial Officer

Steven Blumenfeld, Chief Technology Officer, Phonebites
Liz Janneman, President, Ad Sales
Joshua Katz, President, Marketing
Paul Levine, President, New Media
David Neuman, President, Programming
Courtney Menzel, Executive Vice President, Distribution
Jeanne Meyer, Executive Vice President, Corporate Communications
Joanna Drake Earl, Senior Vice President, Online Studio
Matthew Frankel, Senior Vice President, Corporate Communications
Andrew Stone, Senior Vice President, On-Air Promotions
Frank Lentz, Vice President, Creative Affairs
Patrick Newall, Production Director
Type of service: Digital basic & video on demand.
Operating hours/week: 168.
Programming: Short-form programming targeting the 18-34 year old audience covering a blend of news, culture & viewer-produced video. Current replaced Newsworld International.
Began: August 1, 2005.
Means of Support: Private.
Total subscribers: 51,000,000.
Distribution method: Available to cable systems & satellite providers.
Ownership: Al Gore & Joel Hyatt.

CW11 NEW YORK
220 E 42nd St
New York, NY 10017
Phone: 212-949-1100
Web Site: http://www.wpix.com
Betty Ellen Berlamino, Vice President & General Manager
Bob Marra, General Sales Manager
Karen Scott, News Director
Cathy Davis, Finance Director
Carlos Austin, Local Promotions & Community Affairs Director
V. Jean Maye, Human Resources Director
Steve Schussel, Research Director
Mike Gano, Broadcast Operations & Engineering Director
John Zeigler, Creative Services Director
Laurel Light, Operations Director
Sam Stiers, Webmaster
Type of service: Basic.
Satellites: Spacenet 3, transponder 5.
Operating hours/week: 168.
Programming: Broadcasts movies, sports & syndicated programming.
Began: May 1, 1984, as WPIX, a WB affiliate; re-launched on Sept. 20, 2006.
Means of Support: System pays per subscriber.
Total subscribers: 10,000,000 (Figure includes cable, Canadian, DTH & off-air).
Distribution method: Available to home dish audiences, cable systems & telephone companies.
Equipment: VideoCipher II.

CW+
4000 Warner Blvd
Bldg 168
Burbank, CA 91522
Phones: 818-977-2500; 818-977-5000
Fax: 818-977-5015
Web Site: http://www.cwtv.com
Dawn Ostroff, President, Entertainment
John Maatta, Chief Operating Officer
Michael Roberts, Executive Vice President, Current Programming
Kim Fleary, Executive Vice President, Comedy Development
Rob Tuck, Executive Vice President, Sales & Planning
Paul McGuire, Senior Vice President, Network Communications
Betsy McGowen, Senior Vice President & General Manager, Kids WB! on the CW
Rick Mater, Senior Vice President, Broadcast Standards
Eric Cardinal, Sr. V.P., Research, Senior Vice President, Research
Elizabeth Tumulty, Senior Vice President, Network Distribution
Jennifer Bresnan, Senior Vice President, Alternative Programming
Rich Vokulich, Senior Vice President, Business Affairs
Gaye Hirsch, Vice President, Current Programming
Kevin Levy, Vice President, Program Planning & Scheduling
Joanna Klein, Vice President, Drama Development
Operating hours/week: 30.
Began: September 20, 2006.
Ownership: CBS & Warner Brothers Entertainment.

CYRTV (CHINESE YELLOW RIVER TV) — See KyLinTV.
Programming: Offers programs in Mandarin Chinese which informs and teaches the viewer about Chinese culture.
Began: June 1, 2004, Date shown is of launch in America. Service began in China in 1991.

DALLAS COWBOYS CHANNEL
c/o Comcast Corp.
1500 Market St
Philadelphia, PA 19102
Phone: 215-665-1700
Web Site: http://www.dallascowboys.com
Type of service: Video on demand.
Operating hours/week: 168.
Operating areas: Comcast markets in Texas, Arkansas, New Mexico, Arizona, California.
Programming: Original programming including broadcasts of coach's news conferences & a nightly news show covering practices, player interviews & more.
Began: September 8, 2004.
Total subscribers: 1,300,000.
Ownership: Comcast Corp.

DATING ON DEMAND
1500 Market St
36th Fl E
Philadelphia, PA 19102
Phone: 215-665-1700
Web Site: http://www.datingondemand.com
Page Thompson, Vice President & General Manager, On Demand Programming
Type of service: Digital, video on demand.

Programming: On demand dating profiles.
Began: February 14, 2005.
Distribution method: Available to cable systems.

DAYSTAR TV NETWORK
PO Box 612066
Dallas, TX 75261-2066
Phone: 817-571-7458
Fax: 817-571-1229
E-mail: comments@daystar.com
Web Site: http://www.daystar.com
Marcus Lamb, Founder
Joni Lamb, Founder
Janice Smith, Vice President, Programming
Steve Wilhite, Regional Director, Affiliate Relations
Type of service: Basic, broadband, video on demand & mobile.
Operating hours/week: 168.
Programming: Contemporary, interdenominational, multi-cultural blend of Christian ministry & family-friendly programming including talk-shows, national ministries, children's programming & faith-based original series.
Began: December 31, 1997.
Total subscribers: 60,000,000.
Distribution method: Cable, satellite & broadcast.

DE PELICULA — See Televisa Networks.
E-mail: depelicula@televisanetworks.tv
Programming: Contemporary & classic latin movies.
Began: May 1, 2003, U.S. launch.
Total subscribers: 1,700,000.
Ownership: TuTv, joint venture between Univision & Televisa.

DE PELICULA CLASICO — See Televisa Networks.
E-mail: depeliculaclasico@televisanetworks.tv
Programming: Classic latin movies.
Began: May 1, 2003, U.S. launch.
Total subscribers: 1,600,000.
Ownership: TuTv, joint venture between Univision & Televisa.

DEEP DISH TV
339 Lafayette St
New York, NY 10012
Phone: 212-473-8933
Fax: 212-420-8332
E-mail: deepdish@igc.org
Web Site: http://www.deepdishtv.org
Ron Davis, Chairman
Tom Poole, Vice President
Dee Dee Halleck, Development Coordinator
Type of service: Basic.
Operating hours/week: Varies.
Programming: Non-profit distributor of educational, social activist & arts programming linking independent producers, programmers & community-based activists.
Began: January 1, 1986.
Means of Support: Donations.

THE DENVER CHANNEL - KMGH
123 Speer Blvd
Denver, CO 80203-3417
Phone: 303-832-7777
Fax: 303-832-0119
Web Site: http://www.thedenverchannel.com
Byron Grandy, Vice President & General Manager

DESTINY CHANNEL
140 Broadway
New York, NY 10005
Web Site: http://www.destinychannel.com
Judith Tolkow, Senior Vice President, Programming
David Lenik, Vice President, Production & Network Operations
Type of service: Digital basic.
Operating hours/week: 168.
Programming: Ethics & value-based contemporary content aimed at viewers age 18-34; original programming, films, documentaries & off-network series.
Began: January 1, 2004.

DEUTSCHE WELLE TV
Washington Bureau
2000 M St, Ste 335
Washington, DC 20036
Phone: 202-785-5730
Fax: 202-785-5735
E-mail: news@dwelle-usa.com
Web Site: http://www.dw-world.de/english
Rudiger Lentz, Information Contact
Udo Bauer, Information Contact
Larz LaComa, Chief Engineer
Satellites: GE-1, transponder 22; Intelsat K, transponder 1; PAS-5 (digital), transponder 15 C.
Operating hours/week: 168.
Uplink: Berlin, Germany.
Programming: Current affairs television in English, German & Spanish.
Began: September 1, 1991.
Distribution method: Available to home dish audiences & cable systems.
Ownership: DW-TV.

DIRECT SHOPPING NETWORK
1239 Glendale Ave
Glendale, CA 91205
Phone: 800-818-4376
Fax: 818-550-6111
Web Site: http://www.dsntv.com
Programming: Viewers can purchase gems, jewelry, art, sports media directly from the source.
Began: November 1, 2001.
Total subscribers: 22,000,000.
Distribution method: Satellite.

DIRECT TO YOU
36 Victoria St.
Toronto, ON M5C 1H3
Canada
Phone: 416-864-2212
Fax: 416-864-2220
William Cowan, Sales Director
Jennifer Kochan, Sales Administrator
Type of service: Basic.
Operating hours/week: 168.
Programming: Canadian infomercial service.
Distribution method: Available to cable systems.

DIRECTV CINEMA 3D
2230 E Imperial Hwy
El Segundo, CA 90245
Phone: 310-964-5000
Web Site: http://www.directv.com/3D
Derek Chang, Executive Vice President, Content Strategy & Development
Steven Roberts, Senior Vice President, New Media & Business Development
Type of service: Basic.
Operating areas: Available nationwide.
Programming: 3D movie channel.
Began: July 1, 2010.
Distribution method: Available to home dish audiences.
Ownership: DirecTV.

DISCOVERY CHANNEL
One Discovery Pl
Silver Spring, MD 20910-3354
Phone: 240-662-2000
Web Site: http://dsc.discovery.com
John S. Hendricks, Founder & Chairman
David Zaslav, President & Chief Executive Officer
Peter Liguori, Chief Operating Officer
Eileen O'Neill, Group President, Discovery & TLC Networks
Mark Hollinger, President & Chief Executive Officer, Discovery Networks International
W. Clark Bunting, President & General Manager, Discovery Channel & President, Science Channel
Tom Cosgrove, President & General Manager, Discovery & IMAX 3D Network
Marjorie Kaplan, President, Animal Planet & Science Networks
Laura Michalchyshyn, President & General Manager, Planet Green & FitTV
Henry Schlieff, President & General Manager, Emerging Networks
Edward Sabin, Chief Operating Officer, Discovery & TLC Networks
Bruce Campbell, Chief Development Officer & General Counsel
Kelly Day, Chief Operating Officer, Digital Media & Commerce
Lori McFarling, Chief Marketing Officer, Discovery Education & Domestic Distribution
Ivan Bargueiras, General Manager, US Hispanic Group
Deborah Adler Myers, General Manager, Science Channel
Amy Winter, General Manager & Executive Vice President, TLC
Joe Abruzzese, President, Advertising Sales
Bill Goodwyn, President, Global Distribution, Discovery Communications & Chief Executive Officer, Discovery Education
Carole Tomko, President, Discovery Studios
Adria Alpert-Romm, Senior Executive Vice President, Human Resources & Administration
Lee Bartlett, Executive Vice President, Global Production Management, Business & Legal Affairs
Doug Coblens, Executive Vice President, Business Strategy & New Media
Nancy Daniels, Executive Vice President-Production & Development
Dee Forbes, Executive Vice President & Managing Director, Discovery Networks UK
Joshua Freeman, Executive Vice President, Digital Media
Laurie Goldberg, Executive Vice President, Public Relations, Discovery & TLC Networks
John Honeycutt, Executive Vice President, Head of International Business Operations, Discovery Networks International
Clara Kim, Executive Vice President, Business Affairs
David Leavy, Executive Vice President, Corporate Affairs, Global Communications & Government Relations
Wonya Lucas, Executive Vice President & Chief Operating Officer, Discovery Channel & Science Channel
Glenn Oakley, Executive Vice President, Media Technology, Production & Operations
Luis Silberwasser, Executive Vice President & Chief Content Officer, Production & Development, Discovery Networks International
Marina Anglim, Senior Vice President, Marketing, Discovery & Science Channels
Kevin Bennett, Senior Vice President, Programming
Michael Bremer, Senior Vice President, Chief Financial & Operating Officer, Discovery Networks Latin America
Camilla Carpenter, Senior Vice President, Strategy & Network Operations
Denise Contis, Senior Vice President, Production & Development
Deena Edwards, Senior Vice President, Integrated Content, Discovery & Science Channels
Jocelyn Egan, Senior Vice President, Discovery Solutions
Elisa Freeman, Senior Vice President, Global Distribution & Education Business Development
Michelina Gauthier, Senior Vice President, Talent Business & Legal Affairs
Ed Hersh, Senior Vice President, Startegic Planning, Investigation Discovery
Elizabeth Hillman, Senior Vice President, International Communications
Rob Jacobson, Senior Vice President, Marketing, Planet Green
Maria Kennedy, Senior Vice President, Advertising Sales, Direct Response
Scott Kinney, Senior Vice President, Global Professional Development, Policy & Education Research
Meg Lowe, Senior Vice President, Domestic Distribution
Steve McGowan, Senior Vice President, Research
Stephen Reverend, Senior Vice President, Development & Production for Specials & Events
Guhan Selvaretnam, Senior Vice President, Product, Content & Operations, Discovery Digital Media
Chris Shaw, Senior Vice President, Commercial Development, Discovery Networks International
Robert Voltaggio, Senior Vice President, National Ad Sales & Planning

Branch Office:
LOS ANGELES: 1801 Century Park E, Ste 1430, Los Angeles, CA 90067. Phone: 310-551-1611. Fax: 310-551-1684.
Type of service: Basic.
Satellites: GE Satcom C-4, transponder 21 (east coast); Galaxy V, transponder 12 (west coast).
Operating hours/week: 168.
Uplink: Stamford, CT.
Programming: Non-fiction entertainment covering nature, science & technology, history, adventure & world cultures.
Began: June 17, 1985.
Means of Support: Advertising & subscriber fees.
Total subscribers: 101,000,000.
Distribution method: Available to home dish audiences & cable systems.
Scrambled signal: Yes. Equipment: VideoCipher II; VideoCipher II Plus.
Ownership: Discovery Communications Inc. DCI ownership: Liberty Media, 66%; Advance/Newhouse, 31%; John Hendricks, 1%.

DISCOVERY CHANNEL AFRICA
160 Great Portland St
London W1M 9AB
England
Phone: 44-171-631-1556
Fax: 44-171-631-1558
Satellites: Galaxy 803.
Operating hours/week: 168.
Programming: History, science & technology, human adventure, nature & world culture. Available in 38 Sub-Saharan African countries & Indian Ocean Islands.
Began: January 1, 1996.
Ownership: Discovery Communications Inc.

DISCOVERY CHANNEL ASIA
3 Changi Business Park Vista
#03-00

Singapore 486051
Phone: 65-6510-7500
Fax: 65-548-0598
Tom Keaveny, Executive Vice President & Managing Director, Asia
Satellites: Intelsat 2.
Operating hours/week: 168.
Programming: Available in American Samoa, Atrio Island, Bangladesh, Brunei, China, Fiji, Guam, Hong Kong, Indonesia, Japan, Korea, Macau, Malaysia, Mariana Islands, Marshall Islands, Micronesia, Naura, Palau, Philippines, Papua New Guinea, Singapore, Tahiti, Taiwan, Thailand, & Vietnam.
Began: January 1, 1994.
Total subscribers: 22,000,000 (includes subscribers in Europe, Africa & Middle East).
Scrambled signal: Yes.
Ownership: Discovery Communications Inc.

DISCOVERY CHANNEL AUSTRALIA

117 Harris St
Pyrmont
Sydney, NSW 2009
Australia
Fax: 61-2-9552-2029
Greg Ricca, President & Chief Executive Officer, International Networks
Satellites: Intelsat 2.
Operating hours/week: 168.
Programming: History, science & technology, human adventure, nature & world culture. Available in Australia & New Zealand.
Began: September 1, 1995.
Ownership: Discovery Communications Inc.

DISCOVERY CHANNEL BRAZIL

6505 Blue Lagoon Dr
Miami, FL 33126
Phone: 305-507-1700
Fax: 305-507-1560
Enrique Martinez, Executive Vice President & Managing Director, Latin America
Type of service: Basic.
Satellites: Intelsat III; Pas, transponder 5.
Operating hours/week: 168.
Programming: Programs on science, technology, nature & human adventure; world culture documentaries dubbed in Portuguese.
Began: April 1, 1996.
Ownership: Discovery Communications Inc.

DISCOVERY CHANNEL BEYOND —

See Discovery Channel.
Type of service: Broadband.
Began: April 15, 2006.

DISCOVERY CHANNEL CANADA

9 Channel Nine Ct
Scarborough, ON M4A 2M9
Canada
Phone: 416-332-5000
E-mail: comments@discoverycivilization.ca
Web Site: http://www.discoverychannel.ca
John Hendricks, Chairman & Founder
Trina McQueen, President & General Manager, DSC-Canada
Greg Ricca, President & Chief Executive Officer, Discovery Networks International
Domenick Fioravanti, Senior Vice President, Discovery Networks International
Ken Murphy, Vice President, Production & Administration
Meg Pinto, Vice President, Marketing
Steve Rayment, Senior Manager, Advertising & Communications
Type of service: Basic.
Satellites: Anik E-2.
Operating hours/week: 168.
Programming: Science & technology, human adventure, nature.
Began: January 1, 1995.
Total subscribers: 4,400,000.
Distribution method: Available to cable systems.
Ownership: NetStar Communications Inc., 80% & Discovery Communications Inc., 20%.

DISCOVERY CHANNEL EUROPE

160 Great Portland St
London N1W 9AB
England
Phone: 011-44-171-631-1556
Fax: 011-44-171-631-1558
Joyce Taylor, Managing Director, Discovery Communications Inc. Europe
Nick Comer-Calder, General Manager, Discovery Networks Europe
Chris Abel, Senior Vice President, Marketing
Helen Gladwell, Vice President, Business Affairs & Programming Legal
Chris Haws, Vice President, Commissions, Co-Production & Production
Elizabeth Timms, Public Relations Manager
Satellites: Astra 1-C, transponder 41H; Eutelsat Hotbird 1; Galaxy 601.
Programming: Available in Croatia, Czech Republic, Denmark, Estonia, Finland, Hungary, Iceland, Ireland, Latvia, Luxembourg, The Netherlands, Norway, Poland, Romania, Russia, Slovakia, Sweden, & the United Kingdom.
Began: April 1, 1989.
Total subscribers: 84,000,000.
Distribution method: Available to home dish audiences & cable systems.
Scrambled signal: Yes.
Ownership: Discovery Communications Inc.

DISCOVERY CHANNEL GERMANY

Twyman House
16 Bonny St
London NW1 9PG
England
Fax: 44-171-911-0189
John Hendricks, Founder & Chairman
Greg Ricca, President & Chief Executive Officer, Discovery Networks International
Joyce Taylor, Managing Director, Discovery Communications Europe
Nick Comer-Calder, General Manager, Discovery Networks Europe
Alexander Trauttmansdorff-Weinsberg, Head, Digital Programming, Discovery Channel Germany
Patrick Horl, Head, Programming Discovery Channel Germany
Cornelia Kunze, Marketing Director, Discovery Channel Germany
Type of service: Basic.
Satellites: Astra, transponder 81.
Operating hours/week: 168.
Programming: Programs on nature, history, science, technology & human adventure; world culture documentaries dubbed in German.
Began: July 1, 1996.
Distribution method: Available to cable systems & home dish audiences.
Ownership: Discovery Communications Inc. & Kirch Group.

DISCOVERY CHANNEL HD — See Discovery Channel.

DISCOVERY CHANNEL INDIA

Gopal Das Bldg
28 Barakhamba Rd, 9th Fl
New Delhi 110 001
India
Phone: 91-11-332-9812
Fax: 91-11-332-7891
John Hendricks, Chairman & Founder
Deepak Shourie, Executive Vice President & Managing Director, India
Greg Ricca, President & Chief Executive Officer, Discovery Networks International
Satellites: Intelsat IV.
Operating hours/week: 168.
Programming: History, science & technology, human adventure, wildlife & environment, nature & world culture. Currently available in English with programming blocks dubbed into Hindi.
Began: August 1, 1995.
Total subscribers: 3,000,000.
Ownership: Discovery Communications Inc.

DISCOVERY CHANNEL ITALY

160 Great Portland St
London W1M 9AB
England
Phone: 011-44-171-631-1556
Fax: 011-44-171-631-1558
John Hendricks, Chairman & Founder
Nick Comer-Calder, General Manager, Discovery Networks Europe
Greg Ricca, President & Chief Executive Officer, Discovery Networks International
Satellites: Hotbird I.
Operating hours/week: 168.
Programming: History, science & technology, human adventure, nature & world culture, dubbed in Italian. Available in Italy, Malta, San Marino & Vatican City.
Began: January 1, 1996.
Distribution method: Available to home dish audiences by Telepiu, provider of DSTv direct to home service.
Ownership: Discovery Communications Inc.

DISCOVERY CHANNEL JAPAN

20 Loyang Crescent
50894
Singapore
Phone: 65-548-0588
Fax: 65-548-0598
E-mail: info@discovery.co.jp
John Hendricks, Founder & Chairman
Greg Ricca, President & Chief Executive Officer, Discovery Networks International
Type of service: Basic.
Satellites: JCSat III; TopPas II.
Operating hours/week: 168.
Programming: Documentaries in the genres of nature, history, science, technology, world culture & human adventure with Japanese subtitles.
Began: January 1, 1997.
Distribution method: Available to cable systems & home dish audiences.
Ownership: Discovery Communications Inc.

DISCOVERY CHANNEL MIDDLE EAST

One Discovery Place
Silver Spring, MD 20910-3354
Phone: 240-662-2000
John Hendricks, Chairman & Founder
Greg Ricca, President & Chief Executive Officer, Discovery Networks International
Operating hours/week: 168.
Programming: History, science & technology, human adventure, nature & world culture. Available in Algeria, Bahrain, Chad, Djibouti, Egypt, Iran, Israel, Jordan, Kuwait, Lebanon, Libya, Mauritania, Morocco, Oman, Qatar, Saudi Arabia, Somalia, Sudan, Syria, Tunisia, United Arab Emirates & Yemen.
Began: May 1, 1994.
Ownership: Discovery Communications Inc.

DISCOVERY DIGITAL NETWORKS —

See Discovery Channel.
Programming: Suite is comprised of Science, Planet Green, Military Channel & Discovery en Espanol.
Scrambled signal: Yes.

DISCOVERY EN ESPANOL

6505 Blue Lagoon Dr
Ste 190
Miami, FL 33126
Phone: 786-273-4700
Fax: 786-273-4860
E-mail: Luis_Silberwasser@discovery.com
Web Site: http://www.discovery.com
John Hendricks, Founder & Chairman
Greg Ricca, President & Chief Executive Officer, Discovery Networks International
Enrique Martinez, Executive Vice President & Managing Director, Latin America
Ivan Bargueiras, Senior Vice President, Advertising Sales, Discovery Networks Latin America & General Manager, US Hispanic Networks
Satellites: PanAmSat III; Morclas II; HispaSat; PAS-5.
Operating hours/week: 168.
Programming: Spanish language version of the Discovery Channel, currently available to subscribers in Argentina, Aruba, Bolivia, Brazil, Chile, Colombia, Costa Rica, Dominican Republic, Ecuador, El Salvador, Grand Cayman, Guatemala, Haiti, Honduras, Mexico, Nicaragua, Panana, Paraguay, Peru, Puerto Rico, St. Lucia, Tobago, Trinidad, Uruguay & Venezuela.
Began: February 1, 1994, U.S. launch, June 1998.
Total subscribers: 5,000,000.
Scrambled signal: Yes.
Ownership: Discovery Communications Inc.

DISCOVERY FAMILIA — See Discovery en Espanol.

Web Site: http://www.discoveryfamilia.com
Programming: Spanish language children's programming; lifestyle, food, travel, health & parenting shows.
Began: September 1, 2007.
Total subscribers: 3,000,000.
Scrambled signal: Yes.

DISCOVERY FIT & HEALTH — See Discovery Channel.

Web Site: http://health.discovery.com/
Laura Michalchyshyn, President & General Manager
Programming: Includes forensic mysteries, medical stories, emergency room dramas, baby and pregnancy programming, parenting challenges, and stories of extreme life conditions plus premiere series and specials.

Began: February 1, 2011, as Discovery Fit & Health. Launched January 1, 2003 as FitTV.
Total subscribers: 50,000,000.
Scrambled signal: Yes.

HD THEATER — See Discovery Channel.
Web Site: http://dhd.discovery.com/
Henry S Schleiff, President & General Manager
Type of service: Available to cable systems.
Programming: Brings viewers the wonders of the natural world, explorations of space & beyond, the mysteries of science & world cultures in HD quality. To be rebranded as Velocity in late 2011.
Began: June 1, 2002.
Total subscribers: 36,000,000.
Scrambled signal: Yes.

DISCOVERY HEALTH CHANNEL — See OWN: Oprah Winfrey Network
Web Site: http://health.discovery.com
Replaced on January 1, 2011 by OWN: Oprah Winfrey Network, see listing.

DISCOVERY HEALTH ON CALL — See Discovery Channel.
Type of service: Video on demand.
Programming: Short programs on diet, exercise, disease & conditions.
Began: October 1, 2006.

DISCOVERY HOME CHANNEL — Now Planet Green. See Discovery Channel.

DISCOVERY KIDS CHANNEL — See The Hub.
Began: October 1, 1996, Service rebranded as The Hub October 10, 2010, see listing.

DISCOVERY KIDS EN ESPANOL — See Discovery en Espanol.
John Hendricks, Founder, Chairman & Chief Executive Officer
Donald Wear, Jr., President, Discovery Networks International
Dawn McCall, Senior Vice President & General Manager
Rick Rodriguez, Vice President, Programming
Henry Martinez, Vice President, Affiliate Sales
Cathleen Pratt, Vice President, Advertising Sales
Rosemary Ravinal, Director, Communications
Type of service: Basic.
Satellites: Intelat III; Morelos II.
Operating hours/week: 168.
Operating areas: Available in Central & South America & the Caribbean.
Programming: Spanish & Portuguese dubbed educational programs targeted at children of all ages presented in innovative & creative formats.
Began: June 17, 2005.
Ownership: Discovery Communications Inc.

DISCOVERY KIDS CHANNEL HD — See The Hub

DISCOVERY TIMES CHANNEL — Now ID Investigation Discovery. See Discovery Channel.
Began: January 1, 1996, re-launched 2003 & again on January 27, 2008 as ID Investigation Discovery.
Total subscribers: 73,000,000.

DISCOVERY TRAVEL & LIVING (VIAJAR Y VIVIR)
Discovery U.S. Hispanic Networks Group
6505 Blue Lagoon Dr, Ste 190
Miami, FL 33126
Phone: 786-273-4700
Fax: 786-273-4860
E-mail: l_silberwasser@discovery.com
Luis Silberwasser, Senior Vice President & General Manager, U.S. Hispanic Networks
Began: June 17, 2005.

DISNEY CHANNEL
500 S Buena Vista St
Burbank, CA 91521
Phone: 818-569-7500
E-mail: dlr.media.relations@disney.com
Web Site: http://www.disneychannel.com
Robert A. Iger, President & Chief Executive Officer, Walt Disney Co.
Andy Bird, President, Walt Disney International
Carolina Lightcap, President, Disney Channels Worldwide
Ben Pyne, President, Disney/ESPN Affiliate Sales & Marketing
Rich Ross, Chairman, Walt Disney Studios
George W. Bodenheimer, Co-Chairman, Disney Media Networks
Anne Sweeney, Co-Chairman, Media Networks, Walt Disney Co. & President, Disney-ABC TV Group
Gary Marsh, Chief Creative Officer, Disney Channel Worldwide
Rita Ferro, Executive Vice President, Disney Media Sales & Marketing
Zenia Mucha, Executive Vice President, Corporate Communications, Walt Disney Co.
Preston Padden, Executive Vice President, Special Projects, Walt Disney Co.
Richard Bates, Senior Vice President, Government Relations
Adam Bonnett, Senior Vice President, Original Series
Sean Cocchia, Senior Vice President, General Manager, Radio Disney
Eric Coleman, Senior Vice President, Development
Scott Garner, Senior Vice President, Programming
Nancy Kanter, Senior Vice President, Programming & General Manager, Disney Junior Worldwide
Richard Loomis, Senior Vice President, Marketing & Creative
Susan O'Day, Senior Vice President, Chief Information Officer
Fonda Poston, Senior Vice President, Operations
John M. Renfro, Senior Vice President & Chief Human Resources Officer, Walt Disney Co.
Thomas O. Staggs, Senior Executive Vice President & Chief Financial Officer, Walt Disney Co.
Mark L Walker, Senior Vice President, Disney.com

Affiliate Sales Offices:
CENTRAL: 401 N Michigan Ave, Ste 2000, Chicago, IL 60611. Phone: 312-595-7600.

EASTERN: 500 Park Ave, 7th Floor, New York, NY 10022. Phone: 212-735-5380.

SOUTHEASTERN: 3343 Peachtree Rd NE, East Tower, Ste 600, Atlanta, GA 30326. Phone: 404-262-1227.

SOUTHWESTERN: 5080 Spectrum Dr, Ste 1210 West Tower, Dallas, TX 75248. Phone: 972-851-6000.
Type of service: Basic & pay.
Satellites: Galaxy I-R, transponder 7 (west coast); Galaxy V, transponder 1 (east coast).
Operating hours/week: 168.
Uplink: Burbank, CA.
Programming: Family-oriented programming, including original features, series & specials; acquisitions & Disney library classics.
Began: April 18, 1983.
Means of Support: System fees and advertsing revenue.
Total subscribers: 100,500,000.
Distribution method: Available to cable systems.
Equipment: VideoCipher II.
Ownership: The Walt Disney Co.

DISNEY CHANNEL HD — See Disney Channel.

DISNEY FAMILY MOVIES
500 S Buena Vista St
Burbank, CA 91521
Web Site: http://www.disneyabctv.com
Type of service: Video on demand.
Programming: Disney movies & short animated shows.
Began: N.A.
Distribution method: Available to cable systems.
Scrambled signal: Yes.
Ownership: Disney-ABC Domestic Television.

DISNEY JUNIOR
500 S Buena Vista St
Burbank, CA 91521
Phones: 818-569-7500; 818-569-7574
Web Site: http://disney.go.com/disneyjunior
Joe D'Ambrosia, Vice President, Programming
Type of service: Plans basic.
Operating hours/week: Plans 168.
Operating areas: Will be available nationwide.
Programming: Will offer programs for 2 to 7 year olds.
Scheduled to begin: Plans to launch as a separate channel in 2012. Originally launched February 14, 2011 as a segment on the Disney Channel.
Total subscribers: (Plans to reach 75,000,000 at launch.).
Distribution method: Will be available to cable systems.
Scrambled signal: Planned.
Ownership: Disney/ABC Cable Networks.

DISNEY TRAVEL ON DEMAND
3800 W Alameda Ave
Burbank, CA 91505
Phone: 818-569-7500
Web Site: http://disneyparks.disney.go.com/disneyparks/en_US/index?name=VideoOnDemandPage
Type of service: Digital.
Programming: Interactive, reality & special event shows focused on Disney destinations.
Began: May 1, 2007.
Total subscribers: 9,000,000.
Distribution method: Available to cable systems.

DISNEY XD
500 S Buena Vista St
Burbank, CA 91521
Phone: 818-569-7500
Web Site: http://disney.go.com/disneyxd/#/disneyxd/
Carolina Lightcap, President
David Levine, General Manager & Vice President, Programming
Dina Weinberg, Vice President, Media Relations

Sales Offices:
CENTRAL: 401 N Michigan Ave, Ste 2000, Chicago, IL 60611. Phone: 312-595-7600.

EASTERN: 500 Park Ave, 7th Floor, New York, NY 10022. Phone: 212-735-5380.

SOUTHEASTERN: 3343 Peachtree Rd NE, East Tower, Ste 600, Atlanta, GA 30326. Phone: 404-262-1227.

SOUTHWESTERN: 580 Spectrum Dr, West Tower, Ste 1210, Dallas, TX 75248. Phone: 972-851-6000.
Type of service: Basic.
Satellites: Galaxy VII, transponder 17.
Operating hours/week: 168.
Uplink: Burbank, CA.
Programming: Animated kids shows plus some live action programs and movies.
Began: April 18, 1998, Originally launched as Toon Disney, channel was relaunched as Disney XD February 13, 2009.
Means of Support: Subscriber fees.
Total subscribers: 78,000,000.
Distribution method: Available to cable systems.
Scrambled signal: Yes. Equipment: Available digitally.
Ownership: The Walt Disney Co.

DISNEY XD EN ESPANOL — See Disney XD.

DISNEY XD HD — See Disney XD.

DIVINE — No longer planned.

DIY NETWORK
9721 Sherrill Blvd
Knoxville, TN 37932
Phone: 865-694-2700
Fax: 865-985-7786
Web Site: http://www.diynetwork.com
Ross Babbit, Senior Vice President, Programming Partnerships
Shannon Jamieson Driver, Vice President, Consumer Marketing
Peter Moore, Vice President, Creative Services
Julie Taylor, Vice President, Program Planning
Andy Singer, General Manager
Kent Takano, Executive Producer, Branded Entertainment
Danny Tepper, Programming Director
Dale Robinson, Programming Director
Steven Lerner, Programming Director
Brandii Toby-Leon, Press & Public Relations Director

Branch Office:
NEW YORK: 1180 Avenue of the Americas, New York, NY 10036. Phone: 212-549-4488. Fax: 212-398-9319.
Type of service: Digital basic.
Satellites: Galaxy I-R, transponder 20.
Operating hours/week: 168.
Uplink: Knoxville.
Programming: DIY Network, from the makers of HGTV and Food Network, is the go-to destination for rip-up, knock-out home improvement television. DIY Networks programs and experts answer the most sought-after questions and offer creative projects for do-it-yourself enthusiasts. One of the fastest growing digital networks and currently in more than 53 million homes, DIY Network's programming covers a broad range of categories, including home improvement and landscaping. The network's award-winning website, www.DIYnetwork.com, is a leader in the Nielsen Online Home and Garden category and features multiple resources, including thousands of do-it-yourself home improvement projects, expert advice, how-to videos and images, and user-friendly reference guides with step-by-step instructions.
Began: September 30, 1999.
Means of Support: Advertising & subscriber fees.
Total subscribers: 53,000,000.
Distribution method: Available to cable systems & home dish audiences.
Scrambled signal: Yes.
Ownership: Scripps Networks Interactive.

DIY NETWORK HD — See DIY Network.

DMTV7
400 Robert D Ray Dr
Des Moines, IA 50309
Phone: 515-283-4795
E-mail: pio@dmgov.org
Web Site: https://www.dmgov.org
Total subscribers: 125,000.

DMX CANADA — See DMX Music.
Type of service: Audio.
Operating hours/week: 168.
Programming: 30 channel music service; 15 programmed in Canada, the rest by DMX in Los Angeles, CA.
Began: May 1, 1997.
Means of Support: Subscribers & subscription fees.
Scrambled signal: Yes.
Ownership: Capstar Inc.

DMX MUSIC
1703 W 5th St
Ste 600
Austin, TX 78701
Phone: 512-380-8500
Fax: 512-380-8501
E-mail: info@dmx.com
Web Site: http://www.dmx.com
R. Steven Hicks, Chairman
John D. Cullen, Chief Executive Officer
Paul D. Stone, President
Kimberly K. Shipman, Chief Financial Officer
Tim Seaton, Chief Operating Officer

Branch Offices:
ATLANTA: 3170 Reps Miller Rd, Ste 100, Norcross, GA 30071. Phone: 770-225-2500. Fax: 770-246-3941.

BOSTON: 77 4th Ave, 5th Fl, Waltham, MA 02451. Phone: 508-393-2591. Fax: 508-393-5137.

CHICAGO: 620 Enterprise Dr, Oak Brook, IL 60523. Phones: 847-930-3100; 800-640-2673. Fax: 847-930-3140.

LOS ANGELES: 11150 W Olympic Blvd, Ste 770, Los Angeles, CA 90064. Phones: 310-575-3185; 800-345-5000.

MIAMI: Latin American Offices, 1550 Biscayne Blvd, Miami, FL 33132. Phone: 305-894-2576. Fax: 305-894-4919. E-Mail: gustavo.tonelli@dmx.com.

SEATTLE: 411 First Ave S, Ste 501, Seattle, WA 98104. Phones: 206-329-1400; 800-345-5000. Fax: 206-329-9952.

BRAZIL: Rua dos Bombeiros, 40, CP 04001-100 -Ibriapuera, Sao Paulo, Jardim Paulista 0424-001, Brazil. Phone: 55-11-3884-0150. Fax: 55-11-3457-0653. E-Mail: atendimento@dmxmusic.com.br. Web site: http://dmxmusic.com.br.

CANADA: 7260 12th St SE, Ste 120, Calgary, AB T2H 2S5, Canada. Phones: 403-640-8525; 800-350-0369. Fax: 888-823-0369. E-Mail: dmx.canada@dmx.com. Web site: http://www.dmx.com.

SOUTH AFRICA: Ground Floor Sandown Mews E, 88 Stella St., Sandown, Johannesburg, South Africa. Phone: 27-11-780-3000. Fax: 27-11-780-3001. E-Mail: info@dmx.co.za. Web site: http://http://www.dmx.co.za.
Type of service: Audio.
Satellites: Telstar 402-R; HITS; TVN; TDRSS; Galaxy 605.
Operating hours/week: 168.
Programming: Digital music service offering more than 100 channels of different music formats with on-screen song, artist, & album information.
Total subscribers: 11,000,000.
Distribution method: Available to homes via digital cable, analog cable & direct-to-home via satellite.
Equipment: Scientific-Atlanta; Comstream.
Ownership: Capstar Partners.
Division of DMX Inc.; provides sensory branding, including music design, new media, messaging & scent.

DOCU TVE
Web Site: http://www.rtve.es
Programming: Documentaries, biographies & travel shows.
Began: January 1, 1999, Reflects U.S. launch.
Total subscribers: 700,000 (Reflects U.S. subscribers).
Ownership: RTVE.

DOCUMENTARY CHANNEL
142 8th Ave N
Nashville, TN 37203-3706
Phone: 615-514-2110
Fax: 615-514-2111
E-mail: inquiry@documentarychannel.com
Web Site: http://www.documentarychannel.com
John D. Forbess, Co-Founder
Thomas L. Neff, Co-Founder & Chief Creative Officer
James Ackerman, Chief Executive Officer
Jay Kelley, Senior Vice President, Marketing & Business Development
Robert Edney, Vice President, Advertising Sales
Suzanne Holmes, Program Acquisitions
Type of service: Digital basic.
Operating hours/week: 168.

Programming: Showcase of innovative work of independent, worldwide filmmakers.
Began: January 1, 2006.
Means of Support: Advertising & subscriber fees.
Total subscribers: 26,000,000.
Distribution method: Available to cable & satellite subscribers.
Ownership: Private.

DODGERS ON DEMAND
c/o Time Warner Cable
4344 Eagle Rock Blvd
Los Angeles, CA 90041-3211
Phone: 323-258-3252
Fax: 323-255-1901
Operating areas: California.
Programming: Archived & new programming including game highlights, charity events & press conferences.
Began: August 9, 2006.
Total subscribers: 1,900,000.
Distribution method: Available to cable systems.
Ownership: Time Warner & Los Angeles Dodgers.

DIY NETWORK ON DEMAND — See DIY Network.
Type of service: Video on demand.

DOLPHINS TELEVISION NETWORK
7500 SW 30th St
Davie, FL 33314
Phone: 954-452-7000
Web Site: http://www.miamidolphins.com/esp/news
Jim Rushton, Senior Vice President, Integrated Media & Corporate Partnerships
Bob Lynch, Vice President, Integrated Media Sales
Wayne Partello, Senior Director, Content & Creative
Type of service: Basic.
Operating areas: Southeast, southwest & central Florida.
Programming: Offering detailed and expanded coverage of Miami Dolphins football. Includes expanded preseason coverage plus pre- and post- game analysis. Programming will be in HD and in English and Spanish.
Began: August 13, 2010.
Means of Support: Advertising.
Distribution method: Available to cable subscribers.
Scrambled signal: Yes.
Ownership: MimaimDolphins.

DOMINION SKY ANGEL
3050 N Horseshoe Dr
Ste 290
Naples, FL 34104-7910
Phones: 239-403-9130; 800-759-2643
Web Site: http://www.skyangel.com
Nancy Christopher, Vice President, Public Relations
Operating hours/week: 168.
Programming: Featuring all different ministry styles, program types & Christ-centered denominations.
Began: January 1, 1981.
Distribution method: Satellite.

.2 NETWORK
3948 Townsfair Way
Ste 220
Columbus, OH 43219
Phone: 614-416-6080
Web Site: http://www.dot2network.com
Richard Schilg, Chief Executive Officer
Lee Leddy, Senior Vice President, Network Sales
Marlynda Salas Lecate, Vice President, Network Sales
J. Stuart Stringfellow, Network Sales Consultant & Affiliate Relations Manager
Type of service: Digital.
Operating hours/week: Plans 168.
Programming: Plans movies, original shows, popular television series, children's & lifestyle shows. Also will allow for customizable, local traffic, news, weather & public interest programming.
Distribution method: Will be available to broadcasters & cable systems.
Scrambled signal: Yes.
Ownership: Guardian Enterprise Group Inc.

DRAGONTV
Phone: 877-372-4668
E-mail: support@dragontv.net
Web Site: http://www.dragontv.net
Operating hours/week: 168.
Operating areas: California.
Programming: Combines content from seven Chinese language channels, including: SET International, CTTV ET News, CTTV ET Drama, CTTV ET Global, CTTV ET China, Yo ET YoYo & CTTV4.
Began: October 29, 2003.
Distribution method: Available to Comcast cable subscribers.
Ownership: VideoJump Inc.

DREAM TELEVISION NETWORK
9300 Georgia Ave
Ste 206
Silver Spring, MD 20910
Phone: 301-587-0000
Fax: 301-587-7464
E-mail: draaj@thedreamnetwork.com
Web Site: http://www.thedreamnetwork.com
Dr. Alvin Augustus Jones, President
Randall Williams, Chief Operating Officer
Matt Anderson, Programming Director
Don Kooy, Marketing Director

Branch Offices:
WILLMAR: 2305 62nd St SW, Willmar, MN 56201.

OXFORD: 601 Henderson St, Oxford, NC 27565.

HOLLYWOOD PARK: 326 Sterling Browning Dr, Hollywood Park, TX 78232.
Type of service: Basic.
Satellites: GE 4, transponder 21.
Operating hours/week: 168.
Programming: Urban family programming.
Began: November 4, 1994.
Means of Support: Advertising.

Total subscribers: 37,000,000.
Distribution method: Available to cable systems.
Ownership: Brohein Group LLC.

DRIVE-IN CLASSICS

299 Queen St W
Toronto, ON M5V 2Z5
Canada
Phone: 416-591-7400
Fax: 416-591-0080
E-mail: driveinclassics@driveinclassics.ca
Web Site: http://www.driveinclassics.ca
Type of service: Digital.
Operating hours/week: 168.
Programming: Movies from the 50s, 60s & 70s.
Began: September 7, 2001.

DRIVERTV

435 Hudson St, 6th Fl
New York, NY 10014
Phone: 212-462-1630
E-mail: info@drivertv.com
Web Site: http://www.drivertv.com
Jan Renner, Founder & Chief Executive Officer
Adam Weiner, Chief Operating Officer
Type of service: Video on demand, broadband.
Programming: Research & comparison shopping for automobiles by brand, category or budget.
Began: November 1, 2005.
Total subscribers: 20,000,000.
Distribution method: Available to cable systems.
Scrambled signal: Yes.
Ownership: Radical Media, NBCUniversal LLC (minority interest, 6.5%).

DUBAI TV

PO Box 835
Dubai
UAE
Phone: 971-4-336-9999
Fax: 971-4-336-0060
E-mail: info@dmi.ae
Web Site: http://www.dubaitv.gov.ae
Programming: Arabic-language programming.
Began: June 1, 2004, formerly Emirates Dubai Television.
Distribution method: Available to satellite providers.
Ownership: Dubai Media Inc.

E! ENTERTAINMENT TELEVISION HD — See E! Entertainment Television.

E! ENTERTAINMENT TELEVISION

5750 Wilshire Blvd
Los Angeles, CA 90036-3709
Phone: 323-954-2400
Fax: 323-954-2660
E-mail: amelia.stewart@nbcuni.com
Web Site: http://www.eonline.com
Bonnie Hammer, Chairman, NBC Universal Cable Entertainment & Universal Cable Studios
Suzanne Kolb, President
Steve Dolcemaschio, Chief Operating Officer
Jeff Mayzurk, Chief Technology Officer
Lisa Berger, President, Entertainment Programming
Kevin MacLellan, President, International Media Group & Entertainment Productions
Steve Blue, Executive Vice President, Production & Operations
Duccio Donati, Executive Vice President, International
Sheila Johnson, Executive Vice President, Business & Legal Affairs & General Counsel
Cyndi McClellan, Executive Vice President, Program Strategy & Research
John Najarian, Executive Vice President, Digital Media & Business Development
Bear Fisher, Senior Vice President & Creative Director, E! & Style
Sarah Goldstein, Senior Vice President, Media Relations & Corporate Communications
Eric Gray, Senior Vice President, Finance
Jay James, Senior Vice President, Development
Rob Magdlen, Senior Vice President, Program Planning & Acquisitions
Bruce Perlmutter, Senior Vice President, News & Online
Gary Snegaroff, Senior Vice President, Entertainment Studios
Annemarie Batur, Vice President, Marketing & Advertising
Damla Dogan, Vice President, Original Programming & Series Development

Cable Sales Office:
NEW YORK: 11 W 42nd St, New York, NY 10036.

Branch Offices:
HARTFORD: 10 Columbus Blvd, 8th Floor, Hartford, CT 06106.
Type of service: Linear TV, VOD, HD & mobile.
Satellites: AMC10, transponder C6; AMC11, transponder C8.
Operating hours/week: 168.
Programming: E! is television's top destination for all things entertainment & celebrity. E! is currently available to 97 million cable & satellite subscribers in the U.S. and the E! Everywhere initiative underscores the company's dedication to making E! content available on all new media platforms anytime and anywhere from online to broadband video to wireless to radio to VOD. Popular programming includes E! core franchises, E! News, The Soup, Chelsea Lately and Fashion Police as well as the network's hit series Keeping Up With The Kardashians, Kourtney & Khloe Take Miami, Kourtney & Kim Take New York, Kendra, and Holly's World. Additionally E!'s Live From The Red Carpet signature events keep fans connected to their favorite stars on Hollywood's biggest nights. E! is a network of NBCUniversal Cable Entertainment, a division of NBCUniversal, one of the world's leading media & entertainment companies in the development, production & marketing of entertainment, news & information to a global audience.
Began: June 1, 1990.
Means of Support: Advertising, affiliate sales & international sales.
Total subscribers: 97,000,000.
Distribution method: Available to cable & satellite providers.
Scrambled signal: Yes.
Ownership: NBCUniversal LLC.

EBRU TV

300 Franklin Sq Dr
Somerset, NJ 08873
Phone: 732-560-0800
Fax: 732-560-0801
E-mail: jon@ebru.tv
Web Site: http://www.ebru.tv
Adem Kalac, President & Chief Executive Officer
Jon Omural, Vice President, Business Development & Human Resources
Type of service: Basic.
Satellites: Galaxy 25.
Operating hours/week: 168.
Programming: Offers family oriented lifestyle and culture programming.
Began: November 1, 2006.
Distribution method: Available to cable systems.

ECOLOGY CABLE SERVICE

10763 Folkestone Way
Woodstock, MD 21163
Phone: 410-465-0480
Fax: 410-461-5840
E-mail: eric@ecology.com
Web Site: http://www.ecology.com
Eric McLamb, Founder & President
John H. Hoagland Jr., Vice President & Secretary
Shelley Duvall, Chairman & Chief Executive Officer
Ed Begley, Jr., Chairman, Environmental Advisory Board
Operating hours/week: 168.
Programming: Regional television service operating in affiliation with WETV-Canada. Environmental consumerism, lifestyles & news, home gardening & shopping, children's entertainment & environmental forums.
Began: May 1, 1997.
Scrambled signal: Yes.

ECUAVISIA INTERNACIONAL — See Alterna'TV.

Web Site: http://www.ecuavisa.com
Programming: News, telenovelas, comedy, travel, music, interviews, drama, lifestyle & general entertainment shows from Ecuador.
Ownership: Corporacion Ecuatoriana de Television.

ECUMENICAL TV CHANNEL

PO Box 430
Canfield, OH 44406-0430
Phone: 330-533-2243
E-mail: judyctny@aol.com
Web Site: http://www.doy.org
Bob Gavalier, General Manager
Type of service: Regional.
Operating hours/week: 168.
Operating areas: Northeastern Ohio & western Pennsylvania.
Programming: Educational & family-oriented format representing 13 religious denominations.
Began: January 1, 1985.
Total subscribers: 502,100.
Distribution method: Microwave to cable systems.
Ownership: Diocese of Youngstown.
Religious cable network

EDGETV — No longer planned.

EDUCATIONAL & ENTERTAINMENT NETWORK — No longer planned.

ELECTION CHANNEL

1000 Universal Studios Plaza
Bldg 22-A
Orlando, FL 32819
Phone: 407-224-6848
E-mail: info@electionchannel.com
Web Site: http://www.electionchannel.com
Michael Gerrity, Founder & Chairman
Type of service: Broadband.
Programming: Internet channel offering customized, on demand content from city, county, state or federal election candidates & their platforms.
Began: N.A.
Ownership: Multichannel Ventures Inc.

EMIRATES DUBAI TELEVISION — See Dubai TV.

EMPLOYMENT & CAREER CHANNEL

253 W 51st St
3rd Fl
New York, NY 10019
Phone: 212-445-0754
Fax: 212-445-0760
Web Site: http://www.employ.com
Broderick Byers, Chief Executive Officer
Eric D. Cunningham, Chief Financial Officer
Ernest Feiteira, Chief Operating Officer & General Manager
Jack Wagner, Vice President, Business Development
Type of service: Basic.
Programming: The Employment Channel (TEC) is a multimedia company that creates & distributes employment & career development content in a digital video format for television & the Internet. Programming for all classes of workers, from first-time job seekers to high-income professionals & executives.
Means of Support: Advertsing.
Ownership: Private.

ENCORE

8900 Liberty Cir
Englewood, CO 80112
Phone: 720-852-7700
Fax: 720-852-7710
E-mail: eric.becker@starz.com
Web Site: http://www.encoretv.com
Robert B. Clasen, President & Chief Executive Officer
Jerry Maglio, Executive Vice President, Marketing
Ed Huguez, Executive Vice President, Sales
Bill Myers, Executive Vice President & Chief Financial Officer
Steve Beabout, Executive Vice President, General Counsel & Secretary
Bob Greene, Senior Vice President, Advanced Services
John J. Sie, Founder
John Beyler, Senior Vice President, Technology Operations
Tom Southwick, Senior Vice President, Corporate Communications
David Charmatz, Senior Vice President, Research, Analysis & Strategy
Stephan Shelanski, Senior Vice President, Program Acquisitions, Planning & Scheduling
Debbie Egner, Senior Vice President, Sales & Affiliate Relations
Bill Giorgio, Senior Vice President, Sales & Affiliate Relations
Keno Thomas, Senior Vice President, Sales & Affiliate Relations
Miles McNamee, Senior Vice President, Affiliate Marketing
Type of service: Pay.
Satellites: Galaxy 1-R, transponder 13; Satcom C-4, transponder 5.
Operating hours/week: 168.
Programming: First-run & recent big hit movies, plus great classic films, uncut & commercial free. The network focuses on high-quality movies that received box office success or critical acclaim & include notable stars and/or directors. Additionally, Encore features star interviews, movie trivia & original series.
Began: April 1, 1991, (Encore 2, 3, & 4) September 1, 1994 (Encore 5 & 6). Formerly Encore Movie Networks. Rebranded as Starz Encore Super Pak February 2000.
Means of Support: Subscriber fees.
Total subscribers: 33,100,000.

Distribution method: Available to cable & satellite systems.
Scrambled signal: Yes. Equipment: Digital/ DigiCipher II.
Ownership: Liberty Media Corp.

ENCORE ACTION — See Encore.

ENCORE AVENUE — See Movie Central.
Operating hours/week: 168.
Programming: Movies from the 70's, 80's & 90's. Comprises the 2 channels: EA1 & EA2.
Ownership: Corus Entertainment.

ENCORE DRAMA — See Encore.

ENCORE ESPANOL — See Encore.

ENCORE HD — See Encore.
Began: January 1, 2003, shut down in 2006, relaunched in 2008.

ENCORE LOVE — See Encore.

ENCORE MYSTERY — See Encore.
To be rebranded August 2011 as Encore Suspense.

ENCORE WAM — See Encore.
To be rebranded August 2011 as Encore Family.

ENCORE WESTERNS — See Encore.

ENGLISH ON DEMAND
Comcast Corp
1500 Market St
Philadelphia, PA 19102
Phone: 215-665-1700
Type of service: Digital, video on demand.
Operating hours/week: 4.
Operating areas: New Hampshire, Maine, Vermont, Rhode Island, Connecticut, Massachusetts.
Programming: Basic English language skills. Also focuses on important areas of communication such as job & career advancement, managing family life, utilizing information & civic resources & emphasizes community participation.
Began: September 13, 2007.
Distribution method: Available to cable systems.
Ownership: Comcast Corp.

EPIX
1515 Broadway, 46th Fl
New York, NY 10036-8901
Phone: 212-846-4004
Fax: 212-846-2194
E-mail: nryan@epixhd.com
Web Site: http://www.epixhd.com
Mark Greenberg, President & Chief Executive Officer
Andy Hunter, Chief Marketing Officer
Emil Rensing, Chief Digital Officer
Douglas A Lee, Executive Vice President, Programming Acquisitions, Strategy & Enterprises
LaVerne McKinnon, Executive Vice President, Original Programming
Tim Boell, Group Vice President, Sales & Marketing
Maureen Taran, Vice President, Original Programming, Live Events
Type of service: Pay.
Programming: EPIX, a joint venture between Viacom Inc., its Paramount Pictures unit, Metro-Goldwyn-Mayer Studios Inc. and Lionsgate, is a next-generation multiplatform premium entertainment channel, video-on-demand and online service. Providing an entertainment experience with more feature films on demand and online and more HD movies than any other service, EPIX delivers the latest Hollywood movies, 15,000 films from three of the top motion picture libraries, cutting-edge original programming and special comedy and concert events.
Began: October 30, 2009.
Means of Support: Subscriber fees.
Distribution method: Available to cable systems & online. First offered on FiOS.
Scrambled signal: Yes.
Ownership: Viacom Inc. 42%; Lions Gate Entertainment Corp. 28.6%; Metro-Goldwyn-Mayer Inc. 28.6%.

EPIX HD — See EPIX HD.
Began: October 30, 2009.

EPIX 2 HD — See EPIX.
Began: May 12, 2010.

EQUESTRIAN PLANET
1010 Sherbrooke St W
Ste 2401
Montreal, QC H3A 2R7
Canada
Phone: 514-842-5551
Fax: 514-499-9315
Web Site: http://equestrianplanet.com
Michael Weinberg, Chairman
Murray Shostak, President
Programming: Shows related to the horse world, including racing.
Ownership: Olympic Films.

ES.TV
1925 Century Park E
Ste 1025
Los Angeles, CA 90067
Phone: 310-277-3500
E-mail: eric@es.tv
Web Site: http://www.es.tv
Byron Allen, Chairman & Chief Executive Officer
Darren Galatt, Vice President, Ad Sales
Type of service: Digital broadband.
Operating hours/week: 168.
Operating areas: Available nationwide.
Programming: Features entertainment news, variety shows & celebrity profiles.
Began: May 11, 2009.
Total subscribers: 1,900,000.
Distribution method: Available to Verizon FiOS and Frontier Communications subscribers.
Scrambled signal: No.
Ownership: Entertainment Studios.

ESPN
ESPN Plaza
935 Middle St
Bristol, CT 06010
Phone: 860-766-2000
Fax: 860-766-2400
E-mail: espnpr@espn.com
Web Site: http://www.espn.com
George Bodenheimer, President, ESPN
Ben Pyne, President, Disney & ESPN Affiliate Sales & Marketing
Steve Anderson, Executive Vice President, News Talent & Content Operations
David Berson, Executive Vice President, Program Planning & Strategy
Sean Bratches, Executive Vice President, Sales & Marketing
Christine Driessen, Executive Vice President & Chief Financial Officer
Edwin M. Durso, Executive Vice President, Administration

Eric Johnson, Executive Vice President, Multimedia Sales, ESPN Customer Marketing & Sales
Chuck Pagano, Executive Vice President, Technology
John Skipper, Executive Vice President, Content
Reggie Thomas, Executive Vice President, Operations, Engineering & New Technologies
John A. Walsh, Executive Vice President & Executive Editor
John Wildhack, Executive Vice President, Program Acquisitions & Strategy
Norby Williamson, Executive Vice President, Production
Russell Wolff, Executive Vice President & Managing Director, ESPN International
Rick Barry, Senior Vice President, Programming & Production, Business Operations
Patricia Betron, Senior Vice President & Group Leader, Multimedia Sales
Michael Chico, Senior Vice President, Integrated Sales & Market Research
Marie Ciorciari, Senior Vice President & Group Leader, Multimedia Sales
Keith Clinkscales, Senior Vice President, Content Development & Enterprises
Paul Cushing, Senior Vice President, Information Technology
Leonard DeLuca, Senior Vice President, Programming & Acquisitions, ABC Sports
Pete Dezris, Senior Vice President & General Manager, ESPN Regional TV
Marie Donoghue, Senior Vice President, Business Affairs & Business Development
Jed Drake, Senior Vice President & Executive Producer, Event Production
Carol Fraleigh, Senior Vice President, Technical Operations
Rosa M. Gatti, Senior Vice President, Communications Counsel & Corporate Outreach
Betsy Goff, Senior Vice President, Programming & Talent Negotiations
Mark Gross, Senior Vice President & Managing Editor, Studio Production
Ross Hair, Senior Vice President, ESPN International
Traug Keller, Senior Vice President, Production, Business Divisions
John Kosner, Senior Vice President & General Manager, Digital Media
Carol Kruse, Senior Vice President, Marketing
Aaron Laberge, Senior Vice President, Technology & Product Development
Katie Lacey, Senior Vice President, Marketing
Chris LaPlaca, Senior Vice President, Corporate Communications
Burke Magnus, Senior Vice President, College Sports Programming
Jodi Markley, Senior Vice President, Operations
L. Patrick Mellon, Senior Vice President, Affiliate Sales & Marketing
Laurie Orlando, Senior Vice President, Talent Development & Planning
David Pahl, Senior Vice President & General Counsel
Greg Perrelli, Senior Vice President, Affiliate Sales & Marketing
David Preschlack, Senior Vice President, Affiliate Sales & Marketing
Paul Richardson, Senior Vice President, Human Resources
Jeff Ruhe, Senior Vice President, Event Management
Mark Shapiro, Senior Vice President & General Manager, Programming
Steven Zales, Senior Vice President & General Manager, ESPN Internet Ventures
John Zehr, Senior Vice President, Digital Media Production
Chris Calcinari, Vice President, International & Deportes Production
Cindy Freed, Vice President, Sales Marketing, Customer Marketing & Sales
Tom Gleeson, Vice President, Digital Media
Marcia Keegan, Vice President, Content Integration & Strategic Planning
Rob King, Vice President, Editorial, Digital & Print Media.
Carol Stiff, Vice President, Programming & Acquisitions
Don Ohlmeyer, Ombudsman

Branch Offices:
CHICAGO:, 205 N Michigan Ave, Chicago, IL 60601. Phone: 312-228-5800.

DENVER: 5251 DTC Pkwy, Ste 410, Greenwood Village, CO 80111. Phone: 303-740-8940. Fax: 303-740-9824.

DETROIT: Timberland Office Park, 5445 Corporate Dr, Bldg 5, Troy, MI 48098-2683.

LOS ANGELES: 3800 W Alameda Blvd, 3rd Fl, Burbank, CA 91505.

NEW YORK: 77 W 66th St, New York, NY 10023. Phone: 212-456-7777.
Type of service: Basic.
Satellites: For ESPN, Galaxy V, transponder 9 (main feed); Galaxy I, transponder 14 (alternate feed); for ESPN2, Galaxy V, transponder 14 (main feed); Galaxy I, transponder 9 (alternate feed).
Operating hours/week: 168 (each).
Uplink: Bristol, CT.
Programming: ESPN features men's & women's professional & amateur sports. ESPN2 offers programs targeted to sports enthusiasts with a youthful attitude.
Began: September 7, 1979, (ESPN); October 1, 1993 (ESPN2).
Means of Support: Advertising & affiliate fees.
Total subscribers: 100,122,000 (for ESPN; 100,004,000 for ESPN2.).
Distribution method: Available to home dish audiences, cable systems & SMATVs.
Scrambled signal: Yes.
Ownership: The Walt Disney Co., 80%; Hearst Corp. 20%.

ESPN AMERICA — See ESPN.
Programming: North American sports for european audiences.
Began: February 1, 2009, Originally launched December 5, 2002 as North American Sports Network.

ESPN AMERICA HD — See ESPN.

ESPN CLASSIC HD — See ESPN.

ESPN CLASSIC SPORTS — See ESPN.
Total subscribers: 63,000,000.

ESPN DEPORTES — See ESPN.
Total subscribers: 4,500,000.

ESPN DEPORTES ON DEMAND — See ESPN.
Type of service: Video on demand.

ESPN DEPORTES RADIO — See ESPN.
Began: October 5, 2005.

ESPN EXTRA — See ESPN.

ESPN FULL COURT — See ESPN.

ESPN GAMEPLAN — See ESPN.

ESPN MOBILE TV — See ESPN.
Programming: Live, simulcast sports events, news, commentary, analysis & exclusive mobile programming.
Distribution method: Wireless.

ESPN NOW — See ESPN.

ESPN ON DEMAND — See ESPN.
Type of service: Video on demand.

ESPN/SPORTSTICKER — See ESPN.

ESPN3.COM — See ESPN.
Sean Bratches, Executive Vice President, Sales & Marketing
Damon Phillips, Vice President
Began: April 4, 2010, Formerly known as ESPN360.com.
Distribution method: Available only through ISP providers.

ESPN360.COM — See ESPN.
Rebranded as ESPN3.com April 4, 2010.

ESPN 3D — See ESPN.
Operating hours/week: 168.
Began: June 11, 2010, Converted to 24 hour full-time status February 14, 2011.
Total subscribers: 63,000,000.

ESPN 2 — See ESPN.
Total subscribers: 100,004,000.

ESPN U — See ESPN.
Operating hours/week: 168.
Programming: College sports.
Began: March 4, 2005.
Total subscribers: 20,000,000.

ESPN U ON DEMAND — See ESPN.
Type of service: Video on demand.

ESPNEWS — See ESPN.
Total subscribers: 64,000,000.

ESPNEWS HD — See ESPN.
Began: March 30, 2008.

ESPN HD — See ESPN.

ESPNOL — See ESPN.

ESPN PREMIER LEAGUE — See ESPN.
Programming: Provides coverage of Premier League soccer matches.
Began: August 3, 2009.

ESPN 2 HD — See ESPN.

ESPNU HD — See ESPN.
Began: August 28, 2008.

ESTRELLA TV
1845 Empire Ave
Burbank, CA 91504
Phone: 818-729-5300
E-mail: LBIinfo@lbimedia.com
Web Site: http://www.lbimedia.com
Lenard Liberman, Co-Founder & Executive Vice President, LBI Media
Winter Horton, Chief Operating Officer
Ibra Morales, Vice President, Network Operations
Type of service: Basic.
Satellites: AMC 3, transponder 23.
Sales representative: Spanish Media Rep Team.
Operating hours/week: 168.
Operating areas: Arizona, California, Florida, Nevada, New Mexico, New York, Oregon, Texas & Utah.
Uplink: Dallas, TX.
Programming: Spanish-language entertainment, including musical-variety, comedy, scripted drama, talk and game shows, and features top talent from the United States, Mexico & Latin America.
Began: September 14, 2009.
Means of Support: Advertising & subscriber fees.
Distribution method: Available to satellite systems.
Scrambled signal: Yes. Equipment: Grass Valley, Thomson.
Ownership: LBI Media Inc.

ET-GLOBAL
18430 E San Jose Ave
Ste A
City of Industry, CA 91748
Phones: 626-581-8899; 877-388-8787
Fax: 626-581-8877
E-mail: customer service@ettvamerica.com
Web Site: http://www.ettvamerica.com
May Chiang, Executive Vice President, ETTV
Programming: Offers popular Taiwanese shows including traditional costume dramas, variety shows, continuing series, current affairs programs and local community news.
Means of Support: Subscriber fees.
Distribution method: Available to home dish audiences, cable systems and AT&T's U-verse.
Scrambled signal: No.
Ownership: ETTV America Corp.

ET-NEWS
18430 E San Jose Ave
Ste A
City of Industry, CA 91748
Phones: 626-581-8899; 877-388-8787
Fax: 626-581-8877
E-mail: customer service@ettvamerica.com
Web Site: http://www.ettvamerica.com
May Chiang, Executive Vice President
Programming: Provides breaking international and domestic news for Taiwanese viewers.
Means of Support: Subscriber fees.
Distribution method: Available to home dish audiences, cable systems and AT&T's U-verse.
Scrambled signal: No.
Ownership: ETTV America Corp.

ETERNAL WORD TV NETWORK
5817 Old Leeds Rd
Irondale, AL 35210
Phones: 205-271-2900; 800-447-3986
Fax: 205-271-2925
E-mail: cwegemer@ewtn.com
Web Site: http://www.ewtn.com
Michael Warsaw, President & Chief Executive Officer
Douglas Keck, Executive Vice President & Chief Operating Officer
Terry Borders, Vice President, Engineering
Lisa Gould, Vice President, Viewer Services
Scott Hults, Vice President, Communications
Chris Wegemer, Vice President, Marketing
Patrick Haygood, Human Resources Director
Fred Stok, Marketing Director, U.S.
Tom Wenzel, Marketing Director, North America
Walter Cordova, National Marketing Manager, Spanish Networks
Type of service: Basic.
Satellites: Galaxy 15 (U.S.), transponder 11; IS 9 (Latin America), transponder 8-C; IS 10 (Africa, India), transponder 8-C; IS 8 (Pacific Rim), transponder 12-C; Hot Bird 4 (Europe), transponder III (Galaxy XI, Transponder 11-C (Chnl. 5-US English, Chnl. 4-Canada, Chnl. 3-US Spanish)).
Operating hours/week: 168.
Programming: Family & religious programming from a Catholic viewpoint. Original programming, talk shows, children's animation, teaching series, live coverage of church events & documentaries. EWTN Global Catholic Network provides an affiliate website, www.ewtn.info.
Began: August 15, 1981.
Means of Support: Donations.
Total subscribers: 148,000,000 (Includes international subscribers).
Distribution method: Available to cable systems & dish.

EUROCINEMA
1395 Brickell Ave
Ste 800
Miami, FL 33131
Phone: 305-529-6220
Fax: 305-529-6201
E-mail: ngoesseringer@hotmail.com
Web Site: http://www.eurocinema.com
Sebastien Perioche, Chairman & Chief Executive Officer
Larry Namer, Senior Advisor & Director, U.S. Operations
Ben Evans, Chief Operating Officer
Bruce Rabinowitz, Business & Legal Affairs
Steve Matela, Affiliate Sales & Marketing
Nicole Goesseringer, Media Relations

Branch Offices:
NEW YORK: 387 Park Ave S, 3rd Floor, New York, NY 10016. Phone: 212-763-5533.
Type of service: Basic, video on demand & pay-per-view.
Programming: Award-winning European & international films; documentaries, celebrity guests & coverage of major international film festivals.
Began: June 1, 2004.
Distribution method: Via satellite on select cable systems.

EURONEWS
60 Chemin des Mouilles
BP 161-69131
Lyon Ecully Cedex
France
Phone: 33-4-72-18-80-00
Fax: 33-4-78-33-27-17
Web Site: http://www.euronews.net
Philippe Cayla, President
Michael Peters, Managing Director
Luis Rivas, News & Programmes Director
Olivier de Montchenu, Sales & Marketing Director
Jill Grinda, Worldwide Distribution Dir.
Type of service: Basic & broadband.
Satellites: Noorsat 2, transponder 120.
Operating hours/week: 168.
Programming: International all-news channel covering world events simultaneously in seven languages: English, French, German, Italian, Portuguese, Russian & Spanish.
Began: January 1, 1993.
Total subscribers: 1,605,000 (number includes U.S. subscribers only.).
Distribution method: Broadcast, cable & satellite.

EVENT ENTERTAINMENT
50 Peninsula Center
PMB 110
Rolling Hills Estate, CA 90274-3500
Phone: 310-541-1206
Fax: 310-541-4446
Rick Kulis, President
Judy Kulis, Executive Vice President
Type of service: Basic, Pay, Pay-per-view.
Programming: Distribution & production of pay-per-view sports events to cable & satellite markets. Distribution of soccer, boxing & football programming via closed circuit to bars, restaurants, casinos, racetracks & Hispanic markets.
Means of Support: Subscription fees.

EWTN — See Eternal Word TV Network.

EWTN HD — See Eternal Word TV Network.
Began: December 8, 2009.

EWTN EN ESPANOL — See Eternal Word TV Network.

EXERCISE TV
5750 Wilshire Blvd
3rd Fl
Los Angeles, CA 90036
Phone: 310-575-2960
Fax: 323-634-6007
E-mail: shop@exercisetv.tv
Web Site: http://exercisetv.tv
Chris Mansolillo, President
Kelly Simonich, Senior Director, Programming
Shelly Williams, Senior Director, Integrated Marketing & Promotions
Tendai Muronda, Senior Director, Finance & Operations
Type of service: Video on demand.
Operating hours/week: 168.
Programming: Follow-along fitness workouts, sports instruction & motivational programming.
Began: January 18, 2006.
Total subscribers: 40,000,000.
Distribution method: Available to home dish audiences, cable systems, telcos.
Scrambled signal: Yes.
Ownership: Comcast, Body By Jake, Time Warner Cable and New Balance.

EXPO TV
Expo Communications Inc.
15 W 18th St, 10th Fl
New York, NY 10011
Phone: 212-500-6577
Fax: 212-500-6601
E-mail: brian@expotv.com
Web Site: http://www.expotv.com
Daphne Kwon, Chief Executive Officer
Bill Hildebolt, President
David Becker, Chief Marketing Officer
Peter Gochis, Senior Vice President, Affiliate Sales & Marketing

Rob Golden, Senior Vice President, Content & Technology
Gordon Jones, Vice President, Affiliates Sales & Corporate Development
David Rubenstein, Vice President, Media Sales
Thi Luu, Vice President, Operations & Finance
Jennifer Taylor, Vice President & Creative Director
Type of service: Digital & video on demand.
Operating hours/week: 168.
Programming: Showcases a wide range of as seen on TV products ranging from fitness & entertainment to beauty & sports.
Began: March 1, 2005.
Means of Support: Advertising.
Total subscribers: 25,000,000.

EXXXOTICA
2319 E Valley Pkwy
Ste 127
Escondido, CA 92027
Phone: 800-557-5776
Fax: 619-749-8431
Dan Bender, President, Merlin-Sierra Inc.
Type of service: Pay & Pay-per-view.
Satellites: Telstar 405.
Operating hours/week: 168.
Programming: Adult movies.
Means of Support: Subscription fees.
Distribution method: Available to home dish audiences.
Ownership: Merlin-Sierra Inc.

FAITH TELEVISION NETWORK — See My Family TV.

FALCONSVISION
2925 Courtyards Dr
Norcross, GA 30071
E-mail: falconsvision@falconsvision.com
Web Site: http://www.falconsvision.com
Debra Cramer, General Manager, Channel Operations
Type of service: Digital.
Operating hours/week: 168.
Programming: Coverage of Atlanta Falcons training camps, games & playoffs, as well as players' & coaches' interviews.
Began: July 25, 2003.
Total subscribers: 750,000.
Ownership: Comcast Corp.

FAMILY CHRISTIAN TELEVISION — See OlympuSat Hispanic Pack.

FAMILYLAND TELEVISION NETWORK
3375 County Rd 36
Bloomingdale, OH 43910
Phones: 740-765-5500; 800-773-2645
Fax: 740-765-4971
E-mail: info@familyland.org
Web Site: http://www.familyland.org
Satellites: AMC-4, transponder 21C.
Operating hours/week: 168.
Programming: Family values based entertainment including talk shows, movie classics, commentaries, devotionals, children's shows, home improvement, Christian music, sitcoms & sports.
Distribution method: Available to cable & satellite providers.
Scrambled signal: Yes.

FAMILYNET
3836 DeKalb Technology Pkwy
Bldg 3
Atlanta, GA 30340
Phone: 770-225-1400
Web Site: http://www.familynet.com
Randy D. Singer, President & Chief Executive Officer
R. Martin Coleman, Chief Operating Officer
Ralph W. Turner, Jr., Vice President, Marketing & Distribution
James D. Ingram, Vice President, Production
Ray Raley, Vice President, Engineering & Traffic
Type of service: Basic.
Operating hours/week: 168.
Programming: Family entertainment, inspirational programs, sports & movies.
Began: April 4, 1988.
Total subscribers: 31,000,000.
Distribution method: Available to cable systems.

FANGORIA
1372 Broadway
2nd Fl
New York, NY 10018
Phone: 212-634-0318
Web Site: http://www.fangoriatv.com/info.html
Type of service: Video on demand.
Programming: Classic horror & suspense films, original horror-themed reality shows, independent & mainstream feature films. Available in HD & standard definition.
Began: October 1, 2006.

FANZ-TV
PO Box 7205
Burbank, CA 91510
Phone: 818-237-3809
Web Site: http://www.fanztvnetwork.com
Rod Myers, President & Chief Executive Officer
Satellites: AMC, transponder 3.
Operating hours/week: 168.
Programming: Sports games, news & entertainment.
Began: February 4, 2008.
Distribution method: Available to cable systems & satellite providers.

FASHION NETWORK
1925 Century Park E
Ste 1900
Los Angeles, CA 90067
Phone: 310-208-1888
Fax: 310-208-1717
E-mail: fashiontv@aol.com
James Deutch, Executive Producer
Programming: Fashion, beauty & lifestyle programming.
Began: July 29, 1996.
Means of Support: Advertising, licensing & production.
Ownership: Private investors.

FASHION TELEVISION
c/o City TV
299 Queen St W
Toronto, ON M5V 2Z5
Canada
Phone: 416-591-7400
Fax: 416-591-0080
E-mail: infoft@ftchannel.com
Web Site: http://www.fashiontelevision.com
Type of service: Digital.
Operating hours/week: 168.
Programming: Covers the fashion industry.
Distribution method: Available to cable & satellite programmers.
Ownership: CTVglobemedia.

FASHION TV
Donau City Strasse 11
Ares Tower, 21st Fl
Vienna 1220
Austria

Setting the industry standard...
Communications Daily
Warren Communications News
FREE 30-day trial—call 800-771-9202 or visit www.warren-news.com

Phone: +43 (0)1 5131267
E-mail: ceo@ftv.com
Web Site: http://www.ftv.com
Michel Adam, President & Chief Executive Officer
Satellites: Intelsat 907, transponder T5.
Operating hours/week: 168.
Programming: Fashion shows, trends & beauty oriented entertainment.
Began: January 1, 1997.
Total subscribers: 350,000,000 (Figure includes international subscribers.).
Distribution method: Available to cable & satellite systems.

FASTCOMPANY.TV
7 World Trade Ctr
New York, NY 10007-2195
Phone: 212-389-5300
Fax: 212-389-5496
Web Site: http://www.fastcompany.tv
Robert Scoble, Managing Director
Type of service: Broadband.
Programming: Technology trends & products, executive interviews & lifestyle shows.
Began: March 1, 2008.
Ownership: Mansueto Digital & Fast Company, Inc.

FEARNET
1500 Market St
Philadelphia, PA 19102
Phone: 215-665-1700
Web Site: http://www.fearnet.com
Peter Block, President & General Manager
Ron Garfield, Chief Revenue Officer
Michael Severino, Vice President, Affiliate Sales
Kiesha McCorry, Affiliate Marketing Director
Type of service: Digital, video on demand & broadband.
Programming: Multi-platform offerings of thriller & horror films, tv shows, videos, news & information.
Began: October 31, 2006, as an On-Demand service. Launched October 1, 2010 as a standalone service.
Means of Support: Advertising.
Total subscribers: 28,000,000.
Distribution method: Available to cable systems & online.
Scrambled signal: Yes.
Ownership: NBCUniversal LLC, Sony Pictures Entertainment & Lionsgate Entertainment.

FESTIVAL DIRECT — See Independent Film Channel.
Type of service: Viideo on demand.
Programming: Covers major film festivals in Cannes, Toronto, Venice & Telluride.
Began: February 29, 2008.
Distribution method: Available to cable systems.
Scrambled signal: Yes.

THE FIGHT NETWORK
2844 Dundas St W
2nd Fl
Toronto, ON M6P 1Y7
Canada
Phone: 416-987-2457
Fax: 647-343-4173
E-mail: info@thefightnetwork.com
Web Site: http://www.thefightnetwork.com
Anthony Cicione, General Manager
Chad Midgley, Vice President, Programming
Type of service: Basic, pay-per-view & mobile.
Operating hours/week: 168.
Programming: News, movies, television series, documentaries & other entertainment related to boxing, wrestling, martial arts & other combatant styles.
Distribution method: Available to cable systems.

FIGHT NOW TV
4055 W Sunset Rd
Las Vegas, NV 89118-3894
Phones: 702-616-0275; 702-616-1022
E-mail: info@fightnow.com
Web Site: http://www.fightnow.com
Mike Garrow, General Manager & Co-Founder
Cal Miller, Co-Founder
Romen Podzyhun, Co-Founder
Randy Couture, Spokesperson & Analyst
Type of service: Premium.
Operating hours/week: 168.
Operating areas: Connecticut, New Jersey and New York.
Programming: Combat sports channel available through Cablevision's iO Sports & Entertainment Pak.
Began: May 24, 2011.
Means of Support: Subscriber fees and advertising.
Total subscribers: 130,000 (Number of subscribers to Cablevision's iO Sports & Entertainment Pak.).
Distribution method: Available to Cablevision Systems subscribers.
Ownership: Channel Zero.

FILIPINO CHANNEL
ABS-CBN International
150 Shoreline Dr
Redwood City, CA 94065-1400
Phones: 650-508-6000; 800-345-2465
Fax: 650-508-6001
E-mail: nclemente@abs-cbni.com
Web Site: http://www.abs-cbni.com
Rafael Lopez, Managing Director & Chief Operating Officer
Zenon Carlos, Vice President, Operations
Menchi Orlina, Vice President, Chief Marketing Officer
Tom Consunji, Senior Director, Sales & Mktg.
Marites Militar, Director, Creative Broadcast Group
Type of service: Pay.
Satellites: Telstar 5.
Operating hours/week: 168.
Operating areas: California.
Programming: Showcases award-winning dramas, variety, comedy, news & public affairs programs from the dominant broadcasting company in the Philippines for the Filipino population.
Began: April 3, 1994.
Means of Support: Subscribers.
Total subscribers: 200,000.

Distribution method: Available to home dish audiences (as TFC Direct), cable systems (as The Filipino Channel) & telco providers.
Ownership: ABS-CBN International.

FILIPINO ON DEMAND — See Filipino Channel.

FILM FESTIVAL CHANNEL
PO Box 39349
Los Angeles, CA 90039
Phone: 213-625-1242
E-mail: sundancechnladv@ifcsun.com
Web Site: http://www.filmfestivalchannel.com
Lisa Henschel, President
Type of service: Basic & video on demand.
Programming: Focuses on film festivals; on-air competitions for new filmmakers.
Began: November 1, 2003, on demand service began November 5, 2007.
Distribution method: Available to cable & telco systems.

FILM PRODUCERS PILOT NETWORK — No longer planned.

FINE LIVING NETWORK — See Cooking Channel.
Replaced by the Cooking Channel, May 31, 2010.

FINE LIVING ON DEMAND — See Fine Living.
Type of service: Video on demand.

FIOS1
Verizon Communications
140 W St
New York, NY 10007
Web Site: http://www.verizon.com
Type of service: Digital.
Operating areas: District of Columbia, Maryland & Virginia.
Programming: Local news, sports, weather & community interest.
Began: March 31, 2007.
Distribution method: Available to Verizon systems.
Scrambled signal: Yes.

FITTV — See Discovery Fit & Health
Rebranded February 1, 2011 as Discovery Fit & Health.

5 NEWS
318 N 13st St
Fort Smith, AR 72901
Phone: 479-783-3131
Fax: 479-783-3295
E-mail: news@kfsm.com
Web Site: http://www.5newsonline.com
Van Comer, President & General Manager
Type of service: Basic.
Sales representative: Katz Continental Television.
Operating hours/week: 168.
Operating areas: Arkansas.
Programming: Local news channel.
Began: February 13, 1995.
Means of Support: Advertising.
Total subscribers: 46,000.

Distribution method: Microwave & fiber optic to cable systems.
Scrambled signal: Yes.
Ownership: Local TV Holdings LLC.

5STARMAX — See Cinemax.
Programming: Modern classic movies.
Began: May 1, 2002.

FLIX
Paramount Plaza Bldg
1633 Broadway
New York, NY 10019
Phone: 212-708-1600
Fax: 212-708-1212
E-mail: talk2@showtimeonline.com
Web Site: http:///www.sho.com
Matthew C. Blank, President & Chief Executive Officer
Type of service: Pay.
Satellites: AT&T Telstar 303, transponder 17.
Operating hours/week: 168.
Programming: Movie channel featuring films from the 60s, 70s, 80s & 90s, uncut & commercial-free.
Began: August 1, 1992.
Means of Support: Subscriber fees.
Equipment: VideoCipher II Plus.
Ownership: Showtime Networks.

FLIX ON DEMAND — See Flix.
Type of service: Video on demand.
Began: Unannounced.

FLORIDA CHANNEL
402 S Monroe St
Ste 901, The Capitol Bldg
Tallahassee, FL 32399-1300
Phone: 850-488-1281
Fax: 850-488-4876
E-mail: florida@wfsu.org
Web Site: http://www.wfsu.org/florida_channel
Pat Keating, General Manager
Krysta Brown, News Director
Operating hours/week: 168.
Programming: A public service of the Florida Legislature, WFSU-TV and Florida State University that features programming covering all three branches of state government.
Scrambled signal: Yes.

FMX CABLE FM SYSTEM
c/o Channel & Communications
10715 Cherry Tree Ct
Adelphi, MD 20783
Phones: 301-595-3075; 301-595-5479
Fax: 301-577-4153
William L. Tucker, Jr., President & Chief Executive Officer
Brett-Lydle Martin, Vice President & Controller
Type of service: Pay.
Operating hours/week: 168.
Operating areas: Baltimore, MD & the District of Columbia.
Programming: Audio entertainment & information for cable subscribers & Internet users.
Began: January 1, 1995.

Means of Support: Subscriber fees & advertising.
Distribution method: Available to cable systems & PCs through the Internet.

FOOD NETWORK
75 9th Ave
New York, NY 10011
Phone: 212-398-8836
Fax: 212-736-7716
Web Site: http://www.foodtv.com
Kenneth Lowe, Chairman & Chief Executive Officer
Ed Spray, President, Scripps Networks
Bob Tuschman, General Manager
Heidi Diamond, Senior Vice President, Marketing & Business Development
Karen Grinthal, Senior Vice President, Advertising Sales
Eileen Opatut, Senior Vice President, Programming & Production
Bruce Seidel, Senior Vice President, Program Planning & Special Productions
Christine Barry, Vice President, Direct Response Ads
James Dowdle, Vice President, Midwestern Advertising Sales
Susie Fogelson, Vice President, Marketing
Colleen Griffin, Vice President, Western Region, Advertising Sales
Bill Jarrett, Vice President, Engineering
Bill Kossman, Vice President, Program Planning
Brian Lando, Vice President, Programming & Special Projects
Allison Page, Vice President, Programming
John Paruch, Vice President, Central Region, Advertising Sales
Carrie Welch, Vice President, Public Relations
Melissa Sheldon-Maurer, Director, Ad Sales Research
Type of service: Basic.
Satellites: Galaxy I, transponder 4.
Operating hours/week: 168.
Programming: All things food & related to food, such as nutrition, fitness & food-related features & films.
Began: August 30, 1993.
Means of Support: Advertising.
Total subscribers: 101,000,000.
Distribution method: Available to home dish audiences & cable systems.
Ownership: Scripps Networks Interactive.

FOOD NETWORK HD — See Food Network.

FOOD NETWORK ON DEMAND — See Food Network.
Type of service: Video on demand.

FOX BUSINESS CHANNEL
1211 Avenue of the Americas
21st Fl
New York, NY 10036
Phone: 888-369-4762
E-mail: john.mccann@foxnews.com
Web Site: http://www.foxbusiness.com
Roger Ailes, Chief Executive Officer
Kevin Magee, Executive Vice President
Neil Cavuto, Senior Vice President & Managing Editor, Business News
Brian Jones, Senior Vice President, Operations
Bruce Becker, Vice President, Business News
Alexis Glick, Vice President, Business News
Ray Lambiase, Vice President, Graphics
John McCann, Vice President, Ad Sales
Type of service: Basic.
Operating hours/week: 168.
Programming: Business & financial markets oriented news.

Began: October 15, 2007.
Total subscribers: 45,000,000.
Distribution method: Available to cable systems & satellite providers.

FOX BUSINESS CHANNEL HD — See Fox Business Channel.

FOX COLLEGE SPORTS — See Fox Sports Net.
Began: Formerly FSN Digital.
Total subscribers: 52,000,000 (Includes subscribers for Atlantic, Central & Pacific Fox College Sports channels.).

FOX COLLEGE SPORTS ATLANTIC — See Fox Sports Net.

FOX COLLEGE SPORTS CENTRAL — See Fox Sports Net.

FOX COLLEGE SPORTS PACIFIC — See Fox Sports Net.

FOX DEPORTES
10000 Santa Monica Blvd
Ste 333
Los Angeles, CA 90067
E-mail: matt.grim@foxcable.com
Web Site: http://www.foxcable.com
Vincent Cordero, Executive Vice President & General Manager
Raul de Quesada, Assistant General Manager & Senior Vice President, Marketing, Hispanic Networks
Dermot McQuarrie, Assistant General Manager & Senior Vice President, Production & Programming
Tom Maney, Senior Vice President, Advertising Sales
Matt Grim, Affiliate Sales & Marketing Director
Satellites: Satcom C-1, transponder 16.
Operating hours/week: 168.
Operating areas: Available nationwide.
Programming: National & international Spanish language sports network offering soccer, boxing, football, volleyball, surfing, tennis, auto & horse racing. Formerly known as Prime Deportiva and Fox Sports En Espanol.
Began: March 1, 1995.
Total subscribers: 18,000,000.
Distribution method: Available to cable systems & satellite providers.
Scrambled signal: Yes.
Ownership: Fox Hispanic Media, a subsidiary of News Corp.

FOX ENHANCED TV
10000 Santa Monica Blvd
Los Angeles, CA 90067
Phone: 310-286-3800
Web Site: http://www.fox.com
Programming: Suite of interactive services providing access to breaking news, stats, personalized sports ticker, multiple camera angles & game highlights on demand.
Began: N.A.

FOX HD
10201 W Pico Blvd
Bldg 100, 3rd Fl
Los Angeles, CA 90035
Phone: 310-369-3553
Web Site: http://www.fox.com
Began: January 25, 2006.

FOX MOVIE CHANNEL
10201 W Pico Blvd
Bldg 103

Los Angeles, CA 90035
Phone: 310-369-0923
E-mail: thomas.ruffner@foxmoviechannel.com
Web Site: http://www.foxmoviechannel.com
Peter Rice, Entertainment Chairman
Chuck Saftler, General Manager
Thomas Ruffner, Marketing & Public Relations Manager
Type of service: Pay.
Satellites: Galaxy 11, transponder 6.
Operating hours/week: 168.
Programming: Fox Movie Channel features films ranging from the great titles of the past to the blockbusters of today. Films are unedited, commercial-free and in their original theatrical form. Original programming reveals how Hollywood movies are made today and provides an insightful look at the people who make them.
Began: October 31, 1994, as FXM Movies From FOX. Re-launched as Fox Movie Channel March 1, 2000.
Means of Support: Subscriber fees.
Total subscribers: 30,000,000.
Distribution method: Available to cable systems.
Ownership: News Corp.

FOX NEWS CHANNEL
1211 Avenue of the Americas
21st Fl
New York, NY 10036
Phones: 212-556-2500; 212-685-8400
Fax: 212-301-8274
E-mail: brian.lewis@foxnews.com
Web Site: http://www.foxnews.com
Rupert Murdoch, Chairman & Chief Executive Officer, News Corp. Ltd.
Roger Ailes, Chairman & Chief Executive Officer
Jack Abernathy, Chief Executive Officer, FOX Television Stations
Mark Kranz, Chief Financial Officer
Brian Lewis, Executive Vice President, Corporate Communications
Paul Rittenburg, Executive Vice President, Advertising Sales
Dianne Brandi, Executive Vice President, Legal & Business Affairs
Sharri Berg, Senior Vice President, News Operations
Joel Cheatwood, Senior Vice President, Development
Janet Alshouse, Senior Vice President, International Distribution
Richard O'Brien, Vice President, Creative Director
Frank Sorace, Vice President, Sales Planning & Commercial Operations
John Stack, Vice President, Newsgathering
Greg Ahlquist, Senior Director, Digital Media Productions

Branch Offices:
Los Angeles Bureau: 2044 Armacost Ave, Los Angeles, CA 90025. Phone: 310-571-2000. Fax: 310-571-2009.

Washington, D.C. Bureau: 400 N Capitol St NW, Ste 550, Washington, DC 20001. Phone: 202-824-6300. Fax: 202-824-6426.

New York Bureau: 1211 Ave of the Americas, Concourse 1, New York, NY 10036. Phone: 212-301-3000. Fax: 212-301-4224.
Satellites: Galaxy 11, transponder 6.
Operating hours/week: 168.
Programming: All news channel.
Began: October 7, 1996.
Total subscribers: 93,000,000.
Distribution method: Available to cable systems & mobile video.
Ownership: News Corp. Ltd.

FOX NEWS HD — See Fox News Channel.
Began: May 1, 2008.

FOX REALITY CHANNEL
Programming: Featured original series, specials, rebroadcasts & behind-the-scenes coverage of popular U.S. & international reality TV shows. Replaced by Nat Geo WILD March 29, 2010.

FOX SOCCER — See Fox Sports Net.
1440 S Sepulveda Blvd
Los Angeles, CA 90025
Phone: 310-444-5658
Fax: 310-444-8445
E-mail: comments@foxsoccer.com
Web Site: http://msn.foxsports.com/soccer/fsctv
David Nathanson, Executive Vice President & General Manager
Sean Riley, Senior Vice President, Affiliate Sales & Marketing
Joshua Glassel, Vice President, Programming & Acquisitions
Mike Petruzzi, National Ad Sales Manager
Began: November 1, 1997, as Fox Sports World. Relaunched as Fox Soccer Channel February 7, 2005. Programming exclusively soccer starting in 2006.
Total subscribers: 80,000,000.

FOX SOCCER CHANNEL BROADBAND — See Fox Sports Net.
Web Site: http://foxsoccer.tv/

FOX SOCCER PLUS
1440 S Sepulveda Blvd
Los Angeles, CA 90025
Phone: 310-444-5658
Fax: 310-444-8445
E-mail: comments@foxsoccer.com
Web Site: http://msn.foxsports.com/foxsoccer/plus
David Nathanson, Executive Vice President & General Manager, Fox Soccer Channel
Type of service: Premium.
Operating areas: Available nationwide.
Programming: Offers live, exclusive soccer matches from the best leagues in the world, including England's Barclays Premier League, the UEFA Champions League, England's FA Cup, Coca-Cola Championship, Carling Cup and England Men's National Team as well as Italy's Serie A.
Began: March 1, 2010.
Means of Support: Subscriber fees and advertising.
Distribution method: Available to telcos, home dish audiences & cable systems.
Scrambled signal: Yes.

FOX SPORTS NET
10201 W Pico Blvd
Bldg 101
Los Angeles, CA 90035
Phone: 310-369-1000
E-mail: lou.d'ermilio@fox.com
Web Site: http://www.foxsports.com
Brian C. Mulligan, Chairman, Fox Television
David Hill, Chairman & Chief Executive Officer, Fox Sports Media Group
Ed Goren, Vice Chairman, Fox Sports Media Group
Larry Jones, Chief Operating Officer, Fox Sports
Eric Shanks, President, Fox Sports
Randy Freer, President, Fox Regional Cable Sports Networks
Bob Thompson, President, Fox National Cable Sports Networks

Eric Markgraf, Executive Vice President, Marketing
Guy Sousa, Executive Vice President, Ad Sales
Robert Gottlieb, Senior Vice President, Creative Director
Chris Hannan, Senior Vice President, Marketing, Fox Regional Sports Networks
Adam Shaw, Senior Vice President, Network Development
Sol Doten, Vice President, Affiliate Marketing
Shelly Harper, Vice President, Scheduling & Program Operations
Whit Haskel, Vice President, Marketing & Business Development
David Leepson, Vice President, Development
Matt Cacciato, Regional Vice President, Western Region
Bruce Levinson, Regional Director, Affiliate Sales & Mktg., Southwest Region
Chris Bellitti, Corporate Communications Director
Operating hours/week: 168.
Programming: 24-hour sports network.
Began: November 1, 1996.
Total subscribers: 80,000,000 (Includes subscribers for 20 FSN regional networks and affiliates).
Distribution method: Available to home dish audiences & basic cable systems.
Ownership: News Corp.

FOX SPORTS NET ARIZONA
One Renaissance Square
2 N Central Ave, Ste 1700
Phoenix, AZ 85004
Phone: 602-257-9500
Fax: 602-257-0848
E-mail: fsnarizona@foxsports.com
Web Site: http://msn.foxsports.com/arizona
Cathy Weeden, Vice President & General Manager
Type of service: Basic.
Operating areas: Arizona.
Programming: Regional coverage of area's professional teams, Arizona Diamondbacks baseball & Phoenix Coyotes hockey, as well as coverage of Arizona State & U. of Arizona sports.
Began: September 7, 1996.
Total subscribers: 2,300,000.
Distribution method: Available to cable systems.
Ownership: Cablevision Systems Corp. & Fox Entertainment Group.

FOX SPORTS NET CAROLINAS — See Fox Sports Net South.
Operating areas: North & South Carolina.
Programming: Sub-feed from Fox Sports Net South primarily showing games from Carolina Hurricanes, Charlotte Bobcats and the ACC.
Began: October 27, 2008.
Total subscribers: 4,000,000.
Distribution method: Available to cable & satellite providers.
Scrambled signal: Yes.

FOX SPORTS NET DETROIT
26555 Evergreen
Ste 90
Southfield, MI 48076
Phone: 248-226-9700
Fax: 248-226-9740
E-mail: fsdetroit2009@gmail.com
Web Site: http://www.foxsportsdetroit.com
Greg Hammaren, Vice President & General Manager
Marcia S. Turner, General Sales Manager
Joe Gerzema, National Sales Manager
Samantha Ankeny, Marketing & Sales Promotion Director
Type of service: Expanded basic.
Operating areas: Michigan, portions of northwestern Ohio & northern Indiana.
Programming: Regional sports service offering Detroit Red Wings hockey, Tigers baseball & Pistons basketball.
Began: September 17, 1997.
Total subscribers: 3,200,000.
Distribution method: Available to cable systems and DBS providers.
Scrambled signal: Yes.
Ownership: Fox Entertainment Group.

FOX SPORTS NET FLORIDA
1000 Legion Pl
Ste 1600
Orlando, FL 32801-1060
Phone: 407-648-1150
Fax: 407-245-2571
Web Site: http://www.fsnflorida.com
Steve Liverani, Vice President & General Manager
Neil Davis, General Sales Manager
Jerry Carstens, Finance Director
Tim Ivy, Programming Director
Ken Lehner, Marketing Director
Amy Pempel, Media Relations Director
Ned Tate, Executive Producer

Branch Offices:
SOUTH FLORIDA: 1550 Sawgrass Corporate Pkwy, Ste 350, Sunrise, FL 33323. Phone: 954-845-9994. Fax: 954-845-0923.
Type of service: Regional Sports.
Satellites: GE-1, transponder 4.
Sales representative: Rasco.
Operating hours/week: 168.
Operating areas: Florida.
Programming: Carries Florida Panthers Hockey, Florida Marlins & Tampa Bay Devil Rays Baseball, plus local college football, basketball & baseball; original sports related programming.
Began: January 1, 1997, as SportsChannel Florida.
Means of Support: Subscriber fees & advertising.
Total subscribers: 5,000,000.
Distribution method: Available to cable systems & satellite providers.
Scrambled signal: Yes. Equipment: DSR 4500X.
Ownership: News Corp.

FOX SPORTS NET HOUSTON — See Fox Sports Net Southwest.

FOX SPORTS NET INDIANA — See Fox Sports Net Midwest.

FOX SPORTS NET KANSAS CITY — See Fox Sports Net Midwest.
Jack Donovan, General Manager & Senior Vice President
Operating hours/week: 168.
Operating areas: Kansas & Missouri.
Programming: Royals baseball, University of Missouri, University of Kansas & Kansas State basketball, volleyball & baseball & wrestling, Big 12 women's basketball, baseball & championships, Missouri Valley Conference basketball & championships, college coaches' shows & Missouri high school sports coverage.
Began: April 1, 2008.
Total subscribers: 2,000,000.
Distribution method: Available to cable systems.

FOX SPORTS NET MID-ATLANTIC — See Fox Sports Net.

FOX SPORTS NET MIDWEST
700 St. Louis Union Station
Ste 300
St. Louis, MO 63103
Phone: 314-206-7000
Fax: 314-206-7070
E-mail: midwest@foxsports.net
Web Site: http://www.foxsportsmidwest.com
Jack Donovan, Senior Vice President & General Manager
Robert Adelman, Vice President, Affiliate Sales & Marketing
Matt Riordan, National Sales Manager
Ken Allgeyer, General Sales Manager
Rick Powers, Programming Director
David Pokorny, Marketing Director
Kevin Landy, Executive Producer
Geoff Goldman, Media Relations Manager
Catherine Gamble, Finance Director

Branch Offices:
INDIANAPOLIS: 135 N Pennsylvania St, First Indiana Plaza, Ste 720, Indianapolis, IN 46204. Phone: 317-684-5600. Fax: 317-684-5610.
Type of service: Basic.
Satellites: G7.
Operating hours/week: 168.
Operating areas: Illinois, Indiana, Iowa, Missouri, Nebraska & Kansas.
Programming: Local programming, including St. Louis Cardinals baseball, St. Louis Blues hockey, Kansas City Royals baseball, Indiana Pacers basketball, Indiana Fever basketball, Big 12 football, Big 12 women's basketball, Missouri Valley Conference athletics, U. of Missouri basketball & Kansas State U. sports.
Began: November 1, 1996.
Total subscribers: 5,400,000.
Distribution method: Available to cable systems and satellite.
Scrambled signal: Yes.
Ownership: Fox Entertainment Group.

FOX SPORTS NET MINNESOTA — See Fox Sports Net North.

FOX SPORTS NET NEW YORK — See MSG Plus.

FOX SPORTS NET NORTH
90 S 11th St
Minneapolis, MN 55403
Phone: 612-330-2637
Steve Woelfel, Vice President & General Manager

FOX SPORTS NET NORTHWEST — See Root Sports Northwest.

FOX SPORTS NET OHIO
9200 South Hills Blvd
Ste 200
Broadview Heights, OH 44147
Phone: 440-746-8000
Fax: 440-746-9480
Web Site: http://msn.foxsports.com/regional/ohio
Henry S. Ford, Senior Vice President & General Manager
Jim Cook, Vice President, Sales & Affiliate Relations
Charlie Knudson, Vice President, General Sales Manager
Tom Farmer, Vice President, Programming & Production
Steve Pawlowski, Communications Manager
Satellites: GE-1, transponder 4.
Operating areas: Indiana, Kentucky, western New York, Ohio, western Pennsylvania & West Virginia.
Programming: Regional sports service offering Cleveland Cavaliers basketball, Cleveland Indians, & Cincinnati Reds baseball, Columbus Blue Jackets hockey, plus professional soccer, minor league baseball, basketball, hockey & soccer, college football & basketball, professional golf, tennis, volleyball, motor sports, rugby, and horse racing. Programming includes Beyond the Glory, I, Max, Sports List, and Best Damn Sports Show Period.
Began: February 9, 1989.
Total subscribers: 5,000,000.
Distribution method: Available to cable systems.
Ownership: News Corp.

FOX SPORTS NET PHILADELPHIA — See Fox Sports Net.

FOX SPORTS NET PITTSBURGH — See Root Sports Pittsburgh

FOX SPORTS NET PRIME TICKET
10000 Santa Monica Blvd
Santa Monica, CA 90067
Phone: 310-286-3800
Fax: 310-286-6363
Operating hours/week: 168.
Programming: Focuses on local, original shows & sports coverage.
Began: April 3, 2006, formerly FSN West 2.
Distribution method: Available to cable systems.

FOX SPORTS NET ROCKY MOUNTAIN — See Root Sports Rocky Mountain

FOX SPORTS NET TENNESSEE — See Fox Sports Net South.
Operating areas: Tennessee.
Programming: Sub-feed from Fox Sports Net South focused on Memphis Grizzlies, Nashville Predators & Southeastern Conference sports.
Began: October 27, 2008.
Total subscribers: 1,800,000.
Distribution method: Available to cable & satellite providers.

FOX SPORTS NET UTAH — See Root Sports Rocky Mountain.

FOX SPORTS NET WEST
10000 Santa Monica Blvd
Los Angeles, CA 90067
Phone: 310-286-3800
Fax: 310-286-6363
Steve Simpson, Senior Vice President & General Manager
LaVada Heath, Vice President & General Sales Manager
Brian Decker, Director, Affiliate Relations
Eric Burak, Director, Marketing
Satellites: Satcom C-1, transponder 7 & 21.
Operating hours/week: 168.
Operating areas: California (southern portion).
Programming: Regional sports featuring Los Angeles Lakers & Los Angeles Clippers basketball, Los Angeles Kings hockey, Anaheim Angels & Los Angeles Dodgers baseball, Anaheim Mighty Ducks hockey, Los Angeles Galaxy soccer, USC & UCLA athletics, professional tennis, pro beach volleyball, horse racing, collegiate sports, professional boxing & Fox Sports News.
Began: October 19, 1985.
Means of Support: System fees & advertising.
Total subscribers: 5,000,000.
Distribution method: Available to home dish audiences & cable systems.
Equipment: VideoCipher II.
Ownership: Fox Entertainment Group.

FOX SPORTS NET WEST 2 — See Fox Sports Net Prime Ticket.
Began: January 27, 1997.
Total subscribers: 3,000,000.

FOX SPORTS NET WISCONSIN — See Fox Sports Net North.

FOX SPORTS SOUTHWEST
100 E Royal Ln
Ste 200
Irving, TX 75039
Phone: 972-868-1800
Fax: 972-868-1678
E-mail: ben.rebstock@foxsports.net
Web Site: http://www.foxsportssouthwest.com
Jon Heidtke, Corporate Vice President & General Manager
John Burnett, Vice President & General Sales Manager
Ramon Alvarez, Public Relations Director
Misty Johnson, Marketing Director
Tom Garnier, Programming Manager
Kristi Roberts, Manager, Media Relations

Branch Offices:
HOUSTON: 4261 Southwest Freeway, Houston, TX 77027. Phone: 713-479-2630. Fax: 713-479-2629.

HOUSTON: 5251 Gulfton St, Houston, TX 77027. Phone: 713-821-7500. Fax: 713-661-8378.
Type of service: Basic.
Satellites: Galaxy 7, transponder 23.
Operating hours/week: 168.
Operating areas: Arkansas, Louisiana, New Mexico (portions), Oklahoma & Texas.
Programming: Regional sports service offering Houston Astros & Texas Rangers baseball; Dallas Mavericks, Houston Rockets & Antonio Spurs basketball; Dallas Stars hockey; Big 12 Conference, Conference USA, Southeastern Conference, Western Athletic Conference, Southland Conference & Pacific 10 Conference events; Dallas Burn, Texas high school championship events; regional outdoor shows & regional sports report.
Began: January 4, 1983.
Total subscribers: 6,900,000.
Distribution method: Available to home dish audiences & cable systems.
Equipment: VideoCipher II.
Ownership: Fox Entertainment Group.

FOX SPORTS WORLD — See Fox Soccer.
10000 Santa Monica Blvd
Ste 333
Los Angeles, CA 90067
Phone: 310-286-6300
Fax: 310-286-6375
Web Site: http://www.foxsportsworld.lycos.com
Began: November 1, 1997, Relaunched as Fox Soccer in 2006.

FRANCE 24
5 rue des Nations Unies
Issy-les-Moulineaux 92130
France
Phone: 331-7301-2424
Fax: 331-7301-2456
E-mail: webdesk@france24.com
Web Site: http://www.france24.com
Alain de Pouzilhac, Chairman
Christine Ockrent, Chief Executive Officer
Vincent Giret, General Manager
Philippe Rouxel, Vice President, Worldwide Distribution
Bruno Tezenas du Montcel, Chief Technology Officer
Patrice Begay, Chief Operating Officer of Advertising
Albert Ripamonti, News Director
Anne Kacki, Legal Services Director
Nathalie Lenfant, Communications Director
Stanislas Leridon, Internet & New Media Director
Sophie Letierce, Human Resources Director
Cecile Maries, Administative & Financial Director

Branch Offices:
USA Representative–New Line TV Co: 5731 NW 74th Ave, Miami, FL 33166. Phone: 305-592-1394. Fax: 305-592-1453. E-Mail: distribution@newlinetv.us. Web site: http://http://www.newlinetv.us.
Type of service: Basic.
Operating hours/week: 168.
Programming: An international news channel covering world events from a French perspective and to convey French values throughout the world.
Began: December 6, 2006, in France. Channel launched July 2009 in US.
Means of Support: Advertising.
Distribution method: Available to cable systems.
Ownership: Audiovisuel Exterieur de la France.

FREE SPEECH TV
PO Box 44099
Denver, CO 80201
Phone: 303-442-8445
Fax: 303-442-6472
E-mail: jon@freespeech.org
Web Site: http://www.freespeech.org
Jon Stout, General Manager
Gail Gonzales, Business Manager
Don Rojas, Executive Director
Giselle Diaz Campagna, Development Director
Than Reeder, Operations Director
Leland Rucker, Web Editor
Eric Galatas, Program Manager
Type of service: DISH Network channel 9415; DIRECTV channel 348; Galaxy 18.
Satellites: Galaxy 18.
Operating hours/week: 168.
Programming: An independent, commercial-free television network featuring news, commentary and documentary content addressing a broad range of social, economic, environmental and cultural issues. Signature daily news and talk programs include Democracy Now! and The Thom

Hartmann Program. DISH Network 9514, DIRECTV 348, 200 part-time cable affiliates.
Began: July 1, 1995.
Total subscribers: 22,000,000.
Distribution method: Full-time via DBS on DISH Network & part-time via tape to cable systems.
Scrambled signal: Yes.

FRESH
9242 Beverly Blvd
Beverly Hills, CA 90210
Phone: 310-246-4000
Fax: 310-246-4050
Jim English, President
Brian Quirk, Executive Vice President, Affiliate Sales & Marketing
Claire Zrimc, Vice President, Worldwide Programming & Acquisitions
Marc Brown, Vice President, On-Air Promotions
Andrew Lucas, Operations Director
Scott Barton, Public Relations Director
Type of service: Pay-Per-View.
Satellites: Telstar 5, transponder 5.
Operating hours/week: 168.
Programming: Cable version adult movies & special events.
Began: May 1, 1989, Originially launched as Spice.
Means of Support: Subscriber fees.
Total subscribers: 142,000,000.
Distribution method: Available to home dish audiences & cable systems.
Equipment: DigiCipher II.
Ownership: Playboy Enterprises Inc.

FRIGHT CHANNEL
PO Box 1749
Hollywood, CA 90078
Phone: 323-988-1259
E-mail: caretaker@thefrightchannel.tv
Web Site: http://www.thefrightchannel.tv
Nicholas Psaltos, President & Founder
Vini Bancalari, Programming & Production Director
Josh Davidson, Marketing & Public Relations Director
Neil Jason, Music & Licensing Director
Hirotsugo Aoki, Creative Services Director
Daniel S. Bancalari, Technology & Information Services Director
Type of service: Plans basic & broadband.
Programming: Dedicated to the horror genre; movies, specials & series.
Distribution method: Available to cable systems & online.
Scrambled signal: Yes.

FSN DIGITAL — Relaunched as Fox College Sports in 2004, which is now part of Fox Sports Net.

FSN DIGITAL ATLANTIC — See FSN Digital.

FSN DIGITAL CENTRAL — See FSN Digital.

FSN DIGITAL PACIFIC — See FSN Digital.

FSN HD — See Fox Sports Net.

FTV HD — See Fashion TV.

FUEL TV
1440 S Sepulveda
Los Angeles, CA 90025
Phone: 310-369-1000
Fax: 310-444-8559
E-mail: hookup@fuel.tv
Web Site: http://www.fuel.tv
George Greenberg, Executive Vice President & General Manager
Lorey Zlotnick, Senior Vice President, Marketing
Scott Paridon, Vice President, Production & Development
Peter Vesey, Vice President, Ad Sales
John Stouffer, Public Relations Director
Type of service: Digital basic cable and satellite television.
Operating hours/week: 168.
Operating areas: Nationwide.
Programming: Adrenalin sports, entertainment & music.
Began: July 1, 2003.
Total subscribers: 32,000,000.
Scrambled signal: Yes.
Ownership: FOX Sports Media Group.

FUEL TV HD — See Fuel TV.

FUJIAN STRAITS TV — See KylInTV.
Phone: 0591-8331-0945
Programming: Provides a variety of Chniese programming in Fujianese dialect. Offered by KyLinTV & Dish Network.
Began: October 1, 2005.
Ownership: Fujian Media Group.

FUNIMATION CHANNEL
1200 Lakeside Pkwy
Bldg 1
Flower Mound, TX 75028
Phone: 972-355-7300
E-mail: kim@olympusat.com
Web Site: http://www.funimation.tv
Gen Fukunaga, Chief Executive Officer & President
Kim Reed Fragione, Chief Operating Officer
Bill Saltzgiver, Senior Vice President, Network Operations, Olympusat Inc.
Amanda Nanawa, Director of VOD Operations, Olympusat Inc.

Branch Offices:
Olympusat Inc.: 560 Village Blvd, Ste 250, West Palm Beach, FL 33409. Phone: 561-684-5657. Fax: 561-684-9690.
Type of service: Digital. HD.
Satellites: Intelsat Galaxy 23.
Operating hours/week: 168.
Operating areas: Available nationwide.
Programming: The only anime channel in the United States airing anime programming 24/7 in HD.
Began: September 1, 2005.
Total subscribers: 20,000,000.
Distribution method: Available to cable systems and broadband.
Scrambled signal: Yes.
Ownership: Olympusat Inc. & FUNimation Entertainment.

FUSE
11 Penn Plz
15th Fl
New York, NY 10001
Phone: 212-324-3400
Fax: 212-324-3445
E-mail: fuseinfo@fuse.tv
Web Site: http://www.fuse.tv
James L Dolan, Chairman
Hank J Ratner, Vice Chairman
Eric Sherman, President
David Clark, Executive Vice President & General Manager
Matt Farber, Executive Vice President, Programming, Development & Digital

Brad Samuels, Executive Vice President, Content Distribution
Bob Dahill, Senior Vice President, Affiliate Sales & Marketing
Allan Infeld, Senior Vice President, Ad Sales
Joe Marchese, Senior Vice President, Digital & Marketing Strategy
Jason Million, Senior Vice President, National Ad Sales
Brad Schwartz, Senior Vice President, Programming & Operations
Amy Stevens, Senior Vice President, Strategic Alliances
Barry Watkins, Senior Vice President, Communications
Charlene Weisler, Senior Vice President, Research
Guy Cacciarelli, Vice President, Content Distribution, Western Region
Michael Goldstein, Vice President, Interactive Programming
Sharoan Harris, Vice President, Pricing & Planning
Maggie Helm, Vice President, Ad Sales, West
Brian Hoffman, Vice President, Marketing Solutions
Marcelle Karp, Vice President, Creative Director Creative Services
Beth Lewand, Vice President, Digital Media
Lauren Melone, Vice President, Public Relations
Bob Mitchell, Vice President, Consumer & Affiliate Marketing
Karen Ramspacher, Vice President, Research
Sue Rasmussen, Vice President, Direct-Response Advertising Sales
Michael Roche, Vice President, Ad Sales, East
David Schafer, Vice President, Operations
Norm Schoenfeld, Vice President, Programming
Michelle Solomon, Vice President, Ad Sales Marketing
Peter Tulloch, Vice President, Content Distribution, Eastern Region
Carol Valentine, Vice President, Digital Media Sales
Kim Verkler, Vice President, Ad Sales, Midwest
Lori West, Vice President, Direct Response & Paid Programming
Donna Wolfe, Vice President, Production

Branch Offices:
EASTERN REGION-CORPORATE OFFICE: Rainbow Media Holdings Inc., 200 Jericho Quadrangle, Jericho, NY 11753. Phone: 516-803-4600. Fax: 516-803-4611.

WESTERN REGION: 2425 W Olympic Blvd, Ste 5050W, Santa Monica, CA 90404. Phone: 310-453-4646. Fax: 310-453-6106.

AD SALES: 530 Fifth Ave, 6th Floor, New York, NY 10036.

PROGRAMMING: 708 Third Ave, 7th Floor, New York, NY 10017. Phone: 212-389-6690. Fax: 212-687-2958.
Type of service: Digital.
Satellites: Loral Skynet Telstar 7, transponder 14.
Operating hours/week: 168.
Uplink: Belmont, NY.
Programming: Interactive, live music channel featuring spontaneous appearances by today's superstars & breaking acts of the future.
Began: July 1, 1994.
Means of Support: Advertising.
Total subscribers: 59,500,000 (On Demand service has 18,000,000 subscribers).
Distribution method: Available to home dish audiences & cable systems.
Scrambled signal: Yes. Equipment: VideoCipher II Plus.
Ownership: Cablevision Systems Corp. At the end of 2009 service was spun off from Cablevision to form part of MSG Media which is part of Madison Square Garden LP.

FUSE HD — See Fuse.

FUSE ON DEMAND — See Fuse.
Type of service: Video on demand.
Began: June 1, 2003.

FX
1211 Avenue of the Americas
31st Fl
New York, NY 10036
Phone: 212-822-8625
Fax: 212-822-8628
E-mail: user@fxnetworks.com
Web Site: http://www.fxnetworks.com
Peter Rice, Entertainment Chairman
John Landgraf, President & General Manager, FX Networks
Guy Sousa, Executive Vice President, Fox Channels Group
Lindsay Gardner, Executive Vice President, Affiliate Sales, Fox Channels Group
Kevin Reilly, President, Entertainment
Michael Brochstein, Senior Vice President, Ad Sales
Chris Carlisle, Senior Vice President, Marketing
Mark DeVitre, Senior Vice President, Operations
Gloria Dickey, Senior Vice President, Human Resources, Fox Channels Group
Dennis Farrell, Senior Vice President, Finance, Fox Channels Group
Julie Piepenkotter, Senior Vice President, Research
Chuck Saftler, Senior Vice President, Programming
John Varvi, Senior Vice President, On-Air Promotion
Patrice Callahan, Vice President, Business & Legal Affairs
Elena Gutierrez, Vice President, Ad Sales, Los Angeles
Steve Leblang, Vice President, Strategic Planning & Research
Mike Middeleer, Vice President, On-Air Promotion
Eric Shiu, Vice President, Marketing
Type of service: Basic.
Satellites: Galaxy VII, transponder 4 & 5.
Programming: Original entertainment programming, TV favorites, movies & sports.
Began: June 1, 1994.
Total subscribers: 94,000,000.
Ownership: Fox Entertainment Group.

FX HD — See FX.

FX PREVIEW CHANNEL
c/o Cablevision Inc
1111 Stewart Ave
Bethpage, NY 11714
Phone: 516-803-2300
Web Site: http://www.cablevision.com
Type of service: Video on demand.
Programming: Barker channel for FX cable network.
Distribution method: Available to Cablevision digital cable subscribers.
Ownership: Cablevision, FX Network & Media Storm.

G4
5750 Wilshire Blvd
Los Angeles, CA 90036-3709
Phone: 323-954-2400
Fax: 323-954-2600
E-mail: amelia.stewart@nbcuni.com
Web Site: http://www.g4tv.com
Bonnie Hammer, Chairman, NBC Universal Cable Entertainment & Universal Cable Studios
Neal Tiles, President
Steve Dolcemaschio, Chief Operating Officer
Jeff Mayzurk, Chief Technology Officer
Cyndi McClellan, Executive Vice President, Program Strategy & Research
Sheila Johnson, Executive Vice President, Business & Legal Affairs & General Counsel
Duccio Donati, Executive Vice President, International
John Najarian, Executive Vice President, Digital Media & Business Development
Steve Blue, Executive Vice President, Production & Operations
John Rieber, Senior Vice President, Programming & Production
Sarah Goldstein, Senior Vice President, Media Relations & Corporate Communications
Scott Bantle, Senior Vice President, Creative Services
Eric Gray, Senior Vice President, Finance
Laura Civiello, Vice President, Development
Robert Juster, Vice President, New Media & Interactive
Erika Lewis, Vice President, Current Production
Matt Monos, Vice President, Program Planning & Acquisitions
David Angehrn, Vice President, Marketing & Strategy Planning
Type of service: Linear TV, VOD, HD, mobile.
Operating hours/week: 168.
Programming: G4 offers the last word on gaming, technology, animation, interactivity and geek culture for the male 18-34 demo. The network has given young guys of today's digital generation a television home. G4 is the number 1 podcasted cable network in America and is available in 60 million cable and satellite homes nationwide. The network's popular original programming includes Attack Of The Show!, X-Play, American Ninja Warrior and Campus PD. G4 also continues to expand its live even coverage at CES, Comic-Con, E3, Tokyo Game Show and more. The network's key acquisitions include Heroes & Lost. G4's Multiplex features content on all possible digital platforms, including G4tv.com, G4 Mobile, G4 Podcasts, G4 on Demand, G4 Video Player, G4 Wii Portal & G4 PS3 Portal. G4 is a network of NBCUniversal Cable Entertainment, a division of NBCUniversal, one of the world's leading media and entertainment companies in the development, production, and marketing of entertainment, news, and information to a global audience.
Began: April 1, 2002.
Total subscribers: 59,100,000.
Distribution method: Available to cable & satellite providers.
Scrambled signal: Yes.
Ownership: NBCUniversal LLC.

GALAVISION
605 3rd Ave
12th Fl
New York, NY 10158
Phone: 212-455-5200
Fax: 212-953-0198
Web Site: http://www.galavision.com
Joanne Lynch, Senior Vice President & General Manager
Sebastian Trujillo, Senior Vice President, Operating Manager
Tim Krass, Executive Vice President, Affiliate Relations
Michelle Bella, Vice President, Marketing & Communications
Jasmine Rezai, Vice President, Affiliate Marketing
Tim Spillane, Vice President, Affiliate Sales
Deleela Jones, Director, Marketing
Margarita Black, Programming & Promotions Director

Branch Office:
MIAMI: 9405 NW 41st St, Miami, FL 33178. Phone: 305-471-4021.
Type of service: Basic.
Satellites: Galaxy I-R, transponder 2.
Operating hours/week: 168.
Uplink: Miami, FL.
Programming: Spanish language service providing news, movies, novelas (soap operas), sports, comedy and variety.
Began: October 26, 1979.
Means of Support: Advertising.
Total subscribers: 53,000,000.
Distribution method: Available to cable systems & satellite providers.
Ownership: Univision Inc.

GALAVISION HD — See GalaVision.

GALLERYPLAYER ON DEMAND
411 1st Ave S
Ste 200N
Seattle, WA 98104
Phone: 206-622-4500
Fax: 206-622-4550
E-mail: gpinfo@galleryplayer.com
Web Site: http://www.galleryplayer.com
Kevin Akeroyd, Chief Executive Officer
Bruce Worrall, Chief Operating Officer
Paul Brownlow, Founder & Vice President, Technology
Kirsten Soderlind, Vice President, Creative Development
Rusty Citron, Vice President, Marketing
Type of service: Digital, video on demand.
Programming: Art & photography in high definition from top museums, publishers, artists & photographers.
Began: November 13, 2006.
Distribution method: Available to cable systems.

GAMEHD — See iN DEMAND.

GAME SHOW NETWORK — See GSN.

GAMETAP
c/o Turner Broadcasting Services Inc.
One CNN Center
Atlanta, GA 30303
Phone: 404-827-1700
E-mail: advertise@gametap.com
Web Site: http://www.gametap.com
Stuart Snyder, General Manager
Rick Sanchez, Vice President, Content
Programming: Broadband entertainment network, delivering a variety of games in their original format to players through their personal computers. Also offers exclusive bonus material & special programming about video games.
Began: October 17, 2005.
Ownership: Turner Broadcasting System Inc.

GAMING ENTERTAINMENT TELEVISION
160 Howells Rd
Bayshore, NY 11706
Phone: 631-968-0131
Fax: 631-968-5043
Eric Hughes, Vice President, Marketing
Bill Bridges, Sales
Michele D'Arco, Sales
Bonnie Goldstein, Sales
Type of service: Pay & pay-per-view.
Operating hours/week: 168.
Programming: Lottery, horse & dog racing, interactive games with prizes & pay-per-view entertainment specials.
Means of Support: Subscriber fees & advertising.
Distribution method: Available to home dish audiences & cable systems.
Equipment: VideoCipher.
Ownership: Privately owned.

GAS — Defunct as of December 31, 2007. Replaced by The N.

GAS STATION TV
255 S Old Woodward
Ste 210
Birmingham, MI 48009
Phones: 248-581-3000; 888-581-4788
E-mail: sales@gstv.com
Web Site: http://www.gstv.com
David Leider, Chief Executive Officer
Steve Kuehn, Chief Financial Officer
Jason Brown, Chief Sales Officer
Victor Germaine, Senior Vice President, Business Development
John Caronna, Vice President, Western Region Sales Dir.
Todd W. Rankin, Vice President, Midwest Sales
Robert Fontanella, Vice President, East Coast Sales
Brian Gingrich, Automotive Aftermarket & Local Sales
Programming: GSTV delivers entertaining and informative content with hyper-local targeting down to an individual gas station. Programming includes news and entertainment, ESPN sports, localized AccuWeather, original content and advertising.
Distribution method: Satellite.
Scrambled signal: Yes.

GBH KIDS — See WGBH TV

GEKTV
170 S Spruce Ave
Ste 200
South San Francisco, CA 94080
Phone: 888-435-8866
E-mail: info@gektv.com
Web Site: http://www.gektv.com
Type of service: IPTV & video on demand.
Programming: Package of Asian channels, shows & films. Including content from i-Cable News, i-Cable Entertainment News, Fashion TV-Asia, Pearl River Channel & Setanta Sports Channel.
Began: 39341.

GEM SHOPPING NETWORK
3414 Howell St
Duluth, GA 30096
Phone: 770-622-5505
Fax: 770-622-5503
E-mail: customerservice@gemshopping.com
Web Site: http://www.gemshopping.com
Operating hours/week: 168.
Programming: Television Shopping Channel offering fine gemstones & jewelry.
Began: May 10, 1997.
Total subscribers: 30,000,000.
Distribution method: Available to cable systems & satellite providers.

GEMSTV
1190 Trademark Dr
Ste 107
Reno, NV 89521
Phone: 775-850-8080
Web Site: http://www.gemstv.com
Jason Wai, Chief Executive Officer
Wong Lai Kuen, Chief Financial Officer
Don Rene Kagen, President, Global Merchandising
Frankie Chow, Managing Director, Thailand
Kaori Miwa, Managing Director, GemsLondon
Diane Louie Schneiderjohn, Managing Director, GemsTV, USA
Karen Lesley Wenborn, Managing Director, GemsTV, UK
Type of service: Basic.
Operating hours/week: 168.
Programming: Jewelry & gemstone shopping channel.
Began: November 26, 2006, reflects U.S. launch.
Total subscribers: 15,000,000 (U.S. subcribers only).
Distribution method: Available to cable systems & satellite providers.

GEORGIA PUBLIC BROADCASTING
260 14th St NW
Atlanta, GA 30318
Phones: 404-685-2400; 800-222-6006
Fax: 404-685-2491
E-mail: ask@gpb.org
Web Site: http://www.gpb.org
Teya Ryan, President & Executive Director
Bonnie R. Bean, Chief Financial Officer
Mark Fehlig, Director, Technical & Engineering Services
Melvin Jones, Director, Human Resources
Michael E. Nixon, Director, Education & Technology Services
Robert M. Olive, Assistant General Manager
Operating areas: Georgia.
Programming: Interactive distance learning for public schools, regional libraries & adult technical educations centers.
Began: August 15, 1994.
Distribution method: Satellite, Internet, Open-Air.
Ownership: Georgia Public Broadcasting.

GLOBAL VILLAGE NETWORK
1211 Olino St
Honolulu, HI 96818
Phones: 202-483-4647; 808-423-9642
Fax: 808-423-0565
Gloria Borland, President
Operating areas: Hawaii. Plans nationwide.
Programming: From around the world.
Began: May 1, 1998.

GLOBECAST WORLDTV
5 allee Gustave Eiffel
92136 Issy les Moulineaux
Cedex
France

Phone: 33-1-55-95-26-26
Fax: 33-1-55-95-27-27
E-mail: lisa.coelho@globecast.com
Web Site: http://www.globecastworldtv.com
Lisa Coelho, General Manager
Programming: Packaged international channels.
Distribution method: Satellite.

GMA PINOY TV
GMA Network Center
EDSA Corner Timog Ave.
Diliman, Quezon City
Philippines
Web Site: http://www.gmapinoytv.com
Type of service: Digital.
Operating hours/week: 168.
Programming: News, entertainment & popular series from the Philippines.
Began: August 1, 2005, (U.S. launch).

GMA LIFE TV — See GMA Pinoy TV.

GOD TV
Central Office USA
PO Box 161329
Altamonte Springs, FL 32716
Phone: 407-682-5084
Fax: 407-682-2407
E-mail: info.usa@god.tv
Web Site: http://www.god.tv

Branch Offices:
CAPE TOWN: Box 79, Milnerton, Cape Town 7435, South Africa. Phone: 27-0-21-555-1206. Fax: 27-0-21-555-1207.

INDIA: Box 3455, Anna Nagar, Chennai 600 040, India. Phone: 1600-44-2777. Fax: 91-44-5217-2928.

HONG KONG: Box 35216, King's Rd Post Office, Hong Kong. Phone: 852-3107-8877. Fax: 852-3107-8878.

HAMBURG: Valentinskamp 24, 20354, Hamburg, Germany. Phone: 49-0-40-414-317-314. Fax: 49-0-40-3111-2616.

DENMARK: Box 12, DK 9800, Hjorring, Denmark. Phone: 45-98-90-91-50. Fax: 45-98-91-03-44.

UK & IRELAND: Angel House, Borough Road, Sunderland SR1 1HW. Phone: 44-0-870-60-70-446. Fax: 44-0-191-568-0879.

BROADCAST HQ - ISRAEL: Box 7159, Jerusalem 91071, Israel.
Programming: Offers international Christian programming, including conferences, in depth interviews, youth & music shows featuring prominent Christian leaders & artists from around the world.
Began: January 1, 1995.
Total subscribers: 275,000,000.

GOLDEN EAGLE BROADCASTING
7777 S Lewis Ave
Tulsa, OK 74171
Phones: 918-495-7288; 800-255-4407
Fax: 918-495-7388
E-mail: golden-eagle@oru.edu
Web Site: http://www.goldeneagle.tv
Walter H. Richardson, President
Amy Calvert, Vice President, Marketing & Sales
Bill Lee, Director of Engineering
Satellites: SES-1, transponder 1; Directv channel 363.
Operating hours/week: 168.
Programming: Golden Eagle Broadcasting's family safe programming was launched January 24, 1996. Since that time GEB has provided the finest inspirational and educational television available. Without interruption 24 hours a day, seven days a week. The network provides a unique collection of inspirational, informational, and educational programming for all ages.
Began: January 24, 1996.
Means of Support: Non Commercial.
Distribution method: Available to cable & satellite providers.
Scrambled signal: Yes.

GOLF CHANNEL
7580 Commerce Center Dr
Orlando, FL 32819
Phone: 407-355-4653
Fax: 407-363-7976
E-mail: dhiggins@golfchannel.com
Web Site: http://www.golfchannel.com
Mike McCarley, President
Gene Pizzolato, Chief Revenue & Marketing Officer & Chief Operating Officer, New Media Ventures
Tom Stathakes, Senior Vice President, Programming, Production & Operations
Earl Marshall, Senior Vice President, Finance, Strategy & Business Development
Christopher Murvin, Senior Vice President, Business Affairs
Jeff Foster, Senior Vice President, New Media Sales
Regina O'Brien, Senior Vice President, Marketing
Keith Allo, Vice President, Programming & Original Productions
Linda Wingate, Senior Human Resources Director
Type of service: Basic & video on demand.
Satellites: Galaxy 14; Galaxy 17.
Operating hours/week: 168.
Programming: Live golf tournaments, original programming, daily news shows, celebrity interviews, golf instruction, profiles, and documentaries.
Began: January 17, 1995.
Means of Support: National advertising & subscriber fees.
Total subscribers: 83,000,000.
Distribution method: Available to cable systems and home dish audiences.
Scrambled signal: Yes.
Ownership: Comcast Corp.

GOLF CHANNEL HD — See Golf Channel.
Began: December 9, 2008.
Total subscribers: 12,000,000.

GOLTV
1666 JFK Causeway
Ste 700
North Bay Village, FL 33141
Phones: 305-864-9799; 866-644-6588
Fax: 305-864-7299
E-mail: info@goltv.tv
Web Site: http://www.goltv.tv
Francisco Casal, President
Enzo Francescoli, Chief Executive Officer
Rodrigo Lombello, Chief Operating Officer
Eileen Montalvo, Executive Vice President, Marketing & Sales
Constantino Voulgaris, Vice President, Programming
Steve Soule, Vice President, Affiliate Sales
Didi Montiel, Director, Marketing
Jagdeep Wadhwani, Director, Ad Sales
Type of service: Basic & video on demand.
Operating hours/week: 168.
Programming: Soccer-exclusive satellite & cable network in North America. Over 800 live soccer matches & tournaments a year, plus soccer newscasts & interviews. Available in both Spanish and English.
Began: February 1, 2003, reflects U.S. launch.
Total subscribers: 16,000,000 (includes 6500000 for english language feed).
Ownership: Gol TV Inc.

GONZOX
7007 Winchester Cir
Ste 200
Boulder, CO 80301
Phone: 303-444-0900
Fax: 303-938-8388
Michael Weiner, Chief Executive Officer
Ken Boenish, President
Thomas Nyiri, Vice President, Broadband Communications & Chief Technical Officer
Karyn Miller, Chief Financial & Operating Officer
John Chambliss, Programming Director
Robin Rothman, Media Contact
Mark Grant, Marketing Contact
Type of service: Pay-Per-View & Pay.
Satellites: Telstar 4, transponder 7.
Operating hours/week: 168.
Programming: Adult entertainment.
Began: March 1, 1996.
Distribution method: Available to C-band satellite dish customers.
Ownership: New Frontier Media Inc.

GOOD TV — See KyLinTV.

GOSCOUT HOMES
Cox Communications
1001 Summit Blvd, Ste 1200
Atlanta, GA 30319
855-755-2691
Web Site: http://www.goscouthomes.tv
Programming: Real estate listings available in select Cox Cable markets such as Gainesville, FL; Oklahoma City & Tulsa, OK; Omaha, NE; Phoenix, AZ.
Ownership: Cox Media LLC.

GOSPEL MUSIC CHANNEL
1895 Phoenix Blvd
Ste 355
Atlanta, GA 30354
Phone: 770-969-7936
Fax: 770-969-7906
E-mail: info@gospelmusicchannel.com
Web Site: http://www.gospelmusicchannel.com
Charles Humbard, Founder, President & Chief Executive Officer
Bradley J. Siegel, Vice Chairman
Mary Jeanne Cavanagh, Executive Vice President, Advertising Sales
Leslie Chesloff, Executive Vice President, Programming
Paul Butler, Senior Vice President, General Counsel
Lisa Delligatti, Senior Vice President, Affiliate Sales
Genia Edelman, Senior Vice President, National Accounts
Rick Bell, Vice President, Finance
Philip Manwaring, Vice President, Digital Media
Erin Sullivan, Vice President, West Coast Ad Sales
Matt Turner, Vice President, Eastern Region Ad Sales
Kevin Wagner, Vice President, Creative Services
Jim Weiss, Vice President, Public Relations
Angela Cannon, Senior Director, Affiliate Marketing
Alvin Williams, Senior Director, Music, Talent & Acquisitions
Corey Prince, Director, Human Resources
Tiffany Thorpe, Director, Production Operations
Tammi Weed, Director, Music Industry Development & Program Acquisition
Michael Sinisi, Affiliate Marketing Director
Tracey Tooks, Marketing Manager
Ty Johnson, Manager, National Accounts, Southeast
Melissa Ingram, Counsel, Business Affairs
Type of service: Digital basic & video on demand.
Operating hours/week: 168.
Programming: All-music entertainment network devoted to gospel music; videos, concert series & biographical documentaries.
Began: October 30, 2004.
Means of Support: Advertising.
Total subscribers: 50,000,000.
Distribution method: Satellite & cable systems.
Ownership: Intermedia, Alpine.

GOSPEL MUSIC CHANNEL HD — See Gospel Music Channel.
Began: November 27, 2009.

GOSPEL MUSIC TV
PO Box 217
Gainesville, TX 76241
Phone: 800-665-2334
Web Site: http://www.gmtn.info
Type of service: Basic.
Satellites: Telstar 7, transponder 20; Intelsat Americas 13, transponder 20.
Operating hours/week: 168.
Programming: Gospel music and Christian programming.
Means of Support: Advertising.

GRAN CINE
560 Village Blvd
Ste 250
West Palm Beach, FL 33409
Phone: 866-940-2463
E-mail: opina@grancin
Web Site: http://www.grancine.tv
Maria Gomez-Garcia, Vice President, Network Development
Ivette Mendez, Vice President, Sales & Distribution
Fernanda Merodio, Director, Affiliate Sales & Marketing
Operating hours/week: 168.
Operating areas: Available nationwide plus Puerto Rico.
Programming: Spanish language movies and dramatic series network.

Distribution method: Available to home dish audiences and cable systems.
Scrambled signal: Yes.

GREAT AMERICAN COUNTRY HD — See Great American Country.

GREAT AMERICAN COUNTRY
9721 Sherrill Blvd
PO Box 51850
Knoxville, TN 3932
Phone: 615-327-7525
Fax: 615-329-8770
E-mail: mediarelations@scrippsnetworks.com
Web Site: http://www.gactv.com
Ed Hardy, President
Sarah Trahern, Senior Vice President & General Manager
Suzanne Gordon, Vice President, Programming
Michael O'Brien, Vice President, Sales, Television Division
Stephanie Halouma, Public Affairs Manager
Operating hours/week: 168.
Programming: Provides country music videos, original programming, special musical performances & live concerts; the exclusive television home of the Grand Ole Opry.
Began: December 31, 1995.
Means of Support: Advertising.
Total subscribers: 53,000,000.
Distribution method: Available to cable systems.
Scrambled signal: Yes.
Ownership: Scripps Networks Interactive.

GREEK CHANNEL — See National Greek Television.

GRTV NETWORK
3340 Ocean Park
Ste 3055
Santa Monica, CA 90405
Phone: 310-581-6250
Fax: 310-581-3268
E-mail: akirk@tvn.com
Ian Aaron, TCG President & Chief Operating Officer
Jim Riley, Senior Vice President, Business Development
Brooke Thomas, Senior Vice President, Television & Internet Ad Sales
Laura Barton, Marketing Manager
Dave Bartolone, Engineering Director
Type of service: Basic.
Satellites: Galaxy III-R, transponder 7; Galaxy IX, transponder 13; Galaxy III-R, transponder 8.
Operating hours/week: 168.
Uplink: Burbank, CA.
Programming: Direct response/infomercials.
Began: January 1, 1996.
Means of Support: Advertising, sponsorship & direct response revenue.
Total subscribers: 50,000,000.
Ownership: TVN Entertainment Corp.

GSN
10202 W Washington Blvd
Culver City, CA 90232-3195
Phone: 310-244-2222
Fax: 310-244-2080
E-mail: programming@gsn.com
Web Site: http://www.gsn.com
David Goldhill, President & Chief Executive Officer
Heidi Diamond, Executive Vice President
Chad O'Hara, Executive Vice President, Business & Legal Affairs
Dennis K. Gillespie, Senior Vice President, Distribution
Michael Kohn, Senior Vice President, Business & Legal Affairs
Jamie Roberts, Senior Vice President, Programming
John Zaccario, Senior Vice President, Advertising Sales
Marilyn Berryman, Vice President, National Accounts
Michael Bevan, Vice President, Original Programming
Dick Block, Vice President, Advertising Sales
Frank Cartwright, Vice President, Online Entertainment
Kim Caruso, Executive Director, Ad Sales Research
Kim Cunningham, Vice President, Business Affairs
Anne Droste, Vice President, National Accounts
Linnea Hemenez, Vice President, Creative Services
Sandy McGill, Vice President, National Accounts
Sydney McQuoid, Vice President, Sales, Central Region
Marc Musicus, Vice President, Sales, Eastern Region
Russell H. Myerson, Vice President, Operations
Scott Perlmutter, Vice President, Affiliate Sales, Western Region
Ryan Tredennick, Vice President, Programming Services
Kenneth L. Warun, Vice President, On-Air Promotions
Jean Wiegman, Vice President, Production
Melissa Zimmerman, Vice President, Marketing Solutions
Adam S. Gaynor, Executive Director, Digital Media & Interactive Sales
Joel McGee, Executive Director, Development
Leigh Primack, Executive Director, Distribution
Type of service: Basic.
Satellites: Galaxy VII.
Operating hours/week: 168.
Programming: Contemporary & classic game shows, interactive during morning & primetime hours.
Began: December 1, 1994.
Means of Support: Subscriber fees & advertising.
Total subscribers: 73,000,000.
Ownership: Sony Pictures Entertainment & Liberty Media Corp.

GSN HD — See GSN.
Satellites: Galaxy XIII, transponder 13.
Began: September 15, 2010.

GUANGDONG SOUTHERN TELEVISION (TVS) — See KyLinTV.
No. 331 Huan Shi Dong Road
Guangzhou 510066
China
Phone: 8620-6129-2727
Fax: 8620-8330-3629
Web Site: http://www.tvscn.com/
Type of service: IPTV.
Programming: Shows on Cantonese history, culture, social issues & Chinese news & entertainment. Carried by KyLinTV.
Began: July 1, 2004.
Scrambled signal: Yes.

GUARDIAN TELEVISION NETWORK (GTN)
3948 Townsfair Way
Ste 220
Columbus, OH 43219
Phones: 614-416-6080; 800-517-5151
Fax: 614-416-6345
E-mail: comments@gtn.tv
Web Site: http://www.gtn.tv
Programming: Family entertainment.
Began: January 1, 1976.
Distribution method: Available to cable & satellite systems.

GUNSLINGERS — No longer planned.

GUYTV — No longer in operation; part of Voom HD Networks.

HAHA — No longer planned.

HALLMARK CHANNEL
12700 Ventura Blvd
Studio City, CA 91604
Phones: 818-755-2400; 800-522-5131
Fax: 818-755-2564
Web Site: http://www.hallmarkchannel.com
Bill Abbott, President & Chief Executive Officer
Janice Arouh, Executive Vice President, Network Distribution & Services
Edward Georger, Executive Vice President, Advertising Sales
Joan Gundlach, Executive Vice President, Distribution
Laura Masse, Executive Vice President, Marketing
Brian Stewart, Executive Vice President & Chief Financial Officer
Michelle Vicary, Executive Vice President, Programming
Harriet Beck, Senior Vice President, Legal Affairs
Barbara Fisher, Senior Vice President, Original Programming
Chad Harris, Senior Vice President, Integrated Marketing & New Media
Annie Howell, Senior Vice President, Communications & Media Relations
Mark J. Kern, Senior Vice President, Communications & Media Relations
Len Marino, Senior Vice President, Creative Services & On-Air Promotion
Susanne McAvoy, Senior Vice President, Network Operations
Laura Sillars, Senior Vice President, Lifestyle Programming
Pam Slay, Senior Vice President, Network Program Publicity
Anthony White, Senior Vice President, Marketing
Jess Aguirre, Vice President, Research
Lisa Barroso, Vice President, Distribution
Donovan Batiste, Vice President, Research & Media Planning
Bill Butte, Vice President, Direct Marketing
Roy Cowan, Vice President, Marketing
Shannon Dashiell-Rapp, Vice President, Design
Madeline Di Nonno, Vice President, Marketing Alliances
Whitney Holland, Vice President, Acquisitions
Shira Kalish, Vice President, Ad Sales & Alliance Marketing
Andy Karofsky, Vice President, Marketing
Sean Kelly, Vice President, Western Ad Sales
Erin McIlvain, Vice President, National Accounts
Darren Melameth, Vice President, Program Planning & Scheduling
Hank Smith, Vice President, Human Resources
Ron Stark, Vice President, Affiliate Marketing
Tara Tzirlin, Vice President, Consumer Marketing
Claude Wells, Vice President, Network Distribution & Services
Bob Young, Vice President, Operations
Tara Donnelly, Senior Director, Consumer Marketing
Jaime Sabeirto, Senior Director, Corporate Communications
Allison Bennett, Director, Corporate Communications & Media Relations
Toni Lorusso, Director, Ad Sales Marketing
Seema Patel, Director, Pricing & Planning
Type of service: Basic.
Satellites: Satcom III-R, transponder 5.
Operating hours/week: 168.
Uplink: Denver, CO.
Programming: Family friendly programming.
Began: September 19, 1988, . Formerly Odyssey Network. Re-launched as Hallmark Channel on August 5, 2001.
Means of Support: Advertising & license fees.
Total subscribers: 87,500,000.
Distribution method: Available to cable & home dish audiences.
Scrambled signal: Yes.
Ownership: Crown Media Family Networks.

HALLMARK CHANNEL HD — See Hallmark Channel.
Began: February 1, 2010.

HALLMARK MOVIE CHANNEL — See Hallmark Channel.
Type of service: Digital.
Total subscribers: 40,000,000.
Distribution method: Available to cable, satellite & telco systems.

HALLMARK MOVIE CHANNEL HD — See Hallmark Channel.
Began: April 2, 2008.

HALOGEN NETWORK
3000 WorldReach Dr
Indian Land, SC 29707
Phone: 803-578-1500
Fax: 803-578-1735
E-mail: Karen.davis@halogentv.com
Web Site: http://www.halogentv.com
Rebekah Henderson, General Manager
Kyle Chowning, Vice President, Marketing & Communications
Christie Legg, Vice President, Network Strategy & Partnerships
Kyle Young, Vice President, Business Operations
Marshall Nord, Director of Programming & Acquisitions
John Russo, Director, Sales
Type of service: Digital.
Satellites: HITS POD7.
Operating hours/week: 168.
Programming: Launched in October 2009 to replace Inspirational Life Television (i-Lifetv). Halogen is a socially conscious,

multiplatform television network targeting adults 18-34, that seeks to empower viewers to make positive changes in the world around them. Halogen content includes drama, comedy, reality, documentary, and magazine show genres. Available through the Headend in the Sky service.
Began: October 24, 2009, Originally launched June 4, 1998 as Inspirational Life Television. Rebranded as Halogen Network October 24, 2009.
Total subscribers: 14,000,000.
Distribution method: Available to cable systems.
Scrambled signal: Yes.
Ownership: The Inspiration Networks Inc.

HAVOC TV
880 Apollo St
Ste 239
El Segundo, CA 90245
Phones: 310-563-2613; 310-524-1540
E-mail: ryan@havoctv.com
Web Site: http://www.havoctv.com
Ryan Kresser, Chief Executive Officer & Founder
David Dekadt, President & Founder
Matt Muir, Vice President, Music
Jeff Cutler, Vice President, Action Sports
Dean McCormick, Vice President, Interactive Platforms
Jim Lindberg, Vice President, Marketing & Business Development
Clinton Cox, Vice President, Original Programming
Sam Velde, Director, Programming & Licensing

Branch Offices:
NEW YORK: 41 E 11th St, 11th Floor, New York, NY 10003. Phone: 212-331-1245.

MIAMI: 705 Washington Ave, Miami, FL 33139. Phone: 305-695-6700.
Type of service: Video on demand.
Programming: Action sports & music.
Began: N.A.
Total subscribers: 17,000,000.
Distribution method: Available to cable systems.

HAZARDOUS — See Versus.

HBCU NETWORK
239 Walker St
Atlanta, GA 30310
E-mail: info@hbcunetwork.com
Web Site: http://www.hbcunetwork.com/
Curtis Symonds, Chief Executive Officer
Clint Evans, Executive Vice President, Distribution & Marketing
Candace Walker, Executive Vice President, Programming & Operations
Type of service: Basic.
Operating hours/week: Plans 168.
Operating areas: Plans to serve Mid-Atlantic, Midwest & Southern regions.
Programming: Sports, edutainment and lifestyle network devoted entirely to the four HBCU Conferences (CIAA, MEAC, SIAC, SWAC) and its member and independent universities.
Scheduled to begin: Plans September 2011.
Means of Support: Plans advertising.
Total subscribers: (Plans 10,000,000 at launch.).
Distribution method: Will be available to cable systems.
Scrambled signal: Planned.
Ownership: C3 Media LLC, majority interest; Historically Black Colleges and Universities, 20%.

HBO
1100 Avenue of the Americas
New York, NY 10036
Phone: 212-512-1000
Fax: 212-512-1166
E-mail: admin@hbo.com
Web Site: http://www.homeboxoffice.com
Bill Nelson, Chairman & Chief Executive Officer
Eric Kessler, Co-President
Richard Plepler, Co-President
Colin Callender, President, HBO Films
Henry McGee, President, HBO Home Video
Sue Naegle, President, HBO Entertainment
Sheila Nevins, President, HBO Documentaries & Family
Steven Rosenberg, President, HBO International
Michael Lombardo, President, Programming Group & West Coast Operations
Steve Scheffer, President, Film Programming, Video & Enterprises
David Baldwin, Executive Vice President, Program Planning
Shelley Fischel, Executive Vice President, HR & Administration
Rob Roth, Executive Vice President & Chief Financial Officer
Tom Woodbury, Executive Vice President & General Counsel
Otto Berkes, Senior Vice President, Consumer Technology
Diane Tryneski, Senior Vice President, Studio & Broadcast Operations
Frank Rich, Creative Consultant

Regional Offices:
ATLANTA: Lennox Bldg, 3399 Peachtree Rd NE, Atlanta, GA 30326. Phone: 404-239-6600. Fax: 404-261-4185.

CHICAGO: 6250 N River Rd, Ste 10-300, Rosemont, IL 60018. Phone: 847-318-5100. Fax: 847-825-1333.

DALLAS: 12750 Merit Dr, Ste 1105, Dallas, TX 75251. Phone: 972-450-1000. Fax: 972-387-5670.

DENVER: The Quadrant, 5445 DTC Pkwy, Ste 700, Englewood, CO 80111. Phone: 303-220-2900. Fax: 303-220-9668.

LOS ANGELES: 2049 Century Park E, Ste 4100, Los Angeles, CA 90067. Phone: 310-201-9200. Fax: 310-201-9310.

PHILADELPHIA: 401 City Ave, Ste 620, Bala Cynwyd, PA 19004. Phone: 610-668-6500. Fax: 610-668-9318.

SAN FRANCISCO: 353 Sacramento St, 20th Floor, San Francisco, CA 94111. Phone: 415-765-7700. Fax: 415-788-0183.
Type of service: Pay.
Satellites: Galaxy V, transponder 8 (west coast); Galaxy 111-R, transponder 16 (east coast); Galaxy 111-R, transponder 20 (west coast); Galaxy 111-R, transponder 19 (east coast).
Operating hours/week: 168.
Uplink: Smithtown, NY.
Programming: 24-hour variety programming including movies, entertainment specials, sports, special events, documentaries, children's programming & movies made for HBO.
Began: November 8, 1972.
Means of Support: Subscriber fees.
Total subscribers: 28,200,000 (HBO/Cinemax).
Distribution method: Available to home dish audiences & cable systems.

Scrambled signal: Yes. Equipment: M/A-Com VideoCipher II.
Ownership: Time Warner Entertainment Co.

HBO ASIA
Singapore Pte Ltd.
Lorong Chuan, 04-05 New Tech Park
Singapore 1955
Phone: 65-288-6303
Fax: 65-287-7353
Web Site: http://www.hboasia.com
Dan Murrell, President & Chief Executive Officer
Steve Rosenberg, President, HBO Int'l
Type of service: Pay.
Operating hours/week: 168.
Programming: English language premium service available in Singapore, Thailand, Philippines, Indonesia, Taiwan & Brunei.
Began: June 1, 1992.
Ownership: AOL Time Warner.

HBO COMEDY — See HBO.
Programming: Original comedy series, movies & stand-up specials.
Began: May 1, 1999.

HBO EN ESPANOL — See HBO.

HBO FAMILY — See HBO.
Sheila Nevins, President, HBO Documentary & Family Programming
Delores Morris, Vice President, HBO Family & Documentary Programming
Began: October 1, 1998.
Total subscribers: 30,000,000.

HBO GO
1100 Avenue of the Americas
New York, NY 10036
Phone: 212-512-1000
Fax: 212-512-1166
E-mail: Laura.young@hbo.com
Web Site: http://www.hbogo.com
Eric Kessler, President, HBO
Marti Moore, Vice President, Web Technology, Customer Experience
Type of service: Online video service.
Operating hours/week: 168.
Operating areas: Available nationwide.
Programming: Video streaming service which allows HBO subscribers to watch HBO programming on their PCs.
Began: February 17, 2011.
Distribution method: Available to to all HBO subscribers on Comcast & Verizon FiOS systems.
Scrambled signal: Yes.
Ownership: Home Box Office Inc.

HBO HD — See HBO.

HBO HUNGARY
H-1111 Budapest
Budafoki ut. 59 E-1 ep. 111 em
Hungary
Phone: 011-36-1-365-2466
Web Site: http://www.hbo.hu
Steve Rosenberg, President, HBO Int'l
Type of service: Pay.
Operating hours/week: 72.
Programming: Mix of Hungarian, American & European films.
Began: September 28, 1991.
Ownership: AOL Time Warner & United Communications International (US West & TCI).

HBO INTERNATIONAL
5201 Blue Lagoon Dr
Ste 270
Miami, FL 37736
Phone: 305-266-7763
Fax: 305-266-5898
E-mail: simon.sutton@hbo.com
Web Site: http://www.hbo.com
Simon Sutton, President, HBO Int'l
Type of service: Pay.
Operating hours/week: 168.
Programming: Spanish language premium service available throughout South America, Central America, Mexico & the Caribbean Basin.
Began: October 1, 1991.
Ownership: AOL Time Warner; Ole Communications Inc. & Sony Pictures Entertainment.

HBO LATINO — See HBO.
Programming: U.S. premieres of Spanish-language films, documentaries, music videos, original programming featuring entertainment & cultural issues & a mix of Hollywood movies, HBO Sports & original shows dubbed in Spanish.
Began: November 1, 2000.
Scrambled signal: Yes.
Ownership: Time Warner Inc. 21%; Sony Pictures Entertainment 8%.

HBO ON BROADBAND — See HBO.
Currently only available to Time Warner Cable subscribers in Milwaukee & Green Bay, WI on a trial basis.

HBO ON DEMAND — See HBO.
Type of service: Video on demand.
Programming: Hollywood movies, original programming, kids shows, boxing & episodes from past seasons' series.
Began: January 1, 2001.
Total subscribers: 8,000,000.
Distribution method: Available to cable & satellite providers.

HBO SIGNATURE — See HBO.
Programming: Documentaries, original series & movies targeted to women.
Began: October 1, 1998.

HBO THE WORKS — See HBO.

HBO 2 — See HBO.
Programming: Replays HBO series, movies, sports events & original programming.
Began: October 1, 1998.

HBO ZONE — See HBO.
Programming: Mix of films, music videos & original HBO programming.
Began: May 1, 1999.

HD ON DEMAND — See PBS HD.

HDNET
320 S Walton St
Dallas, TX 75226
Phone: 214-672-1740
Fax: 214-571-9225
E-mail: viewer@hd.net
Web Site: http://www.hd.net
Mark Cuban, Chairman & President
Terdema Ussery, Chief Executive Officer
Philip Garvin, General Manager & Chief Operating Officer
Robert Thoele, Chief Financial Officer & Gen. Counsel
Bill Osborn, Senior Vice President, Marketing
Elisabeth Glass, General Manager & Senior Vice President Programming
Bill Padalino, Managing Director, Affiliate Sales
Colette Carey, Media & Public Relations Director
Rachael Weaver, Networks Programming Director
Lucia F. McCalmont, Program Acquisitions

Branch Offices:
DENVER: 8269 E 23rd Ave, Denver, CO 80238. Phone: 303-542-5600.
Programming: First national television network to broadcast all of its programming in 1080i High Definition; sports, news & entertainment.
Began: September 6, 2001.
Ownership: Mark Cuban.

HDNET MOVIES — See HDNet.

HEADLINE NEWS
One CNN Center NW
Atlanta, GA 30303
Phone: 404-827-1700
E-mail: cnn@cnn.com
Web Site: http://www.cnn.com/hln
Walter Isaacson, President
Greg D'Alba, Executive Vice President & Chief Operating Officer, CNN Sales & Marketing
Rolando Santos, Executive Vice President & General Manager
Jake Carreau, Vice President
David Willis, Vice President & Managing Editor
Stan Anderson, Broadcast Design Director
Type of service: Basic.
Satellites: Galaxy I, transponder 8.
Operating hours/week: 168.
Uplink: Atlanta, GA.
Programming: News-headline service.
Began: December 31, 1981.
Total subscribers: 99,400,000 (Also serves 559,776 subscribers on 68 Canadian systems.).
Distribution method: Available to cable systems.
Equipment: VideoCipher.
Ownership: AOL Time Warner.

HEADLINE NEWS HD — See Headline News.

HEALTHINATION
35 E 21st St
Ste 6E
New York, NY 10010
Phone: 212-633-0007
E-mail: diane@healthination.com
Web Site: http://www.healthination.com
Raj Amin, Chief Executive Officer & Co-Founder
Tony Estrella, Chief Operating Officer & Co-Founder
Holly Atkinson, MD, Chief Medical Officer
Brendan Anderer, Vice President, Programming
Stuart Rohrer, Vice President, Analytics & Technology
Scott Schappell, Vice President, Sales
Michael Stoeckel, Vice President, Client Services
Preeti Parikh, Medical Director of Programming
Diane Hepps, Director, Communications
Type of service: Basic, Video-On-Demand and online.
Operating areas: Available nationwide.
Programming: The channel that educates and inspires people to make healthier choices. The programs cover disease and condition education as well as lifestyle tips, diet and personal stories.
Began: January 30, 2007, on cable.
Means of Support: Advertising and subscriber fees.
Total subscribers: 32,000,000 (Also has over 40000000 unique users online.).
Distribution method: Available to cable systems and FiOS & U-verse subscribers.
Scrambled signal: Yes.
Ownership: Intel Capital & MK Capital.

HEALTHY LIVING CHANNEL
4100 E Mississippi Ave
Ste 1700
Glendale, CO 80246
Phone: 303-839-5303
Fax: 303-839-5335
Web Site: http://www.healthylivingtv.com
Anne Leuthold, Marketing Manager
Wendy Borow Johnson, Programming
Stefania Ascoli, Programming
Programming: Covers topics from fitness & beauty to financial health & relationships.
Total subscribers: 15,000,000.
Ownership: Turner Media Group.

HELENA CIVIC TELEVISION (HCT)
1015 Poplar St
Helena, MT 59601
Phone: 406-447-1608
Fax: 406-447-1609
E-mail: hctv@bresnan.net
Web Site: http://www.helenacivictv.org/
Steven Maly, Executive Director
Kirsten Faubion, Production Director
Jo McLean, Office Manager
Operating hours/week: 168.
Programming: Unedited coverage of local & state government proceedings, public affairs & programs on culture, sports & religion.
Began: January 1, 2001.
Total subscribers: 14,000.

HERE! ON DEMAND — See here! TV.
Type of service: Video on demand.
Programming: Feature films, documentaries, series & specials.
Began: June 1, 2004.

HERE! TV
10990 Wilshire Blvd
Penthouse
Los Angeles, CA 90024
Phone: 310-806-4298
Fax: 310-806-4268
E-mail: info@heretv.com
Web Site: http://www.heretv.com
Paul Colichman, Chief Executive Officer
Andrew Tow, Chief Operating Officer
Mark Reinhart, Executive Vice President, Distribution & Acquisition
Stephen Macias, Senior Vice President, Corporate Communications, Public Relations & Consumer Marketing
Maria Dwyer, Senior Vice President, Distribution Sales & Marketing
Jeff Elgart, Senior Vice President, Corporate Ad Sales & Sponsorships
Meredith Kadlec, Vice President, Original Programming
Cory Sher, Distribution & Marketing Director
Billy Cogar, Development Director

Branch Offices:
NEW YORK: 570 Lexington Ave, 19th Floor, New York, NY 10022.
Type of service: Pay.
Operating hours/week: 168.
Programming: Full-service network offering movies, original series & general entertainment programming targeted to broad-based gay & lesbian audience.
Began: August 29, 2003.
Total subscribers: 40,000,000.
Distribution method: Digital, will also offer broadband.

HGTV
(Home & Garden Television)
9721 Sherrill Blvd
Knoxville, TN 37932
Phones: 865-694-2700; 865-694-7879
Fax: 865-531-8933
E-mail: online-ad@hgtv.com
Web Site: http://www.hgtv.com
Kenneth W. Lowe, President & Chief Executive Officer, E.W. Scripps
Richard A. Boehne, Chief Operating Officer, E.W. Scripps
Jim Samples, President, HGTV
Susan Packard, President, New Ventures Group
Burton Jablin, Executive Vice President
Joseph G. NeCastro, Executive Vice President, Finance & Administration
Lori Asbury, Senior Vice President, Marketing & Creative Services
Mike Boyd, Senior Vice President, Consumer Marketing
Denise Conroy-Galley, Senior Vice President, Marketing & Creative Services
Sarah Cronan, Senior Vice President, Brand Management & Scheduling
A. B. Cruz, III, Senior Vice President & General Counsel
Michael Dingley, Senior Vice President, Programming, Content & Strategy
Lila Reinhard Everett, Senior Vice President, Marketing & Communications
Mark Hale, Senior Vice President, Technical Operations
Freddy P. James, Senior Vice President, Program Development & Production
John Lansing, Senior Vice President & President, Scripps Networks
Jeff Meyer, Senior Vice President, Internet Sales
Donna Stephens, Senior Vice President, Ad Sales
Chad Youngblood, Senior Vice President, Home Category Initiatives
Audrey Adlam, Vice President, Communications
John E. Ajamie, Vice President, Network Operations & Duplication Services
Annette Lindstrom Brun, Vice President, Consumer Marketing
Anna Gecan, Vice President, Programming
Paige Hardwick, Vice President, On-Air Strategy & Media Planning
Doug Hurst, Vice President, Affiliate Marketing
Kristen Jordan, Vice President, International Development
Jennifer Leitman, Vice President, Brand Promotions
Annette Lindstrom, Vice President, Marketing
Chris Moore, Vice President, Creative Director
Robin Pate, Vice President, Program Scheduling
Dusty Schmidt, Vice President, Creative Services
Pamela Treacy, Vice President, New Business & Administration
Karen Wishart, Vice President, Content Planning & Administration
Type of service: Basic.
Satellites: Galaxy I-R, transponder 20.
Operating hours/week: 168.
Programming: Features home repair & remodeling, home decorating, consumer audio, video, garden & lawn care.
Began: December 30, 1994.
Means of Support: Advertising & subscriber fees.
Total subscribers: 100,900,000.
Distribution method: Available to cable systems & home dish audiences.
Ownership: Scripps Networks Interactive.

HGTV CANADA
121 Bloor St E
Ste 1500
Toronto, ON M4W 3M5
Canada
Phone: 416-967-1174
Fax: 416-960-0971
E-mail: feedback@hgtv.ca
Web Site: http://www.hgtv.ca
Alexandra Brown, Senior Vice President
Jim Ericson, Vice President, Programming
Barbara Williams, Vice President, Programming
Type of service: Expanded basic.
Satellites: Anik E-2, transponder 19.
Operating hours/week: 168.
Uplink: Toronto Teleport.
Programming: Provides viewers with home & garden resources & ideas.
Began: October 17, 1997.
Means of Support: Subscriber fees & advertising.
Total subscribers: 5,000,000.
Distribution method: Available to cable systems.
Equipment: DSR 4400.
Ownership: Alliance Atlantis Communications.

HGTV HD — See HGTV.

HGTV ON DEMAND — See HGTV.
Type of service: Video on demand.

HISTORY CHANNEL
235 E 45th St
8th Fl
New York, NY 10017
Phone: 212-210-1400
Fax: 212-907-9481
E-mail: lynn.gardner@aetn.com
Web Site: http://www.history.com
Nancy Dubuc, President & General Manager
Peter Gaffney, Senior Vice President, Programming Strategy, Scheduling & Acquisitions
Dirk Hoogstra, Senior Vice President, Development & Programming
Chris Moseley, Senior Vice President, Marketing
Peter Olsen, Senior Vice President, Ad Sales
Marc Finnegan, Vice President, Scheduling & Acquisitions
Mary Donahue, Vice President, Development & Programming
Julian Hobbs, Vice President, Development & Programming
Matt Ginsberg, Vice President, Development & Programming
Charles Nordlander, Vice President, Development & Programming
Mike Stiller, Vice President, Development & Programming

Type of service: Basic cable & video on demand.
Satellites: Satcom C-3, transponder 12 (analog east); Galaxy IX, transponder 23 (digital); Satcom C-4, transponder 6 (analog west).
Operating hours/week: 168.
Uplink: Stamford, CT.
Programming: Original non-fiction series, specials, event specials and mini-series.
Began: January 1, 1995, History Channel International began on December 1, 1998.
Means of Support: Advertiser & subscriber fees.
Total subscribers: 100,300,000.
Distribution method: Available to cable systems.
Scrambled signal: Yes.
Ownership: Hearst Corp., NBCUniversal LLC & The Walt Disney Co.

HISTORY CHANNEL EN ESPANOL — See History Channel.
Type of service: Basic & video on demand.
Began: June 1, 2004, reflects U.S. launch date.
Total subscribers: 750,000.

HISTORY CHANNEL HD — See History Channel.

HISTORY CHANNEL INTERNATIONAL — See History Channel.

HISTORY TELEVISION
121 Bloor St E
Ste 200
Toronto, ON M4W 3M5
Canada
Phone: 416-967-0022
Fax: 416-967-0044
E-mail: feedback@historytelevision.ca
Web Site: http://www.historytelevision.ca
Phyllis Yaffe, President
Norm Bolen, Vice President, Programming
Janet Eastwood, Vice President, Marketing & Communications
Harvey Rogers, Vice President, Broadcast Operations & Engineering
John Tsagarakis, Vice President, Finance & Business Systems
Type of service: Basic.
Satellites: Anik E-2, transponder 19.
Operating hours/week: 168.
Programming: Documentaries, movies & original historical programming.
Began: October 17, 1997.
Means of Support: Advertising & subscription fees.
Distribution method: Available to cable systems.
Equipment: DigiCipher II.
Ownership: Alliance Communications Corp., 88%; CTV, 12%.

HITN
Brooklyn Navy Yard Bldg 292, Ste 211
63 Flushing Ave, Unit 281
Brooklyn, NY 11205-1078
Phone: 212-966-5660
Fax: 212-966-5725
E-mail: programacion@hitn.org
Web Site: http://www.hitn.org
Jose Luis Rodriguez, President & Chief Executive Officer
Eric Turpin, Vice President, Affiliate Sales & Distribution

Branch Offices:
BROOKLYN NAVY YARD: 63 Flushing Ave, Bldg 292, Ste 326, Brooklyn, NY 11205-1078. Phone: 877-391-4486. Fax: 718-797-2546.
Type of service: Basic & video on demand.
Operating hours/week: 168.
Operating areas: Available nationwide.
Programming: Spanish language, educational programming including documentaries, live interactive programs & original series.
Began: January 1, 1987.
Total subscribers: 40,000,000.
Distribution method: Cable, Satellite.
Scrambled signal: Yes.
Ownership: Privately held.

HITS EN ESPANOL — See HITS (Headend In The Sky).

HITS (HEADEND IN THE SKY)
Comcast Media Center
4100 E Dry Creek Rd
Centennial, CO 80122
Phone: 866-275-4487
E-mail: cmc_denver@cable.comcast.com
Web Site: http://www.HITS.com
Leslie E. Russell, Vice President & General Manager, HITS
Dave Higgins, Vice President, Engineering & Transmission Operations
Programming: Provides digital programming packages to cable operators.

HLN — See Headline News.

HOLLYWOODPRESSTV.COM
Albuquerque Studios, Bldg. D
5650 University Blvd. SE
Albuquerque, NM 87106
E-mail: getmoreinfo@mypresstv.com
Web Site: http://HollywoodPressTV.com
Programming: Online-only movie site. Also offers BroadwayPress TV & EventPress TV.
Began: January 1, 2007.
Means of Support: Subscriber fees.
Total subscribers: 2,000,000.
Distribution method: Available to home dish subscribers.
Scrambled signal: Yes.
Ownership: ReelzChannel.

HOLLYWOOD.COM TV
560 Broadway
Ste 404
New York, NY 10012
Phone: 212-817-9105
E-mail: businessdev@hollywood.com
Web Site: http://www.hollywood.com
Mitchell Rubenstein, Chairman & Chief Executive Officer
Laurie S. Silvers, President
Scott Gomez, Vice President, Finance & Accounting
Type of service: Basic & video on demand.
Programming: Providing interactive access to latest movie releases, showtimes, celebrity interviews and more.
Began: August 1, 2002.
Distribution method: Available to cable & satellite providers.

HOME & GARDEN TELEVISION — See HGTV.

HOME SHOPPING NETWORK EN ESPANOL — See Home Shopping Network.

HOME SHOPPING NETWORK HD — See Home Shopping Network.

HOME SHOPPING NETWORK 2 — See Home Shopping Network.
Type of service: Basic.
Operating hours/week: 168.
Operating areas: Available nationwide.
Programming: Shows mostly taped programs and products from HSN.
Began: August 1, 2010.
Total subscribers: 14,000,000.
Distribution method: Available to home dish audiences.
Scrambled signal: Yes.

HOME THEATRE — See Movie Central.

HOME BOX OFFICE — See HBO.

HOME SHOPPING NETWORK
One HSN Dr.
St. Petersburg, FL 33729
Phone: 727-872-1000
Web Site: http://www.hsn.com
Mindy Grossman, Chief Executive Officer & President
Mark Ethier, Chief Operating Officer
Jill Braff, Executive Vice President, Digital Commerce
Bill Brand, Executive Vice President, Programming & Advanced Services
Greg Henchel, Executive Vice President, General Counsel & Secretary
Lisa Letizio, Executive Vice President, Human Resources
Lynne Ronon, Executive Vice President, Merchandising
Peter Ruben, Executive Vice President, Affiliate Relations Group
Judy Schmeling, Executive Vice President & Chief Financial Officer
Andrew Sheldon, Executive Vice President & Creative Director
Mitchell Hara, Senior Vice President, Corporate Strategy & Mergers and Acquisitions
Arthur Lewis, Senior Vice President, Merchandising, Digital Commerce
Type of service: Basic.
Satellites: Satcom C-4, transponder 10.
Operating hours/week: 168.
Programming: Features live, discount shop-at-home service.
Began: July 1, 1985.
Means of Support: Commissions on merchandise sold.
Total subscribers: 90,600,000.
Distribution method: Available to home dish audiences & cable systems.
Ownership: HSN Inc.
(HSN) Home shopping television network that features a range of products, from electronics & household items to beauty & fashion items.

HOOKS AND BULLETS — See Versus.

HOPE CHANNEL
PO Box 4000
Silver Spring, MD 20914
Phones: 301-680-6689; 800-226-1119
Fax: 301-680-5147
E-mail: info@hopetv.org
Web Site: http://www.hopetv.org

Branch Offices:
ADVENTIST COMMUNICATION NETWORK: 12501 Old Columbia Pike, Silver Spring, MD, 20904. Fax: 301-680-6697.
Type of service: Basic.
Satellites: AMC-4.
Operating hours/week: 168.
Programming: Evangelical series, sermons & education, church news, meetings & sunday school study & programs on public health, family life & special events.
Distribution method: Available to cable systems & satellite audiences.
Ownership: Adventist Television Network.

HORROR CHANNEL — See Fright Channel.

HORROR NET — Launched as FearNet.

HORSETV CHANNEL
4021 Anns Ln
Allen, TX 75002
Phone: 972-633-1133
Fax: 972-578-0675
E-mail: admin@horsetv.com
Web Site: http://www.horsetv.com
Bernard Uechtritz, Executive Chairman
Type of service: Basic.
Operating hours/week: 168.
Programming: Equestrian documentaries, competitions & events; instructional programs; news.
Began: October 27, 2005, Service was shut down due to financial difficulties in December 2007. It was relaunched under new ownership in January 2009.
Distribution method: Available to cable systems & satellite providers.
Scrambled signal: Yes.
Ownership: Private Texas-based investment group.

HOT CHOICE
2029 Century Park E
Ste 2080
Los Angeles, CA 90067
Phone: 310-785-9194
Fax: 310-785-9769
E-mail: pressoffice@indemand.com
Web Site: http://www.indemand.com
Samuel L. Yates, Senior Vice President, Finance & Administration
Greg Rothberg, Vice President, Sales & Marketing
Sandra E. Landau, Vice President & General Counsel
Leigh Bolton, Vice President, Video Promotion
Terry Taylor, Vice President, Affiliate Relations
Michael Klein, Vice President, Programming
John Vartanian, Vice President, Technology & Operations
John Migliacci, Acquisitions Manager
Type of service: Pay-per-view.
Satellites: Satcom C-4, transponder 18.
Operating hours/week: 168.
Programming: Action-adventure and adult-appeal movies & special events.
Began: February 1, 1993.

Equipment: DigiCipher.
Ownership: Comcast, Cox Communications, AT&T Broadband & Internet Services/Liberty Media, Time Warner Cable.

HOWARD TV
iN DEMAND
345 Husdon St, 17th Fl
New York, NY 10014
Phone: 646-638-8200
Fax: 646-486-0855
E-mail: pressoffice@howardtv.com
Web Site: http://www.howardtv.com
Type of service: Video on demand.
Operating hours/week: 160.
Programming: Unlimited & uncensored access to in-studio footage of Howard Stern's satellite radio program, archived programs & other original Howard Stern oriented shows.
Began: N.A.
Distribution method: Available to cable systems.

HOWARD TV ON DEMAND
345 Hudson St
c/o iN DEMAND LLC
New York, NY 10014
Phone: 646-638-8200
Fax: 646-486-0854
Web Site: http://www.howard.tv
Doug Z Goodstein, Executive Producer
Type of service: Subscription video on demand.
Satellites: AMC 10, transponder 18.
Operating hours/week: 168.
Operating areas: Available nationwide on Bright House Networks, Cablevison, Charter, Comcast, Cox & Time Warner Cable systems.
Programming: Offers uncensored unlimited access to all of Howard Stern's television catalog plus original series.
Began: November 18, 2005.
Total subscribers: 40,000,000 (Includes Canadian subscribers through Rogers Cable Systems.).
Distribution method: Available to Bright House Networks, Cablevision, Charter, Comcast, Cox & Time Warner Cable systems subscribers.
Scrambled signal: Yes.
Ownership: iN DEMAND.

HRTV
c/o Santa Anita Park
285 W Huntington Dr
Arcadia, CA 91007
Phones: 866-733-4788; 888-572-8883
E-mail: customerservice@hrtv.com
Web Site: http://www.hrtv.com
Scott Daruty, President & Chief Executive Officer
Jim Bates, Executive Vice President & General Manager
Dennis Murphy, Senior Vice President, Advertising Sales
Christopher Swan, Senior Vice President, Distribution & Business Development
Phil Kubel, Vice President, Post Production & Technology
Stephen Nagler, Vice President, Live Programming
Michael Canale, Senior Producer Live Programming
Type of service: Basic.
Operating hours/week: 168.
Programming: Live thoroughbred & harness racing from tracks across North America. Exclusive coverage of premier tracks like Santa Anita, Gulf Stream, Golden Gate Fields, The Meadows & others. Formerly known as HorseRacing TV.
Began: January 1, 2003.
Means of Support: Advertising.
Total subscribers: 19,000,000.
Scrambled signal: Yes.
Ownership: Magna Entertainment Corp.

HTV MUSICA
404 Washington Ave
Miami Beach, FL 33139
Phone: 305-887-8488
Fax: 305-887-0028
E-mail: contacto@htv.com
Web Site: http://www.htv.com
Daniel Sawicki, President & Chief Executive Officer
Jorge Escasena, Vice President, Affiliate Sales
Gustavo Tonelli, Director, Marketing
Richard Taylor, Director, Advertising Sales
Raquel Bretos Mendez, Manager, Programming

HTV Argentina:
BUENOS AIRES: Avenida Martin Garcia, Piso 7, Dto. A (1268), Buenos Aires, Argentina.
Phone: 54-1-307-2721.
Type of service: Basic.
Satellites: Intelsat 806, transponder 12A; GE-1, transponder 5; Hispasat, transponder 13.
Operating hours/week: 168.
Uplink: Miami, FL.
Programming: Spanish language music videos. Each hour of programming is divided into 4 blocks with different combinations of rhythms.
Began: August 25, 1995.
Means of Support: Advertising & subscriber fees.
Total subscribers: 8,100,000.
Distribution method: Available to cable systems.
Equipment: Scientific-Atlanta; VideoCipher II Plus.
Ownership: Daniel Sawicki & Robert Behar.

HULU
12312 W Olympic Blvd
Los Angeles, CA 90064
Phone: 310-571-4700
Fax: 310-571-4701
E-mail: media@hulu.com
Web Site: http://www.hulu.com
Jason Kilar, Chief Executive Officer
Jean-Paul Colaco, Senior Vice President, Advertising
Andy Forssell, Senior Vice President, Content Acquisition & Distribution
John Foster, Senior Vice President, Talent & Organization
Tom Fuelling, Senior Vice President & Chief Financial Officer
Chadwick Ho, Senior Vice President & General Counsel
Johannes Larcher, Senior Vice President, International
Eugene Wei, Senior Vice President, Audience
Richard Tom, Vice President, Platform Strategies
Type of service: Broadband.
Programming: Full-length movies & tv series from Fox, NBC, Sony Pictures, MGM Studios & others.
Began: October 29, 2007.
Means of Support: Advertising.
Total subscribers: 875,000.
Distribution method: Available online.
Scrambled signal: Yes.
Ownership: NBCUniversal LLC (32%), News Corp. (31%), The Walt Disney Company (27%), Providence Equity Partners (9%) & Hulu employees (1%).

HUNAN SATELLITE TV (HTV) — See KyLinTV.
Phone: 0731-287-1680-8088
Fax: 0731-287-1686-8010
E-mail: web@hunantv.com
Web Site: http://news.hunantv.com/English/
Type of service: IPTV.
Programming: Offers Madarin Chinese language news & entertainment programming. Available on KyLinTV.
Began: January 1, 1997, Date shown is launch date in China.

HUSTLER TV
8484 Wilshire Blvd
Ste 900
Beverly Hills, CA 90211
Phone: 323-651-5400 x7421
Fax: 323-651-0651
Web Site: http://www.hustlertv.com
Michael H. Klein, President
Camila Ipinza, Vice President, Sales & Affiliate Marketing, Western Region
Jim Dettman, Business Development & Distribution Director
David de Beauchamp, Operations Director, LFP Broadcasting
Lillian Martin, Affiliate Sales & Marketing Director
Type of service: Video on demand & pay-per-view.
Satellites: Galaxy 15, transponder Transponder 10.
Programming: Adult entertainment.
Began: October 1, 2004.
Total subscribers: 55,000,000.
Distribution method: Available to cable & satellite systems.
Ownership: LFP Broadcasting.

HWAZAN TV — See KyLinTV.
Type of service: IPTV.
Programming: Buddhist themed shows.

HYPE TV — No longer planned.

IAVC
9550 Flair Dr
Ste 102
El Monte, CA 91731
Phone: 626-337-8889
Web Site: http://www.iavcusa.com
Amanda Lee, Chief Executive Officer
Programming: Exclusive program distributor of Taiwan's major television networks in North America. Available through KyLinTV's IPTV service.
Scrambled signal: Yes.

ICTV
333 W San Carlos St
Ste 400
San Jose, CA 95110
Phone: 408-931-9200
Fax: 408-931-9100
E-mail: info@ictv.com
Web Site: http://www.ictv.com
Robert B. Clasen, Chairman
Wes Hoffman, President & Chief Executive Officer
John Taft, Chief Financial Officer
Jeff Miller, Senior Vice President, Engineering
Stephanie Brownlee, Senior Vice President, Sales
William Zerella, Vice President, Finance
Edith Crowe, Vice President, Marketing
Gary Hamilton, Vice President, Marketing
Stephen Snell, Vice President, Radio Frequency & Video Engineering
Cynthia Smith, Vice President, Sales, Pacific region
Mitchell Askenas, Vice President, Software Engineering
Timothy Dunn, Vice President, Digital Engineering
Shirley Lam, Vice President, SQA
Jonathan Symonds, Vice President, Business Development
Mark Dawson, Vice President, Programming Services
Michael Ivers, Information Contact
Operating areas: Portions of California & Missouri.
Programming: Offers Internet access on customer's TVs via local cable systems. Creator of HeadendWare, the centralized platform for next-generation subscriber services.
Began: October 1, 1998.
Means of Support: Subscriber fees.
Ownership: Cox; IBM & Lauder Partners.

ID INVESTIGATION DISCOVERY — See Discovery Channel.
Web Site: http://investigation.discovery.com/
Programming: America's leading investigation network, Investigation Discovery is the source for fact-based investigative content about culture, history and the human condition.
Began: January 27, 2008, Formerly Discovery Times Channel.
Total subscribers: 73,000,000.

ID INVESTIGATION DISCOVERY HD — See Discovery Channel.

IDEA CHANNEL
2002 Filmore Ave
Erie, PA 16506
Phones: 814-833-7107; 800-388-0662
Fax: 814-833-7415
E-mail: help@freetochoose.tv
Web Site: http://www.ideachannel.com
Bob Chitester, President & Chief Executive Officer
Rick Platt, Vice President
Tara Schupp, Vice President, Administration
Type of service: Basic.
Satellites: Galaxy III, transponder 23.
Operating hours/week: 1.
Programming: Conversational discussions between intellectuals.
Began: October 1, 1992.
Means of Support: Advertising & investments.
Distribution method: Available to cable systems & home dish audiences.
Ownership: Bob Chitester.

IDRIVETV
4100 E Mississippi Ave
Ste 1900
Glendale, CO 80246
Phone: 303-839-5303
Fax: 303-839-5335
E-mail: idrivetv@isafe.org
Web Site: http://www.idrivechannel.com
Programming: Interactive advertising channel focusing on cars, motor boats, motorbikes & airplanes.
Began: November 20, 2005.
Total subscribers: 15,000,000.
Distribution method: Available to Dish Network subscribers.
Ownership: Networks Group.

IFC FILMS ON DEMAND — See Independent Film Channel.

IFC FREE — See Independent Film Channel.
Type of service: Video on demand.

Programming: Offers high-definition debuts of series & episodes before they premiere on IFC.
Total subscribers: 14,600,000.

IFC HD — See Independent Film Channel.

IFC IN THEATERS — See Independent Film Channel.

I-HEALTH — Launched as ION Life.

I-LIFETV — See Halogen Network.

ILLINOIS CHANNEL

PO Box 1856
Springfield, IL 62701
Phone: 217-741-9419
E-mail: illinoischannel@aol.com
Web Site: http://www.illinoischannel.org
Terry Martin, Executive Director
Programming: Gavel to gavel coverage of the three branches of Illinois government.
Began: January 1, 2003.
Total subscribers: 860,000.

IMETRO — See ION Television.

IMPACT

c/o Comast Corp.
One Comcast Ctr
Philadelphia, PA 19103
Phone: 215-286-1700
Web Site: http://www.impactvod.com
Type of service: Video on demand.
Programming: Action movies & shows, including thrillers, spy, crime, westerns, war & martial arts films.
Ownership: Comcast Corp & Metro Goldwyn Mayer Studios.

IN DEMAND

345 Hudson St
17th Fl
New York, NY 10014
Phone: 646-638-8200
Fax: 646-486-0855
E-mail: business@indemand.com
Web Site: http://www.indemand.com
Robert G Benya, President & Chief Executive Officer
John Vartanian, Chief Technology Officer
Michael Berman, Executive Vice President, Programming & General Counsel
Eric Petro, Executive Vice President, Business Development & Chief Financial Officer
Stacie Gray, Chief Creative Director
Susan P. Barnabeo, Senior Vice President, Business Affairs & General Counsel
Mark Boccardi, Senior Vice President, Programming & Business Development
Leigh Bolton, Senior Vice President, Video Promotion
Gavin Harvey, Senior Vice President, Marketing & Brand Director
Claire Kostbar, Senior Vice President, Human Resources & Administration
Lauren LoFrisco, Senior Vice President, Affiliate Marketing
Emilio Nunez, Senior Vice President, Movies & Original Programming
Susan Rynn, Senior Vice President, Research
Susan Scott, Senior Vice President, Distribution
Dan York, Senior Vice President, Programming & Development
Susan Bowlin, Vice President, Broadcast Operations
Ellen Cooper, Vice President, Corporate & Affiliate Communications
Craig Helmstetter, Vice President, Finance
Terri Hyacinth, Vice President, Affiliate Marketing
Sean Murray, Vice President, Audit
Doreen Napolitano, Vice President, Information Systems
Doug Ohlandt, Vice President, Programming & Promotion
Frank Romano, Vice President, Event Sales & Operations
Gregg Rothberg, Vice President, Marketing
Wendy Schaub, Vice President, Video Production
John Schultz, Vice President, Broadcast Operations
Brooke Smarsh, Vice President, Business & Legal Affairs, Assistant General Counsel
Roger Strong, Vice President, Research & Strategy
Bill Wolstromer, Vice President & Controller
Terri B. Hyacinth, Regional Vice President, Affiliate Relations
Emily C. Lewis, Dir., Business Affairs & Sr. Counsel, Business Affairs Director & Senior Counsel

Regional Offices:
ATLANTA: 5 Piedmont Ctr, Ste 402, Atlanta, GA 30305. Phone: 404-760-2843. Fax: 404-760-2841. Ray Monasterski, Information Contact.

DENVER: 4100 E Dry Creek Rd, Littleton, CO 80122. Phone: 303-712-3360. Fax: 303-712-3366.

LOS ANGELES: 2029 Century Park E, One Century Plaza, Ste 2080, Los Angeles, CA 90067. Phone: 310-785-9194. Fax: 310-785-9769.
Type of service: Pay-per-view & video on demand.
Satellites: Satcom C-3; Loral T7, transponder 3; 2 (Chs. 1-22); Satcom C-4; Loral T7, transponder 18; 3 (Chs. 1-30); Telstar 7; Loral T7, transponder 2,3,4; 4 (Chs. 1-34); GE-1, transponder 8,13,14.
Operating hours/week: 168.
Uplink: Denver, CO.
Programming: Pay-per-view network, offering titles from all of the major Hollywood & independent studios, including sports & subscription sports packages & entertainment events through its 60-digital pay-per-view multiplex platform. Also includes three digital barker channels.
Began: November 27, 1985, Formerly Viewer's Choice. Re-branded as iN DEMAND on January 1, 2000.
Means of Support: Pay-per-view & subscription fees.
Total subscribers: 29,000,000 (Figure represents addressable homes.).
Distribution method: Available to cable systems.
Equipment: VideoCipher II Plus; GI DigiCipher II.
Ownership: AT&T Broadband & Internet Services 33%; Time Warner Entertainment-Advance/ Newhouse, 44% jointly; Comcast Corp., MediaOne & Cox Communications, 11% each.

IN2TV

22000 AOL Way
Dulles, VA 20166
Phone: 703-265-1000
E-mail: david.eun@corp.aol.com
Web Site: http://television.aol.com/in2tv
David Eun, President, AOL Media & Studios
Type of service: Broadband.
Programming: Interactive games & six channels featuring episodes of vintage hit television shows on demand, 24/7.
Began: January 1, 2006.
Ownership: AOL Time Warner.

INDEPENDENT FILM CHANNEL

200 Jericho Quadrangle
Jericho, NY 11753
Phone: 516-803-4500
Fax: 516-803-4506
E-mail: webmaster@ifctv.com
Web Site: http://www.ifc.com
Josh Sapan, President & Chief Executive Officer, AMC Networks Inc.
Evan Shapiro, President
Jonathan Sehring, President, IFC Production & Distribution Companies
Joseph A. Cantwell, Executive Vice President, New Media
Jennifer Caserta, Executive Vice President & General Manager
Gregg Hill, Executive Vice President, Affiliate Sales & Marketing
Alan Klein, Executive Vice President, Partnerships & Operations
Lisa Schwartz, Executive Vice President, Distribution Operations & Business Development
Vanessa Benfield, Senior Vice President, Partnership Sales & Integrated Solutions
Caroline Bock, Senior Vice President, Affiliate Marketing & Public Relations
Debbie DeMontreaux, Senior Vice President, Original Programming
Alan Klein, Senior Vice President, Partnerships & Licensing
Kent Rees, Senior Vice President, Marketing, Fox Regional Sports Networks
Lauren Burack, Vice President, Event Marketing & Promotions
Ilene Danuff, Vice President, Branded Content & Integrated Solutions
Elektra Gray, Vice President, Consumer Public Relations
Caroline Kaplan, Vice President, Film & Program Development
Christine Lubrano, Vice President, Non-Fiction Programming
Craig Parks, Vice President, Digital Media
Rachel Smith, Vice President, Fiction Programming
Tony Song, Vice President, Sales & Partnerships, East Coast
Kim Becker, Public Relations Director
Keith Hudson, Senior Manager, Corp. Public Affairs
George Lentz, Manager, Film Acquisitions

Branch Offices:
CENTRAL REGION: 205 N Michigan Ave, Ste 803, Chicago, IL 60601. Phone: 312-938-3134. Fax: 312-729-9370.

SOUTHERN/EASTERN REGION: 3 Village Cir, Ste 208, Westlake, TX 76262. Phone: 817-430-3589. Fax: 817-491-0435.

WESTERN REGION: 2425 W Olympic Blvd, Ste 5050 W, Santa Monica, CA 90404. Phone: 310-828-7005. Fax: 310-828-0375.

EASTERN REGION: 555 Fifth Ave, 3rd Floor, New York, NY 10017. Phone: 917-542-6300.
Type of service: Pay.
Satellites: Galaxy VII, transponder 14.
Operating hours/week: 168.
Programming: Features domestic & international independent films to include documentaries, animation and other creative productions.
Began: September 1, 1994.
Total subscribers: 42,000,000.
Distribution method: Available to cable systems.
Scrambled signal: Yes.
Ownership: AMC Networks Inc. Formerly Rainbow Media Holdings LLC owned by Cablevision Systems Corp., it became a publicly held company under the new name June 30, 2011.

INDEPENDENT MUSIC NETWORK

8424 Santa Monica Blvd S
Ste 776
West Hollywood, CA 90069
Fax: 323-951-0674
E-mail: gary@independentmusicnetwork.com
Web Site: http://www.independentmusicnetwork.com
James Fallacaro, Chairman & President
Anthony L. Escamilla, Executive Vice President
Corinne Fallacaro, Director, Secretary & Treasurer
Christopher Mauritz, Director, Chief Technology Officer
Terry Shea, Public Relations & Marketing
Type of service: Basic & online.
Operating hours/week: 168.
Programming: Independent music video programming featuring amateur & professional musicians.
Began: June 1, 2000.
Distribution method: Available to cable systems and home dish audiences.

INFINITO — See Condista.
Web Site: http://www.infinito.com
Operating hours/week: 168.
Programming: New-age & spiritual lifestyle programming.
Began: March 1, 2003, reflects U.S. launch.
Total subscribers: 15,800,000.
Ownership: Claxson Interactive Group.

INHD — See Mojo HD.

INHD2 — See Mojo HD.

INSP

Inspiration Networks
3000 WorldReach Dr
Indian Land, SC 29707
Phones: 803-578-1000; 800-725-4677
E-mail: info@insp.com
Web Site: http://www.insp.com
David Cerullo, Chairman & Chief Executive Officer
Bill Airy, Chief Strategy Officer
Cecil Elmore, Chief Information Officer
Dale Ardizzone, Executive Vice President, Business Affairs & General Counsel
Marc Favaro, Executive Vice President, Worldwide Sales
Robert I. Brace, Senior Vice President, Finance, Inspiration Ministries

Doug Butts, Senior Vice President, Programming
Jim Goss, Senior Vice President, Creative Services, On-Air Promotions & Short Form Programming
John Roos, Senior Vice President, Corporate Communications
Jenna Czaplinski, Marketing Director
Ken Tolle, Worldwide Distribution Representative
Type of service: Basic, digital, broadband & video on demand.
Satellites: Galaxy 15, transponder 17; Galaxy I-R, transponder 17 (digital).
Operating hours/week: 168.
Uplink: Charlotte, NC.
Programming: Inspirational entertainment including children's programs, music videos, primetime specials, movies, concerts & selected ministry programs. (See also i-LifeTV, LaFamilia, Cosmovision).
Began: September 1, 1990.
Means of Support: Sale of airtime, advertising. Subscriber fees (i-Lifetv, LaFamilia/ Cosmovision).
Total subscribers: 55,000,000.
Distribution method: Available to DBS audiences, telcos & cable systems.
Ownership: The Inspiration Networks Inc.

INSPIRATION ON DEMAND — See INSP.
Type of service: Video on demand & internet.
Satellites: (digital).
Total subscribers: 6,000,000.
Distribution method: Available to cable systems & online.

INTELLICAST — See Weatherscan.
Web Site: http://www.intellicast.com

INTERNATIONAL FAMILY TELEVISION — See KyLinTV.
Type of service: IPTV.
Programming: Dramas, music videos, cooking shows, cartoons, fitness & talk shows for adults & children available in English, Mandarin, Cantonese, Taiwanese, Japanese & Korean.

INTERNATIONAL TELEVISION (ITV)
PO Box 347
East Elmhurst, NY 11369
Phone: 718-784-8555
Fax: 718-784-8901
Web Site: http://www.itvgold.com
Sathya Viswanath, President & Producer
Dr. B. Viswanath, Vice President
Nandini Sikand, Co-Producer
Type of service: Basic, Digital.
Operating hours/week: 24.
Operating areas: New York.
Programming: Indian movies, news, serials, interviews & live shows.
Began: January 1, 1987.
Means of Support: Advertising.
Ownership: Deepak Viswanath, principal.

INTERTAINER
10950 Washington Blvd
3rd Fl
Culver City, CA 90232
Phone: 310-202-2900
Fax: 310-202-2929
E-mail: jenn@intertainer.com
Web Site: http://www.intertainer.com
Richard Baskin, Chairman
Jonathan Taplin, President & Chief Executive Officer
Stephen Ste. Marie, President & Chief Operating Officer
Caroline Beck, Chief Operating Officer
Harvey Finkel, Executive Vice President & Chief Financial Officer
Mark Sonnenberg, Executive Vice President, Content & Marketing
Bonnie Johnson, Executive Vice President, Media Products & Services
Terrence Coles, Senior Vice President, Content
Lauren de la Fuente, Senior Vice President, Marketing
Tim Krass, Senior Vice President, Affiliate Sales & Marketing
Steve Schein, Senior Vice President, Corporate Development & Strategic Planning
Chris Dorr, Senior Vice President, Programming
Bob DePirro, Senior Vice President, Media Technology & Services
Amy Friedlander, Vice President, Business Affairs
Lily Yee, Vice President, Controller
Steven Friedman, Vice President, Telco Sales
Kathy Trullender, Vice President, Affiliate Relations
Carl Segal, Vice President, Production
Tom Meredith, Vice President, Research
Dina Schultz, Special Markets Director
Operating areas: Portions of Colorado & Ohio.
Programming: Provides gateway to movies, music, shopping & information on customer's PC or TV via local cable systems.
Began: October 1, 1998.
Means of Support: Subscriber fees.
Ownership: Comcast Corp. 7%: US West 6.5%; NBC 6%; Intel Corp. 4.5% & Sony Corp. 4.5%.

ION LIFE — See ION Television.
Web Site: http://www.ionlife.tv
Type of service: Digital.
Operating hours/week: 168.
Programming: Healthy lifestyles & personal growth.
Began: February 19, 2007.
Ownership: ION Media Networks.

ION TELEVISION HD — See ION Television.

ION TELEVISION
601 Clearwater Park Rd
West Palm Beach, FL 33401-6233
Phone: 561-659-4122
Fax: 561-659-4252
Web Site: http://www.ionline.tv
Brandon Burgess, Chairman & Chief Executive Officer
Steven P. Appel, Sales & Marketing President
Eleo Hensleigh, Chief Marketing Officer
Richard Garcia, Chief Financial Officer & Senior Vice President
John Heffron, Senior Vice President, Networks Distribution
Adam K. Weinstein, Senior Vice President, Secretary & Chief Legal Officer
Helen C. Karas, Senior Vice President, Network Sales
John Lawon, Executive Vice President, Policy & Strategic Initiatives
Carole Smith, Research Vice President
Emma Cordoba, Vice President & Human Resources Director
Curtis L. Brandon, Controller Vice President
Henry J. Brandon, Director
Type of service: Basic.
Satellites: GE-I, transponder 7.
Operating hours/week: 168.
Programming: Provides ION Television programming to cable systems unable to receive over-the-air signals from an ION Television affiliate.
Began: August 31, 1998, Formerly PAX. Relaunched as i - Independent Television September 25, 2005. Now ION Television.
Means of Support: Advertising.
Total subscribers: 93,000,000.
Distribution method: Available to cable systems.
Ownership: ION Media Networks.

IOWA COMMUNICATIONS NETWORK
400 E 14th St
Grimes State Office Bldg
Des Moines, IA 50319
Phones: 515-725-4692; 877-426-4692
Fax: 515-725-4727
Web Site: http://www.icn.state.ia.us
Bob Montgomery, General Advertising Sales Mgr.
Mike Woody, Local Advertising Sales Manager
Gail Ware, Local Program Manager
Type of service: Basic, microwave.
Operating hours/week: 168.
Operating areas: Iowa.
Programming: Special interest programming including public service shows, talk shows, area sporting events & coach commentary. Network alternately carries CNBC & Country Music TV.
Began: January 1, 1980.
Total subscribers: 166,000.
Ownership: Mediacom.

I-SHOP
4100 E Mississippi Ave
Ste 1700
Glendale, CO 80246
Phone: 303-839-5303
Fax: 303-839-5335
E-mail: gturner@tvmediaworks.com
Web Site: http://www.turnermediagroup.com
Programming: Provides direct response & interactive shopping featuring retailers of fitness, beauty, music, home furnishings & technology.
Total subscribers: 15,000,000.
Ownership: Turner Media Group.

ISRAELI INTERNATIONAL TV — No longer planned.

ITALIAN AMERICAN NETWORK
95 State Hwy 17
Paramus, NJ 07652
Phone: 201-712-5780
Fax: 201-712-5783
E-mail: contact_us@itamnet.com
Web Site: http://www.italianamericannetwork.com
Tony Ceglio, Chief Executive Officer
Fred DiPilla, Chief Financial Officer
Patrick J. Peters, Senior Vice President, Business Development & Marketing
James K. Picinich, Vice President, Programming & Development
Type of service: Digital & broadband.
Programming: Italian culture both in Italy & in America, food, cooking, sports & travel.
Began: June 23, 2008.
Means of Support: Advertising.
Distribution method: Available to cable systems, satellite providers & online.

JACKPOT CHANNEL — No longer planned.

JADE CHANNEL
c/o TVB (USA) Inc.
15411 Blackburn Ave
Norwalk, CA 90650
Phones: 562-802-0220; 877-893-8888
Fax: 562-802-5096
E-mail: jade@tvbusa.com
Web Site: http://www.jworldtv.com
Philip Tam, Senior Vice President TVB-USA
Tracy Lee, Vice President, Advertising
Whayu Lin, Information Contact

Branch Office:
SAN FRANCISCO: 39 Dorman Ave, San Francisco, CA 94124. Phone: 415-282-8228. Fax: 415-282-8226. Karman Liu, Advertising.
Satellites: Galaxy IV.
Operating hours/week: 168.
Operating areas: Los Angeles, San Diego & San Francisco, CA.
Programming: Cantonese & Mandarin language satellite service.
Began: December 1, 1994.
Distribution method: Available to home dish audiences & cable systems.
Ownership: TVB (USA) Inc.

JCTV
PO Box A
Santa Ana, CA 92711
Phone: 714-832-2950
Fax: 714-665-2191
E-mail: jc-tv@jctv.org
Web Site: http://www.jctv.org
Paul Crouch Jr, Vice President, Administration
Bob Higley, Vice President, Cable & Satellite Relations, TBN
Mark McCallie, Vice President, Programming
Type of service: Digital basic.
Satellites: Galaxy 14, transponder 1.
Operating hours/week: 168.
Operating areas: Available nationwide.
Programming: Faith-based music videos, teen talk and reality shows, extreme sports, comedy and concerts all for the 13-29 age category.
Began: January 1, 2002.
Distribution method: Available to cable subscribers.
Scrambled signal: Yes.
Ownership: TBN Networks.

JEWELRY TELEVISION
10001 Kingston Pike
Ste 57
Knoxville, TN 37922
Phone: 865-693-8471
Fax: 865-693-3688
E-mail: kelly.fletcher@jtv.com
Web Site: http://www.jtv.com
Robert Hall, Chief Executive Officer
Joe E. Fields, Chief Operating Officer
Charles A. Wagner, III, Chairman & General Counsel
Wayne Lambert, Chief Information Officer
Crawford Wagner, Chief Financial Officer
William C. Kouns, President

Gerald D. Sisk, Jr., Executive Vice President
Harris Bagley, Executive Vice President, Distribution
Andy Caldwell, Vice President, Affiliate Marketing
Type of service: Basic.
Satellites: Galaxy 13, transponder 21; Galaxy 11.
Operating hours/week: 168.
Uplink: Knoxville, TN.
Programming: Home shopping network dedicated to jewelry & gemstones. The network pays for carriage.
Began: October 15, 1993, as America's Collectibles Network; relaunched as Jewelry TV in 2004.
Means of Support: Shoppers.
Total subscribers: 78,000,000.
Distribution method: Satellite, cable, digital systems.
Scrambled signal: No.

JEWISH LIFE TV

15060 Ventura Blvd
Ste 240
Sherman Oaks, CA 91403
Phone: 818-786-4000
E-mail: info@blazermediagroup.com
Web Site: http://www.jltv.tv
Operating hours/week: 168.
Programming: News, sports, movies, music videos, documentaries & general entertainment.
Began: N.A.
Distribution method: Available to cable systems, satellite providers & online.

JEWISH TELEVISION NETWORK/JTN PRODUCTIONS

13743 Ventura Blvd
Ste 200
Sherman Oaks, CA 91423
Phone: 818-789-5891
E-mail: info@jewishtvnetwork.com
Web Site: http://www.jewishtvnetwork.com
Jay Sanderson, Chief Executive Officer
David Bubis, Executive Vice President
Mike Dewitt, Vice President, Nonfiction Production
Harvey Lehrer, Vice President, Broadband & Production
Type of service: Broadband.
Operating hours/week: 10.
Operating areas: California, District of Columbia & New York.
Programming: National & international news, children's, educational, cultural & community programming, arts & entertainment, documentaries, film & programming from Israel.
Total subscribers: 3,000,000.

JIA YU CHANNEL — See KyLinTV.

No. 1-3,Jalan PJU 8/5H, Bandar Damansara Perd
47820 Petaling Jaya, Selangor Darul Ehsan
Malaysia
Phone: 603-7726-9593
Fax: 603-7710-9363
E-mail: info@jiayu.tv
Web Site: http://www.jiayu.tv
Type of service: IPTV.
Operating hours/week: 168.
Programming: Channel from Malaysia broadcast in Cantonese and Mandarin, offering general entertainment, news, animated & lifestyle programs. Available in the United States through KyLinTV.
Began: January 1, 2004.
Scrambled signal: Yes.

JIANGSU INTERNATIONAL CHANNEL — See KyLinTV.

Type of service: IPTV.
Operating hours/week: 168.
Programming: Focuses on Wuyue culture. The Mandarin Chinese broadcasts are offered through KyLinTV.

JTV

Jackson Television
152 W Michigan Ave
Jackson, MI 49201
Phone: 517-787-8817
Fax: 517-783-5060
Web Site: http://www.jtv.tv
Bart Hawley, President
Kurt Baringer, General Manager
Andy Hawley, Sports Director
Type of service: Basic.
Operating hours/week: 168.
Operating areas: Michigan.
Programming: Offers local daily talk show, cooking, home, design and health programs, plus extensive local high school sports coverage.
Began: July 1, 2000.
Means of Support: Advertising.
Distribution method: Available to cable subscribers.

JUMP TV

463 King St W
3rd Fl
Toronto, ON M5V 1K4
Canada
Phone: 647-426-1310
E-mail: support@jumptv.com
Web Site: http://www.jumptv.com
Blair Baxter, Chief Financial Officer
Scott Paterson, Vice Chairman & President
Elmer Sotto, Vice President, Product & Business Operations
Jay Howard, Vice President & General Counsel

Branch Offices:
UNITED STATES: 45 E 34th St, 5th Floor, New York, NY 10016.
Type of service: Broadband.
Operating hours/week: 168.
Programming: Delivering content from several countries & channels through multiple Internet-enabled devices.

KANSAS NOW 22

807 E Douglas
Wichita, KS 67202
Phone: 316-858-3300
Fax: 316-262-7484
Operating areas: Kansas, Missouri & Oklahoma.
Programming: Local news, national news, weather 24/7.
Total subscribers: 317,400.
Scrambled signal: Yes.
Ownership: Cox Communications Inc. & Gray Television Inc.

KARAOKE CHANNEL

6420-A1 Rea Rd
Ste 161
Charlotte, NC 28277
Phone: 704-817-1530
Fax: 866-932-9024
E-mail: infos@stingray-music.com
Web Site: http://www.stingray-music.com/karaoke_channel.html
Type of service: Basic, broadband & video on demand.
Distribution method: Available to cable & satellite providers.
Ownership: Stingray Digital Media.

KARMALOOP TV

301 Newbury St
Boston, MA 02115
617-369-0100
Web Site: http://www.karmalooptv.com
Greg Selkoe, Chief Executive Officer & Founder
Pharrell Williams, Creative Director, New Programming
Type of service: Broadband.
Operating areas: Available nationwide.
Programming: Provides an insider's look at all elements that fuel cutting edge Verge Culture, the intersection of lifestyle, music and fashion.
Began: January 1, 2008, as an online service.
Scrambled signal: Yes.
Ownership: Greg Selkoe.

KENTUCKY EDUCATIONAL TELEVISION (KET5)

600 Cooper Dr
Lexington, KY 40502
Phone: 859-258-7000
Fax: 859-258-7399
Web Site: http://www.ket.org/legislature
Type of service: Digital.
Programming: Delivers online & cable coverage of the Kentucky General Assembly, including live sessions of Senate, House chambers, committees, program highlights & archives from past sessions & gubernatorial addresses.
Distribution method: Available to cable systems, internet.

KIDCARE TELEVISION NETWORK

8406 Benjamin Rd
Ste C
Tampa, FL 33634
Phone: 800-760-7794
Fax: 813-888-7375
E-mail: info@kidcaretv.com
Web Site: http://www.kidcaretv.com
Philip M. Cohen, Chief Executive Officer
Bernard J. Kouma, Vice President, Subscription Sales
Donald R. Mastropietro, Chief Financial Officer
Type of service: IPTV.
Programming: Place-based network focused on children's health & wellness issues.

KIDSWB.COM

4000 Warner Blvd
Bldg 505
Burbank, CA 91505
Phone: 818-977-9653
Web Site: http://www.kidswb.com
Type of service: Broadband.
Programming: Animation from Warner Brothers, Looney Tunes, Hanna-Barbera & D.C. Comics.
Began: August 1, 2008.
Means of Support: Ad supported.
Distribution method: Available online.

KLRU-TOO

2504-B Whitis Ave
Austin, TX 78712
Phone: 512-471-4811
Fax: 512-475-9090
E-mail: dlauderman@klru.org
Web Site: http://www.klru.org
Bill Stotesbery, Chief Executive Officer, KLRU
Maria Rodriguez, Senior Vice President, Broadcasting
Maury Wright Sullivan, Senior Vice President, Marketing
Type of service: Basic.
Operating areas: Texas.
Programming: KLRU-Q will feature entertaining and inspiring shows about travel, science, nature, history and more. Q will feature blocks of programming throughout the day, with genres chosen specifically for the Austin audience.
Began: February 1, 1988.
Distribution method: Available to cable systems.
Scrambled signal: Yes.
Ownership: Capital of Texas Public Telecommunications Council.

K-MTN TELEVISION

2277 Lake Tahoe Blvd
South Lake Tahoe, CA 96150
Phone: 530-541-8686
Fax: 503-541-7469
Web Site: http://www.kmtn.com
Mike Conway, President
Renee Conway, Assistant
Type of service: Basic.
Operating hours/week: 168.
Operating areas: California & Nevada.
Programming: Focuses on entertainment, local events, family activities, ski reports & other seasonal recreation in the Lake Tahoe area.
Began: January 1, 1984.
Means of Support: Advertising.
Total subscribers: 2,665,000.
Distribution method: Available to cable systems & satellite providers.
Ownership: Mike Conway.

KNOWLEDGE NETWORK

4355 Mathissi Place
Burnaby, BC V5G 4S8
Canada
Phone: 604-431-3222
Fax: 604-431-3387
E-mail: knonline@knowtv.com
Web Site: http://www.knowledgenetwork.ca
Wayne Robert, General Manager
Barb McLean, Vice President, Marketing
Sarah MacDonald, Programming Director
Ron Harrington, Operations & Production Director
Cecilia Garcia, Information Contact
Type of service: Basic.
Satellites: Anik E-1.
Operating hours/week: 168.
Operating areas: Province of British Columbia.
Uplink: Burnaby, BC.
Programming: Kids' shows, how-to programs, documentaries & international specials.
Began: January 1, 1981.
Means of Support: Donations, corporate underwriting & sponsorship, government support.

Distribution method: Available to home dish audiences & cable systems.
Ownership: Publicly owned.

KOREA ONE: CHICAGOLAND KOREAN TV — See Washington Korean TV.

KOREAN CHANNEL
18-38 131 St
College Point, NY 11356
Phone: 718-353-8970
Fax: 718-359-2067
E-mail: info@tkctv.com
Web Site: http://tkctv.com
Sang Ki Han, President
Jaehoo Han, Director
Sue Han, Information Contact
Type of service: Basic.
Operating hours/week: 168.
Programming: Korean entertainment, news, drama & movies.
Began: March 7, 1986.
Total subscribers: 1,000,000.

KTLA LOS ANGELES
UVTV/KTLA
5800 Sunset Blvd
Los Angeles, CA 90028
Phone: 323-460-5500
Fax: 323-460-5994
E-mail: ktla-am-news@tribune.com
Web Site: http://www.ktla.com
Pete Boylan, President & Chief Operating Officer, TV Guide Inc.
Rob Morris, Senior Vice President & General Manager, UVTV
Derk Tenzythoff, Vice President, Programming Services
Type of service: Basic.
Satellites: GE 3, transponder 15.
Operating hours/week: 168.
Programming: CW affiliate in Los Angeles broadcasting movies, sports & syndicated programming.
Began: January 1, 1988.
Means of Support: System pays per subscriber.
Total subscribers: 10,300,000.
Distribution method: Available to home dish audiences.
Equipment: VideoCipher II.
Ownership: Tribune Broadcasting.

KTV - KIDS & TEENS TELEVISION — See Dominion Sky Angel.

KUNLUN THEATER — See KyLinTV.
Programming: Offers male-oriented Chinese language programming. Available through KyLinTV.

KUWAIT TV — See Globecast World TV.
E-mail: info@moinfo.gov.kw
Web Site: http://moinfo.gov.kw
Type of service: Basic.
Operating hours/week: 168.
Programming: Arabic-language family & community programming from Kuwait, including news, music, children's shows, movies & documentaries.
Distribution method: Available through Globecast satellite service.

KYLIN KIDS LEARNING CHINESE — See KyLinTV.

KYLINTV
1600 Old Country Rd
Plainview, NY 11803
Phone: 877-888-8598
Fax: 877-888-8597
E-mail: info@kylintv.com
Web Site: http://www.kylintv.com
Duan Jianbing, President
Programming: Comprised of multiple channels showcasing Chinese culture & history through movies, dramas, documentaries & other entertainment.
Began: September 1, 2005.
Distribution method: IPTV & video on demand.

LA FAMILIA NETWORK — See INSP.
Satellites: Olympusat I, transponder 6; Galaxy 13.
Programming: Hispanic family entertainment including live action & animated children's series, music, concerts, family novelas, news & sports.

LAS VEGAS ONE
3228 Channel 8 Dr
Las Vegas, NV 89109
Phone: 702-792-8888
Fax: 702-696-7222
E-mail: eneilson@klastv.com
Web Site: http://www.8newsnow.com
Emily Neilson, President & General Manager
Robert Stoldal, Vice President, News Operations
Kathy Kramer, Research & Program Director
Ron Comings, News Director
Linda Bonnici, Vice President, Sales
Caroline Bleakley, News Online Manager
Melissa Cipriano, Community Affairs Director
Dan Schwarz, Local Sales Manager
Michael Watkins, General Sales Manager
Chris Palmer, Internet Sales Director
Misty Morgan, National Sales Manager
Doug Kramer, Chief Engineer
Bill Thomas, Human Resource Director
Programming: Original news & talk with rebroadcasts of KLAS-TV's news programming.
Began: January 1, 1998.
Total subscribers: 401,000.

LATELE NOVELA NETWORK
1200 NW 78th St Ave
Ste. 104
Miami, FL 33126
Phone: 561-684-5657
E-mail: info@latelenovela.com
Web Site: http://www.latelenovela.com
Alex Fiore, President
Mercedes Fiore, Senior Vice President
Programming: Latin-American soap operas.
Began: January 1, 2005, Reflects U.S. launch.
Total subscribers: 750,000 (Reflects U.S. subscribers).
Ownership: Latele Novela Network.

LATIN TELEVISION (LTV) — See OlympuSat Hispanic Pack.
Web Site: http://www.ltvtv.com

LATINO AMERICA TV — See Alterna'TV.
Web Site: http://www.latele.tv
Programming: Regional news, soccer, entertainment, telenovelas, interviews, educational & kids programming.
Began: April 1, 2004.
Ownership: ACS Global TV.

LATV NETWORKS
2323 Corinth Ave
West Los Angeles, CA 90064
Phone: 310-943-5288
Fax: 310-943-5299
E-mail: dcrowe@latv.com
Web Site: http://www.latv.com
Luca Bentivoglio, Chief Operating Officer
Natalia Barrios, Manager, Marketing & Affiliate Relations

Branch Offices:
LOS ANGELES: 11835 W Olympic Blvd., Suite 450E, Los Angeles, CA 90064. Phone: 310-943-5303.
Operating hours/week: 168.
Programming: Entertainment, lifestyle & information network targeting Latino youth aged 12-34.
Began: January 1, 2001, launched nationally April 23, 2007.
Total subscribers: 33,000,000.
Distribution method: Cable, satellite & broadcast.

LE CANAL VIE
2100 Rue Sainte-Catherine Ouest
Bureau 700
Montreal, QC H3H 2T3
Canada
Phone: 514-529-3233
Fax: 514-529-3236
Web Site: http://www.canalvie.com
Pierre Roy, President
Lyne Denault, Vice President, Programming
Jean Garneau, Acquisition Director
Type of service: Basic.
Operating hours/week: 168.
Operating areas: Quebec Province.
Uplink: Montreal, QC.
Programming: Regional French language health, life & outdoor channel.
Began: September 8, 1997.
Means of Support: Advertising & subscribers.
Total subscribers: 1,500,000.
Distribution method: Available to home dish audiences & cable systems.
Ownership: Les Chaines Tele Astral.

LE RESEAU DES SPORTS
1755 boul. Rene-Levesque E
Bureau 300
Montreal, QC H2K 4P6
Canada
Phone: 514-599-2244
Fax: 514-599-2249
E-mail: patrick.jutras@rds.ca
Web Site: http://www.rds.ca
Gerry Frappier, President
Lino Bramucci, Senior Vice President & General Manager, Sales
Michel Gagnon, Vice President, Marketing
Francois Messier, Vice President, Programming
Claude Dugre, Vice President, Operations
Maxime Filion, Senior Director, Human Resources
Kevin Dumouchel, Director, Finance & Administration
Patrick Jutras, Sales Director
Satellites: Anik E-2.
Operating hours/week: 168.
Programming: Regional French language sports channel.
Began: September 1, 1989.
Means of Support: Subscriber fees & advertising.
Total subscribers: 2,386,000.
Ownership: CTV.

LEARNING & SKILLS TELEVISION OF ALBERTA
3720 76th Ave
Edmonton, AB T6B 2N9
Canada
Phone: 780-440-7777
Fax: 780-440-8899
E-mail: maryp@chumtv.com
Web Site: http://www.chumlimited.com
Ron Keast, President
Moses Znaimer, Chairman & Executive Producer
Richard Hiron, Sales Director
Tito Margiotta, Operations & Facilities Director
Jill Bonenfant, Programming Director
Todd Babiak, Public Relations Coordinator
John Verburgt, Creative Services Director
Ownership: Chum Ltd.

THE LEARNING CHANNEL
(TLC)
One Discovery Pl
Silver Spring, MD 20910
Phone: 240-662-0000
E-mail: dmr-roman@discovery.com
Web Site: http://tlc.discovery.com
John S. Hendricks, Founder, Chairman & Chief Executive Officer
Eileen O'Neill, President & General Manager
Michela English, President, Discovery Enterprises Worldwide
Bill Goodwyn, President, Domestic Distribution & Enterprises
Greg Moyer, President, Editorial & Creative Officer
Edward Sabin, Chief Operating Officer
Brent Willman, Chief Financial Officer
Regina DiMartino, Executive Vice President, Marketing
Tom Carr, Senior Vice President, Strategic Marketing
Nancy Daniels, Senior Vice President, Production & Development
Laurie Goldberg, Senior Vice President, Communications
Mark Hollinger, Senior Vice President, International Business Development & Gen. Counsel
Chris Lonergan, Senior Vice President, Affiliate Sales & Marketing
Bill McGowan, Senior Vice President, Advertising Sales
Lori McFarling, Senior Vice President, Distribution & Marketing
Deborah Adler Myers, Senior Vice President, Programming
Brant Pinvidie, Senior Vice President, Programming
Laura Staro, Senior Vice President, Research
Amy Winter, Senior Vice President, Marketing, Creative & Operations
Kristin Brown, Vice President, Communications
Howard Lee, Vice President, Production & Development, East Coast
Rita Mullin, Vice President, Development
Clint Stinchcomb, Vice President, New Media Distribution

Branch Office:
LOS ANGELES: 10100 Santa Monica Blvd, Los Angeles, CA 90067. Phone: 310-551-1611. Fax: 310-551-1684.
Type of service: Basic.
Satellites: Satcom C-3, transponder 2.
Operating hours/week: 168.
Uplink: Stamford, CT.
Programming: Documentaries on history, human behavior & science; commercial-free/violence-free programs for preschoolers; how-to programming about cooking, fashion, gardening & home improvement.
Began: November 1, 1980.
Means of Support: Subscribers & advertising.
Total subscribers: 100,000,000.
Distribution method: Available to home dish audiences & cable systems.
Ownership: Discovery Communications Inc.

LEGACY.TV
1925 Century Park E
Ste 1025

Los Angeles, CA 90067
Phone: 310-277-3500
E-mail: eric@es.tv
Web Site: http://www.legacy.tv
Byron Allen, Chair & Chief Executive Officer
Type of service: Planned digital broadband.
Operating hours/week: Plans 168.
Programming: New network will offer programs on African-American history and biographies.
Scheduled to begin: Plans to launch the first quarter of 2012.
Distribution method: Will be available to Verizon FiOS and Frontier Communications subscribers.
Scrambled signal: No.
Ownership: Entertainment Studios.

LEGISLATIVE COUNSEL BUREAU - BROADCAST AND PRODUCTION SERVICES
401 S Carson St
Carson City, NV 89701
Phone: 775-684-6990
Fax: 775-684-6988
E-mail: media@lcb.state.nv.us
Web Site: http://www.leg.state.nv.us/
Programming: Coverage of Nevada state legislative session.
Scrambled signal: Yes.

LIBRARY LITERACY CHANNEL / GHTV
Georgia Highlands College
Heritage Hall, 415 E Third Ave
Rome, GA 30161
Phone: 800-332-2406
E-mail: jbrown@highlands.edu
Web Site: http://www.highlands.edu
Jeff Brown, Channel Director
Type of service: Basic.
Operating areas: Georgia.
Programming: Educational.
Began: January 19, 1991.
Distribution method: Available to Comcast subscribers.
Scrambled signal: Yes.
Ownership: Floyd County/City of Rome.

LIFE NETWORK
121 Bloor St E
Ste 1500
Toronto, ON M4W 3M5
Canada
Phone: 416-967-1174
Fax: 416-960-0971
Web Site: http://www.lifenetwork.ca
Alexandra Brown, Executive Vice President
Barbara Williams, Vice President, Programming
Jim Ericson, Vice President, Programming
Lisa Lyons, Vice President, Distribution & Affiliate Relations
Todd Goldsbie, Vice President, Marketing & Business Development
John Whish, Vice President, Operations
Satellites: Anik E-2, transponder 20-H.
Programming: National English language channel offering tips, ideas & information which viewers can apply to their lives.
Began: January 1, 1995.
Ownership: Alliance Atlantis Communications.

LIFETIME
World Wide Plz
309 W 49th St
New York, NY 10019
Phone: 212-424-7000
Fax: 212-957-4469
Web Site: http://www.lifetimetv.com
Abbe Raven, Chief Executive Officer, A&E Television Networks
Carole Black, Chief Operating Officer, Lifetime Entertainment Services
Nancy Dubuc, President & General Manager
Bob Bibb, Co-Chief Marketing Officer
Lew Goldstein, Co-Chief Marketing Officer
James Wesley, Chief Financial Officer & Exec. V.P.
Lori Conkling, Executive Vice President, Distribution
Mike Greco, Executive Vice President, Research
Rick Haskins, Executive Vice President, Marketing
Patricia Langer, Executive Vice President, Legal, Business Affairs & Human Resources
Robert Sharenow, Executive Vice President, Programming
Dan Suratt, Executive Vice President, Digital Media & Business Development
Meredith Wagner, Executive Vice President, Lifetime Networks
Kelly Abugov, Senior Vice President, Programming
Nancy Alpert, Senior Vice President, Business & Legal Affairs & Deputy General Counsel
Amy Baker, Senior Vice President, Ad Sales
Aviva Bergman, Senior Vice President, Business Affairs, West Coast
Richard Brasso, Senior Vice President, Pricing & Planning
Steven Carcano, Senior Vice President, National Accounts
Danielle Carrig, Senior Vice President, Advocacy & Public Affairs
Amy Genkins, Senior Vice President, Legal Services
Thomas Hanft, Senior Vice President, Marketing, Advertising & Promotion
Paul Jennings, Senior Vice President
Nina Lederman, Senior Vice President, Program Development & Production
Gerald Logue, Senior Vice President, Executive Creative Director
Tanya Lopez, Senior Vice President, Original Movies
Jessica Marshall, Senior Vice President & General Manager, Lifetime Online
Gena McCarthy, Senior Vice President, Reality & Unscripted Programming
Linda Rein, Senior Vice President & General Counsel
Josh Sabarra, Senior Vice President, Corporate Communications & Publicity
Jessica Samet, Senior Vice President, Reality Programming
Jeffrey Schneider, Senior Vice President, Business Affairs & Deputy General Counsel
Dan Thatte, Senior Vice President, Information Technology, Lifetime Entertainment Services

Regional Offices:
ASTORIA: 34-12 36th St, Astoria, NY 11106. Phone: 718-706-3600.

CHICAGO: 435 N Michigan Ave, Ste 902, Chicago, IL 60611. Phone: 312-464-1991.

DETROIT: 555 S Woodward Ave, Ste 705, Birmingham, MI 48009. Phone: 810-646-8282.

LOS ANGELES: 2049 Century Park E, Ste 840, Los Angeles, CA 90067. Phone: 310-556-7500.
Type of service: Basic.
Satellites: Satcom C-4, transponder 4 (east coast); Satcom C-3, transponder 4 (west coast).
Operating hours/week: 168.
Uplink: Glenbrook, CT.

Programming: Informational & entertainment programming targeted to women.
Began: February 1, 1984.
Means of Support: Advertising & affiliate fees.
Total subscribers: 100,900,000.
Distribution method: Available to home dish audiences & cable systems.
Scrambled signal: Yes. Equipment: VideoCipher II.
Ownership: Hearst Corp., NBCUniversal LLC & The Walt Disney Co.

LIFETIME MOVIE NETWORK
309 W 49th St
16th & 17th Fl
New York, NY 10019
Phone: 212-424-7000
Fax: 212-957-4469
Web Site: http://www.lifetimetv.com/lmn
Louise Henry Bryson, Executive Vice President & General Manager & President, Distribution & Affiliate Business Development
Jim Wesley, Chief Financial Officer & Executive Vice President
Susanne Daniels, President, Entertainment, Lifetime Entertainment Services
Carole Black, President & Chief Operating Officer, Lifetime Entertainment Services
Dawn Tarnofsky, Executive Vice President, Entertainment
Meredith Wanger, Senior Vice President, Public Affairs, Lifetime Entertainment Services
Patrick Guy, Senior Vice President, General & Legal Affairs
Nancy Alpert, Senior Vice President, Business & Legal Affairs & Deputy General Counsel
Richard Basso, Vice President, Pricing & Planning
Phil LaGreca, Vice President, Controller
Gwynne McConkey, Vice President, Network Operations & Engineering
Type of service: Basic.
Satellites: Galaxy X, transponder 23.
Operating hours/week: 168.
Programming: Offers miniseries, made for TV movies & theatrical releases.
Began: June 29, 1998.
Means of Support: Advertising.
Total subscribers: 75,000,000.
Distribution method: Available to cable systems & home dish audiences.
Scrambled signal: Yes.
Ownership: Hearst Corp., NBCUniversal LLC & The Walt Disney Co.

LMN ESPANOL ON DEMAND — See Lifetime Movie Network.

LIFETIME MOVIE NETWORK HD — See Lifetime Movie Network.

LIFETIME ON DEMAND — See Lifetime.

LIFETIME REAL WOMEN — See Lifetime.
Total subscribers: 16,000,000.

LIFETIME TELEVISION HD — See Lifetime.
Began: April 17, 2008.

LIGHTSPAN ADVENTURES CHANNEL — No longer planned.

LIME
PO Box 1546
2481 John Nash Blvd
Bluefield, WV 24701
Phones: 304-323-8000; 888-694-7366
Fax: 304-323-2975
E-mail: gaiamlife@gaiam.com
Web Site: http://life.gaiam.com
C.J. Kettler, Chief Executive Officer
Robert Harris, Chief Financial & Administrative Officer
Lee Deboer, Chairman
Noreen O'Loughlin, General Manager
Judith Tolkow, Senior Vice President, Programming
Christine Engelbrechtsen, Vice President, Head of Integrated Sales & Marketing

Branch Office:
NEW YORK: 305 E 46th St, 3rd Floor, New York, NY 10017. Phone: 212-735-5323. Fax: 212-735-5330.
Type of service: Video on demand & broadband.
Satellites: AMC 1, transponder 12; Galaxy 4R, transponder 22.
Programming: Programming devoted to strengthening the body-mind-spirit connection. Formerly Wisdom Television. Linear channel defunct as of February 28, 2007.
Began: July 1, 1997.
Total subscribers: 7,000,000.
Distribution method: Available to cable systems & online.
Ownership: Wisdom Media Group.

LIVETV
700 S Babcock St
Melbourne, FL 32901
Phone: 321-308-3900
Fax: 321-308-3939
E-mail: mike.moeller@livetv.net
Web Site: http://www.livetv.net
Glenn Latta, Co-Founder & President
Neal Pilson, Advisory Board Member
Programming: In-flight entertainment for commercial airlines.
Distribution method: Satellite.
Ownership: JetBlue Airways.

LIVE WELL NETWORK
190 N State St
Chicago, IL 60601
Phone: 312-750-7777
Web Site: http://livewellnetwork.com
Emily Barr, President & General Manager, WLS-TV
Peggy Allen, Vice President, Programming
Kyle Longnecker, Promotion Manager
Type of service: Regional basic.
Operating areas: Illinois, Indiana & Wisconsin.
Programming: Offers programming about the home, your health and a healthy lifestyle.
Began: April 27, 2009.
Distribution method: Available to cable subscribers.
Ownership: Disney Enterprises Inc.

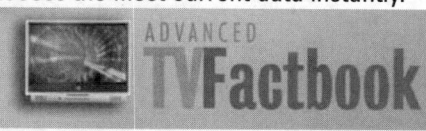

LIVE WELL HD NETWORK
500 S Buena Vista St
Burbank, CA 91521
Phone: 818-260-8766
Web Site: http://livewellhd.com
Type of service: Digital.
Operating hours/week: 168.
Programming: HD subchannel focused on home, lifestyle & health shows.
Began: April 27, 2009.
Scrambled signal: Yes.
Ownership: Disney-ABC Television Group.

LIVEWIRE — See Channel One.
Type of service: Broadband.
Programming: Preview & archived Channel One newsroom shows, expanded footage, interviews, interactive graphics, web-exclusive content, polls, quizzes & user-generated videos.

LIVING FAITH TELEVISION
PO Box 1867
Abingdon, VA 24212
Phones: 276-676-3806; 888-275-9534
Fax: 276-676-3572
E-mail: info@livingfaithtv.com
Web Site: http://www.livingfaithtv.com
J R Linkous, Editor
Type of service: Basic.
Operating hours/week: 168.
Operating areas: Kentucky, North Carolina, Tennessee, Virginia & West Virginia. Available on nationwide.
Programming: Viewer supported Christian television.
Began: January 17, 1995.
Means of Support: Advertising & viewer supported.
Total subscribers: 1,600,000.
Distribution method: Available to cable subscribers and satellite viewers.
Ownership: Living Faith Broadcasting Inc.

LMN HD — See Lifetime Movie Network.

LNC 5
WVEC Television
613 Woodis Ave
Norfolk, VA 23510
Phone: 757-625-1313
Fax: 757-664-5430
Web Site: http://www.wvec.com
Michael Valentine, News Director
Stock Watson, Ad Sales Director
Programming: Local news simulcast/rebroadcast.
Began: January 1, 1997.
Total subscribers: 437,000.
Ownership: Belo Corp.

LO MEJOR ON DEMAND
c/o Time Warner Cable
290 Harbor Dr
Stamford, CT 06902
Phone: 203-328-0600
Monica Talan, Vice President, Corporate Communications, Univision Communications Inc.
Type of service: Free Video On Demand.
Operating hours/week: 168.
Operating areas: Available in California, New York & Texas.
Programming: Offers the best in programming from Galavision, TeleFutura & Univision for Time Warner's digital cable customers.
Began: October 23, 2009.
Distribution method: Available to Time Warner Cable subscribers in Dallas, Los Angeles, New York, San Antonio & San Diego.
Scrambled signal: Yes.
Ownership: Time Warner Cable & Univision Communications Inc.

LOCAL CABLE WEATHER
385 Science Park Rd
State College, PA 16803
Phone: 814-235-8650
Fax: 814-235-8609
E-mail: info@accuwx.com
Web Site: http://www.accuweather.com
Joel N. Myers, President
Michael A. Steinberg, Senior Vice President
Joseph Montler, Director, Television & Broadcasting Sales
Tom Burka, Manager, Cable Product

Branch Office:
PHILADELPHIA AREA: 2 Greenwood Sq, 331 Street Rd, Ste 440, Bensalem, PA 19020. Phone: 888-438-9847. Fax: 215-244-5329.
Type of service: Basic & digital.
Operating hours/week: 168.
Programming: Continuous local weather forecasts from AccuWeather.
Began: April 29, 1996.
Means of Support: Advertising.
Distribution method: Available to cable systems.
Ownership: AccuWeather Inc.

LOCAL NEWS ON CABLE — See LNC 5.

LWS LOCAL WEATHER STATION
1950 N Meridian St
Indianapolis, IN 46202
Phone: 317-923-8888
Fax: 317-926-1144
E-mail: weather@wishtv.com
Web Site: http://www.wishtv.com
Lance Carwile, Program Director
Julie Zoumbaris, General Sales Manager
Carol Sergi, Director, Market Development
Joe Wertenberger, Business Manager
Mike Lopez, Executive Producer
Type of service: Basic & expanded basic.
Operating hours/week: 168.
Operating areas: Illinois, Indiana, Michigan, Texas & Virginia.
Uplink: Local market.
Programming: Continuous local weather programming. Doppler Radar, weather forcasts, current conditions, travel updates & special coverage. Service is offered in markets that have LIN station holdings.
Began: January 1, 1994.
Means of Support: Advertising & subscriber fees.
Total subscribers: 1,423,982.
Distribution method: Available to cable systems via fiber optic, wireless & microwave.
Ownership: LIN Television Corp.

LOGO
c/o MTV Networks
1775 Broadway, 11th Fl
New York, NY 10019
Web Site: http://www.logoonline.com
Lisa Sherman, Executive Vice President & General Manager
Nancy Bennett, Senior Vice President, Creative & Content Development
Type of service: Basic & video on demand.
Programming: Entertainment programming for lesbians & gays. Original programming, movies, documentaries, news & specials. Also available in Mexico & Brazil in pay-per-view format.
Began: June 30, 2005.
Total subscribers: 25,000,000.
Distribution method: Available to cable & satellite providers.
Ownership: Viacom Inc.

LONGHORN NETWORK
2312 San Gabriel St
Ste
Austin, TX 78705
Phone: 512-478-1833
Web Site: http://www.longhornnetwork.com
Dave Brown, Vice President, Programming & Acquisitions
Stephanie Druley, Vice President, Production

Branch Offices:
Production Studios: 3300 N Interstate 35, Austin, TX 78705.
Type of service: Planned regional pay.
Operating hours/week: Plans 168.
Operating areas: Plans Louisiana, New Mexico, Oklahoma & Texas.
Programming: Will offer a variety of content, highlighted by more than 200 exclusive events annually from 20 varsity UT sports, original series and studio shows, historical programming and academic and cultural happenings.
Scheduled to begin: Plans to launch August 26, 2011.
Means of Support: Advertising & subscriber fees.
Distribution method: Will be available to cable systems.
Scrambled signal: Planned.
Ownership: ESPN & U of Texas.

LOTTERY CHANNEL
425 Walnut St
Cincinnati, OH 45202
Phone: 513-381-0777
Fax: 513-721-6035
E-mail: info@lottery.com
Web Site: http://www.lottery.com
Roger Ach, Chairman & Chief Executive Officer
Carol Meinhardt, Executive Vice President
Jeffrey S. Perlee, Managing Director
Operating areas: Rhode Island.
Began: November 8, 1995.
Distribution method: Available to cable systems.

LOUISIANA LEGISLATIVE NETWORK
900 N Third St
PO Box 94062
Baton Rouge, LA 70804
Phone: 225-342-0367
Fax: 225-342-3749
E-mail: pickensp@legis.state.la.us
Web Site: http://www.legis.state.la.us
Type of service: Basic.
Operating hours/week: 28.
Programming: Live & archived coverage of Louisiana legislature meetings & sessions year-round.
Distribution method: Cable, internet.

MAC TV
No. 100, Lane 75
Kang-Ning Rd, Sec 3
Taipei 114
Taiwan, Republic of China
Phone: 8862-2630-1877
Fax: 8862-2630-1895
Web Site: http://www.mactv.com.tw/mactv_en/index.htm
Satellites: JcSat-3A, transponder C3; APSTAR IIR, transponder 7B-2; SuperBird-C, transponder 23D.
Operating hours/week: 168.
Programming: Offers diverse and refined programming to encourage mutual concern among overseas Chinese communities.
Began: March 1, 2000, Date shown is date of inital launch in China.
Distribution method: Available to home dish audiences and cable systems.
Scrambled signal: No.

MACAU ASIA SATELLITE TV (MASTV) — See KyLinTV.
Type of service: IPTV.
Programming: News, global finance, world events, entertainment, cultural shows, sports from Macau. Also features Mandarin dramas & Korean variety shows.

MACTV — See KyLinTV.
Type of service: IPTV.
Programming: Taiwan-centered entertainment shows targeted to overseas Chinese. Carried by KyLinTV.
Began: March 1, 2004.

MADISON SQUARE GARDEN NETWORK — See MSG.

MAG RACK — See Lifeskool.

THE MAJESTIC — See Voom HD Networks.

MALL TV — See i-Shop.

MARIAVISION
E-mail: internacional@mariavision.com
Web Site: http://www.mariavision.com.mx
Programming: Issues related to Catholicism.
Began: January 1, 2003, Reflects U.S. launch.
Ownership: Mariavision Partners.

MARTHA STEWART ON DEMAND
11 W 42nd St
New York, NY 10036
Phone: 212-827-8000
E-mail: television@marthastewart.com
Web Site: http://www.marthastewart.com
Charles Koppelman, Executive Chairman
Lisa Gersh, President & Chief Operating Officer
Janet Balis, Executive Vice President, Media Sales
Missy Foristall, Senior Vice President, Digital Programming & Strategy, Martha Stewart Living Omnimedia
Sarah Gormley, Senior Vice President, Communications & Marketing, Martha Stewart Living Omnimedia
Type of service: Video on demand.
Programming: Season-specific decorating, cooking & entertaining focused how-to shows.
Began: October 1, 2007.
Total subscribers: 14,000,000.
Distribution method: Available to cable systems.
Ownership: Martha Stewart Omnimedia.

MARTIAL ARTS ACTION NETWORK — No longer planned.

MARTIAL ARTS CHANNEL
116 Village Blvd
Ste 200
Princeton, NJ 08540
Phone: 609-524-4003
Web Site: http://www.macexperience.com
R. Anthony Cort, Chief Executive Officer
Mike du Monceau, Programming & Production
Claude J. Wells, Marketing & Communications
Glenn Moss, General Counsel & Business Affairs
Ethan James, Business Development
Type of service: Broadband.

Programming: Martial arts movies, cartoons, instructions, tournaments & documentaries.
Began: July 1, 2006.

MASMUSICA TEVE NETWORK

299 Alhambra Cir
Ste 510
Coral Gables, FL 33134
Phone: 305-648-0065
Fax: 305-648-0068
E-mail: rosamaria@caballero.com
Web Site: http://www.masmusica.tv

Branch Offices:
STUDIO: 3310 Keller Springs Rd, Ste 105, Carrollton, TX 75006. Phone: 972-503-6800. Fax: 972-503-6801.
Type of service: Basic.
Programming: 24-hour broadcast network featuring the latest youth-oriented Spanish-language music programming from a unique mix of the most popular Spanish music formats such as Regional Mexican, Latin Pop, Tropical and Rock en Espanol, including videos, concerts, and interviews.
Means of Support: Advertising.
Scrambled signal: Yes.

MASTV — See KyLinTV.

Programming: Programming for the sophisticated Chinese viewer from Hong Kong, Macao & Taiwan. Provides targeted news, finance & entertainment shows. Offered by KyLinTV.
Scrambled signal: Yes.
Massachusetts Spanish TV Network.

MAVTV

44 Inverness Dr E
Bldg D
Englewood, CO 80112
Phone: 303-471-9242
Fax: 303-799-6643
E-mail: info@mavtv.net
Web Site: http://www.mavtv.com
Steve Severn, Chief Executive Officer
Steve Smith, President, & Chief Operating Officer
Doug Jost, Executive Vice President, Sales & Marketing
David Gluck, Senior Vice President, Business Development
David Boyles, Vice President, Controller
Rob Stevens, Vice President, Programming
Type of service: Premium.
Satellites: Galaxy 11, transponder 21.
Operating hours/week: 168.
Programming: Sports, gaming, business news & entertainment targeted to men 18-54.
Began: October 1, 2004.
Means of Support: Subscription, advertising, sponsorship.
Total subscribers: 6,500,000.

MAX GO

Home Box Office
1100 Avenue of the Americas
New York, NY 10036
Phone: 212-512-1000
Fax: 212-512-1166
E-mail: contactmaxgo@hbo.com
Web Site: http://www.maxgo.com
Shelley Brindle, Senior Vice President, Domestic Network Distribution, HBO
Marti Moore, Vice President, Web Technology, Customer Service
Type of service: Online video service.
Operating hours/week: 168.
Operating areas: Available nationwide.
Programming: Offers over 700 hours of programming to subscribers online.
Began: September 9, 2010.
Distribution method: Available to Cinemax subscribers.
Ownership: Home Box Office Inc.

MAXIMUM TV

PO Box 381
Cypress, TX 77410-0381
E-mail: public.relations@maximum.tv
Web Site: http://www.maximum.tv
Erik Vanderlaan, Chief Technology Officer
Programming: Broadband television service bringing quality and premium programming from Latin America and around the world. Maximum TV delivers a targeted and personalized online television experience via broadband connected devices. Maximum TV's focus is to provide US based Hispanics with television content that is relevant to them, online and on-demand.
Began: January 29, 2010.
Means of Support: Advertising.
Scrambled signal: Yes.

MBC AMERICA

3400 W 6th St
4th Fl
Los Angeles, CA 90020
Phone: 213-487-2345
Fax: 213-736-1555
E-mail: contact@mbc24.com
Web Site: http://mbc-america.com
Bok Haeng Cho, President
Nam Jung Kim, General Director
Nahee Kim, Content Business & Planning Manager
Sung Ho Lee, Broadcast Engineering Manager
Yos Park, Production Manager
James Chong, Ad Manager
Operating hours/week: 168.
Programming: Popular South Korean soap operas, news broadcasts, dramas, current affairs, sports and cultural programs.
Began: September 1, 2002.
Distribution method: Available to cable systems & home dish audiences.
Ownership: Munwha Broadcasting Corp.

MDTV: MEDICAL NEWS NOW

27 North Ave E
Cranford, NJ 07016
Phones: 908-272-6388; 877-638-8669
Fax: 866-329-6388
Web Site: http://www.mdtvnow.com
Paul G. Argen, Chief Executive Officer & Executive Producer
Maria Villalonga, RN, BSN, President
James Walsh, MS, Executive Director
Sean Doran, Senior Producer
Christa B. Kantner, Vice President, Business & Market Development
Programming: Presents technically advanced medical information in an easily understood format. Educates public on today's popular surgical procedures & highlights top surgeons.

ME TELEVISION

1901 E 51st St
Stage 4
Austin, TX 78723
Phone: 512-804-2400
E-mail: info@metelevision.com
Web Site: http://www.metelevision.com
Type of service: Basic, digital.
Operating hours/week: 168.
Operating areas: Texas.
Programming: Showcases regional musical, visual & theatrical artists & touring groups through interviews, live shows, artist information & venue schedules.
Began: October 1, 2005.
Distribution method: Available to cable & satellite systems.
Scrambled signal: Yes.

Setting the industry standard...
Communications Daily
Warren Communications News
FREE 30-day trial—call 800-771-9202 or visit www.warren-news.com

ME-TV

26 N Halsted St
Chicago, IL 60661
Phone: 312-705-2600
Fax: 312-705-2656
E-mail: mkelly@wciu.com
Web Site: http://metvnetwork.com
Norman H Shapiro, President, Weigel Broadcasting Co.
John Bryan, President, Domestic Television Distribution, MGM
Neal Sabin, Executive Vice President, Weigel Broadcasting Co.
Type of service: Basic.
Satellites: AMC-3.
Operating hours/week: 168.
Operating areas: Available nationwide.
Programming: Classic programming from the 1950's to the 1980's.
Began: December 8, 2010.
Means of Support: Advertising.
Distribution method: Available to broadcast stations & cable systems.
Ownership: Weigel Broadcasting Co. Distributed by Metro-Goldwyn-Mayer Studio Inc.

MEADOWS RACING NETWORK — See HorseRacing TV.

MEDIA BROADCAST NETWORK — No longer planned.

MEDIAZONE

One Circle Star Way
Third Fl
San Carlos, CA 94070
Phone: 650-801-3050
E-mail: info@mediazone.com
Web Site: http://www.mediazone.com
Type of service: Broadband & wireless.
Programming: MediaZone is a leading global online broadcaster specializing in professionally-produced sports, international and entertainment video programming. MediaZone has established lasting exclusive partnerships with leading media brands including AOL, NBC Sports and the Shanghai Media Group and is the official online broadcast partner for major events such as Wimbledon, FIBA Basketball and SANZAR Rugby.
Began: N.A.
Scrambled signal: Yes.

MEDIASET ITALIA

4100 E Dry Creek Rd
c/o International Media Distribution
Centennial, CO 80122
Phone: 303-712-5400
Fax: 303-712-5401
Web Site: http://www.imediadistribution.com
Scott Wheeler, Senior Vice President, Network Development
Mike Scott, Vice President, Affiliate Sales & Marketing
Shelly Kurtz, Executive Director, Affiliate Sales & Marketing
Kajsa Moe, Director, Affiliate Sales & Marketing
Nicole Wang, Manager, Affiliate Sales & Marketing
Type of service: Basic.
Operating hours/week: 168.
Operating areas: Available nationwide.
Programming: Mediaset Italia features top Italian programming including drama series, comedies, news, and entertainment shows a few hours/days after airing on its mainstream local TV channels.
Began: June 8, 2011.
Scrambled signal: Yes.
Ownership: Mediaset, owned by Silvio Berlusconi, current Prime Minister of Italy.

MEGA TV

2601 S Bayshore Dr
Ste 2020
Coconut Grove, FL 33133
Phones: 305-441-6901; 305-644-4800
Fax: 786-470-1667
E-mail: info@mega.tv
Web Site: http://www.mega.tv
Raul Alarcon, Jr., Chairman, President & Chief Executive Officer
Pablo Raul Alarcon, Sr., Chairman Emeritus & Director
Joseph A. Garcia, Chief Financial Officer, Executive Vice President & Secretary
Marko Radlovic, Chief Operating Officer & Executive Vice President
Cynthia Hudson Fernandez, Chief Creative Officer & Executive Vice President, SBS; Managing Director, Mega TV
Albert Rodriguez, General Manager
Camilo Bernal, Manager, Affiliate Relations
Rene Rodriguez, Director, Sports Marketing
Operating hours/week: 168.
Programming: Spanish-language programming.
Began: October 17, 2007, reflects nationwide satellite launch.
Distribution method: Available to cable & satellite systems.
Ownership: Spanish Broadcasting System Inc.

MEN7 NETWORK

Phone: 310-442-6630
E-mail: info@men7.tv
Web Site: http://http://www.men7.tv
Type of service: Basic, video on demand, IPTV, mobile.
Programming: Entertainment & lifestyle shows aimed at men between 25-54.
Began: January 25, 2008, Reflects video on demand launch.
Distribution method: Available to cable systems, satellite providers & via broadband.
Scrambled signal: Yes.

MESCAPE — See Mpix.

MEZZO LIVE HD

28 rue Francois 1er
Paris 75008
France
Phone: 33-1-5636-5100
E-mail: contact@mezzo.fr
Web Site: http://www.mezzo.tv

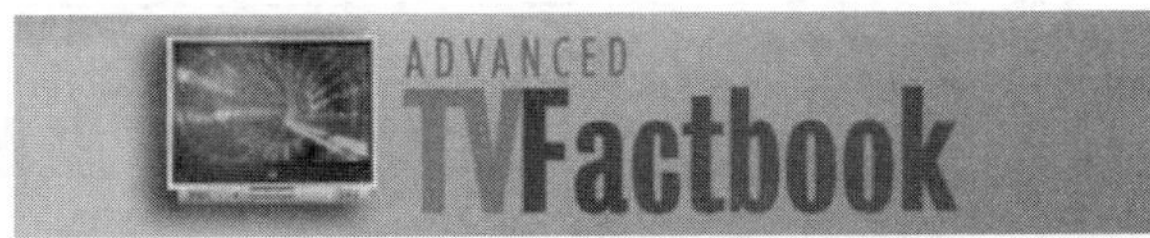

Satellites: Eurobird 9A.
Operating hours/week: 168.
Programming: MEZZO offers all classical music styles and periods: baroque, romantic, classical, contemporary and in all artistic forms: vocal, instrumental, symphonic, polyphonic. MEZZO offers all forms of jazz: ragtime, fusion, soul, electronic. MEZZO embraces all musical styles, plus a major performance nightly.
Began: April 15, 2010.
Distribution method: Availbale to cable systems and satellite providers.
Scrambled signal: Yes.

METEOMEDIA — See Weather Network.
Web Site: http://www.meteomedia.com

METROCHANNELS — See News 12 Traffic & Weather.

METRO SPORTS
6550 Winchester Ave
Kansas City, MO 64133
Phones: 816-358-5360; 816-222-5500
Fax: 816-358-5479
E-mail: kathym.nelson@twcable.com
Web Site: http://www.kcmetrosports.com
John Denison, General Manager
John Sprugel, News/Sports Director & Production Manager
Kathy Nelson, Marketing & Program Director
Steve Kurtenbach, Executive Producer & Remote Production Manager
Type of service: Basic.
Operating hours/week: 168.
Programming: 24-hour regional sports network. Covers professional, college and high school.

MEXICANAL
Av. Salvador Nava Martinez #2850
5to. Piso Colonia del Real, C.P.
San Luis Potosi, SLP 78280
Mexico
Phone: 444-129-2929
Fax: 444-129-2930
Web Site: http://www.mexicanal.com
Luis Torres-Bohl, President
Maruchi Urquiaga, Senior Vice President & General Manager
Chuck Wing, Senior Vice President, Syndication
Edwin Vidal, Director, Operations
Israel Reyero, Assistant Director, Programming & Operations

Branch Offices:
US Offices–Castalia Communciations: 1532 Dunwoody Village Pkwy, Ste 203, Atlanta, GA 30338. Phone: 770-396-7850. Fax: 770-396-3464.
Programming: Regional news, sports news, baseball, interviews, debates, music, travel, kids' & women's shows.
Began: August 1, 2005, Reflects U.S. launch.
Scrambled signal: Yes.
Ownership: Joint venture between Cablecom (Mexican entity) & Castalia Communications.

MGM CHANNEL
MGM Networks
10250 Constellation Blvd
Los Angeles, CA 90067
Phone: 310-449-3000
Web Site: http://www.mgmchannel.com
Gary Barber, Co-Chairman & Chief Executive Officer
Roger Birnbaum, Co-Chairman & Chief Executive Officer
Roma Khanna, President, Television Group & Digital
Gary Marenzi, President, Worldwide Television
Bruce Tuchman, President, MGM Networks
Courtney Williams, Vice President, Sales & Marketing
Steven Bernstein, Vice President, Business Development & Joint Ventures
Gracelyn Brown, Vice President, Programming
Doug Chalfant, Executive Creative Director
Mark Zelenz, Executive Director, Affiliate Sales
Elizabeth Squires, Programming & Marketing Director

Branch Offices:
NEW YORK: 655 3rd Ave, New York, NY 10017. Phone: 212708-0300.
Operating hours/week: 168.
Programming: Popular movies from the MGM film library.
Distribution method: Available to telco, cable & satellite providers.

MGM HD — See MGM Channel.
Programming: Features MGM movies in HD, original shows covering the film industry & red carpet events, movie previews, seasonal promotions & re-mastered classics.
Began: October 10, 2007.
Distribution method: Available to satellite & telco systems.
Ownership: MGM Studios, Inc.

MGM PLUS — See MGM Channel.

MHZ NETWORKS
8101 A Lee Hwy
Falls Church, VA 22042
Phone: 703-770-7100
E-mail: fthomas@mhznetworks.org
Web Site: http://www.mhznetworks.org
Fred Thomas, General Manager
Ann Williams, Station Manager
Jenna Reedy, Marketing Director
Type of service: Basic.
Operating hours/week: 168.
Programming: Independent, public television network focusing on international, educational & arts programming, including unedited international news broadcasts, documentaries, world sports & popular drama series.
Began: January 1, 1983.
Means of Support: Viewer supported.
Total subscribers: 49,000,000.
Distribution method: Broadcast, cable & satellite.
Ownership: Commonwealth Public Broadcasting Corp.

MHZ WORLDVIEW — See MHz Networks.
Began: February 1, 2006.

MI CINE — See Alterna'TV.

MI CINE ON DEMAND — See Alterna'TV.

MICHIGAN GOVERNMENT TELEVISION
George Romney Bldg
111 S Capitol, 4th Fl
Lansing, MI 48933
Phone: 517-373-4250
Fax: 517-335-7342
E-mail: mgtv@mgtv.org
Web Site: http://www.mgtv.org
Bill Trevarthen, Executive Director
Michael Blonde, Senior Producer
Bill Kozdron, Producer
Lois Ewen, Office Manager & Legislative Liaison
Michelle Webb, Operations Manager
Vanessa Ferguson, Writer/Researcher
Type of service: Basic.
Satellites: AMC 3.
Operating areas: Lansing, MI.
Programming: Covers state legislature, executive branch & Michigan Supreme Court.
Began: July 15, 1996.
Total subscribers: 1,400,000.
Distribution method: Available to cable systems.
Scrambled signal: Yes.
Ownership: Michigan Government Television Inc.

MID-ATLANTIC SPORTS NETWORK
(MASN)
333 W Camden St
Baltimore, MD 21201-2435
Phone: 410-625-7100
Web Site: http://www.masn.tv
Jim Cuddihy, Executive Vice President, Programming & Operations
Charlie Dunn, Vice President & General Manager
John McGuinness, Vice President & National Sales Manager
Chris Glass, Executive Producer
Type of service: Basic.
Operating hours/week: 168.
Operating areas: Pennsylvania, Maryland, Virginia, DC, North Carolina, Delaware & West Virginia.
Programming: Regional sports coverage of major & NCAA league baseball, basketball & football games, shows & news. Coverage includes Washington Nationals, Baltimore Orioles, Baltimore Ravens & Georgetown University.
Began: July 31, 2006.
Total subscribers: 6,400,000.
Distribution method: Available to cable systems & satellite providers.
Scrambled signal: Yes.
Ownership: Washington Nationals & Baltimore Orioles.

MIDCO SPORTS NETWORK
425 S 1st Ave
Sioux Falls, SD 57104
Phone: 605-274-7638
E-mail: info@midcosn.com
Web Site: http://www.midcosportsnet.com
Pat McAdaragh, President & Chief Executive Officer, Midcontinent Communications
Wynne Haakenstad, Director of Programming
Tom Nieman, Programming Manager
Type of service: Regional basic.
Operating areas: Available in North Dakota, South Dakota & Minnesota.
Programming: Offers live coverage of regional sporting events from colleges, universities and high schools in North Dakota, South Dakota and Minnesota.
Began: August 18, 2010.
Total subscribers: 250,000.
Distribution method: Available to cable systems.
Ownership: Midcontinent Communications.

MILITARY CHANNEL — See Discovery Channel.
Web Site: http://military.discovery.com
Henry S Schleiff, President & General Manager
Programming: Features real-world stories of heroism, military strategy, technological & historical turning points & all facets of military life & the armed forces.
Began: January 1, 2005, formerly Discovery Wings Channel.
Total subscribers: 57,000,000.

MILITARY HISTORY CHANNEL — See History Channel.

MINNESOTA HOUSE & SENATE TELEVISION
175 State Office Bldg
St. Paul, MN 55155-1298
Phones: 651-296-2146; 800-657-3550
Fax: 651-296-9029; 651-297-3800
Web Site: http://www.house.leg.state.mn.us
Barry LaGrave, Director, House Television
Steve Senyk, Director, Senate Media Services
Type of service: Basic.
Satellites: Telstar 5.
Operating hours/week: 45.
Operating areas: Minnesota.
Uplink: Group W Network Services.
Programming: Live and taped House & Senate committee & floor coverage.
Began: January 7, 1997.
Total subscribers: 200,000.
Distribution method: Available to cable systems.
Ownership: Minnesota Legislature.

MKTV
Media Korea Broadcasting
2025 Center Ave, Ste 120
Ft. Lee, NJ 07204
Phones: 201-363-0707; 800-717-7578
Web Site: http://www.mediakoreatv.com
Operating hours/week: 168.
Operating areas: New York, New Jersey, Connecticut.
Programming: Korean-language news & entertainment.
Began: January 1, 1993.
Distribution method: Available to cable systems.

MLB EXTRA INNINGS — See iN DEMAND.

MLB NETWORK
245 Park Ave
31st Fl
New York, NY 10167
Phone: 212-931-7800
Web Site: http://mlb.mlb.com/index.jsp
Tony Petitti, Chief Executive Officer
Robert McGlarry, Senior Vice President, Programming & Business Affairs
Type of service: Basic.
Operating hours/week: 168.
Programming: Games & highlights, including out of market games.
Began: January 1, 2009.

Total subscribers: 50,000,000.
Distribution method: Available to cable systems & satellite subscribers.
Scrambled signal: Yes.
Ownership: Partnership between Major League Baseball, Comcast (8.34%), Cox & DIRECTV.

MLB NETWORK HD — See MLB Network.

MLS DIRECT KICK — See iN DEMAND.

MNET
19 W 44th St
New York, NY 10036
Phone: 212-869-4288
Fax: 212-239-4071
E-mail: iatvops@gmail.com
Web Site: http://iatv.tv
Adam Ware, Acting President & Chief Executive Officer
J. Edward Lee, Executive Vice President & Chief Operating Officer
Julie Choi, Senior Vice President, Programming & Development
David Chu, Senior Vice President, Programming & Production
Michael Huh, Vice President, Marketing & Strategic Development
Sung Lee, Vice President, Business Development
Thomas Pyun, Vice President, Ad Sales
Alexander Kim, General Counsel
Type of service: Basic, digital basic, broadcast & video on demand.
Programming: Asian-American films, drama, series, sitcom, news, variety & game shows, children's programming, music videos, sports, documentaries. Launched as ImaginAsian TV, rebranded 2011.
Began: August 30, 2004.
Means of Support: Advertising.
Total subscribers: 8,000,000.
Distribution method: Digital, analog.
Scrambled signal: Yes.
Ownership: CJ Media.

MOJO MIX — See iN DEMAND.
Type of service: Video on demand.

MOMENTUM TV
Huitlapexco No. 20
Col. San Miguel Tecamachalco
Naucalpan Edo de Mexico 53970
Mexico
Phone: 52-55-5293-0550
Fax: 52-55-5589-7669
E-mail: mwnetworks@colorado.com.mx
Web Site: http://www.momentum.tv
Programming: Spanish-language documentaries, musicals, biographies, concerts, original shows & series.
Began: Unavailable.

MONSTER ON DEMAND
622 3rd Ave
39th Fl
New York, NY 10017
Phone: 212-351-7000
Fax: 646-658-0541
Web Site: http://www.monsterondemand.com
Type of service: Digital, video on demand.
Programming: Job advertisements.
Began: December 1, 2008.
Total subscribers: 16,500,000.
Distribution method: Available to cable systems.
Ownership: Comcast & Monster Worldwide.

MOODY BROADCASTING NETWORK
820 N LaSalle Blvd
Chicago, IL 60610-3284
Phones: 312-329-4433; 800-621-7031
Fax: 312-329-4339
E-mail: mbn@moody.edu
Web Site: http://www.mbn.org
Dr. Joseph Stowell, III, President
Robert C. Neff, Vice President, Broadcasting
Tom Svoboda, Satellite Operations Manager
Wayne Shepherd, Programming Division Manager
Doug Hastings, Operations Division Manager
David Woodworth, Administrator, Technical Development
Phil Sheppard, Technical Services Division
Type of service: Audio.
Satellites: GE-3, transponder 17; Aurora I, transponder 10.
Operating hours/week: 168.
Programming: Religious format includes music, drama, education & phone-in programs.
Began: May 1, 1982.
Means of Support: Listener contributions & radio affiliate subscriber fees.
Total subscribers: 19,700 (Figure includes Canadian listeners.).
Distribution method: Available on Sky Angel satellite service.
Ownership: Moody Bible Institute of Chicago.

MOREMAX — See Cinemax.
Programming: Popular & rare films to complement Cinemax.
Began: June 1, 1998.

MORE TV CABLE NETWORK — No longer planned.

MOUNTAINWEST SPORTS NETWORK — See The Mtn.

MOVE NETWORKS INC.
796 E Utah Valley Dr
American Fork, UT 84003
Phones: 801-756-5805; 800-515-0395
Fax: 801-756-5806
E-mail: usinfo@movenetworks.com
Web Site: http://www.movenetworks.com
Jason Hodell, Chief Operating & Financial Officer
Drew Major, Chief Technology Officer
Programming: Plans to offer Internet-delivered television, providing nearly 100 channels.
Scheduled to begin: Plans to launch summer 2011.
Ownership: Investors include Benchmark Capital, Hummer Winblad Venture Partners, Microsoft, Steamboat Ventures & Televisa.

MOVIE CENTRAL
64 Jefferson Ave
Unit 18
Toronto, ON M6K 3H4
Canada
Phone: 416-534-1191
E-mail: web.moviecentral@corusent.com
Web Site: http://www.moviecentral.ca
Type of service: Pay.
Operating hours/week: 168.
Programming: New releases, original series & action, thriller, horror, comedy, drama, romance, independent & foreign films. Also includes series & exclusives from HBO & Showtime to Canadian audiences. Comprises 4 channels: MC1, MC2, MC3 & MC4.
Began: April 1, 2001, originally launched as Superchannel on February 1, 1983.
Distribution method: Available to cable providers in Western Canada.
Ownership: Corus Entertainment.

MOVIE CENTRAL EXPRESS — See Movie Central.

MOVIE CENTRAL HD — See Movie Central.

THE MOVIE CHANNEL — See Showtime.

THE MOVIE CHANNEL HD — See Showtime.

THE MOVIE CHANNEL ON DEMAND — See Showtime.
Type of service: Video on demand.

MOVIELINK
2120 Colorado Blvd
4th Fl
Santa Monica, CA 90404
Phone: 310-264-4500
Fax: 310-264-4501
E-mail: bizdev@movielink.com
Web Site: http://www.movielink.com
Operating areas: New York.
Programming: Movie download service with content from film libraries spanning all genres: action, comedy, drama, family, foreign & classics.
Began: January 1, 2002.
Scrambled signal: Yes.
Ownership: Blockbuster Inc.

MOVIEPLEX
8900 Liberty Circle
Englewood, CO 80112
Phone: 720-852-7700
Fax: 720-852-7710
E-mail: eric.becker@starz.com
Web Site: http://www.starz.com
Robert B. Clasen, President & Chief Executive Officer
Ed Huguez, Executive Vice President, Sales
Bill Myers, Senior Vice President, Finance
Tom Southwick, Senior Vice President, Corporate Communications
Eric Becker, Executive Director, Corporate Communications
Type of service: Pay.
Satellites: Satcom C-4, transponder 5 (east/west/MTN).
Operating hours/week: 168.
Programming: MoviePlex provides viewers with a variety of movie entertainment options, including: Encore Love (Monday), Encore (Tuesday), Encore Westerns (Wednesday), Encore Action (Thursday), Encore Mystery (Friday), Encore Drama (Saturday), and Encore Wam (Sunday).
Began: October 1, 1994.
Means of Support: Subscriber fees.
Total subscribers: 5,600,000.
Distribution method: Available to home dish audiences & cable systems.
Equipment: Digital/DigiCipher II.
Ownership: Liberty Media Corp.

MP NETWORK — No longer planned.

MPIX
BCE Place, 181 Bay St
Box 787, Ste 100
Toronto, ON M5J 2T3
Canada
Phone: 416-956-2010
Fax: 416-956-2012; 416-956-2018
E-mail: tmnpix@tmn.ca
Web Site: http://www.moviepix.ca
John Riley, President & Chief Executive Officer
Domenic Vivolo, Senior Vice President, Sales & Marketing
Kevin Wright, Senior Vice President, Programming
Alicia Barin, Vice President, Strategic Planning
Deborah Wilson, Vice President, Communications
Chris Bell, Vice President, Technology
John Pow, Vice President, Finance & Administration
Eric Malette, Vice President, Human Resources
Cecile Chung, Business & Legal Affairs Director
Type of service: Pay.
Satellites: Anik E-2, transponder 27.
Operating hours/week: 168.
Operating areas: Ontario, Quebec, Prince Edward Island, Nova Scotia, New Brunswick & Newfoundland.
Programming: New classic movies, uncut & commercial free.
Began: October 1, 1994.
Means of Support: Subscription fees.
Distribution method: Available to cable systems & home dish audiences.
Ownership: Astral Media Inc.

MSG
11 Penn Plz
New York, NY 10021
Phone: 212-465-6000
Fax: 212-465-6020
E-mail: msgnetpr@msg.com
Web Site: http://www.msg.com
James L Dolan, Chairman
Hank J Ratner, Vice Chairman
Scott O Neil, President, MSG Sports
Mike Bair, President, MSG Media
Melissa Ormond, Chief Operating Officer
Lawrence Burian, Executive Vice President, General Counsel & Secretary
David Clark, Executive Vice President, Sales, MSG Media
Andrea Greenberg, Executive Vice President
Howard Handler, Executive Vice President, Marketing & Sales, MSG Entertainment
Howard Jacobs, Executive Vice President, Marketing & Sales
Joseph Lhota, Executive Vice President, Administration
Robert Pollichino, Executive Vice President & Chief Financial Officer
Carol Albert, Senior Vice President, Marketing
Andrew Biggers, Senior Vice President, Content Distribution, MSG Media
Jeremiah Bosgang, Senior Vice President, Programming & Acquisitions
Felix Ciampa, Senior Vice President, Government Affairs
Casey Coffman, Senior Vice President, Corporate Strategy & Development

Jeff Filippi, Senior Vice President, Executive Producer
Kathryn Kerrigan, Senior Vice President, Planning & Analysis
Mike Ondrejko, Senior Vice President, Corporate Sales & Service
Jerry Passarro, Senior Vice President, Network Operations & Distribution
Donna Randazzo, Senior Vice President, Finance & Controller
Bob Shea, Senior Vice President, Special Projects
Don Simpson, Senior Vice President, Business Development
Gail Stern, Senior Vice President, Merchandising & Licensing
Art Ventura, Senior Vice President, Ad Sales
Lee Weinberg, Senior Vice President, Business & Strategic Planning
Joseph Yospe, Senior Vice President, Controller & Principal Accounting Officer
Dan Ronayne, Vice President & General Manager
Sean Downes, Vice President, Corporate Entertainment
Justin Edelman, Vice President, Communications
Stacey Escudero, Vice President, Business Public Relations
Randy Fibiger, Vice President, Concert Bookings-Theaters
Alison Hellman, Vice President, Affiliate Marketing
Richard McNamara, Vice President, Integrated Media Sales
Heather Pariseau, Vice President, Interactive Programming & Operations
Susan Schroeder, Vice President, Marketing Partnerships & Client Services
Peter Tulloch, Vice President, Advanced Services
Kevin Marotta, Entertainment & Sports Properties Director
Type of service: Regional, video on demand & broadband.
Satellites: GE-1, transponder 18.
Operating hours/week: 168.
Operating areas: Connecticut, New Jersey, New York & Pennsylvania (northeastern portion).
Programming: Sports & entertainment programming, including vintage & current concerts performed at Madison Square Garden.
Means of Support: Advertising & system fees.
Total subscribers: 11,200,000.
Distribution method: Microwave & satellite to home dish audiences & cable systems.
Scrambled signal: Yes.
Ownership: Publicly held. At the end of 2009 service was spun off from Cablevision to form part of MSG Media which is part of Madison Square Garden LP.
(MSG) Madison Square Garden

MSG PLUS

11 Penn Plaza
New York, NY 10121
Phone: 212-465-6000
Fax: 212-465-6020
E-mail: msgnetpr@msg.com
Web Site: http://www.msg.com
James L Dolan, Chairman
Hank J Ratner, Vice Chairman
Mike Bair, President, MSG Media
Scott O'Neil, President, MSG Sports
Type of service: Regional.
Satellites: GE-1, transponder 18.
Operating hours/week: 168.
Operating areas: Connecticut (southern portion), New Jersey & New York.
Programming: Regional sports service offering New York Islanders hockey, New Jersey Devils hockey, plus college basketball & football, professional boxing, tennis, thoroughbred racing, motor racing & other sports programming.
Began: March 10, 2008, formerly Fox Sports Net New York.
Means of Support: System fees & advertising.
Total subscribers: 9,678,000.
Distribution method: Available to home dish audiences & cable systems.
Scrambled signal: Yes.
Ownership: Publicly held.

MSG 3D — See MSG.

Began: March 24, 2010.
Distribution method: Available only to Cablevision Systems Inc. subscribers.

MSG VARSITY

1111 Stewart Ave
Bethpage, NY 11714
Phone: 516-803-2300
Fax: 516-803-2368
Web Site: http://www.msgvarsity.com
Theresa Chillianis, General Manager
Type of service: Regional, video on demand.
Operating hours/week: 168.
Operating areas: Connecticut, New Jersey & New York.
Programming: Offers complete coverage of local high school sports, plus band, dance, debate, drama and student government.
Began: September 24, 2009.
Total subscribers: 3,100,000.
Scrambled signal: Yes.
Ownership: Publicly held.

MSNBC

One MSNBC Plz
Secaucus, NJ 07094
Phone: 212-664-3845
Fax: 212-664-6308
E-mail: mediainquiries@msnbc.com
Web Site: http://www.msnbc.com
Bob Wright, Chairman & Chief Executive Officer, NBC
Phil Griffin, President
Jeremy Gaines, Vice President, Communications, MSNBC
Ray Lambiase, Vice President, Art Production & Design, MSNBC
Barry Margolis, Vice President, NBC News Eastern Sales
Val Nicholas, Vice President, Advertising & Promotions, MSNBC
Sharon Otterman, Vice President & Chief Marketing Officer, MSNBC
Bill Wolff, Vice President Primetime Programming, MSNBC
Leslie Schwartz, Director, Media Relations
Type of service: Basic.
Satellites: 10.
Operating hours/week: 168.
Programming: All news channel featuring packaged news reports, live remotes and analysis of breaking stories.
Began: July 15, 1996.
Means of Support: Advertising.
Total subscribers: 91,600,000.
Distribution method: Available to home dish audiences, cable systems & mobile video.
Scrambled signal: Yes. Equipment: Galaxy IR.
Ownership: NBCUniversal LLC. NBC bought Microsoft's interest in the channel in 2005.

MTC PERSIAN TELEVISION

7355 Canoga Ave
Canoga Park, CA 91304
Phone: 818-703-8212
Fax: 818-887-6080
E-mail: info@mellitv.com
Web Site: http://www.mellitv.com
Operating hours/week: 168.
Programming: Persian variety, news, entertainment & cultural shows.
Distribution method: Available to cable systems & satellite providers.

THE MTN

MountainWest Sports Network
4100 E Dry Creek Rd
Centennial, CO 80122
Phone: 303-267-6900
Fax: 303-267-6960
E-mail: feedback@themtn.tv
Web Site: http://www. themtn.tv
Kim Carver, Vice President & General Manager
Steve Hurlbut, Vice President, Production & Programming
Pam Stinson, Senior Director, Marketing
Brian Tripp, News Director
Type of service: Expanded & digital basic.
Operating hours/week: 133.
Operating areas: Utah, Colorado & New Mexico.
Programming: The MountainWest Sports Network covers live games including conference football, men's and women's basketball, with some coverage of baseball, softball, women's volleyball, women's soccer, gymnastics, track & field, swimming & diving, golf, and tennis. The network also has a comprehensive listing of conference sports shows, news, analysis, commentary and original programming.
Began: September 1, 2006.
Total subscribers: 6,000,000.
Distribution method: Available to cable systems & satellite providers.
Scrambled signal: Yes.
Ownership: NBCUniversal LLC & CBS Sports Network, 50% each.

MTV

MTV Networks Inc.
1515 Broadway, 31st Fl
New York, NY 10036
Phone: 212-258-8000
Fax: 212-846-8759
Web Site: http://www.mtv.com
Stephen K. Friedman, Friedman, President
Billy Dexter, Chief Diversity Officer
Rich Eigendorff, Acting Chief Operating Officer
Harvey Ganot, President, Advertising Sales & Promotions; President, International Advertising Sales
David Janollari, President, Programming
Bob Bakish, President, MTVN International
Doug Herzog, President, MTV Networks Entertainment Group
Abby Terkhuhle, President, MTV Animation, Executive Vice President & Creative Director
Van Toffler, President, MTV Networks Music & Logo Group
Cyma Zarghami, President, MTV Networks Kids & Family
Nicholas Butterworth, Chief Executive Officer, MTVi Group
Alex Ferrari, Chief Operating Officer, MTVN International
Carole Robinson, Executive Vice President & Chief of Staff
Kevin Attix, Executive Vice President, Digital Ad Sales
Gideon Bierer, Executive Vice President, Digital Media
George Cheeks, Executive Vice President, Business Affairs & General Counsel, MTVN Music & Entertainment Group
Greg Clayman, Executive Vice President, Digital Distribution
Denise Dahldorf, Executive Vice President, Affiliate Sales
Scott Davis, Executive Vice President, Operations, Viacom Networks
Colleen Fahey Rush, Executive Vice President & Chief Research Officer
Carl D. Folta, Executive Vice President, Corporate Communications
Richard Gay, Executive Vice President, Strategy & Operations
Tanya Giles, Executive Vice President, Strategic Insights & Research
Brian Graden, Executive Vice President, Programming & Development
Scott Guthrie, Executive Vice President & General Manager, MTV Games
Elizabeth Herbst-Brady, Executive Vice President, Ad Sales Strategy, Music & Entertainment Group
Catherine Houser, Executive Vice President, Human Resources
Leslie Leventman, Executive Vice President, Creative Services, Special Events & Travel Management
Sara Levinson, Executive Vice President, New Business Development
Chris Linn, Executive Vice President, MTV Programming & Head of Production
Nancy Newman, Executive Vice President, Strategy & Organizational Planning, Music/LOGO Group
Casey Patterson, Executive Vice President, Event Production, Talent Development and Studio Relations
Gregory J. Ricca, Executive Vice President & General Counsel, Viacom Networks Group
David Sussman, Executive Vice President, General Counsel, Law & Business Affairs
Sarah Tomassi Lindman, Executive Vice President, Program Strategy
Jacques Tortoli, Executive Vice President & Chief Financial Officer, MTV Networks
Beth Coleman, Senior Vice President, Ad Sales Research
Garrett English, Senior Vice President, Music Production
Jackie French, Senior Vice President, Series Development
Jane Gould, Senior Vice President, Consumer Insights, Nickelodeon & MTVN Kids & Family Group
David Kline, Senior Vice President, Technology & Chief Information Officer, MTV Networks
Type of service: Basic & video on demand.
Satellites: Galaxy III, transponder transponder 17.
Operating hours/week: 168.
Uplink: Network Operations Center, Smithtown, NY.
Programming: All-stereo video music channel including music news, specials, documentaries, original strip programming, promotions & interviews.
Began: August 1, 1981.
Means of Support: Advertising.
Total subscribers: 100,400,000.
Distribution method: Available to cable & satellite providers.
Scrambled signal: Yes. Equipment: VideoCipher II.
Ownership: Viacom Inc.

MTV HITS — See MTV.

Total subscribers: 28,000,000.

MTV JAMS — See MTV.

Total subscribers: 21,000,000.

MTV LATIN AMERICA

1111 Lincoln Rd

6th Fl
Miami Beach, FL 33139
Phone: 305-535-3700
Fax: 305-672-5204
Web Site: http://www.mtvla.com
Scott McBride, Chief Financial Officer
Antoinette Zel, Executive Vice President & Managing Director
Fernando Gaston, Senior Vice President, Creative, Content & Music
Jesus Lara, Senior Vice President, Music & Talent
Jose Tillan, Senior Vice President, Creative, Content & Music
Alina Vogtner, Senior Vice President, Human Resources & Development
Nelson Benedico, Vice President, Marketing Communications
Rita Herring, Vice President, Affiliate Sales
Harry Neuhaus, Vice President, Advertising Sales
Alejandro Pels, Vice President, Programming & Production & Executive Producer
Drana Prekelezaj, Vice President, Programming & Production
Melisa Quinoy, Vice President, Advertising Sales
Pablo Szneiberg, Vice President, Original Content Development
Pablo Yacub, General Counsel
Carole Bardasano, Senior Director, Programming & Acquisitions, MTV & VH1 Latin America
Axel Escudero, Director, Corporate Communications
Pierluigi Gazzolo, Regional Director, Affiliate Sales
Type of service: Basic.
Satellites: Satcom C-3, transponder 19; Morelos; Intelsat.
Operating hours/week: 168.
Uplink: New York.
Programming: Spanish language music videos & other entertainment related shows.
Began: October 1, 1993.
Means of Support: Advertising & subscribers.
Total subscribers: 8,000,000.
Distribution method: Available to home dish audiences, cable systems, MMDS & SMATVs.
Equipment: Decipher/Compression System, General Instrument.
Ownership: Viacom Inc.

MTV NETWORKS DIGITAL SUITE

1515 Broadway
New York, NY 10036
Phones: 212-258-8000; 212-258-8760
Suzanne McDonnell, Senior Vice President, Digital Fusion
Meghann Wu, Vice President, Strategy & Business Development. MTV Networks Entertainment Group
Carole Robinson, Information Contact
Type of service: Basic.
Programming: Packaged Viacom-owned digital channels to include MTV Jams, MTV Hits, MTV Tres (formerly MTV Espanol), VH1 Classic, VH1 Mega Hits, VH1 Soul, VH1 Country, VHUno & Nick Jr.
Began: July 27, 1998.
Distribution method: Available to cable systems.
Scrambled signal: Yes.
Ownership: Viacom Inc.

MTV NETWORKS EUROPE

Corporate Communications
180 Oxford St
London W1D 1D5
United Kingdom
Phone: 44-0-207-478-6000
E-mail: pressinfo@mtvne.com
Web Site: http://www.mtvne.com
Brent Hansen, President & Creative Director, MTV Networks Europe
Frank Brown, Executive Vice President, International, MTV Networks
Anthony Garland, Executive Vice President, International, MTV Networks
Mark Allen, Senior Vice President, Human Resources & Administration
Gil Aronow, Senior Vice President, Business Affairs & General Counsel
Michiel Bakker, Senior Vice President, Network Development
Harriett Brand, Senior Vice President, Talent & Artist Relations
Peter Dougherty, Senior Vice President, Creative & On-Air
Simon Guild, Senior Vice President, Strategy, Planning & Research
Boris Kaz, Senior Vice President, Advertising Sales
Philip McDanell, Senior Vice President & Chief Financial Officer
Iain Renwick, Senior Vice President, Communications
Chris Stephenson, Senior Vice President, Marketing
Peter Einstein, Business Director, MTV Networks Europe

Branch Offices:
AMSTERDAM: Raadhuisstraat 52, 1016 DG Amsterdam, The Netherlands. Phone: 20-620-3393. Fax: 20-620-9310.

MUNICH: Widenmayerstr. 18 RG, 80538 Muenchen, Germany. Phone: 89-212-3060. Fax: 89-298-777.

FRANKFURT: Feldbergstr. 28, 60323 Frankfurt, Germany. Phone: 69-971-14550. Fax: 69-971-145520.

MILAN: Viale Vittorio Veneto 8, 20124 Milano, Italy. Phone: 2-2953-0164. Fax: 2-2953-0166.

PARIS: 12 rue de Florence, 75008 Paris, France. Phone: 1-4293-8283. Fax: 1-4293-8309.

STOCKHOLM: c/o GSP Film AB, Odengatan 104, 11322 Stockholm, Sweden. Phone: 8-337-701. Fax: 8-339-015.
Satellites: Thor; Astra 1A; Astra 1B; Eutelsat II.
Operating hours/week: 168.
Programming: Music, style, news, movie information & comedy.
Began: August 1, 1987.
Means of Support: Advertising & sponsorship.
Total subscribers: 17,000,000 (reflects UK & Ireland subscribers).
Scrambled signal: Yes.
Ownership: Viacom Inc.

MTV NETWORKS HD — See MTV.

Type of service: Digital.
Operating hours/week: 168.
Programming: Music & children's programming.
Began: September 15, 2008.
Total subscribers: 10,000,000.
Ownership: MTV Networks International.

MTV2 — See MTV.

Total subscribers: 71,000,000.

MTVU

c/o MTV Networks
1515 Broadway
New York, NY 10036

Phone: 212-258-8000
E-mail: feedback@mtvu.com
Web Site: http://www.mtvu.com
Van Toffler, President
Stephen Friedman, Executive Vice President
Type of service: Basic.
Operating hours/week: 168.
Programming: Cable channel dedicated to every aspect of college life from music to news to campus life; broadcasts to over 720 colleges & universities.
Began: October 1, 2002, as College Television Network; January 20, 2004 as mtvU.
Total subscribers: 10,100,000 (7,500,000 on-campuses nationwide & 2,600,000 through cable & telco operators in college communities).
Ownership: MTV Networks.

MUCHLOUD

299 Queen St W
Toronto, ON M5V 2Z5
Phone: 416-591-7400
Fax: 416-591-0080
E-mail: muchloud@muchmusic.com
Web Site: http://www.muchmusic.com
Operating hours/week: 168.
Programming: Alternative, hard rock, metal & punk music videos, interviews & specials.

MUCHMORE RETRO

299 Queen St W
Toronto, ON M5V 2Z5
Canada
Phone: 416-591-7400
Fax: 416-591-0080
Web Site: http://www.muchmoreretro.com/
Programming: Music videos from the 80s & 90s.
Began: September 4, 2003.

MUCHMOREMUSIC

299 Queen St W
Toronto, ON M5V 2Z5
Canada
Phone: 416-591-5757
Fax: 416-591-3710
E-mail: muchmoremail@muchmoremusic.com
Web Site: http://www.muchmoremusic.com
Sarah Crawford, Communications Director
Morgan Flury, Senior Producer
John Morrison, Operations Supervisor
Mark Lewis, Information Contact
Programming: Nationwide English language music channel.
Began: September 30, 1998.

MUCHMUSIC NETWORK

299 Queen St W
Toronto, ON M5V 2Z5
Canada
Phone: 416-591-5757
Fax: 416-591-3710
E-mail: muchmail@muchmusic.com
Web Site: http://www.muchmusic.com
Moses Znaimer, President & Executive Producer
Mark Rubenstein, Vice President & General Manager
D. Kirkwood, Vice President, Sales & Marketing
Allan Schwebel, Cable Affiliate Relations Director
Denise Donlon, Music Programming Director

Branch Offices:
LOS ANGELES: Myers Communications, 8439 Sunset Blvd, Los Angeles, CA 90069. Phone: 213-848-3176. Fax: 213-656-4212.

NEW YORK: Myers Marketing & Research, 322 Rte 46 W, Parsippany, NJ 07054. Phone: 973-808-7333. Fax: 973-882-3651. Leah Reznick.
Satellites: Anik E-1, transponder 5.
Operating hours/week: 168.
Programming: Video music channel.
Began: August 31, 1984.
Means of Support: Advertising and system fees.
Total subscribers: 5,613,999.
Distribution method: Available to home dish audiences.
Ownership: CHUM Ltd. & Rainbow Media Holdings Inc.

MULTIMAX — See Cinemax.

Type of service: Pay.
Programming: A package of Cinemax channels including More Max, Action Max, Thriller Max, W Max, @ Max, 5 Max, Outer Max.
Distribution method: Available to cable & satellite providers.

MULTIMEDIOS TELEVISION

Paricutan y 5 de Febrero, No 312
Col. Roma
Monterrey, NL
Mexico
Phone: +52 (81) 8369 9919
Web Site: http://www.multimedios.tv
Operating hours/week: 168.
Programming: Spanish language network that produces news, sports, children's and entertainment programming. Local off-air affiliates also provide material as well.
Means of Support: Advertising and subscriber fees.
Distribution method: Available to cable systems.
Ownership: Grupo Multimedios.

MUN2 TELEVISION

100 Universal City Plz
City Walk Bldg 4525, Ste 2A
Universal City, CA 91608
Phone: 818-622-6862
Fax: 305-889-7212
Web Site: http://www.holamun2.com
Jacqueline Hernandez, Chief Operating Officer, Telemundo
Diana Mogollon, General Manager
Glenn Dryfoos, Senior Vice President & General Counsel
Alejandro Garcia, Senior Vice President, Programming, Telemundo Networks
Mauricio Gerson, Senior Vice President, Programming, Telemundo Networks
Flavio Morales, Senior Vice President, Programming & Production
Alex Alonso, Vice President, Marketing

Hanna Bolte, Vice President, Media & Talent Relations, mun2/Telemundo
Brian Hunt, Vice President, Local Ad Sales
Joe A Bernard, Director, Network Sales
Type of service: Basic.
Satellites: Spacenet 2, transponder 2; Galaxy 332-5, transponder 22; GE 1, transponder 5.
Operating hours/week: 112.
Operating areas: Florida.
Programming: Bilingual general entertainment network for U.S. Hispanics aged 18-34, with original programming that reflects their lifestyles & relevant bilingual content.
Began: October 1, 2001.
Means of Support: Advertising & subscribers.
Total subscribers: 31,000,000.
Distribution method: Available to cable systems & home dish audiences.
Scrambled signal: Yes. Equipment: DigiCipher.
Ownership: Telemundo Group, which is owned by NBCUniversal LLC.

MUSEUM CHANNEL — No longer planned.

MUSIC CHOICE

110 Gibraltar Rd
Ste 200
Horsham, PA 19044
Phone: 215-784-5840
Fax: 215-784-5869
E-mail: comments@musicchoice.com
Web Site: http://www.musicchoice.com
Dave Del Beccaro, President & Chief Executive Officer
Christina Tancredi, Executive Vice President, Marketing
Rick Bergan, Senior Vice President, Distribution
Jeremy Rosenberg, Senior Vice President
Paula T. Calhoun, Vice President & General Counsel
Jim Coleson, Vice President, Commercial Dealer Operations
Mark Melvin, Vice President, National Ad Sales
Anne Thiede, Vice President, Affiliate Sales & Operations
Damon Williams, Vice President, Programming & Production
Nolan Baynes, Director, Marketing
Mike Corry, Director, Advertising Sales
Jason Guarracino, Director, Web & Mobile Application Development

Branch Offices:
Chicago, IL; Los Angeles, CA; Secaucus, NJ.
Type of service: Basic, video on demand & broadband.
Satellites: Satcom C-3, transponder 9; Satcom C-3, transponder 6; Galaxy 3-R (Latin America).
Operating hours/week: 168.
Programming: Offers commercial-free music & music oriented content.
Began: May 1, 1990, Video on demand service began November 2004.
Total subscribers: 20,000,000.
Distribution method: Available to cable systems & mobile video.
Scrambled signal: Yes. Equipment: Jerrold.
Ownership: Partnership between subsidiaries of Microsoft, Motorola, Sony, EMI Music, Adelphia, Comcast (12.4%), Cox & Time Warner Cable.

MUSIC PLUS TELEVISION NETWORK

2116 Bellevue Ave
Los Angeles, CA 90026
Phone: 888-788-7587
Fax: 213-572-0241
Web Site: http://musicplustv.com
Henry Goldman, Business Development Associate
Marc Anthony Cubas, Chief Executive Officer & Chief Financial Officer
Dennis Tzeng, President & Chief Operating Officer
Bernel Nery, Network Operations, Digital Network Productions
Tracy Cayaban, Interactive Programming
Pamela Kerner, Advertising Sales Dir.
Type of service: Broadband & plans basic.
Satellites: Galaxy 13, transponder 1.
Programming: Independent music television network.
Began: January 1, 2005, reflects online operation. Linear cable channel still unannounced.

MUSIMAX & MUSIQUEPLUS

355 Ste. Catherine W
Montreal, QC H3B 1A5
Canada
Phone: 514-284-7587
Fax: 514-284-1889
Web Site: http://www.musimax.com; http://www.musiqueplus.com
Pierre Marchand, President
Type of service: Basic.
Satellites: Anik E-2, transponder 11-A.
Operating hours/week: 168.
Uplink: Montreal Teleport.
Programming: French language music videos.
Began: September 1, 1986.
Means of Support: Advertising & subscribers.
Distribution method: Available to cable systems.
Ownership: CHUM Ltd. & Radio Mutuel Inc.

MUSL TV

14141 Covello St
Ste 10A
Van Nuys, CA 91405
Phone: 818-849-5447
E-mail: info@musltv.com
Web Site: http://www.musltv.com
Richard Wirthlin, Founding Member
Mohamed Mohsen, Chairman
Jacob Arback, President & Chief Executive Officer
Scott Peyton, Chief Financial Officer
Tony Cochi, Executive Vice President, Distribution & Digital Media
Gary Grossman, Executive Vice President, Programming Development
Robb Weller, Executive Vice President, Programming & Production
Bruce Luizzi, Vice President, Corporate Development & Sales
Jason Mathas, Vice President, Competitive Events & Digital Media
Denise Sanchez, Vice President, Events & Network Promotions
Nadim George, Programming & Production Advisor
Type of service: Basic.
Operating hours/week: Plans 168.
Operating areas: Plans nationwide.
Programming: Network will be devoted to fitness, training and competitive performance.
Means of Support: Will be advertiser supported.
Distribution method: Will be available to cable systems.
Scrambled signal: Yes.
Ownership: Privately held.

MXENERGYTV

PO Box 8127
Stamford, CT 06905-8127
Phones: 203-356-1318; 800-785-4373
Fax: 203-425-9562
E-mail: mediarelations@mxenergy.com
Web Site: http://www.mxenergy.com
Jeffrey A Mayer, Prresident & Chief Executive Officer, MXenergy
Chaitu Parikh, Executive Vice President & Chief Financial Officer, MXenergy
Barry Frey, Executive Vice President, Advanced Platform Sales, Cablevision Systems
Type of service: Video on demand.
Operating areas: Connecticut, New Jersey & New York.
Programming: Features programs about saving money and protecting the environment.
Began: November 8, 2010.
Means of Support: Subscriber fees & advertising.
Distribution method: Available to Cablevision Systems subscribers.
Ownership: MXenergy.

MY DAMN CHANNEL

202 W 40th St
16th Fl
New York, NY 10018
Phone: 866-424-8864
E-mail: maria@mydamnchannel.com
Web Site: http://www.mydamnchannel.com
Type of service: Broadband.
Programming: Original comedy & music oriented shows.
Means of Support: Advertising.
Distribution method: Available online.

MYDESTINATION.TV

1925 Century Park E
Ste 1025
Los Angeles, CA 90067
Phone: 310-277-3500
E-mail: eric@es.tv
Web Site: http://www.mydestination.tv
Byron Allen, Chairman & Chief Executive Officer
Darren Galatt, Vice President, Ad Sales
Type of service: Digital broadband.
Operating hours/week: 168.
Operating areas: Available nationwide.
Programming: Focuses on travel shows.
Began: May 11, 2009.
Total subscribers: 1,900,000.
Distribution method: Available to Verizon FiOS and Frontier Communications subscribers.
Scrambled signal: No.
Ownership: Entertainment Studios.

MYNETWORKTV INC.

1211 Avenue of the Americas
21st Fl
New York, NY 10036
Phone: 212-301-3331
Fax: 212-819-0816
E-mail: brian.lewis@foxnews.com
Web Site: http://www.mynetworktv.com
Rupert Murdoch, Chairman & Chief Executive Officer, News Corp., US
James Murdoch, Chairman & Chief Executive Officer, News Corp., Europe & Asia
Arthur M. Siskind, Chief Executive Officer Senior Advisor
Peter Chernin, President & Chief Operating Officer, News Corp.
David F. DeVoe, Senior Executive Vice President & Chief Financial Officer
Lawrence A. Jacobs, Senior Executive Vice President & Group General Counsel
Beryl Cook, Executive Vice President & Chief Human Resources Officer
Anthea Disney, Executive Vice President, Content
Gary Ginsberg, Executive Vice President, Global Marketing & Corporate Affairs
Leon Hertz, Executive Vice President
Brian Lewis, Executive Vice President, Corporate Communications
John Nallen, Executive Vice President & Deputy Chief Financial Officer
Michael Regan, Executive Vice President, Government Affairs
Teri Everett, Senior Vice President, Corporate Affairs & Communications
Genie Gavenchak, Senior Vice President & Deputy General Counsel
Reed Nolte, Senior Vice President, Investor Relations
Tom Mockridge, Chief Executive, European TV
Programming: Original, dramatic series & entertainment.
Began: September 4, 2006.
Ownership: News Corp.

MYX TV

150 Shoreline Dr
Redwood City, CA 94065
Phone: 650-508-6000
Web Site: http://myx.tv/
Miguel Santos, Head of MYX TV
Joy Bovatsek, Head of Programming
Anthony Garcia, Head of Production
Ricky Resurreccion, Head of Ad Sales
Jun Del Rosario, Head of Distribution
Operating hours/week: 168.
Operating areas: Available in Boston, Chicago, Honolulu, Houston, Los Angeles, New York City, San Francisco, Seattle & Washington, DC.
Programming: Music entertainment and lifestyle channel dedicated to the Asian American community.
Began: July 22, 2007.
Means of Support: Advertising.
Total subscribers: 5,000,000.
Distribution method: Available to home dish audiences and cable subscribers.
Scrambled signal: Yes.
Ownership: ABS-CBN Corp.

N3D

2230 E Imperial Hwy
c/o DirecTV
El Segundo, CA 90245-3543
Phone: 310-964-5000
Web Site: http://www.directv.com/3D
Derek Chang, Executive Vice President, Content Strategy & Development
Steven Roberts, Senior Vice President, New Media & Business Development
Type of service: Basic.
Operating hours/week: 168.
Operating areas: Available nationwide.
Programming: Offers exclusive, original 3D programming, plus special events such as NASCAR Coke Zero 400 and the 2010 MLB All Star game.
Began: July 1, 2010.
Distribution method: Available to home dish audiences.
Scrambled signal: Yes.
Ownership: DirecTV.

N3D ON DEMAND

2230 E Imperial Hwy
El Segundo, CA 90245
Phone: 310-964-5000
Web Site: http://www.directv.com/3D
Derek Chang, Executive Vice President, Content Strategy & Development
Steven Roberts, Senior Vice President, New Media & Business Development
Type of service: Video on demand.
Operating areas: Available nationwide.
Began: July 1, 2010.

Distribution method: Available to home dish audiences.
Ownership: DirecTV.

NARRATIVE TELEVISION NETWORK

5840 S Memorial Dr
Ste 312
Tulsa, OK 74145-9082
Phones: 918-627-1000; 800-801-8184
Fax: 918-627-4101
E-mail: info@narrativetv.com
Web Site: http://www.narrativetv.com
Jim Stovall, President
Kathy Harper, Vice President
Kelly Morrison, Marketing Director
Dorothy Thompson, Operations Manager
Clover Nuetzmann, Audience & Industry Relations Manager
Type of service: Basic & video on demand.
Satellites: Galaxy I, transponder 22.
Operating hours/week: 20.
Uplink: Alexandria, VA.
Programming: Provides shows accessible to blind & visually impaired viewers.
Began: January 1, 1988.
Means of Support: Advertising.
Total subscribers: 35,000,000.
Distribution method: Available to home dish audiences & cable systems.

NASA TV

300 E St SW
Code P
Washington, DC 20546
Phone: 202-358-1701
Fax: 202-358-4334
E-mail: public-inquiries@hq.nasa.gov
Web Site: http://www.nasa.gov/multimedia/nasatv/
Joseph N. Benton, Executive Producer
Type of service: Digital.
Satellites: AMC-6, transponder 17C; AMC-7, transponder 18C.
Operating hours/week: 168.
Programming: Covers the entire space program, including launch to landing coverage.
Began: July 1, 1990.
Distribution method: Available to cable & satellite providers.

NASA TV HD — See NASA TV.

Began: July 19, 2010.

NASCAR HOTPASS

2230 E Imperial Hwy
El Segundo, CA 90245
Phone: 310-535-5000
Fax: 310-535-5225
Web Site: http://www.directv.com/DTVAPP/sports/nascar
Programming: A package of five channels featuring behind-the-wheel coverage of individual drivers, real time stats, audio & pit row action.
Began: February 18, 2006, formerly NASCAR In Car.
Distribution method: Available on DirecTV.

NASCAR IN CAR — See NASCAR HotPass.

NAT GEO MUNDO

PO Box 900
Beverly Hills, CA 90213
Phone: 310-369-0745
Web Site: http://www.foxhispanicmedia.com
Hernan Lopez, President & Chief Executive Officer, Fox International Channels
Tom Maney, Senior Vice President, Advertising Sales, Fox Hispanic Media
Sean Riley, Senior Vice President, Distribution, Fox Global Networks
Carmen Larios, General Manager
Matt Grim, Director, Affiliate Sales & Marketing
Operating areas: Available nationwide.
Programming: Nonfiction entertainment network for U.S. Hispanics that will feature high-quality original programming involving nature, science, culture and history.
Began: July 1, 2011.
Means of Support: Advertising.
Total subscribers: 4,000,000.
Distribution method: Available to cable systems & U-verse, Dish Network and FiOS.
Scrambled signal: Yes.
Ownership: Fox Hispanic Media, a subsidiary of News Corp.

NAT GEO WILD

1145 17th St NW
Washington, DC 20036-4688
Phone: 202-857-7000
Fax: 202-912-6602
E-mail: comments@natgeochannel.com
Web Site: http://www.natgeowild.com
John Fahey, President & Chief Executive Officer, National Geographic Society
David Haslingden, Chief Executive Officer, National Geographic Channels Worldwide
Steve Schiffman, President, National Geographic Channels, US
Geoff Daniels, Executive in Charge of Programming
Steve Burns, Executive Vice President, Content
Rich Goldfarb, Senior Vice President, Media Sales
Bridget Whalen Hunnicutt, Senior Vice President, Global Development
Charlie Parsons, Vice President, Global Development
David Lyle, West Coast Development Office
Type of service: Basic.
Operating hours/week: 168.
Programming: A replacement for the Fox Reality Channel, Nat Geo WILD will bring extraordinary natural history programming.
Began: August 1, 2006, Date is of original launch overseas. Launched March 29, 2010 in the United States.
Means of Support: Advertising.
Total subscribers: 40,000,000 (Subscriber figure represents count for Fox Reality Channel, which Nat Geo WILD replaced.).
Distribution method: Available to cable systems.
Scrambled signal: Yes.
Ownership: Fox Cable Networks & National Geographic Ventures.

NAT GEO WILD HD — See Nat Geo WILD.

Began: March 1, 2009, Date is of original launch in the United Kingdom. Launched March 29, 2010 in the United States.

NATIONAL GEOGRAPHIC CHANNEL

1145 17th St NW
Washington, DC 20036
Phone: 202-857-7000
Fax: 202-912-6602
E-mail: comments@natgeochannel.com
Web Site: http://www.nationalgeographic.com/channel
David Haslingden, Chief Executive Officer, National Geographic Channels International & Fox International Channels
John Fahey, President & Chief Executive Officer, National Geographic Society
David Beal, President, National Geographic Entertainment
Tim Kelly, President, National Geographic Global Media

Steve Schiffman, President
Ted Prince Jr, Chief Operating Officer, National Geographic Global Media
Juliet Blake, Senior Vice President, Production & Development
Michael Cascio, Senior Vice President, Special Programming
Brad Dancer, Senior Vice President, Research & Digital Media
Rich Goldfarb, Senior Vice President, Media Sales
Russell Howard, Senior Vice President, Communications Worldwide
Kiera Hynninen, Senior Vice President, Marketing
Heather Moran, Senior Vice President, Programming & Strategic Development
Paul Brake, Vice President, Finance
John Caldwell, Vice President, Strategic Development & Operations
Lisa Clark, Vice President, Consumer Marketing & Media Strategy
John Fletcher, Vice President, Production Services & Network Operations
Malvina Martin, Vice President, Development for Specials
Kevin Mohs, Vice President, Development & Production
Carrie Regan, Vice President, Development for Series
Randy Rylander, Vice President, Programming
Char Serwa, Vice President, Production
Dawn Rodney Tranchitella, Vice President, Creative
Bridget Whalen, Vice President, Development, Co-Productions & Acquisitions
Kim Woodward, Vice President, Development & Production
Cherry Yates, Vice President, Marketing & Communications, National Geographic Channels International
Chris Albert, Executive Director, Communications
David Friedlander, Executive Director, Research
Whit Higgins, Director, Development & Co-Productions
Cindy Linnell, Director, Production Mgmt
Banafsheh Parsee, Director, Business Operations
Joyce Romano, Director, Program Planning & Budget
Matthew Zymet, Director, Digital Media Content
Type of service: Basic.
Operating hours/week: 168.
Programming: National Geographic television programs & documentaries.
Began: January 1, 2001.
Total subscribers: 66,000,000.
Scrambled signal: Yes.
Ownership: Fox Cable Networks & National Geographic Ventures.

NATIONAL GEOGRAPHIC CHANNEL HD NETWORK — See National Geographic Channel.

Began: January 1, 2006.
Total subscribers: 8,500,000.

NATIONAL GEOGRAPHIC CHANNEL ON DEMAND — See National Geographic Channel.

Web Site: http://channel.nationalgeographic.com/channel/vod
Type of service: Video on demand.
Distribution method: Available to select cable operators.

NATIONAL GREEK TELEVISION

30-97 Steinway St
Astoria, NY 11103
Phone: 718-726-0900
Fax: 718-728-3328
E-mail: ngtv@ngtvonline.com
Web Site: http://www.ngtvonline.com
Demetris Kastanas, President
Norma Papamichael, Vice President
Type of service: Pay.
Operating hours/week: 168.
Programming: Greek & Greek-American language & culture programming including news, sports, talk shows, dramas, comedy series, movies & documentaries.
Began: September 1, 1975.
Distribution method: Available to cable systems.

NATIONAL IRANIAN TELEVISION

21050 Erwin St
Woodland Hills, CA 91367
Phone: 818-716-0000
Fax: 818-716-0023
Web Site: http://www.nitv.tv
Zia Atabay, President & Chief Executive Officer
Noureddin Sabet Imani, Vice President & News Director
Type of service: Basic.
Programming: 24-hour Persian programming.
Began: March 1, 2000.

NATIONAL JEWISH TV (NJT)

PO Box 480
Wilton, CT 06897
Phone: 203-834-3799
Joel Levitch, President
Don Humphrey, Chief Executive Officer
Type of service: Basic.
Satellites: Satcom C-1, transponder 18.
Operating hours/week: 3. Sun., 1pm-4pm.
Programming: Cultural, religious & public affairs programming for the Jewish community.
Began: May 1, 1981.
Means of Support: Advertising.
Total subscribers: 10,000,000.

NATIONAL LAMPOON NETWORK

254 W 54th St
Ste 800
New York, NY USA
10019
Phone: 212-471-3532
E-mail: feedback@nationallampoon.com
Web Site: http://nationallampoon.com
Nick DeNinno, Vice President & General Manager
Type of service: Basic.
Operating hours/week: 12.
Programming: Programming aimed at college students (18-24) including comedy, sports, films & talk shows.

Began: January 17, 2003.
Total subscribers: 4,500,000.

NATIVE AMERICAN NATIONS NETWORK — No longer planned.

NATIVE AMERICAN TELEVISION
PO Box 16231
Alexandria, VA 22302
Phone: 202-347-9713
E-mail: rflood@natv.org
Web Site: http://www.natv.org
Type of service: Broadband & plans basic.
Operating areas: Plans California, Arizona & Oklahoma.
Programming: News, specials, cooking shows, documentaries & stand-up comedies targeted to Native Americans in the U.S.
Began: N.A.
Distribution method: Plans availability to cable systems.

NBA LEAGUE PASS — See iN DEMAND.

NBA TV
450 Harmon Meadows Blvd
Secaucus, NJ 07094
Phone: 201-865-1500
Fax: 201-865-2626
Web Site: http://www.nba.com/nbatv
Adam Silver, President & Chief Operating Officer, NBA Entertainment
John Cook, Coordinating Producer
Mike Miller, Coordinating Director
Type of service: Digital.
Operating hours/week: 168.
Programming: Everything NBA to include real time statistics, live look-ins of games in progress, vintage games, highlights, videos & specials.
Began: November 2, 1999.
Total subscribers: 12,500,000.
Distribution method: Available to home dish audiences and cable systems.
Ownership: NBA Enterprises.

NBA TV HD — See NBA TV.

NBC CHICAGO NONSTOP
454 N Columbus Dr
5th Fl
Chicago, IL 60611
Phone: 312-836-5555
Web Site: http://www.nbcchicago.com/shows/nonstop/
Lawrence Wert, President & General Manager, WMAQ-TV
Type of service: Reegional basic.
Operating areas: Illinois, Indiana & Wisconsin.
Programming: 24-hour local news & entertainment channel.
Began: November 1, 2010.
Distribution method: Available to FiOS & cable subscribers.
Ownership: NBCUniversal LLC.

NBC MIAMI NONSTOP
15000 SW 27th St
Miramar, FL 33027
Phone: 954-622-6000
Web Site: http://www.nbcmiami.com
Ardyth Diercks, President & General Manager, NBC Miami
Type of service: Regional basic.
Operating hours/week: 168.
Operating areas: Florida.
Programming: Local information and lifestyle channel offering a wide variety of interesting and relevant programming choices.
Began: May 9, 2011.
Distribution method: Available to local, over the air viewers plus cable subscribers.
Scrambled signal: Yes.
Ownership: NBCUniversal LLC.

NBC NEW YORK NONSTOP
30 Rockefeller Plz
New York, NY 10112
Phone: 212-664-4444
Web Site: http://www.nbcnewyork.com
Michael Jack, President & General Manager, WNBC
Type of service: Regional basic.
Operating areas: Connecticut, New Jersey & New York.
Programming: 24-hour local news & entertainment channel.
Began: March 9, 2009.
Distribution method: Available to FiOS and cable subscribers.
Ownership: NBCUniversal LLC.

NBC PHILADELPHIA NONSTOP
10 Monument Rd
Bala Cynwyd, PA 19004
Phone: 610-668-5510
Web Site: http://www.nbcphiladelphia.com/shows/nonstop/
Dennis Bianchi, President & General Manager, WCAU
Type of service: Regional basic.
Operating areas: Delaware, Maryland & Pennsylvania.
Programming: 24-hour local news & entertainment channel.
Began: October 25, 2010.
Distribution method: Available to FiOS & cable subscribers.
Ownership: NBCUniversal LLC.

NBC WASHINGTON NONSTOP
4001 Nebraska Ave NW
Washington, DC 20016
Phone: 202-885-4000
Web Site: http://www.nbcwashington.com/shows/nonstop/
Jackie Bradford, President & General Manager, WRC-TV
Type of service: Regional basic.
Operating areas: District of Columbia, Maryland & Virginia.
Programming: 24-hour local news & entertainment channel.
Began: October 27, 2010.
Distribution method: Available to FiOS & cable subscribers.
Ownership: NBCUniversal LLC.

NDTV THE DOMINICAN CHANNEL — See Alterna'TV.
Programming: Entertainment, music, news, interviews, food, kids, astrology & educational shows.
Began: April 1, 2004, U.S. launch.
Ownership: Nexus International Broadcasting.

NEO CRICKET
NIMBUS Centre
Oberoi Complex
Andheri West, Mumbai 400 053
India
Phones: 91-22-26352000 ext. 175; 9892438262
Fax: 91-22-26352123
E-mail: manishas@neosports.tv
Web Site: http://www.neosports.tv
Dr. Shan Chandrasekar, President & Chief Executive Officer
Vikram Das, Senior Vice President, International & Syndication
Manisha Sharma, Corporate Communications
Operating hours/week: 168.
Programming: Offers programming on and about cricket. Includes broadcasts of all cricket matches in India.
Began: April 2, 2008, in India. Began service to North America September 30, 2010.
Distribution method: Available to cable subscribers.
Ownership: NEO Sports Broadcast Pvt. Ltd.

NETLINK INTERNATIONAL
7140 S Lewis Ave
Tulsa, OK 74136-5422
Phones: 918-499-6200; 800-488-4806
Fax: 918-488-4278
Peter C. Boylan, Executive Vice President & Chief Operating Officer, TV Guide Inc.
Rob Morris, Senior Vice President & General Manager, UVTV
Derk Tenzythoff, Vice President, Programming Services, UVTV/Netlink
Marian Holland, Compliance Administrator, UVTV/Netlink
Type of service: Basic.
Satellites: Satcom, transponder varies.
Operating hours/week: 168.
Programming: Satellite distribution of Denver TV stations KCNC-TV, KMGH-TV, KUSA, KWGN-TV & KDVR.
Began: January 1, 1987.
Means of Support: Monthly programming fee for services.
Distribution method: Available to home dish audiences & cable systems.
Scrambled signal: Yes. Equipment: VideoCipher II Plus.
Ownership: Netlink/UV.

NETWORK ONE
21111 Erwin St
Woodland Hills, CA 91367
Phones: 818-704-5154; 800-600-6381
Fax: 818-704-3934
Web Site: http://www.networkonetv.com
Garrett Passon, President & Chief Operating Officer
Joe Preston, Chief Executive Officer
Chandos Mahon, Executive Vice President
Jeff Weissner, Vice President, Affiliate Sales & Marketing
Mark Zutz, Vice President, Operations
Alan Maretsky, Programming Director
Lara Sarkissian, Promotions Director
Christina Montesano, Music Programming Director
Gary Eisenberg, Advertising Sales Director
Michael Fahn, Affiliate Sales Director
LaTricia Guyton, Programming Manager
Maureen Cook, Traffic Manager
Tamara Steele, Affiliate Relations Coordinator
Type of service: Basic.
Satellites: Satcom C-1, transponder 11.
Operating hours/week: 168.
Programming: Vintage films & classic t.v. shows from a variety of genres including western, comedy, drama & action.
Began: November 30, 1993.
Means of Support: Advertising.
Total subscribers: 70,000,000 (Figure includes home dish viewers.).
Distribution method: Available to home dish audiences, cable systems & broadcast stations.
Ownership: Network Telephone Services Inc.

THE NEW ENCORE — See Encore.

NEW ENGLAND CABLE NEWS
160 Wells Ave
Newton, MA 02459
Phone: 617-630-5000
Fax: 617-630-5055
E-mail: msegel@necn.com
Web Site: http://www.necn.com
Bill Bridgen, Executive Vice President & General Manager
Type of service: Basic.
Operating hours/week: 168.
Operating areas: Massachusetts, New Hamshire, Connecticut, Maine & Vermont.
Programming: National & local news, weather, sports, informational & talk programming.
Began: March 2, 1992.
Total subscribers: 3,700,000.
Distribution method: Available to cable systems via fiber optics & microwave.
Scrambled signal: Yes.
Ownership: NBCUniversal LLC.

NEW ENGLAND SPORTS NETWORK
480 Arsenal St
Bldg 1
Watertown, MA 02472
Phone: 617-536-9233
Fax: 617-536-7814
E-mail: sports@nesn.com
Web Site: http://www.nesn.com
Susan McGrail, Vice President & General Manager
Raymond Guilbault, Chief Financial Officer
Peter Plaehn, Marketing Director
Robert Whitelaw, Director, Operations
Jerry McAuliffe, Advertising Sales Director
Donald J. Reilly, Business Affairs Director
John Slattery, Advertising & Promotion Director
Michael Hall, New Media Director
Rick Booth, Creative Services Director
Type of service: Regional pay.
Satellites: AMC 11, transponder 14.
Sales representative: Group W Television Sales.
Operating hours/week: 168.
Operating areas: Connecticut (portions), Maine, Massachusetts, New Hampshire, Rhode Island & Vermont.
Uplink: Boston, MA.
Programming: Regional sports service offering Boston Bruins hockey, Boston Red Sox baseball, Hockey East college hockey, New England college football, basketball, soccer & lacrosse, Big Shot Candlepin Bowling, Beanpot Hockey Tournament, boxing, wrestling, outdoor specials, auto racing & sports specials.
Began: April 4, 1984.
Means of Support: Subscriber fees & advertising sales.
Total subscribers: 4,700,000.
Distribution method: Available to home dish audiences & cable systems.
Equipment: VideoCipher II.
Ownership: Boston Red Sox; Boston Bruins.

NEW SCIENCE NETWORK — No longer planned.

NEW YORK NETWORK
Ste 146, S Concourse
Empire State Plaza
Albany, NY 12223
Phone: 518-443-5333
Fax: 518-426-4198
E-mail: contact@nyn.suny.edu
Web Site: http://www.nyn.suny.edu
William F. Snyder, Executive Director
Roy T. Saplin, Administration & Broadcast Services Director
Gary Talkiewicz, Engineering Director
Dave Poplawski, Traffic Director
Type of service: Basic.
Programming: Provides live coverage of major events in Albany as well as instructional programming for educators, students & parents. Offers KU teleport facility. Three digital studios in downtown Albany.

NEW YORK 1 NEWS
75 Ninth Ave
6th Fl
New York, NY 10011
Phone: 212-379-3311
Fax: 212-379-3570
E-mail: ny1foryou@ny1.com
Web Site: http://www.ny1.com
Bernie Man, News Director
Joanna Tombrakes, Ad Sales Dir.
Steve Paulus, General Manager & Senior Vice President, News & Programming
Jeff Polikoff, Technical Operations Director
Peter Landis, News Director
Nikia Redhead, Public Relations Manager
Sales representative: National Cable Advertising Inc.
Began: September 8, 1992.
Means of Support: Advertising.
Total subscribers: 2,200,000.

NEW YORK 1 NOTICIAS — See New York 1 News.
Web Site: http://www.ny1noticias.com

NEW YORK RACING CHANNEL
PO Box 90
Jamaica, NY 11417
Phone: 718-641-4700
Fax: 516-488-6044
E-mail: nyra@nyrainc.com
Web Site: http://www.nyra.com
Rick Marks, Advertising
Bill Nader, Information Contact
Operating hours/week: 25.
Operating areas: New York City & Long Island.
Programming: Races, shows & payoffs.
Began: February 1, 1995.
Distribution method: Microwave to cable systems.
Ownership: New York Racing Assn.

NEW YORK STATE ASSEMBLY RADIO TELEVISION
Room 102 LOB
Albany, NY 12248
Phone: 518-455-4557
Fax: 518-455-5136
E-mail: mergesm@assembly.state.ny.us
Web Site: http://www.assembly.state.ny.us
Type of service: Basic.
Operating areas: New York.
Uplink: Fiber Optic Ring.
Programming: Public affairs & gavel-to-gavel coverage of assembly sessions.
Began: January 1, 2002.
Ownership: New York State.

NEWS 8 AUSTIN
1708 Colorado St
Austin, TX 78701-1131
Phone: 512-531-8800
Fax: 512-531-1234
E-mail: feedback@news8austin.com
Web Site: http://www.austin.ynn.com
Type of service: Basic.
Sales representative: Time Warner Cable Advertising Sales.
Operating hours/week: 168.
Operating areas: Texas.
Programming: 24-hour local news, weather and sports on Time Warner Cable channel 8, or 1508 HD. Other properties include: 24-hour sports channel, YNN Sports ch. 408 or 1509 HD; YNN 24-hour Weather ch. 358 or 1507 HD. YNN Austin is part of the Time Warner Local News Group which has properties in eight (8) markets in Upstate New York, NY1 in Manhattan, and News 14 Carolina in four (4) markets in North Carolina.
Began: September 13, 1999.
Total subscribers: 300,000.
Scrambled signal: Yes.
Ownership: Time Warner Cable Local News Group.

NEWS CHANNEL 5+
474 James Robertson Pkwy
Nashville, TN 37219
Phone: 615-248-5371
Fax: 615-248-5269
E-mail: plus@newschannel5.com
Web Site: http://www.newschannel5.com
Debbie Turner, General Manager
Mike Cutler, News Director
Natalie Ryman, Sales Manager
Michelle Bonnett, Executive Director, News Channel 5+
Mark Binda, Programming Director
Programming: Local news, live call-in shows, weekly business show, public affairs; niche programs, outdoor show; consumer show.
Total subscribers: 500,000.
Ownership: Landmark Communications.

NEWS CHANNEL 3 ANYTIME
803 Channel 3 Dr
Memphis, TN 38103
Phone: 901-543-2333
Web Site: http://www.wreg.com
Ron Walter, General Manager
Robert Eoff, President & General Manager
Operating hours/week: 168.
Began: January 1, 1992.

NEWS NOW 53
777 NW Grand Blvd
Ste 600
Oklahoma City, OK 73118
Phone: 405-600-6600
Web Site: http://www.cox.com/oklahoma
Doug Epperson, General Manager
Type of service: Basic.
Distribution method: Cable.

NEWS ON ONE - WOWT
3501 Farnam St
Omaha, NE 68131-3301
Phone: 402-346-6666
Web Site: http://www.wowt.com
Charlie Peterson, General Manager

NEWS PLUS
The Free Range Group Inc.
628 Virginia Ave
Orlando, FL 32803
Phone: 407-896-7300
Fax: 407-896-7900
Timothy J. Brennan, President
Jeffrey B. Talbert, Vice President
Type of service: Text.
Satellites: Spacenet 3, transponder 4.
Operating hours/week: 168.
Programming: Full-color text and graphic news service, featuring world & national news, financial & business reports, sports scores & highlights; national & international weather conditions.
Began: January 1, 1985.
Means of Support: System pays according to number of subscribers.
Ownership: The Free Range Group Inc.

NEWS 10 NOW — See YNN-Central New York

NEWS 12 BROOKLYN
E 18th St & Ave Z
Brooklyn, NY 11235
Phone: 866-394-7236
Web Site: http://www.news12.com
Began: June 14, 2005.
Total subscribers: 400,000.

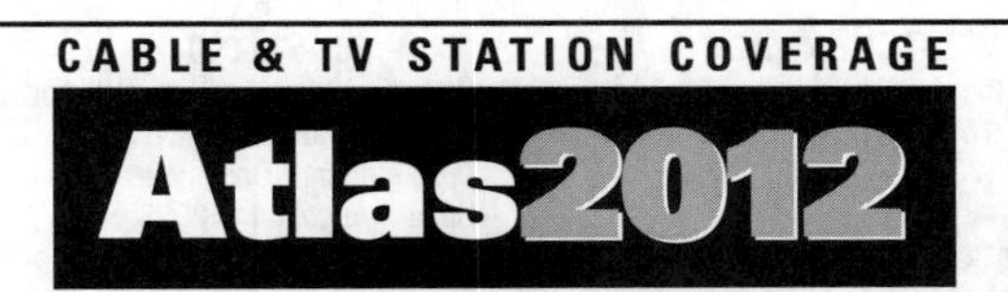
CABLE & TV STATION COVERAGE
Atlas2012
The perfect companion to the Television & Cable Factbook
To order call 800-771-9202 or visit www.warren-news.com

NEWS 12 CONNECTICUT
28 Cross St
Norwalk, CT 06851
Phone: 203-849-1321
Fax: 203-849-1327
E-mail: news12ct@news12.com
Web Site: http://www.news12.com
Tom Appleby, General Manager
John Oleynick, Ad Sales Director
Christopher Sulger, Manager, Affiliate Relations
Betty Prackup, Sales
Carmela Williams, Newsroom Coordinator
Heather Holmes, Promotions Manager
Deborah Gosselin, Marketing Director
Type of service: Basic.
Operating hours/week: 168.
Operating areas: Connecticut.
Programming: Local all-news channel.
Began: June 12, 1995.
Means of Support: Advertising.
Total subscribers: 200,000.
Distribution method: Available to cable systems.
Ownership: Rainbow Media Holdings Inc.

NEWS 12 INTERACTIVE
1 Media Crossways
Woodbury, NY 11797
Web Site: http://www.news12.com
Type of service: Digital.
Programming: Interactive local news programming.
Distribution method: Available to Cablevision subscribers.
Ownership: Rainbow Media.

NEWS 12 LONG ISLAND
One Media Crossways
Woodbury, NY 11797
Phone: 516-393-1200
Fax: 516-393-1456
E-mail: news12li@news12.com
Web Site: http://www.news12.com
Patrick Dolan, President & News Director
James Whiteman, Assistant News Director
Norm Fein, Senior Vice President, News Development
Steve Weinberg, Senior Vice President, Operations
Bob Sullivan, Vice President, Regional Advertising Sales
Alan Goodman, Executive Producer
Ralph Cerenzio, Vice President, Sales, News 12 Networks
Tim Carberry, Local Sales Manager
Deborah Rouer-Feeney, Marketing Director
Type of service: Basic.
Operating hours/week: 168.
Operating areas: New York.
Programming: Local all-news channel.
Began: December 15, 1986.
Means of Support: Advertising.
Total subscribers: 800,000.
Distribution method: Available to cable systems.
Ownership: Rainbow Media Holdings Inc.

NEWS 12 NEW JERSEY
450 Raritan Center Pkwy
Edison, NJ 08837
Phone: 732-346-3200
Fax: 732-417-5155
E-mail: news12nj@news12.com
Web Site: http://www.news12.com
Jonathan Knopf, General Manager
Michael Bartoli, Ad Sales Director
Laura Johnson, Sales Director
Patrick O. Young, Marketing & Promotion Director
Estelle Dziubek, Newsroom Coordinator
Christopher Sulger, Affiliate Relations Manager
Marissa Edelman, Promotion Coordinator
Type of service: Basic.
Operating hours/week: 168.
Operating areas: New Jersey.
Programming: Local & regional news & information.
Began: March 25, 1996.
Means of Support: Advertising.
Total subscribers: 1,800,000.
Distribution method: Available to cable systems by fiber.
Ownership: Rainbow Media Holdings Inc. & The Star-Ledger Co.

NEWS 12 THE BRONX
930 Soundview Ave
Bronx, NY 10473
Phone: 718-861-6800
Fax: 718-328-6790
E-mail: news12bx@news12.com
Web Site: http://www.news12.com
Camilo Pombo, General Manager
Brizm McEntree, Ad Sales Director
Don Meyers, Sales
Elise Agosto, Newsroom Coordinator
Chris Sulger, Affiliate Relations Manager
Deborah Gosselin, Director, Marketing
Type of service: Basic.
Operating hours/week: 168.
Operating areas: Bronx, NY.
Programming: Local all-news channel.
Began: June 1, 1998.
Means of Support: Advertising.
Total subscribers: 260,000.
Distribution method: Available to cable systems.
Ownership: Rainbow Media Holdings Inc.

NEWS 12 TRAFFIC & WEATHER
111 Crossways Park Dr W
Woodbury, NY 11797
Phone: 516-393-9003
E-mail: csanders@news12.com
Web Site: http://www.news12.com
James Dolan, Chief Executive Officer, Cablevision Systems Corp.
Type of service: Basic.
Operating hours/week: 168.
Operating areas: Connecticut, New Jersey & New York.
Programming: Local traffic, transit & weather.
Began: August 5, 1998.
Means of Support: Advertising.
Total subscribers: 2,400,000.
Distribution method: Available on cable systems.
Ownership: Rainbow Media Holdings Inc.

NEWS 12 WESTCHESTER
6 Executive Plaza
Yonkers, NY 10701
Phone: 914-378-8916
Fax: 914-378-8938
E-mail: news12wc@news12.com
Web Site: http://www.news12.com
Janine Rose, General Manager
John Oleynick, Ad Sales Director
Valerie Paul, Newsroom Coordinator
Chris Sulger, Affiliate Relations Manager
Deborah Gosselin, Marketing Director
Mike Menichiello, Promotions Manager
Type of service: Basic.
Operating hours/week: 168.
Operating areas: Westchester, NY.
Programming: Local all-news channel.
Began: November 6, 1995.
Means of Support: Advertising.
Total subscribers: 240,000.
Distribution method: Available to cable systems.
Ownership: Rainbow Media Holdings Inc.

NEWS 14 CAROLINA
2505 Atlantic Ave
Ste 102
Raleigh, NC 27604-1411
Phones: 919-882-4000; 866-328-1414
Fax: 919-882-4015
E-mail: sales@news14.com
Web Site: http://www.news14.com
Alan Mason, Vice President & General Manager
Rick Willis, News Director
Chuck Ward, Advertising Mgr.
Programming: 24-hour regional news in the Raleigh-Durham-Fayetteville / Charlotte / Greensboro-Winston-Salem-High Point markets.
Began: March 1, 2002.
Total subscribers: 485,000.
Ownership: Time Warner.

NEWSCHANNEL 8
1100 Wilson Blvd
6th Fl
Arlington, VA 22209
Phone: 703-236-9628
Fax: 703-236-2345
E-mail: mailus@news8.net
Web Site: http://www.news8.net
John D. Hillis, President
Wayne A. Lynch, Vice President, News & Programming
Eun-Hee Lee, Finance & Administration Director
Fred Ryan, General Manager
Jon DeFeo, News Director
Mitzi Freeberg, Human Resources Director
Mark Olingy, Operations & Engineering Director
Robin Taylor, Marketing & Promotion Director
Amy Wood, General Sales Manager
Type of service: Basic.
Operating hours/week: 168.
Operating areas: District of Columbia, Maryland & Virginia.
Programming: News coverage of the Washington, DC metropolitan area.
Began: October 7, 1991.
Means of Support: Advertising & subscriber fees.
Total subscribers: 1,300,000.
Distribution method: Fiber optic to cable systems.
Ownership: Allbritton Communications Inc.

NEWSDAY TV
c/o Cablevision Corp
1111 Stewart Ave
Bethpage, NY 11714
Phone: 866-575-8000
Web Site: http://www.cablevision.com
Operating hours/week: 168.
Programming: Daily news shows.
Began: August 11, 2008.
Distribution method: Available to cable systmes.
Ownership: Cablevision Corp.

NEWSWATCH 15
1024 N Rampart St
New Orleans, LA 70116-2487
Phone: 504-529-4444
Fax: 504-529-6470
Web Site: http://www.wwltv.com
Bud Brown, President & General Manager
Thomas Planchet, News & Operations Manager
Mike Zikmund, Sales Director
Jim Goodlad, Sales Manager
Type of service: Basic.
Sales representative: TeleRep Inc.
Operating hours/week: 168.
Operating areas: Louisiana.
Programming: Local news coverage every half hour.
Began: October 1, 1989.
Means of Support: Advertising.
Total subscribers: 289,530.
Distribution method: Via coaxial cable & microwave to cable systems.
Ownership: WWL-TV & Cox Cable.

NEW TANG DYNASTY TV
229 W 28th St
Ste 700
New York, NY 10001
Phone: 212-736-8535
Fax: 212-736-8536
E-mail: feedback@ntdtv.com
Web Site: http://www.ntdtv.com
Zhong Lee, President & Chief Executive Officer
Samuel Zhou, Senior Vice President, External Affairs
Keran Feng, Senior Vice President, Marketing & Sales
Mike Chen, Senior Vice President, Multi-language
Yibing Shi, Senior Vice President, Community Outreach
Wanqing Huang, Senior Vice President, Programming

Branch Offices:
CHICAGO: 234 W Cermak Rd, Ste 2F, Chicago, IL 60616. Phone: 312-791-9645. Fax: 312-791-9644.

LOS ANGELES: 9550 Flair Dr, Ste 112, El Monte, CA 91731. Phone: 626-443-2233. Fax: 626-443-2238.

SAN FRANCISCO: 1010 Corporation Way, Palo Alto, CA 94303. Phone: 408-656-6155. Fax: 408-904-5545.

TAIPEI: 6F-3 No. 9 Aiguo W Rd, Zhongzheng District, Taipei, Republic of China. Phone: 886 02 2268 3252. Fax: 886 02 2269 5556.

TORONTO: 420 Consumers Rd, Toronto M2J IP8, Canada. Phone: 416-787-1577. Fax: 416-787-6665.

WASHINGTON: 8927 Shady Grove Ct, Gaithersburg, MD 20877. Phone: 202-449-9480. Fax: 202-449-8566.
Type of service: Digital basic & broadcast.
Satellites: Galaxy 19; Hot Bird 6; ST-1.
Operating hours/week: 168.
Operating areas: Headquartered in New York City, providing TV service nationwide.
Programming: New Tang Dynasty TV (NTDTV) is an independent, nonprofit Chinese language TV network established by overseas Chinese. Non-governmental Chinese language TV network broadcasting uncensored information that reaches tens of millions of people in mainland China.
Began: February 15, 2002, in North America; July 2003 globally.
Total subscribers: 5,300,000.
Distribution method: Available to cable systems.
Scrambled signal: Yes.
Ownership: Non-for-profit 501 c (3).

NFL NETWORK
280 Park Ave
New York, NY 10017
Phone: 212-450-2000
Fax: 212-681-7579
Web Site: http://www.nfl.com/nflnetwork
Steve Bornstein, President & Chief Executive Officer
Ron Furman, Senior Vice President, Media Sales
Dena Kaplan, Senior Vice President, Marketing
Mark Quenzel, Senior Vice President, Programming & Production
Joel Chiodi, Vice President, Marketing & Promotions
John Malkin, Vice President, Affiliate Distribution
Dennis Johnson, Communications Director

Branch Offices:
PRODUCTION: 10950 Washington Blvd, Ste 100, Culver City, CA 90232. Phone: 310-840-4635. Fax: 310-280-1132.
Type of service: Basic.
Operating hours/week: 168.
Programming: First network dedicated solely to the NFL including original programming, NFL films & preseason games.
Began: November 4, 2003.
Total subscribers: 41,000,000.
Ownership: National Football League.

NFL NETWORK HD — See NFL Network.

NFL REDZONE
280 Park Ave
New York, NY 10017
Phone: 212-450-2000
Fax: 212-681-7579
Web Site: http://www.nfl.com/redzonetv
Steve Bornstein, Chief Executive Officer
Type of service: Basic.
Operating areas: Nationwide.
Programming: Service that switches the viewer from game to game when a team is inside the 20-yard line, the 'Red Zone'.
Began: September 13, 2009.
Distribution method: Available to home dish audiences, cable systems and telco-tv providers.
Scrambled signal: Yes.
Ownership: National Football League.

NHK WORLD TV
2-2-1 Jinnan
Shibuya-Ku
Tokyo 150-8001
Japan
Fax: 81-3-5489-8401
E-mail: nhkworld@jibtv.com
Web Site: http://www.nhk.or.jp/nhkworld
Shigehiro Komaru, Chairman
Shigeo Fukuchi, President
Yoshinori Imai, Executive Vice President
Hyuga Hidemi, General Managing Director, Broadcasting
Shin Kanada, General Managing Director, Corporate Planning & Finance
Kenji Nagai, General Managing Director, Engineering
Satellites: Galaxy 13.
Operating hours/week: 168.
Operating areas: District of Columbia & Minnesota.
Programming: NHK's HD English language news/information channel.
Began: April 3, 1995.
Distribution method: Available to home dish audiences and cable systems.
Scrambled signal: Yes.
Ownership: Japan Broadcasting Corp.

NHL CENTER ICE — See iN DEMAND.

NHL NETWORK
9 Channel Nine Ct
Scarborough, ON M1S 4B5
Canada
Phone: 416-384-5000
Fax: 416-384-4675
E-mail: info@nhlnetwork.ca
Web Site: http://www.nhlnetwork.com
Patti Fallick, Vice President, Media Operations & Planning
Jody Shapiro, Group Vice President, Television & Media Ventures
Joe Gabor, Network Director, Canada

Branch Offices:
NEW YORK: NHL Network - USA, 1185 Avenue of the Americas, New York, NY 10020. Phone: 212-789-2000. Fax: 212-789-2020.
Type of service: Digital, video on demand.
Satellites: Galaxy, transponder 15.
Operating hours/week: 168.
Programming: Offers viewers a 24-hour all-access pass to complete hockey coverage both on & off the ice, including live NHL games. The networks daily signature show - NHL On The Fly - offers fans exclusive live look-ins to NHL games, including goals, shootouts, features, interviews, pre- & post-game reports and expert analysis from a variety of hockey insiders & former players, plus special coverage from NHL events. NHL Network is available in the U.S. and Canada by contacting digital cable or satellite providers.
Began: October 1, 2007, reflects U.S. launch. Operational in Canada since 2001.
Total subscribers: 80,000,000.
Distribution method: Available to cable systems.
Scrambled signal: Yes.
Ownership: CTV Globemedia Inc., Comcast Cable Communications Inc. (15.6%).

NHL NETWORK HD — See NHL Network.

NICK AT NITE — See Nickelodeon.
Total subscribers: 99,800,000.

NICK HD — See Nickelodeon.

NICK JR.
c/o MTV Networks
1515 Broadway, 21st Fl
New York, NY 10036
Phone: 212-258-8323
Fax: 212-258-8303
Web Site: http://www.nickjr.com
Cyma Zarghami, President
Brown Johnson, President, Animation, Nickelodeon & MTVN Kids & Family Group
Angela Leaney, Senior Vice President & Creative Director
Tanya Van Court, Senior Vice President & General Manager

Teri Weiss, Senior Vice President, Development & Production
Essie Chambers, Vice President, Development
Kenny Miller, Vice President, Production & Programming
Radha Subramanyam, Vice President, Research & Planning
Type of service: Basic, digital, video on demand & mobile.
Satellites: EchoStar.
Operating hours/week: 168.
Programming: Educational children's programming. Noggin became Nick Jr. September 28, 2009.
Began: February 2, 1999.
Means of Support: Merchandise sales.
Total subscribers: 72,700,000.
Distribution method: Available to home dish audiences & cable systems.
Scrambled signal: Yes.
Ownership: Viacom Inc.

NICK TOO — See Nickelodeon.

NICKELODEON
MTV Networks Inc.
1515 Broadway, 21st Fl
New York, NY 10036
Phone: 212-258-7500
Fax: 212-258-8329
Web Site: http://www.nick.com
Cyma Zarghami, President, Chief Executive Officer, Nickelodeon
Marjorie Cohn, President, Original Programming & Development
Albie Hecht, President, Film & Television Entertainment
Brown Johnson, President, Animation, Nickelodeon & MTVN Kids & Family Group
Pam Kaufman, Chief Marketing Officer
Sarah Kirshbaum Levy, Chief Operating Officer
Tim Quealey, General Manager, Nickelodeon Studios
Fred Seibert, Chairman, Nickelodeon Online
Michael Fleshman, Chief Technology Officer, Nickelodeon Online
Kevin Kay, Executive Vice President, Production
Jim Perry, Executive Vice President, Ad Sales
Julia Pistor, Executive Vice President, Nickelodeon Movies
Andra Shapiro, Executive Vice President, Business Affairs & General Counsel
Marva Smalls, Executive Vice President, Public Affairs & Chief of Staff
Taran Swan, Executive Vice President, Nickelodeon Online
Paul Ward, Executive Vice President, Primetime Acquisitions & Strategy
Steve Youngwood, Executive Vice President, Digital Media
Nelson Boyce, Senior Vice President, Ad Sales Strategy & Business Development
Sharon Cohen, Senior Vice President, Integrated Marketing & Retail Marketing
Doug Cohn, Senior Vice President, Music Marketing & Talent
Sergio Cuan, Senior Vice President, Creative Director
Keith Dawkins, Senior Vice President, Programming Partnerships
Karen Driscoll, Senior Vice President, Marketing & Strategic Planning
Kevin Ellman, Senior Vice President, Business & Legal Affairs
Keiren Fisher, Senior Vice President, Series Production, West Coast
Brenda Freeman, Senior Vice President, Promotions Marketing
Jane Gould, Senior Vice President, Consumer Insights, Nickelodeon & MTVN Kids & Family Group
Kathleen Hricik, Senior Vice President, International Programs Enterprises
Ron Johnson, Senior Vice President, Wal-Mart Retail Development for Nickelodeon & Viacom Consumer Products
Lisa Judson, Senior Vice President, Programming & Executive Creative Director
Tracy Katsky, Senior Vice President, Development & Original Programming
Angela Leaney, Senior Vice President & Creative Director
Jennifer Goodman Linn, Senior Vice President, Brand Marketing, MTVN Kids & Family Group
Katy Loria, Senior Vice President, Digital Ad Sales
Samantha Maltin, Senior Vice President, Nickelodeon Global Partnerships
Dan Martinsen, Senior Vice President, Communications
Sam Moser, Senior Vice President, Advertising Sales, Eastern Region
Anne Mullen, Senior Vice President, On-Air Creative Strategy
Brian Offutt, Senior Vice President, Creative Operations
Antonious Porch, Senior Vice President & Deputy General Counsel, Digital Media
Michelle Raimo, Senior Vice President, Production, Nickelodeon Movies
Marianne Romano, Senior Vice President, Corporate Communications, Kids & Family Group
Jason Root, Senior Vice President, Digital
Frank Tanki, Senior Vice President, Marketing & Operations
Jim Tricarico, Senior Vice President, Ad Sales
Bruce Tuchman, Senior Vice President, New Media Ventures
Tanya Van Court, Senior Vice President, Nickelodeon Divisions
Teri Weiss, Senior Vice President, Development & Production
Marsha Williams, Senior Vice President, Research & Planning

Branch Offices:
CENTRAL: 303 E Wacker Dr, Ste 428, Chicago, IL 60601. Phone: 312-565-2300.

EASTERN: 1775 Broadway, 4th Floor, New York, NY 10036. Phone: 212-713-6400.

SOUTHEASTERN: 3399 Peachtree Rd, Ste 990, Atlanta, GA 30326. Phone: 404-841-3090.

WESTERN: 10 Universal City Plaza, 30th Floor, Universal City, CA 91608. Phone: 818-505-7800.
Type of service: Basic & Video on demand.
Satellites: Galaxy III, transponder 19 & 22.
Operating hours/week: 168.
Operating areas: Available nationwide.
Uplink: Network Operations Center, Smithtown, NY.
Programming: Age specific programming for pre-schoolers through teenagers.
Began: April 1, 1979.
Means of Support: Advertising.
Total subscribers: 101,400,000.
Distribution method: Available to cable systems, satellite & mobile video providers.
Scrambled signal: Yes. Equipment: VideoCipher II.
Ownership: Viacom Inc.

NICKTOONS EN ESPANOL — See NickToons TV.

NICKTOONS TV
c/o Nickelodeon
1515 Broadway

New York, NY 10036
Phone: 212-258-8000
Web Site: http://nicktoons.nick.com
Cyma Zarghami, President
Keith Dawkins, Senior Vice President & General Manager
Type of service: Digital.
Operating hours/week: 168.
Operating areas: Available nationwide.
Programming: Children's shows.
Began: May 1, 2002.
Total subscribers: 57,600,000.
Distribution method: Available to home dish audiences, cable, FiOS & U-verse subscribers.
Scrambled signal: Yes.
Ownership: Viacom Inc.

NIPPON GOLDEN NETWORK
567 S King St
Ste 110
Honolulu, HI 96813
Phone: 808-538-1966
Fax: 808-537-2024
E-mail: nippongon001@hawaii.rr.com
Dr. Dennis M. Ogawa, President

Branch Office:
TOKYO: Higashi Ginza Bldg No. 9-18 Ginza, 3-Chome, Chuo-Ku, Tokyo, Japan.
Type of service: Digital.
Operating hours/week: 168.
Operating areas: Hawaii.
Programming: Japanese dramas, musical & variety shows, documentaries, educational programs & live sumo tournaments.
Began: January 1, 1982.
Means of Support: Subscriber fees & advertising.
Total subscribers: 16,762.
Distribution method: Via tape to cable systems.
Ownership: Nippon Hawaii Cablevision, The Seiyu Ltd., Dentsu Inc. & Television Tokyo Ltd.

NIPPON GOLDEN NETWORK ON DEMAND — See Nippon Golden Network.

NIPPON GOLDEN NETWORK 3 — See Nippon Golden Network.

NIPPON GOLDEN NETWORK 2 — See Nippon Golden Network.

NJTV
25 S Stockton St
Trenton, NJ 08608
Phones: 609-777-5000; 800-792-8645
E-mail: answers@njn.org
Web Site: http://www.njn.net
Neal Shapiro, President & Chief Executive Officer, WNET
Type of service: Basic.
Operating areas: New Jersey, New York & Pennsylvania.
Programming: Offers a lineup of local arts & culture and news & public affiars programming.
Began: July 1, 2011, as NJTV. Began in 1971 as NJN–New Jersey Network.
Distribution method: Available to cable systems.
Scrambled signal: No.
Ownership: Thirteen/WNET, through the non-profit wholly-owned subsidiary Public Media NJ Inc.

NOGGIN — See Nick Jr.

NORTHWEST CABLE NEWS
333 Dexter Ave N
Seattle, WA 98109
Phone: 206-448-3616
Fax: 206-448-3797
E-mail: nwwebmaster@nwcn.com
Web Site: http://www.nwcn.com
Dave Lougee, General Manager
Paul Fry, Vice President & General Manager
Tracey Brogden Miller, News Director
Pam Guinn, General Sales Manager
Larry Blackstock, Operations Director
Kathryn Skinner, Marketing & Affiliate Relations Director
Guy Barbaro, Controller

Branch Offices:
SPOKANE: 4103 S Regal St, Spokane, WA 99203. Phone: 509-838-7387.

BOISE: 5407 Fairview Ave, Boise, ID 83706. Phone: 208-321-5680.

PORTLAND: 1501 SW Jefferson St, Portland, OR 97201. Phone: 503-226-5615.
Type of service: Basic.
Satellites: Satcom C-3.
Sales representative: National Cable Advertising Inc.
Operating areas: Alaska, California, Idaho, Montana, Oregon & Washington.
Programming: Regional all-news channel.
Began: December 18, 1995.
Total subscribers: 2,100,000.
Distribution method: Available to cable systems.
Ownership: Belo Corp.

NTN BUZZTIME
5966 La Place Ct
Ste 100
Carlsbad, CA 92008
Phone: 760-438-7400
Fax: 760-438-3505
E-mail: kendra.berger@ntnbuzztime.com
Web Site: http://www.buzztime.com
Dario Santana, President & Chief Executive Officer
Type of service: Pay.
Programming: Interactive games & shows via America Online, CompuServe & GTE Mainstreet.
Began: January 1, 1985.
Total subscribers: 30,000 (Figure excludes satellite dish subscribers).
Distribution method: Available to home dish audiences & cable systems.

NTN24
Canal Latino International Latino
Americas Av 65-82
Bogata, DC
Colombia

Phone: +57 1 426 9292
Web Site: http://www.ntn24.com
John de Armas, Vice President, World Direct, DirecTV
Operating hours/week: 168.
Operating areas: Available nationwide.
Programming: 24-hour Spanish language international news channel.
Began: October 26, 2009, in the United States on DirecTV. Service launched locally in Colombia November 3, 2008.
Distribution method: Avialble to subscribers of DirecTV through their Mas service.
Scrambled signal: Yes.
Ownership: Carlos Ardila Lulle.

NTV AMERICA

1 Executive Dr
Ste 190
Ft. Lee, NJ 07024
Web Site: http://www.ntvamerica.ntv.ru
Programming: Russian-language news & entertainment.
Distribution method: Available to cable systems & satellite providers.

NTV HAYAT

Avdage Sahinagica 14
Sarajevo 71000
Bosnia and Herzegovina
Web Site: http://www.globecast.com
Elvir Svrakic, Chief Executive Officer
Programming: News, entertainment, music, sports, documentary, children, religious & cultural shows.
Distribution method: Available through GlobeCast satellite service.

NUVO TV

700 N Central Ave
Ste 600
Glendale, CA 91203
Phone: 323-256-8900
Web Site: http://www.mynuvotv.com
Bruce Barshop, Co-Chairman
Jeff Valdez, Co-Chairman
Michael Schwimmer, Chief Executive Officer
Leo Perez, Chief Operating Officer
Craig A Geller, Senior Vice President, Adverisitng Sales
Rafael Oiler, Senior Vice President, Marketing
Marlene Braga, Vice President, Programming & Deevelopment
Carla Lewis-Long, Vice President, Affiliate Distribution
Sara Auspitz, Executive Director, Programming
Jody A. Rose, Executive Director, East Division Affiliate Sales
Anna Rios, Director, Research
Armando Parra, Manager, Affiliate Sales Operations

Branch Offices:
NEW YORK: 450 7th Ave, Ste 1001, New York, NY 10123. Fax: 212-736-3770.
Operating hours/week: 168.
Programming: English-language, Latino-themed programming. On July 4th, 2011 channel was rebranded from Si TV.
Began: February 1, 2003.
Total subscribers: 27,000,000.
Distribution method: Available to dish networks & cable systems.
Scrambled signal: Yes.
Ownership: SCN Enterprises.

NUVO TV HD — See Nuvo TV.

Began: November 7, 2010.

OASIS TV

2029 Century Park E
Ste 1400
Los Angeles, CA 90067
Phone: 310-553-4300
Fax: 310-553-4300
E-mail: info@oasistv.com
Web Site: http://www.oasistv.com
Robert Schnitzer, President & Chief Executive Officer
Gerald Levin, Senior Advisor, Chairman-elect
Reinita Susman, Supervising Producer
Diannah Morgan, Webmaster/IT Director
Type of service: Video on demand and linear.
Operating areas: Nationwide.
Uplink: Avail-TVN.
Programming: Branded Body-Mind-Spirit video programming; content categories include health & healing, metaphysics & spirituality, earth & environment, world peace & current affairs, visionary art & personal growth. Focuses on the following topics: Personal Growth, non-religious Spirituality, Alternative Medicine, Fitness, Current Affairs, Green Technology, Love, Sex and Relationships.
Began: September 1, 1997.
Means of Support: Advertising sales & affiliate fees.
Total subscribers: 10,000,000.
Distribution method: Available to cable systems.
Scrambled signal: Yes.
Ownership: OTV Media Group, Inc.

ODYSSEY TELEVISION NETWORK

437 Danforth Ave
3rd Fl
Toronto, ON M4K 1P1
Canada
Phone: 416-462-1200
Fax: 416-462-1818
E-mail: info@odysseytv.ca
Web Site: http://www.odysseytv.ca
Nick Stuart, President & Chief Executive Officer
Bill Fatsis, Vice President, Sales & Promotions
Type of service: Pay.
Operating hours/week: 168.
Programming: Greek programming, including news, sports, interviews, current affairs, community news, films, drama & comedy series.
Began: December 21, 1998.
Means of Support: Advertising & subscription fees.
Distribution method: Available to home dish audiences & cable systems.
Ownership: Odyssey Television Network Inc.

OHIO CHANNEL

Ohio Government Telecommunications
Ohio Statehouse, Room 013
Columbus, OH 43215
Phones: 614-466-3798; 614-466-9080
E-mail: info@ohiochannel.org
Web Site: http://www.ohiochannel.org
Type of service: Basic.
Operating hours/week: 42.
Programming: Public affairs, documentaries & gavel-to-gavel coverage of legislative session.
Began: January 1, 1996.
Total subscribers: 2,000,000.
Distribution method: Cable, internet.

OHIO NEWS NETWORK

770 Twin Rivers Dr
Columbus, OH 43215
Phone: 614-280-6300
Fax: 614-280-6305
E-mail: barb.geller@ohionewsnow.com
Web Site: http://www.ohionewsnow.com
Tom Griesdom, Vice President & General Manager
Vince Jones, Operations Manager
Barb Geller, Media & Affiliate Relations Manager
Frank Willson, Marketing Director
Chuck DeVendra, Sales Director
Jason Pheister, Programming Director
Greg Fisher, News Director
Scott Heitkamp, Business Manager
Type of service: Basic.
Satellites: Orion 1, transponder 23.
Operating hours/week: 168.
Operating areas: Ohio.
Programming: Local news service.
Began: May 1, 1997.
Means of Support: Advertising & subscriber fees.
Total subscribers: 1,500,000.
Ownership: Dispatch Broadcast Group.

OLEC NETWORK

2205 NW 23rd Ave
Miami, FL 33142
Phone: 305-661-6532
Fax: 305-661-2748
Web Site: http://www.olecnetwork.com
Programming: Packages eight Spanish language channels offering children's programming, animated series, comedies, dramas & reality shows, movies, documentaries, music videos & sporting events.
Distribution method: Available to cable & satellite programmers.

OLELO

1122 Mapunapuna St
Honolulu, HI 96819
Phone: 808-834-0007
Fax: 808-836-2546
E-mail: olelo@olelo.org
Web Site: http://www.olelo.org
Lurline McGregor, Executive Director, President & Chief Executive Officer
Kealii Lopez, Chief Operations Officer
Kit Kawamata, Chief Engineer
Type of service: Basic.
Operating hours/week: 168.
Operating areas: Oahu, HI.
Programming: Public, educational & government access.
Began: January 1, 1991.
Means of Support: Cable franchise fees.
Total subscribers: 235,000.
Distribution method: Available to cable systems.
Ownership: Non-profit organization.

OLE TV

2103 Coral Way
Ste 108
Miami, FL 33145
Phone: 305-856-3311
Fax: 305-856-3366
E-mail: info@oletv.tv
Web Site: http://www.oletv.tv
Toni Elegalde, President
Joseph Roses, Secretary
Gregory Pischner, Production
Amanda Guevara, Programming
Programming: Family-oriented, Hispanic arts, cultural and entertainment network carried by AT&T and Charter currently seen in the South Florida area from Vero Beach to Key West.
Scrambled signal: Yes.

OLYMPUSAT HISPANIC PACK

560 Village Blvd
Ste 250
West Palm Beach, FL 33409
Phone: 561-684-5657
Fax: 561-684-9690
E-mail: colleen@olympusat.com
Web Site: http://www.olympusat.com
Tom Mohler, President
Colleen Glynn, Executive Vice President & General Counsel
Kim Reed Fragione, Chief Operating Officer
Satellites: Galaxy 13, transponder 6.
Ownership: Ocean Communications.

ONCE TV MEXICO

E-mail: oncemexico@mail.oncetv.ipn.mx
Web Site: http://www.oncemexico.tv/
Programming: University-owned educational television network available via satellite from DirecTV and SATMEX Maximo and also various cable outlets in the U.S. and Mexico. Most of its programs are also webcast through the Internet.
University-owned educational television network available via satellite from DirecTV and SATMEX Maximo and also various cable outlets in the U.S. and Mexico. Most of its programs are also webcast through the Internet.

101 NETWORK — See Audience Network

ONSPOT DIGITAL NETWORK

c/o Simon Brand Ventures
115 W Washington St
Indianapolis, IN 46204
Phone: 317-636-1600
Web Site: http://www.simon.com
Simon Badinter, Chairman & Chief Executive Officer
Stewart Stockdale, Chief Marketing Officer
Operating areas: New York, California & Illinois.
Programming: Lifestyle, news, entertainment & shopping center oriented programming & advertising.
Began: May 12, 2006.
Distribution method: Available in shopping malls owned/operated by Simon Property Group.
Scrambled signal: Yes.
Ownership: Publicis Groupe & Simon Property Group.

OPEN STUDENT TELEVISION NETWORK (OSTN)

1940 E 6th St
11th Fl
Cleveland, OH 44114
Phone: 216-586-9626
Fax: 217-586-9636
E-mail: info@ostn.tv
Web Site: http://www.ostn.tv
Arun Kumar, President & Chief Executive Officer
Rich Griffin, Executive Vice President & Director, Technology
Type of service: Broadband.
Operating hours/week: 168.
Programming: Delivered over the Internet2 Network linking academic & research institutions, providing student & faculty produced original shows, projects & fine arts performances.
Began: April 1, 2005.
Total subscribers: 60,000,000.
Scrambled signal: Yes.

OPTIMUM ONLINE

Cablevision Systems Corp.
1111 Stewart Avenue
Bethpage, NY 11714
Web Site: http://www.optimum.net/

OREGON PUBLIC AFFAIRS NETWORK

PO Box 29101

Portland, OR 97296
Phone: 541-737-9562
Fax: 541-737-3453
E-mail: operations@opan.org
Web Site: http://www.opan.org
Type of service: Basic.
Operating hours/week: 10.
Programming: Coverage of public affairs related programming, legislative committees, city clubs, university forums & debates.
Total subscribers: 4,000,000.
Distribution method: Cable, internet.

OUR TIME COMMUNICATIONS — No longer planned.

OUTDOOR CHANNEL
43445 Business Park Dr
Ste 103
Temecula, CA 92590
Phones: 951-699-6991; 800-770-5750
Fax: 951-699-6313
E-mail: info@outdoorchannel.com
Web Site: http://www.outdoorchannel.com
Perry T. Massie, Chairman
Roger L. Werner, Chief Executive Officer & President
Tom Hornish, Chief Operating Officer
Doug Langston, Chief Accounting Officer
Todd Merkow, President, Digital Media
Tom Allen, Executive Vice President & Chief Financial Officer
Randy Brown, Executive Vice President, Affiliate Sales & Marketing
Greg Harrigan, Executive Vice President, Advertising Sales
Thomas H. Massie, Executive Vice President & Secretary
Jason Brist, Senior Vice President, Advertising
John Fabian, Senior Vice President, Advertising Sales, Eastern Region
Gene Brookhart, Vice President, Operations
Chris Chaffin, Vice President, Public Relations & Conservation
Mark C. Corcoran, Vice President, Ad Sales
Michael Kim, Vice President, Affiliate Sales, Western Region
Scott Mann, Vice President, Outdoor Affinity Marketing
Mark Romano, Regional Vice President, Eastern
Daniel Sloane, Regional Vice President, Central
Joe Stretesky, Regional Vice President, Western
David Bolls, Assistant General Counsel
Type of service: Basic, Digital, HD.
Satellites: Galaxy 10-R, transponder 24.
Operating hours/week: 168.
Programming: Focuses on fishing, hunting & all forms of outdoor activities & watersports.
Began: June 1, 1993.
Means of Support: Advertising.
Total subscribers: 35,600,000.
Distribution method: Available to home dish audiences & cable systems.
Ownership: Outdoor Channel Holdings Inc.

OUTDOOR CHANNEL HD — See Outdoor Channel.
Began: June 28, 2010.
Total subscribers: 10,000,000.

OUTDOOR CHANNEL ON DEMAND — See Outdoor Channel.
Type of service: Video on demand.

OUTDOOR CHANNEL 2 HD — See Outdoor Channel.
Began: July 1, 2005.
Total subscribers: 4,000,000.

OUTDOOR LIFE NETWORK (CANADA)
Box 9
Station O
Toronto, ON M4A 2M9
Canada
Phone: 416-332-5640
Fax: 416-332-5624
Web Site: http://www.facetheelements.com
Rick Brace, Senior Vice President
Began: October 17, 1997.

OUTERMAX — See Cinemax.
Programming: Sci-fi, horror & fantasy movies.
Began: May 1, 2001.

OUTLET MALL NETWORK — No longer planned as of 2000.

OUTSIDE TELEVISION
PO Box 7528
Portland, ME 04112
Phone: 207-772-5000
Fax: 207-775-3658
E-mail: info@outsidetelevision.com
Web Site: http://www.outsidetelevision.com
Mark Burchill, Chief Executive Officer
Carmine Parisi, Senior Vice President, Sales
Jeff Dumais, Senior Vice President, Television Properties
Type of service: Basic.
Operating areas: California, Colorado, Florida, Idaho, Maine, New Hampshire, New York, Oregon, South Carolina, Utah & Vermont.
Programming: Active lifestyle entertainment for those passionate about the outdoors. Formerly RSN Resort TV.
Began: January 1, 1985.
Means of Support: Advertising.
Total subscribers: 1,084,119.
Distribution method: Available to cable systems.
Scrambled signal: Yes.

OUTTV
4th Fl, 62 W 8th Ave
Vancouver, BC V5Y 1M6
Canada
Web Site: http://www.outtv.ca
Brad Danks, Chief Operating Officer
Andrew Chang, Chief Financial Officer
Type of service: Basic.
Operating hours/week: 168.
Programming: Gay, lesbian, bisexual & transgender television network: current affairs, documentaries, health & fitness, lifestyle, music, cooking and travel.
Began: September 7, 2001, as PrideVision TV; relaunched April 7, 2005 as Hard on PrideVision & later renamed outTV.

OVATION
2850 Ocean Park Blvd
Santa Monica, CA 90405
Phone: 800-682-8466
Web Site: http://www.ovationtv.com
Ken Solomon, Non-Executive Chairman
Charles Segars, Chief Executive Officer
Chad Gutstein, Executive Vice President
Liz Janneman, Executive Vice President, Ad Sales
Gaynor Strachan Chun, Senior Vice President, Marketing
Ellen Schned, Senior Vice President, Distribution
Kris Slava, Senior Vice President, Programming & Production
Debra Balamos, Vice President, Affiliate & Advertising Sales & Marketing
Frank Bolger, Vice President, Media Sales & Relations
Rob Canter, Vice President, Production & Creative Services
Dan Casciato, Vice President, National Accounts
Lee Lindbloom, Vice President, Technical Services
Sonia Tower, Vice President, Community Relations
Michelle Zajic, Vice President, Programming
Type of service: Basic, digital, video on demand & online.
Satellites: Galaxy VII, transponder 13.
Operating hours/week: 140.
Programming: Visual & performing arts.
Began: April 21, 1996, Re-launched June 20, 2007.
Means of Support: Advertising.
Total subscribers: 42,000,000.
Distribution method: Available to cable systems & home dish audiences.
Equipment: DigiCipher II.
Ownership: Hubbard Media Group, Weinstein Co., Corporate Partners II, Perry Capital & Arcadia Investment Partners.

OWN: OPRAH WINFREY NETWORK
9150 Wilshire Blvd
Ste 240
Beverly Hills, CA 90069
Web Site: http://www.oprah.com/own
Oprah Winfrey, Chief Executive & Creative Officer
Erik Logan, Co-President
Sheri Salata, Co-President
Robert Tercek, President, Digital Media
Brent Willman, Chief Financial Officer
Deborah Myers, Interim General Manager
Kathleen Kayse, Executive Vice President, Ad Sales
Rod Aissa, Senior Vice President, Primetime Programming & Development
Michele Dix, Senior Vice President, Primetime Programming & Development
Scott Garner, Senior Vice President, Scheduling & Acquisitions
Maria Grasso, Senior Vice President, Programming
Glenn Kaino, Senior Vice President, Creative
Jeffrey Meier, Senior Vice President, Scheduling, Acquisitions & Strategy
Nicole Nichols, Senior Vice President, Communications & Strategy
Alan Saxe, Senior Vice President, Business & Legal Affairs
Mauricio Vitale, Senior Vice President, Marketing
Nina Wass, Senior Vice President, Creative Affairs
Doug Levy, Vice President, Operations
Meredith Momoda, Vice President, Integrated Marketing
Greg Neal, Vice President & Creative Director, Marketing
Darrin Oline, Vice President, Digital Media Advertising Sales
Type of service: Basic.
Operating hours/week: 168.
Programming: Replaced Discovery Health Channel. Programming is focused on motivating people to lead healthy lives.
Began: January 1, 2011.
Total subscribers: 80,000,000.
Distribution method: Available to cable systems & satellite providers.
Scrambled signal: Yes.
Ownership: Joint venture between Discovery Communications & Harpo Productions.

OXYGEN
75 9th Ave
New York, NY 10011
Phone: 212-651-2000
E-mail: o2_press@oxygen.com
Web Site: http://www.oxygen.com
Lauren Zalaznick, President, NBC Universal Women & Lifestyle Entertainment Networks
Jason Klarman, President, Oxygen Media
Mary Murano, President, Distribution
Cori Abraham, Senior Vice President, Development
Cameron Blanchard, Senior Vice President, Communications
Tony Cardinale, Senior Vice President, Research & Strategic Insights
Amy Introcaso-Davis, Senior Vice President, Production & Development
Galen Jones, Senior Vice President, Oxygen Research
Jennifer Kavanagh, Senior Vice President, Digital
Susan Malfa, Senior Vice President, Ad Sales
Jane Olson, Senior Vice President, Marketing & Brand Strategy
Cynthia Chu, Vice President & Chief Financial Officer
John Cora, Vice President. Programming Research
Michael DuPont, Vice President, Advertising Sales
Mai Kim Flournoy, Vice President, Strategic Multiplatform Program Planning
David Gross, Vice President, Development
Bryan Hale, Vice President, Original Programming & Development
Elissa Harman, Vice President, Consumer Marketing
Teri Kennedy, Vice President, Current Production
Joseph La Polla, Vice President, Programming
Scott Lewers, Vice President, Multiplatform Program Planning & Acquisitions
Gerry Logue, Vice President, Creative Director
Barbara Shornick, Vice President, Sales & Marketing
Julie Rothman, Vice President, Communications
Juliana Tatlock, Vice President, Programming Strategy
Jennifer Turner, Vice President, Licensing & Strategic Partnerships
Puja Vohra, Vice Prersident, Ad Sales Marketing
Type of service: Basic & video on demand.
Satellites: Satcom C3, transponder 24.
Programming: A network targeted to younger women with original series, specials & movies.
Began: February 2, 2000, relaunched April 23, 2008.
Total subscribers: 76,000,000.
Distribution method: Available to cable systems.
Scrambled signal: Yes.
Ownership: NBCUniversal LLC.

OXYGEN ON DEMAND — See Oxygen.
Began: August 1, 2003.
Total subscribers: 25,000,000.

PAC-12 NETWORK
1350 Treat Blvd
Ste 500
Walnut Creek, CA 94597
Phone: 925-932-4411
Fax: 925-932-4601
E-mail: pac-10@pac-10.org
Web Site: http://www.pac-12.org
Larry Scott, Commissioner
Kevin Weiberg, Deputy Commissioner & Chief Operating Officer
Woodie Dixon, Vice President, Business Affairs & General Counsel
Danette Leighton, Chief Marketing Officer
Ron McQuate, Chief Financial Officer
Dave Hirsch, Vice President, Communications
Kirk Reynolds, Vice President, Public Affairs
Operating areas: Plans Arizona, California, Colorado, Oregon, Utah & Washington.
Programming: Will cover men's & women's sporting events from Pac-12 schools.
Scheduled to begin: Plans to launch in 2012.
Distribution method: Will be available to home dish audiences and cable systems.
Scrambled signal: Planned.
Ownership: Pacific-12 Media Enterprises, which is owned by the Pac-12 Conference.

PACVIA TV
150 S Robles Ave
Ste 470
Pasadena, CA 91101
Phone: 626-304-2685
Operating hours/week: 168.
Programming: Provides dramatic programming in Mandarin Chinese.

PALLADIA — See MTV.
Operating areas: Available nationwide.
Programming: MTV Networks' high-definition music channel.
Began: January 1, 2006, originally as MHD; renamed Palladia on Sept. 1, 2008.
Distribution method: Available to home dish audiences, broadband & cable systems.
Scrambled signal: Yes.

PANDAAMERICA SHOPPING NETWORK
3460 Torrance Blvd
Ste 100
Torrance, CA 90503
Phones: 310-373-9647; 800-959-8889
Fax: 310-678-6024
E-mail: info@pandaamerica.com
Web Site: http://www.pandaamerica.com
Martin Weiss, President
David Connelly, Chief Operating Officer
Mark Miller, Director, Sales & Marketing
Jonathan Aytes, Manager, Production
Type of service: Basic.
Satellites: Galaxy III-R, transponder 8.
Operating hours/week: 168.
Uplink: Burbank, CA.
Programming: Home shopping.
Began: January 1, 1995.
Means of Support: Sale of merchandise.
Distribution method: Available to home dish audiencs & cable systems.

PARENTS TV
Meredith Corporation
1716 Locust St
Des Moines, IA 50309
Phone: 515-284-3000
Fax: 515-284-2700
Web Site: http://www.parents.com/parentstv
Type of service: Broadband & video on demand.
Programming: Features reports & information on child-rearing from Meredith magazines such as Parents, American Baby & Family Circle.
Began: December 1, 2007.
Means of Support: Ad-supported.
Total subscribers: 14,000,000.
Distribution method: Available to cable systems.
Ownership: Meredith Corporation.

PASIONES
7291 NW 74th St
c/o US Imagina LLC
Miami, FL 33166
Phone: 305-777-1900
Fax: 305-820-9046
E-mail: info@imaginaus.com
Web Site: http://www.tvpasiones.com
Programming: Spanish language programming.

PATRIOTS ON DEMAND
c/o Comcast Corp.
1500 Market St
Philadelphia, PA 19102
Web Site: http://www.patriots.com
Type of service: Video on demand.
Programming: Daily team updates, news, analysis & game highlights of the New England Patriots.
Began: October 13, 2005.
Distribution method: Available to cable providers.
Ownership: Comcast Corp.

PAXSON COMMUNICATIONS CORP. — See ION Television.

PB&J
735 Broad St
Ste 304
Chattanooga, TN 37402
Phones: 423-468-5300; 800-294-4800
Neal Ardman, Information Contact
Operating hours/week: Plans 168.
Operating areas: Will be available nationwide.
Programming: Will offer classic cartoon programming from the 1950's to the 1980's.
Scheduled to begin: Plans to launch Summer 2011.
Scrambled signal: Planned.
Ownership: Classic Media & Luken Communications LLC.

PBS HD
2100 Crystal Dr
Arlington, VA 22202
Phone: 703-739-5000
Web Site: http://www.pbs.org
Programming: A mix of new & archived HD & widescreen programs.
Began: March 1, 2004.

PBS KIDS CHANNEL
2100 Crystal Dr
Arlington, VA 22202
Phones: 703-739-5000; 703-739-5773
Fax: 703-739-0775
E-mail: kids@pbs.org
Web Site: http://www.pbs.org
Steven Gray, Vice President, PBS Channels
Stu Kantor, Creative Communications & Editorial Services Director

Branch Office:
NEW YORK: 1790 Broadway, 16th Floor, New York, NY 10019. Phone: 212-708-3000.
Type of service: Digital.
Satellites: Galaxy 3, transponder Ku-20/541.
Operating hours/week: 168.
Uplink: Alexandria, VA.
Programming: 24-hour, interactive, educational, programming for children from preschool through age 12.
Began: January 1, 1999, Video On Demand service began August 1, 2003.
Equipment: Digicipher II.
Ownership: Public Broadcasting Service.

PBS KIDS/PBS KIDS GO!
2100 Crystal Dr
4th Fl
Arlington, VA 22202
Phone: 703-739-5000
Fax: 703-739-5777
Web Site: http://pbskids.org
Lesli Rotenberg, Senior Vice President, PBS Kids Next Generation Media
Type of service: Basic.
Programming: Preschool & elementary aged children's programming.
Scrambled signal: Yes.

PBS KIDS SPROUT
PO Box 288
Fort Washington, PA 19034
Phone: 877-768-8411
E-mail: info@sproutonline.com
Web Site: http://www.sproutonline.com
Sandy Wax, President
Tom Alexander, Senior Vice President, Marketing
Andrew Beecham, Senior Vice President, Programming
David Robinson, Director, Marketing
Type of service: Video on demand.
Operating hours/week: 168.
Programming: Popular preschooler series from PBS Kids, HIT Entertainment & Sesame Street.
Began: September 15, 2005, Video On Demand service launched April 1, 2005.
Total subscribers: 50,000,000 (Includes both basic & video on demand subscribers).
Distribution method: Available to cable & satellite providers.
Scrambled signal: Yes.
Ownership: HIT Entertainment, NBCUniversal LLC, PBS, Sesame Workshop.

PBS WORLD
1320 Braddock Pl
Alexandria, VA 22314
Phone: 703-739-5000
Web Site: http://www.pbs.org
Type of service: Basic & broadcast.
Operating hours/week: 168.
Programming: Non-fiction PBS series & specials including Frontline, American Experience, The News Hour with Jim Lehrer & documentaries by Ken Burns.
Began: August 15, 2007.

PEGASUSTV
516 Villa Ave, Ste 2
c/o Boot Media LLC
Clovis, CA 93612
Phone: 805-630-2242
E-mail: info@pegasustv.com
Web Site: http://www.pegasustv.com
Sally Lasater, National Sales/Advertising
Lesley O'Connor, Texas Sales/Advertising
Charles Smallwood, California Sales/Advertising
Type of service: Free, over-the-air service.
Operating hours/week: 168.
Operating areas: Currently available in California and Texas.
Programming: A television network deciated to equestrian pursuits and country lifestyles. Offers customized programming for individual TV markets.
Began: April 15, 2011.
Means of Support: Advertising.
Total subscribers: 28,600,500.
Distribution method: Available to over the air broadcast stations for digital multicast streams.
Scrambled signal: Yes.
Ownership: Boot Media LLC, majority equity holder and managing member.

PENN NATIONAL RACING ALIVE
(Telebet)
PO Box 32
Grantville, PA 17208
Phone: 717-469-2211
E-mail: fred.lipkin@pngaming.com
Web Site: http://www.pennnational.com/telebet.shtml
Herb Grayek, President
P. T. O'Hara, Jr., Vice President, Operations
Type of service: Regional.
Satellites: Galaxy II (Four nights/week, Sunday afternoon.).
Operating areas: Pennsylvania.
Programming: Live thoroughbred racing with call-in betting.
Began: April 1, 1984.
Means of Support: Percentage of wagers; advertising.
Total subscribers: 400,000.
Equipment: Oak.

PENNSYLVANIA CABLE NETWORK
401 Fallowfield Rd
Camp Hill, PA 17011
Phone: 717-730-6000
Fax: 717-730-6009
Web Site: http://www.pcntv.com
Brian Lockman, President & Chief Executive Officer
Debra Kohr Sheppard, Senior Vice President & Chief Operating Officer
William J. Bova, Senior Vice President, Business Development
Rick Cochran, Vice President, Marketing
Melissa Hiler, Vice President, Controller
Corinna Vescey Wilson, Vice President, Programming
Satellites: GE-2, transponder 13C.
Operating hours/week: 168.
Operating areas: Pennsylvania.
Programming: State public affairs network, with live coverage of Pennsylvania House, Senate, and other governmental activities. Also features state events coverage, high school championship sports & educational programming.
Began: September 4, 1979.
Total subscribers: 3,300,000.

PENTAGON CHANNEL
601 N Fairfax St
Ste 300
Alexandria, VA 22314
Phones: 866-854-3804; 703-428-0200
Fax: 703-428-0466
E-mail: info@pentagonchannel.mil
Web Site: http://www.pentagonchannel.mil
Maxine Teller, Director, Distribution
Type of service: Basic.
Operating hours/week: 168.
Programming: The Pentagon Channel broadcasts military news & information for the members of the U.S. Armed Forces through programming including: Department of Defense news briefings, military news, interviews with top Defense officials, short stories about the work of our military. In addition to enhancing Department of Defense communications with active duty service,

the Pentagon Channel provides the National Guard & Reserve & civilian employees of the Department of Defense more timely access to military information & news.
Began: May 14, 2004.
Distribution method: Available to all cable & satellite providers, American Forces Radio & Television & webcast.

PENTHOUSE HD — See Penthouse TV.
Type of service: Digital and video on demand.
Satellites: Eutelsat Eurobird 9A.
Programming: Adult entertainment available in HD clarity. Penthouse HD is the soft core (erotic) channel. Penthouse HD1 is the hard core adult channel, while Penthouse HD2 offers offset programming from Penthouse HD1.
Began: October 5, 2009.
Distribution method: Available to European cable systems.
Scrambled signal: Yes.

PENTHOUSE TV
7007 Winchester Cir
Ste 200
Boulder, CO 80301
Phones: 303-444-0900; 888-875-0632
Fax: 303-444-0734
Type of service: Digital & video on demand.
Operating hours/week: 168.
Began: December 1, 2006, reflects video on demand service launch.
Total subscribers: 7,000,000.
Distribution method: Cable, satellite & IPTV.
Ownership: Penthouse Media Group, Inc. & New Frontier Media.

PEOPLE'S NETWORK
PO Box 111817
Carrollton, TX 75011-1817
Phone: 214-860-0400
Fax: 214-860-0480
Jeff Olson, Founder
Dale Martin, Ethics & Compliance
Operating hours/week: 35.
Programming: Self-help programs.
Began: February 1, 1995.
Distribution method: Available to home dish audiences.
Ownership: Jeff Olson.

PETCARE TELEVISION NETWORK —
See KidCARE Television Network.

PETS.TV
1925 Century Park E
Ste 1025
Los Angeles, CA 90067
Phone: 310-277-3500
E-mail: eric@es.tv
Web Site: http://www.pets.tv
Byron Allen, Chairman & Chief Executive Officer
Lisa-Renee Ramirez, Executive Vice President & Director Producer
Darren Galatt, Vice President, Ad Sales
Type of service: Digital broadband.
Operating hours/week: 168.
Operating areas: Available nationwide.
Programming: Offers shows on pet care, news, health & lifestyles.
Began: May 11, 2009.
Total subscribers: 1,900,000.
Distribution method: Available to Verizon FiOS and Frontier Communications subscibers.
Scrambled signal: No.
Ownership: Entertainment Studios.

PGA TV
St. James House Oldbury
Bracknell
Berkshire RG12 8th
England
Phone: 0870 142 0755
Type of service: Broadband.
Began: November 15, 2005.
Distribution method: Available only on PGA Broadband.
Ownership: Professional Golfer's Association.

PHILADELPHIA PARK LIVE
PO Box 1000
Bensalem, PA 19020
Phone: 215-639-9000
E-mail: kjones@philadelphiapark.com
Web Site: http://www.philadelphiapark.com
Robert W. Green, Chairman & President, Greenwood Racing, Inc.
Harold G. Handel, Chief Executive Officer
Andrew J. Green, Senior Vice President, Administration
Salvatore Sinatra, Racing Director
Geri Mercer, Simulcasting Director
Type of service: Regional.
Satellites: Satcom IV, transponder 23.
Operating hours/week: 35.
Operating areas: Pennsylvania.
Programming: Thoroughbred racing with commentary & interviews; offered 199 days a year.
Began: September 10, 1985.
Total subscribers: 700,000.

PHOENIX INFO NEWS — See KyLinTV.
No. 9, Tower 1, Seashore Square
18 Defeng Street
Kowloon
Hong Kong
Phone: 852 2621 9888
Fax: 852 2621 9898
Web Site: http://www.pstv-us.net
Operating hours/week: 168.
Programming: All news channel.
Ownership: News Corp., Today's Asia combined own over 75%. 16.4% publicly held.

PHOENIX NORTH AMERICA — See KyLinTV.
Operating hours/week: 168.
Programming: Provides news and entertainment shows from the Asian Pacific Region, including China, Hong Kong, Taiwan and tohers.

PHOENIX PREMIUM CHANNELS —
See KyLinTV.
Programming: Phoenix North America, Phoenix Info News & ATV.

PHOENIX TV
No. 9, Tower 1, Seashore Square
18 Defeng St
Kowloon, Hong Kong
China
Phone: 852-2621-9888
Fax: 852-2621-9898
Liu Chang Le, Chairman & Chief Executive Officer
Chui Keung, Executive Director & Deputy Chief Executive Officer
Yeung Ka Keung, Executive Vice President & Chief Financial Officer
Wang JI Yan, Executive Vice President & Head, Phoenix Chinese Channel
Roger T Uren, Vice President, International Affairs

Branch Offices:
Beijing Office: Room 306, No. 165 Haidian Road, Haidian District, Beijing 100080, China. Phones: 8610-6251-0868; 8610-6251-0869; 8610-6251-0511. Fax: 8610-6251-0484.

Chengdu Office: Room 2405, Commerce Building of Minshan Hotel, 55 Renmin West Road, Chengdu 610016, China. Phones: 8628-8558-8710; 8628-8558-8712. Fax: 8628-8558-8717.

Guangzhou Office: 28/F, Jinde Building, 67-69 Wende Road of Guangzhou, Guangzhou 510030, China. Phones: 020-8322-6130; 020-8322-6120; 020-8322-6366. Fax: 020-8322-6199.

Shanghai Office: Room 2706, CITIC Square, 1168 Nanjing West Road, Shanghai 200041, China. Phone: 8621-5292-5188. Fax: 8621-5292-8670.

Shenzhen Office: China TV Co. Ltd., 10/F Investment Building, 4009 Shen Nan Blvd, Shenzhen, China. Phone: 86755-8290-9001. Fax: 86755-8290-9002.

Wuhan Office: No. 432 of Shangri-La Hotel, 700 Construction Avenue, Wuhan, Hubei Province 430015, China. Phones: 8627-8578-1338; 8627-8578-8228. Fax: 8627-8578-8228.
Type of service: Video on demand.
Satellites: Asia Sat 3S; Eurobird D6.
Operating hours/week: 168.
Programming: Features a mix of programs, ranging from political, economic news and current affairs through talk shows, film and music reviews to movies, and mini series in both Chinese and foreign origins. Channels include Phoenix Chinese Channel, Phoenix Movie Channel, Phoenix InfoNews Channel, Phoenix North America Chinese Channel and Phoenix Chinese News & Entertainment (CNE) Channel.
Began: March 31, 1996, Date shown is date of initial launch in China.
Means of Support: Advertising & subscriber fees.
Distribution method: IPTV & cable systems.
Scrambled signal: No.
Ownership: News Corp. & Today's Asia Ltd., 75%; 16.4% publicly held.

PIKES PEAK COMMUNITY COLLEGE
Distance Education
5675 S Academy Blvd, Campus Box 45
Colorado Springs, CO 80906
Phones: 719-540-7538; 800-456-6847
Fax: 719-540-7532
E-mail: lrc@ppcc.edu
Web Site: http://www.ppcc.edu
Julie Witherow, Distance Education Director
William Wright, Chief Engineer
Type of service: Basic.
Operating hours/week: 64.
Operating areas: Colorado.
Programming: Educational service carried on local cable systems.
Distribution method: Available to cable and wireless cable systems.

PILLSBURY CHANNEL
1111 Stewart Ave
Bethpage, NY 11714
Phone: 516-803-2300
Fax: 516-803-2368
David Kline, President & Chief Operating Officer, Rainbow Advertising Sales Corp.
Barry Frey, Executive Vice President, Advanced Platform Sales, Cablevision
Type of service: Video on demand.
Sales representative: Rainbow Advertising Sales Corp.
Operating hours/week: 168.
Operating areas: Connecticut, New Jersey & New York.
Programming: Branded channel offering Pillsbury products plus longer form programming and interactive shows.
Began: May 4, 2010.
Means of Support: Advertising.
Total subscribers: 2,905,000. Total systems served: 29.
Distribution method: By fiber optics.
Scrambled signal: Yes.
Ownership: General Mills Inc.

PITTSBURGH CABLE NEWS CHANNEL
4145 Evergreen Rd
Pittsburgh, PA 15214-4145
Phones: 412-237-1100; 800-237-9794
Fax: 412-237-1333
E-mail: gm@wpxi.com
Web Site: http://www.wpxi.com/pcnc
Ray Carter, Vice President & General Manager
Mark W. Barash, Station Manager
Mike Goldrick, News Director
Brian Abzanka, Operations Manager & Producer
Maureen O'Connor, Affiliate Relations Representative & Producer
Type of service: Basic & expanded basic.
Sales representative: Linda Hansen.
Operating areas: Pennsylvania, Ohio, West Virginia.
Programming: Cable-exclusive 24-hour local news, talk & information.
Began: January 3, 1994.
Means of Support: Advertising & subscribers fees.
Total subscribers: 850,000. Total systems served: 3.
Distribution method: Via fiber optic to cable systems.
Scrambled signal: Yes.
Ownership: WPXI Inc., Comcast Cable Communications Inc. (30%).

PLANET GREEN — See Discovery Channel.
Web Site: http://planetgreen.discovery.com
Laura Michalchyshyn, President & General Manager
Annie Howell, Senior Vice President, Communications, Public Affairs & Talent Management
Rob Jacobson, Senior Vice President, Marketing
Claire Alexander, Vice President, Operations & Interactive Media
Timothy Kuryak, Vice President, West Coast Development
Operating hours/week: Transitioned from 56 to 168 hours per week March 29, 2010.
Programming: Shows with information for an environmentally conscious lifestyle. Reality

& scripted shows focusing on real estate, design & science.
Began: June 4, 2008, Replaced Discovery Home Channel.
Total subscribers: 56,000,000.
Scrambled signal: Yes.

PLANET GREEN HD — See Discovery Channel.

PLAY & WIN CHANNEL
c/o Booth Communications of Birmingham
645 S Eton St
Birmingham, MI 48009-6829
Phone: 810-540-6110
Fax: 810-540-6739
Hugh Jencks, Information Contact
Operating hours/week: 168.
Operating areas: Michigan.
Programming: General trivia games.
Began: October 15, 1994.
Ownership: Booth Communications Inc.

PLAYBOY EN ESPANOL — See Playboy TV.
Programming: Adult, erotic.
Began: January 1, 2000.
Ownership: Playboy TV International.

PLAYBOY HD — See Playboy TV.

PLAYBOY TV
Playboy Enterprises Inc.
680 N Lake Shore Dr
Chicago, IL 60611
Phone: 312-751-8000
Fax: 312-751-2818
E-mail: cable@playboy.com
Scott Flanders, Chief Executive Officer, Playboy Enterprises
Hugh M Hefner, Chief Creative Officer & Editor-in-Chief, Playboy Enterprises
Jimmy Jellinek, Chief Content Officer, Playboy Enterprises
Tom Hagopian, Executive Vice President & General Manager, Digital Media
Jeffrey M. Jenest, Executive Vice President
Rachel Sagan, Executive Vice President, Business Affairs & General Counsel
Scott Stephen, Executive Vice President, Operations
Sol Weisel, Executive Vice President, Production & Operations
Jeremy S. Westin, Executive Vice President, Business Development
Kendice Briggs, Senior Vice President, Human Resources
Gary Rosenson, Senior Vice President, Affiliate Sales & Marketing
Todd Schwartz, Vice President, Programming
Jim Nagle, Communications Director

Branch Offices:
LOS ANGELES: 3030 Andrita St, Los Angeles, CA 90065. Phone: 323-344-4500.

SANTA MONICA: 2112 Broadway, Santa Monica, CA 90404. Phone: 310-264-6600. Fax: 310-264-1994.

NEW YORK: 730 Fifth Ave, New York, NY 10019. Phone: 212-261-5000. Fax: 212-957-2900.

LOS ANGELES: 2706 Media Center Dr, Los Angeles, CA 90065. Phone: 323-276-4000. Fax: 323-273-4500.

BEVERLY HILLS: 9242 Beverly Blvd, Beverly Hills, CA 90210.
Type of service: Pay & pay-per-view.
Satellites: Galaxy V, transponder 2.
Operating hours/week: 168.
Uplink: Burbank, CA.
Programming: Features original programs & selected erotic films.
Began: November 1, 1982.
Means of Support: Subscriber fees.
Total subscribers: 46,000,000.
Distribution method: Available to home dish audiences & cable systems.
Scrambled signal: Yes. Equipment: VideoCipher II Plus.
Ownership: Icon Acquisition Holdings LP. Hugh M. Hefner & Scott Flanders are among the equity investors.

PLAYERS NETWORK
4620 Polaris Ave
Las Vegas, NV 89103
Phone: 702-895-8884
E-mail: info@playersnetwork.com
Web Site: http://www.playersnetwork.com
Mark Bradley, Chief Executive Officer
Michael Berk, President, Programming
Ed Sullivan, Branding & Design Advisor
John English, Strategic Marketing
Douglas R. Miller, Financial Advisor & Director
Type of service: Basic, video on demand, pay-per-view & broadband.
Operating hours/week: 168.
Programming: Focusing on the gaming lifestyle.
Distribution method: Available to cable, satellite programmers & hotel networks.

PLAYGIRL TV
c/o Trans Digital Media LLC
801 2nd Ave
New York, NY 10017
Phone: 212-867-0234
Fax: 212-682-5278
Web Site: http://www.tdmllc.com
Geoff Lurie, Chief Executive Officer
Type of service: Pay-per-view & video on demand.
Programming: Adult entertainment.
Began: January 1, 2004.
Total subscribers: 20,000,000.
Distribution method: Available to cable & satellite providers.
Ownership: TransDigital Media.

PLAZA TV
Flying J Communications
4185 Harrison Blvd, Ste 301
Ogden, UT 84403
Phones: 801-624-4500; 877-866-7378
Fax: 801-624-4530
Operating hours/week: 168.
Programming: Rebroadcasts major network programming & advertising.

PLEASURE
5435 Airport Blvd
Ste 100
Boulder, CO 80301
Phones: 303-786-8700; 888-728-9993
Fax: 303-938-8388
Mark Kreloff, President & Chief Executive Officer
Michael Weiner, Executive Vice President, Business Affairs
Thomas Nyiri, Chief Technical Officer & V.P., Broadband Communications
Karyn Miller, Chief Financial & Operating Officer
Ken Boenish, Senior Vice President, Sales
Bill Mossa, Vice President, Affiliate Sales
John Chambliss, Programming Director
Robin Rothman, Media Contact
Mark Grant, Marketing Contact
Type of service: Pay-Per-View.
Operating hours/week: 168.
Programming: Adult programming.
Began: June 1, 1999.
Means of Support: PPV; monthly subscription fee.
Distribution method: Available to home dish audience and cable systems.
Ownership: New Frontier Media Inc.

PLUM TV
419 Lafayette St
7th Fl
New York, NY 10003
Phone: 646-292-4200
Fax: 646-292-4201
E-mail: info@plumtv.com
Web Site: http://www.plumtv.com
Jerry Powers, Co-Chairman
Tom Scott, Co-Chairman & Founder
Hanna Gryncwajg, Chief Revenue Officer
Mark Drucker, Vice President, Sales & Marketing, Hamptons
Type of service: Broadcast & video on demand.
Operating areas: Massachusetts, New York, Colorado, Idaho & Florida.
Programming: Focusing on resort events, including film festivals, wine festivals & sporting events at Nantucket, Martha's Vineyard, the Hamptons, Vail, Aspen, Telluride, Sun Valley & Miami Beach.
Began: January 1, 2004.
Distribution method: Available to cable & satellite systems.

POKERTV NETWORK
1555 Flamingo Rd
Ste 315
Las Vegas, NV 89119
Phone: 702-735-7588
Web Site: http://www.pokertvnetwork.com
Programming: News, information, travel, reality & talk shows related to the world of poker.
Began: December 1, 2005.

POPCORNFLIX.COM
757 3rd Ave
3rd Fl
New York, NY 10017
Phone: 212-308-1790
E-mail: info@popcornflix.com
Web Site: http://www.popcornflix.com
Robert Baruc, President, Screen Media Ventures
David Fannon, Executive Vice President, Screen Media Ventures
Gary Delfiner, Senior Vice President, Digital Distribution, Screen Media Ventures
Donna Tracey, Director of Operations, Screen Media Ventures
Type of service: Broadband.
Operating areas: Available nationwide.
Programming: Offers viewers a choice of 176 independent movies free. Plans to have 1,000 films by end of 2011.
Began: March 22, 2011.
Means of Support: Advertising and banner announcements.
Distribution method: Available to PCs and mobile browers.
Scrambled signal: Yes.
Ownership: Screen Media Ventures.

PORTUGUESE CHANNEL
1501 Achushnet Ave
New Bedford, MA 02746-0113
Phone: 508-997-3110
Fax: 508-990-1231
Eduardo Lima, General Manager
Cidolia Silva, Advertising Mgr.
Gary Emken, Accounting

Branch Offices:
STUDIO: 638 Mt. Pleasant St, New Bedford, MA 02745.
Type of service: Basic.
Operating hours/week: 105.
Operating areas: Massachusetts & Rhode Island.
Programming: Portuguese language programs from Brazil & Portugal.
Began: May 1, 1974.
Means of Support: Advertising.
Distribution method: Microwave & coaxial cable to cable systems.
Ownership: Eduardo Lima, Prinicpal.

POWER LINK
Main at Water St
Coudersport, PA 16915
Phone: 814-274-9830
Fax: 814-274-6475; 814-274-8073
John Wattick, Marketing Director
Type of service: Pay.
Operating hours/week: 168.
Programming: Internet access service through cable modems.
Means of Support: Subscription fees.
Distribution method: Available to cable systems.
Ownership: Adelphia Communications Corp.

PRAISE TELEVISION
28059 US Hwy 19N
Ste 300
Clearwater, FL 33761
Phone: 727-536-0036
Fax: 727-530-0671
Web Site: http://www.praisetv.com
Dustin Rubeck, President & Chief Executive Officer
Bob Shreffler, Vice President, Finance
Tim Rasmussen, Senior Producer
Tim Brown, Vice President, News Media
Ken Gibson, Affiliates Director
Satellites: GE-1, transponder 7.
Programming: Contemporary Christian music videos, music specials, movies & concerts.
Began: December 9, 1996.
Distribution method: Available to cable systems, home dish audiences & broadcast stations.
Ownership: Christian Network Inc.

PRAYER CHANNEL
Catholic Diocese of Brooklyn
75 Greene Ave, PO Box C
Brooklyn, NY 11202
Phone: 718-399-5900
Fax: 718-399-5957
E-mail: pastcomm@msn.com
Web Site: http://www.dioceseofbrooklyn.org
M. J. Dempsey, Communications Director
Type of service: Regional.
Operating hours/week: 168.
Operating areas: Boroughs of Brooklyn & Queens, NY.
Programming: Daily mass & evening prayer, Christian music, Bible studies & shows on current events.
Began: March 15, 1988.
Total subscribers: 750,000.
Distribution method: Microwave to cable systems.
Ownership: Office of Pastoral Communications, Catholic Diocese of Brooklyn.

PRIDEVISION TV — See OutTV.

PRIME SPORTS RADIO
100 E Royal Lane
Ste 100
Irving, TX 75039
Phone: 214-402-4500
Fax: 214-831-8329

Jeff Dorf, General Manager
Allen Stone, Program Director
Amy Brown, Promotions Manager
Bob Faulkner, Sales
Type of service: Audio.
Operating hours/week: 168.
Programming: Sports radio network.
Began: September 12, 1994.
Distribution method: Available to cable systems.
Ownership: McMullen Group.

PRIMETIME 24
280 Park Ave
23rd Fl
New York, NY 10017
Phones: 212-702-4637; 212-702-4517
Web Site: http://www.primetime24.net
Type of service: Basic.
Satellites: Galaxy IV, transponder 10, 14 & 22 (east coast); Spacenet 4, transponder 6, 8 & 24 (west coast); Spacenet 4, transponder 10 (FoxNet).
Sales representative: Petry Television Inc.
Operating hours/week: 168.
Programming: Satellite delivery of 7 network stations. East coast feed offers WKRN-TV Nashville, WNBC New York & WSEE-TV Erie. West coast feed offers KOMO-TV Seattle, KPIX-TV San Francisco & KNBC Los Angeles, plus FoxNet. A package of 40 cable channels is also available as AmeriCaPak.
Began: January 1, 1987.
Means of Support: Monthly service charge for cable, SMATV & TVRO.
Total subscribers: 2,000,000.
Distribution method: Available to home dish audiences, cable systems & SMATVs.
Equipment: VideoCipher II Plus.
Ownership: PrimeTime 24 Joint Venture.

PRODUCT INFORMATION NETWORK
2600 Michelson Dr
Ste 1650
Irvine, CA 92612-1594
Phone: 949-263-9900
Fax: 949-757-1526
E-mail: info@pinnet.com
Web Site: http://www.pinnet.com
Mark Russo, Senior Vice President, Operations
Kathy Tran, Affiliate Sales
Jerry Mertes, Long Form & Short Form Ad Sales
Type of service: Basic.
Satellites: Galaxy 11, transponder 9.
Operating hours/week: 168.
Programming: Full-time direct response shopping.
Began: April 1, 1994.
Means of Support: Advertising.
Total subscribers: 23,000,000.
Distribution method: Cable, Broadcast, 4DTV.
Ownership: Private.
(PIN)

PROMOTER
1332 Enterprise Dr
Ste 200
West Chester, PA 19380
Phone: 215-692-5900
Fax: 215-692-6487
Tom Fannell, Vice President, Sales
Bill Higginbotham, Information Contact
Satellites: Satcom C-4, transponder 12.
Uplink: West Chester, PA.
Programming: Provides locally controlled promotion of pay-per-view programming. A digital version is currently being tested in Nashville, TN.
Began: January 1, 1990.

Distribution method: Available to cable systems.
Ownership: StarNet.

PUBLIC INTEREST VIDEO NETWORK
4704 Overbrook Rd
Bethesda, MD 20816
Phone: 301-656-7244
Arlen Slobodow, Director
Type of service: Basic.
Satellites: Westar IV; Satcom 3-R; Galaxy I, transponder varies.
Programming: Public affairs programming offered to public TV & cable systems on ad-hoc basis.
Began: January 1, 1979.

PULSE
Interactive Television Networks Inc.
2010 Main St, Ste 500
Irvine, CA 92614
Phone: 866-988-4988
Fax: 888-886-1305
Web Site: http://www2.pulsetv.com
Operating hours/week: 168.
Programming: IPTV channel showing music videos from several genres including country, rock & hip-hop.
Began: May 1, 2006.
Distribution method: Broadband.

PULSE 24
299 Queen St W
Toronto, ON M5V 2Z5
Canada
Phone: 416-591-5757
Fax: 416-591-8523
E-mail: news@pulse24.com
Mark Lewis, Information Contact
Programming: Regional English language news channel.
Began: January 30, 1998.

PUMA TV — See OlympuSat Hispanic Pack.
Web Site: http://www.pumatv.net
Programming: Music & entertainment.
Began: U.S. launch.
Ownership: El Puma Television.

PUMPTOP TV
18 Morgan
Ste 100
Irvine, CA 92618
Phone: 949-680-4200
Fax: 949-680-4213
E-mail: sales@pumptoptv.com
Web Site: http://www.pumptoptv.com
Programming: ABC news, Google maps, traffic, weather, sports & entertainment.
Ownership: AdtekMedia, Inc.

PUPPY CHANNEL
PO Box 14103
Clearwater, FL 33766
Phone: 727-712-0740
E-mail: fitz@thepuppychannel.com
Web Site: http://www.thepuppychannel.com
Daniel A FitzSimons, Chairman
Carol L. Hudson, Artistic Director
Type of service: Video on demand & broadband.
Programming: Puppy video accompanied by relaxing instrumental music.
Began: March 31, 1999.
Means of Support: Advertising sponsorships, home shopping sales, sales of information, subscriber fees after startup & video sales to non-subscribers.
Distribution method: Home dish & cable systems.

Scrambled signal: Yes.
Ownership: CHANNEMALS LLC.

PURSUIT CHANNEL
122 S LeGrande Ave
Luverne, AL 36049
Phone: 334-335-6926
Fax: 334-335-3361
E-mail: rfaulk@pursuitchannel.com
Web Site: http://www.pursuitchannel.com
Rusty Faulk, Chief Executive Officer
Stewart Thomas, Vice President, Technology
Merrill Sport, Network Distribution
Programming: Hunting and fishing television network.

QATARTV — See GlobeCast WorldTV.
Web Site: http://www.qatar-tv.net
Programming: Pan-Arab culture, religion & family entertainment.
Began: January 1, 2000.

QUBO
601 Clearwater Park Rd
West Palm Beach, FL 33401
Phones: 561-659-4252; 800-700-9789
Web Site: http://www.qubo.com
Brandon Burgess, Chief Executive Officer
Rick Rodriguez, President & General Manager
Dean M. Goodman, President & Chief Executive Officer
Richard Garcia, Senior Vice President & Chief Financial Officer
Adam K. Weinstein, Senior Vice President, Secrtetary & Chief Legal Officer
Kerry J. Hughes, Senior Vice President, Advertising Sales & Sponsorships
Steven J. Friedman, President, Cable
Stephen P. Appel, President, Sales & Marketing
Douglas C. Barker, President, Broadcast Distribution & Southern Region
Type of service: Digital & video on demand.
Operating hours/week: 168.
Programming: Children's oriented programming focusing on education, literacy & values.
Began: January 8, 2007, broadcast launch on Sept. 9, 2006.
Distribution method: Available to cable systems & satellite providers.
Scrambled signal: Yes.
Ownership: Ion Media Networks, Scholastic Corporation, Corus Entertainment Inc. (Nelvana Ltd.), Classic Media LLC & NBCUniversal Media LLC.

QVC
Studio Park
West Chester, PA 19380
Phone: 484-701-1000
Fax: 484-701-1350
E-mail: webmaster@qvc.com
Web Site: http://www.qvc.com
Michael George, President & Chief Executive Officer
Bill Costello, President, QVC International & Chief Financial Officer
Claire Watts, Chief Executive Officer, U.S.
Tom Downs, Executive Vice President, Operations & Services
Angie Simmons, Executive Vice President, Multichannel Platforms
John Sullivan, Executive Vice President & Chief Information Officer
Dave Apostolico, Senior Vice President, Affiliate Sales & Marketing
Robb Cardigan, Senior Vice President, Programming & Broadcasting
Jeff Charney, Senior Vice President, Marketing & Chief Marketing Officer
Francis Edwards, Senior Vice President, International
Rowland Gersen, Senior Vice President & Controller
Neal Grabell, Senior Vice President, General Counsel & Secretary
John Hunter, Senior Vice President, Customer Service
Chuck Pulcini, Senior Vice President, Finance & Treasury
Dennis Reustle, Senior Vice President, Sales & Product Planning
Doug Rose, Senior Vice President, Multichannel Programming & Marketing
Beth Rubino, Senior Vice President, Human Resources
Glenn Thor, Senior Vice President, Finance & Treasury
Dave Caputo, Vice President, Content Production
Fausto Ceballos, Vice President, Creative Services
Andy Cellucci, Vice President, Affiliate Sales & Marketing
Tony Godonis, Vice President, Facilities & Planning
Cherie Grobbel, Vice President, International Finance
Doug Howe, Vice President, Merchandising, Fashion & Beauty
John Kelly, Vice President, Merchandising, Sales & Product Planning
Tim Megaw, Vice President, Broadcasting
Robert Palma, Vice President, Production
Ellen Robin, Vice President, Public Relations
Mark Stieber, Vice President, Corporate Marketing & Business Development
Type of service: Basic.
Satellites: SatCom C4, transponder 9.
Operating hours/week: 168.
Programming: Televised cable shopping, viewer games & sweepstakes.
Began: November 24, 1986.
Means of Support: Revenue from merchandise sold.
Total subscribers: 92,000,000 (reflects U.S. subscribers; 195,000,000 subscribers worldwide.).
Distribution method: Available to home dish audiences.
Ownership: Liberty Media.

QVC HD — See QVC .

R NEWS
c/o Time Warner Communications
71 Mount Hope Ave
Rochester, NY 14620
Phones: 585-756-2424; 888-278-9889
Fax: 585-756-1673
E-mail: mrossney@rnews.com
Web Site: http://www.rnews.com

Ed Buttaccio, News Director
Mark J. Rossney, Webmaster
Type of service: Basic.
Operating hours/week: 168.
Operating areas: Rochester, NY.
Programming: Local news channel.
Began: July 1, 1995.
Means of Support: Advertising & subscriber fees.
Total subscribers: 320,000.
Distribution method: Available to cable systems.
Ownership: Time Warner Communications.

RADAR CHANNEL

619 W College Ave
State College, PA 16801
Phone: 814-234-9601
Fax: 814-231-0453
E-mail: info@accuwx.com
Web Site: http://www.accuweather.com
Andy Hoover, Marketing Manager
Type of service: Basic.
Programming: Continuous weather radar.
Began: February 1, 1997.
Distribution method: Available to cable systems.
Ownership: AccuWeather Inc.

RADIOTV NETWORK — No longer planned.

RAI INTERNATIONAL

32 Avenue of the Americas
New York, NY 10013
Phone: 212-468-2500
Fax: 212-765-1956
E-mail: international@rai.it
Web Site: http://www.international.rai.it
Guido Corso, Vice President, Marketing
Hani Gharbieh, General Manager
Salvatore Vecchuzzio, Manager, Marketing
Type of service: Pay.
Satellites: EchoStar I.
Operating hours/week: 48. Mon.-Sat.
Programming: Italian programming, including soccer games, music, cultural events, movies & historical documentaries.
Began: April 12, 1996.
Means of Support: Subscription fees.
Distribution method: Available to home dish audiences.
Ownership: RAI International.

RAI USA

32 Avenue of the Americas
21st Fl
New York, NY 10019
Phone: 212-468-2500
Fax: 212-765-1956
E-mail: info@raicorp.net
Web Site: http://www.raicorp.net
Guido Corso, President, RAI Corp.
Mario Bona, Chairman & Chief Executive Officer
Rita Basmagian, Vice President, Programming
Marina Giordano, Assistant Program Director
Type of service: Basic.
Satellites: GE 2, transponder 3.
Operating hours/week: 17.
Programming: Italian language programming including news, variety shows, movies, children's specials & live soccer.
Began: February 1, 1987.
Distribution method: Available to over the air & cable systems.

RANG-A-RANG TELEVISION

2221 Chain Bridge Rd
Vienna, VA 22182
Phone: 703-255-5500
Fax: 703-991-2184
Web Site: http://www.rangarangtv.com
Davar Veiseh, Station Manager
Type of service: Basic.
Operating hours/week: 168.
Operating areas: Virginia, Maryland & District of Columbia.
Programming: Persian politics, history, culture, food & health shows.
Began: January 1, 1989.

RCS TELEVISION — See Telelatino Network.
Programming: Coverage of soccer, cricket & rugby matches & other sports related programs.

REACTV

724 A 2nd Ave S
St. Petersburg, FL 33701
Phone: 727-828-3688
Fax: 727-545-2724
E-mail: dd@reactv.com
Web Site: http://www.reactv.com
Frank Maggio, Founder
Type of service: Basic & broadband.
Operating hours/week: 168.
Programming: Interactive game shows. Simulcast on the internet.
Began: August 8, 2006.
Distribution method: Available to cable systems & online.

THE REAL ESTATE CHANNEL

1000 Universal Studios Plaza
Bldg 22A
Orlando, FL 32819
Phone: 407-244-6847
E-mail: info@multichannelventures.com
Web Site: http://www.realestatechannel.com
Michael Gerrity, Founder
Type of service: Broadband.
Programming: Targets global & local real estate markets with sales information, education & promotions from a variety of real esate professionals & services.
Began: April 1, 2007.
Ownership: Multichannel Ventures.

REAL HIP-HOP NETWORK

601 Pennsylvania Ave NW
Ste 900
Washington, DC 20004
Phones: 202-434-8374; 866-887-5249
Fax: 866-887-5249
E-mail: advertising@rhn.tv
Web Site: http://www.rhn.tv
Atonn Muhammad, Chief Executive Officer
Kendrick Lesane, Executive Vice President, Music & Talent
Paul Waters, Chief Operating Officer
Jacqueline Lesane, Corporate Secretary
Lucas Kuria, Executive Vice President, Programming & Development
Jerome Leaks, Greater New York Regional Director
Kevin Brewer, Executive Vice President, Promotions & Marketing
Will Boisture, Executive Vice President, Creative Developing
Type of service: Basic.
Operating hours/week: 168.
Uplink: TA Broadcasting.
Programming: Hip-Hop lifestyle.
Total subscribers: 21,000,000. Total systems served: 2.
Distribution method: Available to cable & satellite programmers.

REAL MADRID TV — Not available in the U.S.

RECIPE.TV

1925 Century Park E
Ste 1025
Los Angeles, CA 90067
Phone: 310-277-3500
E-mail: eric@es.tv
Web Site: http://www.recipe.tv
Byron Allen, Founder & Chief Executive Officer
Cat Santarosa, Executive Vice President & Director Producer
Darren Galatt, Vice President, Ad Sales
Type of service: Digital broadband.
Operating hours/week: 168.
Operating areas: Available nationwide.
Programming: Focuses on food, chefs & recipes.
Began: May 11, 2009.
Total subscribers: 1,900,000.
Distribution method: Available to Verizon FiOS and Frontier Communications subscribers.
Scrambled signal: No.
Ownership: Entertainment Studios.

REELZCHANNEL

1201 W 5th St
Ste T-900
Los Angeles, CA 90017
Phone: 213-443-2400
E-mail: info@reelzchannel.com
Web Site: http://www.reelzchannel.com
Terry O'Reilly, Executive Vice President & General Manager
Bernie Weiss, Executive Vice President, Finance & Administration
Aymon DeMauro, Senior Vice President, Advertising Sales
Mike Smith, Senior Vice President, Programming
Amy Jo Wayne, Senior Vice President, Advertising Sales
Juli Biondi, Vice President, Broadcast Localization
Toni Molle, Vice President, Content Development & Studio Relations
Chris Pulis, Vice President, Production Operations
Keith Till, Vice President, Direct Response
Lori Wallace, Vice President, Advertising Sales & Director
Steve Holzer, Executive Producer, Original Programming
Jeff Otto, Managing Editor
John Halecky, Senior Editor
Rosalie Drake, Director, Ad Sales, Western Region
Robert Ell, Talent Relations Director

Branch Office:
BURBANK: 3500 W Olive Ave, Ste 300, Burbank, CA 91505. Phone: 818-973-2750. Fax: 818-973-2751.
Type of service: Digital.
Operating hours/week: 168.
Programming: Covering movies & the movie industry, including actors, director, reviews & behind-the-scenes looks at new movies & classic films.
Began: September 27, 2006, Formerly Moviewatch.
Means of Support: Ad supported.
Total subscribers: 35,000,000.
Distribution method: Available to cable & satellite providers.
Scrambled signal: Yes.
Ownership: Hubbard Broadcasting Inc.

REGIONAL NEWS NETWORK

721 Broadway
Kingston, NY 12401
Phone: 845-339-6200
Fax: 845-339-6264
E-mail: comments@rnntv.com
Web Site: http://www.rnntv.com
Richard French III, General Manager
Lorri Booth, Administration
Monica Baker, Administration

Branch Offices:
NEW YORK: 437 Fifth Ave, New York, NY 10016. Phone: 212-725-2666. Fax: 212-481-2705.

WESTCHESTER: 800 Westchester Ave, Ste S-640, Rye Brook, NY 10573. Phone: 914-417-2700. Fax: 914-696-0276.
Operating hours/week: 168.
Operating areas: Connecticut, New Jersey & New York.
Programming: Regional news, information & children's educational programming.
Total subscribers: 5,000,000.
Ownership: RNNTV Limited Partnership.

RESEARCH CHANNEL

1201 3rd Ave
Ste 4800
Seattle, WA 98101-3099
Phone: 877-616-7265
E-mail: info@researchchannel.org
Web Site: http://www.researchchannel.org
Amy Philipson, Executive Director
Type of service: Basic & video on demand.
Operating hours/week: 168.
Programming: Peer reviewed research across several disciplines including arts, humanities, business, economics, social, politial & natural sciences.
Began: January 1, 1996.
Total subscribers: 25,000,000.
Distribution method: Available to cable & satellite providers & online.

RESEAU DE L'INFORMATION

Societe Radio-Canada
C.P. 6000, succ. centre-ville
Montreal, QC H3C 3A8
Canada
Phone: 514-597-5551
Fax: 514-597-5289
E-mail: rdicomm@montreal.radio-canada.ca
Web Site: http://www.radio-canada.ca/rdi/
Luce Julien, Senior Director, RDI
Type of service: Basic.
Satellites: Anik E-1; Anik E-2.
Operating hours/week: 168.
Programming: French language news service.
Began: January 1, 1995.
Means of Support: Advertising & subscriber fees.
Distribution method: Available to home dish audiences & cable systems.
Ownership: Societe Radio-Canada.

RFD HD — See RFD-TV.

RFD-TV

3201 Dickerson Pike
Nashville, TN 37207
Phone: 615-227-9292
E-mail: info@rfdtv.com
Web Site: http://www.rfdtv.com
Patrick Gottsch, Founder & President
Ed Frazier, Chief Operating Officer
Steve Campione, Chief Financial Officer
Dave Randell, Senior Vice President, Advertising Sales
Raquel Gottsch, Executive Vice President, Corporate Communications
Gatsby Gottsch, Executive Vice President, Finance
Kelly Kantz, Vice President & General Manager
Type of service: Basic.
Satellites: Galaxy 13, transponder 24.
Sales representative: Ed Frazier.
Operating hours/week: 168.
Operating areas: US, Canada, & Brazil.

Uplink: G-13.
Programming: Services the needs & interests of rural America with programming focused on agriculture, equine & rural lifestyle, along with traditional country music & entertainment.
Began: December 1, 2000.
Means of Support: Carriage fee & Advertising.
Total subscribers: 40,000,000.
Distribution method: Digital satellite. Available to DISH Network and cable subscribers.
Scrambled signal: Yes. Equipment: Scientific Atlanta.
Ownership: Rural Media Group.

RGT — See Alterna'TV.

RHODE ISLAND NEWS CHANNEL
10 Orms St
Providence, RI 02904
Phone: 401-453-8000
Fax: 401-615-1559
E-mail: ctzianabos@abc6.com
Web Site: http://www.abc6.com
Chris Tzianabos, Vice President & General Manager, ABC 6
Marc Fauci, Vice President & Director of Sales
Irene Mahoney-Paige, News Director
Type of service: Basic.
Operating areas: Rhode Island.
Programming: Rhode Island 24-hour news channel.
Began: November 30, 1998.
Means of Support: Advertising.
Total subscribers: 290,000.
Distribution method: Cable.
Ownership: Cox Communications Inc.

RHODE ISLAND STATEWIDE INTERCONNECT
Rhode Island Public Utilities Commission
89 Jefferson Blvd
Warwick, RI 02888
Phone: 401-941-4500
Web Site: http://www.ripuc.org
John A. Notte III, Assoc. Administrator
Type of service: Basic.
Operating hours/week: 133.
Operating areas: Rhode Island & seven Massachusetts communities.
Uplink: Johnston, RI.
Programming: State legislature, college credit courses, cultural, religious & public access of statewide interest.
Began: January 1, 1983.
Means of Support: Cable TV operators.
Total subscribers: 292,000.
Distribution method: Available to cable systems via microwave.
Ownership: Rhode Island cable TV operators.

RIO DE LA PLATA
Desarrollo de Senales Satelitales, Torneos e Competencias
Libertad 565/67, Piso 10
1012 Buenos Aires
Argentina
Phones: 303-771-7700; 541-349-4800
Andres Biernat, Information Contact
Type of service: Pay.
Operating hours/week: 24.
Programming: Variety programming from Argentina. Available on Canales N.
Began: August 1, 1998.
Means of Support: Subscriber fees & advertising.
Distribution method: Available to cable systems.

RITMOSON LATINO
5999 Center Dr
Los Angeles, CA 90045
Phone: 310-348-3373
Web Site: http://www.esmas.com/ritmosonlatino
Marcelo De Antunano, Information Contact
Type of service: Basic.
Uplink: Mexico City.
Programming: Latin music & lifetsyle shows.
Began: May 1, 2003, (U.S. launch).
Means of Support: Advertising & subscriber fees.
Total subscribers: 6,000,000 (reflects U.S. subscribers; 1,300,000 total subscribers worldwide.).
Distribution method: Available to cable systems.
Ownership: Televisa.

RLTV
5525 Research Park Dr
Baltimore, MD 21228
Phones: 410-402-9601; 800-754-8464
Fax: 410-402-9691
E-mail: gbarton@rl.tv
Web Site: http://www.rl.tv
John Erickson, Founder & Executive Chairman
Paul Fitzpatrick, President & Chief Operating Officer
Patrick Baldwin, Senior Vice President, Affiliate Sales
Elliot Jacobson, Senior Vice President, Programming
Gig Barton, Vice President, Ad Sales
Betsy Brightman, Vice President, Affiliate Relations & Distrubution
E J Conlin, Vice President, Marketing
Roy Ennis, Vice President, Finance
Adam Kane, Vice President, Government & Community Affairs
Jonathan Lee, Vice President, Operations
Akin Odulate', Vice President, Business Development
James Peebles, Vice President of Engineering
Type of service: Basic & video on demand.
Operating hours/week: 168.
Programming: Retirement Living TV (RLTV) is the only cable network dedicated to serving the needs of adults 50+ with information and entertainment that inspires and enhances the perception of aging. The network has Emmy award-winning programming that addresses a variety of subjects and genres including health, finance, travel, reality, comedy and drama.
Began: September 5, 2006.
Total subscribers: 29,000,000.
Distribution method: Available to cable systems & online.
Scrambled signal: Yes.
Ownership: John Erickson, Erickson Media & NBCUniversal LLC (minority interest).

ROCHESTER'S CW
WHAM-DT
4225 W Henrietta Rd
Rochester, NY 14623
Phone: 585-334-8700
Web Site: http://www.cwrochester.com
Chuck Samuels, General Manager
Craig Heslor, Operations Director
David DiProsa, General Sales Manager
Type of service: Over the air.
Operating hours/week: 133.
Operating areas: Rochester, NY.
Programming: Local news & syndicated programming; CW Network affiliate.
Began: September 1, 1996, as WRWB-TV, New York's WB affiliate; re-launched on Sept. 20, 2006.
Means of Support: Advertising.
Total subscribers: 272,000.
Distribution method: Available to cable systems.

Scrambled signal: Yes.
Ownership: Newport Television.

ROCK TV — No longer planned.

ROGERS SPORTSNET
9 Channel Nine Ct
Toronto, ON M1S 4B5
Canada
Phone: 416-332-5600
Fax: 416-332-5622
Web Site: http://www.sportsnet.ca
Doug Beeforth, President
Rick Briggs-Jude, Vice President, Production
Type of service: Expanded basic.
Operating hours/week: 168.
Uplink: Toronto, ON.
Programming: Regional sports offering Vancouver Canucks, Edmonton Oilers & Ottawa Senators hockey plus figure skating, NBA basketball, curling, skiing & auto racing.
Began: October 9, 1998.
Means of Support: Advertising & subscription fees.
Total subscribers: 7,500,000.
Distribution method: Available to home dish audiences & cable systems.
Ownership: Rogers Sportsnet Inc.

ROOT SPORTS NORTHWEST
3626 156th Ave SE
Bellevue, WA 98006
Phone: 425-748-3400
Web Site: http://northwest.rootsports.com
Operating areas: Washington, Oregon, Idaho, Montana and Alaska.
Programming: Formerly Fox Sports Net Northwest. Home of the Seattle Mariners, Seattle Sounders FC, Portland Timbers, Washington Huskies, Washington State Cougars, Oregon State Beavers, Gonzaga Bulldogs and Seattle University Redhawks.
Began: April 1, 2011, as Root Sports Northwest. Originally launched in 1987 as Northwest Cable Sports.
Total subscribers: 3,700,000.
Scrambled signal: Yes.
Ownership: DirecTV Sports Networks.

ROOT SPORTS PITTSBURGH
2 Allegheny Center
Ste 1000
Pittsburgh, PA 15212
Phone: 412-322-9500
Fax: 412-237-8439
E-mail: gesmith@directv.com
Web Site: http://pittsburgh.rootsports.com
Ted Black, Senior Vice President & General Manager
Dan Fawcett, Assistant General Manager
Gil Lucas, Executive Producer & Sports Director
Steve Danloff, Vice President & General Sales Manager
David Brugnone, Affiliate Sales
Jeff Butler, Director, Marketing & Public Relations
Joe Coffaro, Operations Manager
Brad Sherwood, Local Sales Manager
Cheryl Pulford, Controller
Jim Herbstritt, Programming
Type of service: Regional.
Satellites: Primestar.
Operating hours/week: 168.
Operating areas: Pennsylvania, West Virginia, Ohio, New York & Maryland.
Programming: Formerly Fox Sports Net Pittsburgh. Regional sporting events including Pittsburgh Pirates, Pittsburgh Penguins, the WPIAL as well as select Big East Conference men's and women's basketball game telecasts.
Began: April 1, 2011, as Root Sports Pittsburgh. Originally launched March 22, 1986 as KBL Entertainment Network.
Means of Support: Advertising & affiliate fees.
Total subscribers: 2,400,000.
Distribution method: Available to home dish audiences & cable systems.
Scrambled signal: Yes. Equipment: Primestar IRD.
Ownership: DirecTV Sports Networks.

ROOT SPORTS ROCKY MOUNTAIN
44 Cook St
Ste 600
Denver, CO 80206
Phone: 303-267-7200
Fax: 303-267-7222
E-mail: twgriggs@directv.com
Web Site: http://rockymountain.rootsports.com
Tim Griggs, Vice President & General Manager
Amy Turner, Director, Public Relations
Operating areas: Colorado, Utah, Wyoming, Idaho, Kansas, Montana, Nebraska, Nevada, New Mexico & South Dakota.
Programming: Formerly Fox Sports Net Rocky Mountain & Fox Sports Net Utah. Regional sports service providing Colorado Rockies, Utah Jazz, University of Colorado, University of Denver, as well as Big 12 football and women's basketball, Pac-10 football and basketball and ACC basketball.
Began: April 1, 2011, as Root Sports Rocky Mountain. Originally launched November 5, 1988 as Prime Sports Rocky Mountain/ Prime Sports Intermountain West.
Total subscribers: 2,600,000.
Distribution method: Available to cable systems.
Scrambled signal: Yes.
Ownership: DirecTV Sports Networks.

ROOT SPORTS UTAH — See Root Sports Rocky Mountain.
Operating hours/week: 168.
Operating areas: Utah, Idaho, Wyoming & Montana.
Programming: Regional sports coverage.
Distribution method: Available to cable systems.

RSC ROMANIA — See GlobeCast WorldTV.
Phone: 877-776-8788
E-mail: support@romsatnet.com
Web Site: http://www.romsatnet.com
Programming: Three channels, RSC1, RSC2 & RSC3, bringing shows from a variety of Romania-based networks to Romanians abroad. Programming from PRIMA TV,

B1TV, MTV Romania, Telesport, EtnoTV & Antena International.
Distribution method: Available to satellite providers.

RSN RESORT TV — See Outside Television

RT
1825 K St NW
Ste 710
Washington, DC 20006
Phone: 202-775-2305
Fax: 202-775-2309
E-mail: rt-us@rttv.ru
Web Site: http://www.rt.com
Margarita Simonyan, Editor in Chief
Denis Trunov, Deputy Editor in Chief
Sergey Maganet, Technical Director
Andrey Bukashkin, Chief Director
Mark Bulla, Chief Engineer
Mark Angelini, Director of Operations
Mindia Gavasheli, Washington DC Contact

Branch Offices:
Moscow Headquarters: Bldg One, 4 Zubovsky Blvd, Moscow 119021, Russia. Phones: 7 (495) 649 89 89; 7 (495) 926 24 50 (press). Fax: 7 (495) 649 89 79. E-Mail: info@rttv.ru; press@rttv.ru.
Operating hours/week: 168.
Operating areas: Available nationwide.
Programming: 24 hour Russian news Channel. Broadcasts in English, Arabic & Spanish.
Began: January 1, 2005.
Distribution method: Available to cable systems, home dish audiences and online.

RTN
735 Broad St
Ste 1204
Chattanooga, AR 37402
Phone: 423-468-5100
E-mail: rtn@myretrotv.com
Web Site: http://www.myretrotv.com
Neal Ardman, Affiliate Relations
Type of service: Digital.
Operating hours/week: 168.
Programming: Classic television serials & shows.
Began: July 1, 2005.
Distribution method: Available to cable systems & satellite providers.
Ownership: Luken Media.

RTN+ — See Russian Television Network.

RTP-USA
283 E Kinney St
Newark, NJ 07105
Phone: 973-344-8888
Anthony Seabra, President
Americo Seabra, Vice President
Adam Seabra, Manager
Programming: Movie service.
Began: January 1, 1984.
Means of Support: Subscriber fees & advertising.

RTR PLANETA — See GlobeCast WorldTV.
Web Site: http://www.rtr-planeta.com
Programming: Russian state television & broadcasting channel providing Russians abroad with Russian culture, history, art, theater, ballet & general entertainment.
Distribution method: Available to satellite providers.

RTR PLANETA SPORT — See GlobeCast WorldTV.
Web Site: http://www.rtr-sport.ru

RTV21 — See GlobeCast WorldTV.
Web Site: http://www.radio21.net
Operating hours/week: 168.
Programming: Albanian-language news & information, movies, serials, sporting & musical events, game & talk shows for Albanians abroad.
Began: January 1, 1998.
Distribution method: Available to satellite providers.

RTVI
304 Hudson St
New York, NY 10013
Phone: 646-292-0290
E-mail: svetlana.rtvi@gmail.com
Michael Galkin, Program Director
Svetlana Ivanova, Vice President, Advertising, Distribution & Special Projects
Programming: Russian-language network providing six newscasts daily, latest TV-series, controversial talk-shows and movies.
Began: January 1, 1997.
Means of Support: Advertising.
Distribution method: Available to cable systems and DirecTV subscribers.

RUSSIA TODAY — See RT.

RUSSIAN TELEVISION NETWORK
Russian Media Group LLC
One Bridge Plaza, Ste 145
Fort Lee, NJ 06901-3518
07024
Phones: 718-745-7000; 800-628-6634
E-mail: info@russianmediagroup.com
Web Site: http://www.russianmediagroup.com
Mark Golub, President & Chief Executive Officer
Evgueni Lvov, Vice President & Chief Operating Officer
Gary Flom, Vice President, Marketing
Vlada Khmelnitskaya, Director, Programming & Manager, Production Department
Michael Paley, Director, Information Technology
Serge Goldberg, Chief Engineer
Operating hours/week: 168.
Programming: RTN offers Russian language newscasts plus concerts, sitcoms and entertainment programs. RTN+ is a Russian language movie channel.
Began: September 1, 1991, for RTN.
Means of Support: Advertising.
Scrambled signal: Yes.
Ownership: Russian Media Group LLC. (RTN).

SAFE TV
3556 Liberty Ave
Springdale, AR 72762
Phones: 479-361-2900; 888-777-9392
Fax: 479-361-2323
E-mail: feedback@safetv.org
Web Site: http://www.safetv.org
Carlos Pardeiro, President & Chief Executive Officer
Rudy Dolinsky, Chief Engineer
Bonnie Dolinsky, Satellite Sales Coordinator
Darlene Doublehead, Administrative Secretary
Dick Shadduck, Community Relations Director
Programming: Family & spiritual entertainment.
Distribution method: Available to cable & satellite providers.

SAIGON BROADCASTING TELEVISION NETWORK
(SBTN)
10501 Garden Grove Blvd
Garden Grove, CA 92843
Phones: 714-636-1121; 877-887-2612
Fax: 714-260-0236
Web Site: http://www.sbtn.net
Truc Ho, Chief Executive Officer
Type of service: Pay.
Satellites: Galaxy 17, transponder 24.
Operating hours/week: 168.
Programming: Vietnamese news, talk shows, sports, children's programming, entertainment, variety, movies, culture & history.
Began: July 1, 2001.
Distribution method: Available to cable systems, satellite & telco providers.
Scrambled signal: Yes.
Ownership: Saigon Broadcasting, NBCUniversal LLC, 50% each.

SALAAM TV — See GlobeCast WorldTV.
Web Site: http://www.salaamtv.com
Programming: Islamic programming.
Distribution method: Available to satellite providers.

SAMANYOLU TV — See GlobeCast WorldTV.
Phone: 732-560-0800
E-mail: izleyicitemsilcisi@samanyolu.tv
Web Site: http://www.samanyolu.tv
Programming: Turkish-language movies, dramas, news, sports, animation & music shows.
Began: January 1, 2000.
Distribution method: Available to satellite providers.

SAN DIEGO NEWS CHANNEL 10 - KGTV
4600 Air Way
San Diego, CA 92102
Phone: 619-237-1010
Fax: 619-262-1302
E-mail: jeff_block@10news.com
Web Site: http://www.10news.com
Jeff Block, General Manager

SAUDITV — See GlobeCast WorldTV.
Phone: 966-1442-8400
Web Site: http://www.saudi1.tv
Programming: Arabic religion, culture, entertainment, music, drama, serials, news, current affairs & children's programming.
Distribution method: Available to satellite providers.

SCHOLASTIC CHANNEL — No longer planned.

SCIENCE — See Discovery Channel.
Web Site: http://science.discovery.com
Deborah Adler Myers, Executive Vice President & General Manager
Programming: The only network devoted entirely to the wonders of science. Formerly known as Science Channel. Rebranding occurred June 8, 2011.
Began: October 1, 1996.
Total subscribers: 68,000,000.
Scrambled signal: Yes.

SCIENCE HD — See Discovery Channel.
Formerly known as Science Channel HD. Rebranding occurred June 8, 2011.

SCIENCE TELEVISION
3930 S Swanson St
Ste 810
Las Vegas, NV 89119
Phone: 702-735-4988
Fax: 702-369-2330
E-mail: rdmassociates@yahoo.com
Robert D. McCracken, Information Contact
Bambi Metscher, National Sales Representative
Jeanne Howerton, National Sales Representative
Type of service: Basic.
Programming: News & information on current issues in science, prominent scientists, new inventions & the future.
Began: March 1, 1996.
Means of Support: Advertising.
Total subscribers: 37,400,000.
Distribution method: Available to LPTVs, telcos, home dish audiences & cable systems.
Ownership: Science Television & Spotlight.

SCI-FI CHANNEL — See Syfy.

SCOLA
21557 270th St
McClelland, IA 51548
Phone: 712-566-2202
Fax: 712-566-2502
E-mail: scola@scola.org
Web Site: http://www.scola.org
Father Lee Lubbers, President & Founder
John Millar, Program Director
Sybil Mahan, Marketing Director
Dan Pike, Telecommunications Manager
Type of service: Basic.
Satellites: Galaxy IV.
Programming: Broadcasts from countries around the world, delivered in native languages.
Began: May 1, 1987.

SCORE
370 King St W
Ste 304, Box 10
Toronto, ON M5V 1J9
Canada
Phone: 416-977-6787
Fax: 416-977-0328
Web Site: http://www.thescore.ca
John Levy, Founder, Chairman & Chief Executive Officer
David Errington, Executive Vice President, Operations
Anthony Cicione, Vice President, Programming & Production
Aaron Holm, Information Systems Director
Barry Crowell, Technical Manager
Benjie Levy, Executive Vice President and Chief Operating Officer
Susan Arthur, Vice President, Marketing & Brand Strategy
Operating hours/week: 168.
Programming: Canadian sports information channel.
Began: May 12, 1997.
Total subscribers: 5,500,000.

SELECT ON DEMAND
1701 JFK Blvd
Philadelphia, PA 19103
Phone: 215-286-8763
Greg Weinstein, Vice President
Type of service: Video on demand.
Programming: Select On Demand is ushering in the next generation of television programming with the development of new digital cable networks designed exclusively for on-demand viewing. With a growing portfolio of digital networks from Anime to Fitness to Home Improvement and Gambling, Select On Demand is revolutionizing a whole new way of watching television through VOD technology.
Began: January 1, 2005.

Scrambled signal: Yes.
Ownership: Comcast Corp.

SEMILLITAS
2601 S Bayshore Dr
Ste 1250
Coconut Grove, FL 33133
Phone: 786-220-0280
Fax: 305-858-7188
E-mail: jespinal@somostv.net
Web Site: http://www.semillitas.tv
Luis Villanueva, President & Chief Executive Officer, SOMOSTV
Type of service: Pay.
Operating hours/week: 168.
Operating areas: Available nationwide.
Programming: Offers culturally relevant, state of the art, nonviolent animation to entertain and educate children 0 to 5 years old, totally in Spanish.
Began: March 15, 2010.
Distribution method: Availble to cable systems.
Scrambled signal: Yes.
Ownership: SOMOSTV.

SEMINAR TV
PO Box 586142
Oceanside, CA 92058-6142
Farhad Sorourifar, Information Contact
Patricia Hampton, Information Contact
Type of service: Basic.
Operating hours/week: 7.
Uplink: Los Angeles, CA.
Programming: Personal & professional development, self-help & personal growth.
Began: August 11, 1997.
Means of Support: Advertising.
Distribution method: Available to home dish audiences, SMATVs, cable systems & broadcast stations.
Ownership: Global Mind Network.

THE SET (SOUTHERN ENTERTAINMENT TV)
752 Commerce Dr
Ste 7
Venice, FL 34292
Phone: 941-488-8088
E-mail: info@theset.net
Web Site: http://www.theset.net
Type of service: Basic.
Satellites: Telstar 7.
Operating hours/week: 168.
Programming: Southern gospel music.
Began: August 1, 2004.

THE SET3 — See The SET.
Programming: Classic Black Gospel.
Began: August 1, 2004.

THE SET2 — See The SET.
Programming: Bluegrass Music.
Began: August 1, 2004.

SETANTA SPORTS USA — See GlobeCast WorldTV.
501 2nd St
Ste 360
San Francisco, CA 94107
Phone: 415-546-1022
Fax: 415-546-1033
Web Site: http://www.setanta.com
Operating hours/week: 168.
Programming: Provides European & international football, rugby & other sports to fans in Canada, Ireland & Australia. Ceased operations in the US February 28, 2010.
Total subscribers: 120,000.
Scrambled signal: Yes.

SEXTV:THE CHANNEL
299 Queen St W
Toronto, ON M5V 2Z5
Canada
Phone: 416-591-7400
Fax: 416-51-0080
Web Site: http://www.sextelevision.net
Programming: Features informative & educational original programming on human sexuality.
Ownership: CHUM Television.

SHALOM TV
PO Box 1989
Fort Lee, NJ 07024
Phone: 201-242-9460
Fax: 201-363-9241
E-mail: mail@shalomtv.com
Web Site: http://www.shalomtv.com
Rabbi Mark Golub, President
David Brugnone, Chief Marketing Officer
Bradford N. Hammer, Chief Operating Officer
Dr. Evgueni Lvov, Vice President, Operations
Edith Samers, Vice President, Marketing
Alan E. Oirich, Director, Production
Jan Weiss, Executive Assistant
Type of service: Free digital video on demand.
Operating areas: North America.
Programming: Free video on demand Jewish television cable network targeted to North American viewers. Offers Jewish-oriented public affairs events such as lectures, forums & observances, along with producing long-format temple tours & interviews of prominent Jewish figures. Also provides produced & acquired English & English-subtitled shows dealing with Jewish life, history & tradition.
Began: July 1, 2003.
Means of Support: Viewer contributions, grants, private funding and sponsorships.
Total subscribers: 30,000,000.
Scrambled signal: Yes.

SHALOM USA AMERICA
1123 Broadway
Ste 817
New York, NY 10010
Phone: 212-627-5522
Fax: 212-627-5802
Shay Bar-Lavi, President
Yael Seinerman, Information Contact
Began: June 1, 1990.

SHANGHAI DRAGON TV
F4 A Section
584 Zhizaoju Rd
Shanghai 200030
China
Phones: 021-3406-1116; 021-5466-6630
Web Site: http://www.smeg.com.cn
Programming: Officers Chinese langauge programming.
Ownership: Shanghai Media & Entertainment Group.

SHARJAHTV — See GlobeCast WorldTV.
Web Site: http://www.sharjahtv.gov.ae
Programming: News, documentaries, movies & children's shows from the United Arab Emirates.
Distribution method: Available to satellite providers.

SHENZHEN SATELLITE TV — See KyLinTV.
Operating hours/week: 168.
Programming: Offers programming that focuses on Hong Kong & Macao. Also provides news and entertainment shows plus some coverage of special events and sports.

SHEPHERDS CHAPEL NETWORK
PO Box 416
Gravette, AR 72736
Phones: 479-787-6026; 479-787-6248
Web Site: http://www.shepherdschapel.com/index.cfm
Arnold Murray, President
Type of service: Basic.
Satellites: Galaxy IV, transponder 16.
Operating hours/week: 168.
Programming: All religious programming, featuring educational & call-in segments.
Began: April 1, 1987.
Means of Support: Donations.
Distribution method: Available to home dish audiences.
Ownership: Shepherd's Chapel.

SHOP AT HOME
5388 Hickory Hollow Pkwy
Nashville, TN 37013
Phones: 615-263-8000; 866-366-4010
Fax: 615-263-8084
E-mail: customerservice@shopathometv.com
Web Site: http://www.shopathometv.com
Joe Fields, Chief Executive Officer
Tim Engle, President
Andy Caldwell, Vice President, Affiliate Marketing

Branch Offices:
HEADQUARTERS: Jewelry Television, 10001 Kingston Pike, Knoxville, TN 37922. Phone: 865-692-6000. Fax: 865-218-5049.
Type of service: Basic.
Satellites: Galaxy VII, transponder 10; Galaxy I, transponder 9, 14.
Operating hours/week: 70.
Uplink: Antioch, TN.
Programming: Showcases a variety of consumer products for purchase.
Began: January 1, 1986.
Means of Support: Merchandise sales.
Total subscribers: 80,000,000.
Distribution method: Available to home dish audiences & cable systems.
Ownership: Jewelry Television.

SHOP LATINO TV
8785 NW 13th Terr
Miami, FL 33172
Phones: 305-593-9003; 866-559-7588
Fax: 305-593-9444
E-mail: info@shoplatinotv.com
Web Site: http://www.shoplatinotv.com
Ciro Espinosa, Chief Operating Officer
Carlos Bejar, Chief Marketing Officer
Bernardo Hasbach, Chief Financial Officer
Adriana Grillet, Senior Vice President, Marketing, Public Relations & Community Affairs
Maria E. Meloni, Vice President, Broadcast Operations, Media & Distribution
Carlos Haas, Vice President, Information Technologies
Frank Maldonado, Vice President, Merchandising
Type of service: Basic.
Satellites: 168.
Programming: Home shopping.
Began: July 7, 2007.
Distribution method: Available to cable & satellite providers.

SHOP TV CANADA
1 Yonge St
9th Fl
Toronto, ON M5E 1E6
Canada
Phone: 416-869-4700
Fax: 416-869-4566
E-mail: info@shoptvcanada.com
Web Site: http://www.shoptvcanada.com
Type of service: Basic.
Programming: Direct response shopping channel promoting products from health & fitness, electronics, sports, recreation and others.
Total subscribers: 1,500,000.

SHOPNBC
6740 Shady Oak Rd
Eden Prairie, MN 55344
Phone: 952-943-6000
Fax: 952-943-6011
E-mail: service@shopnbc.com
Web Site: http://www.shopnbc.com
John Buck, Chairman
Keith Stewart, Chief Executive Officer
Bob Ayd, President, Merchandising, Planning, Programming, Broadcast Operations & On-Air Talent
Bill McGrath, Senior Vice President, Chief Financial Officer
Mark Ahmann, Senior Vice President, Human Resources
Trish Mueller, Senior Vice President, Marketing
Robert Manning, Vice President, Affiliate Relations
Nathan Martin, Vice President, Fulfillment
Type of service: Basic.
Satellites: Galaxy G-1, transponder 12.
Operating hours/week: 168.
Uplink: Minneapolis, MN.
Programming: Shop-at-home. Formerly known as ValueVision.
Began: October 15, 1991.
Means of Support: Product sales.
Total subscribers: 73,000,000.
Distribution method: Available to cable systems & home dish audiences.
Scrambled signal: Yes.
Ownership: ValueVision Media.

SHOPPING CHANNEL
59 Ambassador Dr
Mississauga, ON L5T 2P9
Canada
Phone: 905-565-2600
Fax: 905-565-2641
Web Site: http://www.theshoppingchannel.com
Ted Starkman, Executive Vice President & General Manager
Type of service: Basic.
Satellites: Anik F1, transponder 5.
Operating hours/week: 168.
Programming: Live TV retail service.
Began: January 15, 1987.
Means of Support: Retail sales to cable subscribers.
Total subscribers: 5,600,000.
Distribution method: Available to cable systems.
Ownership: Rogers Media.

SHORT TV
251 53rd St
Brooklyn, NY 11220
Phone: 212-226-6258
Web Site: http://www.shorttv.com
Roland Dib, Founder, President & Chief Executive Officer
Type of service: Basic & broadband.
Operating hours/week: 168.
Operating areas: New York, California, Michigan, Pennsylvania & Florida.
Programming: Independent short films.
Total subscribers: 2,000,000.
Distribution method: Available to cable systems & online.
Scrambled signal: Yes.

SHORTEEZ
9242 Beverly Blvd
Beverly Hills, CA 90210
Phone: 310-246-4000
Fax: 310-246-4050
Web Site: http://www.pbtvnetworks.com
Jim English, President
Brian Quirk, Executive Vice President, Affiliate Sales & Marketing
Claire Zrimc, Vice President, Worldwide Programming & Acquisitions
Marc Brown, Vice President, On-Air Promotions
Scott Barton, Public Relations Director
Andrew Lucas, Operations Director
Type of service: Pay-Per-View.
Satellites: Telstar 5, transponder 5.
Operating hours/week: 168.
Programming: Cable version adult movies & special events.
Began: February 14, 1994, as Adam & Eve; relaunched June 1, 1999 as Spice2.
Means of Support: Subscriber fees.
Distribution method: Available to home dish audiences & cable systems.
Equipment: DigiCipher II.
Ownership: Playboy Enterprises Inc.

SHORTSHD
6 - 8 Luke St
London EC2A 4XY
United Kingdom
Phone: +44 (0) 207-613-5400
Fax: +44 (0) 207-012-1598
Web Site: http://www.shortshd.com
Lucy Daniels, Production
Hans Hagman, Programming
Julien Hossein, Creative Director
Linda Olszewski, US Contact
Susan Petersen, Media Sales
Jenny Taylor, Marketing & Communication
Chris Tidman, Acquisitions

Branch Offices:
Shorts International: 419 Lafayette St, 2nd Fl, New York, NY 10003. Phone: 212-370-6077. Fax: 212-982-1060. E-Mail: susan@shortsinternational.com.

Shorts International: PO Box 2514, Toluca Lake, CA 91610. E-Mail: lindao@shortsinternational.com.
Type of service: Pay.
Programming: Showcases short movies in a range of genres, including action, CGI, cartoon, comedy, drama and horror.
Began: July 20, 2009, Date shown is for launch in United States.
Means of Support: Subscriber fees.
Distribution method: Available to Dish Network & U-verse subscribers.
Scrambled signal: Yes.

SHOWCASE TELEVISION
121 Bloor St E
Ste 200
Toronto, ON M4W 3M5
Canada
Phone: 416-967-0022
Fax: 416-967-0044
Web Site: http://www.showcase.ca
Phyllis Yaffe, President & Chief Executive Officer
Harvey Rogers, Vice President, Broadcast Operations & Engineering
Peter O'Neill, Vice President, Sales
Janet Eastwood, Vice President, Marketing & Communications
Norm Bolen, Vice President, Programming
John Tsagarakis, Vice President, Finance & Business Systems
Type of service: Expanded basic.
Satellites: Anik E-2, transponder 19.
Operating hours/week: 147.
Programming: Movies, series, made-for-television productions & mini-series from Canada & around the world.
Began: January 1, 1995.
Means of Support: Advertising & subscriber fees.
Distribution method: Available to cable systems.
Ownership: Alliance Communications Corp., 99%; Salter Street Films, 1%.

SHOWCASE HD — See Showcase Television.

SHOWTIME
Paramount Plaza Bldg
1633 Broadway, 17th Fl
New York, NY 10019
Phone: 212-708-1600
Fax: 212-708-1212
Web Site: http://www.sho.com
Matthew C. Blank, Chmn. & Chief Exec. Officer, Chairman & Chief Executive Officer, Showtime Networks
David Nevins, President, Entertainment
Len Fogge, Executive Vice President, Creative, Marketing, Research & Digital Media
Ken Hershman, Executive Vice President & General Manager, Showtime Sports & Event Programming
Amy Britt, Senior Vice President, Talent & Casting
Don Buckley, Senior Vice President, Digital Services
Johanna Fuentes, Vice President, Corporate Public Relations
Type of service: Pay.
Operating hours/week: 168.
Programming: Movies & original series.
Began: July 1, 1976.
Total subscribers: 19,500,000.
Ownership: CBS Corp.

SHOWTIME BEYOND — See Showtime.
Programming: Sci-fi, fantasy & horror.

SHOWTIME EN ESPANOL — See Showtime.

SHOWTIME EXTREME — See Showtime.
Programming: Action & martial arts films, gangster movies, thrillers, westerns, & boxing.

SHOWTIME FAMILYZONE — See Showtime.

SHOWTIME HD — See Showtime.

SHOWTIME NEXT — See Showtime.

SHOWTIME ON DEMAND — See Showtime.
Type of service: Video on demand.
Programming: Four categories of programming: SHO Family, SHO Movies, SHO Series & SHO Specials offering a variety of Hollywood movies, original series, family programming, boxing & music events, short films, documentaries & behind-the-scenes extras.
Total subscribers: 6,000,000 (Figure includes The Movie Channel On Demand.).
Distribution method: Available to cable & satellite providers.

SHOWTIME SHOWCASE — See Showtime.

SHOWTIME TOO — See Showtime.

SHOWTIME WOMEN — See Showtime.

SI TV — See Nuvo TV.

SIMAYE AZADI TV — See GlobeCast WorldTV.
Web Site: http://www.iranntv.com
Programming: Persian cultural, social, political & general entertainment, including Arabic, English & Kurdish news reports.
Distribution method: Available to satellite providers.

SINO TV
Multicultural Radio Broadcasting Inc
449 Broadway
New York, NY 10013
Phone: 212-966-1059
Fax: 212-966-9580
E-mail: bettyy@mrbi.net
Web Site: http://www.mrbi.net/sinotv.htm
Operating hours/week: 168.
Programming: Chinese-language news, sports & entertainment.
Distribution method: Available to cable systems.

SIVOO
239 Chestnut St
2nd Fl
Philadelphia, PA 19106
E-mail: help@sivoo.com
Web Site: http://www.sivoo.com
Burhan Fatah, Founder, President & Chief Executive Officer
Christopher Myers, Chief Operating Officer
Philip Ives, Chief Technology Officer
Daniel S. Leon, Vice President, International Programming & Business Development
Jeremy LaCivita, Director, Interactive Development
Eric Pancoast, Director, Core System Development
William D. Fenstermaker, Director, Technology Operations
Type of service: IPTV, video on demand.
Programming: Multicultural entertainment in Spanish, Chinese & Hindi languages. Features movies, TV series & music.
Scrambled signal: Yes.

6 NEWS
609 New Hampshire
PO Box 888
Lawrence, KS 66044
Phone: 785-832-6397
E-mail: news@6newslawrence.com
Web Site: http://www.6newslawrence.com
Type of service: Basic.
Distribution method: Cable.
Ownership: The World Company.

SIX NEWS NOW — See SNN 6.

THE SKI CHANNEL
881 Alma Real Dr
Terrace 8
Pacific Palisades, CA 90272
Phone: 310-230-2050
E-mail: info@theskichannel.com
Web Site: http://www.theskichannel.com
Steve Bellamy, President & Chief Executive Officer
Type of service: Video on demand.
Programming: Focused on year-round mountain sports including skiing, snowboarding, hiking, biking, climbing, caving, camping & kayaking.
Began: December 25, 2008.
Means of Support: Ad-supported.
Total subscribers: 43,000,000.

SKY LINK TV — See KyLinTV.
500 W Montebello Blvd
Rosemead, CA 91770
Phone: 323-888-0028
Fax: 323-888-0029
Web Site: http://www.skylinktv.us
Operating areas: Available nationwide.
Programming: Offers Mandarin language programming through KyLinTV.
Distribution method: Available to home dish audiences, cable systems and internet.
Scrambled signal: Yes.

SKY LINK VOD THEATER — See KyLinTV.

SLEUTH
900 Sylvan Ave
One CNBC Plz
Englewood Cliffs, NJ 07632
Phone: 201-735-3604
Web Site: http://www.sleuthchannel.com
Ryan Sharkey, Senior Vice President, Program Acquisitions & Administration
Type of service: Digital basic.
Satellites: Galaxy 1R, transponder 24.
Operating hours/week: 168.
Operating areas: New York, Texas, Hawaii, Wisconsin & North Carolina.
Programming: Crime, mystery and suspense oriented series, movies & original programming.
Began: January 1, 2006.
Total subscribers: 24,000,000.
Distribution method: Available to cable & satellite programmers.
Scrambled signal: Yes.
Ownership: NBCUniversal LLC.

SLEUTH ON DEMAND — See Sleuth.
Began: June 21, 2007.

SMART LIVING TELEVISION
375 Water St
Ste 375
Vancouver, BC V6B 5C6
Canada
E-mail: pwsoper@smartliving.com
Web Site: http://www.smartlivingmedia.com
Programming: Shows that promote sustainable living from multiple perspectives, including agricultural, financial, ecological, personal & community orientation. Focus on global sustainability interests, trends, conservation, environment, lifestyle choices & public policy.

SMILE OF A CHILD
TBN Networks
2442 Michelle Dr
Tustin, CA 92780
Phones: 714-832-2950; 800-735-5542

Web Site: http://www.smileofachildtv.org
Paul F. Crouch, President & Chief Executive Officer
Rod Henke, Vice President, Broadcast Relations
Bob Higley, Vice President, Cable Sales & Marketing
Ben Miller, Vice President, Engineering
Brenda Rossman, Director, Programming
Type of service: Digital.
Satellites: Galaxy 14, transponder 1.
Operating hours/week: 168.
Operating areas: Available nationwide.
Programming: Offers commercial-free programming that emphasizes faith and values for kids from 2-12.
Began: December 24, 2005.
Total subscribers: 15,000,000.
Distribution method: Available to AT&T U-verse, cable & Verizon FiOS subscribers plus Sky Angel.
Scrambled signal: Yes.
Ownership: TBN Networks.

SMITHSONIAN CHANNEL
Showtime Networks
1633 Broadway
New York, NY 10019
Phone: 212-708-1600
Fax: 212-708-1212
E-mail: contact@smithsoniannetworks.com
Web Site: http://www.smithsonianchannel.com
Tom Hayden, Executive Vice President & General Manager
David Royle, Executive Vice President, Programming & Production
Jeanny Kim, Vice President, Media Services, Smithsonian Business Ventures
Operating hours/week: 168.
Programming: Showcases the Smithsonian's archives & library of history, culture, Americana, music, art & aviation.
Began: September 26, 2007.
Total subscribers: 22,000,000.
Distribution method: Available to cable, telco & satellite providers.
Ownership: Showtime Networks & The Smithsonian Institution.

SMITHSONIAN CHANNEL HD — See Smithsonian Channel.

SMITHSONIAN CHANNEL ON DEMAND — See Smithsonian Channel .

SNEAK PREVUE — See TV Guide Interactive Inc.

SNN 6
1741 Main St
Sarasota, FL 34236
Phone: 941-361-4600
Fax: 941-361-4699
E-mail: news@snn6.com
Web Site: http://www.heraldtribune.com
Lou Ferrara, General Manager
Dennis Newhausel, News Director
Programming: Local news for the Sarasota area.
Total subscribers: 150,000.
Ownership: Sarasota Herald Tribune.

SOAPNET
500 S Buena Vista St
Burbank, CA 91521
Phones: 818-569-7500; 818-569-7574
Web Site: http://www.soapnet.com
Brian Frons, President
Ben Pyne, President, Disney/ESPN Networks Affiliate Sales & Marketing
Heidi Lobel, Senior Vice President, Sales
Sherri York, Senior Vice President, Marketing
Mary Ellen DiPrisco, Vice President, Original Programming
Beth Johnson, Vice President, Digital Media
Jori Peterson, Vice President, Media Relations
Adam Rockmore, Vice President, Marketing
Type of service: Basic analog & digital.
Satellites: Galaxy VII, transponder 14.
Programming: Featuring vintage and recent ABC Network dramas, as well as prime-time dramas, Knots Landing, Falcon Crest and Sisters. Will cease operation in January 2012 and be replaced by Disney Junior, which launched as a program block on the Disney Channel February 14, 2011.
Began: January 24, 2000.
Total subscribers: 75,000,000.
Distribution method: Available to cable systems.
Scrambled signal: Yes.
Ownership: Disney/ABC Cable Networks.

SOCCER TELEVISION — See Telelatino Network.
Programming: Provides coverage of professional & amateur soccer matches, documentaries & news programs dedicated to the sport.

SOCIETY OF PORTUGUESE TELEVISION
c/o Kelly Broadcasting
476 Thomas Blvd
Orange, NJ 07050
Phone: 973-676-0767
Fax: 973-676-2709
Mike Kelly, Information Contact

Main Office:
LISBOA: Eurovideo, R. Viriato, 25 5 Esq., 1050 Lisboa, Portugal.
Type of service: Basic.
Satellites: Telstar 302, transponder 5-V.
Operating hours/week: 168.
Uplink: Orange, NJ.
Programming: Portuguese language shows.
Began: December 1, 1992.
Means of Support: Advertising.
Distribution method: Available to home dish audiences & cable systems.
Ownership: Portuguese Government.

SOL VIDEO ON DEMAND
363 7th Ave
22nd Floor
New York, NY 10001
Phone: 212-983-0219
Fax: 212-983-0524
Type of service: Digital.
Operating hours/week: 168.
Programming: Spanish language movies & animation from Spain & Latin America.
Began: September 1, 2005.
Total subscribers: 5,000,000.
Ownership: Schramm Sports & Entertainment.

SON BROADCASTING
5010 4th St NW
Albuquerque, NM 87107
Phone: 505-345-1991
E-mail: info@sonbroadcasting.cc
Web Site: http://www.kchf.com
Belarmino Gonzalez, Founder & President

SONY ENTERTAINMENT TELEVISION ASIA
550 Madison Ave
New York, NY 10022
Phones: 212-833-7684; 212-833-7834
Fax: 212-833-7862
E-mail: viewer_infoUSA@spe.sony.com

Web Site: http://www.setasia.tv
Type of service: Digital.
Operating hours/week: 168.
Operating areas: California.
Programming: Focused on South Asian dramas, movies, reality-shows, comedies, soaps, talk & game shows.
Began: August 8, 2007, International launch was 1995.
Distribution method: Available to cable systems.
Ownership: Sony Entertainment.

SONY MOVIE CHANNEL
10202 W Washington Blvd
Culver City, CA 90232-3195
Phone: 310-244-4000
Fax: 310-244-1336
Web Site: http://www.sonymoviechannel.com/
Andy Kaplan, President of Networks, Sony Pictures Television
Edward Zimmerman, Vice President, Media Production, Sony Pictures Television
Superna Kalle, General Manager
Type of service: Basic.
Operating hours/week: 168.
Operating areas: Available nationwide.
Programming: Offers uncut and uninterrupted theatrical releases in high definition and 3D.
Began: October 1, 2010.
Distribution method: Available to cable systems.
Ownership: Sony Corp. of America.

SORPRESA
6125 Airport Freeway
Fort Worth, TX 76117
Phone: 817-222-1234
Fax: 817-222-9809
Web Site: http://www.sorpresatv.com
Leonard L. Firestone, Chairman & Chief Executive Officer
Michael C. Fletcher, President
Christopher K. Firestone, Executive Vice President, Operations
Michael Weiden, Senior Vice President, Ad Sales
Maria Badillo, Vice President, Programming
Yolanda Jordana, Vice President, Ad Sales
Jon C. Dubin, Vice President, Ad Sales, West Coast
Type of service: Digital & video on demand.
Satellites: Galaxy 13, transponder 18.
Operating hours/week: 168.
Programming: Spanish language children's programming. Formerly Hispanic Television Network.
Began: December 1, 1999, U.S. launch March 2003.
Total subscribers: 1,600,000.
Distribution method: Available to cable systems.
Ownership: Juniper Content.

SOUNDTRACK CHANNEL
1335 4th St
Ste 400
Santa Monica, CA 90401
Phone: 310-899-1315
Fax: 310-587-3387
Web Site: http://www.soundtrackchannel.com
William Lee, Chief Executive Officer & Co-Founder
Jeff Wishengrad, Co-Founder
Mike Miller, Co-Founder
Denis Leverson, Chief Operating Officer
Glenn Kopelson, Chief Financial Officer
Heather Hull, Affiliate Relations Director, STC U.S.
Type of service: Digital.
Operating hours/week: 168.
Programming: Music videos from movie soundtracks & entertainment-focused programming.
Began: March 1, 2002.
Total subscribers: 6,000,000.
Distribution method: Available to cable, satellite & IPTV operators.

SOUTHEASTERN CHANNEL
Southeastern Louisiana University
SLU Box 12872
Hammond, LA 70402
Phone: 985-549-2418
E-mail: sechannel@selu.edu
Web Site: http://www2.selu.edu/thesoutheasternchannel/
Rick Settoon, General Manager
Steve Zaffuto, Operations Manager
Type of service: Basic.
Operating hours/week: 168.
Operating areas: Louisiana.
Programming: Educational & community programming.
Began: July 9, 2002.
Distribution method: Available to cable systems.

SPACE - THE IMAGINATION STATION
299 Queen St W
Toronto, ON M5V 2Z5
Canada
Phone: 416-591-5757
Fax: 416-591-8523
E-mail: space@spacecast.com
Mark Lewis, Information Contact
Programming: English language science fiction channel.
Began: October 17, 1997.

SPEED
1220 W W T Harris Blvd
Charlotte, NC 28262-8536
Phone: 704-501-5700
E-mail: thomas.tyrer@fox.com
Web Site: http://www.speedtv.com
Bob Thompson, President & Chief Executive Officer, Fox Cable Networks
Hunter Nickell, President
Patti Wheeler, Executive Vice President, Programming & Production
E. Roger Williams, Executive Vice President & Chief Operating Officer
Jack Bonanni, Senior Vice President, Advertising Sales
Lila Everett, Senior Vice President, Marketing
Nickolas Rhodes, Senior Vice President, Business Development
David Safran, Senior Vice President, Sales
John West, Senior Vice President, Ad Sales
Erik Arneson, Vice President, Media Relations
Paul Duong, Vice President, Scheduling & Research

Mike Gannon, Vice President, Advertising Sales
Shari Leventhal, Vice President, Marketing
Nancy MacDonald, Vice President, Marketing & Promotions
Francois McGillicuddy, Vice President, Finance
Bob Scanlon, Vice President, Production & Executive Producer
Cathy Scully, Vice President, Direct Response & Paid Programs
Len Spagnoletti, Vice President, Advertising Sales, Western Region
Helen Tocheff, Vice President, Research & Market Development
John Zabel, Vice President, International Sales & New Business
Mark Mitchell, Executive Director, Digital Media
Tom Livernois, Marketing & Advertising Director
Joe Tripp, Interactive Operations Director
David Harris, Media Relations Manager
Gregory Rondeau, Research Manager
Type of service: Expanded basic.
Satellites: Satcom C-4, transponder 11.
Operating hours/week: 168.
Programming: Automotive, aviation & marine information and entertainment.
Began: February 23, 1996, Formerly known as Speed Channel.
Means of Support: Advertising.
Total subscribers: 80,000,000.
Distribution method: Available to home dish audiences & cable systems.
Ownership: Fox/Liberty Sports, 33.3%; Cox Communications Inc., 33.3%; Comcast Corp., AT&T Broadband & Internet Services, Roger Werner & Daniels Programming, 33.3%.

SPEED HD — See Speed Channel.
Began: February 7, 2008.

SPEED ON DEMAND — See Speed Channel.
Web Site: http://www.speedondemand.com
Type of service: Broadband & video on demand.
Distribution method: Available to cable operators & online.

SPEED2
1220 W W T Harris Blvd
Charlotte, NC 28262-8536
Phone: 704-501-5700
Web Site: http://www.speed2.com
Hunter Nickell, President
Mike Biard, Executive Vice President, Fox Networks Affiliate Sales & Marketing
Kevin Annison, Vice President, Digital & Interactive Media
Type of service: Online.
Programming: Available only to Speed subscribers, the online service offers Formula 1 & 2 racing, plus special competitive events.
Began: July 22, 2010.
Means of Support: Advertising.

SPICE — See Fresh.

SPICE HD — See Fresh.

SPICE HOT — See Fresh.

SPICE LIVE — See Fresh.
Began: December 1, 2003.

SPICE PLATINUM — See Fresh.

SPICE 2 — See Shorteez.

SPICE ULTIMATE — See Fresh.

SPICE: XCESS
9242 Beverly Blvd
Beverly Hills, CA 90210
Phone: 310-246-4000
Fax: 310-246-4050
Type of service: Pay-per-view.
Programming: Adult entertainment. Formerly Hot Zone.
Distribution method: Available to cable systems & satellite providers.

SPIKE TV
1515 Broadway
40th Fl
New York, NY 10036
Phone: 212-258-6000
Fax: 212-846-1923
Web Site: http://www.spiketv.com
Doug Herzog, President, MTVN Entertainment Group
Kevin Kay, President
John Cucci, Chief Operating Officer
David Hall, President, Country Music Television & Sr. V.P., Cable Networks, Opryland USA
Kevin Hale, General Manager, Spike TV & Vice President, Opryland USA
Sharon Levy, Executive Vice President, Original Series & Animation
Niels Schuurman, Executive Vice President, Brand Marketing & Creative
Tim Duffy, Senior Vice President, Original Programming
John Griffin, Senior Vice President, Programming
David Lawenda, Senior Vice President, Ad Sales
Casey Patterson, Senior Vice President, Talent Development & Event Production
Dario Spina, Senior Vice President, Marketing & Promotions
Caleb Weinstein, Senior Vice President, Strategy & Business Development, Entertainment Group
Barbara Zaneri, Senior Vice President, Program Planning & Acquisitions
Todd Ames, Vice President, Consumer Marketing
Michael Berkman, Vice President, Creative Director
Kelleigh Dulany, Vice President, Public Responsibility
Therese Gamba, Vice President, Marketing
Brian Hughes, Vice President, Programming
Sharon Light, Vice President, Ad Sales Research
Chris Martello, Vice President, Sports & Specials
Iness Moskowitz, Vice President, Operations
Tina Potter, Vice President, Brand Central Creative Group
Chris Rantamaki, Vice President, Original Series
Bobby Amirshahi, Corporate Communications Director
Marck Kuchan, Motorsports Director
Nancy Neil, Public Relations Director
Jesse R. Ragan, Research & Scheduling Director
Barrie Hollins, Primetime Programming Manager

Sales, Mktg. & Affiliate Relations Office:
STAMFORD: Group W Satellite Communications, 250 Harbor Dr, Stamford, CT 06904. Phone: 203-965-6000. Fax: 203-965-6315.
Type of service: Basic.
Satellites: Galaxy V, transponder 2.
Operating hours/week: 168.
Programming: Popular, action-oriented movies, series, reality & scripted original shows targeted to men.
Began: March 7, 1983.
Means of Support: Advertising & subscriber fees.
Total subscribers: 100,800,000.
Scrambled signal: Yes.
Ownership: Viacom Inc.

SPIKE TV HD — See Spike TV.

SPIRIT TELEVISION NETWORK
PO Box 1887
Westerville, OH 43086
Phone: 877-474-8700
Fax: 614-839-1329
E-mail: spirit@spirit-television.com
Web Site: http://www.spirit-television.com
Operating hours/week: 168.
Programming: Music videos.
Distribution method: Available to Sky Angel subscribers & online.

SPORTSOUTH
1175 Peachtree St NE
100 Colony Square, Ste 200
Atlanta, GA 30361
Phone: 404-230-7300
Fax: 404-230-7399
Web Site: http://www.turnersouth.com
Jeff Genthner, Senior Vice President & General Manager
Tobie Pate, Senior Vice President, Creative Director
Cheryle Harrison, Vice President, Sales Operations
Sophia Karteris, Vice President, Programming
Steven Raab, Vice President, Marketing
Misty Skedgell, Vice President, Public Relations
Pat Smith, Vice President & Creative Director
Tonya Heath, Information Contact
Type of service: Basic.
Operating hours/week: 168.
Operating areas: Alabama, Georgia, Mississippi, South Carolina, Tennessee and portions of North Carolina.
Uplink: Atlanta, GA.
Programming: Sports & events in the South. Team coverage includes Atlanta, Cincinnati, St. Louis & the Big South & Southern college conferences.
Began: October 1, 1999, as Turner South; relaunched as SportSouth October 13, 2006.
Total subscribers: 9,000,000.
Distribution method: Available to cable systems.
Ownership: Fox Cable Networks.

SPORTING CHANNEL
7172 Hawthorn Ave
Ste 210
Los Angeles, CA 90046
Phone: 213-851-6375
Fax: 213-851-7134
Robert Crawford, Chief Executive Officer
Type of service: Basic & Pay-per-view.
Satellites: Columbia Communications/TDRSS G-7, transponder 10.
Operating hours/week: 4.
Uplink: Denver, CO.
Programming: International sports, including soccer, rugby, baseball, cricket & horse racing.
Began: October 22, 1994.
Means of Support: Advertising & subscribers.
Total subscribers: 6,000,000.
Distribution method: Available to home dish audiences & cable systems.
Equipment: VideoCipher II Plus.

SPORTING NEWS RADIO
1935 Techny Rd
Ste 18
Northbrook, IL 60002
Phone: 847-509-1661
Fax: 847-509-1677
E-mail: webmaster@sportingnews.com
Web Site: http://www.sportingnewsradio.com
Chris Brennan, Chairman, President & Chief Executive Officer
Christopher Canning, Vice President & General Counsel
Beth Roncke, Marketing Manager
Operating hours/week: 168.
Programming: 24-hour sports talk radio network.
Began: January 1, 1994.
Means of Support: Advertising.

SPORTSCHOICE
Oceanic Time Warner
PO Box 30050
Honolulu, HI 96820-0050
Phone: 808-625-2100
Fax: 808-625-5888
Web Site: http://www.oceanic.com
Type of service: Digital.
Operating areas: Hawaii.
Programming: Multiple streams of sports oriented video on a single, interactive tv screen.
Began: November 1, 2006.
Distribution method: Oceanic Time Warner cable system.
Scrambled signal: Yes.

SPORTS GAMING PLAYERS NETWORK — See VSEN-TV.

SPORTS NETWORK
9 Channel Nine Ct
Scarborough, ON M1S 4B5
Canada
Phone: 416-332-5000
Fax: 416-332-7656
E-mail: tluccisano@tsn.ca
Web Site: http://www.tsn.ca
Keith Pelley, President
Jim Newell, Vice President, Finance & Chief Financial Officer
J. Thompson, Vice President & General Manager
Rick Brace, Vice President, Programming
Jake Scudamore, Vice President, Marketing
K. Murphy, Technical Operations Director
Satellites: Anik E-1, transponder 1-B.
Operating hours/week: 168.
Programming: Features professional, college & amateur sports.
Began: September 1, 1984.
Means of Support: Subscriber fees & advertising.
Total subscribers: 7,200,000.
Distribution method: Available to home dish audiences.
Ownership: John Labatt Ltd.

SPORTS PPV
4100 E Dry Creek Rd
Littleton, CO 80122
Phone: 303-486-3938
Fax: 303-486-3951
E-mail: rachel.ford@espn3.com
Web Site: http://www.hits.com
Jon Radloff, New Product Marketing Director
Type of service: PPV/Digital.
Operating hours/week: 24.
Programming: PPV sports & sports barker channel. Part of headend HITS package.
Began: September 4, 1999.
Ownership: ESPN Inc.

SPORTSTIME OHIO
Fastball Sports Productions
1333 Lakeside Avenue
Cleveland, OH 44114
Phone: 216-344-7400
Web Site: http://www.sportstimeohio.com/
Jim Liberatore, President, Fastball Productions
Operating hours/week: 35.
Programming: Featuring Cleveland Indians' games & all Northern Ohio sports. Includes Indians' home games in HD.
Began: March 12, 2006.
Total subscribers: 1,000,000.
Distribution method: Available to cable & satellite providers.
Scrambled signal: Yes.
Ownership: Cleveland Indians.

SPORTSKOOL
100 Cathedral St
Ste 9
Annapolis, MD 21401
Phone: 410-280-8528
Web Site: http://www.sportskool.com
Andrew Walworth, President
John Sorensen, Senior Producer
Type of service: Video on demand.
Programming: The first television network dedicated to delivering in-depth sports expert instruction and coaching for a wide range of sports and athletic activities.
Began: January 1, 2004.
Total subscribers: 25,000,000.
Distribution method: Available to cable systems.
Scrambled signal: Yes.
Ownership: Grace Creek Media.

THE SPORTSMAN CHANNEL
2855 S James Dr
Ste 101
New Berlin, WI 53151
Phones: 262-432-9100; 800-971-2330
Fax: 262-432-9101
E-mail: mscheuermann@thesportsmanchannel.com
Web Site: http://www.thesportsmanchannel.com
Gavin Harvey, Chief Executive Officer
Todd D. Hansen, Chief Operating Officer
Mary Jeanne Cavanagh, Executive Vice President, Advertising Sales
Lisa Delligatti, Senior Vice President, Affiliate Sales
Mark H. Kang, Senior Vice President, Affiliate Relations
Michael Magnotta, Senior Vice President/Creative Director
Ben Lines, Vice President, Marketing
Chris Ozminkowski, Vice President, Affiliate Relations
Michelle Scheuermann, Director, Communications
Lisa Swan, Affiliate Relations Manager, Eastern Region
Sandi Castro, Affiliate Relations Director
Maura Field, Affiliate Planning & Strategy Director
Jim Seeley, Programming Director
Adam King, Affiliate Marketing Manager, Western Region
Alyse Ramer, Affiliate Relations Manager, Southeast Region
Kimberly Hawkins, Senior Coordinator, Affiliate Relations
Type of service: Basic, video on demand & broadband.
Operating hours/week: 168.
Uplink: Chandler, AZ.
Programming: Dedicated exclusively to hunting & fishing.
Began: April 7, 2003.
Total subscribers: 27,000,000.
Ownership: InterMedia Outdoor Holdings, LLC.

THE SPORTSMAN CHANNEL HD —
See The Sportsman Channel.
Began: January 25, 2010.

SPORTSNET NEW YORK
75 Rockefeller Plz
29th Fl
New York, NY 10019
Phone: 212-485-4800
Fax: 212-485-4802
Web Site: http://www.sny.tv
Steve Raab, President
Curt Gowdy, Jr., Senior Vice President, Production & Executive Producer
Scott Weinfeld, Senior Vice President, Finance & Administration
Gary Morgenstern, Senior Vice President, Programming
Andrew Fegyveresi, Vice President, Communications
Marie DeParis, Vice President, Marketing & Business Development
Brad Como, Vice President, News Programming
Brian Erdlen, Chief Revenue Officer
Scott Wilpon, Senior Director, Business Development
Fred Harner, General Manager, Digital Media
Operating hours/week: 168.
Operating areas: New York, New Jersey, Connecticut & Pennsylvania.
Began: March 16, 2006.
Total subscribers: 12,000,000.
Distribution method: Cable, satellite & telecom.
Scrambled signal: Yes.
Ownership: Sterling Entertainment, Time Warner & NBCUniversal LLC (minority interest).

SPORTS VIEW PLUS
Charter Communications
12405 Powerscourt Dr
St. Louis, MO 63131
Phone: 314-965-0555
Web Site: http://http://www.charter.com
Type of service: Digital.
Operating hours/week: 168.
Programming: Combines coverage of baseball, racing, hockey, football, basketball & other sports from cable channels and websites.
Began: March 2, 2009.
Distribution method: Available to Charter systems.

SPORTSVUE
7140 S Lewis Ave
Tulsa, OK 74136
Phone: 800-447-7388
Michael Hanafee, Chief Operating Officer
Dave Sweeney, Senior Vice President
Satellites: Galaxy I, transponder 3.
Operating hours/week: 168.
Programming: Sports information including scores, news & schedules; point spreads from Las Vegas & injury reports.
Began: October 1, 1984.
Means of Support: System fee.
Total subscribers: 1,100,000.
Distribution method: Available to home dish audiences & cable systems.
Ownership: Prevue Network Inc.

STAND UP COMEDY TELEVISION —
No longer planned.

STAR CHINESE CHANNEL — See KyLinTV.
Programming: Provides a wide range of Mandarin-language general entertainment programs including talk shows, game shows, contemporary and costume dramas, lifestyle and variety shows.

STAR INDIA GOLD — See Star India Plus.

STAR INDIA NEWS — See Star India Plus.

STAR INDIA PLUS
8/F 1 Harbourfront
18 Tak Fung St
Hunghom
Hong Kong
Phone: 852-2621-8728
Fax: 852-2621-8620
Web Site: http://www.startv.com
Type of service: Digital.
Operating areas: Massachusetts, Illinois, New York, Pennsylvania & the District of Columbia.
Programming: General entertainment.
Distribution method: Available to cable systems.
Scrambled signal: Yes.

STAR ONE — See Star India Plus.

STARFISH TELEVISION NETWORK
6952 S High Tech Dr
Ste C
Salt Lake City, UT 84047-3772
Phones: 801-567-3180; 800-624-1844
Web Site: http://www.starfishnetwork.org
Joseph G Lake, Chief Executive Officer
John L Marsh, Chief Operating Officer & Founder
Machelle Lake, Vice President, Programming
Andy Carlton, Technical Producer & Chief Engineer
Brenda Marsh, Human Resources & Executive Assistant
Londa Anderson, Program Director
Type of service: Basic.
Operating hours/week: 168.
Programming: Provides airtime to non-profit organizations to allow them to promote their objectives.
Began: April 18, 2007.
Distribution method: Available to cable & satellite providers.

STARSIGHT
39650 Liberty St
3rd Floor
Fremont, CA 94538
Phone: 510-657-9900
Fax: 510-657-5022
Web Site: http://www.starsight.com/
Michael W. Faber, Chairman & Chief Executive Officer
John B. Burns, III, President, StarSight Product Group
Martin W. Henkel, Executive Vice President & Chief Financial Officer
John H. Roop, Senior Vice President, Technology & Development
Jim Miles, Vice President & General Manager, GTE
Gerard Kunkel, Vice President, Product Development
Lisa A. Laury, Corporate Communications Director
Operating areas: East Bay Area, CA & Tampa, FL.
Programming: Interactive on-screen program guide service.
Began: November 1, 1994.
Ownership: StarSight Telecast Inc.

START OVER
1 Time Warner Center
New York, NY 10019-8016
Phone: 212-484-8000
Web Site: http://www.timewarnercable.com/nynj
Type of service: Video on demand.
Programming: Allows subscribers to start at the beginning of a program that is already in progress without an in-home recording device or preplanning.
Began: November 1, 2005.
Scrambled signal: Yes.
Ownership: Time Warner Inc.

STAR!
299 Queen St W
Toronto, ON M5V 2Z5
Canada
Phone: 416-591-5757
Fax: 416-591-8523
E-mail: publicity@star-tv.com
Web Site: http://www.star-tv.com
James Murdoch, Chairman & Chief Executive Officer
Jamie Davis, Senior Vice President, Programming
Mark Lewis, Information Contact
Type of service: Basic and digital basic.
Programming: Canada's national entertainment channel.

STARZ
8900 Liberty Cir
Englewood, CO 80112
Phone: 720-852-7700
Fax: 720-852-7710
E-mail: eric.becker@starz.com
Web Site: http://www.starz.com
Robert B. Clausen, Chairman
Chris Albrecht, President & Chief Executive Officer
Carmi Zlotnick, Managing Director, Starz Media
Steve Beabout, Executive Vice President, General Counsel & Secretary
Glenn Curtis, Executive Vice President & Chief Financial Officer
Gene George, Executive Vice President, Worldwide Distribution
Bob Greene, Executive Vice President, Advanced Services
Edward Huguez, Executive Vice President, Affiliate Sales & Marketing
Nancy McGee, Executive Vice President, Marketing
John Penney, Executive Vice President, Strategy & Business Development

Stephan Shelanski, Executive Vice President, Programming
Michael Thornton, Executive Vice President, Business & Legal Affairs-Programming, Digital & Worldwide Distribution
Sheryl Anderson, Senior Vice President, Human Resources & Administration
Theano Apostolou, Senior Vice President, Corporate Communications
Kelly Bumann, Senior Vice President, Consumer Marketing
Christine Carrier, Senior Vice President, Affiliate Sales
Michelle Parker, Senior Vice President, Business & Legal Affairs
Jonathan Shair, Senior Vice President, Network Operations
Dana Booton, General Manager, Film Roman
Debbie Alther, Vice President, Program & Promotion Planning & Scheduling
Bill Bergmann, Vice President, Finance, Starz Entertainment
Chelsye J. Burrows, Vice President, Programming Publicity
Alecia Dixon, Vice President, Domestic TV Sales
Randall McCurdy, Vice President, Affiliate Sales
Jim Urick, Vice President, Finance, Starz Media
Eric Becker, Executive Director, Corporate Communications
Peter Demas, Executive Director, Key Initiatives
Rachel Falleroni, Executive Director, Program & Promotion Planning & Scheduling
Neal Massey, Executive Director, Marketing, Sales & Corporate Research
Steve Waldo Belgard, Director, Entertainment & Programming Publicity
Type of service: Pay.
Satellites: Galaxy 1-R, transponder 13 (east & west); G1 (east) (Starz! Family), transponder 13 (east) & 5 (west); G1 (Starz! Cinema), transponder 13; Satcom C-4, transponder 5.
Operating hours/week: 168 (Starz! Cinema & Family).
Programming: A first run premium movie channel launched nationwide on February 1, 1994 that offers more first run movies playing in prime time than any other movie channel. Features exclusive first-run releases plus original programming, including STARZ! Pictures world premiere movies.
Began: February 1, 1994, . STARZ!; March 15, 1996, STARZ!2 ; May 1, 1999, STARZ! Cinema & STARZ! Family.
Means of Support: Subscriber fees.
Total subscribers: 18,800,000 (Number includes all Starz channels.).
Distribution method: Available to home dish audiences & cable systems.
Scrambled signal: Yes. Equipment: Digital/DigiCipher II.
Ownership: Liberty Media Corp. (Starz Entertainment).

STARZ CINEMA — See Starz.

STARZ CINEMA HD — See Starz.
Began: June 23, 2010.

STARZ COMEDY — See Starz.

STARZ COMEDY HD — See Starz.
Began: September 1, 2007.

STARZ EDGE — See Starz.

STARZ EDGE HD — See Starz.
Began: September 1, 2007.

STARZ HDTV — See Starz.

STARZ IN BLACK — See Starz.

STARZ IN BLACK HD — See Starz.
Began: June 23, 2010.

STARZ INDIEPLEX — See Starz.

STARZ INDIEPLEX HD — See Starz.
Began: February 11, 2010, Currently available only on Dish Network.

STARZ KIDS & FAMILY — See Starz.

STARZ KIDS & FAMILY HD — See Starz.
Began: September 1, 2007.

STARZ ON DEMAND — See Starz.
Type of service: Video on demand.
Programming: Movies, shorts, behind-the-scenes, interviews & director's cuts.
Total subscribers: 3,700,000.
Distribution method: Available to cable & satellite providers.

STARZ PLAY — See Starz.

STARZ RETROPLEX — See Starz.

STARZ RETROPLEX HD — See Starz.
Began: February 11, 2010, Currently available only on Dish Network.

STARZ TICKET — See Starz.

STUDENT FILM NETWORK

1440 Veteran Ave
Ste 322
Los Angeles, CA 90024
Phone: 310-477-0381
E-mail: stdntflmnt@aol.com
Jonathan Traynham, Executive Producer

Branch Office:
WOODLAND HILLS: Network One, 21111 Erwin St., Woodland Hills, CA 91367. Phone: 818-704-5154.
Type of service: Basic.
Satellites: Satcom C-1, transponder 11.
Operating hours/week: 2.
Uplink: Woodland Hills.
Programming: Short films, VIP interviews & film festival coverage.
Means of Support: Advertising.
Total subscribers: 9,796,625 (Figure includes home dish subscribers).
Distribution method: Available to home dish audiences & cable systems.

STUFF TV — See i-Shop.

STYLE NETWORK

5750 Wilshire Blvd
Los Angeles, CA 90036-3709
Phone: 323-954-2400
Fax: 323-954-2660
E-mail: amelia.stewart@nbcuni.com
Web Site: http://www.mystyle.com
Lauren Zalaznick, Chairman, NBC Universal Entertainment & Digital Networks & Integrated Media
Frances Berwick, President, Style Media
Salaam Coleman Smith, President, Style
Suzanne Kolb, President, Marketing News & Online, E! & Style
Kevin MacLellan, President, International Media Group & Entertainment Productions
Megan Canavan, Chief Financial Officer
Steve Blue, Executive Vice President, Productions & Operations
Duccio Donati, Executive Vice President, International
Sheila Johnson, Executive Vice President, Business & Legal Affairs & General Counsel
Cyndi McClellan, Executive Vice President, Program Strategy & Research
John Najarian, Executive Vice President, Digital Media & Business Development
Katie Ackerman Buchanan, Senior Vice President, Programming & Acquisitions
Bear Fisher, Senior Vice President & Creative Director, E! & Style
Sarah Goldstein, Senior Vice President, Media Relations & Corporate Communications
Eric Gray, Senior Vice President, Finance
Michael Haggerty, Senior Vice President, Research
Sarah Weidmann, Senior Vice President, Series Development & Production
Merah Chung, Vice President, Series Development & Production
Renee Simon, Vice President, Current Programming
Melissa Stone, Vice President, Marketing & Advertising
Type of service: Linear TV, VOD, HD, mobile.
Satellites: AMC10, transponder C6; AMC11, transponder C8.
Operating hours/week: 168.
Programming: The Style Network is the destination for women 18-49 with a passion for the best in relatable, inspiring and transformational lifestyle programming. Style currently counts 65 million cable and satellite subscribers and is one of the fastest growing women's networks in the U.S. Mystyle.com keeps women up-to-date on all of the latest fashion and beauty news on the web. Style's popular series include Ruby, Giuliana & Bill, Clean House, Jerseylicious, Kimora: Life in the Fab Lane, How Do I Look?, The Dish, and Whose Wedding Is It Anyway? The Style Network is a network of NBCUniversal Cable Entertainment, a division of NBCUniversal, one of the world's leading media & entertainment companies in the development, production, and marketing of entertainment, news, and information to a global audience.
Began: October 1, 1998.
Means of Support: Advertising.
Total subscribers: 65,000,000.
Distribution method: Available to cable & satellite providers.
Scrambled signal: Yes. Equipment: Available digitally.
Ownership: NBCUniversal LLC.

SUCCESS CHANNEL — No longer planned.

SUDANTV — See GlobeCast WorldTV.
Web Site: http://www.sudantv.tv

SUDDENLINK2GO

12444 Powerscourt Dr
St Louis, MO 63131
Phones: 314-965-2020; 314-315-9346
Web Site: http://www.suddenlink.com
Jerry Dow, Chief Marketing & Sales Officer
Type of service: Online video service.
Operating hours/week: 168.
Operating areas: Available nationwide.
Programming: Features tens of thousands of full-length TV episodes and shorter video clips, plus more than 1,300 movies.
Began: June 8, 2011.
Distribution method: Available to Suddenlink subscribers.
Scrambled signal: Yes.
Ownership: Cequel Communications LLC.

SUNSPORTS TV

1000 Legion Place
Ste 1600
Orlando, FL 32801-1060
Phone: 407-648-1150
Fax: 407-245-2571
Web Site: http://www.sunsportstv.com
Steve Liverani, Vice President & General Manager
Jerry Carstens, Finance Director
Amy Pempel, Media Relations Director
Tim Ivy, Programming Director
Ken Lehner, Marketing Director
Paul Kennedy, Talent & Sports Director
Neil Davis, General Sales Manager

Branch Offices:
SOUTH FLORIDA: 1550 Sawgrass Corporate Pkwy, Ste 350, Sunrise, FL 33323. Phone: 954-845-9994. Fax: 954-845-0923.

TAMPA: 3001 N Rocky Point Dr E, Ste 236, Tampa, FL 33607. Phone: 813-286-6185. Fax: 813-286-6185.
Type of service: Basic Cable & Satellite.
Sales representative: Fox Sports Sales.
Operating hours/week: 168.
Operating areas: Florida.
Programming: Professional to amateur sports programming focused on local & regional teams & events. Also offers original series targeting Florida sports fans.
Began: March 4, 1988, as Sunshine Network.
Means of Support: Subscriber fees & advertising.
Total subscribers: 6,200,000.
Distribution method: Cable & Satellite.
Scrambled signal: Yes.
Ownership: Fox Channels Group.

SUN-TV — See KyLinTV.
Web Site: http://www.sun-tv.co.jp
Programming: Japanese broadcasting service available on KyLinTV.

SUNDANCE CHANNEL

1633 Broadway
8th Fl
New York, NY 10019
Phone: 917-542-6390
Fax: 212-708-8014
E-mail: katie.lanegran@sundancechannel.com
Web Site: http://www.sundancechannel.com
Josh Sapan, President & Chief Executive Officer, AMC Networks Inc.
Evan Shapiro, President
Sarah Barnett, Executive Vice President & General Manager
Kirk Iwanowski, Executive Vice President, Marketing, Branded Entertainment & Sponsorship
Alan Klein, Executive Vice President, Partnerships & Operations
Christopher Barry, Senior Vice President, Digital Media & Business Strategy
Vanessa Benfield, Senior Vice President, Partnership Sales & Integrated Solutions
Stuart Benson, Senior Vice President & Chief Financial Officer
Timothy Boell, Senior Vice President, Affiliate Sales
Sarah Eaton, Senior Vice President, Public Relations
Michael Klein, Senior Vice President, Original Programming & Development
Shari Weisenberg, Senior Vice President, Marketing
Marco Bresaz, Vice President, Original Programming & Development

J C Cancedda, Vice President, Brand Strategy & Creative
Ilene Danuff, Vice President, Branded Content & Integrated Solutions
Lisa Ellenbogen, Vice President, Consumer Marketing
Kimberly Gabelmann, Vice President, Branded Entertainment & Sponsorship
Andy Hunn, Vice President, Affiliate Sales
Georgia Juvelis, Vice President, Corporate Communications, Rainbow Media Holdings
Jeff Kunken, Vice President, Digital Media & Creative Development
Michael Lehrer, Vice President, Strategic Marketing
Karrin Smoley, Vice President, Affiliate Sales
Tony Song, Vice President, Sales & Partnerships, East Coast
Beth Stein, Vice President, Marketing
Christian Vesper, Vice President, Acquisitions, Program Planning & Scheduling
Lele Engler, Director, Marketing & Media
Type of service: Pay.
Satellites: Satcom C-3, transponder 24 (east); Galaxy 9, transponder 14 (west); HITS, transponder Pod 8.
Operating hours/week: 168.
Programming: Independent features, foreign films, documentaries, shorts, animation & experimental films without commercials.
Began: February 29, 1996.
Means of Support: Subscriber fees.
Total subscribers: 26,000,000.
Distribution method: Available to home dish audiences & cable systems.
Scrambled signal: Yes.
Ownership: AMC Networks Inc. Formerly Rainbow Media Holdings LLC owned by Cablevision Systems Corp., it became a publicly held company under the new name June 30, 2011.

SUNDANCE CHANNEL HD — See Sundance Channel.
Began: April 14, 2010.

SUNDANCE SELECT — See Sundance Channel.
Type of service: Video on demand.
Began: January 1, 2009.

SUPER CHANNEL
5324 Calgary Trail
Ste 200
Edmonton, AB T6H 4J8
Phone: 780-430-2800
Fax: 780.437.8188
E-mail: info@superchannel.ca
Web Site: http://www.superchannel.ca
Type of service: Pay,Video on Demand.
Operating hours/week: 168.
Programming: Comprised of six channels, including 2 in HD. Featuring movies, series, documentaries, concerts, Live Showtime Boxing & Strikeforce MMA.
Began: November 2, 2007.
Distribution method: Available to cable & satellite systems.
Scrambled signal: Yes.
Ownership: Allarco Entertainment 2008 Inc.

SUPERCANAL CARIBE
Santo Domingo
Dominican Republic
Phone: 809-531-3333
Web Site: http://www.supercanal.com
Satellites: AMC, transponder 3.
Operating areas: ME, NH, MA, CT, NY, NJ, FL, PR.
Programming: Spanish-language programming.

SUPERCHANNEL — See Movie Central.

SUPERSTATION WGN — See WGN America.

SUR MEX — See Sur Network.

SUR NETWORK
601 Brickell Key Dr
Ste 100
Miami, FL 33131
Phones: 305-530-3561; 786-236-2207
Fax: 305-373-7811
E-mail: jorge@condista.com
Web Site: http://www.canalsur.com
Arturo Delgado, Chief Executive Officer
Jose Garcia Conde, Chief Financial Officer
Rolando A. Figueroa, Vice President, Marketing
Rafael Manrique, Affiliate Relations

Branch Offices:
BOSTON: 911 Massachusetts Ave, Boston, MA 02118.

FALLS CHURCH: 150 S Washington St, Ste 401, Falls Church, VA 22046.

ST. PETERSBURG: 9455 Koger Blvd, Ste 113, St. Petersburg, FL 33702.
Type of service: Basic.
Satellites: Intelsat 705, transponder 5.
Operating hours/week: 168.
Uplink: Lima, Peru.
Programming: Live newscasts, soccer games & family entertainment from Latin America.
Began: January 1, 1993.
Means of Support: Advertising.
Total subscribers: 1,000,000.
Distribution method: Available to cable systems.
Ownership: Sur Corp.

SUR PERU — See Sur Network.

SWRV
328 W 34th St
New York, NY 10001
Phones: 215-784-5840; 646-458-3357
Fax: 215-784-5869
Web Site: http://www.swrv.tv
Dave Del Beccaro, President & Chief Executive Officer
Type of service: Digital.
Operating hours/week: 168.
Operating areas: Available nationwide.
Programming: Interactive music video network. Each show offers a unique way for viewers to impact what music videos will play next by voting, rating, or commenting via text message or online at swrv.tv.
Began: February 10, 2010.
Distribution method: Available to cable FiOS & U-verse subscribers.
Scrambled signal: Yes.
Ownership: Music Choice.

SYFY
c/o USA Networks
1230 Avenue of the Americas
New York, NY 10020
Phone: 212-413-5236
Fax: 212-413-6515
E-mail: fschwartzfarb@usacable.net
Web Site: http://www.syfy.com
Rod Perth, President, USA Networks Entertainment
Stephen Chao, President, USA Cable
Dave Howe, President, Syfy
Mark Stern, President, Original Programming

Stephen Brenner, Executive Vice President, Business Affairs & General Counsel, USA Networks
Steve Mandala, Executive Vice President, Cable Ad Sales, NBCU
Rafael Pastor, Executive Vice President & Managing Director, USA Networks International
John Silvestri, Executive Vice President, Advertising Sales, USA Networks
Adam Stotsky, Executive Vice President, Global Brand Strategy & Market Development
Thomas P. Vitale, Executive Vice President, Programming & Original Movies
Ted A'Zary, Senior Vice President, Research
Andrew Besch, Senior Vice President, Marketing, USA Networks
Blake Callaway, Senior Vice President, Marketing, Brand & Strategic
Michael Engleman, Senior Vice President, Marketing, Global Brand Strategy & Creative
Craig Engler, Senior Vice President, Syfy Digital
Lucia Gervino, Senior Vice President, Production
Douglas Holloway, Senior Vice President, Affiliate Relations, USA Networks
Tim Krubsack, Senior Vice President, Alternative Programming
Mark Miller, Senior Vice President, Ad Sales
Andrew Plotkin, Senior Vice President, Original Programming
Erik Storey, Senior Vice President, Programming
Douglas Hamilton, Chief Financial Officer & Vice President, Administration, USA Networks
John Doherty, Vice President, Eastern Region Sales
Erika Kennair, Vice President, Original Programming & Development
Susan Lape, Vice President, Primary Research
Sara Morgan Moscowitz, Vice President, Strategic Marketing
Karen O'Hara, Vice President, Original Movies
Tom Olson, Vice President & National Sales Manager
Dana Ortiz, Vice President, Brand Marketing
Chris Sanagustin, Vice President, Development
Scott Silverstein, Vice President & General Sales Manager
Kat Stein, Vice President, Media Relations & Corporate Communications
Scott Vila, Vice President, Current Scripted Programming
Shara Zoll, Vice President, Operations, Syfy.com

Regional Offices:
CENTRAL: 401 N Michigan Ave, Ste 2550, Chicago, IL 60511. Phone: 312-644-5413.

WESTERN: 2049 Century Park E, Los Angeles, CA 90067. Phone: 310-201-2300.

ADVERTISING SALES: 2000 Town Center, Ste 2460, Southfield, MI 40875. Phone: 313-353-1200.
Satellites: Galaxy V, transponder 4.
Operating hours/week: 168.
Programming: Science-fiction/fact, horror & fantasy.
Began: September 24, 1992.
Total subscribers: 95,000,000.
Distribution method: Available to home dish audiences & cable systems.
Scrambled signal: Yes.
Ownership: NBCUniversal LLC.

SYFY HD — See Syfy.

SYRIANTV — See GlobeCast WorldTV.
Phone: 963-01-1372-0700
E-mail: info@syriatel.com.sy
Web Site: http://www.moi.gov.sy/en/
Operating hours/week: 168.
Programming: Arabic-language news, family entertainment, sporting events, comedy shows, cultural, economic, music & social events.

THE SYZYGY NETWORK
593 Wrens Path
Akron, OH 44319
Phone: 330-472-0083
E-mail: info@syzygynetwork.com
Web Site: http://www.syzygynetwork.com
Dave Andrews, Chief Executive Officer
Rob Weiss, President
Larry Nemecek, President, Publishing
Scott Brody, Vice President, Programming
Ron B Moore, Director, Visual Effects
David Reddick, Art Director
Type of service: Plans basic.
Operating areas: Plans nationwide.
Programming: Currently offers InSight program through it's web site. Plans to offer a cable channel catering exclusively to the SciFi and Fantasy fan.
Scheduled to begin: Plans to launch 2012.
Distribution method: Plans.
Scrambled signal: Yes.

TAIWAN MACROVIEW TV — See MAC TV.

TALENTVISION
3300-4151 Hazelbridge Way
Richmond, BC V6X 4J7
Canada
Phone: 604-295-1328
Fax: 604-295-1300
E-mail: info@talentvision.com
Web Site: http://www.talentvisiontv.com
Joseph Chan, President
Calvin Wong, Senior Vice President
Pamela Mooney, Controller, Finance
Louis Tong, Assistant General Manager
Helen Lee, Controller, Marketing & Sales

Branch Offices:
TORONTO: 35 E Bearer Creek Rd, Richmond Hill, ON L4B 1B3. Phone: 905-889-8090. Fax: 905-882-7120.
Type of service: Pay.
Operating hours/week: 127. 98 hrs. Chinese (Mandarin), 15 hrs. Vietnamese & 14 hrs. Korean.
Operating areas: Greater Vancouver, Lower Mainland & Victoria, BC.

Programming: News and current affairs, drama, variety, documentaries.
Began: December 1, 1993.
Means of Support: Subscriber fees & advertising.
Total subscribers: 13,712.
Distribution method: Via tape to cable systems.

TALKLINE COMMUNICATIONS TV NETWORK
Park West Station
PO Box 20108
New York, NY 10025
Phones: 212-769-1925; 866-482-5554
Fax: 212-799-4195
E-mail: tcntalk@aol.com
Web Site: http://talklinecommunications.com/
Zev Brenner, President
Type of service: Basic.
Satellites: Telestar 7.
Operating hours/week: 3.
Programming: Talk shows, news programs & music on & about Jewish life.
Began: August 1, 1981.
Means of Support: Advertising.
Distribution method: Available to cable systems.

TALKLINE COMMUNICATIONS RADIO NETWORK
Park West Station
PO Box 20108
New York, NY 10025
Phone: 212-769-1925
Fax: 212-799-4195
E-mail: tcntalk@aol.com
Web Site: http://talklinecommunications.com/
Zev Brenner, President
Type of service: Audio (radio); basic (TV).
Satellites: Telestar 7, transponder 6 (radio); Galaxy VII, transponder 24 (television).
Operating hours/week: 10.
Programming: Talk shows, news programs & music on & about Jewish life.
Began: August 1, 1981.
Means of Support: Advertising.
Distribution method: Available to cable systems & radio stations.

TAMPA BAY ON DEMAND — See Bay News 9.
Type of service: Video on demand.

TAPESHTV — See GlobeCast WorldTV.
26668 Agoura Rd
Calabasa, CA 91302
Phone: 818-610-0005
Fax: 818-593-4545
Web Site: http://www.tapeshtv.com
Programming: Persian news, movies, music, talk, children's & cooking shows.

TAVSIR IRAN — See GlobeCast WorldTV.
PO Box 1601
Simi Valley, CA 93062
Phone: 818-342-3399
E-mail: info@afnl.com
Web Site: http://www.afnl.com
Operating hours/week: 168.
Began: January 1, 1993.
Distribution method: Farsi-language news & entertainment for Iranian communities in the U.S.

TBN ENLACE USA
2823 W Irving Blvd
Irving, TX 75061
Phone: 972-313-9500
E-mail: cespanol@enlace.org
Web Site: http://www.tbnenlaceusa.tv/
Jonas Gonzalez, President
Bob Higley, Vice President, Affiliate Sales & Marketing
David Adcock, National Director, Affiliate Sales & Relations
Cesar Espanol, National Director, Hispanic Relations
Type of service: Digital basic.
Satellites: Intesat 9; Galaxy Telstar 5; Hispasat 1D; Galaxy 13; Hotbird 6.
Operating hours/week: 168.
Operating areas: Available nationwide.
Programming: features the best inspirational programs from Latin America and the most popular programs from TBN all in Spanish 24 hours a day.
Began: May 1, 2002, (US launch). Available in Central America, South America and Spain since 1997.
Total subscribers: 3,000,000.
Distribution method: Available on DirecTV.
Scrambled signal: Yes.
Ownership: TBN Networks.

TBN HD — See Trinity Broadcasting Network.

TBS IN HD — See TBS Superstation.
Began: September 1, 2007.

TBS SUPERSTATION
One CNN Center
PO Box 105366
Atlanta, GA 30348
Phone: 404-827-1717
Fax: 404-827-3368
Web Site: http://www.tbs.com
Philip I. Kent, Chairman & Chief Executive Officer
Terence F. McGuirk, Vice Chairman, TBS Inc. & Chief Executive Officer, Turner Sports Teams
Andrew Bird, President, TBS International
Andrew T. Heller, President, Domestic Distribution
Garth Ancier, Executive Vice President, Programming
Jeff Gregor, Executive Vice President & Chief Marketing Officer
Jim McCaffrey, Executive Vice President, Operations & Strategy
Victoria W. Miller, Executive Vice President & Chief Financial Officer
Kelly Regal, Executive Vice President, Human Resources & Communications
Louise Sams, Executive Vice President & General Counsel
Scott Teissler, Executive Vice President, Technology & Operations & Chief Technology Officer
Michael Wright, Executive Vice President, Head of Programming
Dennis Adamovich, Senior Vice President & General Manager, Comedy Festivals
Karen Cassell, Senior Vice President, Public Relations, TBS Superstation & TNT
Bill Cox, Senior Vice President, Programming & Public Affairs, TBS Superstation
Laura Dames, Senior Vice President, Marketing Operations, TBS Superstation & TNT
Greg Hughes, Senior Vice President, Entertainment & Sports Media Strategy, TBS Superstation & TNT
Sam Linsky, Senior Vice President, Current Programming
Shirley Powell, Senior Vice President, Corporate Communications, Turner Entertainment Networks
Ken Schwab, Senior Vice President, Programming, Acquisitions & New Media, TBS Superstation & TNT
Robin Thomas, Senior Vice President, Research, TBS Superstation & TNT
Terri Tingle, Senior Vice President, Standards & Practices, TBS Superstation
Molly Battin, Vice President, Brand Development, TBS Superstation
Jeff Carr, Vice President, Programming, TBS Superstation
Julie Crow, Vice President, Marketing Operations, TBS Superstation
Gary Holland, Vice President, Marketing, TBS Superstation
Amy Winter, Vice President, On-Air Promotions, TBS Superstation
Type of service: Basic & video on demand.
Satellites: Galaxy I, transponder 18.
Operating hours/week: 168.
Uplink: Atlanta, GA.
Programming: Sports, movies, children's programming & original series.
Began: December 17, 1976.
Means of Support: System pays common carrier; advertising.
Total subscribers: 101,900,000.
Ownership: Turner Broadcasting & Time Warner.

TEAMHD — See iN DEMAND.

TEENNICK
c/o MTV Networks
1515 Broadway, 21st Fl
New York, NY 10036
Phone: 212-258-8323
Fax: 212-258-8303
Web Site: http://www.teennick.com/
Keith Dawkins, Senior Vice President & General Manager
Laura Molen, Senior Vice President, Ad Sales
Tony Zito, Vice President, The N Online
Type of service: Basic.
Operating hours/week: 168.
Programming: Original shows for pre-teen audience.
Began: April 1, 2002, as The N. Relaunched September 28,2009 as TeenNick.
Total subscribers: 60,000,000.
Distribution method: Available to cable & satellite providers.
Scrambled signal: Yes.

TELE 5 — See GlobeCast WorldTV.
Phone: 847-882-2000
Web Site: http://www.tele5.pl
Programming: Polish-language presentations of world cinema, including European & American films.

TELE PADRE PIO — See GlobeCast WorldTV.
E-mail: info@teleradiopadrepio.it
Web Site: http://www.teleradiopadrepio.it
Programming: Focused on the teachings of Padre Pio, the Gospel & the Catholic Church.
Began: January 1, 2003, reflects international launch; U.S. launch date was December 10, 2007.

TELECARE
1200 Glenn Curtiss Blvd
Uniondale, NY 11553
Phone: 516-538-8700
Fax: 516-489-9701
Web Site: http://www.telecaretv.org
Msgr. James Vlaun, President & Chief Executive Officer
Joseph A. Perrone, General Manager
Type of service: Basic & Expanded basic.
Operating hours/week: 140.
Operating areas: New York.
Programming: Ecumenical, positive programming.
Began: January 1, 1976.
Distribution method: Fiber optic to cable systems.
Ownership: Diocese of Rockville Centre.

TELEFE INTERNATIONAL — See Condista.
Programming: General, Spanish-language entertainment.
Began: January 1, 2001.
Ownership: Television Federal, Buenos Aires.

TELEFORMULA — See Condista.
Web Site: http://www.teleformula.com.mx
Operating hours/week: 168.
Programming: News, sports, finance & entertainment.
Began: January 1, 2002.
Total subscribers: 1,800,000.
Distribution method: Available to satellite.
Ownership: TeleFormula S.A. de C.V.

TELEFUTURA — See Univision.
E-mail: bmedina@univision.net
Web Site: http://www.univision.com
Programming: General entertainment.
Ownership: Univision.

TELEFUTURA HD — See Telefutura.

TELEHIT
5999 Center Dr
Los Angeles, CA 90045
Phone: 310-348-3373
E-mail: correo@telehit.com
Web Site: http://www.esmas.com/telehit
Programming: Spanish & English-language urban music & lifestyle shows.
Began: May 1, 2003, reflects U.S. launch.
Total subscribers: 7,000,000.
Ownership: TuTV.

TELELATINO NETWORK
5125 Steeles Ave W
North York, ON M9L 1R5
Canada
Phones: 416-744-8200; 800-551-8401
Fax: 416-744-0966
E-mail: info@tlntv.com
Web Site: http://www.tlntv.com
Aldo DiFelice, President
John Montesano, Network Development Director
Nick Caccavella, Sales & Marketing Director
Bruce McLeod, Engineering Chief
Agatha Pezzi, Communications & Special Projects Director
Flavio Pincente, Commercial Production & Broadcast Facilities Manager
Rehaz Subdar, Finance Director

Branch Offices:
MONTREAL: 8000 Boulevard Langelier, Bureau 410, St. Leonard, QC H1P 3K2, Canada. Phone: 514-324-4231. Fax: 514-324-8098. E-Mail: montreal@tlntv.com.
Type of service: Basic.
Operating hours/week: 163.
Programming: Spanish & Italian language family entertainment including news, sports, drama, music, kids' & variety shows & local access.
Began: January 1, 1984.
Total subscribers: 3,700,000.

TELEMIAMI
2920 NW 7th St
Miami, FL 33121
Phone: 305-642-7777
Fax: 305-642-0077
E-mail: informacion@telemiami.com
Web Site: http://www.telemiami.com
Paul Stevens, President & Chief Executive Officer

Type of service: Basic.
Operating hours/week: 168.
Operating areas: Florida.
Programming: Entertainment, news, sports; 90% Spanish, 5% Italian, 5% Portuguese.
Began: January 1, 1984.
Means of Support: Advertising.
Total subscribers: 488,000.
Distribution method: Fiber optic to cable systems.
Ownership: United Broadcasting Corp.

TELEMICRO INTERNACIONAL — See Alterna'TV.

Programming: Dominican news & entertainment.

TELEMUNDO

2290 W 8th Ave
Hialeah, FL 33010
Phone: 305-884-8200
E-mail: alfredo.richard@nbcuni.com
Web Site: http://www.telemundo.com
Jacqueline Hernandez, Chief Operating Officer, Telemundo Communications Group
Javier Maynulet, Chief Financial Officer
Patricio Wills, President, Producciones RTI Columbia
Peter Blacker, Executive Vice President, Digital Media & Emerging Businesses
Ramon Escobar, Executive Vice President, Telemundo Network News
Adriana Ibanez, Executive Vice President, Programming
Stephen Levin, Executive Vice President, Sales
Dan Lovinger, Executive Vice President, Ad Sales & Integrated Marketing
Manuel Martinez-Llorian, Executive Vice President, Programming & Production
Michael Rodriguez, Executive Vice President, Multimedia Development & Distribution
Susan Solano Villa, Executive Vice President-Marketing
Aurelio Valcarcel, Executive Vice President, Telemundo Studios, Miami
Karen Barroeta, Senior Vice President, Marketing Creative
Milagros Carrasquillo, Senior Vice President, Research
Anjelica Cohn, Senior Vice President, Business Affairs
Joe Navarro, Senior Vice President, Human Resources
Lynette Pinto, Senior Vice President, Marketing
Ken Wilkey, Senior Vice President, Broadcast Operations
Michelle Alban, Vice President, Corporate Communications & Public Affairs
Maureen Alliegro, Vice President, Network Sales
Michael Alvarez, Vice President, Ad Sales
Andy Barnet, Vice President, National Sales
Hanna Bolte, Vice President, Media & Talent Relations, mun2/Telemundo
Jack Brown, Vice President, Network Sales, Chicago
Carlos Collazo, Vice President, On Air Promotions
Alonso Galvez, Vice President, Production
Ann Gaulke, Vice President, Affiliate Relations
Joshua Mintz, Senior Executive Vice President, Telemundo Entertainment
Jose Morales, Vice President, Content
Borja Perez, Vice President, Integrated Solutions & Digital Media
Joanna Popper, Vice President, Marketing
Christian Riehl, Vice President, Production
Vincent L. Sandusky, Treasurer

Branch Offices:
EAST COAST: 1775 Broadway, Ste 300, New York, NY 10019. Phone: 212-492-5545.

WEST COAST: 6500 Wilshire Blvd, Ste 1200, Los Angeles, CA 90048. Phone: 323-852-5290.

Type of service: Basic & broadband.
Operating hours/week: 168.
Programming: Spanish language programming for the U.S. & international markets.
Began: January 1, 1987.
Means of Support: Advertising.
Total subscribers: 21,600,000.
Distribution method: Available to cable systems.
Scrambled signal: Yes.
Ownership: NBCUniversal LLC.

TELEMUNDO INTERNACIONAL — See Telemundo.

TELEMUNDO NETWORK GROUP

2290 W Eighth Ave
Hialeah, FL 33010
Phone: 305-884-8200
Fax: 305-889-7980
Web Site: http://www.telemundo.com
Jackie Hernandez, Chief Operating Officer
Peter Blacker, Executive Vice President, Digital Media & Emerging Business
Johanna Guerra, Senior Vice President, News
Jorge Hidalgo, Senior Vice President, Sports
Mike Rodriguez, Senior Vice President, Sales

Branch Offices:
FLORIDA: International Program Sales, 2745 de Leon Blvd, Coral Gables, FL 33134. Phone: 305-774-0033. E-Mail: marcus.santana@nbcuni.com. Marcos Santana, President, Telemundo International.

NEW YORK: National Advertising Sales, 30 Rockefeller Plz, New York, NY 10112. Phone: 212-664-7417. E-Mail: michael.rodriguez@nbcuni.com. Michael Rodriguez, Executive Vice President, Multimedia Development & Distribution; Steve Mandala, Senior Vice President, Sales.

Produces, distributes & imports Spanish-language programming worldwide.

TELEMUNDO PUERTO RICO — See Telemundo.

Programming: Offers live news broadcasts directly from Telemundo Puerto Rico (WKAQ-TV), popular Puerto Rican shows, series, sports, music videos, films & specials.
Began: February 1, 2005.
Total subscribers: 3,000,000.
Distribution method: Digital Cable.

TELENOVELAS — See Univision.

E-mail: info@telenovelas.com.ar
Web Site: http://www.telenovelas.com.ar

TELEPACE — See GlobeCast WorldTV.

E-mail: programmi@telepace.it
Web Site: http://www.telepace.it
Programming: Italian-language Catholic programming.

TELEQUEBEC

270 Chemin Sainte-Foy
Quebec, QC G1R 1T3
Canada
Phone: 418-643-5303
Fax: 418-646-1233
E-mail: info@telequebec.tv
Web Site: http://www.telequebec.com
Daniel Le Saunier, Manager

TELETOON

BCE Place, 181 Bay St
Ste 100, Box 787
Toronto, ON M5J 2T3
Canada
Phone: 416-956-2060
Fax: 416-956-2070
Web Site: http://www.teletoon.com
John Riley, President
Darrell Atherley, Vice President, Affiliate Marketing & Sales
Suzanne Carpenter, Vice President, Advertising Sales
Hillary Firestone, Vice President, Network Marketing & Promotions
Kevin Wright, Vice President, Programming
Pascale Guillotte, Communications Director

Branch Office:
MONTREAL: 2100 Ste. Catherine W, 10th Floor, Montreal, QC H3H 2T3, Canada. Phone: 514-939-5016. Fax: 514-939-1515.

Type of service: Basic & Expanded basic.
Satellites: Anik F-1.
Sales representative: Robert Cole Media.
Operating hours/week: 168.
Uplink: Edmonton, AB.
Programming: Nationwide French & English language animated cartoon channels.
Began: October 17, 1997, English language; September 8, 1997, French language.
Means of Support: Advertising & subscribers.
Total subscribers: 6,800,000 ((English); 1,643,000 (French)).
Distribution method: Available to home dish audiences & cable systems.
Equipment: Digicipher II DSR 4400.
Ownership: Family Channel (Canada); YTV Canada; Cinar Films; Nelvana.

TELEVISA NETWORKS

Av. Vasco de Quiroga No. 2000
Edifico C, Piso 3
Col. Santa Fe, DF CP01210
Mexico
Phone: 52-55-5261-2000
Fax: 52-55-5261-3213
Web Site: http://www.televisanetworks.tv
Bruce Boren Krause, Director General
Ana Lydia Montoya, Programming Director
Eduardo Jimenez Machorro, Technical Director
Satellites: Intelsat 3R 8C.

TELEVISION DOMINICANA

E-mail: info@televisiondominicana.tv
Web Site: http://www.televisiondominicana.tv/
Programming: Television Dominicana, presented by the most talented celebrities in the Dominican Republic, offers a wide selection of high quality new, humor and entertainment programming.

TELEVISION KOREA 24

(tvK24)
3435 Wilshire Blvd, 19th Fl
Los Angeles, CA 90010
Phone: 213-382-9600
Fax: 213-382-9601
E-mail: info@tvk24.com
Web Site: http://www.tvk24.com
Eric Yoon, Founder & Chief Executive Officer
Heather Yoon, Broadcasting Director
Taeo Cho, Broadcasting Operations Director
Jeff Limb, Programming Director
Nancy Ahn, Advertising Director
Inwook Kim, News Director
Sang Han, Business Development Director
Type of service: Digital basic & video on demand.
Operating hours/week: 168.
Programming: Korean language news, dramas, movies, sports, business, health, music, children's entertainment, educational programming & game shows.
Began: March 1, 2005.
Total subscribers: 500,000.
Distribution method: Available to cable systems & telco providers.
Scrambled signal: Yes.
Ownership: Eric Yoon, NBCUniversal LLC (minority interest).

TELEVISION SHOPPING MALL — No longer planned.

TEMPO

Tempo Networks, LLC
58 Park Place, Third Floor
Newark, NJ 07102
Phone: 973-508-1000
Web Site: http://www.gottempo.com
Frederick Morton, Senior Vice President & General Manager
Operating hours/week: 168.
Operating areas: Caribbean.
Programming: A mix of original & acquired Caribbean programming, including series, specials, movies, documentaries & sporting events.
Began: November 21, 2005.
Total subscribers: 1,600,000.
Ownership: Private investors.

TEN BLOX — See Penthouse TV.

TEN BLUE — See Penthouse TV.

TEN CLIPS — See Penthouse TV.

TEN MAX — See Penthouse TV.

10 NEWS CHANNEL

4600 Air Way
San Diego, CA 92102
Phone: 619-237-1010
E-mail: jeff_block@10news.com
Web Site: http://www.10news.com
Jeff Block, General Manager
Joel Davis, News Director
Ken Rycyzyn, Ad Sales Director
Michelle Krish, News Editor
Jennifer Brady, Managing Editor
Type of service: Digital.
Operating hours/week: 168.
Operating areas: Southern California.
Programming: Local news service.
Began: September 1, 1996, as News Channel 15; relaunched as 10 News Channel on January 25, 2006.
Means of Support: Advertising.
Total subscribers: 836,000.

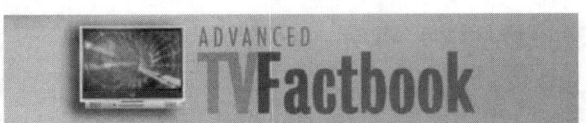

Distribution method: Available to cable systems.
Ownership: McGraw-Hill Companies Inc.

10 NEWS 2
WBIR TV-10
1513 Hutchinson Ave
Knoxville, TN 37917-3851
Phone: 865-637-1010
E-mail: manager@wbir.com
Web Site: http://www.wbir.com
Jeff Lee, General Manager
Operating hours/week: 168.
Total subscribers: 624,163.
Distribution method: Cable, Satellite.
Ownership: Gannett Company Inc.

TEN ON DEMAND — See Penthouse TV.

TEN XTSY — See Penthouse TV.

TENNIS CHANNEL
1531 14th St
Santa Monica, CA 90404
Phone: 310-656-9400
Fax: 310-656-9433
E-mail: ttchr@thetennischannel.com
Web Site: http://www.thetennischannel.tv
Ken Solomon, Chairman & Chief Executive Officer
John Brady, Chief Financial Officer
Bruce Rider, Executive Vice President
Victoria Quoss, Executive Vice President, Programming & Network Strategy
Gary Herman, Senior Vice President, Advertising Sales
Doug Martz, Senior Vice President, Advertising Sales & Alternative Revenue
Larry Meyers, Senior Vice President, Production & Executive Producer
Nancy Pingitore, Senior Vice President, Distribution, Eastern Division
Laura Hockbridge, Vice President, Original Programming
David Scott, Vice President, Programming
Eric Turpin, Vice President, Distribution
Patrick Wilson, Vice President, Distribution
Adonis McReynolds, Traffic Director
Neil Roberts, Marketing Director
Gail Rodriguez, Director, Ad-Sales Marketing
Brian Smejkal, Scheduling Director
Faye Walker, Marketing & Creative Services
Type of service: Basic.
Operating hours/week: 168.
Programming: American & international tennis tournaments & matches, other original tennis-related programs.
Began: May 15, 2003.
Means of Support: Advertising.
Total subscribers: 30,000,000.
Distribution method: Available to cable & satellite providers.

TENNIS CHANNEL HD — See Tennis Channel.
Began: December 31, 2007.

TETRIS TV
One World Financial Center, 27th Fl
c/o Oberon Media
New York, NY 10281
Phone: 646-367-2020
Fax: 212-221-9240
Web Site: http://corp.oberon-media.com
Alexey Pazhitnov, Co-Owner, The Tetris Co. LLC
Henk Rogers, Co-Owner, The Tetris Co. LLC
Tomer Ben-Kiki, Co-Founder, Oberon Media
Tal Kerret, Chairman, Oberon Media
David Lebow, Chief Executive Officer (Acting), Oberon Media
Bob Hayes, Chief Operating Officer, Oberon Media
Bob Sirmans, Senior Vice President, Business Development, Oberon Media
Ari Last, Vice President, Business Development, International, Oberon Media
Jonathan Boltax, Senior Director, ITV Programming & Service Management, Oberon Media
Sharon Rosenman, Senior Director, ITV Business Partnerships, Oberon Media

Branch Offices:
West Coast Office: 2101 4th Ave, Ste 1020, Seattle, WA 98121.
Type of service: Premium.
Operating hours/week: 168.
Operating areas: Available nationwide.
Programming: Interactive TV game service.
Began: February 3, 2010.
Means of Support: Subscriber fees.
Distribution method: Available to DISH Network subscribers.
Scrambled signal: Yes.
Ownership: Oberon Media, in license with The Tetris Company.

TEVE-DE-MENTE — See Alterna'TV.

TEXAS CABLE NEWS
570 Young St
Dallas, TX 75202
Phone: 214-977-4500
Fax: 214-977-4610
E-mail: gerry@dallasnews.com
Web Site: http://www.txcn.com
James T. Aitken, President & General Manager
Steve Ackermann, Executive News Director
Tom Matasso, Engineering Director
Harold Gaar, Sales & Marketing Director
Mark Willenborg, Creative Services Director
Lisa Wegmann, Local Sales Manager
Type of service: Digital.
Operating hours/week: 168.
Operating areas: Texas.
Uplink: Dallas, TX.
Programming: Offers a mixture of news, sports & weather combined with coverage of other important subjects & current events within the state of Texas.
Began: January 1, 1999.
Total subscribers: 1,600,000.
Distribution method: Available to cable systems.
Ownership: Belo Corp.

TEXAS HOUSE OF REPRESENTATIVES VIDEO/AUDIO SERVICES
105 W 15th St
Austin, TX 78701
Phone: 512-463-0903
Fax: 512-463-5729
Web Site: http://www.house.state.tx.us
Type of service: Basic.
Programming: Coverage of House session and committee meetings.
Began: January 1, 1987.
Distribution method: Cable, internet.

TEXAS SENATE MEDIA
PO Box 12068
Austin, TX 78711
Phone: 512-463-0300
E-mail: sharon.scarborough@senate.state.tx.us
Web Site: http://www.senate.state.tx.us/bin/live.php

THE HUB
2950 N Hollywood Way
Ste 100
Burbank, CA 91505
Phone: 818-531-3630
Fax: 818-531-3601
Web Site: http://www.hubworld.com
Brian Goldner, President & Chief Executive Officer, Hasbro Inc.
Margaret Loesch, President & Chief Executive Officer
Amber Fredman-Tarshis, Chief Marketing Officer
Dan Pimentel, Chief Financial Officer
Lorrie Copeland, Senior Vice President, Consumer Rights & Research
Donna Ebbs, Senior Vice President, Programming
Joshua Meyer, Senior Vice President, Business & Legal Affairs
Brooke Goldstein, Senior Vice President, Ad Sales
Jordan Beck, Vice President, Creative Services & On-Air Promotions
Lou Fazio, Vice President, Scheduling, Acquisitions & Planning
Greg Heanue, Vice President, Marketing & Promotions
Fred Poston, Vice President, Operations
Michael Ross, Vice President, Production & Post Production
Michael Grover, Director, Consumer Marketing
J P Shields, Director, Communications & Publicity
Cindy Slocki, Director, Integrated Marketing Solutions
Type of service: Basic.
Operating hours/week: 168.
Operating areas: Available nationwide.
Programming: Formerly Discovery Kids, The Hub offers animated and live-action series, specials and game shows for children 12 and under, plus online activities as well.
Began: October 10, 2010.
Means of Support: Advertising.
Total subscribers: 62,000,000 (Channel is re-branded from Discovery Kids.).
Distribution method: Available to home dish audiences and cable systems, plus FiOS TV.
Scrambled signal: Yes.
Ownership: Discovery Communications, 50%; Hasbro Inc., 50%.

THE JEWISH CHANNEL
Web Site: http://tjctv.com
Type of service: Pay.
Operating areas: New York.
Programming: Jewish news, documentaries, movies & entertainment.
Distribution method: Available to cable systems.

THE N — See TeenNick.
Began: April 1, 2002, Relaunched as TeenNick September 28, 2009.

THEATRE CHANNEL — No longer planned.

THIS TV
10250 Constellation Blvd
Los Angeles, CA 90067-6241
Phone: 310-499-3000
E-mail: comments@thistv.com
Web Site: http://www.thistv.com
Jim Packer, Co-President, MGM Worldwide TV
Jim Marketti, Creative Director
Type of service: Digital.
Satellites: AMC-3.
Operating hours/week: 168.
Programming: Movies & TV shows from the MGM library & children's programming.
Began: November 1, 2008.
Means of Support: Ad-supported.
Scrambled signal: Yes.
Ownership: MGM Studios, 50% & Weigel Broadcasting, 50%.

3 ANGELS BROADCASTING NETWORK
PO Box 220
West Frankfort, IL 62896
Phone: 618-627-4651
Fax: 618-627-2726
Web Site: http://www.3abn.org
Type of service: Basic, broadband & radio.
Operating hours/week: 168.
Programming: Focuses on recovery & rehabilitation, cooking & health, weight loss & smoking cessation, children & family issues, organic gardening, natural home remedies, gospel music & various Bible-themed programs.
Began: November 23, 1986.
Distribution method: Available to cable & satellite providers.

3NET
10202 W Washington Blvd
Culver City, CA 90202
Phone: 310-244-8907
E-mail: rod_riegel@3net.com
Web Site: http://www.3net.com
Bruce Campbell, Chief Development Officer & General Counsel, Discovery Communications Inc.
Andy Kaplan, President of Networks, Sony Pictures Television
Peter Liguori, Chief Operating Officer, Discovery Communications Inc.
Rob Lister, Senior Executive Vice President & General Counsel, IMAX Corp.
Rob Wiesenthal, Executive Vice President & Chief Financial Officer, Sony Corp.; Executive Vice President & Chief Strategy Officer, Sony Entertainment
Tom Cosgrove, President & Chief Executive Officer
Carlos Gutierrez, Vice President, Business Affairs & Legal
Tim Pastore, Vice President, Development & Production
Rod Riegel, Vice President, Marketing & Communications
Type of service: Basic.
Operating hours/week: 168.
Operating areas: Available nationwide.
Programming: First 3D network, offering natural history, documentary, action/adventure, travel, history, hyper-reality, lifestyle and cuisine, concerts, movies, scripted series and more.
Began: February 13, 2011.
Means of Support: Advertising.
Distribution method: Available initially through DirecTV.
Scrambled signal: Yes.
Ownership: Discovery Communications, IMAX Corp. & Sony Corp.

THRILLERMAX — See Cinemax.
Programming: Mystery, suspense, horror & thriller movies, including recent box office hits & independent films.
Began: June 1, 1998.

TIGERVISION
c/o LSU Electronic Media
PO Box 25095
Baton Rouge, LA 70894-1797
Phone: 504-388-1797
Fax: 504-338-1861
E-mail: promotions@lsu.edu
Web Site: http://www.lsusports.net
Type of service: Pay-per-view.
Operating areas: Louisiana.

Programming: LSU football games.
Means of Support: Subscription fees.
Ownership: Louisiana State U.

TIME WARNER CABLE SPORTS

6005 Fair Lakes Rd E
Syracuse, NY 13057
Phone: 315-634-6471
Doug Logan, Director
Tom White, Production & Engineering Manager
Martina St Leger, Operations Manager
Dave Perkins, Sales Manager
Type of service: Basic.
Operating hours/week: 168.
Operating areas: New York.
Programming: Local college & professional sports, recreation & sports related news & entertainment.
Distribution method: Available to cable systems.
Scrambled signal: Yes.

TIME WARNER HITS

1 Time Warner Center
New York, NY 10019
Phone: 212-484-8000
Web Site: http://www.timewarner.com/corp
Type of service: Digital, video on demand.
Programming: Providing instant reruns of popular series & shows previously aired on CBS, ABC, NBC & Fox.
Began: N.A.
Distribution method: Available to cable systems.

TINSELVISION

3130 Fairview Park Dr
Ste 500
Falls Church, VA 22042
Chase Weir, Chairman & Chief Executive Officer

Branch Offices:
INDIA: C-208 Crystal Plaza, New Link Rd, Andheri West, Mumbai 400 053.
Type of service: Video on demand.
Programming: Bollywood & South Asian movies, TV series & sports.
Began: November 21, 2007.
Distribution method: IPTV, broadband.
Scrambled signal: Yes.
Ownership: TinselCinema LLC.

TITAN TV NETWORK

1450 Broadway
30th Fl
New York, NY 10018
Phone: 212-913-0670
Fax: 212-913-0680
E-mail: mktg@titantv.com
Web Site: http://www.titantv.com
Mark Effron, Senior Vice President
Laura van Straaten, Vice President, Content & General Manager
Jon Labes, Executive in Charge of Production, Titan Laughs
Morgan Jones, Production Director

Branch Offices:
CEDAR RAPIDS: TitanTV Media, 818 Dows Rd SE, Cedar Rapids, IA 52403-7000.
Phones: 319-365-5597; 800-365-7629.
Type of service: Broadband.
Programming: Internet broadcast network with channels focusing on the environment, comedy & more. Also provides customizable tv listings.

TKMI LIVE BROADCASTING

PO Box 46
101-115 Buffalo St
Mannington, WV 26582
Phone: 304-986-2896
Fax: 304-986-2895
E-mail: bktkm@westco.net
Web Site: http://www.tkmi.org
Dr. Nicholas Lalli, Founder & President
Pamela Lalli, Vice President & Secretary
Jeff Stacy, Trustee
Tenna Stacy, Trustee
Type of service: Basic.
Operating hours/week: 168.
Operating areas: West Virginia.
Programming: Religious and inspirational shows.
Distribution method: Available over the air and to cable and IP web tv subscribers.
Scrambled signal: No.
Ownership: True Knowledge Ministries International.

TL NOVELAS — See Televisa Networks.

E-mail: tlnovelas@televisanetworks.tv

TLC — See The Learning Channel.

Eileen O'Neill, President & General Manager

TLC HD — See The Learning Channel.

TOTAL LIVING NETWORK

38 S Peoria St
Chicago, IL 60607-2628
Phone: 312-433-3838
Fax: 312-433-3839
E-mail: jrose@tln.com
Web Site: http://www.tln.com
Jerry K. Rose, President
James R. Nichols, Vice President, Finance
Roy Pokorny, Vice President, Sales & Marketing
Dick Rolfe, Vice President, Strategic Initiatives
Peter Edgers, Network Operations Director
Bob Reed, Technical Operations Director
Type of service: Basic.
Satellites: Galaxy 1, transponder 5.
Programming: Christian television program provider.
Began: August 31, 1998.
Total subscribers: 8,000,000.
Ownership: Christian Communications of Chicagoland Inc.

TMC XTRA — See Showtime.

TMN-THE MOVIE NETWORK (1-4)

BCE Place, 181 Bay St
Box 787, Ste 100
Toronto, ON M5J 2T3
Canada
Phone: 416-956-2010
Fax: 416-956-2018
Web Site: http://www.tmn.ca
Andre Bureau, Chief Executive Officer
Lisa de Wilde, President & Chief Operating Officer
Joe Tedesco, Senior Vice President, Finance & Business Affairs
Chris Bell, Vice President, Technology
Satellites: Anik E-2.
Operating hours/week: 168.
Operating areas: New Brunswick, Newfoundland, Nova Scotia, Ontario, Prince Edward Island & Quebec.
Programming: Offers uncut, commercial-free movies.
Began: February 1, 1983.
Means of Support: Subscription fees.
Total subscribers: 500,000.
Distribution method: Available to home dish audiences & cable systems.
Equipment: DigiCipher.
Ownership: Astral Communications Inc.

TNT — See Turner Network TV.

TOO MUCH FOR TV ON DEMAND — See iN DEMAND.

TOON DISNEY — See Disney XD.

Began: April 18, 1998.
Relaunched as Disney XD February 13, 2009.

TOP CHANNEL TV — See GlobeCast WorldTV.

Web Site: http://www.top-channel.tv
Programming: Albanian news, social & economic, films & sports.

TORSTAR MEDIA GROUP TELEVISION (TORONTO STAR TV)

One Yonge St
9th Fl
Toronto, ON M5E 1E6
Canada
Phone: 416-869-4700
Fax: 416-869-4566
E-mail: production@tmgtv.ca
Web Site: http://www.tmgtv.ca
Mark Goodale, Vice President & General Manager
Heather Brunt, Operations Manager
Susan Gouvianakis, Traffic Manager
Deborah Kelly, Production Manager
Type of service: Basic.
Operating hours/week: 24.
Programming: Infomercial channel that airs short & long form infomercials for clients including The Toronto Star.
Began: October 17, 1997.
Means of Support: Advertising.
Total subscribers: 1,400,000.
Distribution method: Available to cable systems.
Ownership: Torstar Corporation.

TRADING DAY — See KyLinTV.

TRAFFIC CHECK — No longer planned.

TRAVEL CHANNEL

5425 Wisconsin Ave
Ste 500
Chevy Chase, MD 20815
Phone: 301-244-7500
Web Site: http://www.travelchannel.com
Laureen Ong, President
Jonathan Sichel, General Manager
Patrick Lafferty, Chief Creative Officer
Shannon O'Neill, Chief Financial Officer
Fred Graver, Senior Vice President, Programming
Lori McFarling, Senior Vice President, Distribution & Marketing
Greg Regis, Senior Vice President, Ad Sales
Patalia Tate, Senior Vice President, Marketing, Creative & Brand Strategy
Elizabeth Browde, Vice President, Programming & Development
Matthew Gould, Vice President, Development
Kerri Hannigan, Vice President, Marketing, Communications & Brand Strategy
Linette Hwu, Vice President, Legal Affairs
Brigitte McCray, Vice President, Programming, Planning & Strategy
Mickey McKenzie, Vice President, Production
Rex Recka, Vice President, Business Affairs
Adam Sutherland, Vice President, Strategy & Business Development
Kay Robinson, Corporate Director, People Services
Type of service: Basic.
Satellites: Satcom F-1R, transponder 9; Satcom C-4, transponder 13; West Coast: AMC-10, transponder 14.
Operating hours/week: 126.
Programming: News & entertainment segments hosted by travel experts, authors, newsmakers & celebrities.
Began: February 1, 1987.
Means of Support: Advertising.
Total subscribers: 95,000,000.
Distribution method: Available to home dish audiences & cable systems.
Scrambled signal: Yes. Equipment: VideoCipher II Plus.
Ownership: Scripps Networks Interactive Inc. 65%; Cox Communications Inc. 35%.

TRAVEL CHANNEL BEYOND — See Travel Channel.

Type of service: Broadband.

TRAVEL CHANNEL HD — See Travel Channel.

Web Site: http://www.travelchannel.com/hd
Began: January 14, 2008.

TRAVEL CHANNEL LATIN AMERICA

Discovery Communications Inc.
6505 Blue Lagoon Dr, Ste 190
Miami, FL 33126
Phone: 786-273-4700
Fax: 786-273-4860
E-mail: dmr_roman@discovery.com
Henry Rodriguez, President
Raul De Quesada, Vice President, Marketing & Communications
Maria Urquiaga, Vice President, Programming & Production
Luis Perez, Vice President, Finance & Advertising Sales
Satellites: Intelsat 601-K.
Operating hours/week: 168.
Programming: Spanish & Portuguese travel & tourism related shows.
Began: October 15, 1995.
Means of Support: Advertising & subscriber fees.
Total subscribers: 5,900,000.
Scrambled signal: Yes.
Ownership: Discovery Communications Inc.

TRAVEL WEATHER NOW — See Bay News 9.

TRAX — No longer planned.

TREEHOUSE TV

64 Jefferson Ave
Unit 18
Toronto, ON M6K 3H3
Canada
Phone: 416-530-5190

Fax: 416-588-9341
Web Site: http://www.treehousetv.com
Susan Ross, Vice President & General Manager, Childrens Television
John Cvecich, Business Director
Type of service: Basic & pay.
Satellites: Anik E2, transponder KU-band.
Operating hours/week: 147.
Programming: Nationwide English language children's channel.
Began: November 1, 1997.
Total subscribers: 6,000,000.
Ownership: Corus Entertainment.

TR3S — See MTV.
MTV Networks
1515 Broadway
New York, NY 10036
Phones: 212-258-8000; 212-258-8760
E-mail: Harry.Neuhaus@mtvstaff.com
Web Site: http://www.tr3s.com
Jose Tillan, Executive Vice President & General Manager
Jesus Lara, Senior Vice President, Music & Talent
Lily Neumeyer, Vice President, Production & Programming
Programming: Music & entertainment for Latino youth.
Began: September 25, 2006.
Total subscribers: 30,000,000.
Ownership: MTV Networks.

TRINITY BROADCASTING NETWORK
PO Box A
Santa Ana, CA 92711
Phone: 714-832-2950
E-mail: bobhigley@tbn.org
Web Site: http://www.tbn.org
David Adcock, National Director, Affiliate Sales & Relations
Cesar Espanol, National Director, Hispanic Relations
Type of service: Basic.
Satellites: Galaxy 14, transponder 1.
Sales representative: Media Services Group Inc.
Operating hours/week: 168.
Uplink: Tustin, CA.
Programming: Religious variety.
Began: May 1, 1973, broadcast TV; May 1, 1978 satellite.
Means of Support: Donations.
Total subscribers: 64,718,049.
Distribution method: Available to cable systems.
Ownership: Non-profit corp.
(TBN)

TROJAN VISION
3131 S Figueroa St
Los Angeles, CA 90089-7756
Phone: 213-743-2731
Fax: 213-743-2767
E-mail: info@trojanvision.com
Web Site: http://www.trojanvision.com
Don Tillman, Executive Director
James Creech, General Manager
Programming: Student-operated programming from USC.
Began: September 15, 1997.
Total subscribers: 1,800,000.

TRUE BLUE
5435 Airport Blvd
Ste 100
Boulder, CO 80301
Phone: 303-786-8700
Fax: 303-938-8388
Mark Kreloff, President & Chief Executive Officer
Michael Weiner, Executive Vice President, Business Affairs
Thomas Nyiri, Vice President, Broadband Communications & Chief Technical Offier
Karyn Miller, Chief Financial & Operating Officer
John Chambliss, Programming Director
Robin Rothman, Media Contact
Mark Grant, Marketing Contact
Type of service: Pay & Pay-per-view.
Satellites: Telstar 5, transponder 14.
Operating hours/week: 168.
Operating areas: Not available in Alabama, Mississippi, North Carolina, Oklahoma, Tennessee or Utah.
Uplink: Ottawa, ON.
Programming: Adult channel offering amateur films, talk shows & American classics.
Began: March 1, 1996.
Distribution method: Available to home dish audiences (C-band) & cable systems.
Scrambled signal: Yes. Equipment: Video Cipher II Plus.
Ownership: New Frontier Media Inc.

TRUTV
600 3rd Ave
2nd Fl
New York, NY 10016
Phones: 212-973-2800; 800-268-7856
Fax: 212-973-3355
Web Site: http://www.trutv.com
Steve Koonin, Chief Executive Officer, truTV & President, Turner Entertainment Networks
Art Bell, President
Marc Juris, Executive Vice President & General Manager
Marlene Dann, Executive Vice President, Daytime Programming
Doug Jacobs, Executive Vice President & General Counsel
Galen Jones, Executive Vice President, Strategy & Planning
Linda Yaccarino, Executive Vice President, Turner Entertainment Sales
Emily Barsh, Senior Vice President, News & Talent Development
Darren Campo, Senior Vice President, Programming, Production & Development
Mary Corigliano, Senior Vice President, Marketing
Claire Cowart, Senior Vice President, Business Development
Anthony Horn, Senior Vice President, Current Programming & Specials
Robyn Hutt, Senior Vice President, Original Programming
John Moran, Senior Vice President
Mary D. Silverman, Senior Vice President, Acquisitions & Development
Susan Abbey, Vice President, Community Affairs
Joseph Alesi, Vice President, Off-Air Creative
Dara Cohen, Vice President, Scripted Programming
Brian Compare, Vice President, Programming & Marketing Research
Emil Freund, Vice President, Information Technology
Glen Freyer, Vice President, Non-Fiction Series Development
Lynne Kirby, Vice President, Development
Michael Lanzillotta, Vice President, Business Affairs
Nancy McKenna, Vice President, Production Operations
Glenn Moss, Vice President, Business & Legal Affairs
Rosalie Muskatt, Vice President, Original Movies
Marissa Ronca, Vice President, Development
Andrew Verderame, Vice President, On-Air Promotions
Fred Graham, Managing Editor
Tim Sullivan, News Editor
Debbie D'Arinzo, Senior Director, Strategy & Planning
Courtney Brown, Ad Sales Marketing Director
Barri Chattman, Daytime Booking & Talent Development Director
Mark Fichandler, Development Director
Linda Finney, Marketing Director
Matt Stueland, Programming Director
Wayne Loewe, Coordinating Producer

Western Regional Office:
BURBANK: 3000 W Alameda Ave, Ste C-185, Burbank, CA 91523. Phone: 818-840-3608. Fax: 818-840-3112.
Type of service: Basic & video on demand.
Satellites: Satcom C-3, transponder 6.
Operating hours/week: 168.
Programming: Live & taped coverage of courtroom trials from across the US; other programs focus on the law & the legal system including movies & non-fiction series.
Began: July 1, 1991, as Court TV; relaunched as truTV on January 1, 2008.
Means of Support: Advertising.
Total subscribers: 90,800,000.
Distribution method: Available to cable systems & mobile video.
Ownership: Turner Broadcasting System Inc.

TRUTV HD — See truTV.

TUFF.TV
225 8th St
Ste 200
Chattanooga, TN 37402
Phone: 423-468-5300
Web Site: http://www.tufftv.com
Lou Seals, Chief Executive Officer, TUFF TV Media Group LLC
Henry Luken, Chief Executive Officer, TUFF TV LLC
Clinton Goodgame, Chief Information Officer, TUFF TV LLC
Neal Ardman, Vice President, Affiliate Sales & Marketing, TUFF TV LLC
Chip Harwood, Vice President, Affiliate Sales & Marketing, TUFF TV Medai Group LLC
Chris Hannaford, Content Acquisitions Manager
Mike Snowden, Content Operations Manager
Cole Sweeton, Creative Services Manager
Andrea Rhum, Senior Account Manager, National Advertising Sales
Anthony Barrett, Account Executive, National Advertising Sales
Cathy Winters, Traffic Coordinator
Type of service: Basic.
Operating areas: Available nationwide.
Uplink: Chattanooga, TN.
Programming: Digital broadcast network offers original programming targeted at men and the specific pursuits, interests, and hobbies. Programming content consists of sports, lifestyle, drama, reality, talk, specials, and movies.
Began: June 30, 2009.
Means of Support: Advertising.
Distribution method: Broadcast television network.
Scrambled signal: Yes.
Ownership: Luken Communications LLC & TUFF TV Media Group.

TURBO — See Discovery Channel.
Type of service: Video on demand & broadband.
Programming: Discovery series & original content focusing on automotive interests.
Began: January 1, 2006.

TURNER CLASSIC MOVIES
(TCM)
One CNN Center, PO Box 105366
Atlanta, GA 30348
Phone: 404-885-5535
Fax: 404-885-5536
Web Site: http://www.tcm.com
Philip Kent, Chairman & Chief Executive Officer, TBS Inc.
Jeff Gregor, Executive Vice President, Chief Marketing Officer & General Manager
Michael Wright, Executive Vice President, Programming
Michael Borza, Senior Vice President, On-Air Creative
Sandra Dewey, Senior Vice President, Original Programming
Katherine Evans, Senior Vice President, TCM Enterprises & New Media
Jim Weiss, Senior Vice President, Public Relations
Tom Brown, Vice President, Program Production
Pola Changnon, Vice President, Creative Director & On-Air Promotions
Jennifer Freeland, Vice President, Public Relations
Darcy Hettrich, Vice President, Talent
Monica Neal, Vice President, Emerging Markets & Partnerships
Fred Spring, Vice President, Research
Charles Tabesh, Vice President, Programming
Began: April 14, 1994.
Total subscribers: 75,000,000.
Distribution method: Available to cable systems.
Ownership: Time Warner Inc.

TURNER CLASSIC MOVIES HD — See Turner Classic Movies.

TURNER NETWORK TV
(TNT)
One CNN Center, PO Box 105366
Atlanta, GA 30348
Phones: 404-885-4570; 404-885-4647
Fax: 404-827-3368
E-mail: privacy.tnt@turner.com
Web Site: http://www.tnt.tv
Philip Kent, Chairman & Chief Executive Officer, TBS Inc.
Steven Koonin, President, Turner Entertainment Networks
Robert DeBitetto, President, Original Programming
Jeff Gregor, Executive Vice President & Chief Marketing Officer
Susan Oman Gross, Executive Vice President, Business Affairs & Distribution
Vicky Miller, Executive Vice President
Julie Weitz, Executive Vice President, Original Programming
Michael Wright, Executive Vice President, Programming
Michael Borza, Senior Vice President, On-Air Production
Karen Cassell, Senior Vice President, Public Relations
Iris Grossman, Senior Vice President, Talent & Casting
David Hudson, Senior Vice President, Late Night & Specials
Sam Linsky, Senior Vice President, Current Programming
Kim Long, Senior Vice President, Production
Christina Miller, Senior Vice President, Turner Sports Strategy/Marketing/Programming & General Manager, NBA Digital
Scot Safon, Senior Vice President, Marketing
Ken Schwab, Senior Vice President, Programming, Acquisitions & New Media
Andrea Taylor, Senior Vice President, Creative Services

Ron Binkowski, Vice President, Post-Production
Nicholas Bogner, Vice President, Original Programming
Tom Carr, Vice President, Entertainment Marketing & Promotions
Laura Dames, Vice President, Marketing Operations
Sandra Dewey, Vice President, Business Affairs
Marc Evans, Vice President, Finance & Strategic Planning
Stan Flowers, Vice President, New Media
Teri Fournier, Vice President, Deputy General Counsel of Turner Entertainment Group
Randy Gragg, Vice President, Print Production
Jonathan Harris, Vice President, Business Affairs
Carrie Henderson, Vice President, Production
Darcy Hettrich, Vice President, Talent for Specials & Live Event Programming
Aaron Khristeus, Vice President & Production Controller
Jeffrey Levine, Vice President, Development
Lillah McCarthy, Vice President, Series Programming
Shannon McGauley, Vice President, Sports Talent Relations, On-Air Creative
Monica Neal, Vice President, Emerging Markets & Partnerships
Betsy Newman, Vice President, Original Programming
Phil Oppenheim, Vice President, Programming
Candace Snyder, Vice President, Post Production
Brett Weitz, Vice President, Series Development
Jim Wilberger, Vice President, Production
Cathy Wischner-Sola, Vice President, Original Programming

Branch Offices:
Chicago, IL; Dallas, TX; Detroit, MI; Los Angeles, CA; New York, NY.
Type of service: Basic & video on demand.
Satellites: Satcom 3-R, transponder 18.
Operating hours/week: 168.
Programming: Offering original motion pictures, miniseries, original series, non-fiction specials & live events, contemporary films, NBA & Wimbledon tennis action & popular television series.
Began: October 3, 1988.
Means of Support: Advertising supported.
Total subscribers: 101,100,000.
Distribution method: Available to home dish audiences & cable systems.
Ownership: Time Warner Inc.

TURNER NETWORK TV HD — See Turner Network TV.

TURNER SOUTH — See SportSouth.

TUTV — See Univision.
Phone: 310-348-3375
E-mail: anerubay@univision.net
Total subscribers: 2,000,000.
Ownership: Univision & Grupo Televisa.
A joint venture between Univision and Televisa

TV ASIA
76 National Rd
Edison, NJ 08817
Phone: 732-650-1100
Fax: 732-650-1112
E-mail: info@tvasiausa.com
Web Site: http://www.tvasiausa.com
H.R. Shah, Founder
Lal Dadlaney, Senior Vice President, Business & Operations
Rohit Vyas, Director, News
Type of service: Pay.
Satellites: Galaxy VI, transponder 12.
Operating hours/week: 168.
Operating areas: California & New Jersey.
Programming: Hindi, Urdu & English, with regional languages such as Punjabi, Gujurati, Bengali & Tamil.
Began: April 1, 1993.
Means of Support: Advertising & subscribers.
Total subscribers: 20,000.
Distribution method: Available to home dish audiences & cable systems.
Ownership: Asia Star Broadcasting Inc.

TV CHILE — See OlympuSat Hispanic Pack.
Type of service: Basic & video on demand.
Programming: Family entertainment, including sports, telenovelas, news & nature shows.
Began: January 1, 1999, reflects U.S. launch.
Total subscribers: 2,400,000.
Ownership: Television Nactional de Chile.

TV COLOMBIA — See OlympuSat Hispanic Pack.

TV GUIDE BROADBAND — See TV Guide Network.
Type of service: Broadband.
Programming: Celebrity interviews, behind-the-scenes shows.

TV GUIDE INTERACTIVE INC.
7140 S Lewis Ave
Tulsa, OK 74136-5422
Phones: 918-488-4450; 800-447-7388
Fax: 918-499-6355
Web Site: http://www.tvguide.com
Jeff Shell, III, Chairman & Chief Executive Officer
Joachim Kiener, Vice Chairman
Charles Butler Ammann, Senior Vice President, Secretary & Gen. Counsel
Craig M. Waggy, Senior Vice President & Chief Financial Officer
Toby DeWeese, Vice President, Corporate Development
Gregory S. Taylor, Tax Officer
Marie-Claude Thomas, Assistant Secretary
Cindy Miles, Assistant Secretary
Satellites: Satcom IV-R, transponder 8.
Operating hours/week: 168.
Programming: Digital interactive program guide.
Began: June 1, 1997.
Means of Support: Subscription fees and ad revenue.
Total subscribers: 14,000,000.
Distribution method: Available to cable systems.
Scrambled signal: Yes.
Ownership: Rovi Corp.

TV GUIDE NETWORK
1211 Avenue of the Americas
21st Fl
New York, NY 10036
Phone: 212-852-7543
Fax: 212-852-4914
E-mail: network.pr@tvguide.com
Web Site: http://www.tvguide.com/channel
Friday Abernethy, Executive Vice President, Affiliate Sales & Marketing
Diane Robina, Executive Vice President, Development, Acquisitions & Programming Strategy
Richy Glassberg, Senior Vice President, Advertising Sales
John High, Senior Vice President, Sales Operations
Leslie Furuta, Vice President, Communications

Timothy Russell, Vice President, National Advertising Sales
Lynn Stepanian, Vice President, Acquisition & Scheduling
Nikki Lichterman, Communications Director

Branch Offices:
CONSHOHOCKEN: 1982 Butler Pike, Ste 4, Conshohocken, PA 19428. Phone: 610-828-9240.

LITTLETON: National Digital TV Center, 4100 E Dry Creek Rd, Littleton Village, CO 80122. Phone: 303-267-6800. Fax: 303-267-6889.

NEW YORK: 369 Lexington Ave, 21st Floor, New York, NY 10017. Phone: 212-370-1799. Fax: 212-370-1698.
Type of service: Basic.
Satellites: Satcom IV-R, transponder 8.
Operating hours/week: 168.
Programming: System-specific on-screen program guide, including video clips, for basic, pay & pay-per-view services. Formerly, Prevue Channel.
Began: February 1, 1988, as Prevue Channel; February 1, 1999 as TV Guide Channel. Renamed TV Guide Network June 4, 2007.
Means of Support: Subscriber fees & advertising.
Total subscribers: 83,000,000.
Distribution method: Available to cable systems & satellite providers.
Ownership: Lionsgate Entertainment.

TV GUIDE NETWORK ON DEMAND — See TV Guide Network.
Means of Support: Ad supported.

TV GUIDE ONLINE
1211 Avenue of the Americas
28th Fl
New York, NY 10036
Phone: 212-852-7543
Fax: 212-852-7363
E-mail: ian.wallin@tvguide.com
Web Site: http://www.tvguide.com
Jeff Shell, Chairman & Chief Executive Officer
Joachim Kiener, Vice Chairman
Charles Butler Ammann, Senior Vice President, Secretary & General Counsel
Craig M. Waggy, Senior Vice President & Chief Financial Officer
Toby DeWeese, Vice President, Corporate Development
Christy Tanner, Vice President, Marketing & Online Development
Gregory S. Taylor, Tax Officer
Marie-Claude Thomas, Assistant Secretary
Cindy Miles, Assistant Secretary

Branch Offices:
LOS ANGELES: 6922 Hollywood Blvd, Hollywood, CA 90028. Fax: 323-817-4673.

CHICAGO: 303 E Wacker Dr, Ste 1116, Chicago, IL 60601. Fax: 312-565-1974.
Operating hours/week: 168.
Programming: Online local television program listings, featuring interactive elements including video, audio & program search, available for local system branding.
Began: March 1, 1997.
Means of Support: Cable systems sponsorships, ad revenue.
Ownership: Lionsgate Entertainment.

TV GUIDE SPOT — See TV Guide Network.
Web Site: http://www.tvguide.com/spot
Type of service: Video on demand.
Programming: Weekly highlights of the best shows, movies & entertainment on television.
Total subscribers: 29,000,000.
Distribution method: Available to select cable providers.

TV JAPAN
100 Broadway
15th Floor
New York, NY 10005
Phone: 212-262-3377
Fax: 212-262-5577
E-mail: tvjapan@tvjapan.net
Web Site: http://www.tvjapan.net
Susumu Tanimura, Chief Executive Officer & President
Masao Watari, Executive Vice President, Programming
Akio Yoshinaka, Senior Vice President, Treasurer & Secretary
Hiroyuki Yamamoto, Senior Vice President
Yoshiaki Iida, Senior Vice President
Sonny Takahashi, Vice President, Sales & Marketing
Type of service: Pay.
Satellites: DISH Network.
Operating hours/week: 161.
Programming: Japanese TV programming created by NHK, including news, sports, drama, education & children's programming.
Began: April 1, 1991.
Total subscribers: 45,000.
Distribution method: Available to home dish audiences, cable & telco systems.
Ownership: Japan Network Group Inc., a joint venture of NHK Group & Itochu Group, in conjunction with 28 Japanese & American companies.

TV LAND
1515 Broadway
48th Fl
New York, NY 10036
Phone: 212-258-8000
Fax: 212-258-1967
E-mail: postmaster@tvland.com
Web Site: http://www.tvland.com
Larry W. Jones, President
John Cucci, Chief Operating Officer
Keith Cox, Executive Vice President, Original Programming
Jaclyn Rann Cohen, Executive Vice President, Program Strategy & Acquisitions
Sal Maniaci, Senior Vice President, Development & Original Production
Casey Patterson, Senior Vice President, Event Production & Talent Development
Kim Rosenblum, Senior Vice President, Marketing & Creative
Rachel Sandler, Senior Vice President, Corporate Communications

Caleb Weinstein, Senior Vice President, Strategy & Business Development, Entertainment Group
Maria Caulfield, Vice President, Affiliate Marketing
Rich Cornish, Vice President, Ad Sales Research
Kelleigh Dulany, Vice President, Public Responsibility
Eliot Goldberg, Vice President, Development & Original Programming
Scott Gregory, Vice President, Programming
Laurel Wichert, Vice President, Research
Rachel Lizerbram Sandler, Head of Communications

Branch Offices:
SANTA MONICA: 2600 Colorado Ave, 2nd Floor, Santa Monica, CA 90404. Fax: 310-752-8850.
Type of service: Expanded basic.
Operating hours/week: 168.
Programming: Classic TV shows.
Began: April 29, 1996.
Means of Support: Advertising.
Total subscribers: 92,000,000.
Distribution method: Available to cable systems.
Scrambled signal: Yes.
Ownership: Viacom Inc.

TV LAND HD — See TV Land.

TV ONE
1010 Wayne Ave
Silver Spring, MD 20910
Phone: 301-755-0400
Fax: 301-755-2883
E-mail: lynn@mcreynoldselek.com
Web Site: http://www.tvoneonline.com
Alfred Liggins, Chairman
Wonya Lucas, President & Chief Executive Officer
Keith Bowen, Chief Revenue Officer
Susan Banks, Executive Vice President, Marketing & Creative Services
Bob Buenting, Executive Vice President, Chief Financial Officer
Jody Drewer, Executive Vice President & Chief Financial Officer
Michelle Rice, Executive Vice President, Affiliate Sales & Marketing
Jay Schneider, Executive Vice President, Operations
Karen Wishart, Executive Vice President, Chief Legal Officer
Kimberly Hulsey, Senior Vice President, Distribution & Strategy
Jeff Meier, Senior Vice President, Programming Strategy & Acquisitions
Toni Judkins, Vice President, Programming & Production
Katrice Jones, Vice President, Digital Media
Laura Lipson, Vice President, Promotion & Marketing
Kinyette Newman, Vice President, Production Management
Scott Perkins, Vice President, Creative Services
Endi Piper, Vice President, Business & Legal Affairs
Seeta Zieger, Vice President, Advertising Sales, Western Region

Branch Offices:
NEW YORK: 1114 Avenue of the Americas, 20th Floor, New York, NY 10036. Phone: 917-934-1023.

CHICAGO: 180 N Stetson St, Ste 3250, Chicago, IL 60601.
Type of service: Basic.
Programming: Targeting African-American adults, TV One offers entertainment & issue oriented original programs, classic series, movies, reality & game shows, entertainment news & music variety programs.
Began: January 19, 2004.
Total subscribers: 53,200,000.
Scrambled signal: Yes.
Ownership: Radio One & NBCUniversal LLC.
Entertainment and lifestyle network targeting African American adults

TV ONE HD — See TV One.
Began: December 17, 2008.

TV ORIENT — See GlobeCast WorldTV.
25835 Southfield Rd
Southfield, MI 48075
Phone: 248-569-2020
E-mail: info@mbnamerica.net
Programming: Arabic-language entertainment, news, sports & cultural programs for viewers in North America.

TV POLONIA
1350 Remington Rd
Schaumburg, IL 60173
Phone: 847-882-2000
Fax: 847-882-2002
E-mail: support@tvpolonia.com
Web Site: http://www.tvpolonia.com
Bob Spanski, President
Bob Pisarek, Vice President
Type of service: Pay.
Operating hours/week: 168.
Programming: Polish-language movies, sports, family entertainment, soap operas, documentaries, masterpiece theater, children's shows, educational programs & newscasts.
Means of Support: N.A.

TV ROMANIA INTERNATIONAL — See GlobeCast WorldTV.
E-mail: tvr@tvr.ro
Web Site: http://www.tvr.ro
Programming: Public television; shows with Romanian point of view on cultural, social, economics & political events.

TV2
1045 Hamilton St
Allentown, PA 18101-1012
Phone: 610-434-7833
Fax: 610-432-6473
Operating hours/week: 35.
Programming: Local sports coverage & sports oriented news & entertainment.
Began: January 1, 1969.
Ownership: Service Electric Cable.

TVE INTERNACIONAL
1100 Ponce de Leon Blvd
Coral Gables, FL 33134
Phones: 305-444-4402; 877-912-7531
Fax: 305-444-6301
E-mail: director_sales.ep@rtve.es
Web Site: http://www.rtve.es

Branch Offices:
Affiliate Sales: Delegacion Comercial America, 1100 Ponce de Leon Blvd, Coral Gables, FL 33154. Phone: 305-444-4402. Fax: 305-444-6301. E-Mail: contacto@rtveamerica.com.
Type of service: Basic.
Satellites: Galaxy, transponder 13.
Operating hours/week: 168.
Programming: Spanish television service available to Puerto Rico & Latin America.
Began: September 1, 1989.
Means of Support: State funding (Spain).
Total subscribers: 2,000,000 (reflects U.S. subscribers only.).
Distribution method: Available to home dish audiences & cable systems.
Ownership: State owned.

TV5, LA TELEVISION INTERNATIONAL
TV5 Quebec Canada
1755 boul Rene-Levesque E, Bureau 101
Montreal, QC H2K 4P6
Canada
Phone: 514-522-5322
Fax: 514-522-6572
E-mail: info@tv5.ca
Web Site: http://www.tv5.ca
Suzanne Gouin, President & Chief Operating Officer
Benoit Beaudoin, Vice President & General Manager
Denis Baby, Sales & Marketing Director
Regis Harrisson, Production & Technology Director
Pierre Gang, Program Director
Francine Grise, Finance & Administration Director
Audrey Schelling, Chief, Communications
Nathalie D'Souza, Chief, Acquisitions & Coproductions
Christina Baldassare, Manager Affiliate Relations
Ruby Dizeal, Chief of Operations
Type of service: Basic.
Satellites: Anik E-2, transponder 10-A.
Operating hours/week: 168.
Uplink: Montreal, QC.
Programming: Rebroadcasts French language programs from Africa, Belgium, Canada, France & Switzerland.
Began: September 1, 1988, in Canada; 1998/01/06 in U.S.
Means of Support: Subscriber fees, government support & advertising.
Total subscribers: 6,168,000.
Distribution method: Available to home dish audiences & cable systems.
Scrambled signal: Yes.
Ownership: Consortium de Television Quebec Canada Inc.

TV5 USA
8733 Sunset Blvd
Ste 202
West Hollywood, CA 90069
Phone: 800-737-0455
E-mail: toutsavoir@eu.tv5.org
Web Site: http://www.tv5.org
Operating hours/week: 168.
Programming: French-language news & entertainment.
Distribution method: Available to satellite providers.

TVG NETWORK
19545 NW Von Neumann Dr
Ste 210
Beaverton, OR 97006
Phone: 888-PLAY-TVG
E-mail: comments@tvgnetwork.com
Web Site: http://www.tvgnetwork.com
Ben Evans, Senior Vice President, Programming & Marketing
Marci Miller, Vice President, Marketing
David Carrico, Vice President, Market Access
Kevin Plate, Vice President, Ad Sales
Rick Baedeker, Media Contact
Jason A. Bulger, Ad Sales Director
Type of service: Basic.
Satellites: GE-1, transponder 23.
Operating hours/week: 168.0.
Programming: 24-hour sports entertainment network featuring five live horse races per hour on average, as well as sports news/commentary, behind-the-scenes footage, and programs with racing themes appealing to both the experienced and novice fan.
Began: July 14, 1999.
Total subscribers: 30,000,000.
Distribution method: Available to home dish audiences and cable systems.
Ownership: Gemstar-TV Guide International.

TVK (CAMBODIAN) — See GlobeCast World TV.
E-mail: info@khmerlive.tv
Programming: Cambodian news, movies, sports, entertainment, educational & game shows.
Began: July 1, 2009.
KhmerLive.TV.

TVK (KOREAN)
3435 Wilshire Blvd
19th Fl
Los Angeles, CA 90010
Phone: 213-382-9600
Fax: 213-382-9601
E-mail: alee@tvk24.com
Web Site: http://www.tvk24.com
H Yoon, Director of Broadcasting
T Cho, Director of Broadcast Operations
A Lee, Director of Advertising
C Park, Director of Operations
J Suk, Director of News
Operating hours/week: 168.
Operating areas: Available nationwide.
Programming: Korean language service that offers up-to-date live news broadcasting three times a day plus original programming produced in-house. TVK2 caters to second generation Korean-Americans in hopes of bridging generational gaps.
Began: March 1, 2005, for TVK, 11/11/2009 for TVK2.
Means of Support: Advertising.
Total subscribers: 8,500,000.
Distribution method: Available to home dish audiences and cable system subscribers.
Scrambled signal: Yes.
Television Korea.

TVK2 — See TVK (Korean).

TVN ENTERTAINMENT
15301 Ventura Blvd
Bldg. E, Ste 3000
Sherman Oaks, CA 91403
Phone: 818-526-5000
Fax: 818-526-5001
E-mail: akan@tvn.com
Web Site: http://www.tvn.com
Doug Sylvester, President & Chief Operating Officer
James P. Riley, Chief Sales & Strategy Officer
Dom Stasi, Chief Technology Officer
Matt Cohen, Senior Vice President, Strategy & Business Development
John Smith, Senior Vice President, Affiliate Sales
Chris Stasi, Senior Vice President, Operations
Marlon Gillett, Vice President, Systems Technology Group
Amy Kan, Vice President, Marketing
Jackie Rome, Vice President, Programming
Sandra Bourbeau, Affiliate Marketing Director

Branch Offices:
OPERATIONS CENTER: 2901 W Alameda Ave, Burbank, CA 91505. Phone: 818-526-5000. Fax: 818-526-5106.
Type of service: Video on demand.
Programming: Works with every major studio, network & telecommunications video

provider in North America. Also provides original on-demand programs & networks.
Began: July 1, 1998.
Means of Support: Subscriber fees.
Total subscribers: 40,000,000.
Distribution method: Via satellite to cable systems, telecommunications companies & DBS providers.
Ownership: TVN Entertainment Corp.

TVU MUSIC TELEVISION
PO Box 1887
Westerville, OH 43086
Phone: 614-839-7100
Fax: 614-839-1329
Web Site: http://www.tvulive.com
Type of service: Basic & online.
Operating hours/week: 168.
Programming: Ecclectic mix of popular music.
Began: January 1, 2001.
Distribution method: Available to cable & satellite providers.
Scrambled signal: Yes.
Ownership: Spirit Communications Inc.

TVW
1058 S Capitol Way
Olympia, WA 98501
Phone: 360-725-3999
Fax: 360-586-5678
E-mail: tvw@tvw.org
Web Site: http://www.tvw.org
Cindy Zehnder, President
Steve Newsom, Chief Engineer
Type of service: Satellite service.
Operating hours/week: 168.
Operating areas: Washington.
Programming: Unedited coverage of Washington State government deliberations, state Supreme Court, state agencies, boards, commissions & public policy events statewide.
Began: April 10, 1995.
Means of Support: Privately & publicly supported.
Total subscribers: 3,000,000.
Distribution method: Cable systems via satellite & fiber optic.
Ownership: Non-profit organization.

24/7 NEWS CHANNEL
5407 Fairview
Boise, ID 83706
Phones: 208-321-5614; 208-375-7277
Fax: 208-378-1762
E-mail: ktvbnews@ktvb.com
Web Site: http://www.ktvb.com
Doug Armstrong, President & General Manager
Type of service: Digital, Basic.
Operating hours/week: 168.
Scrambled signal: Yes.
Ownership: Belo Corp.

29 HD NETWORK
1639 11th St
Ste 258
Santa Monica, CA 90404
Phone: 310-593-4177
Fax: 310-452-8197
E-mail: info@29hdnetwork.com
Web Site: http://www.29hdnetwork.com

Branch Offices:
ASIA: Q3 Green Park Ext, New Delhi 16, India.

U.S.: 1037 Valley Rd, New Canaan, CT 06840.
Type of service: Broadband.
Programming: A high definition network offering a mix of movie & classic programs for the thirty-something audience.

CANAL 22 MEXICO — See Alterna'TV.
Atletas No. 2
Colonia Country Club
Delegacin Coyoacn C.P. 04220
Mxico D.F
Phones: 21-22-96-80; 01-800-22-62-522
Web Site: http://www.canal22.org.mx/index.html
Programming: Documentaries, cultural newscasts & talk shows.

2M MAROC — See GlobeCast WorldTV.
Km 7.3 route de Rabat
Ain Sebaa, Casablanca 20250
Morocco
Phone: 212-22-66-73-73
E-mail: portail@tv2m.co.ma
Web Site: http://www.2m.tv
Type of service: Basic.
Operating hours/week: 168.
Programming: Moroccan news, documentaries, serials, films, cultural & sports events & children's shows.
Distribution method: Available on GlobeCast WorldTV satellite service.

TYC SPORTS
Avenida San Juan 1130
Buenos Aires 1147
Argentina
Phone: 54 11 4300 3800
Fax: 54 11 4300 3499
E-mail: info@tycsports.com.ar
Web Site: http://www.tycsports.com
Satellites: Intelsat 11.
Operating hours/week: 168.
Programming: Sports network from South America. Offers live coverage of the Argentine first-division league soccer league plus soccer from Chile & Paraguay plus boxing, Argentine basketball and auto racing.
Distribution method: Available on FiOS TV and DirecTV.
Scrambled signal: Yes.

UCTV — See KyLinTV.
Type of service: IPTV.
Programming: Chinese-language Buddhist programming.

ULTIMATE SHOPPING NETWORK
2121 Ave. of the Stars
Ste 2920
Los Angeles, CA 90067
Phones: 310-229-2200; 888-881-6736
Web Site: http://www.shopusn.com
Mark J. Miller, Chairman & Chief Executive Officer
Andy Schmidt, Chief Financial Officer
Gary Wolf, Director, USN Corp.
David Norman, Vice President, Merchandising
Steve Parker, General Manager, Broadcasting
Type of service: Basic, broadband & IPTV.
Operating hours/week: 168.
Programming: Home shopping with focus on luxury, upscale items & including a broad range of jewelry, collectibles entertainment products, apparel, housewares & cosmetics.
Began: May 1, 2003.
Total subscribers: 30,000,000.
Distribution method: Available to cable & satellite providers.
Ownership: USN Television Group, Inc.

UNICABLE — See Televisa Networks.
E-mail: unicable@televisanetworks.tv

UNINOVELAS
9405 NW 41st St
Miami, FL 33178
Phone: 305-471-3900

Fax: 305-471-4058
Web Site: http://corporate.univision.com/
Monica Talan, Vice President, Corporate Communications, Univision Communications Inc.
Operating hours/week: Plans 168.
Operating areas: Will be available nationwide.
Programming: Will offer Spanish language dramas and soap operas.
Scheduled to begin: Plans to launch in third quarter of 2011.
Means of Support: Plans advertising.
Distribution method: Will be available to home dish audiences and cable systems.
Scrambled signal: Planned.
Ownership: Univision Communications Inc.

UNION ON DEMAND
570 Lexington Ave
19th Floor
New York, NY 10022
Phone: 212-920-2880
Fax: 212-920-2845
Web Site: http://www.uniondemand.com
Type of service: Basic, broadband, video on demand.
Programming: Action sports film channel, featuring surf, snow, skate, BMX & motorcross events.
Began: April 1, 2006.
Total subscribers: 15,000,000.
Distribution method: Available to cable providers.
Ownership: Quicksilver Entertainment Inc. & Global Media Ventures LLC.

UNIQUE BUSINESS NEWS — See KyLinTV.
No. 33-3, Lane 11
Guangfu N Rd
Taipei
Taiwan, Republic of China
Phone: 02-2766-2888
Fax: 02-2766-2910
Web Site: http://www.ustv.com.tw
Programming: Offers business news from Republic of China. Part of KyLinTV's 'Basic Taiwan Package'.
Scrambled signal: Yes.

UNIQUE SATELLITE TV — See KyLinTV.
No. 33-3, Lane 11
Guangfu N Rd
Taipei
Taiwan, Republic of China
Phone: 02-2766-2888
Fax: 02-2766-2910
Web Site: http://www.ustv.com.tw
Programming: Offers programming from Republic of China. Part of KyLinTV's 'Basic Taiwan Package'.
Scrambled signal: No.

UNIVERSAL HD
900 Sylvan Ave
One CNBC Plz
Englewood Cliffs, NJ 07632
Web Site: http://www.universalhd.com
Ryan Sharkey, Senior Vice President, Program Acquisitions & Administration
Type of service: Digital.
Satellites: AMC 11, transponder 24.
Operating hours/week: 168.
Programming: Offers the best of NBC Universal in 100% 1080i HD, 24/7. Programming includes premiere sporting events, unedited and uninterrupted films and award winning series.
Began: December 1, 2004.
Total subscribers: 55,000,000.
Distribution method: Available to home dish audiences and cable systems.
Scrambled signal: Yes.
Ownership: NBCUniversal LLC.

UNIVERSITY OF CALIFORNIA TV (UCTV)
9500 Gilman Dr
La Jolla, CA 92093-0176T
Phones: 858-534-9412; 888-828-1737
E-mail: knowledge@uctv.com
Web Site: http://www.uctv.tv
Lynn Burnstan, Managing Director
Alison Gang, Communications Manager
Vicky Powell, Special Projects
Steve Anderson, On-Air Operations
Kris Jones, Graphic Design
Melissa McEwen, Web Developer
Type of service: Basic & broadband.
Operating hours/week: 168.
Programming: Public affairs, science, health, humanities & arts programming drawn from 10 UC campuses & includes documentaries, faculty lectures, research symposiums & artistic performances.
Distribution method: Available to cable & satellite providers.

UNIVISION
9405 NW 41st St
Miami, FL 33178
Phone: 305-471-3900
Fax: 305-471-4058
E-mail: afalcon@univision.net
Web Site: http://corporate.univision.com/
Haim Saban, Chairman, Univision
Randy Falco, President & Chief Executive Officer
Cesar Conde, President, Univision Networks
Luis Fernandez, President, Univision Entertainment & Univision Studios
Kevin Cuddihy, President, Univision TV Group
David Lawenda, President, Advertising Sales
Tonia O'Connor, President, Distribution Sales & Marketing
Javier Saralegui, President, Univision Online
Peter Walker, President, Univision Local Media
Andrew W Hobson, Senior Executive Vice President & Chief Financial Officer
Glenn Dryfoos, Executive Vice President, Business Affairs
C. Douglas Kranwinkle, Executive Vice President & General Counsel
Roberto Llamas, Executive Vice President, Chief Human Resources Officer
Peter H Lori, Executive Vice President, Controller & Chief Accounting Officer
Bert Medina, Executive Vice President & Operating Manager, TeleFutura
Rick Alessandri, Senior Vice President, Business Development
Hector Beltran, Senior Vice President & Director, Creative Services

Carlos Deschappelles, Senior Vice President, Sports Sales
David Downs, Senior Vice President, Sports Division
Chris Fager, Senior Vice President, Distribution, National Sales
John Heffron, Senior Vice President, Affiliate Relations, New York Office
German Perez-Hanim, Senior Vice President, Operating Manager, TeleFutura
Jessica Rodriguez, Senior Vice President, Univision Cable Networks
Peter J. Scanlon, Senior Vice President, Network Planning
Dan Thomas, Senior Vice President, Sales Development & Marketing
Nicolas Valls, Senior Vice President, Network Sales & Marketing
Phyllis Verdugo, Senior Vice President, Law Department
Rick Alessandri, Vice President, Business Development
Matt Boxer, Vice President, Marketing & Business Development
Neil Brooks, Vice President, National Sales
Daniel Coronell, Vice President, Univision News
Melinda Duchak, Vice President, Marketing & Research
Maelia Macin, Vice President & General Manager, Los Angeles Stations
Sarah Madigan, Vice President, Business Affairs, Distribution Sales & Marketing
Patricia Marrero, Vice President & Director, Sports Marketing
David Murray, Vice President, Sales Development & Marketing
Peter Pouliopoulos, Vice President, Sales Development & Marketing
Mario Rodriguez, Vice President, Programming
Diego T. Ruiz, Vice President & General Manager, Univision Online
Deborah Shinnick, Vice President & Director, Audience & Programming Analysis
Carole A. Smith, Vice President, Network Research
Adam Stewart, Vice President, Sales Development & Marketing, Western Region
Monica Talan, Vice President, Corporate Communications
Stuart H. Walker, Vice President, Sales Development & Marketing
Type of service: Basic.
Satellites: Galaxy 1-R.
Operating hours/week: 168.
Uplink: Miami, FL.
Programming: News, entertainment & information in Spanish.
Began: September 1, 1961.
Means of Support: Advertising.
Ownership: Perenchio TV Inc.

UNIVISION DEPORTES

9405 NW 41st St
Miami, FL 33178
Phone: 305-471-3900
Fax: 305-471-4058
Web Site: http://corporate.univision.com
Monica Talan, Vice President, Corporate Communications, Univision Communications Inc.
Operating areas: Will be available nationwide.
Programming: Will over coverage of Mexico's national soccer team, the Mexican Soccer League and other sporting events.
Scheduled to begin: Plans to launch the first half of 2012.
Means of Support: Plans advertising.
Distribution method: Will be available to home dish audiences and cable systems.
Scrambled signal: Planned.
Ownership: Univision Communications Inc.

UNIVISION HD — See Univision.

UNIVISION ON DEMAND — See Univision.

Operating hours/week: 168.
Programming: Univision's programming available to DirecTV subscribers.
Began: January 1, 2009, Service began on DirecTV.
Distribution method: Available only to home dish audiences.

UNIVISION STUDIOS

9405 NW 41st St
Miami, FL 33178-2301
Phone: 305-471-3900
Fax: 305-471-4065
Web Site: http://www.univision.com
Luis Fernandez, President
German Perez Nahim, Vice President
Univision Studios produces and co-produces reality shows, dramatic series and other programming formats for Univision Communications' platforms.

UNIVISION 24/7

9405 NW 41st St
Miami, FL 33178
Phone: 305-471-3900
Fax: 305-471-4058
Web Site: http://corporate.univision.com
Monica Talan, Vice President, Corporate Communications, Univision Communications Inc.
Operating hours/week: Plans 168.
Operating areas: Will be available nationwide.
Programming: Will offer round the clock news and information.
Scheduled to begin: Plans to launch in 2012.
Means of Support: Advertising.
Distribution method: Will be available to home dish audiences and cable systems.
Scrambled signal: Planned.
Ownership: Univision Communications Inc.

URBAN AMERICAN TELEVISION NETWORK

2707 S Cooper
Ste 119
Arlington, TX 76015
Phone: 817-303-7449
Fax: 817-459-2942
E-mail: info@uatvn.com
Web Site: http://www.uatvn.com
Jacob R. Miles, III, Chief Executive Officer
Randy Moseley, President & Chief Financial Officer
Ed Maddox, President, National Sales
Bruno Olivieri, Executive Vice President, Affiliate Operations
Sandra Pate, Executive Vice President, Programming & Development
Type of service: Basic.
Satellites: Spacenet 3, transponder 2.
Operating hours/week: 168.
Programming: Family oriented programming, including movies, documentaries, news, talk shows, outdoor programming & home shopping. Targeting urban populations, including African Americans & English speaking Hispanics.
Began: March 14, 1994.
Means of Support: Affiliations, advertising & subscribers.
Total subscribers: 22,000,000.
Distribution method: Available to television stations & cable systems.
Ownership: Private corporation.

U.S. MILITARY TV NETWORK

2973 Harbor Blvd
Ste 276
Costa Mesa, CA 92626
E-mail: info@usmilitary.tv
Web Site: http://www.usmilitary.tv
Lauren Kelly, President & Chief Executive Officer

Branch Offices:
WASHINGTON: Washington Square, 1050 Connecticut Ave NW, Washington, DC 20036.
Operating hours/week: Plans 168.
Programming: Focuses on military personnel & their families through several programs including game shows, intramural sports, political commentary & live newscasts.
Scheduled to begin: Unannounced.
Distribution method: Available to cable & satellite providers.
Scrambled signal: Planned.

USA NETWORK

30 Rockefeller Plz
New York, NY 10112
Phone: 212-664-4444
Fax: 212-408-2711
Web Site: http://www.usanetwork.com
Bonnie Hammer, President, NBC Universal Entertainment & Cable Studio
Chris McCumber, Co-President, USA Network
Jeff Wachtel, Co-President, USA Network
John Larrabee, Chief Information Officer
Mike Sileck, Chief Financial Officer
Dara Khosrowshahi, President, USAi
David Kissinger, President, Programming, Studios USA
Mark Miller, President, Advertising Sales
Richard Sheingold, President, Sales
Jane Blaney, Executive Vice President, Programming, Acquisitions & Scheduling
Jackie de Crinis, Executive Vice President, Original Scripted Programming
Douglas Holloway, Executive Vice President, Network Distribution & Affiliate Relations
Steve Mandala, Executive Vice President, Cable Ad Sales, NBCU
Rafael Pastor, Executive Vice President & Managing Director, USA Networks International
John Silvestri, Executive Vice President, Advertising Sales & General Sales Manager
Rob Sorcher, Executive Vice President, General Manager
Andrew Besch, Senior Vice President, Marketing
Stephen Brenner, Senior Vice President, USAi
Iris Burnett, Senior Vice President, Corporate Communications & Public Affairs
Lonnie Burstein, Senior Vice President, First-Run Development
Ray Giacopelli, Senior Vice President, Research
Liz Korman, Senior Vice President, Advertising Sales
Bill McGoldrick, Senior Vice President, Original Scripted Programming
Heather Olander, Senior Vice President, Alternative Programming
Dick Ross, Senior Vice President, Operations & Production
Donna Rothman, Senior Vice President, Emerging Networks
Peter Ruben, Senior Vice President, National Accounts & Western Division
Adam Shapiro, Senior Vice President, Long-Form Programming
Alexandra Shapiro, Senior Vice President, Brand Marketing & Digital
Ryan Sharkey, Senior Vice President, Program Acquisitions & Administration
Robert West, Senior Vice President, Programming & Scheduling

Regional Offices:
CHICAGO: 401 N Michigan Ave, Ste 3125, Chicago, IL 60611.

DETROIT: 2000 Town Center, Ste 2460, Southfield, MI 48075.

LOS ANGELES: 2049 Century Park E, Ste 2550, Los Angeles, CA 90067.
Type of service: Basic.
Satellites: Galaxy 1R, transponder 24 (east coast); Galaxy 1R, transponder 24 (west coast).
Operating hours/week: 168.
Uplink: Smithtown, NY.
Programming: All entertainment, including original programs, game shows, sitcoms, movies & sports.
Began: April 1, 1977, as Madison Square Garden Network; renamed USA Network April 9, 1979.
Means of Support: System pays per subscriber; advertising.
Total subscribers: 101,200,000.
Distribution method: Available to cable systems.
Scrambled signal: Yes.
Ownership: NBCUniversal LLC.

USA NETWORK HD — See USA Network.

UTH TV

2395 Broadway
Redwood City, CA 94063
Phone: 650-363-1010
Fax: 650-363-1033
Web Site: http://www.uthtv.com
Carl Rosendahl, Chief Executive Officer
Type of service: Broadband.
Programming: Youth produced and oriented music, documentaries, movie reviews & shows about technology, fashion, style & social issues.

UTILISIMA

1440 S Sepulveda Blvd
Los Angeles, CA 10036
Phone: 310-444-8153
Web Site: http://www.utilisima.com
Hernan Lopez, President & Chief Executive Officer, Fox International Channels
Tom Maney, Senior Vice President, Advertising Sales, Fox Hispanic Media
Operating areas: Available nationwide.
Programming: Spanish-language lifestyle programming & female focused entertainment.
Began: January 1, 2008, in the United States. The service began in 1996 in Spain.
Total subscribers: 4,000,000.
Distribution method: Available to cable systems, home dish audiences and FiOS.
Scrambled signal: Yes.
Ownership: Fox Hispanic Media, a subsidiary of News corp.

UTILISIMA US

1440 S Sepulveda Blvd
Los Angeles, CA 90025
Phone: 310-444-8153
E-mail: foxtv.info@fox.com
Web Site: http://www.foxinternationalchannels.com/brands/utilisima
Hernan Lopez, Chief Operating Officer, Fox International Channels
Type of service: Basic.
Operating areas: Available nationwie.
Programming: Spanish language channel dedicated to food, health and family. Programming is heavily lifestyle-driven and showcases everything from cooking and per-

sonal style to decorating, do-it-yourself and home renovation.
Began: July 12, 2010, in Maryland & Virginia on FiOS. Became available nationwide by the end of the week.
Total subscribers: 4,000,000.
Distribution method: Available to FiOS subscribers.
Ownership: News Corp.

VEGAS CHANNEL
(TVC)
6017 Jubilee Gardens
Las Vegas, NV 89131
Phone: 702-395-4040
Fax: 702-645-6876
Web Site: http://www.thevegastvchannel.com
Victoria De Maria, President & Chief Executive Officer
Type of service: Basic, ad-supported, digital, no charge.
Operating hours/week: 168.
Programming: Movies, sports, reality, live events & news all about Las Vegas.
Began: October 27, 2007.

VEHIX TV ON DEMAND
1165 E Wilmington Ave
Ste 200
Salt Lake City, UT 84106
Phones: 801-401-6060; 866-698-3449
E-mail: busdev@vehix.com
Web Site: http://www.vehix.com
Derek Mattsson, Chief Executive Officer
Glenn Morey, Chief Marketing Officer
Rufus S. Frost, V.P., Affiliate Relations, Vice President, Affiliate Relations
Kerry Lehtinen, Vice President, Corporate Communications
Christopher M. Satovick, Vice President, Consumer Products
Michael van Thiel, Vice President, Product Development
Type of service: Video on demand & broadband.
Programming: Automotive video buying guides, test drives, crash tests & reality shows.
Began: January 1, 2006.
Means of Support: Advertising.

VELOCITY
One Discovery Pl
Silver Spring, MD 20910-3354
Phone: 240-662-2000
Web Site: http://dhd.discovery.com/tv/velocity/
Robert S Scanlon, Senior Vice President
Operating hours/week: Plans 168.
Operating areas: Will be available nationwide.
Programming: Will replace Discovery HD Theater. Will feature more than 400 premiere hours of new and returning series and specials showcasing the best of the automotive, sports and leisure, adventure, and travel genres.
Scheduled to begin: Plans to launch late 2011.
Means of Support: Advertising.
Total subscribers: (Plans 40,000,000 at launch.).
Distribution method: Will be available to home dish audiences and cable systems.
Scrambled signal: Planned.
Ownership: Discovery Communications Inc. DCI ownership: Liberty Media, 66%; Advance/Newhouse, 31%; John Hendricks, 1%.

VENEMOVIES
7403 Collins Ave
Miami Beach, FL 33141
Phone: 305-868-6800
Fax: 305-868-6220
E-mail: info@venemovies.com
Web Site: http://www.venemovies.com
Alejandro Parisca, General Manager
Julio Noriega, Vice President, Venevision International
Giselle Trainor, Marketing Director
Type of service: Pay.
Operating hours/week: 168.
Programming: Original, Spanish-language blockbuster movies from Mexico, Colombia, Peru, Venezuela, Argentina, Chile & Spain.
Began: September 1, 2006.
Scrambled signal: Yes.
Ownership: Venevision International, Cisneros Group of Companies.

VERIA TV
701 Highlander Blvd
Ste 200
Arlington, TX 76015
Phones: 817-804-4650; 866-918-3142
Fax: 817-804-4696
E-mail: info@veria.com
Web Site: http://www.veria.com
Gabriella Messina, Head of Programming
Type of service: Basic.
Operating hours/week: 168.
Programming: Natural health & wellness shows.
Began: October 1, 2007.
Distribution method: Available to cable systems & satellite providers.

VERSUS
2 Stamford Plz, 9th Fl
281 Tresser Blvd
Stamford, CT 06901
Phone: 203-406-2500
Fax: 203-406-2530
Web Site: http://www.versus.tv
Jon Litner, President
Marc Fein, Executive Vice President, Programming, Production & Business Operations
Becky Ruthven, Senior Vice President, Affiliate Sales
Leon Schweir, Senior Vice President, Production & Executive Producer
John West, Senior Vice President, Ad Sales
Joe Brown, Vice President, Research
Tripp Dixon, Vice President, Creative Services
Marty Ehrlich, Vice President, Production & Executive Producer
Brad Friedrich, Vice President, Business Development
Jeff Goldberg, Vice President, Programming
Pamela Jensen, Vice President, National Affiliate Sales
Wendy McCoy, Vice President, Marketing
Andrew Meyer, Vice President, Original Programming
Meier Raivich, Vice President, Communications
Neal Scarbrough, Vice President, Digital Media
Mandy Orzo, Acquisitions & Scheduling Director
Greg Trager, Field Sports Programming & Production Director

Branch Offices:
CHICAGO: One IBM Plaza, 330 N Wabash Ave, Ste 2005, Chicago, IL 60611. Phone: 312-832-0808. Fax: 312-832-9485.

DETROIT: 401 S Woodward Ave, Ste 457, Birmingham, MI 48009. Phone: 248-594-0707. Fax: 248-594-1460.

LOS ANGELES: 12100 W Olympic Blvd, Ste 200, Los Angeles, CA 90064. Phone: 310-979-2260. Fax: 310-979-2261.

NEW YORK: 1114 Avenue of the Americas, 20th Floor, New York, NY 10036. Phone: 914-931-1050. Fax: 212-687-1819.

HOUSTON: 133 N Friendswood Dr, Friendswood, TX 77548. Phone: 281-331-7787. Fax: 281-331-7262.
Type of service: Expanded basic.
Satellites: Galaxy 11, transponder 21C.
Operating hours/week: 168.
Programming: Brings scenic outdoor adventure indoors 24 hours a day. Includes family-oriented how-to information for the camper, angler, climber, bicyclist, hunter, photographer, skier, sailor, kayaker and more.
Began: July 1, 1995, as Outdoor Life Network; relaunched as Versus on September 25, 2006. To be rebranded by January 1, 2012.
Total subscribers: 75,000,000.
Distribution method: Available to home dish audiences and cable systems.
Scrambled signal: Yes.
Ownership: NBCUniversal LLC.

VERSUS HD — See Versus.

VERSUS ON DEMAND — See Versus.
Programming: Action sports, fishing, hunting, NHL games, shooting & special events including Tour de France & America's Cup.
Distribution method: Available to cable systems.

VH1 HD — See VH1.

VH1
MTV Networks Inc.
1515 Broadway, 22nd Fl
New York, NY 10036
Phone: 212-258-7800
E-mail: karen.keaney@mtvstaff.com
Web Site: http://www.vh1.com
Tom Calderone, President
Carl D. Folta, Executive Vice President, Corporate Communications
Richard Gay, Executive Vice President, Strategy & Operations
Fred Graver, Executive Vice President, Programming
Rick Krim, Executive Vice President, Talent & Music Programming
Jeff Olde, Executive Vice President, Original Programming & Production
Lee Rolontz, Executive Vice President, Original Production & Development
Ann Sarnoff, Executive Vice President, Chief Operating Officer
Ben Zurier, Executive Vice President, Program Strategy
Robert Natter, Senior Counsel, Business & Legal Affairs
Stacy Alexander, Senior Vice President, Talent & Casting
Michael Benson, Senior Vice President, Promotion & Program Planning
Eddie Dalva, Senior Vice President, Programming, Co-Production & Creative Affairs
Reggie Fils-Aime, Senior Vice President, Marketing
Bill Flanagan, Senior Vice President, Editorial Director
David Giles, Senior Vice President, Research
Bruce Gillmer, Senior Vice President, Music & Talent Relations
Jason Hirschhorn, Senior Vice President & General Manager, VH1 Group
Tina Imm, Senior Vice President & General Manager, VH1 Digital
Susan Kantor, Senior Vice President, Creative Director
Joshua Katz, Senior Vice President, Marketing
John Kelley, Senior Vice President, Communications
Laura Molen, Senior Vice President, Advertising Sales
George Moll, Senior Vice President, Production & Programming
Jill Newfield, Senior Vice President, Business Affairs & General Counsel
Donald Silvey, Senior Vice President, Programming Enterprises & Business Development

Branch Offices:
Atlanta, GA; Dallas, TX; Detroit, MI; Los Angeles, CA; New York, NY.
Type of service: Basic & video on demand.
Satellites: Galaxy III, transponder 15.
Operating hours/week: 168.
Uplink: Network Operations Center, Smithtown, NY.
Programming: Current & classic hit music videos for viewers 25-49.
Began: January 1, 1985.
Means of Support: Advertising.
Total subscribers: 100,000,000.
Distribution method: Available to cable systems & mobile video.
Scrambled signal: Yes. Equipment: M/A-Com; VideoCipher II.
Ownership: Viacom Inc.

VH1 CLASSIC — See VH1.

VH1 COUNTRY — See Country Music TV.
Began: Relaunched as CMT Pure Country on May 26, 2006.

VH1 SOUL — See VH1.
Began: Relaunched on February 1, 2006.
Total subscribers: 20,000,000.

VHUNO — See VH1.

VIDA VISION
2264 NW 94th Ave
Miami, FL 33172
Phones: 305-513-4790; 786-426-9169
Fax: 786-331-8959
E-mail: info@nuestraraza.com
Web Site: http://www.vidavisiontv.com
Ricardo Quintana, President
David R. Hurtado, Chief Operating Officer & Executive Vice President
Operating hours/week: 168.

Programming: Educational, informative & interactive Spanish language programming for young Hispanic families.
Began: January 1, 2002.
Total subscribers: 100,000.
Distribution method: Available to cable & satellite programmers.

VIDEO SEAT
546 E Main St
Lexington, KY 40508
Phone: 859-226-4678
Fax: 859-226-4391
E-mail: cindy.johnson@hostcommunications.com
Web Site: http://www.hostcommunications.com
Thomas J. Stultz, Chief Executive Officer & President
David Cawood, Executive Vice President, Administration & Collegiate Marketing
Fred Erickson, Executive Vice President & Chief Financial Officer
Mike Dodson, Senior Vice President, Broadcast Services
Tim Campbell, Vice President, Media
David Bertram, Marketing & Research Director
Lisa Fluty, Chief Information Officer
Type of service: Pay-per-view.
Programming: College football & basketball on pay-per-view for U. of Tennessee, U. Of Kentucky & Mississippi State.
Means of Support: Subscriber fees.
Ownership: Host Communications Inc.

VIDEO ROLA
Lazaro Cardenas 1710
Guadalajara, Jalisco 44900
Mexico
Phone: 52 333 750 0015
Fax: 52 333 750 0016
E-mail: atanaka@videorola.com
Web Site: http://www.videorola.com
Type of service: Basic.
Sales representative: US - Condista.
Operating hours/week: 168.
Programming: Dedicated to regional Mexican music. 45+ live hours during weekdays, allowing viewers on both sides of the border to interact with the channel and their families. More than 500 new releases every year. Exclusive content.
Began: April 1, 2001, Reflects U.S. launch.
Total subscribers: 1,850,000 (Mexico & U.S.).
Distribution method: Available to cable systems and DTH.
Scrambled signal: Yes.
Ownership: MegaCable.

VIEWER'S CHOICE CANADA
BCE Place, 181 Bay St
PO Box 787, Ste 100
Toronto, ON M5J 2T3
Canada
Phone: 416-956-2010
Fax: 416-956-2055
E-mail: viewerschoice@tv.astral.com
Web Site: http://www.viewerschoice.ca
Lisa de Wilde, President & Chief Executive Officer
Keith McSpurren, Vice President, Marketing
Janet Corcoran, Sales & Marketing Manager
Gillian Harrison, Program & Operations Manager
Mark Waschulzik, Assistant Manager, Marketing
Type of service: Pay-per-view.
Satellites: Anik E-2.
Operating hours/week: 168.
Operating areas: Ontario, Quebec & Atlantic Provinces.
Programming: Movies, live concerts & sports.
Began: September 5, 1991.
Means of Support: Subscriber fees.
Total subscribers: 600,000.
Distribution method: Available to cable systems.
Ownership: Astral Communications Inc., Rogers Pay Per View Inc. & TSN Enterprises.

VIJAY — See Star India Plus.

VISION TV
80 Bond St
Toronto, ON M5B 1X2
Canada
Phone: 416-368-3194
Fax: 416-368-9774
E-mail: visiontv@visiontv.ca
Web Site: http://www.visiontv.ca
Bill Roberts, President & Chief Executive Officer
Mark Prosuhn, Chief Operating Officer
Chris Johnson, Senior Vice President, Programming
Jane Macnaughton, Chief Financial Officer & Vice President, Finance & Administration
Suzanna Mandryk, Vice President, Communications & Marketing
Alberta Nokes, Director, Independent Production
Tony Greco, Director, Affiliate Relations
Pagie Isaac, Director, Business Development
Beverly Shenken, Director, Program Acquistions
Joan Jenkinson, Director, Programming
Brant Kostandoff, General Counsel & Director, Corporate & Regulatory Affairs
Erika Kramer, Director, Technical Operations, Broadcast Systems & Traffic
Marie Lofranco, Manager, Internet Communications
Mulugeta Muru, Manager, IT Services & Programming

Regional Offices:
ATLANTIC REGION: 1318 Main St, Dartmouth, NS B2Z 1B2, Canada. Phone: 902-435-0025. Fax: 902-435-2499. Charles Doucet, Atlantic Representative.

WESTERN REGION: No. 10-671 Fort St, Victoria, BC V8W 1G6, Canada. Phone: 250-360-0848. Fax: 250-360-0870. Maureen Levitt, Western Region Mgr.
Type of service: Basic.
Satellites: Anik E-2, transponder T-5 (east); Anik E-2, transponder T-16 (west).
Operating hours/week: 168.
Programming: Multi-faith, social justice, documentaries & arts.
Means of Support: Advertising & subscriber fees.
Total subscribers: 6,400,000.
Distribution method: Available to home dish audiences & cable systems.
Equipment: DSR 4400.

VIVA TELEVISION NETWORK — See V-me TV.

V-ME KIDS
450 W 33rd St
New York, NY 10001
Phone: 212-560-1313
Web Site: http://www.vmetv.com
Mario Baeza, Chairman & Founder
Carmen M DiRienzo, President & Chief Executive Officer
Andres Cardo, Chief Corporate Development Officer
Guillermo Sierra, Senior Vice President & Chief Content Officer
Richard Taub, Vice President, Business Development
Type of service: Basic.
Operating hours/week: 168.
Operating areas: Available nationwide.
Programming: Offers programming specifically for Hispanic preschoolers.
Began: September 1, 2010.
Distribution method: Available to AT&T U-Verse customers.
Scrambled signal: No.
Ownership: V-me Media Inc. This is a partnership comprised of Thirteen/WNET plus The Baeza Group, Syncom Funds and other private investors.

V-ME TV
450 W 33rd
11th Fl
New York, NY 10001
Phone: 212-273-4800
Fax: 212-273-4802
E-mail: info@vmetv.com
Web Site: http://www.vmetv.com
Carmen DiRienzo, President & Chief Executive Officer
Michael Bollo, Vice President, Sales & Sponsorship
Richard Taub, Vice President, Business Development
Ariel Martinez, Director, Integrated Marketing & Digital Sales
Kim Fabian, Network Sales Manager
Mauricio Gallego, Post-Production Manager
Felix Martinez, IT & Operations Manager
Type of service: Digital broadcast, basic cable & satellite.
Operating hours/week: 168.
Programming: Spanish-language TV, entertains & informs Latino families in Spanish with prime time drama, music, sports, current affairs & Latin cinema, along with world class kids, food, lifestyle & nature programs. The 24-hour network, partnered with public television stations, is one of America's largest Hispanic networks, currently available in over 70% of all Hispanic homes.
Began: March 5, 2007.
Total subscribers: 28,000,000.
Distribution method: Available to cable systems & satellite providers.
Scrambled signal: Yes.
Ownership: V-me Media Inc. (Grupo Prisa, Syncom Funds, Baeza Group, WNET.org).

VOILA — No longer planned.

VOY
330 Madison Ave
6th Fl
New York, NY 10017
Phone: 212-204-8331
Fax: 212-202-5240
Web Site: http://www.voy.tv
Fernando Espuelas, Chairman & Chief Executive Officer

Branch Offices:
VOY PICTURES: 9220 Sunset Blvd, Los Angeles, CA 90069. Phone: 310-550-1019. Fax: 310-388-0775.
Programming: Delivering culturally relevant entertainment & empowering today's new generation of English-speaking Latinos & those discovering Latin culture. The VOY brand connects with its audience through a broad range of emerging & traditional distribution vehicles from broadband & wireless to broadcasting & DVDs.
Scrambled signal: Yes.

VOY TV — See Voy.
Type of service: Broadband.
Programming: Broadband component to Voy satellite channel. Features acquired & original shows, licensed & user-generated video targeted to English-speaking Latinos.
Began: October 11, 2006.
Distribution method: Online.

VSEN-TV
855 E Twain Ave
Ste 159
Las Vegas, NV 89109
Phone: 702-369-3911
E-mail: info@vsentv.com
Web Site: http://www.vsentv.com
Rod Myers, President
Operating hours/week: 168.
Programming: Alternative sports programming.
Began: July 1, 2006.
Distribution method: Available to cable systems & broadcasters.
Ownership: Fuego Entertainment.

VUDU
2980 Bowers Ave
Santa Clara, CA 95051
Phone: 408-492-1010
E-mail: support@vudu.com
Web Site: http://www.vudu.com
Type of service: IPTV.
Programming: Instant home download service of popular movies & shows.

VUTOPIA
345 Hudson St
c/o iN DEMAND LLC
New York, NY 10014
Phone: 646-638-8203
Fax: 646-486-0854
Web Site: http://www.vutopia.com
Matt Tierney, Manager, VOD Programming
Type of service: Subscription video on demand.
Satellites: AMC 10, transponder 18.
Operating hours/week: 168.
Operating areas: Available nationwide on Cox and Time Warner systems.
Programming: Offers a package of commercial-free Hollywood and independent movies and documentaries available on TV and online, all on demand.
Began: April 1, 2010.
Distribution method: Available to Cox and Time Warner cable system subscribers.
Scrambled signal: Yes.
Ownership: iN DEMAND.

WMAX — See Cinemax.
Programming: Dramas, romances & mysteries targeted to women.
Began: May 1, 2001.

W NETWORK
64 Jefferson Ave
Unit 18
Toronto, ON M6K 3H4
Phone: 416-534-1191
E-mail: comments@wnetwork.com
Web Site: http://www.wnetwork.com
Operating hours/week: 168.
Programming: Features Hollywood box-office hits, popular drama series, Canadian & international documentaries & lifestyle information programming from health to home decorating targeted to women.
Began: January 1, 1995, as WTN; relaunched as W Network in April 2002.
Total subscribers: 6,000,000.
Ownership: Corus Entertainment Group.

WALN CABLE RADIO
3028 S Pike Ave
Allentown, PA 18103
Phone: 610-791-1818
Fax: 610-791-9618
E-mail: info@walncableradio.com
Web Site: http://www.walncableradio.com/
Type of service: Basic.
Operating hours/week: 168.
Operating areas: Eastern Pennsylvania & western New Jersey.
Programming: Blend of popular oldies & polka standards, love songs & ballads from the '40s through the '80s.
Means of Support: Advertising.

WAM! AMERICA'S KIDZ NETWORK — See Encore.

WAPA AMERICA
1 Broadcast Center
Chicopee, MA 01013
Phones: 413-377-2054; 888-733-9272
Web Site: http://www.wapaamerica.com
Programming: Current & classic Puerto Rican entertainment shows.
Began: August 23, 2004.
Distribution method: Available to cable systems & satellite providers.
Ownership: LIN TV Corp.

WASHINGTON KOREAN TV
2931-G Eskridge Rd
Fairfax, VA 22031
Phone: 703-560-1590
E-mail: info@wktvusa.com
Web Site: http://www.wktvusa.com
Type of service: Digital.
Operating hours/week: 168.
Programming: Local news, dramas, sports & variety shows.
Began: January 1, 1985.
Distribution method: Available to cable subscribers.

WB.COM
4000 Warner Blvd
Bldg 505
Burbank, CA 91505
Phone: 818-977-9653
Web Site: http://www.thewb.com
Type of service: Broadband.
Programming: Former WB series & original shows available on demand.
Began: August 27, 2008.
Means of Support: Ad supported.
Distribution method: Available online.

WBIR-TV
1513 Hutchinson Ave
Knoxville, TN 37917
Phone: 865-637-1010
Fax: 865-637-6280
E-mail: manager@wbir.com
Web Site: http://www.wbir.com
Jeff Lee, General Manager
Debbie Brizendine, General Sales Manager
Type of service: Basic.
Operating hours/week: 124.
Programming: Local programs & NBC network.
Began: May 2, 1994.
Distribution method: Available to cable systems.
Ownership: Gannett Company Inc.

WCTY CHANNEL 16
200 E Washington St
Room G-19
Indianapolis, IN 46204
Phone: 317-327-2016
Fax: 317-327-2020
E-mail: kmontgom@indygov.org
Web Site: http://www.indygov.org/cable
Ken Montgomery, Station Manager
Angela Gilmer, Producer
Bradley K. Sims, Producer
Alan Dhayer, Systems Administrator
Nick Hess, Producer
Dave Lister, Programming & Promotions Coordinator
Operating hours/week: 168.
Programming: Live & archived coverage of local government meetings, deliberations & community affairs original programming.
Began: January 1, 1984.
Total subscribers: 250,000.

WE ON DEMAND — See WE tv.

WE TV
200 Jericho Quadrangle
Jericho, NY 11753
Phone: 516-803-4400
Fax: 516-803-4399
E-mail: contactwe@rmhi.com
Web Site: http://www.we.tv
Josh Sapan, President & Chief Executive Officer, AMC Networks Inc.
Kim Martin, President
Scott Collins, Executive Vice President, National Advertising Sales
Kenetta Bailey, Senior Vice President, Marketing
Steve Cheskin, Senior Vice President, Programming
Allison Clarke, Senior Vice President, National Advertising Sales, Eastern Region
Stacy Kreisberg, Senior Vice President, Business Affairs
John Miller, Senior Vice President, Original Production & Development
Rosie Pisani, Senior Vice President, Marketing
Jennifer Robertson, Senior Vice President
Joshua Berger, Vice President, Programming Operations
CarolAnne Dolan, Vice President, Nonfiction Development & Production
Elizabeth Doree, Vice President, Acquisitions & Programming Block Strategy
Jennifer Geisser, Vice President, Public Relations
Jennifer Kranz, Vice President, Advertising & Branding
Bob Marino, Vice President, Ad Sales
Andrea Bell Macey, Vice President
Deirdre O'Hearn, Vice President, Development & Talent
Theresa Patiri, Vice President, Production Management & Operations
Gary Pipa, Vice President, Program Planning & Scheduling
Christina Pisano, Vice President, Research
Heather Umen, Vice President, Brand Experience & Events
Elain Waldman, Vice President, Trade Marketing
Jayne Wallace, Vice President, Public Relations
Mike Walton, Vice President, Creative Director, On-Air Promotions
Type of service: Basic.
Satellites: Satcom 3-R, transponder 14.
Operating hours/week: 168.
Uplink: Belmont Racetrack, Long Island, NY.
Programming: Romantic movies, mini-series, celebrity interviews & lifestyle programs.
Began: January 1, 1997, as Romance Classics; re-launched as WE: Women's Entertainment in 2001 and WE tv in 2006.
Means of Support: Subscriber fees.
Total subscribers: 70,000,000 (19,600,000 On Demand subscribers).
Scrambled signal: Yes.

Ownership: AMC Networks Inc. Formerly Rainbow Media Holdings LLC owned by Cablevision Systems Corp., it became a publicly held company under the new name June 30, 2011.

WE TV HD — See WE tv.

WEALTHTV
4757 Morena Blvd
San Diego, CA 92117
Phone: 858-270-6900
Fax: 858-270-6901
Web Site: http://www.wealthtv.net
Robert Herring, Sr., President & Chief Executive Officer
Eric Brown, Executive Vice President
Type of service: Standard Digital and VOD.
Satellites: Galaxy 13.
Programming: Informative shows that provide insights on what every American dreams of, from travel secrets to fast cars, from better etiquette to better investing.
Began: June 1, 2004.
Scrambled signal: Yes.
Ownership: Herring Broadcasting Inc.

WEALTHTV HD — See WealthTV.

WEALTHTV 3D — See WealthTV
Began: July 15, 2010.

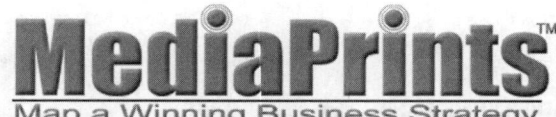

THE WEATHER CHANNEL
(TWC)
300 Interstate N Pkwy
Atlanta, GA 30339-2204
Phone: 770-226-0000
Fax: 770-226-2950
Web Site: http://www.weather.com
Decker Anstrom, Chairman
Bill Burke, President & Chief Executive Officer, The Weather Channel Companies
Jerry Elliott, Chief Financial Officer & Chief Administrative Officer, The Weather Channel Companies
Michael J. Kelly, President & Chief Executive Officer
Lyn Andrews, President, TWC Media Solutions
Lynn Brindell, Executive Vice President, Strategic Marketing
Jennifer Dangar, Executive Vice President, Distribution & Business Development
Geoffrey Darby, Executive Vice President, Programming
Becky Powhatan Kelley, Executive Vice President, Distribution & Business Affairs
Beth Lawrence, Executive Vice President, Advertising Sales & Media Solutions
Shirley Powell, Executive Vice President, Corporate Communications
Ray San, Sr., Executive Vice President, Meteorological Affairs
Sylvia Taylor, Executive Vice President, Human Resources
Bob Walker, Executive Vice President, Marketing & Crossplatform Development
Joe Fiveash, Senior Vice President & General Manager, Weather Channel Interactive
Christopher Raleigh, Senior Vice President & General Sales Manager, TWC Media Solutions
George Callard, Senior Vice President, Legal & Business Affairs
Susan Scott, Senior Vice President, Distribution
Indira Venkat, Senior Vice President, Research
Nancy Apatov, Vice President, Ad Products & Integrated Content, TWC Media Solutions
Pamela Bartino, Vice President & General Manager, Affiliate Sales & TWC Networks
Sheila Buckley, Vice President, National Ad Sales
Cameron Clayton, Vice President, Mobile
Michael Finnerty, Vice President, Web Products
Kathleen Lane, Vice President, Public Relations
Nancy Mazzei, Vice President, Design
Patrick McCormick, Vice President, Mobile & Strategy
Patrick McGalliard, Vice President, Business Development
Reta J Peery, Vice President, Legal & Deputy General Counsel
Mike Pons, Vice President, Corporate Strategy & Development
Megan Rock, Vice President, Partnership Marketing & Operations
Lisa Shankle, Vice President, Business Development
Brittany Smith, Vice President, National Accounts
Meredith Fierman Smith, Vice President, Climate Strategic Marketing
Helen Swenson, Vice President, Live Programming
Liz Wilson Thorington, Vice President, Ad Sales, Southern Region
Kaye Zussman, Vice President, Program Strategy & Development
Jerry Arias, Affiliate Marketing Director
Brad Grant, Video On Demand Director

Regional Offices:
CHICAGO: 180 N Stetson Ave, Ste 3030, Chicago, IL 60601. Phone: 312-946-0892.

DETROIT: 2690 Crooks Rd, Ste 217, Troy, MI 48084. Phone: 810-362-2290.

LOS ANGELES: 1875 Century Park E, Ste 900, Los Angeles, CA 90067. Phone: 310-785-0512.

MIAMI: 777 Brickell Ave, Ste 680, Miami, FL 33131. Phone: 305-375-6100. Fax: 305-375-6110.

NEW YORK: 845 3rd Ave, 11th Floor, New York, NY 10022. Phone: 212-893-2245.
Type of service: Basic.
Satellites: Satcom C-3, transponder 13.
Operating hours/week: 168.
Programming: Local, regional, national & international current & forecast weather information.
Began: May 2, 1982.
Means of Support: Subscriber fees & advertising.
Total subscribers: 101,700,000.
Distribution method: Available to home dish audiences, cable systems & mobile video.

Scrambled signal: Yes.
Ownership: NBCUniversal LLC, Blackstone Group & Bain Capital.

THE WEATHER CHANNEL HD — See The Weather Channel.
Began: October 1, 2007.

WEATHER NETWORK
2655 Bristol Cir
Oakville, ON L6H 7W1
Canada
Phone: 905-829-1156
Web Site: http://www.theweathernetwork.com
Kiko Grusecki, Director, Broadcast Operations
Operating hours/week: 168.
Programming: Weather information & forecasting in both French & English broadcasts.
Distribution method: Available to cable & satellite providers.
Ownership: Pelmorex Communications Inc.

WEATHERNATION
8101 E Prentice Ave
Ste 700
Greenwood Village, CO 80111
Phone: 303-339-7317
Fax: 303-771-5559
E-mail: mnorton@weathernationtv.com
Web Site: http://www.weathernationtv.com/
Douglas Paul Kruhoeffer, Chief Executive Officer
Michael Norton, Vice President
Type of service: Basic.
Operating hours/week: 168.
Programming: Weather channel.
Began: June 13, 2011, Launched 24-hour stream on Facebook July 25, 2011.
Distribution method: Available to cable subscribers.
Scrambled signal: Yes.

WEATHERSCAN
300 Interstate North Pkwy
Atlanta, GA 30339-2204
Phones: 770-226-0000; 770-226-2341
Fax: 770-226-2950
Web Site: http://www.weather.com
Felicia McDade, Business Development Director

Branch Offices:
CHICAGO: 205 N Michigan Ave, Ste 1610, Chicago, IL 60601. Phone: 312-948-0892.

DETROIT: 2690 Crooks Rd, Ste 305, Troy, MI 48084. Phone: 810-362-2290.

LOS ANGELES: 1875 Century Park E, Ste 900, Los Angeles, CA 90067. Phone: 310-785-0512.

NEW YORK: 845 3rd Ave, 11th Floor, New York, NY 10022. Phone: 212-308-3055.
Satellites: Satcom C-3, transponder 13.
Operating hours/week: 168.
Programming: 24-hour, all-local weather available for digital carriage.
Began: July 1, 1998.
Total subscribers: 7,000,000.
Distribution method: Available to home dish audiences & cable systems.
Scrambled signal: Yes.
Ownership: Landmark Communications Inc.

WEATHERVISION
916 Foley St
Jackson, MS 39202
Phones: 601-352-6673; 800-353-9177
Fax: 601-948-6052
E-mail: edward@weathervision.com
Web Site: http://www.weathervision.com
Edward Saint Pe', President
Sales representative: Edward Saint Pe'.
Programming: Customized, local TV weather forecasts.
Began: January 1, 1991.
Distribution method: Via satellite & internet.

WEBMD TELEVISION — No longer operational. See Discovery Health Channel.

WFMT RADIO NETWORKS
5400 N St. Louis Ave
Chicago, IL 60625
Phone: 773-279-2000
Fax: 773-279-2199
E-mail: finearts@wfmt.com
Web Site: http://www.wfmt.com
Daniel J. Schmidt, President & Chief Executive Officer
Reese P. Marcusson, Executive Vice President & Chief Financial Officer
Farrell Frentress, Executive Vice President, Development
Donna L. Davies, Senior Vice President, Development
Parke Richardson, Senior Vice President, Finance & Business Development
V.J. McAleer, Senior Vice President, Production
Joanie Bayhack, Senior Vice President, Corporate Communications & Direct Marketing
Type of service: Audio only.
Satellites: Galaxy IVR, transponder 3, channel B72.0.
Operating hours/week: 168.
Uplink: Chicago, IL.
Programming: Fine arts/classical radio station in Chicago.
Began: March 1, 1979.
Means of Support: Service fees & production contracts.
Total subscribers: 1,900.

WFN HD — See World Fishing Network.

WGBH CREATE — See WGBH-TV.

WGBH HD — See WGBH-TV.

WGBH ON DEMAND — See WGBH-TV.

WGBH-TV
125 Western Ave
Boston, MA 02134
Phone: 617-300-5400
Fax: 617-300-1026
E-mail: access@wgbh.org
Web Site: http://www.wgbh.org
Type of service: Digital.
Programming: News, documentaries, kids' & family, live performances of the arts, series & original programs.
Distribution method: Available to cable subscribers.

WGBH WORLD — See WGBH-TV.

WGN — See WGN America.

WGN AMERICA
2501 W Bradley Pl
Chicago, IL 60618-4718
Phone: 773-528-2311
Fax: 773-883-6299
E-mail: wgnamerica@tribune.com
Web Site: http://www.wgnamerica.com/
Sean Compton, President, Programming
Mr. Julio Marenghi, Executive Vice President & General Manager
Mr. Kevin Connor, Senior Vice President, Affiliate Sales & Marketing
David Rotem, Senior Vice President, Sales
Mr. Marc Drazin, Engineering Director

Branch Offices:
HOLLYWOOD: 5800 Sunset Blvd, Bldg 21, Ste 12H, Hollywood, CA 90028. Phone: 323-460-3861. Fax: 323-460-5299.

NEW YORK: 220 E 42nd St, Ste 400, New York, NY 10017. Phone: 212-210-5900. Fax: 212-210-5905.
Type of service: Basic.
Satellites: Galaxy 14, transponder 13C.
Operating hours/week: 168.
Operating areas: All U.S. states and Canada.
Programming: WGN America is a broad entertainment network consisting of cable exclusives, first-run programs, blockbuster movies and live sports.
Began: November 8, 1978, as Superstation WGN; relaunched as WGN America May 26, 2008.
Means of Support: System pays per subscriber.
Total subscribers: 71,017,000 (Includes cable, Canadian & DTH).
Distribution method: Available to home satellite dish audiences, cable systems & telephone companies.
Scrambled signal: Yes. Equipment: Scientific Atlanta Power Vue H.
Ownership: Tribune Company.

WGN AMERICA HD — See WGN America.

WHEELSTV
289 Great Rd
Acton, MA 01720
Phone: 978-264-4333
Fax: 978-264-9547
E-mail: contact@wheelstv.net
Web Site: http://www.wheelstv.net
Jim Barisano, Chairman & Founder
Type of service: Basic, broadband, IPTV, video on demand.
Operating hours/week: 168.
Programming: Automotive lifestyle entertainment, news & information. Original & acquired programming on cars, trucks & motorcycles; technology, history, international auto shows.
Began: January 1, 2004, reflects video on demand launch. IPTV service launched January 1, 2006.
Ownership: Automotive Networks LLC.

WICKED ON DEMAND
c/o Trans Digital Media LLC
801 2nd Ave
New York, NY 10017
Web Site: http://www.tdmllc.com/tdm_wicked.html
Geoff Lurie, Chief Executive Officer
Type of service: Video on demand.
Programming: Adult entertainment.
Began: January 1, 2005.
Total subscribers: 17,500,000.
Distribution method: Available to cable providers.
Ownership: Joint venture between TransDigital Media & Wicked Pictures.

WILD TV
11263 180th St
Edmonton, AB T5S 0B4
Canada
Phone: 780-444-1512
Fax: 780-443-4591
E-mail: ryan.kohler@wildtv.ca
Web Site: http://www.wildtv.ca
Operating hours/week: 168.
Programming: Hunting & fishing programs.

WINE NETWORK
88 Kearny St
Ste 2100
San Francisco, CA
Phone: 415-772-3639
Fax: 415-288-1371
Web Site: http://www.winetv.tv
Patrick Brunet, Co-Founder & President
Lorie Kim, Co-founder & Executive Vice President
Type of service: Video on demand & IPTV.
Programming: Focusing exclusively on the international world of wine & the wine lover's lifestyle.
Began: September 17, 2004, Reflects international launch.
Distribution method: Available to cable operators.

WISCONSINEYE
122 W Washington Ave
Ste 200
Madison, WI 53703
Phones: 608-316-6850; 866-273-5755
Fax: 608-316-6868
E-mail: info@wiseye.org
Web Site: http://www.wiseye.org
Christopher Long, President & Chief Executive Officer
Type of service: Digital.
Operating areas: Wisconsin.
Programming: Statewide, private nonprofit public affairs network providing unbiased, unedited coverage of state government and public life on cable TV and the Internet.
Began: July 9, 2007.
Distribution method: Available to cable systems and online.
Scrambled signal: Yes.
Ownership: Private, not for profit.

WIZEBUYS TV
790 E Market St
Ste 330
West Chester, PA 19382
Phone: 610-696-1774
Fax: 610-696-8522
Web Site: http://www.wizebuys.tv
Steven R. Conduit, President & Chief Executive Officer
Type of service: Basic.
Operating hours/week: 168.
Programming: National infomercial network.
Began: October 1, 2002.
Total subscribers: 30,000,000.
Distribution method: Satellite.

WKYT-TV
PO Box 55037
2851 Winchester Rd
Lexington, KY 40555
Phone: 859-299-0411
Fax: 859-299-5531
E-mail: wayne.martin@wkyt.com
Web Site: http://www.wkyt.com
Wayne Martin, President & General Manager
Barbara Howard, Program Director
Type of service: Basic.
Programming: CBS affiliate.
Began: May 1, 1995.
Means of Support: Advertising & subscriber fees.
Total subscribers: 445,000.

WOMAN TV — See KyLinTV.
Type of service: IPTV.
Programming: Chinese language talk shows & other programs targeted to women; covers education, occupation, fashion, family

& stories of famous female figures. Carried by KyLinTV.
Began: March 1, 1999.

WOMEN'S TELEVISION NETWORK — See W Network.

THE WORD NETWORK
20733 W Ten Mile
Southfield, MI 48075
Phone: 248-357-4566
Fax: 248-350-3422
E-mail: lewisg@thewordnetwork.org
Web Site: http://www.thewordnetwork.org
Lewis Gibbs, President
John Mattiello, Marketing Director
Thomas Ponsart, Engineering Director
Clara Childs, Affiliate Marketing Manager
Steve Antoniotti, Director, Development
Type of service: Basic.
Satellites: Galaxy 11, transponder 15C.
Operating hours/week: 168.
Programming: Religious programming for the urban African-American community.
Means of Support: Non-profit organization.
Total subscribers: 50,000,000.

WORLD ASIA TELEVISION (WA-TV) — No longer planned.

WORLD CHAMPIONSHIP WRESTLING
One CNN Center
PO Box 105366
Atlanta, GA 30348-5366
Phone: 404-827-2066
Fax: 404-827-2931
Web Site: http://www.wcwwrestling.com
Eric Bischoff, President
Mike Webber, Marketing Director
Alan Sharp, Public Relations Director
Type of service: Pay-per-view.
Programming: Features twelve pay-per-view specials annually.
Began: January 1, 1988.
Means of Support: Subscription fees.
Distribution method: Available to cable systems.
Ownership: Turner Broadcasting System Inc.

WORLD CINEMA HD — Part of Voom HD Networks; no longer in operation.

WORLD FIGHT CHANNEL (WFC)
c/o Minister Joseph A. Hurry Sr.
PO Box 3135
Hollywood, CA 90078
E-mail: admin@worldfightchannel.com
Web Site: http://www.worldfightchannel.com

Branch Offices:
LOS ANGELES: 5751 Venice Blvd, Los Angeles, CA 90018. Phones: 818-201-8598; 702-378-9223.
Type of service: Basic.
Sales representative: Valerie McConnell.
Programming: The World Fight Channel covers all of the different fighting styles in the world. Programs that promote health, strength, and growth of the human body, mind, and spirit.
Began: June 2, 1999.
Distribution method: Internet, Over air, cable, satellite transmission.

WORLD FISHING NETWORK
184 Pearl St, Ste 302
Toronto, ON M5H 1L5
Canada
Phone: 416-593-0915
Web Site: http://www.wfn.tv
Mark Rubenstein, President & Chief Executive Officer
Pete Piper, Senior Director, Advertising & Sponsorship

Branch Offices:
US Office: 360 S. Monroe Street, Suite 230, Denver, CO 80209. Phone: 720-457-2904.
Type of service: Basic.
Operating hours/week: 168.
Operating areas: California, Delaware, Florida, Indiana, Massachusetts, Maryland, New Jersey, New York, Pennsylvania, Rhode Island, Texas, Virginia.
Programming: Angling, saltwater & freshwater fishing, competitions & tournaments, advice & instructional shows & focus on travel destinations.
Began: December 1, 2005.
Total subscribers: 20,000,000.
Distribution method: Available to cable, satellite & telco systems.
Scrambled signal: Yes.
Ownership: Altitude Sports & Entertainment, 50%; Insight Sports Ltd., 50%.

WORLD HARVEST TELEVISION
61300 S Ironwood Rd
South Bend, IN 46614
Phone: 574-291-8200
Fax: 574-291-9043
E-mail: harvest@lesea.com
Web Site: http://www.thenewharvest.com
Peter Sumrall, President & General Manager
Steve Warnecke, General Manager, Affiliate Relations
David Hummel, Senior Program Executive
Type of service: Digital basic.
Satellites: Galaxy IV, transponder 15.
Sales representative: Landin Media Sales.
Operating hours/week: 168.
Programming: Family & religious.
Began: November 1, 2003.
Means of Support: Advertising.
Distribution method: Available to home dish audiences.
Ownership: LeSea Broadcasting.

WORLDGATE SERVICE
3220 Tillman Dr
Ste 300
Bensalem, PA 19020
Phone: 215-633-5100
Fax: 215-633-9590
E-mail: sales@wgate.com
Web Site: http://www.wgate.com
Hal Krisbergh, Chairman & Chief Executive Officer
Joseph Augenbraun, Senior Vice President, Engineering
Paul Zislis, Vice President, Strategic Systems
James McLoughlin, Vice President, Affiliate Sales
Type of service: Pay.
Operating hours/week: 168.
Programming: Full interactive access to Internet for web surfing, e-mail, web-based applications.
Began: April 1, 1998.
Means of Support: Subscriber fees.
Distribution method: Internet via cable head-end systems.
Ownership: Major investors include Motorola, Citicorp, General Instrument & Scientific Atlanta.

WORSHIP NETWORK
2035 Mallory Lane
Franklin, TN 37067
Phone: 615-786-1672
Fax: 615-786-1677
E-mail: askworship@worship.net

Web Site: http://www.worship.net
Bruce Koblish, President & Chief Executive Officer
Bob Shreffler, Vice President, Finance
Tim Brown, Vice President, News Media
Patricia Niedzielski, Vice President, Finance & Administration
Diana Nicholas, Producer
Type of service: Digital & broadband.
Satellites: GE-1, transponder 7.
Operating hours/week: 168.
Uplink: Clearwater, FL.
Programming: Worship & praise music set to scenic nature; music concert specials.
Began: September 28, 1992.
Means of Support: Viewers.
Total subscribers: 70,000,000.
Distribution method: Available to home dish audiences, cable systems & digital broadcast stations.
Ownership: Christian Network Inc.

WPIX — See CW11 New York.

WTBS — See TBS Superstation.

WTEM SPORTS RADIO
8750 Brookville Rd
Silver Spring, MD 20910
Phone: 301-231-7798
Fax: 301-881-8030
Web Site: http://www.espn980.com
Bennett Zier, Executive Vice President & General Manager
Andy Pollin, Sports Director
Tod Castleberry, AM Operations Director
Jim Weiskopf, Station Manager
Yasmin Dorsey, National Sales Manager
Peter Brooks, Promotion Director
Type of service: Audio.
Satellites: Satcom C-4, transponder 6-H.
Operating hours/week: 168.
Programming: All-sports radio service.
Began: May 24, 1992.
Means of Support: Advertising.
Distribution method: Available to cable systems.
Ownership: Clear Channel Communications.

WUCF TV
12443 Research Pkwy
Ste 301
Orlando, FL 32826
Phone: 321-433-7777
Web Site: http://wucftv.org/
Grant J Heston, Assistant Vice President, News & Information, UCF & WUCF TV
Kate Junco, Director, Marketing & Media Relations, Brevard Community College
Type of service: Basic.
Operating areas: Florida.
Programming: A community channel, providing a direct programming schedule from PBS and later introducing other favorite public broadcasting programming and first-class local content about the Central Florida community.
Began: July 1, 2011.
Means of Support: Contributions from members.
Distribution method: Available to Comcast & Bright House Networks cable systems, DIRECTV, Dish Network & U-verse.
Ownership: Brevard Community College & the University of Central Florida.

WWE NETWORK
1241 E Main St
Stamford, CT 06902
Phone: 203-352-8600
Web Site: http://corporate.wwe.com
Kevin Dunn, Executive Vice President, Television Production
Michael Luisi, Executive Vice President, Business Development, General Counsel & Secretary
Stephanie McMahon, Executive Vice President, Creative Development & Operations
Type of service: Plans basic.
Programming: Will offer wrestling plus original and animated programming.
Scheduled to begin: Plans to launch 2012-2013.
Distribution method: Will be available to cable systems.
Scrambled signal: Planned.
Ownership: World Wrestling Entertainment.

WWE 24/7
World Wrestling Entertainment
1241 E Main St
Stamford, CT 06902
Phone: 203-352-8600
Web Site: http://www.wwe.com
Vince McMahon, Chairman & Chief Executive Officer
George Barrios, Chief Financial Officer
Jim Connelly, Executive Vice President, Consumer Products
Brian Kalinowski, Executive Vice President, Digital Media
John Laurinaitus, Executive Vice President, Talent Relations
Stephanie McMahon-Levesque, Executive Vice President, Creative Writing, Talent Relations & Live Events
Michael Pavone, Executive Vice President, WWE Studios
Andrew Whitaker, Executive Vice President, International
Michelle Wilson, Executive Vice President, Marketing
Type of service: Video on demand.
Programming: A subscription video on demand service providing matches, championship bouts, pay-per-view & syndicated series & specials from a variety of wrestling brands including WWE, WCW, ECW & AWA. Also features Hispanic & broadband interactive applications.
Distribution method: Cable.
Scrambled signal: Yes.
Ownership: World Wrestling Entertainment.

XFINITY
One Comcast Center
Philadelphia, PA 19103
Phone: 215-286-1700
Web Site: http://www.comcast.com/Corporate/Learn/overview.html
Programming: Comcast Interactive Media's collection of On Demand shows

and movies available on TV and online. Programming is also available in Spanish through an internet portal.

XFINITY 3D

One Comcast Center
Philadelphia, PA 19103
Phone: 215-286-1700
Marcien Jenckes, Senior Vice President & General Manager, Video Services
Kate Noel, Director, Corporate Communications
Operating hours/week: 168.
Operating areas: Available nationwide.
Programming: Offers concerts from top-tier artists, sporting events, and more than a dozen movies and original programming all in 3D.
Began: February 20, 2011.
Distribution method: Available to Comcast subscribers.
Scrambled signal: Yes.
Ownership: Comcast Corp.

XIAMEN TV — See KyLinTV.

Web Site: http://www.xmg.com.cn/home/
Type of service: IPTV.
Operating hours/week: 168.
Programming: General entertainment channel broadcast in the Minnan dialect.
Ownership: Xiamen Media Group.

XTV

c/o Interactive TV Networks Inc.
23241 Ventura Blvd, Ste 217
Woodland Hills, CA 91364
Phone: 866-988-4988
Helen Wise, President
Carol Gorgichuk, Sales Representative
Type of service: Basic, pay-per-view, broadband & video on demand.
Programming: Adult programming including live TV, pay-per-view & interactive channels made available through IPTV technology.
Means of Support: Subscriber fees.
Distribution method: Available to cable & satellite providers.
Scrambled signal: Yes.

XY.TV

23 Drydock Ave
2nd Fl
Boston, MA 12210
Phone: 617-261-6000
Fax: 617-261-7505
E-mail: contact@xy.tv
Web Site: http://www.xy.tv
John Garabedian, Chief Executive Officer
Dennis Patton, Chief Operating Officer
Beth St. Paul, Vice President, Affiliate Relations
Reed Lewis, Vice President, Technology

Sales Offices:

NEW YORK: 120 E 87th St, Ste P28C, New York, NY 10128. Phone: 212-987-7830. Fax: 212-987-8344.

NEW ORLEANS: 405 Athenia Pkwy, Metairie, LA 70003. Phone: 504-834-9472. Fax: 504-834-5763.

Type of service: Basic.
Operating hours/week: 168.
Programming: Real life television network and web experience for young adults between 12-34. Reality shows, entertainment & lifestyle shows, music videos & celebrities.
Began: December 15, 2003.

YANGTSE RIVER DRAMA — See KyLinTV.

Programming: Offers female-oriented Chinese language programming. Available through KyLinTV.
Scrambled signal: Yes.

YANKEES ENTERTAINMENT & SPORTS

405 Lexington Ave
36th Fl
New York, NY 10174-3699
Phone: 646-487-3600
Fax: 646-487-3612
Web Site: http://web.yesnetwork.com
Leo Hindery Jr., Chairman & Chief Executive Officer
Barbara Wood, Chief Administrative Officer
Matt Bond, Executive Vice President, Affiliate Relations
Derek Chang, Executive Vice President, Development
Grace de Latour, Executive Vice President, Human Resources
Woody Freiman, Executive Vice President, Programming & Production
David Krone, Executive Vice President, Regulatory & Government
Jerry Machovina, Executive Vice President, Media Sales
Howard Levinson, Senior Vice President, Ad Sales
John Brueckner, Vice President, On-Air Promotions
Pat Cavanaugh, Vice President, Finance & Controller
Eric Handler, Vice President, Communications
Michael Spirito, Vice President, Digital Media & Business Development
Mark J. Coleman, General Counsel
Operating hours/week: 168.
Programming: All Yankees games, biography, interview & magazine programs covering the Yankees, as well as other professional & collegiate sports.
Began: March 19, 2002.
Ownership: Yankee Nets.
(YES).

YEMENTV — See GlobeCast WorldTV.

Operating hours/week: 168.
Programming: Yemeni news, movies, serials, talk & game shows, cultural documentaries, political & children's shows for Yemeni communities around the world.
Scrambled signal: Yes.

YES HD — See Yankees Entertainment & Sports.

YES 3D — See Yankees Entertainment & Sports.

Began: July 10, 2010.

YESTERDAY USA

2001 Plymouth Rock
Richardson, TX 75081-3946
Phone: 972-889-9872
Fax: 972-889-2329
E-mail: bill46@yesterdayusa.com
Web Site: http://www.yesterdayusa.com
William J. Bragg, Founder
Satellites: Galaxy I, transponder 24; Galaxy V, transponder 7 (6.8 Wide Band Audio).
Operating hours/week: 168.
Programming: Commercial-free old-time radio shows & music.
Began: January 1, 1985.
Total subscribers: 3,800,000 (Figure includes home dish subscribers.).
Distribution method: Available to home dish audiences & cable systems.

YNN-CENTRAL NEW YORK

815 Erie Blvd E
Syracuse, NY 13210
Phone: 315-234-1000
Fax: 315-234-0635
E-mail: ynncnyinfo@ynn.com
Web Site: http://www.ynn.com
Ron Lombard, General Manager & News Director
Cindy Griffo, Ad Sales Director
Programming: YNN-Central NY is part of the YNN network of 24-hour local newschannels operated by Time Warner Cable throughout Upstate New York. The Central NY-based channel is headquartered in Syracuse and serves more than 600,000 TWC subscribers in a 25-county region, utilizing three separate regional program feeds. Programming follows a one-hour newswheel format, with local weathercasts every ten minutes.
Total subscribers: 600,000.
Scrambled signal: Yes.
Ownership: Time Warner Cable.

YTV CANADA

64 Jefferson Ave
Unit 18
Toronto, ON M6K 3H3
Canada
Phone: 416-534-1191
Fax: 416-588-6987
E-mail: gmackrell@corusent.com
Web Site: http://www.ytv.com
Paul Robertson, President, Television
Gerry MacKrell, Vice President, Sales
Christine Arthur, Sales Manager, Youth Division
Sean Luxton, Director, Distribution & Affiliate Relations
Type of service: Basic.
Satellites: Anik E-2.
Operating hours/week: 168.
Programming: Children's shows.
Total subscribers: 8,200,000 (number includes Canadian households only.).
Distribution method: Available to cable systems.
Ownership: Corus Entertainment.

ZEE CINEMA — See Zee TV USA.

Began: January 1, 1999.

ZEE GOLD — See Zee TV USA.

ZEE TV USA

4100 E Dry Creek Rd
Ste A300
Centennial, CO 80122
Phone: 303-712-5400
Fax: 303-712-5401
E-mail: customerservice@zeetvusa.com
Web Site: http://www.zeetvusa.com
Dheeraj Kapuna, Chief Executive Officer & International Operations
S. Venkatasubramanian, Americas Leader
Type of service: Premium.
Operating hours/week: 168.
Programming: Programming from India & Pakistan including news, movies, dramas, children's programming, sports & talk shows aimed at serving the needs of South Asians living abroad.
Began: July 18, 1998.
Distribution method: Available to cable systems & satellite providers.
Ownership: International Channel Networks.

ZHEJIANG TV

No. 111 Moganshan Road
Hangzhou 310005
China
Web Site: http://www.zjstv.com/
Type of service: INSP.
Operating hours/week: 168.
Programming: Channel broadcast in Mandarin Chinese, the service is intended mainly for Chinese speaking people outside of China. It offers children's programming, current affairs, education, entertainment and news.
Began: October 1, 1960.
Means of Support: Subscriber fees and advertising.

ZHONG TIAN CHANNEL

c/o CTN Channel
1255 Corporate Center Dr, Ste 212
Monterey Park, CA 91754
Phone: 323-415-0068
Fax: 323-415-0038
E-mail: ctitvusa@ctitv.com.tw
Web Site: http://www.ctitv.com
Andy Chuang, General Manager
Type of service: Pay.
Operating hours/week: 168.
Programming: Mandarin Chinese news, variety, sports, dramas, entertainment & information television programming.
Began: August 1, 1999.
Distribution method: Available to cable systems & telco providers.
Ownership: CTI-ZTC.

ZILLIONTV

1170 Kifer Rd
Sunnyvale, CA 94086
Phone: 408-636-5800
Web Site: http://www.zilliontv.tv
Mitchell Berman, Co-Founder & Executive Chairman
David Dozoretz, Chief Creative Officer
Mike Catalano, Chief Technology Officer
Charles Cataldo, Senior Vice President, Digital Entertainment Group
Andrew Robinson, Senior Vice President, Operations
Patrick Gauthier, Senior Vice President, Product Marketing & Strategy
Bonnie Stone, Senior Vice President, Advertising
Liz Seidner Davidoff, Senior Vice President, Global Marketing

Branch Offices:

SANTA MONICA: 100 Willshire Blvd, Suite 750, Santa Monica, CA 940401. Phone: 424-214-2500.

Type of service: Video on demand.
Programming: TV shows, sports, music, movies.

Program Sources & Services

Offering live, film & tape recorders & commercials and production facilities to television stations and cable systems. These listings are based on data supplied by companies known to be serving TV & Cable systems and responding to our questionnaires.

ABC NEWS
77 W 66th St
New York, NY 10023-6201
Phone: 212-456-7297
E-mail: support@abcnews.go.com
Web Site: http://www.abcnews.go.com
David Westin, President

ABC STUDIOS
500 S Buena Vista St
Burbank, CA 91521
Phone: 818-560-1000
Web Site: http://www.abc.com
Howard Davine, Executive Vice President
Develops & produces TV programming.

ACCENTHEALTH
747 Third Ave
New York, NY 10017
Phone: 212-763-5102
Fax: 212-763-5200
E-mail: csr@accenthealth.com
Web Site: http://www.accenthealth.com
Daniel A. Stone, Chief Executive Officer

Branch Offices:
TAMPA: 5440 Beaumont Ctr Blvd, Ste 400, Tampa, FL 33634-5208. Phones: 813-349-7127; 800-235-4930. Fax: 813-349-7299.
Produces AccentHealth Waiting Room TV Network along with CNN. Programming features medical breakthroughs, condition-specific segments, parenting issues, nutrition, etc.

ACCENT MEDIA
1350 Beverly Rd
Stes 213 & 218
McLean, VA 22101
Phone: 703-356-9427
Fax: 703-506-0643
Web Site: http://www.accentmediainc.com
Cecelia Domeyko, President & Director/Producer
Dr. Jack Jorgens, Vice President & Producer
Producer of documentaries & training videos, public service announcements & information campaigns, video news releases, Spanish language productions, media training & museum videos.

ACCESS TELEVISION NETWORK
2600 Michelson Dr
Ste 1650
Irvine, CA 92612
Phones: 949-263-9900; 800-599-7629
Fax: 949-777-1756
Web Site: http://www.accesstv.com
Mark Russo, Senior Vice President, Operations
Provides transactional, direct response & paid programming to cable operators & broadcasters nationwide.

ACCUWEATHER INC.
385 Science Park Rd
State College, PA 16803
Phones: 814-237-0809; 814-235-8650
Fax: 814-235-8609
E-mail: customerservice@accuweather.com
Web Site: http://www.accuweather.com
Dr. Dr. Joel N. Myers, Founder, Chairman & President
Barry Lee Myers, Chiefe Executive Officer
Michael R. Smith, Chief Executive Officer, WeatherData Services Inc.
Dr. Joe Sobel, Senior Vice President
Elliot Abrams, Senior Vice President & Chief Forecaster

Branch Offices:
NEW YORK: Global Sales Office, 1270 Avenue of the Americas, Ste 2330, New York, NY 10020. Phone: 212-554-4750.

WICHITA: WeatherData Services Inc., 100 N Broadway, Ste 750, Wichita, KS 67202. Phone: 316-266-8000.
Provides custom tailored weather forecasts, ready-for-air graphics, graphic access & display systems, real-time weather database & automated weather warning crawl generation system. Local Cable Weather & The Radar Channel give an automated turnkey local weather channel with live video capabilities.

AGENCY FOR INSTRUCTIONAL TECHNOLOGY
1800 N Stonelake Dr
Box A
Bloomington, IN 47402-0120
Phones: 812-339-2203; 800-457-4509
Fax: 812-333-4218
E-mail: info@ait.net
Web Site: http://www.ait.net
Barbara Jackson, Finance Director & Chief Financial Officer
Chuck Wilson, Executive Director
Elaine Larson, Director, Education
Dr. David Gudatis, Executive Producer
Rolanda Kirkley, Warehouse & Facility Manager
Produces & distributes instructional materials including educational videos, computer programming, print materials (guides, workshop handbooks) & digital media; includes resources for Pre-K through adult learners & in all major curriculum areas.

AIRCRAFT MUSIC LIBRARY
162 Columbus Ave
Boston, MA 02116
Phones: 617-303-7600; 800-343-2514
Fax: 617-303-7666
E-mail: info@aircraftmusiclibrary.com
Web Site: http://www.aircraftmusiclibrary.com
Crit Harmon, Producer & Composer
Tim Reppert, Engineer, Composer & Producer
Jennifer Ruggiero, Marketing & Production
Distributes a comprehensive music package encompassing a wide variety of styles for the broadcast, non-broadcast, film & video industries.

ALDEN FILMS/FILMS OF THE NATIONS
PO Box 449
Clarksburg, NJ 08510
Phone: 732-462-3522
Fax: 732-294-0330
E-mail: info@aldenfilms.com
Web Site: http://www.aldenfilms.com
Distributes Jewish, Scandinavian & children's film & video; produces art & flying saucer films & women's self-defense videos.

ALLEGRO PRODUCTIONS INC.
1000 Clint Moore Rd
Boca Raton, FL 33487
Phones: 561-994-9111; 800-232-2133
Fax: 561-241-0707
Web Site: http://www.allegrovideo.com
Scott J. Forman, President
Glenn A. Forman, Vice President
Judith Sitkin, Business Manager
Provides film & video production, animation, CD-ROM/DVD authoring & duplication, high volume videotape duplication & fulfillment & custom music scoring.

ALLIANCE FOR CHRISTIAN MEDIA
644 W Peachtree St
Ste 300
Atlanta, GA 30308-1925
Phones: 404-815-0640; 800-229-3788
Fax: 404-815-0495
E-mail: contact@allianceforchristianmedia.org
Web Site: http://www.allianceforchristianmedia.org
Rev. Canon Louis C. Schueddig, President & Executive Director
Peter Wallace, Executive Producer & Host, Day 1
Tony Callaway, Director, Development
Provides a wide selection of audio/visual resources for Christian education - audio books, videos, tapes & CDs.

ALLIED VAUGHN
7951 Computer Ave
Minneapolis, MN 55435
Phones: 952-832-3100; 800-323-0281
Fax: 952-832-3179
E-mail: avfsales@alliedvaughn.com
Web Site: http://www.alliedvaughn.com
Doug Olzenak, President
Richard Skillman, Vice President, Sales

Branch Offices:
ITASCA: 1310 W Thorndale, Itasca, IL 60143-1159. Phones: 630-919-2120; 800-759-4087. Fax: 847-595-8677.

LIVONIA: 11923 Brookfield, Livonia, MI 48150. Phones: 734-462-5543; 800-462-5543. Fax: 734-462-4004.

ORLANDO: 8812 Torrey Pines Terr, Orlando, FL 32819. Phones: 407-491-7737; 800-877-1778. Fax: 407-876-5388.
Provides video duplication, CD/DVD services, streaming services, Media On-Demand, MediaLinX Online Asset Management, MediaLinX Online Access Management, library management services, fulfillment & distribution services, audiotape duplication, broadcast equipment rental, post production & AVID suites.

ALL MOBILE VIDEO
Chelsea Post
221 W 26th St
New York, NY 10001
Phone: 212-727-1234
Fax: 212-255-6644
Web Site: http://www.allmobilevideo.com
Tom D'Angelo, Rentals
Eric Duke, Mobiles
Richard Duke, Post & Duplication
Lenny Laxer, Transmission
Erik Thielking, Equipment Sales

Branch Offices:
CARTERET: AMV Gateway Teleport, 27 Randolph St, Cateret, NJ 07008. Phone: 732-969-3191. Fax: 732-541-2007.

LODI: AMV Field Operations, 272 State Rte 17 S, Lodi, NJ 07644. Phone: 201-488-4181. Fax: 201-488-3709.

NEW YORK: AMV Unitel, 515 W 57th St, New York, NY 10019. Phones: 212-265-3600; 212-586-8616.
Offers mobile production, post production & uplink solutions.

ALOHA FILMS GROUP INC.
758 S Coast Hwy
Laguna Beach, CA 92651
Phone: 949-494-9840
Fax: 949-494-0573
E-mail: info@alohafilms.com
Web Site: http://www.alohafilms.com
Jimbeau Andrews, Producer
Tim Clohessy, Producer
Shawn Drydahl, Producer
Provides HD production, turn-key post production, motion graphics & web development.

AMAZON INC.
232 E Ohio St
3rd Fl
Chicago, IL 60611
Phone: 312-642-5400
Fax: 312-642-0142
E-mail: info@amazonedit.com
Web Site: http://www.amazonedit.com
Janice Rosenthal, President & Avid Editor
Steve Immer, Avid Editor
Provides offline editing services.

AMC PRODUCTION
5252 Cherokee Ave

Ste 200
Alexandria, VA 22312
Phone: 703-333-2008
Fax: 703-997-7539
E-mail: info@amcproduction.com
Web Site: http://www.amcproduction.com
Produces high-end corporate image, training & educational videos.

AMERICA TEVE
America CV Network LLC
13001 NW 107th Avenue
Hialeah Gardens, FL 33018
Phone: 305-592-4141
Fax: 305-592-3808
Web Site: http://www.americateve.com

AMERICAN JEWISH COMMITTEE
PO Box 705
New York, NY 10150
Phone: 212-751-4000
Fax: 212-891-1450
E-mail: pr@ajc.org
Web Site: http://www.ajc.org
E. Robert Goodkind, President
David A. Harris, Executive Director
Richard Foltin, Director, National & Legislative Affairs
Produces original research, public opinion surveys & programming concerning the Jewish community.

AMERICAN RELIGIOUS TOWN HALL MEETING INC.
745 N Buckner Blvd
Dallas, TX 75218
Phones: 214-328-9828; 800-783-9828
Fax: 214-328-3042
E-mail: tvtelecast@americanreligious.org
Web Site: http://www.americanreligious.org
Elizabeth Ann Leike, President & Chief Executive Officer
Pastor Stephen Gifford, Moderator
Produces religious films & distributes TV film & tape series.

AMERICA'S LEADING INDIES NETWORK (ALIN-TV)
149 Madison Ave
New York, NY 10016
Phone: 212-889-1327
Web Site: http://www.alintv.com
Alan Cohen, President
Syndicator & TV sales representative.

AMIT
817 Broadway
New York, NY 10003
Phones: 212-477-4720; 800-989-2648
Fax: 212-353-2312
E-mail: info@amitchildren.org
Web Site: http://www.amitchildren.org
Dr. Francine S. Stein, President
Arnold Gerson, Executive Vice President

Branch Offices:
BALTIMORE: 2800 Stone Cliff Dr, #112, Baltimore, MD 21202. Phone: 410-484-2223. E-Mail: robbiep@amitchildren.org.

HOLLYWOOD: 2700 N 29th Ave, Ste 203, Hollywood, FL 33020. Phone: 754-922-5100. E-Mail: amitfla@att.net.

LOS ANGELES: 1122 S Robertson Blvd, Ste 9, Los Angeles, CA 90035. Phone: 310-859-4885. Fax: 310-859-4875. E-Mail: jenniferl@amitchildren.org.

SKOKIE: 3856B W Oakton, Skokie, IL 60076. Phone: 847-677-3800. Fax: 847-982-0057. E-Mail: amitchicago@amitchildren.org.

WESTBOROUGH: Seven Brady Rd, Westborough, MA 01581. Phone: 508-870-1571. E-Mail: amitboston@charter.net.

ISRAEL: PO Box 71705, Jerusalem 93420, Israel. Phone: 972-02-673-8360. Fax: 972-02-673-8359. E-Mail: joffice@amit.org.il. Web site: http://http://www.amit.org.il.
Produces & distributes educational films & tape programs on Israel & Amit facilities in Israel.

ANIMATION PEOPLE LTD.
22 Churchmead Close
East Barnet, Herts EN4 8UY
United Kingdom
Phone: 44-20-8449-1601
Web Site: http://www.animationpeople.co.uk
Brian Larkin, Animation Director
Produces traditional hand-drawn animation.

ANOTHER COUNTRY
515 N State St
25th Fl
Chicago, IL 60654
Phone: 312-706-5800
Fax: 312-706-5801
E-mail: will.knelp@anothercountry.net
Web Site: http://www.anothercountry.net
Will Knelp, Director, Business Development
Tim Konn, Executive Producer

APA INTERNATIONAL FILM DISTRIBUTORS INC.
14260 SW 136th St
Ste 16
Miami, FL 33186
Phone: 305-234-4321
Fax: 305-234-7515
Rafael Fusaro, President
Maria Martinez, Senior Vice President
Beatriz Fusaro, Director
Distributes motion pictures, series & cartoons for all Spanish-speaking countries & other nations.

AP TELEVISION NEWS
The Interchange
Oval Rd
Camden Lock, London NW1 7DZ
United Kingdom
Phone: 44-0-20-7482-7400
Fax: 44-0-20-7413-8302
E-mail: aptninfo@ap.org
Web Site: http://www.aptn.com
Daisy Veerasingham, Vice President, EMEA Business Operations
Nigel Baker, Executive Director
Toby Hartwell, Director, Marketing
Sandy MacIntyre, Director, News
Provides breaking global news, sports, entertainment, technology & human interest video content to broadcasters, online & mobile platforms; offices worldwide.

APTINET INC.
130 W 42nd St
20th Fl
New York, NY 10036
Phone: 212-725-7255
Fax: 212-790-2980
E-mail: info@aptinet.com
Web Site: http://www.aptinet.com
Provides interactive & video services for ad agencies & businesses.

AQUARIUS HEALTH CARE MEDIA
18 N Main St
Sherborn, MA 01770
Phones: 508-650-1616; 888-440-2963
Fax: 508-650-1665
E-mail: leslieann@aquariusproductions.com
Web Site: http://www.aquariusproductions.com
Leslie Kussmann, President & Producer
Toni Knights, Distribution Coordinator
Maria McGlone, Media Coordinator
Produces programs to educate, motivate & inspire.

ARCHDIOCESE OF BALTIMORE
1201 S Caton Ave
Baltimore, MD 21227-1092
Phones: 410-646-5102; 800-528-6822
Fax: 410-646-4806
E-mail: mediarch@archbalt.org
Web Site: http://www.archbalt.org
Julia Rogers, Media Director
Nancy Gordy, Media Assistant
Provides print & non-print resources, informational assistance, media consultation & technical assistance to parishes, schools, religious education programs & other organizations.

ARENAS
3375 Barham Blvd
Garden Level
Los Angeles, CA 90068
Phone: 323-785-5555
Fax: 323-785-5560
E-mail: general@arenasgroup.com
Web Site: http://www.arenasgroup.com
Santiago Pozo, Chief Executive Officer
Larry Gleason, President, Distribution
John Butkovich, Executive Vice President, Marketing
Isaac Cuevas, Vice President, Marketing
Leyla Fletcher, Vice President, Marketing Media

Branch Offices:
SPAIN: Estrella 15, 2 Izda, 28004 Madrid, Spain. Phone: 34-609-02-38-55.
Produces, acquires, markets & distributes films in all media including theatrical, video & TV.

ARCTEK SATELLITE PRODUCTIONS
PO Box 14976
Minneapolis, MN 55414
Phones: 612-623-1986; 866-623-1986
Fax: 612-331-2290
E-mail: info@arcteksat.com
Web Site: http://www.arcteksat.com
Todd Hanks, Managing Partner
Brian Stanley, Partner
Provides video production & satellite transmission services - digital or analog.

ARMENIAN FILM FOUNDATION
2219 E Thousand Oaks Blvd
Ste 292
Thousand Oaks, CA 91362
Phone: 805-495-0717
Fax: 805-379-0667
E-mail: info@armenianfilm.org
Web Site: http://www.armenianfilm.org
Dr. J. Michael Hagopian, Chairman
Hratch Karakachian, Treasurer
Produces & distributes documentary & educational films on ethnic subjects concerning Middle Eastern & Armenian cultures.

ARMY & AIR FORCE HOMETOWN NEWS SERVICE
PO Box 3603
New Bern, NC 28564
Phone: 252-633-0161
E-mail: admin@usafns.com
Web Site: http://www.usafns.com
Gerry Proctor, Marketing
Produces & distributes free news & features about American men & women in uniform serving around the world; produces free annual holiday greetings; products distributed to TV stations in service members' hometown.

ARROWDISC
— See listing for Logic General Inc.

ARTBEATS SOFTWARE INC.
PO Box 709
1405 N Myrtle Rd
Myrtle Creek, OR 97457
Phones: 541-863-4429; 800-444-9392
Fax: 541-863-4547
E-mail: info@artbeats.com
Web Site: http://www.artbeats.com
Phil Bates, Founder & President
Provides royalty-free stock footage & still imagery for broadcast, film features, commercial, desktop video, game development & multimedia.

ASCENT MEDIA GROUP
520 Broadway
5th Fl
Santa Monica, CA 90401
Phone: 310-434-7000
E-mail: sales@ascentmedia.com
Web Site: http://www.ascentmedia.com
William Fitzgerald, Chief Executive Officer
Tom Kuehle, Executive Vice President, Strategic Solutions
William Niles, Executive Vice President, General Counsel & Secretary
Douglas Parish, Executive Vice President, Operations
George C. Platisa, Executive Vice President & Chief Financial Officer
David Pruitt, Senior Vice President, Business Development
Bill Romeo, Senior Vice President, Entertainment Television Sales, Creative Group
Provides solutions for the creation, management & distribution of content to major motion picture studios, independent producers, broadcast & programming networks & other companies; systems integration; consulting services; offices worldwide.

ASSOCIATED PRESS BROADCAST
AP Broadcast News Ctr
1100 13th St NW, Ste 700
Washington, DC 20005
Phones: 202-641-9000; 800-821-4747
E-mail: info@ap.org
Web Site: http://www.apbroadcast.com
Bill Burke, Global Director, Online Video Products
Greg Groce, Director, Planning & Analysis
Dave Gwizdowski, Director, Broadcast Markets, The Americas
Lee Perryman, Director, Broadcast Technology & Deputy Director, Broadcast Division
Larry Price, Director, TV Groups & Stations
Kevin Roach, Director, U.S. Broadcast News
Global news network founded in 1846; delivers fast, unbiased news from every corner of the world to all media platforms & formats.

ASSOCIATED TELEVISION INTERNATIONAL
4401 Wilshire Blvd
Los Angeles, CA 90010
Phone: 323-556-5600
Fax: 323-556-5610
E-mail: sales@ati.la
Web Site: http://www.associatedtelevision.com
David McKenzie, President
Murray Drechsler, Chief Financial Officer
Richard Casares, Executive Vice President
Justin Pierce, Senior Vice President

David Stephan, Vice President, Aquisitions & Marketing
Ralitsa Trifonova, Director, International Sales
Produces & distributes movies, TV, radio, interactive media, literature & music.

@RADICAL MEDIA INC.
435 Hudson St
New York, NY 10014
Phone: 212-462-1500
Fax: 212-462-1600
Web Site: http://www.radicalmedia.com
Jon Karmen, Chairman & Chief Executive Officer
Michael Fiore, Chief Operating Officer & Chief Financial Officer
Evan Schnectman, Chief Technical Officer
India Hammer, Head of Operations & Human Resources

Branch Offices:
SANTA MONICA: 1630 12th St, Santa Monica, CA 90404. Phone: 310-664-4500. Fax: 310-664-4600. E-Mail: rubenstein@radicalmedia.com. Frank Scherma, President; Justin Wilkes, Vice President, Media & Entertainment; Liz Friesell-Mason, Managing Director, Post Production.

AUSTRALIA: 85 Commonwealth St, Surry Hills, NSW 2010, Australia. Phone: 61-0-2-9213-6300. Fax: 61-0-2-9213-6399. E-Mail: galluzzo@radicalmedia.com. Rob Galluzzo, Managing Director.

CHINA: 1508 Jiashan Lu, Highstreet Loft, Ste 2405, Shanghai 200031, China. Phone: 86-21-5466-5938. Fax: 86-21-5466-5939. E-Mail: spitzer@radicalmedia.com. Robb Spitzer, Managing Director.

GERMANY: Rueckerstr, Berlin D-10119, Germany. Phone: 49-0-30-233-229-0. Fax: 49-0-30-323-229-1. E-Mail: dressler@radicalmedia.com. Christine Dressler, Managing Director.

UNITED KINGDOM: Scriptor Ct, 155-157 Farringdon Rd, London WC1R 3AD, United Kingdom. Phone: 44-0-20-7462-4070. E-Mail: jodieb@radicalmedia.com. Jodie Brooks, Executive Producer, Sales.
Provides film production, new media, film development, TV programming & animation.

AVENUE — No longer in business.

AWOUNDEDKNEE INDEPENDENT FILMS
48 W 25th St
9th Fl
New York, NY 10010
Phone: 212-255-4440
Fax: 212-255-4494
E-mail: info@awkfilms.com
Web Site: http://www.awkfilms.com
Produces independent films.

AXYZ
477 Richmond St W
10th Fl
Toronto, ON M5V 3EY
Canada
Phones: 416-504-0425; 877-404-0425
Fax: 416-504-0045
Web Site: http://www.axyzfx.com
John Stollar, Executive Vice President
Dave Giles, Executive Producer
Tony de Sousa, Producer
Karen Huybers, Producer
Irene Payne, Producer
Provides post-production services for commercials, TV series & films.

BANDELIER EFX
PO Box 2555
68 Santa Maria
Corrales, NM 87048
Phone: 505-345-8021
Fax: 505-345-8023
E-mail: allans@bandelier.com
Allan Stevens, Director & Producer
Tim Stevens, Animator & Designer
Produces animation & live-action films.

BARBARY POST
435 Pacific Ave
Ste 300
San Francisco, CA 94133
Phone: 415-989-9123
Fax: 415-989-9124
E-mail: contact@barbarypost.com
Web Site: http://www.barbarypost.com
Bob Spector, Director
Kristen Jenkins, Executive Producer
Ian Montgomery, Editor
Daniel Truog, Editor
Provides post production services; specializes in commercial editorial, visual effects & finishing for TV, Web & theatrical.

BARON SERVICES INC.
4930 Research Dr
Huntsville, AL 35805
Phone: 256-881-8811
Fax: 256-881-8283
E-mail: sales@baronservices.com
Web Site: http://www.baronservices.com
Robert O. Baron, President & Chief Executive Officer
John W. Wessinger, Chief Operating Officer
Bob Baron, Jr., Chief Products Officer
Tom Thompson, Executive Vice President, Software Development
Bob Dreisewerd, Vice President & Director, Forecast Services
Kim Grantham, Vice President, Marketing
Bill Walker, Vice President, Radar Division
Provides weather sensing, weather display & meteorological analysis tools.

BASS GROUP — No longer in business.

BATJAC PRODUCTIONS INC.
9595 Wilshire Blvd
Ste 610
Beverly Hills, CA 90212
Phone: 310-278-9870
Fax: 323-272-7381
Gretchen Wayne, President
Produces TV film & tape series & stock footage, mostly John Wayne films.

BAVARIA FILM GMBH
Bavariafilmplatz 7
Geiselgasteig D-82031
Germany
Phone: 49-0-89-6499-0
Fax: 49-0-89-6492-507
E-mail: info@bavaria-film.de
Web Site: http://www.bavaria-film.de
Dr. Norbet Seidel, Chairman
Dr. Matthias Esche, Managing Director
Dr. Achim Rohnke, Managing Director
Produces & distributes cinema, TV, video advertising & industry films.

BBC WORLDWIDE LTD.
Woodlands, 80 Wood Ln
London W12 7TQ
United Kingdom
Phone: 44-0-20-8433-2000
Fax: 44-0-20-8749-0538
Web Site: http://www.bbcworldwide.com
Mark Thompson, Director General & Chairman, Executive Board
Mark Byford, Deputy Director General
Caroline Thomson, Chief Operating Officer
Patrick Younge, Chief Creative Officer, BBC Vision Productions
Sharon Baylay, Director, Marketing Communications & Audiences
Erik Huggers, Director, Future Media & Technology

Branch Offices:
CORAL GABLES: 2332 Galiano St, 2nd Fl, Ste 212, Coral Gables, FL 33134. Phone: 305-443-9808.

LOS ANGELES: 10351 Santa Monica Blvd, Ste 250, Los Angeles, CA 90025. Phone: 310-405-8205.

NEW YORK: 747 Third Ave, New York, NY 10017. Phone: 212-705-9300. Fax: 212-888-0576.

NORTH HOLLYWOOD: 4144 Lankershim Blvd, Ste 200, North Hollywood, CA 91602. Phone: 818-299-9660. Fax: 818-299-9763.

AUSTRALIA: Macquarie Park, Six Eden Park Dr, Level 5, North Sydney, NSW 2113, Australia. Phone: 61-2-9744-4500. Fax: 61-2-9870-7317.

BRAZIL: 1 Andar, Pineheiros, Rua Ferreira de Araujo 741, San Paulo 05428-002, Brazil. Phone: 55-11-2175-7777.

CANADA: 130 Spadina Ave, Ste 401, Toronto, ON M5V 2L4, Canada. Phone: 416-362-3223. Fax: 416-362-3553.

FRANCE: 264 rue du Faubourg Saint-Honore, Paris 75008, France. Phone: 33-1-44-95-84-00. Fax: 33-1-44-95-84-09.

GERMANY: Mediapark 5b, Koln 50670, Germany. Phone: 49-221-454-5580. Fax: 49-221-454-5581.

HONG KONG: Sun Hung Kai Ctr, 30 Harbour Rd, Rooms 2524-2536, Hong Kong, Hong Kong. Phone: 852-2827-2218. Fax: 852-2511-2575.

INDIA: Juhu Tara Rd, Landmark 2nd Fl, Juhu, Mumbau 400049, India. Phone: 91-22-2660-6581. Fax: 91-22-2260-4355.

JAPAN: 7F Akasaka Dai-ichi Bldg, 4-9-17 Akasaka, Minato-ku, Tokyo 107-0052, Japan. Phone: 81-3-3746-4551. Fax: 81-3-3746-4554.

SINGAPORE: 700 Beach Rd, 08-08 199598, Singapore. Phone: 65-6849-5511.
Distributes programming.

BEAST
18 E 16th St
6th Fl
New York, NY 10003
Phone: 212-206-0660
Fax: 212-206-0667
E-mail: ekrajewski@beast.tv
Web Site: http://www.beast.tv
Elizabeth Krajewski, Executive Producer

Branch Offices:
AUSTIN: 512 Rio Grande St, Austin, TX 78701. Phone: 512-583-4567. Fax: 512-610-4600. E-Mail: brent@beast.tv. Brent Holt, Executive Producer.

CHICAGO: 360 N Michigan, Ste 2004, Chicago, IL 60601. Phone: 312-573-2400. Fax: 312-573-2404. E-Mail: mthornley@beast.tv. Melissa Thornley, Executive Producer.

ROYAL OAK: 209 W Sixth St, Royal Oak, MI 48067. Phone: 248-837-2410. Fax: 248-837-2411. E-Mail: mschroeder@beast.tv. Marie Schroeder, Executive Producer.

SANTA MONICA: 1240 Sixth St, Santa Monica, CA 90401. Phone: 310-576-6300. Fax: 310-576-6305. E-Mail: smccarthy@beast.tv. Valerie Petrusson, Managing Director; Sybil McCarthy, Executive Producer.

SAN FRANCISCO: 500 Sansome St, 7th Fl, San Francisco, CA 94111. Phone: 415-392-6300. Fax: 415-392-2600. E-Mail: jettinger@beast.tv. Jon Ettinger, Executive Producer.
Specializes in commercials, web virals & music videos.

DAVE BELL ASSOCIATES INC.
3211 Cahuenga Blvd W
Ste 200
Los Angeles, CA 90068-1372
Phone: 323-851-7801
Dave Bell, Producer
Produces motion picture features, TV movies & specials, documentaries, TV & cable series.

BERKELEY STUDIO — No longer in business.

BERWYN EDITORIAL INC.
350 Hudson St
6th Fl
New York, NY 10014
Phone: 212-519-3800
E-mail: dvd@berwynny.com
Web Site: http://www.berwynny.com
Provides post-production services.

BEST FILM & VIDEO CORP. — No longer in business.

BIG IDEA INC.
230 Franklin Rd
Bldg 2A
Franklin, TX 37064
Phones: 615-224-2200; 800-295-0557
E-mail: customerservice@bigidea.com
Web Site: http://www.bigidea.com
Jenny Kaufman, Director, Licensing
Creates & produces faith-based products reflecting a Judeo-Christian worldview in the family entertainment industry; produces VeggieTales.

BIG SKY EDIT
10 E. 40th St
Ste 1701
New York, NY 10016
Phone: 212-683-4004
Fax: 212-889-6220
Web Site: http://www.bigskyedit.com
Cheryl Panek, Executive Producer

BIJOU ENTERPRISES
805 E Ninth St
Medford, OR 97504
Phone: 541-773-6023
Fax: 541-773-6023
Produces TV film & tape series, documentaries, theatrical shorts, stock footage and products for TV & video.

BIKINI EDIT
39 Wooster St
3rd Fl

New York, NY 10013
Phone: 212-925-4200
Fax: 212-925-6167
E-mail: g@bikinieditorial.com
Web Site: http://www.bikiniedit.com
Gina Pagano, Executive Producer
James Duffy, Editor

BIONIC MEDIA
1375 Broadway
7th Fl
New York, NY 10018
Phone: 212-997-9100
Fax: 212-997-0990
E-mail: info@bionic.tv
Web Site: http://www.bionic.tv
Steve Beal, President
Megan Sweeten, Managing Director
Jim Johnson, Executive Producer
Todd Griffin, Director, Business Development
Victor Newman, Creative Director
Micha Riss, Creative Director
Provides editorial & audio post-production services.

BKN INTERNATIONAL AG
Richmondstr 6
Cologne D-50667
Germany
Phone: 49-0-221-92-0-42-175
Fax: 49-0-221-92-0-42-200
Web Site: http://www.bknkids.com
Sascha Zieman, Chairman & Chief Executive Officer

Branch Offices:
SPAIN: BKN Kids New Media SL, Ave Diagonal, 403, 3-4, Barcelona 08008, Spain. Phone: 34-93-368-05-24. Fax: 34-93-368-04-86.

UNITED KINGDOM: BKN Home Entertainment Ltd./BKN New Media Ltd., 77 Kingsway, London WC2B 6SR, United Kingdom. Phone: 44-0-20-7269-8680. Fax: 44-0-20-7242-8335.
Distributes & markets animated children's TV programs & related consumer products.

BLACKMAGIC DESIGN USA
1551 McCarthy Blvd
Ste 106
Milpitas, CA 95035
Phone: 408-954-0500
Fax: 408-954-0508
E-mail: info-usa@blackmagic-design.com
Web Site: http://www.blackmagic-design.com
Dan May, President, Video Production Sales

Branch Offices:
AUSTRALIA: 11 Gateway Ct, Port Melbourne, VIC 3207, Australia. Phone: 613-9682-4770. Fax: 613-9682-4790. E-Mail: info@blackmagic-design.com.

CHINA: Fortune Mansion, Room 906, No 18 Danling St, Haidian District, Beijing 100080, China. Phone: 86-10-5166-1116. Fax: 86-10-5166-1116, x108. E-Mail: leon_li@blackmagic-design.com. Leon Li, Video Product Sales.

JAPAN: 5F Sotokanda Bldg 4-13, Sotokanda 5-Chome, Chiyoda-ku, Tokyo 101-0021, Japan. Phone: 81-3-5846-6110. Fax: 81-3-5846-6120. E-Mail: info-jp@blackmagic-design.com. Ric Akashi, Video Product Sales.

SINGAPORE: 11 Stamford Rd, #03-05 Capitol Bldg 178884, Singapore. Phone: 65-6338-2696. Fax: 65-6338-2692. E-Mail: richardl@blackmagic-design.com. Richard Linn, Video Product Sales.

UNITED KINGDOM: Mere Hall Business Ctr, Unit 3, Bucklow Hill Ln, Mere, Knutsford, Cheshire WA16 6LE, United Kingdom. Phone: 44-0-1565-830049. Fax: 44-0-1565-830739. E-Mail: info-euro@blackmagic-design.com. Stuart Ashton, Video Product Sales, United Kingdom, Middle East & Africa.
Manufactures high definition video editing technology; equipment includes video recorders, mini converters, broadcast videohubs, monitors & DeckLinks & multibridges.

BLACKSTONE STOCK FOOTAGE
509 Upsall Dr
Antioch, TN 37013
Phone: 615-731-5310
E-mail: g.clifford@worldnet.att.net
Web Site: http://www.blackstonestockfootage.com
Glenda Clifford, President
Offers stock footage; film & computer animation, newsreels & old movies; footage includes sports, cities, scenery, animals, ocean, aviation, military combat, weather & medical.

BLAST DIGITAL
575 Lexington Ave
22nd Fl
New York, NY 10022
Phone: 212-752-4143
Fax: 212-752-4152
Web Site: http://www.blastny.com
Carolyn Mandlavitz, Supervisor, Audio Post Production
Joe O'Connell, Mixer & Sound Designer
Mat Guido, Associate Mixer & Sound Designer
Gerard Collins, Associate Mixer & Sound Designer
Offers full-service audio post-production, specializing in sound engineering, sound design & music production for national TV commercials.

BLUE HIGHWAY
26 Soho St
Ste 303
Toronto, ON M5T 1Z7
Canada
Phone: 416-597-2474
Fax: 416-597-2594
E-mail: mail@bluehighway.ca
Web Site: http://www.bluehighway.ca
Andy Attalai, Partner & Editor
Leo Zaharatos, Partner & Editor
Diana Knegt, Office Manager
Marc Crain, Online Editor
Ralph Floro, Editor
Provides post-production services.

BLUEROCK
575 Lexington Ave
26th Fl
New York, NY 10022
Phone: 212-752-3348
Fax: 212-752-0307
Web Site: http://www.bluerockny.com
Roe Bressan, President & Chief Operations Officer
Cara Cutrone, Executive Producer
Kristin Bilella, Sales

BMG MUSIC PUBLISHING WORLDWIDE
— See listing for Universal Music Publishing Group.

BOND EDIT
665 Broadway
12th Fl
New York, NY 10012
Phone: 212-533-9400
Fax: 212-533-9463
E-mail: info@bondedit.com
Web Site: http://www.bondedit.com
Jeff Beckerman, President & Creative Director
Stephanie Shayne, Executive Producer
Amy Kommatas, Producer
Full-service post-production studio.

BONDED SERVICES
504 Jane St
Ft Lee, NJ 07024
Phone: 201-944-3700
Fax: 201-592-0727
Web Site: http://www.bonded.com

Branch Offices:
BURBANK: 3205 Burton Ave, Burbank, CA 91504. Phone: 818-848-9766. Fax: 818-848-9849.

INGLEWOOD: Freight Division, 441 N Oak St, Inglewood, CA 90302. Phone: 310-680-6830. Fax: 310-680-9099.

CANADA: 288 Judson St, Unit 10, Toronto, ON M8Z 5T6, Canada. Phone: 416-252-5081. Fax: 416-252-3955. E-Mail: darm@bondedservices.com.

HONG KONG: Tung Chun Industrial Bldg, 11-13 Tai Yuen St, Nos 7 & 8, 11th Fl, Block B, Kwai Chung, New Territories, Hong Kong. Phone: 852-2425-6036. Fax: 852-2480-5935. E-Mail: bsi@bonded.com.hk.

THE NETHERLANDS: Tokyostr 13-15, 1175 RB Lijnden, Amsterdam, The Netherlands. Phone: 31-20-6015-031. Fax: 31-20-6041-567. E-Mail: mark_grossouw@bonded.nl.

TURKEY: Dagitim Hizmetleri de Tic AS, Tesvikiye Caddesi Modern, Atp 11/8 Sisli, Istanbul 34367, Turkey. Phone: 92-212-236-68-02. Fax: 92-212-261-62-40. E-Mail: info@bonded.com.tr.

UNITED KINGDOM: Aerodrome Way, Carnford Lane, Hounslow, Middlesex TW5 9QB, United Kingdom. Phone: 44-0-20-8897-7973. Fax: 44-0-20-8897-5539. E-Mail: sales@ftsbonded.com.
Provides storage & distribution of motion picture features, industrial & educational films, picture shorts, foreign language films, TV film & tape series; exports films; film handlers; imports films & TV film series; film rejuvenation & tape evaluation and environmental storage of films & tapes.

BONNEVILLE INTERNATIONAL
55 North 300 West
Salt Lake City, UT 84101
Phone: 801-575-7500
Fax: 801-575-7541
E-mail: bonneville@bonneville.com
Web Site: http://www.bonneville.com
Bruce T. Reese, President & Chief Executive Officer
Robert A. Johnson, Executive Vice President & Chief Operating Officer
Drew M. Horowitz, Executive Vice President, Radio
David Redd, Senior Vice President, Legal & Regulatory Affairs
Designs, produces & places advertising, public service spots & programs.

BOOSEY & HAWKES MUSIC PUBLISHERS LTD.
Aldwych House
71-91 Aldwych
London WC2B 4HN
United Kingdom
Phone: 44-0-20-7054-7200
E-mail: sales@boosey.com
Web Site: http://www.boosey.com
John Minch, President & Chief Executive Officer
Andre de Raaff, Director
Andrew Gummer, Director, Business Affairs
Edward Knighton, Director, Group Finance
Janis Susskino, Publishing Director
Denis Wigman, Director

Branch Offices:
NEW YORK: 35 E 21st St, New York, NY 10010-6212. Phone: 212-358-5300. Fax: 212-358-5305. E-Mail: info.ny@boosey.com. Marc Ostrow, General Manager.

GERMANY: Lutzowufer 26, Berlin 10787, Germany. Phone: 49-0-30-25001300. Fax: 49-0-30-25001399. E-Mail: musikverlag@boosey.com. Winfried Jacobs, Managing Director.
Provides complete music services for all media: from production music to public domain classical works to commercial catalogs & their recordings.

BOSCO PRODUCTIONS
160 E Grand Ave
Chicago, IL 60611
Phone: 312-644-8300
Fax: 312-644-1893
E-mail: angelo@boscoproductions.com
Web Site: http://www.boscoproductions.com
Angela Bosco, President & Chief Executive Officer
Betty Rake, Studio Manager
Iwona Awlasewicz, Video Production Manager
Digital audio production facility; provides casting, production, & trafficking services.

BRAY STUDIOS INC.
— No longer in business.

BREATHE EDITING INC.
12 W 21st St
10th Fl
New York, NY 10010
Phone: 212-947-1748
Fax: 212-947-6397
E-mail: kenny@breatheediting.com
Web Site: http://www.breatheediting.com
Kenny Pedini, Executive Producer
Andy Jennison, Editor
Michael Schwartz, Editor
Provides film editing services.

FRED BRISKIN ASSOCIATES
485 S Robertson Blvd
Beverly Hills, CA 90211-3600
Phone: 310-278-3302
Fred Briskin, President
Independent production of TV & feature films.

BROADCAST MEDIA GROUP INC.
1004 N Jackson St
Starkville, MS 39759
Phones: 662-324-2489; 888-324-2489
Fax: 662-324-2486
E-mail: info@broadcastmediagroup.com
Web Site: http://www.broadcastmediagroup.com
Robbie C. Coblentz, President
Provides videography, editing, DVD creation & duplication services.

BROADCAST MUSIC INC. (BMI)
320 W 57th St
New York, NY 10019-3790
Phone: 212-586-2000
Fax: 212-489-2368

E-mail: newyork@bmi.com
Web Site: http://www.bmi.com
Del Bryant, President & Chief Executive Officer
John E. Cody, Chief Operating Officer & Executive Vice President
Bruce A. Esworthy, Chief Financial Officer & Senior Vice President, Finance
Marvin L. Berenson, Senior Vice President & General Counsel
Fred Cannon, Senior Vice President, Government Relations
Ron Solleveld, Senior Vice President, International

Branch Offices:
ATLANTA: 3340 Peachtree Rd NE, Ste 570, Atlanta, GA 30326. Phone: 404-261-5151.

MIAMI: 1691 Michigan Ave, Ste 350, Miami, FL 33139. Phone: 305-673-5148.

NASHVILLE: 10 Music Sq E, Nashville, TN 37203-4399. Phone: 615-401-2000.

SAN JUAN: 255 Ponce de Leon, MCS Plz, Ste 208, San Juan, PR 00917. Phone: 787-754-6490.

WEST HOLLYWOOD: 8730 Sunset Blvd, 3rd Fl W, West Hollywood, CA 90069-2211. Phone: 310-659-9109.

UNITED KINGDOM: 84 Harley House, Marylebone Rd, London NW1 5HN, United Kingdom. Phone: 44-207486-2036.
Provides music performing rights & copyright clearance services.

BROADCAST NEWS LTD. — No longer in business.

BROADWAY VIDEO ENTERTAINMENT
1619 Broadway
New York, NY 10019-7412
Phone: 212-265-7600
Fax: 212-713-1535
Web Site: http://www.broadwayvideo.com
Lorne Michaels, Founder
Jack Sullivan, Chief Executive Officer
Joseph Brady, Chief Financial Officer
Britta von Schoeler, Senior Vice President & General Manager
Provides post-production services; produces TV & film.

BUENA VISTA HOME ENTERTAINMENT — See listing for Walt Disney Studios.

BUENA VISTA INTERNATIONAL — See listing for Walt Disney Studios..

BUENA VISTA TELEVISION — See listing for Walt Disney Studios.

BUG EDITORIAL INC.
75 Spring St
3rd Fl
New York, NY 10012
Phone: 212-625-1313
Fax: 212-625-1414
E-mail: andreb@bugedit.com
Web Site: http://www.bugedit.com
Andre Betz, Owner & Editor
Jane Weintraub, Executive Producer, New York

Branch Offices:
SANTA MONICA: 225 Santa Monica Blvd, 9th Fl, Santa Monica, CA 90401-2209. Phone: 310-393-2300. Kim Nagel, Executive Producer, Los Angeles; Josh Towvim, Editor, Los Angeles.
Post-production editorial studios.

BUNIM-MURRAY PRODUCTIONS
6007 Sepulveda Blvd
Van Nuys, CA 91411
Phone: 818-756-5150
Fax: 818-756-5140
E-mail: humanresources@bunim-murray.com
Web Site: http://www.bunim-murray.com
Jonathan Murray, Chairman
Gil Goldschein, President
Scott Freeman, Executive Vice President, Current Programming & Development
Fabian Andre, Senior Vice President, Business Development
David Berson, Senior Vice President, Business & Legal Affairs
Jim Johnston, Vice President, Creative Affairs
Bart Peele, Vice President, Operations
Produces reality TV programming.

BURRUD PRODUCTIONS INC.
468 N Camden Dr
2nd Fl
Beverly Hills, CA 90210
Phone: 310-860-5158
Fax: 568-494-6419
E-mail: info@burrud.com
Web Site: http://www.burrud.com
John Burrud, President & Chief Executive Officer

Branch Offices:
SIGNAL HILL: 1905 Redondo Ave, Signal Hill, CA 90755.
Produces film programs on order including documentaries, wildlife, adventure & children's programming; stock footage; multimedia.

BUY THE FARM LLC — No longer in business.
E-mail: info@greenmarkpr.com

BUZZCO ASSOCIATES INC.
33 Bleecker St
New York, NY 10012
Phone: 212-473-8800
Fax: 212-473-8891
E-mail: info@buzzzco.com
Web Site: http://www.buzzzco.com
Vincent Cafarelli, President & Creative Director
Marilyn Kraemer, Principal & General Manager
Candy Kugel, Principal & Producer
Produces film & tape spot commercials, film programs on order, industrial & educational films, open-end film commercials (made for TV), theatrical shorts & animation.

CABLE FILMS/I2BS ONLINE WORLD
Country Club Station 7171
2026 E 63rd St
Mission Hills, KS 66208
Phones: 913-362-2804; 800-514-2804
Fax: 913-341-7365
E-mail: movies@onlineworld.com
Web Site: http://www.onlineworld.com/movies
Herb Miller, President
Distributes 300 motion picture features, industrial & educational films, newsreels, foreign language films, TV film, tape series & theatrical shorts available in PAL, SECAM & NTSC videotape for domestic & international distribution; distributes 30 films based on well-known literature & playwrights for use in libraries & schools.

CAKE EDITORIAL & PI VISUAL EFFECTS
1545 26th St

Ste 300
Santa Monica, CA 90404
Phone: 310-264-5551
Fax: 310-264-5552
Web Site: http://www.cakeshop.tv
Tatiana Derovanessian, President & Executive Producer
Michael Bennet, Director, Marketing
Josh Kirschenbaum, Supervisor, Visual Effects
Provides editorial & visual effects.

CAMPUS GROUP COMPANIES
415 Madison Ave
7th Fl
New York, NY 10017
Phone: 914-961-1900
Fax: 914-961-0882
E-mail: sales@campusgroup.com
Web Site: http://www.campusgroup.com
Steve Campus, President
Produces film & tape spot commercials, film programs on order, TV film & tape series, newsreels, slides, theatrical shorts & multimedia; produces & distributes industrial & educational films & news and teleconference producer & networker.

CAMRAC STUDIOS
1775 Kuenzli St
Reno, NV 89502-1117
Phone: 775-323-0965
Fax: 775-323-1099
E-mail: jim@camrac.com
Web Site: http://www.camrac.com
Jim Mitchell, President
Independent videotape & film production studio; produces & distributes home videos; production; editing; character generation; digital video effects; stereo audio & camera color artwork; duplication; graphics & other services.

CANAL PLUS GROUP
One place due Spectacle
92863 Issy-les-Moulineaux Cedex 9
France
Phone: 33-1-71-35-35-35
Web Site: http://www.canalplusgroup.com
Bertrand Meheut, President
Produces pay-TV channels in France; produces & distributes films.

CANDID CAMERA INC.
PO Box 827
Monterey, CA 93942
Phone: 408-625-3788
Fax: 408-625-3835
E-mail: comments@candidcamera.com
Web Site: http://www.candidcamera.com
Peter Funt, President & Host
Produces Candid Camera & hidden-camera programs & commercials for broadcast & cable outlets.

CANNELL STUDIOS
7083 Hollywood Blvd
Hollywood, CA 90028
Phone: 323-465-5800
Fax: 323-856-7390
E-mail: questions@cannell.com
Web Site: http://www.cannell.com
Stephen J. Cannell, Chief Executive Officer & Chairman
Syndicates & distributes TV programs.

CAPITOL TELEVISION INC. — No longer in business.

CAPTION COLORADO
5690 DTC Blvd
Ste 500W
Englewood, CO 80111
Phones: 720-489-5662; 800-775-7838
Fax: 720-489-5664
Web Site: http://www.captioncolorado.com
R.T. Tad Polumbus, Chief Executive Officer
Troy Greenwood, Chief Operating Officer & Chief Technology Officer
Kurt Suppes, Chief Financial Officer
John Irwin, Senior Vice President, Sales & Marketing
Randy Holyfield, Vice President, Business Development
Mike Lyons, Vice President, Offline Division
Provides real-time closed captioning.

CAPTIONMAX
2438 27th Ave S
Minneapolis, MN 55406
Phone: 612-341-3566
Fax: 612-341-2345
E-mail: donna@captionmax.com
Web Site: http://www.captionmax.com
Gerald Freda, Chief Operating Officer
Max Duckler, President
Donna Horn, Vice President, Business Development
Lindsay Beiriger, Director, Business Development
Maridelle B. Hannah, Director, Business Development
Chris Leininger, Director, Technology
Emily Bell, Manager, Multimedia
Nate Otterdahl, Manager, Real-time Services

Branch Offices:
BURBANK: 441 N Varney, Burbank, CA 91502. Phone: 818-295-2500. Fax: 818-295-2509. Elizabeth Rojas, Project Manager.

NEW YORK: 159 W 25th St, Ste 1009, New York, NY 10001. Phone: 212-462-0060. Fax: 212-462-0061.

SOUTH RIDING: 26171 Glasgow Dr, South Riding, VA 20152. Phone: 703-327-7735. Fax: 703-327-7695.
Provides captioning, subtitling & audio description for all media; FTP services & in-house digital encoding.

CAROUSEL FILM & VIDEO — No longer in business.

CARRAFIELLO, DIEHL & ASSOC. INC.
90 N Broadway
Irvington, NY 10533
Phone: 914-674-3901
E-mail: gcarrafiello@cdamail.com
Web Site: http://www.carrafiellodiehl.com
Gerald Carrafiello, President

CASTLE HILL PRODUCTIONS
36 W 25th St
2nd Fl
New York, NY 10010
Phone: 212-242-1500
Fax: 212-414-5737
Web Site: http://www.castlehillproductions.com
Julian Schlossberg, President & Producer
Provides film production & distribution services.

CASTLE ROCK ENTERTAINMENT
335 N Maple Dr
Beverly Hills, CA 90210
Phone: 310-285-2300
Web Site: http://www.lonestar-movie.com
Martin Shafer, Chairman & Chief Executive Officer
Gregory M. Paul, President & Chief Operating Officer
Glenn Padnick, President, Castle Rock Television
Andrew Scheinman, Creative Director
Rob Reiner, Film Director
Produces feature films; a motion-picture production company. Division of Warner Bros. Pictures.

CATHEDRAL FILMS & VIDEO — No longer in business.

CATHOLIC COMMUNICATION CAMPAIGN
3211 Fourth St NE
Washington, DC 20017-1194
Phone: 202-541-3000
Fax: 202-541-3179
E-mail: ccc@usccb.org
Web Site: http://www.usccb.org/ccc
Rev. Thomas J. Costello, Chairman
Helen Osman, Communications Secretary
Funds & produces documentary & religious programs, public service messages & radio programs; programs available for sale & licensing.

CBC INTERNATIONAL SALES — See listing for Fireworks International.

CBC/RADIO-CANADA
PO Box 3220
Station C
Ottawa, ON K1Y 1E4
Canada
Phones: 613-288-6033; 866-220-6045
Fax: 613-288-6045
E-mail: liaison@radio-canada.ca
Web Site: http://www.cbc.radio-canada.ca
Timothy Casgrain, Chairman
Hubert T. Lacroix, President & Chief Executive Officer
Sylvain Lafrance, Executive Vice President, French Services
Richard Stursberg, Executive Vice President, English Services
Johanne Charbonneau, Vice President & Chief Financial Officer
Raymond Carnovale, Vice President & Chief Technology Officer
William B. Chambers, Vice President, Communications
Reaches Canadians through its national TV and radio networks, specialty cable services, Internet, satellite and podcast services, full service websites, international services, and continuous music network.

C.B. DISTRIBUTION CO. — See listing for Jess S. Morgan & Co.

CBS NEWS INC.
555 W 57th St
New York, NY 10019
Phones: 212-975-3247; 800-777-8398
Fax: 212-975-1893
Web Site: http://www.cbsnews.com
Jeff Fager, Chairman
David Rhodes, President
Paul Friedman, Senior Vice President, CBS News
John Frazee, Senior Vice President, News Services
Linda Mason, Senior Vice President, Standards & Special Projects
Barbara Fedida, Vice President, Talent & Development

CBS TELEVISION DISTRIBUTION
2401 Colorado Ave
Ste 110
Santa Monica, CA 90404
Phone: 310-264-3300
Web Site: http://www.cbstvd.com
John Nogawski, President
Joe DiSalvo, President, Domestic TV Sales
Steven Hirsch, President, Media Sales
Scott Koondel, President, Distribution
Armando Nunez, President, CBS Paramount International TV

Branch Offices:
ATLANTA: 2002 Summit Blvd, Ste 875, Atlanta, GA 30319. Phone: 404-847-9989.

CHICAGO: 455 N Cityfront Plz Dr, Ste 2910, Chicago, IL 60611. Phone: 312-644-3600. Fax: 312-644-7506.

DALLAS: 15303 Dallas Pkwy, Ste 285, Dallas, TX 75001. Phone: 972-960-1996.

NEW YORK: 1700 Broadway, New York, NY 10019. Phone: 212-315-4000.
Produces & distributes first-run series & offers worldwide television syndication. Unit of CBS Corp.

CBS TELEVISION STUDIOS
5555 Melrose Ave
Los Angeles, CA 90038
Phone: 323-956-5000
Web Site: http://www.cbstelevisionstudios.com
David Stapf, Jr., President
Glen Geller, Senior Vice President, Current Programming
Julie McNamara, Senior Vice President, Drama Development
Lauri Metrose, Senior Vice President, Communications
(Formerly CBS Paramount Television.) The television production & distribution arm of CBS Corp.

CENTRAL OFFICE OF INFORMATION
Hercules House
Hercules Rd
London SE1 7DU
United Kingdom
Phone: 44-0-20-7928-2345
Fax: 44-0-20-7928-5037
Web Site: http://www.coi.gov.uk
Mark Lund, Chief Executive Officer
Produces & distributes industrial & educational films (sale or loan); TV film/tape series; distributes motion picture shorts; stock footage; exports films; film buyer.

CHANNEL Z EDIT
15 S Fifth St
Ste 616
Minneapolis, MN 55402
Phone: 612-370-0016
Fax: 612-370-0160
E-mail: ace@channelzedit.com
Web Site: http://www.channelzsucks.com
Ace Allgood, Producer
Amelia Ruth, Producer
Provides creative, editorial & post-production services.

CHAPMAN/LEONARD STUDIO EQUIPMENT INC.
9460 Delegates Dr
Orlando, FL 32837
Phones: 407-851-3456; 888-337-8243
Fax: 407-855-1653
E-mail: cristine@chapman-leonard.com
Web Site: http://www.chapman-leonard.com
Charles Huenergardt, Chief Operating Officer & Coordinator, Special Projects
Christine Chapman-Huenergardt, Vice President, Marketing Director & Sales Representative
Dana Kuprianczyk, Manager, Rental & Customer Service
David Bullard, Supervisor, Equipment & Stage Rental
Gilbert Alvarado, Coordinator, Shipping
Annette Kiatpiriya, Coordinator, Leasing

Branch Offices:
ALBUQUERQUE: 9201 Pan American Frwy NE, Albuquerque, NM 87118. Phone: 888-758-4826.

AUSTIN: 1901 E 51st St, Stage 3, Austin, TX 78723. Phones: 512-473-0084; 888-758-4826. Fax: 512-473-0042.

NEW ORLEANS: 660 Distributors Row, Elmwood Business Park, Sts C & D, New Orleans, LA 70123. Phones: 504-731-6050; 888-758-4826. Fax: 504-731-6051.

NORTH HOLLYWOOD: 12950 Raymer St, North Hollywood, CA 91605. Phones: 818-764-6726; 888-883-6559. Fax: 818-764-6728.

UNITED KINGDOM: Kingley Park, Station Road, Unit 5, Kings Langley WD4 8GW, United Kingdom. Phone: 44-0-1-92-326-5953. Fax: 44-0-1-92-326-8315. Michaela Barnes, Manager; Dennis Fraser, Managing Director.
Manufactures & rents camera support equipment for motion picture & TV use; also offers sound stage & production facility rentals.

CHEMISTRY
99 Madison Ave
7th Fl
New York, NY 10016
Phone: 212-685-7555
Fax: 212-685-8686
Web Site: http://www.chemistryny.com
Stephen Ashkinos, Managing Director & Owner
Suzanne Wlader, Executive Producer
Lauren Basile, Producer
Jennifer Hertslet, Sales

CHINAGRAPH
119 Fifth Ave
6th Fl
New York, NY 10003
Phone: 212-529-1991
Fax: 212-529-1992
E-mail: rquigley@madeinchinagraph.com
Web Site: http://www.madeinchinagraph.com
Anne Gordon, Executive Producer
Rosemary Quigley, Executive Producer

CHRISTIAN CHURCH (DISCIPLES OF CHRIST), COMMUNICATION MINISTRIES
PO Box 1986
Disciples Ctr
Indianapolis, IN 46206-1986
Phone: 317-713-2492
Fax: 317-713-2417
E-mail: wbwills@cm.disciples.org
Web Site: http://www.disciples.org
Wanda Bryant-Wills, Executive Director
Christopher G. Higgins, Manager, Internet & New Media

CHRISTIAN TELEVISION NETWORK
6922 142nd Ave
Largo, FL 33771
Phone: 727-535-5622
Fax: 727-531-2497
E-mail: sales@ctonline.com
Web Site: http://www.ctnonline.com
Bob D'Andrea, President & Founder
Provides 24-hour Christian programming.

THE CHRISTOPHERS
5 Hanover Sq
11th Fl
New York, NY 10004
Phones: 212-759-4050; 888-298-4050
Fax: 212-838-5073
E-mail: mail@christophers.org
Web Site: http://www.christophers.org
Mary Ellen Robinson, Vice President
Produces & distributes syndicated half-hour radio series, one-minute radio spots & quarter-hour radio programs.

CHROME
2044 Broadway
Santa Monica, CA 90404
Phone: 310-264-9700
Fax: 310-264-9701
Web Site: http://www.chrome.tv
Deanne Mehling, Partner & Executive Producer
Cristina Matracia, Senior Producer
Angela Dorian, Producer

CHURCH FEDERATION OF GREATER INDIANAPOLIS INC.
1100 W 42nd St
Ste 345
Indianapolis, IN 46208
Phone: 317-926-5371
Fax: 317-926-5373
E-mail: churches@churchfederationindy.org
Web Site: http://www.churchfederationindy.org
Rev. Dr. Angelique Walker-Smith, Executive Director
Rev. Jim Miller, Associate Director, Programs & Community Ministries
Dr. Ray Marquette, Development & Membership
Produces religious TV programs.

THE CHURCH OF JESUS CHRIST OF LATTER-DAY SAINTS
50 E North Temple St
Salt Lake City, UT 84150
Phone: 801-240-1000
E-mail: 2010550-prs@ldschurch.org
Web Site: http://www.lds.org
Produces religious programming.

CHURCH OF THE NAZARENE
17001 Prairie Star Pkwy
Lenexa, KS 66220
Phone: 913-577-0500
E-mail: gensec@nazarene.org
Web Site: http://www.nazarene.org
David P. Wilson, General Secretary
Produces radio programs in 40 languages, video, broadcast TV, photography, slide shows, multimedia presentations & A/V educational aids.

CHURCH WORLD SERVICE
PO Box 968
28606 Phillips St
Elkhart, IN 46515
Phones: 574-264-3102; 800-297-1516
Fax: 574-262-0966
E-mail: info@churchworldservice.org
Web Site: http://www.churchworldservice.org
Rev. John L. McCullough, Executive Director & Chief Executive Officer
Joanne Rendall, Chief Financial Officer & Deputy Director, Operations
Reginald K. Ingram, Chief Development Officer
Rhonda Hughes, Director, Program Interpretation & Resource Creation
Ann Walle, Director, Marketing & Communications
William E. Wildey, Director, Development
Maurice Bloem, Deputy Director, Programs

Branch Offices:
NEW YORK: 475 Riverside Dr, Ste 700, New York, NY 10115. Phone: 212-870-2061. Fax: 212-870-3523. Lesley Crosson, Media Relations Officer.

WASHINGTON, DC: 110 Maryland Ave NE, Ste 108, Bldg Box 45, Washington, DC 20002. Phone: 202-544-2350. Fax: 202-546-6232.
Produces film/tape spot commercials, development related films & slides.

CINECRAFT PRODUCTIONS INC.
2515 Franklin Blvd
Cleveland, OH 44113
Phone: 216-781-2300
Fax: 216-781-1067
E-mail: info@cinecraft.com
Web Site: http://www.cinecraft.com
Neil G. McCormick, Chairman
Maria E. Keckan, President
Daniel E. Keckan, Vice President, Sales & Marketing
Scott Minium, Executive Producer
Devon Collins, Producer & Editor
Kurt Albrecht, Senior Editor & Cameraman
Mark Conlon, Senior Programmer & IT Specialist
Provides video & film production, CD-ROM, DVD & web development.

CINEGROUPE
1151 rue Alexandre-DeSeve
Montreal, PQ H2L 2T7
Canada
Phone: 514-524-7567
Fax: 514-849-9846
E-mail: info@cinegroupe.ca
Web Site: http://www.cinegroupe.com
Jacques Pettigrew, Founder, President & Chief Executive Officer
Michel Lemire, Executive Vice President, Creative Affairs & Production
Linda Caron, Director, Finance & Administration
Pierre Duff, Director, Information Technologies
Christian Garcia, Director, 3D Studio & Supervisor, CGI
Creates, produces & distributes hit animation & CGI entertainment programming in all media for the worldwide marketplace.

CINEMA ARTS INC.
PO Box 452
Newfoundland, PA 18445
Phone: 570-676-4145
Fax: 570-676-9194
Janice Allen, President
Motion picture laboratory; produces optical transfers for 35mm, 16mm & super 16mm; enlargements & reductions including anamorphic & Vistavision formats; color & black & white; film-to-tape telecine transfer; specializes in shrunken & deteriorating film; stock footage 1895-1965.

CINE MAGNETICS DIGITAL & VIDEO LABORATORIES
100 Business Park Dr
Armonk, NY 10504
Phones: 914-273-7500; 800-431-1102
Fax: 914-273-7575
E-mail: sales@cinemagnetics.com
Web Site: http://www.cinemagnetics.com
Joseph J. Barber, Jr., President
Kenneth Wynne, Vice President & General Manager
Haitham Wahab, Chief Financial Officer

Branch Offices:
CHARLOTTE: 957 Whalley Rd, Charlotte, VT 05445. Phone: 800-431-1102. Fax: 914-273-7575.

OCEANSIDE: 5495 Parrolette Ct, Oceanside, CA 92057. Phone: 760-967-9523. Cindy Taylor, Sales/Client Services.

STUDIO CITY: 3765 Cahuenga Blvd W, Studio City, CA 91604-3504. Phone: 818-623-2560. Fax: 818-623-2565. Tim Willis, Director, Technical.
Provides DVD authoring & compression, DVD & CD replication & duplication, video on demand, video streaming, digital asset management, video duplication, foreign language subtitling & language, replacement & custom design, printing & packaging services.

CINEMA SOURCE — No longer in business.

CLASSICMEDIA
860 Broadway
6th Fl
New York, NY 10003
Phone: 212-659-1959
Fax: 212-659-1958
E-mail: info@classicmedia.tv
Web Site: http://www.classicmedia.tv
Owns & manages feature films, TV, home video & consumer products; product names include Casper the Friendly Ghost, Richie Rich, Rudolph the Red-Nosed Reindeer, Peter Cottontail & Rocky & Bullwinkle.

CNET NETWORKS INC.
235 Second St
San Francisco, CA 94105
Phone: 415-344-2000
Web Site: http://www.cnetnetworks.com

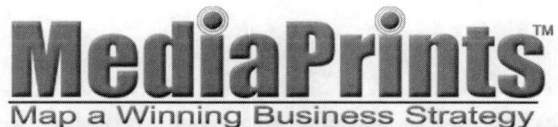

Scott Ard, Editor-in-Chief
Brian Cooley, Editor at Large, CNET TV

Branch Offices:
SOMERVILLE: 55 Davis Sq, Somerville, MA 02144. Phone: 617-284-8633. Fax: 617-284-8688.

NEW YORK: 28 E 28th St, New York, NY 10016. Phone: 646-472-4000. Fax: 646-472-3912.
Division of CBS Interactive Inc.

CNN NEWSOURCE SALES INC.
One CNN Center NW
Atlanta, GA 30303
Phones: 404-827-2085; 404-827-5032
Fax: 404-827-4959; 404-827-3640
Web Site: http://newsource.cnn.com
Provides sales & marketing of CNN Newsource & its services. Division of Turner Broadcasting System Inc.

COASTLINE COMMUNITY COLLEGE CENTER
11460 Warner Ave
Fountain Valley, CA 92708-2597
Phone: 714-546-7600
Web Site: http://coastline.cccd.edu
Ding-Jo Currie, President
Dan Jones, Dean, Instructional Systems Development
Lynn Dahnke, Director, Telecourse Marketing
Michelle Ma, Director, Marketing & Public Relations
Laurie Melby, Director, Telecourse Production & Telemedia
Produces & markets college courses by TV.

COE FILM ASSOCIATES INC. — No longer in business.

COLLEGE BOWL CO.
5900 Canoga Ave
Ste 100
Woodland Hills, CA 91367-5009
Phones: 818-610-8225; 800-234-2695
Fax: 818-610-8230
E-mail: info@collegebowl.com
Web Site: http://www.collegebowl.com
Richard Reid, President
Mary Oberembt, Vice President & General Manager
Franklin J. Gencur, Associate General Manager
Produces TV film & tape series.

COLUMBIA TRISTAR TELEVISION GROUP — See listing for Sony Pictures Television.

COMPANY X
152 W 25th St.
11th Fl
New York, NY 10001
Phone: 212-414-3200
Fax: 212-414-3209
E-mail: rachelle@companyx.tv
Web Site: http://www.companyx.tv
Rachelle Way, Managing Director
Jonlyn Williams, Executive Producer
Jennifer Hertslet, Sales Representative
Provides post-production editing services.

COMPRO PRODUCTIONS INC.
2055 Boar Tusk Rd NE
Conyers, GA 30012-3801
Phone: 770-918-8163
E-mail: steve@compro-atl.com
Web Site: http://www.compro-atl.com
Nels A. Anderson, President & Director
Steve Brinson, Vice President & Producer
Kim Anderson, Chief Financial Officer & Executive Producer
Provides film & video production services; corporate & image films, documentaries, infomercials, episodic television; post production, DVD authoring, streaming video for web, extensive film & tape stock library - international & domestic scenics & culture; aerial & underwater production; outdoor & sports.

COMTEL VIDEO SERVICES INC.
PO Box 1595
Makawao, HI 96768-1595
Phones: 808-270-3065; 808-268-2151
E-mail: info@comtelvideo.com
Web Site: http://www.comtelvideo.com
Robert C. Beggs, President
Provides air checks for advertisers on TV; off-air & off-satellite videotaping; videotape duplication; international standards conversions; closed captioning service.

CONCORDIA PUBLISHING HOUSE
3558 S Jefferson Ave
St Louis, MO 63118-3968
Phones: 314-268-1000; 800-325-3040
E-mail: order@cph.org
Web Site: http://www.cph.org
Bruce G. Kintz, President & Chief Executive Officer
Jonathan D. Schultz, Vice President & Corporate Counsel
Rev. Paul T. McCain, Publisher & Executive Director, Editorial
Peggy Anderson, Executive Director, Finance
Steve Harris, Executive Director, IT
Paul Brunette, Director, Sales
Produces & distributes Christian films & videos.

CONNECTICUT PUBLIC BROADCASTING INC.
1049 Asylum Ave
Hartford, CT 06105
Phones: 860-278-5310; 800-683-1899
E-mail: wherewelive@wnpr.org
Web Site: http://www.cpbi.org
Jerry Franklin, President & Chief Executive Officer
Nancy Bauer, Vice President, Sales & Corporate Sponsorship
Tanya Meck, Director, Leadership Giving
Carol Sisco, Human Resources
Maria Zone, Media Relations

Branch Offices:
NEW HAVEN: 70 Audubon St, New Haven, CT 06510. Phone: 203-776-9677.
Produces public TV programming.

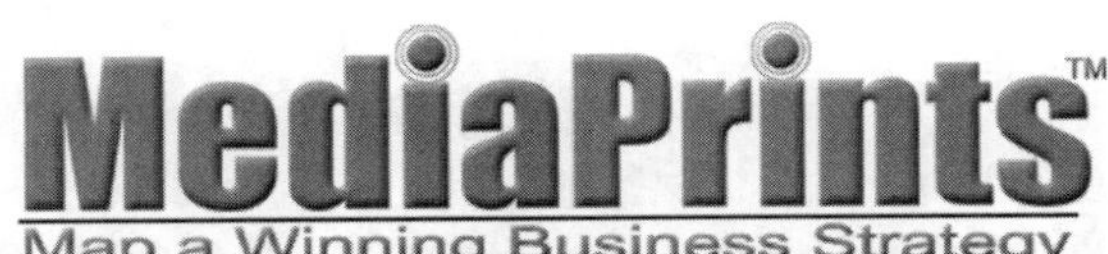
MediaPrints™
Map a Winning Business Strategy
Digital Cable and TV Coverage Maps.
Visit www.warren-news.com/mediaprints.htm

CONSULATE
536 Broadway
9th Fl
New York, NY 10012
Phone: 212-219-0020
Fax: 212-219-0590
E-mail: lisa@consulatefilm.com
Web Site: http://www.consulatefilm.com
Lisa Binassarie, Managing Director
Charlyn Derrick, Senior Producer
Provides film editing services.

CONTINENTAL FILM PRODUCTIONS CORP.
PO Box 5126
4315 N Creek Rd
Chattanooga, TN 37406
Phone: 423-622-1193
Fax: 423-629-0853
E-mail: cfpc@chattanooga.net
Web Site: http://www.continentalfilm.com
Provides production services, including scripting & duplication.

COOKIE JAR ENTERTAINMENT INC.
266 King St W
2nd Fl
Toronto, ON M5V 1H8
Canada
Phone: 416-977-3238
E-mail: info@thecookiejarcompany.com
Web Site: http://www.cjar.com
Michael Hirsh, Chief Executive Officer
Toper Taylor, President & Chief Operating Officer
Aaron Ames, Chief Financial Officer
Jean-Michel Ciszewski, Senior Vice President, Sales & Distribution
Carrie Dumont, Senior Vice President, Business & Legal Affairs
Kenneth Locker, Senior Vice President, Digital Media
Tom Mazza, Worldwide TV Head

Branch Offices:
BURBANK: 4100 W Alameda Ave, Ste 201, Burbank, CA 91505. Phone: 818-955-5400.
Produces, distributes & markets quality children's & family programming; maintains dedicated operations involved in programs & product development/production, merchandising/licensing & marketing/distribution.

CORGAN MEDIA LAB
401 N Houston St
Dallas, TX 75202
Phone: 214-748-2000
Fax: 214-653-8281
E-mail: cml@corgan.com
Web Site: http://www.corganmedialab.com
Shana Valdez, Executive Producer
Creates 3D elements & motion graphics for TV, broadcast & interactive experiences.

COSMO STREET
2036 Broadway
Santa Monica, CA 90404
Phone: 310-828-6666
Fax: 310-453-9699
E-mail: yvette@cosmostreet.com
Web Site: http://www.cosmostreet.com
Yvette Cobarrubias, Executive Producer

Branch Offices:
NEW YORK: 28 W 25th St, New York, NY 10010. Phone: 212-625-6800. Fax: 212-625-6888. Maura Woodward, Executive Producer.

COVENANT HOUSE NEW YORK
460 W 41st St
New York, NY 10036
Phone: 212-613-0300
E-mail: info@covenanthouse.org
Web Site: http://www.covenanthouseny.org
Jerry Kilbane, Executive Director
Georgia Boothe, Associate Executive Director
Dave Gregorio, Director, Support Services
Sal Morgan, Director, Finance
Simore Thompson, Director, Program Operations
Provides video programs for Covenant House events.

CRAVEN FILM
5 W 19th St
New York, NY 10011
Phone: 212-463-7190
E-mail: info@cravenfilms.com
Web Site: http://www.cravenfilms.com
Full service audio-visual producer: industrial, training, educational, fund-raising, governmental, business & informational films & videotapes; commercials & public service announcements; motion picture shorts; foreign language productions.

CREATIVE INTERNATIONAL ACTIVITIES LTD.
372 Central Park W
New York, NY 10025
Phone: 212-663-8944
Fax: 212-724-1436
Klaus J. Lehmann
Provides specials, documentaries, series & children's programming; international barter sales & consulting.

CREW CUTS
28 W 44th St
22nd Fl
New York, NY 10036
Phone: 212-302-2828
Fax: 212-302-9846
E-mail: nancy@crewcuts.com
Web Site: http://www.crewcuts.com
Nancy Shames, Executive Producer
Dani Epstein, Sales Representative
Provides post-production editorial services.

CRN DIGITAL TALK RADIO
10487 Sunland Blvd
Sunland, CA 91040-1905
Phone: 818-352-7152
Fax: 818-352-3229
E-mail: feedback@crni.net
Web Site: http://www.crntalk.com
Michael Horn, President
Erin Farrell, Vice President, Affiliate Relations
Jennifer Horn, Vice President, Marketing & Sales
Paul Stern, Vice President, Operations
Erik Hines, Director, Production
Provides talk radio programming for the telecommunications industry; develops new & unique talk talent & distributes it for use in cable audio packages & as VOD; provides cable systems with a personalized radio station designed to reach customers at the point of sale in a soothing & entertaining environment. Division of Cable Radio Networks.

CROSSPOINT
940 Wadsworth Blvd
2nd Fl
Lakewood, CO 80214
Phone: 303-233-2700
Fax: 303-232-6460
E-mail: info@crosspoint.com
Web Site: http://www.crosspoint.com
Kim Croy, General Manager
Jenn Bang, Manager, Client Services
Corey Hayes, Manager, Business Development
Shawn Roberts, Project Coordinator & Scheduler
Provides production & post-production services; HD production & editing facility; tape-to-tape color correction, non-linear off-line suites, digital image compositing, motion graphics & animation; audio suite for mix, edit, sweetening; local and remote VO record via ISDN, etc.; web site design, video to CD-ROM, CD-ROM duplication, interactive business cards, video for the web, DVD authoring.

CROSSROADS CHRISTIAN COMMUNICATIONS INC.
PO Box 5100
1295 N Service Rd
Burlington, ON L7R 4M2
Canada
Phone: 905-335-7100
Fax: 905-332-6655
E-mail: crossroads@crossroads.ca
Web Site: http://www.crossroads.ca
David Mainse, Founder
Norma-Jean Mainse, Co-founder

Branch Offices:
NEW YORK: PO Box 486, New York, NY 14302.
Provides Christian programming worldwide.

JOHN CROWE PRODUCTIONS — See listing for National Mobile Television.

CROWN INTERNATIONAL PICTURES INC.
8701 Wilshire Blvd
Beverly Hills, CA 90211
Phone: 310-657-6700
Fax: 310-657-4489
E-mail: crown@crownintlpictures.com
Web Site: http://www.crownintlpictures.com
Mark Tenser, President & Chief Executive Officer
Scott E. Schwimer, Senior Vice President
Lisa Agay, Director, Publicity & Advertising
Produces & distributes theatrical feature films.

CRYSTAL CATHEDRAL MINISTRIES
13280 Chapman Ave
Garden Grove, CA 92840
Phone: 714-971-4000
E-mail: info@crystalcathedral.org
Web Site: http://www.crystalcathedral.org
Robert H. Schuller, Founder
Michelle Cavinder, Director, Learning Network & Women's Ministries
Sheila Coleman, Director, Family Ministries
Jim Kok, Director, Care Ministries
Maureen A. Winer, Congregational Life Ministry
Produces & distributes original Christian programming.

CRYSTAL PICTURES INC.
2000 Riverside Dr
Asheville, NC 28804
Phone: 828-285-9995
Fax: 828-285-9997
E-mail: cryspic@aol.com
Joshua Tager, President
Jane Ann Rolston, TV Sales Executive
Produces, distributes & syndicates features, documentaries & shorts.

CTV INC.
PO Box 9
Station O
Scarborough, ON M4A 2M9
Canada
Phones: 416-332-5000; 800-461-1542
Web Site: http://www.ctv.ca
Robert Hurst, President
Alexis Hood, Manager, Communications

Branch Offices:
CANADA: Nine Channel Nine Ct, Scarborough, ON M1S 4B5, Canada.
Produces newsreels; produces & distributes industrial & educational films & TV film/tape series; news; stock footage; imports TV film series.

CUSTOM FILMS/VIDEO INC. — No longer in business.

CUT & RUN
Cinema House
93 Wardour St
London W1F 0UD
United Kingdom
Phone: 44-0-20-7432-9696
Fax: 44-0-20-7432-9697
E-mail: james.tomkinson@cutandrun.tv
Web Site: http://www.cutandrun.tv
James Tomkinson, Managing Director

Branch Offices:
NEW YORK: 599 Broadway, 12th Fl, New York, NY 10012. Phone: 212-260-8900. E-Mail: angie.aguilera@cutandrun.tv. Ran Martin, Executive Producer.

SANTA MONICA: 1635 12th St., Santa Monica, CA 90404. Phone: 310-450-1116. Fax: 310-450-1166. E-Mail: michelle@cutandrun.tv. Michelle Burke, Managing Director.

HONG KONG: 14/F One Hysan Ave, Causeway Bay, Hong Kong. Phone: 852-9184-4813. E-Mail: nick.diss@cutandrun.tv. Nick Diss, Contact.
Provides offline editing.

CUTTERS
515 N State St
25th Fl
Chicago, IL 60654
Phone: 312-644-2500
Fax: 312-644-2501
E-mail: info@cutters.com
Web Site: http://www.cutters.com
John McGrath, General Manager
Phil Barton, Chief Financial Officer
Chuck Silverman, Director, Sales & Marketing
Cindy Duffy, Executive Producer
Nicole Visram, Executive Producer
Arnell Patscott, Chief Engineer

Branch Offices:
SANTA MONICA: 2110 Main St, Ste 207, Santa Monica, CA 90405. Phone: 310-309-3780. Fax: 310-309-3779. E-Mail: infola@cutters.com.
Editorial boutique.

CWK NETWORK INC.
6285 Barfield Rd
3rd Fl
Atlanta, GA 30328
Phones: 404-459-8081; 888-598-5437
E-mail: sales@cwknetwork.com
Web Site: http://www.connectingwithkids.com
Stacey DeWitt, President, Chief Executive Officer & Director
Produces & syndicates programs focusing on the health, education & well-being of children.

DAPTV ASSOCIATES
820 Westbourne Dr
Ste 4
West Hollywood, CA 90069
Phone: 310-867-5881
E-mail: doned1@earthlink.net
Web Site: http://www.daptv.com; http://www.ieditvideo.com
Don Azars, Writer, Director, Editor & Producer
Provides program & video development services & distributes film programs on order.

DAY OF DISCOVERY (RBC MINISTRIES)
3000 Kraft Ave SE
Grand Rapids, MI 49512
Phone: 616-974-2210
Fax: 616-957-5741
Web Site: http://www.rbc.net
Mart De Haan, President

Branch Offices:
CANADA: PO Box 1622, Windsor, ON N9A 6Z7, Canada. Phone: 519-979-1073. E-Mail: canada@rbc.org.
Produces & distributes religious programs; distributes TV film & tape series.

DAY 1
644 W Peachtree St NW
Ste 300
Atlanta, GA 30308
Phone: 404-815-0640
Fax: 404-815-0495
E-mail: pwallace@day1.org
Web Site: http://day1.org
Peter M. Wallace, Executive Producer & Host
Donal A. Jones, Production Coordinator & Audio Engineer
Rebecca Kurziak, Associate Director, Development
Produces the religious radio & TV program, Day 1 (formerly The Protestant Hour). Ministry of the Alliance for Christian Media Inc.

DEBMAR-MERCURY
225 Santa Monica Blvd
8th Fl
Santa Monica, CA 90401
Phone: 310-393-6000
Fax: 310-393-6110
Web Site: http://www.debmarmercury.com
Ira Bernstein, Co-President
Mort Marcus, Co-President
Michael Chinery, Senior Vice President, Sales
Darren Doyle, Vice President, Sales

Branch Offices:
NEW YORK: 75 Rockefeller Plaza, 16th Fl., New York, NY 10010. Phone: 212-669-5025. Fax: 212-962-2872.

UNITED KINGDOM: 163 Holland Park Ave., London W11 4UR, United Kingdom. Phone: 44-0-20-7602-5201.
Provides production & distribution services; specializes in network, cable, syndication, VOD/pay-per-view & pay TV.

DEFENSE MEDIA ACTIVITY
2713 Mitscher Rd SW
Bldg 168
Anacostia Annex, DC 20373-5819
Phone: 703-428-1200
Web Site: http://www.dma.mil
Melvin W. Russell, Senior Executive Service Acting Director
Provides a broad range of multimedia products & services to inform, educate & entertain Department of Defense audiences around the world.

DELUXE LABORATORIES INC.
1377 N Serrano Ave
Hollywood, CA 90027
Phone: 323-960-3600
Fax: 323-960-7016
E-mail: steven.vananda@bydeluxe.com
Web Site: http://www.bydeluxe.com
Cyril Drabinsky, President & Chief Executive Officer, Deluxe Entertainment Services Group
Provides complete film laboratory, post production & digital lab facilities & services; offices worldwide.

DEVILLIER DONEGAN ENTERPRISES LP — No longer in business.

DEWOLFE MUSIC
Shropshire House
11-20 Capper St
London WC1E 6JA
United Kingdom
Phone: 44-0-20-7631-3600
Fax: 44-0-20-7631-3700
E-mail: info@dewolfemusic.co.uk
Web Site: http://www.dewolfemusic.co.uk
Andrew M. Jacobs, Chief Executive Officer
Marcie Jacobs, President
Joel Feinberg, Vice President, Business Development
Jen Paul, Director, Operations
Wilsa Exantus, Manager, Client Service
Valerie Sene, Licensing Coordinator
Brian Hamilton, Senior Sales Consultant
Lauren Pavia, Sales, Licensing & Music
Music library & sound effects specialist for audio-visual & broadcast; classical music; voice recording & mix studio.

DG FASTCHANNEL INC.
750 W John Carpenter Fwy
Ste 700
Irving, TX 75039
Phones: 972-581-2000; 800-324-5672
Fax: 972-581-2001
E-mail: info@dgfastchannel.com
Web Site: http://www.dgfastchannel.com
Scott K. Ginsburg, Chairman & Chief Executive Officer
Omar A. Choucair, Chief Financial Officer
Neil Nguyen, Executive Vice President, Sales & Operations
Pamela Maythenyi, Senior Vice President, Creative Services
Delivers SD & HD advertising via satellite & IP technology; deploys digital media intelligence & asset management tools specifically for the advertising industry; online creative & production resources, rich media video ad serving & digital asset management; offices nationwide.

DIAMOND P SPORTS LLC
14333 Meyer Lake Cir
Clearwater, FL 33760-2839
Phone: 727-530-5000
Produces sports, reality & entertainment programming.

DICK CLARK PRODUCTIONS INC.
2900 Olympic Blvd
Santa Monica, CA 90404
Phone: 310-255-4600
Web Site: http://www.dickclarkproductions.com
Dick Clark, Chief Executive Officer
Produces TV, movies, radio programming & stage performances.

DIGIMATION INC.
115 James Dr W
Ste 140
St Rose, LA 70087
Phones: 504-468-7898; 800-854-4496
Fax: 504-468-5494
E-mail: sales@digimation.com
Web Site: http://www.digimation.com
Provides 3D digital content, creative services & graphics software solutions.

DIGI-ROM — See listing for Play-It Productions Inc.

DIGITAL FORCE
149 Madison Ave
12th Fl
New York, NY 10016
Phones: 212-252-9300; 877-347-2872
Fax: 212-252-7377
E-mail: frontdesk@digitalforce.com
Web Site: http://www.digitalforce.com
Jerome Bunke, President
Provides CD & DVD production services including CD & DVD duplication, replication & copying for audio CDs & data CDs.

DIGITAL JUICE INC.
600 Technology Park
Ste 104
Lake Mary, FL 32746
Phones: 407-531-5540; 800-525-2203
Fax: 407-358-5174
E-mail: info@digitaljuice.com
Web Site: http://www.digitaljuice.com
David Hebel, Chief Executive Officer
Viv Beason, President
Provides royalty-free professional animations, stock footage, music, layered graphics, clip art & templates.

DIGITAL POST SERVICES
2044 Cotner Ave
Los Angeles, CA 90025
Phone: 310-312-9060
Fax: 310-479-5771
Web Site: http://www.digitalpostservices.com
Ryan Noto, Chief Executive Officer
International standards conversion & videotape duplication facility; provides film-to-tape transfers, post-production services & vault storage.

DILIGENT SYSTEMS INC.
726 Rte. 202 S
Ste 320
Bridgewater, NJ 08807
Phone: 908-693-3580
Fax: 908-595-0072
E-mail: info@diligentsystems.com
Web Site: http://www.diligentsystems.com
Herbert Mischel, President & Chief Technology Officer
Charles McMullin, Chief Executive Officer
Peter Strub, Vice President, Business Development
Walt Laskowski, Sales Representative

Branch Offices:
LOS ANGELES: 1110 S Robertson Blvd, Los Angeles, CA 90035.
Provides FAST EDL for TV shows.

DISCOVERY EDUCATION
One Discovery Pl
Silver Spring, MD 20910
Phone: 800-323-9084
Fax: 847-328-6706
Web Site: http://www.discoveryeducation.com
Bill Goodwyn, President, Global Distribution
Kelli Campbell, Senior Vice President, Product & Content Strategy
Publishes & distributes high-quality digital educational resources.

DIVISION X
23689 Industrial Park Dr
Farmington Hills, MI 48335
Phone: 248-471-6010
Fax: 248-471-4692
E-mail: info-x@gw-divisionx.com
Web Site: http://www.gw-divisionx.com
Steven Wild, President
Allan Rothfeder, Executive Vice President & Chief Financial Officer
Provides image creation, production & project supervision, character development, special effects & animation.

DJM
Four E 46th St
New York, NY 10017
Phone: 212-687-0111
Fax: 212-499-9081
E-mail: ed@djmpost.tv
Web Site: http://www.djmpost.tv
Ed Friedman, Owner
Eileen Friedman, Vice President, Distribution
Wilson Converse, Editor & Smoke Artist
Pete Serinita, Digital Audio Post
Danny Breen, Producer/Editor
David Friedman, Editor
Joe Domilici, Editor
Charlie Weissman, Editor
Editing & post production services; audio recording & mixing; duplication & distribution.

DLT ENTERTAINMENT LTD.
124 E 55th St
New York, NY 10022
Phone: 212-245-4680
Fax: 212-315-1132
Web Site: http://www.dltentertainment.com
Don Taffner, President

Branch Offices:
UNITED KINGDOM: UK Headquarters, 10 Bedford Sq, London, England WC1B 3RA, United Kingdom. Phone: 44-0-20-7631-1184. Fax: 44-0-20-7636-4571.

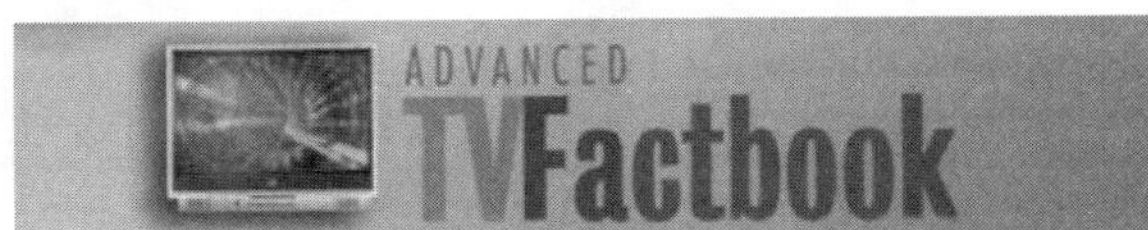

UNITED KINGDOM: The Theatre of Comedy Co., Shaftesbury Theatre, 210 Shaftesbury Ave, London, England WC2H 8DP, United Kingdom. Phone: 44-0-20-7379-3345. Fax: 44-0-20-7836-8181.
Produces & distributes TV programs; first-run syndication; network development; co-production; international syndication sales.

DMX MUSIC
1703 W Fifth St
Ste 600
Austin, TX 78701
Phones: 512-380-8500; 800-345-5000
Fax: 512-380-8501
E-mail: info@dmx.com
Web Site: http://www.dmx.com
R. Steven Hicks, Chairman
Paul D. Stone, President
John D. Cullen, Chief Executive Officer
Tim Seaton, Chief Operating Officer
Kimberly K. Shipman, Chief Financial Officer

Branch Offices:
LOS ANGELES: 11150 W Olympic Blvd, Ste 770, Los Angeles, CA 90064. Phone: 310-575-3185.

MIAMI: Latin America Offices, 1550 Biscayne Blvd, Miami, FL 33132. Phone: 305-894-2576. Fax: 305-894-4919. E-Mail: gustavo.tonelli@dmx.com.

NORCROSS: 3170 Reps Miller Rd, Ste 100, Norcross, GA 30071. Phone: 770-225-2500. Fax: 770-246-3941.

OAKBROOK: 620 Enterprise Dr, Oak Brook, IL 60523. Phones: 847-839-7890; 800-640-2673.

SEATTLE: 411 First Ave, Ste 501, Seattle, WA 94104. Phone: 800-345-5000.

WALTHAM: 77 Fourth Ave, 5th Fl, Waltham, MA 02451. Phone: 508-393-2591. Fax: 508-393-5137.

BRAZIL: Rua dos Bombeiros, 40, Ibirapuero, Sao Paulo 04001-100, Brazil. Phone: 55-11-3884-0150. E-Mail: atendimento@dmx.com. Web site: http://http://www.dmxmusic.com.br.

CANADA: 7260 12th St. SE, #120, Calgary, AB T2H 2S5, Canada. Phones: 403-640-8525; 800-350-0369. Fax: 888-823-0369. E-Mail: dmx.canada@dmx.com. Web site: http://www.dmx.ca.

SOUTH AFRICA: Ground Floor Sandown Mews E, 88 Stella St, Sandown, Johannesburg, South Africa. Phone: 27-11-780-3000. Fax: 27-11-780-3001. E-Mail: info@dmx.co.za. Web site: http://http://www.dmx.co.za.
Sensory branding provider with more than 35 years of industry experience. Services include, music design, new media, messaging & scent. Division of DMX Inc.

DOVE BROADCASTING INC.
3409 Rutherford Rd Ext
Taylors, SC 29687
Phone: 864-244-1616
Fax: 864-292-8481
E-mail: billyrainey16@gmail.com
Web Site: http://www.dovebroadcasting.com
Michele Loftis, Manager, Production
Billy Rainey, Manager, Sales
Produces Christian TV programming.

DOW JONES NEWSWIRES
1211 Ave of the Americas
7th Fl
New York, NY 10036
Phone: 800-223-2274
E-mail: newswires@dowjones.com
Web Site: http://www.dowjones.com
Neal Lipschutz, Senior Vice President & Managing Editor, Dow Jones Newswires
Provides real-time news services.

DREAMWORKS ANIMATION SKG
1000 Flower St
Glendale, CA 91201
Phone: 818-695-5000
Fax: 818-695-3510
Web Site: http://www.dreamworksanimation.com
Jeffrey Katzenberg, Chief Executive Officer & Director
Ann Daly, Chief Operating Officer
Lew Coleman, President & Acting Chief Financial Officer
John Batter, Co-President, Production for Feature Animation
William J. Damaschke, Co-President, Production for Feature Animation & President, Live Theatrical

Branch Offices:
REDWOOD CITY: PDI/DreamWorks, 1800 Seaport Blvd, Redwood City, CA 94063.
Produces & distributes computer-generated animation feature films.

DREAMWORKS STUDIOS SKG
100 Universal Plz
Universal City, CA 91608
Phone: 818-733-9600
E-mail: info@dreamworksstudios.com
Web Site: http://www.dreamworksstudios.com
Steven Spielberg, Principal Partner
Stacey Snider, Principal Partner, Co-Chairman & Chief Financial Officer
Jeff Small, President & Chief Executive Officer
Holly Bario, Co-President, Production
Mark Sourian, Co-President, Production
Develops, produces & distributes films, video games & TV programming.

DREW ASSOCIATES INC.
56 Gay St
PO Box 1702
Sharon, CT 06069
Phone: 860-364-5349
Fax: 860-364-5192
E-mail: info@drewassociates.net
Web Site: http://www.drewassociates.net
Robert L. Drew, President
Anne Drew, Vice President
Produces public affairs & entertainment documentaries, client films & corporate video newsletters.

DRIVER
115 W 27th St
12th Fl
New York, NY 10001
Phone: 212-675-2820
Fax: 212-675-2830
E-mail: info@driver.tv
Web Site: http://www.driver.tv
Linda RaFoss, Partner & Managing Director
Scott Weitz, Executive Producer
J.D. Williams, Executive Producer

Branch Offices:
LOS ANGELES: 842 N Fairfax Ave, Los Angeles, CA 90046.
Provides production services, including agency production, direct production services, in-house edit bays & graphic design; develops content for TV, film & new media.

DUART FILM & VIDEO
245 W 55th St
New York, NY 10019
Phones: 212-757-4580; 800-523-8278
Fax: 212-333-7647
E-mail: info@duart.com
Web Site: http://www.duart.com
Charles Darby, Chief Operating Officer
Steve Blakely, Vice President, Film Lab
Carmen Borgia, Vice President, Audio Production
Joe Monge, Vice President, Video Operations
Videotape post-production facility & film laboratory; provides video editing, tape duplication, film-to-tape & tape-to-film transfers, 16mm & 35mm processing & printing services.

MICHAEL DUNN PRODUCTIONS
2920 Orange Brace Rd
Riverwoods, IL 60015-3724
Phone: 847-940-0150
Fax: 847-940-4144
Michael Dunn, President
Produces motion pictures & videotape.

EDITBAR
240 Newbury St
Ste 304
Boston, MA 02116
Phone: 617-572-3333
Fax: 617-572-3313
E-mail: peterb@editbar.com
Web Site: http://www.editbar.com
Peter Barstis, Editor
Provides editorial services & post-production management for advertising agencies, production companies & filmmakers.

RALPH EDWARDS PRODUCTIONS
6922 Hollywood Blvd
Ste 300
Hollywood, CA 90028-6117
Phone: 323-462-2212
Fax: 323-461-1224
E-mail: info@ralphedwards.com
Web Site: http://www.ralphedwards.com
Barbara Dunn-Leonard, President
Produces & packages network & syndicated TV shows.

89 EDIT
1526 Cloverfield Blvd
Ste E
Santa Monica, CA 90404
Phone: 310-586-2600
Fax: 310-586-0980
E-mail: dan@x-rds.com
Web Site: http://www.89edit.com
Dan Lindau, Managing Partner
Gail Butler, Executive Producer
Nicole Keith, Producer
Kimberley Griswold, Sales
Doug Sherin, Sales

Branch Offices:
NEW YORK: 136 W 21st St, New York, NY 10011. Phone: 212-647-6160. Fax: 212-647-6170. Sharon Lew, Executive Producer; Juliet Conti, Producer; Janice Harryman, Mid-west Sales; Samantha Tuttlebee, Sales.

BERT ELLIOTT SOUND
1752 Harper St NW
Atlanta, GA 30318-3068
Phone: 404-351-9061
Fax: 404-351-6806
E-mail: bertesound@gmail.com
Web Site: http://www.bertelliottsound.com
Bert Elliott, President
Provides audio production; original music for film, video & multimedia productions; desktop audio & video production; 48-track facility.

ELLIS ENTERTAINMENT CORP.
7B Pleasant Blvd
Ste 960
Toronto, ON M4T 1K2
Canada
Phone: 416-924-2186
Fax: 416-444-2473
E-mail: info@ellisent.com
Web Site: http://www.ellisent.com
Stephen Ellis, President
Grace Lo, Manager, Client Service
Distributes non-fiction, wildlife & entertainment TV programming from Britain, Australia & the U.S.

ENCORE ENTERTAINMENT INC. — No longer in business.

ENCYCLOPAEDIA BRITANNICA INC.
331 N La Salle St
Chicago, IL 60610
Phones: 312-347-7159; 800-323-1229
Fax: 312-294-2104
Web Site: http://www.britannica.com
Michael Ross, Senior Vice President

Branch Offices:
AUSTRALIA: Encyclopaedia Britannica Australia Ltd., 90 Mount St, Level 1, North Sydney, NSW 2060, Australia. Phone: 61-2-9923-5600. Fax: 61-2-9929-3753. E-Mail: sales@britannica.com.au. Web site: http://http://www.britannica.com.au.

FRANCE: Encyclopaedia Britannica France Ltd., 9 Rue Antoine Chantin, Cedex 14, Paris 75685, France. Phone: 33-1-45-72-72-72. Fax: 31-1-45-72-03-43. Web site: http://www.britannica.fr.

INDIA: Encyclopaedia Britannica India Pvt. Ltd., 140 Zamrudpur Shopping Complex, N-Block Rd, Greater Kailash-1, New Delhi 110048, India. Phone: 91-11-4653-6450. Fax: 91-11-2924-5116. E-Mail: marketing@ebindia.com. Web site: http://http://www.britannicaindia.com.

ISRAEL: Britannica.com Israel Ltd., 16 Tozeret Ha'aretz St., Tel Aviv 67891, Israel. Phone: 972-3-607-0400. Fax: 972-3-607-0401. Web site: http://www.britannica.co.il.

JAPAN: Britannica Japan Co. Ltd., Da Vinci 2F, 8-3-16 Nishi-Gotanda, Shinagawa, Tokyo 141-0031, Japan. Phone: 81-3-5436-1388. Fax: 81-3-5436-1380. E-Mail: info@britannica.co.jp.

SOUTH KOREA: Korea Britannica Corp., Jeil-sangho B/D 7th Fl, 117 Jangchung-dong 1-ga, Jung-gu, Seoul 100-391, South Korea. Phone: 82-1588-1768. Fax: 82-2-2278-9983. E-Mail: corporate@britannica.co.kr.

TAIWAN: Sec 1, Chungching Rd South, Room 402, #10, Taipei City 100, Taiwan. Phone: 886-2-2311-2592. Fax: 886-2-2311-2595.

UNITED KINGDOM: Encyclopaedia Britannica (UK) Ltd., Mill St, Unity Wharf, 2nd Fl, London SE1 2BH, United Kingom. Phone: 44-20-7500-7800. Fax: 44-20-7500-7878. E-Mail: enquiries@britannica.co.uk. Web site: http://http://www.britannica.co.uk.
Produces & distributes film & video materials for education, business & industry.

ENDEMOL USA
9255 Sunset Blvd
Ste 1100
Los Angeles, CA 90069
Phone: 310-860-9914
Web Site: http://www.endemolusa.tv
David Goldberg, Chairman
Ira Chartoff, Chief Financial Officer
Joerg Bachmeier, Senior Vice President, Digital Media & Business Development
Caroline Baumgard, Senior Vice President, Development
Rob Smith, Senior Vice President, Programming
Produces TV & other audiovisual entertainment; scripted, non-scripted & digital media; offices worldwide. Division of Endemol Group.

ENOKI FILMS USA INC.
16430 Ventura Blvd
Ste 308
Encino, CA 91436
Phone: 818-907-6503
Fax: 818-907-6506
E-mail: info@enokifilmsusa.com
Web Site: http://www.enokifilmsusa.com
Zen Enoki, Chairman
Yoshi Enoki, President
Produces & distributes children's animated series & feature films.

ENVOY PRODUCTIONS
660 Mason Ridge Ctr Dr
St Louis, MO 63141
Phones: 314-317-4100; 888-229-7743
Fax: 314-317-4299
Web Site: http://www.envoyproductions.com
Sandi Clement, Vice President, Sales & Programming
Kurt Sprenger, International Distributor, Life Media International
Produces, distributes & syndicates religious TV series & specials; produces & distributes foreign language TV series & specials; videocassettes; radio; radio syndicated talk show for women; Spanish & French programming.

EPISCOPAL CHURCH CENTER DIGITAL COMMUNICATIONS
815 Second Ave
New York, NY 10017
Phones: 212-922-5385; 800-334-7626
E-mail: arudig@episcopalchurch.org
Web Site: http://www.episcopalchurch.org/communication.htm
Michael F. Collins, Manager, Multimedia Production
Wade Hampton, Art Director & Lead Designer
Barry Merer, Web Producer

THE EPISCOPAL MEDIA CENTER —
See listing for Alliance for Christian Media.

EUE/SCREEN GEMS STUDIOS
222 E 44th St
New York, NY 10017
Phone: 212-450-1600
E-mail: nystudios@euescreengems.com
Web Site: http://www.screengemsstudios.com
Chris Cooney, President & Chief Operating Officer
Ed Branaccio, Chief Technical Officer
Merideth Shapiro, Senior Facility Manager
Paul Gilly, Studio Manager

Branch Offices:
WILMINGTON: 1223 23rd St N, Wilmington, NC 28405. Phone: 910-343-3500. E-Mail: info@screengemsstudios.com. Bill Vasser, Executive Vice President.
Provides video & film production; six sound stages in New York with lighting & grip equipment, two control rooms, prop room, camera room, casting stage, CMX edit room, 35mm & 16mm projection rooms & conference rooms.

EVENING NEWS BROADCASTING CO.
3901 Tunlaw NW
Washington, DC 20007
Phone: 202-333-3007
Independent Washington news bureau, TV, radio & print media production house; provides customized reports, documentaries & coverage for commercial, educational & corporate outlets; offers photojournalism, TV & radio services & studios; tape & film library & satellite uplinks.

FAITH FOR TODAY
PO Box 1000
Thousand Oaks, CA 91359
Phones: 805-955-7777; 888-940-0062
Fax: 805-522-2114
E-mail: info@faithfortoday.tv
Web Site: http://www.faithfortoday.tv
Michael L. Tucker, Executive Producer, Director & Host
Produces Christian TV programming.

FAMILYNET TELEVISION
3836 DeKalb Technology Pkwy
Bldg 3
Atlanta, GA 30340
Phone: 770-225-1400
Fax: 770-936-2755
Web Site: http://www.familynet.com
Provides a blend of family-friendly entertainment to today's family; offered on broadcast stations, cable systems & 4DTV across the U.S.

FAMILY THEATER PRODUCTIONS
7201 Sunset Blvd
Hollywood, CA 90046
Phones: 323-874-6633; 800-874-0999
Fax: 323-874-1168
E-mail: info@familytheater.org
Web Site: http://www.familytheater.org
Father Wilfred J. Raymond, National Director
Dan E. Pitre, Director, Public Relations
Tony Sands, Administrator
David Guffey, Holy Cross Priest
Eleazar Bazini, Sound Engineer & Composer
Produces & distributes faith & values TV programming & films; produces public TV documentaries. Division of Holy Cross Family Ministries.

FARKAS FILMS INC.
385 Third Ave
New York, NY 10016
Phone: 212-679-8212
Fax: 212-889-8354
Rents studio facilities; distributes motion picture & video.

FARMER'S ALMANAC TV — No longer in business.

FARM JOURNAL MEDIA
1500 Market St
Ctr Sq W
Philadelphia, PA 19102
Phone: 215-557-8900
Fax: 215-568-4436
Web Site: http://www.farmjournalmedia.com
Jeff Pence, President
Andy Weber, Chief Executive Officer
Thomas C. Breslin, Chief Financial Officer & Executive Vice President
Steve Custer, Senior Vice President & Publisher
Produces, syndicates & distributes half-hour news, weather, markets & features programs focused on the agriculture industry; topics include production, pricing, food safety, new technologies & environmental matters.

FAST CUTS
1845 Woodall Rodgers Frwy
Ste 200
Dallas, TX 75201
Phone: 214-526-3278
Fax: 214-526-3290
Web Site: http://www.fastcuts.tv
Julie Koellner, Executive Producer
Mimi Hendrix, Senior Producer
Rick Zessar, Senior Producer
P.K. Jones, Audio Producer
Provides post-production services.

TONI FICALORA PRODUCTIONS — No longer in business.

THE FIELD
351 W 22nd St
Ste 2
New York, NY 10011
Phone: 212-253-2888
E-mail: michaelp@thefieldtv.com
Web Site: http://www.thefieldtv.com
Michael Porte, Founder
Mike Siedlecki, Editor
Barrett Heathcote, Editor
Fabrizio Rossetti, Editor
Provides editorial, production & design services for commercials, broadcast, broadband, cinema & emerging media.

FILMACK STUDIOS
223 W Erie St
#4NW
Chicago, IL 60654
Phones: 312-427-3395; 800-345-6225
Fax: 312-427-4866
E-mail: inquiries@filmack.com
Web Site: http://www.filmack.com
Robert Mack, President
Provides specialized 35mm film & video production & duplication services.

FILMCORE
1010 N Highland Ave
Hollywood, CA 90038
Phone: 323-769-8400
E-mail: distribution@filmcore.com
Web Site: http://www.filmcore.net
Steve McCoy, President

Branch Offices:
NEW YORK: 1619 Broadway, Ste 612, New York, NY 10019. Phone: 212-459-0290.

SAN FRANCISCO: 500 Sansome St, 7th Fl, San Francisco, CA 94111. Phone: 415-397-8400. E-Mail: filmcoresf@filmcore.com.
Provides video & non-linear editing, video duplication, trafficking & vault services.

FILMS AFIELD INC. — No longer in business.

FILMS FOR EDUCATORS/FILMS FOR TELEVISION
420 E 55th St
Ste 6U
New York, NY 10022
Phone: 212-486-6577
Fax: 212-980-9826
Rochelle Bebell, President
Distributes film & video programming worldwide; co-production, programming, documentaries & educational features.

FILMS OF INDIA — See listing for 1-World LLC.

FINAL CUT LTD.
Fenton House
55-57 Great Marlborough St
London W1F 7JX
United Kingdom
Phone: 44-20-7556-6300
Fax: 44-20-7287-2824
E-mail: michelle_c@finalcut-uk.com
Web Site: http://www.finalcut-edit.com

Branch Offices:
NEW YORK: 118 W 22nd St, 7th Fl, New York, NY 10011. Phone: 212-375-9800. Fax: 212-375-0256. E-Mail: stephanie_a@finalcut-edit.com.

SANTA MONICA: 1634 Euclid St, Santa Monica, CA 90404-3724. Phone: 310-566-6600. Fax: 310-566-6601. E-Mail: saima_a@finalcut-edit.com.

FINE ART PRODUCTIONS, RICHIE SURACI PICTURES MULTIMEDIA, INTERACTIVE
67 Maple St
Newburgh, NY 12550-4034
Phones: 845-561-5866; 914-527-9740
Fax: 845-561-5866
Web Site: http://users.bsdwebsolutions.com/~rs7fap/OPPS5.html
Richie Suraci, Producer & Director
Produces & distributes film, video, DVD, CD & multimedia programs.

FIRESTONE COMMUNICATIONS INC.
6125 Airport Frwy
Ft Worth, TX 76117
Phone: 817-546-0670

MediaPrints™
Map a Winning Business Strategy
Digital Cable and TV Coverage Maps.
Visit www.warren-news.com/mediaprints.htm

Web Site: http://www.sorpresatv.com
Leonard L. Firestone, Chairman & Chief Executive Officer
Michael G. Fletcher, President
Christopher K. Firestone, Executive Vice President, Operations
J. Romer, Vice President
Francisco Cuevas, Creative Director
Operates SORPRESA, a U.S.-based 24-hr. network dedicated to America's Hispanic children; offers production & creative services.

FIREWORKS INTERNATIONAL
19 Heddon St
London W1B 4BG
United Kingdom
Phone: 44-20-7851-6500
Fax: 44-20-4851-6504
E-mail: info@contentfilm.com
Web Site: http://www.contentfilm.com
Jonathan Ford, Executive Vice President, Digital Acquisitions & Distribution
Bob Kennedy, Executive Vice President, Non-Fiction Programming

Branch Offices:
SANTA MONICA: 225 Arizona Ave, Ste 250, Santa Monica, CA 90401. Phone: 310-576-1059. Fax: 310-576-1859. Saralo MacGregor, Executive Vice President, Worldwide Distribution; Melissa Wohl, Senior Vice President, Worldwide Distribution; Paul Lewis, Vice President, Development; Diana Zakis, Vice President, Sales, Latin America & Asia.

CANADA: 80 Richmond St W, Toronto, ON M5H 24A, Canada. Phone: 416-360-6103. Fax: 416-360-6065. Cameron Wallis, Director, Technical Operations.
International TV & distribution division of Content Film Co.

FIRST LIGHT VIDEO PUBLISHING
2321 Abbot Kinney Blvd
Ste 101
Venice, CA 90291
Phones: 310-577-8581; 800-262-8862
Fax: 310-574-0886
E-mail: sale@firstlightvideo.com
Web Site: http://www.firstlightvideo.com
Michael Bennett, President & Chief Executive Officer
Leslie Collins, Vice President, Sales & Marketing
Largest selection in the nation of high-quality instructional DVD programming in the media arts. Developed specifically for the secondary and higher education markets, the First Light library contains over 400 craft-specific titles, covering film and video production, radio and television broadcasting, editing, media studies, writing, costuming, stagecraft for the theatre & many more topics for media arts courses.

FISCHER EDIT
801 Nicollet Mall
Ste 300W
Minneapolis, MN 55402
Phone: 612-332-4914
Fax: 612-332-4910
E-mail: info@fischeredit.com
Web Site: http://www.fischeredit.com
Tony Fischer, President
Erica Leanna, Producer
Kathy Yerich, Producer
J. Matt Keil, Business Development
Charlotte Peterson, Business Development
Provides creative offline editing services; specializes in TV commercials.

FLUID
532 Broadway
5th Fl
New York, NY 10012
Phone: 212-431-4342
Fax: 212-431-6525
E-mail: info@fluidny.com
Web Site: http://www.fluidny.com
Laura Relovsky, Executive Producer
Provides post-production services, including editorial, original music & sound design, visual effects and design & finishing for film, broadcast & web.

FOLLOW PRODUCTIONS
589 Eighth Ave
12th Fl
New York, NY 10011
Phone: 212-691-1810
Fax: 212-691-1855
E-mail: info@followproductions.com
Web Site: http://www.followproductions.com
Gordon Elliott, Executive Producer
Mark Schneider, Managing Director
Produces TV series for the Food Network.

FOUNDATION POST
200 E Ohio St
2nd Fl
Chicago, IL 60611
Phone: 312-951-8734
Fax: 312-951-8801
Web Site: http://www.foundationpost.com
Tracey Heropkie, Senior Producer
Carrie Lewis, Senior Producer

Branch Offices:
SANTA MONICA: 1669 19th St, Santa Monica, CA 90404. Phone: 424-238-0381.

FOX STUDIOS AUSTRALIA — See listing for Granada Media.

FOX TELEVISION STUDIOS
PO Box 900
Beverly Hills, CA 90213-0900
Phone: 310-295-3415
E-mail: leslie.oren@fox.com
Web Site: http://www.newscorp.com
David Madden, President
Leslie Oren, Senior Vice President, Corporate Communications
Produces TV programming for the U.S. & global markets. Division of News Corp.

SANDY FRANK ENTERTAINMENT INC.
910 Fifth Ave
New York, NY 10021
Phone: 212-772-1889
Fax: 212-772-2297
E-mail: filmsfe@aol.com
Web Site: http://www.sandyfrankentertainment.com
Sandy Frank, Chairman
Rosalie Perrone, Vice President, Business Affairs & Comptroller
Sandy Spidell, Vice President, Operations & Publicity
Nora Maria Diaz, Director, Sales
Susan Piscitello, Director, Creative Affairs
Steve Radosh, Creative Consulting Producer
Barbara Kalicinska, European Sales Representative
Independently produces & distributes syndicated series & format programming worldwide.

FREMANTLE CORP.
23 Lesmill Rd
Ste 201
Toronto, ON M3B 3P6
Phone: 416-443-9204
Fax: 416-443-8685
Web Site: http://www.fremantlecorp.com
Randy Zalken, President
Lisa Dunn, Vice President, Sales & Acquisitions
Marshall Kesten, Director & Officer
Diane Trip, Director, International Sales
Arlene Hay, Manager, Client Services & Contracts
Ann Latham, Manager, Accounting
Sharon Beverley, Administration Sales
Jessie Pirog, Administrative & Marketing Assistant

Branch Offices:
LOS ANGELES: 1575 Westwood Blvd, Ste 301, Los Angeles, CA 90024. Phone: 310-445-0700. Fax: 310-445-0703.

NEW YORK: 1501 Broadway, Ste 1902, New York, NY 10036. Phone: 212-840-6269. Fax: 212-398-9660.
Distributes TV movies, documentaries, tape series & international co-production. Division of Kaleidoscope Entertainment Inc.

FREMANTLE INTERNATIONAL DISTRIBUTION — See listing for FremantleMedia Ltd.

FREMANTLEMEDIA INTERACTIVE — See listing for FremantleMedia Ltd.

FREMANTLEMEDIA LICENSING GROUP — See listing for FremantleMedia Ltd.

FREMANTLEMEDIA LTD.
One Stephen St
London W1T 1AL
United Kingdom
Phone: 44-0-20-7691-6000
Fax: 44-0-20-7691-6100
E-mail: contactus@fremantlemedia.com
Web Site: http://www.fremantlemedia.com
Tony Cohen, Chief Executive Officer
Gary Carter, Chief Operating Officer
Cecile Frot-Coutaz, Chief Executive Officer, FremantleMedia North America
Nicky Gray, Director, Human Resources
Ian Ousey, Director, Financial

Branch Offices:
BURBANK: FremantleMedia North America, 4000 W Alameda Ave, 3rd Fl, Burbank, CA 91505. Phone: 818-748-1100. Fax: 818-563-6410.

MIAMI: Fremantle Productions Latin America, Waterford Bldg, 5200 Blue Lagoon Dr, Ste 200, Miami, FL 33126. Phone: 305-267-0821.

NEW YORK: Fremantle Media North America, 1540 Broadway, 10th Fl, New York, NY 10036. Phone: 212-541-2800. Fax: 212-541-2810.

BRAZIL: FremantleMedia Brazil, Av Professor Manuel Jose Chavez 300, Alto Pinheiros, Sao Paulo 05463-070, Brazil. Phone: 55-11-3846-9100.

MEXICO: FremantleMedia Mexico, Camino al Ajusco #124, Three Col Jardines en la Montana, Tlapan CP 14210, Mexico. Phone: 52-5-55-631-2737.
Produces, licenses & distributes prime time, drama, serial drama & factual entertainment programming to broadcasters worldwide; also develops & produces media entertainment for mobile, broadband, game consoles & Internet protocol TV; company divisions include Fremantle International Distribution, FremantleMedia Interactive & FremantleMedia Licensing Group. Offices worldwide.

CHUCK FRIES PRODUCTIONS
1880 Century Park E
Ste 315
Los Angeles, CA 90067
Phone: 310-203-9520
Fax: 310-203-9519
E-mail: chuckfries@aol.com
Charles W. Fries, Chairman & President
Produces & distributes theatrical, home video, TV & pay TV programming worldwide.

FUMC TELEVISION MINISTRIES
First United Methodist Church
PO Box 1567, Head of Texas St
Shreveport, LA 71165-1567
Phone: 318-424-7771
Fax: 318-429-6888
E-mail: fumc@fumcshreveport.org
Web Site: http://www.fumcshreveport.org
Dr. Pat Day, Senior Pastor
Donna Bell, Administrator, Finance
Jay Sawyer, Administrator, Business
John Mark Wilcox, TV Coordinator
Sunday morning 11am Traditional Worship Service at FUMC airs live on KTBS Channel 3 (the local ABC affiliate) and/or KTBS News Channel 3.3. KTBS Channel 3.3 can be seen on Comcast channel 208 in Shreveport and Suddenlink channel 722 in Bossier City. Worship services at First United Methodist Church in Shreveport, LA are available for free download online at fumcshreveport.org, via iTunes, and on your Android and iPhone. Copies of sermons are also available for purchase on CD or DVD, by contacting the church office.

FUTURE IS NOW (FIN)
119 W 23rd St
Ste 500
New York, NY 10011
Phone: 212-741-9630
Fax: 212-741-9693
E-mail: info@futurenyc.com
Web Site: http://www.futurenyc.com
Gala Verdugo, Founder
Provides professional AVID editing; specializes in commercials, promos, music videos, documentaries & short films.

FUTURE PRODUCTIONS INC. — No longer in business.

FUTURE SOFTWARE LTD.
Grove Business Park
Unit 20
Maidenhead, Berks SL 3LW
United Kingdom
Phone: 44-0-1628-829-811

Fax: 44-0-1628-826-110
E-mail: mail@future-software.co.uk
Web Site: http://www.future-software.co.uk
Develops software for the encoding, transmission & playback of digital media content.

GABBA MEDIA LLC
119 W 23rd St
Ste 500
New York, NY 10011
Phone: 212-741-9630
Fax: 212-741-9693
E-mail: info@gabbamedia.com
Web Site: http://www.gabbamedia.com
Gardiner Welch, Editor
Provides post-production services.

GARI MEDIA GROUP
1532 Falling Star Ave
Westlake Village, CA 91362
Phones: 818-707-4160; 888-424-0007
Fax: 818-707-4161
E-mail: frankg@garimediagroup.com
Web Site: http://www.garimediagroup.com
Frank Gari, President & Chief Executive Officer
Gordon Smith, Chief Operations Officer & Corporate Vice President
Chris Gari, Vice President, Music & Creative Director
Kim Gari, Vice President, Licensing
Jon Herron, Vice President, New Media & Chief Technical Officer
Larry McDaniel, Chief Marketing Officer
Antonio Corcella, Director, Customer Relations
Christine Russell, Director, Sales

Branch Offices:
ATLANTA: 3575 Piedmont Rd, Atlanta, GA 30305. Phone: 404-924-4274. Fax: 404-467-1996.
Full-service creative agency; services includes production for sweep promotion, custom & syndicated music & graphic packages, media buying & strategic marketing.

GATEWAY FILMS/VISION VIDEO
PO Box 540
2030 Wentz Church Rd
Worcester, PA 19490
Phones: 610-584-3500; 800-523-0226
Fax: 610-584-4610
E-mail: info@visionvideo.com
Web Site: http://www.visionvideo.com
A. Kenneth Curtis, President
Produces & distributes Christian videos for family, church or school.

GAVEL TO GAVEL — No longer in business.

GERREN ENTERTAINMENT PRODUCTIONS
3640 W 63rd St
Ste 1A
Los Angeles, CA 90043
Phone: 323-292-1600
E-mail: gerrenproductions@sbcglobal.net
Produces & distributes films & cartoons to LPTV stations; rents audio & video equipment.

GLOBECAST AMERICA
Two World Financial Ctr
225 Liberty St, Ste 4301
New York, NY 10281
Phone: 212-373-5140
Fax: 212-373-5454
Web Site: http://www.globecast.com
Lisa Coelho, Acting Chief Executive Officer
Jeff Casey, Vice President, Media Management

Branch Offices:
CULVER CITY: GlobeCast America, 10525 W Washington Blvd, Culver City, CA 90232. Phone: 310-845-3900. Fax: 310-845-3904.

SUNRISE: 13801 NW 14th St, Sunrise, FL 33323. Phone: 954-514-5209. Fax: 954-514-5223.
Provides content management & worldwide transmission services for professional broadcast delivery; operates a secure global satellite & fiber network to manage and transport 10 million hours of video & other rich media each year, providing ingest, aggregation, transmission & repurposing of content for delivery to direct-to-home satellite platforms; cable, IPTV, mobile & broadband headends. Offices worldwide. Subsidiary of France Telecom.

GLOBO INTERNATIONAL NY LTD.
32 Ave of the Americas
17th Fl
New York, NY 10013
Phone: 917-551-3500
Amauri Soares, Chief Executive Officer
Produces & distributes series & specials.

GOLDEN SQUARE POST PRODUCTION
11 Golden Sq
London W1F 9JB
United Kingdom
Phone: 44-0-20-7300-3555
Fax: 44-0-20-7494-3288
E-mail: info@goldensq.com
Web Site: http://www.goldensq.com
Phil Gillies, Managing Director
Alan Young, Director, Operations
Ewan MacLeod, Executive Producer
Provides post-production services.

SAMUEL GOLDWYN TELEVISION CO. — See listing for MGM Television Entertainment Inc.

GOOD LIFE BROADCASTING INC.
31 Skyline Dr
Lake Mary, FL 32746
Phone: 407-215-6745
Fax: 407-215-6789
E-mail: info@tv45.org
Web Site: http://www.tv45.org
Ken Mikesell, Co-host
Barbara Beck, Co-host
Ed Griffis, Director, Sponsorship
Provides religious, educational & family-oriented programming.

GO ROBOT
56 W 22nd St
11th Fl
New York, NY 10010
Phone: 212-414-4800
Fax: 212-414-0002
E-mail: laura@gorobot.com
Web Site: http://www.gorobot.com
Alisa Sheinberg, Managing Partner
Laura Molinaro, Executive Producer
Provides video post-production services.

GOSPEL COMMUNICATIONS
PO Box 455
Muskegon, MI 49443
Phones: 231-773-3361; 800-253-0413
Fax: 231-777-1847
Web Site: http://www.gospelcommunications.org
Doug DeVos, Co-Chairman
Billy Zeoli, Co-Chairman
J. R. Whitby, President & Chief Executive Officer
Steve Ramsey, Director, North America Ministries
David Zeoli, Director, International Ministries
Kent Vanderwood, Advancement Director
Distributes religious films & videos.

GOULD ENTERTAINMENT CORP. — No longer in business.

GRACE & WILD INC.
23689 Industrial Park Dr
Farmington Hills, MI 48335
Phone: 248-471-6010
Fax: 248-471-2312
E-mail: info-gracewild@gracewild.com
Web Site: http://www.gracewild.com
Steven Wild, President
Allan Rothfeder, Executive Vice President & Chief Financial Officer
Jim Shanley, Executive Director, Business Development
Provides production & post-production services.

GRANADA MEDIA
The London Television Ctr
Upper Ground
London SE1 9LT
United Kingdom
Phone: 44-0-20-7620-1620
Web Site: http://www.granadamedia.com

Branch Offices:
LOS ANGELES: ITV Studios Inc., 15303 Ventura Blvd, Bldg C, Ste 800, Sherman Oaks, CA 91403. Phone: 818-455-4600. Web site: http://http://www.itv-america.com. Paul Buccieri, Chief Executive Officer & President; Sam Zoda, Chief Operating Officer; Colet Abedi, Vice President, Development; Brian Zagorski, Vice President, Current & Programming.

NEW YORK: ITV Studios Inc., 609 Greenwich St, 9th Fl, New York, NY 10014. Phone: 212-905-1700. Web site: http://http://www.itv-america.com. Patrice Andrews, Executive Vice President, Development, Production & Operations.

AUSTRALIA: Granada Australia, 38 Driver Ave, FSA #34, Level 1, Bldg 61, Moore Park, NSW 1363, Australia. Phone: 61-02-9383-4360. Web site: http://http://www.granadaproductions.com.au.

GERMANY: Granada Produktion fur Film & Fernsehen GmbH, Am Coloneum 6, Koln 50829, Germany. Phone: 49-0-221-492-048120. Web site: http://www.granadamedia.de.
Produces & distributes TV programming.

SHERRY GRANT ENTERPRISES INC.
18120 Sweet Elm Dr
Encino, CA 91316-4452
Phone: 818-705-2535
Sherry Grant, President
Produces & distributes short-form TV programs & other special entertainment projects.

GREAT PLAINS NATIONAL
1407 Fleet St
Baltimore, MD 21231
Phone: 800-228-4630
Fax: 800-306-2330
E-mail: askgpn@smarterville.com
Web Site: http://www.shopgpn.com
Distributes & produces educational programming via videocassette or a variety of digital formats. Subsidiary of Smarterville Productions LLC.

THE ART GREENFIELD CO. — No longer in business.

SHERMAN GRINBERG FILM LIBRARIES INC. — No longer in business.

GRIOT EDITORIAL
23475 Northwestern Hwy
Southfield, MI 48075
Phones: 248-355-3330; 877-853-4143
E-mail: info-griot@griotedit.com
Web Site: http://www.gracewild.com/griot
Craig Duncan, General Manager
Provides post-production services.

GUILLOTINE
14 Charles St
Redfern, NSW 2015
Australia
Phone: 61-2-9310-3010
Fax: 61-2-9310-3035
E-mail: lara@guillotinepost.tv
Web Site: http://www.guillotinepost.tv
Provides post-production services.

ALFRED HABER DISTRIBUTION INC.
111 Grand Ave
Ste 203
Palisades Park, NJ 07650
Phone: 201-224-8000
Fax: 201-947-4500
E-mail: info@haberinc.com
Web Site: http://www.alfredhaber.com
Alfred Haber, President
George Scanlon, Chief Financial Officer
Distributes U.S. network (CBS, ABC, NBC & Fox) reality, music & event specials; distributes reality & documentary series, miniseries & made-for-TV motion pictures for the U.S. & international TV marketplace.

LARRY HARMON PICTURES CORP. — No longer in business.

HARMONY GOLD USA INC.
7655 Sunset Blvd
Los Angeles, CA 90046-2700
Phones: 323-851-4900; 323-436-7204
Fax: 323-851-5599
E-mail: sales@harmonygold.com
Web Site: http://www.harmonygold.com
Kathryn Davolio, Reservations Coordinator

Branch Offices:
BURBANK: Dolly Laboratories Inc., 3601 W Alameda Ave, Burbank, CA 91505. Phone: 818-823-2800. Web site: http://http://www.dolby.com.

Produces & distributes animated programs, series, miniseries & documentaries, home video & merchandising; also provides screening room & theatre rentals.

HARPO PRODUCTIONS INC.
110 N Carpenter St
Chicago, IL 60607
Phone: 312-633-1000
Fax: 312-633-1979
Web Site: http://www.oprah.com
Tim Bennett, President
Eric Logan, Executive Vice President
Produces TV talk-shows and feature & made-for-TV films.

HARTLEY FILM FOUNDATION INC.
49 Richmondville Ave
Ste 204
Westport, CT 06880
Phones: 203-226-9500; 800-937-1819
Fax: 203-227-6938
E-mail: info@hartleyfoundation.org
Web Site: http://www.hartleyfoundation.org
Sarah Masters, Managing Director
Laura Healy, Office Manager
Non-profit organization; produces, cultivates, supports & distributes documentaries & audio mediations on world religions, spirituality, ethics & well-being.

HBO ENTERPRISES
1100 Ave of the Americas
New York, NY 10036
Phone: 212-512-1329
Web Site: http://www.hbotvsales.com
Quentin Schaffer, Executive Vice President, Corporate Communications
Jeff Cusson, Senior Vice President
Distributes entertainment TV programming worldwide.

HBO STUDIO PRODUCTIONS
120A E 23rd St
New York, NY 10010
Phone: 212-512-7800
Fax: 212-512-7788
Web Site: http://www.hbostudio.com
Provides video production & post-production services.

HDSTUDIOS
23689 Industrial Park Dr
Farmington Hills, MI 48335
Phone: 248-471-6010
Fax: 248-473-8330
E-mail: info-hd@gw-hdstudios.com
Web Site: http://www.gracewild.com.hdstudios
Kevin Neff, Managing Director & Senior Vice President
Virginia Hart, Vice President, Sales & Production Support Services
Provides DVD authoring & duplication, special effects, audio post, HD-shooting-editing-telecine; sound stage.

HEARST ENTERTAINMENT INC.
300 W 57th St
15th Fl
New York, NY 10019-5238
Phone: 212-969-7553
Fax: 646-280-1553
E-mail: svalenza@hearst.com
Web Site: http://www.hearstent.com
Stacey Valenza, Senior Vice President, Sales & Marketing
Suzanne Grethen, Vice President, Promotion & Marketing, Hearst Television
Produces & distributes made-for-TV movies, first-run entertainment, reality/documentary programming & animated series for the global marketplace.

HEARST TELEVISION INC. — See Hearst Entertainment Inc.

HENNINGER MEDIA SERVICES
2601-A Wilson Blvd
Arlington, VA 22201
Phones: 703-243-3444; 888-243-3444
Fax: 703-243-5697
E-mail: hmsinfo@henninger.com
Web Site: http://www.henninger.com
Robert L. Henninger, President & Chief Executive Officer
Eric Hansen, Executive Vice President & Chief Operating Officer
Sam Crawford, Director, Engineering
Sue O'Hara, Manager, Production
Full-service tele-production facility; provides creative design services; production & multimedia.

HIGH NOON ENTERTAINMENT
12233 W Olympic Blvd
Ste 370
Los Angeles, CA 90064
Phone: 310-820-7500
Web Site: http://www.highnoonentertainment.com
Jim Berger, Chief Executive Officer
Duke Hartman, Chief Operating Officer
Sonny Hutchinson, Chief Creative Officer
Pamela Healey, Senior Vice President, Development
Dana Eller Kopper, Vice President, Production
John Hardy, Vice President, Finance
Rachel Dax, Executive in Charge of Production

Branch Offices:
CENTENNIAL: 4100 E Dry Creek Rd, Centennial, CO 80122. Phone: 303-712-3280.

HOBOKEN: 79 Hudson St, Ste 201, Hoboken, NJ 07030. Phone: 201-850-1441.
Independent production company; produces programming for VH1, TLC, Food Network, HGTV, DIY & History.

HOFFMAN COMMUNICATIONS INC.
2900 Washington Ave N
Minneapolis, MN 55411
Phone: 612-436-3600
Fax: 612-436-3619
Web Site: http://www.hoffmancommunications.com
Mark Hoffman, President
John Sands, Chief Financial Officer
Kathryn Johnson, Director, Client Development
Larry King, Director, Show Operations & Technical
Gary Oseid, Director, IT
Karl Petersen, Director, Production
Jeff Pauley, Business Development
Kelly Verner, Business Administrator
Production, creative & staging company delivering communication solutions for events, training & multimedia production.

HOLLYWOOD NEWSREEL SYNDICATE INC. — No longer in business.

HOLLYWOOD PICTURES
500 S Buena Vista St
Burbank, CA 91521
Phone: 818-560-1000
Produces & distributes motion picture films.

HOLLYWOOD VAULTS INC.
742 Seward St
Hollywood, CA 90038
Phones: 323-461-6464; 800-569-5336
Fax: 323-461-6479
E-mail: vault@hollywoodvaults.com
Web Site: http://www.hollywoodvaults.com
David Wexler, Owner & Founder
Julie Wexler, Vice President
Raymond Barber, Manager, Operations
John Scarff, Office Manager
Provides preservation-quality storage of film, tape & digital media; temperature & humidity controlled, high-security, fire-proof storage with 24-hour access to private, individual vaults.

HOMESTEAD EDITORIAL INC.
48 W 25th St
9th Fl
New York, NY 10010
Phone: 212-255-4440
Fax: 212-255-4494
E-mail: homestead@homesteadedit.com
Web Site: http://www.homesteadedit.com
Lance Doty, Executive Producer
Provides post-production services.

HYENA EDITORIAL INC.
725 Arizona Ave
Ste 100
Santa Monica, CA 90401
Phone: 310-394-1048
Fax: 310-395-5868
E-mail: keith@hyenaedit.com
Web Site: http://www.hyenaedit.com
Keith Salmon, Founder & Editor
Kim Sprouse, Producer
Provides editorial & post-production services.

I-CUBED HYPERMEDIA
11 W Illinois
4th Fl
Chicago, IL 60610
Phone: 312-464-0911
Fax: 312-464-0511
E-mail: info@i-cubedhypermedia.com
Web Site: http://www.i-cubedhypermedia.com
Provides production & post-production services.

IMG WORLD
2049 Century Park E
Ste 2460
Los Angeles, CA 90067
Phone: 424-653-1900
Fax: 424-653-1676
Web Site: http://www.imgworld.com
Theodore J. Forstmann, Chairman & Chief Executive Officer
Ian Todd, President, IMG International

Branch Offices:
NEW YORK: 304 Park Ave S, New York, NY 10010. Phone: 212-489-8300. Fax: 212-246-1596.

SINGAPORE: One Scotts Rd #21-01/03, Shaw Ctr 228208, Singapore. Phone: 65-6505-9300. Fax: 65-6738-3617.

SPAIN: IMG (Overseas) Inc., Via Augusta 200, 4th Fl, Barcelona E-08021, Spain. Phone: 34-93-200-34-55. Fax: 34-93-200-59-24.

UNITED KINGDOM: McCormack House, Hogarth Business Park, Burlington Ln, Chiswick, London W4 2TH, United Kingdom. Phone: 44-208-233-5300. Fax: 44-208-233-5301.
Produces & distributes sports programming

IMPACT PRODUCTIONS
3939 S Harvard Ave
Ste 100
Tulsa, OK 74135
Phone: 918-877-2000
Fax: 918-877-0222
E-mail: mail@impactprod.org
Web Site: http://www.impactprod.org
Tom Newman, Founder & President
Shane Harwell, Marketing Director
Evan Derrick, Chief Editor
Eric Newman, Lead Writer & Director
Cheryl Barnard, Business Development & Post-Production Producer
Jason Stafford, Line Producer & Assistant Director
Produces documentary dramas, TV programming, 3D animation & feature films.

IMPERIA ENTERTAINMENT INC.
190 N Canon Dr
Beverly Hills, CA 90210
Phone: 310-275-0089
Fax: 805-456-0122
E-mail: info@imperiaentertainment.com
Web Site: http://www.imperiaentertainment.com
Kenneth Eade, Chairman
Don Dunn, Film Director
Produces & distributes full-length feature films.

[IN] EXTENSO
2120 Sherbroke E
Office 1005
Montreal, PQ H2K 1C3
Canada
Phone: 514-524-0703
Fax: 514-524-4110
E-mail: info@posttinextenso.com
Web Site: http://www.posttinextenso.com
Stephanie Lestage, President
Angelle Beausoleil, Vice President, Finance
Maude Gelinas, Director, Sales
Provides post-production services.

IN FOCUS COMMUNICATIONS — No longer in business.

INTERACTIVE CONFERENCING NETWORK INC. — No longer in business.

INTERAMA INC. — No longer in business.

INTERCONTINENTAL TELEVIDEO INC. — No longer in business.

INTERNATIONAL CONTACT INC.
351 15th St
Oakland, CA 94612
Phone: 510-836-1180
Fax: 510-835-1314

E-mail: info@intlcontact.com
Web Site: http://www.intlcontact.com
Carla Itzkowich, President
Provides translation, audio, web page localization, video & multimedia production, desktop publishing, research & consultation in all languages.

INTERNATIONAL MEDIA ASSOCIATES — No longer in business.

INTERNATIONAL PROGRAM CONSULTANTS INC.
52 E End Ave
Ste 24
New York, NY 10028
Phone: 212-734-9096
Russell Kagan, President
Produces & distributes TV programming.

INTERNATIONAL TELE-FILM
41 Horner Ave
Unit 3
Etobicoke, ON M8Z 4X4
Canada
Phones: 416-252-1173; 800-561-4300
Fax: 416-252-1676
E-mail: sales@itf.ca
Web Site: http://www.itf.ca
Zena Thomas, Director, Sales
Rachel Ward, Sales
Anne Hamaway, Sales

Branch Offices:
MONTREAL: 7801 Louis H Lafontaine, Ste 104, Anjou, QC H1K 4E4, Canada. Phone: 800-989-8929. Fax: 514-352-5957.
Represents training resource producers; training resources are available in video, DVD, CD-ROM, print-based, simulations & online; many programs are available in other languages.

IRIS FILMS INC. — No longer in business.

IT IS WRITTEN INTERNATIONAL TELEVISION
PO Box O
Thousand Oaks, CA 91359
Phone: 805-433-0210
Fax: 805-433-0218
E-mail: iiw@iiw.org
Web Site: http://www.iiw.org
Shawn Boonstra, Director
Produces & distributes TV programs & video tapes.

IVANHOE BROADCAST NEWS INC.
2745 W Fairbanks Ave
Winter Park, FL 32789
Phone: 407-740-0789
Fax: 407-740-5320
E-mail: mthomas@ivanhoe.com
Web Site: http://www.ivanhoe.com
Bette Bon Fleur, Chief Executive Officer Emeritus
Marjorie Bekhaert Thomas, President & Publisher
John Cherry, President, Sales
Marsha Hitchcock, Director, News
Courtney Hylton, Internet Business Development
Produces & syndicates programming on health, medicine & news for women ages 25-54.

IVI INC.
3213 W Wheeler St
Ste 191
Seattle, WA 98199
Phones: 323-851-6877; 310-210-8011
E-mail: info@ivi.tv
Web Site: http://www.ivi.tv
Ron Erickson, Chairman
Todd Weaver, Founder & Chief Executive Officer
ivi is an Internet television service provider. ivi's service is similar to cable or satellite television but ivi delivers its broadcast television signal over the Internet.

JANUS FILMS CO.
250 E Hartsdale Ave
Ste 4
Hartsdale, NY 10530-3571
Phone: 914-725-7881
Distributes motion picture features & shorts, foreign language films, TV film & tape series; stock footage; film buyer; imports films.

JEWISH CHAUTAUQUA SOCIETY
633 Third Ave
New York, NY 10017
Phones: 212-650-4100; 800-765-6200
Fax: 212-650-4189
E-mail: jcs@urj.org
Web Site: http://www.nftb.org/national_programs/jcs.shtml
Charles Niederman, Chancellor
Produces & distributes educational & religious films.

THE JIM HENSON COMPANY
1416 N LaBrea Ave
Hollywood, CA 90028
Phone: 323-802-1500
Fax: 323-802-1825
E-mail: licensing@henson.com
Web Site: http://www.henson.com
Brian Henson, Chairman
Lisa Henson, Chief Executive Officer
Halle Stanford, Executive Vice President, Children Entertainment
Peter Schube, President & Chief Operating Officer
Laurie Don, Executive Vice President, Operations & Finance
Jason Lust, Senior Vice President, Feature Films
Nicole Goldman, Vice President, Marketing & Public Relations

Branch Offices:
NEW YORK: 37-18 Northern Blvd, Ste 400, Long Island City, NY 11101. Phone: 212-794-2400. Fax: 212-439-7452.
Produces programming.

JIM OWENS ENTERTAINMENT INC.
1110 16th Ave S
Nashville, TN 37212
Phone: 615-256-7700
Fax: 615-256-7779
E-mail: jerryfox@aol.com
Web Site: http://www.crookandchase.com
Jim Owens, President
Jerry Fox, Director, Sales
Produces & distributes music, entertainment & information programming for TV syndication & cable distribution.

JOHNSON PUBLISHING CO. INC.
820 S Michigan Ave
Chicago, IL 60605
Phone: 312-322-9200
Web Site: http://www.johnsonpublishing.com
Linda Johnson Rice, Chairman & Chief Executive Officer
Anne Sempowskiward, President & Chief Operations Officer
Eunice W. Johnson, Secretary & Treasurer

Branch Offices:
NEW YORK: 1270 Ave of the Americas, Ste 1705, New York, NY 10020. Phone: 212-397-4500.

WASHINGTON, DC: 1750 Pennsylvania Ave NW, Ste 1201, Washington, DC 20006. Phone: 202-393-5860.
Produces TV programming.

JUNTUNEN GROUP — See listing for Hoffman Communications.

KABOOM! ENTERTAINMENT INC.
1867 Yonge St
Ste 650
Toronto, ON M4S 1Y5
Canada
Phones: 416-783-8383; 866-495-3650
Fax: 416-783-8384
E-mail: info@phase4films.com
Web Site: http://www.kaboom-ent.com
Berry Meyerowitz, President
David Richardson, Vice President, Sales
Lori Nytko, Coordinator, Operations
Sells, markets, licenses & distributes DVDs, videos & ancillary merchandise. Division of Peace Arch Entertainment Inc.

KAMEN ENTERTAINMENT GROUP INC.
701 Seventh Ave
6th Fl
New York, NY 10036
Phone: 212-575-4660
Fax: 212-575-4799
E-mail: kamen@kamen.com
Web Site: http://www.kamen.com
Marina Kamen, Creative Director & Casting & Senior Music Producer
Roy Kamen, Senior Sound Designer, Radio Producer & Chief Mixer
Provides audio recording services; music library, original music, sound effects, voice-over casting, radio production & direction; 24-track recording studio; live shows.

KILLER TRACKS: NETWORK MUSIC
8750 Wilshire Blvd
Beverly Hills, CA 90211
Phones: 310-358-4455; 800-454-5537
Fax: 310-358-4479
E-mail: sales@killertracks.com
Web Site: http://www.networkmusic.com
Produces & distributes music; sound effects libraries.

KING WORLD PRODUCTIONS INC. — See listing for CBS Television Distribution Media Sales.

KLEIN &
8896 Carson St
Culver City, CA 90232
Phones: 310-317-9599; 310-827-2850
Fax: 310-456-7701
E-mail: bob@lafestival.org
Web Site: http://www.lafestival.org
Robert Klein, President
Markets & promotes electronic media, cable, TV; custom campaigns, including thematic concepts, music, animation & live action.

KULTUR INTERNATIONAL FILMS INC.
195 Hwy 36
West Long Branch, NJ 07764
Phone: 732-229-2343
Fax: 732-229-0066
E-mail: info@kultur.com
Web Site: http://www.kultur.com
Dennis M. Hedlund, Chairman
Distributes performing arts home videos.

KUSA PRODUCTIONS
500 Speer Blvd
Denver, CO 80203
Phones: 303-871-9999; 303-871-1487
E-mail: kusa@9news.com
Web Site: http://www.9news.com
Mark Cornetta, President & General Manager
Provides film & video production & post-production; produces TV commercials, documentaries, industrials & programming.

KUSHNER LOCKE CO. INC.
280 S Beverly Dr
Ste 205
Beverly Hills, CA 90212
Phone: 310-275-7508
Fax: 310-275-7518
E-mail: info@kushnerlocke.com
Web Site: http://www.kushnerlocke.com
Donald Kushner, Co-chairman, Co-chief Executive Officer & Secretary
Peter Locke, Co-chairman & Co-chief Executive Officer
Bruce S. Lilliston, President & Chief Operations Officer
Brett Robinson, Chief Financial Officer & Senior Vice President
Distributes independent lower budget film & TV products; library includes 205 titles with over 1,000 hours of film & TV programming.

N. LEE LACY/ASSOCIATES — No longer in business.

LASERPACIFIC MEDIA CORP.
809 N Cahuenga Blvd
Hollywood, CA 90038
Phone: 323-462-6266
Fax: 323-464-3233
E-mail: info@laserpacific.com
Web Site: http://www.laserpacific.com
Brian Burr, Chief Executive Officer
Provides laser disc & videotape editing facilities; special effects laboratory. Division of Eastman Kodak.

LATHAM FOUNDATION
Latham Plaza Bldg
1826 Clement Ave
Alameda, CA 94501-1397
Phone: 510-521-0920
Fax: 510-521-9861
E-mail: info@latham.org
Web Site: http://www.latham.org
Produces & distributes educational programming, TV films & videos; humane & environmentally oriented; educational foundation; publishes a quarterly newsletter.

LESEA BROADCASTING NETWORK
61300 S Ironwood Rd

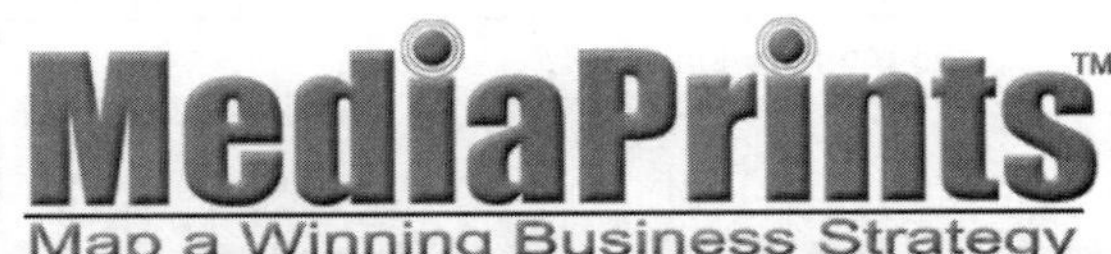
MediaPrints™
Map a Winning Business Strategy
Digital Cable and TV Coverage Maps.
Visit www.warren-news.com/mediaprints.htm

South Bend, IN 46614
Phone: 574-291-8200
Fax: 574-291-9043
Web Site: http://www.lesea.com
Peter Sumrall, President
Produces TV programs, infomercials, documentaries, commercials, corporate communications, live productions/programming & sporting events. Capabilities include video, audio, internet, satellite & multimedia.

LEAR LEVIN PRODUCTIONS INC.
16 W 88th St
New York, NY 10024
Phone: 212-595-5526
Lear Levin, President & Founder
Produces TV commercials.

LIEB PRODUCTIONS — No longer in business.

LIFESTYLE MAGAZINE
PO Box 1000
Thousand Oaks, CA 91359
Phones: 805-955-7680; 888-940-0062
Fax: 805-522-2114
E-mail: info@ffttv.org
Web Site: http://www.lifestyle.org
Mike Tucker, Speaker & Director, Faith For Today Television
Dan Matthews, Co-host
Produces color 30-min. programs on 1-inch videotape, 1/2 & 3/4-inch cassette, DVD & Digibeta.

LINCOLN FINANCIAL SPORTS — See listing for Raycom Sports Inc.

LINSMAN FILM
329 N Windsor Blvd
Los Angeles, CA 90004
Phone: 323-571-4535
Fax: 323-571-1378
E-mail: bill@linsman.com
Web Site: http://www.linsman.com
William D. Linsman, President & Director
Paula Panich, Vice President
Tim Goldberg, Representative
Produces TV commercials & programs. See also Ocean Park Pictures Inc.

LIONSGATE ENTERTAINMENT
2700 Colorado Ave
Santa Monica, CA 90404
Phone: 310-449-9200
Fax: 310-255-3870
E-mail: general-inquiries@lionsgate.com
Web Site: http://www.lionsgate.com
Jon Feltheimer, Co-Chairman & Chief Executive Officer
Michael Burns, Vice Chairman
Steve Beeks, President & Co-Chief Operating Officer
Kevin Beggs, President, Lionsgate Television Group
Joe Drake, President, Motion Picture Group & Co-Chief Operating Officer
Jim Keegan, Chief Financial Officer
Julie Fontaine, Executive Vice President, Theatrical Publicity
Wayne Levin, Executive Vice President, Corporate Operations & General Counsel

Branch Offices:
NEW YORK: 75 Rockefeller Plz, 16th Fl, New York, NY 10007. Phone: 212-577-2400.

CANADA: 2200-1055 W Hastings St., Vancouver, BC V6E 2E9, Canada. Phones: 604-983-5555; 877-848-3866. Fax: 604-983-5554.

AUSTRALIA: Lev 29, Chifley Tower, Two Chifley Sq, Sydney, NSW 2000, Australia.

UNITED KINGDOM: c/o Ariel House, 74A Charlotte St, London E1T 4QJ, United Kingdom. Phone: 44-0-20-7299-8800.
Produces & distributes motion pictures, TV programming, home entertainment, family entertainment & video-on-demand content.

LITTON ENTERTAINMENT
884 Allbritton Blvd.
Ste 200
Mt Pleasant, SC 29464
Phone: 843-883-5060
Fax: 843-883-9957
Web Site: http://www.litton.tv
Dave Morgan, Chief Executive Officer
Pete Sniderman, Chief Operating Officer
Tom Warner, Executive Vice President, Domestic Distribution
Kimi Serrano-Schenck, Senior Vice President, Syndication & New Media
Nancy Smeltzer, Vice President, Operations
(Formerly Litton Worldwide.) Provides strip programming, weekly series, high impact TV specials, theatrical movies & news content; production studio; media sales.

LOGIC GENERAL INC.
26200 SW 95th Ave
Ste 300
Wilsonville, OR 97070
Phone: 503-598-7747
Fax: 503-598-9375
Web Site: http://www.logicgeneral.com
Tara Hagman, Manager, Customer Service

Branch Offices:
SEATTLE: 55 S Atlantic, Ste A-1, Seattle, WA 98134. Phone: 206-973-4200. Fax: 206-973-4201.

TEMPE: 1835 E Sixth St, Ste 1, Tempe, AZ 85281. Phone: 480-736-8959. Fax: 480-736-8961.
Manufactures CDs & DVDs; produces more than 90,000 units per day. Provides a combination of turnkey & media manufacturing resources.

LONDON TELEVISION SERVICE — No longer in business.

LOOK & CO.
280 Park Ave S
New York, NY 10010
Phone: 212-629-7400
Fax: 212-629-3964
Produces original music & sound design for advertising, film & TV.

LUTHERAN CHURCH-MISSOURI SYNOD — See listing for Concordia Publishing House.

LUTHERAN HOUR MINISTRIES — See listing for Envoy Productions.

LYNDAL ENTERTAINMENT INC.
2337 Lemoine Ave
Ste 10
Ft Lee, NJ 07024
Phone: 201-947-7111
Distributes programming.

LYNX IMAGES INC.
PO Box 5961
Station A
Toronto, ON M5W 1P4
Canada
Phone: 416-925-8422
Fax: 416-925-8352
E-mail: website@lynximages.com
Web Site: http://www.lynximages.com
Russell Floren, President & Producer
Barbara Chisholm, Vice President, Production & Publishing
Andrea Gutsche, Vice President, Creative
Produces film, video & TV programming; documentaries include history, nature, travel video & books.

MARYKNOLL WORLD PRODUCTIONS
PO Box 308
Walsh Bldg
Maryknoll, NY 10545
Phones: 914-941-7636 x2558; 800-258-5838
Fax: 914-945-0670
E-mail: syndication@maryknoll.org
Web Site: http://society.maryknoll.org
Produces & distributes educational & religious films, documentary films/videos & TV tape series.

MAYSLES FILMS INC.
343 Lenox Ave
New York, NY 10027
Phone: 212-582-6050
Fax: 212-586-2057
E-mail: info@mayslesfilms.com
Web Site: http://www.mayslesfilms.com
Albert Maysles, Chief Executive Officer
Bradley Kaplan, President
Laura Coxson, General Manager
Chris McCue, Office Manager
Katie Sorohan, Coordinator
Ian Markiewicz, In-house Editor
Produces & distributes documentaries; produces commercials & corporate films.

MCDOUGALL
465 Natoma St
San Francisco, CA 94103
Phone: 415-626-2300
Fax: 415-626-4300
E-mail: info@mcdougall.com
Web Site: http://www.mcdougall.com
Eric McDougall, Founder
Produces color 30-minute programs on 1-inch videotape & 1/2 & 3/4-inch cassette.

MCGUANE STUDIO INC.
36 Horatio St
New York, NY 10014
Phone: 212-463-7259
Jim P. McGuane, President
Produces commercials, industrials, short features, documentaries & music videos.

MEADOWLANE ENTERPRISES INC.
15201 Burbank Blvd
Ste B
Van Nuys, CA 91411
Phone: 818-988-3830
Fax: 818-988-0276
E-mail: meadowlane@sbcglobal.net
Bill Allen, President
Licenses a library of classic TV series.

MEDIALINK WORLDWIDE INC.
The Video News Release Network
708 Third Ave
New York, NY 10017
Phones: 212-682-8300; 800-843-0677
Fax: 212-682-5260
E-mail: LearnMore@synapticdigital.com
Web Site: http://www.synapticdigital.com
Jim Lonergan, President & Chief Executive Officer
Nick G. Abramovich, Chief Operating Officer
Krish M. Menon, Chief Technology Officer
Tom Morrissy, Executive Vice President, Sales
Andrew Lipson, Vice President, Operations
Matt Thomson, Managing Director, Europe

Branch Offices:
CHICAGO: 401 N Michigan Ave, Ste 2100, Chicago, IL 60611. Phone: 312-222-9850. Fax: 312-222-9810. E-Mail: zrobbins@medialink.com.

LOS ANGELES: 6404 Wilshire Blvd, Los Angeles, CA 90048. Phone: 323-653-8535. E-Mail: bmiddleton@medialink.com.

SAN FRANCISCO: 8 California St, Ste 500, San Francisco, CA 94111. Phone: 415-912-1650. E-Mail: sbratman@medialink.com.

WASHINGTON, DC: 529 14th St NW, Ste 450, Washington, DC 20045. Phone: 202-628-3800. Fax: 202-628-2377.

LONDON: 10-11 Percy St, London, England W1T1DN. Phone: +44 20 7580 8330.
Produces & distributes satellite video & audio news releases worldwide; satellite & radio media tours; corporate videos Internet & newswire services.

MEDSTAR TELEVISION INC.
5920 Hamilton Blvd
Allentown, PA 18106
Phone: 610-395-1300
E-mail: Help@medstar.com
Web Site: http://www.medstar.com
Independently produces & syndicates medical news, health & wellness information programming.

LEE MENDELSON FILM PRODUCTIONS INC.
330 Primrose Rd
Ste 215
Burlingame, CA 94010-4028
Phone: 650-342-8284
Fax: 650-342-6170
E-mail: jason@mendelsonproductions.com
Web Site: http://www.mendelsonproductions.com
Produces industrial & educational films, open-end film commercials (made for TV), TV film & tape series & spot commercials, film programs on order & theatrical shorts.

MENNONITE MEDIA — See listing for Third Way Media.

MGM TELEVISION ENTERTAINMENT INC.
10250 Constellation Blvd
Los Angeles, CA 90067
Phone: 310-449-3000

E-mail: mgmonline@mgm.com
Web Site: http://www.mgm.com/tv
Gary Barber, Co-Chairman & Chief Executive Officer, MGM
Roger Birnbaum, Co-Chairman & Chief Executive Officer, MGM
Roma Khanna, President, Television Group & Digital
Gary Marenzi, President, Worldwide Television
John Bryan, President, Domestic Television Dstribution
Chris Ottinger, President, International Television Distribution & Acquisition
Vicky Gregorian, Senior Vice President, Domestic Television Distribution
Susan Hummel, Senior Vice President, US Basic Cable & Canadian Television
Damien Marin, Senior Vice President, Pay Television & Digital Media
Vinicio Espinosa, Vice President, Latin American Television Distribution
Producer & distributor of TV programming.

MIAMI BROADCAST CENTER — No longer in business.

WARREN MILLER ENTERTAINMENT
5720 Flatiron Pkwy
Boulder, CO 80301
Phone: 303-442-3430
E-mail: contact@warrenmillertv.com
Web Site: http://www.warrenmillertv.com
Jeffrey Moore, Senior Executive Producer
Ginger Sheehy, Manager, Development
Josh Haskins, Producer
John Barcklay, Supervisor, Post Production
Provides production & post-production services; fully capable in all media from digital video to full resolution HD; produces for both broadcast & broadband. Division of Bonnier Mountain Group.

MILNER-FENWICK INC.
119 Lakefront Dr
Hunt Valley, MD 21030-2216
Phones: 410-252-1700; 800-432-8433
Fax: 410-252-6316
E-mail: mail@milner-fenwick.com
Web Site: http://www.milner-fenwick.com
David Milner, President
Produces TV film & tape series and film programs on order; produces & distributes industrial & educational films; animation music library, recording facilities, studio facilities for rent & other services.

MIRAMAX FILMS
161 Ave of the Americas
15th Fl
New York, NY 10013
Phone: 917-606-5500
Web Site: http://www.miramax.com
Mike Lang, Chief Executive Officer
Eric Doctorow, Executive Vice President, Worldwide Home Entertainment & Distribution
Joe Patrick, Senior Vice President, Head, TV/ Digital Sales
Bob Cook, Strategic Adviser to Chief Executive Officer
Lindsay Gardner, Strategic Adviser to Chief Executive Officer

Branch Offices:
LOS ANGELES: 8439 W Sunset Blvd, Los Angeles, CA 90069. Phone: 323-650-2937.
Produces & distributes motion picture films.

MODERN SOUND PICTURES INC.
1402 Howard St
Omaha, NE 68102
Phones: 402-341-8476; 800-228-9584
Fax: 402-341-8487
E-mail: info@modernsoundpictures.com
Web Site: http://www.modernsoundpictures.com
Sandra L. Smith, President
Distributes non-theatrical entertainment features & shorts; sells & rents audio/visual equipment.

MOFFITT-LEE PRODUCTIONS
1438 N Gower St
Ste 250
Los Angeles, CA 90028
Phone: 323-382-3469
John Moffitt, President
Produces TV film & tape series.

MONKEYLAND AUDIO INC.
4620 W Magnolia Blvd
Burbank, CA 91505
Phone: 818-553-0955
Fax: 818-553-1155
Web Site: http://www.monkeylandaudio.com
Trip Brock, Principal & Supervising Sound Editor
Rob Embrey, Manager, Scheduling & Operations
Full-service, state-of-the-art digital audio post-production facility. Provides full post sound packages, including sound supervision, editorial, ADR, Foley & re-recording mixing services. Services the audio post-production needs of film studios, TV & cable networks.

JESS S. MORGAN & CO.
5900 Wilshire Blvd
Ste 2300
Los Angeles, CA 90036
Phone: 323-634-2400
Fax: 323-937-6532
Web Site: http://www.jsmco.com
Jess S. Morgan, Owner
Provides TV sales & syndication for Carol Burnett & Friends.

MOVIECRAFT HOME VIDEO
PO Box 438
Orland Park, IL 60462-0438
Phone: 708-460-9082
Fax: 708-460-9099
E-mail: orders@moviecraft.com
Web Site: http://www.moviecraft.com
Larry Urbanski, President
Develops, produces & distributes programming for TV & home video; archival stock footage.

MULLER MEDIA INC. — See listing for Imperia Entertainment Inc.

MULTI-IMAGE NETWORK
312 Otterson Dr
Ste F
Chico, CA 95928-8210
Phone: 530-345-4211
Fax: 530-345-7737
Web Site: http://www.dcsi.net/~min
Creates video publishing channels providing programming for cable TV viewers, develops & sells video publishing software & hardware, still-frame and motion video computer graphics production, editing, bookkeeping & scheduling and digital audio, animation & video switching.

MUSCULAR DYSTROPHY ASSOCIATION
3300 E Sunrise Dr
Tucson, AZ 85718-3208
Phone: 800-572-1717
E-mail: mda@mdausa.org
Web Site: http://www.mdausa.org

Jerry Lewis, National Chairman
National voluntary health agency; produces the annual Jerry Lewis Labor Day Telethon.

MVI POST
6320 Castle Pl
Falls Church, VA 22044
Phone: 703-536-7678
Fax: 703-536-9490
E-mail: m.kohn@mvipost.com
Web Site: http://www.mvipost.com
Frank Maniglia, Sr., Chief Executive Officer
Frank Maniglia, Jr., President
Craig Maniglia, Vice President & Senior Audio Designer
Marc Kohn, Director, Post Production
Provides video & audio post production; music & sound effects libraries; DVD authoring & graphic design.

MYFOOTAGE.COM
244 Fifth Ave
Ste 2768
New York, NY 10001
Phone: 646-450-4768
Web Site: http://www.myfootage.com
Offers a stock footage library & stock photos.

NATIONAL COUNCIL OF CHURCHES
475 Riverside Dr
Ste 880
New York, NY 10115
Phone: 212-870-2228
Fax: 212-870-2030
E-mail: info@ncccusa.org
Web Site: http://www.ncccusa.org
Michael Kinnamon, General Secretary
Claire J. Chapman, Chief Operating Officer
Kurt R. Kaboth, Director, Development
Antonios Kireopoulos, Senior Program Director, Faith & Order & Interfaith Relation
Wesley M. Pattillo, Senior Program Director, Justice, Advocacy & Communication
Garland F. Pierce, Senior Program Director, Education & Leadership Ministries

Branch Offices:
WASHINGTON, DC: 110 Maryland Ave NE, Washington, DC 20002. Phone: 202-544-2350. Fax: 202-543-1297. Cassandra Carmichael, Director.
Distributes religious films & TV film and tape series; produces network religious programs.

NATIONAL FILM BOARD OF CANADA
PO Box 6100
Station Centre-ville
Montreal, PQ H3C 3HS
Canada
Phones: 514-283-9000; 800-267-7710
Fax: 514-283-7564
Web Site: http://www.onf-nfb.gc.ca
Tom Perlmutter, Government Film Commissioner
Claude Joli-Coeur, Assitant Commissioner
Deborah Drisdell, Director General, Accessibility & Digital Enterprises
Luisa Frate, Director General, Finance, Operations & Technology
Monique Simard, Director General, French Program
Cindy Witten, Director General, English Program
Distributes animation, motion picture shorts, foreign language films, theatrical shorts & individual program-documentaries for TV.

NATIONAL GEOGRAPHIC TELEVISION
PO Box 98199
Washington, DC 20090-8199
Phone: 800-647-5463
Web Site: http://www.nationalgeographic.com/tv
Maryanne Culpepper, President
Produces nature, adventure & science films for commercial & non-commercial broadcast TV, cable TV, home video & international TV/video.

NATIONAL MOBILE TELEVISION — No longer in business.

NATIONAL TECHNICAL INFORMATION SERVICE
5285 Port Royal Rd
Springfield, VA 22161
Phones: 703-605-6050; 888-584-8332
Fax: 703-605-6900
E-mail: info@ntis.gov
Web Site: http://www.ntis.gov
Ellen Herbst, Director
Distributes federally produced audiovisual programs including safety & health, medicine, history, social issues, dentistry & geography.

NAVAL MEDIA CENTER — See listing for Defense Media Activity.

NAVY OFFICE OF INFORMATION (OI-03)
Dept. of the Navy
1200 Navy Pentagon
Washington, DC 20350-1200
Phone: 703-692-4724
E-mail: chinfo.dutyoffic.fct@navy.mil
Web Site: http://www.chinfo.navy.mil; http://www.navy.mil/local/chinfo
Rear Adm. Dennis Moynihan, Chief of Information
Lt. Ligia Cohen, Chief of Publicity
William Spencer, Chief of Web & Creative Director
Dick Welsh, Chief of Production
Marie Tillery, Editor, Navy News Service
Produces Dept. of Navy public affairs program.

NBC NEWS
30 Rockefeller Plz
New York, NY 10112
Phone: 212-664-4444
E-mail: nightly@nbc.com
Web Site: http://www.nbc.com/news-sports
Steve Capus, President, NBC News
Cheryl Gould, Senior Vice President
Alexandra Wallace, Senior Vice President
Vivian Schiller, Chief Digital Officer
Produces global news & informational programming for the network's primetime, late-night & daytime schedules. Division of NBC Universal Inc.

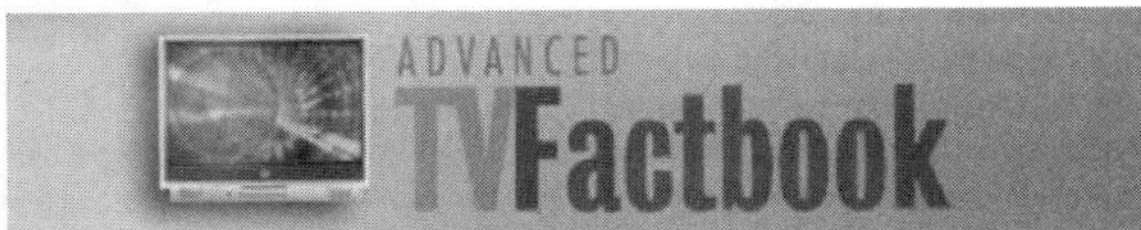

NETHERLANDS CONSULATE GENERAL
Press & Cultural Section
One Rockefeller Pl, 11th Fl
New York, NY 10020-2094
Phone: 877-388-2443
Fax: 212-333-3603
E-mail: nyc-pcz@minbuza.nl
Web Site: http://www.cgny.org
Ferdinand Dorsman, General Director, Cultural Affairs
Robert Kloos, Director, Visual Arts & Architecture
Arthur Kibbelaar, Press & Cultural Affairs Counsel

NETWORK MUSIC — See listing for Killer Tracks: Network Music.

NEWS BROADCAST NETWORK
75 Broad St
15th Fl
New York, NY 10004
Phones: 212-684-8910; 800-920-6397
E-mail: info@newsbroadcastnetwork.com
Web Site: http://www.newsbroadcastnetwork.com
Michael J. Hill, President
Tom Hill, Senior Vice President
Richard M. Neuman, Vice President, Broadcasting/Technology & Executive Producer, Live/Special Events
Steve Gold, Director, NBN Healthcare
Laura Pair, Director, Editorial Operations
Rick Vasta, Director, Video Production Services
Bob Hill, Executive Producer
Produces & distributes video news releases, public service announcements, satellite media tours & marketing productions.

NEWTON MEDIA ASSOCIATES INC.
824 Greenbrier Pkwy
Ste 200
Chesapeake, VA 23320
Phone: 757-547-5400
Fax: 757-547-7383
E-mail: info@newtonmedia.com
Web Site: http://www.newtonmedia.com
Steven M. Newton, President & Chief Executive Officer
Janet Burke, Director, Media
Harry Weimar, Senior Media Sales Consultant
Aimee James, Media Buyer
Aubry Winfrey, Media Buyer
Specializes in creating & managing integrated TV, radio, print & interactive media campaigns for DRTV, corporate, & charitable organizations.

NEW VISIONS SYNDICATION
44895 Hwy 82
Aspen, CO 81611
Phone: 970-925-2640
Fax: 970-925-9369
E-mail: kayla@newvisionssyndication.com
Web Site: http://www.newvisionssyndication.com
Rodney H. Jacobs, Chairman
Kayla B. Hoffman-Cook, Vice President, Syndication
Chris Laursen, Director, Syndication
Produces & distributes entertainment, promotional & educational films; TV syndication, cable distribution, specials & series and stock footage.

NFL FILMS INC.
One NFL Plz
Mt Laurel, NJ 08054
Phone: 856-222-3500
Fax: 856-866-4848
E-mail: sales.facility@nfl.com
Web Site: http://www.nflfilms.com
Steve Sabol, President
Produces educational films, motion picture shorts, TV film & tape series, film programs on order, stock footage & National Football League series, vignettes, footage, films & home video; provides laboratory facilities & services, music library, recording facilities & studio facilities for rent.

NORFLICKS PRODUCTIONS LTD.
124 Dupont St
Toronto, ON M5R 1V2
Canada
Phone: 416-351-7558
Fax: 416-351-8165
E-mail: mail@norflicks.com
Web Site: http://www.norflicks.com
Richard G. Nielsen, President
James Lau, Chief Financial Officer
Marc Ouellet, Manager, Corporate Affairs & Production
Patricia Joyes, Executive Assistant & Producer
Provides production consulting; produces TV series & feature films.

NORTHEAST VIDEO PRODUCTIONS
PO Box 8425
Sleepy Hollow, NY 10591
Phone: 914-631-3850
Fax: 914-631-3850
E-mail: nevsteiner@aol.com
Web Site: http://henrysteiner.com/film.htm
Henry Steiner, President
Provides full-service, script-to-screen video/film production.

NORTHWESTERN INC. — See listing for NW Media.

NTV INTERNATIONAL CORP.
645 Fifth Ave
Ste 303
New York, NY 10022
Phone: 212-660-6900
Fax: 212-660-6998
Jusaburo Hayashi, President & Chief Operating Officer
Leo Lahm, Technical Manager
Tai Takeuchi, Chief Financial Officer & Human Resources
News gathering bureau; provides production services & satellite transmission.

NW MEDIA
106 SE 11th Ave
Portland, OR 97214
Phones: 503-223-5010; 800-547-2252
Fax: 503-223-4737
E-mail: contact@nwmedia.com
Web Site: http://www.nwmedia.com
Jeanne D. Alldredge, President
Stephen P. Wade, Director, Sales
Mark Berry, Manager, Production
Scott Thompson, Manager, Warehouse & Purchasing
Provides complete solutions for CD/DVD manufacturing, digital printing, graphic design & multimedia.

OCEAN PARK PICTURES INC.
1223 Wilshire Blvd
Santa Monica, CA 90403
Phone: 310-450-1220
Fax: 310-450-1451
E-mail: info@oceanparkpix.com
Web Site: http://www.oceanparkpix.com
Film production company; specializes in commercials.

OGLETREE PRODUCTIONS
24 Brentwood Cir
Lubbock, TX 79407
Phone: 806-791-2800
E-mail: oglepro@aol.com
Web Site: http://www.ogletreeproductions.com
Provides HD/SD videography & editing. Produces commercial & industrial videos and video crewing for national clients, broadcast, cable and corporate.

OGM PRODUCTION MUSIC
6464 Sunset Blvd
Ste 790
Hollywood, CA 90028
Phones: 323-461-2701; 800-421-4163
Fax: 323-461-1543
E-mail: info@ogmmusic.com
Web Site: http://www.ogmmusic.com
Ole Georg, President
Offers a library of music for every type of production, including film, TV, video, Internet, interactive & multimedia.

1-WORLD LLC
1605 S Jackson St
Seattle, WA 98144
Fax: 206-781-1401
E-mail: contact1world@1worldfilms.com
Web Site: http://www.1worldfilms.com
Produces & distributes foreign motion pictures.

ON THE AIR STUDIOS
80 Riverside Dr
New York, NY 10024
Phones: 212-362-0830; 800-766-6247
E-mail: onair800@msn.com
Web Site: http://www.ontheairstudios.com
Richard Bianco, Owner & President
Provides demo tapes for voice-over radio, news, local commercials & radio commercials.

OPUS1 MUSIC LIBRARY
12711 Ventura Blvd
Ste 170
Studio City, CA 91604
Phones: 818-508-2040; 888-757-6787
Fax: 818-508-2044
E-mail: office@opus1musiclibrary.com
Web Site: http://www.opus1musiclibrary.com
Alan Ett, President & Chief Executive Officer
Ryan Neill, Vice President, Production
Mitch Rabin, Vice President, Sales & Marketing
Marrsha Sill, Vice President, Film/TV Music
Levon Broussalian, Director, Music Supervision
Production music library representing over 2,000 CDs; creates custom cues & scores.

ORION TELEVISION — See listing for Touchstone Television.

EARL OWENSBY STUDIOS
One Motion Picture Blvd
Shelby, NC 28152
Phone: 704-487-0500
Fax: 704-487-4763
E-mail: earlowensby@bellsouth.net
Web Site: http://www.earlowensby.com
Earl Owensby, President
Motion picture production facilities.

PANTOMIME PICTURES INC.
12144 Riverside Dr
Valley Village, CA 91607-3829
Phone: 818-980-5555
Produces animation for commercial, educational & industrial use, specializes in animation design & conception.

PARAMOUNT LICENSING
5555 Melrose Ave
Hollywood, CA 90038
Phone: 323-956-2244
E-mail: licensing@paramount.com
Web Site: http://www.paramountlicensing.com
Michael Corcoan, President, Consumer Products & Recreation Group
Michael Bartok, Executive Vice President, Licensing
Charles Myers, Senior Vice President, Creative & Development
Lynda Cevallos, Vice President, Licensing
Ryan Gagerman, Vice President, International Licensing
Tom Renger, Vice President, Business Planning & Development
Darren Kyman, Executive Director, Marketing & Retail Development
Handle licensing rights worldwide for properties of Paramount Pictures, Paramount Vantage, Nickelodeon Movies & MTV Films. Division of Paramount Pictures Corp.

PARAMOUNT STUDIOS GROUP — See listing for The Studios at Paramount.

PARAMOUNT TELEVISION GROUP — See listing for CBS Television Studios.

PATHE NEWS INC.
630 Ninth Ave
Ste 305
New York, NY 10036-4751
Phone: 212-489-8669
Fax: 212-489-1416
Provides TV production, stock footage & multimedia services.

PATTERSON STUDIOS INC.
600 Overlook Dr
Winter Haven, FL 33884
Phone: 863-324-3696
Fax: 863-324-0864
E-mail: info@pattersonstudios.com
Web Site: http://www.pattersonstudios.com
John D. Patterson, Founder, Director & Cameraman
Mike Palma, Supervisor, Post Production
Kevin A. Tison, Marketing, Sales & Film Video Production
Produces TV dramas, industrial & documentary programming, commercials & theatrical films & video.

PAULIST PRODUCTIONS
PO Box 1057
17575 Pacific Coast Hwy
Pacific Palisades, CA 90272

Phone: 310-454-0688
Fax: 310-459-6549
E-mail: paulistmail@paulistproductions.org
Web Site: http://www.paulistproductions.org
Frank Desiderio, CSP, President
Barbara M. Gangi, Vice President, Development & Production
Joseph Kim, Vice President, Business Affairs
Enid Sevilla, General Manager & Financial Officer
Michael Kaczmarek, Associate, Marketing & Business Affairs
Produces & distributes religious films.

PBS INTERNATIONAL
10 Guest St
Boston, MD 02135
Phone: 617-300-2000
Fax: 617-779-7900
Web Site: http://www.wgbhinternational.org
Tom Koch, Vice President, Distribution
Charles Schuerhoff, Director, International Aquisitions
Betsy Leblanc, Senior Manager, International Sales
Nanci Barker, Manager, International Sales
Andrew Campana, Manager, International Sales
Jennifer Callahan, Project Manager, Program Development
Produces primetime programming for PBS in the U.S.

PBS VIDEOINDEX
1320 Braddock Pl
Alexandria, VA 22314
Phone: 703-739-5000
Web Site: http://videoindex.pbs.org
Distributes educational & documentary films.

PECKHAM PRODUCTIONS INC.
50 S Buckhout St
Irvington, NY 10533
Phone: 914-591-4140
Fax: 914-591-4149
E-mail: info@peckhampix.com
Web Site: http://www.peckhampix.com
Produces industrial, educational & documentary films, videotapes & TV commercials, programs & promos.

PENNEBAKER ASSOCIATES INC.
262 W 91st St
New York, NY 10024
Phone: 212-496-8195
Fax: 212-496-8915
Fraze Pennebaker, Owner
Produces & distributes music, dance, theatrical drama & general performance films; theatre & TV features & shorts; stock footage.

PERENNIAL PICTURES FILM CORP.
2102 E 52nd St
Indianapolis, IN 46205
Phone: 317-253-1519
E-mail: mail@perennialpictures.com
Web Site: http://www.perennialpictures.com
G. Brian Reynolds, President
Russ Harris, Senior Vice President
Mike Ruggiero, Vice President
Produces animation for TV specials, series & features.

ARCHIE PHILLIPS PRODUCTIONS —
No longer in business.

PHOENIX COMMUNICATIONS GROUP INC.
Three Empire Blvd
South Hackensack, NJ 07606
Phone: 201-807-0888
Web Site: http://www.phoenixcomm.com
Produces Sports NewSatellite, a sports news & highlight feed; video news releases; satellite media tours for distribution.

PHOENIX ENTERTAINMENT GROUP
1732 Aviation Blvd
Ste 131
Redondo Beach, CA 90278
Phone: 310-379-0700
Fax: 888-751-4031
E-mail: sean@phoenixentgroup.com
Web Site: http://www.thephoenixentertainmentgroup.com
Tony Perez, Chief Executive Officer
Specialty entertainment distribution company that produces, markets & distributes urban, Latino, horror, & family/spiritual themed content.

PHOENIX FILMS & VIDEO
2349 Chaffee Dr
St Louis, MO 63146
Phones: 314-569-0211 x105; 800-221-1274
Fax: 314-569-2834
E-mail: info@phoenixlearninggroup.com
Web Site: http://www.phoenixlearninggroup.com
Distributes & produces educational programs. Film library for all ages from 2yrs old through adult. Library includes children's & entertainment programs, curriculum & educational films, documentaries, cultural & art films; programs available for digital streaming. Division of Phoenix Learning Group Inc.

PHOTOBITION BONDED SERVICES —
See listing for Bonded Services.

PILOT PRODUCTIONS INC.
2123 McDaniel Ave
Evanston, IL 60201-2126
Phone: 847-328-3700
Fax: 847-328-3761
Produces video, multimedia & print for business.

PIXAR ANIMATION STUDIOS
1200 Park Ave
Emeryville, CA 94608
Phone: 510-752-3000
Fax: 510-752-3151
E-mail: rmancusp@pixar.com
Web Site: http://www.pixar.com
Dr. Ed Catmull, President
John A. Lasseter, Chief Creative Officer
Produces animated features. Subsidiary of Walt Disney Corp., Walt Disney Studios.

PLAYBOY ENTERTAINMENT GROUP INC.
2706 Media Center Dr
Los Angeles, CA 90065
Phone: 323-276-4000
Fax: 323-276-4500
Web Site: http://www.playboyenterprises.com
Hugh M. Hefner, Editor-in-Chief & Chief Creative Officer
Scott N. Flanders, Chief Executive Officer
Scott Stephen, Executive Vice President, Print/Digital Group
Lorna Donohoe, Senior Vice President, Global Strategic Marketing
Gary Rosenson, Senior Vice President & General Manager, Domestic TV Unit
Develops, produces, acquires & distributes a wide range of high-quality lifestyle & adult programming for domestic & international TV networks.

PLAYHOUSE PICTURES
Wellington
New Zealand

Phones: 64-4-389-4788; 64-21-646-796
E-mail: toby@playhousepictures.com
Web Site: http://www.playhousepictures.com
Produces stop motion animation, music videos, documentaries & short films.

PLAY-IT PRODUCTIONS
259 W 30th St
3rd Fl
New York, NY 10001
Phones: 212-695-6530; 800-815-3444
Fax: 212-695-4304
E-mail: info@play-itproductions.net
Web Site: http://www.play-itproductions.net
Tony Tyler, President
Provides CD & cassette production services; CD-ROM production, authoring & consultation from I-200 CD-ROM or audio CD's overnight. Other services include mastering, replication, duplication, graphic design & printing.

POINT OF VIEW PRODUCTIONS
2477 Folsom St
San Francisco, CA 94110
Phone: 415-821-0435
Fax: 415-821-0434
E-mail: karil@karildaniels.com
Web Site: http://www.karildaniels.com
Karil Daniels, President
Cinematography, videography, photography, script supervision and other production services for corporate programs, commercials, TV shows, feature films.

POTOMAC TELEVISION INC.
1133 19th St SW
Ste 814
Washington, DC 20036
Phones: 202-783-8000; 202-898-8233
Fax: 202-783-1861
Web Site: http://www.potomactv.com
Steve Greenaway, General Manager & Director, Engineering
Kristin Volk, Field Producer & Reporter
Provides video & film production, customized news service, satellite uplink & distribution services.

PRESBYTERIAN CHURCH (U.S.A.)
100 Witherspoon St
Louisville, KY 40202-1396
Phones: 502-569-5000; 888-728-7228
Fax: 502-569-8005
E-mail: presbytel@pcusa.org
Web Site: http://www.pcusa.org
Robert W. Maggs, Jr., President & Chief Executive Officer
Francis E. Maloney, Executive Vice President & Chief Operating Officer
Karen Babik, Communications, Public Relations & Marketing

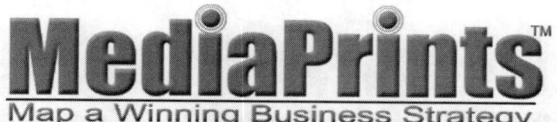

PRODUCTION STUDIO INC.
4930 Illinois Rd
Ste 1-F
Ft Wayne, IN 46804
Phone: 260-432-3601
Fax: 260-436-4800
E-mail: info@productionstudio.com
Web Site: http://www.productionstudio.com
Mark Douglas Fry, Financial Officer
Full service corporate communications company; provides video-film-multimedia beta-sp, 1 in., 0-2 formats, soft image non-linear editing, complete conference planning & design, remote taping, complete post production, graphics & animation.

PROGRAM EXCHANGE
299 W Houston St
New York, NY 10014
Phone: 212-859-1100
Fax: 212-859-1150
E-mail: info@programexchange.com
Web Site: http://www.programexchange.com
Supplies barter TV, sitcoms and children's animated & live programming.

PROMARK TELEVISION INC.
323 S Doheny Dr
Ste 308
Los Angeles, CA 90048
Phones: 760-322-7776; 800-266-6662
Fax: 760-322-5149
E-mail: promarktv@promarktv.com
Web Site: http://www.promarktv.com
David Levine, Founder
TV syndication & national sales.

PSSI GLOBAL SERVICES
7030 Hayvenhurst Ave
Van Nuys, CA 91406
Phones: 310-575-4400; 800-728-5465
Fax: 310-575-4451
E-mail: rlamb@pssiglobal.com
Web Site: http://www.pssiglobal.com

Branch Offices:
LAS VEGAS: 4415 Wagon Tr Ave, Las Vegas, NV 89118. Phone: 702-798-0101. Fax: 702-895-7484. Brian Nelles, Senior Vice President; Joe Kittrell, Vice President, Broadcast Marketing.
PSSI-Strategic Television is a full-service transmission company combining 30 years of operational, project-management, remote production and engineering know-how including a fleet of 27 C- and Ku-band satellite uplink trucks, transportable HD fiber-encoding packages, 3-D mixing, internet streaming, portable flyaway uplinks, downlinks, insert studios, teleport capabilities, distribution from Hawaii & Puerto Rico and communication systems.

PUBLIC MEDIA HOME VISION — No
longer in business.

PYRAMID MEDIA
PO Box 1048
Santa Monica, CA 90406
Phones: 310-828-6149; 800-421-2304
Fax: 310-398-7869
E-mail: info@pyramidmedia.com
Web Site: http://www.pyramidmedia.com
Distributes short films & videotapes, supplies stock footage & licenses programs to cable & pay TV.

QUARTET INTERNATIONAL INC.
20 Butternut Dr
Pearl River, NY 10965
Phone: 845-735-8700

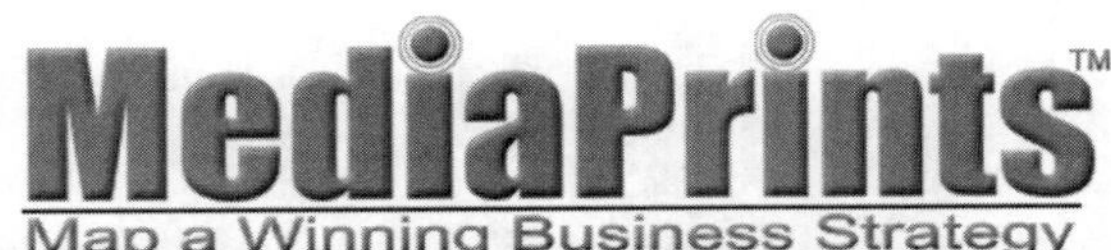
MediaPrints™
Map a Winning Business Strategy
Digital Cable and TV Coverage Maps.
Visit www.warren-news.com/mediaprints.htm

Fax: 845-735-8999
E-mail: tvshowbizz@aol.com
Web Site: http://www.tvshowbiz.com
Harvey Chertok, President
Barbara A. Chertok, Vice President
Produces & distributes films, TV film & tape series; exports films, buys films & imports films & TV film series; TV rights.

RALEIGH STUDIOS
5300 Melrose Ave
Hollywood, CA 90038
Phone: 323-960-3456
E-mail: info@raleighstudios.com
Web Site: http://www.raleighstudios.com
Michael Moore, President
Karin Darrow, Executive Director, Leasing
Jim Fox, Director, Facilities
Yolanda Montellano, Manager, Client Services

Branch Offices:
BATON ROUGE: 10000 Mayfair Dr, Baton Rouge, LA 70809. Phone: 323-960-3456.

MANHATTAN BEACH: 1600 Rosencrans Ave, Manhattan Beach, CA 90266. Phones: 310-727-2700; 310-727-2710. Dana Bromley, Director, Marketing & Client Relations.

PLAYA VISTA: 5600 Campus Ctr Dr, Playa Vista, CA 90266. Phone: 323-960-3456. Willi Schmidt, Vice President, Studio Operations.
Leases film & TV facilities; provides grip & electrical services & post production facilities including screening rooms.

RAYCOM SPORTS INC.
One Julian Price Pl
Charlotte, NC 28208
Phone: 704-378-4400
Fax: 704-378-4465
E-mail: khaines@raycomsports.com
Web Site: http://www.raycomsports.com
Ken Haines, President & Chief Executive Officer
George Johnson, Senior Vice President
Jim Ford, Vice President, Sales
Wyatt Hicks, Vice President, Marketing & ACC Properties
Jimmy Rayborn, Vice President, Operations & Executive Producer
Peter Rolfe, Vice President, Production
Colin Smith, Vice President, Syndication & New Media
Syndicates, distributes & markets national & regional TV events with an emphasis on sporting events.

RCTV INTERNATIONAL
4380 NW 128th St
Miami, FL 33054
Phone: 305-688-7475
Fax: 305-685-5697
E-mail: info@rctvintl.com
Web Site: http://www.rctvintl.com
Daniela Bergami, Chief Executive Officer
Guadalupe D'Agostino, Vice President & General Manager
Jorge Fernandez, Vice President, Finance & Administration
Marc Paneque, Director, International Sales
Amina Galdo, Director, Marketing & Public Relations
Haydee Pabon, Director, International Sales
Markets telenovelas, miniseries, movies, children"s programming, series, documentaries & concerts to the international TV market.

RED RYDER ENTERPRISES INC.
1111 N Westshore Blvd
Ste 604
Tampa, FL 33607
Phone: 813-837-8773
Leases & licenses literary properties.

REEL MEDIA INTERNATIONAL
7000 Independence Pkwy
Ste 160-7
Plano, TX 75025
Phone: 214-521-3301
Fax: 214-522-3448
E-mail: reelmedia@aol.com
Web Site: http://www.reelmediainternational.com
Distributes motion pictures, TV series & specials, including action & adventure films, science-fiction, animation, family, drama, sports & music concerts worldwide.

REELTIME DISTRIBUTING CORP.
353 W 48th St
New York, NY 10036
Phone: 212-582-5380
Produces & distributes R-rated films for theater & video; sound recording.

REMBRANDT FILMS
34 Cross Pond Rd
Pound Ridge, NY 10576
Phones: 914-763-5817; 888-205-8778
E-mail: info@rembrandtfilms.com
Web Site: http://www.rembrandtfilms.com
Adam Snyder, Owner
Provides animation, video production, & business writing through Rembrandt Communications, Rembrandt Films Animation & Rembrandt Video Productions.

RENEGADE
10950 Gilroy Rd
Ste J
Hunt Valley, MD 21031
Phone: 410-667-1400
Fax: 410-667-1482
E-mail: info@getrenegade.com
Web Site: http://www.getrenegade.com
Timothy J. Watkins, President & Chief Executive Officer
Jennifer Leo Stine, Executive Vice President & Chief Operating Officer
Chris Beutler, Vice President, Production & Executive Director, Creative
Robert Taylor, Chief Strategy Officer
Katrina Bartos, Director, Account Services
Noah Thomason, Director, Production
Terri Howard, Office Manager
Full-service advertising agency & production facility; supplies services to cable operators & programmers, including TV & radio spots, web and interactive campaigns, consumer direct mail & marketing, direct sales & customer service training videos and courses.

RHODES PRODUCTIONS
3812 Sepulveda Blvd
Ste 310
Torrance, CA 90505
Phone: 310-791-9933
TV syndication.

RKO PICTURES
1875 Century Park E
Ste 2140
Los Angeles, CA 90067
Phone: 310-277-0707
Fax: 310-226-2490
E-mail: info@rko.com
Web Site: http://www.rko.com
Ted Hartley, Chairman & Chief Executive Officer
Dina Merrill, Vice Chairman
Andrew Matthews, President
Vanessa Coifman, Executive Vice President, Production & Development
Kevin Cornish, Vice President, Development

Branch Offices:
NEW YORK: 750 Lexington Ave, Ste 2200, New York, NY 10022. Phone: 212-644-0600. Fax: 212-644-0384.
Provides multimedia programming, TV & motion picture production, operating entertainment centers & foreign rights sales/acquisitions.

ROBERT KEESHAN ASSOCIATES INC.
c/o MagiKbox LLC
38 Park Ave
Old Greenwich, CT 06870
Phone: 203-422-6111
Fax: 203-422-6116
E-mail: mkeeshan@magikbox.com
Michael Keeshan, Primary Contact
Produced the children's TV show, Captain Kangaroo.

PETER RODGERS ORGANIZATION
6513 Hollywood Blvd
Ste 201
Hollywood, CA 90028
Phone: 323-962-1778
Fax: 323-962-7174
E-mail: info@profilms.com
Web Site: http://www.profilms.com
Stephen M. Rodgers, Chief Executive Officer
Ron Adler, Director, Operations
Distributes TV films & programs worldwide; provides consulting services; representatives.

ROKU CHANNEL STORE
12980 Saratoga Ave
Ste D
Saratoga, CA 95070
Phone: 888-600-7658
Fax: 408-446-1734
E-mail: brian@roku.com
Web Site: http://www.roku.com
Anthony Wood, Founder & Chief Executive Officer
David Krall, President & Chief Operating Officer
Jim Funk, Vice President, Business Development
Mark Goodwin, Vice President, Engineering
Charles Seiber, Vice President, Marketing
James Wong, Vice President, Operations
Ann Hoover, Director, Finance & Operations
Package of video services accessible through digital video player. Offers original programming, sports, video and photo sharing plus music.

ROLAND COMPANY INC.
1202 Bishopsgate Way
Reston, VA 20194
Phone: 703-450-6272
Fax: 703-444-3141
David Roland, President
Provides TV production & publishing services.

ROOSTER POST
40 Spadini Ave
Suite 301
Toronto, ON M5V 2H8
Canada
Phone: 416-977-2401
Fax: 416-977-4910
E-mail: melissa@rooster.ca
Web Site: http://www.rooster.ca
Melissa Kahn, Executive Producer
Provides complete service in editorial, visual design & effects for TV advertising.

ROBERT ROSENHEIM ASSOCIATES
Five Gay St
Sharon, CT 06069
Phone: 860-364-0050
Fax: 860-364-5577
Web Site: http://www.rrallc.com
Robert Rosenheim, President
Classic feature films & older TV series.

JACK ROURKE PRODUCTIONS
PO Box 1705
Burbank, CA 91507
Phone: 818-843-4839
Fax: 818-566-6500
Jack Rourke, President
Produces industrial & educational films, TV film & tape series, spot commercials & live/filmed shows.

RW PRODUCTIONS INC.
2630 Fountainview
Ste 218
Houston, TX 77057
Phones: 713-522-4701; 800-874-2745
Fax: 713-522-0426
E-mail: info@rwvideo.com
Web Site: http://www.rwvideo.com
Bob Willems, Owner
Produces film, video & TV programs; provides motion pictures DVD authoring & CD authoring.

SABAN ENTERTAINMENT — See listing for Walt Disney Studios.

SCENIC CABLE NETWORK & PRODUCTION
PO Box 5678
416 N Oates St
Dothan, AL 36303
Phone: 334-793-2722
Fax: 334-793-4171
E-mail: scenic@sceniccable.com
Web Site: http://www.sceniccable.com
Terry Duffie, President & General Manager
Mit Kirkland, Vice President, Operations
Angela DeLoney, Manager, National Regional Sales
Kim Gantt Martin, Manager, General Sales
Bobby Price, Manager, Systems
Provides cable TV advertising & video production services.

LOU SCHEIMER PRODUCTIONS
20300 Ventura Blvd
Ste 330
Woodland Hills, CA 91364
Phone: 818-884-2810
Fax: 818-884-1824
E-mail: lou@louscheimerproductions.org
Web Site: http://www.louscheimerproductions.org

Lou Scheimer, President
Amy Meyers, Vice President, Development
Animation studio for TV series, feature films, specials & video.

SCOTT & CO. — No longer in business.

SCTN TELEPRODUCTIONS
1900 S Michigan Ave
Ste 3
Chicago, IL 60616
Phone: 312-674-1900
Fax: 312-674-1915
Full-service video production, 30' X 30' studio, CATV programming, infomercials, commercials & industrials.

SEALS COMMUNICATIONS CORP.
3340 Peachtree Rd NE
Ste 1800
Atlanta, GA 30326
Phone: 404-222-6400
E-mail: info@sealsco.com
Web Site: http://www.sealsco.com
E. Lamar Seals, III, Chairman & Chief Executive Officer
John W. Bonner Jr., Co-Chairman
Produces programming; subjects include outdoors, motorsports, health & fitness, music, extreme & action sports, & a wide variety of youth, college & professional sporting events.

SEAR SOUND
353 W 48th St
Studio A
New York, NY 10036
Phone: 212-582-5380
Fax: 212-581-2731
E-mail: waltersear@aol.com
Web Site: http://www.searsound.com
Walter E. Sear, President & Owner
Roberta Findlay, Manager
Chris Allen, Chief Engineer
David Schoenwetter, Assistant Engineer
Forty-eight-track sound recording, digital mastering to CD, audio for video post-production; audio digital editing.

SEPTEMBER PRODUCTIONS
15 Madaket Rd
Nantucket, MA 02554
Phone: 508-228-8073
Fax: 508-228-3853
E-mail: info@september.com
Web Site: http://www.september.com
Sonta Giamber, Executive Producer
Jay Anderson, Midwest Contact
Michael Eha, East Coast Contact
Patricia O'Hara, West Coast Contact
Produces 35mm TV commercials.

SESAME WORKSHOP
One Lincoln Pl
New York, NY 10023
Phone: 212-595-3457
E-mail: press@sesameworkshop.org
Web Site: http://www.sesameworkshop.org
Gary E. Knell, President & Chief Executive Officer
H. Melvin Ming, Chief Operating Officer
Daryl Mintz, Chief Financial Officer
Myung Kang-Huneke, Chief of Staff
Dr. Lewis Bernstein, Executive Vice President, Education, & Research
Terry Fitzpatrick, Executive Vice President, Content Distribution
Susan Kolar, Executive Vice President & Chief Administrative Officer
Sherri Rollins Westin, Executive Vice President & Chief Marketing Officer
Jeanette Betancourt, Senior Vice President, Outreach & Educational Practices
Charlotte Frances Cole, Senior Vice President, Global Education
Anita Stewart, Senior Vice President, Corporate Partnerships
Produces & distributes entertaining & educational programming for children.

SEVEN NETWORK LTD.
PO Box 777
38-42 Pirrama Rd
Pyrmont, NSW 2009
Australia
Phone: 61-02-8777-7777
Fax: 61-02-8777-7181
E-mail: sewood@seven.com.au
Web Site: http://www.sevencorporate.com.au
David Leckie, Chief Executive Officer
Warren Walter Coatsworth, Secretary
Lisa Fitzpatrick, Director, Program Development
Dan Meenan, Director, Factual Programming
Graeme Hill, Manager, Sydney Programming & Communications
Brad Lyons, Manager, Melbourne Programming & Communications
Sonya Wilkes, Executive Producer

Branch Offices:
EPPING: Production Ctr, Mobbs Lane, Epping, NSW 2121, Australia. Phone: 61-02-8777-7777.

SYDNEY: News Central, 52 Martin Pl, Sydney, NSW 2000, Australia. Phone: 61-02-8777-7777.

SYDNEY: Registries Ltd., 207 Kent St, Level 7, Sydney, NSW 2000, Australia. Phone: 61-02-9290-9600.
Australian media company.

SEVENTH-DAY ADVENTIST CHURCH, COMMUNICATIONS DEPARTMENT
12501 Old Columbia Pike
Silver Spring, MD 20904-6600
Phone: 301-680-6300
Fax: 301-680-6312
Web Site: http://www.adventist.org/world_church/communication
Andre Brink, Director, Media Services
Garrett Caldwell, Director, Public Relations
Ansel Oliver, Assistant Director, Adventist News Network
Bryan Collick, Assistant Director, Web Manager
Elizabeth Lechleitner, Editorial Coordinator
Provides media production services; coordinates activities on the Adventist News Network.

SFM ENTERTAINMENT
1180 Ave of the Americas
Ste 2010
New York, NY 10036
Phone: 212-398-4496
Fax: 212-398-5738
E-mail: sfm@sfment.com
Web Site: http://www.sfment.com
Stanley Moger, President & Chief Executive Officer
Michael H. Maizes, Senior Vice President, In-House Counsel & Chief Financial Officer
Creates, sells & distributes programming for syndication.

SHOWCASE PRODUCTIONS INC.
Long Island City Art Ctr
44-02 23rd St-Studio 407
Long Island City, NY 11101
Phone: 212-599-9500

Fax: 212-599-6040
E-mail: alexjr@pipeline.com
Web Site: http://www.producersshowcase.org
Owns or co-owns with NBC more than 800 1950s long format kinescope-preserved programs, all with major stars, directors & writers, from such series as Producers' Showcase, Alcoa/Goodyear, Pontiac Playwrights '56, Kraft, Lux, Robert Montgomery Presents & Hallmark. Related companies own 400 feature films and more than 2,000 hours of 1960s talk radio.

SHOWPLACE TELEVISION SYNDICATION
3023 N Clark St
Ste 890
Chicago, IL 60657-5261
Phone: 773-935-1572
Fax: 206-984-4179
E-mail: sales@showplaceonline.com
Web Site: http://www.showplaceonline.com
Hal Pontious, President
Daren Gaskill, Program Director
Domestic distributor & syndicator. Broadcasting division specializes in sales development, new media, program consulting, research, & database engineering for groups, networks and cable.

62ND STREET PRODUCTIONS
2055 Boar Tusk Rd NE
Conyers, GA 30012-3801
Phone: 770-918-8163
E-mail: steve@compro-atl.com
Web Site: http://www.compro-atl.com
Kim A. Anderson, President
Nels A. Anderson, Director
Steve Brinson, Producer
Produces TV commercials; directors specialize in tabletop, fashion, cars, food, dialogue, humor, time lapse, kids, special effects & music videos.

SKOTLESKI PRODUCTIONS
1001 N Broad St
Ste A
Lansdale, PA 19446
Phones: 215-362-5880; 800-677-8433
Fax: 215-362-5881
E-mail: skotleski@skotleski.com
Web Site: http://www.skotleski.com
Ron Skotleski, President
Provides video production for international, regional & local broadcast & CATV advertising; provides creative strategy development & consulting services.

SKY ANGEL US LLC
1300 Goodlette Rd N
Naples, FL 34102
Phone: 239-963-3200
E-mail: customerrelations@skyangel.com
Web Site: http://www.skyangel.com
Rob Johnson, Chief Executive Officer
Tom Scott, President & Chief Operating Officer
Brian Collins, Executive Vice President, Programming & Media Sales

Branch Offices:
Network Operation Center: 4922 La Collina Way, Ooltewah, TN 37363. Phone: 423-396-8176. Fax: 423-396-8002. E-Mail: master.control@skyangel.com. Web site: http://www.skyangeltech.com.
Two services offered to subscribers: (1) traditional TV service available in the U.S. with over 80 Christian and family-oriented television and radio channels; (2) Web TV service offered worldwide with more than 35 Christian television and radio channels viewed on personal computer.

SOMAT PUBLISHING LTD.
250 W 57th
New York, NY 10107
Phone: 212-586-0660
Produces music.

SONY BMG MUSIC ENTERTAINMENT
550 Madison Ave
New York, NY 10022-3211
Phone: 212-833-8000
Fax: 212-833-4818
Web Site: http://www.sonymusic.com
Andrew Lack, Chairman
Rolf Schmidt-Holtz, Chief Executive Officer
Tim Bowen, Chief Operating Officer
Kevin Kelleher, Executive Vice President & Chief Financial Officer
Music record label.

SONY PICTURES TELEVISION
10202 W Washington Blvd
Culver City, CA 90232
Phone: 310-244-4000
Fax: 310-244-2004
E-mail: spt_webmaster@spe.sony.com
Web Site: http://www.sonypicturestelevision.com
Steve Mosco, President
Andy Kaplan, President, Networks
John Weiser, President, Distribution
Eric Berger, Executive Vice President, Digital Networks
Lucia Cettone, Senior Vice President, Development & Current Programming, Networks
Mark Rodrigue, Vice President, US Cable Sales
Produces & distributes TV film/tape series & film programs on order.

SPANISH BROADCASTING SYSTEM (SBS)
2601 South Bayshore Drive PH2
Coconut Grove, FL 33133
Phone: 305-441-6901
Fax: 305-446-5148
E-mail: idavidson@sbscorporate.com
Web Site: http://www.spanishbroadcasting.com
The largest publicly traded Hispanic-controlled media and entertainment company in the United States. Owns and operates Mega TV, a television operation serving the south Florida market with national distribution through DirectTV.

SPANISH TELEVISION SERVICES INC.
8655 SW 74th Terr

Miami, FL 33143
Phone: 305-596-3140
Fax: 305-596-3198
Hector R. Llorens
International distributor for Ch. 9, Telearte Buenos Aires, Argentina.

SPELLING ENTERTAINMENT — No longer in business.

SPORTS LEGENDS INC./BERL ROTFELD PRODUCTIONS INC. — No longer in business.

MARTY STOUFFER PRODUCTIONS LTD.
15820 Euclid Ave
Chino, CA 91708
Phones: 970-925-5536; 888-925-5536
Fax: 970-920-3820
E-mail: customerservice@wildamerica.com
Web Site: http://www.wildamerica.com
Marty Stouffer, President
Produces film programs; wildlife & natural history subjects.

THE STUDIOS AT PARAMOUNT
5555 Melrose Ave
Los Angeles, CA 90038
Phone: 323-956-5000
Web Site: http://www.paramountstudios.com
Randall Baumberger, President
TV & motion picture studio; provides art, production & post-production services. Division of Paramount Pictures Corp.

SUDBORO PRODUCTIONS — No longer in business.

SUNBOW PRODUCTIONS — No longer in business.

SUNRISE MEDIA LLC
155 W 46th St
2nd Fl
New York, NY 10036
Phone: 212-221-6310
Fax: 212-302-1854
E-mail: info@sunrisemedia.tv
Web Site: http://www.sunrisemedia.tv
Alvin H. Perlmutter, President
Joseph Schroeder, Production Coordinator
Lisa Zbar, Senior Producer & Healthcare Related Production
Morton Silverstein, Special Assignment Producer/Writer
Lorne Lieb, Producer/Administration
Elizabeth Benson, Business Administration
Produces programming for cable, commercial & public TV; home video production; corporate films & medical series. TV, film archives & production.

SWAIN FILM & VIDEO INC.
1404 S Tuttle Ave
Sarasota, FL 34239
Phone: 941-365-8433
Fax: 941-365-5359
E-mail: tony@swainmedia.com
Web Site: http://www.swainmedia.com
Tony Swain, President
Mike Swain, Vice President
Richard Ramsdell, Creative Editor
Offers full service production & post-production facilities in digital video & BetaSP formats; non-linear post-production video for educational & industrial programming, documentaries & commercials; specializes in corporate image video productions; provides sales, marketing & training videos; end products include VHS, CD & DVD as well as video for websites.

ALLEN SWIFT INC. — No longer in business.

TEACHING LEARNING NETWORK — No longer in business.

TECHNICOLOR INC./CFI
4050 Lankershim
North Hollywood, CA 91604
Phones: 818-754-5054; 818-505-2821
Fax: 818-761-4835
Web Site: http://www.technicolor.com
Provides lab services for filmmakers & commercial producers.

TECHNISONIC STUDIOS INC.
500 S Ewing St
Ste G
St Louis, MO 63103
Phone: 314-533-1777
Fax: 314-533-6527
Web Site: http://www.technisonic.tv
Mike Stroot, President
Brad Shelton, Vice President & General Manager
Nancy Aden, Office Manager
Cindy Ogle, Manager, Finance & Accounting
Full service audio, video & film facility; specializes in commercial, industrial & corporate production.

TEL-A-CAST GROUP — No longer in business.

TELECOM PRODUCTIONS
30 Perimeter Park Dr
Ste 101
Atlanta, GA 30341
Phones: 770-455-3569; 800-525-3051
Fax: 770-455-3938
E-mail: budd@tcpatlanta.com
Web Site: http://www.tcpatlanta.com
Budd O. Libby, President
Sales promotion company; creator of Let's Go to the Races.

TELEFILM CANADA
360 Saint Jacques St
Ste 500
Montreal, PQ H2Y 1P5
Canada
Phones: 514-283-6363; 800-567-0890
Fax: 514-283-8212
E-mail: info@telefilm.gc.ca
Web Site: http://www.telefilm.gc.ca
Wayne Clarkson, Executive Director

Branch Offices:
BRITISH COLUMBIA: 609 Granville St, Ste 410, Vancouver, BC V7Y 1G5, Canada. Phones: 604-666-1566; 800-663-7771. Fax: 604-666-7754.

NOVA SCOTIA: 1717 Barrington St, 4th Fl, Halifax, NS B3J 2A4, Canada. Phones: 902-426-8425; 800-565-1773. Fax: 902-426-4445.

ONTARIO: 474 Bathurst St, Ste 100, Toronto, ON M5T 2S6, Canada. Phones: 416-973-4607; 800-463-4607. Fax: 416-973-8606.
Federal cultural agency dedicated to the development & promotion of the Canadian audiovisual industry. Provides financial support to the private sector to create Canadian productions that appeal to domestic & international audiences. The Corporation also administers the funding programs of the Canadian Television Fund.

TELEGENIC PROGRAMS INC.
161 Forest Hill Rd
Toronto, ON M5P 2N3
Canada
Phone: 416-484-8000
Fax: 416-484-8001
H. Lawrence Fein, President & Chief Executive Officer
TV program distribution company.

TELEMUNDO NETWORK GROUP
2290 W Eighth Ave
Hialeah, FL 33010
Phone: 305-884-8200
Fax: 305-889-7980
Web Site: http://www.telemundo.com
Jackie Hernandez, Chief Operating Officer
Peter Blacker, Executive Vice President, Digital Media & Emerging Business
Johanna Guerra, Senior Vice President, News
Jorge Hidalgo, Senior Vice President, Sports
Mike Rodriguez, Senior Vice President, Sales

Branch Offices:
FLORIDA: International Program Sales, 2745 de Leon Blvd, Coral Gables, FL 33134. Phone: 305-774-0033. E-Mail: marcus.santana@nbcuni.com. Marcos Santana, President, Telemundo International.

NEW YORK: National Advertising Sales, 30 Rockefeller Plz, New York, NY 10112. Phone: 212-664-7417. E-Mail: michael.rodriguez@nbcuni.com. Michael Rodriguez, Executive Vice President, Multimedia Development & Distribution; Steve Mandala, Senior Vice President, Sales.
Produces, distributes & imports Spanish-language programming worldwide.

TELEPICTURES PRODUCTIONS
4000 Warner Blvd
Burbank, CA 21522
Phone: 818-972-7073
Web Site: http://www.telepicturestv.com
Estey McLoughlin, President
Develops & produces reality & reality-based programming for the first-run syndication marketplace.

TELEVISION REPRESENTATIVES INC.
9720 Wilshire Blvd
Ste 202
Beverly Hills, CA 90212
Phone: 310-278-4050
TV syndication consultant; home video.

THE TELEVISION SYNDICATION CO. INC.
1520 Sabal Lake Dr.
Ste 105
Longwood, FL 32779
Phone: 407-788-6407
Fax: 407-788-4397
E-mail: tvsco@prodigy.net
Web Site: http://www.tvsco.com
Cassie M. Yde, President
Full-service syndication & distribution organization; provides new product from independent producers to TV, home video & educational outlets worldwide; services include cash & barter market-by-market syndication in the US; cash distribution abroad; acquisition of programs from domestic & international sources; licenses merchandise associated with its programs & co-production of TV series.

THIRD WAY MEDIA
1251 Virginia Ave
Harrisonburg, VA 22802
Phones: 540-434-6701; 800-999-3534
Fax: 540-434-5556
E-mail: info@thirdwaymedia.org
Web Site: http://www.thirdwaymedia.org
Sheri Hartzler, Interim Co-Director & Program Manager
Lowell Hertzler, Interim Co-Director & Business Manager
Lois Hertzler, Coordinator, Marketing/Customer Service
Melodie Davis, Writer/Producer
Wayne Gehman, Media Producer/Photographer
Kimberly Metzler, Finance Assistant & Customer Service
Produces public service spots & video magazine show. Division of Mennonite Mission Network.

THIRTEEN/WNET
450 W 33rd St
New York, NY 10001
Phones: 212-560-1313; 973-643-3315
Fax: 212-560-1314
E-mail: programming@thirteen.org
Web Site: http://www.thirteen.org
Neal Shapiro, President & Chief Executive Officer
Produces & broadcasts public TV.

THOMSON REUTERS CORP.
Three Times Sq
New York, NY 10036
Phone: 646-223-4000
E-mail: general.info@thomsonreuters.com
Web Site: http://thomsonreuters.com
David Thomson, Chairman
Thomas H. Glocer, Chief Executive Officer
Gustav Carlson, Executive Vice President & Chief Marketing Officer
Robert D. Daleo, Executive Vice President & Chief Financial Officer
Stephen Dando, Executive Vice President & Chief Human Resources Officer
Deirdre Stanley, Executive Vice President & General Counsel
(Formerly Reuters Group PLC.) Provides intelligent information for businesses & professionals in the media industry, as well as in financial, legal, tax & accounting, scientific & healthcare markets.

THREE THOUSAND EIGHT
3008 Ross Ave
Dallas, TX 75204
Phone: 214-922-9232
Fax: 214-922-8861
E-mail: ken@3008.com

Web Site: http://www.3008.com
Ken Skaggs, President & Partner
Brent Herrington, Partner & Editor
Soozy Martin, Executive Producer
Provides post production services; specializes in high-end creative editorial.

TM STUDIOS

2002 Academy Ln
Ste 110
Dallas, TX 75234-9220
Phone: 972-406-6800
Fax: 972-406-6890
E-mail: info@tmstudios.com
Web Site: http://www.tmstudios.com
Chris Long, Vice President & General Manager
Marcus Hill, Vice President, Operations
John Kuykendall, Vice President, Facilities
Chris Stevens, Domestic Product Sales
Provides custom & syndicated image packages & production libraries for TV. A Triton Co.

TODAY VIDEO

555 W 57th S
Ste 1420
New York, NY 10019
Phone: 212-307-0707
E-mail: todayvideo@aol.com
Web Site: http://www.todayvideo.com
David Seeger, Chief Executive Officer
Video & film boutique; provides creative solutions for all production & post-production needs, from concept to completion.

TOP KOPY

12 Skyline Dr
Hawthorne, NY 10532
Phone: 914-345-2650
Fax: 914-345-2617
E-mail: info@topkopy.com
Web Site: http://www.topkopy.com
Provides video duplication services for D2, D3, Digital Betacam, DV, one inch, Betacam (SP), MII, U-Matic (SP), VHS, S-VHS, HI-8, 8mm & Betamax formats.

TOUCHSTONE PICTURES/ WALT DISNEY

500 S Buena Vista St
Burbank, CA 91521
Phone: 818-560-1000
Fax: 818-972-5402
Web Site: http://www.touchstonepictures.com
Produces & distributes motion picture films.

TOUCHSTONE TELEVISION — See listing for ABC Studios.

TRACO ADVERTISING INC. — No longer in business.

TRANS WORLD INTERNATIONAL — See listing for IMG World.

TRAVELVIEW INTERNATIONAL

2000 Dairy Ashford
Ste 390
Houston, TX 77077
Phone: 281-679-7619
Fax: 281-679-7658
Web Site: http://www.travelview.com
Darrell Turner, President & Editor-in-Chief
Jim Coulter, Senior Director & Cameraman
Jane Marie Turner, Editorial Director
Michele Blackwell-Moore, Accounting/Office Manager
Marcia Turner, Orders/Shipment/Fulfullment
Produces & distributes travel TV & video programs of destinations, hotels & attractions.

TRIANGLE INC.

420 Pearl St
Malden, MA 02148
Phone: 781-388-4349
Fax: 781-322-0410
E-mail: acarbone@triangle-inc.com
Web Site: http://www.ablevision.org
Ralph Rivkind, President
Michael A. Rodrigues, Chief Executive Officer
Thomas L. Marshall, Chief Operating Officer
Rebecca Beal, Chief Development Officer
Alisa Carbone, Media Producer
Produces Ablevision, a scripted, shot & hosted TV program created and produced entirely by people with disabilities.

TRIBECA FILM CENTER

375 Greenwich St
New York, NY 10013
Phone: 212-941-4000
Fax: 212-941-2012
E-mail: contactus@tribecafilm.com
Web Site: http://www.tribecafilm.com
Robert De Niro, Co-Founder
Jane Rosenthal, Co-Founder
Produces film & tape spot commercials; film handlers.

TRIBUNE ENTERTAINMENT CO. — No longer in business.

TRIBUNE MEDIA SERVICES INC.

435 N Michigan Ave
Ste 1500
Chicago, IL 60611
Phones: 312-222-4444; 800-245-6536
Fax: 312-222-2581
E-mail: info@tms.tribune.com
Web Site: http://www.tms.tribune.com
David D. Williams, President & Chief Executive Officer
Jay Fehnel, Senior Vice President & Chief Operating Officer, Entertainment Products
John Zelenka, Senior Vice President, Business Development & News and Features
Mike Gart, Vice President & Chief Financial Officer
Alexa Bazanos, Vice President, Human Resources
Walter F. Mahoney, Vice President, General Information Services
Stephen P. Tippie, Vice President, Marketing & Licensing

Branch Offices:

ARLINGTON: 2201 N Collins, Ste 210, Arlington, TX 76011. Phone: 817-795-4416. Fax: 817-795-4758.

GLENDALE: 1720 W Florist Ave, Ste 150, Glendale, WI 53209. Phone: 414-352-8700. Fax: 414-352-5694.

LOS ANGELES: 202 W First St, Los Angeles, CA 90012. Phone: 213-237-2140.

QUEENSBURY: 40 Media Dr, Queensbury, NY 12804. Phones: 518-792-4414; 800-833-9581. Fax: 518-792-4414.

JORDAN: Oasis 1 Bldg, A1 - Wakalat St, Office 109, Sweifyah, Jordan. Phone: 962-79-553-9024. Fax: 962-65-824-890.

HONG KONG: 12/F 30 Canton Rd, Unit 1207, Tsim Sha Tsui, Kowloon. Phone: 852-2375-9975. Fax: 852-2865-3238.

THE NETHERLANDS: Orlyplein 10, 25th Fl, Amsterdam 1043 DP, The Netherlands. Phone: 31-0-20-680-2560. Fax: 31-0-20-680-2589.

UNITED KINGDOM: Jupiter House, 14 Finsbury Sq, Triton Ct, Atrium Unit, London EC2A 1BR, United Kingdom. Phone: 44-207-588-7588. Fax: 44-207-638-3011.
Creates, aggregates & distributes news, information & entertainment content that reaches users in print, online & on-screen. Subsidiary of The Tribune Co.

TRIMARK TELEVISION — See listing for Lions Gate Entertainment.

TRISTAR TELEVISION — See listing for Sony Pictures Television.

TROMA ENTERTAINMENT INC.

36-40 11th St
Long Island City, NY 11106
Phone: 718-319-0110
Fax: 718-391-0255
E-mail: internationalsales@troma.com
Web Site: http://www.troma.com
Lloyd Kaufman, President
Independently produces, distributes & syndicates feature films to theatrical & ancillary markets worldwide.

TURNER BROADCASTING SYSTEM INC.

One CNN Ctr
Atlanta, GA 30303
Phone: 404-827-1700
Web Site: http://www.turner.com
Philip I. Kent, Chairman & Chief Executive Officer
David Levy, President, Sales, Distribution & Sports
Scott Teissler, Chief Technical Officer & Chief Digital Technical Strategist
Jack Wakshlag, Chief Research Officer
Jeff Gregor, Execuitve Vice President & Chief Marketing Officer
Walker Jacobs, Executive Vice President, Turner/SI Digital Ad Sales
John E. Kampfe, Executive Vice President & Chief Financial Officer
Jim McCaffrey, Executive Vice President, Operations & Strategy & Chief Strategy Officer
Louise Sams, Executive Vice President & General Counsel
Molly Battin, Senior Vice President, Turner Media Group
Deborah K Bradley, Senior Vice President, Program Acquisitions
Andrea Ching, Senior Vice President, Turner/SI Digital Marketing & Promotions
Jennifer Dorian, Senior Vice President, Strategy Development, Young Adults & Kids Media Group
David Hudson, Senior Vice President, Late Night & Specials
Creates & programs branded news, entertainment, animation & young adult media environments on TV & other platforms.

TVO

PO Box 200
Station Q
Toronto, ON M4T 2T1
Canada
Phones: 416-484-2600; 800-613-0513
E-mail: asktvo@tvo.org
Web Site: http://www.tvontario.org
Lisa de Wilde, Chief Executive Officer
Rob Crocker, Chief Financial Officer
Todd Slivinskas, Chief Technology Officer
Jill Javet, Vice President, Corporate Relations
Erika Kramer, Vice President, Distribution Services
Nancy Chapelle, Managing Director, Content & Programming
Sarah Irwin, Managing Director, Independent Learning Center
Produces & distributes educational TV programming.

TWENTIETH CENTURY FOX FILM CORP.

PO Box 900
Beverly Hills, CA 90213
Phone: 310-277-2211
Fax: 310-203-1558
Web Site: http://www.foxmovies.com
Chris Petri Kin, Senior Vice President, Corporate Communications
Finances, develops, produces, distributes & markets motion pictures, TV & home entertainment programming worldwide.

TWENTIETH CENTURY FOX HOME ENTERTAINMENT

PO Box 900
Beverly Hills, CA 90213-0900
Phone: 877-369-7867
Web Site: http://www.foxconnect.com
Markets, sells & distributes film & TV programming on VHS & DVD.

TWENTIETH CENTURY FOX TELEVISION

10201 W Pico Blvd
Bldg 103, Room 5286
Los Angeles, CA 90064
Phone: 310-369-1000
Fax: 310-369-8726
Web Site: http://www.fox.com
Gary Newman, Chairman
Dana Walden, Chairman
Supplies primetime network & cable series.

TWENTIETH TELEVISION

2121 Ave of the Stars
17th Fl
Los Angeles, CA 90067
Phone: 310-369-1000
Fax: 310-369-3899
Web Site: http://www.fox.com
Greg Meidel, President
Les Eisner, Vice President, Media Relations
Produces & distributes a wide array of first-run & off-network programming, as well as feature film packages.

UNITED CHURCH OF CHRIST, OFFICE OF COMMUNICATIONS

700 Prospect Ave
Cleveland, OH 44115-1100
Phone: 216-736-2173
Fax: 216-736-2223
E-mail: guessb@ucc.org
Web Site: http://www.ucc.org/media-justice
Rev. J. Bennett Guess, Executive Director

MediaPrints™
Map a Winning Business Strategy
Digital Cable and TV Coverage Maps.
Visit www.warren-news.com/mediaprints.htm

Cheryl Leanza, Director, Policy
Barb Powell, Director, Administration
Public relations, news, video, broadcast, radio & media advocacy.

UNITED FILM ENTERPRISES INC.
120 W Park Ave
Ste 309
Long Beach, NY 11561-3301
Phone: 516-431-2687
Fax: 516-431-2805
Nathan Podhorzer, President
Exports & imports films; film buyer; sales representative; producers' representative & purchasing agent for foreign distribution companies.

UNITED LEARNING — See listing for Discovery Education.

UNITED METHODIST COMMUNICATIONS
PO Box 320
Nashville, TN 37202-0320
Phone: 615-742-5400
Fax: 615-742-5423
E-mail: umcom@umcom.org
Web Site: http://www.umcom.org
Fran Coode, Strategic Project Coordinator, UMTV
Produces UMTV & a bi-monthly podcast as well as videos, audio & DVDs.

UNITED NATIONS — See listing for UN Multimedia.

UNITED PRESS INTERNATIONAL
1133 19th St NW
Washington, DC 20036
Phone: 202-898-8000
Fax: 202-898-8048
E-mail: ussales@upi.com
Web Site: http://www.upi.com
Dr. Chung Hwan Kwak, Chairman
Nicholas Chiaia, President
John Hendel, Executive Editor
Marc Oram, General Counsel
Ed Field, Director, Licensing

Branch Offices:
CHILE: Nataniel Cox 47, Piso 9, Santiago, Chile. Phone: 56-2-6570874. Fax: 56-2-6986605. E-Mail: jmolina@upi.com. Juan Molina.

HONG KONG: Wui Tat Centre 18/F, 55 Connaught Rd W, Hong Kong. Phone: 852-2858-2774. Fax: 852-2858-2775.

JAPAN: AH 1 Bldg, 1-9-14 Azabudai, 8th Fl, Minato-ku, Tokyo 106-0041, Japan. Phone: 81-3-3586-2370. Fax: 81-3-3586-2373.

KOREA: 605 Yonhap News Agency Bldg, 85-1 Susong-dong, Chongro-gu, Seoul, Korea. Phone: 82-2-398-3654. Fax: 82-2-737-3654.

LEBANON: Gefinor Ctr, Bloc D, 3rd Fl, Ste 302, Clemenceau, Beirut, Lebanon. Phone: 961-1-745971. Fax: 961-1-745973. E-Mail: mideastsales@upi.com. Rabin Saade.

Provides critical information to media outlets, businesses, governments & researchers worldwide; licenses content directly to print outlets, online media & institutions of all types.

UNIVERSAL MUSIC PUBLISHING GROUP (UMPG)
2100 Colorado Ave
Santa Monica, CA 90404
Phone: 310-235-4700
Fax: 310-235-4900
E-mail: umpg.newmedia@umusic.com
Web Site: http://www.umusicpub.com
David Renzer, Chairman & Chief Executive Officer
Michael J. Sammis, Executive Vice President & Chief Financial Officer
Publishes music; offices worldwide.

UNIVERSAL SPORTS
2900 W Olympic Blvd
Ste 210
Santa Monica, CA 90404
Phone: 310-667-9203
E-mail: info@universalsports.com
Web Site: http://www.universalsports.com
Claude Ruibal, Co-Founder & Chairman
Thomas C Hipkins, Co-Founder
David Sternberg, Chief Executive Officer
Perkins Miller, Chief Operating Officer
Carlos Silva, President
Bo LaMotte, Senior Vice President, Affiliate Relations
T. K. Gore, Director, Marketing & Communications

UNIVERSAL TELEVISION — See listing for NBC News.

UNIVERSITY OF SOUTHERN CALIFORNIA: HUGH M. HEFNER MOVING IMAGE ARCHIVE
School of Cinematic Arts
University Park, NCT 100
Los Angeles, CA 90089-2211
Phone: 213-740-3182
Fax: 213-740-2920
E-mail: filmrequest@cinema.usc.edu
Web Site: http://cinema.usc.edu/about/research-resources/hefner/
Dino Everett, Archivist
An archive for research & study by students & scholars; licenses of USC-produced materials.

UNIVISION STUDIOS
9405 NW 41st St
Miami, FL 33178-2301
Phone: 305-471-3900
Fax: 305-471-4065
Web Site: http://www.univision.com
Luis Fernandez, President
German Perez Nahim, Vice President
Univision Studios produces and co-produces reality shows, dramatic series and other programming formats for Univision Communications' platforms.

UN MULTIMEDIA
Rm S-805A
New York, NY 10017
Phones: 212-963-6953; 212-963-6939
Fax: 212-963-6869
Web Site: http://www.unmultimedia.org
Produces documentaries & TV series; provides live daily feeds.

UNUSUAL FILMS
c/o Bob Jones University
1700 Wade Hampton Blvd
Greenville, SC 29614
Phone: 864-242-5100
Fax: 864-242-5917
E-mail: films@bju.edu
Web Site: http://www.bju.edu
Tim Rogers, Director
Produces & distributes motion picture features & shorts, industrial, educational, religious & foreign language films, animation, TV film series & theatrical shorts.

UPA PRODUCTIONS OF AMERICA
8640 Wilshire Blvd
Beverly Hills, CA 90211
Phone: 310-659-6004
Fax: 310-659-4599
Produces & distributes TV programs, animated programs & feature films to cable, syndication, videocassette & foreign markets; produces industrial films & TV commercials; character licensing & merchandising.

U.S. DEPARTMENT OF AGRICULTURE, OFFICE OF COMMUNICATIONS
Broadcast Media & Technology Ctr
1400 Independence Ave SW, Room 1618-S
Washington, DC 20250-1300
Phone: 202-720-6072
Fax: 202-720-5773
E-mail: david.black@usda.gov
Web Site: http://www.usda.gov
David Black, Center Director
Jordan Alexander, Resource Manager
Anthony Bouldin, Manager, Multimedia
Garth Clark, Manager, Production
Patrick O'Leary, Manager, TV Feature
Larry Holmes, Facility Engineer
Provides full-service digital production facilities to all agencies within the USDA & other federal agencies.

U.S. DIGITAL TELEVISION INC. — No longer in business.

UTV
Ormeau Rd
Belfast BT7 1EB
Northern Ireland
Phone: 44-28-9032-8122
Fax: 44-28-9024-6695
E-mail: info@u.tv
Web Site: http://www.utvplc.com
John McCann, Group Chief Executive
Jim Downey, Group Commercial Director
Provides programming for UK & Ireland.

VALENTINO INC.
7750 Sunset Blvd
Los Angeles, CA 90046
Phones: 310-201-0015; 800-223-6278
Fax: 310-201-0126
E-mail: info@tvmusic.com
Web Site: http://www.tvmusic.com
Production music & sound effects library; subsidiary of Bug Music.

VARSITY MEDIA GROUP INC.
8601 RR 2222
Bldg 3, Ste 120
Austin, TX 78730
Phone: 512-527-2500
Fax: 512-527-2599
E-mail: info@varsitymediagroup.com
Web Site: http://www.varsityworld.com
John Andrews, President & Chief Operating Officer
Provides programming featuring sports series, reality shows, dramas, comedies, music shows, animation & films.

VENARD FILMS LTFD./FARM FILM FOUNDATION — No longer in business.

VENEVISION INTERNATIONAL INC.
121 Alhambra Plz
Ste 1400
Coral Gables, FL 33134
Phone: 305-442-3411
Fax: 305-448-4762
Web Site: http://www.venevisioninternational.com

Branch Offices:
BRAZIL: Jose Hernandez, 2197 BP, Buenos Aires CP 1426, Brazil. Phone: 54-11-4784-0454. Fax: 54-11-4782-5140.

SPAIN: C/Montalban, 5-3 Izq, Madrid 28014, Spain. Phone: 34-91-521-4103. Fax: 34-91-531-1417.

VENEZUELA: Final Ave La Salle, Edf Antarajo, Colina de los Caobos, Caracas DF 1050, Venezuela. Phone: 58-212-708-9164. Fax: 58-212-782-3464.
Produces & distributes Spanish film & TV programming; provides production services.

VERITAS PRODUCTIONS INC.
One Laurie Dr
Englewood Cliffs, NJ 07632
Phone: 201-765-4240
Richard S. Dubelman, Owner
Produces motion pictures, TV commercials & movies; studio rental.

VERTIGO PRODUCTIONS
1678 Lance Point Dr
Maumee, OH 43537
Phone: 416-891-2191
Fax: 416-891-2130
E-mail: contact@vertigocd.com
Web Site: http://www.vertigocd.com
Provides replication services for CD-ROMS, audio CDs & DVDs.

VIACOM INC.
1515 Broadway
New York, NY 10036
Phone: 212-258-6000
Web Site: http://www.viacom.com
Philippe Dauman, President & Chief Executive Officer
Thomas Dooley, Chief Operating Officer & Chief Financial Officer
Carl Folta, Executive Vice President, Corporate Communications
Michael D. Fricklas, Executive Vice President, General Counsel & Secretary
DeDe Lea, Executive Vice President, Government Affairs
Develops, produces & distributes entertainment content.

VICTORY STUDIOS
2247 15th Ave W
Seattle, WA 98119
Phones: 206-282-1776; 888-282-1776
Fax: 206-282-3535
E-mail: info@victorystudios.com
Web Site: http://www.victorystudios.com
Conrad W. Denke, Chief Executive Officer & Owner

Kevin Smith, Senior Vice President
Scott Thomas, Chief Engineer

Branch Offices:
NORTH HOLLYWOOD: 10911 Riverside Dr, Ste 100, North Hollywood, CA 91602. Phone: 818-769-1776. Fax: 818-760-1280. E-Mail: info@victorystudiosla.com.
Full service production & post-production company; Internet and remote productions; HD & SD cameras & editing, studios, full audio services, graphics, color correction, DVD authoring & full video transfers, compression and duplication

VIDEO-CINEMA FILMS INC.
510 E 86th St
Apt 12C
New York, NY 10028
Phone: 212-734-1632
Distributes & licenses motion picture features for TV & video media.

VIDEO ENTERPRISES INC.
575 29th St
Manhattan Beach, CA 90266
Phone: 310-796-5555
Fax: 310-546-2921
E-mail: heidi@videoenterprisesinc.com
Web Site: http://www.videoenterprisesinc.com

Branch Offices:
NEW YORK:. Phone: 914-234-3725. Fax: 914-234-3725. E-Mail: jody@videoenterprisesinc.com.
Provides promotional TV spots & prizes for game, talk, variety & sports shows.

VIDEO EXPRESS PRODUCTIONS
2B Normandy Sq Ct
Silver Spring, MD 20906
Phone: 301-598-6096
Fax: 301-598-6211
E-mail: info@videoexpresspro.com
Web Site: http://www.videoexpresspro.com
Julie Bargeski, President

Branch Offices:
ALEXANDRIA: 1044 N Royal, Alexandria, VA 22314. Phone: 703-836-7626.

MIDDLETOWN: Nine Groff Ct, Middletown, MD 21769. Phone: 301-371-9150.
Provides video production & produces programming.

VIDEO/FASHION NETWORK
611 Broadway
Ste 307
New York, NY 10012
Phone: 212-274-1600
Fax: 212-219-1969
E-mail: info@videofashion.com
Web Site: http://www.videofashion.com
Marlene Cardin, Executive Producer
Produces & distributes fashion, beauty & lifestyle programming for all media markets.

VIDEO ORDNANCE INC.
611 Broadway
Ste 307
New York, NY 10012
Phones: 212-334-3939; 800-377-7773
Fax: 212-219-1969
E-mail: info@videoordnance.com
Web Site: http://www.videoordnance.com
Produces & distributes documentaries concerning aerospace & military technology.

VIDEOWORKS — No longer in business.

VISION DESIGN TELEPRODUCTIONS
555 Broadcast Dr
Mobile, AL 36606
Phone: 251-479-5555
Fax: 251-473-8130
E-mail: tv5@wkrg.com

VISTA STREET ENTERTAINMENT
8700 Venice Blvd
Los Angeles, CA 90034
Phone: 310-280-1184
E-mail: vistastreet@sbcglobal.net
Web Site: http://www.vistastreet.com
Produces cult, horror, witchcraft & action movies.

WADE PRODUCTIONS INC.
493 High Cliffe Ln
Tarrytown, NY 10591
Phone: 914-524-9111
Provides corporate communication production services; meetings, events, entertainment, computer graphic slides, trade shows & training.

WALLACH ENTERTAINMENT
1400 Braeridge Dr
Beverly Hills, CA 90210
Phone: 310-278-4574
Provides sports TV production & sports entertainment management.

WALT DISNEY FEATURE ANIMATION
500 S Buena Vista St
Burbank, CA 91521
Phone: 818-560-1000
Fax: 818-560-1930
Ed Catmull, President
Produces & distributes animated feature films.

WALT DISNEY PICTURES
500 S Buena Vista St
Burbank, CA 91521
Phone: 818-560-5151
Web Site: http://disney.go.com/disneypictures
Oren Aviv, Production President
Produces & distributes motion picture films.

WALT DISNEY STUDIOS
500 S Buena Vista St
Burbank, CA 91521
Phone: 818-560-5151
Web Site: http://studioservice.go.com
Rich Ross, Chairman
Produces & acquires live-action, animated motion pictures, direct-to-DVD & Blu-ray programming, musical recording & live stage plays.

JAY WARD PRODUCTIONS INC. — No longer in business.

WARNER BROS. ANIMATION INC.
15301 Ventura Blvd
Ste 1200
Sherman Oaks, CA 91403
Phone: 818-977-8490
Web Site: http://www.warnerbros.com
Peter Roth, President
Sam Register, Executive Vice President, Creative Affairs
Produces animation TV film/tape series, TV commercials & motion picture cartoon shorts.

WARNER BROS. DOMESTIC CABLE DISTRIBUTION — See listing for Warner Bros. Domestic Television Distribution.

WARNER BROS. DOMESTIC TELEVISION DISTRIBUTION
4000 Warner Blvd
Burbank, CA 91522-1184
Phone: 818-954-6000
Web Site: http://www.warnerbros.com
Ken Werner, President
Andy Lewis, Executive Vice President & General Manager
Gus Lucas, Executive Vice President, Strategic Sales & Planning
Distributes programming to the first-run & off-net syndication marketplaces.

WARNER BROS. INTERNATIONAL TELEVISION DISTRIBUTION
4000 Warner Blvd
Burbank, CA 91522
Phone: 818-954-6000
Fax: 212-954-7667
Web Site: http://www.wbitv.com
Jeffrey Schesinger, President
Malcom Dudley-Smith, Executive Vice President, Sales & Business Development
Andrew Shipps, Senior Vice President, Marketing
Licenses & distributes feature films, TV, programs & animation to the international TV marketplace.

WARNER BROS. PICTURES
4000 Warner Blvd
Burbank, CA 91522
Phone: 818-956-6000
Jeff Robinov, President, Warner Bros. Pictures Group
Kevin McCormick, President, Production
Sue Kroll, President, Worldwide Marketing
Steve Papazian, President, Worldwide Physical Production
Steven Spira, President, Worldwide Business Affairs
Produces & distributes feature films.

WARNER BROS. PICTURES DOMESTIC DISTRIBUTION
4000 Warner Blvd
Burbank, CA 91522
Phone: 818-954-6000
Dan Fellman, President
Distributes theatrical first-run features, classic films, TV product & cartoons to non-theatrical markets; distributes classic films to the domestic theatrical market; sets the release schedule & all exhibition operations.

WARNER BROS. PICTURES INTERNATIONAL
4000 Warner Blvd
Burbank, CA 91522
Phone: 818-954-6222
Fax: 818-954-6488
Veronika Kwan-Rubinek, President, International Distribution
Sue Kroll, President, Worldwide Marketing
David Williamson, Senior Vice President, Finance
Angelina Speare, Executive Vice President, Operations & Finance
Distributes & markets feature films to the overseas marketplace.

WARNER BROS. TELEVISION GROUP
4000 Warner Blvd
Burbank, CA 91522-1703
Phone: 818-954-6000
Fax: 212-954-7667
Web Site: http://www2.warnerbros.com/web/television
Peter Roth, President
Produces primetime series, telefilms & miniseries programming.

WARNER HOME VIDEO
4000 Warner Blvd
Burbank, CA 91522-0001
Phones: 818-954-6000; 866-373-4389
Fax: 818-954-6480
Web Site: http://www.warnervideo.com
Ronald Sanders, President
David Hettler, Executive Vice President, Worldwide Finance & Infomation Technology
Mark Horak, President, North America Operations
Jeffrey Calman, Executive Vice President
Jeff Baker, Senior Vice President, U.S. Sales
Releases & distributes current & library feature films; distributes TV series, direct-to-video hits & special interest lines.

WARNER INDEPENDENT PICTURES
4000 Warner Blvd
Burbank, CA 91522
Phone: 818-954-6000
Fax: 212-954-7667
Web Site: http://wip.warnerbros.com
Polly Cohen, President
Laura Kim, Executive Vice President, Marketing & Publicity
Produces & acquires smaller-budgeted films than those of its parent studio.

WEATHERNEWS INC.
Akabane Bridge Bldg
Tokyo Minato-ku 3-1-14
Tokyo 105-0014
Japan
Phone: 81-43-274-5550
E-mail: internetsales@wni.com
Web Site: http://www.weathernews.com
Chihito Kusabiraki, President

Branch Offices:
NORMAN: Weathernews Americas Inc., 350 David L Boren Blvd, Ste 1000, Norman, OK 73072. Phone: 405-310-2800. Fax: 405-310-2804.
Provides weather forecasts, software & programming (including Internet service) to the broadcast industry, offices worldwide.

EVAN WEINER PRODUCTIONS
370 Claremont Ave
Mount Vernon, NY 10552
Phones: 914-667-9070; 800-965-3347
Fax: 914-667-3043
E-mail: evan4256@aol.com
Evan Weiner, Executive Producer
Produces cable TV & TV station sports talk shows.

WESTERN INSTRUCTIONAL TELEVISION INC.
1438 N Gower St
No. 18
Los Angeles, CA 90028
Phone: 323-466-8601
Fax: 323-466-8895
Donna Matson, President
Produces & distributes educational video programs (lease or purchase); pre-recorded videotapes for in-school use; instructional TV lessons in art, sciences, language arts, social studies & music on videocassettes.

WESTERN INTERNATIONAL SYNDICATION
12100 Wilshire Blvd
Ste 1050
Los Angeles, CA 90025
Phone: 310-820-8485
Fax: 310-820-8376
Web Site: http://www.wistelevision.com
Syndicates & distributes comedy, specials, TV series & sports programming.

WESTON WOODS STUDIOS INC.
143 Main St.
Norwalk, CT 06851-3709
Phones: 203-845-0197; 800-243-5020
Fax: 203-845-0498
Web Site: http://teacher.scholastic.com/products/westonwoods
Linda Lee, Vice President & General Manager
Paul Gagne, Production Director
Kim Hayes-Grimm, Associate Business Manager
Melanie Bishop, Operations Coordinator
Produces & distributes audio/visual materials & videocassettes based on children's books; distributes educational films & motion picture shorts; exports & imports children's films & video programs.

WEST SIDE FILMS/INTERACTIVE — No longer in business.

WGBH INTERNATIONAL — See listing for PBS International.

WORLD CLASS VIDEO
623 Wood Lot Tr
Annapolis, MD 21401
Phone: 410-224-0204
Fax: 410-224-0203
E-mail: bryan@worldclassvideo.com
Web Site: http://www.worldclassvideo.com
Bryan Mong, Founder, Director & Cameraman
Leslie Mong, Manager, Production
David Brillhart, Producer & Editor
Rick Lewis, Producer & Director
TV production company; specializes in HD & in high-end film style video production of magazine features, documentaries & corporate communications; served news organizations, syndicated magazine shows, major broadcast & cable networks, corporations & agencies worldwide.

WORLDVIEW ENTERTAINMENT INC. — No longer in business.

WORLDWIDE ENTERTAINMENT CORP.
135 S McCarty Dr
Ste 101
Beverly Hills, CA 90212
Phone: 310-858-1272
Fax: 310-858-3774
E-mail: jackhh@pacbell.net
Jack H. Harris, President & Owner
Judith Parker Harris, Vice President
Production, distribution, syndication, importation & exportation of theatrical feature films.

WORLD WRESTLING ENTERTAINMENT INC.
1241 E Main St
Stamford, CT 06902
Phone: 203-352-8600
Web Site: http://www.wwe.com
Vincent K. McMahon, Chairman & Chief Executive Officer
George Barrios, Chief Financial Officer
Michelle D. Wilson, Chief Marketing Officer
Kevin Dunn, Executive Vice President, TV Production
Brian Kalinowski, Executive Vice President, Digital Media
John Laurinaitis, Executive Vice President, Talent Relations
Michael Luisi, Executive Vice President, Business Development, General Counsel & Secretary
Stephanie McMahon, Executive Vice President, Creative Development & Operations
Mike Pavone, Executive Vice President, WWE Studios
Andrew Whitaker, Executive Vice President, International
Jim Connelly, Senior Vice President, Consumer Products

Branch Offices:
LOS ANGELES: Digital Sales, 12424 Wilshire Blvd, Ste 1400, Los Angeles, CA 90025. Phone: 310-481-9370.

NEW YORK: 780 Third Ave, Rm 1101, New York, NY 10017. Phone: 212-593-2228.

STAMFORD: TV Production Office, 120 Hamilton Ave, Stamford, CT 06902. Phone: 203-353-2900.

CANADA: Two Lansing Sq, Ste 1003, Willowdale, ON M2J 4PA, Canada. Phone: 418-497-8338.

CHINA: 18F Bund ctr, 22 Yarian Dong Rd, Shanghai 200002, China. Phone: 86-21-6132-3857.

JAPAN: Dongenzaka Imani Bldg 3F, 1-19-12 Gogenzaka, Shibya-ku, Tokyo 150-0043, Japan. Phone: 81-3-5456-6050.

SINGAPORE: Ubi Techpark, 10 Ubi Crescent #04-78 408564, Singapore. Phone: 65-6747-5651.

UNITED KINGDOM: Five Jubilee Pl, London 5W3 3TD, United Kingdom. Phone: 44-0-20-7349-1740.
Produces & distributes sports entertainment events & programs.

WPA FILM LIBRARY
16101 S 108th Ave
Orland Park, IL 60467
Phones: 708-873-3113; 800-777-2223
Fax: 708-460-0187
E-mail: sales@wpafilmlibrary.com
Web Site: http://www.wpafilmlibrary.com
Stock footage library, film archive.

WQED MULTIMEDIA
Content/Product Sales & Client Services
4802 Fifth Ave
Pittsburgh, PA 15213
Phone: 412-622-1300
Fax: 412-622-1488
E-mail: wqed@wqed.org
Web Site: http://www.wqed.org
Deborah L. Acklin, President-elect & Chief Executive Officer
Provides motion picture & TV development services, including set construction, stock footage library, facility rental, studio & sound stage production facilities, post production & teleconference facilities.

WRS MOTION PICTURE & VIDEO LABORATORY
213 Tech Rd
Pittsburgh, PA 15205
Phone: 412-922-1200
Fax: 412-922-1200
E-mail: jackn@wrslabs.com
Web Site: http://www.wrslabs.com
Laboratory facilities & services, editing, processing & recording facilities, videotape-to-film & film-to-tape duplication and Macrovision anti-piracy process.

WTTW LOCAL PRODUCTIONS
5400 N St Louis Ave
Chicago, IL 60625
Phone: 773-583-5000
Web Site: http://www.wttw.com
Creates & distributes local programming. Division of Window to the World Communications Inc.

WTTW NATIONAL PRODUCTIONS
5400 N St Louis Ave
Chicago, IL 60625
Phone: 773-583-5000
Web Site: http://www.wttw.com
Parke Richeson, Senior Vice President & Executive in Charge
Produces original programming for public & commercial TV broadcasting. Division of Window to the World Inc.

Brokerage & Financing

DAVID ABRAHAM & CO. LLC
265 Post Rd W
Westport, CT 06880
Phone: 203-222-1919
E-mail: dabraham@daccapital.com
Web Site: http://www.daccapital.com
David Abraham, President
Provides private-market investment banking for media & communications; equity & debt private placements, merger & acquisition brokerage and financial advisory services.

ALLIED CAPITAL CORP.
1919 Pennsylvania Ave NW
Washington, DC 20006-3434
Phone: 202-721-6100
Fax: 202-721-6101
E-mail: IRARCC@aresmgmt.com
Web Site: http://www.alliedcapital.com
William L. Walton, Chairman & Chief Executive Officer
Joan M. Sweeney, Chief Operating Officer
Penni F. Roll, Chief Financial Officer
Scott S. Binder, Managing Director
Shelley Huchel, Director, Investor Relations

Branch Offices:
CHICAGO: 401 N Michigan Ave, Ste 3310, Chicago, IL 60611. Phone: 312-846-5100. Fax: 312-846-5101.

LOS ANGELES: 11111 Santa Monica Blvd, Ste 2100, Los Angeles, CA 90025. Phone: 310-689-2800. Fax: 310-689-2801.

NEW YORK: 520 Madison Ave, 27th Fl, New York, NY 10022. Phone: 212-822-7800. Fax: 212-822-7801.
Specializes in providing financing to small- & medium-sized growing businesses; finances businesses nationwide in a variety of industries; focuses on three areas of finance: mezzanine finance, small business loans & commercial real estate finance.

ALTA COMMUNICATIONS
100 Federal St
30th Fl
Boston, MA 02116-5021
Phone: 617-262-7770
Fax: 617-262-9779
E-mail: info@altacomm.com
Web Site: http://www.altacomm.com
Timothy L. Dibble, Managing General Partner
Brian W. McNeill, Managing General Partner
Jessica Barry Reed, Vice President
Phillip Dudley, Vice President
Provides debt & equity financing to the media & telecommunications industries.

AUS CONSULTANTS
155 Gaither Dr
Ste A
Mt Laurel, NJ 08054
Phones: 856-234-9200; 800-925-4287
Fax: 856-234-8371
E-mail: aus@ausinc.com
Web Site: http://www.ausinc.com
John L. Ringwood, Chairman & Chief Executive Officer

Branch Offices:
CAMP HILL: 275 Grandview Ave, Ste 100, Camp Hill, PA 17011. Phone: 717-763-9890. Fax: 717-763-9931.

GREENFIELD: 8555 W Forest Ave, Ste 201, Greenfield, WI 53228. Phone: 414-529-5755. Fax: 414-529-5750.
Provides financial consulting services to the CATV industry; expert witness & testimony for presentations to regulatory agencies; valuation & survey research consulting.

AXA FINANCIAL INC.
1290 Ave of the Americas
8th Fl
New York, NY 10104
Phone: 212-554-1234
Web Site: http://www.axaonline.com
Provides wealth protection, asset management & financial planning strategies to individuals & businesses.

BALBOA CAPITAL
2010 Main St
11th Fl
Irvine, CA 92614
Phones: 949-756-0800; 888-225-2621
Fax: 949-756-2565
E-mail: info@balboacapital.com
Web Site: http://www.balboacapital.com
Phil Silva, President
Patrick Ontal, Vice President, Sales
Susan Hooten, Manager, Regional Sales
Matt Lawler, Manager, Sales Support
Tonald Uzzo, Manager, Sales

Branch Offices:
NEW HOLLAND: 912 Main St, Ste 206, New Holland, PA 17557. Phone: 888-915-0900.

SAN FRANCISCO: 601 Montgomery St, Ste 1800, San Francisco, CA 94111. Phone: 800-950-7650.

SCOTTSDALE: 14350 N 87th St, Ste 290, Scottsdale, AZ 85260-2662. Phone: 800-280-5624.
Provides equipment leasing & financing on audio/video, broadcast, computer & other capital equipment.

BANK OF AMERICA
333 S Hope St
13th Fl
Los Angeles, CA 90071
Phone: 213-621-7382
Fax: 213-621-3608
Web Site: http://www.bankofamerica.com
Provides commercial & investment banking services for entertainment & media industries.

BNY MELLON, MEDIA & TECHNOLOGY DIVISION
One Wall St
New York, NY 10286
Phone: 212-495-1784
Web Site: http://www.bnymellon.com
Robert P. Kelly, Chairman & Chief Executive Officer
Gerald L. Hassell, President

Branch Offices:
UNITED KINGDOM: One Canada Sq, London E14 5AL, United Kingdom. Phone: 44-20-7570-1784.
Provides financing for media companies.

BARCLAYS CAPITAL
Five The North Colonnade
Canary Wharf
London E14 4BB
United Kingdom
Phone: 44-0-20-7623-2323
E-mail: corporate.communications@barclayscapital.com
Web Site: http://www.barcap.com
Iain Abrahams, Managing Director, Risk, Liquidity & Private Equity
Gerald A. Donini, Managing Director & Head of Equities
Guglielmo Satori de Borgoricco, Managing Director & Head of Distribution

Branch Offices:
ATLANTA: 3344 Peachtree Rd, Ste 950, Atlanta, GA 30326. Phone: 404-262-4800.

BOSTON: 125 High St, Boston, MA 02110. Phone: 617-330-5800.

CHICAGO: 190 S LaSalle St, Chicago, IL 60603. Phone: 312-609-7200.

DALLAS: 200 Crescent Ct, Ste 400, Dallas, TX 75201. Phone: 214-720-9470.

HOUSTON: Fullbright Tower, 1301 McKinney St, Ste 400, Houston, TX 77010. Phone: 713-401-6800. Fax: 713-401-6752.

LOS ANGELES: 10250 Constellation Blvd, 24th Fl, Los Angeles, CA 90067. Phone: 310-481-2600.

MENLO PARK: 155 Linfield Dr, Menlo Park, CA 94025. Phone: 650-289-6000. Fax: 650-321-2207.

MIAMI: 1111 Brickell Ave, 12th Fl, Miami, FL 33131. Phone: 305-789-8700.

NEW YORK: 200 Park Ave, New York, NY 10166. Phone: 212-412-4000. Fax: 212-412-7300.

PORTLAND: 1001 SW Fifth Ave, Ste 1100, Portland, OR 97204. Phone: 503-535-8062. Fax: 503-535-0714.

SAN FRANCISCO: 555 California St, 30th Fl, San Francisco, CA 94104. Phone: 415-274-3300.

SANTA MONICA: Water Garden Bldg, 1620 26th St, Santa Monica, CA 90404. Phone: 310-907-0510.

SEATTLE: 701 Fifth Ave, Ste 7101, Seattle, WA 98104. Phone: 206-344-5870. Fax: 206-233-2817.

WASHINGTON, DC: 1501 K St NW, Ste 500, Washington, DC 20005. Phone: 202-452-4700.
Provides telecommunications & communications capital marketing & lending.

BARGER BROADCAST BROKERAGE LTD.
8023 Vantage Dr
Ste 840
San Antonio, TX 78230
Phone: 210-340-7080
Fax: 210-341-1777
E-mail: jwbarger@sbcglobal.net
John Barger, President
Provides broadcast brokerage services, appraisals & management consulting; manages San Antonio radio stations: KAHL & KMFR.

BARKER CAPITAL LLC
10 Rockefeller Plz
Ste 910
New York, NY 10020
Phone: 212-332-4318
Fax: 212-332-4315
Web Site: http://www.barkercapital.com
Jacob J. Barker, Founding Partner
Robert B. Crossland III, Managing Director
Sara B. Gochberg, Managing Director
Dale E. Norton, Managing Director & Chief Financial Officer
Timothy P. Olson, Managing Director & General Counsel
Brings specialized investment banking services to underserved media companies with a focus on the broadcasting, publishing, & outdoor advertising sectors; manages an investment fund that provides senior capital to small- to medium-sized media companies & entrepreneurs.

BIA CAPITAL STRATEGIES LLC
15120 Enterprise Ct
Ste 100
Chantilly, VA 20151
Phone: 703-818-8115
Fax: 703-803-3299
E-mail: cwiebe@bia.com
Web Site: http://www.biacapital.com
Thomas J. Buono, Managing Director
Gregg E. Johnson, Managing Director
Lloyd R. Sams, Managing Director
Charles A. Wiebe, Managing Director
Mike Andres, Managing Director

Assists companies in the communications industry to establish strategic, financial & operating objectives and arrange equity, mezzanine & senior debt financing for acquisition & expansion opportunities. Provides clients financial advice, merger/acquisition consulting & access to capital.

BIA DIGITAL PARTNERSHIP LP
15120 Enterprise Ct
Ste 200
Chantilly, VA 20151
Phone: 703-227-9600
Web Site: http://www.biadigitalpartners.com
Lloyd R. Sams, Managing Principal
Gregg E. Johnson, Managing Principal
Provides cost-effective junior capital to growing middle-market companies in the media, entertainment, telecommunications, information & business services sectors.

THE BIA KELSEY GROUP
15120 Enterprise Ct
Ste 100
Chantilly, VA 20151
Phones: 703-818-2425; 800-331-5086
Fax: 703-803-3299
E-mail: info@biakelsey.com
Web Site: http://www.bia.com
Tom J. Buono, Founder & Chief Executive Officerr
Neal Polachek, President
Mark A. Giannini, Chief Operating Officer & Senior Vice President
Rick Ducey, Chief Strategy Officer
Mark Fratrik, Vice President
Bobbi Loy-Luster, Vice President & Senior Analyst
Steve Passwaiter, Vice President, Business Development
Geoff Price, Vice President
Formerly BIA Financial Network LLC. Provides financial intelligence & investment resources to the media, telecommunications, technical & related industries; provides valuation & financial/strategic advisory services; publishes financial reports, yearbooks & pocket guides on the TV industry. Division of BIA Advisory Services.

BLACKBURN & CO. INC.
201 N Union St
Ste 340
Alexandria, VA 22314-2642
Phone: 703-519-3703
Fax: 703-519-9756
E-mail: jimblackburn@msn.com
James W. Blackburn, Jr., Chairman & Chief Executive Officer
Provides brokerage services to TV & radio station owners.

BMO CAPITAL MARKETS, MEDIA & COMMUNICATIONS GROUP
One First Canadian Pl
100 King St W
Toronto, ON M5X 1H3
Canada
Phones: 416-286-9992; 877-225-5266
Web Site: http://www.bmocm.com
Thomas V. Milroy, Chief Executive Officer
Eric C. Tripp, President
Dr. Robert S. Levine, Vice President
Darryl White, Executive Managing Director & Co-Head
Ashi Mathur, Co-Head
Kevin J. Malone, Managing Director

Branch Offices:
NEW YORK: Business Services & Media Group, Three Times Sq, New York, NY 10036. Sandra Andrews, Vice President; Susan Wolford, Managing Director & Group Head.
Formerly BMO Financial Group. Offers comprehensive capital raising and M&A capabilities; provides investors with industry leading equity research, sales & trading for the media, communications & technology sectors.

BOND & PECARO INC.
1920 N St NW
Ste 350
Washington, DC 20036
Phone: 202-775-8870
Fax: 202-775-0175
E-mail: bp@bondpecaro.com
Web Site: http://www.bondpecaro.com
James R. Bond, Jr., Principal
Timothy S. Pecaro, Principal
Jeffrey P. Anderson, Principal
Peter R. Geyer, Principal
John S. Sanders, Principal
Matthew H. Lochte, Principal
Andrew R. Gefen, Principal
Provides financial & management consulting services; specializes in asset appraisals, fair market valuations, expert testimony, impairment testing, feasibility studies, financial consulting, market research & related financial services for broadcasting, cable television, Internet, technology & other media; publishes The Television Industry: A Market-by-Market Review with the NAB.

BOSTON VENTURES MANAGEMENT INC.
125 High St
17th Fl
Boston, MA 02110-2003
Phone: 617-350-1500
Fax: 617-350-1509
E-mail: info@bvlp.com
Web Site: http://www.bostonventures.com
Barry J. Baker, Managing Director & Operating Partner
Gerald S. Hobbs, Managing Director & Operating Partner

Branch Offices:
NEW YORK: 919 Third Ave, Ste 620, New York, NY 10021. Phone: 212-593-0095. Fax: 212-593-0094.
Provides equity & related capital for acquisitions, buyouts & expansions in TV, radio, cable, publishing, outdoor advertising, music and other communications & entertainment industries.

BOWMAN VALUATION SERVICES LLC
706 Duke Street
3rd Fl
Alexandria, VA 22314
Phone: 703-549-5681
Fax: 703-549-5682
E-mail: info@bowmanvaluation.com
Web Site: http://www.bowmanvaluation.com
Peter Bowman, Principal
Chip Snyder, Principal
Provides business valuation & appraisal services for the broadcasting & communications industry.

FRANK BOYLE & CO. LLC
2874 W Main St
2nd Fl
Stratford, CT 06614
Phone: 203-377-3030
Fax: 203-386-9250
E-mail: fboylebrkr@aol.com
Web Site: http://www.flboyle.com
Frank Boyle, President
Provides media brokerage & appraisals for the radio & TV industries.

BREAN MURRAY, CARRET & CO. LLC
570 Lexington Ave
New York, NY 10022-6895
Phone: 212-702-6500
Fax: 212-702-6649
Web Site: http://www.breanmurraycarret.com

Branch Offices:
CHICAGO: 225 W Washington St, 22nd Fl, #2210, Chicago, IL 60606. Phone: 312-924-2892.

SAN FRANCISCO: 580 California St, San Francisco, CA 94104. Phone: 415-283-3325.

CHINA: Capital Tower 3501, No 6 Jia Jianguomenwai Ave, Chaoyang District, Beijing, China. Phone: 86-5971-2880.
Full service, research-driven securities firm.

BULKLEY CAPITAL LP
5949 Sherry Ln
Ste 1370
Dallas, TX 75225
Phone: 214-692-5476
Fax: 214-692-9309
E-mail: info@bulkleycapital.com
Web Site: http://www.bulkleycapital.com
G. Bradford Bulkley, President & Founder
Lisa Bulkley, Vice President
Oliver Cone, Vice President
Gail Quick, Vice President
William Herdrich, Director
Richard W. Gilbert, Director & Advisory Board Member
John A. McKay, Director
William S. Skibitsky, Director
Nancy Wallin, General Manager
Craig R. Lentzsch, Advisory Board Member
William N. Case, Advisor

Branch Offices:
ATLANTA: 3500 Lenox Rd, Ste 1500, Atlanta, GA 30326. Phone: 404-843-2631. Fax: 404-843-2631.

COLUMBIA: 11276 Ridermark Rd, Columbia, MD 21044. Phone: 410-382-4622.
Provides mergers & acquisitions advisory services & private placement of senior & subordinated debt & equity for communications firms.

CHAISSON & CO. INC.
154 Indian Waters Dr
New Canaan, CT 06840
Phone: 203-966-6333
Fax: 203-966-1298
E-mail: rchaisco@aol.com
Robert A. Chaisson, President
Provides brokerage services to radio & TV sales, acquisitions & financing.

CHASE
270 Park Ave
New York, NY 10017-2070
Phone: 212-270-6000
Fax: 800-242-7324
Web Site: http://www.jpmorganchase.com
James Dimon, Chief Executive Officer

CITIBANK N.A.
399 Park Ave
New York, NY 10022
Phone: 800-627-3999
Fax: 212-559-7373
Provides radio, TV & cable financing.

CMS STATION BROKERAGE
1439 Denniston St
Pittsburgh, PA 15217
Phone: 412-421-2600
Fax: 412-421-6001
E-mail: rafson@cmsradio.com
Web Site: http://www.cmsstationbrokerage.com
Roger Rafson, President
Susan Kinger, Office Manager
Provides station brokerage for small & medium-market broadcasters.

COBBCORP LLC
7400 Tamiami Trail N
Ste 102
Naples, FL 34108
Phone: 212-812-5020
Fax: 239-596-0660
E-mail: denisleclair@cobbcorp.com
Web Site: http://www.cobbcorp.com
Brian E. Cobb, President
Denis LeClair, Vice President
Daniel B. Graves, Managing Director
Jeanette Kuszlyk, Controller
Provides brokerage, mergers & acquisition services, private equity, investment & merchant banking.

COMMERCE BANK, MEDIA FINANCE GROUP
— See listing for TD Bank.

COMMUNICATION RESOURCES/MEDIA BROKERS
5343 E 22nd St
Tulsa, OK 74114-2231
Phone: 918-744-6149
Fax: 918-749-3348
Tom Belcher, President
Eileen Belcher, Vice President
Barbara Terry, Secretary-Treasurer
Provides radio, TV, cable & telephony brokerage, acquisitions & mergers.

COMMUNICATIONS EQUITY ASSOCIATES
101 E Kennedy Blvd
Ste 3300
Tampa, FL 33602
Phone: 813-226-8844
Fax: 813-225-1513
E-mail: info@ceaworldwide.com
Web Site: http://www.ceaworldwide.com
J. Patrick Michaels, Jr., Chairman & Chief Executive Officer
Ming Jung, Senior Managing Director & Chief Financial Officer, CEA Cap Advisors
Ken Jones, Senior Vice President & General Counsel
Robert D. Berger, Managing Director
Carsten Philipson, Managing Director
Donald Russell, Managing Director

Branch Offices:
NEW YORK: 54 Thompson St, 4th Fl, New York, NY 10012. Phone: 212-218-5085. Fax:

212-334-5003. Waldo Glasman, Managing Director; John Morrison, Managing Director; Alexander Rossi, Managing Director.

WESTPORT: Principal Advisors Group, 191 Post Rd W, Westport, CT 06880. Phone: 203-221-2662. Fax: 203-221-2663. Dave Moyer, President.

UNITED KINGDOM: 11 Staple Ct, 11 Staple Inn Bldgs, London EC3A 7PT, WC1V 7Q4. Phone: 44-0-207-280-4899. Fax: 44-0-207-280-4899. Martin Farmer, Managing Director. Provides investment banking & brokerage services to CATV, broadcasting, media & entertainment industries; acquisitions, divestitures, mergers & trades; financial placements for equity & debt; joint ventures; appraisals; consultation for tax & estate planning & shareholder negotiations.

CONLEY & ASSOCIATES LLC

1459 Interstate Loop
Bismarck, ND 58503-5560
Phone: 701-222-3902
Fax: 701-258-1937
E-mail: info@conleyassociates.net
Web Site: http://www.conleyassociates.net
Christopher J. Conley, Managing General Partner
Provides management & engineering consulting to the electronic media; specializes in appraisals & valuations; strategic planning & feasibility studies; financial planning & restructuring; contract management; operational evaluations & audits; engineering design & technical evaluations; marketing research & analysis; human resources development & training; franchising & refranchising; regulatory affairs & expert testimony.

COX & COX LLC

2454 Shiva Ct
St. Louis, MO 63011
Phone: 636-458-4780
Fax: 636-458-6323
Web Site: http://www.coxandcoxllc.com
Bob Cox, President
Linda Cox
Provides media brokerage services, specializing in media mergers & acquisitions.

CREDIT SUISSE

Paradeplatz 8
Zurich 8070
Switzerland
Phones: 41-44-212-16-16; 41-44-333-11-11
Fax: 41-44-333-25-87
Web Site: http://www.credit-suisse.com
Walter B. Kielholz, Chairman
Hans-Ulrich Doerig, Vice Chairman
Peter Brabeck-Letmathe, Vice Chairman

Branch Offices:
NEW YORK: 11 Madison Ave, New York, NY 10010-3629. Phone: 212-325-2000. Fax: 212-325-6665.

BRAZIL: Ave Brig Faria Lima, 3064 - 13 andar, Jardim Paulistano, San Paulo 01451-000, Brazil. Phone: 55-11-3841-6000. Fax: 55-11-3841-6900.

HONG KONG: Three Exchange Sq, Eight Connaught Pl Central, 22nd Fl, Hong Kong. Phone: 852-2101-6000. Fax: 852-2101-7990.

JAPAN: Izumi Garden Tower, 6-1 Roppongi 1-Chome, Minato-ku, Tokyo 106-6024, Japan. Phone: 81-3-4550-9000. Fax: 81-3-4550-9800.

SINGAPORE: One Raffles Link 05-02 039393, Singapore. Phone: 65-6212-6000. Fax: 65-6212-6200.

UNITED KINGDOM: One Cabot Sq, London E14 4QJ, United Kingdom. Phone: 44-20-7888-8888. Fax: 44-20-7888-1600.
Provides investment & merchant bank services.

CVC CAPITAL CORP.

131 E 62nd St
New York, NY 10021-7377
Phone: 212-319-7210
Provides investment banking services.

DELOITTE & TOUCHE LLP

1633 Broadway
New York, NY 10019-6754
Phone: 212-489-1600
Fax: 212-489-1687
Web Site: http://www.deloitte.com
Sharon Allen, Chairman
Barry Salzberg, Chief Executive Officer
Provides assurance, advisory, tax & management consulting services; offices in more than 80 cities.

ENVEST MEDIA LLC

6802 Patterson Ave
Richmond, VA 23226
Phone: 804-282-5561
Fax: 804-282-5703
Web Site: http://www.envestmedia.com
Mitt S. Younts, Managing Member

Branch Offices:
ATLANTA: One Glenlake Pkwy, 7th Fl, Ste 700, Alpharetta, GA 30328. Phones: 770-753-9650; 800-808-0130. Fax: 770-753-0089. Jesse Weatherby, Managing Director.
Provides mergers, acquisitions, valuations, financing & strategic consulting services for the radio, TV, newspaper & media industries.

THE EXLINE CO.

4340 Redwood Hwy
Ste F-230
San Rafael, CA 94903
Phone: 415-479-3484
Fax: 415-479-1574
E-mail: exline@pacbell.net
Web Site: http://www.exlinecompany.com
Andrew McClure, President
Judi Lewis, Administrative Coordinator
Provides consulting services in operations, personnel & finance as well as brokerage & appraisals for radio & TV communications companies.

FINOVA GROUP INC. — No longer in business.

RICHARD A. FOREMAN ASSOCIATES INC.

330 Emery Dr E
Stamford, CT 06902
Phone: 203-327-2800
Fax: 203-967-9393
E-mail: raf@rafamedia.com
Web Site: http://www.rafamedia.com
Richard A. Foreman, President
Provides brokerage & consulting services to the radio, TV, digital & entertainment industries.

FBR CAPITAL MARKETS, TECHNOLOGY, MEDIA & TELECOMMUNICATIONS GROUP

1001 19th St N
Arlington, VA 22209
Phones: 703-312-9500; 800-846-5050

Setting the industry standard...
Communications Daily
Warren Communications News
FREE 30-day trial—call 800-771-9202 or visit www.warren-news.com

Fax: 703-312-9501
E-mail: media@fbr.com
Web Site: http://www.fbr.com
David DeRuff, Senior Managing Director & Group Head
Provides creative capital raising, merger & acquisitions and corporate advisory services.

GAMMON MILLER LLC

4806 Vue du Lac Pl
Ste B
Manhattan, KS 66503
Phone: 785-539-1700
Fax: 785-565-0437
Web Site: http://www.gammonmiller.com
Christopher D. Miller, President & Chief Executive Officer

Branch Offices:
CHEVY CHASE: 5600 Wisconsin Ave, Ste 308, Chevy Chase, MD 20815. Phone: 301-332-0904. E-Mail: jgammon@gammonmiller.com. James A. Gammon, Chairman.
Formerly Gammon Media Brokers. Media investment bankers who work buy or sell side assignments. Experience in radio station, television station & newspaper acquisitions or divestitures.

CLIFTON GARDINER & CO. LLC

2437 S Chase Ln
Lakewood, CO 80227
Phone: 303-905-9565
Fax: 303-757-5005
E-mail: cliff@cliftongardiner.com
Web Site: http://www.cliftongardiner.com
Clifton H. Gardiner, Managing Partner
Provides brokerage & investment banking services for media & communications companies.

GE CAPITAL SOLUTIONS

44 Old Ridgebury Rd
Danbury, CT 06810-5105
Phone: 203-796-1000
Web Site: http://www.ge.com/capitalsolutions
Provides equipment leasing & financial services for the entertainment industry.

THE GORDON GROUP

4909 Bears Paw
Springfield, IL 62711
Phone: 217-793-5464
Fax: 217-793-5465
Robert D. Gordon, President

W.B. GRIMES & CO.

24212 Muscari Ct
Gaithersburg, MD 20882
Phone: 301-253-5016
Fax: 240-358-0790
E-mail: info@mediamergers.com
Web Site: http://www.mediamergers.com
Larry Grimes, President

Branch Offices:
COHASSET: 137 N Main St, Cohasset, MA 02025. Phone: 617-480-2217. Fax: 925-263-7017. E-Mail: jbradm@hotmail.com. Brad Murray, Broadcast Brokerage.
Full service merger & acquisition firm.

HADDEN & ASSOCIATES

147 Eastpark Dr
Celebration, FL 34747
Phone: 321-939-3141
Fax: 321-939-3142
E-mail: haddenws@aol.com
Web Site: http://www.haddenonline.com
Doyle Hadden, President
Nationwide media brokers. Provides acquisition, divestiture, appraisal, consulting & financial assistance services.

HENSON MEDIA INC.

455 S 4th Ave
Ste 494
Louisville, KY 40202-2552
Phone: 502-589-0060
Fax: 502-589-0058
E-mail: edhenson1@bellsouth.net
Web Site: http://www.hensonmedia.com
Ed Henson, President
Provides media brokerage services, assists clients in the buying & selling of radio stations & in doing valuations of broadcast facilities; specializes in the midwest & upper south.

R. MILLER HICKS & CO.

1011 W 11th St
Austin, TX 78703
Phone: 512-477-7000
Fax: 512-477-9697
R. Miller Hicks, President
Provides consultation services, appraisals, management & programming.

HOFFMAN-SCHUTZ MEDIA CAPITAL

2044 W California St
San Diego, CA 92110
Phone: 619-291-7070
Web Site: http://www.hs-media.com
David E. Schutz, Founder & President
Provides broadcast station financing, appraisals, financial restructuring & litigation support.

HOLT MEDIA GROUP

2178 Industrial Dr
Ste 914
Bethlehem, PA 18017
Phone: 610-814-2821
Fax: 610-814-2826
Web Site: http://www.holtmedia.com
Arthur H. Holt, President & Chief Executive Officer
Christine Borger, Executive Vice President & Chief Financial Officer
Carl Strandell, Associate
Provides brokerage & acquisitions for internet, radio, TV & cable systems; fair market value, asset & liquidation appraisals; negotiation services & financial planning for sales & acquisitions; management & operations consulting; technical equipment sales & specifications; feasibility analysis & marketing planning for new ventures; expert witness & litigation consulting.

HPC PUCKETT & CO.

PO Box 9063
Rancho Santa Fe, CA 92067

Phone: 858-756-4915
Fax: 858-756-9779
E-mail: tfp@hpcpuckett.com
Web Site: http://www.hpcpuckett.com
Thomas F. Puckett, Chairman
Hunter T. Puckett, Senior Vice President & General Counsel

Branch Offices:
TOPEKA: 5835 SW 29th St, Ste 203, Topeka, KS 66614. Phone: 785-273-0017. Fax: 785-273-5512. Jason A Meyer, Managing Director; Melissa L. Kramer, Vice President.
Provides brokerage services including acquisitions, divestiture, financing & investment banking; specializes in professional services with emphasis on legal procedures, financial analysis, closing procedures & community relations.

ING INVESTMENT MANAGEMENT
230 Park Ave
New York, NY 10169
Phone: 212-309-8200
Web Site: http://www.inginvestment.com
Robert G. Leary, Chairman & Chief Executive Officer
Jeffrey T. Becker, Vice Chairman, Chief Operating Officer & Chief Financial Officer
Frederic A. Nelson, Vice Chairman & Chief Investment Officer
Provides investment banking & corporate finance services.

JONES GROUP LTD.
9697 E Mineral Ave
Englewood, CO 80112-3408
Phones: 303-792-3111; 800-525-7002
Provides brokerage services to buyers & sellers in the communications industry.

JORGENSON BROADCAST BROKERAGE INC.
426 S River Rd
Tryon, NC 28782
Phone: 828-859-6982
Fax: 828-859-6831
Web Site: http://www.radiotvbrokerage.com
Mark W. Jorgenson, Managing Partner

Branch Offices:
CUPERTINO: 19925 Stevens Creek Blvd, Cupertino, CA 95014-2358. Phone: 408-973-7292. Fax: 408-516-9526. E-Mail: pmieuli@att.net. Peter Mieuli, Partner.
Provides broadcast brokerage services nationwide.

KALIL & CO. INC.
6363 N Swan Rd
Ste 200
Tucson, AZ 85718
Phone: 520-795-1050
Fax: 520-322-0584
E-mail: kalil@kalilco.com
Web Site: http://www.kalilco.com
Frank Kalil, President
Provides media brokering services, trust & custodial services, appraisals & assistance with financing & consulting.

KANE REECE ASSOCIATES INC.
822 South Ave W
Westfield, NJ 07090-1460
Phones: 908-317-5757; 800-494-5263
Fax: 908-317-4434
Web Site: http://www.kanereece.com
John E. (Jack) Kane, Founder & Principal
Norval Reece, Co-Founder & Chairman Emeritus
Noah Gottdiener, Chief Executive Officer
Gerry Creagh, President
Dennis Elliott, Managing Director
Provides appraisals & valuations, business plans, engineering consulting, financial & technical due diligence, financing preparations, franchise renewals, litigation support, market/opinion research, management & management consulting, property tax compliance & control, solvency opinions, valuations for buy/sell agreements & workouts. Division of Duff & Phelps Corp.

KEPPER, TUPPER & CO.
2 Galleon
Ste 100
Hilton Head Island, SC 29928
Phone: 203-431-3366
E-mail: keppertup@hotmail.com
Web Site: http://www.kepper-tupper.com
John B. Tupper, Chairman
James R. Kelly, President
Provides investment banking services including domestic & international brokerage of CATV systems & broadcast TV stations; appraisals of electronic media properties for tax & financial reporting; place financing; strategic planning & financial consulting.

KEYCORP.
127 Public Sq
Cleveland, OH 44114-1306
Phones: 216-689-6300; 800-539-2968
Fax: 216-689-0519
Web Site: http://www.key.com
Henry L. Meyer, III, Chairman, Chief Executive Officer & President
Thomas C. Stevens, Vice Chairman & Chief Administrative Officer
Beth Mooney, Vice Chairman, Key Community Banking
Charles S. Hyle, Chief Risk Officer
Provides specialized financing to meet the needs of the broad range of businesses, with specialized products & teams of experts dedicated to specific client segments.

KNOWLES MEDIA BROKERAGE SERVICES
PO Box 9698
Bakersfield, CA 93389
Phones: 661-833-3834; 661-333-9516 (cell phone)
Fax: 661-833-3845
E-mail: gregg.knowles@netzero.com
Web Site: http://www.media-broker.com
Gregg K. Knowles, Broker & Owner
Provides sales, consultation & appraisal services for print media owners nationwide.

KOMPAS GROUP
5235 N 124th St
Ste 262
Butler, WI 53007
Phone: 262-781-0188
Fax: 262-781-5313
E-mail: kompasgroup@toast.net
John Kompas, President
Jackie Kompas, Executive Vice President
Provides consulting, brokerage & representation services as well as provides information for the LPTV industry.

KOZACKO MEDIA SERVICES
PO Box 948
Elmira, NY 14902
Phone: 607-733-7138
Fax: 607-733-1212
E-mail: rkozacko@stny.rr.com
Web Site: http://www.radio4sale.com
Richard L. Kozacko, President

Branch Offices:
TUCSON: PO Box 120-40, 6890 E Sunrise Dr, Tucson, AZ 85750. Phone: 520-299-4869. Fax: 520-844-8559. E-Mail: georgewkimble@aol.com. George W. Kimble, Associate; Pat Anderson, Associate.
Provides brokerage, appraisal & acquisition consulting services for TV & radio stations.

LAZARD
30 Rockefeller Pl
New York, NY 10020
Phone: 212-632-6000
Web Site: http://www.lazard.com
Bruce Wasserstein, Chairman & Chief Executive Officer
Steven J. Golub, Vice Chairman & Chairman, Financial Advisory Group
Charles G. Ward, III, President & Chairman, Asset Management Group
Michael J. Castellano, Chief Financial Officer
Scott D. Hoffman, General Counsel
International financial advisory & asset management firm.

MADISON DEARBORN PARTNERS LLC
Three First National Plz
Ste 4600
Chicago, IL 60602
Phone: 312-895-1000
Fax: 312-895-1001
E-mail: info@mdcp.com
Web Site: http://www.mdcp.com
John A. Canning, Jr., Chairman
Paul J. Finnegan, Co-Chief Executive Officer
Samuel M. Mencoff, Co-Chief Executive Officer
Provides venture capital for TV, radio, CATV, paging, cellular, PCS & SMR acquisitions.

MCG CAPITAL CORP.
1100 Wilson Blvd
Ste 3000
Arlington, VA 22209
Phone: 703-247-7500
Fax: 703-247-7505
E-mail: mcg@mcgcapital.com
Web Site: http://www.mcgcapital.com
Steven F. Tunney, President & Chief Executive Officer
Stephen J. Bacica, Executive Vice President & Chief Financial Officer
Tod K. Reichert, Senior Vice President, Chief Securities & Governance Counsel & Corporate Secretary
Samuel G. Rubenstein, Executive Vice President & General Counsel
B. Hagen Saville, Executive Vice President, Business Development
Derek Thomas, Executive Vice President, Risk Management & Underwriting
Provides capital to support the growth & value creation strategies of small- to mid-sized companies.

MCH ENTERPRISES INC.
179 Niblick Rd
Ste 319
Paso Robles, CA 93446
Phone: 805-237-0952
E-mail: mchenterprises@mchentinc.com
Web Site: http://www.mchentinc.com
Brett E. Miller, Founder
Rosario Miller, President
Sean Miller, Associate
Provides merger & acquisition support to buyers & sellers of broadcast & CATV properties; consulting services include station appraisals, financial planning, transactional management, project management, human resources consulting, website design & maintenance.

M/C VENTURE PARTNERS
75 State St
Ste 2500
Boston, MA 02109
Phone: 617-345-7200
Fax: 617-345-7201
E-mail: mcvp@mcventurepartners.com
Web Site: http://www.mcventurepartners.com
David D. Croll, Managing General Partner
James F. Wade, Managing General Partner
John W. Watkins, Managing General Partner
John D. Patty, Vice President
Edward J. Keefe, Chief Financial Officer

Branch Offices:
SAN FRANCISCO: 235 Pine St, Ste 1675, San Francisco, CA 94104. Phone: 415-438-4875. Fax: 415-296-8901.

UNITED KINGDOM: Charles House, 18b Charles St, London W1J 5DU, United Kingdom. Phone: 44-0-20-7667-6838.
Investment firm; provides equity financing & strategic guidance to entrepreneurial ventures in the media & telecommunications industries, including wireless telephony, CATV, broadcasting & publishing.

R.E. MEADOR & ASSOCIATES INC.
69 Ussery Dr
Lexington, MO 64067
Phone: 660-259-2544
Fax: 660-259-6424
Ralph E. Meador, President
Provides acquisitions & sales services; market studies & appraisals of broadcast properties.

MEDIA SERVICES GROUP INC.
3948 S Third St
Ste 191
Jacksonville Beach, FL 32250
Phone: 904-285-3239
Fax: 904-285-5618
E-mail: info@mediaservicesgroup.com
Web Site: http://www.mediaservicesgroup.com
George Reed, Managing Director

Branch Offices:
COLORADO SPRINGS: 2910 Electra Dr, Colorado Springs, CO 80906-1073. Phone: 719-630-3111. Fax: 719-630-1871. E-Mail: jbmccoy@mediaservicesgroup.com. Jody McCoy, Director.

HIGHLAND PARK: 147 Oak Knoll Ter, Highland Park, IL 60035. Phone: 847-266-9822. Fax: 847-266-9826. E-Mail: robertheymann@comcast.net. Robert L. Heymann, Jr., Director.

LOGAN: 1289 North 1500 East, Logan, UT 84341. Phone: 435-753-8090. E-Mail: merrill.greg@comcast.net. Greg Merrill, Director.

MORRISTOWN: 45 Park Pl S, Ste 146, Morristown, NJ 07960. Phone: 973-631-6612. Fax: 973-631-6633. E-Mail: rtmck2515@aol.com. Tom McKinley, Director.

OVERLAND PARK: 5225 W 122nd St, Overland Park, KS 66209. Phone: 913-498-0040. Fax: 913-498-0041. E-Mail: billlytle8@cs.com. Bill Lytle, Director; Mike Lytle, Associate.

PROVIDENCE: 170 Westminster St, Ste 701, Providence, RI 02903. Phone: 401-454-3130. Fax: 401-454-3131. E-Mail: rmaccini@cox.net. Bob Maccini, Director; Stephan Sloan, Director; Ted Clark, Analyst.

RICHARDSON: 1131 Rockingham Dr, Ste 209, Richardson, TX 75080. Phone: 972-231-4500. Fax: 972-231-4509. E-Mail: whitleytx@cs.com. Bill Whitley, Director.

ST. SIMONS ISLAND: 205 Marina Dr, St Simons Island, GA 31522. Phone: 912-634-6575. Fax: 912-634-5770. E-Mail: eddie@eddieesserman.com. Eddie Esserman, Director.

WAYZATA: 375 Waycliffe Dr S, Wayzata, MN 55391. Phone: 952-404-1104. Fax: 952-404-1102. E-Mail: johncomm88@aol.com. Jerry Johnson, Director.

Provides brokerage services to media, entertainment & communications companies.

MEDIA VENTURE PARTNERS LLC

244 Jackson St
4th Fl
San Francisco, CA 94111
Phone: 415-391-4877
Fax: 415-391-4912
E-mail: pch@mediaventurepartners.com
Web Site: http://www.mediaventurepartners.com
Elliot Evers, Managing Director & Co-Founder
Greg Widroe, Managing Director & Founder, Telecom Group
Brian Pryor, Managing Director
Bill Fanning, Vice President
Sandy Kory, Vice President & Director, New Media Technology
Mike Grobe, Associate

Branch Offices:

BOSTON: 75 State St, Ste 2500, Boston, MA 02109. Phone: 617-345-7316. Fax: 617-507-5667. E-Mail: jhill@mediaventurepartners.com. Jason D. Hill, Managing Director & Co-Founder, Telecom Group; Tim Beach, Vice President.

KANSAS CITY: 1800 Baltimore Ave, Ste 300, Kansas City, MO 64108. Phone: 816-523-8566. Fax: 816-817-0570. E-Mail: cfunk@mediaventurepartners.com. R. Clayton Funk, Managing Director; Jason Nicolay, Associate.

Provides investment banking services to media & emerging telecommunications companies; media brokerage, capital raising, merger & acquisition and strategic consulting services.

MILESTONE COMMUNICATIONS INC.

43 Herrn Ln
Castle Pines, CO 80108
Phone: 303-993-3557
Fax: 303-993-3559
E-mail: michaelwdrake@comcast.net
Michael W. Drake, President
Roxanne Criswell, Associate
Provides brokerage & consulting services, including acquisitions, divestitures & financing, to independent CATV operators.

MMTC MEDIA BROKERS

3636 16th St NW
Suite B-366
Washington, DC 20010
Phone: 202-332-0500
Fax: 202-332-0503
E-mail: info@mmtconline.org
Web Site: http://www.mmtconline.org/brokerage
David Honig, Executive Director
Minority-owned & non-profit media broker; represents buyers & sellers of broadcast & telecom properties; NAMB member.

MYMEDIABROKER.COM

407 Broadmoor
Portales, NM 88130
Phone: 505-356-2000
Fax: 505-356-2003
Web Site: http://www.mymediabroker.com
Sandi Bergman, Founder
Offers acquisition, appraisal & consulting services.

NATIONAL CITY CORP.

National City Ctr
1900 E Ninth St
Cleveland, OH 44114-3484
Phone: 216-222-2000
Web Site: http://www.nationalcity.com
David A. Daberko, Chairman & Chief Executive Officer
Jeffrey D. Kelly, Vice Chairman & Chief Financial Officer
William E. MacDonald, III, Vice Chairman
Peter E. Raskind, Vice Chairman, Consumer & Small Business Financial Services
Thomas A. Richlovsky, Senior Vice President & Treasurer
Provides commercial & retail banking, mortgage financing & servicing, consumer finance & asset management.

NEW COMMERCE COMMUNICATIONS (NCC)

116 Cousley Dr SE
Port Charlotte, FL 33952
Phone: 239-282-5550
Fax: 414-755-1440
E-mail: tomm@com-broker.com
Web Site: http://www.com-broker.com
Tom Millitzer, President
Provides merger & acquisition services to the Internet & telecom industries.

NORMAN FISCHER & ASSOCIATES INC. (NFA INC.)

PO Box 5308
Austin, TX 78763-5308
Phone: 512-476-9457
Fax: 512-476-0540
E-mail: terrill@nfainc.com
Web Site: http://www.nfainc.com
Terrill Fischer, President
Provides management consulting, media brokerage & appraisals.

OPPENHEIMER & CO. INC.

125 Broad St
New York, NY 10004
Phones: 212-668-8000; 800-221-5588
E-mail: info@opco.com
Web Site: http://www.opco.com
Albert Lowenthal, Chairman & Chief Executive Officer
Jeffrey J. Alfano, Executive Vice President & Chief Financial Officer
Provides financial services & advice to high net worth investors, individuals, businesses & institutions.

PATRICK COMMUNICATIONS LLC

6805 Douglas Legum Dr
Ste 100
Elkridge, MD 21075
Phone: 410-799-1740
Fax: 410-799-1705
E-mail: larry@patcomm.com
Web Site: http://www.patcomm.com
W. Lawrence Patrick, Managing Partner
Susan K. Patrick, Managing Partner
Gregory J. Guy, Managing Partner
Vincent A. Pepper, Principal
John Cunney, Principal
Provides station brokerage & investment banking services; fair market & asset appraisals; debt & equity placement; broadcast management & marketing consulting.

JOHN PIERCE & CO. LLC

11 Spiral Dr
Ste 3
Florence, KY 41042
Phone: 859-647-0101
Fax: 859-647-2616
E-mail: ssuts@johnpierceco.com
Web Site: http://www.johnpierceco.com
John Pierce, President
Robin Webster, Vice President, Client Services
Jamie Rasnick, Associate Director
Provides brokerage, appraisal & consulting services to buyers & sellers of radio & TV properties.

PNC FINANCIAL SERVICES GROUP

Steel Plz Office
600 Grant St
Pittsburgh, PA 15219
Phones: 412-762-2000; 888-762-2265
Fax: 412-762-7568
Web Site: http://www.pnc.com
James E. Rohr, Chairman & Chief Executive Officer
Joseph C. Guyaux, President
Michael J. Hannon, Chief Credit Officer
Richard J. Johnson, Chief Financial Officer
Timothy G. Shack, Executive Vice President & Chief Information Officer
Thomas K. Whitford, Executive Vice President & Chief Administrative Officer
John J. Wixted, Jr., Senior Vice President & Chief Regulatory Officer
Provides financial services to communications companies nationwide.

PROVIDENCE EQUITY PARTNERS INC.

50 Kennedy Plz
18th Fl
Providence, RI 02903
Phone: 401-751-1700
Fax: 401-751-1790
E-mail: contact@provequity.com
Web Site: http://www.provequity.com
Jonathan M. Nelson, Chief Executive Officer
Gary S. Weinstein, Chief Operating Officer
Raymond M. Mathieu, Chief Financial Officer
Glenn M. Creamer, Senior Managing Director
Paul J. Salem, Senior Managing Director

Branch Offices:

LOS ANGELES: 1999 Avenue of the Stars, Ste 1250, Los Angeles, CA 90067. Phone: 310-228-5000. Fax: 310-228-5001.

NEW YORK: 9 W 57th St, 390 Park Ave, Ste 4799, New York, NY 10019. Phone: 212-588-5700. Fax: 212-588-6701.

HONG KONG: York House, 18th Fl, 15 Queens Rd, Central, Hong Kong, China. Phone: 852-3653-3800. Fax: 852-3653-3900.

INDIA: Birla Tower, 25 Barakhamba Rd, 6th Fl, New Delhi 110 001, India. Phone: 91-11-3041-9000. Fax: 91-11-3041-9090.

UNITED KINGDOM: 28 St George St, London W1S 2FA, United Kingdom. Phone: 44-0-20-7514-8800. Fax: 44-0-20-7629-2778. E-Mail: info@provequity.co.uk.

Private investment firm; specializes in equity investments in communications & media companies worldwide.

STAN RAYMOND & ASSOCIATES INC.

PO Box 8231
Longboat Key, FL 34228
Phone: 941-383-9404
Fax: 941-383-0132
E-mail: stnray@aol.com
Stan Raymond, President
Provides brokerage & consulting services for radio, TV & cable properties.

RBC DANIELS

3200 Cherry Creek S Dr
Ste 500
Denver, CO 80209
Phone: 303-778-5555
Fax: 303-778-5599
E-mail: info@danielsonline.com
Web Site: http://www.danielsonline.com
Brian Deevy, Chairman & Chief Executive Officer
Brad Busse, President & Chief Operating Officer
Bill Fowler, Chief Financial Officer & Senior Managing Director
Bill Wedum, General Counsel
Greg Ainsworth, Senior Managing Director
Dave Rhodes, Senior Managing Director

Branch Offices:

LOS ANGELES: 11150 Santa Monica Blvd, Ste 1230, Los Angeles, CA 90025. Phone: 310-473-2300. Fax: 310-943-2052.

NEW YORK: 711 Fifth Ave, Ste 405, New York, NY 10022. Phone: 212-935-5900. Fax: 212-863-4859.
Provides mergers & acquisitions, corporate financing & financial advisory services to the cable telecommunications, media & technology industries; member NASD, SIPC.

GORDON RICE ASSOCIATES — No longer in business.

ROBINSON/JEFFREY ASSOCIATES INC.
101 W Long Lake Rd
Bloomfield Hills, MI 48304
Phone: 248-644-0006
Fax: 248-647-2356
E-mail: robinsonjeffreyinc@msn.com
Michael Jeffrey, Principal
Peter Robinson, Principal
Provides investment banking & financial services for the broadband industry.

RUMBAUT & COMPANY
555 NE 34th St
Ste 2701
Miami, FL 33137-4060
Phone: 305-868-0000
Fax: 305-571-0433
E-mail: julio@rumbaut.com
Web Site: http://www.rumbaut.com
Julio Rumbaut, President
Provides media brokerage & consulting services.

SANDLER CAPITAL MANAGEMENT
711 Fifth Ave
15th Fl
New York, NY 10022
Phone: 212-754-8100
Fax: 212-826-0280; 212-826-0281
Web Site: http://www.sandlercap.com
Investment management firm; specializes in the communications industry, targeting public & private companies.

SATTERFIELD & PERRY INC.
7211 Fourth Ave S
St Petersburg, FL 33707
Phone: 727-345-7338
Fax: 727-345-3809
E-mail: eraust@prodigy.net
Web Site: http://www.satterfieldandperry.com
Robert Austin, President
Joe Benkert, Vice President
Jim Birschbach, Vice President

Branch Offices:
AIKEN: 131 Inwood Dr, Aiken, SC 29803. Phone: 803-270-5613. Fax: 803-649-7786. John Willis, Secretary-Treasurer.

COOS BAY: PO Box 362, Coos Bay, OR 97420. Phone: 541-751-0043. Fax: 541-267-5553. Dick McMahon, Vice President.

DENVER: 2020 S Monroe St, Ste 302, Denver, CO 80210. Phone: 303-758-1876. Fax: 303-756-1865. Al Perry, Chairman Emeritus.

OVERLAND PARK: 4918 W 101st Ter, Overland Park, KS 66207. Phone: 913-649-5103. Doug Stephens, Vice President.

WETUMPKA: 169 Mountain Meadows Ln, Wetumpka, AL 36093. Phone: 334-514-2241. Fax: 334-514-2291. Ken Hawkins, Vice President.
Provides TV, cable & radio brokerage services; FDIC approved appraiser.

BURT SHERWOOD & ASSOCIATES INC.
6415 Midnight Pass Rd
Ste 206
Sarasota, FL 34242
Phone: 941-349-2165
Fax: 941-312-0974
Web Site: http://www.burtsherwood.com
Burt Sherwood, Owner, President & Chief Executive Officer
Jason W. Sherwood, Vice President
Provides media brokerage & appraisals for radio, TV & LPTV.

SNL FINANCIAL
One Lower Ragsdale Dr
Bldg 1, Ste 130
Monterey, CA 93940
Phone: 831-624-1536
Fax: 831-625-3225
E-mail: sales@snl.com
Web Site: http://www.snl.com
Derek Baine, Senior Vice President & Senior Analyst
Robin Flynn, Senior Vice President & Senior Analyst
Provides strategic financial planning, customized market & data analyses, regular fair market valuations of media properties.

SNOWDEN ASSOCIATES
PO Box 1966
Washington, NC 27889
Phone: 252-940-1680
Fax: 252-940-1682
E-mail: zophsnowden@embarqmail.com
Zoph Potts, President
Provides media brokerage services, valuations & consulting in Southeastern U.S.

STATE STREET CORP.
State Street Financial Ctr
One Lincoln St
Boston, MA 02111
Phone: 617-786-3000
E-mail: information@statestreet.com
Web Site: http://www.statestreet.com
Joseph L. Hooley, Chairman, President & Chief Executive Officer
Lends to cable, DBS, broadcasting, cellular & long distance resellers, publishing & other media & telecommunications industries; acquisition & expansion financing & refinancing; cash management, investment management, stock transfer, corporate trust & other financial services.

STONEGATE CAPITAL GROUP LLC
20 Stanford Dr
Farmington, CT 06032
Phone: 860-678-7800
Provides investment banking for the broadcast industry.

TD BANK
PO Box 9540
Two Portland Sq
Portland, ME 04112-9540
Phone: 800-462-3666
Web Site: http://www.tdbank.com
Bharat B. Masrani, President & Chief Executive Officer
Stephen J. Boyle, Executive Vice President, Finance & Chief Executive Officer
Walter J. Owens, Executive Vice President, Commercial Banking

Branch Offices:
CHERRY HILL: 1701 Rte 70 E, Cherry Hill, NJ 08034. Phone: 888-751-9000.
Provides commercial banking services.

THE MAHLMAN CO.
Four Midland Gardens
Ste 3F
Bronxville, NY 10708
Phone: 914-793-1577
Fax: 914-793-1587
E-mail: mahlmans@aol.com
Robert O. Mahlman, Founder
Nancy D. Mahlman, Founder
Bill Kehlbeck, Vice President
Specializes in radio station brokerage, appraisal & consulting.

EDWIN TORNBERG & CO.
8917 Cherbourg Dr
Potomac, MD 20854-3104
Phone: 301-983-8700
Ina Tornberg, President
James Weitzman, Vice President
Provides appraisal, brokerage, consulting & merger/acquisition services.

TOTAL TECHNOLOGY VENTURES LLC — See TTV Capital.

TTV CAPITAL
1230 Peachtree St
Promenade II, Ste 1150
Atlanta, GA 30309
Phone: 404-347-8400
Fax: 404-347-8420
E-mail: info@ttvcapital.com
Web Site: http://www.ttvcapital.com
Gardiner W. Garrard III, Co-Founder & Managing Partner
W. Thomas Smith Jr., Co-Founder & Managing Partner
Mark A. Johnson, Partner
Sean M. Banks, Principal
Provides capital to early-to-late stage privately held companies.

UNUM PROVIDENT CORP.
One Fountain Sq
Chattanooga, TN 37402
Phones: 423-294-1011; 866-679-3054
Web Site: http://www.unumprovident.com
Thomas R. Watjen, President & Chief Executive Officer

Branch Offices:
COLUMBIA: 1200 Colonial Life Bldg, Columbia, SC 29230. Phone: 803-798-7000.

GLENDALE: 655 N Central Ave, Ste 900, Glendale, CA 91203. Phone: 800-424-2008.

PORTLAND: 2211 Congress St, Portland, ME 04122. Phone: 207-575-2211.

WORCESTER: 18 Chestnut St, Worcester, MA 01608. Phone: 774-437-4441.

UNITED KINGDOM: Milton Ct, Dorking, Surrey RH4 3LZ, United Kingdom. Phone: 44-1306-887766.
Provides group & individual disability income protection in the U.S. & the United Kingdom.

VALUATION RESEARCH CORP.
330 E Kilbourn Ave
Ste 1020
Milwaukee, WI 53202-4495
Phone: 414-271-8662
Fax: 414-271-2294
Web Site: http://www.valuationresearch.com
Richard B. Nordberg, Senior Vice President, Business Development
Jeffrey N. Trader, Senior Vice President, Business Development

Branch Offices:
BOSTON: 101 Federal St, Ste 1900, Boston, MA 02110. Phone: 617-342-7366. Fax: 617-342-3606. Robert A. Schulte, Senior Vice President, Business Development; Glen J. Hartford, Senior Vice President.

CHICAGO: 200 W Madison St, Ste 2850, Chicago, IL 60606. Phone: 312-957-7500. Fax: 312-422-0035. William J. Hughes, Co-Chief Executive Officer, Managing Director & Senior Executive Vice President.

CINCINNATI: 105 E Fourth St, Ste 1005, Cincinnati, OH 45202. Phone: 513-579-9100. Fax: 513-579-9101. Lawrence E. Van Kirk, III, Senior Vice President; Thomas J. Courtright, Senior Vice President.

EWING: 200 Princeton S Corporate Ctr, Ste 200, Ewing, NJ 08628. Phone: 609-243-7000. Fax: 609-883-7651.

NEW YORK: 500 Fifth Ave, 39th Fl, New York, NY 10110. Phone: 212-983-3370. Fax: 212-278-0675.

SAN FRANCISCO: 50 California St, Ste 3050, San Francisco, CA 94111. Phone: 415-277-1800. Fax: 415-277-2948. Justin E. Johnson, Senior Vice President.

TAMPA: 777 S Harbour Island Blvd., Suite 980, Tampa, FL 33602. Phone: 813-463-8510. Fax: 813-273-6878. Steven Schuetz, Senior Vice President.
Provides fair market appraisals, fairness opinions, capital stock valuations, intangible-asset valuations, pre-acquisition feasibility studies & property tax appraisals.

VANHUSS MEDIA SERVICES INC.
4239 Heyward Pl
Indianapolis, IN 46250
Phone: 317-813-0106
William K. VanHuss, President
Provides brokerage & debt placement services for broadcast & cable industries.

VERONIS SUHLER STEVENSON
350 Park Ave
7th Fl
New York, NY 10022
Phone: 212-935-4990
Fax: 212-381-8168
E-mail: stevensonj@vss.com
Web Site: http://www.vss.com
John S. Suhler, Co-Founder & General Partner
Jeffrey T. Stevenson, Managing Partner
John R. Sinatra, Chief Financial Officer & Managing Director

Marvin L. Shapiro, Managing Director
Scott J. Troeller, Partner

Branch Offices:
UNITED KINGDOM: Buchanan House, Three St James Sq, 8th Fl, London SW1Y 4JU, United Kingdom. Phone: 44-0-20-7484-1400. Fax: 44-0-20-7484-1401. E-Mail: solim@vss.com. Marco Sodi, Partner & Head of Veronis Suhler Stevenson International.
Private equity & mezzanine capital fund management company dedicated to investing in the media, communications, information & education industries in the U.S. & Europe.

WACHOVIA CORP.
One Wachovia Ctr
301 S College St, Ste 4000
Charlotte, NC 28288-0013
Phones: 704-590-0000; 800-922-4684
E-mail: abl.inquiry@wachovia.com
Web Site: http://www.wachovia.com
Robert K. Steel, Chief Executive Officer
Thomas J. Wurtz, Chief Financial Officer
Provides financial services, including asset management, benefits & retirement, mergers & acquisition advisory, lending & financing, risk management, sales & trading; equity & debt offerings.

WALLER CAPITAL PARTNERS
30 Rockefeller Plz
Ste 4350
New York, NY 10112
Phone: 212-632-3600
Fax: 212-632-3607
E-mail: wallercapital@wallercc.com
Web Site: http://www.wallercc.com
John W. Waller, III, Chairman
Garrett M. Baker, President
Jeffrey A. Brandon, Managing Director
Matt Dahl, Managing Director
Michael McHugh, Managing Director
Steven R. Soraparu, Managing Director
Brian Stengel, Managing Director
Provides financing & investment services to the CATV industry; specializes in mergers & acquisitions, buy out financing, raising debt & equity and assisting in development & launching of new cable networks.

WELLS FARGO SECURITIES LLC
420 Montgomery St
San Francisco, CA 97104
Phone: 866-878-5865
Web Site: http://www.wellsfargo.com/securities
Provides equities & sales trading, investment banking & capital markets, fixed income sales sales & trading and integrated research & economics.

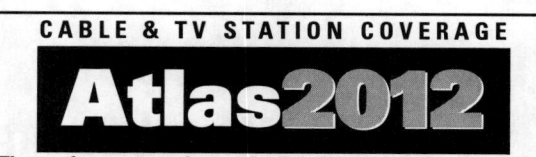

WOOD & CO. INC.
431 Ohio Pike
Ste 200
Cincinnati, OH 45255
Phone: 513-528-7373
Larry C. Wood, President
Provides TV, radio, cable & newspaper brokerage & financing, merger & acquisition negotiation & broadcast station appraisals.

Management & Technical Services

ABI RESEARCH
249 South St
Oyster Bay, NY 11771
Phone: 516-624-2500
Fax: 516-624-2501
Web Site: http://www.abiresearch.com
Tim Archdeacon, President & Chief Executive Officer
Ed Rerisi, Vice President & Chief Operating Officer
Stuart Carlaw, Vice President & Chief Research Officer
Erik Michielsen, Vice President, Sales

Branch Offices:
NEW YORK: 501 Seventh Ave, Ste 205A, New York, NY 10018. Phone: 646-383-8928.

SCOTTSDALE: 14555 N Scottsdale Rd, Ste 150, Scottsdale, AZ 85254. Phone: 480-346-1117.

SINGAPORE: 23 Lorong Telok, Unit 03-01 049035, Singapore. Phone: 65-6534-9329. Fax: 65-6438-6591.

UNITED KINGDOM: 29-30 High Holborn, London WC1V 6AZ, United Kingdom. Phone: 44-0-203-326-0140. Fax: 44-0-203-326-0141.
Assists wireless semiconductor component manufactures in understanding & entering new markets.

ADJOINED CONSULTING — See listing for Capgemini.

A-J CONTRACTING CO. INC. — No longer in business.

AJILON COMMUNICATIONS
Suwanee Ctr, 970 Peachtree Industrial Blvd
Ste 200
Suwanee, GA 30024
Phones: 678-482-5103; 800-843-6910
Fax: 678-482-8849; 800-545-1988
Web Site: http://www.ajiloncom.com
Daniel R. Sims, President & Chief Operating Officer
Walt Strausbaugh, Senior Vice President
Provides telecommunications consulting, technical expertise, program/project management & outsourcing services.

THE AKER PARTNERS INC.
2801 M St NW
Washington, DC 20007
Phones: 202-719-8062; 202-223-4889
Web Site: http://www.akerpartners.com
Colburn Aker, Managing Partner
Carolyn Myles, Senior Partner
David Narsavage, Senior Partner
Sanda Pecina, Partner & Director, Media Relations
Provides communications consulting, public relations & marketing services; specializes in marketing, media relations & public affairs.

ALLISON PAYMENT SYSTEMS LLC
2200 Production Dr
Indianapolis, IN 46241-4912
Phones: 317-808-2400; 800-755-2440
Fax: 317-808-2477
E-mail: sales@apsllc.com
Web Site: http://www.apsllc.com
Joseph H. Thomas, Chairman & Chief Executive Officer
Joseph P. Thomas, President & Chief Operating Officer
Dale J. Eland, Vice President, Manufacturing Services
Brad E. Turner, Vice President, Technical Services
Kevin W. Thomas, Vice President, Customer Relationship Management
Provides payment system products & services, including payment systems, print & mail statements & coupon books.

ALL TV CONNECT — See listing for ATV Broadcast LLC.

ALL TV CONNECT INC. — See listing for ATV Broadcast LLC.

AMDOCS, BROADBAND CABLE & SATELLITE DIVISION
1104 Investment Blvd
El Dorado Hills, CA 95762
Phones: 916-934-7000; 877-878-2122
Fax: 916-934-7054
E-mail: info@amdocs.com
Web Site: http://www.amdocs.com
Brian Shephard, President, Broadband, Cable & Media
Provides customer management & billing services for video, broadband, telecommunications & utilities industries.

AMERICAN EUROPEAN CONSULTING CO. INC.
PO Box 19686
Houston, TX 77224-9686
Phone: 713-464-8711
Fax: 713-464-8711
Arthur Krueger, President
Provides management services, international market research & development.

ANCHOR PACIFIC CORP.
816 Congress Ave
Ste 1100
Austin, TX 78701
Phone: 512-334-6989
C. Ronald Dorchester, President & Chief Executive Officer
Provides management services for CATV, wireless video, etc.

ASCENT MEDIA GROUP
520 Broadway
5th Fl
Santa Monica, CA 90401
Phone: 310-434-7000
E-mail: sales@ascentmedia.com
Web Site: http://www.ascentmedia.com
William Fitzgerald, Chief Executive Officer
Tom Kuehle, Executive Vice President, Strategic Solutions
William Niles, Executive Vice President, General Counsel & Secretary
Douglas Parish, Executive Vice President, Operations
George C. Platisa, Executive Vice President & Chief Financial Officer
David Pruitt, Senior Vice President, Business Development
Bill Romeo, Senior Vice President, Entertainment Television Sales, Creative Group
Provides solutions for the creation, management & distribution of content to major motion picture studios, independent producers, broadcast & programming networks & other companies; systems integration; consulting services; offices worldwide.

ATV BROADCAST LLC
11650 Lantern Road
Ste 104
Fishers, IN 46038
Phone: 317-566-1563
Fax: 317-843-2863
E-mail: info@atvbroadcast.tv
Web Site: http://www.atvbroadcast.tv
Michael N. Ruggiero, Chairman
Douglas A. Smith, Chief Executive Officer & President
Christopher A. Ruggiero, Vice President, Operations
Provides CATV relations for broadcasters; copyright reduction for cable; assists in solving effective competition; syndex & network non-duplication problems; FCC significant viewing filings; channel positioning & implementing Congressional cable bills; must-carry & retransmission consent solutions.

AUDIENCE RESEARCH & DEVELOPMENT LLC
2440 Lofton Terr
Ft Worth, TX 76109
Phone: 817-924-6922
Fax: 817-924-7539
E-mail: info@ar-d.com
Web Site: http://www.ar-d.com
Jerry Gumbert, President & Chief Executive Officer
Jim Willi, Principal & Senior Vice President
Earle Jones, Senior Vice President, Research
Terry Heaton, Senior Vice President, Media 2.0
Provides insight into the development of news, information & entertainment programs in regards to TV & Internet.

THE AUSTIN CO.
6095 Parkland Blvd
Cleveland, OH 44124
Phone: 440-544-2600
Fax: 440-544-2690
E-mail: austin.info@theaustin.com
Web Site: http://www.theaustin.com

Branch Offices:
ATLANTA: 300 Galleria Pkwy, Ste 1600, Atlanta, GA 30339. Phone: 404-564-3950. Fax: 404-564-3951. E-Mail: se@theaustin.com.

IRVINE: 6410 Oak Canyon, Ste 150, Irvine, CA 92618-5201. Phone: 949-451-9000. Fax: 949-451-9011. E-Mail: we@theaustin.com.

PORTAGE: 8135 Cox's Dr, Ste 213, Portage, MI 49002. Phone: 269-329-1170. Fax: 269-329-1417.

TOKYO: 5-11 Akasaka 6-Chome, Minato-ku, Tokyo 1078348, Japan. Phone: 81-090-1547-8903. Fax: 81-03-5544-1754. E-Mail: seiji.ishibashi@theaustin.com.
Consults, designs, engineers & constructs facilities for TV, radio, cable & motion pictures; specializes in broadcast/technical centers, network switching facilities, transmission facilities & executive/administrative facilities.

AZCAR TECHNOLOGIES INC.
3235 14th Ave
Markham, ON L3R 0H3
Canada
Phones: 905-470-2545; 888-694-6623
Fax: 905-470-2559
E-mail: info@azcar.com
Web Site: http://www.azcar.com
Stephen Pumple, Chairman & Chief Executive Officer
Gavin Schutz, President & Chief Operating Officer
William Frazier, Vice President, Business Development
Kenneth C. Fuller, Engineering Director

Branch Offices:
CANONSBURG: AZCAR USA Inc., 121 Hillpointe Dr, Ste 700, Canonsburg, PA 15317. Phones: 724-873-0800; 888-873-0800. Fax: 724-873-4770.
Provides broadcast & multimedia consulting & planning, project management, systems design & integration, equipment procurement & logistics, training and engineering & turnkey integration services; designs & constructs outside broadcast & satellite news gathering vehicles; resells digital audio-video products; offers financing solutions.

BACKCHANNELMEDIA INC.
105 South St
2nd Fl
Boston, MA 02111
Phones: 617-728-3626; 800-578-8283
Fax: 617-517-7777
E-mail: info@backchannelmedia.com
Web Site: http://www.backchannelmedia.com
Daniel Hassan, Chairman & Co-Chief Executive Officer
Michael Kokernak, Co-Chief Executive Officer

Direct response media specialist agency; assists clients & media outlets to understand & capitalize on the changing TV advertising marketplace.

BAKER SCOTT & CO.
34 N Lenhome Dr
Ste 107
Cranford, NJ 07016
Phone: 973-263-3355
Fax: 973-263-9255
E-mail: exec.search@bakerscott.com
Web Site: http://www.bakerscott.com
Provides executive search & organization planning services.

BIA DATAWORLD — See listing for Dataworld.

THE BIA KELSEY GROUP
15120 Enterprise Ct
Ste 100
Chantilly, VA 20151
Phones: 703-818-2425; 800-331-5086
Fax: 703-803-3299
E-mail: info@biakelsey.com
Web Site: http://www.bia.com
Tom J. Buono, Founder & Chief Executive Officerr
Neal Polachek, President
Mark A. Giannini, Chief Operating Officer & Senior Vice President
Rick Ducey, Chief Strategy Officer
Mark Fratrik, Vice President
Bobbi Loy-Luster, Vice President & Senior Analyst
Steve Passwaiter, Vice President, Business Development
Geoff Price, Vice President
Formerly BIA Financial Network LLC. Provides financial intelligence & investment resources to the media, telecommunications, technical & related industries; provides valuation & financial/strategic advisory services; publishes financial reports, yearbooks & pocket guides on the TV industry. Division of BIA Advisory Services.

BITCENTRAL
4340 Von Karman Ave
Ste 410
Newport Beach, CA 92660
Phones: 949-253-9000; 800-214-2828
Fax: 949-253-9004
E-mail: info@bitcentral.com
Web Site: http://www.bitcentral.com
Fred Fourcher, President & Chief Executive Officer
Gary Coats, Chief Operating Officer
Cleve Cushing, Chief Financial Officer
Alex Keighley, Vice President, Sales
John King, Vice President, Professional Engineering Services
Rick Young, Vice President, Product Strategy
Lee Roquet, Vice President, Client Services
Consults, designs, procures & installs complete systems for the transmission & delivery of video, voice & data; provides video content management & distribution solutions.

BOERNER COMMUNICATIONS INC.
215 Park Ave S
10th Fl
New York, NY 10003
Phone: 646-430-8280
E-mail: info@boernercommunications.com
Web Site: http://www.boernercommunications.com
Mary Ann Boerner, President & Chief Executive Officer
Hank Boerner, Senior Strategist & Advisor
Ken Cynar, Senior Strategist & Advisor
Louis Coppola, Vice President, Information Technology
Amy Gallagher, Vice President, Client Services
Provides executive management communications coaching & training; prepares spokespersons, provides seminars in TV news interviewing, government testimony; creative services for video tape presentations, sales & management communications, crisis management, video news releases & documentary production/distribution; Internet & web broadcasting platforms.

BOND & PECARO INC.
1920 N St NW
Ste 350
Washington, DC 20036
Phone: 202-775-8870
Fax: 202-775-0175
E-mail: bp@bondpecaro.com
Web Site: http://www.bondpecaro.com
James R. Bond, Jr., Principal
Timothy S. Pecaro, Principal
Jeffrey P. Anderson, Principal
Peter R. Geyer, Principal
John S. Sanders, Principal
Matthew H. Lochte, Principal
Andrew R. Gefen, Principal
Provides financial & management consulting services; specializes in asset appraisals, fair market valuations, expert testimony, impairment testing, feasibility studies, financial consulting, market research & related financial services for broadcasting, cable television, Internet, technology & other media; publishes The Television Industry: A Market-by-Market Review with the NAB.

BOOTH RESEARCH SERVICES INC.
8046 Roswell Rd
Ste 101C
Atlanta, GA 30350
Phones: 770-992-2200; 800-727-2577
Fax: 770-642-4535
E-mail: brs@boothresearch.com
Web Site: http://www.boothresearch.com
Peter E. Booth, President & Senior Account Director
Scott Booth, Business Development Director
Chrissy Booth Flicker, Project Manager & Programming
Specializes in research for CATV, media & broadcast industries; complete design through analysis; in-house services include telephone (CATI), online, mail, in-person surveys & focus group studies.

BOOZ, ALLEN & HAMILTON INC.
8283 Greensboro Dr
McLean, VA 22102
Phone: 703-902-5000
Fax: 703-902-3333
E-mail: communications@bah.com
Web Site: http://www.boozallen.com
Ralph W. Shrader, Chairman & Chief Executive Officer
Samuel R. Strickland, Executive Vice President & Chief Financial Officer
Provides consulting services to private & government sectors; specializes in strategic, organizational, technological, public management, productivity management & defense technology; offices worldwide.

BORTZ MEDIA & SPORTS GROUP
4582 S Ulster St
Ste 1340
Denver, CO 80237
Phone: 303-893-9902
Fax: 303-893-9913
E-mail: info@bortz.com
Web Site: http://www.bortz.com
Arthur Steiker, Managing Director
James M. Trautman, Managing Director
Mark C. Wyche, Managing Director
Provides domestic & international consulting services for broadcast, cable, new media & professional sports industries; new business planning, fair market valuations of stations, cable systems & program networks; sports media rights analysis; market research & litigation support services.

BRIX NETWORKS — See listing for EXFO.

BROADBANDCAREERS.COM
PO Box 321610
Cocoa Beach, FL 32931
Phone: 877-329-6600
E-mail: sales_team@broadbandcareers.com
Web Site: http://www.broadbandcareers.com
Mark Clancey, Director, Sales & Business Development
Broadband-CATV-IP recruitment advertising; offers association & publisher job banks & a directory of over 8,000 companies.

BROADCAST SERVICES INC.
4801 Industrial Pkwy
Indianapolis, IN 46226
Phone: 317-895-9050
Fax: 317-895-2900
Web Site: http://www.bsiteleplex.com
Tom L. Fitch, President & Chief Executive Officer
Peter Miller, Vice President & General Counsel
Douglas S. Weaver, Vice President, Engineering
Anita Willis, Vice President, Site Development
Provides broadcast & telecommunications antenna site design, development & management services.

BROADVIEW SOFTWARE INC.
207 Adelaide St E
Ste 201
Toronto, ON M5A 1M8
Canada
Phone: 416-778-0623
Fax: 416-778-0648
E-mail: sales@broadviewsoftware.com
Web Site: http://www.broadviewsoftware.com
Arthur Drevnig, Sales & Marketing Director
Provides software that provides TV stations with an integrated solution for program acquisition, ad sales, program scheduling, traffic, master control automation interfacing & reporting.

STUART N. BROTMAN COMMUNICATIONS
47 Baskin Rd
Lexington, MA 02421-6928
Phone: 781-862-8898
Fax: 781-861-0207
E-mail: info@brotman.com
Web Site: http://brotman.com
Stuart N. Brotman, President
Provides strategic corporate, financial, market & regulatory planning for senior management of communications, information & entertainment clients worldwide.

CABLE PARTNERS
Foxglove House
166-168 Piccadilly
London W1J 9EF
United Kingdom
Phone: 44-20-7318-8900
Fax: 44-20-7318-8909
E-mail: askme-sg@synergyonline.com
Web Site: http://www.cablepartners.com
Richard J. Callahan, Chief Executive Officer
Andrew Sukawaty, President

Branch Offices:
DENVER: 3200 Cherry Creek Dr N, Ste 755, Denver, CO 80209. Phone: 303-715-3600. Fax: 303-715-3606.
Provides consulting to cable companies.

CABLE AUDIT ASSOCIATES INC.
5340 S Quebec St
Greenwood Village, CO 80111-1910
Phone: 303-694-0444
Fax: 303-694-2559
E-mail: info@cableaudit.com
Web Site: http://www.cableaudit.com
Bruce Lazarus, Chief Executive Officer
Raoul A. De Sota, Senior Vice President, Strategic Development
John MacDonald, Senior Vice President, Audit Operations
Mitchell Walker, Senior Vice President, Consulting & Technology Services
Greg Bryant, Vice President, Audit Operations & Staff Development
Dona Johnson, Vice President, Premium Services
Mary Miller, Vice President, Client Relations & Contract Compliance
Provides business to business auditing, assurance & revenue systems management services to companies in the media & entertainment industry.

CABLE SYSTEM SERVICES
3588 Kennebec Dr
Eagan, MN 55122
Phone: 651-688-2623
Fax: 651-688-2624
E-mail: cabless@cablesystemservices.com
Web Site: http://www.cablesystemservices.com
Provides broadband fiber design, installation & system management.

CABLE SYSTEM SURVEY CO.
PO Box 311
Tekonsha, MI 49092
Phone: 302-218-4221
E-mail: tntetreault@cablesystemsurveyco.com
Web Site: http://www.cablesystemsurveyco.com
Thomas N. Tetreault, President & Chief Executive Officer

Branch Offices:
WILMINGTON: PO Box 5477, Wilmington, DE 19808. Phone: 302-218 4221. Fax: 302-218-4221.
Provides broadband & fiber optic mapping & design services to MSOs & contractors in the CATV, MATV, private, government business & education networks, CLEC, ILEC & IEC

CAD DRAFTING SERVICES INC.
109 Bank St
Hoopestown, IL 60942
Phone: 815-698-2564
Fax: 815-698-2263

CAPGEMINI, TELECOM, MEDIA & ENTERTAINMENT GROUP
623 Fifth Ave
33rd Fl
New York, NY 10022
Phone: 212-314-8000
Fax: 212-314-8001
Web Site: http://www.us.capgemini.com
Provides consulting, outsourcing & local professional services in more than 36 countries; publishes reports on the telecom, cable, media & entertainment industries.

WILLIAM B. CARR & ASSOCIATES INC.
27 CR310
Dublin, TX 76446
Phone: 254-445-4200
Fax: 254-445-4201
William B. Carr, President
Offers consulting engineering services to the broadcasting & communication industries.

CB COMMUNICATIONS INC.
141 E 55th St
Ste 10-H
New York, NY 10022
Phone: 212-758-7880
Fax: 212-758-7881
Suzan Couch, President
Provides entertainment marketing, including strategic planning, advertising, promotion, traditional & online media and program packaging.

CHADBOURN MARCATH INC.
3318 N Lakeshore Dr
Ste 100
Chicago, IL 60657-3959
Phones: 312-915-0300; 800-223-7828
Fax: 773-525-4898
E-mail: ccs@chadbourn.com
Web Site: http://www.chadbourn.com
James C. Weisberg, President & Chief Technology Officer
Elizabeth Eugenio, Vice President, Business Development
Shelia O'Shaughnessy, Vice President, Marketing
Todd Anderson, Customer Service Director
John Navarra, Systems & Programming Director
Provides telecommunications consulting services.

CHR SOLUTIONS INC.
4424 W Sam Houston Pkwy N
Ste 420
Houston, TX 77041
Phone: 713-995-4778
Fax: 281-754-9170
E-mail: info@chrsolutions.com
Web Site: http://www.chrsolutions.com
Sean Roger Fitzsimmons, Executive Vice President, Client Solutions
Marc Hayden, Executive Vice President, Client Services
Jeff Boozer, Senior Vice President, Business Development
Jay Wempe, Vice President, BPO Services

Branch Offices:
AUSTIN: 5929 Balcones Dr, Ste 200, Austin, TX 78731-1639. Phone: 512-343-2544. Fax: 512-343-0119.

CAMDEN: 110 Harrison Ave SW, Camden, AR 71701. Phone: 870-836-9331. Fax: 870-836-2788.

COLUMBIA: 1805 Burlington St, Columbia, MO 65202. Phone: 573-474-1474. Fax: 573-474-0674.

DALLAS: 2711 LBJ Fwy, Ste 560, Dallas, TX 75234. Phone: 972-484-2323. Fax: 972-243-6139.

HOUSTON: Southwest Corporate Center, 9700 Bissonnet, Ste 2800, Houston, TX 77036.

LUBBOCK: 4747 S Loop 289, Lubbock, TX 79424. Phone: 806-722-7700. Fax: 806-722-7802.

MITCHELL: 1515 N Sanborn Blvd, Mitchell, SD 57301-1021. Phones: 605-996-9646; 877-996-9646. Fax: 605-995-2577.

MOLALLA: 209 Marson Ct, PO Box 543, Molalla, OR 97038. Phones: 503-829-6660; 877-203-1442. Fax: 503-829-5648.

NASHVILLE: BNA Corp Ctr Bldg 100, 402 BNA Dr, Ste 409, Nashville, TN 37217-2542. Phone: 877-996-9646. Fax: 615-365-9052.

SIOUX FALLS: 110 N Minnesota, Ste 300, Sioux Falls, SD 57104-6460. Phone: 605-996-9646. Fax: 605-271-0339.
Single-source provider of business consulting, engineering services, software solutions & technology managed services to clients in all 50 states as well as internationally. Company helps clients grow revenues, reduce costs, improve operations, manage risk & align technology.

COLUMBIA TELECOMMUNICATIONS CORP.
10613 Concord St
Kensington, MD 20895
Phone: 301-933-1488
Fax: 301-933-3340
E-mail: info@ctcnet.us
Web Site: http://www.ctcnet.us
Joanne S. Hovis, President
Andrew L. Afflerbach, PhD, Chief Executive Officer & Director, Engineering
Provides communications engineering consulting services for public sector & non-profit clients nationwide.

COMMUNICATIONS ENGINEERING INC.
8500 Cinder Bed Rd
Ste 100
Newington, VA 22122
Phone: 703-550-5800
Fax: 703-550-5180
E-mail: sales@commeng.com
Web Site: http://www.commeng.com
Lawerence S. Brody, President & Chief Executive Officer
John Wesley Nash, Executive Vice President & Chief Operating Officer
Jim Conley, Senior Vice President, Engineering & Chief Technology Officer
David A. Giblin, Vice President & General Manager
Designs & integrates broadcast & multimedia systems; provides expertise in SD & HD video, multi-format audio, high-speed data networking, asset-management, broadband video transmission, multimedia content, acoustics, space planning & mechanical (HVAC) systems.

COMMUNICATIONS EQUITY ASSOCIATES
101 E Kennedy Blvd
Ste 3300
Tampa, FL 33602
Phone: 813-226-8844
Fax: 813-225-1513
E-mail: info@ceaworldwide.com
Web Site: http://www.ceaworldwide.com
J. Patrick Michaels, Jr., Chairman & Chief Executive Officer
Ming Jung, Senior Managing Director & Chief Financial Officer, CEA Cap Advisors
Ken Jones, Senior Vice President & General Counsel
Robert D. Berger, Managing Director
Carsten Philipson, Managing Director
Donald Russell, Managing Director

Branch Offices:
NEW YORK: 54 Thompson St, 4th Fl, New York, NY 10012. Phone: 212-218-5085. Fax: 212-334-5003. Waldo Glasman, Managing Director; John Morrison, Managing Director; Alexander Rossi, Managing Director.

WESTPORT: Principal Advisors Group, 191 Post Rd W, Westport, CT 06880. Phone: 203-221-2662. Fax: 203-221-2663. Dave Moyer, President.

UNITED KINGDOM: 11 Staple Ct, 11 Staple Inn Bldgs, London EC3A 7PT, WC1V 7Q4. Phone: 44-0-207-280-4899. Fax: 44-0-207-280-4899. Martin Farmer, Managing Director.
Provides investment banking & brokerage services to CATV, broadcasting, media & entertainment industries; acquisitions, divestitures, mergers & trades; financial placements for equity & debt; joint ventures; appraisals; consultation for tax & estate planning & shareholder negotiations.

COMSEARCH
Janelia Technology Park
19700 Janelia Farm Blvd
Ashburn, VA 20147
Phones: 703-726-5500; 800-318-1234
Fax: 703-726-5600
E-mail: sales@comsearch.com
Web Site: http://www.comsearch.com
Douglass Hall, President
Chris Hardy, Vice President & General Manager
Tim Hardy, Vice President, Engineering Solutions
Mark Gibson, Senior Director, Business Development
Brian Downs, Director, Government Solutions
Provides engineering services for mobile, PCS, microwave & satellite industries; includes engineering software, terrain digitizing, propagation analysis, interference analysis, network design, field studies, licensing assistance, demographic studies & market reports. Division of CommScope Inc.

COMSONICS INC.
PO Box 1106
1350 Port Republic Rd
Harrisonburg, VA 22801
Phones: 540-434-5965; 800-336-9681
Fax: 540-432-9794
E-mail: marketing@comsonics.com
Web Site: http://www.comsonics.com
Dennis Zimmerman, Chairman, President & Chief Executive Officer
Donn Meyerhoeffer, Chief Operating Officer
Bret V. Harrison, Director, Repair Services
Manufacturers CATV test & measurement equipment; provides repair services for distribution, headend, test, power supply & fiber optic equipment.

COMTEL VIDEO SERVICES INC.
PO Box 1595
Makawao, HI 96768-1595
Phones: 808-270-3065; 808-268-2151
E-mail: info@comtelvideo.com
Web Site: http://www.comtelvideo.com
Robert C. Beggs, President
Provides air checks for advertisers on TV; off-air & off-satellite videotaping; videotape duplication; international standards conversions; closed captioning service.

CONLEY & ASSOCIATES LLC
1459 Interstate Loop
Bismarck, ND 58503-5560
Phone: 701-222-3902
Fax: 701-258-1937
E-mail: info@conleyassociates.net
Web Site: http://www.conleyassociates.net
Christopher J. Conley, Managing General Partner
Provides management & engineering consulting to the electronic media; specializes in appraisals & valuations; strategic planning & feasibility studies; financial planning & restructuring; contract management; operational evaluations & audits; engineering design & technical evaluations; marketing research & analysis; human resources development & training; franchising & refranchising; regulatory affairs & expert testimony.

CONTEC
1011 State St
Schenectady, NY 12307-1511
Phones: 518-382-8000; 800-382-2723
Fax: 518-382-7680
E-mail: sales@gocontec.com
Web Site: http://www.gocontec.com

Branch Offices:
BROWNSVILLE: WorldWide Digital, 1900 Billy Mitchell Blvd, Brownsville, TX 78521. Phone: 956-541-0600. Fax: 956-831-8310.

SEATTLE: 1250 S 192nd St, Seattle, WA 98148. Phones: 206-244-0604; 888-266-8322. Fax: 206-244-4938.
Provides equipment repair to the broadband industry.

CORNWALL ASSOCIATES
234 N El Molino Ave
Pasadena, CA 91101
Phone: 626-793-5782
Fax: 626-793-7956
E-mail: scornwall@sbcglobal.net
Kent Cornwall, President
J. Shirl Cornwall, Vice President
Provides architecture, interior & technical design & consulting services for production & broadcast facilities.

CREDIT PROTECTION ASSOCIATION INC.
13355 Noel Rd
Ste 2100
Dallas, TX 75230
Phone: 972-233-9614
E-mail: info@creditprotect.com
Web Site: http://www.creditprotect.com
Nate A. Levine, President & Chief Executive Officer
Ann E. Levine, Secretary
Douglas K. Bridges, Vice President & Chief Financial Officer
Full-service national collections company specializing in the CATV industry; offers complete automated submissions of write-off accounts through the major billing services, comprehensive client reports, on-line debtor status inquiry, pro-active customer service, physical recovery & pro-qualified services.

CREWSTAR INC.
Southborough Ctr
One Boston Rd
Southborough, MA 01772
Phones: 508-481-2212; 888-746-6871
Fax: 508-481-7785
E-mail: joe@crewstar.com
Lily Maiella, President
Joseph Maiella, Senior Vice President, Marketing & Sales
Provides clients with video & film crews around the world; provides personalized, accurate crew & talent payroll services for easy production payroll administration & to assure compliance with state & federal guidelines.

CRITICAL MENTION INC. (CLIP SYNDICATE)
1776 Broadway
24th Fl
New York, NY 10019
E-mail: contact@clipsyndicate.com
Web Site: http://www.clipsyndicate.com
Sean Morgan, Founder & Chief Executive Officer
Michael Johnston, Vice President, Network Operations
Jim Pavoldi, Vice President, Business Development & Distribution
Donald Silvey, Vice President, Content Strategy
James Vaughn, Vice President, Software Engineering
Provides a web-based TV search & monitoring service.

CRYSTAL COMPUTER CORP.
4465 Commerce Dr
Ste 107
Buford, GA 30518
Phone: 770-932-0970
Fax: 775-719-3402
E-mail: sales@crystalcc.com
Web Site: http://www.crystalcc.com
Earl Franklin, Chairman
Roger Franklin, President & Chief Executive Officer
Rob Dowd, Senior Vice President, Sales & Marketing
Matthew Frei, Vice President
Tim Johnson, Manager, Sales
Provides turnkey customer-tailored network management & control systems to the satellite & media transmission industries.

CS COMMUNICATIONS INC.
9825 Bridleridge Ct
Vienna, VA 22181
Phone: 703-938-5365
Provides engineering & economic consulting services in DBS & other satellite communication systems, MDS & CATV.

CSG SYSTEMS INC.
9555 Maroon Cir
Englewood, CO 80112
Phones: 303-796-2850; 800-366-2744
Fax: 303-804-4088
E-mail: Sales@csgsystems.com
Web Site: http://www.csgsystems.com
Peter Kalan, President & Chief Executive Officer
Joe Ruble, Executive Vice President, General Counsel & Chief Administration Officer
Randy Wiese, Executive Vice President & Chief Financial Officer
Bret Griess, Executive Vice President & Chief Operating Officer

Branch Offices:
CHICAGO: 33 W Monroe St, Ste 900, Chicago, IL 60603. Phone: 312-660-5600.

OMAHA: North Park NP6, 2525 N 117th St, Omaha, NE 68164. Phone: 402-431-7000.
Provides billing & customer management services for the converging communications industries.

DATAWORLD
15120 Enterprise Ct
Chantilly, VA 20151
Phones: 703-227-9680; 800-331-5086
Fax: 703-803-3299
Web Site: http://www.bia.com/dataworld
Provides engineering & FCC business intelligence to communications industries via a range of data & information services, technical engineering studies & custom mapping. Division of BIA Kelsey Group.

DG FASTCHANNEL INC.
750 W John Carpenter Fwy
Ste 700
Irving, TX 75039
Phones: 972-581-2000; 800-324-5672
Fax: 972-581-2001
E-mail: info@dgfastchannel.com
Web Site: http://www.dgfastchannel.com
Scott K. Ginsburg, Chairman & Chief Executive Officer
Omar A. Choucair, Chief Financial Officer
Neil Nguyen, Executive Vice President, Sales & Operations
Pamela Maythenyi, Senior Vice President, Creative Services
Delivers SD & HD advertising via satellite & IP technology; deploys digital media intelligence & asset management tools specifically for the advertising industry; online creative & production resources, rich media video ad serving & digital asset management; offices nationwide.

DIGITAL GENERATION SYSTEMS —
See listing for DG FastChannel.

DIGITAL PRAXIS LTD.
The Granary
Throcking
Buntingford, Herts SG9 9RU
United Kingdom
Phone: 44-0-1763-281-699
E-mail: steve@digitalpraxis.net
Web Site: http://www.digitalpraxis.net
Steve Shaw, Founder & President
Provides consultation services to companies working in the digital film arena, including technical, operational & creative support.

DIVERSIFIED SYSTEMS INC.
363 Market St
Kenilworth, NJ 07033
Phone: 908-245-4833
Fax: 908-245-0011
E-mail: info@divsystems.com
Web Site: http://www.divsystems.com
Fred D'Alessandro, Founder, President & Chief Executive Officer
Mark M. S. Lee, Executive Vice President, International Growth Market
Kevin Collins, Executive Vice President & Chief Operating Officer
Duane Yoslov, Senior Vice President, Western Region

Branch Offices:
WASHINGTON, DC: 23475 Rockhaven Way, Ste 140, Dulles, VA 20166. Phone: 703-661-8870. Fax: 703-661-1440. E-Mail: t.atkins@divsysinc.com. Tom Atkins, Vice President, Mid-Atlantic Region.

SANTA CLARA: 3275 Edward Ave, Santa Clara, CA 95054. Phone: 408-969-1972. Fax: 408-969-1985. E-Mail: d.yoslov@divsysinc.com. Duane Yoslov, Vice President, West Coast Operations.

SEATTLE: 4000 Aurora Ave N, Ste 225, Seattle, WA 98103. Phone: 206-547-0251. Fax: 206-547-0294. E-Mail: b.fisher@divsysinc.com.
Addresses the technical needs of the broadcast, presentation, cable & telecommunications industry. Provides system consultation, project budgeting, system design, architectural design, system documentation, equipment procurement, custom fabrication, system integration, project commissioning & system training.

EBS INTERNATIONAL (ENTERTAINMENT BUSINESS SERVICES)
1801 Century Park E
Ste 2400
Los Angeles, CA 90067
Phone: 310-284-8780
Fax: 310-284-3430
E-mail: info@ebsinternational.com
Web Site: http://www.ebsinternational.com
Michael R. Zerbib, Founder
Provides research & business services to foreign broadcasters, cable networks, TV & film producers, multimedia & online content developers. Services include film & TV programs acquisition, TV production development & broadband Internet content development.

EDS, COMMUNICATIONS, MEDIA & ENTERTAINMENT — No longer in business

EDX WIRELESS LLC
101 E Broadway
MS305
Eugene, OR 97401
Phone: 541-345-0019
Fax: 541-345-8145
E-mail: info@edx.com
Web Site: http://www.edx.com
Ted G. Hicks, Vice President, Product Management
Scott A. Blumberg, Executive Director, Software Development
Jennifer S. Duncan, Executive Director, Business Development & Strategy
Brian T. Cochran, Director, Support Services
Provides cost effective & technologically advanced wireless network planning, design & management software tools for outdoor & indoor settings, across all frequency bands & in support of advanced air interface standards.

EFFROS COMMUNICATIONS
PO Box 8
Clifton, VA 20124
Phone: 703-631-2099
Fax: 703-631-6999
Web Site: http://www.effros.com
Stephen R. Effros, President
Provides legal consulting services, including strategic analysis & planning.

EQUIDATA
PO Box 6610
724 Thimble Shoals Blvd
Newport News, VA 23606
Phones: 757-873-0519; 800-288-9809
Fax: 757-873-1224
E-mail: info@equidata.com
Web Site: http://www.equidata.com
Provides commercial collection services.

EXFO
400 Godin Ave
Quebec, QC G1M 2K2
Canada
Phones: 418-683-0211; 800-663-3936
Fax: 418-681-3986
E-mail: info@exfo.com
Web Site: http://www.exfo.com
Germain Lamonde, Chairman, President & Chief Executive Officer
Jon Bradley, Vice President, International Telecom Sales
Stephen Bull, Vice President, Research & Development
Etienne Gagnon, Vice President, Product Management & Marketing

Branch Offices:
RICHARDSON: 3400 Waterview Pkwy, Ste 100, Richardson, TX 75080. Phones: 972-761-9271; 800-663-3936. Fax: 972-761-9067.

SINGAPORE: Shaw Tower, 100, Beach Rd, No. 25-01/03 189702, Singapore. Phone: 65-6333-8241. Fax: 65-6333-8242.

UNITED KINGDOM: Omega Enterprise Park, Electron Way, Chandlers Ford, Eastleigh, Hampshire S053 4SE, United Kingdom. Phone: 44-2380-246-800. Fax: 44-2380-246-801.
Provides test & monitoring solutions for network service providers & equipment manufacturers in the global telecommunications industry.

THE EXLINE CO.
4340 Redwood Hwy
Ste F-230
San Rafael, CA 94903
Phone: 415-479-3484
Fax: 415-479-1574
E-mail: exline@pacbell.net
Web Site: http://www.exlinecompany.com
Andrew McClure, President
Judi Lewis, Administrative Coordinator
Provides consulting services in operations, personnel & finance as well as brokerage & appraisals for radio & TV communications companies.

PAUL DEAN FORD
3881 W Dugger Ave
West Terre Haute, IN 47885
Phone: 812-535-3828
E-mail: wpfr@joink.com
Paul Dean Ford, PE
Provides broadcast engineering consulting services.

FORRESTER RESEARCH INC.
400 Technology Sq
Cambridge, MA 02139
Phones: 617-613-6000; 866-367-7378
Fax: 617-613-5200
Web Site: http://www.forrester.com
George F. Colony, Chairman & Chief Executive Officer
Charles Rutstein, Chief Operating Officer
George M. Orlov, Chief Information & Chief Technology Officer
Michael A. Doyle, Chief Financial Officer & Treasurer
Dwight Griesman, Chief Marketing Officer
Elizabeth A. Lemons, Chief People Officer
Gail S. Mann, Chief Legal Officer & Secretary
Greg Nelson, Chief Sales Officer
Mark R. Nemec, Managing Director, Technology Industry Client Group
Dennis van Lingen, Managing Director, Marketing & Strategy Client Group
Tom Pohlmann, Managing Director, Information Technology Client Group

Branch Offices:
DALLAS: 5001 Spring Valley Rd, Ste 200-E, Dallas, TX 75244. Phone: 469-221-5300.

NEW YORK: 160 5th Ave, New York, NY 10010. Phone: 212-857-0700.

SAN FRANCISCO: 150 Spear St, Ste 1100, San Francisco, CA 94105. Phone: 415-355-6000. Fax: 415-503-1936.

WASHINGTON, DC: 8180 Greensboro Dr, Ste 750, McLean, VA 22102. Phone: 703-584-2626.

FRANCE: Forrester Research SAS, 109-111 Rue Victor Hugo, Levallois Perret 92300, France. Phone: 33-01-4758-9300. Fax: 33-01-4758-9301.

GERMANY: Forrester Research GmbH & Co. KG, Eschersheimer Landstr 10, Frankfurt 60322, Germany. Phone: 49-69-9592980. Fax: 49-69-95929810.

THE NETHERLANDS: Forrester Research B.V., Rijnsburgstraat 9-11, Amsterdam 1059 AT, The Netherlands. Phone: 31-20-305-43-49. Fax: 31-20-305-43-333.

UNITED KINGDOM: 265 Strand, London WC2R 1BH, United Kingdom. Phone: 44-0-20-7631-0202. Fax: 44-0-20-7631-5252.
An independent technology & market research company; provides advice to global leaders in business & technology. Proprietary research, consulting, events & peer-to-peer executive programs.

FREEMAN CORP.

1600 Viceroy
Ste 100
Dallas, TX 75235
Phones: 214-445-1000; 800-453-9228
Fax: 214-445-0200
E-mail: pressroom@freemanco.com
Web Site: http://www.freemanco.com
Don Freeman, Chairman & Chief Executive Officer
Joe Popolo, Chief Executive Officer
Carrie Freeman Parsons, Vice Chair
John F. O'Connell Jr, President

Branch Offices:
ALEXANDRIA: 201 N Union St, Ste 210, Alexandria, VA 22314. Phone: 703-739-6620. Fax: 703-739-6627.

CHICAGO: 600 W Chicago Ave, Ste 125, Chicago, IL 60644. Phone: 312-654-8844. Fax: 312-654-8929.

GRAND PRAIRIE: 2940 114th St, Grand Prairie, TX 75050. Phone: 817-607-2600. Fax: 817-633-8392.

MOHAVE VALLEY: 9520 S Vanderslice Rd, Mohave Valley, AZ 86440. Phone: 928-788-4300. Fax: 928-768-6260.
Produces expositions, conventions, corporate events & exhibits

JIM FRENCH DESIGN SHOP

17 E Brady
Tulsa, OK 74103
Phone: 918-583-2926
Fax: 918-583-5905
Jim French, President
Makes custom scenery, displays & props.

PETER FROEHLICH & CO.

PO Box 339
Weatherford, TX 76086
Phones: 817-594-9991; 800-742-4947
Fax: 817-594-1337
E-mail: pfsearch@flash.net
Peter Froehlich, Owner
Offers executive searches specializing in the communications industry; positions are filled at all levels & disciplines.

GELLER MEDIA INTERNATIONAL

666 W End Ave
Ste 11M
New York, NY 10025
Phone: 212-580-3385
Fax: 212-787-6279
E-mail: vgeller@aol.com
Web Site: http://www.gellermedia.com
Valerie Geller, President
Provides broadcasting consulting services; works with broadcasters throughout the world to create news/talk, information & personality radio.

GENCOM TECHNOLOGY LLC

Seven Airborne Rd
Albany, North Shore City
Auckland 0632
New Zealand
Phone: 64-9-913-7500
Fax: 64-9-913-7507
E-mail: info@gencom.com
Web Site: http://www.gencom.com
Provides global media technology solutions, including broadcast TV, multimedia & projection, telecommunications systems, design & consultancy as well as system integration & support.

GEOMART

PO Box 270838
Fort Collins, CO 80527
Phones: 970-416-8340; 800-248-6277
Fax: 970-416-8345; 800-321-6277
E-mail: sales@geomart.com
Web Site: http://www.geomart.com
Provides mapping services, including overnight delivery of any USGS topographic map; complete U.S. coverage of aerial photograph, custom mapping for line of site & cell tower placements, & custom aerial photography for flyovers.

GEORGIA U.S. DATA SERVICES INC.

5672 Peachtree Pkwy
Norcross, GA 30092
Phone: 770-734-0804
Offers subscriber billing services, including mail stream sort, zip + 4 barcode, post office certified reports, cable logo, scan line, sequence number, remarks insert key, insert printing, inserting & delivery to post office.

THE GORDON GROUP

4909 Bears Paw
Springfield, IL 62711
Phone: 217-793-5464
Fax: 217-793-5465
Robert D. Gordon, President

GORMAN & ASSOCIATES

1666 K St NW
Ste 500
Washington, DC 20006
Phone: 202-778-2108
Fax: 202-463-1927
E-mail: info@gormanandassociates.com
Web Site: http://www.gormanandassociates.com
Matthew A. Gorman, Founder & President
Patrick A. Gorman, Vice President
Provides consulting services; specializes in law & the legislative process, communications industry, government relations & operations.

GRAHAM BROCK INC.

PO Box 24466
100 Sylvan Dr, Ste 260
St Simons Island, GA 31522-7466
Phones: 912-638-8028; 202-393-5133
Fax: 912-638-7722
E-mail: jeff@grahambrock.com
Web Site: http://www.grahambrock.com
R. Stuart Graham, President
Jefferson Brock, Vice President
Marilyn Matheny, Secretary-Treasurer
Provides technical broadcast consulting services for AM, FM & TV stations as well as auxiliary services (STL, RPU, LPTV, FM translators).

GREAT LAKES DATA SYSTEMS INC.

5954 Priestly Dr
Carlsbad, CA 92008
Phones: 800-882-7950; 760-602-1900
E-mail: sales@glds.com
Web Site: http://www.glds.com
J. Alonzo Rosado, Chief Executive Officer
Laura Rosado, Chief Executive Officer
Garrick Russell, President & Chief Operating Officer
Gary Schoenfeld, Vice President, Development
Sandi Kruger, Sales Director

Branch Offices:
BEAVER DAM: 306 Seippel Blvd, Beaver Dam, WI 53916. Phones: 920-887-7651; 800-882-7950.
Provides billing, subscriber management & provisioning software.

F.P. HEALY & CO. INC.

307 E 44th St
Ste E
New York, NY 10017
Phone: 212-661-0366
Fax: 212-661-0383
E-mail: fphealy@aol.com
Web Site: http://www.fphealy.com
Frank P. Healy, President
Offers personalized executive & technical search services worldwide.

NORMAN HECHT RESEARCH INC.

33 Queens St
3rd Fl
Syosset, NY 11791
Phone: 516-496-8866
Fax: 516-496-8165
E-mail: nhr@normanhechtresearch.com
Web Site: http://www.normanhechtresearch.com
Norm Hecht, Chief Executive Officer
Laura Greenberg, Co-President & Chief Operating Officer
Dan Greenberg, Co-President
Dennis Regan, Senior Vice President, Research
Provides market & media research to the broadcast, cable, technology, commercial services & communications industries, including news programming & talent research.

HELLERSTEIN & ASSOCIATES

3001 Veazey Terr NW
Ste 1308
Washington, DC 20008
Phone: 202-362-5139
Fax: 646-365-5139
E-mail: judith@jhellerstein.com
Web Site: http://www.jhellerstein.com
Judith Hellerstein, Principal
Provides technology research services; helps companies & governments better understand their markets through ICT & E-Government strategies, market analysis, strategy consulting, next-generation technology strategies, technology assessments & regulatory impact analysis of ICT, telecom & technology issues.

R. MILLER HICKS & CO.

1011 W 11th St
Austin, TX 78703
Phone: 512-477-7000
Fax: 512-477-9697
R. Miller Hicks, President
Provides consultation services, appraisals, management & programming.

HLW INTERNATIONAL LLP

115 Fifth Ave
5th Fl
New York, NY 10003
Phone: 212-353-4600
Fax: 212-353-4666
E-mail: info@hlw.com
Web Site: http://www.hlw.com
John Gering, Managing Partner

Branch Offices:
SANTA MONICA: 1630 Stewart St, Ste 100, Santa Monica, CA 90404. Phone: 310-453-2800. Fax: 310-453-7020. Chari Jalali, Principal.

CHINA: Jiushi Renaissance Mansion, 918 Huai Hai Rd, Section E, 14th Fl, Shanghai 200020, China. Phone: 86-21-6415-9437. Fax: 86-21-6415-9438. Jaiyi Huang, Managing Director.

UNITED KINGDOM: 29/31 Cowper St, London EC24 4AT, United Kingdom. Phone: 44-207-566-6800. Fax: 44-207-253-4628. Andrew Talbot, Managing Director.
Provides architectural & engineering planning, consulting & design services for the broadcast industry.

HORIZON MEDIA INC.

630 Third Ave
New York, NY 10017
Phones: 212-916-8600; 800-633-4201
Fax: 212-916-8653
E-mail: sberwitz@horizonmedia.com
Web Site: http://www.horizonmedia.com
Bill Koenigsberg, Founder, President & Chief Executive Officer
Gabrielle Magnani, Executive Vice President, Marketing & Brand Strategy
Aaron Cohen, Chief Media Negotiating Officer
Zach Rosenberg, General Manager, Western Region
Carl Kotheimer, Strategy & Account Management

Branch Offices:
LOS ANGELES: 1940 Century Park E, Los Angeles, CA 90067. Phone: 310-282-0909. Fax: 310-229-8104.

ORLANDO: 1650 Sand Lake Rd, Ste 225, Orlando, FL 32809. Phone: 407-438-7945. Fax: 407-438-9989.

THE NETHERLANDS: Wilgenweg 28A, Amsterdam 1031 HV, The Netherlands. Phone: 31-20-344-66-33. Fax: 31-20-344-66-34.
Provides brand management, channel planning, research, print negotiation, direct marketing, local market buying, national TV & radio buying.

J.C. HUMKE & ASSOCIATES INC.

5457 S Jericho Way
Centennial, CO 80015-3648
Phone: 303-489-1356
E-mail: joelhumke@comcast.net
Web Site: http://www.rfyellow.com/info/jchumke.html
Joel C. Humke, President
Design & installation services for radio communications users; services include detailed radio coverage & propagation studies from medium wave through microwave frequencies, antenna system design, interface resolution, antenna measurements, cellular telephone, expert witness testimony, TIS information stations, spectrum analysis, ANSI compliance measurements, facility planning, VHF-UHF-microwave & bid specification services.

IDC SERVICES INC.
Five Speen St
Framingham, MA 01701
Phone: 508-872-8200
E-mail: leads@idc.com
Web Site: http://www.idc.com
Kirk Campbell, President & Chief Executive Officer
Crawford Del Prete, Chief Research Officer & Executive Vice President, Worldwide Research Products
Mark Sullivan, Chief Financial Officer
Phillipe de Marcillac, Executive Vice President, International Business Units
John Gantz, Senior Vice President
Frank Gens, Senior Vice President & Chief Analyst
Clare Gillan, Senior Vice President, Executive & Go-To-Market Programs
Vito Mabrucco, Senior Vice President, Worldwide Consulting & Managing Director, IDC Canada
Henry Morris, Senior Vice President, Integration, Development & Applications Strategies Solutions Research
Eric Prothero, Senior Vice President, Worldwide Tracker Research
Brad Thorpe, Senior Vice President, Worldwide Sales
Vernon Turner, Senior Vice President, Enterprise Computing Research
Meredith Whalen, Senior Vice President, U.S. Insights & Vertical Markets Research
Debra Bernardi, Vice President, Human Resources & Education

Branch Offices:
BOULDER: 1750 14th St, Ste 200, Boulder, CO 80302. Phone: 303-385-0327.

DENVER: 16 Market Square, 1400 16th St, Ste 400, Denver, CO 80202. Phone: 508-872-8200.

NEW YORK: 405 Lexington Ave, 25th Fl, New York, NY 10174. Phone: 212-907-6500.

RED BANK: 20 White St, Ste 2B, Red Bank, NJ 07701. Phone: 732-842-0791.

SAN MATEO: 155 Bovet Rd, Ste 800, San Mateo, CA 94402-3115. Phone: 650-653-7000.

WASHINGTON, DC: 211 N Union St, Ste 105, Alexandria, VA 22314. Phone: 571-296-8060.

CANADA: 33 Yonge St, Ste 420, Toronto, ON M5E 1G4, Canada. Phone: 416-369-0033. Fax: 416-369-0033.
Provides market intelligence, advisory services & events for the information, technology, telecommunications & consumer technology markets; offices worldwide.

INFONETICS RESEARCH
900 E Hamilton Ave
Ste 230
Campbell, CA 95008
Phone: 408-583-0011
Fax: 408-583-0031
Web Site: http://www.infonetics.com
J'Amy Napolitan, Co-Founder & Chief Executive Officer
Michael Howard, Co-Founder & Principal Analyst, Carrier/Data Center Networks
Larry Howard, Vice President, Sales
Scott Coyne, Senior Account Director
George Stojsavljecic, Senior Account Director
Stephane Teral, Principal Analyst, Mobile & FMC Infrastructure
Jeff Wilson, Principal Analyst, Security

Branch Offices:
BOSTON: 91 Montvale Ave, Ste 102, Stoneham, MA 02180.

UNITED KINGDOM: Dorchester House, Station Rd, Ste 113, Letchworth Garden City SG6 3AW, United Kingdom. Phone: 44-1462-478900. Fax: 44-1462-482616.
Provides market research & consulting services; offers quarterly market share & forecasting, end-user survey research, service provider survey research & service provider capex analysis.

INFORMA TELECOMS & MEDIA
Mortimer House
37/41 Mortimer St
London W1T 3JH
United Kingdom
Phone: 44-20-7017-5537
Fax: 44-20-7017-4947
E-mail: telecoms.enquiries@informa.com
Web Site: http://www.informatm.com
Ian Hemming, Chief Executive Officer
Mark Bethell, Chief Financial Officer
Mark Newman, Chief Research Officer

Branch Offices:
WESTBOROUGH: One Research Dr, Westborough, MA 01581. Phone: 508-453-4894. E-Mail: charles.bowen@informa.com. Charles Bowen, Account Manager.

SINGAPORE: One Grange Rd, 08-02 Orchard Bldg, Singapore. Phone: 65-6835-5158. E-Mail: giovanni.cerrini@informa.com. Giovanni Cerrini, Director, Asia Pacific Business Development.
Provides strategic advice & forecasting on all aspects of converging mobile, fixed, entertainment & IT markets; publishes reports, magazine, books & directories covering global telecoms & media markets.

INFOSYS TECHNOLOGIES LTD.
Plot 44 & 97A
Hosur Rd
Electronics City, Bangalore 560 100
India
Phone: 91-80-28520261
Fax: 91-80-28520362
E-mail: askus@infosys.com
Web Site: http://www.infosys.com
K. Dinesh, Co-Founder & Board Member
N.R. Narayana Murthy, Chairman & Chief Mentor
S. Gopalakrishnan, Chief Executive Officer & Managing Director
S.D. Shibulal, Chief Operating Officer & Board Member

Branch Offices:
FREMONT: 6607 Kaiser Dr, Fremont, CA 94555. Phone: 510-724-3000. Fax: 510-742-3090.
Provides consulting & IT services; offices worldwide.

INITIATIVE MEDIA WORLDWIDE INC.
One Dag Hammarskjold Pl
No 3
New York, NY 10017-2209
Phone: 212-605-7000
Web Site: http://www.initiative.com
Richard Beaven, Chief Executive Officer
Mauricio Sabogal, President, World Markets
Eric Bader, President, G14 & Chief Strategy Officer, Worldwide
Provides media management & media planning/buying; offices worldwide.

INSIGHT RESEARCH CORP.
718 Main St

Boonton, NJ 07005
Phone: 973-541-9600
E-mail: info@insight-corp.com
Web Site: http://www.insight-corp.com
Provides market research and strategic analysis for the telecom industry; publishes market research reports, executive summaries & an e-mail newsletter.

INTEGRATED ALLIANCE LP
5800 N Interstate 35
Ste 200B
Denton, TX 76207
Phone: 940-565-9415
Fax: 940-383-1876
E-mail: ryoung@integratedalliance.com
Web Site: http://www.integratedalliance.com
Randy Keylor, Chief Executive Officer
Russell Young, Vice President, Marketing
Liz Foster, Human Resources & Operations
Provides inbound & outbound call services for customer care, billing inquiries, technical support & sales/lead generation.

INTERNATIONAL CREATIVE MANAGEMENT INC.
10250 Constellation Blvd
Los Angeles, CA 90067
Phone: 310-550-4000
Fax: 310-555-4100
E-mail: webmaster@icmtalent.com
Web Site: http://www.icmtalent.com
Jeffrey Berg, Chairman & Chief Executive Officer
Richard B. Levy, Chief Operating Officer & General Counsel
Chris Silbermann, President
Esther Newberg, Senior Vice President

Branch Offices:
NEW YORK: 825 Eighth Ave, New York, NY 10019. Phone: 212-556-5600.

UNITED KINGDOM: 61 Frith St, London W1D 3JL, United Kingdom. Phone: 44-207-851-4853.
Represents creative & technical talent in the fields of motion pictures, TV, publishing, music, live performance, commercials & new media.

INTERNATIONAL TECHNOLOGY & TRADE ASSOCIATES INC.
2120 L St. NW
Ste 400
Washington, DC 20037-1527
Phone: 202-828-2614
Fax: 202-828-2617
Web Site: http://www.itta.com
Charles W. Dyke, Chairman & Chief Executive Officer
Eric D. Lundell, President & Chief Operating Officer
Constantine A. Pagedas, Executive Vice President
Provides international business consulting services; assists companies in developing & managing high-technology trades & investments; supports activities such as technology transfer, export promotion & foreign investment in industries including telecommunications, electronics & information technology.

ISUPPLI
1700 E Walnut Ave
Ste 600
El Segundo, CA 90245
Phone: 310-524-4000
Fax: 310-524-4050
E-mail: info@isuppli.com
Web Site: http://www.isuppli.com
Dale Ford, Senior Vice President, Market Intelligence
John Ward, Vice President, Marketing
Provides industry market intelligence & advice; offices worldwide.

JONES/NCTI
9697 E Mineral Ave
Centennial, CO 80112
Phones: 303-797-9393; 866-575-7206
Fax: 303-797-9394
E-mail: info@jonesncti.com
Web Site: http://www.jonesncti.com
Glenn R. Jones, Executive Chairman & Chief & Executive Officer
Robin McVicker, President
Provides workforce performance products, professional services & education to the cable & broadband industry. Products include performance tools & extensive training content in CD/DVD, instructor-led, paper-based & online delivery formats. Provides professional services such as custom curriculum development, e-learning development & conversion, product sales support & customer education & workforce assessments.

KALBA INTERNATIONAL INC.
116 McKinley Ave
New Haven, CT 06515
Phone: 203-397-2199
Fax: 781-240-2657
E-mail: kalba@comcast.net
Web Site: http://www.kalbainternational.com
Kas Kalba, Co-founder
Dr. Yale Braunstein, Senior Advisor
Wes Vivian, Senior Technology Consultant
Provides a wide range of management consulting services covering broadband networks, mobile & internet access products & services, satellite communications & other telecom & multimedia businesses.

KANE REECE ASSOCIATES INC.
822 South Ave W
Westfield, NJ 07090-1460
Phones: 908-317-5757; 800-494-5263
Fax: 908-317-4434
Web Site: http://www.kanereece.com
John E. (Jack) Kane, Founder & Principal
Norval Reece, Co-Founder & Chairman Emeritus
Noah Gottdiener, Chief Executive Officer
Gerry Creagh, President
Dennis Elliott, Managing Director
Provides appraisals & valuations, business plans, engineering consulting, financial & technical due diligence, financing preparations, franchise renewals, litigation support, market/opinion research, management & management consulting, property tax compliance & control, solvency opinions, valuations for buy/sell agreements & workouts. Division of Duff & Phelps Corp.

KHANNA & GUILL INC.
1485 Chain Bridge Rd
Ste 302
McLean, VA 22101-4501
Phone: 703-338-0024
Fax: 703-691-2046
E-mail: info@kgiconsulting.com
Web Site: http://www.kgiconsulting.com
Sid Khanna
Robert Guill
Provides engineering consulting services.

KOMPAS GROUP
5235 N 124th St
Ste 262
Butler, WI 53007
Phone: 262-781-0188
Fax: 262-781-5313
E-mail: kompasgroup@toast.net
John Kompas, President
Jackie Kompas, Executive Vice President
Provides consulting, brokerage & representation services as well as provides information for the LPTV industry.

LEHMANN STROBEL PLC
3613 Anton Farms Rd
Baltimore, MD 21208
Phone: 443-352-8635
E-mail: info@lehmannstrobel.com
Web Site: http://www.lehmannstrobel.com
Walter G. Lehmann, Managing Partner
Sylvia L. Strobel, Senior Partner
Provides expert legal representation & business affairs services to film, TV, video, radio & multimedia professionals & companies.

ARTHUR D. LITTLE INC.
125 High St
High Street Tower, 28th Fl
Boston, MA 02210
Phone: 617-532-9550
Fax: 617-261-6630
Web Site: http://www.adlittle.com
Michael Tram, Chief Executive Officer
Provides management, environmental, health & safety consulting services; technology & product development; offices worldwide.

LNS CAPTIONING
1123 SW Yamhill St
Portland, OR 97205
Phones: 503-299-6200; 800-366-6201
Fax: 503-299-6839
E-mail: officemgr@lnscaptioning.com
Web Site: http://www.lnscaptioning.com
Offers realtime & post-production closed captions for TV, video & webcasting, along with Internet realtime streaming & event captioning.

FRANK N. MAGID ASSOCIATES INC.
One Research Ctr
Marion, IA 52302
Phone: 319-377-7345
Fax: 319-377-5861
E-mail: iowa@magid.com
Web Site: http://www.magid.com
Frank N. Magid, Chairman
Brent Magid, President & Chief Executive Officer
Steve Ridge, President, Television
Marv Danielski, Senior Vice President, Integrated Brand Development
Bill Hague, Senior Vice President

Branch Offices:
MINNEAPOLIS: 8500 Normandale Lake Blvd, Ste 630, Minneapolis, MN 55437. Phone: 952-835-4436. Fax: 952-835-3385. E-Mail: mailmn@magid.com.

NEW YORK: 1775 Broadway, Ste 1401, New York, NY 10019. Phone: 212-515-4520. Fax: 212-515-4540. E-Mail: mailny@magid.com.

SHERMAN OAKS: 15260 Ventura Blvd, Ste 1840, Sherman Oaks, CA 91403. Phone: 818-263-3300. Fax: 818-263-3311. E-Mail: mailla@magid.com.
Provides custom attitudinal research & consultation services for all media; specializes in TV news & programming, audience surveys & complete implementation services including program evaluation, talent coaching & search; publishes daily newsletters & periodic syndicated research papers.

MAGNETIC IMAGE VIDEO
129 Jordan St
San Rafael, CA 94901-3919
Phone: 415-456-7900
Fax: 415-485-3874
E-mail: rentals@mivideo.com
Web Site: http://www.mivideo.com
Larry Kenworthy, President
Cael Hazard, Manager, Production
Rents & repairs NTSC & PAL camera packages, monitors & projectors, equipment & lenses along with multicamera systems with or without crews.

M/A/R/C RESEARCH
1660 N Westridge Cir
Irving, TX 75038
Phone: 800-884-6272
Fax: 972-983-0444
E-mail: marketing@marcresearch.com
Web Site: http://www.marcresearch.com
Merrill Dubrow, President & Chief Executive Officer
Amy Barrentine, Executive Vice President & General Manager
Randall A. Wahl, Executive Vice President
Susan Hurry, Senior Vice President & General Manager
Betsy Sutherland, Senior Vice President & General Manager
Sherri Neuwirth, Senior Vice President

Branch Offices:
BRIDGETON: 3245 Smiley Rd, Bridgeton, MO 63044. Phone: 314-298-1516. Fax: 314-291-5586.

GREENSBORO: 202 CentrePoint Dr, Ste 300, Greensboro, NC 27409. Phone: 800-513-5700. Fax: 336-664-6705.
Provides brand development research & consulting services.

MARKET STRATEGIES
17430 College Pkwy
Livonia, MI 48152
Phone: 734-542-7600
Fax: 734-542-7620
Web Site: http://www.marketstrategies.com
Dr. Andrew James Morrison, Founder, Chairman & Chief Executive Officer
Reginald Baker, PhD, President & Chief Operating Officer
George Wilkerson, Executive Vice President, Communications & Energy Research Division
Leona Foster, Founder & Senior Vice President
Keri Christensen, Vice President, Communications Division
Paul Donagher, Vice President, Communications Division
Pamela S. McGill, Vice President, Communications Division

Branch Offices:
ATLANTA: 834 Inman Village Pkwy, Ste 200, Atlanta, GA 30307. Phone: 404-521-9955. Fax: 404-521-9263.

CLAREMONT: 250 W First St, Ste 304, Claremont, CA 91711. Phone: 909-626-2626. Fax: 909-626-1313.

LITTLE ROCK: 333 Executive Ct, Ste 100, Little Rock, AR 72205. Phone: 501-221-3303. Fax: 501-221-2554.

NEW PROVIDENCE: 571 Central Ave, Ste 115, New Providence, NJ 07974. Phone: 908-739-4500. Fax: 908-739-4519.

PORTLAND: 888 SW Fifth Ave, Ste 790, Portland, OR 97204. Phone: 503-225-0112. Fax: 503-225-8400.

UNITED KINGDOM: 15 Old Bailey, London EC4 M7EF, United Kingdom. Phone: 44-0-20-3178-3537. Fax: 44-0-20-3178-5179.
Provides custom & syndicated research & strategic consulting services.

MARSH & MCLENNAN COS. (MMC)
1166 Ave of the Americas
32nd Fl
New York, NY 10036
Phone: 212-345-8000
Fax: 212-345-8075
Web Site: http://www.mmc.com
Brian Duperreault, President & Chief Executive Officer
Matthew B. Bartley, Executive Vice President & Chief Financial Officer
Peter J. Beshar, Executive Vice President & General Counsel
Orlando D. Ashford, Senior Vice President, Human Resources
E. Scott Gilbert, Senior Vice President & Chief Compliance Officer
Provides management consulting & market research services; offices worldwide.

MATEJKA CABLE RECOVERY INC. —
No longer in business.

MAUCK & ASSOCIATES INC.
718 W Cactus Wren Dr
Phoenix, AZ 85021
Phone: 602-242-9449
Fax: 602-242-9449
Gary Mauck, President
Provides event management; specializes in trade shows, conferences & major promotional events.

B.K. MCINTYRE & ASSOCIATES
1250 24th St NW
Ste 350
Washington, DC 20037-1124
Phone: 202-785-5091
Fax: 202-785-5108
E-mail: bkm@bkmcintyre.com
Web Site: http://www.bkmcintyre.com
Bernice K. McIntyre, President
Meera Ahamed, Associate
Michael H. Pete, Associate
Provides management & regulatory consulting services & expertise to the communications & electric utilities industries.

MEDIASPAN ONLINE SERVICES
333 Jackson Plz
Ann Arbor, MI 48103
Phone: 800-913-1299
Web Site: http://www.mediaspanonline.com
F.R. Frank Campagnoni, President & Chief Executive Officer
William H. (Bud) Owen, Chief Financial Officer
Steven Barth, Executive Vice President & General Manager
Peter Cooper, Vice President, Marketing
Tobey Van Santvoord, Senior Manager

Branch Offices:
IRVINE: 8687 Research Dr, Ste 100, Irvine, CA 92618. Phone: 949-892-2929. Fax: 949-892-2930.

MELBOURNE: Media Software Ctr, 300 North Dr, Ste 100, Melbourne, FL 32934. Phone: 734-887-4400.

NEW YORK: Network Ctr, 41 E 11th St, 11th Fl, New York, NY 10003. Phone: 212-699-6472.
Provides online marketing solutions, including website management, streaming & podcasting tools that empower local media to grow audience & revenue.

MERCER MANAGEMENT CONSULTING INC. —
See listing for Marsh & McLennan Cos. (MMC)

MERIDIAN DESIGN ASSOCIATES ARCHITECTS
1140 Broadway
6th Fl
New York, NY 10001
Phone: 212-431-8643
Fax: 212-431-8775
E-mail: contact@meridiandesign.com
Web Site: http://www.meridiandesign.com
Antonio Argibay, Lead AP Principal
Bice C. Wilson, Principal

Branch Offices:
MIAMI: 10630 NW 27th St, Miami, FL 33172. Phone: 305-362-7663. Fax: 305-362-7675.

BUENOS AIRES: Av Cordoba 1364, Piso 3D, Buenos Aires C1055AAQ, Argentina. Phone: 54-11-4-371-7130. Fax: 54-11-156-893-3722.

SWITZERLAND: 20, rue Boissonas, 1227 Acacias, Geneve, Switzerland. Phone: 41-22-560-88-88. Fax: 41-22-560-88-00. E-Mail: contact@meridiangroup8.com.
Designs media & communications workplaces.

METROWEST CONSULTING GROUP —
No longer in business.

MIDHUDSONMEDIA
315 S 3rd St
PO Box 515
Hudson, NY 12534
Phone: 518-828-2500
Fax: 518-828-0173
E-mail: adsales@midhudsonmedia.com
Web Site: http://midhudsonmedia.com
Media communications company offering marketing, media & Internet communications including video production, cable advertising sales, Internet broadcasting & integrated marketing.

MULTICOMM SCIENCES INTERNATIONAL INC.
266 W Main St
Denville, NJ 07834
Phone: 973-627-7400
Fax: 973-215-2168
E-mail: mail@multicommsciences.com
Web Site: http://www.multicommsciences.com

Offers wireless consulting engineering services from FCC frequency coordination, earth stations, path propagation, RF radiation level analysis & testing, design of microwave systems & mapping of fiber optic & microwave routes.

NATHAN ASSOCIATES INC.
2101 Wilson Blvd
Ste 1200
Arlington, VA 22201
Phone: 703-516-7700
Fax: 703-351-6162
E-mail: jbeyer@nathaninc.com
Web Site: http://www.nathaninc.com
John C. Beyer, Chairman & Chief Executive Officer
Lakhbir Singh, President & Chief Operating Officer
Douglas Young, Principal Economist
Stephen Magiera, Principal Associate

Branch Offices:
IRVINE: 2010 Main St, Ste 700, Irvine, CA 92614. Phone: 949-955-9025. Fax: 949-474-4944. E-Mail: rmangum@nathaninc.com. Russell W. Mangum, III, Vice President & Director, South California Office.

MEMPHIS: 2151 Courtland Pl, Memphis, TN 38104. Phone: 901-725-6732. Fax: 901-725-6734. E-Mail: dsharp@nathaninc.com. David C. Sharp, Director, Memphis Office.

WARWICK: 39 Major Potter Rd, Warwick, RI 02886. Phone: 401-885-0648. Fax: 401-223-9771. E-Mail: sschneider@nathaninc.com. Stephen A. Schneider, Senior Vice President & Managing Director, South New England Office.

INDIA: 45 TTK Rd, George Pnnaiya Bldg, G-C, Ground Fl, Chennai 600 018, India. E-Mail: rtamara@nathaninc.com. Ram Tamara, Managing Director.

UNITED KINGDOM: 3 Millharbour, London E14 9XP, United Kingdom. Phone: 44-207-538-3111. E-Mail: ssinha@emergingmarkets.co.uk. Sunil Sinha, Managing Director.
Provides economic & management consultants services; demand & sales forecasting, market research, survey management, database design & implementation, financial analysis services & expert witness testimony to broadcasting, cable & telecommunications industries.

NATIONAL CAPTIONING INSTITUTE
3725 Concorde Pkwy
Ste 100
Chantilly, VA 20151
Phone: 703-917-7600
Fax: 703-917-9853
E-mail: mail@ncicap.org
Web Site: http://www.ncicap.org
Gene Chao, Chairman, President & Chief Executive Officer
Drake Smith, Chief Technology Officer
Juan Mario Agudelo, Sales & Marketing Director
Beth Nubbe, Off-Line Captioning & Described Media Director
Marc Okrand, Administration & Live Captioning Director

Branch Offices:
BURBANK: 303 N Glenoaks Blvd, Ste 200, Burbank, CA 91502. Phone: 818-238-0068. Fax: 818-238-4266. E-Mail: esarna@ncicap.org. Elissa Sarna, West Coast Sales & Marketing Director.

DALLAS: 7610 N Stemmons Frwy, Ste 200, Dallas, TX 75247. Phone: 214-647-4360. Fax: 214-647-4386. E-Mail: croney@ncicap.org.
Nonprofit firm that launched captioning in 1980; provides captioning & audio description services for broadcast, CATV, web streaming, DVD and government & corporate video programming. Provides subtitling & translation services in over 40 languages.

NATIONAL ECONOMIC RESEARCH ASSOCIATES INC. (NERA)
1166 Ave of the Americas
29th Fl
New York, NY 10036
Phone: 212-345-3000
Fax: 212-345-4650
Web Site: http://www.nera.com
Dr. Andrew Carron, President

Branch Offices:
AUSTIN: 1006 E 39th St, Austin, TX 78751. Phone: 512-371-8995. Fax: 512-371-9612.

BOSTON: 200 Clarendon St, 11th Fl, Boston, MA 02116. Phone: 617-927-4500. Fax: 617-927-4501. Dr. Augustin Ross, Vice President.

ITHACA: 308 N Cayuga St, Ithaca, NY 14850. Phone: 607-277-3007. Fax: 607-277-1581.

CHICAGO: 875 N Michigan Ave, Ste 3650, Chicago, IL 60611. Phone: 312-573-2800. Fax: 312-573-2810.

LOS ANGELES: 777 S Figueroa St, Ste 1950, Los Angeles, CA 90017. Phone: 213-346-3000. Fax: 213-346-3030.

PHILADELPHIA: Two Logan Sq, Ste 800, Philadelphia, PA 19103. Phone: 215-864-3880. Fax: 215-864-3840.

SAN FRANCISCO: One Front St, Ste 260, San Francisco, CA 94111. Phone: 415-291-1000. Fax: 415-291-1020. Dr. Alan Cox, Senior Vice President.

WASHINGTON, DC: 1255 23rd St NW, Ste 600, Washington, DC 20037. Phone: 202-466-3510. Fax: 202-466-3605. Dr. Chantale LaCasse, Senior Vice President; Dr. Richard Rozek, Senior Vice President.

WESTMINSTER: 10955 Westmoor Dr, Ste 400, Westminster, CO 80021. Phone: 303-465-6844. Fax: 303-465-6867.

WHITE PLAINS: 50 Main St, 14th Fl, White Plains, NY 10606. Phone: 914-448-4000. Fax: 914-448-4040.

CANADA: 161 Bay St, 16th Fl, PO Box 501, Toronto, ON M5J 2S5, Canada. Phone: 416-868-7310. Fax: 416-815-3332.
Provides economic research, analysis & consulting services for telephone, radio, TV, cable & common carriers; prepares analyses & expert testimony for judicial, legislative & regulatory proceedings; other services include antitrust, public utility & regulatory economics, public policy & managerial economics; offices worldwide.

NATIONAL TELECONSULTANTS INC.
550 N Brand Blvd
17th Fl
Glendale, CA 91203-1202
Phone: 818-265-4400
Fax: 818-265-4455
E-mail: information@ntc.com
Web Site: http://www.ntc.com

Eric Pohl, Chief Technology Officer
Chuck Phelan, Managing Partner

Branch Offices:
NEW YORK: 45 Rockefeller Plz, 20th Fl, New York, NY 10111-2000. Phone: 212-899-5454. Fax: 212-899-5455.
Provides strategic consulting & engineering design to the media industry.

NORMAN FISCHER & ASSOCIATES INC. (NFA INC.)
PO Box 5308
Austin, TX 78763-5308
Phone: 512-476-9457
Fax: 512-476-0540
E-mail: terrill@nfainc.com
Web Site: http://www.nfainc.com
Terrill Fischer, President
Provides management consulting, media brokerage & appraisals.

NORTHSTAR TELESOLUTIONS
125 Airport Pkwy
Greenwood, IN 46143
Phones: 317-865-2400; 800-466-0900
Fax: 317-865-2426
E-mail: info@northstartele.com
Web Site: http://www.northstartele.com
Josh Thackery, President
Doug Clingman, Information Technology
Jenni Dick, Field Operations
Katy Grogan, Business Development
Kelli Jones, Customer Service
Sherry Rose, Client Support
Provides subscriber management services.

N.S. BIENSTOCK INC.
250 W 57th St
Ste 333
New York, NY 10107
Phone: 212-765-3040
Fax: 212-757-6411
E-mail: nsb@nsbtalent.com
Web Site: http://www.nsbtalent.com
Richard Leibner, President
Jonathan Leibner, General Counsel
Beverly Styles, Office Manager
Talent agency for reality TV & news.

180 CONNECT INC.
6501 E Belleview Ave
Englewood, CO 80111
Phone: 303-395-6001
Fax: 303-395-6197
E-mail: information@180connect.net
Web Site: http://www.180connect.net
Brian Dalmass, President, Network Solutions & Business Development
Mark Morrison, President, Satellite Operations
Provides technical support services, including new installations, reconnections, disconnections, service upgrades/downgrades & service calls for broadband video, data & voice services; also provides management & technical services, including recruiting, training, tooling technical, supporting personnel & providing vehicles outfitted & ready for service; offices nationwide. Division of DIRECTV Inc.

ORC INTERNATIONAL
625 Ave of the Americas
New York, NY 10011
Phone: 212-645-4500
Web Site: http://www.opinionresearch.com
Marc Litvinoff, President
Richard Cornelius, Managing Director, ORC International
Stacy S. Lee, Senior Vice President & Chief Financial Officer
David Magnani, Senior Vice President & General Manager
Jeffrey T. Resnick, Global Managing Director, Innovation & Partnerships
Greg Wayman, Regional Managing Director, Asia Pacific

Branch Offices:
BOSTON: 90 Canal St, Ste 600, Boston, MA 02114. Phone: 617-720-0174.

LOMBARD: 450 E 22nd St, Ste 155, Lombard, IL 60148. Phone: 630-424-6500.

MINNEAPOLIS: 2051 Killebrew Dr, Ste 210, Minneapolis, MN 55425. Phone: 800-367-8358.

WASHINGTON, DC: 900 17th St NW, Ste 850, Washington, DC 20006. Phone: 703-312-6004.
Formerly ORC Research Corp. Provides customized business research on client-specified aspects of TV & cable services industries, specializing in company, product, service or market studies. Confidential, narrow-focused or comprehensive research on merger & acquisition candidates, competitors, targeted markets, products & services, federal & state regulatory & policy activities.

OVATION DATA SERVICES INC.
14199 Westfair E Dr
Houston, TX 77041-1105
Phone: 713-464-1300
Fax: 713-464-1615
E-mail: info@ovationdata.com
Web Site: http://www.ovationdata.com

Branch Offices:
UNITED KINGDOM: UK Data Storage Group, 18 Soho Sq, London W1D 3QL, United Kingdom. Phone: 44-0-207-268-3826.

UNITED KINGDOM: Technology & Service Ctr, Crayfields Industrial Park, Main Rd, Unit 202, St. Paul's Cray, Kent BR5 3HP, United Kingdom. Phone: 44-0-1689-824-777.
Provides digital data management & preservation services; information technology systems.

PATRICK COMMUNICATIONS LLC
6805 Douglas Legum Dr
Ste 100
Elkridge, MD 21075
Phone: 410-799-1740
Fax: 410-799-1705
E-mail: larry@patcomm.com
Web Site: http://www.patcomm.com
W. Lawrence Patrick, Managing Partner
Susan K. Patrick, Managing Partner

Gregory J. Guy, Managing Partner
Vincent A. Pepper, Principal
John Cunney, Principal
Provides station brokerage & investment banking services; fair market & asset appraisals; debt & equity placement; broadcast management & marketing consulting.

PDI CONSTRUCTION
5001 W Watkins St
Phoenix, AZ 85043
Phones: 602-258-7544; 800-894-5601
Fax: 602-254-9309
E-mail: info@pdiconstruction.com
Web Site: http://www.pdiconstruction.com
Charles Campbell, III, President
Ed Campbell, Vice President
Troy Gronsky, Vice President
James Doughton, Technical Project Manager
Provides computer-aided system design, base & strand mapping & technical field support; sweep, proof-of-performance & CLI. Division of Paramount Designs Inc.

PEREGRINE COMMUNICATIONS
14818 W Sixth Ave
Ste 16A
Golden, CO 80401
Phone: 303-278-9660
Fax: 303-278-9685
E-mail: peregrine.info@perecom.com
Web Site: http://www.perecom.com
John Post, President & Chief Executive Officer
Marissa Schubert, Manager, Regional Sales
Systems Integrator.

PINNACLE MEDIA WORLDWIDE
1667 S Mission Rd
Ste E
Fallbrook, CA 92028
Phone: 760-731-1141
Fax: 760-731-1187
E-mail: info@p-m-w.com
Web Site: http://www.p-m-w.com
Bob Lawrence, President & Chief Executive Officer
Mark Carlson, Vice President, Internet
Natalie Gonzalez, Business Manager
Provides strategic and tactical research & analysis services for media companies.

POHLY CO.
99 Bedford St
5th Fl
Boston, MA 02111
Phones: 617-451-1700; 800-383-0888
Fax: 617-338-7767
E-mail: info@pohlyco.com
Web Site: http://www.pohlyco.com
Diana Pohly, President & Chief Executive Officer
David Dalton, Chief Financial Officer
Michael Buller, Vice President & General Manager, Custom Publishing
John Heffernan, Vice President, Purchasing & Operations
Bill Pryor, Vice President & General Manager, Media Sales/Consulting
Kevin Miller, Chief Creative Officer
Provides marketing & publishing services.

POINT OF VIEW PRODUCTIONS
2477 Folsom St
San Francisco, CA 94110
Phone: 415-821-0435
Fax: 415-821-0434
E-mail: karil@karildaniels.com
Web Site: http://www.karildaniels.com
Karil Daniels, President
Cinematography, videography, photography, script supervision and other production services for corporate programs, commercials, TV shows, feature films.

PRICEWATERHOUSECOOPERS
300 Madison Ave
24th Fl
New York, NY 10017
Phone: 646-471-4000
Fax: 646-471-4444
Web Site: http://www.pwcglobal.com
Samuel DiPiazza, Jr., Chief Executive Officer
Provides industry-focused services, including audit & insurance, crisis management, human resources, performance improvement, tax & transactions; offices nationwide.

WARD L. QUAAL CO. — No longer in business.

RAM CONTROL
1334 State Rte 9
Champlain, NY 12919-5007
Phone: 518-298-5736
Fax: 518-298-2089
Leslie Matthews, Owner

RCH CABLE
301 Commerce Dr
Moorestown, NJ 08057
Phone: 856-642-0008
Fax: 856-642-0781
E-mail: rch@rchcable.com
Web Site: http://www.rchcable.net
Robert Halgas, President & Chief Executive Officer
Peter Berkowitz, Chief Technical Officer
Paul Lutes, Chief Financial Officer
Steve Nolfi, Senior Vice President, Sales Operations
Provides custom support solutions, direct sales campaigns, field collections programs, audits of designated market areas or marketing research.

RCW ASSOCIATES
5667 San Pablo Dam Rd
El Sobrante, CA 94803-3414
Phone: 510-223-9700
Fax: 510-223-2390
Robert C. White, Owner & President
Provides collection services.

RFK ENGINEERING SOLUTIONS LLC
1229 19th St NW
Washington, DC 20036-2413
Phone: 202-463-1567
Fax: 202-463-0344
Web Site: http://rkf-eng.com
Philip A. Rubin, President
Ted Kaplan, Chief Operating Officer
Dr. Jeffrey Freedman, Chief Technical Officer
Alex Latker, Director, Regulatory Affairs
Provides telecommunication consulting services addressing system engineering, technical analysis, supporting software development & ITU/FCC regulatory support.

RNL
1050 17th St
Ste A200
Denver, CO 80265
Phone: 303-295-1717
Fax: 303-292-0845
E-mail: denver@rnldesign.com
Web Site: http://www.rnldesign.com
John B. Rogers, Founder
H. Joshua Gould, Chief Executive Officer & Chairman
Richard L. von Luhrte, President
Michael Brendle, Design Director

Branch Offices:
LOS ANGELES: 800 Wilshire Blvd, Ste 400, Los Angeles, CA 90017. Phone: 213-955-9775. Fax: 213-955-9885. E-Mail: losangeles@rnldesign.com.

PHOENIX: 100 W Camelback Rd, Phoenix, AZ 85013. Phone: 602-212-1044. Fax: 602-212-0964. E-Mail: phoenix@rnldesign.com.
Offers architectural design & design/planning of TV & radio broadcasting facilities, including full-service feasibility & site studies, interior space planning, set design & systems integration.

GEORGE RODMAN ASSOCIATES — No longer in business.

SANTIAGO ROI
11054 Ventura Blvd
Ste 466
Los Angeles, CA 91604
Phone: 323-463-4648
E-mail: support@santiagosolutionsgroup.com
Web Site: http://www.santiagosolutionsgroup.com
Carlos Santiago, Founder, Chief Executive Officer, President & Chief Strategist
Steven Petroff, Director, Strategic Planning
Dr. J. C. Alvarez, Director, Retail Marketing & Community Relations
Formerly Santiago Solutions Group. Provides multi-cultural management consulting & business strategy development.

SIEMENS POWER TECHNOLOGIES INTL.
PO Box 1058
1482 Erie Blvd
Schenectady, NY 12301-1058
Phone: 518-395-5000
Fax: 518-346-2777
E-mail: pti-info.ptd@siemens.com
Web Site: http://www.pti-us.com
Dave Pacyna, President & Chief Executive Officer
Michael Edmonds, Vice President & General Manager

Branch Offices:
HOUSTON: 14521 Old Katy Rd, Ste 100, Houston, TX 77079. Phone: 281-497-2422. Fax: 281-497-0316.

LITTLETON: 7810 Shaffer Pkwy, Ste 100, Littleton, CO 80127. Phone: 303-568-7133. Fax: 303-568-7397.

MINNETONKA: 10900 Wayzata Blvd, Ste 400, Minnetonka, MN 55305. Phone: 952-607-2270. Fax: 952-607-2301.

MOUNTAIN VIEW: 1350 Shorebird Way, Mountain View, CA 94043-1338. Phone: 650-694-5096. Fax: 650-365-1356.

GERMANY: Freyeslebenstr 1, Erlangen 91058, Germany. Phone: 49-9131-734-444. Fax: 49-9131-734-445. E-Mail: power-technologies.ptd@siemens.com.

MALAYSIA: 13G Worldwide Business Centre, Block 1, Jalan Tinju 13/50, Shah Alam, Selangor 40675, Malaysia. Phone: 6-03-5511-4800. Fax: 6-03-5511-4801. E-Mail: pti-aps-support.ptd@siemens.com.

UNITED KINGDOM: Sir William Siemens House, Princess Rd, Manchester M20 2UR, United Kingdom. Phone: 44-0-161-446-5200. Fax: 44-0-161-446-6431. E-Mail: pti-service.ptd.uk@siemens.com.
Provides advanced technical consulting services, analytical software programs & professional education in power systems engineering.

SIGNASYS INC.
2158 Paragon Dr
San Jose, CA 95131-1305
Phone: 408-350-7200
Fax: 408-350-7299
Web Site: http://www.signasys.com
Roland Hoffman, President & Chief Executive Officer
Mark Brown, Executive Vice President & Chief Technical Officer
Roberta Friedman, Chief Financial Officer
Helps networks, broadcasters, producers & originators to advance their services/products, increase efficiencies, develop competitive advantages, comply with new legislation & train staff.

SMITH & FISHER
2237 Tackett's Mill Dr
Ste A
Lake Ridge, VA 22192
Phone: 703-494-2101
Fax: 703-494-2132
Web Site: http://www.smithandfisher.com
Neil M. Smith
Kevin T. Fisher
Jeanne F. Smith
Offers Longley-Rice studies, applications for new & changed FM, TV, DTV and LPTV facilities, mapping, expert-witness testimony, field measurement studies, FAA liaison & interference remedies.

SOFTWRIGHT LLC
PO Box 370390
Denver, CO 80237
Phones: 303-344-5486; 800-728-4033
Fax: 303-265-9399
E-mail: sales@softwright.com
Web Site: http://www.softwright.com
Larry D. Ellis, PE, President
Curt Alway, Software Marketing & Sales
Kay Ward, Business Administrator
Michael Wiebe, Software Development
Develops software for evaluating transmitter site coverage; TV/FM, ITFS, PCS, microwave, cellular, paging, & two-way radio system design & site management.

SPANPRO INC.
5495 N Bend Rd
Ste 200
Burlington, KY 41005
Phones: 859-647-2736; 800-647-2790
Fax: 859-746-6245
Craig Wheeler, President
Dan Kerr, Vice President, Technology
Rick Weiss, Vice President, Operations
Dennis Hume, Director, Business Development
Steve Sargent, Director, Engineering
Provides telecommunications engineering construction, maintenance & related applications software development.

STERLING INSTITUTE INC.
12009 Saint Helena Dr
Ste 200
Fairfax, VA 22124-2332
Phone: 703-636-3232
Fax: 703-995-0862
E-mail: si@sterlinginstitute.com
Web Site: http://www.sterlinginstitute.com
Matt Livingston, President
Brandon Scott, Vice President, Learning Technologies
Danielle Lissak, Manager, Client Services
Offers custom-designed executive, management & sales development programs for the broadcasting, cable & publishing industries.

STONE & YOUNGBLOOD
304 Newbury St
Ste 210
Boston, MA 02115
Phone: 617-647-0070
Fax: 781-647-0460
E-mail: sarkis@stoneandyoungblood.com
Stephen Sarkis, President
Provides executive searches & recruiting for advertising, marketing, traditional media (print, radio, cable & broadcast TV industries) and online media.

STRATA MARKETING INC.
30 W Monroe St
Ste 1900
Chicago, IL 60603
Phone: 312-222-1555
Fax: 312-222-2510
E-mail: info@stratag.com
Web Site: http://www.stratag.com
John Shelton, President & Chief Executive Officer
Joy Baer, Executive Vice President
Michael Latulippe, Senior Vice President, Finance & Administration
David Drucker, Vice President & Agency Services Manager
Paul Levy, Vice President, Custom Development
Tom Gombas, Vice President, Cable Division
Mike McHugh, Vice President, Media Sales & Electronic Delivery
Peter Nason, Vice President, Contracts & Marketing
Francine Olson, Vice President, Major Accounts-Cable
Michael Dehler, Vice President, Technical Infrastructure
David Prager, Vice President, e-Business Solutions & Program Management
Develops software for media buying departments, cable systems, TV & radio stations.

STRUCTURAL SYSTEMS TECHNOLOGY INC.
6867 Elm St
Ste 200
McLean, VA 22101-3870
Phones: 703-356-9765; 800-997-6555
Fax: 703-448-0979
E-mail: contact@sst-towers.com
Web Site: http://www.sst-towers.com
Fred W. Purdy, PE, President
Kaveh Mehrnama, PE, Vice President, Engineering
Mary Acker, Executive Secretary & Office Manager
Greg Pleinka, National Sales Manager
Bryan Burton, Chief Designer & Draftsman

Branch Offices:
NEWPORT NEWS: 51 Lakeshore Dr, Newport News, VA 23608. Phones: 757-890-4505; 866-859-5505. Fax: 757-890-4506.
Designs, repairs, inspects & erects tall towers.

S2ONE INC.
9914 E Upriver Dr
Spokane, WA 99206-4415
Phones: 509-891-7362; 800-270-7050
E-mail: info@s2one.com
Web Site: http://www.s2one.com
Mark Hills, President
Installs, maintains & repairs analog & digital transmission equipment throughout the U.S.

SURFXPRESS
470 Vanderbuilt Ave
Brooklyn, NY 11238
Phone: 646-450-3301
Fax: 646-727-4317
E-mail: support@sxpress.com
Web Site: http://www.sxpress.com
Harold Barr, President
Provides co-location; server space & rentals as well as a complete redundant infrastructure. Unlimited bandwidth & interconnects services to the telecommunications industry.

SYNTELLECT INC.
2095 W Pinnacle Peak Rd
Ste 110
Phoenix, AZ 85027
Phone: 800-788-9733
Fax: 602-789-2768
E-mail: info@syntellect.com
Web Site: http://www.syntellect.com
Steve Dodenhoff, President
Bruce Petillo, Manager, Marketing

Branch Offices:
OAKBROOK: 700 Commerce Dr, Oakbrook, IL 60523.

CANADA: 90 Nolan Ct, Ste 1A, Markham, ON L3R 4L9, Canada. Phone: 905-754-4100.

SINGAPORE: 371 Beach Rd #02-26, Keypoint 199597, Singapore. Phone: 65-6392-1833.

UNITED KINGDOM: Technology House, Fleetwood Park, Bartley Way, Fleet, Hamps QU51 2QJ, United Kingdom. Phone: 44-0-1252-61-8853. Fax: 44-0-1252-61-8899.
Operates a transaction-based hosted services center.

SZABO ASSOCIATES INC.
3355 Lenox Rd NE
Ste 945
Atlanta, GA 30326
Phone: 404-266-2464
Fax: 404-266-2165
E-mail: info@szabo.com
Web Site: http://www.szabo.com
Robin Szabo, President
Nolan Childers, Division Manager, Television & Cable
Randy Neff, Division Manager, Radio
Sandi Garris, Manager, Legal Services
Provides collection services exclusively for the media, advertising & entertainment industries; services include credit information system; A/R management; legal sources; corporate management reports; library resource center; bankruptcy assistance; EDI; international services.

TALENT EXCHANGE
PO Box 99
Redondo Beach, CA 90277
Phone: 866-702-2899
Fax: 310-362-8979
E-mail: frontdesk@talent-exchange.com
Web Site: http://www.talent-exchange.com
Streamlines the search for talent & service providers for producers & casting directors & provides a showcase for both working & aspiring actors, models, musicians, dancers, comedians & variety acts.

TC SPECIALTIES
PO Box 192
17 S Main St
Coudersport, PA 16915
Phones: 814-274-8060; 800-458-6074
Fax: 814-274-0690
E-mail: sales@tcspecialties.com
Web Site: http://www.tcspecialties.com
Provides commercial printing services; coupon payment coupons; presort mail facility.

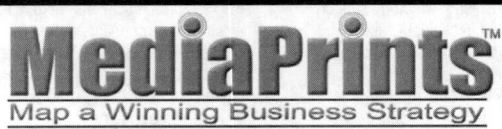

TELAMERICA MEDIA INC.
The Drexel Bldg
1435 Walnut St, 4th Fl
Philadelphia, PA 19102
Phone: 215-568-7066
Fax: 215-564-5388
Web Site: http://www.telamericamedia.com
Lance Funston, Chairman & Chief Executive Officer
Ivan Silverman, Vice President, Media Sales
Brian Walker, Advertising Sales Representative

TELESTRATEGIES INC.
6845 Elm St
Ste 310
McLean, VA 22101
Phone: 703-734-7050
Fax: 703-893-3197
E-mail: info@telestrategies.com
Web Site: http://www.telestrategies.com
Offers telecommunication industry conferences, seminars, tutorials & trade shows.

TELETECH COMMUNICATIONS
2358 Gatetree Ln SE
Grand Rapids, MI 49546
E-mail: teletechcomm@aol.com
John Jones, President
Alan Crispin, Vice President
Provides captioning services to the TV & film industries.

TELETECH INC.
9197 S Peoria St
Englewood, CO 80112-5833
Phones: 303-397-8100; 800-835-3832
Fax: 303-397-8199
E-mail: media@teletech.com
Web Site: http://www.teletech.com
Kenneth Tuchman, Chairman & Chief Executive Officer
James Bartlett, Vice Chairman
Provides communications & media companies with solutions for integrated systems to grow revenue & increase customer retention.

TELVUE CORP.
16000 Horizon Way
Ste 500
Mount Laurel, NJ 08054
Phone: 800-885-8886
Fax: 856-866-7411
E-mail: sales@telvue.com
Web Site: http://www.telvue.com
Jesse Lerman, President & Chief Executive Officer
Paul Andrews, Vice President, Sales & Marketing
John Fell, Secretary & Treasurer
Broadcast technology company that helps hyperlocal television channels achieve professional results at affordable prices. Achieves these results by using our proprietary digital media software & todays open technologies to simplify professional broadcast equipment & workflow. Provides products & solutions for: Video on Demand, Over The Top, Live Streaming, Linear Broadcast & Transcoding.

TIBA SOLUTIONS
201 Brookfield Pkwy
Ste 200
Greenville, SC 29607
Phone: 864-679-4800
E-mail: sales@tibasolutions.com
Web Site: http://www.tibasolutions.com
Ken Brower, President & Chief Operating Officer
Kirk Gollwitzer, Executive Vice President
David Friedline, Director, e-Government Solutions
Doris Rowland, Senior Account Executive
Provides in-house billing & subscriber management & total information systems, featuring order entry, dispatching, marketing support & analysis, sales analysis, outage analysis, addressability, pay-per-view control, receivables processing & inventory management.

EDWIN TORNBERG & CO.
8917 Cherbourg Dr
Potomac, MD 20854-3104
Phone: 301-983-8700
Ina Tornberg, President
James Weitzman, Vice President
Provides appraisal, brokerage, consulting & merger/acquisition services.

TOWERS & PERRIN
335 Madison Ave
New York, NY 10017-4605
Phone: 212-309-3400
Fax: 212-309-0948
Web Site: http://www.towersperrin.com
Mark Mactas, Chairman & Chief Executive Officer
Bob Hogan, Chief Financial Officer
Kevin Young, Secretary & General Counsel
Jim Foreman, Managing Director, Human Capital Group
Tricia Guinn, Managing Director, Risk & Financial Services
Provides solutions to client issues in the areas of human resource strategy, design & management; actuarial & management consulting; reinsurance intermediary services; offices worldwide.

TRANSCOMM INC.
PO Box 2845
Fairfax, VA 22031
Phone: 703-323-5150
Fax: 703-426-4527
E-mail: transcommusa@msn.com
Web Site: http://www.transcommusa.com
Dr. Norman C. Lerner, President
Provides consulting services; specializes in domestic & international financial solutions, economic & business development problems of high technology industries, with emphasis in telecommunications, energy & postal.

TV MAGIC INC.
8112 Engineer Rd
San Diego, CA 92111
Phone: 858-650-3155
Fax: 858-650-3158
E-mail: sales@tvmagic.tv
Web Site: http://www.tvmagic.tv
Stephen D. Rosen, President & Chief Executive Officer

John Mayer, Chief Operating Officer & General Counsel
Pat Thompson, Chief Technology Officer
Gary Stigall, Chief Technical Officer
Bob Anderson, Vice President, Project Management
Benito Behar, Vice President, Sales
Steve Schwartz, Vice President, Service Support Group

Branch Offices:
LOS ANGELES: 107 W Valencia Ave, Burbank, CA 91502. Phone: 818-841-6886. Fax: 818-557-0277. Kevin Bohn, Manager, Engineering.
Full-service consulting & broadcast video engineering company; provides turnkey solutions for broadcasters & other telecommunications entities.

UNITED RECOVERY SYSTEMS
5800 N Course Dr
Houston, TX 77072
Phones: 713-977-1234; 800-568-0399
Fax: 713-977-0119
E-mail: sales@ursi.com
Web Site: http://www.ursi.com
Jim Kelleher, President

Branch Offices:
BRYAN: 4001 E 29th St, Ste 130, Bryan, TX 77802.

TEMPE: 7340 S Kyrene, Tempe, AZ 85283.

TULSA: 6506 S Lewis Ave, Ste 260, Tulsa, OK 74136. Phones: 918-712-0077; 888-593-8401. Fax: 918-712-0606.
Provides adjustment & collection services, insurance services, business facilities oversight, business administration services & management support services.

USA 800 INC.
9808 E 66th Terr
Kansas City, MO 64133
Phone: 800-821-7539
Fax: 816-358-1303
E-mail: sales@usa-800.com
Web Site: http://www.usa-800.com
Tom Davis, President & Chief Executive Officer
Dan Quigley, Chief Operating & Financial Officer
Mike Douglas, Chief Information Officer
Michelle Melland, Vice President, Client Services
Dan Lake, Vice President, Contact Centers
Corey Kramer, Vice President, Business Development
David Labatt, Vice President, Sales
Mike Langel, Vice President, Technology
Jeanne Hicks, Operations Director

Branch Offices:
HALSTEAD: 327 Chestnut St, 2nd Fl, Halstead, KS 67056. Phone: 866-810-1499.

ST. JOSEPH: 5804 Corporate Dr, St. Joseph, MO 64507. Phones: 800-310-6762; 816-676-1020.
Provides customer care, sales & lead acquisition services.

U.S. DEPARTMENT OF COMMERCE
1401 Constitution Ave NW
Washington, DC 20230
Phones: 202-482-2000; 202-482-3548
Fax: 202-482-4128
E-mail: webmaster@doc.gov
Web Site: http://www.commerce.gov
Gary Locke, Commerce Secretary
Ellen Moran, Chief of Staff
Trade Development, International Trade Administration; government point of contact for the telecommunications, aerospace, aircraft & electronic components industries; measuring & controlling instruments, medical & dental; photographic, computer software & business equipment concerning market research, trade & business assistance.

T.J. VAUGHAN & ASSOCIATES
PO Box 440
Rye Beach, NH 03871
Phone: 603-964-6688
Fax: 603-964-5450
Thomas J. Vaughan, President
Provides HDTV feasibility studies, site selection, pattern & antenna analysis, antenna modification, pattern measurements & field tests; RFR measurements.

VCI SOLUTIONS — See listing for Wide-Orbit.

VIDCAD
2010 E Lohman Ave
Ste 2
Las Cruces, NM 88011
Phone: 575-522-0003
Fax: 575-635-4518
E-mail: sales@vidcad.com
Web Site: http://www.vidcad.com
Alex Sotelo, Vice President, Sales
Provides documentation automation software.

VISLINK SERVICES
526 W Blueridge Ave
Orange, CA 92865
Phones: 714-998-2121; 800-870-7570
Fax: 714-998-7808
E-mail: sales@vislinkservices.com
Web Site: http://www.vizlinkservices.com
John Hawkins, Chief Executive Officer & Chairman
Specializes in wireless, video & IP technologies and their supporting management systems. Designs & manufactures radio, satellite transmission & wireless cameras.

VITAC
101 Hillpointe Dr
Canonsburg, PA 15317-9503
Phones: 724-514-4000; 800-278-4822
Fax: 724-514-4111
E-mail: jim-b@vitac.com
Web Site: http://www.vitac.com
Patricia Prozzi, Chief Executive Officer & President
Dwight Wagner, Chief Systems & Technology Officer
Darryn Cleary, Vice President, Sales
Timothy Taylor, Vice President, Engineering & Facility Operations
Debbie Hammond, Manager, Client Services

Branch Offices:
ARLINGTON: 1501 Wilson Blvd, Ste 1003, Arlington, VA 22209. Phone: 703-807-2766. Fax: 703-807-2761. E-Mail: heather-y@vitac.com. Bob Byer, General Manager; Heather York, Director, Marketing.

NORTH HOLLYWOOD: 4605 Lankershim Blvd, Ste 250, North Hollywood, CA 91602. Phones: 818-755-0410; 888-528-4288. Fax: 818-755-0411. E-Mail: jim-b@vitac.com. Jim Ballard, Executive Vice President, Sales & Marketing; Maggie McDermott, Director, West Coast Sales.
Provides captioning & subtitling services for all media formats, including broadcast, corporate & Internet video, subtitling & translation in over 45 languages, realtime English & Spanish captions, audio description, & Internet & streaming media captions.

VOZZCOM INC.
11768 W Sample Rd
Coral Springs, FL 33065
Phones: 954-753-8600; 866-254-8600
Fax: 954-753-5522
E-mail: sales@vozzcom.net
Web Site: http://www.vozzcom.net
Doreen Vozzola, President
David E. Vozzola, Chief Operating Officer
Mark Ecsedy, Vice President, Mid-Atlantic Region
Terry Board, Controller

Branch Offices:
CULVER CITY: 5601 W Slauson Ave, Ste 170, Culver City, CA 90230. Phone: 310-641-1500.
Provides support services to the broadband industry.

V-SOFT COMMUNICATIONS
401 Main St
Ste 213
Cedar Falls, IA 50613
Phones: 319-266-8402; 800-743-3684
Fax: 319-266-9212
E-mail: info@v-soft.com; consulting@v-soft.com
Web Site: http://www.v-soft.com
Doug Vernier, Chief Executive Officer & Owner
John Gray, Vice President, Owner & Research Director
Kate English, Broadcast Engineering Consultant
Lisa Erickson, Technical Support Specialist
Gayle Vernier, Bookkeeper

Branch Offices:
KANSAS CITY:, 15233 W 153rd St, Olathe, KS 66062. Phone: 319-266-8402. Fax: 319-266-9212.

WEST PALM BEACH: 8893 Lakes Blvd, West Palm Beach, FL 33412. Phone: 319-266-8402. Fax: 319-266-9212.
Provides software & support for FCC AM, FM, TV/DTV and microwave allocations & propagation prediction software. Software to prepare custom FCC & Longley-Rice coverage & interference analysis maps, population & demographic studies & frequency searches; Software aids in the preparation of applications to the FCC for AM, FM, LPFM, TV, DTV, TV translators, STLs & other broadcast auxiliaries. Numerous census, terrain, land cover, world polygon mapping, market studies, microwave, AM, FM & TV databases.

WALTERS-STORYK DESIGN GROUP INC.
262 Martin Ave
Highland, NY 12528
Phone: 845-691-9300
Fax: 845-691-9361
E-mail: wsdginfo@wsdg.com
Web Site: http://www.wsdg.com
Beth Walters, Co-founder & Principal
John Storyk, Co-founder & Principal
Nancy Flannery, Chief Financial Officer
Romina Larregina, Senior Project Manager

Branch Offices:
NORTH MIAMI BEACH: 19585 NE 10th Ave, North Miami Beach, FL 33179. Phone: 305-479-2679.

SONOMA: 866 Virginia Ct, Sonoma, CA 95476. Phone: 415-407-6086.

ARGENTINA: Gascon 1364, Buenos Aires C1181 ACZ, Argentina. Phone: 54-11-4865-3111. E-Mail: sergio@wsdg.com. Sergio Molho, Director, International Relations & Partner.

BRAZIL: Rua Rio Grande do Norte 1560, Sala 1107, Savassi, Belo Horizonte MG CEP 30.130-131, Brazil. Phones: 55-31-3225-2766; 55-31-9195-9430. E-Mail: renato@wsdg.com. Renato C.R. Cipriano, Partner & General Manager.

HONG KONG: Ming Pao Industrial Ctr, 18 Ka Yip St, 1910-12, Block B, Chaiwan, Hong Kong. Phone: 852-2898-3133.

MEXICO CITY: Leibnitz 282, Col Nueva Anzures, Mexico City, DF 11590, Mexico. Phone: 5255-5905-0500. Fax: 5255-5905-0506.

SWITZERLAND: Dornacherstr 279, 4053 Basel, Switzerland. Phone: 41-61-903-13-40. Fax: 41-61-903-13-41. E-Mail: europe@wsdg.com. Dirk Noy, Partner & General Manager.
Full-service architectural & acoustic design firm; specializes in professional audio & video production facilities

WARREN & MORRIS LTD.
PO Box 1090
Del Mar, CA 92014-1090
Phone: 858-461-0040
Fax: 858-481-6221
E-mail: cmorris@warrenmorrisltd.com
Web Site: http://www.warrenmorrisltd.com
Scott C. Warren, Senior Partner
Charles C. Morris, Senior Partner
Chip Cossitt, Partner, Wireless Communications
Gary Smetana, Partner, Advanced Technology
Arlon Chaffee, Partner
Amy McCoy, Associate Partner

Branch Offices:
PASADENA: 115 W California Blvd, Ste 268, Pasadena, CA 91105. Phone: 626-584-1155. Fax: 626-568-1260.

PORTSMOUTH: 132 Chapel St, Portsmouth, NH 03801. Phone: 603-431-7929. Fax: 603-431-3460.
Provides executive search services to the digital media, broadband, cable & wireless industries.

WESTERN TECHNICAL SERVICES — See listing for Vislink Services.

WIDEORBIT
1160 Battery St
Ste 300
San Francisco, CA 94111
Phone: 415-675-6700
Fax: 415-675-6701
E-mail: sales@wideorbit.com
Web Site: http://www.wideorbit.com
Eric Mathewson, Founder & Chief Executive Officer
Bruce Roberts, President
Margaret McCarthy, Chief Financial Officer
Nathan Gans, Chief Financial Officer
Eric Moe, Chief Technology Officer
William Offeman, Executive Vice President, Engineering
Mike Zinsmeister, Vice President, Sales
Vijay Komar, Vice President, Engineering
Sean Trigony, General Manager, WO Central
Don Durand, International Sales Director

Branch Offices:
AGAWAM: 67 Hunt St, Ste 106, Agawam, ME 01001. Phone: 413-+272-7220. Fax: 413-272-7222.

DALLAS: 601 Canyon Dr, Ste 101, Coppell, TX 75019. Phone: 214-451-4000.

DENVER: 700 17th St, Ste 1100, Denver, CO 80202. Phone: 720-224-9170. Fax: 720-224-9171.

LYNNWOOD: 3400 188th St SW, Ste 685, Lynnwood, WA 98037. Phone: 425-412-5300. Fax: 425-329-1119.
Provides business management software to media companies. Provides solutions for managing the business of broadcast & cable operations from proposal to order, scheduling to automation, billing & aging. Used by more than 4,000 television stations, radio stations & cable networks around the globe, managing more than $14 billion in advertising revenue. Acquired VCI Solutions in 2010.

WILLIAM MORRIS ENDEAVOR ENTERTAINMENT
One William Morris Pl
Beverly Hills, CA 90212
Phone: 310-859-4000
Fax: 310-859-4440
Web Site: http://www.wmeentertainment.com
Jim Wiatt, Chairman
Ariel Z. Emanuel, Chief Executive Officer
A talent & literary agency that represents clients in all segments of the entertainment industry.

WILLIAMS COMMUNICATIONS INC.
5524 Bee Caves Rd
Ste C-1
Austin, TX 78746
Phone: 512-328-2461
Fax: 512-328-3009
E-mail: info@catvdesign.com
Web Site: http://www.catvdesign.com
Steve Williams, President
Provides engineering services worldwide, RF design, project management & drafting.

ROBERT WOLD CO.
88 Three Vines Ct
Mission Viejo, CA 92694
Phone: 949-363-0993
Fax: 949-363-2093
E-mail: robertnwold@home.com
Robert N. Wold, Owner
Provides consulting services in TV & telecommunications, including domestic & international satellites.

WSI CORP.
400 Minuteman Rd
Andover, MA 01810
Phone: 978-983-6300
Fax: 978-983-6400
E-mail: sales@wsi.com
Web Site: http://www.wsi.com
Mark Gildersleeve, President
Dr. Peter P Neilley, Vice President, Global Forecasting Services
Bill Dow, Vice President & General Manager, Media Division
Mark D. Miller, Vice President & General Manager, Decision Support
Jim Menard, Vice President, Digital Initiatives
John Caffery, Vice President, Human Resources
Linda Maynard, Vice President, Corporate Marketing

Branch Offices:
UNITED KINGDOM: Edgbaston House, 3 Duchess Pl, Hagley Rd, 15th Fl, Birmingham B16 8HN, United Kingdom. Phone: 44-121-233-7600. Fax: 44-121-233-7666.
Provides worldwide weather & weather-related information, mission-critical systems, integration services & presentation services to customers in the media, aviation, industry, government & consumer markets.

JIM YOUNG & ASSOCIATES INC.
1424 Clear Lake Rd
Weatherford, TX 76086
Phone: 817-599-7623
Fax: 817-599-4483
Jim Young, President
Specializes in the placement of CATV, telecommunications, cellular telephone, RF engineering & satellite communications personnel.

ESTIMATED GROWTH OF THE CABLE INDUSTRY

(as of January 1 of each year)

Year	Operating Systems	Total Basic Subscribers
1952	70	14,000
1953	150	30,000
1954	300	65,000
1955	400	150,000
1956	450	300,000
1957	500	350,000
1958	525	450,000
1959	560	550,000
1960	640	650,000
1961	700	725,000
1962	800	850,000
1963	1,000	950,000
1964	1,200	1,085,000
1965	1,325	1,275,000
1966	1,570	1,575,000
1967	1,770	2,100,000
1968	2,000	2,800,000
1969	2,260	3,600,000
1970	2,490	4,500,000
1971	2,639	5,300,000
1972	2,841	6,000,000
1973	2,991	7,300,000
1974	3,158	8,700,000
1975	3,506	9,800,000
1976	3,681	10,800,000
1977	3,832	11,900,000
1978	3,875	13,000,000
1979	4,150	14,100,000
1980	4,225	16,000,000
1981	4,375	18,300,000
1982	4,825	21,000,000
1983	5,600	25,000,000

Year	Operating Systems	Total Basic Subscribers*
1984	6,200	29,000,000
1985	6,600	32,000,000
1986	7,500	37,500,000
1987	7,900	41,000,000
1988	8,500	44,000,000
1989	9,050	47,500,000
1990	9,575	50,000,000
1991	10,704	51,000,000
1992	11,035	53,000,000
1993	11,108	54,200,000
1994	11,214	55,300,000
1995	11,218	56,500,000
1996	11,119	60,280,000
1997	10,050	64,050,000
1998	10,845	64,170,000
1999	10,700	65,500,000
2000	10,400	66,500,000
2001	10,300	67,200,000
2002	9,900	64,500,000
2003	9,400	64,800,000
2004	8,875	65,250,000
2005	8,400	65,300,000
2006	8,000	64,900,000
2007	7,100	66,000,000
2008	6,585	65,190,000
2009	6,050	65,500,000
2010	6,150	65,800,000
2011	6,016	77,750,000
2012	5,575	77,655,000

Note: The change in the number of systems operating each year is determined by three factors: (1) New systems which began operation during the year; (2) older systems coming to the attention of Television & Cable Factbook for the first time and therefore included in the total for the first time; (3) the splitting, combining, or shutting down of systems by operators.

* Includes both analog and digital subscribers.

U.S. CABLE PENETRATION STATE BY STATE

(As of October 2011)

Note: Figures reflect information supplied by system operators and do not include wireless cable systems.

* Basic subscribers, Expanded Basic subscriber, and Pay Unit totals include analog and digital subscribers. Some cable systems have converted to IPTV.

State	Systems	Communities Served	Expanded Basic Subscribers*	Basic Subscribers*	Pay Units*
Alabama	149	629	1,197,393	296,784	158,798
Alaska	30	57	198,187	129,467	95,842
Arizona	57	206	1,485,171	149,964	255,573
Arkansas	169	515	408,628	88,633	81,234
California	177	1,171	8,104,413	1,980,713	1,065,089
Colorado	104	331	1,385,105	64,512	15,607
Connecticut	24	204	1,159,226	288,253	78,812
Delaware	5	80	118,752	156,027	12,363
District of Columbia	20	22	176,000	—	—
Florida	144	792	5,868,214	787,708	514,429
Georgia	184	793	2,194,744	864,846	286,605
Hawaii	6	128	350,115	—	—
Idaho	36	187	234,163	29,460	15,280
Illinois	274	1,297	2,608,692	603,537	310,772
Indiana	116	687	1,418,714	372,802	99,614
Iowa	244	749	697,702	349,013	150,673
Kansas	200	447	652,004	295,029	78,715
Kentucky	149	994	1,017,050	569,794	198,355
Louisiana	102	462	1,055,082	287,831	304,593
Maine	39	354	324,418	224,884	29,553
Maryland	33	414	1,372,603	444,711	177,178
Massachusetts	45	361	1,559,474	255,340	106,873
Michigan	224	1,552	2,314,479	621,564	157,511
Minnesota	274	877	1,342,021	641,147	183,514
Mississippi	115	347	552,660	120,471	46,648
Missouri	187	738	1,519,403	711,732	275,989
Montana	84	147	209,671	121,228	6,014
Nebraska	164	358	551,336	282,488	183,586
Nevada	34	91	590,903	86,778	1,601
New Hampshire	16	199	829,331	120,767	25,786
New Jersey	37	635	2,781,057	672,781	1,231,401
New Mexico	52	146	340,338	198,741	32,013
New York	86	1,567	6,514,574	2,688,409	570,840
North Carolina	104	879	2,308,235	818,134	234,215
North Dakota	72	220	188,103	23,948	15,609
Ohio	168	1,814	3,168,698	528,845	368,658
Oklahoma	230	411	724,901	457,828	212,992
Oregon	82	359	1,085,846	425,128	132,552
Pennsylvania	274	2,582	3,900,520	1,350,957	136,574
Rhode Island	3	45	317,024	272,375	7,000
South Carolina	45	365	1,147,027	628,522	131,170
South Dakota	119	240	210,749	650	34,046
Tennessee	103	551	1,723,046	613,229	353,522
Texas	434	1,392	4,884,775	1,697,144	955,853
Utah	52	210	324,867	143,077	16,851
Vermont	12	236	37,038	73,931	1,180
Virginia	106	572	1,961,115	419,291	390,833
Washington	103	463	1,746,219	552,753	216,507
West Virginia	130	1,020	488,580	212,227	48,585
Wisconsin	173	906	1,749,851	826,768	173,656
Wyoming	53	100	121,468	79,761	17,689
Cuba	1	1	976	—	858
Guam	1	20	48,646	—	2,631
Marianas Islands	1	3	6,500	—	440
Puerto Rico	3	86	339,550	102,000	48,334
Virgin Islands	2	3	42,923	22,622	16,845
TOTAL	**5,851**	**30,015**	**77,658,280**	**23,754,604**	**10,267,461**

LARGEST U.S. CABLE SYSTEMS

(Those with 20,000 or more basic subscribers* as of October 2011)

NEW YORK, NY	2,432,372
LOS ANGELES, CA	1,900,000
SAN FRANCISCO, CA	1,700,000
HOUSTON, TX	1,270,000
SEATTLE, WA	1,188,327
BENSALEM TWP., PA	1,125,000
PHOENIX, AZ	928,298
DENVER, CO	853,827
MIAMI, FL	755,329
HARRISBURG, PA	750,389
ATLANTA (metro area), GA	716,091
MILWAUKEE, WI	709,000
MANCHESTER, NH	700,000
SYRACUSE, NY	700,000
PITTSBURGH, PA	626,604
BEAVERTON, OR	625,811
BOSTON, MA	600,000
DALLAS, TX	600,000
ST. PAUL, MN	600,000
SAN ANTONIO, TX	596,074
COLUMBIA, SC	584,585
TAUNTON, MA	575,000
SAN DIEGO, CA (Cox Communications)	537,000
CINCINNATI, OH	535,000
CHARLOTTE, NC	506,125
PINELLAS COUNTY, FL (Bright House Networks)	504,739
ALBANY, NY	500,074
KANSAS CITY, MO	497,000
ROCHESTER, NY	496,713
INDIANAPOLIS, IN	492,400
SAN DIEGO, CA (Time Warner Cable)	485,000
COLUMBUS, OH (Time Warner Cable)	484,355
GREENSBORO, NC	483,103
CLEVELAND HEIGHTS, OH	481,500
WOODBURY/ISLIP, NY	480,698
OAK BROOK, IL	464,941
WEST PALM BEACH, FL	459,584
NASHVILLE, TN	458,705
LAS VEGAS, NV	430,750
ORLANDO, FL	425,000
RICHMOND, VA	418,000
ORANGE COUNTY, CA	417,940
DAYTON, OH	410,000
WICHITA, KS	410,000
AUSTIN, TX	407,685
HAMPTON ROADS, VA	400,000
ATLANTA (northern portion), GA	396,100
ALHAMBRA, CA	393,500
HILLSBOROUGH COUNTY, FL	381,944
CHICAGO, IL	365,212
FAIRFAX COUNTY, VA	364,637
NAPLES, FL	362,351
STERLING HEIGHTS, MI	362,003
BATON ROUGE, LA	360,988
SCHAUMBURG, IL	351,249
CHICAGO (southern portion), IL	350,000
MILILANI, HI	350,000
LACKAWANNA, NY	334,762
MEMPHIS, TN	315,000
PROVIDENCE, RI	308,944
BROOKLYN, NY	299,226
VINELAND, NJ	289,277
MINNEAPOLIS, MN	284,990
LOUISVILLE, KY	281,083
UNION, NJ	276,830
BRONX, NY	276,209
JACKSONVILLE, FL	273,992
SALT LAKE CITY, UT	272,041
OMAHA, NE	271,382
WILMINGTON, NC	267,000
SACRAMENTO, CA	252,060
SUFFOLK COUNTY, NY	235,885
OKLAHOMA CITY, OK	233,004
GREEN BAY, WI	232,000
BINGHAMTON, NY	230,000
VOORHEES, NJ	229,096
FRESNO, CA	225,375
OAKLAND, NJ	221,209
WARREN, OH	220,000
BALTIMORE COUNTY, MD	218,296
FORT WORTH, TX	215,484
MONTGOMERY COUNTY, MD	215,207
GREENVILLE/SPARTANBURG, SC	204,133
OAKLAND, CA	195,076
DES MOINES, IA	191,517
PENSACOLA, FL	189,944
NEW ORLEANS, LA	185,000
TUCSON, AZ	183,562
DE LAND, FL	183,026
BURLINGTON COUNTY, NJ	179,330
LONG BEACH, CA	178,200
PRINCE GEORGE'S COUNTY, MD	177,817
MELBOURNE, FL	177,694
WASHINGTON, DC	176,000
TULSA, OK	172,000
RARITAN, NJ	168,323
DETROIT, MI	166,926
MONMOUTH COUNTY, NJ (Cablevision Systems Corp.)	164,956
TOLEDO, OH	164,694
PALM BEACH GARDENS, FL	161,785
LINCOLN, NE	157,000
TOMS RIVER, NJ	156,658
COLORADO SPRINGS, CO	151,393
GRAND RAPIDS, MI	150,593
AUBURNDALE, FL	149,194
PEORIA, IL	148,000
MADISON, WI	146,426
LONGMONT, CO	146,378
LEEDS, AL	143,584
PORTLAND, ME	142,700
BALTIMORE, MD	142,385
RENO, NV	141,900
HARLINGEN, TX	141,561
INDIANAPOLIS (portions), IN	141,301
ROCKFORD, IL	141,000
PASCO COUNTY (western portion), FL	140,283
PHILADELPHIA (areas 1, 3 & 4), PA	140,000
SAN JUAN, PR	140,000
CHATTANOOGA, TN	138,324
ALBUQUERQUE, NM	137,000
COVINGTON, KY	136,000
SOUTH BEND, IN	133,804
SPRINGFIELD, MA	132,883
COLUMBUS, OH (Insight Communications)	130,900
WORCESTER, MA	130,889
DELRAY BEACH, FL	130,737
FAYETTEVILLE, NC	130,000
HERNANDO COUNTY, FL	129,881
JOPLIN, MO	128,612
NEWTOWN, CT	128,568
DOVER, NJ	127,059
ANDERSON, IN	126,918
KNOXVILLE, TN	123,579
NORWALK, CT	123,084
LEHIGH VALLEY, PA	121,686
CHARLESTON, SC	121,000
STUART, FL	120,665
EL PASO, TX	120,000

System	Subscribers
BRADENTON, FL	119,782
ANCHORAGE, AK	119,710
HILLSBOROUGH, NJ	115,795
WACO, TX	115,000
LEXINGTON, KY	114,485
AKRON, OH	114,115
BAKERSFIELD, CA	110,000
PONCE, PR	110,000
SAVANNAH, GA	109,859
CEDAR RAPIDS, IA	108,473
GAINESVILLE, FL	107,000
TALLAHASSEE, FL	104,973
RALEIGH, NC	103,690
PIMA COUNTY, AZ	103,364
MAMARONECK, NY	103,340
SPRINGFIELD, IL	99,076
PORTLAND, OR	99,000
GREENVILLE, NC	98,639
BRIDGEPORT, CT	98,100
AUGUSTA, GA	97,000
BIRMINGHAM, AL	97,000
CORPUS CHRISTI, TX	97,000
STOCKTON, CA	94,806
ST. LOUIS, MO	94,652
FLINT, MI	92,232
HARTFORD, CT	91,800
KINGSPORT, TN	91,042
PRINCE WILLIAM COUNTY, VA	90,463
BEAUMONT, TX	90,000
LUQUILLO, PR	89,550
ANN ARBOR, MI	88,058
HATTIESBURG, MS	87,323
TAYLOR, MI	86,672
ROYAL OAK, MI	86,510
MOBILE, AL	85,375
LITTLE ROCK, AR	85,000
LAFAYETTE, IN	84,000
POPLAR BLUFF, MO	83,106
GLENDALE, CA	81,782
HICKORY, NC	81,399
JANESVILLE, WI	81,300
SANTA CRUZ, CA	81,069
MASSILLON, OH	80,881
CANTON, OH	80,225
CHATSWORTH, CA	79,186
ASPEN, CO	79,073
BLOOMINGTON, IN	79,000
CHARLESTON, WV	77,812
MONTGOMERY, AL (Charter Communications)	77,500
PINELLAS COUNTY, FL (Knology)	77,186
CHESTERFIELD, MI	77,043
SAN JOSE, CA	76,691
MONMOUTH COUNTY, NJ (Comcast Cable)	75,460
INDEPENDENCE, MO	75,314
LIVONIA, MI	75,140
JACKSON, MS	75,000
PARMA, OH	75,000
VERO BEACH, FL	75,000
MOLINE, IL	74,910
ANNE ARUNDEL COUNTY, MD	74,189
ROCK HILL, SC	73,907
CELEBRATION, FL	72,940
LUBBOCK, TX	72,428
MIAMI BEACH, FL	72,000
SPRINGFIELD, MO	71,000
HOWARD COUNTY, MD	70,828
SARASOTA, FL	70,605
PLAINVILLE, CT	70,218
MACON, GA	70,000
URBANA, IL	69,500
EAST WINDSOR, NJ	68,463
CHICAGO (southern suburbs), IL	67,174
VALLEY, AL	66,500
MANCHESTER, CT	66,227
SANTA BARBARA, CA	66,000
TRAVERSE CITY, MI	65,926
ROANOKE, VA	65,876
LANSING, MI	65,000
MANSFIELD, OH	65,000
PHILADELPHIA (area 2), PA	65,000
SAN LUIS OBISPO, CA	64,849
YUMA, AZ	64,830
OSSINING, NY	64,217
TARENTUM BOROUGH, PA	64,196
MONTEREY, CA	63,578
ALBERTVILLE, AL	63,257
WHEELING, WV	63,249
FREDERICK, MD	62,896
AMARILLO, TX	62,687
NEW HAVEN, CT	62,227
HOBOKEN, NJ	62,208
MILLERSVILLE, MD	62,000
SHREVEPORT, LA	61,438
BRANFORD, CT	61,075
EVANSVILLE, IN (Insight Communications)	60,458
SPARTA, NJ	60,400
GRAY, TN	60,112
CALDWELL, ID	60,000
MODESTO & OAKDALE, CA	59,905
OLIVETTE, MO	59,403
ASHFORD, CT	59,401
DURHAM, NC	58,969
FARGO, ND	58,713
RIVERSIDE, CA	58,650
BOISE, ID	58,375
TURLOCK, CA	58,297
BLAIRSVILLE, PA	57,711
PONTIAC, MI	57,645
RIVERHEAD, NY	57,410
BERGENFIELD, NJ	57,221
HESPERIA, CA	56,938
VENICE, FL	56,439
SAGINAW, MI	55,949
CHICO, CA	55,483
NEWARK, NJ	54,271
GREENEVILLE, TN	54,077
HARFORD COUNTY, MD	54,000
ROCKLAND, NY	53,872
YONKERS, NY	53,601
EAU CLAIRE, WI	53,386
WALLINGFORD, PA	51,857
BRYAN, TX	51,162
SIOUX FALLS, SD	51,143
ALBANY, GA	50,921
CHICOPEE, MA	50,919
ARLINGTON, VA	50,538
SPOTSYLVANIA/STAFFORD, VA	50,232
PARKERSBURG, WV	50,032
COEUR D'ALENE, ID	50,000
LOUDOUN COUNTY, VA	49,600
COLUMBUS, GA	49,569
BELMONT, NH	49,440
SANTA MARIA, CA	49,001
HAGERSTOWN, MD	49,000
LAWRENCE, KS	48,950
JERSEY CITY, NJ	48,876
SUNBURY, PA	48,844
AGANA, GU	48,646
HOMOSASSA, FL	48,621
DIMONDALE, MI	48,500
MUSKEGON, MI	48,050
ONALASKA, WI	47,555
PANAMA CITY, FL	47,200
ANNISTON, AL	46,540
ST. CHARLES, MO	46,400
KALAMAZOO, MI	46,076
MORGANTOWN, WV	46,069
VIBORG, SD	46,000
LAREDO, TX	45,869
BOWLING GREEN, KY	45,515

NEWARK, OH 45,236
MEDFORD, OR 45,074
PASCO COUNTY (central & eastern portions), FL 45,000
SEYMOUR, CT 43,885
CARMEL, NY 43,759
NEW LONDON, CT 43,648
LONG BEACH, MS 43,401
BILOXI, MS 43,400
HUNTSVILLE, AL (Comcast Cable) 42,708
SLIDELL, LA 42,529
ALTOONA, PA 42,459
AUGUSTA, ME 42,385
TRENTON, NJ 42,048
HOMEWOOD, SC 42,000
GLOUCESTER COUNTY, NJ 41,649
PLYMOUTH, MI 41,618
STROUDSBURG, PA 41,559
SOUTHFIELD, MI 41,466
WILDWOOD, FL 41,335
BECKLEY, WV 41,294
HAMMOND, LA 41,080
PRESCOTT, AZ 40,757
WATERBURY, CT 39,938
TACOMA, WA (Comcast Cable) 39,874
DULUTH, GA 39,790
MERIDEN, CT 39,734
PUEBLO, CO 39,731
BANGOR, ME 39,501
MAZOMANIE, WI 39,413
BILLINGS, MT 39,295
OCEAN COUNTY, NJ 39,269
MIDLAND, TX 39,252
HARRIMAN, TN 39,105
SAN BERNARDINO, CA 38,729
MARYVILLE, IL 38,449
ALEXANDRIA, VA 38,400
LA PORTE, IN 38,030
TUSCALOOSA, AL 38,000
SAN ANGELO, TX 37,872
PORT ORCHARD, WA 37,723
ENFIELD, CT 37,689
HARBORCREEK TWP., PA 37,522
UNIONTOWN, PA 37,369
RANSON, WV 37,353
FORT DODGE, IA 37,222
BEND, OR 37,000
WILKES-BARRE, PA 37,000
WILDWOOD, NJ 36,851
DAGSBORO, DE 36,838
SEMINOLE, TX 36,466
LAKE CHARLES, LA 36,282
ROSEMOUNT, MN 36,180
MACOMB, IL 36,170
GAINESVILLE, GA 36,027
EVANSVILLE, IN (WOW! Internet Cable & Phone) 36,000
KENNEWICK, WA 36,000
WEST MONROE, LA 36,000
COATESVILLE, PA 35,888
CARY, NC 35,831
LIMA, OH 35,732
ABILENE, TX 35,719
CAMBRIDGE, MN 35,700
REHOBOTH BEACH, DE 35,590
PORT CHARLOTTE, FL 35,445
HUNTSVILLE, AL (Knology) 35,269
DEL RIO, TX 35,000
YAKIMA, WA 34,942
COLUMBIA, TN 34,645
ATHENS, GA 34,643
GULF BREEZE, FL 34,522
DOVER, DE 34,424
ODESSA, TX 34,418
JACKSON, MI 34,161
DANBURY, CT 34,142
REDDING, CA 34,019
CHARLOTTESVILLE, VA 33,802
HOUMA, LA 33,750
TYLER, TX 33,445
YORKTOWN, NY 33,436
HAMILTON TWP. (Mercer County), NJ 33,112
EPHRATA, PA 33,000
CLARKSBURG, WV 32,931
OWENSBORO, KY 32,178
BELLEVILLE, IL 32,137
SPOKANE, WA 32,000
SIOUX CITY, IA 31,958
ASHEVILLE, NC 31,700
ANAHEIM, CA 31,642
CARLSTADT BOROUGH, NJ 31,310
ROCHESTER, MN 31,300
OCEAN CITY, MD 31,182
PINEVILLE, LA 31,013
BIRDSBORO, PA 31,000
SMYRNA, GA 30,939
EUREKA, CA 30,912
SHERMAN, TX 30,900
BURLINGTON, IA 30,844
FLORENCE, AL 30,828
PALMERTON, PA 30,748
TEXARKANA, TX 30,737
PEARL, MS 30,736
ST. JOSEPH, MO 30,278
WALLED LAKE, MI 30,248
MERCED, CA 30,198
McKENZIE, TN 30,099
BATTLE CREEK, MI 29,985
JOHNSTOWN, PA 29,865
NEW MIDDLETOWN, OH 29,622
DUBUQUE, IA 29,542
YUBA CITY, CA 29,477
IDAHO FALLS, ID 29,246
LAS CRUCES, NM 29,227
CHARLES COUNTY, MD 29,122
CLINTON, IA 28,585
ALCOA, TN 28,500
MORRISTOWN, TN 28,500
SEBAGO (town), ME 28,446
CORAL SPRINGS, FL 28,329
MANDAN, ND 28,180
BAY CITY, MI 28,129
CHAPEL HILL, NC 28,011
WATERLOO, IA 28,000
GRAND JUNCTION, CO 27,900
TUPELO, MS 27,500
JACKSON, TN 27,454
FOND DU LAC, WI 27,423
DOTHAN, AL 27,400
DULUTH, MN 27,270
MONTGOMERY, AL (Knology) 27,242
NEW PHILADELPHIA, OH 27,196
LITCHFIELD, CT 27,173
MONROEVILLE, PA 27,173
CLARKSVILLE, TN 26,855
OLATHE, KS 26,620
CUMBERLAND, MD 26,612
DENTON, TX 26,600
CAPE GIRARDEAU, MO 26,343
DANVILLE, VA 26,328
STOCKBRIDGE, GA 26,271
VERNON, CT 26,005
WICHITA FALLS, TX 26,000
PATERSON, NJ 25,722
STAUNTON, VA 25,412
WESTMINSTER, MD 25,241
WARWICK, NY 25,056
MACEDONIA, OH 25,000
SHALLOTTE, NC 25,000
TACOMA, WA (Click! Network) 25,000
LONGVIEW, TX 24,930
ORANGE COUNTY (unincorporated areas), FL 24,784

LANCASTER, PA	24,630
MIDDLETOWN, CT	24,558
PORT MURRAY, NJ	24,390
ELIZABETH, NJ	24,357
ROXANA, IL	24,135
WAUSAU, WI	24,100
ALTON, MO	24,000
LAWTON, OK	24,000
HOT SPRINGS, AR	23,971
PADUCAH, KY	23,965
YORK, PA	23,717
TERRE HAUTE, IN	23,638
GOLDSBORO, NC	23,555
COLUMBIA, MO	23,509
CLINTON, CT	23,463
CHEYENNE, WY	23,379
JUNCTION CITY, KS	23,132
AIKEN, SC	23,020
KILLEEN, TX	23,000
GROTON, CT	22,991
WINCHESTER, VA	22,808
PLAINFIELD, NJ	22,740
BETHEL PARK, PA	22,600
WENATCHEE, WA	22,600
SALISBURY, MD	22,542
EAST LANSING, MI	22,516
BRUNSWICK, GA	22,432
TOWANDA, PA	22,359
CARBONDALE, PA	22,300
WEST BEND, WI	22,300
HAROLD, KY	22,131
ALLENDALE, MI	21,686
HUNTINGTON, WV	21,679
LYNCHBURG, VA	21,631
SHEBOYGAN, WI	21,600
JONESBORO, AR	21,433
RICHMOND, KY	21,262
CATSKILL, NY	21,125
CLEVELAND, MS	21,000
VALDOSTA, GA	21,000
KERMIT, WV	20,843
HARRODSBURG, KY	20,462
KENT, OH	20,458
EUGENE, OR	20,036
SAN FRANCISCO (southern portion), CA	20,000
SANDUSKY, OH	20,000

* Total analog and digital basic subscribers.

Nielsen Cable TV Household Estimates

Listed alphabetically by Nielsen Designated Market Area (DMA)

(Data as of October 2011)

DESIGNATED MARKET AREA	*CABLE TV* % RANK*	TV HSHLDS (Jan. 2012)	*CABLE TV* HSEHLDS (Sept. 2011)	*CABLE TV* % of TV HSEHLDS
Abilene-Sweetwater, TX	196	115,630	42,250	37
Albany, GA	143	151,620	77,820	51
Albany-Schenectady-Troy, NY	10	551,120	422,420	77
Albuquerque-Santa Fe, NM	196	710,050	259,450	37
Alexandria, LA	123	90,160	48,910	54
Alpena, MI	84	17,100	10,150	59
Amarillo, TX	174	195,650	85,560	44
Anchorage, AK	58	155,600	98,650	63
Atlanta, GA	77	2,292,640	1,369,740	60
Augusta, GA-Aiken, SC	123	262,560	141,050	54
Austin, TX	61	686,830	424,850	62
Bakersfield, CA	137	221,920	114,880	52
Baltimore, MD	14	1,097,310	819,600	75
Bangor, ME	181	141,580	57,740	41
Baton Rouge, LA	23	333,010	236,030	71
Beaumont-Port Arthur, TX	157	168,420	82,870	49
Bend, OR	51	62,620	39,930	64
Billings, MT	128	109,940	57,780	53
Biloxi-Gulfport, MS	51	128,150	82,520	64
Binghamton, NY	18	136,730	99,170	73
Birmingham (Anniston & Tuscaloosa), AL	157	738,790	361,730	49
Bluefield-Beckley-Oak Hill, WV	47	137,380	88,890	65
Boise, ID	210	261,810	63,910	24
Boston, MA (Manchester, NH)	1	2,379,690	2,122,160	89
Bowling Green, KY	18	79,990	58,340	73
Buffalo, NY	61	645,190	400,370	62
Burlington, VT-Plattsburgh, NY	128	323,750	172,310	53
Butte-Bozeman, MT	177	66,910	28,480	43
Casper-Riverton, WY	67	56,460	34,540	61
Cedar Rapids-Waterloo-Iowa City-Dubuque, IA	94	344,150	198,080	58
Champaign & Springfield-Decatur, IL	94	386,160	223,400	58
Charleston, SC	51	311,260	198,830	64
Charleston-Huntington, WV	118	465,030	256,270	55
Charlotte, NC	94	1,140,900	666,950	58
Charlottesville, VA	128	74,630	39,370	53
Chattanooga, TN	77	366,790	221,670	60
Cheyenne, WY-Scottsbluff, NE	61	56,640	35,180	62
Chicago, IL	61	3,493,480	2,166,190	62
Chico-Redding, CA	205	194,590	65,260	34
Cincinnati, OH	84	896,090	527,700	59
Clarksburg-Weston, WV	128	108,980	57,730	53
Cleveland-Akron (Canton), OH	32	1,514,170	1,050,410	69
Colorado Springs-Pueblo, CO	177	343,160	146,850	43
Columbia, SC	143	404,830	205,040	51
Columbia-Jefferson City, MO	204	176,470	62,020	35
Columbus-Tupelo-West Point-Houston, MS	208	189,910	58,210	31
Columbus, GA (Opelika, AL)	42	215,410	142,420	66
Columbus, OH	37	932,680	624,240	67
Corpus Christi, TX	112	203,550	113,550	56
Dallas-Fort Worth, TX	152	2,571,310	1,282,550	50
Davenport, IA-Rock Island-Moline, IL	112	307,050	171,720	56
Dayton, OH	77	493,600	297,870	60
Denver, CO	157	1,548,570	765,330	49
Des Moines-Ames, IA	169	431,300	200,110	46
Detroit, MI	23	1,842,650	1,308,060	71
Dothan, AL	128	109,080	58,160	53
Duluth, MN-Superior, WI	189	173,710	66,930	39
El Paso, TX (Las Cruces, NM)	185	336,570	135,730	40
Elmira (Corning), NY	32	96,600	67,050	69
Erie, PA	112	157,730	88,810	56
Eugene, OR	143	241,270	123,810	51
Eureka, CA	84	61,180	35,850	59
Evansville, IN	143	287,880	147,640	51
Fairbanks, AK	177	37,010	15,850	43
Fargo-Valley City, ND	123	246,780	134,410	54
Flint-Saginaw-Bay City, MI	67	541,880	276,310	61
Fort Myers-Naples, FL	61	504,240	313,660	62
Fort Smith-Fayetteville-Springdale-Rogers, AR	143	301,120	154,480	51
Fort Wayne, IN	163	267,710	127,660	48
Fresno-Visalia, CA	200	574,800	206,190	36
Gainesville, FL	84	124,730	73,980	59
Glendive, MT	42	4,180	2,740	66
Grand Junction-Montrose, CO	112	72,970	41,130	56
Grand Rapids-Kalamazoo-Battle Creek, MI	94	722,150	419,490	58
Great Falls, MT	163	66,190	31,850	48
Green Bay-Appleton, WI	143	445,760	229,300	51
Greensboro-High Point-Winston Salem, NC	94	691,200	402,820	58
Greenville-New Bern-Washington, NC	152	307,610	153,040	50
Greenville-Spartanburg-Anderson, SC-Asheville, NC	169	860,930	394,690	46
Greenwood-Greenville, MS	84	67,730	39,800	59
Harlingen-Weslaco-Brownsville-McAllen, TX	185	361,820	145,390	40
Harrisburg-Lancaster-Lebanon-York, PA	26	729,440	508,300	70
Harrisonburg, VA	67	91,620	55,780	61
Hartford & New Haven, CT	4	1,006,280	851,060	85
Hattiesburg-Laurel, MS	157	111,560	54,810	49
Helena, MT	123	28,050	15,130	54
Honolulu, HI	1	434,730	387,990	89
Houston, TX	118	2,185,260	1,196,990	55
Huntsville-Decatur (Florence), AL	94	394,010	227,040	58
Idaho Falls-Pocatello, ID (Jackson, WY)	208	128,940	40,610	31
Indianapolis, IN	67	1,109,970	677,270	61
Jackson, MS	185	334,530	135,030	40
Jackson, TN	94	94,650	55,080	58
Jacksonville, FL	77	669,840	399,650	60
Johnstown-Altoona-State College, PA	94	294,770	172,130	58
Jonesboro, AR	67	81,300	49,200	61
Joplin, MO-Pittsburg, KS	196	153,910	56,240	37
Juneau, AK	42	25,500	16,740	66
Kansas City, MO	51	939,740	600,350	64
Knoxville, TN	67	527,790	322,620	61
La Crosse-Eau Claire, WI	118	213,660	117,100	55
Lafayette, IN	37	67,260	44,740	67
Lafayette, LA	84	229,320	136,270	59
Lake Charles, LA	51	94,850	61,110	64
Lansing, MI	137	252,890	132,720	52
Laredo, TX	152	72,060	36,390	50
Las Vegas, NV	84	737,300	433,470	59
Lexington, KY	143	488,850	250,900	51
Lima, OH	16	39,350	28,980	74
Lincoln & Hastings-Kearney, NE	157	280,310	137,360	49
Little Rock-Pine Bluff, AR	180	571,630	242,660	42
Los Angeles, CA	137	5,569,780	2,917,210	52
Louisville, KY	67	674,050	413,900	61
Lubbock, TX	172	160,160	71,900	45
Macon, GA	165	245,910	115,520	47
Madison, WI	137	378,290	195,710	52
Mankato, MN	58	53,720	33,780	63
Marquette, MI	37	85,230	57,530	67
Medford-Klamath Falls, OR	185	170,670	67,600	40
Memphis, TN	152	669,940	336,770	50
Meridian, MS	200	70,190	25,110	36
Miami-Fort Lauderdale, FL	26	1,583,800	1,107,910	70
Milwaukee, WI	77	907,660	542,140	60
Minneapolis-St. Paul, MN	118	1,721,940	947,950	55
Minot-Bismarck-Dickinson (Williston), ND	112	145,480	81,850	56
Missoula, MT	200	114,590	41,020	36
Mobile, AL-Pensacola (Fort Walton Beach), FL	123	527,930	284,600	54
Monroe, LA-El Dorado, AR	174	177,410	78,370	44
Monterey-Salinas, CA	128	223,620	118,660	53
Montgomery-Selma, AL	58	245,100	153,760	63
Myrtle Beach-Florence, SC	42	289,060	191,120	66
Nashville, TN	94	1,024,560	593,430	58
New Orleans, LA	108	643,660	369,110	57
New York, NY	4	7,387,810	6,306,960	85
Norfolk-Portsmouth-Newport News, VA	32	718,750	497,000	69
North Platte, NE	51	15,180	9,640	64

DESIGNATED MARKET AREA	CABLE TV % RANK*	TV HSHLDS (Jan. 2012)	CABLE TV HSEHLDS (Sept. 2011)	CABLE TV % of TV HSEHLDS
Odessa-Midland, TX	77	146,040	87,260	60
Oklahoma City, OK	128	712,630	378,220	53
Omaha, NE	26	415,510	290,540	70
Orlando-Daytona Beach-Melbourne, FL	37	1,465,460	978,040	67
Ottumwa, IA-Kirksville, MO	143	47,810	24,600	51
Paducah, KY-Cape Girardeau, MO-Harrisburg, IL	189	393,330	151,740	39
Palm Springs, CA	14	158,440	118,150	75
Panama City, FL	42	132,120	87,470	66
Parkersburg, WV	18	63,120	46,030	73
Peoria-Bloomington, IL	84	247,850	147,120	59
Philadelphia, PA	7	2,993,370	2,406,070	80
Phoenix (Prescott), AZ	165	1,811,330	855,430	47
Pittsburgh, PA	26	1,171,490	817,130	70
Portland, OR	108	1,190,010	674,530	57
Portland-Auburn, ME	26	401,370	282,710	70
Presque Isle, ME	112	29,850	16,790	56
Providence, RI-New Bedford, MA	3	620,010	536,760	87
Quincy, IL-Hannibal, MO-Keokuk, IA	181	104,790	43,260	41
Raleigh-Durham (Fayetteville), NC	128	1,143,420	606,660	53
Rapid City, SD	67	100,120	61,530	61
Reno, NV	165	271,020	127,840	47
Richmond-Petersburg, VA	108	559,390	320,220	57
Roanoke-Lynchburg, VA	181	455,860	187,840	41
Rochester, MN-Mason City, IA-Austin, MN	94	145,450	84,500	58
Rochester, NY	32	398,790	275,680	69
Rockford, IL	67	184,360	112,560	61
Sacramento-Stockton-Modesto, CA	137	1,388,570	717,610	52
Salisbury, MD	16	159,640	118,410	74
Salt Lake City, UT	174	927,540	410,150	44
San Angelo, TX	94	55,570	32,030	58
San Antonio, TX	118	880,690	484,890	55
San Diego, CA	9	1,077,600	855,710	79
San Francisco-Oakland-San Jose, CA	47	2,506,510	1,631,550	65
Santa Barbara-Santa Maria-San Luis Obispo, CA	84	230,830	136,980	59
Savannah, GA	94	335,080	193,310	58
Seattle-Tacoma, WA	11	1,811,420	1,372,740	76
Sherman, TX-Ada, OK	196	128,790	48,070	37
Shreveport, LA	200	386,150	140,330	36
Sioux City, IA	128	157,060	83,770	53
Sioux Falls (Mitchell), SD	47	261,530	169,100	65
South Bend-Elkhart, IN	172	322,090	143,400	45
Spokane, WA	181	426,690	174,900	41
Springfield, MO	207	423,010	133,970	32
Springfield-Holyoke, MA	4	257,080	217,250	85
St. Joseph, MO	108	46,690	26,530	57
St. Louis, MO	143	1,253,920	635,930	51
Syracuse, NY	11	386,090	294,950	76
Tallahassee, FL-Thomasville, GA	94	272,520	157,540	58
Tampa-St. Petersburg (Sarasota), FL	7	1,788,240	1,432,750	80
Terre Haute, IN	189	142,780	55,390	39
Toledo, OH	37	426,280	284,250	67
Topeka, KS	84	177,710	105,480	59
Traverse City-Cadillac, MI	169	244,050	111,860	46
Tri-Cities, TN-VA	94	323,640	188,660	58
Tucson (Sierra Vista), AZ	152	442,020	219,500	50
Tulsa, OK	157	529,100	259,510	49
Twin Falls, ID	206	65,800	22,000	33
Tyler-Longview (Lufkin & Nacogdoches), TX	194	271,400	102,710	38
Utica, NY	11	104,750	80,130	76
Victoria, TX	77	31,540	18,900	60
Waco-Temple-Bryan, TX	137	353,190	184,310	52
Washington, DC (Hagerstown, MD)	18	2,360,180	1,724,760	73
Watertown, NY	26	93,090	65,400	70
Wausau-Rhinelander, WI	165	181,280	85,770	47
West Palm Beach-Fort Pierce, FL	22	788,020	564,880	72
Wheeling, WV-Steubenville, OH	23	133,120	93,980	71
Wichita Falls, TX & Lawton, OK	189	160,540	63,410	39
Wichita-Hutchinson, KS Plus	67	454,590	278,170	61
Wilkes Barre-Scranton-Hazleton, PA	51	590,740	377,080	64
Wilmington, NC	61	190,730	119,160	62
Yakima-Pasco-Richland-Kennewick, WA	189	230,010	89,420	39
Youngstown, OH	47	263,850	171,470	65
Yuma, AZ-El Centro, CA	194	112,850	43,300	38
Zanesville, OH	36	33,140	22,620	68

* Ranked by Cable TV Penetration, i.e Cable TV Households as % of TV Households.

A. C. Nielsen Co. Cable TV Household Estimates

Alphabetically by State

STATE	CABLE TV % RANK [1]	TV HOUSEHOLDS (Jan. 2012)	CABLE TV (Sept. 2011)	CABLE TV % OF TV HOUSEHOLDS
ALABAMA	38	1,869,030	982,870	53
ALASKA [2]	20	218,110	131,240	60
ARIZONA	44	2,332,510	1,102,430	47
ARKANSAS	46	1,132,360	525,440	46
CALIFORNIA	29	12,303,720	6,949,990	56
COLORADO	41	1,922,350	933,980	49
CONNECTICUT	4	1,332,000	1,141,300	86
DELAWARE	6	340,150	284,980	84
DISTRICT OF COLUMBIA	9	260,050	197,200	76
FLORIDA	12	7,399,920	5,197,580	70
GEORGIA	25	3,538,300	2,047,600	58
HAWAII	2	434,730	387,990	89
IDAHO	51	569,930	157,400	28
ILLINOIS	23	4,755,220	2,808,800	59
INDIANA	29	2,451,650	1,362,620	56
IOWA	38	1,193,880	629,540	53
KANSAS	16	1,085,920	686,070	63
KENTUCKY	28	1,697,310	974,690	57
LOUISIANA	25	1,706,720	997,960	58
MAINE	19	539,170	335,320	62
MARYLAND	10	2,122,870	1,582,730	75
MASSACHUSETTS	1	2,465,820	2,225,310	90
MICHIGAN	16	3,748,210	2,375,630	63
MINNESOTA	31	2,041,050	1,129,710	55
MISSISSIPPI	49	1,100,920	469,420	43
MISSOURI	44	2,342,240	1,108,330	47
MONTANA	48	394,210	173,030	44
NEBRASKA	20	708,540	424,580	60
NEVADA	31	1,000,290	553,250	55
NEW HAMPSHIRE	8	502,730	386,050	77
NEW JERSEY	4	3,142,830	2,694,250	86
NEW MEXICO	50	772,650	292,360	38
NEW YORK	7	7,072,520	5,675,640	80
NORTH CAROLINA	31	3,747,440	2,051,680	55
NORTH DAKOTA	20	277,100	165,200	60
OHIO	14	4,499,700	2,949,660	66
OKLAHOMA	41	1,457,840	710,000	49
OREGON	35	1,477,130	804,530	54
PENNSYLVANIA	11	4,917,250	3,476,240	71
RHODE ISLAND	3	408,310	354,140	87
SOUTH CAROLINA	31	1,796,770	988,310	55
SOUTH DAKOTA	15	318,750	208,700	65
TENNESSEE	23	2,469,050	1,455,150	59
TEXAS	40	8,913,990	4,560,560	51
UTAH	47	864,910	392,630	45
VERMONT	41	242,420	117,810	49
VIRGINIA	16	3,033,490	1,926,120	63
WASHINGTON	13	2,514,670	1,698,160	68
WEST VIRGINIA	25	748,440	433,620	58
WISCONSIN	35	2,242,030	1,200,790	54
WYOMING	35	222,110	120,050	54

[1] Ranked by cable TV penetration, i.e., cable TV households as % of TV households.
[2] Anchorage, Fairbanks and Juneau DMAs only.

U.S. CABLE SYSTEM TOTALS BY STATE

(As of October 2011)

Note: All data is as reported by cable operators or individual cable systems. Not all cable systems or operators report complete data.
* Basic subscriber totals include analog and digital subscribers. Some systems have converted to IPTV.

State	Systems	Communities Served	Franchises Not Yet Operating	Applications Pending	Communities with Applications	Total Basic Subscribers*
Alabama	149	629	0	0	0	1,197,393
Alaska	30	57	0	0	0	198,187
Arizona	57	206	0	0	0	1,485,171
Arkansas	169	515	0	0	0	408,628
California	177	1,171	0	0	0	8,104,413
Colorado	104	331	0	0	0	1,385,105
Connecticut	24	204	0	0	0	1,159,226
Delaware	5	80	0	0	0	118,752
District of Columbia	20	22	0	0	0	176,000
Florida	144	792	0	0	0	5,868,214
Georgia	184	793	0	0	0	2,194,744
Hawaii	6	128	0	0	0	350,115
Idaho	36	187	0	0	0	234,163
Illinois	274	1,297	0	0	0	2,608,692
Indiana	116	687	0	0	0	1,418,714
Iowa	244	749	0	0	0	697,702
Kansas	200	447	0	0	0	652,004
Kentucky	149	994	0	0	0	1,017,050
Louisiana	102	462	0	0	0	1,055,082
Maine	39	354	0	0	0	324,418
Maryland	33	414	0	0	0	1,372,603
Massachusetts	45	361	0	0	0	1,559,474
Michigan	224	1,552	0	0	0	2,314,479
Minnesota	274	877	0	0	0	1,342,021
Mississippi	115	347	0	0	0	552,660
Missouri	187	738	0	0	0	1,519,403
Montana	84	147	0	0	0	209,671
Nebraska	164	358	0	0	0	551,336
Nevada	34	91	0	0	0	590,903
New Hampshire	16	199	0	0	0	829,331
New Jersey	37	635	0	0	0	2,781,057
New Mexico	52	146	0	0	0	340,338
New York	86	1,567	0	0	0	6,514,574
North Carolina	104	879	0	0	0	2,308,235
North Dakota	72	220	0	0	0	188,103
Ohio	168	1,814	0	0	0	3,168,698
Oklahoma	230	411	0	0	0	724,901
Oregon	82	359	0	0	0	1,085,846
Pennsylvania	274	2,582	0	0	0	3,900,520
Rhode Island	3	45	0	0	0	317,024
South Carolina	45	365	0	0	0	1,147,027
South Dakota	119	240	0	0	0	210,749
Tennessee	103	551	0	0	0	1,723,046
Texas	434	1,392	0	0	0	4,884,775
Utah	52	210	0	0	0	324,867
Vermont	12	236	0	0	0	37,038
Virginia	106	572	0	0	0	1,961,115
Washington	103	463	0	0	0	1,746,219
West Virginia	130	1,020	0	0	0	488,580
Wisconsin	173	906	0	0	0	1,749,851
Wyoming	53	100	0	0	0	121,468
TOTAL	**5,851**	**30,015**	**0**	**0**	**0**	**77,658,280**

Commonly Used Initials and Abbreviations

AAAA—American Association of Advertising Agencies

A&E—Arts & Entertainment Network

AAF—American Advertising Federation

ABA—American Bar Association

ABC—American Broadcasting Co.

ABC—Australian Broadcasting Corp.

ABES—Association for Broadcast Engineering Standards

ABS—Association for Broadcast Standards

AC—alternating current

AC-3—Dolby Labs compression system for digital audio

ACA—Association of Canadian Advertisers

ACLU—American Civil Liberties Union

ACRTF—Association Canadienne de la Radio et de la Television de Langue Francaise Inc.

ADI—Area of dominant influence

AeA—American Electronics Association

AFC—automatic frequency control

AFCCE—Association of Federal Communications Consulting Engineers

AFCEA—Armed Forces Communications & Electronics Association

AFL-CIO—American Federation of Labor & Congress of Industrial Organizations

AFM—American Federation of Musicians

AFRTS—American Forces Radio & Television Service

AFT—automatic fine tuning

AFTRA—American Federation of Television & Radio Artists

AFTS—American Forces Television Service

AGMA—American Guild of Musical Artists

AGVA—American Guild of Variety Artists

AIM—Accuracy in Media

AIT—Agency for Instructional TV

ALS—Adult Learning Service (PBS) now

ALS—Advanced Launch System (Air Force)

AM—amplitude modulation

AMA—American Marketing Association

AMC—American Movie Classics

AMP—Association of Media Producers

AMPTP—Association of Motion Picture & Television Producers Inc.

ANA—Association of National Advertisers

ANG—American Newspaper Guild

ANPA—American Newspaper Publishers Association

AP—Associated Press

APA—Administrative Procedures Act

APBI—Associated Press Broadcasters Inc.

APRO—Association of Progressive Rental Organizations

APT—American Public Television

APTS—Association of Public TV Stations

ARF—Advertising Research Foundation

ARPA—Advanced Research Projects Agency

ARRL—American Radio Relay League

ASCAP—American Society of Composers, Authors & Publishers

ASIC—application-specific integrated circuit

ASNE—American Society of News Editors

ASTA—Advertiser Syndicated TV Association

ATIS—Automatic Transmitter Identification System (satellite)

ATSC—Advanced Television Systems Committee

ATV—Associated Television Ltd. (U.K.)

AV—audio-video, audio-visual

AWRT—American Women in Radio & Television

b&w—black & white

BAR—Broadcast Advertisers Reports

BBC—British Broadcasting Corporation

BBM—Bureau of Broadcast Measurement

BCFM—Broadcast Cable Financial Management Association

BEA—Broadcast Education Association

BEMA—Business Equipment Manufacturers Association

BET—Black Entertainment TV

BIAC—Broadcast Interassociation Council

BIB—Board for International Broadcasting

BICIAP—Broadcasting Industry Council to Improve American Productivity

BMI—Broadcast Music Inc.

BOC—Bell Operating Company

BPA—Broadcasters Promotion Association

BREMA—British Radio Equipment Manufacturers Association

BROADCAP—Broadcast Capital Fund Inc.

CAAA—Canadian Association of Advertising Agencies

CAB—Cabletelevision Advertising Bureau

CAB—Canadian Association of Broadcasters

CABLEPAC—Cable Industry Political Action Committee

CAMM—Catholic Apostolate of Mass Media

CARF—Canadian Advertising Research Foundation

CARS—Cable Television Relay Service

CARTA—Catholic Apostolate of Radio, Television & Advertising

CASA—Car Audio Specialists Association

CATV—community antenna TV, cable TV

CB—citizens band

CBA—Catholic Broadcasters Association

CBA—Community Broadcasters Association

CBC—Canadian Broadcasting Corporation

CBO—Congressional Budget Office

CBS—formerly Columbia Broadcasting System

CC—closed captioned

CC—common carrier

CCBS—Clear Channel Broadcasting Service

CCC—Citizens Communications Center

CCD—charge-coupled device

CCIR—International Radio Consultative Committee

CCITT—International Telegraph & Telephone Consultative Committee

CCTA—Canadian Cable TV & Telecom Association

CCTV—closed-circuit television

CD—*Communications Daily*

CD—compact disc digital audio system

CD-E—erasable compact disc

CD+G—compact disc plus graphics

CD-I/CD-i—compact disc-interactive

CD-R—recordable compact disc

CD-ROM—compact disc read-only memory

CDMA—code division multiple access

CE—consumer electronics

CEA—Communications Equity Associates

CED—Committee for Economic Development

CED—*Consumer Electronics Daily*

CEDIA—Custom Electronic Design & Installation Association

CEA—Consumer Electronics Association (EIA)

CEN—Central Educational Network

CEO—chief executive officer

CEPT—Council of European Posts & Telegraph

CES—Consumer Electronics Show

CFA—Consumer Federation of America

CFO—chief financial officer

CHOB—Cannon House Office Building

CIRT—La Camera Nacional de la Industria de Radio y Television (Mexican Association of Broadcasters)

CLeaR-TV—Christian Leaders for Responsible TV

cm—centimeter

CMA—Country Music Association

CMT—Country Music TV

CNN—Cable News Network

CNBC—Consumer News & Business Channel (NBC)

COLTAM—Committee On Local TV Audience Measurements

COMPO—Council of Motion Picture Organizations

CONTAM—Committee on Nationwide TV Audience Measurements

CONUS—contiguous U.S.

COO—chief operating officer

CP—construction permit

CPB—Corporation for Public Broadcasting

CPM—cost per thousand

CPSC—Consumer Product Safety Commission

CPU—central processing unit

CRP—circular polarization

CRT—cathode ray tube

CRTC—Canadian Radio-Television & Telecommunications Commission

CSG—Community Service Grant

C-SPAN—Cable-Satellite Public Affairs Network

CTAC—Cable Technical Advisory Committee

CTAM—Cable & Telecommunications Association for Marketing

CTIA—Cellular Telecommunications & Internet Association

CTIC—Cable TV Information Center

CTV—Canadian TV Network

CTVHH—Cable TV Households

CTW—Children's Television Workshop

CU—Consumers Union

CWA—Communications Workers of America

The CW Network—Television network offering programs from both UPN & The WB networks

D/A—digital-to-analog converter

DAB—digital audio broadcasting

DARS—digital audio radio service

dB—decibel

DBS—Direct Broadcast Satellite

DC—direct current

DCC—Digital Compact Cassette

DFS—Deutsches Fernsehen (Germany)

DGA—Directors Guild of America Inc.

DHS—Department of Homeland Security

DJ—disc jockey

DMA—Designated Market Area

DMX—Digital Music Express

DoD—Department of Defense

DoJ—Department of Justice

DoT—Department of Transportation

DSA—Distinguished Service Award (NAB)

DSI—digital speech interpolation

DSOB—Dirksen Senate Office Building

DSP—digital signal processing

DSR—Statsradiofonien (Denmark)

DSRC—David Sarnoff Research Center

DSS—Digital Satellite System

DTH—direct to home (satellite transmission)

DTV—digital television

DVD—digital versatile disc

DVR—digital video recording, recorder

EBS—Educational Broadband Service

EBS—Emergency Broadcast System

EBS—Emergency Broadcasting Service

EBU—European Broadcasting Union

EEC—European Economic Community

EEN—Eastern Educational Network

EEO—Equal Employment Opportunity

EEOC—Equal Employment Opportunity Commission

EHF—extremely high frequency

EIA—Electronic Industries Association

EIAJ—Electronic Industries Association of Japan

EIAK—Electronic Industries Association of Korea

EIRP—effective isotropically radiated power

EL—electro luminescence

EMRC—Electronic Media Rating Council

ENG—electronic news gathering

EP—extended play

EPA—Environmental Protection Agency

EPG—Electronic Program Guide

ERA—Electronics Representatives Association

ERP—effective radiated power

ESA—European Space Agency

ESPN—Entertainment & Sports Programming Network

ESRB—Entertainment Software Rating Board

ETV—educational television

EUTELSAT—European Telecommunications Satellite Organization

EWTN—Eternal Word TV Network

FAA—Federal Aviation Administration

FAIR—Fairness & Accuracy in Reporting

FB—Factbook

FBA—Federal Bar Association

FBI—Federal Bureau of Investigation

FCBA—Federal Communications Bar Association

FCC—Federal Communications Commission

FDA—Food & Drug Administration

FEA—Federal Energy Administration

FEC—Federal Election Commission

FED—field emitter display

FET—field effect transistor

FM—frequency modulation

FOIA—Freedom of Information Act

FSI—free standing insert

FSS—fixed satellite service

FTC—Federal Trade Commission

FTTH—Fiber to the Home

GAO—General Accounting Office

GATT—General Agreement on Tariffs & Trade

GDP—gross domestic product

GE—General Electric Company (U.S.)

GEC—General Electric Co. Ltd. (U.K.)

GEO—geostationary orbit

GHz—GigaHertz

GNP—gross national product

GPO—Government Printing Office

HBO—Home Box Office

HDTV—high definition television

HGTV—Home & Garden Television

HHS—Department of Health & Human Services

HITS—Headend in the Sky

HRRC—Home Recording Rights Coalition

HRTS—Hollywood Radio & TV Society

HSN—Home Shopping Network

HSOB—Hart Senate Office Building

HUD—Department of Housing & Urban Development

HUR—Households Using Radio

HUT—Households Using TV

Hz—Hertz (cycles per second)

IAAB—Inter-American Association of Broadcasters

IASU—International Association of Satellite Users

IATSE—International Alliance of Theatrical Stage Employees & Moving Picture Machine Operators

IBA—Independent Broadcasting Authority (U.K.)

IBEW—International Brotherhood of Electrical Workers

IBFM—Institute of Broadcasting Financial Management

IBM—International Business Machines

IC—integrated circuit

ICCE—International Conference on Consumer Electronics

IDSA—Interactive Digital Software Association

IEEE—Institute of Electrical & Electronic Engineers

IFA—Internationale Funkausstellung (Berlin consumer electronics show)

IFRB—International Frequency Registration Board

IIA—Information Industry Association

IMA—Interactive Multimedia Association

IMPPA—Independent Motion Picture Producers Association

INMARSAT—International Maritime Satellite Organization

INTELSAT—International Telecommunication Satellite Organization

IPPV—Impulse Pay-Per-View

IPO—initial public offering

ips—inches per second

IPTV—Internet Protocol Television

IRAC—Interdepartment Radio Advisory Committee

IRD—integrated receiver/decoder for satellite reception

IRS—Internal Revenue Service

IRTS—International Radio & Television Society Inc.

ISA—Interactive Services Association

ISCET—International Society of Certified Electronics Technicians

ITA—International Trade Administration

ITC—Independent Television Corporation (U.K.)

ITC—International Trade Commission

ITFS—instructional television fixed service

ITN—Independent TV News Association (U.K.)

ITU—International Telecommunication Union

ITV—industrial TV, institutional TV, instructional TV, interactive TV

ITVA—Interactive TV Association

ITVA—International TV Association

IUE—International Union of Electrical Radio & Machine Workers

JCET—Joint Council on Educational Telecommunications

JEDEC—Joint Electron Device Engineering Council

JPEG—Joint Photographic Experts Group

JTAC—Joint Technical Advisory Council

JVC—Japan Victor Corporation

K—Kelvin (temperature)

kbps—kilobits per second

kHz—kilohertz

km—kilometer

kw—kilowatt

LAN—local area network

LCD—liquid crystal display

LEC—local exchange carrier

LED—light-emitting diode

LEO—low earth orbit

LF—low frequency

LG, LGE—formerly Lucky Goldstar & Goldstar Electronics

LHOB—Longworth House Office Building

LMAC—Land Mobile Advisory Committee

LMA—local marketing agreement

LMDS—Local Multipoint Distribution Service

LNA—low noise amplifier

LNB—low noise block (downconverter)

LPTV—low power TV

m—meter

MAC—multiplexed analog components

MAP—Media Access Project

MB—Media Bureau

Mbps—megabits per second

MCA—formerly Music Corporation of America

MDS—Multipoint Distribution Service

MDU—multiple dwelling unit

MECA—Matsushita Electric Corporation of America

MEI—Matsushita Electric Industries

MF—medium frequency

MFJ—Modified Final Judgment

MGM—Metro-Goldwyn-Mayer

MHz—megahertz

MITI—Ministry of International Trade & Industry (Japan)

mm—millimeter

MMCD—MultiMedia Compact Disc (Sony/Phillips DVD format)

MMDS—Multichannel Multipoint Distribution Service

MOS—metal oxide silicon

MPA—Motion Picture Association

MPAA—Motion Picture Association of America

MPC-1/MPC-2—Multimedia Personal Computer standard configurations

MPEG—Moving Picture Experts Group

MPR—Minnesota Public Radio

MPU—microprocessor unit

mR—milliroentgens

MSG—Madison Square Garden

MSO—multiple system operator (cable TV)

MSGN—Madison Square Garden Network

MTS—multichannel TV sound

MTV—Music Television

MUSE—Multiple Sub-Nyquist Encoding (Japanese high definition satellite transmission system)

NAACP—National Association for the Advancement of Colored People

NAB—National Association of Broadcasters

NABET—National Association of Broadcast Employees & Technicians

NABOB—National Association of Black-Owned Broadcasters

NABUG—National Association of Broadcast Unions & Guilds

NAC—National Association of Counties

NAD 27—North American Datum of 1927

NAFB—National Association of Farm Broadcasters

NAFTA—North American Free Trade Agreement

NAITPD—National Association of Independent Television Producers & Directors

NAM—National Association of Manufacturers

NAMM—National Association of Music Merchants

NARB—National Advertising Review Board

NARBA—North American Radio Broadcasting Agreement

NARDA—National Appliance & Radio-Electronic Dealers Association

NARDA—National Association of Retail Dealers of America

NARM—National Association of Recording Merchandisers

NARUC—National Association of Regulatory Utility Commissioners

NASA—National Aeronautics & Space Administration

NASB—National Association of Spanish Broadcasters

NASRC—National AM Stereo Radio Committee

NATAS—National Academy of Television Arts & Sciences

NATO—National Association of Theater Owners Inc.

NATOA—National Association of Telecommunications Officers & Advisers

NATPE—National Association of Television Program Executives

NATT—National Association of Towns & Townships

NAVA—National Audio-Visual Association Inc.

NAVD—National Association of Video Distributors

NBA—National Basketball Association

NBC—National Broadcasting Company

NBEA—National Broadcast Editorial Association

NBLC—National Black Lawyers Conference

NBMC—National Black Media Coalition

NBN—National Black Network

NCAA—National Collegiate Athletic Association

NCCB—National Citizens Committee for Broadcasting

NCCPTV—National Citizens Committee for Public TV

NCI—National Captioning Institute

NCPAC—National Conservative Political Action Committee

NCRP—National Council for Radiation Protection & Measurements

NCSL—National Conference of State Legislatures

NCTA—National Cable Telecommunications Association

NEA—National Endowment for the Arts

NEC—Nippon Electric Corporation

NEDA—National Electrical Distributors Association

NEH—National Endowment for the Humanities

NEMA—National Electrical Manufacturers Association

NESDA—National Electronics Service Dealers Association

NESN—New England Sports Network

NET—National Educational Television

NEW—National Electronics Week (parts show)

NFA—National Federation of Advertising Agencies

NHK—Nippon Hoso Kyokai (Japan Broadcasting Corporation)

NIAC—National Industry Advisory Committee

NIH—National Institutes of Health

NIMLO—National Institute of Municipal Law Officers

NIST—National Institute for Science & Technology

NLC—National League of Cities

NLRB—National Labor Relations Board

NMPA—National Music Publishers' Association

NNA—National Newspaper Association

NoI—notice of inquiry

NORC—National Opinion & Research Center

NOW—National Organization of Women

NPC—National Press Club

NPR—National Public Radio

NPRM—notice of proposed rule making

NRB—National Religious Broadcasters

NRMA—National Retail Merchants Association

NRSC—National Radio Systems Committee

NRTC—National Rural Telecommunications Cooperative

NSI—Nielsen Station Index

NTA—National Translator Association

NTCA—National Telecommunications Cooperative Association

NTFC—National Television Film Council

NTI—Nielsen TV Index

NTIA—National Telecommunications & Information Administration (Department of Commerce)

NTIS—National Technical Information Service

NTSC—National Television System Committee

NUBA—National UHF Broadcasters Association

o-&-o—owned & operated stations (by network)

OEM—original equipment manufacturer

OEO—Office of Economic Opportunity

OFS—Operational Fixed Service

OMB—Office of Management & Budget

OPP—Office of Plans & Policy (FCC)

OSHA—Occupational Safety & Health Administration

OTA—Office of Technology Assessment

PA—public address (system)

PAL—phase alternation line (European color system)

PAX—PaxNet

PBR—Public Broadcasting Report

PBS—Public Broadcasting Service

PC—personal computer

PCS—personal communications system/service

PEG—public, educational, government cable access channels

PIB—Publishers Information Bureau

PIP—picture in picture

PMN—Pacific Mountain Network

POP—point-of-purchase

PPT—pay-per-transaction

PPV—pay-per-view

PR—public relations

PRI—Public Radio International

PSA—public service announcement

PSA—pre-sunrise authorization

PSSC—Public Service Satellite Consortium

PTA—Parent Teachers Association

PTA—program test authorization

PTAR—prime time access rule

PTL—Public TV Library

PTV—projection TV

PTV—public TV

QVC—Quality, Value, Convenience Inc.

RAB—Radio Advertising Bureau

RADAR—Radio's All-Dimension Audience Research

RAI—Radiotelevisione Italiana

RAM—random access memory

R&D—research & development

RARC—Regional Administrative Radio Conference

RASO—Radio Allocations Study Organization

RF—radio frequency

RFA—Regulatory Flexibility Act

RFE—Radio Free Europe

RHC—regional holding company

RHOB—Rayburn House Office Building

RIAA—Recording Industry Association of America

RIO—Radio Information Office (NAB)

RISC—Reduced Instruction Set Computing

ROM—read-only memory

RSAC—Recreational Software Advisory Council

RSOB—Russell Senate Office Building

RTO—rent-to-own

RTDNA—Radio Television Digital News Association

SAG—Screen Actors Guild

SAP—Separate Audio Program (see MTS)

SBA—Small Business Administration

SBCA—Satellite Broadcasting & Communications Association

SBE—Society of Broadcast Engineers

SBRTC—Southern Baptist Radio-TV Commission

SCA—subsidiary communication authorization

SCTE—Society of Cable Telecommunications Engineers

SD—super density digital compact disk

SEC—Securities & Exchange Commission

SECA—Southern Educational Communications Association

SECAM—sequential couleur a memoire (French color TV system)

SESAC—music licensing society similar to ASCAP & BMI

SHF—super high frequency

SIMPP—Society of Independent Motion Picture Producers

SIP—Station Independence Program

SKU—stock-keeping unit

SMATV—Satellite Master Antenna Television

SMPTE—Society of Motion Picture & TV Engineers

SMR—specialized mobile radio

SMSA—Standard Metropolitan Statistical Area

SOB—Senate Office Building

SPA—Software Publishers Association

SPJ—Society of Professional Journalists

SRA—Station Representatives Association Inc.

SS—solid state

SSB—single side band

STA—special temporary authorization

STL—studio-to-transmitter link

S-VHS—Super VHS

SW—Satellite Week

TARPAC—Television & Radio Political Action Committee

TARPEC—Television & Radio Political Education Committee

TASO—Television Allocations Study Organization

TBA—time brokerage agreement

TBC—time base corrector

TBN—Trinity Broadcasting Network

TBS—Turner Broadcasting System

3DO—a CD multimedia system and company

TI—Texas Instruments

TCM—Turner Classic Movies

TDMA—time division multiple access

TLC—The Learning Channel

TMC—The Movie Channel

TMO—Telemundo

TNE—The New Encore

TNT—Turner Network Television

TPG—Television Producers Guild

TPO—transmitter power output

TR—transponder

TRAFCO—TV, Radio & Film Commission of Methodist Church

TV—television

TVB—Television Bureau of Advertising

TVHH—TV Households

TVI—TV interference

TVRO—TV receive-only earth station

TWC—The Weather Channel

TWTA—traveling wave tube amplifier

UE—United Electrical, Radio & Machine Workers of America

UHF—ultra high frequency

UHF-ICC—UHF Industry Coordinating Committee

UIT—See ITU

UK—United Kingdom

UL—Underwriters' Laboratories Inc.

UNESCO—United Nations Educational, Scientific and Cultural Organization

UNV—Univision

USIA—U.S. Information Agency

USTA—U.S. Telecommunications Association

USTR—United States Trade Representative

VBI—vertical blanking interval

VCPS—Video Copyright Protection Society

VCR—videocassette recorder

VDT—video display terminal

VH1—Video Hits One

VHF—very high frequency

VHS—Video Home System (a VCR format)

VHS-C—compact VHS

VLF—very low frequency

VOA—Voice of America

VOD—Video on-demand

VSB—vestigial sideband

VSDA—Video Software Dealers Association

VTR—videotape recording or video tape recorder

w—watt

"W"—widescreen picture when used in diagonal measurement

WARC—World Administrative Radio Conference

WCA—Wireless Communications Association

WE—Women's Entertainment

WESCON—Western Electronic Show & Convention

WGA—Writers Guild of America

WGAW—Writers Guild of America-West

WIC—Women in Cable & Telecommunications

WID—Washington Internet Daily

W-VHS—Widescreen Video Home System (HDTV recording system)

WWE—World Wrestling Entertainment

XDS—extended data system

Glossary of Cable Television Terms

Derived in part from the glossaries of CableLabs and The National Cable & Telecommunications Association

Access Channels—Channels set aside by the cable operator for use by the public, educational institutions, municipal government or for lease on a non-discriminatory basis.

ACE—See CableACE.

Addressability—The capability of controlling the operation of individual cable subscriber terminals by sending commands from a central computer. See also Two-Way.

Aerial Plant—Cable that is suspended in the air generally on telephone or utility poles.

Affiliate—A TV station which carries, by contractual agreement, network programming. Also, the cable system to which a program service transmits its programming, usually by satellite.

Amplifier—A device that boosts the strength of an electronic signal. Amplifiers are spaced at regular intervals throughout a cable system to maintain the signal strength.

Analog—Transmission of audio and/or video signal by a continually variable waveform signal.

Bandwidth—The portion of the radio spectrum needed to transmit pictures, sound or both. Analog U.S. TV stations use a bandwidth of six million cycles per second (6 MegaHertz).

Basic Cable—Usually the minimum amount of cable TV service available to a subscriber for a standard installation & monthly fee. It generally includes over-the-air broadcast signals & local originations.

Bi-directional—Two way cable communications.

Broadband—A transmission medium that allows transmission of voice, data & video simultaneously at rates of 1.544 Mbps or higher. Broadband transmission media generally can carry multiple channels—each at a different frequency or specific time slot.

C-band—Frequencies in the 4 & 6 GHz regions used in satellite earth station feeds in many television station configurations.

CableACE (Award for Cablecasting Excellence)—The cable TV industry's highest award for original, made-for-cable programming both locally & nationally.

CableCARD—A card that allows consumers to connect to cable TV without a set top box & can provide digital & high definition television service to HDTVs, PCs & DVRs.

Cablecasting—To originate programming over a cable system. Includes public access programming.

Cable Modem—A two-way device allowing the delivery & reception of broadband data to & from a subscriber's PC via cable.

Cable Penetration—The percentage of TV homes subscribing to cable TV.

Cable System—Facility that provides cable service in a given geographic area, comprised of one or more headends.

Cable Television—A communications system that distributes broadcast TV signals plus satellite signals, original programming & other material by means of a coaxial and/or fiber optic cable.

Cable TV Households—An occupied dwelling unit with one or more television sets currently receiving cable television service.

CARS (Cable Television Relay Services)—A microwave system used to relay TV, FM radio, cablecasting & other signals to a terminal for distribution over cable.

Cash Flow—Cash flow is defined as operating income minus interest expense & it basically indicates the amount of cash available before taxes, capital expenditures & debt retirement.

CG (Character Generator)—A device which electronically displays letters & numbers on the TV screen.

Channel Capacity—The maximum number of channels that a system can carry simultaneously.

Churn—The percentage of cable TV subscribers that add or delete program services, or cable service entirely.

Class A Television Service—An FCC classification, created under a November 1999 Act of Congress, of certain qualifying low-power TV stations which have more protection from full service stations than most LPTV stations.

Coaxial Cable—An actual line of transmission for carrying TV signals. Its principal conductor is either a pure copper or copper-coated wire, surrounded by insulation & then encased in aluminum or copper.

Common Carrier—The generic name for any medium which carries messages prepared by others for a fee & is required by law to offer its services on a non-discriminatory basis. Common carriers are regulated by federal & state agencies and exercise no control over message content.

Compression—The act of reducing the amount of bandwidth needed to carry audio and/or video signals. Either analog or digital compression is technically possible.

Converter—A device that, associated with a TV set, can increase the channel capacity of the TV set or convert signals between analog & digital.

DBS (Direct Broadcast Satellite)—A system in which signals are transmitted directly from a satellite to a home receiving dish. DBS refers specifically to high-power transmissions in bands specified by the FCC.

Demographics—The breakdown by age, sex, income levels, education, race, etc. of TV viewers.

Descrambler—An electronic circuit that restores a scrambled video signal to its original form.

Digital—Binary number method for signal and/or data transmission.

Digital Service (contour)—See Noise Limited Contour.

Digital Transmission—A way of increasing channel capacity through digital compression rather than laying new cable. To receive the service, a subscriber needs a digital converter.

Dish—The installation, also called an earth station, for receiving and/or transmitting electronic signals between the earth & communications satellites.

Distant Signal—A TV channel from another market imported & carried by a cable TV system.

DMA (Designated Market Area)—The Nielsen definition of a viewing market for rating & sales purposes. A DMA market is composed of all counties in which commercial stations assigned to the market achieve the largest share of audience.

Downstream—The flow of signals from the cable system headend through the distribution network to the subscriber.

Drop Cable—The small-diameter cable feeding into the subscriber's home.

DVR (Digital Video Recorder)—An electronic device that records video in a digital format. Also referred to as a personal video recorder (PVR).

Earth Station—A structure, including satellite dishes, used for receiving and/or transmitting signals to or from a satellite.

Educational Broadband Service—Channels used to provide educational instruction and cultural & professional development in schools & other institutions, as well as other wireless services. The channels are often used for wireless communications.

Exclusivity—The contractual right to be the sole exhibitor of a program in a particular area during a particular time.

Expanded Basic—Additional cable service or services offered to the subscriber at a charge in addition to the basic cable service.

Fiber Optic Cable—Very thin & pliable cylinders of glass or plastic in a weather-resistant sheathing which carry data as light waves in wide bands of frequencies. Can be used to replace or supplement coaxial cable.

Franchise—The contractual agreement between a cable operator & a governmental body which defines the rights & responsibilities of each in the construction & operation of a cable TV system.

Franchising Authority—The governmental body responsible for specifying the terms of a franchise, awarding it & regulating its operation. While the franchising authority is usually a local city or county body, some areas are regulated on the state level.

FTTx (Fiber to the X)—Generic term for a broadband telecommunications system based on fiber optic cables. Can be Fiber to the Node (FTTN), Fiber to the Curb (FTTC), Fiber to the Building (FTTB), Fiber to the Home (FTTH) or Fiber to the Premises (FTTP), which includes buildings & homes.

Governmental Cablecasting—An opportunity for federal, state & local officials to disseminate information to their constituents via cable TV.

Grandfathering—The situation that exists when a law is passed after a distribution system has begun operating, and the system may be exempt from that law.

Headend—The electronic control center of the cable system. This is the site of the receiving antenna & the signal processing equipment.

Homes Passed—The total number of homes passed by a cable system, thus having the potential of being served promptly.

Hubs—Local distribution centers where signals are taken from a master feed & transmitted over cable to subscribers.

Impulse Pay-Per-View—PPV programming which can be ordered instantly through a remote control or similar device.

Independent—A cable TV system individually owned & operated, not affiliated with a multiple-system operator. Also, a TV station not affiliated with a major network.

Institutional Loop—The upstream transmission of signals from schools, libraries, etc., to the cable headend where the signals are added to the downstream distribution to subscribers. It also can be a separate, closed system interconnecting governmental agencies for sending & receiving voice and data.

Interactive—A sophisticated two-way system which has the capability of connecting more than two points.

Interconnect—The transmission of cable signals or advertising from one cable system to another so that programming & information may be shared.

IPTV (Internet Protocol Television)—Digital television service delivered via a broadband internet connection.

ITFS (Instructional Television Fixed Service)—See Educational Broadband Service.

Ku-band—Frequencies in the 12 GHz band used for business & video satellite services.

Leased Channels—Any channel made available by the operator for a fee.

LMDS (Local Multipoint Distribution Service)—An MDS service which may be used to supplement capacity of wireless cable systems or for non-video data or other purposes.

Local Franchising Authority—Entity granted authority to regulate cable rates in a specified service area according to provisions in the FCC cable rules.

Local Origination Programming (LO)—Programming developed, leased or purchased by a cable TV system for the community it serves.

Local Signals—Over-the-air broadcast signals available within the community, usually carried on a cable system's minimum service level of programming.

Low Power TV (LPTV)—A secondary broadcast television service licensed at a low power. Some LPTV stations provide original programming; some are affiliates of national or regional networks; others operate as translators for full-power TV stations. See also Class A Television Service.

LTE (Long-term Evolution)—Wireless broadband technology that will support speeds of over 300 Mbps downstream & 75 Mbps upstream.

MDS (Multipoint Distribution Service)—A private service utilizing a very high frequency to transmit one TV signal or other services. It is commonly used to broadcast pay TV or as part of a wireless phone system.

Microwave—A transmitting system that relays signals from one tower to another, linking cable systems or other services.

Miles of Plant—The total miles, to the nearest tenth, of coaxial and/or fiber optic cable in use to provide cable in each system's service area.

MMDS (Multichannel Multipoint Distribution Service)—An MDS service with the capability of transmitting more than one TV signal. Also known as wireless cable.

MSO (Multiple System Operator)—A company that owns & operates more than one cable system. Also called group operator.

Multiplexing—Practice of cable programmers, such as HBO & Showtime, of providing multiple channels of different programming simultaneously.

Must Carry—Provision in the Cable Act of 1992 by which a broadcast station is entitled to carriage of its signal by a cable system.

Narrowcasting—The delivery of specialized programming to a specific audience.

NCTA (National Cable Telecommunications Association)—The major trade association for the cable TV industry. See index for complete listing.

Network—An entity that offers programming on a regular basis for 15 hours or more per week to either regional or national affiliates under contract. A network may be either broadcast or cable TV oriented; both are usually delivered via satellite.

Nielsen—A rating service which provides statistical information on viewing habits & demographics.

Non-duplication Rules—Restrictions placed on cable TV systems prohibiting them from importing distant programming which is simultaneously available from local TV stations.

Noise Limited Contour—The area where the predicted field strength of the station's signal exceeds the following levels (these are the levels at which reception of DTV service is limited by noise): Channels 2-6 28 dBu; Channels 7-13 36 dBu; Channels 14-69 41 dBu.

North American Datum of 1927 (NAD-27)—A system of latitude & longitude points established in 1927 which is the standard used by the FCC.

Off-air—Programming received at the cable system headend from over-the-air broadcast signals.

Open Cable—Interoperable digital set-top boxes which will provide greater access to interactive services.

Operating Income—Operating income is the difference between the revenues & direct operating expenses, before interest, depreciation & income taxes.

Ordinance—Enabling legislation passed by a local government to establish guidelines for the franchising process.

Overbuilder—A company that utilizes or builds on to existing infrastructure in areas where there is already cable service.

Pay-Per-View—Cable programming for which subscribers pay on a one-time basis for individual programs, such as prize fights, Broadway & movie premieres.

Pay Programming—Movies, sports & other programs available to the cable subscriber for a charge in addition to the basic fee.

Pay Units—A total count of the number of individual pay subscriptions sold by a cable operator for one or more pay programming services.

Penetration—The ratio of the number of cable subscribers (or pay TV subscribers) to the total number of households passed by the system (or basic subscribers).

Pole Attachments—The cable TV hookups to telephone or utility poles.

Retransmission Consent—Negotiated agreement under terms specified in the Cable Act of 1992 by which a broadcast station may be entitled to some consideration in exchange for carriage of its signal by a cable system.

RFP (Request for Proposals)—The document issued by the franchising authority for the applicant's use. It usually states proposed guidelines, outlines minimum requirements for each applicant & specifies application deadlines.

Satellite—A device in orbit that receives & transmits signals.

Security System—The capability of providing interactive services such as emergency rescue, burglar & fire alarm protection.

Shop-at-Home—Programs allowing subscribers to view products & order them by cable or telephone, including catalogs, shopping, shows, etc.

Significantly Viewed—Television stations achieving a 3% share of weekly viewing hours (2% for independent stations), and a net weekly circulation of 25% (5% for independent stations) in a given community.

Submarine Installation—The laying of cable underwater, as opposed to aerial suspension on poles.

Subscriber—A person who pays cable system or DBS operators for the reception of programs & other electronic services.

Syndicated Exclusivity—An FCC rule requiring cable systems to black out portions of distant signals in order to protect syndicated programming which local TV broadcasters have under an exclusive contract.

Television Households—An occupied dwelling unit with one or more television sets.

Tiered Programming—More than one cable service offered to the subscriber at a charge in addition to the basic cable service.

Total Households—All occupied dwelling units in a given area.

Translator—A small transmitter that picks up a distant TV signal, converts it to another channel to avoid interference & retransmits it into areas the original TV station could not reach.

Transponder—The part of the satellite that receives and re-transmits a signal.

TV Market Ranking—The 35-mile radius zone surrounding a community with an operating commercial station found in the markets listed in Sections 76.51 & 76.53 of the FCC cable rules.

Two-Way—A term used to describe a cable system that enables signals to pass in both directions between the headend and the subscriber.

Underground Installation—The burying of cable underground, as opposed to aerial suspension on poles.

Upstream—The flow of signals from the subscriber or remote origination point to the headend.

Video On-Demand (VOD)—Allows VCR-type control of video or movies offered on PPV basis.

Wide Area Network (WAN)—A computer network which usually spans larger geographic area, such as cities, counties, states, nations & planets. WAN's usually employ telephone-type topologies, like T1, T2, T5, ATM, etc. The Internet is a WAN which is held together by LANs, which network computers.

Wideband—Typically, the term wideband represents a medium intermediate between narrowband & broadband. Wideband is capable of transmitting at more than 64 Kbps & less than 1.5 Mbps.

Wi-Fi (Wireless Fidelity)—A wireless technology brand owned by the Wi-Fi Alliance intended to improve the interoperability of wireless local area network products based on the IEEE 802.11 standards.

WiMAX (Worldwide Interoperability for Microwave Access)—Technology that uses fixed, local radio cells to provide high-speed Internet access via the air interface. A wireless broadband technology with a range of up to 80km and a bandwith of up to 75bps.

Cable Community Index

This is an index of all communities served by cable systems in the Icarus database. The following symbols indicate the type of service. A delta (▲) indicates an operating cable system. An asterisk(*) indicates a cable franchise awarded but not yet operating. A dagger (†) indicates a cable system application has been made. Cross references in all capital letters **(e.g. LAWSON)** indicate communities served by an operating cable system. Cross references with an initial capital letter **(e.g. Williams)** indicate planned service by operating cable systems.

ALABAMA

▲**ABBEVILLE**—Comcast Cable

ABERFOIL—See UNION SPRINGS, AL (Union Springs Telephone Co.)

▲**ABERNANT**—Comcast Cable. Now served by TUSCALOOSA, AL [AL0230]

ABERNANT—See TUSCALOOSA, AL (Comcast Cable)

ADAMSBURG—See FORT PAYNE, AL (Windjammer Cable)

ADAMSVILLE—See LEEDS, AL (Charter Communications)

▲**ADDISON (TOWN)**—Alabama Broadband

▲**AKRON (town)**—Formerly served by CableSouth Inc. No longer in operation

ALABASTER—See LEEDS, AL (Charter Communications)

▲**ALBERTVILLE**—Charter Communications

▲**ALEXANDER CITY**—Charter Communications. Now served by LEEDS, AL [AL0192]

ALEXANDER CITY—See LEEDS, AL (Charter Communications)

▲**ALICEVILLE**—Northland Cable Television

▲**ALLGOOD**—Formerly served by SouthTel Communications LP. No longer in operation

ALPINE—See PELL CITY, AL (Coosa Cable)

▲**ALTOONA**—Rapid Cable

▲**ANDALUSIA**—TV Cable Co. of Andalusia Inc.

ANDERSON—See ELGIN, AL (Cobridge Communications)

ANNISTON ARMY DEPOT—See ANNISTON, AL (Cable One)

▲**ANNISTON**—Cable One

ANTIOCH—See HEATH, AL (Clearview Cable)

▲**APPLETON**—Formerly served by Trust Cable. No longer in operation

ARAB—See ALBERTVILLE, AL (Charter Communications)

▲**ARDMORE**—Mediacom

ARDMORE—See ARDMORE, TN (Mediacom)

ARGO—See MARGARET, AL (Alabama Broadband LLC)

ARITON—See CLIO, AL (Bright House Networks)

▲**ARLEY**—Zoom Media

ASHFORD—See DOTHAN, AL (Comcast Cable)

ASHFORD—See DOTHAN, AL (Knology)

▲**ASHLAND**—CommuniComm Services

▲**ASHVILLE**—Alabama Broadband

▲**ATHENS**—Formerly served by Madison Communications. No longer in operation

▲**ATHENS**—Charter Communications

▲**ATHENS**—Knology

▲**ATMORE**—Mediacom. Now served by GULF BREEZE, FL [FL0070]

▲**ATTALLA**—Comcast Cable

▲**AUBURN**—Charter Communications. Now served by LEEDS, AL [AL0192]

AUBURN—See LEEDS, AL (Charter Communications)

AUTAUGA COUNTY—See MONTGOMERY, AL (Charter Communications)

▲**AUTAUGAVILLE**—Formerly served by NewWave Communications. No longer in operation

AVON—See DOTHAN, AL (Comcast Cable)

BABBIE—See HEATH, AL (Clearview Cable)

▲**BAILEYTON**—Cobridge Communications

▲**BALDWIN COUNTY (northwestern portion)**—Formerly served by Baldwin County Cable. No longer in operation

▲**BALDWIN COUNTY (PORTIONS)**—Cable Options Inc.

BALDWIN COUNTY (PORTIONS)—See DAPHNE, AL (Mediacom)

BALDWIN COUNTY (PORTIONS)—See FAIRHOPE, AL (Mediacom)

BALDWIN COUNTY (PORTIONS)—See ROBERTSDALE, AL (Mediacom)

BARBOUR COUNTY (UNINCORPORATED AREAS)—See EUFAULA, AL (Bright House Networks)

▲**BARNWELL**—Mediacom. Now served by FAIRHOPE (formerly Daphne), AL [AL0124]

BARNWELL—See FAIRHOPE, AL (Mediacom)

BARTON—See CHEROKEE, AL (Ramco Broadband Services)

▲**BAY MINETTE**—Mediacom. Now served by FAIRHOPE (formerly Daphne), AL [AL0124]

BAY MINETTE—See FAIRHOPE, AL (Mediacom)

BAYOU LA BATRE—See MOBILE COUNTY, AL (Mediacom)

BEAR CREEK—See HALEYVILLE, AL (Cobridge Communications)

▲**BEATRICE**—Clearview Cable

BELFOREST—See DAPHNE, AL (Mediacom)

BELK—See FAYETTE, AL (West Alabama TV Cable Co. Inc.)

▲**BELLAMY**—Sky Cablevision

BELLWOOD—See CHANCELLOR, AL (Clearview Cable)

▲**BERRY**—Formerly served by Almega Cable. No longer in operation

BESSEMER (PORTIONS)—See BIRMINGHAM, AL (Bright House Networks)

▲**BEULAH**—Charter Communications

BIBB COUNTY (PORTIONS)—See CENTREVILLE, AL (Sky Cablevision)

▲**BIG COVE**—Mediacom

BIRMINGHAM (PORTIONS)—See LEEDS, AL (Charter Communications)

▲**BIRMINGHAM**—Bright House Networks

BLOUNT COUNTY (NORTHWESTERN PORTION)—See CULLMAN, AL (Windjammer Cable)

▲**BLOUNT COUNTY**—Alabama Broadband LLC

▲**BLOUNTSVILLE**—Time Warner Cable. Now served by CULLMAN, AL [AL0034]

BLOUNTSVILLE—See CULLMAN, AL (Windjammer Cable)

BLUFF PARK—See LEEDS, AL (Charter Communications)

BOAZ—See ALBERTVILLE, AL (Charter Communications)

▲**BOLIGEE**—Sky Cablevision

BON AIR—See LEEDS, AL (Charter Communications)

BON SECOUR—See FOLEY, AL (Riviera Utilities Cable TV)

▲**BOOTH**—Zito Media

BRANCHVILLE—See PELL CITY, AL (Coosa Cable)

BRANTLEY—See LUVERNE, AL (Crenshaw Cable)

BRENT—See CENTREVILLE, AL (Sky Cablevision)

▲**BREWTON**—Mediacom. Now served by GULF BREEZE, FL [FL0070]

▲**BRIDGEPORT**—Charter Communications

BRIGHTON—See BIRMINGHAM, AL (Bright House Networks)

BRILLIANT—See WINFIELD, AL (West Alabama TV Cable Co. Inc.)

BROMPTON—See PELL CITY, AL (Coosa Cable)

BROOKSIDE—See LEEDS, AL (Charter Communications)

▲**BROOKWOOD**—Charter Communications. Now served by LEEDS, AL [AL0192]

BROOKWOOD—See LEEDS, AL (Charter Communications)

BROWNVILLE—See BIRMINGHAM, AL (Bright House Networks)

BRUNDIDGE—See TROY, AL (Cobridge Communications)

BUHL—See LEEDS, AL (Charter Communications)

BUTLER COUNTY (PORTIONS)—See GREENVILLE, AL (Bright House Networks)

▲**BUTLER**—Zito Media

CAHABA HEIGHTS—See LEEDS, AL (Charter Communications)

CALERA—See LEEDS, AL (Charter Communications)

CALHOUN COUNTY (UNINCORPORATED AREAS)—See ANNISTON, AL (Cable One)

▲**CAMDEN**—Mediacom

CAMP HILL—See LEEDS, AL (Charter Communications)

CAPSHAW—See HUNTSVILLE, AL (Mediacom)

CARBON HILL—See JASPER, AL (Charter Communications)

CARROLLTON—See ALICEVILLE, AL (Northland Cable Television)

▲**CASTLEBERRY**—Clearview Cable

▲**CEDAR BLUFF**—Envision Media Inc.

▲**CENTER POINT**—Charter Communications. Now served by LEEDS, AL [AL0192]

CENTER POINT—See LEEDS, AL (Charter Communications)

CENTER STAR—See ELGIN, AL (Cobridge Communications)

▲**CENTRE**—Charter Communications. Now served by PIEDMONT, AL [AL0065]

CENTRE—See PIEDMONT, AL (Charter Communications)

▲**CENTREVILLE**—Sky Cablevision

CHAMBERS COUNTY (PORTIONS)—See LEEDS, AL (Charter Communications)

▲**CHANCELLOR**—Clearview Cable

▲**CHATOM**—Sky Cablevision

CHELSEA—See WESTOVER, AL (Charter Communications)

CHEROKEE COUNTY (PORTIONS)—See PIEDMONT, AL (Charter Communications)

CHEROKEE COUNTY (PORTIONS)—See CEDAR BLUFF, AL (Envision Media Inc.)

▲**CHEROKEE**—Ramco Broadband Services

CHICKASAW—See MOBILE, AL (Comcast Cable)

CHILDERSBURG—See LEEDS, AL (Charter Communications)

CHILTON COUNTY—See CLANTON, AL (Cobridge Communications)

CITRONELLE—See MOBILE COUNTY, AL (Mediacom)

▲**CLANTON**—Cobridge Communications

CLARKE COUNTY (PORTIONS)—See THOMASVILLE, AL (Mediacom)

CLARKE COUNTY (PORTIONS)—See GROVE HILL, AL (Zito Media)

CLAY COUNTY (PORTIONS)—See LEEDS, AL (Charter Communications)

CLAYHATCHEE—See DOTHAN, AL (Time Warner Cable)

▲**CLAYTON (TOWN)**—Comcast Cable

CLEBURNE COUNTY (WESTERN PORTION)—See HEFLIN, AL (Cobridge Communications)

▲**CLIO**—Bright House Networks

▲**CLOVERDALE**—Comcast Cable. Now served by FLORENCE, AL [AL0187]

CLOVERDALE—See FLORENCE, AL (Comcast Cable)

COALING—See LEEDS, AL (Charter Communications)

▲**CODEN**—Mediacom

COFFEE SPRINGS—See CHANCELLOR, AL (Clearview Cable)

▲**COFFEEVILLE**—Sky Cablevision. No longer in operation

COKER—See LEEDS, AL (Charter Communications)

COLBERT COUNTY (UNINCORPORATED AREAS)—See LEIGHTON, AL (Cobridge Communications)

COLBERT COUNTY—See FLORENCE, AL (Comcast Cable)

COLLBRAN—See FORT PAYNE, AL (Windjammer Cable)

▲**COLLINSVILLE**—Collinsville TV Cable

▲**COLUMBIANA**—Cobridge Communications

CONECUH COUNTY (PORTIONS)—See CAMDEN, AL (Mediacom)

COOSA COUNTY (PORTIONS)—See LEEDS, AL (Charter Communications)

COOSA COUNTY (PORTIONS)—See LAKE MARTIN RESORT, AL (Com-Link)

COOSADA—See WETUMPKA, AL (Bright House Networks)

CORDOVA—See JASPER, AL (Charter Communications)

COTACO—See DECATUR, AL (Charter Communications)

COTTONDALE—See LEEDS, AL (Charter Communications)

COTTONWOOD—See DOTHAN, AL (Comcast Cable)

COURTLAND—See LEIGHTON, AL (Cobridge Communications)

COWARTS—See DOTHAN, AL (Comcast Cable)

CREOLA—See MOBILE COUNTY, AL (Mediacom)

▲**CUBA**—Zoom Media

CULLMAN COUNTY (PORTIONS)—See GOOD HOPE, AL (Alabama Broadband LLC)

CULLMAN COUNTY (PORTIONS)—See BAILEYTON, AL (Cobridge Communications)

CULLMAN COUNTY (PORTIONS)—See CULLMAN, AL (Windjammer Cable)

▲**CULLMAN**—Windjammer Cable

▲**CURRY**—Charter Communications

▲**DADEVILLE**—CommuniComm Services

DALE COUNTY—See TROY, AL (Cobridge Communications)

DALE COUNTY—See DOTHAN, AL (Time Warner Cable)

DALEVILLE—See DOTHAN, AL (Time Warner Cable)

▲**DALEVILLE**—Troy Cablevision

DALLAS COUNTY—See SELMA, AL (Charter Communications)

DANVILLE—See DECATUR, AL (Charter Communications)

▲**DAPHNE**—Mediacom

DAPHNE—See FAIRHOPE, AL (Mediacom)

▲**DAUPHIN ISLAND**—Comcast Cable

DE KALB COUNTY (PORTIONS)—See HENAGAR, AL (Cobridge Communications)

DE KALB COUNTY—See FORT PAYNE, AL (Windjammer Cable)

DEATSVILLE—See WETUMPKA, AL (Bright House Networks)

▲**DECATUR**—Charter Communications

DECATUR—See ATHENS, AL (Knology)

DEKALB COUNTY (SOUTHWESTERN PORTION)—See ALBERTVILLE, AL (Charter Communications)

DEKALB COUNTY—See RAINSVILLE, AL (Cobridge Communications)

▲**DEMOPOLIS**—Demopolis CATV Co.

DODGE CITY—See GOOD HOPE, AL (Alabama Broadband LLC)

DORA—See JASPER, AL (Charter Communications)

▲**DOTHAN**—Comcast Cable

▲**DOTHAN**—Knology

▲**DOTHAN**—Time Warner Cable

▲**DOUBLE SPRINGS**—Cobridge Communications

DOUGLAS—See ALBERTVILLE, AL (Charter Communications)

DOZIER—See HEATH, AL (Clearview Cable)

DUNCANVILLE—See LEEDS, AL (Charter Communications)

DUTTON—See RAINSVILLE, AL (Cobridge Communications)

ECLECTIC—See WETUMPKA, AL (Bright House Networks)

EDWARDSVILLE—See HEFLIN, AL (Cobridge Communications)

▲**ELBA**—Charter Communications. Now served by TROY, AL [AL0027]

ELBA—See TROY, AL (Cobridge Communications)

ELBERTA—See FOLEY, AL (Riviera Utilities Cable TV)

ELDRIDGE—See JASPER, AL (Charter Communications)

▲**ELGIN**—Cobridge Communications

ELKMONT—See ATHENS, AL (Charter Communications)

ELKTON—See ARDMORE, TN (Mediacom)

ELMORE COUNTY (PORTIONS)—See WETUMPKA, AL (Bright House Networks)

ELMORE COUNTY—See MONTGOMERY, AL (Charter Communications)

ELROD—See LEEDS, AL (Charter Communications)

▲**ENTERPRISE**—Time Warner Cable

ESTO—See DOTHAN, FL (Comcast Cable)

ETOWAH COUNTY (PORTIONS)—See ALBERTVILLE, AL (Charter Communications)

ETOWAH COUNTY—See ATTALLA, AL (Comcast Cable)

ETOWAH COUNTY—See GADSDEN, AL (Comcast Cable)

▲**EUFAULA**—Bright House Networks

▲**EUTAW**—Sky Cablevision

EVERGREEN—See CAMDEN, AL (Mediacom)

EXCEL—See CAMDEN, AL (Mediacom)

FAIRFIELD (PORTIONS)—See BIRMINGHAM, AL (Bright House Networks)

▲**FAIRFIELD**—Charter Communications

▲**FAIRHOPE**—Mediacom

FAIRVIEW—See CULLMAN, AL (Windjammer Cable)

FALKVILLE—See DECATUR, AL (Charter Communications)

▲**FAYETTE**—West Alabama TV Cable Co. Inc.

FISH RIVER—See FAIRHOPE, AL (Mediacom)

FIVE POINTS—See LEEDS, AL (Charter Communications)

FLINT—See DECATUR, AL (Charter Communications)

▲**FLORALA**—Bright House Networks

▲**FLORENCE**—Comcast Cable

▲**FOLEY**—Riviera Utilities Cable TV

FORESTDALE—See LEEDS, AL (Charter Communications)

▲**FORKLAND**—Sky Cablevision

FORT DEPOSIT—See GREENVILLE, AL (Bright House Networks)

FORT MCCLELLAN—See ANNISTON, AL (Cable One)

FORT MITCHELL—See PHENIX CITY, AL (Cable TV of East Alabama)

FORT MORGAN—See ROBERTSDALE, AL (Mediacom)

▲**FORT PAYNE**—Windjammer Cable

FORT RUCKER—See DOTHAN, AL (Time Warner Cable)

FRANKLIN COUNTY (PORTIONS)—See PHIL CAMPBELL, AL (CommuniComm Services)

FRANKLIN COUNTY—See RUSSELLVILLE, AL (Charter Communications)

▲ **FREEMANVILLE**—Formerly served by CableSouth Inc. No longer in operation

FRISCO CITY—See CAMDEN, AL (Mediacom)

FRUITHURST—See HEFLIN, AL (Cobridge Communications)

FULTONDALE—See LEEDS, AL (Charter Communications)

FYFFE—See RAINSVILLE, AL (Cobridge Communications)

▲ **GADSDEN**—Comcast Cable

GANTT—See HEATH, AL (Clearview Cable)

GARDEN CITY—See CULLMAN, AL (Windjammer Cable)

GARDENDALE—See LEEDS, AL (Charter Communications)

GENEVA COUNTY (PORTIONS)—See CHANCELLOR, AL (Clearview Cable)

GENEVA COUNTY—See GENEVA, AL (Bright House Networks)

GENEVA COUNTY—See DOTHAN, AL (Time Warner Cable)

▲ **GENEVA**—Bright House Networks

GEORGETOWN—See EUFAULA, GA (Bright House Networks)

GEORGIANA—See GREENVILLE, AL (Bright House Networks)

GERALDINE—See ALBERTVILLE, AL (Charter Communications)

GILES COUNTY—See ARDMORE, TN (Mediacom)

GLENCOE—See GADSDEN, AL (Comcast Cable)

GLENWOOD—See LUVERNE, AL (Crenshaw Cable)

▲ **GOOD HOPE**—Alabama Broadband LLC

GOODWATER—See LEEDS, AL (Charter Communications)

GORDO—See ALICEVILLE, AL (Northland Cable Television)

▲ **GORDON**—Formerly served by Gordon Cable TV. No longer in operation

GORDONSVILLE—See LOWNDES COUNTY, AL (Alabama Broadband LLC)

GRAND BAY—See MOBILE COUNTY, AL (Mediacom)

▲ **GRANT**—New Hope Telephone Cooperative. Now served by NEW HOPE, AL [AL0070]

GRANT—See GUNTERSVILLE, AL (Charter Communications)

GRANT—See NEW HOPE, AL (New Hope Telephone Cooperative)

GRAYSON VALLEY—See LEEDS, AL (Charter Communications)

GRAYSVILLE—See LEEDS, AL (Charter Communications)

GREENE COUNTY (UNINCORPORATED AREAS)—See EUTAW, AL (Sky Cablevision)

▲ **GREENSBORO**—Mediacom

▲ **GREENVILLE**—Bright House Networks

GRIMES—See DOTHAN, AL (Time Warner Cable)

▲ **GROVE HILL**—Zito Media

▲ **GUIN**—CommuniComm Services

GULF SHORES—See ROBERTSDALE, AL (Mediacom)

GUNTER AFB—See WETUMPKA, AL (Bright House Networks)

▲ **GUNTERSVILLE**—Charter Communications

GURLEY (UNINCORPORATED AREAS)—See HUNTSVILLE, AL (Mediacom)

▲ **GURLEY**—Charter Communications

▲ **HACKLEBURG**—CommuniComm Services

HALE COUNTY (PORTIONS)—See GREENSBORO, AL (Mediacom)

▲ **HALEYVILLE**—Cobridge Communications

▲ **HAMILTON**—West Alabama TV Cable Co. Inc.

HAMMONDVILLE—See HENAGAR, AL (Cobridge Communications)

HANCEVILLE—See CULLMAN, AL (Windjammer Cable)

HARMONY—See HEATH, AL (Clearview Cable)

HARPERSVILLE—See WESTOVER, AL (Charter Communications)

▲ **HARTSELLE**—Charter Communications. Now served by Decatur, AL [AL0184]

HARTSELLE—See DECATUR, AL (Charter Communications)

HARVEST—See HUNTSVILLE, AL (Mediacom)

HATCHECHUBBEE—See PHENIX CITY, AL (Cable TV of East Alabama)

HAWK PRIDE MOUNTAIN—See FLORENCE, AL (Comcast Cable)

HAYDEN—See BLOUNT COUNTY, AL (Alabama Broadband LLC)

▲ **HAYNEVILLE**—Alabama Broadband LLC

HAZEL GREEN—See HUNTSVILLE, AL (Mediacom)

HEADLAND—See DOTHAN, AL (Comcast Cable)

▲ **HEATH**—Clearview Cable

▲ **HEFLIN**—Cobridge Communications

HELENE—See LEEDS, AL (Charter Communications)

▲ **HENAGAR**—Cobridge Communications

HENRY COUNTY (PORTIONS)—See ABBEVILLE, AL (Comcast Cable)

HENRY COUNTY (SOUTHERN PORTION)—See DOTHAN, AL (Comcast Cable)

HENRY COUNTY (UNINCORPORATED AREAS)—See EUFAULA, AL (Bright House Networks)

HIGDON—See HENAGAR, AL (Cobridge Communications)

▲ **HILLSBORO**—Formerly served by Shoals Cable TV Inc. No longer in operation

HOBSON CITY—See ANNISTON, AL (Cable One)

HOG JAW—See BAILEYTON, AL (Cobridge Communications)

HOKES BLUFF—See SOUTHSIDE, AL (Charter Communications)

▲ **HOLLIS CROSSROADS**—CommuniComm Services

HOLLY POND—See CULLMAN, AL (Windjammer Cable)

HOLLYWOOD—See GUNTERSVILLE, AL (Charter Communications)

HOLMES COUNTY (NORTHERN PORTION)—See DOTHAN, FL (Comcast Cable)

HOMEWOOD—See LEEDS, AL (Charter Communications)

▲ **HOOVER**—Charter Communications. Now served by LEEDS, AL [AL0192]

HOOVER—See LEEDS, AL (Charter Communications)

HORN HILL—See OPP, AL (Opp Cablevision)

HORTON—See GUNTERSVILLE, AL (Charter Communications)

HOUSTON COUNTY (PORTIONS)—See DOTHAN, AL (Comcast Cable)

HOUSTON COUNTY—See DOTHAN, AL (Time Warner Cable)

HUEYTOWN (PORTIONS)—See BIRMINGHAM, AL (Bright House Networks)

HUEYTOWN—See FAIRFIELD, AL (Charter Communications)

HULACO—See BAILEYTON, AL (Cobridge Communications)

▲ **HUNTSVILLE**—Comcast Cable

▲ **HUNTSVILLE**—Knology

▲ **HUNTSVILLE**—Mediacom

HURTSBORO—See PHENIX CITY, AL (Cable TV of East Alabama)

IDER—See HENAGAR, AL (Cobridge Communications)

INDIAN SPRINGS VILLAGE—See LEEDS, AL (Charter Communications)

IRONDALE—See BIRMINGHAM, AL (Bright House Networks)

IRVINGTON—See MOBILE COUNTY, AL (Mediacom)

JACKSON COUNTY (PORTIONS)—See HENAGAR, AL (Cobridge Communications)

JACKSON COUNTY (UNINCORPORATED PORTIONS)—See GUNTERSVILLE, AL (Charter Communications)

JACKSON COUNTY—See GURLEY, AL (Charter Communications)

JACKSON COUNTY—See RAINSVILLE, AL (Cobridge Communications)

JACKSON COUNTY—See DOTHAN, FL (Comcast Cable)

▲ **JACKSON**—Mediacom. Now served by THOMASVILLE, AL [AL0080]

JACKSON—See THOMASVILLE, AL (Mediacom)

JACKSONS' GAP—See LEEDS, AL (Charter Communications)

JACKSONVILLE—See ANNISTON, AL (Cable One)

▲ **JASPER**—Charter Communications

▲ **JASPER**—Zoom Media

JEFFERSON COUNTY (EASTERN PORTION)—See MARGARET, AL (Alabama Broadband LLC)

JEFFERSON COUNTY (PORTIONS)—See BIRMINGHAM, AL (Bright House Networks)

JEFFERSON COUNTY (PORTIONS)—See CULLMAN, AL (Windjammer Cable)

JEFFERSON COUNTY (SOUTHERN PORTION)—See TUSCALOOSA, AL (Comcast Cable)

JEFFERSON COUNTY—See BLOUNT COUNTY, AL (Alabama Broadband LLC)

JEFFERSON COUNTY—See LEEDS, AL (Charter Communications)

JEMISON—See THORSBY, AL (Cobridge Communications)

JOPPA—See BAILEYTON, AL (Cobridge Communications)

KANSAS—See JASPER, AL (Charter Communications)

KENNEDY—See MILLPORT, AL (Northland Cable Television)

KILLEN—See ELGIN, AL (Cobridge Communications)

KIMBERLY—See CULLMAN, AL (Windjammer Cable)

KINSEY—See DOTHAN, AL (Comcast Cable)

KINSTON—See OPP, AL (Opp Cablevision)

LACEYS SPRING—See DECATUR, AL (Charter Communications)

▲ **LAFAYETTE**—CommuniComm Services

LAKE FOREST—See FAIRHOPE, AL (Mediacom)

▲**LAKE MARTIN RESORT**—Com-Link

LAKEVIEW—See ALBERTVILLE, AL (Charter Communications)

LANETT—See VALLEY, AL (Knology)

LAUDERDALE COUNTY (PORTIONS)—See ELGIN, AL (Cobridge Communications)

LAUDERDALE COUNTY—See FLORENCE, AL (Comcast Cable)

LAWRENCE COUNTY (PORTIONS)—See MOULTON, AL (Charter Communications)

LAWRENCE COUNTY (PORTIONS)—See LEIGHTON, AL (Cobridge Communications)

LAWRENCE COUNTY (PORTIONS)—See TRINITY, AL (Coosa Cable)

▲**LAY LAKE**—Cobridge Communications

LEE COUNTY (NORTHEASTERN PORTION)—See BEULAH, AL (Charter Communications)

LEE COUNTY (PORTIONS)—See LEEDS, AL (Charter Communications)

LEE COUNTY (PORTIONS)—See NOTASULGA, AL (Com-Link Inc.)

LEE COUNTY—See PHENIX CITY, AL (Cable TV of East Alabama)

▲**LEEDS**—Charter Communications

▲**LEESBURG**—Envision Media Inc.

▲**LEIGHTON**—Cobridge Communications

LEVEL PLAINS—See DOTHAN, AL (Time Warner Cable)

LEXINGTON—See ELGIN, AL (Cobridge Communications)

LILLIAN—See FAIRHOPE, AL (Mediacom)

LIMESTONE COUNTY (EASTERN PORTION)—See HUNTSVILLE, AL (Knology)

LIMESTONE COUNTY (PORTIONS)—See ATHENS, AL (Charter Communications)

▲**LIMESTONE COUNTY (western portion)**—Charter Communications. Now served by ATHENS, AL [AL0169]

LIMESTONE COUNTY—See ARDMORE, AL (Mediacom)

LINCOLN COUNTY—See ARDMORE, TN (Mediacom)

▲**LINCOLN**—Coosa Cable. Now served by PELL CITY, AL [AL0212]

LINCOLN—See PELL CITY, AL (Coosa Cable)

▲**LINDEN**—Mediacom

LINEVILLE—See ASHLAND, AL (CommuniComm Services)

LIPSCOMB—See BIRMINGHAM, AL (Bright House Networks)

LISMAN—See BUTLER, AL (Zito Media)

LITTLEVILLE—See RUSSELLVILLE, AL (Charter Communications)

▲**LIVINGSTON**—Mediacom

LOACHAPOKA—See NOTASULGA, AL (Com-Link Inc.)

LOCKHART—See FLORALA, AL (Bright House Networks)

▲**LOCUST FORK**—Formerly served by Almega Cable. No longer in operation

LOUISVILLE—See CLIO, AL (Bright House Networks)

▲**LOWNDES COUNTY**—Alabama Broadband LLC

LOXLEY—See ROBERTSDALE, AL (Mediacom)

▲**LUVERNE**—Crenshaw Cable

LYNN—See NAUVOO, AL (Zoom Media)

MACON COUNTY (PORTIONS)—See NOTASULGA, AL (Com-Link Inc.)

MADISON COUNTY (PORTIONS)—See HUNTSVILLE, AL (Knology)

MADISON COUNTY (PORTIONS)—See NEW HOPE, AL (New Hope Telephone Cooperative)

MADISON COUNTY—See HUNTSVILLE, AL (Mediacom)

MADISON—See HUNTSVILLE, AL (Knology)

MAGNOLIA SPRINGS—See FOLEY, AL (Riviera Utilities Cable TV)

MALBIS—See DAPHNE, AL (Mediacom)

MALVERN—See DOTHAN, AL (Time Warner Cable)

▲**MARGARET**—Alabama Broadband LLC

MARION COUNTY (PORTIONS)—See HALEYVILLE, AL (Cobridge Communications)

MARION COUNTY (PORTIONS)—See GUIN, AL (CommuniComm Services)

▲**MARION**—Sky Cablevision

MARLOW—See FAIRHOPE, AL (Mediacom)

MARSHALL COUNTY (NORTHWESTERN PORTION)—See GUNTERSVILLE, AL (Charter Communications)

MARSHALL COUNTY (PORTIONS)—See ALBERTVILLE, AL (Charter Communications)

MARSHALL COUNTY (PORTIONS)—See GUNTERSVILLE, AL (Charter Communications)

MARSHALL COUNTY (PORTIONS)—See NEW HOPE, AL (New Hope Telephone Cooperative)

MARSHALL COUNTY (UNINCORPORATED AREAS)—See BAILEYTON, AL (Cobridge Communications)

MAXWELL AFB—See WETUMPKA, AL (Bright House Networks)

MAXWELL AFB—See MONTGOMERY, AL (Knology)

MAYTOWN—See LEEDS, AL (Charter Communications)

MCINTOSH—See MOBILE COUNTY, AL (Mediacom)

▲**MCKENZIE**—Clearview Cable

▲**MENTONE**—Charter Communications

MERIDIANVILLE—See HUNTSVILLE, AL (Mediacom)

▲**MEXIA**—Formerly served by Galaxy Cablevision. No longer in operation

MIDFIELD—See FAIRFIELD, AL (Charter Communications)

MIDLAND CITY—See DOTHAN, AL (Time Warner Cable)

MIDWAY—See UNION SPRINGS, AL (Union Springs Telephone Co.)

MIFLIN—See FOLEY, AL (Riviera Utilities Cable TV)

MILLBROOK—See WETUMPKA, AL (Bright House Networks)

▲**MILLPORT**—Northland Cable Television

▲**MILLRY**—Sky Cablevision. No longer in operation

▲**MOBILE COUNTY**—Formerly served by Charter Communications. No longer in operation

MOBILE COUNTY—See MOBILE, AL (Comcast Cable)

▲**MOBILE COUNTY**—Mediacom

▲**MOBILE**—Comcast Cable

MONROE COUNTY (PORTIONS)—See CAMDEN, AL (Mediacom)

▲**MONROEVILLE**—Mediacom. Now served by CAMDEN, AL [AL0112]

MONROEVILLE—See CAMDEN, AL (Mediacom)

MONTEVALLO—See LEEDS, AL (Charter Communications)

MONTGOMERY COUNTY—See MONTGOMERY, AL (Charter Communications)

▲**MONTGOMERY**—Charter Communications

▲**MONTGOMERY**—Knology

MONTROSE—See FAIRHOPE, AL (Mediacom)

MOODY—See LEEDS, AL (Charter Communications)

MORGAN CITY (PORTIONS)—See GUNTERSVILLE, AL (Charter Communications)

▲**MORGAN CITY**—Charter Communications. Now served by GUNTERSVILLE, AL [AL0033]

MORGAN COUNTY (EASTERN PORTION)—See GUNTERSVILLE, AL (Charter Communications)

MORGAN COUNTY (PORTIONS)—See BAILEYTON, AL (Cobridge Communications)

MORGAN COUNTY (UNINCORPORATED AREAS)—See DECATUR, AL (Charter Communications)

MORGAN COUNTY—See DECATUR, AL (Charter Communications)

MORRIS—See LEEDS, AL (Charter Communications)

MOSSES—See LOWNDES COUNTY, AL (Alabama Broadband LLC)

▲**MOULTON**—Charter Communications

MOUNDVILLE—See LEEDS, AL (Charter Communications)

MOUNT OLIVE—See LEEDS, AL (Charter Communications)

MOUNT VERNON—See MOBILE COUNTY, AL (Mediacom)

MOUNTAIN BROOK—See LEEDS, AL (Charter Communications)

MOUNTAINBORO—See ALBERTVILLE, AL (Charter Communications)

MULGA—See LEEDS, AL (Charter Communications)

MUNFORD—See ANNISTON, AL (Cable One)

MUSCADINE—See HEFLIN, AL (Cobridge Communications)

MUSCLE SHOALS—See FLORENCE, AL (Comcast Cable)

NAPIER FIELD—See DOTHAN, AL (Time Warner Cable)

▲**NAUVOO**—Zoom Media

NEW BROCKTON—See ENTERPRISE, AL (Time Warner Cable)

▲**NEW HOPE**—New Hope Telephone Cooperative

NEW MARKET—See HUNTSVILLE, AL (Mediacom)

NEW SITE—See LEEDS, AL (Charter Communications)

NEWTON—See DOTHAN, AL (Time Warner Cable)

NEWVILLE—See DOTHAN, AL (Comcast Cable)

NOMA—See DOTHAN, FL (Comcast Cable)

▲**NORTH BREWTON**—Formerly served by CableSouth Inc. No longer in operation

NORTH COURTLAND—See LEIGHTON, AL (Cobridge Communications)

NORTH ROGERSVILLE—See ELGIN, AL (Cobridge Communications)

NORTHPORT—See LEEDS, AL (Charter Communications)

NORTHPORT—See TUSCALOOSA, AL (Comcast Cable)

▲**NOTASULGA**—Com-Link Inc.

OAK GROVE—See LEEDS, AL (Charter Communications)

▲ **OAKMAN**—Formerly served by Almega Cable. No longer in operation

OAKVILLE—See DECATUR, AL (Charter Communications)

▲ **ODENVILLE**—Coosa Cable. Now served by PELL CITY, AL [AL0212]

ODENVILLE—See PELL CITY, AL (Coosa Cable)

OHATCHEE—See ANNISTON, AL (Cable One)

OLEANDER—See GUNTERSVILLE, AL (Charter Communications)

▲ **ONEONTA**—Otelco Telephone Co.

ONYCHA—See OPP, AL (Opp Cablevision)

OPELIKA—See LEEDS, AL (Charter Communications)

▲ **OPP**—Opp Cablevision

ORANGE BEACH—See ROBERTSDALE, AL (Mediacom)

▲ **ORRVILLE**—Zoom Media

▲ **OWENS CROSS ROADS**—New Hope Telephone Cooperative. Now served by NEW HOPE, AL [AL0070]

OWENS CROSS ROADS—See NEW HOPE, AL (New Hope Telephone Cooperative)

OXFORD—See ANNISTON, AL (Cable One)

▲ **OZARK**—Charter Communications. Now served by TROY, AL [AL0027]

OZARK—See TROY, AL (Cobridge Communications)

PAINT ROCK—See GURLEY, AL (Charter Communications)

PARISH—See JASPER, AL (Charter Communications)

PAXTON—See FLORALA, FL (Bright House Networks)

PELHAM—See LEEDS, AL (Charter Communications)

▲ **PELL CITY**—Coosa Cable

PENCE—See DECATUR, AL (Charter Communications)

▲ **PENNINGTON**—Zoom Media

▲ **PERDIDO BEACH**—Mediacom

PERRY COUNTY (UNINCORPORATED AREAS)—See MARION, AL (Sky Cablevision)

PERRY COUNTY—See UNIONTOWN, AL (Alliance Communications)

PETERSON—See LEEDS, AL (Charter Communications)

▲ **PHENIX CITY**—Cable TV of East Alabama

▲ **PHIL CAMPBELL**—CommuniComm Services

PICKENS COUNTY—See ALICEVILLE, AL (Northland Cable Television)

PICKENSVILLE—See ALICEVILLE, AL (Northland Cable Television)

▲ **PIEDMONT**—Charter Communications

PIKE COUNTY—See TROY, AL (Cobridge Communications)

PIKE ROAD—See MONTGOMERY, AL (Knology)

PINCKARD—See DOTHAN, AL (Time Warner Cable)

▲ **PINE HILL**—Zoom Media

PINE RIDGE—See FORT PAYNE, AL (Windjammer Cable)

PINEY WOODS—See JASPER, AL (Zoom Media)

PINSON—See LEEDS, AL (Charter Communications)

PISGAH—See HENAGAR, AL (Cobridge Communications)

PLANTATION HILLS—See DAPHNE, AL (Mediacom)

PLEASANT GROVE—See FAIRFIELD, AL (Charter Communications)

POINT CLEAR—See FAIRHOPE, AL (Mediacom)

▲ **POLLARD**—Formerly served by CableSouth Inc. No longer in operation

POWELL—See RAINSVILLE, AL (Cobridge Communications)

PRATTVILLE—See MONTGOMERY, AL (Charter Communications)

PRATTVILLE—See MONTGOMERY, AL (Knology)

PRICEVILLE (PORTIONS)—See DECATUR, AL (Charter Communications)

PRICHARD—See MOBILE, AL (Comcast Cable)

PROSPECT—See ARDMORE, TN (Mediacom)

▲ **PROVIDENCE**—Sky Cablevision

QUITMAN COUNTY—See EUFAULA, GA (Bright House Networks)

▲ **RAGLAND**—Ragland Telephone Co.

RAINBOW CITY—See GADSDEN, AL (Comcast Cable)

▲ **RAINSVILLE**—Cobridge Communications

▲ **RANBURNE**—Formerly served by Ranburne Cable. No longer in operation

RANDOLPH COUNTY—See ROANOKE, AL (CommuniComm Services)

▲ **RED BAY**—MetroCast Communications

RED LEVEL—See HEATH, AL (Clearview Cable)

REDSTONE ARSENAL—See HUNTSVILLE, AL (Knology)

REECE CITY—See ATTALLA, AL (Comcast Cable)

REFORM—See ALICEVILLE, AL (Northland Cable Television)

REHOBETH—See DOTHAN, AL (Time Warner Cable)

REPTON—See CAMDEN, AL (Mediacom)

RESCUE—See GUNTERSVILLE, AL (Charter Communications)

RIDGEVILLE—See ATTALLA, AL (Comcast Cable)

RIVER FALLS—See HEATH, AL (Clearview Cable)

RIVERCHASE—See LEEDS, AL (Charter Communications)

RIVERSIDE—See PELL CITY, AL (Coosa Cable)

▲ **ROANOKE**—CommuniComm Services

▲ **ROBERTSDALE**—Mediacom

ROCK MILLS—See ROANOKE, AL (CommuniComm Services)

ROCKFORD—See LEEDS, AL (Charter Communications)

ROGERSVILLE—See ELGIN, AL (Cobridge Communications)

ROMAR BEACH—See ROBERTSDALE, AL (Mediacom)

ROOSEVELT CITY—See BIRMINGHAM, AL (Bright House Networks)

RUSSELL COUNTY—See PHENIX CITY, AL (Cable TV of East Alabama)

▲ **RUSSELLVILLE**—Charter Communications

RUTH—See BAILEYTON, AL (Cobridge Communications)

RUTLEDGE—See LUVERNE, AL (Crenshaw Cable)

SALEM—See PHENIX CITY, AL (Cable TV of East Alabama)

▲ **SAMSON**—Bright House Networks

SANFORD—See HEATH, AL (Clearview Cable)

SARALAND—See MOBILE, AL (Comcast Cable)

SARDIS CITY—See ALBERTVILLE, AL (Charter Communications)

SATSUMA—See MOBILE COUNTY, AL (Mediacom)

▲ **SCOTTSBORO**—Charter Communications. Now served by GUNTERSVILLE, AL [AL0033]

SCOTTSBORO—See GUNTERSVILLE, AL (Charter Communications)

▲ **SCOTTSBORO**—Scottsboro Electric Power Board

SEALE—See PHENIX CITY, AL (Cable TV of East Alabama)

SECTION—See RAINSVILLE, AL (Cobridge Communications)

▲ **SELBROOK**—Alabama Broadband LLC

▲ **SELMA**—Charter Communications

SEMMES—See MOBILE COUNTY, AL (Mediacom)

SHADY LAKE TRAILER PARK—See SELBROOK, AL (Alabama Broadband LLC)

SHEFFIELD—See FLORENCE, AL (Comcast Cable)

SHELBY COUNTY (PORTIONS)—See LEEDS, AL (Charter Communications)

SHELBY COUNTY (PORTIONS)—See COLUMBIANA, AL (Cobridge Communications)

SHELBY COUNTY (SOUTHERN PORTION)—See SHELBY LAKE, AL (Charter Communications)

SHELBY COUNTY—See WESTOVER, AL (Charter Communications)

▲ **SHELBY LAKE**—Charter Communications

SHILOH—See RAINSVILLE, AL (Cobridge Communications)

SILVER HILL—See ROBERTSDALE, AL (Mediacom)

SIPSEY—See JASPER, AL (Charter Communications)

▲ **SKYLINE**—Formerly served by Almega Cable. No longer in operation

SMITHS—See PHENIX CITY, AL (Cable TV of East Alabama)

▲ **SOUTHSIDE**—Charter Communications

▲ **SPANISH COVE**—Mediacom. Now served by FAIRHOPE (formerly Daphne), AL [AL0124]

SPANISH COVE—See FAIRHOPE, AL (Mediacom)

SPANISH FORT—See FAIRHOPE, AL (Mediacom)

SPEAKE—See DECATUR, AL (Charter Communications)

SPRING VALLEY—See LEIGHTON, AL (Cobridge Communications)

SPRINGVILLE—See ASHVILLE, AL (Alabama Broadband)

ST. CLAIR COUNTY (PORTIONS)—See ASHVILLE, AL (Alabama Broadband)

ST. CLAIR COUNTY (PORTIONS)—See LEEDS, AL (Charter Communications)

ST. CLAIR COUNTY (PORTIONS)—See PELL CITY, AL (Coosa Cable)

ST. CLAIR COUNTY—See MARGARET, AL (Alabama Broadband LLC)

ST. FLORIAN—See FLORENCE, AL (Comcast Cable)

▲ **STAPLETON**—Mediacom. Now served by FAIRHOPE (formerly Daphne), AL [AL0124]

STAPLETON—See FAIRHOPE, AL (Mediacom)

STEVENSON—See BRIDGEPORT, AL (Charter Communications)

STRAUGHN—See HEATH, AL (Clearview Cable)

▲**SULLIGENT**—CommuniComm Services

SUMITON—See JASPER, AL (Charter Communications)

SUMMERDALE—See FOLEY, AL (Riviera Utilities Cable TV)

▲**SWEET WATER**—Sky Cablevision

SYCAMORE—See LEEDS, AL (Charter Communications)

▲**SYLACAUGA**—Charter Communications. Now served by LEEDS, AL [AL0192]

SYLACAUGA—See LEEDS, AL (Charter Communications)

SYLVAN SPRINGS—See LEEDS, AL (Charter Communications)

SYLVANIA—See HENAGAR, AL (Cobridge Communications)

TALLADEGA COUNTY (PORTIONS)—See LEEDS, AL (Charter Communications)

TALLADEGA COUNTY (PORTIONS)—See PELL CITY, AL (Coosa Cable)

TALLADEGA COUNTY (UNINCORPORATED AREAS)—See ANNISTON, AL (Cable One)

▲**TALLADEGA**—Charter Communications. Now served by LEEDS, AL [AL0192]

TALLADEGA—See LEEDS, AL (Charter Communications)

TALLAPOOSA COUNTY (PORTIONS)—See LEEDS, AL (Charter Communications)

TALLAPOOSA COUNTY (PORTIONS)—See LAKE MARTIN RESORT, AL (Com-Link)

TALLAPOOSA COUNTY (SOUTHERN PORTION)—See WETUMPKA, AL (Bright House Networks)

TALLASSEE—See WETUMPKA, AL (Bright House Networks)

TARRANT CITY—See LEEDS, AL (Charter Communications)

TAYLOR—See DOTHAN, AL (Time Warner Cable)

TAYLORVILLE—See LEEDS, AL (Charter Communications)

THEODORE—See MOBILE COUNTY, AL (Mediacom)

▲**THOMASTON**—Zoom Media

▲**THOMASVILLE**—Mediacom

▲**THORSBY**—Cobridge Communications

TILLMAN'S CORNER—See MOBILE COUNTY, AL (Mediacom)

TONEY (PORTIONS)—See HUNTSVILLE, AL (Mediacom)

TOWN CREEK—See LEIGHTON, AL (Cobridge Communications)

▲**TRAFFORD**—Formerly served by Almega Cable. No longer in operation

▲**TRINITY**—Coosa Cable

▲**TROY**—Cobridge Communications

▲**TROY**—Troy Cablevision & Entertainment

TRUSSVILLE—See MARGARET, AL (Alabama Broadband LLC)

TRUSSVILLE—See LEEDS, AL (Charter Communications)

TUSCALOOSA COUNTY (PORTIONS)—See LEEDS, AL (Charter Communications)

▲**TUSCALOOSA COUNTY**—Charter Communications. Now served by LEEDS, AL [AL0192]

TUSCALOOSA COUNTY—See TUSCALOOSA, AL (Comcast Cable)

TUSCALOOSA—See LEEDS, AL (Charter Communications)

▲**TUSCALOOSA**—Comcast Cable

TUSCUMBIA—See FLORENCE, AL (Comcast Cable)

▲**TUSKEGEE**—Charter Communications. Now served by LEEDS, AL [AL0192]

TUSKEGEE—See LEEDS, AL (Charter Communications)

UNION GROVE—See ALBERTVILLE, AL (Charter Communications)

UNION HILL—See GUNTERSVILLE, AL (Charter Communications)

▲**UNION SPRINGS**—Union Springs Telephone Co.

▲**UNIONTOWN**—Alliance Communications

VALHERMOSO SPRINGS—See DECATUR, AL (Charter Communications)

VALLEY HEAD—See FORT PAYNE, AL (Windjammer Cable)

▲**VALLEY**—Knology

VANCE—See LEEDS, AL (Charter Communications)

VERNON—See SULLIGENT, AL (CommuniComm Services)

VESTAVIA HILLS—See LEEDS, AL (Charter Communications)

VINCENT—See WESTOVER, AL (Charter Communications)

VINEMONT—See CULLMAN, AL (Windjammer Cable)

▲**WADLEY**—CommuniComm Services

WALKER COUNTY (PORTIONS)—See JASPER, AL (Charter Communications)

WALKER COUNTY (PORTIONS)—See NAUVOO, AL (Zoom Media)

WALKER COUNTY—See JASPER, AL (Zoom Media)

WALNUT GROVE—See ALTOONA, AL (Rapid Cable)

▲**WARRIOR**—Time Warner Cable. Now served by CULLMAN, AL [AL0034]

WARRIOR—See CULLMAN, AL (Windjammer Cable)

WASHINGTON COUNTY (UNINCORPORATED AREAS)—See MOBILE COUNTY, AL (Mediacom)

▲**WATERLOO**—Formerly served by North Crossroads Communications Inc. No longer in operation

WEAVER—See ANNISTON, AL (Cable One)

WEBB—See DOTHAN, AL (Comcast Cable)

▲**WEDOWEE**—CommuniComm Services

▲**WEST BLOCTON**—Formerly served by Almega Cable. No longer in operation

WEST END—See LEEDS, AL (Charter Communications)

WEST JEFFERSON—See JASPER, AL (Charter Communications)

WEST KILLEN—See ELGIN, AL (Cobridge Communications)

WEST POINT—See VALLEY, GA (Knology)

WEST POINT—See CULLMAN, AL (Windjammer Cable)

▲**WESTOVER**—Charter Communications

WESTOVER—See LEEDS, AL (Charter Communications)

▲**WETUMPKA**—Bright House Networks

WHATLEY—See GROVE HILL, AL (Zito Media)

WHITE HALL—See LOWNDES COUNTY, AL (Alabama Broadband LLC)

WHITEHOUSE FORKS—See FAIRHOPE, AL (Mediacom)

WHITES CHAPEL—See LEEDS, AL (Charter Communications)

WILCOX COUNTY (PORTIONS)—See CAMDEN, AL (Mediacom)

WILCOX COUNTY—See PINE HILL, AL (Zoom Media)

WILMER—See MOBILE COUNTY, AL (Mediacom)

WILSONVILLE—See COLUMBIANA, AL (Cobridge Communications)

WILTON—See LEEDS, AL (Charter Communications)

▲**WINFIELD**—West Alabama TV Cable Co. Inc.

WINSTON COUNTY (EASTERN PORTION)—See ADDISON (town), AL (Alabama Broadband)

WINSTON COUNTY (PORTIONS)—See HALEYVILLE, AL (Cobridge Communications)

WINSTON COUNTY (SOUTHERN PORTION)—See NAUVOO, AL (Zoom Media)

WINSTON COUNTY—See DOUBLE SPRINGS, AL (Cobridge Communications)

YORK—See LIVINGSTON, AL (Mediacom)

ALASKA

▲**ADAK**—Adak Cablevision

▲**ANCHORAGE**—Formerly served by ACS Television. No longer in operation

▲**ANCHORAGE**—Formerly served by Sprint Corp. No longer in operation

▲**ANCHORAGE**—GCI

▲**ANGOON**—Angoon Cablevision

▲**BARROW**—GCI

▲**BETHEL**—GCI

CHUGIAK—See ANCHORAGE, AK (GCI)

▲**CORDOVA**—GCI

▲**CRAIG**—Craig Cable TV Inc.

▲**DILLINGHAM**—Nushagak Cooperative Inc.

DOUGLAS—See JUNEAU, AK (GCI)

DUTCH HARBOR—See UNALASKA, AK (Eyecom Cable)

EAGLE RIVER—See ANCHORAGE, AK (GCI)

ELELSON AFB—See FAIRBANKS, AK (GCI)

ELMENDORF AFB—See ANCHORAGE, AK (GCI)

FAIRBANKS COUNTY (UNINCORPORATED AREAS)—See FAIRBANKS, AK (GCI)

▲**FAIRBANKS**—GCI

FORT GREELY—See FAIRBANKS, AK (GCI)

FORT RICHARDSON—See ANCHORAGE, AK (GCI)

FORT WAINWRIGHT—See FAIRBANKS, AK (GCI)

▲**GALENA**—Eyecom Cable

▲**GAMBELL**—Formerly served by Frontier Cable Inc. No longer in operation

▲**GIRDWOOD**—Eyecom Cable

▲**HAINES**—Haines Cable TV

▲**HOMER**—GCI

▲**HOONAH**—Formerly served by Hoonah Community TV. No longer in operation

▲**HOOPER BAY**—Formerly served by Frontier Cable Inc. No longer in operation

▲**JUNEAU**—GCI

KACHEMAK CITY—See HOMER, AK (GCI)

KENAI PENINSULA—See SEWARD, AK (GCI)

KENAI—See SOLDOTNA, AK (GCI)

KETCHIKAN GATEWAY BOROUGH—See KETCHIKAN, AK (GCI)

▲**KETCHIKAN**—GCI

▲**KING COVE**—Formerly served by Mount Dutton Cable Corp. No longer in operation

▲**KING SALMON**—Bay Cablevision

▲**KIPNUK**—Formerly served by Frontier Cable Inc. No longer in operation

▲**KODIAK**—GCI

▲**KOTZEBUE**—GCI

MATANUSKA VALLEY—See WASILLA, AK (GCI)

MOUNT EDGECUMBE—See SITKA, AK (GCI)

▲**MOUNTAIN VILLAGE**—Formerly served by Village Cable Co. No longer in operation

NAKNEK—See KING SALMON, AK (Bay Cablevision)

▲**NOME**—GCI

NORTH POLE—See FAIRBANKS, AK (GCI)

NORTH STAR BOROUGH—See FAIRBANKS, AK (GCI)

PALMER—See ANCHORAGE, AK (GCI)

PALMER—See WASILLA, AK (GCI)

PETERS CREEK—See ANCHORAGE, AK (GCI)

▲**PETERSBURG**—GCI

▲**PORT LIONS**—Formerly served by Eyecom Cable. No longer in operation

▲**QUINHAGAK**—Formerly served by Frontier Cable Inc. No longer in operation

RIDGEWAY—See SOLDOTNA, AK (GCI)

▲**SAVOONGA**—Formerly served by Frontier Cable Inc. No longer in operation

SAXMAN—See KETCHIKAN, AK (GCI)

▲**SEWARD**—GCI

SITKA COUNTY—See SITKA, AK (GCI)

▲**SITKA**—GCI

▲**SKAGWAY**—Skagway Cable TV

▲**SOLDOTNA**—GCI

▲**ST. MARY'S**—Formerly served by Frontier Cable Inc. No longer in operation

▲**TANANA**—Supervision Cable TV

▲**THORNE BAY**—Formerly served by Thorne Bay Community TV Inc. No longer in operation

▲**TOGIAK**—Formerly served by Frontier Cable Inc. No longer in operation

▲**TOKSOOK BAY**—Formerly served by Frontier Cable Inc. No longer in operation

▲**TUNUNAK**—Formerly served by Frontier Cable Inc. No longer in operation

▲**UNALAKLEET**—Formerly served by Frontier Cable Inc. No longer in operation

▲**UNALASKA**—Eyecom Cable

▲**VALDEZ**—GCI

WARD COVE—See KETCHIKAN, AK (GCI)

▲**WASILLA**—GCI

WASILLA—See ANCHORAGE, AK (GCI)

▲**WHITTIER**—Supervision Cable TV

▲**WRANGELL**—GCI

ARIZONA

▲**AJO**—Mediacom

▲**ALPINE**—Formerly served by Eagle West Communications Inc. No longer in operation

AMADO—See NOGALES, AZ (Mediacom)

▲**APACHE JUNCTION**—Mediacom

ARIVACA—See NOGALES, AZ (Mediacom)

ARIZONA CITY—See ELOY, AZ (RealStar Communications)

ASH CANYON (UNINCORPORATED AREA)—See SIERRA VISTA, AZ (Cox Communications)

▲**AVONDALE**—Cox Communications. Now served by PHOENIX, AZ [AZ0001]

AVONDALE—See PHOENIX, AZ (Cox Communications)

▲**BAGDAD**—Formerly served by Eagle West Communications. No longer in operation

▲**BENSON**—Cox Communications

▲**BISBEE**—Cable One

▲**BLACK CANYON CITY**—RealStar Communications

BUCKEYE—See PHOENIX, AZ (Cox Communications)

▲**BULLHEAD CITY**—Suddenlink Communications

BUSHMAN ACRES—See SHOW LOW, AZ (Cable One)

▲**BYLAS**—San Carlos Apache Telecom

CAMP VERDE—See SEDONA, AZ (Suddenlink Communications)

▲**CAREFREE**—Cox Communications. Now served by PHOENIX, AZ [AZ0001]

CAREFREE—See PHOENIX, AZ (Cox Communications)

CARR CANYON (UNINCORPORATED AREA)—See SIERRA VISTA, AZ (Cox Communications)

▲**CASA GRANDE (northern portion)**—Formerly served by Eagle West Communications Inc. No longer in operation

▲**CASA GRANDE**—Cox Communications

CASHION—See PHOENIX, AZ (Cox Communications)

CATALINA (PORTIONS)—See PIMA COUNTY, AZ (Comcast Cable)

▲**CAVE CREEK**—Formerly served by Eagle West Communications Inc. No longer in operation

CAVE CREEK—See PHOENIX, AZ (Cox Communications)

CENTRAL HEIGHTS—See GLOBE-MIAMI, AZ (Cable One)

▲**CHANDLER (portions)**—Qwest Choice TV. IPTV service has been discontinued.

CHANDLER—See PHOENIX, AZ (Cox Communications)

▲**CHINLE**—Formerly served by Frontier Communications. No longer in operation

CHINO VALLEY—See PRESCOTT, AZ (Cable One)

CLARKDALE—See COTTONWOOD, AZ (Cable One)

CLAYPOOL—See GLOBE-MIAMI, AZ (Cable One)

▲**CLIFTON**—Cable One

COCHISE COUNTY—See BISBEE, AZ (Cable One)

COCONINO COUNTY—See PAGE, AZ (Cable One)

COCONINO COUNTY—See WILLIAMS, AZ (New Day Broadband)

COCONINO COUNTY—See FLAGSTAFF, AZ (Suddenlink Communications)

▲**CONCHO VALLEY**—Formerly served by Eagle West Communications Inc. No longer in operation

▲**COOLIDGE**—Cable America Corp. Now served by Cox Communications, PHOENIX, AZ [AZ0001]

COOLIDGE—See PHOENIX, AZ (Cox Communications)

▲**CORDES LAKES**—Cordes Lakes Cablevision

CORNVILLE—See COTTONWOOD, AZ (Cable One)

COTTONWOOD (SOUTHEASTERN PORTIONS)—See SEDONA, AZ (Suddenlink Communications)

▲**COTTONWOOD**—Cable One

CRYSTAL BEACH—See LAKE HAVASU CITY, AZ (Suddenlink Communications)

DAVIS-MONTHAN AFB—See TUCSON, AZ (Cox Communications)

DESERT HILLS—See LAKE HAVASU CITY, AZ (Suddenlink Communications)

DEWEY—See PRESCOTT, AZ (Cable One)

▲**DOUGLAS**—Cox Communications

▲**DUDLEYVILLE**—RealStar Communications

▲**EAGAR**—Formerly served by Eagle West Communications Inc. No longer in operation

EARP—See PARKER, CA (Suddenlink Communications)

▲**EAST MESA**—Eagle West Communications Inc

EL MIRAGE—See PHOENIX, AZ (Cox Communications)

▲**ELOY**—RealStar Communications

▲**FLAGSTAFF**—Formerly served by Microwave Communication Services. No longer in operation

▲**FLAGSTAFF**—Suddenlink Communications

▲**FLORENCE GARDEN MOBILE HOME PARK**—Eagle West Communications Inc

FLORENCE—See PHOENIX, AZ (Cox Communications)

FOOTHILLS—See TUCSON, AZ (Cox Communications)

FORT HUACHUCA—See DOUGLAS, AZ (Cox Communications)

FORT HUACHUCA—See SIERRA VISTA, AZ (Cox Communications)

▲**FORT MOHAVE MESA**—Formerly served by Americable International Arizona Inc. No longer in operation

FORT MOHAVE—See BULLHEAD CITY, AZ (Suddenlink Communications)

FOUNTAIN HILLS—See PHOENIX, AZ (Cox Communications)

▲**FREDONIA**—Precis Communications. Now served by KANAB, UT [UT0033]

▲**GILA BEND**—Cox Communications. Now served by PHOENIX, AZ [AZ0001]

GILA BEND—See PHOENIX, AZ (Cox Communications)

GILA COUNTY—See GLOBE-MIAMI, AZ (Cable One)

▲**GILA COUNTY**—San Carlos Apache Telecom

▲**GILBERT (portions)**—Qwest Choice TV. IPTV service has been discontinued

▲**GILBERT**—Cox Communications. Now served by PHOENIX, AZ [AZ0001]

GILBERT—See PHOENIX, AZ (Cox Communications)

▲**GISELA**—Indevideo Co. Inc.

▲**GLENDALE (portions)**—Qwest Choice TV. IPTV service has been discontinued

GLENDALE—See PHOENIX, AZ (Cox Communications)

▲**GLOBE-MIAMI**—Cable One

GOLD CANYON—See APACHE JUNCTION, AZ (Mediacom)

▲**GOLDEN SHORES**—Rapid Cable

▲ **GOLDEN VALLEY**—Golden Valley Cable & Communications

GOODYEAR—See PHOENIX, AZ (Cox Communications)

GRAHAM COUNTY—See SAFFORD, AZ (Cable One)

▲ **GRAND CANYON**—Indevideo Co. Inc.

▲ **GRAND MISSOURI MOBILE HOME PARK**—Formerly served by Sun Valley Cable Inc. No longer in operation

GREEN VALLEY—See TUCSON, AZ (Cox Communications)

GREENLEE COUNTY—See CLIFTON, AZ (Cable One)

GUADALUPE—See PHOENIX, AZ (Cox Communications)

HAYDEN—See DUDLEYVILLE, AZ (RealStar Communications)

▲ **HEBER**—RealStar Communications

HEREFORD—See SIERRA VISTA, AZ (Cox Communications)

▲ **HOLBROOK**—Cable One. Now served by SHOW LOW, AZ [AZ0014]

HOLBROOK—See SHOW LOW, AZ (Cable One)

HORIZAN SIX—See LAKE HAVASU CITY, AZ (Suddenlink Communications)

HUMBOLDT—See PRESCOTT, AZ (Cable One)

ICE HOUSE CANYON—See GLOBE-MIAMI, AZ (Cable One)

INDIAN HILLS—See DUDLEYVILLE, AZ (RealStar Communications)

JOSEPH CITY—See SHOW LOW, AZ (Cable One)

KACHINA—See FLAGSTAFF, AZ (Suddenlink Communications)

▲ **KAYENTA**—Formerly served by Frontier Communications. No longer in operation

▲ **KEARNY**—RealStar Communications

▲ **KINGMAN**—Suddenlink Communications

LA PAZ COUNTY (PORTIONS)—See PARKER, AZ (Suddenlink Communications)

▲ **LAKE HAVASU CITY**—Suddenlink Communications

LAKE MONTEZUMA—See SEDONA, AZ (Suddenlink Communications)

LAKESIDE—See SHOW LOW, AZ (Cable One)

▲ **LEUPP**—Formerly served by Indevideo Co. Inc. No longer in operation

LITCHFIELD PARK—See PHOENIX, AZ (Cox Communications)

▲ **LUKE AFB**—Cox Communications. Now served by PHOENIX, AZ [AZ0001]

LUKE AFB—See PHOENIX, AZ (Cox Communications)

▲ **MAMMOTH**—RealStar Communications

MARANA—See PIMA COUNTY, AZ (Comcast Cable)

MARICOPA COUNTY (PORTIONS)—See PHOENIX, AZ (Cox Communications)

▲ **MARICOPA COUNTY (unincorporated)**—Qwest Choice TV. IPTV service has been discontinued.

▲ **MARICOPA**—Orbitel Communications

MARINE CORPS AIR STATION—See YUMA, AZ (Time Warner Cable)

MAYER—See PRESCOTT, AZ (Cable One)

▲ **MESA**—Cox Communications. Now served by PHOENIX, AZ [AZ0001]

MESA—See PHOENIX, AZ (Cox Communications)

MILLER CANYON (UNINCORPORATED AREA)—See SIERRA VISTA, AZ (Cox Communications)

MOHAVE COUNTY (PORTIONS)—See BULLHEAD CITY, AZ (Suddenlink Communications)

MOHAVE COUNTY (PORTIONS)—See LAKE HAVASU CITY, AZ (Suddenlink Communications)

MOHAVE COUNTY—See KINGMAN, AZ (Suddenlink Communications)

MOHAVE VALLEY—See BULLHEAD CITY, AZ (Suddenlink Communications)

MORENCI—See CLIFTON, AZ (Cable One)

MOUNTAINAIRE—See FLAGSTAFF, AZ (Suddenlink Communications)

▲ **MUNDS PARK**—Suddenlink Communications. Now served by SEDONA, AZ [AZ0025]

MUNDS PARK—See SEDONA, AZ (Suddenlink Communications)

NACO—See BISBEE, AZ (Cable One)

NAVAJO COUNTY (PORTIONS)—See SHOW LOW, AZ (Cable One)

▲ **NOGALES**—Mediacom

OAK CREEK (VILLAGE)—See SEDONA, AZ (Suddenlink Communications)

▲ **ORACLE**—RealStar Communications

ORO VALLEY—See PIMA COUNTY, AZ (Comcast Cable)

OVERGAARD—See HEBER, AZ (RealStar Communications)

PAGE SPRINGS—See COTTONWOOD, AZ (Cable One)

▲ **PAGE**—Cable One

▲ **PARADISE VALLEY (portions)**—Qwest Choice TV. IPTV service has been discontinued.

PARADISE VALLEY—See PHOENIX, AZ (Cox Communications)

▲ **PARKER**—Suddenlink Communications

▲ **PATAGONIA**—Cox Communications. Now served by SIERRA VISTA, AZ [AZ0005]

PATAGONIA—See SIERRA VISTA, AZ (Cox Communications)

▲ **PAYSON (TOWN)**—Suddenlink Communications

▲ **PEACH SPRINGS**—Formerly served by Eagle West Communications Inc. No longer in operation

▲ **PEORIA (portions)**—Qwest Choice TV. IPTV service has been discontinued

PEORIA—See PHOENIX, AZ (Cox Communications)

PERALTA TRAILS—See APACHE JUNCTION, AZ (Mediacom)

PERIDOT—See SAN CARLOS, AZ (San Carlos Apache Telecom)

▲ **PERRYVILLE**—Formerly served by Eagle West Communications Inc. No longer in operation

▲ **PHOENIX (portions)**—Qwest Choice TV. IPTV service has been discontinued

▲ **PHOENIX (portions)**—Qwest Choice TV. This cable system has converted to IPTV. See Phoenix (portions), AZ [AZ5018]

▲ **PHOENIX**—Formerly served by Sprint Corp. No longer in operation

▲ **PHOENIX**—Formerly served by TV Max. No longer in operation

▲ **PHOENIX**—Cox Communications

▲ **PIMA COUNTY**—Comcast Cable

PIMA COUNTY—See TUCSON, AZ (Cox Communications)

PIMA—See SAFFORD, AZ (Cable One)

PINAL COUNTY (PORTIONS)—See APACHE JUNCTION, AZ (Mediacom)

PINAL COUNTY (PORTIONS)—See KEARNY, AZ (RealStar Communications)

PINAL COUNTY—See CASA GRANDE, AZ (Cox Communications)

▲ **PINE**—Suddenlink Communications

PINETOP—See SHOW LOW, AZ (Cable One)

PINEVIEW—See SHOW LOW, AZ (Cable One)

PINEWOOD—See SEDONA, AZ (Suddenlink Communications)

PIRTLEVILLE—See DOUGLAS, AZ (Cox Communications)

▲ **POMERENE**—Formerly served by Midvale Telephone Exchange Inc. No longer in operation

PRESCOTT VALLEY—See PRESCOTT, AZ (Cable One)

▲ **PRESCOTT**—Cable One

▲ **QUARTZSITE**—Formerly served by Americable International Arizona Inc. No longer in operation

QUEEN CREEK—See PHOENIX, AZ (Cox Communications)

QUEEN CREEK—See APACHE JUNCTION, AZ (Mediacom)

QUEEN VALLEY—See APACHE JUNCTION, AZ (Mediacom)

RAMSEY CANYON (UNINCORPORATED AREA)—See SIERRA VISTA, AZ (Cox Communications)

RIO RICO—See NOGALES, AZ (Mediacom)

▲ **RIO VERDE**—Cox Communications. Now served by PHOENIX, AZ [AZ0001]

▲ **RIO VERDE**—Cox Communications. Now served by PHOENIX, AZ [AZ0001]

RIO VERDE—See PHOENIX, AZ (Cox Communications)

RITA RANCH—See TUCSON, AZ (Cox Communications)

▲ **ROBSON RANCH**—Western Broadband

ROCK SHADOWS—See APACHE JUNCTION, AZ (Mediacom)

▲ **ROOSEVELT**—Formerly served by Salt River Cablevision. No longer in operation

▲ **SADDLE MOUNTAIN**—Formerly served by Eagle West Communications Inc. No longer in operation

▲ **SADDLEBROOKE**—Western Broadband

▲ **SAFFORD**—Cable One

SAHUARITA—See TUCSON, AZ (Cox Communications)

▲ **SALOME**—Formerly served by San Carlos Cablevision. No longer in operation

SAN BERNARDINO COUNTY (PORTIONS)—See PARKER, CA (Suddenlink Communications)

▲ **SAN CARLOS**—San Carlos Apache Telecom

SAN LUIS—See YUMA, AZ (Time Warner Cable)

▲ **SAN MANUEL**—RealStar Communications

SAND BANKS—See APACHE JUNCTION, AZ (Mediacom)

SANTA CRUZ COUNTY (PORTIONS)—See NOGALES, AZ (Mediacom)

▲ **SANTA RITA BEL AIRE**—Cox Communications. Now served by TUCSON, AZ [AZ0002]

SANTA RITA BEL AIRE—See TUCSON, AZ (Cox Communications)

SANTO TOMAS—See TUCSON, AZ (Cox Communications)

▲ **SCOTTSDALE (portions)**—Qwest Choice TV. IPTV service has been discontinued

SCOTTSDALE—See PHOENIX, AZ (Cox Communications)

▲ **SEDONA**—Suddenlink Communications

▲ **SELLS**—Formerly served by Red Hawk Cable. No longer in operation

▲ **SHOW LOW**—Cable One

▲ **SIERRA VISTA**—Cox Communications

SIX SHOOTER CANYON—See GLOBE-MIAMI, AZ (Cable One)

SNOWFLAKE—See SHOW LOW, AZ (Cable One)

SOLOMON—See SAFFORD, AZ (Cable One)

SOMERTON—See YUMA, AZ (Time Warner Cable)

SONOITA—See SIERRA VISTA, AZ (Cox Communications)

SOUTH TUCSON—See TUCSON, AZ (Cox Communications)

ST. DAVID—See WILLCOX, AZ (Cox Communications)

▲ **ST. JOHNS**—RealStar Communications

STAR VALLEY—See PAYSON (town), AZ (Suddenlink Communications)

STRAWBERRY—See PINE, AZ (Suddenlink Communications)

STUMP CANYON (UNINCORPORATED AREA)—See SIERRA VISTA, AZ (Cox Communications)

SUN CITY WEST—See PHOENIX, AZ (Cox Communications)

SUN CITY—See PHOENIX, AZ (Cox Communications)

SUN LAKES—See PHOENIX, AZ (Cox Communications)

▲ **SUN LAKES**—Western Broadband

SUNSITES—See WILLCOX, AZ (Cox Communications)

▲ **SUPERIOR**—RealStar Communications

SURPRISE—See PHOENIX, AZ (Cox Communications)

SWIFT TRAIL—See SAFFORD, AZ (Cable One)

TAYLOR—See SHOW LOW, AZ (Cable One)

TEMPE—See PHOENIX, AZ (Cox Communications)

THATCHER—See SAFFORD, AZ (Cable One)

TOLLESON—See PHOENIX, AZ (Cox Communications)

TOLTEC CITY—See ELOY, AZ (RealStar Communications)

TOPOCK—See GOLDEN SHORES, AZ (Rapid Cable)

▲ **TSAILE**—Formerly served by Frontier Communications. No longer in operation

▲ **TUBA CITY**—Indevideo Co. Inc.

TUCSON (PORTIONS)—See PIMA COUNTY, AZ (Comcast Cable)

TUCSON (UNINCORPORATED AREAS)—See PIMA COUNTY, AZ (Comcast Cable)

▲ **TUCSON ESTATES**—Comcast Cable. Now served by PIMA VALLEY, AZ [AZ0003]

TUCSON ESTATES—See PIMA COUNTY, AZ (Comcast Cable)

▲ **TUCSON**—Formerly served by Sprint Corp. No longer in operation

▲ **TUCSON**—Cox Communications

▲ **TUSAYAN**—Indevideo Co. Inc.

VERDE VILLAGE—See SEDONA, AZ (Suddenlink Communications)

WAGON WHEEL—See SHOW LOW, AZ (Cable One)

▲ **WELLTON**—Beamspeed LLC

WHEATFIELDS—See GLOBE-MIAMI, AZ (Cable One)

WHITE MOUNTAIN LAKE—See SHOW LOW, AZ (Cable One)

▲ **WICKENBURG**—Cox Communications. Now served by PHOENIX, AZ [AZ0001]

WICKENBURG—See PHOENIX, AZ (Cox Communications)

▲ **WILLCOX**—Cox Communications

▲ **WILLIAMS**—New Day Broadband

WINKELMAN—See DUDLEYVILLE, AZ (RealStar Communications)

▲ **WINSLOW**—Cable One. Now served by SHOW LOW, AZ [AZ0014]

WINSLOW—See SHOW LOW, AZ (Cable One)

WINTERHAVEN—See YUMA, CA (Time Warner Cable)

▲ **YARNELL**—RealStar Communications

YAVAPAI COUNTY (NORTHEASTERN PORTION)—See COTTONWOOD, AZ (Cable One)

YAVAPAI-APACHE-CLARKSDALE RESERVATION—See COTTONWOOD, AZ (Cable One)

YOUNGTOWN—See PHOENIX, AZ (Cox Communications)

YUMA COUNTY—See YUMA, AZ (Time Warner Cable)

YUMA PROVING GROUND—See YUMA, AZ (Time Warner Cable)

▲ **YUMA**—Time Warner Cable

ARKANSAS

ALBION—See PANGBURN, AR (Indco Cable TV)

ALEXANDER—See SHANNON HILLS, AR (Cobridge Communications)

ALMA—See FORT SMITH, AR (Cox Communications)

▲ **ALMYRA**—Formerly served by Cebridge Connections. No longer in operation

▲ **ALPENA (town)**—Madison County Cable. Now served by WESTERN GROVE, AR [AR0183]

ALPENA—See WESTERN GROVE, AR (Ritter Communications)

▲ **ALTHEIMER**—Almega Cable

ALTUS—See OZARK, AR (Suddenlink Communications)

▲ **AMITY**—Cablevision of Amity

ARBYRD—See MARKED TREE, MO (Ritter Communications)

▲ **ARKADELPHIA**—Suddenlink Communications

▲ **ARKANSAS CITY**—Cablevision of Arkansas City

ARKOLA—See FORT SMITH, AR (Cox Communications)

ARKOMA—See FORT SMITH, OK (Cox Communications)

▲ **ASH FLAT**—Crystal Broadband Networks

▲ **ASHDOWN**—NewWave Communications

▲ **ATKINS**—Suddenlink Communications

AUBREY—See LEE COUNTY (southern portion), AR (Alliance Communications)

▲ **AUGUSTA (town)**—Augusta Video Inc. Now served by SEARCY, AR [AR0017]

AUGUSTA—See SEARCY, AR (White County Cable TV)

AUSTIN—See CABOT, AR (Suddenlink Communications)

BALD KNOB—See SEARCY, AR (White County Cable TV)

BANKS—See HAMPTON, AR (SATCO Cable TV)

BARLING—See FORT SMITH, AR (Cox Communications)

BASSETT—See MARKED TREE, AR (Ritter Communications)

▲ **BATESVILLE**—Suddenlink Communications

BAUXITE—See SHANNON HILLS, AR (Cobridge Communications)

BAXTER COUNTY (PORTIONS)—See MOUNTAIN HOME, AR (Suddenlink Communications)

▲ **BAXTER COUNTY (unincorporated areas)**—Formerly served by Almega Cable. No longer in operation

BAY—See JONESBORO, AR (Suddenlink Communications)

▲ **BEARDEN**—Zoom Media

▲ **BEAVER LAKE**—Cox Communications. Now served by SPRINGDALE, AR [AR0220]

BEAVER LAKE—See SPRINGDALE, AR (Cox Communications)

BEAVER SHORES—See SPRINGDALE, AR (Cox Communications)

BEAVER—See BERRYVILLE, AR (Cox Communications)

BEAVERAMA—See SPRINGDALE, AR (Cox Communications)

▲ **BEEBE**—Cobridge Communications

BELLA VISTA—See SPRINGDALE, AR (Cox Communications)

BELLEFONTE—See HARRISON, AR (Cox Communications)

BELLEVILLE—See DANVILLE, AR (Suddenlink Communications)

▲ **BENTON COUNTY**—Cox Communications. Now served by SPRINGDALE, AR [AR0220]

BENTON COUNTY—See SPRINGDALE, AR (Cox Communications)

BENTON—See SHANNON HILLS, AR (Cobridge Communications)

BENTONVILLE—See SPRINGDALE, AR (Cox Communications)

BERGMAN—See HARRISON, AR (Cox Communications)

▲ **BERRYVILLE**—Cox Communications

BETHEL HEIGHTS TWP.—See SPRINGDALE, AR (Cox Communications)

▲ **BIGGERS**—Boycom Cablevision Inc.

▲ **BISCOE**—Formerly served by Cebridge Connections. No longer in operation

▲ **BISMARCK**—Cablevision of Bismarck

BLACK OAK—See MARKED TREE, AR (Ritter Communications)

▲ **BLACK ROCK**—Indco Cable TV

BLEVINS—See MCCASKILL, AR (Allegiance Communications)

BLOOMER—See FORT SMITH, AR (Cox Communications)

BLUE SPRINGS—See SPRINGDALE, AR (Cox Communications)

▲ **BLYTHEVILLE**—Ritter Communications. Now served by MARKED TREE, AR [AR0072]

BLYTHEVILLE—See MARKED TREE, AR (Ritter Communications)

BONANZA—See FORT SMITH, AR (Cox Communications)

▲ **BONO**—Ritter Communications. Now served by MARKED TREE, AR [AR0072]

BONO—See OAK GROVE HEIGHTS, AR (Fusion Media)

BONO—See MARKED TREE, AR (Ritter Communications)

BOONE COUNTY—See HARRISON, AR (Cox Communications)

▲ **BOONEVILLE HUMAN DEVELOPMENT CENTER**—Formerly served by Eagle Media. No longer in operation

▲ **BOONEVILLE**—Suddenlink Communications

▲ **BRADFORD**—Indco Cable TV

BRADLEY COUNTY—See WARREN, AR (Cablevision of Warren)

▲ **BRADLEY**—Formerly served by Cebridge Connections. No longer in operation

▲ **BRIARCLIFF**—Formerly served by Almega Cable. No longer in operation

▲ **BRINKLEY**—East Arkansas Video Inc.

BROOKLAND—See OAK GROVE HEIGHTS, AR (Fusion Media)

BROOKLAND—See MARKED TREE, AR (Ritter Communications)

BRYANT—See LITTLE ROCK, AR (Comcast Cable)

BUCKNER—See LEWISVILLE, AR (Alliance Communications)

BULL SHOALS—See MOUNTAIN HOME, AR (Suddenlink Communications)

▲ **CABOT**—Suddenlink Communications

CADDO VALLEY—See ARKADELPHIA, AR (Suddenlink Communications)

▲ **CALDWELL**—Indco Cable TV

▲ **CALICO ROCK**—Indco Cable TV

CALION—See SMACKOVER, AR (Zoom Media)

▲ **CAMDEN**—Cam-Tel Co.

CAMMACK VILLAGE—See LITTLE ROCK, AR (Comcast Cable)

CAMPBELL STATION—See NEWPORT, AR (Suddenlink Communications)

CARAWAY—See MARKED TREE, AR (Ritter Communications)

CARDWELL—See MARKED TREE, MO (Ritter Communications)

CARLISLE—See HAZEN, AR (Suddenlink Communications)

▲ **CARPENTER DAM**—Cablevision of Carpenter Dam

CARROLL COUNTY (PORTIONS)—See BERRYVILLE, AR (Cox Communications)

▲ **CARTHAGE**—Formerly served by Almega Cable. No longer in operation

▲ **CARTHAGE**—Formerly served by Almega Cable. No longer in operation

▲ **CASA**—Formerly served by Eagle Media. No longer in operation

CASH—See MARKED TREE, AR (Ritter Communications)

▲ **CAVE CITY**—Indco Cable TV

CAVE SPRINGS—See SPRINGDALE, AR (Cox Communications)

▲ **CEDARVILLE**—Cox Communications. Now served by SPRINGDALE, AR [AR0220]

CEDARVILLE—See SPRINGDALE, AR (Cox Communications)

CENTER POINT—See DIERKS, AR (Allegiance Communications)

CENTERTON—See SPRINGDALE, AR (Cox Communications)

CENTRAL CITY—See FORT SMITH, AR (Cox Communications)

CENTRAL—See FRIENDSHIP, AR (Community Communications Co.)

▲ **CHARLESTON**—Suddenlink Communications

CHEROKEE VILLAGE—See HARDY, AR (Cobridge Communications)

CHERRY VALLEY—See MARKED TREE, AR (Ritter Communications)

CHESTER—See FORT SMITH, AR (Cox Communications)

▲ **CHIDESTER**—Formerly served by Almega Cable. No longer in operation

▲ **CLARENDON**—Zoom Media

▲ **CLARKSVILLE**—Suddenlink Communications

CLAY COUNTY (PORTIONS)—See RECTOR, AR (NewWave Communications)

CLEBURNE COUNTY (PORTIONS)—See FAIRFIELD BAY, AR (Allegiance Communications)

▲ **CLINTON**—Clinton Cablevision Inc.

▲ **COAL HILL**—Suddenlink Communications

COLLEGE CITY—See WALNUT RIDGE, AR (Suddenlink Communications)

COLT—See CALDWELL, AR (Indco Cable TV)

COLUMBIA COUNTY—See MAGNOLIA, AR (Suddenlink Communications)

▲ **CONWAY (eastern portion)**—Alliance Communications. Now served by GREENBRIER, AR [AR0077]

CONWAY (EASTERN PORTION)—See GREENBRIER, AR (Alliance Communications)

CONWAY COUNTY (PORTIONS)—See MORRILTON, AR (Suddenlink Communications)

▲ **CONWAY**—Conway Corp. C.T.S.

▲ **CORNING**—Allegiance Communications

COTTER—See MOUNTAIN HOME, AR (Suddenlink Communications)

CRAIGHEAD COUNTY (NORTHWESTERN PORTION)—See MARKED TREE, AR (Ritter Communications)

CRAIGHEAD COUNTY (PORTIONS)—See OAK GROVE HEIGHTS, AR (Fusion Media)

CRAIGHEAD COUNTY (UNINCORPORATED AREAS)—See GREENE COUNTY (unincorporated areas), AR (Indco Cable TV)

CRAWFORD COUNTY (UNINCORPORATED AREAS)—See SPRINGDALE, AR (Cox Communications)

CRAWFORD COUNTY—See FORT SMITH, AR (Cox Communications)

▲ **CRAWFORDSVILLE (portions)**—Formerly served by Ritter Communications. No longer in operation

CRITTENDEN COUNTY (PORTIONS)—See HUGHES, AR (Suddenlink Communications)

CRITTENDEN COUNTY—See EARLE, AR (Comcast Cable)

▲ **CROSSETT**—Cable South Media

▲ **CURTIS**—Community Communications Co.

▲ **CUSHMAN**—Indco Cable TV

▲ **DAISY**—Allegiance Communications

▲ **DANVILLE**—Suddenlink Communications

DARDANELLE—See RUSSELLVILLE, AR (Suddenlink Communications)

DATTO—See BIGGERS, AR (Boycom Cablevision Inc.)

▲ **DE QUEEN**—Allegiance Communications

DE VALLS BLUFF—See HAZEN, AR (Suddenlink Communications)

▲ **DE WITT**—Suddenlink Communications

DEAN SPRINGS—See FORT SMITH, AR (Cox Communications)

DECATUR—See SILOAM SPRINGS, AR (Cox Communications)

▲ **DELIGHT**—Formerly served by Almega Cable. No longer in operation

DELL—See MARKED TREE, AR (Ritter Communications)

DERMOTT—See McGEHEE, AR (Allegiance Communications)

▲ **DES ARC**—Alliance Communications

DESHA COUNTY—See McGEHEE, AR (Allegiance Communications)

▲ **DIAMOND CITY**—Indco Cable TV

DIAMONDHEAD—See CARPENTER DAM, AR (Cablevision of Carpenter Dam)

DIAZ—See NEWPORT, AR (Suddenlink Communications)

▲ **DIERKS**—Allegiance Communications

DONALDSON—See FRIENDSHIP, AR (Community Communications Co.)

DORA—See FORT SMITH, AR (Cox Communications)

▲ **DOVER**—Suddenlink Communications

DRASCO—See TUMBLING SHOALS, AR (Indco Cable TV)

DREW COUNTY—See MONTICELLO, AR (Cablevision of Monticello)

▲ **DUMAS**—Allegiance Communications

DYER—See FORT SMITH, AR (Cox Communications)

DYESS—See MARKED TREE, AR (Ritter Communications)

▲ **EARLE**—Comcast Cable

▲ **EAST CAMDEN**—Cablevision of East Camden

EAST POCAHONTAS—See POCAHONTAS, AR (Suddenlink Communications)

EDEN ISLE—See HEBER SPRINGS, AR (Suddenlink Communications)

▲ **EL DORADO**—Suddenlink Communications

ELAINE—See LAKE VIEW, AR (Alliance Communications)

ELKINS—See SPRINGDALE, AR (Cox Communications)

ELLIOTT—See SMACKOVER, AR (Zoom Media)

ELM SPRINGS—See SPRINGDALE, AR (Cox Communications)

▲ **EMERSON**—Formerly served by Almega Cable. No longer in operation

▲ **EMMET**—Formerly served by Almega Cable. No longer in operation

▲ **ENGLAND**—Zoom Media

▲ **EUDORA**—Cablevision of Eudora

▲ **EUREKA SPRINGS**—Cox Communications. Now served by BERRYVILLE, AR [AR0221]

EUREKA SPRINGS—See BERRYVILLE, AR (Cox Communications)

▲ **EVENING SHADE**—Indco Cable TV

EVERTON—See WESTERN GROVE, AR (Ritter Communications)

▲ **EXCELSIOR**—Cox Communications. Now served by SPRINGDALE, AR [AR0220]

EXCELSIOR—See SPRINGDALE, AR (Cox Communications)

▲ **FAIRFIELD BAY**—Allegiance Communications

FARMINGTON—See SPRINGDALE, AR (Cox Communications)

FAULKNER COUNTY (PORTIONS)—See MAYFLOWER, AR (Alliance Communications)

FAULKNER COUNTY (PORTIONS)—See CABOT, AR (Suddenlink Communications)

FAULKNER COUNTY (SOUTHEASTERN PORTION)—See VILONIA, AR (Cobridge Communications)

▲ **FAYETTEVILLE**—Cox Communications. Now served by SPRINGDALE, AR [AR0220]

FAYETTEVILLE—See SPRINGDALE, AR (Cox Communications)

FIGURE FIVE—See FORT SMITH, AR (Cox Communications)

FISHER—See MARKED TREE, AR (Ritter Communications)

FLIPPIN—See MOUNTAIN HOME, AR (Suddenlink Communications)

▲ **FORDYCE**—Cable South Media

▲ **FORREST CITY**—East Arkansas Video Inc.

▲ **FORT SMITH**—Cox Communications

▲ **FOUKE**—Rapid Cable

▲ **FOUNTAIN HILL**—Formerly served by Almega Cable. No longer in operation

FRANKLIN COUNTY (WESTERN PORTION)—See FORT SMITH, AR (Cox Communications)

FRANKLIN—See HORSESHOE BEND, AR (Crystal Broadband Networks)

▲ **FRIENDSHIP**—Community Communications Co.

▲ **FULTON**—Allegiance Communications

▲ **GARLAND CITY**—Formerly served by Cebridge Connections. No longer in operation

GARLAND COUNTY—See HOT SPRINGS, AR (Resort TV Cable Co. Inc.)

GARLAND COUNTY—See HOT SPRINGS VILLAGE, AR (Suddenlink Communications)

GARNER—See HIGGINSON, AR (Rapid Cable)

GASSVILLE—See MOUNTAIN HOME, AR (Suddenlink Communications)

GENTRY—See SILOAM SPRINGS, AR (Cox Communications)

▲ **GILLETT**—Cablevision of Gillett

GILMORE—See MARKED TREE, AR (Ritter Communications)

GLENROSE—See SALINE COUNTY (unincorporated areas), AR (Community Cablevision)

▲ **GLENWOOD**—Cablevision of Glenwood

GOOD EARTH—See CAVE CITY, AR (Indco Cable TV)

GOSHEN—See SPRINGDALE, AR (Cox Communications)

▲ **GOSNELL**—Ritter Communications. Now served by MARKED TREE, AR [AR0072]

GOSNELL—See MARKED TREE, AR (Ritter Communications)

▲ **GOULD**—Cablevision of Gould

▲ **GRADY**—Formerly served by Cebridge Connections. No longer in operation

GRANT COUNTY (NORTHERN PORTION)—See SHERIDAN, AR (Zoom Media)

GRANT COUNTY (PORTIONS)—See WHITEHALL, AR (Suddenlink Communications)

GRAVETTE—See SPRINGDALE, AR (Cox Communications)

GREEN FOREST—See BERRYVILLE, AR (Cox Communications)

▲ **GREENBRIER**—Alliance Communications

GREENE COUNTY (PORTIONS)—See OAK GROVE HEIGHTS, AR (Fusion Media)

▲ **GREENE COUNTY (UNINCORPORATED AREAS)**—Indco Cable TV

GREENLAND—See SPRINGDALE, AR (Cox Communications)

GREENWAY—See RECTOR, AR (NewWave Communications)

▲ **GREENWOOD**—Formerly served by Eagle Media. No longer in operation

GREENWOOD—See FORT SMITH, AR (Cox Communications)

▲ **GREERS FERRY**—Formerly served by Alliance Communications. No longer in operation

GRIFFITHVILLE—See HIGGINSON, AR (Rapid Cable)

GRUBBS—See MARKED TREE, AR (Ritter Communications)

▲ **GUION**—Indco Cable TV

GUM SPRINGS—See CURTIS, AR (Community Communications Co.)

▲ **GUM SPRINGS**—Indco Cable TV

▲ **GURDON**—Suddenlink Communications

HACKETT—See FORT SMITH, AR (Cox Communications)

▲ **HAMBURG**—Zoom Media

▲ **HAMPTON**—SATCO Cable TV

HARDIN—See WHITEHALL, AR (Suddenlink Communications)

▲ **HARDY**—Cobridge Communications

HARMON—See SPRINGDALE, AR (Cox Communications)

▲ **HARMONY GROVE**—Formerly served by Almega Cable. No longer in operation

▲ **HARRELL**—Suddenlink Communications

▲ **HARRISBURG**—Ritter Communications. Now served by MARKED TREE, AR [AR0072]

HARRISBURG—See MARKED TREE, AR (Ritter Communications)

▲ **HARRISON**—Cox Communications

HARTFORD—See FORT SMITH, AR (Cox Communications)

HARTMAN—See COAL HILL, AR (Suddenlink Communications)

HASKELL—See SHANNON HILLS, AR (Cobridge Communications)

▲ **HATFIELD**—Formerly served by Allegiance Communications. No longer in operation

HAVANA—See DANVILLE, AR (Suddenlink Communications)

▲ **HAZEN**—Suddenlink Communications

▲ **HEBER SPRINGS**—Suddenlink Communications

▲ **HECTOR**—Suddenlink Communications

▲ **HELENA**—Suddenlink Communications

HEMPSTEAD COUNTY (PORTIONS)—See NASHVILLE, AR (Suddenlink Communications)

HENSLEY—See SHANNON HILLS, AR (Cobridge Communications)

▲ **HERMITAGE**—Formerly served by Almega Cable. No longer in operation

HICKORY RIDGE—See MARKED TREE, AR (Ritter Communications)

▲ **HIGGINSON**—Rapid Cable

HIGHLAND—See HARDY, AR (Cobridge Communications)

HOLIDAY ISLAND—See BERRYVILLE, AR (Cox Communications)

▲ **HOLLY GROVE**—Formerly served by Cebridge Connections. No longer in operation

▲ **HOOKER/LADD**—Community Communications Co.

▲ **HOPE**—Hope Community TV

▲ **HORSESHOE BEND**—Crystal Broadband Networks

HORSESHOE LAKE—See HUGHES, AR (Suddenlink Communications)

▲ **HOT SPRINGS VILLAGE**—Suddenlink Communications

▲ **HOT SPRINGS**—Resort TV Cable Co. Inc.

HOXIE—See WALNUT RIDGE, AR (Suddenlink Communications)

▲ **HUGHES**—Suddenlink Communications

▲ **HUMNOKE**—Formerly served by Cebridge Connections. No longer in operation

▲ **HUMPHREY**—Formerly served by Cebridge Connections. No longer in operation

HUNTINGTON—See FORT SMITH, AR (Cox Communications)

▲ **HUNTSVILLE**—Madison County Cable

▲ **HUTTIG**—Bayou Cable TV

IDA—See TUMBLING SHOALS, AR (Indco Cable TV)

IMBODEN—See BLACK ROCK, AR (Indco Cable TV)

INDEPENDENCE COUNTY (NORTHERN PORTION)—See CAVE CITY, AR (Indco Cable TV)

INDEPENDENCE COUNTY (PORTIONS)—See BATESVILLE, AR (Suddenlink Communications)

INDEPENDENCE COUNTY (UNINCORPORATED AREAS)—See PLEASANT PLAINS, AR (Indco Cable TV)

IZARD COUNTY—See HORSESHOE BEND, AR (Crystal Broadband Networks)

JACKSON COUNTY—See NEWPORT, AR (Suddenlink Communications)

JACKSONPORT—See NEWPORT, AR (Suddenlink Communications)

JACKSONVILLE—See LITTLE ROCK, AR (Comcast Cable)

▲ **JASPER**—Ritter Communications. Now served by WESTERN GROVE, AR [AR0183]

JASPER—See WESTERN GROVE, AR (Ritter Communications)

JEFFERSON COUNTY (PORTIONS)—See PINE BLUFF, AR (Pine Bluff Cable TV Co. Inc.)

JEFFERSON COUNTY (PORTIONS)—See WHITEHALL, AR (Suddenlink Communications)

JEFFERSON COUNTY (PORTIONS)—See PINEBERGEN, AR (Zoom Media LLC)

JOHNSON COUNTY (SOUTHWESTERN PORTION)—See COAL HILL, AR (Suddenlink Communications)

JOHNSON—See SPRINGDALE, AR (Cox Communications)

JOINER—See MARKED TREE, AR (Ritter Communications)

▲ **JONES MILL**—Cablevision of Jones Mill

JONESBORO—See OAK GROVE HEIGHTS, AR (Fusion Media)

▲ **JONESBORO**—Suddenlink Communications

JUDSONIA—See SEARCY, AR (White County Cable TV)

▲ **JUNCTION CITY**—Alliance Communications

JUNCTION CITY—See JUNCTION CITY, LA (Alliance Communications)

KEISER—See MARKED TREE, AR (Ritter Communications)

KENSETT—See SEARCY, AR (White County Cable TV)

KIBLER—See FORT SMITH, AR (Cox Communications)

KIRBY—See DAISY, AR (Allegiance Communications)

KNOB HILL—See SPRINGDALE, AR (Cox Communications)

▲ **KNOBEL**—Formerly served by Cebridge Connections. No longer in operation

▲ **KNOXVILLE**—Formerly served by Quality Entertainment Corp. No longer in operation

LADD—See HOOKER/LADD, AR (Community Communications Co.)

LAFE—See OAK GROVE HEIGHTS, AR (Fusion Media)

LAFE—See RECTOR, AR (NewWave Communications)

▲ **LAKE CITY**—Ritter Communications. Now served by MARKED TREE, AR [AR0072]

LAKE CITY—See MARKED TREE, AR (Ritter Communications)

▲ **LAKE ERLING**—Formerly served by Cebridge Connections. No longer in operation

LAKE FAIRCREST—See EL DORADO, AR (Suddenlink Communications)

LAKE POINSETT—See MARKED TREE, AR (Ritter Communications)

▲ **LAKE VIEW**—Alliance Communications

▲ **LAKE VILLAGE**—Allegiance Communications

LAKEVIEW—See MOUNTAIN HOME, AR (Suddenlink Communications)

LAMAR—See RUSSELLVILLE, AR (Suddenlink Communications)

▲ **LAVACA**—Cox Communications. Now served by FORT SMITH, AR [AR0003]

LAVACA—See FORT SMITH, AR (Cox Communications)

LAWRENCE COUNTY—See WALNUT RIDGE, AR (Suddenlink Communications)

LAWSON—See EL DORADO, AR (Suddenlink Communications)

LE FLORE COUNTY (UNINCORPORATED AREAS)—See FORT SMITH, OK (Cox Communications)

LEACHVILLE—See MARKED TREE, AR (Ritter Communications)

LEAD HILL—See DIAMOND CITY, AR (Indco Cable TV)

LEE COUNTY (PORTIONS)—See FORREST CITY, AR (East Arkansas Video Inc.)

▲ **LEE COUNTY (SOUTHERN PORTION)**—Alliance Communications

▲ **LEOLA**—Formerly served by Cebridge Connections. No longer in operation

LEPANTO—See MARKED TREE, AR (Ritter Communications)

▲ **LESLIE**—Ritter Communications

LETONA—See PANGBURN, AR (Indco Cable TV)

▲ **LEWISVILLE**—Alliance Communications

LEXA—See HELENA, AR (Suddenlink Communications)

LINCOLN COUNTY—See STAR CITY, AR (Cablevision of Star City)

LINCOLN—See SPRINGDALE, AR (Cox Communications)

LITTLE FLOCK—See SPRINGDALE, AR (Cox Communications)

LITTLE RED RIVER—See HEBER SPRINGS, AR (Suddenlink Communications)

LITTLE RIVER COUNTY (PORTIONS)—See ASHDOWN, AR (NewWave Communications)

LITTLE ROCK AFB—See CABOT, AR (Suddenlink Communications)

▲ **LITTLE ROCK**—Formerly served by Charter Communications. No longer in operation

▲ **LITTLE ROCK**—Comcast Cable

▲ **LOCKESBURG**—Formerly served by Lockesburg Cablevision. No longer in operation

▲ **LOCUST BAYOU**—Rapid Cable

▲ **LONDON**—Suddenlink Communications

LONOKE COUNTY (PORTIONS)—See CABOT, AR (Suddenlink Communications)

▲ **LONOKE**—Alliance Communications

LOUANN—See SMACKOVER, AR (Zoom Media)

LOWELL—See SPRINGDALE, AR (Cox Communications)

LUXORA—See MARKED TREE, AR (Ritter Communications)

▲ **LYNN**—Formerly served by Ritter Communications. No longer in operation

MACON—See CABOT, AR (Suddenlink Communications)

MADISON—See HUGHES, AR (Suddenlink Communications)

▲ **MAGAZINE**—Formerly served by Almega Cable. No longer in operation

▲ **MAGIC SPRINGS**—Cablevision of Magic Springs

MAGNESS—See NEWARK, AR (Indco Cable TV)

▲ **MAGNOLIA**—Suddenlink Communications

▲ **MALVERN**—Suddenlink Communications

MANDEVILLE—See FOUKE, AR (Rapid Cable)

▲ **MANILA**—Ritter Communications. Now served by MARKED TREE, AR [AR0072]

MANILA—See MARKED TREE, AR (Ritter Communications)

MANSFIELD—See FORT SMITH, AR (Cox Communications)

MARIANNA—See FORREST CITY, AR (East Arkansas Video Inc.)

MARION COUNTY (PORTIONS)—See MOUNTAIN HOME, AR (Suddenlink Communications)

MARION COUNTY—See YELLVILLE, AR (Indco Cable TV)

▲ **MARKED TREE**—Ritter Communications

MARMADUKE—See OAK GROVE HEIGHTS, AR (Fusion Media)

MARMADUKE—See RECTOR, AR (NewWave Communications)

▲ **MARSHALL**—Alliance Communications

▲ **MARVELL**—Suddenlink Communications

▲ **MAUMELLE**—Cobridge Communications

MAYFIELD—See SPRINGDALE, AR (Cox Communications)

▲ **MAYFLOWER**—Alliance Communications

▲ **MCALMONT**—Cobridge Communications

▲ **MCCASKILL**—Allegiance Communications

▲ **MCCRORY**—Allegiance Communications

▲ **McDOUGAL**—Formerly served by Almega Cable. No longer in operation

▲ **MCGEHEE**—Allegiance Communications

MCRAE—See HIGGINSON, AR (Rapid Cable)

▲ **MELBOURNE**—Indco Cable TV

▲ **MENA**—Allegiance Communications

MENIFEE—See PLUMERVILLE, AR (Alliance Communications)

▲ **MIDLAND**—Cox Communications. Now served by FORT SMITH, AR [AR0003]

▲ **MIDLAND**—Cox Communications. Now served by FORT SMITH, AR [AR0003]

MIDLAND—See FORT SMITH, AR (Cox Communications)

MIDWAY—See MOUNTAIN HOME, AR (Suddenlink Communications)

MILLER COUNTY (UNINCORPORATED AREAS)—See FOUKE, AR (Rapid Cable)

▲ **MINERAL SPRINGS**—Allegiance Communications

MISSISSIPPI COUNTY (PORTIONS)—See MARKED TREE, AR (Ritter Communications)

MITCHELLVILLE—See McGEHEE, AR (Allegiance Communications)

MONETTE—See MARKED TREE, AR (Ritter Communications)

MONTE NE—See SPRINGDALE, AR (Cox Communications)

MONTGOMERY COUNTY (UNINCORPORATED AREAS)—See MOUNT IDA, AR (Suddenlink Communications)

▲ **MONTICELLO**—Cablevision of Monticello

▲ **MONTROSE**—Dean Hill Cable

MOOREFIELD—See BATESVILLE, AR (Suddenlink Communications)

MORGAN—See MAUMELLE, AR (Cobridge Communications)

▲ **MORO**—Indco Cable TV

▲ **MORRILTON**—Suddenlink Communications

▲ **MOUNT IDA**—Suddenlink Communications

▲ **MOUNT PLEASANT**—Indco Cable TV

MOUNTAIN HARBOR RESORT—See MOUNT IDA, AR (Suddenlink Communications)

▲ **MOUNTAIN HOME**—Suddenlink Communications

MOUNTAIN PINE—See HOT SPRINGS, AR (Resort TV Cable Co. Inc.)

▲ **MOUNTAIN VIEW**—Indco Cable TV

MOUNTAINBURG—See FORT SMITH, AR (Cox Communications)

▲ **MULBERRY**—Cox Communications. Now served by FORT SMITH, AR [AR0003]

MULBERRY—See FORT SMITH, AR (Cox Communications)

MULDROW—See FORT SMITH, OK (Cox Communications)

▲ **MURFREESBORO**—Allegiance Communications

▲ **NASHVILLE**—Suddenlink Communications

▲ **NEWARK**—Indco Cable TV

NEWHOPE—See DAISY, AR (Allegiance Communications)

▲ **NEWPORT**—Suddenlink Communications

▲ **NORMAN**—Cablevision of Norman

NORPHLET—See SMACKOVER, AR (Zoom Media)

NORRISTOWN—See RUSSELLVILLE, AR (Suddenlink Communications)

NORTH CROSSETT—See CROSSETT, AR (Cable South Media)

NORTH LITTLE ROCK—See MAUMELLE, AR (Cobridge Communications)

NORTH LITTLE ROCK—See LITTLE ROCK, AR (Comcast Cable)

▲ **O'KEAN**—Formerly served by Cebridge Connections. No longer in operation

▲ **OAK GROVE HEIGHTS**—Fusion Media

OAK GROVE—See MAUMELLE, AR (Cobridge Communications)

▲ **OIL TROUGH**—Indco Cable TV

OLA—See PLAINVIEW, AR (Rapid Cable)

OLD UNION—See EL DORADO, AR (Suddenlink Communications)

OPPELO—See GREENBRIER, AR (Alliance Communications)

▲ **OSCEOLA**—Ritter Communications. Now served by MARKED TREE, AR [AR0072]

OSCEOLA—See MARKED TREE, AR (Ritter Communications)

OUACHITA COUNTY (PORTIONS)—See EAST CAMDEN, AR (Cablevision of East Camden)

OUACHITA COUNTY (PORTIONS)—See SMACKOVER, AR (Zoom Media)

▲ **OXFORD**—Formerly served by Almega Cable. No longer in operation

▲ **OZARK ACRES**—Formerly served by Cebridge Connections. No longer in operation

▲ **OZARK**—Suddenlink Communications

▲ **PALESTINE**—Formerly served by Almega Cable. No longer in operation

▲ **PANGBURN**—Indco Cable TV

PARAGOULD—See OAK GROVE HEIGHTS, AR (Fusion Media)

▲ **PARAGOULD**—Paragould City Light & Water Commission

▲ **PARIS**—Suddenlink Communications

PARKDALE—See WILMOT, AR (Dean Hill Cable)

PARKIN—See EARLE, AR (Comcast Cable)

PATTERSON—See McCRORY, AR (Allegiance Communications)

PEA RIDGE—See SPRINGDALE, AR (Cox Communications)

▲ **PEARCY**—Cablevision of Garland County

PERLA—See MALVERN, AR (Suddenlink Communications)

PERRY—See GREENBRIER, AR (Alliance Communications)

PERRYTOWN—See HOPE, AR (Hope Community TV)

▲ **PERRYVILLE**—Formerly served by Alliance Communications. No longer in operation

PFEIFFER—See CAVE CITY, AR (Indco Cable TV)

PHILLIPS COUNTY—See HELENA, AR (Suddenlink Communications)

PIGGOTT—See RECTOR, AR (NewWave Communications)

PIKE COUNTY (UNINCORPORATED AREAS)—See MURFREESBORO, AR (Allegiance Communications)

▲ **PINE BLUFF (southern portion)**—Formerly served by Almega Cable. No longer in operation

PINE BLUFF ARSENAL—See WHITEHALL, AR (Suddenlink Communications)

▲ **PINE BLUFF**—Pine Bluff Cable TV Co. Inc.

▲ **PINEBERGEN**—Zoom Media LLC

PINEVILLE—See CALICO ROCK, AR (Indco Cable TV)

▲ **PLAINVIEW**—Indco Cable TV

▲ **PLAINVIEW**—Rapid Cable

▲ **PLEASANT PLAINS**—Indco Cable TV

▲ **PLUMERVILLE**—Alliance Communications

▲ **POCAHONTAS**—Suddenlink Communications

POCOLA—See FORT SMITH, OK (Cox Communications)

POLLARD—See RECTOR, AR (NewWave Communications)

POPE COUNTY (PORTIONS)—See ATKINS, AR (Suddenlink Communications)

POPE COUNTY (PORTIONS)—See RUSSELLVILLE, AR (Suddenlink Communications)

POPE COUNTY (UNINCORPORATED AREAS)—See DOVER, AR (Suddenlink Communications)

POPLAR GROVE—See HELENA, AR (Suddenlink Communications)

PORTIA—See BLACK ROCK, AR (Indco Cable TV)

▲ **PORTLAND**—Dean Hill Cable

POTTSVILLE—See RUSSELLVILLE, AR (Suddenlink Communications)

POWHATAN—See BLACK ROCK, AR (Indco Cable TV)

POYEN—See SHERIDAN, AR (Zoom Media)

PRAIRIE COUNTY (PORTIONS)—See DES ARC, AR (Alliance Communications)

PRAIRIE COUNTY (UNINCORPORATED AREAS)—See HAZEN, AR (Suddenlink Communications)

PRAIRIE CREEK—See SPRINGDALE, AR (Cox Communications)

▲ **PRAIRIE GROVE**—Cox Communications. Now served by SPRINGDALE, AR [AR0220]

PRAIRIE GROVE—See SPRINGDALE, AR (Cox Communications)

PRATTSVILLE—See SHERIDAN, AR (Zoom Media)

PRESCOTT—See HOPE, AR (Hope Community TV)

PULASKI COUNTY (EASTERN PORTION)—See McALMONT, AR (Cobridge Communications)

PULASKI COUNTY (PORTIONS)—See LITTLE ROCK, AR (Comcast Cable)

PULASKI COUNTY (PORTIONS)—See CABOT, AR (Suddenlink Communications)

▲ **RATCLIFF**—Formerly served by Eagle Media. No longer in operation

▲ **RAVENDEN SPRINGS**—Formerly served by Cebridge Connections. No longer in operation

RAVENDEN—See BLACK ROCK, AR (Indco Cable TV)

▲ **RECTOR**—NewWave Communications

REDFIELD—See WHITEHALL, AR (Suddenlink Communications)

▲ **REED**—Cablevision of Tillar Reed

REYNO—See BIGGERS, AR (Boycom Cablevision Inc.)

▲ **RISON**—Cablevision of Rison

RIVERCLIFF—See SPRINGDALE, AR (Cox Communications)

ROCHELL—See SPRINGDALE, AR (Cox Communications)

ROCKPORT—See MALVERN, AR (Suddenlink Communications)

▲ **ROGERS**—Cox Communications. Now served by SPRINGDALE, AR [AR0220]

ROGERS—See SPRINGDALE, AR (Cox Communications)

ROLAND—See FORT SMITH, OK (Cox Communications)

RONDO—See LEE COUNTY (southern portion), AR (Alliance Communications)

▲ **ROYAL**—Cablevision of Royal

▲ **RUDY/HIGHWAY 71**—Cox Communications. Now served by FORT SMITH, AR [AR0003]

RUDY—See FORT SMITH, AR (Cox Communications)

▲ **RUSSELL**—Indco Cable TV

▲ **RUSSELLVILLE**—Suddenlink Communications

SALEM—See DAISY, AR (Allegiance Communications)

▲ **SALEM**—Salem Cable Vision

SALINE COUNTY (EASTERN PORTION)—See SHANNON HILLS, AR (Cobridge Communications)

▲ **SALINE COUNTY (UNINCORPORATED AREAS)**—Community Cablevision

SARATOGA—See FULTON, AR (Allegiance Communications)

▲ **SCRANTON**—Formerly served by Eagle Media. No longer in operation

▲ **SEARCY**—White County Cable TV

▲ **SEDGWICK**—Formerly served by Cebridge Connections. No longer in operation

SEQUOYAH COUNTY (SOUTHERN PORTION)—See FORT SMITH, OK (Cox Communications)

SEVIER COUNTY (PORTIONS)—See DIERKS, AR (Allegiance Communications)

SEVIER COUNTY—See DE QUEEN, AR (Allegiance Communications)

▲ **SHANNON HILLS**—Cobridge Communications

SHARP COUNTY (PORTIONS)—See HARDY, AR (Cobridge Communications)

▲ **SHERIDAN**—Zoom Media

SHERWOOD—See McALMONT, AR (Cobridge Communications)

SHERWOOD—See LITTLE ROCK, AR (Comcast Cable)

SHIRLEY—See FAIRFIELD BAY, AR (Allegiance Communications)

▲ **SIDNEY**—Indco Cable TV

▲ **SILOAM SPRINGS**—Cox Communications

▲ **SMACKOVER**—Zoom Media

▲ **SONORA**—Cox Communications. Now served by SPRINGDALE, AR [AR0220]

SONORA—See SPRINGDALE, AR (Cox Communications)

SOUTH BEND—See CABOT, AR (Suddenlink Communications)

SOUTH SIDE—See BATESVILLE, AR (Suddenlink Communications)

▲ **SPRINGDALE**—Cox Communications

ST. FRANCIS COUNTY—See CALDWELL, AR (Indco Cable TV)

ST. FRANCIS—See RECTOR, AR (NewWave Communications)

STAMPS—See LEWISVILLE, AR (Alliance Communications)

▲ **STAR CITY**—Cablevision of Star City

▲ **STEPHENS**—Zoom Media

▲ **STRONG**—Bayou Cable TV

▲ **STUTTGART**—Suddenlink Communications

▲ **SUBIACO**—Formerly served by Eagle Media. No longer in operation

SUCCESS—See BIGGERS, AR (Boycom Cablevision Inc.)

SUGARLOAF LAKE—See FORT SMITH, AR (Cox Communications)

SULPHUR ROCK—See BATESVILLE, AR (Suddenlink Communications)

SULPHUR SPRINGS—See PINEBERGEN, AR (Zoom Media LLC)

SUMMIT—See YELLVILLE, AR (Indco Cable TV)

SWIFTON—See MARKED TREE, AR (Ritter Communications)

▲ **TAYLOR**—Formerly served by Cebridge Connections. No longer in operation

▲ **THORNTON**—Formerly served by Almega Cable. No longer in operation

TILLAR—See REED, AR (Cablevision of Tillar Reed)

TOLETTE—See FULTON, AR (Allegiance Communications)

▲ **TONTITOWN**—Cox Communications. Now served by SPRINGDALE, AR [AR0220]

TONTITOWN—See SPRINGDALE, AR (Cox Communications)

▲ **TRASKWOOD**—Formerly served by Cebridge Connections. No longer in operation

▲ **TRUMANN**—Ritter Communications. Now served by MARKED TREE, AR [AR0072]

TRUMANN—See MARKED TREE, AR (Ritter Communications)

TUCKERMAN—See NEWPORT, AR (Suddenlink Communications)

TULL—See SHANNON HILLS, AR (Cobridge Communications)

▲**TUMBLING SHOALS**—Indco Cable TV

▲**TUPELO**—Indco Cable TV

▲**TURRELL**—Ritter Communications. Now served by MARKED TREE, AR [AR0072]

TURRELL—See MARKED TREE, AR (Ritter Communications)

TYRONZA—See MARKED TREE, AR (Ritter Communications)

UNION COUNTY (PORTIONS)—See SMACKOVER, AR (Zoom Media)

URBANA—See EL DORADO, AR (Suddenlink Communications)

VALLEY SPRINGS—See HARRISON, AR (Cox Communications)

VAN BUREN COUNTY—See CLINTON, AR (Clinton Cablevision Inc.)

▲**VAN BUREN**—Cox Communications. Now served by FORT SMITH, AR [AR0003]

VAN BUREN—See FORT SMITH, AR (Cox Communications)

VILLAGE ESTATES—See SPRINGDALE, AR (Cox Communications)

▲**VILONIA**—Cobridge Communications

▲**VIOLA**—Salem Cable Vision

WABBASEKA—See ALTHEIMER, AR (Almega Cable)

WALDO—See MAGNOLIA, AR (Suddenlink Communications)

▲**WALDRON**—Suddenlink Communications

▲**WALNUT RIDGE**—Suddenlink Communications

WARD—See CABOT, AR (Suddenlink Communications)

WAREAGLE COVE—See SPRINGDALE, AR (Cox Communications)

WAREAGLE—See SPRINGDALE, AR (Cox Communications)

▲**WARREN**—Cablevision of Warren

WASHINGTON COUNTY—See SPRINGDALE, AR (Cox Communications)

▲**WATSON**—Cablevision of Watson

WEAVERS CHAPEL—See CAVE CITY, AR (Indco Cable TV)

WEDINGTON—See SPRINGDALE, AR (Cox Communications)

WEINER—See MARKED TREE, AR (Ritter Communications)

WEST CROSSETT—See CROSSETT, AR (Cable South Media)

▲**WEST FORK**—Cox Communications. Now served by SPRINGDALE, AR [AR0220]

WEST FORK—See SPRINGDALE, AR (Cox Communications)

WEST HELENA—See HELENA, AR (Suddenlink Communications)

WEST POINT—See HIGGINSON, AR (Rapid Cable)

▲**WEST PULASKI**—Cobridge Communications

WEST SILOAM SPRINGS—See SILOAM SPRINGS, OK (Cox Communications)

▲**WESTERN GROVE**—Ritter Communications

▲**WHEATLEY**—Formerly served by Almega Cable. No longer in operation

WHITE COUNTY (PORTIONS)—See HIGGINSON, AR (Rapid Cable)

WHITEHALL (PORTIONS)—See PINE BLUFF, AR (Pine Bluff Cable TV Co. Inc.)

▲**WHITEHALL**—Suddenlink Communications

WIDENER—See HUGHES, AR (Suddenlink Communications)

▲**WILMAR**—Almega Cable

▲**WILMOT**—Dean Hill Cable

WILSON—See MARKED TREE, AR (Ritter Communications)

▲**WINSLOW**—Cox Communications. Now served by SPRINGDALE, AR [AR0220]

WINSLOW—See SPRINGDALE, AR (Cox Communications)

▲**WITCHERVILLE**—Formerly served by Eagle Media. No longer in operation

WITCHERVILLE—See FORT SMITH, AR (Cox Communications)

WOOSTER—See GREENBRIER, AR (Alliance Communications)

WRIGHTSVILLE—See SHANNON HILLS, AR (Cobridge Communications)

WYNNE—See FORREST CITY, AR (East Arkansas Video Inc.)

YELL COUNTY (EASTERN PORTION)—See PLAINVIEW, AR (Rapid Cable)

YELL COUNTY (EASTERN PORTION)—See DANVILLE, AR (Suddenlink Communications)

▲**YELLVILLE**—Indco Cable TV

YORKTOWN—See STAR CITY, AR (Cablevision of Star City)

CALIFORNIA

ACAMPO—See LODI, CA (Comcast Cable)

ACTON—See CHATSWORTH, CA (Time Warner Cable)

ADELANTO—See HESPERIA, CA (Charter Communications)

▲**ADOBE WELLS MOBILE HOME PARK**—Formerly served by Comcast Cable. No longer in operation

AGATE BAY—See NORTHSTAR, CA (Charter Communications)

AGOURA (PORTIONS)—See MALIBU, CA (Charter Communications)

▲**AGOURA HILLS**—Time Warner Cable. Now served by CHATSWORTH, CA [CA0013]

AGOURA HILLS—See MALIBU, CA (Charter Communications)

AGOURA HILLS—See CHATSWORTH, CA (Time Warner Cable)

AHWAHNEE—See OAKHURST, CA (Northland Cable Television)

ALABAMA HILLS—See LONE PINE, CA (Lone Pine TV Inc.)

ALAMEDA COUNTY (UNINCORPORATED AREAS)—See OAKLAND, CA (Comcast Cable)

ALAMEDA COUNTY—See CONCORD, CA (Comcast Cable)

▲**ALAMEDA**—Comcast Cable. Now served by OAKLAND, CA [CA0018]

▲**ALAMEDA**—Formerly served by Alameda Power & Telecom. Now served by OAKLAND, CA [CA0018]

ALAMEDA—See OAKLAND, CA (Comcast Cable)

ALBANY—See OAKLAND, CA (Comcast Cable)

ALBION—See UKIAH, CA (Comcast Cable)

▲**ALHAMBRA**—Charter Communications

ALISO VIEJO—See ORANGE COUNTY, CA (Cox Communications)

ALPINE MEADOWS—See TRUCKEE, CA (Suddenlink Communications)

ALTA LOMA—See ANAHEIM, CA (Time Warner Cable)

ALTA SIERRA ESTATES—See LAKE OF THE PINES, CA (Suddenlink Communications)

ALTA SIERRA—See LAKE OF THE PINES, CA (Suddenlink Communications)

ALTADENA—See ALHAMBRA, CA (Charter Communications)

▲**ALTURAS**—Charter Communications

AMADOR COUNTY (PORTIONS)—See SAN ANDREAS, CA (Comcast Cable)

AMADOR COUNTY—See PINE GROVE, CA (Volcano Vision)

AMERICAN CANYON—See NAPA/SONOMA, CA (Comcast Cable)

ANAHEIM HILLS—See ANAHEIM, CA (Time Warner Cable)

▲**ANAHEIM**—Time Warner Cable

ANDERSON—See REDDING, CA (Charter Communications)

ANDERSON—See PALO CEDRO, CA (New Day Broadband)

ANGELS CAMP—See SAN ANDREAS, CA (Comcast Cable)

ANGELUS OAKS—See FOREST FALLS, CA (Charter Communications)

▲**ANTELOPE**—SureWest Broadband. Formerly served by Sacramento, CA [CA0459]. This cable system has converted to IPTV

ANTIOCH—See CONCORD, CA (Comcast Cable)

APPLE VALLEY—See HESPERIA, CA (Charter Communications)

APTOS—See SANTA CRUZ, CA (Comcast Cable)

AQUA DULCE—See CHATSWORTH, CA (Time Warner Cable)

ARBUCKLE—See WILLIAMS, CA (Comcast Cable)

▲**ARCADIA**—Charter Communications

ARCADIA—See LOS ANGELES, CA (Time Warner Cable)

ARCATA—See EUREKA, CA (Suddenlink Communications)

▲**ARDEN PARK**—SureWest Broadband. Formerly served by Sacramento, CA [CA0459]. This cable system has converted to IPTV

ARGUS—See RIDGECREST, CA (Mediacom)

ARMONA—See FRESNO, CA (Comcast Cable)

ARNOLD—See SAN ANDREAS, CA (Comcast Cable)

AROMAS—See GILROY, CA (Charter Communications)

ARROYO GRANDE—See SAN LUIS OBISPO, CA (Charter Communications)

▲**ARTESIA**—Comcast Cable. No longer in operation

ARVIN—See TEHACHAPI, CA (Bright House Networks)

ATASCADERO—See SAN LUIS OBISPO, CA (Charter Communications)

ATHENS—See LOS ANGELES, CA (Time Warner Cable)

ATHERTON—See SAN JOSE, CA (Comcast Cable)

ATWATER—See MERCED, CA (Comcast Cable)

AUBURN LAKE TRAILS—See PLACERVILLE, CA (Comcast Cable)

▲**AUBURN**—Charter Communications. Now served by PLACER COUNTY (southwestern portion), CA [CA0131]

AUBURN—See PLACER COUNTY (southwestern portion), CA (Wave Broadband)

▲**AVALON/CATALINA ISLAND**—Catalina Cable TV Co.

▲**AVENAL**—Bright House Networks

AVERY—See SAN ANDREAS, CA (Comcast Cable)

AVILA BEACH—See SAN LUIS OBISPO, CA (Charter Communications)

▲ **AZUSA**—Charter Communications

▲ **BAKERSFIELD**—Suddenlink Communications. Now served by BAKERSFIELD, CA [CA0025]

▲ **BAKERSFIELD**—Bright House Networks

BALDWIN HILLS—See LOS ANGELES, CA (Time Warner Cable)

BALDWIN PARK—See LOS ANGELES, CA (Time Warner Cable)

BALLARD—See SANTA MARIA, CA (Comcast Cable)

▲ **BANNING**—Time Warner Cable

▲ **BARSTOW**—Time Warner Cable

BASS LAKE—See OAKHURST, CA (Northland Cable Television)

BAY POINT—See CONCORD, CA (Comcast Cable)

BEALE AFB—See YUBA CITY, CA (Comcast Cable)

BEAR MOUNTAIN—See PALO CEDRO, CA (New Day Broadband)

▲ **BEAR VALLEY**—Formerly served by New Day Broadband. No longer in operation

BEAUMONT—See ANAHEIM, CA (Time Warner Cable)

BEAUMONT—See BANNING, CA (Time Warner Cable)

▲ **BELL**—Formerly served by Comcast Cable. No longer in operation

BELLA VISTA—See PALO CEDRO, CA (New Day Broadband)

BELMONT—See SAN FRANCISCO, CA (Comcast Cable)

BELVEDERE—See NAPA/SONOMA, CA (Comcast Cable)

BEN LOMOND—See SANTA CRUZ, CA (Comcast Cable)

BENBOW—See GARBERVILLE, CA (Wave Broadband)

▲ **BENICIA**—Comcast Cable. Now served by NAPA/SONOMA, CA [CA0038]

BENICIA—See NAPA/SONOMA, CA (Comcast Cable)

BERKELEY—See OAKLAND, CA (Comcast Cable)

BERMUDA DUNES—See PALM DESERT, CA (Time Warner Cable)

BETHEL ISLAND—See CONCORD, CA (Comcast Cable)

BEVERLY HILLS—See CHATSWORTH, CA (Time Warner Cable)

BIG BEAR CITY—See BIG BEAR LAKE, CA (Charter Communications)

▲ **BIG BEAR LAKE**—Charter Communications

BIG BEAR—See HESPERIA, CA (Charter Communications)

BIG OAK FLAT—See GROVELAND, CA (SNC Cable)

BIG PINE—See BISHOP, CA (Suddenlink Communications)

BIG TREES—See SAN ANDREAS, CA (Comcast Cable)

BIGGS—See CHICO, CA (Comcast Cable)

▲ **BISHOP**—Suddenlink Communications

BLACK POINT—See NAPA/SONOMA, CA (Comcast Cable)

BLOOMINGTON—See ANAHEIM, CA (Time Warner Cable)

BLUE JAY—See LAKE ARROWHEAD, CA (Charter Communications)

BLUE LAKE—See EUREKA, CA (Suddenlink Communications)

▲ **BLYTHE**—Suddenlink Communications

BODFISH—See KERNVILLE, CA (Mediacom)

▲ **BOMBAY BEACH**—Cable USA

BONNY DOON—See SANTA CRUZ, CA (Comcast Cable)

BONSALL—See SAN DIEGO, CA (Cox Communications)

▲ **BORON**—Charter Communications

▲ **BORREGO SPRINGS**—Cable USA

BOULDER CREEK—See SANTA CRUZ, CA (Comcast Cable)

▲ **BOX CANYON**—Charter Communications

BOYLE HEIGHTS—See LOS ANGELES, CA (Time Warner Cable)

BRADBURY—See LOS ANGELES, CA (Time Warner Cable)

BRAWLEY—See EL CENTRO, CA (Time Warner Cable)

▲ **BREA**—Formerly served by Adelphia Communications. Now served by ANAHEIM, CA [CA0033]

BREA—See ANAHEIM, CA (Time Warner Cable)

BRENTWOOD—See CONCORD, CA (Comcast Cable)

BRENTWOOD—See LOS ANGELES, CA (Time Warner Cable)

▲ **BRIDGEPORT**—Satview Broadband

BRISBANE—See SAN FRANCISCO, CA (Comcast Cable)

BROCKWAY—See NORTHSTAR, CA (Charter Communications)

BROOKDALE—See SANTA CRUZ, CA (Comcast Cable)

BROOKTRAILS—See UKIAH, CA (Comcast Cable)

BUCK HORN—See PINE GROVE, CA (Volcano Vision)

BUELLTON—See SANTA MARIA, CA (Comcast Cable)

BUENA PARK—See ANAHEIM, CA (Time Warner Cable)

BUENA VISTA—See IONE, CA (Volcano Vision)

BURBANK—See GLENDALE, CA (Charter Communications)

▲ **BURLINGAME**—Comcast Cable. Now served by SAN FRANCISCO, CA [CA0003]

BURLINGAME—See SAN FRANCISCO (southern portion), CA (Astound Broadband)

BURLINGAME—See SAN FRANCISCO, CA (Comcast Cable)

▲ **BURNEY**—Windjammer Cable

BUTTE COUNTY—See CHICO, CA (Comcast Cable)

BUTTONWILLOW—See BAKERSFIELD, CA (Bright House Networks)

BYRON—See CONCORD, CA (Comcast Cable)

▲ **CABAZON**—Formerly served by TV Max. No longer in operation

CALABASAS (UNINCORPORATED AREAS)—See MALIBU, CA (Charter Communications)

CALABASAS PARK—See CHATSWORTH, CA (Time Warner Cable)

▲ **CALABASAS**—Time Warner Cable. Now served by CHATSWORTH, CA [CA0013]

CALABASAS—See MALIBU, CA (Charter Communications)

CALABASAS—See CHATSWORTH, CA (Time Warner Cable)

CALAVERAS COUNTY—See SAN ANDREAS, CA (Comcast Cable)

CALEXICO—See EL CENTRO, CA (Time Warner Cable)

▲ **CALIFORNIA CITY**—Charter Communications

▲ **CALIFORNIA HOT SPRINGS**—Charter Communications

CALIMESA—See ANAHEIM, CA (Time Warner Cable)

▲ **CALIPATRIA**—Cable USA

CALISTOGA—See NAPA/SONOMA, CA (Comcast Cable)

CALPELLA—See UKIAH, CA (Comcast Cable)

▲ **CAMARILLO**—Time Warner Cable. Now served by CHATSWORTH, CA [CA0013]

CAMARILLO—See CHATSWORTH, CA (Time Warner Cable)

CAMBRIA—See SAN LUIS OBISPO, CA (Charter Communications)

CAMERON PARK—See PLACERVILLE, CA (Comcast Cable)

CAMINO—See PLACERVILLE, CA (Comcast Cable)

CAMP MEEKER—See NAPA/SONOMA, CA (Comcast Cable)

CAMP NELSON—See PORTERVILLE, CA (Charter Communications)

CAMP PENDLETON—See SAN DIEGO, CA (Cox Communications)

CAMPBELL—See SAN JOSE, CA (Comcast Cable)

CANOGA PARK—See CHATSWORTH, CA (Time Warner Cable)

▲ **CANYON COUNTRY**—Comcast Cable. Now served by CHATSWORTH, CA [CA0013]

CANYON COUNTRY—See CHATSWORTH, CA (Time Warner Cable)

CANYON LAKE—See ANAHEIM, CA (Time Warner Cable)

▲ **CAPE COD MOBILE HOME PARK**—Formerly served by Comcast Cable. No longer in operation

CAPE COD VILLAGE—See SAN JOSE, CA (Comcast Cable)

CAPITOLA—See WATSONVILLE, CA (Charter Communications)

CARDIFF-BY-THE-SEA—See SAN DIEGO, CA (Cox Communications)

▲ **CARLSBAD**—Time Warner Cable

CARMEL HIGHLANDS—See GILROY, CA (Charter Communications)

CARMEL VALLEY—See MONTEREY, CA (Comcast Cable)

CARMEL-BY-THE-SEA—See MONTEREY, CA (Comcast Cable)

▲ **CARMICHAEL**—SureWest Broadband. Formerly served by Sacramento, CA [CA0459]. This cable system has converted to IPTV

CARNELIAN BAY—See NORTHSTAR, CA (Charter Communications)

CARPINTERIA—See SANTA BARBARA, CA (Cox Communications)

▲ **CARSON**—Comcast Cable. Now served by LOS ANGELES, CA [CA0009]

▲ **CARSON**—Astound Broadband

CARSON—See LOS ANGELES, CA (Time Warner Cable)

▲ **CASA DE AMIGOS MOBILE HOME PARK**—Formerly served by Comcast Cable. No longer in operation

CASITAS SPRINGS—See VENTURA, CA (Charter Communications)

CASPAR—See UKIAH, CA (Comcast Cable)

CASTAIC—See CHATSWORTH, CA (Time Warner Cable)

CASTLE AFB—See MERCED, CA (Comcast Cable)

CASTRO VALLEY—See CONCORD, CA (Comcast Cable)

CASTROVILLE—See GILROY, CA (Charter Communications)

CATALINA ISLAND—See AVALON/CATALINA ISLAND, CA (Catalina Cable TV Co.)

CATHEDRAL CITY—See PALM DESERT, CA (Time Warner Cable)

CAYUCOS—See SAN LUIS OBISPO, CA (Charter Communications)

CAZADERO—See NAPA/SONOMA, CA (Comcast Cable)

CBC NAVAL BASE—See CHATSWORTH, CA (Time Warner Cable)

CEDAR FLAT—See NORTHSTAR, CA (Charter Communications)

CEDAR VALLEY—See OAKHURST, CA (Northland Cable Television)

CEDARPINES PARK—See LAKE ARROWHEAD, CA (Charter Communications)

▲**CEDARVILLE**—Formerly served by Almega Cable. No longer in operation

▲**CENTRAL ORANGE COUNTY**—Time Warner Cable. Now served by ANAHEIM, CA [CA0033]

CERES—See TURLOCK, CA (Charter Communications)

▲**CERRITOS**—Charter Communications

▲**CHALFANT VALLEY**—Formerly served by Satview Broadband. No longer in operation

CHARTER OAK—See LOS ANGELES, CA (Time Warner Cable)

▲**CHATSWORTH**—Time Warner Cable

CHERRY VALLEY (PORTIONS)—See BANNING, CA (Time Warner Cable)

CHESTER—See LAKE ALMANOR, CA (CalNeva Broadband)

▲**CHICO**—Comcast Cable

CHINA LAKE NAVAL WEAPONS CENTER—See RIDGECREST, CA (Mediacom)

CHINO HILLS—See ANAHEIM, CA (Time Warner Cable)

▲**CHINO**—Now served by ANAHEIM, CA [CA0033]

CHINO—See ANAHEIM, CA (Time Warner Cable)

▲**CHOWCHILLA**—Comcast Cable

CHRISTIAN VALLEY (UNINCORPORATED AREAS)—See PLACER COUNTY (southwestern portion), CA (Wave Broadband)

CHRISTIAN VALLEY—See LAKE OF THE PINES, CA (Suddenlink Communications)

CHUALAR—See SOLEDAD, CA (Charter Communications)

CHULA VISTA—See SAN DIEGO, CA (Cox Communications)

▲**CHULA VISTA**—NexHorizon Communications

CITRUS HEIGHTS—See SACRAMENTO, CA (Comcast Cable)

▲**CITRUS HEIGHTS**—SureWest Broadband. Formerly served by Sacramento, CA [CA0459]. This cable system has converted to IPTV

CITRUS—See AZUSA, CA (Charter Communications)

CITY OF COMMERCE—See ALHAMBRA, CA (Charter Communications)

CITY OF INDUSTRY—See LOS ANGELES, CA (Time Warner Cable)

▲**CLAREMONT**—Comcast Cable. Now served by LOS ANGELES, CA [CA0009]

CLAREMONT—See LOS ANGELES, CA (Time Warner Cable)

CLAYTON—See CONCORD, CA (Comcast Cable)

CLEAR CREEK—See LAKE ALMANOR, CA (CalNeva Broadband)

▲**CLEARLAKE OAKS**—Mediacom

CLEARLAKE PARK—See CLEARLAKE OAKS, CA (Mediacom)

CLEARLAKE—See CLEARLAKE OAKS, CA (Mediacom)

CLOVERDALE—See NAPA/SONOMA, CA (Comcast Cable)

CLOVIS—See FRESNO, CA (Comcast Cable)

CLYDE—See CONCORD, CA (Comcast Cable)

COACHELLA—See PALM DESERT, CA (Time Warner Cable)

▲**COALINGA**—Comcast Cable

▲**COARSEGOLD**—Northland Cable Television

COBB—See CLEARLAKE OAKS, CA (Mediacom)

COLD SPRINGS—See PINECREST, CA (SNC Cable)

▲**COLEVILLE**—Satview Broadband

COLFAX—See PLACER COUNTY (southwestern portion), CA (Wave Broadband)

COLMA—See SAN FRANCISCO, CA (Comcast Cable)

▲**COLTON**—Now served by ANAHEIM, CA [CA0033]

COLTON—See ANAHEIM, CA (Time Warner Cable)

COLUMBIA—See TWAIN HARTE, CA (Comcast Cable)

COLUSA—See CHICO, CA (Comcast Cable)

COMMERCE—See ALHAMBRA, CA (Charter Communications)

▲**COMPTON**—Time Warner Cable. Now served by LOS ANGELES, CA [CA0009]

COMPTON—See LOS ANGELES, CA (Time Warner Cable)

▲**CONCORD**—Comcast Cable. Now served by CONCORD (formerly Walnut Creek), CA [CA0101]

▲**CONCORD**—Astound Broadband

▲**CONCORD**—Comcast Cable

CONTRA COSTA COUNTY (PORTIONS)—See OAKLAND, CA (Comcast Cable)

CONTRA COSTA COUNTY (UNINCORPORATED AREAS)—See CONCORD, CA (Astound Broadband)

CONTRA COSTA COUNTY—See CONCORD, CA (Comcast Cable)

COOL—See PLACERVILLE, CA (Comcast Cable)

▲**COPPER COVE COPPEROPOLIS**—Formerly served by Mountain View Cable. No longer in operation

CORCORAN—See FRESNO, CA (Comcast Cable)

CORNING—See CHICO, CA (Comcast Cable)

CORONA DEL MAR—See ANAHEIM, CA (Time Warner Cable)

▲**CORONA**—Time Warner Cable. Now served by ANAHEIM, CA [CA0033]

CORONA—See ANAHEIM, CA (Time Warner Cable)

▲**CORONADO**—Time Warner Cable. Now served by SAN DIEGO, CA [CA0007]

CORONADO—See SAN DIEGO, CA (Time Warner Cable)

CORRALITOS—See WATSONVILLE, CA (Charter Communications)

CORTE MADERA—See NAPA/SONOMA, CA (Comcast Cable)

▲**COSTA MESA**—Time Warner Cable. Now served by ANAHEIM, CA [CA0033]

COSTA MESA—See ANAHEIM, CA (Time Warner Cable)

COTATI—See NAPA/SONOMA, CA (Comcast Cable)

COTTONWOOD—See REDDING, CA (Charter Communications)

COTTONWOOD—See PALO CEDRO, CA (New Day Broadband)

COUNTRY CLUB ESTATES—See SAN LUIS OBISPO, CA (Charter Communications)

▲**COVINA**—Comcast Cable. Now served by LOS ANGELES, CA [CA0009]

COVINA—See ALHAMBRA, CA (Charter Communications)

COVINA—See LOS ANGELES, CA (Time Warner Cable)

CRAGVIEW—See MOUNT SHASTA, CA (Northland Cable Television)

▲**CRESCENT CITY**—Charter Communications

▲**CRESCENT MILLS**—Wave Broadband

CREST—See SAN DIEGO, CA (Cox Communications)

CRESTLINE—See HESPERIA, CA (Charter Communications)

CRESTLINE—See LAKE ARROWHEAD, CA (Charter Communications)

CROCKETT—See OAKLAND, CA (Comcast Cable)

CROW'S LANDING—See NEWMAN, CA (Comcast Cable)

▲**CROWLEY LAKE**—Satview Broadband

CUCAMONGA—See ANAHEIM, CA (Time Warner Cable)

CULVER CITY—See LOS ANGELES, CA (Time Warner Cable)

▲**CUPERTINO**—Matrix Cablevision Inc. Now served by SAN JOSE, CA [CA0004]

CUPERTINO—See SAN JOSE, CA (Comcast Cable)

CUTLER—See PORTERVILLE, CA (Charter Communications)

▲**CYPRESS**—Time Warner Cable. Now served by ANAHEIM, CA [CA0033]

CYPRESS—See ANAHEIM, CA (Time Warner Cable)

DAGGETT—See BARSTOW, CA (Time Warner Cable)

DALY CITY—See SAN FRANCISCO (southern portion), CA (Astound Broadband)

DALY CITY—See SAN FRANCISCO, CA (Comcast Cable)

DANA POINT—See ORANGE COUNTY, CA (Cox Communications)

DANVILLE—See CONCORD, CA (Comcast Cable)

DAVENPORT—See SANTA CRUZ, CA (Comcast Cable)

▲**DAVIS**—Comcast Cable. Now served by SACRAMENTO, CA [CA0002]

DAVIS—See SACRAMENTO, CA (Comcast Cable)

DEL MAR—See CARLSBAD, CA (Time Warner Cable)

DEL MAR—See SAN DIEGO, CA (Time Warner Cable)

DEL MONTE FOREST—See MONTEREY, CA (Comcast Cable)

DEL NORTE COUNTY—See KLAMATH, CA (Almega Cable)

DEL NORTE COUNTY—See CRESCENT CITY, CA (Charter Communications)

▲**DEL PASO HEIGHTS (PORTIONS)**—SureWest Broadband. Formerly served by Sacramento, CA [CA0459]. This cable system has converted to IPTV

DEL REY OAKS—See MONTEREY, CA (Comcast Cable)

DEL RIO—See TURLOCK, CA (Charter Communications)

DELANO—See BAKERSFIELD, CA (Bright House Networks)

DELHI—See TURLOCK, CA (Charter Communications)

DELLEKER—See PORTOLA, CA (Wave Broadband)

DENAIR—See TURLOCK, CA (Charter Communications)

▲ **DESERT CENTER**—Formerly served by American Pacific Co. No longer in operation

▲ **DESERT HOT SPRINGS**—Time Warner Cable. Now served by PALM DESERT, CA [CA0036]

DESERT HOT SPRINGS—See PALM DESERT, CA (Time Warner Cable)

DESERT SHORES—See SALTON SEA BEACH, CA (Cable USA)

DEVORE—See SAN BERNARDINO, CA (Charter Communications)

▲ **DIAMOND BAR**—Time Warner Cable. Now served by LOS ANGELES, CA [CA0009]

DIAMOND BAR—See LOS ANGELES, CA (Time Warner Cable)

DIAMOND SPRINGS—See PLACERVILLE, CA (Comcast Cable)

DILLON BEACH—See POINT REYES STATION, CA (Horizon Cable TV Inc.)

DINUBA—See FRESNO, CA (Comcast Cable)

DISCOVERY BAY—See CONCORD, CA (Comcast Cable)

DIXON—See WEST SACRAMENTO, CA (Wave Broadband)

DONNER LAKE—See TRUCKEE, CA (Suddenlink Communications)

DONNER SUMMIT—See TRUCKEE, CA (Suddenlink Communications)

▲ **DORRIS**—Almega Cable

DOS PALOS—See FRESNO, CA (Comcast Cable)

DOUGLAS COUNTY—See SOUTH LAKE TAHOE, NV (Charter Communications)

DOUGLAS FLAT—See SAN ANDREAS, CA (Comcast Cable)

▲ **DOWNEY**—Comcast Cable. No longer in operation

▲ **DOWNIEVILLE**—Formerly served by Downieville TV Corp. No longer in operation

DUARTE—See AZUSA, CA (Charter Communications)

DUBLIN—See CONCORD, CA (Comcast Cable)

DUCOR—See PORTERVILLE, CA (Charter Communications)

DUNSMUIR—See MOUNT SHASTA, CA (Northland Cable Television)

DURHAM—See CHICO, CA (Comcast Cable)

DYRE MOUNTAIN—See LAKE ALMANOR, CA (CalNeva Broadband)

▲ **EAGLE ROCK**—Time Warner Cable. Now served by LOS ANGELES, CA [CA0009]

EAGLE ROCK—See LOS ANGELES, CA (Time Warner Cable)

▲ **EARLIMART**—Charter Communications. Now served by PORTERVILLE, CA [CA0152]

EARLIMART—See PORTERVILLE, CA (Charter Communications)

EAST BLYTHE—See BLYTHE, CA (Suddenlink Communications)

EAST COMPTON—See LOS ANGELES, CA (Time Warner Cable)

▲ **EAST LOS ANGELES**—Time Warner Cable. Now served by LOS ANGELES, CA [CA0009]

EAST LOS ANGELES—See LOS ANGELES, CA (Time Warner Cable)

EAST PALO ALTO—See SAN JOSE, CA (Comcast Cable)

▲ **EAST SAN FERNANDO VALLEY**—Time Warner Cable. Now served by LOS ANGELES, CA [CA0009]

EAST SAN FERNANDO VALLEY—See LOS ANGELES, CA (Time Warner Cable)

EAST SHORE—See LAKE ALMANOR, CA (CalNeva Broadband)

EDWARDS AFB—See CHATSWORTH, CA (Time Warner Cable)

EHRENBERG—See BLYTHE, AZ (Suddenlink Communications)

EL CAJON—See SAN DIEGO, CA (Cox Communications)

EL CENTRO NAF—See EL CENTRO, CA (Time Warner Cable)

▲ **EL CENTRO**—Time Warner Cable

EL CERRITO—See OAKLAND, CA (Comcast Cable)

EL DORADO COUNTY (PORTIONS)—See MEYERS, CA (Charter Communications)

EL DORADO COUNTY (PORTIONS)—See PLACERVILLE, CA (Comcast Cable)

EL DORADO HILLS—See PLACERVILLE, CA (Comcast Cable)

EL GRANADA—See SAN FRANCISCO, CA (Comcast Cable)

EL MACERO—See SACRAMENTO, CA (Comcast Cable)

▲ **EL MONTE**—Now served by LOS ANGELES, CA [CA0009]

EL MONTE—See LOS ANGELES, CA (Time Warner Cable)

EL RIO—See CHATSWORTH, CA (Time Warner Cable)

EL SEGUNDO—See LOS ANGELES, CA (Time Warner Cable)

EL SOBRANTE—See OAKLAND, CA (Comcast Cable)

ELIZABETH LAKE—See CHATSWORTH, CA (Time Warner Cable)

ELK GROVE—See SACRAMENTO, CA (Comcast Cable)

▲ **ELK GROVE**—SureWest Broadband. Formerly served by Sacramento, CA [CA0459]. This cable system has converted to IPTV

EMERYVILLE—See OAKLAND, CA (Comcast Cable)

EMPIRE—See TURLOCK, CA (Charter Communications)

ENCINITAS (PORTIONS)—See CARLSBAD, CA (Time Warner Cable)

ENCINITAS—See SAN DIEGO, CA (Cox Communications)

ENCINO—See CHATSWORTH, CA (Time Warner Cable)

ESCALON—See TURLOCK, CA (Charter Communications)

ESCONDIDO—See SAN DIEGO, CA (Cox Communications)

ETIWANDA—See ANAHEIM, CA (Time Warner Cable)

▲ **ETNA**—Formerly served by Siskiyou Cablevision Inc. No longer in operation

▲ **EUREKA**—Suddenlink Communications

EXETER—See PORTERVILLE, CA (Charter Communications)

▲ **FAIR OAKS (PORTIONS)**—SureWest Broadband. Formerly served by Sacramento, CA [CA0459]. This cable system has converted to IPTV

FAIRFAX—See NAPA/SONOMA, CA (Comcast Cable)

▲ **FAIRFIELD**—Comcast Cable. Now served by NAPA/SONOMA, CA [CA0038]

FAIRFIELD—See NAPA/SONOMA, CA (Comcast Cable)

▲ **FALL RIVER MILLS**—Almega Cable

FALLBROOK—See CARLSBAD, CA (Time Warner Cable)

FARMERSVILLE—See PORTERVILLE, CA (Charter Communications)

FELTON—See SANTA CRUZ, CA (Comcast Cable)

FERNDALE—See EUREKA, CA (Suddenlink Communications)

FIELDBROOK—See EUREKA, CA (Suddenlink Communications)

FILLMORE—See CHATSWORTH, CA (Time Warner Cable)

FINER LIVING—See REDDING, CA (Charter Communications)

FINLEY—See CLEARLAKE OAKS, CA (Mediacom)

FIREBAUGH—See FRESNO, CA (Comcast Cable)

▲ **FISH CAMP**—Formerly served by Northland Cable Television. No longer in operation

FLORENCE—See LOS ANGELES, CA (Time Warner Cable)

FOLSOM—See SACRAMENTO, CA (Comcast Cable)

FONTANA—See ANAHEIM, CA (Time Warner Cable)

FORD CITY—See TEHACHAPI, CA (Bright House Networks)

▲ **FOREST FALLS**—Charter Communications

FOREST KNOLLS—See NAPA/SONOMA, CA (Comcast Cable)

▲ **FORESTHILL**—Suddenlink Communications

FORESTVILLE—See NAPA/SONOMA, CA (Comcast Cable)

FORT BRAGG—See UKIAH, CA (Comcast Cable)

▲ **FORT IRWIN**—Formerly served by Total TV of Fort Irwin Inc. No longer in operation

▲ **FORT ORD**—Suddenlink Communications

FORTUNA—See EUREKA, CA (Suddenlink Communications)

▲ **FOSTER CITY**—Comcast Cable. Now served by SAN FRANCISCO, CA [CA0003]

FOSTER CITY—See SAN FRANCISCO, CA (Comcast Cable)

FOUNTAIN VALLEY—See ANAHEIM, CA (Time Warner Cable)

FOWLER—See FRESNO, CA (Comcast Cable)

▲ **FRANCISCAN MOBILE HOME PARK**—Comcast Cable

▲ **FRAZIER PARK**—CalNeva Broadband

FREEDOM—See WATSONVILLE, CA (Charter Communications)

▲ **FREMONT**—Comcast Cable. Now served by OAKLAND, CA [CA0018]

FREMONT—See OAKLAND, CA (Comcast Cable)

FRENCH CAMP—See STOCKTON, CA (Comcast Cable)

FRESNO COUNTY—See FRESNO, CA (Comcast Cable)

▲ **FRESNO**—Formerly served by Sprint Corp. No longer in operation

▲ **FRESNO**—Comcast Cable

FULLERTON—See ANAHEIM, CA (Time Warner Cable)

FULTON—See NAPA/SONOMA, CA (Comcast Cable)

GALT—See SACRAMENTO, CA (Comcast Cable)

▲ **GARBERVILLE**—Wave Broadband

GARDEN GROVE—See ANAHEIM, CA (Time Warner Cable)

GARDENA—See CARSON, CA (Astound Broadband)

GARDENA—See LOS ANGELES, CA (Time Warner Cable)

GASQUET—See CRESCENT CITY, CA (Charter Communications)

GEORGETOWN—See PLACERVILLE, CA (Comcast Cable)

▲**GEORGIAN MANOR MOBILE HOME PARK**—Formerly served by Comcast Cable. No longer in operation

GERBER—See TEHAMA, CA (New Day Broadband)

GEYSERVILLE—See NAPA/SONOMA, CA (Comcast Cable)

▲**GILROY**—Charter Communications

GLENBROOK—See SOUTH LAKE TAHOE, NV (Charter Communications)

▲**GLENDALE**—Charter Communications

▲**GLENDORA**—Time Warner Cable. Now served by LOS ANGELES, CA [CA0009]

GLENDORA—See LOS ANGELES, CA (Time Warner Cable)

GLENHAVEN—See CLEARLAKE OAKS, CA (Mediacom)

GLENSHIRE—See TRUCKEE, CA (Suddenlink Communications)

▲**GLENWOOD**—Formerly served by Comcast Cable. No longer in operation

GOLDEN SHORES—See NEEDLES, AZ (CalNeva Broadband)

GOLETA—See SANTA BARBARA, CA (Cox Communications)

GONZALES—See SOLEDAD, CA (Charter Communications)

GRAEAGLE—See PORTOLA, CA (Wave Broadband)

GRANADA HILLS—See CHATSWORTH, CA (Time Warner Cable)

GRAND TERRACE—See ANAHEIM, CA (Time Warner Cable)

GRANGEVILLE—See FRESNO, CA (Comcast Cable)

GRANITE BAY—See PLACER COUNTY (southwestern portion), CA (Wave Broadband)

▲**GRASS VALLEY**—Comcast Cable

GREATER WILLOWBANK—See SACRAMENTO, CA (Comcast Cable)

GREEN BRAE—See NAPA/SONOMA, CA (Comcast Cable)

GREEN VALLEY LAKE—See LAKE ARROWHEAD, CA (Charter Communications)

GREEN VALLEY—See CHATSWORTH, CA (Time Warner Cable)

▲**GREENFIELD**—Charter Communications

GREENVILLE—See CRESCENT MILLS, CA (Wave Broadband)

GRENADA—See YREKA, CA (Northland Cable Television)

GRIDLEY—See CHICO, CA (Comcast Cable)

▲**GROVELAND**—SNC Cable

GROVER BEACH—See SAN LUIS OBISPO, CA (Charter Communications)

▲**GUADALUPE**—Charter Communications. Now served by SAN LUIS OBISPO, CA [CA0045]

GUADALUPE—See SAN LUIS OBISPO, CA (Charter Communications)

GUALALA—See THE SEA RANCH, CA (Central Valley Cable)

GUERNEVILLE—See NAPA/SONOMA, CA (Comcast Cable)

GUSTINE—See NEWMAN, CA (Comcast Cable)

▲**HACIENDA HEIGHTS**—Time Warner Cable. Now served by LOS ANGELES, CA [CA0009]

▲**HACIENDA HEIGHTS**—Time Warner Cable. Now served by LOS ANGELES, CA [CA0009]

HACIENDA HEIGHTS—See LOS ANGELES, CA (Time Warner Cable)

▲**HALF MOON BAY**—Comcast Cable. Now served by SAN FRANCISCO, CA [CA0003]

HALF MOON BAY—See SAN FRANCISCO, CA (Comcast Cable)

HAMILTON BRANCH—See LAKE ALMANOR, CA (CalNeva Broadband)

HAMILTON CITY—See CHICO, CA (Comcast Cable)

HANFORD—See FRESNO, CA (Comcast Cable)

▲**HAPPY CAMP**—Formerly served by Almega Cable. No longer in operation

HARBOR CITY—See LOS ANGELES, CA (Time Warner Cable)

HARDWICK—See FRESNO, CA (Comcast Cable)

HATHAWAY PINES—See SAN ANDREAS, CA (Comcast Cable)

HAWAIIAN GARDENS—See LOS ANGELES, CA (Time Warner Cable)

HAWTHORNE—See LOS ANGELES, CA (Time Warner Cable)

▲**HAYFORK**—New Day Broadband

▲**HAYWARD**—Comcast Cable. Now served by OAKLAND, CA [CA0018]

HAYWARD—See OAKLAND, CA (Comcast Cable)

HEALDSBURG—See NAPA/SONOMA, CA (Comcast Cable)

HEBER—See EL CENTRO, CA (Time Warner Cable)

▲**HEMET**—Time Warner Cable. Now served by ANAHEIM, CA [CA0033]

HEMET—See ANAHEIM, CA (Time Warner Cable)

HERCULES—See OAKLAND, CA (Comcast Cable)

HERITAGE RANCH—See SAN LUIS OBISPO, CA (Charter Communications)

▲**HERLONG**—Formerly served by Almega Cable. No longer in operation

▲**HERMOSA BEACH**—Time Warner Cable. Now served by LOS ANGELES, CA [CA0009]

HERMOSA BEACH—See LOS ANGELES, CA (Time Warner Cable)

▲**HESPERIA**—Charter Communications

HICKMAN—See TURLOCK, CA (Charter Communications)

HIDDEN HILLS—See MALIBU, CA (Charter Communications)

HIDDEN VALLEY LAKE—See CLEARLAKE OAKS, CA (Mediacom)

HIGHLAND—See ANAHEIM, CA (Time Warner Cable)

HILLSBOROUGH—See SAN FRANCISCO, CA (Comcast Cable)

HILMAR—See TURLOCK, CA (Charter Communications)

HOLLISTER—See GILROY, CA (Charter Communications)

HOLLYWOOD—See LOS ANGELES, CA (Time Warner Cable)

HOLTVILLE—See EL CENTRO, CA (Time Warner Cable)

HOMELAND—See ANAHEIM, CA (Time Warner Cable)

HUGHSON—See TURLOCK, CA (Charter Communications)

HUMBOLDT COUNTY—See EUREKA, CA (Suddenlink Communications)

HUNTERS VALLEY—See KLAMATH, CA (Almega Cable)

HUNTINGTON BEACH—See ANAHEIM, CA (Time Warner Cable)

HUNTINGTON PARK—See ALHAMBRA, CA (Charter Communications)

▲**HURON**—Comcast Cable

IDYLLWILD—See ANAHEIM, CA (Time Warner Cable)

IMPERIAL BEACH—See SAN DIEGO, CA (Cox Communications)

IMPERIAL—See EL CENTRO, CA (Time Warner Cable)

INCLINE VILLAGE—See NORTHSTAR, NV (Charter Communications)

INDEPENDENCE—See BISHOP, CA (Suddenlink Communications)

INDIAN WELLS VALLEY—See RIDGECREST, CA (Mediacom)

INDIAN WELLS—See PALM DESERT, CA (Time Warner Cable)

INDIO—See PALM DESERT, CA (Time Warner Cable)

INGLEWOOD—See LOS ANGELES, CA (Time Warner Cable)

INVERNESS—See POINT REYES STATION, CA (Horizon Cable TV Inc.)

INYO COUNTY—See BISHOP, CA (Suddenlink Communications)

INYOKERN—See RIDGECREST, CA (Mediacom)

▲**IONE**—Volcano Vision

IRVINE—See ORANGE COUNTY, CA (Cox Communications)

IRWINDALE—See AZUSA, CA (Charter Communications)

ISLA VISTA—See SANTA BARBARA, CA (Cox Communications)

ISLETON—See SACRAMENTO, CA (Comcast Cable)

IVANHOE—See PORTERVILLE, CA (Charter Communications)

▲**JACK RANCH/POSEY**—Charter Communications

JAMESTOWN—See TWAIN HARTE, CA (Comcast Cable)

JAMUL—See SAN DIEGO, CA (Cox Communications)

JANESVILLE—See SUSANVILLE, CA (Windjammer Cable)

JOHNSON PARK—See BURNEY, CA (Windjammer Cable)

JOHNSTONVILLE—See SUSANVILLE, CA (Windjammer Cable)

JONES VALLEY—See PALO CEDRO, CA (New Day Broadband)

JOSHUA TREE—See YUCCA VALLEY, CA (Time Warner Cable)

▲**JULIAN**—Cable USA

▲**JUNE LAKE**—Suddenlink Communications

JURUPA HILLS—See RIVERSIDE, CA (Charter Communications)

KAGEL CANYON—See CHATSWORTH, CA (Time Warner Cable)

KELSEYVILLE—See CLEARLAKE OAKS, CA (Mediacom)

KENSINGTON—See OAKLAND, CA (Comcast Cable)

KENTFIELD—See NAPA/SONOMA, CA (Comcast Cable)

KENWOOD—See NAPA/SONOMA, CA (Comcast Cable)

KERMAN—See FRESNO, CA (Comcast Cable)

KERN COUNTY (UNINCORPORATED AREAS)—See RIDGECREST, CA (Mediacom)

KERN COUNTY—See BAKERSFIELD, CA (Bright House Networks)

KERN COUNTY—See TEHACHAPI, CA (Bright House Networks)

KERN RIVER VALLEY—See KERNVILLE, CA (Mediacom)

▲**KERNVILLE**—Mediacom

KEYES—See TURLOCK, CA (Charter Communications)

▲**KING CITY**—Charter Communications

KINGS BEACH—See NORTHSTAR, CA (Charter Communications)

KINGS COUNTY—See FRESNO, CA (Comcast Cable)

KINGSBURG—See FRESNO, CA (Comcast Cable)

KIRKWOOD—See PINE GROVE, CA (Volcano Vision)

KLAMATH GLEN—See KLAMATH, CA (Almega Cable)

▲**KLAMATH**—Almega Cable

▲**KNIGHTSEN**—Comcast Cable. Now served by CONCORD, CA [CA0101]

KNIGHTSEN—See CONCORD, CA (Comcast Cable)

KONOCTI BAY—See CLEARLAKE OAKS, CA (Mediacom)

▲**KYBURZ**—Comcast Cable. Now served by PLACERVILLE, CA [CA0108]

KYBURZ—See PLACERVILLE, CA (Comcast Cable)

LA CANADA-FLINTRIDGE—See ALHAMBRA, CA (Charter Communications)

LA CANADA—See GLENDALE, CA (Charter Communications)

LA CONCHITA—See VENTURA, CA (Charter Communications)

LA CRESCENTA—See GLENDALE, CA (Charter Communications)

LA HABRA HEIGHTS—See ANAHEIM, CA (Time Warner Cable)

LA HABRA—See ANAHEIM, CA (Time Warner Cable)

LA HONDA—See SAN FRANCISCO, CA (Comcast Cable)

LA JOLLA—See SAN DIEGO, CA (Time Warner Cable)

LA MESA—See SAN DIEGO, CA (Cox Communications)

LA PALMA—See ANAHEIM, CA (Time Warner Cable)

LA PUENTE—See LOS ANGELES, CA (Time Warner Cable)

LA QUINTA—See PALM DESERT, CA (Time Warner Cable)

LA SELVA BEACH—See SANTA CRUZ, CA (Comcast Cable)

LA VERNE—See LOS ANGELES, CA (Time Warner Cable)

LADERA HEIGHTS—See LOS ANGELES, CA (Time Warner Cable)

LADERA RANCH—See ORANGE COUNTY, CA (Cox Communications)

LADERA—See SAN JOSE, CA (Comcast Cable)

LAFAYETTE—See CONCORD, CA (Comcast Cable)

LAGUNA BEACH—See ORANGE COUNTY, CA (Cox Communications)

LAGUNA HILLS—See ORANGE COUNTY, CA (Cox Communications)

LAGUNA NIGUEL—See ORANGE COUNTY, CA (Cox Communications)

LAGUNITAS—See NAPA/SONOMA, CA (Comcast Cable)

▲**LAKE ALMANOR**—CalNeva Broadband

▲**LAKE ARROWHEAD**—Charter Communications

LAKE ARROWHEAD—See HESPERIA, CA (Charter Communications)

LAKE COUNTY—See CLEARLAKE OAKS, CA (Mediacom)

▲**LAKE ELSINORE**—Comcast Cable. Now served by ANAHEIM, CA [CA0033]

LAKE ELSINORE—See ANAHEIM, CA (Time Warner Cable)

LAKE FOREST—See ORANGE COUNTY, CA (Cox Communications)

▲**LAKE HUGHES**—Formerly served by Lake Hughes Cable TV Service. No longer in operation

LAKE ISABELLA—See KERNVILLE, CA (Mediacom)

▲**LAKE OF THE PINES**—Suddenlink Communications

LAKE TAHOE—See TRUCKEE, CA (Suddenlink Communications)

▲**LAKE WILDWOOD**—Comcast Cable. Now served by GRASS VALLEY, CA [CA0164]

LAKE WILDWOOD—See GRASS VALLEY, CA (Comcast Cable)

LAKEPORT—See CLEARLAKE OAKS, CA (Mediacom)

LAKEVIEW—See ANAHEIM, CA (Time Warner Cable)

▲**LAKEWOOD**—Formerly served by Time Warner Cable. No longer in operation

LAMONT—See TEHACHAPI, CA (Bright House Networks)

LANCASTER—See CHATSWORTH, CA (Time Warner Cable)

LARKSPUR—See NAPA/SONOMA, CA (Comcast Cable)

LAS LOMAS—See GILROY, CA (Charter Communications)

LASSEN COUNTY—See SUSANVILLE, CA (Windjammer Cable)

LATHROP—See STOCKTON, CA (Comcast Cable)

LATON—See FRESNO, CA (Comcast Cable)

LAWNDALE—See LOS ANGELES, CA (Time Warner Cable)

▲**LE GRAND**—Comcast Cable

LEAVITT LAKE—See SUSANVILLE, CA (Windjammer Cable)

LEBEC—See FRAZIER PARK, CA (Cal-Neva Broadband)

▲**LEE VINING**—Formerly served by Satview Broadband. No longer in operation

LEMON GROVE—See SAN DIEGO, CA (Cox Communications)

LEMOORE NAVAL AIR STATION—See FRESNO, CA (Comcast Cable)

LEMOORE—See FRESNO, CA (Comcast Cable)

LENNOX—See LOS ANGELES, CA (Time Warner Cable)

LEONA VALLEY—See CHATSWORTH, CA (Time Warner Cable)

LEUCADIA—See SAN DIEGO, CA (Cox Communications)

▲**LEWISTON**—New Day Broadband

▲**LINCOLN**—SureWest Broadband. Formerly served by Sacramento, CA [CA0459]. This cable system has converted to IPTV

LINCOLN—See PLACER COUNTY (southwestern portion), CA (Wave Broadband)

LINDA—See YUBA CITY, CA (Comcast Cable)

LINDEN—See STOCKTON, CA (Comcast Cable)

LINDSAY—See PORTERVILLE, CA (Charter Communications)

LITTLERIVER—See UKIAH, CA (Comcast Cable)

LITTLEROCK—See CHATSWORTH, CA (Time Warner Cable)

LIVE OAK—See YUBA CITY, CA (Comcast Cable)

LIVERMORE—See CONCORD, CA (Comcast Cable)

LIVINGSTON—See TURLOCK, CA (Charter Communications)

LOCKEFORD—See LODI, CA (Comcast Cable)

▲**LODI**—Comcast Cable

LOMA LINDA—See ANAHEIM, CA (Time Warner Cable)

LOMITA—See LOS ANGELES, CA (Time Warner Cable)

LOMPICO—See SANTA CRUZ, CA (Comcast Cable)

LOMPOC—See SANTA MARIA, CA (Comcast Cable)

▲**LONE PINE**—Lone Pine TV Inc.

▲**LONG BARN**—SNC Cable

▲**LONG BEACH NAVAL BASE**—Formerly served by Americable International. No longer in operation

▲**LONG BEACH**—Charter Communications

LOOMIS—See PLACER COUNTY (southwestern portion), CA (Wave Broadband)

LOS ALAMITOS—See ANAHEIM, CA (Time Warner Cable)

▲**LOS ALAMOS**—Charter Communications

▲**LOS ALTOS HILLS**—Comcast Cable. Now served by SAN FRANCISCO, CA [CA0003]

LOS ALTOS HILLS—See SAN FRANCISCO, CA (Comcast Cable)

LOS ALTOS—See SAN JOSE, CA (Comcast Cable)

▲**LOS ANGELES (south central portion)**—Comcast Cable. Now served by LOS ANGELES, CA [CA0009]

LOS ANGELES (UNINCORPORATED AREAS)—See MALIBU, CA (Charter Communications)

▲**LOS ANGELES (western portion)**—Comcast Cable. Now served by LOS ANGELES, CA [CA0009]

LOS ANGELES COUNTY (PORTIONS)—See BOX CANYON, CA (Charter Communications)

LOS ANGELES COUNTY (PORTIONS)—See MALIBU, CA (Charter Communications)

LOS ANGELES COUNTY (PORTIONS)—See ORANGE COUNTY, CA (Cox Communications)

LOS ANGELES COUNTY (PORTIONS)—See CHATSWORTH, CA (Time Warner Cable)

LOS ANGELES COUNTY (PORTIONS)—See LOS ANGELES, CA (Time Warner Cable)

LOS ANGELES COUNTY—See ALHAMBRA, CA (Charter Communications)

▲**LOS ANGELES**—Comcast Cable. Now served by CHATSWORTH, CA [CA0013]

▲**LOS ANGELES**—Time Warner Cable

LOS BANOS—See NEWMAN, CA (Comcast Cable)

▲**LOS GATOS (unincorporated areas)**—Matrix Cablevision Inc. Now served by SAN JOSE, CA [CA0004]

▲**LOS GATOS**—Comcast Cable. Now served by SAN JOSE, CA [CA0004]

LOS GATOS—See SAN JOSE, CA (Comcast Cable)

LOS MOLINOS—See TEHAMA, CA (New Day Broadband)

LOS OLIVOS—See SANTA MARIA, CA (Comcast Cable)

LOS OSOS—See SAN LUIS OBISPO, CA (Charter Communications)

LOS TRANCOS WOODS—See SAN FRANCISCO, CA (Comcast Cable)

LOST HILLS—See MALIBU, CA (Charter Communications)

LOWER LAKE—See CLEARLAKE OAKS, CA (Mediacom)

LOYALTON—See PORTOLA, CA (Wave Broadband)

LUCERNE—See CLEARLAKE OAKS, CA (Mediacom)

▲**LUSHMEADOWS**—Northland Cable Television

LYTLE CREEK—See ANAHEIM, CA (Time Warner Cable)

MADERA COUNTY (SOUTHERN PORTION)—See FRESNO, CA (Comcast Cable)

MADERA COUNTY (SOUTHWESTERN PORTION)—See CHOWCHILLA, CA (Comcast Cable)

MADERA—See FRESNO, CA (Comcast Cable)

▲**MALIBU**—Charter Communications

▲**MAMMOTH LAKES**—Suddenlink Communications

MANHATTAN BEACH—See LOS ANGELES, CA (Time Warner Cable)

▲**MANTECA**—Comcast Cable. Now served by STOCKTON, CA [CA0028]

MANTECA—See STOCKTON, CA (Comcast Cable)

MARCH AFB—See ANAHEIM, CA (Time Warner Cable)

MARICOPA—See TEHACHAPI, CA (Bright House Networks)

MARIN CITY—See NAPA/SONOMA, CA (Comcast Cable)

MARIN COUNTY (SOUTHEASTERN PORTION)—See NAPA/SONOMA, CA (Comcast Cable)

MARINA DEL RAY—See LOS ANGELES, CA (Time Warner Cable)

MARINA—See MONTEREY, CA (Comcast Cable)

MARIPOSA COUNTY (PORTIONS)—See LUSHMEADOWS, CA (Northland Cable Television)

▲**MARIPOSA**—Northland Cable Television

▲**MARSH CREEK MOTOR HOME PARK**—Formerly served by Comcast Cable. No longer in operation

MARTINEZ—See CONCORD, CA (Comcast Cable)

MARYSVILLE—See YUBA CITY, CA (Comcast Cable)

MAXWELL—See WILLIAMS, CA (Comcast Cable)

MCARTHUR—See FALL RIVER MILLS, CA (Almega Cable)

MCCLELLAN PARK—See SACRAMENTO, CA (Comcast Cable)

▲**MCCLELLAN PARK**—SureWest Broadband. Formerly served by Sacramento, CA [CA0459]. This cable system has converted to IPTV

MCCLOUD—See MOUNT SHASTA, CA (Northland Cable Television)

MCFARLAND—See BAKERSFIELD, CA (Bright House Networks)

▲**MEADOW VISTA**—Formerly served by Cebridge Connections. Now served by LAKE OF THE PINES, CA [CA0202]

MEADOW VISTA—See LAKE OF THE PINES, CA (Suddenlink Communications)

MEADOWVIEW—See SACRAMENTO, CA (Comcast Cable)

▲**MECCA**—Cable USA

MEEKS BAY-TAHOMA AREA—See TRUCKEE, CA (Suddenlink Communications)

MENDOCINO COUNTY—See UKIAH, CA (Comcast Cable)

MENDOCINO—See UKIAH, CA (Comcast Cable)

MENDOTA—See FRESNO, CA (Comcast Cable)

MENIFEE—See ANAHEIM, CA (Time Warner Cable)

▲**MENLO PARK**—Matrix Cablevision Inc. Now served by SAN JOSE, CA [CA0004]

MENLO PARK—See SAN JOSE, CA (Comcast Cable)

MENTONE—See ANAHEIM, CA (Time Warner Cable)

▲**MERCED**—Formerly served by Sprint Corp. No longer in operation

▲**MERCED**—Comcast Cable

▲**MEYERS**—Charter Communications

MI-WUK VILLAGE—See TWAIN HARTE, CA (Comcast Cable)

▲**MIDPINES**—Formerly served by Timber TV. No longer in operation

MIDWAY CITY—See ANAHEIM, CA (Time Warner Cable)

MILL CREEK PARK—See FOREST FALLS, CA (Charter Communications)

MILL VALLEY—See NAPA/SONOMA, CA (Comcast Cable)

MILLBRAE—See SAN FRANCISCO, CA (Comcast Cable)

MILLVILLE—See PALO CEDRO, CA (New Day Broadband)

▲**MILPITAS**—Comcast Cable. Now served by SAN JOSE, CA [CA0004]

MILPITAS—See SAN JOSE, CA (Comcast Cable)

MIRA LOMA—See RIVERSIDE, CA (Charter Communications)

MIRAMAR—See SAN FRANCISCO, CA (Comcast Cable)

▲**MISSION BAY MOBILE HOME PARK**—Formerly served by Comcast Cable. No longer in operation

MISSION HILLS (PORTIONS)—See CHATSWORTH, CA (Time Warner Cable)

MISSION HILLS—See SANTA MARIA, CA (Comcast Cable)

MISSION HILLS—See LOS ANGELES, CA (Time Warner Cable)

MISSION VIEJO—See ORANGE COUNTY, CA (Cox Communications)

▲**MODESTO & OAKDALE**—Comcast Cable

MODOC COUNTY (PORTIONS)—See ALTURAS, CA (Charter Communications)

▲**MOFFETT FIELD NAVAL AIRSTATION**—Formerly served by Americable International-Moffett Inc. No longer in operation

MOHAVE VALLEY—See NEEDLES, CA (CalNeva Broadband)

▲**MOJAVE**—Charter Communications

MOKELUMNE HILL—See SAN ANDREAS, CA (Comcast Cable)

MONO VISTA—See TWAIN HARTE, CA (Comcast Cable)

MONROVIA (SOUTHERN PORTION)—See ALHAMBRA, CA (Charter Communications)

MONROVIA—See ARCADIA, CA (Charter Communications)

MONROVIA—See LOS ANGELES, CA (Time Warner Cable)

MONTAGUE—See YREKA, CA (Northland Cable Television)

MONTARA—See SAN FRANCISCO, CA (Comcast Cable)

MONTCLAIR—See ANAHEIM, CA (Time Warner Cable)

MONTE SERENO—See SAN JOSE, CA (Comcast Cable)

MONTEBELLO—See ALHAMBRA, CA (Charter Communications)

MONTECITO—See SANTA BARBARA, CA (Cox Communications)

MONTEREY COUNTY (PORTIONS)—See GREENFIELD, CA (Charter Communications)

MONTEREY COUNTY (PORTIONS)—See KING CITY, CA (Charter Communications)

MONTEREY COUNTY (PORTIONS)—See SOLEDAD, CA (Charter Communications)

MONTEREY COUNTY (PORTIONS)—See MONTEREY, CA (Comcast Cable)

MONTEREY PARK—See ALHAMBRA, CA (Charter Communications)

▲**MONTEREY**—Formerly served by Sprint Corp. No longer in operation

▲**MONTEREY**—Comcast Cable

MONTROSE—See GLENDALE, CA (Charter Communications)

MOORPARK—See CHATSWORTH, CA (Time Warner Cable)

MORAGA—See CONCORD, CA (Comcast Cable)

MORENO VALLEY—See ANAHEIM, CA (Time Warner Cable)

▲**MORGAN HILL**—Charter Communications. Now served by GILROY, CA [CA0425]

MORGAN HILL—See GILROY, CA (Charter Communications)

MORONGO VALLEY—See YUCCA VALLEY, CA (Time Warner Cable)

MORRO BAY—See SAN LUIS OBISPO, CA (Charter Communications)

MOSS BEACH—See SAN FRANCISCO, CA (Comcast Cable)

MOSS LANDING—See GILROY, CA (Charter Communications)

MOUNT HERMON—See SANTA CRUZ, CA (Comcast Cable)

MOUNT RALSTON—See PLACERVILLE, CA (Comcast Cable)

▲**MOUNT SHASTA**—Northland Cable Television

MOUNTAIN GATE—See PALO CEDRO, CA (New Day Broadband)

▲**MOUNTAIN MEADOWS**—Formerly served by Entertainment Express. No longer in operation

MOUNTAIN MESA—See KERNVILLE, CA (Mediacom)

▲**MOUNTAIN VIEW**—Comcast Cable. Now served by SAN JOSE, CA [CA0004]

MOUNTAIN VIEW—See SAN JOSE, CA (Comcast Cable)

MURPHYS—See SAN ANDREAS, CA (Comcast Cable)

MURRIETA HOT SPRINGS—See ANAHEIM, CA (Time Warner Cable)

MURRIETA—See ANAHEIM, CA (Time Warner Cable)

MUSCOY—See ANAHEIM, CA (Time Warner Cable)

NAPA COUNTY—See NAPA/SONOMA, CA (Comcast Cable)

▲**NAPA/SONOMA**—Comcast Cable

▲**NAPA**—Comcast Cable. Now served by NAPA/SONOMA, CA [CA0038]

NAPA—See NAPA/SONOMA, CA (Comcast Cable)

NATIONAL CITY—See SAN DIEGO, CA (Cox Communications)

NATIONAL CITY—See CHULA VISTA, CA (NexHorizon Communications)

▲**NEEDLES**—CalNeva Broadband

NEVADA CITY—See GRASS VALLEY, CA (Comcast Cable)

NEVADA COUNTY (WESTERN PORTION)—See PLACER COUNTY (southwestern portion), CA (Wave Broadband)

NEVADA COUNTY—See GRASS VALLEY, CA (Comcast Cable)

▲**NEW CUYAMA**—Formerly served by Wave Broadband. No longer in operation

▲**NEWARK**—Comcast Cable. Now served by OAKLAND, CA [CA0018]

NEWARK—See OAKLAND, CA (Comcast Cable)

NEWBURY PARK—See CHATSWORTH, CA (Time Warner Cable)

NEWCASTLE—See PLACER COUNTY (southwestern portion), CA (Wave Broadband)

NEWHALL—See CHATSWORTH, CA (Time Warner Cable)

▲**NEWMAN**—Comcast Cable

▲**NEWPORT BEACH**—Formerly served by Adelphia Communications. Now served by ANAHEIM, CA [CA0033]

NEWPORT BEACH—See ORANGE COUNTY, CA (Cox Communications)

NEWPORT BEACH—See ANAHEIM, CA (Time Warner Cable)

NICE—See CLEARLAKE OAKS, CA (Mediacom)

NILAND—See CALIPATRIA, CA (Cable USA)

NIPOMO—See SAN LUIS OBISPO, CA (Charter Communications)

NORCO—See RIVERSIDE, CA (Charter Communications)

▲**NORTH EDWARDS**—Charter Communications

▲**NORTH FORK**—Ponderosa Cablevision

NORTH HILLS—See CHATSWORTH, CA (Time Warner Cable)

NORTH SMITH RIVER—See CRESCENT CITY, OR (Charter Communications)

NORTHRIDGE—See CHATSWORTH, CA (Time Warner Cable)

▲**NORTHSTAR**—Charter Communications

NORWALK—See ALHAMBRA, CA (Charter Communications)

▲**NOVATO**—Comcast Cable. Now served by NAPA/SONOMA, CA [CA0038]

NOVATO—See NAPA/SONOMA, CA (Comcast Cable)

▲**NOVATO**—Horizon Cable TV Inc.

NUEVO—See ANAHEIM, CA (Time Warner Cable)

OAK CREST MOBLE HOME PARK—See RAINBOW, CA (Venture Communications)

OAK PARK—See SACRAMENTO, CA (Comcast Cable)

OAK PARK—See CHATSWORTH, CA (Time Warner Cable)

OAK RANCH—See PORTERVILLE, CA (Charter Communications)

OAKHILLS—See GILROY, CA (Charter Communications)

▲**OAKHURST**—Northland Cable Television

▲**OAKLAND**—Comcast Cable

OAKLEY—See CONCORD, CA (Comcast Cable)

OAKMONT—See NAPA/SONOMA, CA (Comcast Cable)

OCEANO—See SAN LUIS OBISPO, CA (Charter Communications)

OCEANSIDE—See SAN DIEGO, CA (Cox Communications)

▲**OCOTILLO**—Cable USA

▲**OJAI**—Formerly served by Adelphia Communications. Now served by CHATSWORTH, CA [CA0013]

OJAI—See CHATSWORTH, CA (Time Warner Cable)

OLEMA—See POINT REYES STATION, CA (Horizon Cable TV Inc.)

▲**OLINDA**—Formerly served by Almega Cable. No longer in operation

OLIVEHURST—See YUBA CITY, CA (Comcast Cable)

▲**ONTARIO**—Time Warner Cable. Now served by ANAHEIM, CA [CA0033]

ONTARIO—See ANAHEIM, CA (Time Warner Cable)

ONYX—See KERNVILLE, CA (Mediacom)

ORANGE CITY—See ANAHEIM, CA (Time Warner Cable)

ORANGE COUNTY (UNINCORPORATED AREAS)—See ANAHEIM, CA (Time Warner Cable)

▲**ORANGE COUNTY (western portion)**—Time Warner Cable. Now served by ANAHEIM, CA [CA0033]

▲**ORANGE COUNTY**—Cox Communications

ORANGE COVE—See PORTERVILLE, CA (Charter Communications)

ORCUTT—See SANTA MARIA, CA (Comcast Cable)

▲**ORICK**—Formerly served by Almega Cable. No longer in operation

ORINDA—See CONCORD, CA (Comcast Cable)

ORLAND—See CHICO, CA (Comcast Cable)

OROSI—See PORTERVILLE, CA (Charter Communications)

▲**OROVILLE**—Comcast Cable. Now served by CHICO, CA [CA0066]

OROVILLE—See CHICO, CA (Comcast Cable)

▲**OXNARD**—Time Warner Cable. Now served by CHATSWORTH, CA [CA0013]

OXNARD—See CHATSWORTH, CA (Time Warner Cable)

PACHECO—See CONCORD, CA (Comcast Cable)

PACIFIC BEACH—See SAN DIEGO, CA (Time Warner Cable)

PACIFIC GROVE—See MONTEREY, CA (Comcast Cable)

PACIFIC PALISADES—See LOS ANGELES, CA (Time Warner Cable)

▲**PACIFICA**—Comcast Cable. Now served by SAN FRANCISCO, CA [CA0003]

PACIFICA—See SAN FRANCISCO, CA (Comcast Cable)

PACOIMA—See LOS ANGELES, CA (Time Warner Cable)

PAJARO DUNES—See WATSONVILLE, CA (Charter Communications)

▲**PALM DESERT**—Time Warner Cable

PALM SPRINGS OASIS—See PALM DESERT, CA (Time Warner Cable)

PALM SPRINGS—See PALM DESERT, CA (Time Warner Cable)

▲**PALMDALE**—Time Warner Cable. Now served by CHATSWORTH, CA [CA0013]

PALMDALE—See CHATSWORTH, CA (Time Warner Cable)

PALMS—See LOS ANGELES, CA (Time Warner Cable)

▲**PALO ALTO**—Comcast Cable. Now served by SAN JOSE, CA [CA0004]

PALO ALTO—See SAN JOSE, CA (Comcast Cable)

▲**PALO CEDRO**—New Day Broadband

PALOS VERDES ESTATES—See ORANGE COUNTY, CA (Cox Communications)

▲**PALOS VERDES PENINSULA**—Cox Communications. Now served by ORANGE COUNTY, CA [CA0015]

PALOS VERDES PENINSULA—See ORANGE COUNTY, CA (Cox Communications)

PARADISE—See CHICO, CA (Comcast Cable)

PARLIER—See FRESNO, CA (Comcast Cable)

PASADENA—See ALHAMBRA, CA (Charter Communications)

PASADENA—See ARCADIA, CA (Charter Communications)

PASO ROBLES—See SAN LUIS OBISPO, CA (Charter Communications)

PATTERSON—See NEWMAN, CA (Comcast Cable)

PAUMA VALLEY—See VALLEY CENTER, CA (Mediacom)

PEARBLOSSOM—See CHATSWORTH, CA (Time Warner Cable)

PENN VALLEY—See GRASS VALLEY, CA (Comcast Cable)

PENNGROVE—See NAPA/SONOMA, CA (Comcast Cable)

PENRYN—See PLACER COUNTY (southwestern portion), CA (Wave Broadband)

▲**PERRIS**—Time Warner Cable. Now served by ANAHEIM, CA [CA0033]

PERRIS—See ANAHEIM, CA (Time Warner Cable)

PESCADERO—See SAN FRANCISCO, CA (Comcast Cable)

▲**PETALUMA COAST GUARD STATION**—MWR Cable

▲**PETALUMA**—Comcast Cable. Now served by NAPA/SONOMA, CA [CA0038]

PETALUMA—See NAPA/SONOMA, CA (Comcast Cable)

▲**PHELAN**—Charter Communications

PHOENIX LAKE-CEDAR RIDGE—See TWAIN HARTE, CA (Comcast Cable)

PICO RIVERA—See LOS ANGELES, CA (Time Warner Cable)

PIEDMONT—See OAKLAND, CA (Comcast Cable)

▲**PINE GROVE**—Volcano Vision

PINE MOUNTAIN CLUB—See FRAZIER PARK, CA (CalNeva Broadband)

PINE VALLEY—See SAN DIEGO, CA (Cox Communications)

▲**PINECREST**—SNC Cable

▲**PINOLE**—Comcast Cable. Now served by OAKLAND, CA [CA0018]

PINOLE—See OAKLAND, CA (Comcast Cable)

PIONEER—See PINE GROVE, CA (Volcano Vision)

PISMO/SHELL BEACH—See SAN LUIS OBISPO, CA (Charter Communications)

▲**PITTSBURG**—Comcast Cable. Now served by CONCORD, CA [CA0101]

PITTSBURG—See CONCORD, CA (Comcast Cable)

PITTVILLE—See FALL RIVER MILLS, CA (Almega Cable)

PIXLEY—See PORTERVILLE, CA (Charter Communications)

PLACENTIA—See ANAHEIM, CA (Time Warner Cable)

PLACER COUNTY (EASTERN PORTION)—See NORTHSTAR, CA (Charter Communications)

▲**PLACER COUNTY (SOUTHWESTERN PORTION)**—Wave Broadband

PLACER COUNTY (WESTERN PORTION)—See SACRAMENTO, CA (Comcast Cable)

PLACER COUNTY (WESTERN PORTION)—See PLACER COUNTY (southwestern portion), CA (Wave Broadband)

▲**PLACERVILLE**—Comcast Cable

PLAINVIEW—See PORTERVILLE, CA (Charter Communications)

▲**PLANADA**—Comcast Cable

▲**PLANTATION-BY-THE-SEA**—Formerly served by Cox Communications. No longer in operation

PLAYA DEL RAY—See LOS ANGELES, CA (Time Warner Cable)

PLAYA VISTA—See LOS ANGELES, CA (Time Warner Cable)

▲**PLEASANT HILL**—Comcast Cable. Now served by CONCORD, CA [CA0101]

PLEASANT HILL—See CONCORD, CA (Comcast Cable)

▲**PLEASANTON**—Comcast Cable. Now served by CONCORD, CA [CA0101]

PLEASANTON—See CONCORD, CA (Comcast Cable)

PLUMAS COUNTY—See PORTOLA, CA (Wave Broadband)

▲**POINT MUGU NAVAL AIR STATION**—Communication Services

▲**POINT REYES STATION**—Horizon Cable TV Inc.

POLLOCK PINES—See PLACERVILLE, CA (Comcast Cable)

▲**POMONA**—Comcast Cable. Now served by LOS ANGELES, CA [CA0009]

POMONA—See LOS ANGELES, CA (Time Warner Cable)

POPLAR—See PORTERVILLE, CA (Charter Communications)

PORT HUENEME—See CHATSWORTH, CA (Time Warner Cable)

PORTA COSTA—See OAKLAND, CA (Comcast Cable)

▲**PORTERVILLE**—Charter Communications

▲**PORTOLA VALLEY**—Comcast Cable. Now served by SAN FRANCISCO, CA [CA0003]

PORTOLA VALLEY—See SAN FRANCISCO, CA (Comcast Cable)

▲**PORTOLA**—Wave Broadband

POSEY—See JACK RANCH/POSEY, CA (Charter Communications)

POWAY—See SAN DIEGO, CA (Cox Communications)

POWAY—See SAN DIEGO, CA (Time Warner Cable)

PRESIDIO OF MONTEREY—See FORT ORD, CA (Suddenlink Communications)

PRUNEDALE—See GILROY, CA (Charter Communications)

QUAIL VALLEY—See ANAHEIM, CA (Time Warner Cable)

QUARTZ HILL—See CHATSWORTH, CA (Time Warner Cable)

▲**QUINCY (portions)**—Charter Communications. Now served by PORTOLA, CA [CA0185]

▲**QUINCY**—Formerly served by Quincy Community TV Assn. Inc. No longer in operation

QUINCY—See PORTOLA, CA (Wave Broadband)

▲**RAINBOW**—Venture Communications

RAMONA—See SAN DIEGO, CA (Cox Communications)

RANCHO BERNARDO—See SAN DIEGO, CA (Time Warner Cable)

RANCHO CALAVERAS—See SAN ANDREAS, CA (Comcast Cable)

RANCHO CALIFORNIA—See ANAHEIM, CA (Time Warner Cable)

▲**RANCHO CORDOVA (PORTIONS)**—SureWest Broadband. Formerly served by Sacramento, CA [CA0459]. This cable system has converted to IPTV

▲**RANCHO CORDOVA**—Comcast Cable. Now served by SACRAMENTO, CA [CA0002]

RANCHO CORDOVA—See SACRAMENTO, CA (Comcast Cable)

RANCHO CUCAMONGA—See SAN BERNARDINO, CA (Charter Communications)

RANCHO CUCAMUNGA—See ANAHEIM, CA (Time Warner Cable)

RANCHO MIRAGE—See PALM DESERT, CA (Time Warner Cable)

RANCHO PARK—See LOS ANGELES, CA (Time Warner Cable)

RANCHO SAN DIEGO—See SAN DIEGO, CA (Cox Communications)

RANCHO SANTA FE—See SAN DIEGO, CA (Cox Communications)

RANCHO SANTA MARGARITA—See ORANGE COUNTY, CA (Cox Communications)

▲**RANCHO YOLO MOBILE HOME PARK**—Formerly served by Wave Broadband. No longer in operation

RANCHOS PALOS VERDES—See ORANGE COUNTY, CA (Cox Communications)

▲**RED BLUFF**—Charter Communications

▲**REDDING**—Formerly served by Sprint Corp. No longer in operation

▲**REDDING**—Charter Communications

▲**REDLANDS**—Time Warner Cable. Now served by ANAHEIM, CA [CA0033]

REDLANDS—See ANAHEIM, CA (Time Warner Cable)

▲**REDONDO BEACH**—Time Warner Cable. Now served by LOS ANGELES, CA [CA0009]

REDONDO BEACH—See LOS ANGELES, CA (Time Warner Cable)

REDWAY—See GARBERVILLE, CA (Wave Broadband)

REDWOOD CITY—See SAN FRANCISCO (southern portion), CA (Astound Broadband)

REDWOOD CITY—See SAN FRANCISCO, CA (Comcast Cable)

REDWOOD VALLEY—See UKIAH, CA (Comcast Cable)

REEDLEY—See FRESNO, CA (Comcast Cable)

REQUA—See KLAMATH, CA (Almega Cable)

RESCUE—See PLACERVILLE, CA (Comcast Cable)

RESEDA—See CHATSWORTH, CA (Time Warner Cable)

RIALTO—See ANAHEIM, CA (Time Warner Cable)

RICHMOND—See OAKLAND, CA (Comcast Cable)

▲**RIDGECREST**—Mediacom

RIMFOREST—See LAKE ARROWHEAD, CA (Charter Communications)

RINCON—See VALLEY CENTER, CA (Mediacom)

RIO DEL MAR—See SANTA CRUZ, CA (Comcast Cable)

RIO DELL—See EUREKA, CA (Suddenlink Communications)

RIO NIDO—See NAPA/SONOMA, CA (Comcast Cable)

▲**RIO VISTA**—Comcast Cable. Now served by NAPA/SONOMA, CA [CA0038]

RIO VISTA—See NAPA/SONOMA, CA (Comcast Cable)

▲**RIO VISTA**—Wave Broadband

RIPON—See TURLOCK, CA (Charter Communications)

RIVERBANK—See TURLOCK, CA (Charter Communications)

▲**RIVERDALE**—Comcast Cable

RIVERSIDE COUNTY (EASTERN PORTION)—See BLYTHE, CA (Suddenlink Communications)

RIVERSIDE COUNTY (PORTIONS)—See ANAHEIM, CA (Time Warner Cable)

RIVERSIDE COUNTY (PORTIONS)—See PALM DESERT, CA (Time Warner Cable)

RIVERSIDE COUNTY—See BANNING, CA (Time Warner Cable)

▲**RIVERSIDE**—Formerly served by Cross Country Wireless Cable. No longer in operation

▲**RIVERSIDE**—Charter Communications

ROCKLIN—See PLACER COUNTY (southwestern portion), CA (Wave Broadband)

RODEO—See OAKLAND, CA (Comcast Cable)

▲**ROHNERT PARK**—Comcast Cable. Now served by NAPA/SONOMA, CA [CA0038]

ROHNERT PARK—See NAPA/SONOMA, CA (Comcast Cable)

ROLLING HILLS ESTATES—See ORANGE COUNTY, CA (Cox Communications)

ROLLING HILLS—See ORANGE COUNTY, CA (Cox Communications)

ROMOLAND—See ANAHEIM, CA (Time Warner Cable)

ROSAMOND—See MOJAVE, CA (Charter Communications)

ROSEMEAD—See ALHAMBRA, CA (Charter Communications)

▲**ROSEVILLE**—Comcast Cable. Now served by SACRAMENTO, CA [CA0002]

ROSEVILLE—See SACRAMENTO, CA (Comcast Cable)

▲**ROSEVILLE**—SureWest Broadband. Formerly served by Sacramento, CA [CA0459]. This cable system has converted to IPTV

ROSS—See NAPA/SONOMA, CA (Comcast Cable)

ROSSMOOR—See CONCORD, CA (Comcast Cable)

ROSSMOOR—See ANAHEIM, CA (Time Warner Cable)

ROUND VALLEY—See BISHOP, CA (Suddenlink Communications)

ROWLAND HEIGHTS—See LOS ANGELES, CA (Time Warner Cable)

RUBIDOUX—See RIVERSIDE, CA (Charter Communications)

RUNNING SPRINGS—See LAKE ARROWHEAD, CA (Charter Communications)

SACRAMENTO COUNTY—See SACRAMENTO, CA (Comcast Cable)

▲**SACRAMENTO**—Formerly served by Wireless Broadcasting Services. No longer in operation

▲**SACRAMENTO**—SureWest Broadband. This cable system has converted to IPTV. See Sacramento, CA [CA5597]

▲**SACRAMENTO**—Comcast Cable

▲**SACRAMENTO**—SureWest Broadband. Formerly [CA0459]. This cable system has converted to IPTV

SALIDA—See TURLOCK, CA (Charter Communications)

SALINAS—See MONTEREY, CA (Comcast Cable)

▲ **SALTON CITY**—Cable USA

▲ **SALTON SEA BEACH**—Cable USA

▲ **SAN ANDREAS**—Comcast Cable

SAN ANSELMO—See NAPA/SONOMA, CA (Comcast Cable)

SAN BENITO COUNTY (PORTIONS)—See GILROY, CA (Charter Communications)

SAN BERNARDINO COUNTY (PORTIONS)—See BIG BEAR LAKE, CA (Charter Communications)

SAN BERNARDINO COUNTY (PORTIONS)—See HESPERIA, CA (Charter Communications)

SAN BERNARDINO COUNTY (PORTIONS)—See SAN BERNARDINO, CA (Charter Communications)

SAN BERNARDINO COUNTY—See ANAHEIM, CA (Time Warner Cable)

SAN BERNARDINO COUNTY—See BARSTOW, CA (Time Warner Cable)

▲ **SAN BERNARDINO**—Now served by ANAHEIM, CA [CA0033]

▲ **SAN BERNARDINO**—Now served by ANAHEIM, CA [CA0033]

▲ **SAN BERNARDINO**—Charter Communications

SAN BERNARDINO—See ANAHEIM, CA (Time Warner Cable)

▲ **SAN BRUNO**—City of San Bruno Municipal Cable TV

SAN CARLOS—See SAN FRANCISCO, CA (Comcast Cable)

SAN CLEMENTE—See ORANGE COUNTY, CA (Cox Communications)

SAN DIEGO (UNINCORPORATED AREAS)—See SAN DIEGO, CA (Cox Communications)

SAN DIEGO COUNTY (UNINCORPORATED AREAS)—See CARLSBAD, CA (Time Warner Cable)

SAN DIEGO COUNTY—See SAN DIEGO, CA (Cox Communications)

SAN DIEGO COUNTY—See SAN DIEGO, CA (Time Warner Cable)

▲ **SAN DIEGO NAVAL BASE**—NWS Communications

▲ **SAN DIEGO**—Cox Communications

▲ **SAN DIEGO**—Time Warner Cable

SAN DIMAS—See LOS ANGELES, CA (Time Warner Cable)

SAN FERNANDO—See LOS ANGELES, CA (Time Warner Cable)

▲ **SAN FRANCISCO (SOUTHERN PORTION)**—Astound Broadband

▲ **SAN FRANCISCO**—Formerly served by TV Max. No longer in operation

▲ **SAN FRANCISCO**—Comcast Cable

SAN GABRIEL—See ALHAMBRA, CA (Charter Communications)

SAN GERONIMO—See NAPA/SONOMA, CA (Comcast Cable)

SAN JACINTO—See ANAHEIM, CA (Time Warner Cable)

SAN JOAQUIN (PORTIONS)—See FRESNO, CA (Comcast Cable)

SAN JOAQUIN COUNTY (PORTIONS)—See TURLOCK, CA (Charter Communications)

SAN JOAQUIN COUNTY—See STOCKTON, CA (Comcast Cable)

SAN JOAQUIN COUNTY—See TRACY, CA (Comcast Cable)

▲ **SAN JOSE**—Formerly served by Pacific Bell Video Services. No longer in operation

▲ **SAN JOSE**—Formerly served by TV Max. No longer in operation

▲ **SAN JOSE**—Matrix Cablevision Inc. Now served by SAN JOSE, CA [CA0004]

▲ **SAN JOSE**—Comcast Cable

SAN JUAN BAUTISTA (PORTIONS)—See GILROY, CA (Charter Communications)

SAN JUAN CAPISTRANO—See ORANGE COUNTY, CA (Cox Communications)

SAN LEANDRO—See OAKLAND, CA (Comcast Cable)

SAN LORENZO—See OAKLAND, CA (Comcast Cable)

SAN LUIS OBISPO COUNTY (PORTIONS)—See SAN LUIS OBISPO, CA (Charter Communications)

▲ **SAN LUIS OBISPO**—Formerly served by TVCN. No longer in operation

▲ **SAN LUIS OBISPO**—Charter Communications

SAN MARCOS (PORTIONS)—See CARLSBAD, CA (Time Warner Cable)

SAN MARCOS—See SAN DIEGO, CA (Cox Communications)

SAN MARINO—See LOS ANGELES, CA (Time Warner Cable)

SAN MARTIN—See GILROY, CA (Charter Communications)

SAN MATEO COUNTY (PORTIONS)—See SAN JOSE, CA (Comcast Cable)

SAN MATEO COUNTY—See SAN FRANCISCO, CA (Comcast Cable)

▲ **SAN MATEO**—Comcast Cable. Now served by SAN FRANCISCO, CA [CA0003]

SAN MATEO—See SAN FRANCISCO (southern portion), CA (Astound Broadband)

SAN MATEO—See SAN FRANCISCO, CA (Comcast Cable)

SAN MIGUEL—See SAN LUIS OBISPO, CA (Charter Communications)

▲ **SAN PABLO**—Comcast Cable. Now served by OAKLAND, CA [CA0018]

SAN PABLO—See OAKLAND, CA (Comcast Cable)

SAN PEDRO—See ORANGE COUNTY, CA (Cox Communications)

SAN PEDRO—See LOS ANGELES, CA (Time Warner Cable)

SAN QUENTIN—See NAPA/SONOMA, CA (Comcast Cable)

SAN RAFAEL—See NAPA/SONOMA, CA (Comcast Cable)

SAN RAMON—See CONCORD, CA (Comcast Cable)

▲ **SAN SIMEON ACRES**—San Simeon Community Cable Inc.

SAND CITY—See MONTEREY, CA (Comcast Cable)

SANGER—See FRESNO, CA (Comcast Cable)

▲ **SANTA ANA**—Formerly served by Adelphia Communications. Now served by ANAHEIM, CA [CA0033]

SANTA ANA—See ANAHEIM, CA (Time Warner Cable)

SANTA BARBARA COUNTY (PORTIONS)—See SANTA BARBARA, CA (Cox Communications)

SANTA BARBARA COUNTY—See SANTA MARIA, CA (Comcast Cable)

▲ **SANTA BARBARA**—Cox Communications

SANTA CLARA COUNTY—See SAN JOSE, CA (Comcast Cable)

▲ **SANTA CLARA**—Comcast Cable. Now served by SAN JOSE, CA [CA0004]

SANTA CLARA—See SAN JOSE, CA (Comcast Cable)

▲ **SANTA CLARITA**—Time Warner Cable. Now served by CHATSWORTH, CA [CA0013]

SANTA CLARITA—See CHATSWORTH, CA (Time Warner Cable)

SANTA CRUZ COUNTY (PORTIONS)—See WATSONVILLE, CA (Charter Communications)

SANTA CRUZ COUNTY (UNINCORPORATED AREAS)—See SANTA CRUZ, CA (Comcast Cable)

▲ **SANTA CRUZ**—Comcast Cable

SANTA MARGARITA—See SAN LUIS OBISPO, CA (Charter Communications)

▲ **SANTA MARIA**—Comcast Cable

▲ **SANTA MONICA**—Time Warner Cable. Now served by CHATSWORTH, CA [CA0013]

SANTA MONICA—See CHATSWORTH, CA (Time Warner Cable)

SANTA PAULA—See CHATSWORTH, CA (Time Warner Cable)

▲ **SANTA ROSA**—Comcast Cable. Now served by NAPA/SONOMA, CA [CA0038]

SANTA ROSA—See NAPA/SONOMA, CA (Comcast Cable)

SANTA VENETIA—See NAPA/SONOMA, CA (Comcast Cable)

SANTA YNEZ—See SANTA MARIA, CA (Comcast Cable)

SANTEE—See SAN DIEGO, CA (Cox Communications)

▲ **SARATOGA**—Comcast Cable. Now served by SAN JOSE, CA [CA0004]

SARATOGA—See SAN JOSE, CA (Comcast Cable)

SAUGUS—See CHATSWORTH, CA (Time Warner Cable)

SAUSALITO—See NAPA/SONOMA, CA (Comcast Cable)

SCOTIA—See EUREKA, CA (Suddenlink Communications)

SCOTTS VALLEY—See SANTA CRUZ, CA (Comcast Cable)

▲ **SEAL BEACH**—Formerly served by Adelphia Communications. Now served by ANAHEIM, CA [CA0033]

SEAL BEACH—See ANAHEIM, CA (Time Warner Cable)

SEARLES VALLEY—See RIDGECREST, CA (Mediacom)

SEASIDE—See MONTEREY, CA (Comcast Cable)

SEBASTOPOL—See NAPA/SONOMA, CA (Comcast Cable)

SELMA—See FRESNO, CA (Comcast Cable)

SEPULVEDA—See LOS ANGELES, CA (Time Warner Cable)

SERENE LAKES—See TRUCKEE, CA (Suddenlink Communications)

SHADOW RIDGE CREEK—See PALM DESERT, CA (Time Warner Cable)

SHAFTER—See BAKERSFIELD, CA (Bright House Networks)

SHASTA COUNTY (PORTIONS)—See PALO CEDRO, CA (New Day Broadband)

SHASTA COUNTY—See REDDING, CA (Charter Communications)

▲ **SHAVER LAKE**—Suddenlink Communications

SHERMAN OAKS (PORTIONS)—See CHATSWORTH, CA (Time Warner Cable)

▲ **SHERMAN OAKS**—Time Warner Cable. Now served by CHATSWORTH, CA [CA0013]

SHERMAN OAKS—See CHATSWORTH, CA (Time Warner Cable)

SHINGLE SPRINGS—See PLACERVILLE, CA (Comcast Cable)

SIERRA COUNTY (PORTIONS)—See PORTOLA, CA (Wave Broadband)

▲**SIERRA DAWN ESTATES**—Sierra Dawn Cablevision

▲**SIERRA MADRE**—Now served by LOS ANGELES, CA [CA0009]

SIERRA MADRE—See LOS ANGELES, CA (Time Warner Cable)

SIERRA MEADOWS—See TRUCKEE, CA (Suddenlink Communications)

SIERRA VILLAGE—See TWAIN HARTE, CA (Comcast Cable)

SIGNAL HILL—See LONG BEACH, CA (Charter Communications)

SILVER LAKES—See HESPERIA, CA (Charter Communications)

▲**SIMI VALLEY**—Time Warner Cable. Now served by CHATSWORTH, CA [CA0013]

SIMI VALLEY—See CHATSWORTH, CA (Time Warner Cable)

SISKIYOU COUNTY—See MOUNT SHASTA, CA (Northland Cable Television)

SISKIYOU COUNTY—See YREKA, CA (Northland Cable Television)

SODA SPRINGS—See TRUCKEE, CA (Suddenlink Communications)

SOLANA BEACH—See SAN DIEGO, CA (Cox Communications)

SOLANA BEACH—See CARLSBAD, CA (Time Warner Cable)

SOLANO COUNTY—See NAPA/SONOMA, CA (Comcast Cable)

▲**SOLEDAD**—Charter Communications

SOLVANG—See SANTA MARIA, CA (Comcast Cable)

SONOMA COUNTY—See NAPA/SONOMA, CA (Comcast Cable)

▲**SONORA**—Comcast Cable. Now served by TWAIN HARTE, CA [CA0148]

SONORA—See TWAIN HARTE, CA (Comcast Cable)

SOQUEL—See SANTA CRUZ, CA (Comcast Cable)

SOULSBYVILLE—See TWAIN HARTE, CA (Comcast Cable)

▲**SOUTH GATE**—Time Warner Cable. Now served by LOS ANGELES, CA [CA0009]

SOUTH GATE—See LOS ANGELES, CA (Time Warner Cable)

▲**SOUTH LAKE TAHOE**—Charter Communications

▲**SOUTH NATOMAS**—SureWest Broadband. Formerly served by Sacramento, CA [CA0459]. This cable system has converted to IPTV

▲**SOUTH PASADENA**—Time Warner Cable. Now served by LOS ANGELES, CA [CA0009]

SOUTH PASADENA—See LOS ANGELES, CA (Time Warner Cable)

▲**SOUTH SAN FRANCISCO**—Comcast Cable. Now served by SAN FRANCISCO, CA [CA0003]

SOUTH SAN FRANCISCO—See SAN FRANCISCO (southern portion), CA (Astound Broadband)

SOUTH SAN FRANCISCO—See SAN FRANCISCO, CA (Comcast Cable)

SOUTH SAN GABRIEL—See ALHAMBRA, CA (Charter Communications)

SOUTH TAFT—See TEHACHAPI, CA (Bright House Networks)

SOUTH WHITTIER—See LOS ANGELES, CA (Time Warner Cable)

▲**SPANISH RANCH MOBILE HOME PARK**—Formerly served by Comcast Cable. No longer in operation

SPRING VALLEY LAKE—See HESPERIA, CA (Charter Communications)

SPRING VALLEY—See SAN DIEGO, CA (Cox Communications)

SPRINGVILLE—See PORTERVILLE, CA (Charter Communications)

SQUAW VALLEY—See TRUCKEE, CA (Suddenlink Communications)

ST. HELENA—See NAPA/SONOMA, CA (Comcast Cable)

STANDARD—See TWAIN HARTE, CA (Comcast Cable)

STANFORD—See SAN JOSE, CA (Comcast Cable)

STANISLAUS COUNTY (PORTIONS)—See TURLOCK, CA (Charter Communications)

STANISLAUS COUNTY (PORTIONS)—See NEWMAN, CA (Comcast Cable)

STANISLAUS COUNTY—See MODESTO & OAKDALE, CA (Comcast Cable)

STANTON—See ANAHEIM, CA (Time Warner Cable)

STATELINE—See SOUTH LAKE TAHOE, NV (Charter Communications)

▲**STEVENSON RANCH**—Time Warner Cable. Now served by CHATSWORTH, CA [CA0013]

STEVENSON RANCH—See CHATSWORTH, CA (Time Warner Cable)

STINSON BEACH—See POINT REYES STATION, CA (Horizon Cable TV Inc.)

▲**STOCKTON**—Comcast Cable

STRATHMORE—See PORTERVILLE, CA (Charter Communications)

▲**STRAWBERRY**—Comcast Cable. Now served by PLACERVILLE, CA [CA0108]

STRAWBERRY—See NAPA/SONOMA, CA (Comcast Cable)

STRAWBERRY—See PLACERVILLE, CA (Comcast Cable)

STRAWBERRY—See PINECREST, CA (SNC Cable)

▲**STUDIO CITY**—Formerly served by Adelphia Communications. Now served by CHATSWORTH, CA [CA0013]

STUDIO CITY—See CHATSWORTH, CA (Time Warner Cable)

SUGAR BOWL—See TRUCKEE, CA (Suddenlink Communications)

SUGAR PINE—See TWAIN HARTE, CA (Comcast Cable)

SUISIN CITY—See NAPA/SONOMA, CA (Comcast Cable)

▲**SUN CITY**—Mediacom

SUN VALLEY—See LOS ANGELES, CA (Time Warner Cable)

SUNLAND—See CHATSWORTH, CA (Time Warner Cable)

SUNNYSLOPE—See RIVERSIDE, CA (Charter Communications)

▲**SUNNYVALE**—Comcast Cable. Now served by SAN JOSE, CA [CA0004]

SUNNYVALE—See SAN JOSE, CA (Comcast Cable)

SUNOL—See CONCORD, CA (Comcast Cable)

SUNSET BEACH—See ANAHEIM, CA (Time Warner Cable)

▲**SUSANVILLE**—Windjammer Cable

SUTTER COUNTY (PORTIONS)—See YUBA CITY, CA (Comcast Cable)

SYLMAR—See CHATSWORTH, CA (Time Warner Cable)

TAFT HEIGHTS—See TEHACHAPI, CA (Bright House Networks)

TAFT—See TEHACHAPI, CA (Bright House Networks)

TAHOE CITY (SOUTHEASTERN PORTION)—See TRUCKEE, CA (Suddenlink Communications)

TAHOE CITY—See NORTHSTAR, CA (Charter Communications)

TAHOE DONNER—See TRUCKEE, CA (Suddenlink Communications)

TAHOE PARADISE—See MEYERS, CA (Charter Communications)

TAHOE VISTA—See NORTHSTAR, CA (Charter Communications)

TALMAGE—See UKIAH, CA (Comcast Cable)

TAMALPAIS—See NAPA/SONOMA, CA (Comcast Cable)

TAMELAC—See NAPA/SONOMA, CA (Comcast Cable)

TARZANA—See CHATSWORTH, CA (Time Warner Cable)

▲**TASSAJARA VALLEY**—Formerly served by Comcast Cable. No longer in operation

▲**TEHACHAPI**—Bright House Networks

TEHAMA COUNTY—See REDDING, CA (Charter Communications)

▲**TEHAMA**—New Day Broadband

TEMECULA—See ANAHEIM, CA (Time Warner Cable)

TEMPLE CITY—See ALHAMBRA, CA (Charter Communications)

TEMPLETON—See SAN LUIS OBISPO, CA (Charter Communications)

TERRA BELLA—See PORTERVILLE, CA (Charter Communications)

TERWER VALLEY—See KLAMATH, CA (Almega Cable)

▲**THE SEA RANCH**—Central Valley Cable

▲**THERMAL**—Cable USA

▲**THOUSAND OAKS**—Time Warner Cable. Now served by CHATSWORTH, CA [CA0013]

▲**THOUSAND OAKS**—Charter Communications

THOUSAND OAKS—See CHATSWORTH, CA (Time Warner Cable)

THOUSAND PALMS—See PALM DESERT, CA (Time Warner Cable)

THREE RIVERS—See PORTERVILLE, CA (Charter Communications)

TIBURON—See NAPA/SONOMA, CA (Comcast Cable)

TIPTON—See PORTERVILLE, CA (Charter Communications)

TODD VALLEY—See FORESTHILL, CA (Suddenlink Communications)

TOPANGA—See MALIBU, CA (Charter Communications)

▲**TORRANCE**—Time Warner Cable. Now served by LOS ANGELES, CA [CA0009]

TORRANCE—See LOS ANGELES, CA (Time Warner Cable)

▲**TRACY**—Comcast Cable

▲**TRAVIS AFB**—Comcast Cable. Now served by NAPA/SONOMA, CA [CA0038]

TRAVIS AFB—See NAPA/SONOMA, CA (Comcast Cable)

TREASURE ISLAND NAVAL STATION—See OAKLAND, CA (Comcast Cable)

TRI-PALM ESTATES—See PALM DESERT, CA (Time Warner Cable)

TRINIDAD—See EUREKA, CA (Suddenlink Communications)

▲**TRINITY CENTER**—Formerly served by Almega Cable. No longer in operation

TRONA—See RIDGECREST, CA (Mediacom)

▲**TRUCKEE**—Suddenlink Communications

▲**TUJUNGA**—Time Warner Cable. Now served by CHATSWORTH, CA [CA0013]

TUJUNGA—See CHATSWORTH, CA (Time Warner Cable)

TULARE COUNTY (NORTHEASTERN PORTION)—See PORTERVILLE, CA (Charter Communications)

TULARE COUNTY—See FRESNO, CA (Comcast Cable)

TULARE—See FRESNO, CA (Comcast Cable)

▲ **TULELAKE**—Almega Cable

TUOLUMNE CITY—See TWAIN HARTE, CA (Comcast Cable)

▲ **TURLOCK**—Charter Communications

▲ **TUSTIN**—Comcast Cable. Now served by ANAHEIM, CA [CA0033]

TUSTIN—See ORANGE COUNTY, CA (Cox Communications)

TUSTIN—See ANAHEIM, CA (Time Warner Cable)

▲ **TWAIN HARTE**—Comcast Cable

TWENTYNINE PALMS MARINE CORPS BASE—See YUCCA VALLEY, CA (Time Warner Cable)

TWENTYNINE PALMS—See YUCCA VALLEY, CA (Time Warner Cable)

TWIN BRIDGES—See PLACERVILLE, CA (Comcast Cable)

TWIN PEAKS—See LAKE ARROWHEAD, CA (Charter Communications)

▲ **UKIAH**—Comcast Cable

▲ **UNION CITY**—Comcast Cable. Now served by OAKLAND, CA [CA0018]

UNION CITY—See OAKLAND, CA (Comcast Cable)

UPLAND—See ANAHEIM, CA (Time Warner Cable)

UPPER LAKE—See CLEARLAKE OAKS, CA (Mediacom)

▲ **VACAVILLE**—Comcast Cable. Now served by NAPA/SONOMA, CA [CA0038]

VACAVILLE—See NAPA/SONOMA, CA (Comcast Cable)

VALENCIA—See CHATSWORTH, CA (Time Warner Cable)

VALLECITO—See SAN ANDREAS, CA (Comcast Cable)

▲ **VALLEJO**—Comcast Cable. Now served by NAPA/SONOMA, CA [CA0038]

VALLEJO—See NAPA/SONOMA, CA (Comcast Cable)

▲ **VALLEY CENTER**—Mediacom

VALLEY SPRINGS—See SAN ANDREAS, CA (Comcast Cable)

▲ **VAN NUYS**—Formerly served by Adelphia Communications. Now served by LOS ANGELES, CA [CA0009]

VAN NUYS—See CHATSWORTH, CA (Time Warner Cable)

▲ **VANDENBERG AFB**—Vandenberg Broadband

VANDENBURG VILLAGE—See SANTA MARIA, CA (Comcast Cable)

VENICE—See LOS ANGELES, CA (Time Warner Cable)

VENTURA COUNTY (PORTIONS)—See BOX CANYON, CA (Charter Communications)

VENTURA COUNTY (PORTIONS)—See MALIBU, CA (Charter Communications)

VENTURA COUNTY (PORTIONS)—See SANTA BARBARA, CA (Cox Communications)

VENTURA COUNTY (PORTIONS)—See CHATSWORTH, CA (Time Warner Cable)

VENTURA COUNTY (RINCON AREA)—See VENTURA, CA (Charter Communications)

▲ **VENTURA**—Time Warner Cable. Now served by CHATSWORTH, CA [CA0013]

▲ **VENTURA**—Charter Communications

VENTURA—See CHATSWORTH, CA (Time Warner Cable)

VICTOR—See LODI, CA (Comcast Cable)

▲ **VICTORVILLE**—Charter Communications. Now served by HESPERIA, CA [CA0158]

VICTORVILLE—See HESPERIA, CA (Charter Communications)

VILLA PARK—See ANAHEIM, CA (Time Warner Cable)

▲ **VISALIA**—Formerly served by Sprint Corp. No longer in operation

VISALIA—See FRESNO, CA (Comcast Cable)

VISTA—See SAN DIEGO, CA (Cox Communications)

VISTA—See CARLSBAD, CA (Time Warner Cable)

VOLCANO—See PINE GROVE, CA (Volcano Vision)

WALNUT CREEK—See CONCORD, CA (Astound Broadband)

WALNUT CREEK—See CONCORD, CA (Comcast Cable)

WALNUT PARK—See LOS ANGELES, CA (Time Warner Cable)

WALNUT—See ALHAMBRA, CA (Charter Communications)

WARD VALLEY—See TRUCKEE, CA (Suddenlink Communications)

WASCO—See BAKERSFIELD, CA (Bright House Networks)

WASHOE COUNTY (SOUTHERN PORTION)—See NORTHSTAR, NV (Charter Communications)

WATERFORD—See TURLOCK, CA (Charter Communications)

▲ **WATSONVILLE**—Charter Communications

▲ **WEAVERVILLE**—New Day Broadband

WEED—See MOUNT SHASTA, CA (Northland Cable Television)

WELDON—See KERNVILLE, CA (Mediacom)

WEST COVINA—See ALHAMBRA, CA (Charter Communications)

WEST HILLS—See CHATSWORTH, CA (Time Warner Cable)

▲ **WEST HOLLYWOOD**—Time Warner Cable. Now served by CHATSWORTH, CA [CA0013]

WEST HOLLYWOOD—See CHATSWORTH, CA (Time Warner Cable)

WEST LAKE TAHOE—See TRUCKEE, CA (Suddenlink Communications)

▲ **WEST LOS ANGELES**—Time Warner Cable. Now served by LOS ANGELES, CA [CA0009]

WEST LOS ANGELES—See LOS ANGELES, CA (Time Warner Cable)

WEST POINT—See PINE GROVE, CA (Volcano Vision)

▲ **WEST SACRAMENTO**—Wave Broadband

WEST SAN FERNANDO VALLEY—See CHATSWORTH, CA (Time Warner Cable)

WEST SHORE—See LAKE ALMANOR, CA (CalNeva Broadband)

WESTCHESTER—See LOS ANGELES, CA (Time Warner Cable)

WESTERN VILLAGE—See PALM DESERT, CA (Time Warner Cable)

WESTLAKE VILLAGE—See CHATSWORTH, CA (Time Warner Cable)

WESTMINSTER—See ANAHEIM, CA (Time Warner Cable)

WESTMORLAND—See EL CENTRO, CA (Time Warner Cable)

WESTWOOD—See LAKE ALMANOR, CA (CalNeva Broadband)

WHEATLAND—See YUBA CITY, CA (Comcast Cable)

▲ **WHITTIER**—Charter Communications

WILDOMAR—See ANAHEIM, CA (Time Warner Cable)

▲ **WILLIAMS**—Comcast Cable

WILLITS—See UKIAH, CA (Comcast Cable)

▲ **WILLOW CREEK**—Almega Cable

▲ **WILLOW RANCH MOBILE HOME PARK**—Formerly served by Comcast Cable. No longer in operation

WILLOWBROOK—See LOS ANGELES, CA (Time Warner Cable)

WILLOWS—See CHICO, CA (Comcast Cable)

▲ **WILMINGTON**—Time Warner Cable. Now served by LOS ANGELES, CA [CA0009]

WILMINGTON—See LOS ANGELES, CA (Time Warner Cable)

WILSHIRE—See LOS ANGELES, CA (Time Warner Cable)

WINCHESTER—See ANAHEIM, CA (Time Warner Cable)

WINDSOR HILLS—See LOS ANGELES, CA (Time Warner Cable)

WINDSOR—See NAPA/SONOMA, CA (Comcast Cable)

WINNETKA—See CHATSWORTH, CA (Time Warner Cable)

WINTERS—See WEST SACRAMENTO, CA (Wave Broadband)

WINTON—See MERCED, CA (Comcast Cable)

WOFFORD HEIGHTS—See KERNVILLE, CA (Mediacom)

WOODACRE—See NAPA/SONOMA, CA (Comcast Cable)

WOODBRIDGE—See LODI, CA (Comcast Cable)

WOODCREST—See ANAHEIM, CA (Time Warner Cable)

WOODLAKE—See PORTERVILLE, CA (Charter Communications)

WOODLAND HILLS—See CHATSWORTH, CA (Time Warner Cable)

WOODLAND—See WEST SACRAMENTO, CA (Wave Broadband)

WOODSIDE—See SAN FRANCISCO, CA (Comcast Cable)

WOODVILLE—See PORTERVILLE, CA (Charter Communications)

WRIGHTWOOD—See PHELAN, CA (Charter Communications)

YERMO—See BARSTOW, CA (Time Warner Cable)

YOLO COUNTY—See SACRAMENTO, CA (Comcast Cable)

▲ **YORBA LINDA**—Now served by ANAHEIM, CA [CA0033]

YORBA LINDA—See ANAHEIM, CA (Time Warner Cable)

YOSEMITE LAKE PARK—See COARSEGOLD, CA (Northland Cable Television)

▲ **YOUNTVILLE**—Comcast Cable. Now served by NAPA/SONOMA, CA [CA0038]

YOUNTVILLE—See NAPA/SONOMA, CA (Comcast Cable)

▲ **YREKA**—Northland Cable Television

▲ **YUBA CITY**—Formerly served by Sprint Corp. No longer in operation

▲ **YUBA CITY**—Comcast Cable

YUBA COUNTY (PORTIONS)—See YUBA CITY, CA (Comcast Cable)

YUCAIPA—See FOREST FALLS, CA (Charter Communications)

YUCAIPA—See ANAHEIM, CA (Time Warner Cable)

▲**YUCCA VALLEY**—Time Warner Cable

COLORADO

ADAMS COUNTY—See DENVER (suburbs), CO (Comcast Cable)

▲**AKRON (town)**—CommuniComm Services. Now served by OTIS, CO [CO0128]

AKRON—See OTIS (town), CO (CommuniComm Services)

ALAMOSA COUNTY—See ALAMOSA, CO (Bresnan Communications)

ALAMOSA EAST—See ALAMOSA, CO (Bresnan Communications)

▲**ALAMOSA**—Bresnan Communications

▲**ANTONITO**—Bresnan Communications

APPLE TREE MOBILE HOME PARK—See RIFLE, CO (Comcast Cable)

ARAPAHOE COUNTY—See DENVER (suburbs), CO (Comcast Cable)

ARCHULETA COUNTY—See PAGOSA SPRINGS, CO (Rocky Mountain Cable)

▲**ARRIBA**—Formerly served by Rebeltec Communications. No longer in operation

ARVADA—See DENVER (suburbs), CO (Comcast Cable)

▲**ASPEN**—Comcast Cable

AULT—See EATON, CO (US Cable)

AURORA—See DENVER (suburbs), CO (Comcast Cable)

AURORA—See LAKEWOOD, CO (Comcast Cable)

AUSTIN—See HOTCHKISS, CO (Rocky Mountain Cable)

▲**AVON**—Comcast Cable

▲**BAILEY**—Formerly served by US Cable of Coastal Texas LP. No longer in operation

BASALT—See ASPEN, CO (Comcast Cable)

BATTLEMENT MESA—See PARACHUTE, CO (Comcast Cable)

▲**BAYFIELD**—Rocky Mountain Cable

BEAVER CREEK—See AVON, CO (Comcast Cable)

▲**BENNETT**—Comcast Cable. Now served by DENVER (suburbs), CO [CO0001]

BENNETT—See DENVER (suburbs), CO (Comcast Cable)

BERTHOUD—See LONGMONT, CO (Comcast Cable)

▲**BEULAH**—Beulah Land Communications Inc.

BLACK FOREST—See COLORADO SPRINGS, CO (Comcast Cable)

▲**BLACK HAWK**—Rocky Mountain Cable

▲**BLANCA**—Jade Communications-Direct TV

BLENDE—See PUEBLO, CO (Comcast Cable)

BLUE RIVER—See SILVERTHORNE, CO (Comcast Cable)

▲**BOULDER (portions)**—Qwest Choice TV. IPTV service has been discontinued.

BOULDER COUNTY (PORTIONS)—See DENVER (suburbs), CO (Comcast Cable)

▲**BOULDER**—Comcast Cable. Now served by Denver (suburbs), CO [CO0001]

BOULDER—See DENVER (suburbs), CO (Comcast Cable)

BOW MAR—See DENVER (suburbs), CO (Comcast Cable)

▲**BRECKENRIDGE**—Comcast Cable. Now served by SILVERTHORNE (formerly Dillon), CO [CO0015]

BRECKENRIDGE—See SILVERTHORNE, CO (Comcast Cable)

▲**BRIGHTON**—Comcast Cable. Now served by Denver (suburbs), CO [CO0001]

BRIGHTON—See DENVER (suburbs), CO (Comcast Cable)

BROOKSIDE—See CANON CITY, CO (Bresnan Communications)

▲**BROOMFIELD**—Comcast Cable. Now served by Denver (suburbs), CO [CO0001]

BROOMFIELD—See DENVER (suburbs), CO (Comcast Cable)

BRUSH—See FORT MORGAN, CO (Bresnan Communications)

▲**BUENA VISTA**—Bresnan Communications

▲**BURLINGTON**—Baja Broadband

BYERS—See DENVER (suburbs), CO (Comcast Cable)

▲**CALHAN**—Formerly served by FairPoint Communications. No longer in operation

CAMPION—See LONGMONT, CO (Comcast Cable)

▲**CANON CITY**—Bresnan Communications

▲**CANTERBURY PARK**—Formerly served by Island Cable. No longer in operation

CARBONDALE—See ASPEN, CO (Comcast Cable)

CASCADE—See COLORADO SPRINGS, CO (Comcast Cable)

▲**CASTLE ROCK**—Comcast Cable. Now served by DENVER (suburbs), CO [CO0001]

CASTLE ROCK—See DENVER (suburbs), CO (Comcast Cable)

CEDAREDGE—See HOTCHKISS, CO (Rocky Mountain Cable)

▲**CENTER**—Formerly served by Center Municipal Cable System. No longer in operation

CENTRAL CITY—See BLACK HAWK, CO (Rocky Mountain Cable)

CHAFFEE COUNTY—See BUENA VISTA, CO (Bresnan Communications)

CHAFFEE COUNTY—See SALIDA, CO (Bresnan Communications)

CHAMA—See SAN LUIS, CO (Bresnan Communications)

CHAPPELL—See JULESBURG, NE (PC Telcom)

CHERRY HILLS VILLAGE—See DENVER (suburbs), CO (Comcast Cable)

▲**CHEYENNE WELLS**—NexHorizon Communications

CHIPITA PARK—See COLORADO SPRINGS, CO (Comcast Cable)

CIMARRON HILLS—See COLORADO SPRINGS, CO (Comcast Cable)

CLEAR CREEK COUNTY (EASTERN PORTION)—See CONIFER, CO (US Cable)

CLEAR CREEK COUNTY—See DENVER (suburbs), CO (Comcast Cable)

COAL CREEK—See CANON CITY, CO (Bresnan Communications)

▲**COLLBRAN (TOWN)**—KiRock Communications

▲**COLORADO CITY**—Bresnan Communications

▲**COLORADO SPRINGS**—Formerly served by Sprint Corp. No longer in operation

▲**COLORADO SPRINGS**—Comcast Cable

COLUMBINE VALLEY—See DENVER (suburbs), CO (Comcast Cable)

COMMERCE CITY—See DENVER (suburbs), CO (Comcast Cable)

▲**CONIFER**—US Cable

▲**COPPER MOUNTAIN**—Copper Mountain Consolidated Metropolitan District

▲**CORTEZ**—Baja Broadband

▲**CRAIG**—Bresnan Communications

CRAWFORD—See HOTCHKISS, CO (Rocky Mountain Cable)

▲**CREEDE**—Rocky Mountain Cable

CRESTED BUTTE—See GUNNISON, CO (Time Warner Cable)

▲**CRIPPLE CREEK**—US Cable

▲**CUCHARA VALLEY**—Formerly served by Westcom II LLC. No longer in operation

DACONO—See LONGMONT, CO (Comcast Cable)

▲**DEER TRAIL**—Formerly served by Champion Broadband. No longer in operation

DEER TRAIL—See DENVER (suburbs), CO (Comcast Cable)

▲**DEL NORTE**—Bresnan Communications

DELTA COUNTY—See DELTA, CO (Bresnan Communications)

DELTA COUNTY—See PAONIA, CO (Bresnan Communications)

▲**DELTA**—Bresnan Communications

DENVER (PORTIONS)—See LAKEWOOD, CO (Comcast Cable)

▲**DENVER (SUBURBS)**—Comcast Cable

▲**DENVER**—Formerly served by Sprint Corp. No longer in operation

▲**DENVER**—Comcast Cable

DILLON—See SILVERTHORNE, CO (Comcast Cable)

▲**DOLORES**—Bresnan Communications

DOUGLAS COUNTY—See DENVER (suburbs), CO (Comcast Cable)

▲**DOVE CREEK**—Bresnan Communications

DOWNIEVILLE—See DENVER (suburbs), CO (Comcast Cable)

DUMONT—See DENVER (suburbs), CO (Comcast Cable)

▲**DURANGO WEST**—Bresnan Communications

▲**DURANGO**—Bresnan Communications

▲**EADS**—NexHorizon Communications

EAGLE COUNTY—See ASPEN, CO (Comcast Cable)

▲**EAGLE**—CenturyTel

EAST VAIL—See AVON, CO (Comcast Cable)

▲**EATON**—US Cable

ECKERT—See HOTCHKISS, CO (Rocky Mountain Cable)

EDGEWATER—See DENVER (suburbs), CO (Comcast Cable)

EDWARDS—See AVON, CO (Comcast Cable)

EL JEBEL—See ASPEN, CO (Comcast Cable)

▲**EL PASO COUNTY (EASTERN PORTIONS)**—Falcon PTC. Formerly Falcon, CO [CO0213]. This cable system has converted to IPTV

EL PASO COUNTY—See COLORADO SPRINGS, CO (Comcast Cable)

ELBERT COUNTY—See DENVER (suburbs), CO (Comcast Cable)

ELIZABETH—See DENVER (suburbs), CO (Comcast Cable)

▲ **EMPIRE**—Comcast Cable. Now served by Denver (suburbs), CO [CO0001]

EMPIRE—See DENVER (suburbs), CO (Comcast Cable)

ENGLEWOOD—See DENVER (suburbs), CO (Comcast Cable)

ERIE—See LONGMONT, CO (Comcast Cable)

▲ **ESTES PARK**—Baja Broadband

EVANS—See GREELEY, CO (Comcast Cable)

EVANSTON—See LONGMONT, CO (Comcast Cable)

EVERGREEN (PORTIONS)—See CONIFER, CO (US Cable)

EVERGREEN—See DENVER (suburbs), CO (Comcast Cable)

▲ **FAIRPLAY**—Formerly served by Cebridge Connections. No longer in operation

▲ **FALCON**—Falcon PTC. This cable system has converted to IPTV. See El Paso County (eastern portions), CO [CO5007]

FEDERAL HEIGHTS—See DENVER (suburbs), CO (Comcast Cable)

FIRESTONE—See LONGMONT, CO (Comcast Cable)

▲ **FLAGLER COUNTY (PORTIONS)**—NexHorizon Communications

▲ **FLEMING**—PC Telcom

FLORENCE—See CANON CITY, CO (Bresnan Communications)

▲ **FORT CARSON**—Baja Broadband

▲ **FORT COLLINS**—Formerly served by Sprint Corp. No longer in operation

▲ **FORT COLLINS**—Comcast Cable

FORT GARLAND—See BLANCA, CO (Jade Communications-Direct TV)

▲ **FORT LUPTON**—Comcast Cable. Now served by LONGMONT, CO [CO0011]

FORT LUPTON—See LONGMONT, CO (Comcast Cable)

▲ **FORT MORGAN**—Bresnan Communications

FOUNTAIN—See COLORADO SPRINGS, CO (Comcast Cable)

▲ **FOWLER**—Bresnan Communications. Now served by LA JUNTA, CO [CO0040]

FOWLER—See LA JUNTA, CO (Bresnan Communications)

FOXFIELD—See DENVER (suburbs), CO (Comcast Cable)

FRANKTOWN—See DENVER (suburbs), CO (Comcast Cable)

FRASER—See GRANBY, CO (Comcast Cable)

▲ **FREDERICK**—Comcast Cable. Now served by LONGMONT, CO [CO0011]

FREDERICK—See LONGMONT, CO (Comcast Cable)

FREMONT COUNTY—See CANON CITY, CO (Bresnan Communications)

FRISCO—See SILVERTHORNE, CO (Comcast Cable)

FRUITA—See GRAND JUNCTION, CO (Bresnan Communications)

FRUITVALE—See GRAND JUNCTION, CO (Bresnan Communications)

GARDEN CITY—See GREELEY, CO (Comcast Cable)

GARFIELD COUNTY—See ASPEN, CO (Comcast Cable)

GARFIELD COUNTY—See RIFLE, CO (Comcast Cable)

▲ **GENESEE**—Formerly served by Comcast Cable. No longer in operation

GEORGETOWN—See DENVER (suburbs), CO (Comcast Cable)

▲ **GILCREST**—US Cable

▲ **GILPIN COUNTY**—Formerly served by CAMS Cable. No longer in operation

GLENDALE—See DENVER, CO (Comcast Cable)

▲ **GLENWOOD SPRINGS**—Comcast Cable. Now served by ASPEN, CO [CO0017]

GLENWOOD SPRINGS—See ASPEN, CO (Comcast Cable)

GOLDEN—See DENVER (suburbs), CO (Comcast Cable)

▲ **GRANADA**—NexHorizon Communications

▲ **GRANBY**—Comcast Cable

GRAND COUNTY (UNINCORPORATED AREAS)—See KREMMLING, CO (Comcast Cable)

GRAND COUNTY—See GRANBY, CO (Comcast Cable)

▲ **GRAND JUNCTION**—Bresnan Communications

GRAND LAKE—See GRANBY, CO (Comcast Cable)

▲ **GREELEY**—Comcast Cable

GREEN MOUNTAIN FALLS—See COLORADO SPRINGS, CO (Comcast Cable)

GREENWOOD VILLAGE—See DENVER (suburbs), CO (Comcast Cable)

GUNNISON COUNTY—See GUNNISON, CO (Time Warner Cable)

▲ **GUNNISON**—Time Warner Cable

GYPSUM—See EAGLE, CO (CenturyTel)

HAXTUN—See HOLYOKE, CO (PC Telcom)

▲ **HAYDEN**—Bresnan Communications. Now served by CRAIG, CO [CO0039]

HAYDEN—See CRAIG, CO (Bresnan Communications)

▲ **HERMOSA**—Hermosa Cablevision Inc. Now served by DURANGO, CO [CO0023]

HERMOSA—See DURANGO, CO (Bresnan Communications)

▲ **HIGHLANDS RANCH**—Comcast Cable. Now served by Denver (suburbs), CO [CO0001]

▲ **HIGHLANDS RANCH**—Qwest Choice TV. IPTV service has been discontinued.

▲ **HIGHLANDS RANCH**—Qwest Choice TV. This cable system has converted to IPTV. See Highlands Ranch, CO [CO5003]

HIGHLANDS RANCH—See DENVER (suburbs), CO (Comcast Cable)

▲ **HOLIDAY VILLAGE**—Formerly served by Island Cable. No longer in operation

▲ **HOLLY**—NexHorizon Communications

▲ **HOLYOKE**—PC Telcom

HOT SULPHUR SPRINGS—See GRANBY, CO (Comcast Cable)

▲ **HOTCHKISS**—Rocky Mountain Cable

▲ **HUDSON**—Formerly served by US Cable of Coastal Texas LP. No longer in operation

HUERFANO COUNTY (PORTIONS)—See WALSENBURG, CO (Bresnan Communications)

▲ **HUGO**—NexHorizon Communications

HYGIENE—See LONGMONT, CO (Comcast Cable)

▲ **IDAHO SPRINGS**—Comcast Cable. Now served by DENVER (suburbs), CO [CO0001]

IDAHO SPRINGS—See DENVER (suburbs), CO (Comcast Cable)

IDLEDALE—See DENVER (suburbs), CO (Comcast Cable)

▲ **IGNACIO**—Rural Route Video

INDIAN HILLS—See DENVER (suburbs), CO (Comcast Cable)

JANSEN—See TRINIDAD, CO (Comcast Cable)

JEFFERSON COUNTY (SOUTHERN PORTION)—See CONIFER, CO (US Cable)

JEFFERSON COUNTY—See DENVER (suburbs), CO (Comcast Cable)

JOHNSON VILLAGE—See BUENA VISTA, CO (Bresnan Communications)

▲ **JOHNSTOWN**—US Cable

▲ **JULESBURG**—PC Telcom

▲ **KERSEY**—US Cable. No longer in operation

KEYSTONE—See SILVERTHORNE, CO (Comcast Cable)

KIOWA—See DENVER (suburbs), CO (Comcast Cable)

▲ **KIT CARSON**—Rebeltec Communications

KITTREDGE—See DENVER (suburbs), CO (Comcast Cable)

▲ **KREMMLING**—Comcast Cable

LA JARA—See MANASSA, CO (Bresnan Communications)

▲ **LA JUNTA**—Bresnan Communications

LA PLATA COUNTY—See DURANGO, CO (Bresnan Communications)

LA SALLE—See GREELEY, CO (Comcast Cable)

▲ **LA VETA**—Formerly served by Westcom II LLC. No longer in operation

LAFAYETTE—See LONGMONT, CO (Comcast Cable)

▲ **LAKE CITY**—Rocky Mountain Cable

LAKE COUNTY—See LEADVILLE, CO (Bresnan Communications)

▲ **LAKEWOOD**—Comcast Cable

LAKEWOOD—See DENVER (suburbs), CO (Comcast Cable)

▲ **LAMAR**—Bresnan Communications

▲ **LAPORTE**—US Cable of Coastal Texas LP. Now served by EATON, CO [CO0055]

LAPORTE—See EATON, CO (US Cable)

LARIMER COUNTY (PORTIONS)—See FORT COLLINS, CO (Comcast Cable)

LARIMER COUNTY (PORTIONS)—See EATON, CO (US Cable)

LARIMER COUNTY—See ESTES PARK, CO (Baja Broadband)

LARIMER COUNTY—See LONGMONT, CO (Comcast Cable)

▲ **LARIMER COUNTY**—NexHorizon Communications

LARKSPUR—See DENVER (suburbs), CO (Comcast Cable)

LAS ANIMAS COUNTY (PORTIONS)—See TRINIDAD, CO (Comcast Cable)

▲ **LAS ANIMAS**—Baja Broadband

LAWSON—See DENVER (suburbs), CO (Comcast Cable)

LAZEAR—See HOTCHKISS, CO (Rocky Mountain Cable)

LEADVILLE NORTH—See LEADVILLE, CO (Bresnan Communications)

▲ **LEADVILLE**—Bresnan Communications

▲ **LIMON**—Formerly served by CAMS Cable. No longer in operation

LINCOLN PARK—See CANON CITY, CO (Bresnan Communications)

LITTLETON—See DENVER (suburbs), CO (Comcast Cable)

LOCHBUIE—See DENVER (suburbs), CO (Comcast Cable)

LOG LANE VILLAGE—See FORT MORGAN, CO (Bresnan Communications)

LOGAN COUNTY—See STERLING, CO (Bresnan Communications)

LONE TREE—See DENVER (suburbs), CO (Comcast Cable)

▲**LONGMONT**—Comcast Cable

LOUISVILLE—See LONGMONT, CO (Comcast Cable)

LOUVIERS—See DENVER (suburbs), CO (Comcast Cable)

▲**LOVELAND (Columbine Mobile Home Park)**—Formerly served by US Cable of Coastal Texas LP. No longer in operation

LOVELAND—See LONGMONT, CO (Comcast Cable)

▲**LYONS (TOWN)**—CAMS Cable

▲**MANASSA**—Bresnan Communications

▲**MANCOS**—Bresnan Communications. Now served by DOLORES, CO [CO0106]

MANCOS—See DOLORES, CO (Bresnan Communications)

MANITOU SPRINGS—See COLORADO SPRINGS, CO (Comcast Cable)

▲**MANZANOLA**—Bresnan Communications. Now served by LA JUNTA, CO [CO0040]

MANZANOLA—See LA JUNTA, CO (Bresnan Communications)

MARSHDALE PARK—See CONIFER, CO (US Cable)

▲**MEAD**—K2 Communications

▲**MEEKER**—Bresnan Communications

▲**MERINO**—Kentec Communications

MESA COUNTY—See GRAND JUNCTION, CO (Bresnan Communications)

MILLIKEN—See JOHNSTOWN, CO (US Cable)

MINTURN—See AVON, CO (Comcast Cable)

MOFFAT COUNTY—See CRAIG, CO (Bresnan Communications)

▲**MONTE VISTA**—Bresnan Communications. Now served by ALAMOSA, CO [CO0035]

MONTE VISTA—See ALAMOSA, CO (Bresnan Communications)

MONTROSE COUNTY—See MONTROSE, CO (Bresnan Communications)

▲**MONTROSE**—Bresnan Communications

▲**MONUMENT**—Formerly served by Adelphia Communications. Now served by COLORADO SPRINGS, CO [CO0003]

MONUMENT—See COLORADO SPRINGS, CO (Comcast Cable)

MORGAN COUNTY—See FORT MORGAN, CO (Bresnan Communications)

MORRISON—See DENVER (suburbs), CO (Comcast Cable)

MOUNT CRESTED BUTTE—See GUNNISON, CO (Time Warner Cable)

MOUNTAIN SHADOW SUBDIVISION—See RIFLE, CO (Comcast Cable)

NATURITA—See NUCLA, CO (Bresnan Communications)

▲**NEDERLAND**—Rocky Mountain Cable

▲**NEW CASTLE (town)**—Comcast Cable. Now served by RIFLE, CO [CO0043]

NEW CASTLE—See RIFLE, CO (Comcast Cable)

NIWOT—See DENVER (suburbs), CO (Comcast Cable)

NORTHGLENN—See DENVER (suburbs), CO (Comcast Cable)

▲**NORWOOD**—B & C Cable

▲**NUCLA**—Bresnan Communications

NUNN—See EATON, CO (US Cable)

▲**OAK CREEK**—Formerly served by Westcom II LLC. No longer in operation

▲**OLATHE**—Rocky Mountain Cable

ORCHARD CITY—See HOTCHKISS, CO (Rocky Mountain Cable)

▲**ORDWAY**—NexHorizon Communications

OTERO COUNTY (UNINCORPORATED AREAS)—See LA JUNTA, CO (Bresnan Communications)

▲**OTIS (TOWN)**—CommuniComm Services

OVID—See JULESBURG, CO (PC Telcom)

▲**PAGOSA SPRINGS**—Rocky Mountain Cable

PALISADE—See GRAND JUNCTION, CO (Bresnan Communications)

PALMER LAKE—See COLORADO SPRINGS, CO (Comcast Cable)

PAONIA (UNINCORPORATED PORTIONS)—See HOTCHKISS, CO (Rocky Mountain Cable)

▲**PAONIA**—Bresnan Communications

▲**PARACHUTE**—Comcast Cable

PARK COUNTY (NORTHWESTERN PORTION)—See CONIFER, CO (US Cable)

PARKER—See DENVER (suburbs), CO (Comcast Cable)

▲**PENROSE (unincorporated areas)**—Bresnan Communications. Now served by CANON CITY, CO [CO0016]

PENROSE—See CANON CITY, CO (Bresnan Communications)

▲**PETERSON AFB**—Peterson Broadband

PIERCE—See EATON, CO (US Cable)

PINETOP-DURANGO WEST—See DURANGO WEST, CO (Bresnan Communications)

PITKIN COUNTY—See ASPEN, CO (Comcast Cable)

PLATTEVILLE—See GILCREST, CO (US Cable)

PONCHA SPRINGS—See SALIDA, CO (Bresnan Communications)

POUDRE VALLEY MOBILE HOME PARK—See EATON, CO (US Cable)

PROWERS COUNTY (UNINCORPORATED AREAS)—See LAMAR, CO (Bresnan Communications)

PUEBLO COUNTY—See COLORADO CITY, CO (Bresnan Communications)

PUEBLO COUNTY—See PUEBLO, CO (Comcast Cable)

▲**PUEBLO WEST**—Comcast Cable. Now served by PUEBLO, CO [CO0005]

PUEBLO WEST—See PUEBLO, CO (Comcast Cable)

▲**PUEBLO**—Comcast Cable

▲**RANGELY**—Bresnan Communications

▲**RIFLE**—Comcast Cable

RIO BLANCO COUNTY—See MEEKER, CO (Bresnan Communications)

RIO BLANCO COUNTY—See RANGELY, CO (Bresnan Communications)

RIO GRANDE COUNTY (PORTIONS)—See ALAMOSA, CO (Bresnan Communications)

RIO GRANDE COUNTY—See DEL NORTE, CO (Bresnan Communications)

RIVER VALLEY VILLAGE MOBILE HOME PARK—See WELD COUNTY, CO (NexHorizon Communications)

RIVERBEND—See GUNNISON, CO (Time Warner Cable)

ROCKRIMMON—See COLORADO SPRINGS, CO (Comcast Cable)

ROCKVALE—See CANON CITY, CO (Bresnan Communications)

▲**ROCKY FORD**—Bresnan Communications. Now served by LA JUNTA, CO [CO0040]

ROCKY FORD—See LA JUNTA, CO (Bresnan Communications)

ROGERS MESA—See HOTCHKISS, CO (Rocky Mountain Cable)

ROMEO—See MANASSA, CO (Bresnan Communications)

ROUTT COUNTY—See STEAMBOAT SPRINGS, CO (Comcast Cable)

RYE—See COLORADO CITY, CO (Bresnan Communications)

▲**SAGUACHE**—Rocky Mountain Cable

▲**SALIDA**—Bresnan Communications

▲**SAN LUIS**—Bresnan Communications

SAN PABLO—See SAN LUIS, CO (Bresnan Communications)

SANFORD—See MANASSA, CO (Bresnan Communications)

SEDALIA—See DENVER (suburbs), CO (Comcast Cable)

▲**SEDGWICK**—PC Telcom

▲**SEIBERT**—Formerly served by B & C Cablevision Inc. No longer in operation

SHERIDAN—See DENVER (suburbs), CO (Comcast Cable)

▲**SILT**—Comcast Cable. Now served by RIFLE, CO [CO0043]

SILT—See RIFLE, CO (Comcast Cable)

SILVER CREEK—See GRANBY, CO (Comcast Cable)

SILVER PLUME—See DENVER (suburbs), CO (Comcast Cable)

▲**SILVERTHORNE**—Comcast Cable

▲**SILVERTON**—Rocky Mountain Cable

▲**SIMLA**—Formerly served by FairPoint Communications. No longer in operation

SKYLAND—See GUNNISON, CO (Time Warner Cable)

SNOWMASS VILLAGE—See ASPEN, CO (Comcast Cable)

▲**SOUTH FORK**—Rocky Mountain Cable

SOUTHERN UTE INDIAN RESERVATION—See IGNACIO, CO (Rural Route Video)

▲**SPRINGFIELD**—Baja Broadband

ST. CHARLES MESA—See PUEBLO, CO (Comcast Cable)

▲**STAGECOACH**—Formerly served by Westcom II LLC. No longer in operation

▲**STEAMBOAT SPRINGS**—Comcast Cable

▲**STERLING**—Bresnan Communications

STRASBURG—See DENVER (suburbs), CO (Comcast Cable)

▲**STRATTON**—NexHorizon Communication

▲**SUGAR CITY**—Formerly served by CableDirect. No longer in operation

SUMMIT COUNTY—See SILVERTHORNE, CO (Comcast Cable)

▲**SUNNYSIDE**—Rural Route Video

▲**SUNSET CREEK**—Formerly served by Island Cable. No longer in operation

SUPERIOR—See LONGMONT, CO (Comcast Cable)

SWINK—See LA JUNTA, CO (Bresnan Communications)

▲**TABLE MOUNTAIN**—US Cable

▲**TELLURIDE**—Time Warner Cable

THORNTON—See DENVER (suburbs), CO (Comcast Cable)

TORRES—See SOUTH FORK, CO (Rocky Mountain Cable)

▲**TOWAOC**—Ute Mountain Cable TV

▲**TRINIDAD**—Comcast Cable

VAIL—See AVON, CO (Comcast Cable)

▲**VALDEZ**—Formerly served by Wozniak TV. No longer in operation

▲**VICTOR**—Bresnan Communications

▲**WALDEN**—Bresnan Communications

▲**WALSENBURG**—Bresnan Communications

▲**WALSH**—NexHorizon Communications

WELBY—See DENVER (suburbs), CO (Comcast Cable)

WELD COUNTY (PORTIONS)—See JOHNSTOWN, CO (US Cable)

WELD COUNTY—See GREELEY, CO (Comcast Cable)

▲**WELD COUNTY**—NexHorizon Communications

WELLINGTON—See EATON, CO (US Cable)

▲**WESTCLIFFE**—Formerly served by NexHorizon Communications. No longer in operation

WESTMINSTER—See DENVER (suburbs), CO (Comcast Cable)

WHEAT RIDGE—See DENVER (suburbs), CO (Comcast Cable)

▲**WIGGINS**—Formerly served by Northern Colorado Communications Inc. No longer in operation

▲**WILEY**—NexHorizon Communications. No longer in operation

WILLIAMSBURG—See CANON CITY, CO (Bresnan Communications)

WINDSOR—See GREELEY, CO (Comcast Cable)

▲**WINTER PARK**—Comcast Cable. Now served by GRANBY, CO [CO0021]

WINTER PARK—See GRANBY, CO (Comcast Cable)

▲**WOODLAND PARK**—US Cable

WOODMOOR—See COLORADO SPRINGS, CO (Comcast Cable)

▲**WRAY**—Eagle Communications

▲**YUMA**—CommuniComm Services. Now served by OTIS, CO [CO0128]

YUMA—See OTIS (town), CO (CommuniComm Services)

CONNECTICUT

ANDOVER—See VERNON, CT (Comcast Cable)

ANSONIA—See SEYMOUR, CT (Comcast Cable)

▲**ASHFORD**—Charter Communications

AVON—See PLAINVILLE (town), CT (Comcast Cable)

BANTAM—See LITCHFIELD, CT (Cablevision Systems Corp.)

BARKHAMSTED—See WINSTED, CT (Charter Communications)

BEACON FALLS—See SEYMOUR, CT (Comcast Cable)

BERLIN—See PLAINVILLE (town), CT (Comcast Cable)

BETHANY—See SEYMOUR, CT (Comcast Cable)

BETHEL—See DANBURY, CT (Comcast Cable)

BETHLEHEM—See LITCHFIELD, CT (Cablevision Systems Corp.)

BETHLEHEM—See NEWTOWN (borough), CT (Charter Communications)

BLOOMFIELD—See HARTFORD, CT (Comcast Cable)

▲**BOLTON**—Comcast of Connecticut. Now served by VERNON, CT [CT0034]

BOLTON—See VERNON, CT (Comcast Cable)

BOZRAH—See NORWICH, CT (Comcast Cable)

▲**BRANFORD**—Comcast Cable

▲**BRIDGEPORT**—Cablevision Systems Corp.

BRIDGEWATER—See NEWTOWN (borough), CT (Charter Communications)

BRISTOL—See PLAINVILLE (town), CT (Comcast Cable)

BROOKFIELD—See NEWTOWN (borough), CT (Charter Communications)

BROOKLYN—See ASHFORD, CT (Charter Communications)

BURLINGTON—See PLAINVILLE (town), CT (Comcast Cable)

BURRVILLE—See LITCHFIELD, CT (Cablevision Systems Corp.)

CANAAN—See LAKEVILLE, CT (Comcast Cable)

CANTERBURY—See ASHFORD, CT (Charter Communications)

CANTON—See PLAINVILLE (town), CT (Comcast Cable)

CENTERBROOK—See CLINTON, CT (Comcast Cable)

CENTRAL VILLAGE—See NEW LONDON, CT (MetroCast Communications of Connecticut)

CHAPLIN—See ASHFORD, CT (Charter Communications)

CHESHIRE—See MERIDEN, CT (Cox Communications)

CHESTER—See CLINTON, CT (Comcast Cable)

▲**CLINTON**—Comcast Cable

COLCHESTER—See NORWICH, CT (Comcast Cable)

COLEBROOK—See WINSTED, CT (Charter Communications)

COLUMBIA—See ASHFORD, CT (Charter Communications)

CORNWALL—See LITCHFIELD, CT (Cablevision Systems Corp.)

COVENTRY—See ASHFORD, CT (Charter Communications)

CROMWELL—See MIDDLETOWN, CT (Comcast Cable)

▲**DANBURY**—Comcast Cable

DANIELSON—See NEW LONDON, CT (MetroCast Communications of Connecticut)

DARIEN—See NORWALK, CT (Cablevision Systems Corp.)

DAYVILLE—See NEW LONDON, CT (MetroCast Communications of Connecticut)

DEEP RIVER—See CLINTON, CT (Comcast Cable)

DERBY—See SEYMOUR, CT (Comcast Cable)

DURHAM—See CLINTON, CT (Comcast Cable)

EAST GLASTONBURY—See MANCHESTER, CT (Cox Communications)

EAST GRANBY—See ENFIELD, CT (Cox Communications)

EAST HADDAM—See OLD LYME, CT (Comcast Cable)

EAST HAMPTON—See MIDDLETOWN, CT (Comcast Cable)

EAST HARTFORD—See HARTFORD, CT (Comcast Cable)

EAST HAVEN—See BRANFORD, CT (Comcast Cable)

EAST LYME—See NEW LONDON, CT (MetroCast Communications of Connecticut)

EAST WINDSOR—See ENFIELD, CT (Cox Communications)

EASTFORD—See ASHFORD, CT (Charter Communications)

EASTON—See NORWALK, CT (Cablevision Systems Corp.)

ELLINGTON—See VERNON, CT (Comcast Cable)

▲**ENFIELD**—Cox Communications

ESSEX—See CLINTON, CT (Comcast Cable)

FAIRFIELD COUNTY—See BRIDGEPORT, CT (Cablevision Systems Corp.)

FALLS VILLAGE—See LAKEVILLE, CT (Comcast Cable)

FARMINGTON—See PLAINVILLE (town), CT (Comcast Cable)

FRANKLIN—See NORWICH, CT (Comcast Cable)

GALES FERRY—See GROTON, CT (Comcast Cable)

GLASTONBURY—See MANCHESTER, CT (Cox Communications)

GOSHEN—See LITCHFIELD, CT (Cablevision Systems Corp.)

GOSHEN—See WINSTED, CT (Charter Communications)

GRANBY—See ENFIELD, CT (Cox Communications)

GREENWICH—See NORWALK, CT (Cablevision Systems Corp.)

GRISWOLD—See NEW LONDON, CT (MetroCast Communications of Connecticut)

▲**GROTON**—Comcast Cable

GUILFORD—See BRANFORD, CT (Comcast Cable)

HADDAM NECK—See OLD LYME, CT (Comcast Cable)

HADDAM—See CLINTON, CT (Comcast Cable)

HAMPTON—See ASHFORD, CT (Charter Communications)

▲**HARTFORD**—Comcast Cable

HARTLAND—See ENFIELD, CT (Cox Communications)

HARWINTON—See WINSTED, CT (Charter Communications)

HEBRON—See VERNON, CT (Comcast Cable)

HIGGANUM—See CLINTON, CT (Comcast Cable)

HUNTINGTON—See SEYMOUR, CT (Comcast Cable)

IVORYTON—See CLINTON, CT (Comcast Cable)

KENT—See NEWTOWN (borough), CT (Charter Communications)

KILLINGLY—See NEW LONDON, CT (MetroCast Communications of Connecticut)

KILLINGWORTH—See CLINTON, CT (Comcast Cable)

▲**LAKEVILLE**—Comcast Cable

LEBANON—See ASHFORD, CT (Charter Communications)

LEDYARD—See GROTON, CT (Comcast Cable)

LISBON—See NORWICH, CT (Comcast Cable)

▲**LITCHFIELD**—Cablevision Systems Corp.

LYME—See OLD LYME, CT (Comcast Cable)

MADISON—See BRANFORD, CT (Comcast Cable)

▲**MANCHESTER**—Cox Communications

MANSFIELD—See ASHFORD, CT (Charter Communications)

MARLBOROUGH—See VERNON, CT (Comcast Cable)

▲**MERIDEN**—Cox Communications

MIDDLEBURY—See WATERBURY, CT (Comcast Cable)

MIDDLEFIELD—See MIDDLETOWN, CT (Comcast Cable)

▲**MIDDLETOWN**—Comcast Cable

MILFORD—See BRIDGEPORT, CT (Cablevision Systems Corp.)

MILTON—See LITCHFIELD, CT (Cablevision Systems Corp.)

MONROE—See NEWTOWN (borough), CT (Charter Communications)

MONTVILLE—See NEW LONDON, CT (MetroCast Communications of Connecticut)

MOOSUP—See NEW LONDON, CT (MetroCast Communications of Connecticut)

MORRIS—See LITCHFIELD, CT (Cablevision Systems Corp.)

MYSTIC—See GROTON, CT (Comcast Cable)

NAUGATUCK—See SEYMOUR, CT (Comcast Cable)

NEW BRITAIN—See PLAINVILLE (town), CT (Comcast Cable)

NEW CANAAN—See NORWALK, CT (Cablevision Systems Corp.)

NEW FAIRFIELD—See NEWTOWN (borough), CT (Charter Communications)

NEW HARTFORD—See WINSTED, CT (Charter Communications)

▲**NEW HAVEN**—Comcast Cable

NEW LONDON SUBMARINE BASE—See GROTON, CT (Comcast Cable)

▲**NEW LONDON**—MetroCast Communications of Connecticut

NEW MILFORD—See NEWTOWN (borough), CT (Charter Communications)

NEWINGTON—See MANCHESTER, CT (Cox Communications)

▲**NEWTOWN (BOROUGH)**—Charter Communications

NIANTIC—See NEW LONDON, CT (MetroCast Communications of Connecticut)

NORFOLK—See LAKEVILLE, CT (Comcast Cable)

NORTH BRANFORD—See BRANFORD, CT (Comcast Cable)

NORTH CANAAN—See LAKEVILLE, CT (Comcast Cable)

NORTH HAVEN—See BRANFORD, CT (Comcast Cable)

NORTH STONINGTON—See GROTON, CT (Comcast Cable)

NORTHFIELD—See LITCHFIELD, CT (Cablevision Systems Corp.)

NORTHFORD—See BRANFORD, CT (Comcast Cable)

▲**NORWALK**—Cablevision Systems Corp.

▲**NORWICH**—Comcast Cable

OAKDALE—See NEW LONDON, CT (MetroCast Communications of Connecticut)

OAKVILLE—See LITCHFIELD, CT (Cablevision Systems Corp.)

▲**OLD LYME**—Comcast Cable

OLD MYSTIC—See GROTON, CT (Comcast Cable)

OLD SAYBROOK—See CLINTON, CT (Comcast Cable)

ONECO—See NEW LONDON, CT (MetroCast Communications of Connecticut)

ORANGE—See BRIDGEPORT, CT (Cablevision Systems Corp.)

OXFORD—See SEYMOUR, CT (Comcast Cable)

PAWCATUCK—See GROTON, CT (Comcast Cable)

PLAINFIELD—See NEW LONDON, CT (MetroCast Communications of Connecticut)

▲**PLAINVILLE (TOWN)**—Comcast Cable

PLYMOUTH—See WATERBURY, CT (Comcast Cable)

POMFRET—See ASHFORD, CT (Charter Communications)

PORTLAND—See MIDDLETOWN, CT (Comcast Cable)

PRESTON—See NORWICH, CT (Comcast Cable)

PROSPECT—See WATERBURY, CT (Comcast Cable)

PUTNAM—See NEW LONDON, CT (MetroCast Communications of Connecticut)

QUAKER HILL—See NEW LONDON, CT (MetroCast Communications of Connecticut)

REDDING—See NORWALK, CT (Cablevision Systems Corp.)

RIDGEFIELD—See DANBURY, CT (Comcast Cable)

ROCKFALL—See MIDDLETOWN, CT (Comcast Cable)

ROCKY HILL—See MANCHESTER, CT (Cox Communications)

ROGERS—See NEW LONDON, CT (MetroCast Communications of Connecticut)

ROXBURY—See NEWTOWN (borough), CT (Charter Communications)

SALEM—See OLD LYME, CT (Comcast Cable)

SALISBURY—See LAKEVILLE, CT (Comcast Cable)

SCOTLAND—See ASHFORD, CT (Charter Communications)

▲**SEYMOUR**—Comcast Cable

SHARON—See LAKEVILLE, CT (Comcast Cable)

SHELTON—See SEYMOUR, CT (Comcast Cable)

SHERMAN—See NEWTOWN (borough), CT (Charter Communications)

SIMSBURY—See HARTFORD, CT (Comcast Cable)

SOMERS—See ENFIELD, CT (Cox Communications)

SOUTH GLASTONBURY—See MANCHESTER, CT (Cox Communications)

SOUTH WINDSOR—See MANCHESTER, CT (Cox Communications)

SOUTHBURY—See NEWTOWN (borough), CT (Charter Communications)

SOUTHINGTON—See MERIDEN, CT (Cox Communications)

SPRAGUE—See NORWICH, CT (Comcast Cable)

STAFFORD—See ENFIELD, CT (Cox Communications)

STAMFORD—See NORWALK, CT (Cablevision Systems Corp.)

STERLING—See NEW LONDON, CT (MetroCast Communications of Connecticut)

STONINGTON—See GROTON, CT (Comcast Cable)

STRATFORD—See BRIDGEPORT, CT (Cablevision Systems Corp.)

SUFFIELD—See ENFIELD, CT (Cox Communications)

TERRYVILLE—See WATERBURY, CT (Comcast Cable)

THOMASTON—See LITCHFIELD, CT (Cablevision Systems Corp.)

THOMPSON—See ASHFORD, CT (Charter Communications)

TOLLAND—See VERNON, CT (Comcast Cable)

TORRINGTON—See LITCHFIELD, CT (Cablevision Systems Corp.)

TRUMBULL—See NEWTOWN (borough), CT (Charter Communications)

UNION—See ENFIELD, CT (Cox Communications)

▲**VERNON**—Comcast Cable

VOLUNTOWN—See GROTON, CT (Comcast Cable)

WALLINGFORD—See BRANFORD, CT (Comcast Cable)

WARREN—See LITCHFIELD, CT (Cablevision Systems Corp.)

WASHINGTON—See NEWTOWN (borough), CT (Charter Communications)

▲**WATERBURY**—Comcast Cable

WATERFORD—See NEW LONDON, CT (MetroCast Communications of Connecticut)

WATERTOWN—See LITCHFIELD, CT (Cablevision Systems Corp.)

WAUREGAN—See NEW LONDON, CT (MetroCast Communications of Connecticut)

WEST CORNWALL—See LAKEVILLE, CT (Comcast Cable)

WEST HARTFORD—See HARTFORD, CT (Comcast Cable)

WEST HARTLAND—See WINSTED, CT (Charter Communications)

WESTBROOK—See CLINTON, CT (Comcast Cable)

WESTON—See NORWALK, CT (Cablevision Systems Corp.)

WESTPORT—See NORWALK, CT (Cablevision Systems Corp.)

WETHERSFIELD—See MANCHESTER, CT (Cox Communications)

WILLIMANTIC—See ASHFORD, CT (Charter Communications)

WILLINGTON—See ASHFORD, CT (Charter Communications)

WILTON—See NORWALK, CT (Cablevision Systems Corp.)

WINCHESTER—See WINSTED, CT (Charter Communications)

WINDHAM—See ASHFORD, CT (Charter Communications)

WINDSOR LOCKS—See ENFIELD, CT (Cox Communications)

WINDSOR—See HARTFORD, CT (Comcast Cable)

▲**WINSTED**—Charter Communications

WOLCOTT—See WATERBURY, CT (Comcast Cable)

WOODBRIDGE—See BRIDGEPORT, CT (Cablevision Systems Corp.)

WOODBURY—See NEWTOWN (borough), CT (Charter Communications)

WOODSTOCK—See ASHFORD, CT (Charter Communications)

DELAWARE

ARDEN—See WILMINGTON, DE (Comcast Cable)

ARDENCROFT—See WILMINGTON, DE (Comcast Cable)

ARDENTOWN—See WILMINGTON, DE (Comcast Cable)

BELLEFONTE—See WILMINGTON, DE (Comcast Cable)

BETHANY BEACH—See DAGSBORO, DE (Mediacom)

BETHEL—See REHOBOTH BEACH, DE (Comcast Cable)

BISHOPVILLE—See DAGSBORO, MD (Mediacom)

BLADES—See REHOBOTH BEACH, DE (Comcast Cable)

BOWERS BEACH—See DOVER, DE (Comcast Cable)

BRIDGEVILLE—See REHOBOTH BEACH, DE (Comcast Cable)

CAMDEN—See DOVER, DE (Comcast Cable)

CECIL COUNTY (PORTIONS)—See MIDDLETOWN (town), MD (Atlantic Broadband)

CHESAPEAKE CITY—See MIDDLETOWN (town), MD (Atlantic Broadband)

CHESWOLD—See DOVER, DE (Comcast Cable)

CLARKSVILLE—See DAGSBORO, DE (Mediacom)

CLAYTON—See DOVER, DE (Comcast Cable)

▲ **DAGSBORO**—Mediacom

DELAWARE CITY—See MIDDLETOWN (town), DE (Atlantic Broadband)

DEWEY BEACH—See REHOBOTH BEACH, DE (Comcast Cable)

DOVER AFB—See DOVER, DE (Comcast Cable)

▲ **DOVER**—Comcast Cable

ELKTON (PORTIONS)—See MIDDLETOWN (town), MD (Atlantic Broadband)

ELLENDALE—See REHOBOTH BEACH, DE (Comcast Cable)

ELSMERE—See WILMINGTON, DE (Comcast Cable)

FARMINGTON—See DOVER, DE (Comcast Cable)

FELTON—See DOVER, DE (Comcast Cable)

FRANKFORD—See DAGSBORO, DE (Mediacom)

FREDERICA—See DOVER, DE (Comcast Cable)

GEORGETOWN—See REHOBOTH BEACH, DE (Comcast Cable)

GREENWOOD—See REHOBOTH BEACH, DE (Comcast Cable)

HARRINGTON—See DOVER, DE (Comcast Cable)

HARTLY—See DOVER, DE (Comcast Cable)

HENLOPEN ACRES—See REHOBOTH BEACH, DE (Comcast Cable)

HOUSTON—See DOVER, DE (Comcast Cable)

KENT COUNTY (PORTIONS)—See MIDDLETOWN (town), MD (Atlantic Broadband)

KENT COUNTY (UNINCORPORATED AREAS)—See REHOBOTH BEACH, DE (Comcast Cable)

KENT COUNTY—See DOVER, DE (Comcast Cable)

KENTON—See DOVER, DE (Comcast Cable)

LAUREL—See REHOBOTH BEACH, DE (Comcast Cable)

LEIPSIC—See DOVER, DE (Comcast Cable)

LEWES—See REHOBOTH BEACH, DE (Comcast Cable)

LINCOLN—See REHOBOTH BEACH, DE (Comcast Cable)

LITTLE CREEK—See DOVER, DE (Comcast Cable)

MAGNOLIA—See DOVER, DE (Comcast Cable)

MARYDEL—See DOVER, DE (Comcast Cable)

▲ **MIDDLETOWN (TOWN)**—Atlantic Broadband

MILFORD—See REHOBOTH BEACH, DE (Comcast Cable)

MILLSBORO—See DAGSBORO, DE (Mediacom)

MILLVILLE—See DAGSBORO, DE (Mediacom)

MILTON—See REHOBOTH BEACH, DE (Comcast Cable)

NEW CASTLE COUNTY (SOUTHERN PORTION)—See DOVER, DE (Comcast Cable)

NEW CASTLE COUNTY—See MIDDLETOWN (town), DE (Atlantic Broadband)

NEW CASTLE COUNTY—See WILMINGTON, DE (Comcast Cable)

NEW CASTLE—See WILMINGTON, DE (Comcast Cable)

NEWARK—See WILMINGTON, DE (Comcast Cable)

NEWPORT—See WILMINGTON, DE (Comcast Cable)

OCEAN PINES—See DAGSBORO, MD (Mediacom)

OCEAN VIEW—See DAGSBORO, DE (Mediacom)

ODESSA—See MIDDLETOWN (town), DE (Atlantic Broadband)

PERRY POINT—See MIDDLETOWN (town), MD (Atlantic Broadband)

PERRYVILLE—See MIDDLETOWN (town), MD (Atlantic Broadband)

PITTSVILLE—See DAGSBORO, MD (Mediacom)

PORT DEPOSIT—See MIDDLETOWN (town), MD (Atlantic Broadband)

▲ **REHOBOTH BEACH**—Comcast Cable

ROXANA—See DAGSBORO, DE (Mediacom)

SEAFORD—See REHOBOTH BEACH, DE (Comcast Cable)

SELBYVILLE—See DAGSBORO, DE (Mediacom)

SLAUGHTER BEACH—See REHOBOTH BEACH, DE (Comcast Cable)

SMYRNA—See DOVER, DE (Comcast Cable)

SOUTH BETHANY—See DAGSBORO, DE (Mediacom)

ST. GEORGES—See MIDDLETOWN (town), DE (Atlantic Broadband)

SUSSEX COUNTY (PORTIONS)—See REHOBOTH BEACH, DE (Comcast Cable)

SUSSEX COUNTY—See DAGSBORO, DE (Mediacom)

TOWNSEND—See MIDDLETOWN (town), DE (Atlantic Broadband)

VIOLA—See DOVER, DE (Comcast Cable)

WHALEYSVILLE—See DAGSBORO, MD (Mediacom)

WILLARDS—See DAGSBORO, MD (Mediacom)

▲ **WILMINGTON**—Comcast Cable

WOODSIDE—See DOVER, DE (Comcast Cable)

WYOMING—See DOVER, DE (Comcast Cable)

DISTRICT OF COLUMBIA

▲ **ADAMS MORGAN**—RCN Corp. Formerly [DC0006]. This cable system has converted to IPTV

▲ **ANACOSTIA**—RCN Corp. Formerly [DC0006]. This cable system has converted to IPTV

▲ **BENNING ROAD**—RCN Corp. Formerly [DC0006]. This cable system has converted to IPTV

▲ **BOLLING AFB**—Mid-Atlantic Communications. Now served by WASHINGTON, DC [DC0001]

BOLLING AFB—See WASHINGTON, DC (Comcast Cable)

▲ **BROOKLAND**—RCN Corp. Formerly [DC0006]. This cable system has converted to IPTV

▲ **CAPITOL HILL**—RCN Corp. Formerly [DC0006]. This cable system has converted to IPTV

▲ **CHINATOWN**—RCN Corp. Formerly [DC0006]. This cable system has converted to IPTV

▲ **CLEVELAND PARK**—RCN Corp. Formerly [DC0006]. This cable system has converted to IPTV

▲ **COLUMBIA HEIGHTS**—RCN Corp. Formerly [DC0006]. This cable system has converted to IPTV

▲ **CONGRESS HEIGHTS**—RCN Corp. Formerly [DC0006]. This cable system has converted to IPTV

▲ **DUPONT CIRCLE**—RCN Corp. Formerly [DC0006]. This cable system has converted to IPTV

▲ **FORT TOTTEN**—RCN Corp. Formerly [DC0006]. This cable system has converted to IPTV

▲ **FRIENDSHIP HEIGHTS**—RCN Corp. Formerly [DC0006]. This cable system has converted to IPTV

▲ **GLOVER PARK**—RCN Corp. Formerly [DC0006]. This cable system has converted to IPTV

▲ **MOUNT PLEASANT**—RCN Corp. Formerly [DC0006]. This cable system has converted to IPTV

▲ **MOUNT VERNON SQUARE**—RCN Corp. Formerly [DC0006]. This cable system has converted to IPTV

▲ **PETWORTH**—RCN Corp. Formerly [DC0006]. This cable system has converted to IPTV

▲ **SHAW**—RCN Corp. Formerly [DC0006]. This cable system has converted to IPTV

▲ **TENLEYTOWN**—RCN Corp. Formerly [DC0006]. This cable system has converted to IPTV

▲ **U.S. SOLDIERS' & AIRMEN'S HOME**—Chesapeake Cable Partners. Now served by WASHINGTON, DC [DC0001]

U.S. SOLDIERS' & AIRMEN'S HOME—See WASHINGTON, DC (Comcast Cable)

▲ **VAN NESS**—RCN Corp. Formerly [DC0006]. This cable system has converted to IPTV

▲ **WASHINGTON (northwestern portion)**—RCN Corp. Now served by WASHINGTON (formerly WASHINGTON southeastern portion), DC [DC0006]

▲ **WASHINGTON**—RCN Corp. This cable system has converted to IPTV and has been broken into 19 communities. See [DC5001] through [DC5019]

▲ **WASHINGTON**—Comcast Cable

FLORIDA

▲ **ADVENT CHRISTIAN VILLAGE**—Advent Christian Village Cable TV

ALACHUA COUNTY (PORTIONS)—See GAINESVILLE, FL (Cox Communications)

ALACHUA COUNTY—See ALACHUA, FL (CommuniComm Services)

▲ **ALACHUA**—CommuniComm Services

ALACHUA—See GAINESVILLE, FL (Cox Communications)

ALFORD—See MARIANNA, FL (Comcast Cable)

▲ **ALLIGATOR POINT**—Mediacom. Now served by WEWAHITCHKA, FL [FL0159]

ALLIGATOR POINT—See WEWAHITCHKA, FL (Mediacom)

ALTAMONTE SPRINGS—See ORLANDO, FL (Bright House Networks)

ALTHA—See MARIANNA, FL (Comcast Cable)

ALTOONA—See ASTOR, FL (Florida Cable)

▲ **ALVA**—Time Warner Cable. Now served by NAPLES, FL [FL0029]

ALVA—See NAPLES, FL (Comcast Cable)

AMELIA ISLAND—See JACKSONVILLE, FL (Comcast Cable)

ANNA MARIA—See BRADENTON, FL (Bright House Networks)

ANTHONY—See CITRA, FL (Florida Cable)

▲**APALACHICOLA**—Mediacom. Now served by WEWAHITCHKA, FL [FL0159]

APALACHICOLA—See WEWAHITCHKA, FL (Mediacom)

APOLLO BEACH—See HILLSBOROUGH COUNTY (portions), FL (Bright House Networks)

APOPKA—See ORLANDO, FL (Bright House Networks)

▲**ARCADIA**—Comcast Cable

▲**ARCHER**—Comcast Cable

ASTATULA—See ASTOR, FL (Florida Cable)

▲**ASTOR**—Florida Cable

ATLANTIC BEACH—See JACKSONVILLE, FL (Comcast Cable)

ATLANTIS—See WEST PALM BEACH, FL (Comcast Cable)

ATMORE—See GULF BREEZE, AL (Mediacom)

▲**AUBURNDALE**—Bright House Networks

AVENTURA—See MIAMI BEACH, FL (Atlantic Broadband)

AVENTURA—See MIAMI, FL (Comcast Cable)

AVON PARK AFB—See SEBRING, FL (Comcast Cable)

AVON PARK—See SEBRING, FL (Comcast Cable)

BAKER COUNTY—See MACCLENNY, FL (Comcast Cable)

▲**BAKER**—Mediacom. Now served by MILTON, FL [FL0380]

BAKER—See GULF BREEZE, FL (Mediacom)

BAL HARBOUR—See MIAMI BEACH, FL (Atlantic Broadband)

BALDWIN—See JACKSONVILLE, FL (Comcast Cable)

BALM—See HILLSBOROUGH COUNTY (portions), FL (Bright House Networks)

BAREFOOT BAY—See MELBOURNE, FL (Bright House Networks)

▲**BARTOW**—Comcast Cable

BASCOM—See MARIANNA, FL (Comcast Cable)

BAY COUNTY (PORTIONS)—See WEWAHITCHKA, FL (Mediacom)

BAY COUNTY—See PANAMA CITY, FL (Comcast Cable)

BAY HARBOR ISLANDS—See MIAMI BEACH, FL (Atlantic Broadband)

▲**BAY INDIES MOBILE HOME PARK**—Formerly served by Mobile Home Properties Inc. No longer in operation

BAY PINES—See PINELLAS COUNTY (portions), FL (Bright House Networks)

▲**BELLE GLADE**—Comcast Cable

BELLE ISLE—See ORLANDO, FL (Bright House Networks)

BELLEAIR BEACH—See PINELLAS COUNTY (portions), FL (Bright House Networks)

BELLEAIR BLUFFS—See PINELLAS COUNTY (portions), FL (Bright House Networks)

BELLEAIR SHORES—See PINELLAS COUNTY (portions), FL (Bright House Networks)

BELLEAIR—See PINELLAS COUNTY (portions), FL (Bright House Networks)

BELLEVIEW—See WILDWOOD, FL (Bright House Networks)

▲**BEVERLY BEACH**—Formerly served by TV Max. No longer in operation

BEVERLY BEACH—See DELAND, FL (Bright House Networks)

BEVERLY HILLS—See HOMOSASSA, FL (Bright House Networks)

BEVERLY HILLS—See INVERNESS, FL (Comcast Cable)

BIG COPPITT KEY—See KEY WEST, FL (Comcast Cable)

▲**BIG CYPRESS SEMINOLE INDIAN RESERVATION**—Comcast Cable

BIG PINE KEY—See KEY WEST, FL (Comcast Cable)

BISCAYNE PARK—See MIAMI, FL (Comcast Cable)

BLOOMINGDALE—See HILLSBOROUGH COUNTY (portions), FL (Bright House Networks)

▲**BLOUNTSTOWN**—Bright House Networks

BOCA GRANDE ISLAND—See NAPLES, FL (Comcast Cable)

BOCA GRANDE—See ENGLEWOOD, FL (Comcast Cable)

▲**BOCA RATON**—Comcast Cable. Now served by DELRAY BEACH, FL [FL0091]

▲**BOCA RATON**—Comcast Cable. Now served by DELRAY BEACH, FL [FL0091]

BOCA RATON—See DELRAY BEACH, FL (Comcast Cable)

BOKEELIA—See NAPLES, FL (Comcast Cable)

BONAVENTURE—See BROWARD COUNTY (portions), FL (Comcast Cable)

▲**BONIFAY**—Mediacom. Now served by WEWAHITCHKA, FL [FL0159]

BONIFAY—See WEWAHITCHKA, FL (Mediacom)

BONITA BEACH—See NAPLES, FL (Comcast Cable)

BONITA SPRINGS—See NAPLES, FL (Comcast Cable)

BOSTWICK—See PUTNAM COUNTY (eastern portion), FL (Florida Cable)

▲**BOWLING GREEN**—Comcast Cable

BOYNTON BEACH—See DELRAY BEACH, FL (Comcast Cable)

BOYNTON BEACH—See WEST PALM BEACH, FL (Comcast Cable)

▲**BRADENTON (UNINCORPORATED AREAS)**—Universal Cablevision Inc.

BRADENTON BEACH—See BRADENTON, FL (Bright House Networks)

▲**BRADENTON**—Formerly served by Sprint Corp. No longer in operation

▲**BRADENTON**—Bright House Networks

▲**BRADENTON**—Florida Cable

BRADFORD COUNTY (PORTIONS)—See JACKSONVILLE, FL (Comcast Cable)

BRADFORD COUNTY—See PALATKA, FL (Comcast Cable)

BRADFORD COUNTY—See LAWTEY, FL (Florida Cable)

▲**BRANDON (NORTHERN PORTION)**—Comcast Cable

BRANDON (SOUTHERN PORTION)—See HILLSBOROUGH COUNTY (portions), FL (Bright House Networks)

▲**BRANFORD**—CommuniComm Services

▲**BRATT**—Formerly served by Cable-South Inc. No longer in operation

BREVARD COUNTY (NORTHERN PORTION)—See MIMS, FL (Comcast Cable)

BREVARD COUNTY—See MELBOURNE, FL (Bright House Networks)

BREWTON—See GULF BREEZE, AL (Mediacom)

▲**BRIGHTON SEMINOLE RESERVE**—Comcast Cable

BRISTOL—See BLOUNTSTOWN, FL (Bright House Networks)

▲**BRONSON (TOWN)**—Florida Cable

▲**BROOKER**—New River Cablevision Inc.

BROOKSVILLE (PORTIONS)—See HERNANDO COUNTY, FL (Bright House Networks)

BROOKSVILLE (UNINCORPORATED AREAS)—See HERNANDO COUNTY, FL (Bright House Networks)

BROOKSVILLE—See HERNANDO COUNTY, FL (Florida Cable)

BROWARD COUNTY (PORTIONS)—See CORAL SPRINGS, FL (Advanced Cable Communications)

▲**BROWARD COUNTY (PORTIONS)**—Comcast Cable

BUCKHEAD RIDGE—See OKEECHOBEE, FL (Comcast Cable)

BUNNELL—See DELAND, FL (Bright House Networks)

BUSHNELL—See HERNANDO COUNTY, FL (Florida Cable)

CALHOUN COUNTY (PORTIONS)—See BLOUNTSTOWN, FL (Bright House Networks)

▲**CALLAHAN (town)**—Comcast Cable. Now served by HILLIARD, FL [FL0157]

CALLAHAN—See HILLIARD, FL (Comcast Cable)

CALLAWAY—See PANAMA CITY, FL (Comcast Cable)

▲**CAMPBELLTON**—Campbellton Cable

CANAL POINT—See BELLE GLADE, FL (Comcast Cable)

▲**CANTONMENT**—Bright House Networks

CAPE CANAVERAL—See MELBOURNE, FL (Bright House Networks)

▲**CAPE CORAL**—Time Warner Cable. Now served by NAPLES, FL [FL0029]

CAPE CORAL—See NAPLES, FL (Comcast Cable)

▲**CAPE SAN BLAS**—Mediacom. Now served by WEWAHITCHKA, FL [FL0159]

CAPE SAN BLAS—See WEWAHITCHKA, FL (Mediacom)

CAPTIVA ISLAND—See NAPLES, FL (Comcast Cable)

CARIBBEAN ISLE—See ORLANDO, FL (Bright House Networks)

CARRABELLE—See WEWAHITCHKA, FL (Mediacom)

CASSELBERRY—See ORLANDO, FL (Bright House Networks)

CECIL FIELD NAVAL AIR STATION—See JACKSONVILLE, FL (Comcast Cable)

CEDAR GROVE—See PANAMA CITY, FL (Comcast Cable)

CEDAR GROVE—See SPRINGFIELD, FL (Springfield Cable)

▲**CEDAR KEY**—Bright House Networks

▲**CELEBRATION**—Comcast Cable

▲**CENTURY**—Bright House Networks

CHARLESTON PLACE—See MELBOURNE, FL (Bright House Networks)

CHARLOTTE COUNTY (UNINCORPORATED AREAS)—See PORT CHARLOTTE, FL (Comcast Cable)

▲**CHASEWOOD**—Formerly served by Comcast Cable. No longer in operation

▲ **CHATTAHOOCHEE**—Bright House Networks

▲ **CHIEFLAND**—CommuniComm Services

▲ **CHIPLEY**—Bright House Networks

▲ **CHRISTMAS**—Florida Cable

CINCO BAYOU—See FORT WALTON BEACH, FL (Cox Communications)

▲ **CITRA**—Florida Cable

CITRUS COUNTY (NORTHERN PORTION)—See INVERNESS, FL (Comcast Cable)

CITRUS COUNTY—See HOMOSASSA, FL (Bright House Networks)

CITRUS SPRINGS—See HOMOSASSA, FL (Bright House Networks)

CLAY COUNTY (PORTIONS)—See JACKSONVILLE, FL (Comcast Cable)

CLAY COUNTY—See PALATKA, FL (Comcast Cable)

▲ **CLAY COUNTY**—Florida Cable

CLAY COUNTY—See LAWTEY, FL (Florida Cable)

CLAY HILL—See CLAY COUNTY, FL (Florida Cable)

CLEARWATER—See PINELLAS COUNTY (portions), FL (Bright House Networks)

CLEARWATER—See PINELLAS COUNTY (portions), FL (Knology)

CLERMONT (PORTIONS)—See WILDWOOD, FL (Bright House Networks)

CLERMONT—See ORLANDO, FL (Bright House Networks)

▲ **CLEWISTON**—Now served by BELLE GLADE, FL [FL0073]

CLEWISTON—See BELLE GLADE, FL (Comcast Cable)

CLOUD LAKE—See WEST PALM BEACH, FL (Comcast Cable)

CLOVERLEAF MOBILE HOME PARK—See HERNANDO COUNTY, FL (Bright House Networks)

COCOA BEACH—See MELBOURNE, FL (Bright House Networks)

COCOA—See MELBOURNE, FL (Bright House Networks)

COCONUT CREEK—See BROWARD COUNTY (portions), FL (Comcast Cable)

COLLIER COUNTY—See NAPLES, FL (Comcast Cable)

COLUMBIA COUNTY—See LAKE CITY, FL (Comcast Cable)

CONDO 7—See LIVE OAK, FL (Florida Cable)

COOPER CITY—See BROWARD COUNTY (portions), FL (Comcast Cable)

CORAL GABLES—See MIAMI, FL (Comcast Cable)

▲ **CORAL SPRINGS**—Advanced Cable Communications

COTTAGE HILLS—See CANTONMENT, FL (Bright House Networks)

COTTONDALE—See MARIANNA, FL (Comcast Cable)

▲ **CRAWFORDVILLE**—Comcast Cable. Now served by TALLAHASSEE, FL [FL0283]

CRAWFORDVILLE—See TALLAHASSEE, FL (Comcast Cable)

CRESCENT BEACH—See ST. AUGUSTINE, FL (Comcast Cable)

▲ **CRESCENT CITY**—Comcast Cable

▲ **CRESTVIEW**—Cox Communications. Now served by FORT WALTON BEACH, FL [FL0023]

CRESTVIEW—See FORT WALTON BEACH, FL (Cox Communications)

▲ **CROSS CITY**—CommuniComm Services

CRYSTAL RIVER—See HOMOSASSA, FL (Bright House Networks)

CUTLER RIDGE—See MIAMI, FL (Comcast Cable)

CYPRESS—See MARIANNA, FL (Comcast Cable)

DADE CITY—See PASCO COUNTY (central & eastern portions), FL (Bright House Networks)

DADE COUNTY (PORTIONS)—See MIAMI BEACH, FL (Atlantic Broadband)

DADE COUNTY—See MIAMI, FL (Comcast Cable)

DANIA—See BROWARD COUNTY (portions), FL (Comcast Cable)

DAVENPORT (PORTIONS)—See OSCEOLA COUNTY (western portion), FL (Comcast Cable)

DAVENPORT—See AUBURNDALE, FL (Bright House Networks)

▲ **DAVIE**—Comcast Cable. Now served by BROWARD COUNTY, FL [FL0016]

DAVIE—See BROWARD COUNTY (portions), FL (Comcast Cable)

DAYTONA BEACH SHORES—See DELAND, FL (Bright House Networks)

DAYTONA BEACH—See DELAND, FL (Bright House Networks)

DE BARY (PORTIONS)—See DELAND, FL (Bright House Networks)

▲ **DE FUNIAK SPRINGS**—Bright House Networks

DE LEON SPRINGS—See DELAND, FL (Bright House Networks)

▲ **DEBARY**—Comcast Cable

DEER CREEK GOLF RV PARK—See AUBURNDALE, FL (Bright House Networks)

DEERFIELD BEACH—See BROWARD COUNTY (portions), FL (Comcast Cable)

DEKLE BEACH—See KEATON BEACH, FL (Southeast Cable TV Inc.)

▲ **DELAND**—Bright House Networks

▲ **DELRAY BEACH**—Comcast Cable

DELTONA—See DELAND, FL (Bright House Networks)

DESTIN—See FORT WALTON BEACH, FL (Cox Communications)

DISTRICT FIVE—See DELAND, FL (Bright House Networks)

DISTRICT FOUR—See DELAND, FL (Bright House Networks)

DIXIE COUNTY—See CROSS CITY, FL (CommuniComm Services)

DORAL—See MIAMI, FL (Comcast Cable)

▲ **DOWLING PARK**—Formerly served by KLiP Interactive. No longer in operation

DUCK KEY—See KEY WEST, FL (Comcast Cable)

DUNDEE—See AUBURNDALE, FL (Bright House Networks)

DUNEDIN—See PINELLAS COUNTY (portions), FL (Bright House Networks)

DUNEDIN—See PINELLAS COUNTY (portions), FL (Knology)

▲ **DUNNELLON**—Now served by INVERNESS, FL [FL0319]

DUNNELLON—See INVERNESS, FL (Comcast Cable)

EAGLE LAKE—See AUBURNDALE, FL (Bright House Networks)

EAST BREWTON—See GULF BREEZE, AL (Mediacom)

EAST LAKE WOODLANDS—See PINELLAS COUNTY (portions), FL (Bright House Networks)

▲ **EAST MILTON**—Mediacom. Now served by GULF BREEZE, FL [FL0070]

EAST MILTON—See GULF BREEZE, FL (Mediacom)

EAST PALATKA—See PALATKA, FL (Comcast Cable)

▲ **EASTPOINT**—Mediacom. Now served by WEWAHITCHKA, FL [FL0159]

EASTPOINT—See WEWAHITCHKA, FL (Mediacom)

EATONVILLE—See ORLANDO, FL (Bright House Networks)

EDGEWATER—See DELAND, FL (Bright House Networks)

EDGEWOOD—See ORLANDO, FL (Bright House Networks)

EGLIN AFB—See FORT WALTON BEACH, FL (Cox Communications)

EL PORTAL—See MIAMI, FL (Comcast Cable)

ELFERS—See PASCO COUNTY (western portion), FL (Bright House Networks)

ELLENTON—See BRADENTON, FL (Bright House Networks)

▲ **ENGLEWOOD**—Comcast Cable

ESCAMBIA COUNTY (PORTIONS)—See GULF BREEZE, FL (Mediacom)

ESCAMBIA COUNTY—See CANTONMENT, FL (Bright House Networks)

ESCAMBIA COUNTY—See PENSACOLA, FL (Cox Communications)

ESTERO—See NAPLES, FL (Comcast Cable)

EUREKA—See WILDWOOD, FL (Bright House Networks)

EUSTIS—See LEESBURG, FL (Comcast Cable)

EUSTIS—See ASTOR, FL (Florida Cable)

EUSTIS—See MARION COUNTY (southern portion), FL (Florida Cable)

▲ **EVERGLADES CITY**—Comcast Cable. Now served by NAPLES (formerly BONITA SPRINGS), FL [FL0029]

EVERGLADES CITY—See NAPLES, FL (Comcast Cable)

FAIRFIELD—See PALM CAY, FL (Cablevision of Marion County)

▲ **FANNING SPRINGS**—Florida Cable

FELLSMERE—See VERO BEACH, FL (Comcast Cable)

▲ **FERNANDINA BEACH**—Comcast Cable. Now served by JACKSONVILLE, FL [FL0002]

FERNANDINA BEACH—See JACKSONVILLE, FL (Comcast Cable)

FLAGLER BEACH—See DELAND, FL (Bright House Networks)

FLAGLER COUNTY—See DELAND, FL (Bright House Networks)

FLOMATON—See CENTURY, AL (Bright House Networks)

▲ **FLORAHOME**—Florida Cable

FLORIDA CITY—See MIAMI, FL (Comcast Cable)

▲ **FLORIDA HIGHLANDS**—Formerly served by KLiP Interactive. No longer in operation

▲ **FOREST GLEN**—Formerly served by Comcast Cable. No longer in operation

▲ **FORT LAUDERDALE**—Comcast Cable. Now served by BROWARD COUNTY, FL [FL0016]

FORT LAUDERDALE—See BROWARD COUNTY (portions), FL (Comcast Cable)

FORT MCCOY—See WILDWOOD, FL (Bright House Networks)

FORT MEADE—See BARTOW, FL (Comcast Cable)

FORT MYERS BEACH—See NAPLES, FL (Comcast Cable)

▲**FORT MYERS**—Comcast Cable. Now served by NAPLES (formerly BONITA SPRINGS), FL [FL0029]

FORT MYERS—See NAPLES, FL (Comcast Cable)

FORT OGDEN—See ARCADIA, FL (Comcast Cable)

FORT PIERCE (PORTIONS)—See STUART, FL (Comcast Cable)

▲**FORT PIERCE**—Comcast Cable. Now served by VERO BEACH, FL [FL0040]

▲**FORT PIERCE**—Formerly served by Wireless Broadcasting of Fort Pierce. No longer in operation

FORT PIERCE—See VERO BEACH, FL (Comcast Cable)

▲**FORT WALTON BEACH**—Cox Communications

FRANKLIN COUNTY (PORTIONS)—See WEWAHITCHKA, FL (Mediacom)

▲**FREEPORT**—Cox Communications. Now served by FORT WALTON BEACH, FL [FL0023]

FREEPORT—See FORT WALTON BEACH, FL (Cox Communications)

FROSTPROOF—See LAKE WALES, FL (Comcast Cable)

FRUITLAND PARK—See LEESBURG, FL (Comcast Cable)

▲**FRUITLAND PARK**—Florida Cable

▲**GADSDEN COUNTY (portions)**—Mediacom. Now served by HAVANA, FL [FL0144]

GADSDEN COUNTY (PORTIONS)—See CHATTAHOOCHEE, FL (Bright House Networks)

GADSDEN COUNTY (PORTIONS)—See HAVANA (town), FL (Mediacom)

GADSDEN COUNTY—See TALLAHASSEE, FL (Comcast Cable)

▲**GAINESVILLE**—Cox Communications

GENEVA—See ORLANDO, FL (Bright House Networks)

GEORGETOWN—See WELAKA (town), FL (Comcast Cable)

GIBSONTON—See HILLSBOROUGH COUNTY (portions), FL (Bright House Networks)

GILCHRIST COUNTY (PORTIONS)—See NORTH OLD TOWN, FL (Florida Cable)

GLADES COUNTY (SOUTHERN PORTION)—See NAPLES, FL (Comcast Cable)

GLADES COUNTY—See MOORE HAVEN, FL (Comcast Cable)

GLADES COUNTY—See OKEECHOBEE, FL (Comcast Cable)

GLEN RIDGE—See WEST PALM BEACH, FL (Comcast Cable)

GLEN ST. MARY—See MACCLENNY, FL (Comcast Cable)

GOLDEN BEACH—See MIAMI BEACH, FL (Atlantic Broadband)

▲**GOLDEN GATE**—Time Warner Cable. Now served by NAPLES, FL [FL0029]

GOLDEN GATE—See NAPLES, FL (Comcast Cable)

▲**GOLF VILLAGE**—Now served by DELRAY BEACH, FL [FL0091]

GOLF VILLAGE—See DELRAY BEACH, FL (Comcast Cable)

GOULDS—See MIAMI, FL (Comcast Cable)

GRACEVILLE—See CHIPLEY, FL (Bright House Networks)

GRAND ISLAND—See LEESBURG, FL (Comcast Cable)

GRANDIN—See FLORAHOME, FL (Florida Cable)

GRASSY KEY—See KEY WEST, FL (Comcast Cable)

GREEN COVE SPRINGS—See JACKSONVILLE, FL (Comcast Cable)

▲**GREENACRES CITY**—Now served by WEST PALM BEACH, FL [FL0008]

GREENACRES CITY—See WEST PALM BEACH, FL (Comcast Cable)

▲**GREENSBORO**—Mediacom. Now served by HAVANA, FL [FL0144]

GREENSBORO—See HAVANA (town), FL (Mediacom)

▲**GREENVILLE**—Formerly served by KLiP Interactive. No longer in operation

GREENWOOD MANOR—See MELBOURNE, FL (Bright House Networks)

GREENWOOD VILLAGE—See MELBOURNE, FL (Bright House Networks)

GREENWOOD—See MARIANNA, FL (Comcast Cable)

▲**GRETNA**—Mediacom. Now served by HAVANA, FL [FL0144]

GRETNA—See HAVANA (town), FL (Mediacom)

GROVELAND—See ORLANDO, FL (Bright House Networks)

▲**GULF BREEZE**—Mediacom

GULF COUNTY (PORTIONS)—See WEWAHITCHKA, FL (Mediacom)

GULF STREAM—See DELRAY BEACH, FL (Comcast Cable)

GULFPORT—See PINELLAS COUNTY (portions), FL (Bright House Networks)

HAINES CITY—See AUBURNDALE, FL (Bright House Networks)

HALLANDALE—See BROWARD COUNTY (portions), FL (Comcast Cable)

HAMPTON 2—See HAMPTON, FL (Florida Cable)

▲**HAMPTON**—Florida Cable

HARDEE COUNTY (PORTIONS)—See WAUCHULA, FL (Comcast Cable)

HARTFORD—See DE FUNIAK SPRINGS, AL (Bright House Networks)

▲**HASTINGS**—Comcast Cable

▲**HAVANA (TOWN)**—Mediacom

HAVERHILL—See WEST PALM BEACH, FL (Comcast Cable)

▲**HAWTHORNE**—CommuniComm Services

HAWTHORNE—See PUTNAM COUNTY (western portion), FL (Florida Cable)

HENDRY COUNTY (NORTHEASTERN PORTION)—See BELLE GLADE, FL (Comcast Cable)

HENDRY COUNTY (PORTIONS)—See NAPLES, FL (Comcast Cable)

HERNANDO (PORTIONS)—See INVERNESS, FL (Comcast Cable)

▲**HERNANDO COUNTY**—Bright House Networks

▲**HERNANDO COUNTY**—Florida Cable

HERNANDO—See HOMOSASSA, FL (Bright House Networks)

HIALEAH GARDENS—See MIAMI, FL (Comcast Cable)

▲**HIALEAH**—Comcast Cable. Now served by MIAMI, FL [FL0006]

HIALEAH—See MIAMI, FL (Comcast Cable)

▲**HIDDEN ACRES**—Formerly served by Comcast Cable. No longer in operation

HIDEAWAY MOBILE HOME PARK—See CITRA, FL (Florida Cable)

▲**HIGH SPRINGS**—CommuniComm Services

▲**HIGHLAND BEACH**—Now served by DELRAY BEACH, FL [FL0091]

HIGHLAND BEACH—See DELRAY BEACH, FL (Comcast Cable)

HIGHLANDS COUNTY (PORTIONS)—See SEBRING, FL (Comcast Cable)

HILAND PARK—See SPRINGFIELD, FL (Springfield Cable)

▲**HILLIARD**—Comcast Cable

HILLSBORO BEACH—See BROWARD COUNTY (portions), FL (Comcast Cable)

▲**HILLSBOROUGH COUNTY (PORTIONS)**—Bright House Networks

HOBE SOUND—See STUART, FL (Comcast Cable)

HOLIDAY—See PASCO COUNTY (western portion), FL (Bright House Networks)

HOLLEY (PORTIONS)—See GULF BREEZE, FL (Mediacom)

HOLLISTER—See PALATKA, FL (Comcast Cable)

HOLLY HILL—See DELAND, FL (Bright House Networks)

HOLLYWOOD SEMINOLE RESERVE—See BROWARD COUNTY (portions), FL (Comcast Cable)

HOLLYWOOD—See BROWARD COUNTY (portions), FL (Comcast Cable)

HOLMES BEACH—See BRADENTON, FL (Bright House Networks)

HOLMES COUNTY (PORTIONS)—See WEWAHITCHKA, FL (Mediacom)

▲**HOLOPAW**—Florida Cable

HOMELAND—See BARTOW, FL (Comcast Cable)

HOMESTEAD—See MIAMI, FL (Comcast Cable)

HOMOSASSA SPRINGS—See HOMOSASSA, FL (Bright House Networks)

▲**HOMOSASSA**—Bright House Networks

▲**HOSFORD**—Southeast Cable TV Inc.

HOWEY-IN-THE-HILLS—See LEESBURG, FL (Comcast Cable)

HUDSON—See PASCO COUNTY (western portion), FL (Bright House Networks)

HUNTERS CREEK—See ORLANDO, FL (Bright House Networks)

HURLBURT FIELD—See FORT WALTON BEACH, FL (Cox Communications)

HUTCHINSON ISLAND SOUTH—See STUART, FL (Comcast Cable)

HUTCHINSON—See STUART, FL (Comcast Cable)

HYPOLUXO—See WEST PALM BEACH, FL (Comcast Cable)

▲**IMMOKALEE SEMINOLE INDIAN RESERVATION**—Comcast Cable

▲**IMMOKALEE**—Time Warner Cable. Now served by NAPLES, FL [FL0029]

IMMOKALEE—See NAPLES, FL (Comcast Cable)

INDIAN HARBOR BEACH—See MELBOURNE, FL (Bright House Networks)

INDIAN RIVER COUNTY—See VERO BEACH, FL (Comcast Cable)

INDIAN RIVER SHORES—See VERO BEACH, FL (Comcast Cable)

INDIAN ROCKS BEACH—See PINELLAS COUNTY (portions), FL (Bright House Networks)

INDIAN SHORES—See PINELLAS COUNTY (portions), FL (Bright House Networks)

▲**INDIAN SPRINGS**—Formerly served by Comcast Cable. No longer in operation

▲**INDIANTOWN**—Now served by STUART, FL [FL0024]

INDIANTOWN—See STUART, FL (Comcast Cable)

INDIATLANTIC—See MELBOURNE, FL (Bright House Networks)

INGLIS—See INVERNESS, FL (Comcast Cable)

INTERLACHEN—See PALATKA, FL (Comcast Cable)

INVERNESS—See HOMOSASSA, FL (Bright House Networks)

▲ **INVERNESS**—Comcast Cable

ISLA DEL SOL—See PINELLAS COUNTY (portions), FL (Bright House Networks)

ISLAMORADA—See KEY WEST, FL (Comcast Cable)

JACKSON COUNTY (PORTIONS)—See MARIANNA, FL (Comcast Cable)

JACKSON COUNTY—See CHIPLEY, FL (Bright House Networks)

JACKSONVILLE BEACH—See JACKSONVILLE, FL (Comcast Cable)

JACKSONVILLE NAVAL AIR STATION—See JACKSONVILLE, FL (Comcast Cable)

▲ **JACKSONVILLE**—Comcast Cable

▲ **JASPER**—Comcast Cable

JAY—See CENTURY, FL (Bright House Networks)

JEFFERSON COUNTY—See MONTICELLO, FL (Comcast Cable)

▲ **JENNINGS**—Comcast Cable

JENSEN BEACH—See STUART, FL (Comcast Cable)

JOHNSON—See ORANGE SPRINGS, FL (Florida Cable)

JUNO BEACH—See PALM BEACH GARDENS, FL (Comcast Cable)

JUPITER INLET COLONY—See PALM BEACH GARDENS, FL (Comcast Cable)

JUPITER ISLAND—See PALM BEACH GARDENS, FL (Comcast Cable)

JUPITER—See PALM BEACH GARDENS, FL (Comcast Cable)

▲ **KEATON BEACH**—Southeast Cable TV Inc.

▲ **KENANSVILLE**—Florida Cable

▲ **KENDALL**—Comcast Cable. Now served by MIAMI, FL [FL0006]

KENDALL—See MIAMI, FL (Comcast Cable)

KENNETH CITY—See PINELLAS COUNTY (portions), FL (Bright House Networks)

▲ **KEY COLONY BEACH**—Comcast Cable. Now served by KEY WEST, FL [FL0055]

KEY COLONY BEACH—See KEY WEST, FL (Comcast Cable)

▲ **KEY LARGO**—Comcast Cable. Now served by KEY WEST, FL [FL0055]

KEY LARGO—See KEY WEST, FL (Comcast Cable)

▲ **KEY WEST**—Comcast Cable

KEYSTONE HEIGHTS—See PALATKA, FL (Comcast Cable)

KEYSTONE HEIGHTS—See FLORAHOME, FL (Florida Cable)

KILLEARN LAKES—See MONTICELLO, FL (Comcast Cable)

KINGSLEY LAKE—See LAWTEY, FL (Florida Cable)

KISSIMMEE (PORTIONS)—See OSCEOLA COUNTY (western portion), FL (Comcast Cable)

KISSIMMEE—See ORLANDO, FL (Bright House Networks)

KISSIMMEE—See ORLANDO, FL (Bright House Networks)

▲ **LA BELLE**—Time Warner Cable. Now served by NAPLES, FL [FL0029]

LA BELLE—See NAPLES, FL (Comcast Cable)

LADY LAKE—See LEESBURG, FL (Comcast Cable)

LAKE ALFRED—See AUBURNDALE, FL (Bright House Networks)

▲ **LAKE BUTLER**—Comcast Cable

▲ **LAKE CITY**—Comcast Cable

LAKE CLARKE SHORES—See WEST PALM BEACH, FL (Comcast Cable)

LAKE COUNTY (EASTERN PORTION)—See PAISLEY, FL (Florida Cable)

LAKE COUNTY (NORTHERN PORTIONS)—See WILDWOOD, FL (Bright House Networks)

LAKE COUNTY (SOUTHERN PORTION)—See ORLANDO, FL (Bright House Networks)

LAKE COUNTY (UNINCORPORATED AREAS)—See ASTOR, FL (Florida Cable)

LAKE GENEVA—See PALATKA, FL (Comcast Cable)

LAKE HAMILTON—See AUBURNDALE, FL (Bright House Networks)

LAKE HELEN—See DELAND, FL (Bright House Networks)

▲ **LAKE MARY JANE**—Florida Cable

LAKE MARY—See ORLANDO, FL (Bright House Networks)

LAKE PARK—See PALM BEACH GARDENS, FL (Comcast Cable)

▲ **LAKE PLACID**—Comcast Cablevision of West Florida Inc. Now served by SEBRING, FL [FL0063]

LAKE PLACID—See SEBRING, FL (Comcast Cable)

LAKE WALES (PORTIONS)—See AUBURNDALE, FL (Bright House Networks)

▲ **LAKE WALES**—Comcast Cable

LAKE WORTH—See WEST PALM BEACH, FL (Comcast Cable)

LAKE YALE ESTATES—See MARION COUNTY (southern portion), FL (Florida Cable)

LAKELAND—See AUBURNDALE, FL (Bright House Networks)

LAKEPORT—See OKEECHOBEE, FL (Comcast Cable)

LANARK VILLAGE—See WEWAHITCHKA, FL (Mediacom)

LAND O' LAKES—See PASCO COUNTY (central & eastern portions), FL (Bright House Networks)

LANTANA—See WEST PALM BEACH, FL (Comcast Cable)

LARGO—See PINELLAS COUNTY (portions), FL (Bright House Networks)

LARGO—See PINELLAS COUNTY (portions), FL (Knology)

LAUDERDALE LAKES—See BROWARD COUNTY (portions), FL (Comcast Cable)

LAUDERDALE-BY-THE-SEA—See BROWARD COUNTY (portions), FL (Comcast Cable)

LAUDERHILL—See BROWARD COUNTY (portions), FL (Comcast Cable)

LAUREL—See VENICE, FL (Comcast Cable)

▲ **LAWTEY**—Florida Cable

LAZY LAKE—See BROWARD COUNTY (portions), FL (Comcast Cable)

LECANTO—See HOMOSASSA, FL (Bright House Networks)

LEE COUNTY (UNINCORPORATED AREAS)—See NAPLES, FL (Comcast Cable)

▲ **LEE**—Formerly served by KLiP Interactive. No longer in operation

▲ **LEESBURG LAKESHORE MOBILE HOME PARK**—Leesburg Lakeshore Mobile Home Park Inc. No longer in operation

▲ **LEESBURG**—Comcast Cable

▲ **LEHIGH ACRES**—Comcast Cablevision of West Florida Inc. Now served by NAPLES (formerly BONITA SPRINGS, FL [FL0029]

LEHIGH ACRES—See NAPLES, FL (Comcast Cable)

LEISURE CITY—See MIAMI, FL (Comcast Cable)

LEON COUNTY (PORTIONS)—See MONTICELLO, FL (Comcast Cable)

LEON COUNTY—See TALLAHASSEE, FL (Comcast Cable)

LEVY COUNTY—See WILLISTON, FL (Comcast Cable)

LEVY COUNTY—See BRONSON (town), FL (Florida Cable)

LIBERTY COUNTY—See BLOUNTSTOWN, FL (Bright House Networks)

LIGHTHOUSE POINT—See BROWARD COUNTY (portions), FL (Comcast Cable)

▲ **LITTLE TORCH KEY**—Comcast Cable. Now served by KEY WEST, FL [FL0055]

LITTLE TORCH KEY—See KEY WEST, FL (Comcast Cable)

▲ **LIVE OAK**—Comcast Cable. Now served by LAKE CITY, FL [FL0079]

▲ **LIVE OAK**—Formerly served by KLiP Interactive. No longer in operation

LIVE OAK—See LAKE CITY, FL (Comcast Cable)

▲ **LIVE OAK**—Florida Cable

LONGBOAT KEY—See SARASOTA, FL (Comcast Cable)

LONGWOOD—See ORLANDO, FL (Bright House Networks)

LORIDA—See SPRING LAKE, FL (Comcast Cable)

LOXAHATCHEE—See PALM BEACH GARDENS, FL (Comcast Cable)

LUTZ—See PASCO COUNTY (central & eastern portions), FL (Bright House Networks)

LYNN HAVEN—See PANAMA CITY, FL (Comcast Cable)

LYNNE—See WILDWOOD, FL (Bright House Networks)

▲ **MACCLENNY**—Comcast Cable

MACDILL AFB—See HILLSBOROUGH COUNTY (portions), FL (Bright House Networks)

MACDILL—See HILLSBOROUGH COUNTY (portions), FL (Bright House Networks)

MADEIRA BEACH—See PINELLAS COUNTY (portions), FL (Bright House Networks)

MADISON COUNTY—See MADISON, FL (Comcast Cable)

▲ **MADISON**—Comcast Cable

MAITLAND—See ORLANDO, FL (Bright House Networks)

MALABAR—See MELBOURNE, FL (Bright House Networks)

MALONE—See MARIANNA, FL (Comcast Cable)

MANALAPAN—See WEST PALM BEACH, FL (Comcast Cable)

MANATEE COUNTY (PORTIONS)—See SARASOTA, FL (Comcast Cable)

MANATEE COUNTY—See BRADENTON, FL (Bright House Networks)

MANGONIA PARK—See WEST PALM BEACH, FL (Comcast Cable)

MARATHON SHORES—See KEY WEST, FL (Comcast Cable)

MARATHON—See KEY WEST, FL (Comcast Cable)

MARCO ISLAND—See NAPLES, FL (Comcast Cable)

▲ **MARCO ISLAND**—Marco Island Cable Inc.

▲ **MARGATE**—Comcast Cable. Now served by BROWARD COUNTY, FL [FL0016]

MARGATE—See BROWARD COUNTY (portions), FL (Comcast Cable)

▲ **MARIANNA**—Comcast Cable

MARION COUNTY (NORTHERN PORTION)—See CITRA, FL (Florida Cable)

MARION COUNTY (PORTIONS)—See WILDWOOD, FL (Bright House Networks)

MARION COUNTY (PORTIONS)—See GAINESVILLE, FL (Cox Communications)

MARION COUNTY (PORTIONS)—See ORANGE SPRINGS, FL (Florida Cable)

▲ **MARION COUNTY (SOUTHEASTERN PORTION)**—Cablevision of Marion County

▲ **MARION COUNTY (SOUTHERN PORTION)**—Florida Cable

MARION COUNTY (SOUTHWESTERN PORTION)—See PALM CAY, FL (Cablevision of Marion County)

MARION COUNTY (SOUTHWESTERN PORTION)—See INVERNESS, FL (Comcast Cable)

MARION OAKS—See WILDWOOD, FL (Bright House Networks)

MARTIN COUNTY (SOUTHERN PORTION)—See PALM BEACH GARDENS, FL (Comcast Cable)

MARTIN COUNTY—See STUART, FL (Comcast Cable)

MARTIN COUNTY—See WEST PALM BEACH, FL (Comcast Cable)

MARY ESTHER—See FORT WALTON BEACH, FL (Cox Communications)

MASCOTTE—See ORLANDO, FL (Bright House Networks)

MATLACHA—See NAPLES, FL (Comcast Cable)

▲ **MAYO**—Comcast Cable

MAYPORT NAVAL AIR STATION—See JACKSONVILLE, FL (Comcast Cable)

MCINTOSH—See ORANGE LAKE, FL (CommuniComm Services)

MEDLEY—See MIAMI, FL (Comcast Cable)

MELBOURNE BEACH—See MELBOURNE, FL (Bright House Networks)

MELBOURNE VILLAGE—See MELBOURNE, FL (Bright House Networks)

▲ **MELBOURNE**—Formerly served by Wireless Broadcasting of Melbourne. No longer in operation

▲ **MELBOURNE**—Bright House Networks

MELROSE—See PALATKA, FL (Comcast Cable)

MERRITT ISLAND—See MELBOURNE, FL (Bright House Networks)

▲ **MEXICO BEACH**—Mediacom. Now served by WEWAHITCHKA, FL [FL0159]

MEXICO BEACH—See WEWAHITCHKA, FL (Mediacom)

▲ **MIAMI (PORTIONS)**—Bright House Networks

▲ **MIAMI BEACH**—Atlantic Broadband

MIAMI SHORES—See MIAMI, FL (Comcast Cable)

MIAMI SPRINGS—See MIAMI, FL (Comcast Cable)

▲ **MIAMI**—Comcast Cable. Now served by MIAMI, FL [FL0006]

▲ **MIAMI**—Comcast Cable

▲ **MICANOPY (TOWN)**—CommuniComm Services

MIDDLEBURG—See CLAY COUNTY, FL (Florida Cable)

▲ **MIDWAY**—Comcast Cablevision of Tallahassee Inc. Now served by TALLAHASSEE, FL [FL0283]

MIDWAY—See TALLAHASSEE, FL (Comcast Cable)

▲ **MILTON**—Mediacom. Now served by GULF BREEZE, FL [FL0070]

MILTON—See GULF BREEZE, FL (Mediacom)

▲ **MIMS**—Comcast Cable

MINNEOLA—See ORLANDO, FL (Bright House Networks)

MIRAMAR—See BROWARD COUNTY (portions), FL (Comcast Cable)

MOLINA—See CANTONMENT, FL (Bright House Networks)

MONROE COUNTY (PORTIONS)—See KEY WEST, FL (Comcast Cable)

MONT VERDE—See LEESBURG, FL (Comcast Cable)

MONTEREY LAKES—See ORLANDO, FL (Bright House Networks)

▲ **MONTICELLO**—Comcast Cable

▲ **MOORE HAVEN**—Comcast Cable

MOSS BLUFF—See WILDWOOD, FL (Bright House Networks)

MOUNT DORA—See LEESBURG, FL (Comcast Cable)

MOUNT PLYMOUTH—See LEESBURG, FL (Comcast Cable)

MULBERRY—See AUBURNDALE, FL (Bright House Networks)

▲ **NAPLES**—Comcast Cable. Now served by NAPLES (formerly BONITA SPRINGS), FL [FL0029]

▲ **NAPLES**—Comcast Cable

NARANJA—See MIAMI, FL (Comcast Cable)

NASSAU COUNTY (PORTIONS)—See HILLIARD, FL (Comcast Cable)

NASSAU COUNTY (PORTIONS)—See YULEE, FL (Comcast Cable)

NASSAU COUNTY—See JACKSONVILLE, FL (Comcast Cable)

NAVARRE BEACH—See GULF BREEZE, FL (Mediacom)

NEPTUNE BEACH—See JACKSONVILLE, FL (Comcast Cable)

NEW PORT RICHEY—See PASCO COUNTY (western portion), FL (Bright House Networks)

NEW SMYRNA BEACH—See DELAND, FL (Bright House Networks)

▲ **NEWBERRY**—Cox Communications. Now served by GAINESVILLE, FL [FL0027]

NEWBERRY—See GAINESVILLE, FL (Cox Communications)

NICEVILLE—See FORT WALTON BEACH, FL (Cox Communications)

NOBLETON—See HERNANDO COUNTY, FL (Florida Cable)

NOKOMIS—See VENICE, FL (Comcast Cable)

NORTH BAY VILLAGE—See MIAMI BEACH, FL (Atlantic Broadband)

▲ **NORTH DADE COUNTY**—Comcast Cable. Now served by MIAMI, FL [FL0006]

NORTH FORT MYERS—See NAPLES, FL (Comcast Cable)

NORTH LAUDERDALE—See BROWARD COUNTY (portions), FL (Comcast Cable)

NORTH MIAMI BEACH—See MIAMI, FL (Comcast Cable)

NORTH MIAMI—See MIAMI, FL (Comcast Cable)

▲ **NORTH OLD TOWN**—Florida Cable

NORTH REDINGTON BEACH—See PINELLAS COUNTY (portions), FL (Bright House Networks)

OAK HILL—See DELAND, FL (Bright House Networks)

OAKLAND PARK—See BROWARD COUNTY (portions), FL (Comcast Cable)

OAKLAND—See ORLANDO, FL (Bright House Networks)

▲ **OCALA**—Cox Cable Greater Ocala. Now served by GAINESVILLE, FL [FL0027]

OCALA—See GAINESVILLE, FL (Cox Communications)

OCEAN BREEZE PARK—See STUART, FL (Comcast Cable)

OCEAN REEF CLUB—See KEY WEST, FL (Comcast Cable)

OCEAN RIDGE—See DELRAY BEACH, FL (Comcast Cable)

OCOEE—See ORLANDO, FL (Bright House Networks)

OKALOOSA COUNTY (PORTIONS)—See FORT WALTON BEACH, FL (Cox Communications)

OKALOOSA COUNTY (PORTIONS)—See WEWAHITCHKA, FL (Mediacom)

OKALOOSA ISLAND—See FORT WALTON BEACH, FL (Cox Communications)

▲ **OKEECHOBEE**—Comcast Cable

OLD TOWN—See FANNING SPRINGS, FL (Florida Cable)

OLDSMAR—See PINELLAS COUNTY (portions), FL (Bright House Networks)

OLDSMAR—See PINELLAS COUNTY (portions), FL (Knology)

OPA-LOCKA—See MIAMI, FL (Comcast Cable)

ORANGE CITY—See DELAND, FL (Bright House Networks)

▲ **ORANGE COUNTY (UNINCORPORATED AREAS)**—Comcast Cable

ORANGE COUNTY—See ORLANDO, FL (Bright House Networks)

▲ **ORANGE LAKE**—CommuniComm Services

▲ **ORANGE PARK**—Comcast Cable. Now served by JACKSONVILLE, FL [FL0002]

ORANGE PARK—See JACKSONVILLE, FL (Comcast Cable)

▲ **ORANGE SPRINGS**—Florida Cable

ORCHID—See VERO BEACH, FL (Comcast Cable)

▲ **ORLANDO**—Bright House Networks

▲ **ORLANDO**—Bright House Networks

ORMOND BEACH—See DELAND, FL (Bright House Networks)

ORMOND BY THE SEA—See DELAND, FL (Bright House Networks)

▲ **ORTONA**—Comcast Cable

▲ **OSCEOLA COUNTY (EASTERN PORTION)**—Comcast Cable

▲ **OSCEOLA COUNTY (WESTERN PORTION)**—Comcast Cable

OSCEOLA COUNTY—See ORLANDO, FL (Bright House Networks)

OSCEOLA COUNTY—See ORLANDO, FL (Bright House Networks)

OSTEEN—See DELAND, FL (Bright House Networks)

OVIEDO—See ORLANDO, FL (Bright House Networks)

▲ **OZELLO**—Formerly served by KLiP Interactive. No longer in operation

PAHOKEE—See BELLE GLADE, FL (Comcast Cable)

▲ **PAISLEY**—Florida Cable

▲ **PALATKA**—Comcast Cable

PALATKA—See WELAKA (town), FL (Comcast Cable)

PALATKA—See PUTNAM COUNTY (eastern portion), FL (Florida Cable)

PALM BAY—See MELBOURNE, FL (Bright House Networks)

▲ **PALM BAY**—Comcast Cable

PALM BEACH CITY—See PALM BEACH GARDENS, FL (Comcast Cable)

▲ **PALM BEACH COUNTY (portions)**—Comcast Cable. Now served by WEST PALM BEACH, FL [FL0008]

PALM BEACH COUNTY (PORTIONS)—See BELLE GLADE, FL (Comcast Cable)

PALM BEACH COUNTY (PORTIONS)—See DELRAY BEACH, FL (Comcast Cable)

▲ **PALM BEACH COUNTY (southeastern portion)**—Comcast Cable. Now served by WEST PALM BEACH, FL [FL0008]

PALM BEACH COUNTY—See WEST PALM BEACH, FL (Comcast Cable)

▲ **PALM BEACH GARDENS**—Comcast Cable

PALM BEACH SHORES—See PALM BEACH GARDENS, FL (Comcast Cable)

PALM BEACH—See WEST PALM BEACH, FL (Comcast Cable)

▲ **PALM CAY**—Cablevision of Marion County

▲ **PALM CHASE**—Formerly served by Comcast Cable. No longer in operation

PALM CITY—See STUART, FL (Comcast Cable)

▲ **PALM COAST**—Bright House Networks. Now served by DELAND, FL [FL0033]

PALM COAST—See DELAND, FL (Bright House Networks)

PALM HARBOR—See PINELLAS COUNTY (portions), FL (Bright House Networks)

PALM SHORES MOBILE HOME PARK—See MARION COUNTY (southern portion), FL (Florida Cable)

PALM SHORES—See MELBOURNE, FL (Bright House Networks)

▲ **PALM SPRINGS**—Comcast Cable. Now served by WEST PALM BEACH, FL [FL0008]

PALM SPRINGS—See WEST PALM BEACH, FL (Comcast Cable)

PALMETTO—See BRADENTON, FL (Bright House Networks)

PANAMA CITY (PORTIONS)—See WEWAHITCHKA, FL (Mediacom)

▲ **PANAMA CITY BEACH**—Comcast Cable. Now served by PANAMA CITY, FL [FL0267]

PANAMA CITY BEACH—See PANAMA CITY, FL (Comcast Cable)

▲ **PANAMA CITY BEACH**—Knology

▲ **PANAMA CITY**—Comcast Cable

PARK SOUTH—See ORLANDO, FL (Bright House Networks)

PARKER—See PANAMA CITY, FL (Comcast Cable)

PARKLAND—See BROWARD COUNTY (portions), FL (Comcast Cable)

PARRISH—See BRADENTON, FL (Bright House Networks)

▲ **PASCO COUNTY (CENTRAL & EASTERN PORTIONS)**—Bright House Networks

PASCO COUNTY (SOUTHERN PORTION)—See HILLSBOROUGH COUNTY (portions), FL (Bright House Networks)

▲ **PASCO COUNTY (WESTERN PORTION)**—Bright House Networks

PATRICK AFB—See MELBOURNE, FL (Bright House Networks)

▲ **PEDRO**—Cablevision of Marion County

PEMBROKE PARK—See BROWARD COUNTY (portions), FL (Comcast Cable)

▲ **PEMBROKE PINES**—Comcast Cable. Now served by BROWARD COUNTY, FL [FL0016]

PEMBROKE PINES—See BROWARD COUNTY (portions), FL (Comcast Cable)

PENNBROOK—See WILDWOOD, FL (Bright House Networks)

▲ **PENNEY FARMS**—Florida Cable

PENSACOLA BEACH—See GULF BREEZE, FL (Mediacom)

PENSACOLA NAVAL AIR STATION—See GULF BREEZE, FL (Mediacom)

▲ **PENSACOLA**—Cox Communications

PERRINE—See MIAMI, FL (Comcast Cable)

▲ **PERRY**—Comcast Cable

PIERSON—See ASTOR, FL (Florida Cable)

PINECREST (PORTIONS)—See MIAMI BEACH, FL (Atlantic Broadband)

PINECREST—See MIAMI, FL (Comcast Cable)

PINELAND—See NAPLES, FL (Comcast Cable)

▲ **PINELLAS COUNTY (PORTIONS)**—Bright House Networks

▲ **PINELLAS COUNTY (PORTIONS)**—Knology

PINELLAS COUNTY (UNINCORPORATED AREAS)—See PINELLAS COUNTY (portions), FL (Bright House Networks)

PINELLAS PARK—See PINELLAS COUNTY (portions), FL (Bright House Networks)

PLANT CITY (UNINCORPORATED AREAS)—See BRANDON (northern portion), FL (Comcast Cable)

PLANT CITY—See HILLSBOROUGH COUNTY (portions), FL (Bright House Networks)

PLANTATION—See BROWARD COUNTY (portions), FL (Comcast Cable)

POINCIANA—See ORLANDO, FL (Bright House Networks)

POLK CITY—See AUBURNDALE, FL (Bright House Networks)

POLK COUNTY (NORTHERN PORTION)—See OSCEOLA COUNTY (western portion), FL (Comcast Cable)

▲ **POLK COUNTY (portions)**—Formerly served by People's Wireless Cable. No longer in operation

POLK COUNTY (PORTIONS)—See LAKE WALES, FL (Comcast Cable)

POLK COUNTY—See AUBURNDALE, FL (Bright House Networks)

POLK COUNTY—See ORLANDO, FL (Bright House Networks)

POLO'S OF KISSIMMEE—See ORLANDO, FL (Bright House Networks)

POMONA PARK—See CRESCENT CITY, FL (Comcast Cable)

POMPANO BEACH—See BROWARD COUNTY (portions), FL (Comcast Cable)

PONCE INLET—See DELAND, FL (Bright House Networks)

PONTE VEDRA BEACH—See JACKSONVILLE, FL (Comcast Cable)

▲ **PORT CHARLOTTE**—Comcast Cable

PORT ORANGE—See DELAND, FL (Bright House Networks)

PORT RICHEY—See PASCO COUNTY (western portion), FL (Bright House Networks)

PORT SALERNO—See STUART, FL (Comcast Cable)

▲ **PORT ST. JOE**—Mediacom. Now served by WEWAHITCHKA, FL [FL0159]

PORT ST. JOE—See WEWAHITCHKA, FL (Mediacom)

PORT ST. LUCIE—See STUART, FL (Comcast Cable)

PUNTA GORDA—See NAPLES, FL (Comcast Cable)

PUNTA GORDA—See PORT CHARLOTTE, FL (Comcast Cable)

▲ **PUTNAM COUNTY (EASTERN PORTION)**—Florida Cable

▲ **PUTNAM COUNTY (WESTERN PORTION)**—Florida Cable

▲ **PUTNAM COUNTY**—Formerly served by Florida Cable. No longer in operation

PUTNAM COUNTY—See CRESCENT CITY, FL (Comcast Cable)

▲ **QUINCY**—Comcast Cable. Now served by TALLAHASSEE, FL [FL0283]

QUINCY—See TALLAHASSEE, FL (Comcast Cable)

RAIFORD—See LAWTEY, FL (Florida Cable)

RAINBOW PARK—See WILDWOOD, FL (Bright House Networks)

RAMROD KEY—See KEY WEST, FL (Comcast Cable)

REDDICK—See ORANGE LAKE, FL (CommuniComm Services)

REDINGTON BEACH—See PINELLAS COUNTY (portions), FL (Bright House Networks)

REDINGTON SHORES—See PINELLAS COUNTY (portions), FL (Bright House Networks)

RIDGEWAY—See STUART, FL (Comcast Cable)

RIMA RIDGE—See DELAND, FL (Bright House Networks)

▲ **RIVER RANCH**—SAT STAR Communications

RIVERVIEW—See HILLSBOROUGH COUNTY (portions), FL (Bright House Networks)

RIVIERA BEACH—See WEST PALM BEACH, FL (Comcast Cable)

ROCKLEDGE—See MELBOURNE, FL (Bright House Networks)

ROLLING GREENS—See SILVER SPRINGS SHORES, FL (Comcast Cable)

ROSELAND—See VERO BEACH, FL (Comcast Cable)

ROTONDA—See ENGLEWOOD, FL (Comcast Cable)

ROYAL PALM BEACH—See PALM BEACH GARDENS, FL (Comcast Cable)

RUSKIN—See HILLSBOROUGH COUNTY (portions), FL (Bright House Networks)

SAFETY HARBOR—See PINELLAS COUNTY (portions), FL (Bright House Networks)

SAFETY HARBOR—See PINELLAS COUNTY (portions), FL (Knology)

SALT SPRINGS—See WILDWOOD, FL (Bright House Networks)

▲ **SAMSULA**—Formerly served by Consolidated Cablevision. No longer in operation

SAN ANTONIO—See PASCO COUNTY (central & eastern portions), FL (Bright House Networks)

SAN CARLOS ISLAND—See NAPLES, FL (Comcast Cable)

SAN MATEO—See PALATKA, FL (Comcast Cable)

SAND LAKE POINT—See ORANGE COUNTY (unincorporated areas), FL (Comcast Cable)

▲ **SAND-N-SEA**—Formerly served by Comcast Cable. No longer in operation

▲ **SANDESTIN BEACH RESORT**—Mediacom. Now served by WEWAHITCHKA, FL [FL0159]

SANDESTIN BEACH RESORT—See WEWAHITCHKA, FL (Mediacom)

SANDPIPER MOBILE HOME PARK—See MARION COUNTY (southern portion), FL (Florida Cable)

SANFORD—See ORLANDO, FL (Bright House Networks)

SANIBEL ISLAND—See NAPLES, FL (Comcast Cable)

SANTA ROSA BEACH—See WEWAHITCHKA, FL (Mediacom)

SANTA ROSA COUNTY (NORTHERN PORTIONS)—See CENTURY, FL (Bright House Networks)

SANTA ROSA COUNTY (PORTIONS)—See GULF BREEZE, FL (Mediacom)

▲ **SARALAKE ESTATES MOBILE HOME PARK**—Nalman Electronics

SARASOTA COUNTY (PORTIONS)—See ENGLEWOOD, FL (Comcast Cable)

SARASOTA COUNTY—See SARASOTA, FL (Comcast Cable)

SARASOTA COUNTY—See VENICE, FL (Comcast Cable)

▲ **SARASOTA**—Comcast Cable

SATELLITE BEACH—See MELBOURNE, FL (Bright House Networks)

SATSUMA—See PALATKA, FL (Comcast Cable)

SEA RANCH LAKES—See BROWARD COUNTY (portions), FL (Comcast Cable)

▲ **SEBASTIAN**—Comcast Cable. Now served by VERO BEACH, FL [FL0040]

SEBASTIAN—See VERO BEACH, FL (Comcast Cable)

▲ **SEBRING**—Comcast Cable

SEMINOLE COUNTY—See ORLANDO, FL (Bright House Networks)

SEMINOLE—See PINELLAS COUNTY (portions), FL (Bright House Networks)

SEMINOLE—See PINELLAS COUNTY (portions), FL (Knology)

SEWALL'S POINT—See STUART, FL (Comcast Cable)

SHALIMAR—See FORT WALTON BEACH, FL (Cox Communications)

▲ **SHARPES FERRY**—Florida Cable

SHELL POINT—See TALLAHASSEE, FL (Comcast Cable)

▲ **SILVER SPRINGS SHORES**—Comcast Cable

SILVER SPRINGS—See WILDWOOD, FL (Bright House Networks)

SINGER ISLAND—See WEST PALM BEACH, FL (Comcast Cable)

SLOCOMB—See DE FUNIAK SPRINGS, AL (Bright House Networks)

▲ **SMITH LAKE SHORES MOBILE HOME PARK**—Florida Cable

SNUG HARBOR VILLAGE—See MELBOURNE, FL (Bright House Networks)

SOPCHOPPY—See TALLAHASSEE, FL (Comcast Cable)

SORRENTO—See LEESBURG, FL (Comcast Cable)

SORRENTO—See ASTOR, FL (Florida Cable)

SOUTH BAY—See BELLE GLADE, FL (Comcast Cable)

▲ **SOUTH BROWARD COUNTY**—Comcast Cable. No longer in operation

SOUTH DAYTONA—See DELAND, FL (Bright House Networks)

SOUTH MIAMI HEIGHTS—See MIAMI, FL (Comcast Cable)

SOUTH MIAMI—See MIAMI BEACH, FL (Atlantic Broadband)

SOUTH PALM BEACH—See WEST PALM BEACH, FL (Comcast Cable)

SOUTH PASADENA—See PINELLAS COUNTY (portions), FL (Bright House Networks)

SOUTH ST. PETERSBURG—See PINELLAS COUNTY (portions), FL (Bright House Networks)

SOUTHGATE—See WILDWOOD, FL (Bright House Networks)

▲ **SOUTHPORT**—Mediacom. Now served by WEWAHITCHKA, FL [FL0159]

SOUTHPORT—See WEWAHITCHKA, FL (Mediacom)

SPARR—See CITRA, FL (Florida Cable)

SPRING HILL—See HERNANDO COUNTY, FL (Bright House Networks)

▲ **SPRING LAKE**—Comcast Cable

SPRINGFIELD—See PANAMA CITY, FL (Comcast Cable)

▲ **SPRINGFIELD**—Springfield Cable

▲ **SPRUCE CREEK NORTH**—Formerly served by Galaxy Cablevision. No longer in operation

SPRUCE CREEK—See DELAND, FL (Bright House Networks)

ST. AUGUSTINE BEACH—See ST. AUGUSTINE, FL (Comcast Cable)

▲ **ST. AUGUSTINE**—Comcast Cable

ST. CLOUD—See ORLANDO, FL (Bright House Networks)

ST. GEORGES ISLAND—See WEWAHITCHKA, FL (Mediacom)

ST. JAMES CITY—See NAPLES, FL (Comcast Cable)

ST. JOHNS COUNTY (NORTHERN PORTION)—See JACKSONVILLE, FL (Comcast Cable)

ST. JOHNS COUNTY (UNINCORPORATED AREAS)—See ST. AUGUSTINE, FL (Comcast Cable)

ST. JOHNS COUNTY—See HASTINGS, FL (Comcast Cable)

ST. LEO—See PASCO COUNTY (central & eastern portions), FL (Bright House Networks)

ST. LUCIE COUNTY—See STUART, FL (Comcast Cable)

ST. LUCIE COUNTY—See VERO BEACH, FL (Comcast Cable)

ST. LUCIE VILLAGE—See VERO BEACH, FL (Comcast Cable)

ST. PETERSBURG BEACH—See PINELLAS COUNTY (portions), FL (Bright House Networks)

ST. PETERSBURG—See PINELLAS COUNTY (portions), FL (Bright House Networks)

ST. PETERSBURG—See PINELLAS COUNTY (portions), FL (Knology)

STARKE—See JACKSONVILLE, FL (Comcast Cable)

STARKE—See HAMPTON, FL (Florida Cable)

▲ **STEINHATCHEE**—CommuniComm Services

STOCK ISLAND—See KEY WEST, FL (Comcast Cable)

▲ **STUART**—Comcast Cable

SUGARLOAF KEY—See KEY WEST, FL (Comcast Cable)

SUMMERFIELD—See PEDRO, FL (Cablevision of Marion County)

SUMMERLAND KEY—See KEY WEST, FL (Comcast Cable)

SUMTER COUNTY (PORTIONS)—See WILDWOOD, FL (Bright House Networks)

▲ **SUMTER COUNTY**—Formerly served by Galaxy Cablevision. No longer in operation

SUMTER COUNTY—See HERNANDO COUNTY, FL (Florida Cable)

SUN CITY CENTER—See HILLSBOROUGH COUNTY (portions), FL (Bright House Networks)

▲ **SUNNY HILLS**—Formerly served by Community Cable. No longer in operation

SUNNY ISLES—See MIAMI BEACH, FL (Atlantic Broadband)

SUNRISE—See BROWARD COUNTY (portions), FL (Comcast Cable)

SURFSIDE—See MIAMI BEACH, FL (Atlantic Broadband)

▲ **SUWANNEE CAMPGROUND**—Formerly served by KLiP Interactive. No longer in operation

SUWANNEE COUNTY (PORTIONS)—See LAKE CITY, FL (Comcast Cable)

SUWANNEE COUNTY—See BRANFORD, FL (CommuniComm Services)

▲ **SWEETWATER GOLF & TENNIS CLUB EAST**—Formerly served by Sweetwater Golf & Tennis Club East Inc. No longer in operation

▲ **SWEETWATER OAKS**—Formerly served by Galaxy Cablevision. No longer in operation

SWEETWATER—See MIAMI, FL (Comcast Cable)

TAFT—See ORLANDO, FL (Bright House Networks)

▲ **TALLAHASSEE**—Comcast Cable

TAMARAC—See BROWARD COUNTY (portions), FL (Comcast Cable)

▲ **TAMPA**—Formerly served by V TV Video Television. No longer in operation

TAMPA—See HILLSBOROUGH COUNTY (portions), FL (Bright House Networks)

TARPON SPRINGS—See PINELLAS COUNTY (portions), FL (Bright House Networks)

TARPON SPRINGS—See PINELLAS COUNTY (portions), FL (Knology)

TAVARES—See LEESBURG, FL (Comcast Cable)

TAVERNIER—See KEY WEST, FL (Comcast Cable)

TAYLOR COUNTY—See PERRY, FL (Comcast Cable)

TEMPLE TERRACE—See HILLSBOROUGH COUNTY (portions), FL (Bright House Networks)

▲ **TEQUESTA**—Now served by PALM BEACH GARDENS, FL [FL0030]

TEQUESTA—See PALM BEACH GARDENS, FL (Comcast Cable)

TERRA CEIA—See BRADENTON, FL (Bright House Networks)

THE VILLAGES—See LEESBURG, FL (Comcast Cable)

THREE WORLD RV PARK—See AUBURNDALE, FL (Bright House Networks)

TIERRA VERDE—See PINELLAS COUNTY (portions), FL (Bright House Networks)

TITUSVILLE—See MELBOURNE, FL (Bright House Networks)

TOPSIL—See FORT WALTON BEACH, FL (Cox Communications)

TREASURE ISLAND—See PINELLAS COUNTY (portions), FL (Bright House Networks)

▲ **TRENTON**—Comcast Cable

▲ **TYNDALL AFB**—Mediacom. Now served by WEWAHITCHKA, FL [FL0159]

TYNDALL AFB—See WEWAHITCHKA, FL (Mediacom)

UMATILLA—See LEESBURG, FL (Comcast Cable)

UMATILLA—See MARION COUNTY (southern portion), FL (Florida Cable)

UNION COUNTY—See LAKE BUTLER, FL (Comcast Cable)

UNION COUNTY—See LAWTEY, FL (Florida Cable)

UNIVERSITY OF WEST FLORIDA—See PENSACOLA, FL (Cox Communications)

UPPER MATECUMBE KEY—See KEY WEST, FL (Comcast Cable)

▲**VALPARAISO**—Valparaiso Communications System

VALRICO (SOUTHERN PORTION)—See HILLSBOROUGH COUNTY (portions), FL (Bright House Networks)

VANDERBILT BEACH—See NAPLES, FL (Comcast Cable)

VENICE (PORTIONS)—See PINELLAS COUNTY (portions), FL (Bright House Networks)

▲**VENICE**—Comcast Cable

VERNON—See WEWAHITCHKA, FL (Mediacom)

▲**VERO BEACH**—Comcast Cable

VIERA—See MELBOURNE, FL (Bright House Networks)

VIRGINIA GARDENS—See MIAMI, FL (Comcast Cable)

VOLUSIA COUNTY (PORTIONS)—See DEBARY, FL (Comcast Cable)

VOLUSIA COUNTY (UNINCORPORATED AREAS)—See ASTOR, FL (Florida Cable)

VOLUSIA COUNTY—See DELAND, FL (Bright House Networks)

VOLUSIA—See ASTOR, FL (Florida Cable)

WABASSO—See VERO BEACH, FL (Comcast Cable)

▲**WALDO**—Comcast Cable

WALTON COUNTY (PORTIONS)—See DE FUNIAK SPRINGS, FL (Bright House Networks)

WALTON COUNTY (PORTIONS)—See FORT WALTON BEACH, FL (Cox Communications)

WALTON COUNTY (PORTIONS)—See WEWAHITCHKA, FL (Mediacom)

WASHINGTON COUNTY—See CHIPLEY, FL (Bright House Networks)

▲**WAUCHULA**—Comcast Cable

WEBSTER—See WILDWOOD, FL (Bright House Networks)

WEBSTER—See HERNANDO COUNTY, FL (Florida Cable)

WEEKI WACHEE—See HERNANDO COUNTY, FL (Bright House Networks)

▲**WELAKA (TOWN)**—Comcast Cable

▲**WELLINGTON**—Bright House Networks

WELLINGTON—See WEST PALM BEACH, FL (Comcast Cable)

WESLEY CHAPEL—See PASCO COUNTY (central & eastern portions), FL (Bright House Networks)

WEST DELRAY BEACH—See DELRAY BEACH, FL (Comcast Cable)

WEST MELBOURNE—See MELBOURNE, FL (Bright House Networks)

WEST MIAMI—See MIAMI, FL (Comcast Cable)

▲**WEST PALM BEACH**—Comcast Cable

▲**WESTON**—Advanced Cable Communications

▲**WESTVILLE**—Formerly served by Community Cable. No longer in operation

▲**WEWAHITCHKA**—Mediacom

▲**WHITE SPRINGS**—Southeast Cable TV Inc. No longer in operation

WHITING FIELD NAVAL AIR STATION—See GULF BREEZE, FL (Mediacom)

▲**WILDWOOD**—Bright House Networks

▲**WILLISTON**—Comcast Cable

WILTON MANORS—See BROWARD COUNTY (portions), FL (Comcast Cable)

WIMAUMA—See HILLSBOROUGH COUNTY (portions), FL (Bright House Networks)

WINDERMERE—See ORLANDO, FL (Bright House Networks)

WINTER BEACH—See VERO BEACH, FL (Comcast Cable)

WINTER GARDEN—See ORLANDO, FL (Bright House Networks)

WINTER HAVEN OAKS MOBILE HOME PARK—See AUBURNDALE, FL (Bright House Networks)

WINTER HAVEN—See AUBURNDALE, FL (Bright House Networks)

WINTER PARK—See ORLANDO, FL (Bright House Networks)

WINTER SPRINGS—See ORLANDO, FL (Bright House Networks)

▲**WOODFIELD**—Comcast Cable. Now served by DELRAY BEACH, FL [FL0091]

WORTHINGTON SPRINGS—See BROOKER, FL (New River Cablevision Inc.)

▲**WYNMOOR VILLAGE**—Comcast Cable. Now served by BROWARD COUNTY, FL [FL0016]

WYNMOOR VILLAGE—See BROWARD COUNTY (portions), FL (Comcast Cable)

▲**YANKEETOWN**—Comcast Cable. Now served by INVERNESS, FL [FL0319]

YANKEETOWN—See INVERNESS, FL (Comcast Cable)

YOUNGSTOWN—See PANAMA CITY, FL (Comcast Cable)

▲**YULEE**—Comcast Cable

▲**ZELLWOOD**—Florida Cable

ZEPHYRHILLS—See PASCO COUNTY (central & eastern portions), FL (Bright House Networks)

ZOLFO SPRINGS—See WAUCHULA, FL (Comcast Cable)

GEORGIA

▲**ABBEVILLE**—Bulldog Cable

▲**ACWORTH**—Formerly served by KLiP Interactive. No longer in operation

ACWORTH—See ATLANTA (northern portion), GA (Comcast Cable)

ADAIRSVILLE—See ATLANTA (perimeter north), GA (Comcast Cable)

ADEL—See PEARSON, GA (Mediacom)

▲**ADRIAN**—Comcast Cable

AIKEN COUNTY (PORTIONS)—See AUGUSTA, SC (Comcast Cable)

AILEY—See MOUNT VERNON, GA (Comcast Cable)

ALAMO—See MOUNT VERNON, GA (Comcast Cable)

ALAPAHA—See PEARSON, GA (Mediacom)

▲**ALBANY**—Mediacom

ALDORA—See STOCKBRIDGE, GA (Charter Communications)

ALLENHURST—See HINESVILLE, GA (Comcast Cable)

▲**ALLENTOWN**—Formerly served by KLiP Interactive. No longer in operation

▲**ALMA**—Alma Telephone Co.

ALPHARETTA—See ATLANTA (northern portion), GA (Comcast Cable)

ALTO—See CORNELIA, GA (Windstream)

AMBROSE—See DOUGLAS, GA (Charter Communications)

▲**AMERICUS**—Mediacom

APPLING COUNTY (UNINCORPORATED AREAS)—See SURRENCY, GA (Worth Cable)

▲**ARABI**—Formerly served by Citizens Cable TV. No longer in operation

ARAGON—See ROCKMART, GA (Charter Communications)

ARCADE—See ATLANTA (perimeter north), GA (Comcast Cable)

ARCADE—See JEFFERSON, GA (Windstream)

ARGYLE (PORTIONS)—See HOMERVILLE, GA (Comcast Cable)

ARLINGTON—See CUTHBERT, GA (Mediacom)

▲**ARNOLDSVILLE**—Formerly served by KLiP Interactive. Now served by CRAWFORD, GA [GA0273]

ARNOLDSVILLE—See CRAWFORD, GA (CommuniComm Services)

ASHBURN—See TIFTON, GA (Mediacom)

▲**ATHENS**—Charter Communications

▲**ATLANTA (metro area 2)**—Formerly served by BellSouth Entertainment. No longer in operation

▲**ATLANTA (METRO AREA)**—Comcast Cable

▲**ATLANTA (NORTHERN PORTION)**—Comcast Cable

▲**ATLANTA (PERIMETER NORTH)**—Comcast Cable

▲**ATLANTA (PERIMETER SOUTH)**—Comcast Cable

▲**ATTAPULGUS**—Formerly served by KLiP Interactive. No longer in operation

AUBURN—See ATLANTA (perimeter north), GA (Comcast Cable)

▲**AUGUSTA**—Comcast Cable

▲**AUGUSTA**—Knology

AUSTELL—See ATLANTA (northern portion), GA (Comcast Cable)

▲**AVALON**—Galaxy Cablevision. Now served by HARTWELL (unincorporated areas), GA [GA0293]

AVALON—See HARTWELL (unincorporated areas), GA (Hart Communications)

▲**AVERA**—Formerly served by National Cable Inc. No longer in operation

AVONDALE ESTATES—See ATLANTA (metro area), GA (Comcast Cable)

▲**BACONTON**—Community Network Services

▲**BAINBRIDGE**—Mediacom

▲**BALDWIN COUNTY (eastern portion)**—Formerly served by KLiP Interactive. No longer in operation

▲**BALDWIN COUNTY (NORTHERN PORTION)**—Bulldog Cable

BALDWIN COUNTY—See MILLEDGEVILLE, GA (Charter Communications)

BALDWIN—See CORNELIA, GA (Windstream)

BALL GROUND—See ELLIJAY, GA (Ellijay Telephone Co.)

BANKS COUNTY (PORTIONS)—See COMMERCE, GA (Windstream)

BANKS COUNTY (PORTIONS)—See JEFFERSON, GA (Windstream)

BANKS COUNTY (WESTERN PORTION)—See ATLANTA (perimeter north), GA (Comcast Cable)

BARNESVILLE—See STOCKBRIDGE, GA (Charter Communications)

BARROW COUNTY—See ATLANTA (perimeter north), GA (Comcast Cable)

BARTOW COUNTY—See ATLANTA (perimeter north), GA (Comcast Cable)

BARTOW—See LOUISVILLE, GA (Comcast Cable)

BARWICK—See PAVO, GA (Southeast Cable TV Inc.)

▲ **BAXLEY**—ATC Cable

BEAR CREEK—See NORMAN PARK, GA (Wainwright Cable Inc.)

BELLVILLE—See CLAXTON, GA (Comcast Cable)

BELVEDERE ISLAND—See EULONIA, GA (Comcast Cable)

BEN HILL COUNTY (PORTIONS)—See FITZGERALD, GA (Mediacom)

▲ **BENT TREE COMMUNITY**—Ellijay Telephone Cooperative. Now served by ELLIJAY, GA [GA0044]

BENT TREE—See ELLIJAY, GA (Ellijay Telephone Co.)

BERKELEY LAKE—See ATLANTA (metro area), GA (Comcast Cable)

▲ **BERLIN**—Formerly served by Mega Cable LLC. No longer in operation

BERRIEN COUNTY (PORTIONS)—See PEARSON, GA (Mediacom)

BETHLEHEM—See ATLANTA (perimeter north), GA (Comcast Cable)

BETWEEN—See ATLANTA (perimeter south), GA (Comcast Cable)

BIBB CITY—See COLUMBUS, GA (Charter Communications)

BIBB COUNTY—See MACON, GA (Cox Communications)

▲ **BIG CANOE**—Windstream

▲ **BISHOP**—Formerly served by KLiP Interactive. No longer in operation

▲ **BLACKSHEAR**—ATC Cable

▲ **BLAIRSVILLE**—Windstream

▲ **BLAKELY**—Blakely Cable TV Inc.

BLECKLEY COUNTY (PORTIONS)—See PERRY, GA (ComSouth Telesys Inc.)

BLITCHTON—See SAVANNAH, GA (Comcast Cable)

BLOOMINGDALE—See SAVANNAH, GA (Comcast Cable)

▲ **BLUE RIDGE**—Ellijay Telephone Co.

BLUE RIDGE—See ELLIJAY, GA (Ellijay Telephone Co.)

BLYTHE—See AUGUSTA, GA (Comcast Cable)

BOGART—See ATHENS, GA (Charter Communications)

▲ **BOLINGBROKE**—Reynolds Cable TV Inc.

▲ **BOSTON**—Southeast Cable TV Inc.

BOWDON—See VILLA RICA, GA (Charter Communications)

BOWERSVILLE—See ROYSTON, GA (Northland Cable Television)

▲ **BOWMAN**—Comcast Cablevision of the South. Now served by ELBERTON, GA [GA0192]

BOWMAN—See ELBERTON, GA (Comcast Cable)

BRANTLEY COUNTY (UNINCORPORATED AREAS)—See HOBOKEN, GA (Worth Cable)

BRANTLEY COUNTY (WESTERN PORTION)—See WAYCROSS, GA (Media Stream)

BRASELTON—See ATLANTA (perimeter north), GA (Comcast Cable)

BREMEN—See VILLA RICA, GA (Charter Communications)

BREMEN—See TALLAPOOSA, GA (Comcast Cable)

BRIDGEBORO—See ALBANY, GA (Mediacom)

▲ **BRONWOOD**—Formerly served by Citizens Cable TV. No longer in operation

BROOKLET—See STATESBORO, GA (Northland Cable Television)

BROOKS COUNTY (EASTERN PORTION)—See VALDOSTA, GA (Mediacom)

BROOKS COUNTY (PORTIONS)—See QUITMAN, GA (Comcast Cable)

BROOKS—See ATLANTA (perimeter south), GA (Comcast Cable)

▲ **BROWNS CROSSING**—Formerly served by National Cable Inc. No longer in operation

BROXTON—See DOUGLAS, GA (Charter Communications)

▲ **BRUNSWICK**—Comcast Cable

BRYAN COUNTY (EASTERN PORTION)—See HINESVILLE, GA (Comcast Cable)

BRYAN COUNTY (EASTERN PORTION)—See SAVANNAH, GA (Comcast Cable)

BRYAN COUNTY (NORTHERN PORTION)—See PEMBROKE, GA (Comcast Cable)

BUCHANAN—See VILLA RICA, GA (Charter Communications)

BUCHANAN—See TALLAPOOSA, GA (Comcast Cable)

▲ **BUENA VISTA**—Flint Cable TV

BUFORD—See DULUTH, GA (Charter Communications)

BUFORD—See GAINESVILLE, GA (Charter Communications)

BULLOCH COUNTY—See STATESBORO, GA (Northland Cable Television)

▲ **BURKE COUNTY (PORTIONS)**—Pineland Telephone Coop Inc. Formerly served by Midville, GA [GA0152]. This cable system has converted to IPTV

BURKE COUNTY—See AUGUSTA, GA (Comcast Cable)

▲ **BUTLER**—Flint Cable TV

BUTTS COUNTY (PORTIONS)—See STOCKBRIDGE, GA (Charter Communications)

BYRON—See MACON, GA (Cox Communications)

▲ **CAIRO**—CNS

CAIRO—See THOMASVILLE, GA (Mediacom)

CALDWELL—See RENTZ, GA (Bulldog Cable)

CALHOUN—See ATLANTA (perimeter north), GA (Comcast Cable)

CAMAK—See WARRENTON, GA (Comcast Cable)

CAMDEN COUNTY—See ST. MARY'S, GA (Comcast Cable)

▲ **CAMILLA**—CNS

▲ **CAMILLA**—Mediacom

CANTON—See ATLANTA (perimeter north), GA (Comcast Cable)

CARL—See ATLANTA (perimeter north), GA (Comcast Cable)

▲ **CARNESVILLE**—Carnesville Cable

CARROLL COUNTY (PORTIONS)—See CARROLLTON, GA (Charter Communications)

CARROLL COUNTY (PORTIONS)—See VILLA RICA, GA (Charter Communications)

CARROLL COUNTY (UNINCORPORATED AREAS)—See ATLANTA (perimeter south), GA (Comcast Cable)

▲ **CARROLLTON**—Charter Communications

▲ **CARTERSVILLE**—Now served by ATLANTA (perimeter north), GA [GA0033]

CARTERSVILLE—See ATLANTA (perimeter north), GA (Comcast Cable)

CATAULA—See COLUMBUS, GA (Mediacom)

CATOOSA COUNTY (PORTIONS)—See ROSSVILLE, GA (Comcast Cable)

CATOOSA COUNTY—See RINGGOLD, GA (Charter Communications)

CAVE SPRING—See CEDARTOWN, GA (Charter Communications)

CECIL—See VALDOSTA, GA (Mediacom)

▲ **CEDARTOWN**—Charter Communications

CENTERVILLE—See MACON, GA (Cox Communications)

CENTRALHATCHES—See LAGRANGE, GA (Charter Communications)

CHALYBEATE SPRINGS—See MANCHESTER, GA (Charter Communications)

CHAMBERS COUNTY—See WEST POINT, AL (Charter Communications)

CHAMBLEE—See ATLANTA (metro area), GA (Comcast Cable)

CHARLTON COUNTY—See FOLKSTON, GA (Comcast Cable)

CHATHAM COUNTY (PORTIONS)—See SAVANNAH, GA (Comcast Cable)

CHATHAM COUNTY—See TYBEE ISLAND, GA (Comcast Cable)

▲ **CHATSWORTH**—Charter Communications

CHATTANOOGA VALLEY—See ROSSVILLE, GA (Comcast Cable)

▲ **CHAUNCEY**—Formerly served by KLiP Interactive. No longer in operation

CHEROKEE COUNTY (NORTHERN PORTION)—See ATLANTA (perimeter north), GA (Comcast Cable)

CHEROKEE COUNTY (PORTIONS)—See ELLIJAY, GA (Ellijay Telephone Co.)

CHEROKEE COUNTY (SOUTHERN PORTION)—See ATLANTA (northern portion), GA (Comcast Cable)

CHESTER—See RENTZ, GA (Bulldog Cable)

CHESTNUT MOUNTAIN—See GAINESVILLE, GA (Charter Communications)

CHICKAMAUGA—See ROSSVILLE, GA (Comcast Cable)

CLARKE COUNTY (PORTIONS)—See ATHENS, GA (Charter Communications)

CLARKE COUNTY—See ATLANTA (perimeter north), GA (Comcast Cable)

CLARKESVILLE—See CORNELIA, GA (Windstream)

CLARKSTON—See ATLANTA (metro area), GA (Comcast Cable)

▲ **CLAXTON**—Comcast Cable

CLAY COUNTY—See HIAWASSEE, NC (Windstream)

CLAYTON COUNTY (PORTIONS)—See STOCKBRIDGE, GA (Charter Communications)

CLAYTON COUNTY—See ATLANTA (perimeter south), GA (Comcast Cable)

▲ **CLAYTON**—Northland Cable Television

▲ **CLERMONT**—Now served by ATLANTA (perimeter north), GA [GA0033]

CLERMONT—See ATLANTA (perimeter north), GA (Comcast Cable)

▲ **CLEVELAND**—Windstream

▲ **CLIMAX**—Formerly served by KLiP Interactive. No longer in operation

CLINCH COUNTY (PORTIONS)—See HOMERVILLE, GA (Comcast Cable)

CLYATTVILLE—See LAKE PARK, GA (Cobridge Communications)

COBB COUNTY—See SMYRNA, GA (Charter Communications)

COBB COUNTY—See ATLANTA (northern portion), GA (Comcast Cable)

COBB—See LAKE BLACKSHEAR, GA (Citizens Cable TV)

COBBTOWN—See REIDSVILLE, GA (Kennedy Cablevision Inc.)

COCHRAN—See PERRY, GA (ComSouth Telesys Inc.)

COFFEE COUNTY (UNINCORPORATED AREAS)—See DOUGLAS, GA (Charter Communications)

COHUTTA—See DALTON, GA (Charter Communications)

COLBERT—See ATHENS, GA (Charter Communications)

COLLEGE PARK—See ATLANTA (metro area), GA (Comcast Cable)

▲ **COLLINS**—Worth Cable

▲ **COLONELS ISLAND**—Comcast Cable

COLQUITT COUNTY (PORTIONS)—See MOULTRIE, GA (Mediacom)

▲ **COLQUITT**—Bulldog Cable

COLUMBIA COUNTY (PORTIONS)—See FORT GORDON, GA (Cobridge Communications)

COLUMBIA COUNTY—See AUGUSTA, GA (Comcast Cable)

COLUMBIA—See BLAKELY, AL (Blakely Cable TV Inc.)

▲ **COLUMBUS**—Charter Communications

▲ **COLUMBUS**—Knology

▲ **COLUMBUS**—Mediacom

▲ **COMER**—Charter Communications. Now served by ATHENS, GA [GA0014]

COMER—See ATHENS, GA (Charter Communications)

▲ **COMMERCE**—Windstream

CONCORD—See STOCKBRIDGE, GA (Charter Communications)

▲ **CONCORD**—Georgia Broadband

CONLEY—See ATLANTA (perimeter south), GA (Comcast Cable)

CONYERS—See ATLANTA (perimeter south), GA (Comcast Cable)

COOK COUNTY (PORTIONS)—See PEARSON, GA (Mediacom)

▲ **COOLIDGE**—Southeast Cable TV Inc.

COOPERS—See GORDON, GA (Bulldog Cable)

COPPERHILL—See BLUE RIDGE, TN (Ellijay Telephone Co.)

COPPERHILL—See ELLIJAY, TN (Ellijay Telephone Co.)

▲ **CORDELE**—Mediacom. Now served by FITZGERALD, GA [GA0052]

CORDELE—See FITZGERALD, GA (Mediacom)

CORINTH—See LAGRANGE, GA (Charter Communications)

▲ **CORNELIA**—Windstream

▲ **COVINGTON**—Charter Communications

COWETA COUNTY—See NEWNAN, GA (Charter Communications)

COWETA COUNTY—See ATLANTA (perimeter south), GA (Comcast Cable)

▲ **CRAWFORD COUNTY (Eastern portion)**—Formerly served by Piedmont Cable Corp. No longer in operation

▲ **CRAWFORD COUNTY (PORTIONS)**—Flint Cable TV

▲ **CRAWFORD**—CommuniComm Services

▲ **CRAWFORDVILLE**—Formerly served by CommuniComm Services. No longer in operation

CRESCENT—See EULONIA, GA (Comcast Cable)

CRISP COUNTY (PORTIONS)—See FITZGERALD, GA (Mediacom)

CRISP COUNTY (SOUTHERN PORTION)—See WARWICK, GA (Citizens Cable TV)

CULLODEN—See YATESVILLE, GA (Flint Cable TV)

▲ **CUMMING**—Now served by CANTON, GA [GA0033]

CUMMING—See ATLANTA (perimeter north), GA (Comcast Cable)

▲ **CUSSETA**—Formerly served by Almega Cable. No longer in operation

▲ **CUTHBERT**—Mediacom

DACULA—See DULUTH, GA (Charter Communications)

▲ **DAHLONEGA**—Windstream

DALLAS—See ATLANTA (northern portion), GA (Comcast Cable)

▲ **DALTON**—Charter Communications

DAMASCUS—See COLQUITT, GA (Bulldog Cable)

DANIELSVILLE—See ATHENS, GA (Charter Communications)

▲ **DARIEN**—Comcast Cable

▲ **DARIEN**—Darien Communications

DASHER—See LAKE PARK, GA (Cobridge Communications)

▲ **DAVISBORO**—Formerly served by Walker Cablevision. No longer in operation

DAWSON COUNTY (PORTIONS)—See DAWSONVILLE, GA (Windstream)

DAWSON—See ALBANY, GA (Mediacom)

▲ **DAWSONVILLE**—Windstream

DE SOTO—See LAKE BLACKSHEAR, GA (Citizens Cable TV)

DEARING—See AUGUSTA, GA (Comcast Cable)

DECATUR COUNTY (PORTIONS)—See BAINBRIDGE, GA (Mediacom)

DECATUR—See ATLANTA (metro area), GA (Comcast Cable)

DEKALB COUNTY—See ATLANTA (metro area), GA (Comcast Cable)

DEMOREST—See CORNELIA, GA (Windstream)

DEXTER—See RENTZ, GA (Bulldog Cable)

DILLARD—See CLAYTON, GA (Northland Cable Television)

DODGE COUNTY (PORTIONS)—See MILAN, GA (Bulldog Cable)

DODGE COUNTY (PORTIONS)—See EASTMAN, GA (Mediacom)

▲ **DOERUN**—Doerun Cable TV

▲ **DONALSONVILLE**—Mediacom. Now served by BAINBRIDGE, GA [GA0060]

DONALSONVILLE—See BAINBRIDGE, GA (Mediacom)

DOOLY COUNTY (PORTIONS)—See FITZGERALD, GA (Mediacom)

DORAVILLE—See ATLANTA (metro area), GA (Comcast Cable)

DOUGHERTY COUNTY (PORTIONS)—See ALBANY, GA (Mediacom)

DOUGLAS COUNTY—See ATLANTA (northern portion), GA (Comcast Cable)

▲ **DOUGLAS**—Charter Communications

DOUGLASVILLE—See ATLANTA (northern portion), GA (Comcast Cable)

DRUID HILLS—See ATLANTA (metro area), GA (Comcast Cable)

▲ **DRY BRANCH**—Formerly served by KLiP Interactive. No longer in operation

▲ **DUBLIN**—Charter Communications

DUCKTOWN—See BLUE RIDGE, TN (Ellijay Telephone Co.)

DUCKTOWN—See ELLIJAY, TN (Ellijay Telephone Co.)

▲ **DUDLEY**—Bulldog Cable

▲ **DULUTH**—Charter Communications

DUNWOODY—See ATLANTA (metro area), GA (Comcast Cable)

EARLY COUNTY (PORTIONS)—See COLQUITT, GA (Bulldog Cable)

▲ **EAST DUBLIN**—Charter Communications. Now served by DUBLIN, GA [GA0043]

EAST DUBLIN—See DUBLIN, GA (Charter Communications)

EAST ELLIJAY—See ELLIJAY, GA (Ellijay Telephone Co.)

EAST POINT—See ATLANTA (metro area), GA (Comcast Cable)

EASTANOLLEE (PORTIONS)—See TOCCOA, GA (Northland Cable Television)

▲ **EASTMAN**—Mediacom

▲ **EATONTON**—CommuniComm Services

EDISON—See CUTHBERT, GA (Mediacom)

EFFINGHAM COUNTY (PORTIONS)—See GUYTON, GA (Comcast Cable)

EFFINGHAM COUNTY—See SAVANNAH, GA (Comcast Cable)

ELBERT COUNTY—See ELBERTON, GA (Comcast Cable)

▲ **ELBERTON**—Comcast Cable

▲ **ELBERTON**—ElbertonNet Broadband TV

ELLABELLE—See PEMBROKE, GA (Comcast Cable)

ELLAVILLE—See AMERICUS, GA (Mediacom)

ELLENWOOD—See ATLANTA (perimeter south), GA (Comcast Cable)

ELLERSLIE—See COLUMBUS, GA (Mediacom)

▲ **ELLIJAY**—Ellijay Telephone Co.

EMANUEL COUNTY—See ADRIAN, GA (Comcast Cable)

EMANUEL COUNTY—See SWAINSBORO, GA (Northland Cable Television)

EMERSON—See ATLANTA (perimeter north), GA (Comcast Cable)

▲ **ENIGMA**—Mediacom. Now served by PEARSON, GA [GA0063]

ENIGMA—See PEARSON, GA (Mediacom)

ETON—See CHATSWORTH, GA (Charter Communications)

EUHARLEE—See ATLANTA (perimeter north), GA (Comcast Cable)

▲ **EULONIA**—Comcast Cable

EVANS COUNTY (PORTIONS)—See CLAXTON, GA (Comcast Cable)

EVANS—See AUGUSTA, GA (Comcast Cable)

EVANS—See AUGUSTA, GA (Knology)

▲ **FAIRBURN**—Comcast Cable

FAIRBURN—See ATLANTA (metro area), GA (Comcast Cable)

FAIRFAX—See WEST POINT, AL (Charter Communications)

FAIRVIEW—See ROSSVILLE, GA (Comcast Cable)

FANNIN COUNTY (PORTIONS)—See ELLIJAY, GA (Ellijay Telephone Co.)

FAYETTE COUNTY—See ATLANTA (perimeter south), GA (Comcast Cable)

FAYETTEVILLE—See ATLANTA (perimeter south), GA (Comcast Cable)

▲ **FITZGERALD**—Mediacom

FLEMING—See HINESVILLE, GA (Comcast Cable)

FLEMINGTON—See HINESVILLE, GA (Comcast Cable)

▲**FLINT RIVER**—Formerly served by KLiP Interactive. No longer in operation

FLOVILLA—See STOCKBRIDGE, GA (Charter Communications)

FLOWERY BRANCH—See GAINESVILLE, GA (Charter Communications)

FLOYD COUNTY (PORTIONS)—See ATLANTA (perimeter north), GA (Comcast Cable)

FLOYD—See CEDARTOWN, GA (Charter Communications)

▲**FOLKSTON**—Comcast Cable

FOREST HILLS—See AUGUSTA, GA (Knology)

FOREST PARK—See ATLANTA (perimeter south), GA (Comcast Cable)

FORSYTH COUNTY (WESTERN PORTION)—See ATLANTA (perimeter north), GA (Comcast Cable)

▲**FORSYTH**—Forsyth Cable

▲**FORT BENNING**—Windjammer Cable

FORT GAINES—See CUTHBERT, GA (Mediacom)

FORT GILLEM—See ATLANTA (perimeter south), GA (Comcast Cable)

▲**FORT GORDON**—Cobridge Communications

FORT OGLETHORPE—See ROSSVILLE, GA (Comcast Cable)

FORT STEWART—See HINESVILLE, GA (Comcast Cable)

FORT VALLEY—See PERRY, GA (ComSouth Telesys Inc.)

▲**FORT VALLEY**—ComSouth

FORTSON—See COLUMBUS, GA (Mediacom)

FRANKLIN COUNTY (NORTHERN PORTION)—See HARTWELL (unincorporated areas), GA (Hart Communications)

FRANKLIN COUNTY (PORTIONS)—See CARNESVILLE, GA (Carnesville Cable)

FRANKLIN COUNTY—See ROYSTON, GA (Northland Cable Television)

FRANKLIN SPRINGS—See ROYSTON, GA (Northland Cable Television)

FRANKLIN—See LAGRANGE, GA (Charter Communications)

FULTON COUNTY (NORTHERN PORTION)—See ATLANTA (northern portion), GA (Comcast Cable)

FULTON COUNTY (PORTIONS)—See SMYRNA, GA (Charter Communications)

FULTON COUNTY (SOUTHERN PORTION)—See ATLANTA (metro area), GA (Comcast Cable)

▲**FUNSTON**—Wainwright Cable Inc.

▲**GAINESVILLE**—Charter Communications

GARDEN CITY—See SAVANNAH, GA (Comcast Cable)

GARDI—See HINESVILLE, GA (Comcast Cable)

GEORGIA STATE PRISON—See REIDSVILLE, GA (Kennedy Cablevision Inc.)

▲**GIBSON**—Formerly served by KLiP Interactive. No longer in operation

GILLSVILLE—See ATLANTA (perimeter north), GA (Comcast Cable)

GILMER COUNTY—See ELLIJAY, GA (Ellijay Telephone Co.)

▲**GLENNVILLE**—Comcast Cable

GLENWOOD—See MOUNT VERNON, GA (Comcast Cable)

GLYNN COUNTY—See BRUNSWICK, GA (Comcast Cable)

GOOD HOPE (PORTIONS)—See MONROE, GA (Monroe Utilities Network)

GOOD HOPE—See ATLANTA (perimeter south), GA (Comcast Cable)

GORDON COUNTY (PORTIONS)—See ATLANTA (perimeter north), GA (Comcast Cable)

▲**GORDON**—Bulldog Cable

GRADY COUNTY—See THOMASVILLE, GA (Mediacom)

GRAND RIDGE—See SEMINOLE COUNTY, FL (Bulldog Cable)

GRANTVILLE—See ATLANTA (perimeter south), GA (Comcast Cable)

▲**GRAY**—CommuniComm Services

GRAYSON—See ATLANTA (metro area), GA (Comcast Cable)

▲**GREENE COUNTY (UNINCORPORATED AREAS)**—Plantation Cablevision Inc.

▲**GREENSBORO**—CommuniComm Services

▲**GREENVILLE**—Charter Communications. Now served by STOCKBRIDGE, GA [GA0083]

▲**GREENVILLE**—Formerly served by Almega Cable. No longer in operation

▲**GREENVILLE**—Georgia Broadband

▲**GRIFFIN**—Comcast Cable. Now served by ATLANTA (perimeter south), GA [GA0017]

GRIFFIN—See ATLANTA (perimeter south), GA (Comcast Cable)

GROVETOWN (PORTIONS)—See AUGUSTA, GA (Comcast Cable)

GROVETOWN—See FORT GORDON, GA (Cobridge Communications)

GROVETOWN—See AUGUSTA, GA (Knology)

GUMBRANCH—See HINESVILLE, GA (Comcast Cable)

GUMBRANCH—See SAVANNAH, GA (Comcast Cable)

▲**GUYTON**—Comcast Cable

GWINNETT COUNTY (EASTERN PORTION)—See ATLANTA (perimeter north), GA (Comcast Cable)

GWINNETT COUNTY (PORTIONS)—See DULUTH, GA (Charter Communications)

GWINNETT COUNTY (PORTIONS)—See GAINESVILLE, GA (Charter Communications)

HABERSHAM COUNTY—See CORNELIA, GA (Windstream)

▲**HADDOCK**—Formerly served by KLiP Interactive. No longer in operation

HAGAN—See CLAXTON, GA (Comcast Cable)

HAHIRA—See VALDOSTA, GA (Mediacom)

HALL COUNTY—See GAINESVILLE, GA (Charter Communications)

HALL COUNTY—See ATLANTA (perimeter north), GA (Comcast Cable)

HAMILTON—See PINE MOUNTAIN, GA (Charter Communications)

HAMPTON—See STOCKBRIDGE, GA (Charter Communications)

HAMPTON—See ATLANTA (perimeter south), GA (Comcast Cable)

HANCOCK COUNTY—See SPARTA, GA (Bulldog Cable)

HAPEVILLE—See ATLANTA (metro area), GA (Comcast Cable)

HARALSON COUNTY—See VILLA RICA, GA (Charter Communications)

HARDWICK—See MILLEDGEVILLE, GA (Charter Communications)

HARLEM—See FORT GORDON, GA (Cobridge Communications)

HARRIETTS BLUFF—See WOODBINE, GA (Comcast Cable)

HARRIS COUNTY (SOUTHERN PORTION)—See COLUMBUS, GA (Mediacom)

HARRIS COUNTY (UNINCORPORATED AREAS)—See COLUMBUS, GA (Charter Communications)

HARRIS COUNTY—See PINE MOUNTAIN, GA (Charter Communications)

▲**HARRISON**—Formerly served by Walker Cablevision. No longer in operation

HART COUNTY (PORTIONS)—See ELBERTON, GA (Comcast Cable)

HART COUNTY (PORTIONS)—See ROYSTON, GA (Northland Cable Television)

▲**HARTWELL (UNINCORPORATED AREAS)**—Hart Communications

▲**HARTWELL**—Comcast Cablevision of the South. Now served by ELBERTON, GA [GA0192]

HARTWELL—See ELBERTON, GA (Comcast Cable)

▲**HAWKINSVILLE**—CommuniComm Services. Now served by PERRY, GA [GA0229]

HAWKINSVILLE—See PERRY, GA (ComSouth Telesys Inc.)

HAYESVILLE—See HIAWASSEE, NC (Windstream)

▲**HAYNEVILLE**—ComSouth Telesys Inc. Now served by PERRY, GA [GA0229]

HAYNEVILLE—See PERRY, GA (ComSouth Telesys Inc.)

▲**HAZLEHURST**—Mediacom

HEARD COUNTY (UNINCORPORATED AREAS)—See CARROLLTON, GA (Charter Communications)

▲**HELEN**—Windstream

HELENA—See EASTMAN, GA (Mediacom)

HENRY COUNTY—See STOCKBRIDGE, GA (Charter Communications)

HEPHZIBAH—See AUGUSTA, GA (Comcast Cable)

▲**HIAWASSEE**—Windstream

HIGGSTON—See VIDALIA, GA (Northland Cable Television)

HIGHFALLS—See STOCKBRIDGE, GA (Charter Communications)

▲**HINESVILLE**—Comcast Cable

HINKLES—See TRENTON, GA (Charter Communications)

HIRAM—See ATLANTA (northern portion), GA (Comcast Cable)

▲**HOBOKEN**—Worth Cable

HOGANSVILLE—See ATLANTA (perimeter south), GA (Comcast Cable)

HOLLY SPRINGS—See ATLANTA (perimeter north), GA (Comcast Cable)

HOMELAND—See FOLKSTON, GA (Comcast Cable)

HOMER—See COMMERCE, GA (Windstream)

▲**HOMERVILLE**—Comcast Cable

HOSCHTON—See ATLANTA (perimeter north), GA (Comcast Cable)

HOUSTON COUNTY—See MACON, GA (Cox Communications)

HULL—See ATHENS, GA (Charter Communications)

HUNTER ARMY AIRFIELD—See SAVANNAH, GA (Comcast Cable)

INDIAN LAKE—See NORMAN PARK, GA (Wainwright Cable Inc.)

INDIAN SPRINGS—See STOCKBRIDGE, GA (Charter Communications)

▲**IRON CITY**—Formerly served by KLiP Interactive. No longer in operation

IRWIN COUNTY (PORTIONS)—See FITZGERALD, GA (Mediacom)

▲ **IRWINTON**—Acoucomm Telecommunications

ISLE OF HOPE-DUTCH ISLAND—See SAVANNAH, GA (Comcast Cable)

IVEY—See GORDON, GA (Bulldog Cable)

JACKSON COUNTY (NORTHWESTERN PORTION)—See ATLANTA (perimeter north), GA (Comcast Cable)

JACKSON COUNTY (PORTIONS)—See COMMERCE, GA (Windstream)

JACKSON COUNTY (SOUTHERN PORTION)—See JEFFERSON, GA (Windstream)

▲ **JACKSON COUNTY**—Now served by ATLANTA (perimeter north), GA [GA0033]

JACKSON—See STOCKBRIDGE, GA (Charter Communications)

JASPER—See ELLIJAY, GA (Ellijay Telephone Co.)

JEFF DAVIS COUNTY (PORTIONS)—See HAZLEHURST, GA (Mediacom)

JEFFERSON COUNTY—See LOUISVILLE, GA (Comcast Cable)

▲ **JEFFERSON**—Windstream

▲ **JEFFERSONVILLE**—Windstream

▲ **JEKYLL ISLAND**—Comcast Cable

JENKINS COUNTY (PORTIONS)—See MILLEN, GA (Comcast Cable)

JENKINSBURG—See STOCKBRIDGE, GA (Charter Communications)

JERSEY—See ATLANTA (perimeter south), GA (Comcast Cable)

▲ **JESUP**—Comcast Cable. Now served by HINESVILLE, GA [GA0024]

JESUP—See HINESVILLE, GA (Comcast Cable)

JOHNSON COUNTY—See ADRIAN, GA (Comcast Cable)

JONES COUNTY (PORTIONS)—See MACON, GA (Cox Communications)

JONESBORO—See ATLANTA (perimeter south), GA (Comcast Cable)

KATHLEEN—See PERRY, GA (ComSouth Telesys Inc.)

KENNESAW—See ATLANTA (northern portion), GA (Comcast Cable)

KINGS BAY—See ST. MARY'S, GA (Comcast Cable)

KINGSTON—See ATLANTA (perimeter north), GA (Comcast Cable)

▲ **KITE**—Formerly served by Walker Cablevision. No longer in operation

▲ **LA FAYETTE**—Comcast Cable

▲ **LAGRANGE**—Charter Communications

LAKE ARROWHEAD—See ATLANTA (perimeter north), GA (Comcast Cable)

▲ **LAKE BLACKSHEAR**—Citizens Cable TV

LAKE BLACKSHEAR—See WARWICK, GA (Citizens Cable TV)

LAKE CITY—See ATLANTA (perimeter south), GA (Comcast Cable)

LAKE GEORGE—See HINESVILLE, GA (Comcast Cable)

LAKE OCONEE—See GREENE COUNTY (unincorporated areas), GA (Plantation Cablevision Inc.)

▲ **LAKE PARK**—Cobridge Communications

LAKE RABUN—See CLAYTON, GA (Northland Cable Television)

LAKE SEMINOLE—See SEMINOLE COUNTY, GA (Bulldog Cable)

▲ **LAKELAND**—Mediacom. Now served by PEARSON, GA [GA0063]

LAKELAND—See PEARSON, GA (Mediacom)

LAKEVIEW—See ROSSVILLE, GA (Comcast Cable)

LAMAR COUNTY—See STOCKBRIDGE, GA (Charter Communications)

LANETT—See WEST POINT, AL (Charter Communications)

LANIER COUNTY—See LAKE PARK, GA (Cobridge Communications)

LAURENS COUNTY (EASTERN PORTION)—See RENTZ, GA (Bulldog Cable)

LAURENS COUNTY (PORTIONS)—See DUDLEY, GA (Bulldog Cable)

LAURENS COUNTY—See DUBLIN, GA (Charter Communications)

LAVONIA—See ROYSTON, GA (Northland Cable Television)

LAWRENCEVILLE—See DULUTH, GA (Charter Communications)

▲ **LEARY**—Blakely Cable TV Inc.

LEE COUNTY (PORTIONS)—See ALBANY, GA (Mediacom)

LEE COUNTY—See SMITHVILLE, GA (Citizens Cable TV)

LEESBURG—See ALBANY, GA (Mediacom)

LENOX—See PEARSON, GA (Mediacom)

▲ **LESLIE**—Citizens Cable TV. Now served by LAKE BLACKSHEAR, GA [GA0150]

LESLIE—See LAKE BLACKSHEAR, GA (Citizens Cable TV)

LIBERTY COUNTY (PORTIONS)—See HINESVILLE, GA (Comcast Cable)

LIBERTY COUNTY (SOUTHERN PORTION)—See SAVANNAH, GA (Comcast Cable)

LILBURN—See ATLANTA (metro area), GA (Comcast Cable)

LILLY—See LAKE BLACKSHEAR, GA (Citizens Cable TV)

▲ **LINCOLNTON**—Formerly served by KLiP Interactive. No longer in operation

▲ **LINCOLNTON**—Comcast Cable

LINWOOD—See LA FAYETTE, GA (Comcast Cable)

LITHIA SPRINGS—See ATLANTA (northern portion), GA (Comcast Cable)

LITHONIA—See ATLANTA (metro area), GA (Comcast Cable)

▲ **LIZELLA**—Flint Cable TV

LOCUST GROVE—See STOCKBRIDGE, GA (Charter Communications)

LOGANVILLE—See ATLANTA (perimeter south), GA (Comcast Cable)

LONE OAK—See NEWNAN, GA (Charter Communications)

LONG COUNTY (EASTERN PORTION)—See HINESVILLE, GA (Comcast Cable)

▲ **LOUISVILLE**—Comcast Cable

LOVEJOY—See ATLANTA (perimeter south), GA (Comcast Cable)

LOWNDES COUNTY—See LAKE PARK, GA (Cobridge Communications)

LOWNDES COUNTY—See VALDOSTA, GA (Mediacom)

LUDOWICI—See HINESVILLE, GA (Comcast Cable)

▲ **LULA**—Now served by ATLANTA (perimeter north), GA [GA0033]

LULA—See ATLANTA (perimeter north), GA (Comcast Cable)

LUMBER CITY—See HAZLEHURST, GA (Mediacom)

LUMPKIN COUNTY (PORTIONS)—See DAHLONEGA, GA (Windstream)

LUMPKIN—See CUTHBERT, GA (Mediacom)

LUTHERSVILLE—See NEWNAN, GA (Charter Communications)

▲ **LUTHERSVILLE**—Luthersville Cablevision

LYERLY—See SUMMERVILLE, GA (Charter Communications)

LYONS—See VIDALIA, GA (Northland Cable Television)

MABLETON (PORTIONS)—See SMYRNA, GA (Charter Communications)

MABLETON—See ATLANTA (northern portion), GA (Comcast Cable)

MACON COUNTY (PORTIONS)—See MONTEZUMA, GA (Comcast Cable)

▲ **MACON**—Cox Communications

MADISON COUNTY—See ATHENS, GA (Charter Communications)

MADISON—See EATONTON, GA (CommuniComm Services)

▲ **MANCHESTER**—Charter Communications

MANCHESTER—See LAGRANGE, GA (Charter Communications)

MANSFIELD—See ATLANTA (perimeter south), GA (Comcast Cable)

MARIETTA—See ATLANTA (northern portion), GA (Comcast Cable)

MARION COUNTY—See BUENA VISTA, GA (Flint Cable TV)

MARSHALLVILLE—See PERRY, GA (ComSouth Telesys Inc.)

MARTIN—See HARTWELL (unincorporated areas), GA (Hart Communications)

MARTINEZ—See AUGUSTA, GA (Comcast Cable)

MARTINEZ—See AUGUSTA, GA (Knology)

MAYSVILLE—See ATLANTA (perimeter north), GA (Comcast Cable)

MCCAYSVILLE—See BLUE RIDGE, GA (Ellijay Telephone Co.)

MCDONOUGH—See STOCKBRIDGE, GA (Charter Communications)

MCINTOSH COUNTY—See DARIEN, GA (Comcast Cable)

MCINTOSH COUNTY—See DARIEN, GA (Darien Communications)

MCINTYRE—See IRWINTON, GA (Acoucomm Telecommunications)

MCKAYSVILLE—See ELLIJAY, GA (Ellijay Telephone Co.)

▲ **McRAE**—Mediacom. Now served by EASTMAN, GA [GA0076]

MCRAE—See EASTMAN, GA (Mediacom)

MEANSVILLE—See STOCKBRIDGE, GA (Charter Communications)

MEIGS—See CAMILLA, GA (Mediacom)

MENLO—See SUMMERVILLE, GA (Charter Communications)

MERIDIAN—See EULONIA, GA (Comcast Cable)

MERIWETHER COUNTY—See MANCHESTER, GA (Charter Communications)

MERIWETHER COUNTY—See LUTHERSVILLE, GA (Luthersville Cablevision)

▲ **METTER**—Comcast Cable

▲ **MIDVILLE**—Pineland Telephone Coop Inc. This cable system has converted to IPTV. See Midville, GA [GA5009]

▲ **MIDVILLE**—Pineland Telephone Coop. Inc. Formerly [GA0152]. This cable system has converted to IPTV

MIDWAY-HARDWICK—See MILLEDGEVILLE, GA (Charter Communications)

MIDWAY—See SAVANNAH, GA (Comcast Cable)

▲ **MILAN**—Bulldog Cable

▲ **MILLEDGEVILLE**—Charter Communications

▲ **MILLEN**—Comcast Cable

MILLER COUNTY (PORTIONS)—See COLQUITT, GA (Bulldog Cable)

MILNER—See STOCKBRIDGE, GA (Charter Communications)

MINERAL BLUFF—See BLUE RIDGE, GA (Ellijay Telephone Co.)

MINERAL BLUFF—See ELLIJAY, GA (Ellijay Telephone Co.)

MITCHELL COUNTY (PORTIONS)—See CAMILLA, GA (Mediacom)

MOLENA—See STOCKBRIDGE, GA (Charter Communications)

MONROE COUNTY (NORTHERN PORTION)—See STOCKBRIDGE, GA (Charter Communications)

MONROE COUNTY (PORTIONS)—See MACON, GA (Cox Communications)

▲ **MONROE**—Monroe Utilities Network

▲ **MONTEZUMA**—Comcast Cable

MONTGOMERY COUNTY (PORTIONS)—See MOUNT VERNON, GA (Comcast Cable)

MONTGOMERY COUNTY (PORTIONS)—See UVALDA, GA (Worth Cable)

MONTGOMERY COUNTY—See VIDALIA, GA (Northland Cable Television)

MONTICELLO—See ATLANTA (perimeter south), GA (Comcast Cable)

MOODY AIR FORCE BASE—See LAKE PARK, GA (Cobridge Communications)

MORELAND—See NEWNAN, GA (Charter Communications)

MORGAN COUNTY (PORTIONS)—See EATONTON, GA (CommuniComm Services)

▲ **MORGAN**—Blakely Cable TV Inc.

MORGANTON—See BLUE RIDGE, GA (Ellijay Telephone Co.)

MORGANTON—See ELLIJAY, GA (Ellijay Telephone Co.)

MORROW—See ATLANTA (perimeter south), GA (Comcast Cable)

▲ **MOULTRIE**—CNS

▲ **MOULTRIE**—Mediacom

MOUNT AIRY—See CORNELIA, GA (Windstream)

▲ **MOUNT VERNON**—Comcast Cable

MOUNT ZION—See TALLAPOOSA, GA (Comcast Cable)

MOUNTAIN CITY—See CLAYTON, GA (Northland Cable Television)

MOUNTAIN PARK—See ROSWELL, GA (Charter Communications)

MOXLEY—See LOUISVILLE, GA (Comcast Cable)

MURRAY COUNTY (CENTRAL PORTION)—See CHATSWORTH, GA (Charter Communications)

MURRAYVILLE—See GAINESVILLE, GA (Charter Communications)

▲ **NAHUNTA**—Comcast Cable

NASHVILLE—See PEARSON, GA (Mediacom)

NELSON—See ELLIJAY, GA (Ellijay Telephone Co.)

NEWBORN—See ATLANTA (perimeter south), GA (Comcast Cable)

▲ **NEWNAN**—Charter Communications

▲ **NEWNAN**—NuLink

▲ **NEWTON COUNTY (southern portion)**—Formerly served by KLiP Interactive. No longer in operation

NEWTON COUNTY—See COVINGTON, GA (Charter Communications)

NEWTON COUNTY—See ATLANTA (perimeter south), GA (Comcast Cable)

▲ **NEWTON**—Formerly served by Blakely Cable TV Inc. No longer in operation

NICHOLLS—See DOUGLAS, GA (Charter Communications)

NICHOLSON—See COMMERCE, GA (Windstream)

NORCROSS—See ATLANTA (metro area), GA (Comcast Cable)

▲ **NORMAN PARK**—Wainwright Cable Inc.

NORTH AUGUSTA—See AUGUSTA, SC (Comcast Cable)

▲ **OAK PARK**—Pineland Telephone Coop. Inc. This cable system has converted to IPTV. See Oak Park, GA [GA5010]

▲ **OAK PARK**—Pineland Telephone Coop. Inc. Formerly [GA0224]. This cable system has converted to IPTV

OAKWOOD—See GAINESVILLE, GA (Charter Communications)

▲ **OCHLOCKNEE**—Southeast Cable TV Inc.

OCILLA—See FITZGERALD, GA (Mediacom)

OCONEE COUNTY—See ATHENS, GA (Charter Communications)

OCONEE COUNTY—See ATLANTA (perimeter north), GA (Comcast Cable)

▲ **OCONEE**—Formerly served by National Cable Inc. No longer in operation

ODUM—See HINESVILLE, GA (Comcast Cable)

OFFERMAN—See PATTERSON, GA (ATC Cable)

OGLETHORPE—See MONTEZUMA, GA (Comcast Cable)

OMEGA—See TIFTON, GA (Mediacom)

ORCHARD HILL—See ATLANTA (perimeter south), GA (Comcast Cable)

OXFORD—See COVINGTON, GA (Charter Communications)

PALMETTO—See ATLANTA (metro area), GA (Comcast Cable)

▲ **PATTERSON**—ATC Cable

PAULDING COUNTY—See ATLANTA (northern portion), GA (Comcast Cable)

▲ **PAVO**—Southeast Cable TV Inc.

PAYNE CITY—See MACON, GA (Cox Communications)

PEACH COUNTY (PORTIONS)—See MACON, GA (Cox Communications)

PEACH COUNTY—See FORT VALLEY, GA (ComSouth)

PEACHTREE CITY—See ATLANTA (perimeter south), GA (Comcast Cable)

▲ **PEARSON**—Mediacom

PELHAM—See CAMILLA, GA (Mediacom)

▲ **PEMBROKE**—Comcast Cable

PENDERGRASS—See ATLANTA (perimeter north), GA (Comcast Cable)

▲ **PERRY**—ComSouth Telesys Inc.

PERRY—See MACON, GA (Cox Communications)

PICKENS COUNTY (PORTIONS)—See ELLIJAY, GA (Ellijay Telephone Co.)

PICKENS COUNTY (PORTIONS)—See BIG CANOE, GA (Windstream)

PIEDMONT—See CRAWFORD COUNTY (portions), GA (Flint Cable TV)

PIKE COUNTY (UNINCORPORATED AREAS)—See ZEBULON, GA (Georgia Broadband)

PINE GLEN—See ALBANY, GA (Mediacom)

PINE LAKE—See ATLANTA (metro area), GA (Comcast Cable)

▲ **PINE MOUNTAIN**—Charter Communications

▲ **PINEHURST**—ComSouth Inc. Now served by PERRY, GA [GA0229]

PINEHURST—See PERRY, GA (ComSouth Telesys Inc.)

▲ **PINEVIEW**—Formerly served by KLiP Interactive. No longer in operation

▲ **PITTS**—Formerly served by KLiP Interactive. No longer in operation

▲ **PLAINS**—Citizens Cable TV. Now served by LAKE BLACKSHEAR, GA [GA0150]

PLAINS—See LAKE BLACKSHEAR, GA (Citizens Cable TV)

POLK COUNTY (EASTERN PORTION)—See ROCKMART, GA (Charter Communications)

POLK COUNTY (NORTHEASTERN PORTION)—See ATLANTA (perimeter north), GA (Comcast Cable)

POLK COUNTY—See CEDARTOWN, GA (Charter Communications)

POOLER—See SAVANNAH, GA (Comcast Cable)

▲ **POOLER**—Hargray

▲ **PORT WENTWORTH (portions)**—Comcast Cable. Now served by SAVANNAH, GA [GA0005]

PORT WENTWORTH—See SAVANNAH, GA (Comcast Cable)

▲ **PORTAL**—Formerly served by KLiP Interactive. No longer in operation

PORTERDALE—See COVINGTON, GA (Charter Communications)

POULAN—See ALBANY, GA (Mediacom)

POWDER SPRINGS—See ATLANTA (northern portion), GA (Comcast Cable)

▲ **PRESTON**—Formerly served by Citizens Cable TV. No longer in operation

PULASKI COUNTY (PORTIONS)—See PERRY, GA (ComSouth Telesys Inc.)

PUTNAM COUNTY (PORTIONS)—See EATONTON, GA (CommuniComm Services)

PUTNAM COUNTY (UNINCORPORATED AREAS)—See GREENE COUNTY (unincorporated areas), GA (Plantation Cablevision Inc.)

PUTNAM COUNTY—See BALDWIN COUNTY (northern portion), GA (Bulldog Cable)

PUTNEY—See ALBANY, GA (Mediacom)

▲ **QUITMAN**—Comcast Cable

RADIUM SPRINGS—See ALBANY, GA (Mediacom)

RANDOLPH COUNTY (PORTIONS)—See AMERICUS, GA (Mediacom)

▲ **RANGER**—Formerly served by 3D Cable Inc. No longer in operation

RAY CITY—See PEARSON, GA (Mediacom)

▲ **RAYLE**—Formerly served by KLiP Interactive. No longer in operation

▲ **RAYSVILLE**—Formerly served by KLiP Interactive. No longer in operation

▲ **REBECCA**—Formerly served by KLiP Interactive. No longer in operation

▲ **RECOVERY**—Formerly served by KLiP Interactive. No longer in operation

▲ **REIDSVILLE**—Kennedy Cablevision Inc.

REMERTON—See VALDOSTA, GA (Mediacom)

▲ **RENTZ**—Bulldog Cable

REST HAVEN—See DULUTH, GA (Charter Communications)

▲ **REYNOLDS**—Flint Cable TV

▲ **RHINE**—Formerly served by KLiP Interactive. No longer in operation

RICEBORO—See HINESVILLE, GA (Comcast Cable)

RICHLAND—See CUTHBERT, GA (Mediacom)

RICHMOND COUNTY—See AUGUSTA, GA (Comcast Cable)

RICHMOND HILL—See HINESVILLE, GA (Comcast Cable)

RINCON—See GUYTON, GA (Comcast Cable)

RINCON—See SAVANNAH, GA (Comcast Cable)

▲ **RINGGOLD**—Charter Communications

RISING FAWN—See TRENTON, GA (Charter Communications)

RIVER VIEW—See WEST POINT, AL (Charter Communications)

RIVERDALE—See ATLANTA (perimeter south), GA (Comcast Cable)

▲ **ROBERTA**—Flint Cable TV

ROBINS AFB—See MACON, GA (Cox Communications)

▲ **ROCHELLE**—Bulldog Cable

ROCK SPRING—See LA FAYETTE, GA (Comcast Cable)

ROCKDALE COUNTY (UNINCORPORATED AREAS)—See STOCKBRIDGE, GA (Charter Communications)

ROCKDALE COUNTY—See ATLANTA (perimeter south), GA (Comcast Cable)

▲ **ROCKMART**—Charter Communications

ROME—See ATLANTA (perimeter north), GA (Comcast Cable)

▲ **ROSSVILLE**—Comcast Cable

▲ **ROSWELL**—Charter Communications

ROSWELL—See ATLANTA (northern portion), GA (Comcast Cable)

▲ **ROYSTON**—Northland Cable Television

RUTLEDGE—See GREENSBORO, GA (CommuniComm Services)

▲ **SANDERSVILLE**—Northland Cable Television

SANDY SPRING—See ATLANTA (northern portion), GA (Comcast Cable)

▲ **SANFORD**—Formerly served by KLiP Interactive. No longer in operation

SANTA CLAUS—See VIDALIA, GA (Northland Cable Television)

SAPELO GARDENS—See EULONIA, GA (Comcast Cable)

▲ **SARDIS**—Formerly served by KLiP Interactive. No longer in operation

▲ **SASSER**—Formerly served by Citizens Cable TV. No longer in operation

▲ **SAVANNAH**—Comcast Cable

SCHLEY COUNTY (PORTIONS)—See AMERICUS, GA (Mediacom)

SCREVEN COUNTY (PORTIONS)—See SYLVANIA, GA (Comcast Cable)

SCREVEN—See HINESVILLE, GA (Comcast Cable)

SEMINOLE COUNTY (PORTIONS)—See BAINBRIDGE, GA (Mediacom)

▲ **SEMINOLE COUNTY**—Bulldog Cable

SENOIA—See ATLANTA (perimeter south), GA (Comcast Cable)

SHARPSBURG—See NEWNAN, GA (Charter Communications)

SHAWMUT—See WEST POINT, AL (Charter Communications)

SHELLMAN BLUFF—See EULONIA, GA (Comcast Cable)

SHELLMAN—See AMERICUS, GA (Mediacom)

SHILOH—See MANCHESTER, GA (Charter Communications)

▲ **SKIDAWAY ISLAND**—US Cable of Coastal Texas LP. Now served by SAVANNAH, GA [GA0005]

SKIDAWAY ISLAND—See SAVANNAH, GA (Comcast Cable)

SKY VALLEY—See CLAYTON, GA (Northland Cable Television)

▲ **SMITHVILLE**—Citizens Cable TV

▲ **SMYRNA**—Charter Communications

SNEADS—See SEMINOLE COUNTY, FL (Bulldog Cable)

SNELLVILLE—See ATLANTA (metro area), GA (Comcast Cable)

SOCIAL CIRCLE (PORTIONS)—See MONROE, GA (Monroe Utilities Network)

SOCIAL CIRCLE—See ATLANTA (perimeter south), GA (Comcast Cable)

▲ **SOPERTON**—Comcast Cable

SOUTH AUGUSTA—See AUGUSTA, GA (Comcast Cable)

▲ **SOUTHBRIDGE**—Comcast Cable. Now served by SAVANNAH, GA [GA0005]

SOUTHBRIDGE—See SAVANNAH, GA (Comcast Cable)

SPALDING COUNTY—See ATLANTA (perimeter south), GA (Comcast Cable)

SPARKS—See PEARSON, GA (Mediacom)

▲ **SPARTA**—Bulldog Cable

SPRINGFIELD—See GUYTON, GA (Comcast Cable)

SPRINGFIELD—See SAVANNAH, GA (Comcast Cable)

▲ **ST. MARY'S**—Comcast Cable

▲ **STAPLETON**—Formerly served by KLiP Interactive. No longer in operation

STATENVILLE—See LAKE PARK, GA (Cobridge Communications)

▲ **STATESBORO**—Northland Cable Television

▲ **STATHAM**—Now served by ATLANTA (perimeter north), GA [GA0033]

STATHAM—See ATLANTA (perimeter north), GA (Comcast Cable)

STEPHENS COUNTY (SOUTHERN PORTION)—See HARTWELL (unincorporated areas), GA (Hart Communications)

STEPHENS COUNTY—See TOCCOA, GA (Northland Cable Television)

▲ **STILLMORE**—Pineland Telephone Coop Inc. This cable system has converted to IPTV. See Stillmore, GA [GA5011]

▲ **STILLMORE**—Pineland Telephone Coop. Inc. Formerly [GA0161]. This cable system has converted to IPTV

▲ **STOCKBRIDGE**—Charter Communications

STONE MOUNTAIN—See ATLANTA (metro area), GA (Comcast Cable)

SUGAR HILL—See DULUTH, GA (Charter Communications)

▲ **SUMMERVILLE**—Charter Communications

SUMTER COUNTY (PORTIONS)—See LAKE BLACKSHEAR, GA (Citizens Cable TV)

SUMTER COUNTY (PORTIONS)—See AMERICUS, GA (Mediacom)

SUNNY SIDE—See ATLANTA (perimeter south), GA (Comcast Cable)

▲ **SURRENCY**—Worth Cable

SUWANEE—See DULUTH, GA (Charter Communications)

▲ **SWAINSBORO**—Northland Cable Television

SYCAMORE—See TIFTON, GA (Mediacom)

▲ **SYLVANIA**—Comcast Cable

SYLVESTER—See ALBANY, GA (Mediacom)

TALBOTTON—See LAGRANGE, GA (Charter Communications)

TALBOTTON—See MANCHESTER, GA (Charter Communications)

▲ **TALLAPOOSA**—Comcast Cable

TALMO—See ATLANTA (perimeter north), GA (Comcast Cable)

TATTNALL COUNTY (PORTIONS)—See COLLINS, GA (Worth Cable)

TAYLORSVILLE—See ATLANTA (perimeter north), GA (Comcast Cable)

TELFAIR COUNTY (PORTIONS)—See MILAN, GA (Bulldog Cable)

TELFAIR COUNTY (PORTIONS)—See EASTMAN, GA (Mediacom)

TEMPLE—See VILLA RICA, GA (Charter Communications)

TENNILLE—See SANDERSVILLE, GA (Northland Cable Television)

TERRELL COUNTY (SOUTHERN PORTION)—See ALBANY, GA (Mediacom)

THOMAS COUNTY (PORTIONS)—See CAMILLA, GA (Mediacom)

THOMAS COUNTY—See THOMASVILLE, GA (Mediacom)

▲ **THOMASTON**—Charter Communications

▲ **THOMASVILLE**—CNS

▲ **THOMASVILLE**—Mediacom

THOMSON—See AUGUSTA, GA (Comcast Cable)

THUNDERBOLT—See SAVANNAH, GA (Comcast Cable)

▲ **TIFTON**—Mediacom

TIGER—See CLAYTON, GA (Northland Cable Television)

▲ **TIGNALL**—Formerly served by Almega Cable. No longer in operation

TOCCOA FALLS—See TOCCOA, GA (Northland Cable Television)

▲ **TOCCOA**—Northland Cable Television

TOOMBS COUNTY (PORTIONS)—See UVALDA, GA (Worth Cable)

TOOMBS COUNTY—See VIDALIA, GA (Northland Cable Television)

▲ **TOOMSBORO**—Formerly served by KLiP Interactive. Now served by WILKINSON COUNTY (portions), GA [GA0312]

TOOMSBORO—See WILKINSON COUNTY (portions), GA (Windstream)

TOWNS COUNTY—See HIAWASSEE, GA (Windstream)

TOWNSEND—See EULONIA, GA (Comcast Cable)

▲ **TRENTON**—Charter Communications

TRENTON—See AUGUSTA, SC (Comcast Cable)

TRION—See SUMMERVILLE, GA (Charter Communications)

TROUP COUNTY—See LAGRANGE, GA (Charter Communications)

TROUP COUNTY—See PINE MOUNTAIN, GA (Charter Communications)

TROUP COUNTY—See WEST POINT, GA (Charter Communications)

TUNNEL HILL—See DALTON, GA (Charter Communications)

TURIN—See NEWNAN, GA (Charter Communications)

TURNER COUNTY (SOUTHERN PORTION)—See TIFTON, GA (Mediacom)

TURTLETOWN—See BLUE RIDGE, TN (Ellijay Telephone Co.)

TURTLETOWN—See ELLIJAY, TN (Ellijay Telephone Co.)

TWIGGS COUNTY (PORTIONS)—See JEFFERSONVILLE, GA (Windstream)

▲**TWIN CITY**—Comcast Cable

TY TY—See TIFTON, GA (Mediacom)

▲**TYBEE ISLAND**—Comcast Cable

TYRONE—See ATLANTA (perimeter south), GA (Comcast Cable)

U.S. MARINE LOGISTICS BASE (GOVERNMENT RESERVE)—See ALBANY, GA (Mediacom)

▲**UNADILLA**—CommuniComm Services. Now served by PERRY, GA [GA0229]

UNADILLA—See PERRY, GA (ComSouth Telesys Inc.)

UNION CITY—See ATLANTA (metro area), GA (Comcast Cable)

UNION COUNTY—See BLAIRSVILLE, GA (Windstream)

UNION POINT—See GREENSBORO, GA (CommuniComm Services)

UPSON COUNTY (UNINCORPORATED AREAS)—See THOMASTON, GA (Charter Communications)

▲**UVALDA**—Worth Cable

VALDOSTA (PORTIONS)—See LAKE PARK, GA (Cobridge Communications)

▲**VALDOSTA**—Mediacom

VALLEY—See WEST POINT, AL (Charter Communications)

VARNELL—See DALTON, GA (Charter Communications)

VERNONBURG—See SAVANNAH, GA (Comcast Cable)

▲**VIDALIA**—Northland Cable Television

VIENNA—See FITZGERALD, GA (Mediacom)

▲**VILLA RICA**—Charter Communications

VILLA RICA—See ATLANTA (northern portion), GA (Comcast Cable)

VININGS—See ATLANTA (northern portion), GA (Comcast Cable)

WADLEY—See LOUISVILLE, GA (Comcast Cable)

WALESKA—See ATLANTA (perimeter north), GA (Comcast Cable)

WALKER COUNTY (PORTIONS)—See ROSSVILLE, GA (Comcast Cable)

WALKER—See LA FAYETTE, GA (Comcast Cable)

WALNUT GROVE—See ATLANTA (perimeter south), GA (Comcast Cable)

WALTHOURVILLE—See HINESVILLE, GA (Comcast Cable)

WALTON COUNTY (WESTERN PORTION)—See ATLANTA (perimeter south), GA (Comcast Cable)

WALTON COUNTY—See ATLANTA (perimeter north), GA (Comcast Cable)

WARE COUNTY (EASTERN PORTION)—See WAYCROSS, GA (Media Stream)

WARM SPRINGS—See MANCHESTER, GA (Charter Communications)

WARNER ROBINS—See PERRY, GA (ComSouth Telesys Inc.)

WARNER ROBINS—See MACON, GA (Cox Communications)

WARREN COUNTY (PORTIONS)—See WARRENTON, GA (Comcast Cable)

▲**WARRENTON**—Comcast Cable

▲**WARWICK**—Citizens Cable TV

WASHINGTON COUNTY (PORTIONS)—See SANDERSVILLE, GA (Northland Cable Television)

▲**WASHINGTON**—Comcast Cable

WATKINSVILLE—See ATHENS, GA (Charter Communications)

▲**WAVERLY HALL**—Charter Communications

▲**WAYCROSS**—Media Stream

WAYNE COUNTY (UNINCORPORATED AREAS)—See HINESVILLE, GA (Comcast Cable)

▲**WAYNESBORO**—Comcast Cablevision of the South. Now served by AUGUSTA, GA [GA0004]

WAYNESBORO—See AUGUSTA, GA (Comcast Cable)

▲**WAYNESVILLE**—Comcast Cable

WEST GREEN—See DOUGLAS, GA (Charter Communications)

▲**WEST POINT**—Charter Communications

WHEELER COUNTY (PORTIONS)—See MOUNT VERNON, GA (Comcast Cable)

▲**WHIGHAM**—Formerly served by KLiP Interactive. No longer in operation

WHITE COUNTY (PORTIONS)—See HELEN, GA (Windstream)

WHITE—See ATLANTA (perimeter north), GA (Comcast Cable)

WHITEMARSH ISLAND—See SAVANNAH, GA (Comcast Cable)

WHITESBURG—See TALLAPOOSA, GA (Comcast Cable)

WHITFIELD COUNTY—See DALTON, GA (Charter Communications)

WILDWOOD—See TRENTON, GA (Charter Communications)

▲**WILEY ACRES**—Citizens Cable TV

WILKES COUNTY (PORTIONS)—See WASHINGTON, GA (Comcast Cable)

WILKINSON COUNTY (PORTIONS)—See IRWINTON, GA (Acoucomm Telecommunications)

▲**WILKINSON COUNTY (PORTIONS)**—Windstream

WILKINSON COUNTY—See GORDON, GA (Bulldog Cable)

WILLACOOCHEE—See PEARSON, GA (Mediacom)

WILLIAMSON—See STOCKBRIDGE, GA (Charter Communications)

▲**WILLIAMSON**—Georgia Broadband

WILMINGTON ISLAND—See SAVANNAH, GA (Comcast Cable)

▲**WINDER**—Comcast Cable. Now served by ATLANTA (perimeter north), GA [GA0033]

WINDER—See ATLANTA (perimeter north), GA (Comcast Cable)

WINSTON—See ATLANTA (northern portion), GA (Comcast Cable)

WINTERVILLE—See ATHENS, GA (Charter Communications)

▲**WOODBINE**—Comcast Cable

▲**WOODBURY**—Formerly served by Almega Cable. No longer in operation

▲**WOODBURY**—Georgia Broadband

WOODLAND LAKES RESORT—See HINESVILLE, GA (Comcast Cable)

WOODLAND—See LAGRANGE, GA (Charter Communications)

WOODLAND—See MANCHESTER, GA (Charter Communications)

WOODSTOCK—See ATLANTA (northern portion), GA (Comcast Cable)

WOODVILLE—See GREENSBORO, GA (CommuniComm Services)

WOOLSEY—See ATLANTA (perimeter south), GA (Comcast Cable)

WORTH COUNTY (EASTERN PORTION)—See ALBANY, GA (Mediacom)

WORTH COUNTY—See WARWICK, GA (Citizens Cable TV)

WREN'S QUARTERS—See LOUISVILLE, GA (Comcast Cable)

▲**WRENS**—Bulldog Cable

▲**WRIGHTSVILLE**—Comcast Cable

▲**YATESVILLE**—Flint Cable TV

YOUNG HARRIS—See HIAWASSEE, GA (Windstream)

▲**ZEBULON**—Georgia Broadband

HAWAII

AHUIMANU—See MILILANI, HI (Oceanic Time Warner Cable)

AIEA—See MILILANI, HI (Oceanic Time Warner Cable)

ALIAMANU GOVERNMENT RESERVE—See MILILANI, HI (Oceanic Time Warner Cable)

ANAHOLA—See KAUAI ISLAND, HI (Oceanic Time Warner Cable)

BARKING SANDS NAVAL BASE—See KAUAI ISLAND, HI (Oceanic Time Warner Cable)

▲**BELLOWS AFB**—Oceanic Time Warner Cable

CAPTAIN COOK—See KONA, HI (Oceanic Time Warner Cable)

DIAMOND HEAD/WILHELMINA—See MILILANI, HI (Oceanic Time Warner Cable)

ELEELE—See KAUAI ISLAND, HI (Oceanic Time Warner Cable)

ENCHANTED HILLS—See MILILANI, HI (Oceanic Time Warner Cable)

EWA BEACH—See MILILANI, HI (Oceanic Time Warner Cable)

EWA—See MILILANI, HI (Oceanic Time Warner Cable)

FOSTER VILLAGE—See MILILANI, HI (Oceanic Time Warner Cable)

HAIKU—See MAUI, HI (Oceanic Time Warner Cable)

HALAWA HEIGHTS—See MILILANI, HI (Oceanic Time Warner Cable)

HALEIWA—See MILILANI, HI (Oceanic Time Warner Cable)

HALIIMAILE—See MAUI, HI (Oceanic Time Warner Cable)

HANA—See MAUI, HI (Oceanic Time Warner Cable)

HANALEI—See KAUAI ISLAND, HI (Oceanic Time Warner Cable)

HANAMAULU—See KAUAI ISLAND, HI (Oceanic Time Warner Cable)

HANAPEPE—See KAUAI ISLAND, HI (Oceanic Time Warner Cable)

HAUULA—See MILILANI, HI (Oceanic Time Warner Cable)

▲**HAWAII KAI**—Oceanic Time Warner Cable. Now served by MILILANI (formerly HONOLULU), HI [HI0001]

HAWAII KAI—See MILILANI, HI (Oceanic Time Warner Cable)

▲**HAWI**—Oceanic Time Warner Cable. Now served by KONA (formerly KAILUA KONA), HI [HI0011]

HAWI—See KONA, HI (Oceanic Time Warner Cable)

▲**HICKAM AFB**—Formerly served by Cable TV Services. No longer in operation

▲**HILO**—Oceanic Time Warner Cable

HOLUALOA—See KONA, HI (Oceanic Time Warner Cable)

HONAUNAU—See KONA, HI (Oceanic Time Warner Cable)

HONOKAA—See HILO, HI (Oceanic Time Warner Cable)

HONOKOWAI—See MAUI, HI (Oceanic Time Warner Cable)

▲ **HONOLULU**—Formerly served by Craig Wireless Honolulu Inc. No longer in operation

HONOLULU—See MILILANI, HI (Oceanic Time Warner Cable)

KAAAWA—See MILILANI, HI (Oceanic Time Warner Cable)

KAANAPALI—See MAUI, HI (Oceanic Time Warner Cable)

KAHALUU—See MILILANI, HI (Oceanic Time Warner Cable)

KAHANA—See MAUI, HI (Oceanic Time Warner Cable)

KAHUKU—See MILILANI, HI (Oceanic Time Warner Cable)

KAHULUI—See MAUI, HI (Oceanic Time Warner Cable)

KAIMUKI—See MILILANI, HI (Oceanic Time Warner Cable)

KAINALIU—See KONA, HI (Oceanic Time Warner Cable)

KALAHEO—See KAUAI ISLAND, HI (Oceanic Time Warner Cable)

KALAOA—See KONA, HI (Oceanic Time Warner Cable)

KALAUPAPA—See MAUI, HI (Oceanic Time Warner Cable)

KAMUELA—See KONA, HI (Oceanic Time Warner Cable)

KAPAA—See KAUAI ISLAND, HI (Oceanic Time Warner Cable)

KAPAAU—See KONA, HI (Oceanic Time Warner Cable)

KAPAHULU—See MILILANI, HI (Oceanic Time Warner Cable)

KAPALAMA—See MILILANI, HI (Oceanic Time Warner Cable)

KAPALUA—See MAUI, HI (Oceanic Time Warner Cable)

KAPIOLANI—See MILILANI, HI (Oceanic Time Warner Cable)

▲ **KAUAI ISLAND**—Oceanic Time Warner Cable

KAUMAKANI—See KAUAI ISLAND, HI (Oceanic Time Warner Cable)

KAUNAKAKAI—See MAUI, HI (Oceanic Time Warner Cable)

KAWAIHAE—See KONA, HI (Oceanic Time Warner Cable)

KEALAKEKUA—See KONA, HI (Oceanic Time Warner Cable)

KEALIA—See KAUAI ISLAND, HI (Oceanic Time Warner Cable)

KEAUHOU—See KONA, HI (Oceanic Time Warner Cable)

KEKAHA—See KAUAI ISLAND, HI (Oceanic Time Warner Cable)

KIHEI—See MAUI, HI (Oceanic Time Warner Cable)

KILAUEA MILITARY CAMP—See HILO, HI (Oceanic Time Warner Cable)

KILAUEA—See KAUAI ISLAND, HI (Oceanic Time Warner Cable)

KOHALA—See KONA, HI (Oceanic Time Warner Cable)

KOLOA—See KAUAI ISLAND, HI (Oceanic Time Warner Cable)

▲ **KONA**—Oceanic Time Warner Cable

KULA—See MAUI, HI (Oceanic Time Warner Cable)

KULIOUOU VALLEY—See MILILANI, HI (Oceanic Time Warner Cable)

LAHAINA—See MAUI, HI (Oceanic Time Warner Cable)

LAIE—See MILILANI, HI (Oceanic Time Warner Cable)

LANAI CITY—See MAUI, HI (Oceanic Time Warner Cable)

LAWAI—See KAUAI ISLAND, HI (Oceanic Time Warner Cable)

LIHUE—See KAUAI ISLAND, HI (Oceanic Time Warner Cable)

LOWER PAIA—See MAUI, HI (Oceanic Time Warner Cable)

MAALAEA—See MAUI, HI (Oceanic Time Warner Cable)

MAHINAHINA—See MAUI, HI (Oceanic Time Warner Cable)

MAILI—See MILILANI, HI (Oceanic Time Warner Cable)

MAKAHA—See MILILANI, HI (Oceanic Time Warner Cable)

MAKAKILO CITY—See MILILANI, HI (Oceanic Time Warner Cable)

MAKAWAO—See MAUI, HI (Oceanic Time Warner Cable)

MAKIKI—See MILILANI, HI (Oceanic Time Warner Cable)

MANOA—See MILILANI, HI (Oceanic Time Warner Cable)

MAUI ISLAND—See MAUI, HI (Oceanic Time Warner Cable)

▲ **MAUI**—Formerly served by Maui Cablevision Corp. No longer in operation

▲ **MAUI**—Hawaiian Cablevision. Now served by MAUI (formerly KIHEI), HI [HI0013]

▲ **MAUI**—Oceanic Time Warner Cable

MAUNA KEA—See KONA, HI (Oceanic Time Warner Cable)

MAUNA LANI—See KONA, HI (Oceanic Time Warner Cable)

MAUNAWILI—See MILILANI, HI (Oceanic Time Warner Cable)

MCCULLY—See MILILANI, HI (Oceanic Time Warner Cable)

▲ **MILILANI**—Oceanic Time Warner Cable

MOANALUA—See MILILANI, HI (Oceanic Time Warner Cable)

MOILIILI—See MILILANI, HI (Oceanic Time Warner Cable)

MOKULEIA—See MILILANI, HI (Oceanic Time Warner Cable)

NAALEHU—See KONA, HI (Oceanic Time Warner Cable)

NANAKULI—See MILILANI, HI (Oceanic Time Warner Cable)

NAPILI—See MAUI, HI (Oceanic Time Warner Cable)

NORTH KOHALA DISTRICT—See KONA, HI (Oceanic Time Warner Cable)

NORTH SHORE—See MILILANI, HI (Oceanic Time Warner Cable)

NUUANU—See MILILANI, HI (Oceanic Time Warner Cable)

OMAO—See KAUAI ISLAND, HI (Oceanic Time Warner Cable)

PACIFIC HEIGHTS—See MILILANI, HI (Oceanic Time Warner Cable)

▲ **PAHALA**—Formerly served by Time Warner Cable. No longer in operation

PAHOA—See HILO, HI (Oceanic Time Warner Cable)

PAUOA—See MILILANI, HI (Oceanic Time Warner Cable)

PEARL CITY—See MILILANI, HI (Oceanic Time Warner Cable)

PEARL HARBOR GOVERNMENT RESERVE—See MILILANI, HI (Oceanic Time Warner Cable)

PRINCEVILLE—See KAUAI ISLAND, HI (Oceanic Time Warner Cable)

PUAKO—See KONA, HI (Oceanic Time Warner Cable)

PUKALANI—See MAUI, HI (Oceanic Time Warner Cable)

PUNA—See HILO, HI (Oceanic Time Warner Cable)

PUNCHBOWL—See MILILANI, HI (Oceanic Time Warner Cable)

PUPUKEA—See MILILANI, HI (Oceanic Time Warner Cable)

SOUTH KONA—See KONA, HI (Oceanic Time Warner Cable)

SPRECKELSVILLE—See MAUI, HI (Oceanic Time Warner Cable)

ST. LOUIS HEIGHTS—See MILILANI, HI (Oceanic Time Warner Cable)

SUNSET BEACH—See MILILANI, HI (Oceanic Time Warner Cable)

VOLCANO VILLAGE—See HILO, HI (Oceanic Time Warner Cable)

WAHIAWA—See MILILANI, HI (Oceanic Time Warner Cable)

WAIALUA—See MILILANI, HI (Oceanic Time Warner Cable)

WAIANAE—See MILILANI, HI (Oceanic Time Warner Cable)

WAIHEE—See MAUI, HI (Oceanic Time Warner Cable)

WAIKAPU—See MAUI, HI (Oceanic Time Warner Cable)

WAIKIKI—See MILILANI, HI (Oceanic Time Warner Cable)

WAIKOLOA RESORT—See KONA, HI (Oceanic Time Warner Cable)

WAIKOLOA VILLAGE—See KONA, HI (Oceanic Time Warner Cable)

WAILEA—See MAUI, HI (Oceanic Time Warner Cable)

WAILUA HOMESTEADS—See KAUAI ISLAND, HI (Oceanic Time Warner Cable)

WAILUA—See KAUAI ISLAND, HI (Oceanic Time Warner Cable)

WAILUKU—See MAUI, HI (Oceanic Time Warner Cable)

WAIMANALO—See MILILANI, HI (Oceanic Time Warner Cable)

WAIMEA—See KAUAI ISLAND, HI (Oceanic Time Warner Cable)

WAIOHINU—See HILO, HI (Oceanic Time Warner Cable)

WAIPAHU—See MILILANI, HI (Oceanic Time Warner Cable)

WAIPIO—See MILILANI, HI (Oceanic Time Warner Cable)

IDAHO

▲ **ABERDEEN**—Direct Communications

ADA COUNTY (PORTIONS)—See BOISE, ID (Cable One)

▲ **ADA COUNTY (unincorporated areas)**—Formerly served by Ada Cable Vision Inc. No longer in operation

▲ **ALBION**—Formerly served by Telsat Systems Inc. No longer in operation

ALBION—See MOSCOW, WA (Time Warner Cable)

▲ **AMERICAN FALLS**—Cable One. Now served by POCATELLO, ID [ID0004]

AMERICAN FALLS—See POCATELLO, ID (Cable One)

AMMON—See IDAHO FALLS, ID (Cable One)

▲ **ARCO**—Direct Communications

▲ **ASHTON**—Silver Star Broadband

ASOTIN COUNTY—See LEWISTON, WA (Cable One)

ASOTIN—See LEWISTON, WA (Cable One)

ATHOL—See COEUR D'ALENE, ID (Time Warner Cable)

▲ **AVERY**—Formerly served by Rapid Cable. No longer in operation

BANCROFT—See SODA SPRINGS, ID (Direct Communications)

BANNOCK COUNTY—See POCATELLO, ID (Cable One)

BASALT—See IDAHO FALLS, ID (Cable One)

BAYVIEW—See COEUR D'ALENE, ID (Time Warner Cable)

BELLEVUE—See SUN VALLEY, ID (Cox Communications)

BIG CREEK—See OSBURN, ID (Suddenlink Communications)

BINGHAM COUNTY—See IDAHO FALLS, ID (Cable One)

BLACKFOOT—See IDAHO FALLS, ID (Cable One)

BLAINE COUNTY—See SUN VALLEY, ID (Cox Communications)

▲**BOISE**—Formerly served by Wireless Broadcasting Systems. No longer in operation

▲**BOISE**—Cable One

▲**BONNERS FERRY**—Country Cable

BONNEVILLE COUNTY—See IDAHO FALLS, ID (Cable One)

BOUNDARY COUNTY—See BONNERS FERRY, ID (Country Cable)

▲**BOVILL**—Formerly served by Adelphia Communications. No longer in operation

▲**BOVILL**—Elk River TV Cable Co.

▲**BUHL**—Millennium Digital Media. Now served by TWIN FALLS, ID [ID0088]

BUHL—See TWIN FALLS, ID (Cable One)

BURKE—See OSBURN, ID (Suddenlink Communications)

BURLEY—See TWIN FALLS, ID (Cable One)

▲**CALDWELL**—Cable One

▲**CAMBRIDGE**—Cambridge Cable TV

▲**CASCADE**—Cable One. Now served by CALDWELL, ID [ID0008]

CASCADE—See CALDWELL, ID (Cable One)

CASSIA COUNTY (NORTHERN PORTION)—See TWIN FALLS, ID (Cable One)

▲**CASTLEFORD**—Formerly served by WDB Communications. No longer in operation

CATALDO (PORTIONS)—See OSBURN, ID (Suddenlink Communications)

▲**CATALDO**—Formerly served by Cebridge Connections. Now served by OSBURN, ID [ID0015]

▲**CHALLIS**—Direct Communications

CHUBBOCK—See POCATELLO, ID (Cable One)

CLARKSTON—See LEWISTON, WA (Cable One)

▲**COEUR D'ALENE**—Time Warner Cable

COLTON—See MOSCOW, WA (Time Warner Cable)

COTTONWOOD—See OROFINO, ID (Suddenlink Communications)

▲**COUNCIL**—Cable One

CRAIGMONT—See OROFINO, ID (Suddenlink Communications)

▲**CULDESAC**—Formerly served by Rapid Cable. No longer in operation

DALTON GARDENS—See COEUR D'ALENE, ID (Time Warner Cable)

▲**DEARY**—Elk River TV Cable Co.

▲**DONNELLY**—Cable One. Now served by CALDWELL, ID [ID0008]

DONNELLY—See CALDWELL, ID (Cable One)

DOVER—See SANDPOINT, ID (Northland Cable Television)

▲**DOWNEY**—Independent Cable. Now served by SODA SPRINGS, ID [ID0022]

DOWNEY—See SODA SPRINGS, ID (Direct Communications)

▲**DRIGGS**—Independent Cable. Now served by VICTOR, ID [ID0062]

DRIGGS—See VICTOR, ID (Silver Star Broadband)

EAGLE—See CALDWELL, ID (Cable One)

ELK CREEK—See OSBURN, ID (Suddenlink Communications)

▲**ELK RIVER**—Elk River TV Cable Co.

ELMORE COUNTY—See MOUNTAIN HOME, ID (Windjammer Cable)

▲**EMMETT**—Cable One. Now served by CALDWELL, ID [ID0008]

EMMETT—See CALDWELL, ID (Cable One)

FERNAN LAKE—See COEUR D'ALENE, ID (Time Warner Cable)

FILER—See TWIN FALLS, ID (Cable One)

FIRTH—See IDAHO FALLS, ID (Cable One)

▲**FISH HAVEN**—Independent Cable. Now served by SODA SPRINGS, ID [ID0022]

FISH HAVEN—See SODA SPRINGS, ID (Direct Communications)

FREMONT COUNTY (SOUTHERN PORTION)—See IDAHO FALLS, ID (Cable One)

FRUITLAND—See CALDWELL, ID (Cable One)

GARDEN CITY—See BOISE, ID (Cable One)

GARDEN CITY—See SODA SPRINGS, UT (Direct Communications)

GEM—See OSBURN, ID (Suddenlink Communications)

GENESEE—See MOSCOW, ID (Time Warner Cable)

GEORGETOWN—See SODA SPRINGS, ID (Direct Communications)

▲**GLENNS FERRY**—Rural Telephone Co.

GOODING COUNTY (PORTIONS)—See TWIN FALLS, ID (Cable One)

GOODING—See TWIN FALLS, ID (Cable One)

GRACE—See SODA SPRINGS, ID (Direct Communications)

GRANGEVILLE—See OROFINO, ID (Suddenlink Communications)

GREENLEAF—See CALDWELL, ID (Cable One)

GROVELAND—See IDAHO FALLS, ID (Cable One)

HAGERMAN—See TWIN FALLS, ID (Cable One)

HAILEY—See SUN VALLEY, ID (Cox Communications)

HANSEN—See TWIN FALLS, ID (Cable One)

▲**HARRISON**—Formerly served by Rapid Cable. No longer in operation

HAUSER LAKE—See COEUR D'ALENE, ID (Time Warner Cable)

HAYDEN LAKE—See COEUR D'ALENE, ID (Time Warner Cable)

HAYDEN—See COEUR D'ALENE, ID (Time Warner Cable)

▲**HAZELTON**—Formerly served by WDB Communications. No longer in operation

HEADQUARTERS—See OROFINO, ID (Suddenlink Communications)

HEYBURN—See TWIN FALLS, ID (Cable One)

HOMEDALE—See CALDWELL, ID (Cable One)

HUETTER—See COEUR D'ALENE, ID (Time Warner Cable)

▲**IDAHO CITY**—Idaho City Cable TV

▲**IDAHO FALLS**—Cable One

INKOM—See POCATELLO, ID (Cable One)

IONA—See IDAHO FALLS, ID (Cable One)

JEFFERSON COUNTY—See IDAHO FALLS, ID (Cable One)

JEROME—See TWIN FALLS, ID (Cable One)

JULIAETTA—See MOSCOW, ID (Time Warner Cable)

KAMIAH—See OROFINO, ID (Suddenlink Communications)

KELLOGG—See OSBURN, ID (Suddenlink Communications)

KENDRICK—See MOSCOW, ID (Time Warner Cable)

KETCHUM—See SUN VALLEY, ID (Cox Communications)

KIMBERLY—See TWIN FALLS, ID (Cable One)

KINGSTON—See OSBURN, ID (Suddenlink Communications)

▲**KOOSKIA**—Formerly served by Rapid Cable. No longer in operation

▲**KOOTENAI COUNTY (portions)**—Formerly served by Rapid Cable. No longer in operation

KOOTENAI COUNTY (PORTIONS)—See OSBURN, ID (Suddenlink Communications)

KOOTENAI—See SANDPOINT, ID (Northland Cable Television)

KUNA—See CALDWELL, ID (Cable One)

LATAH COUNTY—See MOSCOW, ID (Time Warner Cable)

▲**LAVA HOT SPRINGS**—Independent Cable. Now served by SODA SPRINGS, ID [ID0022]

LAVA HOT SPRINGS—See SODA SPRINGS, ID (Direct Communications)

LEMHI COUNTY (SOUTHERN PORTION)—See IDAHO FALLS, ID (Cable One)

▲**LEWISTON**—Cable One

▲**MACKAY**—Independent Cable. Now served by ARCO, ID [ID0030]

MACKAY—See ARCO, ID (Direct Communications)

MADISON COUNTY (NORTHERN PORTION)—See IDAHO FALLS, ID (Cable One)

▲**MALAD CITY**—Direct Communications

MARSING—See CALDWELL, ID (Cable One)

▲**McCALL**—Cable One. Now served by CALDWELL, ID [ID0008]

MCCALL—See CALDWELL, ID (Cable One)

▲**McCAMMON**—Independent Cable. Now served by SODA SPRINGS, ID [ID0022]

MCCAMMON—See SODA SPRINGS, ID (Direct Communications)

MERIDIAN—See CALDWELL, ID (Cable One)

MIDDLETON—See CALDWELL, ID (Cable One)

▲**MIDVALE**—Midvale Telephone Exchange Inc.

MILLTOWN—See ST. MARIES, ID (Suddenlink Communications)

MINIDOKA COUNTY (SOUTHERN PORTION)—See TWIN FALLS, ID (Cable One)

MONTPELIER—See SODA SPRINGS, ID (Direct Communications)

MORELAND—See IDAHO FALLS, ID (Cable One)

▲**MOSCOW**—Time Warner Cable

MOUNTAIN HOME AFB—See MOUNTAIN HOME, ID (Windjammer Cable)

▲**MOUNTAIN HOME**—Windjammer Cable

▲**MULLAN**—Mullan Cable TV Inc.

▲**MURRAY**—Formerly served by Rapid Cable. No longer in operation

NAMPA—See CALDWELL, ID (Cable One)

▲ **NEW MEADOWS**—Cable One. Now served by CALDWELL, ID [ID0008]

NEW MEADOWS—See CALDWELL, ID (Cable One)

NEW PLYMOUTH—See CALDWELL, ID (Cable One)

NEZ PERCE COUNTY (PORTIONS)—See LEWISTON, ID (Cable One)

NEZPERCE—See OROFINO, ID (Suddenlink Communications)

NOTUS—See CALDWELL, ID (Cable One)

NYSSA—See CALDWELL, OR (Cable One)

ONAWAY—See MOSCOW, ID (Time Warner Cable)

ONTARIO—See CALDWELL, OR (Cable One)

▲ **OROFINO**—Suddenlink Communications

▲ **OSBURN**—Suddenlink Communications

PAGE—See OSBURN, ID (Suddenlink Communications)

PALOUSE—See MOSCOW, WA (Time Warner Cable)

PARIS—See SODA SPRINGS, ID (Direct Communications)

PARMA—See CALDWELL, ID (Cable One)

PAUL—See TWIN FALLS, ID (Cable One)

PAYETTE—See CALDWELL, ID (Cable One)

PECK—See OROFINO, ID (Suddenlink Communications)

PIERCE—See OROFINO, ID (Suddenlink Communications)

PINEHURST—See OSBURN, ID (Suddenlink Communications)

PLUMMER—See WORLEY, ID (Elk River TV Cable Co.)

▲ **POCATELLO**—Cable One

POLLOCK—See RIGGINS, ID (Elk River TV Cable Co.)

PONDERAY—See SANDPOINT, ID (Northland Cable Television)

POST FALLS—See COEUR D'ALENE, ID (Time Warner Cable)

POTLATCH—See MOSCOW, ID (Time Warner Cable)

▲ **PRESTON**—Direct Communications. Now served by SODA SPRINGS, ID [ID0022]

PRESTON—See SODA SPRINGS, ID (Direct Communications)

▲ **PRICHARD**—Formerly served by Rapid Cable. No longer in operation

PRINCETON—See MOSCOW, WA (Time Warner Cable)

PULLMAN—See MOSCOW, WA (Time Warner Cable)

PURPLE SAGE—See CALDWELL, ID (Cable One)

RATHDRUM—See COEUR D'ALENE, ID (Time Warner Cable)

REXBURG—See IDAHO FALLS, ID (Cable One)

▲ **RICHFIELD**—Formerly served by WDB Communications. No longer in operation

RIGBY—See IDAHO FALLS, ID (Cable One)

▲ **RIGGINS**—Elk River TV Cable Co.

RIRIE—See IDAHO FALLS, ID (Cable One)

RIVERSIDE—See IDAHO FALLS, ID (Cable One)

RUPERT—See TWIN FALLS, ID (Cable One)

SAGLE—See SANDPOINT, ID (Northland Cable Television)

▲ **SALMON**—Custer Telephone Cooperative

SANDPOINT (UNINCORPORATED AREAS)—See SANDPOINT, ID (Northland Cable Television)

▲ **SANDPOINT**—Northland Cable Television

SHELLEY—See IDAHO FALLS, ID (Cable One)

▲ **SHOSHONE**—Millennium Digital Media. Now served by TWIN FALLS, ID [ID0088]

SHOSHONE—See TWIN FALLS, ID (Cable One)

SILVERTON—See OSBURN, ID (Suddenlink Communications)

SMELTERVILLE—See OSBURN, ID (Suddenlink Communications)

▲ **SODA SPRINGS**—Direct Communications

▲ **SPIRIT LAKE**—Formerly served by Cebridge Connections. Now served byTWIN LAKES, ID [ID0092]

SPIRIT LAKE—See TWIN LAKES, ID (Suddenlink Communications)

ST. ANTHONY—See IDAHO FALLS, ID (Cable One)

ST. CHARLES—See SODA SPRINGS, ID (Direct Communications)

▲ **ST. MARIES**—Suddenlink Communications

STAR—See CALDWELL, ID (Cable One)

SUGAR CITY—See IDAHO FALLS, ID (Cable One)

▲ **SUN VALLEY**—Cox Communications

▲ **TROY**—Elk River TV Cable Co.

TWIN FALLS COUNTY (PORTIONS)—See TWIN FALLS, ID (Cable One)

▲ **TWIN FALLS**—Cable One

▲ **TWIN LAKES**—Suddenlink Communications

UCON—See IDAHO FALLS, ID (Cable One)

UNIONTOWN—See MOSCOW, WA (Time Warner Cable)

VALE—See CALDWELL, OR (Cable One)

▲ **VICTOR**—Silver Star Broadband

WALLACE—See OSBURN, ID (Suddenlink Communications)

WARDNER—See OSBURN, ID (Suddenlink Communications)

WEIPPE—See OROFINO, ID (Suddenlink Communications)

▲ **WEISER**—Cable One. Now served by CALDWELL, ID [ID0008]

WEISER—See CALDWELL, ID (Cable One)

WENDELL—See TWIN FALLS, ID (Cable One)

WHITMAN COUNTY (SOUTHEASTERN PORTION)—See MOSCOW, WA (Time Warner Cable)

WILDER—See CALDWELL, ID (Cable One)

WINCHESTER—See OROFINO, ID (Suddenlink Communications)

WOODLAND PARK—See OSBURN, ID (Suddenlink Communications)

▲ **WORLEY**—Elk River TV Cable Co.

ILLINOIS

▲ **ABINGDON**—Mediacom

▲ **ADAIR (unincorporated areas)**—Formerly served by CableDirect. No longer in operation

ADAMS COUNTY—See QUINCY, IL (Comcast Cable)

▲ **ADDIEVILLE**—Charter Communications. Now served by WOODLAWN, IL [IL0067]

ADDIEVILLE—See WOODLAWN, IL (Charter Communications)

ADDISON—See OAK BROOK, IL (Comcast Cable)

ALBANY TWP.—See LENA, WI (Mediacom)

ALBANY—See LENA, WI (Mediacom)

ALBERS—See SCOTT AFB, IL (Charter Communications)

▲ **ALBION**—NewWave Communications

ALEDO—See MINERAL, IL (Mediacom)

▲ **ALEXANDER COUNTY (PORTIONS)**—Zito Media

▲ **ALEXIS**—Mediacom. Now served by MINERAL, IL [IL0170]

ALEXIS—See MINERAL, IL (Mediacom)

ALGONQUIN—See SCHAUMBURG, IL (Comcast Cable)

▲ **ALHAMBRA**—Madison Communications. Now served by STAUNTON, IL [IL0171]

ALHAMBRA—See STAUNTON, IL (Madison Communications)

ALMA—See KINMUNDY, IL (Clearvision Cable Systems Inc.)

ALORTON—See EAST ST. LOUIS, IL (Charter Communications)

▲ **ALPHA**—Diverse Communications Inc.

▲ **ALSEY TWP.**—Formerly served by Longview Communications. No longer in operation

ALSIP—See CHICAGO (southern suburbs), IL (Comcast Cable)

▲ **ALTAMONT**—Mediacom

ALTO PASS—See ZEIGLER, IL (Mediacom)

ALTON—See ROXANA, IL (Charter Communications)

▲ **ALTONA (village)**—Mediacom. Now served by MINERAL, IL [IL0170]

ALTONA—See MINERAL, IL (Mediacom)

▲ **AMBOY**—Comcast Cable

ANDALUSIA TWP.—See MOLINE, IL (Mediacom)

ANDALUSIA—See MOLINE, IL (Mediacom)

▲ **ANDERSONVILLE**—RCN Corp. Formerly served by Chicago (portions), IL [IL0661]. This cable system has converted to IPTV

ANDOVER—See MINERAL, IL (Mediacom)

▲ **ANNA**—NewWave Communications

ANNAWAN—See MINERAL, IL (Mediacom)

▲ **APOLLO ACRES**—Mediacom

APPLE RIVER—See LENA, IL (Mediacom)

ARCOLA—See TUSCOLA, IL (Mediacom)

▲ **ARENZVILLE**—Mediacom

▲ **ARGENTA**—Suddenlink Communications

ARGYLE—See CALEDONIA, IL (Mediacom)

ARGYLE—See LENA, WI (Mediacom)

ARLINGTON HEIGHTS—See SCHAUMBURG, IL (Comcast Cable)

ARLINGTON HEIGHTS—See NAPERVILLE, IL (WOW! Internet Cable & Phone)

▲ **ARMINGTON (VILLAGE)**—Heartland Cable Inc.

▲ **ARMSTRONG**—Park TV & Electronics Inc.

AROMA PARK—See CHICAGO (southern suburbs), IL (Comcast Cable)

AROMA TWP.—See CHICAGO (southern suburbs), IL (Comcast Cable)

ARTHUR—See TUSCOLA, IL (Mediacom)

ASHKUM—See CHICAGO (southern suburbs), IL (Comcast Cable)

ASHLAND—See VIRGINIA, IL (Cass Cable TV Inc.)

ASHLEY—See WOODLAWN, IL (Charter Communications)

ASHMORE—See CHARLESTON, IL (Mediacom)

ASHTON—See FRANKLIN GROVE, IL (Comcast Cable)

ASSUMPTION—See MOWEAQUA, IL (Suddenlink Communications)

▲**ASTORIA**—Mediacom

ATHENS—See WILLIAMSVILLE, IL (Greene County Partners Inc.)

ATKINSON—See MINERAL, IL (Mediacom)

▲**ATLANTA**—Mediacom

ATWOOD—See TUSCOLA, IL (Mediacom)

AUBURN—See VIRDEN, IL (Charter Communications)

▲**AUGUSTA**—Adams Telephone. This cable system has converted to IPTV. See Augusta, IL [IL5282]

▲**AUGUSTA**—Adams Telecom. Formerly [IL0356]. This cable system has converted to IPTV

▲**AURORA**—Comcast Cable. Now served by OAK BROOK, IL [IL0006]

AURORA—See OAK BROOK, IL (Comcast Cable)

▲**AVA**—Formerly served by Longview Communications. No longer in operation

AVISTON—See SCOTT AFB, IL (Charter Communications)

▲**AVON**—Mediacom. Now served by ABINGDON, IL [IL0186]

AVON—See ABINGDON, IL (Mediacom)

BALL TWP.—See SPRINGFIELD, IL (Comcast Cable)

BANNOCKBURN—See SCHAUMBURG, IL (Comcast Cable)

▲**BARDOLPH**—Formerly served by CableDirect. No longer in operation

▲**BARRINGTON HILLS**—Comcast Cable. Now served by SCHAUMBURG, IL [IL0036]

BARRINGTON HILLS—See SCHAUMBURG, IL (Comcast Cable)

BARRINGTON—See SCHAUMBURG, IL (Comcast Cable)

▲**BARRY**—Crystal Broadband Networks

BARSTOW—See MOLINE, IL (Mediacom)

▲**BARTELSO**—Formerly served by CableDirect. No longer in operation

BARTLETT—See OAK BROOK, IL (Comcast Cable)

BARTLETT—See SCHAUMBURG, IL (Comcast Cable)

BARTLETT—See NAPERVILLE, IL (WOW! Internet Cable & Phone)

BARTONVILLE—See PEORIA, IL (Comcast Cable)

▲**BATAVIA**—Comcast Cable. Now served by OAK BROOK, IL [IL0006]

BATAVIA—See OAK BROOK, IL (Comcast Cable)

BATH—See VIRGINIA, IL (Cass Cable TV Inc.)

BAYLES LAKE—See FARMER CITY, IL (Mediacom)

▲**BAYLIS (village)**—Formerly served by Cass Cable TV Inc. No longer in operation

BAYVIEW GARDENS—See ROANOKE, IL (Mediacom)

BEACH PARK—See SCHAUMBURG, IL (Comcast Cable)

BEARDSTOWN—See VIRGINIA, IL (Cass Cable TV Inc.)

BEAUCOUP—See WOODLAWN, IL (Charter Communications)

▲**BEAVERVILLE TWP.**—Formerly served by CableDirect. No longer in operation

BECKEMEYER—See BREESE, IL (Charter Communications)

BEDFORD PARK—See OAK BROOK, IL (Comcast Cable)

▲**BEECHER CITY**—Clearvision Cable Systems Inc.

BEECHER—See CHICAGO (southern suburbs), IL (Comcast Cable)

BELGIUM—See WESTVILLE, IL (Avenue Broadband Communications)

▲**BELLE RIVE**—Formerly served by Longview Communications. No longer in operation

▲**BELLEVILLE**—Charter Communications

BELLEVUE—See PEORIA, IL (Comcast Cable)

BELLFLOWER—See LE ROY, IL (Mediacom)

▲**BELLMONT**—Formerly served by CableDirect. No longer in operation

BELLWOOD—See OAK BROOK, IL (Comcast Cable)

▲**BELVIDERE TWP.**—Mediacom. Now served by POPLAR GROVE, IL [IL0282]

BELVIDERE TWP.—See POPLAR GROVE, IL (Mediacom)

▲**BELVIDERE**—Insight Communications. Now served by ROCKFORD, IL [IL0010]

BELVIDERE—See ROCKFORD, IL (Comcast Cable)

BEMENT—See MONTICELLO, IL (Mediacom)

BENLD—See STAUNTON, IL (Madison Communications)

BENSENVILLE—See OAK BROOK, IL (Comcast Cable)

BENSON—See ROANOKE, IL (Mediacom)

BENTON—See DU QUOIN, IL (Comcast Cable)

BERKELEY—See OAK BROOK, IL (Comcast Cable)

BERLIN—See SPRINGFIELD, IL (Comcast Cable)

BERWYN—See OAK BROOK, IL (Comcast Cable)

BETHALTO—See ROXANA, IL (Charter Communications)

▲**BETHANY**—Suddenlink Communications

BETTENDORF—See MOLINE, IA (Mediacom)

▲**BIGGSVILLE**—Formerly served by CableDirect. No longer in operation

▲**BIRDS**—Park TV & Electronics Inc.

▲**BISMARCK**—Park TV & Electronics Inc.

BISSEL—See SPRINGFIELD, IL (Comcast Cable)

BLAIRSVILLE—See ZEIGLER, IL (Mediacom)

BLANCHARDVILLE—See LENA, WI (Mediacom)

BLANDINSVILLE (VILLAGE)—See MACOMB, IL (Comcast Cable)

BLOOM TWP.—See CHICAGO (southern suburbs), IL (Comcast Cable)

BLOOMINGDALE—See OAK BROOK, IL (Comcast Cable)

▲**BLOOMINGTON**—Comcast Cable

▲**BLUE GRASS**—Mediacom. Now served by MOLINE, IL [IL0011]

BLUE GRASS—See MOLINE, IA (Mediacom)

BLUE ISLAND—See CHICAGO (southern suburbs), IL (Comcast Cable)

▲**BLUE MOUND**—Suddenlink Communications

BLUFF CITY—See VANDALIA, IL (NewWave Communications)

BLUFF SPRINGS—See VIRGINIA, IL (Cass Cable TV Inc.)

▲**BLUFFS**—Crystal Broadband Networks

▲**BLUFORD**—Formerly served by Longview Communications. No longer in operation

BODEN—See MINERAL, IL (Mediacom)

BOLINGBROOK—See OAK BROOK, IL (Comcast Cable)

BOND COUNTY—See GREENVILLE, IL (NewWave Communications)

BONDVILLE (VILLAGE)—See URBANA, IL (Comcast Cable)

▲**BONE GAP**—Formerly served by CableDirect. No longer in operation

▲**BONFIELD (village)**—Formerly served by CableDirect. No longer in operation

▲**BONNIE**—Longview Communications. No longer in operation

▲**BOODY**—Formerly served by CableDirect. No longer in operation

BOONE COUNTY—See ROCKFORD, IL (Comcast Cable)

BOULDER HILL—See OAK BROOK, IL (Comcast Cable)

BOURBONAIS—See CHICAGO (southern suburbs), IL (Comcast Cable)

▲**BOWEN**—Adams Telecom. Formerly served by Golden, IL [IL0257]. This cable system has converted to IPTV

BRACEVILLE (VILLAGE)—See GIBSON CITY, IL (Mediacom)

▲**BRADFORD**—Mediacom. Now served by MINERAL, IL [IL0170]

BRADFORD—See MINERAL, IL (Mediacom)

BRADFORD—See WYOMING, IL (Mediacom)

BRADLEY—See CHICAGO (southern suburbs), IL (Comcast Cable)

▲**BREESE**—Charter Communications

BRERETON—See CANTON, IL (Comcast Cable)

BRIDGEVIEW—See OAK BROOK, IL (Comcast Cable)

▲**BRIGHTON**—BrightGreen Cable

▲**BRIMFIELD**—Mediacom. Now served by BRIMFIELD, IL [IL0201]

▲**BRIMFIELD**—Mediacom

BRIMFIELD—See EDWARDS, IL (Tel-Star Cablevision Inc.)

BROADLANDS—See NEWMAN, IL (Comcast Cable)

BROADVIEW—See OAK BROOK, IL (Comcast Cable)

▲**BROCTON**—Clearvision Cable Systems Inc.

BROOKFIELD—See OAK BROOK, IL (Comcast Cable)

BROWNSTOWN—See VANDALIA, IL (NewWave Communications)

BROWNTOWN—See LENA, WI (Mediacom)

BRUCE TWP.—See STREATOR, IL (Mediacom)

▲**BRYANT (village)**—Formerly served by CableDirect. No longer in operation

▲**BUCKLEY (VILLAGE)**—Park TV & Electronics Inc.

BUCKNER—See DU QUOIN, IL (Comcast Cable)

BUDA—See MINERAL, IL (Mediacom)

BUFFALO GROVE—See SCHAUMBURG, IL (Comcast Cable)

▲ **BUFFALO**—Mediacom. Now served by KINCAID, IL [IL0176]

BUFFALO—See MOLINE, IA (Mediacom)

BUFFALO—See KINCAID, IL (Mediacom)

BULPITT—See KINCAID, IL (Mediacom)

▲ **BUNCOMBE**—Zito Media

BUNKER HILL—See STAUNTON, IL (Madison Communications)

BURBANK—See OAK BROOK, IL (Comcast Cable)

BUREAU COUNTY—See PRINCETON, IL (Comcast Cable)

▲ **BUREAU**—Mediacom. Now served by BRIMFIELD, IL [IL0201]

BUREAU—See BRIMFIELD, IL (Mediacom)

▲ **BURLINGTON (VILLAGE)**—Mediacom

BURNHAM—See CHICAGO (southern suburbs), IL (Comcast Cable)

BURNS HARBOR—See CHICAGO (southern suburbs), IN (Comcast Cable)

BURR RIDGE—See OAK BROOK, IL (Comcast Cable)

BUSH—See ZEIGLER, IL (Mediacom)

▲ **BUSHNELL**—Insight Communications. Now served by MACOMB, IL [IL0076]

BUSHNELL—See MACOMB, IL (Comcast Cable)

BUZZVILLE—See VIRGINIA, IL (Cass Cable TV Inc.)

BYRON—See ROCKFORD, IL (Comcast Cable)

▲ **CAHOKIA**—Charter Communications

▲ **CAIRO**—NewWave Communications

▲ **CALEDONIA**—Mediacom

▲ **CALHOUN COUNTY (portions)**—Formerly served by CableDirect. No longer in operation

CALUMET CITY—See CHICAGO (southern suburbs), IL (Comcast Cable)

CALUMET CITY—See NAPERVILLE, IL (WOW! Internet Cable & Phone)

CALUMET PARK—See CHICAGO (southern suburbs), IL (Comcast Cable)

CAMARGO—See TUSCOLA, IL (Mediacom)

CAMBRIA—See ZEIGLER, IL (Mediacom)

CAMBRIDGE—See MINERAL, IL (Mediacom)

▲ **CAMERON**—Nova Cablevision Inc.

▲ **CAMP POINT**—Adams Telephone. This cable system has converted to IPTV. See Camp Point, IL [IL5313]

▲ **CAMP POINT**—Adams Telecom. Formerly [IL0206]. This cable system has converted to IPTV

CAMPBELLS ISLAND—See MOLINE, IL (Mediacom)

▲ **CAMPTON TWP.**—Comcast Cable. Now served by OAK BROOK, IL [IL0006]

CAMPTON TWP.—See OAK BROOK, IL (Comcast Cable)

CANDLEWICK LAKE—See CALEDONIA, IL (Mediacom)

▲ **CANTON**—Comcast Cable

▲ **CANTRALL**—Mediacom. Now served by DELEVAN, IL [IL0172]

CANTRALL—See DELAVAN, IL (Mediacom)

CAPRON—See POPLAR GROVE, IL (Mediacom)

CARBON CLIFF—See MOLINE, IL (Mediacom)

CARBON HILL—See OAK BROOK, IL (Comcast Cable)

CARBONDALE TWP.—See MURPHYSBORO, IL (Mediacom)

CARBONDALE—See MURPHYSBORO, IL (Mediacom)

▲ **CARLINVILLE**—NewWave Communications

▲ **CARLOCK**—Formerly served by CableDirect. No longer in operation

▲ **CARLYLE**—Charter Communications

▲ **CARMI**—Formerly served by Charter Communications. No longer in operation

CAROL STREAM—See OAK BROOK, IL (Comcast Cable)

▲ **CARPENTERSVILLE**—Comcast Cable. Now served by SCHAUMBURG, IL [IL0036]

CARPENTERSVILLE—See SCHAUMBURG, IL (Comcast Cable)

▲ **CARRIER MILLS**—Zito Media

▲ **CARROLLTON**—Greene County Partners Inc.

CARTERVILLE—See MARION, IL (Mediacom)

▲ **CARTHAGE**—Mediacom

CARY—See SCHAUMBURG, IL (Comcast Cable)

▲ **CASEY**—Mediacom. Now served by MARTINSVILLE, IL [IL0217]

CASEY—See MARTINSVILLE, IL (Mediacom)

CASEYVILLE—See MARYVILLE, IL (Charter Communications)

CATLIN—See WESTVILLE, IL (Avenue Broadband Communications)

▲ **CAVE-IN-ROCK**—Windjammer Cable

CAYUGA—See URBANA, IL (Comcast Cable)

CEDAR GROVE—See FREEMAN SPUR, IL (Zito Media)

CEDAR LAKE—See CHICAGO (southern suburbs), IN (Comcast Cable)

▲ **CEDAR POINT**—Formerly served by McNabb Cable & Satellite Inc. No longer in operation

CEDARVILLE—See FREEPORT, IL (Comcast Cable)

CENTRAL CITY—See OKAWVILLE, IL (Charter Communications)

CENTRALIA—See OKAWVILLE, IL (Charter Communications)

CENTREVILLE—See EAST ST. LOUIS, IL (Charter Communications)

▲ **CERRO GORDO**—Mediacom. Now served by TUSCOLA, IL [IL0135]

CERRO GORDO—See TUSCOLA, IL (Mediacom)

CHADWICK—See LENA, IL (Mediacom)

CHAMPAIGN COUNTY (PORTIONS)—See RANTOUL, IL (Mediacom)

CHAMPAIGN COUNTY—See URBANA, IL (Comcast Cable)

CHAMPAIGN COUNTY—See MAHOMET, IL (Mediacom)

CHAMPAIGN—See URBANA, IL (Comcast Cable)

CHANDLERVILLE—See VIRGINIA, IL (Cass Cable TV Inc.)

CHANNAHON—See OAK BROOK, IL (Comcast Cable)

▲ **CHAPIN**—Mediacom. Now served by JACKSONVILLE, IL [IL0065]

CHAPIN—See JACKSONVILLE, IL (Mediacom)

▲ **CHARLESTON**—Mediacom

▲ **CHATHAM**—Insight Communications. Now served by SPRINGFIELD, IL [IL0016]

CHATHAM—See SPRINGFIELD, IL (Comcast Cable)

CHATSWORTH—See FAIRBURY, IL (Mediacom)

CHEBANSE—See CHICAGO (southern suburbs), IL (Comcast Cable)

▲ **CHEMUNG**—Mediacom. Now served by POPLAR GROVE, IL [IL0282]

CHEMUNG—See POPLAR GROVE, IL (Mediacom)

CHENOA—See FAIRBURY, IL (Mediacom)

CHERRY VALLEY—See ROCKFORD, IL (Comcast Cable)

CHERRY—See LADD, IL (Comcast Cable)

▲ **CHESTER**—Charter Communications. Now served by SPARTA, IL [IL0147]

CHESTER—See SPARTA, IL (NewWave Communications)

▲ **CHESTERFIELD (village)**—Formerly served by CableDirect. No longer in operation

▲ **CHICAGO (area 4)**—Comcast Cable. Now served by CHICAGO, IL [IL0001]

▲ **CHICAGO (area 5)**—Comcast Cable. Now served by CHICAGO, IL [IL0001]

▲ **CHICAGO (areas 1, 4 & 5)**—Comcast Cable. Now served by CHICAGO, IL [IL0001]

▲ **CHICAGO (portions)**—RCN Corp. This cable system has converted to IPTV. See Chicago (portions), IL [IL5236]

▲ **CHICAGO (PORTIONS)**—RCN Corp. Formerly [IL0661]. This cable system has converted to IPTV

▲ **CHICAGO (SOUTHERN PORTION)**—WOW! Internet Cable & Phone

▲ **CHICAGO (SOUTHERN SUBURBS)**—Comcast Cable

CHICAGO HEIGHTS—See CHICAGO (southern suburbs), IL (Comcast Cable)

CHICAGO HEIGHTS—See NAPERVILLE, IL (WOW! Internet Cable & Phone)

CHICAGO RIDGE—See CHICAGO (southern suburbs), IL (Comcast Cable)

▲ **CHICAGO**—Formerly served by Preferred Entertainment of Chicago. No longer in operation

▲ **CHICAGO**—Comcast Cable

▲ **CHILLICOTHE**—Mediacom

CHRISMAN—See URBANA, IL (Comcast Cable)

CHRISTIAN COUNTY (PORTIONS)—See PANA, IL (Charter Communications)

CHRISTIAN COUNTY (PORTIONS)—See TAYLORVILLE, IL (NewWave Communications)

CHRISTOPHER—See DU QUOIN, IL (Comcast Cable)

CICERO—See OAK BROOK, IL (Comcast Cable)

▲ **CISCO (village)**—Formerly served by Longview Communications. No longer in operation

▲ **CISNE**—Wabash Independent Networks

▲ **CISSNA PARK (VILLAGE)**—Park TV & Electronics Inc.

▲ **CLAREMONT**—Formerly served by CableDirect. No longer in operation

CLARENDON HILLS—See OAK BROOK, IL (Comcast Cable)

CLARK COUNTY—See MARTINSVILLE, IL (Mediacom)

▲ **CLAY CITY**—Mediacom

CLAY COUNTY (PORTIONS)—See FLORA, IL (Wabash Independent Networks)

▲ **CLAYTON**—Adams Telecom. Formerly served by Camp Point, IL [IL0206]. This cable system has converted to IPTV

CLEAR LAKE (VILLAGE)—See KINCAID, IL (Mediacom)

CLEVELAND—See MOLINE, IL (Mediacom)

CLIFTON—See CHICAGO (southern suburbs), IL (Comcast Cable)

CLINTON COUNTY—See BREESE, IL (Charter Communications)

CLINTON COUNTY—See OKAWVILLE, IL (Charter Communications)

CLINTON COUNTY—See SCOTT AFB, IL (Charter Communications)

▲**CLINTON**—Mediacom

COAL CITY—See OAK BROOK, IL (Comcast Cable)

COAL VALLEY—See MOLINE, IL (Mediacom)

COALTON—See NOKOMIS, IL (Charter Communications)

▲**COATSBURG**—Adams Telecom. Formerly served by Golden, IL [IL0257]. This cable system has converted to IPTV

▲**COBDEN**—Mediacom. Now served by ZEIGLER, IL [IL0123]

COBDEN—See ZEIGLER, IL (Mediacom)

COELLO/NORTH CITY—See DU QUOIN, IL (Comcast Cable)

▲**COFFEEN**—Mediacom

COLCHESTER—See MACOMB, IL (Comcast Cable)

COLES COUNTY—See MATTOON, IL (Mediacom)

▲**COLFAX**—Mediacom. Now served by LE ROY, IL [IL0539]

COLFAX—See LE ROY, IL (Mediacom)

COLLINSVILLE—See MARYVILLE, IL (Charter Communications)

COLOMA TWP.—See STERLING, IL (Comcast Cable)

COLONA—See MOLINE, IL (Mediacom)

COLP (VILLAGE)—See MARION, IL (Mediacom)

COLUMBIA—See WATERLOO, IL (Charter Communications)

▲**COMPTON**—Formerly served by Compton Cable TV Co. No longer in operation

▲**COMPTON**—Heartland Cable Broadband

▲**CONGERVILLE**—Formerly served by Tel-Star Cablevision Inc. No longer in operation

COOK COUNTY—See SCHAUMBURG, IL (Comcast Cable)

CORDOVA—See MINERAL, IL (Mediacom)

▲**CORNELL**—Mediacom. Now served by PONTIAC, IL [IL0109]

CORNELL—See PONTIAC, IL (Mediacom)

▲**CORTLAND (VILLAGE)**—Mediacom

COTTAGE HILLS—See ROXANA, IL (Charter Communications)

▲**COULTERVILLE**—Mediacom. Now served by COULTERVILLE (formerly RED BUD), IL [IL0152]

▲**COULTERVILLE**—Mediacom

COUNTRY CLUB HILLS—See CHICAGO (southern suburbs), IL (Comcast Cable)

COUNTRYSIDE—See OAK BROOK, IL (Comcast Cable)

▲**COWDEN**—Clearvision Cable Systems Inc.

CRAINVILLE—See MARION, IL (Mediacom)

CRAWFORD COUNTY—See ROBINSON, IL (Mediacom)

CREAL SPRINGS—See LAKE OF EGYPT, IL (Zito Media)

CRESCENT CITY—See WATSEKA, IL (Mediacom)

CREST HILL—See OAK BROOK, IL (Comcast Cable)

CRESTON—See SCHAUMBURG, IL (Comcast Cable)

CRESTWOOD—See CHICAGO (southern suburbs), IL (Comcast Cable)

CRESTWOOD—See NAPERVILLE, IL (WOW! Internet Cable & Phone)

CRETE—See CHICAGO (southern suburbs), IL (Comcast Cable)

CREVE COEUR—See PEORIA, IL (Comcast Cable)

CROWN POINT—See CHICAGO (southern suburbs), IN (Comcast Cable)

CRYSTAL LAKE—See SCHAUMBURG, IL (Comcast Cable)

CUBA—See CANTON, IL (Comcast Cable)

▲**CULLOM**—Mediacom. Now served by PONTIAC, IL [IL0109]

CULLOM—See PONTIAC, IL (Mediacom)

CURRAN TWP.—See SPRINGFIELD, IL (Comcast Cable)

CURRAN—See SPRINGFIELD, IL (Comcast Cable)

▲**CUSTER PARK**—Comcast Cable. Now served by CHICAGO (southern suburbs), IL [IL0008]

CUSTER PARK—See CHICAGO (southern suburbs), IL (Comcast Cable)

▲**DAHLGREN**—Hamilton County Communications. This cable system has converted to IPTV. See Dahlgren, IL [IL5024]

▲**DAHLGREN**—Hamilton County Communications. Formerly [IL0381]. This cable system has converted to IPTV

▲**DALLAS CITY**—Mediacom. Now served by ROSEVILLE, IL [IL0274]

DALLAS CITY—See ROSEVILLE, IL (Mediacom)

DALTON CITY—See BETHANY, IL (Suddenlink Communications)

DALZELL—See LADD, IL (Comcast Cable)

DAMIANSVILLE—See SCOTT AFB, IL (Charter Communications)

DANFORTH—See ONARGA, IL (Comcast Cable)

▲**DANVERS**—Mediacom. Now served by APOLLO ACRES, IL [IL0340]

DANVERS—See APOLLO ACRES, IL (Mediacom)

▲**DANVILLE**—Insight Communications. Now served by URBANA, IL [IL0019]

DANVILLE—See URBANA, IL (Comcast Cable)

DARIEN—See OAK BROOK, IL (Comcast Cable)

DAVENPORT—See MOLINE, IA (Mediacom)

DAVIS JUNCTION—See KIRKLAND, IL (Mediacom)

DAWSON—See KINCAID, IL (Mediacom)

DAYTON TWP.—See STREATOR, IL (Mediacom)

DE LAND—See FARMER CITY, IL (Mediacom)

DE SOTO—See MURPHYSBORO, IL (Mediacom)

DE WITT COUNTY (PORTIONS)—See WARRENSBURG, IL (Crystal Broadcast Networks)

▲**DECATUR**—Insight Communications. Now served by SPRINGFIELD, IL [IL0016]

DECATUR—See SPRINGFIELD, IL (Comcast Cable)

▲**DEER CREEK**—Mediacom. Now served by APOLLO ACRES, IL [IL0340]

DEER CREEK—See APOLLO ACRES, IL (Mediacom)

DEER PARK—See SCHAUMBURG, IL (Comcast Cable)

DEERFIELD—See SCHAUMBURG, IL (Comcast Cable)

DEKALB COUNTY (PORTIONS)—See SUGAR GROVE, IL (Mediacom)

▲**DEKALB**—Comcast Cable. Now served by SCHAUMBURG, IL [IL0036]

DEKALB—See SCHAUMBURG, IL (Comcast Cable)

▲**DELAVAN**—Mediacom

DELAVAN—See DELAVAN, IL (Mediacom)

DEMOTTE—See CHICAGO (southern suburbs), IN (Comcast Cable)

DEPUE—See LADD, IL (Comcast Cable)

DES PLAINES—See SCHAUMBURG, IL (Comcast Cable)

DES PLAINES—See NAPERVILLE, IL (WOW! Internet Cable & Phone)

DIAMOND—See OAK BROOK, IL (Comcast Cable)

DIETERICH—See MONTROSE, IL (Clearvision Cable Systems Inc.)

DIVERNON—See SPRINGFIELD, IL (Comcast Cable)

▲**DIX**—Formerly served by Beck's Cable Systems. No longer in operation

DIXMOOR—See CHICAGO (southern suburbs), IL (Comcast Cable)

▲**DIXON**—Comcast Cable

▲**DOLTON**—Comcast Cable. Now served by CHICAGO (southern suburbs), IL [IL0008]

DOLTON—See CHICAGO (southern suburbs), IL (Comcast Cable)

▲**DONGOLA**—Formerly served by Longview Communications. No longer in operation

▲**DONOVAN TWP.**—Formerly served by CableDirect. No longer in operation

DOUGLAS COUNTY—See NEWMAN, IL (Comcast Cable)

DOWELL—See ZEIGLER, IL (Mediacom)

DOWNERS GROVE—See OAK BROOK, IL (Comcast Cable)

DOWNS—See LE ROY, IL (Mediacom)

▲**DU QUOIN**—Comcast Cable

DUMFERLINE—See ELMWOOD, IL (Mediacom)

DUNDAS—See OLNEY, IL (Comcast Cable)

▲**DUNLAP**—Mediacom. Now served by BRIMFIELD, IL [IL0201]

DUNLAP—See BRIMFIELD, IL (Mediacom)

DUPAGE COUNTY (PORTIONS)—See NAPERVILLE, IL (WOW! Internet Cable & Phone)

DUPAGE COUNTY (UNINCORPORATED AREAS)—See OAK BROOK, IL (Comcast Cable)

DUPO—See MARYVILLE, IL (Charter Communications)

▲**DURAND (village)**—Formerly served by Mediacom. No longer in operation

DURANT—See MOLINE, IA (Mediacom)

▲**DWIGHT**—Mediacom. Now served by PONTIAC, IL [IL0109]

DWIGHT—See PONTIAC, IL (Mediacom)

DYER—See CHICAGO (southern suburbs), IN (Comcast Cable)

EAGLE TWP.—See STREATOR, IL (Mediacom)

EARLVILLE—See SUGAR GROVE, IL (Mediacom)

EAST ALTON—See ROXANA, IL (Charter Communications)

EAST BROOKLYN (VILLAGE)—See GIBSON CITY, IL (Mediacom)

EAST CAPE GIRARDEAU—See ALEXANDER COUNTY (portions), IL (Zito Media)

EAST CHICAGO—See CHICAGO (southern suburbs), IN (Comcast Cable)

▲ **EAST DUBUQUE**—Mediacom. Now served by DUBUQUE, IA [IA0007]

EAST DUNDEE—See SCHAUMBURG, IL (Comcast Cable)

EAST GALESBURG—See GALESBURG, IL (Comcast Cable)

EAST HAZEL CREST—See CHICAGO (southern suburbs), IL (Comcast Cable)

EAST MOLINE—See MOLINE, IL (Mediacom)

EAST PEORIA—See PEORIA, IL (Comcast Cable)

▲ **EAST ST. LOUIS**—Charter Communications

EASTON—See VIRGINIA, IL (Cass Cable TV Inc.)

▲ **EDGEWOOD**—Clearvision Cable Systems Inc.

EDINBURG—See KINCAID, IL (Mediacom)

▲ **EDWARDS**—Tel-Star Cablevision Inc.

EDWARDSVILLE—See MARYVILLE, IL (Charter Communications)

EFFINGHAM COUNTY (UNINCORPORATED AREAS)—See EFFINGHAM, IL (Mediacom)

▲ **EFFINGHAM COUNTY**—Clearvision Cable Systems Inc.

▲ **EFFINGHAM**—Mediacom

EL PASO—See ROANOKE, IL (Mediacom)

ELBURN—See SUGAR GROVE, IL (Mediacom)

ELDORADO—See MARION, IL (Mediacom)

▲ **ELDRED**—Formerly served by Longview Communications. No longer in operation

ELDRIDGE—See MOLINE, IA (Mediacom)

▲ **ELGIN**—Comcast Cable. Now served by OAK BROOK, IL [IL0006]

ELGIN—See OAK BROOK, IL (Comcast Cable)

ELGIN—See NAPERVILLE, IL (WOW! Internet Cable & Phone)

▲ **ELIZABETH**—Formerly served by Mediacom. No longer in operation

ELIZABETHTOWN—See ROSICLARE, IL (Zito Media)

ELK GROVE (VILLAGE)—See SCHAUMBURG, IL (Comcast Cable)

▲ **ELKHART TWP.**—Formerly served by Mediacom. No longer in operation

ELKHART—See DELAVAN, IL (Mediacom)

ELKVILLE—See ZEIGLER, IL (Mediacom)

ELLIOTT—See SIBLEY (village), IL (Heartland Cable Inc.)

ELLSWORTH—See SIBLEY (village), IL (Heartland Cable Inc.)

ELMHURST—See OAK BROOK, IL (Comcast Cable)

ELMWOOD PARK—See OAK BROOK, IL (Comcast Cable)

▲ **ELMWOOD**—Mediacom

ELWOOD—See SENECA, IL (Kraus Electronics Systems Inc.)

EMDEN—See DELAVAN, IL (Mediacom)

ENERGY—See MARION, IL (Mediacom)

▲ **ENFIELD**—NewWave Communications

ESSEX (VILLAGE)—See GIBSON CITY, IL (Mediacom)

EUGENE—See URBANA, IL (Comcast Cable)

EUREKA—See ROANOKE, IL (Mediacom)

EVANSTON—See SCHAUMBURG, IL (Comcast Cable)

▲ **EVANSVILLE**—NewWave Communications

EVERGREEN PARK—See CHICAGO (southern suburbs), IL (Comcast Cable)

EWING—See DU QUOIN, IL (Comcast Cable)

▲ **FAIRBURY**—Mediacom. Now served by FAIRBURY, IL [IL0346]

▲ **FAIRBURY**—Mediacom

▲ **FAIRFIELD**—NewWave Communications

FAIRMONT CITY—See WASHINGTON PARK, IL (Mediacom)

FAIRMOUNT—See URBANA, IL (Comcast Cable)

FAIRVIEW HEIGHTS—See BELLEVILLE, IL (Charter Communications)

▲ **FAIRVIEW**—Mediacom. Now served by ELMWOOD, IL [IL0205]

FAIRVIEW—See ELMWOOD, IL (Mediacom)

FAR HILLS—See ROANOKE, IL (Mediacom)

FARINA—See LOUISVILLE, IL (Mediacom)

▲ **FARMER CITY**—Mediacom

▲ **FARMERSVILLE**—Charter Communications

FARMINGTON—See ELMWOOD, IL (Mediacom)

▲ **FAYETTEVILLE**—Formerly served by CableDirect. No longer in operation

FIATT—See WEE-MA-TUK HILLS, IL (Nova Cablevision Inc.)

▲ **FIELDON**—Formerly served by CableDirect. No longer in operation

▲ **FILLMORE**—Formerly served by CableDirect. No longer in operation

▲ **FINDLAY**—Formerly served by Almega Cable. No longer in operation

FISHER—See MAHOMET, IL (Mediacom)

FITHIAN—See URBANA, IL (Comcast Cable)

▲ **FLANAGAN**—Heartland Cable Inc.

FLAT ROCK—See BIRDS, IL (Park TV & Electronics Inc.)

▲ **FLORA**—Wabash Independent Networks

FLOSSMOOR—See CHICAGO (southern suburbs), IL (Comcast Cable)

FONTANA—See HARVARD, WI (Charter Communications)

FORD HEIGHTS—See CHICAGO (southern suburbs), IL (Comcast Cable)

FOREST CITY—See VIRGINIA, IL (Cass Cable TV Inc.)

FOREST PARK—See OAK BROOK, IL (Comcast Cable)

FOREST VIEW—See OAK BROOK, IL (Comcast Cable)

FORREST—See FAIRBURY, IL (Mediacom)

FORRESTON—See FRANKLIN GROVE, IL (Comcast Cable)

FORSYTH—See SPRINGFIELD, IL (Comcast Cable)

FORT SHERIDAN—See SCHAUMBURG, IL (Comcast Cable)

▲ **FOWLER**—Adams Telecom. Formerly served by Golden, IL [IL0257]. This cable system has converted to IPTV

FOX CREEK—See EDWARDS, IL (Tel-Star Cablevision Inc.)

FOX RIVER GROVE—See SCHAUMBURG, IL (Comcast Cable)

FRANKFORT—See OAK BROOK, IL (Comcast Cable)

FRANKLIN COUNTY—See ZEIGLER, IL (Mediacom)

FRANKLIN COUNTY—See FREEMAN SPUR, IL (Zito Media)

▲ **FRANKLIN GROVE**—Comcast Cable

FRANKLIN PARK—See OAK BROOK, IL (Comcast Cable)

FRANKLIN—See WAVERLY, IL (Crystal Broadband Networks)

FREEBURG—See SCOTT AFB, IL (Charter Communications)

▲ **FREEMAN SPUR**—Zito Media

▲ **FREEPORT**—Comcast Cable

FRYE LAKE—See MINERAL, IL (Mediacom)

FULTON COUNTY—See CANTON, IL (Comcast Cable)

GALATIA—See SALINE COUNTY (portions), IL (Zito Media)

▲ **GALENA**—Mediacom. Now served by DUBUQUE, IA [IA0007]

▲ **GALESBURG**—Comcast Cable

GALVA—See MINERAL, IL (Mediacom)

GANEER TWP.—See CHICAGO (southern suburbs), IL (Comcast Cable)

▲ **GARDEN PRAIRIE**—Mediacom. Now served by POPLAR GROVE, IL [IL0282]

GARDEN PRAIRIE—See POPLAR GROVE, IL (Mediacom)

GARDNER TWP.—See SPRINGFIELD, IL (Comcast Cable)

▲ **GARDNER**—Kraus Electronics Systems Inc.

GARRETT—See TUSCOLA, IL (Mediacom)

GARY—See CHICAGO (southern suburbs), IN (Comcast Cable)

▲ **GAYS (village)**—Formerly served by CableDirect. No longer in operation

▲ **GEFF**—Wabash Independent Networks

▲ **GEM SUBURBAN MOBILE HOME PARK**—Packerland Broadband

GENESEO—See MINERAL, IL (Mediacom)

GENEVA—See OAK BROOK, IL (Comcast Cable)

▲ **GENOA**—Charter Communications. Now served by HARVARD, IL [IL0073]

GENOA—See HARVARD, IL (Charter Communications)

GEORGETOWN—See WESTVILLE, IL (Avenue Broadband Communications)

▲ **GERMAN VALLEY**—Mediacom

GERMANTOWN HILLS—See ROANOKE, IL (Mediacom)

GERMANTOWN—See BREESE, IL (Charter Communications)

▲ **GIBSON CITY**—Mediacom

GIFFORD (VILLAGE)—See RANTOUL, IL (Mediacom)

▲ **GILBERTS**—Mediacom. Now served by CORTLAND (village), IL [IL0485]

GILBERTS—See CORTLAND (village), IL (Mediacom)

▲ **GILLESPIE**—Charter Communications

GILMAN—See ONARGA, IL (Comcast Cable)

▲ **GINGER RIDGE**—Formerly served by Universal Cable Inc. No longer in operation

GIRARD—See VIRDEN, IL (Charter Communications)

▲ **GLADSTONE**—Nova Cablevision Inc.

▲ **GLASFORD**—Mediacom. Now served by ELMWOOD, IL [IL0205]

GLASFORD—See ELMWOOD, IL (Mediacom)

GLEN CARBON—See MARYVILLE, IL (Charter Communications)

GLEN ELLYN—See OAK BROOK, IL (Comcast Cable)

GLEN ELLYN—See NAPERVILLE, IL (WOW! Internet Cable & Phone)

GLENARM—See SPRINGFIELD, IL (Comcast Cable)

GLENCOE—See SCHAUMBURG, IL (Comcast Cable)

▲ **GLENDALE HEIGHTS**—Comcast Cable. Now served by OAK BROOK, IL [IL0006]

GLENDALE HEIGHTS—See OAK BROOK, IL (Comcast Cable)

GLENDALE HEIGHTS—See NAPERVILLE, IL (WOW! Internet Cable & Phone)

GLENVIEW NAVAL AIR STATION—See SCHAUMBURG, IL (Comcast Cable)

▲ **GLENVIEW**—Comcast Cable. Now served by SCHAUMBURG, IL [IL0036]

GLENVIEW—See SCHAUMBURG, IL (Comcast Cable)

GLENVIEW—See NAPERVILLE, IL (WOW! Internet Cable & Phone)

GLENWOOD—See CHICAGO (southern suburbs), IL (Comcast Cable)

GODFREY—See ROXANA, IL (Charter Communications)

GODLEY (VILLAGE)—See GIBSON CITY, IL (Mediacom)

▲ **GOLCONDA**—Zito Media

▲ **GOLD COAST**—RCN Corp. Formerly served by Chicago (portions), IL [IL0661]. This cable system has converted to IPTV

▲ **GOLDEN**—Adams Telephone. This cable system has converted to IPTV. See Golden, IL [IL5317]

▲ **GOLDEN**—Adams Telecom. Formerly [IL0257]. This cable system has converted to IPTV

GOLF—See SCHAUMBURG, IL (Comcast Cable)

▲ **GOOD HOPE**—Mediacom

GOODFIELD—See APOLLO ACRES, IL (Mediacom)

GOOFY RIDGE—See VIRGINIA, IL (Cass Cable TV Inc.)

GOREVILLE—See LAKE OF EGYPT, IL (Zito Media)

▲ **GORHAM TWP.**—Formerly served by CableDirect. No longer in operation

▲ **GRAFTON**—Formerly served by Almega Cable. No longer in operation

▲ **GRAND RIDGE**—Grand Ridge Cable Co. Inc.

▲ **GRAND TOWER (village)**—Formerly served by CableDirect. No longer in operation

GRANDVIEW—See SPRINGFIELD, IL (Comcast Cable)

GRANITE CITY—See MARYVILLE, IL (Charter Communications)

▲ **GRANT PARK (village)**—Mediacom. Now served by ROSELAWN, IN [IN0316]

▲ **GRANTFORK (VILLAGE)**—Clearvision Cable Systems Inc.

GRANVILLE—See BRIMFIELD, IL (Mediacom)

▲ **GRAYVILLE**—NewWave Communications

▲ **GREAT LAKES NAVAL TRAINING CENTER**—Comcast Cable. Now served by SCHAUMBURG, IL [IL0036]

GREAT LAKES NAVAL TRAINING CENTER—See SCHAUMBURG, IL (Comcast Cable)

GREEN ROCK—See MOLINE, IL (Mediacom)

GREEN VALLEY—See DELAVAN, IL (Mediacom)

▲ **GREENFIELD**—BrightGreen Cable

▲ **GREENUP**—Mediacom

▲ **GREENVIEW**—Formerly served by Mediacom. No longer in operation

▲ **GREENVILLE**—NewWave Communications

▲ **GRIDLEY**—Gridley Cable

GRIFFITH—See CHICAGO (southern suburbs), IN (Comcast Cable)

▲ **GRIGGSVILLE**—Crystal Broadband Networks

GROVELAND—See PEKIN, IL (Comcast Cable)

GRUNDY COUNTY—See OAK BROOK, IL (Comcast Cable)

HAINESVILLE—See SCHAUMBURG, IL (Comcast Cable)

▲ **HAMEL**—Madison Communications. Now served by STAUNTON, IL [IL0171]

HAMEL—See STAUNTON, IL (Madison Communications)

HAMMOND—See CHICAGO (southern suburbs), IN (Comcast Cable)

HAMMOND—See TUSCOLA, IL (Mediacom)

▲ **HAMPSHIRE**—Mediacom. Now served by CORTLAND (village), IL [IL0485]

HAMPSHIRE—See CORTLAND (village), IL (Mediacom)

HAMPTON—See MOLINE, IL (Mediacom)

HANNA CITY—See ELMWOOD, IL (Mediacom)

HANNA CITY—See EDWARDS, IL (Tel-Star Cablevision Inc.)

HANOVER PARK—See SCHAUMBURG, IL (Comcast Cable)

▲ **HANOVER**—Mediacom. Now served by LENA, IL [IL0223]

HANOVER—See LENA, IL (Mediacom)

HARDIN COUNTY—See ROSICLARE, IL (Zito Media)

▲ **HARDIN**—BrightGreen Cable

▲ **HARRISBURG**—Mediacom. Now served by MARION, IL [IL0083]

HARRISBURG—See MARION, IL (Mediacom)

HARRISTOWN—See SPRINGFIELD, IL (Comcast Cable)

HARTFORD—See ROXANA, IL (Charter Communications)

▲ **HARTSBURG**—Mediacom. Now served by DELAVAN, IL [IL0172]

HARTSBURG—See DELAVAN, IL (Mediacom)

▲ **HARVARD**—Charter Communications

▲ **HARVEL**—Mediacom. Now served by KINCAID, IL [IL0176]

HARVEL—See KINCAID, IL (Mediacom)

▲ **HARVEY**—Comcast Cable. Now served by CHICAGO (southern suburbs), IL [IL0008]

HARVEY—See CHICAGO (southern suburbs), IL (Comcast Cable)

HARVEY—See NAPERVILLE, IL (WOW! Internet Cable & Phone)

HARWOOD HEIGHTS—See OAK BROOK, IL (Comcast Cable)

HASCA—See OAK BROOK, IL (Comcast Cable)

HAVANA—See VIRGINIA, IL (Cass Cable TV Inc.)

HAWTHORNE WOODS—See SCHAUMBURG, IL (Comcast Cable)

HAZEL CREST—See CHICAGO (southern suburbs), IL (Comcast Cable)

HEARTVILLE—See EFFINGHAM COUNTY, IL (Clearvision Cable Systems Inc.)

▲ **HEBRON (VILLAGE)**—Mediacom

HEBRON—See CHICAGO (southern suburbs), IN (Comcast Cable)

HECKER—See COULTERVILLE, IL (Mediacom)

HEGELER—See WESTVILLE, IL (Avenue Broadband Communications)

HENNEPIN—See BRIMFIELD, IL (Mediacom)

▲ **HENNING**—Formerly served by CableDirect. No longer in operation

HENRY COUNTY (NORTHWESTERN PORTION)—See MOLINE, IL (Mediacom)

HENRY COUNTY (UNINCORPORATED AREAS)—See MINERAL, IL (Mediacom)

HENRY COUNTY—See KEWANEE, IL (Comcast Cable)

HENRY—See CHILLICOTHE, IL (Mediacom)

▲ **HERITAGE LAKE**—Tel-Star Cablevision Inc. Now served by EDWARDS, IL [IL0326]

HERITAGE LAKE—See EDWARDS, IL (Tel-Star Cablevision Inc.)

▲ **HERRICK**—Mediacom

▲ **HERRIN**—Mediacom. Now served by MARION, IL [IL0083]

HERRIN—See MARION, IL (Mediacom)

▲ **HERSCHER**—Formerly served by Comcast Cable. No longer in operation

HERSMAN—See VIRGINIA, IL (Cass Cable TV Inc.)

▲ **HETTICK (village)**—Formerly served by CableDirect. No longer in operation

HEWITTVILLE—See TAYLORVILLE, IL (NewWave Communications)

▲ **HEYWORTH**—Mediacom

HICKORY HILLS—See CHICAGO (southern suburbs), IL (Comcast Cable)

▲ **HIGHLAND PARK**—Comcast Cable. Now served by SCHAUMBURG, IL [IL0036]

HIGHLAND PARK—See SCHAUMBURG, IL (Comcast Cable)

HIGHLAND—See MARYVILLE, IL (Charter Communications)

HIGHWOOD—See SCHAUMBURG, IL (Comcast Cable)

HILLCREST—See SCHAUMBURG, IL (Comcast Cable)

▲ **HILLSBORO**—NewWave Communications

HILLSDALE—See MINERAL, IL (Mediacom)

HILLSIDE—See OAK BROOK, IL (Comcast Cable)

HINCKLEY—See SUGAR GROVE, IL (Mediacom)

HINDSBORO—See TUSCOLA, IL (Mediacom)

HINSDALE—See OAK BROOK, IL (Comcast Cable)

HOBART—See CHICAGO (southern suburbs), IN (Comcast Cable)

HODGKINS—See OAK BROOK, IL (Comcast Cable)

HOFFMAN ESTATES—See SCHAUMBURG, IL (Comcast Cable)

▲ **HOFFMAN**—Formerly served by CableDirect. No longer in operation

HOLIDAY HILLS—See SCHAUMBURG, IL (Comcast Cable)

HOLIDAY SHORES—See STAUNTON, IL (Madison Communications)

HOLLIS TWP.—See PEORIA, IL (Comcast Cable)

HOLLYWOOD HEIGHTS—See MARYVILLE, IL (Charter Communications)

HOME GARDENS—See WESTVILLE, IL (Avenue Broadband Communications)

HOMER GLEN—See OAK BROOK, IL (Comcast Cable)

HOMER—See URBANA, IL (Comcast Cable)

HOMETOWN—See CHICAGO (southern suburbs), IL (Comcast Cable)

▲ **HOMEWOOD**—Comcast Cable. Now served by CHICAGO (southern suburbs), IL [IL0008]

HOMEWOOD—See CHICAGO (southern suburbs), IL (Comcast Cable)

HONEY SCHOOL LOOKOUT—See ALEXANDER COUNTY (portions), IL (Zito Media)

▲ **HOOPESTON**—Avenue Broadband Communications. Now served by WESTVILLE, IL [IL0079]

HOOPESTON—See WESTVILLE, IL (Avenue Broadband Communications)

▲ **HOOPPOLE**—Formerly served by CableDirect. No longer in operation

HOPEDALE—See APOLLO ACRES, IL (Mediacom)

HOPEWELL—See CHILLICOTHE, IL (Mediacom)

HOPKINS TWP.—See STERLING, IL (Comcast Cable)

▲ **HOYLETON**—Formerly served by CableDirect. No longer in operation

▲ **HUDSON**—Mediacom. Now served by APOLLO ACRES, IL [IL0340]

HUDSON—See APOLLO ACRES, IL (Mediacom)

HUMBOLDT—See TUSCOLA, IL (Mediacom)

▲ **HUME (VILLAGE)**—Clearvision Cable Systems Inc.

HUNTLEY—See SCHAUMBURG, IL (Comcast Cable)

HURST—See ZEIGLER, IL (Mediacom)

HUTSONVILLE—See ROBINSON, IL (Mediacom)

▲ **HYDE PARK**—RCN Corp. Formerly served by Chicago (portions), IL [IL0661]. This cable system has converted to IPTV

ILLIOPOLIS—See SPRINGFIELD, IL (Comcast Cable)

▲ **INA**—Formerly served by Longview Communications. No longer in operation

INDIAN CREEK—See SCHAUMBURG, IL (Comcast Cable)

INDIAN HEAD PARK—See CHICAGO (southern suburbs), IL (Comcast Cable)

INDIANOLA—See URBANA, IL (Comcast Cable)

▲ **INDUSTRY**—Mediacom

INVERNESS (VILLAGE)—See SCHAUMBURG, IL (Comcast Cable)

▲ **IPAVA**—Mediacom

▲ **IROQUOIS (village)**—Formerly served by CableDirect. No longer in operation

▲ **IRVING**—Mediacom. Now served by IRVING, IL [IL0687]

▲ **IRVING**—Mediacom

ISLAND LAKE—See SCHAUMBURG, IL (Comcast Cable)

▲ **IUKA**—Formerly served by Advanced Technologies & Technical Resources Inc. No longer in operation

IVESDALE—See TUSCOLA, IL (Mediacom)

JACKSON COUNTY (PORTIONS)—See MURPHYSBORO, IL (Mediacom)

JACKSON COUNTY (PORTIONS)—See ZEIGLER, IL (Mediacom)

▲ **JACKSON COUNTY**—Zito Media

▲ **JACKSONVILLE**—Mediacom

JASPER COUNTY (SOUTHERN PORTION)—See OLNEY, IL (Comcast Cable)

JEFFERSON COUNTY—See WOODLAWN, IL (Charter Communications)

JEISYVILLE—See KINCAID, IL (Mediacom)

JEROME—See SPRINGFIELD, IL (Comcast Cable)

JERSEY COUNTY (PORTIONS)—See JERSEYVILLE, IL (Greene County Partners Inc.)

▲ **JERSEYVILLE**—Greene County Partners Inc.

JOHNSON COUNTY (NORTHERN PORTION)—See LAKE OF EGYPT, IL (Zito Media)

JOHNSON COUNTY (PORTIONS)—See BUNCOMBE, IL (Zito Media)

JOHNSTON CITY—See MARION, IL (Mediacom)

JOLIET—See OAK BROOK, IL (Comcast Cable)

JONESBORO—See ANNA, IL (NewWave Communications)

JUNCTION CITY—See SALEM, IL (Charter Communications)

JUSTICE—See OAK BROOK, IL (Comcast Cable)

▲ **KAMPSVILLE (village)**—Cass Cable TV Inc. No longer in operation

KANE COUNTY (PORTIONS)—See SCHAUMBURG, IL (Comcast Cable)

KANE COUNTY—See OAK BROOK, IL (Comcast Cable)

KANE COUNTY—See SUGAR GROVE, IL (Mediacom)

KANEVILLE—See SUGAR GROVE, IL (Mediacom)

KANGLEY—See STREATOR, IL (Mediacom)

KANKAKEE COUNTY (UNINCORPORATED AREAS)—See CHICAGO (southern suburbs), IL (Comcast Cable)

▲ **KANKAKEE**—Formerly served by Comcast Cable. No longer in operation

KANSAS—See CHARLESTON, IL (Mediacom)

▲ **KARNAK**—Formerly served by Longview Communications. No longer in operation

KEENEYVILLE—See OAK BROOK, IL (Comcast Cable)

▲ **KEITHSBURG**—Nova Cablevision Inc.

KENDALL COUNTY—See OAK BROOK, IL (Comcast Cable)

KENILWORTH (VILLAGE)—See SCHAUMBURG, IL (Comcast Cable)

▲ **KENNEY**—Heartland Cable Inc.

▲ **KEWANEE**—Comcast Cable

▲ **KEYESPORT**—Formerly served by CableDirect. No longer in operation

KICKAPOO TWP.—See PEORIA, IL (Comcast Cable)

KICKAPOO—See EDWARDS, IL (Tel-Star Cablevision Inc.)

KILBOURNE—See VIRGINIA, IL (Cass Cable TV Inc.)

KILDEER—See SCHAUMBURG, IL (Comcast Cable)

▲ **KINCAID**—Mediacom

▲ **KINDERHOOK**—Formerly served by Almega Cable. No longer in operation

▲ **KINGSTON MINES**—KMHC Inc.

▲ **KINGSTON**—Formerly served by Kingston Cable TV Co. No longer in operation

▲ **KINMUNDY**—Clearvision Cable Systems Inc.

▲ **KIRKLAND**—Mediacom

▲ **KIRKWOOD**—Nova Cablevision Inc.

KNOXVILLE—See GALESBURG, IL (Comcast Cable)

LA GRANGE PARK—See CHICAGO (southern suburbs), IL (Comcast Cable)

LA GRANGE—See CHICAGO (southern suburbs), IL (Comcast Cable)

▲ **LA HARPE**—Insight Communications. Now served by MACOMB, IL [IL0076]

LA HARPE—See MACOMB, IL (Comcast Cable)

▲ **LA MOILLE (village)**—Formerly served by CableDirect. No longer in operation

▲ **LA PLACE**—Formerly served by Longview Communications. No longer in operation

▲ **LA ROSE**—Formerly served by Tel-Star Cablevision Inc. No longer in operation

LA SALLE TWP.—See STREATOR, IL (Mediacom)

LA SALLE—See PERU, IL (Comcast Cable)

▲ **LACON**—Mediacom. Now served by LACON, IL [IL0394]

▲ **LACON**—Mediacom

▲ **LADD**—Comcast Cable

LAKE BARRINGTON—See SCHAUMBURG, IL (Comcast Cable)

LAKE BLUFF—See SCHAUMBURG, IL (Comcast Cable)

▲ **LAKE BRACKEN**—Nova Cablevision Inc.

▲ **LAKE CAMELOT**—Tel-Star Cablevision Inc. Now served by EDWARDS, IL [IL0326]

LAKE CAMELOT—See EDWARDS, IL (Tel-Star Cablevision Inc.)

LAKE COUNTY (UNINCORPORATED AREAS)—See CHICAGO (southern suburbs), IN (Comcast Cable)

LAKE COUNTY—See SCHAUMBURG, IL (Comcast Cable)

LAKE FOREST—See SCHAUMBURG, IL (Comcast Cable)

▲ **LAKE HOLIDAY**—Formerly served by Comcast Cable. No longer in operation

LAKE IN THE HILLS—See SCHAUMBURG, IL (Comcast Cable)

▲ **LAKE OF EGYPT**—Zito Media

LAKE OF THE FOUR SEASONS—See CHICAGO (southern suburbs), IN (Comcast Cable)

LAKE OF THE WOODS—See MAHOMET, IL (Mediacom)

LAKE PETERSBURG—See WILLIAMSVILLE, IL (Greene County Partners Inc.)

LAKE SARA—See EFFINGHAM, IL (Mediacom)

LAKE STATION—See CHICAGO (southern suburbs), IN (Comcast Cable)

LAKE WINDERMERE—See EDWARDS, IL (Tel-Star Cablevision Inc.)

▲ **LAKE ZURICH**—Comcast Cable. Now served by SCHAUMBURG, IL [IL0036]

LAKE ZURICH—See SCHAUMBURG, IL (Comcast Cable)

LAKEMOOR—See SCHAUMBURG, IL (Comcast Cable)

▲ **LAKEVIEW**—RCN Corp. Formerly served by Chicago (portions), IL [IL0061]. This cable system has converted to IPTV

LAKEWOOD VILLAGE—See SCHAUMBURG, IL (Comcast Cable)

LAMPLIGHTER—See FAIRBURY, IL (Mediacom)

LANARK—See LENA, IL (Mediacom)

▲ **LANSING**—Comcast Cable. Now served by CHICAGO (southern suburbs), IL [IL0008]

LANSING—See CHICAGO (southern suburbs), IL (Comcast Cable)

LAOMI—See KINCAID, IL (Mediacom)

LATHAM—See WARRENSBURG, IL (Crystal Broadcast Networks)

▲ **LAWRENCEVILLE**—Charter Communications. Now served by VINCENNES, IN [IN0035]

▲ **LE ROY**—Mediacom

▲ **LEAF RIVER**—Grand River Cablevision

LEBANON—See SCOTT AFB, IL (Charter Communications)

LEE COUNTY (SOUTHERN PORTION)—See AMBOY, IL (Comcast Cable)

LEE COUNTY (WESTERN PORTION)—See DIXON, IL (Comcast Cable)

LELAND GROVE—See SPRINGFIELD, IL (Comcast Cable)

LELAND—See SUGAR GROVE, IL (Mediacom)

LEMONT—See OAK BROOK, IL (Comcast Cable)

▲ **LENA**—Mediacom

LENZBURG—See SPARTA, IL (NewWave Communications)

▲ **LEONORE**—HI Cablevision

▲ **LERNA**—Formerly served by CableDirect. No longer in operation

▲ **LEWISTOWN**—Insight Communications. Now served by CANTON, IL [IL0087]

LEWISTOWN—See CANTON, IL (Comcast Cable)

▲ **LEXINGTON**—Mediacom. Now served by FAIRBURY, IL [IL0346]

LEXINGTON—See FAIRBURY, IL (Mediacom)

LEYDEN TWP.—See OAK BROOK, IL (Comcast Cable)

▲ **LIBERTY**—Adams Telephone. This cable system has converted to IPTV. See Liberty, IL [IL5318]

▲ **LIBERTY**—Adams Telecom. Formerly [IL0379]. This cable system has converted to IPTV

▲ **LIBERTYVILLE**—Comcast Cable. Now served by SCHAUMBURG, IL [IL0036]

LIBERTYVILLE—See SCHAUMBURG, IL (Comcast Cable)

LILY LAKE—See OAK BROOK, IL (Comcast Cable)

▲ **LIMA**—Adams Telecom. Formerly served by Golden, IL [IL0257]. This cable system has converted to IPTV

LIMESTONE TWP. (PEORIA COUNTY)—See PEORIA, IL (Comcast Cable)

LIMESTONE TWP.—See CHICAGO (southern suburbs), IL (Comcast Cable)

▲ **LINCOLN PARK**—RCN Corp. Formerly served by Chicago (portions), IL [IL0661]. This cable system has converted to IPTV

▲ **LINCOLN**—Insight Communications. Now served by SPRINGFIELD, IL [IL0016]

LINCOLN—See SPRINGFIELD, IL (Comcast Cable)

LINCOLNSHIRE—See SCHAUMBURG, IL (Comcast Cable)

LINCOLNWOOD—See SCHAUMBURG, IL (Comcast Cable)

LINN (TOWN)—See HARVARD, WI (Charter Communications)

▲ **LISLE**—Comcast Cable. Now served by OAK BROOK, IL [IL0006]

LISLE—See OAK BROOK, IL (Comcast Cable)

▲ **LITCHFIELD**—NewWave Communications

▲ **LITTLE YORK**—Nova Cablevision Inc.

LIVINGSTON—See STAUNTON, IL (Madison Communications)

▲ **LOAMI**—Mediacom. Now served by KINCAID, IL [IL0176]

LOCKPORT—See OAK BROOK, IL (Comcast Cable)

LODA—See FARMER CITY, IL (Mediacom)

LODI—See URBANA, IL (Comcast Cable)

LOGAN COUNTY (PORTIONS)—See SPRINGFIELD, IL (Comcast Cable)

LOMAX—See ROSEVILLE, IL (Mediacom)

LOMBARD—See OAK BROOK, IL (Comcast Cable)

▲ **LONDON MILLS**—Mediacom. Now served by ELMWOOD, IL [IL0205]

LONDON MILLS—See ELMWOOD, IL (Mediacom)

LONG CREEK—See SPRINGFIELD, IL (Comcast Cable)

LONG GROVE—See SCHAUMBURG, IL (Comcast Cable)

LONG GROVE—See MOLINE, IA (Mediacom)

▲ **LONG POINT (village)**—Formerly served by Longview Communications. No longer in operation

▲ **LORAINE**—Adams Telecom. Formerly served by Golden, IL [IL0257]. This cable system has converted to IPTV

▲ **LOSTANT**—HI Cablevision

▲ **LOUISVILLE**—Mediacom

▲ **LOUISVILLE**—Wabash Independent Networks

LOVES PARK—See ROCKFORD, IL (Comcast Cable)

▲ **LOVINGTON**—Moultrie Telecommunications

LOWELL—See CHICAGO (southern suburbs), IN (Comcast Cable)

▲ **LOWPOINT**—Formerly served by Tel-Star Cablevision Inc. No longer in operation

LUDLOW (VILLAGE)—See RANTOUL, IL (Mediacom)

LYONS—See OAK BROOK, IL (Comcast Cable)

MACHESNEY PARK—See ROCKFORD, IL (Comcast Cable)

MACKINAW TRAILER PARK—See APOLLO ACRES, IL (Mediacom)

MACKINAW—See APOLLO ACRES, IL (Mediacom)

▲ **MACOMB**—Comcast Cable

MACON COUNTY (PORTIONS)—See WARRENSBURG, IL (Crystal Broadcast Networks)

MACON COUNTY—See SPRINGFIELD, IL (Comcast Cable)

MACON—See MOWEAQUA, IL (Suddenlink Communications)

MACOUPIN COUNTY (PORTIONS)—See GILLESPIE, IL (Charter Communications)

MADISON COUNTY—See MARYVILLE, IL (Charter Communications)

MADISON COUNTY—See ROXANA, IL (Charter Communications)

MADISON COUNTY—See WASHINGTON PARK, IL (Mediacom)

MADISON—See MARYVILLE, IL (Charter Communications)

▲ **MAHOMET**—Mediacom

▲ **MALDEN**—HI Cablevision

▲ **MALTA**—Mediacom. Now served by KIRKLAND, IL [IL0277]

MALTA—See KIRKLAND, IL (Mediacom)

▲ **MANCHESTER (village)**—Formerly served by Longview Communications. No longer in operation

▲ **MANHATTAN**—Kraus Electronics Systems Inc.

▲ **MANITO**—Cass Cable TV Inc. Now served by VIRGINIA, IL [IL0598]

MANITO—See VIRGINIA, IL (Cass Cable TV Inc.)

▲ **MANLIUS (village)**—Mediacom. Now served by MINERAL, IL [IL0170]

MANLIUS (VILLAGE)—See MINERAL, IL (Mediacom)

▲ **MANSFIELD**—Mediacom. Now served by FARMER CITY, IL [IL0231]

MANSFIELD—See FARMER CITY, IL (Mediacom)

MANTENO—See CHICAGO (southern suburbs), IL (Comcast Cable)

MAPLE PARK (VILLAGE)—See CORTLAND (village), IL (Mediacom)

MAPLETON—See EDWARDS, IL (Tel-Star Cablevision Inc.)

▲ **MAQUON**—Mediacom. Now served by ABINGDON, IL [IL0186]

MAQUON—See ABINGDON, IL (Mediacom)

▲ **MARCELLINE**—Adams Telecom. Formerly served by Golden, IL [IL0257]. This cable system has converted to IPTV

MARENGO—See HARVARD, IL (Charter Communications)

MARINE—See MARYVILLE, IL (Charter Communications)

MARION COUNTY (PORTIONS)—See SALEM, IL (Charter Communications)

MARION COUNTY—See OKAWVILLE, IL (Charter Communications)

▲ **MARION**—Mediacom

MARISSA—See SPARTA, IL (NewWave Communications)

MARK—See BRIMFIELD, IL (Mediacom)

MARKHAM—See CHICAGO (southern suburbs), IL (Comcast Cable)

▲ **MAROA**—Crystal Broadband Networks

MARQUETTE HEIGHTS—See PEKIN, IL (Comcast Cable)

MARSEILLES—See STREATOR, IL (Mediacom)

MARSHALL—See MARTINSVILLE, IL (Mediacom)

▲ **MARTINSVILLE**—Mediacom

▲ **MARTINTON (village)**—Formerly served by CableDirect. No longer in operation

MARTINTOWN—See LENA, WI (Mediacom)

▲ **MARYVILLE**—Charter Communications

MASCOUTAH—See SCOTT AFB, IL (Charter Communications)

▲ **MASON CITY**—Greene County Cable. Now served by VIRGINIA, IL [IL0598]

MASON CITY—See VIRGINIA, IL (Cass Cable TV Inc.)

MASON—See EDGEWOOD, IL (Clearvision Cable Systems Inc.)

MATHERVILLE—See MINERAL, IL (Mediacom)

▲ **MATTESON**—Comcast Cable. Now served by CHICAGO (southern suburbs), IL [IL0008]

MATTESON—See CHICAGO (southern suburbs), IL (Comcast Cable)

▲ **MATTOON**—Mediacom

▲ **MAYWOOD**—Comcast Cable. Now served by OAK BROOK, IL [IL0006]

MAYWOOD—See OAK BROOK, IL (Comcast Cable)

▲ **MAZON (village)**—Formerly served by CableDirect. No longer in operation

MAZON (VILLAGE)—See OAK BROOK, IL (Comcast Cable)

MCCLURE—See ALEXANDER COUNTY (portions), IL (Zito Media)

MCCOLLUM LAKE—See SCHAUMBURG, IL (Comcast Cable)

MCCOOK—See OAK BROOK, IL (Comcast Cable)

MCDONOUGH COUNTY—See MACOMB, IL (Comcast Cable)

▲ **McHENRY**—Comcast Cable. Now served by SCHAUMBURG, IL [IL0036]

MCHENRY—See SCHAUMBURG, IL (Comcast Cable)

MCLEAN COUNTY (PORTIONS)—See LE ROY, IL (Mediacom)

MCLEAN COUNTY—See BLOOMINGTON, IL (Comcast Cable)

MCLEAN—See ATLANTA, IL (Mediacom)

▲ **MCLEANSBORO**—NewWave Communications

▲ **MCNABB**—McNabb Cable & Satellite Inc.

MEADOWS—See GRIDLEY, IL (Gridley Cable)

MECHANICSBURG—See KINCAID, IL (Mediacom)

MEDINA TWP.—See PEORIA, IL (Comcast Cable)

MEDINAH—See OAK BROOK, IL (Comcast Cable)

▲ **MEDORA**—Formerly served by CableDirect. No longer in operation

MELROSE PARK—See OAK BROOK, IL (Comcast Cable)

▲ **MELVIN**—Mediacom. Now served by FARMER CITY, IL [IL0231]

MELVIN—See FARMER CITY, IL (Mediacom)

MENARD COUNTY—See WILLIAMSVILLE, IL (Greene County Partners Inc.)

▲ **MENDON**—Adams Telecom. Formerly served by Golden, IL [IL0257]. This cable system has converted to IPTV

MENDOTA—See PERU, IL (Comcast Cable)

MEREDOSIA—See BLUFFS, IL (Crystal Broadband Networks)

MERRILLVILLE—See CHICAGO (southern suburbs), IN (Comcast Cable)

MERRIONETTE PARK—See CHICAGO (southern suburbs), IL (Comcast Cable)

METAMORA—See ROANOKE, IL (Mediacom)

METCALF (VILLAGE)—See HUME (village), IL (Clearvision Cable Systems Inc.)

▲ **MIDDLETOWN (village)**—Mediacom. Now served by DELAVAN, IL [IL0172]

MIDDLETOWN—See DELAVAN, IL (Mediacom)

MIDLOTHIAN—See CHICAGO (southern suburbs), IL (Comcast Cable)

MILAN—See MOLINE, IL (Mediacom)

MILFORD—See WESTVILLE, IL (Avenue Broadband Communications)

▲ **MILL SHOALS**—Formerly served by CableDirect. No longer in operation

MILLEDGEVILLE—See LENA, IL (Mediacom)

▲ **MILLINGTON**—Comcast Cable. Now served by OAK BROOK, IL [IL0006]

MILLINGTON—See OAK BROOK, IL (Comcast Cable)

MILLSTADT (PORTIONS)—See MARYVILLE, IL (Charter Communications)

▲ **MILTON**—Cass Cable TV Inc. No longer in operation

▲ **MINERAL**—Mediacom

▲ **MINIER**—Mediacom. Now served by APOLLO ACRES, IL [IL0340]

MINIER—See APOLLO ACRES, IL (Mediacom)

MINONK—See ROANOKE, IL (Mediacom)

▲ **MINOOKA**—Comcast Cable. Now served by OAK BROOK, IL [IL0006]

MINOOKA—See OAK BROOK, IL (Comcast Cable)

MINOOKA—See MORRIS, IL (Mediacom)

MOBET—See MINERAL, IL (Mediacom)

MOKENA—See OAK BROOK, IL (Comcast Cable)

▲ **MOLINE**—Mediacom

▲ **MOMENCE**—Mediacom. Now served by ROSELAWN, IN [IN0316]

MONEE—See CHICAGO (southern suburbs), IL (Comcast Cable)

▲ **MONMOUTH**—Comcast Cable

▲ **MONROE CENTER**—Mediacom. Now served by KIRKLAND, IL [IL0277]

MONROE CENTER—See KIRKLAND, IL (Mediacom)

MONROE COUNTY (PORTIONS)—See COULTERVILLE, IL (Mediacom)

MONTGOMERY COUNTY (PORTIONS)—See LITCHFIELD, IL (NewWave Communications)

MONTGOMERY—See OAK BROOK, IL (Comcast Cable)

MONTICELLO (UNINCORPORATED AREAS)—See WHITE HEATH, IL (Full Choice Communications)

▲ **MONTICELLO**—Mediacom

MONTMORENCY TWP.—See STERLING, IL (Comcast Cable)

▲ **MONTROSE**—Clearvision Cable Systems Inc.

MORO TWP.—See ROXANA, IL (Charter Communications)

▲ **MORRIS**—Comcast Cable. Now served by OAK BROOK, IL [IL0006]

MORRIS—See OAK BROOK, IL (Comcast Cable)

▲ **MORRIS**—Mediacom

▲ **MORRISONVILLE**—Mediacom. Now served by KINCAID, IL [IL0176]

MORRISONVILLE—See KINCAID, IL (Mediacom)

▲ **MORTON GROVE**—Comcast Cable. Now served by SHAUMBURG, IL [IL0036]

MORTON GROVE—See SCHAUMBURG, IL (Comcast Cable)

MORTON—See PEKIN, IL (Comcast Cable)

MOUND CITY—See ZEIGLER, IL (Mediacom)

▲ **MOUNDS**—Mediacom. Now served by ZEIGLER, IL [IL0123]

MOUNDS—See ZEIGLER, IL (Mediacom)

▲ **MOUNT AUBURN**—Mediacom. Now served by KINCAID, IL [IL0176]

MOUNT AUBURN—See KINCAID, IL (Mediacom)

▲ **MOUNT CARMEL**—NewWave Communications

▲ **MOUNT CARROLL**—Mediacom. Now served by LENA, IL [IL0223]

MOUNT CARROLL—See LENA, IL (Mediacom)

MOUNT CLARE—See STAUNTON, IL (Madison Communications)

MOUNT JOY—See MOLINE, IA (Mediacom)

MOUNT MORRIS—See ROCKFORD, IL (Comcast Cable)

MOUNT OLIVE—See STAUNTON, IL (Madison Communications)

▲ **MOUNT PROSPECT**—Comcast Cable. Now served by SCHAUMBURG, IL [IL0036]

MOUNT PROSPECT—See SCHAUMBURG, IL (Comcast Cable)

MOUNT PROSPECT—See NAPERVILLE, IL (WOW! Internet Cable & Phone)

▲ **MOUNT PULASKI**—Insight Communications. Now served by SPRINGFIELD, IL [IL0016]

MOUNT PULASKI—See SPRINGFIELD, IL (Comcast Cable)

▲ **MOUNT STERLING**—Cass Cable TV Inc. Now served by VIRGINIA, IL [IL0598]

MOUNT STERLING—See VIRGINIA, IL (Cass Cable TV Inc.)

MOUNT VERNON—See WOODLAWN, IL (Charter Communications)

MOUNT ZION—See SPRINGFIELD, IL (Comcast Cable)

▲ **MOWEAQUA**—Suddenlink Communications

▲ **MULBERRY GROVE**—Clearvision Cable Systems Inc.

MULKEYTOWN—See DU QUOIN, IL (Comcast Cable)

MUNCIE—See URBANA, IL (Comcast Cable)

MUNDELEIN—See SCHAUMBURG, IL (Comcast Cable)

MUNSTER—See CHICAGO (southern suburbs), IN (Comcast Cable)

▲ **MURPHYSBORO**—Mediacom

▲ **MURRAYVILLE**—Formerly served by Almega Cable. No longer in operation

▲ **NAPERVILLE**—Comcast Cable. Now served by OAK BROOK, IL [IL0006]

NAPERVILLE—See OAK BROOK, IL (Comcast Cable)

▲ **NAPERVILLE**—WOW! Internet Cable & Phone

NAPLATE—See STREATOR, IL (Mediacom)

NASHVILLE—See OKAWVILLE, IL (Charter Communications)

▲ **NAUVOO**—Mediacom

NEBO—See PLEASANT HILL, IL (Crystal Broadband Networks)

▲ **NEOGA**—Mediacom

NEPONSET—See MINERAL, IL (Mediacom)

NEW ATHENS—See SPARTA, IL (NewWave Communications)

NEW BADEN—See SCOTT AFB, IL (Charter Communications)

▲ **NEW BERLIN**—Mediacom. Now served by KINCAID, IL [IL0176]

NEW BERLIN—See KINCAID, IL (Mediacom)

▲ **NEW BOSTON**—Nova Cablevision Inc.

NEW CHICAGO—See CHICAGO (southern suburbs), IN (Comcast Cable)

▲ **NEW DOUGLAS**—Madison Communications. Now served by SORENTO/NEW DOUGLAS (formerly Sorento), IL [IL0354]

NEW DOUGLAS—See SORENTO/NEW DOUGLAS, IL (Madison Communications)

▲**NEW HAVEN (village)**—Formerly served by CableDirect. No longer in operation

▲**NEW HOLLAND**—Mediacom. Now served by DELAVAN, IL [IL0172]

NEW HOLLAND—See DELAVAN, IL (Mediacom)

NEW LENOX—See OAK BROOK, IL (Comcast Cable)

NEW MILFORD—See ROCKFORD, IL (Comcast Cable)

NEW TRIER TWP.—See SCHAUMBURG, IL (Comcast Cable)

NEW WINDSOR—See ALPHA, IL (Diverse Communications Inc.)

▲**NEWMAN**—Comcast Cable

▲**NEWTON**—NewWave Communications

NIANTIC—See SPRINGFIELD, IL (Comcast Cable)

NILES—See SCHAUMBURG, IL (Comcast Cable)

NILWOOD—See VIRDEN, IL (Charter Communications)

▲**NOBLE**—Wabash Independent Networks

▲**NOKOMIS**—Charter Communications

NORMAL—See BLOOMINGTON, IL (Comcast Cable)

NORRIDGE—See OAK BROOK, IL (Comcast Cable)

▲**NORRIS CITY**—NewWave Communications

▲**NORRIS**—Insight Communications. Now served by CANTON, IL [IL0087]

NORRIS—See CANTON, IL (Comcast Cable)

NORTH AURORA—See OAK BROOK, IL (Comcast Cable)

NORTH BARRINGTON (VILLAGE)—See SCHAUMBURG, IL (Comcast Cable)

NORTH CHICAGO—See SCHAUMBURG, IL (Comcast Cable)

NORTH HENDERSON—See RIO, IL (Nova Cablevision Inc.)

NORTH PEKIN—See PEKIN, IL (Comcast Cable)

NORTH RIVERSIDE—See OAK BROOK, IL (Comcast Cable)

NORTH UTICA—See PERU, IL (Comcast Cable)

NORTHBROOK—See SCHAUMBURG, IL (Comcast Cable)

NORTHFIELD—See SCHAUMBURG, IL (Comcast Cable)

NORTHLAKE—See OAK BROOK, IL (Comcast Cable)

NORWOOD—See PEORIA, IL (Comcast Cable)

O'FALLON—See BELLEVILLE, IL (Charter Communications)

▲**OAK BROOK**—Comcast Cable

▲**OAK FOREST**—Comcast Cable. Now served by CHICAGO (southern suburbs), IL [IL0008]

OAK FOREST—See CHICAGO (southern suburbs), IL (Comcast Cable)

OAK FOREST—See NAPERVILLE, IL (WOW! Internet Cable & Phone)

OAK GROVE—See MOLINE, IL (Mediacom)

▲**OAK LAWN**—Comcast Cable. Now served by CHICAGO (southern suburbs), IL [IL0008]

OAK LAWN—See CHICAGO (southern suburbs), IL (Comcast Cable)

OAK PARK ESTATES—See BRIMFIELD, IL (Mediacom)

OAK PARK—See OAK BROOK, IL (Comcast Cable)

OAKBROOK TERRACE—See OAK BROOK, IL (Comcast Cable)

OAKFORD (VILLAGE)—See VIRGINIA, IL (Cass Cable TV Inc.)

OAKLAND—See TUSCOLA, IL (Mediacom)

OAKWOOD HILLS—See SCHAUMBURG, IL (Comcast Cable)

OAKWOOD—See URBANA, IL (Comcast Cable)

OBLONG—See ROBINSON, IL (Mediacom)

▲**OCONEE**—Formerly served by Mediacom. No longer in operation

▲**ODELL**—Mediacom. Now served by PONTIAC, IL [IL0109]

ODELL—See PONTIAC, IL (Mediacom)

ODIN—See SALEM, IL (Charter Communications)

OGDEN DUNES—See CHICAGO (southern suburbs), IN (Comcast Cable)

OGDEN—See URBANA, IL (Comcast Cable)

OGLE COUNTY (PORTIONS)—See DIXON, IL (Comcast Cable)

OGLE COUNTY—See ROCKFORD, IL (Comcast Cable)

OGLESBY—See PERU, IL (Comcast Cable)

▲**OKAWVILLE**—Charter Communications

OLIVE BRANCH—See ALEXANDER COUNTY (portions), IL (Zito Media)

OLIVET—See URBANA, IL (Comcast Cable)

OLIVET—See URBANA, IN (Comcast Cable)

▲**OLNEY**—Comcast Cable

OLYMPIA FIELDS—See CHICAGO (southern suburbs), IL (Comcast Cable)

▲**OMAHA**—Formerly served by CableDirect. No longer in operation

▲**ONARGA**—Comcast Cable

▲**ONEIDA**—Oneida Cablevision Inc.

OPHIEM—See ALPHA, IL (Diverse Communications Inc.)

▲**OQUAWKA**—Mediacom. Now served by ROSEVILLE, IL [IL0274]

OQUAWKA—See ROSEVILLE, IL (Mediacom)

ORANGEVILLE—See LENA, IL (Mediacom)

OREANA—See ARGENTA, IL (Suddenlink Communications)

▲**OREGON**—Formerly served by Insight Communications. No longer in operation

ORIENT—See FREEMAN SPUR, IL (Zito Media)

ORION—See MOLINE, IL (Mediacom)

ORLAND HILLS—See CHICAGO (southern suburbs), IL (Comcast Cable)

▲**ORLAND PARK**—Comcast Cable. Now served by CHICAGO (southern suburbs), IL [IL0008]

ORLAND PARK—See CHICAGO (southern suburbs), IL (Comcast Cable)

OSWEGO—See OAK BROOK, IL (Comcast Cable)

▲**OTTAWA**—Mediacom. Now served by STREATOR, IL [IL0069]

OTTAWA—See STREATOR, IL (Mediacom)

OTTER CREEK TWP.—See STREATOR, IL (Mediacom)

OTTO TWP.—See CHICAGO (southern suburbs), IL (Comcast Cable)

OWANECO—See TAYLORVILLE, IL (NewWave Communications)

PALATINE—See SCHAUMBURG, IL (Comcast Cable)

PALESTINE—See ROBINSON, IL (Mediacom)

▲**PALMER**—Mediacom. Now served by KINCAID, IL [IL0176]

PALMER—See KINCAID, IL (Mediacom)

▲**PALMYRA**—Formerly served by Almega Cable. No longer in operation

▲**PALOMA**—Adams Telecom. Formerly served by Golden, IL [IL0257]. This cable system has converted to IPTV

PALOS HEIGHTS—See CHICAGO (southern suburbs), IL (Comcast Cable)

PALOS HILLS—See CHICAGO (southern suburbs), IL (Comcast Cable)

▲**PALOS PARK**—Formerly served by TV Max. No longer in operation

PALOS PARK—See CHICAGO (southern suburbs), IL (Comcast Cable)

PALOS PARK—See NAPERVILLE, IL (WOW! Internet Cable & Phone)

PALOS TWP.—See CHICAGO (southern suburbs), IL (Comcast Cable)

▲**PANA**—Charter Communications

▲**PANAMA**—Formerly served by Beck's Cable Systems. No longer in operation

PANKEYVILLE—See ALEXANDER COUNTY (portions), IL (Zito Media)

PANORAMA PARK—See MOLINE, IA (Mediacom)

▲**PARIS**—Avenue Broadband Communications. Now served by WESTVILLE, IL [IL0079]

PARIS—See WESTVILLE, IL (Avenue Broadband Communications)

▲**PARK FOREST**—Comcast Cable. Now served by CHICAGO (southern suburbs), IL [IL0008]

PARK FOREST—See CHICAGO (southern suburbs), IL (Comcast Cable)

PARK RIDGE—See SCHAUMBURG, IL (Comcast Cable)

PARK VIEW—See MOLINE, IA (Mediacom)

▲**PARKERSBURG**—Formerly served by CableDirect. No longer in operation

▲**PATOKA**—Clearvision Cable Systems Inc.

PAWNEE—See SPRINGFIELD, IL (Comcast Cable)

PAXTON—See FARMER CITY, IL (Mediacom)

▲**PAYSON**—Adams Telephone. This cable system has converted to IPTV. See Payson. IL [IL5323]

▲**PAYSON**—Adams Telecom. Formerly [IL0288]. This cable system has converted to IPTV

▲**PEARL CITY (VILLAGE)**—Mediacom

▲**PECATONICA**—Mediacom. Now served by LENA, IL [IL0223]

PECATONICA—See LENA, IL (Mediacom)

▲**PEKIN**—Comcast Cable

▲**PENFIELD**—Formerly served by CableDirect. No longer in operation

PEORIA COUNTY (PORTIONS)—See EDWARDS, IL (Tel-Star Cablevision Inc.)

PEORIA COUNTY—See CHILLICOTHE, IL (Mediacom)

PEORIA HEIGHTS—See PEORIA, IL (Comcast Cable)

▲**PEORIA**—Comcast Cable

▲**PEOTONE**—Comcast Cable. Now served by CHICAGO (southern suburbs), IL [IL0008]

PEOTONE—See CHICAGO (southern suburbs), IL (Comcast Cable)

PERCY—See SPARTA, IL (NewWave Communications)

PERRY COUNTY—See ZEIGLER, IL (Mediacom)

PERRY TWP.—See GRIGGSVILLE, IL (Crystal Broadband Networks)

▲ **PERU**—Comcast Cable

PESOTUM—See TUSCOLA, IL (Mediacom)

PETERSBURG—See WILLIAMSVILLE, IL (Greene County Partners Inc.)

PHILO—See URBANA, IL (Comcast Cable)

PHOENIX—See CHICAGO (southern suburbs), IL (Comcast Cable)

PIATT COUNTY (EASTERN PORTION)—See WHITE HEATH, IL (Full Choice Communications)

▲ **PIERRON**—Clearvision Cable Systems Inc.

PIERSON—See TUSCOLA, IL (Mediacom)

PINCKNEYVILLE—See DU QUOIN, IL (Comcast Cable)

PINKSTAFF—See BIRDS, IL (Park TV & Electronics Inc.)

▲ **PIPER CITY**—Comcast Cable

PITTSBURG—See WILLIAMSON COUNTY (portions), IL (Zito Media)

▲ **PITTSFIELD**—Cass Cable TV Inc.

▲ **PLAINFIELD**—Comcast Cable. Now served by OAK BROOK, IL [IL0006]

PLAINFIELD—See OAK BROOK, IL (Comcast Cable)

▲ **PLAINVILLE**—Adams Telecom. Formerly served by Payson, IL [IL0288] This cable system has converted to IPTV

▲ **PLANO**—Comcast Cable. Now served by OAK BROOK, IL [IL0006]

PLANO—See OAK BROOK, IL (Comcast Cable)

PLATO TWP.—See OAK BROOK, IL (Comcast Cable)

▲ **PLEASANT HILL**—Crystal Broadband Networks

PLEASANT PLAINS—See VIRGINIA, IL (Cass Cable TV Inc.)

PLEASANT VALLEY—See MOLINE, IA (Mediacom)

▲ **PLYMOUTH**—Adams Telecom. Formerly served by Golden, IL [IL0257]. This cable system has converted to IPTV

POCAHONTAS (UNINCORPORATED AREAS)—See PIERRON, IL (Clearvision Cable Systems Inc.)

▲ **POCAHONTAS**—Clearvision Cable Systems Inc.

POLO—See ROCKFORD, IL (Comcast Cable)

▲ **PONTIAC**—Mediacom

PONTOON BEACH—See MARYVILLE, IL (Charter Communications)

PONTOOSUC—See ROSEVILLE, IL (Mediacom)

▲ **POPLAR GROVE**—Mediacom

PORT BYRON—See MINERAL, IL (Mediacom)

PORTAGE—See CHICAGO (southern suburbs), IN (Comcast Cable)

POSEN—See CHICAGO (southern suburbs), IL (Comcast Cable)

POSEN—See NAPERVILLE, IL (WOW! Internet Cable & Phone)

▲ **POTOMAC (VILLAGE)**—Park TV & Electronics Inc.

▲ **PRAIRIE CITY**—Formerly served by CableDirect. No longer in operation

PRAIRIE CITY—See GOOD HOPE, IL (Mediacom)

PRAIRIE DU ROCHER—See EVANSVILLE, IL (NewWave Communications)

PRAIRIETOWN—See SORENTO/NEW DOUGLAS, IL (Madison Communications)

PREEMPTION—See MINERAL, IL (Mediacom)

▲ **PRINCETON**—Comcast Cable

▲ **PRINCEVILLE**—Mediacom. Now served by BRIMFIELD, IL [IL0201]

PRINCEVILLE—See BRIMFIELD, IL (Mediacom)

PROSPECT HEIGHTS—See SCHAUMBURG, IL (Comcast Cable)

PROSPECT HEIGHTS—See NAPERVILLE, IL (WOW! Internet Cable & Phone)

PROVISO TWP.—See OAK BROOK, IL (Comcast Cable)

PULASKI COUNTY (PORTIONS)—See ZEIGLER, IL (Mediacom)

PULASKI COUNTY—See ALEXANDER COUNTY (portions), IL (Zito Media)

PULASKI—See ALEXANDER COUNTY (portions), IL (Zito Media)

▲ **QUINCY**—Comcast Cable

QUIVER TWP.—See VIRGINIA, IL (Cass Cable TV Inc.)

RALEIGH—See SALINE COUNTY (portions), IL (Zito Media)

▲ **RAMSEY**—NewWave Communications

▲ **RANKIN (VILLAGE)**—Park TV & Electronics Inc.

RANSOM—See GRAND RIDGE, IL (Grand Ridge Cable Co. Inc.)

▲ **RANTOUL**—Mediacom

RAPIDS CITY—See MINERAL, IL (Mediacom)

▲ **RAYMOND**—Charter Communications

READING TWP.—See STREATOR, IL (Mediacom)

RED BUD—See COULTERVILLE, IL (Mediacom)

▲ **REDMON**—Formerly served by CableDirect. No longer in operation

REYNOLDS—See MINERAL, IL (Mediacom)

RICH TWP.—See CHICAGO (southern suburbs), IL (Comcast Cable)

RICHMOND—See SPRING GROVE (village), IL (Mediacom)

RICHTON PARK—See CHICAGO (southern suburbs), IL (Comcast Cable)

▲ **RICHVIEW**—Formerly served by CableDirect. No longer in operation

RICHWOODS TWP.—See PEORIA, IL (Comcast Cable)

▲ **RIDGE FARM**—Insight Communications. Now served by URBANA, IL [IL0019]

RIDGE FARM—See URBANA, IL (Comcast Cable)

RIDOTT TWP.—See GERMAN VALLEY, IL (Mediacom)

RINGWOOD—See SPRING GROVE (village), IL (Mediacom)

▲ **RIO**—Nova Cablevision Inc.

RITCHIE—See CHICAGO (southern suburbs), IL (Comcast Cable)

RIVER FOREST—See OAK BROOK, IL (Comcast Cable)

RIVER GROVE—See OAK BROOK, IL (Comcast Cable)

▲ **RIVER NORTH**—See Chicago (portions), IL [IL5236]

▲ **RIVER OAKS (village)**—Mediacom. Now served by KINCAID, IL [IL0176]

RIVER OAKS (VILLAGE)—See KINCAID, IL (Mediacom)

RIVERDALE—See CHICAGO (southern suburbs), IL (Comcast Cable)

RIVERDALE—See MOLINE, IA (Mediacom)

RIVERSIDE—See CHICAGO (southern suburbs), IL (Comcast Cable)

RIVERTON—See WILLIAMSVILLE, IL (Greene County Partners Inc.)

RIVERWOODS (VILLAGE)—See SCHAUMBURG, IL (Comcast Cable)

▲ **ROANOKE**—Mediacom

ROBBINS (VILLAGE)—See CHICAGO (southern suburbs), IL (Comcast Cable)

▲ **ROBBINS**—Comcast Cable. Now served by CHICAGO (southern suburbs), IL [IL0008]

ROBBINS—See NAPERVILLE, IL (WOW! Internet Cable & Phone)

▲ **ROBINSON**—Mediacom

ROCHELLE—See SCHAUMBURG, IL (Comcast Cable)

ROCHESTER—See SPRINGFIELD, IL (Comcast Cable)

ROCK FALLS—See STERLING, IL (Comcast Cable)

ROCK ISLAND ARSENAL—See MOLINE, IL (Mediacom)

ROCK ISLAND COUNTY—See MOLINE, IL (Mediacom)

▲ **ROCK ISLAND**—Mediacom. Now served by MOLINE, IL [IL0011]

ROCK ISLAND—See MOLINE, IL (Mediacom)

ROCKDALE—See OAK BROOK, IL (Comcast Cable)

ROCKFORD (UNINCORPORATED AREAS)—See POPLAR GROVE, IL (Mediacom)

▲ **ROCKFORD**—Formerly served by Wireless Cable Systems Inc. No longer in operation

▲ **ROCKFORD**—Comcast Cable

▲ **ROGERS PARK (EASTERN PORTION)**—RCN Corp. Formerly served by Chicago (portions), IL [IL0661]. This cable system has converted to IPTV

ROLLING MEADOWS MOBILE HOME PARK—See KIRKLAND, IL (Mediacom)

▲ **ROLLING MEADOWS**—Comcast Cable. Now served by SCHAUMBURG, IL [IL0036]

ROLLING MEADOWS—See SCHAUMBURG, IL (Comcast Cable)

ROME—See CHILLICOTHE, IL (Mediacom)

▲ **ROMEOVILLE**—Comcast Cable. Now served by OAK BROOK, IL [IL0006]

ROMEOVILLE—See OAK BROOK, IL (Comcast Cable)

ROODHOUSE—See CARROLLTON, IL (Greene County Partners Inc.)

▲ **ROSAMOND**—Formerly served by Beck's Cable Systems. No longer in operation

ROSELLE—See OAK BROOK, IL (Comcast Cable)

ROSEMONT—See OAK BROOK, IL (Comcast Cable)

▲ **ROSEVILLE**—Mediacom

ROSEWOOD HEIGHTS—See ROXANA, IL (Charter Communications)

▲ **ROSICLARE**—Zito Media

ROSSVILLE—See WESTVILLE, IL (Avenue Broadband Communications)

ROUND LAKE BEACH—See SCHAUMBURG, IL (Comcast Cable)

ROUND LAKE HEIGHTS—See SCHAUMBURG, IL (Comcast Cable)

ROUND LAKE PARK—See SCHAUMBURG, IL (Comcast Cable)

ROUND LAKE—See SCHAUMBURG, IL (Comcast Cable)

▲ **ROXANA**—Charter Communications

▲ **ROYAL**—Formerly served by CableDirect. No longer in operation

ROYALTON—See ZEIGLER, IL (Mediacom)

RUMA—See EVANSVILLE, IL (NewWave Communications)

▲ **RUSHVILLE**—Cass Cable TV Inc. Now served by VIRGINIA, IL [IL0598]

RUSHVILLE—See VIRGINIA, IL (Cass Cable TV Inc.)

RUTLAND—See FLANAGAN, IL (Heartland Cable Inc.)

▲ **SADORUS**—Formerly served by Longview Communications. No longer in operation

▲ **SALEM**—Charter Communications

▲ **SALINE COUNTY (PORTIONS)**—Zito Media

SALINE COUNTY (PORTIONS)—See CARRIER MILLS, IL (Zito Media)

SAN JOSE—See DELAVAN, IL (Mediacom)

SANDOVAL—See SALEM, IL (Charter Communications)

SANDWICH—See OAK BROOK, IL (Comcast Cable)

SANGAMON COUNTY (PORTIONS)—See DELAVAN, IL (Mediacom)

SANGAMON COUNTY—See SPRINGFIELD, IL (Comcast Cable)

SAUGET—See CAHOKIA, IL (Charter Communications)

SAUK VILLAGE—See CHICAGO (southern suburbs), IL (Comcast Cable)

SAUNEMIN—See PONTIAC, IL (Mediacom)

SAVOY (VILLAGE)—See URBANA, IL (Comcast Cable)

SAWYERVILLE—See STAUNTON, IL (Madison Communications)

▲ **SAYBROOK**—Mediacom. Now served by LE ROY, IL [IL0539]

SAYBROOK—See LE ROY, IL (Mediacom)

▲ **SCALES MOUND**—Mediacom

▲ **SCHAUMBURG**—Comcast Cable

SCHAUMBURG—See NAPERVILLE, IL (WOW! Internet Cable & Phone)

SCHERERVILLE—See CHICAGO (southern suburbs), IN (Comcast Cable)

SCHILLER PARK—See OAK BROOK, IL (Comcast Cable)

SCHRAM CITY—See HILLSBORO, IL (NewWave Communications)

▲ **SCOTT AFB**—Charter Communications

SCOTT COUNTY (PORTIONS)—See MOLINE, IA (Mediacom)

▲ **SEATONVILLE (village)**—Formerly served by CableDirect. No longer in operation

SECOR—See ROANOKE, IL (Mediacom)

▲ **SENECA**—Kraus Electronics Systems Inc.

▲ **SESSER**—NewWave Communications

SEYMOUR (VILLAGE)—See WHITE HEATH, IL (Full Choice Communications)

SHABBONA—See SUGAR GROVE, IL (Mediacom)

SHADY OAKS TRAILER PARK—See MORRIS, IL (Mediacom)

SHANNON—See LENA, IL (Mediacom)

SHARON—See HARVARD, WI (Charter Communications)

▲ **SHAWNEETOWN**—Now served by OWENSBORO, KY [KY0004]

SHEFFIELD—See MINERAL, IL (Mediacom)

SHELBY COUNTY (PORTIONS)—See SHELBYVILLE, IL (Charter Communications)

▲ **SHELBYVILLE**—Charter Communications

SHELDON—See WATSEKA, IL (Mediacom)

▲ **SHERIDAN (village)**—Mediacom. Now served by STREATOR, IL [IL0069]

SHERIDAN—See STREATOR, IL (Mediacom)

SHERMAN—See WILLIAMSVILLE, IL (Greene County Partners Inc.)

SHERRARD—See MINERAL, IL (Mediacom)

SHILOH—See SCOTT AFB, IL (Charter Communications)

▲ **SHIPMAN**—Mediacom

SHOREWOOD—See OAK BROOK, IL (Comcast Cable)

SHUMWAY—See MONTROSE, IL (Clearvision Cable Systems Inc.)

▲ **SIBLEY (VILLAGE)**—Heartland Cable Inc.

▲ **SIDELL (VILLAGE)**—Clearvision Cable Systems Inc.

SIDNEY—See URBANA, IL (Comcast Cable)

SIGEL—See EFFINGHAM, IL (Mediacom)

SILVERWOOD—See URBANA, IL (Comcast Cable)

SILVIS—See MOLINE, IL (Mediacom)

▲ **SIMS**—Formerly served by CableDirect. No longer in operation

▲ **SKOKIE (PORTIONS)**—RCN Corp. Formerly served by Chicago (portions), IL [IL0661]. This cable system has converted to IPTV

▲ **SKOKIE**—Comcast Cable. Now served by SCHAUMBURG, IL [IL0036]

▲ **SKOKIE**—Formerly served by RCN Corp. No longer in operation

SKOKIE—See SCHAUMBURG, IL (Comcast Cable)

SLEEPY HOLLOW—See SCHAUMBURG, IL (Comcast Cable)

▲ **SMITHFIELD**—Formerly served by CableDirect. No longer in operation

SMITHTON—See COULTERVILLE, IL (Mediacom)

SMITHVILLE—See ELMWOOD, IL (Mediacom)

SOLON MILLS—See SPRING GROVE (village), IL (Mediacom)

SOMONAUK—See SUGAR GROVE, IL (Mediacom)

▲ **SORENTO/NEW DOUGLAS**—Madison Communications

SOUTH BARRINGTON (VILLAGE)—See SCHAUMBURG, IL (Comcast Cable)

SOUTH CHICAGO HEIGHTS—See CHICAGO (southern suburbs), IL (Comcast Cable)

SOUTH ELGIN—See OAK BROOK, IL (Comcast Cable)

▲ **SOUTH HOLLAND**—Comcast Cable. Now served by CHICAGO (southern suburbs), IL [IL0008]

SOUTH HOLLAND—See CHICAGO (southern suburbs), IL (Comcast Cable)

SOUTH HOLLAND—See NAPERVILLE, IL (WOW! Internet Cable & Phone)

SOUTH JACKSONVILLE—See JACKSONVILLE, IL (Mediacom)

SOUTH OTTAWA TWP.—See STREATOR, IL (Mediacom)

SOUTH PEKIN—See PEKIN, IL (Comcast Cable)

SOUTH ROXANA—See ROXANA, IL (Charter Communications)

SOUTH WAYNE—See LENA, WI (Mediacom)

▲ **SOUTH WILMINGTON (village)**—Mediacom. Now served by GIBSON CITY, IL [IL0164]

SOUTH WILMINGTON (VILLAGE)—See GIBSON CITY, IL (Mediacom)

SOUTHERN VIEW—See SPRINGFIELD, IL (Comcast Cable)

SPARLAND—See CHILLICOTHE, IL (Mediacom)

▲ **SPARTA**—NewWave Communications

SPAULDING—See SPRINGFIELD, IL (Comcast Cable)

SPILLERTOWN—See FREEMAN SPUR, IL (Zito Media)

SPRING BAY—See ROANOKE, IL (Mediacom)

▲ **SPRING GROVE (VILLAGE)**—Mediacom

SPRING LAKE—See VIRGINIA, IL (Cass Cable TV Inc.)

SPRING VALLEY—See PERU, IL (Comcast Cable)

SPRINGFIELD TWP.—See SPRINGFIELD, IL (Comcast Cable)

▲ **SPRINGFIELD**—Comcast Cable

ST. ANNE—See CHICAGO (southern suburbs), IL (Comcast Cable)

ST. CHARLES—See OAK BROOK, IL (Comcast Cable)

ST. CLAIR COUNTY (UNINCORPORATED PORTIONS)—See WASHINGTON PARK, IL (Mediacom)

ST. CLAIR COUNTY—See BELLEVILLE, IL (Charter Communications)

ST. CLAIR COUNTY—See MARYVILLE, IL (Charter Communications)

ST. CLAIR COUNTY—See SCOTT AFB, IL (Charter Communications)

ST. CLAIR TWP.—See BELLEVILLE, IL (Charter Communications)

ST. CLAIR TWP.—See WASHINGTON PARK, IL (Mediacom)

▲ **ST. DAVID**—Mediacom. Now served by ELMWOOD, IL [IL0205]

ST. DAVID—See ELMWOOD, IL (Mediacom)

ST. ELMO—See ALTAMONT, IL (Mediacom)

▲ **ST. FRANCISVILLE**—Avenue Broadband Communications

ST. JACOB—See MARYVILLE, IL (Charter Communications)

ST. JOHN—See CHICAGO (southern suburbs), IN (Comcast Cable)

ST. JOHNS—See DU QUOIN, IL (Comcast Cable)

ST. JOSEPH—See URBANA, IL (Comcast Cable)

▲ **ST. LIBORY**—Formerly served by CableDirect. No longer in operation

▲ **ST. PETER**—Clearvision Cable Systems Inc.

STANDARD—See BRIMFIELD, IL (Mediacom)

STANFORD—See APOLLO ACRES, IL (Mediacom)

▲ **STAUNTON**—Madison Communications

▲ **STE. MARIE TWP.**—Formerly served by Advanced Technologies & Technical Resources Inc. No longer in operation

STEELEVILLE—See SPARTA, IL (NewWave Communications)

STEGER—See CHICAGO (southern suburbs), IL (Comcast Cable)

STEPHENSON COUNTY—See FREEPORT, IL (Comcast Cable)

STEPHENSON COUNTY—See LENA, IL (Mediacom)

STERLING TWP.—See STERLING, IL (Comcast Cable)

▲**STERLING**—Comcast Cable

STEWARDSON—See NEOGA, IL (Mediacom)

STICKNEY—See OAK BROOK, IL (Comcast Cable)

STILLMAN VALLEY—See ROCKFORD, IL (Comcast Cable)

▲**STOCKTON**—Mediacom. Now served by LENA, IL [IL0223]

STOCKTON—See LENA, IL (Mediacom)

STONE PARK—See OAK BROOK, IL (Comcast Cable)

STONINGTON—See BLUE MOUND, IL (Suddenlink Communications)

STOOKEY TWP.—See BELLEVILLE, IL (Charter Communications)

▲**STRASBURG**—Mediacom. Now served by NEOGA, IL [IL0249]

STRASBURG—See NEOGA, IL (Mediacom)

▲**STREAMWOOD**—Comcast Cable. Now served by SCHAUMBURG, IL [IL0036]

STREAMWOOD—See SCHAUMBURG, IL (Comcast Cable)

STREAMWOOD—See NAPERVILLE, IL (WOW! Internet Cable & Phone)

▲**STREATOR**—Mediacom

▲**STRONGHURST**—Mediacom. Now served by ROSEVILLE, IL [IL0274]

STRONGHURST—See ROSEVILLE, IL (Mediacom)

▲**SUBLETTE (VILLAGE)**—Heartland Cable Broadband

▲**SUGAR GROVE**—Mediacom

▲**SULLIVAN**—Mediacom

SUMMERFIELD—See SCOTT AFB, IL (Charter Communications)

SUMMIT—See OAK BROOK, IL (Comcast Cable)

▲**SUMNER**—Avenue Broadband Communications

SUN RIVER TWP.—See CHICAGO (southern suburbs), IL (Comcast Cable)

SUNNYSIDE—See SCHAUMBURG, IL (Comcast Cable)

SUNSET LAKE—See VIRDEN, IL (Charter Communications)

SWANSEA—See BELLEVILLE, IL (Charter Communications)

SYCAMORE—See SCHAUMBURG, IL (Comcast Cable)

▲**TABLE GROVE**—Mid Century Telephone Cooperative. This cable system has converted to IPTV. See Table Grove, IL [IL5244]

▲**TABLE GROVE**—Mid Century Telephone Cooperative. Formerly [IL0587]. This cable system has converted to IPTV

TALBOTT ADDITION—See VIRGINIA, IL (Cass Cable TV Inc.)

TALLULA—See VIRGINIA, IL (Cass Cable TV Inc.)

TAMAROA—See DU QUOIN, IL (Comcast Cable)

▲**TAMMS**—NewWave Communications

▲**TAMPICO**—Mediacom

TANTARA MOBILE HOME PARK—See JACKSON COUNTY, IL (Zito Media)

TAYLOR RIDGE—See MOLINE, IL (Mediacom)

TAYLOR SPRINGS—See HILLSBORO, IL (NewWave Communications)

▲**TAYLORVILLE**—NewWave Communications

TAZEWELL COUNTY (PORTIONS)—See PEKIN, IL (Comcast Cable)

TAZEWELL TWP.—See PEORIA, IL (Comcast Cable)

TEUTOPOLIS—See EFFINGHAM, IL (Mediacom)

▲**THAWVILLE**—Formerly served by CableDirect. No longer in operation

THAYER—See VIRDEN, IL (Charter Communications)

THEBES—See ALEXANDER COUNTY (portions), IL (Zito Media)

THOMASBORO—See RANTOUL, IL (Mediacom)

THORNTON—See CHICAGO (southern suburbs), IL (Comcast Cable)

TILDEN—See COULTERVILLE, IL (Mediacom)

TILTON—See WESTVILLE, IL (Avenue Broadband Communications)

TIMBER RIDGE—See FAIRBURY, IL (Mediacom)

TINLEY PARK—See CHICAGO (southern suburbs), IL (Comcast Cable)

TISKILWA—See PRINCETON, IL (Comcast Cable)

TOLEDO—See GREENUP, IL (Mediacom)

▲**TOLONO**—Mediacom. Now served by TUSCOLA, IL [IL0135]

TOLONO—See TUSCOLA, IL (Mediacom)

TOLUCA—See ROANOKE, IL (Mediacom)

▲**TONICA**—Heartland Cable Inc.

TOULON—See WYOMING, IL (Mediacom)

TOVEY—See KINCAID, IL (Mediacom)

TOWANDA—See FAIRBURY, IL (Mediacom)

▲**TOWER HILL**—Mediacom

TOWER LAKES—See SCHAUMBURG, IL (Comcast Cable)

TREMONT—See PEKIN, IL (Comcast Cable)

TRENTON—See SCOTT AFB, IL (Charter Communications)

▲**TRIVOLI**—Nova Cablevision Inc.

▲**TROY GROVE (village)**—Formerly served by CableDirect. No longer in operation

TROY—See MARYVILLE, IL (Charter Communications)

▲**TUSCOLA**—Mediacom

ULLIN—See ALEXANDER COUNTY (portions), IL (Zito Media)

UNION COUNTY (PORTIONS)—See ANNA, IL (NewWave Communications)

▲**UNION**—Packerland Broadband

UNIVERSITY PARK—See CHICAGO (southern suburbs), IL (Comcast Cable)

▲**URBANA**—Comcast Cable

▲**URSA**—Adams Telecom. Formerly served by Golden, IL [IL0257]. This cable system has converted to IPTV

UTICA TWP.—See PERU, IL (Comcast Cable)

VALIER—See SESSER, IL (NewWave Communications)

▲**VANDALIA**—NewWave Communications

VARNA—See LACON, IL (Mediacom)

VENICE—See MARYVILLE, IL (Charter Communications)

VERA—See VANDALIA, IL (NewWave Communications)

▲**VERGENNES**—Formerly served by CableDirect. No longer in operation

VERMILION GROVE—See URBANA, IL (Comcast Cable)

▲**VERMILLION (village)**—Formerly served by CableDirect. No longer in operation

▲**VERMONT**—Mediacom

VERNON HILLS—See SCHAUMBURG, IL (Comcast Cable)

VERNON HILLS—See NAPERVILLE, IL (WOW! Internet Cable & Phone)

VERNON—See PATOKA, IL (Clearvision Cable Systems Inc.)

▲**VERSAILLES**—Cass Cable TV Inc. Now served by VIRGINIA, IL [IL0598]

VERSAILLES—See VIRGINIA, IL (Cass Cable TV Inc.)

▲**VICTORIA**—Mediacom

VIENNA—See BUNCOMBE, IL (Zito Media)

VILLA GROVE—See TUSCOLA, IL (Mediacom)

▲**VILLA PARK**—Comcast Cable. Now served by OAK BROOK, IL [IL0006]

VILLA PARK—See OAK BROOK, IL (Comcast Cable)

VIOLA—See MINERAL, IL (Mediacom)

▲**VIRDEN**—Charter Communications

▲**VIRGINIA**—Cass Cable TV Inc.

WABASH COUNTY (PORTIONS)—See MOUNT CARMEL, IL (NewWave Communications)

WALCOTT—See MOLINE, IA (Mediacom)

▲**WALNUT**—Mediacom. Now served by MINERAL, IL [IL0170]

WALNUT—See MINERAL, IL (Mediacom)

▲**WALTONVILLE**—Formerly served by Longview Communications. No longer in operation

WALWORTH—See HARVARD, WI (Charter Communications)

WAMAC—See OKAWVILLE, IL (Charter Communications)

WAPELLA—See CLINTON, IL (Mediacom)

WARREN COUNTY—See MONMOUTH, IL (Comcast Cable)

▲**WARREN**—Mediacom. Now served by LENA, IL [IL0223]

WARREN—See LENA, IL (Mediacom)

▲**WARRENSBURG**—Crystal Broadcast Networks

WARRENVILLE—See OAK BROOK, IL (Comcast Cable)

WASHBURN—See ROANOKE, IL (Mediacom)

WASHINGTON COUNTY—See OKAWVILLE, IL (Charter Communications)

▲**WASHINGTON PARK**—Mediacom

WASHINGTON—See PEORIA, IL (Comcast Cable)

▲**WATAGA**—Formerly served by Mediacom. No longer in operation

▲**WATERLOO**—Charter Communications

WATERMAN—See SUGAR GROVE, IL (Mediacom)

▲**WATSEKA**—Mediacom

WATSON—See EFFINGHAM COUNTY, IL (Clearvision Cable Systems Inc.)

WAUCONDA—See SCHAUMBURG, IL (Comcast Cable)

▲**WAUKEGAN**—Comcast Cable. No longer in operation

▲**WAVERLY**—Crystal Broadband Networks

▲**WAYNE CITY**—NewWave Communications

WAYNE COUNTY (PORTIONS)—See FAIRFIELD, IL (NewWave Communications)

WAYNESVILLE—See ATLANTA, IL (Mediacom)

▲**WEE-MA-TUK HILLS**—Nova Cablevision Inc.

▲ **WELDON**—Mediacom. Now served by FARMER CITY, IL [IL0231]

WELDON—See FARMER CITY, IL (Mediacom)

WELLINGTON—See WESTVILLE, IL (Avenue Broadband Communications)

WENONA—See ROANOKE, IL (Mediacom)

▲ **WEST CHICAGO**—Comcast Cable. Now served by OAK BROOK, IL [IL0006]

WEST CHICAGO—See OAK BROOK, IL (Comcast Cable)

WEST CITY—See DU QUOIN, IL (Comcast Cable)

WEST DUNDEE—See SCHAUMBURG, IL (Comcast Cable)

WEST FRANKFORT—See MARION, IL (Mediacom)

WEST LIBERTY—See OLNEY, IL (Comcast Cable)

WEST PEORIA TWP.—See PEORIA, IL (Comcast Cable)

▲ **WEST SALEM**—Full Choice Communications

▲ **WEST UNION**—Formerly served by Longview Communications. No longer in operation

WESTCHESTER—See OAK BROOK, IL (Comcast Cable)

▲ **WESTERN SPRINGS**—Comcast Cable. Now served by CHICAGO (southern suburbs), IL [IL0008]

WESTERN SPRINGS—See CHICAGO (southern suburbs), IL (Comcast Cable)

WESTFIELD—See CHARLESTON, IL (Mediacom)

WESTMONT—See OAK BROOK, IL (Comcast Cable)

▲ **WESTVILLE**—Avenue Broadband Communications

WHEATLAND—See OAK BROOK, IL (Comcast Cable)

WHEATON—See OAK BROOK, IL (Comcast Cable)

WHEELING—See SCHAUMBURG, IL (Comcast Cable)

WHEELING—See NAPERVILLE, IL (WOW! Internet Cable & Phone)

WHITE HALL—See CARROLLTON, IL (Greene County Partners Inc.)

▲ **WHITE HEATH**—Full Choice Communications

WHITEASH—See MARION, IL (Mediacom)

WHITING—See CHICAGO (southern suburbs), IN (Comcast Cable)

WHITTINGTON—See DU QUOIN, IL (Comcast Cable)

WILL COUNTY (PORTIONS)—See CHICAGO (southern suburbs), IL (Comcast Cable)

WILL COUNTY—See OAK BROOK, IL (Comcast Cable)

WILLIAMS BAY—See HARVARD, WI (Charter Communications)

▲ **WILLIAMSFIELD**—Mediacom. Now served by WYOMING, IL [IL0196]

WILLIAMSFIELD—See WYOMING, IL (Mediacom)

▲ **WILLIAMSON COUNTY (PORTIONS)**—Zito Media

WILLIAMSON COUNTY (SOUTHERN PORTION)—See LAKE OF EGYPT, IL (Zito Media)

WILLIAMSON COUNTY—See MARION, IL (Mediacom)

WILLIAMSON COUNTY—See ZEIGLER, IL (Mediacom)

WILLIAMSON—See STAUNTON, IL (Madison Communications)

▲ **WILLIAMSVILLE**—Greene County Partners Inc.

▲ **WILLOW HILL TWP.**—Formerly served by Advanced Technologies & Technical Resources Inc. No longer in operation

WILLOW SPRINGS—See OAK BROOK, IL (Comcast Cable)

WILLOWBROOK—See OAK BROOK, IL (Comcast Cable)

WILMETTE—See SCHAUMBURG, IL (Comcast Cable)

▲ **WILMINGTON**—Comcast Cable. Now served by OAK BROOK, IL [IL0006]

WILMINGTON—See OAK BROOK, IL (Comcast Cable)

▲ **WILSONVILLE**—Mediacom

WILTON—See MOLINE, IA (Mediacom)

▲ **WINCHESTER**—Crystal Broadband Networks

▲ **WINDSOR**—Mediacom. Now served by NEOGA, IL [IL0249]

WINDSOR—See NEOGA, IL (Mediacom)

WINFIELD—See OAK BROOK, IL (Comcast Cable)

WINFIELD—See CHICAGO (southern suburbs), IN (Comcast Cable)

WINNEBAGO COUNTY (PORTIONS)—See ROCKFORD, IL (Comcast Cable)

WINNETKA—See SCHAUMBURG, IL (Comcast Cable)

▲ **WINSLOW**—Mediacom. Now served by LENA, IL [IL0223]

WINSLOW—See LENA, IL (Mediacom)

WITT—See NOKOMIS, IL (Charter Communications)

▲ **WOLF LAKE**—Formerly served by CableDirect. No longer in operation

WONDER LAKE—See SCHAUMBURG, IL (Comcast Cable)

WOOD DALE—See OAK BROOK, IL (Comcast Cable)

WOOD RIVER—See ROXANA, IL (Charter Communications)

WOODFORD COUNTY—See ROANOKE, IL (Mediacom)

WOODHULL—See ALPHA, IL (Diverse Communications Inc.)

WOODLAND (VILLAGE)—See WATSEKA, IL (Mediacom)

▲ **WOODLAND HEIGHTS**—Tel-Star Cablevision Inc.

▲ **WOODLAWN**—Charter Communications. Now served by WOODLAWN, IL [IL0067]

▲ **WOODLAWN**—Charter Communications

WOODRIDGE—See OAK BROOK, IL (Comcast Cable)

WOODSIDE TWP.—See SPRINGFIELD, IL (Comcast Cable)

▲ **WOODSTOCK**—Comcast Cable. Now served by SCHAUMBURG, IL [IL0036]

WOODSTOCK—See SCHAUMBURG, IL (Comcast Cable)

▲ **WORDEN**—Madison Communications. Now served by STAUNTON, IL [IL0171]

WORDEN—See STAUNTON, IL (Madison Communications)

WORTH—See CHICAGO (southern suburbs), IL (Comcast Cable)

▲ **WRIGLEYVILLE**—See Chicago (portions), IL [IL5236]

WYANET—See PRINCETON, IL (Comcast Cable)

▲ **WYOMING**—Mediacom

▲ **XENIA**—Wabash Independent Networks

YATES CITY—See ELMWOOD, IL (Mediacom)

YORKVILLE—See OAK BROOK, IL (Comcast Cable)

▲ **ZEIGLER**—Mediacom

INDIANA

ADAMS COUNTY—See PORTLAND, IN (Comcast Cable)

ADAMS LAKE—See ROME CITY, IN (Mediacom)

ADAMS TWP.—See FORT WAYNE, IN (Comcast Cable)

ADAMSBORO—See LOGANSPORT, IN (Comcast Cable)

ADVANCE—See JAMESTOWN, IN (Indiana Communications)

▲ **AKRON (town)**—Comcast Cable. Now served by SOUTH BEND, IN [IN0005]

AKRON—See SOUTH BEND, IN (Comcast Cable)

ALBANY—See PORTLAND, IN (Comcast Cable)

ALBION—See LIGONIER, IN (Mediacom)

ALEXANDRIA—See ANDERSON, IN (Comcast Cable)

▲ **ALLEN COUNTY**—Mediacom. Now served by KENDALLVILLE, IN [IN0066]

ALLEN COUNTY—See FORT WAYNE, IN (Comcast Cable)

ALLEN COUNTY—See KENDALLVILLE, IN (Mediacom)

▲ **AMBOY**—Formerly served by CableDirect. No longer in operation

AMERICUS—See LAFAYETTE, IN (Comcast Cable)

AMO—See COATESVILLE, IN (Avenue Broadband Communications)

▲ **ANDERSON**—Formerly served by Broadcast Cable Inc. No longer in operation

▲ **ANDERSON**—Comcast Cable

▲ **ANDREWS**—Formerly served by Longview Communications. No longer in operation

▲ **ANGOLA**—Mediacom

ANTIOCH—See FRANKFORT, IN (Comcast Cable)

ARCADIA—See NOBLESVILLE, IN (Comcast Cable)

▲ **ARGOS**—Mediacom. Now served by NORTH WEBSTER, IN [IN0038]

ARGOS—See NORTH WEBSTER, IN (Mediacom)

ARMSTRONG TWP.—See EVANSVILLE, IN (Insight Communications)

ARTHUR—See WINSLOW, IN (Avenue Broadband Communications)

▲ **ASHLEY**—Formerly served by Longview Communications. No longer in operation

ATLANTA—See NOBLESVILLE, IN (Comcast Cable)

▲ **ATTICA**—Comcast Cable

AUBURN—See KENDALLVILLE, IN (Mediacom)

AURORA—See LAWRENCEBURG, IN (Comcast Cable)

▲ **AVILLA**—Comcast Cable

AVOCA—See BEDFORD, IN (Comcast Cable)

AVON—See INDIANAPOLIS (portions), IN (Bright House Networks)

▲ **BAINBRIDGE**—Formerly served by Global Com Inc. No longer in operation

BARGERSVILLE—See GREENWOOD, IN (Comcast Cable)

BARTHOLOMEW COUNTY—See COLUMBUS, IN (Comcast Cable)

▲ **BATESVILLE**—Comcast Cable

BATTLE GROUND—See LAFAYETTE, IN (Comcast Cable)

▲ **BEDFORD**—Comcast Cable

BEECH GROVE—See INDIANAPOLIS, IN (Comcast Cable)

BENTON COUNTY—See ATTICA, IN (Comcast Cable)

BERNE—See PORTLAND, IN (Comcast Cable)

BEVERLY SHORES—See MICHIGAN CITY, IN (Comcast Cable)

▲ **BICKNELL**—Charter Communications. Now served by VINCENNES, IN [IN0035]

BICKNELL—See VINCENNES, IN (Avenue Broadband Communications)

▲ **BIRDSEYE**—Formerly served by CableDirect. No longer in operation

BLACKFORD COUNTY—See HARTFORD CITY, IN (Comcast Cable)

▲ **BLOOMFIELD**—Insight Communications. Now served by LINTON, IN [IN0052]

BLOOMFIELD—See LINTON, IN (Comcast Cable)

BLOOMINGDALE—See ROCKVILLE, IN (Suddenlink Communications)

▲ **BLOOMINGTON**—Comcast Cable

BLOUNTSVILLE—See ANDERSON, IN (Comcast Cable)

▲ **BLUFFTON**—Mediacom

BOONE COUNTY (PORTIONS)—See JAMESTOWN, IN (Indiana Communications)

BOONE COUNTY—See NOBLESVILLE, IN (Comcast Cable)

▲ **BOONVILLE**—Now served by EVANSVILLE, IN [IN0006]

BOONVILLE—See EVANSVILLE, IN (Insight Communications)

▲ **BOSWELL**—Indiana Communications

▲ **BOURBON**—Mediacom. Now served by NORTH WEBSTER, IN [IN0038]

BOURBON—See NORTH WEBSTER, IN (Mediacom)

▲ **BRAZIL**—Avenue Broadband Communications

▲ **BREMEN**—Mediacom. Now served by NORTH WEBSTER, IN [IN0038]

BREMEN—See NORTH WEBSTER, IN (Mediacom)

BRIDGEPORT—See VINCENNES, IL (Avenue Broadband Communications)

BRIGHT—See LAWRENCEBURG, IN (Comcast Cable)

BRINGHURST—See MONTICELLO, IN (Comcast Cable)

▲ **BRISTOL**—Comcast Cable. Now served by SOUTH BEND, IN [IN0005]

BRISTOL—See SOUTH BEND, IN (Comcast Cable)

BROOK—See KENTLAND, IN (Mediacom)

▲ **BROOKLYN**—Formerly served by CableDirect. No longer in operation

BROOKSTON—See MONTICELLO, IN (Comcast Cable)

▲ **BROOKVILLE (TOWN)**—Comcast Cable

BROWN COUNTY (WESTERN PORTION)—See BLOOMINGTON, IN (Comcast Cable)

BROWN COUNTY—See NASHVILLE, IN (Avenue Broadband Communications)

BROWNSBURG (TOWN)—See INDIANAPOLIS, IN (Comcast Cable)

BROWNSBURG—See INDIANAPOLIS (portions), IN (Bright House Networks)

▲ **BROWNSTOWN**—Comcast Cable

BRUCE LAKE—See WINAMAC, IN (TV Cable of Rensselaer Inc.)

BRUCEVILLE—See VINCENNES, IN (Avenue Broadband Communications)

BRYANT—See PORTLAND, IN (Comcast Cable)

BUCK CREEK—See LAFAYETTE, IN (Comcast Cable)

BUFFALO—See MONTICELLO, IN (Comcast Cable)

BUNKER HILL—See PERU, IN (Comcast Cable)

BURKET—See SOUTH BEND, IN (Comcast Cable)

BURLINGTON—See MONTICELLO, IN (Comcast Cable)

BURNETTSVILLE—See MONTICELLO, IN (Comcast Cable)

▲ **BUTLER**—Mediacom

BUTLERVILLE—See SEYMOUR, IN (Comcast Cable)

CADIZ—See ANDERSON, IN (Comcast Cable)

CAMBRIDGE CITY—See RICHMOND, IN (Comcast Cable)

CAMDEN—See MONTICELLO, IN (Comcast Cable)

▲ **CAMPBELLSBURG**—Insight Communications. Now served by LOUISVILLE, KY [KY0001]

CANNELTON—See TELL CITY, IN (Comcast Cable)

CANTERBURY GREEN—See FORT WAYNE, IN (Comcast Cable)

▲ **CARBON**—Avenue Broadband Communications

▲ **CARLISLE**—Formerly served by Almega Cable. No longer in operation

CARMEL—See INDIANAPOLIS (portions), IN (Bright House Networks)

CARROLL COUNTY—See MONTICELLO, IN (Comcast Cable)

CARTHAGE—See ANDERSON, IN (Comcast Cable)

CASS COUNTY—See KOKOMO, IN (Comcast Cable)

CASS COUNTY—See LOGANSPORT, IN (Comcast Cable)

▲ **CATARACT LAKE**—Formerly served by Longview Communications. No longer in operation

CEDARVILLE—See KENDALLVILLE, IN (Mediacom)

▲ **CENTER POINT**—Formerly served by CableDirect. No longer in operation

CENTER TWP. (VANDERBURGH COUNTY)—See EVANSVILLE, IN (Insight Communications)

▲ **CENTERTON**—Avenue Broadband Communications

CENTERVILLE—See RICHMOND, IN (Comcast Cable)

CEYLON—See PORTLAND, IN (Comcast Cable)

CHALMERS—See MONTICELLO, IN (Comcast Cable)

CHANDLER—See NEWBURGH, IN (Time Warner Cable)

CHESTERFIELD—See ANDERSON, IN (Comcast Cable)

CHESTERTON—See LA PORTE, IN (Comcast Cable)

▲ **CHRISNEY**—Formerly served by CableDirect. No longer in operation

CHRISNEY—See SANTA CLAUS, IN (Avenue Broadband Communications)

CHRISTMAS LAKE VILLAGE—See SANTA CLAUS, IN (Avenue Broadband Communications)

CHURUBUSCO—See LIGONIER, IN (Mediacom)

CICERO—See NOBLESVILLE, IN (Comcast Cable)

CIRCLEVILLE—See RUSHVILLE, IN (Comcast Cable)

CLARKS HILL—See THORNTOWN, IN (Comcast Cable)

▲ **CLAY CITY**—Formerly served by Global Com Inc. No longer in operation

CLAY COUNTY (NORTH CENTRAL PORTION)—See BRAZIL, IN (Avenue Broadband Communications)

CLAY TWP.—See INDIANAPOLIS (portions), IN (Bright House Networks)

CLAYTON—See COATESVILLE, IN (Avenue Broadband Communications)

CLEAR CREEK—See BLOOMINGTON, IN (Comcast Cable)

▲ **CLEAR LAKE**—Longview Communications. Now served by ANGOLA, IN [IN0034]

CLEAR LAKE—See ANGOLA, IN (Mediacom)

CLERMONT—See INDIANAPOLIS, IN (Comcast Cable)

CLIFFORD—See COLUMBUS, IN (Comcast Cable)

CLINTON COUNTY (NORTHWESTERN PORTION)—See LAFAYETTE, IN (Comcast Cable)

CLINTON COUNTY—See FRANKFORT, IN (Comcast Cable)

▲ **CLINTON**—Avenue Broadband Communications

▲ **CLOVERDALE**—Indiana Communications

▲ **COAL CITY**—Formerly served by CableDirect. No longer in operation

COALMONT—See JASONVILLE, IN (Suddenlink Communications)

▲ **COATESVILLE**—Avenue Broadband Communications

COLFAX—See LINDEN, IN (TDS Cable Services)

COLUMBIA CITY—See KENDALLVILLE, IN (Mediacom)

▲ **COLUMBUS**—Comcast Cable

▲ **CONNERSVILLE**—Comcast Cable

CONVERSE—See SWEETSER, IN (Oak Hill Cablevision Inc.)

CORDRY LAKE—See NASHVILLE, IN (Avenue Broadband Communications)

▲ **CORUNNA**—Formerly served by CableDirect. No longer in operation

▲ **COVINGTON**—Comcast Cable

COWAN—See MUNCIE, IN (Comcast Cable)

CRAIGVILLE—See BLUFFTON, IN (Mediacom)

▲ **CRAWFORD COUNTY (portions)**—Charter Communications. Now served by MARENGO, IL [IL0370]

CRAWFORD COUNTY—See MARENGO, IN (Avenue Broadband Communications)

CRAWFORD—See SEYMOUR, IN (Comcast Cable)

▲ **CRAWFORDSVILLE**—Comcast Cable

CROMWELL—See LIGONIER, IN (Mediacom)

CROWS NEST—See INDIANAPOLIS, IN (Comcast Cable)

CULVER—See KNOX, IN (Mediacom)

CUMBERLAND—See INDIANAPOLIS, IN (Comcast Cable)

▲ **CYNTHIANA**—Now served by EVANSVILLE, IN [IN0006]

CYNTHIANA—See EVANSVILLE, IN (Insight Communications)

DALE—See SANTA CLAUS, IN (Avenue Broadband Communications)

DALEVILLE—See MUNCIE, IN (Comcast Cable)

DANVILLE (TOWN)—See INDIANAPOLIS, IN (Comcast Cable)

DANVILLE—See INDIANAPOLIS (portions), IN (Bright House Networks)

▲ **DARLINGTON**—Indiana Communications

DARMSTADT—See EVANSVILLE, IN (Insight Communications)

DAVIESS COUNTY (PORTIONS)—See ODON, IN (Suddenlink Communications)

DAVIESS COUNTY—See VINCENNES, IN (Avenue Broadband Communications)

DAYTON—See LAFAYETTE, IN (Comcast Cable)

DE KALB COUNTY—See KENDALLVILLE, IN (Mediacom)

DE SOTO—See MUNCIE, IN (Comcast Cable)

DEARBORN COUNTY (UNINCORPORATED AREAS)—See LAWRENCEBURG, IN (Comcast Cable)

DECATUR COUNTY (PORTIONS)—See GREENSBURG, IN (Comcast Cable)

DECATUR—See BLUFFTON, IN (Mediacom)

▲ **DECKER**—Formerly served by CableDirect. No longer in operation

DELAWARE COUNTY—See HARTFORD CITY, IN (Comcast Cable)

DELAWARE COUNTY—See MUNCIE, IN (Comcast Cable)

DELPHI—See MONTICELLO, IN (Comcast Cable)

DENVER—See PERU, IN (Comcast Cable)

▲ **DESOTO**—Comcast Cable. Now served by MUNCIE, IN [IN0014]

DILLSBORO—See LAWRENCEBURG, IN (Comcast Cable)

▲ **DISTRICT OF SWEETWATER**—Avenue Broadband Communications. Now served by NASHVILLE, IN [IN0099]

DISTRICT OF SWEETWATER—See NASHVILLE, IN (Avenue Broadband Communications)

DUBLIN—See RICHMOND, IN (Comcast Cable)

DUBOIS COUNTY (PORTIONS)—See JASPER, IN (Avenue Broadband Communications)

▲ **DUBOIS COUNTY**—Formerly served by CableDirect. No longer in operation

DUBOIS COUNTY—See JASPER, IN (Insight Communications)

DUGGER—See JASONVILLE, IN (Suddenlink Communications)

DUNE ACRES—See LA PORTE, IN (Comcast Cable)

DUNELAND BEACH—See MICHIGAN CITY, IN (Comcast Cable)

DUNKIRK—See PORTLAND, IN (Comcast Cable)

DUNREITH—See ANDERSON, IN (Comcast Cable)

▲ **DUPONT**—Formerly served by CableDirect. No longer in operation

EAST GERMANTOWN—See RICHMOND, IN (Comcast Cable)

EATON—See HARTFORD CITY, IN (Comcast Cable)

ECKERTY—See MARENGO, IN (Avenue Broadband Communications)

▲ **ECONOMY**—Formerly served by CableDirect. No longer in operation

EDGEWOOD—See ANDERSON, IN (Comcast Cable)

▲ **EDINBURGH**—Avenue Broadband Communications. Now served by NASHVILLE, IN [IN0099]

EDINBURGH—See NASHVILLE, IN (Avenue Broadband Communications)

EDWARDSPORT—See VINCENNES, IN (Avenue Broadband Communications)

▲ **ELBERFELD**—Avenue Broadband Communications

▲ **ELIZABETH (town)**—Formerly served by Windjammer Cable. No longer in operation

ELIZABETHTOWN—See COLUMBUS, IN (Comcast Cable)

▲ **ELKHART**—Comcast Cable. No longer in operation

ELLETTSVILLE—See BLOOMINGTON, IN (Comcast Cable)

ELNORA—See ODON, IN (Suddenlink Communications)

ELWOOD—See ANDERSON, IN (Comcast Cable)

▲ **ENGLISH**—Avenue Broadband Communications

ETNA GREEN—See SOUTH BEND, IN (Comcast Cable)

▲ **EVANSVILLE**—Insight Communications

▲ **EVANSVILLE**—WOW! Internet Cable & Phone

EVERTON—See CONNERSVILLE, IN (Comcast Cable)

FAIRLAND—See SHELBYVILLE, IN (Comcast Cable)

FAIRMOUNT—See HARTFORD CITY, IN (Comcast Cable)

FAIRVIEW PARK—See CLINTON, IN (Avenue Broadband Communications)

FARMERSBURG—See JASONVILLE, IN (Suddenlink Communications)

FARMLAND—See MUNCIE, IN (Comcast Cable)

FAYETTE COUNTY (PORTIONS)—See CONNERSVILLE, IN (Comcast Cable)

▲ **FERDINAND**—Avenue Broadband Communications

▲ **FILLMORE**—Formerly served by Global Com Inc. No longer in operation

▲ **FISH LAKE**—Formerly served by CableDirect. No longer in operation

FISHERS—See NOBLESVILLE, IN (Comcast Cable)

▲ **FLAT ROCK**—Suscom. Now served by SHELBYVILLE, IN [IN0042]

FLAT ROCK—See SHELBYVILLE, IN (Comcast Cable)

▲ **FLORA**—Comcast Cable

FORT BENJAMIN HARRISON—See INDIANAPOLIS, IN (Comcast Cable)

▲ **FORT BRANCH**—Now served by EVANSVILLE, IN [IN0006]

FORT BRANCH—See EVANSVILLE, IN (Insight Communications)

▲ **FORT WAYNE**—Comcast Cable

FORTVILLE—See INDIANAPOLIS (portions), IN (Bright House Networks)

FOUNTAIN CITY—See RICHMOND, IN (Comcast Cable)

FOUNTAIN COUNTY—See ATTICA, IN (Comcast Cable)

FOWLER—See ATTICA, IN (Comcast Cable)

FOWLERTON—See HARTFORD CITY, IN (Comcast Cable)

▲ **FRANCESVILLE**—Mediacom. Now served by SAN PIERRE, IN [IN0221]

FRANCESVILLE—See SAN PIERRE, IN (Mediacom)

▲ **FRANCISCO**—Formerly served by Almega Cable. No longer in operation

▲ **FRANKFORT**—Comcast Cable

FRANKLIN COUNTY—See BROOKVILLE (town), IN (Comcast Cable)

▲ **FRANKLIN**—Insight Communications. Now served by GREENWOOD, IN [IN0023]

FRANKLIN—See GREENWOOD, IN (Comcast Cable)

▲ **FRANKTON**—Formerly served by Longview Communications. No longer in operation

FREELANDVILLE—See VINCENNES, IN (Avenue Broadband Communications)

▲ **FREETOWN**—Formerly served by CableDirect. No longer in operation

FREMONT—See ANGOLA, IN (Mediacom)

▲ **FRENCH LICK**—Avenue Broadband Communications. Now served by MITCHELL, IN [IN0061]

FRENCH LICK—See MITCHELL, IN (Avenue Broadband Communications)

FULTON COUNTY (WESTERN PORTION)—See WINAMAC, IN (TV Cable of Rensselaer Inc.)

FULTON COUNTY—See SOUTH BEND, IN (Comcast Cable)

GALVESTON—See KOKOMO, IN (Comcast Cable)

GARDEN CITY—See COLUMBUS, IN (Comcast Cable)

GARRETT—See KENDALLVILLE, IN (Mediacom)

▲ **GARY**—Comcast Cable. Now served by CHICAGO (southern suburbs), IL [IL0008]

GAS CITY—See MARION, IN (Bright House Networks)

▲ **GASTON**—Formerly served by Longview Communications. No longer in operation

GEIST LAKE—See NOBLESVILLE, IN (Comcast Cable)

GENEVA—See PORTLAND, IN (Comcast Cable)

GERMAN TWP. (VANDERBURGH COUNTY)—See EVANSVILLE, IN (Insight Communications)

GIBSON COUNTY—See EVANSVILLE, IN (Insight Communications)

▲ **GLENWOOD**—Formerly served by CableDirect. No longer in operation

▲ **GOLDEN LAKE**—Formerly served by CableDirect. No longer in operation

GOODLAND—See KENTLAND, IN (Mediacom)

GOSHEN—See SOUTH BEND, IN (Comcast Cable)

GOSHEN—See NEW PARIS, IN (Quality Cablevision)

▲ **GOSPORT (town)**—Insight Communications. Now served by BLOOMINGTON, IN [IN0016]

GOSPORT—See BLOOMINGTON, IN (Comcast Cable)

GRABILL—See KENDALLVILLE, IN (Mediacom)

GRAND BEACH (VILLAGE)—See MICHIGAN CITY, MI (Comcast Cable)

GRANT COUNTY—See MARION, IN (Bright House Networks)

GRANT COUNTY—See HARTFORD CITY, IN (Comcast Cable)

GRANT PARK (VILLAGE)—See ROSELAWN, IL (Mediacom)

GRANTSBURG—See MARENGO, IN (Avenue Broadband Communications)

▲ **GREENCASTLE**—Comcast Cable

GREENDALE—See LAWRENCEBURG, IN (Comcast Cable)

GREENE COUNTY (EASTERN PORTION)—See BLOOMINGTON, IN (Comcast Cable)

GREENE COUNTY (WESTERN PORTION)—See JASONVILLE, IN (Suddenlink Communications)

GREENE COUNTY—See LINTON, IN (Comcast Cable)

GREENFIELD—See NOBLESVILLE, IN (Comcast Cable)

▲ **GREENS FORK**—Formerly served by CableDirect. No longer in operation

GREENSBORO—See ANDERSON, IN (Comcast Cable)

▲ **GREENSBURG**—Comcast Cable

GREENTOWN—See KOKOMO, IN (Comcast Cable)

▲ **GREENWOOD**—Comcast Cable

▲ **GRIFFIN (town)**—Formerly served by CableDirect. No longer in operation

GRISSOM AFB—See PERU, IN (Comcast Cable)

GROVERTOWN—See SAN PIERRE, IN (Mediacom)

GUILFORD—See LAWRENCEBURG, IN (Comcast Cable)

HAGERSTOWN—See RICHMOND, IN (Comcast Cable)

HAMILTON COUNTY—See INDIANAPOLIS, IN (Comcast Cable)

HAMILTON COUNTY—See NOBLESVILLE, IN (Comcast Cable)

HAMILTON TWP.—See MUNCIE, IN (Comcast Cable)

HAMILTON—See ANGOLA, IN (Mediacom)

▲ **HAMLET**—Formerly served by CableDirect. No longer in operation

▲ **HAMMOND**—Comcast Cable. Now served by CHICAGO (southern suburbs), IL [IL0008]

▲ **HAMMOND**—WOW! Internet Cable & Phone

HANCOCK COUNTY (PORTIONS)—See NOBLESVILLE, IN (Comcast Cable)

HANCOCK COUNTY—See INDIANAPOLIS, IN (Comcast Cable)

HANOVER—See MADISON, IN (Time Warner Cable)

▲ **HARDINSBURG**—Formerly served by CableDirect. No longer in operation

HARLAN—See KENDALLVILLE, IN (Mediacom)

▲ **HARMONY**—Avenue Broadband Communications

HARRISON TWP.—See MUNCIE, IN (Comcast Cable)

▲ **HARTFORD CITY**—Comcast Cable

HARTSVILLE—See COLUMBUS, IN (Comcast Cable)

▲ **HATFIELD**—Now served by OWENSBORO, KY [KY0004]

HAUBSTADT—See EVANSVILLE, IN (Insight Communications)

▲ **HAYDEN**—Formerly served by CableDirect. No longer in operation

▲ **HEBRON**—Comcast Cable. Now served by CHICAGO (southern suburbs), IL [IL0008]

HENDERSON COUNTY (UNINCORPORATED AREAS)—See EVANSVILLE, KY (Insight Communications)

HENDERSON—See EVANSVILLE, KY (Insight Communications)

HENDRICKS COUNTY (PORTIONS)—See MONROVIA, IN (Comcast Cable)

HENDRICKS COUNTY (PORTIONS)—See JAMESTOWN, IN (Indiana Communications)

HENDRICKS COUNTY (SOUTHERN PORTION)—See COATESVILLE, IN (Avenue Broadband Communications)

HENRY COUNTY (PORTIONS)—See ANDERSON, IN (Comcast Cable)

HERBST—See SWAYZEE, IN (The Swayzee Telephone Co.)

▲ **HERITAGE LAKE**—Formerly served by Global Com Inc. No longer in operation

HIDDEN VALLEY LAKE—See LAWRENCEBURG, IN (Comcast Cable)

▲ **HILLSBORO**—Formerly served by Longview Communications. No longer in operation

▲ **HILLSDALE**—Formerly served by CableDirect. No longer in operation

▲ **HOAGLAND**—Formerly served by CableDirect. No longer in operation

▲ **HOLLAND**—Formerly served by CableDirect. No longer in operation

▲ **HOLTON**—Formerly served by CableDirect. No longer in operation

HOMECROFT—See INDIANAPOLIS, IN (Comcast Cable)

HOPE—See SHELBYVILLE, IN (Comcast Cable)

HOWARD COUNTY—See KOKOMO, IN (Comcast Cable)

HOWE—See LAGRANGE, IN (Mediacom)

HUNTERTOWN—See FORT WAYNE, IN (Comcast Cable)

HUNTINGBURG—See JASPER, IN (Insight Communications)

HUNTINGTON COUNTY (PORTIONS)—See FORT WAYNE, IN (Comcast Cable)

HUNTINGTON COUNTY—See HUNTINGTON, IN (Comcast Cable)

▲ **HUNTINGTON**—Comcast Cable

HUNTSVILLE—See ANDERSON, IN (Comcast Cable)

HYMERA—See JASONVILLE, IN (Suddenlink Communications)

IDAVILLE—See MONTICELLO, IN (Comcast Cable)

▲ **INDIANAPOLIS (PORTIONS)**—Bright House Networks

▲ **INDIANAPOLIS**—Formerly served by Sprint Corp. No longer in operation

▲ **INDIANAPOLIS**—Comcast Cable

INGALLS—See INDIANAPOLIS (portions), IN (Bright House Networks)

IRELAND—See JASPER, IN (Avenue Broadband Communications)

JACKSON COUNTY—See SEYMOUR, IN (Comcast Cable)

JALAPA—See SWEETSER, IN (Oak Hill Cablevision Inc.)

▲ **JAMESTOWN**—Indiana Communications

▲ **JASONVILLE**—Suddenlink Communications

JASPER COUNTY (PORTIONS)—See RENSSELAER, IN (TV Cable of Rensselaer Inc.)

JASPER COUNTY (WESTERN PORTION)—See ROSELAWN, IN (Mediacom)

JASPER COUNTY—See MONTICELLO, IN (Comcast Cable)

▲ **JASPER**—Avenue Broadband Communications

▲ **JASPER**—Insight Communications

JAY COUNTY—See PORTLAND, IN (Comcast Cable)

JEFFERSON COUNTY (PORTIONS)—See MADISON, IN (Time Warner Cable)

▲ **JEFFERSON TWP. (Elkhart County)**—Comcast Cable. Now served by SOUTH BEND, IN [IN0005]

JEFFERSON TWP.—See SOUTH BEND, IN (Comcast Cable)

JEFFERSON—See FRANKFORT, IN (Comcast Cable)

▲ **JEFFERSONVILLE**—Insight Communications. Now served by LOUISVILLE, KY [KY0001]

JENNINGS COUNTY—See SEYMOUR, IN (Comcast Cable)

JOHNSON COUNTY—See GREENWOOD, IN (Comcast Cable)

JONESBORO—See MARION, IN (Bright House Networks)

JONESVILLE—See COLUMBUS, IN (Comcast Cable)

KANKAKEE COUNTY—See ROSELAWN, IL (Mediacom)

▲ **KEMPTON**—Formerly served by Country Cablevision. No longer in operation

▲ **KENDALLVILLE**—Mediacom

KENNARD—See NOBLESVILLE, IN (Comcast Cable)

▲ **KENTLAND**—Mediacom

▲ **KEWANNA**—Formerly served by CableDirect. No longer in operation

▲ **KIMMEL**—Formerly served by CableDirect. No longer in operation

▲ **KINGMAN**—Formerly served by CableDirect. No longer in operation

KINGSBURY—See LA PORTE, IN (Comcast Cable)

KINGSFORD HEIGHTS—See LA PORTE, IN (Comcast Cable)

KINGSLAND—See BLUFFTON, IN (Mediacom)

KNIGHT TWP.—See EVANSVILLE, IN (Insight Communications)

▲ **KNIGHTSTOWN**—Insight Communications. Now served by ANDERSON, IN [IN0012]

KNIGHTSTOWN—See ANDERSON, IN (Comcast Cable)

▲ **KNIGHTSVILLE**—Avenue Broadband Communications

KNOX COUNTY (PORTIONS)—See ODON, IN (Suddenlink Communications)

KNOX COUNTY—See VINCENNES, IN (Avenue Broadband Communications)

▲ **KNOX**—Mediacom

▲ **KOKOMO**—Comcast Cable

KOONTZ LAKE—See SAN PIERRE, IN (Mediacom)

KOONTZ LAKE—See WALKERTON, IN (Mediacom)

KOSCIUSKO COUNTY—See SOUTH BEND, IN (Comcast Cable)

KOSCIUSKO COUNTY—See NORTH WEBSTER, IN (Mediacom)

▲ **KOUTS**—Mediacom. Now served by ROSELAWN, IN [IN0316]

KOUTS—See ROSELAWN, IN (Mediacom)

LA CROSSE—See ROSELAWN, IN (Mediacom)

▲ **LA FONTAINE**—Formerly served by Longview Communications. No longer in operation

LA PAZ—See WALKERTON, IN (Mediacom)

LA PORTE COUNTY (UNINCORPORATED AREAS)—See MICHIGAN CITY, IN (Comcast Cable)

▲ **LA PORTE MOBILE HOME PARK**—North American Cablevision. Now served by LA PORTE, IN [IN0009]

▲ **LA PORTE**—Comcast Cable

LADOGA—See ROACHDALE, IN (Indiana Communications)

▲ **LAFAYETTE**—Comcast Cable

▲ **LAGRANGE**—Mediacom

▲ **LAGRO**—Formerly served by CableDirect. No longer in operation

▲ **LAKE CICOTT**—Insight Communications. Now served by LOGANSPORT, IN [IN0037]

LAKE CICOTT—See LOGANSPORT, IN (Comcast Cable)

LAKE COUNTY (SOUTHERN PORTION)—See ROSELAWN, IN (Mediacom)

LAKE HART (TOWN)—See INDIANAPOLIS, IN (Comcast Cable)

▲ **LAKE OF THE FOUR SEASONS**—Comcast Cable. Now served by CHICAGO (southern suburbs), IL [IL0008]

▲ **LAKE SANTEE**—Formerly served by CableDirect. No longer in operation

LAKE VILLAGE—See ROSELAWN, IN (Mediacom)

LAKETON—See NORTH MANCHESTER, IN (Mediacom)

▲ **LAKEVILLE**—Mediacom. Now served by WALKERTON, IN [IN0081]

LAKEVILLE—See WALKERTON, IN (Mediacom)

LAOTTO—See KENDALLVILLE, IN (Mediacom)

▲ **LAPEL**—Formerly served by Longview Communications. No longer in operation

▲ **LARWILL**—Formerly served by CableDirect. No longer in operation

▲ **LAUREL TWP.**—Formerly served by CableDirect. No longer in operation

LAWRENCE COUNTY (NORTHERN PORTION)—See BLOOMINGTON, IN (Comcast Cable)

LAWRENCE COUNTY (PORTIONS)—See VINCENNES, IL (Avenue Broadband Communications)

LAWRENCE COUNTY (PORTIONS)—See BEDFORD, IN (Comcast Cable)

LAWRENCE COUNTY (UNINCORPORATED AREAS)—See MITCHELL, IN (Avenue Broadband Communications)

LAWRENCE—See INDIANAPOLIS, IN (Comcast Cable)

▲ **LAWRENCEBURG**—Comcast Cable

LAWRENCEVILLE—See VINCENNES, IL (Avenue Broadband Communications)

▲ **LEAVENWORTH**—Formerly served by CableDirect. No longer in operation

▲ **LEBANON**—Now served by NOBLESVILLE, IN [IN0020]

LEBANON—See NOBLESVILLE, IN (Comcast Cable)

LEESBURG—See NORTH WEBSTER, IN (Mediacom)

▲ **LEITERS FORD**—Formerly served by CableDirect. No longer in operation

LEO—See KENDALLVILLE, IN (Mediacom)

LEWISVILLE—See ANDERSON, IN (Comcast Cable)

▲ **LIBERTY (TOWN)**—Comcast Cable

LIBERTY CENTER—See BLUFFTON, IN (Mediacom)

▲ **LIBERTY MILLS**—Formerly served by CableDirect. No longer in operation

LIBERTY TWP.—See MUNCIE, IN (Comcast Cable)

▲ **LIGONIER**—Lig TV

▲ **LIGONIER**—Mediacom

▲ **LINDEN**—TDS Cable Services

▲ **LINTON**—Comcast Cable

LIZTON—See INDIANAPOLIS (portions), IN (Bright House Networks)

▲ **LOGANSPORT**—Comcast Cable

LONG BEACH—See MICHIGAN CITY, IN (Comcast Cable)

▲ **LOOGOOTEE**—Avenue Broadband Communications. Now served by VINCENNES, IN [IN0035]

LOOGOOTEE—See VINCENNES, IN (Avenue Broadband Communications)

▲ **LOON LAKE**—Formerly served by CableDirect. No longer in operation

LOSANTVILLE—See ANDERSON, IN (Comcast Cable)

LOST CREEK TWP. (NORTHEASTERN PORTION)—See BRAZIL, IN (Avenue Broadband Communications)

LYNN—See WINCHESTER, IN (Comcast Cable)

▲ **LYNNVILLE**—Formerly served by Avenue Broadband Communications. No longer in operation

▲ **LYONS (town)**—Insight Communications. Now served by BLOOMINGTON, IN [IN0016]

LYONS—See BLOOMINGTON, IN (Comcast Cable)

▲ **MACY**—Formerly served by Longview Communications. No longer in operation

MADISON COUNTY (PORTIONS)—See ANDERSON, IN (Comcast Cable)

▲ **MADISON**—Time Warner Cable

MALDEN—See ROSELAWN, IN (Mediacom)

▲ **MANILLA**—Formerly served by CableDirect. No longer in operation

▲ **MARENGO**—Avenue Broadband Communications

MARIAH HILL—See SANTA CLAUS, IN (Avenue Broadband Communications)

MARION COUNTY—See INDIANAPOLIS, IN (Comcast Cable)

MARION TWP.—See FORT WAYNE, IN (Comcast Cable)

▲ **MARION**—Bright House Networks

▲ **MARKLE**—Formerly served by Longview Communications. No longer in operation

MARKLEVILLE—See ANDERSON, IN (Comcast Cable)

▲ **MARSHALL COUNTY**—Formerly served by Windjammer Cable. No longer in operation

MARSHALL COUNTY—See SOUTH BEND, IN (Comcast Cable)

MARSHALL COUNTY—See WALKERTON, IN (Mediacom)

MARSHALL—See ROCKVILLE, IN (Suddenlink Communications)

▲ **MARTINSVILLE**—Comcast Cable

MCCORDSVILLE—See INDIANAPOLIS (portions), IN (Bright House Networks)

MCCORDSVILLE—See NOBLESVILLE, IN (Comcast Cable)

MECCA—See ROCKVILLE, IN (Suddenlink Communications)

MEDARYVILLE—See SAN PIERRE, IN (Mediacom)

▲ **MEDORA**—Insight Communications. Now served by BEDFORD, IN [IN0033]

MEDORA—See BEDFORD, IN (Comcast Cable)

▲ **MENTONE**—Formerly served by Longview Communications. No longer in operations

MERIDIAN HILLS—See INDIANAPOLIS, IN (Comcast Cable)

▲ **MEROM**—Formerly served by CableDirect. No longer in operation

▲ **MERRILLVILLE**—Comcast Cable. Now served by CHICAGO (southern suburbs), IL [IL0008]

▲ **METAMORA**—Formerly served by CableDirect. No longer in operation

MEXICO—See PERU, IN (Comcast Cable)

MIAMI COUNTY—See KOKOMO, IN (Comcast Cable)

▲ **MIAMI**—Formerly served by CableDirect. No longer in operation

MICHIANA (VILLAGE)—See MICHIGAN CITY, MI (Comcast Cable)

MICHIANA SHORES—See MICHIGAN CITY, IN (Comcast Cable)

▲ **MICHIANA**—Formerly served by Sprint Corp. No longer in operation

▲ **MICHIGAN CITY**—Comcast Cable

▲ **MICHIGANTOWN**—Formerly served by Country Cablevision. No longer in operation

▲ **MIDDLEBURY**—Comcast Cable. Now served by SOUTH BEND, IN [IN0005]

MIDDLEBURY—See SOUTH BEND, IN (Comcast Cable)

▲ **MIDDLETOWN (town)**—Insight Communications. Now served by ANDERSON, IN [IN0012]

MIDDLETOWN—See ANDERSON, IN (Comcast Cable)

MIDLAND—See JASONVILLE, IN (Suddenlink Communications)

MILAN—See LAWRENCEBURG, IN (Comcast Cable)

MILFORD—See NORTH WEBSTER, IN (Mediacom)

MILLERSBURG—See NEW PARIS, IN (Quality Cablevision)

▲ **MILROY**—Formerly served by CableDirect. No longer in operation

MILTON—See RICHMOND, IN (Comcast Cable)

MISHAWAKA—See SOUTH BEND, IN (Comcast Cable)

▲ **MITCHELL**—Avenue Broadband Communications

MODOC—See ANDERSON, IN (Comcast Cable)

MOMENCE—See ROSELAWN, IL (Mediacom)

MONON—See MONTICELLO, IN (Comcast Cable)

▲ **MONROE CITY**—Formerly served by Cebridge Connections. Now served by VINCENNES, IN [IN0035]

MONROE CITY—See VINCENNES, IN (Avenue Broadband Communications)

MONROE COUNTY (PORTIONS)—See BLOOMINGTON, IN (Comcast Cable)

MONROE TWP.—See MUNCIE, IN (Comcast Cable)

MONROE—See BLUFFTON, IN (Mediacom)

▲ **MONROEVILLE (TOWN)**—Comcast Cable

▲ **MONROVIA**—Comcast Cable

▲ **MONTEREY**—Formerly served by CableDirect. No longer in operation

▲ **MONTEZUMA**—Indiana Communications

MONTGOMERY COUNTY (PORTIONS)—See CRAWFORDSVILLE, IN (Comcast Cable)

MONTGOMERY COUNTY (PORTIONS)—See NEW MARKET, IN (Indiana Communications)

▲ **MONTGOMERY**—Formerly served by CableDirect. No longer in operation

▲ **MONTICELLO**—Comcast Cable

MONTPELIER—See PERU, IN (Comcast Cable)

MOONVILLE—See ANDERSON, IN (Comcast Cable)

MOORELAND—See ANDERSON, IN (Comcast Cable)

MOORES HILL—See LAWRENCEBURG, IN (Comcast Cable)

MOORESVILLE—See INDIANAPOLIS, IN (Comcast Cable)

MORGAN COUNTY (NORTHERN PORTION)—See CENTERTON, IN (Avenue Broadband Communications)

MORGAN COUNTY (PORTIONS)—See MONROVIA, IN (Comcast Cable)

MORGAN COUNTY—See INDIANAPOLIS, IN (Comcast Cable)

MORGAN COUNTY—See MARTINSVILLE, IN (Comcast Cable)

▲ **MORGANTOWN**—Avenue Broadband Communications

▲ **MOROCCO**—TV Cable of Rensselaer Inc.

MORRIS—See BATESVILLE, IN (Comcast Cable)

▲ **MORRISTOWN**—Formerly served by Longview Communications. No longer in operation

MOUNT AUBURN—See RICHMOND, IN (Comcast Cable)

MOUNT PLEASANT TWP.—See MUNCIE, IN (Comcast Cable)

▲ **MOUNT SUMMIT**—Now served by ANDERSON, IN [IN0012]

MOUNT SUMMIT—See ANDERSON, IN (Comcast Cable)

▲ **MOUNT VERNON**—Now served by EVANSVILLE, IN [IN0006]

MOUNT VERNON—See EVANSVILLE, IN (Insight Communications)

MULBERRY—See LAFAYETTE, IN (Comcast Cable)

▲ **MUNCIE**—Comcast Cable

MURRAY—See BLUFFTON, IN (Mediacom)

NAPOLEON—See SUNMAN, IN (Enhanced Telecommunications Corp.)

NAPPANEE—See NORTH WEBSTER, IN (Mediacom)

▲ **NASHVILLE**—Avenue Broadband Communications

▲ **NEW ALBANY**—Insight Communications. Now served by LOUISVILLE, KY [KY0001]

NEW BUFFALO TWP.—See MICHIGAN CITY, MI (Comcast Cable)

▲ **NEW CASTLE**—Insight Communications. Now served by ANDERSON, IN [IN0012]

NEW CASTLE—See ANDERSON, IN (Comcast Cable)

NEW DURHAM TWP.—See ROSELAWN, IN (Mediacom)

NEW HARMONY—See WADESVILLE, IN (NewWave Communications)

NEW HAVEN—See FORT WAYNE, IN (Comcast Cable)

▲ **NEW MARKET**—Indiana Communications

NEW PALESTINE (PORTIONS)—See SHELBYVILLE, IN (Comcast Cable)

NEW PALESTINE—See NOBLESVILLE, IN (Comcast Cable)

▲ **NEW PARIS**—Quality Cablevision

NEW POINT—See SUNMAN, IN (Enhanced Telecommunications Corp.)

NEW RICHMOND—See LINDEN, IN (TDS Cable Services)

NEW ROSS—See JAMESTOWN, IN (Indiana Communications)

NEW WAVERLY—See PERU, IN (Comcast Cable)

NEW WHITELAND—See GREENWOOD, IN (Comcast Cable)

NEWBERN—See COLUMBUS, IN (Comcast Cable)

NEWBERRY—See ODON, IN (Suddenlink Communications)

▲ **NEWBURGH**—Time Warner Cable

NEWBURGH—See EVANSVILLE, IN (WOW! Internet Cable & Phone)

▲ **NEWPORT**—Indiana Communications

NEWTON COUNTY (NORTHERN PORTION)—See ROSELAWN, IN (Mediacom)

NOBLE COUNTY (PORTIONS)—See AVILLA, IN (Comcast Cable)

NOBLE COUNTY (PORTIONS)—See KENDALLVILLE, IN (Mediacom)

NOBLE COUNTY—See FORT WAYNE, IN (Comcast Cable)

▲ **NOBLESVILLE**—Comcast Cable

NORTH CROWS NEST—See INDIANAPOLIS, IN (Comcast Cable)

NORTH JUDSON—See KNOX, IN (Mediacom)

NORTH LIBERTY—See WALKERTON, IN (Mediacom)

▲ **NORTH MANCHESTER**—Mediacom

NORTH SALEM—See JAMESTOWN, IN (Indiana Communications)

▲ **NORTH VERNON**—Now served by SEYMOUR, IN [IN0039]

NORTH VERNON—See SEYMOUR, IN (Comcast Cable)

▲ **NORTH WEBSTER**—Mediacom

NORWAY—See MONTICELLO, IN (Comcast Cable)

▲ **OAKLAND CITY**—Charter Communications. Now served by WINSLOW (formerly Petersburg), IN [IN0118]

OAKLAND CITY—See WINSLOW, IN (Avenue Broadband Communications)

▲ **OAKTOWN**—Formerly served by Almega Cable. No longer in operation

OAKVILLE—See MUNCIE, IN (Comcast Cable)

▲ **ODON**—Suddenlink Communications

OGILVILLE—See COLUMBUS, IN (Comcast Cable)

OHIO COUNTY (PORTIONS)—See LAWRENCEBURG, IN (Comcast Cable)

OHIO TWP. (EASTERN PORTION)—See NEWBURGH, IN (Time Warner Cable)

OHIO TWP. (WESTERN PORTION)—See EVANSVILLE, IN (Insight Communications)

OLDENBURG—See BATESVILLE, IN (Comcast Cable)

▲ **OLIVER LAKE**—Formerly served by CableDirect. No longer in operation

OOLITIC—See BEDFORD, IN (Comcast Cable)

ORANGE COUNTY (UNINCORPORATED AREAS)—See MITCHELL, IN (Avenue Broadband Communications)

ORESTES—See ANDERSON, IN (Comcast Cable)

ORLEANS—See MITCHELL, IN (Avenue Broadband Communications)

OSCEOLA—See SOUTH BEND, IN (Comcast Cable)

OSGOOD—See LAWRENCEBURG, IN (Comcast Cable)

OSSIAN (TOWN)—See FORT WAYNE, IN (Comcast Cable)

▲ **OTTER LAKE**—Formerly served by CableDirect. No longer in operation

OTTERBEIN—See LAFAYETTE, IN (Comcast Cable)

▲ **OTWELL**—Formerly served by CableDirect. No longer in operation

OWEN COUNTY (PORTIONS)—See BLOOMINGTON, IN (Comcast Cable)

▲ **OWENSBURG**—Formerly served by CableDirect. No longer in operation

▲ **OWENSVILLE**—Sigecom. Now served by EVANSVILLE, IN [IN0006]

OWENSVILLE—See EVANSVILLE, IN (Insight Communications)

▲ **OXFORD**—Indiana Communications

▲ **PAINT MILL LAKE**—Formerly served by CableDirect. No longer in operation

PAOLI—See MITCHELL, IN (Avenue Broadband Communications)

PARAGON (TOWN)—See INDIANAPOLIS, IN (Comcast Cable)

PARAGON—See MONROVIA, IN (Comcast Cable)

PARK TWP.—See SOUTH BEND, MI (Comcast Cable)

PARKE COUNTY (PORTIONS)—See CLINTON, IN (Avenue Broadband Communications)

PARKE COUNTY (UNINCORPORATED AREAS)—See ROCKVILLE, IN (Suddenlink Communications)

PARKE COUNTY—See MONTEZUMA, IN (Indiana Communications)

PARKER CITY—See MUNCIE, IN (Comcast Cable)

▲ **PATOKA**—Formerly served by Almega Cable. No longer in operation

▲ **PATRICKSBURG**—Formerly served by CableDirect. No longer in operation

PATTON—See MONTICELLO, IN (Comcast Cable)

▲ **PEKIN**—Now served by LOUISVILLE, KY [KY0001]

PENDLETON—See ANDERSON, IN (Comcast Cable)

PENNVILLE—See PORTLAND, IN (Comcast Cable)

PERRY TWP.—See FORT WAYNE, IN (Comcast Cable)

PERRY TWP.—See EVANSVILLE, IN (Insight Communications)

▲ **PERRYSVILLE**—Indiana Communications

PERSHING—See RICHMOND, IN (Comcast Cable)

▲ **PERU**—Comcast Cable

PETERSBURG—See WINSLOW, IN (Avenue Broadband Communications)

PETERSVILLE—See COLUMBUS, IN (Comcast Cable)

PHILADELPHIA—See NOBLESVILLE, IN (Comcast Cable)

PIERCETON—See NORTH WEBSTER, IN (Mediacom)

▲ **PINE VILLAGE**—Formerly served by CableDirect. No longer in operation

PITTSBORO—See INDIANAPOLIS (portions), IN (Bright House Networks)

PITTSBURG—See MONTICELLO, IN (Comcast Cable)

PLAINFIELD—See INDIANAPOLIS (portions), IN (Bright House Networks)

PLAINFIELD—See INDIANAPOLIS, IN (Comcast Cable)

PLAINVILLE—See ODON, IN (Suddenlink Communications)

PLEASANT LAKE—See ANGOLA, IN (Mediacom)

PLEASANT TWP.—See FORT WAYNE, IN (Comcast Cable)

PLYMOUTH—See SOUTH BEND, IN (Comcast Cable)

PONETO—See BLUFFTON, IN (Mediacom)

▲ **PORTAGE**—Comcast Cable. Now served by CHICAGO (southern suburbs), IL [IL0008]

PORTER COUNTY (UNINCORPORATED AREAS)—See MICHIGAN CITY, IN (Comcast Cable)

PORTER—See LA PORTE, IN (Comcast Cable)

▲ **PORTLAND**—Comcast Cable

POSEY COUNTY—See EVANSVILLE, IN (Insight Communications)

POSEY COUNTY—See WADESVILLE, IN (NewWave Communications)

▲ **POSEYVILLE**—Now served by EVANSVILLE, IN [IN0006]

POSEYVILLE—See EVANSVILLE, IN (Insight Communications)

POTTAWATTOMIE PARK—See MICHIGAN CITY, IN (Comcast Cable)

▲ **PRETTY LAKE**—Formerly served by Longview Communications. No longer in operation

▲ **PRINCES LAKES**—Avenue Broadband Communications. Now served by NASHVILLE, IN [IN0099]

PRINCES LAKES—See NASHVILLE, IN (Avenue Broadband Communications)

▲ **PRINCETON**—Now served by EVANSVILLE, IN [IN0006]

PRINCETON—See EVANSVILLE, IN (Insight Communications)

PULASKI COUNTY (SOUTHERN PORTION)—See WINAMAC, IN (TV Cable of Rensselaer Inc.)

PUTNAM COUNTY (PORTIONS)—See GREENCASTLE, IN (Comcast Cable)

QUEENSVILLE—See SEYMOUR, IN (Comcast Cable)

RANDOLPH COUNTY—See MUNCIE, IN (Comcast Cable)

RANDOLPH COUNTY—See PORTLAND, IN (Comcast Cable)

RAVENSWOOD—See INDIANAPOLIS, IN (Comcast Cable)

REDDINGTON—See SEYMOUR, IN (Comcast Cable)

REDKEY—See PORTLAND, IN (Comcast Cable)

REMINGTON—See MONTICELLO, IN (Comcast Cable)

▲**RENSSELAER**—TV Cable of Rensselaer Inc.

REYNOLDS—See MONTICELLO, IN (Comcast Cable)

▲**RICHLAND**—Formerly served by Time Warner Cable. No longer in operation

▲**RICHMOND**—Comcast Cable

RIDGEVILLE—See WINCHESTER, IN (Comcast Cable)

RILEY—See TERRE HAUTE, IN (Time Warner Cable)

RIPLEY COUNTY—See LAWRENCEBURG, IN (Comcast Cable)

RISING SUN—See LAWRENCEBURG, IN (Comcast Cable)

▲**ROACHDALE**—Indiana Communications

▲**ROANN**—Formerly served by CableDirect. No longer in operation

ROANOKE—See FORT WAYNE, IN (Comcast Cable)

ROCHESTER—See SOUTH BEND, IN (Comcast Cable)

ROCKFIELD—See MONTICELLO, IN (Comcast Cable)

ROCKFORD—See SEYMOUR, IN (Comcast Cable)

▲**ROCKPORT**—Now served by OWENSBORO, KY [KY0004]

▲**ROCKVILLE**—Suddenlink Communications

▲**ROME CITY**—Mediacom

ROMNEY—See LINDEN, IN (TDS Cable Services)

▲**ROSEDALE**—Rapid Cable. Now served by CLINTON, IN [IN0049]

ROSEDALE—See CLINTON, IN (Avenue Broadband Communications)

ROSELAND—See SOUTH BEND, IN (Comcast Cable)

▲**ROSELAWN**—Mediacom

ROSEWOOD MANOR—See ROSELAWN, IN (Mediacom)

ROSSTOWN—See COLUMBUS, IN (Comcast Cable)

ROSSVILLE—See MONTICELLO, IN (Comcast Cable)

▲**ROYAL CENTER**—Formerly served by Longview Communications. No longer in operation

RUSH COUNTY (PORTIONS)—See ANDERSON, IN (Comcast Cable)

▲**RUSHVILLE**—Comcast Cable

▲**RUSSELLVILLE**—Formerly served by CableDirect. No longer in operation

RUSSIAVILLE—See KOKOMO, IN (Comcast Cable)

SALEM TWP.—See MUNCIE, IN (Comcast Cable)

▲**SALEM**—Insight Communications. Now served by LOUISVILLE, KY [KY0001]

▲**SAN PIERRE**—Mediacom

SANDBORN—See ODON, IN (Suddenlink Communications)

▲**SANTA CLAUS**—Avenue Broadband Communications

SARATOGA—See WINCHESTER, IN (Comcast Cable)

SCHNEIDER—See ROSELAWN, IN (Mediacom)

SCIPIO—See SEYMOUR, IN (Comcast Cable)

▲**SCOTTSBURG**—Insight Communications. Now served by LOUISVILLE, KY [KY0001]

SEELYVILLE—See BRAZIL, IN (Avenue Broadband Communications)

SELMA—See MUNCIE, IN (Comcast Cable)

▲**SEYMOUR**—Comcast Cable

SHADELAND—See LAFAYETTE, IN (Comcast Cable)

SHAMROCK—See HARTFORD CITY, IN (Comcast Cable)

SHARPSVILLE—See KOKOMO, IN (Comcast Cable)

SHELBURN—See JASONVILLE, IN (Suddenlink Communications)

SHELBY COUNTY—See INDIANAPOLIS, IN (Comcast Cable)

SHELBY—See ROSELAWN, IN (Mediacom)

▲**SHELBYVILLE**—Comcast Cable

▲**SHERIDAN**—Formerly served by Longview Communications. No longer in operation

SHERMAN TWP. (ST. JOSEPH COUNTY)—See SOUTH BEND, MI (Comcast Cable)

▲**SHIPSHEWANA**—Formerly served by Longview Communications. No longer in operation

▲**SHOALS**—Formerly served by Almega Cable. No longer in operation

▲**SILVER LAKE**—Comcast Cable. Now served by SOUTH BEND, IN [IN0005]

SILVER LAKE—See SOUTH BEND, IN (Comcast Cable)

SIMS—See SWAYZEE, IN (The Swayzee Telephone Co.)

SKINNER LAKE—See LIGONIER, IN (Mediacom)

SMITHVILLE—See BLOOMINGTON, IN (Comcast Cable)

▲**SOMERSET**—Formerly served by CableDirect. No longer in operation

▲**SOUTH BEND**—Formerly served by Sprint Corp. No longer in operation

▲**SOUTH BEND**—Comcast Cable

▲**SOUTH WHITLEY**—Mediacom. Now served by LIGONIER, IN [IN0156]

SOUTH WHITLEY—See LIGONIER, IN (Mediacom)

SOUTHPORT—See INDIANAPOLIS, IN (Comcast Cable)

SPEEDWAY—See INDIANAPOLIS, IN (Comcast Cable)

SPENCER COUNTY—See SANTA CLAUS, IN (Avenue Broadband Communications)

▲**SPENCER**—Insight Communications. Now served by BLOOMINGTON, IN [IN0016]

SPENCER—See BLOOMINGTON, IN (Comcast Cable)

SPENCERVILLE—See KENDALLVILLE, IN (Mediacom)

SPICELAND—See ANDERSON, IN (Comcast Cable)

SPRING GROVE—See RICHMOND, IN (Comcast Cable)

SPRING LAKE—See NOBLESVILLE, IN (Comcast Cable)

SPRINGPORT—See ANDERSON, IN (Comcast Cable)

▲**SPURGEON**—Formerly served by CableDirect. No longer in operation

ST. JOE—See KENDALLVILLE, IN (Mediacom)

ST. JOSEPH COUNTY—See SOUTH BEND, IN (Comcast Cable)

ST. JOSEPH COUNTY—See WALKERTON, IN (Mediacom)

ST. JOSEPH TWP.—See FORT WAYNE, IN (Comcast Cable)

ST. LEON—See SUNMAN, IN (Enhanced Telecommunications Corp.)

▲**ST. PAUL**—Formerly served by Longview Communications. No longer in operation

STANFORD—See BLOOMINGTON, IN (Comcast Cable)

STAR CITY—See WINAMAC, IN (TV Cable of Rensselaer Inc.)

STARKE COUNTY—See KNOX, IN (Mediacom)

STAUNTON—See BRAZIL, IN (Avenue Broadband Communications)

STEUBEN COUNTY (PORTIONS)—See ANGOLA, IN (Mediacom)

STILESVILLE—See COATESVILLE, IN (Avenue Broadband Communications)

STINESVILLE—See BLOOMINGTON, IN (Comcast Cable)

STRAUGHN—See ANDERSON, IN (Comcast Cable)

SULLIVAN COUNTY (PORTIONS)—See LINTON, IN (Comcast Cable)

▲**SULLIVAN**—Insight Communications. Now served by LINTON, IN [IN0052]

SULLIVAN—See LINTON, IN (Comcast Cable)

SUMAVA RESORTS—See ROSELAWN, IN (Mediacom)

▲**SUMMITVILLE**—Formerly served by Longview Communications. No longer in operation

SUNMAN (PORTIONS)—See LAWRENCEBURG, IN (Comcast Cable)

▲**SUNMAN**—Enhanced Telecommunications Corp.

▲**SWAYZEE**—The Swayzee Telephone Co.

▲**SWEETSER**—Oak Hill Cablevision Inc.

SWITZ CITY—See BLOOMINGTON, IN (Comcast Cable)

▲**SYRACUSE**—Mediacom. Now served by NORTH WEBSTER, IN [IN0038]

SYRACUSE—See NORTH WEBSTER, IN (Mediacom)

▲**TALMA**—Formerly served by CableDirect. No longer in operation

TASWELL—See MARENGO, IN (Avenue Broadband Communications)

TAYLORSVILLE—See COLUMBUS, IN (Comcast Cable)

▲**TELL CITY**—Comcast Cable

TERRE HAUTE CITY—See BRAZIL, IN (Avenue Broadband Communications)

▲**TERRE HAUTE**—Time Warner Cable

THAYER—See ROSELAWN, IN (Mediacom)

▲**THORNTOWN**—Comcast Cable

TIPPECANOE COUNTY (PORTIONS)—See THORNTOWN, IN (Comcast Cable)

TIPPECANOE COUNTY (SOUTHERN PORTION)—See LINDEN, IN (TDS Cable Services)

TIPPECANOE COUNTY—See LAFAYETTE, IN (Comcast Cable)

TIPPECANOE—See NORTH WEBSTER, IN (Mediacom)

▲TIPTON (portions)—Formerly served by Country Cablevision. No longer in operation

TIPTON COUNTY (PORTIONS)—See ANDERSON, IN (Comcast Cable)

TIPTON COUNTY—See KOKOMO, IN (Comcast Cable)

TIPTON—See NOBLESVILLE, IN (Comcast Cable)

TOCSIN—See BLUFFTON, IN (Mediacom)

▲TOPEKA—Formerly served by Lig TV. No longer in operation

▲TRAFALGAR—Formerly served by CableDirect. No longer in operation

TRAIL CREEK—See MICHIGAN CITY, IN (Comcast Cable)

TRI-LAKES—See LIGONIER, IN (Mediacom)

▲TROY—Formerly served by Avenue Broadband Communications. No longer in operation

▲TWELVE MILE—Formerly served by CableDirect. No longer in operation

▲TWIN LAKES—Formerly served by CableDirect. No longer in operation

ULEN—See NOBLESVILLE, IN (Comcast Cable)

▲UNION CITY—Time Warner Cable. Now served by DAYTON, OH [OH0011]

UNION TWP. (VANDERBURGH COUNTY)—See EVANSVILLE, IN (Insight Communications)

UNIONDALE—See BLUFFTON, IN (Mediacom)

UNIONVILLE—See BLOOMINGTON, IN (Comcast Cable)

UNIVERSAL—See CLINTON, IN (Avenue Broadband Communications)

UPLAND—See HARTFORD CITY, IN (Comcast Cable)

▲URBANA—Formerly served by CableDirect. No longer in operation

VALLONIA—See BEDFORD, IN (Comcast Cable)

VALPARAISO—See LA PORTE, IN (Comcast Cable)

▲VAN BUREN—Formerly served by Longview Communications. No longer in operation

VANDERBURGH COUNTY (PORTIONS)—See EVANSVILLE, IN (Insight Communications)

VANDERBURGH COUNTY (WESTERN PORTION)—See WADESVILLE, IN (NewWave Communications)

▲VEEDERSBURG—Comcast Cable

VERA CRUZ—See BLUFFTON, IN (Mediacom)

VERMILLION COUNTY (PORTIONS)—See CLINTON, IN (Avenue Broadband Communications)

VERNON—See SEYMOUR, IN (Comcast Cable)

VERSAILLES—See LAWRENCEBURG, IN (Comcast Cable)

▲VEVAY—Formerly served by Adelphia Communications. Now served by MADISON, IN [IN0046]

VEVAY—See MADISON, IN (Time Warner Cable)

VIGO COUNTY (PORTIONS)—See BRAZIL, IN (Avenue Broadband Communications)

VIGO COUNTY (PORTIONS)—See CLINTON, IN (Avenue Broadband Communications)

▲VINCENNES—Avenue Broadband Communications

WABASH COUNTY (PORTIONS)—See WABASH, IN (Comcast Cable)

▲WABASH—Comcast Cable

▲WADESVILLE—NewWave Communications

▲WAKARUSA—Comcast Cable. Now served by SOUTH BEND, IN [IN0005]

WAKARUSA—See SOUTH BEND, IN (Comcast Cable)

WALESBORO—See COLUMBUS, IN (Comcast Cable)

▲WALKERTON—Mediacom

▲WALTON—Formerly served by Longview Communications. No longer in operation

▲WANATAH—Mediacom. Now served by ROSELAWN, IN [IN0316]

WANATAH—See ROSELAWN, IN (Mediacom)

WARREN COUNTY—See ATTICA, IN (Comcast Cable)

WARREN PARK—See INDIANAPOLIS, IN (Comcast Cable)

▲WARREN—Warren Cable

WARRICK COUNTY—See EVANSVILLE, IN (Insight Communications)

WARRICK COUNTY—See NEWBURGH, IN (Time Warner Cable)

▲WARSAW—Comcast Cable. Now served by SOUTH BEND, IN [IN0005]

WARSAW—See SOUTH BEND, IN (Comcast Cable)

▲WASHINGTON—Charter Communications. Now served by VINCENNES, IN [IN0035]

WASHINGTON—See VINCENNES, IN (Avenue Broadband Communications)

WATERLOO—See KENDALLVILLE, IN (Mediacom)

▲WAVELAND—Formerly served by CableDirect. No longer in operation

WAYNE COUNTY (NORTHWESTERN PORTION)—See ANDERSON, IN (Comcast Cable)

WAYNE COUNTY—See RICHMOND, IN (Comcast Cable)

WAYNE TWP.—See FORT WAYNE, IN (Comcast Cable)

WAYNESVILLE—See COLUMBUS, IN (Comcast Cable)

▲WAYNETOWN—Indiana Communications

WELLS COUNTY—See FORT WAYNE, IN (Comcast Cable)

WELLS COUNTY—See BLUFFTON, IN (Mediacom)

WEST BADEN SPRINGS—See MITCHELL, IN (Avenue Broadband Communications)

WEST HARRISON—See LAWRENCEBURG, IN (Comcast Cable)

WEST LAFAYETTE—See LAFAYETTE, IN (Comcast Cable)

▲WEST LEBANON—Indiana Communications

WEST TERRE HAUTE—See TERRE HAUTE, IN (Time Warner Cable)

WESTFIELD—See NOBLESVILLE, IN (Comcast Cable)

WESTPHALIA—See ODON, IN (Suddenlink Communications)

▲WESTPORT—Now served by COLUMBUS, IN [IN0022]

WESTPORT—See COLUMBUS, IN (Comcast Cable)

WESTVILLE—See ROSELAWN, IN (Mediacom)

▲WHEATFIELD—Mediacom. Now served by ROSELAWN, IN [IN0316]

WHEATFIELD—See ROSELAWN, IN (Mediacom)

WHITE COUNTY—See MONTICELLO, IN (Comcast Cable)

WHITE COUNTY—See WADESVILLE, IL (NewWave Communications)

WHITELAND—See GREENWOOD, IN (Comcast Cable)

▲WHITESTOWN—Formerly served by Longview Communications. No longer in operation

WHITESTOWN—See INDIANAPOLIS (portions), IN (Bright House Networks)

WHITLEY COUNTY (PORTIONS)—See FORT WAYNE, IN (Comcast Cable)

WILFRED—See JASONVILLE, IN (Suddenlink Communications)

WILKENSON—See NOBLESVILLE, IN (Comcast Cable)

▲WILKINSON—Insight Communications. Now served by NOBLESVILLE, IN [IN0020]

WILLIAMS CREEK—See INDIANAPOLIS, IN (Comcast Cable)

▲WILLIAMSBURG—Formerly served by CableDirect. No longer in operation

▲WILLIAMSBURG—Windjammer Cable

WILLIAMSPORT—See ATTICA, IN (Comcast Cable)

▲WINAMAC—TV Cable of Rensselaer Inc.

▲WINCHESTER—Comcast Cable

WINDFALL—See KOKOMO, IN (Comcast Cable)

WINGATE—See LINDEN, IN (TDS Cable Services)

WINONA LAKE—See SOUTH BEND, IN (Comcast Cable)

▲WINSLOW—Avenue Broadband Communications

WOLCOTT—See MONTICELLO, IN (Comcast Cable)

WOLCOTTVILLE—See ROME CITY, IN (Mediacom)

WOODBURN—See FORT WAYNE, IN (Comcast Cable)

▲WORTHINGTON—Indiana Communications

WYNNEDALE—See INDIANAPOLIS, IN (Comcast Cable)

▲YANKEETOWN—Formerly served by Time Warner Cable. No longer in operation

YEOMAN—See MONTICELLO, IN (Comcast Cable)

YORKTOWN—See MUNCIE, IN (Comcast Cable)

▲YOUNG AMERICA—Formerly served by CableDirect. No longer in operation

▲ZANESVILLE—Formerly served by CableDirect. No longer in operation

ZIONSVILLE—See INDIANAPOLIS (portions), IN (Bright House Networks)

IOWA

ACKLEY—See IOWA FALLS, IA (Mediacom)

ACKWORTH—See DES MOINES, IA (Mediacom)

▲ADAIR—B & L Technologies LLC

▲ADEL—Mediacom. Now served by DES MOINES, IA [IA0001]

ADEL—See DES MOINES, IA (Mediacom)

▲AFTON—B & L Technologies LLC

AGENCY—See OTTUMWA, IA (Mediacom)

▲AINSWORTH—Starwest Inc.

▲AKRON—Premier Communications. Now served by SIOUX CENTER, IA [IA0076]

AKRON—See SIOUX CENTER, IA (Premier Communications)

ALBANY—See CLINTON, IL (Mediacom)

ALBIA—See CENTERVILLE, IA (Mediacom)

▲ALBION—Heart of Iowa Telecommunications. This cable system has converted to IPTV. See Albion, IA [IA5000]

▲**ALBION**—Heart of Iowa Communications. Formerly [IA0623]. This cable system has converted to IPTV

ALBURNETT—See SHELLSBURG, IA (USA Communications)

▲**ALDEN**—Formerly served by Latimer/Coulter Cablevision. No longer in operation

▲**ALEXANDER**—Formerly served by CableDirect. No longer in operation

▲**ALGONA**—Mediacom. Now served by FORT DODGE, IA [IA0011]

▲**ALGONA**—Algona Municipal Utilities

ALGONA—See FORT DODGE, IA (Mediacom)

▲**ALLEMAN**—Formerly served by Huxley Communications Corp. No longer in operation

▲**ALLERTON**—Formerly served by Longview Communications. No longer in operation

ALLISON—See DUMONT, IA (Dumont Cablevision)

▲**ALTA VISTA (TOWN)**—Alta Vista Municipal Cable

▲**ALTA**—ALTA-TEC

ALTA—See FORT DODGE, IA (Mediacom)

ALTON—See ORANGE CITY, IA (Premier Communications)

ALTOONA—See DES MOINES, IA (Mediacom)

AMANA—See CEDAR RAPIDS, IA (Mediacom)

▲**AMES**—Mediacom

ANAMOSA—See CEDAR RAPIDS, IA (Mediacom)

▲**ANDREW**—Andrew Telephone Co. Inc.

▲**ANITA**—WesTel Systems

ANKENY—See DES MOINES, IA (Mediacom)

▲**ANTHON**—Long Lines

APLINGTON—See WAVERLY, IA (Mediacom)

APPANOOSE COUNTY—See CENTERVILLE, IA (Mediacom)

ARCADIA—See BREDA, IA (Western Iowa Networks)

ARCADIA—See WESTSIDE, IA (Western Iowa Networks)

▲**ARLINGTON**—Alpine Communications LC

ARMSTRONG—See SPENCER, IA (Mediacom)

ARNOLDS PARK—See SPIRIT LAKE, IA (Mediacom)

▲**ARTHUR**—Sac County Mutual Telco

ASBURY—See DUBUQUE, IA (Mediacom)

▲**ASHTON**—Premier Communications. Now served by SHELDON, IA [IA0060]

ASHTON—See SHELDON, IA (HTC Cablecom)

ATALISSA—See CEDAR RAPIDS, IA (Mediacom)

▲**ATKINS**—Atkins Cablevision Inc.

▲**ATLANTIC**—Mediacom

AUBURN—See BREDA, IA (Western Iowa Networks)

AUDUBON—See ATLANTIC, IA (Mediacom)

▲**AURELIA**—NU-Telecom. This cable system has converted to IPTV. See Aurelia, IL [IA5021]

▲**AURELIA**—NU-Telecom. Formerly [IA0212]. This cable system has converted to IPTV

▲**AURORA**—Formerly served by Alpine Communications LC. No longer in operation

AVOCA—See ATLANTIC, IA (Mediacom)

AVOCA—See WALNUT, IA (Walnut Communications)

▲**AYRSHIRE**—ATC Cablevision

▲**BADGER**—Goldfield Communication Services Corp.

▲**BAGLEY**—Panora Cooperative Cablevision Assn. Inc.

BANCROFT—See BUFFALO CENTER, IA (Mediacom)

BARNES CITY—See DEEP RIVER, IA (Montezuma Mutual Telephone & Cable Co.)

BARNUM—See FORT DODGE, IA (Mediacom)

▲**BATAVIA**—Formerly served by Westcom. No longer in operation

BATAVIA—See OTTUMWA, IA (Mediacom)

▲**BATTLE CREEK**—Sac County Mutual Telco

BAXTER—See GILMAN, IA (Partner Communications)

▲**BAYARD**—Formerly served by Tele-Services Ltd. No longer in operation

BEACON—See OSKALOOSA, IA (Mediacom)

BEAMAN—See GLADBROOK, IA (Mediacom)

BEDFORD—See ATLANTIC, IA (Mediacom)

BELLE PLAINE—See CEDAR RAPIDS, IA (Mediacom)

▲**BELLEVUE**—IVUE Network. This cable system has converted to IPTV. See Bellevue, IA [IA5033]

▲**BELLEVUE**—IVUE Network. Formerly [IA0553]. This cable system has converted to IPTV

BELMOND—See FORT DODGE, IA (Mediacom)

▲**BENNETT**—F & B Cablevision

BERTRAM—See CEDAR RAPIDS, IA (Mediacom)

▲**BIRMINGHAM**—Starwest Inc. Now served by KEOSAUQUA, IA [IA0186]

BIRMINGHAM—See KEOSAUQUA, IA (Starwest Inc.)

BLACK HAWK COUNTY (PORTIONS)—See WATERLOO, IA (Mediacom)

▲**BLAIRSBURG**—Milford Cable TV

▲**BLAIRSTOWN**—Coon Creek Telephone & Cablevision

▲**BLAKESBURG**—Formerly served by Telnet South LC. No longer in operation

▲**BLENCOE**—Formerly served by Sky Scan Cable Co. No longer in operation

▲**BLENCOE**—Long Lines

▲**BLOCKTON**—B & L Technologies LLC

BLOOMFIELD—See CENTERVILLE, IA (Mediacom)

▲**BODE**—Video Services Ltd.

▲**BONAPARTE**—Mediacom. Now served by KEOSAUQUA, IA [IA0186]

BONAPARTE—See KEOSAUQUA, IA (Starwest Inc.)

BONDURANT—See DES MOINES, IA (Mediacom)

BOONE COUNTY (EASTERN PORTION)—See AMES, IA (Mediacom)

BOONE COUNTY (SOUTHERN PORTION)—See AMES, IA (Mediacom)

BOONE—See AMES, IA (Mediacom)

BOONEVILLE—See DES MOINES, IA (Mediacom)

BOXHOLM—See LEHIGH, IA (Lehigh Services Inc.)

▲**BOYDEN**—Premier Communications. Now served by SIOUX CENTER, IA [IA0076]

BOYDEN—See SIOUX CENTER, IA (Premier Communications)

▲**BRADDYVILLE**—Formerly served by CableDirect. No longer in operation

▲**BRANDON**—Formerly served by New Path Communications LC. No longer in operation

BRAYTON—See ELK HORN, IA (Marne & Elk Horn Telephone Co.)

▲**BREDA**—Western Iowa Networks

▲**BRIGHTON**—Starwest Inc.

▲**BRISTOW**—Dumont Cablevision. Now served by DUMONT, IA [IA0250]

BRISTOW—See DUMONT, IA (Dumont Cablevision)

BRITT—See MASON CITY, IA (Mediacom)

▲**BRONSON**—TelePartners. Now served by LAWTON, IA [IA0330]

BRONSON—See LAWTON, IA (Western Iowa Telephone)

▲**BROOKLYN**—Inter-County Cable Co.

BUENA VISTA COUNTY—See FORT DODGE, IA (Mediacom)

▲**BUFFALO CENTER**—Mediacom

▲**BUFFALO CENTER**—Winnebago Cooperative Telephone Assn.

▲**BURLINGTON**—Mediacom

BURT—See BUFFALO CENTER, IA (Mediacom)

BUSSEY—See DES MOINES, IA (Mediacom)

CALAMUS—See WHEATLAND, IA (F & B Cablevision)

▲**CALHOUN COUNTY (PORTIONS)**—Gowrie Cablevision

CALLENDER—See LEHIGH, IA (Lehigh Services Inc.)

CALMAR—See NEW HAMPTON, IA (Mediacom)

CALUMET—See MARCUS, IA (WesTel Systems)

CAMANCHE—See CLINTON, IA (Mediacom)

▲**CAMBRIDGE**—Huxley Communications Corp.

CANTRIL—See KEOSAUQUA, IA (Starwest Inc.)

CARLISLE—See DES MOINES, IA (Mediacom)

▲**CARROLL**—Mediacom. Now served by ATLANTIC, IA [IA0032]

CARROLL—See ATLANTIC, IA (Mediacom)

▲**CARSON**—Interstate Communications

CARTHAGE—See BURLINGTON, IL (Mediacom)

▲**CASCADE**—Cascade Communications

▲**CASEY**—Casey Cable Co.

▲**CEDAR FALLS**—Cedar Falls Municipal Communications Utility

CEDAR FALLS—See WATERLOO, IA (Mediacom)

▲**CEDAR RAPIDS**—Mediacom

▲**CENTER JUNCTION**—Center Junction Telephone Co.

CENTER POINT—See SHELLSBURG, IA (USA Communications)

▲**CENTERVILLE**—Mediacom

▲**CENTRAL CITY**—USA Communications. Now served by SHELLSBURG, IA [IA0255]

CENTRAL CITY—See SHELLSBURG, IA (USA Communications)

CERRO GORDO—See MASON CITY, IA (Mediacom)

CHARITON—See DES MOINES, IA (Mediacom)

▲ **CHARLES CITY**—Mediacom

CHARLOTTE—See CLINTON, IA (Mediacom)

▲ **CHARTER OAK**—Tip Top Communication. Now served by SCHLESWIG, IA [IA0231]

CHARTER OAK—See SCHLESWIG, IA (Tip Top Communication)

CHEROKEE—See FORT DODGE, IA (Mediacom)

▲ **CHESTER**—Formerly served by CableDirect. No longer in operation

▲ **CHURDAN**—Western Iowa Networks. No longer in operation

▲ **CINCINNATI**—B & L Technologies LLC

CLARE—See FORT DODGE, IA (Mediacom)

▲ **CLARENCE**—Clarence Cablevision

CLARINDA—See ATLANTIC, IA (Mediacom)

CLARION—See FORT DODGE, IA (Mediacom)

CLARKSVILLE—See TRIPOLI, IA (Butler-Bremer Communications)

CLEAR LAKE—See MASON CITY, IA (Mediacom)

▲ **CLEARFIELD**—B & L Technologies LLC

▲ **CLEGHORN**—Wetherell Cable TV System

CLEMONS—See ZEARING, IA (Minerva Valley Cablevision)

▲ **CLERMONT**—Alpine Communications LC. Now served by ARLINGTON, IA [IA0393]

CLERMONT—See ARLINGTON, IA (Alpine Communications LC)

CLINTON COUNTY—See CLINTON, IA (Mediacom)

▲ **CLINTON**—Mediacom

CLIVE—See DES MOINES, IA (Mediacom)

▲ **CLUTIER**—Farmers Cooperative Telephone Co. This cable system has converted to IPTV. See Clutier, IA [IA5077]

▲ **CLUTIER**—Farmers Cooperative Telephone Co. Formerly [IA0413]. This cable system has converted to IPTV

COALVILLE—See FORT DODGE, IA (Mediacom)

▲ **COGGON**—USA Communications

▲ **COLESBURG**—Formerly served by Alpine Communications LC. No longer in operation

COLFAX—See DES MOINES, IA (Mediacom)

▲ **COLLINS**—Formerly served by Huxley Communications Corp. No longer in operation

▲ **COLO**—Colo Telephone Co. This cable system has converted to IPTV. See COLO, IA [IA5003]

▲ **COLO**—Colo Telephone Co. Formerly [IA0416]. This cable system has converted to IPTV

COLUMBUS CITY—See BURLINGTON, IA (Mediacom)

▲ **COLUMBUS JUNCTION**—Mediacom. Now served by BURLINGTON, IA [IA0405]

COLUMBUS JUNCTION—See BURLINGTON, IA (Mediacom)

CONRAD—See GLADBROOK, IA (Mediacom)

▲ **COON RAPIDS**—Coon Rapids Municipal Cable System

CORALVILLE—See CEDAR RAPIDS, IA (Mediacom)

CORLEY—See EARLING, IA (Mutual Communications Services)

CORNELIA—See FORT DODGE, IA (Mediacom)

CORNING—See ATLANTIC, IA (Mediacom)

CORRECTIONVILLE—See SALIX, IA (Long Lines)

▲ **CORWITH**—Communications 1 Cablevision. Now served by KANAWHA, IA [IA0229]

▲ **CORWITH**—Communications 1 Network. Formerly served by Kanawha, IA [IA0229]. This cable system has converted to IPTV

CORYDON—See DES MOINES, IA (Mediacom)

▲ **COULTER**—Formerly served by Latimer/Coulter Cablevision. No longer in operation

CRAWFORD COUNTY (SOUTHERN PORTION)—See ATLANTIC, IA (Mediacom)

▲ **CRESCO**—Mediacom. Now served by OSAGE, IA [IA0085]

CRESCO—See OSAGE, IA (Mediacom)

▲ **CRESTON**—Mediacom. Now served by DES MOINES, IA [IA0001]

CRESTON—See DES MOINES, IA (Mediacom)

CURLEW—See HAVELOCK, IA (Northwest Communications Inc.)

CUSHING—See SCHALLER, IA (Comserv Ltd.)

▲ **CYLINDER**—Formerly served by ATC Cablevision. No longer in operation

DAKOTA CITY—See SIOUX CITY, NE (Cable One)

DAKOTA CITY—See FORT DODGE, IA (Mediacom)

DAKOTA COUNTY (PORTIONS)—See SIOUX CITY, NE (Cable One)

DAKOTA DUNES—See SIOUX CITY, SD (Cable One)

DALLAS CENTER—See DES MOINES, IA (Mediacom)

DALLAS COUNTY—See DES MOINES, IA (Mediacom)

DALLAS—See DES MOINES, IA (Mediacom)

▲ **DANBURY**—Long Lines

DANVILLE—See BURLINGTON, IA (Mediacom)

▲ **DAVIS CITY**—Formerly served by Telnet South LC. No longer in operation

▲ **DAYTON**—Lehigh Services Inc. Now served by LEHIGH, IA [IA0464]

DAYTON—See LEHIGH, IA (Lehigh Services Inc.)

DE WITT—See GRAND MOUND, IA (Grand Mound Cooperative Telephone)

DE WITT—See CLINTON, IA (Mediacom)

▲ **DECATUR**—Telnet South LC. Now served by DES MOINES, IA [IA0001]

DECATUR—See DES MOINES, IA (Mediacom)

▲ **DECORAH**—Mediacom

▲ **DEDHAM**—Templeton Telephone Co. Now served by TEMPLETON, IA [IA0338]

DEDHAM—See TEMPLETON, IA (Templeton Telephone Co.)

▲ **DEEP RIVER**—Montezuma Mutual Telephone & Cable Co.

▲ **DEFIANCE**—Farmers Mutual Telephone Co. Now served by EARLING, IA [IA0302]

DEFIANCE—See EARLING, IA (Mutual Communications Services)

DELAWARE COUNTY (PORTIONS)—See WAVERLY, IA (Mediacom)

▲ **DELHI**—New Century Communications

▲ **DELMAR**—F & B Cablevision

▲ **DELOIT**—Tip Top Communication

▲ **DELTA**—Formerly served by Longview Communications. No longer in operation

DENISON—See ATLANTIC, IA (Mediacom)

▲ **DENMARK**—Formerly served by Longview Communications. No longer in operation

DENVER—See WAVERLY, IA (Mediacom)

▲ **DES MOINES**—Mediacom

DESOTO—See DES MOINES, IA (Mediacom)

DEWAR—See WATERLOO, IA (Mediacom)

DEXTER—See DES MOINES, IA (Mediacom)

▲ **DIAGONAL**—B & L Technologies LLC

▲ **DICKENS**—Premier Communications

DIKE—See WAVERLY, IA (Mediacom)

▲ **DIXON**—Dixon Telephone Co.

▲ **DONAHUE**—Dixon Telephone Co. Now served by DIXON, IA [IA0358]

DONAHUE—See DIXON, IA (Dixon Telephone Co.)

▲ **DONNELLSON**—Formerly served by Longview Communications. No longer in operation

DOON—See SIOUX CENTER, IA (Premier Communications)

▲ **DOW CITY**—Formerly served by Tip Top Communications. No longer in operation

▲ **DOWS**—Dows Cablevision. No longer in operation

DUBUQUE COUNTY—See DUBUQUE, IA (Mediacom)

▲ **DUBUQUE**—Mediacom

▲ **DUMONT**—Dumont Cablevision

DUNCAN—See MASON CITY, IA (Mediacom)

DUNCOMBE—See LEHIGH, IA (Lehigh Services Inc.)

▲ **DUNKERTON**—Dunkerton Telephone Coop. This cable system has converted to IPTV. See Dunkerton, IA [IA5032]

▲ **DUNKERTON**—Dunkerton Telephone Coop. Formerly [IA0428]. This cable system has converted to IPTV

▲ **DUNLAP**—Tip Top Communication

DYERSVILLE—See DUBUQUE, IA (Mediacom)

DYSART—See AMES, IA (Mediacom)

EAGLE GROVE—See FORT DODGE, IA (Mediacom)

EARLHAM—See DES MOINES, IA (Mediacom)

▲ **EARLING**—Mutual Communications Services

▲ **EARLVILLE**—Formerly served by Alpine Communications LC. No longer in operation

EARLY—See CLEGHORN, IA (Wetherell Cable TV System)

EAST DUBUQUE—See DUBUQUE, IL (Mediacom)

▲ **EDDYVILLE**—Mediacom. Now served by CENTERVILLE, IA [IA0039]

EDDYVILLE—See CENTERVILLE, IA (Mediacom)

EDGEWOOD—See WAVERLY, IA (Mediacom)

ELBERON—See KEYSTONE, IA (Keystone Communications)

▲**ELDON**—Mediacom. Now served by CENTERVILLE, IA [IA0039]

ELDON—See CENTERVILLE, IA (Mediacom)

ELDORA—See IOWA FALLS, IA (Mediacom)

ELGIN—See NEW HAMPTON, IA (Mediacom)

▲**ELK HORN**—Marne & Elk Horn Telephone Co.

ELK RUN HEIGHTS—See WATERLOO, IA (Mediacom)

▲**ELKHART**—Huxley Communications Corp.

ELLIOT—See GRISWOLD, IA (Griswold Cable TV)

ELLSWORTH—See STRATFORD, IA (Complete Communications Service)

ELMA—See OSAGE, IA (Mediacom)

ELWOOD—See LOST NATION, IA (LN Satellite Communications Co.)

▲**ELY**—South Slope Coop. Communications Co. Formerly served by North Liberty, IA [IA0432]. This cable system has converted to IPTV

▲**EMERSON**—Interstate Communications

EMMETSBURG—See SPENCER, IA (Mediacom)

EPWORTH—See DUBUQUE, IA (Mediacom)

ERIE—See CLINTON, IL (Mediacom)

ESSEX—See ATLANTIC, IA (Mediacom)

ESTERVILLE—See SPENCER, IA (Mediacom)

EVANSDALE—See WATERLOO, IA (Mediacom)

▲**EXIRA**—Marne & Elk Horn Telephone Co. Now served by ELK HORN, IA [IA0123]

EXIRA—See ELK HORN, IA (Marne & Elk Horn Telephone Co.)

▲**FAIRBANK**—Mediacom. Now served by WAVERLY, IA [IA0021]

FAIRBANK—See WAVERLY, IA (Mediacom)

▲**FAIRFAX**—Formerly served by Starwest Inc. No longer in operation

FAIRFAX—See CEDAR RAPIDS, IA (Mediacom)

FAIRFIELD—See OTTUMWA, IA (Mediacom)

FAIRVIEW—See MARTELLE, IA (Martelle Communications Co-op)

FARLEY—See DUBUQUE, IA (Mediacom)

FARMERSBURG—See MONONA, IA (Northeast Iowa Telephone Co.)

▲**FARMINGTON**—Starwest Inc.

▲**FARRAGUT**—Western Iowa Networks

FAYETTE COUNTY (PORTIONS)—See WAVERLY, IA (Mediacom)

FAYETTE—See NEW HAMPTON, IA (Mediacom)

▲**FENTON**—Fenton Cablevision

▲**FERTILE**—Formerly served by Westcom. No longer in operation

FLOYD COUNTY (PORTIONS)—See CHARLES CITY, IA (Mediacom)

▲**FONDA**—Formerly served by TelePartners. No longer in operation

▲**FONTANELLE**—B & L Technologies LLC

FOREST CITY—See MASON CITY, IA (Mediacom)

▲**FOREST CITY**—Winnebago Cooperative Telephone Assn.

FORT ATKINSON—See NEW HAMPTON, IA (Mediacom)

▲**FORT DODGE**—Mediacom

FORT MADISON—See MOUNT PLEASANT, IA (Mediacom)

FOSTORIA—See MILFORD, IA (Milford Cable TV)

FREDERICKSBURG—See NEW HAMPTON, IA (Mediacom)

FREDERIKA—See TRIPOLI, IA (Butler-Bremer Communications)

FREDONIA—See BURLINGTON, IA (Mediacom)

FREEWAY MOBILE HOME PARK—See SIOUX CITY, NE (Cable One)

▲**FREMONT**—Starwest Inc.

FRUITLAND—See MUSCATINE, IA (MPW Cable)

FULTON—See CLINTON, IL (Mediacom)

GALENA—See DUBUQUE, IL (Mediacom)

GALVA—See CLEGHORN, IA (Wetherell Cable TV System)

▲**GARBER**—Formerly served by Alpine Communications LC. No longer in operation

▲**GARNAVILLO**—Mediacom. Now served by PRAIRIE DU CHIEN, WI [WI0066]

GARNER—See MASON CITY, IA (Mediacom)

GARRISON—See KEYSTONE, IA (Keystone Communications)

GARWIN—See GLADBROOK, IA (Mediacom)

▲**GENEVA**—Dumont Cablevision

▲**GEORGE**—Siebring Cable TV. Now served by SIOUX CENTER, IA [IA0076]

GEORGE—See SIOUX CENTER, IA (Premier Communications)

GILBERT—See STRATFORD, IA (Complete Communications Service)

GILBERTVILLE—See WATERLOO, IA (Mediacom)

▲**GILLETT GROVE**—ATC Cablevision

▲**GILMAN**—Partner Communications

▲**GILMORE CITY**—Mediacom

▲**GLADBROOK**—Mediacom

GLENWOOD—See ATLANTIC, IA (Mediacom)

GLIDDEN—See ATLANTIC, IA (Mediacom)

▲**GOLDFIELD**—Goldfield Communication Services Corp.

▲**GOODELL (village)**—Formerly served by New Path Communications LC. No longer in operation

GOOSE LAKE—See CLINTON, IA (Mediacom)

▲**GOWRIE**—Gowrie Cablevision

GRAETTINGER—See SPENCER, IA (Mediacom)

▲**GRAFTON**—Formerly served by Westcom. No longer in operation

▲**GRAND JUNCTION**—Jefferson Telephone & Cablevision

▲**GRAND MOUND**—Grand Mound Cooperative Telephone

▲**GRAND RIVER**—B & L Technologies LLC

GRANGER—See DES MOINES, IA (Mediacom)

GRANT—See GRISWOLD, IA (Griswold Cable TV)

▲**GRANVILLE**—Premier Communications. Now served by SIOUX CENTER, IA [IA0076]

GRANVILLE—See SIOUX CENTER, IA (Premier Communications)

▲**GRAVITY**—Formerly served by CableDirect. No longer in operation

▲**GREELEY**—Formerly served by Alpine Communications LC. No longer in operation

GREENE COUNTY—See AMES, IA (Mediacom)

▲**GREENE**—Mediacom. Now served by DES MOINES, IA [IA0001]

GREENE—See RUDD, IA (Omnitel Communications)

GREENFIELD—See DES MOINES, IA (Mediacom)

GRIMES—See DES MOINES, IA (Mediacom)

GRINNELL—See DES MOINES, IA (Mediacom)

▲**GRISWOLD**—Griswold Cable TV

▲**GRUNDY CENTER**—Grundy Center Municipal Utilities

GRUNDY CENTER—See IOWA FALLS, IA (Mediacom)

GUTHRIE—See DES MOINES, IA (Mediacom)

▲**HAMBURG**—Our Cable

HAMILTON COUNTY (PORTIONS)—See KEOKUK, IA (Mediacom)

HAMILTON COUNTY—See FORT DODGE, IA (Mediacom)

HAMILTON—See DES MOINES, IA (Mediacom)

HAMILTON—See KEOKUK, IL (Mediacom)

▲**HAMPTON**—Mediacom

HANCOCK COUNTY (PORTIONS)—See KEOKUK, IL (Mediacom)

HANCOCK—See EARLING, IA (Mutual Communications Services)

HARCOURT—See LEHIGH, IA (Lehigh Services Inc.)

HARDIN COUNTY—See IOWA FALLS, IA (Mediacom)

▲**HARLAN**—Harlan Municipal Utilities

HARLAN—See ATLANTIC, IA (Mediacom)

HARPERS FERRY—See LANSING, IA (Mediacom)

HARRIS—See SPIRIT LAKE, IA (Mediacom)

HARRISON COUNTY (UNINCORPORATED AREAS)—See MISSOURI VALLEY, IA (Long Lines)

▲**HARTFORD**—Telnet South LC. Now served by DES MOINES, IA [IA0001]

HARTFORD—See DES MOINES, IA (Mediacom)

HARTLEY—See SANBORN, IA (Community Cable TV Agency of O'Brien County)

HARVESTER COMMUNITY—See GILMAN, IA (Partner Communications)

▲**HAVELOCK**—Northwest Communications Inc.

▲**HAWARDEN**—Mediacom. Now served by ORANGE CITY, IA [IA0488]

▲**HAWARDEN**—HiTec Cable

HAWARDEN—See ORANGE CITY, IA (Premier Communications)

▲**HAWKEYE**—Hawkeye TV Co.

HAZLETON—See WAVERLY, IA (Mediacom)

▲**HEDRICK**—Starwest Inc.

HENRY COUNTY—See MOUNT PLEASANT, IA (Mediacom)

HIAWATHA—See CEDAR RAPIDS, IA (Mediacom)

HILLS—See CEDAR RAPIDS, IA (Mediacom)

▲**HINTON**—Premier Communications. Now served by SIOUX CENTER, IA [IA0076]

HINTON—See SIOUX CENTER, IA (Premier Communications)

▲**HOLLAND**—Formerly served by CableDirect. No longer in operation

HOLSTEIN—See SALIX, IA (Long Lines)

HOLY CROSS—See LUXEMBURG, IA (New Century Communications)

▲ **HOPKINTON**—New Century Communications

▲ **HORNICK**—Telepartners. Now served by LAWTON, IA [IA0330]

HORNICK—See LAWTON, IA (Western Iowa Telephone)

▲ **HOSPERS**—HTC Cablecom. Now served by SHELDON, IA [IA0060]

HOSPERS—See SHELDON, IA (HTC Cablecom)

▲ **HUBBARD**—Hubbard Co-op Cable

▲ **HUDSON**—Mediacom. Now served by INDEPENDENCE, IA [IA0059]

HUDSON—See INDEPENDENCE, IA (Mediacom)

HULL—See SIOUX CENTER, IA (Premier Communications)

HUMBOLDT—See FORT DODGE, IA (Mediacom)

▲ **HUMESTON**—B & L Technologies LLC

▲ **HUXLEY**—Huxley Communications Corp.

HUXLEY—See AMES, IA (Mediacom)

IDA GROVE—See ANTHON, IA (Long Lines)

▲ **INDEPENDENCE**—Independence Light & Power Telecommunications

▲ **INDEPENDENCE**—Mediacom

INDIANOLA—See DES MOINES, IA (Mediacom)

▲ **INWOOD**—Alliance Communications

▲ **IONIA**—Formerly served by Mid-American Cable Systems. No longer in operation

IOWA ARMY MUNITIONS PLANT—See BURLINGTON, IA (Mediacom)

IOWA CITY—See CEDAR RAPIDS, IA (Mediacom)

▲ **IOWA FALLS**—Mediacom

▲ **IRETON**—Premier Communications. Now served by SIOUX CENTER, IA [IA0076]

IRETON—See SIOUX CENTER, IA (Premier Communications)

IRWIN—See EARLING, IA (Mutual Communications Services)

JACKSON COUNTY—See CLINTON, IA (Mediacom)

JACKSONVILLE—See EARLING, IA (Mutual Communications Services)

▲ **JAMAICA**—Panora Cooperative Cablevision Assn. Inc.

JANESVILLE—See WAVERLY, IA (Mediacom)

JASPER COUNTY (CENTRAL PORTION)—See DES MOINES, IA (Mediacom)

JEFFERSON COUNTY—See OTTUMWA, IA (Mediacom)

▲ **JEFFERSON**—Mediacom. Now served by AMES, IA [IA0008]

JEFFERSON—See SALIX, SD (Long Lines)

JEFFERSON—See AMES, IA (Mediacom)

▲ **JESUP**—Jesup Cablevision

JEWELL—See STRATFORD, IA (Complete Communications Service)

JO DAVIESS COUNTY—See DUBUQUE, IL (Mediacom)

JOHNSON COUNTY—See CEDAR RAPIDS, IA (Mediacom)

JOHNSTON—See DES MOINES, IA (Mediacom)

▲ **JOICE (village)**—Formerly served by Westcom. No longer in operation

JONES COUNTY (PORTIONS)—See CEDAR RAPIDS, IA (Mediacom)

KALONA—See CEDAR RAPIDS, IA (Mediacom)

KAMRAR—See STRATFORD, IA (Complete Communications Service)

▲ **KANAWHA**—Communications 1 Network. Formerly [IA0229]. This cable system has converted to IPTV

▲ **KELLERTON**—Telnet South LC. Now served by DES MOINES, IA [IA0001]

KELLERTON—See DES MOINES, IA (Mediacom)

▲ **KELLEY**—Huxley Communications Corp.

KELLOGG—See GILMAN, IA (Partner Communications)

KENSETT—See MASON CITY, IA (Mediacom)

▲ **KEOKUK**—Mediacom

▲ **KEOSAUQUA**—Starwest Inc.

KEOTA—See CEDAR RAPIDS, IA (Mediacom)

▲ **KESWICK**—Formerly served by Longview Communications. No longer in operation

▲ **KEYSTONE**—Keystone Communications

KIMBALLTON—See ELK HORN, IA (Marne & Elk Horn Telephone Co.)

▲ **KINGSLEY**—Evertek Inc.

KIRKMAN—See EARLING, IA (Mutual Communications Services)

KIRON—See SCHALLER, IA (Comserv Ltd.)

▲ **KLEMME**—Communications 1 Cablevision. Now served by KANAWHA, IA [IA0229]

▲ **KLEMME**—Communications 1 Network. Formerly served by Kanawha, IA [IA0229]. This cable system has converted to IPTV

▲ **KNOXVILLE (unincorporated areas)**—Telnet South LC. Now served by DES MOINES, IA [IA0001]

KNOXVILLE (UNINCORPORATED AREAS)—See DES MOINES, IA (Mediacom)

▲ **KNOXVILLE**—Mediacom. Now served by DES MOINES, IA [IA0001]

KNOXVILLE—See DES MOINES, IA (Mediacom)

LA PORTE—See WAVERLY, IA (Mediacom)

▲ **LACONA**—Formerly served by Telnet South LC. No longer in operation

LAKE CITY—See FORT DODGE, IA (Mediacom)

▲ **LAKE MILLS**—Winnebago Cooperative Telephone Assn.

LAKE PANORAMA—See PANORA, IA (Panora Cooperative Cablevision Assn. Inc.)

▲ **LAKE PARK**—Mediacom. Now served by SPIRIT LAKE, IA [IA0036]

LAKE PARK—See SPIRIT LAKE, IA (Mediacom)

▲ **LAKE VIEW**—Corn Belt Telephone Co.

LAKE VILLAGE MOBILE HOME PARK—See SIOUX CITY, NE (Cable One)

LAKESIDE—See FORT DODGE, IA (Mediacom)

LAKEWOOD—See DES MOINES, IA (Mediacom)

▲ **LAKOTA**—Heck's TV & Cable

LAMBS GROVE—See DES MOINES, IA (Mediacom)

▲ **LAMONI**—Telnet South LC. Now served by DES MOINES, IA [IA0001]

LAMONI—See DES MOINES, IA (Mediacom)

▲ **LAMONT**—Formerly served by Alpine Communications LC. No longer in operation

▲ **LANSING**—Mediacom

▲ **LARCHWOOD**—Alliance Communications

LARRABEE—See MARCUS, IA (WesTel Systems)

▲ **LATIMER**—Formerly served by Latimer/Coulter Cablevision. No longer in operation

LAUREL—See GILMAN, IA (Partner Communications)

▲ **LAURENS**—Laurens Municipal Power & Communications

LAURENS—See FORT DODGE, IA (Mediacom)

▲ **LAWLER**—Alpine Communications LC

▲ **LAWTON**—Western Iowa Telephone

▲ **LE MARS**—Premier Communications

▲ **LEDYARD (village)**—Formerly served by New Path Communications LC. No longer in operation

LEE COUNTY (NORTHERN PORTION)—See BURLINGTON, IA (Mediacom)

LEE COUNTY (PORTIONS)—See KEOKUK, IA (Mediacom)

LEE COUNTY (PORTIONS)—See MOUNT PLEASANT, IA (Mediacom)

▲ **LEHIGH**—Lehigh Services Inc.

LELAND—See MASON CITY, IA (Mediacom)

▲ **LENOX**—Lenox Municipal Cablevision

LEON—See DES MOINES, IA (Mediacom)

LEWIS—See GRISWOLD, IA (Griswold Cable TV)

▲ **LIBERTYVILLE**—Formerly served by Westcom. No longer in operation

LIME SPRINGS—See OSAGE, IA (Mediacom)

LINDEN—See PANORA, IA (Panora Cooperative Cablevision Assn. Inc.)

LINN COUNTY (UNINCORPORATED AREAS)—See CEDAR RAPIDS, IA (Mediacom)

LISBON—See CEDAR RAPIDS, IA (Mediacom)

▲ **LISCOMB**—Formerly served by New Path Communications LC. No longer in operation

▲ **LITTLE ROCK**—Premier Communications

▲ **LITTLE SIOUX**—Formerly served by TelePartners. No longer in operation

▲ **LITTLETON**—Farmers Mutual Cooperative Telephone Co. Now served by JESUP, IA [IA0116]

LITTLETON—See JESUP, IA (Jesup Cablevision)

▲ **LIVERMORE**—Milford Cable TV

▲ **LOCKRIDGE**—Formerly served by Westcom. No longer in operation

▲ **LOGAN**—Long Lines

▲ **LOHRVILLE**—Formerly served by Tele-Services Ltd. No longer in operation

LONE TREE—See CEDAR RAPIDS, IA (Mediacom)

LORIMOR—See MURRAY, IA (Interstate Communications)

▲ **LOST NATION**—LN Satellite Communications Co.

LOUISA COUNTY—See BURLINGTON, IA (Mediacom)

LOUISA COUNTY—See MUSCATINE, IA (MPW Cable)

LOVILIA—See DES MOINES, IA (Mediacom)

LOW MOOR—See CLINTON, IA (Mediacom)

▲ **LOWDEN**—F & B Cablevision

▲ **LU VERNE**—Signal Inc.

LUANA—See MONONA, IA (Northeast Iowa Telephone Co.)

▲ **LUCAS**—Telnet South LC. Now served by DES MOINES, IA [IA0001]

LUCAS—See DES MOINES, IA (Mediacom)

▲ **LUXEMBURG**—New Century Communications

LYMAN—See GRISWOLD, IA (Griswold Cable TV)

LYNDON—See CLINTON, IL (Mediacom)

LYNNVILLE—See DES MOINES, IA (Mediacom)

▲ **LYTTON**—Formerly served by TelePartners. No longer in operation

MACEDONIA—See CARSON, IA (Interstate Communications)

MADRID—See AMES, IA (Mediacom)

MAGNOLIA—See LOGAN, IA (Long Lines)

MALCOM—See BROOKLYN, IA (Inter-County Cable Co.)

MALLARD—See HAVELOCK, IA (Northwest Communications Inc.)

▲ **MALVERN**—Our Cable

MANCHESTER—See WAVERLY, IA (Mediacom)

▲ **MANILLA**—Manilla Municipal Cable. Now served by EARLING, IA [IA0302]

MANILLA—See EARLING, IA (Mutual Communications Services)

MANLY—See MASON CITY, IA (Mediacom)

▲ **MANNING**—Manning Municipal Cable TV

MANSON—See FORT DODGE, IA (Mediacom)

▲ **MAPLETON**—Long Lines

MAQUOKETA—See CLINTON, IA (Mediacom)

MARATHON—See CLEGHORN, IA (Wetherell Cable TV System)

▲ **MARBLE ROCK**—Omnitel Communications. Now served by RUDD, IA [IA0503]

MARBLE ROCK—See RUDD, IA (Omnitel Communications)

▲ **MARCUS**—WesTel Systems

MARENGO—See CEDAR RAPIDS, IA (Mediacom)

MARION COUNTY—See DES MOINES, IA (Mediacom)

MARION—See CEDAR RAPIDS, IA (Mediacom)

MARNE—See ELK HORN, IA (Marne & Elk Horn Telephone Co.)

MARSHALL COUNTY—See AMES, IA (Mediacom)

▲ **MARSHALLTOWN**—Mediacom. Now served by AMES, IA [IA0008]

MARSHALLTOWN—See AMES, IA (Mediacom)

▲ **MARTELLE**—Martelle Communications Co-op

▲ **MARTENSDALE**—Interstate Communications. Now served by TRURO, IA [IA0344]

MARTENSDALE—See TRURO, IA (Interstate Communications)

▲ **MASON CITY**—Mediacom

▲ **MASSENA**—B & L Technologies LLC

▲ **MAURICE**—Premier Communications. Now served by SIOUX CENTER, IA [IA0076]

MAURICE—See SIOUX CENTER, IA (Premier Communications)

▲ **MAXWELL**—Formerly served by Huxley Communications Corp. No longer in operation

▲ **MAYNARD**—Mediacom. Now served by WAVERLY, IA [IA0021]

MAYNARD—See WAVERLY, IA (Mediacom)

▲ **MAYSVILLE**—Dixon Telephone Co. Now served by DIXON, IA [IA0358]

MAYSVILLE—See DIXON, IA (Dixon Telephone Co.)

MCCALLSBURG—See ZEARING, IA (Minerva Valley Cablevision)

MCCAUSLAND—See CLINTON, IA (Mediacom)

▲ **MECHANICSVILLE**—Mechanicsville Cablevision

▲ **MEDIAPOLIS**—MTC Technologies

MELBOURNE—See GILMAN, IA (Partner Communications)

MELCHER—See DES MOINES, IA (Mediacom)

▲ **MELVIN**—Premier Communications

▲ **MENLO**—Coon Valley Cooperative Telephone

MERIDEN—See CLEGHORN, IA (Wetherell Cable TV System)

▲ **MERRILL**—Premier Communications. Now served by SIOUX CENTER, IA [IA0076]

MERRILL—See SIOUX CENTER, IA (Premier Communications)

▲ **MESERVEY**—Rockwell Communications Systems Inc.

MIDDLETOWN—See BURLINGTON, IA (Mediacom)

MILES—See CLINTON, IA (Mediacom)

▲ **MILFORD**—Milford Cable TV

MILLS COUNTY (EASTERN PORTION)—See ATLANTIC, IA (Mediacom)

▲ **MILO**—Formerly served by Telnet South LC. No longer in operation

▲ **MILTON**—Starwest Inc. Now served by KEOSAUQUA, IA [IA0186]

MILTON—See KEOSAUQUA, IA (Starwest Inc.)

▲ **MINBURN**—Minburn Cablevision Inc.

▲ **MINDEN**—Walnut Telephone. Now served by WALNUT, IA [IA0241]

MINDEN—See WALNUT, IA (Walnut Communications)

▲ **MINGO**—Formerly served by Huxley Communications Corp. No longer in operation

▲ **MISSOURI VALLEY**—Long Lines

MITCHELLVILLE—See DES MOINES, IA (Mediacom)

▲ **MODALE**—Formerly served by TelePartners. No longer in operation

▲ **MONDAMIN**—Formerly served by TelePartners. No longer in operation

▲ **MONONA**—Northeast Iowa Telephone Co.

MONROE COUNTY (PORTIONS)—See CENTERVILLE, IA (Mediacom)

▲ **MONROE**—Telnet South LC. Now served by DES MOINES, IA [IA0001]

MONROE—See DES MOINES, IA (Mediacom)

MONTEZUMA—See DEEP RIVER, IA (Montezuma Mutual Telephone & Cable Co.)

MONTICELLO—See CEDAR RAPIDS, IA (Mediacom)

MONTOUR—See GILMAN, IA (Partner Communications)

▲ **MONTROSE**—Mediacom. Now served by KEOKUK, IA [IA0612]

MONTROSE—See KEOKUK, IA (Mediacom)

▲ **MOORHEAD**—Soldier Valley Telephone. Now served by SALIX, IA [IA0510]

▲ **MOORHEAD**—Long Lines

MOORLAND—See FORT DODGE, IA (Mediacom)

▲ **MORAVIA**—B & L Technologies LLC

MORLEY—See MARTELLE, IA (Martelle Communications Co-op)

MORNING SUN—See BURLINGTON, IA (Mediacom)

MORRISON—See CLINTON, IL (Mediacom)

▲ **MOULTON**—B & L Technologies LLC

MOUNT AYR—See DES MOINES, IA (Mediacom)

▲ **MOUNT PLEASANT**—Mediacom

MOUNT VERNON—See CEDAR RAPIDS, IA (Mediacom)

▲ **MOVILLE**—Evertek Inc.

▲ **MURRAY**—Interstate Communications

MUSCATINE COUNTY—See MUSCATINE, IA (MPW Cable)

▲ **MUSCATINE**—Mediacom. Now served by MUSCATINE, IA [IA0587]

▲ **MUSCATINE**—MPW Cable

▲ **MYSTIC**—B & L Technologies LLC

NASHUA—See TRIPOLI, IA (Butler-Bremer Communications)

▲ **NEOLA**—Walnut Communications

NEVADA—See AMES, IA (Mediacom)

▲ **NEW ALBIN**—Mediacom

▲ **NEW HAMPTON**—Mediacom

NEW HARTFORD—See WAVERLY, IA (Mediacom)

▲ **NEW LIBERTY**—Dixon Telephone Co. Now served by DIXON, IA [IA0358]

NEW LIBERTY—See DIXON, IA (Dixon Telephone Co.)

NEW LONDON—See MOUNT PLEASANT, IA (Mediacom)

▲ **NEW MARKET**—Farmers Mutual Telephone Co. Now served by STANTON, IA [IA0264]

NEW MARKET—See STANTON, IA (Farmers Mutual Telephone Co)

NEW SHARON—See OSKALOOSA, IA (Mediacom)

NEW VIENNA—See LUXEMBURG, IA (New Century Communications)

▲ **NEW VIRGINIA**—Interstate Communications. Now served by TRURO, IA [IA0344]

NEW VIRGINIA—See TRURO, IA (Interstate Communications)

▲ **NEWELL**—Formerly served by TelePartners. No longer in operation

NEWHALL—See CEDAR RAPIDS, IA (Mediacom)

▲ **NEWTON**—Mediacom. Now served by DES MOINES, IA [IA0001]

NEWTON—See DES MOINES, IA (Mediacom)

▲ **NICHOLS**—Formerly served by PEC Cablevision. No longer in operation

NORA SPRINGS—See RUDD, IA (Omnitel Communications)

NORTH ENGLISH—See CEDAR RAPIDS, IA (Mediacom)

▲ **NORTH LIBERTY**—South Slope Communications Co. This cable system has converted to IPTV. See North Liberty, IA [IA5007]

NORTH LIBERTY—See CEDAR RAPIDS, IA (Mediacom)

▲ **NORTH LIBERTY**—South Slope Coop. Communications Co. Formerly [IA0432]. This cable system has converted to IPTV

NORTH SIOUX CITY—See SIOUX CITY, SD (Cable One)

▲ **NORTHWOOD**—Mediacom. Now served by MASON CITY, IA [IA0010]

NORTHWOOD—See MASON CITY, IA (Mediacom)

NORWALK—See DES MOINES, IA (Mediacom)

NORWAY—See CEDAR RAPIDS, IA (Mediacom)

OAKLAND ACRES—See GILMAN, IA (Partner Communications)

▲ **OAKLAND**—Our Cable

▲ **OAKVILLE**—Formerly served by Longview Communications. No longer in operation

▲ **OCHEYEDAN**—Premier Communications

ODEBOLT—See SCHALLER, IA (Comserv Ltd.)

▲ **OELWEIN**—Mediacom. Now served by WAVERLY, IA [IA0021]

OELWEIN—See WAVERLY, IA (Mediacom)

▲ **OGDEN**—Ogden Telephone Co. Cablevision

OKOBOJI—See SPIRIT LAKE, IA (Mediacom)

▲ **OLDS**—Farmers & Merchants Mutual Telephone. Formerly served by Wayland, IA [IA0525]. This cable system has converted to IPTV.

▲ **OLIN**—Olin Telephone & Cablevision Co.

▲ **ONAWA**—Long Lines

▲ **ONSLOW**—Onslow Cooperative Telephone Assn.

▲ **ORANGE CITY**—Long Lines

▲ **ORANGE CITY**—Premier Communications

ORLEANS—See SPIRIT LAKE, IA (Mediacom)

ORTONVILLE—See DES MOINES, IA (Mediacom)

▲ **OSAGE**—Mediacom

OSCEOLA—See DES MOINES, IA (Mediacom)

▲ **OSKALOOSA**—Mediacom

OSSIAN—See NEW HAMPTON, IA (Mediacom)

OTHO—See LEHIGH, IA (Lehigh Services Inc.)

OTO—See LAWTON, IA (Western Iowa Telephone)

▲ **OTTUMWA**—Mediacom

▲ **OXFORD JUNCTION**—Mediacom. Now served by CEDAR RAPIDS [IA0002]

OXFORD JUNCTION—See LOST NATION, IA (LN Satellite Communications Co.)

OXFORD JUNCTION—See CEDAR RAPIDS, IA (Mediacom)

OXFORD—See CEDAR RAPIDS, IA (Mediacom)

▲ **OXFORD**—South Slope Coop. Communications Co. Formerly served by North Liberty, IA [IA0432]. This cable system has converted to IPTV

OYENS—See LE MARS, IA (Premier Communications)

▲ **PALMER**—Palmer Mutual Telephone Co.

▲ **PALO**—Palo Cooperative Telephone Association. This cable system has converted to IPTV. See Palo, IA [IA5066]

▲ **PALO**—Palo Cooperative Telephone Association. Formerly [IA0319]. This cable system has converted to IPTV

PANAMA—See EARLING, IA (Mutual Communications Services)

▲ **PANORA**—Panora Cooperative Cablevision Assn. Inc.

PARALTA—See SPRINGVILLE, IA (Springville Co-operative Telephone Assn Inc)

PARKERSBURG—See WAVERLY, IA (Mediacom)

▲ **PATON**—Gowrie Cablevision

▲ **PAULINA**—WesTel Systems. Now served by SANBORN, IA [IA0104]

PAULINA—See SANBORN, IA (Community Cable TV Agency of O'Brien County)

PELLA—See DES MOINES, IA (Mediacom)

PERRY—See DES MOINES, IA (Mediacom)

PERSHING—See DES MOINES, IA (Mediacom)

▲ **PERSIA**—TelePartners. Now served by WALNUT, IA [IA0241]

PERSIA—See WALNUT, IA (Walnut Communications)

▲ **PETERSON**—WesTel Systems. Now served by MARCUS, IA [IA0171]

PETERSON—See MARCUS, IA (WesTel Systems)

PIERSON—See CLEGHORN, IA (Wetherell Cable TV System)

PILOT MOUND—See LEHIGH, IA (Lehigh Services Inc.)

▲ **PISGAH**—Formerly served by TelePartners. No longer in operation

PLAINFIELD—See TRIPOLI, IA (Butler-Bremer Communications)

PLEASANT HILL—See DES MOINES, IA (Mediacom)

PLEASANTVILLE—See DES MOINES, IA (Mediacom)

PLOVER—See HAVELOCK, IA (Northwest Communications Inc.)

PLYMOUTH COUNTY—See LE MARS, IA (Premier Communications)

▲ **PLYMOUTH**—Omnitel Communications

PLYMOUTH—See RUDD, IA (Omnitel Communications)

POCAHONTAS—See FORT DODGE, IA (Mediacom)

POLK CITY—See AMES, IA (Mediacom)

POLK COUNTY (NORTHWESTERN PORTION)—See AMES, IA (Mediacom)

POLK—See DES MOINES, IA (Mediacom)

▲ **POMEROY**—Formerly served by TelePartners. No longer in operation

▲ **POSTVILLE**—CenturyTel

PRAIRIE CITY—See DES MOINES, IA (Mediacom)

▲ **PRESTON**—Telnet of Preston. Now served by CLINTON, IA [IA0006]

PRESTON—See CLINTON, IA (Mediacom)

PRIMGHAR—See SANBORN, IA (Community Cable TV Agency of O'Brien County)

PROPHETSTOWN—See CLINTON, IL (Mediacom)

▲ **PROTIVIN**—Protivin Cablevision

QUASQUETON—See WINTHROP, IA (East Buchanan Telephone Cooperative)

▲ **RADCLIFFE**—Radcliffe Cablevision. This cable system has converted to IPTV. See Radcliffe, IA [IA5020]

▲ **RADCLIFFE**—Radcliffe Cablevision. Formerly [IA0265]. This cable system has converted to IPTV

RANDALL—See AMES, IA (Mediacom)

▲ **RANDOLPH**—Formerly served by Westcom. No longer in operation

RAYMOND—See WATERLOO, IA (Mediacom)

▲ **READLYN**—Readlyn Telephone Co.

▲ **RED OAK**—Mediacom. Now served by ATLANTIC, IA [IA0032]

RED OAK—See ATLANTIC, IA (Mediacom)

REDFIELD—See DES MOINES, IA (Mediacom)

REINBECK—See WAVERLY, IA (Mediacom)

REMBRANDT—See CLEGHORN, IA (Wetherell Cable TV System)

REMSEN—See MARCUS, IA (WesTel Systems)

RENWICK (PORTIONS)—See GOLDFIELD, IA (Goldfield Communication Services Corp.)

▲ **RENWICK**—Heck's TV & Cable

RHODES—See GILMAN, IA (Partner Communications)

RICEVILLE—See RUDD, IA (Omnitel Communications)

▲ **RICHLAND**—Starwest Inc.

RICKETTS—See SCHLESWIG, IA (Tip Top Communication)

▲ **RINGSTED**—Ringsted Cablevision

RIVERSIDE—See CEDAR RAPIDS, IA (Mediacom)

ROBINS—See SHELLSBURG, IA (USA Communications)

ROCK CREEK LAKE—See GILMAN, IA (Partner Communications)

▲ **ROCK RAPIDS**—Premier Communications

ROCK VALLEY—See SIOUX CENTER, IA (Premier Communications)

ROCKFORD—See RUDD, IA (Omnitel Communications)

ROCKWELL CITY—See FORT DODGE, IA (Mediacom)

ROCKWELL—See HAMPTON, IA (Mediacom)

RODNEY—See LAWTON, IA (Western Iowa Telephone)

ROLAND—See STRATFORD, IA (Complete Communications Service)

ROLFE—See HAVELOCK, IA (Northwest Communications Inc.)

▲ **ROWLEY (village)**—Formerly served by New Path Communications LC. No longer in operation

▲ **ROYAL**—Royal Telephone Co.

▲ **RUDD**—Omnitel Communications

▲ **RUNNELLS**—Formerly served by Telnet South LC. No longer in operation

▲ **RUSSELL**—Formerly served by Longview Communications. No longer in operation

▲ **RUTHVEN**—Formerly served by Terril Cable Systems. No longer in operation

▲ **RYAN**—USA Communications

SABULA—See CLINTON, IA (Mediacom)

SAC CITY—See FORT DODGE, IA (Mediacom)

SAGEVILLE—See DUBUQUE, IA (Mediacom)

▲ **SALEM**—Formerly served by Longview Communications. No longer in operation

▲ **SALIX**—Long Lines

▲ **SANBORN**—Community Cable TV Agency of O'Brien County

SANBORN—See SIOUX CENTER, IA (Premier Communications)

SAVANNA—See CLINTON, IL (Mediacom)

SAYLORVILLE—See DES MOINES, IA (Mediacom)

▲ **SCHALLER**—Comserv Ltd.

▲ **SCHLESWIG**—Tip Top Communication

▲ **SCRANTON**—Scranton Community Antenna Television

SERGEANT BLUFF—See SIOUX CITY, IA (Cable One)

▲**SEYMOUR**—Formerly served by Longview Communications. No longer in operation

SHEFFIELD—See HAMPTON, IA (Mediacom)

▲**SHELBY**—Walnut Telephone Co. Now served by WALNUT, IA [IA0241]

SHELBY—See WALNUT, IA (Walnut Communications)

SHELDAHL—See AMES, IA (Mediacom)

▲**SHELDON**—HTC Cablecom

SHELL ROCK—See WAVERLY, IA (Mediacom)

▲**SHELLSBURG**—USA Communications

SHENANDOAH—See ATLANTIC, IA (Mediacom)

▲**SHERRILL**—Formerly served by Alpine Communications LC. No longer in operation

▲**SHUEYVILLE**—South Slope Coop. Communications Co. Formerly served by North Liberty, IA [IA0432]. This cable system has converted to IPTV

▲**SIBLEY**—HTC Cablecom. Now served by SHELDON, IA [IA0060]

SIBLEY—See SHELDON, IA (HTC Cablecom)

▲**SIDNEY**—Our Cable

▲**SIGOURNEY**—Mediacom. Now served by CEDAR RAPIDS, IA [IA0002]

SIGOURNEY—See CEDAR RAPIDS, IA (Mediacom)

▲**SILVER CITY**—Formerly served by Interstate Communications. No longer in operation

▲**SIOUX CENTER**—Premier Communications

▲**SIOUX CITY**—Cable One

SIOUX COUNTY—See ORANGE CITY, IA (Premier Communications)

▲**SIOUX RAPIDS**—WesTel Systems. Now served by MARCUS, IA [IA0171]

SIOUX RAPIDS—See MARCUS, IA (WesTel Systems)

SLATER—See AMES, IA (Mediacom)

SLOAN—See SALIX, IA (Long Lines)

▲**SMITHLAND**—TelePartners. Now served by LAWTON, IA [IA0330]

SMITHLAND—See LAWTON, IA (Western Iowa Telephone)

▲**SOLDIER**—Soldier Valley Telephone. Now served by SALIX, IA [IA0510]

▲**SOLDIER**—Long Lines

SOLON MILLS—See CEDAR RAPIDS, IA (Mediacom)

▲**SOLON**—South Slope Coop. Communications Co. Formerly served by North Liberty, IA [IA0432]. This cable system has converted to IPTV

SOUTH SIOUX CITY—See SIOUX CITY, NE (Cable One)

▲**SPENCER**—Mediacom

▲**SPENCER**—SMU Cable TV

SPILLVILLE—See NEW HAMPTON, IA (Mediacom)

▲**SPIRIT LAKE**—Mediacom

▲**SPRINGVILLE**—Springville Co-operative Telephone Assn Inc

ST. ANSGAR—See RUDD, IA (Omnitel Communications)

ST. ANTHONY—See ZEARING, IA (Minerva Valley Cablevision)

▲**ST. CHARLES**—Interstate Communications. Now served by TRURO, IA [IA0344]

ST. CHARLES—See TRURO, IA (Interstate Communications)

▲**ST. LUCAS**—Alpine Communications LC. Now served by LAWLER, IA [IA0462]

ST. LUCAS—See LAWLER, IA (Alpine Communications LC)

ST. MARYS—See TRURO, IA (Interstate Communications)

ST. OLAF—See MONONA, IA (Northeast Iowa Telephone Co.)

STACEYVILLE—See RUDD, IA (Omnitel Communications)

STANHOPE—See STRATFORD, IA (Complete Communications Service)

▲**STANTON**—Farmers Mutual Telephone Co

▲**STANWOOD**—Clarence Cablevision

▲**STATE CENTER**—Partner Communications. Now served by GILMAN, IA [IA0128]

STATE CENTER—See GILMAN, IA (Partner Communications)

▲**STEAMBOAT ROCK**—Formerly served by Steamboat Rock Cablevision. No longer in operation

STOCKPORT—See KEOSAUQUA, IA (Starwest Inc.)

STONE CITY—See MARTELLE, IA (Martelle Communications Co-op)

▲**STORM LAKE**—Mediacom. Now served by FORT DODGE, IA [IA0011]

▲**STORM LAKE**—Knology

STORM LAKE—See FORT DODGE, IA (Mediacom)

STORY CITY—See AMES, IA (Mediacom)

STORY COUNTY—See AMES, IA (Mediacom)

▲**STRATFORD**—Complete Communications Service

▲**STRAWBERRY POINT**—Mediacom. Now served by WAVERLY, IA [IA0021]

STRAWBERRY POINT—See WAVERLY, IA (Mediacom)

STUART—See DES MOINES, IA (Mediacom)

SULLY—See DES MOINES, IA (Mediacom)

SUMMERSET—See DES MOINES, IA (Mediacom)

SUMNER—See NEW HAMPTON, IA (Mediacom)

▲**SUN VALLEY LAKE**—Interstate Communications

▲**SUTHERLAND**—WesTel Systems. Now served by MARCUS, IA [IA0171]

SUTHERLAND—See MARCUS, IA (WesTel Systems)

▲**SWALEDALE (village)**—Formerly served by New Path Communications LC. No longer in operation

▲**SWEA CITY**—Mediacom

SWISHER—See CEDAR RAPIDS, IA (Mediacom)

▲**TABOR**—Our Cable

TAMA—See AMES, IA (Mediacom)

▲**TEMPLETON**—Templeton Telephone Co.

TENNANT—See EARLING, IA (Mutual Communications Services)

▲**TERRIL**—Terril Cable Systems

▲**THOMPSON**—Winnebago Cooperative Telephone Assn.

THOMSON—See CLINTON, IL (Mediacom)

▲**THOR**—Milford Cable TV

▲**THORNTON**—Rockwell Communications Systems Inc.

▲**THURMAN**—Formerly served by Tele-Services Ltd. No longer in operation

TIFFIN—See CEDAR RAPIDS, IA (Mediacom)

▲**TIFFIN**—South Slope Coop. Communications Co. Formerly served by North Liberty, IA [IA0432]. This cable system has converted to IPTV

TIPTON—See CEDAR RAPIDS, IA (Mediacom)

▲**TITONKA**—Titonka-Burt Communications

TODDVILLE—See CEDAR RAPIDS, IA (Mediacom)

▲**TOLEDO**—Mediacom. Now served by AMES, IA [IA0008]

TOLEDO—See AMES, IA (Mediacom)

TOMPKINS MOBILE HOME PARK—See SIOUX CITY, NE (Cable One)

▲**TORONTO**—F & B Cablevision

▲**TRAER**—Mediacom. Now served by AMES, IA [IA0008]

TRAER—See AMES, IA (Mediacom)

▲**TREYNOR**—Our Cable

▲**TRIPOLI**—Butler-Bremer Communications

▲**TRURO**—Interstate Communications

▲**UNDERWOOD**—TelePartners. Now served by WALNUT, IA [IA0241]

UNDERWOOD—See WALNUT, IA (Walnut Communications)

UNION COUNTY (PORTIONS)—See SIOUX CITY, SD (Cable One)

▲**UNION GROVE VILLAGE**—Heart of Iowa Telecommunications. This cable system has converted to IPTV. See Union, IA [IA5001]

▲**UNION**—Heart of Iowa Communications. Formerly [IA0521]. This cable system has converted to IPTV.

UNIVERSITY HEIGHTS—See CEDAR RAPIDS, IA (Mediacom)

UNIVERSITY PARK—See OSKALOOSA, IA (Mediacom)

URBANA—See SHELLSBURG, IA (USA Communications)

URBANDALE—See DES MOINES, IA (Mediacom)

▲**UTE**—Long Lines

▲**VAIL**—Tip Top Communications. Now served by DELOIT, IA [IA0422]

VAIL—See DELOIT, IA (Tip Top Communication)

▲**VAN HORNE**—Van Horne Telephone Co.

VAN METER—See DES MOINES, IA (Mediacom)

▲**VAN WERT**—B & L Technologies LLC

VENTURA—See MASON CITY, IA (Mediacom)

VILLISCA—See ATLANTIC, IA (Mediacom)

VINCENT—See THOR, IA (Milford Cable TV)

VINTON—See CEDAR RAPIDS, IA (Mediacom)

VIOLA—See SPRINGVILLE, IA (Springville Co-operative Telephone Assn Inc)

▲**VOLGA**—Alpine Communications LC. Now served by ARLINGTON, IA [IA0393]

VOLGA—See ARLINGTON, IA (Alpine Communications LC)

▲**WADENA (village)**—Alpine Communications LC. Now served by ARLINGTON, IA [IA0393]

WADENA (VILLAGE)—See ARLINGTON, IA (Alpine Communications LC)

WAHPETON—See SPIRIT LAKE, IA (Mediacom)

▲**WALFORD**—South Slope Coop. Communications Inc. Formerly served by North Liberty, IA [IA0432]. This

cable system has converted to IPTV

▲ **WALKER**—Formerly served by Mid American Cable Systems. No longer in operation

▲ **WALL LAKE**—Corn Belt Telephone Co.

WALL LAKE—See LAKE VIEW, IA (Corn Belt Telephone Co.)

WALLINGFORD—See SPENCER, IA (Mediacom)

▲ **WALNUT**—Walnut Communications

WAPELLO COUNTY—See OTTUMWA, IA (Mediacom)

WAPPELLO—See BURLINGTON, IA (Mediacom)

WARREN COUNTY (PORTIONS)—See DES MOINES, IA (Mediacom)

WARSAW—See KEOKUK, IL (Mediacom)

WASHBURN—See WATERLOO, IA (Mediacom)

WASHINGTON—See CEDAR RAPIDS, IA (Mediacom)

WASHTA—See CLEGHORN, IA (Wetherell Cable TV System)

▲ **WATERLOO**—Formerly served by Wireless Cable TV of Waterloo. No longer in operation

▲ **WATERLOO**—Mediacom

WAUKEE (EASTERN PORTION)—See DES MOINES, IA (Mediacom)

WAUKEE—See DES MOINES, IA (Mediacom)

WAUKON JUNCTION—See LANSING, IA (Mediacom)

▲ **WAVERLY**—Mediacom

▲ **WAYLAND**—Farmers & Merchants Mutual Telephone. This cable system has converted to IPTV. See Olds, IA [IA5075] & Wayland, IA [IA5076]

▲ **WAYLAND**—Farmers & Merchants Mutual Telephone. Formerly [IA0525]. This cable system has converted to IPTV.

WEBB—See DICKENS, IA (Premier Communications)

WEBSTER CITY—See FORT DODGE, IA (Mediacom)

WEBSTER COUNTY—See FORT DODGE, IA (Mediacom)

WELDON—See VAN WERT, IA (B & L Technologies LLC)

WELLMAN—See CEDAR RAPIDS, IA (Mediacom)

▲ **WELLSBURG**—Formerly served by Union Cablevision. No longer in operation

▲ **WESLEY**—Communications 1 Cablevision. Now served by KANAWHA, IA [IA0229]

▲ **WESLEY**—Communications 1 Cablevision. Formerly Kanawha, IA. This cable system has converted to IPTV. See Kanawha, IA [IA5095]

WEST BEND—See HAVELOCK, IA (Northwest Communications Inc.)

WEST BRANCH—See CEDAR RAPIDS, IA (Mediacom)

WEST BURLINGTON—See BURLINGTON, IA (Mediacom)

WEST DES MOINES—See DES MOINES, IA (Mediacom)

WEST LIBERTY—See CEDAR RAPIDS, IA (Mediacom)

WEST OKOBOJI—See SPIRIT LAKE, IA (Mediacom)

WEST POINT—See MOUNT PLEASANT, IA (Mediacom)

WEST UNION—See NEW HAMPTON, IA (Mediacom)

▲ **WESTGATE (village)**—Formerly served by Alpine Communications LC. No longer in operation

WESTPHALIA—See EARLING, IA (Mutual Communications Services)

▲ **WESTSIDE**—Western Iowa Networks

WESTWOOD—See MOUNT PLEASANT, IA (Mediacom)

WHAT CHEER—See CEDAR RAPIDS, IA (Mediacom)

▲ **WHEATLAND**—F & B Cablevision

WHITESIDE COUNTY (PORTIONS)—See CLINTON, IL (Mediacom)

▲ **WHITING**—Long Lines

▲ **WHITTEMORE**—ATC Cablevision

WHITTIER—See SPRINGVILLE, IA (Springville Co-operative Telephone Assn Inc)

▲ **WILLIAMS**—Formerly served by Williams Cablevision. No longer in operation

▲ **WILLIAMSBURG**—Mediacom. Now served by CEDAR RAPIDS, IA [IA0002]

WILLIAMSBURG—See CEDAR RAPIDS, IA (Mediacom)

WINDSOR HEIGHTS—See DES MOINES, IA (Mediacom)

▲ **WINFIELD**—Formerly served by Longview Communications. No longer in operation

WINTERSET—See DES MOINES, IA (Mediacom)

▲ **WINTHROP**—East Buchanan Telephone Cooperative

▲ **WODEN**—Formerly served by Heck's TV & Cable. No longer in operation

WOODBINE—See LOGAN, IA (Long Lines)

▲ **WOODBURN**—Telnet South LC. Now served by DES MOINES, IA [IA0001]

WOODBURN—See DES MOINES, IA (Mediacom)

WOODBURY COUNTY—See SIOUX CITY, IA (Cable One)

WOODWARD—See AMES, IA (Mediacom)

▲ **WOOLSTOCK**—Goldfield Communication Services Corp.

▲ **WORTHINGTON**—New Century Communications. Now served by LUXEMBURG, IA [IA0554]

▲ **WORTHINGTON**—New Century Communications

WRIGHT COUNTY (CENTRAL PORTION)—See FORT DODGE, IA (Mediacom)

WYOMING—See CEDAR RAPIDS, IA (Mediacom)

YALE—See PANORA, IA (Panora Cooperative Cablevision Assn. Inc.)

▲ **ZEARING**—Minerva Valley Cablevision

KANSAS

▲ **ABBYVILLE**—Formerly served by Cox Communications. No longer in operation

▲ **ABILENE**—Eagle Communications

ALBERT—See RUSH CENTER, KS (GBT Communications Inc.)

ALLEN COUNTY (PORTIONS)—See IOLA, KS (Cox Communications)

▲ **ALMA**—Zito Media

▲ **ALMENA**—Nex-Tech. This cable system has converted to IPTV. See Almena, KS [KS5146]

▲ **ALMENA**—Nex-Tech. Formerly [KS0360]. This cable system has converted to IPTV

▲ **ALTA VISTA**—Formerly served by Galaxy Cablevision. No longer in operation

▲ **ALTAMONT**—Wave Wireless

▲ **ALTON**—Nex-Tech. Formerly served by Edmond, KS [KS0450]. This cable system has converted to IPTV

▲ **ALTOONA**—Mediacom

▲ **AMERICUS**—Zito Media

▲ **ANDALE**—Formerly served by Almega Cable. No longer in operation

ANDOVER—See WICHITA, KS (Cox Communications)

▲ **ANTHONY**—Suddenlink Communications

▲ **ARCADIA**—Formerly served by National Cable Inc. No longer in operation

▲ **ARGONIA**—Formerly served by Almega Cable. No longer in operation

ARKANSAS CITY—See WICHITA, KS (Cox Communications)

▲ **ARLINGTON**—Formerly served by Almega Cable. No longer in operation

ARMA—See PITTSBURG, KS (Cox Communications)

▲ **ASHLAND**—Formerly served by Cebridge Connections. Now served by CIMARRON, KS [KS0126]

ASHLAND—See CIMARRON, KS (United Communications Assn. Inc.)

▲ **ASSARIA**—Home Communications Inc. This cable system has converted to IPTV. See Assaria, KS [KS5062]

▲ **ASSARIA**—Home Communications Inc. Formerly [KS0363]. This cable system has converted to IPTV

ATCHISON COUNTY (PORTIONS)—See ATCHISON, KS (Allegiance Communications)

▲ **ATCHISON**—Allegiance Communications

ATLANTA—See CLEARWATER, KS (SKT Entertainment)

▲ **ATTICA**—Formerly served by Almega Cable. No longer in operation

▲ **ATWOOD**—Atwood Cable Systems Inc.

AUBURN—See TOPEKA, KS (Cox Communications)

AUGUSTA—See WICHITA, KS (Cox Communications)

▲ **AXTELL**—Blue Valley Telecommunications. This cable system has converted to IPTV. See Axtell, KS [KS5019]

▲ **AXTELL**—Blue Valley Telecommunications. Formerly [KS0242]. This cable system has converted to IPTV

▲ **BAILEYVILLE**—Rainbow Communications

▲ **BALDWIN CITY**—Mediacom

BARBER COUNTY (PORTIONS)—See MEDICINE LODGE, KS (Allegiance Communications)

▲ **BARNARD**—Twin Valley Communications. Formerly served by Bennington, KS [KS0214]. This cable system has converted to IPTV

▲ **BARNES**—Formerly served by Eagle Communications. No longer in operation

BARTON COUNTY—See GREAT BEND, KS (Cox Communications)

▲ **BASEHOR**—Knology (Formerly Sunflower Broadband). Now served by LAWRENCE, KS [KS0004]

BASEHOR—See LAWRENCE, KS (Knology)

▲ **BAXTER SPRINGS**—City of Baxter Springs

▲ **BAZINE**—Formerly served by Cebridge Connections. Now served by RUSH CENTER, KS [KS0418]

BAZINE—See RUSH CENTER, KS (GBT Communications Inc.)

▲**BEATTIE**—Allegiance Communications

BEL AIRE—See WICHITA, KS (Cox Communications)

▲**BELLE PLAINE**—SKT Entertainment. Now served by CLEARWATER, KS [KS0136]

BELLE PLAINE—See CLEARWATER, KS (SKT Entertainment)

▲**BELLEVILLE**—Cunningham Cable TV. Now served by WASHINGTON (formerly Glen Elder), KS [KS0228]

BELLEVILLE—See WASHINGTON, KS (Blue Valley Tele-Communications)

▲**BELOIT**—Cunningham Cable TV. Now served by WASHINGTON (formerly Glen Elder), KS [KS0228]

BELOIT—See WASHINGTON, KS (Blue Valley Tele-Communications)

▲**BELVUE**—Formerly served by Giant Communications. No longer in operation

▲**BENNINGTON**—Twin Valley Communications. This system has converted to IPTV. See Bennington, KS [KS5025]

▲**BENNINGTON**—Twin Valley Communications. Formerly [KS0214]. This cable system has converted to IPTV

▲**BENTLEY**—Blue Sky Cable LLC

▲**BERN**—Formerly served by Rainbow Communications. No longer in operation

BERRYTON—See TOPEKA, KS (Cox Communications)

▲**BEVERLY**—Twin Valley Communications. Formerly served by Bennington, KS [KS0214]. This cable system has converted to IPTV

BIG BOW—See ULYSSES, KS (Pioneer Communications)

BIRD CITY—See McDONALD, KS (Eagle Communications)

BISON—See RUSH CENTER, KS (GBT Communications Inc.)

▲**BLUE MOUND**—Formerly served by National Cable Inc. No longer in operation

▲**BLUE RAPIDS**—Zito Media

BOGUE—See LENORA, KS (Nex-Tech)

BOURBON COUNTY (UNINCORPORATED AREAS)—See FORT SCOTT, KS (Suddenlink Communications)

▲**BREWSTER**—S&T Cable

▲**BROOKVILLE**—Wilson Communications. Now served by WILSON, KS [KS0162].

BROOKVILLE—See WILSON, KS (Wilson Communications)

BUCHANAN COUNTY—See ATCHISON, MO (Allegiance Communications)

▲**BUCKLIN**—United Communications Assn. Inc.

BUCKLIN—See CIMARRON, KS (United Communications Assn. Inc.)

▲**BUFFALO**—Formerly served by National Cable Inc. No longer in operation

▲**BUHLER**—Allegiance Communications

▲**BURDEN**—SKT Entertainment. Now served by CLEARWATER, KS [KS0136]

BURDEN—See CLEARWATER, KS (SKT Entertainment)

BURDETT—See RUSH CENTER, KS (GBT Communications Inc.)

BURLINGAME—See BURLINGTON, KS (Mediacom)

▲**BURLINGTON**—Mediacom

▲**BURNS**—Formerly served by Blue Sky Cable LLC. No longer in operation

▲**BURR OAK**—Nex-Tech. This cable system has converted to IPTV. See Burr Oak, KS [KS5042]

▲**BURR OAK**—Nex-Tech. Formerly [KS0265]. This cable system has converted to IPTV

▲**BURRTON**—Formerly served by Cebridge Connections. No longer in operation

BURRTON—See WICHITA, KS (Cox Communications)

BUSHTON—See HOLYROOD, KS (H & B Cable Service Inc.)

BUTLER COUNTY (PORTIONS)—See WICHITA, KS (Cox Communications)

▲**CALDWELL**—Formerly served by Almega Cable. No longer in operation

CANEY—See COFFEYVILLE, KS (Cox Communications)

▲**CANTON**—Formerly served by Cox Communications. No longer in operation

▲**CANTON**—Home Communications Inc

CARBONDALE—See BURLINGTON, KS (Mediacom)

▲**CAWKER CITY**—City of Cawker City. Now served by WASHINGTON, KS [KS0228]

CAWKER CITY—See WASHINGTON, KS (Blue Valley Tele-Communications)

CEDAR VALE—See CLEARWATER, KS (SKT Entertainment)

▲**CENTRALIA**—Blue Valley Tele-Communications

▲**CHANUTE**—Cable One

▲**CHAPMAN**—Eagle Communications

CHASE—See HOLYROOD, KS (H & B Cable Service Inc.)

CHENEY—See WICHITA, KS (Cox Communications)

CHEROKEE COUNTY (NORTHERN PORTION)—See PITTSBURG, KS (Cox Communications)

CHERRYVALE—See COFFEYVILLE, KS (Cox Communications)

▲**CHETOPA**—Allegiance Communications

CHICOPEE—See PITTSBURG, KS (Cox Communications)

▲**CIMARRON**—United Communications Assn. Inc.

CIRCLEVILLE—See HOLTON, KS (Giant Communications)

CLAFLIN—See HOLYROOD, KS (H & B Cable Service Inc.)

▲**CLAY CENTER**—Eagle Communications

CLAY COUNTY (PORTIONS)—See CLAY CENTER, KS (Eagle Communications)

CLAY COUNTY—See CLIFTON, KS (Zito Media)

▲**CLEARWATER**—SKT Entertainment

▲**CLIFTON**—Zito Media

CLOUD COUNTY (PORTIONS)—See CONCORDIA, KS (Cunningham Cable TV)

CLYDE—See CLIFTON, KS (Zito Media)

▲**COFFEYVILLE**—Cox Communications

▲**COLBY**—S&T Cable

▲**COLDWATER**—United Communications Assn. Inc. Now served by CIMARRON, KS [KS0126]

COLDWATER—See CIMARRON, KS (United Communications Assn. Inc.)

▲**COLUMBUS**—Columbus Telephone Co. This cable system has converted to IPTV. See Columbus, KS [KS5041]

▲**COLUMBUS**—Columbus Telephone Co. Formerly [KS0056]. This cable system has converted to IPTV

▲**COLWICH**—Formerly served by Almega Cable. No longer in operation

▲**CONCORDIA**—Cunningham Cable TV

▲**CONWAY SPRINGS**—Allegiance Communications

COOLIDGE—See ULYSSES, KS (Pioneer Communications)

▲**COPELAND**—United Communications Assn. Inc. Now served by CIMARRON, KS [KS0126]

COPELAND—See CIMARRON, KS (United Communications Assn. Inc.)

COTTONWOOD FALLS—See STRONG CITY, KS (Zito Media)

▲**COUNCIL GROVE**—Council Grove Telecommunications Inc.

▲**COURTLAND**—Nex-Tech. This cable system has converted to IPTV. See Courtland, KS [KS5043]

▲**COURTLAND**—Nex-Tech. Formerly [KS0271]. This cable system has converted to IPTV

CRAWFORD COUNTY (EASTERN PORTION)—See PITTSBURG, KS (Cox Communications)

▲**CUBA**—Eagle Communications

▲**CUNNINGHAM**—Cox Communications. Now served by WICHITA, KS [KS0001]

CUNNINGHAM—See WICHITA, KS (Cox Communications)

▲**DEARING**—SKT Entertainment. Now served by COFFEYVILLE, KS [KS0016]

DEARING—See COFFEYVILLE, KS (Cox Communications)

DEERFIELD—See ULYSSES, KS (Pioneer Communications)

▲**DELPHOS**—Cunningham Cable TV. No longer in operation

▲**DENISON**—Rainbow Communications

DERBY—See WICHITA, KS (Cox Communications)

DETROIT—See CHAPMAN, KS (Eagle Communications)

DEXTER—See CLEARWATER, KS (SKT Entertainment)

DICKINSON COUNTY—See HERINGTON, KS (Allegiance Communications)

DICKINSON COUNTY—See ABILENE, KS (Eagle Communications)

▲**DIGHTON**—S&T Cable

▲**DODGE CITY**—Cox Communications

DORRANCE—See HOLYROOD, KS (H & B Cable Service Inc.)

DOUGLAS COUNTY (UNINCORPORATED AREAS)—See LAWRENCE, KS (Knology)

▲**DOUGLASS**—Allegiance Communications

▲**DOWNS**—Cunningham Cable TV. Now served by WASHINGTON (formerly Glen Elder), KS [KS0228]

▲**DOWNS**—Formerly served by Cebridge Connections. Now served by WASHINGTON (formerly GLEN ELDER), KS [KS0228]

DOWNS—See WASHINGTON, KS (Blue Valley Tele-Communications)

▲**DURHAM**—Formerly served by Eagle Communications. No longer in operation

▲**DWIGHT**—Formerly served by Eagle Communications. No longer in operation

EASTBOROUGH—See WICHITA, KS (Cox Communications)

▲**EASTON**—Formerly served by Giant Communications. No longer in operation

EDGERTON—See BALDWIN CITY, KS (Mediacom)

▲**EDMOND**—Nex-Tech. Formerly [KS0450]. This cable system has converted to IPTV

▲ **EDNA**—Formerly served by Craw-Kan Telephone Co-op. No longer in operation

▲ **EDNA**—Formerly served by GIRARD, KS [KS0446]. Craw-Kan Telephone Co-op. This cable system has converted to IPTV

▲ **EFFINGHAM**—Rainbow Communications

EL DORADO—See WICHITA, KS (Cox Communications)

▲ **ELK CITY**—Formerly served by SKT Entertainment. No longer in operation

ELK COUNTY—See CLEARWATER, KS (SKT Entertainment)

▲ **ELKHART**—Epic Touch Co.

▲ **ELLINWOOD**—Allegiance Communications

ELLIS—See HAYS, KS (Eagle Communications)

ELLIS—See RUSH CENTER, KS (GBT Communications Inc.)

▲ **ELLSWORTH**—Eagle Communications

ELWOOD—See HIAWATHA, KS (Rainbow Communications)

▲ **EMMETT**—Rainbow Communications

▲ **EMPORIA**—Cable One

▲ **ENSIGN**—United Communications Assn. Inc. Now served by CIMARRON, KS [KS0126]

ENSIGN—See CIMARRON, KS (United Communications Assn. Inc.)

ENTERPRISE—See CHAPMAN, KS (Eagle Communications)

ERIE—See IOLA, KS (Cox Communications)

▲ **ESBON**—Nex-Tech. Formerly served by Lebanon, KS [KS0397]. This cable system has converted to IPTV

▲ **ESKRIDGE**—Zito Media

EUDORA—See LAWRENCE, KS (Knology)

▲ **EUREKA**—Mediacom

EVEREST—See HIAWATHA, KS (Rainbow Communications)

▲ **FAIRVIEW**—Carson Communications. Now served by HIAWATHA, KS [KS0059]

FAIRVIEW—See HIAWATHA, KS (Rainbow Communications)

FINNEY COUNTY—See GARDEN CITY, KS (Cox Communications)

FLORENCE—See MARION, KS (Eagle Communications)

FORD COUNTY—See DODGE CITY, KS (Cox Communications)

▲ **FORD**—United Communications Assn. Inc. Now served by CIMARRON, KS [KS0126]

FORD—See CIMARRON, KS (United Communications Assn. Inc.)

▲ **FORMOSO**—Cunningham Cable TV. Now served by WASHINGTON (formerly Glen Elder), KS [KS0228]

FORMOSO—See WASHINGTON, KS (Blue Valley Tele-Communications)

▲ **FORT RILEY**—Allegiance Communications

▲ **FORT SCOTT**—Suddenlink Communications

FOWLER—See MEADE, KS (Allegiance Communications)

▲ **FRANKFORT**—Blue Valley Tele-Communications

FRANKLIN—See PITTSBURG, KS (Cox Communications)

▲ **FREDONIA**—Allegiance Communications

▲ **FRONTENAC**—Formerly served by Almega Cable. No longer in operation

FRONTENAC—See PITTSBURG, KS (Cox Communications)

▲ **GALENA**—Mediacom. Now served by CARL JUNCTION, MO [MO0094]

▲ **GALVA**—Home Communications Inc

▲ **GARDEN CITY**—Cox Communications

GARDEN PLAIN (PORTIONS)—See WICHITA, KS (Cox Communications)

▲ **GARDEN PLAIN**—Formerly served by Cebridge Connections. No longer in operation

GARFIELD—See RUSH CENTER, KS (GBT Communications Inc.)

GARNETT—See OTTAWA, KS (Allegiance Communications)

GAS—See IOLA, KS (Cox Communications)

▲ **GENESEO**—Formerly served by Eagle Communications. No longer in operation

▲ **GIRARD**—Craw-Kan Telephone Co-op. This cable system has converted to IPTV. See GIRARD, KS [KS5099]

▲ **GIRARD**—Formerly served by Craw-Kan Telephone Co-op. No longer in operation

▲ **GIRARD**—Formerly [KS0446]. Craw-Kan Telephone Coop. This cable system has converted to IPTV

▲ **GLASCO**—Cunningham Cable TV. No longer in operation

GLEN ELDER—See WASHINGTON, KS (Blue Valley Tele-Communications)

GODDARD—See WICHITA, KS (Cox Communications)

▲ **GOESSEL**—Mid-Kansas Cable Services Inc.

▲ **GOFF**—Rainbow Communications

▲ **GOODLAND**—Eagle Communications

▲ **GOODLAND**—S&T Cable

▲ **GORHAM**—Nex-Tech. Now served by LENORA, KS [KS0450]

GORHAM—See LENORA, KS (Nex-Tech)

GRANDVIEW PLAZA—See JUNCTION CITY, KS (Cox Communications)

▲ **GRANTVILLE**—SCI Cable

▲ **GREAT BEND**—Cox Communications

GREELEY COUNTY (PORTIONS)—See ULYSSES, KS (Pioneer Communications)

▲ **GREEN**—Formerly served by Eagle Communications. No longer in operation

▲ **GREENLEAF**—Allegiance Communications

GRENOLA—See CLEARWATER, KS (SKT Entertainment)

GRIDLEY—See BURLINGTON, KS (Mediacom)

GRINNELL—See BREWSTER, KS (S&T Cable)

▲ **GYPSUM**—Home Communications Inc

▲ **HADDAM**—Formerly served by West-com. No longer in operation

HALSTEAD—See WICHITA, KS (Cox Communications)

▲ **HAMILTON**—Mediacom. Now served by EUREKA, KS [KS0058]

HAMILTON—See EUREKA, KS (Mediacom)

▲ **HANOVER**—Blue Valley Tele-Communications

▲ **HANSTON**—United Communications Assn. Inc. Now served by CIMARRON, KS [KS0126]

HANSTON—See CIMARRON, KS (United Communications Assn. Inc.)

▲ **HARPER**—Allegiance Communications

▲ **HARTFORD**—Zito Media

HARVEY COUNTY (UNINCORPORATED AREAS)—See WICHITA, KS (Cox Communications)

▲ **HARVEYVILLE**—Formerly served by Galaxy Cablevision. No longer in operation

▲ **HAVEN**—Allegiance Communications

▲ **HAVENSVILLE**—Blue Valley Telecommunications. Formerly served by Onaga, KS [KS0407]. This cable system has converted to IPTV

▲ **HAVENSVILLE**—Rainbow Communications

▲ **HAVILAND**—Haviland Cable-Vision

▲ **HAYS**—Eagle Communications

HAYSVILLE—See WICHITA, KS (Cox Communications)

▲ **HEALY**—S&T Cable

▲ **HERINGTON**—Allegiance Communications

▲ **HERNDON**—Formerly served by Pinpoint Cable TV. No longer in operation

HESSTON—See WICHITA, KS (Cox Communications)

▲ **HIAWATHA**—Rainbow Communications

HIGHLAND—See HIAWATHA, KS (Rainbow Communications)

▲ **HILL CITY**—Nex-Tech. Now served by LENORA, KS [KS0450]

HILL CITY—See LENORA, KS (Nex-Tech)

HILLSBORO—See MARION, KS (Eagle Communications)

HOISINGTON—See GREAT BEND, KS (Cox Communications)

HOLCOMB—See ULYSSES, KS (Pioneer Communications)

▲ **HOLTON**—Giant Communications

▲ **HOLYROOD**—H & B Cable Service Inc.

▲ **HOME TWP.**—Blue Valley Telecommunications. Formerly [KS0424]. This cable system has converted to IPTV

▲ **HOME**—Blue Valley Telecommunications. Formerly [KS0424]. This cable system has converted to IPTV. See Home, KS [K5022]

▲ **HOPE**—Eagle Communications

HORTON—See HIAWATHA, KS (Rainbow Communications)

HOWARD—See CLEARWATER, KS (SKT Entertainment)

▲ **HOXIE**—Eagle Communications

▲ **HOYT**—Giant Communications

HUGOTON—See ULYSSES, KS (Pioneer Communications)

HUMBOLDT—See IOLA, KS (Cox Communications)

▲ **HUTCHINSON**—Cox Communications. Now served by WICHITA, KS [KS0001]

HUTCHINSON—See WICHITA, KS (Cox Communications)

▲ **INDEPENDENCE**—Cable One

▲ **INGALLS**—United Communications Assn. Inc. Now served by CIMARRON, KS [KS0126]

INGALLS—See CIMARRON, KS (United Communications Assn. Inc.)

INMAN—See BUHLER, KS (Allegiance Communications)

▲ **IOLA**—Cox Communications

▲ **IUKA**—Formerly served by Cox Communications. No longer in operation

▲ **JAMESTOWN**—Cunningham Cable TV. Now served by WASHINGTON (formerly Glen Elder), KS [KS0228]

JAMESTOWN—See WASHINGTON, KS (Blue Valley Tele-Communications)

▲ **JETMORE**—United Communications Assn. Inc. Now served by CIMARRON, KS [KS0126]

JETMORE—See CIMARRON, KS (United Communications Assn. Inc.)

▲ **JEWELL**—Cunningham Cable TV. Now served by WASHINGTON (formerly Glen Elder), KS [KS0228]

JEWELL—See WASHINGTON, KS (Blue Valley Tele-Communications)

JOHNSON COUNTY (SOUTHERN PORTION)—See PAOLA, KS (Suddenlink Communications)

JOHNSON COUNTY—See OLATHE, KS (Comcast Cable)

JOHNSON—See ULYSSES, KS (Pioneer Communications)

▲ **JUNCTION CITY**—Cox Communications

KANOPOLIS—See ELLSWORTH, KS (Eagle Communications)

KANORADO—See BREWSTER, KS (S&T Cable)

▲ **KANSAS CITY (unincorporated areas)**—Charter Communications. Now served by LAWRENCE, KS [KS0004]

KANSAS CITY (UNINCORPORATED AREAS)—See LAWRENCE, KS (Knology)

KANSAS STATE UNIVERSITY—See JUNCTION CITY, KS (Cox Communications)

KECHI—See WICHITA, KS (Cox Communications)

KENDALL—See ULYSSES, KS (Pioneer Communications)

▲ **KENSINGTON**—Cunningham Cable TV. Now served by EDMOND, KS [KS0450]

KEYES—See ELKHART, OK (Epic Touch Co.)

KINGMAN COUNTY—See WICHITA, KS (Cox Communications)

KINGMAN—See WICHITA, KS (Cox Communications)

▲ **KINSLEY**—Cox Communications

▲ **KIOWA**—Formerly served by Almega Cable. No longer in operation

▲ **KIRWIN**—Nex-Tech. This cable system has converted to IPTV. See Kirwin, KS [KS5075]

▲ **KIRWIN**—Nex-Tech. Formerly [KS0287]. This cable system has converted to IPTV

KISMET—See MEADE, KS (Allegiance Communications)

▲ **LA CROSSE**—Cox Communications. Now served by RUSH CENTER, KS [KS0418]

LA CROSSE—See RUSH CENTER, KS (GBT Communications Inc.)

▲ **LA CYGNE**—Formerly served by Almega Cable. No longer in operation

▲ **LA HARPE**—Formerly served by CableDirect. No longer in operation

▲ **LAKE DABINAWA**—Rainbow Communications

▲ **LAKE OF THE FOREST**—Time Warner Cable. Now served by KANSAS CITY, MO [MO0001]

▲ **LAKE WABAUNSEE**—Formerly served by Galaxy Cablevision. No longer in operation

LAKEWOOD HILLS—See LAKE DABINAWA, KS (Rainbow Communications)

LAKIN—See ULYSSES, KS (Pioneer Communications)

LANCASTER—See ATCHISON, KS (Allegiance Communications)

▲ **LANE**—Formerly served by National Cable Inc. No longer in operation

LARNED—See GREAT BEND, KS (Cox Communications)

▲ **LAWRENCE**—Knology

LE ROY—See BURLINGTON, KS (Mediacom)

LEAVENWORTH COUNTY (UNINCORPORATED AREAS)—See LAWRENCE, KS (Knology)

▲ **LEBANON**—Nex-Tech. This cable system has converted to IPTV. See Lebanon, KS [KS5049]

▲ **LEBANON**—Nex-Tech. Formerly [KS0397]. This cable system has converted to IPTV

LEBO—See BURLINGTON, KS (Mediacom)

LECOMPTON—See PERRY, KS (SCI Cable)

▲ **LEHIGH**—Formerly served by Eagle Communications. No longer in operation

▲ **LENEXA**—SureWest Broadband. This cable system has converted to IPTV. See Lenexa, KS [KS5122]

▲ **LENEXA**—Formerly [KS0462]. SureWest Broadband. This cable system has converted to IPTV

▲ **LENORA**—Nex-Tech

LEON—See CLEARWATER, KS (SKT Entertainment)

▲ **LEONARDVILLE**—Formerly served by Giant Communications. No longer in operation

▲ **LEOTI**—Formerly served by Cebridge Connections. Now served by ULYSSES, KS [KS0044]

LEOTI—See ULYSSES, KS (Pioneer Communications)

LEVANT—See BREWSTER, KS (S&T Cable)

LEWIS & CLARK VILLAGE—See ATCHISON, MO (Allegiance Communications)

LEWIS—See RUSH CENTER, KS (GBT Communications Inc.)

▲ **LIBERAL**—Windjammer Cable

LIEBENTHAL—See RUSH CENTER, KS (GBT Communications Inc.)

▲ **LINCOLN**—Eagle Communications

LINCOLNVILLE—See MARION, KS (Eagle Communications)

▲ **LINN**—Allegiance Communications

▲ **LINSBORG**—Cox Communications. Now served by WICHITA, KS [KS0001]

LINSBORG—See WICHITA, KS (Cox Communications)

LINWOOD—See LAWRENCE, KS (Knology)

LITTLE RIVER—See HOLYROOD, KS (H & B Cable Service Inc.)

LOGAN—See LENORA, KS (Nex-Tech)

LONGTON—See CLEARWATER, KS (SKT Entertainment)

LORRAINE—See HOLYROOD, KS (H & B Cable Service Inc.)

▲ **LOUISBURG**—Formerly served by Almega Cable. No longer in operation

▲ **LOUISVILLE**—WTC Communications. Formerly served by Wamego, KS [KS0057]. This cable system has converted to IPTV

▲ **LOWELL**—Formerly served by Riverton-Lowell Cablevision. No longer in operation

▲ **LUCAS**—Wilson Communications. Now served by WILSON, KS

LUCAS—See WILSON, KS (Wilson Communications)

▲ **LURAY**—Gorham Telephone Co. This cable system has converted to IPTV. See Luray, KS [KS5094]

▲ **LURAY**—Gorham Telephone Co. Formerly [KS0298]. This cable system has converted to IPTV

LYNDON—See BURLINGTON, KS (Mediacom)

▲ **LYON COUNTY**—Formerly served by Galaxy Cablevision. No longer in operation

LYON COUNTY—See EMPORIA, KS (Cable One)

▲ **LYONS**—Cox Communications. Now served by GREAT BEND, KS [KS0012]

LYONS—See GREAT BEND, KS (Cox Communications)

▲ **MACKSVILLE**—Formerly served by Almega Cable. No longer in operation

▲ **MADISON**—Mediacom. Now served by EUREKA, KS [KS0058]

MADISON—See EUREKA, KS (Mediacom)

▲ **MAHASKA**—Formerly served by Westcom. No longer in operation

MAIZE—See WICHITA, KS (Cox Communications)

MANHATTAN (PORTIONS)—See ST. GEORGE, KS (SCI Cable)

MANHATTAN—See JUNCTION CITY, KS (Cox Communications)

▲ **MANKATO**—Cunningham Cable TV. Now served by WASHINGTON (formerly Glen Elder), KS [KS0228]

MANKATO—See WASHINGTON, KS (Blue Valley Tele-Communications)

MANTER—See ULYSSES, KS (Pioneer Communications)

▲ **MAPLE HILL**—Zito Media

MARIENTHAL—See ULYSSES, KS (Pioneer Communications)

MARION COUNTY (SOUTHERN PORTION)—See WICHITA, KS (Cox Communications)

MARION COUNTY—See MARION, KS (Eagle Communications)

▲ **MARION**—Eagle Communications

▲ **MARQUETTE**—Blue Sky Cable LLC

MARSHALL COUNTY (PORTIONS)—See MARYSVILLE, KS (Blue Valley Tele-Communications)

▲ **MARYSVILLE**—Blue Valley Tele-Communications

▲ **MAYETTA**—Giant Communications

MCCONNELL AFB—See WICHITA, KS (Cox Communications)

MCCRACKEN—See RUSH CENTER, KS (GBT Communications Inc.)

▲ **McCUNE**—Formerly served by Craw-Kan Telephone Co-op. No longer in operation

▲ **MCCUNE**—Formerly served by GIRARD, KS [KS0446]. Craw-Kan Telephone Co-op. This cable system has converted to IPTV

▲ **MCDONALD**—Eagle Communications

▲ **McFARLAND**—Formerly served by Galaxy Cablevision. No longer in operation

▲ **MCLOUTH**—Giant Communications

MCPHERSON COUNTY (PORTIONS)—See WICHITA, KS (Cox Communications)

▲ **McPHERSON**—Cox Communications. Now served by WICHITA, KS [KS0001]

MCPHERSON—See WICHITA, KS (Cox Communications)

▲ **MEADE**—Allegiance Communications

▲ **MEDICINE LODGE**—Allegiance Communications

▲ **MELVERN**—Zito Media

MERIDEN (PORTIONS)—See GRANTVILLE, KS (SCI Cable)

▲ **MERIDEN**—SCI Cable

MIAMI COUNTY (UNINCORPORATED AREAS)—See PAOLA, KS (Suddenlink Communications)

MILFORD (PORTIONS)—See JUNCTION CITY, KS (Cox Communications)

▲ **MILFORD**—Eagle Communications

▲ **MILTONVALE**—Twin Valley Communications. Formerly served by Bennington, KS [KS0214]. This cable system has converted to IPTV

▲ **MINNEAPOLIS**—Eagle Communications

MINNEOLA—See MEADE, KS (Allegiance Communications)

MITCHELL COUNTY (PORTIONS)—See WASHINGTON, KS (Blue Valley Tele-Communications)

MOLINE—See CLEARWATER, KS (SKT Entertainment)

▲ **MONTEZUMA**—United Communications Assn. Inc. Now served by CIMARRON, KS [KS0126]

MONTEZUMA—See CIMARRON, KS (United Communications Assn. Inc.)

MONTGOMERY COUNTY (PORTIONS)—See INDEPENDENCE, KS (Cable One)

MONTGOMERY COUNTY (PORTIONS)—See COFFEYVILLE, KS (Cox Communications)

▲ **MORGANVILLE**—Formerly served by Eagle Communications. No longer in operation

▲ **MORRILL**—Rainbow Communications

MORRIS COUNTY (PORTIONS)—See COUNCIL GROVE, KS (Council Grove Telecommunications Inc.)

▲ **MORROWVILLE**—Formerly served by Diode Cable Co. No longer in operation

MOSCOW—See ULYSSES, KS (Pioneer Communications)

▲ **MOUND VALLEY**—Formerly served by National Cable Inc. No longer in operation

▲ **MOUNDRIDGE**—Mid-Kansas Cable Services Inc.

▲ **MOUNT HOPE**—Formerly served by Almega Cable. No longer in operation

▲ **MULLINVILLE**—Formerly served by Mullinville Cable TV. No longer in operation

▲ **MULVANE (unincorporated areas)**—Formerly served by CableDirect. No longer in operation

▲ **MULVANE**—Cox Communications. Now served by WICHITA, KS [KS0001]

MULVANE—See WICHITA, KS (Cox Communications)

▲ **MUNDEN**—Formerly served by Westcom. No longer in operation

▲ **MUNJOR**—Nex-Tech

▲ **MUSCOTAH**—Rainbow Communications

▲ **NARKA**—Formerly served by Westcom. No longer in operation

▲ **NATOMA**—Eagle Communications. Now served by EDMOND, KS [KS0450]

▲ **NEODESHA**—Cable One. Now served by INDEPENDENCE, KS [KS0022]

NEODESHA—See INDEPENDENCE, KS (Cable One)

NEOSHO COUNTY (PORTIONS)—See IOLA, KS (Cox Communications)

▲ **NEOSHO RAPIDS**—Zito Media

▲ **NESS CITY**—Formerly served by Cebridge Connections. Now served by RUSH CENTER, KS [KS0418]

NESS CITY—See RUSH CENTER, KS (GBT Communications Inc.)

NEW STRAWN—See BURLINGTON, KS (Mediacom)

▲ **NEWTON**—Cox Communications. Now served by WICHITA, KS [KS0001]

NEWTON—See WICHITA, KS (Cox Communications)

NICKERSON—See WICHITA, KS (Cox Communications)

▲ **NORCATUR**—Formerly served by Pinpoint Cable TV. No longer in operation

NORTH NEWTON—See WICHITA, KS (Cox Communications)

▲ **NORTON**—Nex-Tech. This cable system has converted to IPTV. See Norton, KS [KS5050]

▲ **NORTON**—Nex-Tech. Formerly [KS0050]. This cable system has converted to IPTV

▲ **NORTONVILLE**—Giant Communications

▲ **NORWICH**—Formerly served by Almega Cable. No longer in operation

▲ **OAKLEY**—S&T Cable

▲ **OBERLIN**—Eagle Communications

▲ **OFFERLE**—GBT Communications Inc.

OGDEN—See JUNCTION CITY, KS (Cox Communications)

▲ **OKETO**—Blue Valley Tele-Communications. Formerly served by Home, KS [KS0424]. This cable system has converted to IPTV

▲ **OLATHE**—Comcast Cable

▲ **OLPE**—Zito Media

▲ **OLSBURG**—Formerly served by Giant Communications. No longer in operation

▲ **ONAGA**—Blue Valley Telecommunications

▲ **OSAGE CITY**—Mediacom. Now served by BURLINGTON, KS [KS0064]

OSAGE CITY—See BURLINGTON, KS (Mediacom)

▲ **OSAGE COUNTY**—Formerly served by Galaxy Cablevision. No longer in operation

OSAWATOMIE—See PAOLA, KS (Suddenlink Communications)

OSBORNE—See LENORA, KS (Nex-Tech)

▲ **OSKALOOSA**—Giant Communications. Now served by McLOUTH, KS [KS0191]

OSKALOOSA—See McLOUTH, KS (Giant Communications)

▲ **OSWEGO**—Mediacom

OTIS—See RUSH CENTER, KS (GBT Communications Inc.)

▲ **OTTAWA**—Allegiance Communications

▲ **OVERBROOK**—Zito Media

▲ **OVERLAND PARK**—Time Warner Cable of Johnson County. No longer in operation

▲ **OVERLAND PARK**—Formerly served by LENEXA, KS [KS0462]. SureWest Broadband. This cable system has converted to IPTV

▲ **OXFORD**—Allegiance Communications

▲ **OZAWKIE**—Giant Communications

▲ **PALMER**—Formerly served by Eagle Communications. No longer in operation

▲ **PAOLA**—Suddenlink Communications

PARK CITY—See WICHITA, KS (Cox Communications)

▲ **PARKER**—Formerly served by National Cable Inc. No longer in operation

▲ **PARSONS**—Cable One

▲ **PARTRIDGE**—Formerly served by CableDirect. No longer in operation

PAULINE—See TOPEKA, KS (Cox Communications)

▲ **PAWNEE ROCK**—Golden Belt Telephone Association Inc. Now served by RUSH CENTER, KS [KS0418]

PAWNEE ROCK—See RUSH CENTER, KS (GBT Communications Inc.)

▲ **PAXICO**—Zito Media

▲ **PEABODY**—Allegiance Communications

▲ **PERRY**—SCI Cable

▲ **PHILLIPSBURG**—Nex-Tech

▲ **PITTSBURG**—Cox Communications

PLAINS—See MEADE, KS (Allegiance Communications)

▲ **PLAINVILLE**—Nex-Tech

PLATTE COUNTY—See ATCHISON, MO (Allegiance Communications)

▲ **PLEASANTON**—Formerly served by Almega Cable. No longer in operation

▲ **POMONA**—Zito Media

▲ **POTTAWATOMIE COUNTY (PORTIONS)**—WTC Communications. Formerly served by Wamego, KS [KS0057]. This cable system has converted to IPTV

POTTAWATOMIE COUNTY (SOUTHEASTERN PORTION)—See JUNCTION CITY, KS (Cox Communications)

PRATT COUNTY—See WICHITA, KS (Cox Communications)

▲ **PRATT**—Cox Communications. Now served by WICHITA, KS [KS0001]

PRATT—See WICHITA, KS (Cox Communications)

▲ **PRESCOTT**—Craw-Kan Telephone Co-op. This cable system has converted to IPTV. See PRESCOTT, KS [KS5101]

▲ **PRESCOTT**—Formerly [KS0446]. Craw-Kan Telephone Coop. This cable system has converted to IPTV

▲ **PRETTY PRAIRIE**—Formerly served by Almega Cable. No longer in operation

▲ **PRINCETON**—Formerly served by CableDirect. No longer in operation

▲ **PROTECTION**—United Communications Assn. Inc. Now served by CIMARRON, KS [KS0126]

PROTECTION—See CIMARRON, KS (United Communications Assn. Inc.)

▲ **QUENEMO**—Formerly served by Galaxy Cablevision. No longer in operation

▲ **QUINTER**—Quinter Cable Co. Now served by EDMUND, KS [KS0450]

▲ **RANDALL**—Cunningham Cable TV. Now served by WASHINGTON (formerly Glen Elder), KS [KS0228]

RANDALL—See WASHINGTON, KS (Blue Valley Tele-Communications)

▲ **RANDOLPH**—Rainbow Communications

RANSOM—See RUSH CENTER, KS (GBT Communications Inc.)

▲ **READING**—Formerly served by Galaxy Cablevision. No longer in operation

RENO COUNTY (PORTIONS)—See WICHITA, KS (Cox Communications)

▲ **REPUBLIC**—Formerly served by Diode Cable Co. No longer in operation

▲ **RESERVE**—Rainbow Communications

RICE COUNTY—See GREAT BEND, KS (Cox Communications)

RICHFIELD—See ULYSSES, KS (Pioneer Communications)

▲ **RICHMOND**—Zito Media

RILEY COUNTY (SOUTHERN PORTION)—See JUNCTION CITY, KS (Cox Communications)

▲ **RILEY**—Eagle Communications

ROBINSON—See HIAWATHA, KS (Rainbow Communications)

ROLLA—See ULYSSES, KS (Pioneer Communications)

▲ **ROSALIA**—Formerly served by CableDirect. No longer in operation

ROSE HILL—See WICHITA, KS (Cox Communications)

▲ **ROSSVILLE**—Zito Media

ROZEL—See RUSH CENTER, KS (GBT Communications Inc.)

▲ **RUSH CENTER**—GBT Communications Inc.

RUSHVILLE—See ATCHISON, MO (Allegiance Communications)

RUSSELL SPRINGS—See BREWSTER, KS (S&T Cable)

▲ **RUSSELL**—Eagle Communications

SABETHA—See HIAWATHA, KS (Rainbow Communications)

▲ **SALINA**—Formerly served by TVCN. No longer in operation

▲ **SALINA**—Cox Communications

SALINE COUNTY (PORTIONS)—See SALINA, KS (Cox Communications)

SATANTA—See ULYSSES, KS (Pioneer Communications)

▲ **SCANDIA**—Cunningham Cable TV. Now served by WASHINGTON (formerly Glen Elder), KS [KS0228]

SCANDIA—See WASHINGTON, KS (Blue Valley Tele-Communications)

SCHOENCHEN—See RUSH CENTER, KS (GBT Communications Inc.)

▲ **SCOTT CITY**—Pioneer Communications. Now served by ULYSSES, KS [KS0044]

SCOTT CITY—See ULYSSES, KS (Pioneer Communications)

SCRANTON—See BURLINGTON, KS (Mediacom)

▲ **SEDAN**—Allegiance Communications

▲ **SEDGWICK COUNTY (portions)**—Formerly served by Westcom. No longer in operation

SEDGWICK COUNTY (PORTIONS)—See WICHITA, KS (Cox Communications)

SEDGWICK—See WICHITA, KS (Cox Communications)

▲ **SENECA**—Carson Communications. Now served by HIAWATHA, KS [KS0059]

SENECA—See HIAWATHA, KS (Rainbow Communications)

SEVERY—See CLEARWATER, KS (SKT Entertainment)

SEWARD COUNTY (PORTIONS)—See MEADE, KS (Allegiance Communications)

▲ **SHARON SPRINGS**—Formerly served by Cebridge Connections. Now served by ULYSSES, KS [KS0044]

SHARON SPRINGS—See ULYSSES, KS (Pioneer Communications)

▲ **SHARON**—Allegiance Communications

SHAWNEE COUNTY—See TOPEKA, KS (Cox Communications)

▲ **SHAWNEE**—Formerly served by LENEXA, KS [KS0462]. SureWest Broadband. This cable system has converted to IPTV

SILVER LAKE—See ROSSVILLE, KS (Zito Media)

▲ **SMITH CENTER**—Nex-Tech

▲ **SMOLAN**—Home Communications Inc

▲ **SOLOMON**—Eagle Communications

SOUTH COFFEYVILLE—See COFFEYVILLE, OK (Cox Communications)

▲ **SOUTH HAVEN**—Formerly served by Almega Cable. No longer in operation

SOUTH HUTCHINSON—See WICHITA, KS (Cox Communications)

▲ **SPEARVILLE**—United Communications Assn. Inc. Now served by CIMARRON, KS [KS0126]

SPEARVILLE—See CIMARRON, KS (United Communications Assn. Inc.)

▲ **SPRING HILL**—Formerly served by Cebridge Connections. Now served by PAOLA, KS [KS0029]

SPRING HILL—See PAOLA, KS (Suddenlink Communications)

▲ **ST. FRANCIS**—Eagle Communications

▲ **ST. GEORGE**—SCI Cable

▲ **ST. JOHN**—GBT Communications Inc.

▲ **ST. MARY'S**—WTC Communications. Formerly served by Wamego, KS [KS0057]. This cable system has converted to IPTV

▲ **ST. PAUL**—Cable TV of St. Paul

▲ **STAFFORD**—Allegiance Communications

▲ **STERLING**—Eagle Communications. Now served by GREAT BEND, KS [KS0012]

STERLING—See GREAT BEND, KS (Cox Communications)

▲ **STOCKTON**—Nex-Tech. This cable system has converted to IPTV. See Stockton, KS [KS5055]

▲ **STOCKTON**—Nex-Tech. Formerly [KS0051]. This cable system has converted to IPTV

▲ **STRONG CITY**—Zito Media

SUBLETTE—See ULYSSES, KS (Pioneer Communications)

▲ **SUMMERFIELD**—Blue Valley Tele-Communications. This cable system has converted to IPTV. See Summerfield, KS [KS5015]

▲ **SUMMERFIELD**—Blue Valley Telecommunications. Formerly [KS0452]. This cable system has converted to IPTV

▲ **SYLVAN GROVE**—Wilson Communications. Now served by WILSON, KS [KS0162]

SYLVAN GROVE—See WILSON, KS (Wilson Communications)

▲ **SYLVIA**—Formerly served by Cox Communications. No longer in operation

SYRACUSE—See ULYSSES, KS (Pioneer Communications)

▲ **TAMPA**—Formerly served by Eagle Communications. No longer in operation

TECUMSEH—See TOPEKA, KS (Cox Communications)

▲ **TESCOTT**—Twin Valley Communications. Formerly served by Bennington, KS [KS0214]. This cable system has converted to IPTV

▲ **THAYER**—Mediacom

TIMKEN—See RUSH CENTER, KS (GBT Communications Inc.)

▲ **TIPTON**—Wilson Communications. Now served by WILSON, KS [KS0162]

TIPTON—See WILSON, KS (Wilson Communications)

TONGANOXIE—See LAWRENCE, KS (Knology)

▲ **TOPEKA**—Cox Communications

▲ **TORONTO**—Mediacom

TOWANDA—See WICHITA, KS (Cox Communications)

▲ **TRIBUNE**—Formerly served by Cebridge Connections. Now served by ULYSSES, KS [KS0044]

TRIBUNE—See ULYSSES, KS (Pioneer Communications)

TROY—See HIAWATHA, KS (Rainbow Communications)

▲ **TURON**—Formerly served by Cox Communications. No longer in operation

TYRO (PORTIONS)—See COFFEYVILLE, KS (Cox Communications)

▲ **UDALL**—Wheat State Telecable Inc.

▲ **ULYSSES**—Pioneer Communications

▲ **UNIONTOWN**—Craw-Kan Telephone Co-op. This cable system has converted to IPTV. See UNIONTOWN, KS [KS5100]

▲ **UNIONTOWN**—Craw-Kan Telephone Co-op. This cable system has converted to IPTV

UTICA—See RUSH CENTER, KS (GBT Communications Inc.)

VALLEY CENTER—See WICHITA, KS (Cox Communications)

▲ **VALLEY FALLS**—Giant Communications

▲ **VERMILLION**—Blue Valley Telecommunications. This cable system has converted to IPTV. See Vermillion, KS [KS5016]

▲ **VERMILLION**—Blue Valley Telecommunications. Formerly [KS0339]. This cable system has converted to IPTV

▲ **VICTORIA**—Nex-Tech. Now served by LENORA, KS [KS0450]

VICTORIA—See LENORA, KS (Nex-Tech)

VINING—See CLIFTON, KS (Zito Media)

VIOLA—See CLEARWATER, KS (SKT Entertainment)

▲ **WAKEENEY**—Eagle Communications

▲ **WAKEFIELD**—Eagle Communications

▲ **WALNUT**—Craw-Kan Telephone Co-op. This cable system has converted to IPTV. See WALNUT, KS [KS5103]

▲ **WALNUT**—Craw-Kan Telephone Co-op. This cable system has converted to IPTV

▲ **WALTON**—Formerly served by Galaxy Cablevision. No longer in operation

▲ **WAMEGO**—WTC Communications. This cable system has converted to IPTV. See Wamego, KA [KS5017]

▲ **WAMEGO**—WTC Communications. Formerly [KS0057]. This cable system has converted to IPTV

▲ **WASHINGTON**—Cunningham Cable TV. Now served by WASHINGTON (formerly Glen Elder), KS [KS0228]

▲ **WASHINGTON**—Blue Valley Tele-Communications

▲ **WATERVILLE**—Blue Valley Tele-Communications

WATHENA—See HIAWATHA, KS (Rainbow Communications)

▲ **WAVERLY**—Zito Media

▲ **WEIR**—Formerly served by WSC Cablevision. No longer in operation

▲ **WELLINGTON**—Sumner Cable TV Inc.

WELLSVILLE—See BALDWIN CITY, KS (Mediacom)

▲ **WESTMORELAND**—Formerly served by Giant Communications. No longer in operation

▲ **WETMORE**—Rainbow Communications

▲ **WHITE CITY**—Eagle Communications

▲ **WHITE CLOUD**—Rainbow Communications

▲ **WHITING**—Rainbow Communications

▲ **WICHITA**—Formerly served by Sprint Corp. No longer in operation

▲ **WICHITA**—Cox Communications

▲ **WILLIAMSBURG**—Zito Media

WILLOWBROOK—See WICHITA, KS (Cox Communications)

▲ **WILSEY**—Formerly served by CableDirect. No longer in operation

WILSON COUNTY—See FREDONIA, KS (Allegiance Communications)

▲ **WILSON**—Wilson Communications

▲ **WINCHESTER**—Giant Communications

WINFIELD—See WICHITA, KS (Cox Communications)

WINONA—See BREWSTER, KS (S&T Cable)

▲ **WOODBINE**—Eagle Communications

WYANDOTTE COUNTY (PORTIONS)—See LAWRENCE, KS (Knology)

YATES CENTER—See IOLA, KS (Cox Communications)

KENTUCKY

ABERDEEN—See MORGANTOWN, KY (Mediacom)

ADAIR COUNTY (PORTIONS)—See COLUMBIA, KY (Duo County Telecom)

▲ **ADAIRVILLE**—Suddenlink Communications

AGES—See BLACK MOUNTAIN, KY (Zito Media)

AIRPORT GARDENS—See BULAN, KY (NewWave Communications)

▲ **ALBANY**—Mediacom. Now served by TOMPKINSVILLE, KY [KY0092]

ALBANY—See TOMPKINSVILLE, KY (Mediacom)

ALEXANDRIA—See COVINGTON, KY (Insight Communications)

ALLEN—See HAROLD, KY (Inter Mountain Cable Inc.)

ALMO—See CALLOWAY COUNTY, KY (Mediacom)

▲ **ALTRO**—Formerly served by Altro TV Inc. No longer in operation

ALVATON—See BOWLING GREEN, KY (Insight Communications)

ANCHORAGE—See LOUISVILLE, KY (Insight Communications)

ANDERSON COUNTY (EASTERN PORTION)—See HARRODSBURG, KY (Time Warner Cable)

▲ **ANNVILLE**—C & W Cable

ARGO—See HAROLD, KY (Inter Mountain Cable Inc.)

ARJAY—See MIDDLESBORO, KY (NewWave Communications)

ARLINGTON—See WICKLIFFE, KY (Zito Media)

ARTEMUS—See BARBOURVILLE, KY (Barbourville Utility Commission)

▲ **ASHLAND**—Formerly served by Adelphia Communications. No longer in operation

▲ **ASHLAND**—Time Warner Cable

ATHOL—See BEATTYVILLE, KY (Crystal Broadband Networks)

▲ **AUBURN**—Formerly served by Cebridge Connections. Now served by RUSSELLVILLE, KY [KY0032]

AUBURN—See RUSSELLVILLE, KY (Suddenlink Communications)

AUDUBON PARK—See LOUISVILLE, KY (Insight Communications)

▲ **AUGUSTA**—Bracken County Cablevision Inc. Now served by MAYSVILLE, KY [KY0033]

AUGUSTA—See MAYSVILLE, KY (Limestone Bracken Cablevision)

AURORA—See MARSHALL COUNTY, KY (Mediacom)

AUSTIN—See LOUISVILLE, IN (Insight Communications)

AUXIER—See VAN LEAR, KY (Big Sandy Broadband)

AVAWAM—See LESLIE COUNTY (northern portion), KY (Windjammer Cable)

BAILEY'S SWITCH—See GRAY, KY (Eastern Cable Corp.)

BALLARD COUNTY (PORTIONS)—See GRAVES COUNTY, KY (Zito Media)

BANCROFT—See LOUISVILLE, KY (Insight Communications)

BANNER—See HAROLD, KY (Inter Mountain Cable Inc.)

BARBOURMEADE—See LOUISVILLE, KY (Insight Communications)

▲ **BARBOURVILLE**—Barbourville Utility Commission

▲ **BARDSTOWN**—Bardstown Cable TV

BARDWELL—See WICKLIFFE, KY (Zito Media)

BARLOW—See WICKLIFFE, KY (Zito Media)

BARRALLTON—See BROOKS, KY (Windjammer Cable)

BARREN COUNTY (PORTIONS)—See SUMMER SHADE, KY (Mediacom)

BASKETT—See OWENSBORO, KY (Time Warner Cable)

BAUGHMAN—See FLAT LICK, KY (NewWave Communications)

BAXTER—See HARLAN, KY (Harlan Community TV Inc.)

BAXTER—See BLACK MOUNTAIN, KY (Zito Media)

BEALS—See OWENSBORO, KY (Time Warner Cable)

▲ **BEATTYVILLE**—Crystal Broadband Networks

▲ **BEAVER DAM**—NewWave Communications

BEDFORD—See LOUISVILLE, KY (Insight Communications)

BEE SPRING—See MORGANTOWN, KY (Mediacom)

BEECH CREEK—See GREENVILLE, KY (Comcast Cable)

BEECHMONT—See GREENVILLE, KY (Comcast Cable)

BEECHWOOD VILLAGE—See LOUISVILLE, KY (Insight Communications)

BELFRY—See HAROLD, KY (Inter Mountain Cable Inc.)

BELL COUNTY (PORTIONS)—See PINEVILLE, KY (NewWave Communications)

BELL COUNTY (SOUTHEASTERN PORTION)—See MIDDLESBORO, KY (NewWave Communications)

BELL COUNTY (SOUTHERN PORTION)—See GREASY CREEK, KY (Suddenlink Communications)

BELLEFONTE—See ASHLAND, KY (Time Warner Cable)

BELLEMEADE—See LOUISVILLE, KY (Insight Communications)

BELLEVUE—See COVINGTON, KY (Insight Communications)

BELLEWOOD—See LOUISVILLE, KY (Insight Communications)

BELTON—See GREENVILLE, KY (Comcast Cable)

▲ **BENHAM**—Tri-Star Communications. No longer in operation

▲ **BENTON**—Charter Communications. Now served by MAYFIELD, KY [KY0037]

BENTON—See MAYFIELD, KY (NewWave Communications)

BEREA—See RICHMOND, KY (Time Warner Cable)

BETHEL—See MOUNT STERLING, KY (Windjammer Cable)

BETSY LAYNE—See HAROLD, KY (Inter Mountain Cable Inc.)

BEVINSVILLE—See HAROLD, KY (Inter Mountain Cable Inc.)

▲ **BIG CLIFTY**—Mediacom. Now served by CANEYVILLE, KY [KY0291]

BIG CLIFTY—See CANEYVILLE, KY (Mediacom)

BIG CREEK—See GARRARD, KY (NewWave Communications)

BIGHILL—See McKEE, KY (Peoples Telecom)

BIMBLE—See FLAT LICK, KY (NewWave Communications)

▲ **BLACK MOUNTAIN**—Zito Media

BLACKBERRY CITY—See HAROLD, WV (Inter Mountain Cable Inc.)

BLACKBERRY CREEK—See HAROLD, KY (Inter Mountain Cable Inc.)

BLACKEY—See HINDMAN, KY (TV Service Inc.)

▲ **BLAINE**—Formerly served by Lycom Communications. No longer in operation

BLAIR TOWN—See HAROLD, KY (Inter Mountain Cable Inc.)

BLAIR—See CUMBERLAND, KY (Access Cable Television Inc.)

BLEDSOE—See MOZELLE, KY (Windjammer Cable)

▲ **BLOOMFIELD**—Insight Communications

BLUE BANK—See MOREHEAD, KY (Time Warner Cable)

BLUE RIDGE MANOR—See LOUISVILLE, KY (Insight Communications)

BLUE RIVER—See HAROLD, KY (Inter Mountain Cable Inc.)

BLUFF CITY—See OWENSBORO, KY (Time Warner Cable)

BOBS CREEK—See BLACK MOUNTAIN, KY (Zito Media)

BOLDMAN—See HAROLD, KY (Inter Mountain Cable Inc.)

BONNIEVILLE—See MUNFORDVILLE, KY (Mediacom)

▲ **BONNYMAN**—Bonnyman TV. Now served by HINDMAN, KY [KY0027]

BONNYMAN—See HINDMAN, KY (TV Service Inc.)

BOONE COUNTY—See COVINGTON, KY (Insight Communications)

BOONE HEIGHTS—See BARBOURVILLE, KY (Barbourville Utility Commission)

BOONEVILLE—See BEATTYVILLE, KY (Crystal Broadband Networks)

▲ **BOONEVILLE**—Peoples Telecom

BOONS CAMP—See VAN LEAR, KY (Big Sandy Broadband)

BORDEN—See LOUISVILLE, KY (Insight Communications)

BOTTOM—See JENKINS, KY (Inter Mountain Cable Inc.)

▲ **BOWLING GREEN**—Insight Communications

BOYD COUNTY (PORTIONS)—See ASHLAND, KY (Time Warner Cable)

BOYLE COUNTY (PORTIONS)—See HARRODSBURG, KY (Time Warner Cable)

▲ **BRADFORDSVILLE**—Formerly served by Charter Communications. No longer in operation

BRANDENBURG—See LOUISVILLE, KY (Insight Communications)

BRANHAM VILLAGE—See VAN LEAR, KY (Big Sandy Broadband)

BRECKINRIDGE COUNTY (PORTIONS)—See CLOVERPORT, KY (Windjammer Cable)

BRECKINRIDGE COUNTY—See HARDINSBURG, KY (Windjammer Cable)

▲ **BREMEN**—Crystal Broadband Networks

BRIARWOOD—See LOUISVILLE, KY (Insight Communications)

BROAD BOTTOM—See HAROLD, KY (Inter Mountain Cable Inc.)

BRODHEAD—See LINCOLN COUNTY (eastern portion), KY (Mediacom)

▲ **BRODHEAD**—Wilcop Cable TV

BROECK POINTE—See LOUISVILLE, KY (Insight Communications)

BROMLEY—See COVINGTON, KY (Insight Communications)

BRONSTON—See SOMERSET, KY (NewWave Communications)

BROOKPORT—See PADUCAH, IL (Comcast Cable)

▲ **BROOKS**—Windjammer Cable

BROOKSIDE—See BLACK MOUNTAIN, KY (Zito Media)

▲ **BROOKSVILLE**—Bracken County Cablevision Inc. Now served by MAYSVILLE, KY [KY0033]

BROOKSVILLE—See MAYSVILLE, KY (Limestone Bracken Cablevision)

BROWDER—See GREENVILLE, KY (Comcast Cable)

BROWNS FORK—See HINDMAN, KY (TV Service Inc.)

BROWNS FORK—See LESLIE COUNTY (northern portion), KY (Windjammer Cable)

BROWNSBORO FARM—See LOUISVILLE, KY (Insight Communications)

BROWNSBORO VILLAGE—See LOUISVILLE, KY (Insight Communications)

▲ **BROWNSVILLE**—Mediacom. Now served by MORGANTOWN, KY [KY0096]

BROWNSVILLE—See MORGANTOWN, KY (Mediacom)

BRYANTS STORE—See WHITLEY COUNTY, KY (Zito Media)

▲ **BRYANTSVILLE**—Formerly served by Charter Communications. No longer in operation

BUCHANAN COUNTY—See HAROLD, VA (Inter Mountain Cable Inc.)

BUCKNER—See LOUISVILLE, KY (Insight Communications)

▲ **BULAN**—NewWave Communications

BULLITT COUNTY—See LOUISVILLE, KY (Insight Communications)

▲ **BULLSKIN CREEK**—Formerly served by Bullskin Cable TV. No longer in operation

BURDINE—See JENKINS, KY (Inter Mountain Cable Inc.)

BURGIN—See HARRODSBURG, KY (Time Warner Cable)

▲ **BURKESVILLE**—Mediacom

BURLINGTON—See COVINGTON, KY (Insight Communications)

▲ **BURNSIDE**—Charter Communications. Now served by SOMERSET, KY [KY0021]

BURNSIDE—See SOMERSET, KY (NewWave Communications)

BURTONVILLE—See MOREHEAD, KY (Time Warner Cable)

BUSY—See HINDMAN, KY (TV Service Inc.)

BUTLER—See COVINGTON, KY (Insight Communications)

▲ **CADIZ**—Mediacom

CALDWELL COUNTY—See DAWSON SPRINGS, KY (Insight Communications)

CALDWELL COUNTY—See MARION, KY (Mediacom)

CALHOUN—See LIVERMORE, KY (Time Warner Cable)

▲ **CALLOWAY COUNTY**—Mediacom

CALLOWAY COUNTY—See MURRAY, KY (NewWave Communications)

▲ **CALVERT CITY**—Charter Communications. Now served by MAYFIELD, KY [KY0037]

CALVERT CITY—See MAYFIELD, KY (NewWave Communications)

CALVIN—See MIDDLESBORO, KY (NewWave Communications)

CAMARGO—See MOUNT STERLING, KY (Windjammer Cable)

CAMBRIDGE—See LOUISVILLE, KY (Insight Communications)

CAMP SPRINGS—See COVINGTON, KY (Insight Communications)

CAMPBELL COUNTY—See COVINGTON, KY (Insight Communications)

CAMPBELLSBURG—See LOUISVILLE, KY (Insight Communications)

▲ **CAMPBELLSVILLE**—Comcast Cablevision of the South. Now served by ELIZABETHTOWN, KY [KY0012]

CAMPBELLSVILLE—See ELIZABETHTOWN, KY (Comcast Cable)

▲ **CAMPTON**—Windjammer Cable

CANADA—See HAROLD, KY (Inter Mountain Cable Inc.)

▲ **CANEYVILLE**—Mediacom

CANNEL CITY—See WEST LIBERTY, KY (Mountain Telephone)

CANNON—See GRAY, KY (Eastern Cable Corp.)

CARLISLE COUNTY (PORTIONS)—See GRAVES COUNTY, KY (Zito Media)

CARLISLE COUNTY—See WICKLIFFE, KY (Zito Media)

▲ **CARLISLE**—Now served by MOUNT STERLING, KY [KY0046]

CARLISLE—See MOUNT STERLING, KY (Windjammer Cable)

CARROLLTON—See LOUISVILLE, KY (Insight Communications)

CARTER COUNTY (SOUTHWESTERN PORTION)—See MOREHEAD, KY (Time Warner Cable)

CARTER COUNTY—See GRAYSON, KY (Suddenlink Communications)

CASEY COUNTY (SOUTHERN PORTION)—See RUSSELL COUNTY (unincorporated areas), KY (Mediacom)

▲ **CASEY COUNTY (SOUTHWESTERN PORTION)**—Mediacom

CASEY COUNTY—See LIBERTY, KY (NewWave Communications)

CATHRON'S CREEK—See HARLAN, KY (Harlan Community TV Inc.)

CAVE CITY—See HORSE CAVE, KY (Comcast Cable)

CAWOOD—See BLACK MOUNTAIN, KY (Zito Media)

CENTERTOWN—See BEAVER DAM, KY (NewWave Communications)

CENTRAL CITY (UNINCORPORATED AREAS)—See NELSON, KY (Time Warner Cable)

CENTRAL CITY—See GREENVILLE, KY (Comcast Cable)

CHAPMAN—See LAWRENCE COUNTY (southern portion), KY (Lycom Communications)

CHARLESTOWN—See LOUISVILLE, KY (Insight Communications)

CHAVIES—See HINDMAN, KY (TV Service Inc.)

CHENOA—See FRAKES, KY (Suddenlink Communications)

CHERRYVILLE—See LAWRENCE COUNTY (southern portion), KY (Lycom Communications)

CHEVROLET—See BLACK MOUNTAIN, KY (Zito Media)

CHRISTIAN COUNTY—See NORTONVILLE, KY (Mediacom)

CHRISTIAN COUNTY—See TRENTON, KY (Mediacom)

CHRISTOPHER—See HINDMAN, KY (TV Service Inc.)

CLAIBORNE COUNTY (PORTIONS)—See FRAKES, TN (Suddenlink Communications)

CLAIRFIELD—See FRAKES, TN (Suddenlink Communications)

CLARK COUNTY—See RICHMOND, KY (Time Warner Cable)

CLARKSON—See LEITCHFIELD, KY (Comcast Cable)

CLARKSVILLE—See LOUISVILLE, KY (Insight Communications)

CLARYVILLE—See COVINGTON, KY (Insight Communications)

CLAY CITY—See MOUNT STERLING, KY (Windjammer Cable)

CLAY COUNTY (PORTIONS)—See ANNVILLE, KY (C & W Cable)

▲ **CLAY**—Now served by DIXON, KY [KY0218]

CLAY—See DIXON, KY (Time Warner Cable)

CLEAR CREEK—See PINEVILLE, KY (NewWave Communications)

CLEATON—See GREENVILLE, KY (Comcast Cable)

CLINTON COUNTY (PORTIONS)—See TOMPKINSVILLE, KY (Mediacom)

▲ **CLINTON COUNTY**—Mediacom. Now served by TOMPKINSVILLE, KY [KY0092]

CLINTON—See WICKLIFFE, KY (Zito Media)

CLOSPLINT—See BLACK MOUNTAIN, KY (Zito Media)

▲ **CLOVER BOTTOM**—McKee TV Enterprises Inc. Now served by McKEE, KY [KY0113]

CLOVER BOTTOM—See McKEE, KY (Peoples Telecom)

▲ **CLOVERPORT**—Windjammer Cable

COAL GROVE—See ASHLAND, OH (Time Warner Cable)

COAL RUN—See HAROLD, KY (Inter Mountain Cable Inc.)

COALGOOD—See BLACK MOUNTAIN, KY (Zito Media)

COLD SPRING—See COVINGTON, KY (Insight Communications)

COLDIRON—See WALLINS CREEK, KY (Zito Media)

COLLIER CREEK—See JENKINS, KY (Inter Mountain Cable Inc.)

COLONY—See LONDON, KY (Time Warner Cable)

COLSON—See HINDMAN, KY (TV Service Inc.)

▲ **COLUMBIA**—Duo County Telecom

COMBS—See LESLIE COUNTY (northern portion), KY (Windjammer Cable)

CONGLETON—See BEATTYVILLE, KY (Crystal Broadband Networks)

▲ **CORBIN**—NewWave Communications

▲ **CORINTH**—Windjammer Cable

▲ **CORYDON**—Now served by OWENSBORO, KY [KY0004]

CORYDON—See LOUISVILLE, IN (Insight Communications)

CORYDON—See OWENSBORO, KY (Time Warner Cable)

▲ **COVINGTON**—Insight Communications

COWAN CREEK—See HINDMAN, KY (TV Service Inc.)

COWAN—See MOREHEAD, KY (Time Warner Cable)

COXTON—See BLACK MOUNTAIN, KY (Zito Media)

▲ **CRAB ORCHARD**—Wilcop Cable TV. Now served by BRODHEAD, KY [KY0173]

CRAB ORCHARD—See BRODHEAD, KY (Wilcop Cable TV)

CRANKS—See BLACK MOUNTAIN, KY (Zito Media)

CREEKSIDE—See LOUISVILLE, KY (Insight Communications)

CRESCENT PARK—See COVINGTON, KY (Insight Communications)

CRESCENT SPRINGS—See COVINGTON, KY (Insight Communications)

CRESTVIEW HILLS—See COVINGTON, KY (Insight Communications)

CRITTENDEN COUNTY—See MARION, KY (Mediacom)

▲ **CRITTENDEN**—Insight Communications. Now served by COVINGTON, KY [KY0002]

CRITTENDEN—See COVINGTON, KY (Insight Communications)

CROFTON—See NORTONVILLE, KY (Mediacom)

CROMONA—See HINDMAN, KY (TV Service Inc.)

▲ **CROMWELL**—Windjammer Cable

CROSSGATE—See LOUISVILLE, KY (Insight Communications)

CROTHERSVILLE—See LOUISVILLE, IN (Insight Communications)

CRUMMIES—See BLACK MOUNTAIN, KY (Zito Media)

CUBAGE—See MIDDLESBORO, KY (NewWave Communications)

CUMBERLAND COUNTY (PORTIONS)—See BURKESVILLE, KY (Mediacom)

▲ **CUMBERLAND**—Access Cable Television Inc.

CUNNINGHAM—See GRAVES COUNTY, KY (Zito Media)

▲ **CUTSHIN**—Craft Cable Service. Now served by HINDMAN, KY [KY0027]

CUTSHIN—See HINDMAN, KY (TV Service Inc.)

▲ **CYNTHIANA**—Time Warner Cable

▲ **DANVILLE**—Now served by HARRODSBURG, KY [KY0231]

DANVILLE—See HARRODSBURG, KY (Time Warner Cable)

DARFORK—See BULAN, KY (NewWave Communications)

DAVID—See HAROLD, KY (Inter Mountain Cable Inc.)

DAVIESS COUNTY (PORTIONS)—See WHITESVILLE, KY (Mediacom)

DAVIESS COUNTY—See OWENSBORO, KY (Time Warner Cable)

DAVISBURG—See FRAKES, KY (Suddenlink Communications)

▲ **DAWSON SPRINGS**—Insight Communications

DAYHOIT—See WALLINS CREEK, KY (Zito Media)

DEANE—See JENKINS, KY (Inter Mountain Cable Inc.)

DENVER—See VAN LEAR, KY (Big Sandy Broadband)

DEPOY—See GREENVILLE, KY (Comcast Cable)

DEVONDALE—See LOUISVILLE, KY (Insight Communications)

DEWITT—See FLAT LICK, KY (NewWave Communications)

DEXTER—See CALLOWAY COUNTY, KY (Mediacom)

DIONE—See BLACK MOUNTAIN, KY (Zito Media)

▲ **DIXON**—Time Warner Cable

DIZNEY—See BLACK MOUNTAIN, KY (Zito Media)

DORTON—See HAROLD, KY (Inter Mountain Cable Inc.)

DOUGLASS HILLS—See LOUISVILLE, KY (Insight Communications)

DOVER—See TRENTON, TN (Mediacom)

DRAKESBORO—See GREENVILLE, KY (Comcast Cable)

DRUID HILLS—See LOUISVILLE, KY (Insight Communications)

DRY FORK—See HINDMAN, KY (TV Service Inc.)

DRY RIDGE—See COVINGTON, KY (Insight Communications)

▲ **DUNMOR**—Windjammer Cable

DUNNVILLE—See LIBERTY, KY (NewWave Communications)

DWALE—See HAROLD, KY (Inter Mountain Cable Inc.)

EAGAN—See FRAKES, TN (Suddenlink Communications)

EARLINGTON—See MADISONVILLE, KY (NewWave Communications)

EAST BERNSTADT—See LONDON, KY (Time Warner Cable)

EAST PINEVILLE—See PINEVILLE, KY (NewWave Communications)

EAST POINT—See VAN LEAR, KY (Big Sandy Broadband)

EASTERN—See HAROLD, KY (Inter Mountain Cable Inc.)

EDDYVILLE—See KUTTAWA, KY (Zito Media)

EDGEWOOD—See COVINGTON, KY (Insight Communications)

EDMONSON COUNTY—See MORGANTOWN, KY (Mediacom)

EDMONTON—See SUMMER SHADE, KY (Mediacom)

▲ **ELIZABETHTOWN**—Comcast Cable

ELIZAVILLE—See MOREHEAD, KY (Time Warner Cable)

▲ **ELKHORN CITY**—Formerly served by Cebridge Connections. Now served by PIKEVILLE, KY [KY0045]

ELKHORN CITY—See PIKEVILLE, KY (Suddenlink Communications)

▲ **ELKTON**—Mediacom. Now served by TRENTON, KY [KY0101]

ELKTON—See TRENTON, KY (Mediacom)

ELSMERE—See COVINGTON, KY (Insight Communications)

EMINENCE—See LOUISVILLE, KY (Insight Communications)

EMMA—See HAROLD, KY (Inter Mountain Cable Inc.)

ENTERPRISE—See MOREHEAD, KY (Time Warner Cable)

▲ **EOLIA**—Charter Communications. Now served by JENKINS, KY [KY0041]

EOLIA—See JENKINS, KY (Inter Mountain Cable Inc.)

EPWORTH—See MOREHEAD, KY (Time Warner Cable)

EQUALITY—See OWENSBORO, IL (Time Warner Cable)

ERLANGER—See COVINGTON, KY (Insight Communications)

ERMINE—See HINDMAN, KY (TV Service Inc.)

ESTILL COUNTY—See IRVINE, KY (Irvine Community TV Inc.)

ESTILL—See HINDMAN, KY (TV Service Inc.)

EUBANK—See SOMERSET, KY (NewWave Communications)

▲ **EVARTS**—Evarts TV Inc.

EVERSOLE—See JENKINS, KY (Inter Mountain Cable Inc.)

EWING—See MOREHEAD, KY (Time Warner Cable)

EZEL—See FRENCHBURG, KY (Windjammer Cable)

FALCON—See SALYERSVILLE, KY (Frank Howard's TV Cable)

▲ **FALLSBURG**—Inter Mountain Cable Inc.

▲ **FALMOUTH**—Insight Communications. Now served by COVINGTON, KY [KY0002]

FALMOUTH—See COVINGTON, KY (Insight Communications)

FANCY FARM—See GRAVES COUNTY, KY (Zito Media)

FAYETTE COUNTY—See LEXINGTON, KY (Insight Communications)

▲ **FEDSCREEK**—Fuller's TV. Now served by HAROLD, KY [KY0006]

FEDSCREEK—See HAROLD, KY (Inter Mountain Cable Inc.)

FERGUSON—See SOMERSET, KY (NewWave Communications)

FERNDALE—See PINEVILLE, KY (NewWave Communications)

FINCASTLE—See LOUISVILLE, KY (Insight Communications)

FISTY—See BULAN, KY (NewWave Communications)

FITCH—See MOREHEAD, KY (Time Warner Cable)

FIVE FORKS—See LAWRENCE COUNTY (southern portion), KY (Lycom Communications)

▲ **FIVE STAR**—Insight Communications. Now served by LOUISVILLE, KY [KY0001]

FIVE STAR—See LOUISVILLE, KY (Insight Communications)

▲ **FLAT LICK**—NewWave Communications

FLATWOODS—See ASHLAND, KY (Time Warner Cable)

FLEMING COUNTY—See MOREHEAD, KY (Time Warner Cable)

FLEMING—See JENKINS, KY (Inter Mountain Cable Inc.)

▲ **FLEMINGSBURG**—Formerly served by Adelphia Communications. Now served by MOREHEAD, KY [KY0031]

FLEMINGSBURG—See MOREHEAD, KY (Time Warner Cable)

FLORENCE—See COVINGTON, KY (Insight Communications)

FLOYD COUNTY—See LOUISVILLE, IN (Insight Communications)

FLOYD COUNTY—See HAROLD, KY (Inter Mountain Cable Inc.)

FLOYDS KNOBS—See LOUISVILLE, IN (Insight Communications)

FOGERTOWN—See GARRARD, KY (NewWave Communications)

FORDSVILLE—See WHITESVILLE, KY (Mediacom)

▲ **FORT CAMPBELL**—Comcast Cable

FORT KNOX—See LOUISVILLE, KY (Insight Communications)

FORT MITCHELL—See COVINGTON, KY (Insight Communications)

FORT THOMAS—See COVINGTON, KY (Insight Communications)

FORT WRIGHT—See COVINGTON, KY (Insight Communications)

FOURMILE—See PINEVILLE, KY (NewWave Communications)

FOXPORT—See MOREHEAD, KY (Time Warner Cable)

▲ **FRAKES**—Suddenlink Communications

FRANKFORT (UNINCORPORATED AREAS)—See FRANKFORT/STONEWALL, KY (Windjammer Cable)

▲ **FRANKFORT/STONEWALL**—Windjammer Cable

▲ **FRANKFORT**—Frankfort Plant Board Cable Service

FRANKLIN COUNTY (SOUTHERN PORTION)—See HARRODSBURG, KY (Time Warner Cable)

FRANKLIN FURNACE—See ASHLAND, OH (Time Warner Cable)

▲ **FRANKLIN**—Comcast Cable. Now served by NASHVILLE, TN [TN0002]

FREDONIA—See MARION, KY (Mediacom)

FREEBURN—See HAROLD, KY (Inter Mountain Cable Inc.)

▲ **FRENCHBURG**—Windjammer Cable

▲ **FULTON**—NewWave Communications

GALENA—See LOUISVILLE, IN (Insight Communications)

GALVESTON—See HAROLD, KY (Inter Mountain Cable Inc.)

GAMALIEL—See TOMPKINSVILLE, KY (Mediacom)

▲ **GARRARD**—NewWave Communications

GARRETT—See HAROLD, KY (Inter Mountain Cable Inc.)

▲ **GARRISON**—Formerly served by Adelphia Communications. Now served by VANCEBURG, KY [KY0286]

GARRISON—See VANCEBURG, KY (Time Warner Cable)

GEORGETOWN—See LOUISVILLE, IN (Insight Communications)

▲ **GEORGETOWN**—Time Warner Cable

GERMANTOWN—See MAYSVILLE, KY (Limestone Bracken Cablevision)

GHENT—See LOUISVILLE, KY (Insight Communications)

GIBBO—See JENKINS, KY (Inter Mountain Cable Inc.)

GILBERTSVILLE—See MARSHALL COUNTY, KY (Mediacom)

GIRDLER—See GRAY, KY (Eastern Cable Corp.)

▲ **GLASGOW**—Glasgow Electric Power Board-CATV Division. This cable system has converted to IPTV. See Glasgow, KY [KY5022]

▲ **GLASGOW**—Glasgow EPB. Formerly [KY0038]. This cable system has converted to IPTV.

GLENVIEW HILLS—See LOUISVILLE, KY (Insight Communications)

GLENVIEW MANOR—See LOUISVILLE, KY (Insight Communications)

GLOBE—See MOREHEAD, KY (Time Warner Cable)

GOOSE CREEK—See LOUISVILLE, KY (Insight Communications)

GOOSE ROCK—See GARRARD, KY (NewWave Communications)

GRAEFENBURG—See FRANKFORT, KY (Frankfort Plant Board Cable Service)

GRAHAM—See GREENVILLE, KY (Comcast Cable)

GRAND RIVERS—See KUTTAWA, KY (Zito Media)

GRANGERTOWN—See OWENSBORO, KY (Time Warner Cable)

GRANT COUNTY—See COVINGTON, KY (Insight Communications)

GRAVES COUNTY—See PADUCAH, KY (Comcast Cable)

▲ **GRAVES COUNTY**—Zito Media

GRAY HAWK—See McKEE, KY (Peoples Telecom)

▲ **GRAY**—Eastern Cable Corp.

GRAYMOOR—See LOUISVILLE, KY (Insight Communications)

GRAYS KNOB—See HARLAN, KY (Harlan Community TV Inc.)

GRAYSON COUNTY (PORTIONS)—See CANEYVILLE, KY (Mediacom)

▲ **GRAYSON**—Suddenlink Communications

▲ **GREASY CREEK**—Suddenlink Communications

GREEN COUNTY (PORTIONS)—See GREENSBURG, KY (Access Cable Television Inc.)

GREEN SPRING—See LOUISVILLE, KY (Insight Communications)

▲ **GREENSBURG**—Access Cable Television Inc.

GREENUP COUNTY (PORTIONS)—See ASHLAND, KY (Time Warner Cable)

GREENUP COUNTY (UNINCORPORATED AREAS)—See MALONETON, KY (Time Warner Cable)

▲ **GREENUP**—Charter Communications. Now served by SOUTH POINT, OH [WV0011]

▲ **GREENVILLE**—Comcast Cable

GREENVILLE—See LOUISVILLE, IN (Insight Communications)

GRETHEL—See HAROLD, KY (Inter Mountain Cable Inc.)

GULSTON—See HARLAN, KY (Harlan Community TV Inc.)

GUTHRIE—See TRENTON, KY (Mediacom)

HAGERHILL—See VAN LEAR, KY (Big Sandy Broadband)

HALDEMAN—See MOREHEAD, KY (Time Warner Cable)

HAMLIN TOWN—See FRAKES, TN (Suddenlink Communications)

HANGING ROCK—See ASHLAND, OH (Time Warner Cable)

HANSON—See MADISONVILLE, KY (NewWave Communications)

HARDBURLY—See BULAN, KY (NewWave Communications)

HARDIN COUNTY (NORTHERN PORTION)—See LOUISVILLE, KY (Insight Communications)

HARDIN COUNTY (SOUTHEASTERN PORTION)—See MUNFORDVILLE, KY (Mediacom)

HARDIN—See MARSHALL COUNTY, KY (Mediacom)

▲ **HARDINSBURG**—Windjammer Cable

HARDSHELL—See BULAN, KY (NewWave Communications)

HARDY—See HAROLD, KY (Inter Mountain Cable Inc.)

HARLAN COUNTY (PORTIONS)—See CUMBERLAND, KY (Access Cable Television Inc.)

HARLAN COUNTY (UNINCORPORATED AREAS)—See EVARTS, KY (Evarts TV Inc.)

HARLAN COUNTY—See HARLAN, KY (Harlan Community TV Inc.)

▲ **HARLAN**—Harlan Community TV Inc.

▲ **HAROLD**—Inter Mountain Cable Inc.

HARRISON COUNTY—See LOUISVILLE, IN (Insight Communications)

▲ **HARRODSBURG**—Time Warner Cable

HART COUNTY—See MUNFORDVILLE, KY (Mediacom)

HARTFORD—See BEAVER DAM, KY (NewWave Communications)

HATFIELD BOTTOM—See HAROLD, WV (Inter Mountain Cable Inc.)

HATFIELD—See OWENSBORO, IN (Time Warner Cable)

▲ **HAWESVILLE**—Crystal Broadband Networks

HAYMOND—See HINDMAN, KY (TV Service Inc.)

HAYWARD—See MOREHEAD, KY (Time Warner Cable)

▲ **HAZARD**—Hazard TV Cable Co. Inc.

HAZARD—See LESLIE COUNTY (northern portion), KY (Windjammer Cable)

HAZEL GREEN—See CAMPTON, KY (Windjammer Cable)

▲ **HAZEL**—Zito Media

HEBBERDSVILLE—See OWENSBORO, KY (Time Warner Cable)

HEBRON—See COVINGTON, KY (Insight Communications)

HEIDELBERG—See BEATTYVILLE, KY (Crystal Broadband Networks)

HEIDRICK—See BARBOURVILLE, KY (Barbourville Utility Commission)

HELTON—See MOZELLE, KY (Windjammer Cable)

▲ **HENDERSON (SOUTHERN PORTION)**—Mediacom

▲ **HENDERSON (town)**—Now served by OWENSBORO, KY [KY0004]

HENDERSON (TOWN)—See OWENSBORO, KY (Time Warner Cable)

HENDERSON COUNTY (PORTIONS)—See HENDERSON (southern portion), KY (Mediacom)

HENDERSON COUNTY (PORTIONS)—See OWENSBORO, KY (Time Warner Cable)

▲ **HENDERSON**—Now served by EVANSVILLE, IN [IN0006]

HENRY COUNTY—See LOUISVILLE, KY (Insight Communications)

HENRYVILLE—See LOUISVILLE, KY (Insight Communications)

HI HAT—See HAROLD, KY (Inter Mountain Cable Inc.)

▲ **HICKMAN**—Zito Media

HICKORY HILL—See LOUISVILLE, KY (Insight Communications)

HICKORY—See GRAVES COUNTY, KY (Zito Media)

HIGHLAND HEIGHTS—See COVINGTON, KY (Insight Communications)

HILLS AND DALES—See LOUISVILLE, KY (Insight Communications)

HILLSBORO—See MOREHEAD, KY (Time Warner Cable)

HILLVIEW—See LOUISVILLE, KY (Insight Communications)

HIMA—See GARRARD, KY (NewWave Communications)

HIMYAR—See FLAT LICK, KY (NewWave Communications)

▲ **HINDMAN**—TV Service Inc.

HIPPO—See HAROLD, KY (Inter Mountain Cable Inc.)

HIRAM—See CUMBERLAND, KY (Access Cable Television Inc.)

HISEVILLE—See HORSE CAVE, KY (Comcast Cable)

HITCHINS—See GRAYSON, KY (Suddenlink Communications)

HITE—See HAROLD, KY (Inter Mountain Cable Inc.)

▲ **HODGENVILLE**—Comcast Cablevision of the South. Now served by ELIZABETHTOWN, KY [KY0012]

HODGENVILLE—See ELIZABETHTOWN, KY (Comcast Cable)

HOLLOW CREEK—See LOUISVILLE, KY (Insight Communications)

HOLLYVILLA—See LOUISVILLE, KY (Insight Communications)

HOLMES MILL—See BLACK MOUNTAIN, KY (Zito Media)

HOPKINS COUNTY (PORTIONS)—See NORTONVILLE, KY (Mediacom)

HOPKINS COUNTY (PORTIONS)—See MADISONVILLE, KY (NewWave Communications)

HOPKINS COUNTY—See DAWSON SPRINGS, KY (Insight Communications)

HOPKINS COUNTY—See NEBO, KY (Mediacom)

HOPKINSVILLE—See TRENTON, KY (Mediacom)

▲ **HOPKINSVILLE**—NewWave Communications

▲ **HORSE CAVE**—Comcast Cable

HOUSTON ACRES—See LOUISVILLE, KY (Insight Communications)

HUEYSVILLE—See HAROLD, KY (Inter Mountain Cable Inc.)

HULEN—See PINEVILLE, KY (NewWave Communications)

HUNTER—See HAROLD, KY (Inter Mountain Cable Inc.)

HUNTERS HOLLOW—See LOUISVILLE, KY (Insight Communications)

HURLEY—See HAROLD, VA (Inter Mountain Cable Inc.)

HURSTBOURNE ACRES—See LOUISVILLE, KY (Insight Communications)

▲ **HUSTONVILLE**—Access Cable Television Inc.

▲ **HYDEN**—Bowling Corp.

INDEPENDENCE—See COVINGTON, KY (Insight Communications)

INDIAN HILLS-CHEROKEE—See LOUISVILLE, KY (Insight Communications)

INDIAN HILLS—See LOUISVILLE, KY (Insight Communications)

▲ **INEZ**—Charter Communications. Now served by KERMIT, WV [WV0038]

INGRAM—See GREASY CREEK, KY (Suddenlink Communications)

IRONTON—See ASHLAND, OH (Time Warner Cable)

▲ **IRVINE**—Irvine Community TV Inc.

IRVINGTON (VILLAGE)—See IRVINGTON, KY (Windjammer Cable)

▲ **IRVINGTON**—Windjammer Cable

▲ **ISLAND CITY**—Formerly served by City TV Cable. No longer in operation

ISLAND CREEK—See HAROLD, KY (Inter Mountain Cable Inc.)

▲ **ISLAND**—Windjammer Cable

ISOM—See HINDMAN, KY (TV Service Inc.)

IVEL—See HAROLD, KY (Inter Mountain Cable Inc.)

IVYTON—See SALYERSVILLE, KY (Frank Howard's TV Cable)

JACKHORN—See JENKINS, KY (Inter Mountain Cable Inc.)

JACKSON COUNTY (PORTIONS)—See ANNVILLE, KY (C & W Cable)

JACKSON COUNTY—See McKEE, KY (Peoples Telecom)

▲ **JACKSON**—Windjammer Cable

JAMESTOWN (PORTIONS)—See RUSSELL SPRINGS, KY (Duo County Telecom)

JAMESTOWN—See RUSSELL COUNTY (unincorporated areas), KY (Mediacom)

JARVIS—See GRAY, KY (Eastern Cable Corp.)

JEFF—See HINDMAN, KY (TV Service Inc.)

JEFFERSON COUNTY—See LOUISVILLE, KY (Insight Communications)

JEFFERSONTOWN—See LOUISVILLE, KY (Insight Communications)

JEFFERSONVILLE—See LOUISVILLE, KY (Insight Communications)

JEFFERSONVILLE—See MOUNT STERLING, KY (Windjammer Cable)

▲ **JENKINS**—Inter Mountain Cable Inc.

JEREMIAH—See HINDMAN, KY (TV Service Inc.)

JESSAMINE COUNTY (NORTHERN PORTION)—See LEXINGTON, KY (Insight Communications)

JESSAMINE COUNTY—See NICHOLASVILLE, KY (Time Warner Cable)

JOHNNY YOUNG BRANCH—See VARNEY, KY (Inter Mountain Cable Inc.)

JOHNSON COUNTY—See HAROLD, KY (Inter Mountain Cable Inc.)

JUNCTION CITY—See HARRODSBURG, KY (Time Warner Cable)

JUNCTION—See OWENSBORO, IL (Time Warner Cable)

KAYJAY—See GREASY CREEK, KY (Suddenlink Communications)

KEAVY—See LONDON, KY (Time Warner Cable)

KEITH—See HARLAN, KY (Harlan Community TV Inc.)

KENTON COUNTY—See COVINGTON, KY (Insight Communications)

KENTON VALE—See COVINGTON, KY (Insight Communications)

KENVIR—See BLACK MOUNTAIN, KY (Zito Media)

KETTLE ISLAND—See MIDDLESBORO, KY (NewWave Communications)

KEVIL—See PADUCAH, KY (Comcast Cable)

KIMPER—See HAROLD, KY (Inter Mountain Cable Inc.)

KINGS CREEK—See HINDMAN, KY (TV Service Inc.)

KINGSLEY—See LOUISVILLE, KY (Insight Communications)

KINGSTON—See RICHMOND, KY (Time Warner Cable)

KIRKSEY—See CALLOWAY COUNTY, KY (Mediacom)

KIRKSVILLE—See RICHMOND, KY (Time Warner Cable)

KITTS HILL—See ASHLAND, OH (Time Warner Cable)

KNOTT COUNTY (PORTIONS)—See HAROLD, KY (Inter Mountain Cable Inc.)

KNOTT COUNTY—See HINDMAN, KY (TV Service Inc.)

KNOX COUNTY (EASTERN PORTION)—See FLAT LICK, KY (NewWave Communications)

KNOX COUNTY—See BARBOURVILLE, KY (Barbourville Utility Commission)

KNOX COUNTY—See CORBIN, KY (NewWave Communications)

KONA—See HINDMAN, KY (TV Service Inc.)

▲ **KUTTAWA**—Zito Media

LA CENTER—See WICKLIFFE, KY (Zito Media)

LADEN—See BLACK MOUNTAIN, KY (Zito Media)

▲ **LAFAYETTE**—Formerly served by Adelphia Communications. No longer in operation

LAFAYETTE—See SCOTTSVILLE, KY (North Central Communications)

LAKE CITY—See KUTTAWA, KY (Zito Media)

LAKE MALONE—See DUNMOR, KY (Windjammer Cable)

LAKESIDE PARK—See COVINGTON, KY (Insight Communications)

LANCASTER—See HARRODSBURG, KY (Time Warner Cable)

LANDSAW—See CAMPTON, KY (Windjammer Cable)

LANESVILLE—See LOUISVILLE, IN (Insight Communications)

LANGDON PLACE—See LOUISVILLE, KY (Insight Communications)

LARUE COUNTY (UNINCORPORATED AREAS)—See ELIZABETHTOWN, KY (Comcast Cable)

LARUE COUNTY (WESTERN PORTION)—See MUNFORDVILLE, KY (Mediacom)

LATONIA LAKES—See COVINGTON, KY (Insight Communications)

LAUREL COUNTY—See CORBIN, KY (NewWave Communications)

LAUREN COUNTY (PORTIONS)—See ANNVILLE, KY (C & W Cable)

▲ **LAWRENCE COUNTY (SOUTHERN PORTION)**—Lycom Communications

▲ **LAWRENCEBURG**—Now served by HARRODSBURG, KY [KY0231]

LAWRENCEBURG—See HARRODSBURG, KY (Time Warner Cable)

LAWTON—See MOREHEAD, KY (Time Warner Cable)

LEBANON JUNCTION—See LOUISVILLE, KY (Insight Communications)

▲ **LEBANON**—Time Warner Cable

LEDBETTER—See PADUCAH, KY (Comcast Cable)

LEE CITY—See VANCLEVE, KY (TV Service Inc.)

LEFT FORK—See MIDDLESBORO, KY (NewWave Communications)

▲ **LEITCHFIELD**—Comcast Cable

LEJUNIOR—See BLACK MOUNTAIN, KY (Zito Media)

LEON—See GRAYSON, KY (Suddenlink Communications)

▲ **LEROSE**—Phil's Cablevision

▲ **LESLIE COUNTY (NORTHERN PORTION)**—Windjammer Cable

LESLIE COUNTY (PORTIONS)—See HYDEN, KY (Bowling Corp.)

LETCHER COUNTY (PORTIONS)—See WHITESBURG, KY (Comcast Cable)

LEWIS CREEK—See JENKINS, KY (Inter Mountain Cable Inc.)

LEWISBURG—See DUNMOR, KY (Windjammer Cable)

▲ **LEWISPORT**—Crystal Broadband Networks

▲ **LEXINGTON**—Formerly served by Wireless Associates LP. No longer in operation

LEXINGTON—See LOUISVILLE, IN (Insight Communications)

▲ **LEXINGTON**—Insight Communications

▲ **LIBERTY**—NewWave Communications

LICKBURG—See SALYERSVILLE, KY (Frank Howard's TV Cable)

LILY—See CORBIN, KY (NewWave Communications)

LIMESTONE—See MOREHEAD, KY (Time Warner Cable)

▲ **LINCOLN COUNTY (EASTERN PORTION)**—Mediacom

LINCOLN COUNTY (EASTERN PORTION)—See LIBERTY, KY (NewWave Communications)

LINCOLN COUNTY (NORTHERN PORTION)—See HARRODSBURG, KY (Time Warner Cable)

LINCOLN COUNTY—See SOMERSET, KY (NewWave Communications)

LINCOLNSHIRE—See LOUISVILLE, KY (Insight Communications)

LINEFORK—See HINDMAN, KY (TV Service Inc.)

LITTLE MUD CREEK—See HAROLD, KY (Inter Mountain Cable Inc.)

LITTLE ROBINSON—See HAROLD, KY (Inter Mountain Cable Inc.)

LITTLE YORK—See LOUISVILLE, IN (Insight Communications)

▲ **LIVERMORE**—Time Warner Cable

LIVINGSTON COUNTY (PORTIONS)—See KUTTAWA, KY (Zito Media)

LIVINGSTON COUNTY—See PADUCAH, KY (Comcast Cable)

LOG MOUNTAIN—See PINEVILLE, KY (NewWave Communications)

LOGAN COUNTY—See RUSSELLVILLE, KY (Suddenlink Communications)

▲ **LONDON**—Time Warner Cable

LONE—See BEATTYVILLE, KY (Crystal Broadband Networks)

LORETTO—See LEBANON, KY (Time Warner Cable)

LOST CREEK—See BULAN, KY (NewWave Communications)

LOTHAIR—See HINDMAN, KY (TV Service Inc.)

LOTTS CREEK—See BULAN, KY (NewWave Communications)

LOUELLEN—See BLACK MOUNTAIN, KY (Zito Media)

▲ **LOUISA**—Lycom Communications

▲ **LOUISVILLE**—Insight Communications

LOVELACEVILLE—See GRAVES COUNTY, KY (Zito Media)

▲ **LOWMANSVILLE**—Inter Mountain Cable Inc.

LOYALL—See HARLAN, KY (Harlan Community TV Inc.)

LUDLOW—See COVINGTON, KY (Insight Communications)

▲ **LYNCH**—Tri-Star Communications. No longer in operation

LYNDON—See LOUISVILLE, KY (Insight Communications)

LYNN—See HAROLD, WV (Inter Mountain Cable Inc.)

LYNNVIEW—See LOUISVILLE, KY (Insight Communications)

LYON COUNTY—See KUTTAWA, KY (Zito Media)

MACES CREEK—See HINDMAN, KY (TV Service Inc.)

MADISON COUNTY—See RICHMOND, KY (Time Warner Cable)

▲ **MADISONVILLE**—NewWave Communications

MAGOFFIN COUNTY—See SALYERSVILLE, KY (Frank Howard's TV Cable)

MAGOFFIN—See HAROLD, KY (Inter Mountain Cable Inc.)

MAJESTIC—See HAROLD, KY (Inter Mountain Cable Inc.)

MALONE—See WEST LIBERTY, KY (Mountain Telephone)

▲ **MALONETON**—Time Warner Cable

▲ **MANCHESTER**—C & W Cable. Now served by ANNVILLE, KY [KY0122]

MANCHESTER—See ANNVILLE, KY (C & W Cable)

MANOR CREEK—See LOUISVILLE, KY (Insight Communications)

MANTON—See HAROLD, KY (Inter Mountain Cable Inc.)

MARION COUNTY—See LEBANON, KY (Time Warner Cable)

▲ **MARION**—Mediacom

MARROWBONE—See BURKESVILLE, KY (Mediacom)

MARSHALL COUNTY—See PADUCAH, KY (Comcast Cable)

▲ **MARSHALL COUNTY**—Mediacom

MARSHES SIDING—See WHITLEY CITY, KY (Access Cable Television Inc.)

MARTIN—See HAROLD, KY (Inter Mountain Cable Inc.)

▲ **MARTINS FORK**—Formerly served by Tri-State Cable TV. No longer in operation

MARYHILL ESTATES—See LOUISVILLE, KY (Insight Communications)

MASON COUNTY—See MAYSVILLE, KY (Limestone Bracken Cablevision)

MASSAC COUNTY—See PADUCAH, IL (Comcast Cable)

MATEWAN—See HAROLD, WV (Inter Mountain Cable Inc.)

▲ **MAYFIELD**—NewWave Communications

MAYKING—See HINDMAN, KY (TV Service Inc.)

▲ **MAYSVILLE**—Limestone Bracken Cablevision

MAYTOWN—See HAROLD, KY (Inter Mountain Cable Inc.)

MCCARR—See HAROLD, KY (Inter Mountain Cable Inc.)

MCCRACKEN COUNTY—See PADUCAH, KY (Comcast Cable)

MCDANIELS—See CANEYVILLE, KY (Mediacom)

MCHENRY—See BEAVER DAM, KY (NewWave Communications)

▲ **MCKEE**—Peoples Telecom

▲ **MCKINNEY**—NewWave Communications

MCLEAN COUNTY—See LIVERMORE, KY (Time Warner Cable)

MCROBERTS—See JENKINS, KY (Inter Mountain Cable Inc.)

MCVEIGH—See HAROLD, KY (Inter Mountain Cable Inc.)

MEADE COUNTY (PORTIONS)—See LOUISVILLE, KY (Insight Communications)

MEADOW VALE—See LOUISVILLE, KY (Insight Communications)

MEADOWBROOK FARM—See LOUISVILLE, KY (Insight Communications)

MEADOWVIEW ESTATES—See LOUISVILLE, KY (Insight Communications)

MEADS BRANCH—See LAWRENCE COUNTY (southern portion), KY (Lycom Communications)

MEALLY—See VAN LEAR, KY (Big Sandy Broadband)

MEANS—See FRENCHBURG, KY (Windjammer Cable)

MELBER—See GRAVES COUNTY, KY (Zito Media)

MELBOURNE—See COVINGTON, KY (Insight Communications)

MELVIN—See HAROLD, KY (Inter Mountain Cable Inc.)

MENIFEE COUNTY (UNINCORPORATED AREAS)—See CAMPTON, KY (Windjammer Cable)

MERCER COUNTY—See HARRODSBURG, KY (Time Warner Cable)

META—See HAROLD, KY (Inter Mountain Cable Inc.)

METROPOLIS—See PADUCAH, IL (Comcast Cable)

MIDDLEBURG—See LIBERTY, KY (NewWave Communications)

▲ **MIDDLESBORO**—NewWave Communications

MIDDLETOWN—See LOUISVILLE, KY (Insight Communications)

▲ **MIDWAY**—Now served by GEORGETOWN, KY [KY0044]

MIDWAY—See GEORGETOWN, KY (Time Warner Cable)

MILLERSBURG—See MOUNT STERLING, KY (Windjammer Cable)

MILLSTONE—See HINDMAN, KY (TV Service Inc.)

▲ **MILLVILLE**—Formerly served by Chumley's Antenna Systems Inc. No longer in operation

MILLVILLE—See FRANKFORT, KY (Frankfort Plant Board Cable Service)

MILLWOOD—See CANEYVILLE, KY (Mediacom)

MINGO COUNTY—See HAROLD, WV (Inter Mountain Cable Inc.)

MINOR LANE HEIGHTS—See LOUISVILLE, KY (Insight Communications)

MIRACLE—See MIDDLESBORO, KY (NewWave Communications)

MISLAND—See KUTTAWA, KY (Zito Media)

MIZE—See WEST LIBERTY, KY (Mountain Telephone)

MOCKINGBIRD VALLEY—See LOUISVILLE, KY (Insight Communications)

MONROE COUNTY (PORTIONS)—See TOMPKINSVILLE, KY (Mediacom)

MONTGOMERY COUNTY—See MOUNT STERLING, KY (Windjammer Cable)

▲ **MONTICELLO**—Community Telecom Services

MOORLAND—See LOUISVILLE, KY (Insight Communications)

▲ **MOREHEAD STATE UNIVERSITY**—Morehead State University

▲ **MOREHEAD**—Time Warner Cable

MORELAND—See HUSTONVILLE, KY (Access Cable Television Inc.)

MORGAN COUNTY—See CAMPTON, KY (Windjammer Cable)

MORGANFIELD—See OWENSBORO, KY (Time Warner Cable)

▲ **MORGANTOWN**—Mediacom

MORNING VIEW—See COVINGTON, KY (Insight Communications)

MORRELL—See McKEE, KY (Peoples Telecom)

MORTONS GAP—See MADISONVILLE, KY (NewWave Communications)

MOUNT CARMEL—See MOREHEAD, KY (Time Warner Cable)

▲ **MOUNT OLIVET**—Bracken County Cablevision Inc.

▲ **MOUNT STERLING**—Windjammer Cable

▲ **MOUNT VERNON**—Charter Communications. Now served by SOMERSET, KY [KY0021]

MOUNT VERNON—See SOMERSET, KY (NewWave Communications)

MOUNT WASHINGTON—See LOUISVILLE, KY (Insight Communications)

▲ **MOZELLE**—Windjammer Cable

MUD LICK—See MOREHEAD, KY (Time Warner Cable)

MUHLENBERG COUNTY (SOUTHERN PORTION)—See DUNMOR, KY (Windjammer Cable)

MULDRAUGH—See LOUISVILLE, KY (Insight Communications)

▲ **MUNFORDVILLE**—Mediacom

▲ **MURRAY**—Murray Electric System

▲ **MURRAY**—NewWave Communications

MYRA—See HAROLD, KY (Inter Mountain Cable Inc.)

NANCY—See SOMERSET, KY (NewWave Communications)

▲ **NEBO**—Mediacom

NELSON COUNTY—See BARDSTOWN, KY (Bardstown Cable TV)

NELSON COUNTY—See LEBANON, KY (Time Warner Cable)

▲**NELSON**—Time Warner Cable

NEON—See JENKINS, KY (Inter Mountain Cable Inc.)

NEPTON—See MOREHEAD, KY (Time Warner Cable)

NEW ALBANY—See LOUISVILLE, IN (Insight Communications)

NEW CASTLE—See LOUISVILLE, KY (Insight Communications)

▲**NEW HAVEN**—Formerly served by Adelphia Communications. Now served by LEBANON, KY [KY0049]

NEW HAVEN—See LEBANON, KY (Time Warner Cable)

NEW WASHINGTON—See LOUISVILLE, KY (Insight Communications)

▲**NEWPORT**—Insight Communications. Now served by COVINGTON, KY [KY0002]

NEWPORT—See COVINGTON, KY (Insight Communications)

NEWTOWN—See HAROLD, WV (Inter Mountain Cable Inc.)

NICHOLAS COUNTY—See MOUNT STERLING, KY (Windjammer Cable)

▲**NICHOLASVILLE**—Time Warner Cable

NOCTOR (PORTIONS)—See JACKSON, KY (Windjammer Cable)

NOLANSBURG—See BLACK MOUNTAIN, KY (Zito Media)

NORBOURNE ESTATES—See LOUISVILLE, KY (Insight Communications)

NORTH MATEWAN—See HAROLD, WV (Inter Mountain Cable Inc.)

▲**NORTH MIDDLETOWN**—Now served by GEORGETOWN, KY [KY0044]

NORTH MIDDLETOWN—See MOUNT STERLING, KY (Windjammer Cable)

NORTHFIELD—See LOUISVILLE, KY (Insight Communications)

▲**NORTONVILLE**—Mediacom

NORWOOD—See LOUISVILLE, KY (Insight Communications)

▲**OAK GROVE**—Mediacom. Now served by TRENTON, KY [KY0101]

OAK GROVE—See TRENTON, KY (Mediacom)

OAKLAND—See BOWLING GREEN, KY (Insight Communications)

OBION COUNTY (PORTIONS)—See FULTON, TN (NewWave Communications)

OHIO COUNTY (PORTIONS)—See WHITESVILLE, KY (Mediacom)

OHIO COUNTY—See BEAVER DAM, KY (NewWave Communications)

OLD BROWNSBORO PLACE—See LOUISVILLE, KY (Insight Communications)

OLD SHAWNEETOWN—See OWENSBORO, IL (Time Warner Cable)

▲**OLIVE HILL**—Now served by MOOREHEAD, KY [KY0031]

OLIVE HILL—See MOREHEAD, KY (Time Warner Cable)

ONEIDA—See GARRARD, KY (NewWave Communications)

OTISCO—See LOUISVILLE, KY (Insight Communications)

OVEN FORK—See JENKINS, KY (Inter Mountain Cable Inc.)

▲**OWENSBORO**—Time Warner Cable

▲**OWINGSVILLE**—Now served by MOOREHEAD, KY [KY0031]

OWINGSVILLE—See MOREHEAD, KY (Time Warner Cable)

OWSLEY COUNTY (PORTIONS)—See BOONEVILLE, KY (Peoples Telecom)

PACTOLUS—See GRAYSON, KY (Suddenlink Communications)

▲**PADUCAH**—Formerly served by NDW II Inc. No longer in operation

▲**PADUCAH**—Comcast Cable

PAGE—See PINEVILLE, KY (NewWave Communications)

▲**PAINTSVILLE**—Charter Communications. Now served by KERMIT, WV [WV0038]

▲**PARIS**—Now served by GEORGETOWN, KY [KY0044]

PARIS—See GEORGETOWN, KY (Time Warner Cable)

▲**PARK CITY**—Mediacom

PARK HILLS—See COVINGTON, KY (Insight Communications)

▲**PARKSVILLE**—Formerly served by Charter Communications. No longer in operation

PARKWAY VILLAGE—See LOUISVILLE, KY (Insight Communications)

PARTRIDGE—See JENKINS, KY (Inter Mountain Cable Inc.)

▲**PATHFORK**—Formerly served by Cebridge Connections. Now served by GREASY CREEK, KY [KY0239]

PATHFORK—See GREASY CREEK, KY (Suddenlink Communications)

PAYNE GAP—See JENKINS, KY (Inter Mountain Cable Inc.)

PEKIN—See LOUISVILLE, IN (Insight Communications)

PEMBROKE—See TRENTON, KY (Mediacom)

PENROD—See DUNMOR, KY (Windjammer Cable)

PEOPLES—See ANNVILLE, KY (C & W Cable)

▲**PERRYVILLE**—Now served by HARRODSBURG, KY [KY0231]

PERRYVILLE—See HARRODSBURG, KY (Time Warner Cable)

PETER FORK—See HAROLD, KY (Inter Mountain Cable Inc.)

PEWEE VALLEY—See LOUISVILLE, KY (Insight Communications)

PHELPS—See HAROLD, KY (Inter Mountain Cable Inc.)

PHILPOT—See PLEASANT RIDGE, KY (Windjammer Cable)

PHYLLIS—See HAROLD, KY (Inter Mountain Cable Inc.)

PICKETT COUNTY (PORTIONS)—See TOMPKINSVILLE, TN (Mediacom)

PIKE COUNTY (PORTIONS)—See PIKEVILLE, KY (Suddenlink Communications)

PIKE COUNTY—See HAROLD, KY (Inter Mountain Cable Inc.)

PIKEVILLE—See HAROLD, KY (Inter Mountain Cable Inc.)

▲**PIKEVILLE**—Suddenlink Communications

▲**PINE HILL**—Now served by MOOREHEAD, KY [KY0031]

PINE HILL—See MOREHEAD, KY (Time Warner Cable)

PINE KNOT—See WHITLEY CITY, KY (Access Cable Television Inc.)

▲**PINEVILLE**—NewWave Communications. Now served by PINEVILLE, KY [KY0063]. Communities previously served by this system are now served by MIDDLESBORO, KY [KY0034]

▲**PINEVILLE**—NewWave Communications

PINSONFORK—See HAROLD, KY (Inter Mountain Cable Inc.)

PIONEER VILLAGE—See LOUISVILLE, KY (Insight Communications)

PIPPA PASSES—See HINDMAN, KY (TV Service Inc.)

PLANO—See BOWLING GREEN, KY (Insight Communications)

PLANTATION—See LOUISVILLE, KY (Insight Communications)

PLEASANT HILL—See SALYERSVILLE, KY (Frank Howard's TV Cable)

▲**PLEASANT RIDGE**—Windjammer Cable

PLEASUREVILLE—See LOUISVILLE, KY (Insight Communications)

PLUM SPRINGS—See BOWLING GREEN, KY (Insight Communications)

POPLAR GROVE—See MOREHEAD, KY (Time Warner Cable)

POUND—See JENKINS, VA (Inter Mountain Cable Inc.)

POWDERLY—See GREENVILLE, KY (Comcast Cable)

POWELL COUNTY (UNINCORPORATED AREAS)—See STANTON, KY (Crystal Broadband Networks)

PRATER CREEK—See HAROLD, KY (Inter Mountain Cable Inc.)

PRATER FORK—See HAROLD, KY (Inter Mountain Cable Inc.)

PRESTONSBURG—See HAROLD, KY (Inter Mountain Cable Inc.)

▲**PRESTONSBURG**—Suddenlink Communications

PRIMROSE—See BEATTYVILLE, KY (Crystal Broadband Networks)

▲**PRINCETON**—Mediacom. Now served by MARION, KY [KY0071]

PRINCETON—See MARION, KY (Mediacom)

PRINTER—See HAROLD, KY (Inter Mountain Cable Inc.)

PROCTOR—See BEATTYVILLE, KY (Crystal Broadband Networks)

PROSPECT—See LOUISVILLE, KY (Insight Communications)

▲**PROVIDENCE**—Insight Communications

PULASKI COUNTY—See SOMERSET, KY (NewWave Communications)

PURYEAR—See HAZEL, TN (Zito Media)

PUTNEY—See BLACK MOUNTAIN, KY (Zito Media)

PYRAMID—See HAROLD, KY (Inter Mountain Cable Inc.)

QUICKSAND—See JACKSON, KY (Windjammer Cable)

QUINCY—See VANCEBURG, KY (Time Warner Cable)

RACELAND—See ASHLAND, KY (Time Warner Cable)

RADCLIFF—See LOUISVILLE, KY (Insight Communications)

RADO HOLLOW—See JENKINS, KY (Inter Mountain Cable Inc.)

RANSOM—See HAROLD, KY (Inter Mountain Cable Inc.)

RATFORD—See MIDDLESBORO, KY (NewWave Communications)

RAVEN—See HINDMAN, KY (TV Service Inc.)

RAVENNA—See IRVINE, KY (Irvine Community TV Inc.)

RED BOILING SPRINGS—See SCOTTSVILLE, TN (North Central Communications)

RED JACKET—See HAROLD, WV (Inter Mountain Cable Inc.)

REDBUD—See BLACK MOUNTAIN, KY (Zito Media)

REDFOX—See HINDMAN, KY (TV Service Inc.)

REED—See OWENSBORO, KY (Time Warner Cable)

RENFRO VALLEY—See SOMERSET, KY (NewWave Communications)

REO—See OWENSBORO, IN (Time Warner Cable)

REVELO—See WHITLEY CITY, KY (Access Cable Television Inc.)

RIBOLT—See MOREHEAD, KY (Time Warner Cable)

RICHLAWN—See LOUISVILLE, KY (Insight Communications)

▲**RICHMOND**—Time Warner Cable

RIDGWAY—See OWENSBORO, IL (Time Warner Cable)

RINGOS MILLS—See MOREHEAD, KY (Time Warner Cable)

RISNER—See HAROLD, KY (Inter Mountain Cable Inc.)

RIVER BLUFF—See LOUISVILLE, KY (Insight Communications)

RIVER RIDGE—See LOUISVILLE, KY (Insight Communications)

RIVERWOOD—See LOUISVILLE, KY (Insight Communications)

ROBERTS BRANCH—See JENKINS, KY (Inter Mountain Cable Inc.)

ROBINETTE KNOB—See VARNEY, KY (Inter Mountain Cable Inc.)

ROBINSON CREEK—See HAROLD, KY (Inter Mountain Cable Inc.)

▲**ROCHESTER**—Windjammer Cable

ROCKCASTLE COUNTY (WESTERN PORTION)—See LINCOLN COUNTY (eastern portion), KY (Mediacom)

ROCKCASTLE COUNTY—See SOMERSET, KY (NewWave Communications)

ROCKFIELD—See BOWLING GREEN, KY (Insight Communications)

ROCKHOLDS—See WHITLEY COUNTY, KY (Zito Media)

ROCKHOUSE—See VARNEY, KY (Inter Mountain Cable Inc.)

ROCKPORT—See BEAVER DAM, KY (NewWave Communications)

ROCKPORT—See OWENSBORO, IN (Time Warner Cable)

ROLLING FIELDS—See LOUISVILLE, KY (Insight Communications)

ROLLING HILLS—See LOUISVILLE, KY (Insight Communications)

ROSSPOINT—See BLACK MOUNTAIN, KY (Zito Media)

▲**ROUGH RIVER DAM**—Mediacom. Now served by CANEYVILLE, KY [KY0291]

ROUGH RIVER DAM—See CANEYVILLE, KY (Mediacom)

ROWAN COUNTY—See MOREHEAD, KY (Time Warner Cable)

ROWDY—See BULAN, KY (NewWave Communications)

RUMSEY—See LIVERMORE, KY (Time Warner Cable)

▲**RUSSELL COUNTY (UNINCORPORATED AREAS)**—Mediacom

RUSSELL COUNTY—See RUSSELL SPRINGS, KY (Duo County Telecom)

▲**RUSSELL SPRINGS**—Duo County Telecom

RUSSELL—See ASHLAND, KY (Time Warner Cable)

▲**RUSSELLVILLE**—Suddenlink Communications

RYLAND HEIGHTS—See COVINGTON, KY (Insight Communications)

SACRAMENTO—See BREMEN, KY (Crystal Broadband Networks)

SALEM—See LOUISVILLE, IN (Insight Communications)

SALEM—See MARION, KY (Mediacom)

SALT GUM—See FLAT LICK, KY (NewWave Communications)

SALT LICK—See MOREHEAD, KY (Time Warner Cable)

▲**SALYERSVILLE**—Frank Howard's TV Cable

SANDGAP—See McKEE, KY (Peoples Telecom)

▲**SANDY HOOK**—Formerly served by Windjammer Cable. No longer in operation

SASSAFRAS—See HINDMAN, KY (TV Service Inc.)

SCALF—See FLAT LICK, KY (NewWave Communications)

SCIENCE HILL—See SOMERSET, KY (NewWave Communications)

SCOTT COUNTY—See GEORGETOWN, KY (Time Warner Cable)

SCOTTSBURG—See LOUISVILLE, IN (Insight Communications)

▲**SCOTTSVILLE**—North Central Communications

▲**SEBREE**—NewWave Communications

SECO—See HINDMAN, KY (TV Service Inc.)

SECOND CREEK—See BULAN, KY (NewWave Communications)

SEDALIA—See GRAVES COUNTY, KY (Zito Media)

SELLERSBURG—See LOUISVILLE, KY (Insight Communications)

SENECA GARDENS—See LOUISVILLE, KY (Insight Communications)

SHARKEY—See MOREHEAD, KY (Time Warner Cable)

▲**SHARPSBURG**—Formerly served by Adelphia Communications. Now served by MOUNT STERLING, KY [KY0046]

SHARPSBURG—See MOUNT STERLING, KY (Windjammer Cable)

SHAWNEETOWN—See OWENSBORO, IL (Time Warner Cable)

SHELBY COUNTY—See FRANKFORT, KY (Frankfort Plant Board Cable Service)

SHELBY COUNTY—See LOUISVILLE, KY (Insight Communications)

SHELBY GAP—See HAROLD, KY (Inter Mountain Cable Inc.)

▲**SHELBYVILLE**—Insight Communications. Now served by LOUISVILLE, KY [KY0001]

SHELBYVILLE—See LOUISVILLE, KY (Insight Communications)

▲**SHEPHERDSVILLE**—Inside Connect Cable

SHEPHERDSVILLE—See LOUISVILLE, KY (Insight Communications)

SHEPHERDSVILLE—See BROOKS, KY (Windjammer Cable)

SHIVELY—See LOUISVILLE, KY (Insight Communications)

SILER—See WHITLEY COUNTY, KY (Zito Media)

SILICA—See MOREHEAD, KY (Time Warner Cable)

SILOAM—See SCOTTSVILLE, TN (North Central Communications)

SILVER GROVE—See COVINGTON, KY (Insight Communications)

SIMPSONVILLE—See LOUISVILLE, KY (Insight Communications)

▲**SITKA**—Sitka TV Cable

▲**SLAUGHTERS**—Windjammer Cable

SLOANS VALLEY—See SOMERSET, KY (NewWave Communications)

SMILAX—See HINDMAN, KY (TV Service Inc.)

SMITH MILLS BOROUGH—See OWENSBORO, KY (Time Warner Cable)

SMITHLAND—See KUTTAWA, KY (Zito Media)

SMITHS GROVE—See BOWLING GREEN, KY (Insight Communications)

▲**SOLDIER**—Now served by MOOREHEAD, KY [KY0031]

SOLDIER—See MOREHEAD, KY (Time Warner Cable)

▲**SOMERSET**—NewWave Communications

SONORA—See MUNFORDVILLE, KY (Mediacom)

SOUTH BEATTYVILLE—See BEATTYVILLE, KY (Crystal Broadband Networks)

SOUTH CARROLLTON—See GREENVILLE, KY (Comcast Cable)

SOUTH FULTON—See FULTON, TN (NewWave Communications)

SOUTH PARK VIEW—See LOUISVILLE, KY (Insight Communications)

SOUTH PIKEVILLE—See PIKEVILLE, KY (Suddenlink Communications)

SOUTH SHORE—See MALONETON, KY (Time Warner Cable)

SOUTHGATE—See COVINGTON, KY (Insight Communications)

SPENCER COUNTY (PORTIONS)—See LOUISVILLE, KY (Insight Communications)

SPENCER COUNTY (PORTIONS)—See OWENSBORO, IN (Time Warner Cable)

SPOTTSVILLE—See OWENSBORO, KY (Time Warner Cable)

SPRINGFIELD—See LEBANON, KY (Time Warner Cable)

ST. CHARLES—See DAWSON SPRINGS, KY (Insight Communications)

ST. HELENS—See BEATTYVILLE, KY (Crystal Broadband Networks)

ST. MATTHEWS—See LOUISVILLE, KY (Insight Communications)

ST. PAUL—See CANEYVILLE, KY (Mediacom)

ST. REGIS PARK—See LOUISVILLE, KY (Insight Communications)

STAMPING GROUND—See GEORGETOWN, KY (Time Warner Cable)

▲**STANFORD**—Now served by HARRODSBURG, KY [KY0231]

STANFORD—See HARRODSBURG, KY (Time Warner Cable)

▲**STANTON**—Crystal Broadband Networks

STANVILLE—See HAROLD, KY (Inter Mountain Cable Inc.)

STEARNS—See WHITLEY CITY, KY (Access Cable Television Inc.)

STEWART COUNTY—See TRENTON, TN (Mediacom)

STINNETT (PORTIONS)—See LESLIE COUNTY (northern portion), KY (Windjammer Cable)

STONE COAL—See HAROLD, KY (Inter Mountain Cable Inc.)

STONEWALL—See FRANKFORT/STONEWALL, KY (Windjammer Cable)

STONEY FORK—See MIDDLESBORO, KY (NewWave Communications)

STOPOVER—See HAROLD, KY (Inter Mountain Cable Inc.)

STRATHMOOR MANOR—See LOUISVILLE, KY (Insight Communications)

STRATHMOOR VILLAGE—See LOUISVILLE, KY (Insight Communications)

STRAY CREEK—See MIDDLESBORO, KY (NewWave Communications)

▲**STURGIS**—Now served by OWENSBORO, KY [KY0004]

STURGIS—See OWENSBORO, KY (Time Warner Cable)

SULLIVAN—See OWENSBORO, KY (Time Warner Cable)

▲ **SUMMER SHADE**—Mediacom

▲ **SUMMERSVILLE**—NewWave Communications. Now served by GREENSBURG, KY [KY0110]

SUMMERSVILLE—See GREENSBURG, KY (Access Cable Television Inc.)

▲ **SYCAMORE CREEK**—Formerly served by Inter Mountain Cable Inc. No longer in operation

SYCAMORE—See LOUISVILLE, KY (Insight Communications)

SYMSONIA—See GRAVES COUNTY, KY (Zito Media)

TALLEGA—See BEATTYVILLE, KY (Crystal Broadband Networks)

TATEVILLE—See SOMERSET, KY (NewWave Communications)

TAYLOR COUNTY—See ELIZABETHTOWN, KY (Comcast Cable)

TAYLOR MILL—See COVINGTON, KY (Insight Communications)

▲ **TAYLORSVILLE**—Insight Communications. Now served by LOUISVILLE, KY [KY0001]

TAYLORSVILLE—See LOUISVILLE, KY (Insight Communications)

TEABERRY—See HAROLD, KY (Inter Mountain Cable Inc.)

TEN BROECK—See LOUISVILLE, KY (Insight Communications)

THACKER—See HAROLD, WV (Inter Mountain Cable Inc.)

THORNHILL—See LOUISVILLE, KY (Insight Communications)

THORNTON—See HINDMAN, KY (TV Service Inc.)

TODD COUNTY—See TRENTON, KY (Mediacom)

TOLER CREEK—See HAROLD, KY (Inter Mountain Cable Inc.)

▲ **TOLLESBORO**—Formerly served by Adelphia Communications. Now served by MOREHEAD, KY [KY0031]

TOLLESBORO—See MOREHEAD, KY (Time Warner Cable)

▲ **TOMPKINSVILLE**—Mediacom

TOPMOST—See HINDMAN, KY (TV Service Inc.)

TOTZ—See BLACK MOUNTAIN, KY (Zito Media)

TRAM—See HAROLD, KY (Inter Mountain Cable Inc.)

▲ **TRENTON**—Mediacom

TRIBBEY—See BULAN, KY (NewWave Communications)

TRIGG COUNTY—See CADIZ, KY (Mediacom)

TRIMBLE COUNTY (EASTERN PORTION)—See LOUISVILLE, KY (Insight Communications)

TRIPLETT—See MOREHEAD, KY (Time Warner Cable)

TURKEY CREEK—See FLAT LICK, KY (NewWave Communications)

▲ **TUTOR KEY**—P & W TV Cable

TYNER—See ANNVILLE, KY (C & W Cable)

UNDERWOOD—See LOUISVILLE, KY (Insight Communications)

UNION—See COVINGTON, KY (Insight Communications)

UNIONTOWN—See OWENSBORO, KY (Time Warner Cable)

UPPER JOHNS CREEK—See HAROLD, KY (Inter Mountain Cable Inc.)

UPPER TYGART—See MOREHEAD, KY (Time Warner Cable)

▲ **UPTON/SONORA**—Mediacom. Now served by MUNFORDVILLE, KY [KY0086]

UPTON—See MUNFORDVILLE, KY (Mediacom)

UTICA—See LOUISVILLE, KY (Insight Communications)

UTICA—See PLEASANT RIDGE, KY (Windjammer Cable)

▲ **VAN LEAR**—Big Sandy Broadband

▲ **VANCEBURG**—Time Warner Cable

▲ **VANCLEVE**—TV Service Inc.

▲ **VARNEY**—Inter Mountain Cable Inc.

VERDA—See BLACK MOUNTAIN, KY (Zito Media)

▲ **VERSAILLES**—Now served by HARRODSBURG, KY [KY0231]

VERSAILLES—See HARRODSBURG, KY (Time Warner Cable)

VICCO—See HINDMAN, KY (TV Service Inc.)

VIENNA—See LOUISVILLE, IN (Insight Communications)

VILLA HILLS—See COVINGTON, KY (Insight Communications)

VINE GROVE—See ELIZABETHTOWN, KY (Comcast Cable)

VIPER—See HINDMAN, KY (TV Service Inc.)

VISALIA—See COVINGTON, KY (Insight Communications)

WACO—See RICHMOND, KY (Time Warner Cable)

WALKER—See FLAT LICK, KY (NewWave Communications)

▲ **WALKERTOWN**—Community TV Inc.

WALLINGFORD—See MOREHEAD, KY (Time Warner Cable)

▲ **WALLINS CREEK**—Zito Media

WALLINS—See WALLINS CREEK, KY (Zito Media)

WALTON—See COVINGTON, KY (Insight Communications)

WANETA—See McKEE, KY (Peoples Telecom)

WARREN COUNTY—See BOWLING GREEN, KY (Insight Communications)

▲ **WARSAW**—Insight Communications

WASHINGTON COUNTY—See LOUISVILLE, IN (Insight Communications)

WASHINGTON—See MAYSVILLE, KY (Limestone Bracken Cablevision)

WATERGAP—See HAROLD, KY (Inter Mountain Cable Inc.)

WATTERSON PARK—See LOUISVILLE, KY (Insight Communications)

WAVERLY—See OWENSBORO, KY (Time Warner Cable)

WAYLAND—See HINDMAN, KY (TV Service Inc.)

WAYNE COUNTY—See MONTICELLO, KY (Community Telecom Services)

WAYNESBURG—See SOMERSET, KY (NewWave Communications)

WEBSTER COUNTY (SOUTHERN PORTION)—See PROVIDENCE, KY (Insight Communications)

WEEKSBURY—See HAROLD, KY (Inter Mountain Cable Inc.)

▲ **WELCHS CREEK**—Windjammer Cable

WELLS ADDITION—See HAROLD, KY (Inter Mountain Cable Inc.)

WEST BUECHEL—See LOUISVILLE, KY (Insight Communications)

▲ **WEST LIBERTY**—Mountain Telephone

WEST POINT—See LOUISVILLE, KY (Insight Communications)

WEST POINT—See BROOKS, KY (Windjammer Cable)

WEST PRESTONSBURG—See HAROLD, KY (Inter Mountain Cable Inc.)

WEST VAN LEAR—See VAN LEAR, KY (Big Sandy Broadband)

WESTMORELAND—See SCOTTSVILLE, TN (North Central Communications)

WESTWOOD—See ASHLAND, KY (Time Warner Cable)

WHEATCROFT—See DIXON, KY (Time Warner Cable)

WHEELWRIGHT—See HAROLD, KY (Inter Mountain Cable Inc.)

WHITE HALL—See RICHMOND, KY (Time Warner Cable)

WHITE PLAINS—See MADISONVILLE, KY (NewWave Communications)

▲ **WHITESBURG**—Comcast Cable

WHITESVILLE (UNINCORPORATED AREAS)—See PLEASANT RIDGE, KY (Windjammer Cable)

▲ **WHITESVILLE**—Mediacom

▲ **WHITLEY CITY**—Access Cable Television Inc.

WHITLEY COUNTY—See CORBIN, KY (NewWave Communications)

▲ **WHITLEY COUNTY**—Zito Media

▲ **WICKLIFFE**—Zito Media

WILDER—See COVINGTON, KY (Insight Communications)

WILDWOOD—See LOUISVILLE, KY (Insight Communications)

▲ **WILLIAMSBURG**—NewWave Communications

WILLIAMSPORT—See VAN LEAR, KY (Big Sandy Broadband)

▲ **WILLIAMSTOWN**—Williamstown Cable

▲ **WILLISBURG**—Formerly served by Windjammer Cable. No longer in operation

WILMORE—See NICHOLASVILLE, KY (Time Warner Cable)

▲ **WINCHESTER**—Now served by RICHMOND, KY [KY0008]

WINCHESTER—See RICHMOND, KY (Time Warner Cable)

WINDSOR—See RUSSELL COUNTY (unincorporated areas), KY (Mediacom)

WINDY HILL—See LOUISVILLE, KY (Insight Communications)

WINGO—See GRAVES COUNTY, KY (Zito Media)

WISE COUNTY (NORTHERN PORTION)—See JENKINS, VA (Inter Mountain Cable Inc.)

WISEMANTOWN—See IRVINE, KY (Irvine Community TV Inc.)

WOLFE COUNTY (UNINCORPORATED AREAS)—See CAMPTON, KY (Windjammer Cable)

WOODBINE—See WILLIAMSBURG, KY (NewWave Communications)

WOODBURN—See BOWLING GREEN, KY (Insight Communications)

WOODFORD COUNTY (EASTERN PORTION)—See HARRODSBURG, KY (Time Warner Cable)

WOODLAND HILLS—See LOUISVILLE, KY (Insight Communications)

WOODLAWN PARK—See LOUISVILLE, KY (Insight Communications)

WOODLAWN—See COVINGTON, KY (Insight Communications)

WOODSON BEND—See SOMERSET, KY (NewWave Communications)

WORTHINGTON HILLS—See LOUISVILLE, KY (Insight Communications)

WORTHINGTON—See ASHLAND, KY (Time Warner Cable)

WORTHVILLE—See LOUISVILLE, KY (Insight Communications)

WYNN—See OWENSBORO, KY (Time Warner Cable)

YANCY—See HARLAN, KY (Harlan Community TV Inc.)

YOSEMITE—See LIBERTY, KY (NewWave Communications)

ZEBULON—See HAROLD, KY (Inter Mountain Cable Inc.)

ZION—See OWENSBORO, KY (Time Warner Cable)

LOUISIANA

▲**ABBEVILLE**—Cox Communications. Now served by BATON ROUGE, LA [LA0003]

ABBEVILLE—See BATON ROUGE, LA (Cox Communications)

ABITA SPRINGS—See SLIDELL, LA (Charter Communications)

▲**ACADIA PARISH (portions)**—Formerly served by Almega Cable. No longer in operation

ADDIS—See BATON ROUGE, LA (Cox Communications)

ALBANY—See HAMMOND, LA (Charter Communications)

ALEXANDRIA—See PINEVILLE, LA (Suddenlink Communications)

ALLEN PARISH—See BUNKIE, LA (Charter Communications)

AMELIA—See BOURG, LA (Charter Communications)

AMITE CITY—See HAMMOND, LA (Charter Communications)

AMITE—See BOGALUSA, LA (Charter Communications)

ANACOCO—See FORT POLK, LA (Suddenlink Communications)

ANGLE—See BOGALUSA, LA (Charter Communications)

▲**ANGOLA**—Audubon Cablevision Inc.

ARABI—See NEW ORLEANS, LA (Cox Communications)

▲**ARCADIA**—Alliance Communications

ARNAUDVILLE—See GRAND COTEAU, LA (Allen's TV Cable Service Inc.)

ASCENSION PARISH—See BATON ROUGE, LA (Cox Communications)

ASSUMPTION PARISH (SOUTHERN PORTION)—See THIBODAUX, LA (Charter Communications)

AVOYELLES PARISH—See MOREAUVILLE, LA (Suddenlink Communications)

BAKER—See BATON ROUGE, LA (Cox Communications)

BALDWIN—See BATON ROUGE, LA (Cox Communications)

BALL—See PINEVILLE, LA (Suddenlink Communications)

BANKS SPRINGS—See COLUMBIA, LA (CMA Cablevision)

BARKSDALE AFB—See BOSSIER CITY, LA (Suddenlink Communications)

▲**BASILE**—Alliance Communications

▲**BASTROP**—Suddenlink Communications

▲**BATON ROUGE**—Cox Communications

BAYOU BLACK—See BOURG, LA (Charter Communications)

BAYOU CANE—See HOUMA, LA (Comcast Cable)

▲**BAYOU L'OURSE**—Allen's TV Cable Service Inc. Now served by MORGAN CITY, LA [LA0188]

BAYOU L'OURSE—See MORGAN CITY, LA (Allens TV Cable Service Inc.)

BAYOU PIGEON—See BATON ROUGE, LA (Cox Communications)

BAYOU SORREL—See BATON ROUGE, LA (Cox Communications)

BAYOU VISTA—See BATON ROUGE, LA (Cox Communications)

BEAUREGARD PARISH—See DE RIDDER, LA (Suddenlink Communications)

BELCHER—See HOSSTON, LA (Comcast Cable)

BELL CITY—See IOWA, LA (Suddenlink Communications)

▲**BELLE CHASSE**—CMA Cablevision

BELLE ROSE (PORTIONS)—See THIBODAUX, LA (Charter Communications)

BENTLEY—See DRY PRONG, LA (Zoom Media)

▲**BENTON**—Zoom Media

▲**BERNICE**—Alliance Communications

BERWICK—See MORGAN CITY, LA (Allens TV Cable Service Inc.)

BETHANY—See SHREVEPORT, LA (Comcast Cable)

BIENVILLE PARISH (NORTHWESTERN PORTION)—See SIBLEY, LA (Suddenlink Communications)

BIENVILLE PARISH (PORTIONS)—See ARCADIA, LA (Alliance Communications)

▲**BLANCHARD**—CMA Cablevision

▲**BOGALUSA**—Charter Communications

BONITA—See COLLINSTON, LA (Northeast Tel)

BOOTHEVILLE—See BELLE CHASSE, LA (CMA Cablevision)

BORDELONVILLE—See MOREAUVILLE, LA (Suddenlink Communications)

▲**BOSSIER CITY**—Suddenlink Communications

BOSSIER PARISH (NORTHERN PORTION)—See PLAIN DEALING, LA (Alliance Communications)

BOSSIER PARISH—See BOSSIER CITY, LA (Suddenlink Communications)

BOSSIER PARISH—See BENTON, LA (Zoom Media)

▲**BOURG**—Charter Communications

BOUTTE—See NEW ORLEANS, LA (Cox Communications)

▲**BOYCE**—Suddenlink Communications

▲**BRAITHWAITE**—Formerly served by CMA Cablevision. No longer in operation

BREAUX BRIDGE—See BATON ROUGE, LA (Cox Communications)

▲**BROUILLETTE**—Formerly served by Almega Cable. No longer in operation

BROUSSARD—See BATON ROUGE, LA (Cox Communications)

BRUSLY—See BATON ROUGE, LA (Cox Communications)

▲**BUNKIE**—Charter Communications

BURAS—See BELLE CHASSE, LA (CMA Cablevision)

CADDO PARISH—See BLANCHARD, LA (CMA Cablevision)

CADDO PARISH—See SHREVEPORT, LA (Comcast Cable)

CALCASIEU PARISH (PORTIONS)—See SULPHUR, LA (Suddenlink Communications)

CALCASIEU PARISH—See LAKE CHARLES, LA (Suddenlink Communications)

▲**CALHOUN**—CMA Cablevision

CALHOUN—See WEST MONROE, LA (Comcast Cable)

▲**CALVIN**—Formerly served by Cebridge Connections. No longer in operation

▲**CAMERON**—Formerly served by Charter Communications. No longer in operation

CAMERON—See CARLYSS, LA (Cameron Communications)

▲**CAMPTI**—Red River Cable TV

CARENCRO—See BATON ROUGE, LA (Cox Communications)

▲**CARLYSS**—Cameron Communications

CARVILLE—See BATON ROUGE, LA (Cox Communications)

CATAHOULA PARISH—See WALLACE RIDGE, LA (Zoom Media)

CECELIA—See BATON ROUGE, LA (Cox Communications)

▲**CECILIA (northern portion)**—Formerly served by Trust Cable. No longer in operation

CENTERVILLE—See BATON ROUGE, LA (Cox Communications)

CENTRAL—See BATON ROUGE, LA (Cox Communications)

CHACKBAY—See THIBODAUX, LA (Charter Communications)

CHALMETTE—See NEW ORLEANS, LA (Cox Communications)

CHARENTON—See BATON ROUGE, LA (Cox Communications)

CHATAIGNIER—See ST. LANDRY PARISH, LA (Charter Communications)

▲**CHATHAM**—Formerly served by Chatham CATV. No longer in operation

CHAUVIN—See BOURG, LA (Charter Communications)

CHENEYVILLE—See LECOMPTE, LA (Suddenlink Communications)

▲**CHOUDRANT**—Formerly served by Almega Cable. No longer in operation

CHURCH POINT—See ST. LANDRY PARISH, LA (Charter Communications)

▲**CLARENCE**—Red River Cable TV

▲**CLAYTON (TOWN)**—Zoom Media

▲**CLINTON**—Trust Cable. Now served by ETHEL, LA [LA0160]

CLINTON—See ETHEL, LA (Trust Cable)

▲**CLOUTIERVILLE**—Formerly served by Almega Cable. No longer in operation

▲**COLFAX**—Alliance Communications

▲**COLLINSTON**—Northeast Tel

COLUMBIA HEIGHTS—See COLUMBIA, LA (CMA Cablevision)

▲**COLUMBIA**—CMA Cablevision

CONCORDIA PARISH—See FERRIDAY, LA (Cable South Media)

CORBIN—See HAMMOND, LA (Charter Communications)

▲**COTEAU HOLMES**—Formerly served by Trust Cable. No longer in operation

▲**COTTON VALLEY**—Zoom Media

COTTONPORT—See MOREAUVILLE, LA (Suddenlink Communications)

▲**COUSHATTA**—Red River Cable TV

COVINGTON—See SLIDELL, LA (Charter Communications)

CREOLE—See CARLYSS, LA (Cameron Communications)

▲**CROWLEY**—Cox Communications. Now served by BATON ROUGE, LA [LA0003]

CROWLEY—See BATON ROUGE, LA (Cox Communications)

CULLEN—See SPRINGHILL, LA (CMA Cablevision)

CUT OFF—See GOLDEN MEADOW, LA (Vision Communications)

▲**DE QUINCY**—CommuniComm Services. Now served by VINTON, LA [LA0064]

DE QUINCY—See VINTON (town), LA (CommuniComm Services)

▲**DE RIDDER**—Suddenlink Communications

DE SOTO PARISH (PORTIONS)—See SHREVEPORT, LA (Comcast Cable)

DELCAMBRE—See BATON ROUGE, LA (Cox Communications)

▲ **DELHI**—CMA Cablevision

DENHAM SPRINGS—See BATON ROUGE, LA (Cox Communications)

DESTREHAN—See NEW ORLEANS, LA (Cox Communications)

▲ **DIXIE INN**—Formerly served by PC One Cable. No longer in operation

▲ **DODSON**—Formerly served by Cebridge Connections. No longer in operation

DONALDSONVILLE—See THIBODAUX, LA (Charter Communications)

DONALDSONVILLE—See BATON ROUGE, LA (Cox Communications)

DOYLINE—See SIBLEY, LA (Suddenlink Communications)

▲ **DRY PRONG**—Zoom Media

DUBACH—See BERNICE, LA (Alliance Communications)

DUBBERLY—See SIBLEY, LA (Suddenlink Communications)

DULAC—See BOURG, LA (Charter Communications)

DULARGE—See BOURG, LA (Charter Communications)

DUPLESSIS—See BATON ROUGE, LA (Cox Communications)

DUSON—See BATON ROUGE, LA (Cox Communications)

EAST BATON ROUGE PARISH—See BATON ROUGE, LA (Cox Communications)

EAST HODGE—See JONESBORO, LA (Suddenlink Communications)

EBARB—See MANY, LA (Suddenlink Communications)

ECHO—See MOREAUVILLE, LA (Suddenlink Communications)

EDGARD—See LA PLACE, LA (Comcast Cable)

▲ **EFFIE**—Zoom Media

▲ **EGAN**—Formerly served by Trust Cable. No longer in operation

ELIZABETH—See BUNKIE, LA (Charter Communications)

ELTON—See KINDER, LA (Communi-Comm Services)

EMPIRE—See BELLE CHASSE, LA (CMA Cablevision)

ENGLAND AUTHORITY—See PINEVILLE, LA (Suddenlink Communications)

ERATH—See BATON ROUGE, LA (Cox Communications)

ERWINVILLE—See BATON ROUGE, LA (Cox Communications)

▲ **ESTHERWOOD**—Formerly served by Alliance Communications Network. No longer in operation

▲ **ETHEL**—Trust Cable

EUNICE—See ST. LANDRY PARISH, LA (Charter Communications)

EVANGELINE PARISH—See VILLE PLATTE, LA (Suddenlink Communications)

EVERGREEN—See BUNKIE, LA (Charter Communications)

▲ **FARMERVILLE**—CMA Cablevision

▲ **FERRIDAY**—Cable South Media

FILLMORE—See BOSSIER CITY, LA (Suddenlink Communications)

FISHER—See MANY, LA (Suddenlink Communications)

FLORIEN—See MANY, LA (Suddenlink Communications)

▲ **FOLSOM**—Charter Communications. Now served by SLIDELL (formerly St. Tammany Parish), LA [LA0182]

FOLSOM—See SLIDELL, LA (Charter Communications)

FORDOCHE—See MARINGOUIN, LA (Spillway Communications Inc.)

FOREST HILL—See LECOMPTE, LA (Suddenlink Communications)

▲ **FORKED ISLAND**—Kaplan Telephone Co. Formerly served by Kaplan, LA [LA0162]. This cable system has converted to IPTV

▲ **FORT POLK**—Suddenlink Communications

▲ **FOUR CORNERS**—Formerly served by CableSouth Inc. No longer in operation

FOURCHON—See GOLDEN MEADOW, LA (Vision Communications)

▲ **FRANKLIN**—Cox Communications. Now served by BATON ROUGE, LA [LA0003]

FRANKLIN—See BATON ROUGE, LA (Cox Communications)

FRANKLINTON—See BOGALUSA, LA (Charter Communications)

FRENCH SETTLEMENT—See HAMMOND, LA (Charter Communications)

FROST—See HAMMOND, LA (Charter Communications)

GALLIANO—See GOLDEN MEADOW, LA (Vision Communications)

GARDEN CITY—See BATON ROUGE, LA (Cox Communications)

GARYVILLE—See LA PLACE, LA (Comcast Cable)

▲ **GEORGETOWN**—Formerly served by Almega Cable. No longer in operation

GHEENS—See GOLDEN MEADOW, LA (Vision Communications)

▲ **GIBSLAND**—Alliance Communications

GIBSON—See BOURG, LA (Charter Communications)

GILBERT—See WISNER, LA (CMA Cablevision)

GILLIAM—See HOSSTON, LA (Comcast Cable)

GLENMORA—See LECOMPTE, LA (Suddenlink Communications)

▲ **GOLDEN MEADOW**—Vision Communications

GONZALES—See BATON ROUGE, LA (Cox Communications)

GOOD PINE—See JENA, LA (Cable South Media)

GRAMBLING—See RUSTON, LA (Suddenlink Communications)

▲ **GRAMERCY**—Cox Communications. Now served by BATON ROUGE, LA [LA0003]

GRAMERCY—See BATON ROUGE, LA (Cox Communications)

GRAND CAILLOU—See BOURG, LA (Charter Communications)

GRAND CANE—See MANSFIELD, LA (CMA Cablevision)

▲ **GRAND CHENIER**—CableSouth Inc. Now served by CARLYSS, LA [LA0063]

GRAND CHENIER—See CARLYSS, LA (Cameron Communications)

▲ **GRAND COTEAU**—Allen's TV Cable Service Inc.

GRAND ISLE—See GOLDEN MEADOW, LA (Vision Communications)

▲ **GRAND LAKE**—CableSouth Inc. Now served by CARLYSS, LA [LA0063]

GRAND LAKE—See CARLYSS, LA (Cameron Communications)

GRANT PARISH (PORTIONS)—See DRY PRONG, LA (Zoom Media)

GRANT PARISH—See PINEVILLE, LA (Suddenlink Communications)

GRAY—See HOUMA, LA (Comcast Cable)

GRAYSON—See COLUMBIA, LA (CMA Cablevision)

▲ **GREENSBURG**—Formerly served by Almega Cable. No longer in operation

GREENWOOD—See SHREVEPORT, LA (Comcast Cable)

GRETNA—See NEW ORLEANS, LA (Cox Communications)

GROSSE TETE—See BATON ROUGE, LA (Cox Communications)

▲ **HACKBERRY**—Formerly served by Charter Communications. No longer in operation

HACKBERRY—See CARLYSS, LA (Cameron Communications)

HAHNVILLE—See NEW ORLEANS, LA (Cox Communications)

▲ **HALL SUMMIT**—Formerly served by Red River Cable TV. No longer in operation

▲ **HAMMOND**—Charter Communications

HARAHAN—See NEW ORLEANS, LA (Cox Communications)

▲ **HAUGHTON**—Formerly served by Cebridge Connections. No longer in operation

HAUGHTON—See BOSSIER CITY, LA (Suddenlink Communications)

HAYES—See IOWA, LA (Suddenlink Communications)

▲ **HAYNESVILLE**—CMA Cablevision. Now served by HOMER, LA [LA0062]

HAYNESVILLE—See HOMER, LA (CMA Cablevision)

HEFLIN—See SIBLEY, LA (Suddenlink Communications)

HENDERSON—See BATON ROUGE, LA (Cox Communications)

▲ **HENRY**—Formerly served by Cable-South Inc. No longer in operation

HESSMER—See MARKSVILLE, LA (Charter Communications)

HODGE—See JONESBORO, LA (Suddenlink Communications)

HOLDEN—See HAMMOND, LA (Charter Communications)

▲ **HOMER**—CMA Cablevision

▲ **HOSSTON**—Comcast Cable

HOTWELLS—See BOYCE, LA (Suddenlink Communications)

HOUMA—See BOURG, LA (Charter Communications)

▲ **HOUMA**—Comcast Cable

IBERIA PARISH (PORTIONS)—See NEW IBERIA, LA (Suddenlink Communications)

IBERIA PARISH—See BATON ROUGE, LA (Cox Communications)

IBERVILLE PARISH (PORTIONS)—See MARINGOUIN, LA (Spillway Communications Inc.)

IBERVILLE PARISH—See BATON ROUGE, LA (Cox Communications)

IBERVILLE—See BATON ROUGE, LA (Cox Communications)

INDEPENDENCE—See HAMMOND, LA (Charter Communications)

▲ **INNIS**—Formerly served by Spillway Communications Inc. No longer in operation

▲ **IOTA**—Charter Communications. Now served by ST. LANDRY PARISH, LA [LA0022]

IOTA—See ST. LANDRY PARISH, LA (Charter Communications)

▲ **IOWA**—Suddenlink Communications

JACKSON PARISH (PORTIONS)—See JONESBORO, LA (Suddenlink Communications)

JACKSON—See ETHEL, LA (Trust Cable)

JEAN LAFITTE—See NEW ORLEANS, LA (Cox Communications)

JEANERETTE—See BATON ROUGE, LA (Cox Communications)

JEFFERSON PARISH (PORTIONS)—See NEW ORLEANS, LA (Cox Communications)

▲**JENA**—Cable South Media

JENNINGS—See ST. LANDRY PARISH, LA (Charter Communications)

JOAQUIN—See LOGANSPORT, TX (CMA Cablevision)

JOHNSONS BAYOU—See CARLYSS, LA (Cameron Communications)

▲**JONESBORO**—Suddenlink Communications

▲**JONESVILLE**—Cable South Media

JONESVILLE—See WALLACE RIDGE, LA (Zoom Media)

JOYCE—See WINNFIELD, LA (Suddenlink Communications)

▲**KAPLAN**—Kaplan Telephone Co. This cable system has converted to IPTV. See Kaplan, LA [LA5021]

KAPLAN—See BATON ROUGE, LA (Cox Communications)

▲**KAPLAN**—Kaplan Telephone Co. Formery [LA0162]. This cable system has converted to IPTV

KENNER—See NEW ORLEANS, LA (Cox Communications)

▲**KENTWOOD**—Alliance Communications

▲**KILBOURNE**—Community Communications Co.

KILLIAN—See HAMMOND, LA (Charter Communications)

▲**KINDER**—CommuniComm Services

KOLIN—See LECOMPTE, LA (Suddenlink Communications)

▲**KROTZ SPRINGS**—Spillway Cablevision Inc.

▲**LA PLACE**—Comcast Cable

LA SALLE PARISH—See JENA, LA (Cable South Media)

LABADIEVILLE—See THIBODAUX, LA (Charter Communications)

LACASSINE—See IOWA, LA (Suddenlink Communications)

LACOMBE—See SLIDELL, LA (Charter Communications)

LAFAYETTE PARISH—See BATON ROUGE, LA (Cox Communications)

▲**LAFAYETTE**—Cox Communications. Now served by BATON ROUGE, LA [LA0003]

LAFAYETTE—See BATON ROUGE, LA (Cox Communications)

LAFOURCHE PARISH (WESTERN PORTION)—See THIBODAUX, LA (Charter Communications)

LAFOURCHE PARISH—See HOUMA, LA (Comcast Cable)

LAFOURCHE PARISH—See GOLDEN MEADOW, LA (Vision Communications)

▲**LAKE ARTHUR**—CommuniComm Services

LAKE BISTINEAU—See SIBLEY, LA (Suddenlink Communications)

LAKE BRUIN—See ST. JOSEPH, LA (Suddenlink Communications)

▲**LAKE CHARLES**—Suddenlink Communications

▲**LAKE CLAIBORNE**—Formerly served by Almega Cable. No longer in operation

LAKE COTILE—See BOYCE, LA (Suddenlink Communications)

▲**LAKE PROVIDENCE**—CMA Cablevision

▲**LAKE ST. JOHN**—Formerly served by Almega Cable. No longer in operation

LAKESHORE—See WEST MONROE, LA (Comcast Cable)

LAROSE—See GOLDEN MEADOW, LA (Vision Communications)

LE BLEU—See IOWA, LA (Suddenlink Communications)

▲**LECOMPTE**—Suddenlink Communications

▲**LEESVILLE**—Suddenlink Communications

LEEVILLE—See GOLDEN MEADOW, LA (Vision Communications)

LEONVILLE—See ST. LANDRY PARISH, LA (Charter Communications)

LIBUSE (PORTIONS)—See PINEVILLE, LA (Suddenlink Communications)

LINCOLN PARISH (PORTIONS)—See BERNICE, LA (Alliance Communications)

LINCOLN PARISH—See RUSTON, LA (Suddenlink Communications)

LIVINGSTON PARISH (PORTIONS)—See HAMMOND, LA (Charter Communications)

LIVINGSTON—See HAMMOND, LA (Charter Communications)

LIVONIA—See MARINGOUIN, LA (Spillway Communications Inc.)

LOCKHART—See HAMMOND, LA (Charter Communications)

LOCKPORT—See GOLDEN MEADOW, LA (Vision Communications)

▲**LOGANSPORT**—CMA Cablevision

LOREAUVILLE—See BATON ROUGE, LA (Cox Communications)

LOUISIANA STATE PENITENTIARY—See ANGOLA, LA (Audubon Cablevision Inc.)

LULING—See NEW ORLEANS, LA (Cox Communications)

LUTCHER—See BATON ROUGE, LA (Cox Communications)

LYDIA—See NEW IBERIA, LA (Suddenlink Communications)

MADISON PARISH—See TALLULAH, LA (CMA Cablevision)

MADISONVILLE—See SLIDELL, LA (Charter Communications)

MAMOU—See VILLE PLATTE, LA (Suddenlink Communications)

MANDEVILLE—See SLIDELL, LA (Charter Communications)

▲**MANGHAM**—Formerly served by Almega Cable. No longer in operation

▲**MANSFIELD**—CMA Cablevision

MANSURA—See MARKSVILLE, LA (Charter Communications)

▲**MANY**—Suddenlink Communications

▲**MARINGOUIN**—Spillway Communications Inc.

▲**MARION**—Bayou Cable TV

▲**MARKSVILLE**—Charter Communications

▲**MARKSVILLE**—Zoom Media

MATHEWS—See GOLDEN MEADOW, LA (Vision Communications)

MAURICE—See BATON ROUGE, LA (Cox Communications)

▲**MCINTYRE**—Formerly served by Almega Cable. No longer in operation

MCNARY—See LECOMPTE, LA (Suddenlink Communications)

▲**MELVILLE**—Alliance Communications Network

MER ROUGE—See BASTROP, LA (Suddenlink Communications)

MERAUX—See NEW ORLEANS, LA (Cox Communications)

▲**MERRYVILLE**—Alliance Communications

MIDWAY—See JENA, LA (Cable South Media)

MILTON—See BATON ROUGE, LA (Cox Communications)

▲**MINDEN**—Suddenlink Communications

▲**MIRE**—Formerly served by Trust Cable. No longer in operation

▲**MONROE**—CMA Cablevision

MONROE—See WEST MONROE, LA (Comcast Cable)

MONTEGUT—See BOURG, LA (Charter Communications)

▲**MONTEREY**—Formerly served by Almega Cable. No longer in operation

▲**MONTGOMERY**—Alliance Communications

MONTZ—See NEW ORLEANS, LA (Cox Communications)

MOORINGSPORT—See BLANCHARD, LA (CMA Cablevision)

▲**MOREAUVILLE**—Suddenlink Communications

MOREHOUSE PARISH (PORTIONS)—See BASTROP, LA (Suddenlink Communications)

MOREHOUSE PARISH (UNINCORPORATED AREAS)—See COLLINSTON, LA (Northeast Tel)

▲**MORGAN CITY**—Allens TV Cable Service Inc.

MORGANZA—See POINTE COUPEE, LA (Cobridge Communications)

MOSS BLUFF—See WESTLAKE, LA (CommuniComm Services)

MOSSVILLE—See SULPHUR, LA (Suddenlink Communications)

NAPOLEONVILLE—See THIBODAUX, LA (Charter Communications)

▲**NATCHEZ**—Alliance Communications

▲**NATCHITOCHES (portions)**—Rapid Cable. Now served by NATCHEZ, LA [LA0122]

NATCHITOCHES PARISH—See NATCHITOCHES, LA (Suddenlink Communications)

▲**NATCHITOCHES**—Suddenlink Communications

NEGREET—See MANY, LA (Suddenlink Communications)

▲**NEW IBERIA**—Cox Communications. Now served by BATON ROUGE, LA [LA0003]

NEW IBERIA—See BATON ROUGE, LA (Cox Communications)

▲**NEW IBERIA**—Suddenlink Communications

▲**NEW ORLEANS**—Cox Communications

NEW ROADS—See POINTE COUPEE, LA (Cobridge Communications)

▲**NEWELLTON**—Alliance Communications

NEWLLANO—See LEESVILLE, LA (Suddenlink Communications)

NORCO—See NEW ORLEANS, LA (Cox Communications)

NORTH HODGE—See JONESBORO, LA (Suddenlink Communications)

NORTH MONROE—See MONROE, LA (CMA Cablevision)

▲**NORWOOD**—Trust Cable. Now served by ETHEL, LA [LA0160]

NORWOOD—See ETHEL, LA (Trust Cable)

▲**OAK GROVE**—CMA Cablevision of Lake Providence. Now served by LAKE PROVIDENCE, LA [LA0053]

OAK GROVE—See LAKE PROVIDENCE, LA (CMA Cablevision)

▲**OAK RIDGE**—Formerly served by Charter Communications. No longer in operation

OAKDALE—See BUNKIE, LA (Charter Communications)

OBERLIN—See KINDER, LA (CommuniComm Services)

OIL CITY—See BLANCHARD, LA (CMA Cablevision)

▲ **OLLA**—Alliance Communications

OPELOUSAS—See ST. LANDRY PARISH, LA (Charter Communications)

ORLEANS PARISH—See NEW ORLEANS, LA (Cox Communications)

OUACHITA PARISH (NORTHERN PORTION)—See WEST MONROE, LA (Comcast Cable)

PAINCOURTVILLE—See THIBODAUX, LA (Charter Communications)

▲ **PALMETTO**—Formerly served by Village Cable Co. No longer in operation

PARKS—See BATON ROUGE, LA (Cox Communications)

PATTERSON—See BATON ROUGE, LA (Cox Communications)

PAULINA—See THIBODAUX, LA (Charter Communications)

PEARL RIVER—See SLIDELL, LA (Charter Communications)

▲ **PECANIERE**—CableSouth Inc. No longer in operation

▲ **PIERRE PART**—Allen's TV Cable Service Inc. Now served by MORGAN CITY, LA [LA0188]

PIERRE PART—See MORGAN CITY, LA (Allens TV Cable Service Inc.)

▲ **PINE PRAIRIE**—Charter Communications

▲ **PINEVILLE**—Suddenlink Communications

▲ **PLAIN DEALING**—Alliance Communications

PLAQUEMINE—See BATON ROUGE, LA (Cox Communications)

PLAUCHEVILLE—See MOREAUVILLE, LA (Suddenlink Communications)

▲ **POINTE A LA HACHE**—Formerly served by CMA Cablevision. No longer in operation

POINTE COUPEE PARISH—See POINTE COUPEE, LA (Cobridge Communications)

POINTE COUPEE PARISH—See MARINGOUIN, LA (Spillway Communications Inc.)

▲ **POINTE COUPEE**—Cobridge Communications

POLLOCK—See PINEVILLE, LA (Suddenlink Communications)

PONCHATOULA—See HAMMOND, LA (Charter Communications)

PORT ALLEN—See BATON ROUGE, LA (Cox Communications)

▲ **PORT BARRE**—Allen's TV Cable Service Inc. Now served by GRAND COTEAU, LA [LA0207]

PORT BARRE—See GRAND COTEAU, LA (Allen's TV Cable Service Inc.)

PORT SULPHUR—See BELLE CHASSE, LA (CMA Cablevision)

PORT VINCENT—See HAMMOND, LA (Charter Communications)

PORTERVILLE—See SPRINGHILL, LA (CMA Cablevision)

PRINCETON—See BOSSIER CITY, LA (Suddenlink Communications)

QUITMAN—See JONESBORO, LA (Suddenlink Communications)

RACELAND—See THIBODAUX, LA (Charter Communications)

RACELAND—See GOLDEN MEADOW, LA (Vision Communications)

RAPIDES PARISH (PORTIONS)—See LECOMPTE, LA (Suddenlink Communications)

RAPIDES PARISH (PORTIONS)—See MOREAUVILLE, LA (Suddenlink Communications)

RAPIDES PARISH—See PINEVILLE, LA (Suddenlink Communications)

RAYNE—See BATON ROUGE, LA (Cox Communications)

▲ **RAYVILLE**—Formerly served by Cotton Country Cable. No longer in operation

RAYVILLE—See DELHI, LA (CMA Cablevision)

REDDELL—See VILLE PLATTE, LA (Suddenlink Communications)

RESERVE—See LA PLACE, LA (Comcast Cable)

RICHMOND—See TALLULAH, LA (CMA Cablevision)

RIDGECREST—See FERRIDAY, LA (Cable South Media)

RINGGOLD—See SIBLEY, LA (Suddenlink Communications)

ROANOKE—See LAKE ARTHUR, LA (CommuniComm Services)

▲ **ROBELINE**—Formerly served by MARBAC Communications. No longer in operation

▲ **ROCKY BRANCH**—Bayou Cable TV

▲ **RODESSA**—Formerly served by Almega Cable. No longer in operation

ROSEDALE—See BATON ROUGE, LA (Cox Communications)

ROSELAND—See HAMMOND, LA (Charter Communications)

ROSEPINE—See DE RIDDER, LA (Suddenlink Communications)

▲ **RUSTON**—Suddenlink Communications

SABINE PARISH—See MANY, LA (Suddenlink Communications)

SAREPTA—See COTTON VALLEY, LA (Zoom Media)

SATSUMA—See HAMMOND, LA (Charter Communications)

SCHRIEVER—See BOURG, LA (Charter Communications)

SCHRIEVER—See HOUMA, LA (Comcast Cable)

SCOTT—See BATON ROUGE, LA (Cox Communications)

▲ **SHREVEPORT**—Comcast Cable

▲ **SIBLEY**—Suddenlink Communications

▲ **SICILY ISLAND**—Formerly served by Almega Cable. No longer in operation

SIMMESPORT—See MOREAUVILLE, LA (Suddenlink Communications)

▲ **SIMPSON**—Zoom Media

SIMSBORO—See RUSTON, LA (Suddenlink Communications)

SLAGLE—See SIMPSON, LA (Zoom Media)

SLAUGHTER—See BATON ROUGE, LA (Cox Communications)

▲ **SLIDELL**—Charter Communications

SORRENTO—See BATON ROUGE, LA (Cox Communications)

SOUTH MANSFIELD—See MANSFIELD, LA (CMA Cablevision)

SOUTH MONROE—See MONROE, LA (CMA Cablevision)

SPRINGFIELD—See HAMMOND, LA (Charter Communications)

▲ **SPRINGHILL**—CMA Cablevision

▲ **ST. BERNARD PARISH**—Cox Communications. Now served by NEW ORLEANS, LA [LA0001]

ST. BERNARD PARISH—See NEW ORLEANS, LA (Cox Communications)

ST. CHARLES PARISH (PORTIONS)—See NEW ORLEANS, LA (Cox Communications)

▲ **ST. FRANCISVILLE**—Audubon Cablevision Inc.

ST. GABRIEL—See BATON ROUGE, LA (Cox Communications)

ST. JAMES PARISH (SOUTHERN PORTION)—See THIBODAUX, LA (Charter Communications)

ST. JAMES PARISH—See BATON ROUGE, LA (Cox Communications)

ST. JAMES—See THIBODAUX, LA (Charter Communications)

ST. JOHN THE BAPTIST PARISH (EASTERN PORTION)—See LA PLACE, LA (Comcast Cable)

▲ **ST. JOSEPH**—Suddenlink Communications

ST. LANDRY PARISH (PORTIONS)—See GRAND COTEAU, LA (Allen's TV Cable Service Inc.)

ST. LANDRY PARISH (PORTIONS)—See KROTZ SPRINGS, LA (Spillway Cablevision Inc.)

▲ **ST. LANDRY PARISH**—Charter Communications

ST. MARTIN PARISH (PORTIONS)—See GRAND COTEAU, LA (Allen's TV Cable Service Inc.)

ST. MARTIN PARISH (PORTIONS)—See NEW IBERIA, LA (Suddenlink Communications)

ST. MARTIN PARISH—See BATON ROUGE, LA (Cox Communications)

▲ **ST. MARTINVILLE**—Cox Communications. Now served by BATON ROUGE, LA [LA0003]

ST. MARTINVILLE—See BATON ROUGE, LA (Cox Communications)

ST. MARY PARISH—See MORGAN CITY, LA (Allens TV Cable Service Inc.)

ST. MARY PARISH—See BATON ROUGE, LA (Cox Communications)

ST. ROSE—See NEW ORLEANS, LA (Cox Communications)

ST. TAMMANY PARISH (UNINCORPORATED AREAS)—See SLIDELL, LA (Charter Communications)

STANLEY—See LOGANSPORT, LA (CMA Cablevision)

▲ **START**—Formerly served by Almega Cable. No longer in operation

STEPHENSVILLE—See MORGAN CITY, LA (Allens TV Cable Service Inc.)

▲ **STERLINGTON**—Bayou Cable TV

STONEWALL—See SHREVEPORT, LA (Comcast Cable)

▲ **SULPHUR**—Suddenlink Communications

SUNSET—See GRAND COTEAU, LA (Allen's TV Cable Service Inc.)

SUNSHINE—See BATON ROUGE, LA (Cox Communications)

SUPREME—See THIBODAUX, LA (Charter Communications)

SWARTZ—See WEST MONROE, LA (Comcast Cable)

SWEETWATER CREEK—See BOGALUSA, LA (Charter Communications)

▲ **SWEETWATER**—Charter Communications. Now served by BOGALUSA, LA [LA0023]

▲ **TALLULAH**—CMA Cablevision

TANGIPAHOA PARISH—See HAMMOND, LA (Charter Communications)

▲ **TANGIPAHOA**—Formerly served by Almega Cable. No longer in operation

TENSAS PARISH (PORTIONS)—See ST. JOSEPH, LA (Suddenlink Communications)

TERREBONNE PARISH—See BOURG, LA (Charter Communications)

TERREBONNE PARISH—See HOUMA, LA (Comcast Cable)

THERIOT—See BOURG, LA (Charter Communications)

▲ **THIBODAUX**—Charter Communications

TICKFAW—See HAMMOND, LA (Charter Communications)

TRIUMPH—See BELLE CHASSE, LA (CMA Cablevision)

TULLOS—See OLLA, LA (Alliance Communications)

▲**TURKEY CREEK**—Formerly served by Alliance Communications Network. No longer in operation

UNION PARISH (PORTIONS)—See BERNICE, LA (Alliance Communications)

URANIA—See OLLA, LA (Alliance Communications)

VACHERIE—See THIBODAUX, LA (Charter Communications)

▲**VARNADO**—Charter Communications. Now served by BOGALUSA, LA [LA0023]

VARNADO—See BOGALUSA, LA (Charter Communications)

VENICE—See BELLE CHASSE, LA (CMA Cablevision)

VERDUNVILLE—See BATON ROUGE, LA (Cox Communications)

VERMILION PARISH (PORTIONS)—See NEW IBERIA, LA (Suddenlink Communications)

VERMILION PARISH—See BATON ROUGE, LA (Cox Communications)

VERNON PARISH (SOUTHEASTERN PORTION)—See BUNKIE, LA (Charter Communications)

VERNON PARISH—See DE RIDDER, LA (Suddenlink Communications)

VERNON PARISH—See LEESVILLE, LA (Suddenlink Communications)

VIDRINE—See VILLE PLATTE, LA (Suddenlink Communications)

VIENNA—See RUSTON, LA (Suddenlink Communications)

▲**VILLE PLATTE**—Suddenlink Communications

▲**VINTON (TOWN)**—CommuniComm Services

VIOLET—See NEW ORLEANS, LA (Cox Communications)

VIVIAN—See BLANCHARD, LA (CMA Cablevision)

WALKER (PORTIONS)—See BATON ROUGE, LA (Cox Communications)

WALKER—See HAMMOND, LA (Charter Communications)

▲**WALLACE RIDGE**—Zoom Media

WASHINGTON PARISH—See BOGALUSA, LA (Charter Communications)

WASHINGTON—See ST. LANDRY PARISH, LA (Charter Communications)

WASKOM—See SHREVEPORT, TX (Comcast Cable)

▲**WATERPROOF**—Alliance Communications Network

WATSON—See BATON ROUGE, LA (Cox Communications)

WEBSTER PARISH (SOUTHERN PORTION)—See SIBLEY, LA (Suddenlink Communications)

WEBSTER PARISH (UNINCORPORATED AREAS)—See SPRINGHILL, LA (CMA Cablevision)

WEBSTER PARISH—See MINDEN, LA (Suddenlink Communications)

▲**WELSH**—CommuniComm Services. Now served by LAKE ARTHUR, LA [LA0078]

WELSH—See LAKE ARTHUR, LA (CommuniComm Services)

WEST BATON ROUGE PARISH—See BATON ROUGE, LA (Cox Communications)

WEST FELICIANA PARISH (PORTIONS)—See ANGOLA, LA (Audubon Cablevision Inc.)

WEST FELICIANA PARISH—See ST. FRANCISVILLE, LA (Audubon Cablevision Inc.)

▲**WEST MONROE**—Comcast Cable

▲**WESTLAKE**—CommuniComm Services

WESTWEGO—See NEW ORLEANS, LA (Cox Communications)

WHITE CASTLE—See BATON ROUGE, LA (Cox Communications)

▲**WILSON**—CableSouth Inc. Now served by ETHEL, LA [LA0160]

WILSON—See ETHEL, LA (Trust Cable)

WINN PARISH—See WINNFIELD, LA (Suddenlink Communications)

▲**WINNFIELD**—Suddenlink Communications

WINNSBORO TWP.—See WINNSBORO, LA (Cable South Media)

▲**WINNSBORO**—Cable South Media

▲**WISNER**—CMA Cablevision

WOODWORTH—See LECOMPTE, LA (Suddenlink Communications)

YOUNGSVILLE—See BATON ROUGE, LA (Cox Communications)

ZACHARY—See BATON ROUGE, LA (Cox Communications)

ZWOLLE—See MANY, LA (Suddenlink Communications)

MAINE

ACTON—See SANFORD, ME (MetroCast Cablevision)

▲**ADDISON (TOWN)**—Time Warner Cable

ALBION—See AUGUSTA, ME (Time Warner Cable)

ALBION—See WATERVILLE, ME (Time Warner Cable)

ALFRED—See SEBAGO (town), ME (Time Warner Cable)

ALLAGASH (TOWN)—See MADAWASKA, ME (Time Warner Cable)

ALLAGASH—See MADAWASKA, ME (Time Warner Cable)

ALNA—See AUGUSTA, ME (Time Warner Cable)

ANSON—See MADISON, ME (Bee Line Cable TV)

AROOSTOOK COUNTY (PORTIONS)—See MONTICELLO (town), ME (Polaris Cable Services)

▲**AROOSTOOK COUNTY**—Time Warner Cable

ARUNDEL—See SEBAGO (town), ME (Time Warner Cable)

▲**ASHLAND**—Time Warner Cable. Now served by AROOSTOOK COUNTY, ME [ME0008]

ASHLAND—See AROOSTOOK COUNTY, ME (Time Warner Cable)

AUBURN—See AUGUSTA, ME (Time Warner Cable)

▲**AUGUSTA**—Time Warner Cable

▲**AVON**—Now served by NORTH ANSON, ME [ME0062]

AVON—See NORTH ANSON, ME (Time Warner Cable)

BAILEY ISLAND—See BRUNSWICK (town), ME (Comcast Cable)

BAILEYVILLE—See CALAIS, ME (Time Warner Cable)

BALDWIN—See SEBAGO (town), ME (Time Warner Cable)

▲**BANGOR**—Time Warner Cable

BAR HARBOR—See BANGOR, ME (Time Warner Cable)

BAR MILLS—See SEBAGO (town), ME (Time Warner Cable)

BARING—See CALAIS, ME (Time Warner Cable)

BASS HARBOR—See BANGOR, ME (Time Warner Cable)

BATH—See BRUNSWICK (town), ME (Comcast Cable)

BEALS—See JONESPORT, ME (Time Warner Cable)

BELFAST—See BANGOR, ME (Time Warner Cable)

BELGRADE (TOWN)—See AUGUSTA, ME (Time Warner Cable)

BELGRADE LAKES—See AUGUSTA, ME (Time Warner Cable)

▲**BELGRADE**—Now served by AUGUSTA, ME [ME0004]

BELMONT (TOWN)—See BANGOR, ME (Time Warner Cable)

BENTON—See AUGUSTA, ME (Time Warner Cable)

BENTON—See WATERVILLE, ME (Time Warner Cable)

BERNARD—See BANGOR, ME (Time Warner Cable)

▲**BETHEL**—Formerly served by Adelphia Communications. Now served by SEBAGO (town), ME [ME0107]

BETHEL—See SEBAGO (town), ME (Time Warner Cable)

BIDDEFORD—See YORK, ME (Time Warner Cable)

▲**BINGHAM**—Moosehead Enterprises

BLAINE—See AROOSTOOK COUNTY, ME (Time Warner Cable)

▲**BLUE HILL (town)**—Formerly served by Adelphia Communications. Now served by BANGOR, ME [ME0002]

BLUE HILL (TOWN)—See BANGOR, ME (Time Warner Cable)

BOOTHBAY HARBOR—See AUGUSTA, ME (Time Warner Cable)

▲**BOOTHBAY**—Formerly served by Adelphia Communications. Now served by AUGUSTA, ME [ME0004]

BOOTHBAY—See AUGUSTA, ME (Time Warner Cable)

BOWDOIN (TOWN)—See BRUNSWICK (town), ME (Comcast Cable)

BOWDOINHAM (TOWN)—See BRUNSWICK (town), ME (Comcast Cable)

BRADLEY—See BANGOR, ME (Time Warner Cable)

BREWER—See BANGOR, ME (Time Warner Cable)

BRIDGEWATER (TOWN)—See MONTICELLO (town), ME (Polaris Cable Services)

▲**BRIDGTON**—Now served by SEBAGO (town), ME [ME0107]

BRIDGTON—See SEBAGO (town), ME (Time Warner Cable)

BRISTOL (TOWN)—See AUGUSTA, ME (Time Warner Cable)

▲**BRISTOL**—Now served by AUGUSTA, ME [ME0004]

BROWNVILLE—See MILO, ME (Time Warner Cable)

▲**BRUNSWICK (TOWN)**—Comcast Cable

BRYANT POND—See SEBAGO (town), ME (Time Warner Cable)

BUCKFIELD (TOWN)—See AUGUSTA, ME (Time Warner Cable)

▲**BUCKFIELD**—Formerly served by Adelphia Communications. Now served by AUGUSTA, ME [ME0004]

BUCKSPORT—See BANGOR, ME (Time Warner Cable)

▲**BUXTON**—Now served by SEBAGO (town), ME [ME0107]

BUXTON—See SEBAGO (town), ME (Time Warner Cable)

▲**CALAIS**—Time Warner Cable

CAMDEN—See AUGUSTA, ME (Time Warner Cable)

CANAAN—See BANGOR, ME (Time Warner Cable)

▲ **CANTON (town)**—Now served by AUGUSTA, ME [ME0004]

CANTON (TOWN)—See AUGUSTA, ME (Time Warner Cable)

CAPE ELIZABETH—See PORTLAND, ME (Time Warner Cable)

CAPE PORPOISE—See SEBAGO (town), ME (Time Warner Cable)

CARIBOU—See AROOSTOOK COUNTY, ME (Time Warner Cable)

CARMEL—See BANGOR, ME (Time Warner Cable)

▲ **CARRABASSETT VALLEY**—Now served by NORTH ANSON, ME [ME0062]

CARRABASSETT VALLEY—See NORTH ANSON, ME (Time Warner Cable)

CASCO—See PORTLAND, ME (Time Warner Cable)

▲ **CASTINE**—Formerly served by Adelphia Communications. Now served by BANGOR, ME [ME0002]

CASTINE—See BANGOR, ME (Time Warner Cable)

▲ **CASTLE HILL**—Time Warner Cable. Now served by AROOSTOOK COUNTY, ME [ME0008]

CASTLE HILL—See AROOSTOOK COUNTY, ME (Time Warner Cable)

CASWELL (TOWN)—See AROOSTOOK COUNTY, ME (Time Warner Cable)

CHELSEA—See AUGUSTA, ME (Time Warner Cable)

▲ **CHERRYFIELD**—Time Warner Cable

CHINA—See AUGUSTA, ME (Time Warner Cable)

CHINA—See WATERVILLE, ME (Time Warner Cable)

CLINTON—See AUGUSTA, ME (Time Warner Cable)

CLINTON—See WATERVILLE, ME (Time Warner Cable)

COLUMBIA FALLS—See ADDISON (town), ME (Time Warner Cable)

CONNOR (PORTIONS)—See AROOSTOOK COUNTY, ME (Time Warner Cable)

COPLIN—See NORTH ANSON, ME (Time Warner Cable)

CORINNA—See BANGOR, ME (Time Warner Cable)

CORINTH (TOWN)—See BANGOR, ME (Time Warner Cable)

▲ **CORNISH (town)**—Now served by SEBAGO (town), ME [ME0107]

CORNISH (TOWN)—See SEBAGO (town), ME (Time Warner Cable)

CUMBERLAND—See PORTLAND, ME (Time Warner Cable)

CUSHING (TOWN)—See AUGUSTA, ME (Time Warner Cable)

DAMARISCOTTA—See AUGUSTA, ME (Time Warner Cable)

▲ **DANFORTH**—Polaris Cable Services

DAYTON—See SEBAGO (town), ME (Time Warner Cable)

DEDHAM (TOWN)—See BANGOR, ME (Time Warner Cable)

DEER ISLE (TOWN)—See BANGOR, ME (Time Warner Cable)

DENMARK (TOWN)—See SEBAGO (town), ME (Time Warner Cable)

▲ **DENMARK**—Now served by SEBAGO (town), ME [ME0107]

DETROIT (TOWN)—See BANGOR, ME (Time Warner Cable)

DEXTER—See BANGOR, ME (Time Warner Cable)

DIXFIELD—See AUGUSTA, ME (Time Warner Cable)

DOVER-FOXCROFT—See BANGOR, ME (Time Warner Cable)

DRESDEN—See AUGUSTA, ME (Time Warner Cable)

DURHAM (TOWN)—See BRUNSWICK (town), ME (Comcast Cable)

DYER BROOK—See OAKFIELD, ME (Polaris Cable Services)

▲ **EAGLE LAKE**—Formerly served by Adelphia Communications. Now served by MADAWASKA, ME [ME0026]

EAGLE LAKE—See MADAWASKA, ME (Time Warner Cable)

EAST BALDWIN—See SEBAGO (town), ME (Time Warner Cable)

EAST BOOTHBAY—See AUGUSTA, ME (Time Warner Cable)

EAST DIXFIELD—See AUGUSTA, ME (Time Warner Cable)

EAST LEBANON—See SANFORD, ME (MetroCast Cablevision)

▲ **EAST MACHIAS**—Formerly served by Pine Tree Cablevision. No longer in operation

EAST MILLINOCKET—See MILLINOCKET, ME (Bee Line Cable TV)

▲ **EASTON**—Time Warner Cable. Now served by AROOSTOOK COUNTY, ME [ME0008]

EASTON—See AROOSTOOK COUNTY, ME (Time Warner Cable)

EDDINGTON—See BANGOR, ME (Time Warner Cable)

EDGECOMB—See AUGUSTA, ME (Time Warner Cable)

ELLSWORTH—See BANGOR, ME (Time Warner Cable)

EMBDEN—See NORTH ANSON, ME (Time Warner Cable)

ENFIELD—See HOWLAND, ME (Polaris Cable Services)

EUSTIS—See NORTH ANSON, ME (Time Warner Cable)

FAIRFIELD—See WATERVILLE, ME (Time Warner Cable)

FALMOUTH—See PORTLAND, ME (Time Warner Cable)

FARMINGDALE—See AUGUSTA, ME (Time Warner Cable)

FARMINGTON—See MADISON, ME (Bee Line Cable TV)

FORT FAIRFIELD—See AROOSTOOK COUNTY, ME (Time Warner Cable)

▲ **FORT KENT**—Formerly served by Adelphia Communications. Now served by MADAWASKA, ME [ME0026]

FORT KENT—See MADAWASKA, ME (Time Warner Cable)

▲ **FRANKLIN (town)**—Now served by BANGOR, ME [ME0002]

FRANKLIN (TOWN)—See BANGOR, ME (Time Warner Cable)

FRANKLIN—See BANGOR, ME (Time Warner Cable)

FREEPORT (TOWN)—See BRUNSWICK (town), ME (Comcast Cable)

FRENCHVILLE—See MADAWASKA, ME (Time Warner Cable)

▲ **FRIENDSHIP (town)**—Now served by AUGUSTA, ME [ME0004]

FRIENDSHIP (TOWN)—See AUGUSTA, ME (Time Warner Cable)

GARDINER—See AUGUSTA, ME (Time Warner Cable)

▲ **GLENBURN (town)**—Now served by BANGOR, ME [ME0002]

GLENBURN—See BANGOR, ME (Time Warner Cable)

GORHAM—See PORTLAND, ME (Time Warner Cable)

GOULDSBORO—See CHERRYFIELD, ME (Time Warner Cable)

GRAND ISLE—See MADAWASKA, ME (Time Warner Cable)

GRAY (TOWN)—See PORTLAND, ME (Time Warner Cable)

▲ **GREENBUSH (town)**—Formerly served by Argent Communications. No longer in operation

▲ **GREENE (town)**—Time Warner Cable. Now served by AUGUSTA, ME [ME0004]

GREENE (TOWN)—See AUGUSTA, ME (Time Warner Cable)

▲ **GREENVILLE**—Moosehead Enterprises

GREENWOOD—See SEBAGO (town), ME (Time Warner Cable)

▲ **GUILFORD**—Moosehead Enterprises

HALLOWELL—See AUGUSTA, ME (Time Warner Cable)

HAMLIN (TOWN)—See MADAWASKA, ME (Time Warner Cable)

HAMPDEN—See BANGOR, ME (Time Warner Cable)

▲ **HANCOCK**—Now served by BANGOR, ME [ME0002]

HANCOCK—See BANGOR, ME (Time Warner Cable)

HANOVER (TOWN)—See AUGUSTA, ME (Time Warner Cable)

HARPSWELL—See BRUNSWICK (town), ME (Comcast Cable)

HARRINGTON—See ADDISON (town), ME (Time Warner Cable)

HARRISON—See SEBAGO (town), ME (Time Warner Cable)

HARTLAND—See BANGOR, ME (Time Warner Cable)

▲ **HERMON**—Now served by BANGOR, ME [ME0002]

HERMON—See BANGOR, ME (Time Warner Cable)

HINKLEY—See WATERVILLE, ME (Time Warner Cable)

HIRAM—See SEBAGO (town), ME (Time Warner Cable)

HODGDON—See HOULTON, ME (Polaris Cable Services)

HOLDEN—See BANGOR, ME (Time Warner Cable)

HOLLIS—See SEBAGO (town), ME (Time Warner Cable)

HOPE (TOWN)—See LINCOLNVILLE, ME (Lincolnville Communications)

▲ **HOULTON**—Polaris Cable Services

▲ **HOWLAND**—Polaris Cable Services

INDUSTRY—See MADISON, ME (Bee Line Cable TV)

▲ **ISLAND FALLS**—Polaris Cable Services

▲ **JACKMAN**—Moosehead Enterprises

▲ **JAY (town)**—Now served by AUGUSTA, ME [ME0004]

JAY—See AUGUSTA, ME (Time Warner Cable)

JEFFERSON (TOWN)—See AUGUSTA, ME (Time Warner Cable)

▲ **JONESPORT**—Time Warner Cable

▲ **KENDUSKEAG**—Now served by BANGOR, ME [ME0002]

KENDUSKEAG—See BANGOR, ME (Time Warner Cable)

▲ **KENNEBUNK**—Time Warner Cable. Now served by SEBAGO (town), ME [ME0107]

KENNEBUNK—See SEBAGO (town), ME (Time Warner Cable)

KENNEBUNKPORT—See SEBAGO (town), ME (Time Warner Cable)

KEZAR FALLS—See SEBAGO (town), ME (Time Warner Cable)

KINGFIELD—See NORTH ANSON, ME (Time Warner Cable)

LAMOINE—See BANGOR, ME (Time Warner Cable)

LEEDS—See AUGUSTA, ME (Time Warner Cable)

LEVANT—See BANGOR, ME (Time Warner Cable)

▲**LEWISTON**—Time Warner Cable. Now served by AUGUSTA, ME [ME0004]

LEWISTON—See AUGUSTA, ME (Time Warner Cable)

LIMERICK—See SEBAGO (town), ME (Time Warner Cable)

LIMESTONE—See AROOSTOOK COUNTY, ME (Time Warner Cable)

LIMINGTON—See SEBAGO (town), ME (Time Warner Cable)

▲**LINCOLN**—Time Warner Cable

▲**LINCOLNVILLE**—Lincolnville Communications

LISBON FALLS—See AUGUSTA, ME (Time Warner Cable)

LISBON—See AUGUSTA, ME (Time Warner Cable)

LITCHFIELD—See AUGUSTA, ME (Time Warner Cable)

LITTLETON (TOWN)—See MONTICELLO (town), ME (Polaris Cable Services)

LIVERMORE FALLS—See AUGUSTA, ME (Time Warner Cable)

LIVERMORE—See AUGUSTA, ME (Time Warner Cable)

LOCKE MILLS—See SEBAGO (town), ME (Time Warner Cable)

▲**LOVELL (town)**—Formerly served by Adelphia Communications. Now served by CONWAY, NH [NH0038]

LOWELL—See HOWLAND, ME (Polaris Cable Services)

▲**LUBEC**—Now served by Pine Tree Cablevision. No longer in operation

LYMAN—See SEBAGO (town), ME (Time Warner Cable)

▲**MACHIAS**—Formerly served by Pine Tree Cablevision. No longer in operation

▲**MADAWASKA**—Time Warner Cable

▲**MADISON**—Bee Line Cable TV

MANCHESTER—See AUGUSTA, ME (Time Warner Cable)

MANSET—See BANGOR, ME (Time Warner Cable)

MAPLETON—See AROOSTOOK COUNTY, ME (Time Warner Cable)

▲**MARS HILL**—Time Warner Cable. Now served by AROOSTOOK COUNTY, ME [ME0008]

MARS HILL—See AROOSTOOK COUNTY, ME (Time Warner Cable)

▲**MATTAWAMKEAG (TOWN)**—Mattawamkeag Cablevision

MATTAWAMKEAG—See MATTAWAMKEAG (town), ME (Mattawamkeag Cablevision)

MECHANIC FALLS—See AUGUSTA, ME (Time Warner Cable)

▲**MEDWAY**—Polaris Cable Services

MERRILL—See OAKFIELD, ME (Polaris Cable Services)

MEXICO—See AUGUSTA, ME (Time Warner Cable)

MILBRIDGE—See CHERRYFIELD, ME (Time Warner Cable)

MILFORD—See BANGOR, ME (Time Warner Cable)

▲**MILLINOCKET**—Bee Line Cable TV

▲**MILO**—Time Warner Cable

MINOT—See AUGUSTA, ME (Time Warner Cable)

MONMOUTH—See AUGUSTA, ME (Time Warner Cable)

▲**MONSON**—Moosehead Enterprises

▲**MONTICELLO (TOWN)**—Polaris Cable Services

MONTICELLO—See MONTICELLO (town), ME (Polaris Cable Services)

MOODY—See YORK, ME (Time Warner Cable)

MOOSE RIVER—See JACKMAN, ME (Moosehead Enterprises)

▲**MOUNT DESERT (town)**—Formerly served by Adelphia Communications. Now served by BANGOR, ME [ME0002]

MOUNT DESERT (TOWN)—See BANGOR, ME (Time Warner Cable)

MOUNT VERNON (TOWN)—See AUGUSTA, ME (Time Warner Cable)

NAPLES—See SEBAGO (town), ME (Time Warner Cable)

NEW GLOUCESTER (TOWN)—See PORTLAND, ME (Time Warner Cable)

NEW HARBOR—See AUGUSTA, ME (Time Warner Cable)

NEW PORTLAND—See NORTH ANSON, ME (Time Warner Cable)

▲**NEW SHARON (town)**—Formerly served by Argent Communications. No longer in operation

NEW SWEDEN (PORTIONS)—See AROOSTOOK COUNTY, ME (Time Warner Cable)

NEW VINEYARD—See NORTH ANSON, ME (Time Warner Cable)

▲**NEWCASTLE**—Time Warner Cable. Now served by AUGUSTA, ME [ME0004]

NEWCASTLE—See AUGUSTA, ME (Time Warner Cable)

NEWPORT—See BANGOR, ME (Time Warner Cable)

NEWRY—See SEBAGO (town), ME (Time Warner Cable)

NOBLEBORO—See AUGUSTA, ME (Time Warner Cable)

NORRIDGEWOCK—See NORTH ANSON, ME (Time Warner Cable)

▲**NORTH ANSON**—Time Warner Cable

NORTH BERWICK—See YORK, ME (Time Warner Cable)

NORTH MONMOUTH—See AUGUSTA, ME (Time Warner Cable)

NORTH NEW PORTLAND—See NORTH ANSON, ME (Time Warner Cable)

NORTH VASSALBORO—See AUGUSTA, ME (Time Warner Cable)

NORTH YARMOUTH—See PORTLAND, ME (Time Warner Cable)

▲**NORWAY**—Now served by SEBAGO (town), ME [ME0107]

NORWAY—See SEBAGO (town), ME (Time Warner Cable)

▲**OAKFIELD**—Polaris Cable Services

OAKLAND—See WATERVILLE, ME (Time Warner Cable)

OGUNQUIT—See YORK, ME (Time Warner Cable)

OLD ORCHARD BEACH—See YORK, ME (Time Warner Cable)

OLD TOWN—See BANGOR, ME (Time Warner Cable)

ORONO—See BANGOR, ME (Time Warner Cable)

ORRINGTON—See BANGOR, ME (Time Warner Cable)

ORRS ISLAND—See BRUNSWICK (town), ME (Comcast Cable)

OWLS HEAD—See AUGUSTA, ME (Time Warner Cable)

OXFORD—See AUGUSTA, ME (Time Warner Cable)

PALMYRA—See BANGOR, ME (Time Warner Cable)

PARIS—See SEBAGO (town), ME (Time Warner Cable)

PARSONFIELD—See SEBAGO (town), ME (Time Warner Cable)

PASSADUMKEAG—See HOWLAND, ME (Polaris Cable Services)

▲**PATTEN**—Polaris Cable Services

PEAKS ISLAND—See PORTLAND, ME (Time Warner Cable)

PEMAQUID—See AUGUSTA, ME (Time Warner Cable)

▲**PEMBROKE**—Formerly served by Pine Tree Cablevision. No longer in operation

PERU—See AUGUSTA, ME (Time Warner Cable)

PHILLIPS—See NORTH ANSON, ME (Time Warner Cable)

PHIPPSBURG (TOWN)—See BRUNSWICK (town), ME (Comcast Cable)

▲**PITTSFIELD**—Time Warner Cable. Now served by BANGOR, ME [ME0002]

PITTSFIELD—See BANGOR, ME (Time Warner Cable)

PITTSTON—See AUGUSTA, ME (Time Warner Cable)

PLANTATION ST. JOHN—See MADAWASKA, ME (Time Warner Cable)

▲**PLEASANT RIDGE PLANTATION**—Formerly served by Pleasant Ridge Cablevision Inc. No longer in operation

▲**POLAND**—Formerly served by Adelphia Communications. No longer in operation

PORT CLYDGE—See AUGUSTA, ME (Time Warner Cable)

▲**PORTAGE**—Time Warner Cable. Now served by AROOSTOOK COUNTY, ME [ME0008]

PORTAGE—See AROOSTOOK COUNTY, ME (Time Warner Cable)

PORTER—See SEBAGO (town), ME (Time Warner Cable)

▲**PORTLAND**—Time Warner Cable

PORTLAND—See AUGUSTA, ME (Time Warner Cable)

POWNAL—See PORTLAND, ME (Time Warner Cable)

PRESQUE ISLE—See AROOSTOOK COUNTY, ME (Time Warner Cable)

PRINCETON—See CALAIS, ME (Time Warner Cable)

RANDOLPH—See AUGUSTA, ME (Time Warner Cable)

▲**RANGELEY (TOWN)**—Argent Communications

RAYMOND—See PORTLAND, ME (Time Warner Cable)

READFIELD (TOWN)—See AUGUSTA, ME (Time Warner Cable)

RICHMOND—See AUGUSTA, ME (Time Warner Cable)

▲**ROCKLAND**—Time Warner Cable. Now served by AUGUSTA, ME [ME0004]

ROCKLAND—See AUGUSTA, ME (Time Warner Cable)

ROCKPORT (TOWN)—See AUGUSTA, ME (Time Warner Cable)

▲**ROCKWOOD**—Moosehead Enterprises

ROME (TOWN)—See AUGUSTA, ME (Time Warner Cable)

ROUND POND—See AUGUSTA, ME (Time Warner Cable)

ROXBURY (TOWN)—See AUGUSTA, ME (Time Warner Cable)

▲**RUMFORD**—Formerly served by Adelphia Communications. Now served by AUGUSTA, ME [ME0004]

RUMFORD—See AUGUSTA, ME (Time Warner Cable)

SABATTUS—See AUGUSTA, ME (Time Warner Cable)

SACO—See YORK, ME (Time Warner Cable)

▲**SANFORD**—MetroCast Cablevision

SANGERVILLE—See GUILFORD, ME (Moosehead Enterprises)

SCARBOROUGH—See PORTLAND, ME (Time Warner Cable)

▲**SEARSMONT**—Windjammer Cable

SEARSPORT—See BANGOR, ME (Time Warner Cable)

▲**SEBAGO (TOWN)**—Time Warner Cable

SEBASCO ESTATES—See BRUNSWICK (town), ME (Comcast Cable)

SHAPLEIGH—See SANFORD, ME (MetroCast Cablevision)

SHAWMUT—See WATERVILLE, ME (Time Warner Cable)

SHERMAN MILLS—See SHERMAN, ME (Sherman Cablevision)

▲**SHERMAN**—Sherman Cablevision

▲**SIDNEY (town)**—Now served by AUGUSTA, ME [ME0004]

SIDNEY (TOWN)—See AUGUSTA, ME (Time Warner Cable)

SKOWHEGAN—See MADISON, ME (Bee Line Cable TV)

▲**SMITHFIELD (town)**—Now served by NORTH ANSON, ME [ME0062]

SMITHFIELD (TOWN)—See NORTH ANSON, ME (Time Warner Cable)

SMYRNA—See OAKFIELD, ME (Polaris Cable Services)

SOLON—See NORTH ANSON, ME (Time Warner Cable)

▲**SORRENTO**—Now served by BANGOR, ME [ME0002]

SORRENTO—See BANGOR, ME (Time Warner Cable)

SOUTH BRISTOL (TOWN)—See AUGUSTA, ME (Time Warner Cable)

SOUTH PARIS—See SEBAGO (town), ME (Time Warner Cable)

SOUTH PORTLAND—See PORTLAND, ME (Time Warner Cable)

SOUTH THOMASTON (TOWN)—See AUGUSTA, ME (Time Warner Cable)

SOUTHPORT (TOWN)—See AUGUSTA, ME (Time Warner Cable)

SOUTHWEST HARBOR—See BANGOR, ME (Time Warner Cable)

SPRINGVALE—See SANFORD, ME (MetroCast Cablevision)

SPRUCE HEAD—See AUGUSTA, ME (Time Warner Cable)

ST. AGATHA—See MADAWASKA, ME (Time Warner Cable)

ST. ALBANS—See BANGOR, ME (Time Warner Cable)

ST. FRANCIS TWP.—See MADAWASKA, ME (Time Warner Cable)

▲**ST. FRANCIS**—Formerly served by Adelphia Communications. Now served by MADAWASKA, ME [ME0026]

ST. FRANCIS—See MADAWASKA, ME (Time Warner Cable)

ST. GEORGE (TOWN)—See AUGUSTA, ME (Time Warner Cable)

ST. JOHN—See MADAWASKA, ME (Time Warner Cable)

STACYVILLE—See SHERMAN, ME (Sherman Cablevision)

STANDISH—See SEBAGO (town), ME (Time Warner Cable)

STEEP FALLS—See SEBAGO (town), ME (Time Warner Cable)

▲**STOCKHOLM (town)**—Formerly served by Argent Communications. No longer in operations

▲**STOCKTON SPRINGS**—Now served by BANGOR, ME [ME0002]

STOCKTON SPRINGS—See BANGOR, ME (Time Warner Cable)

▲**STONINGTON**—Formerly served by Adelphia Communications. Now served by BANGOR, ME [ME0002]

STONINGTON—See BANGOR, ME (Time Warner Cable)

STRATTON—See NORTH ANSON, ME (Time Warner Cable)

STRONG—See NORTH ANSON, ME (Time Warner Cable)

SULLIVAN—See BANGOR, ME (Time Warner Cable)

SURRY—See BANGOR, ME (Time Warner Cable)

▲**TEMPLE (TOWN)**—Windjammer Cable

TENANTS HARBOR—See AUGUSTA, ME (Time Warner Cable)

THOMASTON—See AUGUSTA, ME (Time Warner Cable)

TOPSHAM—See BRUNSWICK (town), ME (Comcast Cable)

TREMONT—See BANGOR, ME (Time Warner Cable)

▲**TRENTON**—Now served by BANGOR, ME [ME0002]

TRENTON—See BANGOR, ME (Time Warner Cable)

TREVETT—See AUGUSTA, ME (Time Warner Cable)

TURNER—See AUGUSTA, ME (Time Warner Cable)

▲**UNION (town)**—Now served by AUGUSTA, ME [ME0004]

UNION (TOWN)—See AUGUSTA, ME (Time Warner Cable)

▲**VAN BUREN**—Time Warner Cable. Now served by MADAWASKA, ME [ME0026]

VAN BUREN—See MADAWASKA, ME (Time Warner Cable)

VASSALBORO—See AUGUSTA, ME (Time Warner Cable)

VASSALBORO—See WATERVILLE, ME (Time Warner Cable)

VEAZIE—See BANGOR, ME (Time Warner Cable)

VERONA—See BANGOR, ME (Time Warner Cable)

▲**VINALHAVEN**—Now served by AUGUSTA, ME [ME0004]

VINALHAVEN—See AUGUSTA, ME (Time Warner Cable)

WALDOBORO—See AUGUSTA, ME (Time Warner Cable)

WALES—See AUGUSTA, ME (Time Warner Cable)

WALLAGRASS—See MADAWASKA, ME (Time Warner Cable)

▲**WARREN (town)**—Now served by AUGUSTA , ME [ME0004]

WARREN (TOWN)—See AUGUSTA, ME (Time Warner Cable)

▲**WASHBURN**—Time Warner Cable. Now served by AROOSTOOK COUNTY, ME [ME0008]

WASHBURN—See AROOSTOOK COUNTY, ME (Time Warner Cable)

WATERBORO—See SEBAGO (town), ME (Time Warner Cable)

WATERFORD (TOWN)—See SEBAGO (town), ME (Time Warner Cable)

▲**WATERVILLE**—Time Warner Cable

WAYNE—See AUGUSTA, ME (Time Warner Cable)

▲**WELD**—Formerly served by Argent Communications. No longer in operation

WELLS—See YORK, ME (Time Warner Cable)

WEST BALDWIN—See SEBAGO (town), ME (Time Warner Cable)

WEST BATH—See BRUNSWICK (town), ME (Comcast Cable)

WEST ENFIELD—See HOWLAND, ME (Polaris Cable Services)

WEST GARDINER—See AUGUSTA, ME (Time Warner Cable)

WEST PARIS—See SEBAGO (town), ME (Time Warner Cable)

WEST SOUTHPORT—See AUGUSTA, ME (Time Warner Cable)

WESTBROOK—See PORTLAND, ME (Time Warner Cable)

WESTFIELD—See AROOSTOOK COUNTY, ME (Time Warner Cable)

WESTON—See DANFORTH, ME (Polaris Cable Services)

WESTPORT ISLE—See AUGUSTA, ME (Time Warner Cable)

WHITEFIELD (TOWN)—See AUGUSTA, ME (Time Warner Cable)

▲**WILTON/FARMINGTON**—Bee Line Cable TV. Now served by MADISON, ME [ME0018]

WILTON—See MADISON, ME (Bee Line Cable TV)

▲**WINDHAM**—Now served by PORTLAND, ME [ME0001]

WINDHAM—See PORTLAND, ME (Time Warner Cable)

WINDSOR (TOWN)—See AUGUSTA, ME (Time Warner Cable)

WINN—See MATTAWAMKEAG (town), ME (Mattawamkeag Cablevision)

WINSLOW—See WATERVILLE, ME (Time Warner Cable)

▲**WINTER HARBOR**—Pine Tree Cablevision. Now served by CHERRYFIELD, ME [ME0111]

WINTER HARBOR—See CHERRYFIELD, ME (Time Warner Cable)

WINTERPORT—See BANGOR, ME (Time Warner Cable)

WINTHROP—See AUGUSTA, ME (Time Warner Cable)

WISCASSET—See AUGUSTA, ME (Time Warner Cable)

WOODLAND—See AROOSTOOK COUNTY, ME (Time Warner Cable)

WOODLAND—See CALAIS, ME (Time Warner Cable)

WOODSTOCK—See SEBAGO (town), ME (Time Warner Cable)

WOOLWICH—See BRUNSWICK (town), ME (Comcast Cable)

WYMAN—See NORTH ANSON, ME (Time Warner Cable)

YARMOUTH—See PORTLAND, ME (Time Warner Cable)

▲**YORK**—Time Warner Cable

MARYLAND

ABELL—See ST. MARY'S COUNTY, MD (MetroCast Communications)

ABERDEEN—See HARFORD COUNTY, MD (Comcast Cable)

ABINGDON—See HARFORD COUNTY, MD (Comcast Cable)

ACCIDENT—See DEEP CREEK LAKE, MD (Comcast Cable)

ACCOKEEK—See PRINCE GEORGE'S COUNTY (portions), MD (Comcast Cable)

ADAMSTOWN—See FREDERICK, MD (Comcast Cable)

ALLEGANY COUNTY (EASTERN PORTION)—See OLDTOWN, MD (Oldtown Community Systems Inc.)

ALLEGANY COUNTY—See CUMBERLAND, MD (Atlantic Broadband)

ANDREWS AFB—See PRINCE GEORGE'S COUNTY (portions), MD (Comcast Cable)

▲**ANNAPOLIS (portions)**—Comcast Cable. Now served by ANNE ARUNDEL COUNTY, MD [MD0006]

ANNAPOLIS (PORTIONS)—See ANNE ARUNDEL COUNTY (portions), MD (Comcast Cable)

ANNAPOLIS JUNCTION—See MILLERSVILLE, MD (Broadstripe)

ANNE ARUNDEL COUNTY (NORTHERN PORTION)—See MILLERSVILLE, MD (Broadstripe)

▲**ANNE ARUNDEL COUNTY (PORTIONS)**—Comcast Cable

ARBUTUS—See BALTIMORE COUNTY, MD (Comcast Cable)

ARNOLD—See MILLERSVILLE, MD (Broadstripe)

ARNOLD—See ANNE ARUNDEL COUNTY (portions), MD (Comcast Cable)

AVENUE—See ST. MARY'S COUNTY, MD (MetroCast Communications)

▲**BALTIMORE (Inner Harbor)**—Formerly served by Flight Systems Cablevision. No longer in operation

▲**BALTIMORE COUNTY**—Comcast Cable

▲**BALTIMORE**—Formerly served by Sprint Corp. No longer in operation

▲**BALTIMORE**—Comcast Cable

BARCLAY—See GRASONVILLE, MD (Atlantic Broadband)

BARNESVILLE—See MONTGOMERY COUNTY (portions), MD (Comcast Cable)

BAYARD—See OAKLAND, WV (Shentel)

▲**BEL AIR**—Armstrong Cable Services

BEL AIR—See HARFORD COUNTY, MD (Comcast Cable)

BEL ALTON—See CHARLES COUNTY, MD (Comcast Cable)

BELCAMP—See HARFORD COUNTY, MD (Comcast Cable)

BENEDICT—See CHARLES COUNTY, MD (Comcast Cable)

BERKELEY SPRINGS—See HANCOCK, WV (Comcast Cable)

BERKELEY—See HANCOCK, WV (Comcast Cable)

BERLIN—See OCEAN CITY, MD (Comcast Cable)

BERWYN HEIGHTS—See PRINCE GEORGE'S COUNTY (portions), MD (Comcast Cable)

BETHESDA—See MONTGOMERY COUNTY (portions), MD (Comcast Cable)

▲**BETHESDA**—RCN Corp. Formerly [MD0054]. This cable system has converted to IPTV

BETHLEHEM—See CAMBRIDGE, MD (Comcast Cable)

BETTERTON—See GRASONVILLE, MD (Atlantic Broadband)

BLADENSBURG—See PRINCE GEORGE'S COUNTY (portions), MD (Comcast Cable)

BOLIVAR—See HAGERSTOWN, MD (Antietam Cable TV)

BOONSBORO—See HAGERSTOWN, MD (Antietam Cable TV)

BOWIE—See PRINCE GEORGE'S COUNTY (portions), MD (Comcast Cable)

BOYDS—See MONTGOMERY COUNTY (portions), MD (Comcast Cable)

BOYNTON—See GRANTSVILLE, PA (Comcast Cable)

BRADDOCK HEIGHTS—See FREDERICK, MD (Comcast Cable)

BRANDYWINE—See PRINCE GEORGE'S COUNTY (portions), MD (Comcast Cable)

BRENTWOOD—See PRINCE GEORGE'S COUNTY (portions), MD (Comcast Cable)

BROOKEVILLE—See MONTGOMERY COUNTY (portions), MD (Comcast Cable)

BROOKLYN PARK—See MILLERSVILLE, MD (Broadstripe)

BROOKLYN PARK—See ANNE ARUNDEL COUNTY (portions), MD (Comcast Cable)

BROOKLYN—See ANNE ARUNDEL COUNTY (portions), MD (Comcast Cable)

BROOKVIEW—See CAMBRIDGE, MD (Comcast Cable)

BRUNSWICK—See FREDERICK, MD (Comcast Cable)

BRYANS ROAD—See CHARLES COUNTY, MD (Comcast Cable)

BRYANTOWN—See CHARLES COUNTY, MD (Comcast Cable)

BURKITTSVILLE—See FREDERICK, MD (Comcast Cable)

BURTONSVILLE—See MONTGOMERY COUNTY (portions), MD (Comcast Cable)

BUSHWOOD—See ST. MARY'S COUNTY, MD (MetroCast Communications)

CABIN JOHN—See MONTGOMERY COUNTY (portions), MD (Comcast Cable)

CALIFORNIA—See ST. MARY'S COUNTY, MD (MetroCast Communications)

CALLAWAY—See ST. MARY'S COUNTY, MD (MetroCast Communications)

CALVERT BEACH—See PRINCE FREDERICK, MD (Comcast Cable)

▲**CAMBRIDGE**—Comcast Cable

CAPE ST. CLAIRE—See ANNE ARUNDEL COUNTY (portions), MD (Comcast Cable)

CAPITOL HEIGHTS—See PRINCE GEORGE'S COUNTY (portions), MD (Comcast Cable)

CARDIFF—See BEL AIR, MD (Armstrong Cable Services)

CAROLINE COUNTY—See CAMBRIDGE, MD (Comcast Cable)

CARPENDALE—See CUMBERLAND, WV (Atlantic Broadband)

CARROLL COUNTY—See WESTMINSTER, MD (Comcast Cable)

CATONSVILLE—See BALTIMORE COUNTY, MD (Comcast Cable)

CECIL COUNTY—See ELKTON, MD (Comcast Cable)

▲**CECILTON**—Comcast Cable

CENTREVILLE—See GRASONVILLE, MD (Atlantic Broadband)

CHAPTICO—See ST. MARY'S COUNTY, MD (MetroCast Communications)

▲**CHARLES COUNTY**—Comcast Cable

CHARLESTOWN—See ELKTON, MD (Comcast Cable)

▲**CHESAPEAKE BEACH**—Comcast Cable. Now served by PRINCE FREDERICK, MD [MD0016]

CHESAPEAKE BEACH—See PRINCE FREDERICK, MD (Comcast Cable)

CHESAPEAKE CITY—See SALISBURY, MD (Comcast Cable)

CHESTERTOWN—See GRASONVILLE, MD (Atlantic Broadband)

CHEVERLY—See PRINCE GEORGE'S COUNTY (portions), MD (Comcast Cable)

CHEVY CHASE—See MONTGOMERY COUNTY (portions), MD (Comcast Cable)

▲**CHEVY CHASE**—RCN Corp. Formerly [MD0054]. This cable system has converted to IPTV

CHURCH CREEK—See CAMBRIDGE, MD (Comcast Cable)

CHURCH HILL—See GRASONVILLE, MD (Atlantic Broadband)

CHURCHVILLE—See HARFORD COUNTY, MD (Comcast Cable)

CLARKSVILLE—See HOWARD COUNTY (portions), MD (Comcast Cable)

CLEAR SPRING—See HAGERSTOWN, MD (Antietam Cable TV)

CLEARVILLE—See CUMBERLAND, PA (Atlantic Broadband)

CLEMENTS—See ST. MARY'S COUNTY, MD (MetroCast Communications)

CLEWSVILLE—See HAGERSTOWN, MD (Antietam Cable TV)

CLINTON—See PRINCE GEORGE'S COUNTY (portions), MD (Comcast Cable)

COBB ISLAND—See CHARLES COUNTY, MD (Comcast Cable)

COCKEYSVILLE—See BALTIMORE COUNTY, MD (Comcast Cable)

COLLEGE PARK—See PRINCE GEORGE'S COUNTY (portions), MD (Comcast Cable)

COLMAR MANOR—See PRINCE GEORGE'S COUNTY (portions), MD (Comcast Cable)

COLTONS POINT—See ST. MARY'S COUNTY, MD (MetroCast Communications)

COLUMBIA—See HOWARD COUNTY (portions), MD (Comcast Cable)

COMPTON—See ST. MARY'S COUNTY, MD (MetroCast Communications)

COOKSVILLE—See HOWARD COUNTY (portions), MD (Comcast Cable)

CORRIGANVILLE—See CUMBERLAND, MD (Atlantic Broadband)

COTTAGE CITY—See PRINCE GEORGE'S COUNTY (portions), MD (Comcast Cable)

CRELLIN—See OAKLAND, MD (Shentel)

CRESAPTOWN—See CUMBERLAND, MD (Atlantic Broadband)

▲**CRISFIELD**—Charter Communications

CROFTON—See ANNE ARUNDEL COUNTY (portions), MD (Comcast Cable)

CROWNSVILLE—See ANNE ARUNDEL COUNTY (portions), MD (Comcast Cable)

CUMBERLAND VALLEY TWP.—See CUMBERLAND, PA (Atlantic Broadband)

▲**CUMBERLAND**—Atlantic Broadband

DAMASCUS—See MONTGOMERY COUNTY (portions), MD (Comcast Cable)

DAMERON—See ST. MARY'S COUNTY, MD (MetroCast Communications)

DARLINGTON—See BEL AIR, MD (Armstrong Cable Services)

DAVIDSONVILLE—See ANNE ARUNDEL COUNTY (portions), MD (Comcast Cable)

DAVIS—See CUMBERLAND, WV (Atlantic Broadband)

DAYTON—See HOWARD COUNTY (portions), MD (Comcast Cable)

DEALE—See ANNE ARUNDEL COUNTY (portions), MD (Comcast Cable)

▲**DEEP CREEK LAKE**—Comcast Cable

DEEP CREEK—See OAKLAND, MD (Shentel)

DEER PARK—See OAKLAND, MD (Shentel)

DELMAR—See SALISBURY, DE (Comcast Cable)

DELMAR—See SALISBURY, MD (Comcast Cable)

DENTON—See CAMBRIDGE, MD (Comcast Cable)

DERWOOD—See MONTGOMERY COUNTY (portions), MD (Comcast Cable)

DISTRICT HEIGHTS—See PRINCE GEORGE'S COUNTY (portions), MD (Comcast Cable)

DORCHESTER COUNTY (WESTERN PORTION)—See CAMBRIDGE, MD (Comcast Cable)

DRYDEN—See ST. MARY'S COUNTY, MD (MetroCast Communications)

DUNDALK—See BALTIMORE COUNTY, MD (Comcast Cable)

DUNKIRK—See PRINCE FREDERICK, MD (Comcast Cable)

EARLEVILLE—See SALISBURY, MD (Comcast Cable)

EAST NEW MARKET—See CAMBRIDGE, MD (Comcast Cable)

▲**EASTON**—Easton Cable

ECKHART MINES—See CUMBERLAND, MD (Atlantic Broadband)

EDGEWOOD ARSENAL—See HARFORD COUNTY, MD (Comcast Cable)

EDMONDSTON—See PRINCE GEORGE'S COUNTY (portions), MD (Comcast Cable)

ELDORADO—See CAMBRIDGE, MD (Comcast Cable)

ELK GARDEN—See OAKLAND, WV (Shentel)

▲**ELKTON**—Comcast Cable

ELLERSLIE—See CUMBERLAND, MD (Atlantic Broadband)

ELLICOTT CITY—See HOWARD COUNTY (portions), MD (Comcast Cable)

EMMITSBURG—See FREDERICK, MD (Comcast Cable)

ESSEX—See BALTIMORE COUNTY, MD (Comcast Cable)

FAIRMOUNT HEIGHTS—See PRINCE GEORGE'S COUNTY (portions), MD (Comcast Cable)

FALLSTON—See BEL AIR, MD (Armstrong Cable Services)

FALLSTON—See HARFORD COUNTY, MD (Comcast Cable)

FAULKNER—See CHARLES COUNTY, MD (Comcast Cable)

FEDERALSBURG—See CAMBRIDGE, MD (Comcast Cable)

FENWICK ISLAND—See OCEAN CITY, DE (Comcast Cable)

FLINTSTONE—See CUMBERLAND, MD (Atlantic Broadband)

FLINTSTONE—See OLDTOWN, MD (Oldtown Community Systems Inc.)

FOREST HEIGHTS—See PRINCE GEORGE'S COUNTY (portions), MD (Comcast Cable)

FOREST HILL—See BEL AIR, MD (Armstrong Cable Services)

FOREST HILL—See HARFORD COUNTY, MD (Comcast Cable)

FORESTVILLE—See PRINCE GEORGE'S COUNTY (portions), MD (Comcast Cable)

FORT ASHBY—See CUMBERLAND, WV (Atlantic Broadband)

FORT DETRICK—See FREDERICK, MD (Comcast Cable)

FORT MEADE—See ANNE ARUNDEL COUNTY (portions), MD (Comcast Cable)

FORT WASHINGTON—See PRINCE GEORGE'S COUNTY (portions), MD (Comcast Cable)

FOXVILLE—See HAGERSTOWN, MD (Antietam Cable TV)

FREDERICK COUNTY—See FREDERICK, MD (Comcast Cable)

▲**FREDERICK**—Comcast Cable

FRIENDSVILLE—See DEEP CREEK LAKE, MD (Comcast Cable)

FROSTBURG—See CUMBERLAND, MD (Atlantic Broadband)

FRUITLAND—See SALISBURY, MD (Comcast Cable)

FULTON—See HOWARD COUNTY (portions), MD (Comcast Cable)

FUNKSTOWN—See HAGERSTOWN, MD (Antietam Cable TV)

▲**GAITHERSBURG (PORTIONS)**—RCN Corp. Formerly [MD0054]. This cable system has converted to IPTV

GAITHERSBURG—See MONTGOMERY COUNTY (portions), MD (Comcast Cable)

GALENA—See SALISBURY, MD (Comcast Cable)

GALESTOWN—See CAMBRIDGE, MD (Comcast Cable)

GALESVILLE—See ANNE ARUNDEL COUNTY (portions), MD (Comcast Cable)

GAMBRILLS—See MILLERSVILLE, MD (Broadstripe)

GAMBRILLS—See ANNE ARUNDEL COUNTY (portions), MD (Comcast Cable)

GARRETT COUNTY (UNINCORPORATED AREAS)—See DEEP CREEK LAKE, MD (Comcast Cable)

GARRETT PARK—See MONTGOMERY COUNTY (portions), MD (Comcast Cable)

GERMANTOWN—See MONTGOMERY COUNTY (portions), MD (Comcast Cable)

GIBSON ISLAND—See ANNE ARUNDEL COUNTY (portions), MD (Comcast Cable)

GLEN BURNIE—See MILLERSVILLE, MD (Broadstripe)

GLEN BURNIE—See ANNE ARUNDEL COUNTY (portions), MD (Comcast Cable)

GLEN ECHO—See MONTGOMERY COUNTY (portions), MD (Comcast Cable)

GLENARDEN—See PRINCE GEORGE'S COUNTY (portions), MD (Comcast Cable)

GLENELG—See HOWARD COUNTY (portions), MD (Comcast Cable)

GLENWOOD—See HOWARD COUNTY (portions), MD (Comcast Cable)

GOLDSBORO—See CAMBRIDGE, MD (Comcast Cable)

GORMANIA—See OAKLAND, WV (Shentel)

▲**GRANTSVILLE**—Comcast Cable

▲**GRASONVILLE**—Atlantic Broadband

GREAT CACAPON—See HANCOCK, WV (Comcast Cable)

GREAT MILLS—See ST. MARY'S COUNTY, MD (MetroCast Communications)

GREENBELT—See PRINCE GEORGE'S COUNTY (portions), MD (Comcast Cable)

GREENSBORO—See CAMBRIDGE, MD (Comcast Cable)

▲**HAGERSTOWN**—Antietam Cable TV

HALFWAY—See HAGERSTOWN, MD (Antietam Cable TV)

HAMBLETON—See CUMBERLAND, WV (Atlantic Broadband)

HAMPSHIRE COUNTY—See CUMBERLAND, WV (Atlantic Broadband)

HAMPSTEAD—See WESTMINSTER, MD (Comcast Cable)

▲**HANCOCK**—Comcast Cable

HANOVER—See MILLERSVILLE, MD (Broadstripe)

HANOVER—See ANNE ARUNDEL COUNTY (portions), MD (Comcast Cable)

HARFORD COUNTY (PORTIONS)—See BEL AIR, MD (Armstrong Cable Services)

▲**HARFORD COUNTY**—Comcast Cable

HARMANS—See MILLERSVILLE, MD (Broadstripe)

HARMANS—See ANNE ARUNDEL COUNTY (portions), MD (Comcast Cable)

HARMONY—See CAMBRIDGE, MD (Comcast Cable)

HARWOOD—See ANNE ARUNDEL COUNTY (portions), MD (Comcast Cable)

HAVRE DE GRACE—See HARFORD COUNTY, MD (Comcast Cable)

HEBRON—See SALISBURY, MD (Comcast Cable)

HELEN—See ST. MARY'S COUNTY, MD (MetroCast Communications)

HENDERSON—See CAMBRIDGE, MD (Comcast Cable)

HENDRICKS—See CUMBERLAND, WV (Atlantic Broadband)

HIGHLAND—See HOWARD COUNTY (portions), MD (Comcast Cable)

HILLSBORO—See CAMBRIDGE, MD (Comcast Cable)

HOLLYWOOD—See ST. MARY'S COUNTY, MD (MetroCast Communications)

▲**HOWARD COUNTY (portions)**—Mid-Atlantic Communications. Now served by HOWARD COUNTY, MD [MD0008]

▲**HOWARD COUNTY (PORTIONS)**—Comcast Cable

HUGHESVILLE—See CHARLES COUNTY, MD (Comcast Cable)

HUNTINGTOWN—See PRINCE FREDERICK, MD (Comcast Cable)

HURLOCK—See CAMBRIDGE, MD (Comcast Cable)

HYATTSVILLE—See PRINCE GEORGE'S COUNTY (portions), MD (Comcast Cable)

HYNDMAN—See CUMBERLAND, PA (Atlantic Broadband)

INDIAN HEAD—See CHARLES COUNTY, MD (Comcast Cable)

IRONSIDES—See CHARLES COUNTY, MD (Comcast Cable)

ISSUE—See CHARLES COUNTY, MD (Comcast Cable)

JARRETTSVILLE—See BEL AIR, MD (Armstrong Cable Services)

JEFFERSON—See FREDERICK, MD (Comcast Cable)

JESSUP—See MILLERSVILLE, MD (Broadstripe)

JESSUP—See ANNE ARUNDEL COUNTY (portions), MD (Comcast Cable)

JOPPA—See HARFORD COUNTY, MD (Comcast Cable)

KENSINGTON—See MONTGOMERY COUNTY (portions), MD (Comcast Cable)

KENT COUNTY (PORTIONS)—See GRASONVILLE, MD (Atlantic Broadband)

KITZMILLER—See OAKLAND, MD (Shentel)

LA PLATA—See CHARLES COUNTY, MD (Comcast Cable)

LANDOVER HILLS—See PRINCE GEORGE'S COUNTY (portions), MD (Comcast Cable)

LANSDOWNE—See BALTIMORE COUNTY, MD (Comcast Cable)

LARGO—See PRINCE GEORGE'S COUNTY (portions), MD (Comcast Cable)

LAUREL—See MILLERSVILLE, MD (Broadstripe)

LAUREL—See ANNE ARUNDEL COUNTY (portions), MD (Comcast Cable)

LAUREL—See HOWARD COUNTY (portions), MD (Comcast Cable)

LAUREL—See PRINCE GEORGE'S COUNTY (portions), MD (Comcast Cable)

LEONARDTOWN—See ST. MARY'S COUNTY, MD (MetroCast Communications)

▲**LEXINGTON PARK**—GMP Cable TV. Now served by ST. MARYS COUNTY, MD [MD0024]

LEXINGTON PARK—See ST. MARY'S COUNTY, MD (MetroCast Communications)

LIBERTYTOWN—See FREDERICK, MD (Comcast Cable)

LINTHICUM HEIGHTS—See ANNE ARUNDEL COUNTY (portions), MD (Comcast Cable)

LINTHICUM—See MILLERSVILLE, MD (Broadstripe)

LINTHICUM—See ANNE ARUNDEL COUNTY (portions), MD (Comcast Cable)

LISBON—See HOWARD COUNTY (portions), MD (Comcast Cable)

LOCH LYNN HEIGHTS—See OAKLAND, MD (Shentel)

LONDONDERRY TWP. (BEDFORD COUNTY)—See CUMBERLAND, PA (Atlantic Broadband)

▲**LOTHIAN**—Comcast Cable. Now served by ANNE ARUNDEL COUNTY, MD [MD0006]

LOTHIAN—See ANNE ARUNDEL COUNTY (portions), MD (Comcast Cable)

LOVEVILLE—See ST. MARY'S COUNTY, MD (MetroCast Communications)

LUSBY—See PRINCE FREDERICK, MD (Comcast Cable)

MANCHESTER—See WESTMINSTER, MD (Comcast Cable)

MARBURY—See CHARLES COUNTY, MD (Comcast Cable)

MARDELA SPRINGS—See SALISBURY, MD (Comcast Cable)

MARRIOTTSVILLE—See WESTMINSTER, MD (Comcast Cable)

MARSHALL HALL—See CHARLES COUNTY, MD (Comcast Cable)

MARYDEL—See CAMBRIDGE, MD (Comcast Cable)

MARYLAND CITY—See ANNE ARUNDEL COUNTY (portions), MD (Comcast Cable)

MCHENRY—See DEEP CREEK LAKE, MD (Comcast Cable)

MECHANICSVILLE—See PRINCE FREDERICK, MD (Comcast Cable)

MECHANICSVILLE—See ST. MARY'S COUNTY, MD (MetroCast Communications)

MIDDLE RIVER—See BALTIMORE COUNTY, MD (Comcast Cable)

MIDDLETOWN—See FREDERICK, MD (Comcast Cable)

▲**MILLERSVILLE**—Broadstripe

MILLERSVILLE—See ANNE ARUNDEL COUNTY (portions), MD (Comcast Cable)

MILLINGTON—See GRASONVILLE, MD (Atlantic Broadband)

MINERAL COUNTY—See CUMBERLAND, WV (Atlantic Broadband)

MONKTON—See BEL AIR, MD (Armstrong Cable Services)

▲**MONTGOMERY COUNTY (portions)**—RCN Corp. This cable system has converted to IPTV. See Bethesda, MD [MD5097], Chevy Chase, MD [MD5098], Gaithersburg, MD [MD5099] & Takoma Park, MD [MD5102]

▲**MONTGOMERY COUNTY (PORTIONS)**—Comcast Cable

MONTPELIER—See PRINCE GEORGE'S COUNTY (portions), MD (Comcast Cable)

MORGAN COUNTY (PORTIONS)—See HANCOCK, WV (Comcast Cable)

MORGANZA—See ST. MARY'S COUNTY, MD (MetroCast Communications)

MORNINGSIDE—See PRINCE GEORGE'S COUNTY (portions), MD (Comcast Cable)

MOUNT AIRY—See FREDERICK, MD (Comcast Cable)

MOUNT PLEASANT—See FREDERICK, MD (Comcast Cable)

MOUNT RAINIER—See PRINCE GEORGE'S COUNTY (portions), MD (Comcast Cable)

MOUNT SAVAGE—See CUMBERLAND, MD (Atlantic Broadband)

MOUNT VICTORIA—See CHARLES COUNTY, MD (Comcast Cable)

MOUNTAIN LAKE PARK—See OAKLAND, MD (Shentel)

MYERSVILLE—See FREDERICK, MD (Comcast Cable)

NANJEMOY—See CHARLES COUNTY, MD (Comcast Cable)

NEW CARROLLTON—See PRINCE GEORGE'S COUNTY (portions), MD (Comcast Cable)

NEW MARKET—See FREDERICK, MD (Comcast Cable)

NEW WINDSOR—See WESTMINSTER, MD (Comcast Cable)

NEWBURG—See CHARLES COUNTY, MD (Comcast Cable)

NORTH BEACH—See PRINCE FREDERICK, MD (Comcast Cable)

NORTH BRENTWOOD—See PRINCE GEORGE'S COUNTY (portions), MD (Comcast Cable)

NORTH EAST—See ELKTON, MD (Comcast Cable)

▲**OAKLAND**—Shentel

▲**OCEAN CITY**—Comcast Cable

ODENTON—See MILLERSVILLE, MD (Broadstripe)

ODENTON—See ANNE ARUNDEL COUNTY (portions), MD (Comcast Cable)

▲**OLDTOWN**—Oldtown Community Systems Inc.

OLNEY—See MONTGOMERY COUNTY (portions), MD (Comcast Cable)

OWINGS MILLS—See BALTIMORE COUNTY, MD (Comcast Cable)

OWINGS—See PRINCE FREDERICK, MD (Comcast Cable)

OXFORD—See GRASONVILLE, MD (Atlantic Broadband)

OXON HILL—See PRINCE GEORGE'S COUNTY (portions), MD (Comcast Cable)

PARK HALL—See ST. MARY'S COUNTY, MD (MetroCast Communications)

PARKVILLE—See BALTIMORE COUNTY, MD (Comcast Cable)

PARSONS—See CUMBERLAND, WV (Atlantic Broadband)

PASADENA—See MILLERSVILLE, MD (Broadstripe)

PASADENA—See ANNE ARUNDEL COUNTY (portions), MD (Comcast Cable)

PATUXENT HEIGHTS—See ST. MARY'S COUNTY, MD (MetroCast Communications)

PATUXENT RIVER—See ST. MARY'S COUNTY, MD (MetroCast Communications)

PERRY HALL—See BALTIMORE COUNTY, MD (Comcast Cable)

PERRYMAN—See HARFORD COUNTY, MD (Comcast Cable)

PIKESVILLE—See BALTIMORE COUNTY, MD (Comcast Cable)

PINESBURG—See HAGERSTOWN, MD (Antietam Cable TV)

PINEY POINT—See ST. MARY'S COUNTY, MD (MetroCast Communications)

PINTO—See CUMBERLAND, MD (Atlantic Broadband)

PISGAH—See CHARLES COUNTY, MD (Comcast Cable)

▲**POCOMOKE**—Comcast Cable. Now served by SALISBURY, MD [MD0015]

POCOMOKE—See SALISBURY, MD (Comcast Cable)

POINT OF ROCKS—See FREDERICK, MD (Comcast Cable)

POMFRET—See CHARLES COUNTY, MD (Comcast Cable)

POOLESVILLE—See MONTGOMERY COUNTY (portions), MD (Comcast Cable)

PORT TOBACCO—See CHARLES COUNTY, MD (Comcast Cable)

POTOMAC—See MONTGOMERY COUNTY (portions), MD (Comcast Cable)

PRESTON—See CAMBRIDGE, MD (Comcast Cable)

▲**PRINCE FREDERICK**—Comcast Cable

▲**PRINCE GEORGE'S COUNTY (northern portion)**—Comcast Cable. Now served by PRINCE GEORGE'S COUNTY (formerly southern portion), MD [MD0005]

▲**PRINCE GEORGE'S COUNTY (PORTIONS)**—Comcast Cable

PRINCESS ANNE—See SALISBURY, MD (Comcast Cable)

PYLESVILLE—See BEL AIR, MD (Armstrong Cable Services)

QUEEN ANNE'S COUNTY (PORTIONS)—See GRASONVILLE, MD (Atlantic Broadband)

QUEEN ANNE'S COUNTY (PORTIONS)—See CAMBRIDGE, MD (Comcast Cable)

QUEEN ANNE'S—See CAMBRIDGE, MD (Comcast Cable)

QUEENSTOWN—See GRASONVILLE, MD (Atlantic Broadband)

RANDALLSTOWN—See BALTIMORE COUNTY, MD (Comcast Cable)

RAWLINGS—See CUMBERLAND, MD (Atlantic Broadband)

REISTERSTOWN—See BALTIMORE COUNTY, MD (Comcast Cable)

RHODESDALE—See CAMBRIDGE, MD (Comcast Cable)

RIDGE—See ST. MARY'S COUNTY, MD (MetroCast Communications)

RIDGELEY—See CUMBERLAND, WV (Atlantic Broadband)

RIDGELY—See CAMBRIDGE, MD (Comcast Cable)

RIO VISTA—See GRASONVILLE, MD (Atlantic Broadband)

RISON—See CHARLES COUNTY, MD (Comcast Cable)

RIVERDALE—See PRINCE GEORGE'S COUNTY (portions), MD (Comcast Cable)

RIVIERA BEACH—See ANNE ARUNDEL COUNTY (portions), MD (Comcast Cable)

ROCK HALL—See GRASONVILLE, MD (Atlantic Broadband)

ROCK POINT—See CHARLES COUNTY, MD (Comcast Cable)

ROCKVILLE—See MONTGOMERY COUNTY (portions), MD (Comcast Cable)

ROMNEY—See CUMBERLAND, WV (Atlantic Broadband)

ROSEDALE—See BALTIMORE COUNTY, MD (Comcast Cable)

ROSEMONT—See FREDERICK, MD (Comcast Cable)

▲**SALISBURY**—Comcast Cable

SALISBURY—See GRANTSVILLE, PA (Comcast Cable)

SEAT PLEASANT—See PRINCE GEORGE'S COUNTY (portions), MD (Comcast Cable)

SECRETARY—See CAMBRIDGE, MD (Comcast Cable)

SEVERN—See MILLERSVILLE, MD (Broadstripe)

SEVERN—See ANNE ARUNDEL COUNTY (portions), MD (Comcast Cable)

SEVERNA PARK—See MILLERSVILLE, MD (Broadstripe)

SEVERNA PARK—See ANNE ARUNDEL COUNTY (portions), MD (Comcast Cable)

SHALLMAR—See OAKLAND, MD (Shentel)

SHARPTOWN—See SALISBURY, MD (Comcast Cable)

SHERWOOD FOREST—See ANNE ARUNDEL COUNTY (portions), MD (Comcast Cable)

SILVER SPRING—See MONTGOMERY COUNTY (portions), MD (Comcast Cable)

SMITHSBURG—See HAGERSTOWN, MD (Antietam Cable TV)

SNOW HILL—See SALISBURY, MD (Comcast Cable)

SOMERSET COUNTY—See CRISFIELD, MD (Charter Communications)

SOMERSET COUNTY—See SALISBURY, MD (Comcast Cable)

SOMERSET—See MONTGOMERY COUNTY (portions), MD (Comcast Cable)

SOUTHAMPTON TWP. (BEDFORD COUNTY)—See CUMBERLAND, PA (Atlantic Broadband)

SPRING GAP—See OLDTOWN, MD (Oldtown Community Systems Inc.)

ST. CHARLES—See CHARLES COUNTY, MD (Comcast Cable)

ST. INIGOES—See ST. MARY'S COUNTY, MD (MetroCast Communications)

▲**ST. MARY'S COUNTY**—MetroCast Communications

ST. MICHAELS—See GRASONVILLE, MD (Atlantic Broadband)

STEVENSVILLE—See GRASONVILLE, MD (Atlantic Broadband)

STREET—See BEL AIR, MD (Armstrong Cable Services)

SUDLERSVILLE—See GRASONVILLE, MD (Atlantic Broadband)

SUSSEX COUNTY—See OCEAN CITY, DE (Comcast Cable)

SUSSEX COUNTY—See SALISBURY, DE (Comcast Cable)

SYKESVILLE—See WESTMINSTER, MD (Comcast Cable)

TAKOMA PARK—See MONTGOMERY COUNTY (portions), MD (Comcast Cable)

TAKOMA PARK—See PRINCE GEORGE'S COUNTY (portions), MD (Comcast Cable)

▲**TAKOMA PARK**—RCN Corp. Formerly [MD0054]. This cable system has converted to IPTV

TALBOT COUNTY (PORTIONS)—See GRASONVILLE, MD (Atlantic Broadband)

TALL TIMBERS—See ST. MARY'S COUNTY, MD (MetroCast Communications)

TANEYTOWN—See WESTMINSTER, MD (Comcast Cable)

TEMPLEVILLE—See GRASONVILLE, MD (Atlantic Broadband)

THOMAS—See CUMBERLAND, WV (Atlantic Broadband)

THURMONT—See FREDERICK, MD (Comcast Cable)

TIMONIUM-LUTHERVILLE—See BALTIMORE COUNTY, MD (Comcast Cable)

TOWSON—See BALTIMORE COUNTY, MD (Comcast Cable)

TRAPPE—See GRASONVILLE, MD (Atlantic Broadband)

TUCKER COUNTY—See CUMBERLAND, WV (Atlantic Broadband)

UNION BRIDGE—See WESTMINSTER, MD (Comcast Cable)

UNIVERSITY PARK—See PRINCE GEORGE'S COUNTY (portions), MD (Comcast Cable)

UPPER MARLBORO—See PRINCE GEORGE'S COUNTY (portions), MD (Comcast Cable)

URBANA—See FREDERICK, MD (Comcast Cable)

VALLEY LEE—See ST. MARY'S COUNTY, MD (MetroCast Communications)

VIENNA—See CAMBRIDGE, MD (Comcast Cable)

WALDORF—See CHARLES COUNTY, MD (Comcast Cable)

WALKERSVILLE—See FREDERICK, MD (Comcast Cable)

▲**WARWICK**—Mid-Atlantic Communications. Now served by SALISBURY, MD [MD0015]

WARWICK—See SALISBURY, MD (Comcast Cable)

WASHINGTON COUNTY (UNINCORPORATED AREAS)—See FREDERICK, MD (Comcast Cable)

WASHINGTON COUNTY—See HAGERSTOWN, MD (Antietam Cable TV)

WASHINGTON GROVE—See MONTGOMERY COUNTY (portions), MD (Comcast Cable)

WELCOME—See CHARLES COUNTY, MD (Comcast Cable)

WEST BETHESDA—See MONTGOMERY COUNTY (portions), MD (Comcast Cable)

WEST FRIENDSHIP—See HOWARD COUNTY (portions), MD (Comcast Cable)

WEST SALISBURY—See GRANTSVILLE, PA (Comcast Cable)

▲**WESTMINSTER**—Comcast Cable

WHEATON—See MONTGOMERY COUNTY (portions), MD (Comcast Cable)

WHITE HALL—See BEL AIR, MD (Armstrong Cable Services)

WHITE PLAINS—See CHARLES COUNTY, MD (Comcast Cable)

WICOMICO COUNTY (SOUTHWESTERN PORTION)—See CAMBRIDGE, MD (Comcast Cable)

WICOMICO COUNTY—See SALISBURY, MD (Comcast Cable)

WILEY FORD—See CUMBERLAND, WV (Atlantic Broadband)

WILLIAMSPORT—See HAGERSTOWN, MD (Antietam Cable TV)

WOODBINE—See HOWARD COUNTY (portions), MD (Comcast Cable)

WOODLAWN—See BALTIMORE COUNTY, MD (Comcast Cable)

WOODSBORO—See FREDERICK, MD (Comcast Cable)

WORCESTER COUNTY—See OCEAN CITY, MD (Comcast Cable)

WORCESTER COUNTY—See SALISBURY, MD (Comcast Cable)

WYE MILLS—See GRASONVILLE, MD (Atlantic Broadband)

MASSACHUSETTS

ABINGTON—See TAUNTON, MA (Comcast Cable)

ACTON—See WESTFORD, MA (Comcast Cable)

ACUSHNET—See TAUNTON, MA (Comcast Cable)

ADAMS—See PITTSFIELD, MA (Time Warner Cable)

AGAWAM—See SPRINGFIELD, MA (Comcast Cable)

ALLSTON—See BOSTON, MA (Comcast Cable)

▲**ALLSTON**—RCN Corp. Formerly served by Boston, MA [MA0105]. This cable system has converted to IPTV

▲**AMESBURY**—Formerly served by Comcast Cable. No longer in operation

▲**AMHERST**—Comcast Cable. Now served by SPRINGFIELD, MA [MA0005]

AMHERST—See SPRINGFIELD, MA (Comcast Cable)

▲**ANDOVER**—Comcast Cable. Now served by WESTFORD, MA [MA0093]

ANDOVER—See WESTFORD, MA (Comcast Cable)

▲**ARLINGTON**—Comcast Cable. Now served by BOSTON, MA [MA0001]

ARLINGTON—See BOSTON, MA (Comcast Cable)

▲**ARLINGTON**—RCN Corp. Formerly served by Boston, MA [MA0105]. This cable system has converted to IPTV

ASHBURNHAM—See WESTFORD, MA (Comcast Cable)

ASHBY (TOWN)—See WESTFORD, MA (Comcast Cable)

ASHLAND—See BOSTON, MA (Comcast Cable)

ASSONET—See TAUNTON, MA (Comcast Cable)

▲**ATHOL**—Time Warner Cable

ATTLEBORO—See TAUNTON, MA (Comcast Cable)

AUBURN—See WORCESTER, MA (Charter Communications)

AVON—See TAUNTON, MA (Comcast Cable)

AYER—See WESTFORD, MA (Comcast Cable)

BALDWINVILLE—See WESTFORD, MA (Comcast Cable)

BARNSTABLE—See TAUNTON, MA (Comcast Cable)

BARRE (TOWN)—See RUTLAND (town), MA (Charter Communications)

BEDFORD—See WESTFORD, MA (Comcast Cable)

▲ **BELCHERTOWN**—Charter Communications

BELLINGHAM—See TAUNTON, MA (Comcast Cable)

BELMONT—See BOSTON, MA (Comcast Cable)

BERKLEY—See TAUNTON, MA (Comcast Cable)

BERLIN—See PEPPERELL, MA (Charter Communications)

▲ **BERNARDSTON**—Comcast Cable. Now served by SPRINGFIELD, MA [MA0005]

BERNARDSTON—See SPRINGFIELD, MA (Comcast Cable)

▲ **BEVERLY**—Comcast Cable. Now served by BOSTON, MA [MA0001]

BEVERLY—See BOSTON, MA (Comcast Cable)

BILLERICA—See WESTFORD, MA (Comcast Cable)

BLACKSTONE—See TAUNTON, MA (Comcast Cable)

BOLTON—See WESTFORD, MA (Comcast Cable)

BONDSVILLE—See SPRINGFIELD, MA (Comcast Cable)

▲ **BOSTON**—RCN Corp. This cable system has converted to IPTV. See Boston, MA [MA5096]

▲ **BOSTON**—Comcast Cable

▲ **BOSTON**—RCN Corp. Formerly [MA0105]. This cable system has converted to IPTV

BOURNE—See TAUNTON, MA (Comcast Cable)

BOXBOROUGH—See WESTFORD, MA (Comcast Cable)

BOXFORD—See WESTFORD, MA (Comcast Cable)

BOYLSTON—See WORCESTER, MA (Charter Communications)

▲ **BRAINTREE**—Comcast Cable. Now served by TAUNTON, MA [MA0033]

▲ **BRAINTREE**—Beld Broadband. Formerly [MA0106]. This cable system has converted to IPTV

▲ **BRAINTREE**—BELD Broadband

BRAINTREE—See TAUNTON, MA (Comcast Cable)

BREWSTER—See TAUNTON, MA (Comcast Cable)

BRIDGEWATER—See TAUNTON, MA (Comcast Cable)

BRIGHTON—See BOSTON, MA (Comcast Cable)

▲ **BRIGHTON**—RCN Corp. Formerly served by Boston, MA [MA0105]. This cable system has converted to IPTV

BRIMFIELD—See WALES, MA (Charter Communications)

▲ **BROCKTON**—Comcast Cable. Now served by TAUNTON, MA [MA0033]

BROCKTON—See TAUNTON, MA (Comcast Cable)

BROOKFIELD—See CHARLTON, MA (Charter Communications)

BROOKLINE—See PEPPERELL, NH (Charter Communications)

BROOKLINE—See BOSTON, MA (Comcast Cable)

▲ **BROOKLINE**—RCN Corp. Formerly served by Boston, MA [MA0105]. This cable system has converted to IPTV

BUCKLAND—See SPRINGFIELD, MA (Comcast Cable)

BURLINGTON—See BOSTON, MA (Comcast Cable)

▲ **BURLINGTON**—RCN Corp. Formerly served by Boston, MA [MA0105]. This cable system has converted to IPTV

CAMBRIDGE—See BOSTON, MA (Comcast Cable)

CANTON—See TAUNTON, MA (Comcast Cable)

CARLISLE (TOWN)—See WESTFORD, MA (Comcast Cable)

CARVER—See TAUNTON, MA (Comcast Cable)

CENTERVILLE—See TAUNTON, MA (Comcast Cable)

CHARLESTOWN—See BOSTON, MA (Comcast Cable)

▲ **CHARLTON**—Charter Communications

CHATHAM—See TAUNTON, MA (Comcast Cable)

CHELMSFORD—See WESTFORD, MA (Comcast Cable)

CHELSEA—See BOSTON, MA (Comcast Cable)

CHESHIRE—See PITTSFIELD, MA (Time Warner Cable)

▲ **CHESTER**—Comcast Cable. Now served by SPRINGFIELD, MA [MA0005]

CHESTER—See SPRINGFIELD, MA (Comcast Cable)

▲ **CHICOPEE**—Charter Communications

CHILMARK—See TAUNTON, MA (Comcast Cable)

CLARKSBURG—See PITTSFIELD, MA (Time Warner Cable)

CLINTON—See WESTFORD, MA (Comcast Cable)

COHASSET—See TAUNTON, MA (Comcast Cable)

CONCORD—See WESTFORD, MA (Comcast Cable)

▲ **CONWAY**—Comcast Cable. Now served by SPRINGFIELD, MA [MA0005]

CONWAY—See SPRINGFIELD, MA (Comcast Cable)

COTUIT—See TAUNTON, MA (Comcast Cable)

DALTON—See PITTSFIELD, MA (Time Warner Cable)

▲ **DANVERS**—Formerly served by Comcast Cable. No longer in operation

DARTMOUTH—See TAUNTON, MA (Comcast Cable)

▲ **DEDHAM**—Comcast Cable. Now served by BOSTON, MA [MA0001]

DEDHAM—See BOSTON, MA (Comcast Cable)

▲ **DEDHAM**—RCN Corp. Formerly served by Boston, MA [MA0105]. This cable system has converted to IPTV

DEERFIELD—See SPRINGFIELD, MA (Comcast Cable)

DENNIS PORT—See TAUNTON, MA (Comcast Cable)

DENNIS—See TAUNTON, MA (Comcast Cable)

DIGHTON—See TAUNTON, MA (Comcast Cable)

DORCHESTER—See BOSTON, MA (Comcast Cable)

▲ **DORCHESTER**—RCN Corp. Formerly served by Boston, MA [MA0105]. This cable system has converted to IPTV

DOUGLAS (TOWN)—See UXBRIDGE, MA (Charter Communications)

DOVER—See BOSTON, MA (Comcast Cable)

DRACUT—See WESTFORD, MA (Comcast Cable)

DUDLEY—See WORCESTER, MA (Charter Communications)

DUNSTABLE—See PEPPERELL, MA (Charter Communications)

DUXBURY—See TAUNTON, MA (Comcast Cable)

EAST BOSTON—See BOSTON, MA (Comcast Cable)

EAST BRIDGEWATER—See TAUNTON, MA (Comcast Cable)

EAST BROOKFIELD (TOWN)—See CHARLTON, MA (Charter Communications)

EAST BROOKFIELD—See CHARLTON, MA (Charter Communications)

EAST DENNIS—See TAUNTON, MA (Comcast Cable)

EAST FALMOUTH—See TAUNTON, MA (Comcast Cable)

EAST HARWICH—See TAUNTON, MA (Comcast Cable)

EAST LONGMEADOW—See CHICOPEE, MA (Charter Communications)

EAST TEMPLETON—See WESTFORD, MA (Comcast Cable)

EASTHAM—See TAUNTON, MA (Comcast Cable)

EASTHAMPTON—See CHICOPEE, MA (Charter Communications)

EASTON—See TAUNTON, MA (Comcast Cable)

EDGARTOWN—See TAUNTON, MA (Comcast Cable)

ERVING—See SPRINGFIELD, MA (Comcast Cable)

ESSEX—See BOSTON, MA (Comcast Cable)

EVERETT—See BOSTON, MA (Comcast Cable)

▲ **FAIRHAVEN**—Comcast Cable. Now served by TAUNTON, MA [MA0033]

FAIRHAVEN—See TAUNTON, MA (Comcast Cable)

FALL RIVER—See TAUNTON, MA (Comcast Cable)

FALMOUTH—See TAUNTON, MA (Comcast Cable)

FITCHBURG—See WESTFORD, MA (Comcast Cable)

▲ **FORT DEVONS**—Formerly served by Americable International. No longer in operation

▲ **FOXBOROUGH**—Comcast Cable. Now served by TAUNTON, MA [MA0033]

FOXBOROUGH—See TAUNTON, MA (Comcast Cable)

▲ **FRAMINGHAM**—Comcast Cable. Now served by BOSTON, MA [MA0001]

FRAMINGHAM—See BOSTON, MA (Comcast Cable)

▲ **FRAMINGHAM**—RCN Corp. Formerly served by Boston, MA [MA0105]. This cable system has converted to IPTV

FRANKLIN—See BOSTON, MA (Comcast Cable)

FRANKLIN—See TAUNTON, MA (Comcast Cable)

FREETOWN—See TAUNTON, MA (Comcast Cable)

GARDNER—See WESTFORD, MA (Comcast Cable)

GEORGETOWN—See WESTFORD, MA (Comcast Cable)

GILBERTVILLE—See SPRINGFIELD, MA (Comcast Cable)

GILL—See SPRINGFIELD, MA (Comcast Cable)

▲ **GLOUCESTER**—Comcast Cable. Now served by BOSTON, MA [MA0001]

GLOUCESTER—See BOSTON, MA (Comcast Cable)

GRAFTON—See WORCESTER, MA (Charter Communications)

GRANBY—See SPRINGFIELD, MA (Comcast Cable)

GRANVILLE—See SPRINGFIELD, MA (Comcast Cable)

GREAT BARRINGTON—See PITTSFIELD, MA (Time Warner Cable)

GREENFIELD—See SPRINGFIELD, MA (Comcast Cable)

GROTON—See PEPPERELL, MA (Charter Communications)

GROVELAND—See WESTFORD, MA (Comcast Cable)

HADLEY—See BELCHERTOWN, MA (Charter Communications)

HALIFAX—See TAUNTON, MA (Comcast Cable)

HAMILTON—See BOSTON, MA (Comcast Cable)

HAMPDEN—See CHICOPEE, MA (Charter Communications)

HANOVER—See TAUNTON, MA (Comcast Cable)

HANSCOM AFB—See BOSTON, MA (Comcast Cable)

HANSON—See TAUNTON, MA (Comcast Cable)

HARDWICK—See SPRINGFIELD, MA (Comcast Cable)

HARVARD—See PEPPERELL, MA (Charter Communications)

HARWICH PORT—See TAUNTON, MA (Comcast Cable)

HARWICH—See TAUNTON, MA (Comcast Cable)

▲**HAVERHILL**—Comcast Cable. Now served by WESTFORD, MA [MA0093]

HAVERHILL—See WESTFORD, MA (Comcast Cable)

HINGHAM—See TAUNTON, MA (Comcast Cable)

▲**HINSDALE**—Charter Communications

HOLBROOK—See TAUNTON, MA (Comcast Cable)

HOLDEN—See WORCESTER, MA (Charter Communications)

▲**HOLLAND**—Cox Communications

HOLLIS—See PEPPERELL, NH (Charter Communications)

HOLLISTON—See BOSTON, MA (Comcast Cable)

HOLYOKE—See SPRINGFIELD, MA (Comcast Cable)

HOPEDALE—See TAUNTON, MA (Comcast Cable)

▲**HOPKINTON**—Comcast Cable. Now served by BOSTON, MA [MA0001]

HOPKINTON—See BOSTON, MA (Comcast Cable)

HOUSATONIC—See PITTSFIELD, MA (Time Warner Cable)

HUBBARDSTON—See RUTLAND (town), MA (Charter Communications)

HUDSON—See WESTFORD, MA (Comcast Cable)

HULL—See TAUNTON, MA (Comcast Cable)

HUNTINGTON—See SPRINGFIELD, MA (Comcast Cable)

HYANNIS—See TAUNTON, MA (Comcast Cable)

HYDE PARK—See BOSTON, MA (Comcast Cable)

▲**HYDE PARK**—RCN Corp. Formerly served by Boston, MA [MA0105]. This cable system has converted to IPTV

IPSWICH—See BOSTON, MA (Comcast Cable)

JAMAICA PLAIN—See BOSTON, MA (Comcast Cable)

KINGSTON—See TAUNTON, MA (Comcast Cable)

LAKEVILLE—See TAUNTON, MA (Comcast Cable)

LANCASTER—See WESTFORD, MA (Comcast Cable)

▲**LANESBORO**—Charter Communications

▲**LAWRENCE**—Comcast Cable. Now served by WESTFORD, MA [MA0093]

LAWRENCE—See WESTFORD, MA (Comcast Cable)

▲**LEE**—Time Warner Cable. Now served by PITTSFIELD, MA [MA0090]

LEE—See PITTSFIELD, MA (Time Warner Cable)

LEICESTER—See WORCESTER, MA (Charter Communications)

LENOX—See PITTSFIELD, MA (Time Warner Cable)

▲**LEOMINSTER**—Comcast Cable. Now served by WESTFORD, MA [MA0093]

LEOMINSTER—See WESTFORD, MA (Comcast Cable)

▲**LEXINGTON**—Comcast Cable. Now served by BOSTON, MA [MA0001]

LEXINGTON—See BOSTON, MA (Comcast Cable)

▲**LEXINGTON**—RCN Corp. Formerly served by Boston, MA [MA0105]. This cable system has converted to IPTV

LINCOLN (TOWN)—See WESTFORD, MA (Comcast Cable)

LITTLETON (TOWN)—See WESTFORD, MA (Comcast Cable)

▲**LONGMEADOW**—Comcast Cable. Now served by SPRINGFIELD, MA [MA0005]

LONGMEADOW—See SPRINGFIELD, MA (Comcast Cable)

▲**LOWELL**—Comcast Cable. Now served by WESTFORD, MA [MA0093]

LOWELL—See WESTFORD, MA (Comcast Cable)

LUDLOW—See CHICOPEE, MA (Charter Communications)

LUNENBURG—See WESTFORD, MA (Comcast Cable)

LYNN—See BOSTON, MA (Comcast Cable)

LYNNFIELD—See BOSTON, MA (Comcast Cable)

▲**MALDEN**—Comcast Cable. Now served by BOSTON, MA [MA0001]

MALDEN—See BOSTON, MA (Comcast Cable)

MANCHESTER—See BOSTON, MA (Comcast Cable)

MANSFIELD—See TAUNTON, MA (Comcast Cable)

MARBLEHEAD—See BOSTON, MA (Comcast Cable)

▲**MARION**—Comcast Cable. Now served by TAUNTON, MA [MA0033]

MARION—See TAUNTON, MA (Comcast Cable)

▲**MARLBOROUGH**—Comcast Cable. Now served by WESTFORD, MA [MA0093]

MARLBOROUGH—See WESTFORD, MA (Comcast Cable)

▲**MARSHFIELD**—Comcast Cable. Now served by TAUNTON, MA [MA0033]

MARSHFIELD—See TAUNTON, MA (Comcast Cable)

MARSTON MILLS—See TAUNTON, MA (Comcast Cable)

▲**MARTHA'S VINEYARD**—Comcast Cable. Now served by TAUNTON, MA [MA0033]

MARTHA'S VINEYARD—See TAUNTON, MA (Comcast Cable)

▲**MASHPEE**—Comcast Cable. Now served by TAUNTON, MA [MA0033]

MASHPEE—See TAUNTON, MA (Comcast Cable)

MATTAPAN—See BOSTON, MA (Comcast Cable)

MATTAPOISETT—See TAUNTON, MA (Comcast Cable)

▲**MAYNARD**—Comcast Cable. Now served by WESTFORD, MA [MA0093]

MAYNARD—See WESTFORD, MA (Comcast Cable)

MEDFIELD—See BOSTON, MA (Comcast Cable)

MEDFORD—See BOSTON, MA (Comcast Cable)

MEDWAY—See BOSTON, MA (Comcast Cable)

MELROSE—See BOSTON, MA (Comcast Cable)

MENDON—See TAUNTON, MA (Comcast Cable)

MENEMSHA—See TAUNTON, MA (Comcast Cable)

MERRIMAC—See WESTFORD, MA (Comcast Cable)

METHUEN—See WESTFORD, MA (Comcast Cable)

▲**MIDDLEBOROUGH**—Comcast Cable. Now served by TAUNTON, MA [MA0033]

MIDDLEBOROUGH—See TAUNTON, MA (Comcast Cable)

MIDDLETON—See WESTFORD, MA (Comcast Cable)

▲**MILFORD**—Formerly served by Comcast Cable. No longer in operation

MILLBURY—See WORCESTER, MA (Charter Communications)

MILLERS FALLS—See SPRINGFIELD, MA (Comcast Cable)

MILLIS—See BOSTON, MA (Comcast Cable)

MILLVILLE—See UXBRIDGE, MA (Charter Communications)

MINTON—See TAUNTON, MA (Comcast Cable)

MONSON—See SPRINGFIELD, MA (Comcast Cable)

MONTAGUE—See SPRINGFIELD, MA (Comcast Cable)

NAHANT—See BOSTON, MA (Comcast Cable)

▲**NANTUCKET**—Comcast Cable. Now served by TAUNTON, MA [MA0033]

NANTUCKET—See TAUNTON, MA (Comcast Cable)

▲**NATICK**—Comcast Cable. Now served by BOSTON, MA [MA0001]

NATICK—See BOSTON, MA (Comcast Cable)

▲**NATICK**—RCN Corp. Formerly served by Boston, MA [MA0105]. This cable system has converted to IPTV

▲**NEEDHAM**—Comcast Cable. Now served by BOSTON, MA [MA0001]

NEEDHAM—See BOSTON, MA (Comcast Cable)

▲**NEEDHAM**—RCN Corp. Formerly served by Boston, MA [MA0105]. This cable system has converted to IPTV

▲**NEW BEDFORD**—Comcast Cable. Now served by TAUNTON, MA [MA0033]

NEW BEDFORD—See TAUNTON, MA (Comcast Cable)

NEWBURY—See BOSTON, MA (Comcast Cable)

▲**NEWBURYPORT**—Comcast Cable. Now served by BOSTON, MA [MA0001]

NEWBURYPORT—See BOSTON, MA (Comcast Cable)

NEWTON—See BOSTON, MA (Comcast Cable)

▲**NEWTON**—RCN Corp. Formerly served by Boston, MA [MA0105]. This cable system has converted to IPTV

NORFOLK—See TAUNTON, MA (Comcast Cable)

▲**NORTH ADAMS**—Time Warner Cable. Now served by PITTSFIELD, MA [MA0090]

NORTH ADAMS—See PITTSFIELD, MA (Time Warner Cable)

▲**NORTH ANDOVER**—Comcast Cable. Now served by WESTFORD, MA [MA0093]

NORTH ANDOVER—See WESTFORD, MA (Comcast Cable)

NORTH ATTLEBORO—See TAUNTON, MA (Comcast Cable)

NORTH BROOKFIELD (TOWN)—See CHARLTON, MA (Charter Communications)

NORTH BROOKFIELD—See CHARLTON, MA (Charter Communications)

NORTH CHATHAM—See TAUNTON, MA (Comcast Cable)

NORTH HARWICH—See TAUNTON, MA (Comcast Cable)

NORTH READING—See BOSTON, MA (Comcast Cable)

NORTH SCITUATE—See TAUNTON, MA (Comcast Cable)

NORTHAMPTON—See SPRINGFIELD, MA (Comcast Cable)

NORTHBOROUGH—See WORCESTER, MA (Charter Communications)

NORTHBRIDGE—See WORCESTER, MA (Charter Communications)

NORTHFIELD—See SPRINGFIELD, MA (Comcast Cable)

NORTON—See TAUNTON, MA (Comcast Cable)

▲**NORWOOD**—Comcast Cable. Now served by BOSTON, MA [MA0001[

NORWOOD—See BOSTON, MA (Comcast Cable)

OAK BLUFFS—See TAUNTON, MA (Comcast Cable)

OAKHAM—See RUTLAND (town), MA (Charter Communications)

ORANGE—See ATHOL, MA (Time Warner Cable)

▲**ORLEANS**—Comcast Cable. Now served by TAUNTON, MA [MA0033]

ORLEANS—See TAUNTON, MA (Comcast Cable)

OSTERVILLE—See TAUNTON, MA (Comcast Cable)

OTTER RIVER—See WESTFORD, MA (Comcast Cable)

OXFORD—See WORCESTER, MA (Charter Communications)

PALMER—See SPRINGFIELD, MA (Comcast Cable)

PAXTON—See WORCESTER, MA (Charter Communications)

▲**PEABODY**—Comcast Cable. Now served by BOSTON, MA [MA0001]

PEABODY—See BOSTON, MA (Comcast Cable)

PELHAM—See SPRINGFIELD, MA (Comcast Cable)

▲**PEMBROKE**—Comcast Cable. Now served by TAUNTON, MA [MA0033]

PEMBROKE—See TAUNTON, MA (Comcast Cable)

▲**PEPPERELL**—Charter Communications

▲**PHILLIPSTON**—Comcast Cable. Now served by WESTFORD, MA [MA0093]

PHILLIPSTON—See WESTFORD, MA (Comcast Cable)

▲**PITTSFIELD**—Time Warner Cable

PLAINVILLE—See TAUNTON, MA (Comcast Cable)

▲**PLYMOUTH**—Comcast Cable. Now served by TAUNTON, MA [MA0033]

PLYMOUTH—See TAUNTON, MA (Comcast Cable)

PLYMPTON—See TAUNTON, MA (Comcast Cable)

PROVINCETOWN—See TAUNTON, MA (Comcast Cable)

▲**QUINCY**—Comcast Cable. Now served by TAUNTON, MA [MA0033]

QUINCY—See TAUNTON, MA (Comcast Cable)

RAYNHAM—See TAUNTON, MA (Comcast Cable)

READING—See BOSTON, MA (Comcast Cable)

REHOBOTH—See TAUNTON, MA (Comcast Cable)

REVERE—See BOSTON, MA (Comcast Cable)

RICHMOND—See PITTSFIELD, MA (Time Warner Cable)

ROCHESTER—See TAUNTON, MA (Comcast Cable)

ROCKLAND—See TAUNTON, MA (Comcast Cable)

ROCKPORT—See BOSTON, MA (Comcast Cable)

ROSLINDALE—See BOSTON, MA (Comcast Cable)

ROWLEY—See BOSTON, MA (Comcast Cable)

ROXBURY—See BOSTON, MA (Comcast Cable)

RUDOLPH—See TAUNTON, MA (Comcast Cable)

▲**RUSSELL**—Russell Municipal Cable TV

▲**RUTLAND (TOWN)**—Charter Communications

SALEM—See BOSTON, MA (Comcast Cable)

SALISBURY—See WESTFORD, MA (Comcast Cable)

SANDWICH—See TAUNTON, MA (Comcast Cable)

▲**SAUGUS**—Comcast Cable. Now served by BOSTON, MA [MA0001]

SAUGUS—See BOSTON, MA (Comcast Cable)

▲**SCITUATE**—Comcast Cable. Now served by TAUNTON, MA [MA0033]

SCITUATE—See TAUNTON, MA (Comcast Cable)

SEEKONK—See TAUNTON, MA (Comcast Cable)

SHEFFIELD (TOWN)—See PITTSFIELD, MA (Time Warner Cable)

SHELBURNE FALLS—See SPRINGFIELD, MA (Comcast Cable)

SHELBURNE—See SPRINGFIELD, MA (Comcast Cable)

SHERBORN—See BOSTON, MA (Comcast Cable)

SHIRLEY (TOWN)—See WESTFORD, MA (Comcast Cable)

▲**SHREWSBURY**—Shrewsbury's Community Cablevision

SIASCONSET—See TAUNTON, MA (Comcast Cable)

SOMERSET—See TAUNTON, MA (Comcast Cable)

SOMERVILLE—See BOSTON, MA (Comcast Cable)

▲**SOMERVILLE**—RCN Corp. Formerly served by Boston, MA [MA0105]. This cable system has converted to IPTV

SOUTH BOSTON—See BOSTON, MA (Comcast Cable)

▲**SOUTH BOSTON**—RCN Corp. Formerly served by Boston, MA [MA0105]. This cable system has converted to IPTV

SOUTH CHATHAM—See TAUNTON, MA (Comcast Cable)

SOUTH DEERFIELD—See SPRINGFIELD, MA (Comcast Cable)

SOUTH DENNIS—See TAUNTON, MA (Comcast Cable)

SOUTH HADLEY—See SPRINGFIELD, MA (Comcast Cable)

SOUTH HAMPTON (TOWN)—See WESTFORD, NH (Comcast Cable)

SOUTH HARWICH—See TAUNTON, MA (Comcast Cable)

▲**SOUTH YARMOUTH**—Comcast Cable. Now served by TAUNTON, MA [MA0033]

SOUTH YARMOUTH—See TAUNTON, MA (Comcast Cable)

SOUTHAMPTON—See CHICOPEE, MA (Charter Communications)

SOUTHBOROUGH—See WORCESTER, MA (Charter Communications)

SOUTHBRIDGE—See WORCESTER, MA (Charter Communications)

SOUTHWICK—See SPRINGFIELD, MA (Comcast Cable)

SPENCER—See WORCESTER, MA (Charter Communications)

▲**SPRINGFIELD**—Comcast Cable

▲**STERLING**—Comcast Cable. Now served by WESTFORD, MA [MA0093]

STERLING—See WESTFORD, MA (Comcast Cable)

STOCKBRIDGE—See PITTSFIELD, MA (Time Warner Cable)

STONEHAM—See BOSTON, MA (Comcast Cable)

▲**STONEHAM**—RCN Corp. Formerly served by Boston, MA [MA0105]. This cable system has converted to IPTV

▲**STOUGHTON**—Comcast Cable. Now served by TAUNTON, MA [MA0033]

STOUGHTON—See TAUNTON, MA (Comcast Cable)

STOW—See BOSTON, MA (Comcast Cable)

STURBRIDGE—See WORCESTER, MA (Charter Communications)

SUDBURY—See WESTFORD, MA (Comcast Cable)

SUNDERLAND—See SPRINGFIELD, MA (Comcast Cable)

SUTTON—See UXBRIDGE, MA (Charter Communications)

SWAMPSCOTT—See BOSTON, MA (Comcast Cable)

SWANSEA—See TAUNTON, MA (Comcast Cable)

▲**TAUNTON**—Comcast Cable

TEMPLETON—See WESTFORD, MA (Comcast Cable)

TEWKSBURY—See WESTFORD, MA (Comcast Cable)

THORNDIKE—See SPRINGFIELD, MA (Comcast Cable)

THREE RIVERS—See SPRINGFIELD, MA (Comcast Cable)

TISBURY—See TAUNTON, MA (Comcast Cable)

TOPSFIELD—See WESTFORD, MA (Comcast Cable)

TOWNSEND (TOWN)—See WESTFORD, MA (Comcast Cable)

TRURO—See TAUNTON, MA (Comcast Cable)

TURNERS FALLS—See SPRINGFIELD, MA (Comcast Cable)

TYNGSBOROUGH—See WESTFORD, MA (Comcast Cable)

UPTON—See WORCESTER, MA (Charter Communications)

▲**UXBRIDGE**—Charter Communications

VINEYARD HAVEN—See TAUNTON, MA (Comcast Cable)

WAKEFIELD—See BOSTON, MA (Comcast Cable)

▲**WAKEFIELD**—RCN Corp. Formerly served by Boston, MA [MA0105]. This cable system has converted to IPTV

▲**WALES**—Charter Communications

WALPOLE—See TAUNTON, MA (Comcast Cable)

▲**WALTHAM**—Comcast Cable. Now served by BOSTON, MA [MA0001]

WALTHAM—See BOSTON, MA (Comcast Cable)

▲**WALTHAM**—RCN Corp. Formerly served by Boston, MA [MA0105]. This cable system has converted to IPTV

WAQUOIT—See TAUNTON, MA (Comcast Cable)

WARE—See SPRINGFIELD, MA (Comcast Cable)

WAREHAM—See TAUNTON, MA (Comcast Cable)

WARREN—See SPRINGFIELD, MA (Comcast Cable)

▲**WATERTOWN**—Comcast Cable. Now served by BOSTON, MA [MA0001]

WATERTOWN—See BOSTON, MA (Comcast Cable)

▲**WATERTOWN**—RCN Corp. Formerly served by Boston, MA [MA0105]. This cable system has converted to IPTV

WAYLAND—See BOSTON, MA (Comcast Cable)

WEBSTER—See WORCESTER, MA (Charter Communications)

WELLESLEY—See BOSTON, MA (Comcast Cable)

WELLFLEET—See TAUNTON, MA (Comcast Cable)

WENHAM—See BOSTON, MA (Comcast Cable)

WEST BARNSTABLE—See TAUNTON, MA (Comcast Cable)

WEST BOYLSTON—See WORCESTER, MA (Charter Communications)

WEST BRIDGEWATER—See TAUNTON, MA (Comcast Cable)

WEST BROOKFIELD—See WORCESTER, MA (Charter Communications)

WEST CHATHAM—See TAUNTON, MA (Comcast Cable)

WEST DENNIS—See TAUNTON, MA (Comcast Cable)

WEST HARWICH—See TAUNTON, MA (Comcast Cable)

WEST NEWBURY—See BOSTON, MA (Comcast Cable)

WEST ROXBURY—See BOSTON, MA (Comcast Cable)

▲**WEST ROXBURY**—RCN Corp. Formerly served by Boston, MA [MA0105]. This cable system has converted to IPTV

WEST SPRINGFIELD—See SPRINGFIELD, MA (Comcast Cable)

▲**WEST STOCKBRIDGE**—Charter Communications

WEST TISBURY—See TAUNTON, MA (Comcast Cable)

WESTBOROUGH—See WORCESTER, MA (Charter Communications)

▲**WESTFIELD**—Comcast Cable. Now served by SPRINGFIELD, MA [MA0005]

WESTFIELD—See SPRINGFIELD, MA (Comcast Cable)

▲**WESTFORD**—Comcast Cable

WESTHAMPTON—See SPRINGFIELD, MA (Comcast Cable)

WESTMINSTER—See WESTFORD, MA (Comcast Cable)

WESTON—See BOSTON, MA (Comcast Cable)

▲**WESTPORT**—Charter Communications

WESTWOOD—See BOSTON, MA (Comcast Cable)

▲**WEYMOUTH**—Comcast Cable. Now served by TAUNTON, MA [MA0033]

WEYMOUTH—See TAUNTON, MA (Comcast Cable)

WHATELY—See SPRINGFIELD, MA (Comcast Cable)

WHITMAN—See TAUNTON, MA (Comcast Cable)

WILBRAHAM—See CHICOPEE, MA (Charter Communications)

WILLIAMSTOWN—See PITTSFIELD, MA (Time Warner Cable)

WILMINGTON—See BOSTON, MA (Comcast Cable)

▲**WINCHENDON**—Comcast Cable. Now served by WESTFORD, MA [MA0093]

WINCHENDON—See WESTFORD, MA (Comcast Cable)

WINCHESTER—See BOSTON, MA (Comcast Cable)

WINTHROP—See BOSTON, MA (Comcast Cable)

▲**WOBURN**—Comcast Cable. Now served by BOSTON, MA [MA0001]

WOBURN—See BOSTON, MA (Comcast Cable)

▲**WOBURN**—RCN Corp. Formerly served by Boston, MA [MA0105]. This cable system has converted to IPTV

▲**WORCESTER**—Charter Communications

WRENTHAM—See TAUNTON, MA (Comcast Cable)

YARMOUTH (PORT)—See TAUNTON, MA (Comcast Cable)

YARMOUTH (TOWN)—See TAUNTON, MA (Comcast Cable)

YARMOUTH—See TAUNTON, MA (Comcast Cable)

MICHIGAN

ACADIA TWP.—See TRAVERSE CITY, MI (Charter Communications)

ACME TWP.—See TRAVERSE CITY, MI (Charter Communications)

ADA—See GRAND RAPIDS, MI (Comcast Cable)

ADAMS TWP. (HILLSDALE COUNTY)—See HILLSDALE, MI (Comcast Cable)

ADAMS TWP. (HOUGHTON COUNTY)—See HOUGHTON, MI (Charter Communications)

▲**ADDISON (VILLAGE)**—Comcast Cable

ADDISON TWP.—See OXFORD, MI (Charter Communications)

▲**ADRIAN**—Formerly served by Comcast Cable. No longer in operation

AETNA TWP. (MECOSTA COUNTY)—See HOWARD CITY, MI (Charter Communications)

AGATE HARBOR—See EAGLE HARBOR TWP., MI (Cable America Corp.)

AHMEEK—See HOUGHTON, MI (Charter Communications)

AKRON (VILLAGE)—See AKRON/FAIRGROVE, MI (Pine River Cable)

AKRON TWP.—See AKRON/FAIRGROVE, MI (Pine River Cable)

▲**AKRON/FAIRGROVE**—Pine River Cable

ALABASTER TWP.—See OSCODA, MI (Charter Communications)

ALAIEDON TWP. (PORTIONS)—See EAST LANSING, MI (Comcast Cable)

ALAIEDON TWP.—See DIMONDALE, MI (Broadstripe)

ALAIEDON TWP.—See LANSING, MI (Comcast Cable)

ALAMO TWP.—See ALLEGAN, MI (Charter Communications)

ALAMO TWP.—See KALAMAZOO, MI (Charter Communications)

ALANSON (VILLAGE)—See INDIAN RIVER, MI (Charter Communications)

▲**ALBA**—Charter Communications. Now served by TRAVERSE CITY, MI [MI0026]

ALBA—See TRAVERSE CITY, MI (Charter Communications)

ALBEE TWP.—See SAGINAW, MI (Charter Communications)

ALBERT TWP.—See LEWISTON, MI (Lewiston Communications)

ALBION—See DIMONDALE, MI (Broadstripe)

ALCONA TWP.—See OSCODA, MI (Charter Communications)

ALGANSEE TWP.—See COLDWATER, MI (Charter Communications)

ALGOMA TWP.—See ROCKFORD, MI (Charter Communications)

ALGONAC—See CHESTERFIELD TWP., MI (Comcast Cable)

ALLEGAN COUNTY (PORTIONS)—See ALLENDALE, MI (Charter Communications)

ALLEGAN TWP.—See ALLEGAN, MI (Charter Communications)

▲**ALLEGAN**—Charter Communications

▲**ALLEN (village)**—Formerly served by CableDirect. No longer in operation

ALLEN PARK—See TAYLOR, MI (Comcast Cable)

ALLEN PARK—See DETROIT, MI (WOW! Internet Cable & Phone)

ALLEN—See HILLSDALE, MI (Comcast Cable)

▲**ALLENDALE**—Charter Communications

ALLOUEZ TWP.—See HOUGHTON, MI (Charter Communications)

▲**ALMA**—Charter Communications

ALMENA TWP.—See LAWTON, MI (Comcast Cable)

ALMENA TWP.—See MATTAWAN, MI (Mediacom)

ALMER TWP.—See VASSAR, MI (Charter Communications)

ALMIRA TWP.—See TRAVERSE CITY, MI (Charter Communications)

ALMONT TWP.—See ALMONT, MI (Charter Communications)

▲**ALMONT**—Charter Communications

ALOHA TWP.—See CHEBOYGAN, MI (Charter Communications)

▲**ALPENA**—Charter Communications

▲**ALPHA (VILLAGE)**—Upper Peninsula Communications

ALPINE TWP. (PORTIONS)—See GRAND RAPIDS, MI (Comcast Cable)

ALPINE TWP.—See ROCKFORD, MI (Charter Communications)

▲**AMASA**—Upper Peninsula Communications

AMBER TWP.—See LUDINGTON, MI (Charter Communications)

▲**AMBOY TWP.**—Formerly served by CableDirect. No longer in operation

▲**ANN ARBOR**—Comcast Cable

ANTWERP TWP.—See LAWTON, MI (Comcast Cable)

ANTWERP TWP.—See MATTAWAN, MI (Mediacom)

▲**APPLEGATE**—Formerly served by Cablevision Systems Corp. No longer in operation

ARBELA TWP.—See THETFORD TWP., MI (Charter Communications)

ARCADA TWP.—See ALMA, MI (Charter Communications)

ARCADIA TWP. (LAPEER COUNTY)—See NORTH BRANCH TWP., MI (Charter Communications)

ARENAC TWP.—See OMER, MI (Charter Communications)

ARGENTINE TWP.—See FENTON, MI (Charter Communications)

ARLINGTON TWP.—See BLOOMINGDALE, MI (Bloomingdale Communications Inc.)

ARLINGTON TWP.—See SOUTH HAVEN, MI (Comcast Cable)

ARMADA (VILLAGE)—See CHESTERFIELD TWP., MI (Comcast Cable)

ARMADA TWP.—See CHESTERFIELD TWP., MI (Comcast Cable)

▲**ARNOLD LAKE**—Charter Communications

ASH TWP.—See MONROE, MI (Charter Communications)

ASHLAND TWP.—See GRANT, MI (Charter Communications)

▲**ASHLEY**—Pine River Cable

ASHTON—See LE ROY (village), MI (Pine River Cable)

ATHENS—See DIMONDALE, MI (Broadstripe)

ATHENS—See UNION CITY, MI (Broadstripe)

▲**ATLANTA**—Formerly served by Northwoods Cable Inc. No longer in operation

ATLAS TWP.—See DAVISON, MI (Charter Communications)

▲**ATTICA TWP.**—Charter Communications. Now served by NORTH BRANCH TWP., MI [MI0337]

ATTICA TWP.—See NORTH BRANCH TWP., MI (Charter Communications)

▲**AU GRES**—Charter Communications

AU SABLE TWP. (IOSCO COUNTY)—See OSCODA, MI (Charter Communications)

AU TRAIN TWP.—See MARQUETTE, MI (Charter Communications)

AUBURN HILLS—See ROYAL OAK, MI (Comcast Cable)

AUBURN—See BAY CITY, MI (Charter Communications)

AUGUSTA TWP.—See TAYLOR, MI (Comcast Cable)

AUGUSTA—See RICHLAND, MI (Comcast Cable)

AURELIUS TWP.—See DIMONDALE, MI (Broadstripe)

AURORA—See IRON MOUNTAIN, WI (Charter Communications)

AUSTIN TWP. (MECOSTA COUNTY)—See CANADIAN LAKES, MI (Charter Communications)

AUSTIN TWP. (MECOSTA COUNTY)—See HOWARD CITY, MI (Charter Communications)

BACKUS TWP.—See HOUGHTON LAKE, MI (Charter Communications)

▲**BAD AXE**—Comcast Cable. Now served by PIGEON, MI [MI0375]

BAD AXE—See PIGEON, MI (Comcast Cable)

BAGLEY TWP.—See TRAVERSE CITY, MI (Charter Communications)

BAINBRIDGE TWP.—See ST. JOSEPH TWP., MI (Comcast Cable)

▲**BALDWIN (VILLAGE)**—Charter Communications

BALDWIN TWP. (IOSCO COUNTY)—See OSCODA, MI (Charter Communications)

BANCROFT—See DURAND, MI (Charter Communications)

BANGOR TWP. (BAY COUNTY)—See BAY CITY, MI (Charter Communications)

BANGOR—See SOUTH HAVEN, MI (Comcast Cable)

BARAGA—See HOUGHTON, MI (Charter Communications)

BARK RIVER TWP.—See ESCANABA, MI (Charter Communications)

BARODA (VILLAGE)—See ST. JOSEPH TWP., MI (Comcast Cable)

BARRY TWP. (PORTIONS)—See DELTON, MI (Charter Communications)

BARRY TWP. (PORTIONS)—See RICHLAND, MI (Comcast Cable)

▲**BARRYTON**—Pine River Cable

▲**BARTON CITY**—Pine River Cable

BARTON HILLS (VILLAGE)—See ANN ARBOR, MI (Comcast Cable)

BATAVIA TWP.—See COLDWATER, MI (Charter Communications)

BATES TWP.—See IRON RIVER, MI (Iron River Cable)

BATH TWP.—See DIMONDALE, MI (Broadstripe)

▲**BATTLE CREEK**—Comcast Cable

▲**BAY CITY**—Charter Communications

BAY MILLS TWP.—See SAULT STE. MARIE, MI (Charter Communications)

BAY PORT VILLAGE—See PIGEON, MI (Comcast Cable)

BAY SHORE—See TRAVERSE CITY, MI (Charter Communications)

BAY TWP.—See TRAVERSE CITY, MI (Charter Communications)

BAY VIEW—See TRAVERSE CITY, MI (Charter Communications)

BEAL CITY—See WEIDMAN, MI (Charter Communications)

BEAR CREEK TWP.—See TRAVERSE CITY, MI (Charter Communications)

▲**BEAR LAKE**—Charter Communications. Now served by TRAVERSE CITY, MI [MI0026]

BEAR LAKE—See TRAVERSE CITY, MI (Charter Communications)

BEAUGRAND TWP.—See CHEBOYGAN, MI (Charter Communications)

BEAVER CREEK TWP.—See GRAYLING, MI (Charter Communications)

▲**BEAVER ISLAND**—Pine River Cable

▲**BEAVER TWP. (BAY COUNTY)**—Charter Communications. Now served by BAY CITY, MI [MI0018]

BEAVER TWP.—See BAY CITY, MI (Charter Communications)

BEAVERTON—See ST. HELEN, MI (Charter Communications)

BEDFORD TWP. (CALHOUN COUNTY)—See BATTLE CREEK, MI (Comcast Cable)

BELDING—See GREENVILLE, MI (Charter Communications)

BELLAIRE (VILLAGE)—See TRAVERSE CITY, MI (Charter Communications)

BELLEVILLE—See PLYMOUTH TWP., MI (Comcast Cable)

BELLEVUE—See DIMONDALE, MI (Broadstripe)

BELVIDERE TWP.—See LAKEVIEW, MI (Charter Communications)

BENNINGTON TWP.—See OWOSSO, MI (Charter Communications)

BENONA TWP.—See HART, MI (Charter Communications)

▲**BENTON HARBOR**—Comcast Cable

BENTON HARBOR—See ST. JOSEPH TWP., MI (Comcast Cable)

BENTON TWP. (BERRIEN COUNTY)—See BENTON HARBOR, MI (Comcast Cable)

BENTON TWP. (CHEBOYGAN COUNTY)—See CHEBOYGAN, MI (Charter Communications)

BENTON TWP. (EATON COUNTY)—See DIMONDALE, MI (Broadstripe)

BENZIE COUNTY (PORTIONS)—See TRAVERSE CITY, MI (Charter Communications)

BENZONIA—See TRAVERSE CITY, MI (Charter Communications)

BERGLAND TWP.—See IRONWOOD, MI (Charter Communications)

▲**BERGLAND**—Charter Communications. Now served by IRONWOOD, MI [MI0064]

BERGLAND—See IRONWOOD, MI (Charter Communications)

BERKLEY—See ROYAL OAK, MI (Comcast Cable)

BERKLEY—See DETROIT, MI (WOW! Internet Cable & Phone)

BERLIN TWP. (IONIA COUNTY)—See IONIA, MI (Charter Communications)

BERLIN TWP. (MONROE COUNTY)—See MONROE, MI (Charter Communications)

BERLIN TWP. (MONROE COUNTY)—See TAYLOR, MI (Comcast Cable)

▲**BERLIN TWP. (ST. CLAIR COUNTY)**—Charter Communications

BERRIEN SPRINGS—See ST. JOSEPH TWP., MI (Comcast Cable)

BERRIEN TWP.—See ST. JOSEPH TWP., MI (Comcast Cable)

BERTRAND TWP.—See NILES, MI (Comcast Cable)

BESSEMER—See IRONWOOD, MI (Charter Communications)

BETHANY TWP.—See ALMA, MI (Charter Communications)

BETHEL TWP.—See COLDWATER, MI (Charter Communications)

BEULAH—See TRAVERSE CITY, MI (Charter Communications)

BEVERLY HILLS—See SOUTHFIELD, MI (Comcast Cable)

BIG CREEK TWP.—See MIO, MI (Charter Communications)

▲**BIG PRAIRIE TWP.**—Charter Communications

▲**BIG RAPIDS**—Charter Communications

▲**BIG STAR LAKE**—Charter Communications

▲**BILLINGS**—Charter Communications

BINGHAM FARMS—See SOUTHFIELD, MI (Comcast Cable)

BINGHAM TWP. (LEELANAU COUNTY)—See TRAVERSE CITY, MI (Charter Communications)

BINGHAM TWP.—See ST. JOHNS, MI (Charter Communications)

BIRCH RUN—See SAGINAW, MI (Charter Communications)

▲ **BIRMINGHAM**—Comcast Cable. Now served by SOUTHFIELD, MI [MI0009]

BIRMINGHAM—See SOUTHFIELD, MI (Comcast Cable)

BITELY—See LILLEY TWP., MI (Charter Communications)

BLACKMAN TWP.—See JACKSON, MI (Comcast Cable)

BLAIR TWP.—See TRAVERSE CITY, MI (Charter Communications)

BLENDON TWP.—See ALLENDALE, MI (Charter Communications)

BLISSFIELD TWP.—See MONROE, MI (Charter Communications)

BLISSFIELD—See MONROE, MI (Charter Communications)

BLISSFIELD—See PETERSBURG, MI (D & P Cable)

BLOOMER TWP.—See CARSON CITY, MI (Pine River Cable)

BLOOMFIELD HILLS—See SOUTHFIELD, MI (Comcast Cable)

BLOOMFIELD TWP. (OAKLAND COUNTY)—See SOUTHFIELD, MI (Comcast Cable)

BLOOMINGDALE TWP. (VAN BUREN COUNTY)—See BLOOMINGDALE, MI (Bloomingdale Communications Inc.)

▲ **BLOOMINGDALE**—Bloomingdale Communications Inc.

BLUE LAKE TWP. (MUSKEGON COUNTY)—See WHITEHALL, MI (Charter Communications)

BLUE LAKE TWP.—See TRAVERSE CITY, MI (Charter Communications)

BLUMFIELD TWP.—See SAGINAW, MI (Charter Communications)

▲ **BOARDMAN TWP. (SOUTHERN PORTION)**—Pine River Cable

BOSTON TWP.—See DIMONDALE, MI (Broadstripe)

BOURRET TWP.—See BUTMAN TWP., MI (Charter Communications)

BOWNE TWP.—See MIDDLEVILLE/ CALEDONIA, MI (Charter Communications)

BOYNE CITY—See TRAVERSE CITY, MI (Charter Communications)

BOYNE FALLS—See TRAVERSE CITY, MI (Charter Communications)

BOYNE VALLEY TWP.—See TRAVERSE CITY, MI (Charter Communications)

BRADY TWP. (KALAMAZOO COUNTY)—See THREE RIVERS, MI (Comcast Cable)

BRADY TWP. (SAGINAW COUNTY)—See CHESANING, MI (Charter Communications)

BRAMPTON TWP.—See ESCANABA, MI (Charter Communications)

BRANCH TWP. (MASON CO.)—See CUSTER, MI (Charter Communications)

BRANDON TWP.—See OXFORD, MI (Charter Communications)

BRECKENRIDGE—See ALMA, MI (Charter Communications)

BREITUNG TWP.—See IRON MOUNTAIN, MI (Charter Communications)

▲ **BRETHREN**—Pine River Cable

BRIDGEHAMPTON TWP.—See DECKERVILLE, MI (Comcast Cable)

BRIDGEPORT (PORTIONS)—See SAGINAW, MI (Charter Communications)

BRIDGEPORT CHARTER TWP.—See SAGINAW, MI (Charter Communications)

▲ **BRIDGEPORT TWP.**—Charter Communications. Now served by SAGINAW, MI [MI0013]

BRIDGEPORT TWP.—See SAGINAW, MI (Charter Communications)

BRIDGMAN—See ST. JOSEPH TWP., MI (Comcast Cable)

▲ **BRIGHTON**—Comcast Cable. Now served by ANN ARBOR, MI [MI0006]

BRIGHTON—See ANN ARBOR, MI (Comcast Cable)

BRIMLEY—See SAULT STE. MARIE, MI (Charter Communications)

BRITTANY PARK—See CHESTERFIELD TWP., MI (Comcast Cable)

BRITTON—See ADDISON (village), MI (Comcast Cable)

BRITTON—See PETERSBURG, MI (D & P Cable)

BROCKWAY—See YALE, MI (Comcast Cable)

BROHMAN—See LILLEY TWP., MI (Charter Communications)

▲ **BRONSON TWP. (portions)**—Formerly served by CableDirect. No longer in operation

BRONSON—See COLDWATER, MI (Charter Communications)

BROOKFIELD TWP. (EATON COUNTY)—See SPRINGPORT TWP., MI (Springport Telephone Co.)

BROOKFIELD TWP.—See PIGEON, MI (Comcast Cable)

▲ **BROOKLYN (IRISH HILLS)**—Comcast Cable. Now served by JACKSON, MI [MI0039]

BROOKLYN (IRISH HILLS)—See JACKSON, MI (Comcast Cable)

BROOKS TWP. (PORTIONS)—See GRANT, MI (Charter Communications)

BROOKS TWP. (PORTIONS)—See MUSKEGON, MI (Comcast Cable)

BROOMFIELD TWP.—See WEIDMAN, MI (Charter Communications)

▲ **BROOMFIELD VALLEY TRAILER PARK**—Charter Communications

▲ **BROWN CITY**—Comcast Cable

BROWNSTOWN TWP.—See TAYLOR, MI (Comcast Cable)

BRUCE TWP. (MACOMB COUNTY)—See CHESTERFIELD TWP., MI (Comcast Cable)

▲ **BRUTUS**—Pine River Cable

BUCHANAN—See NILES, MI (Comcast Cable)

BUCKEYE TWP.—See ST. HELEN, MI (Charter Communications)

BUCKLEY—See TRAVERSE CITY, MI (Charter Communications)

BUEL TWP.—See LEXINGTON, MI (Comcast Cable)

BUENA VISTA TWP.—See SAGINAW, MI (Charter Communications)

BUNKER HILL TWP.—See DIMONDALE, MI (Broadstripe)

BURLEIGH TWP.—See WHITTEMORE, MI (Charter Communications)

BURLINGTON (VILLAGE)—See COLDWATER, MI (Charter Communications)

BURLINGTON TWP. (CALHOUN COUNTY)—See UNION CITY, MI (Broadstripe)

BURLINGTON TWP.—See DIMONDALE, MI (Broadstripe)

BURNS TWP.—See DURAND, MI (Charter Communications)

BURR OAK—See COLDWATER, MI (Charter Communications)

BURT TWP.—See INDIAN RIVER, MI (Charter Communications)

▲ **BURT**—Charter Communications. Now served by SAGINAW, MI [MI0013]

BURT—See SAGINAW, MI (Charter Communications)

BURTCHVILLE TWP.—See CHESTERFIELD TWP., MI (Comcast Cable)

BURTON—See FLINT, MI (Comcast Cable)

▲ **BUTMAN TWP.**—Charter Communications

BYRON TWP.—See GRAND RAPIDS, MI (Comcast Cable)

BYRON—See DURAND, MI (Charter Communications)

▲ **CADILLAC**—Charter Communications

CALDWELL TWP.—See TRAVERSE CITY, MI (Charter Communications)

CALEDONIA TWP. (KENT COUNTY)—See MIDDLEVILLE/CALEDONIA, MI (Charter Communications)

CALEDONIA TWP. (SHIAWASSEE COUNTY)—See OWOSSO, MI (Charter Communications)

CALEDONIA TWP.—See OSCODA, MI (Charter Communications)

CALEDONIA—See GRAND RAPIDS, MI (Comcast Cable)

CALUMET—See HOUGHTON, MI (Charter Communications)

CALVIN TWP.—See CASSOPOLIS, MI (Comcast Cable)

▲ **CAMBRIA TWP.**—Formerly served by CableDirect. No longer in operation

CAMBRIA TWP.—See HILLSDALE, MI (Comcast Cable)

CAMBRIDGE TWP.—See JACKSON, MI (Comcast Cable)

CAMPBELL TWP.—See DIMONDALE, MI (Broadstripe)

▲ **CANADIAN LAKES**—Charter Communications

CANNON TWP.—See GRAND RAPIDS, MI (Comcast Cable)

CANNON—See ROCKFORD, MI (Charter Communications)

CANTON TWP.—See PLYMOUTH TWP., MI (Comcast Cable)

CANTON TWP.—See DETROIT, MI (WOW! Internet Cable & Phone)

▲ **CAPAC**—Comcast Cable

CARLETON (VILLAGE)—See MONROE, MI (Charter Communications)

CARLTON TWP.—See FREEPORT, MI (Lewiston Communications)

CARMEL TWP.—See DIMONDALE, MI (Broadstripe)

CARNEY—See POWERS, MI (Upper Peninsula Communications)

▲ **CARO**—Charter Communications. Now served by VASSAR, MI [MI0131]

CARO—See VASSAR, MI (Charter Communications)

CARP LAKE—See IRONWOOD, MI (Charter Communications)

CARP LAKE—See LEVERING, MI (Charter Communications)

CARROLLTON—See SAGINAW, MI (Charter Communications)

▲ **CARSON CITY**—Pine River Cable

CARSONVILLE—See DECKERVILLE, MI (Comcast Cable)

CASCADE TWP.—See MIDDLEVILLE/ CALEDONIA, MI (Charter Communications)

CASCADE TWP.—See GRAND RAPIDS, MI (Comcast Cable)

CASCO TWP. (ALLEGAN COUNTY)—See SOUTH HAVEN, MI (Comcast Cable)

CASCO TWP. (ST. CLAIR COUNTY)—See CHESTERFIELD TWP., MI (Comcast Cable)

CASEVILLE (VILLAGE)—See PIGEON, MI (Comcast Cable)

▲ **CASEVILLE**—Comcast Cable. Now served by PIGEON, MI [MI0375]

CASNOVIA (VILLAGE)—See GRANT, MI (Charter Communications)

▲ **CASPIAN**—Caspian Community TV Corp.

▲ **CASS CITY**—Charter Communications. Now served by VASSAR, MI [MI0131]

CASS CITY—See VASSAR, MI (Charter Communications)

▲**CASSOPOLIS**—Comcast Cable

CATO TWP.—See LAKEVIEW, MI (Charter Communications)

CEDAR CREEK TWP. (MUSKEGON COUNTY)—See MUSKEGON, MI (Comcast Cable)

CEDAR CREEK TWP.—See TRAVERSE CITY, MI (Charter Communications)

CEDAR SPRINGS—See ROCKFORD, MI (Charter Communications)

CEMENT CITY (VILLAGE)—See JACKSON, MI (Comcast Cable)

CENTER LINE—See STERLING HEIGHTS, MI (Comcast Cable)

CENTER LINE—See DETROIT, MI (WOW! Internet Cable & Phone)

CENTERVILLE TWP.—See TRAVERSE CITY, MI (Charter Communications)

CENTRAL LAKE—See TRAVERSE CITY, MI (Charter Communications)

CENTREVILLE—See THREE RIVERS, MI (Comcast Cable)

CERESCO—See BATTLE CREEK, MI (Comcast Cable)

▲**CHAMPION TWP.**—Upper Peninsula Communications

CHARLESTON TWP. (PORTIONS)—See CLIMAX TWP., MI (Climax Telephone Co.)

CHARLESTON TWP. (PORTIONS)—See RICHLAND, MI (Comcast Cable)

CHARLEVOIX TWP.—See TRAVERSE CITY, MI (Charter Communications)

▲**CHARLEVOIX**—Charter Communications. Now served by TRAVERSE CITY, MI [MI0026]

CHARLEVOIX—See TRAVERSE CITY, MI (Charter Communications)

CHARLOTTE—See DIMONDALE, MI (Broadstripe)

CHASSELL TWP.—See HOUGHTON, MI (Charter Communications)

CHATHAM—See MARQUETTE, MI (Charter Communications)

▲**CHEBOYGAN**—Charter Communications

CHELSEA—See ANN ARBOR, MI (Comcast Cable)

CHERRY GROVE TWP.—See CADILLAC, MI (Charter Communications)

▲**CHESANING**—Charter Communications

CHESHIRE TWP.—See BLOOMINGDALE, MI (Bloomingdale Communications Inc.)

▲**CHESTER TWP. (OTTAWA COUNTY)**—Charter Communications

CHESTER TWP.—See TRAVERSE CITY, MI (Charter Communications)

▲**CHESTERFIELD TWP.**—Comcast Cable

CHESTONIA TWP.—See TRAVERSE CITY, MI (Charter Communications)

CHIKAMING TWP.—See ST. JOSEPH TWP., MI (Comcast Cable)

CHINA TWP.—See CHESTERFIELD TWP., MI (Comcast Cable)

▲**CHIPPEWA TWP. (ISABELLA COUNTY)**—Charter Communications

CHIPPEWA TWP. (MECOSTA COUNTY)—See CANADIAN LAKES, MI (Charter Communications)

CHOCOLAY TWP.—See MARQUETTE, MI (Charter Communications)

CHRISTMAS—See MARQUETTE, MI (Charter Communications)

CHURCHILL TWP.—See SKIDWAY LAKE, MI (Charter Communications)

CLAM LAKE TWP.—See CADILLAC, MI (Charter Communications)

▲**CLARE**—Charter Communications. Now served by MOUNT PLEASANT, MI [MI0069]

CLARE—See MOUNT PLEASANT, MI (Charter Communications)

CLARENCE TWP.—See SPRINGPORT TWP., MI (Springport Telephone Co.)

▲**CLARK TWP.**—Formerly served by Northwoods Cable Inc. No longer in operation

▲**CLARKSTON**—Comcast Cable. Now served by PONTIAC, MI [MI0017]

CLARKSTON—See PONTIAC, MI (Comcast Cable)

CLARKSVILLE—See DIMONDALE, MI (Broadstripe)

CLAWSON—See ROYAL OAK, MI (Comcast Cable)

CLAWSON—See DETROIT, MI (WOW! Internet Cable & Phone)

CLAY TWP.—See CHESTERFIELD TWP., MI (Comcast Cable)

CLAYTON TWP. (GENESEE COUNTY)—See DURAND, MI (Charter Communications)

CLAYTON TWP. (GENESEE COUNTY)—See LENNON, MI (Lennon Telephone Co.)

CLEAR LAKE—See WEST BRANCH, MI (Pine River Cable)

CLEARWATER TWP.—See TRAVERSE CITY, MI (Charter Communications)

CLEMENT TWP.—See BUTMAN TWP., MI (Charter Communications)

▲**CLEON TWP.**—Ace Communications. Formerly served by Thompsonville, MI [MI0230]. This cable system has converted to IPTV

CLEVELAND TWP.—See TRAVERSE CITY, MI (Charter Communications)

CLIFFORD—See NORTH BRANCH TWP., MI (Charter Communications)

▲**CLIMAX TWP.**—Climax Telephone Co.

CLINTON COUNTY—See LANSING, MI (Comcast Cable)

CLINTON TWP.—See STERLING HEIGHTS, MI (Comcast Cable)

CLINTON—See ANN ARBOR, MI (Comcast Cable)

CLINTON—See DETROIT, MI (WOW! Internet Cable & Phone)

CLIO—See FLINT, MI (Comcast Cable)

CLYDE TWP. (ALLEGAN COUNTY)—See SAUGATUCK, MI (Comcast Cable)

CLYDE TWP. (ST. CLAIR COUNTY)—See CHESTERFIELD TWP., MI (Comcast Cable)

COE TWP.—See MOUNT PLEASANT, MI (Charter Communications)

COLD SPRINGS TWP.—See TRAVERSE CITY, MI (Charter Communications)

▲**COLDWATER**—Charter Communications

▲**COLDWATER**—Coldwater Board of Public Utilities

▲**COLEMAN**—Charter Communications

COLFAX TWP. (PORTIONS)—See PIGEON, MI (Comcast Cable)

COLOMA TWP.—See WATERVLIET, MI (Comcast Cable)

COLOMA—See WATERVLIET, MI (Comcast Cable)

COLON—See COLDWATER, MI (Charter Communications)

COLUMBIA TWP. (VAN BUREN COUNTY)—See BLOOMINGDALE, MI (Bloomingdale Communications Inc.)

COLUMBIA TWP.—See JACKSON, MI (Comcast Cable)

COLUMBIAVILLE—See LAPEER, MI (Charter Communications)

COLUMBUS TWP. (ST. CLAIR COUNTY)—See CHESTERFIELD TWP., MI (Comcast Cable)

COMINS TWP.—See MIO, MI (Charter Communications)

COMMERCE TWP.—See WALLED LAKE, MI (Comcast Cable)

COMMONWEALTH—See IRON MOUNTAIN, WI (Charter Communications)

COMSTOCK TWP. (PORTIONS)—See CLIMAX TWP., MI (Climax Telephone Co.)

COMSTOCK TWP. (PORTIONS)—See RICHLAND, MI (Comcast Cable)

COMSTOCK TWP.—See KALAMAZOO, MI (Charter Communications)

CONCORD—See DIMONDALE, MI (Broadstripe)

CONSTANTINE—See THREE RIVERS, MI (Comcast Cable)

CONVIS TWP.—See DIMONDALE, MI (Broadstripe)

CONWAY—See TRAVERSE CITY, MI (Charter Communications)

COOPER TWP.—See ALLEGAN, MI (Charter Communications)

COOPERSVILLE—See ALLENDALE, MI (Charter Communications)

▲**COPEMISH**—Ace Communication. Formerly served by Thompsonville, MI [MI0230]. This cable system has converted to IPTV

COPPER CITY—See HOUGHTON, MI (Charter Communications)

CORUNNA—See OWOSSO, MI (Charter Communications)

CORUNNA—See LENNON, MI (Lennon Telephone Co.)

CORWITH TWP.—See TRAVERSE CITY, MI (Charter Communications)

COTTRELLVILLE TWP.—See CHESTERFIELD TWP., MI (Comcast Cable)

COUNTRY ACRES MOBILE HOME PARK—See ALLENDALE, MI (Charter Communications)

▲**COUNTRY ACRES**—Charter Communications. Now served by ALLENDALE, MI [MI0094]

COURTLAND TWP.—See ROCKFORD, MI (Charter Communications)

COVERT TWP.—See SOUTH HAVEN, MI (Comcast Cable)

CRAWFORD COUNTY (PORTIONS)—See HIGGINS LAKE, MI (Charter Communications)

CROCKERY TWP.—See ALLENDALE, MI (Charter Communications)

CROSWELL—See LEXINGTON, MI (Comcast Cable)

CROTON TWP.—See GRANT, MI (Charter Communications)

▲**CRYSTAL FALLS**—City of Crystal Falls

CRYSTAL LAKE—See TRAVERSE CITY, MI (Charter Communications)

▲**CRYSTAL TWP.**—Formerly served by Great Lakes Communication. No longer in operation

CUMMING TWP.—See ROSE CITY, MI (Charter Communications)

CURTISVILLE—See GLENNIE (village), MI (Pine River Cable)

▲**CUSTER**—Charter Communications

DAFTER TWP.—See SAULT STE. MARIE, MI (Charter Communications)

DAGGETT—See STEPHENSON, MI (Howard Cable)

DALTON TWP. (PORTIONS)—See WHITEHALL, MI (Charter Communications)

DALTON TWP.—See MUSKEGON, MI (Comcast Cable)

DANBY TWP.—See DIMONDALE, MI (Broadstripe)

DANSVILLE (VILLAGE)—See DIMONDALE, MI (Broadstripe)

▲ **DAVISON**—Charter Communications

DAY TWP.—See IONIA, MI (Charter Communications)

DAYTON TWP. (NEWAYGO COUNTY) (PORTIONS)—See MUSKEGON, MI (Comcast Cable)

DAYTON TWP. (TUSCOLA COUNTY)—See NORTH BRANCH TWP., MI (Charter Communications)

▲ **DE TOUR (VILLAGE)**—Upper Peninsula Communications

DE WITT TWP.—See LANSING, MI (Comcast Cable)

DE WITT—See LANSING, MI (Comcast Cable)

▲ **DEARBORN HEIGHTS**—Comcast Cable. Now served by PLYMOUTH, MI [MI0012]

DEARBORN HEIGHTS—See PLYMOUTH TWP., MI (Comcast Cable)

DEARBORN HEIGHTS—See DETROIT, MI (WOW! Internet Cable & Phone)

▲ **DEARBORN**—Comcast Cable. Now served by PLYMOUTH, MI [MI0012]

DEARBORN—See PLYMOUTH TWP., MI (Comcast Cable)

DEARBORN—See DETROIT, MI (WOW! Internet Cable & Phone)

DECATUR (VILLAGE)—See LAWTON, MI (Comcast Cable)

▲ **DECKERVILLE**—Comcast Cable

DEEP RIVER TWP.—See BAY CITY, MI (Charter Communications)

DEERFIELD TWP. (LAPEER COUNTY)—See LAPEER, MI (Charter Communications)

DEERFIELD TWP. (LAPEER COUNTY)—See NORTH BRANCH TWP., MI (Charter Communications)

DEERFIELD TWP. (LENAWEE COUNTY)—See MONROE, MI (Charter Communications)

DEERFIELD TWP. (MECOSTA COUNTY)—See HOWARD CITY, MI (Charter Communications)

DEERFIELD—See FENTON, MI (Charter Communications)

DEERFIELD—See PETERSBURG, MI (D & P Cable)

DELHI TWP.—See LANSING, MI (Comcast Cable)

DELTA TWP.—See LANSING, MI (Comcast Cable)

▲ **DELTON**—Charter Communications

DENMARK TWP.—See SAGINAW, MI (Charter Communications)

DENTON TWP.—See HOUGHTON LAKE, MI (Charter Communications)

DENVER TWP. (ISABELLA COUNTY)—See CHIPPEWA TWP. (Isabella County), MI (Charter Communications)

▲ **DETROIT**—Formerly served by Sprint Corp. No longer in operation

▲ **DETROIT**—Comcast Cable

▲ **DETROIT**—WOW! Internet Cable & Phone

DEXTER TWP.—See LIVINGSTON COUNTY, MI (Charter Communications)

DEXTER—See ANN ARBOR, MI (Comcast Cable)

DICKSON TWP.—See BRETHREN, MI (Pine River Cable)

▲ **DIMONDALE**—Broadstripe

DOLLAR BAY—See HOUGHTON, MI (Charter Communications)

DORR TWP. (PORTIONS)—See MIDDLEVILLE/CALEDONIA, MI (Charter Communications)

DORR TWP. (PORTIONS)—See GRAND RAPIDS, MI (Comcast Cable)

DOUGLAS—See SAUGATUCK, MI (Comcast Cable)

DOUGLASS TWP.—See IONIA, MI (Charter Communications)

DOVER TWP.—See ADDISON (village), MI (Comcast Cable)

DOVER—See ADDISON (village), MI (Comcast Cable)

▲ **DOWAGIAC**—Comcast Cable. Now served by CASSOPOLIS, MI [MI0168]

DOWAGIAC—See CASSOPOLIS, MI (Comcast Cable)

▲ **DRUMMOND ISLAND**—Formerly served by Northwoods Cable Inc. No longer in operation

DRYDEN TWP.—See ALMONT, MI (Charter Communications)

DRYDEN—See ALMONT, MI (Charter Communications)

DUNDEE (VILLAGE)—See TAYLOR, MI (Comcast Cable)

DUNDEE TWP.—See MONROE, MI (Charter Communications)

DUNDEE—See PETERSBURG, MI (D & P Cable)

▲ **DURAND**—Charter Communications

DURAND—See LENNON, MI (Lennon Telephone Co.)

DWIGHT TWP.—See PIGEON, MI (Comcast Cable)

EAGLE (VILLAGE)—See DIMONDALE, MI (Broadstripe)

▲ **EAGLE HARBOR TWP.**—Cable America Corp.

EAGLE TWP.—See DIMONDALE, MI (Broadstripe)

EAST BAY TWP.—See TRAVERSE CITY, MI (Charter Communications)

EAST CHINA TWP.—See CHESTERFIELD TWP., MI (Comcast Cable)

EAST GRAND RAPIDS—See GRAND RAPIDS, MI (Comcast Cable)

▲ **EAST JORDAN**—Charter Communications. Now served by TRAVERSE CITY, MI [MI0026]

EAST JORDAN—See TRAVERSE CITY, MI (Charter Communications)

EAST LAKE—See TRAVERSE CITY, MI (Charter Communications)

▲ **EAST LANSING**—Comcast Cable

EAST LEROY—See BATTLE CREEK, MI (Comcast Cable)

EAST TAWAS—See OSCODA, MI (Charter Communications)

EASTON TWP.—See IONIA, MI (Charter Communications)

EASTPOINTE—See STERLING HEIGHTS, MI (Comcast Cable)

EASTPOINTE—See DETROIT, MI (WOW! Internet Cable & Phone)

▲ **EATON RAPIDS**—Comcast Cable. Now served by LANSING, MI [MI0007]

EATON RAPIDS—See LANSING, MI (Comcast Cable)

EATON TWP.—See DIMONDALE, MI (Broadstripe)

EBEN JUNCTION—See MARQUETTE, MI (Charter Communications)

ECKFORD TWP.—See DIMONDALE, MI (Broadstripe)

ECORSE—See TAYLOR, MI (Comcast Cable)

EDENVILLE TWP.—See HOPE TWP. (Midland County), MI (Charter Communications)

EDENVILLE TWP.—See MIDLAND, MI (Charter Communications)

EDMORE—See IONIA, MI (Charter Communications)

EDWARDS TWP.—See WEST BRANCH, MI (Pine River Cable)

▲ **EDWARDSBURG**—Comcast Cable. Now served by THREE RIVERS, MI [MI0050]

EDWARDSBURG—See THREE RIVERS, MI (Comcast Cable)

EGELSTON TWP.—See MUSKEGON, MI (Comcast Cable)

ELBA TWP. (LAPEER COUNTY)—See LAPEER, MI (Charter Communications)

ELBERTA—See TRAVERSE CITY, MI (Charter Communications)

ELK RAPIDS (TOWN)—See TRAVERSE CITY, MI (Charter Communications)

ELK RAPIDS (VILLAGE)—See TRAVERSE CITY, MI (Charter Communications)

ELK RAPIDS TWP.—See TRAVERSE CITY, MI (Charter Communications)

ELK RAPIDS—See TRAVERSE CITY, MI (Charter Communications)

ELK TWP.—See YALE, MI (Comcast Cable)

ELKHART—See THREE RIVERS, IN (Comcast Cable)

ELKLAND TWP.—See VASSAR, MI (Charter Communications)

ELKTON VILLAGE—See PIGEON, MI (Comcast Cable)

ELLINGTON TWP.—See VASSAR, MI (Charter Communications)

ELMER TWP.—See MIO, MI (Charter Communications)

ELMIRA TWP.—See TRAVERSE CITY, MI (Charter Communications)

ELMWOOD TWP. (LEELANAU COUNTY)—See TRAVERSE CITY, MI (Charter Communications)

ELMWOOD TWP.—See PIGEON, MI (Comcast Cable)

▲ **ELSIE**—Charter Communications

ELY TWP.—See MARQUETTE, MI (Charter Communications)

EMERSON TWP.—See ALMA, MI (Charter Communications)

EMPIRE TWP.—See TRAVERSE CITY, MI (Charter Communications)

EMPIRE—See TRAVERSE CITY, MI (Charter Communications)

▲ **ENGADINE**—Upper Peninsula Communications

ENSLEY TWP.—See HOWARD CITY, MI (Charter Communications)

ERIE TWP.—See MONROE, MI (Charter Communications)

ERWIN TWP.—See IRONWOOD, MI (Charter Communications)

▲ **ESCANABA**—Charter Communications

ESSEXVILLE—See BAY CITY, MI (Charter Communications)

ESTRAL BEACH—See MONROE, MI (Charter Communications)

EUREKA TWP.—See GREENVILLE, MI (Charter Communications)

EVANGELINE TWP.—See TRAVERSE CITY, MI (Charter Communications)

▲ **EVART**—Charter Communications

EVELINE TWP.—See TRAVERSE CITY, MI (Charter Communications)

EVERETT TWP.—See GRANT, MI (Charter Communications)

EVERGREEN TWP.—See IONIA, MI (Charter Communications)

▲ **EWEN**—Charter Communications. Now served by IRONWOOD, MI [MI0064]

EWEN—See IRONWOOD, MI (Charter Communications)

EXCELSIOR TWP.—See TRAVERSE CITY, MI (Charter Communications)

EXETER TWP.—See MONROE, MI (Charter Communications)

EXETER TWP.—See TAYLOR, MI (Comcast Cable)

FABIUS TWP.—See THREE RIVERS, MI (Comcast Cable)

FAIRFIELD—See ADDISON (village), MI (Comcast Cable)

FAIRGROVE (VILLAGE)—See AKRON/FAIRGROVE, MI (Pine River Cable)

FAIRGROVE TWP.—See AKRON/FAIRGROVE, MI (Pine River Cable)

FAIRHAVEN TWP.—See PIGEON, MI (Comcast Cable)

FAIRVIEW—See MIO, MI (Charter Communications)

▲**FALMOUTH**—Pine River Cable

FARMINGTON HILLS—See LIVONIA, MI (Bright House Networks)

▲**FARMINGTON**—Bright House Networks. Now served by LIVONIA, MI [MI0019]

FARMINGTON—See LIVONIA, MI (Bright House Networks)

FARWELL—See MOUNT PLEASANT, MI (Charter Communications)

FAWN RIVER TWP.—See COLDWATER, MI (Charter Communications)

FAYETTE TWP.—See HILLSDALE, MI (Comcast Cable)

FENNVILLE—See SAUGATUCK, MI (Comcast Cable)

FENTON TWP.—See FENTON, MI (Charter Communications)

▲**FENTON**—Charter Communications

FERNDALE—See ROYAL OAK, MI (Comcast Cable)

FERNDALE—See DETROIT, MI (WOW! Internet Cable & Phone)

FERRYSBURG—See MUSKEGON, MI (Comcast Cable)

FIFE LAKE TWP.—See TRAVERSE CITY, MI (Charter Communications)

▲**FIFE LAKE**—Charter Communications. Now served by TRAVERSE CITY, MI [MI0026]

FIFE LAKE—See TRAVERSE CITY, MI (Charter Communications)

FILER TWP.—See TRAVERSE CITY, MI (Charter Communications)

FILLMORE TWP. (NORTHWEST PORTION)—See ALLENDALE, MI (Charter Communications)

▲**FINE LAKE**—Pine River Cable

FLAT ROCK—See TAYLOR, MI (Comcast Cable)

FLINT TWP.—See FLINT, MI (Comcast Cable)

▲**FLINT**—Comcast Cable

FLORENCE—See IRON MOUNTAIN, WI (Charter Communications)

FLOWERFIELD TWP.—See THREE RIVERS, MI (Comcast Cable)

FLUSHING TWP.—See FLINT, MI (Comcast Cable)

FLUSHING—See FLINT, MI (Comcast Cable)

FORD RIVER TWP.—See ESCANABA, MI (Charter Communications)

FOREST HOME TWP.—See TRAVERSE CITY, MI (Charter Communications)

FOREST TWP. (GENESEE COUNTY)—See DAVISON, MI (Charter Communications)

FOREST TWP.—See TRAVERSE CITY, MI (Charter Communications)

▲**FORESTER TWP.**—Formerly served by Cablevision Systems Corp. No longer in operation

▲**FORESTVILLE**—Formerly served by Cablevision Systems Corp. No longer in operation

FORSYTH TWP.—See MARQUETTE, MI (Charter Communications)

FORT GRATIOT TWP.—See CHESTERFIELD TWP., MI (Comcast Cable)

FOUNTAIN—See CUSTER, MI (Charter Communications)

▲**FOWLER**—Charter Communications. Now served by ST. JOHNS, MI [MI0353]

FOWLER—See ST. JOHNS, MI (Charter Communications)

FOWLERVILLE—See DIMONDALE, MI (Broadstripe)

FRANKENLUST TWP.—See BAY CITY, MI (Charter Communications)

FRANKENMUTH—See SAGINAW, MI (Charter Communications)

FRANKFORT—See TRAVERSE CITY, MI (Charter Communications)

FRANKLIN TWP.—See JACKSON, MI (Comcast Cable)

FRANKLIN—See SOUTHFIELD, MI (Comcast Cable)

▲**FRASER TWP.**—Charter Communications

FRASER—See STERLING HEIGHTS, MI (Comcast Cable)

FRASER—See DETROIT, MI (WOW! Internet Cable & Phone)

▲**FREDERIC TWP.**—Charter Communications

FREDONIA TWP.—See DIMONDALE, MI (Broadstripe)

FREDONIA TWP.—See COLDWATER, MI (Charter Communications)

▲**FREE SOIL**—Formerly served by Charter Communications. No longer in operation

FREELAND—See SAGINAW, MI (Charter Communications)

FREEMAN TWP.—See LAKE GEORGE, MI (Charter Communications)

FREEMONT TWP.—See NORTH BRANCH TWP., MI (Charter Communications)

FREEPORT CITY—See FREEPORT, MI (Lewiston Communications)

▲**FREEPORT**—Lewiston Communications

FREMONT—See MUSKEGON, MI (Comcast Cable)

FRENCHTOWN TWP.—See MONROE, MI (Charter Communications)

FRENCHTOWN TWP.—See TAYLOR, MI (Comcast Cable)

▲**FROST TWP.**—Charter Communications. Now served by MOUNT PLEASANT, MI [MI0069]

FROST TWP.—See MOUNT PLEASANT, MI (Charter Communications)

FRUITLAND TWP.—See MUSKEGON, MI (Comcast Cable)

FRUITLAND—See WHITEHALL, MI (Charter Communications)

FRUITPORT CHARTER TWP. (PORTIONS)—See ALLENDALE, MI (Charter Communications)

FRUITPORT CHARTER TWP. (PORTIONS)—See MUSKEGON, MI (Comcast Cable)

FRUITPORT VILLAGE—See ALLENDALE, MI (Charter Communications)

GAASTRA—See CASPIAN, MI (Caspian Community TV Corp.)

▲**GAGETOWN**—Comcast Cable. Now served by PIGEON, MI [MI0375]

GAGETOWN—See PIGEON, MI (Comcast Cable)

GAINES TWP. (GENESEE COUNTY)—See DURAND, MI (Charter Communications)

GAINES TWP. (GENESEE COUNTY)—See LENNON, MI (Lennon Telephone Co.)

GAINES TWP. (KENT COUNTY)—See MIDDLEVILLE/CALEDONIA, MI (Charter Communications)

GAINES TWP. (KENT COUNTY)—See GRAND RAPIDS, MI (Comcast Cable)

GAINES—See DURAND, MI (Charter Communications)

GALESBURG—See RICHLAND, MI (Comcast Cable)

GANGES TWP.—See SAUGATUCK, MI (Comcast Cable)

GARDEN CITY—See TAYLOR, MI (Comcast Cable)

GARDEN CITY—See DETROIT, MI (WOW! Internet Cable & Phone)

▲**GARDEN TWP.**—Upper Peninsula Communications

GARFIELD TWP. (BAY COUNTY)—See HOPE TWP. (Midland County), MI (Charter Communications)

▲**GARFIELD TWP. (Clare County)**—Charter Communications. Now served by MOUNT PLEASANT, MI [MI0069]

GARFIELD TWP. (CLARE COUNTY)—See MOUNT PLEASANT, MI (Charter Communications)

GARFIELD TWP. (GRAND TRAVERSE COUNTY)—See TRAVERSE CITY, MI (Charter Communications)

GARFIELD TWP. (NEWAYGO COUNTY) (PORTIONS)—See MUSKEGON, MI (Comcast Cable)

GARFIELD TWP. (NEWAYGO COUNTY)—See GRANT, MI (Charter Communications)

GARFIELD TWP.—See BAY CITY, MI (Charter Communications)

▲**GAYLORD**—Charter Communications. Now served by TRAVERSE CITY, MI [MI0026]

GAYLORD—See TRAVERSE CITY, MI (Charter Communications)

GENESEE COUNTY (PORTIONS)—See THETFORD TWP., MI (Charter Communications)

GENESEE TWP.—See FLINT, MI (Comcast Cable)

GENEVA TWP. (MIDLAND COUNTY)—See CHIPPEWA TWP. (Isabella County), MI (Charter Communications)

GENEVA TWP. (VAN BUREN COUNTY)—See SOUTH HAVEN, MI (Comcast Cable)

GENOA TWP.—See ANN ARBOR, MI (Comcast Cable)

GEORGETOWN TWP.—See GRAND RAPIDS, MI (Comcast Cable)

▲**GERMFASK**—Upper Peninsula Communications

GERRISH TWP. (PORTIONS)—See HIGGINS LAKE, MI (Charter Communications)

GERRISH TWP. (PORTIONS)—See ROSCOMMON, MI (Charter Communications)

GIBRALTAR—See TAYLOR, MI (Comcast Cable)

▲**GILEAD**—Formerly served by CableDirect. No longer in operation

GILMORE TWP. (BENZIE COUNTY)—See TRAVERSE CITY, MI (Charter Communications)

▲**GILMORE TWP. (Isabella County)**—Charter Communications. Now served by MOUNT PLEASANT, MI [MI0069]

GILMORE TWP. (ISABELLA COUNTY)—See MOUNT PLEASANT, MI (Charter Communications)

GIRARD TWP.—See COLDWATER, MI (Charter Communications)

GLADSTONE—See ESCANABA, MI (Charter Communications)

GLADWIN—See ST. HELEN, MI (Charter Communications)

GLEN ARBOR TWP.—See TRAVERSE CITY, MI (Charter Communications)

GLENN—See SOUTH HAVEN, MI (Comcast Cable)

▲**GLENNIE (VILLAGE)**—Pine River Cable

GOBLES CITY—See ALLEGAN, MI (Charter Communications)

GOLDEN TWP.—See MEARS, MI (Lewiston Communications)

GOODAR TWP.—See ROSE CITY, MI (Charter Communications)

▲**GOODELLS**—Formerly served by Cablevision Systems Corp. No longer in operation

GOODRICH—See DAVISON, MI (Charter Communications)

GORE TWP.—See PIGEON, MI (Comcast Cable)

GRAND BLANC TWP.—See FLINT, MI (Comcast Cable)

GRAND BLANC—See FLINT, MI (Comcast Cable)

GRAND HAVEN—See ALLENDALE, MI (Charter Communications)

GRAND ISLAND TWP.—See MARQUETTE, MI (Charter Communications)

▲**GRAND LAKE**—Charter Communications

GRAND LEDGE—See LANSING, MI (Comcast Cable)

▲**GRAND MARAIS**—Cable America Corp.

GRAND RAPIDS TWP.—See GRAND RAPIDS, MI (Comcast Cable)

▲**GRAND RAPIDS**—Comcast Cable

GRANDVILLE—See GRAND RAPIDS, MI (Comcast Cable)

GRANT TWP. (GRAND TRAVERSE COUNTY)—See TRAVERSE CITY, MI (Charter Communications)

GRANT TWP. (IOSCO COUNTY)—See OSCODA, MI (Charter Communications)

GRANT TWP. (NEWAYGO COUNTY)—See GRANT, MI (Charter Communications)

GRANT TWP. (OCEANA COUNTY)—See WHITEHALL, MI (Charter Communications)

GRANT TWP. (PORTIONS)—See MOUNT PLEASANT, MI (Charter Communications)

▲**GRANT**—Charter Communications

GRASS LAKE TWP.—See DIMONDALE, MI (Broadstripe)

▲**GRASS LAKE**—Millennium Digital Media. Now served by DIMONDALE, MI [MI0136]

GRASS LAKE—See DIMONDALE, MI (Broadstripe)

GRATTAN TWP.—See GRAND RAPIDS, MI (Comcast Cable)

▲**GRAYLING**—Charter Communications

GREEN LAKE TWP.—See TRAVERSE CITY, MI (Charter Communications)

GREEN OAK TWP.—See DIMONDALE, MI (Broadstripe)

GREEN OAK TWP.—See LIVINGSTON COUNTY, MI (Charter Communications)

GREEN OAK TWP.—See ANN ARBOR, MI (Comcast Cable)

GREEN TWP. (ALPENA COUNTY)—See ALPENA, MI (Charter Communications)

GREEN TWP. (MECOSTA COUNTY)—See BIG RAPIDS, MI (Charter Communications)

GREENBUSH TWP. (ALCONA COUNTY)—See OSCODA, MI (Charter Communications)

GREENDALE TWP.—See CHIPPEWA TWP. (Isabella County), MI (Charter Communications)

GREENLAND TWP.—See IRONWOOD, MI (Charter Communications)

▲**GREENVILLE**—Charter Communications

GREENWOOD TWP. (OSCODA COUNTY)—See LEWISTON, MI (Lewiston Communications)

GROSSE ILE—See TAYLOR, MI (Comcast Cable)

GROSSE ILE—See DETROIT, MI (WOW! Internet Cable & Phone)

GROSSE POINTE FARMS—See STERLING HEIGHTS, MI (Comcast Cable)

GROSSE POINTE PARK—See STERLING HEIGHTS, MI (Comcast Cable)

GROSSE POINTE SHORES—See STERLING HEIGHTS, MI (Comcast Cable)

GROSSE POINTE WOODS—See STERLING HEIGHTS, MI (Comcast Cable)

GROSSE POINTE—See STERLING HEIGHTS, MI (Comcast Cable)

GROUT TWP.—See SAGE TWP., MI (Charter Communications)

GROUT TWP.—See ST. HELEN, MI (Charter Communications)

GROVELAND TWP.—See PONTIAC, MI (Comcast Cable)

GUNPLAIN TWP.—See ALLEGAN, MI (Charter Communications)

GWINN—See MARQUETTE, MI (Charter Communications)

HADLEY TWP.—See OXFORD, MI (Charter Communications)

HAGAR TWP.—See WATERVLIET, MI (Comcast Cable)

▲**HALE**—Charter Communications

HAMBURG TWP.—See LIVINGSTON COUNTY, MI (Charter Communications)

HAMILTON TWP. (CLARE COUNTY)—See SAGE TWP., MI (Charter Communications)

▲**HAMLIN TWP. (MASON COUNTY)**—Charter Communications

HAMLIN TWP. (PORTIONS)—See LANSING, MI (Comcast Cable)

HAMPTON TWP.—See BAY CITY, MI (Charter Communications)

HAMTRAMCK—See DETROIT, MI (Comcast Cable)

HANCOCK—See HOUGHTON, MI (Charter Communications)

HANDY TWP.—See DIMONDALE, MI (Broadstripe)

HANOVER TWP.—See TRAVERSE CITY, MI (Charter Communications)

HANOVER—See DIMONDALE, MI (Broadstripe)

▲**HARBOR BEACH**—Comcast Cable. Now served by PIGEON, MI [MI0375]

HARBOR BEACH—See PIGEON, MI (Comcast Cable)

HARBOR SPRINGS—See TRAVERSE CITY, MI (Charter Communications)

HARING TWP.—See CADILLAC, MI (Charter Communications)

HARPER WOODS—See STERLING HEIGHTS, MI (Comcast Cable)

HARRIS TWP.—See ESCANABA, MI (Charter Communications)

HARRISON TWP.—See CHESTERFIELD TWP., MI (Comcast Cable)

HARRISON TWP.—See DETROIT, MI (WOW! Internet Cable & Phone)

HARRISON—See MOUNT PLEASANT, MI (Charter Communications)

HARRISVILLE—See OSCODA, MI (Charter Communications)

HARSEN'S ISLAND—See CHESTERFIELD TWP., MI (Comcast Cable)

HART TWP.—See HART, MI (Charter Communications)

▲**HART**—Charter Communications

HARTFORD TWP. (WESTERN PORTION)—See WATERVLIET, MI (Comcast Cable)

HARTFORD—See SOUTH HAVEN, MI (Comcast Cable)

▲**HARTLAND**—Comcast Cable

HARVEY—See MARQUETTE, MI (Charter Communications)

HASLETT—See EAST LANSING, MI (Comcast Cable)

HASTINGS TWP.—See DIMONDALE, MI (Broadstripe)

HASTINGS—See DIMONDALE, MI (Broadstripe)

HATTON TWP.—See MOUNT PLEASANT, MI (Charter Communications)

HAWES TWP.—See OSCODA, MI (Charter Communications)

HAY TWP.—See BILLINGS, MI (Charter Communications)

HAYES TWP. (CLARE COUNTY)—See MOUNT PLEASANT, MI (Charter Communications)

HAYES TWP.—See TRAVERSE CITY, MI (Charter Communications)

▲**HAZEL PARK**—Comcast Cable. Now served by STERLING HEIGHTS, MI [MI0002]

HAZEL PARK—See STERLING HEIGHTS, MI (Comcast Cable)

HAZEL PARK—See DETROIT, MI (WOW! Internet Cable & Phone)

HAZELTON TWP.—See LENNON, MI (Lennon Telephone Co.)

HEATH TWP.—See ALLEGAN, MI (Charter Communications)

HELENA TWP.—See TRAVERSE CITY, MI (Charter Communications)

HEMLOCK—See SAGINAW, MI (Charter Communications)

HENRIETTA TWP.—See DIMONDALE, MI (Broadstripe)

HERMANSVILLE—See IRON MOUNTAIN, MI (Charter Communications)

HERSEY—See REED CITY, MI (Charter Communications)

▲**HESPERIA**—Charter Communications

HIAWATHA TWP.—See ESCANABA, MI (Charter Communications)

▲**HIGGINS LAKE**—Charter Communications

HIGGINS TWP.—See ROSCOMMON, MI (Charter Communications)

▲**HIGHLAND PARK**—Charter Communications

HIGHLAND TWP. (OAKLAND COUNTY)—See WALLED LAKE, MI (Comcast Cable)

HILL TWP.—See HALE, MI (Charter Communications)

HILL TWP.—See ROSE CITY, MI (Charter Communications)

▲**HILLMAN TWP.**—Formerly served by Northwoods Cable Inc. No longer in operation

▲**HILLSDALE**—Comcast Cable

HOLLAND TWP.—See ALLENDALE, MI (Charter Communications)

▲**HOLLAND**—Comcast Cable

HOLLY VILLAGE—See FLINT, MI (Comcast Cable)

HOLTON TWP.—See MUSKEGON, MI (Comcast Cable)

HOME TWP.—See IONIA, MI (Charter Communications)

HOME TWP.—See RIVERDALE, MI (Charter Communications)

HOMER—See DIMONDALE, MI (Broadstripe)

HOMESTEAD TWP.—See TRAVERSE CITY, MI (Charter Communications)

HONOR—See TRAVERSE CITY, MI (Charter Communications)

HOPE TWP. (BARRY COUNTY)—See DELTON, MI (Charter Communications)

▲**HOPE TWP. (MIDLAND COUNTY)**—Charter Communications

HOPKINS—See ALLEGAN, MI (Charter Communications)

HORTON—See DIMONDALE, MI (Broadstripe)

▲**HOUGHTON LAKE**—Charter Communications

▲**HOUGHTON**—Charter Communications

▲**HOWARD CITY**—Charter Communications

HOWARD TWP.—See NILES, MI (Comcast Cable)

HOWELL TWP.—See HARTLAND, MI (Comcast Cable)

HOWELL—See ANN ARBOR, MI (Comcast Cable)

HUBBELL—See HOUGHTON, MI (Charter Communications)

▲**HUDSON**—Comcast Cable

HUDSON—See ADDISON (village), MI (Comcast Cable)

HUDSONVILLE—See ALLENDALE, MI (Charter Communications)

HUMBOLDT TWP.—See CHAMPION TWP., MI (Upper Peninsula Communications)

HUME TWP.—See PIGEON, MI (Comcast Cable)

HUNTINGTON WOODS—See ROYAL OAK, MI (Comcast Cable)

HUNTINGTON WOODS—See DETROIT, MI (WOW! Internet Cable & Phone)

HURLEY—See IRONWOOD, WI (Charter Communications)

HURON TWP. (WAYNE COUNTY)—See MONROE, MI (Charter Communications)

HURON TWP.—See PIGEON, MI (Comcast Cable)

IDA TWP.—See MONROE, MI (Charter Communications)

▲**IMLAY CITY**—Charter Communications. Now served by ALMONT, MI [MI0257]

IMLAY CITY—See ALMONT, MI (Charter Communications)

IMLAY TWP.—See ALMONT, MI (Charter Communications)

INDEPENDENCE TWP.—See PONTIAC, MI (Comcast Cable)

▲**INDIAN RIVER**—Charter Communications

INDIANFIELDS TWP.—See VASSAR, MI (Charter Communications)

INGERSOLL TWP.—See MIDLAND, MI (Charter Communications)

INGHAM TWP.—See DIMONDALE, MI (Broadstripe)

INKSTER—See TAYLOR, MI (Comcast Cable)

INLAND TWP.—See TRAVERSE CITY, MI (Charter Communications)

INVERNESS TWP.—See CHEBOYGAN, MI (Charter Communications)

IONIA TWP.—See IONIA, MI (Charter Communications)

▲**IONIA**—Charter Communications

IRA TWP.—See CHESTERFIELD TWP., MI (Comcast Cable)

▲**IRON MOUNTAIN**—Charter Communications

▲**IRON MOUNTAIN**—Northside T.V. Corp.

IRON RIVER TWP.—See IRON RIVER, MI (Iron River Cable)

▲**IRON RIVER**—Iron River Cable

▲**IRONWOOD**—Charter Communications

IRVING TWP.—See FREEPORT, MI (Lewiston Communications)

ISABELLA TWP.—See MOUNT PLEASANT, MI (Charter Communications)

ISHPEMING—See MARQUETTE, MI (Charter Communications)

ITHACA—See ALMA, MI (Charter Communications)

▲**JACKSON**—Comcast Cable. Now served by JACKSON, MI [MI0039]

▲**JACKSON**—Formerly served by Wireless Cable Systems Inc. No longer in operation

▲**JACKSON**—Comcast Cable

JAMES TWP.—See SAGINAW, MI (Charter Communications)

JAMESTOWN TWP. (PORTIONS)—See ALLENDALE, MI (Charter Communications)

JAMESTOWN TWP. (PORTIONS)—See GRAND RAPIDS, MI (Comcast Cable)

▲**JAMESTOWN TWP.**—Charter Communications. Now served by ALLENDALE, MI [MI0094]

JEFFERSON TWP. (CASS COUNTY)—See CASSOPOLIS, MI (Comcast Cable)

JEFFERSON TWP. (HILLSDALE COUNTY)—See HILLSDALE, MI (Comcast Cable)

JOHNSTOWN TWP.—See DELTON, MI (Charter Communications)

▲**JONES**—Comcast Cable. Now served by THREE RIVERS, MI [MI0050]

JONES—See THREE RIVERS, MI (Comcast Cable)

JONESFIELD TWP.—See SAGINAW, MI (Charter Communications)

JONESVILLE VILLAGE—See HILLSDALE, MI (Comcast Cable)

JOYFIELD TWP.—See TRAVERSE CITY, MI (Charter Communications)

KALAMAZOO TWP. (WESTERN PORTION)—See KALAMAZOO, MI (Charter Communications)

▲**KALAMAZOO**—Charter Communications

KALAMAZOO—See RICHLAND, MI (Comcast Cable)

▲**KALEVA (VILLAGE)**—Pine River Cable

KALEVA—See KALEVA (village), MI (Pine River Cable)

KALKASKA—See TRAVERSE CITY, MI (Charter Communications)

KASSON TWP.—See TRAVERSE CITY, MI (Charter Communications)

KAWKAWLIN TWP. (SOUTHERN PORTION)—See BAY CITY, MI (Charter Communications)

KAWKAWLIN TWP.—See FRASER TWP., MI (Charter Communications)

KEARNEY TWP.—See TRAVERSE CITY, MI (Charter Communications)

KEEGO HARBOR—See WEST BLOOMFIELD TWP., MI (Comcast Cable)

▲**KEELER TWP.**—Sister Lakes Cable TV

KENT CITY—See ROCKFORD, MI (Charter Communications)

KENTWOOD—See GRAND RAPIDS, MI (Comcast Cable)

KIMBALL TWP.—See CHESTERFIELD TWP., MI (Comcast Cable)

▲**KINCHELOE**—Charter Communications

KINDE—See PIGEON, MI (Comcast Cable)

▲**KINDERHOOK TWP.**—Formerly served by CableDirect. No longer in operation

KINDERHOOK TWP.—See COLDWATER, MI (Charter Communications)

KINGSFORD—See IRON MOUNTAIN, MI (Charter Communications)

KINGSLEY—See TRAVERSE CITY, MI (Charter Communications)

KINGSTON (VILLAGE)—See ALMONT, MI (Charter Communications)

▲**KINGSTON TWP.**—Charter Communications. Now served by NORTH BRANCH TWP., MI [MI0337]

KINGSTON TWP.—See ALMONT, MI (Charter Communications)

KINGSTON TWP.—See NORTH BRANCH TWP., MI (Charter Communications)

KINROSS—See KINCHELOE, MI (Charter Communications)

KNIGHT (TOWN)—See IRONWOOD, WI (Charter Communications)

KOCHVILLE TWP. (PORTIONS)—See SAGINAW, MI (Charter Communications)

KOYLTON TWP.—See NORTH BRANCH TWP., MI (Charter Communications)

KRAKOW—See GRAND LAKE, MI (Charter Communications)

L'ANSE—See HOUGHTON, MI (Charter Communications)

LA PORTE COUNTY (PORTIONS)—See ST. JOSEPH TWP., IN (Comcast Cable)

LA SALLE TWP.—See MONROE, MI (Charter Communications)

LAGRANGE COUNTY—See THREE RIVERS, IN (Comcast Cable)

LAGRANGE—See CASSOPOLIS, MI (Comcast Cable)

LAINGSBURG—See DIMONDALE, MI (Broadstripe)

LAKE ANGELUS—See PONTIAC, MI (Comcast Cable)

LAKE ANN (VILLAGE)—See TRAVERSE CITY, MI (Charter Communications)

LAKE ANN—See TRAVERSE CITY, MI (Charter Communications)

LAKE CITY—See TRAVERSE CITY, MI (Charter Communications)

LAKE COUNTY (PORTIONS)—See WOLF LAKE, MI (Pine River Cable)

▲**LAKE GEORGE**—Charter Communications

LAKE LINDEN—See HOUGHTON, MI (Charter Communications)

LAKE ODESSA—See DIMONDALE, MI (Broadstripe)

LAKE ORION—See PONTIAC, MI (Comcast Cable)

LAKE TWP. (BENZIE COUNTY)—See TRAVERSE CITY, MI (Charter Communications)

LAKE TWP. (LAKE COUNTY)—See BIG STAR LAKE, MI (Charter Communications)

LAKE TWP. (ROSCOMMON COUNTY)—See HIGGINS LAKE, MI (Charter Communications)

LAKE TWP.—See TRAVERSE CITY, MI (Charter Communications)

LAKE TWP.—See ST. JOSEPH TWP., MI (Comcast Cable)

LAKETON TWP.—See MUSKEGON, MI (Comcast Cable)

LAKETOWN TWP.—See ALLENDALE, MI (Charter Communications)

▲**LAKEVIEW**—Charter Communications

LAKEVILLE—See OXFORD, MI (Charter Communications)

LAKEWOOD (VILLAGE)—See WHITEHALL, MI (Charter Communications)

LANSING TWP.—See LANSING, MI (Comcast Cable)

▲**LANSING**—Formerly served by Sprint Corp. No longer in operation

▲**LANSING**—Comcast Cable

LAPEER TWP.—See LAPEER, MI (Charter Communications)

▲ **LAPEER**—Charter Communications

LARKIN TWP.—See MIDLAND, MI (Charter Communications)

LATHRUP VILLAGE—See SOUTHFIELD, MI (Comcast Cable)

LAURIUM—See HOUGHTON, MI (Charter Communications)

LAWRENCE—See LAWTON, MI (Comcast Cable)

LAWRENCE—See SOUTH HAVEN, MI (Comcast Cable)

LAWTON (VILLAGE)—See LAWTON, MI (Comcast Cable)

▲ **LAWTON**—Comcast Cable

▲ **LE ROY (VILLAGE)**—Pine River Cable

LEE TWP. (ALLEGAN COUNTY)—See BLOOMINGDALE, MI (Bloomingdale Communications Inc.)

LEE TWP.—See MIDLAND, MI (Charter Communications)

LEELANAU TWP.—See TRAVERSE CITY, MI (Charter Communications)

LEIGHTON TWP.—See MIDDLEVILLE/CALEDONIA, MI (Charter Communications)

LELAND TWP.—See TRAVERSE CITY, MI (Charter Communications)

LENNON—See DURAND, MI (Charter Communications)

▲ **LENNON**—Lennon Telephone Co.

LENOX TWP.—See CHESTERFIELD TWP., MI (Comcast Cable)

LEONARD—See OXFORD, MI (Charter Communications)

LEONI TWP.—See JACKSON, MI (Comcast Cable)

LESLIE TWP.—See DIMONDALE, MI (Broadstripe)

▲ **LEVERING**—Charter Communications

▲ **LEWISTON**—Lewiston Communications

▲ **LEXINGTON**—Comcast Cable

LIBERTY TWP. (JACKSON COUNTY)—See JACKSON, MI (Comcast Cable)

LIBERTY TWP.—See DIMONDALE, MI (Broadstripe)

LIBERTY TWP.—See TRAVERSE CITY, MI (Charter Communications)

▲ **LILLEY TWP.**—Charter Communications

LIMA TWP.—See ANN ARBOR, MI (Comcast Cable)

LINCOLN PARK—See TAYLOR, MI (Comcast Cable)

LINCOLN PARK—See DETROIT, MI (WOW! Internet Cable & Phone)

LINCOLN TWP. (BERRIEN COUNTY)—See ST. JOSEPH TWP., MI (Comcast Cable)

LINCOLN TWP. (CLARE COUNTY)—See LAKE GEORGE, MI (Charter Communications)

LINCOLN TWP.—See BAY CITY, MI (Charter Communications)

LINCOLN—See OSCODA, MI (Charter Communications)

LINDEN—See FENTON, MI (Charter Communications)

LINWOOD—See FRASER TWP., MI (Charter Communications)

LITCHFIELD—See COLDWATER, MI (Charter Communications)

LITTLE LAKE—See MARQUETTE, MI (Charter Communications)

LITTLEFIELD TWP.—See INDIAN RIVER, MI (Charter Communications)

LITTLEFIELD TWP.—See TRAVERSE CITY, MI (Charter Communications)

▲ **LIVINGSTON COUNTY**—Charter Communications

LIVINGSTON TWP.—See TRAVERSE CITY, MI (Charter Communications)

▲ **LIVONIA**—Bright House Networks

LOCKPORT TWP.—See THREE RIVERS, MI (Comcast Cable)

LODI TWP.—See ANN ARBOR, MI (Comcast Cable)

LOGAN TWP.—See SKIDWAY LAKE, MI (Charter Communications)

LONDON TWP.—See MONROE, MI (Charter Communications)

LONDON TWP.—See TAYLOR, MI (Comcast Cable)

LONG LAKE TWP.—See TRAVERSE CITY, MI (Charter Communications)

LONG LAKE—See OSCODA, MI (Charter Communications)

LONG RAPIDS TWP.—See ALPENA, MI (Charter Communications)

LOWELL TWP.—See LOWELL, MI (Comcast Cable)

▲ **LOWELL**—Comcast Cable

▲ **LUDINGTON**—Charter Communications

LUNA PIER—See MONROE, MI (Charter Communications)

LUPTON—See ROSE CITY, MI (Charter Communications)

LUTHER (VILLAGE)—See LE ROY (village), MI (Pine River Cable)

▲ **LUZERNE**—Pine River Cable

LYON TWP. (OAKLAND COUNTY)—See WALLED LAKE, MI (Comcast Cable)

LYON TWP. (ROSCOMMON COUNTY)—See HIGGINS LAKE, MI (Charter Communications)

LYONS TWP.—See DIMONDALE, MI (Broadstripe)

LYONS TWP.—See IONIA, MI (Charter Communications)

LYONS VILLAGE—See IONIA, MI (Charter Communications)

▲ **MACKINAC ISLAND**—Charter Communications

▲ **MACKINAW CITY**—Charter Communications

MACKINAW TWP.—See MACKINAW CITY, MI (Charter Communications)

MACOMB TWP.—See STERLING HEIGHTS, MI (Comcast Cable)

▲ **MADISON HEIGHTS**—Comcast Cable. Now served by STERLING HEIGHTS, MI [MI0002]

MADISON HEIGHTS—See STERLING HEIGHTS, MI (Comcast Cable)

MADISON HEIGHTS—See DETROIT, MI (WOW! Internet Cable & Phone)

MADISON TWP.—See ADDISON (village), MI (Comcast Cable)

MANCELONA TWP.—See TRAVERSE CITY, MI (Charter Communications)

▲ **MANCELONA**—Charter Communications. Now served by TRAVERSE CITY, MI [MI0026]

MANCELONA—See TRAVERSE CITY, MI (Charter Communications)

MANCHESTER—See ANN ARBOR, MI (Comcast Cable)

MANISTEE TWP.—See TRAVERSE CITY, MI (Charter Communications)

▲ **MANISTEE**—Charter Communications. Now served by TRAVERSE CITY, MI [MI0026]

MANISTEE—See TRAVERSE CITY, MI (Charter Communications)

MANISTIQUE—See ESCANABA, MI (Charter Communications)

MANITOU BEACH—See ADDISON (village), MI (Comcast Cable)

MANLIUS TWP.—See ALLEGAN, MI (Charter Communications)

MANLIUS TWP.—See SAUGATUCK, MI (Comcast Cable)

▲ **MANTON**—Charter Communications. Now served by TRAVERSE CITY, MI [MI0026]

MANTON—See TRAVERSE CITY, MI (Charter Communications)

MAPLE GROVE TWP. (MANISTEE COUNTY)—See KALEVA (village), MI (Pine River Cable)

MAPLE GROVE TWP.—See SAGINAW, MI (Charter Communications)

▲ **MAPLE RAPIDS**—Pine River Cable

MAPLE RIDGE TWP. (ALPENA COUNTY)—See ALPENA, MI (Charter Communications)

MAPLE VALLEY TWP. (MONTCALM COUNTY)—See HOWARD CITY, MI (Charter Communications)

MARATHON TWP.—See LAPEER, MI (Charter Communications)

MARATHON—See NORTH BRANCH TWP., MI (Charter Communications)

▲ **MARCELLUS**—Mediacom

MARENGO TWP.—See DIMONDALE, MI (Broadstripe)

▲ **MARENISCO TWP.**—Upper Peninsula Communications

MARINE CITY—See CHESTERFIELD TWP., MI (Comcast Cable)

MARION TWP. (LIVINGSTON COUNTY)—See LIVINGSTON COUNTY, MI (Charter Communications)

MARION TWP. (OSCEOLA COUNTY)—See MARION, MI (Pine River Cable)

MARION TWP.—See TRAVERSE CITY, MI (Charter Communications)

▲ **MARION**—Pine River Cable

MARKEY TWP.—See HOUGHTON LAKE, MI (Charter Communications)

MARLETTE TWP.—See BROWN CITY, MI (Comcast Cable)

MARLETTE—See BROWN CITY, MI (Comcast Cable)

▲ **MARQUETTE**—Charter Communications

MARSHALL (PORTIONS)—See BATTLE CREEK, MI (Comcast Cable)

MARSHALL—See DIMONDALE, MI (Broadstripe)

MARTIN (VILLAGE)—See ALLEGAN, MI (Charter Communications)

MARTIN TWP.—See ALLEGAN, MI (Charter Communications)

MARTIN TWP.—See MIDDLEVILLE/CALEDONIA, MI (Charter Communications)

MARTINY TWP. (SOUTHERN PORTION)—See CANADIAN LAKES, MI (Charter Communications)

MARTINY TWP.—See MECOSTA, MI (Charter Communications)

MARYSVILLE—See CHESTERFIELD TWP., MI (Comcast Cable)

MASON TWP. (ARENAC COUNTY)—See OMER, MI (Charter Communications)

MASON—See DIMONDALE, MI (Broadstripe)

▲ **MASON**—West Shore Cable TV Inc.

MASONVILLE TWP. (SOUTHERN PORTION)—See ESCANABA, MI (Charter Communications)

▲ **MASS CITY**—Charter Communications. Now served by IRONWOOD, MI [MI0064]

MASS CITY—See IRONWOOD, MI (Charter Communications)

▲ **MATTAWAN**—Mediacom

MAYBEE—See MONROE, MI (Charter Communications)

MAYFIELD TWP. (GRAND TRAVERSE COUNTY)—See TRAVERSE CITY, MI (Charter Communications)

MAYFIELD TWP. (LAPEER COUNTY)—See LAPEER, MI (Charter Communications)

MAYFIELD—See TRAVERSE CITY, MI (Charter Communications)

▲**MAYVILLE**—Charter Communications. Now served by NORTH BRANCH TWP., MI [MI0337]

MAYVILLE—See NORTH BRANCH TWP., MI (Charter Communications)

▲**MCBAIN**—Pine River Cable

MCBRIDES VILLAGE—See IONIA, MI (Charter Communications)

MCKINLEY TWP.—See PELLSTON, MI (Charter Communications)

MCKINLEY TWP.—See PIGEON, MI (Comcast Cable)

MCMILLAN TWP. (LUCE COUNTY)—See NEWBERRY, MI (Charter Communications)

MEADE TWP.—See PIGEON, MI (Comcast Cable)

▲**MEARS**—Lewiston Communications

▲**MECOSTA**—Charter Communications

▲**MELLEN TWP.**—Packerland Broadband

MELROSE TWP.—See TRAVERSE CITY, MI (Charter Communications)

MELVINDALE—See TAYLOR, MI (Comcast Cable)

MELVINDALE—See DETROIT, MI (WOW! Internet Cable & Phone)

MEMPHIS—See CHESTERFIELD TWP., MI (Comcast Cable)

▲**MENDON (VILLAGE)**—Mediacom

MENDON TWP.—See THREE RIVERS, MI (Comcast Cable)

MENTOR TWP.—See MIO, MI (Charter Communications)

MERIDIAN TWP.—See EAST LANSING, MI (Comcast Cable)

MERRILL—See SAGINAW, MI (Charter Communications)

▲**MERRITT TWP.**—Formerly served by Cablevision Systems Corp. No longer in operation

▲**MESICK**—Pine River Cable

METAMORA TWP.—See OXFORD, MI (Charter Communications)

METAMORA—See OXFORD, MI (Charter Communications)

METRO TOWERS—See CHESTERFIELD TWP., MI (Comcast Cable)

MEYER TWP.—See IRON MOUNTAIN, MI (Charter Communications)

▲**MICHIGAMME**—Upper Peninsula Communications

MIDDLEBURY TWP.—See ELSIE, MI (Charter Communications)

MIDDLETON—See PERRINTON, MI (Pine River Cable)

▲**MIDDLEVILLE/CALEDONIA**—Charter Communications

MIDLAND TWP.—See MIDLAND, MI (Charter Communications)

▲**MIDLAND**—Charter Communications

▲**MIKADO TWP.**—Pine River Cable

MILFORD TWP.—See WALLED LAKE, MI (Comcast Cable)

MILFORD—See WALLED LAKE, MI (Comcast Cable)

MILLEN TWP.—See BARTON CITY, MI (Pine River Cable)

MILLINGTON TWP.—See VASSAR, MI (Charter Communications)

MILLINGTON—See VASSAR, MI (Charter Communications)

MILLS TWP. (MIDLAND COUNTY)—See HOPE TWP. (Midland County), MI (Charter Communications)

MILLS TWP. (OGEMAW COUNTY)—See SKIDWAY LAKE, MI (Charter Communications)

MILTON TWP. (ANTRIM COUNTY)—See TRAVERSE CITY, MI (Charter Communications)

MILTON TWP. (CASS COUNTY)—See NILES, MI (Comcast Cable)

▲**MINDEN CITY**—Formerly served by Cablevision Systems Corp. No longer in operation

▲**MIO**—Charter Communications

MISSAUKEE COUNTY (PORTIONS)—See TRAVERSE CITY, MI (Charter Communications)

▲**MISSAUKEE COUNTY (UNINCORPORATED AREAS)**—Pine River Cable

MOLINE—See MIDDLEVILLE/CALEDONIA, MI (Charter Communications)

MOLTKE TWP.—See ROGERS CITY, MI (Charter Communications)

MONITOR TWP.—See BAY CITY, MI (Charter Communications)

MONROE TWP. (MONROE COUNTY)—See MONROE, MI (Charter Communications)

MONROE TWP.—See TAYLOR, MI (Comcast Cable)

▲**MONROE**—Comcast Cable. Now served by TAYLOR, MI [MI0008]

▲**MONROE**—Charter Communications

MONROE—See TAYLOR, MI (Comcast Cable)

MONTAGUE—See WHITEHALL, MI (Charter Communications)

MONTCALM TWP. (NORTHERN PORTION)—See IONIA, MI (Charter Communications)

MONTCALM TWP.—See GREENVILLE, MI (Charter Communications)

MONTMORENCY COUNTY—See LEWISTON, MI (Lewiston Communications)

MONTREAL—See IRONWOOD, WI (Charter Communications)

MONTROSE TWP.—See MONTROSE, MI (Charter Communications)

▲**MONTROSE**—Charter Communications

MORAN—See SAULT STE. MARIE, MI (Charter Communications)

MORENCI—See PETERSBURG, MI (D & P Cable)

MORLEY—See HOWARD CITY, MI (Charter Communications)

MORRICE—See DIMONDALE, MI (Broadstripe)

MORTON TWP.—See CANADIAN LAKES, MI (Charter Communications)

MOTTVILLE TWP.—See THREE RIVERS, MI (Comcast Cable)

MOUNT CLEMENS—See STERLING HEIGHTS, MI (Comcast Cable)

MOUNT CLEMENS—See DETROIT, MI (WOW! Internet Cable & Phone)

MOUNT HALEY TWP.—See MIDLAND, MI (Charter Communications)

MOUNT MORRIS TWP.—See FLINT, MI (Comcast Cable)

MOUNT MORRIS—See FLINT, MI (Comcast Cable)

▲**MOUNT PLEASANT**—Charter Communications

MUIR—See IONIA, MI (Charter Communications)

MULLET LAKE—See CHEBOYGAN, MI (Charter Communications)

▲**MULLETT TWP.**—Formerly served by Northwoods Cable Inc. No longer in operation

MULLIKEN—See DIMONDALE, MI (Broadstripe)

MUNDY TWP.—See FLINT, MI (Comcast Cable)

MUNISING—See MARQUETTE, MI (Charter Communications)

MUSKEGON HEIGHTS—See MUSKEGON, MI (Comcast Cable)

▲**MUSKEGON**—Comcast Cable

NADEAU—See POWERS, MI (Upper Peninsula Communications)

NAPOLEON TWP.—See JACKSON, MI (Comcast Cable)

▲**NASHVILLE**—Pine River Cable

NAUBINWAY—See ENGADINE, MI (Upper Peninsula Communications)

NEGAUNEE—See MARQUETTE, MI (Charter Communications)

▲**NEGAUNEE**—City of Negaunee Cable TV

NELSON TWP. (PORTIONS)—See HOWARD CITY, MI (Charter Communications)

NELSON TWP. (PORTIONS)—See ROCKFORD, MI (Charter Communications)

NEW BALTIMORE—See CHESTERFIELD TWP., MI (Comcast Cable)

NEW CARLISLE—See ST. JOSEPH TWP., IN (Comcast Cable)

NEW ERA (VILLAGE)—See WHITEHALL, MI (Charter Communications)

NEW HAVEN (VILLAGE)—See CHESTERFIELD TWP., MI (Comcast Cable)

NEW HAVEN—See CHESTERFIELD TWP., MI (Comcast Cable)

NEW LOTHROP—See LENNON, MI (Lennon Telephone Co.)

NEWARK TWP.—See ALMA, MI (Charter Communications)

NEWAYGO COUNTY—See MUSKEGON, MI (Comcast Cable)

NEWAYGO—See GRANT, MI (Charter Communications)

NEWBERG TWP.—See THREE RIVERS, MI (Comcast Cable)

▲**NEWBERRY**—Charter Communications

NEWFIELD TWP.—See HESPERIA, MI (Charter Communications)

NEWTON TWP.—See BATTLE CREEK, MI (Comcast Cable)

NILES TWP.—See NILES, MI (Comcast Cable)

▲**NILES**—Comcast Cable

NORMAN TWP.—See WELLSTON, MI (Pine River Cable)

NORTH ADAMS VILLAGE—See HILLSDALE, MI (Comcast Cable)

NORTH BRANCH (VILLAGE)—See ALMONT, MI (Charter Communications)

▲**NORTH BRANCH TWP.**—Charter Communications

NORTH MUSKEGON—See MUSKEGON, MI (Comcast Cable)

NORTH PLAINS TWP.—See DIMONDALE, MI (Broadstripe)

NORTH STAR TWP.—See ALMA, MI (Charter Communications)

NORTHFIELD TWP.—See LIVINGSTON COUNTY, MI (Charter Communications)

NORTHPORT—See TRAVERSE CITY, MI (Charter Communications)

NORTHVILLE TWP.—See DETROIT, MI (WOW! Internet Cable & Phone)

NORTHVILLE—See PLYMOUTH TWP., MI (Comcast Cable)

NORTHVILLE—See DETROIT, MI (WOW! Internet Cable & Phone)

NORTON SHORES—See MUSKEGON, MI (Comcast Cable)

NORVELL TWP.—See JACKSON, MI (Comcast Cable)

NORWAY TWP.—See NORWAY, MI (City of Norway CATV)

▲**NORWAY**—City of Norway CATV

NORWOOD—See TRAVERSE CITY, MI (Charter Communications)

NOTTAWA TWP. (ISABELLA COUNTY)—See WEIDMAN, MI (Charter Communications)

NOTTAWA TWP. (ST. JOSEPH COUNTY)—See THREE RIVERS, MI (Comcast Cable)

NOVESTA TWP.—See NORTH BRANCH TWP., MI (Charter Communications)

NOVI—See LIVONIA, MI (Bright House Networks)

OAK PARK—See SOUTHFIELD, MI (Comcast Cable)

OAKLAND TWP.—See ROYAL OAK, MI (Comcast Cable)

OAKLEY (VILLAGE)—See CHESANING, MI (Charter Communications)

OCEOLA TWP.—See ANN ARBOR, MI (Comcast Cable)

OCEOLA TWP.—See HARTLAND, MI (Comcast Cable)

ODEN—See TRAVERSE CITY, MI (Charter Communications)

ODESSA TWP.—See DIMONDALE, MI (Broadstripe)

OGEMAW COUNTY (UNINCORPORATED AREAS)—See HALE, MI (Charter Communications)

OGEMAW TWP.—See WEST BRANCH, MI (Pine River Cable)

OKEMOS—See EAST LANSING, MI (Comcast Cable)

▲ **OLIVE TWP. (Ottawa County)**—Charter Communications. Now served by ALLENDALE, MI [MI0094]

OLIVE TWP. (OTTAWA COUNTY)—See ALLENDALE, MI (Charter Communications)

OLIVER TWP.—See PIGEON, MI (Comcast Cable)

OLIVET—See DIMONDALE, MI (Broadstripe)

▲ **OMER**—Charter Communications

▲ **ONAWAY**—Formerly served by Northwoods Cable Inc. No longer in operation

ONEIDA CHARTER TWP.—See DIMONDALE, MI (Broadstripe)

ONEIDA TWP.—See LANSING, MI (Comcast Cable)

ONEKAMA (VILLAGE)—See TRAVERSE CITY, MI (Charter Communications)

ONONDAGA TWP.—See DIMONDALE, MI (Broadstripe)

ONSTED (VILLAGE)—See JACKSON, MI (Comcast Cable)

▲ **ONTONAGON**—Charter Communications. Now served by IRONWOOD, MI [MI0064]

ONTONAGON—See IRONWOOD, MI (Charter Communications)

ORANGE TWP. (KALKASKA COUNTY)—See BOARDMAN TWP. (southern portion), MI (Pine River Cable)

ORANGEVILLE TWP.—See MIDDLEVILLE/CALEDONIA, MI (Charter Communications)

ORCHARD LAKE—See WEST BLOOMFIELD TWP., MI (Comcast Cable)

OREGON TWP.—See DAVISON, MI (Charter Communications)

OREGON TWP.—See LAPEER, MI (Charter Communications)

ORION TWP.—See PONTIAC, MI (Comcast Cable)

ORLEANS TWP. (PORTIONS)—See GREENVILLE, MI (Charter Communications)

ORLEANS TWP. (PORTIONS)—See IONIA, MI (Charter Communications)

ORONOKO TWP.—See ST. JOSEPH TWP., MI (Comcast Cable)

ORTONVILLE—See OXFORD, MI (Charter Communications)

OSCEOLA TWP. (HOUGHTON COUNTY)—See HOUGHTON, MI (Charter Communications)

OSCEOLA TWP. (OSCEOLA COUNTY)—See EVART, MI (Charter Communications)

OSCODA TWP.—See OSCODA, MI (Charter Communications)

▲ **OSCODA**—Charter Communications

OSHTEMO TWP.—See KALAMAZOO, MI (Charter Communications)

▲ **OSHTEMO TWP.**—Comcast Cable

OSSINEKE TWP.—See ALPENA, MI (Charter Communications)

OTISCO TWP.—See GREENVILLE, MI (Charter Communications)

OTISVILLE—See DAVISON, MI (Charter Communications)

OTSEGO CITY—See ALLEGAN, MI (Charter Communications)

OTTER LAKE—See NORTH BRANCH TWP., MI (Charter Communications)

OVERISEL TWP.—See ALLEGAN, MI (Charter Communications)

OVID TWP.—See COLDWATER, MI (Charter Communications)

OVID VILLAGE—See ELSIE, MI (Charter Communications)

OWENDALE—See PIGEON, MI (Comcast Cable)

OWOSSO TWP.—See OWOSSO, MI (Charter Communications)

▲ **OWOSSO**—Charter Communications

OXFORD (VILLAGE)—See OXFORD, MI (Charter Communications)

OXFORD TWP.—See OXFORD, MI (Charter Communications)

▲ **OXFORD**—Charter Communications

PALMER—See MARQUETTE, MI (Charter Communications)

PALMYRA TWP.—See MONROE, MI (Charter Communications)

PALMYRA TWP.—See ADDISON (village), MI (Comcast Cable)

PARADISE TWP.—See TRAVERSE CITY, MI (Charter Communications)

PARCHMENT—See KALAMAZOO, MI (Charter Communications)

PARIS TWP.—See BIG RAPIDS, MI (Charter Communications)

PARK TWP. (OTTAWA COUNTY)—See ALLENDALE, MI (Charter Communications)

PARMA TWP.—See SPRINGPORT TWP., MI (Springport Telephone Co.)

PARMA—See DIMONDALE, MI (Broadstripe)

PAVILION TWP. (PORTIONS)—See CLIMAX TWP., MI (Climax Telephone Co.)

PAVILION TWP.—See KALAMAZOO, MI (Charter Communications)

PAVILION TWP.—See THREE RIVERS, MI (Comcast Cable)

PAW PAW (VILLAGE)—See LAWTON, MI (Comcast Cable)

PECK—See YALE, MI (Comcast Cable)

▲ **PELLSTON**—Charter Communications

PENCE—See IRONWOOD, WI (Charter Communications)

PENINSULA TWP.—See TRAVERSE CITY, MI (Charter Communications)

PENN TWP.—See CASSOPOLIS, MI (Comcast Cable)

PENNFIELD TWP.—See BATTLE CREEK, MI (Comcast Cable)

PENTLAND TWP.—See NEWBERRY, MI (Charter Communications)

▲ **PENTWATER**—Charter Communications

PERE MARQUETTE TWP.—See LUDINGTON, MI (Charter Communications)

▲ **PERRINTON**—Pine River Cable

PERRY—See DIMONDALE, MI (Broadstripe)

PETERSBURG—See MONROE, MI (Charter Communications)

▲ **PETERSBURG**—D & P Cable

▲ **PETOSKEY**—Charter Communications. Now served by TRAVERSE CITY, MI [MI0026]

PETOSKEY—See TRAVERSE CITY, MI (Charter Communications)

PEWAMO—See DIMONDALE, MI (Broadstripe)

▲ **PICKFORD TWP.**—Sunrise Communications LLC

PIERSON (VILLAGE)—See HOWARD CITY, MI (Charter Communications)

▲ **PIGEON**—Comcast Cable

PINCKNEY—See LIVINGSTON COUNTY, MI (Charter Communications)

PINCONNING TWP.—See BAY CITY, MI (Charter Communications)

PINCONNING—See BAY CITY, MI (Charter Communications)

PINE GROVE TWP.—See ALLEGAN, MI (Charter Communications)

PINE RIVER TWP.—See ALMA, MI (Charter Communications)

PINE TWP.—See HOWARD CITY, MI (Charter Communications)

PINE TWP.—See IONIA, MI (Charter Communications)

PINEWOOD CREEK—See CHESTERFIELD TWP., MI (Comcast Cable)

PIPESTONE TWP.—See WATERVLIET, MI (Comcast Cable)

PITTSFIELD TWP.—See ANN ARBOR, MI (Comcast Cable)

PITTSFORD TWP.—See HILLSDALE, MI (Comcast Cable)

PLAINFIELD TWP. (IOSCO COUNTY)—See OSCODA, MI (Charter Communications)

PLAINFIELD TWP. (KENT COUNTY) (PORTIONS)—See GRAND RAPIDS, MI (Comcast Cable)

PLAINFIELD TWP. (KENT COUNTY)—See ROCKFORD, MI (Charter Communications)

PLAINWELL CITY—See ALLEGAN, MI (Charter Communications)

PLEASANT LAKE—See DIMONDALE, MI (Broadstripe)

PLEASANT RIDGE—See ROYAL OAK, MI (Comcast Cable)

PLEASANT RIDGE—See DETROIT, MI (WOW! Internet Cable & Phone)

PLEASANT VIEW TWP.—See TRAVERSE CITY, MI (Charter Communications)

PLEASANTON TWP.—See TRAVERSE CITY, MI (Charter Communications)

▲ **PLYMOUTH TWP.**—Comcast Cable

PLYMOUTH TWP.—See DETROIT, MI (WOW! Internet Cable & Phone)

PLYMOUTH—See DETROIT, MI (WOW! Internet Cable & Phone)

POINTE AUX BARQUES TWP.—See PIGEON, MI (Comcast Cable)

POKAGON TWP. (PORTIONS)—See CASSOPOLIS, MI (Comcast Cable)

POLKTON TWP.—See ALLENDALE, MI (Charter Communications)

▲ **PONTIAC**—Comcast Cable

▲ **PORT AUSTIN**—Comcast Cable. Now served by PIGEON, MI [MI0375]

PORT AUSTIN—See PIGEON, MI (Comcast Cable)

▲ **PORT HOPE**—Comcast Cable. Now served by PIGEON, MI [MI0375]

PORT HOPE—See PIGEON, MI (Comcast Cable)

PORT HURON TWP.—See CHESTERFIELD TWP., MI (Comcast Cable)

PORT HURON—See CHESTERFIELD TWP., MI (Comcast Cable)

PORT SANILAC—See DECKERVILLE, MI (Comcast Cable)

PORT SHELDON TWP.—See ALLENDALE, MI (Charter Communications)

PORTAGE (NORTHEASTERN PORTION)—See KALAMAZOO, MI (Charter Communications)

PORTAGE (PORTIONS)—See OSHTEMO TWP., MI (Comcast Cable)

PORTAGE (SOUTHERN PORTION)—See THREE RIVERS, MI (Comcast Cable)

▲**PORTAGE TWP.**—Upper Peninsula Communications

PORTER TWP. (VAN BUREN COUNTY)—See LAWTON, MI (Comcast Cable)

PORTER TWP.—See THREE RIVERS, MI (Comcast Cable)

PORTLAND—See DIMONDALE, MI (Broadstripe)

PORTSMOUTH TWP.—See BAY CITY, MI (Charter Communications)

▲**POSEN**—Sunrise Communications LLC

POTTERVILLE—See DIMONDALE, MI (Broadstripe)

▲**POWERS**—Upper Peninsula Communications

PRAIRIE RONDE TWP.—See THREE RIVERS, MI (Comcast Cable)

PRAIRIE RONDE—See THREE RIVERS, MI (Comcast Cable)

PRAIRIEVILLE TWP. (PORTIONS)—See DELTON, MI (Charter Communications)

PRAIRIEVILLE TWP. (PORTIONS)—See RICHLAND, MI (Comcast Cable)

▲**PRESCOTT (village)**—Formerly served by Charter Communications. No longer in operation

PRESQUE ISLE TWP.—See GRAND LAKE, MI (Charter Communications)

PRINCETON—See MARQUETTE, MI (Charter Communications)

PULASKI TWP.—See DIMONDALE, MI (Broadstripe)

PULASKI TWP.—See POSEN, MI (Sunrise Communications LLC)

PULAWSKI TWP.—See GRAND LAKE, MI (Charter Communications)

PUTNAM TWP.—See LIVINGSTON COUNTY, MI (Charter Communications)

QUAIL RUN—See CHESTERFIELD TWP., MI (Comcast Cable)

QUINCY—See COLDWATER, MI (Charter Communications)

RAISIN TWP.—See ADDISON (village), MI (Comcast Cable)

RAISINVILLE TWP.—See MONROE, MI (Charter Communications)

RAISINVILLE TWP.—See TAYLOR, MI (Comcast Cable)

RAPID RIVER TWP.—See TRAVERSE CITY, MI (Charter Communications)

RAPID RIVER—See ESCANABA, MI (Charter Communications)

RAVENNA—See CHESTER TWP. (Ottawa County), MI (Charter Communications)

RAY TWP.—See CHESTERFIELD TWP., MI (Comcast Cable)

RAY TWP.—See STERLING HEIGHTS, MI (Comcast Cable)

READING—See COLDWATER, MI (Charter Communications)

▲**REDFORD**—Bright House Networks. Now served by LIVONIA, MI [MI0019]

REDFORD—See LIVONIA, MI (Bright House Networks)

▲**REED CITY**—Charter Communications

REEDER TWP.—See TRAVERSE CITY, MI (Charter Communications)

▲**REESE**—Charter Communications. Now served by SAGINAW, MI [MI0013]

REESE—See SAGINAW, MI (Charter Communications)

▲**REMUS**—Charter Communications

▲**REPUBLIC TWP.**—Cable America Corp.

RESORT TWP.—See TRAVERSE CITY, MI (Charter Communications)

REYNOLDS TWP.—See HOWARD CITY, MI (Charter Communications)

RICHFIELD TWP. (GENESEE COUNTY)—See DAVISON, MI (Charter Communications)

RICHFIELD TWP. (ROSCOMMON COUNTY)—See ST. HELEN, MI (Charter Communications)

RICHLAND TWP. (MONTCALM COUNTY)—See RIVERDALE, MI (Charter Communications)

▲**RICHLAND TWP.**—Comcast Cable. Now served by RICHLAND (formerly Kalamazoo), MI [MI0316]

RICHLAND TWP.—See SAGINAW, MI (Charter Communications)

RICHLAND TWP.—See RICHLAND, MI (Comcast Cable)

▲**RICHLAND**—Comcast Cable

RICHMOND TWP. (MACOMB COUNTY)—See CHESTERFIELD TWP., MI (Comcast Cable)

RICHMOND TWP. (OSCEOLA COUNTY)—See REED CITY, MI (Charter Communications)

RICHMOND—See CHESTERFIELD TWP., MI (Comcast Cable)

RIDGEWAY TWP.—See ADDISON (village), MI (Comcast Cable)

RIGA TWP.—See MONROE, MI (Charter Communications)

RILEY TWP.—See CHESTERFIELD TWP., MI (Comcast Cable)

RIPLEY—See HOUGHTON, MI (Charter Communications)

RIVER ROUGE—See TAYLOR, MI (Comcast Cable)

▲**RIVERDALE**—Charter Communications

RIVERSIDE TWP.—See MCBAIN, MI (Pine River Cable)

RIVERVIEW—See TAYLOR, MI (Comcast Cable)

RIVERVIEW—See DETROIT, MI (WOW! Internet Cable & Phone)

▲**RIVES JUNCTION**—Formerly served by Cablevision Systems Corp. No longer in operation

RIVES TWP.—See JACKSON, MI (Comcast Cable)

ROBINSON TWP.—See ALLENDALE, MI (Charter Communications)

ROCHESTER HILLS—See ROYAL OAK, MI (Comcast Cable)

ROCHESTER HILLS—See DETROIT, MI (WOW! Internet Cable & Phone)

ROCHESTER—See ROYAL OAK, MI (Comcast Cable)

ROCHESTER—See DETROIT, MI (WOW! Internet Cable & Phone)

ROCK RIVER TWP.—See MARQUETTE, MI (Charter Communications)

▲**ROCKFORD**—Charter Communications

ROCKLAND TWP.—See IRONWOOD, MI (Charter Communications)

ROCKWOOD—See TAYLOR, MI (Comcast Cable)

▲**ROGERS CITY**—Charter Communications

ROGERS TWP.—See ROGERS CITY, MI (Charter Communications)

ROLLIN—See ADDISON (village), MI (Comcast Cable)

ROMEO—See CHESTERFIELD TWP., MI (Comcast Cable)

▲**ROMULUS**—Comcast Cable. Now served by PLYMOUTH TWP., MI [MI0012]

ROMULUS—See PLYMOUTH TWP., MI (Comcast Cable)

RONALD TWP.—See IONIA, MI (Charter Communications)

ROOSEVELT PARK—See MUSKEGON, MI (Comcast Cable)

ROSCOMMON (VILLAGE)—See ROSCOMMON, MI (Charter Communications)

▲**ROSCOMMON**—Charter Communications

▲**ROSE CITY**—Charter Communications

ROSE TWP. (OAKLAND COUNTY)—See PONTIAC, MI (Comcast Cable)

ROSE TWP. (OGEMAW COUNTY)—See ROSE CITY, MI (Charter Communications)

▲**ROSEBUSH**—Charter Communications. Now served by MOUNT PLEASANT, MI [MI0069]

ROSEBUSH—See MOUNT PLEASANT, MI (Charter Communications)

▲**ROSEVILLE**—Comcast Cable. Now served by STERLING HEIGHTS, MI [MI0002]

ROSEVILLE—See STERLING HEIGHTS, MI (Comcast Cable)

ROSEVILLE—See DETROIT, MI (WOW! Internet Cable & Phone)

ROSS TWP.—See RICHLAND, MI (Comcast Cable)

ROTHBURY—See WHITEHALL, MI (Charter Communications)

ROXANNE TWP.—See DIMONDALE, MI (Broadstripe)

ROYAL OAK TWP.—See SOUTHFIELD, MI (Comcast Cable)

▲**ROYAL OAK**—Comcast Cable

ROYAL OAK—See DETROIT, MI (WOW! Internet Cable & Phone)

ROYALTON TWP.—See ST. JOSEPH TWP., MI (Comcast Cable)

RUBICON TWP.—See PIGEON, MI (Comcast Cable)

RUDYARD TWP.—See KINCHELOE, MI (Charter Communications)

RUSH TWP.—See OWOSSO, MI (Charter Communications)

▲**RUTLAND TWP.**—Charter Communications

▲**SAGE TWP.**—Charter Communications

SAGINAW TWP.—See SAGINAW, MI (Charter Communications)

▲**SAGINAW**—Charter Communications

SAGOLA TWP.—See IRON MOUNTAIN, MI (Charter Communications)

SALEM TWP. (WASHTENAW COUNTY)—See LIVINGSTON COUNTY, MI (Charter Communications)

▲**SALINE**—Comcast Cable. Now served by ANN ARBOR, MI [MI0006]

SALINE—See ANN ARBOR, MI (Comcast Cable)

SANBORN TWP.—See ALPENA, MI (Charter Communications)

SAND BEACH TWP.—See PIGEON, MI (Comcast Cable)

SAND LAKE—See HOWARD CITY, MI (Charter Communications)

SANDS TWP.—See MARQUETTE, MI (Charter Communications)

SANDSTONE TWP. (PORTIONS)—See JACKSON, MI (Comcast Cable)

▲ **SANDUSKY**—Comcast Cable

▲ **SANFORD**—Formerly served by Charter Communications. No longer in operation

SANILAC TWP.—See DECKERVILLE, MI (Comcast Cable)

SARANAC—See DIMONDALE, MI (Broadstripe)

▲ **SAUGATUCK**—Comcast Cable

▲ **SAULT STE. MARIE**—Charter Communications

SCHOOLCRAFT—See THREE RIVERS, MI (Comcast Cable)

SCIO TWP.—See ANN ARBOR, MI (Comcast Cable)

SCIOTA TWP.—See DIMONDALE, MI (Broadstripe)

SCIPIO TWP.—See HILLSDALE, MI (Comcast Cable)

SCOTTS—See CLIMAX TWP., MI (Climax Telephone Co.)

SCOTTVILLE—See LUDINGTON, MI (Charter Communications)

▲ **SEBEWAING**—Comcast Cable. Now served by PIGEON, MI [MI0375]

SEBEWAING—See PIGEON, MI (Comcast Cable)

SECORD TWP.—See BUTMAN TWP., MI (Charter Communications)

SELFRIDGE AFB—See CHESTERFIELD TWP., MI (Comcast Cable)

SELMA TWP.—See CADILLAC, MI (Charter Communications)

▲ **SENEY TWP.**—Cable America Corp.

SEVILLE TWP.—See RIVERDALE, MI (Charter Communications)

SHAFTSBURG—See DIMONDALE, MI (Broadstripe)

SHELBY (UNINCORPORATED AREAS)—See HART, MI (Charter Communications)

SHELBY TWP.—See STERLING HEIGHTS, MI (Comcast Cable)

SHELBY TWP.—See DETROIT, MI (WOW! Internet Cable & Phone)

SHEPHERD—See MOUNT PLEASANT, MI (Charter Communications)

SHERIDAN TWP. (NEWAYGO COUNTY)—See MUSKEGON, MI (Comcast Cable)

SHERIDAN TWP.—See DIMONDALE, MI (Broadstripe)

SHERIDAN—See IONIA, MI (Charter Communications)

SHERMAN TWP. (ISABELLA COUNTY)—See WEIDMAN, MI (Charter Communications)

SHERMAN TWP. (MASON COUNTY)—See CUSTER, MI (Charter Communications)

SHERMAN TWP. (NEWAYGO COUNTY)—See MUSKEGON, MI (Comcast Cable)

▲ **SHERWOOD TWP.**—Formerly served by CableDirect. No longer in operation

SHERWOOD TWP.—See UNION CITY, MI (Broadstripe)

SHERWOOD—See DIMONDALE, MI (Broadstripe)

SHIAWASSEE TWP.—See DURAND, MI (Charter Communications)

▲ **SHINGLETON**—Cable America Corp.

SHOREHAM—See ST. JOSEPH TWP., MI (Comcast Cable)

SIDNEY TWP.—See IONIA, MI (Charter Communications)

SILVER CREEK TWP. (PORTIONS)—See CASSOPOLIS, MI (Comcast Cable)

SILVER CREEK TWP.—See KEELER TWP., MI (Sister Lakes Cable TV)

SIMS TWP.—See AU GRES, MI (Charter Communications)

SISTER LAKES—See KEELER TWP., MI (Sister Lakes Cable TV)

SIX LAKES—See LAKEVIEW, MI (Charter Communications)

SKANDIA TWP.—See MARQUETTE, MI (Charter Communications)

▲ **SKIDWAY LAKE**—Charter Communications

SODUS TWP.—See ST. JOSEPH TWP., MI (Comcast Cable)

SOLON TWP. (KENT COUNTY)—See ROCKFORD, MI (Charter Communications)

SOLON TWP. (LEELANAU COUNTY)—See TRAVERSE CITY, MI (Charter Communications)

SOMERSET TWP.—See JACKSON, MI (Comcast Cable)

SOO TWP.—See SAULT STE. MARIE, MI (Charter Communications)

SOUTH ARM TWP.—See TRAVERSE CITY, MI (Charter Communications)

SOUTH BRANCH TWP.—See ROSCOMMON, MI (Charter Communications)

SOUTH HAVEN TWP.—See SOUTH HAVEN, MI (Comcast Cable)

▲ **SOUTH HAVEN**—Comcast Cable

SOUTH LYON—See DIMONDALE, MI (Broadstripe)

SOUTH RANGE—See HOUGHTON, MI (Charter Communications)

SOUTH ROCKWOOD—See TAYLOR, MI (Comcast Cable)

▲ **SOUTHFIELD**—Comcast Cable

SOUTHGATE—See TAYLOR, MI (Comcast Cable)

SOUTHGATE—See DETROIT, MI (WOW! Internet Cable & Phone)

SPARTA TWP.—See ROCKFORD, MI (Charter Communications)

SPARTA—See ROCKFORD, MI (Charter Communications)

SPAULDING TWP.—See SAGINAW, MI (Charter Communications)

SPEAKER TWP.—See YALE, MI (Comcast Cable)

SPENCER TWP.—See GREENVILLE, MI (Charter Communications)

SPRING ARBOR TWP.—See DIMONDALE, MI (Broadstripe)

SPRING ARBOR TWP.—See JACKSON, MI (Comcast Cable)

SPRING LAKE—See ALLENDALE, MI (Charter Communications)

▲ **SPRINGDALE TWP.**—Ace Communications. Formerly served by Thompsonville, MI [MI0230]. This cable system has converted to IPTV

▲ **SPRINGFIELD TWP. (Oakland County)**—Comcast Cable. Now served by PONTIAC, MI [MI0017]

SPRINGFIELD TWP.—See TRAVERSE CITY, MI (Charter Communications)

SPRINGFIELD TWP.—See PONTIAC, MI (Comcast Cable)

SPRINGFIELD—See BATTLE CREEK, MI (Comcast Cable)

SPRINGPORT (VILLAGE)—See SPRINGPORT TWP., MI (Springport Telephone Co.)

▲ **SPRINGPORT TWP.**—Springport Telephone Co.

SPRINGVALE TWP.—See TRAVERSE CITY, MI (Charter Communications)

SPRINGVILLE TWP.—See MESICK, MI (Pine River Cable)

ST. CHARLES (VILLAGE)—See SAGINAW, MI (Charter Communications)

ST. CHARLES TWP.—See SAGINAW, MI (Charter Communications)

ST. CLAIR SHORES—See STERLING HEIGHTS, MI (Comcast Cable)

ST. CLAIR SHORES—See DETROIT, MI (WOW! Internet Cable & Phone)

ST. CLAIR TWP.—See CHESTERFIELD TWP., MI (Comcast Cable)

ST. CLAIR—See CHESTERFIELD TWP., MI (Comcast Cable)

▲ **ST. HELEN**—Charter Communications

ST. IGNACE TWP.—See SAULT STE. MARIE, MI (Charter Communications)

▲ **ST. IGNACE**—Charter Communications. Now served by SAULT STE. MARIE, MI [MI0090]

ST. IGNACE—See SAULT STE. MARIE, MI (Charter Communications)

ST. JAMES TWP.—See BEAVER ISLAND, MI (Pine River Cable)

▲ **ST. JOHNS**—Charter Communications

▲ **ST. JOSEPH TWP.**—Comcast Cable

ST. JOSEPH—See BENTON HARBOR, MI (Comcast Cable)

ST. LOUIS—See ALMA, MI (Charter Communications)

STAMBAUGH TWP.—See IRON RIVER, MI (Iron River Cable)

STAMBAUGH—See CASPIAN, MI (Caspian Community TV Corp.)

STANDISH TWP.—See BAY CITY, MI (Charter Communications)

▲ **STANDISH**—Charter Communications. Now served by BAY CITY, MI [MI0018]

STANDISH—See BAY CITY, MI (Charter Communications)

STANNARD TWP.—See IRONWOOD, MI (Charter Communications)

▲ **STANTON**—Charter Communications. Now served by IONIA, MI [MI0091]

STANTON—See IONIA, MI (Charter Communications)

STANWOOD—See HOWARD CITY, MI (Charter Communications)

STAR LAKE—See BIG STAR LAKE, MI (Charter Communications)

STAR TWP.—See TRAVERSE CITY, MI (Charter Communications)

▲ **STEPHENSON**—Howard Cable

▲ **STEPHENSON**—Packerland Broadband

▲ **STERLING HEIGHTS**—Comcast Cable

STERLING HEIGHTS—See DETROIT, MI (WOW! Internet Cable & Phone)

STERLING VILLAGE—See STERLING, MI (Pine River Cable)

▲ **STERLING**—Pine River Cable

STEVENSVILLE—See ST. JOSEPH TWP., MI (Comcast Cable)

STOCKBRIDGE—See DIMONDALE, MI (Broadstripe)

STRONACH TWP.—See TRAVERSE CITY, MI (Charter Communications)

STURGIS—See COLDWATER, MI (Charter Communications)

SULLIVAN TWP.—See MUSKEGON, MI (Comcast Cable)

SUMMERFIELD TWP. (MONROE COUNTY)—See MONROE, MI (Charter Communications)

SUMMIT TWP. (JACKSON COUNTY)—See JACKSON, MI (Comcast Cable)

SUMMIT TWP. (MASON CO.)—See LUDINGTON, MI (Charter Communications)

SUMMIT-LEONI—See JACKSON, MI (Comcast Cable)

SUMNER TWP.—See ALMA, MI (Charter Communications)

SUMNER TWP.—See RIVERDALE, MI (Charter Communications)

SUMPTER TWP.—See TAYLOR, MI (Comcast Cable)

SUNFIELD—See DIMONDALE, MI (Broadstripe)

SUPERIOR TWP. (CHIPPEWA COUNTY)—See SAULT STE. MARIE, MI (Charter Communications)

SUPERIOR TWP. (WASHTENAW COUNTY)—See ANN ARBOR, MI (Comcast Cable)

SURREY TWP.—See MOUNT PLEASANT, MI (Charter Communications)

SUTTONS BAY TWP.—See TRAVERSE CITY, MI (Charter Communications)

SUTTONS BAY—See TRAVERSE CITY, MI (Charter Communications)

SWAN CREEK TWP.—See SAGINAW, MI (Charter Communications)

SWARTZ CREEK—See FLINT, MI (Comcast Cable)

SWEETWATER TWP. (LAKE COUNTY)—See CUSTER, MI (Charter Communications)

SYLVAN LAKE—See WEST BLOOMFIELD TWP., MI (Comcast Cable)

SYLVAN TWP.—See ANN ARBOR, MI (Comcast Cable)

TALLMADGE TWP. (PORTIONS)—See GRAND RAPIDS, MI (Comcast Cable)

TALLMADGE TWP.—See ALLENDALE, MI (Charter Communications)

TAWAS CITY—See OSCODA, MI (Charter Communications)

TAWAS TWP.—See OSCODA, MI (Charter Communications)

▲**TAYLOR**—Comcast Cable

TAYLOR—See DETROIT, MI (WOW! Internet Cable & Phone)

TAYMOUTH TWP.—See SAGINAW, MI (Charter Communications)

TECUMSEH—See ADDISON (village), MI (Comcast Cable)

TEKONSHA—See COLDWATER, MI (Charter Communications)

TEXAS TWP.—See OSHTEMO TWP., MI (Comcast Cable)

THE HOMESTEAD—See TRAVERSE CITY, MI (Charter Communications)

▲**THETFORD TWP.**—Charter Communications

▲**THOMAS TWP.**—Charter Communications. Now served by SAGINAW, MI [MI0013]

THOMAS TWP.—See SAGINAW, MI (Charter Communications)

THOMPSON TWP.—See ESCANABA, MI (Charter Communications)

▲**THOMPSONVILLE**—Ace Communications. This cable system has converted to IPTV. See Thompsonville, MI [MI5027]

▲**THOMPSONVILLE**—Ace Communications. Formerly [MI0230]. This cable system has converted to IPTV

THORNAPPLE TWP.—See MIDDLEVILLE/CALEDONIA, MI (Charter Communications)

▲**THREE OAKS**—Comcast Cable. Now served by ST. JOSEPH TWP., MI [MI0051]

THREE OAKS—See ST. JOSEPH TWP., MI (Comcast Cable)

▲**THREE RIVERS**—Comcast Cable

TILDEN TWP.—See MARQUETTE, MI (Charter Communications)

TITTABAWASSEE TWP.—See SAGINAW, MI (Charter Communications)

TOBACCO TWP.—See BILLINGS, MI (Charter Communications)

TORCH LAKE TWP. (ANTRIM COUNTY)—See TRAVERSE CITY, MI (Charter Communications)

TORCH LAKE TWP. (HOUGHTON COUNTY)—See HOUGHTON, MI (Charter Communications)

▲**TRAVERSE CITY**—Charter Communications

TRENTON—See TAYLOR, MI (Comcast Cable)

TRENTON—See DETROIT, MI (WOW! Internet Cable & Phone)

TROWBRIDGE TWP.—See ALLEGAN, MI (Charter Communications)

TROY—See ROYAL OAK, MI (Comcast Cable)

TROY—See DETROIT, MI (WOW! Internet Cable & Phone)

TURNER TWP.—See OMER, MI (Charter Communications)

TURNER VILLAGE—See OMER, MI (Charter Communications)

TUSCARORA TWP.—See INDIAN RIVER, MI (Charter Communications)

TUSCOLA TWP.—See VASSAR, MI (Charter Communications)

TUSTIN (VILLAGE)—See LE ROY (village), MI (Pine River Cable)

TWINING—See OMER, MI (Charter Communications)

TYRONE TWP. (KENT COUNTY)—See ROCKFORD, MI (Charter Communications)

TYRONE TWP. (LIVINGSTON COUNTY)—See FENTON, MI (Charter Communications)

▲**UBLY**—Comcast Cable. Now served by PIGEON, MI [MI0375]

UBLY—See PIGEON, MI (Comcast Cable)

UNADILLA TWP.—See LIVINGSTON COUNTY, MI (Charter Communications)

▲**UNION CITY**—Broadstripe

UNION CITY—See DIMONDALE, MI (Broadstripe)

UNION TWP. (ISABELLA COUNTY)—See MOUNT PLEASANT, MI (Charter Communications)

UNIONVILLE VILLAGE—See UNIONVILLE, MI (Pine River Cable)

▲**UNIONVILLE**—Pine River Cable

UTICA—See STERLING HEIGHTS, MI (Comcast Cable)

UTICA—See DETROIT, MI (WOW! Internet Cable & Phone)

VALLEY TWP.—See ALLEGAN, MI (Charter Communications)

VAN BUREN COUNTY (PORTIONS)—See BLOOMINGDALE, MI (Bloomingdale Communications Inc.)

VAN BUREN—See PLYMOUTH TWP., MI (Comcast Cable)

VANDALIA (VILLAGE)—See CASSOPOLIS, MI (Comcast Cable)

VANDERBILT—See TRAVERSE CITY, MI (Charter Communications)

VASSAR TWP.—See VASSAR, MI (Charter Communications)

▲**VASSAR**—Charter Communications

VENICE TWP.—See DURAND, MI (Charter Communications)

VENICE TWP.—See LENNON, MI (Lennon Telephone Co.)

VERGENNES TWP.—See GRAND RAPIDS, MI (Comcast Cable)

VERGENNES TWP.—See LOWELL, MI (Comcast Cable)

▲**VERMONTVILLE**—Broadstripe

VERNON (VILLAGE)—See DURAND, MI (Charter Communications)

VERNON TWP. (SHIAWASSEE COUNTY)—See DURAND, MI (Charter Communications)

VERNON TWP.—See MOUNT PLEASANT, MI (Charter Communications)

VERNON TWP.—See LENNON, MI (Lennon Telephone Co.)

VERONA TWP.—See PIGEON, MI (Comcast Cable)

VEVAY TWP.—See DIMONDALE, MI (Broadstripe)

VICKSBURG—See THREE RIVERS, MI (Comcast Cable)

VICTOR TWP.—See DIMONDALE, MI (Broadstripe)

VIENNA TWP. (GENESEE COUNTY)—See FLINT, MI (Comcast Cable)

VIENNA TWP. (PORTIONS)—See THETFORD TWP., MI (Charter Communications)

WAKEFIELD—See IRONWOOD, MI (Charter Communications)

▲**WALDRON VILLAGE**—Comcast Cable

WALKER—See GRAND RAPIDS, MI (Comcast Cable)

WALLACE—See STEPHENSON, MI (Packerland Broadband)

▲**WALLED LAKE**—Comcast Cable

WALTON TWP.—See DIMONDALE, MI (Broadstripe)

WARREN TWP.—See COLEMAN, MI (Charter Communications)

WARREN—See STERLING HEIGHTS, MI (Comcast Cable)

WARREN—See DETROIT, MI (WOW! Internet Cable & Phone)

WASHINGTON TWP. (MACOMB COUNTY)—See CHESTERFIELD TWP., MI (Comcast Cable)

WASHINGTON—See THREE RIVERS, MI (Comcast Cable)

WATERFORD TWP.—See PONTIAC, MI (Comcast Cable)

WATERLOO TWP.—See DIMONDALE, MI (Broadstripe)

▲**WATERSMEET**—Charter Communications. Now served by IRONWOOD, MI [MI0064]

WATERSMEET—See IRONWOOD, MI (Charter Communications)

WATERTOWN TWP. (CLINTON COUNTY)—See DIMONDALE, MI (Broadstripe)

WATERTOWN TWP. (CLINTON COUNTY)—See LANSING, MI (Comcast Cable)

WATERTOWN TWP. (SANILAC COUNTY)—See SANDUSKY, MI (Comcast Cable)

WATERTOWN TWP. (TUSCOLA COUNTY)—See NORTH BRANCH TWP., MI (Charter Communications)

▲**WATERVLIET**—Comcast Cable

WATSON TWP.—See ALLEGAN, MI (Charter Communications)

WAUCEDAH TWP.—See IRON MOUNTAIN, MI (Charter Communications)

WAVERLY TWP. (VAN BUREN COUNTY)—See BLOOMINGDALE, MI (Bloomingdale Communications Inc.)

WAVERLY TWP. (VAN BUREN COUNTY)—See LAWTON, MI (Comcast Cable)

WAWATAM TWP.—See MACKINAW CITY, MI (Charter Communications)

WAYLAND—See MIDDLEVILLE/CALEDONIA, MI (Charter Communications)

WAYNE TWP.—See CASSOPOLIS, MI (Comcast Cable)

▲**WAYNE**—Comcast Cable. Now served by PLYMOUTH, MI [MI0012]

WAYNE—See PLYMOUTH TWP., MI (Comcast Cable)

WAYNE—See DETROIT, MI (WOW! Internet Cable & Phone)

WEBBERVILLE—See DIMONDALE, MI (Broadstripe)

WEBSTER TWP.—See LIVINGSTON COUNTY, MI (Charter Communications)

WEBSTER TWP.—See ANN ARBOR, MI (Comcast Cable)

WEESAW—See ST. JOSEPH TWP., MI (Comcast Cable)

▲ **WEIDMAN**—Charter Communications

WELLS TWP.—See ESCANABA, MI (Charter Communications)

▲ **WELLSTON**—Pine River Cable

▲ **WEST BLOOMFIELD TWP.**—Comcast Cable

▲ **WEST BRANCH**—Pine River Cable

WEST TRAVERSE TWP.—See TRAVERSE CITY, MI (Charter Communications)

WESTLAND—See PLYMOUTH TWP., MI (Comcast Cable)

WESTLAND—See DETROIT, MI (WOW! Internet Cable & Phone)

WESTPHALIA—See DIMONDALE, MI (Broadstripe)

WETMORE—See MARQUETTE, MI (Charter Communications)

WHEATFIELD TWP. (PORTIONS)—See EAST LANSING, MI (Comcast Cable)

WHEATFIELD TWP.—See DIMONDALE, MI (Broadstripe)

WHEATLAND TWP. (MECOSTA COUNTY)—See REMUS, MI (Charter Communications)

WHEELER TWP.—See ALMA, MI (Charter Communications)

WHEELER—See ALMA, MI (Charter Communications)

▲ **WHITE CLOUD**—Charter Communications

WHITE LAKE—See WALLED LAKE, MI (Comcast Cable)

WHITE PIGEON TWP. (EASTERN PORTION)—See COLDWATER, MI (Charter Communications)

WHITE PIGEON—See THREE RIVERS, MI (Comcast Cable)

WHITE PINE—See IRONWOOD, MI (Charter Communications)

WHITE RIVER TWP.—See WHITEHALL, MI (Charter Communications)

▲ **WHITEHALL**—Charter Communications

WHITEWATER TWP.—See TRAVERSE CITY, MI (Charter Communications)

WHITMORE LAKE—See LIVINGSTON COUNTY, MI (Charter Communications)

WHITNEY TWP.—See AU GRES, MI (Charter Communications)

▲ **WHITTEMORE**—Charter Communications

WILBER TWP.—See OSCODA, MI (Charter Communications)

WILCOX TWP.—See WHITE CLOUD, MI (Charter Communications)

WILLIAMS TWP. (EASTERN PORTION)—See BAY CITY, MI (Charter Communications)

WILLIAMS TWP. (WESTERN PORTION)—See MIDLAND, MI (Charter Communications)

WILLIAMSTON—See DIMONDALE, MI (Broadstripe)

WILLIAMSTOWN TWP.—See DIMONDALE, MI (Broadstripe)

WILSON TWP.—See TRAVERSE CITY, MI (Charter Communications)

WINDSOR CHARTER TWP.—See LANSING, MI (Comcast Cable)

WINDSOR TWP.—See DIMONDALE, MI (Broadstripe)

WINFIELD TWP.—See HOWARD CITY, MI (Charter Communications)

WINSOR TWP.—See PIGEON, MI (Comcast Cable)

WISE TWP.—See MOUNT PLEASANT, MI (Charter Communications)

▲ **WISNER (village)**—Formerly served by Northwoods Cable Inc. No longer in operation

WIXOM—See WALLED LAKE, MI (Comcast Cable)

▲ **WOLF LAKE**—Pine River Cable

▲ **WOLVERINE (VILLAGE)**—Upper Peninsula Communications

WOLVERINE LAKE—See WALLED LAKE, MI (Comcast Cable)

WOODCREEK MANOR—See DURAND, MI (Charter Communications)

▲ **WOODHAVEN**—Comcast Cable. Now served by TAYLOR, MI [MI0008]

WOODHAVEN—See TAYLOR, MI (Comcast Cable)

WOODHAVEN—See DETROIT, MI (WOW! Internet Cable & Phone)

WOODHULL TWP.—See DIMONDALE, MI (Broadstripe)

▲ **WOODLAND (VILLAGE)**—Pine River Cable

WOODSTOCK TWP.—See ADDISON (village), MI (Comcast Cable)

WORTH TWP.—See LEXINGTON, MI (Comcast Cable)

WRIGHT TWP. (OTTAWA COUNTY) (PORTIONS)—See GRAND RAPIDS, MI (Comcast Cable)

WRIGHT TWP. (PORTIONS)—See ALLENDALE, MI (Charter Communications)

▲ **WYANDOTTE**—Wyandotte Municipal Services

WYOMING—See GRAND RAPIDS, MI (Comcast Cable)

▲ **YALE**—Comcast Cable

YANKEE SPRINGS TWP.—See MIDDLEVILLE/CALEDONIA, MI (Charter Communications)

▲ **YORK TWP.**—Comcast Cable. Now served by TAYLOR, MI [MI0008]

YORK TWP.—See TAYLOR, MI (Comcast Cable)

YPSILANTI—See ANN ARBOR, MI (Comcast Cable)

ZEELAND TWP.—See ALLENDALE, MI (Charter Communications)

ZILWAUKEE—See SAGINAW, MI (Charter Communications)

MINNESOTA

▲ **ADA**—Loretel Cablevision

▲ **ADAMS**—Now served by CHATFIELD, MN [MN0111]

ADAMS—See CHATFIELD, MN (Mediacom)

▲ **ADRIAN**—Knology

AFTON—See ST. PAUL, MN (Comcast Cable)

▲ **AITKIN**—Charter Communications. Now served by Brainerd, MN [MN0022]

AITKIN—See BRAINERD, MN (Charter Communications)

▲ **AKELEY TWP.**—ACS Video. Formerly served by Perham, MN [MN0050]. This cable system has converted to IPTV

AKELEY—See PERHAM, MN (ACS Video)

▲ **ALBANY**—Charter Communications

▲ **ALBERT LEA**—Charter Communications

ALBERTVILLE—See BUFFALO, MN (Charter Communications)

▲ **ALDEN**—US Cable

▲ **ALEXANDRIA**—Formerly served by Viking Vision. No longer in operation

▲ **ALEXANDRIA**—Charter Communications

▲ **ALTURA**—Midcontinent Communications

▲ **ALVARADO**—Stephen Cable TV Inc.

AMBOY—See GOOD THUNDER, MN (Woodstock LLC)

AMOR TWP.—See PERHAM, MN (ACS Video)

ANDOVER—See ST. PAUL, MN (Comcast Cable)

▲ **ANNANDALE**—Heart of the Lakes Cable System Inc.

ANOKA—See ST. PAUL, MN (Comcast Cable)

APPLE VALLEY—See ROSEMOUNT, MN (Charter Communications)

▲ **APPLETON**—Mediacom

ARDEN HILLS—See ST. PAUL, MN (Comcast Cable)

▲ **ARGYLE**—Stephen Cable TV Inc.

ARLINGTON—See REDWOOD FALLS, MN (Mediacom)

ASKOV—See SANDSTONE, MN (Savage Communications Inc.)

ATWATER—See CLARA CITY, MN (Mediacom)

AUDUBON—See PERHAM, MN (ACS Video)

AURDAL TWP.—See FERGUS FALLS, MN (Charter Communications)

AURORA—See EVELETH, MN (Mediacom)

▲ **AUSTIN**—Charter Communications

▲ **AVON**—US Cable of Coastal Texas LP. Now served by CAMBRIDGE, MN [MN0016]

AVON—See CAMBRIDGE, MN (US Cable)

▲ **BABBITT**—Midcontinent Communications

BACKUS—See PEQUOT LAKES, MN (Charter Communications)

BADGER TWP.—See ERSKINE, MN (Garden Valley Telephone Co.)

▲ **BADGER**—Sjoberg's Cable TV Inc.

▲ **BAGLEY**—Bagley Public Utilities

▲ **BALATON**—Midcontinent Communications

BALDWIN TWP.—See CAMBRIDGE, MN (US Cable)

▲ **BALL CLUB**—Paul Bunyan Communications. Formerly served by Deer River, MN [MN0180]. This cable system has converted to IPTV

BARCLAY TWP.—See PEQUOT LAKES, MN (Charter Communications)

▲ **BARNESVILLE**—Formerly served by Sprint Corp. No longer in operation

▲ **BARNESVILLE**—Barnesville Cable TV

▲ **BARNUM**—Savage Communications Inc.

▲ **BARRETT**—Runestone Cable TV

BASS BROOK TWP.—See GRAND RAPIDS, MN (Mediacom)

BATTLE LAKE—See PERHAM, MN (ACS Video)

▲ **BAUDETTE**—Sjoberg's Cable TV Inc.

BAXTER—See BRAINERD, MN (Charter Communications)

BAY LAKE—See BRAINERD, MN (Charter Communications)

BAYPORT—See ST. PAUL, MN (Comcast Cable)

BEAVER BAY—See SILVER BAY, MN (Mediacom)

BECKER—See CAMBRIDGE, MN (US Cable)

BELGRADE TWP.—See MANKATO, MN (Charter Communications)

▲**BELGRADE**—Now served by CHOKIO, MN [MN0210]

BELGRADE—See CHOKIO, MN (Mediacom)

▲**BELLE PLAINE**—Now served by WASECA, MN [MN0043]

BELLE PLAINE—See WASECA, MN (Mediacom)

BELLE PRAIRIE TWP.—See LITTLE FALLS, MN (Charter Communications)

▲**BELLECHESTER**—Sleepy Eye Telephone. Formerly served by Goodhue, MN [MN0208]. This cable system has converted to IPTV

BELTRAMI COUNTY—See BEMIDJI, MN (Midcontinent Communications)

▲**BELVIEW**—Clara City Telephone Co.

▲**BEMIDJI**—Midcontinent Communications

▲**BENSON**—Charter Communications. Now served by WILLMAR, MN [MN0018]

BENSON—See WILLMAR, MN (Charter Communications)

BERTHA—See PERHAM, MN (ACS Video)

BETHEL—See CAMBRIDGE, MN (US Cable)

▲**BIG FALLS**—North American Communications Corp.

BIG LAKE—See BUFFALO, MN (Charter Communications)

▲**BIGELOW**—Formerly served by American Telecasting of America Inc. No longer in operation

▲**BIGFORK**—North American Communications Corp.

BIRCH LAKE TWP.—See PEQUOT LAKES, MN (Charter Communications)

BIRCHWOOD VILLAGE—See ST. PAUL, MN (Comcast Cable)

BIRD ISLAND—See OLIVIA, MN (Mediacom)

BIWABIK—See EVELETH, MN (Mediacom)

▲**BLACKDUCK**—Paul Bunyan Communications. This cable system has converted to IPTV. See Blackduck, MN [MN5315]

▲**BLACKDUCK**—Paul Bunyan Communications. Formerly [MN0164]. This cable system has converted to IPTV

BLAINE—See ST. PAUL, MN (Comcast Cable)

▲**BLOOMING PRAIRIE**—Mediacom. Now served by Dodge Center, MN [MN0093]

BLOOMING PRAIRIE—See DODGE CENTER, MN (Mediacom)

▲**BLOOMINGTON**—Time Warner Cable. Now served by MINNEAPOLIS, MN [MN0001]

BLOOMINGTON—See MINNEAPOLIS, MN (Comcast Cable)

▲**BLUE EARTH**—Bevcomm Inc.

BLUE HILL TWP.—See CAMBRIDGE, MN (US Cable)

▲**BLUEBERRY TWP.**—Formerly served by MENAHGA, MN [MN0118]. West Central Telephone Assn. This cable system has converted to IPTV

BLUFFTON (VILLAGE)—See PERHAM, MN (ACS Video)

▲**BLUFFTON TWP**—ACS Video. Formerly served by Perham, MN [MN0050]. This cable system has converted to IPTV

BORUP—See ADA, MN (Loretel Cablevision)

▲**BOVEY**—North American Communications Corp.

BRADFORD TWP.—See CAMBRIDGE, MN (US Cable)

BRAHAM—See CAMBRIDGE, MN (US Cable)

▲**BRAINERD**—Charter Communications

BRANSVOLD TWP.—See ERSKINE, MN (Garden Valley Telephone Co.)

BREEZY POINT—See PEQUOT LAKES, MN (Charter Communications)

▲**BREWSTER**—US Cable

▲**BRICELYN**—Bevcomm Inc.

BRIDGEWATER TWP.—See ROSEMOUNT, MN (Charter Communications)

BROOKLYN CENTER—See ST. PAUL, MN (Comcast Cable)

▲**BROOKLYN PARK**—Comcast Cable. Now served by ST. PAUL (formerly Roseville), MN [MN0002]

BROOKLYN PARK—See ST. PAUL, MN (Comcast Cable)

▲**BROOTEN**—Now served by CHOKIO, MN [MN0210]

BROOTEN—See CHOKIO, MN (Mediacom)

▲**BROWERVILLE**—Charter Communications. Now served by BRAINERD, MN [MN0022]

BROWERVILLE—See BRAINERD, MN (Charter Communications)

▲**BROWNS VALLEY**—Midcontinent Communications

BROWNSDALE—See DODGE CENTER, MN (Mediacom)

▲**BROWNSVILLE**—Now served by CALEDONIA, MN [MN0086]

BROWNSVILLE—See CALEDONIA, MN (Mediacom)

▲**BROWNTON**—Mediacom

BUFFALO LAKE—See BROWNTON, MN (Mediacom)

▲**BUFFALO**—Charter Communications

BUHL—See EVELETH, MN (Mediacom)

BURNSVILLE—See ST. PAUL, MN (Comcast Cable)

BUSE TWP.—See FERGUS FALLS, MN (Charter Communications)

BUTTERFIELD—See WASECA, MN (Mediacom)

BYRON—See ROCHESTER, MN (Charter Communications)

▲**CALEDONIA**—Mediacom

CALLAWAY—See PERHAM, MN (ACS Video)

CALUMET—See HIBBING, MN (Mediacom)

▲**CAMBRIDGE**—US Cable

▲**CANBY**—Midcontinent Communications

▲**CANNON FALLS**—Mediacom

▲**CANOSIA TWP.**—New Century Communications

CANTERBURY ESTATES—See PRIOR LAKE, MN (Mediacom)

▲**CANTON**—Now served by CALEDONIA, MN [MN0086]

CANTON—See CALEDONIA, MN (Mediacom)

▲**CARLOS**—DVSI Cable Television. Now served by PARKERS PRAIRIE, MN [MN0346]

CARLOS—See PARKERS PRAIRIE, MN (ACS Video)

CARLOS—See ALEXANDRIA, MN (Charter Communications)

CARLTON—See CLOQUET, MN (Mediacom)

CARVER COUNTY (UNINCORPORATED AREAS)—See MINNEAPOLIS, MN (Comcast Cable)

CARVER—See MINNEAPOLIS, MN (Comcast Cable)

CASCADE TWP.—See ROCHESTER, MN (Charter Communications)

CASS LAKE—See BEMIDJI, MN (Midcontinent Communications)

CENTER CITY—See CAMBRIDGE, MN (US Cable)

CENTER TWP.—See PEQUOT LAKES, MN (Charter Communications)

CENTERVILLE—See ST. PAUL, MN (Comcast Cable)

▲**CEYLON**—US Cable

CHAMPLIN—See ST. PAUL, MN (Comcast Cable)

CHANHASSEN—See LAKE MINNETONKA, MN (Mediacom)

▲**CHASKA**—Time Warner Cable. Now served by MINNEAPOLIS, MN [MN0001]

CHASKA—See MINNEAPOLIS, MN (Comcast Cable)

▲**CHATFIELD**—Mediacom

CHICKAMAW BEACH—See PEQUOT LAKES, MN (Charter Communications)

▲**CHISAGO CITY**—Now served by CAMBRIDGE, MN [MN0016]

CHISAGO CITY—See CAMBRIDGE, MN (US Cable)

CHISHOLM—See EVELETH, MN (Mediacom)

▲**CHOKIO**—Mediacom

CIRCLE PINES—See ST. PAUL, MN (Comcast Cable)

▲**CLARA CITY**—Mediacom

CLAREMONT—See ALDEN, MN (US Cable)

CLARISSA—See BRAINERD, MN (Charter Communications)

CLARKFIELD—See MINNEOTA, MN (US Cable)

CLARKS GROVE—See ALDEN, MN (US Cable)

CLEAR LAKE—See CAMBRIDGE, MN (US Cable)

▲**CLEARBROOK**—Garden Valley Telephone Co.

CLEARWATER—See CAMBRIDGE, MN (US Cable)

▲**CLEMENTS**—Clara City Telephone Co.

CLEVELAND—See WASECA, MN (Mediacom)

CLIMAX—See ADA, MN (Loretel Cablevision)

▲**CLINTON**—Now served by APPLETON, MN [MN0106]

CLINTON—See APPLETON, MN (Mediacom)

CLITHERALL (VILLAGE)—See PERHAM, MN (ACS Video)

CLITHERALL TWP.—See PERHAM, MN (ACS Video)

▲**CLOQUET**—Mediacom

COATES—See VERMILLION, MN (Bevcomm Inc.)

COKATO—See BUFFALO, MN (Charter Communications)

COLD SPRING—See CAMBRIDGE, MN (US Cable)

▲**COLERAINE**—Jaguar Communications

COLERAINE—See BOVEY, MN (North American Communications Corp.)

▲**COLOGNE**—Nu-Telecom

COLUMBIA HEIGHTS—See ST. PAUL, MN (Comcast Cable)

COLUMBUS TWP.—See CAMBRIDGE, MN (US Cable)

▲ **COMFREY**—Clara City Telephone Co.

▲ **CONCORD**—Mediacom. Now served by Dodge Center, MN [MN0093]

CONCORD—See DODGE CENTER, MN (Mediacom)

▲ **COOK**—Mediacom

COON RAPIDS—See ST. PAUL, MN (Comcast Cable)

CORCORAN—See ST. PAUL, MN (Comcast Cable)

CORINNA TWP.—See ANNANDALE, MN (Heart of the Lakes Cable System Inc.)

▲ **CORLISS TWP.**—ACS Video. Formerly served by Perham, MN [MN0050]. This cable system has converted to IPTV

CORMORANT LAKE (EASTERN PORTION)—See PELICAN LAKE, MN (Loretel Cablevision)

CORMORANT TWP.—See PERHAM, MN (ACS Video)

CORMORANT TWP.—See PELICAN LAKE, MN (Loretel Cablevision)

▲ **COSMOS**—Now served by CLARA CITY, MN [MN0125]

COSMOS—See CLARA CITY, MN (Mediacom)

COTTAGE GROVE—See ST. PAUL, MN (Comcast Cable)

▲ **COTTONWOOD**—Charter Communications

▲ **COURTLAND**—NU-Telecom. Formerly served by New Ulm, MN [MN0285]. This cable system has converted to IPTV

CREDIT RIVER—See PRIOR LAKE, MN (Mediacom)

▲ **CROOKED LAKE TWP.**—Emily Cooperative Telephone. Formerly served by Emily, MN [MN0081]. This cable system has converted to IPTV

▲ **CROOKSTON**—Midcontinent Communications. Now served by GRAND FORKS, ND [ND0003]

CROSBY—See BRAINERD, MN (Charter Communications)

▲ **CROSSLAKE**—Crosslake Communications

CROW WING COUNTY (NORTHERN PORTION)—See PEQUOT LAKES, MN (Charter Communications)

CROW WING COUNTY (UNINCORPORATED AREAS)—See BRAINERD, MN (Charter Communications)

CRYSTAL—See ST. PAUL, MN (Comcast Cable)

CURRIE—See MARSHALL, MN (Knology)

CUYUNA—See BRAINERD, MN (Charter Communications)

CYRUS—See BARRETT, MN (Runestone Cable TV)

DAKOTA COUNTY (PORTIONS)—See ST. PAUL, MN (Comcast Cable)

▲ **DAKOTA**—Now served by CALEDONIA, MN [MN0086]

DAKOTA—See CALEDONIA, MN (Mediacom)

DANE PRAIRIE TWP.—See FERGUS FALLS, MN (Charter Communications)

DANUBE—See OLIVIA, MN (Mediacom)

DASSEL—See BUFFALO, MN (Charter Communications)

▲ **DAWSON**—Now served by APPLETON, MN [MN0106]

DAWSON—See APPLETON, MN (Mediacom)

DAYTON—See BUFFALO, MN (Charter Communications)

DEAD LAKE TWP.—See PERHAM, MN (ACS Video)

DEEPHAVEN—See LAKE MINNETONKA, MN (Mediacom)

▲ **DEER CREEK TWP.**—ACS Video. Formerly served by Perham, MN [MN0050]. This cable system has converted to IPTV

DEER CREEK—See PERHAM, MN (ACS Video)

▲ **DEER RIVER**—Paul Bunyan Communications. This cable system has converted to IPTV. See Deer River, MN [MN5345]

▲ **DEER RIVER**—Paul Bunyan Communications

DEERWOOD TWP.—See KARLSTAD, MN (Sjoberg's Cable TV Inc.)

DEERWOOD—See BRAINERD, MN (Charter Communications)

DELANO—See BUFFALO, MN (Charter Communications)

DELAVAN—See MINNESOTA LAKE, MN (Bevcomm TV)

▲ **DELAVAN**—North American Communications Corp.

DELLWOOD—See ST. PAUL, MN (Comcast Cable)

DENMARK TWP.—See ST. PAUL, MN (Comcast Cable)

DENT—See PERHAM, MN (ACS Video)

DETROIT LAKES—See PERHAM, MN (ACS Video)

DETROIT TWP.—See PERHAM, MN (ACS Video)

▲ **DEXTER**—North American Communications Corp.

▲ **DILWORTH**—Loretel Cablevision. Now served by FARGO, ND [ND0001]

▲ **DODGE CENTER**—Mediacom

DONNELLY—See BARRETT, MN (Runestone Cable TV)

▲ **DORA TWP.**—ACS Video. Formerly served by Perham, MN [MN0050]. This cable system has converted to IPTV

DOVER TWP.—See CHATFIELD, MN (Mediacom)

DOVER—See CHATFIELD, MN (Mediacom)

DRESBACH—See CALEDONIA, MN (Mediacom)

DULUTH (UNINCORPORATED AREAS)—See CANOSIA TWP., MN (New Century Communications)

▲ **DULUTH**—Charter Communications

DUNDAS—See ROSEMOUNT, MN (Charter Communications)

▲ **DUNDEE**—Formerly served by American Telecasting of America Inc. No longer in operation

DUNN TWP.—See PELICAN LAKE, MN (Loretel Cablevision)

▲ **DUNNELL**—US Cable

EAGAN—See ST. PAUL, MN (Comcast Cable)

EAGLE BEND—See PARKERS PRAIRIE, MN (ACS Video)

EAGLE LAKE—See MANKATO, MN (Charter Communications)

EAST BETHEL—See CAMBRIDGE, MN (US Cable)

▲ **EAST GULL LAKE**—Savage Communications Inc. Now served by PILLAGER, MN [MN0230]

EAST GULL LAKE—See PILLAGER, MN (Savage Communications Inc.)

EASTON—See MINNESOTA LAKE, MN (Bevcomm TV)

▲ **EASTON**—North American Communications Corp.

▲ **ECHO**—Clara City Telephone Co.

EDEN PRAIRIE—See MINNEAPOLIS, MN (Comcast Cable)

EDGERTON—See ADRIAN, MN (Knology)

EDINA—See MINNEAPOLIS, MN (Comcast Cable)

▲ **EDNA TWP.**—ACS Video. Formerly served by Perham, MN [MN0050]. This cable system has converted to IPTV

▲ **EITZEN**—Ace Communications Group. This cable system has converted to IPTV. See Eitzen, MN [MN5143]

▲ **EITZEN**—Ace Communications. Formerly [MN0294]. This cable system has converted to IPTV

▲ **ELBOW LAKE**—Runestone Cable TV. Now served by BARRETT, MN [MN0233]

ELBOW LAKE—See BARRETT, MN (Runestone Cable TV)

ELGIN—See PLAINVIEW, MN (US Cable)

ELK RIVER—See BUFFALO, MN (Charter Communications)

▲ **ELKO**—Mediacom

ELLENDALE—See ALDEN, MN (US Cable)

▲ **ELLSWORTH**—Knology

ELMORE—See BLUE EARTH, MN (Bevcomm Inc.)

ELMWOOD TWP.—See SABIN, MN (Midcontinent Communications)

▲ **ELY**—Midcontinent Communications

ELYSIAN—See ALDEN, MN (US Cable)

▲ **EMILY**—Emily Cooperative Telephone. This cable system has converted to IPTV. See Emily, MN [MN5256]

▲ **EMILY**—Emily Cooperative Telephone. Formerly [MS0081]. This cable system has converted to IPTV

▲ **EMMONS**—Heck's TV & Cable

EMPIRE TWP.—See ROSEMOUNT, MN (Charter Communications)

ERDAHL—See BARRETT, MN (Runestone Cable TV)

▲ **ERIE TWP.**—ACS Video. Formerly served by Perham, MN [MN0050]. This cable system has converted to IPTV

▲ **ERSKINE**—Garden Valley Telephone Co.

ESKO—See CLOQUET, MN (Mediacom)

▲ **ESSING**—NU-Telecom. Formerly served by New Ulm, MN [MN0285]. This cable system has converted to IPTV

▲ **EVELETH**—Mediacom

EVERTS TWP.—See PERHAM, MN (ACS Video)

EXCELSIOR—See LAKE MINNETONKA, MN (Mediacom)

EYOTA—See ROCHESTER, MN (Charter Communications)

FAIRFAX—See REDWOOD FALLS, MN (Mediacom)

▲ **FAIRMONT**—Midcontinent Communications

FAIRVIEW TWP.—See PEQUOT LAKES, MN (Charter Communications)

FALCON HEIGHTS—See ST. PAUL, MN (Comcast Cable)

▲ **FARIBAULT**—Charter Communications

FARMINGTON—See ROSEMOUNT, MN (Charter Communications)

FAYAL TWP.—See EVELETH, MN (Mediacom)

FELTON—See ADA, MN (Loretel Cablevision)

▲**FERGUS FALLS**—Charter Communications

▲**FERTILE**—Loretel Cablevision

▲**FIFTY LAKES**—Emily Cooperative Telephone. Formerly served by Emily, MN [MN0081]. This cable system has converted to IPTV

▲**FINLAND**—Formerly served by New Century Communications. No longer in operation

FISHER—See ADA, MN (Loretel Cablevision)

▲**FLOODWOOD**—Savage Communications Inc.

FLORENCE TWP.—See LAKE CITY, MN (Mediacom)

FOLEY—See CAMBRIDGE, MN (US Cable)

FOREST LAKE—See CAMBRIDGE, MN (US Cable)

FORESTON—See CAMBRIDGE, MN (US Cable)

▲**FOSSTON**—City of Fosston Cable TV

▲**FOUNTAIN**—North American Communications Corp.

FRANKLIN—See REDWOOD FALLS, MN (Mediacom)

FRAZEE—See PERHAM, MN (ACS Video)

FREEBORN—See ALDEN, MN (US Cable)

▲**FRENCH RIVER TWP.**—Formerly served by New Century Communications. No longer in operation

▲**FRIDLEY**—Time Warner Cable. Now served by MINNEAPOLIS, MN [MN0001]

FRIDLEY—See MINNEAPOLIS, MN (Comcast Cable)

FRONTENAC—See LAKE CITY, MN (Mediacom)

FROST—See BRICELYN, MN (Bevcomm Inc.)

▲**FULDA**—Now served by PIPESTONE, MN [MN0348]

FULDA—See PIPESTONE, MN (Mediacom)

▲**GARDEN CITY**—North American Communications Corp.

▲**GARY**—Loretel Cablevision

▲**GAYLORD**—Now served by REDWOOD FALLS, MN [MN0057]

GAYLORD—See REDWOOD FALLS, MN (Mediacom)

GEM LAKE—See ST. PAUL, MN (Comcast Cable)

GENEVA—See ALDEN, MN (US Cable)

GHENT—See MINNEOTA, MN (US Cable)

GIBBON—See REDWOOD FALLS, MN (Mediacom)

GILBERT—See EVELETH, MN (Mediacom)

▲**GIRARD TWP.**—ACS Video. Formerly served by Perham, MN [MN0050]. This cable system has converted to IPTV

▲**GLENCOE**—Nu-Telecom (Formerly Midcontinent Communications). This cable system has converted to IPTV. See Glencoe, MN [MN5329]

▲**GLENVILLE**—US Cable

▲**GLENWOOD**—Charter Communications

GODFREY TWP.—See ERSKINE, MN (Garden Valley Telephone Co.)

GODFREY—See ERSKINE, MN (Garden Valley Telephone Co.)

GOLDEN VALLEY—See ST. PAUL, MN (Comcast Cable)

GONVICK—See CLEARBROOK, MN (Garden Valley Telephone Co.)

▲**GOOD THUNDER**—Woodstock LLC

▲**GOODHUE**—Sleepy Eye Telephone. This cable system has converted to IPTV. See Goodhue, MN [MN5120]

▲**GOODHUE**—Sleepy Eye Telephone. Formerly [MN0208]. This cable system has converted to IPTV

GOODVIEW—See WINONA, MN (Charter Communications)

▲**GOODVIEW**—Hiawatha Broadband. Formerly served by Winona, MN [MN0398]. This cable system has converted to IPTV

▲**GORMAN TWP.**—ACS Video. Formerly served by Perham, MN [MN0050]. This cable system has converted to IPTV

▲**GRACEVILLE**—Now served by APPLETON, MN [MN0106]

GRACEVILLE—See APPLETON, MN (Mediacom)

▲**GRANADA**—US Cable

▲**GRAND MARAIS**—Mediacom

▲**GRAND MEADOW**—Southern Cablevision Inc.

GRAND PRAIRIE—See GRAND RAPIDS, MN (Mediacom)

GRAND RAPIDS TWP.—See GRAND RAPIDS, MN (Mediacom)

▲**GRAND RAPIDS**—Mediacom

▲**GRANITE FALLS**—Now served by CLARA CITY, MN [MN0125]

GRANITE FALLS—See CLARA CITY, MN (Mediacom)

GRANT TWP.—See ST. PAUL, MN (Comcast Cable)

▲**GREEN ISLE**—North American Communications Corp.

GREEN LAKE TWP.—See WILLMAR, MN (Charter Communications)

GREEN PRAIRIE TWP.—See LITTLE FALLS, MN (Charter Communications)

▲**GREENBUSH**—Sjoberg's Cable TV Inc.

GREENWOOD—See LAKE MINNETONKA, MN (Mediacom)

GREY CLOUD ISLAND—See ST. PAUL, WI (Comcast Cable)

▲**GREY EAGLE**—diversiCOM. This cable system has converted to IPTV. See Grey Eagle, MN [MN5142]

▲**GREY EAGLE**—diversiCOM. Formerly [MN0232]. This cable system has converted to IPTV

▲**GROVE CITY**—Now served by CLARA CITY, MN [MN0125]

GROVE CITY—See CLARA CITY, MN (Mediacom)

GROVE PARK TWP.—See ERSKINE, MN (Garden Valley Telephone Co.)

GROVE PARK—See ERSKINE, MN (Garden Valley Telephone Co.)

▲**GRYGLA**—Garden Valley Telephone Co.

GULDRID—See BAUDETTE, MN (Sjoberg's Cable TV Inc.)

HACKENSACK—See PEQUOT LAKES, MN (Charter Communications)

▲**HALLOCK**—Midcontinent Communications

HALSTAD—See ADA, MN (Loretel Cablevision)

HAM LAKE—See ST. PAUL, MN (Comcast Cable)

HAMBURG—See NORWOOD, MN (Mediacom)

▲**HAMPTON**—Cannon Valley Cablevision. Now served by VERMILLION, MN [MN0391]

HAMPTON—See VERMILLION, MN (Bevcomm Inc.)

▲**HANCOCK**—Now served by CHOKIO, MN [MN0210]

HANCOCK—See CHOKIO, MN (Mediacom)

▲**HANLEY FALLS**—Farmers Mutual Telephone Co.

HANOVER—See ST. PAUL, MN (Comcast Cable)

▲**HANSKA**—Formerly served by Clara City Telephone Co. No longer in operation

▲**HANSKA**—Sleepy Eye Telephone. Formerly served by Goodhue, MN [MN0208]. This cable system has converted to IPTV

▲**HARMONY**—Harmony Cable Inc.

HARRIS TWP.—See GRAND RAPIDS, MN (Mediacom)

HARRIS—See CAMBRIDGE, MN (US Cable)

HARRISON TWP.—See WILLMAR, MN (Charter Communications)

HARTLAND—See ALDEN, MN (US Cable)

HASSAN TWP.—See BUFFALO, MN (Charter Communications)

HASTINGS—See ST. PAUL, MN (Comcast Cable)

HAUGEN TWP.—See ROUND LAKE TWP., MN (New Century Communications)

HAVEN TWP.—See ST. CLOUD, MN (Charter Communications)

HAVEN TWP.—See CAMBRIDGE, MN (US Cable)

HAVERHILL TWP.—See ROCHESTER, MN (Charter Communications)

▲**HAWLEY**—Loretel Systems

▲**HAYFIELD**—Mediacom. Now served by Dodge Center, MN [MN0093]

HAYFIELD—See DODGE CENTER, MN (Mediacom)

▲**HAYWARD**—North American Communications Corp.

▲**HECTOR**—Now served by BROWNTON, MN [MN0145]

HECTOR—See BROWNTON, MN (Mediacom)

HENDERSON—See WASECA, MN (Mediacom)

▲**HENDRICKS**—Formerly served by US Cable of Coastal Texas LP. No longer in operation

▲**HENDRICKS**—ITC. Formerly served by Clear Lake, SD [SD0047]. This cable system has converted to IPTV

HENDRUM—See ADA, MN (Loretel Cablevision)

▲**HENNING TWP.**—ACS Video. Formerly served by Perham, MN [MN0050]. This cable system has converted to IPTV

HENNING—See PERHAM, MN (ACS Video)

▲**HENRIETTA TWP.**—ACS Video. Formerly served by Perham, MN [MN0050]. This cable system has converted to IPTV

HEREIM TWP.—See GREENBUSH, MN (Sjoberg's Cable TV Inc.)

HERMAN—See BARRETT, MN (Runestone Cable TV)

HERMANTOWN—See CLOQUET, MN (Mediacom)

▲**HERON LAKE**—US Cable

HEWITT—See PERHAM, MN (ACS Video)

▲**HIBBING**—Mediacom

▲**HILL CITY**—Savage Communications Inc.

HILL RIVER TWP.—See ERSKINE, MN (Garden Valley Telephone Co.)

▲**HILLS**—Alliance Communications

HILLTOP—See ST. PAUL, MN (Comcast Cable)

HINCKLEY—See SANDSTONE, MN (Savage Communications Inc.)

HIRAM TWP.—See PEQUOT LAKES, MN (Charter Communications)

HITTERDAL—See ULEN, MN (Loretel Cablevision)

HOFFMAN—See BARRETT, MN (Runestone Cable TV)

▲**HOKAH**—Now served by CALEDONIA, MN [MN0086]

HOKAH—See CALEDONIA, MN (Mediacom)

HOLDINGFORD—See CAMBRIDGE, MN (US Cable)

HOLLAND—See RUTHTON, MN (K-Communications Inc.)

HOLLANDALE—See ALDEN, MN (US Cable)

HOLMESVILLE TWP.—See PERHAM, MN (ACS Video)

HOLT—See THIEF RIVER FALLS, MN (Sjoberg's Cable TV Inc.)

HOMER TWP.—See WINONA, MN (Charter Communications)

▲**HOMER**—Hiawatha Broadband. Formerly served by Winona, MN [MN0398]. This cable system has converted to IPTV

HOPKINS—See MINNEAPOLIS, MN (Comcast Cable)

▲**HOUSTON**—Now served by CALEDONIA, MN [MN0086]

HOUSTON—See CALEDONIA, MN (Mediacom)

▲**HOWARD LAKE**—Mediacom

HOYT LAKES—See EVELETH, MN (Mediacom)

▲**HUBBARD**—Paul Bunyan Communications

HUDSON TWP.—See ALEXANDRIA, MN (Charter Communications)

HUDSON—See ST. PAUL, WI (Comcast Cable)

HUGO—See ST. PAUL, MN (Comcast Cable)

▲**HUTCHINSON**—Now served by BROWNTON, MN [MN0145]

HUTCHINSON—See BROWNTON, MN (Mediacom)

▲**INTERNATIONAL FALLS**—Midcontinent Communications

INVER GROVE HEIGHTS—See ST. PAUL, MN (Comcast Cable)

▲**IONA**—Formerly served by American Telecasting of America Inc. No longer in operation

IRONDALE—See BRAINERD, MN (Charter Communications)

IRONTON—See BRAINERD, MN (Charter Communications)

IRVING TWP.—See WILLMAR, MN (Charter Communications)

ISANTI—See CAMBRIDGE, MN (US Cable)

ISLE HARBOR—See ISLE, MN (Savage Communications Inc.)

▲**ISLE**—Savage Communications Inc.

▲**IVANHOE**—Mediacom

▲**JACKSON**—Jackson Municipal TV System

JAMESON—See INTERNATIONAL FALLS, MN (Midcontinent Communications)

▲**JANESVILLE**—Now served by WASECA, MN [MN0043]

JANESVILLE—See WASECA, MN (Mediacom)

▲**JASPER**—Knology

▲**JEFFERS**—NU-Telecom

JENKINS—See PEQUOT LAKES, MN (Charter Communications)

▲**JORDAN**—Time Warner Cable. Now served by MINNEAPOLIS, MN [MN0001]

JORDAN—See MINNEAPOLIS, MN (Comcast Cable)

KANDIYOHI—See WILLMAR, MN (Charter Communications)

▲**KARLSTAD**—Sjoberg's Cable TV Inc.

KASOTA—See WASECA, MN (Mediacom)

KASOTA—See MADISON LAKE, MN (North American Communications Corp.)

KASSON—See ROCHESTER, MN (Charter Communications)

▲**KEEWATIN**—Now served by GRAND RAPIDS, MN [MN0038]

KEEWATIN—See GRAND RAPIDS, MN (Mediacom)

▲**KEGO TWP.**—ACS Video. Formerly served by Perham, MN [MN0050]. This cable system has converted to IPTV

▲**KELLIHER**—Formerly served by North American Communications Corp. No longer in operation

KELLOGG—See WABASHA, MN (US Cable)

▲**KENNEDY**—Stephen Cable TV Inc.

KENSINGTON—See BARRETT, MN (Runestone Cable TV)

▲**KENYON**—Now served by DODGE CENTER, MN [MN0093]

KENYON—See DODGE CENTER, MN (Mediacom)

▲**KERKHOVEN**—Charter Communications. Now served by WILLMAR, MN [MN0018]

KERKHOVEN—See WILLMAR, MN (Charter Communications)

KIESTER—See BRICELYN, MN (Bevcomm Inc.)

KING TWP.—See ERSKINE, MN (Garden Valley Telephone Co.)

KINNEY—See EVELETH, MN (Mediacom)

▲**KNIFE LAKE TWP.**—New Century Communications

▲**KNIFE RIVER**—New Century Communications

KNUTE TWP.—See ERSKINE, MN (Garden Valley Telephone Co.)

KOOCHICHING COUNTY—See INTERNATIONAL FALLS, MN (Midcontinent Communications)

LA GRAND TWP.—See ALEXANDRIA, MN (Charter Communications)

LA PRAIRIE TWP.—See GRAND RAPIDS, MN (Mediacom)

▲**LAFAYETTE**—Now served by WASECA, MN [MN0043]

LAFAYETTE—See WASECA, MN (Mediacom)

LAKE BENTON—See IVANHOE, MN (Mediacom)

▲**LAKE BRONSON**—Stephen Cable TV Inc.

▲**LAKE CITY**—Mediacom

LAKE COUNTY (WESTERN PORTION)—See EVELETH, MN (Mediacom)

LAKE COUNTY—See SILVER BAY, MN (Mediacom)

▲**LAKE CRYSTAL**—Now served by WASECA, MN [MN0043]

LAKE CRYSTAL—See WASECA, MN (Mediacom)

LAKE EDWARDS TWP.—See PEQUOT LAKES, MN (Charter Communications)

LAKE ELMO—See ST. PAUL, MN (Comcast Cable)

LAKE EUNICE TWP.—See PERHAM, MN (ACS Video)

LAKE LIDA—See PELICAN LAKE, MN (Loretel Cablevision)

▲**LAKE LILLIAN**—Farmers Mutual Telephone Co.

▲**LAKE MINNETONKA**—Mediacom

LAKE PARK—See PERHAM, MN (ACS Video)

LAKE SHORE—See BRAINERD, MN (Charter Communications)

LAKE ST. CROIX BEACH—See ST. PAUL, MN (Comcast Cable)

LAKE TWP.—See LAKE CITY, MN (Mediacom)

LAKE TWP.—See WARROAD, MN (Sjoberg's Cable TV Inc.)

LAKE VALLEY—See APPLETON, MN (Mediacom)

LAKE WILSON—See ADRIAN, MN (Knology)

▲**LAKEFIELD**—Lakefield Cable TV

LAKELAND SHORES—See ST. PAUL, MN (Comcast Cable)

LAKELAND—See ST. PAUL, MN (Comcast Cable)

LAKEVIEW TWP.—See PERHAM, MN (ACS Video)

LAKEVILLE—See ROSEMOUNT, MN (Charter Communications)

▲**LAMBERTON**—Lamberton TV Cable Co.

▲**LANCASTER**—Stephen Cable TV Inc.

LANDFALL—See ST. PAUL, MN (Comcast Cable)

▲**LANESBORO**—Now served by CALEDONIA, MN [MN0086]

LANESBORO—See CALEDONIA, MN (Mediacom)

LANGOLA (PORTIONS)—See RICE, MN (Benton Cablevision Inc.)

LANSING—See MAPLEVIEW, MN (North American Communications Corp.)

LAUDERDALE—See ST. PAUL, MN (Comcast Cable)

LE CENTER—See ALDEN, MN (US Cable)

▲**LE ROY**—Mediacom. Now served by CHATFIELD, MN [MN0111]

LE ROY—See CHATFIELD, MN (Mediacom)

LE SAUK TWP.—See ST. CLOUD, MN (Charter Communications)

▲**LE SUEUR**—Now served by WASECA, MN [MN0043]

LE SUEUR—See WASECA, MN (Mediacom)

LEECH LAKE TWP.—See PERHAM, MN (ACS Video)

LENT TWP.—See CAMBRIDGE, MN (US Cable)

▲**LEOTA**—Formerly served by American Telecasting of America Inc. No longer in operation

LESSOR TWP.—See ERSKINE, MN (Garden Valley Telephone Co.)

▲**LESTER PRAIRIE**—Now served by BROWNTON, MN [MN0145]

LESTER PRAIRIE—See BROWNTON, MN (Mediacom)

LEWISTON—See STOCKTON, MN (Midcontinent Communications)

▲**LEWISVILLE**—North American Communications Corp.

LEXINGTON—See ST. PAUL, MN (Comcast Cable)

LIDA TWP.—See PERHAM, MN (ACS Video)

LILYDALE—See ST. PAUL, MN (Comcast Cable)

LIME TWP.—See MANKATO, MN (Charter Communications)

LINDSTROM—See CAMBRIDGE, MN (US Cable)

LINO LAKES—See ST. PAUL, MN (Comcast Cable)

LINWOOD TWP.—See CAMBRIDGE, MN (US Cable)

LINWOOD—See CAMBRIDGE, MN (US Cable)

▲**LISMORE**—K-Communications Inc.

▲**LITCHFIELD**—Now served by BROWNTON, MN [MN0145]

LITCHFIELD—See BROWNTON, MN (Mediacom)

LITTLE CANADA—See ST. PAUL, MN (Comcast Cable)

LITTLE FALLS TWP.—See LITTLE FALLS, MN (Charter Communications)

▲**LITTLE FALLS**—Charter Communications

▲**LITTLEFORK**—Midcontinent Communications

LIVONIA TWP.—See CAMBRIDGE, MN (US Cable)

LONG BEACH—See GLENWOOD, MN (Charter Communications)

LONG LAKE—See LAKE MINNETONKA, MN (Mediacom)

▲**LONG LAKE**—New Century Communications

▲**LONG PRAIRIE**—Charter Communications. Now served by BRAINERD, MN [MN0022]

LONG PRAIRIE—See BRAINERD, MN (Charter Communications)

LONGVILLE—See PERHAM, MN (ACS Video)

LONSDALE—See WASECA, MN (Mediacom)

LOON LAKE TWP.—See PEQUOT LAKES, MN (Charter Communications)

LORETTO—See LAKE MINNETONKA, MN (Mediacom)

LOWER SIOUX—See REDWOOD FALLS, MN (Mediacom)

▲**LOWRY**—Lowry Telephone Co. Now served by BARRETT, MN [MN0233]

LOWRY—See BARRETT, MN (Runestone Cable TV)

▲**LUVERNE**—Now served by WORTHINGTON, MN [MN0041]

LUVERNE—See ADRIAN, MN (Knology)

LUVERNE—See WORTHINGTON, MN (Mediacom)

LYND—See MINNEOTA, MN (US Cable)

▲**MABEL**—Now served by CALEDONIA, MN [MN0086]

MABEL—See CALEDONIA, MN (Mediacom)

▲**MADELIA**—Time Warner Cable. Now served by MINNEAPOLIS, MN [MN0001]

MADELIA—See MINNEAPOLIS, MN (Comcast Cable)

▲**MADISON LAKE**—North American Communications Corp.

▲**MADISON**—Now served by APPLETON, MN [MN0106]

MADISON—See APPLETON, MN (Mediacom)

▲**MAGNOLIA**—Formerly served by American Telecasting of America Inc. No longer in operation

▲**MAHNOMEN**—Loretel Cablevision

MAHTOMEDI—See ST. PAUL, MN (Comcast Cable)

MAINE—See PERHAM, MN (ACS Video)

MANHATTAN BEACH—See CROSSLAKE, MN (Crosslake Communications)

MANKATO TWP.—See MANKATO, MN (Charter Communications)

▲**MANKATO**—Charter Communications

MANTORVILLE—See DODGE CENTER, MN (Mediacom)

MANTRAP TWP.—See PERHAM, MN (ACS Video)

MAPLE GROVE—See ST. PAUL, MN (Comcast Cable)

MAPLE LAKE—See BUFFALO, MN (Charter Communications)

MAPLE PLAIN—See LAKE MINNETONKA, MN (Mediacom)

MAPLETON—See ALDEN, MN (US Cable)

▲**MAPLEVIEW**—North American Communications Corp.

MAPLEWOOD—See ST. PAUL, MN (Comcast Cable)

▲**MARBLE**—Marble Cable TV Systems. Now served by HIBBING, MN [MN0027]

MARBLE—See HIBBING, MN (Mediacom)

MARINE ON THE ST. CROIX—See CAMBRIDGE, MN (US Cable)

MARION TWP.—See ROCHESTER, MN (Charter Communications)

▲**MARSHALL**—Charter Communications

▲**MARSHALL**—Knology

MARSHAN TWP.—See ST. PAUL, MN (Comcast Cable)

MAY TWP.—See CAMBRIDGE, MN (US Cable)

▲**MAYER**—Nu-Telecom

MAYNARD—See CLARA CITY, MN (Mediacom)

▲**MAZEPPA**—Formerly served by US Cable of Coastal Texas LP. No longer in operation

▲**MAZEPPA**—Sleepy Eye Telephone. Formerly served by Goodhue, MN [MN0208]. This cable system has converted to IPTV

MCGREGOR (UNINCORPORATED AREAS)—See ROUND LAKE TWP., MN (New Century Communications)

▲**MCGREGOR**—Savage Communications Inc.

MCINTOSH—See ERSKINE, MN (Garden Valley Telephone Co.)

MEDFORD—See ALDEN, MN (US Cable)

MEDICINE LAKE—See ST. PAUL, MN (Comcast Cable)

MEDINA—See LAKE MINNETONKA, MN (Mediacom)

▲**MELROSE**—Charter Communications

▲**MENAGHA**—West Central Telephone Assn. This cable system has converted to IPTV. See Menagha, MN [MN5130]

▲**MENAHGA**—West Central Telephone Assn. This cable system has converted to IPTV

MENDOTA HEIGHTS—See ST. PAUL, MN (Comcast Cable)

MENDOTA—See ST. PAUL, MN (Comcast Cable)

MENTOR—See ERSKINE, MN (Garden Valley Telephone Co.)

MERDOCK—See WILLMAR, MN (Charter Communications)

▲**MIDDLE RIVER**—Sjoberg's Cable TV Inc.

MIDDLE RIVER—See ARGYLE, MN (Stephen Cable TV Inc.)

MIDWAY TWP.—See CLOQUET, MN (Mediacom)

MILACA—See CAMBRIDGE, MN (US Cable)

MILAN—See WATSON, MN (Farmers Mutual Telephone Co.)

MILROY—See MINNEOTA, MN (US Cable)

MILTONA—See PARKERS PRAIRIE, MN (ACS Video)

MINDEN TWP.—See ST. CLOUD, MN (Charter Communications)

▲**MINNEAPOLIS**—Comcast Cable

▲**MINNEOTA**—US Cable

MINNESOTA CITY—See WINONA, MN (Charter Communications)

▲**MINNESOTA CITY**—Hiawatha Broadband. Formerly served by Winona, MN [MN0398]. This cable system has converted to IPTV

▲**MINNESOTA LAKE**—Bevcomm TV

MINNETONKA BEACH—See LAKE MINNETONKA, MN (Mediacom)

MINNETONKA—See MINNEAPOLIS, MN (Comcast Cable)

MINNETRISTA—See LAKE MINNETONKA, MN (Mediacom)

▲**MISSION TWP.**—Crosslake Communications. Formerly served by Crosslake, MN [MN0069]. This cable system has converted to IPTV

▲**MONTEVIDEO**—Charter Communications

▲**MONTGOMERY**—Mediacom

MONTICELLO—See BUFFALO, MN (Charter Communications)

▲**MONTROSE**—Time Warner Cable. Now served by MINNEAPOLIS, MN [MN0001]

MONTROSE—See MINNEAPOLIS, MN (Comcast Cable)

MOOSE LAKE TWP.—See MOOSE LAKE, MN (Mediacom)

▲**MOOSE LAKE**—Mediacom

MORA—See CAMBRIDGE, MN (US Cable)

MORGAN—See MINNEOTA, MN (US Cable)

▲**MORRIS**—Now served by CHOKIO, MN [MN0210]

MORRIS—See CHOKIO, MN (Mediacom)

▲**MORRISTOWN**—Bevcomm Inc.

▲**MORSE TWP.**—Paul Bunyan Communications. Formerly served by Deer River [MN0180]. This cable system has converted to IPTV

MORTON—See REDWOOD FALLS, MN (Mediacom)

▲**MOTLEY**—Savage Communications Inc. Now served by PILLAGER, MN [MN0230]

MOTLEY—See PILLAGER, MN (Savage Communications Inc.)

MOUND—See LAKE MINNETONKA, MN (Mediacom)

MOUNDS VIEW—See ST. PAUL, MN (Comcast Cable)

MOUNT PLEASANT TWP.—See LAKE CITY, MN (Mediacom)

MOUNTAIN IRON—See EVELETH, MN (Mediacom)

▲**MOUNTAIN LAKE**—Mediacom

NASHWAUK—See GRAND RAPIDS, MN (Mediacom)

NESSEL TWP.—See CAMBRIDGE, MN (US Cable)

▲**NEVIS TWP.**—ACS Video. Formerly served by Perham, MN [MN0050]. This cable system has converted to

IPTV

NEVIS—See PERHAM, MN (ACS Video)

▲ **NEW AUBURN**—North American Communications Corp.

NEW BRIGHTON—See ST. PAUL, MN (Comcast Cable)

NEW GERMANY—See MAYER, MN (Nu-Telecom)

NEW HOPE—See ST. PAUL, MN (Comcast Cable)

NEW LONDON TWP.—See WILLMAR, MN (Charter Communications)

NEW LONDON—See WILLMAR, MN (Charter Communications)

NEW MARKET TWP.—See ELKO, MN (Mediacom)

▲ **NEW MARKET**—North American Communications Corp.

▲ **NEW PRAGUE**—Time Warner Cable. Now served by MINNEAPOLIS, MN [MN0001]

NEW PRAGUE—See MINNEAPOLIS, MN (Comcast Cable)

NEW RICHLAND—See ALDEN, MN (US Cable)

NEW SCANDIA TWP.—See CAMBRIDGE, MN (US Cable)

▲ **NEW ULM**—NU-Telecom. This cable system has converted to IPTV. See New Ulm, MN [MN5117]

▲ **NEW ULM**—Time Warner Cable. Now served by MINNEAPOLIS, MN [MN0001]

NEW ULM—See MINNEAPOLIS, MN (Comcast Cable)

▲ **NEW ULM**—NU-Telecom. Formerly [MN0285]. This cable system has converted to IPTV

NEW YORK MILLS—See PERHAM, MN (ACS Video)

▲ **NEWFOLDEN**—Sjoberg's Cable TV Inc.

NEWPORT—See ST. PAUL, MN (Comcast Cable)

▲ **NEWTON TWP**—ACS Video. Formerly served by Perham, MN [MN0050]. This cable system has converted to IPTV

▲ **NICOLLET**—Clara City Telephone Co.

NIDAROS TWP.—See PERHAM, MN (ACS Video)

NISSWA—See BRAINERD, MN (Charter Communications)

NORCROSS—See BARRETT, MN (Runestone Cable TV)

NORTH BRANCH—See CAMBRIDGE, MN (US Cable)

NORTH HUDSON—See ST. PAUL, WI (Comcast Cable)

NORTH MANKATO—See MANKATO, MN (Charter Communications)

NORTH OAKS—See ST. PAUL, MN (Comcast Cable)

NORTH REDWOOD—See REDWOOD FALLS, MN (Mediacom)

NORTH ST. PAUL—See ST. PAUL, MN (Comcast Cable)

NORTHFIELD—See ROSEMOUNT, MN (Charter Communications)

▲ **NORTHROP**—US Cable

▲ **NORWOOD**—Mediacom

OAK GROVE—See ST. PAUL, MN (Comcast Cable)

OAK LAWN TWP.—See BRAINERD, MN (Charter Communications)

OAK PARK HEIGHTS—See ST. PAUL, MN (Comcast Cable)

OAKDALE—See ST. PAUL, MN (Comcast Cable)

▲ **OAKPORT**—Loretel Cablevision. Now served by FARGO, ND [ND0001]

OGILVIE—See CAMBRIDGE, MN (US Cable)

OKABENA—See HERON LAKE, MN (US Cable)

▲ **OKLEE**—Garden Valley Telephone Co.

▲ **OLIVIA**—Mediacom

▲ **ONAMIA**—Savage Communications Inc. Now served by ISLE, MN [MN0313]

ONAMIA—See ISLE, MN (Savage Communications Inc.)

ORONO—See LAKE MINNETONKA, MN (Mediacom)

ORONOCO TWP.—See ROCHESTER, MN (Charter Communications)

ORONOCO—See PINE ISLAND, MN (Pine Island Telephone Co.)

▲ **ORTONVILLE**—Midcontinent Communications. Now served by WATERTOWN, SD [SD0004]

▲ **OSAGE TWP.**—ACS Video. Formerly served by Perham, MN [MN0050]. This cable system has converted to IPTV

OSAGE—See PERHAM, MN (ACS Video)

▲ **OSAKIS**—Charter Communications. Now served by ALEXANDRIA, MN [MN0031]

OSAKIS—See ALEXANDRIA, MN (Charter Communications)

▲ **OSLO**—Midcontinent Communications

OSSEO—See ST. PAUL, MN (Comcast Cable)

▲ **OSTRANDER**—North American Communications Corp.

OTSEGO—See BUFFALO, MN (Charter Communications)

▲ **OTTERTAIL TWP.**—ACS Video. Formerly served by Perham, MN [MN0050]. This cable system has converted to IPTV

OTTERTAIL—See PERHAM, MN (ACS Video)

▲ **OTTO TWP.**—ACS Video. Formerly served by Perham, MN [MN0050]. This cable system has converted to IPTV

▲ **OUTING**—Emily Cooperative Telephone. Formerly served by Emily, MN [MN001]. This cable system has converted to IPTV

▲ **OWATONNA**—Charter Communications

PALMER TWP.—See CAMBRIDGE, MN (US Cable)

▲ **PARK RAPIDS**—Charter Communications

PARKERS PRAIRIE TWP.—See PARKERS PRAIRIE, MN (ACS Video)

▲ **PARKERS PRAIRIE**—ACS Video

PARKVILLE—See EVELETH, MN (Mediacom)

▲ **PAYNESVILLE**—Now served by CLARA CITY, MN [MN0125]

PAYNESVILLE—See CLARA CITY, MN (Mediacom)

▲ **PELICAN LAKE**—Loretel Cablevision

▲ **PELICAN RAPIDS**—Loretel Systems

▲ **PENGILLY**—Savage Communications Inc.

PENNOCK—See WILLMAR, MN (Charter Communications)

▲ **PEQUOT LAKES**—Charter Communications

PERHAM (VILLAGE)—See PERHAM, MN (ACS Video)

▲ **PERHAM TWP.**—ACS Video. Formerly served by Perham, MN [MN0050]. This cable system has converted to IPTV

▲ **PERHAM**—ACS Video

PERRY LAKE TWP.—See BRAINERD, MN (Charter Communications)

▲ **PETERSON**—Now served by CALEDONIA, MN [MN0086]

PETERSON—See CALEDONIA, MN (Mediacom)

PIERZ—See CAMBRIDGE, MN (US Cable)

PIKE CREEK TWP.—See LITTLE FALLS, MN (Charter Communications)

▲ **PILLAGER**—Savage Communications Inc.

PINE CITY—See CAMBRIDGE, MN (US Cable)

▲ **PINE ISLAND**—Pine Island Telephone Co.

▲ **PINE LAKE TWP.**—ACS Video. Formerly served by Perham, MN [MN0050]. This cable system has converted to IPTV

PINE RIVER—See PEQUOT LAKES, MN (Charter Communications)

PINE SPRINGS—See ST. PAUL, MN (Comcast Cable)

PIPESTONE—See ADRIAN, MN (Knology)

▲ **PIPESTONE**—Mediacom

▲ **PLAINVIEW**—US Cable

▲ **PLATO**—North American Communications Corp.

PLUMMER—See OKLEE, MN (Garden Valley Telephone Co.)

PLYMOUTH—See ST. PAUL, MN (Comcast Cable)

PORTER—See MINNEOTA, MN (US Cable)

POWERS TWP.—See PEQUOT LAKES, MN (Charter Communications)

PRESCOTT—See ST. PAUL, WI (Comcast Cable)

PRESTON—See CHATFIELD, MN (Mediacom)

PRINCETON—See CAMBRIDGE, MN (US Cable)

▲ **PRIOR LAKE**—Mediacom

▲ **PROCTOR**—Now served by CLOQUET, MN [MN0042]

PROCTOR—See CLOQUET, MN (Mediacom)

RABBIT LAKE TWP.—See BRAINERD, MN (Charter Communications)

▲ **RACINE**—North American Communications Corp.

RAMSEY COUNTY—See ST. PAUL, MN (Comcast Cable)

RAMSEY—See ST. PAUL, MN (Comcast Cable)

▲ **RANDALL**—Consolidated Telecommunications Co. This cable system has converted to IPTV. See RANDALL, MN [MN5026]

▲ **RANDALL**—Consolidated Telecommunications Co. Formerly [MN0202]. This cable system has converted to IPTV

RANDOLPH TWP.—See VERMILLION, MN (Bevcomm Inc.)

▲ **RANDOLPH**—Cannon Valley Cablevision. Now served by VERMILLION, MN [MN0391]

RANDOLPH—See VERMILLION, MN (Bevcomm Inc.)

RANIER—See INTERNATIONAL FALLS, MN (Midcontinent Communications)

▲ **RAVENNA**—Cannon Valley Cablevision. Now served by VERMILLION, MN [MN0391]

RAVENNA—See VERMILLION, MN (Bevcomm Inc.)

▲**RAYMOND**—Farmers Mutual Telephone Co.

▲**READING**—Formerly served by American Telecasting of Minnesota Inc. No longer in operation

READS LANDING—See WABASHA, MN (US Cable)

▲**RED LAKE FALLS**—Sjoberg's Cable TV Inc.

RED LAKE TWP.—See RED LAKE FALLS, MN (Sjoberg's Cable TV Inc.)

▲**RED ROCK**—North American Communications Corp.

▲**RED WING**—Charter Communications

▲**REDEYE TWP.**—Formerly served by MENAGHA, MN [MN0112]. West Central Telephone Assn. This cable system has converted to IPTV

▲**REDWOOD FALLS**—Mediacom

▲**REDWOOD FALLS**—NU-Telecom. Formerly served by New Ulm, MN [MN0285]. This cable system has converted to IPTV

▲**REMER**—Eagle Cablevision Inc.

RENVILLE—See MINNEOTA, MN (US Cable)

▲**REVERE**—Revere TV Cable Co.

RICE (VILLAGE)—See RICE, MN (Benton Cablevision Inc.)

RICE COUNTY—See FARIBAULT, MN (Charter Communications)

RICE LAKE TWP.—See DULUTH, MN (Charter Communications)

▲**RICE**—Benton Cablevision Inc.

RICHFIELD—See MINNEAPOLIS, MN (Comcast Cable)

RICHMOND—See CAMBRIDGE, MN (US Cable)

RICHVILLE—See PERHAM, MN (ACS Video)

RICHWOOD TWP.—See PERHAM, MN (ACS Video)

RIVER FALLS—See ST. PAUL, WI (Comcast Cable)

RIVERTON—See BRAINERD, MN (Charter Communications)

ROBBINSDALE—See ST. PAUL, MN (Comcast Cable)

▲**ROCHESTER**—Charter Communications

ROCKFORD—See BUFFALO, MN (Charter Communications)

ROCKVILLE—See CAMBRIDGE, MI (US Cable)

ROGERS—See ST. PAUL, MN (Comcast Cable)

▲**ROLLINGSTONE**—Charter Communications. Now served by STOCKTON, MN [MN0369]

ROLLINGSTONE—See STOCKTON, MN (Midcontinent Communications)

▲**ROSE CREEK**—North American Communications Corp.

▲**ROSEAU**—Sjoberg's Cable TV Inc.

▲**ROSEMOUNT**—Charter Communications

ROSEVILLE—See ST. PAUL, MN (Comcast Cable)

▲**ROUND LAKE TWP.**—New Century Communications

▲**ROUND LAKE**—US Cable

ROYALTON—See CAMBRIDGE, MN (US Cable)

RUSH CITY—See CAMBRIDGE, MN (US Cable)

▲**RUSH LAKE TWP.**—ACS Video. Formerly served by Perham, MN [MN0050]. This cable system has converted to IPTV

RUSH LAKE—See CAMBRIDGE, MN (US Cable)

RUSHFORD VILLAGE—See CHATFIELD, MN (Mediacom)

RUSHFORD—See CHATFIELD, MN (Mediacom)

▲**RUSHMORE**—K-Communications Inc.

RUSSELL—See MINNEOTA, MN (US Cable)

▲**RUTHTON**—K-Communications Inc.

▲**RUTLEDGE (village)**—Formerly served by New Century Communications. No longer in operation

▲**SABIN**—Midcontinent Communications

SACRED HEART—See MINNEOTA, MN (US Cable)

SAGINAW—See CANOSIA TWP., MN (New Century Communications)

▲**SANBORN**—Formerly served by NU-Telecom. No longer in operation

▲**SANBORN**—NU-Telecom. Formerly served by New Ulm, MN [MN0285]. This cable system has converted to IPTV

▲**SANDSTONE**—Savage Communications Inc.

SARTELL—See ST. CLOUD, MN (Charter Communications)

SAUK CENTRE TWP.—See SAUK CENTRE, MN (Charter Communications)

▲**SAUK CENTRE**—Charter Communications

SAUK RAPIDS (PORTIONS)—See RICE, MN (Benton Cablevision Inc.)

SAUK RAPIDS—See ST. CLOUD, MN (Charter Communications)

SAVAGE—See PRIOR LAKE, MN (Mediacom)

SCAMBLER TWP.—See PELICAN LAKE, MN (Loretel Cablevision)

SCANDIA—See CAMBRIDGE, MN (US Cable)

SCANLON—See CLOQUET, MN (Mediacom)

▲**SEARLES**—NU-Telecom. Formerly served by New Ulm, MN [MN0285]. This cable system has converted to IPTV

▲**SEBEKA**—Formerly served by MENAGHA, MN [MN0118]. West Central Telephone Assn. This cable system has converted to IPTV

SHAFER—See CAMBRIDGE, MN (US Cable)

▲**SHAKOPEE**—Time Warner Cable. Now served by MINNEAPOLIS, MN [MN0001]

SHAKOPEE—See MINNEAPOLIS, MN (Comcast Cable)

SHELLY—See ADA, MN (Loretel Cablevision)

SHERBURN—See FAIRMONT, MN (Midcontinent Communications)

▲**SHEVLIN**—Garden Valley Telephone Co.

SHINGOBEE TWP.—See PERHAM, MN (ACS Video)

SHOREVIEW—See ST. PAUL, MN (Comcast Cable)

SHOREWOOD—See LAKE MINNETONKA, MN (Mediacom)

▲**SHULTZ LAKE TWP.**—Formerly served by New Century Communications. No longer in operation

▲**SILVER BAY**—Mediacom

SILVER CREEK TWP.—See SILVER BAY, MN (Mediacom)

SILVER LAKE—See BROWNTON, MN (Mediacom)

SKYLINE—See MANKATO, MN (Charter Communications)

▲**SLAYTON**—Now served by PIPESTONE, MN [MN0348]

SLAYTON—See MARSHALL, MN (Knology)

SLAYTON—See PIPESTONE, MN (Mediacom)

SLEEPY EYE—See REDWOOD FALLS, MN (Mediacom)

▲**SLEEPY EYE**—Sleepy Eye Telephone. Formerly served by Goodhue, MN [MN0208]. This cable system has converted to IPTV

SLETTEN TWP.—See ERSKINE, MN (Garden Valley Telephone Co.)

SOUDAN—See TOWER, MN (Midcontinent Communications)

SOUTH BEND TWP.—See MANKATO, MN (Charter Communications)

SOUTH HARBOR—See ISLE, MN (Savage Communications Inc.)

SOUTH INTERNATIONAL FALLS—See INTERNATIONAL FALLS, MN (Midcontinent Communications)

SOUTH ST. PAUL—See ST. PAUL, MN (Comcast Cable)

SPICER—See WILLMAR, MN (Charter Communications)

SPOONER—See BAUDETTE, MN (Sjoberg's Cable TV Inc.)

▲**SPRING GROVE**—Now served by CALEDONIA, MN [MN0086]

SPRING GROVE—See CALEDONIA, MN (Mediacom)

SPRING LAKE PARK—See ST. PAUL, MN (Comcast Cable)

SPRING LAKE TWP.—See PRIOR LAKE, MN (Mediacom)

SPRING PARK—See LAKE MINNETONKA, MN (Mediacom)

SPRING VALLEY—See CHATFIELD, MN (Mediacom)

▲**SPRINGFIELD**—Now served by REDWOOD FALLS, MN [MN0057]

▲**SPRINGFIELD**—NU-Telecom. This cable system has converted to IPTV. See Springfield, MN [MN5118]

SPRINGFIELD—See REDWOOD FALLS, MN (Mediacom)

▲**SPRINGFIELD**—NU-Telecom. Formerly [MN0396]. This cable system has converted to IPTV

SPRUCE VALLEY TWP.—See MIDDLE RIVER, MN (Sjoberg's Cable TV Inc.)

ST. ANTHONY—See ST. PAUL, MN (Comcast Cable)

ST. AUGUSTA—See CAMBRIDGE, MN (US Cable)

ST. BONIFACIUS—See LAKE MINNETONKA, MN (Mediacom)

▲**ST. CHARLES**—Hiawatha Broadband. This cable system has converted to IPTV. See St. Charles, MN [MN5158]

▲**ST. CHARLES**—Hiawatha Broadband. Formerly [MN0397]. This cable system has converted to IPTV

ST. CHARLES—See CHATFIELD, MN (Mediacom)

ST. CLAIR—See ALDEN, MN (US Cable)

▲**ST. CLOUD**—Formerly served by Astound Broadband. No longer in operation

▲**ST. CLOUD**—Charter Communications

▲**ST. CROIX**—Comcast Cable. Now served by ST. PAUL (formerly Roseville), MN [MN0002]

ST. CROIX—See ST. PAUL, MN (Comcast Cable)

ST. FRANCIS—See CAMBRIDGE, MN (US Cable)

▲ **ST. HILAIRE**—Garden Valley Telephone Co.

▲ **ST. JAMES**—Now served by WASECA, MN [MN0043]

ST. JAMES—See WASECA, MN (Mediacom)

ST. JOHNS TWP.—See WILLMAR, MN (Charter Communications)

▲ **ST. JOSEPH**—Formerly served by Astound Communications. No longer in operation

ST. JOSEPH—See CAMBRIDGE, MN (US Cable)

▲ **ST. LOUIS PARK**—Time Warner Cable. Now served by MINNEAPOLIS, MN [MN0001]

ST. LOUIS PARK—See MINNEAPOLIS, MN (Comcast Cable)

ST. MARYS POINT—See ST. PAUL, MN (Comcast Cable)

ST. MICHAEL—See BUFFALO, MN (Charter Communications)

ST. PAUL PARK—See ST. PAUL, MN (Comcast Cable)

▲ **ST. PAUL**—Comcast Cable. Now served by St. PAUL, MN (formerly ROSEVILLE, MN) [MN0002]

▲ **ST. PAUL**—Comcast Cable

▲ **ST. PETER**—Now served by WASECA, MN [MN0043]

ST. PETER—See WASECA, MN (Mediacom)

ST. STEPHEN—See CAMBRIDGE, MN (US Cable)

ST. WENDEL TWP.—See CAMBRIDGE, MN (US Cable)

▲ **STACY**—Now served by CAMBRIDGE, MN [MN0016]

STACY—See CAMBRIDGE, MN (US Cable)

STANFORD TWP.—See CAMBRIDGE, MN (US Cable)

STAPLES (VILLAGE)—See PERHAM, MN (ACS Video)

▲ **STAPLES**—Charter Communications. Now served by BRAINERD, MN [MN0022]

STAPLES—See BRAINERD, MN (Charter Communications)

▲ **STAR LAKE TWP.**—ACS Video. Formerly served by Perham, MN [MN0050]. This cable system has converted to IPTV

▲ **STARBUCK**—Mediacom. Now served by CHOKIO, MN [MN0210]

STARBUCK—See CHOKIO, MN (Mediacom)

▲ **STEPHEN**—Stephen Cable TV Inc.

STEWART—See BROWNTON, MN (Mediacom)

STEWARTVILLE—See ROCHESTER, MN (Charter Communications)

STILLWATER—See ST. PAUL, MN (Comcast Cable)

▲ **STOCKTON**—Midcontinent Communications

▲ **STORDEN**—US Cable

▲ **STOWE PRAIRIE TWP.**—ACS Video. Formerly served by Perham, MN [MN0050]. This cable system has converted to IPTV

SUNFISH LAKE—See ST. PAUL, MN (Comcast Cable)

SUPERIOR (VILLAGE)—See DULUTH, WI (Charter Communications)

SVERDRUP TWP.—See PERHAM, MN (ACS Video)

▲ **SWANVILLE**—Formerly served by 391 Satellite LLC. No longer in operation

▲ **TACONITE**—City of Taconite Cable TV. Now served by HIBBING, MN [MN0027]

TACONITE—See HIBBING, MN (Mediacom)

TAUNTON—See MINNEOTA, MN (US Cable)

▲ **TAYLORS FALLS**—Now served by CAMBRIDGE, MN [MN0016]

TAYLORS FALLS—See CAMBRIDGE, MN (US Cable)

▲ **THIEF RIVER FALLS**—Sjoberg's Cable TV Inc.

THOMSON—See CLOQUET, MN (Mediacom)

TINTAH—See BARRETT, MN (Runestone Cable TV)

TONKA BAY—See LAKE MINNETONKA, MN (Mediacom)

▲ **TOWER**—Midcontinent Communications

▲ **TRACY**—Charter Communications

TRACY—See MARSHALL, MN (Knology)

▲ **TRIMONT**—Terril Cable Systems

TROY—See ST. PAUL, WI (Comcast Cable)

▲ **TRUMAN**—Terril Cable Systems

▲ **TURTLE LAKE TWP.**—ACS Video. Formerly served by Perham, MN [MN0050]. This cable system has converted to IPTV

TURTLE RIVER—See BEMIDJI, MN (Midcontinent Communications)

▲ **TWIN VALLEY**—ACS Video. Formerly served by Perham, MN [MN0050]. This cable system has converted to IPTV

TWO HARBORS (UNINCORPORATED AREAS)—See KNIFE RIVER, MN (New Century Communications)

▲ **TWO HARBORS**—Now served by SILVER BAY, MN [MN0084]

TWO HARBORS—See SILVER BAY, MN (Mediacom)

TYLER—See IVANHOE, MN (Mediacom)

▲ **ULEN**—Loretel Cablevision

URBANK—See PARKERS PRAIRIE, MN (ACS Video)

VADNAIS HEIGHTS—See ST. PAUL, MN (Comcast Cable)

▲ **VERMILLION**—Bevcomm Inc.

▲ **VERNDALE**—Savage Communications Inc.

▲ **VERNON CENTER**—North American Communications Corp.

VICTORIA—See LAKE MINNETONKA, MN (Mediacom)

VIKING—See THIEF RIVER FALLS, MN (Sjoberg's Cable TV Inc.)

VINING (VILLAGE)—See PERHAM, MN (ACS Video)

VIRGINIA—See EVELETH, MN (Mediacom)

WABANICA—See BAUDETTE, MN (Sjoberg's Cable TV Inc.)

▲ **WABASHA**—Hiawatha Broadband. This cable system has converted to IPTV. See Wabasha, MN [MN5160]

▲ **WABASHA**—Hiawatha Broadband. Formerly [MN0399]. This cable system has converted to IPTV

▲ **WABASHA**—US Cable

▲ **WABASSO**—Clara City Telephone Co.

▲ **WABEDO TWP.**—ACS Video. Formerly served by Perham, MN [MN0050]. This cable system has converted to IPTV

WACONIA—See LAKE MINNETONKA, MN (Mediacom)

WADENA—See PERHAM, MN (ACS Video)

▲ **WADENA**—Charter Communications

WAHKON—See ISLE, MN (Savage Communications Inc.)

WAITE PARK—See ST. CLOUD, MN (Charter Communications)

WAKEFIELD TWP—See CAMBRIDGE, MN (US Cable)

WALCOTT TWP.—See FARIBAULT, MN (Charter Communications)

WALDEN TWP.—See PEQUOT LAKES, MN (Charter Communications)

▲ **WALDORF**—Dynax Communications Inc. Now served by WASECA, MN [MN0043]

WALDORF—See WASECA, MN (Mediacom)

WALKER—See PERHAM, MN (ACS Video)

▲ **WALNUT GROVE**—Walnut Grove Cable TV

WALTHAM—See DODGE CENTER, MN (Mediacom)

▲ **WANAMINGO**—US Cable

▲ **WARREN**—Sjoberg's Cable TV Inc.

▲ **WARROAD**—Sjoberg's Cable TV Inc.

WARSAW—See MORRISTOWN, MN (Bevcomm Inc.)

▲ **WARSAW**—North American Communications Corp.

▲ **WASECA**—Mediacom

WASHINGTON COUNTY (PORTIONS)—See ST. PAUL, MN (Comcast Cable)

WASHINGTON TWP.—See MADISON LAKE, MN (North American Communications Corp.)

WATAB TWP.—See RICE, MN (Benton Cablevision Inc.)

WATERTOWN—See BUFFALO, MN (Charter Communications)

WATERVILLE—See ALDEN, MN (US Cable)

▲ **WATSON**—Farmers Mutual Telephone Co.

WAUBUN—See PERHAM, MN (ACS Video)

WAVERLY—See MINNEAPOLIS, MN (Comcast Cable)

WAYZATA—See LAKE MINNETONKA, MN (Mediacom)

WEBSTER TWP.—See ELKO, MN (Mediacom)

▲ **WELCOME**—Terril Cable Systems

WELLS TWP.—See WARSAW, MN (North American Communications Corp.)

▲ **WELLS**—Now served by WASECA, MN [MN0043]

WELLS—See WASECA, MN (Mediacom)

WENDELL—See BARRETT, MN (Runestone Cable TV)

WEST CONCORD—See DODGE CENTER, MN (Mediacom)

WEST LAKELAND—See ST. PAUL, MN (Comcast Cable)

WEST ST. PAUL—See ST. PAUL, MN (Comcast Cable)

▲ **WESTBROOK**—Formerly served by US Cable of Coastal Texas LP. No longer in operation

▲ **WESTBROOK**—Westbrook Public Utilities

▲ **WHEATON**—Now served by APPLETON, MN [MN0106]

WHEATON—See APPLETON, MN (Mediacom)

WHEELER—See BAUDETTE, MN (Sjoberg's Cable TV Inc.)

WHITE BEAR LAKE—See ST. PAUL, MN (Comcast Cable)

WHITE BEAR TWP.—See ST. PAUL, MN (Comcast Cable)

▲ **WHITE OAK TWP.**—ACS Video. Formerly served by Perham, MN [MN0050]. This cable system has converted to IPTV

WHYTE TWP.—See EVELETH, MN (Mediacom)

WILLERNIE—See ST. PAUL, MN (Comcast Cable)

▲ **WILLMAR**—Charter Communications

▲ **WILLOW RIVER**—Formerly served by New Century Communications. No longer in operation

▲ **WILMONT**—K-Communications Inc.

WILSON TWP.—See PEQUOT LAKES, MN (Charter Communications)

WILSON—See WINONA, MN (Charter Communications)

WILTON—See BEMIDJI, MN (Midcontinent Communications)

WINDERMERE TWP.—See MOOSE LAKE, MN (Mediacom)

▲ **WINDOM**—Windom Telecommunications. This cable system has converted to IPTV. See Windom, MN [MN5119]

▲ **WINDOM**—Windom Telecomunications. Formerly [MN0066]. This cable system has converted to IPTV

WINGER—See ERSKINE, MN (Garden Valley Telephone Co.)

▲ **WINNEBAGO**—Now served by WASECA, MN [MN0043]

WINNEBAGO—See WASECA, MN (Mediacom)

▲ **WINONA**—Hiawatha Broadband. This cable system has converted to IPTV. See Winona, MN [MN5161]

▲ **WINONA**—Charter Communications

▲ **WINONA**—Hiawatha Broadband. Formerly Winona, MN [MN0398]. This cable system has converted to IPTV

WINSTED—See BROWNTON, MN (Mediacom)

WINTHROP—See REDWOOD FALLS, MN (Mediacom)

WINTON—See ELY, MN (Midcontinent Communications)

WOLFORD—See BRAINERD, MN (Charter Communications)

▲ **WOOD LAKE**—Clara City Telephone Co.

WOODBURY—See ST. PAUL, MN (Comcast Cable)

WOODLAND—See LAKE MINNETONKA, MN (Mediacom)

WOODSIDE TWP.—See ERSKINE, MN (Garden Valley Telephone Co.)

WOODSIDE—See ERSKINE, MN (Garden Valley Telephone Co.)

WOODSTOCK—See RUTHTON, MN (K-Communications Inc.)

WORTHINGTON—See ADRIAN, MN (Knology)

▲ **WORTHINGTON**—Mediacom

▲ **WRENSHALL**—Formerly served by New Century Communications. No longer in operation

▲ **WYKOFF**—North American Communications Corp.

WYOMING—See CAMBRIDGE, MN (US Cable)

YOUNG AMERICA—See NORWOOD, MN (Mediacom)

ZIMMERMAN—See CAMBRIDGE, MN (US Cable)

ZUMBROTA—See ROCHESTER, MN (Charter Communications)

MISSISSIPPI

ABBEVILLE—See OXFORD, MS (MetroCast Communications)

▲ **ABERDEEN**—MetroCast Communications

ADAMS COUNTY—See NATCHEZ, MS (Cable One)

ALCORN COUNTY—See CORINTH, MS (Zoom Media)

▲ **AMORY**—MetroCast Communications

▲ **ANGUILLA**—CMA Cablevision

▲ **ARCOLA**—CMA Cablevision

▲ **ARTESIA**—Cable TV Inc.

▲ **ASHLAND**—MetroCast Communications

ATTALA COUNTY (UNINCORPORATED AREAS)—See KOSCIUSKO, MS (MetroCast Communications)

▲ **BALDWYN**—MetroCast Communications

▲ **BASSFIELD**—Alliance Communications

BATESVILLE—See CLEVELAND, MS (Cable One)

▲ **BAY SPRINGS**—Video Inc.

▲ **BAY ST. LOUIS**—Mediacom. Now served by WAVELAND, MS [MS0022]

BAY ST. LOUIS—See WAVELAND, MS (Mediacom)

▲ **BEAUMONT**—Mediacom

BECKER—See AMORY, MS (MetroCast Communications)

BELDEN—See TUPELO, MS (Comcast Cable)

▲ **BELMONT**—Formerly served by Almega Cable. No longer in operation

▲ **BELZONI**—Cable TV of Belzoni Inc.

▲ **BENOIT**—Formerly served by J & L Cable. No longer in operation

▲ **BENTONIA**—Comcast Cable

BIGGERSVILLE—See CORINTH, MS (Zoom Media)

▲ **BILOXI**—Cable One

BISSELL—See TUPELO, MS (Comcast Cable)

BLUE MOUNTAIN—See RIPLEY, MS (Ripley Video Cable Co. Inc.)

BOLTON—See JACKSON, MS (Comcast Cable)

▲ **BOONEVILLE**—MetroCast Communications

BOYLE—See CLEVELAND, MS (Cable One)

BRANDON—See PEARL, MS (Comcast Cable)

▲ **BROOKHAVEN**—Cable One

BROOKSVILLE—See MACON, MS (Cable TV Inc.)

▲ **BRUCE**—MetroCast Communications

BUCKATUNNA—See WAYNESBORO, MS (CMA Cablevision)

▲ **BUDE**—Franklin Telephone SnapVision. Formerly [MS0069]. This cable system has converted to IPTV

▲ **BURNSVILLE**—Formerly served by Almega Cable. No longer in operation

CALEDONIA—See COLUMBUS, MS (Cable One)

▲ **CALHOUN CITY**—MetroCast Communications

CALHOUN COUNTY—See CALHOUN CITY, MS (MetroCast Communications)

CALHOUN—See LAUREL, MS (Comcast Cable)

▲ **CANTON**—Comcast Cable

▲ **CARRIERRE**—Charter Communications. Now served by PICAYUNE, MS [MS0023]

CARRIERRE—See PICAYUNE, MS (Charter Communications)

CARROLLTON—See WINONA, MS (Cable One)

▲ **CARTHAGE**—MetroCast Communications

▲ **CARY**—Formerly served by J & L Cable. No longer in operation

▲ **CENTREVILLE**—Trust Cable

▲ **CHARLESTON**—Cable One. Now served by WINONA, MS [MS0014]

CHARLESTON—See WINONA, MS (Cable One)

CHICKASAW—See TUPELO, MS (Comcast Cable)

CHOCTAW INDIAN RESERVATION—See PHILADELPHIA, MS (MetroCast Communications)

▲ **CHUNKY**—Zoom Media

▲ **CLARKSDALE**—Cable One

CLAY COUNTY—See TUPELO, MS (Comcast Cable)

▲ **CLEVELAND**—Cable One

CLINTON—See JACKSON, MS (Comcast Cable)

COAHOMA COUNTY—See CLARKSDALE, MS (Cable One)

▲ **COFFEEVILLE**—MetroCast Communications

▲ **COLES POINT**—Formerly served by Foster Communications Inc. No longer in operation

▲ **COLLINS**—Collins Communications

▲ **COLUMBIA**—Cable South Media

COLUMBUS AFB—See COLUMBUS, MS (Cable One)

▲ **COLUMBUS**—Cable One

CONCORDIA PARISH (PORTIONS)—See NATCHEZ, LA (Cable One)

COPIAH COUNTY—See CRYSTAL SPRINGS, MS (Bailey Cable TV Inc.)

▲ **CORINTH**—Zoom Media

COURTLAND—See CLEVELAND, MS (Cable One)

COVINGTON COUNTY (PORTIONS)—See COLLINS, MS (Collins Communications)

COVINGTON COUNTY (PORTIONS)—See SEMINARY, MS (Home Cable Entertainment)

▲ **CRAWFORD**—Cable TV Inc.

▲ **CROSBY**—Telapex. No longer in operation

▲ **CROSBY**—Franklin Telephone SnapVision. Formerly served by Meadville-Bude, MS [MS0069]. This cable system has converted to IPTV

▲ **CROWDER**—Alliance Communications

▲ **CRYSTAL SPRINGS**—Bailey Cable TV Inc.

D'IBERVILLE—See BILOXI, MS (Cable One)

D'LO—See MENDENHALL, MS (Bailey Cable TV Inc.)

DALEWOOD—See MERIDIAN, MS (Comcast Cable)

▲ **DE KALB**—Zoom Media

▲ **DECATUR (town)**—Mediacom. Now served by LOUISVILLE, MS [MS0038]

DECATUR—See UNION, MS (Mediacom)

DERMA—See CALHOUN CITY, MS (MetroCast Communications)

DIAMONDHEAD—See LONG BEACH, MS (Cable One)

DIXIE—See MCLAURIN, MS (Home Cable Entertainment)

DREW—See CLEVELAND, MS (Cable One)

DUCK HILL—See WINONA, MS (Cable One)

DUNCAN—See CLARKSDALE, MS (Cable One)

DURANT—See WINONA, MS (Cable One)

▲ **EAGLE LAKE**—Delta Telephone Co. This cable system has converted to IPTV. See Eagle Lake, MS [MS5023]

▲ **EAGLE LAKE**—Delta Telephone SnapVision. This cable system has converted to IPTV

ECRU—See NEW ALBANY, MS (MetroCast Communications)

EDWARDS—See JACKSON, MS (Comcast Cable)

ELIZABETH—See LELAND, MS (CMA Cablevision)

ELLISVILLE—See LAUREL, MS (Comcast Cable)

ENTERPRISE—See QUITMAN, MS (CMA Cablevision)

ESCATAWPA—See PASCAGOULA, MS (Cable One)

▲ **EUPORA**—Cable TV Inc.

▲ **EVERGREEN**—Formerly served by SouthTel Communications LP. No longer in operation

FALKNER—See RIPLEY, MS (Ripley Video Cable Co. Inc.)

FANNIN—See PEARL, MS (Comcast Cable)

▲ **FAYETTE**—Formerly served by Almega Cable. No longer in operation

FERNWOOD—See BROOKHAVEN, MS (Cable One)

▲ **FLORA (PORTIONS)**—Telepak Network SnapVision. Formerly [MS0148]. This cable system has converted to IPTV

▲ **FLORA**—Telepak Networks SnapVision. This cable system has converted to IPTV. See Flora, MS [MS5019]

FLORENCE (PORTIONS)—See PEARL, MS (Comcast Cable)

FLORENCE—See JACKSON, MS (Comcast Cable)

FLOWOOD—See PEARL, MS (Comcast Cable)

▲ **FOREST**—MetroCast Communications

FOREST—See LAKE, MS (Zoom Media)

FORREST COUNTY—See HATTIESBURG, MS (Comcast Cable)

FORREST COUNTY—See MACEDONIA, MS (Zoom Media)

▲ **FRANKLIN CREEK**—Formerly served by CableSouth Inc. No longer in operation

FRIARS POINT—See JONESTOWN, MS (Alliance Communications)

▲ **FULTON**—Comcast Cable. Now served by TUPELO, MS [MS0009]

FULTON—See TUPELO, MS (Comcast Cable)

GAUTIER—See PASCAGOULA, MS (Cable One)

GEORGE COUNTY—See LUCEDALE, MS (Mediacom)

GLEN—See CORINTH, MS (Zoom Media)

▲ **GLOSTER**—Trust Cable. Now served by CENTREVILLE, MS [MS0048]

GLOSTER—See CENTREVILLE, MS (Trust Cable)

GOODMAN—See WINONA, MS (Cable One)

▲ **GREENVILLE**—Suddenlink Communications

▲ **GREENWOOD**—Suddenlink Communications

GRENADA COUNTY—See CLEVELAND, MS (Cable One)

▲ **GRENADA**—Cable One. Now served by CLEVELAND, MS [MS0019]

GRENADA—See CLEVELAND, MS (Cable One)

GULFPORT—See LONG BEACH, MS (Cable One)

▲ **GUNNISON**—Formerly served by J & L Cable. No longer in operation

GUNTOWN—See BALDWYN, MS (MetroCast Communications)

GUYS—See CORINTH, TN (Zoom Media)

HAMILTON—See COLUMBUS, MS (Cable One)

HANCOCK COUNTY (PORTIONS)—See LONG BEACH, MS (Cable One)

HANCOCK COUNTY (PORTIONS)—See WAVELAND, MS (Mediacom)

HARRISON COUNTY—See BILOXI, MS (Cable One)

HARRISON COUNTY—See LONG BEACH, MS (Cable One)

HATLEY—See AMORY, MS (MetroCast Communications)

▲ **HATTIESBURG**—Comcast Cable

▲ **HAZLEHURST/TERRY**—Bailey Cable TV Inc. Now served by CRYSTAL SPRINGS, MS [MS0143]

HAZLEHURST—See CRYSTAL SPRINGS, MS (Bailey Cable TV Inc.)

HEIDELBERG—See HATTIESBURG, MS (Comcast Cable)

▲ **HICKORY FLAT**—MetroCast Communications

HICKORY—See CHUNKY, MS (Zoom Media)

HINDS COUNTY—See JACKSON, MS (Comcast Cable)

▲ **HOLLANDALE**—CMA Cablevision

▲ **HOLLY SPRINGS**—MetroCast Communications

▲ **HOUSTON**—Mediacom. Now served by PONTOTOC, MS [MS0045]

HOUSTON—See PONTOTOC, MS (MetroCast Communications)

▲ **HUMPHREYS COUNTY (PORTIONS)**—Delta Telephone SnapVision. Formerly served by Isola-Inverness, MS [MS0080]. This cable system has converted to IPTV

HURLEY—See PASCAGOULA, MS (Cable One)

▲ **INDIANOLA**—Formerly served by Adelphia Communications. Now served by GREENWOOD, MS [MS0151]

INDIANOLA—See GREENWOOD, MS (Suddenlink Communications)

INGOMAR—See NEW ALBANY, MS (MetroCast Communications)

▲ **INVERNESS**—Telepak Networks SnapVision. Formerly [MS0080]. This cable system has converted to IPTV

▲ **ISOLA-INVERNESS**—Telepak Networks. This cable system has converted to IPTV. See Isola, MS [MS5011] and Inverness, MS [MS5007]

▲ **ISOLA**—Delta Telephone SnapVision. Formerly [MS0080]. This cable system has converted to IPTV

▲ **ITTA BENA**—Cable One. Now served by WINONA, MS [MS0014]

ITTA BENA—See WINONA, MS (Cable One)

▲ **IUKA**—MetroCast Communications

JACKSON COUNTY—See BILOXI, MS (Cable One)

JACKSON COUNTY—See PASCAGOULA, MS (Cable One)

▲ **JACKSON**—Comcast Cable

JASPER COUNTY (UNINCORPORATED AREAS)—See HATTIESBURG, MS (Comcast Cable)

JOHNS—See PUCKETT, MS (Comcast Cable)

JONES COUNTY (PORTIONS)—See HATTIESBURG, MS (Comcast Cable)

JONES COUNTY (PORTIONS)—See SEMINARY, MS (Home Cable Entertainment)

JONES COUNTY—See LAUREL, MS (Comcast Cable)

▲ **JONESTOWN**—Alliance Communications

▲ **JUMPERTOWN**—Vista III Media. Now served by BOONEVILLE, MS [MS0133]

JUMPERTOWN—See BOONEVILLE, MS (MetroCast Communications)

KEESLER AFB—See BILOXI, MS (Cable One)

KILMICHAEL—See WINONA, MS (Cable One)

▲ **KILN**—Formerly served by Trust Cable. No longer in operation

▲ **KOSCIUSKO**—MetroCast Communications

▲ **KOSSUTH**—Time Warner Cable. Now served by CORINTH, MS [MS0016]

KOSSUTH—See CORINTH, MS (Zoom Media)

LACKEY—See COLUMBUS, MS (Cable One)

LAFAYETTE COUNTY—See OXFORD, MS (MetroCast Communications)

▲ **LAKE**—Zoom Media

LAMAR COUNTY—See HATTIESBURG, MS (Comcast Cable)

LAMBERT—See CLEVELAND, MS (Cable One)

LAUDERDALE COUNTY—See MERIDIAN, MS (Comcast Cable)

▲ **LAUDERDALE**—Comcast Cable. Now served by MERIDIAN, MS [MS0007]

LAUDERDALE—See MERIDIAN, MS (Comcast Cable)

▲ **LAUREL**—Comcast Cable

▲ **LEAKESVILLE**—Alliance Communications

LEE COUNTY (PORTIONS)—See NETTLETON, MS (MetroCast Communications)

LEE COUNTY (UNINCORPORATED AREAS)—See PONTOTOC, MS (Zoom Media)

LEE COUNTY—See TUPELO, MS (Comcast Cable)

LEE COUNTY—See BALDWYN, MS (MetroCast Communications)

LEFLORE COUNTY—See WINONA, MS (Cable One)

LEFLORE COUNTY—See GREENWOOD, MS (Suddenlink Communications)

▲ **LELAND**—CMA Cablevision

▲ **LEXINGTON**—CableSouth Media. Now served by WINONA, MS [MS0014]

LEXINGTON—See WINONA, MS (Cable One)

▲ **LIBERTY**—Trust Cable. Now served by CENTREVILLE, MS [MS0048]

LIBERTY—See CENTREVILLE, MS (Trust Cable)

LINCOLN COUNTY (PORTIONS)—See BROOKHAVEN, MS (Cable One)

▲ **LONG BEACH**—Cable One

▲ **LOUISE**—Delta Telephone SnapVision. Formerly Branch Cable Inc. served by Meadville-Bude, MS [MS0069]. This cable system has converted to IPTV.

LOUISVILLE—See UNION, MS (Mediacom)

LOWNDES COUNTY—See COLUMBUS, MS (Cable One)

▲ **LUCEDALE**—Mediacom

LULA—See JONESTOWN, MS (Alliance Communications)

▲**LUMBERTON**—Zito Media

LYON—See CLARKSDALE, MS (Cable One)

▲**MABEN**—MetroCast Communications

▲**MACEDONIA**—Zoom Media

▲**MACON**—Cable TV Inc.

MADISON COUNTY—See CANTON, MS (Comcast Cable)

MADISON COUNTY—See JACKSON, MS (Comcast Cable)

MADISON—See JACKSON, MS (Comcast Cable)

▲**MAGEE**—Bailey Cable TV Inc.

MAGNOLIA—See BROOKHAVEN, MS (Cable One)

MANATACHIE—See TUPELO, MS (Comcast Cable)

MARIETTA—See TUPELO, MS (Comcast Cable)

MARION COUNTY (PORTIONS)—See COLUMBIA, MS (Cable South Media)

MARION—See MERIDIAN, MS (Comcast Cable)

MARKS—See CLEVELAND, MS (Cable One)

MARSHALL COUNTY—See POTTS CAMP, MS (MetroCast Communications)

MATHISTON—See MABEN, MS (MetroCast Communications)

▲**MAYERSVILLE**—Formerly served by J & L Cable. No longer in operation

MCADAMS—See KOSCIUSKO, MS (MetroCast Communications)

MCCOMB—See BROOKHAVEN, MS (Cable One)

▲**MCLAURIN**—Home Cable Entertainment

MCNAIRY COUNTY—See CORINTH, TN (Zoom Media)

MCNEILL—See PICAYUNE, MS (Charter Communications)

▲**MEADVILLE-BUDE**—Branch Cable Inc. This cable system has converted to IPTV. See Bude, MS [MS5016] & Meadville, MS [MS5012]

▲**MEADVILLE**—Franklin Telephone SnapVision. Formerly [MS0069]. This cable system has converted to IPTV

▲**MENDENHALL**—Bailey Cable TV Inc.

▲**MERIDIAN NAVAL AIR STATION**—Zito Media

▲**MERIDIAN**—Comcast Cable

MERIGOLD—See CLEVELAND, MS (Cable One)

METCALFE—See GREENVILLE, MS (Suddenlink Communications)

MICHIE—See CORINTH, TN (Zoom Media)

MISSISSIPPI STATE UNIVERSITY—See STARKVILLE, MS (MetroCast Communications)

MIZE—See MAGEE, MS (Bailey Cable TV Inc.)

MONTGOMERY COUNTY (PORTIONS)—See WINONA, MS (Cable One)

▲**MONTICELLO**—Zoom Media

MOON LAKE—See JONESTOWN, MS (Alliance Communications)

▲**MOOREVILLE**—Formerly served by Foster Communications Inc. No longer in operation

▲**MOOREVILLE**—Formerly served by SouthTel Communications LP. No longer in operation

MOOREVILLE—See TUPELO, MS (Comcast Cable)

MOORHEAD—See GREENWOOD, MS (Suddenlink Communications)

MORTON—See FOREST, MS (MetroCast Communications)

MOSS POINT—See PASCAGOULA, MS (Cable One)

▲**MOUND BAYOU**—Galaxy Cablevision. Now served by CLEVELAND, MS [MS0019]

MOUND BAYOU—See CLEVELAND, MS (Cable One)

MOUNT OLIVE—See MAGEE, MS (Bailey Cable TV Inc.)

MYRTLE—See NEW ALBANY, MS (MetroCast Communications)

▲**NATCHEZ**—Cable One

NESHOBA COUNTY (UNINCORPORATED AREAS)—See PHILADELPHIA, MS (MetroCast Communications)

▲**NETTLETON**—MetroCast Communications

▲**NEW ALBANY**—MetroCast Communications

▲**NEW AUGUSTA**—Formerly served by Telepex. No longer in operation

▲**NEW AUGUSTA**—Franklin Telephone SnapVision. Formerly served by Meadville-Bude, MS [MS0069]. This cable system has converted to IPTV

▲**NEW HEBRON**—Branch Cable Inc. This cable system has converted to IPTV. See New Hebron, MS [MS5014]

▲**NEW HEBRON**—Franklin Telephone SnapVision. Formerly served by Branch Cable Inc. [MS0171]. This cable system has converted to IPTV

NEW HOPE—See COLUMBUS, MS (Cable One)

NEW SIGHT—See BROOKHAVEN, MS (Cable One)

NEWTON COUNTY (PORTIONS)—See CHUNKY, MS (Zoom Media)

NEWTON COUNTY (PORTIONS)—See LAKE, MS (Zoom Media)

▲**NEWTON**—Mediacom. Now served by LOUISVILLE, MS [MS0038]

NEWTON—See UNION, MS (Mediacom)

NORTH CARROLLTON—See WINONA, MS (Cable One)

NOXAPATER—See UNION, MS (Mediacom)

OAK GROVE—See HATTIESBURG, MS (Comcast Cable)

▲**OAKLAND**—Formerly served by L & J Cable. No longer in operation

OCEAN SPRINGS—See BILOXI, MS (Cable One)

OCEAN SPRINGS—See ST. ANDREWS, MS (Mediacom)

OKOLONA—See TUPELO, MS (Comcast Cable)

OKTIBBEHA COUNTY (PORTIONS)—See STARKVILLE, MS (MetroCast Communications)

▲**OKTIBBEHA COUNTY**—Cable TV Inc.

▲**OSAGE COUNTY**—Formerly served by Galaxy Cablevision. No longer in operation

▲**OSYKA**—Formerly served by Almega Cable. No longer in operation

▲**OXFORD**—MetroCast Communications

PACE—See CLEVELAND, MS (Cable One)

▲**PACHUTA**—Formerly served by Galaxy Cablevision. No longer in operation

▲**PASCAGOULA**—Cable One

PASS CHRISTIAN—See LONG BEACH, MS (Cable One)

▲**PAULDING**—Comcast Cable

PEARL RIVER COUNTY—See PICAYUNE, MS (Charter Communications)

▲**PEARL**—Comcast Cable

▲**PEARLINGTON**—Mediacom. Now served by WAVELAND, MS [MS0022]

PEARLINGTON—See WAVELAND, MS (Mediacom)

PELAHATCHIE—See PEARL, MS (Comcast Cable)

PENDORFF—See LAUREL, MS (Comcast Cable)

PERRY COUNTY—See MACEDONIA, MS (Zoom Media)

PETAL—See HATTIESBURG, MS (Comcast Cable)

PETAL—See MACEDONIA, MS (Zoom Media)

▲**PHILADELPHIA**—MetroCast Communications

▲**PICAYUNE**—Charter Communications

PICKENS—See WINONA, MS (Cable One)

PIKE COUNTY—See BROOKHAVEN, MS (Cable One)

PINE GROVE—See RIPLEY, MS (Ripley Video Cable Co. Inc.)

PITTSBORO—See BRUCE, MS (MetroCast Communications)

PLANTERSVILLE—See TUPELO, MS (Comcast Cable)

PONTOTOC COUNTY (PORTIONS)—See TUPELO, MS (Comcast Cable)

▲**PONTOTOC**—MetroCast Communications

▲**PONTOTOC**—Zoom Media

POPE—See CLEVELAND, MS (Cable One)

▲**POPLARVILLE**—Zito Media

▲**PORT GIBSON**—Bailey Cable TV Inc.

▲**POTTS CAMP**—MetroCast Communications

PRENTISS COUNTY—See BOONEVILLE, MS (MetroCast Communications)

▲**PRENTISS**—Zoom Media

▲**PUCKETT**—Comcast Cable

PURVIS—See HATTIESBURG, MS (Comcast Cable)

▲**QUITMAN**—CMA Cablevision

▲**RALEIGH**—MetroCast Communications

RANKIN COUNTY (PORTIONS)—See PEARL, MS (Comcast Cable)

RANKIN COUNTY—See JACKSON, MS (Comcast Cable)

RAWLS SPRINGS—See HATTIESBURG, MS (Comcast Cable)

RAYMOND—See JACKSON, MS (Comcast Cable)

RENOVA—See CLEVELAND, MS (Cable One)

RICHLAND—See JACKSON, MS (Comcast Cable)

▲**RICHTON**—Alliance Communications

RIDGELAND—See JACKSON, MS (Comcast Cable)

▲**RIENZI**—Formerly served by Adelphia Communications. Now served by CORINTH, MS [MS0016]

RIENZI—See CORINTH, MS (Zoom Media)

▲**RIPLEY**—Ripley Video Cable Co. Inc.

▲**ROLLING FORK**—RF Cable LLC

▲**ROSEDALE**—Cablevision of Rosedale

▲**ROXIE**—Telepak Networks SnapVision. Formerly Branch Cable Inc. served by MEADVILLE-BUDE, MS [MS0069]. This cable system has converted to IPTV.

RULEVILLE—See CLEVELAND, MS (Cable One)

RUNNELSTOWN—See MACEDONIA, MS (Zoom Media)

RURAL HILL—See COLUMBUS, MS (Cable One)

RUSSELL—See MERIDIAN, MS (Comcast Cable)

SALTILLO—See TUPELO, MS (Comcast Cable)

SALTILLO—See BALDWYN, MS (MetroCast Communications)

SANDERSVILLE—See HATTIESBURG, MS (Comcast Cable)

▲**SANFORD**—Home Cable Entertainment

SAUCIER—See LONG BEACH, MS (Cable One)

▲**SCOOBA**—Cable TV Inc.

SCOTT COUNTY (PORTIONS)—See LAKE, MS (Zoom Media)

SCOTT COUNTY (UNINCORPORATED AREAS)—See FOREST, MS (MetroCast Communications)

▲**SEMINARY**—Home Cable Entertainment

SHADY GROVE (PORTIONS)—See LAUREL, MS (Comcast Cable)

SHANNON—See NETTLETON, MS (MetroCast Communications)

SHAW (PORTIONS)—See CLEVELAND, MS (Cable One)

▲**SHELBY**—Galaxy Cablevision. Now served by CLEVELAND, MS [MS0019]

SHELBY—See CLEVELAND, MS (Cable One)

SHERMAN—See TUPELO, MS (Comcast Cable)

▲**SHUBUTA**—Alliance Communications

SHUQUALAK—See MACON, MS (Cable TV Inc.)

SIDON—See GREENWOOD, MS (Suddenlink Communications)

SILVER CREEK—See PRENTISS, MS (Zoom Media)

SIMPSON COUNTY—See MENDENHALL, MS (Bailey Cable TV Inc.)

SMITHVILLE—See AMORY, MS (MetroCast Communications)

SNOW LAKE SHORES—See ASHLAND, MS (MetroCast Communications)

SOSO—See BAY SPRINGS, MS (Video Inc.)

▲**ST. ANDREWS**—Mediacom

STAR—See PEARL, MS (Comcast Cable)

▲**STARKVILLE**—MetroCast Communications

▲**STATE LINE**—Zoom Media

STEENS—See COLUMBUS, MS (Cable One)

STONE COUNTY (PORTIONS)—See WIGGINS, MS (Mediacom)

STONEWALL—See QUITMAN, MS (CMA Cablevision)

STRICKLAND—See CORINTH, MS (Zoom Media)

SUMMIT—See BROOKHAVEN, MS (Cable One)

▲**SUMNER**—Formerly served by Cable One. No longer in operation

▲**SUMRALL**—Alliance Communications

SUNFLOWER COUNTY—See GREENWOOD, MS (Suddenlink Communications)

▲**SUNFLOWER**—Sledge Cable. This cable system has converted to IPTV. See Sunflower, MS [MS5031]

▲**SUNFLOWER**—Sledge Cable. Formerly [MS0195]. This cable system has converted to IPTV

▲**SUNRISE**—Home Cable Entertainment

SWIFTWATER—See GREENVILLE, MS (Suddenlink Communications)

SYMONDS—See CLEVELAND, MS (Cable One)

TALLAHATCHIE COUNTY—See WINONA, MS (Cable One)

▲**TAYLORSVILLE**—Zoom Media

TCHULA—See WINONA, MS (Cable One)

TERRY—See CRYSTAL SPRINGS, MS (Bailey Cable TV Inc.)

THEO—See CORINTH, MS (Zoom Media)

TISHOMINGO COUNTY—See IUKA, MS (MetroCast Communications)

TOOMSUBA—See MERIDIAN, MS (Comcast Cable)

TREMONT—See TUPELO, MS (Comcast Cable)

▲**TUPELO**—Comcast Cable

TUTWILER—See WINONA, MS (Cable One)

▲**TYLERTOWN**—Zito Media

UNION COUNTY (PORTIONS)—See TUPELO, MS (Comcast Cable)

UNION COUNTY—See NEW ALBANY, MS (MetroCast Communications)

▲**UNION**—Mediacom. Now served by LOUISVILLE, MS [MS0038]

▲**UNION**—Mediacom

UNION—See UNION, MS (Mediacom)

UNIVERSITY OF MISSISSIPPI—See OXFORD, MS (MetroCast Communications)

VAIDEN—See WINONA, MS (Cable One)

VAN CLEAVE—See BILOXI, MS (Cable One)

VARDAMAN—See CALHOUN CITY, MS (MetroCast Communications)

VERONA—See TUPELO, MS (Comcast Cable)

▲**VICKSBURG**—Vicksburg Video Inc.

VIDALIA—See NATCHEZ, LA (Cable One)

WADE—See PASCAGOULA, MS (Cable One)

▲**WATER VALLEY**—Mediacom. Now served by PONTOTOC, MS [MS0045]

WATER VALLEY—See PONTOTOC, MS (MetroCast Communications)

▲**WAVELAND**—Mediacom

WAYNE COUNTY—See WAYNESBORO, MS (CMA Cablevision)

▲**WAYNESBORO**—CMA Cablevision

WAYSIDE—See GREENVILLE, MS (Suddenlink Communications)

WEBB—See WINONA, MS (Cable One)

WEBSTER COUNTY—See EUPORA, MS (Cable TV Inc.)

▲**WEIR**—Delta Telephone SnapVision. This cable system has converted to IPTV. See Weir, MS [MS5013]

▲**WEIR**—Delta Telephone SnapVision. Formerly [MS0126]. This cable system has converted to IPTV

WEST POINT—See TUPELO, MS (Comcast Cable)

▲**WIGGINS**—Mediacom

▲**WINONA**—Cable One

WINSTON COUNTY (PORTIONS)—See UNION, MS (Mediacom)

▲**WINSTONVILLE**—Formerly served by J & L Cable. No longer in operation

▲**WOODVILLE**—Trust Cable. Now served by WOODVILLE, MS [MS0048]

WOODVILLE—See CENTREVILLE, MS (Trust Cable)

YALOBUSHA COUNTY—See COFFEEVILLE, MS (MetroCast Communications)

YAZOO CITY—See CLEVELAND, MS (Cable One)

MISSOURI

ADAIR COUNTY—See KIRKSVILLE, MO (Cable One)

▲**ADRIAN**—Provincial Cable & Data

▲**ADVANCE**—Formerly served by Cebridge Connections. Now served by MORLEY, MO [MO0171]

ADVANCE—See MORLEY, MO (Semo Communications Corp.)

AFFTON—See OLIVETTE, MO (Charter Communications)

AGENCY—See ST. JOSEPH, MO (Suddenlink Communications)

AIRPORT DRIVE VILLAGE—See CARL JUNCTION, MO (Mediacom)

▲**ALBA**—Mediacom. Now served by CARL JUNCTION, MO [MO0094]

ALBA—See CARL JUNCTION, MO (Mediacom)

▲**ALBANY**—Mediacom

▲**ALMA**—Citizens Telephone Co

▲**ALTON**—Boycom Cablevision Inc.

▲**AMAZONIA**—Formerly served by CableDirect. No longer in operation

▲**AMSTERDAM**—Craw-Kan Telephone Co-op. This cable system has converted to IPTV. See Amsterdam, MO [MO5189]

▲**AMSTERDAM**—Craw-Kan Telephone Co-op. Formerly [MO0383]. This cable system has converted to IPTV

▲**ANDERSON**—Mediacom. Now served by GRANBY, MO [MO0156]

ANDERSON—See GRANBY, MO (Mediacom)

▲**ANNAPOLIS**—Formerly served by Charter Communications. No longer in operation

ANNISTON—See MORLEY, MO (Semo Communications Corp.)

▲**APPLETON CITY**—Mediacom

ARCADIA—See FARMINGTON, MO (Charter Communications)

▲**ARCHIE**—Mediacom. Now served by BUTLER, MO [MO0097]

ARCHIE—See BUTLER, MO (Mediacom)

▲**ARGYLE**—Formerly served by First Cable of Missouri Inc. No longer in operation

▲**ARMSTRONG**—Formerly served by Cebridge Connections. No longer in operation

ARNOLD—See IMPERIAL, MO (Charter Communications)

ASH GROVE—See EVERTON, MO (Mediacom)

ASHLAND—See COLUMBIA, MO (Charter Communications)

ATCHISON COUNTY—See ROCKPORT, MO (Rockport Cablevision)

▲**ATLANTA**—Formerly served by CableDirect. No longer in operation

AUDRAIN COUNTY (PORTIONS)—See MEXICO, MO (US Cable)

AUNT'S CREEK—See NIXA, MO (Suddenlink Communications)

AURORA—See MONETT, MO (Suddenlink Communications)

AUXVASSE—See FULTON, MO (Charter Communications)

▲**AVA**—Mediacom. Now served by SEYMOUR, MO [MO0172]

AVA—See SEYMOUR, MO (Mediacom)

AVONDALE—See KANSAS CITY, MO (Time Warner Cable)

BAGNELL—See OSAGE BEACH, MO (Charter Communications)

BALDWIN PARK—See INDEPENDENCE, MO (Comcast Cable)

BALLWIN—See OLIVETTE, MO (Charter Communications)

▲**BARING**—Formerly served by CableDirect. No longer in operation

▲**BARNARD**—Formerly served by CableDirect. No longer in operation

▲**BARNHART**—Charter Communications

BATES CITY—See INDEPENDENCE, MO (Comcast Cable)

BATTLEFIELD—See SPRINGFIELD, MO (Mediacom)

BEL-NOR—See FERGUSON, MO (Charter Communications)

BEL-RIDGE—See FERGUSON, MO (Charter Communications)

▲**BELL CITY**—Semo Communications Corporation. Now served by MORLEY, MO [MO0171]

BELL CITY—See MORLEY, MO (Semo Communications Corp.)

BELLA VILLA—See OLIVETTE, MO (Charter Communications)

▲**BELLE**—Formerly served by Almega Cable. No longer in operation

BELLEFONTAINE NEIGHBORS—See OVERLAND, MO (Charter Communications)

BELLERIVE—See FERGUSON, MO (Charter Communications)

BELLFLOWER—See MEXICO, MO (US Cable)

BELTON—See KANSAS CITY, MO (Time Warner Cable)

▲**BENTON**—Charter Communications. Now served by CAPE GIRARDEAU, MO [MO0018]

BENTON—See CAPE GIRARDEAU, MO (Charter Communications)

BERKELEY—See FERGUSON, MO (Charter Communications)

▲**BERNIE**—Formerly served by Cebridge Connections. Now served by DEXTER, MO [MO0039]

BERNIE—See DEXTER, MO (NewWave Communications)

BERTRAND—See CAPE GIRARDEAU, MO (Charter Communications)

▲**BETHANY**—Mediacom

BEVERLY HILLS—See FERGUSON, MO (Charter Communications)

▲**BEVIER**—Chariton Valley Communications Corp. Now served by MACON, MO [MO0071]

BEVIER—See MACON, MO (Chariton Valley Cablevision)

▲**BILLINGS**—Mediacom. Now served by SEYMOUR, MO [MO0172]. Previously served by FORSYTH, MO [MO0126]

BILLINGS—See SEYMOUR, MO (Mediacom)

▲**BIRCH TREE**—Boycom Cablevision Inc.

▲**BISMARCK**—Charter Communications. Now served by FARMINGTON, MO [MO0035]

BISMARCK—See FARMINGTON, MO (Charter Communications)

BLACK JACK—See OLIVETTE, MO (Charter Communications)

BLACKBURN—See ALMA, MO (Citizens Telephone Co)

BLODGETT—See MORLEY, MO (Semo Communications Corp.)

BLOOMFIELD—See DEXTER, MO (NewWave Communications)

BLUE EYE—See LAMPE, AR (Crystal Broadband Networks)

BLUE EYE—See LAMPE, MO (Crystal Broadband Networks)

BLUE SPRINGS—See INDEPENDENCE, MO (Comcast Cable)

▲**BOGARD**—Formerly served by CableDirect. No longer in operation

▲**BOLCKOW**—Formerly served by CableDirect. No longer in operation

▲**BOLIVAR**—Windstream

BONNE TERRE—See FARMINGTON, MO (Charter Communications)

BONNER SPRINGS—See KANSAS CITY, KS (Time Warner Cable)

BOONE COUNTY (PORTIONS)—See COLUMBIA, MO (Mediacom)

BOONE COUNTY—See COLUMBIA, MO (Charter Communications)

▲**BOONVILLE**—Suddenlink Communications

▲**BOSWORTH**—Formerly served by CableDirect. No longer in operation

BOURBON—See SULLIVAN, MO (Charter Communications)

▲**BOWLING GREEN**—Crystal Broadband Networks

BRANSON VIEW ESTATES—See BRANSON, MO (Suddenlink Communications)

BRANSON WEST—See NIXA, MO (Suddenlink Communications)

▲**BRANSON**—Suddenlink Communications

▲**BRAYMER**—Allegiance Communications

BRECKENRIDGE HILLS—See OVERLAND, MO (Charter Communications)

BRENTWOOD—See OVERLAND, MO (Charter Communications)

BRIDGETON TERRACE—See OLIVETTE, MO (Charter Communications)

BRIDGETON—See OLIVETTE, MO (Charter Communications)

▲**BROOKFIELD**—Suddenlink Communications

BROOKING PARK—See SMITHTON, MO (Provincial Cable & Data)

BROOKLINE (PORTIONS)—See SPRINGFIELD, MO (Mediacom)

BROOKLYN HEIGHTS—See CARTHAGE, MO (Suddenlink Communications)

▲**BROWNING**—Formerly served by CableDirect. No longer in operation

BROWNWOOD—See MORLEY, MO (Semo Communications Corp.)

▲**BRUNSWICK**—Mediacom. Now served by SALISBURY, MO [MO0155]

BRUNSWICK—See SALISBURY, MO (Mediacom)

BUCKLIN—See MACON, MO (Chariton Valley Cablevision)

BUCKNER—See INDEPENDENCE, MO (Comcast Cable)

▲**BUFFALO**—Provincial Cable & Data

BULL CREEK—See BRANSON, MO (Suddenlink Communications)

▲**BUNCETON**—Otelco

▲**BUNKER**—Formerly served by Cebridge Connections. No longer in operation

▲**BURLINGTON JUNCTION**—B & L Technologies LLC

BUTLER COUNTY (NORTHERN PORTION)—See WAPPAPELLO, MO (Boycom Cablevision Inc.)

BUTLER COUNTY (PORTIONS)—See POPLAR BLUFF, MO (City Cable)

▲**BUTLER COUNTY**—Boycom Cablevision Inc.

▲**BUTLER**—Mediacom

BYRNES MILLS—See BARNHART, MO (Charter Communications)

▲**CABOOL**—Mediacom. Now served by SEYMOUR, MO [MO0172]

CABOOL—See SEYMOUR, MO (Mediacom)

▲**CAINSVILLE**—Formerly served by Longview Communications. No longer in operation

▲**CAIRO**—Formerly served by Almega Cable. No longer in operation

▲**CALIFORNIA**—Crystal Broadband Networks

CALLAO—See MACON, MO (Chariton Valley Cablevision)

CALLAWAY COUNTY (PORTIONS)—See FULTON, MO (Charter Communications)

CALLAWAY COUNTY—See JEFFERSON CITY, MO (Mediacom)

CALVERTON PARK—See FERGUSON, MO (Charter Communications)

CAMDEN COUNTY (PORTIONS)—See PORTER MILLS, MO (Lake Communications)

CAMDEN COUNTY—See OSAGE BEACH, MO (Charter Communications)

▲**CAMDEN POINT**—Allegiance Communications

CAMDENTON—See OSAGE BEACH, MO (Charter Communications)

▲**CAMERON**—Mediacom

CAMPBELL—See DEXTER, MO (NewWave Communications)

CANALOU—See MORLEY, MO (Semo Communications Corp.)

▲**CANTON**—Formerly served by Westcom. No longer in operation

▲**CAPE GIRARDEAU**—Charter Communications

▲**CARL JUNCTION**—Mediacom

▲**CARROLLTON**—Mediacom

CARTERVILLE—See JOPLIN, MO (Cable One)

▲**CARTHAGE**—Suddenlink Communications

▲**CARUTHERSVILLE**—Mediacom

▲**CASS COUNTY (northwestern portion)**—Formerly served by Cass County Cable. No longer in operation

▲**CASS COUNTY**—Formerly served by Longview Communications. No longer in operation

▲**CASSVILLE**—Mediacom

CEDAR HILL LAKES—See BARNHART, MO (Charter Communications)

CEDAR HILL—See BARNHART, MO (Charter Communications)

CENTERTOWN—See COLE COUNTY (portions), MO (Suddenlink Communications)

▲**CENTERVIEW**—Formerly served by CableDirect. No longer in operation

▲**CENTRALIA**—US Cable. Now served by MEXICO, MO [MO0033]

CENTRALIA—See MEXICO, MO (US Cable)

CHAFFEE—See CAPE GIRARDEAU, MO (Charter Communications)

▲**CHAMOIS**—Mid Missouri Broadband

CHARLACK—See OLIVETTE, MO (Charter Communications)

▲**CHARLESTON**—Charter Communications. Now served by CAPE GIRARDEAU, MO [MO0018]

CHARLESTON—See CAPE GIRARDEAU, MO (Charter Communications)

▲**CHESTERFIELD**—Charter Communications. Now served by OLIVETTE, MO [MO0009]

CHESTERFIELD—See OLIVETTE, MO (Charter Communications)

CHESTERFIELD—See OVERLAND, MO (Charter Communications)

▲**CHILHOWEE**—Formerly served by National Cable Inc. No longer in operation

▲ **CHILLICOTHE**—Windjammer Cable

CHRISTIAN COUNTY—See NIXA, MO (Suddenlink Communications)

▲ **CHULA**—Formerly served by CableDirect. No longer in operation

▲ **CLARENCE**—Milan Interactive Communications

CLARK—See STURGEON, MO (Provincial Cable & Data)

▲ **CLARKSBURG**—Formerly served by First Cable of Missouri Inc. No longer in operation

▲ **CLARKSDALE**—Formerly served by CableDirect. No longer in operation

CLARKSON VALLEY—See OLIVETTE, MO (Charter Communications)

▲ **CLARKSVILLE**—First Cable of Missouri Inc.

▲ **CLARKTON**—NewWave Communications

CLAYCOMO—See KANSAS CITY, MO (Time Warner Cable)

CLAYTON—See OVERLAND, MO (Charter Communications)

▲ **CLEARMONT**—Formerly served by Longview Communications. No longer in operation

CLEVER—See REPUBLIC, MO (Cable America Corp.)

▲ **CLEVER**—Suddenlink Communications

CLIFF VILLAGE—See JOPLIN, MO (Cable One)

▲ **CLINTON**—Charter Communications

CLYDE—See CONCEPTION JUNCTION, MO (B & L Technologies LLC)

COBALT VILLAGE—See FARMINGTON, MO (Charter Communications)

▲ **COFFMAN BEND**—Formerly served by Almega Cable. No longer in operation

▲ **COLE CAMP**—Provincial Cable & Data

COLE COUNTY (PORTIONS)—See JEFFERSON CITY, MO (Mediacom)

▲ **COLE COUNTY (PORTIONS)**—Suddenlink Communications

▲ **COLUMBIA**—Charter Communications

▲ **COLUMBIA**—Mediacom

COMPTON RIDGE—See BRANSON, MO (Suddenlink Communications)

▲ **CONCEPTION JUNCTION**—B & L Technologies LLC

CONCEPTION—See CONCEPTION JUNCTION, MO (B & L Technologies LLC)

CONCORDIA—See ALMA, MO (Citizens Telephone Co)

▲ **CONWAY**—Fidelity Communications

COOL VALLEY—See FERGUSON, MO (Charter Communications)

COOPER COUNTY (PORTIONS)—See BOONVILLE, MO (Suddenlink Communications)

CORDER—See ALMA, MO (Citizens Telephone Co)

COTTLEVILLE—See ST. CHARLES, MO (Charter Communications)

COUNTRY CLUB HILLS—See OVERLAND, MO (Charter Communications)

COUNTRY CLUB VILLAGE—See ST. JOSEPH, MO (Suddenlink Communications)

COUNTRY LIFE ACRES—See OLIVETTE, MO (Charter Communications)

COUNTRYSIDE—See KANSAS CITY, KS (Time Warner Cable)

▲ **COWGILL**—GH Technologies. This cable system has converted to IPTV. See Cowgill, MO [MO5188]

▲ **COWGILL**—GH Technologies. Formerly [MO0445]. This cable system has converted to IPTV

▲ **CRAIG**—Formerly served by CableDirect. No longer in operation

▲ **CRANE**—Mediacom. Now served by SEYMOUR, MO [MO0126]. Previously served by FORSYTH, MO [MO0126]

CRANE—See SEYMOUR, MO (Mediacom)

CRAWFORD COUNTY—See SULLIVAN, MO (Charter Communications)

▲ **CREIGHTON**—Formerly served by CableDirect. No longer in operation

CRESTWOOD—See OLIVETTE, MO (Charter Communications)

CREVE COEUR—See OLIVETTE, MO (Charter Communications)

CREVE COEUR—See OVERLAND, MO (Charter Communications)

▲ **CROCKER**—Formerly served by Longview Communications. No longer in operation

CRYSTAL CITY—See IMPERIAL, MO (Charter Communications)

CRYSTAL LAKE PARK—See OLIVETTE, MO (Charter Communications)

CRYSTAL LAKES—See EXCELSIOR SPRINGS, MO (Mediacom)

▲ **CUBA**—Formerly served by Charter Communications. No longer in operation

CUBA—See SULLIVAN, MO (Charter Communications)

▲ **CURRYVILLE**—Formerly served by First Cable of Missouri Inc. No longer in operation

DARDENNE PRAIRIE—See LAKE ST. LOUIS, MO (Charter Communications)

DARDENNE PRAIRIE—See ST. CHARLES, MO (Charter Communications)

▲ **DE KALB**—Formerly served by CableDirect. No longer in operation

DE SOTO—See IMPERIAL, MO (Charter Communications)

DE SOTO—See KANSAS CITY, KS (Time Warner Cable)

DEARBORN—See CAMDEN POINT, MO (Allegiance Communications)

DEFIANCE—See LAKE SHERWOOD, MO (Cable America Corp.)

DELLWOOD—See FERGUSON, MO (Charter Communications)

DELTA—See MORLEY, MO (Semo Communications Corp.)

DENT COUNTY—See SALEM, MO (Fidelity Communications)

DES PERES—See OLIVETTE, MO (Charter Communications)

DESLOGE—See FARMINGTON, MO (Charter Communications)

▲ **DEXTER**—NewWave Communications

▲ **DIAMOND**—Mediacom. Now served by GRANBY, MO [MO0156]

DIAMOND—See GRANBY, MO (Mediacom)

▲ **DIXON**—Cable America Corp. Now served by WAYNESVILLE (formerly ST. ROBERT), MO [MO0023]

DIXON—See WAYNESVILLE, MO (Cable America Corp.)

DOE RUN—See FARMINGTON, MO (Charter Communications)

▲ **DONIPHAN**—Boycom Cablevision Inc.

▲ **DOOLITTLE**—Cable America Corp. Now served by WAYNESVILLE (formerly ST. ROBERT), MO [MO0023]

DOOLITTLE—See WAYNESVILLE, MO (Cable America Corp.)

▲ **DOWNING**—Formerly served by Longview Communications. No longer in operation

▲ **DREXEL**—Formerly served by Almega Cable. No longer in operation

▲ **DUDLEY**—Boycom Cablevision Inc.

DUENWEG—See CARL JUNCTION, MO (Mediacom)

DUNKLIN COUNTY (PORTIONS)—See DEXTER, MO (NewWave Communications)

DUNKLIN COUNTY—See CLARKTON, MO (NewWave Communications)

DUNKLIN COUNTY—See KENNETT, MO (Windjammer Cable)

▲ **DUQUESNE**—Mediacom. Now served by CARL JUNCTION, MO [MO0094]

DUQUESNE—See CARL JUNCTION, MO (Mediacom)

▲ **DURHAM**—Formerly served by CableDirect. No longer in operation

▲ **EAGLEVILLE**—Formerly served by Longview Communications. No longer in operation

EAST BONNE—See FARMINGTON, MO (Charter Communications)

▲ **EAST LYNNE**—Formerly served by CableDirect. No longer in operation

EAST PRAIRIE—See CAPE GIRARDEAU, MO (Charter Communications)

▲ **EASTON**—Formerly served by First Cable of Missouri Inc. No longer in operation

EDGERTON—See CAMDEN POINT, MO (Allegiance Communications)

▲ **EDINA**—US Cable

EDMUNDSON—See OVERLAND, MO (Charter Communications)

EDWARDSVILLE PARK—See KANSAS CITY, KS (Time Warner Cable)

EDWARDSVILLE—See KANSAS CITY, KS (Time Warner Cable)

▲ **EL DORADO SPRINGS**—Cobridge Communications

▲ **ELDON**—Charter Communications. Now served by OSAGE BEACH, MO [MO0017]

ELDON—See OSAGE BEACH, MO (Charter Communications)

▲ **ELLINGTON**—Boycom Cablevision Inc.

ELLISVILLE—See OLIVETTE, MO (Charter Communications)

▲ **ELLSINORE**—Boycom Cablevision Inc.

▲ **ELMO**—Formerly served by CableDirect. No longer in operation

▲ **ELSBERRY**—Crystal Broadband Networks

ELVINS—See FARMINGTON, MO (Charter Communications)

▲ **EMINENCE**—Boycom Cablevision Inc.

EMMA—See ALMA, MO (Citizens Telephone Co)

▲ **EOLIA**—Formerly served by First Cable of Missouri Inc. No longer in operation

▲ **ESSEX**—Formerly served by Cebridge Connections. Now served by DEXTER, MO [MO0039]

ESSEX—See DEXTER, MO (NewWave Communications)

ESTHER—See FARMINGTON, MO (Charter Communications)

▲ **EUGENE**—Formerly served by First Cable of Missouri Inc. No longer in operation

EUREKA—See OLIVETTE, MO (Charter Communications)

▲ **EVERTON**—Mediacom

▲ **EWING**—Formerly served by CableDirect. No longer in operation

EXCELSIOR ESTATES—See EXCELSIOR SPRINGS, MO (Mediacom)

▲ **EXCELSIOR SPRINGS**—Mediacom

EXETER—See CASSVILLE, MO (Mediacom)

▲**FAIR GROVE**—Fidelity Communications

▲**FAIR PLAY**—Formerly served by Cebridge Connections. No longer in operation

FAIRFAX—See ROCKPORT, MO (Rockport Cablevision)

FAIRWAY—See KANSAS CITY, KS (Time Warner Cable)

▲**FARBER**—US Cable. Now served by MEXICO, MO [MO0033]

FARBER—See MEXICO, MO (US Cable)

▲**FARMINGTON**—Charter Communications

▲**FAUCETT**—Formerly served by CableDirect. No longer in operation

▲**FAYETTE**—Suddenlink Communications

FENTON—See OLIVETTE, MO (Charter Communications)

▲**FERGUSON**—Charter Communications

FERRELVIEW—See KANSAS CITY, MO (Time Warner Cable)

FESTUS—See IMPERIAL, MO (Charter Communications)

▲**FISK**—Boycom Cablevision Inc.

▲**FLAT RIVER**—Charter Communications. Now served by FARMINGTON, MO [MO0035]

FLAT RIVER—See FARMINGTON, MO (Charter Communications)

FLINT HILL—See LAKE ST. LOUIS, MO (Charter Communications)

FLORDELL HILLS—See OVERLAND, MO (Charter Communications)

FLORISSANT—See OLIVETTE, MO (Charter Communications)

FOLEY—See WINFIELD, MO (US Cable)

▲**FORDLAND**—Formerly served by Cebridge Connections. No longer in operation

FOREST CITY—See OREGON, MO (South Holt Cablevision Inc.)

▲**FORSYTH**—Mediacom

FORT LEAVENWORTH—See KANSAS CITY, KS (Time Warner Cable)

FORT LEONARD WOOD—See WAYNESVILLE, MO (Cable America Corp.)

FRANKCLAY—See FARMINGTON, MO (Charter Communications)

▲**FRANKFORD**—Formerly served by Westcom. No longer in operation

FRANKLIN COUNTY (NORTHEASTERN PORTION)—See BARNHART, MO (Charter Communications)

FRANKLIN COUNTY (SOUTHWESTERN PORTION)—See SULLIVAN, MO (Charter Communications)

▲**FREDERICKTOWN**—Charter Communications. Now served by FARMINGTON, MO [MO0035]

FREDERICKTOWN—See FARMINGTON, MO (Charter Communications)

▲**FREEBURG**—Formerly served by CableDirect. No longer in operation

▲**FREMONT**—Formerly served by Cebridge Connections. No longer in operation

FRISBEE—See CLARKTON, MO (NewWave Communications)

FRONTENAC—See OLIVETTE, MO (Charter Communications)

FRUITLAND—See MORLEY, MO (Semo Communications Corp.)

▲**FULTON**—Charter Communications

▲**GAINESVILLE**—Formerly served by Almega Cable. No longer in operation

▲**GALENA**—Formerly served by Almega Cable. No longer in operation

GALENA—See CARL JUNCTION, KS (Mediacom)

▲**GALLATIN**—Formerly served by Longview Communications. No longer in operation

▲**GALT**—Formerly served by CableDirect. No longer in operation

▲**GARDEN CITY**—Formerly served by Longview Communications. No longer in operation

GARDNER—See KANSAS CITY, KS (Time Warner Cable)

▲**GASCONADE**—Formerly served by First Cable of Missouri Inc. No longer in operation

▲**GERALD**—Fidelity Communications

GIBSON—See CLARKTON, MO (NewWave Communications)

GIDEON—See CLARKTON, MO (NewWave Communications)

GILLIAM—See ALMA, MO (Citizens Telephone Co)

GLADSTONE—See KANSAS CITY, MO (Time Warner Cable)

▲**GLASGOW**—Suddenlink Communications

GLEN ECHO PARK—See FERGUSON, MO (Charter Communications)

GLENAIRE—See KANSAS CITY, MO (Time Warner Cable)

GLENALLEN—See MARBLE HILL, MO (Boycom Cablevision Inc.)

GLENDALE—See OLIVETTE, MO (Charter Communications)

GOLDEN CITY—See EVERTON, MO (Mediacom)

▲**GOODMAN**—Mediacom. Now served by GRANBY, MO [MO0156]

GOODMAN—See GRANBY, MO (Mediacom)

▲**GOWER**—Allegiance Communications

GRAHAM—See MAITLAND, MO (Holway Telephone Co.)

GRAIN VALLEY—See INDEPENDENCE, MO (Comcast Cable)

▲**GRANBY**—Mediacom

GRANDIN—See ELLSINORE, MO (Boycom Cablevision Inc.)

GRANDVIEW—See KANSAS CITY, MO (Time Warner Cable)

▲**GRANT CITY**—B & L Technologies LLC

GRANTWOOD VILLAGE—See OLIVETTE, MO (Charter Communications)

▲**GRAVOIS MILLS**—Lake Communications

GRAY SUMMIT—See BARNHART, MO (Charter Communications)

▲**GREEN CASTLE**—Formerly served by Longview Communications. No longer in operation

GREEN PARK—See OLIVETTE, MO (Charter Communications)

▲**GREEN RIDGE**—Formerly served by CableDirect. No longer in operation

GREENDALE—See FERGUSON, MO (Charter Communications)

GREENE COUNTY (PORTIONS)—See FAIR GROVE, MO (Fidelity Communications)

GREENE COUNTY (PORTIONS)—See SPRINGFIELD, MO (Mediacom)

GREENE COUNTY (SOUTHWESTERN PORTION)—See REPUBLIC, MO (Cable America Corp.)

GREENE COUNTY (UNINCORPORATED AREAS)—See EVERTON, MO (Mediacom)

GREENFIELD—See EVERTON, MO (Mediacom)

▲**GREENTOP**—Formerly served by Longview Communications. No longer in operation

GREENVIEW—See PORTER MILLS, MO (Lake Communications)

▲**GREENVILLE**—Formerly served by Almega Cable. No longer in operation

GREENWOOD—See INDEPENDENCE, MO (Comcast Cable)

GRUNDY COUNTY—See TRENTON, MO (Suddenlink Communications)

▲**HALLSVILLE**—Longview Communications. Now served by STURGEON, MO [MO0395]

HALLSVILLE—See STURGEON, MO (Provincial Cable & Data)

▲**HAMILTON**—Allegiance Communications

HANLEY HILLS—See OLIVETTE, MO (Charter Communications)

▲**HANNIBAL**—US Cable

▲**HARRISBURG**—Formerly served by First Cable of Missouri Inc. No longer in operation

▲**HARRISONVILLE**—Cobridge Communications

▲**HARTVILLE**—Formerly served by Cebridge Connections. No longer in operation

HARVESTER—See ST. CHARLES, MO (Charter Communications)

▲**HAWK POINT**—Formerly served by First Cable of Missouri Inc. No longer in operation

HAYTI HEIGHTS—See CARUTHERSVILLE, MO (Mediacom)

HAYTI—See CARUTHERSVILLE, MO (Mediacom)

HAYWOOD CITY—See MORLEY, MO (Semo Communications Corp.)

HAZELWOOD—See OLIVETTE, MO (Charter Communications)

HENRIETTA—See RICHMOND, MO (Mediacom)

HENRY COUNTY—See CLINTON, MO (Charter Communications)

HERCULANEUM—See IMPERIAL, MO (Charter Communications)

▲**HERMANN**—Mediacom

HERMITAGE—See POMME DE TERRE, MO (American Broadband)

HICKORY COUNTY—See POMME DE TERRE, MO (American Broadband)

▲**HIGBEE**—Formerly served by Longview Communications. No longer in operation

HIGGINSVILLE—See ALMA, MO (Citizens Telephone Co)

HIGH RIDGE—See BARNHART, MO (Charter Communications)

HIGH RIDGE—See IMPERIAL, MO (Charter Communications)

HIGHLANDVILLE—See NIXA, MO (Suddenlink Communications)

▲**HIGHWAY DD**—Formerly served by Cebridge Connections. Now served by NIXA, MO [MO0068]

HIGHWAY DD—See NIXA, MO (Suddenlink Communications)

HILLSBORO—See IMPERIAL, MO (Charter Communications)

HILLSDALE—See FERGUSON, MO (Charter Communications)

HOLCOMB—See CLARKTON, MO (NewWave Communications)

▲**HOLDEN**—Crystal Broadband Networks

HOLLISTER—See BRANSON, MO (Suddenlink Communications)

▲**HOLT**—Formerly served by CableDirect. No longer in operation

▲**HOLTS SUMMIT**—Mediacom. Now served by JEFFERSON CITY, MO [MO0020]

HOLTS SUMMIT—See JEFFERSON CITY, MO (Mediacom)

HOMESTEAD VILLAGE—See EXCELSIOR SPRINGS, MO (Mediacom)

▲**HOPKINS**—B & L Technologies LLC

▲**HORNERSVILLE**—Base Cablevision

HOUSE SPRINGS—See BARNHART, MO (Charter Communications)

HOUSTON LAKE—See KANSAS CITY, MO (Time Warner Cable)

▲**HOUSTON**—Houston Cable Inc. Now served by WAYNESVILLE, MO [MO0023]

HOUSTON—See WAYNESVILLE, MO (Cable America Corp.)

HOUSTONIA—See ALMA, MO (Citizens Telephone Co)

HOWARDVILLE—See NEW MADRID, MO (Charter Communications)

HOWELL COUNTY—See ALTON, MO (Boycom Cablevision Inc.)

HOWELL COUNTY—See WEST PLAINS, MO (Cobridge Communications)

HUMANSVILLE—See POMME DE TERRE, MO (American Broadband)

▲**HUME**—Formerly served by Midwest Cable Inc. No longer in operation

HUNTLEIGH—See OLIVETTE, MO (Charter Communications)

HUNTSVILLE—See MOBERLY, MO (US Cable)

▲**HURDLAND**—Formerly served by CableDirect. No longer in operation

▲**IBERIA**—Formerly served by Longview Communications. No longer in operation

ILLMO—See CAPE GIRARDEAU, MO (Charter Communications)

▲**IMPERIAL**—Charter Communications

▲**INDEPENDENCE**—Comcast Cable

INDEPENDENCE—See KANSAS CITY, MO (Time Warner Cable)

INDIAN POINT—See BRANSON, MO (Suddenlink Communications)

IRON CITY—See FARMINGTON, MO (Charter Communications)

IRON MOUNTAIN LAKE—See FARMINGTON, MO (Charter Communications)

▲**IRONTON**—Charter Communications. Now served by FARMINGTON, MO [MO0035]

IRONTON—See FARMINGTON, MO (Charter Communications)

▲**IVY BEND**—Formerly served by Almega Cable. No longer in operation

JACKSON COUNTY—See INDEPENDENCE, MO (Comcast Cable)

JACKSON—See CAPE GIRARDEAU, MO (Charter Communications)

▲**JACKSONVILLE**—Formerly served by First Cable of Missouri Inc. No longer in operation

▲**JAMESPORT**—Formerly served by CableDirect. No longer in operation

JASPER COUNTY—See CARL JUNCTION, MO (Mediacom)

▲**JASPER**—Mediacom. Now served by GRANBY, MO [MO0156]

JASPER—See GRANBY, MO (Mediacom)

▲**JEFFERSON CITY**—Mediacom

JEFFERSON COUNTY (UNINCORPORATED AREAS)—See BARNHART, MO (Charter Communications)

JEFFERSON COUNTY—See IMPERIAL, MO (Charter Communications)

JENNINGS—See OVERLAND, MO (Charter Communications)

JOHN KNOX VILLAGE—See KANSAS CITY, MO (Time Warner Cable)

JOHNSON COUNTY (NORTHEASTERN PORTION)—See KANSAS CITY, KS (Time Warner Cable)

JOHNSON COUNTY (PORTIONS)—See WARRENSBURG, MO (Charter Communications)

▲**JONESBURG**—US Cable

▲**JOPLIN (northwest)**—Formerly served by Almega Cable. No longer in operation

▲**JOPLIN**—Cable One

JUNCTION CITY—See FARMINGTON, MO (Charter Communications)

▲**KAHOKA**—Formerly served by Almega Cable. No longer in operation

KANSAS CITY (PORTIONS)—See INDEPENDENCE, MO (Comcast Cable)

▲**KANSAS CITY (PORTIONS)**—Formerly served by Lenexa, KS [KS0462]. SureWest Broadband. This cable system has converted to IPTV

KANSAS CITY (SOUTH OF KAW RIVER)—See KANSAS CITY, KS (Time Warner Cable)

▲**KANSAS CITY**—Formerly served by People's Choice TV. No longer in operation

▲**KANSAS CITY**—Time Warner Cable

KEARNEY—See KANSAS CITY, MO (Time Warner Cable)

KELSO—See CAPE GIRARDEAU, MO (Charter Communications)

▲**KENNETT**—Windjammer Cable

▲**KEYTESVILLE**—Formerly served by Longview Communications. No longer in operation

▲**KIMBERLING CITY**—Mediacom. Now served by FORSYTH, MO [MO0126]

KIMBERLING CITY—See FORSYTH, MO (Mediacom)

KIMBERLING CITY—See NIXA, MO (Suddenlink Communications)

KIMMSWICK—See BARNHART, MO (Charter Communications)

▲**KING CITY**—Formerly served by Longview Communications. No longer in operation

KINGDOM CITY—See FULTON, MO (Charter Communications)

▲**KINGSTON**—Formerly served by First Cable of Missouri Inc. No longer in operation

▲**KINLOCH**—Formerly served by Data Cablevision. No longer in operation

▲**KIRKSVILLE**—Cable One

KIRKWOOD—See OLIVETTE, MO (Charter Communications)

▲**KNOB NOSTER**—Charter Communications. Now served by WARRENSBURG, OH [MO0425]

KNOB NOSTER—See WARRENSBURG, MO (Charter Communications)

▲**KNOX CITY**—Formerly served by CableDirect. No longer in operation

▲**LA BELLE**—Formerly served by Westcom. No longer in operation

▲**LA MONTE**—Provincial Cable & Data

▲**LA PLATA**—Formerly served by Almega Cable. No longer in operation

LACLEDE COUNTY—See LEBANON, MO (Fidelity Communications)

▲**LACLEDE**—Longview Communications. No longer in operation

LADDONIA—See MEXICO, MO (US Cable)

LADUE—See OLIVETTE, MO (Charter Communications)

LAKE LOTAWANO—See INDEPENDENCE, MO (Comcast Cable)

LAKE OF THE FOREST—See KANSAS CITY, KS (Time Warner Cable)

LAKE OZARK—See OSAGE BEACH, MO (Charter Communications)

LAKE QUIVERA—See KANSAS CITY, KS (Time Warner Cable)

LAKE QUIVERA—See KANSAS CITY, MO (Time Warner Cable)

▲**LAKE SHERWOOD**—Cable America Corp.

▲**LAKE ST. LOUIS**—Charter Communications

LAKE TAPAWINGO—See INDEPENDENCE, MO (Comcast Cable)

▲**LAKE VIKING**—Formerly served by First Cable of Missouri Inc. No longer in operation

LAKE WAUKOMIS—See KANSAS CITY, MO (Time Warner Cable)

LAKE WINNEBAGO—See INDEPENDENCE, MO (Comcast Cable)

LAKELAND—See OSAGE BEACH, MO (Charter Communications)

LAKESHIRE—See OLIVETTE, MO (Charter Communications)

LAKEVIEW—See NIXA, MO (Suddenlink Communications)

LAMAR HEIGHTS—See LAMAR, MO (Suddenlink Communications)

▲**LAMAR**—Suddenlink Communications

LAMBERT—See CAPE GIRARDEAU, MO (Charter Communications)

▲**LAMPE**—Crystal Broadband Networks

LANAGAN—See NOEL, MO (Crystal Broadband Networks)

▲**LANCASTER**—Formerly served by Longview Communications. No longer in operation

LANSING—See KANSAS CITY, KS (Time Warner Cable)

▲**LATHROP**—Allegiance Communications

LAURIE—See OSAGE BEACH, MO (Charter Communications)

LAWSON—See EXCELSIOR SPRINGS, MO (Mediacom)

LEADINGTON—See FARMINGTON, MO (Charter Communications)

LEADWOOD—See FARMINGTON, MO (Charter Communications)

LEAVENWORTH COUNTY (PORTIONS)—See KANSAS CITY, KS (Time Warner Cable)

LEAVENWORTH—See KANSAS CITY, KS (Time Warner Cable)

LEAWOOD—See JOPLIN, MO (Cable One)

LEAWOOD—See KANSAS CITY, KS (Time Warner Cable)

▲**LEBANON**—Fidelity Communications

LEE'S SUMMIT—See KANSAS CITY, MO (Time Warner Cable)

LEES SUMMIT—See INDEPENDENCE, MO (Comcast Cable)

▲**LEETON**—Formerly served by CableDirect. No longer in operation

LEMAY—See OLIVETTE, MO (Charter Communications)

LENEXA—See KANSAS CITY, KS (Time Warner Cable)

▲**LESTERVILLE**—Formerly served by Almega Cable. No longer in operation

▲**LEXINGTON**—Suddenlink Communications

▲**LIBERAL**—Mediacom. Now served by GRANBY, MO [MO0156]

LIBERAL—See GRANBY, MO (Mediacom)

LIBERTY—See KANSAS CITY, MO (Time Warner Cable)

▲**LICKING**—Licking Cable. Now served by WAYNESVILLE, MO [MO0023]

LICKING—See WAYNESVILLE, MO (Cable America Corp.)

LILBOURN—See NEW MADRID, MO (Charter Communications)

LINCOLN COUNTY (SOUTHEASTERN PORTION)—See WINFIELD, MO (US Cable)

LINCOLN COUNTY—See WARRENTON, MO (Charter Communications)

▲ **LINCOLN**—Provincial Cable & Data

LINN COUNTY—See BROOKFIELD, MO (Suddenlink Communications)

LINN CREEK—See OSAGE BEACH, MO (Charter Communications)

▲ **LINN**—Mid Missouri Broadband

LIVINGSTON COUNTY (PORTIONS)—See CHILLICOTHE, MO (Windjammer Cable)

LOCKWOOD—See EVERTON, MO (Mediacom)

LOHMAN—See COLE COUNTY (portions), MO (Suddenlink Communications)

LONE JACK—See KANSAS CITY, MO (Time Warner Cable)

▲ **LOOSE CREEK**—Mid Missouri Broadband

▲ **LOUISIANA**—US Cable

▲ **LOWRY CITY**—Mediacom

MACKENZIE—See OLIVETTE, MO (Charter Communications)

▲ **MACKS CREEK**—Formerly served by Almega Cable. No longer in operation

▲ **MACON**—Chariton Valley Cablevision

▲ **MADISON**—US Cable

▲ **MAITLAND**—Holway Telephone Co.

▲ **MAITLAND**—N.W. Communications

▲ **MALDEN**—NewWave Communications. Now served by DEXTER, MO [MO0039]

MALDEN—See DEXTER, MO (NewWave Communications)

MALTA BEND—See ALMA, MO (Citizens Telephone Co)

MAMMOTH SPRING—See THAYER, AR (Cobridge Communications)

MANCHESTER—See OLIVETTE, MO (Charter Communications)

▲ **MANSFIELD**—Mediacom. Now served by SEYMOUR, MO [MO0172]

MANSFIELD—See SEYMOUR, MO (Mediacom)

MAPLEWOOD—See OVERLAND, MO (Charter Communications)

▲ **MARBLE HILL**—Boycom Cablevision Inc.

▲ **MARCELINE**—Mediacom

MARIONVILLE—See MONETT, MO (Suddenlink Communications)

MARLBOROUGH—See OLIVETTE, MO (Charter Communications)

▲ **MARSHALL**—Windjammer Cable

▲ **MARSHFIELD**—Mediacom. Now served by SEYMOUR, MO [MO0172]

MARSHFIELD—See SEYMOUR, MO (Mediacom)

MARSTON—See NEW MADRID, MO (Charter Communications)

MARTHASVILLE—See LAKE SHERWOOD, MO (Cable America Corp.)

MARTINSBURG—See MEXICO, MO (US Cable)

▲ **MARYLAND HEIGHTS**—Cable America Corp.

MARYLAND HEIGHTS—See OVERLAND, MO (Charter Communications)

MARYVILLE UNIVERSITY—See MARYVILLE, MO (Suddenlink Communications)

▲ **MARYVILLE**—Suddenlink Communications

MATTHEWS—See MORLEY, MO (Semo Communications Corp.)

▲ **MAYSVILLE**—Allegiance Communications

▲ **MAYVIEW**—Formerly served by CableDirect. No longer in operation

MCDONALD COUNTY (PORTIONS)—See NOEL, MO (Crystal Broadband Networks)

▲ **MEADVILLE**—Formerly served by Longview Communications. No longer in operation

MEHLVILLE—See OLIVETTE, MO (Charter Communications)

▲ **MEMPHIS**—Formerly served by Longview Communications. No longer in operation

▲ **MERCER**—Formerly served by Telnet South LC. No longer in operation

MERRIAM WOODS—See BRANSON, MO (Suddenlink Communications)

MERRIAM—See KANSAS CITY, KS (Time Warner Cable)

▲ **META**—Formerly served by CableDirect. No longer in operation

▲ **MEXICO**—US Cable

MIDDLEBROOK—See FARMINGTON, MO (Charter Communications)

▲ **MIDDLETOWN (town)**—Formerly served by First Cable of Missouri Inc. No longer in operation

▲ **MILAN**—Milan Interactive Services

MILL SPRING—See PIEDMONT, MO (Boycom Cablevision Inc.)

MILLER COUNTY (PORTIONS)—See OSAGE BEACH, MO (Charter Communications)

MILLER—See EVERTON, MO (Mediacom)

▲ **MINDENMINES**—Formerly served by Cebridge Connections. No longer in operation

MINER—See CAPE GIRARDEAU, MO (Charter Communications)

MISSION HILLS—See KANSAS CITY, KS (Time Warner Cable)

MISSION WOODS—See KANSAS CITY, KS (Time Warner Cable)

MISSION—See KANSAS CITY, KS (Time Warner Cable)

▲ **MISSIONARY**—Crystal Broadband

MISSISSIPPI COUNTY (CENTRAL PORTION)—See CAPE GIRARDEAU, MO (Charter Communications)

▲ **MOBERLY**—US Cable

▲ **MOKANE**—Formerly served by First Cable of Missouri Inc. No longer in operation

MOLINE ACRES—See OVERLAND, MO (Charter Communications)

▲ **MONETT**—Suddenlink Communications

MONITEAU COUNTY (PORTIONS)—See CALIFORNIA, MO (Crystal Broadband Networks)

▲ **MONROE CITY**—US Cable of Coastal Texas LP. Now served by HANNIBAL, MO [MO0021]

MONROE CITY—See HANNIBAL, MO (US Cable)

▲ **MONTGOMERY CITY**—US Cable. Now served by MEXICO, MO [MO0033]

MONTGOMERY CITY—See MEXICO, MO (US Cable)

▲ **MONTICELLO**—Formerly served by CableDirect. No longer in operation

MOREHOUSE COLONY—See MORLEY, MO (Semo Communications Corp.)

MOREHOUSE—See CAPE GIRARDEAU, MO (Charter Communications)

MORGAN COUNTY (PORTIONS)—See OSAGE BEACH, MO (Charter Communications)

▲ **MORLEY**—Semo Communications Corp.

MOSCOW MILLS—See WARRENTON, MO (Charter Communications)

▲ **MOUND CITY**—Formerly served by Longview Communications. No longer in operation

MOUNT VERNON—See EVERTON, MO (Mediacom)

▲ **MOUNTAIN GROVE**—Almega Cable. Now served by WAYNESVILLE, MO [MO0023]

MOUNTAIN GROVE—See WAYNESVILLE, MO (Cable America Corp.)

▲ **MOUNTAIN VIEW**—Boycom Cablevision Inc.

MULBERRY—See GRANBY, MO (Mediacom)

NAPOLEON—See LEXINGTON, MO (Suddenlink Communications)

▲ **NAYLOR**—Boycom Cablevision Inc.

NECK CITY—See CARL JUNCTION, MO (Mediacom)

NEELYVILLE—See NAYLOR, MO (Boycom Cablevision Inc.)

▲ **NEOSHO**—Suddenlink Communications

▲ **NEVADA**—Cobridge Communications

▲ **NEW BLOOMFIELD**—Formerly served by Longview Communications. No longer in operation

▲ **NEW CAMBRIA**—Chariton Valley Communications Corp. Now served by MACON, MO [MO0071]

NEW CAMBRIA—See MACON, MO (Chariton Valley Cablevision)

NEW FLORENCE—See MEXICO, MO (US Cable)

▲ **NEW FRANKLIN**—Formerly served by Longview Communications. No longer in operation

NEW HAMBURG—See CAPE GIRARDEAU, MO (Charter Communications)

▲ **NEW HAVEN**—Fidelity Communications

NEW MADRID COUNTY (NORTHERN PORTION)—See MORLEY, MO (Semo Communications Corp.)

NEW MADRID COUNTY—See NEW MADRID, MO (Charter Communications)

NEW MADRID COUNTY—See PORTAGEVILLE, MO (NewWave Communications)

▲ **NEW MADRID**—Charter Communications

NEW MELLE—See LAKE SHERWOOD, MO (Cable America Corp.)

▲ **NEWBURG**—Cable America Corp. Now served by WAYNESVILLE (formerly ST. ROBERT), MO [MO0023]

NEWBURG—See WAYNESVILLE, MO (Cable America Corp.)

NEWTON COUNTY (PORTIONS)—See NEOSHO, MO (Suddenlink Communications)

NEWTON COUNTY—See JOPLIN, MO (Cable One)

▲ **NEWTON**—Formerly served by Midwest Cable Inc. No longer in operation

NEWTONIA—See GRANBY, MO (Mediacom)

▲ **NIANGUA**—Formerly served by Almega Cable. No longer in operation

▲ **NIANGUA**—Formerly served by Cebridge Connections. Now served by PORTER MILLS, MO [MO0090]

NIANGUA—See PORTER MILLS, MO (Lake Communications)

▲ **NIXA**—Suddenlink Communications

NODAWAY COUNTY (PORTIONS)—See MARYVILLE, MO (Suddenlink Communications)

▲ **NOEL**—Crystal Broadband Networks

▲ **NORBORNE**—GH Technologies. This cable system has converted to IPTV. See Norborne, MO [MO5171]

▲ **NORBORNE**—GH Technologies. Formerly [MO0469]. This cable system has converted to IPTV

▲ **NORBORNE**—Mediacom

NORMANDY—See FERGUSON, MO (Charter Communications)

NORTH KANSAS CITY—See KANSAS CITY, MO (Time Warner Cable)

NORTH LILBOURN—See NEW MADRID, MO (Charter Communications)

NORTHMOOR—See KANSAS CITY, MO (Time Warner Cable)

▲ **NORTHSHORE**—Formerly served by Almega Cable. No longer in operation

NORTHWOODS—See OVERLAND, MO (Charter Communications)

NORWOOD COURT—See FERGUSON, MO (Charter Communications)

▲ **NORWOOD**—Formerly served by Cebridge Connections. No longer in operation

▲ **NOVINGER**—Formerly served by Longview Communications. No longer in operation

O'FALLON—See LAKE ST. LOUIS, MO (Charter Communications)

O'FALLON—See ST. CHARLES, MO (Charter Communications)

OAK GROVE—See INDEPENDENCE, MO (Comcast Cable)

OAK GROVE—See LAMPE, AR (Crystal Broadband Networks)

OAKLAND—See OLIVETTE, MO (Charter Communications)

OAKS VILLAGE—See KANSAS CITY, MO (Time Warner Cable)

OAKVIEW—See KANSAS CITY, MO (Time Warner Cable)

OAKVILLE—See OLIVETTE, MO (Charter Communications)

OAKWOOD PARK—See KANSAS CITY, MO (Time Warner Cable)

OAKWOOD—See KANSAS CITY, MO (Time Warner Cable)

ODESSA—See INDEPENDENCE, MO (Comcast Cable)

OLD MONROE—See WINFIELD, MO (US Cable)

▲ **OLIVETTE**—Charter Communications

OLYMPIAN VILLAGE—See BARNHART, MO (Charter Communications)

ORAN—See CAPE GIRARDEAU, MO (Charter Communications)

▲ **OREGON**—South Holt Cablevision Inc.

ORONOGO—See CARL JUNCTION, MO (Mediacom)

▲ **OSAGE BEACH**—Charter Communications

OSAGE COUNTY (NORTHWESTERN PORTION)—See LOOSE CREEK, MO (Mid Missouri Broadband)

▲ **OSCEOLA**—Mediacom

▲ **OTTERVILLE**—Formerly served by CableDirect. No longer in operation

OVERLAND PARK—See KANSAS CITY, KS (Time Warner Cable)

▲ **OVERLAND**—Charter Communications

OZARK BEACH (PORTIONS)—See FORSYTH, MO (Mediacom)

OZARK—See NIXA, MO (Suddenlink Communications)

▲ **PACIFIC**—Charter Communications. Now served by BARNHART, MO [MO0385]

PACIFIC—See BARNHART, MO (Charter Communications)

PAGEDALE—See FERGUSON, MO (Charter Communications)

▲ **PALMYRA**—Cass Cable TV Inc. Now served by HANNIBAL, MO [MO0021]

PALMYRA—See HANNIBAL, MO (US Cable)

▲ **PARIS**—US Cable. Now served by HANNIBAL, MO [MO0021]

PARIS—See HANNIBAL, MO (US Cable)

PARK HILLS—See FARMINGTON, MO (Charter Communications)

PARKVILLE—See KANSAS CITY, MO (Time Warner Cable)

PARKWAY—See SULLIVAN, MO (Charter Communications)

▲ **PARMA**—NewWave Communications

▲ **PARNELL**—B & L Technologies LLC

PASADENA HILLS—See FERGUSON, MO (Charter Communications)

PASADENA PARK—See FERGUSON, MO (Charter Communications)

PATTERSON—See PIEDMONT, MO (Boycom Cablevision Inc.)

PECULIAR—See INDEPENDENCE, MO (Comcast Cable)

PEMISCOT COUNTY—See PORTAGEVILLE, MO (NewWave Communications)

PEMISCOT COUNTY—See STEELE, MO (NewWave Communications)

PERRY COUNTY (PORTIONS)—See PERRYVILLE, MO (Charter Communications)

▲ **PERRY**—US Cable

▲ **PERRYVILLE**—Charter Communications

PERSIMMON HOLLOW—See LAMPE, MO (Crystal Broadband Networks)

PETTIS COUNTY—See WARRENSBURG, MO (Charter Communications)

PEVELY—See IMPERIAL, MO (Charter Communications)

PHELPS COUNTY (PORTIONS)—See WAYNESVILLE, MO (Cable America Corp.)

PHELPS COUNTY (PORTIONS)—See SULLIVAN, MO (Charter Communications)

PHILLIPSBURG—See LEBANON, MO (Fidelity Communications)

▲ **PIEDMONT**—Boycom Cablevision Inc.

PIERCE CITY—See MONETT, MO (Suddenlink Communications)

▲ **PILOT GROVE**—Otelco

PILOT KNOB—See FARMINGTON, MO (Charter Communications)

PINE LAWN—See OVERLAND, MO (Charter Communications)

PINEVILLE—See NOEL, MO (Crystal Broadband Networks)

PITTSBURG—See POMME DE TERRE, MO (American Broadband)

PLATTE CITY—See KANSAS CITY, MO (Time Warner Cable)

PLATTE COUNTY (PORTIONS)—See KANSAS CITY, MO (Time Warner Cable)

PLATTE WOODS—See KANSAS CITY, MO (Time Warner Cable)

▲ **PLATTSBURG**—Allegiance Communications

PLEASANT HILL—See INDEPENDENCE, MO (Comcast Cable)

▲ **PLEASANT HOPE**—Fidelity Communications

PLEASANT VALLEY—See KANSAS CITY, MO (Time Warner Cable)

▲ **POCAHONTAS**—Semo Communications Corp.. Now served by MORLEY, MO [MO0171]

POCAHONTAS—See MORLEY, MO (Semo Communications Corp.)

POLK COUNTY—See BOLIVAR, MO (Windstream)

▲ **POMME DE TERRE**—American Broadband

▲ **POPLAR BLUFF**—City Cable

▲ **PORTAGE DES SIOUX**—Cable America Corp.

▲ **PORTAGEVILLE**—NewWave Communications

▲ **PORTER MILLS**—Lake Communications

▲ **POTOSI**—Crystal Broadband Networks

▲ **POWERSITE**—Formerly served by Almega Cable. No longer in operation

PRAIRIE VILLAGE—See KANSAS CITY, KS (Time Warner Cable)

▲ **PRINCETON**—Formerly served by Longview Communications. No longer in operation

PULASKI COUNTY (PORTIONS)—See WAYNESVILLE, MO (Cable America Corp.)

PURCELL—See CARL JUNCTION, MO (Mediacom)

▲ **PURDY**—Mediacom. Now served by CASSVILLE, MO [MO0118]

PURDY—See CASSVILLE, MO (Mediacom)

▲ **PUXICO**—Boycom Cablevision Inc.

▲ **QULIN**—Boycom Cablevision Inc.

RANDOLPH COUNTY—See MOBERLY, MO (US Cable)

▲ **RAVENWOOD**—B & L Technologies LLC

RAYMORE—See INDEPENDENCE, MO (Comcast Cable)

RAYTOWN—See INDEPENDENCE, MO (Comcast Cable)

REDINGS MILL—See JOPLIN, MO (Cable One)

REEDS SPRING—See NIXA, MO (Suddenlink Communications)

▲ **RENICK**—Charter Communications. No longer in operation

▲ **RENICK**—Milan Interactive Communications

▲ **REPUBLIC**—Cable America Corp.

REYNOLDS COUNTY—See ELLINGTON, MO (Boycom Cablevision Inc.)

▲ **RICH HILL**—N.W. Communications

RICHARDS-GEBAUR AFB—See KANSAS CITY, MO (Time Warner Cable)

▲ **RICHLAND**—Cable America Corp. Now served by WAYNESVILLE (formerly ST. ROBERT), MO [MO0023]

RICHLAND—See WAYNESVILLE, MO (Cable America Corp.)

RICHMOND HEIGHTS—See OLIVETTE, MO (Charter Communications)

▲ **RICHMOND**—Mediacom

RISCO—See PARMA, MO (NewWave Communications)

RIVERMINES—See FARMINGTON, MO (Charter Communications)

RIVERSIDE—See KANSAS CITY, MO (Time Warner Cable)

RIVERVIEW—See OVERLAND, MO (Charter Communications)

ROCHEPORT—See COLUMBIA, MO (Charter Communications)

ROCK HILL—See OLIVETTE, MO (Charter Communications)

▲ **ROCKAWAY BEACH**—Cox Communications. Now served by BRANSON, MO [MO0038]

ROCKAWAY BEACH—See BRANSON, MO (Suddenlink Communications)

▲ **ROCKPORT**—Rockport Cablevision

▲ **ROCKVILLE**—Formerly served by N.W. Communications. No longer in operation

ROELAND PARK—See KANSAS CITY, KS (Time Warner Cable)

▲ **ROGERSVILLE**—Mediacom. Now served by SEYMOUR, MO [MO0172]

ROGERSVILLE—See SEYMOUR, MO (Mediacom)

▲ **ROLLA**—Phelps County Cable. Now served by WAYNESVILLE, MO [MO0023]

ROLLA—See WAYNESVILLE, MO (Cable America Corp.)

ROLLA—See SULLIVAN, MO (Fidelity Communications)

ROSEBUD—See GERALD, MO (Fidelity Communications)

▲ **RUSSELLVILLE**—Formerly served by Longview Communications. No longer in operation

SAGINAW—See JOPLIN, MO (Cable One)

▲ **SALEM**—Fidelity Communications

▲ **SALISBURY**—Mediacom

SAPPINGTON—See OLIVETTE, MO (Charter Communications)

▲ **SARCOXIE**—Mediacom. Now served by GRANBY, MO [MO0156]

SARCOXIE—See GRANBY, MO (Mediacom)

SAVANNAH—See ST. JOSEPH, MO (Suddenlink Communications)

▲ **SCHELL CITY**—N.W. Communications

SCOTT CITY—See CAPE GIRARDEAU, MO (Charter Communications)

SCOTT COUNTY (SOUTHERN PORTION)—See MORLEY, MO (Semo Communications Corp.)

SCOTT COUNTY—See CAPE GIRARDEAU, MO (Charter Communications)

▲ **SEDALIA**—Charter Communications. Now served by WARRENSBURG, MO [MO0425]

SEDALIA—See WARRENSBURG, MO (Charter Communications)

▲ **SELIGMAN**—Allegiance Communications

SENATH—See KENNETT, MO (Windjammer Cable)

▲ **SENECA**—Crystal Broadband Networks

▲ **SEYMOUR**—Mediacom

SHAWNEE—See KANSAS CITY, KS (Time Warner Cable)

▲ **SHELBINA**—US Cable. Now served by HANNIBAL, MO [MO0021]

SHELBINA—See HANNIBAL, MO (US Cable)

SHELBYVILLE—See HANNIBAL, MO (US Cable)

▲ **SHELDON**—Formerly served by Cebridge Connections. No longer in operation

▲ **SHERIDAN**—B & L Technologies LLC

SHOAL CREEK DRIVE—See JOPLIN, MO (Cable One)

SHREWSBURY—See OLIVETTE, MO (Charter Communications)

SIBLEY—See INDEPENDENCE, MO (Comcast Cable)

SIKESTON—See CAPE GIRARDEAU, MO (Charter Communications)

▲ **SILEX**—Formerly served by First Cable of Missouri Inc. No longer in operation

SILVER CREEK—See JOPLIN, MO (Cable One)

▲ **SKIDMORE**—Holway Telephone Co. Now served by MAITLAND, MO [MO0336]

SKIDMORE—See MAITLAND, MO (Holway Telephone Co.)

SLATER—See ALMA, MO (Citizens Telephone Co)

▲ **SMITHTON**—Provincial Cable & Data

SMITHVILLE—See KANSAS CITY, MO (Time Warner Cable)

SOUTH WEST CITY—See NOEL, MO (Crystal Broadband Networks)

SPANISH LAKE—See OLIVETTE, MO (Charter Communications)

▲ **SPARTA**—Formerly served by Almega Cable. No longer in operation

▲ **SPRING CITY**—Formerly served by Almega Cable. No longer in operation

▲ **SPRINGFIELD**—Mediacom

ST. ANN—See OVERLAND, MO (Charter Communications)

ST. CHARLES COUNTY (UNINCORPORATED AREAS)—See PORTAGE DES SIOUX, MO (Cable America Corp.)

ST. CHARLES COUNTY—See LAKE SHERWOOD, MO (Cable America Corp.)

ST. CHARLES COUNTY—See LAKE ST. LOUIS, MO (Charter Communications)

ST. CHARLES COUNTY—See ST. CHARLES, MO (Charter Communications)

▲ **ST. CHARLES**—Charter Communications

▲ **ST. CLAIR**—Charter Communications. Now served by SULLIVAN (formerly WASHINGTON), MO [MO0030]

ST. CLAIR—See SULLIVAN, MO (Charter Communications)

ST. GEORGE—See OLIVETTE, MO (Charter Communications)

▲ **ST. JAMES**—Charter Communications. Now served by SULLIVAN (formerly WASHINGTON), MO [MO0030]

ST. JAMES—See SULLIVAN, MO (Charter Communications)

ST. JOHN—See OLIVETTE, MO (Charter Communications)

▲ **ST. JOSEPH**—Suddenlink Communications

ST. LOUIS COUNTY (NORTHERN PORTIONS)—See OVERLAND, MO (Charter Communications)

ST. LOUIS COUNTY—See OLIVETTE, MO (Charter Communications)

▲ **ST. LOUIS**—Formerly served by Sprint Corp. No longer in operation

▲ **ST. LOUIS**—Charter Communications

ST. MARTINS—See COLE COUNTY (portions), MO (Suddenlink Communications)

ST. PAUL—See LAKE ST. LOUIS, MO (Charter Communications)

ST. PETERS—See ST. CHARLES, MO (Charter Communications)

ST. ROBERT—See WAYNESVILLE, MO (Cable America Corp.)

▲ **ST. THOMAS**—Formerly served by First Cable of Missouri Inc. No longer in operation

▲ **STANBERRY**—Formerly served by Longview Communications. No longer in operation

STARK CITY—See GRANBY, MO (Mediacom)

▲ **STE. GENEVIEVE**—Formerly served by Charter Communications. No longer in operation

▲ **STE. GENEVIEVE**—Charter Communications

▲ **STEELE**—NewWave Communications

▲ **STEELVILLE**—Charter Communications. Now served by SULLIVAN (formerly WASHINGTON), MO [MO0030]

STEELVILLE—See SULLIVAN, MO (Charter Communications)

▲ **STOCKTON**—Windstream

STODDARD COUNTY (PORTIONS)—See DEXTER, MO (NewWave Communications)

STONE COUNTY (PORTIONS)—See NIXA, MO (Suddenlink Communications)

▲ **STOTTS CITY**—Formerly served by Cebridge Connections. No longer in operation

▲ **STOVER**—Provincial Cable & Data

▲ **STRAFFORD**—Mediacom. Now served by SEYMOUR, MO [MO0172]

STRAFFORD—See SEYMOUR, MO (Mediacom)

▲ **STURGEON**—Provincial Cable & Data

SUGAR CREEK—See INDEPENDENCE, MO (Comcast Cable)

▲ **SULLIVAN**—Charter Communications. Now served by SULLIVAN (formerly WASHINGTON), MO [MO0030]

▲ **SULLIVAN**—Charter Communications

▲ **SULLIVAN**—Fidelity Communications

SULPHUR SPRINGS—See NOEL, AR (Crystal Broadband Networks)

▲ **SUMMERSVILLE**—Formerly served by Almega Cable. No longer in operation

SUNRISE BEACH—See OSAGE BEACH, MO (Charter Communications)

SUNSET HILLS—See OLIVETTE, MO (Charter Communications)

SWEET SPRINGS—See ALMA, MO (Citizens Telephone Co)

SYCAMORE HILLS—See OLIVETTE, MO (Charter Communications)

▲ **SYRACUSE**—Formerly served by First Cable of Missouri Inc. No longer in operation

TABLE ROCK—See NIXA, MO (Suddenlink Communications)

TALLAPOOSA—See PARMA, MO (NewWave Communications)

TANEY COUNTY (PORTIONS)—See BRANSON, MO (Suddenlink Communications)

▲ **TAOS**—Formerly served by Longview Communications. No longer in operation

TARKIO—See ROCKPORT, MO (Rockport Cablevision)

▲ **TERRE DU LAC**—Charter Communications. Now served by FARMINGTON, MO [MO0035]

TERRE DU LAC—See FARMINGTON, MO (Charter Communications)

▲ **THAYER**—Cobridge Communications

TIMES BEACH—See OLIVETTE, MO (Charter Communications)

▲ **TINA**—GH Technologies. This cable system has converted to IPTV. See Tina, MO [MO5178]

▲ **TINA**—GH Technologies. Formerly [MO0375]. This cable system has converted to IPTV

▲ **TIPTON**—Charter Communications. No longer in operation

▲ **TIPTON**—Crystal Broadband Networks

TOWN & COUNTRY—See OLIVETTE, MO (Charter Communications)

TRACY—See KANSAS CITY, MO (Time Warner Cable)

▲ **TRENTON**—Suddenlink Communications

▲ **TRIMBLE**—Time Warner Cable. Now served by KANSAS CITY, MO [MO0001]

TRIMBLE—See KANSAS CITY, MO (Time Warner Cable)

▲ **TROY**—Charter Communications. Now served by WARRENTON, MO [MO0065]

TROY—See WARRENTON, MO (Charter Communications)

TRUESDALE—See WARRENTON, MO (Charter Communications)

TWINS OAKS—See OLIVETTE, MO (Charter Communications)

UNION STAR—See ST. JOSEPH, MO (Suddenlink Communications)

UNION—See SULLIVAN, MO (Charter Communications)

▲ **UNIONVILLE**—Unionville Missouri CATV

UNITY VILLAGE—See KANSAS CITY, MO (Time Warner Cable)

UNIVERSITY CITY—See OVERLAND, MO (Charter Communications)

UPLANDS PARK—See FERGUSON, MO (Charter Communications)

▲ **URBANA**—Formerly served by Cebridge Connections. No longer in operation

▲ **URICH**—Formerly served by CableDirect. No longer in operation

▲ **UTICA (village)**—Formerly served by Green Hills Communications Inc. No longer in operation

VALLEY PARK—See OLIVETTE, MO (Charter Communications)

▲ **VAN BUREN**—Boycom Cablevision Inc.

▲ **VANDALIA**—Crystal Broadband Networks

VANDIVER—See MEXICO, MO (US Cable)

VANDUSER—See MORLEY, MO (Semo Communications Corp.)

VELDA CITY—See FERGUSON, MO (Charter Communications)

VELDA VILLAGE HILLS—See FERGUSON, MO (Charter Communications)

VENICE ON THE LAKE—See BRANSON, MO (Suddenlink Communications)

VERONA—See MONETT, MO (Suddenlink Communications)

▲ **VERSAILLES**—Crystal Broadband Networks

▲ **VIBURNUM**—Crystal Broadband Networks

▲ **VIENNA**—Formerly served by Longview Communications. No longer in operation

▲ **VILLA RIDGE**—Charter Communications. Now served by BARNHART, MO [MO0385]

VILLA RIDGE—See BARNHART, MO (Charter Communications)

VILLAGE OF FOUR SEASONS—See OSAGE BEACH, MO (Charter Communications)

VINITA PARK—See OLIVETTE, MO (Charter Communications)

VINITA TERRACE—See FERGUSON, MO (Charter Communications)

WALNUT GROVE—See EVERTON, MO (Mediacom)

WALNUT HILLS—See WARRENSBURG, MO (Charter Communications)

▲ **WAPPAPELLO**—Boycom Cablevision Inc.

▲ **WARDELL**—Formerly served by Almega Cable. No longer in operation

WARDSVILLE—See COLE COUNTY (portions), MO (Suddenlink Communications)

WARREN COUNTY—See LAKE SHERWOOD, MO (Cable America Corp.)

▲ **WARRENSBURG**—Charter Communications

▲ **WARRENTON**—Charter Communications

▲ **WARSAW**—Crystal Broadband Networks

WARSON WOODS—See OLIVETTE, MO (Charter Communications)

WASHBURN—See SELIGMAN, MO (Allegiance Communications)

WASHINGTON—See SULLIVAN, MO (Charter Communications)

WAVERLY—See ALMA, MO (Citizens Telephone Co)

WAYNE COUNTY (PORTIONS)—See PIEDMONT, MO (Boycom Cablevision Inc.)

WAYNE COUNTY (SOUTHERN PORTION)—See WAPPAPELLO, MO (Boycom Cablevision Inc.)

▲ **WAYNESVILLE**—Cable America Corp.

WEATHERBY LAKE—See KANSAS CITY, MO (Time Warner Cable)

WEAUBLEAU—See POMME DE TERRE, MO (American Broadband)

WEBB CITY—See JOPLIN, MO (Cable One)

WEBSTER GROVES—See OLIVETTE, MO (Charter Communications)

WELDON SPRING HEIGHTS—See LAKE ST. LOUIS, MO (Charter Communications)

WELDON SPRING—See LAKE ST. LOUIS, MO (Charter Communications)

WELDON SPRING—See ST. CHARLES, MO (Charter Communications)

WELLINGTON—See LEXINGTON, MO (Suddenlink Communications)

▲ **WELLSTON**—Formerly served by Data Cablevision. No longer in operation

WELLSVILLE—See MEXICO, MO (US Cable)

WENTZVILLE—See LAKE ST. LOUIS, MO (Charter Communications)

▲ **WEST PLAINS**—Cobridge Communications

▲ **WESTBORO**—Formerly served by CableDirect. No longer in operation

WESTON—See KANSAS CITY, MO (Time Warner Cable)

▲ **WESTPHALIA**—Formerly served by CableDirect. No longer in operation

WESTWOOD HILLS—See KANSAS CITY, KS (Time Warner Cable)

WESTWOOD—See KANSAS CITY, KS (Time Warner Cable)

WHEATLAND—See POMME DE TERRE, MO (American Broadband)

▲ **WHEELING**—Formerly served by Longview Communications. No longer in operation

WHITE BRANCH—See WARSAW, MO (Crystal Broadband Networks)

WHITEMAN AFB—See WARRENSBURG, MO (Charter Communications)

WILBUR PARK—See OLIVETTE, MO (Charter Communications)

WILDWOOD—See OLIVETTE, MO (Charter Communications)

WILLARD—See EVERTON, MO (Mediacom)

▲ **WILLIAMSVILLE**—Formerly served by Almega Cable. No longer in operation

▲ **WILLOW SPRINGS**—Almega Cable. Now served by WAYNESVILLE, MO [MO0023]

WILLOW SPRINGS—See WAYNESVILLE, MO (Cable America Corp.)

▲ **WILSON BEND**—Formerly served by Almega Cable. No longer in operation

WILSON CITY—See MORLEY, MO (Semo Communications Corp.)

WINCHESTER—See OLIVETTE, MO (Charter Communications)

▲ **WINDSOR**—Crystal Broadband Networks

▲ **WINFIELD**—US Cable

▲ **WINONA**—Boycom Cablevision Inc.

WOODS HEIGHTS—See EXCELSIOR SPRINGS, MO (Mediacom)

WOODSON TERRACE—See OLIVETTE, MO (Charter Communications)

WRIGHT CITY—See WARRENTON, MO (Charter Communications)

▲ **WYACONDA**—Formerly served by CableDirect. No longer in operation

WYANDOTTE COUNTY (PORTIONS)—See KANSAS CITY, KS (Time Warner Cable)

WYATT—See MORLEY, MO (Semo Communications Corp.)

MONTANA

▲ **ABSAROKEE**—Cable Montana

▲ **ALBERTON**—Bresnan Communications

ALHAMBRA—See HELENA, MT (Bresnan Communications)

▲ **ANACONDA**—Bresnan Communications

▲ **ARLEE**—Formerly served by Bresnan Communications. No longer in operation

▲ **BAKER**—Mid-Rivers Communications

BEAVERHEAD COUNTY (PORTIONS)—See DILLON, MT (Bresnan Communications)

▲ **BELFRY**—Belfry Cable TV

BELGRADE—See BOZEMAN, MT (Bresnan Communications)

▲ **BELT**—Formerly served by KLiP Interactive. No longer in operation

▲ **BIG FLAT**—Formerly served by Bresnan Communications. No longer in operation

▲ **BIG SKY**—Bulldog Cable

▲ **BIG TIMBER**—Cable Montana

BIGFORK—See KALISPELL, MT (Bresnan Communications)

▲ **BILLINGS (WESTERN PORTION)**—Cable Montana

▲ **BILLINGS**—Formerly served by USA Digital TV. No longer in operation

▲ **BILLINGS**—Bresnan Communications

BLACK EAGLE—See GREAT FALLS, MT (Bresnan Communications)

BLAINE COUNTY (NORTHERN PORTION)—See CHINOOK, MT (Bresnan Communications)

BONNER—See MISSOULA, MT (Bresnan Communications)

▲ **BOULDER**—Bresnan Communications

▲ **BOZEMAN**—Bresnan Communications

▲ **BRIDGER**—Bridger Cable TV

▲ **BROADUS**—Skyview TV Inc.

BROADWATER COUNTY—See TOWNSEND, MT (Bresnan Communications)

▲ **BUTTE**—Bresnan Communications

CASCADE COUNTY—See GREAT FALLS, MT (Bresnan Communications)

▲ **CASCADE**—Bresnan Communications

▲ **CHARLO**—Formerly served by KLiP Interactive. No longer in operation

▲ **CHESTER**—Formerly served by KLiP Interactive. No longer in operation

▲ **CHINOOK**—Bresnan Communications

▲ **CHOTEAU**—3 Rivers Communications

▲ **CIRCLE**—Mid-Rivers Communications

CLANCY—See HELENA, MT (Bresnan Communications)

CLINTON—See MISSOULA, MT (Bresnan Communications)

▲ **COLSTRIP**—Cable Montana

COLUMBIA FALLS—See KALISPELL, MT (Bresnan Communications)

▲**COLUMBUS**—Cable Montana. Now served by LAUREL, MT [MT0023]

COLUMBUS—See LAUREL, MT (Cable Montana)

▲**CONRAD**—3 Rivers Communications

CORVALLIS—See HAMILTON, MT (Bresnan Communications)

▲**CROW AGENCY**—Crow Cable TV

CROW INDIAN RESERVATION—See CROW AGENCY, MT (Crow Cable TV)

▲**CULBERTSON**—Bulldog Cable

CUSTER COUNTY—See MILES CITY, MT (Mid-Rivers Communications)

▲**CUT BANK**—Bresnan Communications

▲**DARBY (town)**—Formerly served by KLiP Interactive. No longer in operation

DAWSON COUNTY—See GLENDIVE, MT (Mid-Rivers Communications)

DEER LODGE COUNTY—See ANACONDA, MT (Bresnan Communications)

▲**DEER LODGE**—Bresnan Communications

▲**DILLON**—Bresnan Communications

▲**DRUMMOND**—Drummond Cable TV

▲**DUTTON**—Formerly served by KLiP Interactive. No longer in operation

EAST HELENA—See HELENA, MT (Bresnan Communications)

▲**EKALAKA**—Mid-Rivers Communications

▲**ENNIS**—Bulldog Cable

▲**EUREKA**—Tobacco Valley Communications

EVERGREEN—See KALISPELL, MT (Bresnan Communications)

FAIRFIELD—See CHOTEAU, MT (3 Rivers Communications)

▲**FAIRVIEW**—Mid-Rivers Communications

FALLON—See TERRY, MT (Mid-Rivers Communications)

FERGUS COUNTY—See LEWISTOWN, MT (Mid-Rivers Communications)

FLATHEAD COUNTY—See KALISPELL, MT (Bresnan Communications)

FLORENCE—See MISSOULA, MT (Bresnan Communications)

▲**FORSYTH**—Cable Montana

▲**FORT BENTON**—Bresnan Communications

▲**FOUR CORNERS**—Formerly served by Northwestern Communications Corp. No longer in operation

▲**FROMBERG**—Cable Montana

GALLATIN COUNTY—See BOZEMAN, MT (Bresnan Communications)

▲**GARDINER**—Formerly served by North Yellowstone Cable TV. No longer in operation

GLACIER COUNTY—See CUT BANK, MT (Bresnan Communications)

▲**GLASGOW**—Bresnan Communications

▲**GLENDIVE**—Mid-Rivers Communications

▲**GRANT CREEK**—Bresnan Communications. Now served by MISSOULA, MT [MT0002]

GRANT CREEK—See MISSOULA, MT (Bresnan Communications)

▲**GREAT FALLS**—Bresnan Communications

▲**HAMILTON**—Bresnan Communications

▲**HARDIN**—Cable Montana

▲**HARLEM**—Bresnan Communications

▲**HARLOWTON**—Mid-Rivers Communications

▲**HAVRE**—Bresnan Communications

HELENA VALLEY—See HELENA, MT (Bresnan Communications)

▲**HELENA**—Bresnan Communications

HILL COUNTY—See HAVRE, MT (Bresnan Communications)

▲**HOT SPRINGS**—Hot Springs Telephone Co.

▲**HYSHAM**—Mid-Rivers Communications

JEFFERSON COUNTY (UNINCORPORATED AREAS)—See HELENA, MT (Bresnan Communications)

▲**JOLIET**—Cable Montana

▲**JORDAN**—Mid-Rivers Communications

▲**KALISPELL**—Bresnan Communications

LAKE COUNTY—See POLSON, MT (Bresnan Communications)

▲**LAME DEER**—Eagle Cablevision Inc.

▲**LAUREL**—Cable Montana

▲**LAVINA**—Mid-Rivers Communications

LEWIS & CLARK COUNTY—See HELENA, MT (Bresnan Communications)

▲**LEWISTOWN**—Mid-Rivers Communications

▲**LIBBY**—Windjammer Cable

LINCOLN COUNTY—See LIBBY, MT (Windjammer Cable)

▲**LINCOLN**—Lincoln Cable TV

▲**LIVINGSTON**—Bresnan Communications

LOCKWOOD—See BILLINGS, MT (Bresnan Communications)

▲**LODGE GRASS**—Eagle Cablevision Inc.

▲**LOLO**—Bresnan Communications. Now served by MISSOULA, MT [MT0002]

LOLO—See MISSOULA, MT (Bresnan Communications)

MALMSTROM AFB—See GREAT FALLS, MT (Bresnan Communications)

▲**MALTA**—Bresnan Communications

▲**MANHATTAN**—Bresnan Communications. Now served by BOZEMAN, MT [MT0007]

MANHATTAN—See BOZEMAN, MT (Bresnan Communications)

▲**MARION**—Formerly served by Mallard Cablevision. No longer in operation

▲**MELSTONE**—Formerly served by Mel-View Cable TV. No longer in operation

▲**MILES CITY**—Mid-Rivers Communications

▲**MILLTOWN**—Bresnan Communications. Now served by MISSOULA, MT [MT0002]

MILLTOWN—See MISSOULA, MT (Bresnan Communications)

MISSOULA COUNTY—See MISSOULA, MT (Bresnan Communications)

MISSOULA SOUTH—See MISSOULA, MT (Bresnan Communications)

▲**MISSOULA**—Cable Montana. Now served by MISSOULA, MT [MT0002]

▲**MISSOULA**—Bresnan Communications

MONTANA CITY—See HELENA, MT (Bresnan Communications)

▲**NINE MILE**—Formerly served by Bresnan Communications. No longer in operation

▲**OPPORTUNITY**—Western Cable TV

ORCHARD HOMES (PORTIONS)—See MISSOULA, MT (Bresnan Communications)

PABLO—See POLSON, MT (Bresnan Communications)

▲**PARADISE**—Formerly served by KLiP Interactive. No longer in operation

▲**PARK CITY**—Cable Montana. Now served by LAUREL, MT [MT0023]

PARK CITY—See LAUREL, MT (Cable Montana)

PARK COUNTY—See LIVINGSTON, MT (Bresnan Communications)

▲**PHILIPSBURG**—Formerly served by Eagle Cablevision Inc. No longer in operation

▲**PLAINS**—Western Montana Community Telephone

▲**PLENTYWOOD**—Bulldog Cable

▲**POLSON**—Bresnan Communications

PONDERA COUNTY—See CONRAD, MT (3 Rivers Communications)

▲**POPLAR**—Bulldog Cable

POWELL COUNTY—See DEER LODGE, MT (Bresnan Communications)

RATTLESNAKE VALLEY—See MISSOULA, MT (Bresnan Communications)

RATTLESNAKE—See MISSOULA, MT (Bresnan Communications)

RAVALLI COUNTY—See HAMILTON, MT (Bresnan Communications)

RAVALLI COUNTY—See STEVENSVILLE, MT (Bresnan Communications)

▲**RED LODGE**—Cable Montana

▲**RICHEY**—Mid-Rivers Communications

▲**RIVERSIDE GREENS**—Formerly served by Northwestern Communications Corp. No longer in operation

▲**RONAN**—Bresnan Communications. Now served by POLSON, MT [MT0016]

RONAN—See POLSON, MT (Bresnan Communications)

ROOSEVELT COUNTY—See WOLF POINT, MT (Nemont)

▲**ROUNDUP**—Mid-Rivers Communications

▲**RYEGATE**—Mid-Rivers Communications

▲**SAVAGE**—Mid-Rivers Communications

▲**SCOBEY**—Bulldog Cable

▲**SEELEY LAKE**—Western Montana Community Telephone

▲**SHELBY**—3 Rivers Communications

▲**SHERIDAN**—Formerly served by Ruby Valley Cable Co. Inc. No longer in operation

▲**SIDNEY**—Mid-Rivers Communications

SILVER BOW COUNTY—See BUTTE, MT (Bresnan Communications)

▲**ST. IGNATIUS**—Western Montana Community Telephone

▲**ST. REGIS**—Formerly served by KLiP Interactive. No longer in operation

▲**STANFORD**—Formerly served by B.E.K. Inc. No longer in operation

▲**STEVENSVILLE**—Bresnan Communications

STEVENSVILLE—See MISSOULA, MT (Bresnan Communications)

▲**SUN PRAIRIE**—Charter Communications

▲**SUPERIOR**—Western Montana Community Telephone

▲**TERRY**—Mid-Rivers Communications

TETON COUNTY—See CHOTEAU, MT (3 Rivers Communications)

▲**THOMPSON FALLS**—Western Montana Community Telephone

TOOLE COUNTY—See CUT BANK, MT (Bresnan Communications)

▲**TOWNSEND**—Bresnan Communications

▲**TROY**—Windjammer Cable

▲**TWIN BRIDGES**—Formerly served by Twin Bridges Cable TV Inc. No longer in operation

▲**VALIER**—Formerly served by KLiP Interactive. No longer in operation

VALLEY COUNTY—See GLASGOW, MT (Bresnan Communications)

VAUGHN—See SUN PRAIRIE, MT (Charter Communications)

▲**VICTOR**—Formerly served by Bresnan Communications. No longer in operation

WALKERVILLE—See BUTTE, MT (Bresnan Communications)

▲**WEST YELLOWSTONE**—Bulldog Cable

▲**WHITE SULPHUR SPRINGS**—Formerly served by Eagle Cablevision Inc. No longer in operation

WHITEFISH—See KALISPELL, MT (Bresnan Communications)

▲**WHITEHALL**—Whitehall Cable TV

▲**WIBAUX**—Mid-Rivers Communications

▲**WOLF POINT**—Nemont

YELLOWSTONE COUNTY—See BILLINGS, MT (Bresnan Communications)

NEBRASKA

ADAMS COUNTY—See HASTINGS, NE (Charter Communications)

▲**AINSWORTH**—Cable Nebraska

▲**ALBION**—Cable Nebraska

ALDA—See GRAND ISLAND, NE (Charter Communications)

▲**ALEXANDRIA**—Comstar Cable TV Inc.

▲**ALLEN (village)**—CenCom Inc. This cable system has converted to IPTV. See Allen (vlllage), NE [NE5002]

▲**ALLEN (VILLAGE)**—CenCom NNTV. Formerly [NE0258]. This cable system has converted to IPTV

▲**ALLIANCE**—Charter Communications

▲**ALMA TWP.**—Pinpoint Cable TV

AMHERST—See KEARNEY, NE (Charter Communications)

ANSELMO—See DUNNING, NE (Consolidated Cable Inc.)

▲**ANSLEY**—NCTC Cable

▲**ARAPAHOE**—ATC Communications

▲**ARCADIA**—NCTC Cable

ARLINGTON—See BLAIR, NE (American Broadband)

▲**ARNOLD**—Great Plains Communications

ARTHUR—See HYANNIS, NE (Consolidated Cable Inc.)

▲**ASHLAND**—Charter Communications. Now served by SPRINGFIELD (formerly Plattsmouth), NE [NE0020]

ASHLAND—See SPRINGFIELD, NE (Charter Communications)

▲**ASHTON**—NCTC Cable

▲**ATKINSON**—Fort Randall Cable

▲**AUBURN**—Time Warner Cable

▲**AURORA**—Mid-State Community TV

▲**AVOCA**—Formerly served by CableDirect. No longer in operation

AXTELL—See KEARNEY, NE (Charter Communications)

▲**BANCROFT**—Great Plains Communications

BARTLEY—See CAMBRIDGE, NE (Pinpoint Cable TV)

▲**BASSETT**—American Broadband

BATTLE CREEK—See NORFOLK, NE (Cable One)

▲**BAYARD**—Charter Communications. Now served by SCOTTSBLUFF, NE [NE0008]

BAYARD—See SCOTTSBLUFF, NE (Charter Communications)

▲**BEATRICE**—Charter Communications

▲**BEAVER CITY**—Pinpoint Cable TV

▲**BEAVER CROSSING**—Zito Media

▲**BEAVER LAKE**—Our Cable

▲**BEE (village)**—Formerly served by TelePartners. No longer in operation

▲**BEEMER**—TelePartners. Now served by NORFOLK, NE [NE0006]

BEEMER—See NORFOLK, NE (Cable One)

BELDEN—See WAYNE, NE (American Broadband)

BELLEVUE—See OMAHA, NE (Cox Communications)

▲**BELLWOOD**—Cable Nebraska

▲**BENEDICT**—Formerly served by Galaxy Cablevision. No longer in operation

▲**BENKELMAN**—BWTelcom

BENNET—See SYRACUSE, NE (Zito Media)

▲**BENNINGTON**—Cox Communications. Now served by OMAHA, NE [NE0001]

BENNINGTON—See OMAHA, NE (Cox Communications)

BERTRAND—See KEARNEY, NE (Charter Communications)

▲**BIG SPRINGS**—Consolidated Cable Inc.

BLADEN—See BLUE HILL, NE (Glenwood Telecommunications)

▲**BLAIR**—American Broadband

▲**BLOOMFIELD**—Great Plains Communications

▲**BLUE HILL**—Glenwood Telecommunications

BLUE SPRINGS—See WILBER, NE (Zito Media)

▲**BOELUS**—NCTC Cable

BOX BUTTE COUNTY (PORTIONS)—See SCOTTSBLUFF, NE (Charter Communications)

▲**BRADSHAW**—Zito Media

BRADY—See MAXWELL, NE (Consolidated Cable Inc.)

▲**BRAINARD**—Zito Media

▲**BRIDGEPORT**—Charter Communications. Now served by SCOTTSBLUFF, NE [NE0008]

BRIDGEPORT—See SCOTTSBLUFF, NE (Charter Communications)

▲**BRISTOW TWP.**—Formerly served by Sky Scan Cable Co. No longer in operation

▲**BROCK**—Formerly served by CableDirect. No longer in operation

▲**BROKEN BOW**—Great Plains Communications. Now served by ARNOLD, NE [NE0114]

BROKEN BOW—See ARNOLD, NE (Great Plains Communications)

▲**BRULE**—Peregrine Communications

▲**BRUNSWICK (village)**—Formerly served by Sky Scan Cable Co. No longer in operation

▲**BURWELL**—NCTC Cable

▲**BUTTE (VILLAGE)**—CenCom NNTV. Formerly [NE0157]. This cable system has converted to IPTV

▲**BUTTE**—CenCom Inc. This cable system has converted to IPTV. See Butte (village), NE [NE5005]

▲**BYRON**—Zito Media

CAIRO—See KEARNEY, NE (Charter Communications)

CALLAWAY—See ARNOLD, NE (Great Plains Communications)

▲**CAMBRIDGE**—Pinpoint Cable TV

CAMPBELL—See BLUE HILL, NE (Glenwood Telecommunications)

CARROLL—See WAYNE, NE (American Broadband)

CARTER LAKE—See OMAHA, IA (Cox Communications)

CASS COUNTY (PORTIONS)—See SYRACUSE, NE (Zito Media)

CASS COUNTY—See SPRINGFIELD, NE (Charter Communications)

▲**CEDAR BLUFFS**—Formerly served by TelePartners. No longer in operation

▲**CEDAR CREEK**—Formerly served by Westcom. No longer in operation

▲**CEDAR RAPIDS**—Cable Nebraska

CENTER—See BLOOMFIELD, NE (Great Plains Communications)

▲**CENTRAL CITY**—Cable Nebraska

▲**CERESCO**—Zito Media

▲**CHADRON**—Great Plains Communications

▲**CHAMBERS**—Formerly served by Sky Scan Cable Co. No longer in operation

▲**CHAPMAN**—Great Plains Communications

▲**CHAPPELL**—Charter Communications. Now served by JULESBURG, CO [CO0084]

CHASE COUNTY—See WAUNETA, NE (BWTelcom)

▲**CHESTER**—Zito Media

CHEYENNE COUNTY—See SIDNEY, NE (Charter Communications)

▲**CLARKS (VILLAGE)**—CenCom NNTV. Formerly [NE0189]. This cable system has converted to IPTV

▲**CLARKS**—CenCom Inc. (formerly Clarks Cable TV). This cable system has converted to IPTV. See Clarks (village), NE [NE5006]

▲**CLARKSON**—Formerly served by TelePartners. No longer in operation

CLATONIA—See WILBER, NE (Zito Media)

▲**CLAY CENTER**—Zito Media

▲**CLEARWATER (VILLAGE)**—CenCom NNTV. Formerly [NE0144]. This cable system has converted to IPTV

▲**CLEARWATER**—CenCom Inc. This cable system has converted to IPTV. See Clearwater (village), NE [NE5014]

▲**CODY**—Midcontinent Communications

▲**COLERIDGE (VILLAGE)**—CenCom NNTV. Formerly [NE0113]. This cable system has converted to IPTV

▲**COLERIDGE**—CenCom Inc. This cable system has converted to IPTV. See Coleridge (village), NE [NE5001]

▲**COLUMBUS (portions)**—Formerly served by Sky Scan Cable Co. No longer in operation

▲**COLUMBUS**—Time Warner Cable

▲**COMSTOCK**—Formerly served by Consolidated Cable Inc. No longer in operation

▲**CONCORD (VILLAGE)**—CenCom NNTV. Formerly [NE0385]. This cable system has converted to IPTV

COOK—See SYRACUSE, NE (Zito Media)

▲**CORTLAND**—Formerly served by Great Plains Communications. No longer in operation

COUNCIL BLUFFS—See OMAHA, IA (Cox Communications)

▲**COZAD**—Charter Communications. Now served by KEARNEY, NE [NE0011]

COZAD—See KEARNEY, NE (Charter Communications)

▲**CRAWFORD**—Mobius Communications Co. No longer in operation

CREIGHTON—See BLOOMFIELD, NE (Great Plains Communications)

▲**CRESTON**—Formerly served by Sky Scan Cable Co. No longer in operation

CRETE—See LINCOLN, NE (Time Warner Cable)

CROFTON—See BLOOMFIELD, NE (Great Plains Communications)

▲**CULBERTSON**—Pinpoint Cable TV

▲**CURTIS**—Consolidated Cable Inc.

▲**DALTON**—Dalton Telephone Co.

▲**DANNEBROG**—NCTC Cable

▲**DAVEY (village)**—Formerly served by TelePartners. No longer in operation

▲**DAVID CITY**—Time Warner Cable. Now served by COLUMBUS, NE [NE0015]

DAVID CITY—See COLUMBUS, NE (Time Warner Cable)

DAWSON COUNTY (PORTIONS)—See KEARNEY, NE (Charter Communications)

▲**DAWSON**—Formerly served by CableDirect. No longer in operation

▲**DAYKIN**—Comstar Cable TV Inc.

DE WITT—See WILBER, NE (Zito Media)

▲**DECATUR (village)**—CenCom Inc. This cable system has converted to IPTV. See Decatur (village), IL [NE5016]

▲**DECATUR (VILLAGE)**—CenCom NNTV. Formerly [NE0145]. This cable system has converted to IPTV

DENTON—See LINCOLN, NE (Time Warner Cable)

▲**DESHLER**—Zito Media

▲**DILLER**—Diode Telecom Inc

▲**DIX**—HunTel Cablevision. Now served by DALTON, NE [NE0240]

DIX—See DALTON, NE (Dalton Telephone Co.)

▲**DIXON (VILLAGE)**—CenCom NNTV. Formerly [NE0385]. This cable system has converted to IPTV.

▲**DIXON/CONCORD**—CenCom Inc. This cable system has converted to IPTV. See Dixon (village), NE [NE5016] & Concord (village), NE [NE5013]

DODGE COUNTY—See FREMONT, NE (Time Warner Cable)

▲**DODGE**—Great Plains Communications. Now served by NORTH BEND, NE [NE0080]

DODGE—See NORTH BEND, NE (Great Plains Communications)

▲**DONIPHAN**—Mid-State Community TV. Now served by AURORA, NE [NE0033]

DONIPHAN—See AURORA, NE (Mid-State Community TV)

DORCHESTER—See WILBER, NE (Zito Media)

DOUGLAS COUNTY (PORTIONS)—See GRETNA, NE (Zito Media)

DOUGLAS COUNTY—See OMAHA, NE (Cox Communications)

▲**DUBOIS**—Formerly served by CableDirect. No longer in operation

▲**DUNCAN**—Cable Nebraska

▲**DUNNING**—Consolidated Cable Inc.

▲**DWIGHT (village)**—Formerly served by TelePartners. No longer in operation

EAGLE—See SYRACUSE, NE (Zito Media)

EDGAR—See CLAY CENTER, NE (Zito Media)

▲**ELBA**—NCTC Cable

▲**ELGIN**—Great Plains Communications

ELKHORN—See OMAHA, NE (Cox Communications)

ELKHORN—See GRETNA, NE (Zito Media)

ELM CREEK—See KEARNEY, NE (Charter Communications)

ELMWOOD—See SYRACUSE, NE (Zito Media)

▲**ELSIE**—Elsie Communications Inc.

ELWOOD—See ARAPAHOE, NE (ATC Communications)

EMERSON—See WAYNE, NE (American Broadband)

▲**ENDICOTT**—Formerly served by Westcom. No longer in operation

EUSTIS—See FARNAM, NE (Consolidated Cable Inc.)

▲**EWING**—Great Plains Cable TV. Now served by ELGIN, NE [NE0282]

EWING—See ELGIN, NE (Great Plains Communications)

▲**FAIRBURY**—Time Warner Cable

FAIRFIELD—See CLAY CENTER, NE (Zito Media)

▲**FALLS CITY**—Time Warner Cable

▲**FARNAM**—Consolidated Cable Inc.

▲**FAWN HEIGHTS**—Formerly served by TelePartners. No longer in operation

▲**FILLEY**—Comstar Cable TV Inc.

FORT CALHOUN—See BLAIR, NE (American Broadband)

▲**FRANKLIN**—Formerly served by Pinpoint Cable TV. No longer in operation

▲**FREMONT**—Time Warner Cable

FRIEND—See WILBER, NE (Zito Media)

▲**FULLERTON**—Cable Nebraska

▲**FUNK**—Glenwood Telecommunications. Now served by BLUE HILL, NE [NE0093]

FUNK—See BLUE HILL, NE (Glenwood Telecommunications)

▲**GARLAND**—Zito Media

▲**GENEVA**—Formerly served by Sprint Corp. No longer in operation

▲**GENEVA**—Zito Media

▲**GENOA**—Cable Nebraska

GERING—See SCOTTSBLUFF, NE (Charter Communications)

GIBBON—See GRAND ISLAND, NE (Charter Communications)

▲**GILTNER**—Mid-State Community TV. Now served by AURORA, NE [NE0033]

GILTNER—See AURORA, NE (Mid-State Community TV)

▲**GINGER COVE**—Formerly served by TelePartners. No longer in operation

▲**GLENVILLE**—Zito Media

▲**GOEHNER (village)**—Formerly served by TelePartners. No longer in operation

▲**GORDON**—Great Plains Communications. Now served by CHADRON, NE [NE0024]

GORDON—See CHADRON, NE (Great Plains Communications)

▲**GOTHENBURG**—Charter Communications. Now served by KEARNEY, NE [NE0011]

GOTHENBURG—See KEARNEY, NE (Charter Communications)

▲**GRAND ISLAND**—Charter Communications

▲**GRAND ISLAND**—Zito Media

GRANT COUNTY (PORTIONS)—See HYANNIS, NE (Consolidated Cable Inc.)

▲**GRANT**—Great Plains Communications

▲**GREELEY**—Center Cable Co.

▲**GREENWOOD**—Charter Communications. Now served by SPRINGFIELD (formerly Plattsmouth), NE [NE0020]

GREENWOOD—See SPRINGFIELD, NE (Charter Communications)

▲**GRESHAM**—Zito Media

▲**GRETNA**—Zito Media

▲**GUIDE ROCK**—Glenwood Telecommunications

GURLEY—See DALTON, NE (Dalton Telephone Co.)

▲**HADAR**—Sky Scan Cable Co. Now served by NORFOLK, NE [NE0006]

HADAR—See NORFOLK, NE (Cable One)

▲**HAIGLER**—BWTelcom

HALL COUNTY—See GRAND ISLAND, NE (Charter Communications)

HALLAM—See WILBER, NE (Zito Media)

HALSEY—See DUNNING, NE (Consolidated Cable Inc.)

HAMPTON—See AURORA, NE (Mid-State Community TV)

▲**HARDY**—Formerly served by Diode Cable Co. No longer in operation

▲**HARRISON**—Windbreak Cable TV

▲**HARTINGTON**—CedarVision Inc.

HARVARD—See CLAY CENTER, NE (Zito Media)

HASTINGS AFB—See HASTINGS, NE (Charter Communications)

▲**HASTINGS**—Charter Communications

▲**HAY SPRINGS**—Great Plains Communications. Now served by CHADRON, NE [NE0024]

HAY SPRINGS—See CHADRON, NE (Great Plains Communications)

HAYES CENTER—See GRANT, NE (Great Plains Communications)

▲**HEBRON**—Diode Telecom Inc.

▲**HEMINGFORD**—Formerly served by Mobius Communications Co. No longer in operation

▲**HENDERSON**—Mainstay Cable TV

HERMAN—See BLAIR, NE (American Broadband)

HERSHEY—See SUTHERLAND, NE (Great Plains Communications)

HICKMAN—See WILBER, NE (Zito Media)

HILDRETH—See KEARNEY, NE (Charter Communications)

HOLBROOK—See ARAPAHOE, NE (ATC Communications)

HOLDREDGE—See KEARNEY, NE (Charter Communications)

▲**HOLDREGE**—Charter Communications. Now served by KEARNEY, NE [NE0011]

HOLSTEIN—See BLUE HILL, NE (Glenwood Telecommunications)

▲**HOMER**—HunTel Cablevision. Now served by WAYNE, NE [NE0374]

HOMER—See WAYNE, NE (American Broadband)

▲**HOOPER**—WesTel Systems

▲**HORDVILLE**—Mid-State Community TV. Now served by AURORA, NE [NE0033]

HORDVILLE—See AURORA, NE (Mid-State Community TV)

HOSKINS—See NORFOLK, NE (Cable One)

▲ **HOWELLS**—Formerly served by TelePartners. No longer in operation

▲ **HUBBARD (VILLAGE)**—CenCom NNTV. Formerly [NE0375]. This cable system has converted to IPTV

▲ **HUBBARD**—CenCom Inc. This cable system has converted to IPTV. See Hubbard (village), NE [NE5018]

HUMBOLDT—See FALLS CITY, NE (Time Warner Cable)

▲ **HUMPHREY**—Cable Nebraska

▲ **HYANNIS**—Consolidated Cable Inc.

IMPERIAL—See GRANT, NE (Great Plains Communications)

INDIAN HILLS—See NORTH PLATTE, NE (Charter Communications)

▲ **INDIANOLA**—Pinpoint Cable TV. Now served by CAMBRIDGE, NE [NE0269]

INDIANOLA—See CAMBRIDGE, NE (Pinpoint Cable TV)

INGLEWOOD—See FREMONT, NE (Time Warner Cable)

▲ **JANSEN**—Formerly served by Diode Cable Co. No longer in operation

▲ **JOHNSON LAKE**—Charter Communications. Now served by KEARNEY, NE [NE0011]

JOHNSON LAKE—See KEARNEY, NE (Charter Communications)

JOHNSON—See SYRACUSE, NE (Zito Media)

▲ **JUNIATA**—Charter Communications

▲ **KEARNEY**—Charter Communications

KEITH COUNTY—See OGALLALA, NE (Charter Communications)

▲ **KENESAW**—Charter Communications

KENNARD—See BLAIR, NE (American Broadband)

KIMBALL COUNTY—See KIMBALL, NE (Charter Communications)

▲ **KIMBALL**—Charter Communications

LA VISTA—See OMAHA, NE (Cox Communications)

▲ **LAKE CUNNINGHAM**—Formerly served by TelePartners. No longer in operation

▲ **LAKE MALONEY**—Charter Communications. Now served by NORTH PLATTE, NE [NE0009]

LAKE MALONEY—See NORTH PLATTE, NE (Charter Communications)

▲ **LAKE VENTURA**—Formerly served by Charter Communications. No longer in operation

▲ **LAKE WACONDA**—Formerly served by Westcom. No longer in operation

LANCASTER COUNTY—See LINCOLN, NE (Time Warner Cable)

▲ **LAUREL**—American Broadband

LAWRENCE—See BLUE HILL, NE (Glenwood Telecommunications)

▲ **LEIGH**—Formerly served by TelePartners. No longer in operation

▲ **LEWELLEN**—Formerly served by Consolidated Cable Inc. No longer in operation

▲ **LEXINGTON**—Charter Communications. Now served by KEARNEY, NE [NE0011]

LEXINGTON—See KEARNEY, NE (Charter Communications)

LINCOLN COUNTY—See NORTH PLATTE, NE (Charter Communications)

▲ **LINCOLN**—Formerly served by Sprint Corp. No longer in operation

▲ **LINCOLN**—Time Warner Cable

▲ **LINDSAY**—Formerly served by TelePartners. No longer in operation

LITCHFIELD—See KEARNEY, NE (Charter Communications)

▲ **LOCHLAND**—Glenwood Telecommunications. Now served by BLUE HILL, NE [NE0093]

LOCHLAND—See BLUE HILL, NE (Glenwood Telecommunications)

LODGEPOLE—See DALTON, NE (Dalton Telephone Co.)

LONG PINE—See AINSWORTH, NE (Cable Nebraska)

LOOMIS—See KEARNEY, NE (Charter Communications)

LOUISVILLE—See SPRINGFIELD, NE (Charter Communications)

LOUP CITY—See KEARNEY, NE (Charter Communications)

▲ **LYMAN**—Windbreak Cable TV

▲ **LYNCH**—Formerly served by TelePartners. No longer in operation

▲ **LYONS**—American Broadband

MADISON—See NORFOLK, NE (Cable One)

▲ **MADRID**—Consolidated Cable Inc. Now served by WALLACE, NE [NE0336]

MADRID—See WALLACE, NE (Consolidated Cable Inc.)

▲ **MALCOLM**—Zito Media

▲ **MARQUETTE**—Mid-State Community TV. Now served by AURORA, NE [NE0033]

MARQUETTE—See AURORA, NE (Mid-State Community TV)

▲ **MARTINSBURG (village)**—CenCom Inc. This cable system has converted to IPTV. See Martinsburg (village), NE [NE5022]

▲ **MARTINSBURG (VILLAGE)**—CenCom NNTV. Formerly [NE0388]. This cable system has converted to IPTV

▲ **MASKELL (VILLAGE)**—CenCom NNTV. Formerly [NE0387]. This cable system has converted to IPTV

▲ **MASON CITY**—NCTC Cable

▲ **MAXWELL**—Consolidated Cable Inc.

MAYWOOD—See CURTIS, NE (Consolidated Cable Inc.)

▲ **MCCOOK**—Great Plains Communications

▲ **MEAD**—Formerly served by TelePartners. No longer in operation

▲ **MEADOW GROVE**—Cable Nebraska

MELBETA—See SCOTTSBLUFF, NE (Charter Communications)

MERNA—See DUNNING, NE (Consolidated Cable Inc.)

MILFORD—See WILBER, NE (Zito Media)

MILLER (UNINCORPORATED AREAS)—See KEARNEY, NE (Charter Communications)

▲ **MINATARE**—Charter Communications. Now served by SCOTTSBLUFF, NE [NE0008]

MINATARE—See SCOTTSBLUFF, NE (Charter Communications)

▲ **MINDEN**—Charter Communications. Now served by KEARNEY, NE [NE0011]

MINDEN—See KEARNEY, NE (Charter Communications)

▲ **MITCHELL**—Charter Communications. Now served by SCOTTSBLUFF, NE [NE0008]

MITCHELL—See SCOTTSBLUFF, NE (Charter Communications)

▲ **MONROE**—Cable Nebraska

▲ **MORRILL**—Charter Communications. Now served by SCOTTSBLUFF, NE [NE0008]

MORRILL—See SCOTTSBLUFF, NE (Charter Communications)

MULLEN—See HYANNIS, NE (Consolidated Cable Inc.)

MURDOCK—See SYRACUSE, NE (Zito Media)

MURRAY—See SYRACUSE, NE (Zito Media)

▲ **NAPER**—Cable Nebraska

NEBRASKA CITY—See AUBURN, NE (Time Warner Cable)

▲ **NEHAWKA**—Formerly served by Westcom. No longer in operation

NELIGH—See ELGIN, NE (Great Plains Communications)

▲ **NELSON**—Zito Media

NEMAHA COUNTY (PORTIONS)—See SYRACUSE, NE (Zito Media)

▲ **NEWCASTLE (village)**—CenCom Inc. This cable system has converted to IPTV. See Newcastle (village), NE [NE5025]

▲ **NEWCASTLE (VILLAGE)**—CenCom NNTV. Formerly [NE0198]. This cable system has converted to IPTV

▲ **NEWMAN GROVE**—Cable Nebraska

▲ **NICKERSON**—Formerly served by TelePartners. No longer in operation

NIOBRARA—See BLOOMFIELD, NE (Great Plains Communications)

▲ **NORFOLK**—Cable One

NORMAN—See BLUE HILL, NE (Glenwood Telecommunications)

▲ **NORTH BEND**—Great Plains Communications

▲ **NORTH LOUP**—NCTC Cable

▲ **NORTH PLATTE**—Charter Communications

▲ **O'NEILL**—Cable Nebraska

OAKDALE—See ELGIN, NE (Great Plains Communications)

▲ **OAKLAND**—American Broadband

▲ **OBERT (VILLAGE)**—CenCom NNTV. Formerly [NE0387]. This cable system has converted to IPTV

▲ **OBERT/MASKELL**—CenCom Inc. This cable system has converted to IPTV. See Obert, NE [NE5027] & Maskell, NE [NE5023]

▲ **OCONTO**—Great Plains Cable TV. Now served by ARNOLD, NE [NE0114]

OCONTO—See ARNOLD, NE (Great Plains Communications)

ODELL—See DILLER, NE (Diode Telecom Inc)

ODESSA—See KEARNEY, NE (Charter Communications)

▲ **OGALLALA**—Charter Communications

▲ **OMAHA (western portion)**—Qwest Choice TV. This cable system has converted to IPTV. See Omaha, NE [NE5000]

▲ **OMAHA (WESTERN PORTION)**—CenturyLink. Formerly [NE0377]. This cable system has converted to IPTV.

▲ **OMAHA**—Formerly served by Digital Broadcast Corp. No longer in operation

▲ **OMAHA**—Cox Communications

▲ **ORCHARD**—Formerly served by TelePartners. No longer in operation

▲ **ORD**—Charter Communications. Now served by KEARNEY, NE [NE0011]

ORD—See KEARNEY, NE (Charter Communications)

▲ **ORLEANS**—Formerly served by Pinpoint Cable TV. No longer in operation

▲ **OSCEOLA**—Cable Nebraska

▲ **OSHKOSH**—Windbreak Cable TV

▲ **OSMOND**—HunTel Cablevision. Now served by WAYNE, NE [NE0374]

OSMOND—See WAYNE, NE (American Broadband)

▲ **OTOE**—Formerly served by CableDirect. No longer in operation

OVERTON—See KEARNEY, NE (Charter Communications)

▲ **OXFORD**—Pinpoint Cable TV

▲ **PAGE (village)**—Formerly served by Sky Scan Cable Co. No longer in operation

PALISADE—See GRANT, NE (Great Plains Communications)

▲ **PALMER**—Cable Nebraska

PALMYRA—See SYRACUSE, NE (Zito Media)

PAPILLION—See OMAHA, NE (Cox Communications)

PAWNEE CITY—See FALLS CITY, NE (Time Warner Cable)

▲ **PAXTON**—Peregrine Communications

▲ **PENDER**—HunTel Cablevision. Now served by WAYNE, NE [NE0374]

PENDER—See WAYNE, NE (American Broadband)

▲ **PERU**—Zito Media

PETERSBURG—See ELGIN, NE (Great Plains Communications)

PHILLIPS—See KEARNEY, NE (Charter Communications)

▲ **PICKRELL**—Comstar Cable TV Inc.

PIERCE—See NORFOLK, NE (Cable One)

▲ **PILGER**—Sky Scan Cable Co. Now served by NORFOLK, NE [NE0006]

PILGER—See NORFOLK, NE (Cable One)

PLAINVIEW—See BLOOMFIELD, NE (Great Plains Communications)

▲ **PLATTE CENTER**—Formerly served by TelePartners. No longer in operation

▲ **PLATTE CENTER**—Cable Nebraska

PLATTE COUNTY (PORTIONS)—See RICHLAND, NE (Cable Nebraska)

PLATTSMOUTH—See SPRINGFIELD, NE (Charter Communications)

PLEASANT DALE—See WILBER, NE (Zito Media)

PLEASANTON—See KEARNEY, NE (Charter Communications)

PLYMOUTH—See WILBER, NE (Zito Media)

▲ **POLK**—Cable Nebraska

▲ **PONCA**—Great Plains Communications. Now served by BLOOMFIELD, NE [NE0065]

PONCA—See BLOOMFIELD, NE (Great Plains Communications)

POTTER—See DALTON, NE (Dalton Telephone Co.)

▲ **PRAGUE (village)**—Formerly served by Westcom. No longer in operation

RANDOLPH—See NORFOLK, NE (Cable One)

RAVENNA—See KEARNEY, NE (Charter Communications)

▲ **RAYMOND**—Zito Media

▲ **RED CLOUD**—Formerly served by Pinpoint Cable TV. No longer in operation

▲ **REPUBLICAN CITY**—Formerly served by Pinpoint Cable TV. No longer in operation

▲ **RICHLAND**—Cable Nebraska

RIVERDALE (VILLAGE)—See KEARNEY, NE (Charter Communications)

ROCK COUNTY—See BASSETT, NE (American Broadband)

ROSELAND—See BLUE HILL, NE (Glenwood Telecommunications)

▲ **RULO**—Formerly served by CableDirect. No longer in operation

RUSHVILLE—See CHADRON, NE (Great Plains Communications)

▲ **RUSKIN**—Formerly served by Diode Cable Co. No longer in operation

▲ **SALEM**—Formerly served by CableDirect. No longer in operation

▲ **SARGENT**—NCTC Cable

SARPY COUNTY (PORTIONS)—See GRETNA, NE (Zito Media)

SARPY COUNTY (UNINCORPORATED AREAS)—See OMAHA, NE (Cox Communications)

▲ **SCHUYLER**—Cable Nebraska

▲ **SCOTIA**—NCTC Cable

SCOTTS BLUFF COUNTY—See SCOTTSBLUFF, NE (Charter Communications)

▲ **SCOTTSBLUFF**—Charter Communications

SCRIBNER—See NORTH BEND, NE (Great Plains Communications)

SEWARD COUNTY—See LINCOLN, NE (Time Warner Cable)

SEWARD—See LINCOLN, NE (Time Warner Cable)

▲ **SHELBY**—Cable Nebraska

SHELTON—See GRAND ISLAND, NE (Charter Communications)

▲ **SHUBERT**—Formerly served by CableDirect. No longer in operation

▲ **SIDNEY**—Charter Communications

▲ **SILVER CREEK**—Cable Nebraska

SNYDER—See NORTH BEND, NE (Great Plains Communications)

▲ **SPALDING**—Cable Nebraska

▲ **SPENCER (VILLAGE)**—CenCom NNTV. Formerly [NE0147]. This cable system has converted to IPTV

▲ **SPENCER**—CenCom Inc. This cable system has converted to IPTV. See Spencer (village), NE [NE5026]

▲ **SPRINGFIELD (portions)**—Formerly served by TelePartners. No longer in operation

▲ **SPRINGFIELD**—Charter Communications

SPRINGVIEW—See AINSWORTH, NE (Cable Nebraska)

▲ **ST. EDWARD**—Cable Nebraska

ST. LIBORY—See GRAND ISLAND, NE (Charter Communications)

ST. LIBORY—See KEARNEY, NE (Charter Communications)

ST. PAUL—See GRAND ISLAND, NE (Charter Communications)

▲ **STAMFORD**—Formerly served by Pinpoint Cable TV. No longer in operation

▲ **STANTON**—Stanton Telecom

▲ **STAPLEHURST (VILLAGE)**—Zita Media

STAPLETON—See ARNOLD, NE (Great Plains Communications)

▲ **STEINAUER**—Formerly served by CableDirect. No longer in operation

▲ **STELLA**—Formerly served by StellaVision. No longer in operation

STERLING—See SYRACUSE, NE (Zito Media)

▲ **STRATTON**—Peregrine Communications

▲ **STROMSBURG**—Cable Nebraska

▲ **STUART**—CenCom Inc. This cable system has converted to IPTV. See Stuart (village), NE [NE5030]

▲ **STUART**—CenCom NNTV. Formerly [NE0135]. This cable system has converted to IPTV

SUMNER—See KEARNEY, NE (Charter Communications)

▲ **SUPERIOR**—Glenwood Telecommunications

▲ **SUTHERLAND**—Great Plains Communications

SUTTON—See CLAY CENTER, NE (Zito Media)

▲ **SWANTON**—Comstar Cable TV Inc.

▲ **SYRACUSE**—Zito Media

TABLE ROCK—See FALLS CITY, NE (Time Warner Cable)

▲ **TALMAGE**—Formerly served by Great Plains Communications. No longer in operation

▲ **TAYLOR**—NCTC Cable

TECUMSEH—See AUBURN, NE (Time Warner Cable)

▲ **TEKAMAH**—American Broadband

TERRYTOWN—See SCOTTSBLUFF, NE (Charter Communications)

THEDFORD—See DUNNING, NE (Consolidated Cable Inc.)

TILDEN—See NORFOLK, NE (Cable One)

▲ **TOBIAS**—Formerly served by CableDirect. No longer in operation

▲ **TRENTON**—Great Plains Communications

▲ **TRUMBULL**—Mid-State Community TV. Now served by AURORA, NE [NE0033]

TRUMBULL—See AURORA, NE (Mid-State Community TV)

UEHLING—See HOOPER, NE (WesTel Systems)

▲ **ULYSSES**—Zito Media

UNADILLA—See SYRACUSE, NE (Zito Media)

▲ **UNION**—Formerly served by Westcom. No longer in operation

UPLAND—See BLUE HILL, NE (Glenwood Telecommunications)

UTICA—See WACO, NE (Zito Media)

▲ **VALENTINE**—Cable Nebraska

VALLEY—See GRETNA, NE (Zito Media)

▲ **VALPARAISO**—Zito Media

VENANGO—See GRANT, NE (Great Plains Communications)

VERDIGRE—See BLOOMFIELD, NE (Great Plains Communications)

▲ **VERDON**—Formerly served by CableDirect. No longer in operation

▲ **WACO**—Zito Media

▲ **WAHOO**—Charter Communications. Now served by SPRINGFIELD (formerly Plattsmouth), NE [NE0020]

WAHOO—See SPRINGFIELD, NE (Charter Communications)

WAKEFIELD—See WAYNE, NE (American Broadband)

▲ **WALLACE**—Consolidated Cable Inc.

▲ **WALTHILL**—HunTel Cablevision. Now served by WAYNE, NE [NE0374]

WALTHILL—See WAYNE, NE (American Broadband)

▲ **WASHINGTON (village)**—Formerly served by TelePartners. No longer in operation

WASHINGTON COUNTY—See BLAIR, NE (American Broadband)

WATERLOO—See GRETNA, NE (Zito Media)

▲ **WAUNETA**—BWTelcom

WAUSA—See BLOOMFIELD, NE (Great Plains Communications)

WAVERLY—See SPRINGFIELD, NE (Charter Communications)

▲ **WAYNE**—American Broadband

WEEPING WATER—See SYRACUSE, NE (Zito Media)

WEST POINT—See NORFOLK, NE (Cable One)

▲ **WESTERN**—Zito Media

▲**WESTON (village)**—Formerly served by Westcom. No longer in operation

▲**WILBER**—Zito Media

WILCOX—See KEARNEY, NE (Charter Communications)

WINNETOON—See BLOOMFIELD, NE (Great Plains Communications)

▲**WINSIDE (village)**—CenCom Inc. This cable system has converted to IPTV. See Winside (village), NW [NE5033]

▲**WINSIDE (village)**—Formerly served by Sky Scan Cable Co. No longer in operation

▲**WINSIDE (VILLAGE)**—CenCom NNTV. Formerly [NE0386]. This cable system has converted to IPTV

WINSLOW—See HOOPER, NE (WesTel Systems)

WISNER—See NORFOLK, NE (Cable One)

▲**WOLBACH**—Great Plains Communications

WOOD RIVER—See GRAND ISLAND, NE (Charter Communications)

▲**WOODCLIFF LAKES**—Time Warner Cable. Now served by FREMONT, NE [NE0007]

WOODCLIFF LAKES—See FREMONT, NE (Time Warner Cable)

WYMORE—See WILBER, NE (Zito Media)

▲**WYNOT**—CenCom Inc. No longer in operation

▲**YORK**—Time Warner Cable

▲**YUTAN**—Formerly served by TelePartners. No longer in operation

NEVADA

▲**ALAMO**—Rainbow Cable

BABBITT ARMY BASE—See HAWTHORNE, NV (Charter Communications)

▲**BATTLE MOUNTAIN**—Baja Broadband

▲**BEATTY**—Formerly served by Eagle West Communications. No longer in operation

▲**BLUE DIAMOND**—Formerly served by Eagle West Communications Inc. No longer in operation

▲**BOULDER CITY (northern portion)**—Formerly served by Eagle West Communications. No longer in operation

BOULDER CITY—See LAS VEGAS, NV (Cox Communications)

BUNKERVILLE—See MESQUITE, NV (Baja Broadband)

▲**CALIENTE**—Rainbow Cable. Now served by PANACA, NV [NV0047]

CALIENTE—See PANACA, NV (Rainbow Cable)

▲**CALLVILLE BAY**—Formerly served by Eagle West Communications Inc. No longer in operation

▲**CARLIN**—Baja Broadband

▲**CARSON CITY**—Formerly served by Quadravision. No longer in operation

▲**CARSON CITY**—Charter Communications

CENTERVILLE—See GARDNERVILLE, NV (Charter Communications)

CHURCHILL COUNTY—See FALLON, NV (Charter Communications)

CLARK COUNTY—See LAS VEGAS, NV (Cox Communications)

COLD SPRINGS—See RENO, NV (Charter Communications)

CREECH AFB—See INDIAN SPRINGS, NV (United Cable Management)

▲**CRYSTAL BAY**—Charter Communications

DAYTON—See CARSON CITY, NV (Charter Communications)

DESERT SKIES RV PARK—See MESQUITE, AZ (Baja Broadband)

ELKO COUNTY (PORTIONS)—See ELKO, NV (Baja Broadband)

▲**ELKO**—Baja Broadband

▲**ELY**—Central Telcom Services

▲**EMPIRE**—Formerly served by United States Gypsum Co. No longer in operation

ESMERALDA COUNTY (PORTIONS)—See TONOPAH, NV (RealStar Communications)

▲**EUREKA**—Central Telcom Services

FALLON STATION—See FALLON, NV (Charter Communications)

▲**FALLON**—Charter Communications

▲**FERNLEY**—Charter Communications

▲**GARDNERVILLE**—Charter Communications

GENOA—See GARDNERVILLE, NV (Charter Communications)

GOLD HILL—See VIRGINIA CITY, NV (Comstock Community TV Inc.)

GOLDEN VALLEY—See RENO, NV (Charter Communications)

▲**GOLDFIELD**—Formerly served by Eagle West Communications Inc. No longer in operation

GREEN VALLEY—See LAS VEGAS, NV (Cox Communications)

▲**HAWTHORNE**—Charter Communications

HENDERSON—See LAS VEGAS, NV (Cox Communications)

HIDDEN VALLEY—See RENO, NV (Charter Communications)

HOLBROOK JUNCTION—See TOPAZ LAKE, NV (Satview Broadband)

HUMBOLDT COUNTY (PORTIONS)—See WINNEMUCCA, NV (CalNeva Broadband)

▲**INDIAN SPRINGS AFB**—Formerly served by United Cable Management. No longer in operation

▲**INDIAN SPRINGS**—United Cable Management

▲**JACKPOT**—Satview Broadband

JACKS VALLEY—See GARDNERVILLE, NV (Charter Communications)

▲**LAS VEGAS**—Formerly served by Sprint Corp. No longer in operation

▲**LAS VEGAS**—Cox Communications

▲**LAUGHLIN**—CMA Cablevision

LEMMON VALLEY—See RENO, NV (Charter Communications)

▲**LOCKWOOD**—Charter Communications. Now served by RENO, NV [NV0002]

LOCKWOOD—See RENO, NV (Charter Communications)

▲**LOGANDALE**—Baja Broadband

▲**LOVELOCK**—Lovelock Cable TV

LYON COUNTY (NORTHERN PORTION)—See FERNLEY, NV (Charter Communications)

LYON COUNTY (NORTHWESTERN PORTION)—See CARSON CITY, NV (Charter Communications)

▲**MCGILL**—Central Telcom Services

▲**MESQUITE**—Baja Broadband

MINDEN—See GARDNERVILLE, NV (Charter Communications)

MOGUL—See RENO, NV (Charter Communications)

▲**NELLIS AFB**—Bluebird Communications

NORTH LAS VEGAS—See LAS VEGAS, NV (Cox Communications)

OVERTON—See LOGANDALE, NV (Baja Broadband)

▲**PAHRUMP**—CMA Cablevision

▲**PANACA**—Rainbow Cable

PANTHER VALLEY—See RENO, NV (Charter Communications)

PEAVINE—See RENO, CA (Charter Communications)

▲**PIOCHE**—Rainbow Cable. Now served by PANACA, NV [NV0047]

PIOCHE—See PANACA, NV (Rainbow Cable)

PLACER COUNTY (EASTERN PORTION)—See CRYSTAL BAY, CA (Charter Communications)

PYRAMID LAKE—See FERNLEY, NV (Charter Communications)

RED ROCK—See RENO, NV (Charter Communications)

RENO CASCADE—See RENO, NV (Charter Communications)

▲**RENO**—Formerly served by Quadravision. No longer in operation

▲**RENO**—Charter Communications

▲**RUTH**—Central Telcom Services

SEARCHLIGHT—See LAUGHLIN, NV (CMA Cablevision)

SHERIDAN—See GARDNERVILLE, NV (Charter Communications)

SIERRA—See RENO, NV (Charter Communications)

▲**SILVER SPRINGS**—Charter Communications

SPANISH SPRINGS—See RENO, NV (Charter Communications)

SPARKS—See RENO, NV (Charter Communications)

SPRING CREEK—See ELKO, NV (Baja Broadband)

STAGECOACH—See SILVER SPRINGS, NV (Charter Communications)

STEAMBOAT—See RENO, NV (Charter Communications)

STOREY COUNTY (SOUTHERN PORTION)—See CARSON CITY, NV (Charter Communications)

SUN VALLEY—See RENO, NV (Charter Communications)

▲**TONOPAH**—RealStar Communications

▲**TOPAZ LAKE**—Satview Broadband

TOPAZ RANCH ESTATES—See TOPAZ LAKE, NV (Satview Broadband)

VERDI—See RENO, NV (Charter Communications)

▲**VERDI**—Suddenlink Communications

▲**VIRGINIA CITY**—Comstock Community TV Inc.

WADSWORTH—See FERNLEY, NV (Charter Communications)

WALKER—See TOPAZ LAKE, CA (Satview Broadband)

WASHOE COUNTY—See CRYSTAL BAY, NV (Charter Communications)

WASHOE COUNTY—See RENO, NV (Charter Communications)

▲**WELLINGTON**—Satview Broadband

▲**WELLS**—Satview Broadband

▲**WENDOVER**—Central Telcom Services

WENDOVER—See WENDOVER, UT (Central Telcom Services)

▲**WINNEMUCCA**—CalNeva Broadband

YERINGTON—See FALLON, NV (Charter Communications)

NEW HAMPSHIRE

ACTON (TOWN)—See CONWAY, ME (Time Warner Cable)

ALBANY—See CONWAY, NH (Time Warner Cable)

ALEXANDRIA—See BELMONT, NH (MetroCast Cablevision)

ALLENSTOWN—See MANCHESTER, NH (Comcast Cable)

ALSTEAD (TOWN)—See MANCHESTER, NH (Comcast Cable)

ALSTEAD CENTER—See MANCHESTER, NH (Comcast Cable)

▲**ALSTEAD**—Formerly served by Adelphia Communications. Now served by MANCHESTER, NH [NH0048]

ALSTEAD—See MANCHESTER, NH (Comcast Cable)

ALTON—See BELMONT, NH (MetroCast Cablevision)

AMHERST—See MANCHESTER, NH (Comcast Cable)

▲**ANDOVER (town)**—Formerly served by Adelphia Communications. Now served by BURLINGTON, VT [VT0001]

ANTRIM—See MANCHESTER, NH (Comcast Cable)

ASHLAND—See PLYMOUTH, NH (Time Warner Cable)

ATKINSON—See MANCHESTER, NH (Comcast Cable)

AUBURN—See MANCHESTER, NH (Comcast Cable)

BARNSTEAD—See BELMONT, NH (MetroCast Cablevision)

BARRINGTON—See ROCHESTER, NH (MetroCast Cablevision)

BARTLETT—See CONWAY, NH (Time Warner Cable)

▲**BATH (village)**—Formerly served by Adelphia Communications. Now served by LITTLETON, NH [NH0020]

BATH (VILLAGE)—See LITTLETON, NH (Time Warner Cable)

BEDFORD—See MANCHESTER, NH (Comcast Cable)

▲**BELMONT**—MetroCast Cablevision

BENNINGTON—See MANCHESTER, NH (Comcast Cable)

▲**BERLIN**—Time Warner Cable

BETHLEHEM (TOWN)—See LITTLETON, NH (Time Warner Cable)

BOSCAWEN—See MANCHESTER, NH (Comcast Cable)

BOW—See MANCHESTER, NH (Comcast Cable)

BRADFORD—See WARNER TWP., NH (TDS Telecom)

BRENTWOOD—See MANCHESTER, NH (Comcast Cable)

BRIDGEWATER—See BELMONT, NH (MetroCast Cablevision)

BRISTOL—See BELMONT, NH (MetroCast Cablevision)

BROOKFIELD (TOWN)—See CONWAY, NH (Time Warner Cable)

▲**CAMPTON**—Formerly served by Adelphia Communications. Now served by PLYMOUTH, NH [NH0055]

CAMPTON—See PLYMOUTH, NH (Time Warner Cable)

CANDIA—See MANCHESTER, NH (Comcast Cable)

CANTERBURY—See MANCHESTER, NH (Comcast Cable)

▲**CARROLL**—Formerly served by Adelphia Communications. Now served by LITTLETON, NH [NH0020]

CARROLL—See LITTLETON, NH (Time Warner Cable)

CENTER HARBOR—See BELMONT, NH (MetroCast Cablevision)

CENTER OSSIPEE—See CONWAY, NH (Time Warner Cable)

CHESTER (TOWN)—See MANCHESTER, NH (Comcast Cable)

CHESTER—See MANCHESTER, NH (Comcast Cable)

CHESTERFIELD—See SPOFFORD, NH (Argent Communications)

CHESTERFIELD—See MANCHESTER, NH (Comcast Cable)

CHICHESTER (TOWN)—See MANCHESTER, NH (Comcast Cable)

▲**CLAREMONT**—Comcast Cable. Now served by BURLINGTON, VT [VT0001]

▲**CONCORD**—Comcast Cable. Now served by MANCHESTER, NH [NH0048]

CONCORD—See MANCHESTER, NH (Comcast Cable)

▲**CONWAY**—Time Warner Cable

▲**CORNISH**—Formerly served by Adelphia Communications. Now served by BURLINGTON, VT [VT0001]

DALTON—See BERLIN, NH (Time Warner Cable)

DANVILLE—See MANCHESTER, NH (Comcast Cable)

DEERFIELD—See BELMONT, NH (MetroCast Cablevision)

DEERING—See MANCHESTER, NH (Comcast Cable)

▲**DERRY**—Comcast Cable. Now served by MANCHESTER, NH [NH0048]

DERRY—See MANCHESTER, NH (Comcast Cable)

DORCHESTER (TOWN)—See PLYMOUTH, NH (Time Warner Cable)

DREWSVILLE—See MANCHESTER, NH (Comcast Cable)

EAST KINGSTON—See MANCHESTER, NH (Comcast Cable)

EAST ROCHESTER—See ROCHESTER, NH (MetroCast Cablevision)

EAST WESTMORELAND—See SPOFFORD, NH (Argent Communications)

EATON (TOWN)—See CONWAY, NH (Time Warner Cable)

EFFINGHAM—See CONWAY, NH (Time Warner Cable)

EPPING—See MANCHESTER, NH (Comcast Cable)

EPSOM—See BELMONT, NH (MetroCast Cablevision)

EXETER—See MANCHESTER, NH (Comcast Cable)

FARMINGTON—See ROCHESTER, NH (MetroCast Cablevision)

FITZWILLIAM—See TROY, NH (Argent Communications)

FRANCESTOWN—See MANCHESTER, NH (Comcast Cable)

FRANCONIA—See LITTLETON, NH (Time Warner Cable)

FRANKLIN—See BELMONT, NH (MetroCast Cablevision)

▲**FREEDOM (town)**—Formerly served by Adelphia Communications. Now served by CONWAY, NH [NH0038]

FREEDOM (TOWN)—See CONWAY, NH (Time Warner Cable)

FREMONT (TOWN)—See MANCHESTER, NH (Comcast Cable)

FREMONT—See MANCHESTER, NH (Comcast Cable)

FRYEBURG—See CONWAY, ME (Time Warner Cable)

GILFORD—See BELMONT, NH (MetroCast Cablevision)

GILMANTON—See BELMONT, NH (MetroCast Cablevision)

GLEN—See CONWAY, NH (Time Warner Cable)

GOFFSTOWN—See MANCHESTER, NH (Comcast Cable)

GONIC—See ROCHESTER, NH (MetroCast Cablevision)

GORHAM—See BERLIN, NH (Time Warner Cable)

▲**GRANTHAM**—Formerly served by Adelphia Communications. Now served by BURLINGTON, VT [VT0001]

GREENLAND—See MANCHESTER, NH (Comcast Cable)

▲**GREENVILLE**—Formerly served by Adelphia Communications. Now served by MANCHESTER, NH [NH0048]

GREENVILLE—See MANCHESTER, NH (Comcast Cable)

GROTON (TOWN)—See PLYMOUTH, NH (Time Warner Cable)

GROVETON—See STRATFORD (town), NH (Argent Communications)

GROVETON—See BERLIN, NH (Time Warner Cable)

HAMPSTEAD—See MANCHESTER, NH (Comcast Cable)

HAMPTON FALLS—See MANCHESTER, NH (Comcast Cable)

HAMPTON—See MANCHESTER, NH (Comcast Cable)

HANCOCK—See MANCHESTER, NH (Comcast Cable)

HARRISVILLE (TOWN)—See NELSON (town), NH (Argent Communications)

HEBRON—See BELMONT, NH (MetroCast Cablevision)

HENNIKER—See MANCHESTER, NH (Comcast Cable)

▲**HILL (town)**—Formerly served by Adelphia Communications. Now served by BURLINGTON, VT [VT0001]

HILLSBOROUGH COUNTY—See MANCHESTER, NH (Comcast Cable)

HILLSBOROUGH—See MANCHESTER, NH (Comcast Cable)

▲**HINSDALE**—Formerly served by Adelphia Communications. No longer in operation

HOLDERNESS (PORTIONS)—See PLYMOUTH, NH (Time Warner Cable)

HOOKSETT—See MANCHESTER, NH (Comcast Cable)

HOPKINTON—See MANCHESTER, NH (Comcast Cable)

HUDSON—See MANCHESTER, NH (Comcast Cable)

JACKSON—See CONWAY, NH (Time Warner Cable)

JEFFERSON (TOWN)—See CONWAY, NH (Time Warner Cable)

KEARSARGE—See CONWAY, NH (Time Warner Cable)

▲**KEENE**—Time Warner Cable

KENSINGTON—See MANCHESTER, NH (Comcast Cable)

KINGSTON—See MANCHESTER, NH (Comcast Cable)

LACONIA—See BELMONT, NH (MetroCast Cablevision)

LANCASTER—See BERLIN, NH (Time Warner Cable)

LANGDON—See MANCHESTER, NH (Comcast Cable)

LEBANON (PORTIONS)—See ROCHESTER, ME (MetroCast Cablevision)

▲**LEBANON**—Comcast Cable. Now served by BURLINGTON, VT [VT0001]

▲**LINCOLN**—Formerly served by Adelphia Communications. Now served by PLYMOUTH, NH [NH0055]

LINCOLN—See PLYMOUTH, NH (Time Warner Cable)

LISBON—See LITTLETON, NH (Time Warner Cable)

LITCHFIELD—See MANCHESTER, NH (Comcast Cable)

▲**LITTLETON**—Time Warner Cable

▲**LONDONDERRY**—Comcast Cable. Now served by MANCHESTER, NH [NH0048]

LONDONDERRY—See MANCHESTER, NH (Comcast Cable)

LOUDON (TOWN)—See MANCHESTER, NH (Comcast Cable)

LOVELL (TOWN)—See CONWAY, ME (Time Warner Cable)

▲**MADISON (town)**—Formerly served by Adelphia Communications. Now served by CONWAY, NH [NH0038]

MADISON (TOWN)—See CONWAY, NH (Time Warner Cable)

▲**MANCHESTER**—Comcast Cable

MARLBOROUGH—See KEENE, NH (Time Warner Cable)

MARLOW—See STODDARD, NH (Argent Communications)

MEREDITH—See BELMONT, NH (MetroCast Cablevision)

▲**MERRIMACK**—Formerly served by Adelphia Communications. Now served by MANCHESTER, NH [NH0048]

MERRIMACK—See MANCHESTER, NH (Comcast Cable)

MIDDLETON (TOWN)—See CONWAY, NH (Time Warner Cable)

▲**MILAN (TOWN)**—Argent Communications

MILFORD—See MANCHESTER, NH (Comcast Cable)

MILTON MILLS—See ROCHESTER, NH (MetroCast Cablevision)

MILTON—See ROCHESTER, NH (MetroCast Cablevision)

▲**MONROE (town)**—Formerly served by Adelphia Communications. Now served by LITTLETON, NH [NH0020]

MONROE (TOWN)—See LITTLETON, NH (Time Warner Cable)

▲**MOULTONBOROUGH (town)**—Formerly served by Adelphia Communications. Now served by CONWAY, NH [NH0038]

MOULTONBOROUGH (TOWN)—See CONWAY, NH (Time Warner Cable)

MOUNT VERNON—See MANCHESTER, NH (Comcast Cable)

▲**NASHUA**—Comcast Cable. Now served by MANCHESTER, NH [NH0048]

NASHUA—See MANCHESTER, NH (Comcast Cable)

▲**NELSON (TOWN)**—Argent Communications

NEW BOSTON (TOWN)—See MANCHESTER, NH (Comcast Cable)

▲**NEW BOSTON**—Formerly served by Adelphia Communications. Now served by MANCHESTER, NH [NH0048]

NEW BOSTON—See MANCHESTER, NH (Comcast Cable)

NEW CASTLE—See MANCHESTER, NH (Comcast Cable)

NEW DURHAM—See BELMONT, NH (MetroCast Cablevision)

NEW HAMPTON—See BELMONT, NH (MetroCast Cablevision)

NEW IPSWICH—See MANCHESTER, NH (Comcast Cable)

▲**NEW LONDON**—Formerly served by Adelphia Communications. Now served by BURLINGTON, VT [VT0001]

NEWBURY—See WARNER TWP., NH (TDS Telecom)

NEWFIELDS—See MANCHESTER, NH (Comcast Cable)

NEWINGTON (TOWN)—See MANCHESTER, NH (Comcast Cable)

NEWMARKET—See MANCHESTER, NH (Comcast Cable)

▲**NEWPORT**—Formerly served by Adelphia Communications. Now served by BURLINGTON, VT [VT0001]

NEWTON—See MANCHESTER, NH (Comcast Cable)

NORTH CONWAY—See CONWAY, NH (Time Warner Cable)

NORTH HAMPTON—See MANCHESTER, NH (Comcast Cable)

NORTH WALPOLE—See MANCHESTER, NH (Comcast Cable)

NORTH WOODSTOCK—See PLYMOUTH, NH (Time Warner Cable)

NORTHFIELD (TOWN)—See BELMONT, NH (MetroCast Cablevision)

NORTHFIELD—See BELMONT, NH (MetroCast Cablevision)

NORTHUMBERLAND (TOWN)—See BERLIN, NH (Time Warner Cable)

NORTHWOOD—See BELMONT, NH (MetroCast Cablevision)

NOTTINGHAM (TOWN)—See MANCHESTER, NH (Comcast Cable)

NOTTINGHAM—See MANCHESTER, NH (Comcast Cable)

OSSIPEE (TOWN)—See CONWAY, NH (Time Warner Cable)

PELHAM—See MANCHESTER, NH (Comcast Cable)

PEMBROKE—See MANCHESTER, NH (Comcast Cable)

▲**PETERBOROUGH**—Formerly served by Adelphia Communications. Now served by MANCHESTER, NH [NH0048]

PETERBOROUGH—See MANCHESTER, NH (Comcast Cable)

PITTSFIELD—See BELMONT, NH (MetroCast Cablevision)

▲**PLAINFIELD (town)**—Formerly served by Adelphia Communications. Now served by BURLINGTON, VT [VT0001]

PLAISTOW—See MANCHESTER, NH (Comcast Cable)

▲**PLYMOUTH**—Time Warner Cable

▲**PORTSMOUTH**—Comcast Cable. Now served by MANCHESTER, NH [NH0048]

PORTSMOUTH—See MANCHESTER, NH (Comcast Cable)

RANDOLPH—See BERLIN, NH (Time Warner Cable)

RAYMOND—See MANCHESTER, NH (Comcast Cable)

RICHMOND (TOWN)—See KEENE, NH (Time Warner Cable)

RINDGE—See TROY, NH (Argent Communications)

▲**ROCHESTER**—MetroCast Cablevision

ROXBURY (TOWN)—See KEENE, NH (Time Warner Cable)

RUMNEY (TOWN)—See PLYMOUTH, NH (Time Warner Cable)

RYE—See MANCHESTER, NH (Comcast Cable)

SALEM (TOWN)—See MANCHESTER, NH (Comcast Cable)

SANBORNTON (TOWN)—See BELMONT, NH (MetroCast Cablevision)

SANBORNVILLE—See CONWAY, NH (Time Warner Cable)

SANDOWN—See MANCHESTER, NH (Comcast Cable)

SEABROOK—See MANCHESTER, NH (Comcast Cable)

SOUTH CHARLESTOWN—See MANCHESTER, NH (Comcast Cable)

▲**SPOFFORD**—Argent Communications

▲**STODDARD**—Argent Communications

STRAFFORD (TOWN-PORTIONS)—See BELMONT, NH (MetroCast Cablevision)

STRAFFORD (TOWN-PORTIONS)—See ROCHESTER, NH (MetroCast Cablevision)

▲**STRATFORD (TOWN)**—Argent Communications

STRATHAM—See MANCHESTER, NH (Comcast Cable)

▲**SUGAR HILL (town)**—Formerly served by Adelphia Communications. Now served by LITTLETON, NH [NH0020]

SUGAR HILL (TOWN)—See LITTLETON, NH (Time Warner Cable)

SULLIVAN (TOWN)—See NELSON (town), NH (Argent Communications)

SURRY—See KEENE, NH (Time Warner Cable)

SUTTON (TOWN)—See WARNER TWP., NH (TDS Telecom)

SWANZEY—See KEENE, NH (Time Warner Cable)

TAMWORTH (TOWN)—See CONWAY, NH (Time Warner Cable)

TEMPLE—See MANCHESTER, NH (Comcast Cable)

THORNTON—See PLYMOUTH, NH (Time Warner Cable)

TILTON—See BELMONT, NH (MetroCast Cablevision)

▲**TROY**—Argent Communications

TUFTONBORO (TOWN)—See CONWAY, NH (Time Warner Cable)

▲**WAKEFIELD (town)**—Formerly served by Adelphia Communications. Now served by CONWAY, NH [NH0038]

WAKEFIELD (TOWN)—See CONWAY, NH (Time Warner Cable)

WALPOLE—See MANCHESTER, NH (Comcast Cable)

▲**WARNER TWP.**—TDS Telecom

WARREN (TOWN)—See PLYMOUTH, NH (Time Warner Cable)

WATERVILLE VALLEY (TOWN)—See WATERVILLE VALLEY, NH (SkiSat Cable TV)

▲**WATERVILLE VALLEY**—SkiSat Cable TV

WEARE—See MANCHESTER, NH (Comcast Cable)

WEBSTER—See MANCHESTER, NH (Comcast Cable)

▲**WENTWORTH (town)**—Formerly served by Adelphia Communications. Now served by PLYMOUTH, NH [NH0055]

WENTWORTH (TOWN)—See PLYMOUTH, NH (Time Warner Cable)

WEST CHESTERFIELD—See SPOFFORD, NH (Argent Communications)

WEST CHESTERFIELD—See MANCHESTER, NH (Comcast Cable)

▲**WEST STEWARTSTOWN**—Formerly served by White Mountain Cablevision. No longer in operation

WESTMORELAND—See SPOFFORD, NH (Argent Communications)

WHITEFIELD—See BERLIN, NH (Time Warner Cable)

WILTON—See MANCHESTER, NH (Comcast Cable)

WINDHAM—See MANCHESTER, NH (Comcast Cable)

WOLFEBORO—See BELMONT, NH (MetroCast Cablevision)

WOODSTOCK—See PLYMOUTH, NH (Time Warner Cable)

NEW JERSEY

ABERDEEN TWP.—See RARITAN, NJ (Cablevision Systems Corp.)

ABSECON—See VINELAND, NJ (Comcast Cable)

ALEXANDRIA TWP.—See HUNTERDON COUNTY, NJ (Service Electric Cable TV of Hunterdon Inc.)

▲**ALLAMUCHY TWP.**—Cablevision Systems Corp. Now served by DOVER, NJ [NJ0005]

ALLAMUCHY TWP.—See DOVER, NJ (Cablevision Systems Corp.)

ALLENDALE—See OAKLAND, NJ (Cablevision Systems Corp.)

ALLENHURST—See MONMOUTH COUNTY, NJ (Comcast Cable)

ALLENTOWN—See HAMILTON TWP. (Mercer County), NJ (Cablevision Systems Corp.)

ALLOWAY TWP.—See VINELAND, NJ (Comcast Cable)

ALPHA BORO—See HUNTERDON COUNTY, NJ (Service Electric Cable TV of Hunterdon Inc.)

ALPINE—See OAKLAND, NJ (Cablevision Systems Corp.)

ANDOVER BOROUGH—See SPARTA, NJ (Service Electric Cable company)

ANDOVER TWP.—See SPARTA, NJ (Service Electric Cable company)

ANNANDALE—See HILLSBOROUGH, NJ (Comcast Cable)

ASBURY PARK—See MONMOUTH COUNTY, NJ (Cablevision Systems Corp.)

▲**ATLANTIC CITY**—Formerly served by OrionVision. No longer in operation

ATLANTIC CITY—See VINELAND, NJ (Comcast Cable)

ATLANTIC HIGHLANDS—See MONMOUTH COUNTY, NJ (Comcast Cable)

AUDUBON PARK—See VOORHEES, NJ (Comcast Cable)

AUDUBON—See VOORHEES, NJ (Comcast Cable)

▲**AVALON**—Comcast Cable. Now served by AVALON (formerly Rio Grande), NJ [NJ0018]

▲**AVALON**—Comcast Cable

AVON-BY-THE-SEA—See MONMOUTH COUNTY, NJ (Cablevision Systems Corp.)

BARNEGAT LIGHT—See LONG BEACH TWP., NJ (Comcast Cable)

BARNEGAT TWP.—See TOMS RIVER, NJ (Comcast Cable)

BARRINGTON—See VOORHEES, NJ (Comcast Cable)

BASS RIVER TWP.—See VINELAND, NJ (Comcast Cable)

BAY HEAD—See OCEAN COUNTY, NJ (Comcast Cable)

▲**BAYONNE**—Cablevision Systems Corp.

BEACH HAVEN—See LONG BEACH TWP., NJ (Comcast Cable)

BEACHWOOD—See TOMS RIVER, NJ (Comcast Cable)

BEDMINSTER (PORTIONS)—See RARITAN, NJ (Cablevision Systems Corp.)

BEDMINSTER TWP.—See LONG HILL TWP., NJ (Comcast Cable)

BEDMINSTER—See LONG HILL TWP., NJ (Comcast Cable)

BELLE MEAD—See HILLSBOROUGH, NJ (Comcast Cable)

BELLEVILLE TWP.—See UNION, NJ (Comcast Cable)

BELLMAWR—See VOORHEES, NJ (Comcast Cable)

BELMAR—See MONMOUTH COUNTY, NJ (Cablevision Systems Corp.)

BELVIDERE—See PORT MURRAY, NJ (Comcast Cable)

▲**BERGENFIELD**—Cablevision Systems Corp.

BERKELEY HEIGHTS TWP.—See UNION, NJ (Comcast Cable)

BERKELEY TWP.—See TOMS RIVER, NJ (Comcast Cable)

BERKLEY TWP.—See MONMOUTH COUNTY, NJ (Cablevision Systems Corp.)

BERLIN TWP.—See VOORHEES, NJ (Comcast Cable)

BERLIN—See VOORHEES, NJ (Comcast Cable)

BERNARDS TWP.—See RARITAN, NJ (Cablevision Systems Corp.)

BERNARDSVILLE—See LONG HILL TWP., NJ (Comcast Cable)

BETHLEHEM TWP.—See HILLSBOROUGH, NJ (Comcast Cable)

BEVERLY—See BURLINGTON COUNTY, NJ (Comcast Cable)

BLAIRSTOWN TWP.—See SPARTA, NJ (Service Electric Cable company)

BLAWENBURG—See HILLSBOROUGH, NJ (Comcast Cable)

BLOOMFIELD TWP.—See UNION, NJ (Comcast Cable)

BLOOMINGDALE—See OAKLAND, NJ (Cablevision Systems Corp.)

BLOOMSBURY—See HUNTERDON COUNTY, NJ (Service Electric Cable TV of Hunterdon Inc.)

BOGOTA—See OAKLAND, NJ (Cablevision Systems Corp.)

BOONTON TWP.—See DOVER, NJ (Cablevision Systems Corp.)

BOONTON—See DOVER, NJ (Cablevision Systems Corp.)

BORDENTOWN TWP.—See BURLINGTON COUNTY, NJ (Comcast Cable)

BORDENTOWN—See BURLINGTON COUNTY, NJ (Comcast Cable)

BOUND BROOK—See RARITAN, NJ (Cablevision Systems Corp.)

BRADLEY BEACH—See MONMOUTH COUNTY, NJ (Cablevision Systems Corp.)

BRANCHBURG TWP.—See HILLSBOROUGH, NJ (Comcast Cable)

BRANCHVILLE—See SPARTA, NJ (Service Electric Cable company)

BRICK TWP.—See OCEAN COUNTY, NJ (Comcast Cable)

BRIDGETON—See VINELAND, NJ (Comcast Cable)

BRIDGEWATER—See RARITAN, NJ (Cablevision Systems Corp.)

BRIELLE—See MONMOUTH COUNTY, NJ (Cablevision Systems Corp.)

BRIGANTINE—See VINELAND, NJ (Comcast Cable)

BROOKLAWN—See MAPLE SHADE, NJ (Comcast Cable)

BROWNS MILLS—See VOORHEES, NJ (Comcast Cable)

BUENA VISTA TWP.—See VINELAND, NJ (Comcast Cable)

BUENA—See VINELAND, NJ (Comcast Cable)

BURLINGTON CITY—See BURLINGTON COUNTY, NJ (Comcast Cable)

▲**BURLINGTON COUNTY**—Comcast Cable

BURLINGTON TWP.—See BURLINGTON COUNTY, NJ (Comcast Cable)

BUTLER—See OAKLAND, NJ (Cablevision Systems Corp.)

BYRAM TWP.—See SPARTA, NJ (Service Electric Cable company)

CALDWELL—See UNION, NJ (Comcast Cable)

CALIFON—See PORT MURRAY, NJ (Comcast Cable)

CAMDEN—See VOORHEES, NJ (Comcast Cable)

CAPE MAY POINT—See WILDWOOD, NJ (Comcast Cable)

CAPE MAY—See WILDWOOD, NJ (Comcast Cable)

▲**CARLSTADT BOROUGH**—Comcast Cable

CARNEYS POINT TWP.—See VINELAND, NJ (Comcast Cable)

CARTERET—See UNION, NJ (Comcast Cable)

CEDAR GROVE TWP.—See OAKLAND, NJ (Cablevision Systems Corp.)

CHADWICK BEACH—See MONMOUTH COUNTY, NJ (Cablevision Systems Corp.)

CHATHAM TWP.—See LONG HILL TWP., NJ (Comcast Cable)

CHATHAM—See DOVER, NJ (Cablevision Systems Corp.)

CHERRY HILL—See VOORHEES, NJ (Comcast Cable)

CHESILHURST—See VINELAND, NJ (Comcast Cable)

CHESTER BOROUGH—See LONG HILL TWP., NJ (Comcast Cable)

CHESTER TWP.—See LONG HILL TWP., NJ (Comcast Cable)

CHESTERFIELD TWP.—See VOORHEES, NJ (Comcast Cable)

CINNAMINSON TWP.—See BURLINGTON COUNTY, NJ (Comcast Cable)

CLARK TWP.—See UNION, NJ (Comcast Cable)

CLARKSBURG—See MONMOUTH COUNTY, NJ (Cablevision Systems Corp.)

CLAYTON—See GLOUCESTER COUNTY, NJ (Comcast Cable)

CLEMENTON—See VOORHEES, NJ (Comcast Cable)

CLIFFSIDE PARK—See PALISADES PARK, NJ (Time Warner Cable)

CLIFFWOOD BEACH—See RARITAN, NJ (Cablevision Systems Corp.)

CLIFFWOOD—See RARITAN, NJ (Cablevision Systems Corp.)

CLIFTON—See OAKLAND, NJ (Cablevision Systems Corp.)

CLINTON TWP.—See HILLSBOROUGH, NJ (Comcast Cable)

CLINTON—See HILLSBOROUGH, NJ (Comcast Cable)

CLOSTER—See BERGENFIELD, NJ (Cablevision Systems Corp.)

COLLINGSWOOD—See VOORHEES, NJ (Comcast Cable)

COLTS NECK—See MONMOUTH COUNTY, NJ (Cablevision Systems Corp.)

COMMERCIAL TWP.—See VINELAND, NJ (Comcast Cable)

CORBIN CITY—See VINELAND, NJ (Comcast Cable)

CRANBURY TWP.—See EAST WINDSOR, NJ (Comcast Cable)

CRANFORD TWP.—See UNION, NJ (Comcast Cable)

CRESSKILL—See BERGENFIELD, NJ (Cablevision Systems Corp.)

CRESTWOOD VILLAGE—See TOMS RIVER, NJ (Comcast Cable)

DEAL—See MONMOUTH COUNTY, NJ (Comcast Cable)

DEERFIELD TWP.—See VINELAND, NJ (Comcast Cable)

DELANCO TWP.—See BURLINGTON COUNTY, NJ (Comcast Cable)

DELAWARE TWP. (PORTIONS)—See LAMBERTVILLE, NJ (Comcast Cable)

DELAWARE TWP.—See HILLSBOROUGH, NJ (Comcast Cable)

DELRAN TWP.—See BURLINGTON COUNTY, NJ (Comcast Cable)

DEMAREST—See BERGENFIELD, NJ (Cablevision Systems Corp.)

DENNIS TWP.—See VINELAND, NJ (Comcast Cable)

DENVILLE—See DOVER, NJ (Cablevision Systems Corp.)

DEPTFORD TWP.—See GLOUCESTER COUNTY, NJ (Comcast Cable)

DOVER TWP. (PORTIONS)—See MONMOUTH COUNTY, NJ (Cablevision Systems Corp.)

DOVER TWP. (PORTIONS)—See TOMS RIVER, NJ (Comcast Cable)

▲**DOVER**—Cablevision Systems Corp.

DOWNE TWP.—See VINELAND, NJ (Comcast Cable)

DUMONT—See BERGENFIELD, NJ (Cablevision Systems Corp.)

DUNELLEN—See RARITAN, NJ (Cablevision Systems Corp.)

EAGLESWOOD TWP.—See TOMS RIVER, NJ (Comcast Cable)

EAST AMWELL TWP.—See HILLSBOROUGH, NJ (Comcast Cable)

EAST BRUNSWICK TWP.—See EAST WINDSOR, NJ (Comcast Cable)

EAST BRUNSWICK—See EAST WINDSOR, NJ (Comcast Cable)

EAST GREENWICH TWP.—See GLOUCESTER COUNTY, NJ (Comcast Cable)

EAST HANOVER TWP.—See DOVER, NJ (Cablevision Systems Corp.)

EAST NEWARK BOROUGH—See CARLSTADT BOROUGH, NJ (Comcast Cable)

EAST ORANGE—See UNION, NJ (Comcast Cable)

EAST RUTHERFORD BOROUGH—See CARLSTADT BOROUGH, NJ (Comcast Cable)

EAST WINDSOR TWP.—See EAST WINDSOR, NJ (Comcast Cable)

▲**EAST WINDSOR**—Comcast Cable

EASTAMPTON TWP.—See VOORHEES, NJ (Comcast Cable)

EATONTOWN—See MONMOUTH COUNTY, NJ (Comcast Cable)

EDGEWATER PARK TWP.—See BURLINGTON COUNTY, NJ (Comcast Cable)

EDGEWATER—See PALISADES PARK, NJ (Time Warner Cable)

EDISON—See RARITAN, NJ (Cablevision Systems Corp.)

EGG HARBOR CITY—See VINELAND, NJ (Comcast Cable)

EGG HARBOR TWP.—See VINELAND, NJ (Comcast Cable)

▲**ELIZABETH**—Cablevision Systems Corp.

ELK TWP.—See VINELAND, NJ (Comcast Cable)

ELMER—See VINELAND, NJ (Comcast Cable)

ELMWOOD PARK—See OAKLAND, NJ (Cablevision Systems Corp.)

ELSINBORO TWP.—See VINELAND, NJ (Comcast Cable)

EMERSON—See BERGENFIELD, NJ (Cablevision Systems Corp.)

ENGLEWOOD CLIFFS—See PALISADES PARK, NJ (Time Warner Cable)

ENGLEWOOD—See PALISADES PARK, NJ (Time Warner Cable)

ENGLISHTOWN—See MONMOUTH COUNTY, NJ (Cablevision Systems Corp.)

ESSEX FELLS—See UNION, NJ (Comcast Cable)

EVESHAM TWP.—See VOORHEES, NJ (Comcast Cable)

EWING TWP.—See TRENTON, NJ (Comcast Cable)

FAIR HAVEN—See MONMOUTH COUNTY, NJ (Comcast Cable)

FAIR LAWN—See BERGENFIELD, NJ (Cablevision Systems Corp.)

FAIRFIELD TWP. (CUMBERLAND COUNTY)—See VINELAND, NJ (Comcast Cable)

FAIRFIELD TWP.—See UNION, NJ (Comcast Cable)

FAIRVIEW—See PALISADES PARK, NJ (Time Warner Cable)

FANWOOD—See UNION, NJ (Comcast Cable)

FAR HILLS BOROUGH—See LONG HILL TWP., NJ (Comcast Cable)

FARMINGDALE—See MONMOUTH COUNTY, NJ (Cablevision Systems Corp.)

FIELDSBORO—See VOORHEES, NJ (Comcast Cable)

FLAGTOWN—See HILLSBOROUGH, NJ (Comcast Cable)

FLEMINGTON—See HILLSBOROUGH, NJ (Comcast Cable)

FLORENCE TWP.—See VOORHEES, NJ (Comcast Cable)

FLORHAM PARK—See DOVER, NJ (Cablevision Systems Corp.)

FOLSOM—See VINELAND, NJ (Comcast Cable)

FORT DIX—See VOORHEES, NJ (Comcast Cable)

FORT LEE—See PALISADES PARK, NJ (Time Warner Cable)

FORT MONMOUTH—See MONMOUTH COUNTY, NJ (Comcast Cable)

FRANKFORD TWP.—See SPARTA, NJ (Service Electric Cable company)

FRANKLIN LAKES—See OAKLAND, NJ (Cablevision Systems Corp.)

FRANKLIN PARK—See HILLSBOROUGH, NJ (Comcast Cable)

FRANKLIN TWP. (GLOUCESTER COUNTY)—See VINELAND, NJ (Comcast Cable)

FRANKLIN TWP.—See PORT MURRAY, NJ (Comcast Cable)

FRANKLIN—See SPARTA, NJ (Service Electric Cable company)

FRANKLINVILLE—See VINELAND, NJ (Comcast Cable)

FREDON—See SPARTA, NJ (Service Electric Cable company)

FREEHOLD TWP.—See MONMOUTH COUNTY, NJ (Cablevision Systems Corp.)

▲**FREEHOLD**—Cablevision Systems Corp. Now served by MAMMOTH, NJ [NJ0012]

FREEHOLD—See MONMOUTH COUNTY, NJ (Cablevision Systems Corp.)

FREEHOLD—See MONMOUTH COUNTY, NJ (Comcast Cable)

FRELINGHYUSEN TWP.—See SPARTA, NJ (Service Electric Cable company)

FRENCHTOWN BORO—See HUNTERDON COUNTY, NJ (Service Electric Cable TV of Hunterdon Inc.)

GALLOWAY TWP.—See VINELAND, NJ (Comcast Cable)

GARFIELD—See OAKLAND, NJ (Cablevision Systems Corp.)

GARWOOD—See UNION, NJ (Comcast Cable)

GIBBSBORO—See VOORHEES, NJ (Comcast Cable)

GILLETTE—See LONG HILL TWP., NJ (Comcast Cable)

GLASSBORO—See GLOUCESTER COUNTY, NJ (Comcast Cable)

GLEN GARDNER—See PORT MURRAY, NJ (Comcast Cable)

GLEN RIDGE TWP.—See UNION, NJ (Comcast Cable)

GLEN ROCK—See OAKLAND, NJ (Cablevision Systems Corp.)

▲**GLOUCESTER COUNTY**—Comcast Cable

GLOUCESTER TWP.—See VOORHEES, NJ (Comcast Cable)

GLOUCESTER—See MAPLE SHADE, NJ (Comcast Cable)

GREEN BROOK—See RARITAN, NJ (Cablevision Systems Corp.)

GREEN TWP.—See SPARTA, NJ (Service Electric Cable company)

GREENWICH TWP.—See GLOUCESTER COUNTY, NJ (Comcast Cable)

GREENWICH TWP.—See HUNTERDON COUNTY, NJ (Service Electric Cable TV of Hunterdon Inc.)

GUTTENBERG—See PALISADES PARK, NJ (Time Warner Cable)

HACKENSACK—See OAKLAND, NJ (Cablevision Systems Corp.)

HACKETTSTOWN—See PORT MURRAY, NJ (Comcast Cable)

HADDON HEIGHTS—See VOORHEES, NJ (Comcast Cable)

HADDON TWP.—See VOORHEES, NJ (Comcast Cable)

HADDONFIELD—See VOORHEES, NJ (Comcast Cable)

HAINESPORT TWP.—See VOORHEES, NJ (Comcast Cable)

HALEDON—See OAKLAND, NJ (Cablevision Systems Corp.)

HAMBURG—See SPARTA, NJ (Service Electric Cable company)

▲**HAMILTON TWP. (MERCER COUNTY)**—Cablevision Systems Corp.

HAMILTON TWP.—See VINELAND, NJ (Comcast Cable)

HAMMONTON—See VINELAND, NJ (Comcast Cable)

HAMPTON TWP.—See SPARTA, NJ (Service Electric Cable company)

HAMPTON—See PORT MURRAY, NJ (Comcast Cable)

HANOVER TWP.—See DOVER, NJ (Cablevision Systems Corp.)

HARDING TWP.—See LONG HILL TWP., NJ (Comcast Cable)

HARDWICK TWP.—See SPARTA, NJ (Service Electric Cable company)

HARDYSTON TWP.—See SPARTA, NJ (Service Electric Cable company)

HARMONY TWP.—See HUNTERDON COUNTY, NJ (Service Electric Cable TV of Hunterdon Inc.)

HARRINGTON PARK—See BERGENFIELD, NJ (Cablevision Systems Corp.)

HARRISON TWP. (GLOUCESTER COUNTY)—See VINELAND, NJ (Comcast Cable)

HARRISON—See UNION, NJ (Comcast Cable)

HARVEY CEDARS—See LONG BEACH TWP., NJ (Comcast Cable)

HASBROUCK HEIGHTS—See OAKLAND, NJ (Cablevision Systems Corp.)

HAWORTH—See BERGENFIELD, NJ (Cablevision Systems Corp.)

HAWTHORNE—See OAKLAND, NJ (Cablevision Systems Corp.)

HAZLET TWP.—See MONMOUTH COUNTY, NJ (Comcast Cable)

HELMETTA—See EAST WINDSOR, NJ (Comcast Cable)

HI-NELLA—See VOORHEES, NJ (Comcast Cable)

HIGH BRIDGE—See PORT MURRAY, NJ (Comcast Cable)

HIGHLAND PARK—See RARITAN, NJ (Cablevision Systems Corp.)

HIGHLANDS—See MONMOUTH COUNTY, NJ (Comcast Cable)

HIGHTSTOWN—See EAST WINDSOR, NJ (Comcast Cable)

▲**HILLSBOROUGH**—Comcast Cable

HILLSDALE—See BERGENFIELD, NJ (Cablevision Systems Corp.)

HILLSDALE—See PARAMUS, NJ (US Cable of Paramus-Hillsdale)

HILLSIDE TWP.—See UNION, NJ (Comcast Cable)

HO-HO-KUS—See OAKLAND, NJ (Cablevision Systems Corp.)

▲**HOBOKEN**—Cablevision Systems Corp.

HOLLAND TWP.—See HUNTERDON COUNTY, NJ (Service Electric Cable TV of Hunterdon Inc.)

HOLMDEL TWP.—See MONMOUTH COUNTY, NJ (Comcast Cable)

HOPATCONG—See DOVER, NJ (Cablevision Systems Corp.)

HOPE—See SPARTA, NJ (Service Electric Cable company)

HOPEWELL BOROUGH—See TRENTON, NJ (Comcast Cable)

HOPEWELL TWP. (CUMBERLAND COUNTY)—See VINELAND, NJ (Comcast Cable)

HOPEWELL TWP. (MERCER COUNTY)—See LAMBERTVILLE, NJ (Comcast Cable)

HOWELL TWP.—See MONMOUTH COUNTY, NJ (Cablevision Systems Corp.)

HOWELL—See MONMOUTH COUNTY, NJ (Cablevision Systems Corp.)

▲**HUNTERDON COUNTY**—Service Electric Cable TV of Hunterdon Inc.

INDEPENDENCE TWP.—See PORT MURRAY, NJ (Comcast Cable)

INTERLAKEN—See MONMOUTH COUNTY, NJ (Cablevision Systems Corp.)

IRVINGTON TWP.—See UNION, NJ (Comcast Cable)

ISLAND HEIGHTS—See TOMS RIVER, NJ (Comcast Cable)

JACKSON TWP.—See MONMOUTH COUNTY, NJ (Cablevision Systems Corp.)

JACKSON—See MONMOUTH COUNTY, NJ (Cablevision Systems Corp.)

JAMESBURG—See EAST WINDSOR, NJ (Comcast Cable)

JEFFERSON TWP.—See DOVER, NJ (Cablevision Systems Corp.)

JEFFERSON TWP.—See SPARTA, NJ (Service Electric Cable company)

▲**JERSEY CITY**—Comcast Cable

KEANSBURG—See RARITAN, NJ (Cablevision Systems Corp.)

KEARNY—See CARLSTADT BOROUGH, NJ (Comcast Cable)

KENILWORTH—See UNION, NJ (Comcast Cable)

KEYPORT—See RARITAN, NJ (Cablevision Systems Corp.)

KINGSTON—See HILLSBOROUGH, NJ (Comcast Cable)

KINGWOOD TWP.—See HUNTERDON COUNTY, NJ (Service Electric Cable TV of Hunterdon Inc.)

KINNELON—See OAKLAND, NJ (Cablevision Systems Corp.)

KNOWLTON—See SPARTA, NJ (Service Electric Cable company)

LACEY TWP.—See TOMS RIVER, NJ (Comcast Cable)

LAFAYETTE TWP.—See SPARTA, NJ (Service Electric Cable company)

LAKE COMO—See MONMOUTH COUNTY, NJ (Cablevision Systems Corp.)

LAKEHURST—See TOMS RIVER, NJ (Comcast Cable)

LAKEWOOD TWP.—See MONMOUTH COUNTY, NJ (Cablevision Systems Corp.)

LAKEWOOD—See MONMOUTH COUNTY, NJ (Cablevision Systems Corp.)

▲**LAMBERTVILLE**—Comcast Cable

LAUREL LAKE—See VINELAND, NJ (Comcast Cable)

LAUREL SPRINGS—See VOORHEES, NJ (Comcast Cable)

LAVALLETTE—See MONMOUTH COUNTY, NJ (Cablevision Systems Corp.)

LAWNSIDE—See VOORHEES, NJ (Comcast Cable)

LAWRENCE TWP. (CUMBERLAND COUNTY)—See VINELAND, NJ (Comcast Cable)

LAWRENCE TWP.—See TRENTON, NJ (Comcast Cable)

LAWRENCEVILLE—See TRENTON, NJ (Comcast Cable)

LEBANON BOROUGH—See HILLSBOROUGH, NJ (Comcast Cable)

LEBANON TWP.—See PORT MURRAY, NJ (Comcast Cable)

LEONIA—See PALISADES PARK, NJ (Time Warner Cable)

LIBERTY TWP.—See PORT MURRAY, NJ (Comcast Cable)

LINCOLN PARK—See OAKLAND, NJ (Cablevision Systems Corp.)

LINDEN—See UNION, NJ (Comcast Cable)

LINDENWOLD—See VOORHEES, NJ (Comcast Cable)

LINWOOD—See VINELAND, NJ (Comcast Cable)

LITTLE EGG HARBOR TWP.—See TOMS RIVER, NJ (Comcast Cable)

LITTLE FALLS TWP.—See OAKLAND, NJ (Cablevision Systems Corp.)

LITTLE FERRY—See PALISADES PARK, NJ (Time Warner Cable)

LITTLE SILVER—See MONMOUTH COUNTY, NJ (Comcast Cable)

LIVINGSTON TWP.—See UNION, NJ (Comcast Cable)

LOCH ARBOUR—See MONMOUTH COUNTY, NJ (Comcast Cable)

LODI—See OAKLAND, NJ (Cablevision Systems Corp.)

LOGAN TWP.—See VINELAND, NJ (Comcast Cable)

▲**LONG BEACH TWP.**—Comcast Cable

LONG BRANCH—See MONMOUTH COUNTY, NJ (Comcast Cable)

▲**LONG HILL TWP.**—Comcast Cable

LONGPORT—See VINELAND, NJ (Comcast Cable)

LOPATCONG TWP.—See HUNTERDON COUNTY, NJ (Service Electric Cable TV of Hunterdon Inc.)

LOWER ALLOWAYS CREEK TWP.—See VINELAND, NJ (Comcast Cable)

LOWER TWP.—See WILDWOOD, NJ (Comcast Cable)

LUMBERTON—See VOORHEES, NJ (Comcast Cable)

LYNDHURST TWP.—See CARLSTADT BOROUGH, NJ (Comcast Cable)

MADISON—See DOVER, NJ (Cablevision Systems Corp.)

MAGNOLIA—See VOORHEES, NJ (Comcast Cable)

MANAHAWKIN—See TOMS RIVER, NJ (Comcast Cable)

MANALAPAN TWP.—See MONMOUTH COUNTY, NJ (Cablevision Systems Corp.)

MANASQUAN—See MONMOUTH COUNTY, NJ (Cablevision Systems Corp.)

MANCHESTER TWP.—See TOMS RIVER, NJ (Comcast Cable)

MANNINGTON TWP.—See VINELAND, NJ (Comcast Cable)

MANSFIELD TWP. (BURLINGTON COUNTY)—See VOORHEES, NJ (Comcast Cable)

MANSFIELD TWP.—See PORT MURRAY, NJ (Comcast Cable)

MANTOLOKING—See OCEAN COUNTY, NJ (Comcast Cable)

MANTUA TWP.—See GLOUCESTER COUNTY, NJ (Comcast Cable)

MANVILLE—See RARITAN, NJ (Cablevision Systems Corp.)

MAPLE SHADE TWP.—See MAPLE SHADE, NJ (Comcast Cable)

▲**MAPLE SHADE**—Comcast Cable

MAPLEWOOD TWP.—See UNION, NJ (Comcast Cable)

MARGATE CITY—See VINELAND, NJ (Comcast Cable)

MARLBORO TWP.—See MONMOUTH COUNTY, NJ (Cablevision Systems Corp.)

MATAWAN—See RARITAN, NJ (Cablevision Systems Corp.)

MAURICE RIVER TWP.—See VINELAND, NJ (Comcast Cable)

MAYS LANDING—See VINELAND, NJ (Comcast Cable)

MAYWOOD—See OAKLAND, NJ (Cablevision Systems Corp.)

MCGUIRE AFB—See VOORHEES, NJ (Comcast Cable)

MEDFORD LAKES—See VOORHEES, NJ (Comcast Cable)

MEDFORD TWP.—See VOORHEES, NJ (Comcast Cable)

MENDHAM—See LONG HILL TWP., NJ (Comcast Cable)

MERCHANTVILLE—See VOORHEES, NJ (Comcast Cable)

METUCHEN—See RARITAN, NJ (Cablevision Systems Corp.)

MIDDLE TWP.—See AVALON, NJ (Comcast Cable)

MIDDLE TWP.—See WILDWOOD, NJ (Comcast Cable)

MIDDLESEX—See RARITAN, NJ (Cablevision Systems Corp.)

MIDDLETOWN TWP.—See MONMOUTH COUNTY, NJ (Comcast Cable)

MIDLAND PARK—See OAKLAND, NJ (Cablevision Systems Corp.)

MILFORD BORO—See HUNTERDON COUNTY, NJ (Service Electric Cable TV of Hunterdon Inc.)

MILLBURN TWP.—See UNION, NJ (Comcast Cable)

MILLINGTON—See LONG HILL TWP., NJ (Comcast Cable)

▲**MILLSTONE TWP.**—Cablevision Systems Corp. Now served by MONMOUTH, NJ [NJ0012]

MILLSTONE TWP.—See MONMOUTH COUNTY, NJ (Cablevision Systems Corp.)

MILLSTONE—See HILLSBOROUGH, NJ (Comcast Cable)

MILLTOWN—See RARITAN, NJ (Cablevision Systems Corp.)

MILLVILLE—See VINELAND, NJ (Comcast Cable)

MINE HILL TWP.—See DOVER, NJ (Cablevision Systems Corp.)

MONMOUTH BEACH—See MONMOUTH COUNTY, NJ (Comcast Cable)

▲ **MONMOUTH COUNTY**—Cablevision Systems Corp.

▲ **MONMOUTH COUNTY**—Comcast Cable

MONROE TWP. (GLOUCESTER COUNTY)—See VINELAND, NJ (Comcast Cable)

MONROE TWP.—See EAST WINDSOR, NJ (Comcast Cable)

MONTCLAIR TWP.—See UNION, NJ (Comcast Cable)

MONTGOMERY TWP.—See HILLSBOROUGH, NJ (Comcast Cable)

MONTVILLE TWP. (NORTHEASTERN PORTION)—See OAKLAND, NJ (Cablevision Systems Corp.)

MONTVILLE TWP.—See DOVER, NJ (Cablevision Systems Corp.)

MOONACHIE—See PALISADES PARK, NJ (Time Warner Cable)

MOORESTOWN TWP.—See VOORHEES, NJ (Comcast Cable)

MORRIS PLAINS—See DOVER, NJ (Cablevision Systems Corp.)

MORRIS TWP.—See DOVER, NJ (Cablevision Systems Corp.)

MORRISTOWN—See DOVER, NJ (Cablevision Systems Corp.)

MOUNT ARLINGTON—See DOVER, NJ (Cablevision Systems Corp.)

MOUNT EPHRAIM—See MAPLE SHADE, NJ (Comcast Cable)

MOUNT HOLLYTWP.—See VOORHEES, NJ (Comcast Cable)

MOUNT LAUREL TWP.—See VOORHEES, NJ (Comcast Cable)

MOUNT OLIVE TWP.—See DOVER, NJ (Cablevision Systems Corp.)

MOUNT OLIVE TWP.—See PORT MURRAY, NJ (Comcast Cable)

MOUNTAIN LAKES—See DOVER, NJ (Cablevision Systems Corp.)

MOUNTAINSIDE—See UNION, NJ (Comcast Cable)

MULLICA TWP. (ATLANTIC COUNTY)—See VINELAND, NJ (Comcast Cable)

NATIONAL PARK—See GLOUCESTER COUNTY, NJ (Comcast Cable)

NEPTUNE TWP.—See MONMOUTH COUNTY, NJ (Cablevision Systems Corp.)

NEPTUNE—See MONMOUTH COUNTY, NJ (Cablevision Systems Corp.)

NESHANIC STATION—See HILLSBOROUGH, NJ (Comcast Cable)

NETCONG—See DOVER, NJ (Cablevision Systems Corp.)

NEW BRUNSWICK—See RARITAN, NJ (Cablevision Systems Corp.)

NEW HANOVER TWP.—See VOORHEES, NJ (Comcast Cable)

NEW MILFORD—See BERGENFIELD, NJ (Cablevision Systems Corp.)

NEW PROVIDENCE—See UNION, NJ (Comcast Cable)

▲ **NEWARK**—Cablevision Systems Corp.

NEWFIELD—See VINELAND, NJ (Comcast Cable)

NEWTON—See SPARTA, NJ (Service Electric Cable company)

NORMANDY BEACH—See MONMOUTH COUNTY, NJ (Cablevision Systems Corp.)

NORTH ARLINGTON BOROUGH—See CARLSTADT BOROUGH, NJ (Comcast Cable)

NORTH BERGEN—See HOBOKEN, NJ (Cablevision Systems Corp.)

NORTH BRANCH—See HILLSBOROUGH, NJ (Comcast Cable)

NORTH BRUNSWICK TWP.—See RARITAN, NJ (Cablevision Systems Corp.)

NORTH CALDWELL—See OAKLAND, NJ (Cablevision Systems Corp.)

NORTH HALEDON—See OAKLAND, NJ (Cablevision Systems Corp.)

NORTH HANOVER TWP.—See VOORHEES, NJ (Comcast Cable)

NORTH PLAINFIELD—See PLAINFIELD, NJ (Comcast Cable)

NORTH WILDWOOD—See WILDWOOD, NJ (Comcast Cable)

NORTHFIELD—See VINELAND, NJ (Comcast Cable)

NORTHVALE—See BERGENFIELD, NJ (Cablevision Systems Corp.)

NORWOOD—See BERGENFIELD, NJ (Cablevision Systems Corp.)

NUTLEY TWP.—See OAKLAND, NJ (Cablevision Systems Corp.)

▲ **OAKLAND**—Cablevision Systems Corp.

OAKLYN—See VOORHEES, NJ (Comcast Cable)

OCEAN BEACH—See MONMOUTH COUNTY, NJ (Cablevision Systems Corp.)

OCEAN CITY—See VINELAND, NJ (Comcast Cable)

▲ **OCEAN COUNTY**—Comcast Cable

OCEAN GATE—See TOMS RIVER, NJ (Comcast Cable)

OCEAN TWP.—See MONMOUTH COUNTY, NJ (Cablevision Systems Corp.)

OCEAN TWP.—See TOMS RIVER, NJ (Comcast Cable)

OCEANPORT—See MONMOUTH COUNTY, NJ (Comcast Cable)

OGDENSBURG—See SPARTA, NJ (Service Electric Cable company)

OLD BRIDGE—See RARITAN, NJ (Cablevision Systems Corp.)

OLD TAPPAN—See BERGENFIELD, NJ (Cablevision Systems Corp.)

OLDMANS TWP.—See VINELAND, NJ (Comcast Cable)

ORADELL—See BERGENFIELD, NJ (Cablevision Systems Corp.)

ORANGE—See UNION, NJ (Comcast Cable)

ORTLEY BEACH—See MONMOUTH COUNTY, NJ (Cablevision Systems Corp.)

OXFORD TWP.—See PORT MURRAY, NJ (Comcast Cable)

▲ **PALISADES PARK**—Time Warner Cable

PALMYRA—See BURLINGTON COUNTY, NJ (Comcast Cable)

PARAMUS—See BERGENFIELD, NJ (Cablevision Systems Corp.)

▲ **PARAMUS**—US Cable of Paramus-Hillsdale

PARK RIDGE—See OAKLAND, NJ (Cablevision Systems Corp.)

PARLIN—See RARITAN, NJ (Cablevision Systems Corp.)

PARSIPPANY-TROY HILLS TWP.—See DOVER, NJ (Cablevision Systems Corp.)

PARSIPPANY—See DOVER, NJ (Cablevision Systems Corp.)

PASSAIC—See OAKLAND, NJ (Cablevision Systems Corp.)

▲ **PATERSON**—Cablevision Systems Corp.

PAULSBORO—See GLOUCESTER COUNTY, NJ (Comcast Cable)

PEAPACK-GLADSTONE—See LONG HILL TWP., NJ (Comcast Cable)

PELICAN ISLAND—See MONMOUTH COUNTY, NJ (Cablevision Systems Corp.)

PEMBERTON TWP.—See VOORHEES, NJ (Comcast Cable)

PEMBERTON—See VOORHEES, NJ (Comcast Cable)

PENNINGTON BOROUGH—See TRENTON, NJ (Comcast Cable)

PENNS GROVE—See VINELAND, NJ (Comcast Cable)

PENNSAUKEN TWP.—See VOORHEES, NJ (Comcast Cable)

PENNSVILLE TWP.—See VINELAND, NJ (Comcast Cable)

PEQUANNOCK TWP.—See OAKLAND, NJ (Cablevision Systems Corp.)

PERRINEVILLE—See MONMOUTH COUNTY, NJ (Cablevision Systems Corp.)

PERTH AMBOY—See UNION, NJ (Comcast Cable)

▲ **PHILLIPSBURG**—Service Electric Cable TV of Hunterdon Inc. Now served by HUNTERDON COUNTY, NJ [NJ0067]

PHILLIPSBURG—See HUNTERDON COUNTY, NJ (Service Electric Cable TV of Hunterdon Inc.)

PICATINNY ARSENAL—See DOVER, NJ (Cablevision Systems Corp.)

PILESGROVE TWP.—See VINELAND, NJ (Comcast Cable)

PINE BEACH—See TOMS RIVER, NJ (Comcast Cable)

PINE HILL—See VOORHEES, NJ (Comcast Cable)

PINEHURST—See VINELAND, NJ (Comcast Cable)

PISCATAWAY—See RARITAN, NJ (Cablevision Systems Corp.)

PITMAN—See VOORHEES, NJ (Comcast Cable)

PITTSGROVE TWP.—See VINELAND, NJ (Comcast Cable)

▲ **PLAINFIELD**—Comcast Cable

PLAINSBORO TWP.—See EAST WINDSOR, NJ (Comcast Cable)

▲ **PLEASANTVILLE**—Comcast Cable. Now served by VINELAND, NJ [NJ0034]

PLEASANTVILLE—See VINELAND, NJ (Comcast Cable)

PLUMSTED TWP.—See VOORHEES, NJ (Comcast Cable)

POHATCONG TWP.—See HUNTERDON COUNTY, NJ (Service Electric Cable TV of Hunterdon Inc.)

POINT PLEASANT BEACH—See OCEAN COUNTY, NJ (Comcast Cable)

POINT PLEASANT—See OCEAN COUNTY, NJ (Comcast Cable)

POMPTON LAKES—See OAKLAND, NJ (Cablevision Systems Corp.)

▲ **PORT MURRAY**—Comcast Cable

PORT REPUBLIC—See VINELAND, NJ (Comcast Cable)

PRINCETON JUNCTION—See EAST WINDSOR, NJ (Comcast Cable)

PRINCETON TWP.—See PRINCETON, NJ (Comcast Cable)

▲ **PRINCETON**—Comcast Cable

PROSPECT PARK—See OAKLAND, NJ (Cablevision Systems Corp.)

QUINTON TWP.—See VINELAND, NJ (Comcast Cable)

RAHWAY—See UNION, NJ (Comcast Cable)

RAMSEY—See OAKLAND, NJ (Cablevision Systems Corp.)

RANDOLPH TWP.—See DOVER, NJ (Cablevision Systems Corp.)

RARITAN TWP.—See HILLSBOROUGH, NJ (Comcast Cable)

▲**RARITAN**—Cablevision Systems Corp.

READINGTON TWP.—See HILLSBOROUGH, NJ (Comcast Cable)

RED BANK—See MONMOUTH COUNTY, NJ (Comcast Cable)

RIDGEFIELD PARK—See PALISADES PARK, NJ (Time Warner Cable)

RIDGEFIELD—See PALISADES PARK, NJ (Time Warner Cable)

RIDGEWOOD—See OAKLAND, NJ (Cablevision Systems Corp.)

RINGWOOD—See OAKLAND, NJ (Cablevision Systems Corp.)

RIO GRANDE—See AVALON, NJ (Comcast Cable)

RIVER EDGE—See OAKLAND, NJ (Cablevision Systems Corp.)

RIVER VALE TWP.—See BERGENFIELD, NJ (Cablevision Systems Corp.)

RIVERDALE—See OAKLAND, NJ (Cablevision Systems Corp.)

RIVERSIDE TWP.—See BURLINGTON COUNTY, NJ (Comcast Cable)

RIVERTON—See BURLINGTON COUNTY, NJ (Comcast Cable)

ROBBINSVILLE—See HAMILTON TWP. (Mercer County), NJ (Cablevision Systems Corp.)

ROBBINSVILLE—See MONMOUTH COUNTY, NJ (Cablevision Systems Corp.)

ROCHELLE PARK—See OAKLAND, NJ (Cablevision Systems Corp.)

ROCKAWAY TWP.—See DOVER, NJ (Cablevision Systems Corp.)

ROCKAWAY—See DOVER, NJ (Cablevision Systems Corp.)

ROCKLEIGH—See BERGENFIELD, NJ (Cablevision Systems Corp.)

ROCKY HILL—See HILLSBOROUGH, NJ (Comcast Cable)

ROOSEVELT—See EAST WINDSOR, NJ (Comcast Cable)

ROSELAND—See UNION, NJ (Comcast Cable)

ROSELLE PARK—See UNION, NJ (Comcast Cable)

ROSELLE—See UNION, NJ (Comcast Cable)

ROXBURY TWP.—See DOVER, NJ (Cablevision Systems Corp.)

RUMSON—See MONMOUTH COUNTY, NJ (Comcast Cable)

RUNNEMEDE—See VOORHEES, NJ (Comcast Cable)

RUTHERFORD BOROUGH—See CARLSTADT BOROUGH, NJ (Comcast Cable)

SADDLE BROOK TWP.—See OAKLAND, NJ (Cablevision Systems Corp.)

SADDLE RIVER—See BERGENFIELD, NJ (Cablevision Systems Corp.)

SALEM—See VINELAND, NJ (Comcast Cable)

SANDYSTON TWP.—See SPARTA, NJ (Service Electric Cable company)

SAYREVILLE—See RARITAN, NJ (Cablevision Systems Corp.)

SCOTCH PLAINS TWP.—See UNION, NJ (Comcast Cable)

SEA BRIGHT—See MONMOUTH COUNTY, NJ (Comcast Cable)

SEA GIRT—See MONMOUTH COUNTY, NJ (Cablevision Systems Corp.)

SEA ISLE CITY—See AVALON, NJ (Comcast Cable)

SEASIDE HEIGHTS—See MONMOUTH COUNTY, NJ (Cablevision Systems Corp.)

SEASIDE PARK—See MONMOUTH COUNTY, NJ (Cablevision Systems Corp.)

SECAUCUS—See UNION, NJ (Comcast Cable)

SHAMONG TWP.—See VOORHEES, NJ (Comcast Cable)

SHILOH—See VINELAND, NJ (Comcast Cable)

SHIP BOTTOM—See LONG BEACH TWP., NJ (Comcast Cable)

SHORT HILLS—See UNION, NJ (Comcast Cable)

SHREWSBURY TWP.—See MONMOUTH COUNTY, NJ (Comcast Cable)

SHREWSBURY—See MONMOUTH COUNTY, NJ (Comcast Cable)

SKILLMAN—See HILLSBOROUGH, NJ (Comcast Cable)

SOMERDALE—See VOORHEES, NJ (Comcast Cable)

SOMERS POINT—See VINELAND, NJ (Comcast Cable)

SOMERSET—See HILLSBOROUGH, NJ (Comcast Cable)

SOMERVILLE—See RARITAN, NJ (Cablevision Systems Corp.)

SOUTH AMBOY—See RARITAN, NJ (Cablevision Systems Corp.)

SOUTH BOUND BROOK—See RARITAN, NJ (Cablevision Systems Corp.)

SOUTH BRANCH—See HILLSBOROUGH, NJ (Comcast Cable)

SOUTH BRUNSWICK TWP.—See EAST WINDSOR, NJ (Comcast Cable)

SOUTH HACKENSACK TWP.—See OAKLAND, NJ (Cablevision Systems Corp.)

SOUTH HARRISON TWP.—See VINELAND, NJ (Comcast Cable)

SOUTH ORANGE—See NEWARK, NJ (Cablevision Systems Corp.)

SOUTH PLAINFIELD—See PLAINFIELD, NJ (Comcast Cable)

SOUTH RIVER—See UNION, NJ (Comcast Cable)

SOUTH SEASIDE PARK—See MONMOUTH COUNTY, NJ (Cablevision Systems Corp.)

SOUTH TOMS RIVER—See TOMS RIVER, NJ (Comcast Cable)

SOUTHAMPTON TWP.—See VOORHEES, NJ (Comcast Cable)

SPARTA TWP.—See SPARTA, NJ (Service Electric Cable company)

▲**SPARTA**—Service Electric Cable company

SPOTSWOOD—See EAST WINDSOR, NJ (Comcast Cable)

SPRING LAKE HEIGHTS—See MONMOUTH COUNTY, NJ (Cablevision Systems Corp.)

SPRING LAKE—See MONMOUTH COUNTY, NJ (Cablevision Systems Corp.)

SPRINGFIELD TWP.—See UNION, NJ (Comcast Cable)

SPRINGFIELD TWP.—See VOORHEES, NJ (Comcast Cable)

STAFFORD TWP.—See TOMS RIVER, NJ (Comcast Cable)

STANHOPE—See DOVER, NJ (Cablevision Systems Corp.)

STILLWATER TWP.—See SPARTA, NJ (Service Electric Cable company)

STIRLING—See LONG HILL TWP., NJ (Comcast Cable)

STOCKTON—See LAMBERTVILLE, NJ (Comcast Cable)

STONE HARBOR—See AVALON, NJ (Comcast Cable)

STRATFORD—See VOORHEES, NJ (Comcast Cable)

STRATHMERE—See AVALON, NJ (Comcast Cable)

SUMMIT—See UNION, NJ (Comcast Cable)

SURF CITY—See LONG BEACH TWP., NJ (Comcast Cable)

SUSSEX—See SPARTA, NJ (Service Electric Cable company)

SWAINTON—See AVALON, NJ (Comcast Cable)

SWEDESBORO—See VINELAND, NJ (Comcast Cable)

TABERNACLE TWP.—See VOORHEES, NJ (Comcast Cable)

TAVISTOCK—See VOORHEES, NJ (Comcast Cable)

TEANECK—See OAKLAND, NJ (Cablevision Systems Corp.)

TENAFLY—See BERGENFIELD, NJ (Cablevision Systems Corp.)

TETERBORO—See PALISADES PARK, NJ (Time Warner Cable)

TEWKSBURY TWP.—See HILLSBOROUGH, NJ (Comcast Cable)

THREE BRIDGES—See HILLSBOROUGH, NJ (Comcast Cable)

TINTON FALLS—See MONMOUTH COUNTY, NJ (Comcast Cable)

TITUSVILLE—See LAMBERTVILLE, NJ (Comcast Cable)

▲**TOMS RIVER**—Comcast Cable

TOTOWA—See OAKLAND, NJ (Cablevision Systems Corp.)

▲**TRENTON**—Comcast Cable

TUCKERTON—See TOMS RIVER, NJ (Comcast Cable)

TURNERSVILLE—See VINELAND, NJ (Comcast Cable)

UNION BEACH—See RARITAN, NJ (Cablevision Systems Corp.)

UNION CITY—See HOBOKEN, NJ (Cablevision Systems Corp.)

UNION TWP.—See HILLSBOROUGH, NJ (Comcast Cable)

UNION TWP.—See UNION, NJ (Comcast Cable)

▲**UNION**—Comcast Cable

UPPER DEERFIELD TWP.—See VINELAND, NJ (Comcast Cable)

UPPER FREEHOLD TWP.—See MONMOUTH COUNTY, NJ (Cablevision Systems Corp.)

UPPER PITTSGROVE TWP.—See VINELAND, NJ (Comcast Cable)

UPPER SADDLE RIVER—See OAKLAND, NJ (Cablevision Systems Corp.)

UPPER TWP.—See AVALON, NJ (Comcast Cable)

UPPER TWP.—See VINELAND, NJ (Comcast Cable)

VENTNOR CITY—See VINELAND, NJ (Comcast Cable)

VERNON TWP.—See SPARTA, NJ (Service Electric Cable company)

VERONA TWP.—See UNION, NJ (Comcast Cable)

VICTORY GARDENS—See DOVER, NJ (Cablevision Systems Corp.)

VILLAS—See AVALON, NJ (Comcast Cable)

▲**VINELAND**—Comcast Cable

VOORHEES TWP.—See VOORHEES, NJ (Comcast Cable)

▲**VOORHEES**—Comcast Cable

WALDWICK—See OAKLAND, NJ (Cablevision Systems Corp.)

WALL TWP.—See MONMOUTH COUNTY, NJ (Cablevision Systems Corp.)

WALL—See MONMOUTH COUNTY, NJ (Cablevision Systems Corp.)

WALLINGTON BOROUGH—See CARLSTADT BOROUGH, NJ (Comcast Cable)

WANAQUE—See OAKLAND, NJ (Cablevision Systems Corp.)

WANTAGE TWP.—See SPARTA, NJ (Service Electric Cable company)

WARETOWN—See TOMS RIVER, NJ (Comcast Cable)

WARREN TWP.—See RARITAN, NJ (Cablevision Systems Corp.)

WASHINGTON TWP. (BERGEN COUNTY)—See OAKLAND, NJ (Cablevision Systems Corp.)

WASHINGTON TWP. (GLOUCESTER COUNTY)—See VINELAND, NJ (Comcast Cable)

WASHINGTON TWP. (MERCER COUNTY)—See HAMILTON TWP. (Mercer County), NJ (Cablevision Systems Corp.)

WASHINGTON TWP. (MORRIS COUNTY)—See PORT MURRAY, NJ (Comcast Cable)

WASHINGTON TWP. (WARREN COUNTY)—See PORT MURRAY, NJ (Comcast Cable)

WASHINGTON—See PORT MURRAY, NJ (Comcast Cable)

WATCHUNG—See RARITAN, NJ (Cablevision Systems Corp.)

WATERFORD TWP.—See VINELAND, NJ (Comcast Cable)

WAYNE—See OAKLAND, NJ (Cablevision Systems Corp.)

WEEHAWKEN—See HOBOKEN, NJ (Cablevision Systems Corp.)

WENONAH—See GLOUCESTER COUNTY, NJ (Comcast Cable)

WEST AMWELL TWP.—See LAMBERTVILLE, NJ (Comcast Cable)

WEST BERLIN—See VOORHEES, NJ (Comcast Cable)

WEST CALDWELL TWP.—See UNION, NJ (Comcast Cable)

WEST CAPE MAY—See WILDWOOD, NJ (Comcast Cable)

WEST DEPTFORD TWP.—See GLOUCESTER COUNTY, NJ (Comcast Cable)

WEST LONG BRANCH—See MONMOUTH COUNTY, NJ (Comcast Cable)

WEST NEW YORK—See HOBOKEN, NJ (Cablevision Systems Corp.)

WEST ORANGE—See UNION, NJ (Comcast Cable)

WEST PATERSON—See OAKLAND, NJ (Cablevision Systems Corp.)

WEST TRENTON—See TRENTON, NJ (Comcast Cable)

WEST WILDWOOD—See WILDWOOD, NJ (Comcast Cable)

WEST WINDSOR TWP.—See EAST WINDSOR, NJ (Comcast Cable)

WESTAMPTON TWP.—See BURLINGTON COUNTY, NJ (Comcast Cable)

WESTAMPTON TWP.—See VOORHEES, NJ (Comcast Cable)

WESTFIELD—See UNION, NJ (Comcast Cable)

WESTVILLE—See GLOUCESTER COUNTY, NJ (Comcast Cable)

WESTWOOD—See OAKLAND, NJ (Cablevision Systems Corp.)

WEYMOUTH CITY—See VINELAND, NJ (Comcast Cable)

WHARTON—See DOVER, NJ (Cablevision Systems Corp.)

WHITE HOUSE STATION—See HILLSBOROUGH, NJ (Comcast Cable)

WHITE TWP.—See PORT MURRAY, NJ (Comcast Cable)

WILDWOOD CREST—See WILDWOOD, NJ (Comcast Cable)

▲**WILDWOOD**—Comcast Cable

WILLINGBORO TWP.—See BURLINGTON COUNTY, NJ (Comcast Cable)

WINFIELD TWP.—See UNION, NJ (Comcast Cable)

WINSLOW TWP.—See VINELAND, NJ (Comcast Cable)

WOOD-RIDGE—See OAKLAND, NJ (Cablevision Systems Corp.)

WOODBINE—See VINELAND, NJ (Comcast Cable)

WOODBRIDGE TWP.—See UNION, NJ (Comcast Cable)

WOODBURY HEIGHTS—See GLOUCESTER COUNTY, NJ (Comcast Cable)

WOODBURY—See GLOUCESTER COUNTY, NJ (Comcast Cable)

WOODCLIFF LAKE—See BERGENFIELD, NJ (Cablevision Systems Corp.)

WOODLAND TWP.—See VOORHEES, NJ (Comcast Cable)

WOODLYNNE—See VOORHEES, NJ (Comcast Cable)

WOODSTOWN—See VINELAND, NJ (Comcast Cable)

WOOLWICH BOROUGH (GLOUCESTER COUNTY)—See VINELAND, NJ (Comcast Cable)

WOOLWICH TWP.—See VINELAND, NJ (Comcast Cable)

WRIGHTSTOWN—See VOORHEES, NJ (Comcast Cable)

WYCKOFF—See OAKLAND, NJ (Cablevision Systems Corp.)

YARDVILLE—See HAMILTON TWP. (Mercer County), NJ (Cablevision Systems Corp.)

NEW MEXICO

▲**ALAMOGORDO**—Baja Broadband

▲**ALBUQUERQUE**—Formerly served by Multimedia Development Corp. No longer in operation

▲**ALBUQUERQUE**—Comcast Cable

ALTO—See RUIDOSO, NM (Baja Broadband)

ANACONDA—See GRANTS, NM (Comcast Cable)

▲**ANGEL FIRE**—Comcast Cable

ARENAS VALLEY—See SILVER CITY, NM (Comcast Cable)

▲**ARTESIA**—PVT

AZTEC—See FARMINGTON, NM (Comcast Cable)

BAYARD—See SILVER CITY, NM (Comcast Cable)

BELEN—See LOS LUNAS, NM (Comcast Cable)

BERNALILLO COUNTY (PORTION)—See ALBUQUERQUE, NM (Comcast Cable)

BERNALILLO—See ALBUQUERQUE, NM (Comcast Cable)

BLOOMFIELD—See FARMINGTON, NM (Comcast Cable)

BLUEWATER—See GRANTS, NM (Comcast Cable)

BOLES ACRES—See ALAMOGORDO, NM (Baja Broadband)

BOSQUE FARMS—See ALBUQUERQUE, NM (Comcast Cable)

▲**BRAZOS**—Formerly served by US Cable of Coastal Texas LP. No longer in operation

CANNON AFB—See CLOVIS, NM (Suddenlink Communications)

CANON—See TAOS, NM (Comcast Cable)

CAPITAN—See RUIDOSO, NM (Baja Broadband)

▲**CARLSBAD**—US Cable of Coastal Texas LP

▲**CARRIZOZO**—Baja Broadband

CERRO—See QUESTA, NM (Comcast Cable)

▲**CHAMA**—US Cable of Coastal Texas LP

CHAVES COUNTY—See ROSWELL, NM (Cable One)

▲**CIMARRON**—Comcast Cable

▲**CLAYTON (TOWN)**—Baja Broadband

▲**CLOUDCROFT**—PVTV Cable Services. Now served by ARTESIA, NM [NM0016]

CLOUDCROFT—See ARTESIA, NM (PVT)

▲**CLOVIS**—Suddenlink Communications

CORRALES—See ALBUQUERQUE, NM (Comcast Cable)

▲**CROWNPOINT**—Formerly served by Crownpoint Cable TV Inc. No longer in operation

▲**CUBA**—Formerly served by Sun Valley Cable Inc. No longer in operation

DEL CERRO ESTATES—See LA MESA, NM (Windjammer Cable)

▲**DEMING**—Comcast Cable

DEXTER—See ARTESIA, NM (PVT)

▲**DIXON**—US Cable of Coastal Texas LP

DONA ANA COUNTY (PORTIONS)—See LAS CRUCES, NM (Comcast Cable)

DONA ANA—See LAS CRUCES, NM (Comcast Cable)

EDDY COUNTY (PORTIONS)—See ARTESIA, NM (PVT)

EDDY COUNTY—See CARLSBAD, NM (US Cable of Coastal Texas LP)

EDGEWOOD—See ALBUQUERQUE, NM (Comcast Cable)

EL PRADO—See TAOS, NM (Comcast Cable)

ELDORADO—See SANTA FE, NM (Comcast Cable)

▲**ELEPHANT BUTTE**—PVT

▲**ESPANOLA**—US Cable of Coastal Texas LP

▲**ESTANCIA**—Formerly served by Chamisa Futurevision. No longer in operation

▲**EUNICE**—US Cable of Coastal Texas LP. Now served by HOBBS, NM [NM0006]

EUNICE—See HOBBS, NM (US Cable of Coastal Texas LP)

▲**FARMINGTON**—Comcast Cable

FARWELL—See CLOVIS, TX (Suddenlink Communications)

FORT BAYARD—See SILVER CITY, NM (Comcast Cable)

▲**FORT SUMNER**—Rapid Cable

▲**FOUR HILLS**—Formerly served by JRC Telecommunications. No longer in operation

▲**GALLUP**—Comcast Cable

GAMERCO—See GALLUP, NM (Comcast Cable)

GRANT COUNTY (PORTIONS)—See SILVER CITY, NM (Comcast Cable)

▲**GRANTS**—Comcast Cable

HAGERMAN—See ARTESIA, NM (PVT)

▲**HATCH**—Comcast Cable

▲**HIGH ROLLS MOUNTAIN PARK**—Baja Broadband

▲**HOBBS**—US Cable of Coastal Texas LP

HOLLOMAN AFB—See ALAMOGORDO, NM (Baja Broadband)

HURLEY—See SILVER CITY, NM (Comcast Cable)

ISLETA—See ALBUQUERQUE, NM (Comcast Cable)

▲**JAL**—US Cable of Coastal Texas LP

KIRTLAND AFB—See ALBUQUERQUE, NM (Comcast Cable)

KIRTLAND—See FARMINGTON, NM (Comcast Cable)

LA LUZ—See ALAMOGORDO, NM (Baja Broadband)

▲**LA MESA**—Windjammer Cable

▲**LAS CRUCES**—Formerly served by Santa Fe Wireless Cable TV. No longer in operation

▲**LAS CRUCES**—Comcast Cable

▲**LAS VEGAS**—Comcast Cable

LEA COUNTY—See LOVINGTON, NM (Comcast Cable)

LEA COUNTY—See HOBBS, NM (US Cable of Coastal Texas LP)

LLANO—See TAOS, NM (Comcast Cable)

▲**LOGAN**—Baja Broadband

▲**LORDSBURG**—City TV Cable Service. No longer in operation

LOS ALAMOS COUNTY—See LOS ALAMOS, NM (Comcast Cable)

▲**LOS ALAMOS**—Comcast Cable

LOS CHAVEZ—See LOS LUNAS, NM (Comcast Cable)

▲**LOS LUNAS**—Comcast Cable

▲**LOS OJOS**—Formerly served by US Cable of Coastal Texas LP. No longer in operation

LOS RANCHOS DE ALBUQUERQUE—See ALBUQUERQUE, NM (Comcast Cable)

LOVING—See CARLSBAD, NM (US Cable of Coastal Texas LP)

▲**LOVINGTON**—Comcast Cable

▲**MAXWELL**—Formerly served by Rocky Mountain Cable. No longer in operation

MCKINLEY COUNTY (PORTIONS)—See THOREAU, NM (Comcast Cable)

MCKINLEY COUNTY (SOUTH CENTRAL PORTION)—See GRANTS, NM (Comcast Cable)

▲**MELROSE**—Rapid Cable

MESCALERO APACHE INDIAN RESERVATION (PORTIONS)—See RUIDOSO, NM (Baja Broadband)

MESILLA—See LAS CRUCES, NM (Comcast Cable)

MESQUITE—See LA MESA, NM (Windjammer Cable)

MILAN—See GRANTS, NM (Comcast Cable)

▲**MORA**—Formerly served by Rocky Mountain Cable. No longer in operation

MORIARTY—See ALBUQUERQUE, NM (Comcast Cable)

▲**MOUNTAINAIR**—Formerly served by Chamisa Futurevision. No longer in operation

NAMBE—See POJOAQUE, NM (Comcast Cable)

▲**NAVAJO**—Formerly served by Frontier Communications. No longer in operation

▲**PECOS**—Comcast Cable

▲**PENASCO**—US Cable of Coastal Texas LP

PERALTA—See ALBUQUERQUE, NM (Comcast Cable)

PICURIS—See PENASCO, NM (US Cable of Coastal Texas LP)

PLACITAS—See ALBUQUERQUE, NM (Comcast Cable)

PLACITAS—See HATCH, NM (Comcast Cable)

▲**PLAYAS**—Formerly served by Playas CATV. No longer in operation

▲**POJOAQUE**—Comcast Cable

▲**PORTALES**—Comcast Cable

QUAY COUNTY—See TUCUMCARI, NM (Comcast Cable)

▲**QUESTA**—Comcast Cable

▲**RAMAH**—Formerly served by Navajo Communications. No longer in operation

RANCHOS DE TAOS—See TAOS, NM (Comcast Cable)

▲**RATON**—Comcast Cable

▲**RED RIVER**—Comcast Cable

▲**RESERVE**—Formerly served by Eagle West Communications Inc. No longer in operation

RIO ARRIBA COUNTY (SOUTHEASTERN PORTION)—See SANTA CLARA INDIAN RESERVATION, NM (US Cable of Coastal Texas LP)

RIO ARRIBA COUNTY—See CHAMA, NM (US Cable of Coastal Texas LP)

▲**RIO RANCHO**—Cable One

RODEY—See HATCH, NM (Comcast Cable)

ROOSEVELT COUNTY—See PORTALES, NM (Comcast Cable)

▲**ROSWELL**—Formerly served by Microwave Communication Services. No longer in operation

▲**ROSWELL**—Cable One

RUIDOSO DOWNS—See RUIDOSO, NM (Baja Broadband)

▲**RUIDOSO**—Baja Broadband

▲**SAN ANTONIO**—Formerly served by Sun Valley Cable Inc. No longer in operation

SAN ILDEFONSO PUEBLO—See POJOAQUE, NM (Comcast Cable)

▲**SAN JON**—Elk River TV Cable Co.

SAN JUAN PUEBLO—See SANTA CLARA INDIAN RESERVATION, NM (US Cable of Coastal Texas LP)

SAN MIGUEL COUNTY—See LAS VEGAS, NM (Comcast Cable)

SAN MIGUEL—See LA MESA, NM (Windjammer Cable)

SAN RAFAEL—See GRANTS, NM (Comcast Cable)

SANDIA KNOLL—See ALBUQUERQUE, NM (Comcast Cable)

SANDOVAL COUNTY (PORTIONS)—See ALBUQUERQUE, NM (Comcast Cable)

▲**SANTA BARBARA**—Formerly served by JRC Telecommunications. No longer in operation

▲**SANTA CLARA INDIAN RESERVATION**—US Cable of Coastal Texas LP

SANTA CLARA—See SILVER CITY, NM (Comcast Cable)

SANTA FE COUNTY (NORTHERN PORTION)—See SANTA CLARA INDIAN RESERVATION, NM (US Cable of Coastal Texas LP)

SANTA FE COUNTY—See ALBUQUERQUE, NM (Comcast Cable)

SANTA FE COUNTY—See SANTA FE, NM (Comcast Cable)

▲**SANTA FE**—Formerly served by Santa Fe Wireless Cable TV. No longer in operation

▲**SANTA FE**—Comcast Cable

▲**SANTA ROSA**—Rapid Cable

▲**SHIPROCK**—Formerly served by Frontier Communications. No longer in operation

SIERRA COUNTY (UNINCORPORATED AREAS)—See TRUTH OR CONSEQUENCES, NM (Baja Broadband)

▲**SILVER CITY**—Comcast Cable

▲**SOCORRO**—Comcast Cable

▲**SPRINGER**—Comcast Cable

TALPA—See TAOS, NM (Comcast Cable)

TAOS COUNTY (PORTIONS)—See RED RIVER, NM (Comcast Cable)

▲**TAOS**—Comcast Cable

▲**TATUM**—Rapid Cable

TEUSQUE PUEBLO—See SANTA FE, NM (Comcast Cable)

TEUSQUE—See SANTA FE, NM (Comcast Cable)

TEXICO—See CLOVIS, NM (Suddenlink Communications)

▲**THOREAU**—Comcast Cable

TIJERAS—See ALBUQUERQUE, NM (Comcast Cable)

▲**TOHATCHI**—Formerly served by Frontier Communications. No longer in operation

▲**TRUTH OR CONSEQUENCES**—Baja Broadband

▲**TUCUMCARI**—Comcast Cable

TULAROSA—See ALAMOGORDO, NM (Baja Broadband)

▲**TWIN FORKS**—PVTV Cable Services. Now served by ARTESIA, NM [NM0016]

TWIN FORKS—See ARTESIA, NM (PVT)

TYRONE—See SILVER CITY, NM (Comcast Cable)

VADO—See LA MESA, NM (Windjammer Cable)

VALENCIA COUNTY (PORTIONS)—See GRANTS, NM (Comcast Cable)

VALENCIA COUNTY (PORTIONS)—See LOS LUNAS, NM (Comcast Cable)

VANADIUM (UNINCORPORATED AREAS)—See SILVER CITY, NM (Comcast Cable)

▲**VAUGHN**—Formerly served by Cebridge Connections. No longer in operation

▲**WAGON MOUND**—Formerly served by Rocky Mountain Cable. No longer in operation

WHITE ROCK—See LOS ALAMOS, NM (Comcast Cable)

WHITE SANDS—See LAS CRUCES, NM (Comcast Cable)

WILLIAMSBURG—See TRUTH OR CONSEQUENCES, NM (Baja Broadband)

▲**YAH-TA-HEY**—Formerly served by Frontier Communications. No longer in operation

▲**ZUNI**—Formerly served by Frontier Communications. No longer in operation

NEW YORK

▲**ADAMS (town)**—Time Warner Cable. No longer in operation

ADAMS (VILLAGE)—See WATERTOWN, NY (Time Warner Cable)

ADAMS CENTER—See WATERTOWN, NY (Time Warner Cable)

AFTON—See ONEONTA, NY (Time Warner Cable)

AIRMONT (VILLAGE)—See ROCKLAND, NY (Cablevision Systems Corp.)

AKRON (VILLAGE)—See BATAVIA, NY (Time Warner Cable)

ALABAMA (TOWN)—See BATAVIA, NY (Time Warner Cable)

▲**ALBANY**—Time Warner Cable

ALBERTSON—See WOODBURY, NY (Cablevision Systems Corp.)

ALBION (VILLAGE)—See BATAVIA, NY (Time Warner Cable)

▲**ALBION**—Time Warner Cable. Now served by BATAVIA (formerly Stafford), NY [NY0249]

ALBION—See BATAVIA, NY (Time Warner Cable)

▲**ALDEN**—Time Warner Cable. Now served by BATAVIA (formerly Stafford), NY [NY0249]

ALDEN—See BATAVIA, NY (Time Warner Cable)

ALEXANDER (VILLAGE)—See BATAVIA, NY (Time Warner Cable)

ALEXANDRIA (TOWN)—See ALEXANDRIA BAY, NY (Cass Cable TV Inc.)

ALEXANDRIA (TOWN)—See WATERTOWN, NY (Time Warner Cable)

▲**ALEXANDRIA BAY**—Cass Cable TV Inc.

▲**ALFRED**—Formerly served by Alfred Cable System Inc. No longer in operation

ALFRED—See HORNELL, NY (Time Warner Cable)

ALLEGANY (TOWN)—See OLEAN, NY (Time Warner Cable)

ALLEGANY (VILLAGE)—See OLEAN, NY (Time Warner Cable)

ALPINE—See SPENCER, NY (Haefele TV Inc.)

ALPLAUS—See ALBANY, NY (Time Warner Cable)

ALTAMONT—See ALBANY, NY (Time Warner Cable)

ALTONA—See CHAMPLAIN, NY (Time Warner Cable)

AMAGANSETT—See RIVERHEAD, NY (Cablevision Systems Corp.)

AMENIA (TOWN)—See DOVER PLAINS, NY (Cablevision Systems Corp.)

AMES (VILLAGE)—See ALBANY, NY (Time Warner Cable)

AMHERST—See LACKAWANNA, NY (Time Warner Cable)

AMITY (TOWN)—See OLEAN, NY (Time Warner Cable)

AMITYVILLE—See WOODBURY, NY (Cablevision Systems Corp.)

▲**AMSTERDAM**—Time Warner Cable. Now served by ALBANY, NY [NY0014]

AMSTERDAM—See ALBANY, NY (Time Warner Cable)

ANCRAM (TOWN)—See CHATHAM, NY (Charter Communications)

▲**ANDES**—MTC Cable. Now served by MARGARETVILLE, NY [NY0155]

ANDES—See MARGARETVILLE, NY (MTC Cable)

ANDOVER (TOWN)—See OLEAN, NY (Time Warner Cable)

ANDOVER (VILLAGE)—See OLEAN, NY (Time Warner Cable)

▲**ANGELICA**—Time Warner Cable. Now served by HORNELL, NY [NY0076]

ANGELICA—See HORNELL, NY (Time Warner Cable)

ANGOLA—See LACKAWANNA, NY (Time Warner Cable)

ANNSVILLE—See ROME, NY (Time Warner Cable)

ANTWERP (VILLAGE)—See WATERTOWN, NY (Time Warner Cable)

APULIA STATION—See CORTLAND, NY (Time Warner Cable)

AQUEBOGUE—See RIVERHEAD, NY (Cablevision Systems Corp.)

ARCADE (TOWN)—See OLEAN, NY (Time Warner Cable)

ARCADE (VILLAGE)—See OLEAN, NY (Time Warner Cable)

ARCADIA (TOWN)—See GENEVA, NY (Time Warner Cable)

ARDSLEY—See MAMARONECK, NY (Cablevision Systems Corp.)

▲**ARGYLE**—Now served by QUEENSBURY, NY [NY0042]

ARGYLE—See ALBANY, NY (Time Warner Cable)

ARKVILLE—See MARGARETVILLE, NY (MTC Cable)

ARKWRIGHT—See DUNKIRK, NY (Time Warner Cable)

ARMONK—See OSSINING, NY (Cablevision Systems Corp.)

ASHAROKEN—See WOODBURY, NY (Cablevision Systems Corp.)

ASHLAND (TOWN) (GREENE COUNTY)—See CATSKILL, NY (Mid-Hudson Cablevision Inc.)

▲**ASTORIA**—RCN Corp. Formerly served by Queens, NY [NY0283]. This cable system has converted to IPTV

ASTORIA—See NEW YORK, NY (Time Warner Cable)

ATHENS (TOWN)—See CATSKILL, NY (Mid-Hudson Cablevision Inc.)

ATHENS (VILLAGE)—See CATSKILL, NY (Mid-Hudson Cablevision Inc.)

ATLANTIC BEACH—See WOODBURY, NY (Cablevision Systems Corp.)

ATTICA (VILLAGE)—See BATAVIA, NY (Time Warner Cable)

AU SABLE (TOWN)—See PLATTSBURGH, NY (Charter Communications)

▲**AUBURN**—Time Warner Cable

▲**AUGUSTA (town)**—Chain Lakes Cablevision. Now served by ROME, NY [NY0037]

AUGUSTA (TOWN)—See ROME, NY (Time Warner Cable)

AURELIUS (TOWN)—See GENEVA, NY (Time Warner Cable)

AURORA (CAYUGA COUNTY)—See GENEVA, NY (Time Warner Cable)

AUSTERLITZ (TOWN)—See CHATHAM, NY (Charter Communications)

AVA (TOWN)—See ROME, NY (Time Warner Cable)

AVERILL PARK—See ALBANY, NY (Time Warner Cable)

▲**AVOCA**—Time Warner Cable. Now served by HORNELL, NY [NY0076]

AVOCA—See HORNELL, NY (Time Warner Cable)

AVON (VILLAGE)—See BATAVIA, NY (Time Warner Cable)

BABYLON (VILLAGE)—See WOODBURY, NY (Cablevision Systems Corp.)

BABYLON—See WOODBURY, NY (Cablevision Systems Corp.)

▲**BAINBRIDGE**—Time Warner Cable. Now served by ONEONTA, NY [NY0065]

BAINBRIDGE—See ONEONTA, NY (Time Warner Cable)

BAITING HOLLOW—See RIVERHEAD, NY (Cablevision Systems Corp.)

BALDWIN—See WOODBURY, NY (Cablevision Systems Corp.)

▲**BALDWINSVILLE**—Time Warner Cable. Now served by SYRACUSE, NY [NY0013]

BALDWINSVILLE—See SYRACUSE (suburbs), NY (Time Warner Cable)

BALLSTON LAKE—See ALBANY, NY (Time Warner Cable)

BALLSTON SPA—See ALBANY, NY (Time Warner Cable)

BALLSTON—See ALBANY, NY (Time Warner Cable)

BANGOR—See MASSENA, NY (Time Warner Cable)

BARKER—See LACKAWANNA, NY (Time Warner Cable)

BARNEVELD (VILLAGE)—See UTICA, NY (Time Warner Cable)

BARRYVILLE—See HUDSON VALLEY, NY (Time Warner Cable)

BARTON (TOWN)—See SPENCER, NY (Haefele TV Inc.)

▲**BATAVIA**—Time Warner Cable

▲**BATH**—Time Warner Cable. Now served by HORNELL, NY [NY0076]

BATH—See HORNELL, NY (Time Warner Cable)

BAXTER ESTATES—See WOODBURY, NY (Cablevision Systems Corp.)

BAY POINT—See RIVERHEAD, NY (Cablevision Systems Corp.)

BAY RIDGE—See NEW YORK, NY (Time Warner Cable)

BAY SHORE—See WOODBURY, NY (Cablevision Systems Corp.)

BAYSIDE—See NEW YORK, NY (Time Warner Cable)

BAYVILLE—See WOODBURY, NY (Cablevision Systems Corp.)

BEACON—See OSSINING, NY (Cablevision Systems Corp.)

BEDFORD HILLS—See OSSINING, NY (Cablevision Systems Corp.)

BEDFORD—See OSSINING, NY (Cablevision Systems Corp.)

BEECHHURST—See NEW YORK, NY (Time Warner Cable)

BEEKMAN (TOWN)—See CARMEL, NY (Comcast Cable)

BEEKMANTOWN—See PLATTSBURGH, NY (Charter Communications)

BELFAST—See HORNELL, NY (Time Warner Cable)

BELLE TERRE—See SUFFOLK COUNTY, NY (Cablevision Systems Corp.)

BELLEROSE (NASSAU COUNTY)—See WOODBURY, NY (Cablevision Systems Corp.)

BELLEROSE (QUEENS COUNTY)—See NEW YORK, NY (Time Warner Cable)

BELLEVILLE—See WATERTOWN, NY (Time Warner Cable)

BELLMORE—See WOODBURY, NY (Cablevision Systems Corp.)

BELLPORT—See SUFFOLK COUNTY, NY (Cablevision Systems Corp.)

BELMONT (VILLAGE)—See OLEAN, NY (Time Warner Cable)

BEMUS POINT (VILLAGE)—See JAMESTOWN, NY (Time Warner Cable)

BENNINGTON—See BATAVIA, NY (Time Warner Cable)

BENTON—See GENEVA, NY (Time Warner Cable)

BERGEN (VILLAGE)—See BATAVIA, NY (Time Warner Cable)

BERKSHIRE (TOWN)—See SPENCER, NY (Haefele TV Inc.)

▲**BERKSHIRE**—Haefele TV Inc. Now served by SPENCER, NY [NY0145]

BERKSHIRE—See SPENCER, NY (Haefele TV Inc.)

▲**BERLIN (TOWN)**—Charter Communications

BERNE (TOWN)—See ALBANY, NY (Time Warner Cable)

BETHANY (TOWN)—See BATAVIA, NY (Time Warner Cable)

BETHEL (TOWN)—See HUDSON VALLEY, NY (Time Warner Cable)

BETHLEHEM (TOWN)—See CATSKILL, NY (Mid-Hudson Cablevision Inc.)

BETHLEHEM—See ALBANY, NY (Time Warner Cable)

BETHPAGE—See WOODBURY, NY (Cablevision Systems Corp.)

BIG INDIAN—See HUDSON VALLEY, NY (Time Warner Cable)

▲ **BINGHAMTON**—Time Warner Cable

BLACK BROOK (TOWN)—See PLATTSBURGH, NY (Charter Communications)

BLACK RIVER (VILLAGE)—See WATERTOWN, NY (Time Warner Cable)

BLASDELL—See LACKAWANNA, NY (Time Warner Cable)

BLOOMING GROVE (TOWN)—See HUDSON VALLEY, NY (Time Warner Cable)

BLOOMINGBURG (VILLAGE)—See HUDSON VALLEY, NY (Time Warner Cable)

BLOOMINGDALE—See SARANAC LAKE, NY (Time Warner Cable)

BLOOMINGTON—See HUDSON VALLEY, NY (Time Warner Cable)

▲ **BLOOMVILLE**—DTC Cable Inc.

BLUE MOUNTAIN LAKE—See INDIAN LAKE (town), NY (Hamilton County Cable TV Inc.)

BLUE POINT—See SUFFOLK COUNTY, NY (Cablevision Systems Corp.)

BOICEVILLE—See HUDSON VALLEY, NY (Time Warner Cable)

▲ **BOLIVAR**—Time Warner Cable. Now served by HORNELL, NY [NY0076].

BOLIVAR—See HORNELL, NY (Time Warner Cable)

BOLTON—See ALBANY, NY (Time Warner Cable)

BOMBAY (TOWN)—See MASSENA, NY (Time Warner Cable)

BOONVILLE—See ROME, NY (Time Warner Cable)

BOSTON—See LACKAWANNA, NY (Time Warner Cable)

▲ **BOVINA (TOWN)**—DTC Cable Inc.

BRADFORD (TOWN)—See ENFIELD, NY (Haefele TV Inc.)

BRANCHPORT—See GENEVA, NY (Time Warner Cable)

BRANT (TOWN)—See LACKAWANNA, NY (Time Warner Cable)

BRASHER—See MASSENA, NY (Time Warner Cable)

BREWSTER—See CARMEL, NY (Comcast Cable)

BRIARCLIFF MANOR—See OSSINING, NY (Cablevision Systems Corp.)

BRIDGEHAMPTON—See RIVERHEAD, NY (Cablevision Systems Corp.)

BRIDGEWATER—See ILION, NY (Time Warner Cable)

BRIGHTON—See ROCHESTER, NY (Time Warner Cable)

BRIGHTWATERS—See SUFFOLK COUNTY, NY (Cablevision Systems Corp.)

BRISTOL—See ROCHESTER, NY (Time Warner Cable)

BROADALBIN—See ALBANY, NY (Time Warner Cable)

BROCKPORT—See ROCHESTER, NY (Time Warner Cable)

BROCTON (VILLAGE)—See JAMESTOWN, NY (Time Warner Cable)

▲ **BRONX**—Cablevision Systems Corp.

BRONXVILLE—See MAMARONECK, NY (Cablevision Systems Corp.)

BROOKFIELD—See ILION, NY (Time Warner Cable)

BROOKHAVEN (TOWN)—See SUFFOLK COUNTY, NY (Cablevision Systems Corp.)

▲ **BROOKHAVEN**—Cablevision Systems Corp. Now served by SUFFOLK COUNTY, NY [NY0006]

BROOKHAVEN—See SUFFOLK COUNTY, NY (Cablevision Systems Corp.)

BROOKLYN (WESTERN PORTION)—See NEW YORK, NY (Time Warner Cable)

BROOKLYN HEIGHTS—See NEW YORK, NY (Time Warner Cable)

BROOKLYN NAVY YARD—See NEW YORK, NY (Time Warner Cable)

▲ **BROOKLYN**—Formerly served by Cellularvision of New York. No longer in operation

▲ **BROOKLYN**—Cablevision Systems Corp.

BROOKVILLE (VILLAGE)—See WOODBURY, NY (Cablevision Systems Corp.)

BROWNVILLE (VILLAGE)—See WATERTOWN, NY (Time Warner Cable)

BRUNSWICK—See ALBANY, NY (Time Warner Cable)

BRUSHTON—See MASSENA, NY (Time Warner Cable)

BRUTUS—See SYRACUSE (suburbs), NY (Time Warner Cable)

BUCHANAN—See OSSINING, NY (Cablevision Systems Corp.)

▲ **BUFFALO**—Now served by LACKAWANNA, NY [NY0216]

BUFFALO—See LACKAWANNA, NY (Time Warner Cable)

BURDETT (VILLAGE)—See ENFIELD, NY (Haefele TV Inc.)

▲ **BURDETT**—Haefele TV Inc. Now served by ENFIELD, NY [NY0152]

BURDETT—See ENFIELD, NY (Haefele TV Inc.)

BURKE (VILLAGE)—See MASSENA, NY (Time Warner Cable)

▲ **BURLINGTON (town)**—Chain Lakes Cable. Now served by ROME, NY [NY0037]

BURLINGTON (TOWN)—See ROME, NY (Time Warner Cable)

BURNT HILLS—See ALBANY, NY (Time Warner Cable)

BUSTI (TOWN)—See JAMESTOWN, NY (Time Warner Cable)

BUTTERNUTS—See ONEONTA, NY (Time Warner Cable)

BYRON (TOWN)—See ROCHESTER, NY (Time Warner Cable)

CADOSIA—See HANCOCK, NY (Hancock Video)

CAIRO (TOWN)—See CATSKILL, NY (Mid-Hudson Cablevision Inc.)

CAIRO—See HUDSON VALLEY, NY (Time Warner Cable)

CALEDONIA (VILLAGE)—See BATAVIA, NY (Time Warner Cable)

CALLICOON (TOWN)—See HUDSON VALLEY, NY (Time Warner Cable)

CALVERTON—See SUFFOLK COUNTY, NY (Cablevision Systems Corp.)

CAMBRIA HEIGHTS—See NEW YORK, NY (Time Warner Cable)

CAMBRIA—See LACKAWANNA, NY (Time Warner Cable)

CAMBRIDGE (VILLAGE)—See ALBANY, NY (Time Warner Cable)

CAMDEN—See ROME, NY (Time Warner Cable)

CAMILLUS—See SYRACUSE (suburbs), NY (Time Warner Cable)

CANAAN (TOWN)—See CHATHAM, NY (Charter Communications)

CANADICE—See ROCHESTER, NY (Time Warner Cable)

▲ **CANAJOHARIE (village)**—Time Warner Cable. Now served by ALBANY, NY [NY0014]

CANAJOHARIE (VILLAGE)—See ALBANY, NY (Time Warner Cable)

CANANDAIGUA—See GENEVA, NY (Time Warner Cable)

CANASERAGA—See HORNELL, NY (Time Warner Cable)

CANASTOTA (VILLAGE)—See ROME, NY (Time Warner Cable)

CANDOR (PORTIONS)—See SPENCER, NY (Haefele TV Inc.)

CANDOR (VILLAGE)—See ITHACA, NY (Time Warner Cable)

CANOE PLACE—See RIVERHEAD, NY (Cablevision Systems Corp.)

CANTON (VILLAGE)—See MASSENA, NY (Time Warner Cable)

CAPE VINCENT (VILLAGE)—See WATERTOWN, NY (Time Warner Cable)

CARLTON (TOWN)—See BATAVIA, NY (Time Warner Cable)

▲ **CARMEL**—Comcast Cable

CAROLINE (TOWN)—See SPENCER, NY (Haefele TV Inc.)

CAROLINE—See ITHACA, NY (Time Warner Cable)

CARROLL (TOWN)—See JAMESTOWN, NY (Time Warner Cable)

CARROLLTON (TOWN)—See LIMESTONE, NY (Atlantic Broadband)

CARTHAGE—See WATERTOWN, NY (Time Warner Cable)

CASSADAGA (VILLAGE)—See JAMESTOWN, NY (Time Warner Cable)

CASTILE (TOWN)—See BATAVIA, NY (Time Warner Cable)

CASTLETON-ON-HUDSON—See ALBANY, NY (Time Warner Cable)

CASTORLAND—See WATERTOWN, NY (Time Warner Cable)

CATHARINE (TOWN)—See SPENCER, NY (Haefele TV Inc.)

▲ **CATO (town)**—Time Warner Cable. Now served by SYRACUSE, NY [NY0013]

CATO—See SYRACUSE (suburbs), NY (Time Warner Cable)

CATSKILL (TOWN)—See CATSKILL, NY (Mid-Hudson Cablevision Inc.)

CATSKILL (TOWN)—See HUDSON VALLEY, NY (Time Warner Cable)

CATSKILL (VILLAGE)—See CATSKILL, NY (Mid-Hudson Cablevision Inc.)

▲ **CATSKILL**—Mid-Hudson Cablevision Inc.

CATTARAUGUS—See OLEAN, NY (Time Warner Cable)

CAYUGA (VILLAGE)—See GENEVA, NY (Time Warner Cable)

CAYUGA HEIGHTS—See ITHACA, NY (Time Warner Cable)

CAYUTA (TOWN)—See SPENCER, NY (Haefele TV Inc.)

CAZENOVIA—See SYRACUSE (suburbs), NY (Time Warner Cable)

CEDARHURST—See WOODBURY, NY (Cablevision Systems Corp.)

CELORON (VILLAGE)—See JAMESTOWN, NY (Time Warner Cable)

CENTER MORICHES—See SUFFOLK COUNTY, NY (Cablevision Systems Corp.)

CENTEREACH—See SUFFOLK COUNTY, NY (Cablevision Systems Corp.)

CENTERPORT—See WOODBURY, NY (Cablevision Systems Corp.)

▲ **CENTRAL SQUARE**—Time Warner Cable. Now served by OSWEGO, NY [NY0061]

CENTRAL SQUARE—See OSWEGO, NY (Time Warner Cable)

CENTRE ISLAND—See WOODBURY, NY (Cablevision Systems Corp.)

CERES TWP.—See OLEAN, PA (Time Warner Cable)

CHAFFEE (TOWN)—See OLEAN, NY (Time Warner Cable)

CHAMPION—See WATERTOWN, NY (Time Warner Cable)

CHAMPLAIN (VILLAGE)—See CHAMPLAIN, NY (Time Warner Cable)

▲ **CHAMPLAIN**—Time Warner Cable

CHARLOTTEVILLE—See SUMMIT (town), NY (Chain Lakes Cablevision)

CHARLTON—See ALBANY, NY (Time Warner Cable)

CHATEAUGAY (VILLAGE)—See MASSENA, NY (Time Warner Cable)

▲ **CHATHAM**—Charter Communications

CHAUMONT—See WATERTOWN, NY (Time Warner Cable)

CHAUTAUQUA—See DUNKIRK, NY (Time Warner Cable)

CHAZY (TOWN)—See CHAMPLAIN, NY (Time Warner Cable)

CHEEKTOWAGA—See LACKAWANNA, NY (Time Warner Cable)

CHERRY CREEK—See JAMESTOWN, NY (Time Warner Cable)

CHERRY VALLEY (VILLAGE)—See ALBANY, NY (Time Warner Cable)

CHESTER (TOWN) (ORANGE COUNTY)—See WARWICK, NY (Cablevision Systems Corp.)

CHESTER (VILLAGE)—See WARWICK, NY (Cablevision Systems Corp.)

CHESTERFIELD (TOWN)—See PLATTSBURGH, NY (Charter Communications)

CHESTERTOWN—See JOHNSBURG (town), NY (Hamilton County Cable TV Inc.)

CHESTNUT RIDGE—See RAMAPO (town), NY (Cablevision Systems Corp.)

CHESTNUT RIDGE—See ROCKLAND, NY (Cablevision Systems Corp.)

CHICHESTER—See HUDSON VALLEY, NY (Time Warner Cable)

CHILI—See ROCHESTER, NY (Time Warner Cable)

CHITTENANGO—See ROME, NY (Time Warner Cable)

CHURCHVILLE (VILLAGE)—See BATAVIA, NY (Time Warner Cable)

CICERO—See SYRACUSE (suburbs), NY (Time Warner Cable)

▲ **CINCINNATUS**—Chain Lakes Cablevision. Now served by CORTLAND, NY [NY0062]

CINCINNATUS—See CORTLAND, NY (Time Warner Cable)

CLARENDON—See ROCHESTER, NY (Time Warner Cable)

CLARKSON (TOWN)—See ROCHESTER, NY (Time Warner Cable)

CLARKSTOWN—See ROCKLAND, NY (Cablevision Systems Corp.)

CLAVERACK—See CATSKILL, NY (Mid-Hudson Cablevision Inc.)

CLAY—See SYRACUSE (suburbs), NY (Time Warner Cable)

CLAYTON—See WATERTOWN, NY (Time Warner Cable)

CLAYVILLE (VILLAGE)—See UTICA, NY (Time Warner Cable)

CLEARVIEW—See NEW YORK, NY (Time Warner Cable)

CLERMONT—See GERMANTOWN, NY (GTel Teleconnections)

CLEVELAND (VILLAGE)—See ROME, NY (Time Warner Cable)

CLIFTON PARK—See ALBANY, NY (Time Warner Cable)

CLIFTON SPRINGS (VILLAGE)—See GENEVA, NY (Time Warner Cable)

CLINTON (TOWN)—See DOVER PLAINS, NY (Cablevision Systems Corp.)

CLINTON (VILLAGE)—See UTICA, NY (Time Warner Cable)

CLYDE (VILLAGE)—See GENEVA, NY (Time Warner Cable)

CLYMER (TOWN)—See JAMESTOWN, NY (Time Warner Cable)

▲ **CLYMER**—Time Warner Cable. Now served by JAMESTOWN, NY [NY0030]

▲ **COBLESKILL (town)**—Time Warner Cable. Now served by ALBANY, NY [NY0014]

COBLESKILL (VILLAGE)—See ALBANY, NY (Time Warner Cable)

COBLESKILL—See ALBANY, NY (Time Warner Cable)

COCHECTON—See HUDSON VALLEY, NY (Time Warner Cable)

COEYMANS—See CATSKILL, NY (Mid-Hudson Cablevision Inc.)

▲ **COHOCTON**—Time Warner Cable. Now served by HORNELL, NY [NY0076]

COHOCTON—See HORNELL, NY (Time Warner Cable)

COHOES—See ALBANY, NY (Time Warner Cable)

COLCHESTER TWP.—See HUDSON VALLEY, NY (Time Warner Cable)

COLD BROOK—See UTICA, NY (Time Warner Cable)

COLD SPRING HARBOR—See WOODBURY, NY (Cablevision Systems Corp.)

COLDEN—See LACKAWANNA, NY (Time Warner Cable)

COLDSPRING (TOWN)—See OLEAN, NY (Time Warner Cable)

COLLEGE POINT—See NEW YORK, NY (Time Warner Cable)

COLLINS (TOWN)—See OLEAN, NY (Time Warner Cable)

COLLINS CENTER (TOWN)—See OLEAN, NY (Time Warner Cable)

COLONIE (VILLAGE)—See ALBANY, NY (Time Warner Cable)

COLTON—See MASSENA, NY (Time Warner Cable)

COLUMBIA (TOWN)—See ILION, NY (Time Warner Cable)

COLUMBIAVILLE—See CATSKILL, NY (Mid-Hudson Cablevision Inc.)

COLUMBUS (TOWN)—See ONEONTA, NY (Time Warner Cable)

COMMACK—See SUFFOLK COUNTY, NY (Cablevision Systems Corp.)

CONCORD (TOWN)—See OLEAN, NY (Time Warner Cable)

CONESUS (TOWN)—See BATAVIA, NY (Time Warner Cable)

CONEWANGO—See OLEAN, NY (Time Warner Cable)

CONSTABLE (TOWN)—See MASSENA, NY (Time Warner Cable)

CONSTABLEVILLE—See ROME, NY (Time Warner Cable)

▲ **CONSTANTIA (town)**—Time Warner Cable. Now served by ROME, NY [NY0037]

CONSTANTIA (TOWN)—See ROME, NY (Time Warner Cable)

▲ **COOPERSTOWN**—Time Warner Cable. Now served by ONEONTA, NY [NY0065]

COOPERSTOWN—See ONEONTA, NY (Time Warner Cable)

COPAKE (TOWN)—See CHATHAM, NY (Charter Communications)

COPENHAGEN—See WATERTOWN, NY (Time Warner Cable)

COPIAGUE—See WOODBURY, NY (Cablevision Systems Corp.)

CORAM—See SUFFOLK COUNTY, NY (Cablevision Systems Corp.)

CORFU (VILLAGE)—See BATAVIA, NY (Time Warner Cable)

CORINTH (VILLAGE)—See ALBANY, NY (Time Warner Cable)

CORNING—See ELMIRA/CORNING, NY (Time Warner Cable)

CORNWALL (TOWN)—See HUDSON VALLEY, NY (Time Warner Cable)

CORNWALLVILLE—See DURHAM, NY (Mid-Hudson Cablevision Inc.)

▲ **CORONA**—RCN Corp. Formerly served by Queens, NY [NY0283]. This cable system has converted to IPTV

CORONA—See NEW YORK, NY (Time Warner Cable)

▲ **CORTLAND**—Time Warner Cable

CORTLANDT—See OSSINING, NY (Cablevision Systems Corp.)

CORTLANDVILLE—See CORTLAND, NY (Time Warner Cable)

COTTEKILL—See HUDSON VALLEY, NY (Time Warner Cable)

COVE NECK—See WOODBURY, NY (Cablevision Systems Corp.)

COVENTRY (TOWN)—See ONEONTA, NY (Time Warner Cable)

COVERT (TOWN)—See GENEVA, NY (Time Warner Cable)

COVERT (TOWN)—See ITHACA, NY (Time Warner Cable)

COVINGTON (TOWN)—See BATAVIA, NY (Time Warner Cable)

COXSACKIE (TOWN)—See CATSKILL, NY (Mid-Hudson Cablevision Inc.)

COXSACKIE (VILLAGE)—See CATSKILL, NY (Mid-Hudson Cablevision Inc.)

CRAWFORD (TOWN)—See HUDSON VALLEY, NY (Time Warner Cable)

CROGHAN (VILLAGE)—See WATERTOWN, NY (Time Warner Cable)

CROSS RIVER—See YORKTOWN, NY (Cablevision Systems Corp.)

CROTON-ON-HUDSON—See OSSINING, NY (Cablevision Systems Corp.)

CROWN POINT (TOWN)—See PORT HENRY (village), NY (Time Warner Cable)

CUBA (TOWN)—See OLEAN, NY (Time Warner Cable)

CUBA (VILLAGE)—See OLEAN, NY (Time Warner Cable)

CUTCHOGUE—See RIVERHEAD, NY (Cablevision Systems Corp.)

▲ **CUYLER**—Chain Lakes Cable. Now served by CORTLAND, NY [NY0062]

CUYLER—See CORTLAND, NY (Time Warner Cable)

DANBY—See ITHACA, NY (Time Warner Cable)

DANNEMORA (VILLAGE)—See PLATTSBURGH, NY (Charter Communications)

▲ **DANSVILLE**—Time Warner Cable. Now served by HORNELL, NY [NY0076]

DANSVILLE—See HORNELL, NY (Time Warner Cable)

DANUBE (TOWN)—See ILION, NY (Time Warner Cable)

DARIEN—See BATAVIA, NY (Time Warner Cable)

DAVENPORT—See ONEONTA, NY (Time Warner Cable)

DAY—See ALBANY, NY (Time Warner Cable)

DAYTON (TOWN)—See JAMESTOWN, NY (Time Warner Cable)

DE KALB (TOWN)—See MASSENA, NY (Time Warner Cable)

DE LANCEY—See HAMDEN, NY (DTC Cable Inc.)

▲ **DE RUYTER**—Chain Lakes Cablevision. No longer in operation

DE WITT—See SYRACUSE (suburbs), NY (Time Warner Cable)

DEANSBORO—See ROME, NY (Time Warner Cable)

DEER PARK—See WOODBURY, NY (Cablevision Systems Corp.)

DEERFIELD TWP.—See ELMIRA/CORNING, PA (Time Warner Cable)

DEERFIELD—See UTICA, NY (Time Warner Cable)

DEFERIET—See WATERTOWN, NY (Time Warner Cable)

DEFREESTVILLE—See ALBANY, NY (Time Warner Cable)

DELANSON—See ALBANY, NY (Time Warner Cable)

DELAWARE (TOWN)—See HUDSON VALLEY, NY (Time Warner Cable)

DELEVAN (VILLAGE)—See OLEAN, NY (Time Warner Cable)

DELHI (VILLAGE)—See ONEONTA, NY (Time Warner Cable)

▲**DELHI**—Time Warner Cable. Now served by ONEONTA, NY [NY0065]

▲**DELHI**—DTC Cable Inc.

DELMAR—See ALBANY, NY (Time Warner Cable)

DENMARK (TOWN)—See WATERTOWN, NY (Time Warner Cable)

DENNING (UNINCORPORATED AREAS)—See HUDSON VALLEY, NY (Time Warner Cable)

DENVER—See HUDSON VALLEY, NY (Time Warner Cable)

DEPEW—See LACKAWANNA, NY (Time Warner Cable)

▲**DEPOSIT**—Formerly served by Adams Cable TV. Now served by CARBONDALE, PA [PA0067]

DERING HARBOR—See RIVERHEAD, NY (Cablevision Systems Corp.)

DEXTER (VILLAGE)—See WATERTOWN, NY (Time Warner Cable)

DIANA (TOWN)—See WATERTOWN, NY (Time Warner Cable)

DIX HILLS—See WOODBURY, NY (Cablevision Systems Corp.)

DIX—See GENEVA, NY (Time Warner Cable)

DOBBS FERRY—See MAMARONECK, NY (Cablevision Systems Corp.)

DOLGEVILLE—See ILION, NY (Time Warner Cable)

DOUGLASTON—See NEW YORK, NY (Time Warner Cable)

DOVER (TOWN)—See DOVER PLAINS, NY (Cablevision Systems Corp.)

▲**DOVER PLAINS**—Cablevision Systems Corp.

▲**DOWNSVILLE**—Formerly served by Downsville Community Antenna. No longer in operation

DOWNSVILLE—See MARGARETVILLE, NY (MTC Cable)

▲**DRESDEN**—Time Warner Cable. Now served by GENEVA, NY [NY0218]

DRESDEN—See GENEVA, NY (Time Warner Cable)

DRYDEN (VILLAGE)—See ITHACA, NY (Time Warner Cable)

DUANESBURG—See PRINCETOWN (town), NY (Princetown Cable Co.)

DUANESBURG—See ALBANY, NY (Time Warner Cable)

▲**DUNDEE**—Time Warner Cable. Now served by ELMIRA/CORNING, NY [NY0057]

DUNDEE—See ELMIRA/CORNING, NY (Time Warner Cable)

DUNKIRK (TOWN)—See DUNKIRK, NY (Time Warner Cable)

▲**DUNKIRK**—Time Warner Cable

▲**DURHAM**—Mid-Hudson Cablevision Inc.

DUTCHESS COUNTY—See HUDSON VALLEY, NY (Time Warner Cable)

EAGLE BAY—See UTICA, NY (Time Warner Cable)

EARLVILLE (VILLAGE)—See ILION, NY (Time Warner Cable)

EAST AURORA—See LACKAWANNA, NY (Time Warner Cable)

EAST BLOOMFIELD (TOWN)—See GENEVA, NY (Time Warner Cable)

EAST BRANCH—See HANCOCK, NY (Hancock Video)

EAST CARTHAGE—See WATERTOWN, NY (Time Warner Cable)

EAST CONCORD TWP.—See OLEAN, NY (Time Warner Cable)

EAST DURHAM—See DURHAM, NY (Mid-Hudson Cablevision Inc.)

EAST ELMHURST—See NEW YORK, NY (Time Warner Cable)

EAST FISHKILL—See OSSINING, NY (Cablevision Systems Corp.)

EAST GREENBUSH—See ALBANY, NY (Time Warner Cable)

EAST GUILFORD—See ONEONTA, NY (Time Warner Cable)

▲**EAST HAMPTON**—Cablevision Systems Corp. Now served by RIVERHEAD, NY [NY0024]

EAST HAMPTON—See RIVERHEAD, NY (Cablevision Systems Corp.)

EAST HILLS—See WOODBURY, NY (Cablevision Systems Corp.)

EAST LAWRENCE TWP.—See ELMIRA/CORNING, PA (Time Warner Cable)

EAST MARION—See RIVERHEAD, NY (Cablevision Systems Corp.)

EAST MORICHES—See SUFFOLK COUNTY, NY (Cablevision Systems Corp.)

EAST NORTHPORT—See WOODBURY, NY (Cablevision Systems Corp.)

EAST QUOGUE—See RIVERHEAD, NY (Cablevision Systems Corp.)

EAST RANDOLPH (VILLAGE)—See OLEAN, NY (Time Warner Cable)

EAST ROCHESTER—See ROCHESTER, NY (Time Warner Cable)

EAST ROCKAWAY—See WOODBURY, NY (Cablevision Systems Corp.)

EAST SYRACUSE—See SYRACUSE (suburbs), NY (Time Warner Cable)

EAST WILLISTON—See WOODBURY, NY (Cablevision Systems Corp.)

EASTCHESTER—See MAMARONECK, NY (Cablevision Systems Corp.)

EASTON (TOWN)—See ALBANY, NY (Time Warner Cable)

EASTPORT—See SUFFOLK COUNTY, NY (Cablevision Systems Corp.)

EATON—See ILION, NY (Time Warner Cable)

EDEN—See LACKAWANNA, NY (Time Warner Cable)

▲**EDINBURG (town)**—Formerly served by Adelphia Communications. Now served by ALBANY, NY [NY0014]

EDINBURG (TOWN)—See ALBANY, NY (Time Warner Cable)

EDMESTON—See ONEONTA, NY (Time Warner Cable)

ELBA (VILLAGE)—See BATAVIA, NY (Time Warner Cable)

ELBRIDGE—See SYRACUSE (suburbs), NY (Time Warner Cable)

ELDRED BOROUGH—See OLEAN, PA (Time Warner Cable)

ELDRED TWP.—See OLEAN, PA (Time Warner Cable)

ELDRED—See HUDSON VALLEY, NY (Time Warner Cable)

ELIZABETHTOWN—See PLATTSBURGH, NY (Charter Communications)

ELKLAND—See ELMIRA/CORNING, PA (Time Warner Cable)

ELLENBURG—See CHAMPLAIN, NY (Time Warner Cable)

▲**ELLENVILLE**—Time Warner Cable. Now served by HUDSON VALLEY (formerly Middletown), NY [NY0231]

ELLENVILLE—See HUDSON VALLEY, NY (Time Warner Cable)

ELLERY (TOWN)—See JAMESTOWN, NY (Time Warner Cable)

ELLICOTT (TOWN)—See JAMESTOWN, NY (Time Warner Cable)

ELLICOTTVILLE (TOWN)—See OLEAN, NY (Time Warner Cable)

ELLICOTTVILLE (VILLAGE)—See OLEAN, NY (Time Warner Cable)

ELLINGTON (TOWN)—See JAMESTOWN, NY (Time Warner Cable)

ELLISBURG—See WATERTOWN, NY (Time Warner Cable)

ELMA—See LACKAWANNA, NY (Time Warner Cable)

▲**ELMHURST**—RCN Corp. Formerly served by Queens, NY [NY0283]. This cable system has converted to IPTV

▲**ELMIRA/CORNING**—Time Warner Cable

▲**ELMIRA**—Time Warner Cable. Now served by ELMIRA/CORNING (formerly Corning), NY [NY0057]

ELMONT—See WOODBURY, NY (Cablevision Systems Corp.)

ELMSFORD—See MAMARONECK, NY (Cablevision Systems Corp.)

ELWOOD—See WOODBURY, NY (Cablevision Systems Corp.)

ENFIELD (TOWN)—See ENFIELD, NY (Haefele TV Inc.)

▲**ENFIELD**—Haefele TV Inc.

ESOPUS—See HUDSON VALLEY, NY (Time Warner Cable)

ESPERANCE (VILLAGE)—See ALBANY, NY (Time Warner Cable)

ESSEX (TOWN)—See WILLSBORO (town), NY (Cable Communications of Willsboro)

ESSEX—See WILLSBORO (town), NY (Cable Communications of Willsboro)

EVANS (TOWN)—See LACKAWANNA, NY (Time Warner Cable)

EVANS MILLS (VILLAGE)—See WATERTOWN, NY (Time Warner Cable)

EXETER (TOWN)—See ROME, NY (Time Warner Cable)

EXETER—See ONEONTA, NY (Time Warner Cable)

FABIUS (VILLAGE)—See CORTLAND, NY (Time Warner Cable)

FAIR HAVEN—See OSWEGO, NY (Time Warner Cable)

FAIRPORT—See ROCHESTER, NY (Time Warner Cable)

FALCONER (VILLAGE)—See JAMESTOWN, NY (Time Warner Cable)

FALLSBURG (TOWN)—See HUDSON VALLEY, NY (Time Warner Cable)

FARMINGDALE—See WOODBURY, NY (Cablevision Systems Corp.)

FARMINGTON (TOWN)—See GENEVA, NY (Time Warner Cable)

FARMINGVILLE—See SUFFOLK COUNTY, NY (Cablevision Systems Corp.)

FARNHAM (VILLAGE)—See LACKAWANNA, NY (Time Warner Cable)

FAYETTE (TOWN)—See GENEVA, NY (Time Warner Cable)

FAYETTEVILLE—See SYRACUSE (suburbs), NY (Time Warner Cable)

FENNER (TOWN)—See ROME, NY (Time Warner Cable)

FENNER (TOWN)—See SYRACUSE (suburbs), NY (Time Warner Cable)

FILLMORE—See BATAVIA, NY (Time Warner Cable)

FISHKILL (VILLAGE)—See OSSINING, NY (Cablevision Systems Corp.)

FISHS EDDY—See HANCOCK, NY (Hancock Video)

FLANDERS—See RIVERHEAD, NY (Cablevision Systems Corp.)

FLEISCHMANNS—See HUDSON VALLEY, NY (Time Warner Cable)

FLEMING—See AUBURN, NY (Time Warner Cable)

FLORAL PARK—See WOODBURY, NY (Cablevision Systems Corp.)

FLORAL PARK—See NEW YORK, NY (Time Warner Cable)

FLORIDA (VILLAGE)—See WARWICK, NY (Cablevision Systems Corp.)

FLOWER HILL—See WOODBURY, NY (Cablevision Systems Corp.)

FLOYD—See ROME, NY (Time Warner Cable)

FLUSHING—See NEW YORK, NY (Time Warner Cable)

FONDA—See ALBANY, NY (Time Warner Cable)

FOREST HILLS—See NEW YORK, NY (Time Warner Cable)

FORESTBURGH (TOWN)—See HUDSON VALLEY, NY (Time Warner Cable)

▲**FORESTPORT**—Now served by UTICA, NY [NY0022]

FORESTPORT—See UTICA, NY (Time Warner Cable)

FORESTVILLE—See DUNKIRK, NY (Time Warner Cable)

FORT ANN (VILLAGE)—See ALBANY, NY (Time Warner Cable)

FORT COVINGTON—See MASSENA, NY (Time Warner Cable)

FORT DRUM—See WATERTOWN, NY (Time Warner Cable)

FORT EDWARD (VILLAGE)—See ALBANY, NY (Time Warner Cable)

FORT HAMILTON ARMY BASE—See NEW YORK, NY (Time Warner Cable)

FORT JOHNSON—See ALBANY, NY (Time Warner Cable)

FORT PLAIN (VILLAGE)—See ALBANY, NY (Time Warner Cable)

FORT SALONGA—See SUFFOLK COUNTY, NY (Cablevision Systems Corp.)

FOWLER (TOWN)—See MASSENA, NY (Time Warner Cable)

FRANKFORT (TOWN)—See UTICA, NY (Time Warner Cable)

FRANKFORT (VILLAGE)—See ILION, NY (Time Warner Cable)

FRANKLIN (VILLAGE)—See ONEONTA, NY (Time Warner Cable)

FRANKLIN SQUARE—See WOODBURY, NY (Cablevision Systems Corp.)

FRANKLINVILLE (TOWN)—See OLEAN, NY (Time Warner Cable)

FRANKLINVILLE (VILLAGE)—See OLEAN, NY (Time Warner Cable)

FRASER—See HAMDEN, NY (DTC Cable Inc.)

▲**FREDONIA (village)**—Time Warner Cable. Now served by JAMESTOWN, NY [NY0030]

FREDONIA (VILLAGE)—See JAMESTOWN, NY (Time Warner Cable)

FREEDOM (TOWN)—See OLEAN, NY (Time Warner Cable)

FREEPORT—See WOODBURY, NY (Cablevision Systems Corp.)

FREEVILLE—See ITHACA, NY (Time Warner Cable)

FREMONT—See HUDSON VALLEY, NY (Time Warner Cable)

FRENCH CREEK—See JAMESTOWN, NY (Time Warner Cable)

▲**FRESH MEADOWS**—RCN Corp. Formerly served by Queens, NY [NY0283]. This cable system has converted to IPTV

FRESH MEADOWS—See NEW YORK, NY (Time Warner Cable)

▲**FRIENDSHIP**—Time Warner Cable. Now served by HORNELL, NY [NY0076]

FRIENDSHIP—See HORNELL, NY (Time Warner Cable)

▲**FULTON**—Time Warner Cable. Now served by OSWEGO, NY [NY0061]

FULTON—See OSWEGO, NY (Time Warner Cable)

FULTONVILLE—See ALBANY, NY (Time Warner Cable)

GAINES (TOWN)—See BATAVIA, NY (Time Warner Cable)

GAINESVILLE (TOWN)—See BATAVIA, NY (Time Warner Cable)

GALEN (VILLAGE)—See GENEVA, NY (Time Warner Cable)

GALLATIN—See CATSKILL, NY (Mid-Hudson Cablevision Inc.)

GALWAY—See ALBANY, NY (Time Warner Cable)

GARDEN CITY—See WOODBURY, NY (Cablevision Systems Corp.)

GARDINER (TOWN)—See HUDSON VALLEY, NY (Time Warner Cable)

GARRATTSVILLE—See ROME, NY (Time Warner Cable)

GARRISON—See OSSINING, NY (Cablevision Systems Corp.)

GATES—See ROCHESTER, NY (Time Warner Cable)

GEDDES—See SYRACUSE (suburbs), NY (Time Warner Cable)

GENESEE FALLS (TOWN)—See BATAVIA, NY (Time Warner Cable)

GENESEO (VILLAGE)—See BATAVIA, NY (Time Warner Cable)

GENEVA (TOWN)—See GENEVA, NY (Time Warner Cable)

▲**GENEVA**—Time Warner Cable

GENOA TWP.—See MORAVIA, NY (Southern Cayuga County Cablevision)

GEORGETOWN (TOWN)—See CORTLAND, NY (Time Warner Cable)

GERMAN FLATTS—See ILION, NY (Time Warner Cable)

▲**GERMANTOWN**—GTel Teleconnections

GERRY (TOWN)—See JAMESTOWN, NY (Time Warner Cable)

GHENT (TOWN)—See CHATHAM, NY (Charter Communications)

GILBERTSVILLE—See ONEONTA, NY (Time Warner Cable)

GLEN (TOWN)—See ALBANY, NY (Time Warner Cable)

GLEN COVE—See WOODBURY, NY (Cablevision Systems Corp.)

GLEN OAKS—See NEW YORK, NY (Time Warner Cable)

GLEN PARK (VILLAGE)—See WATERTOWN, NY (Time Warner Cable)

GLEN SPEY—See HUDSON VALLEY, NY (Time Warner Cable)

GLENDALE—See NEW YORK, NY (Time Warner Cable)

GLENFIELD—See WATERTOWN, NY (Time Warner Cable)

▲**GLENS FALLS**—Time Warner Cable. Now served by ALBANY, NY [NY0014]

GLENS FALLS—See ALBANY, NY (Time Warner Cable)

GLENVILLE—See ALBANY, NY (Time Warner Cable)

GLOVERSVILLE—See ALBANY, NY (Time Warner Cable)

GORHAM—See GENEVA, NY (Time Warner Cable)

GOSHEN (VILLAGE)—See HUDSON VALLEY, NY (Time Warner Cable)

GOUVERNEUR (VILLAGE)—See MASSENA, NY (Time Warner Cable)

GOWANDA (VILLAGE)—See OLEAN, NY (Time Warner Cable)

GRAHAMSVILLE (TOWN)—See HUDSON VALLEY, NY (Time Warner Cable)

GRANBY—See OSWEGO, NY (Time Warner Cable)

GRAND GORGE—See HUDSON VALLEY, NY (Time Warner Cable)

GRAND ISLAND—See LACKAWANNA, NY (Time Warner Cable)

GRAND VIEW-ON-HUDSON—See ROCKLAND, NY (Cablevision Systems Corp.)

GRANVILLE—See ALBANY, NY (Time Warner Cable)

GREAT NECK ESTATES—See WOODBURY, NY (Cablevision Systems Corp.)

GREAT NECK PLAZA (VILLAGE)—See WOODBURY, NY (Cablevision Systems Corp.)

GREAT NECK—See WOODBURY, NY (Cablevision Systems Corp.)

GREAT VALLEY (TOWN)—See OLEAN, NY (Time Warner Cable)

GREAT VALLEY—See SALAMANCA, NY (Atlantic Broadband)

GREECE—See ROCHESTER, NY (Time Warner Cable)

GREEN ISLAND—See ALBANY, NY (Time Warner Cable)

GREENBURGH—See MAMARONECK, NY (Cablevision Systems Corp.)

GREENE (TOWN)—See SMITHVILLE, NY (Haefele TV Inc.)

GREENE COUNTY (PORTIONS)—See HUDSON VALLEY, NY (Time Warner Cable)

▲**GREENE**—Time Warner Cable. Now served by BINGHAMTON, NY [NY0016]

GREENE—See BINGHAMTON, NY (Time Warner Cable)

GREENFIELD—See ALBANY, NY (Time Warner Cable)

GREENLAWN—See WOODBURY, NY (Cablevision Systems Corp.)

GREENPOINT—See NEW YORK, NY (Time Warner Cable)

GREENPORT (COLUMBIA COUNTY)—See CATSKILL, NY (Mid-Hudson Cablevision Inc.)

GREENPORT—See RIVERHEAD, NY (Cablevision Systems Corp.)

GREENVILLE—See CATSKILL, NY (Mid-Hudson Cablevision Inc.)

GREENWICH (VILLAGE)—See ALBANY, NY (Time Warner Cable)

GREENWOOD LAKE (VILLAGE)—See WARWICK, NY (Cablevision Systems Corp.)

GREENWOOD LAKE—See WARWICK, NY (Cablevision Systems Corp.)

▲**GREIG**—Time Warner Cable. Now served by CARTHAGE, NY [NY0206]

GREIG—See WATERTOWN, NY (Time Warner Cable)

GROTON (VILLAGE)—See ITHACA, NY (Time Warner Cable)

GROVELAND (TOWN)—See HORNELL, NY (Time Warner Cable)

GUILDERLAND—See ALBANY, NY (Time Warner Cable)

JAY—See PLATTSBURGH, NY (Charter Communications)

JEFFERSON (TOWN)—See SUMMIT (town), NY (Chain Lakes Cablevision)

JEFFERSONVILLE (VILLAGE)—See HUDSON VALLEY, NY (Time Warner Cable)

JERICHO—See WOODBURY, NY (Cablevision Systems Corp.)

JEWETT—See HUDSON VALLEY, NY (Time Warner Cable)

▲**JOHNSBURG (TOWN)**—Hamilton County Cable TV Inc.

▲**JOHNSTOWN (city)**—Time Warner Cable. Now served by AMSTERDAM, NY [NY0047]

JOHNSTOWN (CITY)—See ALBANY, NY (Time Warner Cable)

JOHNSTOWN (TOWN)—See ALBANY, NY (Time Warner Cable)

JORDAN—See SYRACUSE (suburbs), NY (Time Warner Cable)

JUNCTION—See ALBANY, NY (Time Warner Cable)

KATONAH—See OSSINING, NY (Cablevision Systems Corp.)

KEENE (TOWN)—See KEENE VALLEY, NY (Keene Valley Video Inc.)

▲**KEENE VALLEY**—Keene Valley Video Inc.

KEESEVILLE (VILLAGE)—See PLATTSBURGH, NY (Charter Communications)

KENDALL—See BATAVIA, NY (Time Warner Cable)

KENMORE (VILLAGE)—See LACKAWANNA, NY (Time Warner Cable)

KENSINGTON (VILLAGE)—See WOODBURY, NY (Cablevision Systems Corp.)

KEW GARDEN HILLS—See NEW YORK, NY (Time Warner Cable)

KIANTONE (TOWN)—See JAMESTOWN, NY (Time Warner Cable)

KILLAWOG—See BINGHAMTON, NY (Time Warner Cable)

KING FERRY—See MORAVIA, NY (Southern Cayuga County Cablevision)

KINGS PARK—See SUFFOLK COUNTY, NY (Cablevision Systems Corp.)

KINGS POINT—See WOODBURY, NY (Cablevision Systems Corp.)

KINGSBURY (TOWN)—See ALBANY, NY (Time Warner Cable)

▲**KINGSTON**—Time Warner Cable. Now served by HUDSON VALLEY (formerly Middletown), NY [NY0231]

KINGSTON—See HUDSON VALLEY, NY (Time Warner Cable)

KIRKLAND (TOWN)—See ROME, NY (Time Warner Cable)

KIRKLAND (TOWN)—See UTICA, NY (Time Warner Cable)

KNOX (TOWN)—See ALBANY, NY (Time Warner Cable)

KORTRIGHT—See ONEONTA, NY (Time Warner Cable)

LA FAYETTE—See SYRACUSE (suburbs), NY (Time Warner Cable)

LA GRANGE (TOWN)—See HUDSON VALLEY, NY (Time Warner Cable)

LA GRANGE—See OSSINING, NY (Cablevision Systems Corp.)

▲**LACKAWANNA**—Time Warner Cable

LACONA—See OSWEGO, NY (Time Warner Cable)

LAGRANGEVILLE—See OSSINING, NY (Cablevision Systems Corp.)

LAKE GEORGE (VILLAGE)—See ALBANY, NY (Time Warner Cable)

LAKE GROVE (VILLAGE)—See SUFFOLK COUNTY, NY (Cablevision Systems Corp.)

LAKE PLACID—See SARANAC LAKE, NY (Time Warner Cable)

LAKE PLEASANT—See WELLS, NY (Hamilton County Cable TV Inc.)

LAKE RONKONKAMA—See SUFFOLK COUNTY, NY (Cablevision Systems Corp.)

LAKE SUCCESS (VILLAGE)—See WOODBURY, NY (Cablevision Systems Corp.)

LAKEWOOD (VILLAGE)—See JAMESTOWN, NY (Time Warner Cable)

▲**LANCASTER (town)**—Now served by LACKAWANNA, NY [NY0216]

LANCASTER (VILLAGE)—See LACKAWANNA, NY (Time Warner Cable)

LANSING (VILLAGE)—See ITHACA, NY (Time Warner Cable)

LARCHMONT (VILLAGE)—See MAMARONECK, NY (Cablevision Systems Corp.)

LATTINGTOWN—See WOODBURY, NY (Cablevision Systems Corp.)

LAUREL HOLLOW—See WOODBURY, NY (Cablevision Systems Corp.)

LAUREL—See RIVERHEAD, NY (Cablevision Systems Corp.)

LAURELTON—See NEW YORK, NY (Time Warner Cable)

LAURENS (VILLAGE)—See ONEONTA, NY (Time Warner Cable)

LAWRENCE TWP.—See ELMIRA/CORNING, PA (Time Warner Cable)

LAWRENCE—See WOODBURY, NY (Cablevision Systems Corp.)

LAWTONS (TOWN)—See OLEAN, NY (Time Warner Cable)

LAYTON—See WARWICK, NJ (Cablevision Systems Corp.)

LE RAY (TOWN)—See WATERTOWN, NY (Time Warner Cable)

LE ROY (VILLAGE)—See BATAVIA, NY (Time Warner Cable)

LEBANON—See ILION, NY (Time Warner Cable)

LEDYARD—See GENEVA, NY (Time Warner Cable)

LEE—See ROME, NY (Time Warner Cable)

LEICESTER (VILLAGE)—See BATAVIA, NY (Time Warner Cable)

LENOX (TOWN)—See ROME, NY (Time Warner Cable)

LEONARDSVILLE—See ILION, NY (Time Warner Cable)

LEVITTOWN—See WOODBURY, NY (Cablevision Systems Corp.)

LEWIS—See PLATTSBURGH, NY (Charter Communications)

LEWISBORO—See YORKTOWN, NY (Cablevision Systems Corp.)

LEWISTON (VILLAGE)—See LACKAWANNA, NY (Time Warner Cable)

LEXINGTON—See HUDSON VALLEY, NY (Time Warner Cable)

LEYDEN—See ROME, NY (Time Warner Cable)

LIBERTY (VILLAGE)—See HUDSON VALLEY, NY (Time Warner Cable)

LIMA (VILLAGE)—See BATAVIA, NY (Time Warner Cable)

▲**LIMESTONE**—Atlantic Broadband

LINCOLN (TOWN)—See ROME, NY (Time Warner Cable)

LINDEN HILL—See NEW YORK, NY (Time Warner Cable)

LINDENHURST—See WOODBURY, NY (Cablevision Systems Corp.)

LINDLEY (TOWN)—See ELMIRA/CORNING, NY (Time Warner Cable)

LISBON—See MASSENA, NY (Time Warner Cable)

LISLE (VILLAGE)—See BINGHAMTON, NY (Time Warner Cable)

LITCHFIELD (TOWN)—See ILION, NY (Time Warner Cable)

LITTLE FALLS—See ILION, NY (Time Warner Cable)

LITTLE NECK—See NEW YORK, NY (Time Warner Cable)

LITTLE VALLEY (TOWN)—See SALAMANCA, NY (Atlantic Broadband)

LITTLE VALLEY (VILLAGE)—See SALAMANCA, NY (Atlantic Broadband)

LIVERPOOL—See SYRACUSE (suburbs), NY (Time Warner Cable)

LIVINGSTON (TOWN)—See CATSKILL, NY (Mid-Hudson Cablevision Inc.)

LIVINGSTON MANOR (TOWN)—See HUDSON VALLEY, NY (Time Warner Cable)

LIVONIA (VILLAGE)—See BATAVIA, NY (Time Warner Cable)

LLOYD HARBOR—See WOODBURY, NY (Cablevision Systems Corp.)

LLOYD—See OSSINING, NY (Cablevision Systems Corp.)

LOCKE TWP.—See MORAVIA, NY (Southern Cayuga County Cablevision)

LOCKPORT—See LACKAWANNA, NY (Time Warner Cable)

LOCUST VALLEY—See WOODBURY, NY (Cablevision Systems Corp.)

LODI (VILLAGE)—See GENEVA, NY (Time Warner Cable)

LONG BEACH—See WOODBURY, NY (Cablevision Systems Corp.)

▲**LONG ISLAND CITY**—RCN Corp. Formerly served by Queens, NY [NY0283]. This cable system has converted to IPTV

LONG ISLAND CITY—See NEW YORK, NY (Time Warner Cable)

▲**LONG LAKE**—Chain Lakes Cablevision

LOUISVILLE—See MASSENA, NY (Time Warner Cable)

LOWVILLE—See WATERTOWN, NY (Time Warner Cable)

LUMBERLAND—See HUDSON VALLEY, NY (Time Warner Cable)

LYME (TOWN)—See WATERTOWN, NY (Time Warner Cable)

▲**LYNBROOK**—Cablevision Systems Corp. Now served by WOODBURY/ISLIP, NY [NY0001]

LYNBROOK—See WOODBURY, NY (Cablevision Systems Corp.)

LYNDONVILLE—See BATAVIA, NY (Time Warner Cable)

LYONS (VILLAGE)—See GENEVA, NY (Time Warner Cable)

LYONS FALLS—See ROME, NY (Time Warner Cable)

LYONSDALE (TOWN)—See ROME, NY (Time Warner Cable)

LYONSDALE—See ROME, NY (Time Warner Cable)

LYSANDER (TOWN)—See SYRACUSE (suburbs), NY (Time Warner Cable)

MACEDON (VILLAGE)—See GENEVA, NY (Time Warner Cable)

MACHIAS (TOWN)—See OLEAN, NY (Time Warner Cable)

MADISON (VILLAGE)—See ROME, NY (Time Warner Cable)

MADISON—See ILION, NY (Time Warner Cable)

MADRID (TOWN)—See MASSENA, NY (Time Warner Cable)

MAHOPAC—See CARMEL, NY (Comcast Cable)

MAHWAH TWP.—See RAMAPO (town), NJ (Cablevision Systems Corp.)

MURRAY (TOWN)—See ROCHESTER, NY (Time Warner Cable)

MURRAY HILL—See NEW YORK, NY (Time Warner Cable)

MUTTONTOWN—See WOODBURY, NY (Cablevision Systems Corp.)

NANUET—See ROCKLAND, NY (Cablevision Systems Corp.)

NAPANOCH—See HUDSON VALLEY, NY (Time Warner Cable)

▲ **NAPLES**—Time Warner Cable. Now served by GENEVA, NY [NY0218]

NAPLES—See GENEVA, NY (Time Warner Cable)

NARROWSBURG—See HUDSON VALLEY, NY (Time Warner Cable)

NASSAU (VILLAGE)—See ALBANY, NY (Time Warner Cable)

NELLISTON (VILLAGE)—See ALBANY, NY (Time Warner Cable)

NELSON (TOWN)—See SYRACUSE (suburbs), NY (Time Warner Cable)

NELSON TWP.—See ELMIRA/CORNING, PA (Time Warner Cable)

NELSONVILLE—See OSSINING, NY (Cablevision Systems Corp.)

NESCONSET—See SUFFOLK COUNTY, NY (Cablevision Systems Corp.)

NEVERSINK (TOWN)—See HUDSON VALLEY, NY (Time Warner Cable)

NEW ALBION (TOWN)—See OLEAN, NY (Time Warner Cable)

NEW BALTIMORE—See CATSKILL, NY (Mid-Hudson Cablevision Inc.)

NEW BERLIN (VILLAGE)—See ONEONTA, NY (Time Warner Cable)

▲ **NEW BERLIN**—Time Warner Cable. Now served by ONEONTA, NY [NY0065]

NEW BREMEN—See WATERTOWN, NY (Time Warner Cable)

NEW CASTLE—See OSSINING, NY (Cablevision Systems Corp.)

NEW HARTFORD (VILLAGE)—See UTICA, NY (Time Warner Cable)

NEW HAVEN—See OSWEGO, NY (Time Warner Cable)

NEW HEMPSTEAD—See ROCKLAND, NY (Cablevision Systems Corp.)

NEW HYDE PARK—See WOODBURY, NY (Cablevision Systems Corp.)

NEW LEBANON (TOWN)—See CHATHAM, NY (Charter Communications)

NEW LISBON—See ROME, NY (Time Warner Cable)

NEW PALTZ (VILLAGE)—See HUDSON VALLEY, NY (Time Warner Cable)

▲ **NEW PALTZ**—Time Warner Cable. Now served by HUDSON VALLEY (formerly Middletown), NY [NY0231]

NEW ROCHELLE—See MAMARONECK, NY (Cablevision Systems Corp.)

NEW SCOTLAND—See ALBANY, NY (Time Warner Cable)

NEW WINDSOR—See HUDSON VALLEY, NY (Time Warner Cable)

NEW YORK MILLS (VILLAGE)—See UTICA, NY (Time Warner Cable)

▲ **NEW YORK**—Time Warner Cable

NEWARK (VILLAGE)—See GENEVA, NY (Time Warner Cable)

▲ **NEWARK VALLEY (town)**—Time Warner Binghamton. Now served by BINGHAMTON, NY [NY0016]

NEWARK VALLEY (TOWN)—See SPENCER, NY (Haefele TV Inc.)

NEWARK VALLEY (VILLAGE)—See BINGHAMTON, NY (Time Warner Cable)

▲ **NEWBURGH**—Time Warner Cable. Now served by HUDSON VALLEY (formerly Middletown), NY [NY0231]

NEWBURGH—See HUDSON VALLEY, NY (Time Warner Cable)

▲ **NEWCOMB**—Chain Lakes Cablevision

NEWFANE (TOWN)—See LACKAWANNA, NY (Time Warner Cable)

NEWFIELD—See ITHACA, NY (Time Warner Cable)

NEWPORT (VILLAGE)—See UTICA, NY (Time Warner Cable)

NEWSTEAD (TOWN)—See BATAVIA, NY (Time Warner Cable)

NIAGARA (TOWN)—See LACKAWANNA, NY (Time Warner Cable)

▲ **NIAGARA FALLS**—Now served by LACKAWANNA, NY [NY0216]

NIAGARA FALLS—See LACKAWANNA, NY (Time Warner Cable)

NISKAYUNA—See ALBANY, NY (Time Warner Cable)

NISSEQUOGUE—See SUFFOLK COUNTY, NY (Cablevision Systems Corp.)

NORFOLK—See MASSENA, NY (Time Warner Cable)

NORTH BRANCH—See HUDSON VALLEY, NY (Time Warner Cable)

NORTH CASTLE—See MAMARONECK, NY (Cablevision Systems Corp.)

NORTH CASTLE—See OSSINING, NY (Cablevision Systems Corp.)

NORTH CLYMER—See JAMESTOWN, NY (Time Warner Cable)

NORTH COLLINS (TOWN)—See OLEAN, NY (Time Warner Cable)

NORTH COLLINS (VILLAGE)—See OLEAN, NY (Time Warner Cable)

NORTH CREEK—See JOHNSBURG (town), NY (Hamilton County Cable TV Inc.)

NORTH DANSVILLE (TOWN)—See HORNELL, NY (Time Warner Cable)

NORTH EAST (TOWN)—See DOVER PLAINS, NY (Cablevision Systems Corp.)

NORTH ELBA—See SARANAC LAKE, NY (Time Warner Cable)

NORTH GREENBUSH—See ALBANY, NY (Time Warner Cable)

NORTH HARMONY (TOWN)—See DUNKIRK, NY (Time Warner Cable)

NORTH HARMONY (TOWN)—See JAMESTOWN, NY (Time Warner Cable)

NORTH HAVEN—See RIVERHEAD, NY (Cablevision Systems Corp.)

NORTH HEMPSTEAD—See WOODBURY, NY (Cablevision Systems Corp.)

NORTH HILLS (VILLAGE)—See WOODBURY, NY (Cablevision Systems Corp.)

NORTH HOOSICK—See ALBANY, NY (Time Warner Cable)

NORTH NORWICH—See ONEONTA, NY (Time Warner Cable)

NORTH PITCHER—See CORTLAND, NY (Time Warner Cable)

▲ **NORTH SALEM**—Cablevision Systems Corp. Now served by YORKTOWN, NY [NY0050]

NORTH SALEM—See YORKTOWN, NY (Cablevision Systems Corp.)

NORTH SEA—See RIVERHEAD, NY (Cablevision Systems Corp.)

NORTH SYRACUSE—See SYRACUSE (suburbs), NY (Time Warner Cable)

NORTH TARRYTOWN—See OSSINING, NY (Cablevision Systems Corp.)

NORTH TONAWANDA—See LACKAWANNA, NY (Time Warner Cable)

NORTH WOODMERE—See WOODBURY, NY (Cablevision Systems Corp.)

NORTHAMPTON—See RIVERHEAD, NY (Cablevision Systems Corp.)

NORTHPORT—See WOODBURY, NY (Cablevision Systems Corp.)

NORTHUMBERLAND (TOWN)—See ALBANY, NY (Time Warner Cable)

▲ **NORTHVILLE**—Formerly served by Adelphia Communications. Now served by ALBANY, NY [NY0014]

NORTHVILLE—See ALBANY, NY (Time Warner Cable)

▲ **NORWICH**—Time Warner Cable. Now served by ONEONTA, NY [NY0065]

NORWICH—See ONEONTA, NY (Time Warner Cable)

NORWOOD—See MASSENA, NY (Time Warner Cable)

NOYAC—See RIVERHEAD, NY (Cablevision Systems Corp.)

NUNDA (VILLAGE)—See BATAVIA, NY (Time Warner Cable)

NYACK—See ROCKLAND, NY (Cablevision Systems Corp.)

OAK HILL—See DURHAM, NY (Mid-Hudson Cablevision Inc.)

OAKFIELD (VILLAGE)—See BATAVIA, NY (Time Warner Cable)

OAKLAND GARDENS—See NEW YORK, NY (Time Warner Cable)

OCEANSIDE—See WOODBURY, NY (Cablevision Systems Corp.)

ODESSA (VILLAGE)—See GENEVA, NY (Time Warner Cable)

OGDEN (TOWN)—See ROCHESTER, NY (Time Warner Cable)

▲ **OGDENSBURG**—Time Warner Cable. Now served by MASSENA, NY [NY0072]

OGDENSBURG—See MASSENA, NY (Time Warner Cable)

OLD BETHPAGE—See WOODBURY, NY (Cablevision Systems Corp.)

OLD BROOKVILLE—See WOODBURY, NY (Cablevision Systems Corp.)

OLD FIELD—See SUFFOLK COUNTY, NY (Cablevision Systems Corp.)

▲ **OLD FORGE**—Formerly served by Adelphia Communications. Now served by UTICA, NY [NY0022]

OLD FORGE—See UTICA, NY (Time Warner Cable)

OLD WESTBURY—See WOODBURY, NY (Cablevision Systems Corp.)

OLEAN (TOWN)—See OLEAN, NY (Time Warner Cable)

▲ **OLEAN**—Time Warner Cable

▲ **OLIVE**—Time Warner Cable. Now served by HUDSON VALLEY (formerly Middletown), NY [NY0231]

OLIVE—See HUDSON VALLEY, NY (Time Warner Cable)

OLIVEBRIDGE—See HUDSON VALLEY, NY (Time Warner Cable)

OLIVEREA—See HUDSON VALLEY, NY (Time Warner Cable)

ONEIDA CASTLE (VILLAGE)—See ROME, NY (Time Warner Cable)

▲ **ONEIDA**—Time Warner Cable. Now served by ROME, NY [NY0037]

ONEIDA—See ROME, NY (Time Warner Cable)

▲ **ONEONTA**—Time Warner Cable

ONONDAGA—See SYRACUSE (suburbs), NY (Time Warner Cable)

ONTARIO (TOWN)—See GENEVA, NY (Time Warner Cable)

ORANGE (TOWN)—See ENFIELD, NY (Haefele TV Inc.)

ORANGETOWN (TOWN)—See ROCKLAND, NY (Cablevision Systems Corp.)

ORANGEVILLE (TOWN)—See BATAVIA, NY (Time Warner Cable)

ORCHARD PARK (VILLAGE)—See LACKAWANNA, NY (Time Warner Cable)

ORIENT POINT—See RIVERHEAD, NY (Cablevision Systems Corp.)

ORIENT—See RIVERHEAD, NY (Cablevision Systems Corp.)

ORISKANY FALLS—See ROME, NY (Time Warner Cable)

ORISKANY—See UTICA, NY (Time Warner Cable)

ORLEANS—See WATERTOWN, NY (Time Warner Cable)

ORWELL (TOWN)—See SYRACUSE (suburbs), NY (Time Warner Cable)

OSCEOLA—See ELMIRA/CORNING, PA (Time Warner Cable)

▲ **OSSINING**—Cablevision Systems Corp.

OSWEGATCHIE—See MASSENA, NY (Time Warner Cable)

▲ **OSWEGO**—Time Warner Cable

OTEGO (VILLAGE)—See ONEONTA, NY (Time Warner Cable)

OTISCO (TOWN)—See SYRACUSE (suburbs), NY (Time Warner Cable)

OTISVILLE (VILLAGE)—See HUDSON VALLEY, NY (Time Warner Cable)

OTSEGO—See ONEONTA, NY (Time Warner Cable)

OTSELIC (TOWN)—See CORTLAND, NY (Time Warner Cable)

▲ **OTSELIC**—Chain Lakes Cable. Now served by CORTLAND, NY [NY0062]

OVID (TOWN)—See GENEVA, NY (Time Warner Cable)

OVID (VILLAGE)—See GENEVA, NY (Time Warner Cable)

OWASCO—See AUBURN, NY (Time Warner Cable)

▲ **OWEGO (village)**—Time Warner Cable. Now served by BINGHAMTON, NY [NY0016]

OWEGO (VILLAGE)—See BINGHAMTON, NY (Time Warner Cable)

▲ **OXFORD (town)**—Time Warner Cable. Now served by ONEONTA, NY [NY0065]

OXFORD (VILLAGE)—See ONEONTA, NY (Time Warner Cable)

OYSTER BAY COVE—See WOODBURY, NY (Cablevision Systems Corp.)

OYSTER BAY—See WOODBURY, NY (Cablevision Systems Corp.)

OZONE PARK—See NEW YORK, NY (Time Warner Cable)

PALATINE (TOWN)—See ALBANY, NY (Time Warner Cable)

PALATINE BRIDGE (TOWN)—See ALBANY, NY (Time Warner Cable)

PALENVILLE—See HUDSON VALLEY, NY (Time Warner Cable)

PALERMO—See OSWEGO, NY (Time Warner Cable)

PALMYRA (TOWN)—See GENEVA, NY (Time Warner Cable)

PALMYRA (VILLAGE)—See GENEVA, NY (Time Warner Cable)

PAMELIA (TOWN)—See WATERTOWN, NY (Time Warner Cable)

PANAMA (VILLAGE)—See JAMESTOWN, NY (Time Warner Cable)

PARIS (TOWN)—See UTICA, NY (Time Warner Cable)

PARISH (VILLAGE)—See OSWEGO, NY (Time Warner Cable)

PARISHVILLE—See MASSENA, NY (Time Warner Cable)

PARK SLOPE—See NEW YORK, NY (Time Warner Cable)

PARMA—See ROCHESTER, NY (Time Warner Cable)

PATCHOGUE (VILLAGE)—See SUFFOLK COUNTY, NY (Cablevision Systems Corp.)

PATTERSON—See CARMEL, NY (Comcast Cable)

PAWLING (VILLAGE)—See CARMEL, NY (Comcast Cable)

PECONIC—See RIVERHEAD, NY (Cablevision Systems Corp.)

PEEKSKILL—See OSSINING, NY (Cablevision Systems Corp.)

PELHAM MANOR—See MAMARONECK, NY (Cablevision Systems Corp.)

PELHAM—See MAMARONECK, NY (Cablevision Systems Corp.)

PEMBROKE (TOWN)—See BATAVIA, NY (Time Warner Cable)

PENDLETON—See LACKAWANNA, NY (Time Warner Cable)

PENFIELD—See ROCHESTER, NY (Time Warner Cable)

▲ **PENN YAN**—Time Warner Cable. Now served by GENEVA, NY [NY0218]

PENN YAN—See GENEVA, NY (Time Warner Cable)

PENNELLVILLE—See SYRACUSE (suburbs), NY (Time Warner Cable)

PERINTON—See ROCHESTER, NY (Time Warner Cable)

PERKINSVILLE—See HORNELL, NY (Time Warner Cable)

PERRY (VILLAGE)—See BATAVIA, NY (Time Warner Cable)

PERRYSBURG (TOWN)—See OLEAN, NY (Time Warner Cable)

PERRYSBURG (VILLAGE)—See OLEAN, NY (Time Warner Cable)

PERSIA (TOWN)—See OLEAN, NY (Time Warner Cable)

PERTH—See ALBANY, NY (Time Warner Cable)

PERU (TOWN)—See PLATTSBURGH, NY (Charter Communications)

▲ **PETERBORO**—Chain Lakes Cablevision. Now served by ROME, NY [NY0037]

PETERBORO—See ROME, NY (Time Warner Cable)

PETERSBURG—See BERLIN (town), NY (Charter Communications)

PETERSBURGH (TOWN)—See BERLIN (town), NY (Charter Communications)

PHELPS (TOWN)—See GENEVA, NY (Time Warner Cable)

PHELPS (VILLAGE)—See GENEVA, NY (Time Warner Cable)

PHILADELPHIA (VILLAGE)—See WATERTOWN, NY (Time Warner Cable)

PHILIPSTOWN—See OSSINING, NY (Cablevision Systems Corp.)

PHILMONT—See CATSKILL, NY (Mid-Hudson Cablevision Inc.)

▲ **PHOENICIA**—Time Warner Cable. Now served by HUDSON VALLEY (formerly Middletown), NY [NY0231]

PHOENICIA—See HUDSON VALLEY, NY (Time Warner Cable)

PHOENIX—See SYRACUSE (suburbs), NY (Time Warner Cable)

PIERMONT—See ROCKLAND, NY (Cablevision Systems Corp.)

PIERREPONT MANOR—See WATERTOWN, NY (Time Warner Cable)

PIERREPONT—See MASSENA, NY (Time Warner Cable)

▲ **PINE HILL**—Time Warner Cable. Now served by HUDSON VALLEY (formerly Middletown), NY [NY0231]

PINE HILL—See HUDSON VALLEY, NY (Time Warner Cable)

PINE NECK—See RIVERHEAD, NY (Cablevision Systems Corp.)

PINE PLAINS (TOWN)—See DOVER PLAINS, NY (Cablevision Systems Corp.)

PITCAIRN (TOWN)—See WATERTOWN, NY (Time Warner Cable)

PITCHER (TOWN)—See CORTLAND, NY (Time Warner Cable)

PITTSFIELD—See ONEONTA, NY (Time Warner Cable)

PITTSFORD (VILLAGE)—See ROCHESTER, NY (Time Warner Cable)

PITTSTOWN (TOWN)—See ALBANY, NY (Time Warner Cable)

PLAINEDGE—See WOODBURY, NY (Cablevision Systems Corp.)

PLAINFIELD—See ILION, NY (Time Warner Cable)

PLAINVIEW—See WOODBURY, NY (Cablevision Systems Corp.)

PLANDOME (VILLAGE)—See WOODBURY, NY (Cablevision Systems Corp.)

PLANDOME HEIGHTS (VILLAGE)—See WOODBURY, NY (Cablevision Systems Corp.)

PLANDOME MANOR—See WOODBURY, NY (Cablevision Systems Corp.)

PLATTEKILL—See OSSINING, NY (Cablevision Systems Corp.)

▲ **PLATTSBURGH**—Charter Communications

PLEASANT VALLEY (PORTIONS)—See HUDSON VALLEY, NY (Time Warner Cable)

PLEASANTVILLE—See OSSINING, NY (Cablevision Systems Corp.)

PLESSIS—See ALEXANDRIA BAY, NY (Cass Cable TV Inc.)

PLYMOUTH (TOWN)—See ONEONTA, NY (Time Warner Cable)

POESTENKILL—See ALBANY, NY (Time Warner Cable)

POLAND—See UTICA, NY (Time Warner Cable)

POMFRET (TOWN)—See JAMESTOWN, NY (Time Warner Cable)

POMFRET—See DUNKIRK, NY (Time Warner Cable)

POMONA—See OSSINING, NY (Cablevision Systems Corp.)

POMONOK—See NEW YORK, NY (Time Warner Cable)

POMPEY—See SYRACUSE (suburbs), NY (Time Warner Cable)

POND EDDY—See HUDSON VALLEY, NY (Time Warner Cable)

POQUOTT (VILLAGE)—See SUFFOLK COUNTY, NY (Cablevision Systems Corp.)

PORT BYRON—See SYRACUSE (suburbs), NY (Time Warner Cable)

▲ **PORT CHESTER**—Cablevision Systems Corp.

▲ **PORT HENRY (VILLAGE)**—Time Warner Cable

PORT JEFFERSON STATION—See SUFFOLK COUNTY, NY (Cablevision Systems Corp.)

PORT JEFFERSON—See SUFFOLK COUNTY, NY (Cablevision Systems Corp.)

▲ **PORT JERVIS**—Time Warner Cable. Now served by HUDSON VALLEY (formerly Middletown), NY [NY0231]

PORT JERVIS—See HUDSON VALLEY, NY (Time Warner Cable)

PORT LEYDEN—See ROME, NY (Time Warner Cable)

PORT WASHINGTON—See WOODBURY, NY (Cablevision Systems Corp.)

PORTAGE—See BATAVIA, NY (Time Warner Cable)

PORTER—See LACKAWANNA, NY (Time Warner Cable)

PORTLAND (PORTIONS)—See JAMESTOWN, NY (Time Warner Cable)

PORTLAND—See DUNKIRK, NY (Time Warner Cable)

PORTVILLE (TOWN)—See OLEAN, NY (Time Warner Cable)

PORTVILLE (VILLAGE)—See OLEAN, NY (Time Warner Cable)

POTSDAM (VILLAGE)—See MASSENA, NY (Time Warner Cable)

▲**POTSDAM**—Time Warner Cable. Now served by MASSENA, NY [NY0072]

▲**POUGHKEEPSIE**—Time Warner Cable. Now served by HUDSON VALLEY (formerly Middletown), NY [NY0231]

POUGHKEEPSIE—See OSSINING, NY (Cablevision Systems Corp.)

POUGHKEEPSIE—See HUDSON VALLEY, NY (Time Warner Cable)

POUND RIDGE—See YORKTOWN, NY (Cablevision Systems Corp.)

PRATTSBURGH (TOWN)—See GENEVA, NY (Time Warner Cable)

PRATTSVILLE (TOWN)—See CATSKILL, NY (Mid-Hudson Cablevision Inc.)

PREBLE (TOWN)—See CORTLAND, NY (Time Warner Cable)

PRESHO—See ELMIRA/CORNING, NY (Time Warner Cable)

PRESTON HOLLOW—See DURHAM, NY (Mid-Hudson Cablevision Inc.)

▲**PRINCETOWN (TOWN)**—Princetown Cable Co.

PRINCETOWN—See PRINCETOWN (town), NY (Princetown Cable Co.)

PROSPECT (VILLAGE)—See UTICA, NY (Time Warner Cable)

PULASKI—See OSWEGO, NY (Time Warner Cable)

PULTENEY—See GENEVA, NY (Time Warner Cable)

PURCHASE—See PORT CHESTER, NY (Cablevision Systems Corp.)

PUTNAM VALLEY (TOWN)—See CARMEL, NY (Comcast Cable)

PUTNAM VALLEY—See YORKTOWN, NY (Cablevision Systems Corp.)

PUTNAM—See PORT HENRY (village), NY (Time Warner Cable)

QUEENS VILLAGE—See NEW YORK, NY (Time Warner Cable)

▲**QUEENS**—RCN Corp. This cable system has converted to IPTV. See Queens, NY [NY5321]

▲**QUEENS**—RCN Corp. Formerly [NY0283]. This cable system has converted to IPTV

QUEENS—See NEW YORK, NY (Time Warner Cable)

▲**QUEENSBURY**—Formerly served by Adelphia Communications. No longer in operation

QUOGUE—See RIVERHEAD, NY (Cablevision Systems Corp.)

▲**RAMAPO (TOWN)**—Cablevision Systems Corp.

RAMAPO (TOWN)—See ROCKLAND, NY (Cablevision Systems Corp.)

RAMAPO CORRIDOR—See ROCKLAND, NY (Cablevision Systems Corp.)

RANDOLPH (TOWN)—See OLEAN, NY (Time Warner Cable)

RANDOLPH (VILLAGE)—See OLEAN, NY (Time Warner Cable)

RANSOMVILLE—See LACKAWANNA, NY (Time Warner Cable)

RAVENA (VILLAGE)—See CATSKILL, NY (Mid-Hudson Cablevision Inc.)

READING (TOWN)—See GENEVA, NY (Time Warner Cable)

READING—See ENFIELD, NY (Haefele TV Inc.)

RED CREEK (VILLAGE)—See GENEVA, NY (Time Warner Cable)

RED HOOK (VILLAGE)—See HUDSON VALLEY, NY (Time Warner Cable)

REDWOOD—See ALEXANDRIA BAY, NY (Cass Cable TV Inc.)

▲**REGO PARK**—RCN Corp. Formerly served by Queens, NY [NY0283]. This cable system has converted to IPTV

REGO PARK—See NEW YORK, NY (Time Warner Cable)

REMSEN (VILLAGE)—See UTICA, NY (Time Warner Cable)

REMSENBURG—See RIVERHEAD, NY (Cablevision Systems Corp.)

RENSSELAER FALLS—See MASSENA, NY (Time Warner Cable)

▲**RENSSELAER**—Time Warner Cable. Now served by ALBANY, NY [NY0014]

RENSSELAER—See ALBANY, NY (Time Warner Cable)

RENSSELAERVILLE—See DURHAM, NY (Mid-Hudson Cablevision Inc.)

▲**RHINEBECK (town)**—Time Warner Cable. Now served by HUDSON VALLEY (formerly Middletown), NY [NY0231]

RHINEBECK (VILLAGE)—See HUDSON VALLEY, NY (Time Warner Cable)

RHINECLIFF—See HUDSON VALLEY, NY (Time Warner Cable)

RICHFIELD SPRINGS—See ONEONTA, NY (Time Warner Cable)

RICHFIELD—See ONEONTA, NY (Time Warner Cable)

RICHFORD (TOWN)—See SPENCER, NY (Haefele TV Inc.)

RICHLAND (TOWN)—See OSWEGO, NY (Time Warner Cable)

RICHMOND HILL—See NEW YORK, NY (Time Warner Cable)

RICHMOND—See ROCHESTER, NY (Time Warner Cable)

RICHMONDVILLE (VILLAGE)—See ALBANY, NY (Time Warner Cable)

RICHVILLE (VILLAGE)—See MASSENA, NY (Time Warner Cable)

RIDGEWAY (TOWN)—See BATAVIA, NY (Time Warner Cable)

RIDGEWOOD—See NEW YORK, NY (Time Warner Cable)

RIGA (TOWN)—See BATAVIA, NY (Time Warner Cable)

RIGA (TOWN)—See ROCHESTER, NY (Time Warner Cable)

RIPLEY—See DUNKIRK, NY (Time Warner Cable)

▲**RIVERHEAD**—Cablevision Systems Corp.

▲**ROCHESTER**—Time Warner Cable

ROCKAWAY BEACH—See NEW YORK, NY (Time Warner Cable)

ROCKAWAY PARK—See NEW YORK, NY (Time Warner Cable)

ROCKAWAY POINT—See NEW YORK, NY (Time Warner Cable)

ROCKDALE—See ONEONTA, NY (Time Warner Cable)

ROCKLAND (TOWN)—See HUDSON VALLEY, NY (Time Warner Cable)

ROCKLAND COUNTY (UNINCORPORATED AREAS)—See ROCKLAND, NY (Cablevision Systems Corp.)

▲**ROCKLAND**—Cablevision Systems Corp.

ROCKVILLE CENTRE—See WOODBURY, NY (Cablevision Systems Corp.)

RODMAN (TOWN)—See WATERTOWN, NY (Time Warner Cable)

▲**ROME**—Time Warner Cable

ROMULUS (TOWN)—See GENEVA, NY (Time Warner Cable)

ROOSEVELT ISLAND—See NEW YORK, NY (Time Warner Cable)

ROOSEVELT—See WOODBURY, NY (Cablevision Systems Corp.)

ROOT (TOWN)—See ALBANY, NY (Time Warner Cable)

ROSE (TOWN)—See GENEVA, NY (Time Warner Cable)

ROSEDALE—See NEW YORK, NY (Time Warner Cable)

▲**ROSENDALE**—Time Warner Cable. Now served by HUDSON VALLEY (formerly Middletown), NY [NY0231]

ROSENDALE—See HUDSON VALLEY, NY (Time Warner Cable)

ROSLYN ESTATES—See WOODBURY, NY (Cablevision Systems Corp.)

ROSLYN HARBOR (VILLAGE)—See WOODBURY, NY (Cablevision Systems Corp.)

ROSLYN—See WOODBURY, NY (Cablevision Systems Corp.)

ROTTERDAM (PORTIONS)—See PRINCETOWN (town), NY (Princetown Cable Co.)

ROTTERDAM—See ALBANY, NY (Time Warner Cable)

ROUND LAKE—See ALBANY, NY (Time Warner Cable)

ROUND TOP—See HUDSON VALLEY, NY (Time Warner Cable)

ROUSES POINT—See CHAMPLAIN, NY (Time Warner Cable)

ROXBURY—See HUDSON VALLEY, NY (Time Warner Cable)

ROYALTON (TOWN)—See BATAVIA, NY (Time Warner Cable)

RUSH (TOWN)—See BATAVIA, NY (Time Warner Cable)

RUSHFORD—See LIMESTONE, NY (Atlantic Broadband)

RUSHVILLE—See GENEVA, NY (Time Warner Cable)

RUSSELL (TOWN)—See MASSENA, NY (Time Warner Cable)

RUSSELL GARDENS (VILLAGE)—See WOODBURY, NY (Cablevision Systems Corp.)

RUSSIA (TOWN)—See UTICA, NY (Time Warner Cable)

RUTLAND (TOWN)—See WATERTOWN, NY (Time Warner Cable)

RYE (CITY)—See MAMARONECK, NY (Cablevision Systems Corp.)

RYE BROOK (VILLAGE)—See MAMARONECK, NY (Cablevision Systems Corp.)

SACKETS HARBOR (VILLAGE)—See WATERTOWN, NY (Time Warner Cable)

SADDLE ROCK (VILLAGE)—See WOODBURY, NY (Cablevision Systems Corp.)

SAG HARBOR—See RIVERHEAD, NY (Cablevision Systems Corp.)

SAGAPONACK—See RIVERHEAD, NY (Cablevision Systems Corp.)

SALAMANCA (TOWN)—See SALAMANCA, NY (Atlantic Broadband)

▲**SALAMANCA**—Atlantic Broadband

SALEM (VILLAGE)—See ALBANY, NY (Time Warner Cable)

SALINA—See SYRACUSE (suburbs), NY (Time Warner Cable)

SALISBURY (TOWN)—See ILION, NY (Time Warner Cable)

SAN REMO—See SUFFOLK COUNTY, NY (Cablevision Systems Corp.)

SANBORN—See LACKAWANNA, NY (Time Warner Cable)

SAND LAKE—See ALBANY, NY (Time Warner Cable)

SANDS POINT—See WOODBURY, NY (Cablevision Systems Corp.)

SANDUSKY (TOWN)—See OLEAN, NY (Time Warner Cable)

SANDY CREEK (VILLAGE)—See OSWEGO, NY (Time Warner Cable)

SANDY CREEK—See OSWEGO, NY (Time Warner Cable)

SANDYSTON TWP.—See WARWICK, NJ (Cablevision Systems Corp.)

SANGERFIELD—See ROME, NY (Time Warner Cable)

SARANAC (TOWN)—See PLATTSBURGH, NY (Charter Communications)

▲ **SARANAC LAKE**—Time Warner Cable

SARATOGA (TOWN)—See ALBANY, NY (Time Warner Cable)

▲ **SARATOGA SPRINGS**—Time Warner Cable. Now served by ALBANY, NY [NY0014]

SARATOGA SPRINGS—See ALBANY, NY (Time Warner Cable)

SARDINIA (TOWN)—See OLEAN, NY (Time Warner Cable)

▲ **SAUGERTIES (town)**—Time Warner Cable. Now served by HUDSON VALLEY (formerly Middletown), NY [NY0231]

SAUGERTIES (VILLAGE)—See HUDSON VALLEY, NY (Time Warner Cable)

SAVANNAH (TOWN)—See GENEVA, NY (Time Warner Cable)

SCARSDALE—See MAMARONECK, NY (Cablevision Systems Corp.)

SCHAGTICOKE (VILLAGE)—See ALBANY, NY (Time Warner Cable)

▲ **SCHENECTADY**—Time Warner Cable. Now served by ALBANY, NY [NY0014]

SCHENECTADY—See ALBANY, NY (Time Warner Cable)

SCHENEVUS—See ONEONTA, NY (Time Warner Cable)

SCHODACK—See ALBANY, NY (Time Warner Cable)

SCHOHARIE (VILLAGE)—See ALBANY, NY (Time Warner Cable)

▲ **SCHROEPPEL**—Time Warner Cable. Now served by SYRACUSE, NY [NY0013]

SCHROEPPEL—See SYRACUSE (suburbs), NY (Time Warner Cable)

▲ **SCHROON (town)**—Time Warner Cable. Now served by PORT HENRY (village), NY [NY0123]

SCHROON LAKE—See PORT HENRY (village), NY (Time Warner Cable)

SCHROON—See PORT HENRY (village), NY (Time Warner Cable)

SCHUYLER FALLS (TOWN)—See PLATTSBURGH, NY (Charter Communications)

SCHUYLER—See UTICA, NY (Time Warner Cable)

SCHUYLERVILLE—See ALBANY, NY (Time Warner Cable)

SCIO—See OLEAN, NY (Time Warner Cable)

SCIOTA—See CHAMPLAIN, NY (Time Warner Cable)

SCOTIA—See ALBANY, NY (Time Warner Cable)

SCOTT (TOWN)—See CORTLAND, NY (Time Warner Cable)

SCOTTSVILLE (VILLAGE)—See BATAVIA, NY (Time Warner Cable)

SCRIBA—See OSWEGO, NY (Time Warner Cable)

SEA CLIFF—See WOODBURY, NY (Cablevision Systems Corp.)

SEAFORD—See WOODBURY, NY (Cablevision Systems Corp.)

SELDEN—See SUFFOLK COUNTY, NY (Cablevision Systems Corp.)

SENECA (TOWN)—See GENEVA, NY (Time Warner Cable)

SENECA COUNTY (SOUTHERN PORTION)—See GENEVA, NY (Time Warner Cable)

SENECA FALLS (VILLAGE)—See GENEVA, NY (Time Warner Cable)

SENNETT—See AUBURN, NY (Time Warner Cable)

SETAUKET—See SUFFOLK COUNTY, NY (Cablevision Systems Corp.)

SEWARD—See ALBANY, NY (Time Warner Cable)

SHANDAKEN—See HUDSON VALLEY, NY (Time Warner Cable)

SHARON SPRINGS—See ALBANY, NY (Time Warner Cable)

SHARON—See ALBANY, NY (Time Warner Cable)

SHAWANGUNK (TOWN)—See HUDSON VALLEY, NY (Time Warner Cable)

SHELBY (TOWN)—See BATAVIA, NY (Time Warner Cable)

SHELDON (TOWN)—See BATAVIA, NY (Time Warner Cable)

SHELTER ISLAND—See RIVERHEAD, NY (Cablevision Systems Corp.)

SHERBURNE (VILLAGE)—See ILION, NY (Time Warner Cable)

SHERIDAN (TOWN)—See DUNKIRK, NY (Time Warner Cable)

SHERMAN—See DUNKIRK, NY (Time Warner Cable)

SHERRILL (VILLAGE)—See ROME, NY (Time Warner Cable)

SHIRLEY—See SUFFOLK COUNTY, NY (Cablevision Systems Corp.)

SHOKAN—See HUDSON VALLEY, NY (Time Warner Cable)

SHORTSVILLE (VILLAGE)—See GENEVA, NY (Time Warner Cable)

▲ **SIDNEY**—Time Warner Cable. Now served by ONEONTA, NY [NY0065]

SIDNEY—See ONEONTA, NY (Time Warner Cable)

▲ **SILVER CREEK**—Time Warner Cable. Now served by DUNKIRK, NY [NY0064]

SILVER CREEK—See DUNKIRK, NY (Time Warner Cable)

SILVER SPRINGS—See BATAVIA, NY (Time Warner Cable)

SINCLAIRVILLE (VILLAGE)—See JAMESTOWN, NY (Time Warner Cable)

SKANEATELES (VILLAGE)—See AUBURN, NY (Time Warner Cable)

SLOAN—See LACKAWANNA, NY (Time Warner Cable)

SLOATSBURG—See RAMAPO (town), NY (Cablevision Systems Corp.)

SMITHBORO—See SPENCER, NY (Haefele TV Inc.)

SMITHFIELD (TOWN)—See ROME, NY (Time Warner Cable)

SMITHTOWN—See SUFFOLK COUNTY, NY (Cablevision Systems Corp.)

SMITHVILLE FLATS—See SMITHVILLE, NY (Haefele TV Inc.)

▲ **SMITHVILLE**—Haefele TV Inc.

SMYRNA—See ILION, NY (Time Warner Cable)

SODUS (TOWN)—See GENEVA, NY (Time Warner Cable)

SODUS (VILLAGE)—See GENEVA, NY (Time Warner Cable)

SODUS POINT (VILLAGE)—See GENEVA, NY (Time Warner Cable)

SOLVAY—See SYRACUSE (suburbs), NY (Time Warner Cable)

SOMERS (TOWN)—See CARMEL, NY (Comcast Cable)

SOMERS—See YORKTOWN, NY (Cablevision Systems Corp.)

SOMERSET—See LACKAWANNA, NY (Time Warner Cable)

SOUTH BRISTOL (TOWN)—See GENEVA, NY (Time Warner Cable)

SOUTH DAYTON (VILLAGE)—See JAMESTOWN, NY (Time Warner Cable)

SOUTH FLORAL PARK—See WOODBURY, NY (Cablevision Systems Corp.)

SOUTH GLENS FALLS (VILLAGE)—See ALBANY, NY (Time Warner Cable)

SOUTH JAMESPORT—See RIVERHEAD, NY (Cablevision Systems Corp.)

SOUTH NYACK—See ROCKLAND, NY (Cablevision Systems Corp.)

SOUTHAMPTON (VILLAGE)—See RIVERHEAD, NY (Cablevision Systems Corp.)

SOUTHAMPTON—See RIVERHEAD, NY (Cablevision Systems Corp.)

SOUTHEAST (TOWN)—See CARMEL, NY (Comcast Cable)

SOUTHFIELDS—See RAMAPO (town), NY (Cablevision Systems Corp.)

SOUTHOLD—See RIVERHEAD, NY (Cablevision Systems Corp.)

SPAFFORD—See AUBURN, NY (Time Warner Cable)

SPARTA (TOWN)—See HORNELL, NY (Time Warner Cable)

SPECULATOR—See WELLS, NY (Hamilton County Cable TV Inc.)

SPENCER (TOWN)—See SPENCER, NY (Haefele TV Inc.)

▲ **SPENCER**—Haefele TV Inc.

SPENCERPORT—See ROCHESTER, NY (Time Warner Cable)

SPRING VALLEY—See ROCKLAND, NY (Cablevision Systems Corp.)

SPRINGFIELD GARDENS—See NEW YORK, NY (Time Warner Cable)

SPRINGFIELD—See ONEONTA, NY (Time Warner Cable)

SPRINGPORT—See GENEVA, NY (Time Warner Cable)

SPRINGS—See RIVERHEAD, NY (Cablevision Systems Corp.)

▲ **SPRINGVILLE (village)**—Now served by OLEAN, NY [NY0056]

SPRINGVILLE (VILLAGE)—See OLEAN, NY (Time Warner Cable)

SPRINGWATER—See HORNELL, NY (Time Warner Cable)

ST. ARMAND—See SARANAC LAKE, NY (Time Warner Cable)

ST. JAMES—See SUFFOLK COUNTY, NY (Cablevision Systems Corp.)

ST. JOHNSVILLE (VILLAGE)—See ALBANY, NY (Time Warner Cable)

STAFFORD—See BATAVIA, NY (Time Warner Cable)

▲ **STAMFORD**—Time Warner Cable. Now served by ONEONTA, NY [NY0065]

STAMFORD—See ONEONTA, NY (Time Warner Cable)

STANFORD (TOWN)—See DOVER PLAINS, NY (Cablevision Systems Corp.)

STARKEY (TOWN)—See ELMIRA/CORNING, NY (Time Warner Cable)

▲ **STATEN ISLAND**—Time Warner Cable

STERLING—See OSWEGO, NY (Time Warner Cable)

STEWART MANOR—See WOODBURY, NY (Cablevision Systems Corp.)

STILLWATER (VILLAGE)—See ALBANY, NY (Time Warner Cable)

STOCKBRIDGE (TOWN)—See ROME, NY (Time Warner Cable)

STOCKHOLM—See MASSENA, NY (Time Warner Cable)

STOCKPORT (TOWN)—See CATSKILL, NY (Mid-Hudson Cablevision Inc.)

STOCKPORT—See CATSKILL, NY (Mid-Hudson Cablevision Inc.)

STOCKTON (TOWN)—See JAMESTOWN, NY (Time Warner Cable)

STONE RIDGE—See HUDSON VALLEY, NY (Time Warner Cable)

STONY BROOK—See SUFFOLK COUNTY, NY (Cablevision Systems Corp.)

STONY POINT—See OSSINING, NY (Cablevision Systems Corp.)

STOTTVILLE—See CATSKILL, NY (Mid-Hudson Cablevision Inc.)

STUYVESANT—See ALBANY, NY (Time Warner Cable)

SUFFERN—See RAMAPO (town), NY (Cablevision Systems Corp.)

▲ **SUFFOLK COUNTY**—Cablevision Systems Corp.

SUGAR LOAF—See WARWICK, NY (Cablevision Systems Corp.)

▲ **SULLIVAN (town)**—Time Warner Cable. Now served by ROME, NY [NY0037]

SULLIVAN (TOWN)—See ROME, NY (Time Warner Cable)

SULLIVAN COUNTY (PORTIONS)—See HUDSON VALLEY, NY (Time Warner Cable)

▲ **SULLIVAN COUNTY**—Time Warner Cable. Now served by HUDSON VALLEY (formerly Middletown), NY [NY0231]

▲ **SUMMIT (TOWN)**—Chain Lakes Cablevision

SUNSET PARK—See NEW YORK, NY (Time Warner Cable)

SWEDEN (TOWN)—See ROCHESTER, NY (Time Warner Cable)

SYLVAN BEACH—See ROME, NY (Time Warner Cable)

SYOSSET—See WOODBURY, NY (Cablevision Systems Corp.)

▲ **SYRACUSE (SUBURBS)**—Time Warner Cable

▲ **SYRACUSE**—Time Warner Cable

TANNERSVILLE—See HUDSON VALLEY, NY (Time Warner Cable)

TARRYTOWN—See OSSINING, NY (Cablevision Systems Corp.)

TAYLOR (TOWN)—See CORTLAND, NY (Time Warner Cable)

THENDARA—See UTICA, NY (Time Warner Cable)

THERESA (TOWN)—See ALEXANDRIA BAY, NY (Cass Cable TV Inc.)

THERESA (VILLAGE)—See WATERTOWN, NY (Time Warner Cable)

THOMASTON (VILLAGE)—See WOODBURY, NY (Cablevision Systems Corp.)

THOMPSON (TOWN)—See HUDSON VALLEY, NY (Time Warner Cable)

THROOP—See AUBURN, NY (Time Warner Cable)

TIANA—See RIVERHEAD, NY (Cablevision Systems Corp.)

TICONDEROGA (TOWN)—See PORT HENRY (village), NY (Time Warner Cable)

TILLSON—See HUDSON VALLEY, NY (Time Warner Cable)

TIOGA—See SPENCER, NY (Haefele TV Inc.)

TIOGA—See ELMIRA/CORNING, PA (Time Warner Cable)

TIVOLI (VILLAGE)—See HUDSON VALLEY, NY (Time Warner Cable)

TOMPKINS (TOWN)—See HANCOCK, NY (Hancock Video)

▲ **TOMPKINS COUNTY**—Time Warner Cable. Now served by ITHACA, NY [NY0028]

TOMPKINS COUNTY—See ITHACA, NY (Time Warner Cable)

TONAWANDA—See LACKAWANNA, NY (Time Warner Cable)

TRENTON (TOWN) (PORTIONS)—See ROME, NY (Time Warner Cable)

TRENTON (TOWN)—See UTICA, NY (Time Warner Cable)

TRIANGLE (TOWN)—See BINGHAMTON, NY (Time Warner Cable)

▲ **TROUPSBURG**—Time Warner Cable. Now served by HORNELL, NY [NY0076]

TROUPSBURG—See HORNELL, NY (Time Warner Cable)

▲ **TROY**—Time Warner Cable. Now served by ALBANY, NY [NY0014]

TROY—See ALBANY, NY (Time Warner Cable)

TRUMANSBURG (VILLAGE)—See ITHACA, NY (Time Warner Cable)

TRUXTON (TOWN)—See CORTLAND, NY (Time Warner Cable)

TUCKAHOE—See MAMARONECK, NY (Cablevision Systems Corp.)

TULLY (TOWN)—See CORTLAND, NY (Time Warner Cable)

TULLY—See SYRACUSE (suburbs), NY (Time Warner Cable)

TUPPER LAKE—See SARANAC LAKE, NY (Time Warner Cable)

▲ **TURIN (town)**—Turin Cable TV. Now served by ROME, NY [NY0037]

TURIN (TOWN)—See ROME, NY (Time Warner Cable)

TURIN—See ROME, NY (Time Warner Cable)

▲ **TUSTEN**—Tiime Warner Cable. Now served by HUDSON VALLEY (formerly Middletown), NY [NY0231]

TUSTEN—See HUDSON VALLEY, NY (Time Warner Cable)

TUXEDO PARK—See RAMAPO (town), NY (Cablevision Systems Corp.)

TUXEDO—See RAMAPO (town), NY (Cablevision Systems Corp.)

TYRONE—See GENEVA, NY (Time Warner Cable)

ULSTER (TOWN)—See HUDSON VALLEY, NY (Time Warner Cable)

ULYSSES (TOWN)—See ITHACA, NY (Time Warner Cable)

UNADILLA (VILLAGE)—See ONEONTA, NY (Time Warner Cable)

UNION SPRINGS—See GENEVA, NY (Time Warner Cable)

UNION VALE (TOWN)—See DOVER PLAINS, NY (Cablevision Systems Corp.)

UNIONDALE—See WOODBURY, NY (Cablevision Systems Corp.)

UNIONVILLE—See WARWICK, NY (Cablevision Systems Corp.)

UPPER BROOKVILLE—See WOODBURY, NY (Cablevision Systems Corp.)

UPPER NYACK—See ROCKLAND, NY (Cablevision Systems Corp.)

▲ **UTICA**—Time Warner Cable

UTOPIA—See NEW YORK, NY (Time Warner Cable)

VALATIE—See ALBANY, NY (Time Warner Cable)

VALLEY FALLS (VILLAGE)—See ALBANY, NY (Time Warner Cable)

VALLEY STREAM—See WOODBURY, NY (Cablevision Systems Corp.)

VAN BUREN (TOWN)—See SYRACUSE (suburbs), NY (Time Warner Cable)

VAN ETTEN (VILLAGE)—See SPENCER, NY (Haefele TV Inc.)

VARICK (TOWN)—See GENEVA, NY (Time Warner Cable)

VERBANK—See DOVER PLAINS, NY (Cablevision Systems Corp.)

VERMONTVILLE—See SARANAC LAKE, NY (Time Warner Cable)

VERNON (VILLAGE)—See ROME, NY (Time Warner Cable)

VERONA (TOWN)—See ROME, NY (Time Warner Cable)

VICTOR (VILLAGE)—See GENEVA, NY (Time Warner Cable)

VICTORY MILLS—See ALBANY, NY (Time Warner Cable)

VIENNA—See ROME, NY (Time Warner Cable)

VILLAGE OF THE BRANCH—See SUFFOLK COUNTY, NY (Cablevision Systems Corp.)

VILLENOVA (TOWN)—See JAMESTOWN, NY (Time Warner Cable)

VIRGIL (TOWN)—See SPENCER, NY (Haefele TV Inc.)

VIRGIL (TOWN)—See CORTLAND, NY (Time Warner Cable)

VOLNEY—See OSWEGO, NY (Time Warner Cable)

VOORHEESVILLE—See ALBANY, NY (Time Warner Cable)

WADDINGTON (VILLAGE)—See MASSENA, NY (Time Warner Cable)

WADHAMS—See PLATTSBURGH, NY (Charter Communications)

WADING RIVER—See RIVERHEAD, NY (Cablevision Systems Corp.)

WAINSCOTT—See RIVERHEAD, NY (Cablevision Systems Corp.)

WALDEN (VILLAGE)—See HUDSON VALLEY, NY (Time Warner Cable)

▲ **WALDEN**—Time Warner Cable. Now served by HUDSON VALLEY (formerly Middletown), NY [NY0231]

WALES—See LACKAWANNA, NY (Time Warner Cable)

WALLKILL (TOWN)—See HUDSON VALLEY, NY (Time Warner Cable)

▲ **WALTON (village)**—Time Warner Cable. Now served by ONEONTA, NY [NY0065]

WALTON (VILLAGE)—See ONEONTA, NY (Time Warner Cable)

WALWORTH (TOWN)—See GENEVA, NY (Time Warner Cable)

WAMPSVILLE—See ROME, NY (Time Warner Cable)

WANTAGH—See WOODBURY, NY (Cablevision Systems Corp.)

WAPPINGER (TOWN)—See OSSINING, NY (Cablevision Systems Corp.)

WAPPINGERS FALLS—See OSSINING, NY (Cablevision Systems Corp.)

WARRENSBURG (TOWN)—See ALBANY, NY (Time Warner Cable)

▲ **WARSAW (village)**—Time Warner. Now served by BATAVIA (formerly Stafford), NY [NY0249]

WARSAW (VILLAGE)—See BATAVIA, NY (Time Warner Cable)

WARWICK (VILLAGE)—See WARWICK, NY (Cablevision Systems Corp.)

WARWICK TWP.—See WARWICK, NY (Cablevision Systems Corp.)

▲ **WARWICK**—Cablevision Systems Corp.

WASHINGTON (TOWN)—See DOVER PLAINS, NY (Cablevision Systems Corp.)

WASHINGTONVILLE (VILLAGE)—See HUDSON VALLEY, NY (Time Warner Cable)

▲ **WASHINGTONVILLE**—Time Warner Cable. Now served by HUDSON VALLEY (formerly Middletown), NY [NY0231]

WATER MILL—See RIVERHEAD, NY (Cablevision Systems Corp.)

WATERLOO (VILLAGE)—See GENEVA, NY (Time Warner Cable)

▲**WATERTOWN**—Time Warner Cable. Now served by CARTHAGE, NY [NY0206]

▲**WATERTOWN**—Time Warner Cable

WATERVILLE—See ROME, NY (Time Warner Cable)

WATERVLIET—See ALBANY, NY (Time Warner Cable)

WATKINS GLEN (VILLAGE)—See ELMIRA/CORNING, NY (Time Warner Cable)

WATKINS GLEN—See GENEVA, NY (Time Warner Cable)

WATSON—See WATERTOWN, NY (Time Warner Cable)

WAWARSING—See HUDSON VALLEY, NY (Time Warner Cable)

WAWAYANDA (TOWN)—See HUDSON VALLEY, NY (Time Warner Cable)

WAYLAND—See HORNELL, NY (Time Warner Cable)

WAYNE—See GENEVA, NY (Time Warner Cable)

WEBSTER (VILLAGE)—See ROCHESTER, NY (Time Warner Cable)

WEEDSPORT—See SYRACUSE (suburbs), NY (Time Warner Cable)

▲**WELLESLEY ISLAND**—Time Warner Cable. Now served by CARTHAGE, NY [NY0206]

WELLESLEY ISLAND—See WATERTOWN, NY (Time Warner Cable)

▲**WELLS**—Hamilton County Cable TV Inc.

WELLSVILLE (TOWN)—See OLEAN, NY (Time Warner Cable)

WELLSVILLE (VILLAGE)—See OLEAN, NY (Time Warner Cable)

▲**WELLSVILLE**—Now served by OLEAN, NY [NY0056]

WELLSVILLE—See OLEAN, NY (Time Warner Cable)

WESLEY HILLS—See ROCKLAND, NY (Cablevision Systems Corp.)

WEST BLOOMFIELD (TOWN)—See BATAVIA, NY (Time Warner Cable)

WEST CARTHAGE—See WATERTOWN, NY (Time Warner Cable)

WEST CHAZY—See CHAMPLAIN, NY (Time Warner Cable)

WEST HARRISON—See PORT CHESTER, NY (Cablevision Systems Corp.)

WEST HAVERSTRAW—See OSSINING, NY (Cablevision Systems Corp.)

WEST HURLEY—See HUDSON VALLEY, NY (Time Warner Cable)

WEST LEYDEN—See ROME, NY (Time Warner Cable)

WEST MILFORD—See WARWICK, NJ (Cablevision Systems Corp.)

WEST MONROE (TOWN)—See ROME, NY (Time Warner Cable)

WEST NYACK—See ROCKLAND, NY (Cablevision Systems Corp.)

WEST POINT MILITARY ACADEMY—See HUDSON VALLEY, NY (Time Warner Cable)

WEST POINT—See HUDSON VALLEY, NY (Time Warner Cable)

WEST SENECA—See LACKAWANNA, NY (Time Warner Cable)

WEST SHOKAN—See HUDSON VALLEY, NY (Time Warner Cable)

WEST SPARTA (TOWN)—See HORNELL, NY (Time Warner Cable)

WEST TIANA—See RIVERHEAD, NY (Cablevision Systems Corp.)

WEST TURIN—See ROME, NY (Time Warner Cable)

WEST VALLEY—See LIMESTONE, NY (Atlantic Broadband)

WEST WINFIELD—See ILION, NY (Time Warner Cable)

WESTBURY—See WOODBURY, NY (Cablevision Systems Corp.)

WESTERLO—See CATSKILL, NY (Mid-Hudson Cablevision Inc.)

WESTERN—See ROME, NY (Time Warner Cable)

▲**WESTFIELD**—Time Warner Cable

WESTHAMPTON BEACH—See RIVERHEAD, NY (Cablevision Systems Corp.)

WESTHAMPTON—See RIVERHEAD, NY (Cablevision Systems Corp.)

WESTMORELAND—See ROME, NY (Time Warner Cable)

WESTMORELAND—See UTICA, NY (Time Warner Cable)

WESTPORT (TOWN)—See PLATTSBURGH, NY (Charter Communications)

WESTTOWN—See WARWICK, NY (Cablevision Systems Corp.)

WESTVILLE—See MASSENA, NY (Time Warner Cable)

WHEATFIELD—See LACKAWANNA, NY (Time Warner Cable)

WHEATLAND (TOWN)—See BATAVIA, NY (Time Warner Cable)

WHEATLEY HEIGHTS—See WOODBURY, NY (Cablevision Systems Corp.)

WHITE PLAINS—See MAMARONECK, NY (Cablevision Systems Corp.)

▲**WHITEHALL (town)**—Time Warner Cable. Now served by ALBANY, NY [NY0014]

WHITEHALL (TOWN)—See ALBANY, NY (Time Warner Cable)

WHITESBORO (VILLAGE)—See UTICA, NY (Time Warner Cable)

WHITESTONE—See NEW YORK, NY (Time Warner Cable)

WHITESTOWN—See ROME, NY (Time Warner Cable)

WHITESTOWN—See UTICA, NY (Time Warner Cable)

▲**WHITESVILLE**—Fitzpatrick Cable TV

▲**WHITNEY POINT (village)**—Time Warner Cable. Now served by BINGHAMTON, NY [NY0016]

WHITNEY POINT (VILLAGE)—See BINGHAMTON, NY (Time Warner Cable)

WILLET—See CORTLAND, NY (Time Warner Cable)

WILLIAMSBURG—See NEW YORK, NY (Time Warner Cable)

WILLIAMSON (TOWN)—See GENEVA, NY (Time Warner Cable)

WILLIAMSVILLE—See LACKAWANNA, NY (Time Warner Cable)

WILLING—See OLEAN, NY (Time Warner Cable)

WILLISTON PARK—See WOODBURY, NY (Cablevision Systems Corp.)

▲**WILLSBORO (TOWN)**—Cable Communications of Willsboro

WILLSBORO BAY—See WILLSBORO (town), NY (Cable Communications of Willsboro)

WILLSBORO POINT—See WILLSBORO (town), NY (Cable Communications of Willsboro)

WILLSBORO—See WILLSBORO (town), NY (Cable Communications of Willsboro)

WILNA—See WATERTOWN, NY (Time Warner Cable)

WILSON (VILLAGE)—See LACKAWANNA, NY (Time Warner Cable)

WILTON—See ALBANY, NY (Time Warner Cable)

WINDHAM (TOWN)—See CATSKILL, NY (Mid-Hudson Cablevision Inc.)

▲**WINDSOR (town)**—Formerly served by Adams Cable. Now served by CARBONDALE, PA [PA0067]

WINFIELD—See ILION, NY (Time Warner Cable)

WINGDALE—See DOVER PLAINS, NY (Cablevision Systems Corp.)

WOLCOTT (VILLAGE)—See GENEVA, NY (Time Warner Cable)

▲**WOODBURY**—Cablevision Systems Corp.

WOODBURY—See OSSINING, NY (Cablevision Systems Corp.)

▲**WOODHULL**—Time Warner Cable. Now served by HORNELL, NY [NY0076]

WOODHULL—See HORNELL, NY (Time Warner Cable)

WOODMERE—See WOODBURY, NY (Cablevision Systems Corp.)

▲**WOODRIDGE (village)**—Time Warner Cable. Now served by HUDSON VALLEY (formerly Middletown), NY [NY0231]

WOODRIDGE—See HUDSON VALLEY, NY (Time Warner Cable)

WOODSBURGH—See WOODBURY, NY (Cablevision Systems Corp.)

▲**WOODSIDE**—RCN Corp. Formerly served by Queens, NY [NY0283]. This cable system has converted to IPTV

WOODSIDE—See NEW YORK, NY (Time Warner Cable)

▲**WOODSTOCK (town)**—Time Warner Cable. Now served by HUDSON VALLEY (formerly Middletown), NY [NY0231]

WOODSTOCK (TOWN)—See HUDSON VALLEY, NY (Time Warner Cable)

WORCESTER—See ONEONTA, NY (Time Warner Cable)

WURTSBORO (VILLAGE)—See HUDSON VALLEY, NY (Time Warner Cable)

WYANDANCH—See WOODBURY, NY (Cablevision Systems Corp.)

WYOMING—See BATAVIA, NY (Time Warner Cable)

YAPHANK—See SUFFOLK COUNTY, NY (Cablevision Systems Corp.)

YATES (TOWN)—See BATAVIA, NY (Time Warner Cable)

▲**YONKERS**—Cablevision Systems Corp.

YORK (TOWN)—See BATAVIA, NY (Time Warner Cable)

YORKSHIRE (TOWN)—See OLEAN, NY (Time Warner Cable)

▲**YORKTOWN**—Cablevision Systems Corp.

YORKVILLE (VILLAGE)—See UTICA, NY (Time Warner Cable)

YOUNGSTOWN (VILLAGE)—See LACKAWANNA, NY (Time Warner Cable)

YULAN—See HUDSON VALLEY, NY (Time Warner Cable)

NORTH CAROLINA

ABERDEEN—See SOUTHERN PINES, NC (Time Warner Cable)

ACME—See RIEGELWOOD, NC (Time Warner Cable)

ADVANCE—See GREENSBORO, NC (Time Warner Cable)

▲**AHOSKIE**—Formerly served by Adelphia Communications. Now served by MURFREESBORO, NC [NC0144]

AHOSKIE—See MURFREESBORO, NC (Time Warner Cable)

ALAMANCE (VILLAGE)—See GREENSBORO, NC (Time Warner Cable)

ALAMANCE COUNTY—See GREENSBORO, NC (Time Warner Cable)

▲**ALBEMARLE**—Time Warner Cable

ALEXANDER COUNTY—See HICKORY, NC (Charter Communications)

ALEXANDER MILLS—See FOREST CITY, NC (Northland Cable Television)

ALLEGHANY COUNTY (UNINCORPORATED AREAS)—See NORTH WILKESBORO, NC (Charter Communications)

ALLIANCE—See PAMLICO COUNTY, NC (Time Warner Cable)

▲**ANDERSON CREEK TWP.**—Charter Communications. Now served by BUIES CREEK, NC [NC0194]

ANDERSON CREEK TWP.—See BUIES CREEK, NC (Charter Communications)

▲**ANDREWS**—Cable TV of Andrews. Now served by MURPHY, NC [NC0079]

ANDREWS—See MURPHY, NC (Cable TV of Cherokee County)

ANGIER—See BUIES CREEK, NC (Charter Communications)

ANSON COUNTY (UNINCORPORATED AREAS)—See MORVEN, NC (WFL Cable Television Associates Inc.)

ANSON COUNTY—See WADESBORO, NC (Time Warner Cable)

ANSONVILLE—See WADESBORO, NC (Time Warner Cable)

APEX—See CARY, NC (Time Warner Cable)

ARAPAHOE—See PAMLICO COUNTY, NC (Time Warner Cable)

ARCADIA—See GREENSBORO, NC (Time Warner Cable)

ARCHDALE—See GREENSBORO, NC (Time Warner Cable)

ARLINGTON—See GREENSBORO, NC (Time Warner Cable)

ARMOUR—See RIEGELWOOD, NC (Time Warner Cable)

▲**ARROWHEAD BEACH**—Mediacom. Now served by EDENTON, NC [NC0076]

ARROWHEAD BEACH—See EDENTON, NC (Mediacom)

ASH—See SHALLOTTE, NC (Atlantic Telephone Membership Corp.)

ASHE COUNTY—See BOONE, NC (Charter Communications)

ASHE COUNTY—See WEST JEFFERSON, NC (Morris Broadband)

▲**ASHEBORO**—Time Warner Cable. Now served by GREENSBORO, NC [NC0006]

ASHEBORO—See GREENSBORO, NC (Time Warner Cable)

▲**ASHEVILLE**—Charter Communications

ATLANTIC BEACH—See NEWPORT, NC (Time Warner Cable)

ATLANTIC—See NEWPORT, NC (Time Warner Cable)

▲**AULANDER**—Formerly served by Adelphia Communications. Now served by MURFREESBORO, NC [NC0144]

AULANDER—See MURFREESBORO, NC (Time Warner Cable)

AURORA—See PAMLICO COUNTY, NC (Time Warner Cable)

AUTRYVILLE—See FAYETTEVILLE, NC (Time Warner Cable)

AVERY COUNTY—See BOONE, NC (Charter Communications)

AVON—See MANTEO, NC (Charter Communications)

AYDEN—See GREENVILLE, NC (Suddenlink Communications)

AYDLETT—See CAMDEN/CURRITUCK, NC (Mediacom)

BADIN—See ALBEMARLE, NC (Time Warner Cable)

▲**BAILEY**—Time Warner Cable

BAKERSVILLE—See BURNSVILLE, NC (Charter Communications)

▲**BALD HEAD ISLAND**—Tele-Media

BANNER ELK—See BOONE, NC (Charter Communications)

BARNARDSVILLE—See ASHEVILLE, NC (Charter Communications)

BAT CAVE—See FOREST CITY, NC (Northland Cable Television)

▲**BATH**—Red's TV Cable Inc.

BATTLEBORO—See GREENVILLE, NC (Suddenlink Communications)

BAYBORO—See PAMLICO COUNTY, NC (Time Warner Cable)

BEACON RIDGE—See SOUTHERN PINES, NC (Time Warner Cable)

BEARGRASS—See PARMELE, NC (Suddenlink Communications)

BEAUFORT COUNTY (UNINCORPORATED AREAS)—See BATH, NC (Red's TV Cable Inc.)

BEAUFORT COUNTY (UNINCORPORATED AREAS)—See PAMLICO COUNTY, NC (Time Warner Cable)

BEAUFORT COUNTY—See WASHINGTON, NC (Suddenlink Communications)

BEAUFORT—See NEWPORT, NC (Time Warner Cable)

BEAVER CREEK—See WEST JEFFERSON, NC (Morris Broadband)

BEECH MOUNTAIN—See BOONE, NC (Charter Communications)

▲**BELHAVEN**—Belhaven Cable TV

▲**BELHAVEN**—TriCounty Telecom

BELMONT—See GASTONIA, NC (Time Warner Cable)

BELWOOD—See SHELBY, NC (Time Warner Cable)

▲**BENSON**—Charter Communications. Now served by BUIES CREEK, NC [NC0194]

BENSON—See BUIES CREEK, NC (Charter Communications)

BERMUDA RUN—See GREENSBORO, NC (Time Warner Cable)

BERTIE COUNTY (EASTERN PORTION)—See PLYMOUTH (town), NC (Mediacom)

BERTIE COUNTY (PORTIONS)—See MURFREESBORO, NC (Time Warner Cable)

BERTIE COUNTY (WESTHERN PORTION)—See RICH SQUARE, NC (Mediacom)

BESSEMER CITY—See GASTONIA, NC (Time Warner Cable)

BETHANIA (PORTIONS)—See GREENSBORO, NC (Time Warner Cable)

BETHEL—See PARMELE, NC (Suddenlink Communications)

BETHLEHEM—See HICKORY, NC (Charter Communications)

BEULAVILLE—See HOLLY RIDGE, NC (Charter Communications)

BILTMORE FOREST—See ASHEVILLE, NC (Charter Communications)

BISCOE—See GREENSBORO, NC (Time Warner Cable)

BLACK CREEK—See WILSON, NC (Time Warner Cable)

▲**BLACK MOUNTAIN**—Tri-Star Communications. No longer in operation

BLACK MOUNTAIN—See ASHEVILLE, NC (Charter Communications)

BLADEN COUNTY (PORTIONS)—See ELIZABETHTOWN, NC (Time Warner Cable)

BLADEN COUNTY (PORTIONS)—See RIEGELWOOD, NC (Time Warner Cable)

BLADENBORO—See ELIZABETHTOWN, NC (Time Warner Cable)

BLOWING ROCK—See BOONE, NC (Charter Communications)

BOILING SPRINGS—See SHELBY, NC (Time Warner Cable)

BOLIVIA—See SHALLOTTE, NC (Atlantic Telephone Membership Corp.)

BOLLING SPRING LAKES—See WILMINGTON, NC (Time Warner Cable)

BOLTON—See RIEGELWOOD, NC (Time Warner Cable)

BONNIE DOONE—See FAYETTEVILLE, NC (Time Warner Cable)

▲**BOONE**—Charter Communications

BOONVILLE—See GREENSBORO, NC (Time Warner Cable)

BOSTIC—See FOREST CITY, NC (Northland Cable Television)

BOWLING GREEN—See GASTONIA, SC (Time Warner Cable)

▲**BREVARD**—Comporium Communications

BRICK LANDING—See SHALLOTTE, NC (Atlantic Telephone Membership Corp.)

BRIDGETON—See GREENVILLE, NC (Suddenlink Communications)

BROADWAY—See BUIES CREEK, NC (Charter Communications)

BROOKFORD—See HICKORY, NC (Charter Communications)

BRUNSWICK COUNTY (PORTIONS)—See RIEGELWOOD, NC (Time Warner Cable)

BRUNSWICK COUNTY (UNINCORPORATED AREAS)—See SHALLOTTE, NC (Atlantic Telephone Membership Corp.)

BRUNSWICK—See ELIZABETHTOWN, NC (Time Warner Cable)

▲**BRYSON CITY**—Zito Media

BUCKHEAD—See RIEGELWOOD, NC (Time Warner Cable)

▲**BUIES CREEK**—Charter Communications

▲**BUNCOMBE COUNTY (northern portion)**—Charter Communications. Now served by ASHEVILLE, NC [NC0012]

BUNCOMBE COUNTY (NORTHERN PORTION)—See ASHEVILLE, NC (Charter Communications)

▲**BUNN**—Formerly served by Adelphia Communications. Now served by HENDERSON, NC [NC0062]

BUNN—See HENDERSON, NC (Time Warner Cable)

▲**BUNNLEVEL**—Carolina Cable Partnership. Now served by BUIES CREEK, NC [NC0194]

BUNNLEVEL—See BUIES CREEK, NC (Charter Communications)

BURGAW—See WILMINGTON, NC (Time Warner Cable)

▲**BURKE COUNTY**—Charter Communications. Now served by HICKORY, NC [NC0009]

BURKE COUNTY—See HICKORY, NC (Charter Communications)

▲**BURLINGTON**—Time Warner Cable. Now served by GREENSBORO, NC [NC0006]

BURLINGTON—See GREENSBORO, NC (Time Warner Cable)

▲**BURNSVILLE**—Charter Communications

▲**BURNSVILLE**—Country Cablevision Inc.

BUTNER—See DURHAM, NC (Time Warner Cable)

▲**BUXTON**—Charter Communications. Now served by MANTEO, NC [NC0118]

BUXTON—See MANTEO, NC (Charter Communications)

BYNUM—See CHAPEL HILL, NC (Time Warner Cable)

CABARRUS COUNTY (PORTIONS)—See ALBEMARLE, NC (Time Warner Cable)

CABARRUS COUNTY—See KANNAPOLIS, NC (Time Warner Cable)

CABARRUS—See CHARLOTTE, NC (Time Warner Cable)

CAJAH'S MOUNTAIN—See HICKORY, NC (Charter Communications)

CALABASH—See SHALLOTTE, NC (Atlantic Telephone Membership Corp.)

CALDWELL COUNTY—See BOONE, NC (Charter Communications)

CALDWELL COUNTY—See HICKORY, NC (Charter Communications)

CALYPSO—See HOLLY RIDGE, NC (Charter Communications)

▲**CAMDEN COUNTY**—Mediacom. Now served by CAMDEN/CURRITUCK (formerly Currituck County, southern portion), NC [NC0083]

CAMDEN COUNTY—See CAMDEN/CURRITUCK, NC (Mediacom)

▲**CAMDEN/CURRITUCK**—Mediacom

CAMP LEACH—See BELHAVEN, NC (TriCounty Telecom)

▲**CAMP LEJEUNE**—Charter Communications. Now served by HOLLY RIDGE, NC [NC0069]

CAMP LEJEUNE—See HOLLY RIDGE, NC (Charter Communications)

▲**CAMP WESLEY**—Now served by GOLD HILL, NC [NC0140]

CAMP WESLEY—See SALISBURY, NC (Time Warner Cable)

CANDLER—See ASHEVILLE, NC (Charter Communications)

CANDOR—See GREENSBORO, NC (Time Warner Cable)

CANTON (CRUSO/BETHEL)—See WAYNESVILLE, NC (Carolina Mountain Cablevision Inc.)

CANTON—See WAYNESVILLE, NC (Charter Communications)

CAPE CARTERET—See NEWPORT, NC (Time Warner Cable)

▲**CAROLINA BEACH**—Charter Communications. Now served by HOLLY RIDGE, NC [NC0069]

CAROLINA BEACH—See HOLLY RIDGE, NC (Charter Communications)

▲**CARRBORO**—Time Warner Cable

CARTER COUNTY—See BOONE, TN (Charter Communications)

CARTERET COUNTY—See NEWPORT, NC (Time Warner Cable)

CARTHAGE—See SOUTHERN PINES, NC (Time Warner Cable)

▲**CARY**—Time Warner Cable

CASAR—See SHELBY, NC (Time Warner Cable)

CASHIERS—See HIGHLANDS, NC (Northland Cable Television)

CASTALIA—See NASH COUNTY, NC (Crystal Broadband Networks)

CASTLE HAYNE—See WILMINGTON, NC (Time Warner Cable)

CASWELL BEACH—See WILMINGTON, NC (Time Warner Cable)

CASWELL COUNTY (PORTIONS)—See ROXBORO, NC (Charter Communications)

CATAWBA (NORTHERN PORTION)—See HICKORY, NC (Charter Communications)

CATAWBA COUNTY—See HICKORY, NC (Charter Communications)

CEDAR CREEK RESORTS—See HIGHLANDS, NC (Northland Cable Television)

▲**CEDAR ISLAND**—Time Warner Cable

CEDAR POINT—See NEWPORT, NC (Time Warner Cable)

CERRO GORDO—See ELIZABETHTOWN, NC (Time Warner Cable)

CHADBOURN—See ELIZABETHTOWN, NC (Time Warner Cable)

▲**CHAPEL HILL**—Time Warner Cable

▲**CHARLOTTE**—Time Warner Cable

CHATHAM COUNTY (UNINCORPORATED AREAS)—See BUIES CREEK, NC (Charter Communications)

CHATHAM COUNTY—See CHAPEL HILL, NC (Time Warner Cable)

CHEROKEE COUNTY (PORTIONS)—See MURPHY, NC (Cable TV of Cherokee County)

▲**CHEROKEE INDIAN RESERVATION**—Cherokee Cablevision

▲**CHERRY POINT**—Time Warner Cable. Now served by NEWPORT, NC [NC0013]

CHERRY POINT—See NEWPORT, NC (Time Warner Cable)

CHERRYVILLE—See GASTONIA, NC (Time Warner Cable)

CHIMNEY ROCK—See FOREST CITY, NC (Northland Cable Television)

CHINA GROVE—See KANNAPOLIS, NC (Time Warner Cable)

▲**CHINQUAPIN**—Charter Communications. Now served by HOLLY RIDGE, NC [NC0069]

CHINQUAPIN—See HOLLY RIDGE, NC (Charter Communications)

CHOCOWINITY—See WASHINGTON, NC (Suddenlink Communications)

CHOWAN BEACH—See EDENTON, NC (Mediacom)

CHOWAN COUNTY—See EDENTON, NC (Mediacom)

CHURCHLAND—See REEDS CROSS ROADS, NC (Piedmont Communications Services, Inc.)

CLAREMONT—See HICKORY, NC (Charter Communications)

CLARKTON—See ELIZABETHTOWN, NC (Time Warner Cable)

CLAYTON—See SELMA/GARNER, NC (Time Warner Cable)

CLEMMONS—See GREENSBORO, NC (Time Warner Cable)

CLEVELAND COUNTY—See SHELBY, NC (Time Warner Cable)

CLEVELAND—See SALISBURY, NC (Time Warner Cable)

CLIFFSIDE—See FOREST CITY, NC (Northland Cable Television)

▲**CLINTON**—StarVision

CLOVER—See GASTONIA, SC (Time Warner Cable)

CLYDE—See WAYNESVILLE, NC (Carolina Mountain Cablevision Inc.)

CLYDE—See WAYNESVILLE, NC (Charter Communications)

COATS—See BUIES CREEK, NC (Charter Communications)

COFIELD—See MURFREESBORO, NC (Time Warner Cable)

COINJOCK—See CAMDEN/CURRITUCK, NC (Mediacom)

COLERAIN—See PLYMOUTH (town), NC (Mediacom)

COLERIDGE—See GREENSBORO, NC (Time Warner Cable)

COLFAX—See GREENSBORO, NC (Time Warner Cable)

COLINGTON—See MANTEO, NC (Charter Communications)

▲**COLUMBIA**—Mediacom. Now served by PLYMOUTH, NC [NC0085]

COLUMBIA—See PLYMOUTH (town), NC (Mediacom)

▲**COLUMBUS COUNTY (central portion)**—Formerly served by Carolina Cable Partnership. No longer in operation

COLUMBUS COUNTY (PORTIONS)—See LAKE WACCAMAW, NC (Time Warner Cable)

COLUMBUS COUNTY (PORTIONS)—See RIEGELWOOD, NC (Time Warner Cable)

▲**COLUMBUS COUNTY (UNINCORPORATED AREAS)**—Time Warner Cable

CONCORD—See KANNAPOLIS, NC (Time Warner Cable)

CONETOE—See GREENVILLE, NC (Suddenlink Communications)

CONNELLY SPRINGS—See HICKORY, NC (Charter Communications)

CONOVER—See HICKORY, NC (Charter Communications)

▲**CONWAY**—Mediacom. Now served by RICH SQUARE, NC [NC0115]

CONWAY—See RICH SQUARE, NC (Mediacom)

COOLEEMEE—See GREENSBORO, NC (Time Warner Cable)

CORNELIUS—See MOORESVILLE, NC (MI-Connection)

▲**COROLLA**—Charter Communications. Now served by MANTEO, NC [NC0118]

COROLLA—See MANTEO, NC (Charter Communications)

COURTNEY—See GREENSBORO, NC (Time Warner Cable)

CRAMERTON—See GASTONIA, NC (Time Warner Cable)

CRAVEN COUNTY—See GREENVILLE, NC (Suddenlink Communications)

CRAVEN COUNTY—See NEWPORT, NC (Time Warner Cable)

▲**CRAVEN**—Now served by GOLD HILL, NC [NC0140]

CRAVEN—See SALISBURY, NC (Time Warner Cable)

CREEDMOOR—See DURHAM, NC (Time Warner Cable)

▲**CRESTON (SOUTHERN PORTION)**—Zito Media

CRESWELL—See PLYMOUTH (town), NC (Mediacom)

CRICKET—See NORTH WILKESBORO, NC (Charter Communications)

CRISP—See PINETOPS, NC (Crystal Broadband Networks)

CROSSNORE—See BOONE, NC (Charter Communications)

CROUSE—See HICKORY, NC (Charter Communications)

▲**CRUSO**—Carolina Mountain Cable. Now served by WAYNESVILLE, NC [NC0127]

CRUSO—See WAYNESVILLE, NC (Carolina Mountain Cablevision Inc.)

CULLOWHEE—See FRANKLIN/SYLVA, NC (Morris Broadband)

CUMBERLAND COUNTY—See FAYETTEVILLE, NC (Time Warner Cable)

CURRITUCK COUNTY (SOUTHERN PORTION)—See CAMDEN/CURRITUCK, NC (Mediacom)

DALLAS—See HICKORY, NC (Charter Communications)

DANA—See HENDERSONVILLE, NC (Morris Broadband)

DANBURY—See GREENSBORO, NC (Time Warner Cable)

DARE COUNTY (PORTIONS)—See MANTEO, NC (Charter Communications)

DAVIDSON COUNTY (WESTERN PORTION)—See REEDS CROSS ROADS, NC (Piedmont Communications Services, Inc.)

▲**DAVIDSON COUNTY**—Time Warner Cable. Now served by GREENSBORO, NC [NC0006]

DAVIDSON COUNTY—See GREENSBORO, NC (Time Warner Cable)

▲**DAVIDSON COUNTY**—Windstream Communications

DAVIDSON—See MOORESVILLE, NC (MI-Connection)

DAVIE COUNTY (PORTIONS)—See GREENSBORO, NC (Time Warner Cable)

DEEP GAP—See BOONE, NC (Charter Communications)

DELCO—See RIEGELWOOD, NC (Time Warner Cable)

DENTON—See GREENSBORO, NC (Time Warner Cable)

DENVER—See HICKORY, NC (Charter Communications)

DILLSBORO—See FRANKLIN/SYLVA, NC (Morris Broadband)

DOBBINS HEIGHTS—See ROCKINGHAM, NC (Time Warner Cable)

▲**DOBSON**—Time Warner Cable. Now served by GREENSBORO, NC [NC0006]

DOBSON—See GREENSBORO, NC (Time Warner Cable)

DORTCHES—See NASH COUNTY, NC (Crystal Broadband Networks)

DOUGLAS CROSSROADS—See BELHAVEN, NC (TriCounty Telecom)

▲**DOVER**—Formerly served by Johnston County Cable LP. No longer in operation

DREXEL—See HICKORY, NC (Charter Communications)

DUBLIN—See ELIZABETHTOWN, NC (Time Warner Cable)

DUCK—See MANTEO, NC (Charter Communications)

▲**DUNCAN**—Carolina Cable Partnership. No longer in operation

DUNN—See FAYETTEVILLE, NC (Time Warner Cable)

DUPLIN COUNTY—See HOLLY RIDGE, NC (Charter Communications)

DURHAM COUNTY (PORTIONS)—See DURHAM, NC (Time Warner Cable)

DURHAM COUNTY—See CHAPEL HILL, NC (Time Warner Cable)

▲**DURHAM**—Time Warner Cable

EARL—See SHELBY, NC (Time Warner Cable)

EAST ARCADIA—See RIEGELWOOD, NC (Time Warner Cable)

EAST BEND—See GREENSBORO, NC (Time Warner Cable)

EAST FLAT ROCK—See HENDERSONVILLE, NC (Morris Broadband)

EAST ROCKINGHAM—See ROCKINGHAM, NC (Time Warner Cable)

EAST SPENCER—See SALISBURY, NC (Time Warner Cable)

EDEN—See GREENSBORO, NC (Time Warner Cable)

▲**EDENTON**—Mediacom

EDGECOMBE COUNTY (EASTERN PORTION)—See GREENVILLE, NC (Suddenlink Communications)

EDGECOMBE COUNTY (PORTIONS)—See NASH COUNTY, NC (Crystal Broadband Networks)

EDGECOMBE COUNTY (PORTIONS)—See OAK CITY, NC (Crystal Broadband Networks)

EDGECOMBE COUNTY (PORTIONS)—See WHITAKERS, NC (Crystal Broadband Networks)

EDGECOMBE COUNTY (PORTIONS)—See MID LAKES TRAILER PARK, NC (Windjammer Cable)

EDWARD—See PAMLICO COUNTY, NC (Time Warner Cable)

▲**ELIZABETH CITY**—Time Warner Cable

▲**ELIZABETHTOWN**—Time Warner Cable

ELK PARK—See BOONE, NC (Charter Communications)

▲**ELKIN**—Time Warner Cable. Now served by MOUNT AIRY, NC [NC0075]

ELKIN—See GREENSBORO, NC (Time Warner Cable)

ELLENBORO—See FOREST CITY, NC (Northland Cable Television)

ELLERBE—See ROCKINGHAM, NC (Time Warner Cable)

ELLERBE—See WADESBORO, NC (Time Warner Cable)

ELM CITY—See WILSON, NC (Time Warner Cable)

ELON COLLEGE—See GREENSBORO, NC (Time Warner Cable)

EMERALD ISLE—See NEWPORT, NC (Time Warner Cable)

EMMA—See ASHEVILLE, NC (Charter Communications)

▲**ENFIELD**—Suddenlink Communications

ENGELHARD—See BELHAVEN, NC (Belhaven Cable TV)

ENKA—See ASHEVILLE, NC (Charter Communications)

ENOCHVILLE—See KANNAPOLIS, NC (Time Warner Cable)

ERWIN—See BUIES CREEK, NC (Charter Communications)

ERWIN—See FAYETTEVILLE, NC (Time Warner Cable)

EUREKA—See WAYNE COUNTY (northern portion), NC (Time Warner Cable)

EVERETTS—See PARMELE, NC (Suddenlink Communications)

▲**FAIR BLUFF**—Formerly served by MIM Cable. No longer in operation

FAIRFIELD MOUNTAIN—See FOREST CITY, NC (Northland Cable Television)

FAIRFIELD—See BELHAVEN, NC (Belhaven Cable TV)

FAIRMONT—See LUMBERTON, NC (Time Warner Cable)

FAIRPLAINS—See NORTH WILKESBORO, NC (Charter Communications)

FAIRVIEW (PORTIONS)—See ASHEVILLE, NC (Charter Communications)

FAIRVIEW (TOWN)—See MONROE, NC (Time Warner Cable)

▲**FAISON**—Charter Communications. Now served by HOLLY RIDGE, NC [NC0069]

FAISON—See HOLLY RIDGE, NC (Charter Communications)

FAITH—See SALISBURY, NC (Time Warner Cable)

FALCON—See FAYETTEVILLE, NC (Time Warner Cable)

FALLSTON—See SHELBY, NC (Time Warner Cable)

▲**FARMVILLE**—Time Warner Cable

▲**FAYETTEVILLE**—Time Warner Cable

FLAT ROCK—See HENDERSONVILLE, NC (Morris Broadband)

FLETCHER—See ASHEVILLE, NC (Charter Communications)

FLETCHER—See HENDERSONVILLE, NC (Morris Broadband)

▲**FOREST CITY**—Northland Cable Television

FOREST HILLS—See FRANKLIN/SYLVA, NC (Morris Broadband)

FORSYTH COUNTY—See GREENSBORO, NC (Time Warner Cable)

FORT BRAGG—See FAYETTEVILLE, NC (Time Warner Cable)

FORT FISHER AFB—See HOLLY RIDGE, NC (Charter Communications)

FOSCOE—See BOONE, NC (Charter Communications)

▲**FOUNTAIN**—Windjammer Cable

FOUR OAKS—See SELMA/GARNER, NC (Time Warner Cable)

FOXFIRE VILLAGE—See SOUTHERN PINES, NC (Time Warner Cable)

FRANKLIN COUNTY (PORTIONS)—See HENDERSON, NC (Time Warner Cable)

FRANKLIN COUNTY (PORTIONS)—See RALEIGH, NC (Time Warner Cable)

▲**FRANKLIN/SYLVA**—Morris Broadband

FRANKLINTON—See RALEIGH, NC (Time Warner Cable)

FRANKLINVILLE—See GREENSBORO, NC (Time Warner Cable)

FREMONT—See GOLDSBORO, NC (Time Warner Cable)

FRISCO—See MANTEO, NC (Charter Communications)

FUQUAY-VARINA—See CARY, NC (Time Warner Cable)

GAMEWELL—See HICKORY, NC (Charter Communications)

GARLAND—See CLINTON, NC (StarVision)

GARYSBURG—See ROANOKE RAPIDS, NC (Charter Communications)

GASTON COUNTY—See HICKORY, NC (Charter Communications)

GASTON COUNTY—See GASTONIA, NC (Time Warner Cable)

GASTON—See ROANOKE RAPIDS, NC (Charter Communications)

▲**GASTONIA**—Time Warner Cable

▲**GATES COUNTY**—Charter Communications

GATESVILLE—See GATES COUNTY, NC (Charter Communications)

GERMANTON—See GREENSBORO, NC (Time Warner Cable)

GERTON—See FOREST CITY, NC (Northland Cable Television)

GIBSONVILLE—See GREENSBORO, NC (Time Warner Cable)

GLEN ALPINE—See HICKORY, NC (Charter Communications)

GLEN RAVEN—See GREENSBORO, NC (Time Warner Cable)

GLOUCESTER—See NEWPORT, NC (Time Warner Cable)

GODWIN—See FAYETTEVILLE, NC (Time Warner Cable)

▲**GOLD HILL**—Time Warner Cable. Now served by SALISBURY, NC [NC0022]

GOLD HILL—See SALISBURY, NC (Time Warner Cable)

▲**GOLDSBORO**—Time Warner Cable

▲**GOLDSTON**—Formerly served by Main Street Broadband. No longer in operation

GORMAN—See DURHAM, NC (Time Warner Cable)

GRAHAM COUNTY (CENTRAL PORTION)—See ROBBINSVILLE, NC (Zito Media)

GRAHAM—See GREENSBORO, NC (Time Warner Cable)

GRANDFATHER MOUNTAIN—See BOONE, NC (Charter Communications)

GRANDY—See CAMDEN/CURRITUCK, NC (Mediacom)

GRANITE FALLS—See HICKORY, NC (Charter Communications)

GRANITE QUARRY—See SALISBURY, NC (Time Warner Cable)

GRANTSBORO—See PAMLICO COUNTY, NC (Time Warner Cable)

GRANVILLE COUNTY (PORTIONS)—See DURHAM, NC (Time Warner Cable)

GRANVILLE COUNTY (PORTIONS)—See HENDERSON, NC (Time Warner Cable)

GRANVILLE COUNTY (PORTIONS)—See RALEIGH, NC (Time Warner Cable)

GREENE COUNTY (PORTIONS)—See SNOW HILL, NC (MediaCast)

▲ **GREENSBORO**—Time Warner Cable

▲ **GREENVILLE**—Suddenlink Communications

GRIMESLAND—See SIMPSON, NC (Suddenlink Communications)

GROVER—See SHELBY, NC (Time Warner Cable)

GUILFORD COUNTY (PORTIONS)—See DAVIDSON COUNTY, NC (Windstream Communications)

HALIFAX COUNTY (PORTIONS)—See OAK CITY, NC (Crystal Broadband Networks)

HALIFAX COUNTY—See ROANOKE RAPIDS, NC (Charter Communications)

▲ **HALIFAX**—Crystal Broadband Networks

HALLSBORO—See LAKE WACCAMAW, NC (Time Warner Cable)

HAMILTON—See OAK CITY, NC (Crystal Broadband Networks)

HAMLET—See ROCKINGHAM, NC (Time Warner Cable)

HAMPSTEAD—See HOLLY RIDGE, NC (Charter Communications)

HARBINGER—See CAMDEN/CURRITUCK, NC (Mediacom)

HARKERS ISLAND—See NEWPORT, NC (Time Warner Cable)

▲ **HARRIS**—Northland Cable Television

HARRISBURG—See KANNAPOLIS, NC (Time Warner Cable)

HASSEL—See OAK CITY, NC (Crystal Broadband Networks)

HATTERAS—See MANTEO, NC (Charter Communications)

HAVELOCK—See NEWPORT, NC (Time Warner Cable)

HAW RIVER—See GREENSBORO, NC (Time Warner Cable)

HAYS—See NORTH WILKESBORO, NC (Charter Communications)

HAYWOOD COUNTY (UNINCORPORATED AREAS)—See WAYNESVILLE, NC (Carolina Mountain Cablevision Inc.)

HAYWOOD COUNTY—See WAYNESVILLE, NC (Charter Communications)

HAZELWOOD—See WAYNESVILLE, NC (Charter Communications)

HEMBY BRIDGE—See MONROE, NC (Time Warner Cable)

HENDERSON COUNTY (NORTHEASTERN PORTION)—See FOREST CITY, NC (Northland Cable Television)

HENDERSON COUNTY—See HENDERSONVILLE, NC (Morris Broadband)

▲ **HENDERSON**—Time Warner Cable

▲ **HENDERSONVILLE**—Morris Broadband

HENRICO—See LAKE GASTON, NC (Time Warner Cable)

HERTFORD COUNTY (PORTIONS)—See MURFREESBORO, NC (Time Warner Cable)

HERTFORD—See EDENTON, NC (Mediacom)

▲ **HICKORY**—Charter Communications

HIDDENITE—See HICKORY, NC (Charter Communications)

▲ **HIGH POINT**—Time Warner Cable. Now served by GREENSBORO, NC [NC0006]

HIGH POINT—See GREENSBORO, NC (Time Warner Cable)

HIGH POINT—See DAVIDSON COUNTY, NC (Windstream Communications)

HIGH SHOALS—See HICKORY, NC (Charter Communications)

▲ **HIGHLANDS**—Northland Cable Television

HILDEBRAN—See HICKORY, NC (Charter Communications)

HILLSBOROUGH—See CARRBORO, NC (Time Warner Cable)

HOBGOOD—See OAK CITY, NC (Crystal Broadband Networks)

HOBUCKEN—See PAMLICO COUNTY, NC (Time Warner Cable)

HOFFMAN—See ROCKINGHAM, NC (Time Warner Cable)

HOLDEN BEACH—See WILMINGTON, NC (Time Warner Cable)

▲ **HOLLISTER**—Crystal Broadband Networks

▲ **HOLLY RIDGE**—Charter Communications

HOLLY SPRINGS—See CARY, NC (Time Warner Cable)

HOOKERTON—See SNOW HILL, NC (MediaCast)

HOPE MILLS—See FAYETTEVILLE, NC (Time Warner Cable)

HUBERT—See NEWPORT, NC (Time Warner Cable)

HUDSON—See HICKORY, NC (Charter Communications)

HUNTERSVILLE—See CHARLOTTE, NC (Time Warner Cable)

HURDLE MILLS—See ROXBORO, NC (Charter Communications)

HYDE COUNTY (PORTIONS)—See BELHAVEN, NC (TriCounty Telecom)

ICARD—See HICKORY, NC (Charter Communications)

INDIAN BEACH—See NEWPORT, NC (Time Warner Cable)

INDIAN TRAIL—See MONROE, NC (Time Warner Cable)

IREDELL COUNTY (PORTIONS)—See STATESVILLE, NC (Time Warner Cable)

▲ **IRONDUFF**—Carolina Mountain Cable. Now served by WAYNESVILLE, NC [NC0127]

IRONDUFF—See WAYNESVILLE, NC (Carolina Mountain Cablevision Inc.)

JACKSON COUNTY (PORTIONS)—See HIGHLANDS, NC (Northland Cable Television)

JACKSON COUNTY (UNINCORPORATED AREAS)—See FRANKLIN/SYLVA, NC (Morris Broadband)

JACKSON—See RICH SQUARE, NC (Mediacom)

▲ **JACKSONVILLE**—Time Warner Cable

JAMES CITY—See GREENVILLE, NC (Suddenlink Communications)

JAMESTOWN—See GREENSBORO, NC (Time Warner Cable)

JAMESVILLE—See PLYMOUTH (town), NC (Mediacom)

JARVISBURG—See CAMDEN/CURRITUCK, NC (Mediacom)

JEFFERSON—See WEST JEFFERSON, NC (Morris Broadband)

JOHNSONVILLE TWP.—See BUIES CREEK, NC (Charter Communications)

JOHNSTON COUNTY (PORTIONS)—See CARY, NC (Time Warner Cable)

JOHNSTON COUNTY (PORTIONS)—See RALEIGH, NC (Time Warner Cable)

JOHNSTON COUNTY (PORTIONS)—See SELMA/GARNER, NC (Time Warner Cable)

JOHNSTON COUNTY (PORTIONS)—See WAYNE COUNTY (northern portion), NC (Time Warner Cable)

JOHNSTON COUNTY—See KENLY, NC (Charter Communications)

JONATHAN CREEK—See WAYNESVILLE, NC (Carolina Mountain Cablevision Inc.)

JONES COUNTY (PORTIONS)—See JACKSONVILLE, NC (Time Warner Cable)

JONESVILLE—See GREENSBORO, NC (Time Warner Cable)

JULLAN—See GREENSBORO, NC (Time Warner Cable)

JUPITER—See ASHEVILLE, NC (Charter Communications)

▲ **KANNAPOLIS**—Time Warner Cable

KELFORD—See RICH SQUARE, NC (Mediacom)

KENANSVILLE—See HOLLY RIDGE, NC (Charter Communications)

▲ **KENLY**—Charter Communications

KERNERSVILLE—See GREENSBORO, NC (Time Warner Cable)

KILL DEVIL HILLS—See MANTEO, NC (Charter Communications)

▲ **KING**—Time Warner Cable. Now served by GREENSBORO, NC [NC0006]

KING—See GREENSBORO, NC (Time Warner Cable)

KINGS CREEK—See HICKORY, NC (Charter Communications)

KINGS MOUNTAIN—See SHELBY, NC (Time Warner Cable)

KINGSTOWN—See SHELBY, NC (Time Warner Cable)

▲ **KINSTON**—Cox Communications. Now served by GREENVILLE, NC [NC0014]

KINSTON—See GREENVILLE, NC (Suddenlink Communications)

KIPLING—See BUIES CREEK, NC (Charter Communications)

KITTRELL—See HENDERSON, NC (Time Warner Cable)

KITTY HAWK—See MANTEO, NC (Charter Communications)

KNIGHTDALE—See RALEIGH, NC (Time Warner Cable)

KURE BEACH—See HOLLY RIDGE, NC (Charter Communications)

LA GRANGE—See GREENVILLE, NC (Suddenlink Communications)

▲ **LAKE GASTON**—Time Warner Cable

LAKE JUNALUSKA—See WAYNESVILLE, NC (Charter Communications)

LAKE LURE—See FOREST CITY, NC (Northland Cable Television)

▲ **LAKE NORMAN**—Now served by MOORESVILLE, NC [NC0207]

LAKE PARK—See MONROE, NC (Time Warner Cable)

▲ **LAKE TOXAWAY**—Comporium Communications. Now served by BREVARD, NC [NC0053]

LAKE TOXAWAY—See BREVARD, NC (Comporium Communications)

▲ **LAKE WACCAMAW**—Time Warner Cable

LAKE WYLIE—See GASTONIA, SC (Time Warner Cable)

LANCASTER—See CHARLOTTE, NC (Time Warner Cable)

LANDIS—See KANNAPOLIS, NC (Time Warner Cable)

▲ **LANSING**—Mediacom. Now served by WEST JEFFERSON, NC [NC0098]

LANSING—See WEST JEFFERSON, NC (Morris Broadband)

LASKER—See RICH SQUARE, NC (Mediacom)

LATTIMORE—See SHELBY, NC (Time Warner Cable)

LAUREL PARK—See HENDERSONVILLE, NC (Morris Broadband)

▲ **LAURINBURG**—Time Warner Cable. Now served by MYRTLE BEACH, SC [SC0007]

LAWNDALE—See SHELBY, NC (Time Warner Cable)

LEASBURG—See ROXBORO, NC (Charter Communications)

LEE COUNTY (PORTIONS)—See BUIES CREEK, NC (Charter Communications)

LEICESTER—See ASHEVILLE, NC (Charter Communications)

LELAND—See WILMINGTON, NC (Time Warner Cable)

LENOIR COUNTY (PORTIONS)—See SNOW HILL, NC (MediaCast)

LENOIR—See HICKORY, NC (Charter Communications)

LEWISTON—See RICH SQUARE, NC (Mediacom)

LEWISVILLE—See GREENSBORO, NC (Time Warner Cable)

LEXINGTON—See GREENSBORO, NC (Time Warner Cable)

LIBERTY—See GREENSBORO, NC (Time Warner Cable)

LIGHT OAK—See SHELBY, NC (Time Warner Cable)

LILESVILLE—See WADESBORO, NC (Time Warner Cable)

LILLINGTON—See BUIES CREEK, NC (Charter Communications)

LINCOLN COUNTY—See HICKORY, NC (Charter Communications)

LINCOLNTON—See HICKORY, NC (Charter Communications)

LINVILLE RIDGE—See BOONE, NC (Charter Communications)

LITTLE SWITZERLAND—See BURNSVILLE, NC (Country Cablevision Inc.)

▲ **LITTLETON**—Time Warner Cable

LOCUST—See ALBEMARLE, NC (Time Warner Cable)

LONE HICKORY—See GREENSBORO, NC (Time Warner Cable)

LONG BEACH—See WILMINGTON, NC (Time Warner Cable)

LONGVIEW—See HICKORY, NC (Charter Communications)

LONGWOOD—See SHALLOTTE, NC (Atlantic Telephone Membership Corp.)

LOUISBURG—See HENDERSON, NC (Time Warner Cable)

LOWELL—See GASTONIA, NC (Time Warner Cable)

LOWLAND—See PAMLICO COUNTY, NC (Time Warner Cable)

LUCAMA—See KENLY, NC (Charter Communications)

LUMBER BRIDGE (PORTIONS)—See LUMBERTON, NC (Time Warner Cable)

▲ **LUMBERTON**—Time Warner Cable

MACCLESFIELD—See PINETOPS, NC (Crystal Broadband Networks)

MACCRIPINES—See PINETOPS, NC (Crystal Broadband Networks)

MACON COUNTY (EASTERN PORTION)—See HIGHLANDS, NC (Northland Cable Television)

MACON COUNTY—See FRANKLIN/SYLVA, NC (Morris Broadband)

MADISON COUNTY—See BURNSVILLE, NC (Country Cablevision Inc.)

MADISON—See GREENSBORO, NC (Time Warner Cable)

MAGGIE VALLEY—See WAYNESVILLE, NC (Carolina Mountain Cablevision Inc.)

MAGGIE VALLEY—See WAYNESVILLE, NC (Charter Communications)

MAGNOLIA—See HOLLY RIDGE, NC (Charter Communications)

MAIDEN—See HICKORY, NC (Charter Communications)

MAMERS—See BUIES CREEK, NC (Charter Communications)

MANNS HARBOR—See MANTEO, NC (Charter Communications)

MANSON—See HENDERSON, NC (Time Warner Cable)

▲ **MANTEO**—Charter Communications

MARBLE—See MURPHY, NC (Cable TV of Cherokee County)

▲ **MARION**—Charter Communications

MARS HILL—See ASHEVILLE, NC (Charter Communications)

MARSHALL—See ASHEVILLE, NC (Charter Communications)

MARSHALLBERG—See NEWPORT, NC (Time Warner Cable)

MARSHVILLE—See MONROE, NC (Time Warner Cable)

MARSTON—See ROCKINGHAM, NC (Time Warner Cable)

MARTIN COUNTY (CENTRAL PORTION)—See PARMELE, NC (Suddenlink Communications)

MARTIN COUNTY (PORTIONS)—See PLYMOUTH (town), NC (Mediacom)

MARTIN COUNTY (UNINCORPORATED AREAS)—See OAK CITY, NC (Crystal Broadband Networks)

MARVIN—See MONROE, NC (Time Warner Cable)

MATTHEWS—See CHARLOTTE, NC (Time Warner Cable)

MAURY—See SNOW HILL, NC (MediaCast)

MAYSVILLE—See JACKSONVILLE, NC (Time Warner Cable)

MCADENVILLE—See GASTONIA, NC (Time Warner Cable)

MCDOWELL COUNTY (CENTRAL PORTION)—See MARION, NC (Charter Communications)

MEAT CAMP—See BOONE, NC (Charter Communications)

▲ **MEBANE**—Time Warner Cable. Now served by GREENSBORO, NC [NC0006]

MEBANE—See GREENSBORO, NC (Time Warner Cable)

MECKLENBURG COUNTY (UNINCORPORATED AREAS)—See MOORESVILLE, NC (MI-Connection)

MECKLENBURG COUNTY (UNINCORPORATED AREAS)—See CHARLOTTE, NC (Time Warner Cable)

MERRITT—See PAMLICO COUNTY, NC (Time Warner Cable)

MESIC—See PAMLICO COUNTY, NC (Time Warner Cable)

MICAVILLE—See BURNSVILLE, NC (Charter Communications)

MICRO—See KENLY, NC (Charter Communications)

▲ **MID LAKES TRAILER PARK**—Windjammer Cable

MIDDLEBURG—See HENDERSON, NC (Time Warner Cable)

MIDDLESEX—See BAILEY, NC (Time Warner Cable)

MIDLAND—See KANNAPOLIS, NC (Time Warner Cable)

MIDWAY PARK—See JACKSONVILLE, NC (Time Warner Cable)

MILDRED—See GREENVILLE, NC (Suddenlink Communications)

MILLERS CREEK—See NORTH WILKESBORO, NC (Charter Communications)

MILLS RIVER—See HENDERSONVILLE, NC (Morris Broadband)

MILTON—See ROXBORO, NC (Charter Communications)

MINERAL SPRINGS (TOWN)—See MONROE, NC (Time Warner Cable)

MINNESOTT BEACH—See PAMLICO COUNTY, NC (Time Warner Cable)

MINT HILL—See CHARLOTTE, NC (Time Warner Cable)

MITCHELL COUNTY—See BURNSVILLE, NC (Charter Communications)

MITCHELL COUNTY—See BURNSVILLE, NC (Country Cablevision Inc.)

▲ **MOCKSVILLE**—Time Warner Cable. Now served by GREENSBORO, NC [NC0006]

MOCKSVILLE—See GREENSBORO, NC (Time Warner Cable)

MOMEYER—See SPRING HOPE, NC (Time Warner Cable)

▲ **MONROE**—Time Warner Cable

MONTGOMERY COUNTY (PORTIONS)—See ALBEMARLE, NC (Time Warner Cable)

MONTREAT—See ASHEVILLE, NC (Charter Communications)

MOORE COUNTY (PORTIONS)—See SOUTHERN PINES, NC (Time Warner Cable)

MOORE COUNTY (PORTIONS)—See ROBBINS, NC (Windjammer Cable)

MOORE COUNTY—See BUIES CREEK, NC (Charter Communications)

MOORESBORO—See SHELBY, NC (Time Warner Cable)

▲ **MOORESVILLE**—MI-Connection

MORAVIAN FALLS—See NORTH WILKESBORO, NC (Charter Communications)

MOREHEAD CITY—See NEWPORT, NC (Time Warner Cable)

▲ **MORGANTON**—CoMPAS-City of Morganton Public Antenna System

MORRISVILLE—See CARY, NC (Time Warner Cable)

▲ **MORVEN**—WFL Cable Television Associates Inc.

▲ **MOUNT AIRY**—Time Warner Cable. Now served by GREENSBORO, NC [NC0006]

MOUNT AIRY—See GREENSBORO, NC (Time Warner Cable)

MOUNT GILEAD—See ALBEMARLE, NC (Time Warner Cable)

MOUNT HOLLY—See GASTONIA, NC (Time Warner Cable)

MOUNT OLIVE—See GOLDSBORO, NC (Time Warner Cable)

MOUNT PLEASANT—See KANNAPOLIS, NC (Time Warner Cable)

MOUNTAIN VIEW—See HICKORY, NC (Charter Communications)

MULBERRY—See NORTH WILKESBORO, NC (Charter Communications)

▲ **MURFREESBORO**—Time Warner Cable

▲ **MURPHY**—Cable TV of Cherokee County

NAGS HEAD—See MANTEO, NC (Charter Communications)

NASH COUNTY (PORTIONS)—See WHITAKERS, NC (Crystal Broadband Networks)

NASH COUNTY (SOUTHWESTERN PORTION)—See BAILEY, NC (Time Warner Cable)

▲ **NASH COUNTY**—Crystal Broadband Networks

NASH COUNTY—See GREENVILLE, NC (Suddenlink Communications)

NASHVILLE—See GREENVILLE, NC (Suddenlink Communications)

NAVASSA—See WILMINGTON, NC (Time Warner Cable)

▲ **NEBO**—Morris Broadband

NEBRASKA—See BELHAVEN, NC (Belhaven Cable TV)

▲ **NEW BERN**—Cox Communications. Now served by GREENVILLE, NC [NC0014]

NEW BERN—See GREENVILLE, NC (Suddenlink Communications)

NEW HANOVER COUNTY (UNINCORPORATED AREAS)—See HOLLY RIDGE, NC (Charter Communications)

NEW HANOVER COUNTY—See WILMINGTON, NC (Time Warner Cable)

NEW LONDON—See ALBEMARLE, NC (Time Warner Cable)

NEWLAND—See BOONE, NC (Charter Communications)

▲ **NEWPORT**—Time Warner Cable

▲ **NEWTON GROVE**—Charter Communications. Now served by BUIES CREEK, NC [NC0194]

NEWTON GROVE—See BUIES CREEK, NC (Charter Communications)

NEWTON—See HICKORY, NC (Charter Communications)

NORLINA—See HENDERSON, NC (Time Warner Cable)

NORTH HICKORY—See HICKORY, NC (Charter Communications)

NORTH TOPSAIL BEACH—See HOLLY RIDGE, NC (Charter Communications)

▲ **NORTH WILKESBORO**—Charter Communications

NORTHAMPTON COUNTY (PORTIONS)—See LAKE GASTON, NC (Time Warner Cable)

NORTHAMPTON COUNTY—See ROANOKE RAPIDS, NC (Charter Communications)

NORTHAMPTON COUNTY—See RICH SQUARE, NC (Mediacom)

NORTHLAKES—See HICKORY, NC (Charter Communications)

NORTHWEST NAVAL BASE—See CAMDEN/CURRITUCK, VA (Mediacom)

NORTHWEST—See RIEGELWOOD, NC (Time Warner Cable)

NORWOOD—See ALBEMARLE, NC (Time Warner Cable)

▲ **OAK CITY**—Crystal Broadband Networks

OAK RIDGE—See GREENSBORO, NC (Time Warner Cable)

OAKBORO—See ALBEMARLE, NC (Time Warner Cable)

▲ **OCEAN ISLE BEACH/BRICK LANDING**—Tele-Media. Now served by SHALLOTTE, NC [NC0050]

OCEAN ISLE BEACH—See SHALLOTTE, NC (Atlantic Telephone Membership Corp.)

OCEAN ISLE BEACH—See WILMINGTON, NC (Time Warner Cable)

OCRACOKE ISLAND—See BELHAVEN, NC (Belhaven Cable TV)

OLD FORT—See MARION, NC (Charter Communications)

OLDE POINT—See HOLLY RIDGE, NC (Charter Communications)

▲ **OLDE POINTE**—Charter Communications. Now served by HOLLY RIDGE, NC [NC0069]

ONSLOW COUNTY—See HOLLY RIDGE, NC (Charter Communications)

ORANGE COUNTY (PORTIONS)—See DURHAM, NC (Time Warner Cable)

ORANGE COUNTY—See CHAPEL HILL, NC (Time Warner Cable)

ORIENTAL—See PAMLICO COUNTY, NC (Time Warner Cable)

▲ **ORRUM**—Formerly served by Carolina Cable Partnership. No longer in operation

OXFORD—See HENDERSON, NC (Time Warner Cable)

PAMLICO BEACH—See BELHAVEN, NC (TriCounty Telecom)

▲ **PAMLICO COUNTY**—Time Warner Cable

PANTEGO—See BELHAVEN, NC (Tri-County Telecom)

PARKTON—See FAYETTEVILLE, NC (Time Warner Cable)

▲ **PARMELE**—Suddenlink Communications

PASQUOTANK COUNTY—See ELIZABETH CITY, NC (Time Warner Cable)

PATTERSON SPRINGS—See SHELBY, NC (Time Warner Cable)

PATTERSON—See HICKORY, NC (Charter Communications)

PEACHLAND—See MORVEN, NC (WFL Cable Television Associates Inc.)

PELETIER—See NEWPORT, NC (Time Warner Cable)

▲ **PEMBROKE**—Formerly served by Carolina Cable Partnership. No longer in operation

PEMBROKE—See LUMBERTON, NC (Time Warner Cable)

PENDER COUNTY (PORTIONS)—See HOLLY RIDGE, NC (Charter Communications)

PENDER COUNTY—See WILMINGTON, NC (Time Warner Cable)

PENSACOLA—See BURNSVILLE, NC (Charter Communications)

PERQUIMANS COUNTY—See EDENTON, NC (Mediacom)

PERSON COUNTY—See ROXBORO, NC (Charter Communications)

PFAFFTOWN—See GREENSBORO, NC (Time Warner Cable)

PIKE ROAD—See BELHAVEN, NC (Tri-County Telecom)

PIKEVILLE—See GOLDSBORO, NC (Time Warner Cable)

PILOT MOUNTAIN—See GREENSBORO, NC (Time Warner Cable)

PINE HALL—See GREENSBORO, NC (Time Warner Cable)

PINE KNOLL SHORES—See NEWPORT, NC (Time Warner Cable)

PINE LEVEL—See SELMA/GARNER, NC (Time Warner Cable)

PINEBLUFF—See SOUTHERN PINES, NC (Time Warner Cable)

PINEHURST—See SOUTHERN PINES, NC (Time Warner Cable)

▲ **PINETOPS**—Crystal Broadband Networks

PINETOWN—See BELHAVEN, NC (Tri-County Telecom)

PINEVILLE (PORTIONS)—See CHARLOTTE, NC (Time Warner Cable)

PINEWILD—See SOUTHERN PINES, NC (Time Warner Cable)

▲ **PINK HILL**—Time Warner Cable

PINNACLE—See GREENSBORO, NC (Time Warner Cable)

PISGAH FOREST—See BREVARD, NC (Comporium Communications)

PITT COUNTY (PORTIONS)—See SNOW HILL, NC (MediaCast)

PITT COUNTY (PORTIONS)—See SIMPSON, NC (Suddenlink Communications)

PITT COUNTY—See GREENVILLE, NC (Suddenlink Communications)

PITT COUNTY—See FARMVILLE, NC (Time Warner Cable)

PITTSBORO—See CHAPEL HILL, NC (Time Warner Cable)

PLAINVIEW—See BUIES CREEK, NC (Charter Communications)

PLEASANT GARDEN—See GREENSBORO, NC (Time Warner Cable)

▲ **PLYMOUTH (TOWN)**—Mediacom

POINT HARBOR—See CAMDEN/CURRITUCK, NC (Mediacom)

POLK COUNTY (NORTHERN PORTION)—See FOREST CITY, NC (Northland Cable Television)

POLKTON—See MORVEN, NC (WFL Cable Television Associates Inc.)

POLKVILLE—See SHELBY, NC (Time Warner Cable)

POLLOCKSVILLE—See JACKSONVILLE, NC (Time Warner Cable)

POPE AFB—See FAYETTEVILLE, NC (Time Warner Cable)

POPLAR BRANCH—See CAMDEN/CURRITUCK, NC (Mediacom)

POPLAR TENT—See KANNAPOLIS, NC (Time Warner Cable)

POWELLS POINT—See CAMDEN/CURRITUCK, NC (Mediacom)

▲ **POWELLSVILLE**—Mediacom. Now served by WINDSOR, NC [NC0111]

POWELLSVILLE—See PLYMOUTH (town), NC (Mediacom)

▲ **PRINCETON**—Southern Cablevision. Now served by KENLY, NC [NC0148]

PRINCETON—See KENLY, NC (Charter Communications)

PRINCEVILLE—See GREENVILLE, NC (Suddenlink Communications)

QUALLA—See CHEROKEE INDIAN RESERVATION, NC (Cherokee Cablevision)

▲ **RAEFORD**—Time Warner Cable

▲ **RALEIGH**—Time Warner Cable

RAMSEUR—See GREENSBORO, NC (Time Warner Cable)

RANDLEMAN—See GREENSBORO, NC (Time Warner Cable)

RANDOLPH COUNTY (PORTIONS)—See GREENSBORO, NC (Time Warner Cable)

▲ **RANGER**—Haywood Cablevision. Now served by MURPHY, NC [NC0079]

RANGER—See MURPHY, NC (Cable TV of Cherokee County)

RANLO—See GASTONIA, NC (Time Warner Cable)

RED OAK—See NASH COUNTY, NC (Crystal Broadband Networks)

RED SPRINGS—See LUMBERTON, NC (Time Warner Cable)

▲ **REEDS CROSS ROADS**—Piedmont Communications Services, Inc.

▲ **REIDSVILLE**—Time Warner Cable. Now served by GREENSBORO, NC [NC0006]

REIDSVILLE—See GREENSBORO, NC (Time Warner Cable)

RENNERT—See LUMBERTON, NC (Time Warner Cable)

RHODHISS—See HICKORY, NC (Charter Communications)

▲ **RICH SQUARE**—Mediacom

RICHFIELD—See ALBEMARLE, NC (Time Warner Cable)

RICHLANDS—See HOLLY RIDGE, NC (Charter Communications)

RICHLANDS—See JACKSONVILLE, NC (Time Warner Cable)

RICHMOND COUNTY (UNINCORPORATED AREAS)—See WADESBORO, NC (Time Warner Cable)

RICHMOND COUNTY—See ROCKINGHAM, NC (Time Warner Cable)

▲ **RIEGELWOOD**—Time Warner Cable

RIVER BEND—See GREENVILLE, NC (Suddenlink Communications)

RIVER ROAD—See WASHINGTON, NC (Suddenlink Communications)

ROAN MOUNTAIN—See BOONE, TN (Charter Communications)

▲ **ROANOKE RAPIDS**—Charter Communications

▲ **ROARING FORK**—Formerly served by Almega Cable. No longer in operation

ROARING GAP—See NORTH WILKESBORO, NC (Charter Communications)

ROARING RIVER—See NORTH WILKESBORO, NC (Charter Communications)

▲ **ROBBINS**—Windjammer Cable

▲ **ROBBINSVILLE**—Zito Media

ROBERSONVILLE—See PARMELE, NC (Suddenlink Communications)

▲ **ROBESON COUNTY (western portion)**—Formerly served by Carolina Cable Partnerships. No longer in operation

ROBESON COUNTY—See LUMBERTON, NC (Time Warner Cable)

ROCKINGHAM COUNTY (PORTIONS)—See GREENSBORO, NC (Time Warner Cable)

▲ **ROCKINGHAM**—Time Warner Cable

ROCKWELL—See SALISBURY, NC (Time Warner Cable)

▲ **ROCKY MOUNT**—Cox Communications. Now served by GREENVILLE, NC [NC0014]

ROCKY MOUNT—See GREENVILLE, NC (Suddenlink Communications)

RODANTHE—See MANTEO, NC (Charter Communications)

ROLESVILLE—See RALEIGH, NC (Time Warner Cable)

RONDA—See NORTH WILKESBORO, NC (Charter Communications)

ROPER—See PLYMOUTH (town), NC (Mediacom)

ROSE HILL—See HOLLY RIDGE, NC (Charter Communications)

▲ **ROSEBORO**—StarVision. Now served by CLINTON, NC [NC0070]

ROSEBORO—See CLINTON, NC (StarVision)

ROSMAN—See BREVARD, NC (Comporium Communications)

ROWAN COUNTY—See KANNAPOLIS, NC (Time Warner Cable)

ROWAN COUNTY—See SALISBURY, NC (Time Warner Cable)

▲ **ROWLAND**—Time Warner Cable. Now served by MYRTLE BEACH, SC [SC0007]

▲ **ROXBORO**—Charter Communications

ROXOBEL—See RICH SQUARE, NC (Mediacom)

RURAL HALL—See GREENSBORO, NC (Time Warner Cable)

RUTH—See FOREST CITY, NC (Northland Cable Television)

RUTHERFORD COLLEGE—See HICKORY, NC (Charter Communications)

RUTHERFORD COUNTY (PORTIONS)—See FOREST CITY, NC (Northland Cable Television)

RUTHERFORDTON—See FOREST CITY, NC (Northland Cable Television)

SALEMBURG—See CLINTON, NC (StarVision)

▲ **SALISBURY**—Time Warner Cable

SALTER PATH—See NEWPORT, NC (Time Warner Cable)

SALVO—See MANTEO, NC (Charter Communications)

SAMPSON COUNTY—See CLINTON, NC (StarVision)

SANDY CREEK—See RIEGELWOOD, NC (Time Warner Cable)

SANDY MUSH—See FOREST CITY, NC (Northland Cable Television)

SANDY RIDGE—See GREENSBORO, NC (Time Warner Cable)

▲ **SANFORD**—Charter Communications. Now served by BUIES CREEK, NC [NC0194]

SANFORD—See BUIES CREEK, NC (Charter Communications)

SANTEETLAH—See ROBBINSVILLE, NC (Zito Media)

▲ **SANTREE MOBILE HOME PARK**—Formerly served by Adelphia Communications. No longer in operation

SAPPHIRE VALLEY—See HIGHLANDS, NC (Northland Cable Television)

SAPPHIRE—See HIGHLANDS, NC (Northland Cable Television)

SARATOGA—See WILSON, NC (Time Warner Cable)

SAWMILLS—See HICKORY, NC (Charter Communications)

SAXAPAHAW—See GREENSBORO, NC (Time Warner Cable)

▲ **SCOTLAND NECK**—Suddenlink Communications

SEABOARD—See RICH SQUARE, NC (Mediacom)

SEAGROVE—See GREENSBORO, NC (Time Warner Cable)

SEALEVEL—See NEWPORT, NC (Time Warner Cable)

▲ **SELMA/GARNER**—Time Warner Cable

SEMORA—See ROXBORO, NC (Charter Communications)

SEVEN DEVILS—See BOONE, NC (Charter Communications)

SEVEN LAKES—See SOUTHERN PINES, NC (Time Warner Cable)

SEVERN—See RICH SQUARE, NC (Mediacom)

SEYMOUR JOHNSON AFB—See GOLDSBORO, NC (Time Warner Cable)

▲ **SHALLOTTE**—Atlantic Telephone Membership Corp.

SHANNON—See LUMBERTON, NC (Time Warner Cable)

SHARPSBURG—See GREENVILLE, NC (Suddenlink Communications)

▲ **SHELBY**—Time Warner Cable

SILER CITY—See BUIES CREEK, NC (Charter Communications)

▲ **SIMPSON**—Suddenlink Communications

SIMS—See BAILEY, NC (Time Warner Cable)

SIX POINTS—See FOREST CITY, NC (Northland Cable Television)

▲ **SMITHFIELD**—Johnston County Cable LP. Now served by SELMA/GARNER (formerly Garner), NC [NC0032]

SMITHFIELD—See SELMA/GARNER, NC (Time Warner Cable)

SMITHTON—See BELHAVEN, NC (Tri-County Telecom)

SMYRNA—See NEWPORT, NC (Time Warner Cable)

SNEADS FERRY—See HOLLY RIDGE, NC (Charter Communications)

▲ **SNOW HILL**—MediaCast

SOUTH GASTONIA—See GASTONIA, NC (Time Warner Cable)

▲ **SOUTHERN PINES**—Time Warner Cable

SOUTHERN SHORES—See MANTEO, NC (Charter Communications)

SOUTHMONT—See GREENSBORO, NC (Time Warner Cable)

SOUTHPORT—See WILMINGTON, NC (Time Warner Cable)

▲ **SPARTA**—Alleghany Cablevision Inc.

SPENCER MOUNTAIN—See GASTONIA, NC (Time Warner Cable)

SPENCER—See SALISBURY, NC (Time Warner Cable)

SPINDALE—See FOREST CITY, NC (Northland Cable Television)

SPIVEY'S CORNER—See BUIES CREEK, NC (Charter Communications)

▲ **SPRING HOPE**—Time Warner Cable

SPRING LAKE—See FAYETTEVILLE, NC (Time Warner Cable)

SPRUCE PINE—See BURNSVILLE, NC (Charter Communications)

SPRUCE PINE—See BURNSVILLE, NC (Country Cablevision Inc.)

ST. HELENA—See WILMINGTON, NC (Time Warner Cable)

ST. PAULS—See LUMBERTON, NC (Time Warner Cable)

STACY—See NEWPORT, NC (Time Warner Cable)

STALLINGS—See MONROE, NC (Time Warner Cable)

STANFIELD—See ALBEMARLE, NC (Time Warner Cable)

STANLEY—See GASTONIA, NC (Time Warner Cable)

STANLY COUNTY—See ALBEMARLE, NC (Time Warner Cable)

STANTONSBURG—See WILSON, NC (Time Warner Cable)

STAR—See GREENSBORO, NC (Time Warner Cable)

▲ **STATESVILLE**—Formerly served by Adelphia Communications. No longer in operation

▲ **STATESVILLE**—Time Warner Cable

STEDMAN—See FAYETTEVILLE, NC (Time Warner Cable)

STELLA—See NEWPORT, NC (Time Warner Cable)

STERN—See DURHAM, NC (Time Warner Cable)

STOKES COUNTY (PORTIONS)—See GREENSBORO, NC (Time Warner Cable)

STOKESDALE—See GREENSBORO, NC (Time Warner Cable)

STONEVILLE—See GREENSBORO, NC (Time Warner Cable)

STONEWALL—See PAMLICO COUNTY, NC (Time Warner Cable)

STONY POINT—See HICKORY, NC (Charter Communications)

STOVALL—See HENDERSON, NC (Time Warner Cable)

STUMPY POINT—See MANTEO, NC (Charter Communications)

SUGAR GROVE—See BOONE, NC (Charter Communications)

SUGAR MOUNTAIN—See BOONE, NC (Charter Communications)

SUMMERFIELD—See GREENSBORO, NC (Time Warner Cable)

SUNSET BEACH—See SHALLOTTE, NC (Atlantic Telephone Membership Corp.)

▲ **SUNSET HARBOR**—Tele-Media. Now served by SHALLOTTE, NC [NC0050]

SUNSET HARBOR—See SHALLOTTE, NC (Atlantic Telephone Membership Corp.)

▲ **SUPPLY**—Tele-Media. Now served by SHALLOTTE, NC [NC0050]

SUPPLY—See SHALLOTTE, NC (Atlantic Telephone Membership Corp.)

SURF CITY—See HOLLY RIDGE, NC (Charter Communications)

SURRY COUNTY—See GREENSBORO, NC (Time Warner Cable)

SWAN QUARTER—See BELHAVEN, NC (Belhaven Cable TV)

SWANCREEK—See GREENSBORO, NC (Time Warner Cable)

SWANNANOA—See ASHEVILLE, NC (Charter Communications)

SWANSBORO—See NEWPORT, NC (Time Warner Cable)

SWEPSONVILLE—See GREENSBORO, NC (Time Warner Cable)

▲ **SYLVA**—Mediacom. Now served by FRANKLIN/SYLVA (formerly Franklin), NC [NC0087]

TABOR CITY—See COLUMBUS COUNTY (unincorporated areas), NC (Time Warner Cable)

TARAWA TERRACE—See HOLLY RIDGE, NC (Charter Communications)

TARBORO—See GREENVILLE, NC (Suddenlink Communications)

TAYLORSVILLE—See HICKORY, NC (Charter Communications)

TAYLORTOWN—See SOUTHERN PINES, NC (Time Warner Cable)

TEACHEY—See HOLLY RIDGE, NC (Charter Communications)

TERRA CEIA—See BELHAVEN, NC (Tri-County Telecom)

THOMASVILLE—See GREENSBORO, NC (Time Warner Cable)

THURMOND—See NORTH WILKESBORO, NC (Charter Communications)

TIMBERLAKE—See ROXBORO, NC (Charter Communications)

TOAST—See GREENSBORO, NC (Time Warner Cable)

TOBACCOVILLE—See GREENSBORO, NC (Time Warner Cable)

TOPSAIL BEACH—See HOLLY RIDGE, NC (Charter Communications)

TOPTON—See MURPHY, NC (Cable TV of Cherokee County)

TOWNSVILLE—See HENDERSON, NC (Time Warner Cable)

TRADE—See BOONE, TN (Charter Communications)

TRANSYLVANIA COUNTY—See BREVARD, NC (Comporium Communications)

TRAPHILL—See NORTH WILKESBORO, NC (Charter Communications)

TRENT WOODS—See GREENVILLE, NC (Suddenlink Communications)

TRINITY—See GREENSBORO, NC (Time Warner Cable)

TROUTMAN—See STATESVILLE, NC (Time Warner Cable)

▲ **TROY**—Charter Communications

▲ **TRYON**—Charter Communications. Now served by GREENVILLE/SPARTANBURG, SC [SC0003]

TYRO—See REEDS CROSS ROADS, NC (Piedmont Communications Services, Inc.)

TYRRELL COUNTY (PORTIONS)—See PLYMOUTH (town), NC (Mediacom)

UNION COUNTY—See MONROE, NC (Time Warner Cable)

UNIONVILLE (TOWN)—See MONROE, NC (Time Warner Cable)

VALDESE—See HICKORY, NC (Charter Communications)

VALE—See HICKORY, NC (Charter Communications)

VALLE CRUCIS—See BOONE, NC (Charter Communications)

VANCE COUNTY (PORTIONS)—See HENDERSON, NC (Time Warner Cable)

VANCEBORO—See GREENVILLE, NC (Suddenlink Communications)

VANDEMERE—See PAMLICO COUNTY, NC (Time Warner Cable)

▲ **VASS**—Charter Communications. Now served by BUIES CREEK, NC [NC0194]

VASS—See BUIES CREEK, NC (Charter Communications)

VILAS—See BOONE, NC (Charter Communications)

WACO—See SHELBY, NC (Time Warner Cable)

WADE—See FAYETTEVILLE, NC (Time Warner Cable)

▲ **WADESBORO**—Time Warner Cable

▲ **WAGRAM**—Formerly served by Wagram Cable TV. No longer in operation

WAKE COUNTY (PORTIONS)—See CARY, NC (Time Warner Cable)

WAKE COUNTY (PORTIONS)—See DURHAM, NC (Time Warner Cable)

WAKE COUNTY (PORTIONS)—See RALEIGH, NC (Time Warner Cable)

WAKE COUNTY (PORTIONS)—See SELMA/GARNER, NC (Time Warner Cable)

WAKE FORREST—See RALEIGH, NC (Time Warner Cable)

WALKERTOWN—See GREENSBORO, NC (Time Warner Cable)

WALLACE—See HOLLY RIDGE, NC (Charter Communications)

WALLBURG—See GREENSBORO, NC (Time Warner Cable)

WALNUT COVE—See GREENSBORO, NC (Time Warner Cable)

WALSTONBURG—See SNOW HILL, NC (MediaCast)

WANCHESE—See MANTEO, NC (Charter Communications)

WARREN COUNTY (EASTERN PORTION)—See LITTLETON, NC (Time Warner Cable)

WARREN COUNTY (PORTIONS)—See HENDERSON, NC (Time Warner Cable)

WARREN COUNTY (PORTIONS)—See LAKE GASTON, NC (Time Warner Cable)

WARRENSVILLE—See WEST JEFFERSON, NC (Morris Broadband)

WARRENTON—See HENDERSON, NC (Time Warner Cable)

▲ **WARSAW**—Charter Communications. Now served by HOLLY RIDGE, NC [NC0069]

WARSAW—See HOLLY RIDGE, NC (Charter Communications)

WASHINGTON COUNTY—See PLYMOUTH (town), NC (Mediacom)

WASHINGTON PARK—See WASHINGTON, NC (Suddenlink Communications)

▲ **WASHINGTON**—Suddenlink Communications

WATAUGA COUNTY—See BOONE, NC (Charter Communications)

WATHA—See WILMINGTON, NC (Time Warner Cable)

WAVES—See MANTEO, NC (Charter Communications)

WAXHAW—See MONROE, NC (Time Warner Cable)

▲ **WAYNE COUNTY (NORTHERN PORTION)**—Time Warner Cable

WAYNE COUNTY (PORTIONS)—See GREENVILLE, NC (Suddenlink Communications)

WAYNE COUNTY (PORTIONS)—See GOLDSBORO, NC (Time Warner Cable)

▲ **WAYNESVILLE**—Carolina Mountain Cablevision Inc.

▲ **WAYNESVILLE**—Charter Communications

WEAVERVILLE—See ASHEVILLE, NC (Charter Communications)

WEBSTER—See FRANKLIN/SYLVA, NC (Morris Broadband)

WEDDINGTON—See CHARLOTTE, NC (Time Warner Cable)

WELCOME—See GREENSBORO, NC (Time Warner Cable)

WELDON—See ROANOKE RAPIDS, NC (Charter Communications)

WENDELL—See RALEIGH, NC (Time Warner Cable)

WESLEY CHAPEL—See MONROE, NC (Time Warner Cable)

WEST CANTON—See WAYNESVILLE, NC (Charter Communications)

WEST END—See SOUTHERN PINES, NC (Time Warner Cable)

▲ **WEST JEFFERSON**—Morris Broadband

WESTFIELD—See GREENSBORO, NC (Time Warner Cable)

WHISPERING PINES—See BUIES CREEK, NC (Charter Communications)

▲ **WHITAKERS**—Crystal Broadband Networks

WHITE LAKE—See ELIZABETHTOWN, NC (Time Warner Cable)

WHITE PLAINS—See GREENSBORO, NC (Time Warner Cable)

WHITE POST—See BELHAVEN, NC (Tri-County Telecom)

▲ **WHITEVILLE**—Time Warner Cable. Now served by ELIZABETHTOWN/WHITEVILLE, NC (formerly Bladenboro) [NC0071]

WHITEVILLE—See ELIZABETHTOWN, NC (Time Warner Cable)

WHITNEL—See HICKORY, NC (Charter Communications)

WHITSETT—See GREENSBORO, NC (Time Warner Cable)

WHITTIER—See BRYSON CITY, NC (Zito Media)

WILKES COUNTY—See NORTH WILKESBORO, NC (Charter Communications)

WILKES COUNTY—See GREENSBORO, NC (Time Warner Cable)

WILKESBORO—See NORTH WILKESBORO, NC (Charter Communications)

WILLIAMSTON—See PARMELE, NC (Suddenlink Communications)

WILLISTON—See NEWPORT, NC (Time Warner Cable)

▲ **WILMINGTON**—Formerly served by Microwave Communication Services. No longer in operation

▲ **WILMINGTON**—Time Warner Cable

WILSON COUNTY (NORTHWESTERN PORTION)—See BAILEY, NC (Time Warner Cable)

WILSON COUNTY (PORTIONS)—See WAYNE COUNTY (northern portion), NC (Time Warner Cable)

▲ **WILSON**—Time Warner Cable

▲**WINDSOR**—Mediacom. Now served by PLYMOUTH, NC [NC0085]

WINDSOR—See PLYMOUTH (town), NC (Mediacom)

WINFALL—See EDENTON, NC (Mediacom)

WINGATE—See MONROE, NC (Time Warner Cable)

▲**WINSTON-SALEM**—Time Warner Cable. Now served by GREENSBORO, NC [NC0006]

WINSTON-SALEM—See GREENSBORO, NC (Time Warner Cable)

WINTERVILLE—See GREENVILLE, NC (Suddenlink Communications)

WINTON—See MURFREESBORO, NC (Time Warner Cable)

WISE—See HENDERSON, NC (Time Warner Cable)

WOODFIN—See ASHEVILLE, NC (Charter Communications)

WOODLAND—See RICH SQUARE, NC (Mediacom)

WRIGHTSVILLE BEACH—See WILMINGTON, NC (Time Warner Cable)

YADKIN COUNTY—See GREENSBORO, NC (Time Warner Cable)

YANCEY COUNTY (PORTIONS)—See BURNSVILLE, NC (Charter Communications)

YANCEY COUNTY—See BURNSVILLE, NC (Country Cablevision Inc.)

YAUPON BEACH—See WILMINGTON, NC (Time Warner Cable)

YOUNGSVILLE—See RALEIGH, NC (Time Warner Cable)

ZEBULON—See RALEIGH, NC (Time Warner Cable)

ZIONVILLE—See BOONE, NC (Charter Communications)

NORTH DAKOTA

ACRES-A-PLENTY—See MANDAN, ND (Midcontinent Communications)

ADAMS—See PEMBINA, ND (Polar Cablevision)

ALEXANDER—See WATFORD CITY, ND (Reservation Telephone Cooperative)

ANAMOOSE—See HARVEY, ND (Midcontinent Communications)

ANETA—See COOPERSTOWN, ND (Midcontinent Communications)

ANTLER—See VELVA, ND (SRT Communications)

ARNEGARD—See WATFORD CITY, ND (Reservation Telephone Cooperative)

ARTHUR—See CASSELTON, ND (Midcontinent Communications)

▲**ARVILLA**—Midcontinent Communications

BARLOW—See CARRINGTON, ND (Midcontinent Communications)

▲**BEACH**—Midcontinent Communications

BELFIELD—See SOUTH HEART, ND (Midcontinent Communications)

▲**BERTHOLD**—SRT Communications. Now served by VELVA, ND [ND0059]

BERTHOLD—See VELVA, ND (SRT Communications)

▲**BEULAH**—Midcontinent Communications

BINFORD—See COOPERSTOWN, ND (Midcontinent Communications)

BISBEE—See ROLETTE, ND (Midcontinent Communications)

BISMARCK—See MANDAN, ND (Midcontinent Communications)

BOTTINEAU—See ROLETTE, ND (Midcontinent Communications)

BOWBELLS—See RAY, ND (Northwest Communications Cooperative)

▲**BOWDON**—Dakota Central Telecommunications. This cable system has converted to IPTV. See Bowdon, ND [ND5000]

▲**BOWDON**—Dakota Central Telecommunications. Formerly [ND0139]. This cable system has converted to IPTV

▲**BOWMAN**—Midcontinent Communications

BRECKENRIDGE—See WAHPETON, MN (Midcontinent Communications)

BRIARWOOD—See FARGO, ND (Cable One)

BUFFALO—See CASSELTON, ND (Midcontinent Communications)

BURLINGTON—See MINOT, ND (Midcontinent Communications)

BUTTE—See VELVA, ND (SRT Communications)

BUXTON—See GRAND FORKS, ND (Midcontinent Communications)

CANDO—See DEVILS LAKE, ND (Midcontinent Communications)

▲**CARPIO**—SRT Communications. Now served by VELVA, ND [ND0059]

CARPIO—See VELVA, ND (SRT Communications)

▲**CARRINGTON**—Midcontinent Communications

▲**CARSON**—Formerly served by Northland Communications. No longer in operation

CASS COUNTY (PORTIONS)—See FARGO, ND (Cable One)

▲**CASSELTON**—Midcontinent Communications

CAVALIER AIR FORCE STATION—See PEMBINA, ND (Polar Cablevision)

CAVALIER—See PEMBINA, ND (Polar Cablevision)

CENTER—See BEULAH, ND (Midcontinent Communications)

▲**CLEVELAND**—Dakota Central Telecommunications. This cable system has converted to IPTV. See Cleveland, ND [ND5002]

▲**CLEVELAND**—Dakota Central Telecommunications. Formerly [ND0162]. This cable system has converted to IPTV

COLUMBUS—See RAY, ND (Northwest Communications Cooperative)

▲**COOPERSTOWN**—Midcontinent Communications

CROOKSTON—See GRAND FORKS, MN (Midcontinent Communications)

CROSBY—See RAY, ND (Northwest Communications Cooperative)

CRYSTAL—See PEMBINA, ND (Polar Cablevision)

DEERING—See VELVA, ND (SRT Communications)

DES LACS—See VELVA, ND (SRT Communications)

▲**DEVILS LAKE**—Midcontinent Communications

▲**DICKINSON**—Consolidated Telecommunications Co.

DILWORTH—See FARGO, MN (Cable One)

DODGE—See BEULAH, ND (Midcontinent Communications)

DONNYBROOK—See VELVA, ND (SRT Communications)

DRAKE—See HARVEY, ND (Midcontinent Communications)

DRAYTON—See GRAFTON, ND (Midcontinent Communications)

▲**DUNN CENTER**—Formerly served by Eagle Cablevision Inc. No longer in operation

DUNSEITH—See ROLETTE, ND (Midcontinent Communications)

EAST GRAND FORKS—See GRAND FORKS, MN (Midcontinent Communications)

▲**EDGELEY**—Dickey Rural Networks. This cable system has converted to IPTV. See Edgeley, ND [ND5020]

▲**EDGELEY**—Dickey Rural Networks. Formerly [ND0182]. This cable system has converted to IPTV

EDINBURG—See PEMBINA, ND (Polar Cablevision)

EDMORE—See DEVILS LAKE, ND (Midcontinent Communications)

▲**ELGIN**—Formerly served by Northland Communications. No longer in operation

▲**ELLENDALE**—Dickey Rural Networks. Formerly served by Oakes, ND [ND0026]. This cable system has converted to IPTV

EMERADO—See GRAND FORKS, ND (Midcontinent Communications)

▲**ENDERLIN**—MLGC

▲**ESMOND**—Midcontinent Communications

FAIRMOUNT—See HANKINSON, ND (Midcontinent Communications)

▲**FARGO**—Cable One

FESSENDEN—See HARVEY, ND (Midcontinent Communications)

▲**FINLEY**—MLGC

▲**FLASHER**—Formerly served by Flasher Cablevision Inc. No longer in operation

FLAXTON—See RAY, ND (Northwest Communications Cooperative)

FORDVILLE—See PEMBINA, ND (Polar Cablevision)

▲**FOREST RIVER**—Midcontinent Communications

▲**FORMAN**—Dickey Rural Networks. Formerly served by Milnor, ND [ND0067]. This cable system has converted to IPTV

FRONTIER—See FARGO, ND (Cable One)

▲**GACKLE**—Midcontinent Communications

GALESBURG—See GRAND FORKS, ND (Midcontinent Communications)

▲**GARRISON**—Reservation Telephone Cooperative

▲**GILBY**—Formerly served by Midcontinent Communications. No longer in operation

GILBY—See PEMBINA, ND (Polar Cablevision)

GLADSTONE—See BEULAH, ND (Midcontinent Communications)

GLEN ULLIN—See BEULAH, ND (Midcontinent Communications)

GLENBURN—See MINOT, ND (Midcontinent Communications)

▲**GLENFIELD**—Formerly served by Dakota Central Telecommunications. No longer in operation

GOLDEN VALLEY—See BEULAH, ND (Midcontinent Communications)

GOODRICH—See MCCLUSKY, ND (Midcontinent Communications)

▲**GRAFTON**—Midcontinent Communications

GRAND FORKS AFB—See GRAND FORKS, ND (Midcontinent Communications)

▲**GRAND FORKS**—Formerly served by Microwave Communication Services. No longer in operation

▲**GRAND FORKS**—Midcontinent Communications

GRANDIN—See GRAND FORKS, ND (Midcontinent Communications)

▲**RUGBY**—Midcontinent Communications

RUTHVILLE—See MINOT, ND (Midcontinent Communications)

RYDER—See PARSHALL, ND (Reservation Telephone Cooperative)

▲**SANBORN**—Formerly served by Cable Services Inc. No longer in operation

▲**SAWYER**—Formerly served by Sawyer CATV. No longer in operation

SAWYER—See VELVA, ND (SRT Communications)

SCRANTON—See BOWMAN, ND (Midcontinent Communications)

▲**SELFRIDGE**—West River Cable Television

▲**SHERWOOD**—SRT Communications. Now served by VELVA, ND [ND0059]

SHERWOOD—See VELVA, ND (SRT Communications)

▲**SHEYENNE**—Dakota Central Telecommunications

▲**SOLEN**—Formerly served by Midcontinent Communications. No longer in operation

▲**SOURIS**—United Telephone Mutual Aid Corp.

▲**SOUTH HEART**—Midcontinent Communications

ST. JOHN—See ROLETTE, ND (Midcontinent Communications)

ST. THOMAS—See PEMBINA, ND (Polar Cablevision)

▲**STANLEY**—Stanley Cablevision Inc.

STANTON—See BEULAH, ND (Midcontinent Communications)

STARKWEATHER—See DEVILS LAKE, ND (Midcontinent Communications)

STREETER—See GACKLE, ND (Midcontinent Communications)

SURREY—See MINOT, ND (Midcontinent Communications)

▲**SYKESON**—Dakota Central Telecommunications. This cable system has converted to IPTV. See Sykeston, ND [ND5010]

▲**SYKESTON**—Dakota Central Telecommunications. Formerly [ND0152]. This cable system has converted to IPTV

▲**TAYLOR**—Consolidated Telecommunications Co. Now served by DICKINSON, ND [ND0005]

TAYLOR—See DICKINSON, ND (Consolidated Telecommunications Co.)

THOMPSON—See GRAND FORKS, ND (Midcontinent Communications)

TIOGA—See RAY, ND (Northwest Communications Cooperative)

TOLLEY—See VELVA, ND (SRT Communications)

TOWNER—See RUGBY, ND (Midcontinent Communications)

TURTLE LAKE—See BEULAH, ND (Midcontinent Communications)

UNDERWOOD—See BEULAH, ND (Midcontinent Communications)

▲**UPHAM**—RAE Cable. Now served by NEWBURG, ND [ND0059]

UPHAM—See VELVA, ND (SRT Communications)

▲**VALLEY CITY**—Cable Services Inc.

▲**VELVA**—SRT Communications

▲**WAHPETON**—Midcontinent Communications

WALHALLA—See LANGDON, ND (Midcontinent Communications)

WARD COUNTY (PORTIONS)—See MINOT, ND (Midcontinent Communications)

WASHBURN—See BEULAH, ND (Midcontinent Communications)

▲**WATFORD CITY**—Reservation Telephone Cooperative

WEST FARGO—See FARGO, ND (Cable One)

▲**WESTHOPE**—SRT Communications. Now served by VELVA, ND [ND0059]

WESTHOPE—See VELVA, ND (SRT Communications)

WILDROSE—See RAY, ND (Northwest Communications Cooperative)

WILLISTON TWP. (PORTIONS)—See WILLISTON, ND (Midcontinent Communications)

▲**WILLISTON**—Midcontinent Communications

WILLOW CITY—See ROLETTE, ND (Midcontinent Communications)

WILTON—See BEULAH, ND (Midcontinent Communications)

WIMBLEDON—See COOPERSTOWN, ND (Midcontinent Communications)

▲**WISHEK**—Midcontinent Communications

▲**WOODWORTH**—Dakota Central Telecommunications. This cable system has converted to IPTV. See Woodworth, ND [ND5013]

▲**WOODWORTH**—Dakota Central Telecommunications. Formerly [ND0168]. This cable system has converted to IPTV

▲**WYNDMERE**—Dickey Rural Networks

▲**YPSILANTI**—Dakota Central Telecommunications. This cable system has converted to IPTV. See Ypsilanti, ND [ND5104]

▲**YPSILANTI**—Dakota Central Telecommunications. Formerly [ND0169]. This cable system has converted to IPTV

ZAP—See BEULAH, ND (Midcontinent Communications)

ZEELAND—See WISHEK, ND (Midcontinent Communications)

OHIO

▲**ADA**—Time Warner Cable. Now served by KENTON, OH [OH0128]

ADA—See KENTON, OH (Time Warner Cable)

ADAMS COUNTY (PORTIONS)—See CINCINNATI, OH (Time Warner Cable)

ADAMS TWP. (CLINTON COUNTY)—See CINCINNATI, OH (Time Warner Cable)

ADAMS TWP. (DARKE COUNTY)—See DAYTON, OH (Time Warner Cable)

ADAMS TWP. (GUERNSEY COUNTY)—See NEWARK, OH (Time Warner Cable)

ADAMS TWP. (SENECA COUNTY)—See BELLEVUE, OH (Time Warner Cable)

ADAMS TWP. (WASHINGTON COUNTY)—See BEVERLY, OH (Time Warner Cable)

ADAMS TWP.—See DAYTON, OH (Time Warner Cable)

ADAMSVILLE—See ZANESVILLE, OH (Time Warner Cable)

ADELPHI—See CHILLICOTHE, OH (Time Warner Cable)

▲**ADENA**—Comcast Cable. Now served by WHEELING, WV [WV0004]

ADRIAN—See SYCAMORE, OH (Time Warner Cable)

▲**AKRON**—Time Warner Cable

▲**ALBANY**—Time Warner Cable. Now served by JACKSON, OH [OH0098]

ALBANY—See ATHENS, OH (Time Warner Cable)

ALBANY—See JACKSON, OH (Time Warner Cable)

ALEXANDER TWP.—See ATHENS, OH (Time Warner Cable)

ALEXANDRIA—See MOUNT VERNON, OH (Time Warner Cable)

ALGER—See KENTON, OH (Time Warner Cable)

ALLEN COUNTY (PORTIONS)—See LIMA, OH (Time Warner Cable)

ALLEN TWP. (DARKE COUNTY)—See DAYTON, OH (Time Warner Cable)

ALLEN TWP. (HANCOCK COUNTY)—See FINDLAY, OH (Time Warner Cable)

ALLEN TWP. (OTTAWA COUNTY)—See CLAY CENTER/GIBSONBURG, OH (Time Warner Cable)

ALLIANCE—See CANTON, OH (Time Warner Cable)

AMANDA TWP. (FAIRFIELD COUNTY)—See COLUMBUS, OH (Insight Communications)

AMANDA TWP. (FAIRFIELD COUNTY)—See CHILLICOTHE, OH (Time Warner Cable)

AMANDA—See OAKLAND, OH (Time Warner Cable)

AMBERLEY—See CINCINNATI, OH (Time Warner Cable)

AMBOY TWP.—See WAUSEON, OH (Time Warner Cable)

▲**AMELIA**—Formerly served by Adelphia Communications. No longer in operation

AMERICAN TWP. (ALLEN COUNTY)—See LIMA, OH (Time Warner Cable)

▲**AMESVILLE**—Formerly served by Riley Video Services. No longer in operation

AMHERST TWP.—See CLEVELAND HEIGHTS, OH (Time Warner Cable)

AMHERST—See CLEVELAND HEIGHTS, OH (Time Warner Cable)

▲**AMSTERDAM**—Windjammer Cable

ANDERSON TWP. (HAMILTON COUNTY)—See CINCINNATI, OH (Time Warner Cable)

ANDOVER TWP. (PORTIONS)—See VERNON, OH (S. Bryer Cable TV Corp.)

▲**ANDOVER**—Formerly served by Cebridge Connections. Now served by MEADVILLE, PA [PA0062]

ANNA—See DAYTON, OH (Time Warner Cable)

ANSONIA—See DAYTON, OH (Time Warner Cable)

ANTRIM TWP.—See UPPER SANDUSKY, OH (Time Warner Cable)

ANTWERP—See HICKSVILLE, OH (Mediacom)

APPLE CREEK—See WOOSTER, OH (Clear Picture Inc.)

AQUILLA—See CLEVELAND HEIGHTS, OH (Time Warner Cable)

ARCADIA—See FOSTORIA, OH (Time Warner Cable)

ARCANUM—See DAYTON, OH (Time Warner Cable)

ARCHBOLD—See BRYAN, OH (Time Warner Cable)

ARLINGTON HEIGHTS—See CINCINNATI, OH (Time Warner Cable)

ARLINGTON—See FINDLAY, OH (Time Warner Cable)

ASHLAND (PORTIONS)—See SOUTH POINT, KY (Armstrong Cable Services)

ASHLAND COUNTY (PORTIONS)—See POLK, OH (Time Warner Cable)

▲**ASHLAND**—Armstrong Cable Services

ASHLAND—See MANSFIELD, OH (Time Warner Cable)

▲**ASHLEY CORNER**—Time Warner Cable

▲**BLOOMINGDALE**—Suddenlink Communications

BLOOMVILLE—See SYCAMORE, OH (Time Warner Cable)

BLUE ASH—See CINCINNATI, OH (Time Warner Cable)

BLUE WATER MANOR—See NELSON TWP., OH (Suddenlink Communications)

▲**BLUFFTON**—Time Warner Cable. Now served by LIMA, OH [OH0020]

BLUFFTON—See LIMA, OH (Time Warner Cable)

▲**BOARDMAN**—Armstrong Cable Services

BOKESCREEK TWP.—See COLUMBUS, OH (Time Warner Cable)

▲**BOLIVAR**—Now served by NEW PHILADELPHIA, OH [OH0030]

BOLIVAR—See NEW PHILADELPHIA, OH (Time Warner Cable)

BOSTON HEIGHTS—See MACEDONIA, OH (Time Warner Cable)

BOSTON TWP. (SUMMIT COUNTY)—See AKRON, OH (Time Warner Cable)

BOTKINS—See DAYTON, OH (Time Warner Cable)

BOURNEVILLE—See BAINBRIDGE, OH (Time Warner Cable)

BOWERSTON—See LEESVILLE, OH (Time Warner Cable)

BOWERSVILLE—See CINCINNATI, OH (Time Warner Cable)

BOWLING GREEN TWP. (LICKING COUNTY)—See ZANESVILLE, OH (Time Warner Cable)

▲**BOWLING GREEN**—Time Warner Cable

BOYD COUNTY—See SOUTH POINT, KY (Armstrong Cable Services)

BRACEVILLE TWP. (TRUMBULL COUNTY)—See WARREN, OH (Time Warner Cable)

BRADFORD—See DAYTON, OH (Time Warner Cable)

BRADNER—See CLAY CENTER/GIBSONBURG, OH (Time Warner Cable)

BRADY LAKE VILLAGE—See KENT, OH (Time Warner Cable)

BRADY TWP. (WILLIAMS COUNTY)—See BRYAN, OH (Time Warner Cable)

BRATENAHL—See EAST CLEVELAND, OH (East Cleveland Cable TV & Communications LLC)

BRATENAHL—See CLEVELAND HEIGHTS, OH (Time Warner Cable)

BRECKSVILLE—See CLEVELAND HEIGHTS, OH (Time Warner Cable)

BRECKSVILLE—See CLEVELAND, OH (WOW! Internet Cable & Phone)

BREMAN—See LANCASTER, OH (Time Warner Cable)

BREWSTER—See MASSILLON, OH (Massillon Cable TV Inc.)

BRIARWOOD BEACH—See LODI, OH (Time Warner Cable)

BRICE—See COLUMBUS, OH (Insight Communications)

BRICE—See COLUMBUS, OH (WOW! Internet Cable & Phone)

BRIGHTON TWP.—See WELLINGTON, OH (GLW Broadband)

BRIMFIELD TWP. (PORTAGE COUNTY)—See KENT, OH (Time Warner Cable)

BRISTOL TWP.—See WARREN, OH (Time Warner Cable)

BROADVIEW HEIGHTS—See PARMA, OH (Cox Communications)

BRONSON TWP.—See NORWALK, OH (Time Warner Cable)

BROOK PARK—See CLEVELAND HEIGHTS, OH (Time Warner Cable)

BROOK PARK—See CLEVELAND, OH (WOW! Internet Cable & Phone)

▲**BROOKFIELD TWP. (TRUMBULL COUNTY)**—Northeast Cable TV

BROOKLYN HEIGHTS—See PARMA, OH (Cox Communications)

BROOKLYN—See CLEVELAND HEIGHTS, OH (Time Warner Cable)

BROOKLYN—See CLEVELAND, OH (WOW! Internet Cable & Phone)

BROOKVILLE—See DAYTON, OH (Time Warner Cable)

BROWN TWP. (CARROLL COUNTY)—See CANTON, OH (Time Warner Cable)

BROWN TWP. (CARROLL COUNTY)—See MINERVA, OH (Time Warner Cable)

BROWN TWP. (DARKE COUNTY)—See DAYTON, OH (Time Warner Cable)

BROWN TWP. (DELAWARE COUNTY)—See COLUMBUS, OH (Insight Communications)

BROWNHELM TWP.—See WELLINGTON, OH (GLW Broadband)

BROWNHELM TWP.—See CLEVELAND HEIGHTS, OH (Time Warner Cable)

BROWNSVILLE—See ZANESVILLE, OH (Time Warner Cable)

BRUNERSBURG—See DEFIANCE, OH (Time Warner Cable)

BRUNSWICK HILLS—See BRUNSWICK, OH (Time Warner Cable)

▲**BRUNSWICK**—Time Warner Cable

▲**BRYAN**—Bryan Municipal Utilities

▲**BRYAN**—Time Warner Cable

BUCHTEL—See NELSONVILLE, OH (Nelsonville TV Cable)

BUCKEYE LAKE—See LANCASTER, OH (Time Warner Cable)

▲**BUCYRUS**—Time Warner Cable

BUFFALO—See SENECAVILLE, OH (Suddenlink Communications)

BURBANK—See LODI, OH (Time Warner Cable)

BURGOON (VILLAGE)—See CLAY CENTER/GIBSONBURG, OH (Time Warner Cable)

BURKETSVILLE—See DAYTON, OH (Time Warner Cable)

BURLINGTON TWP.—See NEWARK, OH (Time Warner Cable)

BURLINGTON—See SOUTH POINT, OH (Armstrong Cable Services)

BURTON CITY (PORTIONS)—See ORRVILLE, OH (Armstrong Cable Services)

BURTON TWP.—See CLEVELAND HEIGHTS, OH (Time Warner Cable)

BURTON—See CLEVELAND HEIGHTS, OH (Time Warner Cable)

BUSHCREEK TWP. (MUSKINGUM COUNTY)—See ZANESVILLE, OH (Time Warner Cable)

BUTLER COUNTY (PORTIONS)—See CINCINNATI, OH (Time Warner Cable)

BUTLER TWP. (COLUMBIANA COUNTY)—See SALEM, OH (Time Warner Cable)

BUTLER TWP. (MERCER COUNTY)—See CELINA, OH (Time Warner Cable)

BUTLER TWP. (RICHLAND COUNTY)—See ASHLAND, OH (Armstrong Cable Services)

BUTLER—See MANSFIELD, OH (Time Warner Cable)

BUTLERVILLE—See CINCINNATI, OH (Time Warner Cable)

BYESVILLE—See SENECAVILLE, OH (Suddenlink Communications)

▲**CADIZ**—Time Warner Cable

CAESARS CREEK TWP.—See CINCINNATI, OH (Time Warner Cable)

CAIRO—See LIMA, OH (Time Warner Cable)

CALDWELL—See NEWARK, OH (Time Warner Cable)

▲**CALEDONIA**—Now served by MARION, OH [OH0040]

CALEDONIA—See MARION, OH (Time Warner Cable)

▲**CAMBRIDGE**—Time Warner Cable. Now served by NEWARK, OH [OH0019]

CAMBRIDGE—See NEWARK, OH (Time Warner Cable)

CAMDEN TWP.—See WELLINGTON, OH (GLW Broadband)

CAMDEN—See DAYTON, OH (Time Warner Cable)

▲**CAMERON**—Formerly served by Cebridge Connections. No longer in operation

CAMPBELL—See BOARDMAN, OH (Armstrong Cable Services)

CANAAN TWP. (ATHENS COUNTY)—See ATHENS, OH (Time Warner Cable)

▲**CANAAN TWP. (Madison County)**—Time Warner Cable. Now served by COLUMBUS, OH [OH0002]

CANAAN TWP. (MADISON COUNTY)—See COLUMBUS, OH (Time Warner Cable)

CANAAN TWP. (WAYNE COUNTY)—See WOOSTER, OH (Clear Picture Inc.)

CANAAN TWP. (WAYNE COUNTY)—See LODI, OH (Time Warner Cable)

CANAL FULTON—See MASSILLON, OH (Massillon Cable TV Inc.)

CANAL WINCHESTER—See COLUMBUS, OH (Insight Communications)

CANAL WINCHESTER—See COLUMBUS, OH (WOW! Internet Cable & Phone)

CANFIELD TWP.—See BOARDMAN, OH (Armstrong Cable Services)

CANFIELD TWP.—See BERLIN TWP. (Mahoning County), OH (Shentel)

CANFIELD—See BOARDMAN, OH (Armstrong Cable Services)

▲**CANTON**—Time Warner Cable

CARBON HILL—See NELSONVILLE, OH (Nelsonville TV Cable)

CARDINGTON—See MOUNT GILEAD, OH (Time Warner Cable)

▲**CAREY**—Time Warner Cable. Now served by SYCAMORE, OH [OH0215]

CAREY—See SYCAMORE, OH (Time Warner Cable)

CARLISLE TWP. (LORAIN COUNTY)—See CLEVELAND HEIGHTS, OH (Time Warner Cable)

CARLISLE—See CINCINNATI, OH (Time Warner Cable)

CAROLINE—See SYCAMORE, OH (Time Warner Cable)

CARROLL TWP. (OTTAWA COUNTY)—See PORT CLINTON, OH (Time Warner Cable)

CARROLL—See LANCASTER, OH (Time Warner Cable)

▲**CARROLLTON**—Time Warner Cable. Now served by MINERVA, OH [OH0132]

CARROLLTON—See MINERVA, OH (Time Warner Cable)

CARROTHERS—See SYCAMORE, OH (Time Warner Cable)

CARTHAGENA—See CELINA, OH (Time Warner Cable)

CASS TWP. (HANCOCK COUNTY)—See FINDLAY, OH (Time Warner Cable)

CASS TWP.—See WILLARD, OH (Time Warner Cable)

CASSTOWN—See DAYTON, OH (Time Warner Cable)

CASTALIA—See SANDUSKY, OH (Buckeye Cable System)

CASTINE—See DAYTON, OH (Time Warner Cable)

CATAWBA (VILLAGE)—See DAYTON, OH (Time Warner Cable)

CATAWBA ISLAND TWP. (OTTAWA COUNTY)—See PORT CLINTON, OH (Time Warner Cable)

CATLETTSBURG—See SOUTH POINT, KY (Armstrong Cable Services)

CECIL—See PAULDING, OH (Time Warner Cable)

CEDARVILLE—See DAYTON, OH (Time Warner Cable)

▲**CELINA**—Time Warner Cable

CENTER TWP. (COLUMBIANA COUNTY)—See SALEM, OH (Time Warner Cable)

CENTER TWP. (WILLIAMS COUNTY)—See BRYAN, OH (Time Warner Cable)

CENTER TWP. (WOOD COUNTY)—See BOWLING GREEN, OH (Time Warner Cable)

CENTER TWP.—See NEWARK, OH (Time Warner Cable)

CENTERBURG—See MOUNT VERNON, OH (Time Warner Cable)

CENTERVILLE—See DAYTON, OH (Time Warner Cable)

CEREDO—See SOUTH POINT, WV (Armstrong Cable Services)

CHAGRIN FALLS—See CLEVELAND HEIGHTS, OH (Time Warner Cable)

CHAMPAIGN COUNTY (PORTIONS)—See DAYTON, OH (Time Warner Cable)

CHAMPION TWP. (TRUMBULL COUNTY)—See WARREN, OH (Time Warner Cable)

▲**CHANDLERSVILLE**—Now served by NEWARK, OH [OH0019]

CHANDLERSVILLE—See NEWARK, OH (Time Warner Cable)

CHARDON TWP.—See CLEVELAND HEIGHTS, OH (Time Warner Cable)

CHARDON—See CLEVELAND HEIGHTS, OH (Time Warner Cable)

CHARLESTOWN TWP.—See ATWATER TWP., OH (Time Warner Cable)

CHATFIELD—See SYCAMORE, OH (Time Warner Cable)

CHATHAM TWP.—See LODI, OH (Time Warner Cable)

CHAUNCEY—See NELSONVILLE, OH (Nelsonville TV Cable)

CHERRY FORK—See CINCINNATI, OH (Time Warner Cable)

CHESAPEAKE—See SOUTH POINT, OH (Armstrong Cable Services)

CHESTER TWP. (WAYNE COUNTY)—See WOOSTER, OH (Clear Picture Inc.)

CHESTER TWP.—See BEVERLY, OH (Time Warner Cable)

CHESTERLAND—See CLEVELAND HEIGHTS, OH (Time Warner Cable)

CHESTERVILLE—See MOUNT GILEAD, OH (Time Warner Cable)

CHEVIOT—See CINCINNATI, OH (Time Warner Cable)

CHICKASAW—See MINSTER, OH (Time Warner Cable)

▲**CHILLICOTHE**—Time Warner Cable

CHIPPEWA LAKE—See LODI, OH (Time Warner Cable)

CHIPPEWA TWP. (WAYNE COUNTY)—See AKRON, OH (Time Warner Cable)

▲**CHIPPEWA TWP.**—Time Warner Cable. Now served by AKRON, OH [OH0005]

CHIPPEWA TWP.—See DOYLESTOWN, OH (Doylestown Communications)

CHRISTIANSBURG—See DAYTON, OH (Time Warner Cable)

▲**CINCINNATI**—Time Warner Cable

▲**CIRCLEVILLE**—Time Warner Communications. Now served by COLUMBUS, OH [OH0002]

▲**CIRCLEVILLE**—Time Warner Cable

CLARIDON TWP.—See MARION, OH (Time Warner Cable)

CLARIDON—See CLEVELAND HEIGHTS, OH (Time Warner Cable)

CLARIDON—See THOMPSON TWP. (Geauga County), OH (Zito Media)

CLARINGTON—See HANNIBAL, OH (Windjammer Cable)

CLARK TWP. (BROWN COUNTY)—See CINCINNATI, OH (Time Warner Cable)

CLARK TWP. (CLINTON COUNTY)—See CINCINNATI, OH (Time Warner Cable)

CLARK TWP. (HOLMES COUNTY)—See NEW PHILADELPHIA, OH (Time Warner Cable)

CLARKSBURG—See NEW HOLLAND, OH (Time Warner Cable)

CLARKSFIELD—See NEW LONDON, OH (Time Warner Cable)

▲**CLAY CENTER/GIBSONBURG**—Time Warner Cable

CLAY TWP. (AUGLAIZE COUNTY)—See WAYNESFIELD, OH (Time Warner Cable)

CLAY TWP. (KNOX COUNTY)—See MOUNT VERNON, OH (Time Warner Cable)

CLAY TWP. (MONTGOMERY COUNTY)—See DAYTON, OH (Time Warner Cable)

CLAY TWP. (OTTAWA COUNTY)—See CLAY CENTER/GIBSONBURG, OH (Time Warner Cable)

CLAY TWP. (SCIOTO COUNTY)—See LUCASVILLE, OH (Time Warner Cable)

CLAY TWP. (SCIOTO COUNTY)—See PORTSMOUTH, OH (Time Warner Cable)

CLAY TWP.—See CROWN CITY, OH (Windjammer Cable)

CLAYTON TWP.—See THORNVILLE, OH (Time Warner Cable)

CLAYTON—See DAYTON, OH (Time Warner Cable)

CLEARCREEK TWP. (FAIRFIELD COUNTY)—See CHILLICOTHE, OH (Time Warner Cable)

CLERMONT COUNTY (PORTIONS)—See CINCINNATI, OH (Time Warner Cable)

CLEVELAND HEIGHTS (PORTIONS)—See CLEVELAND, OH (WOW! Internet Cable & Phone)

▲**CLEVELAND HEIGHTS**—Time Warner Cable

▲**CLEVELAND**—Time Warner Cable (formerly Adelphia Cable). Now served by CLEVELAND HEIGHTS, OH [OH0006]

CLEVELAND—See CLEVELAND HEIGHTS, OH (Time Warner Cable)

▲**CLEVELAND**—WOW! Internet Cable & Phone

CLIFTON (VILLAGE)—See DAYTON, OH (Time Warner Cable)

CLINTON COUNTY (PORTIONS)—See CINCINNATI, OH (Time Warner Cable)

CLINTON TWP. (FRANKLIN COUNTY)—See COLUMBUS, OH (Insight Communications)

CLINTON TWP. (WAYNE COUNTY)—See WOOSTER, OH (Clear Picture Inc.)

CLINTON TWP.—See COLUMBUS, OH (WOW! Internet Cable & Phone)

CLINTON—See GREEN, OH (Time Warner Cable)

CLOVERDALE—See OTTOVILLE, OH (OTEC Communication Co.)

CLYDE—See BELLEVUE, OH (Time Warner Cable)

COAL RUN—See BEVERLY, OH (Time Warner Cable)

COAL TWP. (JACKSON COUNTY)—See JACKSON, OH (Time Warner Cable)

COAL TWP. (PERRY COUNTY)—See CORNING, OH (Zito Media)

COALTON—See JACKSON, OH (Time Warner Cable)

▲**COITSVILLE TWP.**—Shentel

COLDWATER—See CELINA, OH (Time Warner Cable)

COLEBROOK—See ORWELL, OH (FairPoint Communications)

COLERAIN TWP. (HAMILTON COUNTY)—See CINCINNATI, OH (Time Warner Cable)

COLERAIN TWP. (ROSS COUNTY)—See CHILLICOTHE, OH (Time Warner Cable)

COLLEGE CORNER—See DAYTON, IN (Time Warner Cable)

COLLEGE TWP. (KNOX COUNTY)—See MOUNT VERNON, OH (Time Warner Cable)

COLLINS—See CLEVELAND HEIGHTS, OH (Time Warner Cable)

▲**COLLINSVILLE**—Formerly served by Time Warner Cable. No longer in operation

COLUMBIA TWP. (HAMILTON COUNTY)—See CINCINNATI, OH (Time Warner Cable)

COLUMBIA—See NEW PHILADELPHIA, OH (Time Warner Cable)

▲**COLUMBUS GROVE (VILLAGE)**—FairPoint Communications

COLUMBUS GROVE—See OTTAWA, OH (Time Warner Cable)

▲**COLUMBUS**—Formerly served by Sprint Corp. No longer in operation

▲**COLUMBUS**—Insight Communications

▲**COLUMBUS**—Time Warner Cable

▲**COLUMBUS**—WOW! Internet Cable & Phone

▲**COMMERCIAL POINT**—Time Warner Cable

▲**CONCORD TWP. (Lake County)**—Time Warner Cable. Now served by CLEVELAND HEIGHTS, OH [OH0006]

CONCORD TWP. (LAKE COUNTY)—See CLEVELAND HEIGHTS, OH (Time Warner Cable)

CONCORD TWP.—See COLUMBUS, OH (Time Warner Cable)

CONESVILLE—See NEWARK, OH (Time Warner Cable)

▲**CONGRESS TWP.**—Time Warner Cable

CONNEAUT—See ASHTABULA, OH (Time Warner Cable)

CONTINENTAL—See COLUMBUS GROVE (village), OH (FairPoint Communications)

▲**CONVOY**—Comcast Cable

COOLVILLE—See BEVERLY, OH (Time Warner Cable)

COPLEY TWP.—See CLEVELAND HEIGHTS, OH (Time Warner Cable)

COPLEY—See AKRON, OH (Time Warner Cable)

▲**CORNING**—Zito Media

CORTLAND—See WARREN, OH (Time Warner Cable)

CORTSVILLE TWP. (PORTIONS)—See STRUTHERS, OH (Time Warner Cable)

CORWIN (VILLAGE)—See DAYTON, OH (Time Warner Cable)

▲ **COSHOCTON**—Formerly served by Time Warner Cable. No longer in operation

COSTONIA—See TORONTO, OH (Jefferson County Cable Inc.)

COVENTRY TWP. (SUMMIT COUNTY)—See AKRON, OH (Time Warner Cable)

COVENTRY TWP. (SUMMIT COUNTY)—See GREEN, OH (Time Warner Cable)

▲ **CRAIG BEACH**—Time Warner Cable

CRANBERRY TWP.—See SYCAMORE, OH (Time Warner Cable)

CRANE TWP. (PAULDING COUNTY)—See VAN WERT, OH (Time Warner Cable)

CRANE TWP. (WYANDOT COUNTY)—See UPPER SANDUSKY, OH (Time Warner Cable)

CRAWFORD TWP.—See SYCAMORE, OH (Time Warner Cable)

CRESCENT—See BARTON, OH (Powhatan Point Cable Co.)

CRESTLINE—See GALION, OH (Time Warner Cable)

CRESTON—See LODI, OH (Time Warner Cable)

▲ **CRIDERSVILLE**—Time Warner Cable. Now served by LIMA, OH [OH0020]

CRIDERSVILLE—See LIMA, OH (Time Warner Cable)

▲ **CROOKSVILLE**—Time Warner Cable. Now served by ZANESVILLE, OH [OH0037]

CROOKSVILLE—See ZANESVILLE, OH (Time Warner Cable)

CROSBY TWP. (HAMILTON COUNTY)—See CINCINNATI, OH (Time Warner Cable)

CROTON—See MOUNT VERNON, OH (Time Warner Cable)

▲ **CROWN CITY**—Windjammer Cable

▲ **CRYSTAL LAKE MOBILE HOME PARK**—Time Warner Cable. Now served by COLUMBUS, OH [OH0002]

CRYSTAL LAKE MOBILE HOME PARK—See COLUMBUS, OH (Time Warner Cable)

▲ **CUMBERLAND**—Formerly served by Almega Cable. No longer in operation

CURTICE—See CLAY CENTER/GIBSONBURG, OH (Time Warner Cable)

CUSTAR (VILLAGE)—See BOWLING GREEN, OH (Time Warner Cable)

CUYAHOGA FALLS—See AKRON, OH (Time Warner Cable)

CUYAHOGA FALLS—See CLEVELAND HEIGHTS, OH (Time Warner Cable)

CUYAHOGA HEIGHTS—See CLEVELAND HEIGHTS, OH (Time Warner Cable)

CUYAHOGA HEIGHTS—See CLEVELAND, OH (WOW! Internet Cable & Phone)

CYGNET—See BOWLING GREEN, OH (Time Warner Cable)

CYNTHIAN TWP.—See MINSTER, OH (Time Warner Cable)

DALTON—See ORRVILLE, OH (Armstrong Cable Services)

DANBURY TWP. (OTTAWA COUNTY)—See PORT CLINTON, OH (Time Warner Cable)

DANVILLE—See MOUNT VERNON, OH (Time Warner Cable)

DARBY TWP. (PICKAWAY COUNTY)—See COLUMBUS, OH (Time Warner Cable)

DARBYVILLE—See COMMERCIAL POINT, OH (Time Warner Cable)

DARRTOWN—See CINCINNATI, OH (Time Warner Cable)

▲ **DAYTON**—Time Warner Cable

DE GRAFF—See DAYTON, OH (Time Warner Cable)

DECATUR TWP. (LAWRENCE COUNTY)—See PEDRO, OH (Windjammer Cable)

DEER CREEK TWP.—See COLUMBUS, OH (Time Warner Cable)

DEER PARK—See CINCINNATI, OH (Time Warner Cable)

DEERCREEK TWP. (PICKAWAY COUNTY)—See NEW HOLLAND, OH (Time Warner Cable)

DEERFIELD TWP. (PORTAGE COUNTY)—See ATWATER TWP., OH (Time Warner Cable)

DEERFIELD TWP. (WARREN COUNTY)—See CINCINNATI, OH (Time Warner Cable)

DEFIANCE COUNTY (PORTIONS)—See DEFIANCE, OH (Time Warner Cable)

▲ **DEFIANCE**—Time Warner Cable

DELAWARE TWP. (DELAWARE COUNTY)—See COLUMBUS, OH (Insight Communications)

▲ **DELHI TWP.**—Formerly served by Adelphia Communications. No longer in operation

▲ **DELLROY**—Now served by NEW PHILADELPHIA, OH [OH0030]

DELLROY—See NEW PHILADELPHIA, OH (Time Warner Cable)

▲ **DELPHOS**—Time Warner Cable

DELTA—See WAUSEON, OH (Time Warner Cable)

▲ **DENMARK TWP.**—Zito Media

DENNISON—See NEW PHILADELPHIA, OH (Time Warner Cable)

DERWENT—See SENECAVILLE, OH (Suddenlink Communications)

▲ **DESHLER**—Time Warner Cable

DEXTER CITY—See WARNER, OH (Zito Media)

DINSMORE TWP.—See DAYTON, OH (Time Warner Cable)

DODSON TWP.—See CINCINNATI, OH (Time Warner Cable)

DONNELSVILLE—See DAYTON, OH (Time Warner Cable)

DORSET TWP.—See DENMARK TWP., OH (Zito Media)

DOVER TWP. (ATHENS COUNTY)—See ATHENS, OH (Time Warner Cable)

DOVER TWP. (FULTON COUNTY)—See DEFIANCE, OH (Time Warner Cable)

DOVER—See NEW PHILADELPHIA, OH (Time Warner Cable)

▲ **DOYLESTOWN**—Doylestown Communications

DOYLESTOWN—See AKRON, OH (Time Warner Cable)

▲ **DRESDEN**—Time Warner Cable. Now served by ZANESVILLE, OH [OH0037]

DRESDEN—See ZANESVILLE, OH (Time Warner Cable)

DUBLIN—See COLUMBUS, OH (Time Warner Cable)

DUBLIN—See COLUMBUS, OH (WOW! Internet Cable & Phone)

DUCHOQUET TWP. (SOUTHERN PORTION)—See WAPAKONETA, OH (Time Warner Cable)

DUDLEY—See WARNER, OH (Zito Media)

DUNBRIDGE—See BOWLING GREEN, OH (Time Warner Cable)

DUNCAN FALLS—See ZANESVILLE, OH (Time Warner Cable)

▲ **DUNKIRK**—Time Warner Cable. Now served by KENTON, OH [OH0128]

DUNKIRK—See KENTON, OH (Time Warner Cable)

EAGLE TWP. (HANCOCK COUNTY)—See FINDLAY, OH (Time Warner Cable)

EAST CANTON—See CANTON, OH (Time Warner Cable)

▲ **EAST CLEVELAND**—East Cleveland Cable TV & Communications LLC

EAST FULTONHAM—See ZANESVILLE, OH (Time Warner Cable)

EAST LIBERTY—See COLUMBUS, OH (Time Warner Cable)

▲ **EAST LIVERPOOL**—Comcast Cable

▲ **EAST PALESTINE**—Comcast Cable. Now served by NEW MIDDLETOWN, OH (formerly Springfield Twp.) [OH0145]

EAST PALESTINE—See NEW MIDDLETOWN, OH (Comcast Cable)

EAST SPARTA—See CANTON, OH (Time Warner Cable)

EAST UNION TWP. (WAYNE COUNTY)—See WOOSTER, OH (Clear Picture Inc.)

EASTLAKE—See CLEVELAND HEIGHTS, OH (Time Warner Cable)

EATON TWP. (LORAIN COUNTY)—See WELLINGTON, OH (GLW Broadband)

▲ **EATON**—Time Warner Cable. Now served by DAYTON, OH [OH0011]

EATON—See DAYTON, OH (Time Warner Cable)

EDEN TWP. (SENECA COUNTY)—See FOSTORIA, OH (Time Warner Cable)

EDEN TWP. (WYANDOT COUNTY)—See UPPER SANDUSKY, OH (Time Warner Cable)

EDEN TWP.—See NEWARK, OH (Time Warner Cable)

EDGERTON—See BRYAN, OH (Time Warner Cable)

EDINBURG TWP.—See ATWATER TWP., OH (Time Warner Cable)

EDINBURG—See NEW MIDDLETOWN, PA (Comcast Cable)

EDISON—See MOUNT GILEAD, OH (Time Warner Cable)

▲ **EDON**—Windjammer Cable

ELBA—See WARNER, OH (Zito Media)

ELDORADO—See DAYTON, OH (Time Warner Cable)

ELIDA—See LIMA, OH (Time Warner Cable)

ELIZABETH TWP. (LAWRENCE COUNTY)—See PEDRO, OH (Windjammer Cable)

ELIZABETH TWP. (MIAMI COUNTY)—See DAYTON, OH (Time Warner Cable)

ELLSWORTH TWP.—See BERLIN TWP. (Mahoning County), OH (Shentel)

ELMORE—See CLAY CENTER/GIBSONBURG, OH (Time Warner Cable)

ELMWOOD PLACE—See CINCINNATI, OH (Time Warner Cable)

ELYRIA TWP. (LORAIN COUNTY)—See CLEVELAND HEIGHTS, OH (Time Warner Cable)

▲ **ELYRIA**—Time Warner Cable. Now served by CLEVELAND HEIGHTS, OH [OH0006]

ELYRIA—See CLEVELAND HEIGHTS, OH (Time Warner Cable)

EMERALD TWP.—See PAULDING, OH (Time Warner Cable)

EMPIRE—See TORONTO, OH (Jefferson County Cable Inc.)

ENGLEWOOD—See DAYTON, OH (Time Warner Cable)

ENON—See DAYTON, OH (Time Warner Cable)

ERIE TWP. (OTTAWA COUNTY)—See PORT CLINTON, OH (Time Warner Cable)

ERIE TWP. (PORTIONS)—See TOLEDO, MI (Buckeye Cable System Inc)

ETNA TWP.—See COLUMBUS, OH (Insight Communications)

ETNA TWP.—See MOUNT VERNON, OH (Time Warner Cable)

EUCLID—See CLEVELAND HEIGHTS, OH (Time Warner Cable)

▲ **EUREKA**—Windjammer Cable

EVENDALE—See CINCINNATI, OH (Time Warner Cable)

▲ **FAIRBORN**—Time Warner Cable. Now served by DAYTON, OH [OH0011]

FAIRBORN—See DAYTON, OH (Time Warner Cable)

FAIRFAX—See CINCINNATI, OH (Time Warner Cable)

▲ **FAIRFIELD (Butler County)**—Formerly served by Adelphia Communications. Now served by CINCINNATI, OH [OH0001]

FAIRFIELD COUNTY (PORTIONS)—See OAKLAND, OH (Time Warner Cable)

FAIRFIELD TWP. (HURON COUNTY)—See WILLARD, OH (Time Warner Cable)

FAIRFIELD—See CINCINNATI, OH (Time Warner Cable)

FAIRLAWN—See AKRON, OH (Time Warner Cable)

FAIRPOINT HARBOR—See CLEVELAND HEIGHTS, OH (Time Warner Cable)

FAIRVIEW PARK—See PARMA, OH (Cox Communications)

FAIRVIEW PARK—See CLEVELAND, OH (WOW! Internet Cable & Phone)

FALLS TWP. (HOCKING COUNTY)—See LOGAN, OH (Time Warner Cable)

FARMERSVILLE—See DAYTON, OH (Time Warner Cable)

FARMINGTON TWP.—See WARREN, OH (Time Warner Cable)

FARMINGTON—See NELSON TWP., OH (Suddenlink Communications)

FAYETTE TWP.—See SOUTH POINT, OH (Armstrong Cable Services)

▲ **FAYETTE**—Formerly served by Adelphia Communications. Now served by WAUSEON, OH [OH0106]

FAYETTE—See WAUSEON, OH (Time Warner Cable)

FAYETTEVILLE—See CINCINNATI, OH (Time Warner Cable)

▲ **FINDLAY**—Time Warner Cable

FLATROCK TWP.—See NAPOLEON, OH (Time Warner Cable)

FLATWOODS—See SOUTH POINT, KY (Armstrong Cable Services)

FLETCHER—See DAYTON, OH (Time Warner Cable)

FLORENCE TWP. (ERIE COUNTY)—See CLEVELAND HEIGHTS, OH (Time Warner Cable)

FLORIDA—See DEFIANCE, OH (Time Warner Cable)

FLORIDA—See NAPOLEON, OH (Time Warner Cable)

▲ **FLUSHING**—Comcast Cable. Now served by WHEELING, WV [WV0004]

FOREST PARK—See CINCINNATI, OH (Time Warner Cable)

▲ **FOREST**—Time Warner Cable. Now served by KENTON, OH [OH0128]

FOREST—See KENTON, OH (Time Warner Cable)

▲ **FORT JENNINGS**—Fort Jennings Telephone Co.

FORT LORAMIE—See NEW KNOXVILLE, OH (NKTelco Services)

FORT LORAMIE—See MINSTER, OH (Time Warner Cable)

▲ **FORT RECOVERY (VILLAGE)**—Comcast Cable

FORT SENECA—See CLAY CENTER/GIBSONBURG, OH (Time Warner Cable)

FORT SHAWNEE—See LIMA, OH (Time Warner Cable)

▲ **FOSTORIA**—Time Warner Cable

FOUNTAIN PLACE—See MARION, OH (Time Warner Cable)

FOWLER TWP.—See WARREN, OH (Time Warner Cable)

▲ **FRANKFORT**—Formerly served by Adelphia Communications. Now served by CHILLICOTHE, OH [OH0033]

FRANKFORT—See CHILLICOTHE, OH (Time Warner Cable)

▲ **FRANKLIN FURNACE**—Formerly served by Adelphia Communications. Now served by ASHLAND, KY [KY0326]

FRANKLIN TWP. (MERCER COUNTY)—See CELINA, OH (Time Warner Cable)

FRANKLIN TWP. (PORTAGE COUNTY)—See KENT, OH (Time Warner Cable)

FRANKLIN TWP. (SUMMIT COUNTY)—See GREEN, OH (Time Warner Cable)

FRANKLIN TWP. (WAYNE COUNTY)—See WOOSTER, OH (Clear Picture Inc.)

FRANKLIN TWP.—See COLUMBUS, OH (WOW! Internet Cable & Phone)

FRANKLIN—See CINCINNATI, OH (Time Warner Cable)

▲ **FRAZEYBURG**—Time Warner Cable. Now served by ZANESVILLE, OH [OH0037]

FRAZEYBURG—See ZANESVILLE, OH (Time Warner Cable)

FREDERICKSBURG—See NEW PHILADELPHIA, OH (Time Warner Cable)

▲ **FREDERICKTOWN**—Time Warner Cable. Now served by MOUNT VERNON, OH [OH0095]

FREDERICKTOWN—See MOUNT VERNON, OH (Time Warner Cable)

FREEDOM TWP. (PORTAGE COUNTY)—See NELSON TWP., OH (Suddenlink Communications)

▲ **FREEPORT TWP.**—Windjammer Cable

FREEPORT—See FREEPORT TWP., OH (Windjammer Cable)

▲ **FREMONT**—Time Warner Cable. Now served by BELLEVUE, OH [OH0086]

FREMONT—See BELLEVUE, OH (Time Warner Cable)

▲ **FRIENDSHIP**—Time Warner Cable

▲ **FULTON TWP.**—Formerly served by Adelphia Communications. Now served by WAUSEON, OH [OH0106]

FULTON TWP.—See WAUSEON, OH (Time Warner Cable)

FULTON—See MOUNT GILEAD, OH (Time Warner Cable)

FULTONHAM—See ZANESVILLE, OH (Time Warner Cable)

GAHANNA (FRANKLIN COUNTY)—See COLUMBUS, OH (Insight Communications)

GAHANNA—See COLUMBUS, OH (WOW! Internet Cable & Phone)

GALENA—See COLUMBUS, OH (Time Warner Cable)

▲ **GALION**—Time Warner Cable

GALLIA COUNTY (UNINCORPORATED AREAS)—See CROWN CITY, OH (Windjammer Cable)

▲ **GALLIPOLIS**—Zito Media

GAMBIER—See MOUNT VERNON, OH (Time Warner Cable)

GARFIELD HEIGHTS—See CLEVELAND HEIGHTS, OH (Time Warner Cable)

GARFIELD HEIGHTS—See CLEVELAND, OH (WOW! Internet Cable & Phone)

GARRETTSVILLE—See WARREN, OH (Time Warner Cable)

GATES MILLS—See CLEVELAND HEIGHTS, OH (Time Warner Cable)

GEAUGA COUNTY (PORTIONS)—See NELSON TWP., OH (Suddenlink Communications)

GENEVA TWP. (ASHTABULA COUNTY)—See ASHTABULA, OH (Time Warner Cable)

GENEVA-ON-THE-LAKE—See ASHTABULA, OH (Time Warner Cable)

GENEVA—See ASHTABULA, OH (Time Warner Cable)

GENOA TWP. (DELAWARE COUNTY)—See COLUMBUS, OH (Insight Communications)

GENOA—See CLAY CENTER/GIBSONBURG, OH (Time Warner Cable)

GERMAN (VILLAGE)—See BLOOMINGDALE, OH (Suddenlink Communications)

GERMAN TWP. (AUGLAIZE COUNTY)—See MINSTER, OH (Time Warner Cable)

GERMAN TWP. (FULTON COUNTY)—See BRYAN, OH (Time Warner Cable)

GERMAN TWP. (MONTGOMERY COUNTY)—See DAYTON, OH (Time Warner Cable)

GERMAN TWP.—See DAYTON, OH (Time Warner Cable)

▲ **GERMANTOWN**—Time Warner Cable. Now served by DAYTON, OH [OH0011]

GERMANTOWN—See DAYTON, OH (Time Warner Cable)

GETTYSBURG—See DAYTON, OH (Time Warner Cable)

GIBSONBURG—See CLAY CENTER/GIBSONBURG, OH (Time Warner Cable)

GILBOA—See COLUMBUS GROVE (village), OH (FairPoint Communications)

GILEAD TWP.—See MOUNT GILEAD, OH (Time Warner Cable)

GIRARD—See WARREN, OH (Time Warner Cable)

GLANDORF (VILLAGE)—See OTTAWA, OH (Time Warner Cable)

▲ **GLENCOE**—Comcast Cable. Now served by WHEELING, WV [WV0004]

GLENDALE—See CINCINNATI, OH (Time Warner Cable)

GLENFORD—See THORNVILLE, OH (Time Warner Cable)

▲ **GLENMONT**—Now served by NEW PHILADELPHIA, OH [OH0030]

GLENMONT—See NEW PHILADELPHIA, OH (Time Warner Cable)

GLENWILLOW—See CLEVELAND HEIGHTS, OH (Time Warner Cable)

GLORIA GLENS—See LODI, OH (Time Warner Cable)

GLOUSTER—See NELSONVILLE, OH (Nelsonville TV Cable)

GNADENHUTTON—See NEW PHILADELPHIA, OH (Time Warner Cable)

GOLF MANOR—See CINCINNATI, OH (Time Warner Cable)

GOMER—See LIMA, OH (Time Warner Cable)

GOOD HOPE TWP.—See LOGAN, OH (Time Warner Cable)

GORDON—See DAYTON, OH (Time Warner Cable)

▲ **GOSHEN TWP. (Clermont County)**—Tiime Warner Cable. Now served by CINCINNATI, OH [OH0001]

GOSHEN TWP. (CLERMONT COUNTY)—See CINCINNATI, OH (Time Warner Cable)

GOSHEN TWP. (MAHONING COUNTY)—See BERLIN TWP. (Mahoning County), OH (Shentel)

GRAFTON TWP.—See WELLINGTON, OH (GLW Broadband)

▲**GRAFTON**—Grafton Cable Communications. Now served by WELLINGTON, OH [OH0189]

GRAFTON—See WELLINGTON, OH (GLW Broadband)

GRAND PRAIRIE TWP.—See MARION, OH (Time Warner Cable)

GRAND RAPIDS—See WATERVILLE, OH (Time Warner Cable)

GRAND RIVER—See CLEVELAND HEIGHTS, OH (Time Warner Cable)

GRANDVIEW HEIGHTS—See COLUMBUS, OH (Time Warner Cable)

GRANDVIEW HEIGHTS—See COLUMBUS, OH (WOW! Internet Cable & Phone)

GRANGER TWP.—See CLEVELAND HEIGHTS, OH (Time Warner Cable)

GRANVILLE TWP. (MERCER COUNTY)—See CELINA, OH (Time Warner Cable)

GRANVILLE—See NEWARK, OH (Time Warner Cable)

GRATIOT—See ZANESVILLE, OH (Time Warner Cable)

GRATIS—See DAYTON, OH (Time Warner Cable)

GRAYTOWN—See PORT CLINTON, OH (Time Warner Cable)

GREEN CAMP—See MARION, OH (Time Warner Cable)

GREEN CREEK TWP. (SANDUSKY COUNTY)—See BELLEVUE, OH (Time Warner Cable)

▲**GREEN MEADOWS**—Time Warner Entertainment Co. LP. Now served by DAYTON, OH [OH0011]

GREEN MEADOWS—See DAYTON, OH (Time Warner Cable)

GREEN SPRINGS—See BELLEVUE, OH (Time Warner Cable)

GREEN TWP. (BROWN COUNTY)—See CINCINNATI, OH (Time Warner Cable)

GREEN TWP. (CLARK COUNTY)—See DAYTON, OH (Time Warner Cable)

▲**GREEN TWP. (Hamilton County)**—Time Warner Cable. Now served by CINCINNATI, OH [OH0001]

GREEN TWP. (HAMILTON COUNTY)—See CINCINNATI, OH (Time Warner Cable)

GREEN TWP. (MAHONING COUNTY)—See BERLIN TWP. (Mahoning County), OH (Shentel)

GREEN TWP. (MAHONING COUNTY)—See SALEM, OH (Time Warner Cable)

GREEN TWP. (WAYNE COUNTY)—See ORRVILLE, OH (Armstrong Cable Services)

▲**GREEN**—Time Warner Cable

▲**GREENFIELD ESTATES**—Formerly served by World Cable. No longer in operation

GREENFIELD TWP. (FAIRFIELD COUNTY)—See COLUMBUS, OH (Insight Communications)

GREENFIELD TWP. (HURON COUNTY)—See WILLARD, OH (Time Warner Cable)

▲**GREENFIELD**—Formerly served by Adelphia Communications. Now served by WASHINGTON COURT HOUSE, OH [OH0070]

GREENFIELD—See WASHINGTON COURT HOUSE, OH (Time Warner Cable)

GREENHILLS—See CINCINNATI, OH (Time Warner Cable)

GREENSBURG TWP.—See KALIDA, OH (Kalida Telephone Co.)

GREENUP COUNTY (EASTERN PORTION)—See SOUTH POINT, KY (Armstrong Cable Services)

GREENUP COUNTY—See PORTSMOUTH, KY (Time Warner Cable)

GREENUP—See SOUTH POINT, KY (Armstrong Cable Services)

▲**GREENVILLE**—Time Warner Cable. Now served by DAYTON, OH [OH0011]

GREENVILLE—See DAYTON, OH (Time Warner Cable)

GREENWICH—See WILLARD, OH (Time Warner Cable)

▲**GREENWOOD (village)**—Formerly served by Adelphia Communications. No longer in operation

GROTON TWP. (ERIE COUNTY)—See SANDUSKY, OH (Buckeye Cable System)

GROVE CITY—See COLUMBUS, OH (Time Warner Cable)

GROVE CITY—See COLUMBUS, OH (WOW! Internet Cable & Phone)

GROVEPORT—See COLUMBUS, OH (Time Warner Cable)

GROVER HILL—See OTTOVILLE, OH (OTEC Communication Co.)

▲**GUERNSEY COUNTY (portions)**—Now served by NEWARK, OH [OH0019]

GUERNSEY COUNTY (PORTIONS)—See NEWARK, OH (Time Warner Cable)

▲**GUILFORD LAKE**—Time Warner Cable. Now served by SALEM, OH [OH0096]

GUILFORD LAKE—See SALEM, OH (Time Warner Cable)

GUILFORD TWP.—See LODI, OH (Time Warner Cable)

▲**GUYSVILLE**—Formerly served by Adelphia Communications. Now served by WATERTOWN, OH [OH0175]

GUYSVILLE—See BEVERLY, OH (Time Warner Cable)

HALE TWP.—See KENTON, OH (Time Warner Cable)

HALLSVILLE—See CHILLICOTHE, OH (Time Warner Cable)

HAMBDEN TWP. (GEAUGA COUNTY)—See THOMPSON TWP. (Geauga County), OH (Zito Media)

HAMBDEN TWP.—See CLEVELAND HEIGHTS, OH (Time Warner Cable)

HAMDEN—See JACKSON, OH (Time Warner Cable)

HAMER TWP.—See CINCINNATI, OH (Time Warner Cable)

HAMILTON TWP. (FRANKLIN COUNTY)—See COLUMBUS, OH (Insight Communications)

HAMILTON TWP. (FRANKLIN COUNTY)—See COLUMBUS, OH (Time Warner Cable)

HAMILTON TWP. (WARREN COUNTY)—See CINCINNATI, OH (Time Warner Cable)

▲**HAMILTON**—Time Warner Cable. Now served by CINCINNATI, OH [OH0001]

HAMILTON—See CINCINNATI, OH (Time Warner Cable)

HAMLER—See DESHLER, OH (Time Warner Cable)

▲**HANNIBAL**—Windjammer Cable

HANOVER TWP. (COLUMBIANA COUNTY)—See SALEM, OH (Time Warner Cable)

HANOVER TWP.—See CINCINNATI, OH (Time Warner Cable)

HANOVER—See NEWARK, OH (Time Warner Cable)

HANOVERTON—See SALEM, OH (Time Warner Cable)

HARBOR VIEW—See TOLEDO, OH (Buckeye Cable System Inc)

HARDING TWP.—See WAUSEON, OH (Time Warner Cable)

HARLAN TWP.—See CINCINNATI, OH (Time Warner Cable)

HARLEM TWP. (DELAWARE COUNTY)—See COLUMBUS, OH (Insight Communications)

HARLEM TWP. (DELAWARE COUNTY)—See COLUMBUS, OH (Time Warner Cable)

HARMONY TWP.—See DAYTON, OH (Time Warner Cable)

HARMONY TWP.—See MOUNT GILEAD, OH (Time Warner Cable)

HARPERSFIELD TWP. (ASHTABULA COUNTY)—See ASHTABULA, OH (Time Warner Cable)

HARPSTER—See UPPER SANDUSKY, OH (Time Warner Cable)

HARRIS TWP. (OTTAWA COUNTY)—See CLAY CENTER/GIBSONBURG, OH (Time Warner Cable)

HARRISBURG—See COLUMBUS, OH (Time Warner Cable)

▲**HARRISON TWP. (Carroll County)**—Time Warner Cable. Now served by NEW PHILADELPHIA, OH [OH0030]

HARRISON TWP. (CARROLL COUNTY)—See NEW PHILADELPHIA, OH (Time Warner Cable)

HARRISON TWP. (PICKAWAY COUNTY)—See COLUMBUS, OH (Insight Communications)

HARRISON—See CINCINNATI, OH (Time Warner Cable)

HARRISVILLE—See DAYTON, IN (Time Warner Cable)

HARROD—See LIMA, OH (Time Warner Cable)

HARTLAND TWP.—See NORWALK, OH (Time Warner Cable)

HARTSGROVE—See THOMPSON TWP. (Geauga County), OH (Zito Media)

HARTVILLE—See CANTON, OH (Time Warner Cable)

HASKINS—See WATERVILLE, OH (Time Warner Cable)

▲**HAYDEN HEIGHTS**—Formerly served by Time Warner Cable. No longer in operation

HAYDENVILLE—See NELSONVILLE, OH (Nelsonville TV Cable)

HAYESVILLE—See ASHLAND, OH (Armstrong Cable Services)

HEATH—See NEWARK, OH (Time Warner Cable)

HELENA (VILLAGE)—See CLAY CENTER/GIBSONBURG, OH (Time Warner Cable)

HEMLOCK—See CORNING, OH (Zito Media)

HENRIETTA TWP.—See WELLINGTON, OH (GLW Broadband)

HENRY TWP. (WOOD COUNTY)—See BOWLING GREEN, OH (Time Warner Cable)

HESSVILLE—See CLAY CENTER/GIBSONBURG, OH (Time Warner Cable)

▲**HICKSVILLE**—Mediacom

▲**HIDE-A-WAY HILLS**—Time Warner Cable

HIGHLAND HEIGHTS—See CLEVELAND HEIGHTS, OH (Time Warner Cable)

HIGHLAND HILLS—See CLEVELAND HEIGHTS, OH (Time Warner Cable)

HIGHLAND—See CINCINNATI, OH (Time Warner Cable)

HILLGROVE—See DAYTON, OH (Time Warner Cable)

HILLIAR TWP. (KNOX COUNTY)—See MOUNT VERNON, OH (Time Warner Cable)

HILLIARD—See COLUMBUS, OH (WOW! Internet Cable & Phone)

HILLS & DALES (VILLAGE)—See CANTON, OH (Time Warner Cable)

▲**HILLSBORO**—Time Warner Cable. Now served by CINCINNATI, OH [OH0001]

HILLSBORO—See CINCINNATI, OH (Time Warner Cable)

HILLSVILLE—See NEW MIDDLETOWN, PA (Comcast Cable)

HINCKLEY TWP.—See CLEVELAND HEIGHTS, OH (Time Warner Cable)

HIRAM—See MACEDONIA, OH (Time Warner Cable)

HOAGLIN TWP. (VAN WERT COUNTY)—See OTTOVILLE, OH (OTEC Communication Co.)

HOAGLIN TWP. (VAN WERT COUNTY)—See VAN WERT, OH (Time Warner Cable)

HOCKING COUNTY (UNINCORPORATED AREAS)—See MURRAY CITY, OH (Time Warner Cable)

HOCKING COUNTY—See CORNING, OH (Zito Media)

HOCKING TWP. (FAIRFIELD COUNTY)—See CHILLICOTHE, OH (Time Warner Cable)

HOCKINGPORT—See BEVERLY, OH (Time Warner Cable)

HOLGATE—See DESHLER, OH (Time Warner Cable)

HOLLAND—See TOLEDO, OH (Buckeye Cable System Inc)

HOLLANSBURG—See DAYTON, OH (Time Warner Cable)

HOLMES TWP.—See BUCYRUS, OH (Time Warner Cable)

HOLMESVILLE—See NEW PHILADELPHIA, OH (Time Warner Cable)

HOMER TWP. (MEDINA COUNTY)—See LODI, OH (Time Warner Cable)

▲**HOPEDALE**—Time Warner Cable

HOPEWELL TWP. (MERCER COUNTY)—See CELINA, OH (Time Warner Cable)

HOPEWELL TWP. (MUSKINGUM COUNTY)—See ZANESVILLE, OH (Time Warner Cable)

HOPEWELL TWP. (SENECA COUNTY)—See FOSTORIA, OH (Time Warner Cable)

HOWARD TWP. (KNOX COUNTY)—See MOUNT VERNON, OH (Time Warner Cable)

▲**HOWARD**—Formerly served by Adelphia Communications. Now served by NEWARK, OH [OH0019]

HOWARD—See NEWARK, OH (Time Warner Cable)

HOWLAND TWP. (TRUMBULL COUNTY)—See WARREN, OH (Time Warner Cable)

▲**HUBBARD TWP. (TRUMBULL COUNTY)**—Northeast Cable TV

HUBBARD TWP. (TRUMBULL COUNTY)—See COITSVILLE TWP., OH (Shentel)

HUBBARD TWP. (TRUMBULL COUNTY)—See WARREN, OH (Time Warner Cable)

HUBBARD TWP.—See YOUNGSTOWN, OH (Northeast Cable TV)

HUBBARD—See WARREN, OH (Time Warner Cable)

HUBER HEIGHTS—See DAYTON, OH (Time Warner Cable)

HUDSON TWP. (SUMMIT COUNTY)—See MACEDONIA, OH (Time Warner Cable)

HUDSON VILLAGE—See MACEDONIA, OH (Time Warner Cable)

HUDSON—See MACEDONIA, OH (Time Warner Cable)

HUNTING VALLEY—See CLEVELAND HEIGHTS, OH (Time Warner Cable)

HUNTINGTON TWP. (ROSS COUNTY)—See CHILLICOTHE, OH (Time Warner Cable)

▲**HUNTINGTON TWP.**—Formerly served by Adelphia Communications. Now served by CHILLICOTHE, OH [OH0033]

HUNTSBURG TWP.—See THOMPSON TWP. (Geauga County), OH (Zito Media)

HUNTSVILLE (VILLAGE)—See BELLEFONTAINE, OH (Time Warner Cable)

HURON TWP. (ERIE COUNTY)—See SANDUSKY, OH (Buckeye Cable System)

HURON—See SANDUSKY, OH (Buckeye Cable System)

IBERIA—See GALION, OH (Time Warner Cable)

INDEPENDENCE—See CLEVELAND HEIGHTS, OH (Time Warner Cable)

INDEPENDENCE—See CLEVELAND, OH (WOW! Internet Cable & Phone)

INDIAN HILL—See CINCINNATI, OH (Time Warner Cable)

INDIAN SPRINGS—See CINCINNATI, OH (Time Warner Cable)

▲**IRONDALE**—Comcast Cable. Now served by WHEELING, WV [WV0004]

▲**IRONTON**—Formerly served by Adelphia Communications. Now served by HUNTINGTON, WV [WV0002]

IRONVILLE—See SOUTH POINT, KY (Armstrong Cable Services)

ISLAND CREEK TWP. (JEFFERSON COUNTY)—See KNOXVILLE, OH (Suddenlink Communications)

ITHACA—See DAYTON, OH (Time Warner Cable)

JACKSON CENTER—See DAYTON, OH (Time Warner Cable)

JACKSON COUNTY (PORTIONS)—See JACKSON, OH (Time Warner Cable)

JACKSON TWP. (ALLEN COUNTY)—See LIMA, OH (Time Warner Cable)

JACKSON TWP. (GUERNSEY COUNTY)—See SENECAVILLE, OH (Suddenlink Communications)

JACKSON TWP. (MAHONING COUNTY)—See BERLIN TWP. (Mahoning County), OH (Shentel)

JACKSON TWP. (NOBLE COUNTY)—See WARNER, OH (Zito Media)

JACKSON TWP. (PUTNAM COUNTY)—See KALIDA, OH (Kalida Telephone Co.)

JACKSON TWP. (PUTNAM COUNTY)—See OTTOVILLE, OH (OTEC Communication Co.)

JACKSON TWP. (STARK COUNTY)—See MASSILLON, OH (Massillon Cable TV Inc.)

JACKSON TWP. (STARK COUNTY)—See CANTON, OH (Time Warner Cable)

JACKSON TWP. (VAN WERT COUNTY)—See OTTOVILLE, OH (OTEC Communication Co.)

JACKSON TWP.—See COLUMBUS, OH (WOW! Internet Cable & Phone)

▲**JACKSON**—Time Warner Cable

JACKSONBURG (VILLAGE)—See CINCINNATI, OH (Time Warner Cable)

JACKSONTOWN—See THORNVILLE, OH (Time Warner Cable)

JACKSONTOWN—See ZANESVILLE, OH (Time Warner Cable)

JACKSONVILLE—See NELSONVILLE, OH (Nelsonville TV Cable)

JAMESTOWN (VILLAGE)—See DAYTON, OH (Time Warner Cable)

JASPER TWP. (FAYETTE COUNTY)—See WASHINGTON COURT HOUSE, OH (Time Warner Cable)

▲**JASPER**—Time Warner Cable

JEFFERSON TWP. (ASHTABULA COUNTY)—See ASHTABULA, OH (Time Warner Cable)

JEFFERSON TWP. (ASHTABULA COUNTY)—See DENMARK TWP., OH (Zito Media)

JEFFERSON TWP. (FAYETTE COUNTY)—See WASHINGTON COURT HOUSE, OH (Time Warner Cable)

JEFFERSON TWP. (FRANKLIN COUNTY)—See COLUMBUS, OH (Insight Communications)

JEFFERSON TWP. (ROSS COUNTY)—See CHILLICOTHE, OH (Time Warner Cable)

JEFFERSON TWP. (SCIOTO COUNTY)—See LUCASVILLE, OH (Time Warner Cable)

JEFFERSON—See ASHTABULA, OH (Time Warner Cable)

JEFFERSONVILLE—See WASHINGTON COURT HOUSE, OH (Time Warner Cable)

JENERA—See FINDLAY, OH (Time Warner Cable)

JENNINGS TWP. (PUTNAM COUNTY)—See OTTOVILLE, OH (OTEC Communication Co.)

JENNINGS TWP.—See ROCKFORD, OH (Time Warner Cable)

JEROME TWP.—See COLUMBUS, OH (Time Warner Cable)

▲**JEROMESVILLE**—Time Warner Cable

JERRY CITY—See BOWLING GREEN, OH (Time Warner Cable)

JERSEY TWP.—See COLUMBUS, OH (Insight Communications)

JERUSALEM—See MALAGA TWP., OH (Richards TV Cable)

▲**JEWETT**—Time Warner Cable

JOHNSTON TWP.—See WARREN, OH (Time Warner Cable)

JOHNSTOWN—See MOUNT VERNON, OH (Time Warner Cable)

JUNCTION CITY—See THORNVILLE, OH (Time Warner Cable)

▲**KALIDA**—Kalida Telephone Co.

KEENE TWP.—See NEWARK, OH (Time Warner Cable)

KENOVA—See SOUTH POINT, WV (Armstrong Cable Services)

▲**KENT**—Time Warner Cable

▲**KENTON**—Time Warner Cable

▲**KETTERING**—Time Warner Cable. Now served by DAYTON, OH [OH0011]

KETTERING—See DAYTON, OH (Time Warner Cable)

KETTLERSVILLE—See MINSTER, OH (Time Warner Cable)

▲**KEY**—Comcast Cable. Now served by WHEELING, WV [WV0004]

KILBOURNE—See COLUMBUS, OH (Insight Communications)

KILLBUCK—See NEW PHILADELPHIA, OH (Time Warner Cable)

KIMBOLTON—See NEWARK, OH (Time Warner Cable)

▲**KINGSTON**—Formerly served by Adelphia Communications. Now served by CHILLICOTHE, OH [OH0033]

KINGSTON—See CHILLICOTHE, OH (Time Warner Cable)

KINGSVILLE—See ASHTABULA, OH (Time Warner Cable)

▲ **KINSMAN**—Formerly served by Cebridge Connections. Now served by MEADVILLE, PA [PA0062]

KIPLING—See SENECAVILLE, OH (Suddenlink Communications)

KIPTON (VILLAGE)—See WELLINGTON, OH (GLW Broadband)

▲ **KIRKERSVILLE**—Time Warner Cable. Now served by MOUNT VERNON, OH [OH0095]

KIRKERSVILLE—See MOUNT VERNON, OH (Time Warner Cable)

KIRTLAND HILLS—See CLEVELAND HEIGHTS, OH (Time Warner Cable)

KIRTLAND—See CLEVELAND HEIGHTS, OH (Time Warner Cable)

KNOX TWP. (COLUMBIANA COUNTY)—See MINERVA, OH (Time Warner Cable)

KNOX TWP. (JEFFERSON COUNTY)—See KNOXVILLE, OH (Suddenlink Communications)

▲ **KNOXVILLE**—Suddenlink Communications

▲ **LA RUE**—Time Warner Cable. Now served by KENTON, OH [OH0128]

LA RUE—See KENTON, OH (Time Warner Cable)

LACARNE—See PORT CLINTON, OH (Time Warner Cable)

LAFAYETTE TWP. (MEDINA COUNTY)—See LODI, OH (Time Warner Cable)

LAFAYETTE—See LIMA, OH (Time Warner Cable)

LAGRANGE (VILLAGE)—See WELLINGTON, OH (GLW Broadband)

LAGRANGE TWP.—See WELLINGTON, OH (GLW Broadband)

LAGRANGE—See WELLINGTON, OH (GLW Broadband)

LAKE BUCKHORN—See NEW PHILADELPHIA, OH (Time Warner Cable)

LAKE TWP. (STARK COUNTY)—See CANTON, OH (Time Warner Cable)

LAKE TWP. (WOOD COUNTY)—See CLAY CENTER/GIBSONBURG, OH (Time Warner Cable)

LAKE WHITE—See CHILLICOTHE, OH (Time Warner Cable)

LAKELINE—See CLEVELAND HEIGHTS, OH (Time Warner Cable)

LAKEMORE—See AKRON, OH (Time Warner Cable)

LAKESIDE—See PORT CLINTON, OH (Time Warner Cable)

LAKEVIEW (LOGAN COUNTY)—See BELLEFONTAINE, OH (Time Warner Cable)

LAKEVIEW (LOGAN COUNTY)—See WAYNESFIELD, OH (Time Warner Cable)

LAKEVILLE—See JEROMESVILLE, OH (Time Warner Cable)

LAKEWOOD (CUYAHOGA COUNTY)—See PARMA, OH (Cox Communications)

LAKEWOOD—See CLEVELAND HEIGHTS, OH (Time Warner Cable)

LAMBERTVILLE—See TOLEDO, MI (Buckeye Cable System Inc)

▲ **LANCASTER**—Time Warner Cable

LATTY TWP.—See OTTOVILLE, OH (OTEC Communication Co.)

LATTY—See PAULDING, OH (Time Warner Cable)

LAURELVILLE—See CHILLICOTHE, OH (Time Warner Cable)

LAWRENCE TWP. (STARK COUNTY)—See MASSILLON, OH (Massillon Cable TV Inc.)

LAWRENCE TWP.—See NEW PHILADELPHIA, OH (Time Warner Cable)

LAWRENCEVILLE—See DAYTON, OH (Time Warner Cable)

LEAVITTSBURG—See WARREN, OH (Time Warner Cable)

▲ **LEBANON**—Formerly served by Adelphia Communications. Now served by CINCINNATI, OH [OH0001]

▲ **LEBANON**—Cincinnati Bell Extended Territories

LEBANON—See CINCINNATI, OH (Time Warner Cable)

LEE TWP. (MONROE COUNTY)—See HANNIBAL, OH (Windjammer Cable)

LEESBURG TWP.—See COLUMBUS, OH (Time Warner Cable)

▲ **LEESBURG**—Time Warner Cable. Now served by CINCINNATI, OH [OH0001]

LEESBURG—See CINCINNATI, OH (Time Warner Cable)

▲ **LEESVILLE**—Time Warner Cable

LEESVILLE—See COLUMBUS, OH (Time Warner Cable)

▲ **LEIPSIC**—Orwell Cable TV Co. Now served by COLUMBUS GROVE, OH [OH0402]

LEIPSIC—See COLUMBUS GROVE (village), OH (FairPoint Communications)

LEMON TWP.—See CINCINNATI, OH (Time Warner Cable)

LEMOYNE—See WATERVILLE, OH (Time Warner Cable)

LENOX TWP.—See ASHTABULA, OH (Time Warner Cable)

LEROY TWP. (LAKE COUNTY)—See CLEVELAND HEIGHTS, OH (Time Warner Cable)

LEROY TWP. (LAKE COUNTY)—See THOMPSON TWP. (Geauga County), OH (Zito Media)

LEWIS CENTER—See COLUMBUS, OH (Insight Communications)

LEWIS COUNTY (PORTIONS)—See PORTSMOUTH, KY (Time Warner Cable)

LEWISBURG—See DAYTON, OH (Time Warner Cable)

LEWISVILLE—See WOODSFIELD, OH (City of Woodsfield)

LEXINGTON (RICHLAND COUNTY)—See MANSFIELD, OH (Time Warner Cable)

LEXINGTON TWP.—See CANTON, OH (Time Warner Cable)

LIBERTY CENTER—See DEFIANCE, OH (Time Warner Cable)

▲ **LIBERTY TWP. (Butler County)**—Time Warner Cable. Now served by CINCINNATI, OH [OH0001]

LIBERTY TWP. (BUTLER COUNTY)—See CINCINNATI, OH (Time Warner Cable)

LIBERTY TWP. (CLINTON COUNTY)—See CINCINNATI, OH (Time Warner Cable)

LIBERTY TWP. (CRAWFORD COUNTY)—See BUCYRUS, OH (Time Warner Cable)

LIBERTY TWP. (DARKE COUNTY)—See DAYTON, OH (Time Warner Cable)

LIBERTY TWP. (DELAWARE COUNTY)—See COLUMBUS, OH (Time Warner Cable)

LIBERTY TWP. (FAIRFIELD COUNTY)—See COLUMBUS, OH (Insight Communications)

LIBERTY TWP. (FAIRFIELD COUNTY)—See CHILLICOTHE, OH (Time Warner Cable)

LIBERTY TWP. (GUERNSEY COUNTY)—See NEWARK, OH (Time Warner Cable)

LIBERTY TWP. (HANCOCK COUNTY)—See BENTON RIDGE, OH (B. R. Cablevision Co.)

LIBERTY TWP. (HANCOCK COUNTY)—See FINDLAY, OH (Time Warner Cable)

LIBERTY TWP. (HARDIN COUNTY)—See KENTON, OH (Time Warner Cable)

LIBERTY TWP. (HENRY COUNTY)—See DEFIANCE, OH (Time Warner Cable)

LIBERTY TWP. (HIGHLAND COUNTY)—See CINCINNATI, OH (Time Warner Cable)

LIBERTY TWP. (JACKSON COUNTY)—See JACKSON, OH (Time Warner Cable)

LIBERTY TWP. (KNOX COUNTY)—See MOUNT VERNON, OH (Time Warner Cable)

LIBERTY TWP. (ROSS COUNTY)—See CHILLICOTHE, OH (Time Warner Cable)

LIBERTY TWP. (SENECA COUNTY)—See CLAY CENTER/GIBSONBURG, OH (Time Warner Cable)

LIBERTY TWP. (TRUMBULL COUNTY)—See WARREN, OH (Time Warner Cable)

LIBERTY TWP. (UNION COUNTY)—See COLUMBUS, OH (Time Warner Cable)

LIBERTY TWP. (VAN WERT COUNTY)—See VAN WERT, OH (Time Warner Cable)

LIBERTY TWP. (WOOD COUNTY)—See BOWLING GREEN, OH (Time Warner Cable)

LIBERTY TWP.—See DAYTON, OH (Time Warner Cable)

LIBERTY TWP.—See NEWARK, OH (Time Warner Cable)

LICK TWP. (JACKSON COUNTY)—See JACKSON, OH (Time Warner Cable)

▲ **LICKING COUNTY**—Now served by NEWARK, OH [OH0019]

LICKING COUNTY—See NEWARK, OH (Time Warner Cable)

LICKING TWP. (MUSKINGUM COUNTY)—See ZANESVILLE, OH (Time Warner Cable)

▲ **LIMA**—Time Warner Cable

LIMAVILLE—See CANTON, OH (Time Warner Cable)

LINCOLN HEIGHTS—See CINCINNATI, OH (Time Warner Cable)

LINCOLN TWP.—See MOUNT GILEAD, OH (Time Warner Cable)

LINDALE—See CINCINNATI, OH (Time Warner Cable)

▲ **LINDSEY (Sandusky County)**—Tiime Warner Cable. Now served by CLAY CENTER/GIBSONBURG (formerly Allen Twp.), OH [OH0071]

LINDSEY—See CLAY CENTER/GIBSONBURG, OH (Time Warner Cable)

LINNDALE—See CLEVELAND HEIGHTS, OH (Time Warner Cable)

LINNDALE—See CLEVELAND, OH (WOW! Internet Cable & Phone)

LINTON TWP.—See NEWARK, OH (Time Warner Cable)

▲ **LISBON**—Time Warner Cable. Now served by SALEM, OH [OH0096]

LISBON—See SALEM, OH (Time Warner Cable)

LITCHFIELD TWP. (PORTIONS)—See MEDINA, OH (Armstrong Cable Services)

LITHOPOLIS—See COLUMBUS, OH (Insight Communications)

LITTLE HOCKING—See BEVERLY, OH (Time Warner Cable)

LIVERPOOL TWP.—See MEDINA, OH (Armstrong Cable Services)

LIVERPOOL TWP.—See EAST LIVERPOOL, OH (Comcast Cable)

OAKWOOD (PAULDING COUNTY)—See COLUMBUS GROVE (village), OH (FairPoint Communications)

OAKWOOD—See CLEVELAND HEIGHTS, OH (Time Warner Cable)

OAKWOOD—See DAYTON, OH (Time Warner Cable)

▲ **OBERLIN**—Cable Co-op Inc.

OBETZ—See COLUMBUS, OH (Time Warner Cable)

OBETZ—See COLUMBUS, OH (WOW! Internet Cable & Phone)

OCTA—See WASHINGTON COURT HOUSE, OH (Time Warner Cable)

OHIO CITY—See VAN WERT, OH (Time Warner Cable)

OHIO TWP. (MONROE COUNTY)—See HANNIBAL, OH (Windjammer Cable)

OLD FORT—See CLAY CENTER/GIBSONBURG, OH (Time Warner Cable)

OLD WASHINGTON—See SENECAVILLE, OH (Suddenlink Communications)

OLIVE TWP. (MEIGS COUNTY)—See BEVERLY, OH (Time Warner Cable)

OLIVE TWP. (NOBLE COUNTY)—See NEWARK, OH (Time Warner Cable)

OLIVESBURG—See ASHLAND, OH (Armstrong Cable Services)

OLMSTED FALLS—See PARMA, OH (Cox Communications)

▲ **OLMSTED TWP.**—Olmsted Cable Co. Corp. Now served by PARMA, OH [OH0009]

OLMSTED TWP.—See PARMA, OH (Cox Communications)

ONTARIO—See MANSFIELD, OH (Time Warner Cable)

ORANGE TWP. (ASHLAND COUNTY)—See ASHLAND, OH (Armstrong Cable Services)

ORANGE TWP. (DELAWARE COUNTY)—See COLUMBUS, OH (Insight Communications)

ORANGE—See CLEVELAND HEIGHTS, OH (Time Warner Cable)

OREGON—See TOLEDO, OH (Buckeye Cable System Inc)

ORIENT—See COLUMBUS, OH (Time Warner Cable)

▲ **ORRVILLE**—Armstrong Cable Services

▲ **ORWELL**—FairPoint Communications

OSGOOD—See VERSAILLES, OH (Time Warner Cable)

OSNABURG TWP. (STARK COUNTY)—See CANTON, OH (Time Warner Cable)

OTTAWA HILLS—See TOLEDO, OH (Buckeye Cable System Inc)

OTTAWA LAKE—See TOLEDO, MI (Buckeye Cable System Inc)

▲ **OTTAWA**—Time Warner Cable

▲ **OTTOVILLE**—OTEC Communication Co.

▲ **OWENSVILLE**—Time Warner Cable. Now served by CINCINNATI, OH [OH0001]

OWENSVILLE—See CINCINNATI, OH (Time Warner Cable)

OXFORD TWP. (BUTLER COUNTY)—See CINCINNATI, OH (Time Warner Cable)

OXFORD TWP. (ERIE COUNTY)—See SANDUSKY, OH (Buckeye Cable System)

OXFORD TWP. (ERIE COUNTY)—See NORWALK, OH (Time Warner Cable)

OXFORD TWP. (TUSCARAWAS COUNTY)—See NEW PHILADELPHIA, OH (Time Warner Cable)

▲ **OXFORD**—Time Warner Cable. Now served by DAYTON, OH [OH0011]

OXFORD—See DAYTON, OH (Time Warner Cable)

PAINESVILLE TWP. (LAKE COUNTY)—See CLEVELAND HEIGHTS, OH (Time Warner Cable)

PAINESVILLE—See CLEVELAND HEIGHTS, OH (Time Warner Cable)

PAINT TWP. (FAYETTE COUNTY)—See WASHINGTON COURT HOUSE, OH (Time Warner Cable)

PAINT TWP. (HIGHLAND COUNTY)—See WASHINGTON COURT HOUSE, OH (Time Warner Cable)

PALESTINE—See DAYTON, OH (Time Warner Cable)

PALMYRA TWP. (PORTIONS)—See ATWATER TWP., OH (Time Warner Cable)

PALMYRA TWP. (PORTIONS)—See CRAIG BEACH, OH (Time Warner Cable)

PANDORA—See COLUMBUS GROVE (village), OH (FairPoint Communications)

PARIS TWP. (PORTAGE COUNTY)—See NELSON TWP., OH (Suddenlink Communications)

PARIS TWP. (STARK COUNTY)—See CANTON, OH (Time Warner Cable)

PARKMAN TWP.—See NELSON TWP., OH (Suddenlink Communications)

PARKMAN—See NELSON TWP., OH (Suddenlink Communications)

PARMA HEIGHTS—See PARMA, OH (Cox Communications)

▲ **PARMA**—Cox Communications

PARRAL—See NEW PHILADELPHIA, OH (Time Warner Cable)

▲ **PATASKALA**—Time Warner Cable. Now served by MOUNT VERNON, OH [OH0095]

PATASKALA—See MOUNT VERNON, OH (Time Warner Cable)

PATTERSON—See KENTON, OH (Time Warner Cable)

PAULDING TWP. (PAULDING COUNTY)—See PAULDING, OH (Time Warner Cable)

▲ **PAULDING**—Time Warner Cable

PAXTON TWP.—See BAINBRIDGE, OH (Time Warner Cable)

▲ **PAYNE**—Comcast Cable

PEBBLE TWP. (PIKE COUNTY)—See CHILLICOTHE, OH (Time Warner Cable)

▲ **PEDRO**—Windjammer Cable

PEE PEE TWP. (PIKE COUNTY)—See CHILLICOTHE, OH (Time Warner Cable)

▲ **PEEBLES**—Time Warner Cable. Now served by CINCINNATI, OH [OH0001]

PEEBLES—See CINCINNATI, OH (Time Warner Cable)

PEMBERVILLE—See CLAY CENTER/GIBSONBURG, OH (Time Warner Cable)

PENFIELD TWP.—See WELLINGTON, OH (GLW Broadband)

PENN TWP.—See CINCINNATI, OH (Time Warner Cable)

PEPPER PIKE—See CLEVELAND HEIGHTS, OH (Time Warner Cable)

PERKINS TWP. (ERIE COUNTY)—See SANDUSKY, OH (Buckeye Cable System)

PERRY COUNTY (PORTIONS)—See ZANESVILLE, OH (Time Warner Cable)

PERRY TWP. (COLUMBIANA COUNTY)—See SALEM, OH (Time Warner Cable)

PERRY TWP. (FRANKLIN COUNTY)—See COLUMBUS, OH (Time Warner Cable)

PERRY TWP. (LAWRENCE COUNTY)—See SOUTH POINT, OH (Armstrong Cable Services)

PERRY TWP. (LOGAN COUNTY)—See COLUMBUS, OH (Time Warner Cable)

PERRY TWP. (PICKAWAY COUNTY)—See NEW HOLLAND, OH (Time Warner Cable)

PERRY TWP. (PUTNAM COUNTY)—See OTTOVILLE, OH (OTEC Communication Co.)

PERRY TWP. (RICHLAND COUNTY)—See MANSFIELD, OH (Time Warner Cable)

PERRY TWP. (STARK COUNTY)—See MASSILLON, OH (Massillon Cable TV Inc.)

PERRY TWP. (STARK COUNTY)—See CANTON, OH (Time Warner Cable)

PERRY TWP.—See COLUMBUS, OH (WOW! Internet Cable & Phone)

PERRY—See CLEVELAND HEIGHTS, OH (Time Warner Cable)

PERRYSBURG TWP. (WOOD COUNTY)—See CLAY CENTER/GIBSONBURG, OH (Time Warner Cable)

PERRYSBURG TWP.—See TOLEDO, OH (Buckeye Cable System Inc)

PERRYSBURG—See WATERVILLE, OH (Time Warner Cable)

PERRYSVILLE—See JEROMESVILLE, OH (Time Warner Cable)

PERU TWP. (HURON COUNTY)—See NORWALK, OH (Time Warner Cable)

PERU TWP.—See MOUNT GILEAD, OH (Time Warner Cable)

PETERSBURG—See NEW MIDDLETOWN, OH (Comcast Cable)

PETTISVILLE—See DEFIANCE, OH (Time Warner Cable)

PHILLIPSBURG—See DAYTON, OH (Time Warner Cable)

▲ **PHILO (portions)**—Time Warner Cable. Now served by ZANESVILLE, OH [OH0037]

PHILO—See ZANESVILLE, OH (Time Warner Cable)

PICKAWAY COUNTY—See COLUMBUS, OH (Time Warner Cable)

PICKAWAY TWP. (PICKAWAY COUNTY)—See CHILLICOTHE, OH (Time Warner Cable)

PICKERINGTON—See COLUMBUS, OH (Insight Communications)

PIERPONT TWP.—See DENMARK TWP., OH (Zito Media)

PIKE COUNTY—See CHILLICOTHE, OH (Time Warner Cable)

PIKE TWP. (BROWN COUNTY)—See CINCINNATI, OH (Time Warner Cable)

PIKE TWP. (PERRY COUNTY)—See THORNVILLE, OH (Time Warner Cable)

PIKE TWP. (STARK COUNTY)—See CANTON, OH (Time Warner Cable)

PIKE TWP.—See DAYTON, OH (Time Warner Cable)

PIKE TWP.—See WAUSEON, OH (Time Warner Cable)

▲ **PIKETON**—Time Warner Cable

▲ **PINE LAKE TRAILER PARK**—Formerly served by Marshall County Cable. No longer in operation

▲ **PIONEER**—Formerly served by Windjammer Cable. No longer in operation

▲ **PIQUA**—Time Warner Cable. No longer in operation

PITSBURG—See DAYTON, OH (Time Warner Cable)

PITT TWP.—See UPPER SANDUSKY, OH (Time Warner Cable)

PITTSFIELD TWP.—See WELLINGTON, OH (GLW Broadband)

PLAIN CITY—See COLUMBUS, OH (Time Warner Cable)

PLAIN GROVE TWP.—See NEW MIDDLETOWN, PA (Comcast Cable)

PLAIN TWP. (FRANKLIN COUNTY)—See COLUMBUS, OH (Insight Communications)

PLAIN TWP. (STARK COUNTY)—See CANTON, OH (Time Warner Cable)

PLAIN TWP. (WAYNE COUNTY)—See WOOSTER, OH (Clear Picture Inc.)

PLAIN TWP. (WOOD COUNTY)—See BOWLING GREEN, OH (Time Warner Cable)

PLAINFIELD—See NEWARK, OH (Time Warner Cable)

PLEASANT CITY—See SENECAVILLE, OH (Suddenlink Communications)

PLEASANT HILL (JEFFERSON COUNTY)—See TORONTO, OH (Jefferson County Cable Inc.)

PLEASANT PLAIN—See CINCINNATI, OH (Time Warner Cable)

PLEASANT TWP. (FAIRFIELD COUNTY)—See LANCASTER, OH (Time Warner Cable)

PLEASANT TWP. (FRANKLIN COUNTY)—See COLUMBUS, OH (Time Warner Cable)

PLEASANT TWP. (HANCOCK COUNTY)—See FINDLAY, OH (Time Warner Cable)

PLEASANT TWP. (HARDIN COUNTY)—See KENTON, OH (Time Warner Cable)

PLEASANT TWP. (HENRY COUNTY)—See DESHLER, OH (Time Warner Cable)

PLEASANT TWP. (KNOX COUNTY)—See MOUNT VERNON, OH (Time Warner Cable)

PLEASANT TWP. (MARION COUNTY)—See MARION, OH (Time Warner Cable)

PLEASANT TWP. (PERRY COUNTY)—See CORNING, OH (Zito Media)

PLEASANT TWP. (PUTNAM COUNTY)—See OTTAWA, OH (Time Warner Cable)

PLEASANT TWP. (SENECA COUNTY)—See BELLEVUE, OH (Time Warner Cable)

PLEASANT TWP. (VAN WERT COUNTY)—See VAN WERT, OH (Time Warner Cable)

PLEASANT TWP.—See DAYTON, OH (Time Warner Cable)

PLEASANTVILLE—See LANCASTER, OH (Time Warner Cable)

PLYMOUTH TWP. (ASHTABULA COUNTY)—See ASHTABULA, OH (Time Warner Cable)

PLYMOUTH TWP. (ASHTABULA COUNTY)—See DENMARK TWP., OH (Zito Media)

PLYMOUTH—See WILLARD, OH (Time Warner Cable)

POLAND TWP. (MAHONING COUNTY)—See BOARDMAN, OH (Armstrong Cable Services)

POLAND TWP. (MAHONING COUNTY)—See STRUTHERS, OH (Time Warner Cable)

POLAND—See BOARDMAN, OH (Armstrong Cable Services)

POLK TWP.—See GALION, OH (Time Warner Cable)

▲**POLK**—Time Warner Cable

▲**PORT CLINTON**—Time Warner Cable

PORT JEFFERSON—See DAYTON, OH (Time Warner Cable)

PORT WASHINGTON—See NEW PHILADELPHIA, OH (Time Warner Cable)

▲**PORT WILLIAM**—Time Warner Cable. Now served by CINCINNATI, OH [OH0001]

PORT WILLIAM—See CINCINNATI, OH (Time Warner Cable)

PORTAGE COUNTY (PORTIONS)—See WARREN, OH (Time Warner Cable)

PORTAGE TWP. (OTTAWA COUNTY)—See PORT CLINTON, OH (Time Warner Cable)

PORTAGE—See BOWLING GREEN, OH (Time Warner Cable)

PORTER TWP. (DELAWARE COUNTY)—See COLUMBUS, OH (Time Warner Cable)

PORTER TWP. (SCIOTO COUNTY)—See PORTSMOUTH, OH (Time Warner Cable)

▲**PORTERFIELD**—Formerly served by Adelphia Communications. No longer in operation

▲**PORTSMOUTH**—Time Warner Cable

POTTERY ADDITION—See TORONTO, OH (Jefferson County Cable Inc.)

POWELL (VILLAGE)—See COLUMBUS, OH (Time Warner Cable)

▲**POWHATAN POINT**—Powhatan Point Cable Co.

PRAIRIE TWP. (FRANKLIN COUNTY)—See COLUMBUS, OH (Time Warner Cable)

PRAIRIE TWP.—See COLUMBUS, OH (WOW! Internet Cable & Phone)

PROCTORVILLE (PORTIONS)—See SOUTH POINT, OH (Armstrong Cable Services)

▲**PROCTORVILLE**—Formerly served by Lycom Communications. No longer in operation

PROSPECT TWP. (MARION COUNTY)—See MARION, OH (Time Warner Cable)

PROVIDENCE TWP.—See WAUSEON, OH (Time Warner Cable)

PULASKI TWP. (WILLIAMS COUNTY)—See BRYAN, OH (Time Warner Cable)

PUSHETA TWP.—See WAPAKONETA, OH (Time Warner Cable)

▲**PUT IN BAY**—Time Warner Cable

PYMATUNING STATE PARK—See VERNON, OH (S. Bryer Cable TV Corp.)

QUAKER CITY—See SENECAVILLE, OH (Suddenlink Communications)

QUINCY—See DAYTON, OH (Time Warner Cable)

RACCOON TWP.—See RIO GRANDE, OH (Time Warner Cable)

▲**RAINSBORO**—Formerly served by Adelphia Communications. Now served by WASHINGTON COURT HOUSE, OH [OH0070]

RAINSBORO—See WASHINGTON COURT HOUSE, OH (Time Warner Cable)

RANDOLPH TWP. (PORTAGE COUNTY)—See ATWATER TWP., OH (Time Warner Cable)

RAVENNA—See KENT, OH (Time Warner Cable)

RAWSON—See FINDLAY, OH (Time Warner Cable)

RAYMOND—See COLUMBUS, OH (Time Warner Cable)

READING—See CINCINNATI, OH (Time Warner Cable)

REED TWP.—See SYCAMORE, OH (Time Warner Cable)

REEDSVILLE—See BEVERLY, OH (Time Warner Cable)

REESE STATION—See COLUMBUS, OH (Time Warner Cable)

REILY TWP.—See CINCINNATI, OH (Time Warner Cable)

REMINDERVILLE—See MACEDONIA, OH (Time Warner Cable)

RENDVILLE—See CORNING, OH (Zito Media)

REPUBLIC—See SYCAMORE, OH (Time Warner Cable)

REYNOLDSBURG—See COLUMBUS, OH (Insight Communications)

REYNOLDSBURG—See COLUMBUS, OH (WOW! Internet Cable & Phone)

RICE TWP.—See PORT CLINTON, OH (Time Warner Cable)

RICH HILL TWP.—See ZANESVILLE, OH (Time Warner Cable)

RICHFIELD (VILLAGE)—See CLEVELAND HEIGHTS, OH (Time Warner Cable)

RICHFIELD TWP. (SUMMIT COUNTY)—See CLEVELAND HEIGHTS, OH (Time Warner Cable)

RICHLAND COUNTY—See MANSFIELD, OH (Time Warner Cable)

RICHLAND TWP. (ALLEN COUNTY)—See LIMA, OH (Time Warner Cable)

RICHLAND TWP. (CLINTON COUNTY)—See WASHINGTON COURT HOUSE, OH (Time Warner Cable)

RICHLAND TWP. (DEFIANCE COUNTY)—See DEFIANCE, OH (Time Warner Cable)

RICHLAND TWP. (FAIRFIELD COUNTY)—See THORNVILLE, OH (Time Warner Cable)

RICHLAND TWP. (GUERNSEY COUNTY)—See SENECAVILLE, OH (Suddenlink Communications)

RICHLAND TWP. (LOGAN COUNTY)—See KENTON, OH (Time Warner Cable)

RICHLAND TWP. (WYANDOT COUNTY)—See KENTON, OH (Time Warner Cable)

RICHLAND TWP.—See MARION, OH (Time Warner Cable)

RICHLAND TWP.—See NEW PHILADELPHIA, OH (Time Warner Cable)

▲**RICHMOND DALE**—Formerly served by Adelphia Communications. Now served by CHILLICOTHE, OH [OH0033]

RICHMOND DALE—See CHILLICOTHE, OH (Time Warner Cable)

RICHMOND HEIGHTS—See CLEVELAND HEIGHTS, OH (Time Warner Cable)

RICHVILLE—See MASSILLON, OH (Massillon Cable TV Inc.)

RICHWOOD—See COLUMBUS, OH (Time Warner Cable)

RIDGE TWP. (VAN WERT COUNTY)—See VAN WERT, OH (Time Warner Cable)

RIDGEFIELD TWP. (HURON COUNTY)—See NORWALK, OH (Time Warner Cable)

▲**RIDGEVILLE TWP.**—RTEC Communications

RIDGEWAY—See KENTON, OH (Time Warner Cable)

RIGA TWP. (PORTIONS)—See TOLEDO, MI (Buckeye Cable System Inc)

RILEY TWP. (SANDUSKY COUNTY)—See BELLEVUE, OH (Time Warner Cable)

▲**RIO GRANDE**—Time Warner Cable

▲**RIPLEY (Brown County)**—Formerly served by Adelphia Communications. Now served by CINCINNATI, OH [OH0001]

RIPLEY TWP. (PORTIONS)—See WILLARD, OH (Time Warner Cable)

RIPLEY—See CINCINNATI, OH (Time Warner Cable)

▲**RISING SUN**—Time Warner Cable. Now served by CLAY CENTER/GIBSONBURG (formerly Allen Twp.), OH [OH0071]

RISING SUN—See CLAY CENTER/GIBSONBURG, OH (Time Warner Cable)

RITTMAN—See LODI, OH (Time Warner Cable)

RIVERLEA—See COLUMBUS, OH (Time Warner Cable)

RIVERLEA—See COLUMBUS, OH (WOW! Internet Cable & Phone)

▲ **RIVERSIDE**—Now served by DAYTON, OH [OH0011]

RIVERSIDE—See DAYTON, OH (Time Warner Cable)

ROAMING SHORES—See ROCK CREEK, OH (Zito Media)

▲ **ROBBINS MOBILE HOME PARK**—Time Warner Cable. Now served by KENT, OH [OH0034]

ROBIN MOBILE HOME PARK—See KENT, OH (Time Warner Cable)

ROCHESTER (VILLAGE)—See WELLINGTON, OH (GLW Broadband)

ROCHESTER TWP.—See WELLINGTON, OH (GLW Broadband)

▲ **ROCK CREEK**—Zito Media

ROCKBRIDGE—See LOGAN, OH (Time Warner Cable)

ROCKDALE—See SOUTH POINT, KY (Armstrong Cable Services)

▲ **ROCKFORD**—Time Warner Cable

ROCKY RIDGE—See PORT CLINTON, OH (Time Warner Cable)

ROCKY RIVER—See PARMA, OH (Cox Communications)

ROGERS—See NELSON TWP., OH (Suddenlink Communications)

ROME TWP. (ATHENS COUNTY)—See BEVERLY, OH (Time Warner Cable)

ROME TWP. (LAWRENCE COUNTY)—See SOUTH POINT, OH (Armstrong Cable Services)

ROME TWP.—See ORWELL, OH (FairPoint Communications)

ROOTSTOWN TWP. (PORTAGE COUNTY)—See KENT, OH (Time Warner Cable)

ROSEVILLE—See ZANESVILLE, OH (Time Warner Cable)

ROSEWOOD (VILLAGE)—See DAYTON, OH (Time Warner Cable)

ROSS COUNTY (PORTIONS)—See CHILLICOTHE, OH (Time Warner Cable)

▲ **ROSS TWP. (Butler County)**—Formerly served by Adelphia Communications. Now served by CINCINNATI, OH [OH0001]

ROSS TWP. (BUTLER COUNTY)—See CINCINNATI, OH (Time Warner Cable)

ROSS TWP. (JEFFERSON COUNTY)—See BLOOMINGDALE, OH (Suddenlink Communications)

ROSSBURG—See DAYTON, OH (Time Warner Cable)

ROSSFORD—See TOLEDO, OH (Buckeye Cable System Inc)

ROSWELL—See NEW PHILADELPHIA, OH (Time Warner Cable)

ROUNDHEAD TWP.—See WAYNESFIELD, OH (Time Warner Cable)

ROWSBURG—See JEROMESVILLE, OH (Time Warner Cable)

ROYALTON—See WAUSEON, OH (Time Warner Cable)

RUSH CREEK TWP. (FAIRFIELD COUNTY)—See LANCASTER, OH (Time Warner Cable)

RUSH CREEK TWP. (LOGAN COUNTY)—See KENTON, OH (Time Warner Cable)

RUSH CREEK TWP.—See HIDE-A-WAY HILLS, OH (Time Warner Cable)

▲ **RUSH RUN**—Jefferson County Cable Inc.

RUSH TWP. (SCIOTO COUNTY)—See LUCASVILLE, OH (Time Warner Cable)

RUSHSYLVANIA—See KENTON, OH (Time Warner Cable)

RUSHVILLE—See THORNVILLE, OH (Time Warner Cable)

RUSSELL TWP.—See CLEVELAND HEIGHTS, OH (Time Warner Cable)

RUSSELLS POINT—See BELLEFONTAINE, OH (Time Warner Cable)

RUSSIA—See VERSAILLES, OH (Time Warner Cable)

RUTLAND—See SCIPIO TWP. (Meigs County), OH (Time Warner Cable)

SABINA—See WASHINGTON COURT HOUSE, OH (Time Warner Cable)

SAGAMORE HILLS TWP. (SUMMIT COUNTY)—See MACEDONIA, OH (Time Warner Cable)

SALEM TWP. (COLUMBIANA COUNTY)—See SALEM, OH (Time Warner Cable)

SALEM TWP. (JEFFERSON COUNTY)—See BLOOMINGDALE, OH (Suddenlink Communications)

SALEM TWP. (OTTAWA COUNTY)—See PORT CLINTON, OH (Time Warner Cable)

SALEM TWP. (WASHINGTON COUNTY)—See WARNER, OH (Zito Media)

▲ **SALEM**—Time Warner Cable

SALESVILLE—See SENECAVILLE, OH (Suddenlink Communications)

SALINE TWP.—See KNOXVILLE, OH (Suddenlink Communications)

▲ **SALINEVILLE**—Windjammer Cable

SALISBURY TWP.—See SCIPIO TWP. (Meigs County), OH (Time Warner Cable)

SALT CREEK TWP. (PICKAWAY COUNTY)—See CHILLICOTHE, OH (Time Warner Cable)

SALT CREEK TWP.—See NEWARK, OH (Time Warner Cable)

SALT LICK TWP.—See CORNING, OH (Zito Media)

SALTCREEK TWP. (PICKAWAY COUNTY)—See CHILLICOTHE, OH (Time Warner Cable)

SANDUSKY TWP. (RICHLAND COUNTY)—See MANSFIELD, OH (Time Warner Cable)

SANDUSKY TWP. (SANDUSKY COUNTY)—See PORT CLINTON, OH (Time Warner Cable)

SANDUSKY TWP.—See BELLEVUE, OH (Time Warner Cable)

▲ **SANDUSKY**—Buckeye Cable System

SANDY TWP. (STARK COUNTY)—See CANTON, OH (Time Warner Cable)

SANDY TWP. (TUSCARAWAS COUNTY)—See CANTON, OH (Time Warner Cable)

▲ **SARAHSVILLE**—Formerly served by Cebridge Connections. No longer in operation

▲ **SARDINIA**—Formerly served by Crystal Broadband Networks. No longer in operation

SARDINIA—See CINCINNATI, OH (Time Warner Cable)

SARDIS—See HANNIBAL, OH (Windjammer Cable)

SAVANNAH—See NEW LONDON, OH (Time Warner Cable)

SAYBROOK TWP. (ASHTABULA COUNTY)—See ASHTABULA, OH (Time Warner Cable)

▲ **SCIO**—Time Warner Cable

SCIOTO COUNTY (PORTIONS)—See LUCASVILLE, OH (Time Warner Cable)

SCIOTO TWP. (PICKAWAY COUNTY)—See COMMERCIAL POINT, OH (Time Warner Cable)

SCIOTO TWP. (ROSS COUNTY)—See CHILLICOTHE, OH (Time Warner Cable)

SCIOTOVILLE—See PORTSMOUTH, OH (Time Warner Cable)

▲ **SCIPIO TWP. (MEIGS COUNTY)**—Time Warner Cable

SCIPIO TWP. (SENECA COUNTY)—See SYCAMORE, OH (Time Warner Cable)

▲ **SCOTT (village)**—Formerly served by CableDirect. No longer in operation

SCOTT TWP. (LAWRENCE COUNTY)—See NEW MIDDLETOWN, PA (Comcast Cable)

SEAL TWP. (PIKE COUNTY)—See PIKETON, OH (Time Warner Cable)

▲ **SEAMAN**—Time Warner Cable. Now served by CINCINNATI, OH [OH0001]

SEAMAN—See CINCINNATI, OH (Time Warner Cable)

▲ **SEBRING**—Time Warner Cable. Now served by MINERVA, OH [OH0132]

SEBRING—See MINERVA, OH (Time Warner Cable)

SENECA TWP. (SENECA COUNTY)—See SYCAMORE, OH (Time Warner Cable)

▲ **SENECAVILLE**—Suddenlink Communications

SEVEN HILLS—See PARMA, OH (Cox Communications)

SEVEN MILE—See CINCINNATI, OH (Time Warner Cable)

SEVILLE—See LODI, OH (Time Warner Cable)

SHAKER HEIGHTS—See CLEVELAND HEIGHTS, OH (Time Warner Cable)

SHAKER HEIGHTS—See CLEVELAND, OH (WOW! Internet Cable & Phone)

SHALERSVILLE TWP.—See MACEDONIA, OH (Time Warner Cable)

SHARON TWP. (FRANKLIN COUNTY)—See COLUMBUS, OH (Insight Communications)

SHARON TWP. (MEDINA COUNTY)—See CLEVELAND HEIGHTS, OH (Time Warner Cable)

SHARON TWP.—See COLUMBUS, OH (Time Warner Cable)

SHARON TWP.—See COLUMBUS, OH (WOW! Internet Cable & Phone)

SHARONVILLE—See CINCINNATI, OH (Time Warner Cable)

SHAWNEE HILLS—See COLUMBUS, OH (Time Warner Cable)

SHAWNEE TWP. (ALLEN COUNTY)—See LIMA, OH (Time Warner Cable)

SHAWNEE—See CORNING, OH (Zito Media)

SHEFFIELD LAKE—See CLEVELAND HEIGHTS, OH (Time Warner Cable)

SHEFFIELD TWP. (ASHTABULA COUNTY)—See ASHTABULA, OH (Time Warner Cable)

SHEFFIELD TWP. (ASHTABULA COUNTY)—See DENMARK TWP., OH (Zito Media)

SHEFFIELD TWP. (LORAIN COUNTY)—See CLEVELAND HEIGHTS, OH (Time Warner Cable)

SHEFFIELD—See CLEVELAND HEIGHTS, OH (Time Warner Cable)

▲ **SHELBY**—Time Warner Cable

SHERMAN TWP. (HURON COUNTY)—See BELLEVUE, OH (Time Warner Cable)

SHERRODSVILLE—See NEW PHILADELPHIA, OH (Time Warner Cable)

▲ **SHERWOOD**—Shertel Cable. This cable system has converted to IPTV. See Sherwood, OH [OH5191]

▲ **SHERWOOD**—Formerly served by Shertel Cable [OH0365]. This cable system has converted to IPTV

SHILOH—See WILLARD, OH (Time Warner Cable)

SHOALS—See SOUTH POINT, WV (Armstrong Cable Services)

▲ **SHREVE**—Time Warner Cable. Now served by JEROMESVILLE, OH [OH0266]

SHREVE—See JEROMESVILLE, OH (Time Warner Cable)

SIAM—See SYCAMORE, OH (Time Warner Cable)

▲ **SIDNEY**—Time Warner Cable. Now served by DAYTON, OH [OH0011]

SIDNEY—See DAYTON, OH (Time Warner Cable)

SILVER LAKE—See AKRON, OH (Time Warner Cable)

SILVERCREEK TWP.—See DAYTON, OH (Time Warner Cable)

SILVERTON—See CINCINNATI, OH (Time Warner Cable)

SMITH TWP. (MAHONING COUNTY)—See ATWATER TWP., OH (Time Warner Cable)

SMITH TWP. (MAHONING COUNTY)—See MINERVA, OH (Time Warner Cable)

SMITH TWP. (PORTIONS) (MAHONING COUNTY)—See BERLIN TWP. (Mahoning County), OH (Shentel)

SMITHFIELD—See TORONTO, OH (Jefferson County Cable Inc.)

SMITHVILLE—See WOOSTER, OH (Clear Picture Inc.)

SOLON—See CLEVELAND HEIGHTS, OH (Time Warner Cable)

▲ **SOMERSET**—Time Warner Communications. Now served by THORNVILLE, OH [OH0154]

SOMERSET—See THORNVILLE, OH (Time Warner Cable)

SOMERVILLE—See CINCINNATI, OH (Time Warner Cable)

SONORA—See ZANESVILLE, OH (Time Warner Cable)

SOUTH AMHERST—See CLEVELAND HEIGHTS, OH (Time Warner Cable)

SOUTH BLOOMFIELD—See CIRCLEVILLE, OH (Time Warner Cable)

SOUTH BLOOMFIELD—See COLUMBUS, OH (Time Warner Cable)

SOUTH CHARLESTON—See DAYTON, OH (Time Warner Cable)

SOUTH EUCLID—See CLEVELAND HEIGHTS, OH (Time Warner Cable)

SOUTH LEBANON—See CINCINNATI, OH (Time Warner Cable)

SOUTH NEW CASTLE—See NEW MIDDLETOWN, PA (Comcast Cable)

▲ **SOUTH POINT**—Armstrong Cable Services

SOUTH PORTSMOUTH—See PORTSMOUTH, KY (Time Warner Cable)

SOUTH RUSSELL—See CLEVELAND HEIGHTS, OH (Time Warner Cable)

SOUTH SALEM—See CHILLICOTHE, OH (Time Warner Cable)

SOUTH SHORE—See PORTSMOUTH, KY (Time Warner Cable)

SOUTH SOLON—See DAYTON, OH (Time Warner Cable)

SOUTH VIENNA—See DAYTON, OH (Time Warner Cable)

SOUTH VINEMONT—See DAYTON, OH (Time Warner Cable)

SOUTH WEBSTER (VILLAGE)—See PORTSMOUTH, OH (Time Warner Cable)

SOUTH ZANESVILLE—See ZANESVILLE, OH (Time Warner Cable)

SOUTHINGTON TWP.—See WARREN, OH (Time Warner Cable)

SPARTA—See MOUNT GILEAD, OH (Time Warner Cable)

SPENCER TWP. (ALLEN COUNTY)—See LIMA, OH (Time Warner Cable)

SPENCER TWP. (LUCAS COUNTY)—See WATERVILLE, OH (Time Warner Cable)

SPENCER—See LODI, OH (Time Warner Cable)

SPENCERVILLE—See LIMA, OH (Time Warner Cable)

SPRING LAKES MOBILE HOME PARK—See KENT, OH (Time Warner Cable)

SPRING VALLEY—See SOUTH POINT, WV (Armstrong Cable Services)

SPRING VALLEY—See DAYTON, OH (Time Warner Cable)

SPRINGBORO—See DAYTON, OH (Time Warner Cable)

SPRINGCREEK TWP.—See DAYTON, OH (Time Warner Cable)

SPRINGDALE—See CINCINNATI, OH (Time Warner Cable)

SPRINGFIELD TWP. (HAMILTON COUNTY)—See CINCINNATI, OH (Time Warner Cable)

SPRINGFIELD TWP. (JEFFERSON COUNTY)—See BLOOMINGDALE, OH (Suddenlink Communications)

SPRINGFIELD TWP. (MAHONING COUNTY)—See BOARDMAN, OH (Armstrong Cable Services)

SPRINGFIELD TWP. (PORTIONS)—See AMSTERDAM, OH (Windjammer Cable)

SPRINGFIELD TWP. (RICHLAND COUNTY)—See MANSFIELD, OH (Time Warner Cable)

SPRINGFIELD TWP. (SUMMIT COUNTY)—See AKRON, OH (Time Warner Cable)

SPRINGFIELD TWP.—See DAYTON, OH (Time Warner Cable)

▲ **SPRINGFIELD**—Time Warner Cable. Now served by DAYTON, OH [OH0011]

SPRINGFIELD—See DAYTON, OH (Time Warner Cable)

ST. ALBANS TWP. (LICKING COUNTY)—See COLUMBUS, OH (Insight Communications)

ST. ALBANS TWP.—See MOUNT VERNON, OH (Time Warner Cable)

ST. BERNARD—See CINCINNATI, OH (Time Warner Cable)

ST. CLAIR TWP. (COLUMBIANA COUNTY)—See EAST LIVERPOOL, OH (Comcast Cable)

ST. CLAIR TWP.—See CINCINNATI, OH (Time Warner Cable)

ST. HENRY—See CELINA, OH (Time Warner Cable)

ST. JOHNS—See WAYNESFIELD, OH (Time Warner Cable)

ST. JOSEPH TWP. (WILLIAMS COUNTY)—See BRYAN, OH (Time Warner Cable)

ST. LOUISVILLE—See NEWARK, OH (Time Warner Cable)

ST. MARTIN—See CINCINNATI, OH (Time Warner Cable)

▲ **ST. MARY'S**—Time Warner Cable

▲ **ST. PARIS**—Time Warner Communications. Now served by DAYTON, OH [OH0011]

ST. PARIS—See DAYTON, OH (Time Warner Cable)

STARK COUNTY (PORTIONS)—See CANTON, OH (Time Warner Cable)

STAUNTON TWP.—See DAYTON, OH (Time Warner Cable)

STERLING TWP. (BROWN COUNTY)—See CINCINNATI, OH (Time Warner Cable)

STERLING—See LODI, OH (Time Warner Cable)

▲ **STEUBENVILLE**—Comcast Cable. Now served by WHEELING, WV [WV0004]

STEWART—See BEVERLY, OH (Time Warner Cable)

STOCKPORT—See BEVERLY, OH (Time Warner Cable)

STOKES TWP. (LOGAN COUNTY)—See BELLEFONTAINE, OH (Time Warner Cable)

STOKES TWP. (LOGAN COUNTY)—See WAYNESFIELD, OH (Time Warner Cable)

STOKES TWP.—See DAYTON, OH (Time Warner Cable)

STONELICK TWP.—See CINCINNATI, OH (Time Warner Cable)

STONY RIDGE—See WATERVILLE, OH (Time Warner Cable)

STOUTSVILLE—See CHILLICOTHE, OH (Time Warner Cable)

STOW—See AKRON, OH (Time Warner Cable)

STRASBURG—See NEW PHILADELPHIA, OH (Time Warner Cable)

STRATTON—See TORONTO, OH (Jefferson County Cable Inc.)

STREETSBORO—See KENT, OH (Time Warner Cable)

STRONGSVILLE—See CLEVELAND HEIGHTS, OH (Time Warner Cable)

STRONGSVILLE—See CLEVELAND, OH (WOW! Internet Cable & Phone)

▲ **STRUTHERS**—Time Warner Cable

STRYKER—See BRYAN, OH (Time Warner Cable)

SUFFIELD TWP.—See KENT, OH (Time Warner Cable)

SUGAR BUSH KNOLLS—See KENT, OH (Time Warner Cable)

SUGAR CREEK TWP. (ALLEN COUNTY)—See LIMA, OH (Time Warner Cable)

SUGAR CREEK TWP. (PUTNAM COUNTY)—See KALIDA, OH (Kalida Telephone Co.)

SUGAR CREEK TWP. (STARK COUNTY)—See MASSILLON, OH (Massillon Cable TV Inc.)

SUGAR CREEK TWP. (WAYNE COUNTY)—See ORRVILLE, OH (Armstrong Cable Services)

SUGAR CREEK TWP. (WAYNE COUNTY)—See WOOSTER, OH (Clear Picture Inc.)

SUGAR CREEK TWP.—See LIMA, OH (Time Warner Cable)

SUGAR GROVE—See LANCASTER, OH (Time Warner Cable)

SUGARCREEK—See NEW PHILADELPHIA, OH (Time Warner Cable)

SULLIVAN TWP.—See ASHLAND, OH (Armstrong Cable Services)

SULPHUR SPRINGS—See BUCYRUS, OH (Time Warner Cable)

▲ **SUMMERFIELD (village)**—Formerly served by Almega Cable. No longer in operation

SUMMIT COUNTY (SOUTHWESTERN PORTION)—See MASSILLON, OH (Massillon Cable TV Inc.)

▲ **SUNBURY**—Time Warner Cable. Now served by COLUMBUS, OH [OH0002]

SUNBURY—See COLUMBUS, OH (Time Warner Cable)

SUNFISH TWP.—See CHILLICOTHE, OH (Time Warner Cable)

SWAN CREEK TWP.—See WAUSEON, OH (Time Warner Cable)

WARD TWP.—See MURRAY CITY, OH (Time Warner Cable)

▲**WARNER**—Zito Media

WARREN COUNTY (PORTIONS)—See CINCINNATI, OH (Time Warner Cable)

▲**WARREN TWP. (TRUMBULL COUNTY)**—Northeast Cable TV

WARREN TWP. (TRUMBULL COUNTY)—See WARREN, OH (Time Warner Cable)

WARREN TWP.—See YOUNGSTOWN, OH (Northeast Cable TV)

▲**WARREN**—Time Warner Cable

WARRENSVILLE HEIGHTS—See CLEVELAND HEIGHTS, OH (Time Warner Cable)

▲**WASHINGTON COURT HOUSE**—Time Warner Cable

WASHINGTON TWP. (DARKE COUNTY)—See DAYTON, OH (Time Warner Cable)

WASHINGTON TWP. (MONTGOMERY COUNTY)—See DAYTON, OH (Time Warner Cable)

WASHINGTON TWP. (MUSKINGUM COUNTY)—See ZANESVILLE, OH (Time Warner Cable)

WASHINGTON TWP. (PAULDING COUNTY)—See OTTOVILLE, OH (OTEC Communication Co.)

WASHINGTON TWP. (RICHLAND COUNTY)—See MANSFIELD, OH (Time Warner Cable)

WASHINGTON TWP. (SHELBY COUNTY)—See DAYTON, OH (Time Warner Cable)

WASHINGTON TWP. (STARK COUNTY)—See CANTON, OH (Time Warner Cable)

WATERFORD TWP.—See BEVERLY, OH (Time Warner Cable)

WATERTOWN—See BEVERLY, OH (Time Warner Cable)

WATERVILLE TWP. (LUCAS COUNTY)—See TOLEDO, OH (Buckeye Cable System Inc)

WATERVILLE—See TOLEDO, OH (Buckeye Cable System Inc)

▲**WATERVILLE**—Time Warner Cable

▲**WAUSEON**—Time Warner Cable

▲**WAVERLY**—Formerly served by Adelphia Communications. Now served by CHILLICOTHE, OH [OH0033]

WAVERLY—See CHILLICOTHE, OH (Time Warner Cable)

WAYNE COUNTY (EASTERN PORTION)—See MASSILLON, OH (Massillon Cable TV Inc.)

WAYNE COUNTY (NORTHERN PORTION)—See SOUTH POINT, WV (Armstrong Cable Services)

WAYNE COUNTY (SOUTHEASTERN PORTION)—See WOOSTER, OH (Clear Picture Inc.)

WAYNE LAKES (VILLAGE)—See DAYTON, OH (Time Warner Cable)

WAYNE TWP. (JEFFERSON COUNTY)—See BLOOMINGDALE, OH (Suddenlink Communications)

WAYNE TWP. (WAYNE COUNTY)—See WOOSTER, OH (Clear Picture Inc.)

WAYNE—See CLAY CENTER/GIBSONBURG, OH (Time Warner Cable)

WAYNESBURG (VILLAGE)—See CANTON, OH (Time Warner Cable)

▲**WAYNESFIELD**—Time Warner Cable

WAYNESVILLE—See DAYTON, OH (Time Warner Cable)

WEATHERSFIELD TWP. (TRUMBULL COUNTY)—See BOARDMAN, OH (Armstrong Cable Services)

WEATHERSFIELD TWP. (TRUMBULL COUNTY)—See WARREN, OH (Time Warner Cable)

▲**WEATHERSFIELD TWP.**—Northeast Cable TV

WEBSTER TWP. (WOOD COUNTY)—See BOWLING GREEN, OH (Time Warner Cable)

WELLER TWP. (RICHLAND COUNTY)—See ASHLAND, OH (Armstrong Cable Services)

WELLINGTON (VILLAGE)—See WELLINGTON, OH (GLW Broadband)

WELLINGTON TWP.—See WELLINGTON, OH (GLW Broadband)

▲**WELLINGTON**—GLW Broadband

WELLSTON—See JACKSON, OH (Time Warner Cable)

WELLSVILLE—See EAST LIVERPOOL, OH (Comcast Cable)

WEST ALEXANDRIA—See DAYTON, OH (Time Warner Cable)

WEST CARROLLTON—See DAYTON, OH (Time Warner Cable)

WEST CHESTER TWP. (BUTLER COUNTY)—See CINCINNATI, OH (Time Warner Cable)

WEST ELKTON—See DAYTON, OH (Time Warner Cable)

WEST FARMINGTON—See WARREN, OH (Time Warner Cable)

WEST JEFFERSON—See COLUMBUS, OH (Time Warner Cable)

▲**WEST LAFAYETTE**—Time Warner Cable. Now served by NEWARK, OH [OH0019]

WEST LAFAYETTE—See NEWARK, OH (Time Warner Cable)

WEST LEIPSIC (VILLAGE)—See COLUMBUS GROVE (village), OH (FairPoint Communications)

▲**WEST LIBERTY (VILLAGE)**—Champaign Telephone Co. Formerly served by Urbana, OH [OH0443]. This cable system has converted to IPTV

WEST LIBERTY—See DAYTON, OH (Time Warner Cable)

WEST MANCHESTER—See DAYTON, OH (Time Warner Cable)

▲**WEST MANSFIELD**—Time Warner Cable. Now served by COLUMBUS, OH [OH0002]

WEST MANSFIELD—See COLUMBUS, OH (Time Warner Cable)

WEST MILLGROVE—See CLAY CENTER/GIBSONBURG, OH (Time Warner Cable)

WEST MILTON TWP.—See DAYTON, OH (Time Warner Cable)

WEST RUSHVILLE—See THORNVILLE, OH (Time Warner Cable)

WEST SALEM—See LODI, OH (Time Warner Cable)

WEST TWP.—See MINERVA, OH (Time Warner Cable)

▲**WEST UNION**—Time Warner Cable. Now served by CINCINNATI, OH [OH0001]

WEST UNION—See CINCINNATI, OH (Time Warner Cable)

WEST UNITY—See BRYAN, OH (Time Warner Cable)

WESTBORO—See CINCINNATI, OH (Time Warner Cable)

WESTERVILLE (DELAWARE & FRANKLIN COUNTIES)—See COLUMBUS, OH (Insight Communications)

WESTERVILLE—See COLUMBUS, OH (WOW! Internet Cable & Phone)

WESTFIELD CENTER—See LODI, OH (Time Warner Cable)

WESTLAKE—See CLEVELAND HEIGHTS, OH (Time Warner Cable)

WESTLAKE—See CLEVELAND, OH (WOW! Internet Cable & Phone)

WESTON—See BOWLING GREEN, OH (Time Warner Cable)

WHARTON—See KENTON, OH (Time Warner Cable)

WHEELERSBURG—See PORTSMOUTH, OH (Time Warner Cable)

WHEELING TWP. (GUERNSEY COUNTY)—See NEWARK, OH (Time Warner Cable)

WHETSTONE TWP.—See GALION, OH (Time Warner Cable)

WHIPPLE—See WARNER, OH (Zito Media)

WHITE COTTAGE—See ZANESVILLE, OH (Time Warner Cable)

WHITE OAK TWP.—See CINCINNATI, OH (Time Warner Cable)

WHITEFORD TWP.—See TOLEDO, MI (Buckeye Cable System Inc)

WHITEFORD—See TOLEDO, MI (Buckeye Cable System Inc)

WHITEHALL—See COLUMBUS, OH (Insight Communications)

WHITEHALL—See COLUMBUS, OH (WOW! Internet Cable & Phone)

WHITEHOUSE—See WATERVILLE, OH (Time Warner Cable)

WICKLIFFE—See CLEVELAND HEIGHTS, OH (Time Warner Cable)

WILBERFORCE—See DAYTON, OH (Time Warner Cable)

▲**WILLARD**—Time Warner Cable

WILLIAMSFIELD—See VERNON, OH (S. Bryer Cable TV Corp.)

WILLIAMSPORT—See NEW HOLLAND, OH (Time Warner Cable)

WILLISTON—See CLAY CENTER/GIBSONBURG, OH (Time Warner Cable)

WILLOUGHBY HILLS—See CLEVELAND HEIGHTS, OH (Time Warner Cable)

WILLOUGHBY—See CLEVELAND HEIGHTS, OH (Time Warner Cable)

WILLOWICK—See CLEVELAND HEIGHTS, OH (Time Warner Cable)

▲**WILLOWS MOBILE HOME PARK**—Time Warner Cable. Now served by AKRON, OH [OH0005]

WILLOWS MOBILE HOME PARK—See AKRON, OH (Time Warner Cable)

WILLS TWP.—See SENECAVILLE, OH (Suddenlink Communications)

WILLSHIRE—See ROCKFORD, OH (Time Warner Cable)

WILMINGTON TWP. (LAWRENCE COUNTY)—See NEW MIDDLETOWN, PA (Comcast Cable)

▲**WILMINGTON**—Time Warner Cable. Now served by CINCINNATI, OH [OH0001]

WILMINGTON—See CINCINNATI, OH (Time Warner Cable)

WILMOT—See NEW PHILADELPHIA, OH (Time Warner Cable)

WILSON—See MALAGA TWP., OH (Richards TV Cable)

WINCHESTER—See CINCINNATI, OH (Time Warner Cable)

WINDHAM (PORTAGE COUNTY)—See NELSON TWP., OH (Suddenlink Communications)

WINDHAM TWP.—See NELSON TWP., OH (Suddenlink Communications)

WINDHAM—See WARREN, OH (Time Warner Cable)

WINDSOR—See ORWELL, OH (FairPoint Communications)

WINDSOR—See THOMPSON TWP. (Geauga County), OH (Zito Media)

▲**WINESBURG**—Formerly served by National Cable Inc. No longer in operation

WINONA—See SALEM, OH (Time Warner Cable)

WOOD VALLEY MOBILE HOME PARK—See MARION, OH (Time Warner Cable)

WOOD VALLEY—See MARION, OH (Time Warner Cable)

WOODLAWN—See CINCINNATI, OH (Time Warner Cable)

WOODMERE—See CLEVELAND HEIGHTS, OH (Time Warner Cable)

▲ **WOODSFIELD**—City of Woodsfield

WOODSTOCK—See DAYTON, OH (Time Warner Cable)

WOODVILLE—See CLAY CENTER/GIBSONBURG, OH (Time Warner Cable)

WOOSTER TWP. (WAYNE COUNTY)—See WOOSTER, OH (Clear Picture Inc.)

▲ **WOOSTER**—Clear Picture Inc.

WORTHINGTON—See COLUMBUS, OH (Time Warner Cable)

WORTHINGTON—See COLUMBUS, OH (WOW! Internet Cable & Phone)

WREN—See ROCKFORD, OH (Time Warner Cable)

WRIGHT-PATTERSON—See DAYTON, OH (Time Warner Cable)

WURTLAND—See SOUTH POINT, KY (Armstrong Cable Services)

WYOMING—See CINCINNATI, OH (Time Warner Cable)

XENIA—See DAYTON, OH (Time Warner Cable)

YELLOW CREEK—See EAST LIVERPOOL, OH (Comcast Cable)

▲ **YELLOW SPRINGS**—Time Warner Cable Communications Inc. Now served by DAYTON, OH [OH0011]

YELLOW SPRINGS—See DAYTON, OH (Time Warner Cable)

YORK TWP. (FULTON COUNTY)—See WAUSEON, OH (Time Warner Cable)

YORK TWP. (MUSKINGUM COUNTY)—See ZANESVILLE, OH (Time Warner Cable)

YORK TWP. (SANDUSKY COUNTY)—See BELLEVUE, OH (Time Warner Cable)

YORK TWP.—See MEDINA, OH (Armstrong Cable Services)

YORKSHIRE—See VERSAILLES, OH (Time Warner Cable)

▲ **YOUNGSTOWN**—Formerly served by Sprint Corp. No longer in operation

▲ **YOUNGSTOWN**—Northeast Cable TV

▲ **YOUNGSTOWN**—Time Warner Cable

ZALESKI—See JACKSON, OH (Time Warner Cable)

ZANE TWP. (LOGAN COUNTY)—See COLUMBUS, OH (Time Warner Cable)

ZANESFIELD (VILLAGE)—See BELLEFONTAINE, OH (Time Warner Cable)

▲ **ZANESVILLE**—Time Warner Cable

ZOAR—See NEW PHILADELPHIA, OH (Time Warner Cable)

OKLAHOMA

▲ **ACHILLE**—CommuniComm Services. Now served by TISHOMINGO, OK [OK0064]

ACHILLE—See TISHOMINGO, OK (CommuniComm Services)

▲ **ADA**—Cable One

▲ **ADAIR**—Allegiance Communications

AFTON—See KETCHUM, OK (Allegiance Communications)

▲ **AGRA**—Formerly served by Allegiance Communications. No longer in operation

ALDERSON—See McALESTER, OK (Allegiance Communications)

▲ **ALEX**—Southern Plains Cable

▲ **ALINE (town)**—Formerly served by Blue Sky Cable LLC. No longer in operation

▲ **ALLEN (TOWN)**—Allegiance Communications

ALMA—See VELMA, OK (Reach Broadband)

ALTUS AFB—See ALTUS, OK (Cable One)

▲ **ALTUS**—Cable One

▲ **ALVA**—Suddenlink Communications

▲ **AMES**—Pioneer Telephone Coop. This cable system has converted to IPTV. See Ames, OK [OK5062]

▲ **AMES**—Pioneer Telephone Coop. Formerly [OK0370]. This cable system has converted to IPTV

▲ **ANADARKO**—Suddenlink Communications

▲ **ANTLERS**—Alliance Communications

▲ **APACHE**—Southern Plains Cable

▲ **ARAPAHO**—Full Circle Communications

▲ **ARDMORE/LONE GROVE**—Cable One

ARMSTRONG—See DURANT, OK (CommuniComm Services)

▲ **ARNETT**—Pioneer Telephone Coop. This cable system has converted to IPTV. See Arnett, OK [OK5012]

▲ **ARNETT**—Pioneer Telephone Coop. Formerly [OK0261]. This cable system has converted to IPTV

ARPELAR—See STUART, OK (Allegiance Communications)

▲ **ASHER**—Formerly served by CableDirect. No longer in operation

▲ **ATOKA**—CommuniComm Services. Now served by COALGATE, OK [OK0120]

ATOKA—See COALGATE, OK (CommuniComm Services)

▲ **AVANT**—Community Cablevision Co.

▲ **BARNSDALL**—Community Cablevision Co.

▲ **BARTLESVILLE**—Cable One

▲ **BEAVER**—Panhandle Telephone Coop. Inc.

▲ **BEGGS**—Allegiance Communications

▲ **BENNINGTON**—Formerly served by Allegiance Communications. No longer in operation

BERNICE—See KETCHUM, OK (Allegiance Communications)

▲ **BESSIE**—Formerly served by Cebridge Connections. No longer in operation

BETHANY—See OKLAHOMA CITY, OK (Cox Communications)

BETHEL ACRES—See SHAWNEE, OK (Allegiance Communications)

▲ **BILLINGS**—Formerly served by Cebridge Connections. No longer in operation

▲ **BINGER**—Cable West

BIXBY—See TULSA, OK (Cox Communications)

▲ **BLACKWELL**—Suddenlink Communications

▲ **BLAIR**—LakeView Cable

▲ **BLANCHARD**—Pioneer Telephone Coop. This cable system has converted to IPTV. See Blanchard, OK [OK5015]

▲ **BLANCHARD**—Pioneer Telephone Coop. Formerly [OK0391]. This cable system has converted to IPTV

▲ **BOISE CITY**—Panhandle Telephone Coop. Inc.

BOKCHITO—See TISHOMINGO, OK (CommuniComm Services)

▲ **BOSHOKE**—Formerly served by Cebridge Connections. No longer in operation

▲ **BOSWELL**—Allegiance Communications

▲ **BOYNTON**—Formerly served by Allegiance Communications. No longer in operation

▲ **BRAGGS**—Allegiance Communications

▲ **BRECKINRIDGE**—Formerly served by Cebridge Connections. No longer in operation

BRIDGEPORT—See HINTON, OK (Hinton CATV Co.)

▲ **BRISTOW**—Allegiance Communications

BROKEN ARROW—See TULSA, OK (Cox Communications)

▲ **BROKEN BOW**—Broken Bow TV Cable Co. Inc.

BROOKEN—See LONGTOWN, OK (Allegiance Communications)

BRYAN COUNTY—See DURANT, OK (CommuniComm Services)

▲ **BUFFALO**—Pioneer Telephone Coop. This cable system has converted to IPTV. See Buffalo, OK [OK5091]

▲ **BUFFALO**—Pioneer Telephone Coop. Formerly [OK0151]. This cable system has converted to IPTV

BUNCOMBE CREEK—See TISHOMINGO, OK (CommuniComm Services)

▲ **BURNS FLAT**—Full Circle Communications

▲ **BUTLER**—Formerly served by Basic Cable Services Inc. No longer in operation

▲ **BYARS**—Formerly served by Cebridge Connections. No longer in operation

BYNG—See ADA, OK (Cable One)

▲ **CACHE**—LakeView Cable

CALERA—See DURANT, OK (CommuniComm Services)

▲ **CALUMET**—Pioneer Telephone Coop. This cable system has converted to IPTV. See Calumet, OK [OK5063]

▲ **CALUMET**—Pioneer Telephone Coop. Formerly [OK0238]. This cable system has converted to IPTV

▲ **CALVIN**—Allegiance Communications

▲ **CAMARGO**—Formerly served by Cebridge Connections. No longer in operation

▲ **CAMERON**—Allegiance Communications

▲ **CANADIAN**—Lakeland Cable TV Inc.

▲ **CANEY**—Formerly served by Allegiance Communications. No longer in operation

▲ **CANTON**—Formerly served by Blue Sky Cable LLC. No longer in operation

▲ **CANUTE**—Full Circle Communications

▲ **CARMEN**—Pioneer Telephone Coop. This cable system has converted to IPTV. See CARMEN, OK [OK5092]

▲ **CARMEN**—Pioneer Telephone Coop. Formerly [OK0234]. This cable system has converted to IPTV

▲ **CARNEGIE**—Carnegie Cable

▲ **CARNEY**—Formerly served by Allegiance Communications. No longer in operation

CARTER COUNTY—See ARDMORE/LONE GROVE, OK (Cable One)

▲ **CARTER**—Formerly served by CableDirect. No longer in operation

▲ **CASHION**—Formerly served by Cebridge Connections. No longer in operation

CATOOSA—See TULSA, OK (Cox Communications)

▲ **CATOOSA**—Pine River Cable

CEDAR LAKE—See HINTON, OK (Hinton CATV Co.)

▲ **CEMENT**—Southern Plains Cable

▲ **CHANDLER**—Allegiance Communications

▲ **CHATTANOOGA**—Formerly served by Southern Plains Cable. No longer in operation

CHECOTAH—See EUFAULA, OK (Reach Broadband)

▲ **CHELSEA**—Charter Communications. Now served by KETCHUM, OK [OK0179]

CHELSEA—See KETCHUM, OK (Allegiance Communications)

▲ **CHEROKEE**—Formerly served by Alliance Communications Network. No longer in operation

▲ **CHEYENNE**—James Mogg TV

▲ **CHICKASHA**—Suddenlink Communications

▲ **CHICKEN CREEK**—Formerly served by Eagle Media. No longer in operation

CHOCTAW COUNTY (PORTIONS)—See HUGO, OK (Suddenlink Communications)

CHOCTAW COUNTY (UNINCORPORATED AREAS)—See BOSWELL, OK (Allegiance Communications)

CHOCTAW—See OKLAHOMA CITY, OK (Cox Communications)

▲ **CHOUTEAU**—Charter Communications. Now served by KETCHUM, OK [OK0179]

CHOUTEAU—See KETCHUM, OK (Allegiance Communications)

CLAREMORE—See TULSA, OK (Cox Communications)

▲ **CLAREMORE**—Zoom Media

▲ **CLAYTON (TOWN)**—Allegiance Communications

▲ **CLEO SPRINGS**—Formerly served by Blue Sky Cable LLC. No longer in operation

CLEVELAND—See MANNFORD, OK (Cim Tel Cable Inc.)

CLINTON—See ELK CITY, OK (Cable One)

▲ **COALGATE**—CommuniComm Services

▲ **COLBERT**—CommuniComm Services. Now served by TISHOMINGO, OK [OK0064]

COLBERT—See TISHOMINGO, OK (CommuniComm Services)

▲ **COLCORD**—Allegiance Communications

▲ **COLLINSVILLE**—Community Cablevision Co.

COLONY—See HINTON, OK (Hinton CATV Co.)

▲ **COMANCHE COUNTY (UNINCORPORATED AREA)**—LakeView Cable

COMANCHE COUNTY—See LAWTON, OK (Fidelity Communications)

▲ **COMANCHE**—Pioneer Telephone Coop. This cable system has converted to IPTV. See Comanche, OK [OK5022]

▲ **COMANCHE**—Pioneer Telephone Coop. Formerly [OK0177]. This cable system has converted to IPTV

COMMERCE—See MIAMI, OK (Cable One)

▲ **COOKSON**—Formerly served by Eagle Media. No longer in operation

▲ **COPAN**—Community Cablevision Co.

CORDELL—See ELK CITY, OK (Cable One)

▲ **CORN**—Cable West

CORNISH—See HEALDTON, OK (Suddenlink Communications)

COTTONWOOD—See COALGATE, OK (CommuniComm Services)

COUNTYLINE—See VELMA, OK (Reach Broadband)

▲ **COVINGTON**—Pioneer Telephone Coop. This cable system has converted to IPTV. See Covington, OK [OK5064]

▲ **COVINGTON**—Pioneer Telephone Coop. Formerly [OK0203]. This cable system has converted to IPTV

COWETA—See TULSA, OK (Cox Communications)

COYLE—See LANGSTON, OK (Allegiance Communications)

CRAIG COUNTY—See VINITA, OK (Cable One)

CREEK COUNTY (PORTIONS)—See TULSA, OK (Cox Communications)

CREEK COUNTY (PORTIONS)—See TULSA COUNTY (western portion), OK (Pine River Cable)

▲ **CRESCENT**—Suddenlink Communications

▲ **CROMWELL**—Allegiance Communications

CROWDER—See CANADIAN, OK (Lakeland Cable TV Inc.)

▲ **CUSHING**—Suddenlink Communications

▲ **CUSTER CITY**—Pioneer Telephone Coop. This cable system has converted to IPTV. See Custer City, OK [OK5066]

▲ **CUSTER CITY**—Pioneer Telephone Coop. Formerly [OK0277]. This cable system has converted to IPTV

▲ **CYRIL**—Alliance Cable Network

▲ **DACOMA**—Pioneer Telephone Coop. This cable system has converted to IPTV. See Dacoma, OK [OK5093]

▲ **DACOMA**—Pioneer Telephone Coop. Formerly [OK0278]. This cable system has converted to IPTV

DALE—See SHAWNEE, OK (Allegiance Communications)

▲ **DAVENPORT**—Vi-Tel Inc.

▲ **DAVIDSON**—Formerly served by CableDirect. No longer in operation

DAVIS—See ADA, OK (Cable One)

▲ **DEER CREEK**—Formerly served by CableDirect. No longer in operation

DEL CITY—See OKLAHOMA CITY, OK (Cox Communications)

DELAWARE COUNTY (NORTHERN PORTION)—See GROVE, OK (Suddenlink Communications)

▲ **DELAWARE**—Allegiance Communications

▲ **DEPEW**—Allegiance Communications

DEWAR—See OKMULGEE, OK (Suddenlink Communications)

DEWEY—See BARTLESVILLE, OK (Cable One)

DICKSON—See ARDMORE/LONE GROVE, OK (Cable One)

▲ **DILL CITY**—Cable West

▲ **DISNEY**—Omni III Cable TV Inc.

▲ **DOVER**—Pioneer Telephone Coop. This cable system has converted to IPTV. See Dover, OK [OK5099]

▲ **DOVER**—Pioneer Telephone Coop. Formerly [OK0250]. This cable system has converted to IPTV

▲ **DRUMMOND**—Pioneer Telephone Coop. This cable system has converted to IPTV. See Drummond, OK [OK5094]

▲ **DRUMMOND**—Pioneer Telephone Coop. Formerly [OK0281]. This cable system has converted to IPTV

▲ **DRUMRIGHT**—Suddenlink Communications

▲ **DUKE**—Formerly served by CableDirect. No longer in operation

▲ **DUNCAN**—Cable One

▲ **DURANT**—CommuniComm Services

▲ **DUSTIN**—Allegiance Communications

EAGLETOWN—See BROKEN BOW, OK (Broken Bow TV Cable Co. Inc.)

▲ **EAKLY**—Hinton CATV Co. Now served by HINTON, OK [OK0140]

EAKLY—See HINTON, OK (Hinton CATV Co.)

EARLSBORO—See SHAWNEE, OK (Allegiance Communications)

EDMOND—See OKLAHOMA CITY, OK (Cox Communications)

EL RENO—See OKLAHOMA CITY, OK (Cox Communications)

▲ **ELDORADO**—Formerly served by Cable West. No longer in operation

ELGIN—See FLETCHER, OK (Reach Broadband)

▲ **ELK CITY**—Cable One

▲ **ELK CREEK**—Formerly served by Eagle Media. No longer in operation

ELMORE CITY—See ADA, OK (Cable One)

▲ **ENID**—Suddenlink Communications

ENTERPRISE—See LONGTOWN, OK (Allegiance Communications)

▲ **ERICK**—Reach Broadband

ERIN SPRINGS—See LINDSAY, OK (Suddenlink Communications)

▲ **EUFAULA**—Reach Broadband

▲ **FAIRFAX**—Cim Tel Cable Inc. Now served by MANNFORD, OK [OK0296]

FAIRFAX—See MANNFORD, OK (Cim Tel Cable Inc.)

FAIRLAND—See KETCHUM, OK (Allegiance Communications)

▲ **FAIRVIEW**—Suddenlink Communications

▲ **FARGO**—Pioneer Telephone Coop. This cable system has converted to IPTV. See Fargo, OK [OK5096]

▲ **FARGO**—Pioneer Telephone Coop. Formerly [OK0345]. This cable system has converted to IPTV

▲ **FLETCHER**—Reach Broadband

FOREST PARK—See OKLAHOMA CITY, OK (Cox Communications)

FORGAN—See BEAVER, OK (Panhandle Telephone Coop. Inc.)

▲ **FORT COBB**—Cable West

▲ **FORT GIBSON**—Allegiance Communications

▲ **FORT SILL**—Suddenlink Communications

▲ **FORT SUPPLY**—Formerly served by CableDirect. No longer in operation

FOX—See VELMA, OK (Reach Broadband)

FRANCIS—See ADA, OK (Cable One)

▲ **FREDERICK**—Cable One. Now served by ALTUS, OK [OK0017]

FREDERICK—See ALTUS, OK (Cable One)

▲ **FREEDOM**—Formerly served by Pioneer Telephone Coop. No longer in operation

▲ **GAGE**—Pioneer Telephone Coop. Formerly served by Shattuck, OK [OK0135]. This cable system has converted to IPTV

▲ **GANS**—Allegiance Communications

▲ **GARBER**—Formerly served by Longview Communications. No longer in operation

GARFIELD COUNTY—See ENID, OK (Suddenlink Communications)

GARVIN COUNTY (UNINCORPORATED AREAS)—See PAULS VALLEY, OK (Suddenlink Communications)

▲ **GEARY**—Formerly served by Cebridge Connections. No longer in operation

▲ **GERONIMO**—Formerly served by CableDirect. No longer in operation

▲ **GERONIMO**—LakeView Cable

▲ **GLENCOE**—Allegiance Communications

▲ **GLENPOOL (southern portion)**—Formerly served by Titan Broadband Services. No longer in operation

GLENPOOL—See TULSA, OK (Cox Communications)

▲ **GOLTRY**—Formerly served by Cebridge Connections. No longer in operation

▲ **GOODWELL**—Allegiance Communications

▲ **GORE**—Allegiance Communications

▲ **GOTEBO**—Formerly served by Basic Cable Services Inc. No longer in operation

▲ **GOULD**—Pioneer Telephone Coop. Formerly served by Hollis, OK [OK0087]. This cable system has converted to IPTV

▲ **GRACEMONT**—Cable West

GRADY COUNTY (PORTIONS)—See CHICKASHA, OK (Suddenlink Communications)

GRAND LAKE—See KETCHUM, OK (Allegiance Communications)

▲ **GRANDFIELD**—Southern Plains Cable

▲ **GRANITE**—Cable West

GROVE—See KETCHUM, OK (Allegiance Communications)

▲ **GROVE**—Suddenlink Communications

GUTHRIE—See OKLAHOMA CITY, OK (Cox Communications)

▲ **GUYMON**—Allegiance Communications

HAILEYVILLE—See HARTSHORNE, OK (Allegiance Communications)

▲ **HAMMON**—Formerly served by Rapid Cable. No longer in operation

▲ **HARDESTY**—Panhandle Telephone Coop. Inc. This cable system has converted to IPTV. See Hardesty, OK [OK5032]

▲ **HARDESTY**—Panhandle Telephone Coop. Inc. Formerly [OK0373]. This cable system has converted to IPTV

HARRAH—See OKLAHOMA CITY, OK (Cox Communications)

▲ **HARTSHORNE**—Allegiance Communications

HASKELL COUNTY—See STIGLER, OK (Allegiance Communications)

▲ **HASKELL**—Allegiance Communications

HAWORTH—See BROKEN BOW, OK (Broken Bow TV Cable Co. Inc.)

HAYWOOD—See STUART, OK (Allegiance Communications)

▲ **HEALDTON**—Suddenlink Communications

▲ **HEAVENER**—Suddenlink Communications

▲ **HECTORVILLE**—Quality Cablevision of Oklahoma Inc. No longer in operation

▲ **HELENA**—Pioneer Telephone Coop. This cable system has converted to IPTV. See Helena, OK [OK5072]

▲ **HELENA**—Pioneer Telephone Coop. Formerly [OK0153]. This cable system has converted to IPTV

▲ **HENNESSEY**—Pioneer Telephone Coop. This cable system has converted to IPTV. See Hennessey, OK [OK5087]

▲ **HENNESSEY**—Pioneer Telephone Coop. Formerly [OK0113]. This cable system has converted to IPTV

▲ **HENRYETTA**—Suddenlink Communications. Now served by OKMULGEE, OK [OK0026]

HENRYETTA—See OKMULGEE, OK (Suddenlink Communications)

▲ **HINTON**—Hinton CATV Co.

▲ **HOBART**—Cable One

HOCHATOWA—See BROKEN BOW, OK (Broken Bow TV Cable Co. Inc.)

▲ **HOLDENVILLE**—Allegiance Communications

▲ **HOLLIS**—Pioneer Telephone Coop. This cable system has converted to IPTV. See Hollis, OK [OK5086]

▲ **HOLLIS**—Pioneer Telephone Coop. Formerly [OK0087]. This cable system has converted to IPTV

▲ **HOMINY**—Community Cablevision Co.

▲ **HOOKER**—Panhandle Telephone Coop. Inc.

▲ **HOWE**—Allegiance Communications

▲ **HUGO**—Suddenlink Communications

▲ **HULBERT**—Allegiance Communications

▲ **HUNTER**—Formerly served by Pioneer Telephone Coop. No longer in operation

HYDRO—See WEATHERFORD, OK (Suddenlink Communications)

IDABEL (SHULTZ COMMUNITY)—See BROKEN BOW, OK (Broken Bow TV Cable Co. Inc.)

▲ **IDABEL**—Suddenlink Communications

INDIAHOMA—See CACHE, OK (LakeView Cable)

INDIANOLA—See CANADIAN, OK (Lakeland Cable TV Inc.)

▲ **INOLA**—Allegiance Communications

JACKSON COUNTY—See ALTUS, OK (Cable One)

JAY—See DISNEY, OK (Omni III Cable TV Inc.)

JENKS—See TULSA, OK (Cox Communications)

JENNINGS—See MANNFORD, OK (Cim Tel Cable Inc.)

▲ **JET**—Formerly served by Cebridge Connections. No longer in operation

JOHNSTON COUNTY (PORTIONS)—See TISHOMINGO, OK (CommuniComm Services)

▲ **JONES**—Formerly served by Almega Cable. No longer in operation

▲ **KANSAS**—Allegiance Communications

▲ **KAW CITY**—Community Cablevision Co.

KAY COUNTY (PORTIONS)—See PONCA CITY, OK (Cable One)

▲ **KELLYVILLE**—Allegiance Communications

▲ **KEOTA**—Allegiance Communications

▲ **KETCHUM**—Allegiance Communications

KIEFER—See TULSA, OK (Cox Communications)

▲ **KINGFISHER**—Pioneer Telephone Coop. This cable system has converted to IPTV. See Kingfisher, OK [OK5074]

▲ **KINGFISHER**—Pioneer Telephone Coop. Formerly [OK0800]. This cable system has converted to IPTV

▲ **KINGSTON**—CommuniComm Services. Now served by TISHOMINGO, OK [OK0064]

KINGSTON—See TISHOMINGO, OK (CommuniComm Services)

KINTA—See QUINTON, OK (Allegiance Communications)

KIOWA COUNTY (PORTIONS)—See HOBART, OK (Cable One)

KIOWA—See SAVANNA, OK (Allegiance Communications)

▲ **KONAWA**—Allegiance Communications

KREBS—See McALESTER, OK (Allegiance Communications)

▲ **KREMLIN**—Formerly served by Cebridge Connections. No longer in operation

▲ **LAHOMA**—Pioneer Telephone Coop. This cable system has converted to IPTV. See Lahoma, OK [OK5097]

▲ **LAHOMA**—Pioneer Telephone Coop. Formerly [OK0298]. This cable system has converted to IPTV

▲ **LAKE ELLSWORTH**—LakeView Cable

▲ **LAKE LAWTONKA**—LakeView Cable

▲ **LAKE TENKILLER**—Formerly served by Cox Communications. No longer in operation

▲ **LAMONT**—Formerly served by Blue Sky Cable LLC. No longer in operation

LANGLEY—See KETCHUM, OK (Allegiance Communications)

▲ **LANGSTON**—Allegiance Communications

▲ **LAVERNE**—Panhandle Telephone Coop. Inc.

▲ **LAWTON**—Fidelity Communications

LE FLORE COUNTY (UNINCORPORATED AREAS)—See PANAMA, OK (Allegiance Communications)

▲ **LEEDEY**—Formerly served by Rapid Cable. No longer in operation

LENAPAH—See DELAWARE, OK (Allegiance Communications)

LEXINGTON—See PURCELL, OK (Suddenlink Communications)

▲ **LINDSAY**—Suddenlink Communications

LOCUST GROVE—See SALINA, OK (Allegiance Communications)

LONE GROVE—See ARDMORE/LONE GROVE, OK (Cable One)

▲ **LONE WOLF**—Formerly served by Cable West. No longer in operation

▲ **LONGDALE**—LongView Communications. No longer in operation

▲ **LONGTOWN**—Allegiance Communications

LOOKEBA—See HINTON, OK (Hinton CATV Co.)

LUKFATA—See BROKEN BOW, OK (Broken Bow TV Cable Co. Inc.)

▲ **LUTHER**—Allegiance Communications

MADILL—See ARDMORE/LONE GROVE, OK (Cable One)

▲ **MANGUM**—Cable One. Now served by ELK CITY, OK [OK0032]

MANGUM—See ELK CITY, OK (Cable One)

▲ **MANNFORD**—Cim Tel Cable Inc.

MARIETTA—See ARDMORE/LONE GROVE, OK (Cable One)

▲ **MARLAND**—Formerly served by Allegiance Communications. No longer in operation

MARLOW—See DUNCAN, OK (Cable One)

MARSHALL COUNTY (NORTHERN PORTION)—See ARDMORE/LONE GROVE, OK (Cable One)

▲ **MARSHALL**—Pioneer Telephone Coop. This cable system has converted to IPTV. See Marshall, OK [OK5076]

▲ **MARSHALL**—Pioneer Telephone Coop. Formerly [OK0298]. This cable system has converted to IPTV

▲ **MARTHA**—Formerly served by CableDirect. No longer in operation

▲ **MAUD**—Allegiance Communications

MAYES COUNTY (PORTIONS)—See PRYOR, OK (Alliance Communications)

MAYES COUNTY (WESTERN PORTION)—See ROGERS COUNTY (northern portion), OK (Time Warner Cable)

MAYSVILLE—See PURCELL, OK (Suddenlink Communications)

MCALESTER ARMY AMMUNITION PLANT—See SAVANNA, OK (Allegiance Communications)

▲ **MCALESTER**—Allegiance Communications

MCCLAIN COUNTY—See PURCELL, OK (Suddenlink Communications)

MCCURTAIN COUNTY (PORTIONS)—See BROKEN BOW, OK (Broken Bow TV Cable Co. Inc.)

▲ **MCCURTAIN**—Allegiance Communications

MCINTOSH COUNTY (PORTIONS)—See EUFAULA, OK (Reach Broadband)

MCLOUD—See SHAWNEE, OK (Allegiance Communications)

▲ **MEDICINE PARK**—LakeView Cable

MEEKER—See SHAWNEE, OK (Allegiance Communications)

▲ **MENO**—Formerly served by CableDirect. No longer in operation

▲ **MIAMI**—Cable One

MIDWEST CITY—See OKLAHOMA CITY, OK (Cox Communications)

▲ **MILBURN**—Formerly served by Allegiance Communications. No longer in operation

MONKEY ISLAND—See KETCHUM, OK (Allegiance Communications)

MOORE—See OKLAHOMA CITY, OK (Cox Communications)

▲ **MOORELAND**—Pioneer Telephone Coop. This cable system has converted to IPTV. See Mooreland, OK [OK5043]

▲ **MOORELAND**—Pioneer Telephone Coop. Formerly [OK0392]. This cable system has converted to IPTV

▲ **MORRIS**—Allegiance Communications

▲ **MORRISON**—Allegiance Communications

▲ **MOUNDS**—Allegiance Communications

▲ **MOUNTAIN PARK**—LakeView Cable

▲ **MOUNTAIN VIEW**—Mountain View Cable TV

MUSKOGEE COUNTY—See MUSKOGEE, OK (Suddenlink Communications)

▲ **MUSKOGEE**—Suddenlink Communications

MUSTANG—See OKLAHOMA CITY, OK (Cox Communications)

▲ **NASH**—Pioneer Telephone Coop. This cable system has converted to IPTV. See Nash, OK [OK5100]

▲ **NASH**—Pioneer Telephone Coop. Formerly [OK0301]. This cable system has converted to IPTV

▲ **NEWCASTLE**—Pioneer Telephone Coop. This cable system has converted to IPTV. See Newcastle, OK [OK5095]

▲ **NEWCASTLE**—Pioneer Telephone Coop. Formerly [OK0302]. This cable system has converted to IPTV

▲ **NEWKIRK**—Allegiance Communications

NICHOLS HILLS—See OKLAHOMA CITY, OK (Cox Communications)

▲ **NINNEKAH**—Formerly served by Cable West. No longer in operation

NOBLE COUNTY (PORTIONS)—See PERRY, OK (Suddenlink Communications)

▲ **NOBLE**—Formerly served by Cebridge Connections. Now served by PURCELL, OK [OK0048]

NOBLE—See PURCELL, OK (Suddenlink Communications)

NORMAN—See OKLAHOMA CITY, OK (Cox Communications)

NORTH ENID—See ENID, OK (Suddenlink Communications)

NORTH MIAMI—See MIAMI, OK (Cable One)

NOWATA COUNTY—See BARTLESVILLE, OK (Cable One)

▲ **NOWATA**—Cable One. Now served by BARTLESVILLE, OK [OK0010]

NOWATA—See BARTLESVILLE, OK (Cable One)

OAK HILL—See BROKEN BOW, OK (Broken Bow TV Cable Co. Inc.)

OAKLAND—See ARDMORE/LONE GROVE, OK (Cable One)

▲ **OCHELATA**—Community Cablevision Co.

▲ **OILTON**—Community Cablevision Co.

▲ **OKARCHE**—Pioneer Telephone Coop. This cable system has converted to IPTV. See Okarche, OK [OK5079]

▲ **OKARCHE**—Pioneer Telephone Coop. Formerly [OK0176]. This cable system has converted to IPTV

▲ **OKAY**—Allegiance Communications

▲ **OKEENE**—Pioneer Telephone Coop. This cable system has converted to IPTV. See Okeene, OK [OK5090]

▲ **OKEENE**—Pioneer Telephone Coop. Formerly [OK0146]. This cable system has converted to IPTV

▲ **OKEMAH**—Allegiance Communications

▲ **OKLAHOMA CITY**—Formerly served by WANTV of OKC. No longer in operation

▲ **OKLAHOMA CITY**—Cox Communications

OKMULGEE COUNTY (CENTRAL PORTION)—See OKMULGEE, OK (Suddenlink Communications)

▲ **OKMULGEE**—Suddenlink Communications

▲ **OLUSTEE**—Formerly served by Basic Cable Services Inc. No longer in operation

▲ **OOLOGAH**—Allegiance Communications

▲ **ORLANDO**—Formerly served by CableDirect. No longer in operation

OSAGE COUNTY (PORTIONS)—See PONCA CITY, OK (Cable One)

OSAGE COUNTY (PORTIONS)—See TULSA, OK (Cox Communications)

OSAGE COUNTY (PORTIONS)—See TULSA COUNTY (western portion), OK (Pine River Cable)

OSAGE—See MANNFORD, OK (Cim Tel Cable Inc.)

OTTAWA COUNTY—See MIAMI, OK (Cable One)

OWASSO—See TULSA, OK (Cox Communications)

▲ **PANAMA**—Allegiance Communications

▲ **PAOLI**—Formerly served by Cebridge Connections. No longer in operation

▲ **PARADISE HILL**—Formerly served by Eagle Media. No longer in operation

▲ **PARK HILL**—Formerly served by Eagle Media. No longer in operation

PARK HILL—See TAHLEQUAH, OK (Tahlequah Cable TV Inc.)

▲ **PAULS VALLEY**—Suddenlink Communications

▲ **PAWHUSKA**—Allegiance Communications

▲ **PAWNEE**—Now served by MANNFORD, OK [OK0296]

PAWNEE—See MANNFORD, OK (Cim Tel Cable Inc.)

PERKINS—See STILLWATER, OK (Suddenlink Communications)

▲ **PERRY**—Suddenlink Communications

▲ **PICHER**—Formerly served by Mediacom. No longer in operation

▲ **PIEDMONT**—Formerly served by Almega Cable. No longer in operation

▲ **POCASSET**—Formerly served by CableDirect. No longer in operation

▲ **POCOLA**—Cox Communications. Now served by FORT SMITH, AR [AR0003]

▲ **PONCA CITY**—Cable One

▲ **POND CREEK**—Pioneer Telephone Coop. This cable system has converted to IPTV. See Pond Creek, OK [OK5081]

▲ **POND CREEK**—Pioneer Telephone Coop. Formerly [OK0185]. This cable system has converted to IPTV

PONTOTOC COUNTY—See ADA, OK (Cable One)

▲ **PORTER**—Allegiance Communications

▲ **PORUM LANDING**—Allegiance Communications

▲ **PORUM**—Allegiance Communications

▲ **POTEAU**—Suddenlink Communications

PRAGUE—See SHAWNEE, OK (Allegiance Communications)

▲ **PRESTON**—Formerly served by Quality Cablevision of Oklahoma Inc. No longer in operation

PRUE—See MANNFORD, OK (Cim Tel Cable Inc.)

PRUITT CITY—See VELMA, OK (Reach Broadband)

▲ **PRYOR (outside areas)**—Formerly served by Time Warner Cable. No longer in operation

▲ **PRYOR**—Alliance Communications

▲ **PURCELL**—Suddenlink Communications

▲ **QUINTON**—Allegiance Communications

▲ **RALSTON**—Allegiance Communications

▲ **RAMONA**—Community Cablevision Co.

▲ **RANDLETT**—Formerly served by Cable Television Inc. No longer in operation

RATLIFF CITY—See VELMA, OK (Reach Broadband)

▲ **RATTAN**—Allegiance Communications

RAVIA—See TISHOMINGO, OK (CommuniComm Services)

RED OAK—See WILBURTON, OK (Allegiance Communications)

▲ **RED ROCK**—Formerly served by Blue Sky Cable LLC. No longer in operation

RINGLING—See HEALDTON, OK (Suddenlink Communications)

▲ **RINGWOOD**—Pioneer Telephone Coop. This cable system has converted to IPTV. See Ringwood, OK [OK5082]

▲ **RINGWOOD**—Pioneer Telephone Coop. Formerly [OK0375]. This cable system has converted to IPTV

▲ **RIPLEY**—Formerly served by CableDirect. No longer in operation

▲**ROCKY**—Formerly served by CableDirect. No longer in operation

ROFF—See ADA, OK (Cable One)

▲**ROGERS COUNTY (NORTHERN PORTION)**—Time Warner Cable

ROGERS COUNTY (PORTIONS)—See TULSA, OK (Cox Communications)

ROGERS COUNTY (PORTIONS)—See CATOOSA, OK (Pine River Cable)

ROLLING HILLS—See TULSA, OK (Cox Communications)

▲**ROOSEVELT TWP.**—Cable West

▲**RUSH SPRINGS**—Reach Broadband

▲**RYAN**—Formerly served by Almega Cable. No longer in operation

▲**SALINA**—Allegiance Communications

▲**SALLISAW**—Suddenlink Communications

▲**SAND POINT**—CommuniComm Services

SAND SPRINGS—See TULSA, OK (Cox Communications)

SAPULPA—See TULSA, OK (Cox Communications)

▲**SAVANNA**—Allegiance Communications

SAYRE—See ELK CITY, OK (Cable One)

▲**SCHULTER**—Allegiance Communications

▲**SEILING**—Pioneer Telephone Coop. This cable system has converted to IPTV. See Seiling, OK [OK5088]

▲**SEILING**—Pioneer Telephone Coop. Formerly [OK0122]. This cable system has converted to IPTV

SEMINOLE COUNTY (SOUTHERN PORTION)—See KONAWA, OK (Allegiance Communications)

▲**SEMINOLE**—Suddenlink Communications

▲**SENTINEL**—Cable West

SEQUOYAH COUNTY (UNINCORPORATED AREAS)—See GANS, OK (Allegiance Communications)

SHADY POINT—See PANAMA, OK (Allegiance Communications)

▲**SHATTUCK**—Pioneer Telephone Coop. This cable system has converted to IPTV. See Shattuck, OK [OK5089]

▲**SHATTUCK**—Pioneer Telephone Coop. Formerly [OK0135]. This cable system has converted to IPTV

▲**SHAWNEE**—Allegiance Communications

▲**SHIDLER**—Community Cablevision Co.

SICKLES—See HINTON, OK (Hinton CATV Co.)

▲**SKIATOOK**—Community Cablevision Co.

▲**SNYDER**—LongView Communications. Now served by MOUNTAIN PARK, OK [OK0300]

SNYDER—See MOUNTAIN PARK, OK (LakeView Cable)

▲**SOPER**—Soper Cable TV

SPAVINAW—See KETCHUM, OK (Allegiance Communications)

SPENCER—See OKLAHOMA CITY, OK (Cox Communications)

SPERRY—See SKIATOOK, OK (Community Cablevision Co.)

▲**SPIRO**—Suddenlink Communications

▲**STERLING**—Southern Plains Cable

▲**STIGLER**—Allegiance Communications

▲**STILLWATER**—Suddenlink Communications

▲**STILWELL**—Allegiance Communications

▲**STONEWALL**—CommuniComm Services. Now served by COALGATE, OK [OK0120]

STONEWALL—See COALGATE, OK (CommuniComm Services)

▲**STRANG**—Allegiance Communications

▲**STRATFORD**—Allegiance Communications

▲**STRINGTOWN**—CommuniComm Services

▲**STROUD**—Allegiance Communications

▲**STUART**—Allegiance Communications

SULPHUR—See ADA, OK (Cable One)

▲**TAHLEQUAH**—Tahlequah Cable TV Inc.

▲**TALALA**—Formerly served by Quality Cablevision of Oklahoma Inc. No longer in operation

▲**TALIHINA**—Allegiance Communications

▲**TALOGA**—Taloga Cable TV

TECUMSEH—See SHAWNEE, OK (Allegiance Communications)

TEMPLE—See WALTERS, OK (Alliance Communications)

▲**TERRAL**—Formerly served by Almega Cable. No longer in operation

THE VILLAGE—See OKLAHOMA CITY, OK (Cox Communications)

▲**THOMAS**—Pioneer Telephone Coop. This cable system has converted to IPTV. See Thomas, OK [OK5083]

▲**THOMAS**—Pioneer Telephone Coop. Formerly served by [OK0155]. This cable system has converted to IPTV.

▲**TIPTON**—LakeView Cable

▲**TISHOMINGO**—CommuniComm Services

TONKAWA—See PONCA CITY, OK (Cable One)

▲**TRYON**—Allegiance Communications

TULSA (NORTHWESTERN PORTION)—See ROGERS COUNTY (northern portion), OK (Time Warner Cable)

▲**TULSA COUNTY (WESTERN PORTION)**—Pine River Cable

▲**TULSA**—Cox Communications

TUPELO—See COALGATE, OK (CommuniComm Services)

▲**TURPIN**—Allegiance Communications

TUSHKA—See COALGATE, OK (CommuniComm Services)

▲**TUTTLE**—Formerly served by Vidia Communications. No longer in operation

▲**TYRONE**—Allegiance Communications

▲**UNION CITY**—Formerly served by Vidia Communications. No longer in operation

VALLEY BROOK—See OKLAHOMA CITY, OK (Cox Communications)

▲**VALLIANT**—Allegiance Communications

VANCE AFB—See ENID, OK (Suddenlink Communications)

▲**VELMA**—Reach Broadband

▲**VERDEN**—Cable West

▲**VERDIGRIS**—Allegiance Communications

▲**VIAN**—Allegiance Communications

▲**VICI**—Formerly served by Rapid Cable. No longer in operation

▲**VINITA**—Cable One

WAGONER COUNTY (EASTERN PORTION)—See MUSKOGEE, OK (Suddenlink Communications)

WAGONER COUNTY (PORTIONS)—See HASKELL, OK (Allegiance Communications)

WAGONER COUNTY (PORTIONS)—See TULSA, OK (Cox Communications)

WAGONER COUNTY (PORTIONS)—See CATOOSA, OK (Pine River Cable)

WAGONER—See MUSKOGEE, OK (Suddenlink Communications)

▲**WAKITA**—Pioneer Telephone Coop. This cable system has converted to IPTV. See Wakita, OK [OK5084]

▲**WAKITA**—Pioneer Telephone Coop. Formerly served by [OK0226]. This cable system has converted to IPTV.

▲**WALTERS**—Alliance Communications

▲**WANETTE**—Formerly served by Cebridge Connections. No longer in operation

▲**WAPANUCKA**—CommuniComm Services

▲**WARNER**—Cross Cable TV

WARR ACRES—See OKLAHOMA CITY, OK (Cox Communications)

▲**WASHINGTON**—Formerly served by Cebridge Connections. No longer in operation

▲**WATONGA**—Pioneer Telephone Coop. This cable system has converted to IPTV. See Watonga, OK [OK5085]

▲**WATONGA**—Pioneer Telephone Coop. Formerly served by [OK0082]. This cable system has converted to IPTV.

WATTS—See WESTVILLE, OK (Allegiance Communications)

▲**WAUKOMIS**—Formerly served by Adelphia Cable. No longer in operation

▲**WAURIKA**—Alliance Communications

WAYNE—See PURCELL, OK (Suddenlink Communications)

▲**WAYNOKA**—Formerly served by Waynoka Community TV. No longer in operation

▲**WEATHERFORD**—Suddenlink Communications

WEBBERS FALLS—See GORE, OK (Allegiance Communications)

▲**WELCH**—Allegiance Communications

▲**WELEETKA**—Allegiance Communications

▲**WELLSTON**—Allegiance Communications

WESTPORT—See MANNFORD, OK (Cim Tel Cable Inc.)

▲**WESTVILLE**—Allegiance Communications

▲**WETUMKA**—Allegiance Communications

▲**WEWOKA**—Formerly served by Cebridge Connections. Now served by SEMINOLE, OK [OK0042]

WEWOKA—See SEMINOLE, OK (Suddenlink Communications)

▲**WHITE HORN COVE**—Formerly served by Lake Area TV Cable. No longer in operation

WHITEFIELD—See STIGLER, OK (Allegiance Communications)

▲**WILBURTON**—Allegiance Communications

WILSON—See HEALDTON, OK (Suddenlink Communications)

▲**WISTER**—Allegiance Communications

▲**WOODALL**—Formerly served by Eagle Media. No longer in operation

WOODS COUNTY (EASTERN PORTION)—See ALVA, OK (Suddenlink Communications)

▲**WOODWARD**—Suddenlink Communications

▲**WRIGHT CITY**—Allegiance Communications

▲**WYANDOTTE**—Allegiance Communications

WYNNEWOOD—See PAULS VALLEY, OK (Suddenlink Communications)

▲ **WYNONA**—Community Cablevision Co.

▲ **YALE**—Community Cablevision Co.

YUKON—See OKLAHOMA CITY, OK (Cox Communications)

OREGON

ADAIR VILLAGE—See CORVALLIS, OR (Comcast Cable)

ADAMS—See WESTON, OR (Rapid Cable)

ALBANY—See CORVALLIS, OR (Comcast Cable)

ALOHA—See BEAVERTON, OR (Comcast Cable)

ALVADORE—See EUGENE, OR (Comcast Cable)

AMITY—See SALEM, OR (Comcast Cable)

APPLEGATE—See MEDFORD, OR (Charter Communications)

ARCH CAPE—See ASTORIA, OR (Charter Communications)

▲ **ARLINGTON**—Arlington TV Cooperative Inc.

▲ **ASHLAND**—Ashland TV. This cable system has converted to IPTV. See Ashland, OR [OR5023]

ASHLAND—See MEDFORD, OR (Charter Communications)

▲ **ASHLAND**—Formerly served by Ashland TV [OR0174]. This cable system has converted to IPTV

▲ **ASTORIA**—Charter Communications

ATHENA—See WESTON, OR (Rapid Cable)

AUMSVILLE—See STAYTON, OR (Wave Broadband)

AURORA—See WOODBURN, OR (Wave Broadband)

BAKER CITY—See LA GRANDE, OR (Charter Communications)

BAKER COUNTY (NORTHERN PORTION)—See LA GRANDE, OR (Charter Communications)

BANDON—See COOS BAY, OR (Charter Communications)

BANKS—See BEAVERTON, OR (Comcast Cable)

BARLOW—See WOODBURN, OR (Wave Broadband)

BAY CITY—See LINCOLN CITY, OR (Charter Communications)

BEAVER—See LINCOLN CITY, OR (Charter Communications)

▲ **BEAVERCREEK**—Beaver Creek Telephone Co.

▲ **BEAVERTON**—Comcast Cable

▲ **BEND**—Formerly served by WANTV. No longer in operation

▲ **BEND**—Bend Broadband

BENTON COUNTY—See CORVALLIS, OR (Comcast Cable)

BINGEN—See THE DALLES, WA (Charter Communications)

BLACK BUTTE RANCH—See BEND, OR (Bend Broadband)

▲ **BLY**—Formerly served by Bly Cable Co. No longer in operation

▲ **BOARDMAN**—Rapid Cable

▲ **BONANZA**—Formerly served by Almega Cable. No longer in operation

▲ **BORING**—Formerly served by Community Cable Inc. No longer in operation

BRIGHTWOOD—See THE DALLES, OR (Charter Communications)

▲ **BROOKINGS**—Charter Communications

▲ **BROOKS**—Formerly served by Country Cablevision Ltd. No longer in operation

▲ **BROWNSVILLE**—Rapid Cable

▲ **BURNS**—Charter Communications

▲ **BUTTE FALLS**—Almega Cable

▲ **CANBY**—Wave Broadband. Now served by WOODBURN, OR [OR0023]

CANBY—See WOODBURN, OR (Wave Broadband)

CANNON BEACH—See ASTORIA, OR (Charter Communications)

CANYON CITY—See MOUNT VERNON, OR (Blue Mountain TV Cable Co.)

CANYONVILLE—See ROSEBURG, OR (Charter Communications)

CAPE MEARES—See LINCOLN CITY, OR (Charter Communications)

CARLTON—See SALEM, OR (Comcast Cable)

▲ **CASCADE LOCKS**—City of Cascade Locks Cable TV

CATHLAMET—See ASTORIA, WA (Charter Communications)

▲ **CAVE JUNCTION**—Formerly served by Almega Cable. No longer in operation

CENTRAL POINT—See MEDFORD, OR (Charter Communications)

▲ **CHILOQUIN**—Almega Cable

CLACKAMAS COUNTY (PORTIONS)—See BEAVERCREEK, OR (Beaver Creek Telephone Co.)

CLACKAMAS COUNTY (PORTIONS)—See SANDY, OR (Wave Broadband)

CLACKAMAS COUNTY (PORTIONS)—See WOODBURN, OR (Wave Broadband)

CLACKAMAS COUNTY—See PORTLAND, OR (Comcast Cable)

CLACKAMAS COUNTY—See ESTACADA, OR (Reliance Connects)

CLACKAMAS—See WOODBURN, OR (Wave Broadband)

CLATSKANIE—See ASTORIA, OR (Charter Communications)

CLATSOP COUNTY—See ASTORIA, OR (Charter Communications)

CLOVERDALE—See LINCOLN CITY, OR (Charter Communications)

COBURG—See COTTAGE GROVE, OR (Charter Communications)

▲ **COLTON**—ColtonTel

COLTON—See ESTACADA, OR (Reliance Connects)

COLUMBIA CITY—See BEAVERTON, OR (Comcast Cable)

COLUMBIA COUNTY (NORTHERN PORTION)—See ASTORIA, OR (Charter Communications)

COLUMBIA COUNTY (PORTIONS)—See BEAVERTON, OR (Comcast Cable)

▲ **CONDON**—J & N Cable

▲ **COOS BAY**—Charter Communications

COOS COUNTY (NORTHERN PORTION)—See COOS BAY, OR (Charter Communications)

COQUILLE—See COOS BAY, OR (Charter Communications)

CORBETT—See PORTLAND, OR (Comcast Cable)

CORBETT—See ESTACADA, OR (Reliance Connects)

CORNELIUS—See BEAVERTON, OR (Comcast Cable)

▲ **CORVALLIS**—Comcast Cable

▲ **COTTAGE GROVE**—Charter Communications

▲ **COVE**—Formerly served by Almega Cable. No longer in operation

CRESCENT—See GILCHRIST, OR (Country Cablevision Ltd.)

CRESWELL—See COTTAGE GROVE, OR (Charter Communications)

CULVER—See MADRAS, OR (Crestview Cable TV)

CURRY COUNTY (PORTIONS)—See BROOKINGS, OR (Charter Communications)

▲ **DALLAS**—Charter Communications

DALLESPORT—See THE DALLES, WA (Charter Communications)

DAYTON—See SALEM, OR (Comcast Cable)

▲ **DAYVILLE**—Blue Mountain TV Cable Co.

▲ **DEPOE BAY**—Broadstripe

DEXTER—See COTTAGE GROVE, OR (Charter Communications)

DILLARD—See ROSEBURG, OR (Charter Communications)

DONALD—See WOODBURN, OR (Wave Broadband)

DOUGLAS COUNTY (NORTHERN PORTION)—See COTTAGE GROVE, OR (Charter Communications)

DOUGLAS COUNTY (PORTIONS)—See ROSEBURG, OR (Charter Communications)

DRAIN—See COTTAGE GROVE, OR (Charter Communications)

▲ **DUFUR**—Northstate Cablevision

DUNDEE—See SALEM, OR (Comcast Cable)

DUNES CITY—See FLORENCE, OR (Charter Communications)

DUNTHORPE—See PORTLAND, OR (Comcast Cable)

DURHAM—See BEAVERTON, OR (Comcast Cable)

EAGLE CREEK—See PORTLAND, OR (Comcast Cable)

EAGLE CREEK—See ESTACADA, OR (Reliance Connects)

EAGLE POINT—See MEDFORD, OR (Charter Communications)

ECHO—See PENDLETON, OR (Charter Communications)

▲ **ELGIN**—Elgin TV Assn. Inc.

ELMIRA—See COTTAGE GROVE, OR (Charter Communications)

▲ **ENTERPRISE**—Almega Cable

▲ **ESTACADA**—Reliance Connects

▲ **EUGENE**—Comcast Cable

FAIRVIEW—See PORTLAND, OR (Comcast Cable)

FALLS CITY—See DALLAS, OR (Charter Communications)

▲ **FLORENCE**—Charter Communications

FOREST GROVE—See BEAVERTON, OR (Comcast Cable)

▲ **FOSSIL**—Fossil Community TV Inc.

GARDINER—See COOS BAY, OR (Charter Communications)

GARIBALDI—See LINCOLN CITY, OR (Charter Communications)

GASTON—See BEAVERTON, OR (Comcast Cable)

GATES—See STAYTON, OR (Wave Broadband)

GEARHART—See ASTORIA, OR (Charter Communications)

GERVAIS—See WOODBURN, OR (Wave Broadband)

▲ **GILCHRIST**—Country Cablevision Ltd.

GLADSTONE—See PORTLAND, OR (Comcast Cable)

▲ **GLENDALE**—Almega Cable

GLENEDEN BEACH—See DEPOE BAY, OR (Broadstripe)

GLENWOOD—See EUGENE, OR (Comcast Cable)

▲**GLIDE**—Glide Cablevision

▲**GOLD BEACH**—Charter Communications

GOLD HILL—See MEDFORD, OR (Charter Communications)

▲**GOVERNMENT CAMP**—CharlieVision

GRAND RONDE—See SHERIDAN, OR (Wave Broadband)

▲**GRANTS PASS**—Charter Communications

▲**GREEN ACRES**—Greenacres TV Cable

GRESHAM—See PORTLAND, OR (Comcast Cable)

▲**HAINES**—Formerly served by Almega Cable. No longer in operation

▲**HALFWAY**—Formerly served by Charter Communications. No longer in operation

▲**HALSEY**—Roome Telecommunications Inc.

HAMMOND—See ASTORIA, OR (Charter Communications)

HAPPY VALLEY—See PORTLAND, OR (Comcast Cable)

HARNEY COUNTY (PORTIONS)—See BURNS, OR (Charter Communications)

HARRISBURG—See EUGENE, OR (Comcast Cable)

HEBO—See LINCOLN CITY, OR (Charter Communications)

▲**HELIX**—Helix Communications

▲**HEPPNER**—Heppner TV Inc.

HERMISTON—See PENDLETON, OR (Charter Communications)

HILLSBORO—See BEAVERTON, OR (Comcast Cable)

HINES—See BURNS, OR (Charter Communications)

HOOD RIVER COUNTY—See THE DALLES, OR (Charter Communications)

HOOD RIVER—See THE DALLES, OR (Charter Communications)

HUBBARD—See WOODBURN, OR (Wave Broadband)

▲**IDANHA**—Formerly served by Wave Broadband. No longer in operation

IDLEYLD PARK—See GLIDE, OR (Glide Cablevision)

ILWACO—See ASTORIA, WA (Charter Communications)

▲**IMBLER**—Formerly served by Almega Cable. No longer in operation

INDEPENDENCE—See DALLAS, OR (Charter Communications)

▲**IONE**—Ione TV Co-op. Now served by HEPPNER, OR [OR0077]

IONE—See HEPPNER, OR (Heppner TV Inc.)

IRRIGON—See UMATILLA, OR (Rapid Cable)

ISLAND CITY—See LA GRANDE, OR (Charter Communications)

JACKSON COUNTY—See MEDFORD, OR (Charter Communications)

JACKSONVILLE—See MEDFORD, OR (Charter Communications)

JASPER—See COTTAGE GROVE, OR (Charter Communications)

JEFFERSON—See DALLAS, OR (Charter Communications)

JOHN DAY—See MOUNT VERNON, OR (Blue Mountain TV Cable Co.)

JOHNSON CITY—See PORTLAND, OR (Comcast Cable)

JOSEPH—See ENTERPRISE, OR (Almega Cable)

JOSEPHINE COUNTY—See GRANTS PASS, OR (Charter Communications)

JUNCTION CITY—See EUGENE, OR (Comcast Cable)

KEIZER—See SALEM, OR (Comcast Cable)

KENO—See KLAMATH FALLS, OR (Charter Communications)

KERNVILLE—See DEPOE BAY, OR (Broadstripe)

KING CITY—See BEAVERTON, OR (Comcast Cable)

KLAMATH COUNTY (UNINCORPORATED AREAS)—See KLAMATH FALLS, OR (Charter Communications)

▲**KLAMATH FALLS**—Charter Communications

KLICKITAT COUNTY (PORTIONS)—See THE DALLES, WA (Charter Communications)

KLICKITAT—See THE DALLES, WA (Charter Communications)

▲**KNAPPA**—Rapid Cable

▲**LA GRANDE**—Charter Communications

▲**LA PINE**—Crestview Cable TV

▲**LACOMBE**—Wave Broadband

LAFAYETTE—See SALEM, OR (Comcast Cable)

LAKE COUNTY (PORTIONS)—See LAKEVIEW, OR (Charter Communications)

LAKE OSWEGO—See BEAVERTON, OR (Comcast Cable)

LAKESIDE—See COOS BAY, OR (Charter Communications)

▲**LAKEVIEW**—Charter Communications

LANE COUNTY (PORTIONS)—See COTTAGE GROVE, OR (Charter Communications)

LANE COUNTY (PORTIONS)—See FLORENCE, OR (Charter Communications)

LANE COUNTY—See EUGENE, OR (Comcast Cable)

LEABURG—See COTTAGE GROVE, OR (Charter Communications)

▲**LEBANON**—Comcast Cable. Now served by CORVALLIS, OR [OR0008]

LEBANON—See CORVALLIS, OR (Comcast Cable)

LEBANON—See LACOMBE, OR (Wave Broadband)

LEXINGTON—See HEPPNER, OR (Heppner TV Inc.)

LINCOLN BEACH—See DEPOE BAY, OR (Broadstripe)

▲**LINCOLN CITY**—Charter Communications

LINCOLN COUNTY (PORTIONS)—See WALDPORT, OR (Alsea River Cable Co.)

LINCOLN COUNTY (PORTIONS)—See DEPOE BAY, OR (Broadstripe)

LINCOLN COUNTY (PORTIONS)—See LINCOLN CITY, OR (Charter Communications)

LINN COUNTY (WESTERN PORTION)—See CORVALLIS, OR (Comcast Cable)

LINNTON—See PORTLAND, OR (Comcast Cable)

LONG BEACH—See ASTORIA, WA (Charter Communications)

LOSTINE—See ENTERPRISE, OR (Almega Cable)

LOWELL—See COTTAGE GROVE, OR (Charter Communications)

LYONS—See STAYTON, OR (Wave Broadband)

▲**MACLEAY**—Country Cablevision Ltd.

▲**MADRAS**—Crestview Cable TV

▲**MALIN**—Almega Cable

MANZANITA—See LINCOLN CITY, OR (Charter Communications)

▲**MAPLETON**—Rapid Cable

MARCOLA—See COTTAGE GROVE, OR (Charter Communications)

MARION COUNTY (PORTIONS)—See SALEM, OR (Comcast Cable)

MARION COUNTY (PORTIONS)—See MACLEAY, OR (Country Cablevision Ltd.)

MARION COUNTY (PORTIONS)—See SILVERTON, OR (Wave Broadband)

MARION COUNTY (PORTIONS)—See WOODBURN, OR (Wave Broadband)

MARION COUNTY (SOUTHWESTERN PORTION)—See DALLAS, OR (Charter Communications)

MARION—See MACLEAY, OR (Country Cablevision Ltd.)

MAYWOOD PARK—See PORTLAND, OR (Comcast Cable)

MCKENZIE—See COTTAGE GROVE, OR (Charter Communications)

MCMINNVILLE—See SALEM, OR (Comcast Cable)

▲**MEDFORD**—Charter Communications

MEHAMA—See STAYTON, OR (Wave Broadband)

MERLIN—See GRANTS PASS, OR (Charter Communications)

▲**MERRILL**—Almega Cable

METOLIUS—See MADRAS, OR (Crestview Cable TV)

MIDLAND—See KLAMATH FALLS, OR (Charter Communications)

MILL CITY—See STAYTON, OR (Wave Broadband)

MILLERSBURG—See CORVALLIS, OR (Comcast Cable)

▲**MILTON-FREEWATER**—Charter Communications. Now served by WALLA WALLA, WA [WA0016]

▲**MILWAUKIE**—Comcast Cable. Now served by PORTLAND, OR [OR0001]

MILWAUKIE—See PORTLAND, OR (Comcast Cable)

MOLALLA—See WOODBURN, OR (Wave Broadband)

MONMOUTH—See DALLAS, OR (Charter Communications)

▲**MONROE**—Monroe Telephone Co. This cable system has converted to IPTV. See Monroe, OR [OR5001]

▲**MONROE**—Monroe Telephone. Formerly [OR0105]. This cable system has converted to IPTV

▲**MORO**—J & N Cable

MOUNT ANGEL—See SILVERTON, OR (Wave Broadband)

MOUNT HOOD—See PARKDALE, OR (Valley TV Co-op Inc.)

▲**MOUNT VERNON**—Blue Mountain TV Cable Co.

MULINO—See BEAVERCREEK, OR (Beaver Creek Telephone Co.)

MULINO—See WOODBURN, OR (Wave Broadband)

MULTNOMAH COUNTY (UNINCORPORATED AREAS)—See PORTLAND, OR (Comcast Cable)

▲**MYRTLE CREEK**—Charter Communications. Now served by ROSEBURG, OR [OR0016]

MYRTLE CREEK—See ROSEBURG, OR (Charter Communications)

MYRTLE POINT—See COOS BAY, OR (Charter Communications)

NAHCOTTA—See ASTORIA, WA (Charter Communications)

NASELLE—See ASTORIA, WA (Charter Communications)

NEEDY—See WOODBURN, OR (Wave Broadband)

NEHALEM—See LINCOLN CITY, OR (Charter Communications)

NEOTSU—See LINCOLN CITY, OR (Charter Communications)

NESKOWIN—See LINCOLN CITY, OR (Charter Communications)

NETARTS—See LINCOLN CITY, OR (Charter Communications)

NEW BRIDGE—See RICHLAND, OR (Eagle Valley Communications)

▲ **NEWBERG**—Comcast Cable. Now served by SALEM, OR [OR0005]

NEWBERG—See SALEM, OR (Comcast Cable)

NEWPORT—See LINCOLN CITY, OR (Charter Communications)

NORTH ALBANY—See CORVALLIS, OR (Comcast Cable)

NORTH BEND—See COOS BAY, OR (Charter Communications)

NORTH PLAINS—See BEAVERTON, OR (Comcast Cable)

▲ **NORTH POWDER**—Formerly served by Almega Cable. No longer in operation

NOTI—See COTTAGE GROVE, OR (Charter Communications)

OAKLAND—See ROSEBURG, OR (Charter Communications)

OAKRIDGE—See COTTAGE GROVE, OR (Charter Communications)

OAKVILLE—See CORVALLIS, OR (Comcast Cable)

OCEAN PARK—See ASTORIA, WA (Charter Communications)

OCEANSIDE—See LINCOLN CITY, OR (Charter Communications)

▲ **ODELL**—Valley TV Co-op Inc.

OREGON CITY (PORTIONS)—See WOODBURN, OR (Wave Broadband)

▲ **OREGON CITY (UNINCORPORATED AREAS)**—Clear Creek Telephone & TeleVision

OREGON CITY—See BEAVERCREEK, OR (Beaver Creek Telephone Co.)

OREGON CITY—See PORTLAND, OR (Comcast Cable)

ORIENT—See PORTLAND, OR (Comcast Cable)

▲ **OTIS**—Broadstripe

OTTER ROCK—See LINCOLN CITY, OR (Charter Communications)

OYSTERVILLE—See ASTORIA, WA (Charter Communications)

PACIFIC CITY—See LINCOLN CITY, OR (Charter Communications)

PACIFIC COUNTY—See ASTORIA, WA (Charter Communications)

▲ **PARKDALE**—Valley TV Co-op Inc.

▲ **PENDLETON**—Charter Communications

PHILOMATH—See CORVALLIS, OR (Comcast Cable)

PHOENIX—See MEDFORD, OR (Charter Communications)

PILOT ROCK—See PENDLETON, OR (Charter Communications)

PLEASANT HILL—See COTTAGE GROVE, OR (Charter Communications)

POLK COUNTY (PORTIONS)—See DALLAS, OR (Charter Communications)

POLK COUNTY (PORTIONS)—See SALEM, OR (Comcast Cable)

PORT ORFORD—See COOS BAY, OR (Charter Communications)

▲ **PORTLAND (western portion)**—Comcast Cable. Now served by PORTLAND, OR [OR0001]

▲ **PORTLAND**—Comcast Cable

▲ **POWERS**—Formerly served by Charter Communications. No longer in operation

▲ **PRAIRIE CITY**—Blue Mountain TV Cable Co.

▲ **PRINEVILLE**—Formerly served by Central Vision. No longer in operation

PRINEVILLE—See BEND, OR (Bend Broadband)

▲ **PRINEVILLE**—Crestview Cable TV

▲ **PROSPECT**—Almega Cable

▲ **RAINIER**—J & N Cable

REDLAND—See OREGON CITY (unincorporated areas), OR (Clear Creek Telephone & TeleVision)

▲ **REDMOND**—Formerly served by Central Vision. No longer in operation

REDMOND—See BEND, OR (Bend Broadband)

REEDSPORT—See COOS BAY, OR (Charter Communications)

RHODODENDRON—See THE DALLES, OR (Charter Communications)

▲ **RICHLAND**—Eagle Valley Communications

RICKREALL—See DALLAS, OR (Charter Communications)

RIDDLE—See ROSEBURG, OR (Charter Communications)

RIETH—See PENDLETON, OR (Charter Communications)

RIVERDALE—See PORTLAND, OR (Comcast Cable)

RIVERGROVE—See BEAVERTON, OR (Comcast Cable)

ROCKAWAY BEACH—See LINCOLN CITY, OR (Charter Communications)

ROGUE RIVER—See GRANTS PASS, OR (Charter Communications)

▲ **ROSE LODGE**—Millennium Digital Media. Now served by DEPOE BAY, OR [OR0134]

ROSE LODGE—See DEPOE BAY, OR (Broadstripe)

▲ **ROSEBURG**—Charter Communications

▲ **SALEM (southeastern portion)**—Formerly served by Mill Creek Cable TV Inc. No longer in operation

▲ **SALEM**—Comcast Cable

SALMON RIVER—See DEPOE BAY, OR (Broadstripe)

▲ **SANDY**—Wave Broadband

SANTA CLARA—See EUGENE, OR (Comcast Cable)

SCAPPOOSE—See BEAVERTON, OR (Comcast Cable)

▲ **SCIO**—Scio Cablevision Inc.

SEAL ROCK—See DEPOE BAY, OR (Broadstripe)

SEASIDE—See ASTORIA, OR (Charter Communications)

SEAVIEW—See ASTORIA, WA (Charter Communications)

▲ **SENECA**—Blue Mountain TV Cable Co.

▲ **SHADY COVE**—Almega Cable

SHAW—See MACLEAY, OR (Country Cablevision Ltd.)

▲ **SHERIDAN**—Wave Broadband

SHERWOOD—See BEAVERTON, OR (Comcast Cable)

SILETZ RIVER—See DEPOE BAY, OR (Broadstripe)

▲ **SILETZ**—Millennium Digital Media. Now served by DEPOE BAY, OR [OR0134]

SILETZ—See DEPOE BAY, OR (Broadstripe)

▲ **SILVERTON**—Wave Broadband

SISTERS—See BEND, OR (Bend Broadband)

SODAVILLE—See CORVALLIS, OR (Comcast Cable)

SOUTH BEACH—See DEPOE BAY, OR (Broadstripe)

▲ **SOUTH SALEM**—Formerly served by Country Cablevision Ltd. No longer in operation

▲ **SOUTHBEACH**—Millennium Digital Media. Now served by DEPOE BAY, OR [OR0134]

SPRING RIVER—See SUNRIVER, OR (Chambers Cable of Sunriver Inc.)

SPRINGDALE—See PORTLAND, OR (Comcast Cable)

SPRINGFIELD—See EUGENE, OR (Comcast Cable)

▲ **ST. HELENS**—Comcast Cable. Now served by BEAVERTON, OR [OR0002]

ST. HELENS—See BEAVERTON, OR (Comcast Cable)

▲ **ST. PAUL (town)**—Formerly served by St. Paul Cooperative Telephone Assoc. No longer in operation

STANFIELD—See PENDLETON, OR (Charter Communications)

▲ **STAYTON**—Wave Broadband

SUBLIMITY—See STAYTON, OR (Wave Broadband)

▲ **SUMPTER**—Formerly served by Almega Cable. No longer in operation

▲ **SUNRIVER**—Chambers Cable of Sunriver Inc.

SUTHERLIN—See ROSEBURG, OR (Charter Communications)

SVENSEN—See KNAPPA, OR (Rapid Cable)

SWEET HOME—See CORVALLIS, OR (Comcast Cable)

SYLVAN—See PORTLAND, OR (Comcast Cable)

TALENT—See MEDFORD, OR (Charter Communications)

TANGENT—See CORVALLIS, OR (Comcast Cable)

TERREBONNE—See BEND, OR (Bend Broadband)

▲ **THE DALLES**—Charter Communications

TIGARD—See BEAVERTON, OR (Comcast Cable)

TILLAMOOK COUNTY (PORTIONS)—See LINCOLN CITY, OR (Charter Communications)

TILLAMOOK—See LINCOLN CITY, OR (Charter Communications)

TOLEDO—See LINCOLN CITY, OR (Charter Communications)

TRAIL—See SHADY COVE, OR (Almega Cable)

TRI-CITY—See ROSEBURG, OR (Charter Communications)

TROUTDALE—See PORTLAND, OR (Comcast Cable)

TUALATIN—See BEAVERTON, OR (Comcast Cable)

TUMALO—See BEND, OR (Bend Broadband)

TURNER—See STAYTON, OR (Wave Broadband)

▲ **TYGH VALLEY**—Formerly served by J & N Cable. No longer in operation

UMATILLA COUNTY (PORTIONS)—See PENDLETON, OR (Charter Communications)

UMATILLA COUNTY (UNINCORPORATED AREAS)—See UMATILLA, OR (Rapid Cable)

▲ **UMATILLA**—Rapid Cable

UNION COUNTY—See LA GRANDE, OR (Charter Communications)

UNION—See LA GRANDE, OR (Charter Communications)

VENETA—See COTTAGE GROVE, OR (Charter Communications)

▲ **VERNONIA**—Vernonia CATV Inc.

▲ **WALDPORT**—Alsea River Cable Co.

WALLOWA LAKE—See ENTERPRISE, OR (Almega Cable)

WALLOWA—See ENTERPRISE, OR (Almega Cable)

WALTERVILLE—See COTTAGE GROVE, OR (Charter Communications)

▲ **WARM SPRINGS**—Formerly served by American Telecasting. No longer in operation

WARREN—See BEAVERTON, OR (Comcast Cable)

WARRENTON—See ASTORIA, OR (Charter Communications)

WASCO COUNTY—See THE DALLES, OR (Charter Communications)

▲ **WASCO**—J & N Cable

WASHINGTON COUNTY—See BEAVERTON, OR (Comcast Cable)

WASHINGTON COUNTY—See PORTLAND, OR (Comcast Cable)

WATERLOO—See CORVALLIS, OR (Comcast Cable)

WELCHES—See THE DALLES, OR (Charter Communications)

WEMME—See SANDY, OR (Wave Broadband)

WEST LINN—See PORTLAND, OR (Comcast Cable)

WEST STAYTON—See MACLEAY, OR (Country Cablevision Ltd.)

WESTFIR—See COTTAGE GROVE, OR (Charter Communications)

▲ **WESTON**—Rapid Cable

▲ **WESTPORT**—Formerly served by Almega Cable. No longer in operation

WHEELER—See LINCOLN CITY, OR (Charter Communications)

WHITE CITY—See MEDFORD, OR (Charter Communications)

WHITE SALMON—See THE DALLES, WA (Charter Communications)

WILLAMINA—See SHERIDAN, OR (Wave Broadband)

WILSONVILLE—See BEAVERTON, OR (Comcast Cable)

WINCHESTER BAY—See COOS BAY, OR (Charter Communications)

WINSTON—See ROSEBURG, OR (Charter Communications)

WOOD VILLAGE—See PORTLAND, OR (Comcast Cable)

▲ **WOODBURN**—Wave Broadband

YACHATS—See LINCOLN CITY, OR (Charter Communications)

YAMHILL—See SALEM, OR (Comcast Cable)

YONCALLA—See COTTAGE GROVE, OR (Charter Communications)

PENNSYLVANIA

AARONSBURG—See MILLHEIM, PA (Millheim TV Transmission Co.)

ABBOTTSTOWN—See YORK, PA (Comcast Cable)

ABINGTON TWP. (MONTGOMERY COUNTY)—See WILLOW GROVE, PA (Comcast Cable)

ACCIDENT (UNINCORPORATED AREAS)—See ADDISON TWP. (southern portion), MD (Somerfield Cable TV Co.)

ACME—See CONNELLSVILLE, PA (Armstrong Cable Services)

ACOSTA—See CONNELLSVILLE, PA (Armstrong Cable Services)

ACRE LAKE—See LOOMIS LAKE, PA (Adams Digital Cable)

ADAMS TWP. (BUTLER COUNTY)—See ZELIENOPLE, PA (Armstrong Cable Services)

▲ **ADAMS TWP. (CAMBRIA COUNTY)**—Comcast Cable

ADAMSBURG—See GREENSBURG, PA (Comcast Cable)

ADAMSTOWN—See EPHRATA, PA (Blue Ridge Communications)

▲ **ADDISON TWP. (SOUTHERN PORTION)**—Somerfield Cable TV Co.

ADDISON—See ADDISON TWP. (southern portion), PA (Somerfield Cable TV Co.)

ADRIAN—See KISKIMINETAS TWP., PA (Comcast Cable)

AFTON (SOUTHWESTERN PORTION)—See CARBONDALE, NY (Adams Digital Cable)

AKRON—See EPHRATA, PA (Blue Ridge Communications)

ALBA—See CANTON, PA (Zito Media)

ALBANY TWP.—See MESHOPPEN, PA (Blue Ridge Communications)

ALBION—See HARBORCREEK TWP., PA (Time Warner Cable)

ALBRIGHTSVILLE—See PALMERTON, PA (Blue Ridge Communications)

ALBRIGHTSVILLE—See POCONO, PA (MetroCast Communications)

ALBURTIS—See LEHIGH VALLEY, PA (Service Electric Cable TV & Communications)

ALDAN—See WALLINGFORD, PA (Comcast Cable)

ALDENVILLE—See CARBONDALE, PA (Adams Digital Cable)

ALEXANDRIA—See HUNTINGDON, PA (Comcast Cable)

ALIQUIPPA—See PITTSBURGH, PA (Comcast Cable)

ALLEGHENY COUNTY—See PITTSBURGH, PA (Comcast Cable)

ALLEGHENY TWP. (BLAIR COUNTY)—See ALTOONA, PA (Atlantic Broadband)

ALLEGHENY TWP. (SOMERSET COUNTY)—See NEW BALTIMORE, PA (Laurel Cable LP)

▲ **ALLEN TWP.**—RCN Corp. Formerly served by NORTHAMPTON BOROUGH, PA [PA0008]. This cable system has converted to IPTV

ALLEN TWP.—See LEHIGH VALLEY, PA (Service Electric Cable TV & Communications)

ALLENPORT—See CONNELLSVILLE, PA (Armstrong Cable Services)

▲ **ALLENSVILLE**—Formerly served by Valley Cable Systems. No longer in operation

▲ **ALLENTOWN**—RCN Corp. Formerly served by NORTHAMPTON BOROUGH, PA [PA0008]. This cable system has converted to IPTV

ALLENTOWN—See LEHIGH VALLEY, PA (Service Electric Cable TV & Communications)

ALLENWOOD—See WILLIAMSPORT, PA (Comcast Cable)

ALSACE TWP.—See READING, PA (Comcast Cable)

▲ **ALTOONA**—Atlantic Broadband

ALUM BANK—See BEDFORD, PA (Comcast Cable)

AMBLER—See LANSDALE, PA (Comcast Cable)

AMBRIDGE—See PITTSBURGH, PA (Comcast Cable)

AMITY TWP. (BERKS COUNTY)—See BIRDSBORO, PA (Service Electric Cablevision)

AMITY—See PITTSBURGH, PA (Comcast Cable)

AMWELL TWP.—See PITTSBURGH, PA (Comcast Cable)

AMWELL TWP.—See BENTLEYVILLE, PA (FairPoint Communications)

ANDOVER BORO—See MEADVILLE, OH (Armstrong Cable Services)

ANDOVER TWP. (ASHTABULA COUNTY)—See MEADVILLE, OH (Armstrong Cable Services)

ANDOVER VILLAGE—See MEADVILLE, OH (Armstrong Cable Services)

ANDOVER—See MEADVILLE, OH (Armstrong Cable Services)

ANNIN TWP.—See COUDERSPORT, PA (Zito Media)

ANNVILLE TWP.—See LEBANON, PA (Comcast Cable)

ANTHONY TWP.—See LEWIS TWP., PA (Eagles Mere & La Porte Cablevision Inc.)

ANTIS TWP.—See ALTOONA, PA (Atlantic Broadband)

ANTRIM TWP.—See SHIPPENSBURG, PA (Comcast Cable)

APOLLO—See KISKIMINETAS TWP., PA (Comcast Cable)

APPLEWOLD—See KISKIMINETAS TWP., PA (Comcast Cable)

ARARAT TWP.—See CARBONDALE, PA (Adams Digital Cable)

ARCHBALD—See DUNMORE, PA (Comcast Cable)

ARENDTSVILLE—See GETTYSBURG, PA (Comcast Cable)

ARISTES—See SUNBURY, PA (Service Electric Cablevision)

▲ **ARMAGH**—Comcast Cable

ARMSTRONG TWP. (LYCOMING COUNTY)—See WILLIAMSPORT, PA (Comcast Cable)

ARNOLD—See TARENTUM BOROUGH, PA (Comcast Cable)

▲ **ARNOT**—Blue Ridge Communications

ARONA—See GREENSBURG, PA (Comcast Cable)

ASHLAND—See MAHANOY CITY, PA (Service Electric Cable Company)

ASHLEY—See WILKES-BARRE, PA (Service Electric Cable Company)

ASHVILLE—See CRESSON, PA (Comcast Cable)

ASPINWALL—See PITTSBURGH, PA (Comcast Cable)

ASTON TWP.—See WALLINGFORD, PA (Comcast Cable)

ASYLUM TWP.—See TOWANDA, PA (Comcast Cable)

ATGLEN (CHESTER COUNTY)—See COATESVILLE, PA (Comcast Cable)

ATLASBURG—See BURGETTSTOWN, PA (Blue Devil Cable TV Inc.)

▲ **AUBURN**—Comcast Cable

▲ **AULTMAN**—Formerly served by Adelphia Communications. Now served by BLAIRSVILLE, PA [PA0320]

AULTMAN—See BLAIRSVILLE, PA (Comcast Cable)

AUSTIN BOROUGH—See COUDERSPORT, PA (Zito Media)

AUSTINVILLE TWP.—See TROY, PA (Blue Ridge Communications)

AVALON—See PITTSBURGH, PA (Comcast Cable)

▲ **AVELLA**—Blue Devil Cable TV Inc.

AVIS—See WILLIAMSPORT, PA (Comcast Cable)

AVOCA—See SCRANTON, PA (Comcast Cable)

AVONDALE—See KENNETT SQUARE, PA (Comcast Cable)

AVONMORE—See KISKIMINETAS TWP., PA (Comcast Cable)

AYR TWP.—See SHIPPENSBURG, PA (Comcast Cable)

BADEN—See PITTSBURGH, PA (Comcast Cable)

BAIRDFORD—See TARENTUM BOROUGH, PA (Comcast Cable)

BALA CYNWYD—See LOWER MERION TWP., PA (Comcast Cable)

BALD EAGLE TWP. (CLINTON COUNTY)—See LOCK HAVEN, PA (Comcast Cable)

BALD EAGLE TWP. (CLINTON COUNTY)—See WILLIAMSPORT, PA (Comcast Cable)

BALDWIN—See PITTSBURGH, PA (Comcast Cable)

BALLY—See POTTSTOWN, PA (Comcast Cable)

BANGOR BORO—See LEHIGH VALLEY, PA (Service Electric Cable TV & Communications)

▲**BANGOR BOROUGH**—RCN Corp. Formerly served by NORTHAMPTON BOROUGH, PA [PA0008]. This cable system has converted to IPTV

BANKS TWP. (CARBON COUNTY)—See HAZLETON, PA (Service Electric Cablevision)

BANKS TWP.—See BLAIRSVILLE, PA (Comcast Cable)

BARBOURS—See ELDRED TWP., PA (Herr Cable Co.)

BAREVILLE—See LANCASTER, PA (Comcast Cable)

BARKEYVILLE—See GROVE CITY, PA (Armstrong Cable Services)

BARNES—See SHEFFIELD, PA (WestPA.net Inc.)

BARR TWP.—See BLAIRSVILLE, PA (Comcast Cable)

BARRETT TWP.—See STROUDSBURG, PA (Blue Ridge Communications)

BARRY TWP.—See MAHANOY CITY, PA (Service Electric Cable Company)

BART TWP.—See LANCASTER, PA (Comcast Cable)

▲**BASTRESS TWP.**—Formerly served by Bastress TV Cable Association. No longer in operation

BATH BORO—See LEHIGH VALLEY, PA (Service Electric Cable TV & Communications)

▲**BATH BOROUGH**—Formerly served by NORTHAMPTON BOROUGH, PA [PA0008]. RCN Corp. This cable system has converted to IPTV

BEACH HAVEN—See BERWICK, PA (MetroCast Communications)

▲**BEACH LAKE**—Blue Ridge Communications

BEALLSVILLE—See UNIONTOWN, PA (Atlantic Broadband)

BEAR CREEK TWP.—See WILKES-BARRE, PA (Service Electric Cable Company)

▲**BEAVER FALLS**—Comcast Cable

BEAVER MEADOWS—See HAZLETON, PA (Service Electric Cablevision)

▲**BEAVER SPRINGS**—Service Electric Cable TV & Communications. Now served by SUNBURY, PA [PA0029]

BEAVER TWP. (SNYDER COUNTY)—See SUNBURY, PA (Service Electric Cablevision)

▲**BEAVER VALLEY**—Comcast Cable

BEAVER—See ROCHESTER, PA (Comcast Cable)

BEAVERDALE—See ADAMS TWP. (Cambria County), PA (Comcast Cable)

BEAVERTOWN BOROUGH—See SUNBURY, PA (Service Electric Cablevision)

▲**BEAVERTOWN**—Formerly served by Nittany Media Inc. No longer in operation

BECCARIA TWP.—See COALPORT, PA (Comcast Cable)

BECHTELSVILLE—See POTTSTOWN, PA (Comcast Cable)

▲**BEDFORD**—Comcast Cable

BEDMINSTER TWP.—See SELLERSVILLE, PA (Comcast Cable)

BEECH CREEK—See WILLIAMSPORT, PA (Comcast Cable)

BELL ACRES—See PITTSBURGH, PA (Comcast Cable)

BELL TWP. (CLEARFIELD COUNTY)—See PUNXSUTAWNEY, PA (Comcast Cable)

BELL TWP. (JEFFERSON COUNTY)—See PUNXSUTAWNEY, PA (Comcast Cable)

BELLE VERNON—See PITTSBURGH, PA (Comcast Cable)

BELLEFONTE—See STATE COLLEGE, PA (Comcast Cable)

▲**BELLEVILLE**—Zampelli Electronics

BELLEVUE—See PITTSBURGH, PA (Comcast Cable)

BELLWOOD—See ALTOONA, PA (Atlantic Broadband)

BEN AVON HEIGHTS—See PITTSBURGH, PA (Comcast Cable)

BEN AVON—See PITTSBURGH, PA (Comcast Cable)

BENDERSVILLE—See GETTYSBURG, PA (Comcast Cable)

BENNER TWP.—See STATE COLLEGE, PA (Comcast Cable)

▲**BENSALEM TWP.**—Comcast Cable

BENSON—See JOHNSTOWN, PA (Atlantic Broadband)

▲**BENTLEY CREEK**—Blue Ridge Communications

BENTLEYVILLE—See UNIONTOWN, PA (Atlantic Broadband)

▲**BENTLEYVILLE**—FairPoint Communications

BENTON—See BERWICK, PA (MetroCast Communications)

BENZINGER TWP.—See ST. MARY'S, PA (Zito Media)

BERLIN BOROUGH—See CENTRAL CITY BOROUGH, PA (Comcast Cable)

BERLIN TWP. (WAYNE COUNTY)—See BEACH LAKE, PA (Blue Ridge Communications)

BERLIN TWP. (WAYNE COUNTY)—See HONESDALE, PA (Blue Ridge Communications)

BERN TWP. (BERKS COUNTY)—See READING, PA (Comcast Cable)

BERNVILLE—See READING, PA (Comcast Cable)

BERRYSBURG—See LYKENS, PA (Comcast Cable)

▲**BERWICK**—MetroCast Communications

BETHANY—See HONESDALE, PA (Blue Ridge Communications)

▲**BETHEL PARK**—Comcast Cable

BETHEL TWP. (BERKS COUNTY)—See LEBANON, PA (Comcast Cable)

BETHELEM TWP.—See LEHIGH VALLEY, PA (Service Electric Cable TV & Communications)

▲**BETHLEHEM TWP.**—Formerly served by NORTHAMPTON BOROUGH, PA [PA0008]. RCN Corp. This cable system has converted to IPTV

▲**BETHLEHEM**—Formerly served by NORTHAMPTON BOROUGH, PA [PA0008]. RCN Corp. This cable system has converted to IPTV

BETHLEHEM—See LEHIGH VALLEY, PA (Service Electric Cable TV & Communications)

BEYER—See KISKIMINETAS TWP., PA (Comcast Cable)

BIG BEAVER—See ZELIENOPLE, PA (Armstrong Cable Services)

BIG BEAVER—See BEAVER FALLS, PA (Comcast Cable)

▲**BIG POND**—Formerly served by Barrett's TV Cable System. No longer in operation

BIG RUN—See PUNXSUTAWNEY, PA (Comcast Cable)

▲**BIGLER TWP.**—Comcast Cable. Now served by PHILLIPSBURG, PA [PA0109]

BIGLER TWP.—See PHILIPSBURG BOROUGH, PA (Comcast Cable)

BIGLERVILLE—See GETTYSBURG, PA (Comcast Cable)

▲**BIRDSBORO**—Service Electric Cablevision

BIRMINGHAM BOROUGH—See ALTOONA, PA (Atlantic Broadband)

BLACK LICK TWP.—See ADAMS TWP. (Cambria County), PA (Comcast Cable)

BLACK LICK TWP.—See BLAIRSVILLE, PA (Comcast Cable)

BLACK TWP.—See CENTRAL CITY BOROUGH, PA (Comcast Cable)

BLACKSVILLE—See BRAVE, WV (Zito Media)

BLAINE TWP.—See PITTSBURGH, PA (Comcast Cable)

BLAIR TWP. (BLAIR COUNTY)—See ALTOONA, PA (Atlantic Broadband)

BLAIRS MILLS—See DOYLESBURG, PA (Valley Cable Systems)

▲**BLAIRSVILLE**—Comcast Cable

BLAKELY—See DUNMORE, PA (Comcast Cable)

BLAKESLEE—See POCONO, PA (MetroCast Communications)

BLAWNOX BOROUGH—See TARENTUM BOROUGH, PA (Comcast Cable)

BLOOMFIELD TWP.—See ALTOONA, PA (Atlantic Broadband)

BLOOMING VALLEY—See MEADVILLE, PA (Armstrong Cable Services)

BLOOMINGTON—See CLEARFIELD, PA (Atlantic Broadband)

▲**BLOOMSBURG**—Service Electric Cable TV & Communications. Now served by SUNBURY, PA [PA0029]

BLOOMSBURG—See BERWICK, PA (MetroCast Communications)

BLOOMSBURG—See SUNBURY, PA (Service Electric Cablevision)

▲**BLOSSBURG**—Formerly served by Williamson Road TV Co. Inc. No longer in operation

BLUE BALL—See LANCASTER, PA (Comcast Cable)

BLUE RIDGE SUMMIT—See SHIPPENSBURG, PA (Comcast Cable)

BOBTOWN—See UNIONTOWN, PA (Atlantic Broadband)

BOGGS TWP. (CENTRE COUNTY)—See STATE COLLEGE, PA (Comcast Cable)

BOGGS TWP. (CLEARFIELD COUNTY)—See CLEARFIELD, PA (Atlantic Broadband)

BOGGS TWP. (CLEARFIELD COUNTY)—See SNOW SHOE, PA (Tele-Media)

BOILING SPRINGS—See SHIPPENSBURG, PA (Comcast Cable)

BOLIVAR—See BLAIRSVILLE, PA (Comcast Cable)

BONNEAUVILLE—See GETTYSBURG, PA (Comcast Cable)

BOSWELL—See JOHNSTOWN, PA (Atlantic Broadband)

BOSWELL—See CENTRAL CITY BOROUGH, PA (Comcast Cable)

▲**CARLISLE**—Comcast Cable. Now served by SHIPPENSBURG, PA [PA0066]

CARLISLE—See SHIPPENSBURG, PA (Comcast Cable)

CARMICHAELS—See UNIONTOWN, PA (Atlantic Broadband)

▲**CARNEGIE**—Comcast Cable. Now served by PITTSBURGH, PA [PA0001]

CARNEGIE—See PITTSBURGH, PA (Comcast Cable)

CARROLL TWP. (PERRY COUNTY)—See DUNCANNON, PA (Blue Ridge Communications)

CARROLL TWP. (PERRY COUNTY)—See SHIPPENSBURG, PA (Comcast Cable)

CARROLL TWP. (WASHINGTON COUNTY)—See PITTSBURGH, PA (Comcast Cable)

CARROLL TWP.—See GETTYSBURG, PA (Comcast Cable)

CARROLL VALLEY—See GETTYSBURG, PA (Comcast Cable)

▲**CARROLLTOWN BOROUGH**—Formerly served by Adelphia Communications. Now served by BLAIRSVILLE, PA [PA0320]

CARROLLTOWN BOROUGH—See BLAIRSVILLE, PA (Comcast Cable)

▲**CARROLLTOWN**—Formerly served by Adelphia Communications. Now served by BLAIRSVILLE, PA [PA0320]

CASCADE—See SHIPPENSBURG, MD (Comcast Cable)

CASS TWP. (HUNTINGDON COUNTY)—See UNION TWP. (Huntingdon County), PA (Atlantic Broadband)

CASS TWP. (SCHUYLKILL COUNTY)—See POTTSVILLE, PA (Comcast Cable)

CASS TWP. (SCHUYLKILL COUNTY)—See PRIMROSE, PA (J. B. Cable)

CASSANDRA—See CRESSON, PA (Comcast Cable)

CASSELMAN—See CENTRAL CITY BOROUGH, PA (Comcast Cable)

CASSVILLE BOROUGH—See UNION TWP. (Huntingdon County), PA (Atlantic Broadband)

CASTANEA TWP.—See LOCK HAVEN, PA (Comcast Cable)

▲**CASTLE SHANNON**—Comcast Cable. Now served by PITTSBURGH, PA [PA0001]

CASTLE SHANNON—See PITTSBURGH, PA (Comcast Cable)

CATASAUQUA BORO—See LEHIGH VALLEY, PA (Service Electric Cable TV & Communications)

▲**CATASAUQUA BOROUGH**—Formerly served by NORTHAMPTON BOROUGH, PA [PA0008]. RCN Corp. This cable system has converted to IPTV

CATAWISSA BOROUGH—See SUNBURY, PA (Service Electric Cablevision)

CATAWISSA TWP.—See SUNBURY, PA (Service Electric Cablevision)

CATHERINE TWP.—See ALTOONA, PA (Atlantic Broadband)

CATHERINE TWP.—See HUNTINGDON, PA (Comcast Cable)

CATLIN HOLLOW—See WELLSBORO, PA (Blue Ridge Communications)

CECIL COUNTY (PORTIONS)—See OXFORD, MD (Armstrong Cable Services)

CENTER TWP. (BEAVER COUNTY)—See PITTSBURGH, PA (Comcast Cable)

CENTER TWP. (BUTLER COUNTY)—See BUTLER, PA (Armstrong Cable Services)

CENTER TWP. (SNYDER COUNTY)—See SUNBURY, PA (Service Electric Cablevision)

CENTER TWP.—See WAYNESBURG, PA (Comcast Cable)

CENTERPORT—See READING, PA (Comcast Cable)

CENTERVILLE (BRADFORD COUNTY)—See BENTLEY CREEK, PA (Blue Ridge Communications)

CENTERVILLE (CRAWFORD COUNTY)—See MEADVILLE, PA (Armstrong Cable Services)

▲**CENTRAL CITY BOROUGH**—Comcast Cable

CENTRAL CITY—See CENTRAL CITY BOROUGH, PA (Comcast Cable)

CENTRE HALL—See STATE COLLEGE, PA (Comcast Cable)

CENTRE TWP.—See READING, PA (Comcast Cable)

CHADDS FORD TWP.—See KENNETT SQUARE, PA (Comcast Cable)

CHALFANT—See PITTSBURGH, PA (Comcast Cable)

CHALFONT—See JAMISON, PA (Comcast Cable)

CHALK HILL—See MARKLEYSBURG, PA (Comcast Cable)

CHAMBERSBURG—See SHIPPENSBURG, PA (Comcast Cable)

CHAMPION—See INDIAN CREEK, PA (Laurel Highland Television Co.)

CHAPMAN BORO—See LEHIGH VALLEY, PA (Service Electric Cable TV & Communications)

▲**CHAPMAN BOROUGH**—Formerly served by NORTHAMPTON BOROUGH, PA [PA0008]. RCN Corp. This cable system has converted to IPTV

CHARLEROI—See PITTSBURGH, PA (Comcast Cable)

CHARLESTOWN TWP.—See COATESVILLE, PA (Comcast Cable)

CHARTIERS TWP. (WASHINGTON COUNTY)—See PITTSBURGH, PA (Comcast Cable)

CHELTENHAM TWP.—See WILLOW GROVE, PA (Comcast Cable)

CHERRY RIDGE TWP. (WAYNE COUNTY)—See GREENTOWN, PA (Blue Ridge Communications)

CHERRY RIDGE TWP. (WAYNE COUNTY)—See HONESDALE, PA (Blue Ridge Communications)

CHERRY TREE—See BLAIRSVILLE, PA (Comcast Cable)

CHERRY TWP. (SULLIVAN COUNTY)—See DUSHORE, PA (Blue Ridge Communications)

CHERRY TWP.—See BUTLER, PA (Armstrong Cable Services)

CHERRYHILL TWP.—See BLAIRSVILLE, PA (Comcast Cable)

CHESTER COUNTY—See COATESVILLE, PA (Comcast Cable)

CHESTER HEIGHTS—See WALLINGFORD, PA (Comcast Cable)

CHESTER HILL—See PHILIPSBURG BOROUGH, PA (Comcast Cable)

CHESTER TWP. (DELAWARE COUNTY)—See WALLINGFORD, PA (Comcast Cable)

CHESTER—See WALLINGFORD, PA (Comcast Cable)

CHESTNUT HILL TWP.—See STROUDSBURG, PA (Blue Ridge Communications)

CHESWICK—See TARENTUM BOROUGH, PA (Comcast Cable)

▲**CHICORA**—Armstrong Cable Services. Now served by BUTLER, PA [PA0044]

CHICORA—See BUTLER, PA (Armstrong Cable Services)

CHINCHILLA—See DUNMORE, PA (Comcast Cable)

CHIPPEWA TWP.—See BEAVER FALLS, PA (Comcast Cable)

CHRISTIANA BOROUGH—See LANCASTER, PA (Comcast Cable)

CHURCHILL—See MONROEVILLE, PA (Comcast Cable)

CLAIRTON—See PITTSBURGH, PA (Comcast Cable)

CLARENCE—See SNOW SHOE, PA (Tele-Media)

CLARENDON HEIGHTS—See CLARENDON, PA (Clarendon TV Association)

▲**CLARENDON**—Clarendon TV Association

▲**CLARION BOROUGH**—Comcast Cable

CLARK—See MERCER COUNTY, PA (Time Warner Cable)

CLARK—See SHARON, PA (Time Warner Cable)

CLARKS GREEN—See DUNMORE, PA (Comcast Cable)

CLARKS SUMMIT—See DUNMORE, PA (Comcast Cable)

CLARKSBURG—See BLAIRSVILLE, PA (Comcast Cable)

CLARKSVILLE—See UNIONTOWN, PA (Atlantic Broadband)

CLAY TWP. (HUNTINGDON COUNTY)—See THREE SPRINGS, PA (MetroCast Communications)

CLAY TWP. (LANCASTER COUNTY)—See EPHRATA, PA (Blue Ridge Communications)

CLAYSBURG—See ALTOONA, PA (Atlantic Broadband)

▲**CLAYSVILLE**—Blue Devil Cable TV Inc.

CLEARFIELD COUNTY (PORTIONS)—See PUNXSUTAWNEY, PA (Comcast Cable)

CLEARFIELD COUNTY—See CRESSON, PA (Comcast Cable)

▲**CLEARFIELD**—Atlantic Broadband

CLEONA—See LEBANON, PA (Comcast Cable)

CLEVELAND TWP.—See SUNBURY, PA (Service Electric Cablevision)

CLIFFORD TWP. (SUSQUEHANNA COUNTY)—See CARBONDALE, PA (Adams Digital Cable)

CLIFTON HEIGHTS—See WALLINGFORD, PA (Comcast Cable)

▲**CLIFTON HEIGHTS**—RCN Corp. Formerly served by Philadelphia (suburbs), PA [PA0447]. This cable system has converted to IPTV

CLINTON TWP. (BUTLER COUNTY)—See ZELIENOPLE, PA (Armstrong Cable Services)

CLINTON TWP. (VENANGO COUNTY)—See GROVE CITY, PA (Armstrong Cable Services)

CLINTON TWP. (WAYNE COUNTY)—See CARBONDALE, PA (Adams Digital Cable)

CLINTON TWP.—See TARENTUM BOROUGH, PA (Comcast Cable)

▲**CLINTONVILLE**—Armstrong Utilities Inc. Now served by GROVE CITY, PA [PA0089]

CLINTONVILLE—See GROVE CITY, PA (Armstrong Cable Services)

CLOVER TWP.—See PUNXSUTAWNEY, PA (Comcast Cable)

CLYMER—See BLAIRSVILLE, PA (Comcast Cable)

COAL CENTER—See CONNELLSVILLE, PA (Armstrong Cable Services)

DALLAS—See BERWICK, PA (Metro-Cast Communications)

DALLASTOWN—See YORK, PA (Comcast Cable)

DALMATIA—See LEBANON, PA (Comcast Cable)

DALTON—See DUNMORE, PA (Comcast Cable)

DAMASCUS TWP.—See BEACH LAKE, PA (Blue Ridge Communications)

▲ **DANVILLE**—CATV Service Inc.

DARBY TWP.—See WALLINGFORD, PA (Comcast Cable)

▲ **DARBY TWP.**—RCN Corp. Formerly served by Philadelphia (suburbs), PA [PA5259]. This cable system has converted to IPTV

DARBY—See WALLINGFORD, PA (Comcast Cable)

▲ **DARBY**—RCN Corp. Formerly served by Philadelphia (suburbs), PA [PA5259]. This cable system has converted to IPTV

▲ **DARLINGTON TWP. (Beaver County)**—Comcast Cable. Now served by BEAVER FALLS, PA [PA0065]

DARLINGTON TWP. (BEAVER COUNTY)—See BEAVER FALLS, PA (Comcast Cable)

DARLINGTON—See BEAVER FALLS, PA (Comcast Cable)

DAUGHERTY TWP.—See ZELIENOPLE, PA (Armstrong Cable Services)

DAUGHERTY TWP.—See BEAVER FALLS, PA (Comcast Cable)

DAUPHIN—See HARRISBURG, PA (Comcast Cable)

DAVIDSVILLE—See JOHNSTOWN, PA (Atlantic Broadband)

DAWSON—See UNIONTOWN, PA (Atlantic Broadband)

DAYBROOK—See BRAVE, WV (Zito Media)

DAYTON BOROUGH—See KISKIMINETAS TWP., PA (Comcast Cable)

DEAN TWP. (CAMBRIA COUNTY)—See COALPORT, PA (Comcast Cable)

DEAN TWP. (CAMBRIA COUNTY)—See CRESSON, PA (Comcast Cable)

DECATUR TWP. (MIFFLIN COUNTY)—See MIFFLINBURG, PA (Atlantic Broadband)

DECATUR—See DERRY/DECATUR, PA (Atlantic Broadband)

DEEMSTON—See UNIONTOWN, PA (Atlantic Broadband)

DELANO—See MAHANOY CITY, PA (Service Electric Cable Company)

DELAWARE TWP. (MERCER COUNTY)—See GREENVILLE, PA (Time Warner Cable)

DELAWARE TWP. (NORTHUMBERLAND COUNTY)—See WILLIAMSPORT, PA (Comcast Cable)

DELAWARE TWP. (NORTHUMBERLAND COUNTY)—See LEWIS TWP., PA (Eagles Mere & La Porte Cablevision Inc.)

DELAWARE WATER GAP—See STROUDSBURG, PA (Blue Ridge Communications)

DENVER—See EPHRATA, PA (Blue Ridge Communications)

DEPOSIT—See CARBONDALE, NY (Adams Digital Cable)

DERRY TWP. (MIFFLIN COUNTY)—See LEWISTOWN, PA (Comcast Cable)

DERRY TWP. (WESTMORELAND COUNTY)—See GREENSBURG, PA (Comcast Cable)

▲ **DERRY/DECATUR**—Atlantic Broadband

DERRY—See BLAIRSVILLE, PA (Comcast Cable)

DICKINSON TWP. (CUMBERLAND COUNTY)—See SHIPPENSBURG, PA (Comcast Cable)

DICKSON CITY—See SCRANTON, PA (Comcast Cable)

▲ **DILLSBURG**—Formerly served by Adelphia Communications. Now served by HIGHROCK, PA [PA0106]

DILLSBURG—See GETTYSBURG, PA (Comcast Cable)

DIMOCK TWP.—See MONTROSE, PA (Time Warner Cable)

DINGMAN TWP.—See MILFORD, PA (Blue Ridge Communications)

DISTANT—See KISKIMINETAS TWP., PA (Comcast Cable)

DISTRICT TWP.—See BIRDSBORO, PA (Service Electric Cablevision)

DIXONVILLE (INDIANA COUNTY)—See BLAIRSVILLE, PA (Comcast Cable)

DONEGAL TWP. (WASHINGTON COUNTY)—See WEST ALEXANDER, PA (Comcast Cable)

DONEGAL TWP. (WESTMORELAND COUNTY)—See INDIAN CREEK, PA (Laurel Highland Television Co.)

DONEGAL—See INDIAN CREEK, PA (Laurel Highland Television Co.)

DONORA—See PITTSBURGH, PA (Comcast Cable)

DORMONT—See PITTSBURGH, PA (Comcast Cable)

DORRANCE TWP.—See HAZLETON, PA (Service Electric Cablevision)

DORRANCE—See BERWICK, PA (MetroCast Communications)

DOUGLASS TWP. (MONTGOMERY COUNTY)—See POTTSTOWN, PA (Comcast Cable)

DOVER TWP.—See GETTYSBURG, PA (Comcast Cable)

DOVER—See YORK, PA (Comcast Cable)

DOWNINGTOWN—See COATESVILLE, PA (Comcast Cable)

▲ **DOYLESBURG**—Valley Cable Systems

DOYLESTOWN—See JAMISON, PA (Comcast Cable)

DRAVOSBURG—See BETHEL PARK, PA (Comcast Cable)

DREHER TWP.—See HAWLEY, PA (Blue Ridge Communications)

DRIFTING—See SNOW SHOE, PA (Tele-Media)

DRUMORE TWP.—See LANCASTER, PA (Comcast Cable)

▲ **DU BOIS**—Formerly served by Adelphia Communications. Now served by PUNXSUTAWNEY, PA [PA0397]

DU BOIS—See PUNXSUTAWNEY, PA (Comcast Cable)

DUBLIN BOROUGH—See SELLERSVILLE, PA (Comcast Cable)

DUBLIN TWP. (HUNTINGDON COUNTY)—See SHADE GAP, PA (Shade Gap TV Assn.)

DUBOISTOWN—See WILLIAMSPORT, PA (Comcast Cable)

DUDLEY—See HUNTINGDON, PA (Comcast Cable)

DUKE CENTER—See SMETHPORT, PA (Comcast Cable)

DUNBAR TWP.—See CONNELLSVILLE, PA (Armstrong Cable Services)

DUNBAR—See CONNELLSVILLE, PA (Armstrong Cable Services)

▲ **DUNCANNON**—Blue Ridge Communications

DUNCANSVILLE—See ALTOONA, PA (Atlantic Broadband)

DUNKARD TWP.—See UNIONTOWN, PA (Atlantic Broadband)

DUNLEVY—See CONNELLSVILLE, PA (Armstrong Cable Services)

▲ **DUNMORE**—Comcast Cable

DUNNSTABLE TWP. (EASTERN PORTION)—See LOCK HAVEN, PA (Comcast Cable)

DUNNSTABLE TWP.—See WILLIAMSPORT, PA (Comcast Cable)

DUPONT—See DUNMORE, PA (Comcast Cable)

DUQUESNE—See BETHEL PARK, PA (Comcast Cable)

DURHAM TWP.—See LEHIGH VALLEY, PA (Service Electric Cable TV & Communications)

DURYEA—See SCRANTON, PA (Comcast Cable)

▲ **DUSHORE**—Blue Ridge Communications

DYBERRY TWP.—See CARBONDALE, PA (Adams Digital Cable)

EAGLES MERE BOROUGH—See LA PORTE BOROUGH, PA (Comcast Cable)

EARL TWP. (BERKS COUNTY)—See POTTSTOWN, PA (Comcast Cable)

EARL TWP. (LANCASTER COUNTY)—See EPHRATA, PA (Blue Ridge Communications)

EARL TWP. (LANCASTER COUNTY)—See LANCASTER, PA (Comcast Cable)

EARL TWP. (LANCASTER COUNTY)—See BIRDSBORO, PA (Service Electric Cablevision)

▲ **EAST ALLEN TWP.**—Formerly served by NORTHAMPTON BOROUGH, PA [PA0008]. RCN Corp. This cable system has converted to IPTV

EAST ALLEN TWP.—See LEHIGH VALLEY, PA (Service Electric Cable TV & Communications)

EAST BANGOR BORO—See LEHIGH VALLEY, PA (Service Electric Cable TV & Communications)

EAST BERLIN—See GETTYSBURG, PA (Comcast Cable)

EAST BETHLEHEM TWP. (WASHINGTON COUNTY)—See UNIONTOWN, PA (Atlantic Broadband)

EAST BRADFORD TWP. (CHESTER COUNTY)—See COATESVILLE, PA (Comcast Cable)

EAST BRADY—See BUTLER, PA (Armstrong Cable Services)

EAST BRADY—See CLARION BOROUGH, PA (Comcast Cable)

EAST BRANDYWINE TWP.—See COATESVILLE, PA (Comcast Cable)

EAST BRUNSWICK TWP.—See MAHANOY CITY, PA (Service Electric Cable Company)

EAST BUFFALO TWP.—See DANVILLE, PA (CATV Service Inc.)

EAST BUTLER—See BUTLER, PA (Armstrong Cable Services)

EAST CALN TWP.—See COATESVILLE, PA (Comcast Cable)

EAST CAMERON TWP.—See SUNBURY, PA (Service Electric Cablevision)

EAST CANTON—See CANTON, PA (Zito Media)

EAST CARROLL TWP.—See BLAIRSVILLE, PA (Comcast Cable)

EAST COCALICO TWP.—See EPHRATA, PA (Blue Ridge Communications)

▲ **EAST CONEMAUGH**—Formerly served by Adelphia Communications. Now served by BLAIRSVILLE, PA [PA0320]

EAST CONEMAUGH—See BLAIRSVILLE, PA (Comcast Cable)

EAST COVENTRY TWP.—See POTTSTOWN, PA (Comcast Cable)

EAST DEER TWP.—See TARENTUM BOROUGH, PA (Comcast Cable)

EAST DONEGAL TWP.—See ELIZABETHTOWN, PA (Comcast Cable)

EAST DRUMORE TWP.—See LANCASTER, PA (Comcast Cable)

EAST EARL TWP. (PORTIONS)—See EPHRATA, PA (Blue Ridge Communications)

EAST EARL TWP. (SOUTHERN PORTION)—See LANCASTER, PA (Comcast Cable)

EAST FALLOWFIELD TWP. (CHESTER COUNTY)—See COATESVILLE, PA (Comcast Cable)

EAST GOSHEN TWP. (CHESTER COUNTY)—See COATESVILLE, PA (Comcast Cable)

EAST GOSHEN TWP.—See COATESVILLE, PA (Comcast Cable)

EAST GREENVILLE—See POTTSTOWN, PA (Comcast Cable)

EAST HANOVER TWP. (DAUPHIN COUNTY)—See LEBANON, PA (Comcast Cable)

EAST HANOVER TWP. (LEBANON COUNTY)—See LEBANON, PA (Comcast Cable)

EAST HANOVER TWP. (LEBANON COUNTY)—See FORT INDIANTOWN GAP, PA (Gap Cable TV Inc.)

EAST HEMPFIELD TWP. (LANCASTER COUNTY)—See LANCASTER, PA (Comcast Cable)

EAST HICKORY—See MEADVILLE, PA (Armstrong Cable Services)

EAST HUNTINGDON TWP. (PORTIONS)—See GREENSBURG, PA (Comcast Cable)

EAST HUNTINGDON TWP.—See CONNELLSVILLE, PA (Armstrong Cable Services)

EAST KANE—See KANE, PA (Comcast Cable)

EAST LACKAWANNOCK TWP. (PORTIONS)—See GROVE CITY, PA (Armstrong Cable Services)

EAST LAMPETER TWP. (LANCASTER COUNTY)—See LANCASTER, PA (Comcast Cable)

EAST LANSDOWNE—See WALLINGFORD, PA (Comcast Cable)

▲**EAST LANSDOWNE**—RCN Corp. Formerly served by Philadelphia (suburbs), PA [PA5259]. This cable system has converted to IPTV

EAST MANCHESTER TWP. (YORK COUNTY)—See YORK, PA (Comcast Cable)

EAST MARLBOROUGH TWP.—See KENNETT SQUARE, PA (Comcast Cable)

EAST MCKEESPORT—See MONROEVILLE, PA (Comcast Cable)

EAST NANTHEAL TWP.—See BIRDSBORO, PA (Service Electric Cablevision)

EAST NANTMEAL TWP.—See COATESVILLE, PA (Comcast Cable)

EAST NORRITON TWP.—See NORRISTOWN, PA (Comcast Cable)

EAST NORWEGIAN TWP. (SCHUYLKILL COUNTY)—See POTTSVILLE, PA (Comcast Cable)

EAST NOTTINGHAM TWP.—See OXFORD, PA (Armstrong Cable Services)

EAST PENN TWP.—See PALMERTON, PA (Blue Ridge Communications)

EAST PENNSBORO TWP. (CUMBERLAND COUNTY)—See HARRISBURG, PA (Comcast Cable)

EAST PETERSBURG—See LANCASTER, PA (Comcast Cable)

EAST PIKELAND TWP.—See POTTSTOWN, PA (Comcast Cable)

EAST PITTSBURGH—See MONROEVILLE, PA (Comcast Cable)

EAST PROSPECT—See YORK, PA (Comcast Cable)

EAST PROVIDENCE TWP.—See BEDFORD, PA (Comcast Cable)

EAST ROCHESTER—See ROCHESTER, PA (Comcast Cable)

EAST ROCKHILL TWP.—See SELLERSVILLE, PA (Comcast Cable)

EAST SIDE—See POCONO, PA (MetroCast Communications)

▲**EAST SMITHFIELD**—Community Cable Corp.

EAST ST. CLAIR TWP. (BEDFORD COUNTY)—See WOODBURY, PA (Atlantic Broadband)

EAST ST. CLAIR TWP. (BEDFORD COUNTY)—See BEDFORD, PA (Comcast Cable)

EAST STROUDSBURG—See STROUDSBURG, PA (Blue Ridge Communications)

EAST TAYLOR TWP.—See JOHNSTOWN, PA (Atlantic Broadband)

EAST TROY—See TROY, PA (Blue Ridge Communications)

EAST UNION TWP.—See SHENANDOAH, PA (Shen-Heights TV Assoc. Inc.)

EAST VANDERGRIFT—See KISKIMINETAS TWP., PA (Comcast Cable)

EAST VINCENT TWP.—See POTTSTOWN, PA (Comcast Cable)

EAST WASHINGTON—See PITTSBURGH, PA (Comcast Cable)

▲**EAST WATERFORD**—Formerly served by Valley Cable Systems. No longer in operation

EAST WHEATFIELD TWP.—See ARMAGH, PA (Comcast Cable)

EAST WHITELAND TWP.—See COATESVILLE, PA (Comcast Cable)

▲**EASTON**—Service Electric Cable TV & Communcations. Now served by LEHIGH VALLEY, PA [PA0006]

▲**EASTON**—Formerly served by NORTHAMPTON BOROUGH, PA [PA0008]. RCN Corp. This cable system has converted to IPTV

EASTON—See LEHIGH VALLEY, PA (Service Electric Cable TV & Communications)

EASTTOWN TWP.—See COATESVILLE, PA (Comcast Cable)

EASTVALE—See BEAVER FALLS, PA (Comcast Cable)

▲**EASTVILLE**—Eastville TV Cable. No longer in operation

EATON TWP.—See MESHOPPEN, PA (Blue Ridge Communications)

EATONVILLE—See MESHOPPEN, PA (Blue Ridge Communications)

▲**EAU CLAIRE**—Formerly served by Cebridge Connections. Now served by GROVE CITY, PA [PA0089]

EAU CLAIRE—See GROVE CITY, PA (Armstrong Cable Services)

EBENSBURG—See BLAIRSVILLE, PA (Comcast Cable)

ECONOMY—See PITTSBURGH, PA (Comcast Cable)

EDDYSTONE (DELAWARE COUNTY)—See WALLINGFORD, PA (Comcast Cable)

▲**EDDYSTONE**—RCN Corp. Formerly served by Philadelphia (suburbs), PA [PA0447]. This cable system has converted to IPTV

EDEN TWP.—See LANCASTER, PA (Comcast Cable)

EDGEMONT TWP.—See COATESVILLE, PA (Comcast Cable)

EDGEWOOD—See PITTSBURGH, PA (Comcast Cable)

EDGEWORTH—See PITTSBURGH, PA (Comcast Cable)

▲**EDINBORO**—Coaxial Cable TV Corp.

EDMON—See KISKIMINETAS TWP., PA (Comcast Cable)

EDWARDSVILLE—See SCRANTON, PA (Comcast Cable)

EDWARDSVILLE—See BERWICK, PA (MetroCast Communications)

EHRENFELD—See ADAMS TWP. (Cambria County), PA (Comcast Cable)

ELCO—See CONNELLSVILLE, PA (Armstrong Cable Services)

▲**ELDERTON BOROUGH**—Comcast Cable. Now served by KISKIMINETAS TWP., PA [PA0074]

ELDERTON BOROUGH—See KISKIMINETAS TWP., PA (Comcast Cable)

ELDERTON—See KISKIMINETAS TWP., PA (Comcast Cable)

ELDRED TWP. (JEFFERSON COUNTY)—See CLARION BOROUGH, PA (Comcast Cable)

ELDRED TWP. (SCHUYLKILL COUNTY)—See PALMERTON, PA (Blue Ridge Communications)

▲**ELDRED TWP.**—Herr Cable Co.

ELDRED—See SMETHPORT, PA (Comcast Cable)

ELGIN—See CORRY, PA (Time Warner Cable)

ELIMSPORT—See WILLIAMSPORT, PA (Comcast Cable)

ELIZABETH TWP. (LANCASTER COUNTY)—See EPHRATA, PA (Blue Ridge Communications)

▲**ELIZABETHTOWN**—Comcast Cable

ELIZABETHVILLE—See LYKENS, PA (Comcast Cable)

ELK CREEK TWP.—See HARBORCREEK TWP., PA (Time Warner Cable)

ELK TWP. (CHESTER COUNTY)—See OXFORD, PA (Armstrong Cable Services)

ELK TWP. (CLARION COUNTY)—See SHIPPENVILLE, PA (Atlantic Broadband)

ELK TWP. (CLARION COUNTY)—See SHIPPENVILLE, PA (Atlantic Broadband)

▲**ELKLAND**—Time Warner Cable. Now served by ELMIRA/CORNING, NY [NY0057]

ELLIOTTSBURG—See PERRY COUNTY, PA (Kuhn Communications)

ELLPORT—See ZELIENOPLE, PA (Armstrong Cable Services)

ELLSWORTH—See UNIONTOWN, PA (Atlantic Broadband)

ELLSWORTH—See BENTLEYVILLE, PA (FairPoint Communications)

ELLWOOD CITY—See ZELIENOPLE, PA (Armstrong Cable Services)

ELMHURST TWP.—See DUNMORE, PA (Comcast Cable)

ELTON—See ADAMS TWP. (Cambria County), PA (Comcast Cable)

ELVERSON BOROUGH—See BIRDSBORO, PA (Service Electric Cablevision)

ELYSBURG—See SUNBURY, PA (Service Electric Cablevision)

EMLENTON—See SHIPPENVILLE, PA (Atlantic Broadband)

EMLENTON—See CLARION BOROUGH, PA (Comcast Cable)

▲**EMMAUS**—Service Electric Cable TV & Communications. Now served by LEHIGH VALLEY, PA [PA0006]

EMMAUS—See LEHIGH VALLEY, PA (Service Electric Cable TV & Communications)

EMPORIUM—See COUDERSPORT, PA (Zito Media)

EMSWORTH—See PITTSBURGH, PA (Comcast Cable)

ENON VALLEY—See BEAVER FALLS, PA (Comcast Cable)

EPHRATA TWP. (LANCASTER COUNTY)—See EPHRATA, PA (Blue Ridge Communications)

▲**EPHRATA**—Blue Ridge Communications

ERDENHEIM—See LANSDALE, PA (Comcast Cable)

▲**ERIE**—Time Warner Cable

ERNEST—See BLAIRSVILLE, PA (Comcast Cable)

ESTELLA—See ROME, PA (Beaver Valley Cable Co.)

ETNA—See PITTSBURGH, PA (Comcast Cable)

EVANS CITY—See ZELIENOPLE, PA (Armstrong Cable Services)

EVERETT—See BEDFORD, PA (Comcast Cable)

EVERSON—See CONNELLSVILLE, PA (Armstrong Cable Services)

EXETER BOROUGH (PORTIONS)—See DUNMORE, PA (Comcast Cable)

EXETER TWP. (BERKS COUNTY)—See BIRDSBORO, PA (Service Electric Cablevision)

EXTON—See COATESVILLE, PA (Comcast Cable)

EYNON—See DUNMORE, PA (Comcast Cable)

FACTORYVILLE—See DUNMORE, PA (Comcast Cable)

FAIRBANK—See UNIONTOWN, PA (Atlantic Broadband)

FAIRCHANCE—See UNIONTOWN, PA (Atlantic Broadband)

FAIRFIELD—See GETTYSBURG, PA (Comcast Cable)

FAIRMONT CITY—See LIMESTONE, PA (Atlantic Broadband)

FAIRMOUNT CITY—See PUNXSUTAWNEY, PA (Comcast Cable)

FAIRVIEW (ERIE COUNTY)—See HARBORCREEK TWP., PA (Time Warner Cable)

FAIRVIEW TWP. (ERIE COUNTY)—See HARBORCREEK TWP., PA (Time Warner Cable)

FAIRVIEW TWP. (LUZERNE COUNTY)—See WILKES-BARRE, PA (Service Electric Cable Company)

FAIRVIEW TWP. (YORK COUNTY)—See NEWBERRY TWP., PA (Blue Ridge Communications)

FALLOWFIELD TWP.—See PITTSBURGH, PA (Comcast Cable)

FALLOWFIELD TWP.—See BENTLEYVILLE, PA (FairPoint Communications)

FALLS CREEK—See PUNXSUTAWNEY, PA (Comcast Cable)

FALLS TWP. (BUCKS COUNTY)—See BENSALEM TWP., PA (Comcast Cable)

FALLS TWP. (WYOMING COUNTY)—See MESHOPPEN, PA (Blue Ridge Communications)

FALLS TWP. (WYOMING COUNTY)—See DUNMORE, PA (Comcast Cable)

FALLSTON—See BEAVER FALLS, PA (Comcast Cable)

FANNETT TWP. (FRANKLIN COUNTY)—See DOYLESBURG, PA (Valley Cable Systems)

▲**FANNETTSBURG**—Fannettsburg Cable TV Co. No longer in operation

FARMINGTON TWP. (CLARION COUNTY)—See NORTH CLARION, PA (Armstrong Cable Services)

FARRELL—See MERCER COUNTY, PA (Time Warner Cable)

FARRELL—See SHARON, PA (Time Warner Cable)

FARVIEW STATE HOSPITAL—See CARBONDALE, PA (Adams Digital Cable)

FASSETT—See BENTLEY CREEK, PA (Blue Ridge Communications)

▲**FAWN GROVE**—Formerly served by Armstrong Cable Services. No longer in operation

FAWN TWP. (ALLEGHENY COUNTY)—See TARENTUM BOROUGH, PA (Comcast Cable)

FAYETTE CITY (FAYETTE COUNTY)—See UNIONTOWN, PA (Atlantic Broadband)

FAYETTE COUNTY (UNINCORPORATED AREAS)—See MARKLEYSBURG, PA (Comcast Cable)

FELL TWP. (LACKAWANNA COUNTY)—See CARBONDALE, PA (Adams Digital Cable)

FELTON—See YORK, PA (Comcast Cable)

FERGUSON TWP.—See STATE COLLEGE, PA (Comcast Cable)

FERMANAGH TWP.—See LEWISTOWN, PA (Nittany Media Inc.)

FERN GLEN—See BERWICK, PA (MetroCast Communications)

FERNDALE (CAMBRIA COUNTY)—See JOHNSTOWN, PA (Atlantic Broadband)

FINDLAY TWP. (ALLEGHENY COUNTY)—See PITTSBURGH, PA (Comcast Cable)

FINDLEY TWP. (MERCER COUNTY)—See GROVE CITY, PA (Armstrong Cable Services)

FISHERTOWN—See BEDFORD, PA (Comcast Cable)

FLEETWOOD—See BIRDSBORO, PA (Service Electric Cablevision)

FLEMING BOROUGH—See UNION TWP. (Centre County), PA (Country Cable)

FLEMINGTON—See LOCK HAVEN, PA (Comcast Cable)

FLOURTOWN—See LANSDALE, PA (Comcast Cable)

FOLCROFT—See WALLINGFORD, PA (Comcast Cable)

▲**FOLCROFT**—RCN Corp. Formerly served by Philadelphia (suburbs), PA [PA0447]. This cable system has converted to IPTV

FORD CITY—See KISKIMINETAS TWP., PA (Comcast Cable)

▲**FOREST CITY**—Formerly served by Adams Cable Service. Now served by CARBONDALE, PA [PA0067]

FOREST CITY—See CARBONDALE, PA (Adams Digital Cable)

FOREST HILLS—See PITTSBURGH, PA (Comcast Cable)

▲**FORKS TWP.**—Formerly served by NORTHAMPTON BOROUGH, PA [PA0008]. RCN Corp. This cable system has converted to IPTV

FORKS TWP.—See LEHIGH VALLEY, PA (Service Electric Cable TV & Communications)

FORKSTON TWP.—See MESHOPPEN, PA (Blue Ridge Communications)

▲**FORT INDIANTOWN GAP**—Gap Cable TV Inc.

▲**FORT LOUDON**—Comcast Cable. Now served by CHAMBERSBURG, PA [PA0066]

FORT LOUDON—See SHIPPENSBURG, PA (Comcast Cable)

FORTY FORT—See SCRANTON, PA (Comcast Cable)

FORWARD TWP. (ALLEGHENY COUNTY)—See PITTSBURGH, PA (Comcast Cable)

FORWARD TWP.—See BUTLER, PA (Armstrong Cable Services)

FORWARD—See ZELIENOPLE, PA (Armstrong Cable Services)

FOSTER TWP. (LUZERNE COUNTY)—See HAZLETON, PA (Service Electric Cablevision)

FOSTER TWP. (MCKEAN COUNTY)—See BRADFORD, PA (Atlantic Broadband)

FOSTER TWP. (MCKEAN COUNTY)—See SMETHPORT, PA (Comcast Cable)

FOSTER TWP. (SCHUYLKILL COUNTY)—See PRIMROSE, PA (J. B. Cable)

FOUNTAIN HILL BORO—See LEHIGH VALLEY, PA (Service Electric Cable TV & Communications)

▲**FOUNTAIN HILL BOROUGH**—Formerly served by NORTHAMPTON BOROUGH, PA [PA0008]. RCN Corp. This cable system has converted to IPTV

FOX CHAPEL—See PITTSBURGH, PA (Comcast Cable)

FOX TWP. (ELK COUNTY)—See ST. MARY'S, PA (Zito Media)

FOXBURG—See CLARION BOROUGH, PA (Comcast Cable)

FRACKVILLE—See MAHANOY CITY, PA (Service Electric Cable Company)

FRAILEY TWP.—See TREMONT, PA (Wire Television Corp.)

FRANCONIA—See SELLERSVILLE, PA (Comcast Cable)

FRANKLIN (CAMBRIA COUNTY)—See JOHNSTOWN, PA (Atlantic Broadband)

FRANKLIN (VENANGO COUNTY)—See MEADVILLE, PA (Armstrong Cable Services)

▲**FRANKLIN (VENANGO COUNTY)**—Time Warner Cable

FRANKLIN COUNTY—See SHIPPENSBURG, PA (Comcast Cable)

FRANKLIN PARK—See PITTSBURGH, PA (Comcast Cable)

FRANKLIN TWP. (BEAVER COUNTY)—See ZELIENOPLE, PA (Armstrong Cable Services)

FRANKLIN TWP. (CARBON COUNTY)—See PALMERTON, PA (Blue Ridge Communications)

FRANKLIN TWP. (COLUMBIA COUNTY)—See SUNBURY, PA (Service Electric Cablevision)

FRANKLIN TWP. (ERIE COUNTY)—See EDINBORO, PA (Coaxial Cable TV Corp.)

FRANKLIN TWP. (HUNTINGDON COUNTY)—See SPRUCE CREEK TWP., PA (MetroCast Communications)

FRANKLIN TWP. (NORTHUMBERLAND COUNTY)—See SUNBURY, PA (Service Electric Cablevision)

FRANKLIN TWP. (SNYDER COUNTY)—See SUNBURY, PA (Service Electric Cablevision)

FRANKLINDALE TWP.—See TROY, PA (Blue Ridge Communications)

FRANKLINTOWN—See GETTYSBURG, PA (Comcast Cable)

FRANKSTOWN TWP. (BLAIR COUNTY)—See ALTOONA, PA (Atlantic Broadband)

FRANKSTOWN TWP.—See ALTOONA, PA (Atlantic Broadband)

FRANKSTOWN—See ALTOONA, PA (Atlantic Broadband)

FREDERICKTOWN—See UNIONTOWN, PA (Atlantic Broadband)

FREDONIA—See GREENVILLE, PA (Time Warner Cable)

FREEBURG—See SUNBURY, PA (Service Electric Cablevision)

FREEDOM TWP. (BLAIR COUNTY)—See ALTOONA, PA (Atlantic Broadband)

FREEDOM—See ROCHESTER, PA (Comcast Cable)

FREELAND—See POCONO, PA (MetroCast Communications)

FREELAND—See HAZLETON, PA (Service Electric Cablevision)

FREEMANSBURG BORO—See LEHIGH VALLEY, PA (Service Electric Cable TV & Communications)

▲**FREEMANSBURG BOROUGH**—Formerly served by NORTHAMPTON BOROUGH, PA [PA0008]. RCN Corp. This cable system has converted to IPTV

▲**FREEPORT**—Formerly served by Adelphia Communications. Now served by KISKIMINETAS TWP., PA [PA0074]

FREEPORT—See KISKIMINETAS TWP., PA (Comcast Cable)

FRENCHCREEK TWP. (VENANGO COUNTY)—See FRANKLIN (Venango County), PA (Time Warner Cable)

FRIEDENS—See CONNELLSVILLE, PA (Armstrong Cable Services)

FRIEDENSBURG—See POTTSVILLE, PA (Comcast Cable)

FRIENDSVILLE (UNINCORPORATED AREAS)—See ADDISON TWP. (southern portion), MD (Somerfield Cable TV Co.)

FRYBURG—See NORTH CLARION, PA (Armstrong Cable Services)

FULTON COUNTY (PORTIONS)—See SHIPPENSBURG, PA (Comcast Cable)

FULTON TWP.—See LANCASTER, PA (Comcast Cable)

GAINES TWP. (TIOGA COUNTY)—See GAINES, PA (Gaines-Watrous TV Inc.)

▲**GAINES**—Gaines-Watrous TV Inc.

▲**GALETON**—Blue Ridge Communications

GALLITZIN BOROUGH—See CRESSON, PA (Comcast Cable)

GALLITZIN—See ALTOONA, PA (Atlantic Broadband)

GAP—See LANCASTER, PA (Comcast Cable)

▲**GARLAND**—Formerly served by Cebridge Connections. No longer in operation

GARRETT COUNTY (PORTIONS)—See ADDISON TWP. (southern portion), MD (Somerfield Cable TV Co.)

GASKILL TWP.—See PUNXSUTAWNEY, PA (Comcast Cable)

GEISTOWN—See JOHNSTOWN, PA (Atlantic Broadband)

GENESEE—See OSWAYO, PA (Zito Media)

GEORGES TWP. (FAYETTE COUNTY)—See UNIONTOWN, PA (Atlantic Broadband)

GERMAN TWP. (FAYETTE COUNTY)—See UNIONTOWN, PA (Atlantic Broadband)

GERMANY TWP.—See GETTYSBURG, PA (Comcast Cable)

▲**GETTYSBURG**—Comcast Cable

GIBSON TWP.—See CARBONDALE, PA (Adams Digital Cable)

GILBERTON—See MAHANOY CITY, PA (Service Electric Cable Company)

GILPIN TWP.—See KISKIMINETAS TWP., PA (Comcast Cable)

GIRARD BOROUGH—See HARBORCREEK TWP., PA (Time Warner Cable)

GIRARD TWP. (ERIE COUNTY)—See HARBORCREEK TWP., PA (Time Warner Cable)

GIRARDVILLE—See MAHANOY CITY, PA (Service Electric Cable Company)

GLADE TWP. (WARREN COUNTY)—See WARREN, PA (Atlantic Broadband)

GLADWYNE—See LOWER MERION TWP., PA (Comcast Cable)

GLASGOW—See BEAVER FALLS, PA (Comcast Cable)

GLASSPORT—See PITTSBURGH, PA (Comcast Cable)

GLEN CAMPBELL—See BLAIRSVILLE, PA (Comcast Cable)

GLEN HOPE—See COALPORT, PA (Comcast Cable)

GLEN LYON—See BERWICK, PA (MetroCast Communications)

GLEN RICHEY—See CLEARFIELD, PA (Atlantic Broadband)

▲**GLEN ROCK**—Formerly served by Adelphia Communications. Now served by HIGHROCK, PA [PA0106]

GLEN ROCK—See GETTYSBURG, PA (Comcast Cable)

GLENBURN TWP. (LACKAWANNA COUNTY)—See DUNMORE, PA (Comcast Cable)

GLENDON—See LEHIGH VALLEY, PA (Service Electric Cable TV & Communications)

GLENFIELD—See PITTSBURGH, PA (Comcast Cable)

GLENIRON—See MIFFLINBURG, PA (Atlantic Broadband)

GLENOLDEN—See WALLINGFORD, PA (Comcast Cable)

▲**GLENOLDEN**—RCN Corp. Formerly served by Philadelphia (suburbs), PA [PA0447]. This cable system has converted to IPTV

GOLDSBORO—See YORK, PA (Comcast Cable)

GORDON—See MAHANOY CITY, PA (Service Electric Cable Company)

▲**GRAHAM TWP.**—Tele-Media. Now served by SNOW SHOE, PA [PA0188]

GRAHAM TWP.—See SNOW SHOE, PA (Tele-Media)

▲**GRAMPIAN**—Atlantic Broadband

GRANTSVILLE (UNINCORPORATED AREAS)—See ADDISON TWP. (southern portion), MD (Somerfield Cable TV Co.)

▲**GRANVILLE TWP.**—Nittany Media Inc. Now served by LEWISTOWN (formerly McAlisterville), PA [PA0365]

GRANVILLE TWP.—See LEWISTOWN, PA (Comcast Cable)

GRANVILLE TWP.—See LEWISTOWN, PA (Nittany Media Inc.)

GRASSFLAT—See SNOW SHOE, PA (Tele-Media)

GRATERFORD—See KING OF PRUSSIA, PA (Comcast Cable)

GRATZ—See LYKENS, PA (Comcast Cable)

GRAY—See CONNELLSVILLE, PA (Armstrong Cable Services)

GREAT BEND BOROUGH—See CARBONDALE, PA (Adams Digital Cable)

GREAT BEND TWP.—See CARBONDALE, PA (Adams Digital Cable)

GREAT BEND—See CARBONDALE, PA (Adams Digital Cable)

GREEN LANE BOROUGH—See SELLERSVILLE, PA (Comcast Cable)

GREEN TREE—See PITTSBURGH, PA (Comcast Cable)

▲**GREEN TWP. (Indiana County)**—Formerly served by Adelphia Communications. Now served by BLAIRSVILLE, PA [PA0320]

GREEN TWP. (INDIANA COUNTY)—See BLAIRSVILLE, PA (Comcast Cable)

▲**GREENBURR**—Formerly served by Greenburr TV Cable. No longer in operation

GREENCASTLE—See SHIPPENSBURG, PA (Comcast Cable)

▲**GREENE COUNTY**—Formerly served by DuCom Cable TV. No longer in operation

GREENE COUNTY—See WAYNESBURG, PA (Comcast Cable)

GREENE TWP. (BEAVER COUNTY)—See BEAVER VALLEY, PA (Comcast Cable)

GREENE TWP. (CLINTON COUNTY)—See WILLIAMSPORT, PA (Comcast Cable)

GREENE TWP. (ERIE COUNTY)—See HARBORCREEK TWP., PA (Time Warner Cable)

GREENE TWP. (FRANKLIN COUNTY)—See SHIPPENSBURG, PA (Comcast Cable)

GREENE TWP. (PIKE COUNTY)—See GREENTOWN, PA (Blue Ridge Communications)

GREENFIELD TWP. (BLAIR COUNTY)—See ALTOONA, PA (Atlantic Broadband)

GREENFIELD TWP. (LACKAWANNA COUNTY)—See CARBONDALE, PA (Adams Digital Cable)

GREENSBORO—See UNIONTOWN, PA (Atlantic Broadband)

▲**GREENSBURG**—Comcast Cable

▲**GREENTOWN**—Blue Ridge Communications

GREENVILLE TWP.—See GREENVILLE, PA (Time Warner Cable)

▲**GREENVILLE**—Time Warner Cable

GREENWICH TWP.—See READING, PA (Comcast Cable)

GREENWICH TWP.—See LEHIGH VALLEY, PA (Service Electric Cable TV & Communications)

GREENWOOD TWP. (PERRY COUNTY)—See ELIZABETHTOWN, PA (Comcast Cable)

GREGG TWP. (UNION COUNTY)—See WILLIAMSPORT, PA (Comcast Cable)

GRINDSTONE—See UNIONTOWN, PA (Atlantic Broadband)

▲**GROVE CITY**—Armstrong Cable Services

GROVER—See CANTON, PA (Zito Media)

GUILFORD TWP.—See SHIPPENSBURG, PA (Comcast Cable)

GULICH TWP.—See PHILIPSBURG BOROUGH, PA (Comcast Cable)

GUYS MILLS—See MEADVILLE, PA (Armstrong Cable Services)

HALFMOON TWP.—See STATE COLLEGE, PA (Comcast Cable)

HALIFAX—See LEBANON, PA (Comcast Cable)

HALLAM BOROUGH—See YORK, PA (Comcast Cable)

HALLSTEAD (SUSQUEHANNA COUNTY)—See CARBONDALE, PA (Adams Digital Cable)

HALLSTEAD—See CARBONDALE, PA (Adams Digital Cable)

▲**HAMBURG**—Comcast Cable. Now served by READING, PA [PA0012]

HAMBURG—See READING, PA (Comcast Cable)

HAMILTON TWP. (MONROE COUNTY)—See STROUDSBURG, PA (Blue Ridge Communications)

HAMILTONBAN TWP.—See GETTYSBURG, PA (Comcast Cable)

HAMLIN TWP.—See KANE, PA (Comcast Cable)

HAMLIN—See CARBONDALE, PA (Adams Digital Cable)

HAMPDEN TWP. (CUMBERLAND COUNTY)—See HARRISBURG, PA (Comcast Cable)

HAMPTON TWP. (ALLEGHENY COUNTY)—See ZELIENOPLE, PA (Armstrong Cable Services)

HAMPTON TWP. (ALLEGHENY COUNTY)—See TARENTUM BOROUGH, PA (Comcast Cable)

▲**HAMPTON TWP.**—Comcast Cable. Now served by TARENTUM BOROUGH, PA [PA0424]

HAMPTON TWP.—See TARENTUM BOROUGH, PA (Comcast Cable)

▲**HANOVER TWP. (LEHIGH COUNTY)**—Formerly served by NORTHAMPTON BOROUGH, PA [PA0008]. RCN Corp. This cable system has converted to IPTV

HANOVER TWP. (LUZERNE COUNTY)—See WILKES-BARRE, PA (Service Electric Cable Company)

▲**HANOVER TWP. (NORTHAMPTON COUNTY)**—Formerly served by NORTHAMPTON BOROUGH, PA [PA0008]. RCN Corp. This cable system has converted to IPTV

HANOVER TWP.—See LEHIGH VALLEY, PA (Service Electric Cable TV & Communications)

HANOVER—See YORK, PA (Comcast Cable)

▲**HARBORCREEK TWP.**—Time Warner Cable

HARFORD TWP.—See LOOMIS LAKE, PA (Adams Digital Cable)

HARFORD—See LOOMIS LAKE, PA (Adams Digital Cable)

HARMAR TWP.—See TARENTUM BOROUGH, PA (Comcast Cable)

HARMONY TWP.—See CARBONDALE, PA (Adams Digital Cable)

HARMONY—See ZELIENOPLE, PA (Armstrong Cable Services)

HARRIS TWP. (CENTRE COUNTY)—See STATE COLLEGE, PA (Comcast Cable)

▲**HARRISBURG**—Formerly served by Gap Cable TV. No longer in operation

▲**HARRISBURG**—Comcast Cable

HARRISVILLE—See GROVE CITY, PA (Armstrong Cable Services)

HARTFORD TWP.—See MERCER COUNTY, OH (Time Warner Cable)

HARTFORD TWP.—See SHARON, OH (Time Warner Cable)

HARTLETON—See MIFFLINBURG, PA (Atlantic Broadband)

HARTLEY TWP.—See MIFFLINBURG, PA (Atlantic Broadband)

▲**HARTSLOG**—Formerly served by Milestone Communications LP. No longer in operation

HARVEYS LAKE BOROUGH—See DALLAS, PA (Comcast Cable)

HARWICK—See TARENTUM BOROUGH, PA (Comcast Cable)

HASTINGS—See BLAIRSVILLE, PA (Comcast Cable)

HATBORO—See LANSDALE, PA (Comcast Cable)

HATFIELD—See SELLERSVILLE, PA (Comcast Cable)

HAVERFORD TWP.—See LANSDALE, PA (Comcast Cable)

▲**HAWLEY**—Blue Ridge Communications

HAWTHORN—See PUNXSUTAWNEY, PA (Comcast Cable)

HAYCOCK TWP.—See LEHIGH VALLEY, PA (Service Electric Cable TV & Communications)

HAYSVILLE—See PITTSBURGH, PA (Comcast Cable)

HAZEL HURST—See KANE, PA (Comcast Cable)

▲**HAZEN**—Zito Media

HAZLE TWP.—See HAZLETON, PA (Service Electric Cablevision)

▲**HAZLETON**—Service Electric Cablevision

HEGINS TWP.—See LYKENS, PA (Comcast Cable)

HEIDELBERG TWP. (LEHIGH COUNTY)—See PALMERTON, PA (Blue Ridge Communications)

HEIDELBERG TWP. (YORK COUNTY)—See YORK, PA (Comcast Cable)

▲**HEIDELBERG TWP.**—Formerly served by NORTHAMPTON BOROUGH, PA [PA0008]. RCN Corp. This cable system has converted to IPTV

HEIDELBURG—See PITTSBURGH, PA (Comcast Cable)

HELLAM (YORK COUNTY)—See LANCASTER, PA (Comcast Cable)

HELLAM TWP. (YORK COUNTY)—See LANCASTER, PA (Comcast Cable)

HELLAM TWP. (YORK COUNTY)—See YORK, PA (Comcast Cable)

HELLERTOWN BORO—See LEHIGH VALLEY, PA (Service Electric Cable TV & Communications)

▲**HELLERTOWN BOROUGH**—Formerly served by NORTHAMPTON BOROUGH, PA [PA0008]. RCN Corp. This cable system has converted to IPTV

▲**HEMLOCK FARMS DEVELOPMENT**—Blue Ridge Communications

HEMLOCK TWP.—See SUNBURY, PA (Service Electric Cablevision)

HEMPFIELD TWP. (MERCER COUNTY)—See GREENVILLE, PA (Time Warner Cable)

HEMPFIELD TWP. (WESTMORELAND COUNTY)—See GREENSBURG, PA (Comcast Cable)

HENDERSON TWP. (HUNTINGDON COUNTY)—See HUNTINGDON, PA (Comcast Cable)

HENDERSON TWP. (JEFFERSON COUNTY)—See PUNXSUTAWNEY, PA (Comcast Cable)

HENRY CLAY TWP.—See MARKLEYSBURG, PA (Comcast Cable)

HEPBURN TWP.—See WILLIAMSPORT, PA (Comcast Cable)

HEPBURNVILLE—See COGAN STATION, PA (Zito Media)

HEREFORD TWP. (BERKS COUNTY)—See POTTSTOWN, PA (Comcast Cable)

HEREFORD TWP. (BERKS COUNTY)—See LEHIGH VALLEY, PA (Service Electric Cable TV & Communications)

HERMITAGE—See MERCER COUNTY, PA (Time Warner Cable)

HERMITAGE—See SHARON, PA (Time Warner Cable)

▲**HERNDON**—Formerly served by Pike's Peak TV Association. No longer in operation

HERRICK TWP.—See CARBONDALE, PA (Adams Digital Cable)

▲**HERSHEY**—Comcast Cable. Now served by LEBANON, PA [PA0024]

HERSHEY—See LEBANON, PA (Comcast Cable)

HIDDEN VALLEY—See CONNELLSVILLE, PA (Armstrong Cable Services)

HIGHLAND TWP. (CHESTER COUNTY)—See OXFORD, PA (Armstrong Cable Services)

HIGHLAND TWP. (ELK COUNTY)—See KANE, PA (Comcast Cable)

HIGHROCK—See GETTYSBURG, PA (Comcast Cable)

HIGHSPIRE—See HARRISBURG, PA (Comcast Cable)

HILLIARDS—See GROVE CITY, PA (Armstrong Cable Services)

HILLSGROVE—See ELDRED TWP., PA (Herr Cable Co.)

HILLTOWN TWP.—See SELLERSVILLE, PA (Comcast Cable)

▲**HOLLAND**—Comcast Cable. Now served by JAMISON, PA [PA0033]

HOLLAND—See JAMISON, PA (Comcast Cable)

HOLLIDAYSBURG—See ALTOONA, PA (Atlantic Broadband)

HOLLISTERVILLE—See CARBONDALE, PA (Adams Digital Cable)

HOLLSOPPLE—See JOHNSTOWN, PA (Atlantic Broadband)

HOME—See KISKIMINETAS TWP., PA (Comcast Cable)

HOMER CITY—See BLAIRSVILLE, PA (Comcast Cable)

HOMESTEAD—See BETHEL PARK, PA (Comcast Cable)

HOMEWOOD—See ZELIENOPLE, PA (Armstrong Cable Services)

▲**HONESDALE**—Blue Ridge Communications

HONEY BROOK BOROUGH—See BIRDSBORO, PA (Service Electric Cablevision)

▲**HONEY GROVE**—Formerly served by Nittany Media. No longer in operation

HONEYBROOK TWP. (CHESTER COUNTY)—See BIRDSBORO, PA (Service Electric Cablevision)

HOOKSTOWN—See BEAVER VALLEY, PA (Comcast Cable)

HOOVERSVILLE—See CENTRAL CITY BOROUGH, PA (Comcast Cable)

HOP BOTTOM—See LOOMIS LAKE, PA (Adams Digital Cable)

HOPEWELL TWP.—See WALNUT BOTTOM, PA (Kuhn Communications)

HOPEWELL—See HUNTINGDON, PA (Comcast Cable)

HORSHAM TWP.—See LANSDALE, PA (Comcast Cable)

HORTON TWP. (ELK COUNTY)—See BROCKWAY, PA (Brockway TV Inc.)

HORTON TWP. (ELK COUNTY)—See PUNXSUTAWNEY, PA (Comcast Cable)

HOUTZDALE—See PHILIPSBURG BOROUGH, PA (Comcast Cable)

HOVEY TWP.—See CLARION BOROUGH, PA (Comcast Cable)

HOWARD—See STATE COLLEGE, PA (Comcast Cable)

HOWE TWP.—See ELIZABETHTOWN, PA (Comcast Cable)

HUBBARD TWP.—See MERCER COUNTY, OH (Time Warner Cable)

HUBLERSBURG—See ZION, PA (Tele-Media)

HUBLEY TWP.—See LYKENS, PA (Comcast Cable)

HUEFNER—See NORTH CLARION, PA (Armstrong Cable Services)

HUEY—See CLARION BOROUGH, PA (Comcast Cable)

HUGHESTOWN—See DUNMORE, PA (Comcast Cable)

HUGHESVILLE—See WILLIAMSPORT, PA (Comcast Cable)

HULMEVILLE—See LEVITTOWN, PA (Comcast Cable)

HUMMELSTOWN—See LEBANON, PA (Comcast Cable)

HUNKER—See GREENSBURG, PA (Comcast Cable)

HUNLOCK CREEK—See MESHOPPEN, PA (Blue Ridge Communications)

HUNLOCK CREEK—See BERWICK, PA (MetroCast Communications)

HUNTINGDON—See McALEVYS FORT, PA (Atlantic Broadband)

▲ **HUNTINGDON**—Comcast Cable

▲ **HUNTINGTON TWP. (Luzerne County)**—Formerly served by Comcast Cable. No longer in operation

HUSTON TWP. (BLAIR COUNTY)—See ALTOONA, PA (Atlantic Broadband)

HUSTON TWP. (CENTRE COUNTY)—See UNION TWP. (Centre County), PA (Country Cable)

HUSTON TWP. (CLEARFIELD COUNTY)—See SABULA, PA (Zito Media)

HYDE PARK—See KISKIMINETAS TWP., PA (Comcast Cable)

HYDE—See CLEARFIELD, PA (Atlantic Broadband)

HYDETOWN—See MEADVILLE, PA (Armstrong Cable Services)

▲ **HYNDMAN BOROUGH**—Formerly served by Adelphia Communications. Now served by CENTRAL CITY BOROUGH, PA [PA0132]

HYNDMAN BOROUGH—See CENTRAL CITY BOROUGH, PA (Comcast Cable)

▲ **ICKESBURG**—Nittany Media Inc. Now served by LEWISTOWN (formerly McAlisterville), PA [PA0365]

ICKESBURG—See LEWISTOWN, PA (Nittany Media Inc.)

IMLER—See ALTOONA, PA (Atlantic Broadband)

INDEPENDENT LAKE—See CARBONDALE, PA (Adams Digital Cable)

▲ **INDIAN CREEK**—Laurel Highland Television Co.

INDIAN HEAD—See INDIAN CREEK, PA (Laurel Highland Television Co.)

INDIAN LAKE—See CENTRAL CITY BOROUGH, PA (Comcast Cable)

INDIAN ORCHARD—See HONESDALE, PA (Blue Ridge Communications)

▲ **INDIANA**—Formerly served by Adelphia Communications. Now served by BLAIRSVILLE, PA [PA0320]

INDIANA—See BLAIRSVILLE, PA (Comcast Cable)

INDIANOLA—See TARENTUM BOROUGH, PA (Comcast Cable)

INDUSTRY—See BEAVER FALLS, PA (Comcast Cable)

INGRAM—See PITTSBURGH, PA (Comcast Cable)

IRVINE—See YOUNGSVILLE, PA (Youngsville TV Corp.)

IRVONA—See COALPORT, PA (Comcast Cable)

IRWIN TWP. (VENANGO COUNTY)—See GROVE CITY, PA (Armstrong Cable Services)

IRWIN—See GREENSBURG, PA (Comcast Cable)

IVYLAND (PORTIONS)—See JAMISON, PA (Comcast Cable)

JACKSON CENTER BOROUGH—See GROVE CITY, PA (Armstrong Cable Services)

JACKSON CENTER—See GROVE CITY, PA (Armstrong Cable Services)

JACKSON TWP. (BUTLER COUNTY)—See GROVE CITY, PA (Armstrong Cable Services)

JACKSON TWP. (BUTLER COUNTY)—See ZELIENOPLE, PA (Armstrong Cable Services)

JACKSON TWP. (CAMBRIA COUNTY)—See JOHNSTOWN, PA (Atlantic Broadband)

JACKSON TWP. (COLUMBIA COUNTY)—See BERWICK, PA (MetroCast Communications)

JACKSON TWP. (MONROE COUNTY)—See STROUDSBURG, PA (Blue Ridge Communications)

JACKSON TWP. (NORTHUMBERLAND COUNTY)—See SUNBURY, PA (Service Electric Cablevision)

JACKSON TWP. (SNYDER COUNTY)—See SUNBURY, PA (Service Electric Cablevision)

JACKSON TWP.—See CARBONDALE, PA (Adams Digital Cable)

JACOBUS—See YORK, PA (Comcast Cable)

JAMES CITY—See KANE, PA (Comcast Cable)

▲ **JAMESTOWN**—Formerly served by Cebridge Connections. Now served by MEADVILLE, PA [PA0062]

JAMESTOWN—See MEADVILLE, PA (Armstrong Cable Services)

▲ **JAMISON**—Comcast Cable

JAY TWP.—See WEEDVILLE, PA (Zito Media)

JEANNETTE—See GREENSBURG, PA (Comcast Cable)

JEDDO BOROUGH—See HAZLETON, PA (Service Electric Cablevision)

JEFFERSON (GREENE COUNTY)—See UNIONTOWN, PA (Atlantic Broadband)

JEFFERSON COUNTY—See PUNXSUTAWNEY, PA (Comcast Cable)

JEFFERSON TWP. (LACKAWANNA COUNTY)—See CARBONDALE, PA (Adams Digital Cable)

JEFFERSON TWP.—See SHARON, PA (Time Warner Cable)

JENKINS TWP. (LUZERNE COUNTY)—See DUNMORE, PA (Comcast Cable)

JENKINTOWN BOROUGH—See WILLOW GROVE, PA (Comcast Cable)

JENNER TWP. (SOMERSET COUNTY)—See JOHNSTOWN, PA (Atlantic Broadband)

JENNERS—See CENTRAL CITY BOROUGH, PA (Comcast Cable)

JENNERSTOWN—See CENTRAL CITY BOROUGH, PA (Comcast Cable)

JERMYN—See CARBONDALE, PA (Adams Digital Cable)

JEROME—See JOHNSTOWN, PA (Atlantic Broadband)

JERSEY SHORE—See WILLIAMSPORT, PA (Comcast Cable)

JESSUP—See DUNMORE, PA (Comcast Cable)

JIM THORPE—See PALMERTON, PA (Blue Ridge Communications)

JOFFRE—See BURGETTSTOWN, PA (Blue Devil Cable TV Inc.)

▲ **JOHNSONBURG**—Johnsonburg Community TV Co.

▲ **JOHNSONBURG**—Zito Media

▲ **JOHNSTOWN**—Atlantic Broadband

JONESTOWN (COLUMBIA COUNTY)—See DUSHORE, PA (Blue Ridge Communications)

JONESTOWN (LEBANON COUNTY)—See LEBANON, PA (Comcast Cable)

JULIAN—See UNION TWP. (Centre County), PA (Country Cable)

JUNIATA TERRACE—See LEWISTOWN, PA (Comcast Cable)

JUNIATA TWP. (BLAIR COUNTY)—See ALTOONA, PA (Atlantic Broadband)

JUNIATA TWP. (HUNTINGDON COUNTY)—See HUNTINGDON, PA (Comcast Cable)

JUNIATA TWP. (PERRY COUNTY)—See ELIZABETHTOWN, PA (Comcast Cable)

▲ **KANE**—Comcast Cable

KARNS CITY—See BUTLER, PA (Armstrong Cable Services)

KARTHAUS TWP.—See SNOW SHOE, PA (Tele-Media)

KASKA—See SCHUYLKILL TWP., PA (MetroCast Communications)

KEISTERVILLE—See UNIONTOWN, PA (Atlantic Broadband)

▲ **KELLETTVILLE**—Formerly served by Cebridge Connections. No longer in operation

KELLY TWP. (UNION COUNTY)—See DANVILLE, PA (CATV Service Inc.)

KENHORST—See READING, PA (Comcast Cable)

KENNEDYVILLE—See WELLSBORO, PA (Blue Ridge Communications)

KENNERDELL—See GROVE CITY, PA (Armstrong Cable Services)

▲ **KENNETT SQUARE**—Comcast Cable

KENNETT TWP.—See KENNETT SQUARE, PA (Comcast Cable)

KERSEY—See ST. MARY'S, PA (Zito Media)

KIDDER TWP. (CARBON COUNTY)—See PALMERTON, PA (Blue Ridge Communications)

KILBUCK—See PITTSBURGH, PA (Comcast Cable)

KIMMELL TWP.—See ALTOONA, PA (Atlantic Broadband)

▲ **KING OF PRUSSIA**—Comcast Cable

KING TWP.—See WOODBURY, PA (Atlantic Broadband)

KINGSLEY—See LOOMIS LAKE, PA (Adams Digital Cable)

KINGSTON (LUZERNE COUNTY)—See WILKES-BARRE, PA (Service Electric Cable Company)

KINGSTON TWP.—See DALLAS, PA (Comcast Cable)

KINSMAN TWP.—See MEADVILLE, OH (Armstrong Cable Services)

KINSMAN—See MEADVILLE, OH (Armstrong Cable Services)

KINZERS—See LANCASTER, PA (Comcast Cable)

KIRKWOOD (PORTIONS)—See CARBONDALE, NY (Adams Digital Cable)

▲ **KISKIMINETAS TWP.**—Comcast Cable

KISTLER—See PHILIPSBURG BOROUGH, PA (Comcast Cable)

▲ **KITTANNING**—Comcast Cable. Now served by KISKIMINETAS TWP., PA [PA0074]

KITTANNING—See KISKIMINETAS TWP., PA (Comcast Cable)

KLINE TWP.—See HAZLETON, PA (Service Electric Cablevision)

KNOX TWP. (CLARION COUNTY)—See SHIPPENVILLE, PA (Atlantic Broadband)

KNOX TWP.—See CLEARFIELD, PA (Atlantic Broadband)

KNOX TWP.—See PUNXSUTAWNEY, PA (Comcast Cable)

KNOX—See SHIPPENVILLE, PA (Atlantic Broadband)

KOPPEL—See ZELIENOPLE, PA (Armstrong Cable Services)

KOSSUTH—See SHIPPENVILLE, PA (Atlantic Broadband)

KREAMER—See SUNBURY, PA (Service Electric Cablevision)

KULPMONT (NORTHUMBERLAND COUNTY)—See SUNBURY, PA (Service Electric Cablevision)

KUNKLE—See MESHOPPEN, PA (Blue Ridge Communications)

▲ **KUTZTOWN**—Hometown Utilicom. This cable system has converted to IPTV. See Kutztown, PA [PA5144]

▲ **KUTZTOWN**—Hometown Utilicom. Formerly [PA0452]. This cable system has converted to IPTV

KUTZTOWN—See BIRDSBORO, PA (Service Electric Cablevision)

▲ **KYLERTOWN**—Tele-Media. Now served by SNOWSHOE, PA [PA0188]

KYLERTOWN—See SNOW SHOE, PA (Tele-Media)

LA BELLE—See UNIONTOWN, PA (Atlantic Broadband)

LA PLUME—See DUNMORE, PA (Comcast Cable)

▲ **LA PORTE BOROUGH**—Comcast Cable

LACEYVILLE—See MESHOPPEN, PA (Blue Ridge Communications)

LACKAWAXEN TWP.—See MILFORD, PA (Blue Ridge Communications)

LACKAWONNOCK TWP.—See SHARON, PA (Time Warner Cable)

LAFLIN BOROUGH—See DUNMORE, PA (Comcast Cable)

▲ **LAIRDSVILLE**—Formerly served by Ralph Herr TV. No longer in operation

LAKE ARIEL—See CARBONDALE, PA (Adams Digital Cable)

LAKE CAREY—See MESHOPPEN, PA (Blue Ridge Communications)

LAKE CITY—See HARBORCREEK TWP., PA (Time Warner Cable)

LAKE COMO (VILLAGE)—See LAKEWOOD, PA (Hancock Video)

LAKE HARMONY—See POCONO, PA (MetroCast Communications)

LAKE LATONKA BOROUGH—See GROVE CITY, PA (Armstrong Cable Services)

LAKE LORAIN—See CARBONDALE, PA (Adams Digital Cable)

LAKE TWP. (MERCER COUNTY)—See GROVE CITY, PA (Armstrong Cable Services)

LAKE TWP. (WAYNE COUNTY)—See CARBONDALE, PA (Adams Digital Cable)

LAKE WINOLA—See MESHOPPEN, PA (Blue Ridge Communications)

LAKE WYNONAH—See AUBURN, PA (Comcast Cable)

LAKEVILLE—See CARBONDALE, PA (Adams Digital Cable)

▲ **LAKEWOOD**—Hancock Video

LAMAR TWP. (CLINTON COUNTY)—See WILLIAMSPORT, PA (Comcast Cable)

LAMARTINE—See SHIPPENVILLE, PA (Atlantic Broadband)

LAMBS CREEK—See WELLSBORO, PA (Blue Ridge Communications)

LANCASTER TWP. (BUTLER COUNTY)—See ZELIENOPLE, PA (Armstrong Cable Services)

▲ **LANCASTER**—Comcast Cable

LANDINGVILLE—See POTTSVILLE, PA (Comcast Cable)

LANDISBURG—See PERRY COUNTY, PA (Kuhn Communications)

LANESBORO—See CARBONDALE, PA (Adams Digital Cable)

LANGELOTH—See BURGETTSTOWN, PA (Blue Devil Cable TV Inc.)

LANGHORNE MANOR—See LEVITTOWN, PA (Comcast Cable)

LANGHORNE—See LEVITTOWN, PA (Comcast Cable)

▲ **LANSDALE**—Comcast Cable

LANSDOWNE—See WALLINGFORD, PA (Comcast Cable)

▲ **LANSDOWNE**—RCN Corp. Formerly served by Philadelphia (suburbs), PA [PA0447]. This cable system has converted to IPTV

LANSE—See SNOW SHOE, PA (Tele-Media)

LANSFORD—See PALMERTON, PA (Blue Ridge Communications)

LAPORTE TWP. (SULLIVAN COUNTY)—See LA PORTE BOROUGH, PA (Comcast Cable)

LARKSVILLE—See BERWICK, PA (MetroCast Communications)

LATHROP TWP.—See LOOMIS LAKE, PA (Adams Digital Cable)

LATIMORE TWP—See GETTYSBURG, PA (Comcast Cable)

▲ **LATROBE**—Comcast Cable. Now served by BLAIRSVILLE, PA [PA0320]

LATROBE—See BLAIRSVILLE, PA (Comcast Cable)

LAUREL MOUNTAIN—See BLAIRSVILLE, PA (Comcast Cable)

LAUREL RUN—See WILKES-BARRE, PA (Service Electric Cable Company)

LAURELDALE—See READING, PA (Comcast Cable)

▲ **LAURELTON**—Formerly served by D&E Communications. No longer in operation

LAURELTON—See MIFFLINBURG, PA (Atlantic Broadband)

LAVEROCK—See LANSDALE, PA (Comcast Cable)

LAWRENCE COUNTY (SOUTHERN PORTION)—See ZELIENOPLE, PA (Armstrong Cable Services)

LAWRENCE TWP. (CLEARFIELD COUNTY)—See CLEARFIELD, PA (Atlantic Broadband)

▲ **LAWRENCEVILLE**—Formerly served by Time Warner Cable. No longer in operation

LAYTON—See MATAMORAS, NJ (Cablevision Systems Corp.)

LE RAYSVILLE BOROUGH—See ROME, PA (Beaver Valley Cable Co.)

LE RAYSVILLE—See ROME, PA (Beaver Valley Cable Co.)

LEACOCK TWP. (LANCASTER COUNTY)—See LANCASTER, PA (Comcast Cable)

▲ **LEBANON**—Comcast Cable

LECONTES MILLS—See SNOW SHOE, PA (Tele-Media)

LEECHBURG—See KISKIMINETAS TWP., PA (Comcast Cable)

LEEPER—See NORTH CLARION, PA (Armstrong Cable Services)

LEESPORT—See READING, PA (Comcast Cable)

LEET TWP.—See PITTSBURGH, PA (Comcast Cable)

LEETSDALE—See PITTSBURGH, PA (Comcast Cable)

LEHIGH TWP. (NORTHAMPTON COUNTY)—See PALMERTON, PA (Blue Ridge Communications)

▲ **LEHIGH TWP.**—Formerly served by NORTHAMPTON BOROUGH, PA [PA0008]. RCN Corp. This cable system has converted to IPTV

▲ **LEHIGH VALLEY**—Service Electric Cable TV & Communications

LEHIGHTON—See PALMERTON, PA (Blue Ridge Communications)

LEHMAN TWP. (LUZERNE COUNTY)—See DALLAS, PA (Comcast Cable)

LEHMAN TWP. (PIKE COUNTY)—See STROUDSBURG, PA (Blue Ridge Communications)

LEMON TWP.—See MESHOPPEN, PA (Blue Ridge Communications)

LEMOYNE—See HARRISBURG, PA (Comcast Cable)

LENHARTSVILLE—See READING, PA (Comcast Cable)

LENOX TWP. (SUSQUEHANNA COUNTY)—See CARBONDALE, PA (Adams Digital Cable)

LEOLA—See LANCASTER, PA (Comcast Cable)

▲ **LEROY TWP.**—Blue Ridge Communications

LETTERKENNY TWP. (FRANKLIN COUNTY)—See SHIPPENSBURG, PA (Comcast Cable)

LETTERKENNY TWP.—See WALNUT BOTTOM, PA (Kuhn Communications)

▲ **LEVITTOWN**—Comcast Cable

LEWIS RUN—See BRADFORD, PA (Atlantic Broadband)

LEWIS TWP. (UNION COUNTY)—See MIFFLINBURG, PA (Atlantic Broadband)

▲ **LEWIS TWP.**—Eagles Mere & La Porte Cablevision Inc.

LEWISBERRY—See NEWBERRY TWP., PA (Blue Ridge Communications)

▲ **LEWISBURG**—Lewisburg CATV. Now served by DANVILLE, PA [PA0054]

▲ **LEWISBURG**—Windstream (formerly D&E Communications.) This cable system has converted to IPTV. See Lewisburg, PA [PA5118]

LEWISBURG—See DANVILLE, PA (CATV Service Inc.)

▲ **LEWISBURG**—Windstream. Formerly [PA0390]. This cable system has converted to IPTV

LEWISTOWN—See DERRY/DECATUR, PA (Atlantic Broadband)

▲ **LEWISTOWN**—Comcast Cable

▲ **LEWISTOWN**—Nittany Media Inc.

LIBERTY TWP. (BEDFORD COUNTY)—See HUNTINGDON, PA (Comcast Cable)

LIBERTY TWP. (MERCER COUNTY)—See GROVE CITY, PA (Armstrong Cable Services)

LIBERTY TWP. (MONTOUR COUNTY)—See DANVILLE, PA (CATV Service Inc.)

LIBERTY—See PITTSBURGH, PA (Comcast Cable)

LICKINGVILLE—See NORTH CLARION, PA (Armstrong Cable Services)

LIGONIER TWP.—See BLAIRSVILLE, PA (Comcast Cable)

▲ **LIGONIER**—Formerly served by Adelphia Communications. Now served by BLAIRSVILLE, PA [PA0320]

LILLY—See CRESSON, PA (Comcast Cable)

LIMERICK TWP.—See POTTSTOWN, PA (Comcast Cable)

▲ **LIMESTONE TWP. (Lycoming County)**—Comcast Cable. Now served by WILLIAMSPORT, PA [PA0040]

LIMESTONE TWP. (MONTOUR COUNTY)—See DANVILLE, PA (CATV Service Inc.)

LIMESTONE TWP. (MONTOUR COUNTY)—See LEWIS TWP., PA (Eagles Mere & La Porte Cablevision Inc.)

LIMESTONE TWP. (UNION COUNTY)—See MIFFLINBURG, PA (Atlantic Broadband)

LIMESTONE TWP. (UNION COUNTY)—See SUNBURY, PA (Service Electric Cablevision)

LIMESTONE TWP.—See PUNXSUTAWNEY, PA (Comcast Cable)

LIMESTONE TWP.—See WILLIAMSPORT, PA (Comcast Cable)

▲ **LIMESTONE**—Atlantic Broadband

LINCOLN FALLS—See ROME, PA (Beaver Valley Cable Co.)

LINCOLN—See CENTRAL CITY BOROUGH, PA (Comcast Cable)

▲ **LINESVILLE**—Formerly served by Cebridge Connections. No longer in operation

LISTIE—See CONNELLSVILLE, PA (Armstrong Cable Services)

LITITZ—See EPHRATA, PA (Blue Ridge Communications)

LITTLE BRITAIN TWP.—See LANCASTER, PA (Comcast Cable)

LITTLE MAHANOY TWP.—See SUNBURY, PA (Service Electric Cablevision)

LITTLE MEADOWS BOROUGH—See ROME, PA (Beaver Valley Cable Co.)

LITTLE MEADOWS—See ROME, PA (Beaver Valley Cable Co.)

LITTLESTOWN—See GETTYSBURG, PA (Comcast Cable)

LITTLESTOWN—See YORK, PA (Comcast Cable)

▲ **LIVERPOOL**—Zampelli Electronics

LLEWELLYN—See POTTSVILLE, PA (Comcast Cable)

LLOYDELL—See ADAMS TWP. (Cambria County), PA (Comcast Cable)

▲ **LOCK HAVEN**—Comcast Cable

LOCUST TWP.—See SUNBURY, PA (Service Electric Cablevision)

LOGAN TWP. (BLAIR COUNTY)—See ALTOONA, PA (Atlantic Broadband)

LOGAN TWP. (HUNTINGDON COUNTY)—See HUNTINGDON, PA (Comcast Cable)

LOGANTON—See WILLIAMSPORT, PA (Comcast Cable)

▲ **LOGANTON**—TV Cable Associates Inc.

LOGANVILLE—See YORK, PA (Comcast Cable)

LONDON BRITAIN TWP.—See KENNETT SQUARE, PA (Comcast Cable)

LONDON GROVE TWP.—See KENNETT SQUARE, PA (Comcast Cable)

▲ **LONDONDERRY TWP. (BEDFORD COUNTY)**—Leap Cable TV

LONDONDERRY TWP. (CHESTER COUNTY)—See OXFORD, PA (Armstrong Cable Services)

LONDONDERRY TWP. (DAUPHIN COUNTY)—See LEBANON, PA (Comcast Cable)

LONG BRANCH—See CONNELLSVILLE, PA (Armstrong Cable Services)

LONG POND—See POCONO, PA (MetroCast Communications)

LONGSWAMP TWP.—See LEHIGH VALLEY, PA (Service Electric Cable TV & Communications)

LONGSWAMP TWP.—See BIRDSBORO, PA (Service Electric Cablevision)

▲ **LOOMIS LAKE**—Adams Digital Cable

LORAIN—See JOHNSTOWN, PA (Atlantic Broadband)

LORETTO—See CRESSON, PA (Comcast Cable)

LOWBER—See BETHEL PARK, PA (Comcast Cable)

LOWER ALLEN TWP.—See HARRISBURG, PA (Comcast Cable)

LOWER ALSACE TWP.—See READING, PA (Comcast Cable)

LOWER BURRELL—See TARENTUM BOROUGH, PA (Comcast Cable)

LOWER CHICHESTER TWP.—See WALLINGFORD, PA (Comcast Cable)

LOWER FRANKFORD TWP.—See SHIPPENSBURG, PA (Comcast Cable)

LOWER FREDERICK—See SELLERSVILLE, PA (Comcast Cable)

LOWER GWYNEDD TWP. (MONTGOMERY COUNTY)—See LANSDALE, PA (Comcast Cable)

LOWER GWYNEDD TWP. (MONTGOMERY COUNTY)—See NORRISTOWN, PA (Comcast Cable)

LOWER HEIDELBERG TWP. (BERKS COUNTY)—See READING, PA (Comcast Cable)

▲ **LOWER MACUNGIE TWP.**—Formerly served by NORTHAMPTON BOROUGH, PA [PA0008]. RCN Corp. This cable system has converted to IPTV

LOWER MACUNGIE TWP.—See LEHIGH VALLEY, PA (Service Electric Cable TV & Communications)

LOWER MAHANOY TWP.—See SUNBURY, PA (Service Electric Cablevision)

LOWER MAKEFIELD TWP.—See LEVITTOWN, PA (Comcast Cable)

▲ **LOWER MERION TWP.**—Comcast Cable

LOWER MIFFLIN TWP.—See SHIPPENSBURG, PA (Comcast Cable)

LOWER MORELAND TWP.—See WILLOW GROVE, PA (Comcast Cable)

LOWER MOUNT BETHEL TWP.—See LEHIGH VALLEY, PA (Service Electric Cable TV & Communications)

▲ **LOWER NAZARETH TWP.**—Formerly served by NORTHAMPTON BOROUGH, PA [PA0008]. RCN Corp. This cable system has converted to IPTV

LOWER NAZARETH TWP.—See LEHIGH VALLEY, PA (Service Electric Cable TV & Communications)

LOWER OXFORD TWP.—See OXFORD, PA (Armstrong Cable Services)

LOWER PAXTON TWP. (DAUPHIN COUNTY)—See HARRISBURG, PA (Comcast Cable)

LOWER POTTSGROVE TWP.—See POTTSTOWN, PA (Comcast Cable)

LOWER PROVIDENCE TWP.—See NORRISTOWN, PA (Comcast Cable)

LOWER SALFORD—See SELLERSVILLE, PA (Comcast Cable)

▲ **LOWER SAUCON TWP.**—Formerly served by NORTHAMPTON BOROUGH, PA [PA0008]. RCN Corp. This cable system has converted to IPTV

LOWER SAUCON TWP.—See LEHIGH VALLEY, PA (Service Electric Cable TV & Communications)

LOWER SOUTHAMPTON—See BENSALEM TWP., PA (Comcast Cable)

LOWER SWATARA TWP.—See HARRISBURG, PA (Comcast Cable)

LOWER TOWAMENSING TWP.—See PALMERTON, PA (Blue Ridge Communications)

LOWER TURKEYFOOT TWP.—See MARKLEYSBURG, PA (Comcast Cable)

LOWER TYRONE TWP.—See UNIONTOWN, PA (Atlantic Broadband)

LOWER WINDSOR TWP. (YORK COUNTY)—See YORK, PA (Comcast Cable)

LOWER YODER TWP.—See JOHNSTOWN, PA (Atlantic Broadband)

▲ **LOWHILL TWP.**—Formerly served by NORTHAMPTON BOROUGH, PA [PA0008]. RCN Corp. This cable system has converted to IPTV

LOWHILL TWP.—See LEHIGH VALLEY, PA (Service Electric Cable TV & Communications)

LOWVILLE—See MEADVILLE, PA (Armstrong Cable Services)

LOYALHANNA TWP. (WESTMORELAND COUNTY)—See BLAIRSVILLE, PA (Comcast Cable)

LOYALHANNA TWP.—See KISKIMINETAS TWP., PA (Comcast Cable)

LOYALSOCK TWP.—See WILLIAMSPORT, PA (Comcast Cable)

LOYSVILLE—See PERRY COUNTY, PA (Kuhn Communications)

LUCINDA—See NORTH CLARION, PA (Armstrong Cable Services)

LUDLOW—See SHEFFIELD, PA (WestPA.net Inc.)

LUNDYS LANE—See HARBORCREEK TWP., PA (Time Warner Cable)

LUZERNE—See SCRANTON, PA (Comcast Cable)

LYCOMING TWP.—See WILLIAMSPORT, PA (Comcast Cable)

LYKENS TWP.—See LYKENS, PA (Comcast Cable)

▲ **LYKENS**—Comcast Cable

LYNN TWP. (LEHIGH COUNTY)—See PALMERTON, PA (Blue Ridge Communications)

LYON STATION—See BIRDSBORO, PA (Service Electric Cablevision)

MACUNGIE—See LEHIGH VALLEY, PA (Service Electric Cable TV & Communications)

MADISON TWP. (COLUMBIA COUNTY)—See LEWIS TWP., PA (Eagles Mere & La Porte Cablevision Inc.)

MADISON TWP. (LACKAWANNA COUNTY)—See CARBONDALE, PA (Adams Digital Cable)

MADISON—See GREENSBURG, PA (Comcast Cable)

▲ **MAHAFFEY**—Formerly served by Adelphia Communications. Now served by PUNXSUTAWNEY, PA [PA0397]

MAHAFFEY—See PUNXSUTAWNEY, PA (Comcast Cable)

▲ **MAHANOY CITY**—Service Electric Cable Company

MAHANOY TWP.—See MAHANOY CITY, PA (Service Electric Cable Company)

MAHONING TWP. (CARBON COUNTY)—See PALMERTON, PA (Blue Ridge Communications)

MAHONING TWP. (LAWRENCE COUNTY)—See PULASKI, PA (Comcast Cable)

MAHONING TWP. (MONTOUR COUNTY)—See DANVILLE, PA (CATV Service Inc.)

MAIDENCREEK TWP. (BERKS COUNTY)—See READING, PA (Comcast Cable)

MAIDENCREEK TWP.—See BIRDSBORO, PA (Service Electric Cablevision)

MAIDENCREEK—See BIRDSBORO, PA (Service Electric Cablevision)

MAIN TWP.—See SUNBURY, PA (Service Electric Cablevision)

MAINESBURG—See WELLSBORO, PA (Blue Ridge Communications)

MAINSVILLE—See SHIPPENSBURG, PA (Comcast Cable)

MALVERN BOROUGH—See COATESVILLE, PA (Comcast Cable)

▲**MALVERN**—Comcast Cable. Now served by COATESVILLE (formerly Chester County), PA [PA0014]

MALVERN—See COATESVILLE, PA (Comcast Cable)

▲**MAMMOTH**—Citizens Cable Communications. This cable system has converted to IPTV. See Mammoth, PA [PA5000]

▲**MAMMOTH**—Citizens Cable Communications. Formerly [PA0400]. This cable system has converted to IPTV

MANCHESTER—See YORK, PA (Comcast Cable)

MANHEIM—See EPHRATA, PA (Blue Ridge Communications)

MANNS CHOICE—See BEDFORD, PA (Comcast Cable)

MANOR—See GREENSBURG, PA (Comcast Cable)

MANORVILLE—See KISKIMINETAS TWP., PA (Comcast Cable)

MANSFIELD—See WELLSBORO, PA (Blue Ridge Communications)

MAR LIN—See POTTSVILLE, PA (Comcast Cable)

MARBLE—See NORTH CLARION, PA (Armstrong Cable Services)

MARCUS HOOK—See WALLINGFORD, PA (Comcast Cable)

MARIANNA—See UNIONTOWN, PA (Atlantic Broadband)

▲**MARIENVILLE**—Formerly served by Cebridge Connections. Now served by MEADVILLE, PA [PA0062]

MARIENVILLE—See MEADVILLE, PA (Armstrong Cable Services)

MARIETTA—See ELIZABETHTOWN, PA (Comcast Cable)

MARION CENTER—See BLAIRSVILLE, PA (Comcast Cable)

MARION HEIGHTS—See SUNBURY, PA (Service Electric Cablevision)

MARION TWP. (BUTLER COUNTY)—See ZELIENOPLE, PA (Armstrong Cable Services)

MARION TWP. (CLARION COUNTY)—See CLARION BOROUGH, PA (Comcast Cable)

MARKLESBURG—See HUNTINGDON, PA (Comcast Cable)

MARKLETON—See CONNELLSVILLE, PA (Armstrong Cable Services)

▲**MARKLEYSBURG**—Comcast Cable

MARLBOROUGH TWP.—See SELLERSVILLE, PA (Comcast Cable)

MARPLE TWP. (DELAWARE COUNTY)—See LANSDALE, PA (Comcast Cable)

MARS—See ZELIENOPLE, PA (Armstrong Cable Services)

MARSHALL TWP.—See ZELIENOPLE, PA (Armstrong Cable Services)

MARTIC TWP.—See LANCASTER, PA (Comcast Cable)

MARTINSBURG—See ALTOONA, PA (Atlantic Broadband)

MARY D—See SCHUYLKILL TWP., PA (MetroCast Communications)

MARYSVILLE—See HARRISBURG, PA (Comcast Cable)

MASONTOWN—See UNIONTOWN, PA (Atlantic Broadband)

▲**MATAMORAS**—Cablevision Systems Corp.

MATHER—See UNIONTOWN, PA (Atlantic Broadband)

MATTAWANA—See McVEYTOWN, PA (Zampelli Electronics)

MAXATAWNY TWP.—See BIRDSBORO, PA (Service Electric Cablevision)

MAYBERRY TWP. (MONTOUR COUNTY)—See DANVILLE, PA (CATV Service Inc.)

MAYFIELD—See CARBONDALE, PA (Adams Digital Cable)

MAYPORT—See LIMESTONE, PA (Atlantic Broadband)

MAYTOWN—See ELIZABETHTOWN, PA (Comcast Cable)

MCADOO BOROUGH—See HAZLETON, PA (Service Electric Cablevision)

▲**MCALEVYS FORT**—Atlantic Broadband

MCALISTERVILLE—See LEWISTOWN, PA (Nittany Media Inc.)

MCCALMONT TWP.—See PUNXSUTAWNEY, PA (Comcast Cable)

MCCANDLESS—See PITTSBURGH, PA (Comcast Cable)

MCCLELLANDTOWN—See UNIONTOWN, PA (Atlantic Broadband)

MCCLURE—See DERRY/DECATUR, PA (Atlantic Broadband)

▲**MCCLURE**—Nittany Media Inc.

▲**McCONNELLSBURG**—Comcast Cable. Now served by SHIPPENSBURG, PA [PA0066]

MCCONNELLSBURG—See SHIPPENSBURG, PA (Comcast Cable)

MCDONALD—See BETHEL PARK, PA (Comcast Cable)

MCDONALD—See PITTSBURGH, PA (Comcast Cable)

MCEWENSVILLE—See DANVILLE, PA (CATV Service Inc.)

MCGRANN—See KISKIMINETAS TWP., PA (Comcast Cable)

MCINTYRE—See BLAIRSVILLE, PA (Comcast Cable)

MCKEAN BOROUGH—See HARBORCREEK TWP., PA (Time Warner Cable)

MCKEAN TWP. (ERIE COUNTY)—See HARBORCREEK TWP., PA (Time Warner Cable)

MCKEES ROCKS—See PITTSBURGH, PA (Comcast Cable)

MCKEESPORT—See PITTSBURGH, PA (Comcast Cable)

MCSHERRYSTOWN—See YORK, PA (Comcast Cable)

▲**MCVEYTOWN**—Zampelli Electronics

MEAD TWP. (WARREN COUNTY)—See WARREN, PA (Atlantic Broadband)

▲**MEADVILLE**—Armstrong Cable Services

MECHANICSBURG—See HARRISBURG, PA (Comcast Cable)

MECHANICSVILLE—See JAMISON, PA (Comcast Cable)

MEDIA (DELAWARE COUNTY)—See WALLINGFORD, PA (Comcast Cable)

MEHOOPANY—See MESHOPPEN, PA (Blue Ridge Communications)

MELCROFT—See INDIAN CREEK, PA (Laurel Highland Television Co.)

MENALLEN TWP. (FAYETTE COUNTY)—See UNIONTOWN, PA (Atlantic Broadband)

MENALLEN TWP.—See GETTYSBURG, PA (Comcast Cable)

▲**MERCER COUNTY**—Time Warner Cable

MERCER TWP. (PORTIONS)—See GROVE CITY, PA (Armstrong Cable Services)

MERCER—See GROVE CITY, PA (Armstrong Cable Services)

MERCERSBURG—See SHIPPENSBURG, PA (Comcast Cable)

MERRITTSTOWN—See UNIONTOWN, PA (Atlantic Broadband)

MESHOPPEN BOROUGH—See MESHOPPEN, PA (Blue Ridge Communications)

MESHOPPEN TWP.—See MESHOPPEN, PA (Blue Ridge Communications)

▲**MESHOPPEN**—Blue Ridge Communications

▲**METAL TWP.**—Valley Cable Systems

▲**MEYERSDALE**—Comcast Cable

MIDDLE PAXTON—See HARRISBURG, PA (Comcast Cable)

MIDDLE SMITHFIELD TWP.—See STROUDSBURG, PA (Blue Ridge Communications)

MIDDLE SMITHFIELD—See STROUDSBURG, PA (Blue Ridge Communications)

MIDDLE TAYLOR TWP.—See JOHNSTOWN, PA (Atlantic Broadband)

MIDDLEBURG BOROUGH—See SUNBURY, PA (Service Electric Cablevision)

MIDDLEBURG—See SUNBURY, PA (Service Electric Cablevision)

MIDDLEBURY—See WELLSBORO, PA (Blue Ridge Communications)

MIDDLECREEK TWP.—See SUNBURY, PA (Service Electric Cablevision)

MIDDLEPORT—See SCHUYLKILL TWP., PA (MetroCast Communications)

MIDDLESEX TWP. (CUMBERLAND COUNTY)—See SHIPPENSBURG, PA (Comcast Cable)

MIDDLETOWN TWP. (BUCKS COUNTY)—See LEVITTOWN, PA (Comcast Cable)

MIDDLETOWN—See HARRISBURG, PA (Comcast Cable)

▲**MIDLAND**—Comcast Cable. Now served by BEAVER FALLS, PA [PA0065]

MIDLAND—See BEAVER FALLS, PA (Comcast Cable)

▲**MIDWAY**—Formerly served by Adelphia Communications. Now served by BETHEL PARK, PA [PA0318]

MIDWAY—See BETHEL PARK, PA (Comcast Cable)

MIFFLIN—See LEWISTOWN, PA (Nittany Media Inc.)

▲**MIFFLINBURG (PORTIONS)**—Windstream. Formerly served by Lewisburg, PA [PA0390]. This cable system has converted to IPTV

▲**MIFFLINBURG**—Atlantic Broadband

▲**MIFFLINTOWN**—Nittany Media Inc. Now served by LEWISTOWN (formerly McAlisterville), PA [PA0365]

MIFFLINTOWN—See LEWISTOWN, PA (Nittany Media Inc.)

MIFFLINVILLE—See BERWICK, PA (MetroCast Communications)

MILESBURG—See STATE COLLEGE, PA (Comcast Cable)

MILFORD (PORTIONS)—See MATAMORAS, PA (Cablevision Systems Corp.)

MILFORD SQUARE—See NEWTOWN, PA (Comcast Cable)

MILFORD TWP. (PIKE COUNTY)—See MILFORD, PA (Blue Ridge Communications)

MILFORD TWP.—See LEWISTOWN, PA (Nittany Media Inc.)

▲**MILFORD**—Blue Ridge Communications

MILL CREEK—See HUNTINGDON, PA (Comcast Cable)

MILL HALL—See WILLIAMSPORT, PA (Comcast Cable)

MILL RUN—See INDIAN CREEK, PA (Laurel Highland Television Co.)

▲**MILL VILLAGE**—Formerly served by Cebridge Connections. Now served by MEADVILLE, PA [PA0062]

MILL VILLAGE—See MEADVILLE, PA (Armstrong Cable Services)

MILLBOURNE (DELAWARE COUNTY)—See WALLINGFORD, PA (Comcast Cable)

▲**MILLBOURNE**—RCN Corp. Formerly served by Philadelphia (suburbs), PA [PA0447]. This cable system has converted to IPTV

MILLCREEK TWP. (LEBANON COUNTY)—See LEBANON, PA (Comcast Cable)

MILLER TWP. (HUNTINGDON COUNTY)—See HUNTINGDON, PA (Comcast Cable)

MILLER TWP. (PERRY COUNTY)—See DUNCANNON, PA (Blue Ridge Communications)

▲**MILLERSBURG**—Comcast Cable. Now served by LEBANON, PA [PA0024]

MILLERSBURG—See LEBANON, PA (Comcast Cable)

MILLERSTOWN—See ELIZABETHTOWN, PA (Comcast Cable)

MILLERSVILLE—See LANCASTER, PA (Comcast Cable)

▲**MILLHEIM**—Millheim TV Transmission Co.

▲**MILLMONT**—Formerly served by D&E Communications. No longer in operation

MILLMONT—See MIFFLINBURG, PA (Atlantic Broadband)

MILLRIFT—See MATAMORAS, PA (Cablevision Systems Corp.)

MILLSBORO—See UNIONTOWN, PA (Atlantic Broadband)

MILLVALE—See PITTSBURGH, PA (Comcast Cable)

MILLVIEW—See ROME, PA (Beaver Valley Cable Co.)

MILLVILLE—See BERWICK, PA (MetroCast Communications)

MILROY—See REEDSVILLE, PA (Comcast Cable)

MILTON—See DANVILLE, PA (CATV Service Inc.)

MINERAL POINT—See JOHNSTOWN, PA (Atlantic Broadband)

MINERAL TWP.—See FRANKLIN (Venango County), PA (Time Warner Cable)

MINERSVILLE—See POTTSVILLE, PA (Comcast Cable)

MINGOVILLE—See ZION, PA (Tele-Media)

MOCANAQUA—See BERWICK, PA (MetroCast Communications)

MODENA—See COATESVILLE, PA (Comcast Cable)

MOHNTON—See READING, PA (Comcast Cable)

MONACA—See ROCHESTER, PA (Comcast Cable)

MONAGHAN TWP.—See GETTYSBURG, PA (Comcast Cable)

MONESSEN—See PITTSBURGH, PA (Comcast Cable)

MONONGAHELA TWP.—See UNIONTOWN, PA (Atlantic Broadband)

MONONGAHELA—See PITTSBURGH, PA (Comcast Cable)

MONROE (CLARION COUNTY)—See LIMESTONE, PA (Atlantic Broadband)

MONROE TWP. (SNYDER COUNTY)—See SUNBURY, PA (Service Electric Cablevision)

MONROE TWP.—See MESHOPPEN, PA (Blue Ridge Communications)

MONROE—See MOUNT PLEASANT MILLS, PA (Zampelli Electronics)

MONROETON BOROUGH—See TOWANDA, PA (Comcast Cable)

▲**MONROEVILLE**—Comcast Cable

MONROEVILLE—See BLAIRSVILLE, PA (Comcast Cable)

MONT ALTO—See SHIPPENSBURG, PA (Comcast Cable)

MONTAGUE TWP.—See MATAMORAS, NJ (Cablevision Systems Corp.)

▲**MONTGOMERY**—Comcast Cable. Now served by WILLIAMSPORT, PA [PA0040]

MONTGOMERY—See WILLIAMSPORT, PA (Comcast Cable)

MONTGOMERYVILLE—See LANSDALE, PA (Comcast Cable)

MONTOUR COUNTY—See DANVILLE, PA (CATV Service Inc.)

MONTOUR TWP. (COLUMBIA COUNTY)—See SUNBURY, PA (Service Electric Cablevision)

MONTOURSVILLE—See WILLIAMSPORT, PA (Comcast Cable)

▲**MONTROSE**—Time Warner Cable

▲**MONUMENT**—Formerly served by Monument TV. No longer in operation

MOON TWP.—See PITTSBURGH, PA (Comcast Cable)

▲**MOORE TWP.**—Formerly served by NORTHAMPTON BOROUGH, PA [PA0008]. RCN Corp. This cable system has converted to IPTV

MOORE TWP.—See LEHIGH VALLEY, PA (Service Electric Cable TV & Communications)

MOORESVILLE—See BRAVE, WV (Zito Media)

MOOSIC—See SCRANTON, PA (Comcast Cable)

MORGAN—See PITTSBURGH, PA (Comcast Cable)

MORRIS TWP.—See HUNTINGDON, PA (Comcast Cable)

MORRISDALE—See SNOW SHOE, PA (Tele-Media)

MORRISVILLE—See BENSALEM TWP., PA (Comcast Cable)

MORTON TWP.—See WALLINGFORD, PA (Comcast Cable)

▲**MORTON**—RCN Corp. Formerly served by Philadelphia (suburbs), PA [PA0447]. This cable system has converted to IPTV

MOSCOW (LACKAWANNA COUNTY)—See DUNMORE, PA (Comcast Cable)

MOUNT CARBON—See POTTSVILLE, PA (Comcast Cable)

MOUNT CARMEL BOROUGH—See SUNBURY, PA (Service Electric Cablevision)

MOUNT CARMEL TWP. (NORTHUMBERLAND COUNTY)—See SUNBURY, PA (Service Electric Cablevision)

MOUNT GRETNA—See LEBANON, PA (Comcast Cable)

MOUNT HOLLY SPRINGS—See SHIPPENSBURG, PA (Comcast Cable)

MOUNT JEWETT—See KANE, PA (Comcast Cable)

MOUNT LEBANON TWP.—See BETHEL PARK, PA (Comcast Cable)

▲**MOUNT MORRIS**—Comcast Cable. Now served by WAYNESBURG, PA [PA0134]

MOUNT MORRIS—See WAYNESBURG, PA (Comcast Cable)

▲**MOUNT OLIVER**—Mount Oliver TV Cable/Adelphia Cable. Now served by BETHEL PARK, PA [PA0318]

MOUNT OLIVER—See BETHEL PARK, PA (Comcast Cable)

MOUNT PENN—See READING, PA (Comcast Cable)

▲**MOUNT PLEASANT MILLS**—Zampelli Electronics

MOUNT PLEASANT TWP. (COLUMBIA COUNTY)—See SUNBURY, PA (Service Electric Cablevision)

MOUNT PLEASANT TWP. (WAYNE COUNTY)—See CARBONDALE, PA (Adams Digital Cable)

MOUNT PLEASANT TWP. (WESTMORELAND COUNTY)—See CONNELLSVILLE, PA (Armstrong Cable Services)

MOUNT PLEASANT—See GREENSBURG, PA (Comcast Cable)

MOUNT POCONO—See STROUDSBURG, PA (Blue Ridge Communications)

MOUNT UNION—See PHILIPSBURG BOROUGH, PA (Comcast Cable)

MOUNT WOLF—See YORK, PA (Comcast Cable)

MOUNTAIN TOP—See BERWICK, PA (MetroCast Communications)

MOUNTAIN TOP—See WILKES-BARRE, PA (Service Electric Cable Company)

MOUNTVILLE—See LANCASTER, PA (Comcast Cable)

MUDDYCREEK TWP.—See ZELIENOPLE, PA (Armstrong Cable Services)

MUHLENBERG TWP.—See READING, PA (Comcast Cable)

MUHLENBERG—See MESHOPPEN, PA (Blue Ridge Communications)

MUNCY CREEK TWP.—See WILLIAMSPORT, PA (Comcast Cable)

MUNCY VALLEY—See DUSHORE, PA (Blue Ridge Communications)

MUNCY—See WILLIAMSPORT, PA (Comcast Cable)

MUNHALL—See BETHEL PARK, PA (Comcast Cable)

▲**MURRYSVILLE**—Formerly served by Adelphia Communications. No longer in operation

MYERSTOWN—See LEBANON, PA (Comcast Cable)

NANTICOKE—See SCRANTON, PA (Comcast Cable)

NANTICOKE—See BERWICK, PA (MetroCast Communications)

▲**NANTY GLO**—Formerly served by Adelphia Communications. Now served by ADAMS TWP. (Cambria County), PA [PA0133]

NANTY GLO—See ADAMS TWP. (Cambria County), PA (Comcast Cable)

NANTY-GLO (PORTIONS)—See JOHNSTOWN, PA (Atlantic Broadband)

NAPIER TWP. (BEDFORD COUNTY)—See BEDFORD, PA (Comcast Cable)

NARBERTH BOROUGH—See LOWER MERION TWP., PA (Comcast Cable)

NARVON—See LANCASTER, PA (Comcast Cable)

NATRONA HEIGHTS—See TARENTUM BOROUGH, PA (Comcast Cable)

NAZARETH BORO—See LEHIGH VALLEY, PA (Service Electric Cable TV & Communications)

▲**NAZARETH BOROUGH**—Formerly served by NORTHAMPTON BOROUGH, PA [PA0008]. RCN Corp. This cable system has converted to IPTV

▲**NEELYTON**—Formerly served by Valley Cable Systems. No longer in operation

NEMACOLIN—See UNIONTOWN, PA (Atlantic Broadband)

NESCOPECK—See BERWICK, PA (MetroCast Communications)

NESQUEHONING—See PALMERTON, PA (Blue Ridge Communications)

NETHER PROVIDENCE TWP.—See WALLINGFORD, PA (Comcast Cable)

NEVILLE TWP.—See PITTSBURGH, PA (Comcast Cable)

NEW ALBANY—See DUSHORE, PA (Blue Ridge Communications)

NEW ALEXANDRIA—See GREENSBURG, PA (Comcast Cable)

▲**NEW BALTIMORE**—Laurel Cable LP

NEW BEAVER—See ZELIENOPLE, PA (Armstrong Cable Services)

NEW BEAVER—See BEAVER FALLS, PA (Comcast Cable)

NEW BERLIN—See SUNBURY, PA (Service Electric Cablevision)

▲**NEW BETHLEHEM**—Formerly served by Adelphia Communications. Now served by PUNXSUTAWNEY, PA [PA0397]

NEW BETHLEHEM—See LIMESTONE, PA (Atlantic Broadband)

NEW BETHLEHEM—See PUNXSUTAWNEY, PA (Comcast Cable)

▲**NEW BLOOMFIELD**—Nittany Media Inc. Now served by LEWISTOWN (formerly McAlisterville), PA [PA0365]

NEW BLOOMFIELD—See LEWISTOWN, PA (Nittany Media Inc.)

NEW BRIGHTON—See BEAVER FALLS, PA (Comcast Cable)

NEW BRITAIN—See JAMISON, PA (Comcast Cable)

NEW BUFFALO (PORTIONS)—See DUNCANNON, PA (Blue Ridge Communications)

▲**NEW CASTLE**—Comcast Cable. Now served by NEW MIDDLETOWN, OH [OH0145]

NEW COLUMBIA TWP.—See DANVILLE, PA (CATV Service Inc.)

▲**NEW COLUMBIA**—Formerly served by D&E Communications. No longer in operation

NEW CUMBERLAND—See HARRISBURG, PA (Comcast Cable)

NEW EAGLE—See PITTSBURGH, PA (Comcast Cable)

NEW FLORENCE—See ARMAGH, PA (Comcast Cable)

NEW FREEDOM—See GETTYSBURG, PA (Comcast Cable)

NEW GALILEE—See BEAVER FALLS, PA (Comcast Cable)

NEW GARDEN TWP.—See KENNETT SQUARE, PA (Comcast Cable)

NEW GRENADA—See WATERFALL, PA (Waterfall Community TV)

NEW HANOVER TWP. (MONTGOMERY COUNTY)—See POTTSTOWN, PA (Comcast Cable)

NEW HOLLAND—See LANCASTER, PA (Comcast Cable)

NEW HOPE (BUCKS COUNTY)—See NEWTOWN, PA (Comcast Cable)

NEW KENSINGTON—See TARENTUM BOROUGH, PA (Comcast Cable)

NEW LONDON TWP.—See KENNETT SQUARE, PA (Comcast Cable)

NEW MILFORD (SUSQUEHANNA COUNTY)—See CARBONDALE, PA (Adams Digital Cable)

NEW MILFORD BOROUGH—See CARBONDALE, PA (Adams Digital Cable)

▲**NEW MILFORD TWP.**—Formerly served by Adams Cable Service. Now served by CARBONDALE, PA [PA0067]

NEW MILFORD TWP.—See CARBONDALE, PA (Adams Digital Cable)

NEW OXFORD—See GETTYSBURG, PA (Comcast Cable)

NEW PARIS—See BEDFORD, PA (Comcast Cable)

NEW PHILADELPHIA—See SCHUYLKILL TWP., PA (MetroCast Communications)

NEW RINGGOLD—See MAHANOY CITY, PA (Service Electric Cable Company)

NEW SEWICKLEY TWP.—See ZELIENOPLE, PA (Armstrong Cable Services)

NEW SEWICKLEY TWP.—See PITTSBURGH, PA (Comcast Cable)

NEW STANTON—See GREENSBURG, PA (Comcast Cable)

▲**NEW WILMINGTON**—Armstrong Cable Services

▲**NEWBERRY TWP.**—Blue Ridge Communications

▲**NEWBURG**—Kuhn Communications. Now served by WALNUT BOTTOM, PA [PA0220]

NEWBURG—See WALNUT BOTTOM, PA (Kuhn Communications)

NEWELL—See CONNELLSVILLE, PA (Armstrong Cable Services)

NEWPORT TWP.—See BERWICK, PA (MetroCast Communications)

▲**NEWPORT**—Comcast Cable

NEWRY—See ALTOONA, PA (Atlantic Broadband)

NEWTON HAMILTON—See PHILIPSBURG BOROUGH, PA (Comcast Cable)

NEWTON TWP. (LACKAWANNA COUNTY)—See MESHOPPEN, PA (Blue Ridge Communications)

NEWTON TWP. (LACKAWANNA COUNTY)—See DUNMORE, PA (Comcast Cable)

NEWTOWN TWP.—See COATESVILLE, PA (Comcast Cable)

▲**NEWTOWN**—Comcast Cable

NEWVILLE—See SHIPPENSBURG, PA (Comcast Cable)

NICHOLSON BOROUGH—See DUNMORE, PA (Comcast Cable)

NINEVAH—See SHIPPENVILLE, PA (Atlantic Broadband)

NINEVEH—See SHIPPENVILLE, PA (Atlantic Broadband)

NIPPENOSE TWP.—See WILLIAMSPORT, PA (Comcast Cable)

NORMALVILLE—See INDIAN CREEK, PA (Laurel Highland Television Co.)

▲**NORRISTOWN**—Comcast Cable

NORTH ABINGTON TWP.—See DUNMORE, PA (Comcast Cable)

NORTH ANNVILLE TWP.—See LEBANON, PA (Comcast Cable)

NORTH APOLLO—See KISKIMINETAS TWP., PA (Comcast Cable)

NORTH BEAVER TWP. (LAWRENCE COUNTY)—See ZELIENOPLE, PA (Armstrong Cable Services)

NORTH BELLE VERNON—See PITTSBURGH, PA (Comcast Cable)

NORTH BEND—See WILLIAMSPORT, PA (Comcast Cable)

NORTH BETHLEHEM TWP. (PORTIONS)—See UNIONTOWN, PA (Atlantic Broadband)

NORTH BETHLEHEM TWP.—See BENTLEYVILLE, PA (FairPoint Communications)

NORTH BRADDOCK—See MONROEVILLE, PA (Comcast Cable)

NORTH BUFFALO TWP.—See KISKIMINETAS TWP., PA (Comcast Cable)

NORTH CATASAUQUA BORO—See LEHIGH VALLEY, PA (Service Electric Cable TV & Communications)

▲**NORTH CATASAUQUA BOROUGH**—Formerly served by NORTHAMPTON BOROUGH, PA [PA0008]. RCN Corp. This cable system has converted to IPTV

NORTH CENTRE (PORTIONS)—See SUNBURY, PA (Service Electric Cablevision)

NORTH CHARLEROI—See PITTSBURGH, PA (Comcast Cable)

▲**NORTH CLARION**—Armstrong Cable Services

NORTH CODORUS TWP.—See GETTYSBURG, PA (Comcast Cable)

NORTH CORNWALL TWP.—See LEBANON, PA (Comcast Cable)

NORTH COVENTRY TWP.—See POTTSTOWN, PA (Comcast Cable)

NORTH EAST—See HARBORCREEK TWP., PA (Time Warner Cable)

NORTH FAYETTE TWP. (ALLEGHENY COUNTY)—See PITTSBURGH, PA (Comcast Cable)

NORTH FRANKLIN TWP.—See PITTSBURGH, PA (Comcast Cable)

NORTH HEIDELBERG—See READING, PA (Comcast Cable)

NORTH HUNTINGDON TWP. (WESTMORELAND COUNTY)—See GREENSBURG, PA (Comcast Cable)

NORTH IRWIN—See GREENSBURG, PA (Comcast Cable)

NORTH LEBANON TWP.—See LEBANON, PA (Comcast Cable)

NORTH LONDONDERRY TWP.—See LEBANON, PA (Comcast Cable)

NORTH MANHEIM TWP.—See POTTSVILLE, PA (Comcast Cable)

NORTH MIDDLETON TWP. (CUMBERLAND COUNTY)—See SHIPPENSBURG, PA (Comcast Cable)

NORTH NEWTON TWP.—See SHIPPENSBURG, PA (Comcast Cable)

NORTH ORWELL—See ROME, PA (Beaver Valley Cable Co.)

NORTH ROME—See ROME, PA (Beaver Valley Cable Co.)

NORTH SEWICKLEY TWP.—See ZELIENOPLE, PA (Armstrong Cable Services)

NORTH TOWANDA TWP.—See TOWANDA, PA (Comcast Cable)

NORTH VERSAILLES TWP.—See MONROEVILLE, PA (Comcast Cable)

NORTH WALES—See LANSDALE, PA (Comcast Cable)

▲**NORTH WHITEHALL TWP.**—Formerly served by NORTHAMPTON BOROUGH, PA [PA0008]. RCN Corp. This cable system has converted to IPTV

NORTH WOODBURY TWP.—See ALTOONA, PA (Atlantic Broadband)

NORTH YORK—See YORK, PA (Comcast Cable)

▲**NORTHAMPTON BOROUGH**—Formerly [PA0008]. RCN Corp. This cable system has converted to IPTV

▲**NORTHAMPTON**—RCN Corp. This cable system has converted to IPTV. See Northampton Borough, PA [PA5228]

NORTHEAST TWP. (ERIE COUNTY)—See HARBORCREEK TWP., PA (Time Warner Cable)

NORTHMORELAND TWP.—See DALLAS, PA (Comcast Cable)

NORTHUMBERLAND COUNTY (PORTIONS)—See LEWIS TWP., PA (Eagles Mere & La Porte Cablevision Inc.)

NORTHUMBERLAND—See SUNBURY, PA (Service Electric Cablevision)

NORVELT—See CONNELLSVILLE, PA (Armstrong Cable Services)

NORWEGIAN TWP. (SCHUYLKILL COUNTY)—See POTTSVILLE, PA (Comcast Cable)

▲ **PHILADELPHIA (AREA 2)**—Comcast Cable

▲ **PHILADELPHIA (AREAS 1, 3 & 4)**—Comcast Cable

▲ **PHILADELPHIA (SUBURBS)**—RCN Corp. Formerly [PA0447]. This cable system has converted to IPTV

▲ **PHILIPSBURG BOROUGH**—Comcast Cable

PHILIPSBURG—See PHILIPSBURG BOROUGH, PA (Comcast Cable)

PHOENIXVILLE—See POTTSTOWN, PA (Comcast Cable)

PIATT TWP. (LYCOMING COUNTY)—See WILLIAMSPORT, PA (Comcast Cable)

PICTURE ROCKS—See WILLIAMSPORT, PA (Comcast Cable)

PIKE TWP. (CLEARFIELD COUNTY)—See CLEARFIELD, PA (Atlantic Broadband)

PIKE TWP. (POTTER COUNTY)—See GALETON, PA (Blue Ridge Communications)

PIKE TWP. (POTTER COUNTY)—See GAINES, PA (Gaines-Watrous TV Inc.)

PIKE TWP.—See BIRDSBORO, PA (Service Electric Cablevision)

PILLOW—See LYKENS, PA (Comcast Cable)

PINE CREEK TWP.—See WILLIAMSPORT, PA (Comcast Cable)

PINE GROVE (SCHUYLKILL COUNTY)—See POTTSVILLE, PA (Comcast Cable)

PINE GROVE TWP. (WARREN COUNTY)—See WARREN, PA (Atlantic Broadband)

PINE RIDGE—See STROUDSBURG, PA (Blue Ridge Communications)

PINE TWP. (ALLEGHENY COUNTY)—See ZELIENOPLE, PA (Armstrong Cable Services)

PINE TWP. (BUTLER COUNTY)—See ZELIENOPLE, PA (Armstrong Cable Services)

PINE TWP. (INDIANA COUNTY)—See BLAIRSVILLE, PA (Comcast Cable)

PINE TWP. (MERCER COUNTY)—See GROVE CITY, PA (Armstrong Cable Services)

PINE TWP.—See KISKIMINETAS TWP., PA (Comcast Cable)

PINECREEK—See HAZEN, PA (Zito Media)

PINEVILLE—See NEWTOWN, PA (Comcast Cable)

PINEY TWP.—See CLARION BOROUGH, PA (Comcast Cable)

PINEY—See LIMESTONE, PA (Atlantic Broadband)

▲ **PINOAK**—Formerly served by Cebridge Connections. Now served by MEADVILLE, PA [PA0062]

PIONEER PARK CAMPGROUND—See CONNELLSVILLE, PA (Armstrong Cable Services)

PIPERSVILLE—See NEWTOWN, PA (Comcast Cable)

▲ **PITCAIRN**—Pitcairn Community Cable System

▲ **PITTSBURGH**—Comcast Cable

PITTSFIELD—See YOUNGSVILLE, PA (Youngsville TV Corp.)

PITTSTON TWP.—See DUNMORE, PA (Comcast Cable)

PITTSTON—See DUNMORE, PA (Comcast Cable)

▲ **PLAINFIELD TWP.**—Formerly served by NORTHAMPTON BOROUGH, PA [PA0008]. RCN Corp. This cable system has converted to IPTV

PLAINFIELD TWP.—See LEHIGH VALLEY, PA (Service Electric Cable TV & Communications)

PLAINS TWP. (LUZERNE COUNTY)—See SCRANTON, PA (Comcast Cable)

PLATEA BORO—See HARBORCREEK TWP., PA (Time Warner Cable)

PLEASANT HILLS—See PITTSBURGH, PA (Comcast Cable)

PLEASANT MOUNT—See CARBONDALE, PA (Adams Digital Cable)

PLEASANT TWP. (WARREN COUNTY)—See WARREN, PA (Atlantic Broadband)

PLEASANTVILLE—See MEADVILLE, PA (Armstrong Cable Services)

▲ **PLUM**—Comcast Cable. Now served by MONROEVILLE, PA [PA0023]

PLUM—See MONROEVILLE, PA (Comcast Cable)

PLUMCREEK TWP.—See KISKIMINETAS TWP., PA (Comcast Cable)

▲ **PLUMER**—Formerly served by Cebridge Connections. No longer in operation

PLUMVILLE—See KISKIMINETAS TWP., PA (Comcast Cable)

PLYMOUTH MEETING—See LANSDALE, PA (Comcast Cable)

PLYMOUTH TWP. (LUZERNE COUNTY)—See BERWICK, PA (MetroCast Communications)

PLYMOUTH—See SCRANTON, PA (Comcast Cable)

POCONO LAKE—See STROUDSBURG, PA (Blue Ridge Communications)

POCONO TWP.—See STROUDSBURG, PA (Blue Ridge Communications)

▲ **POCONO**—MetroCast Communications

POCOPSON TWP.—See COATESVILLE, PA (Comcast Cable)

POCOPSON TWP.—See KENNETT SQUARE, PA (Comcast Cable)

POINT MARION—See UNIONTOWN, PA (Atlantic Broadband)

POINT TWP. (MONTOUR COUNTY)—See SUNBURY, PA (Service Electric Cablevision)

POLK TWP. (JEFFERSON COUNTY)—See HAZEN, PA (Zito Media)

POLK TWP. (MONROE COUNTY)—See STROUDSBURG, PA (Blue Ridge Communications)

POLK—See FRANKLIN (Venango County), PA (Time Warner Cable)

PORT ALLEGANY—See COUDERSPORT, PA (Zito Media)

PORT CARBON—See POTTSVILLE, PA (Wire Television Corp.)

PORT CLINTON—See READING, PA (Comcast Cable)

PORT MATILDA—See STATE COLLEGE, PA (Comcast Cable)

▲ **PORT ROYAL**—Nittany Media Inc. Now served by LEWISTOWN (formerly McAlisterville), PA [PA0365]

PORT ROYAL—See LEWISTOWN, PA (Nittany Media Inc.)

PORT TREVORTON—See MOUNT PLEASANT MILLS, PA (Zampelli Electronics)

PORT VUE—See PITTSBURGH, PA (Comcast Cable)

PORTAGE (BOROUGH)—See ADAMS TWP. (Cambria County), PA (Comcast Cable)

▲ **PORTAGE**—Formerly served by Adelphia Communications. Now served by ADAMS TWP. (Cambria County), PA [PA0133]

PORTER TWP. (CLARION COUNTY)—See LIMESTONE, PA (Atlantic Broadband)

PORTER TWP. (SCHUYLKILL COUNTY)—See LYKENS, PA (Comcast Cable)

PORTERSVILLE—See ZELIENOPLE, PA (Armstrong Cable Services)

PORTLAND BORO—See LEHIGH VALLEY, PA (Service Electric Cable TV & Communications)

POTTER TWP. (BEAVER COUNTY)—See BEAVER VALLEY, PA (Comcast Cable)

POTTER TWP. (CENTRE COUNTY)—See STATE COLLEGE, PA (Comcast Cable)

POTTERVILLE—See ROME, PA (Beaver Valley Cable Co.)

▲ **POTTSTOWN**—Comcast Cable

▲ **POTTSVILLE**—Comcast Cable

▲ **POTTSVILLE**—Wire Television Corp.

POWELL TWP.—See TROY, PA (Blue Ridge Communications)

POWELL—See TROY, PA (Blue Ridge Communications)

POYNTELLE—See CARBONDALE, PA (Adams Digital Cable)

PRESTO—See PITTSBURGH, PA (Comcast Cable)

PRESTON PARK (VILLAGE)—See LAKEWOOD, PA (Hancock Video)

PRESTON TWP.—See CARBONDALE, PA (Adams Digital Cable)

PRICE TWP. (MONROE COUNTY)—See STROUDSBURG, PA (Blue Ridge Communications)

▲ **PRIMROSE**—J. B. Cable

PRINGLE—See WILKES-BARRE, PA (Service Electric Cable Company)

PROMPTON—See CARBONDALE, PA (Adams Digital Cable)

PROSPECT PARK—See WALLINGFORD, PA (Comcast Cable)

▲ **PROSPECT PARK**—RCN Corp. Formerly served by Philadelphia (suburbs), PA [PA0447]. This cable system has converted to IPTV

PROSPECT—See BUTLER, PA (Armstrong Cable Services)

PROVIDENCE TWP. (LANCASTER COUNTY)—See LANCASTER, PA (Comcast Cable)

PULASKI TWP. (LAWRENCE COUNTY)—See PULASKI, PA (Comcast Cable)

▲ **PULASKI**—Comcast Cable

▲ **PUNXSUTAWNEY**—Comcast Cable

PUTNAM TWP.—See WELLSBORO, PA (Blue Ridge Communications)

PYMATUNING TWP.—See MERCER COUNTY, PA (Time Warner Cable)

PYMATUNING TWP.—See SHARON, PA (Time Warner Cable)

QUAKERTOWN—See SELLERSVILLE, PA (Comcast Cable)

QUARRYVILLE—See LANCASTER, PA (Comcast Cable)

QUECREEK—See CONNELLSVILLE, PA (Armstrong Cable Services)

QUEEN—See ALTOONA, PA (Atlantic Broadband)

QUEMAHONING TWP. (SOMERSET COUNTY)—See JOHNSTOWN, PA (Atlantic Broadband)

QUEMAHONING TWP. (SOMERSET COUNTY)—See CENTRAL CITY BOROUGH, PA (Comcast Cable)

QUIGGLEVILLE—See COGAN STATION, PA (Zito Media)

QUINOY TWP.—See SHIPPENSBURG, PA (Comcast Cable)

RACCOON TWP. (SOUTHERN PORTION)—See BEAVER VALLEY, PA (Comcast Cable)

RAHNS—See KING OF PRUSSIA, PA (Comcast Cable)

RAILROAD—See GETTYSBURG, PA (Comcast Cable)

RUSH TWP. (SCHUYLKILL COUNTY)—See MAHANOY CITY, PA (Service Electric Cable Company)

RUSH TWP.—See PALMERTON, PA (Blue Ridge Communications)

RUSSELLTON—See TARENTUM BOROUGH, PA (Comcast Cable)

RUTLEDGE (DELAWARE COUNTY)—See WALLINGFORD, PA (Comcast Cable)

▲**RUTLEDGE**—RCN Corp. Formerly served by Philadelphia (suburbs), PA [PA0447]. This cable system has converted to IPTV

RYE TWP.—See DUNCANNON, PA (Blue Ridge Communications)

▲**SABULA**—Zito Media

SADSBURY TWP. (CHESTER COUNTY)—See COATESVILLE, PA (Comcast Cable)

SADSBURY TWP. (LANCASTER COUNTY)—See LANCASTER, PA (Comcast Cable)

SAEGERTOWN—See MEADVILLE, PA (Armstrong Cable Services)

SAGAMORE—See KISKIMINETAS TWP., PA (Comcast Cable)

SALEM TWP. (CLARION COUNTY)—See SHIPPENVILLE, PA (Atlantic Broadband)

SALEM TWP. (WAYNE COUNTY)—See CARBONDALE, PA (Adams Digital Cable)

SALEM TWP. (WESTMORELAND COUNTY)—See GREENSBURG, PA (Comcast Cable)

SALFORD—See SELLERSVILLE, PA (Comcast Cable)

SALINA—See KISKIMINETAS TWP., PA (Comcast Cable)

SALISBURY TWP. (LANCASTER COUNTY)—See LANCASTER, PA (Comcast Cable)

▲**SALISBURY TWP.**—Formerly served by NORTHAMPTON BOROUGH, PA [PA0008]. RCN Corp. This cable system has converted to IPTV

SALISBURY TWP.—See LEHIGH VALLEY, PA (Service Electric Cable TV & Communications)

SALIX—See ADAMS TWP. (Cambria County), PA (Comcast Cable)

SALLADASBURG—See WILLIAMSPORT, PA (Comcast Cable)

▲**SALTILLO**—Saltillo TV Cable Corp.

SALTLICK TWP. (FAYETTE COUNTY)—See CONNELLSVILLE, PA (Armstrong Cable Services)

SALTLICK TWP. (FAYETTE COUNTY)—See INDIAN CREEK, PA (Laurel Highland Television Co.)

SALTSBURG—See BLAIRSVILLE, PA (Comcast Cable)

SALTSBURG—See KISKIMINETAS TWP., PA (Comcast Cable)

SANDY CREEK TWP. (VENANGO COUNTY)—See FRANKLIN (Venango County), PA (Time Warner Cable)

SANDY LAKE TWP.—See GROVE CITY, PA (Armstrong Cable Services)

▲**SANDY LAKE**—Formerly served by Cebridge Connections. Now served by GROVE CITY, PA [PA0089]

SANDY LAKE—See GROVE CITY, PA (Armstrong Cable Services)

▲**SANDY TWP. (Clearfield County)**—Formerly served by Satterlee Leasing Inc. No longer in operation

SANDY TWP.—See PUNXSUTAWNEY, PA (Comcast Cable)

SANDYSTON TWP.—See MATAMORAS, NJ (Cablevision Systems Corp.)

SANFORD—See CARBONDALE, NY (Adams Digital Cable)

SANKERTOWN—See CRESSON, PA (Comcast Cable)

SARVER—See KISKIMINETAS TWP., PA (Comcast Cable)

SAW CREEK ESTATES—See STROUDSBURG, PA (Blue Ridge Communications)

SAW CREEK—See STROUDSBURG, PA (Blue Ridge Communications)

SAXONBURG—See BUTLER, PA (Armstrong Cable Services)

SAXTON—See HUNTINGDON, PA (Comcast Cable)

SAYBROOK—See SHEFFIELD, PA (WestPA.net Inc.)

SAYBROOK—See SHEFFIELD, PA (WestPA.net Inc.)

▲**SAYRE**—Time Warner Cable

SCALP LEVEL—See ADAMS TWP. (Cambria County), PA (Comcast Cable)

SCENERY HILL—See BENTLEYVILLE, PA (FairPoint Communications)

SCHELLSBURG—See BEDFORD, PA (Comcast Cable)

SCHUYLKILL COUNTY—See POTTSVILLE, PA (Comcast Cable)

SCHUYLKILL HAVEN—See POTTSVILLE, PA (Comcast Cable)

SCHUYLKILL TWP. (CHESTER COUNTY)—See POTTSTOWN, PA (Comcast Cable)

▲**SCHUYLKILL TWP.**—MetroCast Communications

SCHWENKSVILLE—See TRAPPE, PA (Comcast Cable)

SCOTT TWP. (ALLEGHENY TWP.)—See PITTSBURGH, PA (Comcast Cable)

SCOTT TWP. (COLUMBIA COUNTY)—See SUNBURY, PA (Service Electric Cablevision)

SCOTT TWP. (LACKAWANNA COUNTY)—See DUNMORE, PA (Comcast Cable)

SCOTT TWP. (WAYNE COUNTY)—See CARBONDALE, PA (Adams Digital Cable)

SCOTTDALE—See CONNELLSVILLE, PA (Armstrong Cable Services)

▲**SCRANTON**—Comcast Cable

SEELYVILLE (WAYNE COUNTY)—See CARBONDALE, PA (Adams Digital Cable)

SELINSGROVE—See SUNBURY, PA (Service Electric Cablevision)

▲**SELLERSVILLE**—Comcast Cable

SELTZER—See POTTSVILLE, PA (Comcast Cable)

SEMINOLE—See KISKIMINETAS TWP., PA (Comcast Cable)

SEVEN FIELDS—See ZELIENOPLE, PA (Armstrong Cable Services)

SEVEN VALLEYS—See GETTYSBURG, PA (Comcast Cable)

SEWARD—See ARMAGH, PA (Comcast Cable)

SEWICKLEY HEIGHTS—See PITTSBURGH, PA (Comcast Cable)

SEWICKLEY HILLS—See PITTSBURGH, PA (Comcast Cable)

SEWICKLEY—See PITTSBURGH, PA (Comcast Cable)

▲**SHADE GAP**—Shade Gap TV Assn.

SHADE TWP. (SOMERSET COUNTY)—See CENTRAL CITY BOROUGH, PA (Comcast Cable)

SHADY GROVE—See SHIPPENSBURG, PA (Comcast Cable)

SHALER TWP.—See PITTSBURGH, PA (Comcast Cable)

SHAMOKIN DAM—See SUNBURY, PA (Service Electric Cablevision)

SHAMOKIN TWP.—See SUNBURY, PA (Service Electric Cablevision)

SHAMOKIN—See SUNBURY, PA (Service Electric Cablevision)

SHARON HILL—See WALLINGFORD, PA (Comcast Cable)

▲**SHARON HILL**—RCN Corp. Formerly served by Philadelphia (suburbs), PA [PA0447]. This cable system has converted to IPTV

▲**SHARON**—Time Warner Cable

SHARON—See MERCER COUNTY, PA (Time Warner Cable)

SHARPSBURG—See PITTSBURGH, PA (Comcast Cable)

SHARPSVILLE—See MERCER COUNTY, PA (Time Warner Cable)

SHARPSVILLE—See SHARON, PA (Time Warner Cable)

SHARTLESVILLE—See READING, PA (Comcast Cable)

SHAVERTOWN—See BERWICK, PA (MetroCast Communications)

SHEAKLEYVILLE TWP.—See MEADVILLE, PA (Armstrong Cable Services)

▲**SHEFFIELD**—South Side TV Assn. Now served by SHEFFIELD, PA [PA0242]

▲**SHEFFIELD**—WestPA.net Inc.

▲**SHEFFIELD**—WestPA.net Inc.

SHELOCTA—See KISKIMINETAS TWP., PA (Comcast Cable)

▲**SHENANDOAH**—Shen-Heights TV Assoc. Inc.

SHENANGO TWP. (LAWRENCE COUNTY)—See ZELIENOPLE, PA (Armstrong Cable Services)

SHENANGO TWP. (MERCER COUNTY)—See MEADVILLE, PA (Armstrong Cable Services)

SHENANGO TWP.—See MERCER COUNTY, PA (Time Warner Cable)

SHENANGO TWP.—See SHARON, PA (Time Warner Cable)

SHEPPTON—See SHENANDOAH, PA (Shen-Heights TV Assoc. Inc.)

SHERMANS DALE—See SHIPPENSBURG, PA (Comcast Cable)

SHICKSHINNY—See BERWICK, PA (MetroCast Communications)

SHILLINGTON—See READING, PA (Comcast Cable)

SHIPPEN TWP. (CAMERON COUNTY)—See COUDERSPORT, PA (Zito Media)

SHIPPEN TWP. (TIOGA COUNTY)—See WELLSBORO, PA (Blue Ridge Communications)

SHIPPEN—See COUDERSPORT, PA (Zito Media)

▲**SHIPPENSBURG**—Comcast Cable

▲**SHIPPENVILLE**—Atlantic Broadband

▲**SHIPPENVILLE**—Atlantic Broadband

▲**SHIPPINGPORT BOROUGH**—Comcast Cable. Now served by BEAVER FALLS, PA [PA0065]

SHIPPINGPORT BOROUGH—See BEAVER FALLS, PA (Comcast Cable)

SHIREMANSTOWN—See HARRISBURG, PA (Comcast Cable)

▲**SHIRLEY TWP.**—Formerly served by Adelphia Communications. Now served by PHILIPSBURG BOROUGH, PA [PA0109]

SHIRLEY TWP.—See PHILIPSBURG BOROUGH, PA (Comcast Cable)

SHIRLEYSBURG—See PHILIPSBURG BOROUGH, PA (Comcast Cable)

SHOEMAKERSVILLE—See READING, PA (Comcast Cable)

SHOHOLA TWP.—See MILFORD, PA (Blue Ridge Communications)

SPRINGFIELD TWP. (DELAWARE COUNTY)—See WALLINGFORD, PA (Comcast Cable)

SPRINGFIELD TWP. (MERCER COUNTY)—See GROVE CITY, PA (Armstrong Cable Services)

SPRINGFIELD TWP.—See LEHIGH VALLEY, PA (Service Electric Cable TV & Communications)

SPRINGFIELD TWP.—See HARBORCREEK TWP., PA (Time Warner Cable)

SPRINGHILL TWP. (FAYETTE COUNTY)—See UNIONTOWN, PA (Atlantic Broadband)

SPRINGHILL TWP. (GREENE COUNTY)—See UNIONTOWN, PA (Atlantic Broadband)

SPRINGVILLE—See MONTROSE, PA (Time Warner Cable)

SPROUL—See ALTOONA, PA (Atlantic Broadband)

▲ **SPRUCE CREEK TWP.**—MetroCast Communications

SPRUCE LAKE—See CARBONDALE, PA (Adams Digital Cable)

ST. CLAIR (BEDFORD COUNTY)—See WOODBURY, PA (Atlantic Broadband)

ST. CLAIR (SCHUYLKILL COUNTY)—See MAHANOY CITY, PA (Service Electric Cable Company)

ST. CLAIRSVILLE—See WOODBURY, PA (Atlantic Broadband)

ST. LAWRENCE—See BIRDSBORO, PA (Service Electric Cablevision)

▲ **ST. MARY'S**—Zito Media

ST. MICHAEL—See ADAMS TWP. (Cambria County), PA (Comcast Cable)

ST. PETERSBURG—See CLARION BOROUGH, PA (Comcast Cable)

ST. THOMAS TWP. (FRANKLIN COUNTY)—See SHIPPENSBURG, PA (Comcast Cable)

STAHLSTOWN—See INDIAN CREEK, PA (Laurel Highland Television Co.)

STARFORD—See BLAIRSVILLE, PA (Comcast Cable)

STARLIGHT (VILLAGE)—See LAKEWOOD, PA (Hancock Video)

STARRUCCA—See CARBONDALE, PA (Adams Digital Cable)

▲ **STATE COLLEGE**—Formerly served by D&E Communications. No longer in operation

▲ **STATE COLLEGE**—Windstream (formerly D&E Communications.) This cable system has converted to IPTV. See State College, PA [PA5280]

▲ **STATE COLLEGE**—Comcast Cable

STATE LINE—See SHIPPENSBURG, PA (Comcast Cable)

STEELTON—See HARRISBURG, PA (Comcast Cable)

STERLING TWP. (WAYNE COUNTY)—See CARBONDALE, PA (Adams Digital Cable)

STERLING—See CARBONDALE, PA (Adams Digital Cable)

STILLWATER—See BERWICK, PA (MetroCast Communications)

STOCKDALE—See CONNELLSVILLE, PA (Armstrong Cable Services)

▲ **STOCKERTOWN BOROUGH**—Formerly served by NORTHAMPTON BOROUGH, PA [PA0008]. RCN Corp. This cable system has converted to IPTV

STOCKERTOWN—See LEHIGH VALLEY, PA (Service Electric Cable TV & Communications)

STONEBORO—See GROVE CITY, PA (Armstrong Cable Services)

STONEHAM—See CLARENDON, PA (Clarendon TV Association)

STONYCREEK TWP. (CAMBRIA COUNTY)—See JOHNSTOWN, PA (Atlantic Broadband)

STONYCREEK TWP. (SOMERSET COUNTY)—See CENTRAL CITY BOROUGH, PA (Comcast Cable)

STOYSTOWN—See CENTRAL CITY BOROUGH, PA (Comcast Cable)

STRABAN TWP.—See GETTYSBURG, PA (Comcast Cable)

STRASBURG—See LANCASTER, PA (Comcast Cable)

STRATTANVILLE—See CLARION BOROUGH, PA (Comcast Cable)

STRATTONVILLE—See LIMESTONE, PA (Atlantic Broadband)

STRAUSSTOWN—See READING, PA (Comcast Cable)

STRONG—See SUNBURY, PA (Service Electric Cablevision)

STROUD TWP. (MONROE COUNTY)—See STROUDSBURG, PA (Blue Ridge Communications)

▲ **STROUDSBURG**—Blue Ridge Communications

SUGAR GROVE TWP.—See GREENVILLE, PA (Time Warner Cable)

▲ **SUGAR GROVE**—MetroCast Communications

SUGAR NOTCH—See WILKES-BARRE, PA (Service Electric Cable Company)

SUGARCREEK (VENANGO COUNTY)—See MEADVILLE, PA (Armstrong Cable Services)

SUGARCREEK (VENANGO COUNTY)—See OIL CITY, PA (Comcast Cable)

SUGARCREEK (VENANGO COUNTY)—See FRANKLIN (Venango County), PA (Time Warner Cable)

▲ **SUGARLOAF TWP.**—MetroCast Communications. Now served by BERWICK, PA [PA0094]

SUGARLOAF TWP.—See BERWICK, PA (MetroCast Communications)

SUGARLOAF TWP.—See HAZLETON, PA (Service Electric Cablevision)

SUGARLOAF—See BERWICK, PA (MetroCast Communications)

SULLIVAN TWP.—See WELLSBORO, PA (Blue Ridge Communications)

SUMMERHILL (PORTIONS)—See JOHNSTOWN, PA (Atlantic Broadband)

SUMMERHILL—See ADAMS TWP. (Cambria County), PA (Comcast Cable)

▲ **SUMMERVILLE**—Formerly served by Adelphia Communications. Now served by PUNXSUTAWNEY, PA [PA0397]

SUMMERVILLE—See LIMESTONE, PA (Atlantic Broadband)

SUMMERVILLE—See PUNXSUTAWNEY, PA (Comcast Cable)

SUMMIT HILL—See PALMERTON, PA (Blue Ridge Communications)

SUMMIT LAKE—See CARBONDALE, PA (Adams Digital Cable)

SUMMIT TWP. (ERIE COUNTY)—See HARBORCREEK TWP., PA (Time Warner Cable)

SUMMIT TWP. (SOMERSET COUNTY)—See MEYERSDALE, PA (Comcast Cable)

▲ **SUNBURY**—Service Electric Cablevision

SUSQUEHANNA DEPOT BOROUGH—See CARBONDALE, PA (Adams Digital Cable)

SUTERSVILLE—See BETHEL PARK, PA (Comcast Cable)

SWARTHMORE—See WALLINGFORD, PA (Comcast Cable)

SWATARA—See HARRISBURG, PA (Comcast Cable)

SWEET VALLEY—See MESHOPPEN, PA (Blue Ridge Communications)

▲ **SWENGEL**—Formerly served by D&E Communications. No longer in operation

SWENGEL—See MIFFLINBURG, PA (Atlantic Broadband)

SWISSVALE—See MONROEVILLE, PA (Comcast Cable)

SWOYERSVILLE—See SCRANTON, PA (Comcast Cable)

SYKESVILLE—See PUNXSUTAWNEY, PA (Comcast Cable)

SYLVANIA BOROUGH—See TROY, PA (Blue Ridge Communications)

SYLVANIA—See TROY, PA (Blue Ridge Communications)

TAMAQUA—See SCHUYLKILL TWP., PA (MetroCast Communications)

TAMAQUA—See MAHANOY CITY, PA (Service Electric Cable Company)

▲ **TARENTUM BOROUGH**—Comcast Cable

TATAMY BORO—See LEHIGH VALLEY, PA (Service Electric Cable TV & Communications)

▲ **TATAMY BOROUGH**—Formerly served by NORTHAMPTON BOROUGH, PA [PA0008]. RCN Corp. This cable system has converted to IPTV

TAYLOR TWP. (BLAIR COUNTY)—See ALTOONA, PA (Atlantic Broadband)

TAYLOR TWP. (LAWRENCE COUNTY)—See ZELIENOPLE, PA (Armstrong Cable Services)

TAYLOR—See SCRANTON, PA (Comcast Cable)

TELFORD—See SELLERSVILLE, PA (Comcast Cable)

TELL TWP.—See DOYLESBURG, PA (Valley Cable Systems)

TEMPLE—See READING, PA (Comcast Cable)

TEMPLETON—See KISKIMINETAS TWP., PA (Comcast Cable)

TERRE HILL—See EPHRATA, PA (Blue Ridge Communications)

TERRY TWP.—See MESHOPPEN, PA (Blue Ridge Communications)

TEXAS TWP. (WAYNE COUNTY)—See HONESDALE, PA (Blue Ridge Communications)

THE FALLS—See STROUDSBURG, PA (Blue Ridge Communications)

THE HIDEOUT—See CARBONDALE, PA (Adams Digital Cable)

THOMPSON BOROUGH—See CARBONDALE, PA (Adams Digital Cable)

▲ **THOMPSON TWP.**—Adams Cable Service. Now served by Carbondale, PA [PA0067]

THOMPSON TWP.—See CARBONDALE, PA (Adams Digital Cable)

▲ **THOMPSONTOWN**—Nittany Media Inc. Now served by LEWISTOWN (formerly McAlisterville), PA [PA0365]

THOMPSONTOWN—See LEWISTOWN, PA (Nittany Media Inc.)

THORNBURG—See PITTSBURGH, PA (Comcast Cable)

THORNBURY TWP. (CHESTER COUNTY)—See COATESVILLE, PA (Comcast Cable)

THORNBURY TWP. (DELAWARE COUNTY)—See COATESVILLE, PA (Comcast Cable)

▲ **THREE SPRINGS**—MetroCast Communications

THROOP—See SCRANTON, PA (Comcast Cable)

▲**TIDIOUTE**—Formerly served by Cebridge Connections. No longer in operation

TILDEN TWP.—See READING, PA (Comcast Cable)

▲**TIMBLIN BOROUGH**—Formerly served by Adelphia Communications. Now served by PUNXSUTAWNEY, PA [PA0397]

TIMBLIN—See PUNXSUTAWNEY, PA (Comcast Cable)

TIMOTHY LAKE—See STROUDSBURG, PA (Blue Ridge Communications)

TINGLEY LAKE—See LOOMIS LAKE, PA (Adams Digital Cable)

TINICUM TWP. (DELAWARE COUNTY)—See WALLINGFORD, PA (Comcast Cable)

TINICUM TWP.—See LEHIGH VALLEY, PA (Service Electric Cable TV & Communications)

▲**TINICUM**—RCN Corp. Formerly served by Philadelphia (suburbs), PA [PA0447]. This cable system has converted to IPTV

TIONA—See SHEFFIELD, PA (WestPA.net Inc.)

TIONESTA TWP.—See NORTH CLARION, PA (Armstrong Cable Services)

TIONESTA—See NORTH CLARION, PA (Armstrong Cable Services)

TIRE HILL—See JOHNSTOWN, PA (Atlantic Broadband)

▲**TITUSVILLE**—Formerly served by Cebridge Connections. Now served by MEADVILLE, PA [PA0062]

TITUSVILLE—See MEADVILLE, PA (Armstrong Cable Services)

▲**TOBY TWP.**—Formerly served by Adelphia Communications. Now served by CLARION BOROUGH, PA [PA0137]

TOBY TWP.—See CLARION BOROUGH, PA (Comcast Cable)

TOBY—See ST. MARY'S, PA (Zito Media)

TOBYHANNA TWP. (MONROE COUNTY)—See STROUDSBURG, PA (Blue Ridge Communications)

TODD TWP. (HUNTINGDON COUNTY)—See UNION TWP. (Huntingdon County), PA (Atlantic Broadband)

TODD TWP.—See HUNTINGDON, PA (Comcast Cable)

TODD—See UNION TWP. (Huntingdon County), PA (Atlantic Broadband)

TOPTON—See BIRDSBORO, PA (Service Electric Cablevision)

TOWAMENCIN—See LANSDALE, PA (Comcast Cable)

TOWAMENSING TWP.—See PALMERTON, PA (Blue Ridge Communications)

▲**TOWANDA**—Comcast Cable

TOWER CITY—See LYKENS, PA (Comcast Cable)

▲**TOWNVILLE**—Formerly served by Cebridge Connections. Now served by MEADVILLE, PA [PA0062]

TOWNVILLE—See MEADVILLE, PA (Armstrong Cable Services)

TOWNVILLE—See EDINBORO, PA (Coaxial Cable TV Corp.)

TRAFFORD—See MONROEVILLE, PA (Comcast Cable)

TRAINER—See WALLINGFORD, PA (Comcast Cable)

▲**TRAPPE**—Comcast Cable

▲**TREASURE LAKE**—Zito Media

TREDYFFRIN TWP.—See COATESVILLE, PA (Comcast Cable)

TREESDALE—See ZELIENOPLE, PA (Armstrong Cable Services)

TREMONT TWP.—See POTTSVILLE, PA (Comcast Cable)

▲**TREMONT**—Wire Television Corp.

TRENT—See CONNELLSVILLE, PA (Armstrong Cable Services)

TROUT RUN—See COGAN STATION, PA (Zito Media)

TROUTVILLE—See PUNXSUTAWNEY, PA (Comcast Cable)

TROY TWP.—See TROY, PA (Blue Ridge Communications)

▲**TROY**—Blue Ridge Communications

TRUMBAUERSVILLE—See SELLERSVILLE, PA (Comcast Cable)

TULLYTOWN—See BENSALEM TWP., PA (Comcast Cable)

TULPEHOCKEN TWP.—See LEBANON, PA (Comcast Cable)

TUNKHANNOCK BOROUGH—See MESHOPPEN, PA (Blue Ridge Communications)

TUNKHANNOCK TWP. (WYOMING COUNTY)—See MESHOPPEN, PA (Blue Ridge Communications)

TUNNELHILL—See CRESSON, PA (Comcast Cable)

TURBETT TWP.—See LEWISTOWN, PA (Nittany Media Inc.)

TURBOT TWP. (NORTHUMBERLAND COUNTY)—See DANVILLE, PA (CATV Service Inc.)

TURBOT TWP. (NORTHUMBERLAND COUNTY)—See LEWIS TWP., PA (Eagles Mere & La Porte Cablevision Inc.)

TURBOTVILLE—See DANVILLE, PA (CATV Service Inc.)

TURKEY CITY—See SHIPPENVILLE, PA (Atlantic Broadband)

TURTLE CREEK—See MONROEVILLE, PA (Comcast Cable)

TUSCARORA TWP. (BRADFORD COUNTY)—See MESHOPPEN, PA (Blue Ridge Communications)

TUSCARORA—See SCHUYLKILL TWP., PA (MetroCast Communications)

TWILIGHT—See PITTSBURGH, PA (Comcast Cable)

TWIN ROCKS—See ADAMS TWP. (Cambria County), PA (Comcast Cable)

TYLERSBURG—See NORTH CLARION, PA (Armstrong Cable Services)

▲**TYLERSVILLE**—Tylersville Community TV Cable Assoc.

TYRONE TWP. (BLAIR COUNTY)—See ALTOONA, PA (Atlantic Broadband)

▲**TYRONE**—Formerly served by Adelphia Communications. Now served by STATE COLLEGE, PA [PA0037]

TYRONE—See ALTOONA, PA (Atlantic Broadband)

TYRONE—See STATE COLLEGE, PA (Comcast Cable)

ULSTER—See ROME, PA (Beaver Valley Cable Co.)

▲**ULYSSES**—Time Warner Cable

UNION CITY—See CORRY, PA (Time Warner Cable)

UNION COUNTY—See MIFFLINBURG, PA (Atlantic Broadband)

UNION TWP. (BERKS COUNTY)—See BIRDSBORO, PA (Service Electric Cablevision)

▲**UNION TWP. (CENTRE COUNTY)**—Country Cable

UNION TWP. (ERIE COUNTY)—See CORRY, PA (Time Warner Cable)

▲**UNION TWP. (HUNTINGDON COUNTY)**—Atlantic Broadband

UNION TWP. (JEFFERSON COUNTY)—See CLARION BOROUGH, PA (Comcast Cable)

UNION TWP. (LEBANON COUNTY)—See LEBANON, PA (Comcast Cable)

UNION TWP. (LEBANON COUNTY)—See FORT INDIANTOWN GAP, PA (Gap Cable TV Inc.)

UNION TWP. (SCHUYLKILL COUNTY)—See SHENANDOAH, PA (Shen-Heights TV Assoc. Inc.)

UNION TWP. (UNION COUNTY)—See SUNBURY, PA (Service Electric Cablevision)

UNION TWP. (WASHINGTON COUNTY)—See BETHEL PARK, PA (Comcast Cable)

UNION TWP.—See MESHOPPEN, PA (Blue Ridge Communications)

UNION TWP.—See HUNTINGDON, PA (Comcast Cable)

UNION TWP.—See PUNXSUTAWNEY, PA (Comcast Cable)

UNION TWP.—See YORK, PA (Comcast Cable)

UNIONDALE—See CARBONDALE, PA (Adams Digital Cable)

▲**UNIONTOWN**—Atlantic Broadband

UNITY TWP. (WESTMORELAND COUNTY)—See BLAIRSVILLE, PA (Comcast Cable)

UPLAND—See WALLINGFORD, PA (Comcast Cable)

UPPER ALLEN TWP.—See HARRISBURG, PA (Comcast Cable)

UPPER AUGUSTA TWP.—See SUNBURY, PA (Service Electric Cablevision)

UPPER BERN TWP.—See READING, PA (Comcast Cable)

UPPER BURRELL TWP.—See MONROEVILLE, PA (Comcast Cable)

UPPER CHICHESTER TWP.—See WALLINGFORD, PA (Comcast Cable)

UPPER DARBY TWP.—See WALLINGFORD, PA (Comcast Cable)

▲**UPPER DARBY**—RCN Corp. Formerly served by Philadelphia (suburbs), PA [PA0447]. This cable system has converted to IPTV

UPPER DUBLIN TWP.—See LANSDALE, PA (Comcast Cable)

UPPER FREDERICK TWP.—See SELLERSVILLE, PA (Comcast Cable)

UPPER GWYNEDD TWP.—See LANSDALE, PA (Comcast Cable)

UPPER HANOVER TWP.—See POTTSTOWN, PA (Comcast Cable)

UPPER LEACOCK TWP.—See LANCASTER, PA (Comcast Cable)

▲**UPPER MACUNGIE TWP.**—Formerly served by NORTHAMPTON BOROUGH, PA [PA0008]. RCN Corp. This cable system has converted to IPTV

UPPER MACUNGIE TWP.—See LEHIGH VALLEY, PA (Service Electric Cable TV & Communications)

UPPER MAHANOY TWP.—See SUNBURY, PA (Service Electric Cablevision)

UPPER MAHANTANGO TWP.—See LYKENS, PA (Comcast Cable)

UPPER MAKEFIELD TWP.—See NEWTOWN, PA (Comcast Cable)

UPPER MERION TWP.—See KING OF PRUSSIA, PA (Comcast Cable)

UPPER MILFORD TWP.—See LEHIGH VALLEY, PA (Service Electric Cable TV & Communications)

UPPER MORELAND TWP.—See WILLOW GROVE, PA (Comcast Cable)

UPPER MOUNT BETHEL TWP.—See LEHIGH VALLEY, PA (Service Electric Cable TV & Communications)

▲**UPPER NAZARETH TWP.**—Formerly served by NORTHAMPTON BOR-

OUGH, PA [PA0008]. RCN Corp. This cable system has converted to IPTV

UPPER NAZARETH TWP.—See LEHIGH VALLEY, PA (Service Electric Cable TV & Communications)

UPPER OXFORD TWP.—See OXFORD, PA (Armstrong Cable Services)

UPPER OXFORD TWP.—See KENNETT SQUARE, PA (Comcast Cable)

UPPER PAXTON TWP. (DAUPHIN COUNTY)—See LEBANON, PA (Comcast Cable)

UPPER PAXTON TWP. (DAUPHIN COUNTY)—See LYKENS, PA (Comcast Cable)

UPPER POTTSGROVE—See POTTSTOWN, PA (Comcast Cable)

UPPER PROVIDENCE TWP. (DELAWARE COUNTY)—See WALLINGFORD, PA (Comcast Cable)

UPPER SALFORD—See SELLERSVILLE, PA (Comcast Cable)

▲**UPPER SAUCON TWP.**—Formerly served by NORTHAMPTON BOROUGH, PA [PA0008]. RCN Corp. This cable system has converted to IPTV

UPPER SAUCON TWP.—See LEHIGH VALLEY, PA (Service Electric Cable TV & Communications)

UPPER SOUTHAMPTON—See BENSALEM TWP., PA (Comcast Cable)

UPPER ST. CLAIR TWP.—See BETHEL PARK, PA (Comcast Cable)

UPPER UWCHLAN TWP. (CHESTER COUNTY)—See COATESVILLE, PA (Comcast Cable)

UPPER YODER TWP.—See JOHNSTOWN, PA (Atlantic Broadband)

URSINA—See MARKLEYSBURG, PA (Comcast Cable)

UTICA—See MEADVILLE, PA (Armstrong Cable Services)

UWCHLAN TWP.—See COATESVILLE, PA (Comcast Cable)

VALENCIA—See ZELIENOPLE, PA (Armstrong Cable Services)

VALLEY TWP. (CHESTER COUNTY)—See COATESVILLE, PA (Comcast Cable)

VALLEY TWP. (MONTOUR COUNTY)—See DANVILLE, PA (CATV Service Inc.)

VANDERBILT—See CONNELLSVILLE, PA (Armstrong Cable Services)

VANDERGRIFT—See KISKIMINETAS TWP., PA (Comcast Cable)

VANDLING—See CARBONDALE, PA (Adams Digital Cable)

VANPORT TWP.—See ROCHESTER, PA (Comcast Cable)

VENANGO TWP. (BUTLER COUNTY)—See GROVE CITY, PA (Armstrong Cable Services)

VENANGO TWP. (CRAWFORD COUNTY)—See EDINBORO, PA (Coaxial Cable TV Corp.)

VENANGO—See EDINBORO, PA (Coaxial Cable TV Corp.)

VENUS—See NORTH CLARION, PA (Armstrong Cable Services)

VERONA BOROUGH—See TARENTUM BOROUGH, PA (Comcast Cable)

VERSAILLES—See PITTSBURGH, PA (Comcast Cable)

VESTABURG—See UNIONTOWN, PA (Atlantic Broadband)

▲**VICKSBURG**—Formerly served by D&E Communications. No longer in operation

VINTONDALE—See ADAMS TWP. (Cambria County), PA (Comcast Cable)

VOLANT BOROUGH—See GROVE CITY, PA (Armstrong Cable Services)

VOWINCKEL—See NORTH CLARION, PA (Armstrong Cable Services)

W. SUNBURY—See BUTLER, PA (Armstrong Cable Services)

WADESTOWN—See BRAVE, WV (Zito Media)

WALKER TWP. (SCHUYLKILL COUNTY)—See PALMERTON, PA (Blue Ridge Communications)

WALLACE TWP.—See COATESVILLE, PA (Comcast Cable)

WALLACETON—See SNOW SHOE, PA (Tele-Media)

WALLENPAUPACK LAKE ESTATES—See CARBONDALE, PA (Adams Digital Cable)

▲**WALLINGFORD**—Comcast Cable

▲**WALNUT BOTTOM**—Kuhn Communications

▲**WALNUT**—Formerly served by Penn CATV of Walnut. No longer in operation

WALNUTPORT—See PALMERTON, PA (Blue Ridge Communications)

WALSTON—See PUNXSUTAWNEY, PA (Comcast Cable)

WAMPUM—See ZELIENOPLE, PA (Armstrong Cable Services)

WANA—See BRAVE, WV (Zito Media)

WAPWALLOPEN—See BERWICK, PA (MetroCast Communications)

WARMINSTER—See BENSALEM TWP., PA (Comcast Cable)

WARREN CENTER TWP.—See ROME, PA (Beaver Valley Cable Co.)

WARREN COUNTY—See WARREN, PA (Atlantic Broadband)

▲**WARREN**—Atlantic Broadband

WARRINGTON TWP. (BUCKS COUNTY)—See JAMISON, PA (Comcast Cable)

WARRINGTON TWP. (YORK COUNTY)—See NEWBERRY TWP., PA (Blue Ridge Communications)

WARRINGTON TWP.—See GETTYSBURG, PA (Comcast Cable)

WARRIOR RUN BOROUGH—See WILKES-BARRE, PA (Service Electric Cable Company)

▲**WARRIORS MARK**—Atlantic Broadband. Now served by ALTOONA, PA [PA0018]

WARRIORS MARK—See ALTOONA, PA (Atlantic Broadband)

WARSAW TWP.—See HAZEN, PA (Zito Media)

WARWICK TWP. (BERKS COUNTY)—See BIRDSBORO, PA (Service Electric Cablevision)

WARWICK TWP. (BUCKS COUNTY)—See JAMISON, PA (Comcast Cable)

WARWICK TWP. (CHESTER COUNTY)—See BIRDSBORO, PA (Service Electric Cablevision)

WARWICK TWP. (LANCASTER COUNTY)—See EPHRATA, PA (Blue Ridge Communications)

WARWICK—See BIRDSBORO, PA (Service Electric Cablevision)

WASHINGTON COUNTY—See SHIPPENSBURG, MD (Comcast Cable)

WASHINGTON TWP. (CARBON COUNTY)—See PALMERTON, PA (Blue Ridge Communications)

WASHINGTON TWP. (CLARION COUNTY)—See NORTH CLARION, PA (Armstrong Cable Services)

WASHINGTON TWP. (ERIE COUNTY)—See EDINBORO, PA (Coaxial Cable TV Corp.)

WASHINGTON TWP. (JEFFERSON COUNTY)—See BROCKWAY, PA (Brockway TV Inc.)

WASHINGTON TWP. (JEFFERSON COUNTY)—See HAZEN, PA (Zito Media)

WASHINGTON TWP. (LAWRENCE COUNTY)—See GROVE CITY, PA (Armstrong Cable Services)

WASHINGTON TWP. (NORTHUMBERLAND COUNTY)—See SUNBURY, PA (Service Electric Cablevision)

WASHINGTON TWP. (SNYDER COUNTY)—See SUNBURY, PA (Service Electric Cablevision)

WASHINGTON TWP. (WYOMING COUNTY)—See MESHOPPEN, PA (Blue Ridge Communications)

WASHINGTON TWP. (YORK COUNTY)—See LANCASTER, PA (Comcast Cable)

▲**WASHINGTON TWP.**—Formerly served by NORTHAMPTON BOROUGH, PA [PA0008]. RCN Corp. This cable system has converted to IPTV

WASHINGTON TWP.—See LEHIGH VALLEY, PA (Service Electric Cable TV & Communications)

▲**WASHINGTON**—Comcast Cable. Now served by PITTSBURGH, PA [PA0001]

WASHINGTON—See PITTSBURGH, PA (Comcast Cable)

WASHINGTONVILLE—See DANVILLE, PA (CATV Service Inc.)

▲**WATERFALL**—Waterfall Community TV

WATERFORD (ERIE COUNTY)—See HARBORCREEK TWP., PA (Time Warner Cable)

WATERFORD TWP. (ERIE COUNTY)—See HARBORCREEK TWP., PA (Time Warner Cable)

WATSON TWP.—See WILLIAMSPORT, PA (Comcast Cable)

WATSONTOWN—See DANVILLE, PA (CATV Service Inc.)

WATTS TWP.—See DUNCANNON, PA (Blue Ridge Communications)

▲**WATTSBURG**—Formerly served by Cebridge Connections. Now served by MEADVILLE, PA [PA0062]

WATTSBURG—See MEADVILLE, PA (Armstrong Cable Services)

WAYMART—See CARBONDALE, PA (Adams Digital Cable)

WAYNE HEIGHTS—See SHIPPENSBURG, PA (Comcast Cable)

WAYNE TWP. (ERIE COUNTY)—See CORRY, PA (Time Warner Cable)

WAYNE TWP. (LAWRENCE COUNTY)—See ZELIENOPLE, PA (Armstrong Cable Services)

WAYNE TWP.—See BRAVE, PA (Zito Media)

WAYNE—See KING OF PRUSSIA, PA (Comcast Cable)

WAYNESBORO—See SHIPPENSBURG, PA (Comcast Cable)

▲**WAYNESBURG**—Comcast Cable

WEATHERLY—See POCONO, PA (MetroCast Communications)

▲**WEEDVILLE**—Zito Media

WEIKERT—See MIFFLINBURG, PA (Atlantic Broadband)

WEISENBERG TWP.—See LEHIGH VALLEY, PA (Service Electric Cable TV & Communications)

WEISSPORT—See PALMERTON, PA (Blue Ridge Communications)

WELDBANK—See SHEFFIELD, PA (WestPA.net Inc.)

WELLS TANNERY—See WATERFALL, PA (Waterfall Community TV)

WELLS TWP.—See HUNTINGDON, PA (Comcast Cable)

▲**WELLSBORO**—Blue Ridge Communications

WELLSVILLE—See NEWBERRY TWP., PA (Blue Ridge Communications)

WERNERSVILLE—See READING, PA (Comcast Cable)

WESLEYVILLE—See HARBORCREEK TWP., PA (Time Warner Cable)

▲**WEST ALEXANDER**—Comcast Cable

WEST BETHLEHEM TWP.—See UNIONTOWN, PA (Atlantic Broadband)

WEST BRADFORD TWP.—See COATESVILLE, PA (Comcast Cable)

WEST BRANCH TWP. (POTTER COUNTY)—See GALETON, PA (Blue Ridge Communications)

WEST BRANDYWINE TWP.—See COATESVILLE, PA (Comcast Cable)

WEST BROWNSVILLE—See CONNELLSVILLE, PA (Armstrong Cable Services)

WEST BRUNSWICK TWP.—See POTTSVILLE, PA (Comcast Cable)

WEST BUFFALO TWP. (PORTIONS)—See MIFFLINBURG, PA (Atlantic Broadband)

▲**WEST BURLINGTON TWP.**—Formerly served by Barrett's TV Cable System. No longer in operation

WEST CALN TWP.—See COATESVILLE, PA (Comcast Cable)

WEST CAMERON TWP.—See SUNBURY, PA (Service Electric Cablevision)

WEST CARROLL TWP.—See BLAIRSVILLE, PA (Comcast Cable)

WEST CHESTER—See COATESVILLE, PA (Comcast Cable)

WEST CHILLISQUAQUE TWP. (PORTIONS)—See DANVILLE, PA (CATV Service Inc.)

WEST COCALICO TWP.—See EPHRATA, PA (Blue Ridge Communications)

WEST CONSHOHOCKEN—See NORRISTOWN, PA (Comcast Cable)

WEST CORNWALL TWP.—See LEBANON, PA (Comcast Cable)

WEST DEER TWP. (PORTIONS)—See ZELIENOPLE, PA (Armstrong Cable Services)

▲**WEST DEER TWP.**—Comcast Cable. Now served by TARENTUM BOROUGH, PA [PA0424]

WEST DEER TWP.—See TARENTUM BOROUGH, PA (Comcast Cable)

WEST DONEGAL TWP.—See ELIZABETHTOWN, PA (Comcast Cable)

WEST EARL TWP. (NORTHERN PORTION)—See EPHRATA, PA (Blue Ridge Communications)

WEST EARL TWP.—See LANCASTER, PA (Comcast Cable)

▲**WEST EASTON BOROUGH**—Formerly served by NORTHAMPTON BOROUGH, PA [PA0008]. RCN Corp. This cable system has converted to IPTV

WEST EASTON—See LEHIGH VALLEY, PA (Service Electric Cable TV & Communications)

WEST ELIZABETH—See PITTSBURGH, PA (Comcast Cable)

WEST FAIRVIEW—See HARRISBURG, PA (Comcast Cable)

WEST FALLOWFIELD TWP.—See OXFORD, PA (Armstrong Cable Services)

WEST GOSHEN—See COATESVILLE, PA (Comcast Cable)

WEST GROVE—See KENNETT SQUARE, PA (Comcast Cable)

WEST HANOVER TWP. (DAUPHIN COUNTY)—See HARRISBURG, PA (Comcast Cable)

WEST HAZLETON BOROUGH—See HAZLETON, PA (Service Electric Cablevision)

WEST HEMLOCK TWP.—See DANVILLE, PA (CATV Service Inc.)

WEST HEMPFIELD TWP. (LANCASTER COUNTY)—See LANCASTER, PA (Comcast Cable)

WEST HICKORY—See MEADVILLE, PA (Armstrong Cable Services)

WEST HOMESTEAD—See BETHEL PARK, PA (Comcast Cable)

WEST KITTANNING—See KISKIMINETAS TWP., PA (Comcast Cable)

WEST LAMPETER TWP.—See LANCASTER, PA (Comcast Cable)

WEST LAWN—See READING, PA (Comcast Cable)

WEST LEECHBURG—See KISKIMINETAS TWP., PA (Comcast Cable)

WEST MAHANOY TWP.—See SHENANDOAH, PA (Shen-Heights TV Assoc. Inc.)

WEST MAHANOY—See MAHANOY CITY, PA (Service Electric Cable Company)

WEST MANCHESTER TWP.—See YORK, PA (Comcast Cable)

WEST MANHEIM TWP.—See GETTYSBURG, PA (Comcast Cable)

WEST MANHEIM TWP.—See YORK, PA (Comcast Cable)

WEST MAYFIELD—See BEAVER FALLS, PA (Comcast Cable)

WEST MEAD TWP.—See MEADVILLE, PA (Armstrong Cable Services)

WEST MIDDLESEX—See MERCER COUNTY, PA (Time Warner Cable)

WEST MIDDLESEX—See SHARON, PA (Time Warner Cable)

▲**WEST MIFFLIN**—Formerly served by Adelphia Communications. Now served by BETHEL PARK, PA [PA0318]

WEST MIFFLIN—See BETHEL PARK, PA (Comcast Cable)

WEST NANTICOKE—See BERWICK, PA (MetroCast Communications)

WEST NANTMEAL—See COATESVILLE, PA (Comcast Cable)

▲**WEST NEWTON**—Formerly served by Adelphia Communications. Now served by BETHEL PARK, PA [PA0318]

WEST NEWTON—See BETHEL PARK, PA (Comcast Cable)

WEST NORRITON TWP.—See NORRISTOWN, PA (Comcast Cable)

WEST NOTTINGHAM TWP.—See OXFORD, PA (Armstrong Cable Services)

WEST PENN TWP. (NORTHWESTERN PORTION)—See MAHANOY CITY, PA (Service Electric Cable Company)

WEST PENN TWP. (SOUTHEASTERN PORTION)—See PALMERTON, PA (Blue Ridge Communications)

WEST PENNSBORO TWP. (CUMBERLAND COUNTY)—See SHIPPENSBURG, PA (Comcast Cable)

WEST PERRY TWP.—See MOUNT PLEASANT MILLS, PA (Zampelli Electronics)

WEST PIKE RUN TWP.—See CONNELLSVILLE, PA (Armstrong Cable Services)

WEST PIKE RUN TWP.—See BENTLEYVILLE, PA (FairPoint Communications)

WEST PIKELAND TWP. (PORTIONS)—See COATESVILLE, PA (Comcast Cable)

WEST PITTSTON—See DUNMORE, PA (Comcast Cable)

WEST POTTSGROVE TWP.—See POTTSTOWN, PA (Comcast Cable)

WEST PROVIDENCE TWP.—See BEDFORD, PA (Comcast Cable)

WEST READING—See READING, PA (Comcast Cable)

WEST ROCKHILL TWP.—See SELLERSVILLE, PA (Comcast Cable)

WEST SADSBURY TWP. (CHESTER COUNTY)—See COATESVILLE, PA (Comcast Cable)

WEST SALEM TWP.—See GREENVILLE, PA (Time Warner Cable)

WEST SHENANGO TWP.—See MEADVILLE, PA (Armstrong Cable Services)

WEST ST. CLAIR—See BEDFORD, PA (Comcast Cable)

WEST TAYLOR TWP.—See JOHNSTOWN, PA (Atlantic Broadband)

WEST VIEW—See PITTSBURGH, PA (Comcast Cable)

WEST VINCENT TWP.—See COATESVILLE, PA (Comcast Cable)

WEST WHEATFIELD TWP. (INDIANA COUNTY)—See BLAIRSVILLE, PA (Comcast Cable)

WEST WHEATFIELD TWP.—See ARMAGH, PA (Comcast Cable)

WEST WHITEHEAD TWP. (CHESTER COUNTY)—See COATESVILLE, PA (Comcast Cable)

WEST WHITELAND TWP.—See COATESVILLE, PA (Comcast Cable)

WEST WYOMING—See SCRANTON, PA (Comcast Cable)

WEST YORK—See YORK, PA (Comcast Cable)

WESTFALL TWP. (PORTIONS)—See MATAMORAS, PA (Cablevision Systems Corp.)

WESTFIELD TWP.—See WESTFIELD, PA (Westfield Community Antenna)

▲**WESTFIELD**—Westfield Community Antenna

▲**WESTLINE**—Keystone Wilcox Cable TV Inc.

WESTMONT (CAMBRIA COUNTY)—See JOHNSTOWN, PA (Atlantic Broadband)

WESTMORELAND CITY—See GREENSBURG, PA (Comcast Cable)

WESTON—See BERWICK, PA (MetroCast Communications)

WESTTOWN TWP.—See COATESVILLE, PA (Comcast Cable)

WETMORE TWP.—See KANE, PA (Comcast Cable)

WHARTON TWP.—See MARKLEYSBURG, PA (Comcast Cable)

WHEATFIELD TWP.—See DUNCANNON, PA (Blue Ridge Communications)

WHEATLAND—See MERCER COUNTY, PA (Time Warner Cable)

WHEATLAND—See SHARON, PA (Time Warner Cable)

WHITAKER—See BETHEL PARK, PA (Comcast Cable)

WHITE DEER TWP.—See DANVILLE, PA (CATV Service Inc.)

WHITE HAVEN—See POCONO, PA (MetroCast Communications)

WHITE MILLS—See HONESDALE, PA (Blue Ridge Communications)

WHITE TWP. (CAMBRIA COUNTY)—See COALPORT, PA (Comcast Cable)

▲**WHITEHALL TWP.**—Formerly served by NORTHAMPTON BOROUGH, PA [PA0008]. RCN Corp. This cable system has converted to IPTV

WHITEHALL TWP.—See LEHIGH VALLEY, PA (Service Electric Cable TV & Communications)

WHITEHALL—See PITTSBURGH, PA (Comcast Cable)

WHITEMARSH TWP. (SOUTHERN PORTION)—See NORRISTOWN, PA (Comcast Cable)

WHITEMARSH TWP.—See LANSDALE, PA (Comcast Cable)

WHITPAIN TWP. (PORTIONS)—See LANSDALE, PA (Comcast Cable)

WHITPAIN TWP.—See NORRISTOWN, PA (Comcast Cable)

WICONISCO TWP.—See LYKENS, PA (Comcast Cable)

WIDNOON—See KISKIMINETAS TWP., PA (Comcast Cable)

▲**WILCOX**—Zito Media

WILKES-BARRE TWP.—See WILKES-BARRE, PA (Service Electric Cable Company)

▲**WILKES-BARRE**—Service Electric Cable Company

WILKINS TWP.—See MONROEVILLE, PA (Comcast Cable)

WILKINSBURG—See PITTSBURGH, PA (Comcast Cable)

WILLIAMS TWP. (DAUPHIN COUNTY)—See LYKENS, PA (Comcast Cable)

▲**WILLIAMS TWP.**—Formerly served by NORTHAMPTON BOROUGH, PA [PA0008]. RCN Corp. This cable system has converted to IPTV

WILLIAMS TWP.—See LEHIGH VALLEY, PA (Service Electric Cable TV & Communications)

▲**WILLIAMSBURG (Blair County)**—Formerly served by Adelphia Communications. Now served by HUNTINGDON, PA [PA0107]

WILLIAMSBURG—See HUNTINGDON, PA (Comcast Cable)

▲**WILLIAMSPORT**—Comcast Cable

WILLIAMSTOWN (DAUPHIN COUNTY)—See LYKENS, PA (Comcast Cable)

WILLISTOWN TWP.—See COATESVILLE, PA (Comcast Cable)

▲**WILLOW GROVE**—Comcast Cable

WILMINGTON TWP. (MERCER COUNTY)—See MERCER COUNTY, PA (Time Warner Cable)

WILMINGTON TWP.—See SHARON, PA (Time Warner Cable)

WILMORE—See ADAMS TWP. (Cambria County), PA (Comcast Cable)

WILMOT TWP.—See MESHOPPEN, PA (Blue Ridge Communications)

▲**WILSON BOROUGH**—Formerly served by NORTHAMPTON BOROUGH, PA [PA0008]. RCN Corp. This cable system has converted to IPTV

WILSON—See LEHIGH VALLEY, PA (Service Electric Cable TV & Communications)

WINBURNE—See SNOW SHOE, PA (Tele-Media)

WIND GAP BORO—See LEHIGH VALLEY, PA (Service Electric Cable TV & Communications)

▲**WIND GAP BOROUGH**—Formerly served by NORTHAMPTON BOROUGH, PA [PA0008]. RCN Corp. This cable system has converted to IPTV

WINDBER—See JOHNSTOWN, PA (Atlantic Broadband)

WINDBER—See ADAMS TWP. (Cambria County), PA (Comcast Cable)

WINDHAM TWP.—See MESHOPPEN, PA (Blue Ridge Communications)

WINDSOR (BROOME COUNTY)—See CARBONDALE, NY (Adams Digital Cable)

WINDSOR (VILLAGE)—See CARBONDALE, NY (Adams Digital Cable)

WINDSOR—See YORK, PA (Comcast Cable)

▲**WINFIELD**—Formerly served by D&E Communications. No longer in operation

WINONA LAKES (MONROE & PIKE COUNTIES)—See STROUDSBURG, PA (Blue Ridge Communications)

WINSLOW TWP. (PORTIONS)—See PUNXSUTAWNEY, PA (Comcast Cable)

WOLF CREEK TWP.—See GROVE CITY, PA (Armstrong Cable Services)

WOLF TWP.—See WILLIAMSPORT, PA (Comcast Cable)

WOMELSDORF—See LEBANON, PA (Comcast Cable)

WOOD TWP.—See HUNTINGDON, PA (Comcast Cable)

WOODBURY TWP. (BEDFORD COUNTY)—See WOODBURY, PA (Atlantic Broadband)

WOODBURY TWP.—See ALTOONA, PA (Atlantic Broadband)

WOODBURY TWP.—See HUNTINGDON, PA (Comcast Cable)

▲**WOODBURY**—Atlantic Broadband

WOODCOCK BOROUGH—See EDINBORO, PA (Coaxial Cable TV Corp.)

WOODWARD TWP. (LYCOMING COUNTY)—See WILLIAMSPORT, PA (Comcast Cable)

WORCESTER TWP. (MONTGOMERY COUNTY)—See NORRISTOWN, PA (Comcast Cable)

WORCESTER—See POTTSTOWN, PA (Comcast Cable)

WORMLEYSBURG—See HARRISBURG, PA (Comcast Cable)

WORTH TWP.—See ZELIENOPLE, PA (Armstrong Cable Services)

WORTH TWP.—See STATE COLLEGE, PA (Comcast Cable)

WORTHINGTON—See KISKIMINETAS TWP., PA (Comcast Cable)

WORTHVILLE—See PUNXSUTAWNEY, PA (Comcast Cable)

WRIGHT TWP.—See WILKES-BARRE, PA (Service Electric Cable Company)

WRIGHTER LAKE—See CARBONDALE, PA (Adams Digital Cable)

WRIGHTSTOWN TWP.—See NEWTOWN, PA (Comcast Cable)

WRIGHTSVILLE—See LANCASTER, PA (Comcast Cable)

WYALUSING BOROUGH—See MESHOPPEN, PA (Blue Ridge Communications)

WYALUSING TWP.—See MESHOPPEN, PA (Blue Ridge Communications)

WYNDMOOR—See LANSDALE, PA (Comcast Cable)

WYOMING COUNTY—See MESHOPPEN, PA (Blue Ridge Communications)

WYOMING—See SCRANTON, PA (Comcast Cable)

WYOMISSING HILLS—See READING, PA (Comcast Cable)

WYOMISSING—See READING, PA (Comcast Cable)

WYSOX TWP.—See TOWANDA, PA (Comcast Cable)

YANKEE LAKE—See MERCER COUNTY, OH (Time Warner Cable)

YANKEE LAKE—See SHARON, OH (Time Warner Cable)

YARDLEY—See LEVITTOWN, PA (Comcast Cable)

YATESBORO—See KISKIMINETAS TWP., PA (Comcast Cable)

YATESVILLE—See DUNMORE, PA (Comcast Cable)

YEADON—See WALLINGFORD, PA (Comcast Cable)

▲**YEADON**—RCN Corp. Formerly served by Philadelphia (suburbs), PA [PA0447]. This cable system has converted to IPTV

YOE—See YORK, PA (Comcast Cable)

YORK HAVEN (YORK COUNTY)—See NEWBERRY TWP., PA (Blue Ridge Communications)

YORK HAVEN (YORK COUNTY)—See YORK, PA (Comcast Cable)

YORK SPRINGS—See GETTYSBURG, PA (Comcast Cable)

▲**YORK**—Comcast Cable

YORKANA—See YORK, PA (Comcast Cable)

YOUNG TWP. (INDIANA COUNTY)—See BLAIRSVILLE, PA (Comcast Cable)

YOUNG TWP. (JEFFERSON COUNTY)—See PUNXSUTAWNEY, PA (Comcast Cable)

YOUNGSTOWN—See BLAIRSVILLE, PA (Comcast Cable)

▲**YOUNGSVILLE**—Youngsville TV Corp.

YOUNGWOOD—See GREENSBURG, PA (Comcast Cable)

▲**ZELIENOPLE**—Armstrong Cable Services

ZERBE TWP.—See SUNBURY, PA (Service Electric Cablevision)

ZERBE—See TREMONT, PA (Wire Television Corp.)

ZION GROVE—See BERWICK, PA (MetroCast Communications)

▲**ZION**—Tele-Media

ZULINGER—See SHIPPENSBURG, PA (Comcast Cable)

PUERTO RICO

ADJUNTAS—See PONCE, PR (Choice Cable)

AGUADA—See PONCE, PR (Choice Cable)

AGUADILLA—See PONCE, PR (Choice Cable)

AGUAS BUENAS—See LUQUILLO, PR (Liberty Cablevision of Puerto Rico)

AIBONITO—See LUQUILLO, PR (Liberty Cablevision of Puerto Rico)

ANASCO—See PONCE, PR (Choice Cable)

ARECIBO—See LUQUILLO, PR (Liberty Cablevision of Puerto Rico)

ARROYO—See PONCE, PR (Choice Cable)

BARCELONETA—See LUQUILLO, PR (Liberty Cablevision of Puerto Rico)

BARRANQUITAS—See LUQUILLO, PR (Liberty Cablevision of Puerto Rico)

BAYAMON—See SAN JUAN, PR (OneLink Communications)

CABA ROJO—See PONCE, PR (Choice Cable)

CAGUAS—See LUQUILLO, PR (Liberty Cablevision of Puerto Rico)

CAMUY—See LUQUILLO, PR (Liberty Cablevision of Puerto Rico)

CANOVANAS—See LUQUILLO, PR (Liberty Cablevision of Puerto Rico)

CAROLINA—See SAN JUAN, PR (OneLink Communications)

CATANO—See SAN JUAN, PR (OneLink Communications)

CAYEY—See LUQUILLO, PR (Liberty Cablevision of Puerto Rico)

▲**CEIBA NAVAL BASE**—Formerly served by Americable International. No longer in operation

CEIBA—See LUQUILLO, PR (Liberty Cablevision of Puerto Rico)

CIALES—See LUQUILLO, PR (Liberty Cablevision of Puerto Rico)

CIDRA—See LUQUILLO, PR (Liberty Cablevision of Puerto Rico)

COAMO—See PONCE, PR (Choice Cable)

COMERIO—See LUQUILLO, PR (Liberty Cablevision of Puerto Rico)

COROZAL—See LUQUILLO, PR (Liberty Cablevision of Puerto Rico)

DORADO—See LUQUILLO, PR (Liberty Cablevision of Puerto Rico)

FAJARDO—See LUQUILLO, PR (Liberty Cablevision of Puerto Rico)

GUANICA—See PONCE, PR (Choice Cable)

GUAYAMA—See PONCE, PR (Choice Cable)

GUAYANILLA—See PONCE, PR (Choice Cable)

GUAYNABO—See SAN JUAN, PR (OneLink Communications)

GURABO—See LUQUILLO, PR (Liberty Cablevision of Puerto Rico)

HATILLO—See LUQUILLO, PR (Liberty Cablevision of Puerto Rico)

HORMIGUEROS—See PONCE, PR (Choice Cable)

HUMACAO—See LUQUILLO, PR (Liberty Cablevision of Puerto Rico)

ISABELA—See PONCE, PR (Choice Cable)

JAYUYA—See PONCE, PR (Choice Cable)

JUANA DIAZ—See PONCE, PR (Choice Cable)

JUNCOS—See LUQUILLO, PR (Liberty Cablevision of Puerto Rico)

LAJAS—See PONCE, PR (Choice Cable)

LARES—See LUQUILLO, PR (Liberty Cablevision of Puerto Rico)

LAS MARIAS—See PONCE, PR (Choice Cable)

LAS PIEDRAS—See LUQUILLO, PR (Liberty Cablevision of Puerto Rico)

▲ **LEVITTOWN**—OneLink Communications. Now served by SAN JUAN, PR [PR0001]

LEVITTOWN—See SAN JUAN, PR (OneLink Communications)

LOIZA—See LUQUILLO, PR (Liberty Cablevision of Puerto Rico)

▲ **LUQUILLO**—Liberty Cablevision of Puerto Rico

MANATI—See LUQUILLO, PR (Liberty Cablevision of Puerto Rico)

MARICAO—See PONCE, PR (Choice Cable)

MAUNABO—See PONCE, PR (Choice Cable)

MAYAGUEZ—See PONCE, PR (Choice Cable)

▲ **MERCEDITA**—Centennial de Puerto Rico. Now served by MAYAGUEZ, PR [PR0008]

MERCEDITA—See PONCE, PR (Choice Cable)

MOCA—See PONCE, PR (Choice Cable)

MOROVIS—See LUQUILLO, PR (Liberty Cablevision of Puerto Rico)

NAGUABO—See LUQUILLO, PR (Liberty Cablevision of Puerto Rico)

NARANJITO—See LUQUILLO, PR (Liberty Cablevision of Puerto Rico)

OROCOVIS—See LUQUILLO, PR (Liberty Cablevision of Puerto Rico)

PATILLAS—See PONCE, PR (Choice Cable)

PENUELAS—See PONCE, PR (Choice Cable)

PLAYA DE PONCE—See PONCE, PR (Choice Cable)

▲ **PONCE**—Choice Cable

QUEBRADILLAS—See PONCE, PR (Choice Cable)

RINCON—See PONCE, PR (Choice Cable)

RIO GRANDE—See LUQUILLO, PR (Liberty Cablevision of Puerto Rico)

SABANNA GRANDE—See PONCE, PR (Choice Cable)

SALINAS—See PONCE, PR (Choice Cable)

SAN GERMAN—See PONCE, PR (Choice Cable)

▲ **SAN JUAN**—OneLink Communications

SAN LORENZO—See LUQUILLO, PR (Liberty Cablevision of Puerto Rico)

SAN SEBASTION—See LUQUILLO, PR (Liberty Cablevision of Puerto Rico)

SANTA ISABEL—See PONCE, PR (Choice Cable)

TALLABOA—See PONCE, PR (Choice Cable)

TOA ALTA—See SAN JUAN, PR (OneLink Communications)

TOA BAJA—See SAN JUAN, PR (OneLink Communications)

TRUJILLO ALTO—See SAN JUAN, PR (OneLink Communications)

UTUADO—See LUQUILLO, PR (Liberty Cablevision of Puerto Rico)

VEGA ALTA—See LUQUILLO, PR (Liberty Cablevision of Puerto Rico)

VEGA BAJA—See LUQUILLO, PR (Liberty Cablevision of Puerto Rico)

VILLALBA—See PONCE, PR (Choice Cable)

YABUCOA—See LUQUILLO, PR (Liberty Cablevision of Puerto Rico)

YAUCO—See PONCE, PR (Choice Cable)

RHODE ISLAND

ASHAWAY—See PROVIDENCE, RI (Cox Communications)

BARRINGTON—See PROVIDENCE, RI (Cox Communications)

BARRINGTON—See WARREN, RI (Full Channel TV Inc.)

BRADFORD—See PROVIDENCE, RI (Cox Communications)

BRISTOL COUNTY—See PROVIDENCE, RI (Cox Communications)

BRISTOL COUNTY—See WARREN, RI (Full Channel TV Inc.)

BRISTOL—See NEWPORT, RI (Cox Communications)

BRISTOL—See WARREN, RI (Full Channel TV Inc.)

▲ **BURRILLVILLE (town)**—Cox Communications. Now served by PROVIDENCE, RI [RI0001]

BURRILLVILLE (TOWN)—See PROVIDENCE, RI (Cox Communications)

CENTRAL FALLS—See PROVIDENCE, RI (Cox Communications)

CHARLESTOWN—See PROVIDENCE, RI (Cox Communications)

COVENTRY—See PROVIDENCE, RI (Cox Communications)

▲ **CRANSTON**—Cox Communications. Now served by PROVIDENCE, RI [RI0001]

CRANSTON—See PROVIDENCE, RI (Cox Communications)

CUMBERLAND—See PROVIDENCE, RI (Cox Communications)

EAST GREENWICH—See PROVIDENCE, RI (Cox Communications)

EAST PROVIDENCE—See PROVIDENCE, RI (Cox Communications)

EXETER (TOWN)—See PROVIDENCE, RI (Cox Communications)

GLOCESTER (TOWN)—See PROVIDENCE, RI (Cox Communications)

HOPKINTON—See PROVIDENCE, RI (Cox Communications)

JAMESTOWN—See PROVIDENCE, RI (Cox Communications)

JOHNSTON—See PROVIDENCE, RI (Cox Communications)

LINCOLN—See PROVIDENCE, RI (Cox Communications)

LITTLE COMPTON—See NEWPORT, RI (Cox Communications)

MIDDLETOWN—See NEWPORT, RI (Cox Communications)

NARRAGANSETT—See PROVIDENCE, RI (Cox Communications)

▲ **NEW SHOREHAM**—Formerly served by Block Island Cable TV. No longer in operation

▲ **NEWPORT & LINCOLN**—Cox Communications. Now served by PROVIDENCE, RI [RI0001]

NEWPORT COUNTY—See PROVIDENCE, RI (Cox Communications)

NEWPORT NAVAL BASE—See NEWPORT, RI (Cox Communications)

▲ **NEWPORT**—Cox Communications

NEWPORT—See PROVIDENCE, RI (Cox Communications)

NORTH KINGSTOWN—See PROVIDENCE, RI (Cox Communications)

NORTH PROVIDENCE—See PROVIDENCE, RI (Cox Communications)

NORTH SMITHFIELD—See PROVIDENCE, RI (Cox Communications)

PAWTUCKET—See PROVIDENCE, RI (Cox Communications)

PROVIDENCE COUNTY—See PROVIDENCE, RI (Cox Communications)

▲ **PROVIDENCE**—Cox Communications

RICHMOND—See PROVIDENCE, RI (Cox Communications)

SCITUATE (TOWN)—See PROVIDENCE, RI (Cox Communications)

SMITHFIELD—See PROVIDENCE, RI (Cox Communications)

SOUTH KINGSTOWN—See PROVIDENCE, RI (Cox Communications)

TIVERTON—See PROVIDENCE, RI (Cox Communications)

▲ **WARREN**—Full Channel TV Inc.

WARWICK—See PROVIDENCE, RI (Cox Communications)

WEST GREENWICH—See PROVIDENCE, RI (Cox Communications)

WEST WARWICK—See PROVIDENCE, RI (Cox Communications)

▲ **WESTERLY**—Cox Communications. Now served by PROVIDENCE, RI [RI0001]

WESTERLY—See PROVIDENCE, RI (Cox Communications)

WOONSOCKET—See PROVIDENCE, RI (Cox Communications)

SOUTH CAROLINA

ABBEVILLE COUNTY (PORTIONS)—See SPARTANBURG, SC (Charter Communications)

ABBEVILLE COUNTY (PORTIONS)—See CALHOUN FALLS, SC (Comcast Cable)

ABBEVILLE COUNTY (UNINCORPORATED AREAS)—See GREENWOOD, SC (Northland Cable Television)

▲ **ABBEVILLE**—Charter Communications. Now served by GREENVILLE/ SPARTANBURG, SC [SC0003]

ABBEVILLE—See SPARTANBURG, SC (Charter Communications)

AIKEN COUNTY (PORTIONS)—See GILBERT, SC (Comporium Cable)

▲ **AIKEN**—Atlantic Broadband

ALLENDALE COUNTY—See ALLENDALE, SC (Atlantic Broadband)

▲**ALLENDALE**—Atlantic Broadband

▲**ANCHOR POINT**—Charter Communications

ANDERSON COUNTY (PORTIONS)—See SPARTANBURG, SC (Charter Communications)

ANDERSON COUNTY (UNINCORPORATED AREAS)—See ANCHOR POINT, SC (Charter Communications)

▲**ANDERSON**—Charter Communications. Now served by GREENVILLE/SPARTANBURG, SC [SC0003]

ANDERSON—See SPARTANBURG, SC (Charter Communications)

ANDREWS—See MYRTLE BEACH, SC (Time Warner Cable)

ARCADIA LAKES—See COLUMBIA, SC (Time Warner Cable)

ATLANTIC BEACH—See MYRTLE BEACH, SC (Time Warner Cable)

▲**AWENDAW**—US Cable of Coastal Texas LP. Now served by CHARLESTON, SC [SC0001]

AWENDAW—See CHARLESTON, SC (Comcast Cable)

AYNOR—See HOMEWOOD, SC (Horry Telephone Coop.)

BAMBERG COUNTY—See BAMBERG, SC (Atlantic Broadband)

▲**BAMBERG**—Atlantic Broadband

BARNWELL COUNTY—See BARNWELL, SC (Atlantic Broadband)

▲**BARNWELL**—Atlantic Broadband

BATESBURG—See COLUMBIA, SC (Time Warner Cable)

BATH—See AIKEN, SC (Atlantic Broadband)

BEAUFORT COUNTY (SOUTHERN PORTION)—See BLUFFTON, SC (Hargray)

BEAUFORT COUNTY—See BEAUFORT, SC (Hargray)

BEAUFORT COUNTY—See MYRTLE BEACH, SC (Time Warner Cable)

▲**BEAUFORT USMC AIR STATION**—Comcast Cable

▲**BEAUFORT**—Hargray

▲**BELTON**—Charter Communications. Now served by GREENVILLE/SPARTANBURG, SC [SC0003]

▲**BENNETTSVILLE**—MetroCast Communications

BERKELEY COUNTY (PORTIONS)—See MYRTLE BEACH, SC (Time Warner Cable)

BERKELEY COUNTY (UNINCORPORATED AREAS)—See MONCKS CORNER, SC (Home Telecom)

BERKELEY COUNTY—See CHARLESTON, SC (Comcast Cable)

▲**BETHUNE**—Formerly served by Pine Tree Cablevision. No longer in operation

▲**BISHOPVILLE**—Time Warner. Now served by COLUMBIA, SC [SC0002]

BISHOPVILLE—See COLUMBIA, SC (Time Warner Cable)

BLACKSBURG—See SPARTANBURG, SC (Charter Communications)

BLACKVILLE—See BARNWELL, SC (Atlantic Broadband)

BLUE RIDGE—See SPARTANBURG, SC (Charter Communications)

▲**BLUFFTON**—Hargray

BLYTHEWOOD—See COLUMBIA, SC (Time Warner Cable)

BONNEAU—See MONCKS CORNER, SC (Home Telecom)

▲**BOWMAN**—Almega Cable

BRANCHVILLE—See BOWMAN, SC (Almega Cable)

BREVARD—See ROCK HILL, NC (Comporium Communications)

▲**BRIARCLIFF ACRES**—Cablevision Industries Inc. Now served by MYRTLE BEACH, SC [SC0007]

BRIARCLIFF ACRES—See MYRTLE BEACH, SC (Time Warner Cable)

▲**BRISSEY ROCK**—Formerly served by KLiP Interactive. No longer in operation

▲**BROWNS FERRY**—Time Warner Cable. Now served by MYRTLE BEACH, SC [SC0007]

BROWNS FERRY—See MYRTLE BEACH, SC (Time Warner Cable)

BRUNSON—See HAMPTON, SC (Comcast Cable)

BUCKSPORT—See HOMEWOOD, SC (Horry Telephone Coop.)

BUFFALO—See SPARTANBURG, SC (Charter Communications)

BURNETTOWN—See AIKEN, SC (Atlantic Broadband)

CALHOUN COUNTY (PORTIONS)—See COLUMBIA, SC (Time Warner Cable)

▲**CALHOUN FALLS**—Comcast Cable

▲**CAMDEN**—TruVista Communications

▲**CAMERON**—Formerly served by Almega Cable. No longer in operation

CAMPOBELLO—See SPARTANBURG, SC (Charter Communications)

CASSATT—See CAMDEN, SC (TruVista Communications)

CAYCE—See COLUMBIA, SC (Time Warner Cable)

CENTRAL PACOLET—See SPARTANBURG, SC (Charter Communications)

CENTRAL—See SENECA, SC (Northland Cable Television)

CHAPIN—See COLUMBIA, SC (Time Warner Cable)

CHARLESTON COUNTY (NORTHERN PORTION)—See CHARLESTON, SC (Comcast Cable)

CHARLESTON COUNTY (UNINCORPORATED AREAS)—See McCLELLANVILLE, SC (Windjammer Cable)

▲**CHARLESTON**—Comcast Cable

▲**CHARLESTON**—Knology

▲**CHERAW**—Time Warner Cable. Now served by MYRTLE BEACH, SC [SC0007]

CHERAW—See MYRTLE BEACH, SC (Time Warner Cable)

CHEROKEE COUNTY (UNINCORPORATED AREAS)—See SPARTANBURG, SC (Charter Communications)

CHESNEE—See SPARTANBURG, SC (Charter Communications)

CHESTER COUNTY (UNINCORPORATED AREAS)—See SPARTANBURG, SC (Charter Communications)

CHESTER COUNTY (UNINCORPORATED AREAS)—See ROCK HILL, SC (Comporium Communications)

CHESTER COUNTY (UNINCORPORATED AREAS)—See CHESTER, SC (TruVista Communications)

▲**CHESTER**—TruVista Communications

▲**CHESTERFIELD (TOWN)**—NewWave Communications

CHESTERFIELD COUNTY (PORTIONS)—See CHESTERFIELD (town), SC (NewWave Communications)

CHESTERFIELD COUNTY—See MYRTLE BEACH, SC (Time Warner Cable)

CHOPPEE—See MYRTLE BEACH, SC (Time Warner Cable)

CLARENDON COUNTY—See COLUMBIA, SC (Time Warner Cable)

CLEMSON—See SENECA, SC (Northland Cable Television)

CLINTON—See SPARTANBURG, SC (Charter Communications)

CLIO—See BENNETTSVILLE, SC (MetroCast Communications)

COLLETON COUNTY—See WALTERBORO, SC (Comcast Cable)

▲**COLUMBIA**—Time Warner Cable

COLUMBUS—See SPARTANBURG, NC (Charter Communications)

CONWAY—See HOMEWOOD, SC (Horry Telephone Coop.)

CONWAY—See MYRTLE BEACH, SC (Time Warner Cable)

CORDOVA (SOUTHWESTERN PORTION)—See COLUMBIA, SC (Time Warner Cable)

▲**COTTAGEVILLE**—Formerly served by Pine Tree Cablevision. No longer in operation

COWPENS—See SPARTANBURG, SC (Charter Communications)

▲**CROSS HILL**—Formerly served by KLiP Interactive. No longer in operation

▲**CROSS**—Formerly served by Pine Tree Cablevision. No longer in operation

CROSS—See MONCKS CORNER, SC (Home Telecom)

DALZELL—See COLUMBIA, SC (Time Warner Cable)

▲**DANIEL ISLAND**—Home Telecom. See North Charleston, SC [SC5008]

DARLINGTON COUNTY—See MYRTLE BEACH, SC (Time Warner Cable)

DARLINGTON—See MYRTLE BEACH, SC (Time Warner Cable)

DATAW ISLAND—See LADY'S ISLAND, SC (Comcast Cable)

▲**DAUFUSKIE ISLAND**—Resorts Cable TV

DAVIS STATION—See SUMMERTON, SC (Almega Cable)

▲**DEBORDIEU COLONY**—Time Warner Cable. Now served by MYRTLE BEACH, SC [SC0007]

DEBORDIEU COLONY—See MYRTLE BEACH, SC (Time Warner Cable)

DENMARK—See BARNWELL, SC (Atlantic Broadband)

DILLON COUNTY—See MYRTLE BEACH, SC (Time Warner Cable)

▲**DILLON**—Formerly served by Adelphia Communications. Now served by MYRTLE BEACH, SC [SC0007]

DILLON—See MYRTLE BEACH, SC (Time Warner Cable)

DONALDS—See SPARTANBURG, SC (Charter Communications)

DORCHESTER COUNTY (PORTIONS)—See MYRTLE BEACH, SC (Time Warner Cable)

DORCHESTER COUNTY (UNINCORPORATED AREAS)—See ST. GEORGE, SC (Almega Cable)

DUE WEST—See SPARTANBURG, SC (Charter Communications)

DUNBAR—See MYRTLE BEACH, SC (Time Warner Cable)

DUNCAN—See SPARTANBURG, SC (Charter Communications)

EASLEY—See SPARTANBURG, SC (Charter Communications)

EAST LAURINBURG—See MYRTLE BEACH, NC (Time Warner Cable)

EASTOVER—See COLUMBIA, SC (Time Warner Cable)

EBENEZER—See SPARTANBURG, SC (Charter Communications)

EDGEFIELD COUNTY (PORTIONS)—See GREENWOOD, SC (Northland Cable Television)

EDGEFIELD—See GREENWOOD, SC (Northland Cable Television)

▲**EHRHARDT**—Formerly served by Almega Cable. No longer in operation

ELGIN—See COLUMBIA, SC (Time Warner Cable)

ELKO—See BARNWELL, SC (Atlantic Broadband)

▲**ELLOREE**—Formerly served by Pine Tree Cablevision. No longer in operation

ENOREE—See SPARTANBURG, SC (Charter Communications)

▲**ESTILL**—Hargray

EUTAWVILLE—See HOLLY HILL, SC (Almega Cable)

FAIRFAX—See ALLENDALE, SC (Atlantic Broadband)

FAIRFIELD COUNTY (NORTHERN PORTION)—See ROCK HILL, SC (Comporium Communications)

FAIRFIELD COUNTY (PORTIONS)—See WINNSBORO, SC (TruVista Communications)

FAIRFIELD—See SPARTANBURG, SC (Charter Communications)

▲**FIVE POINTS**—Northland Cable Television

FLORENCE COUNTY—See MYRTLE BEACH, SC (Time Warner Cable)

▲**FLORENCE**—Time Warner Cable. Now served by MYRTLE BEACH, SC [SC0007]

FLORENCE—See MYRTLE BEACH, SC (Time Warner Cable)

▲**FOLLY BEACH**—US Cable of Coastal Texas LP. Now served by CHARLESTON, SC [SC0001]

FOLLY BEACH—See CHARLESTON, SC (Comcast Cable)

FOREST ACRES—See COLUMBIA, SC (Time Warner Cable)

FORESTBROOK—See MYRTLE BEACH, SC (Time Warner Cable)

FORT JACKSON—See COLUMBIA, SC (Time Warner Cable)

FORT LAWN—See ROCK HILL, SC (Comporium Communications)

▲**FORT MILL**—Comporium Communications. Now served by ROCK HILL, SC [SC0138]

FORT MILL—See ROCK HILL, SC (Comporium Communications)

FOUNTAIN INN—See SPARTANBURG, SC (Charter Communications)

FRIPP ISLAND—See LADY'S ISLAND, SC (Comcast Cable)

▲**GAFFNEY**—Charter Communications. Now served by GREENVILLE/SPARTANBURG, SC [SC0003]

GAFFNEY—See SPARTANBURG, SC (Charter Communications)

GARDEN CITY BEACH—See MYRTLE BEACH, SC (Time Warner Cable)

▲**GASTON**—Formerly served by Pine Tree Cablevision. No longer in operation

GEORGETOWN COUNTY (PORTIONS)—See HOMEWOOD, SC (Horry Telephone Coop.)

GEORGETOWN COUNTY—See MYRTLE BEACH, SC (Time Warner Cable)

GEORGETOWN—See MYRTLE BEACH, SC (Time Warner Cable)

GIBSON—See MYRTLE BEACH, NC (Time Warner Cable)

▲**GILBERT**—Comporium Cable

GLOVERVILLE—See AIKEN, SC (Atlantic Broadband)

GOAT ISLAND RESORT—See SUMMERTON, SC (Almega Cable)

GOOSE CREEK—See CHARLESTON, SC (Comcast Cable)

GRANITEVILLE—See AIKEN, SC (Atlantic Broadband)

▲**GRAY COURT**—Charter Communications. Now served by GREENVILLE/SPARTANBURG, SC [SC0003]

GRAY COURT—See SPARTANBURG, SC (Charter Communications)

GREAT FALLS—See ROCK HILL, SC (Comporium Communications)

▲**GREENVILLE COUNTY**—Formerly served by KLiP Interactive. No longer in operation

GREENVILLE COUNTY—See SPARTANBURG, SC (Charter Communications)

GREENWOOD COUNTY—See GREENWOOD, SC (Northland Cable Television)

▲**GREENWOOD**—Northland Cable Television

▲**GREER**—Charter Communications. Now served by GREENVILLE/SPARTANBURG, SC [SC0003]

GREER—See SPARTANBURG, SC (Charter Communications)

HAMPTON COUNTY (PORTIONS)—See HAMPTON, SC (Comcast Cable)

▲**HAMPTON**—Comcast Cable

HANAHAN—See CHARLESTON, SC (Comcast Cable)

HARBISON—See COLUMBIA, SC (Time Warner Cable)

▲**HARDEEVILLE**—Hargray

HARLEYVILLE—See MONCKS CORNER, SC (Home Telecom)

▲**HARTSVILLE**—Time Warner Cable. Now served by MYRTLE BEACH, SC [SC0007]

HARTSVILLE—See MYRTLE BEACH, SC (Time Warner Cable)

▲**HARTWELL VILLAS**—Charter Communications

HEATH SPRINGS—See ROCK HILL, SC (Comporium Communications)

HEMINGWAY—See MYRTLE BEACH, SC (Time Warner Cable)

HICKORY GROVE—See ROCK HILL, SC (Comporium Communications)

▲**HILDA**—Formerly served by Pine Tree Cablevision. No longer in operation

▲**HILTON HEAD ISLAND**—Time Warner Cable. Now served by MYRTLE BEACH, SC [SC0007]

HILTON HEAD ISLAND—See MYRTLE BEACH, SC (Time Warner Cable)

HODGES—See GREENWOOD, SC (Northland Cable Television)

▲**HOLLY HILL**—Almega Cable

▲**HOLLYWOOD**—US Cable of Coastal Texas LP. Now served by CHARLESTON, SC [SC0001]

HOLLYWOOD—See CHARLESTON, SC (Comcast Cable)

▲**HOMEWOOD**—Horry Telephone Coop.

▲**HOPKINS**—Formerly served by Pine Tree Cablevision. No longer in operation

HORNEA PATH—See SPARTANBURG, SC (Charter Communications)

HORRY COUNTY (PORTIONS)—See HOMEWOOD, SC (Horry Telephone Coop.)

HORRY COUNTY—See MYRTLE BEACH, SC (Time Warner Cable)

INMAN—See SPARTANBURG, SC (Charter Communications)

IRMO—See COLUMBIA, SC (Time Warner Cable)

ISLE OF PALMS—See CHARLESTON, SC (Comcast Cable)

▲**IVA**—Charter Communications. Now served by GREENVILLE/SPARTANBURG, SC [SC0003]

IVA—See SPARTANBURG, SC (Charter Communications)

JACKSON—See AIKEN, SC (Atlantic Broadband)

JAMES ISLAND—See CHARLESTON, SC (Comcast Cable)

▲**JEFFERSON**—Formerly served by Pine Tree Cablevision. No longer in operation

JOANNA—See SPARTANBURG, SC (Charter Communications)

▲**JOHNS ISLAND**—US Cable of Coastal Texas LP. Now served by CHARLESTON, SC [SC0001]

JOHNS ISLAND—See CHARLESTON, SC (Comcast Cable)

▲**JOHNSONVILLE**—Time Warner Cable. Now served by MYRTLE BEACH, SC [SC0007]

JOHNSONVILLE—See MYRTLE BEACH, SC (Time Warner Cable)

JOHNSTON—See GREENWOOD, SC (Northland Cable Television)

JONESVILLE—See SPARTANBURG, SC (Charter Communications)

KELLYTOWN—See MYRTLE BEACH, SC (Time Warner Cable)

KEOWEE KEY—See SPARTANBURG, SC (Charter Communications)

KERSHAW COUNTY—See CAMDEN, SC (TruVista Communications)

KERSHAW—See ROCK HILL, SC (Comporium Communications)

KIAWAH ISLAND—See CHARLESTON, SC (Comcast Cable)

KINGSTREE—See MYRTLE BEACH, SC (Time Warner Cable)

LA FRANCE—See ANCHOR POINT, SC (Charter Communications)

LADSON—See CHARLESTON, SC (Knology)

▲**LADY'S ISLAND**—Comcast Cable

LADY'S ISLAND—See BEAUFORT, SC (Hargray)

▲**LAKE CITY**—Time Warner Cable. Now served by MYRTLE BEACH, SC [SC0007]

LAKE CITY—See MYRTLE BEACH, SC (Time Warner Cable)

LAKE MURRAY—See GILBERT, SC (Comporium Cable)

LAKE MURRAY—See COLUMBIA, SC (Time Warner Cable)

▲**LAKE VIEW**—Time Warner Cable. Now served by MYRTLE BEACH, SC [SC0007]

LAKE VIEW—See MYRTLE BEACH, SC (Time Warner Cable)

LAKE WYLIE WOODS—See ROCK HILL, SC (Comporium Communications)

▲**LAMAR**—Formerly served by Pine Tree Cablevision. No longer in operation

LAMBERTOWN—See MYRTLE BEACH, SC (Time Warner Cable)

LANCASTER COUNTY (PORTIONS)—See ROCK HILL, SC (Comporium Communications)

▲**LANCASTER**—Comporium Communications. Now served by ROCK HILL, SC [SC0138]

LANCASTER—See ROCK HILL, SC (Comporium Communications)

LANDRAN—See SPARTANBURG, NC (Charter Communications)

LANDRUM—See SPARTANBURG, SC (Charter Communications)

▲**LANE**—Time Warner Cable. Now served by MYRTLE BEACH, SC [SC0007]

LANE—See MYRTLE BEACH, SC (Time Warner Cable)

LANGLEY—See AIKEN, SC (Atlantic Broadband)

LATTA—See MYRTLE BEACH, SC (Time Warner Cable)

LAURENS COUNTY (PORTIONS)—See SPARTANBURG, SC (Charter Communications)

LAURENS COUNTY (PORTIONS)—See GREENWOOD, SC (Northland Cable Television)

▲**LAURENS**—Charter Communications. Now served by GREENVILLE/SPARTANBURG, SC [SC0003]

LAURENS—See SPARTANBURG, SC (Charter Communications)

LAURINBURG—See MYRTLE BEACH, NC (Time Warner Cable)

LEE COUNTY—See COLUMBIA, SC (Time Warner Cable)

LEESVILLE—See COLUMBIA, SC (Time Warner Cable)

LEXINGTON COUNTY (NORTHWESTERN PORTION)—See GILBERT, SC (Comporium Cable)

LEXINGTON COUNTY—See COLUMBIA, SC (Time Warner Cable)

LEXINGTON—See COLUMBIA, SC (Time Warner Cable)

LIBERTY—See SENECA, SC (Northland Cable Television)

LITCHFIELD BEACH—See MYRTLE BEACH, SC (Time Warner Cable)

LITTLE MOUNTAIN—See COLUMBIA, SC (Time Warner Cable)

▲**LITTLE RIVER**—Time Warner Cable. Now served by MYRTLE BEACH, SC [SC0007]

LITTLE RIVER—See MYRTLE BEACH, SC (Time Warner Cable)

▲**LOCKHART**—Charter Communications. Now served by GREENVILLE/SPARTANBURG, SC [SC0003]

LOCKHART—See SPARTANBURG, SC (Charter Communications)

LONGS—See HOMEWOOD, SC (Horry Telephone Coop.)

LORIS—See HOMEWOOD, SC (Horry Telephone Coop.)

▲**LUGOFF**—Formerly served by Pine Tree Cablevision. No longer in operation

LUGOFF—See CAMDEN, SC (TruVista Communications)

LYMAN—See SPARTANBURG, SC (Charter Communications)

LYNN—See SPARTANBURG, NC (Charter Communications)

MANNING—See SUMMERTON, SC (Almega Cable)

MANNING—See COLUMBIA, SC (Time Warner Cable)

MARIETTA—See SPARTANBURG, SC (Charter Communications)

MARION COUNTY—See MYRTLE BEACH, SC (Time Warner Cable)

MARION—See MYRTLE BEACH, SC (Time Warner Cable)

MARLBORO COUNTY—See BENNETTSVILLE, SC (MetroCast Communications)

MAULDIN—See SPARTANBURG, SC (Charter Communications)

MAXTON—See MYRTLE BEACH, NC (Time Warner Cable)

MAYESVILLE—See COLUMBIA, SC (Time Warner Cable)

▲**MCCLELLANVILLE**—Windjammer Cable

MCCOLL—See BENNETTSVILLE, SC (MetroCast Communications)

▲**McCORMICK COUNTY**—Formerly served by KLiP Interactive. No longer in operation

▲**McCORMICK**—Formerly served by McCormick Cable. No longer in operation

▲**MONCKS CORNER**—Home Telecom

MONTMORENCI—See AIKEN, SC (Atlantic Broadband)

▲**MOUNT PLEASANT (portions)**—Comcast Cable. Now served by CHARLESTON, SC [SC0001]

MOUNT PLEASANT—See CHARLESTON, SC (Comcast Cable)

MOUNT PLEASANT—See CHARLESTON, SC (Knology)

▲**MULLINS**—Time Warner Cable. Now served by MYRTLE BEACH, SC [SC0007]

MULLINS—See MYRTLE BEACH, SC (Time Warner Cable)

MURRELLS INLET—See HOMEWOOD, SC (Horry Telephone Coop.)

MURRELLS INLET—See MYRTLE BEACH, SC (Time Warner Cable)

▲**MYRTLE BEACH**—Time Warner Cable

NEW ELLENTON—See AIKEN, SC (Atlantic Broadband)

NEWBERRY COUNTY (UNINCORPORATED AREAS)—See WHITMIRE, SC (Charter Communications)

NEWBERRY COUNTY—See NEWBERRY, SC (Comcast Cable)

▲**NEWBERRY**—Comcast Cable

NINETY-SIX—See GREENWOOD, SC (Northland Cable Television)

NORRIS—See SENECA, SC (Northland Cable Television)

NORTH CHARLESTON—See CHARLESTON, SC (Comcast Cable)

NORTH CHARLESTON—See CHARLESTON, SC (Knology)

NORTH CHARLESTON—See MYRTLE BEACH, SC (Time Warner Cable)

NORTH MYRTLE BEACH (PORTIONS)—See HOMEWOOD, SC (Horry Telephone Coop.)

NORTH MYRTLE BEACH—See MYRTLE BEACH, SC (Time Warner Cable)

NORTH SANTEE—See MYRTLE BEACH, SC (Time Warner Cable)

NORTH STONE—See MYRTLE BEACH, SC (Time Warner Cable)

▲**NORTH**—Formerly served by Pine Tree Cablevision. No longer in operation

▲**NORWAY**—Formerly served by Almega Cable. No longer in operation

OCONEE COUNTY (PORTIONS)—See FIVE POINTS, SC (Northland Cable Television)

OCONEE COUNTY (PORTIONS)—See SENECA, SC (Northland Cable Television)

OCONEE COUNTY (UNINCORPORATED AREAS)—See SPARTANBURG, SC (Charter Communications)

OKATIE—See BLUFFTON, SC (Hargray)

▲**OLANTA**—FTC Vision. Formerly served by Turbeville, SC [SC0085]. This cable system has converted to IPTV

ORANGEBURG COUNTY (PORTIONS)—See COLUMBIA, SC (Time Warner Cable)

ORANGEBURG COUNTY (UNINCORPORATED AREAS)—See HOLLY HILL, SC (Almega Cable)

ORANGEBURG COUNTY—See BOWMAN, SC (Almega Cable)

ORANGEBURG COUNTY—See SANTEE, SC (Almega Cable)

ORANGEBURG—See COLUMBIA, SC (Time Warner Cable)

OWINGS—See SPARTANBURG, SC (Charter Communications)

PACOLET MILLS—See SPARTANBURG, SC (Charter Communications)

PACOLET—See SPARTANBURG, SC (Charter Communications)

▲**PAGELAND**—NewWave Communications

PAPLICO—See MYRTLE BEACH, SC (Time Warner Cable)

PARRIS ISLAND—See BEAUFORT, SC (Hargray)

PAWLEY'S ISLAND—See MYRTLE BEACH, SC (Time Warner Cable)

PELION—See COLUMBIA, SC (Time Warner Cable)

PELZER—See SPARTANBURG, SC (Charter Communications)

PENDLETON—See SENECA, SC (Northland Cable Television)

PICKENS COUNTY (PORTIONS)—See SPARTANBURG, SC (Charter Communications)

PICKENS COUNTY—See SENECA, SC (Northland Cable Television)

▲**PICKENS**—Charter Communications. Now served by GREENVILLE/SPARTANBURG, SC [SC0003]

PICKENS—See SPARTANBURG, SC (Charter Communications)

PICKENS—See SENECA, SC (Northland Cable Television)

PICKETT POST—See SPARTANBURG, SC (Charter Communications)

PINERIDGE—See COLUMBIA, SC (Time Warner Cable)

PINERIDGE—See MYRTLE BEACH, SC (Time Warner Cable)

PINEWOOD—See COLUMBIA, SC (Time Warner Cable)

PORT ROYAL—See BEAUFORT, SC (Hargray)

POTATO CREEK—See SUMMERTON, SC (Almega Cable)

PROSPERITY—See NEWBERRY, SC (Comcast Cable)

QUINBY—See MYRTLE BEACH, SC (Time Warner Cable)

RAVENEL—See CHARLESTON, SC (Comcast Cable)

RAVENWOOD—See COLUMBIA, SC (Time Warner Cable)

REEVESVILLE—See ST. GEORGE, SC (Almega Cable)

▲**REGENT PARK**—Comporium Communications. Now served by ROCK HILL, SC [SC0138]

REGENT PARK—See ROCK HILL, SC (Comporium Communications)

RICHBURG—See ROCK HILL, SC (Comporium Communications)

RICHLAND COUNTY—See COLUMBIA, SC (Time Warner Cable)

RIDGE SPRING—See GILBERT, SC (Comporium Cable)

▲**RIDGELAND**—Hargray

▲**RIDGEVILLE**—Time Warner Cable. Now served by MYRTLE BEACH, SC [SC0007]

RIDGEVILLE—See MYRTLE BEACH, SC (Time Warner Cable)

RIDGEWAY—See WINNSBORO, SC (TruVista Communications)

RIVER HILLS—See ROCK HILL, SC (Comporium Communications)

ROBESON COUNTY—See MYRTLE BEACH, NC (Time Warner Cable)

▲**ROCK HILL**—Comporium Communications

▲**ROWESVILLE**—Formerly served by Almega Cable. No longer in operation

ROWLAND—See MYRTLE BEACH, NC (Time Warner Cable)

RUBY—See CHESTERFIELD (town), SC (NewWave Communications)

▲**SALEM**—Charter Communications. Now served by GREENVILLE/SPARTANBURG, SC [SC0003]

SALEM—See SPARTANBURG, SC (Charter Communications)

SALUDA COUNTY (EASTERN PORTION)—See GILBERT, SC (Comporium Cable)

SALUDA COUNTY (PORTIONS)—See GREENWOOD, SC (Northland Cable Television)

SALUDA COUNTY (PORTIONS)—See COLUMBIA, SC (Time Warner Cable)

SALUDA—See SPARTANBURG, NC (Charter Communications)

SALUDA—See GREENWOOD, SC (Northland Cable Television)

▲**SAMPIT**—Time Warner Cable. Now served by MYRTLE BEACH, SC [SC0007]

SAMPIT—See MYRTLE BEACH, SC (Time Warner Cable)

SANDY SPRINGS—See ANCHOR POINT, SC (Charter Communications)

▲**SANTEE**—Almega Cable

SCOTLAND COUNTY—See MYRTLE BEACH, NC (Time Warner Cable)

SCRANTON—See MYRTLE BEACH, SC (Time Warner Cable)

SEABROOK ISLAND—See CHARLESTON, SC (Comcast Cable)

▲**SENECA**—Northland Cable Television

SHARON—See ROCK HILL, SC (Comporium Communications)

SHAW AFB—See COLUMBIA, SC (Time Warner Cable)

SIMPSONVILLE—See SPARTANBURG, SC (Charter Communications)

SIX MILE—See SENECA, SC (Northland Cable Television)

SNELLING—See BARNWELL, SC (Atlantic Broadband)

SOCASTEE—See HOMEWOOD, SC (Horry Telephone Coop.)

SOCASTEE—See MYRTLE BEACH, SC (Time Warner Cable)

SOUTH CONGAREE—See COLUMBIA, SC (Time Warner Cable)

SOUTH SANTEE—See McCLELLANVILLE, SC (Windjammer Cable)

SPARTANBURG COUNTY—See SPARTANBURG, SC (Charter Communications)

▲**SPARTANBURG**—Charter Communications. Now served by GREENVILLE/SPARTANBURG, SC [SC0003]

▲**SPARTANBURG**—Charter Communications

SPRINGDALE—See COLUMBIA, SC (Time Warner Cable)

▲**SPRINGFIELD**—Formerly served by Almega Cable. No longer in operation

▲**ST. GEORGE**—Almega Cable

ST. HELENA ISLAND—See LADY'S ISLAND, SC (Comcast Cable)

ST. MATTHEWS—See COLUMBIA, SC (Time Warner Cable)

▲**ST. STEPHEN**—Formerly served by Pine Tree Cablevision. No longer in operation

STARR—See SPARTANBURG, SC (Charter Communications)

SULLIVAN'S ISLAND—See CHARLESTON, SC (Comcast Cable)

▲**SUMMERTON**—Almega Cable

SUMMERTON—See COLUMBIA, SC (Time Warner Cable)

▲**SUMMERVILLE**—Time Warner Cable. Now served by MYRTLE BEACH, SC [SC0007]

SUMMERVILLE—See CHARLESTON, SC (Comcast Cable)

SUMMERVILLE—See CHARLESTON, SC (Knology)

SUMMERVILLE—See MYRTLE BEACH, SC (Time Warner Cable)

SUMMIT—See GILBERT, SC (Comporium Cable)

SUMTER COUNTY—See COLUMBIA, SC (Time Warner Cable)

SUMTER—See COLUMBIA, SC (Time Warner Cable)

▲**SURFSIDE BEACH**—Time Warner Cable. Now served by MYRTLE BEACH, SC [SC0007]

SURFSIDE BEACH—See MYRTLE BEACH, SC (Time Warner Cable)

▲**SWANSEA**—Formerly served by Pine Tree Cablevision. No longer in operation

TATUM—See BENNETTSVILLE, SC (MetroCast Communications)

TAW CAW—See SUMMERTON, SC (Almega Cable)

TEGA CAY—See ROCK HILL, SC (Comporium Communications)

▲**THE SUMMIT**—Formerly served by Adelphia Communications. No longer in operation

TIMMONSVILLE—See MYRTLE BEACH, SC (Time Warner Cable)

TOWNVILLE—See ANCHOR POINT, SC (Charter Communications)

▲**TRAVELERS REST**—Charter Communications. Now served by GREENVILLE/SPARTANBURG, SC [SC0003]

TRAVELERS REST—See SPARTANBURG, SC (Charter Communications)

TRYON—See SPARTANBURG, NC (Charter Communications)

▲**TURBEVILLE**—FTC Vision. This cable system has converted to IPTV. See Turbeville, SC [SC5029] & Olanta, SC [SC5027]

▲**TURBEVILLE**—FTC Vision. Formerly [SC0085]. This cable system has converted to IPTV

UNION COUNTY (PORTIONS)—See SPARTANBURG, SC (Charter Communications)

UNION COUNTY (UNINCORPORATED AREAS)—See WHITMIRE, SC (Charter Communications)

▲**UNION**—Charter Communications. Now served by GREENVILLE/SPARTANBURG, SC [SC0003]

UNION—See SPARTANBURG, SC (Charter Communications)

VANCE—See SANTEE, SC (Almega Cable)

VARNVILLE—See HAMPTON, SC (Comcast Cable)

VAUCLUSE—See AIKEN, SC (Atlantic Broadband)

WADMALAW ISLAND—See CHARLESTON, SC (Comcast Cable)

▲**WAGENER**—Formerly served by Pine Tree Cablevision. No longer in operation

WALHALLA—See FIVE POINTS, SC (Northland Cable Television)

▲**WALTERBORO**—Comcast Cable

WAMPEE—See HOMEWOOD, SC (Horry Telephone Coop.)

WARE SHOALS—See GREENWOOD, SC (Northland Cable Television)

WARRENVILLE—See AIKEN, SC (Atlantic Broadband)

WELLFORD—See SPARTANBURG, SC (Charter Communications)

WEST COLUMBIA—See COLUMBIA, SC (Time Warner Cable)

▲**WEST PELZER**—Charter Communications. Now served by GREENVILLE/SPARTANBURG, SC [SC0003]

WEST PELZER—See SPARTANBURG, SC (Charter Communications)

WEST UNION—See SENECA, SC (Northland Cable Television)

WESTMINSTER—See FIVE POINTS, SC (Northland Cable Television)

▲**WHITMIRE**—Charter Communications

▲**WILD DUNES**—US Cable of Coastal Texas. Now served by CHARLESTON, SC [SC0001]

WILLIAMSBURG COUNTY—See MYRTLE BEACH, SC (Time Warner Cable)

▲**WILLIAMSTON**—Charter Communications. Now served by GREENVILLE/SPARTANBURG, SC [SC0003]

WILLIAMSTON—See SPARTANBURG, SC (Charter Communications)

WILLISTON—See BARNWELL, SC (Atlantic Broadband)

▲**WINNSBORO**—TruVista Communications

WOODRUFF—See SPARTANBURG, SC (Charter Communications)

YORK COUNTY—See ROCK HILL, SC (Comporium Communications)

YORK—See ROCK HILL, SC (Comporium Communications)

SOUTH DAKOTA

▲**ABERDEEN TWP.**—Midcontinent Communications

▲**ABERDEEN**—Formerly served by ITC. No longer in operation

ALCESTER—See VIBORG, SD (Knology)

▲**ALEXANDRIA**—TrioTel Communications Inc.

ALLEN—See WALL, SD (Golden West Telecommunications)

▲**ALPENA (TOWN)**—Santel Communications. Formerly served by Mount Vernon, SD [SD0188]. This cable system has converted to IPTV

ARLINGTON—See BROOKINGS, SD (Mediacom)

▲**ARMOUR**—Golden West Telecommunications

▲**ARTESIAN**—Santel Communications. Formerly served by Mount Vernon, SD [SD0188]. This cable system has converted to IPTV

▲**ASHTON**—Midcontinent Communications

▲**ASTORIA**—Satellite Cable Services Inc. Now served by CLEAR LAKE, SD [SD0047]

▲**ASTORIA**—ITC. Formerly served by Clear Lake, SD [SD0047]. This cable system has converted to IPTV

▲**AURORA**—ITC. Formerly served by Clear Lake, SD [SD0047]. This cable system has converted to IPTV

AURORA—See BROOKINGS, SD (Mediacom)

▲**AVON**—Golden West Telecommunications

BALTIC—See SIOUX FALLS, SD (Midcontinent Communications)

BATH—See ABERDEEN TWP., SD (Midcontinent Communications)

BEADLE COUNTY—See HURON, SD (Midcontinent Communications)

BELLE FOURCHE—See SPEARFISH, SD (Midcontinent Communications)

▲**BERESFORD**—Beresford Cablevision Inc.

BIG STONE CITY—See WATERTOWN, MN (Midcontinent Communications)

BIG STONE TWP.—See WATERTOWN, MN (Midcontinent Communications)

▲**BISON**—West River Cable Television

BLACK HAWK—See RAPID CITY, SD (Midcontinent Communications)

BLUNT—See HIGHMORE, SD (Venture Communications Cooperative)

BONESTEEL—See FAIRFAX, SD (Golden West Telecommunications)

▲**BOULDER CANYON**—Midcontinent Communications

BOWDLE—See ABERDEEN TWP., SD (Midcontinent Communications)

BOX ELDER—See RAPID CITY, SD (Midcontinent Communications)

▲**BRADLEY**—ITC. Formerly served by Clear Lake, SD [SD0047]. This cable system has converted to IPTV

BRANDON—See GARRETSON, SD (Alliance Communications)

▲**BRANDT**—ITC. Formerly served by Clear Lake, SD [SD0047]. This cable system has converted to IPTV

BRIDGEWATER—See FREEMAN, SD (Mediacom)

BRISTOL—See ABERDEEN TWP., SD (Midcontinent Communications)

▲**BRITTON**—Venture Communications Cooperative

▲**BROOKINGS (RURAL)**—ITC. Formerly served by Clear Lake, SD [SD0047]. This cable system has converted to IPTV

▲**BROOKINGS**—Mediacom

BROWN COUNTY—See ABERDEEN TWP., SD (Midcontinent Communications)

▲**BRUCE**—Mediacom. Now served by BROOKINGS, SD [SD0005]

BRUCE—See BROOKINGS, SD (Mediacom)

▲**BRYANT**—Satellite Cable Services Inc. Now served by CLEAR LAKE, SD [SD0047]

▲**BRYANT**—ITC. Formerly served by Clear Lake, SD [SD0047]. This cable system has converted to IPTV

BUFFALO GAP—See CUSTER, SD (Golden West Telecommunications)

▲**BUFFALO**—West River Cable Television. No longer in operation

BUFFALO—See BISON, SD (West River Cable Television)

▲**BURKE**—Golden West Telecommunications

CANISTOTA—See FREEMAN, SD (Mediacom)

CANOVA—See ALEXANDRIA, SD (TrioTel Communications Inc.)

CANTON (PORTIONS)—See VIBORG, SD (Knology)

CANTON—See SIOUX FALLS, SD (Midcontinent Communications)

▲**CARTHAGE**—Alliance Communications. This cable system has converted to IPTV. See Carthage, SD [SD5079]

▲**CARTHAGE**—Alliance Communications. Formerly [SD0244]. This cable system has converted to IPTV

▲**CASTLEWOOD**—Mediacom. Now served by BROOKINGS, SD [SD0005]

▲**CASTLEWOOD**—ITC. Formerly served by Clear Lake, SD [SD0047]. This cable system has converted to IPTV

CASTLEWOOD—See BROOKINGS, SD (Mediacom)

▲**CAVOUR**—Midcontinent Communications

CENTERVILLE—See VIBORG, SD (Knology)

CENTRAL CITY—See SPEARFISH, SD (Midcontinent Communications)

CHAMBERLAIN—See WHITE LAKE, SD (Midstate Communications)

CHANCELLOR—See VIBORG, SD (Knology)

▲**CHERRY CREEK**—Formerly served by Cheyenne River Sioux Tribe Telephone Authority. No longer in operation

▲**CHESTER (RURAL)**—ITC. Formerly served by Clear Lake, SD [SD0047]. This cable system has converted to IPTV

▲**CHESTER**—Satellite Cable Services Inc. Now served by CLEAR LAKE, SD [SD0047]

▲**CLARK TWP.**—Satellite Cable Services Inc. Now served by CLEAR LAKE, SD [SD0047]

▲**CLARK**—ITC. Formerly served by Clear Lake, SD [SD0047]. This cable system has converted to IPTV

▲**CLEAR LAKE**—Formerly served by HD Electric Cooperative. No longer in operation

▲**CLEAR LAKE**—ITC. This cable system has converted to IPTV. See Clear Lake, SD [SD5042]

▲**CLEAR LAKE**—ITC. Formerly [SD0047]. This cable system has converted to IPTV

CODINGTON COUNTY (PORTIONS)—See WATERTOWN, SD (Midcontinent Communications)

▲**COLMAN**—Mediacom. Now served by BROOKINGS, SD [SD0005]

▲**COLMAN**—Knology

COLMAN—See BROOKINGS, SD (Mediacom)

COLOME—See WINNER, SD (Golden West Telecommunications)

COLTON—See SIOUX FALLS, SD (Midcontinent Communications)

▲**CONDE**—Satellite Cable Services Inc. Now served by GROTON, SD [SD0030]

▲**CORSICA**—Golden West Telecommunications

CORSON—See GARRETSON, SD (Alliance Communications)

COUNTRYSIDE MOBILE HOME PARK—See RAPID CITY, SD (Midcontinent Communications)

CRESBARD—See FAULKTON, SD (Western Telephone Company)

CROOKS—See SIOUX FALLS, SD (Midcontinent Communications)

CUSTER COUNTY (UNINCORPORATED AREAS)—See CUSTER, SD (Golden West Telecommunications)

▲**CUSTER**—Golden West Telecommunications

▲**DAKOTA DUNES**—Long Lines

DE SMET—See BROOKINGS, SD (Mediacom)

DEADWOOD—See SPEARFISH, SD (Midcontinent Communications)

▲**DELL RAPIDS**—Golden West Telecommunications

▲**DELMONT**—Midstate Communications. Now served by PLATTE, SD [SD0049]

DELMONT—See PLATTE, SD (Midstate Communications)

DOLAND—See ABERDEEN TWP., SD (Midcontinent Communications)

DRAPER—See WALL, SD (Golden West Telecommunications)

▲**DUPREE**—Cheyenne River Sioux Tribe Telephone Authority. Formerly served by Eagle Butte, SD [SD0164]. This cable system has converted to IPTV

▲**EAGLE BUTTE**—Cheynne River Sioux Tribe Telephone. This cable system has converted to IPTV. See Eagle Butte, CA [SD5048]

▲**EAGLE BUTTE**—Cheyenne River Sioux Tribe Telephone Authority. Formerly [SD0164]. This cable system has converted to IPTV

▲**EDEN**—Venture Communications Cooperative. Now served by BRITTON, SD [SD0041]

EDEN—See BRITTON, SD (Venture Communications Cooperative)

▲**EDGEMONT**—Golden West Cablevision. Now served by WALL, SD [SD0068]

EDGEMONT—See CUSTER, SD (Golden West Telecommunications)

EGAN—See BROOKINGS, SD (Mediacom)

ELK POINT—See VIBORG, SD (Knology)

▲**ELKTON (RURAL)**—ITC. Formerly served by Clear Lake, SD [SD0047]. This cable system has converted to IPTV

ELKTON—See BROOKINGS, SD (Mediacom)

ELLSWORTH AFB—See RAPID CITY, SD (Midcontinent Communications)

▲**EMERY**—Emery Cable Vision Inc. Now served by ALEXANDRIA, SD [SD0097]

EMERY—See ALEXANDRIA, SD (TrioTel Communications Inc.)

▲**ESTELLINE**—Mediacom. Now served by BROOKINGS, SD [SD0005]

▲**ESTELLINE**—ITC. Formerly served by Clear Lake, SD [SD0047]. This cable system has converted to IPTV

ESTELLINE—See BROOKINGS, SD (Mediacom)

▲**ETHAN**—Santel Communications. Now served by MOUNT VERNON, SD [SD0188]

▲**ETHAN**—Santel Communications. Formerly served by Mount Vernon, SD [SD0188]. This cable system has converted to IPTV

▲**EUREKA**—Valley Cable. Now served by HERREID, SD [SD0091]

▲**EUREKA**—Valley Telecommunications Coop. Assn. Formerly served by Herreid, SD [SD0091]. This cable system has converted to IPTV

EVERGREEN HOUSING—See WALL, SD (Golden West Telecommunications)

▲**FAIRFAX**—Golden West Telecommunications

▲**FAITH**—West River Cable Television

FALL RIVER COUNTY—See CUSTER, SD (Golden West Telecommunications)

▲**FAULKTON**—Western Telephone Company

FLANDREAU—See COLMAN, SD (Knology)

FLANDREAU—See BROOKINGS, SD (Mediacom)

▲**FLORENCE**—Satellite Cable Services Inc. Now served by CLEAR LAKE, SD [SD0047]

▲**FLORENCE**—ITC. Formerly served by Clear Lake, SD [SD0047]. This cable system has converted to IPTV

▲**FORT PIERRE**—Midcontinent Communications

▲**FRANKFORT**—James Valley Telecommunications. Now served by GROTON, SD [SD0030]

FREDERICK—See ABERDEEN TWP., SD (Midcontinent Communications)

▲**FREEMAN**—Mediacom

▲**GARRETSON**—Alliance Communications

▲**GARY**—Satellite Cable Services Inc. Now served by CLEAR LAKE, SD [SD0047]

▲**GARY**—ITC. Formerly served by Clear Lake, SD [SD0047]. This cable system has converted to IPTV

GAYVILLE—See VIBORG, SD (Knology)

▲ **GAYVILLE**—Midcontinent Communications

▲ **GEDDES**—Midstate Communications. Now served by PLATTE, SD [SD0049]

GEDDES—See PLATTE, SD (Midstate Communications)

▲ **GETTYSBURG**—Venture Communications Cooperative

▲ **GLENHAM**—Valley Cable. Now served by HERREID, SD [SD0091]

▲ **GLENHAM**—Valley Telecommunications Coop. Assn. Formerly served by Herreid, SD [SD0091]. This cable system has converted to IPTV

▲ **GOODWIN**—ITC. Formerly served by Clear Lake, SD [SD0047]. This cable system has converted to IPTV

GRANT COUNTY—See WATERTOWN, SD (Midcontinent Communications)

▲ **GREGORY**—Golden West Telecommunications

▲ **GROTON**—James Valley Telecommunications. This cable system has converted to IPTV. See Groton, SD [SD5005]

▲ **GROTON**—James Valley Telecommunications. Formerly [SD0030]. This cable system has converted to IPTV

HARRISBURG—See VIBORG, SD (Knology)

HARROLD—See HIGHMORE, SD (Venture Communications Cooperative)

▲ **HART RANCH**—Midcontinent Communications

▲ **HARTFORD**—Golden West Telecommunications

▲ **HAYTI**—Mediacom. Now served by BROOKINGS, SD [SD0005]

▲ **HAYTI**—ITC. Formerly served by Clear Lake, SD [SD0047]. This cable system has converted to IPTV

HAYTI—See BROOKINGS, SD (Mediacom)

▲ **HENRY**—Satellite Cable Services Inc. Now served by CLEAR LAKE, SD [SD0047]

▲ **HENRY**—ITC. Formerly served by Clear Lake, SD [SD0047]. This cable system has converted to IPTV

▲ **HERREID**—Valley Telecommunications Coop. Assn. This cable system has converted to IPTV. See Herreid, SD [SD5032]

▲ **HERREID**—Valley Telecommunications Coop. Assn. Formerly [SD0091]. This cable system has converted to IPTV

▲ **HIGHMORE**—Venture Communications Cooperative

▲ **HILL CITY**—Golden West Cablevision. Now served by CUSTER, SD [SD0034]

HILL CITY—See CUSTER, SD (Golden West Telecommunications)

HITCHCOCK—See WESSINGTON, SD (Venture Communications Cooperative)

HORSE CREEK HOUSING—See WALL, SD (Golden West Telecommunications)

▲ **HOSMER**—Valley Cable & Satellite Communications, Inc. Now served by HERREID, SD [SD0091]

▲ **HOSMER**—Valley Telecommunications Coop. Assn. Formerly served by Herreid, SD [SD0091]. This cable system has converted to IPTV

▲ **HOT SPRINGS**—Golden West Telecommunications. Now served by CUSTER, SD [SD0034]

HOT SPRINGS—See CUSTER, SD (Golden West Telecommunications)

▲ **HOVEN**—Venture Communications Cooperative. Now served by GETTYSBURG, SD [SD0036]

HOVEN—See GETTYSBURG, SD (Venture Communications Cooperative)

▲ **HOWARD**—Alliance Communications. This cable system has converted to IPTV. See Howard, SD [SD5082]

▲ **HOWARD**—Alliance Communications. Formerly [SD0052]. This cable system has converted to IPTV

▲ **HUDSON**—Alliance Communications. This cable system has converted to IPTV. See Hudson, SD [SD5083]

▲ **HUDSON**—Sioux Valley Wireless. Now served by HUDSON, SD [SD0254]

HUMBOLDT—See SIOUX FALLS, SD (Midcontinent Communications)

HURLEY—See VIBORG, SD (Knology)

▲ **HURON**—Midcontinent Communications

IPSWICH—See ABERDEEN TWP., SD (Midcontinent Communications)

IRENE—See VIBORG, SD (Knology)

▲ **IROQUOIS**—Midcontinent Communications

JAVA—See ABERDEEN TWP., SD (Midcontinent Communications)

▲ **JEFFERSON**—Jefferson Satellite Telecommunications Inc. Now served by SALIX, IA [IA0510]

KADOKA—See WALL, SD (Golden West Telecommunications)

▲ **KENNEBEC**—Kennebec Telephone Co. Inc.

▲ **KIMBALL**—Midstate Communications. Now served by WHITE LAKE, SD [SD0026]

KIMBALL—See WHITE LAKE, SD (Midstate Communications)

KYLE—See WALL, SD (Golden West Telecommunications)

▲ **LAKE ANDES**—Satellite Cable Services Inc. Now served by TRIPP, SD [SD0087]

LAKE ANDES—See TRIPP, SD (Fort Randall Cable)

▲ **LAKE BENTON**—ITC. Formerly served by Clear Lake, SD [SD0047]. This cable system has converted to IPTV

▲ **LAKE NORDEN**—Mediacom. Now served by BROOKINGS, SD [SD0005]

▲ **LAKE NORDEN**—ITC. Formerly served by Clear Lake, SD [SD0047]. This cable system has converted to IPTV

LAKE NORDEN—See BROOKINGS, SD (Mediacom)

LAKE PRESTON—See BROOKINGS, SD (Mediacom)

LAKE WAGGONER—See WALL, SD (Golden West Telecommunications)

▲ **LANGFORD**—Venture Communications Cooperative. Now served by BRITTON, SD [SD0041]

LANGFORD—See BRITTON, SD (Venture Communications Cooperative)

LAWRENCE COUNTY (NORTHERN PORTION)—See SPEARFISH, SD (Midcontinent Communications)

LAWRENCE COUNTY (PORTIONS)—See RAPID CITY, SD (Knology)

LEAD—See SPEARFISH, SD (Midcontinent Communications)

▲ **LEMMON**—West River Cable TV. Now served by BISON, SD [SD0103]

LEMMON—See BISON, SD (West River Cable Television)

LENNOX—See VIBORG, SD (Knology)

▲ **LEOLA**—Valley Cable & Satellite Communications Inc. Now served by HERREID, SD [SD0091]

▲ **LEOLA**—Valley Telecommunications Coop. Assn. Formerly served by Herreid, SD [SD0091]. This cable system has converted to IPTV

▲ **LETCHER**—Santel Communications. Formerly served by Mount Vernon, SD [SD0188]. This cable system has converted to IPTV

▲ **LOWER BRULE**—Golden West Telecommunications

MADISON—See COLMAN, SD (Knology)

MADISON—See SIOUX FALLS, SD (Midcontinent Communications)

MANDERSON-WHITE HORSE CREEK—See WALL, SD (Golden West Telecommunications)

MARION—See FREEMAN, SD (Mediacom)

MARTIN—See WALL, SD (Golden West Telecommunications)

▲ **McINTOSH**—West River Cable Television. Now served by BISON, SD [SD0103]

MCINTOSH—See BISON, SD (West River Cable Television)

▲ **MCLAUGHLIN**—West River Cable Television

MEADE COUNTY (PORTIONS)—See RAPID CITY, SD (Knology)

MEADE COUNTY (PORTIONS)—See RAPID CITY, SD (Midcontinent Communications)

MEADE COUNTY (WESTERN PORTION)—See SPEARFISH, SD (Midcontinent Communications)

▲ **MELLETTE**—Satellite Cable Services Inc. Now served by GROTON, SD [SD0030]

MENNO—See FREEMAN, SD (Mediacom)

MIDLAND—See WALL, SD (Golden West Telecommunications)

MILBANK—See WATERTOWN, SD (Midcontinent Communications)

MILLER—See HURON, SD (Midcontinent Communications)

MINA—See ABERDEEN TWP., SD (Midcontinent Communications)

MINNEHAHA COUNTY (SOUTHERN PORTION)—See HARTFORD, SD (Golden West Telecommunications)

MINNEHAHA COUNTY—See DELL RAPIDS, SD (Golden West Telecommunications)

▲ **MISSION TWP.**—Golden West Telecommunications

▲ **MITCHELL**—Midcontinent Communications

▲ **MOBRIDGE**—Midcontinent Communications

▲ **MONROE**—Formerly served by Sioux Valley Wireless. No longer in operation

▲ **MONTROSE**—Golden West Telecommunications

▲ **MOUND CITY**—Valley Telecommunications Coop. Assn. Formerly served by Herreid, SD [SD0091]. This cable system has converted to IPTV

▲ **MOUNT VERNON**—Santel Communications. This cable system has converted to IPTV. See Mount Vernon, SD [SD5013]

▲ **MOUNT VERNON**—Santel Communications. Formerly served by Mount Vernon, SD [SD0188]. This cable system has converted to IPTV

MURDO—See WALL, SD (Golden West Telecommunications)

▲ **NEW EFFINGTON**—RCTV

NEW UNDERWOOD—See WALL, SD (Golden West Telecommunications)

▲ **NEWELL**—West River Cable Television. No longer in operation

NEWELL—See BISON, SD (West River Cable Television)

▲ **NUNDA (RURAL)**—ITC. Formerly served by Clear Lake, SD [SD0047]. This cable system has converted to IPTV

▲ **OACOMA**—Midstate Communications. Now served by WHITE LAKE, SD [SD0026]

OACOMA—See WHITE LAKE, SD (Midstate Communications)

▲ **OELRICHS**—Golden West Cablevision. Now served by WALL, SD [SD0068]

OELRICHS—See CUSTER, SD (Golden West Telecommunications)

▲ **OLDHAM**—Alliance Communications. This cable system has converted to IPTV. See Oldham, SD [SD5010]

▲ **OLDHAM**—Alliance Communications. Formerly [SD0191]. This cable system has converted to IPTV.

OLIVET—See FREEMAN, SD (Mediacom)

ONAKA—See HIGHMORE, SD (Venture Communications Cooperative)

▲ **ONIDA**—Venture Communications Cooperative

ORTONVILLE TWP.—See WATERTOWN, MN (Midcontinent Communications)

ORTONVILLE—See WATERTOWN, MN (Midcontinent Communications)

PARKER—See VIBORG, SD (Knology)

PARKSTON—See FREEMAN, SD (Mediacom)

▲ **PARKSTON**—Santel Communications. Formerly served by Mount Vernon, SD [SD0188]. This cable system has converted to IPTV

PENNINGTON COUNTY (PORTIONS)—See RAPID CITY, SD (Knology)

PENNINGTON COUNTY (PORTIONS)—See RAPID CITY, SD (Midcontinent Communications)

PHILIP—See WALL, SD (Golden West Telecommunications)

▲ **PICKSTOWN**—Satellite Cable Services Inc. Now served by TRIPP, SD [SD0087]

PICKSTOWN—See TRIPP, SD (Fort Randall Cable)

PIEDMONT—See RAPID CITY, SD (Midcontinent Communications)

▲ **PIERPONT**—Venture Communications Cooperative. Now served by BRITTON, SD [SD0041]

PIERPONT—See BRITTON, SD (Venture Communications Cooperative)

PIERRE—See FORT PIERRE, SD (Midcontinent Communications)

▲ **PINE RIDGE**—Golden West Telecommunications

▲ **PLANKINTON**—Golden West Telecommunications

▲ **PLATTE**—Midstate Communications

▲ **POLLOCK**—Valley Cable & Satellite Communications Inc. Now served by HERREID, SD [SD0091]

▲ **POLLOCK**—Valley Telecommunications Coop. Assn. Formerly served by Herreid, SD [SD0091]. This cable system has converted to IPTV

PORCUPINE—See WALL, SD (Golden West Telecommunications)

▲ **PRAIRIE ACRES ESTATES**—Comcast Cable. Now served by RAPID CITY, SD [SD0002]

PRAIRIE ACRES ESTATES—See RAPID CITY, SD (Midcontinent Communications)

▲ **PRAIRIEWOOD VILLAGE**—Midcontinent Communications

PRESHO—See KENNEBEC, SD (Kennebec Telephone Co. Inc.)

PUKWANA—See WHITE LAKE, SD (Midstate Communications)

▲ **RAPID CITY**—Formerly served by USA Digital TV. No longer in operation

▲ **RAPID CITY**—Knology

▲ **RAPID CITY**—Midcontinent Communications

▲ **RAYMOND**—Satellite Cable Services Inc. Now served by CLEAR LAKE, SD [SD0047]

▲ **RAYMOND**—ITC. Formerly served by Clear Lake, SD [SD0047]. This cable system has converted to IPTV

▲ **REDFIELD**—Spink Electric. No longer in operation

REDFIELD—See ABERDEEN TWP., SD (Midcontinent Communications)

REE HEIGHTS—See HIGHMORE, SD (Venture Communications Cooperative)

▲ **RELIANCE**—Golden West Telecommunications

RENNER—See SIOUX FALLS, SD (Midcontinent Communications)

▲ **RIMROCK**—Midcontinent Communications. Now served by RAPID CITY, SD [SD0002]

RIMROCK—See RAPID CITY, SD (Midcontinent Communications)

ROSCOE—See ABERDEEN TWP., SD (Midcontinent Communications)

▲ **ROSEBUD**—Golden West Telecommunications

▲ **ROSHOLT**—Venture Communications Cooperative

ROSLYN—See ABERDEEN TWP., SD (Midcontinent Communications)

SALEM—See FREEMAN, SD (Mediacom)

SCOTLAND—See FREEMAN, SD (Mediacom)

SELBY—See ABERDEEN TWP., SD (Midcontinent Communications)

SENECA—See HIGHMORE, SD (Venture Communications Cooperative)

▲ **SHERMAN**—Alliance Communications. Formerly served by Garretson, SD [SD0016]. This cable system has converted to IPTV

▲ **SINAI (RURAL)**—ITC. Formerly served by Clear Lake, SD [SD0047]. This cable system has converted to IPTV

SIOUX CITY (NORTHERN PORTION)—See VIBORG, IA (Knology)

▲ **SIOUX FALLS**—Midcontinent Communications

▲ **SISSETON**—Venture Communications Cooperative

▲ **SPEARFISH**—Midcontinent Communications

SPENCER—See ALEXANDRIA, SD (Trio-Tel Communications Inc.)

▲ **SPRINGFIELD**—Golden West Telecommunications

▲ **ST. FRANCIS**—Golden West Telecommunications

ST. LAWRENCE—See HURON, SD (Midcontinent Communications)

STICKNEY—See WHITE LAKE, SD (Midstate Communications)

STURGIS—See SPEARFISH, SD (Midcontinent Communications)

▲ **SUMMIT (town)**—Satellite Cable Services Inc. Now served by WILMOT, SD [SD0089]

▲ **TABOR**—Satellite Cable Services Inc. Now served by TRIPP, SD [SD0087]

TABOR—See TRIPP, SD (Fort Randall Cable)

▲ **TAKINI**—Formerly served by Cheyenne River Sioux Tribe Telephone Authority. No longer in operation

TEA—See VIBORG, SD (Knology)

▲ **TIMBER LAKE**—West River Cable Television

TOLSTOY—See HIGHMORE, SD (Venture Communications Cooperative)

▲ **TORONTO**—Satellite Cable Services Inc. Now served by CLEAR LAKE, SD [SD0047]

▲ **TORONTO**—ITC. Formerly served by Clear Lake, SD [SD0047]. This cable system has converted to IPTV

▲ **TRENT**—Golden West Telecommunications

▲ **TRIPP**—Fort Randall Cable

▲ **TRIPP**—Santel Communications. Formerly served by Mount Vernon, SD [SD0188]. This cable system has converted to IPTV

TULARE—See WESSINGTON, SD (Venture Communications Cooperative)

TUTHILL—See WALL, SD (Golden West Telecommunications)

▲ **TYNDALL**—Satellite Cable Services Inc. Now served by TRIPP, SD [SD0087]

TYNDALL—See TRIPP, SD (Fort Randall Cable)

▲ **VALLEY SPRINGS**—Alliance Communications. This cable system has converted to IPTV. See Valley Springs, SD [SD5089]

▲ **VALLEY SPRINGS**—Alliance Communications. Formerly [SD0084]. This cable system has converted to IPTV

VEBLEN—See NEW EFFINGTON, SD (RCTV)

▲ **VERMILLION**—Mediacom. Now served by GAYVILLE (formerly Yankton), SD [SD0009]

VERMILLION—See GAYVILLE, SD (Midcontinent Communications)

VETAL—See WALL, SD (Golden West Telecommunications)

▲ **VIBORG**—Knology

VOLGA—See BROOKINGS, SD (Mediacom)

▲ **WAGNER**—Satellite Cable Services Inc. Now served by TRIPP, SD [SD0087]

WAGNER—See TRIPP, SD (Fort Randall Cable)

WAKONDA—See VIBORG, SD (Knology)

▲ **WALL**—Golden West Telecommunications

WALWORTH COUNTY—See MOBRIDGE, SD (Midcontinent Communications)

WANBLEE—See WALL, SD (Golden West Telecommunications)

WARNER—See ABERDEEN TWP., SD (Midcontinent Communications)

▲ **WATERTOWN**—Knology

▲ **WATERTOWN**—Midcontinent Communications

▲ **WAUBAY**—ITC. Formerly served by Clear Lake, SD [SD0047]. This cable system has converted to IPTV

WAUBAY—See ABERDEEN TWP., SD (Midcontinent Communications)

▲ **WEBSTER**—ITC. Formerly served by Clear Lake, SD [SD0047]. This cable system has converted to IPTV

WEBSTER—See ABERDEEN TWP., SD (Midcontinent Communications)

▲ **WENTWORTH (RURAL)**—ITC. Formerly served by Clear Lake, SD [SD0047]. This cable system has converted to IPTV

▲ **WENTWORTH**—Satellite Cable Services Inc. Now served by CLEAR LAKE, SD [SD0047]

▲ **WESSINGTON SPRINGS**—Venture Communications Cooperative

▲ **WESSINGTON**—Venture Communications Cooperative

▲ **WEST WHITLOCK**—Formerly served by Western Telephone Company. No longer in operation

▲ **WHITE LAKE**—Midstate Communications

WHITE RIVER—See WALL, SD (Golden West Telecommunications)

▲ **WHITE**—Mediacom. Now served by BROOKINGS, SD [SD0005]

▲ **WHITE**—ITC. Formerly served by Clear Lake, SD [SD0047]. This cable system has converted to IPTV

WHITE—See BROOKINGS, SD (Mediacom)

▲ **WHITEWOOD**—Midcontinent Communications

▲ **WILLOW LAKE**—Satellite Cable Services Inc. Now served by CLEAR LAKE, SD [SD0047]

▲ **WILLOW LAKE**—ITC. Formerly served by Clear Lake, SD [SD0047]. This cable system has converted to IPTV

▲ **WILMOT**—Formerly served by RCTV. No longer in operation

▲ **WINNER**—Golden West Telecommunications

WOLSEY—See HURON, SD (Midcontinent Communications)

▲ **WOLSEY**—Santel Communications. Formerly served by Mount Vernon, SD [SD0188]. This cable system has converted to IPTV

▲ **WOONSOCKET**—Santel Communications. This cable system has converted to IPTV. See Mount Vernon, SD [SD5013]

▲ **WOONSOCKET**—Santel Communications. Formerly served by Mount Vernon, SD [SD0188]. This cable system has converted to IPTV

WORTHING—See VIBORG, SD (Knology)

▲ **YALE**—Midcontinent Communications

YANKTON—See VIBORG, SD (Knology)

YANKTON—See GAYVILLE, SD (Midcontinent Communications)

TENNESSEE

ADAMSVILLE—See SELMER, TN (Charter Communications)

AFTON—See GREENEVILLE, TN (Comcast Cable)

ALAMO—See JACKSON, TN (Charter Communications)

▲ **ALCOA**—Charter Communications

ALCORN COUNTY (UNINCORPORATED AREAS)—See MEMPHIS, MS (Comcast Cable)

ALEXANDRIA—See LEBANON, TN (Charter Communications)

ALGOOD—See COOKEVILLE, TN (Charter Communications)

ALLARDT—See JAMESTOWN, TN (Comcast Cable)

▲ **ALTAMONT**—Charter Communications. Now served by MONTEAGLE, TN [TN0016]

ALTAMONT—See MONTEAGLE, TN (Charter Communications)

ANDERSON COUNTY (PORTIONS)—See HARRIMAN, TN (Comcast Cable)

ANDERSON COUNTY (PORTIONS)—See OAK RIDGE, TN (Comcast Cable)

ARLINGTON—See MEMPHIS, TN (Comcast Cable)

ARTHUR—See NEW TAZEWELL, TN (Communicomm Services)

ASHLAND CITY—See CLARKSVILLE, TN (Charter Communications)

▲ **ASHLAND CITY**—Comcast Cable

▲ **ATHENS**—Comcast Cable

ATOKA—See MILLINGTON, TN (Millington CATV Inc.)

ATWOOD—See MCKENZIE, TN (Charter Communications)

BAILEYTON—See GREENEVILLE, TN (Comcast Cable)

BANEBERRY—See MORRISTOWN, TN (Charter Communications)

BARTLETT—See MEMPHIS, TN (Comcast Cable)

BAXTER—See COOKEVILLE, TN (Charter Communications)

BEAN STATION—See MORRISTOWN, TN (Charter Communications)

BEDFORD COUNTY (PORTIONS)—See LEWISBURG, TN (Charter Communications)

BEDFORD COUNTY (PORTIONS)—See TULLAHOMA, TN (Charter Communications)

BEDFORD COUNTY (UNINCORPORATED AREAS)—See CHAPEL HILL, TN (Small Town Cable)

BEERSHEBA SPRINGS—See MONTEAGLE, TN (Charter Communications)

BELFAST—See LEWISBURG, TN (Charter Communications)

BELL BUCKLE—See TULLAHOMA, TN (Charter Communications)

BELLEVUE—See NASHVILLE, TN (Comcast Cable)

BELLS—See JACKSON, TN (Charter Communications)

▲ **BENTON**—Comcast Cablevision of the South. Now served by ATHENS, TN [TN0024]

BENTON—See ATHENS, TN (Comcast Cable)

BETHEL SPRINGS—See SELMER, TN (Charter Communications)

BLAINE—See KNOXVILLE, TN (Comcast Cable)

▲ **BLEDSOE COUNTY (CENTRAL PORTIONS)**—Bledsoe Telephone Coop. Formerly served by Pikeville, TN [TN0158]. This cable system has converted to IPTV

BLOUNT COUNTY (PORTIONS)—See ALCOA, TN (Charter Communications)

BLOUNT COUNTY (PORTIONS)—See KNOXVILLE, TN (Comcast Cable)

BLOUNT COUNTY (PORTIONS)—See WALDEN CREEK, TN (Comcast Cable)

BLOUNTVILLE—See KINGSPORT, TN (Charter Communications)

BLUFF CITY—See KINGSPORT, TN (Charter Communications)

▲ **BOLIVAR**—NewWave Communications

BON AQUA—See NASHVILLE, TN (Comcast Cable)

BRADEN—See MEMPHIS, TN (Comcast Cable)

▲ **BRADFORD**—NewWave Communications. Now served by DYER, TN [TN0057]

BRADFORD—See DYER, TN (NewWave Communications)

BRADLEY COUNTY—See CLEVELAND, TN (Charter Communications)

BRADYVILLE—See WOODBURY, TN (Comcast Cable)

BRAEMAR—See GRAY, TN (Comcast Cable)

BRENTWOOD—See NASHVILLE, TN (Comcast Cable)

BRIGHTON—See COVINGTON, TN (Comcast Cable)

▲ **BRISTOL**—Charter Communications. Now served by KINGSPORT, TN [TN0007]

BRISTOL—See KINGSPORT, TN (Charter Communications)

BRISTOL—See KINGSPORT, VA (Charter Communications)

BROWNFIELD—See MEMPHIS, MS (Comcast Cable)

▲ **BROWNSVILLE**—NewWave Communications

BRUCETON—See MCKENZIE, TN (Charter Communications)

BUCHANAN—See MCKENZIE, TN (Charter Communications)

BULLS GAP—See GREENEVILLE, TN (Comcast Cable)

BURLISON—See COVINGTON, TN (Comcast Cable)

BURNS—See NASHVILLE, TN (Comcast Cable)

BURRVILLE—See WARTBURG, TN (Comcast Cable)

BYHALIA—See MEMPHIS, MS (Comcast Cable)

▲ **BYRDSTOWN**—Celina Cable

▲ **CALHOUN**—Charter Communications. Now served by CLEVELAND, TN [TN0013]

CALHOUN—See CLEVELAND, TN (Charter Communications)

CAMDEN—See PARIS, TN (Charter Communications)

CAMPBELL COUNTY—See LA FOLLETTE, TN (Comcast Cable)

CANNON COUNTY—See WOODBURY, TN (Comcast Cable)

CARTER COUNTY (PORTIONS)—See KINGSPORT, TN (Charter Communications)

CARTER COUNTY—See GRAY, TN (Comcast Cable)

▲ **CARTHAGE**—Comcast Cable. Now served by NASHVILLE, TN [TN0002]

CARTHAGE—See NASHVILLE, TN (Comcast Cable)

▲ **CARTWRIGHT**—Bledsoe Telephone Coop. Formerly served by Dunlap, TN [TN0040]. This cable system has converted to IPTV

CARYVILLE—See LA FOLLETTE, TN (Comcast Cable)

▲ **CELINA**—Celina Cable

CENTERTOWN—See TULLAHOMA, TN (Charter Communications)

▲ **CENTERVILLE**—Charter Communications

▲ **CHAPEL HILL**—Small Town Cable

CHARLESTON—See CLEVELAND, TN (Charter Communications)

▲ **CHATTANOOGA**—Comcast Cable

CHEATHAM COUNTY (PORTIONS)—See NASHVILLE, TN (Comcast Cable)

CHEATHAM COUNTY—See ASHLAND CITY, TN (Comcast Cable)

CHESTER COUNTY (PORTIONS)—See JACKSON, TN (Charter Communications)

CHUCKEY—See GREENEVILLE, TN (Comcast Cable)

CHURCH HILL—See KINGSPORT, TN (Charter Communications)

CLARKRANGE—See GRIMSLEY, TN (Comcast Cable)

CLARKSBURG—See MCKENZIE, TN (Charter Communications)

▲ **CLARKSVILLE**—Formerly served by Virginia Communications Inc. No longer in operation

▲ **CLARKSVILLE**—Charter Communications

CLAY COUNTY (UNINCORPORATED AREAS)—See CELINA, TN (Celina Cable)

▲ **CLEVELAND**—Charter Communications

▲ **CLIFTON**—Charter Communications

CLINTON—See OAK RIDGE, TN (Comcast Cable)

COALFIELD—See WARTBURG, TN (Comcast Cable)

COALMONT—See MONTEAGLE, TN (Charter Communications)

▲ **COBBLY NOB**—Comcast Cable. Now served by WALDEN CREEK, TN [TN0031]

COBBLY NOB—See WALDEN CREEK, TN (Comcast Cable)

COCKE COUNTY—See MORRISTOWN, TN (Charter Communications)

COFFEE COUNTY (PORTIONS)—See TULLAHOMA, TN (Charter Communications)

COLDWATER—See MEMPHIS, MS (Comcast Cable)

COLLEGE GROVE—See COLUMBIA, TN (Charter Communications)

COLLEGEDALE—See CHATTANOOGA, TN (Comcast Cable)

COLLIERVILLE—See MEMPHIS, TN (Comcast Cable)

COLLINWOOD—See WAYNESBORO, TN (Charter Communications)

COLONIAL HEIGHTS—See KINGSPORT, TN (Charter Communications)

▲ **COLUMBIA**—Charter Communications

▲ **COLUMBIA**—CPWS Broadband

COMO—See MEMPHIS, MS (Comcast Cable)

CONCORD—See LOUDON, TN (Charter Communications)

▲ **COOKEVILLE**—Charter Communications

COOPERTOWN—See CLARKSVILLE, TN (Charter Communications)

COOPERTOWN—See NASHVILLE, TN (Comcast Cable)

▲ **CORNERSVILLE**—Small Town Cable. Now served by CHAPEL HILL, TN [TN0089]

CORNERSVILLE—See CHAPEL HILL, TN (Small Town Cable)

COSBY—See WALDEN CREEK, TN (Comcast Cable)

COTTONTOWN—See NASHVILLE, TN (Comcast Cable)

▲ **COUNCE**—Pickwick Cablevision

▲ **COVINGTON**—Comcast Cable

COWAN—See LYNCHBURG, TN (Comcast Cable)

CRAB ORCHARD—See CUMBERLAND COUNTY, TN (Spirit Broadband)

CRENSHAW—See MEMPHIS, MS (Comcast Cable)

CRITTENDEN COUNTY (EASTERN PORTION)—See MEMPHIS, AR (Comcast Cable)

CROCKETT COUNTY (PORTIONS)—See JACKSON, TN (Charter Communications)

CROSS PLAINS—See NASHVILLE, TN (Comcast Cable)

CROSSVILLE (UNINCORPORATED AREAS)—See FAIRFIELD GLADE, TN (Comcast Cable)

▲ **CROSSVILLE**—Charter Communications

CROSSVILLE—See CUMBERLAND COUNTY, TN (Spirit Broadband)

CRUMP—See SAVANNAH, TN (Charter Communications)

CUMBERLAND COUNTY—See CROSSVILLE, TN (Charter Communications)

▲ **CUMBERLAND COUNTY**—Spirit Broadband

CUMBERLAND GAP—See NEW TAZEWELL, TN (Communicomm Services)

CUNNINGHAM—See CLARKSVILLE, TN (Charter Communications)

DADE COUNTY (UNINCORPORATED AREAS)—See CHATTANOOGA, GA (Comcast Cable)

DANDRIDGE—See MORRISTOWN, TN (Charter Communications)

▲ **DANDRIDGE**—Haywood Cablevision

DAVIDSON COUNTY—See NASHVILLE, TN (Comcast Cable)

▲ **DAYTON**—Charter Communications. Now served by CLEVELAND, TN [TN0013]

DAYTON—See CLEVELAND, TN (Charter Communications)

DECATUR COUNTY—See LEXINGTON, TN (Charter Communications)

▲ **DECATUR**—Charter Communications. Now served by CLEVELAND, TN [TN0013]

DECATUR—See CLEVELAND, TN (Charter Communications)

DECATURVILLE—See LEXINGTON, TN (Charter Communications)

DECHERD—See LYNCHBURG, TN (Comcast Cable)

DEER LODGE—See WARTBURG, TN (Comcast Cable)

DEKALB COUNTY—See SMITHVILLE, TN (Comcast Cable)

DELANO—See ATHENS, TN (Comcast Cable)

DESOTO COUNTY (UNINCORPORTED AREAS)—See MEMPHIS, MS (Comcast Cable)

DICKSON COUNTY—See NASHVILLE, TN (Comcast Cable)

DICKSON—See NASHVILLE, TN (Comcast Cable)

▲ **DOVER**—Mediacom. Now served by PEMBROKE, KY [KY0101]

DOWELLTOWN—See LEBANON, TN (Charter Communications)

DOYLE—See COOKEVILLE, TN (Charter Communications)

▲ **DRESDEN**—Dresden Cable Inc.

DRUMMONDS—See MILLINGTON, TN (Millington CATV Inc.)

▲ **DUNLAP**—Bledsoe Telephone Coop. This cable system has converted to IPTV. See Dunlap, TN [TN5004]

▲ **DUNLAP**—Bledsoe Telephone Coop. Formerly [TN0040]. This cable system has converted to IPTV

DYER COUNTY—See DYERSBURG, TN (Cable One)

▲ **DYER**—NewWave Communications

▲ **DYERSBURG**—Cable One

▲ **EAGLEVILLE**—Small Town Cable. Now served by CHAPEL HILL, TN [TN0089]

EAGLEVILLE—See CHAPEL HILL, TN (Small Town Cable)

EAST RIDGE—See CHATTANOOGA, TN (Comcast Cable)

▲ **ELIZABETHTON**—Charter Communications. Now served by KINGSPORT, TN [TN0007]

ELIZABETHTON—See KINGSPORT, TN (Charter Communications)

ELMWOOD—See NASHVILLE, TN (Comcast Cable)

EMLYN—See JELLICO, KY (Access Cable Television Inc.)

ENGLEWOOD—See ATHENS, TN (Comcast Cable)

ERIN—See TENNESSEE RIDGE, TN (Peoples CATV Inc.)

ERWIN—See GRAY, TN (Comcast Cable)

ERWIN—See UNICOI, TN (Shentel)

ESTILL SPRINGS—See LYNCHBURG, TN (Comcast Cable)

ETHRIDGE—See SUMMERTOWN, TN (Small Town Cable)

ETOWAH—See ATHENS, TN (Comcast Cable)

▲ **FAIRFIELD GLADE**—Comcast Cable

FAIRVIEW—See NASHVILLE, TN (Comcast Cable)

FALL BRANCH—See GRAY, TN (Comcast Cable)

FARRAGUT—See LOUDON, TN (Charter Communications)

FAYETTE COUNTY (UNINCORPORATED AREAS)—See MEMPHIS, TN (Comcast Cable)

▲ **FAYETTEVILLE**—Charter Communications

▲ **FAYETTEVILLE**—Fayette Public Utilities

FENTRESS COUNTY—See JAMESTOWN, TN (Comcast Cable)

FINLEY—See DYERSBURG, TN (Cable One)

▲ **FLINTVILLE**—Charter Communications

FRANKLIN COUNTY (PORTIONS)—See TULLAHOMA, TN (Charter Communications)

FRANKLIN COUNTY—See LYNCHBURG, TN (Comcast Cable)

FRANKLIN—See NASHVILLE, KY (Comcast Cable)

FRANKLIN—See NASHVILLE, TN (Comcast Cable)

FRIENDSHIP—See DYERSBURG, TN (Cable One)

▲ **FRIENDSVILLE**—Comcast Cable

GADSDEN—See JACKSON, TN (Charter Communications)

GALLATIN—See NASHVILLE, TN (Comcast Cable)

GALLAWAY—See MEMPHIS, TN (Comcast Cable)

GARLAND—See COVINGTON, TN (Comcast Cable)

GATES—See BROWNSVILLE, TN (NewWave Communications)

▲ **GATLINBURG**—Charter Communications

GERMANTOWN—See MEMPHIS, TN (Comcast Cable)

GIBSON COUNTY—See MCKENZIE, TN (Charter Communications)

GIBSON COUNTY—See DYER, TN (NewWave Communications)

GIBSON—See MCKENZIE, TN (Charter Communications)

GILES COUNTY (PORTIONS)—See COLUMBIA, TN (Charter Communications)

GILES COUNTY (UNINCORPORATED AREAS)—See MINOR HILL, TN (Small Town Cable)

GILT EDGE—See COVINGTON, TN (Comcast Cable)

GLEASON—See MCKENZIE, TN (Charter Communications)

GOODLETTSVILLE—See NASHVILLE, TN (Comcast Cable)

GORDONSVILLE—See LEBANON, TN (Charter Communications)

GRAINGER COUNTY (NORTHEASTERN PORTION)—See MORRISTOWN, TN (Charter Communications)

GRAND JUNCTION—See MEMPHIS, TN (Comcast Cable)

▲**GRAY**—Comcast Cable

GRAYSVILLE—See CLEVELAND, TN (Charter Communications)

GREENBACK—See FRIENDSVILLE, TN (Comcast Cable)

GREENBRIER—See NASHVILLE, TN (Comcast Cable)

GREENE COUNTY—See GREENEVILLE, TN (Comcast Cable)

▲**GREENEVILLE**—Comcast Cable

GREENFIELD—See MARTIN, TN (Charter Communications)

▲**GRIMSLEY**—Comcast Cable

GRUETLI-LAAGER—See MONTEAGLE, TN (Charter Communications)

GRUNDY COUNTY (PORTIONS)—See MONTEAGLE, TN (Charter Communications)

HALLS—See BROWNSVILLE, TN (NewWave Communications)

HAMBLEN COUNTY—See MORRISTOWN, TN (Charter Communications)

HAMBLEN COUNTY—See GREENEVILLE, TN (Comcast Cable)

HAMILTON COUNTY—See CHATTANOOGA, TN (Comcast Cable)

HAMPTON—See GRAY, TN (Comcast Cable)

HAMPTON—See SIMMERLY CREEK, TN (Zito Media)

HARDEMAN COUNTY (PORTIONS)—See BOLIVAR, TN (NewWave Communications)

HARDEMAN COUNTY (UNINCORPORATED AREAS)—See MEMPHIS, TN (Comcast Cable)

HARDIN COUNTY (PORTIONS)—See COUNCE, TN (Pickwick Cablevision)

HARDIN COUNTY—See SAVANNAH, TN (Charter Communications)

HARMONTOWN—See MEMPHIS, MS (Comcast Cable)

HARMONY—See GRAY, TN (Comcast Cable)

▲**HARRIMAN**—Comcast Cable

HARROGATE—See NEW TAZEWELL, TN (Communicomm Services)

▲**HARTSVILLE**—Comcast Cable. Now served by NASHVILLE, TN [TN0002]

HARTSVILLE—See NASHVILLE, TN (Comcast Cable)

HAWKINS COUNTY (CENTRAL PORTION)—See ROGERSVILLE, TN (Small Town Cable)

HAWKINS COUNTY—See KINGSPORT, TN (Charter Communications)

HAWKINS COUNTY—See GREENEVILLE, TN (Comcast Cable)

HAYWOOD COUNTY (PORTIONS)—See BROWNSVILLE, TN (NewWave Communications)

HAYWOOD COUNTY (UNINCORPORATED AREAS)—See MEMPHIS, TN (Comcast Cable)

HENDERSON COUNTY—See LEXINGTON, TN (Charter Communications)

▲**HENDERSON**—Charter Communications. Now served by JACKSON, TN [TN0008]

HENDERSON—See JACKSON, TN (Charter Communications)

HENDERSONVILLE—See NASHVILLE, TN (Comcast Cable)

HENNING—See BROWNSVILLE, TN (NewWave Communications)

HENRY COUNTY (UNINCORPORATED AREAS)—See PARIS, TN (Charter Communications)

▲**HENRY**—Peoples CATV Inc.

HERMITAGE—See NASHVILLE, TN (Comcast Cable)

HERNANDO—See MEMPHIS, MS (Comcast Cable)

▲**HOHENWALD**—Charter Communications. Now served by COLUMBIA, TN [TN0017]

HOHENWALD—See COLUMBIA, TN (Charter Communications)

HOLLOW ROCK—See MCKENZIE, TN (Charter Communications)

HOLSTON VALLEY—See KINGSPORT, VA (Charter Communications)

HORN LAKE—See MEMPHIS, MS (Comcast Cable)

HORNBEAK—See TIPTONVILLE, TN (NewWave Communications)

▲**HUMBOLDT**—Infostructure Cable

HUMPHREYS COUNTY (PORTIONS)—See NASHVILLE, TN (Comcast Cable)

HUNTINGDON—See MCKENZIE, TN (Charter Communications)

▲**HUNTLAND**—Mediacom

▲**HUNTSVILLE**—Comcast Cable

IRON CITY—See LORETTO, TN (Charter Communications)

JACKSBORO—See LA FOLLETTE, TN (Comcast Cable)

▲**JACKSON**—Charter Communications

▲**JAMESTOWN**—Comcast Cable

▲**JASPER**—Charter Communications

JEFFERSON CITY—See MORRISTOWN, TN (Charter Communications)

JEFFERSON COUNTY—See MORRISTOWN, TN (Charter Communications)

▲**JELLICO**—Access Cable Television Inc.

JOELTON—See NASHVILLE, TN (Comcast Cable)

JOHNSON CITY (SOUTHWESTERN PORTION)—See GRAY, TN (Comcast Cable)

▲**JOHNSON CITY**—Charter Communications. Now served by KINGSPORT, TN [TN0007]

JOHNSON CITY—See KINGSPORT, TN (Charter Communications)

JOHNSON COUNTY—See MOUNTAIN CITY, TN (Charter Communications)

JONESBOROUGH—See GRAY, TN (Comcast Cable)

KENTON—See DYER, TN (NewWave Communications)

KIMBALL—See JASPER, TN (Charter Communications)

▲**KINGSPORT**—Charter Communications

KINGSTON SPRINGS—See NASHVILLE, TN (Comcast Cable)

KINGSTON—See TEN MILE, TN (Charter Communications)

KINGSTON—See HARRIMAN, TN (Comcast Cable)

KNOX COUNTY—See LOUDON, TN (Charter Communications)

KNOX COUNTY—See KNOXVILLE, TN (Comcast Cable)

▲**KNOXVILLE**—Formerly served by Tennessee Wireless Inc. No longer in operation

▲**KNOXVILLE**—Comcast Cable

▲**KNOXVILLE**—Knology

▲**KODAK**—Comcast Cable

▲**LA FOLLETTE**—Comcast Cable

LA GRANGE—See MEMPHIS, TN (Comcast Cable)

LA VERGNE—See NASHVILLE, TN (Comcast Cable)

▲**LAFAYETTE**—Comcast Cable. Now served by SCOTTSVILLE, KY [KY0073]

LAKE CITY—See LA FOLLETTE, TN (Comcast Cable)

LAKE COUNTY—See TIPTONVILLE, TN (NewWave Communications)

LAKE TANSI—See CROSSVILLE, TN (Charter Communications)

LAKELAND—See MEMPHIS, TN (Comcast Cable)

LAKESITE—See CHATTANOOGA, TN (Comcast Cable)

LANCING—See WARTBURG, TN (Comcast Cable)

LAUDERDALE COUNTY (PORTIONS)—See LORETTO, AL (Charter Communications)

LAUDERDALE COUNTY (UNINCORPORATED AREAS)—See BROWNSVILLE, TN (NewWave Communications)

▲**LAUREL BLOOMERY**—Charter Communications. Now served by MOUNTAIN CITY, TN [TN0067]

LAUREL BLOOMERY—See MOUNTAIN CITY, TN (Charter Communications)

LAWRENCE COUNTY (PORTIONS)—See LAWRENCEBURG, TN (Charter Communications)

LAWRENCE COUNTY (PORTIONS)—See LORETTO, TN (Charter Communications)

LAWRENCE COUNTY (UNINCORPORATED AREAS)—See SUMMERTOWN, TN (Small Town Cable)

▲**LAWRENCEBURG**—Charter Communications

▲**LEBANON**—Charter Communications

LENOIR CITY—See LOUDON, TN (Charter Communications)

LENOX—See DYERSBURG, TN (Cable One)

LEWIS COUNTY (PORTIONS)—See COLUMBIA, TN (Charter Communications)

▲**LEWISBURG**—Charter Communications

▲**LEXINGTON**—Charter Communications

LIBERTY—See LEBANON, TN (Charter Communications)

LINCOLN COUNTY (PORTIONS)—See FAYETTEVILLE, TN (Charter Communications)

▲**LINDEN**—Two Rivers Media

▲**LIVINGSTON**—Comcast Cable

▲**LOBELVILLE**—Two Rivers Media

LONE MOUNTAIN—See NEW TAZEWELL, TN (Communicomm Services)

LOOKOUT MOUNTAIN—See CHATTANOOGA, GA (Comcast Cable)

LOOKOUT MOUNTAIN—See CHATTANOOGA, TN (Comcast Cable)

▲**LORETTO**—Charter Communications

LOUDON COUNTY (PORTIONS)—See FRIENDSVILLE, TN (Comcast Cable)

LOUDON COUNTY—See LOUDON, TN (Charter Communications)

▲**LOUDON**—Charter Communications

LOUISVILLE—See ALCOA, TN (Charter Communications)

LUTTRELL—See KNOXVILLE, TN (Comcast Cable)

LYLES—See NASHVILLE, TN (Comcast Cable)

▲**LYNCHBURG**—Comcast Cable

LYNN GARDEN—See KINGSPORT, TN (Charter Communications)

▲**LYNNVILLE**—Formerly served by Small Town Cable. No longer in operation

MACON COUNTY—See NASHVILLE, TN (Comcast Cable)

MADISON COUNTY (PORTIONS)—See JACKSON, TN (Charter Communications)

▲**MADISONVILLE**—Charter Communications

MANCHESTER—See TULLAHOMA, TN (Charter Communications)

MARION COUNTY (UNINCORPORATED AREAS)—See CHATTANOOGA, TN (Comcast Cable)

MARION COUNTY—See JASPER, TN (Charter Communications)

MARION—See MEMPHIS, AR (Comcast Cable)

MARSHALL COUNTY (PORTIONS)—See LEWISBURG, TN (Charter Communications)

MARSHALL COUNTY (UNINCORPORATED AREAS)—See MEMPHIS, MS (Comcast Cable)

▲**MARTIN**—Charter Communications

MARYVILLE—See ALCOA, TN (Charter Communications)

MASON—See MEMPHIS, TN (Comcast Cable)

MAURY CITY—See JACKSON, TN (Charter Communications)

MAURY COUNTY (PORTIONS)—See COLUMBIA, TN (Charter Communications)

▲**MAYNARDVILLE**—Comcast Cablevision of the South. Now served by KNOXVILLE, TN [TN0004]

MAYNARDVILLE—See KNOXVILLE, TN (Comcast Cable)

MCDONALD—See CLEVELAND, TN (Charter Communications)

▲**MCEWEN**—Charter Communications

▲**MCKENZIE**—Charter Communications

MCLEMORESVILLE—See MCKENZIE, TN (Charter Communications)

MCMINN COUNTY (PORTIONS)—See ATHENS, TN (Comcast Cable)

MCMINN COUNTY—See CLEVELAND, TN (Charter Communications)

MCMINNVILLE—See TULLAHOMA, TN (Charter Communications)

MCNAIRY COUNTY (PORTIONS)—See SELMER, TN (Charter Communications)

MCNAIRY—See SELMER, TN (Charter Communications)

MEDINA—See HUMBOLDT, TN (Infostructure Cable)

▲**MEMPHIS**—Comcast Cable

MIDDLETON—See MEMPHIS, TN (Comcast Cable)

MIDWAY—See TEN MILE, TN (Charter Communications)

MIDWAY—See GREENEVILLE, TN (Comcast Cable)

MILAN—See MCKENZIE, TN (Charter Communications)

MILLEDGEVILLE—See SAVANNAH, TN (Charter Communications)

MILLERSVILLE—See NASHVILLE, TN (Comcast Cable)

▲**MILLINGTON**—Millington CATV Inc.

▲**MINOR HILL**—Small Town Cable

MITCHELLVILLE—See NASHVILLE, TN (Comcast Cable)

MONROE COUNTY—See MADISONVILLE, TN (Charter Communications)

▲**MONTEAGLE**—Charter Communications

MONTEREY—See COOKEVILLE, TN (Charter Communications)

▲**MONTGOMERY COUNTY (portions)**—Charter Communications. Now served by CLARKSVILLE, TN [TN0009]

MONTGOMERY COUNTY—See CLARKSVILLE, TN (Charter Communications)

MOORE COUNTY (PORTIONS)—See TULLAHOMA, TN (Charter Communications)

MOORE COUNTY (PORTIONS)—See LYNCHBURG, TN (Comcast Cable)

MOORESBURG—See MORRISTOWN, TN (Charter Communications)

MORGAN COUNTY—See WARTBURG, TN (Comcast Cable)

MORRISON—See TULLAHOMA, TN (Charter Communications)

▲**MORRISTOWN**—Charter Communications

MOSCOW—See MEMPHIS, TN (Comcast Cable)

MOSHEIM—See GREENEVILLE, TN (Comcast Cable)

MOUNT CARMEL—See KINGSPORT, TN (Charter Communications)

MOUNT JULIET—See NASHVILLE, TN (Comcast Cable)

MOUNT PLEASANT—See COLUMBIA, TN (Charter Communications)

▲**MOUNTAIN CITY**—Charter Communications

MOUNTAIN CITY—See GRAY, TN (Comcast Cable)

MUNFORD—See MILLINGTON, TN (Millington CATV Inc.)

MURFREESBORO—See NASHVILLE, TN (Comcast Cable)

▲**NASHVILLE**—Comcast Cable

NEW DEAL—See NASHVILLE, TN (Comcast Cable)

NEW HOPE—See JASPER, TN (Charter Communications)

NEW MARKET—See MORRISTOWN, TN (Charter Communications)

▲**NEW TAZEWELL**—Communicomm Services

▲**NEWBERN**—Charter Communications. Now served by NEWBERN, TN [TN0206]

▲**NEWBERN**—Charter Communications

NEWCOMB—See JELLICO, TN (Access Cable Television Inc.)

NEWPORT—See MORRISTOWN, TN (Charter Communications)

▲**NEWPORT**—Haywood Cablevision

NIOTA—See VONORE, TN (Comcast Cable)

NOLENSVILLE—See NASHVILLE, TN (Comcast Cable)

▲**NORRIS**—Comcast Cable

NORTHAVEN—See MILLINGTON, TN (Millington CATV Inc.)

▲**OAK RIDGE**—Comcast Cable

OAKDALE—See WARTBURG, TN (Comcast Cable)

OAKLAND—See MEMPHIS, TN (Comcast Cable)

OBION COUNTY (UNINCORPORATED AREAS)—See MARTIN, TN (Charter Communications)

OBION COUNTY—See DYER, TN (NewWave Communications)

OBION—See MARTIN, TN (Charter Communications)

OCOEE—See ATHENS, TN (Comcast Cable)

OLD HICKORY—See NASHVILLE, TN (Comcast Cable)

OLDFORT—See ATHENS, TN (Comcast Cable)

OLIVE BRANCH—See MEMPHIS, MS (Comcast Cable)

OLIVER SPRINGS—See OAK RIDGE, TN (Comcast Cable)

ONEIDA—See HUNTSVILLE, TN (Comcast Cable)

ORLINDA—See NASHVILLE, TN (Comcast Cable)

OSWEGO—See JELLICO, TN (Access Cable Television Inc.)

▲**OVERTON COUNTY (PORTIONS)**—Overton County Cable

PALMER—See MONTEAGLE, TN (Charter Communications)

▲**PARIS**—Charter Communications

▲**PARSONS**—Charter Communications. Now served by LEXINGTON, TN [TN0047]

PARSONS—See LEXINGTON, TN (Charter Communications)

PEGRAM—See NASHVILLE, TN (Comcast Cable)

PETROS—See WARTBURG, TN (Comcast Cable)

PHILADELPHIA—See LOUDON, TN (Charter Communications)

PICKETT COUNTY—See BYRDSTOWN, TN (Celina Cable)

PICKWICK DAM—See COUNCE, TN (Pickwick Cablevision)

PIGEON FORGE—See GATLINBURG, TN (Charter Communications)

PIGEON FORGE—See WALDEN CREEK, TN (Comcast Cable)

▲**PIKEVILLE**—Bledsoe Telephone Coop. This cable system has converted to IPTV. See Pikeville, TN [TN5005]

▲**PIKEVILLE**—Bledsoe Telephone Coop. Formerly [TN0158]. This cable system has converted to IPTV

PIPERTON—See MEMPHIS, TN (Comcast Cable)

PLEASANT HILL—See CUMBERLAND COUNTY, TN (Spirit Broadband)

PLEASANT VIEW—See CLARKSVILLE, TN (Charter Communications)

POLK COUNTY (PORTIONS)—See ATHENS, TN (Comcast Cable)

▲**PORTLAND**—Comcast Cable. Now served by NASHVILLE, TN [TN0002]

PORTLAND—See NASHVILLE, TN (Comcast Cable)

POWELL—See KNOXVILLE, TN (Comcast Cable)

POWELLS CROSSROADS—See JASPER, TN (Charter Communications)

▲**PULASKI**—Charter Communications. Now served by COLUMBIA, TN [TN0017]

PULASKI—See COLUMBIA, TN (Charter Communications)

PUTNAM COUNTY (PORTIONS)—See COOKEVILLE, TN (Charter Communications)

RED BANK—See CHATTANOOGA, TN (Comcast Cable)

▲**RED BOILING SPRINGS**—Celina Cable. Now served by SCOTTSVILLE, KY [KY0073]

RHEA COUNTY—See SPRING CITY, TN (Spring City Cable TV Inc.)

RHEATOWN—See GREENEVILLE, TN (Comcast Cable)

RICEVILLE—See ATHENS, TN (Comcast Cable)

RIDGELY—See TIPTONVILLE, TN (NewWave Communications)

RIDGESIDE—See CHATTANOOGA, TN (Comcast Cable)

▲**RIPLEY**—NewWave Communications. Now served by BROWNSVILLE, TN [TN0054]

RIPLEY—See BROWNSVILLE, TN (NewWave Communications)

RIVES—See MARTIN, TN (Charter Communications)

ROAN MOUNTAIN—See SIMMERLY CREEK, TN (Zito Media)

ROANE COUNTY—See HARRIMAN, TN (Comcast Cable)

ROANE COUNTY—See OAK RIDGE, TN (Comcast Cable)

ROBERTSON COUNTY (PORTIONS)—See NASHVILLE, TN (Comcast Cable)

ROBINSONVILLE—See MEMPHIS, MS (Comcast Cable)

ROCKFORD—See KNOXVILLE, TN (Comcast Cable)

ROCKWOOD—See HARRIMAN, TN (Comcast Cable)

ROELLEN—See DYERSBURG, TN (Cable One)

▲**ROGERSVILLE (PORTIONS)**—Charter Communications

▲**ROGERSVILLE**—Small Town Cable

ROSSVILLE—See MEMPHIS, TN (Comcast Cable)

RUSSELLVILLE—See GREENEVILLE, TN (Comcast Cable)

RUTHERFORD COUNTY—See NASHVILLE, TN (Comcast Cable)

RUTHERFORD—See DYER, TN (NewWave Communications)

RUTLEDGE—See MORRISTOWN, TN (Charter Communications)

SALTILLO—See SAVANNAH, TN (Charter Communications)

SAMBURG—See TIPTONVILLE, TN (NewWave Communications)

SARDIS—See MEMPHIS, MS (Comcast Cable)

SAULSBURY—See MEMPHIS, TN (Comcast Cable)

▲**SAVANNAH**—Charter Communications

SCOTT COUNTY (PORTIONS)—See KINGSPORT, VA (Charter Communications)

SCOTT COUNTY—See HUNTSVILLE, TN (Comcast Cable)

▲**SCOTTS HILL**—Two Rivers Media

▲**SELMER**—Charter Communications

SENATOBIA—See MEMPHIS, MS (Comcast Cable)

▲**SEQUATCHIE COUNTY (PORTIONS)**—Bledsoe Telephone Coop. Formerly served by Dunlap, TN [TN0040]. This cable system has converted to IPTV

SEQUATCHIE COUNTY (UNINCORPORATED AREAS)—See CHATTANOOGA, TN (Comcast Cable)

SEQUATCHIE—See JASPER, TN (Charter Communications)

SEVIERVILLE—See GATLINBURG, TN (Charter Communications)

SEVIERVILLE—See WALDEN CREEK, TN (Comcast Cable)

SEWANEE—See MONTEAGLE, TN (Charter Communications)

SEYMOUR—See ALCOA, TN (Charter Communications)

SHARON—See MARTIN, TN (Charter Communications)

SHAWANEE—See NEW TAZEWELL, TN (Communicomm Services)

SHELBY COUNTY (UNINCORPORATED AREAS)—See MEMPHIS, TN (Comcast Cable)

SHELBYVILLE—See TULLAHOMA, TN (Charter Communications)

SIGNAL MOUNTAIN—See CHATTANOOGA, TN (Comcast Cable)

▲**SIMMERLY CREEK**—Zito Media

SIMPSON COUNTY—See NASHVILLE, KY (Comcast Cable)

SLEDGE—See MEMPHIS, MS (Comcast Cable)

SMITH COUNTY (UNINCORPORATED AREAS)—See LEBANON, TN (Charter Communications)

SMITH COUNTY—See NASHVILLE, TN (Comcast Cable)

▲**SMITHVILLE**—Comcast Cable

SMYRNA—See NASHVILLE, TN (Comcast Cable)

▲**SNEEDVILLE**—Zito Media

SODDY DAISY—See CHATTANOOGA, TN (Comcast Cable)

SOMERVILLE—See MEMPHIS, TN (Comcast Cable)

SOUTH CARTHAGE—See NASHVILLE, TN (Comcast Cable)

SOUTH PITTSBURG—See JASPER, TN (Charter Communications)

SOUTHAVEN—See MEMPHIS, MS (Comcast Cable)

SOUTHSIDE—See CLARKSVILLE, TN (Charter Communications)

SPARTA—See COOKEVILLE, TN (Charter Communications)

SPEEDWELL—See NEW TAZEWELL, TN (Communicomm Services)

SPENCER—See TULLAHOMA, TN (Charter Communications)

▲**SPRING CITY**—Spring City Cable TV Inc.

SPRING HILL—See COLUMBIA, TN (Charter Communications)

SPRINGFIELD—See NASHVILLE, TN (Comcast Cable)

SPRINGVILLE—See MCKENZIE, TN (Charter Communications)

ST. JOSEPH—See LORETTO, TN (Charter Communications)

STANTON—See MEMPHIS, TN (Comcast Cable)

▲**STONEY CREEK**—Charter Communications

SULLIVAN COUNTY—See KINGSPORT, TN (Charter Communications)

▲**SUMMERTOWN**—Small Town Cable

SUMNER COUNTY (PORTIONS)—See NASHVILLE, TN (Comcast Cable)

SUNBRIGHT—See WARTBURG, TN (Comcast Cable)

SUNSET—See MEMPHIS, AR (Comcast Cable)

SURGOINSVILLE—See ROGERSVILLE, TN (Small Town Cable)

SWEETWATER—See MADISONVILLE, TN (Charter Communications)

TALBOTT—See MORRISTOWN, TN (Charter Communications)

▲**TALBOTT**—Haywood Cablevision

TATE COUNTY (UNINCORPORATED ARES)—See MEMPHIS, MS (Comcast Cable)

TAZEWELL—See NEW TAZEWELL, TN (Communicomm Services)

TELLICO PLAINS—See VONORE, TN (Comcast Cable)

▲**TEN MILE**—Charter Communications

▲**TENNESSEE RIDGE**—Peoples CATV Inc.

THOMPSON'S STATION—See COLUMBIA, TN (Charter Communications)

TIGRETT—See DYERSBURG, TN (Cable One)

TIPPAH COUNTY (UNINCORPORATED AREAS)—See MEMPHIS, MS (Comcast Cable)

TIPTON COUNTY (SOUTHEASTERN PORTION)—See MEMPHIS, TN (Comcast Cable)

TIPTON COUNTY—See COVINGTON, TN (Comcast Cable)

▲**TIPTONVILLE**—NewWave Communications

TOWNSEND—See WALDEN CREEK, TN (Comcast Cable)

TRACY CITY—See MONTEAGLE, TN (Charter Communications)

▲**TRENTON**—Trenton TV Cable Co.

TREZEVANT—See MCKENZIE, TN (Charter Communications)

TRIMBLE—See MCKENZIE, TN (Charter Communications)

TROY—See MARTIN, TN (Charter Communications)

▲**TULLAHOMA**—Charter Communications

TUNICA COUNTY (UNINCORPORATED AREAS)—See MEMPHIS, MS (Comcast Cable)

TUNICA—See MEMPHIS, MS (Comcast Cable)

▲**TURTLETOWN**—Kudzu Cable TV Inc. Now served by BLUE RIDGE, GA [GA0075]

TUSCULUM—See GREENEVILLE, TN (Comcast Cable)

UNICOI COUNTY (PORTIONS)—See UNICOI, TN (Shentel)

UNICOI COUNTY—See GRAY, TN (Comcast Cable)

▲**UNICOI**—Shentel

▲**UNION CITY**—Formerly served by MetroVision. No longer in operation

UNION CITY—See MARTIN, TN (Charter Communications)

UNION COUNTY (PORTIONS)—See KNOXVILLE, TN (Comcast Cable)

UNIONVILLE—See CHAPEL HILL, TN (Small Town Cable)

VALLEY FORGE—See GRAY, TN (Comcast Cable)

VAN BUREN COUNTY (PORTIONS)—See TULLAHOMA, TN (Charter Communications)

VIOLA—See TULLAHOMA, TN (Charter Communications)

▲**VONORE**—Comcast Cable

▲**WALDEN CREEK**—Comcast Cable

WALDEN—See CHATTANOOGA, TN (Comcast Cable)

WALLS—See MEMPHIS, MS (Comcast Cable)

WALNUT—See MEMPHIS, MS (Comcast Cable)

WARREN COUNTY (PORTIONS)—See TULLAHOMA, TN (Charter Communications)

▲**WARTBURG**—Comcast Cable

WARTRACE—See TULLAHOMA, TN (Charter Communications)

WASHINGTON COUNTY (PORTIONS)—See KINGSPORT, VA (Charter Communications)

WASHINGTON COUNTY—See GRAY, TN (Comcast Cable)

WATERTOWN—See LEBANON, TN (Charter Communications)

WAUTAUGA—See KINGSPORT, TN (Charter Communications)

▲**WAVERLY**—Comcast Cable. Now served by NASHVILLE, TN [TN0002]

WAVERLY—See NASHVILLE, TN (Comcast Cable)

WAYNE COUNTY (PORTIONS)—See WAYNESBORO, TN (Charter Communications)

▲**WAYNESBORO**—Charter Communications

WEST MEMPHIS—See MEMPHIS, AR (Comcast Cable)

▲**WESTMORELAND**—Comcast Cable. Now served by SCOTTSVILLE, KY [KY0073]

▲**WESTPOINT**—Charter Communications. Now served by LORETTO, TN [TN0068]

WESTPOINT—See LORETTO, TN (Charter Communications)

WHITE BLUFF—See NASHVILLE, TN (Comcast Cable)

WHITE COUNTY (PORTIONS)—See COOKEVILLE, TN (Charter Communications)

▲**WHITE HOUSE**—Comcast Cable. Now served by NASHVILLE, TN [TN0002]

WHITE HOUSE—See NASHVILLE, TN (Comcast Cable)

WHITE PINE—See MORRISTOWN, TN (Charter Communications)

WHITES CREEK—See NASHVILLE, TN (Comcast Cable)

▲**WHITESBURG**—Formerly served by Adelphia Communications. Now served GREENEVILLE, TN [TN0022]

WHITESBURG—See GREENEVILLE, TN (Comcast Cable)

WHITESIDE—See JASPER, TN (Charter Communications)

WHITEVILLE—See MEMPHIS, TN (Comcast Cable)

WHITLEY COUNTY (SOUTHERN PORTION)—See JELLICO, KY (Access Cable Television Inc.)

WHITWELL—See JASPER, TN (Charter Communications)

WILLIAMSON COUNTY (PORTIONS)—See COLUMBIA, TN (Charter Communications)

WILLIAMSON COUNTY (PORTIONS)—See NASHVILLE, TN (Comcast Cable)

WILLIAMSON COUNTY (UNINCORPORATED AREAS)—See CHAPEL HILL, TN (Small Town Cable)

WILLISTON—See MEMPHIS, TN (Comcast Cable)

WILSON COUNTY (PORTIONS)—See LEBANON, TN (Charter Communications)

▲**WINCHESTER**—Formerly served by Comcast Cable. No longer in operation

WINCHESTER—See LYNCHBURG, TN (Comcast Cable)

WINFIELD—See HUNTSVILLE, TN (Comcast Cable)

▲**WOODBURY**—Comcast Cable

WOODLAND MILLS—See MARTIN, TN (Charter Communications)

WYNNBURG—See TIPTONVILLE, TN (NewWave Communications)

TEXAS

▲**ABERNATHY**—Reach Broadband

▲**ABILENE**—Suddenlink Communications

▲**ACE**—Formerly served by Jones Broadcasting. No longer in operation

▲**ACKERLY**—Formerly served by National Cable Inc. No longer in operation

ADDISON—See CARROLLTON, TX (Charter Communications)

ADDISON—See DALLAS, TX (Time Warner Cable)

▲**ADKINS**—Formerly served by Almega Cable. No longer in operation

▲**ADRIAN**—Formerly served by Sunset Cablevision. No longer in operation

ALAMO HEIGHTS—See SAN ANTONIO, TX (Grande Communications)

ALAMO HEIGHTS—See SAN ANTONIO, TX (Time Warner Cable)

ALAMO—See HARLINGEN, TX (Time Warner Cable)

▲**ALBA**—Formerly served by Almega Cable. No longer in operation

▲**ALBANY**—Suddenlink Communications

ALEDO—See FORT WORTH (northern portions), TX (Charter Communications)

▲**ALGOA**—Formerly served by Almega Cable. No longer in operation

ALICE (UNINCORPORATED AREAS)—See ALICE, TX (Time Warner Cable)

▲**ALICE**—Time Warner Cable

▲**ALLEN**—Time Warner Cable. Now served by DALLAS, TX [TX0003]

ALLEN—See DALLAS (northwest suburbs), TX (Grande Communications)

ALLEN—See DALLAS, TX (Time Warner Cable)

▲**ALLENDALE**—Formerly served by Cebridge Connections. No longer in operation

ALMA—See ENNIS, TX (Charter Communications)

▲**ALPINE**—US Cable of Coastal Texas LP

▲**ALTO**—Almega Cable

▲**ALTON**—Time Warner Communications. Now served by PHARR, TX [TX0017]

ALTON—See HARLINGEN, TX (Time Warner Cable)

▲**ALUM CREEK**—Time Warner Cable. No longer in operation

▲**ALVARADO**—Almega Cable

ALVIN (UNINCORPORATED AREAS)—See HEIGHTS (unincorporated areas), TX (Almega Cable)

ALVIN—See HOUSTON, TX (Comcast Cable)

ALVORD—See DECATUR, TX (CommuniComm Services)

▲**AMARILLO**—Suddenlink Communications

AMHERST—See MULESHOE, TX (Reach Broadband)

▲**ANAHUAC**—Formerly served by Carrell Communications. No longer in operation

ANDERSON COUNTY (UNINCORPORATED AREAS)—See LAKE PALESTINE WEST, TX (Northland Cable Television)

ANDERSON COUNTY—See PALESTINE, TX (Windjammer Cable)

▲**ANDERSON**—Formerly served by National Cable Inc. No longer in operation

ANDREWS COUNTY—See ANDREWS, TX (Suddenlink Communications)

▲**ANDREWS**—Suddenlink Communications

ANGELINA COUNTY (PORTIONS)—See CENTRAL, TX (Almega Cable)

ANGELINA COUNTY (PORTIONS)—See HOMER, TX (Almega Cable)

ANGELINA COUNTY (PORTIONS)—See ZAVALLA, TX (Almega Cable)

ANGELINA COUNTY—See CORRIGAN, TX (Suddenlink Communications)

▲**ANGLETON**—CMA Communications

▲**ANNA**—Formerly served by Cebridge Connections. Now served by PILOT POINT, TX [TX0286]

ANNA—See PILOT POINT, TX (Suddenlink Communications)

ANNETTA NORTH—See FORT WORTH (northern portions), TX (Charter Communications)

ANNETTA SOUTH—See FORT WORTH (northern portions), TX (Charter Communications)

ANNETTA—See FORT WORTH (northern portions), TX (Charter Communications)

ANNONA—See CLARKSVILLE, TX (Suddenlink Communications)

▲**ANSON**—Suddenlink Communications

ANTHONY—See EL PASO, NM (Time Warner Cable)

ANTHONY—See EL PASO, TX (Time Warner Cable)

▲**ANTON**—Reach Broadband

APRIL SOUND SUBDIVISION—See WALDEN, TX (Suddenlink Communications)

AQUA DULCE—See ALICE, TX (Time Warner Cable)

▲**AQUA VISTA**—Formerly served by Cebridge Connections. No longer in operation

ARANSAS COUNTY—See ARANSAS PASS, TX (Cable One)

▲**ARANSAS PASS**—Cable One

ARBOR VINEYARD—See HOUSTON, TX (Comcast Cable)

▲**ARCHER CITY**—Time Warner Cable. Now served by WICHITA FALLS, TX [TX0026]

ARCHER CITY—See WICHITA FALLS, TX (Time Warner Cable)

▲**ARCOLA**—Formerly served by Almega Cable. No longer in operation

▲**ARGYLE**—Formerly served by South-Tel Communications LP. No longer in operation

ARGYLE—See DALLAS (northwest suburbs), TX (Grande Communications)

▲**ARLINGTON**—Time Warner Cable. Now served by DALLAS, TX [TX0003]

ARLINGTON—See DALLAS (northwest suburbs), TX (Grande Communications)

ARLINGTON—See DALLAS, TX (Time Warner Cable)

▲**ARP**—Zoom Media

▲**ASHERTON**—Time Warner Cable. Now served by CRYSTAL CITY, TX [TX0147]

ASHERTON—See CRYSTAL CITY, TX (Time Warner Cable)

ASHFORD PARK—See HOUSTON, TX (Comcast Cable)

▲**ASPERMONT**—Alliance Communications

ATASCOSA COUNTY—See POTEET, TX (Alliance Communications)

ATASCOSA COUNTY—See CHARLOTTE, TX (Zoom Media)

▲**ATASCOSA**—Almega Cable

▲**ATHENS**—Suddenlink Communications

▲**ATLANTA**—Cobridge Communications

AUBREY—See PILOT POINT, TX (Suddenlink Communications)

▲**AUSTIN**—Grande Communications

▲**AUSTIN**—Time Warner Cable

AUTUMN RUN—See HOUSTON, TX (Comcast Cable)

AVERY—See CLARKSVILLE, TX (Suddenlink Communications)

▲**AVINGER**—Formerly served by Almega Cable. No longer in operation

▲**AZTEC**—Formerly served by Cebridge Connections. No longer in operation

BACLIFF—See HOUSTON, TX (Comcast Cable)

BAGWELL—See CLARKSVILLE, TX (Suddenlink Communications)

BAILEY'S PRAIRIE—See ANGLETON, TX (CMA Communications)

▲**BAIRD**—Formerly served by Brownwood TV Cable Service Inc. No longer in operation

BALCH SPRINGS—See TERRELL, TX (Suddenlink Communications)

BALCONES HEIGHTS—See SAN ANTONIO, TX (Grande Communications)

BALCONES HEIGHTS—See SAN ANTONIO, TX (Time Warner Cable)

BALD HILL—See HOMER, TX (Almega Cable)

▲**BALLINGER**—Allegiance Communications

▲**BALMORHEA**—Balmorhea TV Cable

BAMMEL OAKS—See HOUSTON, TX (Comcast Cable)

▲**BANDERA**—Zoom Media

BANQUETE—See CORPUS CHRISTI, TX (Time Warner Cable)

BARKER'S LANDING—See HOUSTON, TX (Comcast Cable)

BARRETT STATION—See HOUSTON, TX (Comcast Cable)

▲**BARSTOW**—Formerly served by Almega Cable. No longer in operation

▲**BARTLETT**—Zoom Media

BASTROP—See AUSTIN, TX (Time Warner Cable)

▲**BATESVILLE**—Formerly served by Almega Cable. No longer in operation

▲**BAY CITY**—Mid-Coast Cablevision

BAYOU VISTA—See HOUSTON, TX (Comcast Cable)

BAYTOWN—See HOUSTON, TX (Comcast Cable)

▲**BEACH CITY**—Formerly served by Carrell Communications. No longer in operation

BEAR CREEK FARMS—See HOUSTON, TX (Comcast Cable)

BEASLEY—See PLEAK, TX (Almega Cable)

▲**BEAUMONT COLONY**—Formerly served by Carrell Communications. No longer in operation

▲**BEAUMONT**—Time Warner Cable

BECKVILLE—See LAKE CHEROKEE, TX (Alliance Communications)

▲**BEDFORD**—Time Warner Cable. Now served by DALLAS, TX [TX0003]

BEDFORD—See DALLAS, TX (Time Warner Cable)

▲**BEDIAS**—Formerly served by Almega Cable. No longer in operation

BEE CAVES—See AUSTIN, TX (Time Warner Cable)

BEE COUNTY—See BEEVILLE, TX (Time Warner Cable)

▲**BEEVILLE**—Time Warner Cable

BELL COUNTY—See KILLEEN, TX (Time Warner Cable)

BELLAIRE—See HOUSTON, TX (Comcast Cable)

▲**BELLEVUE**—Formerly served by Cebridge Connections. No longer in operation

BELLMEAD—See WACO, TX (Time Warner Cable)

BELLS—See SHERMAN, TX (Cable One)

▲**BELLVILLE**—CMA Cablevision

BELTON—See KILLEEN, TX (Time Warner Cable)

▲**BEN BOLT**—National Cable Inc. Now served by ALICE, TX [TX0102]

BEN BOLT—See ALICE, TX (Time Warner Cable)

▲**BEN WHEELER**—Zoom Media

▲**BENAVIDES**—Time Warner Cable. Now served by ALICE, TX [TX0102]

BENAVIDES—See ALICE, TX (Time Warner Cable)

BENBROOK—See FORT WORTH (northern portions), TX (Charter Communications)

▲**BENJAMIN**—Formerly served by Jayroc Cablevision. No longer in operation

▲**BENTSEN GROVE**—Formerly served by CableDirect. No longer in operation

BERMUDA BEACH—See HOUSTON, TX (Comcast Cable)

BERRYVILLE—See LAKE PALESTINE WEST, TX (Northland Cable Television)

BERTRAM—See AUSTIN, TX (Time Warner Cable)

BEVERLY HILLS—See WACO, TX (Time Warner Cable)

BEVIL OAKS—See SOUR LAKE, TX (CMA Communications)

BEXAR COUNTY (PORTIONS)—See LAS GALLINAS, TX (Almega Cable)

▲**BEXAR COUNTY (PORTIONS)**—GVTC Communications. Formerly served by Boerne (portions), TX [TX0315]. This cable system has converted to IPTV

BEXAR COUNTY—See SAN ANTONIO, TX (Time Warner Cable)

BIG EDDY—See LAKE PALESTINE EAST, TX (Northland Cable Television)

▲**BIG LAKE**—Suddenlink Communications

BIG SANDY—See HAWKINS, TX (Suddenlink Communications)

▲**BIG SPRING**—Suddenlink Communications

▲**BIG WELLS**—Formerly served by Almega Cable. No longer in operation

BIGGS AIRFIELD—See EL PASO, TX (Time Warner Cable)

▲**BIRCH CREEK**—Reveille Broadband

▲**BISHOP**—Time Warner Cable. Now served by CORPUS CHRISTI, TX [TX0010]

BISHOP—See CORPUS CHRISTI, TX (Time Warner Cable)

BLACKHORSE RANCH—See HOUSTON, TX (En-Touch Systems Inc.)

▲**BLACKWELL**—CMA Cablevision

▲**BLANCO**—Zoom Media

▲**BLANKET**—Formerly served by National Cable Inc. No longer in operation

▲**BLESSING**—Bay City Cablevision

▲**BLOOMING GROVE**—Formerly served by Almega Cable. No longer in operation

▲**BLOOMINGTON**—Almega Cable

BLOSSOM—See CLARKSVILLE, TX (Suddenlink Communications)

BLUE BELL—See HOUSTON, TX (Comcast Cable)

BLUE MOUND—See FORT WORTH (northern portions), TX (Charter Communications)

▲**BOERNE (portions)**—GVTV Communications. Formerly [TX0315]. This cable system has converted to IPTV. See Boerne (portions) [TX5465]

▲**BOERNE (PORTIONS)**—GVTV Communications. Formerly [TX0315]. This cable system has converted to IPTV

BOERNE (PORTIONS)—See BOERNE (portions), TX (GVTV Communications. Formerly [TX0315]. This cable system has converted to IPTV)

BOGATA—See CLARKSVILLE, TX (Suddenlink Communications)

▲**BOLING**—Formerly served by Cebridge Connections. No longer in operation

BONHAM—See SHERMAN, TX (Cable One)

▲**BOOKER**—Panhandle Telephone Coop. Inc.

▲**BORGER**—Cable One

BOVINA—See FRIONA, TX (Reach Broadband)

BOWIE COUNTY (NORTHERN PORTION)—See NEW BOSTON, TX (Allegiance Communications)

BOWIE COUNTY (PORTIONS)—See REDWATER, TX (Almega Cable)

BOWIE COUNTY—See DE KALB, TX (Allegiance Communications)

BOWIE COUNTY—See HOOKS, TX (Allegiance Communications)

BOWIE COUNTY—See MAUD, TX (Allegiance Communications)

BOWIE COUNTY—See TEXARKANA, TX (Cable One)

▲**BOWIE**—CommuniComm Services

▲**BOYD**—Formerly served by South-Tel Communications LP. No longer in operation

▲**BRACKETTVILLE**—Almega Cable

▲**BRADY**—Suddenlink Communications

BRAZORIA COUNTY (PORTIONS)—See OYSTER CREEK, TX (Almega Cable)

BRAZORIA COUNTY—See HOUSTON, TX (Comcast Cable)

BRAZORIA COUNTY—See BRAZORIA, TX (Suddenlink Communications)

▲**BRAZORIA**—Suddenlink Communications

BRAZOS COUNTY (UNINCORPORATED AREAS)—See BRYAN, TX (Suddenlink Communications)

▲**BRECKENRIDGE**—Suddenlink Communications

▲**BREMOND**—Zito Media

▲**BRENHAM**—Suddenlink Communications

BRIAR CREEK—See HOUSTON, TX (Comcast Cable)

BRIAR HILLS—See HOUSTON, TX (Comcast Cable)

BRIARCLIFF—See AUSTIN, TX (Time Warner Cable)

▲**BRIDGE CITY**—Time Warner Cable. Now served by BEAUMONT, TX [TX0022]

BRIDGE CITY—See BEAUMONT, TX (Time Warner Cable)

BRIDGEPORT—See DECATUR, TX (CommuniComm Services)

BROKEN BAYOU—See HOUSTON, TX (Comcast Cable)

BRONTE—See ROBERT LEE, TX (CMA Cablevision)

BROOK HOLLOW WEST—See HOUSTON, TX (Comcast Cable)

▲**BROOKELAND**—Formerly served by Cebridge Connections. No longer in operation

BROOKS AFB—See SAN ANTONIO, TX (Time Warner Cable)

▲**BROOKSHIRE**—Formerly served by Northland Cable Television. No longer in operation

BROOKSIDE VILLAGE—See HOUSTON, TX (Comcast Cable)

▲**BROWNFIELD**—Reach Broadband

BROWNSBORO—See BEN WHEELER, TX (Zoom Media)

▲**BROWNSVILLE**—Time Warner Communications. Now served by PHARR, TX [TX0017]

BROWNSVILLE—See HARLINGEN, TX (Time Warner Cable)

▲**BROWNWOOD**—Formerly served by Brownwood TV Cable Service Inc. No longer in operation

BRUCEVILLE-EDDY—See WACO, TX (Time Warner Cable)

▲**BRUNI**—Windjammer Cable

▲**BRYAN**—Suddenlink Communications

BRYSON—See JACKSBORO, TX (CommuniComm Services)

BUCHANAN—See REDWATER, TX (Almega Cable)

▲ **BUCKHOLTS**—Formerly served by National Cable Inc. No longer in operation

BUDA—See AUSTIN, TX (Time Warner Cable)

BUFFALO GAP—See TUSCOLA, TX (CMA Cablevision)

▲ **BUFFALO SPRINGS LAKE**—Formerly served by Almega Cable. No longer in operation

▲ **BUFFALO**—Northland Cable Television

BULLARD—See LAKE PALESTINE EAST, TX (Northland Cable Television)

BULVERDE—See SAN ANTONIO, TX (Time Warner Cable)

▲ **BUNA**—Formerly served by Cable Plus Inc. No longer in operation

BUNKER HILL—See HOUSTON, TX (Comcast Cable)

BURGER ESTATES—See HOUSTON, TX (Comcast Cable)

▲ **BURKBURNETT**—Suddenlink Communications

BURKE—See CORRIGAN, TX (Suddenlink Communications)

BURLESON CITY—See JOSHUA, TX (Almega Cable)

BURLESON COUNTY (PORTIONS)—See LYONS, TX (Reveille Broadband)

▲ **BURLESON**—Pathway. This cable system has converted to IPTV. See Burleson, TX [TX5530] & Joshua, TX [TX5531]

BURLESON—See FORT WORTH (northern portions), TX (Charter Communications)

▲ **BURLESON**—Pathway. Formerly [TX0103]. This cable system has converted to IPTV

BURNET—See MARBLE FALLS, TX (Northland Cable Television)

BURNET—See AUSTIN, TX (Time Warner Cable)

▲ **BURTON**—Formerly served by Reveille Broadband. No longer in operation

▲ **BYERS**—Formerly served by Byers-Petrolia Cable TV/North Texas Telephone Co. No longer in operation

▲ **CACTUS**—Elk River TV Cable Co.

CADDO MILLS—See QUINLAN, TX (Zoom Media)

▲ **CADDO PEAK**—North Texas Broadband

▲ **CALDWELL**—Suddenlink Communications

CALHOUN COUNTY—See PORT LAVACA, TX (Cable One)

▲ **CALVERT**—Zito Media

▲ **CAMERON COUNTY (southern portion)**—Formerly served by Ridgewood Cablevision. No longer in operation

CAMERON COUNTY—See HARLINGEN, TX (Time Warner Cable)

▲ **CAMERON**—Zito Media

CAMP COUNTY (PORTIONS)—See PITTSBURG, TX (Suddenlink Communications)

▲ **CAMP WOODS**—Formerly served by Cebridge Connections. No longer in operation

▲ **CAMPBELL**—Formerly served by CableSouth Inc. No longer in operation

▲ **CANADIAN**—Suddenlink Communications

CANEY CITY—See MALAKOFF, TX (Northland Cable Television)

▲ **CANTON**—East Texas Cable Co.

CANUTILLO—See EL PASO, TX (Time Warner Cable)

▲ **CANYON LAKE**—GVTC Communications

CANYON—See AMARILLO, TX (Suddenlink Communications)

▲ **CARLSBAD**—Formerly served by Cebridge Connections. No longer in operation

CARLTON—See WAXAHACHIE, TX (Charter Communications)

▲ **CARMINE**—Formerly served by Reveille Broadband. No longer in operation

▲ **CAROLINA COVE**—Cablevision of Walker County

CARRIZO SPRINGS—See CRYSTAL CITY, TX (Time Warner Cable)

▲ **CARROLLTON**—Charter Communications

CARROLLTON—See DALLAS (northwest suburbs), TX (Grande Communications)

CARROLLTON—See DALLAS, TX (Time Warner Cable)

▲ **CARTHAGE**—Cobridge Communications

CASON—See DAINGERFIELD, TX (Suddenlink Communications)

CASS COUNTY (PORTIONS)—See ATLANTA, TX (Cobridge Communications)

CASTLE HILLS—See SAN ANTONIO, TX (Grande Communications)

CASTLE HILLS—See SAN ANTONIO, TX (Time Warner Cable)

▲ **CASTROVILLE**—Charter Communications. Now served by HONDO, TX [TX0218]

CASTROVILLE—See HONDO, TX (Reach Broadband)

▲ **CEDAR CREEK**—Formerly served by Trust Cable. No longer in operation

CEDAR HILL—See DALLAS, TX (Time Warner Cable)

CEDAR PARK—See AUSTIN, TX (Time Warner Cable)

▲ **CEDAR SPRINGS**—Formerly served by Cebridge Connections. No longer in operation

CELESTE—See LEONARD, TX (Zoom Media)

CELINA—See PILOT POINT, TX (Suddenlink Communications)

▲ **CENTER POINT**—Almega Cable

▲ **CENTER**—Suddenlink Communications

▲ **CENTERVILLE**—Formerly served by Almega Cable. No longer in operation

▲ **CENTRAL**—Almega Cable

CHAMBERS COUNTY (WESTERN PORTION)—See HOUSTON, TX (Comcast Cable)

CHAMBERS COUNTY (WESTERN PORTION)—See MONT BELVIEU, TX (Suddenlink Communications)

CHANDLER—See LAKE PALESTINE WEST, TX (Northland Cable Television)

CHANNELVIEW—See HOUSTON, TX (Comcast Cable)

▲ **CHANNING**—Formerly served by Sunset Cablevision. No longer in operation

▲ **CHAPPELL HILL**—Formerly served by Reveille Broadband. No longer in operation

▲ **CHARLOTTE**—Zoom Media

▲ **CHEEK**—Formerly served by Cebridge Connections. No longer in operation

▲ **CHEROKEE COUNTY (NORTHERN PORTIONS)**—Reach Broadband

CHEROKEE COUNTY (PORTIONS)—See RUSK, TX (Suddenlink Communications)

CHEROKEE COUNTY—See JACKSONVILLE, TX (Suddenlink Communications)

▲ **CHESTER**—Formerly served by Cebridge Connections. No longer in operation

CHICO—See DECATUR, TX (Communi-Comm Services)

CHILDRESS COUNTY—See WELLINGTON, TX (Suddenlink Communications)

▲ **CHILDRESS**—Formerly served by Cebridge Connections. Now served by WELLINGTON, TX [TX0313]

CHILDRESS—See WELLINGTON, TX (Suddenlink Communications)

▲ **CHILLICOTHE**—Formerly served by Almega Cable. No longer in operation

▲ **CHILTON**—Formerly served by Galaxy Cablevision. No longer in operation

CHIMNEY HILL—See HOUSTON, TX (Comcast Cable)

CHINA GROVE—See SAN ANTONIO, TX (Time Warner Cable)

CHINA SPRING—See WACO, TX (Time Warner Cable)

▲ **CHINA**—CMA Cablevision. Now served by SOUR LAKE, TX [TX0162]

CHINA—See SOUR LAKE, TX (CMA Communications)

▲ **CHRISTOVAL**—Formerly served by Almega Cable. No longer in operation

CIBOLO—See SAN ANTONIO, TX (Time Warner Cable)

CISCO—See EASTLAND, TX (Suddenlink Communications)

▲ **CLARENDON**—Suddenlink Communications

CLARKSVILLE CITY—See GLADEWATER, TX (Suddenlink Communications)

▲ **CLARKSVILLE**—Suddenlink Communications

▲ **CLAUDE**—Formerly served by Almega Cable. No longer in operation

CLAWSON—See CENTRAL, TX (Almega Cable)

CLEAR LAKE SHORES—See HOUSTON, TX (Comcast Cable)

▲ **CLEBURNE**—Charter Communications

▲ **CLEVELAND**—CMA Cablevision

▲ **CLIFTON**—Reach Broadband

CLINT—See EL PASO, TX (Time Warner Cable)

CLUTE—See HOUSTON, TX (Comcast Cable)

COAHOMA—See BIG SPRING, TX (Suddenlink Communications)

COCKRELL HILL—See DALLAS, TX (Time Warner Cable)

COLDSPRING—See LAKE LIVINGSTON, TX (Suddenlink Communications)

▲ **COLEMAN**—Reach Broadband

COLES CROSSING—See HOUSTON, TX (En-Touch Systems Inc.)

▲ **COLETO CREEK**—Formerly served by National Cable Inc. No longer in operation

COLLEGE STATION—See BRYAN, TX (Suddenlink Communications)

COLLEYVILLE—See DALLAS, TX (Time Warner Cable)

COLLIN COUNTY (PORTIONS)—See LUCAS, TX (Suddenlink Communications)

COLLIN COUNTY (PORTIONS)—See TERRELL, TX (Suddenlink Communications)

COLLINGSWORTH COUNTY—See WELLINGTON, TX (Suddenlink Communications)

COLLINSVILLE—See VALLEY VIEW, TX (Nortex Communications)

▲ **COLMESNEIL**—Formerly served by Carrell Communications. No longer in operation

COLONIES—See HOUSTON, TX (Comcast Cable)

▲ **COLORADO CITY**—Cobridge Communications

COLUMBIA LAKES—See WEST COLUMBIA, TX (Texas Mid-Gulf Cablevision)

▲ **COLUMBUS**—Time Warner Cable

COMAL COUNTY (PORTIONS)—See CANYON LAKE, TX (GVTC Communications)

COMAL COUNTY—See SAN ANTONIO, TX (Time Warner Cable)

▲ **COMANCHE**—Reach Broadband

COMBES—See HARLINGEN, TX (Time Warner Cable)

▲ **COMBINE**—Formerly served by Charter Communications. No longer in operation

▲ **COMFORT**—Formerly served by Cebridge Connections. No longer in operation

▲ **COMFORT**—Comfort Cable Co.

CONCHO COUNTY (PORTIONS)—See EDEN, TX (Reach Broadband)

CONCORD COLONY—See HOUSTON, TX (Comcast Cable)

CONROE (UNINCORPORATED AREAS)—See MAGNOLIA, TX (Versalink Media)

▲ **CONROE WEST**—Suddenlink Communications

▲ **CONROE**—Suddenlink Communications

CONVERSE—See SAN ANTONIO, TX (Time Warner Cable)

COOKE COUNTY—See GAINESVILLE, TX (Suddenlink Communications)

▲ **COOLIDGE**—Northland Cable Television

▲ **COOPER**—Alliance Communications

COPPELL—See DALLAS, TX (Time Warner Cable)

COPPERAS COVE—See KILLEEN, TX (Time Warner Cable)

COPPERFIELD—See HOUSTON, TX (Comcast Cable)

CORINTH—See DENTON, TX (Charter Communications)

CORNERSTONE VILLAGE NORTH—See HOUSTON, TX (Comcast Cable)

CORPUS CHRISTI NAVAL AIR STATION—See CORPUS CHRISTI, TX (Time Warner Cable)

▲ **CORPUS CHRISTI**—Grande Communications

▲ **CORPUS CHRISTI**—Time Warner Cable

▲ **CORRIGAN**—Suddenlink Communications

▲ **CORSICANA**—Northland Cable Television

CORYELL COUNTY (UNINCORPORATED AREAS)—See KILLEEN, TX (Time Warner Cable)

COTTONWOOD SHORES—See MARBLE FALLS, TX (Northland Cable Television)

COTTONWOOD—See HOUSTON, TX (Comcast Cable)

▲ **COTULLA**—Time Warner Cable. Now served by PEARSALL, TX [TX0196]

COTULLA—See PEARSALL, TX (Time Warner Cable)

▲ **COUNTRY CLUB SHORES**—Formerly served by CableSouth Inc. No longer in operation

▲ **COUNTRY HAVEN**—Formerly served by Cebridge Connections. No longer in operation

▲ **CRANDALL**—Formerly served by Almega Cable. No longer in operation

▲ **CRANE**—Suddenlink Communications

▲ **CRANFILLS GAP**—Formerly served by National Cable Inc. No longer in operation

▲ **CRAWFORD**—Zito Media

▲ **CROCKETT**—Northland Cable Television

CROSBY—See HOUSTON, TX (Comcast Cable)

▲ **CROSBYTON**—Reach Broadband

▲ **CROWELL**—Alliance Communications

CROWLEY—See FORT WORTH (northern portions), TX (Charter Communications)

▲ **CRYSTAL BEACH**—Formerly served by Rapid Cable. No longer in operation

▲ **CRYSTAL CITY**—Time Warner Cable

▲ **CUERO**—Time Warner Cable. Now served by GONZALES, TX [TX0209]

CUERO—See GONZALES, TX (Time Warner Cable)

▲ **CUMBY**—Formerly served by Cebridge Connections. No longer in operation

▲ **CUSHING**—Almega Cable

▲ **CUT AND SHOOT**—Northland Cable Television

CYPRESS TRAILS—See HOUSTON, TX (Comcast Cable)

▲ **CYPRESS**—Formerly served by Almega Cable. No longer in operation

▲ **DAINGERFIELD**—Suddenlink Communications

▲ **DALHART**—XIT Communications. This cable system has converted to IPTV. See Dalhart, TX [TX5049]

▲ **DALHART**—Allegiance Communications

▲ **DALHART**—XIT Communications. Formerly [TX1023]. This cable system has converted to IPTV

DALLAM COUNTY—See DALHART, TX (Allegiance Communications)

▲ **DALLAS (NORTHWEST SUBURBS)**—Grande Communications

DALLAS COUNTY (PORTIONS)—See TERRELL, TX (Suddenlink Communications)

DALLAS COUNTY—See DALLAS, TX (Time Warner Cable)

▲ **DALLAS**—Time Warner Cable

DALWORTHINGTON GARDENS—See DALLAS, TX (Time Warner Cable)

DANBURY—See ANGLETON, TX (CMA Communications)

▲ **DARROUZETT**—Panhandle Telephone Coop. Inc.

DAWSON COUNTY (UNINCORPORATED AREAS)—See LAMESA, TX (Northland Cable Television)

DAWSON—See HUBBARD, TX (Almega Cable)

DAYTON—See HOUSTON, TX (Comcast Cable)

▲ **DE KALB**—Allegiance Communications

▲ **DE LEON**—Reach Broadband

▲ **DE SOTO**—Time Warner Cable. Now served by DALLAS, TX [TX0003]

DE SOTO—See DALLAS, TX (Time Warner Cable)

▲ **DECATUR**—CommuniComm Services

DEER PARK—See HOUSTON, TX (Comcast Cable)

DEERFIELD VILLAGE—See HOUSTON, TX (Comcast Cable)

▲ **DEL RIO**—Time Warner Cable

DENISON—See SHERMAN, TX (Cable One)

DENNISON—See EAST GRAYSON COUNTY, TX (TV Cable of Grayson County)

▲ **DENTON**—Charter Communications

DENTON—See DALLAS (northwest suburbs), TX (Grande Communications)

DENVER CITY—See SEMINOLE, TX (US Cable of Coastal Texas LP)

DEPORT—See CLARKSVILLE, TX (Suddenlink Communications)

DETROIT—See CLARKSVILLE, TX (Suddenlink Communications)

▲ **DEVINE**—Reach Broadband

DEWITT COUNTY—See GONZALES, TX (Time Warner Cable)

DIALVILLE—See RUSK, TX (Suddenlink Communications)

▲ **DIANA**—Almega Cable

DIBOLL—See CORRIGAN, TX (Suddenlink Communications)

▲ **DICKENS**—Formerly served by Almega Cable. No longer in operation

DICKINSON—See HOUSTON, TX (Comcast Cable)

▲ **DILLEY**—Time Warner Cable. Now served by PEARSALL, TX [TX0196]

DILLEY—See PEARSALL, TX (Time Warner Cable)

▲ **DIME BOX**—Formerly served by Reveille Broadband. No longer in operation

DIMMIT COUNTY—See CRYSTAL CITY, TX (Time Warner Cable)

▲ **DIMMITT**—Suddenlink Communications

▲ **DIXIE**—Formerly served by Northland Communications Corp. No longer in operation

DOMINION—See SAN ANTONIO, TX (Time Warner Cable)

DONA ANA COUNTY (PORTIONS)—See EL PASO, NM (Time Warner Cable)

DONNA—See HARLINGEN, TX (Time Warner Cable)

DOUBLE OAK—See DALLAS, TX (Time Warner Cable)

DRIPPING SPRINGS—See AUSTIN, TX (Time Warner Cable)

▲ **DRISCOLL**—Time Warner Cable. Now served by CORPUS CHRISTI, TX [TX0010]

DRISCOLL—See CORPUS CHRISTI, TX (Time Warner Cable)

▲ **DUBLIN**—Northland Cable Television

DUMAS—See BORGER, TX (Cable One)

▲ **DUNCANVILLE**—Charter Communications

DUVAL COUNTY (NORTHERN PORTION)—See FREER, TX (Allegiance Communications)

DUVAL COUNTY (PORTIONS)—See ALICE, TX (Time Warner Cable)

DYESS AFB—See ABILENE, TX (Suddenlink Communications)

▲ **EAGLE LAKE**—Time Warner Cable. Now served by COLUMBUS, TX [TX0257]

EAGLE LAKE—See COLUMBUS, TX (Time Warner Cable)

▲ **EAGLE PASS**—Time Warner Cable

EARTH—See MULESHOE, TX (Reach Broadband)

▲ **EAST GRAYSON COUNTY**—TV Cable of Grayson County

▲ **EAST MOUNTAIN**—Gilmer Cable

EAST TAWAKONI—See QUINLAN, TX (Zoom Media)

EASTLAND COUNTY—See EASTLAND, TX (Suddenlink Communications)

▲ **EASTLAND**—Suddenlink Communications

EASTON COMMON VILLAGE—See HOUSTON, TX (Comcast Cable)

EASTON—See LAKE CHEROKEE, TX (Alliance Communications)

▲ **ECTOR COUNTY (PORTIONS)**—Ridgewood Cablevision

ECTOR COUNTY—See ODESSA, TX (Cable One)

ECTOR COUNTY—See WEST ODESSA, TX (US Cable of Coastal Texas LP)

▲ **ECTOR**—TV Cable of Grayson County

ED-LOU—See HOUSTON, TX (Comcast Cable)

▲ **EDCOUCH**—Time Warner Communications. Now served by PHARR, TX [TX0017]

EDCOUCH—See HARLINGEN, TX (Time Warner Cable)

▲ **EDEN**—Reach Broadband

EDGECLIFF VILLAGE—See FORT WORTH (northern portions), TX (Charter Communications)

EDGEWOOD—See WILLS POINT, TX (Zoom Media)

EDINBURG—See HARLINGEN, TX (Time Warner Cable)

▲ **EDNA**—Mid-Coast Cablevision

EDOM—See BEN WHEELER, TX (Zoom Media)

EGAN COUNTY (PORTIONS)—See EGAN, TX (North Texas Broadband)

▲ **EGAN**—North Texas Broadband

▲ **EL CAMPO**—Mid-Coast Cablevision

EL LAGO—See HOUSTON, TX (Comcast Cable)

EL PASO COUNTY—See EL PASO, TX (Time Warner Cable)

▲ **EL PASO**—Time Warner Cable

▲ **ELDORADO**—Reach Broadband

▲ **ELECTRA**—Suddenlink Communications

ELGIN—See AUSTIN, TX (Time Warner Cable)

ELKHART—See PALESTINE, TX (Windjammer Cable)

ELKINS LAKE—See HUNTSVILLE, TX (Suddenlink Communications)

▲ **ELLINGER**—Formerly served by National Cable Inc. No longer in operation

ELLIS COUNTY—See WAXAHACHIE, TX (Charter Communications)

ELM MOTT—See WACO, TX (Time Warner Cable)

ELMENDORF—See SAN ANTONIO, TX (Time Warner Cable)

▲ **ELMO**—Formerly served by Almega Cable. No longer in operation

ELSA—See HARLINGEN, TX (Time Warner Cable)

EMERALD BAY—See LAKE PALESTINE EAST, TX (Northland Cable Television)

▲ **EMORY**—Formerly served by Alliance Communications. No longer in operation

ENCHANTED OAKS—See GUN BARREL CITY, TX (Northland Cable Television)

▲ **ENCINAL**—Windjammer Cable

ENCLAVE AT PAVILLION—See HOUSTON, TX (Comcast Cable)

▲ **ENNIS**—Charter Communications

ESCOBARES—See HARLINGEN, TX (Time Warner Cable)

ETTER—See CACTUS, TX (Elk River TV Cable Co.)

EULESS—See DALLAS, TX (Time Warner Cable)

▲ **EVANT**—Formerly served by Almega Cable. No longer in operation

EVERMAN—See FORT WORTH (northern portions), TX (Charter Communications)

FABENS—See EL PASO, TX (Time Warner Cable)

▲ **FAIR OAKS RANCH**—GVTC Communications. Formerly served by Boerne (portions), TX [TX0315]. This cable system has converted to IPTV

FAIR OAKS RANCH—See FAIR OAKS RANCH, TX (GVTC Communications. Formerly served by Boerne (portions), TX [TX0315]. This cable system has converted to IPTV)

▲ **FAIRFIELD**—Northland Cable Television

FAIRVIEW—See LUCAS, TX (Suddenlink Communications)

▲ **FALFURRIAS**—Time Warner Cable. Now served by ALICE, TX [TX0102]

FALFURRIAS—See ALICE, TX (Time Warner Cable)

▲ **FANNETT**—Almega Cable

FANNIN COUNTY—See SHERMAN, TX (Cable One)

FARMERS BRANCH—See DALLAS, TX (Time Warner Cable)

▲ **FARMERSVILLE**—Time Warner Cable

FATE—See TERRELL, TX (Suddenlink Communications)

▲ **FAYETTEVILLE**—Grisham TV Cable Co.

▲ **FENTRESS**—Formerly served by National Cable Inc. No longer in operation

FERRIS—See WAXAHACHIE, TX (Charter Communications)

▲ **FLAT**—Formerly served by National Cable Inc. No longer in operation

▲ **FLATONIA**—Almega Cable

FLEETWOOD OAKS—See HOUSTON, TX (Comcast Cable)

FLEETWOOD—See HOUSTON, TX (Comcast Cable)

FLINT (UNINCORPORATED AREAS)—See LAKE PALESTINE EAST, TX (Northland Cable Television)

▲ **FLORENCE**—Windjammer Cable

▲ **FLORESVILLE**—Formerly served by Clear Vu Cable. No longer in operation

▲ **FLOWER MOUND**—Time Warner Cable. Now served by DALLAS, TX [TX0003]

FLOWER MOUND—See DALLAS, TX (Time Warner Cable)

▲ **FLOYDADA**—Suddenlink Communications

▲ **FOLLETT**—Panhandle Telephone Coop. Inc.

FOREST BEND—See HOUSTON, TX (Comcast Cable)

FOREST HILL—See FORT WORTH (northern portions), TX (Charter Communications)

FORNEY—See TERRELL, TX (Suddenlink Communications)

▲ **FORSAN**—Formerly served by National Cable Inc. No longer in operation

▲ **FORT BEND COUNTY (portions)**—Rapid Cable. Now served by ARCOLA, TX [TX0243]

FORT BEND COUNTY (PORTIONS)—See HOUSTON, TX (Phonoscope Ltd.)

FORT BEND COUNTY (UNINCORPORATED AREAS)—See PLEAK, TX (Almega Cable)

FORT BEND COUNTY—See HOUSTON, TX (Comcast Cable)

FORT BLISS—See EL PASO, TX (Time Warner Cable)

FORT CLARK SPRINGS—See BRACKETTVILLE, TX (Almega Cable)

▲ **FORT DAVIS**—Fort Davis TV Cable

FORT GATES—See GATESVILLE, TX (Suddenlink Communications)

FORT HOOD—See KILLEEN, TX (Time Warner Cable)

FORT SAM HOUSTON—See SAN ANTONIO, TX (Time Warner Cable)

▲ **FORT STOCKTON**—US Cable of Coastal Texas LP

▲ **FORT WORTH (NORTHERN PORTIONS)**—Charter Communications

FRANKLIN COUNTY (PORTIONS)—See MOUNT VERNON, TX (Suddenlink Communications)

FRANKLIN COUNTY—See MINEOLA, TX (Suddenlink Communications)

▲ **FRANKLIN**—Zito Media

FRANKSTON—See LAKE PALESTINE WEST, TX (Northland Cable Television)

▲ **FREDERICKSBURG**—Time Warner Cable. Now served by AUSTIN, TX [TX0005]

FREDERICKSBURG—See AUSTIN, TX (Time Warner Cable)

FREEPORT—See HOUSTON, TX (Comcast Cable)

▲ **FREER**—Allegiance Communications

FRICK ROAD PARK—See HOUSTON, TX (Comcast Cable)

FRIENDSWOOD—See HOUSTON, TX (Comcast Cable)

FRIO COUNTY—See PEARSALL, TX (Time Warner Cable)

▲ **FRIONA**—Reach Broadband

FRISCO—See DALLAS (northwest suburbs), TX (Grande Communications)

FRISCO—See DALLAS, TX (Time Warner Cable)

FRITCH—See BORGER, TX (Cable One)

▲ **FRUITVALE**—Formerly served by Almega Cable. No longer in operation

FULLER SPRINGS—See CORRIGAN, TX (Suddenlink Communications)

FULTON—See ROCKPORT, TX (Cobridge Communications)

▲ **GAINESVILLE**—Suddenlink Communications

GALENA PARK—See HOUSTON, TX (Comcast Cable)

GALVESTON COUNTY—See HOUSTON, TX (Comcast Cable)

GALVESTON—See HOUSTON, TX (Comcast Cable)

▲ **GANADO**—Mid-Coast Cablevision

GARCENO—See HARLINGEN, TX (Time Warner Cable)

GARCIASVILLE—See HARLINGEN, TX (Time Warner Cable)

▲ **GARDEN CITY**—Formerly served by National Cable Inc. No longer in operation

GARDEN RIDGE—See SAN ANTONIO, TX (Time Warner Cable)

▲ **GARDENDALE**—Formerly served by Cebridge Connections. No longer in operation

GARFIELD—See STONY POINT, TX (Almega Cable)

▲ **GARLAND**—Time Warner Cable. Now served by DALLAS, TX [TX0003]

GARLAND—See DALLAS, TX (Time Warner Cable)

GARRETT—See ENNIS, TX (Charter Communications)

▲ **GARRISON**—Almega Cable

▲ **GARWOOD**—Formerly served by National Cable Inc. No longer in operation

▲ **GARY**—Formerly served by Almega Cable. No longer in operation

▲ **GATESVILLE**—Suddenlink Communications

▲ **GAUSE**—Formerly served by National Cable Inc. No longer in operation

▲ **GEORGE WEST**—Time Warner Cable

▲ **GEORGETOWN**—Suddenlink Communications

GERONIMO—See SAN ANTONIO, TX (Time Warner Cable)

GIDDINGS—See LA GRANGE, TX (CMA Cablevision)

GILLESPIE COUNTY (PORTIONS)—See AUSTIN, TX (Time Warner Cable)

▲ **GILMER**—Gilmer Cable

▲ **GLADEWATER**—Suddenlink Communications

GLADEWATER—See HAWKINS, TX (Suddenlink Communications)

GLEANNLOCK FARMS—See HOUSTON, TX (En-Touch Systems Inc.)

▲ **GLEN ROSE**—Formerly served by Glen Rose CATV. No longer in operation

GLEN ROSE—See GRANBURY, TX (Charter Communications)

GLENN HEIGHTS—See WAXAHACHIE, TX (Charter Communications)

GLENWOOD ACRES—See EAST MOUNTAIN, TX (Gilmer Cable)

GLENWOOD—See EAST MOUNTAIN, TX (Gilmer Cable)

▲ **GODLEY**—Formerly served by Almega Cable. No longer in operation

▲ **GOLDEN**—Formerly served by Almega Cable. No longer in operation

▲ **GOLDSMITH**—Formerly served by Cebridge Connections. No longer in operation

▲ **GOLDTHWAITE**—Almega Cable

▲ **GOLIAD**—Reach Broadband

▲ **GOLINDA**—Formerly served by National Cable Inc. No longer in operation

▲ **GONZALES**—Time Warner Cable

GOODFELLOW AFB—See SAN ANGELO, TX (Suddenlink Communications)

▲ **GOODRICH**—Versalink Media

▲ **GORDON**—Formerly served by Mallard Cablevision. No longer in operation

GORDONVILLE—See SHERWOOD SHORES, TX (TV Cable of Grayson County)

▲ **GOREE**—Formerly served by Jayroc Cablevision. No longer in operation

▲ **GORMAN**—Reach Broadband

GRAFORD—See JACKSBORO, TX (CommuniComm Services)

▲ **GRAHAM**—Windjammer Cable

▲ **GRANADA HILLS**—Time Warner Cable. Now served by AUSTIN, TX [TX0005]

GRANADA HILLS—See AUSTIN, TX (Time Warner Cable)

GRANADA—See HOUSTON, TX (Comcast Cable)

▲ **GRANBURY**—Charter Communications

▲ **GRAND PRAIRIE**—Time Warner Cable. Now served by DALLAS, TX [TX0003]

GRAND PRAIRIE—See DALLAS, TX (Time Warner Cable)

GRAND SALINE—See MINEOLA, TX (Suddenlink Communications)

▲ **GRANDFALLS**—Formerly served by Almega Cable. No longer in operation

GRANDVIEW—See ALVARADO, TX (Almega Cable)

GRANGER—See BARTLETT, TX (Zoom Media)

GRANGERLAND—See NEW CANEY, TX (Northland Cable Television)

GRANITE SHOALS—See MARBLE FALLS, TX (Northland Cable Television)

▲ **GRAPE CREEK**—CMA Cablevision

▲ **GRAPELAND**—Suddenlink Communications

GRAPEVINE—See DALLAS, TX (Time Warner Cable)

GRAYSON COUNTY (NORTHERN PORTION)—See SHERMAN, TX (Cable One)

GRAYSON COUNTY (PORTIONS)—See SHERWOOD SHORES, TX (TV Cable of Grayson County)

▲ **GREENVILLE**—GEUS

▲ **GREENVILLE**—Time Warner Cable

▲ **GREENWOOD**—Ridgewood Cablevision

GREGG COUNTY (PORTIONS)—See KILGORE, TX (Almega Cable)

GREGG COUNTY (PORTIONS)—See HAWKINS, TX (Suddenlink Communications)

GREGORY—See ARANSAS PASS, TX (Cable One)

GRESHAM (UNINCORPORATED AREAS)—See LAKE PALESTINE EAST, TX (Northland Cable Television)

GREY FOREST—See SAN ANTONIO, TX (Time Warner Cable)

GROESBECK—See MEXIA, TX (Northland Cable Television)

▲ **GROOM**—Formerly served by Almega Cable. No longer in operation

GROVES—See BEAUMONT, TX (Time Warner Cable)

▲ **GROVETON**—Formerly served by Almega Cable. No longer in operation

▲ **GRUVER**—Elk River TV Cable Co.

GUADALUPE COUNTY—See SAN ANTONIO, TX (Time Warner Cable)

▲ **GUN BARREL CITY**—Northland Cable Television

GUNTER—See PILOT POINT, TX (Suddenlink Communications)

▲ **GUSTINE**—Formerly served by Cable Unlimited. No longer in operation

▲ **GUY**—Formerly served by Cebridge Connections. No longer in operation

▲ **HALE CENTER**—Reach Broadband

HALE COUNTY—See PLAINVIEW, TX (Suddenlink Communications)

HALL COUNTY (PORTIONS)—See MEMPHIS, TX (Reach Broadband)

HALLETTSVILLE—See LA GRANGE, TX (CMA Cablevision)

HALLSVILLE—See MARSHALL, TX (Cobridge Communications)

HALTOM CITY—See FORT WORTH (northern portions), TX (Charter Communications)

▲ **HAMILTON**—Northland Cable Television

▲ **HAMLIN**—Suddenlink Communications

HAMSHIRE—See BEAUMONT, TX (Time Warner Cable)

HAPPY COUNTRY HOMES—See TERRELL, TX (Suddenlink Communications)

▲ **HAPPY**—Formerly served by Almega Cable. No longer in operation

▲ **HARBOR POINT**—Formerly served by CableSouth Inc. No longer in operation

HARDIN COUNTY (PORTIONS)—See OKLAHOMA, TX (Suddenlink Communications)

HARKER HEIGHTS—See KILLEEN, TX (Time Warner Cable)

▲ **HARLINGEN**—Time Warner Communications. Now served by PHARR, TX [TX0017]

▲ **HARLINGEN**—Time Warner Cable

▲ **HARPER**—Formerly served by Cable Comm Ltd. No longer in operation

HARRIS COUNTY (NORTHEASTERN PORTION)—See NEW CANEY, TX (Northland Cable Television)

▲ **HARRIS COUNTY (northern portion)**—Charter Communications. Now served by SPRING, TX [TX0044]

HARRIS COUNTY (NORTHERN PORTION)—See SPRING, TX (Charter Communications)

HARRIS COUNTY (PORTIONS)—See HOUSTON, TX (En-Touch Systems Inc.)

HARRIS COUNTY (SOUTHEASTERN PORTION)—See MONT BELVIEU, TX (Suddenlink Communications)

HARRIS COUNTY—See HOUSTON, TX (Comcast Cable)

HARRISON COUNTY (PORTIONS)—See MARSHALL, TX (Cobridge Communications)

HARRISON COUNTY (PORTIONS)—See LANSING, TX (Zoom Media)

▲ **HART**—Reach Broadband

HARTLEY COUNTY—See DALHART, TX (Allegiance Communications)

HARVEST ACRES—See SAN ANGELO, TX (Suddenlink Communications)

▲ **HASKELL**—Alliance Communications

HASLET—See FORT WORTH (northern portions), TX (Charter Communications)

▲ **HASSE**—Formerly served by Cable Unlimited. No longer in operation

▲ **HAWKINS**—Suddenlink Communications

▲ **HAWLEY**—Formerly served by Jayroc Cablevision. No longer in operation

HAYS COUNTY (NORTHEASTERN PORTION)—See AUSTIN, TX (Time Warner Cable)

HAYS—See AUSTIN, TX (Time Warner Cable)

▲ **HEARNE**—Suddenlink Communications

HEARTHSTONE GREEN—See HOUSTON, TX (Comcast Cable)

HEARTHSTONE—See HOUSTON, TX (Comcast Cable)

HEATH—See TERRELL, TX (Suddenlink Communications)

HEATHERGLEN—See HOUSTON, TX (Comcast Cable)

▲ **HEBBRONVILLE**—Alliance Communications

HEBRON—See DALLAS, TX (Time Warner Cable)

▲ **HEDLEY**—Formerly served by Almega Cable. No longer in operation

HEDWIG—See HOUSTON, TX (Comcast Cable)

▲ **HEIGHTS (UNINCORPORATED AREAS)**—Almega Cable

HELOTES—See SAN ANTONIO, TX (Time Warner Cable)

HEMPHILL COUNTY (PORTIONS)—See CANADIAN, TX (Suddenlink Communications)

▲ **HEMPHILL**—Almega Cable

▲ **HEMPSTEAD**—CMA Cablevision

HENDERSON COUNTY (PORTIONS)—See BEN WHEELER, TX (Zoom Media)

HENDERSON COUNTY—See ATHENS, TX (Suddenlink Communications)

▲ **HENDERSON**—Suddenlink Communications

HENDRIX—See EAST GRAYSON COUNTY, OK (TV Cable of Grayson County)

▲**HENRIETTA**—Suddenlink Communications

▲**HEREFORD**—XIT Communications

HERITAGE PARK—See HOUSTON, TX (Comcast Cable)

HERMLEIGH—See SNYDER, TX (Suddenlink Communications)

HEWITT—See WACO, TX (Grande Communications)

HEWITT—See WACO, TX (Time Warner Cable)

HICKORY CREEK—See DENTON, TX (Charter Communications)

▲**HICO**—Northland Cable Television

HIDALGO COUNTY—See HARLINGEN, TX (Time Warner Cable)

▲**HIDALGO**—Time Warner Communications. Now served by PHARR, TX [TX0017]

HIDALGO—See HARLINGEN, TX (Time Warner Cable)

▲**HIGGINS**—Formerly served by Almega Cable. No longer in operation

HIGHLAND HAVEN—See MARBLE FALLS, TX (Northland Cable Television)

HIGHLAND PARK—See UNIVERSITY PARK, TX (Charter Communications)

▲**HIGHLAND RANGE**—Formerly served by Highland Cable. No longer in operation

HIGHLAND VILLAGE—See DALLAS, TX (Time Warner Cable)

HIGHLANDS—See HOUSTON, TX (Comcast Cable)

HILL COUNTRY VILLAGE—See SAN ANTONIO, TX (Time Warner Cable)

HILLCREST VILLAGE—See HOUSTON, TX (Comcast Cable)

▲**HILLSBORO**—Northland Cable Television

HILLSHIRE—See HOUSTON, TX (Comcast Cable)

HITCHCOCK—See HOUSTON, TX (Comcast Cable)

HOCKLEY COUNTY—See LEVELLAND, TX (Cobridge Communications)

HOCKLEY—See MONTGOMERY COUNTY (unincorporated areas), TX (Versalink Media)

HOLIDAY BEACH—See ROCKPORT, TX (Cobridge Communications)

▲**HOLIDAY LAKES**—Formerly served by Cebridge Connections. No longer in operation

HOLLAND—See KILLEEN, TX (Time Warner Cable)

▲**HOLLIDAY**—Time Warner Cable. Now served by WICHITA FALLS, TX [TX0026]

HOLLIDAY—See WICHITA FALLS, TX (Time Warner Cable)

HOLLYWOOD PARK—See SAN ANTONIO, TX (Time Warner Cable)

▲**HOMER**—Almega Cable

▲**HONDO**—Reach Broadband

▲**HONEY GROVE**—Suddenlink Communications

HOOD COUNTY—See GRANBURY, TX (Charter Communications)

▲**HOOKS**—Allegiance Communications

HOPKINS COUNTY—See SULPHUR SPRINGS, TX (Suddenlink Communications)

HORIZON CITY—See EL PASO, TX (Time Warner Cable)

HORSESHOE BAY—See MARBLE FALLS, TX (Northland Cable Television)

HOUSTON (EASTERN & WESTERN SUBURBS)—See HOUSTON, TX (Comcast Cable)

▲**HOUSTON**—Formerly served by Sprint Corp. No longer in operation

▲**HOUSTON**—Comcast Cable

▲**HOUSTON**—En-Touch Systems Inc.

▲**HOUSTON**—Phonoscope Ltd.

▲**HOUSTON**—TV Max

HOWARD COUNTY—See BIG SPRING, TX (Suddenlink Communications)

▲**HOWARDWICK**—Formerly served by Almega Cable. No longer in operation

HOWE—See SHERMAN, TX (Cable One)

▲**HUBBARD**—Almega Cable

HUDSON OAKS—See FORT WORTH (northern portions), TX (Charter Communications)

▲**HUDSON**—Suddenlink Communications

HUFFMAN—See NEW CANEY, TX (Northland Cable Television)

HUGHES SPRINGS—See DAINGERFIELD, TX (Suddenlink Communications)

▲**HULL**—Formerly served by Carrell Communications. No longer in operation

HUMBLE—See HOUSTON, TX (Comcast Cable)

HUNGERFORD—See PLEAK, TX (Almega Cable)

HUNT COUNTY (PORTIONS)—See QUINLAN, TX (Zoom Media)

HUNT—See INGRAM, TX (Suddenlink Communications)

HUNTER CREEK—See HOUSTON, TX (Comcast Cable)

▲**HUNTINGTON**—Formerly served by CommuniComm Services. No longer in operation

▲**HUNTSVILLE**—Suddenlink Communications

HURST—See FORT WORTH (northern portions), TX (Charter Communications)

HUTCHINS—See DALLAS, TX (Time Warner Cable)

HUTTO—See AUSTIN, TX (Time Warner Cable)

▲**IDALOU**—Reach Broadband

▲**IMPERIAL**—Formerly served by Cebridge Connections. No longer in operation

INDIAN LAKE—See HARLINGEN, TX (Time Warner Cable)

INDIAN SHORE—See NEW CANEY, TX (Northland Cable Television)

▲**INDIAN SPRINGS**—Formerly served by Cebridge Connections. No longer in operation

INGLESIDE ON THE BAY—See ARANSAS PASS, TX (Cable One)

INGLESIDE—See ARANSAS PASS, TX (Cable One)

▲**INGRAM**—Suddenlink Communications

INKS LAKE—See LAKE BUCHANAN, TX (Northland Cable Television)

▲**IOLA**—Formerly served by National Cable Inc. No longer in operation

▲**IOWA PARK**—Formerly served by Cebridge Connections. Now served by BURKBURNETT, TX [TX0154]

IOWA PARK—See BURKBURNETT, TX (Suddenlink Communications)

▲**IRAAN**—US Cable of Coastal Texas LP

IRION COUNTY (PORTIONS)—See MERTZON, TX (Reach Broadband)

▲**IRVING**—Time Warner Cable. Now served by DALLAS, TX [TX0003]

IRVING—See DALLAS, TX (Time Warner Cable)

▲**ITALY**—Formerly served by Almega Cable. No longer in operation

ITASCA—See ALVARADO, TX (Almega Cable)

JACINTO CITY—See HOUSTON, TX (Comcast Cable)

▲**JACKSBORO**—CommuniComm Services

JACKSON'S LANDING (UNINCORPORATED ARESAS)—See LAKE PALESTINE WEST, TX (Northland Cable Television)

▲**JACKSONVILLE**—Suddenlink Communications

JAMAICA BEACH—See HOUSTON, TX (Comcast Cable)

JAMESTOWN COLONY—See HOUSTON, TX (Comcast Cable)

▲**JARRELL**—Suddenlink Communications

▲**JASPER**—CMA Cablevision

▲**JAYTON**—Formerly served by Jayroc Cablevision. No longer in operation

JEFFERSON COUNTY (PORTIONS)—See FANNETT, TX (Almega Cable)

JEFFERSON COUNTY (PORTIONS)—See SOUR LAKE, TX (CMA Communications)

JEFFERSON—See MARSHALL, TX (Cobridge Communications)

JERSEY VILLAGE—See HOUSTON, TX (Comcast Cable)

▲**JEWETT**—Northland Cable Television

▲**JOHNSON CITY**—Almega Cable

JOHNSON COUNTY (PORTIONS)—See JOSHUA, TX (Almega Cable)

JOHNSON COUNTY (PORTIONS)—See CADDO PEAK, TX (North Texas Broadband)

JONES COUNTY (PORTIONS)—See ANSON, TX (Suddenlink Communications)

JONES COUNTY (PORTIONS)—See HAMLIN, TX (Suddenlink Communications)

JONES CREEK—See BRAZORIA, TX (Suddenlink Communications)

JONESTOWN—See AUSTIN, TX (Time Warner Cable)

▲**JOSEPHINE**—Formerly served by Almega Cable. No longer in operation

▲**JOSHUA**—Almega Cable

▲**JOSHUA**—Pathway. Formerly served by Burleson, TX [TX0103]. This cable system has converted to IPTV

JOURDANTON—See POTEET, TX (Alliance Communications)

▲**JUNCTION**—Suddenlink Communications

KARNES CITY—See KENEDY, TX (Reach Broadband)

▲**KATY (southern portion)**—Formerly served by Cebridge Connections. No longer in operation

KATY—See HOUSTON, TX (Comcast Cable)

KAUFMAN COUNTY—See TERRELL, TX (Suddenlink Communications)

▲**KAUFMAN**—Northland Cable Television

KEEGANS GLEN—See HOUSTON, TX (Comcast Cable)

KEENE—See ALVARADO, TX (Almega Cable)

KELLER—See FORT WORTH (northern portions), TX (Charter Communications)

KELLY AFB—See SAN ANTONIO, TX (Time Warner Cable)

KEMAH—See HOUSTON, TX (Comcast Cable)

KEMP—See EAST GRAYSON COUNTY, OK (TV Cable of Grayson County)

▲ **KEMPNER**—Formerly served by National Cable Inc. No longer in operation

KEMPNER—See KILLEEN, TX (Time Warner Cable)

▲ **KENDALL COUNTY (PORTIONS)**—GVTV Communications. Formerly served by Boerne (portions), TX [TX0315]. This cable system has converted to IPTV

KENDLETON—See PLEAK, TX (Almega Cable)

▲ **KENEDY**—Reach Broadband

▲ **KENEFICK**—Formerly served by Carrell Communications. No longer in operation

KENNEDALE—See FORT WORTH (northern portions), TX (Charter Communications)

▲ **KERENS**—Northland Cable Television

▲ **KERMIT**—Suddenlink Communications

KERR COUNTY (PORTIONS)—See INGRAM, TX (Suddenlink Communications)

KERR COUNTY—See KERRVILLE, TX (Time Warner Cable)

▲ **KERRVILLE**—Time Warner Cable

▲ **KILGORE**—Almega Cable

▲ **KILGORE**—Kilgore Cable TV Co.

▲ **KILLEEN**—Time Warner Cable

KIMBLE COUNTY (PORTIONS)—See JUNCTION, TX (Suddenlink Communications)

KINGSLAND—See MARBLE FALLS, TX (Northland Cable Television)

▲ **KINGSVILLE**—CMA Cablevision

▲ **KINGWOOD**—Suddenlink Communications

KIRBY—See SAN ANTONIO, TX (Time Warner Cable)

▲ **KIRBYVILLE**—Formerly served by CommuniComm Services. No longer in operation

KLIENBROOK—See HOUSTON, TX (Comcast Cable)

KNIPPA—See UVALDE, TX (Time Warner Cable)

KNOLLWOOD—See SHERMAN, TX (Cable One)

▲ **KNOX CITY**—Alliance Communications

▲ **KOUNTZE**—Time Warner Cable. Now served by BEAUMONT, TX [TX0022]

KOUNTZE—See BEAUMONT, TX (Time Warner Cable)

▲ **KRESS**—Formerly served by Almega Cable. No longer in operation

KRUGERVILLE—See PILOT POINT, TX (Suddenlink Communications)

▲ **KRUM**—Suddenlink Communications

KYLE—See AUSTIN, TX (Time Warner Cable)

LA COSTE—See SAN ANTONIO, TX (Time Warner Cable)

LA FERIA—See HARLINGEN, TX (Time Warner Cable)

▲ **LA GRANGE**—CMA Cablevision

▲ **LA GRULLA**—Time Warner Cable. Now served by PHARR, TX [TX0017]

LA GRULLA—See HARLINGEN, TX (Time Warner Cable)

LA JOYA—See HARLINGEN, TX (Time Warner Cable)

LA MARQUE—See HOUSTON, TX (Comcast Cable)

LA PORTE—See HOUSTON, TX (Comcast Cable)

▲ **LA PRYOR**—Formerly served by Almega Cable. No longer in operation

LA ROSITA—See HARLINGEN, TX (Time Warner Cable)

LA SALLE COUNTY (PORTIONS)—See PEARSALL, TX (Time Warner Cable)

LA SALLE COUNTY (SOUTHERN PORTION)—See ENCINAL, TX (Windjammer Cable)

LA VILLA—See HARLINGEN, TX (Time Warner Cable)

LACKLAND AFB—See SAN ANTONIO, TX (Time Warner Cable)

LACY-LAKEVIEW—See WACO, TX (Time Warner Cable)

LADONIA—See WOLFE CITY, TX (Zoom Media)

LAGO VISTA—See AUSTIN, TX (Time Warner Cable)

LAGUNA HEIGHTS—See HARLINGEN, TX (Time Warner Cable)

LAGUNA VISTA—See HARLINGEN, TX (Time Warner Cable)

▲ **LAKE ARROWHEAD**—Windjammer Cable

LAKE BRIDGEPORT—See DECATUR, TX (CommuniComm Services)

▲ **LAKE BROWNWOOD**—Formerly served by National Cable Inc. No longer in operation

▲ **LAKE BUCHANAN**—Northland Cable Television

▲ **LAKE CHEROKEE**—Alliance Communications

LAKE CITY—See MATHIS, TX (Time Warner Cable)

LAKE COLORADO CITY—See COLORADO CITY, TX (Cobridge Communications)

LAKE CONROE EAST—See WALDEN, TX (Suddenlink Communications)

LAKE DALLAS—See DENTON, TX (Charter Communications)

LAKE DALLAS—See DALLAS (northwest suburbs), TX (Grande Communications)

▲ **LAKE GRAHAM**—TGN Cable

▲ **LAKE HILLS**—Zoom Media

LAKE JACKSON—See HOUSTON, TX (Comcast Cable)

LAKE KIOWA—See VALLEY VIEW, TX (Nortex Communications)

LAKE L.B. JOHNSON—See MARBLE FALLS, TX (Northland Cable Television)

▲ **LAKE LIVINGSTON**—Suddenlink Communications

LAKE MEXIA—See MEXIA, TX (Northland Cable Television)

▲ **LAKE PALESTINE EAST**—Northland Cable Television

▲ **LAKE PALESTINE WEST**—Northland Cable Television

LAKE TANGLEWOOD—See AMARILLO, TX (Suddenlink Communications)

LAKE THUNDERBIRD ESTATES—See SMITHVILLE, TX (Reveille Broadband)

LAKE TYLER—See LAKE PALESTINE EAST, TX (Northland Cable Television)

LAKE WHITNEY—See WHITNEY, TX (Reach Broadband)

LAKE WORTH—See FORT WORTH (northern portions), TX (Charter Communications)

LAKEPORT—See LAKE CHEROKEE, TX (Alliance Communications)

LAKESIDE CITY—See WICHITA FALLS, TX (Time Warner Cable)

LAKEWAY—See AUSTIN, TX (Time Warner Cable)

LAKEWOOD VILLAGE—See PILOT POINT, TX (Suddenlink Communications)

LAKEWOOD—See NEW CANEY, TX (Northland Cable Television)

LAKEWOOD—See OKLAHOMA, TX (Suddenlink Communications)

LAMAR COUNTY (PORTIONS)—See POWDERLY, TX (Almega Cable)

LAMAR COUNTY (PORTIONS)—See CLARKSVILLE, TX (Suddenlink Communications)

LAMAR COUNTY (UNINCORPORATED AREAS)—See PARIS, TX (Suddenlink Communications)

▲ **LAMESA**—Northland Cable Television

LAMPASAS COUNTY (UNINCORPORATED AREAS)—See KILLEEN, TX (Time Warner Cable)

LAMPASAS COUNTY—See LAMPASAS, TX (Suddenlink Communications)

▲ **LAMPASAS**—Suddenlink Communications

LANCASTER—See DALLAS, TX (Time Warner Cable)

▲ **LANEVILLE**—Formerly served by Cebridge Connections. No longer in operation

LANGHAM COLONY—See HOUSTON, TX (Comcast Cable)

▲ **LANSING**—Zoom Media

▲ **LAREDO**—Time Warner Cable

LAS COLINAS—See DALLAS, TX (Time Warner Cable)

▲ **LAS GALLINAS**—Almega Cable

LAS MILPAS—See HARLINGEN, TX (Time Warner Cable)

LATEXO—See GRAPELAND, TX (Suddenlink Communications)

LAUGHLIN AFB—See DEL RIO, TX (Time Warner Cable)

▲ **LAVERNIA**—Comfort Cable Co.

LEAGUE CITY—See HOUSTON, TX (Comcast Cable)

▲ **LEANDER**—Suddenlink Communications

LEANDER—See AUSTIN, TX (Time Warner Cable)

LEARY—See REDWATER, TX (Almega Cable)

▲ **LEFORS**—Formerly served by Almega Cable. No longer in operation

LEON VALLEY—See SAN ANTONIO, TX (Time Warner Cable)

▲ **LEONA**—Formerly served by Charter Communications. No longer in operation

▲ **LEONARD**—Zoom Media

▲ **LEVELLAND**—Cobridge Communications

LEWISVILLE—See DALLAS (northwest suburbs), TX (Grande Communications)

LEWISVILLE—See DALLAS, TX (Time Warner Cable)

▲ **LEXINGTON**—Reveille Broadband

LIBERTY CITY—See GLADEWATER, TX (Suddenlink Communications)

LIBERTY COUNTY (PORTIONS)—See SPLENDORA, TX (Almega Cable)

LIBERTY COUNTY (SOUTHEASTERN PORTION)—See MONT BELVIEU, TX (Suddenlink Communications)

LIBERTY HILL—See AUSTIN, TX (Time Warner Cable)

▲ **LIBERTY**—Time Warner Cable. Now served by HOUSTON, TX [TX0001]

LIBERTY—See HOUSTON, TX (Comcast Cable)

LINDALE—See MINEOLA, TX (Suddenlink Communications)

▲ **LINDEN**—Reach Broadband

LINDSAY—See VALLEY VIEW, TX (Nortex Communications)

▲ **LIPAN**—Formerly served by Almega Cable. No longer in operation

LITTLE ELM—See PILOT POINT, TX (Suddenlink Communications)

LITTLE FLOCK—See HOMER, TX (Almega Cable)

▲ **LITTLE RIVER-ACADEMY**—Centrovision Inc.

LITTLEFIELD—See LEVELLAND, TX (Cobridge Communications)

LIVE OAK—See SAN ANTONIO, TX (Time Warner Cable)

▲ **LIVERPOOL**—Almega Cable

▲ **LIVINGSTON**—Suddenlink Communications

LIVINGSTON—See GOODRICH, TX (Versalink Media)

▲ **LLANO**—Northland Cable Television

▲ **LOCKHART**—Time Warner Cable. Now served by AUSTIN, TX [TX0005]

LOCKHART—See AUSTIN, TX (Time Warner Cable)

▲ **LOCKNEY**—Reach Broadband

LOG CABIN—See MALAKOFF, TX (Northland Cable Television)

▲ **LOLITA**—Formerly served by Clearview Cable. No longer in operation

▲ **LOMETA**—Almega Cable

LONE OAK—See QUINLAN, TX (Zoom Media)

LONE STAR—See DAINGERFIELD, TX (Suddenlink Communications)

▲ **LONGVIEW**—Longview Cable Television

▲ **LOOP**—Formerly served by National Cable Inc. No longer in operation

LOPEZVILLE—See HARLINGEN, TX (Time Warner Cable)

▲ **LORAINE (town)**—Formerly served by Almega Cable. No longer in operation

▲ **LORENA**—Time Warner Cable. Now served by WACO, TX [TX0015]

LORENA—See WACO, TX (Time Warner Cable)

▲ **LORENZO**—Formerly served by Almega Cable. No longer in operation

LOS BARRERAS—See HARLINGEN, TX (Time Warner Cable)

▲ **LOS FRESNOS**—Time Warner Communications. Now served by PHARR, TX [TX0017]

LOS FRESNOS—See HARLINGEN, TX (Time Warner Cable)

LOS MORENOS—See HARLINGEN, TX (Time Warner Cable)

LOS SAENZ—See HARLINGEN, TX (Time Warner Cable)

▲ **LOST PINES**—Suddenlink Communications

▲ **LOTT**—Zito Media

▲ **LOUISE**—Mid-Coast Cablevision

▲ **LOVELADY**—Formerly served by Almega Cable. No longer in operation

▲ **LOWRY CROSSING**—Suddenlink Communications

LUBBOCK COUNTY (PORTIONS)—See LUBBOCK, TX (Reach Broadband)

▲ **LUBBOCK COUNTY (southeastern portion)**—Formerly served by Almega Cable. No longer in operation

▲ **LUBBOCK**—Reach Broadband

▲ **LUBBOCK**—Suddenlink Communications

▲ **LUCAS**—Suddenlink Communications

▲ **LUEDERS**—Formerly served by Jayroc Cablevision. No longer in operation

LUFKIN—See CORRIGAN, TX (Suddenlink Communications)

▲ **LULING**—Time Warner Cable. Now served by AUSTIN, TX [TX0005]

LULING—See AUSTIN, TX (Time Warner Cable)

LUMBERTON—See BEAUMONT, TX (Time Warner Cable)

LYFORD—See HARLINGEN, TX (Time Warner Cable)

▲ **LYONS**—Reveille Broadband

LYTLE—See DEVINE, TX (Reach Broadband)

MABANK—See GUN BARREL CITY, TX (Northland Cable Television)

MADISON COUNTY—See MADISONVILLE, TX (Northland Cable Television)

▲ **MADISONVILLE**—Northland Cable Television

MAGNOLIA—See HOUSTON, TX (Comcast Cable)

▲ **MAGNOLIA**—Versalink Media

▲ **MALAKOFF**—Northland Cable Television

▲ **MANOR**—Formerly served by Almega Cable. No longer in operation

MANOR—See AUSTIN, TX (Time Warner Cable)

MANSFIELD—See FORT WORTH (northern portions), TX (Charter Communications)

MANVEL (UNINCORPORATED AREAS)—See HEIGHTS (unincorporated areas), TX (Almega Cable)

▲ **MANVEL**—Texas Mid-Gulf Cablevision

MAPLE LEAF GARDENS—See HOUSTON, TX (Comcast Cable)

▲ **MARATHON**—Marathon TV Cable

▲ **MARBLE FALLS**—Northland Cable Television

MARBLE FALLS—See AUSTIN, TX (Time Warner Cable)

▲ **MARFA**—Marfa TV Cable Co. Inc.

MARION COUNTY (PORTIONS)—See ORE CITY, TX (Reach Broadband)

MARION COUNTY—See MARSHALL, TX (Cobridge Communications)

MARION—See SAN ANTONIO, TX (Time Warner Cable)

MARKHAM—See BAY CITY, TX (Mid-Coast Cablevision)

▲ **MARLIN**—Northland Cable Television

MARSHALL CREEK—See FORT WORTH (northern portions), TX (Charter Communications)

▲ **MARSHALL**—Cobridge Communications

▲ **MART**—Rapid Cable

MARTINDALE—See AUSTIN, TX (Time Warner Cable)

MASON COUNTY (PORTIONS)—See MASON, TX (Reach Broadband)

▲ **MASON**—Reach Broadband

▲ **MATADOR (TOWN)**—Reach Broadband

MATAGORDA COUNTY (PORTIONS)—See BLESSING, TX (Bay City Cablevision)

MATAGORDA COUNTY (UNINCORPORATED AREAS)—See BAY CITY, TX (Mid-Coast Cablevision)

MATAGORDA—See BAY CITY, TX (Mid-Coast Cablevision)

▲ **MATHIS**—Time Warner Cable

▲ **MAUD**—Allegiance Communications

▲ **MAURICEVILLE**—Formerly served by Cebridge Connections. No longer in operation

MAVERICK COUNTY—See EAGLE PASS, TX (Time Warner Cable)

▲ **MAY**—Formerly served by Cable Unlimited. No longer in operation

MAYPEARL—See ALVARADO, TX (Almega Cable)

MCALLEN—See HARLINGEN, TX (Time Warner Cable)

▲ **MCCAMEY**—US Cable of Coastal Texas LP

MCCLENDON-CHISOLM—See TERRELL, TX (Suddenlink Communications)

MCCULLOCH COUNTY (PORTIONS)—See BRADY, TX (Suddenlink Communications)

MCDADE—See AUSTIN, TX (Time Warner Cable)

MCGREGOR—See WACO, TX (Time Warner Cable)

MCKINNEY—See DALLAS (northwest suburbs), TX (Grande Communications)

MCKINNEY—See DALLAS, TX (Time Warner Cable)

MCLEAN—See BORGER, TX (Cable One)

MCLENNAN COUNTY (PORTIONS)—See WACO, TX (Time Warner Cable)

MEADOW—See LUBBOCK, TX (Reach Broadband)

MEADOWLAKES—See MARBLE FALLS, TX (Northland Cable Television)

MEDINA COUNTY (PORTIONS)—See DEVINE, TX (Reach Broadband)

▲ **MEDINA**—Formerly served by Medina Cable Ltd. No longer in operation

MELISSA—See PILOT POINT, TX (Suddenlink Communications)

MEMORIAL THICKET—See HOUSTON, TX (Comcast Cable)

▲ **MEMPHIS**—Reach Broadband

MENARD COUNTY (PORTIONS)—See MENARD, TX (Reach Broadband)

▲ **MENARD**—Reach Broadband

MERCEDES—See HARLINGEN, TX (Time Warner Cable)

▲ **MERIDIAN**—Formerly served by Almega Cable. No longer in operation

▲ **MERKEL**—CMA Cablevision

▲ **MERTZON**—Reach Broadband

MESQUITE—See DALLAS, TX (Time Warner Cable)

▲ **MEXIA**—Northland Cable Television

▲ **MIAMI**—Elk River TV Cable Co.

MIDLAND COUNTY (PORTIONS)—See MIDLAND, TX (Suddenlink Communications)

MIDLAND—See ODESSA, TX (Grande Communications)

▲ **MIDLAND**—Suddenlink Communications

MIDLOTHIAN—See WAXAHACHIE, TX (Charter Communications)

▲ **MIDWAY**—Formerly served by Almega Cable. No longer in operation

MILAM COUNTY (PORTIONS)—See CAMERON, TX (Zito Media)

▲ **MILES**—Allegiance Communications

MILLER COUNTY—See TEXARKANA, AR (Cable One)

MILLS WALK—See HOUSTON, TX (Comcast Cable)

▲ **MILLSAP**—Formerly served by Mallard Cablevision. No longer in operation

▲ **MINEOLA**—Suddenlink Communications

▲ **MINERAL WELLS**—Suddenlink Communications

MIRANDO CITY—See OILTON, TX (Windjammer Cable)

MISSION BEND—See HOUSTON, TX (Comcast Cable)

MISSION DORADO—See ODESSA, TX (Cable One)

MISSION—See HARLINGEN, TX (Time Warner Cable)

MISSOURI CITY—See HOUSTON, TX (Comcast Cable)

MITCHELL COUNTY—See COLORADO CITY, TX (Cobridge Communications)

MOBILE CITY—See TERRELL, TX (Suddenlink Communications)

MODOT VILLAGE—See HOUSTON, TX (Comcast Cable)

▲ **MONAHANS**—Suddenlink Communications

▲ **MONT BELVIEU**—Suddenlink Communications

▲ **MONTAGUE**—Formerly served by Cebridge Connections. No longer in operation

MONTGOMERY (UNINCORPORATED AREAS)—See CONROE WEST, TX (Suddenlink Communications)

MONTGOMERY COUNTY (PORTIONS)—See SPLENDORA, TX (Almega Cable)

MONTGOMERY COUNTY (PORTIONS)—See OKLAHOMA, TX (Suddenlink Communications)

MONTGOMERY COUNTY (PORTIONS)—See PORTER, TX (Suddenlink Communications)

MONTGOMERY COUNTY (PORTIONS)—See MAGNOLIA, TX (Versalink Media)

▲ **MONTGOMERY COUNTY (UNINCORPORATED AREAS)**—Versalink Media

MONTGOMERY COUNTY (UNINCORPORATED ARES)—See CUT AND SHOOT, TX (Northland Cable Television)

MONTGOMERY COUNTY—See HOUSTON, TX (Comcast Cable)

MONTGOMERY COUNTY—See CONROE, TX (Suddenlink Communications)

MONTGOMERY COUNTY—See WALDEN, TX (Suddenlink Communications)

MONTGOMERY—See WALDEN, TX (Suddenlink Communications)

▲ **MOODY**—Centrovision Inc.

MOON CITY—See EL PASO, TX (Time Warner Cable)

▲ **MORAN**—Formerly served by Jayroc Cablevision. No longer in operation

▲ **MORGAN'S POINT RESORT**—Centrovision Inc.

MORGANS POINT—See HOUSTON, TX (Comcast Cable)

MORRIS COUNTY—See DAINGERFIELD, TX (Suddenlink Communications)

MORTON—See LEVELLAND, TX (Cobridge Communications)

▲ **MOSS BLUFF**—Formerly served by Carrell Communications. No longer in operation

▲ **MOULTON**—Formerly served by National Cable Inc. No longer in operation

▲ **MOUND**—Formerly served by National Cable Inc. No longer in operation

▲ **MOUNT ENTERPRISE**—Formerly served by Cebridge Connections. No longer in operation

▲ **MOUNT PLEASANT**—Suddenlink Communications

▲ **MOUNT VERNON**—Suddenlink Communications

MOUNTAIN CITY—See AUSTIN, TX (Time Warner Cable)

MUENSTER—See VALLEY VIEW, TX (Nortex Communications)

▲ **MULESHOE**—Reach Broadband

▲ **MUNDAY**—Alliance Communications

MURCHISON—See BEN WHEELER, TX (Zoom Media)

MURPHY—See DALLAS, TX (Time Warner Cable)

▲ **MUSTANG RIDGE**—Formerly served by Almega Cable. No longer in operation

▲ **MYRTLE SPRINGS**—Formerly served by Cebridge Connections. No longer in operation

NACOGDOCHES COUNTY—See NACOGDOCHES, TX (Suddenlink Communications)

▲ **NACOGDOCHES**—Suddenlink Communications

▲ **NAPLES**—Alliance Communications

NASH—See TEXARKANA, TX (Cable One)

NASSAU BAY—See HOUSTON, TX (Comcast Cable)

NATALIA—See DEVINE, TX (Reach Broadband)

▲ **NAVASOTA**—Suddenlink Communications

▲ **NAZARETH**—Elk River TV Cable Co.

NEDERLAND—See BEAUMONT, TX (Time Warner Cable)

NEEDVILLE—See HOUSTON, TX (Comcast Cable)

▲ **NEW BOSTON**—Allegiance Communications

NEW BRAUNFELS—See SAN ANTONIO, TX (Time Warner Cable)

▲ **NEW CANEY**—Northland Cable Television

NEW CHAPEL HILL—See LAKE PALESTINE EAST, TX (Northland Cable Television)

NEW DEAL—See LUBBOCK, TX (Reach Broadband)

NEW HOPE—See LOWRY CROSSING, TX (Suddenlink Communications)

NEW LONDON—See ARP, TX (Zoom Media)

▲ **NEW SUMMERFIELD**—Formerly served by Almega Cable. No longer in operation

▲ **NEW ULM**—Formerly served by National Cable Inc. No longer in operation

▲ **NEW WAVERLY**—Cablevision of Walker County

▲ **NEWCASTLE**—TGN Cable

▲ **NIXON**—Almega Cable

▲ **NOCONA**—Suddenlink Communications

NOLAN COUNTY (NORTHERN PORTION)—See SWEETWATER, TX (Suddenlink Communications)

NOLANVILLE—See KILLEEN, TX (Time Warner Cable)

▲ **NOME**—Formerly served by Carrell Communications. No longer in operation

NOONDAY—See LAKE PALESTINE EAST, TX (Northland Cable Television)

▲ **NORDHEIM**—Formerly served by National Cable Inc. No longer in operation

▲ **NORMANGEE**—Formerly served by Almega Cable. No longer in operation

NORTH CLIFFE MANOR—See HOUSTON, TX (Comcast Cable)

NORTH PINES RANCHETTS—See HOUSTON, TX (Comcast Cable)

NORTH RICHLAND HILLS—See FORT WORTH (northern portions), TX (Charter Communications)

▲ **NORTH SILSBEE**—Formerly served by Carrell Communications. No longer in operation

▲ **NORTH ZULCH**—Formerly served by Almega Cable. No longer in operation

NORTHCLIFF—See SAN ANTONIO, TX (Time Warner Cable)

NORTHCREST—See WACO, TX (Time Warner Cable)

NORTHWEST GREEN—See HOUSTON, TX (Comcast Cable)

NORTHWEST PARK—See HOUSTON, TX (Comcast Cable)

NUECES COUNTY—See CORPUS CHRISTI, TX (Time Warner Cable)

▲ **NURSERY**—Formerly served by National Cable Inc. No longer in operation

O'BRIEN—See KNOX CITY, TX (Alliance Communications)

▲ **O'DONNELL**—Reach Broadband

OAK GROVE—See KAUFMAN, TX (Northland Cable Television)

OAK LEAF—See WAXAHACHIE, TX (Charter Communications)

OAK POINT—See PILOT POINT, TX (Suddenlink Communications)

OAK RIDGE NORTH—See SPRING, TX (Charter Communications)

OAK RIDGE—See GAINESVILLE, TX (Suddenlink Communications)

OAKLAND VILLAGE—See HOUSTON, TX (Comcast Cable)

▲ **OAKWOOD**—Formerly served by Charter Communications. No longer in operation

ODEM—See CORPUS CHRISTI, TX (Time Warner Cable)

▲ **ODESSA**—Cable One

▲ **ODESSA**—Grande Communications

▲ **OILTON**—Windjammer Cable

▲ **OKLAHOMA**—Suddenlink Communications

OLD RIVER-WINFREE—See MONT BELVIEU, TX (Suddenlink Communications)

OLDEN—See EASTLAND, TX (Suddenlink Communications)

OLMITO—See HARLINGEN, TX (Time Warner Cable)

OLMOS PARK—See SAN ANTONIO, TX (Time Warner Cable)

▲ **OLNEY**—Suddenlink Communications

▲ **OLTON**—Reach Broadband

OMAHA—See NAPLES, TX (Alliance Communications)

OMEGA BAY—See HOUSTON, TX (Comcast Cable)

ONALASKA—See LAKE LIVINGSTON, TX (Suddenlink Communications)

▲ **ORANGE GROVE**—Time Warner Cable

▲ **ORANGE**—Time Warner Cable. Now served by BEAUMONT, TX [TX0022]

ORANGE—See BEAUMONT, TX (Time Warner Cable)

▲ **ORE CITY**—Reach Broadband

OVERTON—See ARP, TX (Zoom Media)

OVILLA—See WAXAHACHIE, TX (Charter Communications)

▲ **OYSTER CREEK**—Almega Cable

▲ **OZONA**—Circle Bar Cable TV Inc.

PADDOCK—See HOUSTON, TX (Comcast Cable)

▲ **PADUCAH (TOWN)**—Suddenlink Communications

▲ **PALACIOS**—Bay City Cablevision

▲ **PALESTINE**—Windjammer Cable

PALM VALLEY—See HARLINGEN, TX (Time Warner Cable)

PALMER—See WAXAHACHIE, TX (Charter Communications)

PALMHURST—See HARLINGEN, TX (Time Warner Cable)

PALMVIEW—See HARLINGEN, TX (Time Warner Cable)

PALO PINTO COUNTY (PORTIONS)—See MINERAL WELLS, TX (Suddenlink Communications)

▲**PALO PINTO**—Formerly served by Mallard Cablevision. No longer in operation

PAMPA—See BORGER, TX (Cable One)

PANHANDLE—See BORGER, TX (Cable One)

PANORAMA VILLAGE—See CONROE, TX (Suddenlink Communications)

PANTEGO—See DALLAS, TX (Time Warner Cable)

▲**PARADISE**—Formerly served by CableSouth Inc. No longer in operation

▲**PARIS**—Suddenlink Communications

PARKER COUNTY (PORTIONS)—See FORT WORTH (northern portions), TX (Charter Communications)

PARKER—See DALLAS, TX (Time Warner Cable)

▲**PARKWAY VILLAGE**—Time Warner Cable. No longer in operation

PASADENA—See HOUSTON, TX (Comcast Cable)

PATTON VILLAGE—See NEW CANEY, TX (Northland Cable Television)

PAYNE SPRINGS—See GUN BARREL CITY, TX (Northland Cable Television)

PEARLAND—See HOUSTON, TX (Comcast Cable)

▲**PEARSALL**—Time Warner Cable

PECAN HILL—See WAXAHACHIE, TX (Charter Communications)

▲**PECOS**—Suddenlink Communications

▲**PELICAN BAY**—Formerly served by SouthTel Communications LP. No longer in operation

PENITAS—See HARLINGEN, TX (Time Warner Cable)

▲**PERRIN**—Formerly served by Mallard Cablevision. No longer in operation

▲**PERRYTON**—Allegiance Communications

▲**PETERSBURG**—Formerly served by Almega Cable. No longer in operation

▲**PETTUS**—Formerly served by National Cable Inc. No longer in operation

▲**PFLUGERVILLE**—Suddenlink Communications

PHARR—See HARLINGEN, TX (Time Warner Cable)

PHILLIPS—See BORGER, TX (Cable One)

▲**PILOT POINT**—Suddenlink Communications

PINE FOREST—See BEAUMONT, TX (Time Warner Cable)

PINEDALE—See HOUSTON, TX (Comcast Cable)

PINEHURST—See MONTGOMERY COUNTY (unincorporated areas), TX (Versalink Media)

PINELAND—See HEMPHILL, TX (Almega Cable)

PINEY POINT—See HOUSTON, TX (Comcast Cable)

PIRATE BEACH—See HOUSTON, TX (Comcast Cable)

PIRATE COVE—See HOUSTON, TX (Comcast Cable)

▲**PITTSBURG**—Suddenlink Communications

▲**PLACEDO**—Formerly served by National Cable Inc. No longer in operation

▲**PLAINS**—Almega Cable

▲**PLAINVIEW**—Suddenlink Communications

▲**PLANO**—Time Warner Cable. Now served by DALLAS, TX [TX0003]

PLANO—See DALLAS (northwest suburbs), TX (Grande Communications)

PLANO—See DALLAS, TX (Time Warner Cable)

▲**PLEAK**—Almega Cable

▲**PLEASANT VALLEY**—Formerly served by CableDirect. No longer in operation

▲**PLEASANTON**—Reach Broadband

▲**PLUM GROVE**—Formerly served by Carrell Communications. No longer in operation

POINT BLANK—See LAKE LIVINGSTON, TX (Suddenlink Communications)

POINT COMFORT—See PORT LAVACA, TX (Cable One)

POINT VENTURE—See AUSTIN, TX (Time Warner Cable)

POLK COUNTY (PORTIONS)—See CORRIGAN, TX (Suddenlink Communications)

POLK COUNTY (PORTIONS)—See LIVINGSTON, TX (Suddenlink Communications)

▲**PONDER**—Formerly served by SouthTel Communications LP. No longer in operation

PORT ACRES—See BEAUMONT, TX (Time Warner Cable)

▲**PORT ARANSAS**—Charter Communications. Now served by ROCKPORT, TX [TX0116]

PORT ARANSAS—See ROCKPORT, TX (Cobridge Communications)

▲**PORT ARTHUR**—Time Warner Cable. Now served by BEAUMONT, TX [TX0022]

PORT ARTHUR—See BEAUMONT, TX (Time Warner Cable)

▲**PORT ISABEL**—Time Warner Communications. Now served by PHARR, TX [TX0017]

PORT ISABEL—See HARLINGEN, TX (Time Warner Cable)

▲**PORT LAVACA**—Cable One

PORT NECHES—See BEAUMONT, TX (Time Warner Cable)

▲**PORT O'CONNOR**—Time Warner Cable

PORTER HEIGHTS (UNINCORPORATED AREAS)—See NEW CANEY, TX (Northland Cable Television)

▲**PORTER**—Suddenlink Communications

PORTER—See KINGWOOD, TX (Suddenlink Communications)

▲**PORTLAND**—Charter Communications. Now served by ROCKPORT, TX [TX0116]

PORTLAND—See ROCKPORT, TX (Cobridge Communications)

POSSUM KINGDOM LAKE—See JACKSBORO, TX (CommuniComm Services)

▲**POST**—Suddenlink Communications

▲**POTEET**—Alliance Communications

▲**POTOSI**—Formerly served by Jayroc Cablevision. No longer in operation

▲**POTTSBORO**—TV Cable of Grayson County

▲**POWDERLY**—Almega Cable

PRAIRIE VIEW—See WALLER, TX (Suddenlink Communications)

▲**PREMONT**—Time Warner Cable. Now served by ALICE, TX [TX0102]

PREMONT—See ALICE, TX (Time Warner Cable)

▲**PRESIDIO**—Presidio TV Cable

▲**PRESTON PENINSULA**—Allegiance Communications

▲**PRICE**—Formerly served by Almega Cable. No longer in operation

PRIMERA—See HARLINGEN, TX (Time Warner Cable)

PRINCETON—See DALLAS, TX (Time Warner Cable)

▲**PROGRESO**—Formerly served by CableDirect. No longer in operation

PROSPER—See PILOT POINT, TX (Suddenlink Communications)

▲**QUANAH**—Suddenlink Communications

QUEEN CITY—See ATLANTA, TX (Cobridge Communications)

▲**QUEMADO**—Time Warner Cable

▲**QUINLAN**—Zoom Media

▲**QUITAQUE**—Formerly served by Almega Cable. No longer in operation

QUITMAN—See MINEOLA, TX (Suddenlink Communications)

RAINS COUNTY (PORTIONS)—See QUINLAN, TX (Zoom Media)

▲**RALLS**—Reach Broadband

RANCHO VIEJO—See HARLINGEN, TX (Time Warner Cable)

RANDOLPH AFB—See SAN ANTONIO, TX (Time Warner Cable)

RANGER—See EASTLAND, TX (Suddenlink Communications)

▲**RANKIN**—US Cable of Coastal Texas LP

RAYFORD FOREST—See SPRING, TX (Charter Communications)

▲**RAYMONDVILLE**—Time Warner Communications. Now served by PHARR, TX [TX0017]

RAYMONDVILLE—See HARLINGEN, TX (Time Warner Cable)

▲**RAYWOOD**—Formerly served by Cebridge Connections. No longer in operation

▲**REALITOS**—Formerly served by National Cable Inc. No longer in operation

RED ACKERS—See LAKE PALESTINE WEST, TX (Northland Cable Television)

RED LICK—See TEXARKANA, TX (Cable One)

RED OAK—See WAXAHACHIE, TX (Charter Communications)

RED RIVER ARMY DEPOT—See HOOKS, TX (Allegiance Communications)

REDLAND—See CENTRAL, TX (Almega Cable)

▲**REDWATER**—Almega Cable

REESE AFB—See LUBBOCK, TX (Reach Broadband)

REEVES COUNTY (PORTIONS)—See PECOS, TX (Suddenlink Communications)

▲**REFUGIO**—Time Warner Cable. Now served by MATHIS, TX [TX0216]

REFUGIO—See MATHIS, TX (Time Warner Cable)

REID ESTATES—See HOUSTON, TX (Comcast Cable)

▲**REKLAW**—Formerly served by Almega Cable. No longer in operation

RENO (LAMAR COUNTY)—See PARIS, TX (Suddenlink Communications)

▲**RENO (Parker County)**—Formerly served by Almega County. No longer in operation

▲**RICARDO**—Formerly served by Riviera Cable TV. No longer in operation

RICHARDSON—See DALLAS, TX (Time Warner Cable)

RICHLAND HILLS—See FORT WORTH (northern portions), TX (Charter Communications)

▲**RICHLAND SPRINGS**—Formerly served by Almega Cable. No longer in operation

RICHMOND—See HOUSTON, TX (Comcast Cable)

RICHMOND—See HOUSTON, TX (Phonoscope Ltd.)

RICHWOOD—See HOUSTON, TX (Comcast Cable)

▲**RIESEL**—Formerly served by Cabletex Systems Inc. No longer in operation

RIO BRAVO—See LAREDO, TX (Time Warner Cable)

RIO DEL SOL—See HARLINGEN, TX (Time Warner Cable)

▲**RIO GRANDE CITY**—Time Warner Communications. Now served by PHARR, TX [TX0017]

RIO GRANDE CITY—See HARLINGEN, TX (Time Warner Cable)

RIO HONDO—See HARLINGEN, TX (Time Warner Cable)

▲**RIO VISTA**—Formerly served by National Cable Inc. No longer in operation

▲**RISING STAR**—Formerly served by Brownwood TV Cable Service Inc. No longer in operation

▲**RIVER OAKS (Tarrant County)**—Charter Communications. Now served by FORT WORTH, TX [TX0008]

RIVER OAKS—See FORT WORTH (northern portions), TX (Charter Communications)

▲**RIVERSIDE**—Formerly served by Almega Cable. No longer in operation

▲**RIVIERA**—Formerly served by Riviera Cable TV. No longer in operation

ROANOKE—See FORT WORTH (northern portions), TX (Charter Communications)

ROANOKE—See DALLAS (northwest suburbs), TX (Grande Communications)

▲**ROARING SPRINGS (town)**—Formerly served by Almega Cable. No longer in operation

▲**ROBERT LEE**—CMA Cablevision

ROBINSON—See WACO, TX (Time Warner Cable)

ROBSTOWN—See CORPUS CHRISTI, TX (Time Warner Cable)

▲**ROBY**—Formerly served by Almega Cable. No longer in operation

▲**ROCHESTER**—Formerly served by Jayroc Cablevision. No longer in operation

▲**ROCKDALE**—Suddenlink Communications

ROCKETT—See WAXAHACHIE, TX (Charter Communications)

▲**ROCKPORT**—Cobridge Communications

▲**ROCKSPRINGS**—Formerly served by Almega Cable. No longer in operation

ROCKWALL COUNTY (PORTIONS)—See TERRELL, TX (Suddenlink Communications)

▲**ROCKWALL**—Charter Communications

▲**ROGERS**—Centrovision Inc.

ROLLING FORK—See HOUSTON, TX (Comcast Cable)

ROLLING HILLS—See AMARILLO, TX (Suddenlink Communications)

ROLLINGWOOD—See AUSTIN, TX (Time Warner Cable)

▲**ROMA**—Time Warner Communications. Now served by PHARR, TX [TX0017]

ROMA—See HARLINGEN, TX (Time Warner Cable)

ROMAN FOREST—See NEW CANEY, TX (Northland Cable Television)

ROPESVILLE—See LUBBOCK, TX (Reach Broadband)

▲**ROSCOE**—CMA Cablevision

▲**ROSE CITY**—Formerly served by Cebridge Connections. No longer in operation

▲**ROSEBUD**—DMS Cable TV

ROSENBERG—See HOUSTON, TX (Comcast Cable)

ROSENBERG—See HOUSTON, TX (Phonoscope Ltd.)

▲**ROTAN**—Suddenlink Communications

ROUND ROCK—See AUSTIN, TX (Time Warner Cable)

ROWLETT—See DALLAS, TX (Time Warner Cable)

ROXTON—See PARIS, TX (Suddenlink Communications)

▲**ROYSE CITY**—Formerly served by Cebridge Connections. Now served by TERRELL, TX [TX0920]

ROYSE CITY—See TERRELL, TX (Suddenlink Communications)

▲**RULE**—Alliance Communications

RUNAWAY BAY—See DECATUR, TX (CommuniComm Services)

▲**RUNGE**—Formerly served by Almega Cable. No longer in operation

RUSK COUNTY—See HENDERSON, TX (Suddenlink Communications)

▲**RUSK**—Suddenlink Communications

▲**SABINAL**—Almega Cable

SABINE PASS—See BEAUMONT, TX (Time Warner Cable)

SACHSE—See DALLAS, TX (Time Warner Cable)

SADLER—See WHITESBORO, TX (Suddenlink Communications)

SAGINAW—See FORT WORTH (northern portions), TX (Charter Communications)

▲**SALADO**—Centrovision Inc.

▲**SAN ANGELO**—Suddenlink Communications

▲**SAN ANTONIO**—Grande Communications

▲**SAN ANTONIO**—Time Warner Cable

▲**SAN AUGUSTINE**—Formerly served by Cebridge Connections. Now served by CENTER, TX [TX0192]

SAN AUGUSTINE—See CENTER, TX (Suddenlink Communications)

SAN BENITO—See HARLINGEN, TX (Time Warner Cable)

▲**SAN CARLOS**—Formerly served by CableDirect. No longer in operation

SAN DIEGO—See ALICE, TX (Time Warner Cable)

SAN ELIZARIO—See EL PASO, TX (Time Warner Cable)

SAN JACINTO COUNTY (PORTIONS)—See WATERWOOD, TX (Cablevision of Walker County)

SAN JUAN (HIDALGO COUNTY)—See HARLINGEN, TX (Time Warner Cable)

SAN LEANNA—See AUSTIN, TX (Time Warner Cable)

▲**SAN LEON**—Almega Cable

▲**SAN MARCOS**—Grande Communications. Now served by AUSTIN, TX [TX0989]

▲**SAN MARCOS**—Time Warner Cable. Now served by AUSTIN, TX [TX0005]

SAN MARCOS—See AUSTIN, TX (Grande Communications)

SAN MARCOS—See AUSTIN, TX (Time Warner Cable)

▲**SAN PATRICIO COUNTY**—Time Warner Cable. Now served by CORPUS CHRISTI, TX [TX0010]

SAN PATRICIO COUNTY—See ARANSAS PASS, TX (Cable One)

SAN PATRICIO COUNTY—See CORPUS CHRISTI, TX (Time Warner Cable)

▲**SAN SABA**—Suddenlink Communications

▲**SAN YGNACIO**—Time Warner Cable

▲**SANDERSON**—US Cable of Coastal Texas LP

▲**SANDIA**—Formerly served by National Cable Inc. No longer in operation

SANGER—See PILOT POINT, TX (Suddenlink Communications)

SANSOM PARK—See FORT WORTH (northern portions), TX (Charter Communications)

▲**SANTA ANNA**—Formerly served by Brownwood TV Cable Service Inc. No longer in operation

SANTA CRUZ—See HARLINGEN, TX (Time Warner Cable)

▲**SANTA FE (unincorporated areas)**—Formerly served by Almega Cable. No longer in operation

SANTA FE—See HOUSTON, TX (Comcast Cable)

SANTA ROSA—See HARLINGEN, TX (Time Warner Cable)

SANTA TERESA—See EL PASO, NM (Time Warner Cable)

▲**SARGENT**—Formerly served by Almega Cable. No longer in operation

SAVOY—See SHERMAN, TX (Cable One)

SCHERTZ—See SAN ANTONIO, TX (Time Warner Cable)

SCHLEIDER COUNTY (PORTIONS)—See ELDORADO, TX (Reach Broadband)

SCHULENBURG—See LA GRANGE, TX (CMA Cablevision)

SCURRY COUNTY—See SNYDER, TX (Suddenlink Communications)

SEABROOK—See HOUSTON, TX (Comcast Cable)

▲**SEADRIFT**—Time Warner Cable

SEAGOVILLE—See TERRELL, TX (Suddenlink Communications)

SEAGRAVES—See SEMINOLE, TX (US Cable of Coastal Texas LP)

▲**SEALY**—CMA Cablevision. Now served by BELLVILLE, TX [TX0292]

SEALY—See BELLVILLE, TX (CMA Cablevision)

SEGUIN—See SAN ANTONIO, TX (Time Warner Cable)

SELMA—See SAN ANTONIO, TX (Time Warner Cable)

▲**SEMINOLE**—US Cable of Coastal Texas LP

SEPCO PARK—See HOUSTON, TX (Comcast Cable)

SETTLERS VILLAGE—See HOUSTON, TX (Comcast Cable)

▲**SEVEN POINTS (northern portion)**—Formerly served by Trust Cable. No longer in operation

SEVEN POINTS (SOUTHERN PORTION)—See GUN BARREL CITY, TX (Northland Cable Television)

▲**SEYMOUR**—Suddenlink Communications

SHADY SHORES—See DENTON, TX (Charter Communications)

SHALLOWATER—See LUBBOCK, TX (Reach Broadband)

▲**SHAMROCK**—Suddenlink Communications

SHAVANO PARK—See SAN ANTONIO, TX (Time Warner Cable)

▲**SHEFFIELD**—Formerly served by Ector Cable. No longer in operation

SHENANDOAH (UNINCORPORATED AREAS)—See HOUSTON, TX (Comcast Cable)

SHENANDOAH—See SPRING, TX (Charter Communications)

SHEPHERD—See LAKE LIVINGSTON, TX (Suddenlink Communications)

SHEPPARD AFB—See WICHITA FALLS, TX (Time Warner Cable)

▲ **SHERIDAN**—Formerly served by National Cable Inc. No longer in operation

▲ **SHERMAN**—Cable One

▲ **SHERWOOD SHORES**—TV Cable of Grayson County

SHERWOOD—See MERTZON, TX (Reach Broadband)

SHILOH—See MEXIA, TX (Northland Cable Television)

▲ **SHINER**—Almega Cable

SHOREACRES—See HOUSTON, TX (Comcast Cable)

SIENNA PLANTATION—See HOUSTON, TX (En-Touch Systems Inc.)

▲ **SIERRA BLANCA**—Formerly served by Sierra Cable TV. No longer in operation

▲ **SILSBEE**—Time Warner Cable. Now served by BEAUMONT, TX [TX0022]

SILSBEE—See BEAUMONT, TX (Time Warner Cable)

▲ **SILVERTON**—Reach Broadband

▲ **SINTON**—Charter Communications. Now served by ROCKPORT, TX [TX0116]

SINTON—See ROCKPORT, TX (Cobridge Communications)

▲ **SKELLYTOWN**—Formerly served by Almega Cable. No longer in operation

SKIDMORE—See BEEVILLE, TX (Time Warner Cable)

▲ **SLATON**—Cobridge Communications

▲ **SMILEY**—Formerly served by National Cable Inc. No longer in operation

SMITH (UNINCORPORATED AREAS)—See LAKE PALESTINE EAST, TX (Northland Cable Television)

SMITH COUNTY (PORTIONS)—See HAWKINS, TX (Suddenlink Communications)

SMITH COUNTY (SOUTHERN PORTION)—See CHEROKEE COUNTY (northern portions), TX (Reach Broadband)

SMITH COUNTY—See MINEOLA, TX (Suddenlink Communications)

SMITH COUNTY—See TYLER, TX (Suddenlink Communications)

▲ **SMITHVILLE**—Reveille Broadband

SMITHVILLE—See AUSTIN, TX (Time Warner Cable)

SMYER—See LUBBOCK, TX (Reach Broadband)

▲ **SNOOK**—Formerly served by National Cable Inc. No longer in operation

▲ **SNYDER**—Formerly served by Snyder Microwave Communications LC. No longer in operation

▲ **SNYDER**—Suddenlink Communications

SOCORRO—See EL PASO, TX (Time Warner Cable)

SOMERSET—See SAN ANTONIO, TX (Time Warner Cable)

SOMERVELL COUNTY—See GRANBURY, TX (Charter Communications)

SOMERVILLE—See LYONS, TX (Reveille Broadband)

SOMMERALL—See HOUSTON, TX (Comcast Cable)

▲ **SONORA**—Suddenlink Communications

▲ **SOUR LAKE**—CMA Communications

SOUTH CREEK—See HOUSTON, TX (Comcast Cable)

SOUTH HOUSTON—See HOUSTON, TX (Comcast Cable)

SOUTH PADRE ISLAND—See HARLINGEN, TX (Time Warner Cable)

▲ **SOUTH SHORES**—Formerly served by Cable Unlimited. No longer in operation

▲ **SOUTH SILSBEE**—Formerly served by Cebridge Connections. No longer in operation

SOUTHLAKE—See FORT WORTH (northern portions), TX (Charter Communications)

SOUTHMAYD—See WEST GRAYSON COUNTY, TX (TV Cable of Grayson County)

▲ **SPEARMAN**—Panhandle Telephone Coop. Inc.

▲ **SPICEWOOD BEACH**—Formerly served by Charter Communications. No longer in operation

SPICEWOOD—See AUSTIN, TX (Time Warner Cable)

▲ **SPLENDORA**—Almega Cable

SPLENDORA—See NEW CANEY, TX (Northland Cable Television)

SPRING VALLEY CREEK—See HOUSTON, TX (Comcast Cable)

SPRING VALLEY—See HOUSTON, TX (Comcast Cable)

▲ **SPRING**—Charter Communications

▲ **SPRINGTOWN**—CommuniComm Services

▲ **SPUR**—Almega Cable

▲ **SPURGER**—Formerly served by Carrell Communications. No longer in operation

▲ **ST. FRANCIS VILLAGE**—Formerly served by National Cable Inc. No longer in operation

▲ **ST. JO**—Rapid Cable. Now served by VALLEY VIEW, TX [TX0792]

ST. JO—See VALLEY VIEW, TX (Nortex Communications)

ST. PAUL—See DALLAS, TX (Time Warner Cable)

STABLEGATE—See HOUSTON, TX (En-Touch Systems Inc.)

STAFFORD—See HOUSTON, TX (Comcast Cable)

▲ **STAMFORD**—Alliance Communications

▲ **STANTON**—Formerly served by Almega Cable. No longer in operation

STAR HARBOR—See MALAKOFF, TX (Northland Cable Television)

STARR COUNTY—See HARLINGEN, TX (Time Warner Cable)

▲ **STEPHENVILLE**—Northland Cable Television

▲ **STERLING CITY**—Reach Broadband

STINNETT—See BORGER, TX (Cable One)

▲ **STOCKDALE**—Windjammer Cable

STONE CREEK—See HOUSTON, TX (Comcast Cable)

STONEBRIDGE RANCH—See DALLAS, TX (Time Warner Cable)

STONEHENGE—See HOUSTON, TX (Comcast Cable)

▲ **STONY POINT**—Almega Cable

▲ **STRATFORD**—Almega Cable

▲ **STRAWN**—Strawn TV Cable Inc.

SUDAN—See MULESHOE, TX (Reach Broadband)

SUFFOLK CHASE—See HOUSTON, TX (Comcast Cable)

SUGAR LAND—See HOUSTON, TX (Comcast Cable)

▲ **SULLIVAN CITY**—Time Warner Communications. Now served by PHARR, TX [TX0017]

SULLIVAN CITY—See HARLINGEN, TX (Time Warner Cable)

▲ **SULPHUR SPRINGS**—Suddenlink Communications

SUMMERWOOD—See HOUSTON, TX (En-Touch Systems Inc.)

▲ **SUNDOWN**—Formerly served by Almega Cable. No longer in operation

SUNDOWN—See HOUSTON, TX (Comcast Cable)

SUNLAND PARK—See EL PASO, NM (Time Warner Cable)

SUNNYVALE—See DALLAS, TX (Time Warner Cable)

SUNRAY—See BORGER, TX (Cable One)

SUNRISE BEACH—See MARBLE FALLS, TX (Northland Cable Television)

SUNSET VALLEY—See AUSTIN, TX (Time Warner Cable)

SURFSIDE BEACH—See OYSTER CREEK, TX (Almega Cable)

▲ **SWEENY**—Texas Mid-Gulf Cablevision

▲ **SWEETWATER**—Suddenlink Communications

TAFT—See ARANSAS PASS, TX (Cable One)

▲ **TAHOKA**—Reach Broadband

TALCO—See CLARKSVILLE, TX (Suddenlink Communications)

TALLOWOOD—See HOUSTON, TX (Comcast Cable)

▲ **TARKINGTON PRAIRIE**—Formerly served by Jones Broadcasting. No longer in operation

TARRANT COUNTY (PORTIONS)—See CADDO PEAK, TX (North Texas Broadband)

TATUM—See LAKE CHEROKEE, TX (Alliance Communications)

TAYLOR COUNTY (NORTHERN PORTION)—See ABILENE, TX (Suddenlink Communications)

TAYLOR LAKE VILLAGE—See HOUSTON, TX (Comcast Cable)

TAYLOR—See AUSTIN, TX (Time Warner Cable)

TEAGUE—See FAIRFIELD, TX (Northland Cable Television)

TEHUACANA—See MEXIA, TX (Northland Cable Television)

▲ **TEMPLE**—Centrovision Inc.

TEMPLE—See KILLEEN, TX (Time Warner Cable)

▲ **TENAHA**—Almega Cable

TERRELL HILLS—See SAN ANTONIO, TX (Grande Communications)

TERRELL HILLS—See SAN ANTONIO, TX (Time Warner Cable)

▲ **TERRELL**—Suddenlink Communications

TERRY COUNTY—See BROWNFIELD, TX (Reach Broadband)

TEXARKANA—See TEXARKANA, AR (Cable One)

▲ **TEXARKANA**—Cable One

TEXAS CITY—See HOUSTON, TX (Comcast Cable)

▲ **TEXHOMA**—Panhandle Telephone Coop. Inc.

▲ **TEXLINE**—Baja Broadband

THE COLONY—See DALLAS, TX (Time Warner Cable)

THE HILLS—See AUSTIN, TX (Time Warner Cable)

THE MEADOWS—See HOUSTON, TX (Comcast Cable)

THE WOODLANDS—See HOUSTON, TX (Comcast Cable)

THORNDALE—See AUSTIN, TX (Time Warner Cable)

THORNHILL APARTMENTS—See HOUSTON, TX (Comcast Cable)

▲THORNTON—Formerly served by National Cable Inc. No longer in operation

THORNTONVILLE—See MONAHANS, TX (Suddenlink Communications)

THRALL—See AUSTIN, TX (Time Warner Cable)

▲THREE RIVERS—Reach Broadband

▲THROCKMORTON—TGN Cable

▲THUNDERBIRD BAY—Formerly served by Cable Unlimited. No longer in operation

TIKI ISLAND—See HOUSTON, TX (Comcast Cable)

▲TILDEN—Formerly served by Almega Cable. No longer in operation

▲TIMPSON—Almega Cable

TIOGA—See PILOT POINT, TX (Suddenlink Communications)

TITUS COUNTY (PORTIONS)—See MOUNT PLEASANT, TX (Suddenlink Communications)

▲TOLAR—Formerly served by Charter Communications. No longer in operation

▲TOLEDO VILLAGE—Formerly served by Carrell Communications. No longer in operation

TOM BEAN—See SHERMAN, TX (Cable One)

TOM GREEN COUNTY (PORTIONS)—See ROBERT LEE, TX (CMA Cablevision)

TOMBALL—See HOUSTON, TX (Comcast Cable)

TOMBALL—See MONTGOMERY COUNTY (unincorporated areas), TX (Versalink Media)

TOOL—See GUN BARREL CITY, TX (Northland Cable Television)

TRAVIS COUNTY—See AUSTIN, TX (Time Warner Cable)

▲TRENT—Formerly served by Jayroc Cablevision. No longer in operation

TRINIDAD—See MALAKOFF, TX (Northland Cable Television)

▲TRINITY—Formerly served by Cebridge Connections. Now served by LAKE LIVINGSTON (formerly SHEPHERD), TX [TX0851]

TRINITY—See LAKE LIVINGSTON, TX (Suddenlink Communications)

TROPHY CLUB—See FORT WORTH (northern portions), TX (Charter Communications)

TROUP—See ARP, TX (Zoom Media)

▲TROY—Centrovision Inc.

TRUMBULL—See WAXAHACHIE, TX (Charter Communications)

▲TULETA—Formerly served by National Cable Inc. No longer in operation

▲TULIA—Suddenlink Communications

▲TURKEY—Elk River TV Cable Co.

TURNERTOWN—See ARP, TX (Zoom Media)

TURTLE LAKE—See HOUSTON, TX (Comcast Cable)

▲TUSCOLA—CMA Cablevision

TYE—See ABILENE, TX (Suddenlink Communications)

▲TYLER—Suddenlink Communications

TYNAN—See MATHIS, TX (Time Warner Cable)

UNION GROVE—See GLADEWATER, TX (Suddenlink Communications)

UNIVERSAL CITY—See SAN ANTONIO, TX (Time Warner Cable)

▲UNIVERSITY PARK—Charter Communications

UPSHUR COUNTY (PORTIONS)—See DIANA, TX (Almega Cable)

UVALDE COUNTY (PORTIONS)—See UVALDE, TX (Time Warner Cable)

▲UVALDE—Time Warner Cable

▲VALENTINE—Valentine TV Cable

▲VALLEY MILLS—Reach Broadband

▲VALLEY VIEW—Nortex Communications

VAN ALSTYNE—See SHERMAN, TX (Cable One)

▲VAN HORN—US Cable of Coastal Texas LP

VAN VLECK—See BAY CITY, TX (Mid-Coast Cablevision)

VAN ZANDT COUNTY (PORTIONS)—See BEN WHEELER, TX (Zoom Media)

VAN ZANDT COUNTY—See MINEOLA, TX (Suddenlink Communications)

VAN—See BEN WHEELER, TX (Zoom Media)

▲VEGA—XIT Communications. Now served by HEREFORD, TX [TX0125]

▲VEGA—XIT Communications. Formerly served by Hereford, TX [TX0125]. This cable system has converted to IPTV

VENUS—See ALVARADO, TX (Almega Cable)

▲VERNON—Suddenlink Communications

VICTORIA COUNTY (UNINCORPORATED AREAS)—See VICTORIA, TX (Suddenlink Communications)

▲VICTORIA—Suddenlink Communications

▲VIDOR (southern portion)—Formerly served by Cebridge Connections. No longer in operation

▲VIDOR—Time Warner Cable. Now served by BEAUMONT, TX [TX0022]

VIDOR—See BEAUMONT, TX (Time Warner Cable)

VINTON—See EL PASO, TX (Time Warner Cable)

VOLENTE—See AUSTIN, TX (Time Warner Cable)

▲WACO—Grande Communications

▲WACO—Time Warner Cable

▲WAELDER—Formerly served by National Cable Inc. No longer in operation

WAKE VILLAGE—See TEXARKANA, TX (Cable One)

▲WALDEN—Suddenlink Communications

WALKER COUNTY (PORTIONS)—See CAROLINA COVE, TX (Cablevision of Walker County)

WALKER COUNTY—See HUNTSVILLE, TX (Suddenlink Communications)

WALLER COUNTY—See HOUSTON, TX (Comcast Cable)

▲WALLER—Suddenlink Communications

▲WALLIS—Formerly served by Rapid Cable. No longer in operation

▲WALNUT SPRINGS—Formerly served by National Cable Inc. No longer in operation

WARD COUNTY—See MONAHANS, TX (Suddenlink Communications)

WARREN CITY—See GLADEWATER, TX (Suddenlink Communications)

WASHINGTON COUNTY (PORTIONS)—See BRENHAM, TX (Suddenlink Communications)

WATAUGA—See FORT WORTH (northern portions), TX (Charter Communications)

▲WATERWOOD—Cablevision of Walker County

▲WAXAHACHIE—Charter Communications

▲WEATHERFORD—Charter Communications

WEBB COUNTY—See LAREDO, TX (Time Warner Cable)

WEBSTER—See HOUSTON, TX (Comcast Cable)

WEDGEWOOD—See HOUSTON, TX (Comcast Cable)

WEIMAR—See LA GRANGE, TX (CMA Cablevision)

▲WEINERT—Formerly served by Jayroc Cablevision. No longer in operation

▲WELCH—Formerly served by National Cable Inc. No longer in operation

▲WELLINGTON—Suddenlink Communications

▲WELLMAN—Formerly served by National Cable Inc. No longer in operation

▲WELLS—Formerly served by Cebridge Connections. No longer in operation

▲WESLACO—Time Warner Communications. Now served by PHARR, TX [TX0017]

WESLACO—See HARLINGEN, TX (Time Warner Cable)

▲WEST COLUMBIA—Texas Mid-Gulf Cablevision

▲WEST GRAYSON COUNTY—TV Cable of Grayson County

WEST HOLLOW VILLA—See HOUSTON, TX (Comcast Cable)

WEST HOLLOW—See HOUSTON, TX (Comcast Cable)

WEST LAKE HILLS—See AUSTIN, TX (Time Warner Cable)

WEST LUBBOCK—See LUBBOCK, TX (Reach Broadband)

WEST MOUNTAIN—See EAST MOUNTAIN, TX (Gilmer Cable)

▲WEST ODESSA—US Cable of Coastal Texas LP

WEST ORANGE—See BEAUMONT, TX (Time Warner Cable)

WEST TAWAKONI—See QUINLAN, TX (Zoom Media)

WEST TRAILS—See HOUSTON, TX (Comcast Cable)

WEST UNIVERSITY PLACE—See HOUSTON, TX (Comcast Cable)

▲WEST—Reach Broadband

▲WESTBROOK—Formerly served by National Cable Inc. No longer in operation

WESTGATE—See HOUSTON, TX (En-Touch Systems Inc.)

▲WESTHOFF—Formerly served by National Cable Inc. No longer in operation

WESTLAKE—See FORT WORTH (northern portions), TX (Charter Communications)

WESTOVER HILLS—See FORT WORTH (northern portions), TX (Charter Communications)

WESTWORTH VILLAGE—See FORT WORTH (northern portions), TX (Charter Communications)

▲WHARTON—Texas Mid-Gulf Cablevision

▲WHEELER—Elk River TV Cable Co.

WHITE DEER—See BORGER, TX (Cable One)

WHITE OAK MANOR—See HOUSTON, TX (Comcast Cable)

WHITE OAK—See GLADEWATER, TX (Suddenlink Communications)

WHITE SETTLEMENT—See FORT WORTH (northern portions), TX (Charter Communications)

▲ **WHITEFACE**—Formerly served by Cebridge Connections. No longer in operation

WHITEHOUSE—See TYLER, TX (Suddenlink Communications)

▲ **WHITESBORO**—Suddenlink Communications

WHITEWRIGHT—See SHERMAN, TX (Cable One)

▲ **WHITNEY**—Reach Broadband

WICHITA COUNTY (UNINCORPORATED AREAS)—See WICHITA FALLS, TX (Time Warner Cable)

▲ **WICHITA FALLS**—Time Warner Cable

▲ **WICKETT**—Formerly served by Almega Cable. No longer in operation

▲ **WILDWOOD**—Daybreak Communications

WILLACY COUNTY—See HARLINGEN, TX (Time Warner Cable)

WILLIS—See CONROE, TX (Suddenlink Communications)

▲ **WILLOW PARK**—Mallard Cablevision. Now served by FORT WORTH, TX [TX0008]

WILLOW PARK—See FORT WORTH (northern portions), TX (Charter Communications)

WILLOW POINT—See HOUSTON, TX (Comcast Cable)

▲ **WILLS POINT**—Zoom Media

▲ **WILMER**—Formerly served by Metro Cable. No longer in operation

▲ **WILSON**—Formerly served by Charter Communications. No longer in operation

WIMBERLEY—See AUSTIN, TX (Time Warner Cable)

WINDCREST—See SAN ANTONIO, TX (Time Warner Cable)

WINDFERN MANOR—See HOUSTON, TX (Comcast Cable)

WINDFERN MEADOW—See HOUSTON, TX (Comcast Cable)

WINDFERN—See HOUSTON, TX (Comcast Cable)

▲ **WINK**—Almega Cable

WINKLER COUNTY (PORTIONS)—See KERMIT, TX (Suddenlink Communications)

▲ **WINNIE**—Time Warner Cable. Now served by BEAUMONT, TX [TX0022]

WINNIE—See BEAUMONT, TX (Time Warner Cable)

▲ **WINNSBORO**—Suddenlink Communications

WINONA—See HAWKINS, TX (Suddenlink Communications)

▲ **WINTERS**—Allegiance Communications

▲ **WODEN**—Formerly served by Almega Cable. No longer in operation

▲ **WOLFE CITY**—Zoom Media

WOLFFORTH—See LUBBOCK, TX (Reach Broadband)

WOOD COUNTY (PORTIONS)—See HAWKINS, TX (Suddenlink Communications)

WOOD COUNTY—See MINEOLA, TX (Suddenlink Communications)

WOODBRANCH VILLAGE—See NEW CANEY, TX (Northland Cable Television)

WOODCREEK—See AUSTIN, TX (Time Warner Cable)

WOODFERN MANOR—See HOUSTON, TX (Comcast Cable)

WOODFERN—See HOUSTON, TX (Comcast Cable)

WOODGATE—See HOUSTON, TX (Comcast Cable)

WOODLOCH—See SPRING, TX (Charter Communications)

▲ **WOODROW**—Formerly served by Cebridge Connections. No longer in operation

WOODS—See CENTER POINT, TX (Almega Cable)

WOODSBORO—See MATHIS, TX (Time Warner Cable)

▲ **WOODVILLE**—CMA Cablevision

WOODWAY—See WACO, TX (Grande Communications)

WOODWAY—See WACO, TX (Time Warner Cable)

▲ **WORTHAM (TOWN)**—Northland Cable Television

▲ **WYLIE**—Time Warner Cable. Now served by DALLAS, TX [TX0003]

WYLIE—See DALLAS, TX (Time Warner Cable)

▲ **YOAKUM**—Time Warner Cable. Now served by GONZALES, TX [TX0209]

YOAKUM—See GONZALES, TX (Time Warner Cable)

YORKSHIRE—See HOUSTON, TX (Comcast Cable)

▲ **YORKTOWN**—Almega Cable

YOUNG COUNTY (PORTIONS)—See OLNEY, TX (Suddenlink Communications)

YOUNG COUNTY—See GRAHAM, TX (Windjammer Cable)

▲ **ZAPATA**—Time Warner Cable

ZAVALA COUNTY—See CRYSTAL CITY, TX (Time Warner Cable)

▲ **ZAVALLA**—Almega Cable

▲ **ZION HILL**—Formerly served by National Cable Inc. No longer in operation

UTAH

ALPINE—See SALT LAKE CITY, UT (Comcast Cable)

AMERICAN FORK—See SALT LAKE CITY, UT (Comcast Cable)

ANNABELLA—See GUNNISON, UT (Central Telcom Services (CUTV))

AURORA—See GUNNISON, UT (Central Telcom Services (CUTV))

AUSTIN—See GUNNISON, UT (Central Telcom Services (CUTV))

BEAR RIVER CITY—See LOGAN, UT (Comcast Cable)

▲ **BEAVER**—South Central Communications

BICKNELL—See LYMAN, UT (South Central Communications)

▲ **BLANDING**—Emery Telcom

BLUFFDALE—See SALT LAKE CITY, UT (Comcast Cable)

BOUNTIFUL—See OGDEN, UT (Comcast Cable)

BOX ELDER COUNTY (UNINCORPORATED AREAS)—See OGDEN, UT (Comcast Cable)

▲ **BRIAN HEAD**—South Central Communications

▲ **BRIGHAM CITY**—Comcast Cable. Now served by OGDEN (formerly HOOPER), UT [UT0008]

BRIGHAM CITY—See OGDEN, UT (Comcast Cable)

BRYCE—See PANGUITCH, UT (South Central Communications)

CACHE COUNTY (PORTIONS)—See LOGAN, UT (Comcast Cable)

CARBON COUNTY (PORTIONS)—See PRICE, UT (Emery Telcom)

▲ **CASTLE DALE**—Emery Telcom

▲ **CEDAR CITY**—Bresnan Communications

CENTERFIELD—See GUNNISON, UT (Central Telcom Services (CUTV))

CENTERVILLE—See OGDEN, UT (Comcast Cable)

▲ **CENTRAL**—Central Telcom Services (CUTV). Now served by GUNNISON, UT [UT0037]

CENTRAL—See GUNNISON, UT (Central Telcom Services (CUTV))

CIRCLEVILLE—See PANGUITCH, UT (South Central Communications)

CLARKSTON—See LOGAN, UT (Comcast Cable)

CLEARFIELD—See OGDEN, UT (Comcast Cable)

▲ **CLEVELAND**—Emery Telcom

CLINTON—See OGDEN, UT (Comcast Cable)

▲ **COALVILLE**—Comcast Cable

COLUMBIA—See EAST CARBON, UT (Emery Telcom)

CORINNE—See LOGAN, UT (Comcast Cable)

DAVIS COUNTY (PORTIONS)—See OGDEN, UT (Comcast Cable)

▲ **DELTA**—Satview Broadband

DEWEYVILLE—See LOGAN, UT (Comcast Cable)

DRAPER—See SALT LAKE CITY, UT (Comcast Cable)

▲ **DUCHESNE**—Strata Networks

▲ **DUGWAY**—Central Telcom Services (CUTV)

▲ **EAST CARBON**—Emery Telcom

EDEN—See HUNTSVILLE, UT (HLS Communications)

ELK RIDGE—See PROVO, UT (Comcast Cable)

ELMO—See CLEVELAND, UT (Emery Telcom)

ELSINORE—See GUNNISON, UT (Central Telcom Services (CUTV))

EMERY COUNTY—See CASTLE DALE, UT (Emery Telcom)

EMERY COUNTY—See GREEN RIVER, UT (Emery Telcom)

▲ **ENOCH**—South Central Communications

▲ **ENTERPRISE**—South Central Communications

▲ **EPHRAIM**—Central Telcom Services (CUTV). Now served by GUNNISON, UT [UT0037]

EPHRAIM—See GUNNISON, UT (Central Telcom Services (CUTV))

▲ **ESCALANTE**—South Central Communications

▲ **EUREKA**—Central Telcom Services (CUTV). Now served by GUNNISON, UT [UT0037]

EUREKA—See GUNNISON, UT (Central Telcom Services (CUTV))

FAIRVIEW—See GUNNISON, UT (Central Telcom Services (CUTV))

▲ **FARMINGTON**—Comcast Cable. Now served by OGDEN (formerly HOOPER), UT [UT0008]

FARMINGTON—See OGDEN, UT (Comcast Cable)

FARR WEST—See OGDEN, UT (Comcast Cable)

▲ **FERRON**—Emery Telcom

▲ **FIELDING**—Comcast Cable. Now served by LOGAN, UT [UT0006]

FIELDING—See LOGAN, UT (Comcast Cable)

▲ **FILLMORE**—Satview Broadband

FOUNTAIN GREEN—See GUNNISON, UT (Central Telcom Services (CUTV))

▲ **FRANCIS (TOWN)**—All West Communications. Formerly served by Kamas, UT [UT0053]. This cable system has converted to IPTV

FREDONIA—See KANAB, AZ (South Central Communications)

FRUIT HEIGHTS—See OGDEN, UT (Comcast Cable)

GARLAND—See LOGAN, UT (Comcast Cable)

▲**GLENWOOD**—Central Telcom Services (CUTV)

▲**GOSHEN**—Central Telcom Services (CUTV). Now served by GUNNISON, UT [UT0037]

GOSHEN—See GUNNISON, UT (Central Telcom Services (CUTV))

GRAND COUNTY—See MOAB, UT (Emery Telcom)

GRANTSVILLE—See SALT LAKE CITY, UT (Comcast Cable)

▲**GREEN RIVER**—Emery Telcom

▲**GUNNISON**—Central Telcom Services (CUTV)

HARRISBURG JUNCTION—See ST. GEORGE, UT (Baja Broadband)

HARRISVILLE—See OGDEN, UT (Comcast Cable)

▲**HEBER CITY**—Comcast Cable

HELPER—See PRICE, UT (Emery Telcom)

HERRIMAN—See SALT LAKE CITY, UT (Comcast Cable)

HIGHLAND—See SALT LAKE CITY, UT (Comcast Cable)

HILL AFB—See OGDEN, UT (Comcast Cable)

HONEYVILLE—See LOGAN, UT (Comcast Cable)

HOOPER—See OGDEN, UT (Comcast Cable)

HUNTINGTON—See CASTLE DALE, UT (Emery Telcom)

▲**HUNTSVILLE**—HLS Communications

▲**HURRICANE**—Charter Communications. Now served by ST. GEORGE, UT [UT0007]

HURRICANE—See ST. GEORGE, UT (Baja Broadband)

HYDE PARK—See LOGAN, UT (Comcast Cable)

HYRUM—See LOGAN, UT (Comcast Cable)

IVINS—See ST. GEORGE, UT (Baja Broadband)

▲**KAMAS**—All West Communications. This cable system has converted to IPTV. See Kamas, UT [UT5013]

▲**KAMAS**—All West Communications. Formerly [UT0053]. This cable system has converted to IPTV

▲**KANAB**—South Central Communications

▲**KANARRAVILLE**—South Central Communications

KAYSVILLE—See OGDEN, UT (Comcast Cable)

KENILWORTH—See PRICE, UT (Emery Telcom)

LA VERKIN—See ST. GEORGE, UT (Baja Broadband)

LAYTON—See OGDEN, UT (Comcast Cable)

LEEDS—See ST. GEORGE, UT (Baja Broadband)

LEHI—See SALT LAKE CITY, UT (Comcast Cable)

LEWISTON—See LOGAN, UT (Comcast Cable)

▲**LINDON**—Formerly served by Nuvont Communications. IPTV service no longer in operation

LINDON—See SALT LAKE CITY, UT (Comcast Cable)

▲**LINDON**—UTOPIA

LOA—See LYMAN, UT (South Central Communications)

▲**LOGAN**—Comcast Cable

▲**LYMAN**—South Central Communications

▲**MANILA**—Formerly served by Myvocom. No longer in operation

MANTI—See GUNNISON, UT (Central Telcom Services (CUTV))

MAPLETON—See SALT LAKE CITY, UT (Comcast Cable)

▲**MARION**—All West Communications. Formerly served by Kamas, UT [UT0053]. This cable system has converted to IPTV

▲**MAYFIELD**—Central Telcom Services (CUTV). Now served by GUNNISON, UT [UT0037]

MAYFIELD—See GUNNISON, UT (Central Telcom Services (CUTV))

MENDON—See LOGAN, UT (Comcast Cable)

▲**MIDVALE**—Formerly served by Nuvont Communications. IPTV operations no longer in operation

MIDVALE—See SALT LAKE CITY, UT (Comcast Cable)

MIDVALE—See LINDON, UT (UTOPIA)

MIDWAY—See HEBER CITY, UT (Comcast Cable)

▲**MILFORD**—South Central Communications

MILLVILLE—See LOGAN, UT (Comcast Cable)

▲**MINERSVILLE**—South Central Communications

▲**MOAB**—Emery Telcom

▲**MONA**—Central Telcom Services (CUTV)

MONROE—See GUNNISON, UT (Central Telcom Services (CUTV))

▲**MONTICELLO**—Emery Telcom

▲**MORGAN CITY**—Comcast Cable

MORGAN COUNTY—See MORGAN CITY, UT (Comcast Cable)

▲**MORONI**—Central Telcom Services (CUTV). Now served by GUNNISON, UT [UT0037]

MORONI—See GUNNISON, UT (Central Telcom Services (CUTV))

▲**MOUNT PLEASANT**—Central Telcom Services (CUTV). Now served by GUNNISON, UT [UT0037]

MOUNT PLEASANT—See GUNNISON, UT (Central Telcom Services (CUTV))

▲**MURRAY**—Formerly served by Nuvont Communications. IPTV service no longer in operation

MURRAY—See SALT LAKE CITY, UT (Comcast Cable)

MURRAY—See LINDON, UT (UTOPIA)

▲**NEPHI**—Comcast Cable

▲**NEW HARMONY**—Formerly served by South Central Communications. No longer in operation

NEWTON—See LOGAN, UT (Comcast Cable)

NIBLEY—See LOGAN, UT (Comcast Cable)

NORTH LOGAN—See LOGAN, UT (Comcast Cable)

NORTH OGDEN—See OGDEN, UT (Comcast Cable)

NORTH SALT LAKE—See OGDEN, UT (Comcast Cable)

▲**OAKLEY**—All West Communications. Formerly served by Kamas, UT [UT0053]. This cable system has converted to IPTV

▲**OGDEN**—Comcast Cable

ORANGEVILLE—See CASTLE DALE, UT (Emery Telcom)

▲**OREM**—Formerly served by Nuvont Communications. IPTV service no longer in operation

OREM—See SALT LAKE CITY, UT (Comcast Cable)

OREM—See LINDON, UT (UTOPIA)

▲**PANGUITCH (portions)**—South Central Communications. Now served by PANGUITCH, UT [UT0043]

▲**PANGUITCH**—South Central Communications

PARADISE—See LOGAN, UT (Comcast Cable)

▲**PARAGONAH**—South Central Communications. Now served by PAROWAN, UT [UT0034]

PARAGONAH—See PAROWAN, UT (South Central Communications)

▲**PARK CITY**—Comcast Cable. Now served by SALT LAKE CITY, UT [UT0001]

PARK CITY—See SALT LAKE CITY, UT (Comcast Cable)

▲**PAROWAN**—South Central Communications

▲**PAYSON**—Formerly served by Nuvont Communications. IPTV service no longer in operation

PAYSON—See PROVO, UT (Comcast Cable)

PAYSON—See LINDON, UT (UTOPIA)

▲**PEOA**—All West Communications. Formerly served by Kamas, UT [UT0053]. This cable system has converted to IPTV

PERRY—See OGDEN, UT (Comcast Cable)

PLAIN CITY—See OGDEN, UT (Comcast Cable)

PLEASANT GROVE—See SALT LAKE CITY, UT (Comcast Cable)

PLEASANT VIEW—See OGDEN, UT (Comcast Cable)

PLYMOUTH—See LOGAN, UT (Comcast Cable)

▲**PRICE**—Emery Telcom

PROVIDENCE—See LOGAN, UT (Comcast Cable)

▲**PROVO**—Formerly served by Nuvont Communications. IPTV service no longer in operation

▲**PROVO**—Formerly served by Provo Cable. No longer in operation

▲**PROVO**—Comcast Cable

▲**RANDOLPH TWP.**—All West Communications. This cable system has converted to IPTV. See Randolph, UT [UT5015]

▲**RANDOLPH**—All West Communications. Formerly [UT0066]. This cable system has converted to IPTV

REDMOND—See GUNNISON, UT (Central Telcom Services (CUTV))

▲**RICHFIELD**—Central Telcom Services (CUTV). Now served by GUNNISON, UT [UT0037]

RICHFIELD—See GUNNISON, UT (Central Telcom Services (CUTV))

▲**RICHMOND**—Comcast Cable. Now served by LOGAN, UT [UT0006]

RICHMOND—See LOGAN, UT (Comcast Cable)

RIVER HEIGHTS—See LOGAN, UT (Comcast Cable)

▲**RIVERDALE**—Comcast Cable. Now served by OGDEN (formerly HOOPER), UT [UT0008]

RIVERDALE—See OGDEN, UT (Comcast Cable)

RIVERTON—See SALT LAKE CITY, UT (Comcast Cable)

▲**ROCKVILLE**—Baja Broadband

▲**ROOSEVELT**—Strata Networks

ROY—See OGDEN, UT (Comcast Cable)

▲**SALEM**—Comcast Cable. Now served by PROVO, UT [UT0005]

SALEM—See PROVO, UT (Comcast Cable)

▲**SALINA**—Central Telcom Services (CUTV). Now served by GUNNISON, UT [UT0037]

SALINA—See GUNNISON, UT (Central Telcom Services (CUTV))

▲**SALT LAKE CITY**—Formerly served by TechnoVision Inc. No longer in operation

▲**SALT LAKE CITY**—Comcast Cable

SALT LAKE COUNTY—See SALT LAKE CITY, UT (Comcast Cable)

▲**SANDY**—Comcast Cable. Now served by SALT LAKE CITY, UT [UT0001]

SANDY—See SALT LAKE CITY, UT (Comcast Cable)

SANPETE COUNTY—See GUNNISON, UT (Central Telcom Services (CUTV))

SANTA CLARA—See ST. GEORGE, UT (Baja Broadband)

▲**SANTAQUIN**—Central Telcom Services (CUTV). Now served by GUNNISON, UT [UT0037]

SANTAQUIN—See GUNNISON, UT (Central Telcom Services (CUTV))

SEVIER COUNTY—See GUNNISON, UT (Central Telcom Services (CUTV))

SMITHFIELD—See LOGAN, UT (Comcast Cable)

▲**SOUTH JORDAN**—Qwest Choice TV. This cable system has converted to IPTV. See Randolph, UT [UT5021]

▲**SOUTH JORDAN**—CenturyLink. Formerly [UT0091]. This cable system has converted to IPTV.

SOUTH JORDAN—See SALT LAKE CITY, UT (Comcast Cable)

SOUTH OGDEN—See OGDEN, UT (Comcast Cable)

SOUTH SALT LAKE CITY—See SALT LAKE CITY, UT (Comcast Cable)

SOUTH WEBER—See OGDEN, UT (Comcast Cable)

SPANISH FORK CITY—See PROVO, UT (Comcast Cable)

SPANISH FORK—See PROVO, UT (Comcast Cable)

▲**SPANISH FORK**—Spanish Fork Community Network

SPRING CITY—See GUNNISON, UT (Central Telcom Services (CUTV))

SPRINGDALE—See ROCKVILLE, UT (Baja Broadband)

SPRINGVILLE—See SALT LAKE CITY, UT (Comcast Cable)

▲**ST. GEORGE**—Baja Broadband

SUMMIT COUNTY (PORTIONS)—See COALVILLE, UT (Comcast Cable)

SUMMIT COUNTY (PORTIONS)—See SALT LAKE CITY, UT (Comcast Cable)

SUNNYSIDE—See EAST CARBON, UT (Emery Telcom)

SUNSET—See OGDEN, UT (Comcast Cable)

SYRACUSE—See OGDEN, UT (Comcast Cable)

TAYLORSVILLE—See SALT LAKE CITY, UT (Comcast Cable)

TOOELE COUNTY—See SALT LAKE CITY, UT (Comcast Cable)

▲**TOOELE**—Comcast Cable. Now served by SALT LAKE CITY, UT [UT0001]

TOOELE—See SALT LAKE CITY, UT (Comcast Cable)

TOQUERVILLE—See ST. GEORGE, UT (Baja Broadband)

TREMONTON—See LOGAN, UT (Comcast Cable)

TROPIC—See PANGUITCH, UT (South Central Communications)

UINTAH CITY—See OGDEN, UT (Comcast Cable)

UTAH COUNTY (PORTIONS)—See GUNNISON, UT (Central Telcom Services (CUTV))

UTAH COUNTY (PORTIONS)—See PROVO, UT (Comcast Cable)

UTAH COUNTY (UNINCORPORATED AREAS)—See SALT LAKE CITY, UT (Comcast Cable)

▲**VERNAL**—Bresnan Communications. No longer in operation

WASATCH COUNTY—See HEBER CITY, UT (Comcast Cable)

WASHINGTON TERRACE—See OGDEN, UT (Comcast Cable)

WASHINGTON—See ST. GEORGE, UT (Baja Broadband)

WEBER COUNTY (PORTIONS)—See OGDEN, UT (Comcast Cable)

WELLINGTON—See PRICE, UT (Emery Telcom)

WELLSVILLE—See LOGAN, UT (Comcast Cable)

▲**WENDOVER**—Precis Communications. Now served by WENDOVER, NV [NV0054]

WEST BOUNTIFUL—See OGDEN, UT (Comcast Cable)

WEST HAVEN—See OGDEN, UT (Comcast Cable)

WEST JORDAN—See SALT LAKE CITY, UT (Comcast Cable)

WEST POINT—See OGDEN, UT (Comcast Cable)

▲**WEST VALLEY CITY**—Formerly served by Nuvont Communications. IPTV service no longer in operation

WEST VALLEY CITY—See SALT LAKE CITY, UT (Comcast Cable)

WEST VALLEY CITY—See LINDON, UT (UTOPIA)

WILLARD—See OGDEN, UT (Comcast Cable)

▲**WINCHESTER**—Formerly served by South Central Communications. No longer in operation

▲**WOODLAND**—All West Communications. Formerly served by Kamas, UT [UT0053]. This cable system has converted to IPTV

▲**WOODRUFF (TOWN)**—All West Communications. Formerly served by Randolph, UT [UT0066]. This cable system has converted to IPTV

WOODS CROSS—See OGDEN, UT (Comcast Cable)

VERMONT

ANDOVER (TOWN)—See BURLINGTON, NH (Comcast Cable)

ARLINGTON—See BENNINGTON, VT (Comcast Cable)

ATHENS—See BRATTLEBORO, VT (Comcast Cable)

BAKERSFIELD—See ENOSBURG FALLS, VT (Comcast Cable)

BARNET—See DANVILLE (town), VT (Charter Communications)

▲**BARRE**—Charter Communications. Now served by DANVILLE (TOWN) (formerly St. Johnsbury), VT [VT0009]

BARRE—See DANVILLE (town), VT (Charter Communications)

BARTON—See BURLINGTON, VT (Comcast Cable)

BATH—See DANVILLE (town), NH (Charter Communications)

BEEBE PLAIN—See BURLINGTON, VT (Comcast Cable)

BELLOWS FALLS—See BRATTLEBORO, VT (Comcast Cable)

▲**BENNINGTON**—Comcast Cable

▲**BERLIN**—Comcast Cable. Now served by BURLINGTON, VT [VT0001]

BERLIN—See BURLINGTON, VT (Comcast Cable)

BETHEL—See BURLINGTON, VT (Comcast Cable)

▲**BLOOMFIELD TWP.**—Formerly served by Adelphia Communications. No longer in operation

BOMOSEEN—See BURLINGTON, VT (Comcast Cable)

BONDVILLE—See BENNINGTON, VT (Comcast Cable)

▲**BRADFORD**—Charter Communications. Now served by DANVILLE (TOWN) (formerly St. Johnsbury), VT [VT0009]

BRADFORD—See DANVILLE (town), VT (Charter Communications)

▲**BRAINTREE**—Formerly served by Adelphia Cable-Berlin. Now served by BURLINGTON, VT [VT0001]

BRAINTREE—See BURLINGTON, VT (Comcast Cable)

BRANDON—See BURLINGTON, VT (Comcast Cable)

▲**BRATTLEBORO**—Comcast Cable

BRIDGEWATER—See BURLINGTON, VT (Comcast Cable)

BRISTOL—See BURLINGTON, VT (Comcast Cable)

BURKE—See DANVILLE (town), VT (Charter Communications)

▲**BURLINGTON**—Comcast Cable

CABOT TWP.—See BURLINGTON, VT (Comcast Cable)

CABOT—See BURLINGTON, VT (Comcast Cable)

CALAIS—See BURLINGTON, VT (Comcast Cable)

CAMBRIDGE JUNCTION—See JEFFERSONVILLE, VT (Jeffersonville Cable TV Corp.)

CAMBRIDGE—See JEFFERSONVILLE, VT (Jeffersonville Cable TV Corp.)

CAMBRIDGEPORT—See BRATTLEBORO, VT (Comcast Cable)

CANAAN (TOWN)—See BURLINGTON, NH (Comcast Cable)

CASTLETON—See BURLINGTON, VT (Comcast Cable)

CAVENDISH—See BURLINGTON, VT (Comcast Cable)

▲**CHARLESTON**—Comcast Cable. Now served by BURLINGTON, VT [VT0001]

CHARLESTON—See BURLINGTON, VT (Comcast Cable)

CHARLOTTE—See BURLINGTON, VT (Comcast Cable)

▲**CHELSEA**—Charter Communications. Now served by DANVILLE (TOWN) (formerly St. Johnsbury), VT [VT0009]

CHELSEA—See DANVILLE (town), VT (Charter Communications)

CHESTER DEPOT (VILLAGE)—See BURLINGTON, VT (Comcast Cable)

CHESTER—See BURLINGTON, VT (Comcast Cable)

CHITTENDEN—See BURLINGTON, VT (Comcast Cable)

CLAREMONT—See BURLINGTON, NH (Comcast Cable)

CLARENDON TWP.—See BURLINGTON, VT (Comcast Cable)

COLCHESTER—See BURLINGTON, VT (Comcast Cable)

CONCORD—See DANVILLE (town), VT (Charter Communications)

CORNISH (TOWN)—See BURLINGTON, NH (Comcast Cable)

CORNISH FLAT—See BURLINGTON, NH (Comcast Cable)

▲ **COVENTRY TWP.**—Formerly served by Adelphia Communications. No longer in operation

COVENTRY—See BURLINGTON, VT (Comcast Cable)

DANBURY (TOWN)—See BURLINGTON, NH (Comcast Cable)

DANBY—See BURLINGTON, VT (Comcast Cable)

▲ **DANVILLE (TOWN)**—Charter Communications

DERBY CENTER—See BURLINGTON, VT (Comcast Cable)

DERBY LINE—See BURLINGTON, VT (Comcast Cable)

▲ **DERBY**—Comcast Cable. Now served by BURLINGTON, VT [VT0001]

DERBY—See BURLINGTON, VT (Comcast Cable)

DORSET—See BENNINGTON, VT (Comcast Cable)

DUMMERSTON—See PUTNEY, VT (Southern Vermont Cable Co.)

DUXBURY—See BURLINGTON, VT (Comcast Cable)

EAST ARLINGTON—See BENNINGTON, VT (Comcast Cable)

EAST BARRE—See DANVILLE (town), VT (Charter Communications)

EAST BERKSHIRE—See ENOSBURG FALLS, VT (Comcast Cable)

EAST BURKE—See DANVILLE (town), VT (Charter Communications)

▲ **EAST CORINTH**—Formerly served by Olsen TV. No longer in operation

EAST FAIRFIELD—See ENOSBURG FALLS, VT (Comcast Cable)

EAST HARDWICK—See BURLINGTON, VT (Comcast Cable)

EAST JAMAICA—See PUTNEY, VT (Southern Vermont Cable Co.)

EAST MIDDLEBURY—See BURLINGTON, VT (Comcast Cable)

EAST MONTPELIER—See BURLINGTON, VT (Comcast Cable)

EAST POULTNEY—See BURLINGTON, VT (Comcast Cable)

EAST PUTNEY—See PUTNEY, VT (Southern Vermont Cable Co.)

EAST RYEGATE—See DANVILLE (town), VT (Charter Communications)

EAST ST. JOHNSBURY—See DANVILLE (town), VT (Charter Communications)

ENFIELD—See BURLINGTON, NH (Comcast Cable)

▲ **ENOSBURG FALLS**—Comcast Cable

ENOSBURG—See ENOSBURG FALLS, VT (Comcast Cable)

ESSEX JUNCTION—See BURLINGTON, VT (Comcast Cable)

ESSEX—See BURLINGTON, VT (Comcast Cable)

FAIR HAVEN—See BURLINGTON, VT (Comcast Cable)

FAYSTON—See WAITSFIELD, VT (Waitsfield Cable Co.)

FERRISBURG—See BURLINGTON, VT (Comcast Cable)

FOREST DALE—See BURLINGTON, VT (Comcast Cable)

GEORGIA—See BURLINGTON, VT (Comcast Cable)

GLOVER—See BURLINGTON, VT (Comcast Cable)

GRAFTON—See BRATTLEBORO, VT (Comcast Cable)

GRANITEVILLE—See DANVILLE (town), VT (Charter Communications)

GRANTHAM—See BURLINGTON, NH (Comcast Cable)

GROTON—See DANVILLE (town), VT (Charter Communications)

GUILFORD TWP.—See BRATTLEBORO, VT (Comcast Cable)

HANOVER—See BURLINGTON, NH (Comcast Cable)

HARDWICK—See BURLINGTON, VT (Comcast Cable)

HAVERHILL—See DANVILLE (town), NH (Charter Communications)

HILL (TOWN)—See BURLINGTON, NH (Comcast Cable)

HINESBURG—See BURLINGTON, VT (Comcast Cable)

HUNTINGTON—See BURLINGTON, VT (Comcast Cable)

HYDE PARK—See BURLINGTON, VT (Comcast Cable)

HYDEVILLE—See BURLINGTON, VT (Comcast Cable)

▲ **IRASBURG TWP.**—Formerly served by Adelphia Communications. No longer in operation

IRASBURG—See BURLINGTON, VT (Comcast Cable)

▲ **JACKSONVILLE**—Formerly served by Area Telecable. No longer in operation

▲ **JAMAICA TWP.**—Southern Vermont Cable Co. Now served by PUTNEY, VT [VT0067]

JAMAICA TWP.—See PUTNEY, VT (Southern Vermont Cable Co.)

▲ **JEFFERSONVILLE**—Jeffersonville Cable TV Corp.

JERICHO—See BURLINGTON, VT (Comcast Cable)

JOHNSON—See BURLINGTON, VT (Comcast Cable)

KILLINGTON—See BURLINGTON, VT (Comcast Cable)

KIRBY—See DANVILLE (town), VT (Charter Communications)

LEBANON—See BURLINGTON, NH (Comcast Cable)

LONDONDERRY—See BURLINGTON, VT (Comcast Cable)

LUDLOW—See BURLINGTON, VT (Comcast Cable)

LYNDON CENTER—See DANVILLE (town), VT (Charter Communications)

LYNDON CORNERS—See DANVILLE (town), VT (Charter Communications)

LYNDON—See DANVILLE (town), VT (Charter Communications)

LYNDONVILLE—See DANVILLE (town), VT (Charter Communications)

MANCHESTER CENTER—See BENNINGTON, VT (Comcast Cable)

▲ **MANCHESTER**—Formerly served by Adelphia Communications. Now served BENNINGTON, VT [VT0004]

MANCHESTER—See BENNINGTON, VT (Comcast Cable)

MARSHFIELD TWP.—See BURLINGTON, VT (Comcast Cable)

MARSHFIELD—See DANVILLE (town), VT (Charter Communications)

MCINDOE FALLS—See DANVILLE (town), VT (Charter Communications)

MENDON—See BURLINGTON, VT (Comcast Cable)

MERIDEN—See BURLINGTON, NH (Comcast Cable)

MIDDLEBURY—See BURLINGTON, VT (Comcast Cable)

MIDDLESEX—See BURLINGTON, VT (Comcast Cable)

MILTON—See BURLINGTON, VT (Comcast Cable)

MONTGOMERY—See ENOSBURG FALLS, VT (Comcast Cable)

MONTPELIER—See BURLINGTON, VT (Comcast Cable)

MORETOWN—See BURLINGTON, VT (Comcast Cable)

MORETOWN—See WAITSFIELD, VT (Waitsfield Cable Co.)

MORRISTOWN—See BURLINGTON, VT (Comcast Cable)

MORRISVILLE—See BURLINGTON, VT (Comcast Cable)

▲ **MOUNT ASCUTNEY**—Formerly served by New England Wireless Inc. No longer in operation

MOUNT TABOR—See BURLINGTON, VT (Comcast Cable)

NEW LONDON—See BURLINGTON, NH (Comcast Cable)

NEWBURY—See DANVILLE (town), VT (Charter Communications)

▲ **NEWFANE**—Comcast Cable. Now served by PUTNEY, VT [VT0067]

NEWFANE—See PUTNEY, VT (Southern Vermont Cable Co.)

NEWPORT CENTER—See BURLINGTON, VT (Comcast Cable)

NEWPORT—See BURLINGTON, NH (Comcast Cable)

NEWPORT—See BURLINGTON, VT (Comcast Cable)

NORTH BENNINGTON—See BENNINGTON, VT (Comcast Cable)

NORTH DANVILLE—See DANVILLE (town), VT (Charter Communications)

NORTH HAVERHILL—See DANVILLE (town), NH (Charter Communications)

NORTH TROY—See BURLINGTON, VT (Comcast Cable)

NORTH WESTMINSTER—See BRATTLEBORO, VT (Comcast Cable)

NORTHFIELD (TOWN)—See NORTHFIELD (village), VT (Trans-Video Inc.)

▲ **NORTHFIELD (VILLAGE)**—Trans-Video Inc.

OLD BENNINGTON—See BENNINGTON, VT (Comcast Cable)

ORANGE (TOWN)—See DANVILLE (town), VT (Charter Communications)

ORLEANS—See BURLINGTON, VT (Comcast Cable)

PASSUMPSIC—See DANVILLE (town), VT (Charter Communications)

PAWLET—See BURLINGTON, VT (Comcast Cable)

PEACHAM—See DANVILLE (town), VT (Charter Communications)

PERKINSVILLE—See BURLINGTON, VT (Comcast Cable)

PERU—See BENNINGTON, VT (Comcast Cable)

PIERMONT—See DANVILLE (town), NH (Charter Communications)

PIKE—See DANVILLE (town), NH (Charter Communications)

PITTSFORD (VILLAGE)—See BURLINGTON, VT (Comcast Cable)

PITTSFORD—See BURLINGTON, VT (Comcast Cable)

PLAINFIELD (TOWN)—See BURLINGTON, NH (Comcast Cable)

PLAINFIELD TWP.—See BURLINGTON, VT (Comcast Cable)

PLAINFIELD—See DANVILLE (town), VT (Charter Communications)

PLYMOUTH—See BURLINGTON, VT (Comcast Cable)

POULTNEY—See BURLINGTON, VT (Comcast Cable)

POWNAL—See BENNINGTON, VT (Comcast Cable)

PROCTOR TWP.—See BURLINGTON, VT (Comcast Cable)

PROCTORSVILLE—See BURLINGTON, VT (Comcast Cable)

▲**PUTNEY**—Southern Vermont Cable Co.

RANDOLPH—See BURLINGTON, VT (Comcast Cable)

RAWSONVILLE—See PUTNEY, VT (Southern Vermont Cable Co.)

READING—See BURLINGTON, VT (Comcast Cable)

RICHFORD—See ENOSBURG FALLS, VT (Comcast Cable)

▲**RICHMOND**—Formerly served by Adelphia Communications. Now served by BURLINGTON, VT [VT0001]

RICHMOND—See BURLINGTON, VT (Comcast Cable)

RIVERTON—See NORTHFIELD (village), VT (Trans-Video Inc.)

▲**ROCHESTER**—Formerly served by Adelphia Communications. Now served by BURLINGTON, VT [VT0001]

ROCHESTER—See BURLINGTON, VT (Comcast Cable)

ROCKINGHAM—See BRATTLEBORO, VT (Comcast Cable)

▲**RUTLAND**—Comcast Cable. Now served by BURLINGTON, VT [VT0001]

▲**RUTLAND**—Formerly served by Satellite Signals of New England. No longer in operation

RUTLAND—See BURLINGTON, VT (Comcast Cable)

RYEGATE—See DANVILLE (town), VT (Charter Communications)

SALISBURY (TOWN)—See BURLINGTON, NH (Comcast Cable)

SANDGATE—See BENNINGTON, VT (Comcast Cable)

SAXTONS RIVER—See BRATTLEBORO, VT (Comcast Cable)

SHAFTSBURY—See BENNINGTON, VT (Comcast Cable)

SHEFFIELD—See DANVILLE (town), VT (Charter Communications)

SHELBURNE—See BURLINGTON, VT (Comcast Cable)

SHERBURNE (TOWN)—See BURLINGTON, VT (Comcast Cable)

SMUGGLERS NOTCH—See JEFFERSONVILLE, VT (Jeffersonville Cable TV Corp.)

SOUTH BURLINGTON—See BURLINGTON, VT (Comcast Cable)

SOUTH DORSET—See BENNINGTON, VT (Comcast Cable)

SOUTH LONDONDERRY—See BURLINGTON, VT (Comcast Cable)

SOUTH NEWFANE—See PUTNEY, VT (Southern Vermont Cable Co.)

SOUTH ROYALTON—See DANVILLE (town), VT (Charter Communications)

SOUTH RYEGATE—See DANVILLE (town), VT (Charter Communications)

▲**SPRINGFIELD**—Comcast Cable. Now served by BURLINGTON, VT [VT0001]

SPRINGFIELD—See BURLINGTON, VT (Comcast Cable)

ST. ALBANS (CITY)—See BURLINGTON, VT (Comcast Cable)

ST. GEORGE (TOWN)—See BURLINGTON, VT (Comcast Cable)

ST. JOHNSBURY CENTER—See DANVILLE (town), VT (Charter Communications)

ST. JOHNSBURY—See DANVILLE (town), VT (Charter Communications)

STARKSBORO TWP.—See BURLINGTON, VT (Comcast Cable)

▲**STOWE**—Stowe Cablevision, Inc.

STRATTON MOUNTAIN—See BENNINGTON, VT (Comcast Cable)

STRATTON—See BENNINGTON, VT (Comcast Cable)

SUNAPEE—See BURLINGTON, NH (Comcast Cable)

SUNDERLAND—See BENNINGTON, VT (Comcast Cable)

SUTTON—See DANVILLE (town), VT (Charter Communications)

SWANTON (VILLAGE)—See BURLINGTON, VT (Comcast Cable)

TAFTSVILLE—See BURLINGTON, VT (Comcast Cable)

▲**TOWNSHEND**—Southern Vermont Cable Co.

TROY TWP.—See BURLINGTON, VT (Comcast Cable)

TYSON—See BURLINGTON, VT (Comcast Cable)

UNDERHILL (TOWN)—See BURLINGTON, VT (Comcast Cable)

VERGENNES—See BURLINGTON, VT (Comcast Cable)

VERNON—See BRATTLEBORO, VT (Comcast Cable)

▲**WAITSFIELD**—Waitsfield Cable Co.

WALLINGFORD TWP.—See BURLINGTON, VT (Comcast Cable)

WARDSBORO TWP.—See WILMINGTON, VT (Duncan Cable TV Service)

WARREN—See WAITSFIELD, VT (Waitsfield Cable Co.)

WASHINGTON (TOWN)—See DANVILLE (town), VT (Charter Communications)

WASHINGTON COUNTY (PORTIONS)—See WAITSFIELD, VT (Waitsfield Cable Co.)

WATERBURY—See BURLINGTON, VT (Comcast Cable)

WATERFORD—See DANVILLE (town), VT (Charter Communications)

WEBSTERVILLE—See DANVILLE (town), VT (Charter Communications)

WELLS RIVER—See DANVILLE (town), VT (Charter Communications)

WEST ARLINGTON (PORTIONS)—See BENNINGTON, VT (Comcast Cable)

WEST BURKE—See DANVILLE (town), VT (Charter Communications)

▲**WEST DOVER**—Duncan Cable TV (formerly Area Telecable). Now served by WILMINGTON, VT [VT0017]

WEST DOVER—See WILMINGTON, VT (Duncan Cable TV Service)

WEST DUMMERSTON—See PUTNEY, VT (Southern Vermont Cable Co.)

WEST LEBANON—See BURLINGTON, NH (Comcast Cable)

WEST PAWLET—See BURLINGTON, VT (Comcast Cable)

WEST RUTLAND TWP.—See BURLINGTON, VT (Comcast Cable)

WEST TOWNSHEND—See TOWNSHEND, VT (Southern Vermont Cable Co.)

WESTMINSTER TWP.—See BRATTLEBORO, VT (Comcast Cable)

WESTON—See BURLINGTON, VT (Comcast Cable)

WEYBRIDGE (PORTIONS)—See BURLINGTON, VT (Comcast Cable)

WHEELOCK—See DANVILLE (town), VT (Charter Communications)

▲**WHITINGHAM**—Formerly served by Area Telecable. No longer in operation

▲**WILLIAMSTOWN (portions)**—Formerly served by North Valley Cable Systems Inc. No longer in operation

WILLIAMSTOWN—See DANVILLE (town), VT (Charter Communications)

WILLIAMSVILLE—See PUTNEY, VT (Southern Vermont Cable Co.)

WILLISTON—See BURLINGTON, VT (Comcast Cable)

▲**WILMINGTON**—Duncan Cable TV Service

WILMOT (TOWN)—See BURLINGTON, NH (Comcast Cable)

WINDSOR—See BURLINGTON, VT (Comcast Cable)

WINHALL—See BENNINGTON, VT (Comcast Cable)

WINOOSKI—See BURLINGTON, VT (Comcast Cable)

WOODBURY—See BURLINGTON, VT (Comcast Cable)

WOODFORD—See BENNINGTON, VT (Comcast Cable)

WOODSTOCK—See BURLINGTON, VT (Comcast Cable)

WOODSVILLE—See DANVILLE (town), NH (Charter Communications)

WORCESTER—See BURLINGTON, VT (Comcast Cable)

VIRGINIA

ABINGDON—See GLADE SPRING, VA (Comcast Cable)

▲**ACCOMAC**—Charter Communications

ACCOMACK COUNTY—See ACCOMAC, VA (Charter Communications)

ALBEMARLE COUNTY (PORTIONS)—See SCOTTSVILLE, VA (Nelson Cable)

ALBEMARLE COUNTY—See CHARLOTTESVILLE, VA (Comcast Cable)

ALBERTA—See LAWRENCEVILLE, VA (Shentel)

ALEXANDRIA (PORTIONS)—See FAIRFAX COUNTY, VA (Cox Communications)

▲**ALEXANDRIA**—Comcast Cable

ALLEGHANY COUNTY—See COVINGTON, VA (Shentel)

ALLEGHANY SPRINGS—See BLACKSBURG, VA (Comcast Cable)

ALTA VISTA—See RUSTBURG, VA (Shentel)

▲**ALTAVISTA**—Formerly served by Adelphia Communications. Now served by DANVILLE, VA [VA0012]

ALTAVISTA—See DANVILLE, VA (Comcast Cable)

▲**AMELIA COUNTY (PORTIONS)**—Comcast Cable

▲**AMHERST COUNTY (SOUTHERN PORTION)**—Comcast Cable

AMHERST—See AMHERST COUNTY (southern portion), VA (Comcast Cable)

ANNANDALE—See FAIRFAX COUNTY, VA (Cox Communications)

APPALACHIA—See NORTON, VA (Comcast Cable)

APPOMATTOX COUNTY (PORTIONS)—See RUSTBURG, VA (Shentel)

▲**APPOMATTOX**—Jet Broadband. Now served by RUSTBURG (formerly Timberlake), VA [VA0128]

APPOMATTOX—See RUSTBURG, VA (Shentel)

▲**ARLINGTON**—Comcast Cable

ASHLAND—See RICHMOND, VA (Comcast Cable)

ATKINS—See MARION, VA (Comcast Cable)

AUGUSTA COUNTY (PORTIONS)—See STAUNTON, VA (Comcast Cable)

AUGUSTA COUNTY (PORTIONS)—See WINTERGREEN, VA (Nelson Cable)

AUGUSTA SPRINGS—See STAUNTON, VA (Comcast Cable)

AUGUSTA—See STAUNTON, VA (Comcast Cable)

▲**AUSTINVILLE**—Citizens Telephone Coop. Now served by FORT CHISWELL, VA [VA0066]

AUSTINVILLE—See FORT CHISWELL, VA (Citizens Telephone Coop.)

AXTON—See MARTINSVILLE, VA (Comcast Cable)

AYLETT—See KING WILLIAM (portions), VA (Comcast Cable)

BACHELOR'S HALL—See BROSVILLE, VA (Chatmoss Cablevision)

BACOVA—See HOT SPRINGS, VA (Comcast Cable)

BALLSVILLE—See POWHATAN, VA (Comcast Cable)

BANDY—See RICHLANDS, VA (Time Warner Cable)

BANNER—See NORTON, VA (Comcast Cable)

BARBOURSVILLE—See RUCKERSVILLE, VA (Comcast Cable)

▲**BARREN SPRINGS**—Citizens Telephone Coop. Now served by FORT CHISWELL, VA [VA0066]

BARREN SPRINGS—See FORT CHISWELL, VA (Citizens Telephone Coop.)

BASSETT—See MARTINSVILLE, VA (Comcast Cable)

▲**BASTIAN**—Formerly served by Almega Cable. No longer in operation

BATH COUNTY—See HOT SPRINGS, VA (Comcast Cable)

BEALETON—See WARRENTON, VA (Comcast Cable)

BEDFORD COUNTY (NORTHERN PORTION)—See RUSTBURG, VA (Shentel)

BEDFORD COUNTY (PORTIONS)—See LYNCHBURG, VA (Comcast Cable)

BEDFORD COUNTY (PORTIONS)—See TROUTVILLE, VA (Comcast Cable)

BEDFORD COUNTY (SOUTHWESTERN PORTION)—See REDWOOD, VA (Suddenlink Communications)

▲**BEDFORD**—Charter Communications. Now served by REDWOOD (formerly Franklin County), VA [VA0033]

BEDFORD—See TROUTVILLE, VA (Comcast Cable)

BEDFORD—See REDWOOD, VA (Suddenlink Communications)

BELFAST MILLS—See ROSEDALE, VA (Cable Plus)

▲**BELLE HAVEN**—Charter Communications. Now served by ACCOMAC, VA [VA0158]

BELLE HAVEN—See ACCOMAC, VA (Charter Communications)

▲**BEN HUR**—Formerly served by Adelphia Communications. Now served by NORTON, VA [VA0157]

BEN HUR—See NORTON, VA (Comcast Cable)

BENTONVILLE—See FRONT ROYAL, VA (Comcast Cable)

BERRYVILLE—See WINCHESTER, VA (Comcast Cable)

BIG ROCK—See GRUNDY, VA (Time Warner Cable)

BIG STONE GAP—See NORTON, VA (Comcast Cable)

▲**BISHOP**—Bishop TV Club Inc. Now served by RICHLANDS, VA [VA0041]

BISHOP—See RICHLANDS, VA (Time Warner Cable)

▲**BLACKSBURG**—Comcast Cable

▲**BLACKSTONE**—Nesbe Cable TV. Now served by CREWE, VA [VA0099]

BLACKSTONE—See CREWE, VA (Shentel)

BLOXOM—See ACCOMAC, VA (Charter Communications)

BLUE RIDGE—See TROUTVILLE, VA (Comcast Cable)

BOLD CAMP—See NORTON, VA (Comcast Cable)

BOND TOWN—See NORTON, VA (Comcast Cable)

BOONES MILL—See REDWOOD, VA (Suddenlink Communications)

BOTETOURT COUNTY—See TROUTVILLE, VA (Comcast Cable)

▲**BOWLING GREEN**—MetroCast

BOYCE—See WINCHESTER, VA (Comcast Cable)

BOYDTON—See SOUTH HILL, VA (Comcast Cable)

BOYKINS—See SUFFOLK, VA (Charter Communications)

BRACEY—See LAKE GASTON, VA (CWA Cable)

BRANCHVILLE—See SUFFOLK, VA (Charter Communications)

BREAKS INTERSTATE PARK—See ROSEDALE, VA (Cable Plus)

BRIDGEWATER—See HARRISONBURG, VA (Comcast Cable)

▲**BRISTOL (portions)**—BVU OptiNet. This cable system has converted to IPTV. See Bristol (portions), VA [VA5201]

▲**BRISTOL**—Formerly [VA0190]. BVU OptiNet. This cable system has converted to IPTV

BRISTOW—See PRINCE WILLIAM COUNTY, VA (Comcast Cable)

BROADWAY—See HARRISONBURG, VA (Comcast Cable)

▲**BROOKNEAL**—Comcast Cable

▲**BROSVILLE**—Chatmoss Cablevision

BRUNSWICK COUNTY (PORTIONS)—See LAKE GASTON, VA (CWA Cable)

BRUNSWICK COUNTY—See LAWRENCEVILLE, VA (Shentel)

▲**BUCHANAN**—Shentel

BUCKINGHAM COUNTY (PORTIONS)—See DILLWYN, VA (Comcast Cable)

BUCKINGHAM COUNTY (PORTIONS)—See SCOTTSVILLE, VA (Nelson Cable)

▲**BUENA VISTA**—Formerly served by Adelphia Communications. Now served by LEXINGTON, VA [VA0147]

BUENA VISTA—See LEXINGTON, VA (Comcast Cable)

BURGESS—See NORTHUMBERLAND COUNTY, VA (MetroCast Communications)

BURKE—See FAIRFAX COUNTY, VA (Cox Communications)

BURKEVILLE—See CREWE, VA (Shentel)

▲**CALLAGHAN**—Clearview TV Cable

CALLAO—See NORTHUMBERLAND COUNTY, VA (MetroCast Communications)

CAMPBELL COUNTY—See LYNCHBURG, VA (Comcast Cable)

CARBO—See LEBANON (portions), VA (Almega Cable)

CAROLINE COUNTY (UNINCORPORATED AREAS)—See KING GEORGE, VA (MetroCast Communications)

CAROLINE COUNTY—See BOWLING GREEN, VA (MetroCast)

CARROLL COUNTY (PORTIONS)—See FORT CHISWELL, VA (Citizens Telephone Coop.)

CARROLL COUNTY (PORTIONS)—See GALAX, VA (Comcast Cable)

CARROLLTON—See SUFFOLK, VA (Charter Communications)

CASCADE—See BROSVILLE, VA (Chatmoss Cablevision)

CASTLETON—See FRONT ROYAL, VA (Comcast Cable)

CASTLEWOOD—See LEBANON (portions), VA (Almega Cable)

CASTLEWOOD—See LEBANON, VA (Shentel)

CASWELL COUNTY (PORTIONS)—See DANVILLE, NC (Comcast Cable)

CATHARPIN—See PRINCE WILLIAM COUNTY, VA (Comcast Cable)

CATLETT—See WARRENTON, VA (Comcast Cable)

CEDAR BLUFF—See RICHLANDS, VA (Time Warner Cable)

CENTRAL GARAGE—See KING WILLIAM (portions), VA (Comcast Cable)

CENTREVILLE—See FAIRFAX COUNTY, VA (Cox Communications)

CHAMBLISSBURG—See TROUTVILLE, VA (Comcast Cable)

CHANTILLY—See FAIRFAX COUNTY, VA (Cox Communications)

▲**CHARLES CITY COUNTY (PORTIONS)**—Comcast Cable

CHARLOTTE COUNTY (EASTERN PORTION)—See KEYSVILLE, VA (Shentel)

CHARLOTTE COURT HOUSE—See KEYSVILLE, VA (Shentel)

▲**CHARLOTTESVILLE**—Formerly served by NTELOS. No longer in operation

▲**CHARLOTTESVILLE**—Comcast Cable

▲**CHASE CITY**—Formerly served by Adelphia Communications. Now served by SOUTH HILL, VA [VA0062]

CHASE CITY—See SOUTH HILL, VA (Comcast Cable)

CHATHAM—See DANVILLE, VA (Comcast Cable)

CHERITON—See ACCOMAC, VA (Charter Communications)

▲**CHESAPEAKE**—Mediacom. Now served by CAMDEN/CURRITUCK (formerly Currituck County, southern portion), NC [NC0083]

CHESAPEAKE—See HAMPTON ROADS, VA (Cox Communications)

CHESTER GAP—See FRONT ROYAL, VA (Comcast Cable)

▲**CHESTERFIELD COUNTY**—Comcast Cable. Now served by RICHMOND, VA [VA0004]

CHESTERFIELD COUNTY—See RICHMOND, VA (Comcast Cable)

CHILHOWIE—See GLADE SPRING, VA (Comcast Cable)

▲**CHINCOTEAGUE ISLAND**—Charter Communications

CHRISTIANSBURG—See BLACKSBURG, VA (Comcast Cable)

CHRISTIANSBURG—See RADFORD, VA (Shentel)

CHURCHVILLE—See STAUNTON, VA (Comcast Cable)

▲**CLARAVILLE**—Formerly served by Adelphia Communications. No longer in operation

CLARION—See RUSTBURG, VA (Shentel)

CLARKE COUNTY—See WINCHESTER, VA (Comcast Cable)

▲**CLARKSVILLE**—Shentel

CLEVELAND—See LEBANON (portions), VA (Almega Cable)

CLIFTON FORGE—See COVINGTON, VA (Shentel)

CLIFTON—See FAIRFAX COUNTY, VA (Cox Communications)

CLINCHCO—See NORTON, VA (Comcast Cable)

CLINCHFIELD—See LEBANON (portions), VA (Almega Cable)

CLINCHPORT (PORTIONS)—See NORTON, VA (Comcast Cable)

▲**CLINTWOOD**—Formerly served by Adelphia Communications. Now served by NORTON, VA [VA0157]

CLINTWOOD—See NORTON, VA (Comcast Cable)

CLOVERDALE—See TROUTVILLE, VA (Comcast Cable)

COEBURN—See NORTON, VA (Comcast Cable)

COLLINSVILLE—See MARTINSVILLE, VA (Comcast Cable)

▲**COLONIAL BEACH**—MetroCast

COLONIAL HEIGHTS—See PETERSBURG, VA (Comcast Cable)

CONCORD—See RUSTBURG, VA (Shentel)

COURTLAND—See SUFFOLK, VA (Charter Communications)

▲**COVINGTON**—Shentel

CRAB ORCHARD—See NORTON, VA (Comcast Cable)

CRAIG COUNTY (PORTIONS)—See NEW CASTLE (town), VA (Citizens Telephone Coop.)

▲**CRAIGSVILLE**—Formerly served by Adelphia Communications. Now served by STAUNTON, VA [VA0026]

CRAIGSVILLE—See STAUNTON, VA (Comcast Cable)

▲**CRAWFORD MANOR**—Crawford Manor Cable TV

▲**CREWE**—Shentel

CRIMORA—See STAUNTON, VA (Comcast Cable)

CROCKETT—See SPEEDWELL, VA (R&S Communications LLC)

▲**CROZET**—Formerly served by Adelphia Communications. Now served by CHARLOTTESVILLE, VA [VA0131]

CROZET—See CHARLOTTESVILLE, VA (Comcast Cable)

▲**CULPEPER COUNTY**—Comcast Cable

▲**CULPEPER**—Formerly served by Adelphia Communications. Now served by CULPEPER COUNTY, VA [VA0182]

CULPEPER—See CULPEPER COUNTY, VA (Comcast Cable)

CUMBERLAND COUNTY (SOUTHWESTERN PORTION)—See FARMVILLE, VA (Shentel)

DAHLGREN—See KING GEORGE, VA (MetroCast Communications)

DALE CITY—See PRINCE WILLIAM COUNTY, VA (Comcast Cable)

DALEVILLE—See TROUTVILLE, VA (Comcast Cable)

▲**DAMASCUS**—Zito Media

DANIEL BOONE—See GATE CITY, VA (Scott Telecom & Electronics)

DANTE—See LEBANON, VA (Shentel)

▲**DANVILLE**—Comcast Cable

DAYTON—See HARRISONBURG, VA (Comcast Cable)

DELTAVILLE—See MIDDLESEX COUNTY, VA (MetroCast Communications)

DESKINS—See GRUNDY, VA (Time Warner Cable)

DICKENSON COUNTY—See NORTON, VA (Comcast Cable)

▲**DILLWYN**—Comcast Cable

DINWIDDIE—See PETERSBURG (unincorporated areas), VA (Comcast Cable)

DORAN—See RICHLANDS, VA (Time Warner Cable)

DRAKES BRANCH—See KEYSVILLE, VA (Shentel)

DRY FORK—See BROSVILLE, VA (Chatmoss Cablevision)

DUBLIN—See PULASKI, VA (Comcast Cable)

▲**DUFFIELD**—Formerly served by Adelphia Communications. Now served by NORTON, VA [VA0157]

DUFFIELD—See NORTON, VA (Comcast Cable)

DUMFRIES—See PRINCE WILLIAM COUNTY, VA (Comcast Cable)

EASTVILLE—See ACCOMAC, VA (Charter Communications)

▲**EDINBURG**—Shentel

EDWARDSVILLE—See NORTHUMBERLAND COUNTY, VA (MetroCast Communications)

ELKTON—See HARRISONBURG, VA (Comcast Cable)

ELLISTON—See BLACKSBURG, VA (Comcast Cable)

ELTHAM—See HAMPTON ROADS, VA (Cox Communications)

▲**EMPORIA**—Comcast Cable

ESSERVILLE—See NORTON, VA (Comcast Cable)

ESSEX COUNTY (PORTIONS)—See TAPPAHANNOCK, VA (MetroCast)

EVINGTON—See RUSTBURG, VA (Shentel)

▲**EWING**—Zito Media

EXMORE—See ACCOMAC, VA (Charter Communications)

▲**FAIRFAX COUNTY**—Cox Communications

FAIRFAX STATION—See FAIRFAX COUNTY, VA (Cox Communications)

FAIRFAX—See FAIRFAX COUNTY, VA (Cox Communications)

FAIRLAWN—See RADFORD, VA (Shentel)

▲**FALLS CHURCH**—RCN Corp. This cable system has converted to IPTV. See Falls Church, VA [VA5184]

FALLS CHURCH—See FAIRFAX COUNTY, VA (Cox Communications)

▲**FALLS CHURCH**—RCN Corp. Formerly [VA0194]. This cable system has converted to IPTV

▲**FARMVILLE**—Shentel

FERRUM—See REDWOOD, VA (Suddenlink Communications)

FIELDALE—See MARTINSVILLE, VA (Comcast Cable)

FINCASTLE—See TROUTVILLE, VA (Comcast Cable)

FISHERSVILLE—See STAUNTON, VA (Comcast Cable)

FLAT ROCK—See POWHATAN, VA (Comcast Cable)

FLOYD COUNTY—See FLOYD, VA (Citizens Telephone Coop.)

▲**FLOYD**—Citizens Telephone Coop.

FLUVANNA COUNTY (PORTIONS)—See SCOTTSVILLE, VA (Nelson Cable)

FOREST—See RUSTBURG, VA (Shentel)

▲**FORT A.P. HILL**—GMP Communications LP. Now served by KING GEORGE, VA [VA0058]

FORT A.P. HILL—See KING GEORGE, VA (MetroCast Communications)

▲**FORT BELVOIR ARMY BASE**—Comcast Cable

▲**FORT CHISWELL**—Citizens Telephone Coop. Now served by FORT CHISWELLI, VA [VA0066]

▲**FORT CHISWELL**—Citizens Telephone Coop.

FORT EUSTIS ARMY BASE—See HAMPTON ROADS, VA (Cox Communications)

FORT LEE—See PETERSBURG, VA (Comcast Cable)

FORT MONROE—See HAMPTON ROADS, VA (Cox Communications)

FORT MYER ARMY BASE—See ARLINGTON, VA (Comcast Cable)

FORT STORY—See HAMPTON ROADS, VA (Cox Communications)

FRANKLIN COUNTY (PORTIONS)—See FLOYD, VA (Citizens Telephone Coop.)

FRANKLIN COUNTY—See REDWOOD, VA (Suddenlink Communications)

▲**FRANKLIN**—Charter Communications. Now served by SUFFOLK, VA [VA0025]

FRANKLIN—See SUFFOLK, VA (Charter Communications)

FREDERICK COUNTY—See WINCHESTER, VA (Comcast Cable)

▲**FREDERICKSBURG**—Cox Communications

FRIES—See GALAX, VA (Comcast Cable)

▲**FRONT ROYAL**—Comcast Cable

GAINESVILLE—See PRINCE WILLIAM COUNTY, VA (Comcast Cable)

▲**GALAX**—Comcast Cable

GARRISONVILLE—See SPOTSYLVANIA, VA (Comcast Cable)

▲**GATE CITY**—Scott Telecom & Electronics

▲**GLADE SPRING**—Comcast Cable

GLADEHILL—See REDWOOD, VA (Suddenlink Communications)

▲**GLASGOW**—Formerly served by Adelphia Communications. Now served by LEXINGTON, VA [VA0147]

GLASGOW—See LEXINGTON, VA (Comcast Cable)

GLENWOOD—See DANVILLE, VA (Comcast Cable)

▲**GLOUCESTER COUNTY**—Cox Communications. Now served by HAMPTON ROADS (formerly Virginia Beach), VA [VA0002]

GLOUCESTER COUNTY—See HAMPTON ROADS, VA (Cox Communications)

GOOCHLAND COUNTY—See RICHMOND, VA (Comcast Cable)

GOOCHLAND—See RICHMOND, VA (Comcast Cable)

GOODE—See RUSTBURG, VA (Shentel)

GOODVIEW—See TROUTVILLE, VA (Comcast Cable)

▲**GORDONSVILLE**—Comcast Cable

▲**GOSHEN**—Comcast Cable

GRAFTON—See HAMPTON ROADS, VA (Cox Communications)

GRATTON—See RICHLANDS, VA (Time Warner Cable)

GRAYSON COUNTY (PORTIONS)—See GALAX, VA (Comcast Cable)

GREAT FALLS—See FAIRFAX COUNTY, VA (Cox Communications)

GREENE COUNTY—See RUCKERSVILLE, VA (Comcast Cable)

GREENSVILLE COUNTY—See EMPORIA, VA (Comcast Cable)

GREENVILLE—See STAUNTON, VA (Comcast Cable)

GRETNA—See DANVILLE, VA (Comcast Cable)

GROTTOES—See STAUNTON, VA (Comcast Cable)

▲**GRUNDY**—Time Warner Cable

HALIFAX COUNTY—See SOUTH BOSTON, VA (Comcast Cable)

HALIFAX—See SOUTH BOSTON, VA (Comcast Cable)

HALLWOOD—See ACCOMAC, VA (Charter Communications)

HAMILTON—See LOUDOUN COUNTY, VA (Comcast Cable)

HAMPDEN SYDNEY—See FARMVILLE, VA (Shentel)

▲**HAMPTON ROADS**—Cox Communications

HAMPTON—See HAMPTON ROADS, VA (Cox Communications)

HANOVER COUNTY (PORTIONS)—See RICHMOND, VA (Comcast Cable)

HANSONVILLE—See LEBANON (portions), VA (Almega Cable)

HARMAN—See GRUNDY, VA (Time Warner Cable)

▲**HARRISONBURG**—Formerly served by NTELOS. No longer in operation

▲**HARRISONBURG**—Comcast Cable

HARRISTON—See STAUNTON, VA (Comcast Cable)

HAYMARKET—See PRINCE WILLIAM COUNTY, VA (Comcast Cable)

▲**HAYSI**—Formerly served by K & V Cable TV Co. No longer in operation

HEATHSVILLE—See NORTHUMBERLAND COUNTY, VA (MetroCast Communications)

HENRICO COUNTY (PORTIONS)—See RICHMOND, VA (Comcast Cable)

▲**HENRICO COUNTY**—Comcast Cable. Now served by RICHMOND, VA [VA0004]

HENRY COUNTY—See MARTINSVILLE, VA (Comcast Cable)

HERNDON—See FAIRFAX COUNTY, VA (Cox Communications)

HILLSVILLE—See GALAX, VA (Comcast Cable)

HILTONS—See GATE CITY, VA (Scott Telecom & Electronics)

HONAKER—See LEBANON, VA (Shentel)

HOPEWELL—See PETERSBURG, VA (Comcast Cable)

HORSE PASTURE—See MARTINSVILLE, VA (Comcast Cable)

HOT SPRINGS—See CALLAGHAN, VA (Clearview TV Cable)

▲**HOT SPRINGS**—Comcast Cable

HUDDLESTON—See TROUTVILLE, VA (Comcast Cable)

HUNTLY—See FRONT ROYAL, VA (Comcast Cable)

HURLEY—See GRUNDY, VA (Time Warner Cable)

▲**HURT**—Formerly served by Adelphia Communications. Now served by DANVILLE, VA [VA0012]

HURT—See DANVILLE, VA (Comcast Cable)

▲**INDEPENDENCE**—Formerly served by Adelphia Communications. Now served by GALAX, VA [VA0140]

INDEPENDENCE—See GALAX, VA (Comcast Cable)

INDIAN CREEK—See NORTON, VA (Comcast Cable)

IRON GATE—See COVINGTON, VA (Shentel)

IRVINGTON (TOWN)—See LANCASTER COUNTY, VA (MetroCast Communications)

ISLE OF WIGHT COUNTY—See SUFFOLK, VA (Charter Communications)

▲**IVANHOE**—Citizens Telephone Coop. Now served by FORT CHISWELL, VA [VA0066]

IVANHOE—See FORT CHISWELL, VA (Citizens Telephone Coop.)

IVOR—See SUFFOLK, VA (Charter Communications)

▲**JAMES CITY COUNTY**—Cox Communications. Now served by HAMPTON ROADS (formerly Virginia Beach), VA [VA0002]

JAMES CITY COUNTY—See HAMPTON ROADS, VA (Cox Communications)

▲**JARRATT**—CWA Cable

JASPER (PORTIONS)—See NORTON, VA (Comcast Cable)

JEFFERSON—See POWHATAN, VA (Comcast Cable)

JOHNSON CREEK—See CALLAGHAN, VA (Clearview TV Cable)

▲**JONESVILLE**—CC & S Cable TV. Now served by NORTON, VA [VA0157]

JONESVILLE—See NORTON, VA (Comcast Cable)

JOSEPHINE—See NORTON, VA (Comcast Cable)

▲**KEEN MOUNTAIN**—Time Warner Cable

KELLER—See ACCOMAC, VA (Charter Communications)

▲**KENBRIDGE**—Shentel

KEOKEE—See NORTON, VA (Comcast Cable)

▲**KEYSVILLE**—Shentel

KILMARNOCK (TOWN)—See LANCASTER COUNTY, VA (MetroCast Communications)

KING & QUEEN COUNTY (PORTIONS)—See HAMPTON ROADS, VA (Cox Communications)

▲**KING GEORGE**—MetroCast Communications

▲**KING WILLIAM (PORTIONS)**—Comcast Cable

LA CROSSE—See SOUTH HILL, VA (Comcast Cable)

▲**LACEY SPRING**—Formerly served by Adelphia Communications. Now served by HARRISONBURG, VA [VA0016]

LACEY SPRING—See HARRISONBURG, VA (Comcast Cable)

LADYSMITH—See RUTHER GLEN, VA (Comcast Cable)

LAFAYETTE—See BLACKSBURG, VA (Comcast Cable)

▲**LAKE GASTON**—CWA Cable

LAKE MONTICELLO—See CHARLOTTESVILLE, VA (Comcast Cable)

LAKE OF THE WOODS—See SPOTSYLVANIA, VA (Comcast Cable)

LAKE RIDGE—See PRINCE WILLIAM COUNTY, VA (Comcast Cable)

▲**LANCASTER COUNTY**—MetroCast Communications

LANEXA—See HAMPTON ROADS, VA (Cox Communications)

▲**LANGLEY AFB**—Cox Communications. Now served by HAMPTON ROADS (formerly Virginia Beach), VA [VA0002]

LANGLEY AFB—See HAMPTON ROADS, VA (Cox Communications)

▲**LAWRENCEVILLE**—Shentel

▲**LEBANON (PORTIONS)**—Almega Cable

▲**LEBANON**—Shentel

LEE COUNTY—See NORTON, VA (Comcast Cable)

LEESBURG—See LOUDOUN COUNTY, VA (Comcast Cable)

LEWISETTA—See NORTHUMBERLAND COUNTY, VA (MetroCast Communications)

▲**LEXINGTON**—Comcast Cable

LORTON—See FAIRFAX COUNTY, VA (Cox Communications)

LOTTSBURG—See NORTHUMBERLAND COUNTY, VA (MetroCast Communications)

▲**LOUDOUN COUNTY**—Comcast Cable

LOUISA COUNTY—See RICHMOND, VA (Comcast Cable)

▲**LOUISA**—Comcast Cable. Now served by RICHMOND, VA [VA0004]

LOUISA—See RICHMOND, VA (Comcast Cable)

LOVETTSVILLE—See LOUDOUN COUNTY, VA (Comcast Cable)

▲**LOVINGSTON/SHIPMAN**—Nelson Cable

LUNENBURG COUNTY (PORTIONS)—See SOUTH HILL, VA (Comcast Cable)

LUNENBURG COUNTY (PORTIONS)—See KENBRIDGE, VA (Shentel)

▲**LURAY**—Comcast Cable

▲**LYNCHBURG**—Comcast Cable

MACON—See POWHATAN, VA (Comcast Cable)

MADISON COUNTY—See MADISON, VA (Comcast Cable)

▲**MADISON**—Comcast Cable

MANASSAS—See PRINCE WILLIAM COUNTY, VA (Comcast Cable)

▲**MARION**—Comcast Cable

MARSHALL—See WARRENTON, VA (Comcast Cable)

▲**MARTINSVILLE**—Comcast Cable

MATHEWS COUNTY—See MATHEWS, VA (Comcast Cable)

▲**MATHEWS**—Comcast Cable

MATTAPONI—See HAMPTON ROADS, VA (Cox Communications)

MAURERTOWN—See EDINBURG, VA (Shentel)

MAVISDALE—See KEEN MOUNTAIN, VA (Time Warner Cable)

▲**MAX MEADOWS**—See Fort Chiswell, VA [VA0066]

MAX MEADOWS—See FORT CHISWELL, VA (Citizens Telephone Coop.)

MAXIE—See GRUNDY, VA (Time Warner Cable)

MAYTOWN—See NORTON, VA (Comcast Cable)

MCGAHEYSVILLE—See HARRISONBURG, VA (Comcast Cable)

▲**MCKENNEY**—Formerly served by Adelphia Communications. Now served by PETERSBURG (unincorporated areas), VA [VA0186]

MCKENNEY—See PETERSBURG (unincorporated areas), VA (Comcast Cable)

MCLEAN—See FAIRFAX COUNTY, VA (Cox Communications)

MECKLENBURG COUNTY (PORTIONS)—See LAKE GASTON, VA (CWA Cable)

MECKLENBURG COUNTY (PORTIONS)—See CLARKSVILLE, VA (Shentel)

MECKLENBURG COUNTY—See SOUTH HILL, VA (Comcast Cable)

MELFA—See ACCOMAC, VA (Charter Communications)

MIDDLEBURG—See LOUDOUN COUNTY, VA (Comcast Cable)

▲**MIDDLESEX COUNTY**—MetroCast Communications

MINERAL—See RICHMOND, VA (Comcast Cable)

MINT SPRING—See STAUNTON, VA (Comcast Cable)

MONETA—See TROUTVILLE, VA (Comcast Cable)

MONETA—See REDWOOD, VA (Suddenlink Communications)

MONTCLAIR—See PRINCE WILLIAM COUNTY, VA (Comcast Cable)

▲**MONTEREY**—Formerly served by Highland Communications. No longer in operation

MONTGOMERY COUNTY (PORTIONS)—See FLOYD, VA (Citizens Telephone Coop.)

MONTGOMERY COUNTY—See BLACKSBURG, VA (Comcast Cable)

MONTGOMERY COUNTY—See RADFORD, VA (Shentel)

MONTROSS—See WESTMORELAND COUNTY, VA (Comcast Cable)

MONTVALE—See TROUTVILLE, VA (Comcast Cable)

▲ **MOUNT CLINTON**—Formerly served by Adelphia Communications. Now served by HARRISONBURG, VA [VA0016]

MOUNT CLINTON—See HARRISONBURG, VA (Comcast Cable)

MOUNT CRAWFORD—See HARRISONBURG, VA (Comcast Cable)

MOUNT JACKSON—See EDINBURG, VA (Shentel)

MOUNT SIDNEY—See LURAY, VA (Comcast Cable)

NACE—See TROUTVILLE, VA (Comcast Cable)

NASSAWODOX—See ACCOMAC, VA (Charter Communications)

NELSON COUNTY (PORTIONS)—See WINTERGREEN, VA (Nelson Cable)

▲ **NEW CASTLE (TOWN)**—Citizens Telephone Coop.

NEW HOPE—See STAUNTON, VA (Comcast Cable)

NEW KENT COUNTY (PORTIONS)—See HAMPTON ROADS, VA (Cox Communications)

▲ **NEW KENT**—Cox Communications. Now served by HAMPTON ROADS (formerly Virginia Beach), VA [VA0002]

NEW KENT—See HAMPTON ROADS, VA (Cox Communications)

NEW MARKET—See EDINBURG, VA (Shentel)

NEWPORT NEWS—See HAMPTON ROADS, VA (Cox Communications)

NEWSOMS—See SUFFOLK, VA (Charter Communications)

▲ **NICKELSVILLE**—Formerly served by Scott Telecom & Electronics. No longer in operation

NICKELSVILLE—See GATE CITY, VA (Scott Telecom & Electronics)

NOKESVILLE—See PRINCE WILLIAM COUNTY, VA (Comcast Cable)

NORFOLK NAVAL BASE/SOUTHSIDE HAMPTON ROADS—See HAMPTON ROADS, VA (Cox Communications)

NORFOLK—See HAMPTON ROADS, VA (Cox Communications)

NORTH TAZEWELL—See RICHLANDS, VA (Time Warner Cable)

NORTHAMPTON COUNTY—See ACCOMAC, VA (Charter Communications)

NORTHUMBERLAND COUNTY (PORTIONS)—See LANCASTER COUNTY, VA (MetroCast Communications)

▲ **NORTHUMBERLAND COUNTY**—MetroCast Communications

▲ **NORTON**—Comcast Cable

OAKTON—See FAIRFAX COUNTY, VA (Cox Communications)

OAKWOOD—See KEEN MOUNTAIN, VA (Time Warner Cable)

OCCOQUAN—See PRINCE WILLIAM COUNTY, VA (Comcast Cable)

OLDTOWN—See GALAX, VA (Comcast Cable)

ONANCOCK—See ACCOMAC, VA (Charter Communications)

ONLEY—See ACCOMAC, VA (Charter Communications)

OPHELIA—See NORTHUMBERLAND COUNTY, VA (MetroCast Communications)

ORANGE COUNTY (EASTERN PORTION)—See SPOTSYLVANIA, VA (Comcast Cable)

ORANGE COUNTY (PORTIONS)—See GORDONSVILLE, VA (Comcast Cable)

ORANGE COUNTY—See ORANGE, VA (Comcast Cable)

▲ **ORANGE**—Comcast Cable

PAGE CITY—See LURAY, VA (Comcast Cable)

PAGE COUNTY (PORTIONS)—See HARRISONBURG, VA (Comcast Cable)

PAINT LICK—See RICHLANDS, VA (Time Warner Cable)

PAINTER—See ACCOMAC, VA (Charter Communications)

▲ **PALMYRA**—Comcast Cable

PAMPLIN—See CREWE, VA (Shentel)

PARKSLEY—See ACCOMAC, VA (Charter Communications)

PATRICK COUNTY (PORTIONS)—See FLOYD, VA (Citizens Telephone Coop.)

PATRICK SPRINGS—See STUART, VA (Comcast Cable)

▲ **PEARISBURG**—Charter Communications. Now served by BECKLEY, WV [WV0005]

PENHOOK—See REDWOOD, VA (Suddenlink Communications)

▲ **PENNINGTON GAP**—Formerly served by Adelphia Communications. Now served by NORTON, VA [VA0157]

PENNINGTON GAP—See NORTON, VA (Comcast Cable)

▲ **PETERSBURG (UNINCORPORATED AREAS)**—Comcast Cable

▲ **PETERSBURG**—Comcast Cable

PHENIX—See KEYSVILLE, VA (Shentel)

PILGRIMS KNOB—See KEEN MOUNTAIN, VA (Time Warner Cable)

PITTSYLVANIA COUNTY (NORTHWESTERN PORTION)—See REDWOOD, VA (Suddenlink Communications)

PITTSYLVANIA COUNTY—See DANVILLE, VA (Comcast Cable)

POOR VALLEY—See NORTON, VA (Comcast Cable)

▲ **POQUOSON**—Cox Communications. Now served by HAMPTON ROADS (formerly Virginia Beach), VA [VA0002]

POQUOSON—See HAMPTON ROADS, VA (Cox Communications)

PORT ROYAL—See KING GEORGE, VA (MetroCast Communications)

PORTSMOUTH—See HAMPTON ROADS, VA (Cox Communications)

POUNDING MILL—See RICHLANDS, VA (Time Warner Cable)

POWHATAN COUNTY—See POWHATAN, VA (Comcast Cable)

▲ **POWHATAN**—Comcast Cable

PRINCE EDWARD COUNTY (NORTHWESTERN PORTION)—See FARMVILLE, VA (Shentel)

PRINCE GEORGE COUNTY (PORTIONS)—See PETERSBURG, VA (Comcast Cable)

▲ **PRINCE GEORGE**—Formerly served by Adelphia Communications. Now served by PETERSBURG, VA [VA0015]

PRINCE GEORGE—See PETERSBURG, VA (Comcast Cable)

▲ **PRINCE WILLIAM COUNTY**—Comcast Cable

PROVIDENCE FORGE—See HAMPTON ROADS, VA (Cox Communications)

PROVOST—See POWHATAN, VA (Comcast Cable)

PULASKI COUNTY (PORTIONS)—See RADFORD, VA (Shentel)

PULASKI COUNTY—See PULASKI, VA (Comcast Cable)

▲ **PULASKI**—Comcast Cable

PURCELLVILLE—See LOUDOUN COUNTY, VA (Comcast Cable)

QUANTICO—See PRINCE WILLIAM COUNTY, VA (Comcast Cable)

QUINTON—See HAMPTON ROADS, VA (Cox Communications)

▲ **RADFORD**—Shentel

RAVEN—See RICHLANDS, VA (Time Warner Cable)

RAWLEY SPRINGS—See HARRISONBURG, VA (Comcast Cable)

RED ASH—See RICHLANDS, VA (Time Warner Cable)

▲ **REDWOOD**—Suddenlink Communications

REEDVILLE—See NORTHUMBERLAND COUNTY, VA (MetroCast Communications)

REMINGTON—See WARRENTON, VA (Comcast Cable)

▲ **RESTON**—Comcast Cable

▲ **RICHLANDS**—Time Warner Cable

▲ **RICHMOND**—Formerly served by NTELOS. No longer in operation

▲ **RICHMOND**—Comcast Cable

RIDGEWAY—See MARTINSVILLE, VA (Comcast Cable)

RINGGOLD—See DANVILLE, VA (Comcast Cable)

▲ **RIVER OAKS**—Comcast Cable. Now served by PRINCE WILLIAM COUNTY (formerly Manassas), VA [VA0148]

RIVER OAKS—See PRINCE WILLIAM COUNTY, VA (Comcast Cable)

RIVERTON—See FRONT ROYAL, VA (Comcast Cable)

RIVERVIEW—See NORTON, VA (Comcast Cable)

ROANOKE COUNTY—See SALEM, VA (Comcast Cable)

ROANOKE COUNTY—See ROANOKE, VA (Cox Communications)

▲ **ROANOKE**—Formerly served by NTELOS. No longer in operation

▲ **ROANOKE**—Cox Communications

ROCKBRIDGE COUNTY—See LEXINGTON, VA (Comcast Cable)

ROCKFISH—See WINTERGREEN, VA (Nelson Cable)

ROCKINGHAM COUNTY—See HARRISONBURG, VA (Comcast Cable)

▲ **ROCKINGHAM**—Formerly served by Adelphia Communications. Now served by HARRISONBURG, VA [VA0016]

ROCKINGHAM—See HARRISONBURG, VA (Comcast Cable)

ROCKY MOUNT—See REDWOOD, VA (Suddenlink Communications)

ROSE HILL—See EWING, VA (Zito Media)

▲ **ROSEDALE**—Cable Plus

ROUND HILL—See LOUDOUN COUNTY, VA (Comcast Cable)

ROYAL CITY—See RICHLANDS, VA (Time Warner Cable)

▲ **RUCKERSVILLE**—Comcast Cable

RURAL RETREAT (PORTIONS)—See SPEEDWELL, VA (R&S Communications LLC)

▲ **RURAL RETREAT**—Rural Retreat Cable TV Inc.

RUSHMERE—See SUFFOLK, VA (Charter Communications)

RUSSELL COUNTY—See LEBANON, VA (Shentel)

▲ **RUSTBURG**—Shentel

▲ **RUTHER GLEN**—Comcast Cable

▲ **SALEM**—Comcast Cable

SALTVILLE—See GLADE SPRING, VA (Comcast Cable)

SALUDA—See MIDDLESEX COUNTY, VA (MetroCast Communications)

▲ **SANDY RIDGE**—Scott Telecom & Electronics

SAXIS—See ACCOMAC, VA (Charter Communications)

▲ **SCOTTSVILLE**—Nelson Cable

SCRUGGS—See REDWOOD, VA (Suddenlink Communications)

SEVEN MILE FORD—See GLADE SPRING, VA (Comcast Cable)

SHACKLEFORDS—See HAMPTON ROADS, VA (Cox Communications)

SHAWSVILLE—See BLACKSBURG, VA (Comcast Cable)

SHENANDOAH COUNTY—See EDINBURG, VA (Shentel)

▲ **SHENANDOAH**—Formerly served by Adelphia Communications. Now served by HARRISONBURG, VA [VA0016]

SHENANDOAH—See HARRISONBURG, VA (Comcast Cable)

SHIPMAN—See LOVINGSTON/SHIPMAN, VA (Nelson Cable)

SMITH MOUNTAIN LAKE—See REDWOOD, VA (Suddenlink Communications)

SMITHFIELD—See SUFFOLK, VA (Charter Communications)

SMYTH COUNTY—See GLADE SPRING, VA (Comcast Cable)

SMYTH COUNTY—See MARION, VA (Comcast Cable)

▲ **SOUTH BOSTON**—Comcast Cable

▲ **SOUTH HILL**—Comcast Cable

SOUTHAMPTON COUNTY—See SUFFOLK, VA (Charter Communications)

SOUTHRIDGE—See PRINCE WILLIAM COUNTY, VA (Comcast Cable)

▲ **SPEEDWELL**—R&S Communications LLC

SPOTSYLVANIA COUNTY (NORTHERN PORTION)—See SPOTSYLVANIA, VA (Comcast Cable)

SPOTSYLVANIA COUNTY—See FREDERICKSBURG, VA (Cox Communications)

▲ **SPOTSYLVANIA**—Comcast Cable

SPRING CITY—See LEBANON (portions), VA (Almega Cable)

SPRINGFIELD—See FAIRFAX COUNTY, VA (Cox Communications)

ST. PAUL—See LEBANON, VA (Shentel)

STACY—See GRUNDY, VA (Time Warner Cable)

STAFFORD COUNTY (NORTHERN PORTION)—See SPOTSYLVANIA, VA (Comcast Cable)

STAFFORD COUNTY (SOUTHERN PORTION)—See FREDERICKSBURG, VA (Cox Communications)

STANARDSVILLE—See RUCKERSVILLE, VA (Comcast Cable)

STANLEY—See LURAY, VA (Comcast Cable)

STANLEYTOWN—See MARTINSVILLE, VA (Comcast Cable)

▲ **STAUNTON**—Comcast Cable

STEELBURG—See RICHLANDS, VA (Time Warner Cable)

STEELES TAVERN—See STAUNTON, VA (Comcast Cable)

STEPHENS CITY—See WINCHESTER, VA (Comcast Cable)

STEPHENS—See NORTON, VA (Comcast Cable)

STERLING—See LOUDOUN COUNTY, VA (Comcast Cable)

STEWARTSVILLE—See TROUTVILLE, VA (Comcast Cable)

STRASBURG—See EDINBURG, VA (Shentel)

▲ **STUART**—Comcast Cable

STUARTS DRAFT—See STAUNTON, VA (Comcast Cable)

▲ **SUFFOLK**—Charter Communications

SUGAR GROVE—See GLADE SPRING, VA (Comcast Cable)

SUSSEX COUNTY—See SUFFOLK, VA (Charter Communications)

SWORDS CREEK—See LEBANON, VA (Shentel)

SWORDS CREEK—See RICHLANDS, VA (Time Warner Cable)

▲ **TANGIER ISLAND**—Charter Communications

▲ **TAPPAHANNOCK**—MetroCast

▲ **TAZEWELL**—Formerly served by Adelphia Communications. Now served by RICHLANDS, VA [VA0041]

TAZEWELL—See RICHLANDS, VA (Time Warner Cable)

THAXTON—See TROUTVILLE, VA (Comcast Cable)

TIMBERLAKE—See RUSTBURG, VA (Shentel)

TIMBERVILLE—See HARRISONBURG, VA (Comcast Cable)

TIPTOP—See RICHLANDS, VA (Time Warner Cable)

TOMS BROOK—See EDINBURG, VA (Shentel)

TRIANGLE—See PRINCE WILLIAM COUNTY, VA (Comcast Cable)

▲ **TROUTVILLE**—Comcast Cable

TUNSTALL (PITTSYLVANIA COUNTY)—See BROSVILLE, VA (Chatmoss Cablevision)

U.S. COAST GUARD 5TH DISTRICT—See HAMPTON ROADS, VA (Cox Communications)

U.S. COAST GUARD SUPPORT CENTER—See HAMPTON ROADS, VA (Cox Communications)

UNION HALL—See REDWOOD, VA (Suddenlink Communications)

URBANNA—See MIDDLESEX COUNTY, VA (MetroCast Communications)

VANDOLA—See BROSVILLE, VA (Chatmoss Cablevision)

VANSANT—See GRUNDY, VA (Time Warner Cable)

VERONA—See STAUNTON, VA (Comcast Cable)

▲ **VICTORIA**—Formerly served by Adelphia Communications. Now served by SOUTH HILL, VA [VA0062]

VICTORIA—See SOUTH HILL, VA (Comcast Cable)

VIENNA—See FAIRFAX COUNTY, VA (Cox Communications)

VILLA HEIGHTS—See MARTINSVILLE, VA (Comcast Cable)

VINTON—See ROANOKE, VA (Cox Communications)

VIRGINIA BEACH—See HAMPTON ROADS, VA (Cox Communications)

WACHAPREAGUE—See ACCOMAC, VA (Charter Communications)

WAKEFIELD—See SUFFOLK, VA (Charter Communications)

WALMSLEY—See NORTHUMBERLAND COUNTY, VA (MetroCast Communications)

WARDELL—See RICHLANDS, VA (Time Warner Cable)

WARM SPRINGS—See HOT SPRINGS, VA (Comcast Cable)

WARREN COUNTY—See FRONT ROYAL, VA (Comcast Cable)

▲ **WARRENTON**—Comcast Cable

▲ **WARSAW**—MetroCast

▲ **WASHINGTON COUNTY (PORTIONS)**—Formerly served by BRISTOL (portions), VA [VA0190]. BVU OptiNet. This cable system has converted to IPTV

WASHINGTON COUNTY—See GLADE SPRING, VA (Comcast Cable)

WASHINGTON—See FRONT ROYAL, VA (Comcast Cable)

WATER VIEW—See MIDDLESEX COUNTY, VA (MetroCast Communications)

WAVERLY—See SUFFOLK, VA (Charter Communications)

WAYNESBORO—See STAUNTON, VA (Comcast Cable)

WEBER CITY—See GATE CITY, VA (Scott Telecom & Electronics)

WEST POINT—See HAMPTON ROADS, VA (Cox Communications)

WESTMORELAND COUNTY (UNINCORPORATED AREAS)—See COLONIAL BEACH, VA (MetroCast)

▲ **WESTMORELAND COUNTY**—Comcast Cable

WESTMORELAND SHORES—See COLONIAL BEACH, VA (MetroCast)

WESTMORELAND—See WESTMORELAND COUNTY, VA (Comcast Cable)

WESTOVER HILLS—See DANVILLE, VA (Comcast Cable)

WEYERS CAVE—See LURAY, VA (Comcast Cable)

WHITE STONE (TOWN)—See LANCASTER COUNTY, VA (MetroCast Communications)

WHITEWOOD—See KEEN MOUNTAIN, VA (Time Warner Cable)

WHITMELL—See BROSVILLE, VA (Chatmoss Cablevision)

WICOMICO CHURCH—See NORTHUMBERLAND COUNTY, VA (MetroCast Communications)

▲ **WILLIAMSBURG**—Cox Communications. Now served by HAMPTON ROADS (formerly Virginia Beach), VA [VA0002]

WILLIAMSBURG—See HAMPTON ROADS, VA (Cox Communications)

▲ **WINCHESTER**—Comcast Cable

WINDSOR—See SUFFOLK, VA (Charter Communications)

▲ **WINTERGREEN**—Nelson Cable

WIRTZ—See REDWOOD, VA (Suddenlink Communications)

WISE COUNTY—See NORTON, VA (Comcast Cable)

WISE—See NORTON, VA (Comcast Cable)

WISE—See LEBANON, VA (Shentel)

WOLFORD—See GRUNDY, VA (Time Warner Cable)

WOODBRIDGE—See PRINCE WILLIAM COUNTY, VA (Comcast Cable)

WOODFORD—See RUTHER GLEN, VA (Comcast Cable)

WOODLAWN—See GALAX, VA (Comcast Cable)

WOODSTOCK—See EDINBURG, VA (Shentel)

▲ **WYTHE COUNTY**—Citizens Telephone Coop. Now served byy FORT CHISWELL, VA [VA0066]

WYTHE COUNTY—See WYTHEVILLE, VA (Shentel)

WYTHEVILLE—See FORT CHISWELL, VA (Citizens Telephone Coop.)

▲**WYTHEVILLE**—Shentel

YANCEYVILLE—See DANVILLE, NC (Comcast Cable)

YORK COUNTY—See HAMPTON ROADS, VA (Cox Communications)

YORKTOWN NAVAL WEAPONS STATION—See HAMPTON ROADS, VA (Cox Communications)

▲**YORKTOWN**—Cox Communications. Now served by HAMPTON ROADS (formerly Virginia Beach), VA [VA0002]

YORKTOWN—See HAMPTON ROADS, VA (Cox Communications)

YUMA—See GATE CITY, VA (Scott Telecom & Electronics)

WASHINGTON

▲**ABERDEEN**—Comcast Cable. Now served by TACOMA, WA [WA0003]

ABERDEEN—See TACOMA, WA (Comcast Cable)

ADAMS COUNTY—See OTHELLO, WA (Northland Cable Television)

AGATE—See UNION, WA (Hood Canal Communications)

AIRWAY HEIGHTS—See SPOKANE, WA (Comcast Cable)

ALGONA—See AUBURN, WA (Comcast Cable)

ALLYN (PORTIONS)—See PORT ORCHARD, WA (Wave Broadband)

▲**ALMIRA**—Formerly served by Almega Cable. No longer in operation

AMES LAKE—See DUVALL, WA (Broadstripe)

ANACORTES—See BELLINGHAM, WA (Comcast Cable)

▲**ANDERSON ISLAND**—Millennium Digital Media/Broadstripe

ARLINGTON (NORTHWESTERN PORTION)—See CAMANO ISLAND, WA (Wave Broadband)

▲**ARLINGTON**—Comcast Cable. Now served by SEATTLE, WA [WA0001]

ARLINGTON—See SEATTLE, WA (Comcast Cable)

▲**AUBURN**—Comcast Cable

▲**BAINBRIDGE ISLAND**—Comcast Cable. Now served by TACOMA, WA [WA0003]

BAINBRIDGE ISLAND—See TACOMA, WA (Comcast Cable)

BANGOR SUBMARINE BASE—See PORT ORCHARD, WA (Wave Broadband)

BATTLE GROUND—See VANCOUVER, WA (Comcast Cable)

▲**BAYVIEW**—Wave Broadband. Now served by CAMANO ISLAND, WA [WA0046]

BAYVIEW—See CAMANO ISLAND, WA (Wave Broadband)

BEAUX ARTS VILLAGE—See SEATTLE, WA (Comcast Cable)

BEAVER—See FORKS, WA (Millennium Digital Media/Broadstripe)

BELFAIR—See PORT ORCHARD, WA (Wave Broadband)

▲**BELLEVUE**—Comcast Cable. Now served by SEATTLE, WA [WA0001]

BELLEVUE—See SEATTLE, WA (Comcast Cable)

▲**BELLINGHAM**—Comcast Cable

▲**BELLINGHAM**—Millennium Digital Media/Broadstripe

BENTON CITY—See WEST RICHLAND, WA (Charter Communications)

BENTON COUNTY—See KENNEWICK, WA (Charter Communications)

BENTON COUNTY—See WEST RICHLAND, WA (Charter Communications)

▲**BIG LAKE**—Wave Broadband. Now served by CAMANO ISLAND, WA [WA0046]

BIG LAKE—See CAMANO ISLAND, WA (Wave Broadband)

BLACK DIAMOND—See AUBURN, WA (Comcast Cable)

BLAINE—See BELLINGHAM, WA (Comcast Cable)

BONNER COUNTY (UNINCORPORATED AREAS)—See NEWPORT, ID (Concept Cable)

BONNEY LAKE—See TACOMA, WA (Comcast Cable)

BOTHELL—See SEATTLE, WA (Comcast Cable)

▲**BREMERTON**—Comcast Cable. No longer in operation

▲**BREWSTER**—Millennium Digital Media/Broadstripe

▲**BRIDGEHAVEN**—Millennium Digital Media/Broadstripe

BRIDGEPORT BAR—See BREWSTER, WA (Millennium Digital Media/Broadstripe)

BRIDGEPORT—See BREWSTER, WA (Millennium Digital Media/Broadstripe)

BRIER—See SEATTLE, WA (Comcast Cable)

BRINNON—See PORT TOWNSEND, WA (Millennium Digital Media/Broadstripe)

BRYANT—See CAMANO ISLAND, WA (Wave Broadband)

BUCKLEY—See TACOMA, WA (Comcast Cable)

▲**BURIEN**—Comcast Cable. Now served by AUBURN, WA [WA0211]

BURIEN—See AUBURN, WA (Comcast Cable)

▲**BURLINGTON**—Comcast Cable. Now served by SEATTLE, WA [WA0001]

BURLINGTON—See SEATTLE, WA (Comcast Cable)

▲**CAMANO ISLAND**—Wave Broadband

CAMAS—See VANCOUVER, WA (Comcast Cable)

CARBONADO—See TACOMA, WA (Comcast Cable)

CARNATION—See DUVALL, WA (Broadstripe)

CARNATION—See SEATTLE, WA (Comcast Cable)

CARROLLS—See LONGVIEW, WA (Comcast Cable)

▲**CARSON**—Millennium Digital Media/Broadstripe

CASCADE-FAIRWOOD—See SEATTLE, WA (Comcast Cable)

CASHMERE—See WENATCHEE, WA (Charter Communications)

CASTLE ROCK—See LONGVIEW, WA (Comcast Cable)

CENTRAL PARK—See TACOMA, WA (Comcast Cable)

▲**CENTRALIA-CHEHALIS**—Comcast Cable. Now served by TACOMA, WA [WA0003]

CENTRALIA-CHEHALIS—See TACOMA, WA (Comcast Cable)

CENTRALIA—See EATONVILLE, WA (Rainier Cable)

▲**CHATTAROY**—Formerly served by Almega Cable. No longer in operation

CHEHALIS—See EATONVILLE, WA (Rainier Cable)

CHELAN COUNTY—See WENATCHEE, WA (Charter Communications)

CHELAN FALLS—See CHELAN, WA (Millennium Digital Media/Broadstripe)

▲**CHELAN**—Millennium Digital Media/Broadstripe

▲**CHENEY**—Formerly served by Wave Broadband. No longer in operation

CHEWELAH—See WENATCHEE, WA (Charter Communications)

▲**CHINOOK PASS**—Formerly served by Almega Cable. No longer in operation

▲**CHINOOK**—Chinook Progressive Club TV

▲**CLALLAM BAY**—Formerly served by Wave Broadband. No longer in operation

CLALLAM COUNTY (SOUTHEASTERN PORTION)—See FORKS, WA (Millennium Digital Media/Broadstripe)

CLALLAM COUNTY (UNINCORPORATED AREAS)—See PORT ANGELES, WA (Wave Broadband)

CLARK COUNTY (UNINCORPORATED AREAS)—See VANCOUVER, WA (Comcast Cable)

CLARK COUNTY (URBAN AREAS)—See VANCOUVER, WA (Comcast Cable)

CLARK FORK—See NEWPORT, ID (Concept Cable)

▲**CLE ELUM**—R & R Cable

CLEAR LAKE—See CAMANO ISLAND, WA (Wave Broadband)

CLINTON—See SEATTLE, WA (Comcast Cable)

CLYDE HILL—See SEATTLE, WA (Comcast Cable)

▲**COLFAX**—Colfax Highline Cable Co.

COLLEGE PLACE—See WALLA WALLA, WA (Charter Communications)

COLONY SURF—See UNION, WA (Hood Canal Communications)

▲**COLVILLE**—Charter Communications

▲**CONCRETE**—Millennium Digital Media/Broadstripe

▲**CONNELL**—Northstar Broadband

CONWAY—See CAMANO ISLAND, WA (Wave Broadband)

COPALIS BEACH—See OCEAN SHORES, WA (Coast Communications Co. Inc.)

COPALIS CROSSING—See OCEAN SHORES, WA (Coast Communications Co. Inc.)

COSMOPOLIS—See TACOMA, WA (Comcast Cable)

▲**COULEE CITY**—Formerly served by Almega Cable. No longer in operation

▲**COULEE DAM**—Country Cable

▲**COUPEVILLE**—Comcast Cable. Now served by SEATTLE, WA [WA0001]

COUPEVILLE—See SEATTLE, WA (Comcast Cable)

COVINGTON—See AUBURN, WA (Comcast Cable)

COWICHE—See NACHES, WA (J & N Cable)

COWLITZ COUNTY—See LONGVIEW, WA (Comcast Cable)

CRESCENT BAR—See QUINCY, WA (J & N Cable)

▲**CRESTON**—Millennium Digital Media/Broadstripe

▲**DARRINGTON**—Millennium Digital Media/Broadstripe

▲**DAVENPORT**—Northstar Communications

▲**DAYTON**—Touchet Valley TV Inc.

DEER LAKE—See WENATCHEE, WA (Charter Communications)

▲**DEER PARK**—Northstar Broadband

DEMING—See BELLINGHAM, WA (Comcast Cable)

DES MOINES—See AUBURN, WA (Comcast Cable)

DES MOINES—See SEATTLE, WA (Comcast Cable)

▲ DIAMOND LAKE—Northstar Broadband

DIXIE—See WALLA WALLA, WA (Charter Communications)

DOTY—See PE ELL, WA (Millennium Digital Media/Broadstripe)

DOUGLAS COUNTY—See WENATCHEE, WA (Charter Communications)

DRYAD—See PE ELL, WA (Millennium Digital Media/Broadstripe)

DU PONT—See TACOMA, WA (Comcast Cable)

▲ DUVALL—Broadstripe

EAST SEATTLE—See SEATTLE, WA (Comcast Cable)

EAST WENATCHEE—See WENATCHEE, WA (Charter Communications)

▲ EASTON—Millennium Digital Media/Broadstripe

EATONVILLE—See TACOMA, WA (Comcast Cable)

▲ EATONVILLE—Rainier Cable

▲ ECHO LAKE/SNOHOMISH—Millennium Digital Media/Broadstripe

EDGEWOOD—See TACOMA, WA (Comcast Cable)

▲ EDMONDS—Comcast Cable. Now served by SEATTLE, WA [WA0001]

EDMONDS—See SEATTLE, WA (Comcast Cable)

ELECTRIC CITY—See GRAND COULEE, WA (Charter Communications)

▲ ELLENSBURG—Charter Communications

ELMA—See TACOMA, WA (Comcast Cable)

ELMER CITY—See GRAND COULEE, WA (Charter Communications)

ENDICOTT—See ST. JOHN, WA (St. John Cable Co. Inc.)

▲ ENTIAT—Millennium Digital Media/Broadstripe

ENUMCLAW—See AUBURN, WA (Comcast Cable)

▲ EPHRATA—Northland Cable Television

▲ EVERETT—Comcast Cable. Now served by SEATTLE, WA [WA0001]

EVERETT—See SEATTLE, WA (Comcast Cable)

EVERSON—See BELLINGHAM, WA (Comcast Cable)

▲ FAIRCHILD AFB—Cable Montana. Now served by SPOKANE, WA [WA0004]

FAIRCHILD AFB—See SPOKANE, WA (Comcast Cable)

▲ FAIRFIELD—Elk River TV Cable Co.

FALL CITY—See AUBURN, WA (Comcast Cable)

FEDERAL WAY—See AUBURN, WA (Comcast Cable)

FERNDALE—See BELLINGHAM, WA (Comcast Cable)

FIFE—See TACOMA, WA (Comcast Cable)

FIFE—See EATONVILLE, WA (Rainier Cable)

FIRCREST—See TACOMA, WA (Comcast Cable)

▲ FORKS—Millennium Digital Media/Broadstripe

FORT LEWIS—See TACOMA, WA (Comcast Cable)

FOX ISLAND—See TACOMA, WA (Comcast Cable)

FRANKLIN COUNTY—See KENNEWICK, WA (Charter Communications)

▲ FREELAND—Comcast Cable. Now served by SEATTLE, WA [WA0001]

FREELAND—See SEATTLE, WA (Comcast Cable)

▲ FRIDAY HARBOR—Windjammer Cable

GAMBLEWOOD—See TACOMA, WA (Comcast Cable)

▲ GARFIELD—Elk River TV Cable Co.

GEORGE—See QUINCY, WA (J & N Cable)

GIG HARBOR—See TACOMA, WA (Comcast Cable)

GLEED—See NACHES, WA (J & N Cable)

GLEN MOBILE HOME PARK—See BELLINGHAM, WA (Comcast Cable)

GLENOMA—See RANDLE, WA (Millennium Digital Media/Broadstripe)

GOLDBAR—See SEATTLE, WA (Comcast Cable)

▲ GOLDENDALE—J & N Cable

GRAHAM—See TACOMA, WA (Comcast Cable)

GRAHAM—See EATONVILLE, WA (Rainier Cable)

▲ GRAND COULEE—Charter Communications

▲ GRANDVIEW—Charter Communications. Now served by YAKIMA, WA [WA0009]

GRANDVIEW—See YAKIMA, WA (Charter Communications)

GRANGER—See YAKIMA, WA (Charter Communications)

GRANITE FALLS—See SEATTLE, WA (Comcast Cable)

GRANT COUNTY—See GRAND COULEE, WA (Charter Communications)

GRANT COUNTY—See EPHRATA, WA (Northland Cable Television)

GRANT COUNTY—See MOSES LAKE, WA (Northland Cable Television)

GRAYLAND—See TACOMA, WA (Comcast Cable)

GRAYS HARBOR COUNTY—See OCEAN SHORES, WA (Coast Communications Co. Inc.)

GRAYS HARBOR COUNTY—See TACOMA, WA (Comcast Cable)

GRAYS HARBOR—See TACOMA, WA (Comcast Cable)

▲ GREENBANK—Millennium Digital Media/Broadstripe

▲ GUEMES ISLAND—Index Cable TV Inc.

HAMILTON—See CONCRETE, WA (Millennium Digital Media/Broadstripe)

HANSVILLE—See TACOMA, WA (Comcast Cable)

▲ HARRINGTON—Elk River TV Cable Co.

HAYDEN ISLAND—See VANCOUVER, OR (Comcast Cable)

HERRON ISLAND—See ANDERSON ISLAND, WA (Millennium Digital Media/Broadstripe)

HOGAN'S CORNER—See OCEAN SHORES, WA (Coast Communications Co. Inc.)

HOLLY—See PORT ORCHARD, WA (Wave Broadband)

HOOD CANAL—See BRIDGEHAVEN, WA (Millennium Digital Media/Broadstripe)

HOODSPORT—See UNION, WA (Hood Canal Communications)

HOQUAIM—See TACOMA, WA (Comcast Cable)

▲ INDEX—Iron Goat Networks LLC

INDIAN BEACH—See CAMANO ISLAND, WA (Wave Broadband)

INDIANOLA (UNINCORPORATED AREAS)—See TACOMA, WA (Comcast Cable)

INGLEWOOD-FINN HILL—See SEATTLE, WA (Comcast Cable)

▲ IONE—Northstar Broadband

ISLAND COUNTY (PORTIONS)—See BELLINGHAM, WA (Comcast Cable)

ISLAND COUNTY—See SEATTLE, WA (Comcast Cable)

ISSAQUAH (SOUTHEASTERN PORTION)—See DUVALL, WA (Broadstripe)

ISSAQUAH—See AUBURN, WA (Comcast Cable)

JACKSON PARK—See PORT ORCHARD, WA (Wave Broadband)

▲ KAHLOTUS—Formerly served by Community Cable Service. No longer in operation

▲ KALA POINT—Millennium Digital Media/Broadstripe

KALAMA—See LONGVIEW, WA (Comcast Cable)

KELSO—See LONGVIEW, WA (Comcast Cable)

KENMORE—See SEATTLE, WA (Comcast Cable)

▲ KENNEWICK—Charter Communications

KENT—See AUBURN, WA (Comcast Cable)

KETTLE FALLS—See COLVILLE, WA (Charter Communications)

KEY PENINSULA—See ANDERSON ISLAND, WA (Millennium Digital Media/Broadstripe)

KEYPORT NAVAL BASE—See PORT ORCHARD, WA (Wave Broadband)

KEYPORT—See PORT ORCHARD, WA (Wave Broadband)

KING COUNTY—See SEATTLE, WA (Comcast Cable)

KINGSTON—See TACOMA, WA (Comcast Cable)

KIRKLAND—See SEATTLE, WA (Comcast Cable)

KITSAP COUNTY—See TACOMA, WA (Comcast Cable)

KITSAP LAKE—See PORT ORCHARD, WA (Wave Broadband)

KITTITAS COUNTY (NORTHERN PORTION)—See CLE ELUM, WA (R & R Cable)

KITTITAS COUNTY (PORTIONS)—See EASTON, WA (Millennium Digital Media/Broadstripe)

KITTITAS—See ELLENSBURG, WA (Charter Communications)

LA CENTER—See VANCOUVER, WA (Comcast Cable)

▲ LA CONNER—Wave Broadband. Now served by CAMANO ISLAND, WA [WA0046]

LA CONNER—See CAMANO ISLAND, WA (Wave Broadband)

LACEY—See TACOMA, WA (Comcast Cable)

LACROSSE—See ST. JOHN, WA (St. John Cable Co. Inc.)

▲ LAKE BAY—Millennium Digital Media/Broadstripe

LAKE CLE ELUM—See ROSLYN, WA (R & R Cable)

LAKE CREEK—See FORKS, WA (Millennium Digital Media/Broadstripe)

LAKE CUSHMAN—See UNION, WA (Hood Canal Communications)

LAKE FOREST PARK—See SEATTLE, WA (Comcast Cable)

▲ LAKE GOODWIN—Wave Broadband. Now served by CAMANO ISLAND, WA [WA0046]

LAKE GOODWIN—See CAMANO ISLAND, WA (Wave Broadband)

LAKE HOLIDAY—See TACOMA, WA (Comcast Cable)

LAKE STEVENS—See SEATTLE, WA (Comcast Cable)

LAKE SYMINGTON—See PORT ORCHARD, WA (Wave Broadband)

LAKE TAHUYA—See PORT ORCHARD, WA (Wave Broadband)

LAKEBAY—See TACOMA, WA (Comcast Cable)

LAKEWOOD CENTER—See TACOMA, WA (Comcast Cable)

LAKEWOOD—See EATONVILLE, WA (Rainier Cable)

LAKEWOOD—See CAMANO ISLAND, WA (Wave Broadband)

LANGLEY—See SEATTLE, WA (Comcast Cable)

LEAVNWORTH—See WENATCHEE, WA (Charter Communications)

LEWIS COUNTY—See MORTON, WA (Broadstripe)

LEWIS COUNTY—See MOSSYROCK, WA (Comcast Cable)

LEWIS COUNTY—See TACOMA, WA (Comcast Cable)

▲**LIBERTY LAKE**—Northstar Broadband

LILLIWAUP FALLS—See UNION, WA (Hood Canal Communications)

▲**LIND**—Northstar Broadband

LITTLE BOSTON—See TACOMA, WA (Comcast Cable)

LOFALL—See TACOMA, WA (Comcast Cable)

LONE PINE—See COULEE DAM, WA (Country Cable)

LONG POINT—See SEATTLE, WA (Comcast Cable)

▲**LONGVIEW**—Comcast Cable

▲**LOOMIS**—Formerly served by JKA Cable Systems. No longer in operation

▲**LOON LAKE**—Charter Communications. Now served by WENATCHEE, WA [WA0015]

LOON LAKE—See WENATCHEE, WA (Charter Communications)

LOST LAKE—See CAMANO ISLAND, WA (Wave Broadband)

LOWER HOOD CANAL—See UNION, WA (Hood Canal Communications)

LUMMI INDIAN RESERVATION—See BELLINGHAM, WA (Comcast Cable)

▲**LUMMI INDIAN RESERVATION**—San Juan Cable & Construction

▲**LYLE**—J & N Cable

LYMAN—See CONCRETE, WA (Millennium Digital Media/Broadstripe)

LYNDEN—See BELLINGHAM, WA (Comcast Cable)

LYNWOOD—See SEATTLE, WA (Comcast Cable)

MADRONA BEACH—See CAMANO ISLAND, WA (Wave Broadband)

MADRONA—See SEATTLE, WA (Comcast Cable)

▲**MALAGA**—Formerly served by Almega Cable. No longer in operation

MANCHESTER—See PORT ORCHARD, WA (Wave Broadband)

▲**MANSFIELD**—Millennium Digital Media/Broadstripe

▲**MANSON**—Millennium Digital Media. Now served by CHELAN, WA [WA0058]

MANSON—See CHELAN, WA (Millennium Digital Media/Broadstripe)

MAPLE FALLS—See BELLINGHAM, WA (Comcast Cable)

MAPLE VALLEY—See AUBURN, WA (Comcast Cable)

▲**MARBLEMOUNT**—Millennium Digital Media/Broadstripe

MARYSVILLE—See SEATTLE, WA (Comcast Cable)

MASON COUNTY (SOUTHWESTERN PORTION)—See TACOMA, WA (Comcast Cable)

MASON COUNTY—See PORT ORCHARD, WA (Wave Broadband)

▲**MATTAWA**—Formerly served by Almega Cable. No longer in operation

▲**MAXWELTON**—Comcast Cable. Now served by SEATTLE, WA [WA0001]

MAXWELTON—See SEATTLE, WA (Comcast Cable)

MAYFIELD LAKE—See MOSSYROCK, WA (Comcast Cable)

MCCHORD AFB—See TACOMA, WA (Comcast Cable)

▲**McCHORD AIR FORCE BASE**—Comcast Cable. Now served by TACOMA, WA [WA0003]

MCCLEARY—See TACOMA, WA (Comcast Cable)

MCKENNA—See TACOMA, WA (Comcast Cable)

▲**MEDICAL LAKE**—Formerly served by Wave Broadband. No longer in operation

MEDINA—See SEATTLE, WA (Comcast Cable)

MERCER ISLAND—See SEATTLE, WA (Comcast Cable)

▲**METALINE FALLS**—Northstar Broadband

METALINE—See METALINE FALLS, WA (Northstar Broadband)

MILL CREEK—See SEATTLE, WA (Comcast Cable)

MILLWOOD—See SPOKANE, WA (Comcast Cable)

MILTON-FREEWATER—See WALLA WALLA, OR (Charter Communications)

MILTON—See TACOMA, WA (Comcast Cable)

▲**MINERAL**—Comcast Cable

MONROE—See SEATTLE, WA (Comcast Cable)

▲**MONTESANO**—Comcast Cable. Now served by TACOMA, WA [WA0003]

MONTESANO—See TACOMA, WA (Comcast Cable)

▲**MORTON**—Broadstripe

▲**MOSES LAKE**—Northland Cable Television

▲**MOSSYROCK**—Comcast Cable

MOUNT VERNON—See SEATTLE, WA (Comcast Cable)

MOUNTLAKE TERRACE—See SEATTLE, WA (Comcast Cable)

MOXEE CITY—See YAKIMA, WA (Charter Communications)

MUKITEO—See SEATTLE, WA (Comcast Cable)

▲**NACHES**—J & N Cable

▲**NAPAVINE**—Millennium Digital Media/Broadstripe

▲**NESPELEM**—Formerly served by Country Cable. No longer in operation

NEWCASTLE—See AUBURN, WA (Comcast Cable)

▲**NEWPORT**—Concept Cable

NOOKSACK—See BELLINGHAM, WA (Comcast Cable)

NORMANDY PARK—See AUBURN, WA (Comcast Cable)

▲**NORTH BONNEVILLE**—North Bonneville Community Cable TV System

NORTH SHORE—See PORT ORCHARD, WA (Wave Broadband)

▲**NORTHPORT**—Formerly served by Almega Cable. No longer in operation

OAK HARBOR—See SEATTLE, WA (Comcast Cable)

▲**OAKESDALE**—Elk River TV Cable Co.

OAKVILLE—See TACOMA, WA (Comcast Cable)

OCEAN CITY—See OCEAN SHORES, WA (Coast Communications Co. Inc.)

▲**OCEAN SHORES**—Coast Communications Co. Inc.

▲**ODESSA (TOWN)**—Northstar Broadband

OKANOGAN COUNTY (UNINCORPORATED AREAS)—See WENATCHEE, WA (Charter Communications)

▲**OKANOGAN**—Charter Communications. Now served by WENATCHEE, WA [WA0015]

OKANOGAN—See WENATCHEE, WA (Charter Communications)

OLALLA—See PORT ORCHARD, WA (Wave Broadband)

OLDTOWN—See NEWPORT, ID (Concept Cable)

▲**OLYMPIA**—Comcast Cable. Now served by TACOMA, WA [WA0003]

OLYMPIA—See TACOMA, WA (Comcast Cable)

OMAK—See WENATCHEE, WA (Charter Communications)

▲**ORCAS ISLAND**—Almega Cable

▲**OROVILLE**—Charter Communications. Now served by WENATCHEE, WA [WA0015]

OROVILLE—See WENATCHEE, WA (Charter Communications)

ORTING—See TACOMA, WA (Comcast Cable)

▲**OTHELLO**—Northland Cable Television

PACIFIC BEACH—See OCEAN SHORES, WA (Coast Communications Co. Inc.)

PACIFIC COUNTY—See TACOMA, WA (Comcast Cable)

PACIFIC—See AUBURN, WA (Comcast Cable)

▲**PACKWOOD**—Millennium Digital Media/Broadstripe

PASCO—See KENNEWICK, WA (Charter Communications)

PATEROS—See BREWSTER, WA (Millennium Digital Media/Broadstripe)

▲**PE ELL**—Millennium Digital Media/Broadstripe

PEND OREILLE COUNTY—See NEWPORT, WA (Concept Cable)

PESHASTIN—See WENATCHEE, WA (Charter Communications)

PHILLIPS LAKE—See UNION, WA (Hood Canal Communications)

PICKERING—See UNION, WA (Hood Canal Communications)

PINE LAKE—See SEATTLE, WA (Comcast Cable)

▲**POINT ROBERTS**—Delta Cable Vision

▲**POMEROY**—Formerly served by Almega Cable. No longer in operation

▲**PORT ANGELES**—Wave Broadband

PORT HADLOCK—See PORT TOWNSEND, WA (Millennium Digital Media/Broadstripe)

PORT LUDLOW—See PORT TOWNSEND, WA (Millennium Digital Media/Broadstripe)

▲**PORT ORCHARD**—Wave Broadband

▲**PORT TOWNSEND**—Millennium Digital Media/Broadstripe

POULSBO—See TACOMA, WA (Comcast Cable)

▲ **PRESCOTT**—Formerly served by Charter Communications. No longer in operation

PRESTON—See AUBURN, WA (Comcast Cable)

PRIEST RIVER—See NEWPORT, ID (Concept Cable)

PROSSER—See YAKIMA, WA (Charter Communications)

PUGET SOUND NAVAL SHIPYARD—See PORT ORCHARD, WA (Wave Broadband)

PUYALLUP—See TACOMA, WA (Comcast Cable)

PUYALLUP—See EATONVILLE, WA (Rainier Cable)

QUILCENE—See PORT TOWNSEND, WA (Millennium Digital Media/Broadstripe)

▲ **QUINCY**—J & N Cable

RAINIER—See TACOMA, WA (Comcast Cable)

RANDLE (PORTIONS)—See PACKWOOD, WA (Millennium Digital Media/Broadstripe)

▲ **RANDLE**—Millennium Digital Media/Broadstripe

▲ **RAYMOND**—Comcast Cable. Now served by TACOMA, WA [WA0003]

RAYMOND—See TACOMA, WA (Comcast Cable)

▲ **REARDAN**—Elk River TV Cable Co.

▲ **REDMOND**—Comcast Cable. Now served by SEATTLE, WA [WA0001]

REDMOND—See DUVALL, WA (Broadstripe)

REDMOND—See SEATTLE, WA (Comcast Cable)

RENTON—See AUBURN, WA (Comcast Cable)

▲ **REPUBLIC**—Television Assn. of Republic

RICHLAND—See KENNEWICK, WA (Charter Communications)

RICHMOND BEACH—See SEATTLE, WA (Comcast Cable)

RIDGEFIELD—See VANCOUVER, WA (Comcast Cable)

▲ **RITZVILLE**—Northstar Broadband

▲ **ROCHESTER**—Comcast Cable. Now served by TACOMA, WA [WA0003]

ROCHESTER—See TACOMA, WA (Comcast Cable)

ROCK ISLAND—See WENATCHEE, WA (Charter Communications)

ROCKFORD—See FAIRFIELD, WA (Elk River TV Cable Co.)

RONALD—See ROSLYN, WA (R & R Cable)

▲ **ROSALIA**—Elk River TV Cable Co.

ROSE VALLEY—See LONGVIEW, WA (Comcast Cable)

▲ **ROSLYN**—R & R Cable

ROY—See TACOMA, WA (Comcast Cable)

▲ **ROYAL CITY**—Formerly served by Almega Cable. No longer in operation

▲ **RUSTON**—Comcast Cable. Now served by TACOMA, WA [WA0003]

RUSTON—See TACOMA, WA (Comcast Cable)

▲ **RYDERWOOD**—Comcast Cable

SAHALEE—See DUVALL, WA (Broadstripe)

SAMISH LAKE—See BELLINGHAM, WA (Comcast Cable)

SAN JUAN COUNTY (PORTIONS)—See FRIDAY HARBOR, WA (Windjammer Cable)

SANDY HOOK—See TACOMA, WA (Comcast Cable)

SEABECK—See PORT ORCHARD, WA (Wave Broadband)

SEATAC—See AUBURN, WA (Comcast Cable)

▲ **SEATTLE (SURROUNDING AREAS)**—Wave Broadband

▲ **SEATTLE**—Formerly served by Sprint Corp. No longer in operation

▲ **SEATTLE**—Comcast Cable

SEDRO WOOLLEY—See SEATTLE, WA (Comcast Cable)

▲ **SEQUIM**—Wave Broadband. Now served by PORT ANGELES, WA [WA0020]

SEQUIM—See PORT ANGELES, WA (Wave Broadband)

SEVEN LAKES—See CAMANO ISLAND, WA (Wave Broadband)

SHELTER BAY—See CAMANO ISLAND, WA (Wave Broadband)

▲ **SHELTON**—Comcast Cable. Now served by TACOMA, WA [WA0003]

SHELTON—See TACOMA, WA (Comcast Cable)

SHELTON—See UNION, WA (Hood Canal Communications)

SHORELINE—See SEATTLE, WA (Comcast Cable)

SILVER BROOK—See PACKWOOD, WA (Millennium Digital Media/Broadstripe)

SILVER LAKE—See LONGVIEW, WA (Comcast Cable)

SILVERDALE—See PORT ORCHARD, WA (Wave Broadband)

SKAGIT COUNTY (PORTIONS)—See BELLINGHAM, WA (Comcast Cable)

SKAGIT COUNTY (PORTIONS)—See GUEMES ISLAND, WA (Index Cable TV Inc.)

SKAGIT COUNTY—See SEATTLE, WA (Comcast Cable)

SKAMANIA—See CARSON, WA (Millennium Digital Media/Broadstripe)

▲ **SKAMOKAWA**—Formerly served by Wright Cablevision. No longer in operation

SKOKOMISH VALLEY—See UNION, WA (Hood Canal Communications)

SNOHOMISH COUNTY (NORTHWESTERN PORTION)—See CAMANO ISLAND, WA (Wave Broadband)

SNOHOMISH COUNTY (SOUTHWESTERN PORTIONS)—See Echo Lake/Snohomish, WA (Millennium Digital Media/Broadstripe)

SNOHOMISH COUNTY—See SEATTLE, WA (Comcast Cable)

SNOHOMISH COUNTY—See INDEX, WA (Iron Goat Networks LLC)

SNOHOMISH—See SEATTLE, WA (Comcast Cable)

SNOQUALMIE VALLEY—See DUVALL, WA (Broadstripe)

SNOQUALMIE—See AUBURN, WA (Comcast Cable)

SOAP LAKE—See EPHRATA, WA (Northland Cable Television)

SOUTH BEND—See TACOMA, WA (Comcast Cable)

SOUTH CLE ELUM—See CLE ELUM, WA (R & R Cable)

SOUTH KITSAP—See PORT ORCHARD, WA (Wave Broadband)

SOUTH PRAIRIE—See TACOMA, WA (Comcast Cable)

SPANAWAY—See TACOMA, WA (Comcast Cable)

SPANAWAY—See EATONVILLE, WA (Rainier Cable)

▲ **SPANGLE**—Formerly served by Elk River TV Cable Co. No longer in operation

SPOKANE COUNTY—See SPOKANE, WA (Comcast Cable)

▲ **SPOKANE**—Formerly served by Video Wave Television. No longer in operation

▲ **SPOKANE**—Comcast Cable

▲ **SPRAGUE**—Elk River TV Cable Co.

▲ **SPRINGDALE**—Elk River TV Cable Co.

▲ **ST. JOHN**—St. John Cable Co. Inc.

STANWOOD—See CAMANO ISLAND, WA (Wave Broadband)

▲ **STARBUCK**—Formerly served by Charter Communications. No longer in operation

STARTUP—See SEATTLE, WA (Comcast Cable)

STEILACOOM—See TACOMA, WA (Comcast Cable)

STEPTOE—See COLFAX, WA (Colfax Highline Cable Co.)

STEVENSON—See CARSON, WA (Millennium Digital Media/Broadstripe)

▲ **SUDDEN VALLEY**—Comcast Cable. No longer in operation

SULTAN—See SEATTLE, WA (Comcast Cable)

▲ **SUMAS**—City of Sumas TV Cable System

SUMMIT—See TACOMA, WA (Comcast Cable)

SUMNER—See TACOMA, WA (Comcast Cable)

▲ **SUNCREST**—TV Max. Now served by SPOKANE, WA [WA0004]

SUNCREST—See SPOKANE, WA (Comcast Cable)

▲ **SUNNYSIDE**—Charter Communications. Now served by YAKIMA, WA [WA0009]

SUNNYSIDE—See YAKIMA, WA (Charter Communications)

SUQUAMISH (UNINCORPORATED AREAS)—See TACOMA, WA (Comcast Cable)

SWINOMISH INDIAN RESERVATION—See CAMANO ISLAND, WA (Wave Broadband)

▲ **TACOMA**—Click! Network

▲ **TACOMA**—Comcast Cable

TACOMA—See EATONVILLE, WA (Rainier Cable)

TAHUYA—See PORT ORCHARD, WA (Wave Broadband)

▲ **TEKOA**—Northstar Broadband

TENINO—See TACOMA, WA (Comcast Cable)

▲ **THORP**—Millennium Digital Media/Broadstripe

THURSTON COUNTY—See TACOMA, WA (Comcast Cable)

TIETON—See NACHES, WA (J & N Cable)

TIMBER LAKES—See UNION, WA (Hood Canal Communications)

TOKELAND—See TACOMA, WA (Comcast Cable)

▲ **TOLEDO**—Formerly served by RGA Cable TV. No longer in operation

TONASKET—See WENATCHEE, WA (Charter Communications)

TOPPENISH—See YAKIMA, WA (Charter Communications)

TOUTLE—See LONGVIEW, WA (Comcast Cable)

TRACYTON—See TACOMA, WA (Comcast Cable)

TUKWILA—See AUBURN, WA (Comcast Cable)

▲ **TULALIP INDIAN RESERVATION**—Tulalip Tribes Broadband

TURNWATER—See TACOMA, WA (Comcast Cable)

▲**TWISP**—Millennium Digital Media/Broadstripe

UMATILLA COUNTY (UNINCORPORATED AREAS)—See WALLA WALLA, OR (Charter Communications)

UNION GAP—See YAKIMA, WA (Charter Communications)

▲**UNION**—Hood Canal Communications

UNIVERSITY PLACE—See TACOMA, WA (Comcast Cable)

UNIVERSITY PLACE—See EATONVILLE, WA (Rainier Cable)

UPPER SOUTH SHORE—See CHELAN, WA (Millennium Digital Media/Broadstripe)

UTSALADY—See CAMANO ISLAND, WA (Wave Broadband)

▲**VADER**—Formerly served by Millennium Digital Media. No longer in operation

▲**VANCOUVER**—Comcast Cable

VASHON ISLAND—See TACOMA, WA (Comcast Cable)

VASHON—See TACOMA, WA (Comcast Cable)

▲**WAITSBURG**—Charter Communications. Now served by WALLA WALLA, WA [WA0016]

WAITSBURG—See WALLA WALLA, WA (Charter Communications)

WALLA WALLA COUNTY (PORTIONS)—See WALLA WALLA, WA (Charter Communications)

WALLA WALLA COUNTY—See KENNEWICK, WA (Charter Communications)

▲**WALLA WALLA**—Charter Communications

WAPATO—See YAKIMA, WA (Charter Communications)

▲**WARDEN**—Northstar Broadband

WASHOUGAL—See VANCOUVER, WA (Comcast Cable)

▲**WASHTUCNA**—Formerly served by Charter Communications. No longer in operation

▲**WATERVILLE**—Millennium Digital Media/Broadstripe

▲**WENATCHEE**—Charter Communications

▲**WEST RICHLAND**—Charter Communications

▲**WESTPORT**—Comcast Cable. Now served by TACOMA, WA [WA0003]

WESTPORT—See TACOMA, WA (Comcast Cable)

WHATCOM COUNTY (PORTIONS)—See BELLINGHAM, WA (Millennium Digital Media/Broadstripe)

WHATCOM COUNTY (SOUTHERN PORTION)—See CAMANO ISLAND, WA (Wave Broadband)

WHATCOM COUNTY—See BELLINGHAM, WA (Comcast Cable)

WHIDBEY ISLAND NAVAL AIR STATION—See SEATTLE, WA (Comcast Cable)

WHIDBEY ISLAND—See SEATTLE, WA (Comcast Cable)

▲**WHIDBEY ISLAND**—Millennium Digital Media/Broadstripe

▲**WILBUR**—Northstar Broadband

WILKESON—See TACOMA, WA (Comcast Cable)

▲**WILSON CREEK**—Formerly served by Almega Cable. No longer in operation

▲**WINLOCK**—Comcast Cable

WINTHROP—See TWISP, WA (Millennium Digital Media/Broadstripe)

▲**WISHRAM**—Formerly served by J & N Cable. No longer in operation

WOODINVILLE—See DUVALL, WA (Broadstripe)

WOODINVILLE—See SEATTLE, WA (Comcast Cable)

WOODLAND—See LONGVIEW, WA (Comcast Cable)

WOODWAY—See SEATTLE, WA (Comcast Cable)

▲**YACOLT**—J & N Cable

YAKIMA COUNTY (UNINCORPORATED AREAS)—See NACHES, WA (J & N Cable)

YAKIMA COUNTY—See YAKIMA, WA (Charter Communications)

YAKIMA INDIAN RESERVATION—See YAKIMA, WA (Charter Communications)

▲**YAKIMA**—Formerly served by Wireless Broadcasting Systems of Yakima Inc. No longer in operation

▲**YAKIMA**—Charter Communications

YARROW POINT—See SEATTLE, WA (Comcast Cable)

YELM—See TACOMA, WA (Comcast Cable)

ZILLAH—See YAKIMA, WA (Charter Communications)

WEST VIRGINIA

ACME—See CHARLESTON, WV (Suddenlink Communications)

ADDISON TWP.—See PARKERSBURG, OH (Suddenlink Communications)

ADENA—See WHEELING, OH (Comcast Cable)

ADRIAN—See BUCKHANNON, WV (Suddenlink Communications)

AFLEX—See KERMIT, KY (Suddenlink Communications)

ALBRIGHT—See KINGWOOD, WV (Atlantic Broadband)

▲**ALDERSON**—Charter Communications. Now served by BECKLEY, WV [WV0005]

ALDERSON—See BECKLEY, WV (Suddenlink Communications)

ALDERSON—See ASBURY, WV (Windjammer Cable)

ALGOMA—See NORTHFORK, WV (Shentel)

ALKOL—See CHARLESTON, WV (Suddenlink Communications)

ALLEGANY COUNTY (PORTIONS)—See KEYSER, MD (Comcast Cable)

ALLEN JUNCTION—See BECKLEY, WV (Suddenlink Communications)

ALPOCA (PORTIONS)—See PINEVILLE, WV (Shentel)

ALTA—See CHARLESTON, WV (Suddenlink Communications)

▲**ALUM BRIDGE**—Rapid Cable. Now served by WESTON, WV [WV0034]

ALUM BRIDGE—See WESTON, WV (Shentel)

AMES HEIGHTS—See ANSTED, WV (Shentel)

AMIGO—See BECKLEY, WV (Suddenlink Communications)

AMMA—See LEFT HAND, WV (Econoco Inc.)

AMONATE—See NORTHFORK, VA (Shentel)

ANMOORE—See CLARKSBURG, WV (Time Warner Cable)

▲**ANSTED**—Shentel

▲**ANTHONY CREEK**—Windjammer Cable

ANTHONY—See FRANKFORD, WV (Clearview TV Cable)

▲**APPLE GROVE**—Windjammer Cable

ARBORVALE—See DURBIN, WV (Milestone Communications LP)

ARBUCKLE—See LEON, WV (Vital Communications Group)

ARNETT—See BECKLEY, WV (Suddenlink Communications)

ARNETT—See CHARLESTON, WV (Suddenlink Communications)

▲**ARNETTSVILLE**—Formerly served by Adelphia Communications. No longer in operation

ARNOLDSBURG—See NEBO, WV (Windjammer Cable)

ARTHURDALE—See KINGWOOD, WV (Atlantic Broadband)

▲**ASBURY**—Windjammer Cable

ASCO—See NORTHFORK, WV (Shentel)

ASHFORD—See CHARLESTON, WV (Suddenlink Communications)

ATENVILLE—See WAYNE, WV (Suddenlink Communications)

ATHENS—See BECKLEY, WV (Suddenlink Communications)

▲**AUBURN**—Formerly served by Cebridge Connections. No longer in operation

▲**AUGUSTA**—Comcast Cable

AVONDALE—See IAEGER, WV (Shentel)

BAISDEN—See OMAR, WV (Colane Cable TV Inc.)

BALD KNOB—See VAN, WV (Colane Cable TV)

▲**BALLARD**—Windjammer Cable

BANCROFT—See RED HOUSE, WV (Comcast Cable)

BANDYTOWN—See VAN, WV (Colane Cable TV)

BANNOCK—See WHEELING, OH (Comcast Cable)

BARBOUR COUNTY (PORTIONS)—See PHILIPPI, WV (Philippi Communications System)

BARBOUR COUNTY—See BELINGTON, WV (Shentel)

BARBOURSVILLE—See HUNTINGTON, WV (Comcast Cable)

BARBOURSVILLE—See MILTON, WV (Suddenlink Communications)

BARNABUS—See OMAR, WV (Colane Cable TV Inc.)

BARNESVILLE—See WHEELING, OH (Comcast Cable)

BARRACKVILLE—See CLARKSBURG, WV (Time Warner Cable)

BARTON—See KEYSER, MD (Comcast Cable)

BARTOW—See DURBIN, WV (Milestone Communications LP)

BAXTER—See GRANT TOWN, WV (Atlantic Broadband)

BEARTOWN—See IAEGER, WV (Shentel)

BEASLEY HOLLOW—See CHARLESTON, WV (Suddenlink Communications)

BEAUTY—See KERMIT, KY (Suddenlink Communications)

▲**BECKLEY**—Suddenlink Communications

▲**BEECH BOTTOM**—Blue Devil Cable TV Inc.

BEECH BOTTOM—See WARWOOD, WV (Centre TV Cable)

▲**BEECH CREEK**—Colane Cable TV Inc.

BEECH GLEN—See CHARLESTON, WV (Suddenlink Communications)

BELCHER ROAD—See CHARLESTON, WV (Suddenlink Communications)

▲**BELINGTON**—Shentel

BELINGTON—See ELLAMORE, WV (Windjammer Cable)

BELLAIRE—See WHEELING, OH (Comcast Cable)

BELLE—See CHARLESTON, WV (Suddenlink Communications)

BELLEVILLE—See PARKERSBURG (southern portion), WV (Community Antenna Service)

BELLVIEW—See MORGANTOWN, WV (Comcast Cable)

BELMONT COUNTY—See WHEELING, OH (Comcast Cable)

BELMONT—See WHEELING, OH (Comcast Cable)

BELMONT—See PARKERSBURG, WV (Suddenlink Communications)

BELPRE—See PARKERSBURG, OH (Suddenlink Communications)

BELVA—See CHARLESTON, WV (Suddenlink Communications)

▲**BENS CREEK**—Charter Communications. Now served by OMAR, WV [WV0191]

BENS CREEK—See OMAR, WV (Colane Cable TV Inc.)

BENTREE—See CHARLESTON, WV (Suddenlink Communications)

BENWOOD—See WHEELING, WV (Comcast Cable)

▲**BERGOO**—Charter Communications. Now served by WEBSTER SPRINGS, WV [WV0080]

BERGOO—See WEBSTER SPRINGS, WV (Shentel)

BERKELEY COUNTY (PORTIONS)—See RANSON, WV (Comcast Cable)

▲**BETHANY**—Comcast Cable

BETHESDA—See WHEELING, OH (Comcast Cable)

BETHLEHEM—See WHEELING, WV (Comcast Cable)

▲**BEVERLY**—Suddenlink Communications

BICKMORE—See CHARLESTON, WV (Suddenlink Communications)

BIG CHIMNEY—See CHARLESTON, WV (Suddenlink Communications)

BIG CREEK—See HARTS, WV (Shentel)

BIG SANDY—See IAEGER, WV (Shentel)

▲**BIRCH RIVER**—Windjammer Cable

BLAINE—See WHEELING, OH (Comcast Cable)

BLAIR—See KERMIT, WV (Suddenlink Communications)

BLAKELEY—See CHARLESTON, WV (Suddenlink Communications)

BLAND COUNTY (PORTIONS)—See BLUEFIELD, VA (Comcast Cable)

BLOOMINGROSE—See CHARLESTON, WV (Suddenlink Communications)

BLOOMINGTON—See KEYSER, MD (Comcast Cable)

BLUE CREEK—See CHARLESTON, WV (Suddenlink Communications)

▲**BLUEFIELD**—Comcast Cable

BLUEWELL—See BLUEFIELD, WV (Comcast Cable)

BLUNT—See CHARLESTON, WV (Suddenlink Communications)

BOAZ—See PARKERSBURG, WV (Suddenlink Communications)

BOLIVAR—See RANSON, WV (Comcast Cable)

▲**BOMONT**—Vital Communications Group

BOOMER—See CHARLESTON, WV (Suddenlink Communications)

BOONE COUNTY (PORTIONS)—See VAN, WV (Colane Cable TV)

BOONE COUNTY (PORTIONS)—See CHARLESTON, WV (Suddenlink Communications)

▲**BOONE COUNTY (UNINCORPORATED AREAS)**—Shentel

BOONE COUNTY—See KERMIT, WV (Suddenlink Communications)

BOOTH—See MORGANTOWN, WV (Comcast Cable)

BORDERLAND—See KERMIT, WV (Suddenlink Communications)

BOYD COUNTY (SOUTHERN PORTION)—See PRICHARD, KY (Windjammer Cable)

BRADLEY—See PARKERSBURG, WV (Suddenlink Communications)

BRADSHAW—See IAEGER, WV (Shentel)

BRANCHLAND—See HARTS, WV (Shentel)

▲**BRANDYWINE**—Formerly served by Brandywine Cablevision. No longer in operation

BRANHAM HEIGHTS—See CHARLESTON, WV (Suddenlink Communications)

BRAXTON COUNTY—See GASSAWAY, WV (Shentel)

BREEDEN—See DINGESS, WV (Shentel)

BRENTON—See PINEVILLE, WV (Shentel)

BRETZ—See KINGWOOD, WV (Atlantic Broadband)

BRIAR CREEK—See PINEVILLE, WV (Shentel)

BRIDGEPORT—See WHEELING, OH (Comcast Cable)

BRIDGEPORT—See CLARKSBURG, WV (Time Warner Cable)

BRILLIANT—See WHEELING, OH (Comcast Cable)

BRISTOL—See SALEM, WV (Shentel)

▲**BROAD RUN**—Rapid Cable. Now served by WESTON, WV [WV0034]

BROAD RUN—See WESTON, WV (Shentel)

BROOKE COUNTY (PORTIONS)—See BETHANY, WV (Comcast Cable)

BROOKE COUNTY (PORTIONS)—See WHEELING, WV (Comcast Cable)

BROOKE COUNTY—See NEW CUMBERLAND, WV (Comcast Cable)

▲**BROOKHAVEN**—Formerly served by Adelphia Communications. No longer in operation

BROOKSIDE—See WHEELING, OH (Comcast Cable)

BROWNSVILLE—See CHARLESTON, WV (Suddenlink Communications)

BROWNTON—See FLEMINGTON, WV (Suddenlink Communications)

▲**BRUNO**—Colane Cable TV Inc.

BRUSH CREEK—See CHARLESTON, WV (Suddenlink Communications)

BUCKEYE—See MARLINGTON (town), WV (Shentel)

BUCKHANNON (PORTIONS)—See ELLAMORE, WV (Windjammer Cable)

▲**BUCKHANNON**—Suddenlink Communications

BUD (PORTIONS)—See PINEVILLE, WV (Shentel)

▲**BUD**—Formerly served by Bud-Alpoca TV Cable Club Inc. No longer in operation

BUFFALO—See RED HOUSE, WV (Comcast Cable)

BULL CREEK—See PANTHER, WV (Shentel)

BURLINGTON—See KEYSER, WV (Comcast Cable)

BURNAUGH—See PRICHARD, KY (Windjammer Cable)

▲**BURNSVILLE**—Charter Communications. Now served by WESTON, WV [WV0034]

BURNSVILLE—See WESTON, WV (Shentel)

BURNWELL—See KERMIT, KY (Suddenlink Communications)

BURTON—See LITTLETON, WV (Zito Media)

CABELL COUNTY (UNINCORPORATED AREAS)—See APPLE GROVE, WV (Windjammer Cable)

CABELL COUNTY (UNINCORPORATED AREAS)—See SALT ROCK, WV (Windjammer Cable)

CABELL COUNTY—See MILTON, WV (Suddenlink Communications)

CABIN CREEK—See CHARLESTON, WV (Suddenlink Communications)

▲**CAIRO**—Formerly served by Almega Cable. No longer in operation

CALHOUN COUNTY—See GRANTSVILLE, WV (Shentel)

CALVIN—See NETTIE, WV (Windjammer Cable)

CAMDEN (TOWN)—See WEBSTER SPRINGS, WV (Shentel)

▲**CAMDEN ON GAULEY**—Charter Communications. Now served by WEBSTER SPRINGS, WV [WV0080]

CAMDEN ON GAULEY—See WEBSTER SPRINGS, WV (Shentel)

CAMDEN—See WESTON, WV (Shentel)

▲**CAMERON**—Zito Media

CAMP CREEK—See CHARLESTON, WV (Suddenlink Communications)

CAMPBELLS CREEK—See CHARLESTON, WV (Suddenlink Communications)

CAMPBELLTOWN—See MARLINGTON (town), WV (Shentel)

CANE FORK—See CHARLESTON, WV (Suddenlink Communications)

CANEBRAKE—See NORTHFORK, WV (Shentel)

CANEY—See KERMIT, KY (Suddenlink Communications)

▲**CANVAS**—Econoco Inc.

CAPELS—See NORTHFORK, WV (Shentel)

▲**CAPON BRIDGE**—Formerly served by Valley Cable Systems. No longer in operation

CARBON—See CHARLESTON, WV (Suddenlink Communications)

CARETTA—See NORTHFORK, WV (Shentel)

▲**CASS**—Milestone Communications LP

CASSVILLE—See MORGANTOWN, WV (Comcast Cable)

CEDAR GROVE—See CHARLESTON, WV (Suddenlink Communications)

CENTERVILLE—See PRICHARD, WV (Windjammer Cable)

▲**CHAPEL**—Windjammer Cable

CHAPMANVILLE (PORTIONS)—See CRAWLEY CREEK ROAD, WV (Colane Cable)

CHAPMANVILLE—See HARTS, WV (Shentel)

CHAPMANVILLE—See KERMIT, WV (Suddenlink Communications)

CHARLES TOWN—See RANSON, WV (Comcast Cable)

▲**CHARLESTON**—Suddenlink Communications

CHARLTON HEIGHTS—See CHARLESTON, WV (Suddenlink Communications)

CHARMCO—See BECKLEY, WV (Suddenlink Communications)

▲**CHATTAROY**—Charter Communications. Now served by KERMIT, WV [WV0038]

CHATTAROY—See KERMIT, WV (Suddenlink Communications)

CHELYAN—See CHARLESTON, WV (Suddenlink Communications)

CHESAPEAKE—See CHARLESTON, WV (Suddenlink Communications)

CHESHIRE TWP.—See PARKERSBURG, OH (Suddenlink Communications)

CHESHIRE—See PARKERSBURG, OH (Suddenlink Communications)

▲ **CHESTER**—Comcast Cable

CHLOE—See NEBO, WV (Windjammer Cable)

CINCO—See CHARLESTON, WV (Suddenlink Communications)

▲ **CLARKSBURG**—Formerly served by Adelphia Communications. Now served by MORGANTOWN, WV [WV0198]

CLARKSBURG—See MORGANTOWN, WV (Comcast Cable)

▲ **CLARKSBURG**—Country Cable

▲ **CLARKSBURG**—Time Warner Cable

▲ **CLAY (TOWN)**—Shentel

CLAY COUNTY (SOUTHERN PORTION)—See CHARLESTON, WV (Suddenlink Communications)

CLAY COUNTY (UNINCORPORATED AREAS)—See BIRCH RIVER, WV (Windjammer Cable)

CLAY—See NEBO, WV (Windjammer Cable)

CLEAR FORK—See PINEVILLE, WV (Shentel)

CLEARVIEW—See WHEELING, WV (Comcast Cable)

CLENDENIN—See CHARLESTON, WV (Suddenlink Communications)

CLINTONVILLE—See ASBURY, WV (Windjammer Cable)

CLOVER DRIVE—See CHARLESTON, WV (Suddenlink Communications)

COAL CITY—See BECKLEY, WV (Suddenlink Communications)

COAL FORK—See CHARLESTON, WV (Suddenlink Communications)

▲ **COALTON**—Country Cable

COALTON—See ELLAMORE, WV (Windjammer Cable)

COLDWATER CREEK—See KERMIT, KY (Suddenlink Communications)

COLERAIN TWP.—See WHEELING, OH (Comcast Cable)

▲ **COLFAX**—Formerly served by Adelphia Communications. Now served by MORGANTOWN, WV [WV0198]

COLFAX—See MORGANTOWN, WV (Comcast Cable)

▲ **COLLIERS**—Jefferson County Cable Inc.

COLUMBIA—See CHARLESTON, WV (Suddenlink Communications)

COMFORT—See CHARLESTON, WV (Suddenlink Communications)

CONNORSVILLE—See WHEELING, OH (Comcast Cable)

COONSKIN DRIVE—See CHARLESTON, WV (Suddenlink Communications)

COOPERTOWN—See CHARLESTON, WV (Suddenlink Communications)

CORE—See MORGANTOWN, WV (Comcast Cable)

CORINNE—See PINEVILLE, WV (Shentel)

CORRINNE—See BECKLEY, WV (Suddenlink Communications)

CORTON—See BOMONT, WV (Vital Communications Group)

COSTA—See CHARLESTON, WV (Suddenlink Communications)

▲ **COTTAGEVILLE**—Community Antenna Service

COTTLE—See CRAIGSVILLE, WV (Shentel)

COVE GAP—See WAYNE, WV (Suddenlink Communications)

COVEL—See HERNDON, WV (Shentel)

COVEL—See PINEVILLE, WV (Shentel)

COW CREEK—See OMAR, WV (Colane Cable TV Inc.)

▲ **COWEN**—Charter Communications. Now served by WEBSTER SPRINGS, WV [WV0080]

COWEN—See WEBSTER SPRINGS, WV (Shentel)

CRABTREE—See WAYNE, WV (Suddenlink Communications)

▲ **CRAIGSVILLE**—Shentel

▲ **CRAWLEY CREEK ROAD**—Colane Cable

CREDE—See CHARLESTON, WV (Suddenlink Communications)

CRICHTON—See BECKLEY, WV (Suddenlink Communications)

CROOKED RUN—See CLARKSBURG, WV (Country Cable)

CROSS CREEK TWP. (JEFFERSON COUNTY)—See WHEELING, OH (Comcast Cable)

CROSS LANES—See CHARLESTON, WV (Suddenlink Communications)

▲ **CROSSROADS**—Formerly served by Crossroads TV Cable. No longer in operation

CROWN HILL—See CHARLESTON, WV (Suddenlink Communications)

CRUM—See KERMIT, WV (Suddenlink Communications)

CRUMPLER—See NORTHFORK, WV (Shentel)

CUCUMBER—See NORTHFORK, WV (Shentel)

CULLODEN—See MILTON, WV (Suddenlink Communications)

CUNARD—See BECKLEY, WV (Suddenlink Communications)

▲ **CURTIN**—Charter Communications. Now served by WEBSTER SPRINGS, WV [WV0080]

CURTIN—See WEBSTER SPRINGS, WV (Shentel)

CYCLONE—See PINEVILLE, WV (Shentel)

CYCLONE—See KERMIT, WV (Suddenlink Communications)

CYRUS—See PRICHARD, KY (Windjammer Cable)

DALLISON—See PARKERSBURG (southern portion), WV (Community Antenna Service)

DAMERON—See CHARLESTON, WV (Suddenlink Communications)

DANESE—See MEADOW BRIDGE, WV (Vital Communications Group)

DANVILLE—See MADISON, WV (Suddenlink Communications)

DAVELLA—See KERMIT, KY (Suddenlink Communications)

DAVIS CREEK—See CHARLESTON, WV (Suddenlink Communications)

DAVISVILLE—See PARKERSBURG (southern portion), WV (Community Antenna Service)

DAVY—See NORTHFORK, WV (Shentel)

DAWES—See CHARLESTON, WV (Suddenlink Communications)

▲ **DAWSON**—Econoco Inc.

DEBORD—See KERMIT, KY (Suddenlink Communications)

DECOTA—See CHARLESTON, WV (Suddenlink Communications)

DEEPWATER—See CHARLESTON, WV (Suddenlink Communications)

▲ **DELBARTON**—Colane Cable TV Inc. Now served by OMAR, WV [WV0191]

DELBARTON—See OMAR, WV (Colane Cable TV Inc.)

DENVER—See TUNNELTON, WV (Community Antenna Service)

DIAMOND—See CHARLESTON, WV (Suddenlink Communications)

▲ **DIANA**—Country Cable

DILLE—See BIRCH RIVER, WV (Windjammer Cable)

DILLONVALE—See WHEELING, OH (Comcast Cable)

▲ **DINGESS**—Shentel

DIXIE—See CHARLESTON, WV (Suddenlink Communications)

▲ **DORCAS**—C T & R Cable

▲ **DOROTHY**—Charter Communications. Now served by BECKLEY, WV [WV0005]

DOROTHY—See BECKLEY, WV (Suddenlink Communications)

DOTHAN—See SCARBRO, WV (Shentel)

▲ **DRENNEN**—Shentel

DRY BRANCH DRIVE—See CHARLESTON, WV (Suddenlink Communications)

DRYBRANCH—See CHARLESTON, WV (Suddenlink Communications)

DUCK—See NEBO, WV (Windjammer Cable)

DUNBAR—See CHARLESTON, WV (Suddenlink Communications)

▲ **DUNLOW**—Formerly served by Almega Cable. No longer in operation

DUPONT CITY—See CHARLESTON, WV (Suddenlink Communications)

▲ **DURBIN**—Milestone Communications LP

DURGON—See MOOREFIELD, WV (Atlantic Broadband)

DUTCH ROAD—See CHARLESTON, WV (Suddenlink Communications)

EAST BANK—See CHARLESTON, WV (Suddenlink Communications)

EAST DAILEY—See BEVERLY, WV (Suddenlink Communications)

EAST KERMIT—See KERMIT, WV (Suddenlink Communications)

EAST LOVELY—See KERMIT, WV (Suddenlink Communications)

EAST LYNN—See WAYNE, WV (Suddenlink Communications)

EAST PEA RIDGE—See HUNTINGTON, WV (Comcast Cable)

▲ **EASTON**—Formerly served by Adelphia Communications. No longer in operation

ECCLES—See BECKLEY, WV (Suddenlink Communications)

ECKMAN—See NORTHFORK, WV (Shentel)

EDRAY—See MARLINGTON (town), WV (Shentel)

EDWIGHT—See CHARLESTON, WV (Suddenlink Communications)

ELEANOR—See RED HOUSE, WV (Comcast Cable)

ELGOOD—See OAKVALE, WV (Shentel)

ELIZABETH—See PARKERSBURG, WV (Suddenlink Communications)

ELK CREEK—See KERMIT, KY (Suddenlink Communications)

ELK FOREST—See CHARLESTON, WV (Suddenlink Communications)

ELK HILLS—See CHARLESTON, WV (Suddenlink Communications)

ELK TWO MILE—See CHARLESTON, WV (Suddenlink Communications)

ELKHORN—See NORTHFORK, WV (Shentel)

ELKINS—See BEVERLY, WV (Suddenlink Communications)

ELKRIDGE—See CHARLESTON, WV (Suddenlink Communications)

ELKVIEW—See CHARLESTON, WV (Suddenlink Communications)

ELKVIEW—See FRAME, WV (Windjammer Cable)

▲ **ELLAMORE**—Windjammer Cable

▲ **ELLENBORO**—Charter Communications. Now served by WESTON, WV [WV0034]

ELLENBORO—See WESTON, WV (Shentel)

ELSINORE—See RED HOUSE, WV (Comcast Cable)

ENTERPRISE—See SHINNSTON, WV (Suddenlink Communications)

ESKDALE—See CHARLESTON, WV (Suddenlink Communications)

EUNICE—See CHARLESTON, WV (Suddenlink Communications)

EVANS—See COTTAGEVILLE, WV (Community Antenna Service)

EVERETTVILLE—See MORGANTOWN, WV (Comcast Cable)

EVERGREEN HILL—See COTTAGEVILLE, WV (Community Antenna Service)

FAIRDALE—See BECKLEY, WV (Suddenlink Communications)

FAIRLEA—See BECKLEY, WV (Suddenlink Communications)

▲ **FAIRMONT**—Time Warner Cable. Now served by CLARKSBURG, WV [WV0010]

FAIRMONT—See MORGANTOWN, WV (Comcast Cable)

FAIRMONT—See CLARKSBURG, WV (Time Warner Cable)

FAIRPLAIN—See SANDYVILLE, WV (Windjammer Cable)

FAIRPOINT—See WHEELING, OH (Comcast Cable)

FAIRVIEW—See GRANT TOWN, WV (Atlantic Broadband)

FAIRVIEW—See KERMIT, KY (Suddenlink Communications)

FALLING ROCK—See CHARLESTON, WV (Suddenlink Communications)

FALLSVIEW—See CHARLESTON, WV (Suddenlink Communications)

FANROCK—See PINEVILLE, WV (Shentel)

FARMINGTON—See SHINNSTON, WV (Suddenlink Communications)

FAYETTEVILLE—See BECKLEY, WV (Suddenlink Communications)

FELLOWSVILLE—See TUNNELTON, WV (Community Antenna Service)

FENWICK—See RICHWOOD, WV (Shentel)

FERRELLSBURG—See WAYNE, WV (Suddenlink Communications)

▲ **FLAT ROCK**—Time Warner Cable

FLAT TOP—See BECKLEY, WV (Suddenlink Communications)

FLATWOODS—See GASSAWAY, WV (Shentel)

▲ **FLEMINGTON**—Suddenlink Communications

FLUSHING—See WHEELING, OH (Comcast Cable)

FOLA—See CHARLESTON, WV (Suddenlink Communications)

FOLLANSBEE—See WHEELING, WV (Comcast Cable)

▲ **FOLSOM**—Jones TV Cable & Satellite Systems Inc.

FORT GAY—See WAYNE, WV (Suddenlink Communications)

FORT SPRING—See ASBURY, WV (Windjammer Cable)

FOSTERVILLE—See CHARLESTON, WV (Suddenlink Communications)

FOUR STATES—See SHINNSTON, WV (Suddenlink Communications)

▲ **FRAME**—Windjammer Cable

▲ **FRAMETOWN**—Windjammer Cable

FRANK—See DURBIN, WV (Milestone Communications LP)

▲ **FRANKFORD**—Clearview TV Cable

▲ **FRANKLIN**—Shentel

FRAZIERS BOTTOM—See PLINY, WV (Bradley Communications)

FRENCH CREEK—See BUCKHANNON, WV (Suddenlink Communications)

▲ **FRIENDLY**—Windjammer Cable

FRONTAGE ROAD—See MADISON, WV (Suddenlink Communications)

FROSTBURG—See KEYSER, MD (Comcast Cable)

GALLAGHER—See CHARLESTON, WV (Suddenlink Communications)

GALLIPOLIS FERRY—See PARKERSBURG, WV (Suddenlink Communications)

GALLIPOLIS—See PARKERSBURG, OH (Suddenlink Communications)

GALLOWAY—See FLEMINGTON, WV (Suddenlink Communications)

▲ **GANDEEVILLE**—Econoco Inc.

GARRISON—See CHARLESTON, WV (Suddenlink Communications)

GARWOOD—See HERNDON, WV (Shentel)

GARWOOD—See PINEVILLE, WV (Shentel)

▲ **GASSAWAY**—Shentel

GAULEY BRIDGE—See CHARLESTON, WV (Suddenlink Communications)

▲ **GENOA**—Lycom Communications

GEORGES CREEK—See CHARLESTON, WV (Suddenlink Communications)

▲ **GILBERT**—Colane Cable TV Inc. Now served by OMAR, WV [WV0191]

GILBERT—See OMAR, WV (Colane Cable TV Inc.)

▲ **GILBOA**—Shentel

GILES COUNTY (PORTIONS)—See BECKLEY, VA (Suddenlink Communications)

GILES—See CHARLESTON, WV (Suddenlink Communications)

GILLIAM—See NORTHFORK, WV (Shentel)

GLASGOW—See CHARLESTON, WV (Suddenlink Communications)

▲ **GLEN DALE**—Comcast Cable. Now served by WHEELING, WV [WV0004]

GLEN DALE—See WHEELING, WV (Comcast Cable)

GLEN FERRIS—See CHARLESTON, WV (Suddenlink Communications)

GLEN FORK—See PINEVILLE, WV (Shentel)

GLEN JEAN—See SCARBRO, WV (Shentel)

GLEN LYN—See BECKLEY, VA (Suddenlink Communications)

GLEN ROBBINS—See WHEELING, OH (Comcast Cable)

GLEN ROGERS—See PINEVILLE, WV (Shentel)

GLEN WHITE—See BECKLEY, WV (Suddenlink Communications)

GLEN—See BOMONT, WV (Vital Communications Group)

GLENCOE—See WHEELING, OH (Comcast Cable)

▲ **GLENHAYES**—Formerly served by Lycom Communications. No longer in operation

▲ **GLENVILLE**—Rapid Cable. Now served by WESTON, WV [WV0034]

GLENVILLE—See WESTON, WV (Shentel)

GLENWOOD—See APPLE GROVE, WV (Windjammer Cable)

▲ **GOLDTOWN**—Econoco Inc.

GOODY—See KERMIT, KY (Suddenlink Communications)

GORDON—See VAN, WV (Colane Cable TV)

GOSHEN TWP. (BELMONT COUNTY)—See WHEELING, OH (Comcast Cable)

▲ **GRAFTON**—Comcast Cable. Now served by MORGANTOWN, WV [WV0198]

GRAFTON—See MORGANTOWN, WV (Comcast Cable)

▲ **GRANT TOWN**—Atlantic Broadband

▲ **GRANTSVILLE**—Shentel

GRANVILLE—See MORGANTOWN, WV (Comcast Cable)

GRASSY CREEK—See DIANA, WV (Country Cable)

▲ **GRAYSVILLE**—Windjammer Cable

▲ **GREEN ACRES**—Formerly served by Almega Cable. No longer in operation

GREEN BANK—See DURBIN, WV (Milestone Communications LP)

GREEN BOTTOM—See APPLE GROVE, WV (Windjammer Cable)

GREEN SPRING—See SPRINGFIELD, WV (Comcast Cable)

GREEN VALLEY—See BLUEFIELD, WV (Comcast Cable)

GREENBRIER COUNTY (PORTIONS)—See BECKLEY, WV (Suddenlink Communications)

GREENTOWN—See MORGANTOWN, WV (Comcast Cable)

GREENVIEW—See SIX MILE, WV (Colane Cable)

GREY EAGLE—See KERMIT, WV (Suddenlink Communications)

GUYAN ESTATES—See HUNTINGTON, WV (Comcast Cable)

GYPSY—See SHINNSTON, WV (Suddenlink Communications)

▲ **HAMLIN**—Armstrong Cable Services

HAMMONDSVILLE—See WHEELING, OH (Comcast Cable)

▲ **HAMPDEN**—Colane Cable TV Inc. Now served by OMAR, WV [WV0191]

HAMPDEN—See OMAR, WV (Colane Cable TV Inc.)

HAMPSHIRE COUNTY (PORTIONS)—See AUGUSTA, WV (Comcast Cable)

HANCOCK COUNTY (PORTIONS)—See CHESTER, WV (Comcast Cable)

HANCOCK COUNTY (PORTIONS)—See NEW CUMBERLAND, WV (Comcast Cable)

HANDLEY—See CHARLESTON, WV (Suddenlink Communications)

▲ **HANOVER**—Colane Cable TV Inc.

HANSFORD—See CHARLESTON, WV (Suddenlink Communications)

HARDY COUNTY—See MOOREFIELD, WV (Atlantic Broadband)

HARDY—See OAKVALE, WV (Shentel)

▲ **HARMAN**—Formerly served by Harman Cable Corp. No longer in operation

HARPERS FERRY—See RANSON, WV (Comcast Cable)

HARRISON COUNTY (PORTIONS)—See BUCKHANNON, WV (Suddenlink Communications)

HARRISON COUNTY (PORTIONS)—See FLEMINGTON, WV (Suddenlink Communications)

HARRISON COUNTY (RURAL AREAS)—See CLARKSBURG, WV (Time Warner Cable)

HARRISON COUNTY—See SALEM, WV (Shentel)

▲ **HARRISVILLE**—Rapid Cable. Now served by WESTON, WV [WV0034]

HARRISVILLE—See WHEELING, OH (Comcast Cable)

HARRISVILLE—See WESTON, WV (Shentel)

HARTFORD—See PARKERSBURG, WV (Suddenlink Communications)

▲ **HARTS**—Shentel

HARTWELL—See NORTHFORK, WV (Shentel)

HARVEY—See SCARBRO, WV (Shentel)

HASTINGS—See PINE GROVE, WV (Zito Media)

HATFIELD—See KERMIT, KY (Suddenlink Communications)

HAVACO—See NORTHFORK, WV (Shentel)

HAYWOOD—See SHINNSTON, WV (Suddenlink Communications)

HEDGESVILLE—See RANSON, WV (Comcast Cable)

HELEN—See BECKLEY, WV (Suddenlink Communications)

HEMPHILL—See NORTHFORK, WV (Shentel)

HENDERSON—See PARKERSBURG, WV (Suddenlink Communications)

HENSLEY—See IAEGER, WV (Shentel)

HEPZIBAH—See SHINNSTON, WV (Suddenlink Communications)

▲ **HERNDON**—Shentel

HERNSHAW—See CHARLESTON, WV (Suddenlink Communications)

▲ **HEWETT**—Colane Cable TV

HILLSBORO—See MARLINGTON (town), WV (Shentel)

HILLTOP—See SCARBRO, WV (Shentel)

HINES—See BECKLEY, WV (Suddenlink Communications)

▲ **HINTON**—Charter Communications. Now served by BECKLEY, WV [WV0005]

HINTON—See BECKLEY, WV (Suddenlink Communications)

HINTON—See TALCOTT, WV (Windjammer Cable)

HODE—See KERMIT, KY (Suddenlink Communications)

HODGESVILLE—See BUCKHANNON, WV (Suddenlink Communications)

HOLCOMB—See RICHWOOD, WV (Shentel)

HOLLOWAY—See WHEELING, OH (Comcast Cable)

HOLLY LAWN—See CHARLESTON, WV (Suddenlink Communications)

HOLLY—See CHARLESTON, WV (Suddenlink Communications)

HOMETOWN—See RED HOUSE, WV (Comcast Cable)

HOTCHKISS—See PINEVILLE, WV (Shentel)

HUBBALL—See WAYNE, WV (Suddenlink Communications)

HUDDY—See KERMIT, KY (Suddenlink Communications)

HUGHESTON—See CHARLESTON, WV (Suddenlink Communications)

HUNDRED—See LITTLETON, WV (Zito Media)

HUNTER ROAD—See CHARLESTON, WV (Suddenlink Communications)

▲ **HUNTERSVILLE**—Milestone Communications LP

▲ **HUNTINGTON**—Comcast Cable

HURRICANE—See MILTON, WV (Suddenlink Communications)

▲ **HUTCHINSON**—Formerly served by Adelphia Communications. Now served by MORGANTOWN, WV [WV0198]

HUTCHINSON—See MORGANTOWN, WV (Comcast Cable)

HUTTONSVILLE—See BEVERLY, WV (Suddenlink Communications)

▲ **IAEGER**—Shentel

IDAMAY—See SHINNSTON, WV (Suddenlink Communications)

INDEPENDENCE—See KINGWOOD, WV (Atlantic Broadband)

INDORE—See CHARLESTON, WV (Suddenlink Communications)

INDUSTRIAL—See SALEM, WV (Shentel)

INEZ—See KERMIT, KY (Suddenlink Communications)

INGLESIDE—See OAKVALE, WV (Shentel)

INGRAM BRANCH—See PAGE, WV (Shentel)

▲ **INWOOD**—Formerly served by Adelphia Communications. Now served by SHEPHERDSTOWN, WV [WV0016]

INWOOD—See RANSON, WV (Comcast Cable)

IRONDALE—See WHEELING, OH (Comcast Cable)

ISAACS CREEK—See CLARKSBURG, WV (Country Cable)

ISABAN—See PANTHER, WV (Shentel)

ISLAND CREEK TWP. (JEFFERSON COUNTY)—See WHEELING, OH (Comcast Cable)

ITMANN—See PINEVILLE, WV (Shentel)

IVYDALE—See NEBO, WV (Windjammer Cable)

JACKSONBURG—See PINE GROVE, WV (Zito Media)

JANE LEW—See WESTON, WV (Shentel)

JANIE—See CHARLESTON, WV (Suddenlink Communications)

JEFFERSON COUNTY—See RANSON, WV (Comcast Cable)

JEFFREY—See HEWETT, WV (Colane Cable TV)

▲ **JENKINJONES**—Formerly served by Obey's TV Cable. No longer in operation

JESSE—See PINEVILLE, WV (Shentel)

JODIE—See CHARLESTON, WV (Suddenlink Communications)

JOHNSON BRANCH—See PAGE, WV (Shentel)

JOHNSON COUNTY (PORTIONS)—See KERMIT, KY (Suddenlink Communications)

JOHNSON RUN—See PETERSBURG, WV (Shentel)

JOLO—See IAEGER, WV (Shentel)

JULIAN—See CHARLESTON, WV (Suddenlink Communications)

JUMBO—See DIANA, WV (Country Cable)

JUMPING BRANCH—See BECKLEY, WV (Suddenlink Communications)

JUNIOR—See BELINGTON, WV (Shentel)

JUSTICE—See OMAR, WV (Colane Cable TV Inc.)

KANAWHA COUNTY—See CHARLESTON, WV (Suddenlink Communications)

KANAWHA FALLS—See CHARLESTON, WV (Suddenlink Communications)

KATY LICK—See CLARKSBURG, WV (Country Cable)

KAYFORD—See CHARLESTON, WV (Suddenlink Communications)

KEARNEYSVILLE—See RANSON, WV (Comcast Cable)

KEEDYSVILLE—See RANSON, MD (Comcast Cable)

KEITH—See CHARLESTON, WV (Suddenlink Communications)

KELLYSVILLE—See OAKVALE, WV (Shentel)

KENNA—See GOLDTOWN, WV (Econoco Inc.)

▲ **KERMIT**—Suddenlink Communications

KESLING MILL—See BUCKHANNON, WV (Suddenlink Communications)

KEY—See WHEELING, OH (Comcast Cable)

▲ **KEYSER**—Comcast Cable

▲ **KIMBALL**—Comcast Cable. Now served by NORTHFORK, WV [WV0045]

KIMBALL—See NORTHFORK, WV (Shentel)

KIMBERLY—See CHARLESTON, WV (Suddenlink Communications)

KINCAID—See PAGE, WV (Shentel)

KINGSTON—See SCARBRO, WV (Shentel)

▲ **KINGWOOD**—Atlantic Broadband

KINGWOOD—See TUNNELTON, WV (Community Antenna Service)

KITCHEN—See WAYNE, WV (Suddenlink Communications)

KNOWLWOOD—See CHARLESTON, WV (Suddenlink Communications)

KOPPERSTOWN—See PINEVILLE, WV (Shentel)

KYLE—See NORTHFORK, WV (Shentel)

LAFFERTY—See WHEELING, OH (Comcast Cable)

LAING—See CHARLESTON, WV (Suddenlink Communications)

LAKE—See HEWETT, WV (Colane Cable TV)

LANDRAFF—See NORTHFORK, WV (Shentel)

LANSING VALLEY—See WHEELING, OH (Comcast Cable)

LANSING—See ANSTED, WV (Shentel)

LAUREL FORK—See CHARLESTON, WV (Suddenlink Communications)

LAUREL POINT—See MORGANTOWN, WV (Comcast Cable)

LAVALETTE—See WAYNE, WV (Suddenlink Communications)

LAWRENCE COUNTY (PORTIONS)—See OMAR, KY (Colane Cable TV Inc.)

LAWRENCEVILLE—See CHESTER, WV (Comcast Cable)

LAYLAND—See MEADOW BRIDGE, WV (Vital Communications Group)

LECKIE—See NORTHFORK, WV (Shentel)

LECKIEVILLE—See KERMIT, KY (Suddenlink Communications)

LEEVALE—See CHARLESTON, WV (Suddenlink Communications)

LEEWOOD—See CHARLESTON, WV (Suddenlink Communications)

▲ **LEFT HAND**—Econoco Inc.

LEIVASY—See NETTIE, WV (Windjammer Cable)

▲ **LENORE**—Charter Communications. Now served by KERMIT, WV [WV0038]

LENORE—See KERMIT, WV (Suddenlink Communications)

▲ **LEON**—Vital Communications Group

LESAGE—See HUNTINGTON, WV (Comcast Cable)

LESAGE—See APPLE GROVE, WV (Windjammer Cable)

LESLIE—See BECKLEY, WV (Suddenlink Communications)

MOUNDSVILLE—See WHEELING, WV (Comcast Cable)

MOUNT CARBON—See CHARLESTON, WV (Suddenlink Communications)

MOUNT GAY—See DINGESS, WV (Shentel)

MOUNT HOPE—See BECKLEY, WV (Suddenlink Communications)

▲**MOUNT LOOKOUT**—Econoco Inc.

MOUNT NEBO—See MOUNT LOOKOUT, WV (Econoco Inc.)

MOUNT PLEASANT—See WHEELING, OH (Comcast Cable)

▲**MOUNT STORM**—Formerly served by Almega Cable. No longer in operation

MOUNT ZION—See GRANTSVILLE, WV (Shentel)

MOZART—See WHEELING, WV (Comcast Cable)

▲**MUD RIVER**—Colane Cable TV

MUDFORK—See DINGESS, WV (Shentel)

MULBERRY—See CHARLESTON, WV (Suddenlink Communications)

▲**MULLENS**—Jet Broadband. Now served by PINEVILLE, WV [WV0204]

MULLENS—See PINEVILLE, WV (Shentel)

MURPHYTOWN—See PARKERSBURG (southern portion), WV (Community Antenna Service)

MYRTLE—See KERMIT, WV (Suddenlink Communications)

NABOB—See CHARLESTON, WV (Suddenlink Communications)

NALLEN—See MOUNT LOOKOUT, WV (Econoco Inc.)

NARROWS—See BECKLEY, VA (Suddenlink Communications)

NATIONAL—See MORGANTOWN, WV (Comcast Cable)

NAUGATUCK—See KERMIT, WV (Suddenlink Communications)

▲**NEBO**—Windjammer Cable

NEFFS—See WHEELING, OH (Comcast Cable)

NEIBERT—See LYBURN, WV (Colane Cable TV)

NELLIS—See CHARLESTON, WV (Suddenlink Communications)

▲**NETTIE**—Windjammer Cable

NEW ALEXANDRIA—See WHEELING, OH (Comcast Cable)

NEW CREEK—See KEYSER, WV (Comcast Cable)

▲**NEW CUMBERLAND**—Comcast Cable

NEW HAVEN—See PARKERSBURG, WV (Suddenlink Communications)

NEW HOPE—See RICHWOOD, WV (Shentel)

NEW MANCHESTER—See NEW CUMBERLAND, WV (Comcast Cable)

▲**NEW MARTINSVILLE**—Charter Communications. Now served by PARKERSBURG, WV [WV0003]

NEW MARTINSVILLE—See PARKERSBURG, WV (Suddenlink Communications)

NEW RICHMOND—See PINEVILLE, WV (Shentel)

NEWBURG—See KINGWOOD, WV (Atlantic Broadband)

NEWELL—See CHESTER, WV (Comcast Cable)

NEWHALL—See NORTHFORK, WV (Shentel)

NEWTON—See LEFT HAND, WV (Econoco Inc.)

NICHOLAS COUNTY—See SUMMERSVILLE, WV (Shentel)

NIMITZ—See BECKLEY, WV (Suddenlink Communications)

NITRO (PORTIONS)—See RED HOUSE, WV (Comcast Cable)

▲**NITRO**—Charter Communications. Now served by CHARLESTON, (formerly Chelyan) WV [WV0006]

NITRO—See CHARLESTON, WV (Suddenlink Communications)

NOAMA—See CHARLESTON, WV (Suddenlink Communications)

NOLAN—See KERMIT, WV (Suddenlink Communications)

NORTH FORK—See PETERSBURG, WV (Shentel)

NORTH HILLS—See PARKERSBURG, WV (Suddenlink Communications)

NORTH PAGE—See PAGE, WV (Shentel)

NORTH WELCH—See NORTHFORK, WV (Shentel)

▲**NORTHFORK**—Shentel

▲**NORTON**—Formerly served by Adelphia Communications. Now served by ELLAMORE, WV [WV0125]

NORTON—See ELLAMORE, WV (Windjammer Cable)

NUTTER FORT—See CLARKSBURG, WV (Time Warner Cable)

▲**OAK HILL**—Charter Communications. Now served by BECKLEY, WV [WV0005]

OAK HILL—See BECKLEY, WV (Suddenlink Communications)

▲**OAKVALE**—Shentel

OCEANA—See PINEVILLE, WV (Shentel)

OHIO COUNTY—See WHEELING, WV (Comcast Cable)

OHLEY—See CHARLESTON, WV (Suddenlink Communications)

▲**OMAR**—Colane Cable TV Inc.

ONA—See MILTON, WV (Suddenlink Communications)

OPPY—See KERMIT, KY (Suddenlink Communications)

ORGAS—See CHARLESTON, WV (Suddenlink Communications)

ORMA—See NEBO, WV (Windjammer Cable)

OSAGE—See MORGANTOWN, WV (Comcast Cable)

OTTAWA—See KERMIT, WV (Suddenlink Communications)

PACKS BRANCH—See CHARLESTON, WV (Suddenlink Communications)

PACKSVILLE—See CHARLESTON, WV (Suddenlink Communications)

PADEN CITY—See PARKERSBURG, WV (Suddenlink Communications)

▲**PAGE**—Shentel

PAGETON—See NORTHFORK, WV (Shentel)

PAINT CREEK (PORTIONS)—See CHARLESTON, WV (Suddenlink Communications)

PAINTSVILLE—See KERMIT, KY (Suddenlink Communications)

▲**PANTHER**—Shentel

PARCOAL—See WEBSTER SPRINGS, WV (Shentel)

▲**PARKERSBURG (SOUTHERN PORTION)**—Community Antenna Service

▲**PARKERSBURG**—Suddenlink Communications

▲**PAW PAW**—Atlantic Broadband

▲**PAX**—Charter Communications. Now served by BECKLEY, WV [WV0005]

PAX—See BECKLEY, WV (Suddenlink Communications)

PAYTONA—See CHARLESTON, WV (Suddenlink Communications)

PEARISBURG—See BECKLEY, VA (Suddenlink Communications)

PEASE TWP. (BELMONT COUNTY)—See WHEELING, OH (Comcast Cable)

PEMBROKE—See BECKLEY, VA (Suddenlink Communications)

PENDLETON COUNTY—See FRANKLIN, WV (Shentel)

▲**PENNSBORO**—Shentel

PEORA—See WYATT, WV (Country Cable)

▲**PETERSBURG**—Shentel

▲**PETERSTOWN**—Charter Communications. Now served by BECKLEY, WV [WV0005]

PETERSTOWN—See BECKLEY, WV (Suddenlink Communications)

PETTUS—See CHARLESTON, WV (Suddenlink Communications)

▲**PHILIPPI**—Philippi Communications System

PIEDMONT—See KEYSER, WV (Comcast Cable)

PIERPOINT—See PINEVILLE, WV (Shentel)

PIKE COUNTY (PORTIONS)—See OMAR, KY (Colane Cable TV Inc.)

PIKE COUNTY (UNINCORPORATED AREAS)—See KERMIT, KY (Suddenlink Communications)

PILGRIM—See KERMIT, KY (Suddenlink Communications)

PINCH—See CHARLESTON, WV (Suddenlink Communications)

PINE BLUFF—See WYATT, WV (Country Cable)

PINE GROVE—See DURBIN, WV (Milestone Communications LP)

▲**PINE GROVE**—Zito Media

▲**PINEVILLE**—Shentel

▲**PIPESTEM**—Charter Communications. Now served by BECKLEY, WV [WV0005]

PIPESTEM—See BECKLEY, WV (Suddenlink Communications)

PLEASANT VALLEY—See MORGANTOWN, WV (Comcast Cable)

PLEASANT VALLEY—See CLARKSBURG, WV (Time Warner Cable)

PLEASANT VIEW (LINCOLN COUNTY)—See HAMLIN, WV (Armstrong Cable Services)

PLEASANTS COUNTY—See PARKERSBURG, WV (Suddenlink Communications)

▲**PLINY**—Bradley Communications

POCA—See RED HOUSE, WV (Comcast Cable)

POCA—See CHARLESTON, WV (Suddenlink Communications)

POCAHONTAS—See BLUEFIELD, VA (Comcast Cable)

POCATALICO—See SISSONVILLE, WV (Suddenlink Communications)

POE—See GILBOA, WV (Shentel)

POINT LICK—See CHARLESTON, WV (Suddenlink Communications)

▲**POINT PLEASANT**—Charter Communications. Now served by PARKERSBURG, WV [WV0003]

POINT PLEASANT—See PARKERSBURG, WV (Suddenlink Communications)

POMEROY—See PARKERSBURG, OH (Suddenlink Communications)

POND CREEK—See KERMIT, KY (Suddenlink Communications)

POND GAP—See CHARLESTON, WV (Suddenlink Communications)

PORT AMHERST—See CHARLESTON, WV (Suddenlink Communications)

POSEY—See CHARLESTON, WV (Suddenlink Communications)

SLAB FORK—See PINEVILLE, WV (Shentel)

SLATER'S BRANCH—See KERMIT, KY (Suddenlink Communications)

SLATYFORK—See SNOWSHOE, WV (Windjammer Cable)

SMITH TWP.—See WHEELING, OH (Comcast Cable)

SMITHERS—See CHARLESTON, WV (Suddenlink Communications)

SMITHFIELD TWP. (JEFFERSON COUNTY)—See WHEELING, OH (Comcast Cable)

▲ **SMITHFIELD**—Formerly served by Almega Cable. No longer in operation

SNOW HILL—See CHARLESTON, WV (Suddenlink Communications)

▲ **SNOWSHOE**—Windjammer Cable

SOPHIA—See BECKLEY, WV (Suddenlink Communications)

SOUTH CHARLESTON—See CHARLESTON, WV (Suddenlink Communications)

SOUTH WILLIAMSON—See KERMIT, KY (Suddenlink Communications)

SPELTER—See SHINNSTON, WV (Suddenlink Communications)

▲ **SPENCER**—Charter Communications. Now served by PARKERSBURG, WV [WV0003]

SPENCER—See PARKERSBURG, WV (Suddenlink Communications)

SPRIGG—See KERMIT, WV (Suddenlink Communications)

SPRING FORK—See CHARLESTON, WV (Suddenlink Communications)

SPRINGFIELD TWP.—See PARKERSBURG, OH (Suddenlink Communications)

▲ **SPRINGFIELD**—Comcast Cable

SPRINGFIELD—See CHARLESTON, WV (Suddenlink Communications)

SQUIRE—See NORTHFORK, WV (Shentel)

ST. ALBANS (PORTIONS)—See RED HOUSE, WV (Comcast Cable)

ST. ALBANS—See CHARLESTON, WV (Suddenlink Communications)

ST. CLAIRSVILLE—See WHEELING, OH (Comcast Cable)

▲ **ST. MARY'S**—Charter Communications. Now served by PARKERSBURG, WV [WV0003]

ST. MARYS—See WESTON, WV (Shentel)

ST. MARYS—See PARKERSBURG, WV (Suddenlink Communications)

STAR CITY—See MORGANTOWN, WV (Comcast Cable)

STATON—See KERMIT, KY (Suddenlink Communications)

STEPHENSON—See BECKLEY, WV (Suddenlink Communications)

STEUBENVILLE—See WHEELING, OH (Comcast Cable)

STICKNEY—See CHARLESTON, WV (Suddenlink Communications)

STIRRAT—See OMAR, WV (Colane Cable TV Inc.)

STONE—See KERMIT, KY (Suddenlink Communications)

STONEWOOD—See CLARKSBURG, WV (Time Warner Cable)

STOVER—See CHARLESTON, WV (Suddenlink Communications)

STRANGE CREEK—See FRAMETOWN, WV (Windjammer Cable)

SUMMERLEE—See BECKLEY, WV (Suddenlink Communications)

SUMMERS COUNTY (PORTIONS)—See TALCOTT, WV (Windjammer Cable)

SUMMERS COUNTY (UNINCORPORATED AREAS)—See BECKLEY, WV (Suddenlink Communications)

SUMMERSVILLE (PORTIONS)—See NETTIE, WV (Windjammer Cable)

▲ **SUMMERSVILLE**—Shentel

SUMMIT POINT—See RANSON, WV (Comcast Cable)

SUMMITVIEW—See TALCOTT, WV (Windjammer Cable)

SUNDIAL—See CHARLESTON, WV (Suddenlink Communications)

SUTTON—See GASSAWAY, WV (Shentel)

SUTTON—See BIRCH RIVER, WV (Windjammer Cable)

SWISS—See CHARLESTON, WV (Suddenlink Communications)

SWITCHBACK—See NORTHFORK, WV (Shentel)

SYLVESTER—See CHARLESTON, WV (Suddenlink Communications)

SYRACUSE—See PARKERSBURG, OH (Suddenlink Communications)

TAD—See CHARLESTON, WV (Suddenlink Communications)

▲ **TALCOTT**—Windjammer Cable

▲ **TANNER**—Windjammer Cable

TAYLOR COUNTY (EASTERN PORTION)—See SHINNSTON, WV (Suddenlink Communications)

TAYLOR COUNTY (PORTIONS)—See MORGANTOWN, WV (Comcast Cable)

TAYLOR COUNTY (PORTIONS)—See CLARKSBURG, WV (Time Warner Cable)

TAZEWELL COUNTY (PORTIONS)—See BLUEFIELD, VA (Comcast Cable)

TENNERTON—See BUCKHANNON, WV (Suddenlink Communications)

TERRA ALTA—See KINGWOOD, WV (Atlantic Broadband)

TILTONSVILLE—See WHEELING, OH (Comcast Cable)

TOLER—See KERMIT, KY (Suddenlink Communications)

TOMAHAWK—See KERMIT, KY (Suddenlink Communications)

TRIADELPHIA—See WHEELING, WV (Comcast Cable)

TRIPP—See KERMIT, WV (Suddenlink Communications)

TROY—See WESTON, WV (Shentel)

▲ **TUNNELTON**—Community Antenna Service

TURKEY CREEK—See KERMIT, KY (Suddenlink Communications)

▲ **TURTLE CREEK**—Colane Cable

TWENTYMILE—See CHARLESTON, WV (Suddenlink Communications)

TWILIGHT—See VAN, WV (Colane Cable TV)

TWIN BRANCH—See NORTHFORK, WV (Shentel)

TYLER COUNTY (PORTIONS)—See PARKERSBURG, WV (Suddenlink Communications)

UNEEDA—See MADISON, WV (Suddenlink Communications)

UNION ADDITION—See CHARLESTON, WV (Suddenlink Communications)

▲ **UNION**—Vital Communications Group

▲ **UPPER TRACT**—Formerly served by Cebridge Connections. No longer in operation

UPPERGLADE—See WEBSTER SPRINGS, WV (Shentel)

UPSHUR COUNTY—See BUCKHANNON, WV (Suddenlink Communications)

VALLEY BEND—See BEVERLY, WV (Suddenlink Communications)

VALLEY FORK—See MAYSEL, WV (Econoco Inc.)

VALLEY GROVE—See WHEELING, WV (Comcast Cable)

VALLSCREEK—See NORTHFORK, WV (Shentel)

▲ **VAN**—Colane Cable TV

▲ **VARNEY**—Colane Cable TV Inc. Now served by OMAR, WV [WV0191]

VARNEY—See OMAR, WV (Colane Cable TV Inc.)

VAUGHAN—See CHARLESTON, WV (Suddenlink Communications)

VERDUNVILLE—See DINGESS, WV (Shentel)

VICTOR—See ANSTED, WV (Shentel)

VIENNA—See PARKERSBURG, WV (Suddenlink Communications)

VIVIAN—See NORTHFORK, WV (Shentel)

WALKER—See PARKERSBURG (southern portion), WV (Community Antenna Service)

▲ **WALKERSVILLE**—Formerly served by Almega Cable. No longer in operation

WALLACE—See FOLSOM, WV (Jones TV Cable & Satellite Systems Inc.)

WALLBACK—See MAYSEL, WV (Econoco Inc.)

▲ **WALTON**—Formerly served by Windjammer Cable. No longer in operation

▲ **WAR**—Suddenlink Communications. Now served by NORTHFORK, WV [WV0045]

WAR—See NORTHFORK, WV (Shentel)

▲ **WARDENSVILLE**—Formerly served by Valley Cable Systems. No longer in operation

WARFIELD—See KERMIT, KY (Suddenlink Communications)

WARREN TWP. (BELMONT COUNTY)—See WHEELING, OH (Comcast Cable)

▲ **WARWOOD**—Centre TV Cable

WASHINGTON COUNTY—See PARKERSBURG, OH (Suddenlink Communications)

WASHINGTON—See PARKERSBURG (southern portion), WV (Community Antenna Service)

WAVERLY—See PARKERSBURG, WV (Suddenlink Communications)

WAYNE COUNTY (NORTHWESTERN PORTION)—See HUNTINGTON, WV (Comcast Cable)

WAYNE COUNTY (PORTIONS)—See OMAR, WV (Colane Cable TV Inc.)

WAYNE COUNTY (UNINCORPORATED AREAS)—See PRICHARD, WV (Windjammer Cable)

▲ **WAYNE**—Suddenlink Communications

WEBSTER COUNTY (PORTIONS)—See WEBSTER SPRINGS, WV (Shentel)

WEBSTER COUNTY (UNINCORPORATED AREAS)—See DIANA, WV (Country Cable)

▲ **WEBSTER SPRINGS**—Shentel

WEIRTON—See NEW CUMBERLAND, WV (Comcast Cable)

▲ **WELCH**—Jet Broadband. Now served by NORTHFORK, WV [WV0045]

WELCH—See NORTHFORK, WV (Shentel)

WELLSBURG—See WHEELING, WV (Comcast Cable)

WEST BELLE—See CHARLESTON, WV (Suddenlink Communications)

WEST HAMLIN—See HAMLIN, WV (Armstrong Cable Services)

▲ **WEST LIBERTY (town)**—Comcast Cable. Now served by WHEELING, WV [WV0004]

WEST LIBERTY—See WHEELING, WV (Comcast Cable)

WEST LOGAN—See KERMIT, WV (Suddenlink Communications)

▲**WEST MILFORD**—Formerly served by Cebridge Connections. Now served by BUCKHANNON, WV [WV0024]

WEST MILFORD—See BUCKHANNON, WV (Suddenlink Communications)

WEST PEA RIDGE—See HUNTINGTON, WV (Comcast Cable)

▲**WEST UNION**—Shentel

WESTERNPORT—See KEYSER, MD (Comcast Cable)

▲**WESTON**—Shentel

▲**WESTOVER**—Formerly served by Adelphia Communications. Now served by MORGANTOWN, WV [WV0198]

WESTOVER—See MORGANTOWN, WV (Comcast Cable)

WETZEL COUNTY (PORTIONS)—See PARKERSBURG, WV (Suddenlink Communications)

WETZEL COUNTY—See PINE GROVE, WV (Zito Media)

WEVACO—See CHARLESTON, WV (Suddenlink Communications)

WHARNCLIFFE—See OMAR, WV (Colane Cable TV Inc.)

WHARTON—See VAN, WV (Colane Cable TV)

WHEELING TWP.—See WHEELING, OH (Comcast Cable)

▲**WHEELING**—Comcast Cable

▲**WHITE SULPHUR SPRINGS**—Charter Communications. Now served by BECKLEY, WV [WV0005]

WHITE SULPHUR SPRINGS—See BECKLEY, WV (Suddenlink Communications)

WHITE SULPHUR SPRINGS—See ANTHONY CREEK, WV (Windjammer Cable)

▲**WHITEHALL**—Formerly served by Adelphia Communications. Now served by MORGANTOWN, WV [WV0198]

WHITEHALL—See MORGANTOWN, WV (Comcast Cable)

WHITESVILLE—See CHARLESTON, WV (Suddenlink Communications)

WIDEN—See BIRCH RIVER, WV (Windjammer Cable)

▲**WILEYVILLE**—Formerly served by Almega Cable. No longer in operation

WILLIAMSBURG—See FRANKFORD, WV (Clearview TV Cable)

▲**WILLIAMSON**—Charter Communications. Now served by KERMIT, WV [WV0038]

WILLIAMSON—See KERMIT, WV (Suddenlink Communications)

WILLIAMSTOWN—See PARKERSBURG, WV (Suddenlink Communications)

WILLOWTON—See OAKVALE, WV (Shentel)

WINDSOR HEIGHTS—See WARWOOD, WV (Centre TV Cable)

WINFIELD—See RED HOUSE, WV (Comcast Cable)

WINIFREDE—See CHARLESTON, WV (Suddenlink Communications)

WINTERSVILLE—See WHEELING, OH (Comcast Cable)

WITCHER—See CHARLESTON, WV (Suddenlink Communications)

WOLF CREEK—See KERMIT, KY (Suddenlink Communications)

WOOD COUNTY—See PARKERSBURG, WV (Suddenlink Communications)

WOODVILLE—See CHARLESTON, WV (Suddenlink Communications)

WORTH—See NORTHFORK, WV (Shentel)

▲**WORTHINGTON**—Formerly served by Adelphia Communications. Now served by MORGANTOWN, WV [WV0198]

WORTHINGTON—See MORGANTOWN, WV (Comcast Cable)

WORTHINGTON—See SHINNSTON, WV (Suddenlink Communications)

WRISTON—See PAGE, WV (Shentel)

▲**WYATT**—Country Cable

WYATT—See SHINNSTON, WV (Suddenlink Communications)

WYCO—See BECKLEY, WV (Suddenlink Communications)

WYOMING COUNTY (PORTIONS)—See PINEVILLE, WV (Shentel)

WYOMING COUNTY (PORTIONS)—See BECKLEY, WV (Suddenlink Communications)

WYOMING COUNTY (PORTIONS)—See KERMIT, WV (Suddenlink Communications)

WYOMING COUNTY—See HANOVER, WV (Colane Cable TV Inc.)

YOLYN—See KERMIT, WV (Suddenlink Communications)

YORKVILLE—See WHEELING, OH (Comcast Cable)

YOUNGS BOTTOM—See CHARLESTON, WV (Suddenlink Communications)

WISCONSIN

ABBOTSFORD—See SPENCER, WI (Charter Communications)

▲**ADAMS**—Charter Communications

ADAMS—See ONALASKA, WI (Charter Communications)

ADDISON (TOWN)—See WEST BEND, WI (Charter Communications)

ADELL—See RANDOM LAKE, WI (Time Warner Cable)

AFTON—See JANESVILLE, WI (Charter Communications)

▲**ALBANY**—Mediacom

ALBION—See JANESVILLE, WI (Charter Communications)

ALGOMA—See FOND DU LAC, WI (Charter Communications)

ALGOMA—See TWO RIVERS, WI (Charter Communications)

ALLENTON—See WEST BEND, WI (Charter Communications)

ALLOUEZ—See GREEN BAY, WI (Time Warner Cable)

▲**ALMA (TOWN)**—US Cable

ALMA CENTER—See INDEPENDENCE, WI (Western Wisconsin Communications Cooperative)

ALMENA—See DALLAS, WI (Mosaic Media)

▲**ALMOND**—New Century Communications

ALTOONA—See EAU CLAIRE, WI (Charter Communications)

▲**AMBERG**—Packerland Broadband

▲**AMERY**—Northwest Community Communications

▲**AMHERST (village)**—Amherst Telephone. This cable system has converted to IPTV. See Amherst (village), WI [WI5372]

▲**ANGELICA**—Northern Lakes Cable TV. Now served by KRAKOW, WI [WI0327]

ANGELICA—See KRAKOW, WI (Packerland Broadband)

ANGELO—See ONALASKA, WI (Charter Communications)

ANIWA (VILLAGE)—See WAUSAU, WI (Charter Communications)

ANSON (TOWN)—See EAU CLAIRE, WI (Charter Communications)

▲**ANTIGO**—Charter Communications

APPLETON—See GREEN BAY, WI (Time Warner Cable)

ARBOR VITAE—See MINOCQUA, WI (Charter Communications)

ARCADIA—See INDEPENDENCE, WI (Western Wisconsin Communications Cooperative)

ARENA (TOWN)—See MAZOMANIE, WI (Charter Communications)

ARGONNE—See RHINELANDER, WI (Charter Communications)

▲**ARGYLE**—Mediacom

▲**ARKANSAW**—Chippewa Valley Cable Co. Inc.

ARLINGTON—See MADISON, WI (Charter Communications)

ARLINGTON—See MAZOMANIE, WI (Charter Communications)

ARPIN (VILLAGE)—See VESPER, WI (Packerland Broadband)

ASHIPPUN—See MILWAUKEE, WI (Time Warner Cable)

▲**ASHLAND**—Charter Communications

ASHWAUBENON—See GREEN BAY, WI (Time Warner Cable)

ATHENS—See SPENCER, WI (Charter Communications)

▲**AUBURNDALE**—Packerland Broadband

▲**AUGUSTA**—Packerland Broadband

AURORA (TOWN)—See FOND DU LAC, WI (Charter Communications)

▲**AVOCA**—Packerland Broadband

AZTALAN—See JANESVILLE, WI (Charter Communications)

▲**BAGLEY (VILLAGE)**—Dairyland Cable Systems Inc.

BAILEYS HARBOR—See SISTER BAY, WI (Charter Communications)

▲**BALDWIN (TOWN)**—Baldwin Telecom Inc. Formerly served by Baldwin (village), WI [WI0079]. This cable system has converted to IPTV

▲**BALDWIN (village)**—Baldwin Telecom Inc. This cable system has converted to IPTV. See Baldwin (village), WI [WI5355]

▲**BALDWIN (VILLAGE)**—Baldwin Telecom Inc. Formerly served by Baldwin (village), WI [WI0079]. This cable system has converted to IPTV

BALSAM LAKE—See MILLTOWN, WI (Lakeland Communications)

▲**BANCROFT**—New Century Communications

BANGOR—See ONALASKA, WI (Charter Communications)

BARABOO—See MAZOMANIE, WI (Charter Communications)

BARKSDALE (TOWN)—See ASHLAND, WI (Charter Communications)

BARNEVELD—See MAZOMANIE, WI (Charter Communications)

BARRE—See ONALASKA, WI (Charter Communications)

BARRON—See RICE LAKE, WI (Charter Communications)

BARRON—See DALLAS, WI (Mosaic Media)

BARTON (TOWN)—See WEST BEND, WI (Charter Communications)

BASS LAKE (TOWN)—See HAYWARD, WI (Charter Communications)

▲**BAY CITY**—US Cable

BAYFIELD—See ASHLAND, WI (Charter Communications)

BAYSIDE—See MILWAUKEE, WI (Time Warner Cable)

▲**BEAR CREEK**—Charter Communications

BEAVER DAM—See HUSTISFORD, WI (Charter Communications)

BEECHER—See PEMBINE, WI (Packerland Broadband)

BELGIUM—See RANDOM LAKE, WI (Time Warner Cable)

▲**BELL CENTER**—Richland-Grant Telephone Co-op. This cable system has converted to IPTV. See Bell Center, WI [WI5364]

▲**BELL CENTER**—Richland-Grant Telephone Co-op. Formerly [WI0228]. This cable system has converted to IPTV

BELLE PLAINE—See CLINTONVILLE, WI (Charter Communications)

▲**BELLEVILLE**—Charter Communications. Now served by MADISON, WI[WI0002]

BELLEVILLE—See MADISON, WI (Charter Communications)

BELLEVUE—See GREEN BAY, WI (Time Warner Cable)

BELMONT—See CUBA CITY, WI (Mediacom)

BELOIT—See JANESVILLE, WI (Charter Communications)

BENTON—See CUBA CITY, WI (Mediacom)

BERGEN—See WAUSAU, WI (Charter Communications)

BERLIN—See FOND DU LAC, WI (Charter Communications)

BEVENT—See WITTENBERG, WI (Wittenberg Cable TV)

BIG BEND—See MILWAUKEE, WI (Time Warner Cable)

BIRCHWOOD—See MIKANA, WI (S & K TV Systems)

BIRNAMWOOD—See WAUSAU, WI (Charter Communications)

BIRON—See WISCONSIN RAPIDS, WI (Charter Communications)

BLACK CREEK—See CLINTONVILLE, WI (Charter Communications)

BLACK EARTH—See MAZOMANIE, WI (Charter Communications)

▲**BLACK RIVER FALLS**—Charter Communications. Now served by ONALASKA, WI [WI0024]

BLACK RIVER FALLS—See ONALASKA, WI (Charter Communications)

BLACK WOLF (TOWN)—See FOND DU LAC, WI (Charter Communications)

BLAIR—See INDEPENDENCE, WI (Western Wisconsin Communications Cooperative)

▲**BLANCHARDVILLE**—Mediacom

BLOOMER—See ELMWOOD, WI (Celect Communications)

BLOOMER—See EAU CLAIRE, WI (Charter Communications)

BLOOMFIELD (TOWN)—See TUSTIN, WI (New Century Communications)

BLOOMFIELD—See KENOSHA, WI (Time Warner Cable)

BLOOMING GROVE—See MADISON, WI (Charter Communications)

▲**BLOOMINGDALE**—Formerly served by Midwest Cable Inc. No longer in operation

BLOOMINGTON—See LANCASTER, WI (Charter Communications)

BLUE MOUNDS—See MAZOMANIE, WI (Charter Communications)

▲**BLUE RIVER (VILLAGE)**—Dairyland Cable Systems Inc.

▲**BLUFFVIEW MOBILE HOME PARK**—HLM Cable Corp. Now served by MERRIMAC, WI [WI0154]

BLUFFVIEW MOBILE HOME PARK—See MERRIMAC, WI (Merrimac Cable)

▲**BOAZ**—Village of Boaz

▲**BONDUEL**—Packerland Broadband

BOSCOBEL—See PRAIRIE DU CHIEN, WI (Mediacom)

▲**BOULDER JUNCTION**—Karban TV Systems Inc.

BOVINA—See CLINTONVILLE, WI (Charter Communications)

BOWLER (VILLAGE)—See WAUSAU, WI (Charter Communications)

BOYCEVILLE—See GLENWOOD CITY, WI (Nextgen Communications)

▲**BOYD/CADOTT**—Charter Communications. Now served by EAU CLAIRE, WI [WI0011]

BOYD—See EAU CLAIRE, WI (Charter Communications)

BRADFORD—See JANESVILLE, WI (Charter Communications)

BRADLEY (TOWN)—See RHINELANDER, WI (Charter Communications)

BRANDON—See FOND DU LAC, WI (Charter Communications)

BRIDGEPORT (TOWN)—See PRAIRIE DU CHIEN, WI (Mediacom)

▲**BRIGGSVILLE**—New Century Communications

BRILLION—See TWO RIVERS, WI (Charter Communications)

BRISTOL—See KENOSHA, WI (Time Warner Cable)

BROCKWAY—See ONALASKA, WI (Charter Communications)

BRODHEAD—See JANESVILLE, WI (Charter Communications)

BROKAW—See WAUSAU, WI (Charter Communications)

▲**BROOKFIELD**—Time Warner Cable. Now served by MILWAUKEE, WI [WI0001]

BROOKFIELD—See MILWAUKEE, WI (Time Warner Cable)

BROOKLYN (TOWN)—See FOND DU LAC, WI (Charter Communications)

BROOKLYN—See MADISON, WI (Charter Communications)

BROOKVIEW TRAILER COURT—See CASHTON, WI (Mediacom)

BROWN DEER—See MILWAUKEE, WI (Time Warner Cable)

BROWNSVILLE—See KNOWLES, WI (Packerland Broadband)

BRUCE—See ELMWOOD, WI (Celect Communications)

BRUCE—See LADYSMITH, WI (Charter Communications)

BRUNSWICK TWP.—See EAU CLAIRE, WI (Charter Communications)

BUCHANAN (TOWN)—See GREEN BAY, WI (Time Warner Cable)

BUDNICK PARK—See MERRIMAC, WI (Merrimac Cable)

BUFFALO—See ALMA (town), WI (US Cable)

BURKE—See MADISON, WI (Charter Communications)

▲**BURLINGTON**—Time Warner Cable. Now served by MILWAUKEE, WI [WI0001]

BURLINGTON—See MILWAUKEE, WI (Time Warner Cable)

BURNETT (TOWN)—See HUSTISFORD, WI (Charter Communications)

BUTLER (VILLAGE)—See MILWAUKEE, WI (Time Warner Cable)

BUTTE DES MORTS—See FOND DU LAC, WI (Charter Communications)

▲**BUTTERNUT**—Packerland Broadband

CADOTT—See EAU CLAIRE, WI (Charter Communications)

CALAMUS—See HUSTISFORD, WI (Charter Communications)

CALEDONIA (TOWN)—See MERRIMAC, WI (Merrimac Cable)

CALEDONIA—See KENOSHA, WI (Time Warner Cable)

CALUMET (TOWN)—See FOND DU LAC, WI (Charter Communications)

CAMBRIA—See RANDOLPH, WI (CenturyTel)

CAMBRIDGE—See MADISON, WI (Charter Communications)

CAMERON (TOWN)—See MARSHFIELD, WI (Charter Communications)

CAMERON—See RICE LAKE, WI (Charter Communications)

CAMERON—See DALLAS, WI (Mosaic Media)

CAMP DOUGLAS—See MAUSTON, WI (Mediacom)

CAMPBELL—See ONALASKA, WI (Charter Communications)

CAMPBELLSPORT—See FOND DU LAC, WI (Charter Communications)

CARLTON (TOWN)—See TWO RIVERS, WI (Charter Communications)

CAROLINE—See CLINTONVILLE, WI (Charter Communications)

CASCADE—See MILWAUKEE, WI (Time Warner Cable)

CASCO (TOWN)—See CASCO, WI (CenturyTel)

CASCO (VILLAGE)—See CASCO, WI (CenturyTel)

▲**CASCO**—CenturyTel

▲**CASHTON**—Mediacom

CASSIAN (TOWN)—See RHINELANDER, WI (Charter Communications)

CASSVILLE—See LANCASTER, WI (Charter Communications)

CATO—See MANITOWOC, WI (Comcast Cable)

▲**CAZENOVIA**—Community Antenna System Inc.

CEDAR GROVE—See RANDOM LAKE, WI (Time Warner Cable)

▲**CEDARBURG**—Time Warner Cable. Now served by MILWAUKEE, WI [WI0001]

CEDARBURG—See MILWAUKEE, WI (Time Warner Cable)

CENTER (TOWN)—See JANESVILLE, WI (Charter Communications)

CENTER—See GREEN BAY, WI (Time Warner Cable)

CENTURIA—See MILLTOWN, WI (Lakeland Communications)

CHARLESTOWN—See FOND DU LAC, WI (Charter Communications)

CHASE—See GREEN BAY, WI (Time Warner Cable)

▲**CHASEBURG**—Mediacom. Now served by COON VALLEY, WI [WI0171]

CHASEBURG—See COON VALLEY, WI (Mediacom)

CHENEQUA—See MILWAUKEE, WI (Time Warner Cable)

CHESTER—See HUSTISFORD, WI (Charter Communications)

CHETEK—See RICE LAKE, WI (Charter Communications)

CHILTON—See FOND DU LAC, WI (Charter Communications)

CHIPPEWA FALLS—See EAU CLAIRE, WI (Charter Communications)

CHRISTIANA—See MADISON, WI (Charter Communications)

CLARNO—See JANESVILLE, WI (Charter Communications)

CLAYTON (POLK COUNTY)—See AMERY, WI (Northwest Community Communications)

CLAYTON (WINNEBAGO COUNTY)—See GREEN BAY, WI (Time Warner Cable)

CLAYTON COUNTY—See PRAIRIE DU CHIEN, IA (Mediacom)

CLAYTON—See PRAIRIE DU CHIEN, IA (Mediacom)

CLEVELAND—See RANDOM LAKE, WI (Time Warner Cable)

CLINTON (VILLAGE)—See JANESVILLE, WI (Charter Communications)

▲ **CLINTONVILLE**—Charter Communications

CLOVERLEAF LAKES—See CLINTONVILLE, WI (Charter Communications)

CLYMAN—See HUSTISFORD, WI (Charter Communications)

COBB—See MAZOMANIE, WI (Charter Communications)

COCHRANE—See ALMA (town), WI (US Cable)

COLBY—See SPENCER, WI (Charter Communications)

▲ **COLEMAN**—Packerland Broadband

COLFAX—See MENOMONIE, WI (Charter Communications)

COLGATE—See WEST BEND, WI (Charter Communications)

COLOMA—See WAUTOMA, WI (Charter Communications)

COLUMBIA COUNTY—See MAZOMANIE, WI (Charter Communications)

COLUMBUS—See MADISON, WI (Charter Communications)

COMBINED LOCKS—See GREEN BAY, WI (Time Warner Cable)

▲ **COON VALLEY**—Mediacom

COOPERSTOWN (TOWN)—See TWO RIVERS, WI (Charter Communications)

CORNELL—See EAU CLAIRE, WI (Charter Communications)

COURTLAND—See RANDOLPH, WI (CenturyTel)

CRANDON—See RHINELANDER, WI (Charter Communications)

CRAWFORD COUNTY (PORTIONS)—See COON VALLEY, WI (Mediacom)

CRAWFORD COUNTY (UNINCORPORATED AREAS)—See PRAIRIE DU CHIEN, WI (Mediacom)

CRESCENT—See RHINELANDER, WI (Charter Communications)

▲ **CRIVITZ**—Howard Cable

CROSS PLAINS (VILLAGE)—See MADISON, WI (Charter Communications)

▲ **CUBA CITY**—Mediacom

CUDAHY—See MILWAUKEE, WI (Time Warner Cable)

CUMBERLAND—See RICE LAKE, WI (Charter Communications)

CUSHING—See MILLTOWN, WI (Lakeland Communications)

DACADA VILLAGE—See RANDOM LAKE, WI (Time Warner Cable)

DAKOTA (TOWN)—See WAUTOMA, WI (Charter Communications)

DALE—See GREEN BAY, WI (Time Warner Cable)

▲ **DALLAS**—Mosaic Media

▲ **DALTON**—New Century Communications

DANE—See MAZOMANIE, WI (Charter Communications)

▲ **DARIEN**—Packerland Broadband

DARLINGTON—See CUBA CITY, WI (Mediacom)

DAYTON (TOWN)—See CLINTONVILLE, WI (Charter Communications)

DE FOREST—See MADISON, WI (Charter Communications)

DE PERE—See GREEN BAY, WI (Time Warner Cable)

DECATUR—See JANESVILLE, WI (Charter Communications)

DEER PARK—See AMERY, WI (Northwest Community Communications)

DEERFIELD—See MADISON, WI (Charter Communications)

DEKORRA (TOWN)—See MAZOMANIE, WI (Charter Communications)

DELAFIELD—See MILWAUKEE, WI (Time Warner Cable)

▲ **DELAVAN**—Charter Communications

DENMARK—See TWO RIVERS, WI (Charter Communications)

DICKEYVILLE—See LANCASTER, WI (Charter Communications)

DODGEVILLE—See MAZOMANIE, WI (Charter Communications)

DORCHESTER—See SPENCER, WI (Charter Communications)

DOUSMAN—See MILWAUKEE, WI (Time Warner Cable)

DOVER (TOWN)—See MILWAUKEE, WI (Time Warner Cable)

DOWNING—See GLENWOOD CITY, WI (Nextgen Communications)

DOWNSVILLE—See ELMWOOD, WI (Celect Communications)

DOWNSVILLE—See MENOMONIE, WI (Charter Communications)

▲ **DOYLESTOWN**—Formerly served by New Century Communications. No longer in operation

▲ **DRESSER**—Charter Communications

DUNKIRK—See MADISON, WI (Charter Communications)

DUNN (TOWN)—See MAZOMANIE, WI (Charter Communications)

DUNN—See MADISON, WI (Charter Communications)

DURAND—See ARKANSAW, WI (Chippewa Valley Cable Co. Inc.)

EAGLE POINT—See EAU CLAIRE, WI (Charter Communications)

▲ **EAGLE RIVER**—Charter Communications

EAGLE—See MILWAUKEE, WI (Time Warner Cable)

EAST TROY—See MILWAUKEE, WI (Time Warner Cable)

EASTMAN (UNINCORPORATED AREAS)—See SENECA (village), WI (Dairyland Cable Systems Inc.)

▲ **EAU CLAIRE**—Charter Communications

EAU GALLE—See ARKANSAW, WI (Chippewa Valley Cable Co. Inc.)

EDEN (VILLAGE)—See FOND DU LAC, WI (Charter Communications)

EDGAR—See SPENCER, WI (Charter Communications)

EDGERTON—See JANESVILLE, WI (Charter Communications)

EDGEWATER—See MIKANA, WI (S & K TV Systems)

EDMUND—See MAZOMANIE, WI (Charter Communications)

EGG HARBOR—See STURGEON BAY, WI (Charter Communications)

EILEEN (TOWN)—See ASHLAND, WI (Charter Communications)

EISENSTEIN—See PARK FALLS, WI (Charter Communications)

ELAND—See WITTENBERG, WI (Wittenberg Cable TV)

ELBA (TOWN)—See MADISON, WI (Charter Communications)

▲ **ELCHO (TOWN)**—Packerland Broadband

ELDERDON—See WITTENBERG, WI (Wittenberg Cable TV)

ELDORADO (TOWN)—See FOND DU LAC, WI (Charter Communications)

ELEVA—See INDEPENDENCE, WI (Western Wisconsin Communications Cooperative)

ELK MOUND (VILLAGE)—See EAU CLAIRE, WI (Charter Communications)

ELKADER—See PRAIRIE DU CHIEN, IA (Mediacom)

ELKHART LAKE—See RANDOM LAKE, WI (Time Warner Cable)

ELKHORN—See SUGAR CREEK (town), WI (Mediacom)

ELKHORN—See MILWAUKEE, WI (Time Warner Cable)

ELLINGTON—See GREEN BAY, WI (Time Warner Cable)

▲ **ELLSWORTH**—US Cable

ELM GROVE (VILLAGE)—See MILWAUKEE, WI (Time Warner Cable)

ELMWOOD PARK—See KENOSHA, WI (Time Warner Cable)

▲ **ELMWOOD**—Celect Communications

▲ **ELROY**—Community Antenna System Inc.

EMBARRASS—See CLINTONVILLE, WI (Charter Communications)

EMPIRE (TOWN)—See FOND DU LAC, WI (Charter Communications)

▲ **ENDEAVOR**—New Century Communications

EPHRAIM—See SISTER BAY, WI (Charter Communications)

ETTRICK—See INDEPENDENCE, WI (Western Wisconsin Communications Cooperative)

EVANSVILLE—See JANESVILLE, WI (Charter Communications)

EVERGREEN TRAILER COURT—See PLATTEVILLE, WI (CenturyLink)

EXELAND—See RADISSON, WI (S & K TV Systems)

EXETER—See MADISON, WI (Charter Communications)

FAIRCHILD—See INDEPENDENCE, WI (Western Wisconsin Communications Cooperative)

▲ **FAIRWATER**—Formerly served by CenturyTel. No longer in operation

▲ **FALL CREEK**—Packerland Broadband

FALL RIVER—See RANDOLPH, WI (CenturyTel)

FARMERSVILLE—See KNOWLES, WI (Packerland Broadband)

FARMINGTON (TOWN)—See CLINTONVILLE, WI (Charter Communications)

FARMINGTON (TOWN)—See WEST BEND, WI (Charter Communications)

▲ **FENNIMORE**—Mediacom

FERRYVILLE—See COON VALLEY, WI (Mediacom)

▲ **FIFIELD**—Packerland Broadband

FISH CREEK—See SISTER BAY, WI (Charter Communications)

FITCHBURG—See MAZOMANIE, WI (Charter Communications)

FLAMBEAU—See LADYSMITH, WI (Charter Communications)

▲ **FOND DU LAC**—Charter Communications

FOOTVILLE—See ORFORDVILLE, WI (Mediacom)

FORESTVILLE (VILLAGE)—See CASCO, WI (CenturyTel)

FORT ATKINSON—See JANESVILLE, WI (Charter Communications)

▲ **FORT MCCOY**—Mediacom

FORT WINNEBAGO—See RANDOLPH, WI (CenturyTel)

▲**FOUNTAIN CITY**—Charter Communications

FOUNTAIN PRAIRIE—See RANDOLPH, WI (CenturyTel)

FOX CREEK—See MILLTOWN, WI (Lakeland Communications)

FOX LAKE TWP.—See RANDOLPH, WI (CenturyTel)

FOX LAKE—See HUSTISFORD, WI (Charter Communications)

FOX POINT—See MILWAUKEE, WI (Time Warner Cable)

FRANCIS CREEK—See TWO RIVERS, WI (Charter Communications)

FRANKLIN—See MILWAUKEE, WI (Time Warner Cable)

FREDERIC—See MILLTOWN, WI (Lakeland Communications)

FREDONIA—See RANDOM LAKE, WI (Time Warner Cable)

FREEDOM—See GREEN BAY, WI (Time Warner Cable)

▲**FREMONT**—Mediacom

FRIENDSHIP (TOWN)—See FOND DU LAC, WI (Charter Communications)

FRIENDSHIP—See ADAMS, WI (Charter Communications)

FULTON—See JANESVILLE, WI (Charter Communications)

GALESVILLE—See INDEPENDENCE, WI (Western Wisconsin Communications Cooperative)

GALLOWAY—See WITTENBERG, WI (Wittenberg Cable TV)

GARNAVILLO—See PRAIRIE DU CHIEN, IA (Mediacom)

GAYS MILLS—See CASHTON, WI (Mediacom)

GENESEE (TOWN)—See MILWAUKEE, WI (Time Warner Cable)

GENEVA—See KENOSHA, WI (Time Warner Cable)

▲**GENOA CITY**—Charter Communications

GERMANTOWN (VILLAGE)—See MILWAUKEE, WI (Time Warner Cable)

GERMANTOWN—See MAUSTON, WI (Mediacom)

GIBRALTAR (TOWN)—See SISTER BAY, WI (Charter Communications)

GIBSON (TOWN)—See TWO RIVERS, WI (Charter Communications)

▲**GILLETT**—Packerland Broadband

▲**GILMAN**—S & K TV Systems

GILMANTON—See ARKANSAW, WI (Chippewa Valley Cable Co. Inc.)

GLENBEULAH—See RANDOM LAKE, WI (Time Warner Cable)

GLENDALE—See MILWAUKEE, WI (Time Warner Cable)

▲**GLENWOOD CITY**—Nextgen Communications

▲**GLIDDEN**—Packerland Broadband

▲**GOODMAN**—Packerland Broadband

GOTHAM—See MAZOMANIE, WI (Charter Communications)

GRAFTON—See MILWAUKEE, WI (Time Warner Cable)

GRAND CHUTE (TOWN)—See GREEN BAY, WI (Time Warner Cable)

GRAND RAPIDS—See WISCONSIN RAPIDS, WI (Charter Communications)

GRANT COUNTY (UNINCORPORATED AREAS)—See PRAIRIE DU CHIEN, WI (Mediacom)

GRANT—See LADYSMITH, WI (Charter Communications)

GRANT—See WISCONSIN RAPIDS, WI (Charter Communications)

▲**GRANTON**—New Century Communications

▲**GRANTSBURG**—Grantsburg Telcom

GREEN BAY TWP.—See CASCO, WI (CenturyTel)

▲**GREEN BAY**—Formerly served by Sprint Corp. No longer in operation

▲**GREEN BAY**—Time Warner Cable

GREEN LAKE—See FOND DU LAC, WI (Charter Communications)

GREEN VALLEY—See GILLETT, WI (Packerland Broadband)

GREENBUSH (TOWN)—See RANDOM LAKE, WI (Time Warner Cable)

GREENDALE—See MILWAUKEE, WI (Time Warner Cable)

GREENFIELD (LA CROSSE COUNTY)—See CASHTON, WI (Mediacom)

▲**GREENFIELD (Milwaukee County)**—Time Warner Cable. Now served by MILWAUKEE, WI [WI0001]

GREENFIELD (TOWN)—See MAZOMANIE, WI (Charter Communications)

GREENFIELD (TOWN)—See ONALASKA, WI (Charter Communications)

GREENFIELD—See MILWAUKEE, WI (Time Warner Cable)

▲**GREENLEAF**—Formerly served by CenturyTel. No longer in operation

GREENVILLE (TOWN)—See GREEN BAY, WI (Time Warner Cable)

▲**GREENWOOD**—Packerland Broadband

GRESHAM—See CLINTONVILLE, WI (Charter Communications)

GUTTENBERG—See PRAIRIE DU CHIEN, IA (Mediacom)

HAGER CITY—See PEPIN, WI (US Cable)

HALES CORNERS—See MILWAUKEE, WI (Time Warner Cable)

HALLIE—See EAU CLAIRE, WI (Charter Communications)

HAMILTON—See ONALASKA, WI (Charter Communications)

▲**HAMMOND (VILLAGE)**—Baldwin Telecom Inc. Formerly served by Baldwin (village), WI [WI0079]. This cable system has converted to IPTV

HANCOCK—See WAUTOMA, WI (Charter Communications)

HARLEM TWP.—See JANESVILLE, IL (Charter Communications)

HARMONY—See JANESVILLE, WI (Charter Communications)

HARRISON (TOWN)—See GREEN BAY, WI (Time Warner Cable)

HARTFORD—See WEST BEND, WI (Charter Communications)

HARTLAND (VILLAGE)—See MILWAUKEE, WI (Time Warner Cable)

HATLEY (VILLAGE)—See WAUSAU, WI (Charter Communications)

HAUGEN—See RICE LAKE, WI (Charter Communications)

▲**HAWKINS (VILLAGE)**—Packerland Broadband

HAYWARD (TOWN)—See HAYWARD, WI (Charter Communications)

▲**HAYWARD**—Charter Communications

HAZEL GREEN—See CUBA CITY, WI (Mediacom)

HEAFFORD JUNCTION—See RHINELANDER, WI (Charter Communications)

HERMAN—See RANDOM LAKE, WI (Time Warner Cable)

HEWITT—See AUBURNDALE, WI (Packerland Broadband)

HIGHLAND—See MAZOMANIE, WI (Charter Communications)

HILBERT (VILLAGE)—See GREEN BAY, WI (Time Warner Cable)

▲**HILLSBORO**—Community Antenna System Inc.

HILLSDALE—See DALLAS, WI (Mosaic Media)

HIXTON—See INDEPENDENCE, WI (Western Wisconsin Communications Cooperative)

HOBART—See GREEN BAY, WI (Time Warner Cable)

HOLLAND (TOWN)—See GREEN BAY, WI (Time Warner Cable)

HOLLAND TWP.—See RANDOM LAKE, WI (Time Warner Cable)

HOLLAND—See ONALASKA, WI (Charter Communications)

▲**HOLLANDALE**—Packerland Broadband

HOLMEN—See ONALASKA, WI (Charter Communications)

HORICON—See HUSTISFORD, WI (Charter Communications)

HORTONIA (TOWN)—See CLINTONVILLE, WI (Charter Communications)

HORTONVILLE—See CLINTONVILLE, WI (Charter Communications)

HOWARD (VILLAGE)—See GREEN BAY, WI (Time Warner Cable)

▲**HOWARDS GROVE**—Time Warner Cable. Now served by RANDOM LAKE, WI [WI0059]

HOWARDS GROVE—See RANDOM LAKE, WI (Time Warner Cable)

HUBBARD—See HUSTISFORD, WI (Charter Communications)

HUBERTUS—See WEST BEND, WI (Charter Communications)

▲**HUDSON (town)**—Baldwin Telecom Inc. Formerly served by Baldwin (village), WI [WI0126]. This cable system has converted to IPTV. See Hudson Twp., WI [WI5044]

▲**HUDSON (TOWN)**—Baldwin Telecom Inc. Formerly served by Baldwin (village), WI [WI0079]. This cable system has converted to IPTV

HULL—See STEVENS POINT, WI (Charter Communications)

HUMBIRD—See INDEPENDENCE, WI (Western Wisconsin Communications Cooperative)

▲**HUSTISFORD**—Charter Communications

HUSTLER—See MAUSTON, WI (Mediacom)

▲**INDEPENDENCE**—Western Wisconsin Communications Cooperative

INGALLSTON TWP.—See MARINETTE, MI (Time Warner Cable)

▲**IOLA**—Mediacom

IRON RIDGE—See HUSTISFORD, WI (Charter Communications)

▲**IRONTON**—Formerly served by Dairyland Cable Systems Inc. No longer in operation

IXONIA—See MILWAUKEE, WI (Time Warner Cable)

JACKSON—See WEST BEND, WI (Charter Communications)

JACKSONPORT—See STURGEON BAY, WI (Charter Communications)

▲**JANESVILLE**—Formerly served by Wireless Cable Systems Inc. No longer in operation

▲**JANESVILLE**—Charter Communications

JEFFERSON—See JANESVILLE, WI (Charter Communications)

JIM FALLS—See EAU CLAIRE, WI (Charter Communications)

JOHNSON CREEK—See JANESVILLE, WI (Charter Communications)

▲**JUNCTION CITY**—Packerland Broadband

JUNEAU COUNTY (UNINCORPORATED AREAS)—See MAUSTON, WI (Mediacom)

JUNEAU—See HUSTISFORD, WI (Charter Communications)

KAUKAUNA—See GREEN BAY, WI (Time Warner Cable)

KEKOSKEE—See KNOWLES, WI (Packerland Broadband)

▲**KELLNERSVILLE**—New Century Communications

▲**KENDALL**—Community Antenna System Inc.

▲**KENOSHA**—Time Warner Cable

KEWASKUM—See WEST BEND, WI (Charter Communications)

KEWAUNEE—See TWO RIVERS, WI (Charter Communications)

KIEL—See FOND DU LAC, WI (Charter Communications)

KIMBERLY—See GREEN BAY, WI (Time Warner Cable)

KING—See CLINTONVILLE, WI (Charter Communications)

▲**KINGSTON**—New Century Communications

▲**KNAPP (village)**—Baldwin Telecom Inc. No longer in operation

▲**KNAPP (VILLAGE)**—Baldwin Telecom Inc. Formerly served by Baldwin (village), WI [WI0079]. This cable system has converted to IPTV

▲**KNOWLES**—Packerland Broadband

KOHLER—See SHEBOYGAN, WI (Charter Communications)

KOSHKONONG—See JANESVILLE, WI (Charter Communications)

KOSSUTH (TOWN)—See TWO RIVERS, WI (Charter Communications)

▲**KRAKOW**—Packerland Broadband

KRONENWETTER—See WAUSAU, WI (Charter Communications)

LA CRESCENT—See ONALASKA, MN (Charter Communications)

▲**LA CROSSE**—Charter Communications. Now served by ONALASKA, WI [WI0024]

LA CROSSE—See ONALASKA, WI (Charter Communications)

LA CROSSE—See CASHTON, WI (Mediacom)

LA FARGE—See CASHTON, WI (Mediacom)

LA GRANGE (TOWN)—See ONALASKA, WI (Charter Communications)

LA GRANGE TWP.—See SUGAR CREEK (town), WI (Mediacom)

LA GRANGE—See MILWAUKEE, WI (Time Warner Cable)

▲**LA VALLE (VILLAGE)**—Packerland Broadband

▲**LAC DU FLAMBEAU**—Formerly served by Gauthier Cablevision. No longer in operation

▲**LADYSMITH**—Charter Communications

LAFAYETTE TWP.—See SUGAR CREEK (town), WI (Mediacom)

LAFAYETTE—See EAU CLAIRE, WI (Charter Communications)

LAFAYETTE—See MILWAUKEE, WI (Time Warner Cable)

LAKE DELTON—See MAZOMANIE, WI (Charter Communications)

LAKE GENEVA—See KENOSHA, WI (Time Warner Cable)

▲**LAKE HOLCOMBE**—S & K TV Systems

LAKE MILLS—See JANESVILLE, WI (Charter Communications)

▲**LAKE NEBAGAMON**—Charter Communications

LAKE NOQUEBAY—See CRIVITZ, WI (Howard Cable)

LAKE WISSOTA—See EAU CLAIRE, WI (Charter Communications)

LAKE—See PARK FALLS, WI (Charter Communications)

LAKETOWN—See DRESSER, WI (Charter Communications)

▲**LANCASTER**—Charter Communications

▲**LAND O'LAKES**—Karban TV Systems Inc.

LANNON—See MILWAUKEE, WI (Time Warner Cable)

▲**LAONA**—Packerland Broadband

LARRABEE (TOWN)—See CLINTONVILLE, WI (Charter Communications)

LAWRENCE (TOWN)—See GREEN BAY, WI (Time Warner Cable)

LEBANON (TOWN)—See CLINTONVILLE, WI (Charter Communications)

LEDGEVIEW (TOWN)—See GREEN BAY, WI (Time Warner Cable)

▲**LENA**—Packerland Broadband

LEON—See ONALASKA, WI (Charter Communications)

LEROY—See KNOWLES, WI (Packerland Broadband)

LIBERTY (TOWN)—See CLINTONVILLE, WI (Charter Communications)

LIBERTY GROVE (TOWN)—See SISTER BAY, WI (Charter Communications)

LIMA (TOWN)—See SHEBOYGAN, WI (Charter Communications)

LIMA—See RANDOM LAKE, WI (Time Warner Cable)

LINCOLN (TOWN)—See MARSHFIELD, WI (Charter Communications)

LINCOLN TWP.—See INDEPENDENCE, WI (Western Wisconsin Communications Cooperative)

LINCOLN—See EAGLE RIVER, WI (Charter Communications)

LINCOLN—See RHINELANDER, WI (Charter Communications)

LIND (TOWN)—See CLINTONVILLE, WI (Charter Communications)

LINDEN—See MAZOMANIE, WI (Charter Communications)

LINN—See KENOSHA, WI (Time Warner Cable)

LINWOOD—See STEVENS POINT, WI (Charter Communications)

LISBON—See MILWAUKEE, WI (Time Warner Cable)

LITTLE CHUTE—See GREEN BAY, WI (Time Warner Cable)

LITTLE SUAMICO—See GREEN BAY, WI (Time Warner Cable)

LITTLE WOLF—See MANAWA, WI (Manawa Telecom Cable TV)

LIVINGSTON—See MAZOMANIE, WI (Charter Communications)

LODI—See MAZOMANIE, WI (Charter Communications)

▲**LOGANVILLE (VILLAGE)**—Dairyland Cable Systems Inc.

LOHRVILLE—See WAUTOMA, WI (Charter Communications)

LOMIRA—See FOND DU LAC, WI (Charter Communications)

LONE ROCK—See MAZOMANIE, WI (Charter Communications)

LOWELL—See HUSTISFORD, WI (Charter Communications)

LOWVILLE TWP.—See RANDOLPH, WI (CenturyTel)

LOYAL—See SPENCER, WI (Charter Communications)

LUCK—See MILLTOWN, WI (Lakeland Communications)

LUXEMBURG (TOWN)—See CASCO, WI (CenturyTel)

LUXEMBURG (VILLAGE)—See CASCO, WI (CenturyTel)

LYNDON—See RANDOM LAKE, WI (Time Warner Cable)

LYNXVILLE (UNINCORPORATED AREAS)—See SENECA (village), WI (Dairyland Cable Systems Inc.)

LYONS—See KENOSHA, WI (Time Warner Cable)

LYONS—See MILWAUKEE, WI (Time Warner Cable)

▲**MADISON**—Charter Communications

MAINE—See WAUSAU, WI (Charter Communications)

MALIBEKA—See MILWAUKEE, WI (Time Warner Cable)

▲**MANAWA**—Manawa Telecom Cable TV

MANITOWOC (TOWN)—See MANITOWOC, WI (Comcast Cable)

MANITOWOC RAPIDS—See MANITOWOC, WI (Comcast Cable)

▲**MANITOWOC**—Comcast Cable

MAPLE BLUFF—See MADISON, WI (Charter Communications)

MAPLE CREEK (TOWN)—See CLINTONVILLE, WI (Charter Communications)

MARATHON CITY—See WAUSAU, WI (Charter Communications)

MARCELLON—See RANDOLPH, WI (CenturyTel)

MARIBEL—See TWO RIVERS, WI (Charter Communications)

▲**MARINETTE**—Time Warner Cable

MARION (TOWN)—See WAUTOMA, WI (Charter Communications)

MARION—See CLINTONVILLE, WI (Charter Communications)

MARKESAN—See FOND DU LAC, WI (Charter Communications)

MARQUETTE—See PRAIRIE DU CHIEN, IA (Mediacom)

▲**MARQUETTE**—New Century Communications

MARSHALL—See MADISON, WI (Charter Communications)

MARSHFIELD (PORTIONS)—See AUBURNDALE, WI (Packerland Broadband)

▲**MARSHFIELD**—Charter Communications

MATTESON (TOWN)—See CLINTONVILLE, WI (Charter Communications)

MATTOON (VILLAGE)—See WAUSAU, WI (Charter Communications)

▲**MAUSTON**—Mediacom

MAYVILLE—See HUSTISFORD, WI (Charter Communications)

▲**MAZOMANIE**—Charter Communications

MCFARLAND (VILLAGE)—See MADISON, WI (Charter Communications)

MCGREGOR—See PRAIRIE DU CHIEN, IA (Mediacom)

MCMILLAN (TOWN)—See MARSHFIELD, WI (Charter Communications)

MEDARY—See ONALASKA, WI (Charter Communications)

▲**MEDFORD**—Charter Communications

MEDINA—See GREEN BAY, WI (Time Warner Cable)

▲**MELLEN**—Packerland Broadband

▲ **MELROSE**—Charter Communications. Now served by ONALASKA, WI [WI0024]

MELROSE—See ONALASKA, WI (Charter Communications)

▲ **MELVINA**—Formerly served by Midwest Cable Inc. No longer in operation

MENASHA (TOWN)—See GREEN BAY, WI (Time Warner Cable)

MENOMINEE (TOWN)—See MARINETTE, WI (Time Warner Cable)

MENOMINEE TWP.—See MARINETTE, MI (Time Warner Cable)

▲ **MENOMONEE FALLS**—Time Warner Cable. Now served by MILWAUKEE, WI [WI0001]

MENOMONEE FALLS—See MILWAUKEE, WI (Time Warner Cable)

MENOMONIE (TOWN)—See MENOMONIE, WI (Charter Communications)

▲ **MENOMONIE**—Charter Communications

▲ **MEQUON**—Time Warner Cable. Now served by MILWAUKEE, WI [WI0001]

MEQUON—See MILWAUKEE, WI (Time Warner Cable)

▲ **MERCER**—Karban TV Systems Inc.

MERILLAN—See INDEPENDENCE, WI (Western Wisconsin Communications Cooperative)

▲ **MERRILL**—Charter Communications

MERRIMAC (TOWN)—See MERRIMAC, WI (Merrimac Cable)

▲ **MERRIMAC**—Merrimac Cable

MERTON (TOWN)—See MILWAUKEE, WI (Time Warner Cable)

MIDDLETON—See MADISON, WI (Charter Communications)

▲ **MIKANA**—S & K TV Systems

MILFORD—See JANESVILLE, WI (Charter Communications)

▲ **MILLADORE (TOWN)**—New Century Communications

▲ **MILLTOWN**—Lakeland Communications

MILTON (TOWN)—See JANESVILLE, WI (Charter Communications)

▲ **MILWAUKEE**—Time Warner Cable

▲ **MINDORO**—Charter Communications. Now served by ONALASKA, WI [WI0024]

MINDORO—See ONALASKA, WI (Charter Communications)

MINERAL POINT—See MAZOMANIE, WI (Charter Communications)

▲ **MINOCQUA**—Charter Communications

▲ **MINONG**—S & K TV Systems

MISHICOT—See TWO RIVERS, WI (Charter Communications)

MONDOVI—See ARKANSAW, WI (Chippewa Valley Cable Co. Inc.)

MONFORT—See MAZOMANIE, WI (Charter Communications)

MONICO—See RHINELANDER, WI (Charter Communications)

MONONA—See MADISON, WI (Charter Communications)

MONROE—See JANESVILLE, WI (Charter Communications)

▲ **MONTELLO**—Charter Communications

▲ **MONTICELLO**—Mediacom

MORRISONVILLE—See MADISON, WI (Charter Communications)

MORTON (TOWN)—See MILWAUKEE, WI (Time Warner Cable)

MOSEL—See RANDOM LAKE, WI (Time Warner Cable)

MOSINEE—See WAUSAU, WI (Charter Communications)

MOUNT CALVARY—See FOND DU LAC, WI (Charter Communications)

MOUNT HOREB—See MAZOMANIE, WI (Charter Communications)

MOUNT PLEASANT—See KENOSHA, WI (Time Warner Cable)

MOUNT STERLING (UNINCORPORATED AREAS)—See SENECA (village), WI (Dairyland Cable Systems Inc.)

MUKWA (TOWN)—See CLINTONVILLE, WI (Charter Communications)

MUKWONAGO—See MILWAUKEE, WI (Time Warner Cable)

MUSCODA TWP.—See FENNIMORE, WI (Mediacom)

MUSCODA—See FENNIMORE, WI (Mediacom)

▲ **MUSKEGO**—Time Warner Cable. Now served by MILWAUKEE, WI [WI0001]

MUSKEGO—See MILWAUKEE, WI (Time Warner Cable)

NASAWAPI—See STURGEON BAY, WI (Charter Communications)

NASHOTA (TOWN)—See MILWAUKEE, WI (Time Warner Cable)

NECEDAH—See MAUSTON, WI (Mediacom)

NEENAH (TOWN)—See GREEN BAY, WI (Time Warner Cable)

NEILLSVILLE—See SPENCER, WI (Charter Communications)

NEKIMI (TOWN)—See FOND DU LAC, WI (Charter Communications)

NEKOOSA—See WISCONSIN RAPIDS, WI (Charter Communications)

NELSON—See PEPIN, WI (US Cable)

NEOSHO—See HUSTISFORD, WI (Charter Communications)

NESHKORO—See WAUTOMA, WI (Charter Communications)

NEW AUBURN—See ELMWOOD, WI (Celect Communications)

NEW AUBURN—See EAU CLAIRE, WI (Charter Communications)

▲ **NEW BERLIN**—Time Warner Cable. Now served by MILWAUKEE, WI [WI0001]

NEW BERLIN—See MILWAUKEE, WI (Time Warner Cable)

▲ **NEW FRANKEN**—CenturyLink. Now served by CASCO, WI [WI0115]

NEW FRANKEN—See CASCO, WI (CenturyTel)

NEW GLARUS—See JANESVILLE, WI (Charter Communications)

NEW HOLSTEIN—See FOND DU LAC, WI (Charter Communications)

NEW LISBON—See MAUSTON, WI (Mediacom)

NEW LONDON—See CLINTONVILLE, WI (Charter Communications)

▲ **NEW RICHMOND**—Northwest Community Communications

NEWBOLD—See RHINELANDER, WI (Charter Communications)

▲ **NEWBURG**—Tiime Warner Cable. Now served by MILWAUKEE, WI [WI0001]

NEWBURG—See MILWAUKEE, WI (Time Warner Cable)

NEWTON (TOWN)—See MANITOWOC, WI (Comcast Cable)

NIAGARA (TOWN)—See NIAGARA, WI (Niagara Community TV Co-op)

▲ **NIAGARA**—Niagara Community TV Co-op

▲ **NICHOLS**—Packerland Broadband

NOKOMIS—See RHINELANDER, WI (Charter Communications)

NORTH BAY—See KENOSHA, WI (Time Warner Cable)

NORTH FOND DU LAC—See FOND DU LAC, WI (Charter Communications)

▲ **NORTH FREEDOM**—Charter Communications. Now served by MAZOMANIE, WI [WI0116]

NORTH FREEDOM—See MAZOMANIE, WI (Charter Communications)

▲ **NORTH PRAIRIE**—Time Warner Cable. Now served by MILWAUKEE, WI [WI0001]

NORTH PRAIRIE—See MILWAUKEE, WI (Time Warner Cable)

NORTHFIELD—See INDEPENDENCE, WI (Western Wisconsin Communications Cooperative)

▲ **NORWALK**—Mediacom. Now served by ONTARIO, WI [WI0303]

NORWALK—See ONTARIO, WI (Mediacom)

NORWAY—See MILWAUKEE, WI (Time Warner Cable)

OAK CREEK—See MILWAUKEE, WI (Time Warner Cable)

OAKDALE—See ONALASKA, WI (Charter Communications)

OAKFIELD—See FOND DU LAC, WI (Charter Communications)

OAKLAND (TOWN)—See MADISON, WI (Charter Communications)

OCONOMOWOC (TOWN)—See MILWAUKEE, WI (Time Warner Cable)

▲ **OCONOMOWOC LAKE**—Time Warner Cable. Now served by MILWAUKEE, WI [WI0001]

OCONOMOWOC LAKE—See MILWAUKEE, WI (Time Warner Cable)

OCONOMOWOC—See JANESVILLE, WI (Charter Communications)

▲ **OCONTO FALLS**—Oconto Falls Cable TV

▲ **OCONTO**—Charter Communications

OMRO—See FOND DU LAC, WI (Charter Communications)

▲ **ONALASKA**—Charter Communications

ONEIDA COUNTY (PORTIONS)—See ELCHO (town), WI (Packerland Broadband)

ONEIDA—See GREEN BAY, WI (Time Warner Cable)

▲ **ONTARIO**—Mediacom

OOSTBURG—See RANDOM LAKE, WI (Time Warner Cable)

OREGON (VILLAGE)—See MADISON, WI (Charter Communications)

▲ **ORFORDVILLE**—Mediacom

OSCEOLA—See DRESSER, WI (Charter Communications)

OSHKOSH—See GREEN BAY, WI (Time Warner Cable)

OSSEO—See INDEPENDENCE, WI (Western Wisconsin Communications Cooperative)

OTSEGO—See RANDOLPH, WI (CenturyTel)

OTTAWA (TOWN)—See MILWAUKEE, WI (Time Warner Cable)

OWEN—See SPENCER, WI (Charter Communications)

▲ **OXFORD**—New Century Communications

PACIFIC TWP.—See RANDOLPH, WI (CenturyTel)

▲ **PACKWAUKEE**—New Century Communications

PADDOCK LAKE—See KENOSHA, WI (Time Warner Cable)

PALMYRA (VILLAGE)—See JANESVILLE, WI (Charter Communications)

PARDEEVILLE—See RANDOLPH, WI (CenturyTel)

▲ **PARK FALLS**—Charter Communications

PARK RIDGE (VILLAGE)—See STEVENS POINT, WI (Charter Communications)

PATCH GROVE—See LANCASTER, WI (Charter Communications)

PELICAN—See RHINELANDER, WI (Charter Communications)

PELL LAKE—See GENOA CITY, WI (Charter Communications)

▲ **PEMBINE**—Packerland Broadband

▲ **PEPIN**—US Cable

PESHTIGO—See MARINETTE, WI (Time Warner Cable)

PEWAUKEE—See MILWAUKEE, WI (Time Warner Cable)

▲ **PHELPS**—Upper Peninsula Communications

▲ **PHILLIPS**—Price County Telephone Co. This cable system has converted to IPTV. See Phillips, WI [WI5049]

▲ **PHILLIPS**—Price County Telephone Co. Formerly [WI5049]. This cable system has converted to IPTV

PIERCE—See TWO RIVERS, WI (Charter Communications)

PIGEON FALLS—See INDEPENDENCE, WI (Western Wisconsin Communications Cooperative)

PIGEON—See INDEPENDENCE, WI (Western Wisconsin Communications Cooperative)

PINE LAKE—See RHINELANDER, WI (Charter Communications)

PITTSFIELD—See GREEN BAY, WI (Time Warner Cable)

▲ **PITTSVILLE**—Packerland Broadband

PLAIN—See MAZOMANIE, WI (Charter Communications)

PLAINFIELD—See WAUTOMA, WI (Charter Communications)

PLATTEVILLE TWP. (EASTERN PORTION)—See PLATTEVILLE, WI (CenturyLink)

▲ **PLATTEVILLE**—Formerly served by Mediacom. No longer in operation

▲ **PLATTEVILLE**—CenturyLink

PLEASANT PRAIRIE—See KENOSHA, WI (Time Warner Cable)

PLEASANT SPRINGS (TOWN)—See MADISON, WI (Charter Communications)

PLOVER (VILLAGE)—See STEVENS POINT, WI (Charter Communications)

PLOVER—See STEVENS POINT, WI (Charter Communications)

PLUM CITY—See ARKANSAW, WI (Chippewa Valley Cable Co. Inc.)

▲ **PLYMOUTH**—Time Warner Cable. Now served by RANDOM LAKE, WI [WI0059]

PLYMOUTH—See RANDOM LAKE, WI (Time Warner Cable)

POLK COUNTY (PORTIONS)—See AMERY, WI (Northwest Community Communications)

POLK—See WEST BEND, WI (Charter Communications)

PORT EDWARDS (VILLAGE)—See WISCONSIN RAPIDS, WI (Charter Communications)

PORT EDWARDS—See WISCONSIN RAPIDS, WI (Charter Communications)

PORT WASHINGTON—See MILWAUKEE, WI (Time Warner Cable)

PORTAGE—See MAZOMANIE, WI (Charter Communications)

PORTERFIELD—See MARINETTE, WI (Time Warner Cable)

PORTLAND (TOWN)—See JANESVILLE, WI (Charter Communications)

POTOSI—See CUBA CITY, WI (Mediacom)

POTTER—See TWO RIVERS, WI (Charter Communications)

POUND—See COLEMAN, WI (Packerland Broadband)

POY SIPPI—See GREEN BAY, WI (Time Warner Cable)

POYNETTE—See MAZOMANIE, WI (Charter Communications)

▲ **PRAIRIE DU CHIEN**—Mediacom

PRAIRIE DU SAC—See MAZOMANIE, WI (Charter Communications)

PRAIRIE FARM—See DALLAS, WI (Mosaic Media)

PRAIRIE LAKE (TOWN)—See RICE LAKE, WI (Charter Communications)

▲ **PRENTICE**—Packerland Broadband

PRESTON—See ADAMS, WI (Charter Communications)

PRINCETON—See FOND DU LAC, WI (Charter Communications)

▲ **PULASKI**—Nsight Teleservices. This cable system has converted to IPTV. See Pulaski, WI [WI5377]

▲ **PULASKI**—Nsight. Formerly [WI0114]. This cable system has converted to IPTV

RACINE—See KENOSHA, WI (Time Warner Cable)

▲ **RADISSON**—S & K TV Systems

RANDALL (TOWN)—See KENOSHA, WI (Time Warner Cable)

RANDALL—See KENOSHA, WI (Time Warner Cable)

▲ **RANDOLPH**—CenturyTel

▲ **RANDOM LAKE**—Time Warner Cable

RANTOUL (TOWN)—See TWO RIVERS, WI (Charter Communications)

RAYMOND (TOWN)—See KENOSHA, WI (Time Warner Cable)

READSTOWN—See CASHTON, WI (Mediacom)

RED CEDAR (TOWN)—See MENOMONIE, WI (Charter Communications)

RED CLIFF—See ASHLAND, WI (Charter Communications)

RED RIVER TWP.—See CASCO, WI (CenturyTel)

REDGRANITE—See WAUTOMA, WI (Charter Communications)

REEDSBURG—See MAZOMANIE, WI (Charter Communications)

REEDSVILLE—See GREEN BAY, WI (Time Warner Cable)

REESEVILLE—See HUSTISFORD, WI (Charter Communications)

REID—See WITTENBERG, WI (Wittenberg Cable TV)

RHINE (TOWN)—See RANDOM LAKE, WI (Time Warner Cable)

▲ **RHINELANDER**—Charter Communications

▲ **RIB LAKE**—Formerly served by Citizens Communications. No longer in operation

RIB MOUNTAIN—See WAUSAU, WI (Charter Communications)

▲ **RICE LAKE**—Charter Communications

RICHFIELD—See WEST BEND, WI (Charter Communications)

RICHLAND CENTER—See MAZOMANIE, WI (Charter Communications)

▲ **RICHLAND CENTER**—Richland Center Cable TV

RICHMOND (TOWN)—See CLINTONVILLE, WI (Charter Communications)

RICHMOND—See GENOA CITY, IL (Charter Communications)

RICHMOND—See NEW RICHMOND, WI (Northwest Community Communications)

RIDGELAND—See DALLAS, WI (Mosaic Media)

RIDGEWAY—See MAZOMANIE, WI (Charter Communications)

RINGLE (TOWN)—See WAUSAU, WI (Charter Communications)

RIO—See RANDOLPH, WI (CenturyTel)

RIPON—See FOND DU LAC, WI (Charter Communications)

RIVER HILLS—See MILWAUKEE, WI (Time Warner Cable)

▲ **ROBERTS (VILLAGE)**—Baldwin Telecom Inc. Formerly served by Baldwin (village), WI [WI0079]. This cable system has converted to IPTV

ROCHESTER—See MILWAUKEE, WI (Time Warner Cable)

ROCK SPRINGS—See MAZOMANIE, WI (Charter Communications)

ROCK—See JANESVILLE, WI (Charter Communications)

ROCKLAND—See ONALASKA, WI (Charter Communications)

ROCKTON—See JANESVILLE, IL (Charter Communications)

ROLLING (TOWN)—See ANTIGO, WI (Charter Communications)

▲ **ROME TWP.**—Solarus

ROSCOE TWP.—See JANESVILLE, IL (Charter Communications)

ROSCOE—See JANESVILLE, IL (Charter Communications)

ROSENDALE—See FOND DU LAC, WI (Charter Communications)

▲ **ROSHOLT**—New Century Communications

ROTHSCHILD—See WAUSAU, WI (Charter Communications)

ROXBURY—See MAZOMANIE, WI (Charter Communications)

ROYALTON (TOWN)—See CLINTONVILLE, WI (Charter Communications)

ROYALTON TWP.—See MANAWA, WI (Manawa Telecom Cable TV)

▲ **ROZELLVILLE**—New Century Communications

RUBICON—See WEST BEND, WI (Charter Communications)

RUDOLPH (TOWN)—See WISCONSIN RAPIDS, WI (Charter Communications)

▲ **RUDOLPH**—Charter Communications

RUSSELL (TOWN)—See ASHLAND, WI (Charter Communications)

SALEM—See KENOSHA, WI (Time Warner Cable)

SAND CREEK—See DALLAS, WI (Mosaic Media)

SAND LAKE—See HAYWARD, WI (Charter Communications)

SARATOGA—See WISCONSIN RAPIDS, WI (Charter Communications)

SAUK CITY—See MAZOMANIE, WI (Charter Communications)

SAUKVILLE (VILLAGE)—See MILWAUKEE, WI (Time Warner Cable)

▲ **SAXEVILLE**—New Century Communications

SCANDINAVIA—See IOLA, WI (Mediacom)

SCHLESWIG (TOWN)—See FOND DU LAC, WI (Charter Communications)

SCHOFIELD—See WAUSAU, WI (Charter Communications)

SCOTT TWP.—See CASCO, WI (CenturyTel)

▲ **SENECA (VILLAGE)**—Dairyland Cable Systems Inc.

SENECA—See WISCONSIN RAPIDS, WI (Charter Communications)

SEVASTAPOL—See STURGEON BAY, WI (Charter Communications)

SEXTONVILLE—See MAZOMANIE, WI (Charter Communications)

▲ **SHARON**—Charter Communications. Now served by HARVARD, IL [IL0073]

SHAWANO—See CLINTONVILLE, WI (Charter Communications)

SHEBOYGAN FALLS—See SHEBOYGAN, WI (Charter Communications)

▲ **SHEBOYGAN**—Charter Communications

SHELBY—See ONALASKA, WI (Charter Communications)

SHELBY—See CASHTON, WI (Mediacom)

SHELL LAKE—See SPOONER, WI (Charter Communications)

SHERMAN TWP.—See RANDOM LAKE, WI (Time Warner Cable)

SHERWOOD (VILLAGE)—See GREEN BAY, WI (Time Warner Cable)

SHIOCTIN—See CLINTONVILLE, WI (Charter Communications)

SHOREWOOD HILLS—See MADISON, WI (Charter Communications)

SHOREWOOD—See MILWAUKEE, WI (Time Warner Cable)

SHULLSBURG—See CUBA CITY, WI (Mediacom)

SILVER LAKE—See KENOSHA, WI (Time Warner Cable)

▲ **SIREN**—Siren Communications

▲ **SISTER BAY**—Charter Communications

SLINGER—See WEST BEND, WI (Charter Communications)

SOLDIER'S GROVE—See CASHTON, WI (Mediacom)

▲ **SOLON SPRINGS**—Northwest Community Communications

SOMERS—See KENOSHA, WI (Time Warner Cable)

▲ **SOMERSET**—Northwest Community Communications

SOMERSET—See AMERY, WI (Northwest Community Communications)

SOUTH BELOIT—See JANESVILLE, IL (Charter Communications)

SOUTH BYRON—See KNOWLES, WI (Packerland Broadband)

SOUTH MILWAUKEE—See MILWAUKEE, WI (Time Warner Cable)

▲ **SPARTA**—Charter Communications. Now served by ONALASKA, WI [WI0024]

SPARTA—See ONALASKA, WI (Charter Communications)

▲ **SPENCER**—Charter Communications

▲ **SPOONER**—Charter Communications

SPRING GREEN—See MAZOMANIE, WI (Charter Communications)

SPRING PRAIRIE—See KENOSHA, WI (Time Warner Cable)

SPRING VALLEY—See ELMWOOD, WI (Celect Communications)

SPRINGFIELD (TOWN)—See MAZOMANIE, WI (Charter Communications)

ST. CLOUD—See FOND DU LAC, WI (Charter Communications)

ST. CROIX FALLS—See DRESSER, WI (Charter Communications)

ST. FRANCIS—See MILWAUKEE, WI (Time Warner Cable)

▲ **ST. JOSEPH TWP.**—Formerly served by Tele-Communications Cable Co. No longer in operation

ST. NAZIANZ—See GREEN BAY, WI (Time Warner Cable)

STANLEY—See EAU CLAIRE, WI (Charter Communications)

STANTON—See NEW RICHMOND, WI (Northwest Community Communications)

STAR PRAIRIE (TOWN)—See NEW RICHMOND, WI (Northwest Community Communications)

STAR PRAIRIE (VILLAGE)—See NEW RICHMOND, WI (Northwest Community Communications)

STELLA—See RHINELANDER, WI (Charter Communications)

▲ **STETSONVILLE**—Charter Communications

STETTIN—See WAUSAU, WI (Charter Communications)

▲ **STEUBEN**—Formerly served by Steuben Community TV System. No longer in operation

▲ **STEVENS POINT**—Charter Communications

STOCKBRIDGE—See GREEN BAY, WI (Time Warner Cable)

STOCKTON (TOWN)—See STEVENS POINT, WI (Charter Communications)

▲ **STODDARD**—Mediacom. Now served by COON VALLEY, WI [WI0171]

STODDARD—See COON VALLEY, WI (Mediacom)

STONE LAKE—See HAYWARD, WI (Charter Communications)

STOUGHTON—See MADISON, WI (Charter Communications)

STRATFORD—See SPENCER, WI (Charter Communications)

STRUM—See INDEPENDENCE, WI (Western Wisconsin Communications Cooperative)

▲ **STURGEON BAY**—Charter Communications

STURTEVANT—See KENOSHA, WI (Time Warner Cable)

SUAMICO—See GREEN BAY, WI (Time Warner Cable)

▲ **SUGAR CREEK (TOWN)**—Mediacom

SULLIVAN—See JANESVILLE, WI (Charter Communications)

SUMMIT (TOWN)—See MILWAUKEE, WI (Time Warner Cable)

SUMNER—See JANESVILLE, WI (Charter Communications)

SUMPTER (TOWN)—See MERRIMAC, WI (Merrimac Cable)

SUN PRAIRIE—See MADISON, WI (Charter Communications)

SUSSEX—See MILWAUKEE, WI (Time Warner Cable)

TAINTER (TOWN)—See MENOMONIE, WI (Charter Communications)

TAYCHEEDAH (TOWN)—See FOND DU LAC, WI (Charter Communications)

TAYLOR—See INDEPENDENCE, WI (Western Wisconsin Communications Cooperative)

TENNYSON—See CUBA CITY, WI (Mediacom)

TEXAS (TOWN)—See WAUSAU, WI (Charter Communications)

THEINSVILLE (VILLAGE)—See MILWAUKEE, WI (Time Warner Cable)

THERESA—See HUSTISFORD, WI (Charter Communications)

▲ **THORP**—CenturyTel

▲ **THREE LAKES**—Karban TV Systems Inc.

▲ **TIGERTON**—Wittenberg Cable TV. Now served by WITTENBERG, WI [WI0158]

TIGERTON—See WITTENBERG, WI (Wittenberg Cable TV)

TILDEN—See EAU CLAIRE, WI (Charter Communications)

▲ **TOMAH**—Charter Communications. Now served by ONALASKA, WI [WI0024]

TOMAH—See ONALASKA, WI (Charter Communications)

TOMAHAWK—See RHINELANDER, WI (Charter Communications)

TONY (VILLAGE)—See LADYSMITH, WI (Charter Communications)

TREGO—See MINONG, WI (S & K TV Systems)

TREMPEALEAU COUNTY—See INDEPENDENCE, WI (Western Wisconsin Communications Cooperative)

TRENTON (TOWN)—See WEST BEND, WI (Charter Communications)

TROY (TOWN)—See KENOSHA, WI (Time Warner Cable)

TURTLE (TOWN)—See JANESVILLE, WI (Charter Communications)

TURTLE LAKE—See AMERY, WI (Northwest Community Communications)

▲ **TUSTIN**—New Century Communications

TWIN LAKES—See GENOA CITY, WI (Charter Communications)

▲ **TWO RIVERS**—Charter Communications

UNDERHILL—See GILLETT, WI (Packerland Broadband)

UNION CENTER—See WONEWOC, WI (Packerland Broadband)

UNION GROVE—See MILWAUKEE, WI (Time Warner Cable)

UNION—See EAU CLAIRE, WI (Charter Communications)

UNION—See JANESVILLE, WI (Charter Communications)

UNITY—See SPENCER, WI (Charter Communications)

VALDERS—See GREEN BAY, WI (Time Warner Cable)

VAN DYNE—See FOND DU LAC, WI (Charter Communications)

VANDENBROEK—See GREEN BAY, WI (Time Warner Cable)

VERNON—See MILWAUKEE, WI (Time Warner Cable)

VERONA—See MAZOMANIE, WI (Charter Communications)

▲ **VESPER**—Packerland Broadband

VIENNA (TOWN)—See MAZOMANIE, WI (Charter Communications)

VINLAND (TOWN)—See GREEN BAY, WI (Time Warner Cable)

VIOLA—See CASHTON, WI (Mediacom)

VIROQUA—See CASHTON, WI (Mediacom)

▲ **WABENO**—Packerland Broadband

WALDO—See MILWAUKEE, WI (Time Warner Cable)

▲ **WARRENS**—Charter Communications. Now served by ONALASKA, WI [WI0024]

WARRENS—See ONALASKA, WI (Charter Communications)

WASHBURN—See ASHLAND, WI (Charter Communications)

WASHINGTON (TOWN)—See CLINTONVILLE, WI (Charter Communications)

WASHINGTON—See EAGLE RIVER, WI (Charter Communications)

WATERFORD—See MILWAUKEE, WI (Time Warner Cable)

WATERLOO—See JANESVILLE, WI (Charter Communications)

WATERTOWN—See JANESVILLE, WI (Charter Communications)

WAUKECHON (TOWN)—See CLINTONVILLE, WI (Charter Communications)

WAUKEON—See PRAIRIE DU CHIEN, IA (Mediacom)

WAUKESHA—See MILWAUKEE, WI (Time Warner Cable)

WAUNAKEE—See MAZOMANIE, WI (Charter Communications)

WAUPACA—See CLINTONVILLE, WI (Charter Communications)

WAUPUN—See HUSTISFORD, WI (Charter Communications)

▲ **WAUSAU**—Charter Communications

WAUTOMA (TOWN)—See WAUTOMA, WI (Charter Communications)

▲ **WAUTOMA**—Charter Communications

▲ **WAUWATOSA**—Time Warner Cable. Now served by MILWAUKEE, WI [WI0001]

WAUWATOSA—See MILWAUKEE, WI (Time Warner Cable)

▲ **WAUZEKA**—Packerland Broadband

WEBSTER—See SIREN, WI (Siren Communications)

WESCOTT (TOWN)—See CLINTONVILLE, WI (Charter Communications)

WEST ALLIS—See MILWAUKEE, WI (Time Warner Cable)

WEST BARABOO—See MAZOMANIE, WI (Charter Communications)

▲ **WEST BEND**—Charter Communications

WEST MILWAUKEE (VILLAGE)—See MILWAUKEE, WI (Time Warner Cable)

WEST POINT (TOWN)—See MAZOMANIE, WI (Charter Communications)

WEST SALEM—See ONALASKA, WI (Charter Communications)

WESTBY—See CASHTON, WI (Mediacom)

WESTFIELD—See WAUTOMA, WI (Charter Communications)

WESTON—See WAUSAU, WI (Charter Communications)

WESTPORT (TOWN)—See MADISON, WI (Charter Communications)

WESTPORT (TOWN)—See MAZOMANIE, WI (Charter Communications)

WEYAUWEGA—See CLINTONVILLE, WI (Charter Communications)

▲ **WEYERHAEUSER**—Formerly served by S & K TV Systems. No longer in operation

WHEATFIELD—See KENOSHA, WI (Time Warner Cable)

WHEATLAND—See KENOSHA, WI (Time Warner Cable)

WHEATON—See EAU CLAIRE, WI (Charter Communications)

WHEELER—See MENOMONIE, WI (Charter Communications)

▲ **WHITE LAKE**—Packerland Broadband

WHITEFISH BAY—See MILWAUKEE, WI (Time Warner Cable)

WHITEHALL—See INDEPENDENCE, WI (Western Wisconsin Communications Cooperative)

WHITELAW—See MANITOWOC, WI (Comcast Cable)

▲ **WHITEWATER**—Charter Communications. Now served by JANESVILLE, WI [WI0007]

WHITEWATER—See JANESVILLE, WI (Charter Communications)

WHITING (VILLAGE)—See STEVENS POINT, WI (Charter Communications)

WILD ROSE—See WAUTOMA, WI (Charter Communications)

WILLIAMSTOWN—See HUSTISFORD, WI (Charter Communications)

▲ **WILTON**—Mediacom. Now served by ONTARIO, WI [WI0303]

WILTON—See ONTARIO, WI (Mediacom)

WINCHESTER (TOWN)—See GREEN BAY, WI (Time Warner Cable)

WIND LAKE—See MILWAUKEE, WI (Time Warner Cable)

WIND POINT—See KENOSHA, WI (Time Warner Cable)

WINDSOR (TOWN)—See MADISON, WI (Charter Communications)

WINNECONNE (VILLAGE)—See FOND DU LAC, WI (Charter Communications)

WINTER—See RADISSON, WI (S & K TV Systems)

WISCONSIN DELLS—See MAZOMANIE, WI (Charter Communications)

▲ **WISCONSIN RAPIDS**—Charter Communications

WITHEE—See SPENCER, WI (Charter Communications)

▲ **WITTENBERG**—Wittenberg Cable TV

▲ **WOLF RIVER**—New Century Communications

▲ **WONEWOC**—Packerland Broadband

WOODBORO (TOWN)—See RHINELANDER, WI (Charter Communications)

▲ **WOODMAN**—Formerly served by Woodman TV Cable System. No longer in operation

WOODRUFF—See MINOCQUA, WI (Charter Communications)

WOODVILLE (TOWN)—See GREEN BAY, WI (Time Warner Cable)

▲ **WOODVILLE (VILLAGE)**—Baldwin Telecom Inc. Formerly served by Baldwin (village), WI [WI0079]. This cable system has converted to IPTV

WRIGHTSTOWN—See GREEN BAY, WI (Time Warner Cable)

WYOCENA TWP.—See RANDOLPH, WI (CenturyTel)

YORKVILLE—See MILWAUKEE, WI (Time Warner Cable)

WYOMING

▲ **AFTON (town)**—Formerly served by KLiP Interactive. No longer in operation

ALBANY COUNTY—See LARAMIE, WY (Bresnan Communications)

BAR NUNN—See CASPER, WY (Bresnan Communications)

▲ **BASIN**—TCT West Inc. This cable system has converted to IPTV. See Basin, WY [WY5003]

BASIN—See GREYBULL, WY (Bresnan Communications)

▲ **BASIN**—TCT West Inc. This cable system has converted to IPTV

BIG HORN COUNTY—See GREYBULL, WY (Bresnan Communications)

▲ **BUFFALO**—Bresnan Communications

▲ **BURLINGTON**—Formerly served by Basin, WY [WY0072]. TCT West Inc. This cable system has converted to IPTV

▲ **BURNS**—B & C Cablevision Inc.

▲ **BYRON**—Formerly served by Byron Cable TV. No longer in operation

▲ **BYRON**—Formerly served by Basin, WY [WY0072]. TCT West Inc. This cable system has converted to IPTV

CAMPBELL COUNTY—See GILLETTE, WY (Bresnan Communications)

CARBON COUNTY (PORTIONS)—See SARATOGA, WY (CommuniComm Services)

▲ **CASPER**—Bresnan Communications

▲ **CHEYENNE**—Bresnan Communications

▲ **CODY**—Bresnan Communications

▲ **COKEVILLE (TOWN)**—All West Communications. Formerly [WY0054]. This cable system has converted to IPTV

▲ **COKEVILLE**—All West Communications. This cable system has converted to IPTV. See Cokeville (town), WY [WY5014]

▲ **COWLEY**—Formerly served by Cowley Telecable Inc. No longer in operation

▲ **COWLEY**—Formerly served by Basin, WY [WY0072]. TCT West Inc. This cable system has converted to IPTV

DAYTON—See RANCHESTER, WY (Tongue River Communications)

▲ **DOUGLAS**—CommuniComm Services

▲ **DUBOIS**—Formerly served by KLiP Interactive. No longer in operation

EAST THERMOPOLIS—See THERMOPOLIS, WY (Bresnan Communications)

▲ **EDGERTON**—Formerly served by Tongue River Cable TV Inc. No longer in operation

▲ **EMBLEM**—Formerly served by Basin, WY [WY0072]. TCT West Inc. This cable system has converted to IPTV

▲ **ENCAMPMENT**—CommuniComm Services

▲ **EVANSTON (PORTIONS)**—Windjammer Cable

EVANSVILLE—See CASPER, WY (Bresnan Communications)

FORT LARAMIE—See GUERNSEY, WY (CAMS Cable)

FOX FARM COLLEGE—See CHEYENNE, WY (Bresnan Communications)

▲ **FRANNIE**—Formerly served by Basin, WY [WY0072]. TCT West Inc. This cable system has converted to IPTV

FREMONT COUNTY—See RIVERTON, WY (Bresnan Communications)

▲ **GILLETTE**—Bresnan Communications

▲ **GLENDO**—Formerly served by CommuniComm Services. No longer in operation

▲ **GLENROCK**—CommuniComm Services

GOSHEN COUNTY (UNINCORPORATED AREAS)—See TORRINGTON, WY (CommuniComm Services)

▲ **GREEN RIVER**—Sweetwater Cable TV Co. Inc.

▲ **GREYBULL**—Bresnan Communications

▲ **GREYBULL**—Formerly served by Basin, WY [WY0072]. TCT West Inc. This cable system has converted to IPTV

▲ **GUERNSEY**—CAMS Cable

HANNA—See SARATOGA, WY (CommuniComm Services)

HARTVILLE—See GUERNSEY, WY (CAMS Cable)

HOT SPRINGS COUNTY—See THERMOPOLIS, WY (Bresnan Communications)

▲ **HULETT**—Tongue River Communications

▲ **JACKSON (TOWN)**—Bresnan Communications

JAMES TOWN—See GREEN RIVER, WY (Sweetwater Cable TV Co. Inc.)

JOHNSON COUNTY—See BUFFALO, WY (Bresnan Communications)

▲ **KEMMERER**—Formerly served by KLiP Interactive. No longer in operation

▲ **LANDER**—Bresnan Communications. Now served by RIVERTON, WY [WY0059]

LANDER—See RIVERTON, WY (Bresnan Communications)

LARAMIE COUNTY—See CHEYENNE, WY (Bresnan Communications)

▲ **LARAMIE**—Bresnan Communications

LINGLE—See TORRINGTON, WY (CommuniComm Services)

▲ **LOVELL**—TCT West Inc. This cable system has converted to IPTV. See Lovell, WY [WY5009]

▲ **LOVELL**—Formerly [WY0024]. TCT West Inc. This cable system has converted to IPTV

▲ **LUSK**—CommuniComm Services

▲ **MAMMOTH HOT SPRINGS**—Formerly served by North Yellowstone Cable TV. No longer in operation

▲ **MANDERSON**—Formerly served by Basin, WY [WY0072]. TCT West Inc. This cable system has converted to IPTV

▲ **MEDICINE BOW**—Medicine Bow Cable

▲ **MEETEETSE**—Formerly served by Basin, WY [WY0072]. TCT West Inc. This cable system has converted to IPTV

▲ **MEETEETSE**—Formerly served by KLiP Interactive. No longer in operation

MILLS—See CASPER, WY (Bresnan Communications)

▲ **MOORCROFT**—Tongue River Communications

MOUNTAIN VIEW (NATRONA COUNTY)—See CASPER, WY (Bresnan Communications)

▲ **MOUNTAIN VIEW (UINTA COUNTY)**—Union Cable Co.

NATRONA COUNTY—See CASPER, WY (Bresnan Communications)

▲ **NEWCASTLE**—Bresnan Communications

NORTH ROCK SPRINGS—See ROCK SPRINGS, WY (Sweetwater Cable TV Co. Inc.)

OLD BALDY—See SARATOGA, WY (CommuniComm Services)

▲ **OSAGE**—Formerly served by Tongue River Cable TV Inc. No longer in operation

▲ **OTTO**—Formerly served by Basin, WY [WY0072]. TCT West Inc. This cable system has converted to IPTV

PARADISE VALLEY—See CASPER, WY (Bresnan Communications)

PARK COUNTY—See CODY, WY (Bresnan Communications)

▲ **PINE BLUFFS**—CAMS Cable

▲ **PINE HAVEN**—Tongue River Communications

▲ **PINEDALE**—Formerly served by KLiP Interactive. No longer in operation

PLATTE COUNTY (UNINCORPORATED AREAS)—See WHEATLAND, WY (CommuniComm Services)

▲ **POWELL**—Bresnan Communications

RAFTER J RANCH—See JACKSON (town), WY (Bresnan Communications)

▲ **RANCHESTER**—Tongue River Communications

▲ **RAWLINS**—Bresnan Communications

RELIANCE—See ROCK SPRINGS, WY (Sweetwater Cable TV Co. Inc.)

RENO JUNCTION—See WRIGHT, WY (Bresnan Communications)

RIVERSIDE—See ENCAMPMENT, WY (CommuniComm Services)

▲ **RIVERTON**—Bresnan Communications

▲ **ROCK SPRINGS**—Sweetwater Cable TV Co. Inc.

ROLLING HILLS—See GLENROCK, WY (CommuniComm Services)

▲ **SARATOGA**—CommuniComm Services

▲ **SHELL**—Formerly served by Basin, WY [WY0072]. TCT West Inc. This cable system has converted to IPTV

SHERIDAN COUNTY—See SHERIDAN, WY (Bresnan Communications)

▲ **SHERIDAN**—Formerly served by Sprint Corp. No longer in operation

▲ **SHERIDAN**—Bresnan Communications

▲ **SHOSHONI**—Formerly served by Winhill Corp. No longer in operation

SINCLAIR—See RAWLINS, WY (Bresnan Communications)

SLEEPY HOLLOW—See GILLETTE, WY (Bresnan Communications)

SOUTH GREELEY—See CHEYENNE, WY (Bresnan Communications)

SOUTH PARK—See JACKSON (town), WY (Bresnan Communications)

▲ **STORY**—Tongue River Communications

▲ **SUNDANCE**—Tongue River Communications

SWEETWATER COUNTY (UNINCORPORATED AREAS)—See ROCK SPRINGS, WY (Sweetwater Cable TV Co. Inc.)

SWEETWATER COUNTY—See GREEN RIVER, WY (Sweetwater Cable TV Co. Inc.)

▲ **TEN SLEEP**—TCT West. No longer in operation

▲ **TEN SLEEP**—Formerly served by Basin, WY [WY0072]. TCT West Inc. This cable system has converted to IPTV

TETON COUNTY—See JACKSON (town), WY (Bresnan Communications)

TETON VILLAGE—See JACKSON (town), WY (Bresnan Communications)

▲ **THERMOPOLIS**—Bresnan Communications

▲ **TORRINGTON**—CommuniComm Services

UINTA COUNTY (PORTIONS)—See EVANSTON (portions), WY (Windjammer Cable)

▲ **UPTON**—Tongue River Communications

▲ **WAMSUTTER**—Formerly served by Sweetwater Cable TV Co. Inc. No longer in operation

WARREN AFB—See CHEYENNE, WY (Bresnan Communications)

WASHAKIE COUNTY—See WORLAND, WY (Bresnan Communications)

WESTON COUNTY—See NEWCASTLE, WY (Bresnan Communications)

▲ **WHEATLAND**—CommuniComm Services

WILSON—See JACKSON (town), WY (Bresnan Communications)

▲ **WORLAND**—Bresnan Communications

▲ **WRIGHT**—Bresnan Communications

▲ **WYODAK**—Formerly served by Tongue River Cable TV Inc. No longer in operation

GUAM

AGANA HEIGHTS—See AGANA, GU (MCV Broadband)

▲ **AGANA**—MCV Broadband

AGAT—See AGANA, GU (MCV Broadband)

ASAN-MAINA—See AGANA, GU (MCV Broadband)

BARRIGADA—See AGANA, GU (MCV Broadband)

CHALAN PAGO-ORDOT—See AGANA, GU (MCV Broadband)

DEDEDO—See AGANA, GU (MCV Broadband)

HAGATNA—See AGANA, GU (MCV Broadband)

INARAJAN—See AGANA, GU (MCV Broadband)

MANGILAO—See AGANA, GU (MCV Broadband)

MERIZO—See AGANA, GU (MCV Broadband)

MONGMONG-TOTO-MAITE—See AGANA, GU (MCV Broadband)

PITI—See AGANA, GU (MCV Broadband)

SANTA RITA—See AGANA, GU (MCV Broadband)

SINAJANA—See AGANA, GU (MCV Broadband)

TALOFOFO—See AGANA, GU (MCV Broadband)

TAMUNING—See AGANA, GU (MCV Broadband)

UMATAC—See AGANA, GU (MCV Broadband)

YIGO—See AGANA, GU (MCV Broadband)

YONA—See AGANA, GU (MCV Broadband)

MARIANA ISLANDS

ROTA—See SAIPAN (MCV Broadband)

▲ **SAIPAN**—MCV Broadband

TINIAN—See SAIPAN (MCV Broadband)

VIRGIN ISLANDS

▲ **ST. CROIX**—Innovative Cable TV St. Croix

ST. JOHN—See ST. THOMAS, VI (Innovative Cable TV St. Thomas-St. John)

▲ **ST. THOMAS**—Innovative Cable TV St. Thomas-St. John

CUBA

▲ **GUANTANAMO BAY**—Phoenix Cable

OTHER U.S. TERRITORIES AND POSSESSIONS

AGANA HEIGHTS—See AGANA, GU (MCV Broadband)

▲ **AGANA**—MCV Broadband

AGAT—See AGANA, GU (MCV Broadband)

ASAN-MAINA—See AGANA, GU (MCV Broadband)

BARRIGADA—See AGANA, GU (MCV Broadband)

CHALAN PAGO-ORDOT—See AGANA, GU (MCV Broadband)

DEDEDO—See AGANA, GU (MCV Broadband)

HAGATNA—See AGANA, GU (MCV Broadband)

INARAJAN—See AGANA, GU (MCV Broadband)

MANGILAO—See AGANA, GU (MCV Broadband)

MERIZO—See AGANA, GU (MCV Broadband)

MONGMONG-TOTO-MAITE—See AGANA, GU (MCV Broadband)

Index to Sections
Television & Cable Factbook No. 80

TV STATIONS VOLUME

Section A

Section B

Section C – Charts

CABLE SYSTEMS VOLUME

Section D

Section E

Section F – Charts

Cable Systems State Index